2016 County and City Extra
Annual Metro, City, and County Data Book
24th Edition

2016 County and City Extra

Annual Metro, City, and County Data Book

24th Edition

Edited by Deirdre A. Gaquin
and Mary Meghan Ryan

Bernan Press

Lanham, MD

Published by Bernan Press
An imprint of
The Rowman & Littlefield Publishing Group, Inc.
4501 Forbes Boulevard, Lanham, Maryland 20706

www.rowman.com
800-462-6420
info@bernan.com

ISBN: 978-159888-869-0

E-ISBN: 978-159888-870-6

ISSN: 1059-9096

∞ ™ The paper used in this publication meets the minimum requirements of American National Standard for Information Sciences—Permanence of Paper for Printed Library Materials, ANSI/NISO Z39.48-1992. Manufactured in the United States of America.

Contents

INTRODUCTION

County and City Extra is an annual publication that provides the most up-to-date statistical information available for every state, county, metropolitan area, and congressional district, as well as all cities in the United States with a 2010 census population of 25,000 or more. Data for places, including towns and cities with populations of fewer than 25,000 people are published by Bernan Press in a separate companion volume, *Places, Towns and Townships,* recently released in its sixth edition. These two volumes are designed to meet the needs of libraries, businesses, and other organizations or individuals who desire convenient and timely sources of the most frequently sought information about geographic entities within the United States. The annual updating of *County and City Extra* for more than 20 years ensures its stature as a reliable and authoritative source for statistical information.

Bernan Press also publishes a companion volume, the *State and Metropolitan Area Data Book,* previously published by the Census Bureau. That edition provides an expanded collection of data about states and metropolitan areas, including micropolitan areas and their component counties. Another recent addition is the *County and City Extra: Special Historical Edition, 1790–2010* with data from the earliest days of the nation, and states, counties, and cities from their beginnings.

County and City Extra, Places, Towns and Townships, and *State and Metropolitan Area Data Book* are large volumes, but are not big enough to accommodate the wealth of information from the decennial census and the American Community Survey. Two additional volumes in the *County and City Extra* series include this information. *County and City Extra—Special Decennial Census Edition* provides detailed population and housing data from the 2010 census and was published by Bernan Press in December 2011. *The Who, What, and Where of America—Understanding the American Community Survey,* soon to be released in its fifth edition, includes social and economic details from the ongoing American Community Survey, and the *County and City Extra* Series includes additional books on special topics, such as the recently published *Families in America.*

The American Community Survey (ACS) is a national survey that has replaced the census long form as the key source of detailed social and economic data. *County and City Extra* includes data from both the 2010 census and the ACS.

New and Updated Information for the 2016 Edition

County and City Extra includes data from the 2012 Economic Census, recently released for states, counties, metropolitan areas, and cities. Table E has been expanded to include newly available County Business Patterns data for

congressional districts. Updated data include 2015 population estimates for states, counties, metropolitan areas, and cities. Also included are the latest available data for education, vital statistics, income and poverty, employment and unemployment, residential construction, production by industry, health resources, crime, land use, city government finances, and many other topics.

Table E (Congressional Districts) includes a wide selection of 2014 American Community Survey data, Social Security data, and data from the 2012 Census of Agriculture for the congressional districts of the 114th Congress, along with the 114th Congressional representatives.

In February 2013, the Office of Management and Budget released a completely new list of Core Based Statistical Areas (metropolitan and micropolitan areas) based on the 2010 census and some changes in the way these areas are defined. These metropolitan areas are used in Table C. Appendixes B and C provide details about the component counties of these metropolitan and micropolitan areas and their 2010 census and 2015 estimated populations. Appendix D has a map for each state showing the metropolitan and micropolitan areas.

This edition includes data from the 2010 census, 2014 and 2015 population estimates, and the ACS. Annual ACS data are available for all states and almost all metropolitan areas (all geographic areas with populations of 65,000 or more), but five years are needed to build a sample large enough for reliable estimates for all counties and all the cities in this book. The Census Bureau no longer releases 3-year data which were previously available for areas with populations of 20,000 or more.

With the now annual release of 1-year and 5-year estimates, *County and City Extra* uses ACS data for all geographic areas. ACS 1-year data for 2014 are included in Table A (States), Table C (metropolitan areas) and Table E (Congressional Districts)—all areas with populations of 65,000 or more. Table B (Counties) and Table D (cities) include 5-year data (2010–2014). The release of 5-year data for even the smallest geographic areas means that annual social and economic characteristics are available for all counties and cities.

Although some of the state data are also included in Table B (States and Counties), the separate state data table offers several important features:

- Additional data not available at the county level are provided. Examples include population projections, health insurance coverage, number of immigrants, personal tax payments, information about health service firms not subject to federal tax, and exports by state of origin.

- Additional data that exceeds the space limitations for counties can be found for states. Examples are age of householder, more detailed information about employment in retail trade and services, and the expanded presentation of federal payments to individuals by type.

- State totals can be found more quickly and compared more readily.

Appendix F, **Source Notes and Explanations**, includes internet references for all data sources. This is especially helpful in today's environment where the data sources are updated at a faster pace. The sources referenced here can be used to track down additional information too cumbersome for this book. Some of the data can be directly found in data tables on the websites; some can be assembled through on-line access tools; others can be obtained by downloading files and processing them with statistical software; and some need to be ordered from the agencies.

Rankings

The rankings present the geography types by various subjects, including population, land area, population density, population change, age, immigration, birth rate, housing characteristics, race, Hispanic origin, educational attainment, income, unemployment rate, per capita local taxes, poverty rate, defense contracts, value of agricultural products, and violent crime rate.

Subjects Covered and Volume Organization

A summary of the **subjects covered** in each of the five tables appears on **page xi**. The **colored map** portfolio begins on **page xiii**.

The main body of this volume contains five basic parts. Each part includes a table that is preceded by highlights and rankings, as well as the complete column headings for the table. **Part A**, which begins on **page 1**, contains data for states. **Part B**, beginning on **page 51**, contains information for states and counties. The county geography codes include county typology codes from the Economic Research Service of the Department of Agriculture. These codes characterize counties by size of the largest place as well as by other criteria for nonmetropolitan counties. (See Appendix A for the definition of each code.) **Part C**, beginning on **page 773**, contains information for metropolitan areas. Statistics for cities with a 2010 census population of 25,000 or more can be found in **Part D**, which begins on **page 895**. **Part E**, beginning on **page 1175**, contains data for the congressional districts of the 114th Congress.

A contents page preceding tables B through E lists the page number on which the data for a given geographic area begin. Counties and cities are listed alphabetically by state. Metropolitan areas are listed alphabetically, except that metropolitan divisions are listed alphabetically within the metropolitan

statistical area of which they are components. Congressional districts are listed in numeric order within states.

The appendixes include definitions of geographic concepts (**Appendix A**), sources and definitions of each data item included in this volume (**Appendix F**), an alphabetical listing of metropolitan areas with their component counties delineated as of February 2013, with 2010 census populations (**Appendix B**), a listing of metropolitan and micropolitan areas and their component counties as of February 2013, with 2010 census populations and 2015 estimated populations (**Appendix C**), a list of cities by county (**Appendix E**), and maps showing congressional districts in the United States and metropolitan areas, counties, and selected places within each state (**Appendix D**).

Symbols

D Indicates that the number has been withheld to avoid disclosure of information pertaining to a specific organization or individual, or because the number does not meet statistical standards for publication.

NA Indicates that data are not available.

X Indicates that data are not applicable or are not meaningful for this geographic unit.

In this volume, a figure that is less than half the unit of measure shown will appear as zero.

Sources

The great majority of the data in this volume have been obtained from federal government sources. A few items are obtained from private sources that are widely recognized as reliable basic sources of those particular data items. For a complete list of these sources, see **Appendix F**.

Data included in this volume meet the publication standards established by the U.S. Census Bureau and the other federal statistical agencies from which they were obtained. Every effort has been made to select data that are accurate, meaningful, and useful. All data from censuses, surveys, and administrative records are subject to errors arising from factors such as sampling variability, reporting errors, incomplete coverage, nonresponse, imputations, and processing error. Responsibility of the editors and publishers of this volume is limited to reasonable care in the reproduction and presentation of data obtained from sources believed to be reliable.

County and City Extra: Annual Metro, City, and County Data Book is part of Bernan Press's *County and City Extra* series. The editors of *County and City Extra* acknowledge the contributions of Courtenay Slater and the late George Hall, the originators of this publication. Their initial contributions continue to enrich the *County and City Extra* series. As always, we are especially grateful to the many federal agency personnel who assisted us in obtaining the data, provided excellent resources on their websites, and patiently answered questions.

Deirdre A. Gaquin has been a data use consultant to private organizations, government agencies, and universities for over 30 years. Prior to that, she was Director of Data Access Services at Data Use & Access Laboratories, a pioneer in private sector distribution of federal statistical data. A former President of the Association of Public Data Users, Ms. Gaquin has served on numerous boards, panels, and task forces concerned with federal statistical data and has worked on five decennial censuses. She holds a Master of Urban Planning (MUP) degree from Hunter College. Ms. Gaquin is also an editor of Bernan Press's *The Who, What, and Where of America: Understanding the American Community Survey*; *Places, Towns and Townships*; *The Congressional District Atlas*, *The Almanac of American Education, Race and Employment in America,* and *the State and Metropolitan Area Data Book.*

Mary Meghan Ryan is the senior research editor for Bernan Press. She is also the editor for the *Handbook of U.S. Labor Statistics*, *State Profiles*, and the associate editor for *Business Statistics of the United States*.

SUBJECTS COVERED, BY GEOGRAPHY TYPE

State data begin on page 1
County data begin on page 51
Metropolitan area data begin on page 773
City data begin on page 895
Congressional district data begin on page 1175

Subject	Column Number				
	Table A. States	Table B. States and Counties	Table C. Metropolitan Areas	Table D. Cities	Table E. Congressional Districts
Land area	1	1	1	1	1
Population					
Total persons, 1990	31				
Total persons, 2000	32	20	20	23	
Total persons, 2010	33	21	21	24	
Total persons, 2014					2
Total persons, 2015	2	2	2	2	
Rank, 2015	3	3	3	3	
Persons per square kilometer	4	4	4	4	
Race and Hispanic or Latino origin, 2010	45–50				
Race and Hispanic or Latino origin, 2014	5–9	5–9	5–9		4–11
Race and Hispanic or Latino origin, 2010–2014				5–10	
Percent female	21	19	19	22	12
Foreign-born population	22			11	13
Percent born in state of residence	23				14
Immigrants	24				
Age distribution, 2010	52–61				
Age distribution, 2014	10–19	10–18	10–18		15–23
Age distribution, 2010–2014				12–20	
Median age	20, 62			21	24
Percent population change, 1990–2000	34				
Percent population change, 2000–2010	35	22	22	25	
Percent population change, 2010–2015	36	23	23	26	
Components of population change	37–41	24–26	24–26		
Daytime population		33–34	33–34		
Population projections	42–44				
Households					
Total households, 2010	64	27	27		
Total households, 2014	25				28
Total households, 2010–2014		27–31			
Total households, 2010–2014				27	
Percent change in number of households	26, 65			29–30	
Household type	28–30, 67–68	29–31	29–31		30–33
Persons per household	27, 66	28	28	28	29
Persons in group quarters		32	32	31–34	34–39
Housing					
Housing units in 2010	69–78			47–49	
Housing units in 2014	79–92		89–96		40–45
Housing units in 2015		87–88	87–88		
Housing units in 2010–2014		89–96			
Housing units in 2010–2014				50–58	
Percent change in number of housing units	70, 80	88	88	48	
Housing costs	73–77, 83–90	91–95	91–95	52–57	43–45
Substandard housing units	78, 91	96	96		
Percent with no vehicle available				58	
Percent who lived in same house one year ago	92			59	
Percent who lived outside city one year ago				60	
New residential construction	93–95	169–170	169–170	69–71	
Manufactured housing	96				
Vital statistics					
Births	97–98	35–36	35–36		
Deaths	99–103	37–38	37–38		

SUBJECTS COVERED, BY GEOGRAPHY TYPE — Continued

State data begin on page 1
County data begin on page 51
Metropolitan area data begin on page 773
City data begin on page 895
Congressional district data begin on page 1175

Subject	Column Number				
	Table A. States	Table B. States and Counties	Table C. Metropolitan Areas	Table D. Cities	Table E. Congressional Districts
Health					
Persons in nursing facilities				33	37
Medicare enrollees	106	41–43	41–43		
Persons lacking health insurance	104–105	39–40	39–40		59
Crime	107–110	44–47	44–47	35–38	
Education					
School enrollment	111–112	48–49	48–49		25
Educational attainment	113–116	50–51	50–51	39–41	26–27
Expenditures for education	117–118	52–53	52–53		
Income					
Personal income	134–149	62–71	62–71		
Per capita income	122, 136, 149	54, 64	54, 64	42	46
Household income	123–126	55–58	55–58	43–45	47–48
Poverty	127–133	59–61	59–61	46	49–50
Food stamps					51
Personal income by type	138–140	66–70	66–70		
Earnings by industry	150–158	72–83	72–83		
Transfer payments	141–146	71	71		
Gross state product	159				
Personal tax payments	147				
Disposable personal income	148–149				
Social Security	160–162	84–86	84–86		60–62
Labor Force and Employment					
Labor force and unemployment	167–171	97–100	97–100	61–68	52–54
Employment in selected occupations	163–166	101–103	101–103		55–58
Employment by industry	172–183, 207–216	104–112	104–112		73–84
Exports of goods produced	119–121				
Establishments, employment, sales, and payroll					
Manufacturing	207–216	151–154	151–154	88–91	
Construction	217–221				
Wholesale trade	222–226	135–138	135–138	72–75	
Retail trade	227–235	139–142	139–142	76–79	
Information	236–246				
Utilities	247–251				
Transportation and warehousing	252–256				
Finance and insurance	257–261				
Real estate and rental and leasing	262–266	143–146	143–146	80–83	
Professional, scientific, and technical services	267–275	147–150	147–150	84–87	
Health care and social assistance	276–289	159–162	159–162	100–103	
Arts, entertainment and recreation	290–294			96–99	
Accommodation and food services	295–300	155–158	155–158	92–95	
Other services, except public administration	301–308	163–166	163–166	104–108	
Nonemployer businesses		167–168	167–168		
Government employment	309–314	171, 194–196	171, 194–196	108	
Government payroll	315–330	172–179	172–179	109–116	
Government finances	331–350	180–193	180–193	117–139	

State data begin on page 1
County data begin on page 51
Metropolitan area data begin on page 773
City data begin on page 895
Congressional district data begin on page 1175

Subject	Column Number				
	Table A. States	Table B. States and Counties	Table C. Metropolitan Areas	Table D. Cities	Table E. Congressional Districts
Agriculture	184–202	113–132	113–132		63–72
Land and water	203–206	133–134	133–134		
Voting and elections	351–355	197–199	197–199		
Climate				140–146	

Population Change
2010–2015

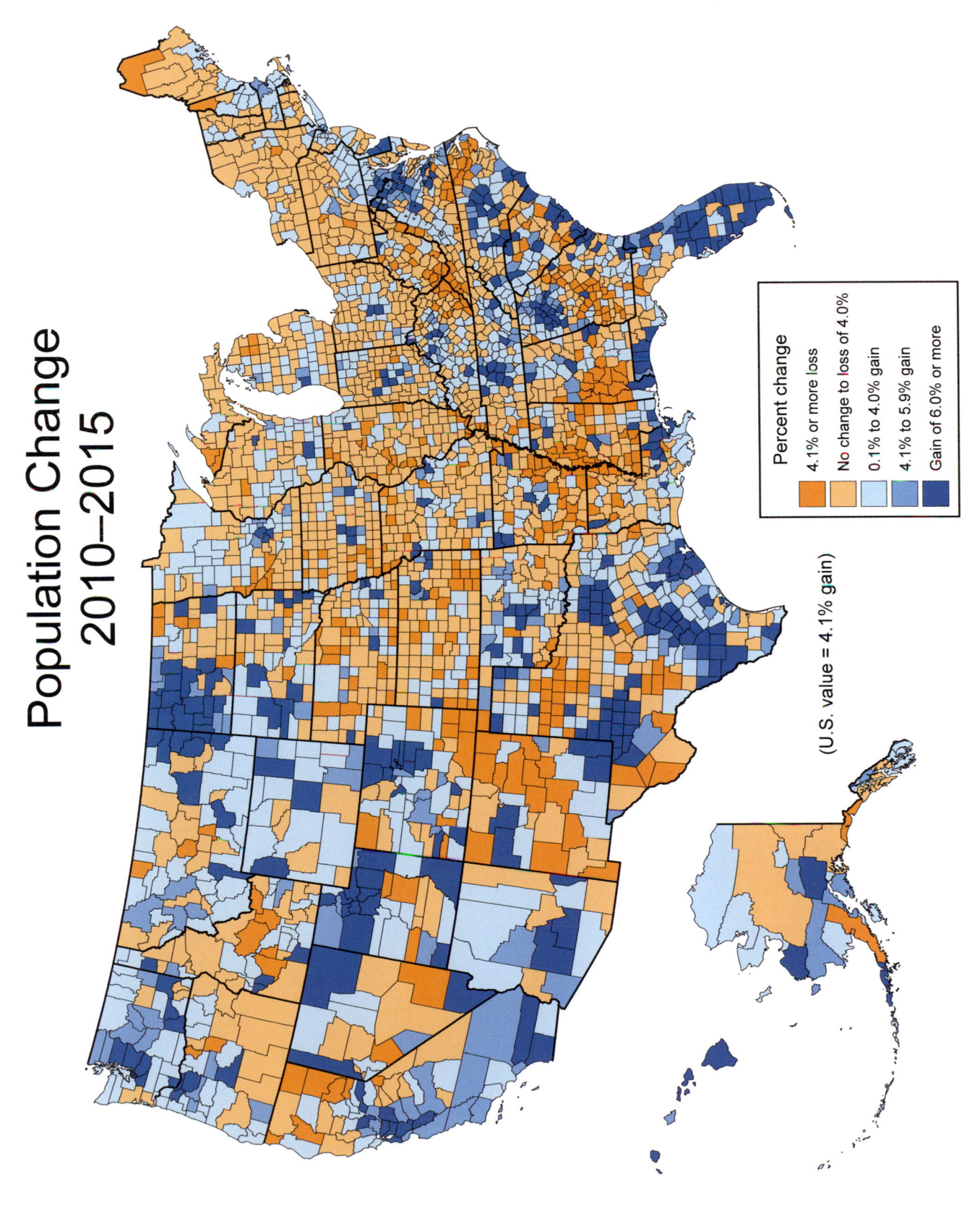

Percent change

	4.1% or more loss
	No change to loss of 4.0%
	0.1% to 4.0% gain
	4.1% to 5.9% gain
	Gain of 6.0% or more

(U.S. value = 4.1% gain)

Black, Not Hispanic or Latino, Population 2014

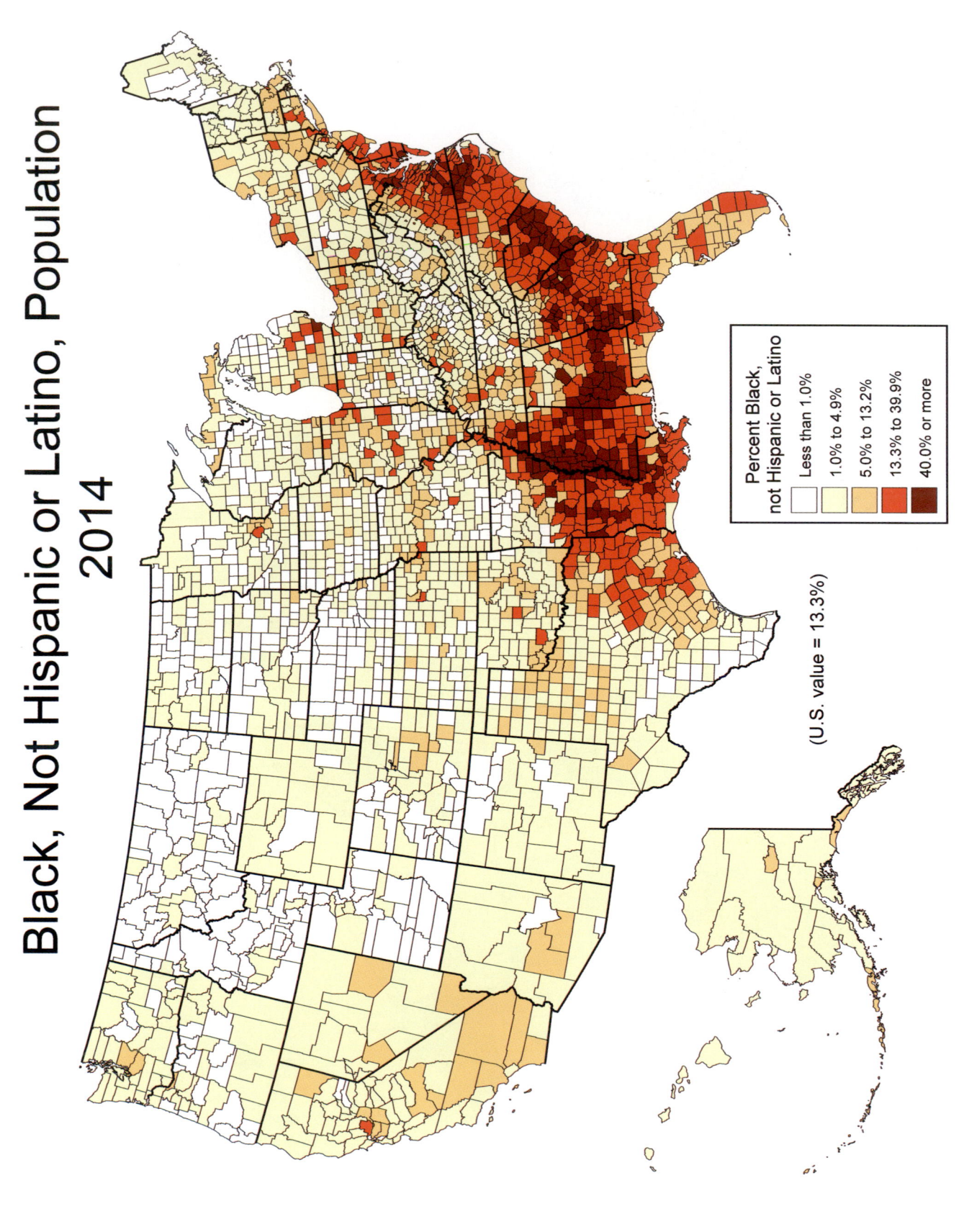

Percent Black, not Hispanic or Latino

- Less than 1.0%
- 1.0% to 4.9%
- 5.0% to 13.2%
- 13.3% to 39.9%
- 40.0% or more

(U.S. value = 13.3%)

Hispanic or Latino Population 2014

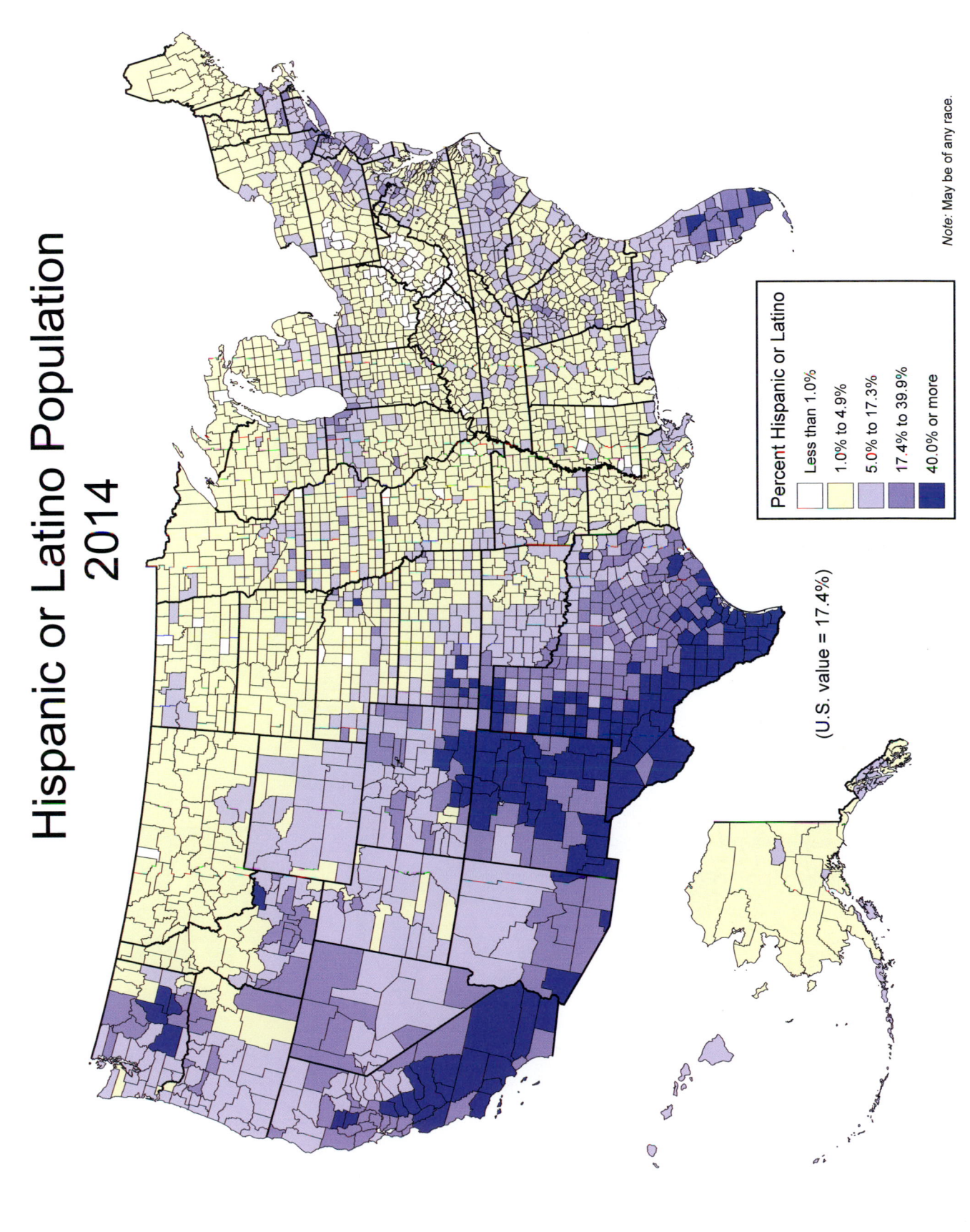

Percent Hispanic or Latino

- Less than 1.0%
- 1.0% to 4.9%
- 5.0% to 17.3%
- 17.4% to 39.9%
- 40.0% or more

(U.S. value = 17.4%)

Note: May be of any race.

xv

Population Under 18 Years Old
2014

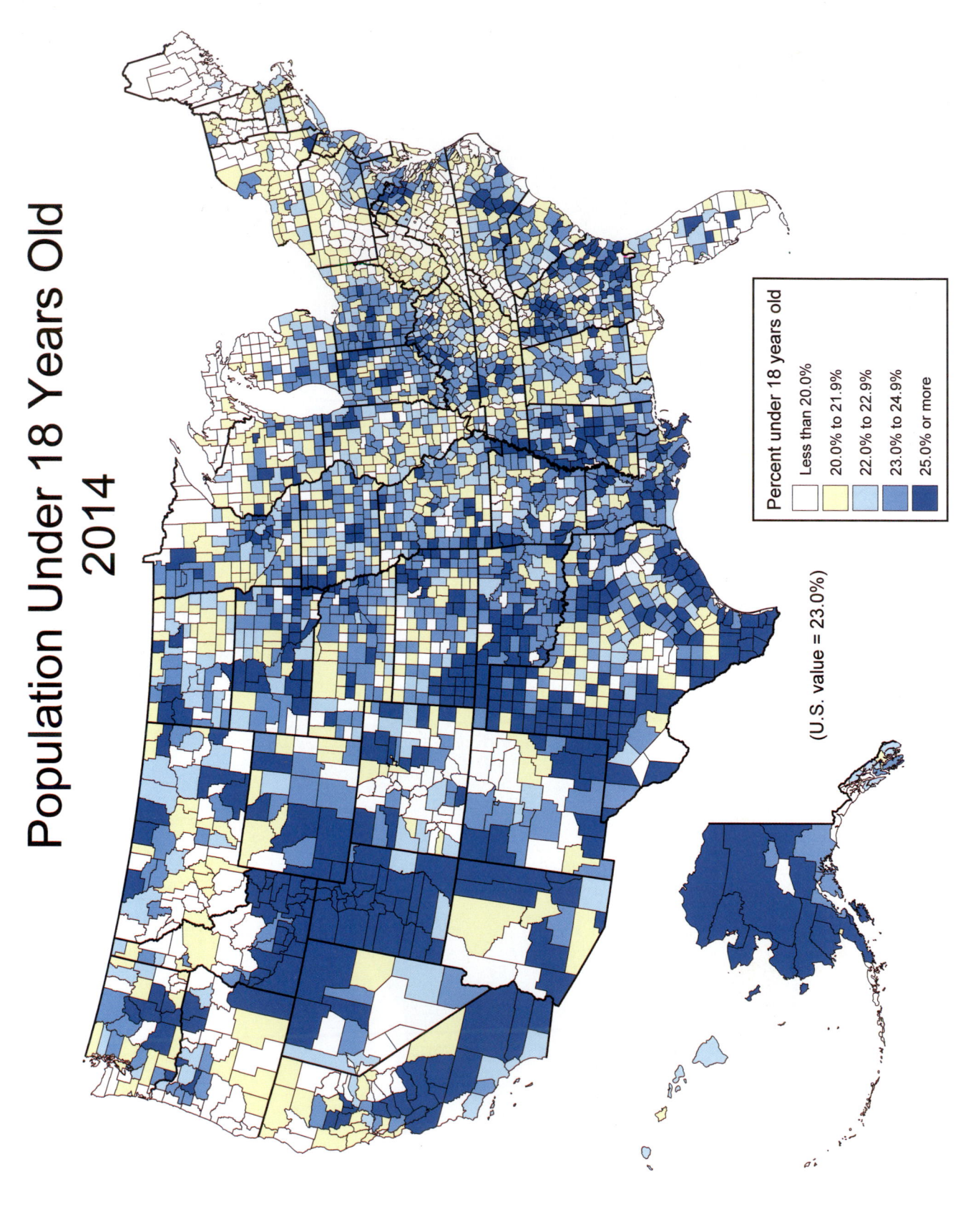

Percent under 18 years old

- Less than 20.0%
- 20.0% to 21.9%
- 22.0% to 22.9%
- 23.0% to 24.9%
- 25.0% or more

(U.S. value = 23.0%)

Population 65 Years Old and Over
2014

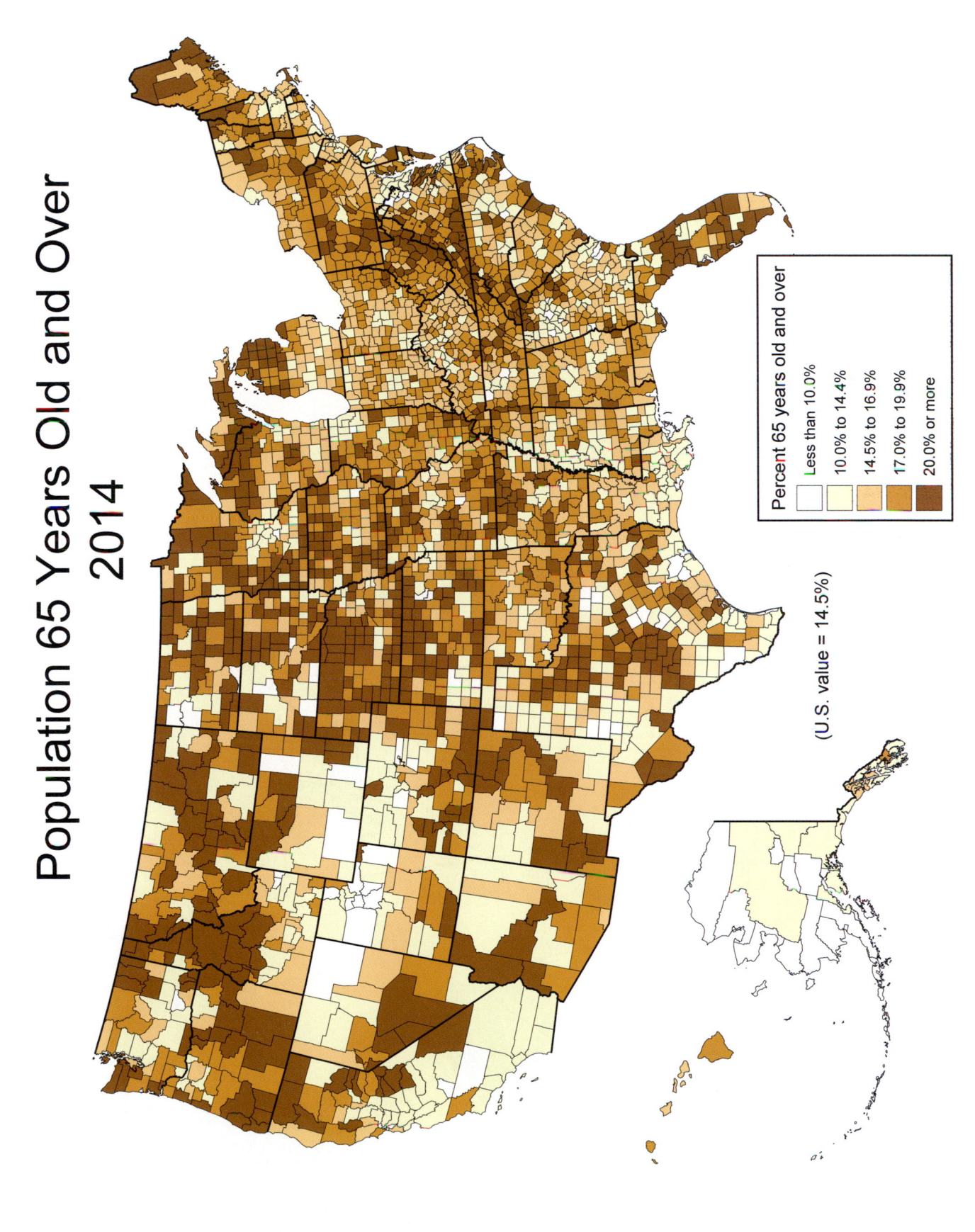

Percent 65 years old and over

Percent 65 years old and over
- Less than 10.0%
- 10.0% to 14.4%
- 14.5% to 16.9%
- 17.0% to 19.9%
- 20.0% or more

(U.S. value = 14.5%)

Population Density
2015

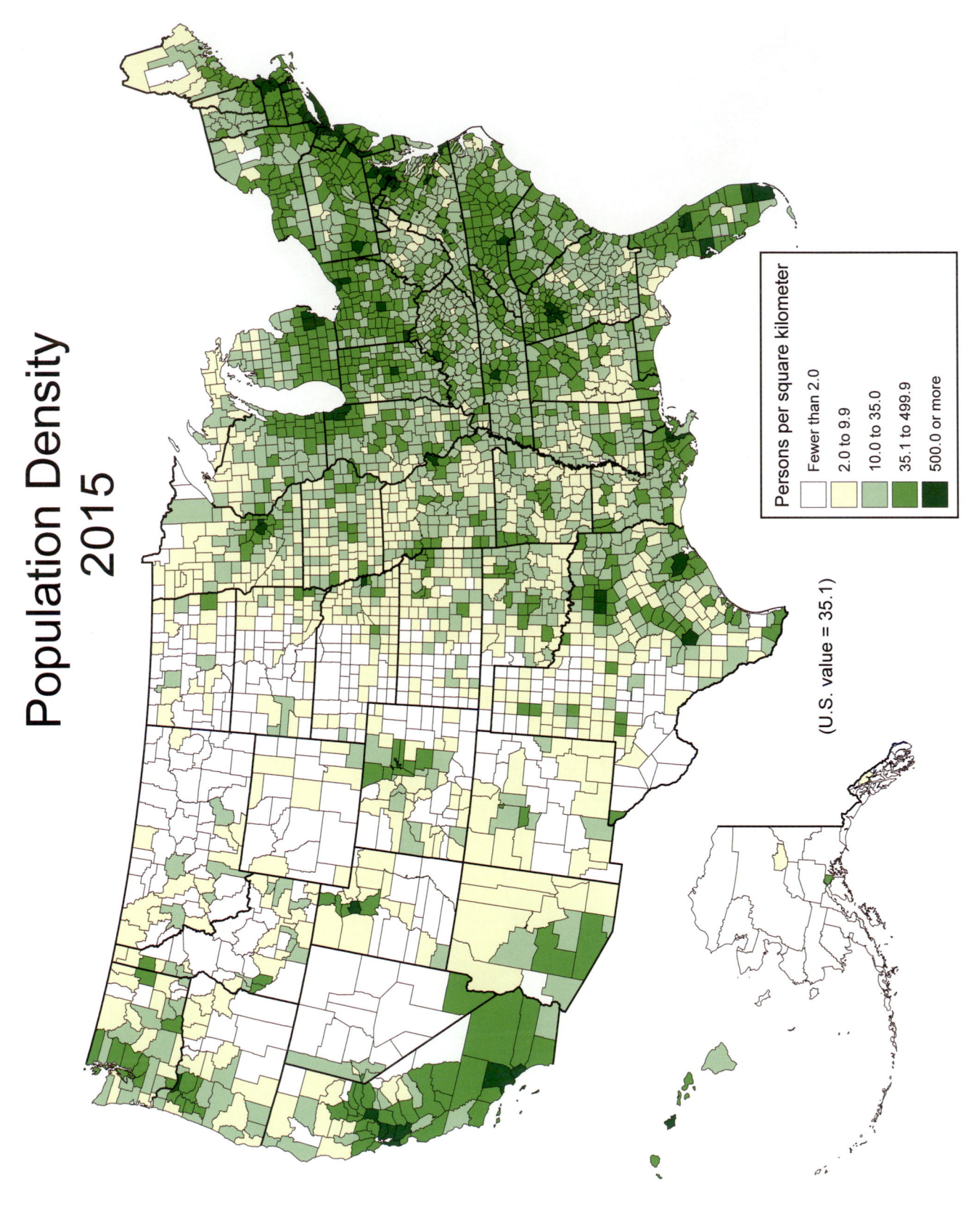

Persons per square kilometer

Fewer than 2.0
2.0 to 9.9
10.0 to 35.0
35.1 to 499.9
500.0 or more

(U.S. value = 35.1)

Unemployment Rate
2015

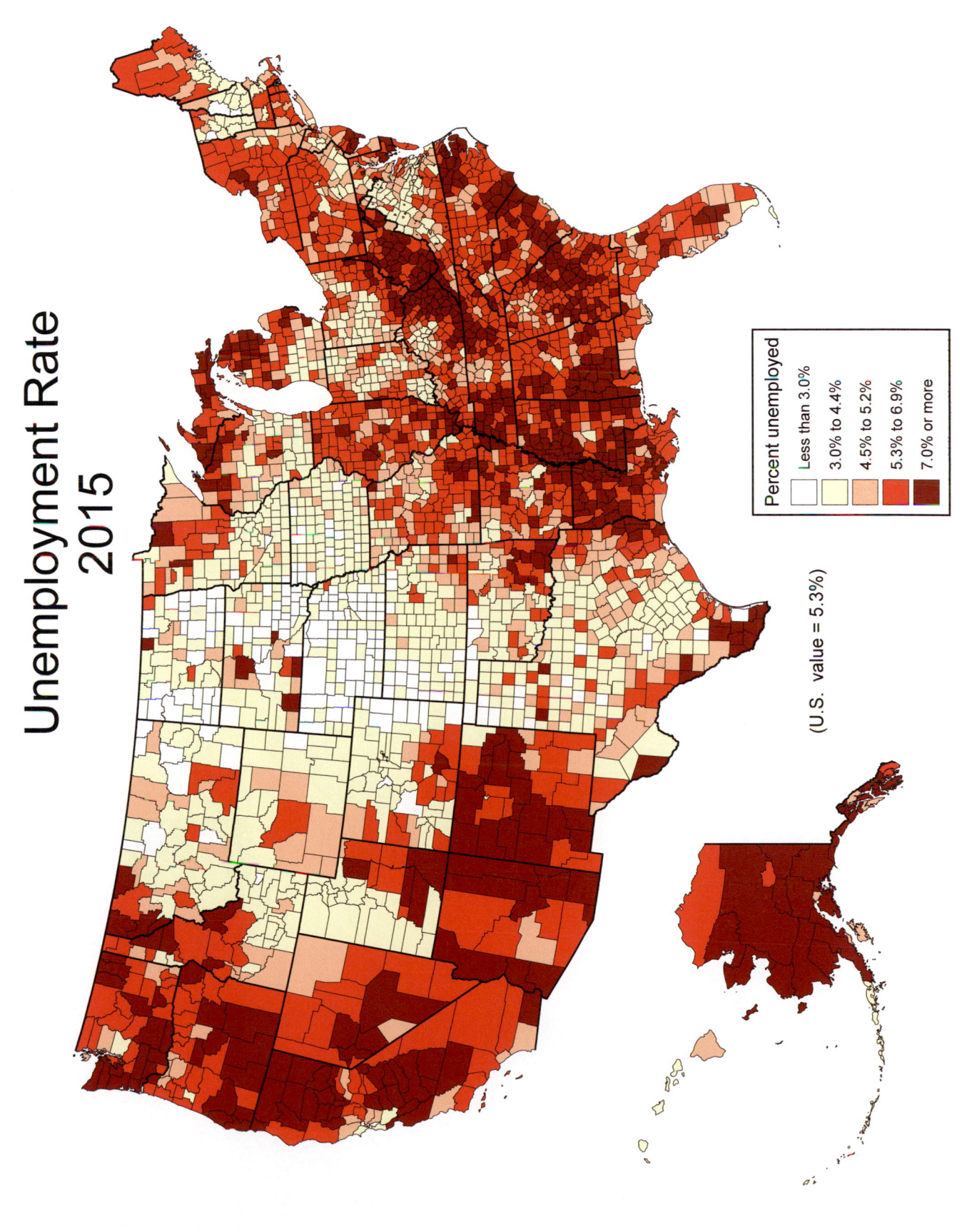

Percent unemployed

- Less than 3.0%
- 3.0% to 4.4%
- 4.5% to 5.2%
- 5.3% to 6.9%
- 7.0% or more

(U.S. value = 5.3%)

Educational Expenditures Per Student
2012–2013

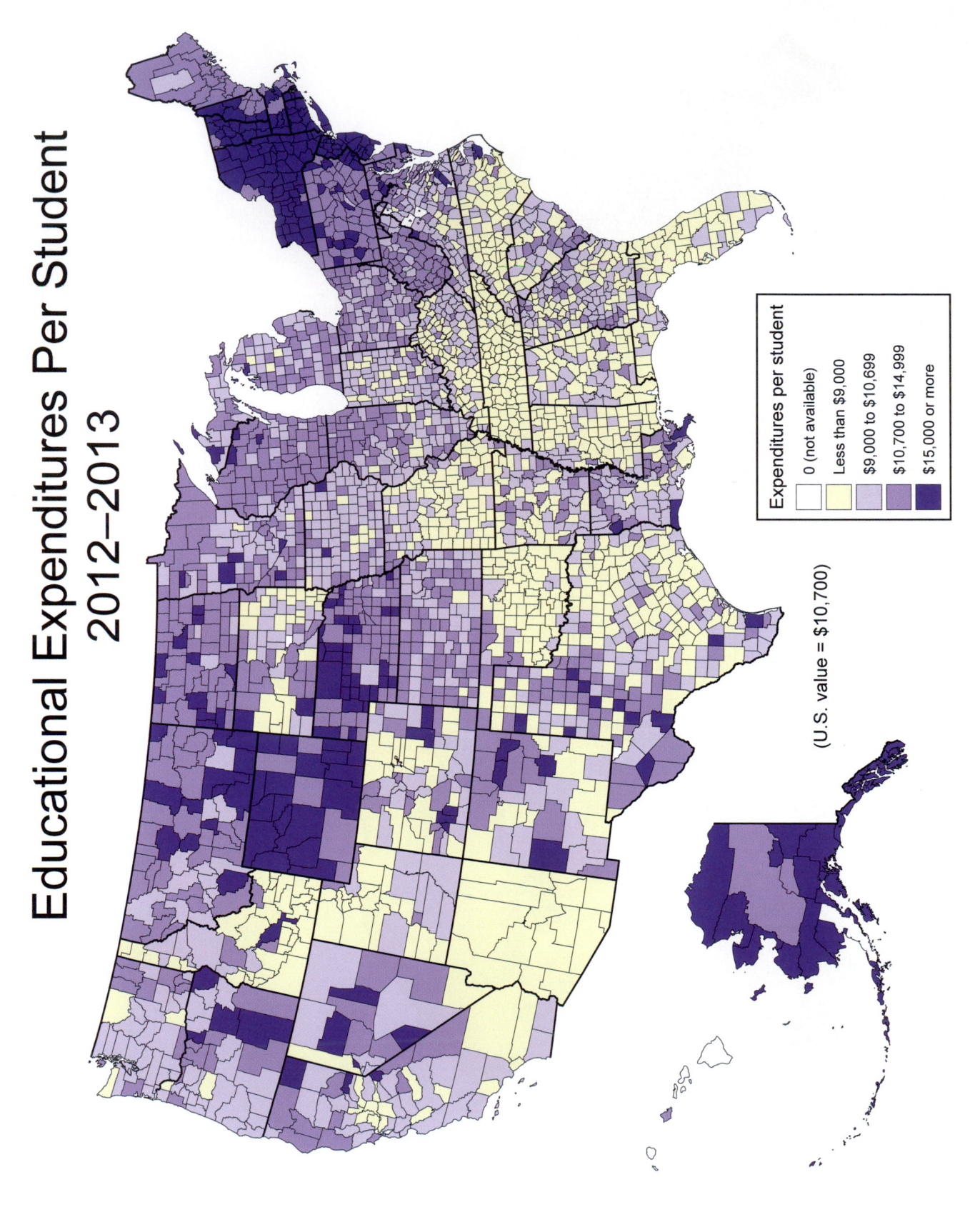

Expenditures per student

- 0 (not available)
- Less than $9,000
- $9,000 to $10,699
- $10,700 to $14,999
- $15,000 or more

(U.S. value = $10,700)

Population with High School Diploma or Less
2010–2014

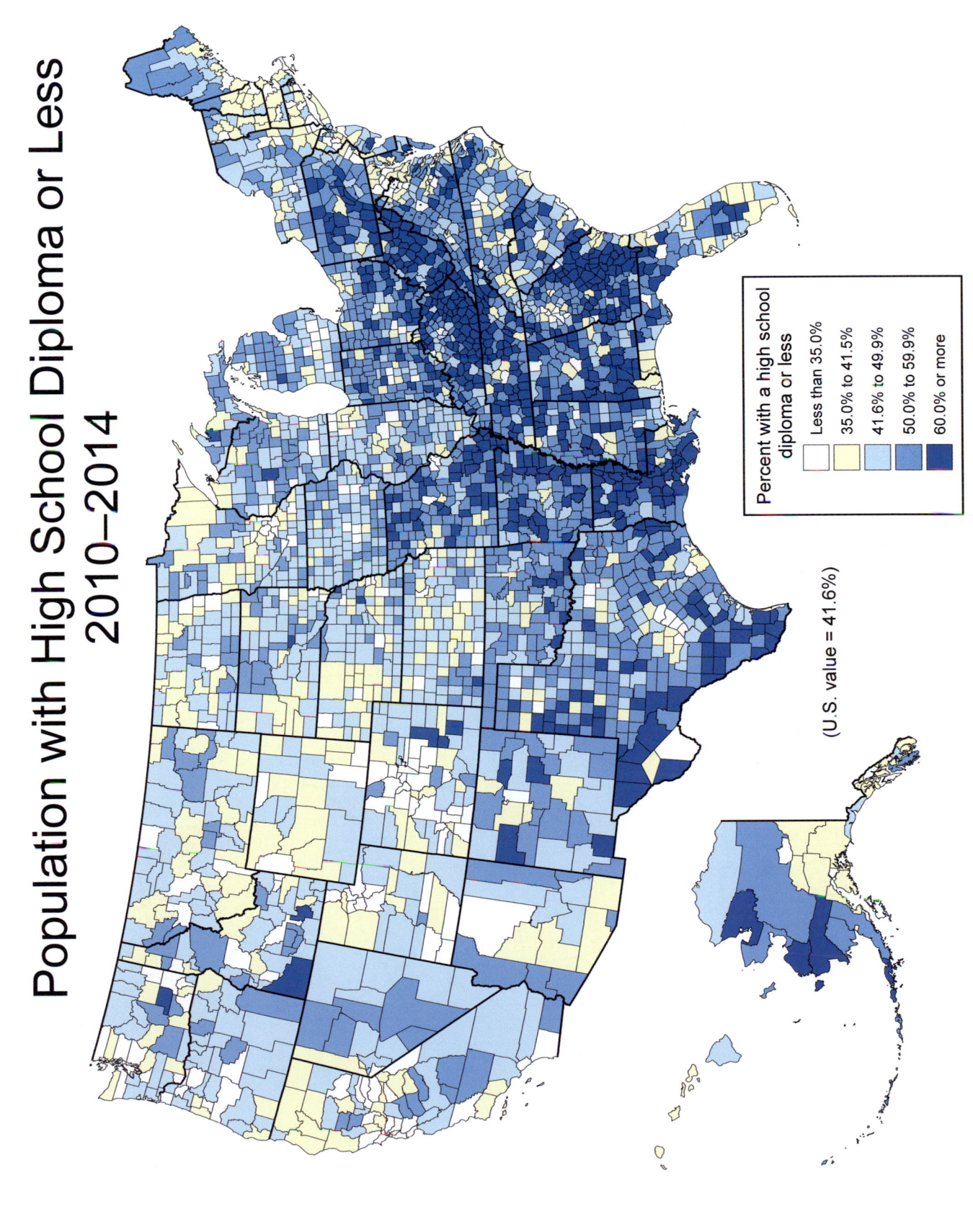

Percent with a high school diploma or less

- Less than 35.0%
- 35.0% to 41.5%
- 41.6% to 49.9%
- 50.0% to 59.9%
- 60.0% or more

(U.S. value = 41.6%)

Earnings from Manufacturing 2014

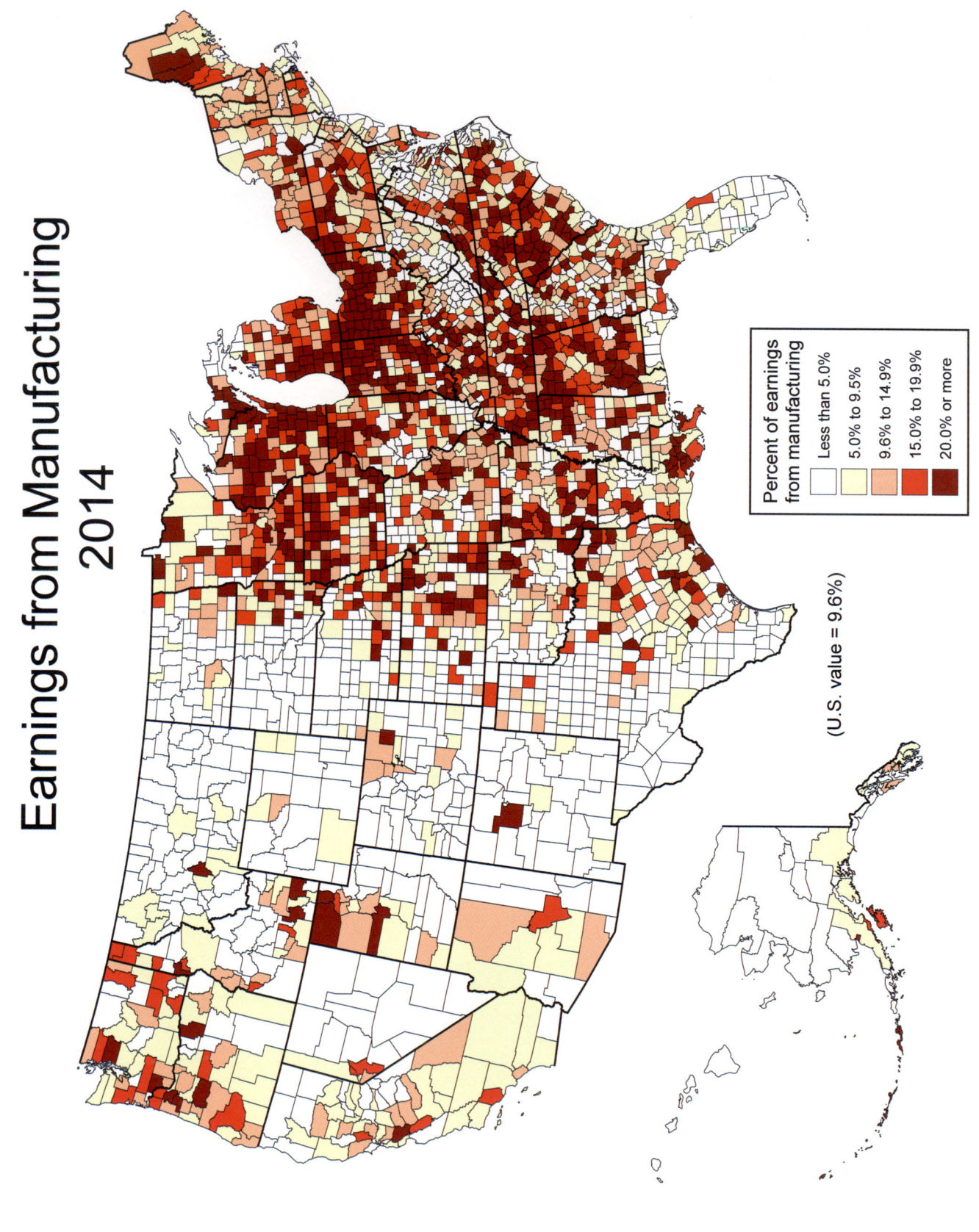

Percent of earnings from manufacturing

- Less than 5.0%
- 5.0% to 9.5%
- 9.6% to 14.9%
- 15.0% to 19.9%
- 20.0% or more

(U.S. value = 9.6%)

Employment in Management, Business, Science, and Arts Occupations: 2010–2014

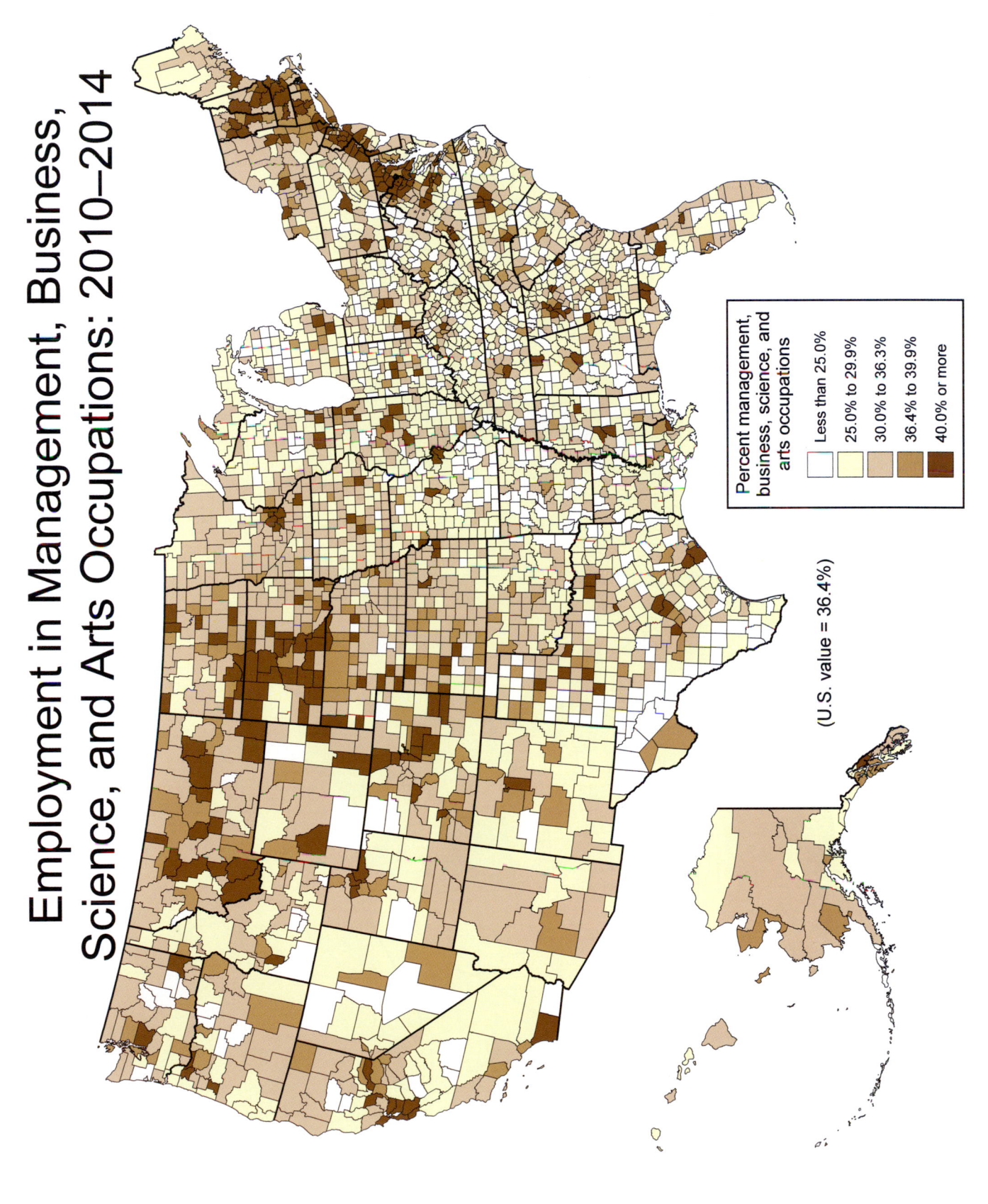

Percent management, business, science, and arts occupations

- Less than 25.0%
- 25.0% to 29.9%
- 30.0% to 36.3%
- 36.4% to 39.9%
- 40.0% or more

(U.S. value = 36.4%)

Land in Farms 2012

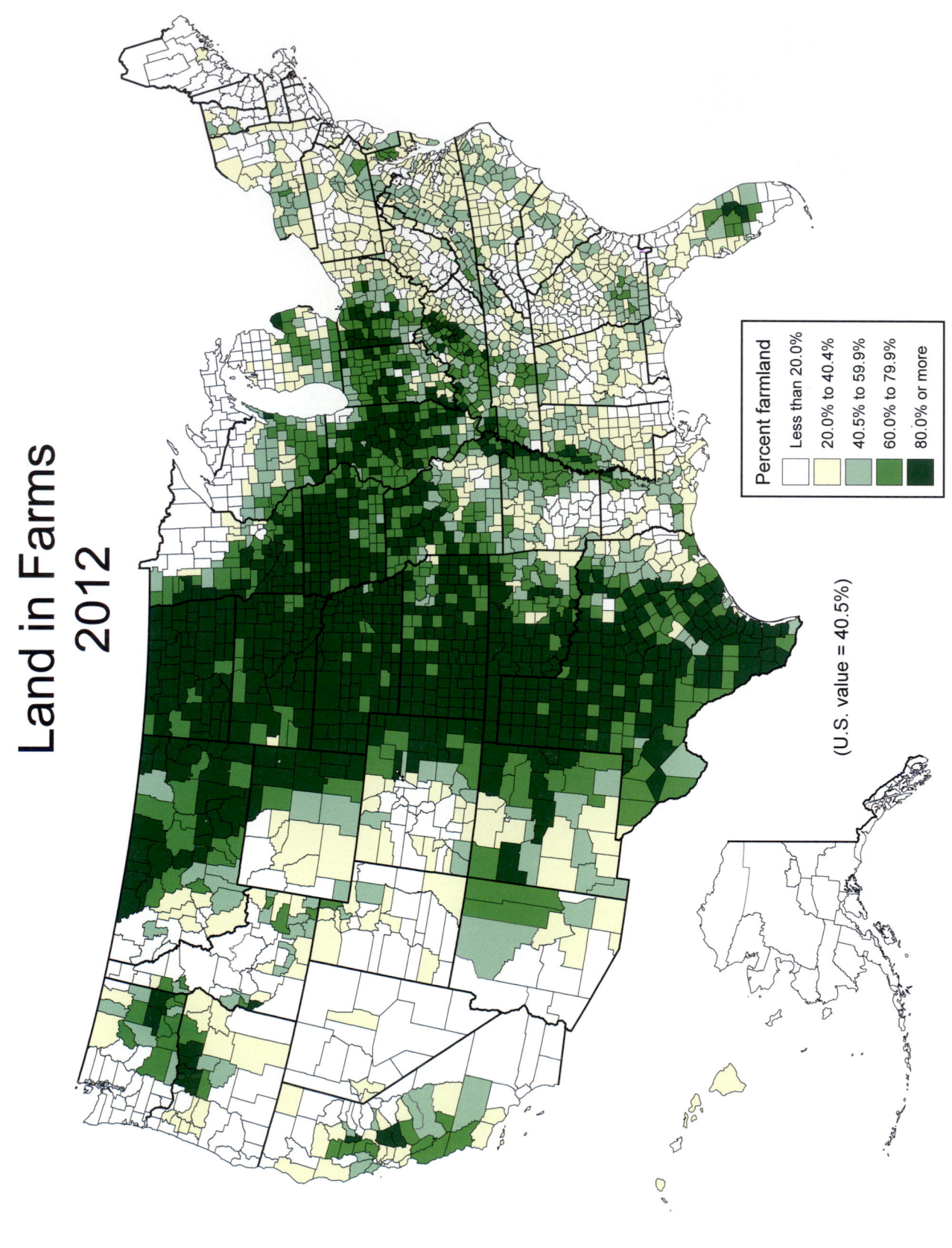

Percent farmland

- Less than 20.0%
- 20.0% to 40.4%
- 40.5% to 59.9%
- 60.0% to 79.9%
- 80.0% or more

(U.S. value = 40.5%)

Persons Under Age 65 with No Health Insurance
2014

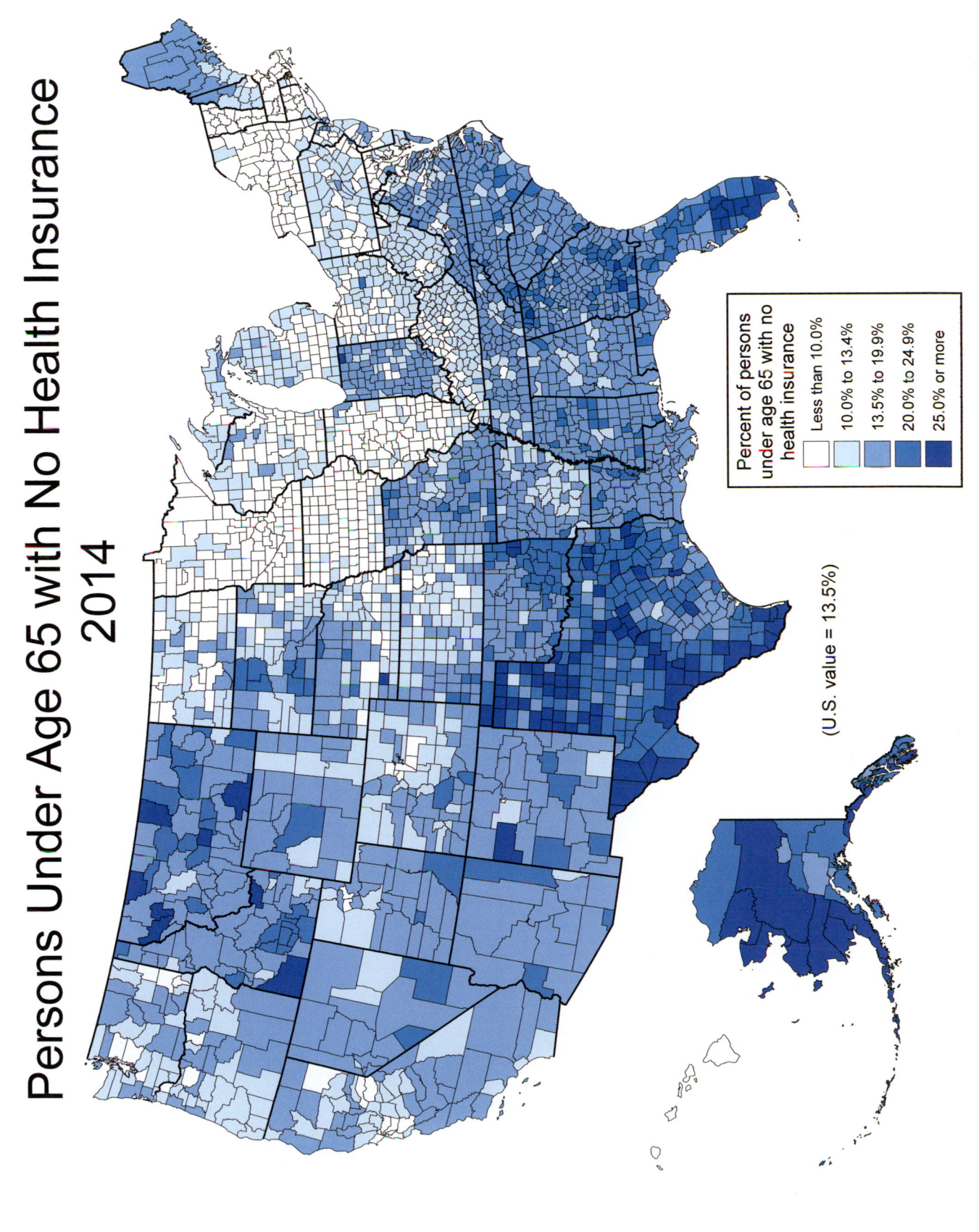

Percent of persons under age 65 with no health insurance

- Less than 10.0%
- 10.0% to 13.4%
- 13.5% to 19.9%
- 20.0% to 24.9%
- 25.0% or more

(U.S. value = 13.5%)

Median Household Income
2014

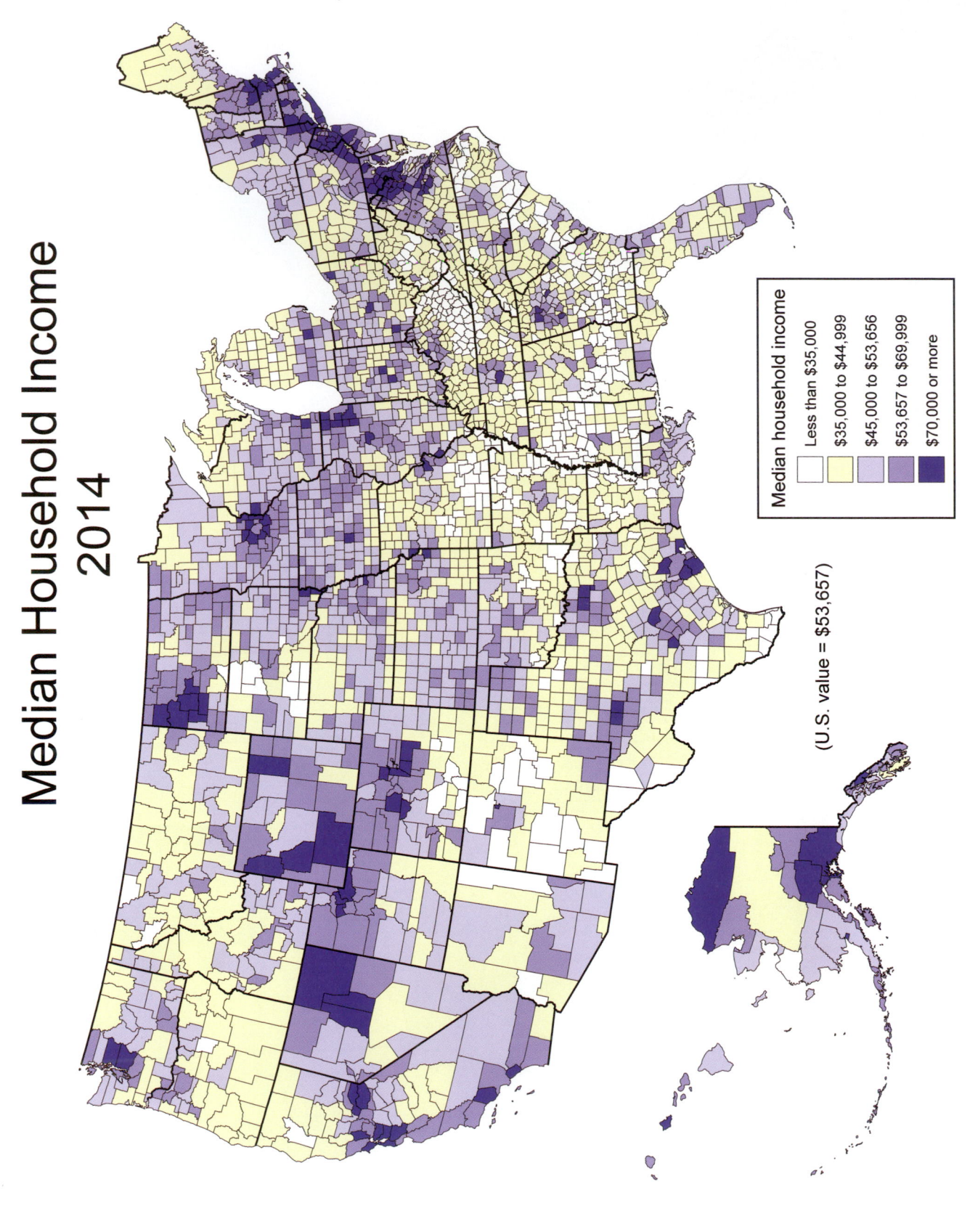

Median household income

☐	Less than $35,000
☐	$35,000 to $44,999
☐	$45,000 to $53,656
☐	$53,657 to $69,999
☐	$70,000 or more

(U.S. value = $53,657)

Percent in Poverty
2014

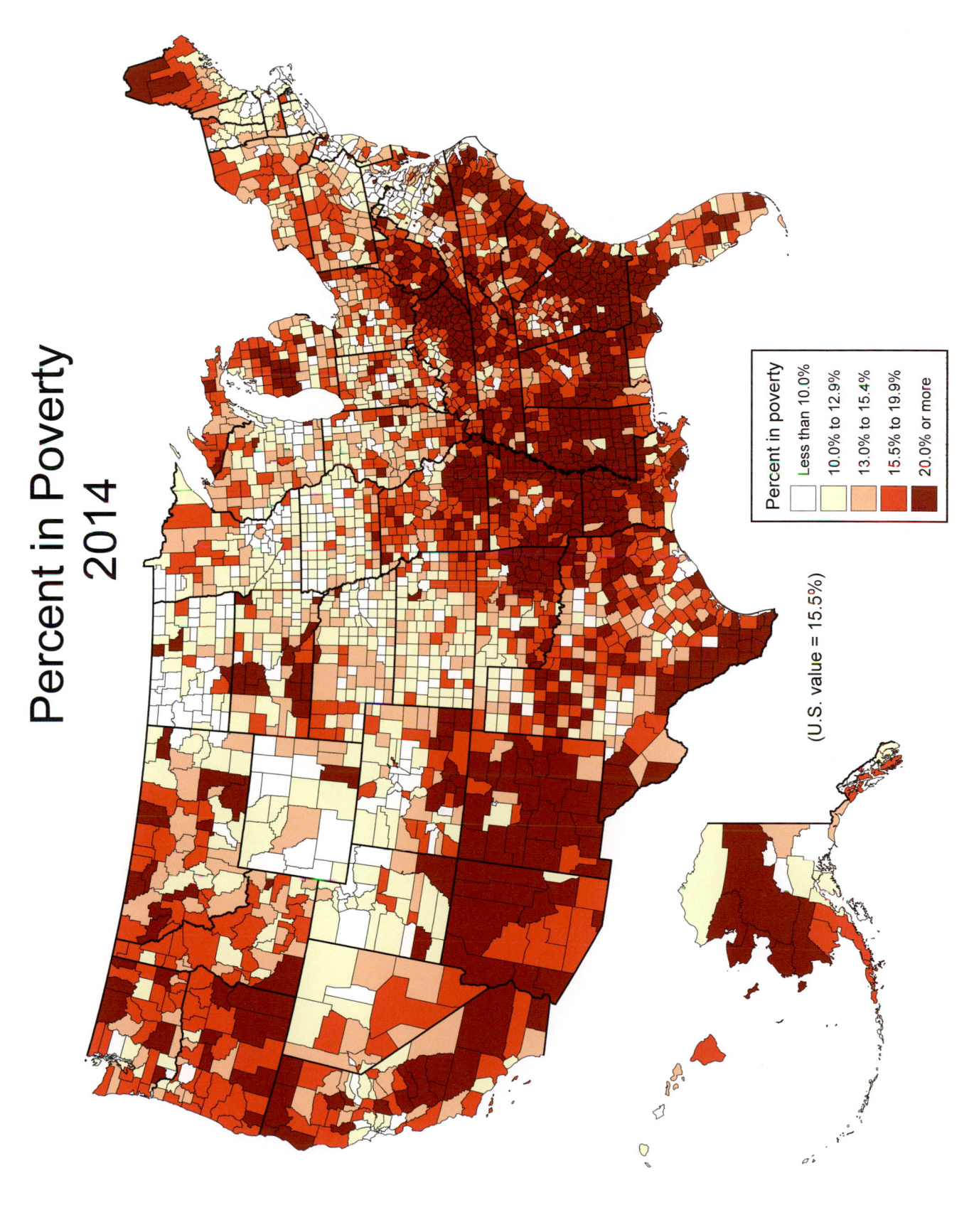

Percent in poverty

Less than 10.0%
10.0% to 12.9%
13.0% to 15.4%
15.5% to 19.9%
20.0% or more

(U.S. value = 15.5%)

Vote for President Obama
2012

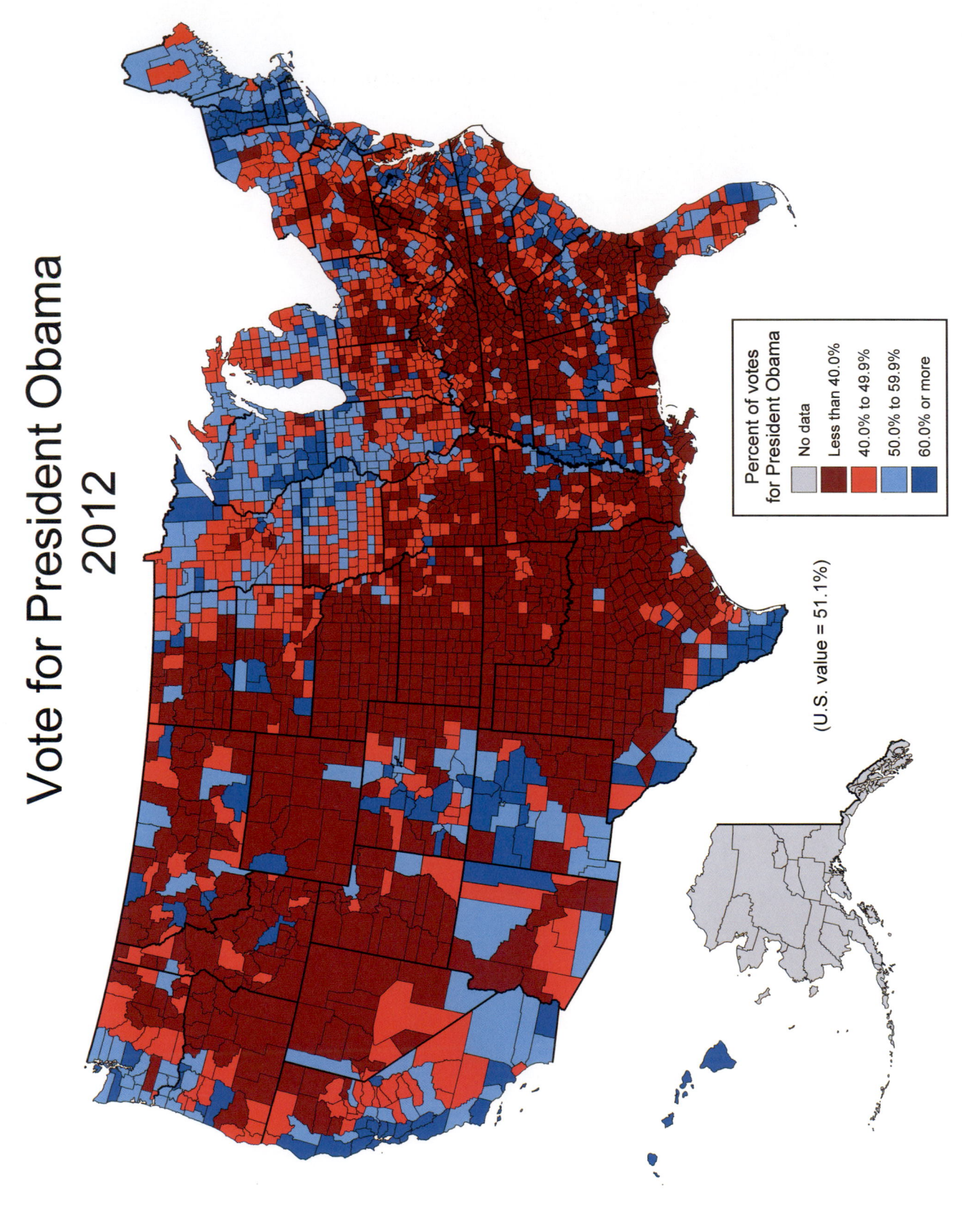

Percent of votes
for President Obama

No data
Less than 40.0%
40.0% to 49.9%
50.0% to 59.9%
60.0% or more

(U.S. value = 51.1%)

States

(For explanation of symbols, see page viii)

State Highlights and Rankings

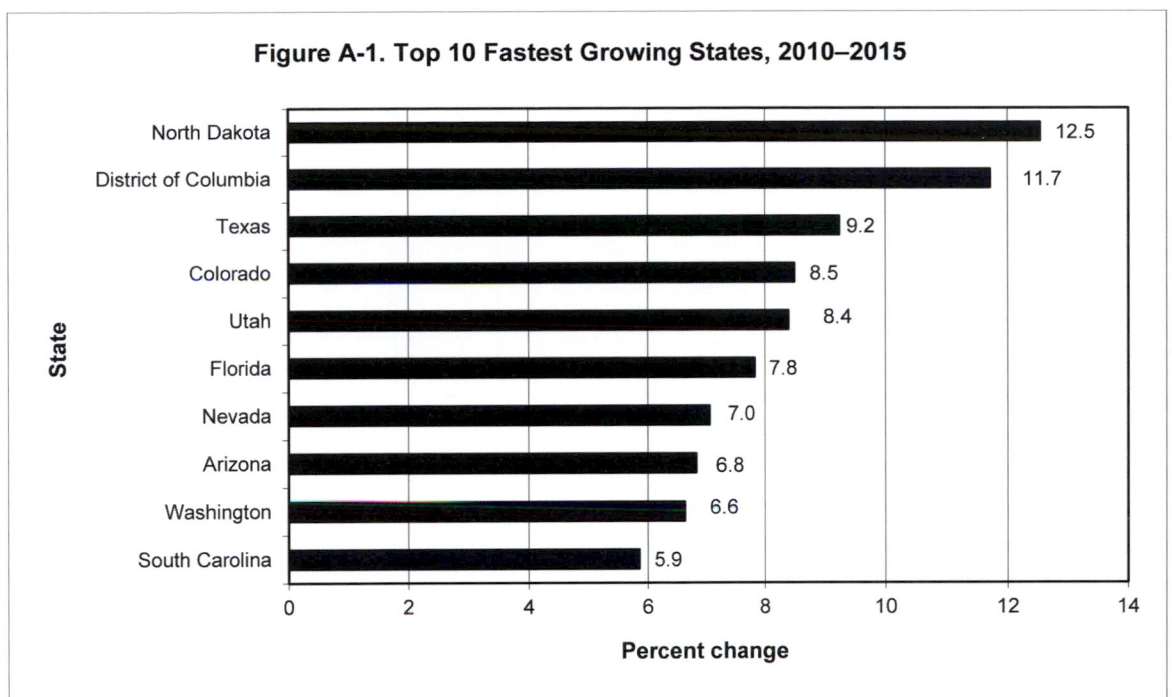

Figure A-1. Top 10 Fastest Growing States, 2010–2015

There is no simple relationship between population size and land area for most of the geographic entities included in this publication. According to the Census Bureau's 2015 estimates, state populations ranged from a high of over 39 million in California to a low of 586,107 in Wyoming. (The median population for states—with half having a larger population and half having a smaller population—was over 4.4 million people.) California was also one of the largest states in land area (ranking third). Alaska was by far the largest state in area; it was more than twice the size of Texas, the second-largest state, even though its population rank was close to the bottom (ranked 48th). Texas was also the second-largest state in terms of total population with over 27.0 million residents. At the other end of the geographic size spectrum were many of the New England states (with Rhode Island ranking as the smallest), plus Delaware, Hawaii, and New Jersey. As a consequence of differing area size and population rank, New Jersey was the most densely settled state, with 470.3 persons per square kilometer, while Alaska was the least densely settled, with about 0.5 persons per square kilometer. California, which had the largest population and third-largest land area, ranked 12th in terms of population density (97 persons per square kilometer). The 15 most populous states remained almost unchanged between 2010 and 2015—Arizona moved into the top 15 while Indiana dropped out—but there were changes within their ranks. Florida became the 3rd most populous state, pushing ahead of New York while Georgia became the 8th most populous state. North Carolina moved up to 9th place while Michigan dropped to 10th.

Not surprisingly, states with higher population density also had higher proportions of developed land. According to the Department of Agriculture's most recent National Resources Inventory, 35.4 percent of New Jersey's land was developed. Connecticut had the second highest proportion with 33.9 percent, followed by Massachusetts at 33.1 percent. Among the reporting states, Nevada had the lowest proportion of developed land, at just 0.8 percent, followed by Montana and Wyoming, with 1.1 percent

and 1.2 percent of their land developed. Nearly 85 percent of Nevada's land was owned by the federal government. This was by far the highest percentage in the nation. Federal land accounted for almost 21 percent of the United States' total land area. (Estimates are not available for Alaska, and the District of Columbia. See Appendix F for definitions and additional information.)

The total population of the United States increased 4.1 percent between 2010 and 2015, with 21 states matching or exceeding this rate of growth and the remainder growing more slowly. North Dakota and the District of Columbia experienced the highest growth rates (12.5 and 11.7 percent) even though they ranked 47th and 49th respectively in population among all the states. Despite its growth, North Dakota ranked 47th for total population and 48th for density. It was among 5 states with population densities of fewer than 5 persons per square kilometer. Texas and Florida ranked among the top 10 states for total population and for population growth from 2010 to 2015. Texas, with the second-largest population, grew by 9.2 percent, increasing its population by over 2.3 million people. Rhode Island and Vermont both ranked among the 10 least populous states, as well as among the 10 states with the lowest population growth between 2010 and 2015. While most states have increased their populations in the five years, West Virginia's population declined by a small amount. Nine other states experienced increases below one percent. Louisiana's population has rebounded from a loss of about 250,000 residents after Hurricane Katrina hit the state in August 2005. Its 2015 population of over 4.6 million is slightly higher than its 2005 estimated population on July 1 of that year.

States and the District of Columbia, Selected Rankings

Population, 2015			Land area, 2010				Population density, 2015			
Popu-lation rank	State	Popu-lation [col 2]	Popu-lation rank	Land area rank	State	Land area (square kilometers) [col 1]	Popu-lation rank	Density rank	State	Density (per square kilometer) [col 4]
	United States	321 418 820			United States	9 147 593			United States	35.1
1	California	39 144 818	48	1	Alaska	1 477 953	49	1	District of Columbia	4 254.6
2	Texas	27 469 114	2	2	Texas	676 587	11	2	New Jersey	470.3
3	Florida	20 271 272	1	3	California	403 466	43	3	Rhode Island	394.4
4	New York	19 795 791	44	4	Montana	376 962	15	4	Massachusetts	336.3
5	Illinois	12 859 995	36	5	New Mexico	314 161	29	5	Connecticut	286.3
6	Pennsylvania	12 802 503	14	6	Arizona	294 207	19	6	Maryland	238.9
7	Ohio	11 613 423	35	7	Nevada	284 332	45	7	Delaware	187.4
8	Georgia	10 214 860	22	8	Colorado	268 431	4	8	New York	162.2
9	North Carolina	10 042 802	51	9	Wyoming	251 470	3	9	Florida	146.0
10	Michigan	9 922 576	27	10	Oregon	248 608	6	10	Pennsylvania	110.5
11	New Jersey	8 958 013	39	11	Idaho	214 045	7	11	Ohio	109.7
12	Virginia	8 382 993	31	12	Utah	212 818	1	12	California	97.0
13	Washington	7 170 351	34	13	Kansas	211 754	5	13	Illinois	89.4
14	Arizona	6 828 065	21	14	Minnesota	206 232	40	14	Hawaii	86.1
15	Massachusetts	6 794 422	37	15	Nebraska	198 974	12	15	Virginia	82.0
16	Indiana	6 619 680	46	16	South Dakota	196 350	9	16	North Carolina	79.8
17	Tennessee	6 600 299	47	17	North Dakota	178 711	16	17	Indiana	71.3
18	Missouri	6 083 672	18	18	Missouri	178 040	8	18	Georgia	68.6
19	Maryland	6 006 401	28	19	Oklahoma	177 660	10	19	Michigan	67.8
20	Wisconsin	5 771 337	13	20	Washington	172 119	23	20	South Carolina	62.9
21	Minnesota	5 489 594	8	21	Georgia	148 959	17	21	Tennessee	61.8
22	Colorado	5 456 574	10	22	Michigan	146 435	41	22	New Hampshire	57.4
23	South Carolina	4 896 146	30	23	Iowa	144 669	26	23	Kentucky	43.3
24	Alabama	4 858 979	5	24	Illinois	143 793	25	24	Louisiana	41.7
25	Louisiana	4 670 724	20	25	Wisconsin	140 268	13	24	Washington	41.7
26	Kentucky	4 425 092	3	26	Florida	138 887	20	26	Wisconsin	41.1
27	Oregon	4 028 977	33	27	Arkansas	134 771	2	27	Texas	40.6
28	Oklahoma	3 911 338	24	28	Alabama	131 171	24	28	Alabama	37.0
29	Connecticut	3 590 886	9	29	North Carolina	125 920	18	29	Missouri	34.2
30	Iowa	3 123 899	4	30	New York	122 057	38	30	West Virginia	29.6
31	Utah	2 995 919	32	31	Mississippi	121 531	21	31	Minnesota	26.6
32	Mississippi	2 992 333	6	32	Pennsylvania	115 883	50	32	Vermont	26.2
33	Arkansas	2 978 204	25	33	Louisiana	111 898	32	33	Mississippi	24.6
34	Kansas	2 911 641	17	34	Tennessee	106 798	14	34	Arizona	23.2
35	Nevada	2 890 845	7	35	Ohio	105 829	33	35	Arkansas	22.1
36	New Mexico	2 085 109	12	36	Virginia	102 279	28	36	Oklahoma	22.0
37	Nebraska	1 896 190	26	37	Kentucky	102 269	30	37	Iowa	21.6
38	West Virginia	1 844 128	16	38	Indiana	92 789	22	38	Colorado	20.3
39	Idaho	1 654 930	42	39	Maine	79 883	42	39	Maine	16.6
40	Hawaii	1 431 603	23	40	South Carolina	77 857	27	40	Oregon	16.2
41	New Hampshire	1 330 608	38	41	West Virginia	62 259	31	41	Utah	14.1
42	Maine	1 329 328	19	42	Maryland	25 142	34	42	Kansas	13.8
43	Rhode Island	1 056 298	50	43	Vermont	23 871	35	43	Nevada	10.2
44	Montana	1 032 949	41	44	New Hampshire	23 187	37	44	Nebraska	9.5
45	Delaware	945 934	15	45	Massachusetts	20 202	39	45	Idaho	7.7
46	South Dakota	858 469	11	46	New Jersey	19 047	36	46	New Mexico	6.6
47	North Dakota	756 927	40	47	Hawaii	16 635	46	47	South Dakota	4.4
48	Alaska	738 432	29	48	Connecticut	12 542	47	48	North Dakota	4.2
49	District of Columbia	672 228	45	49	Delaware	5 047	44	49	Montana	2.7
50	Vermont	626 042	43	50	Rhode Island	2 678	51	50	Wyoming	2.3
51	Wyoming	586 107	49	51	District of Columbia	158	48	51	Alaska	0.5

States and the District of Columbia, Selected Rankings

	Percent population change, 2010-2015				Percent under 18 years old, 2014				Percent 65 years old and over, 2014		
Population rank	Percent change rank	State	Percent change [col 36]	Population rank	Under 18 years old rank	State	Percent under 18 years old [cols 10 + 11]	Population rank	65 years old and over rank	State	Percent 65 years old and over [cols 17 + 18 + 19]
		United States	4.1			United States	23.0			United States	14.5
47	1	North Dakota	12.5	31	1	Utah	30.8	3	1	Florida	19.1
49	2	District of Columbia	11.7	39	2	Idaho	26.4	42	2	Maine	18.4
2	3	Texas	9.2	2	2	Texas	26.4	38	3	West Virginia	17.8
22	4	Colorado	8.5	48	4	Alaska	25.3	50	4	Vermont	17.0
31	5	Utah	8.4	34	5	Kansas	24.9	6	5	Pennsylvania	16.7
3	6	Florida	7.8	37	6	Nebraska	24.8	44	6	Montana	16.6
35	7	Nevada	7.0	8	7	Georgia	24.7	45	7	Delaware	16.4
14	8	Arizona	6.8	46	7	South Dakota	24.7	40	8	Hawaii	16.0
13	9	Washington	6.6	28	9	Oklahoma	24.5	14	9	Arizona	15.9
23	10	South Carolina	5.9	32	10	Mississippi	24.4	41	9	New Hampshire	15.9
39	11	Idaho	5.6	14	11	Arizona	24.1	27	9	Oregon	15.9
8	12	Georgia	5.4	36	11	New Mexico	24.1	33	12	Arkansas	15.8
46	12	South Dakota	5.4	16	13	Indiana	24.0	30	12	Iowa	15.8
45	14	Delaware	5.3	33	14	Arkansas	23.9	43	12	Rhode Island	15.8
9	14	North Carolina	5.3	25	14	Louisiana	23.9	23	12	South Carolina	15.8
40	16	Hawaii	5.2	1	16	California	23.6	7	16	Ohio	15.6
27	16	Oregon	5.2	51	16	Wyoming	23.6	29	17	Connecticut	15.5
1	18	California	5.1	21	18	Minnesota	23.5	10	18	Michigan	15.4
12	19	Virginia	4.8	30	19	Iowa	23.4	18	18	Missouri	15.4
44	20	Montana	4.4	22	20	Colorado	23.3	24	20	Alabama	15.3
28	21	Oklahoma	4.3	35	20	Nevada	23.3	36	20	New Mexico	15.3
48	22	Alaska	4.0	5	22	Illinois	23.2	46	22	South Dakota	15.2
19	22	Maryland	4.0	26	23	Kentucky	23.0	20	22	Wisconsin	15.2
17	22	Tennessee	4.0	18	23	Missouri	23.0	17	24	Tennessee	15.1
51	22	Wyoming	4.0	9	23	North Carolina	23.0	15	25	Massachusetts	15.0
15	26	Massachusetts	3.8	24	26	Alabama	22.9	26	26	Kentucky	14.8
37	26	Nebraska	3.8	47	27	North Dakota	22.8	11	27	New Jersey	14.7
21	28	Minnesota	3.5	7	27	Ohio	22.8	4	27	New York	14.7
25	29	Louisiana	3.0	17	27	Tennessee	22.8	9	27	North Carolina	14.7
30	30	Iowa	2.5	13	30	Washington	22.7	28	30	Oklahoma	14.5
4	31	New York	2.2	19	31	Maryland	22.6	37	31	Nebraska	14.4
33	32	Arkansas	2.1	11	31	New Jersey	22.6	39	32	Idaho	14.3
16	32	Indiana	2.1	20	31	Wisconsin	22.6	34	32	Kansas	14.3
34	32	Kansas	2.1	10	34	Michigan	22.5	32	32	Mississippi	14.3
26	35	Kentucky	2.0	12	34	Virginia	22.5	16	35	Indiana	14.2
11	36	New Jersey	1.9	23	36	South Carolina	22.4	21	35	Minnesota	14.2
24	37	Alabama	1.7	44	37	Montana	22.0	35	37	Nevada	14.1
18	38	Missouri	1.6	45	38	Delaware	21.8	47	37	North Dakota	14.1
20	39	Wisconsin	1.5	40	39	Hawaii	21.7	13	37	Washington	14.1
36	40	New Mexico	1.3	29	40	Connecticut	21.6	51	40	Wyoming	14.0
41	41	New Hampshire	1.1	27	40	Oregon	21.6	5	41	Illinois	13.9
32	42	Mississippi	0.8	4	42	New York	21.4	12	41	Virginia	13.9
6	42	Pennsylvania	0.8	6	43	Pennsylvania	21.1	19	43	Maryland	13.8
7	44	Ohio	0.7	15	44	Massachusetts	20.6	25	44	Louisiana	13.6
29	45	Connecticut	0.5	38	45	West Virginia	20.5	1	45	California	12.9
10	46	Michigan	0.4	3	46	Florida	20.4	22	46	Colorado	12.7
43	46	Rhode Island	0.4	41	47	New Hampshire	20.2	8	47	Georgia	12.4
5	48	Illinois	0.2	43	47	Rhode Island	20.2	2	48	Texas	11.5
42	49	Maine	0.1	42	49	Maine	19.5	49	49	District of Columbia	11.3
50	50	Vermont	0.0	50	49	Vermont	19.5	31	50	Utah	10.1
38	51	West Virginia	-0.5	49	51	District of Columbia	17.5	48	51	Alaska	9.4

States and the District of Columbia, Selected Rankings

Percent born in state of residence, 2014				Number of immigrants, 2014				Birth rate, 2014			
Popu-lation rank	Born in state of residence rank	State	Percent born in state of residence [col 23]	Popu-lation rank	Immigrant rank	State	Number of immigrants [col 24]	Popu-lation rank	Birth rate rank	State	Birth rate (per 1,000 population) [col 98]
		United States	58.7			United States	1 016 518			United States	12.5
25	1	Louisiana	77.7	1	1	California	198 379	31	1	Utah	17.4
10	2	Michigan	76.7	4	2	New York	141 406	48	2	Alaska	15.5
7	3	Ohio	75.1	3	3	Florida	109 310	47	3	North Dakota	15.4
6	4	Pennsylvania	73.4	2	4	Texas	95 295	2	4	Texas	14.8
32	5	Mississippi	71.5	11	5	New Jersey	51 609	49	5	District of Columbia	14.4
30	6	Iowa	71.2	5	6	Illinois	36 535	46	5	South Dakota	14.4
20	7	Wisconsin	71.2	15	7	Massachusetts	29 776	37	7	Nebraska	14.2
24	8	Alabama	70.3	12	8	Virginia	28 477	39	8	Idaho	14.0
38	9	West Virginia	70.2	19	9	Maryland	24 787	25	9	Louisiana	13.9
26	10	Kentucky	69.6	6	10	Pennsylvania	23 944	28	10	Oklahoma	13.8
16	11	Indiana	68.3	8	11	Georgia	23 792	34	11	Kansas	13.5
21	12	Minnesota	68.2	13	12	Washington	22 710	51	12	Wyoming	13.2
5	13	Illinois	67.3	10	13	Michigan	18 185	40	13	Hawaii	13.1
18	14	Missouri	66.1	9	14	North Carolina	17 152	33	14	Arkansas	13.0
37	15	Nebraska	65.2	14	15	Arizona	16 908	1	14	California	13.0
46	16	South Dakota	65.1	7	16	Ohio	14 641	8	14	Georgia	13.0
47	17	North Dakota	65.0	21	17	Minnesota	13 764	14	17	Arizona	12.9
42	18	Maine	63.3	29	18	Connecticut	11 252	32	17	Mississippi	12.9
4	19	New York	63.3	22	19	Colorado	10 872	30	19	Iowa	12.8
31	20	Utah	62.2	35	20	Nevada	10 089	21	19	Minnesota	12.8
15	21	Massachusetts	61.8	17	21	Tennessee	8 507	16	21	Indiana	12.7
33	22	Arkansas	61.1	16	22	Indiana	8 008	26	21	Kentucky	12.7
17	23	Tennessee	60.9	27	23	Oregon	7 379	35	23	Nevada	12.6
28	24	Oklahoma	60.8	18	24	Missouri	6 419	36	24	New Mexico	12.5
2	25	Texas	60.1	31	25	Utah	6 166	17	24	Tennessee	12.5
34	26	Kansas	58.6	20	26	Wisconsin	5 997	13	24	Washington	12.5
43	27	Rhode Island	58.3	40	27	Hawaii	5 741	19	27	Maryland	12.4
23	28	South Carolina	57.7	26	28	Kentucky	5 634	18	27	Missouri	12.4
9	29	North Carolina	57.5	34	29	Kansas	4 861	12	27	Virginia	12.4
8	30	Georgia	55.6	37	30	Nebraska	4 442	24	30	Alabama	12.3
29	31	Connecticut	55.4	28	31	Oklahoma	4 441	22	30	Colorado	12.3
1	32	California	55.0	25	32	Louisiana	4 382	5	30	Illinois	12.3
44	33	Montana	54.3	23	33	South Carolina	4 233	9	33	North Carolina	12.2
40	34	Hawaii	53.1	30	34	Iowa	4 225	44	34	Montana	12.1
36	35	New Mexico	52.9	24	35	Alabama	3 685	4	34	New York	12.1
11	36	New Jersey	52.7	36	36	New Mexico	3 359	7	36	Ohio	12.0
50	37	Vermont	52.3	43	37	Rhode Island	3 297	23	37	South Carolina	11.9
12	38	Virginia	49.2	49	38	District of Columbia	3 169	45	38	Delaware	11.7
39	39	Idaho	48.5	33	39	Arkansas	2 793	20	38	Wisconsin	11.7
13	40	Washington	47.7	39	40	Idaho	2 202	11	40	New Jersey	11.6
19	41	Maryland	47.5	41	41	New Hampshire	2 103	10	41	Michigan	11.5
27	42	Oregon	46.0	45	42	Delaware	2 085	27	41	Oregon	11.5
45	43	Delaware	45.6	32	43	Mississippi	1 587	3	43	Florida	11.1
22	44	Colorado	42.9	48	44	Alaska	1 505	6	43	Pennsylvania	11.1
41	45	New Hampshire	42.7	42	45	Maine	1 382	38	45	West Virginia	11.0
48	46	Alaska	41.3	47	46	North Dakota	1 351	15	46	Massachusetts	10.7
51	47	Wyoming	41.0	46	47	South Dakota	1 108	43	47	Rhode Island	10.3
14	48	Arizona	39.0	50	48	Vermont	791	29	48	Connecticut	10.1
49	49	District of Columbia	36.2	38	49	West Virginia	783	50	49	Vermont	9.8
3	50	Florida	36.1	44	50	Montana	451	42	50	Maine	9.5
35	51	Nevada	25.8	51	51	Wyoming	414	41	51	New Hampshire	9.3

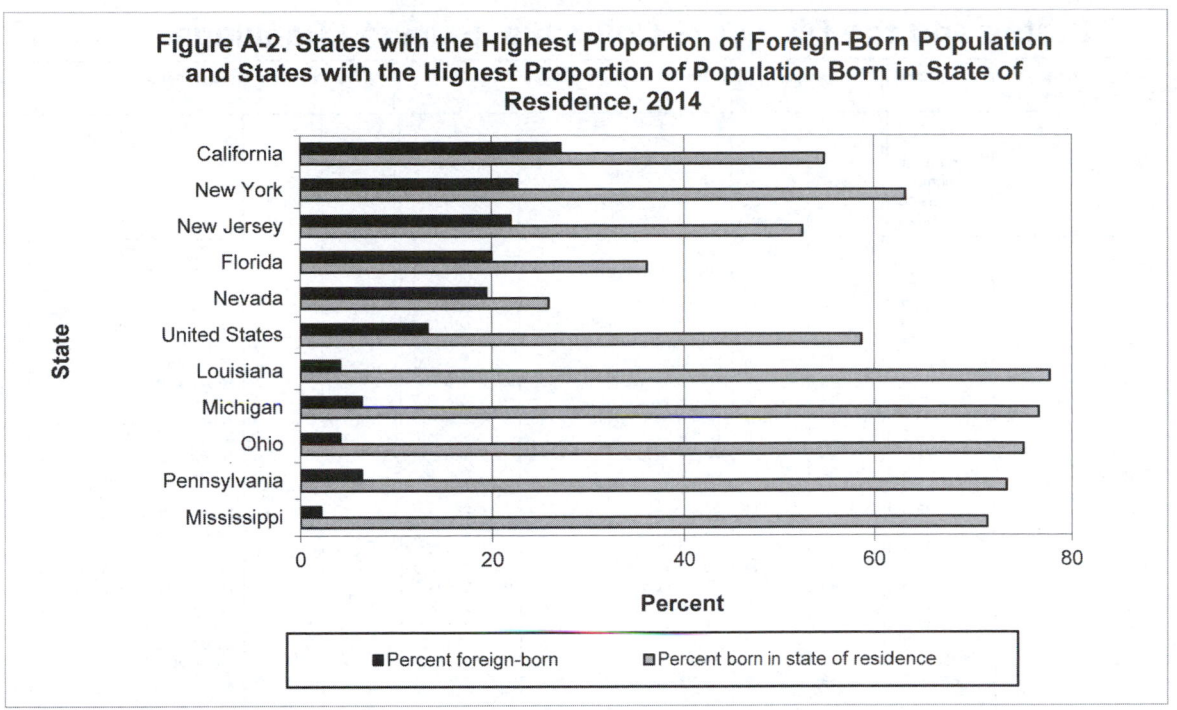

Figure A-2. States with the Highest Proportion of Foreign-Born Population and States with the Highest Proportion of Population Born in State of Residence, 2014

■ Percent foreign-born   □ Percent born in state of residence

The U.S. median age increased slightly from 37.2 years in 2010 to 37.7 years in 2014, primarily caused by the aging Baby Boomer population. This increase was much less than the jump from 32.1 years to 35.3 years between 1990 and 2000. From 2010 to 2014, the population between 65 and 74 years showed the largest proportional increase, while the proportion between 5 and 17 and 45 and 54 showed the largest decrease. There were small increases in the young adult age groups, ages 18 to 34, with the 25 to 34 Millennial group now proportionally equal to the younger Baby Boomers in the 45 to 54 age group and outnumbering the peak Baby Boomers in the 55 to 64 age group. The median age by state ranged from 30.5 years in Utah to 44.2 years in Maine. Utah had the highest proportion of young residents; in 2014, 31.5 percent of the state's population was younger than 18 years old. The population age 65 years and over ranged from 7.7 percent in Alaska to 17.3 percent in Florida. Alaska, North Dakota, Wyoming, and Nevada had the lowest proportions of female residents, and were among just nine states in which men outnumbered women. District of Columbia had the highest proportion of female residents with 52.8 percent, followed by Rhode Island with 51.7 percent.

Natural growth is the difference between the number of births and the number of deaths. Vermont had the fewest births between 2010 and 2015. Maine and West Virginia were the only states to have more deaths than births. A net migration of more than 2,898 people prevented Maine from having a population loss from 2010 to 2015 but West Virginia did experience a population decline. California, the largest state in the nation, had over 1.3 million more births than deaths and 568,884 new residents through net migration. From 2010 to 2015, California gained 834,999 residents from foreign countries and lost 266,155 residents to other states. Texas and Florida each had a net gain of over 1.1 million new residents during this period. In Texas, 61.4 percent of these new residents were from other states; in Florida, over half were from other states. Fourteen states had a net loss of residents due to migration including New York which lost over 653,000 residents to other states but gained over 630,000 new residents from other countries.

In nine states, 70 percent or more of the residents were born in that same state. Louisiana ranked highest with 77.7 percent. The ten highest rates were mainly in the Midwest and the South. Thirteen states and the District of Columbia had proportions less than 50 percent. Nevada had the lowest proportion by far, with just 25.8 percent of its residents having been born in the state. Nationally, 58.7 percent of Americans lived in the state of their birth.

The U.S. birth rate in 2014 was 12.5 per 1,000 population, a slight increase from 2013 and the first increase in several years. Utah had the highest birth rate in the nation, with 17.4 births per 1,000 population. Alaska had the second highest birth rate at 15.5 followed by North Dakota with a birth rate of 15.4. Maine, Vermont, and New Hampshire had the lowest birth rates in the nation, all below 10 births per 1,000 population. Alaska had the lowest crude death rate with 5.4 deaths per 1,000 population followed by Utah at 5.6 deaths. However, both states had relatively young populations (In Utah, 43.0 percent of the population was under 25 years old while 36.9 percent of the population was under 25 in Alaska). Once adjusted for age, Alaska's death rate increased to 7.2, and Utah's to 7.1, just under the U.S. rate of 7.3. West Virginia, Alabama, and Arkansas had the highest crude death rates in the nation. Mississippi had the highest age-adjusted death rate followed by Alabama, both with a mix of younger and older residents. Florida had, by far, the highest proportion of senior citizens. However, Florida also had a high proportion of younger people, which helped give the state a crude death rate of 9.3 per 1,000 population, ranking it 15th among the states. When Florida's death rate was age-adjusted, it dropped to 6.6, which was well below the national age-adjusted rate of 7.3 and among the lowest 8 states. Hawaii had the lowest age-adjusted death rate at 5.9, one of 13 states with rates below 7.0. Mississippi, Louisiana, and Alabama, had the highest infant mortality rates, while Iowa, Massachusetts, and Vermont had the lowest infant death rates.

States and the District of Columbia, Selected Rankings

Percent of owners with a mortgage paying 30 percent or more of income for housing expenses, 2014				Median value of owner-occupied housing units, 2014				Median gross rent of renter-occupied housing units, 2014			
Popu-lation rank	Percent of income for housing rank	State	Percent of income for housing [col 83]	Popu-lation rank	Median value rank	State	Median value (dollars) [col 88]	Popu-lation rank	Median rent rank	State	Median rent (dollars) [col 90]
		United States	30.7			United States	181 200			United States	934
1	1	California	40.3	40	1	Hawaii	528 000	40	1	Hawaii	1 448
40	1	Hawaii	40.3	49	2	District of Columbia	486 900	49	2	District of Columbia	1 360
11	3	New Jersey........................	39.3	1	3	California	412 700	1	3	California	1 268
4	4	New York	37.1	15	4	Massachusetts..................	338 900	19	4	Maryland	1 242
3	5	Florida	36.9	11	5	New Jersey.......................	313 200	11	5	New Jersey.......................	1 202
43	6	Rhode Island	36.8	19	6	Maryland	288 500	48	6	Alaska	1 183
50	7	Vermont	35.4	4	7	New York	279 100	4	7	New York	1 148
29	8	Connecticut	34.0	29	8	Connecticut.......................	267 200	12	8	Virginia	1 116
27	9	Oregon	32.7	13	9	Washington	266 200	15	9	Massachusetts..................	1 107
15	10	Massachusetts..................	32.5	22	10	Colorado	255 200	29	10	Connecticut.......................	1 076
41	10	New Hampshire	32.5	48	11	Alaska	254 500	13	11	Washington	1 032
36	12	New Mexico.......................	32.1	12	12	Virginia	247 800	45	12	Delaware	1 024
35	13	Nevada..............................	32.0	27	13	Oregon	239 800	22	13	Colorado	1 020
13	14	Washington........................	31.5	41	14	New Hampshire.................	236 400	3	14	Florida	1 003
5	15	Illinois...............................	31.4	43	15	Rhode Island	236 000	41	15	New Hampshire.................	994
42	15	Maine	31.4	45	16	Delaware	230 500	35	16	Nevada..............................	955
45	17	Delaware...........................	31.1	31	17	Utah	223 200	43	17	Rhode Island	934
19	18	Maryland	30.9	50	18	Vermont	214 600	27	18	Oregon	924
44	19	Montana	30.5	51	19	Wyoming	201 000	50	19	Vermont	917
32	20	Mississippi	30.4	44	20	Montana............................	196 800	14	20	Arizona	916
8	21	Georgia	29.4	35	21	Nevada	192 100	5	21	Illinois...............................	905
23	22	South Carolina..................	29.3	21	22	Minnesota	188 300	2	22	Texas................................	896
14	23	Arizona	29.1	14	23	Arizona	176 700	31	23	Utah	886
17	24	Tennessee	29.0	42	24	Maine	174 800	8	24	Georgia	882
22	25	Colorado	28.9	5	25	Illinois...............................	171 900	21	25	Minnesota	859
6	26	Pennsylvania	28.5	6	26	Pennsylvania	165 400	6	26	Pennsylvania	848
12	26	Virginia	28.5	39	27	Idaho................................	165 300	9	27	North Carolina	803
9	28	North Carolina	28.3	20	28	Wisconsin	164 700	25	28	Louisiana	801
25	29	Louisiana	28.1	3	29	Florida	162 700	51	29	Wyoming	792
24	30	Alabama............................	28.0	47	30	North Dakota	161 800	23	30	South Carolina..................	791
20	31	Wisconsin	27.9	36	31	New Mexico.......................	158 400	10	31	Michigan	788
31	32	Utah	27.3	9	32	North Carolina	155 000	20	32	Wisconsin	782
39	33	Idaho................................	27.1	8	33	Georgia	147 900	36	33	New Mexico.......................	777
2	34	Texas................................	27.0	25	34	Louisiana	143 600	42	34	Maine	776
48	35	Alaska	26.9	17	35	Tennessee	142 900	34	35	Kansas..............................	773
49	36	District of Columbia	26.4	46	36	South Dakota....................	142 300	17	36	Tennessee	770
10	36	Michigan	26.4	23	37	South Carolina..................	140 000	39	37	Idaho................................	755
26	38	Kentucky	25.7	2	38	Texas................................	139 600	18	38	Missouri	754
18	39	Missouri	25.2	18	39	Missouri	138 500	16	39	Indiana	753
21	40	Minnesota	24.8	37	40	Nebraska	133 800	37	40	Nebraska	742
7	41	Ohio..................................	24.7	30	41	Iowa	133 100	28	41	Oklahoma	737
28	42	Oklahoma	24.6	34	42	Kansas..............................	132 100	7	42	Ohio..................................	735
33	43	Arkansas...........................	24.4	7	43	Ohio..................................	129 100	47	43	North Dakota	728
51	44	Wyoming	23.6	10	44	Michigan	125 700	24	44	Alabama............................	717
34	45	Kansas..............................	23.5	24	45	Alabama	125 600	30	45	Iowa	711
37	46	Nebraska	22.9	16	46	Indiana	124 300	32	45	Mississippi	711
38	47	West Virginia	22.7	26	47	Kentucky	123 800	44	45	Montana	711
16	48	Indiana	22.6	28	48	Oklahoma	119 800	33	48	Arkansas...........................	683
46	49	South Dakota	22.5	33	49	Arkansas...........................	112 500	26	49	Kentucky	678
30	50	Iowa	20.8	32	50	Mississippi	104 000	38	50	West Virginia	656
47	51	North Dakota	16.3	38	51	West Virginia	103 900	46	51	South Dakota....................	647

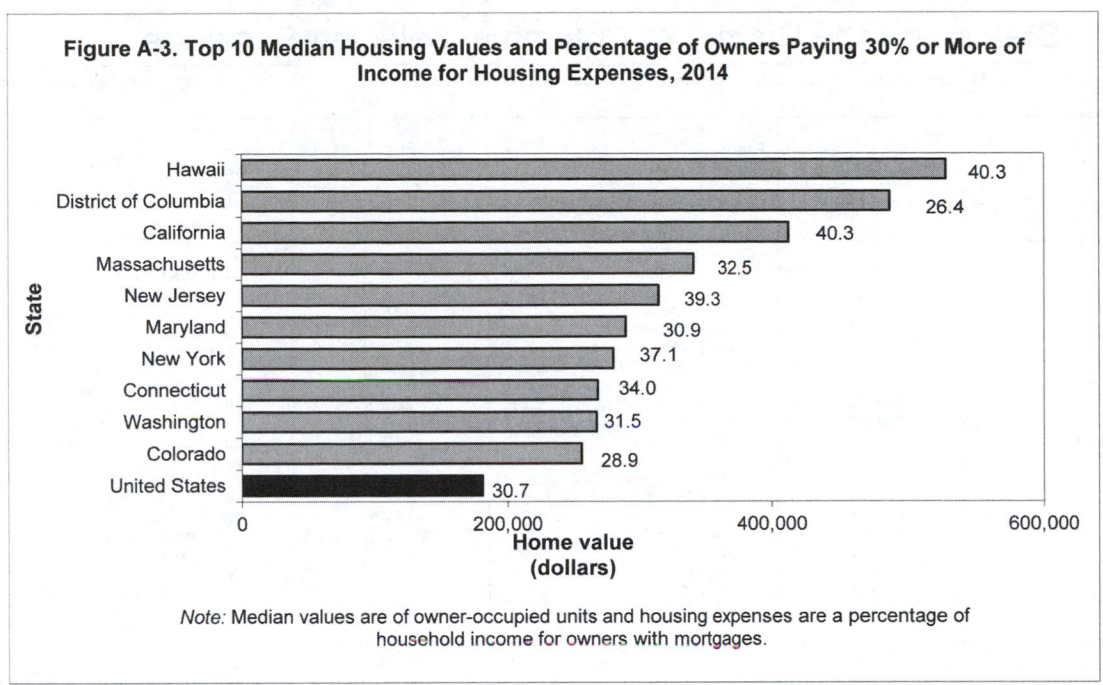

Figure A-3. Top 10 Median Housing Values and Percentage of Owners Paying 30% or More of Income for Housing Expenses, 2014

State	Percentage
Hawaii	40.3
District of Columbia	26.4
California	40.3
Massachusetts	32.5
New Jersey	39.3
Maryland	30.9
New York	37.1
Connecticut	34.0
Washington	31.5
Colorado	28.9
United States	30.7

Home value (dollars)

Note: Median values are of owner-occupied units and housing expenses are a percentage of household income for owners with mortgages.

In 2014, homeowners with mortgages paid a median of 22.5 percent of their incomes for monthly owner costs (mortgage, insurance, taxes, utilities, fuel, etc.). This ranged from a high of 26.7 percent in Hawaii to 18.1 percent in North Dakota. Nationally, 30.7 percent of owners with a mortgage paid 30 percent or more of income for housing expenses in 2014. California and Hawaii had the highest proportion of mortgage holders paying 30 percent or more of their income with 40.3 percent, followed by New Jersey at 39.3 percent, New York at 37.1 percent and Florida at 36.9 percent. In 30 states and the District of Columbia, less than 30 percent of all mortgaged owners paid this high level of owner costs. North Dakota had the lowest proportion in the nation with 16.3 percent. Four states and the District of Columbia had median home values exceeding $300,000 in 2014, led by Hawaii with a median home value of $528,000. Nationally, the median value of owner-occupied housing units was $181,200. Hawaii also had the highest median gross rent, at $1,448. The District of Columbia, Hawaii, California, Maryland, and New Jersey all had median gross monthly rents exceeding $1,200.

Many minority groups had above average growth rates since 2000. Currently, in four states and the District of Columbia, the minority population outnumbers the non-Hispanic White population. Nationally, 63.8 percent of the U.S. population was non-Hispanic White alone or in combination, but the racial and ethnic compositions of the states varied widely. In Hawaii, the state with the highest proportion of minorities, Asian and Pacific Islander alone or in combination was the largest race group, representing 74 percent of the state's population. Hispanic or Latino residents made up over 47 percent of New Mexico's population and over 38 percent of residents in both California and Texas. The District of Columbia had the highest proportion of Black residents at just under half the population at 48.7 percent, down from 60.5 percent in 2000. Among the states, Mississippi and Louisiana ranked first and second, with Black populations of 37.8 and 32.8 percent, respectively. Alaska had the highest proportion of American Indians and Alaska Natives, who made up 18.4 percent of the population. Montana, New Mexico, and South Dakota all had high proportions of American Indian populations. As might be expected, the states with the largest number of minorities were among the states with the

highest total populations. New York was home to approximately 3.1 million Black residents, and California had the largest number of Hispanics, Asian and Pacific Islanders, and American Indians and Alaska Natives. California had over 390,000 non-Hispanic American Indian and Alaska Native residents, though they made up just 1.0 percent of the state's population. Despite having only about 82,000 Native American residents, South Dakota had the second highest proportion in the nation.

States and the District of Columbia, Selected Rankings

Percent White, not Hispanic or Latino, alone or in combination, 2014				Percent Black, not Hispanic or Latino, alone or in combination, 2014				Percent Hispanic or Latino,[1] 2014			
Population rank	Percent White rank	State	Percent White [col 5]	Population rank	Percent Black rank	State	Percent Black [col 6]	Population rank	Hispanic or Latino rank	State	Percent Hispanic or Latino [col 9]
		United States	63.8			United States	13.3			United States	17.4
42	1	Maine	95.2	49	1	District of Columbia	48.7	36	1	New Mexico	47.7
50	2	Vermont	95.1	32	2	Mississippi	37.8	1	2	California	38.6
38	3	West Virginia	94.0	25	3	Louisiana	32.8	2	2	Texas	38.6
41	4	New Hampshire	92.6	8	4	Georgia	31.7	14	4	Arizona	30.6
44	5	Montana	89.0	19	5	Maryland	30.6	35	5	Nevada	27.8
30	6	Iowa	88.5	23	6	South Carolina	28.2	3	6	Florida	24.1
47	7	North Dakota	88.2	24	7	Alabama	27.1	22	7	Colorado	21.2
26	8	Kentucky	86.9	45	8	Delaware	22.6	11	8	New Jersey	19.3
51	9	Wyoming	85.6	9	9	North Carolina	22.4	4	9	New York	18.6
46	10	South Dakota	84.9	12	10	Virginia	20.2	5	10	Illinois	16.7
39	11	Idaho	84.6	17	11	Tennessee	17.6	29	11	Connecticut	15.1
20	12	Wisconsin	83.6	3	12	Florida	16.4	43	12	Rhode Island	14.0
21	13	Minnesota	83.4	33	13	Arkansas	16.1	31	13	Utah	13.5
37	14	Nebraska	82.0	4	14	New York	15.5	27	14	Oregon	12.5
16	15	Indiana	81.9	10	15	Michigan	15.0	13	15	Washington	12.2
18	15	Missouri	81.9	5	16	Illinois	14.9	39	16	Idaho	12.0
7	15	Ohio	81.9	11	17	New Jersey	13.6	34	17	Kansas	11.4
31	18	Utah	81.1	7	18	Ohio	13.5	15	18	Massachusetts	10.8
27	19	Oregon	79.9	6	19	Pennsylvania	12.8	49	19	District of Columbia	10.4
6	20	Pennsylvania	79.2	18	20	Missouri	12.5	37	20	Nebraska	10.2
34	21	Kansas	79.0	2	21	Texas	12.3	40	21	Hawaii	10.1
10	22	Michigan	77.6	29	22	Connecticut	10.8	28	22	Oklahoma	9.8
43	23	Rhode Island	76.2	16	23	Indiana	10.2	51	22	Wyoming	9.8
17	24	Tennessee	76.1	35	24	Nevada	9.4	8	24	Georgia	9.3
15	25	Massachusetts	75.7	26	25	Kentucky	9.0	19	24	Maryland	9.3
33	26	Arkansas	75.0	15	26	Massachusetts	7.6	9	26	North Carolina	9.0
13	27	Washington	73.8	20	27	Wisconsin	7.1	45	27	Delaware	8.9
28	28	Oklahoma	71.9	34	28	Kansas	7.0	12	27	Virginia	8.9
22	29	Colorado	70.9	43	29	Rhode Island	6.8	33	29	Arkansas	7.0
29	30	Connecticut	70.3	21	30	Minnesota	6.7	48	30	Alaska	6.8
48	31	Alaska	67.7	1	31	California	6.5	16	31	Indiana	6.6
24	32	Alabama	67.5	37	32	Nebraska	5.5	6	31	Pennsylvania	6.6
9	33	North Carolina	65.6	14	33	Arizona	4.9	20	33	Wisconsin	6.5
45	34	Delaware	65.5	13	33	Washington	4.9	30	34	Iowa	5.6
12	35	Virginia	65.3	48	35	Alaska	4.8	23	35	South Carolina	5.4
23	36	South Carolina	65.2	22	35	Colorado	4.8	21	36	Minnesota	5.1
5	37	Illinois	63.6	38	37	West Virginia	4.4	17	37	Tennessee	5.0
25	38	Louisiana	60.5	30	38	Iowa	4.1	25	38	Louisiana	4.8
32	39	Mississippi	58.2	40	39	Hawaii	3.2	10	38	Michigan	4.8
14	40	Arizona	58.0	28	40	Oklahoma	2.9	24	40	Alabama	4.1
11	40	New Jersey	58.0	47	41	North Dakota	2.5	18	41	Missouri	4.0
4	42	New York	57.8	46	42	South Dakota	2.4	46	42	South Dakota	3.6
3	43	Florida	57.1	36	43	New Mexico	2.3	44	43	Montana	3.5
8	44	Georgia	55.8	42	44	Maine	1.8	7	43	Ohio	3.5
19	45	Maryland	54.5	51	44	Wyoming	1.8	26	45	Kentucky	3.4
35	46	Nevada	54.1	41	46	New Hampshire	1.7	41	46	New Hampshire	3.3
2	47	Texas	44.7	50	46	Vermont	1.7	47	47	North Dakota	3.2
1	48	California	40.7	31	48	Utah	1.5	32	48	Mississippi	3.0
36	49	New Mexico	40.2	39	49	Idaho	1.1	50	49	Vermont	1.8
49	50	District of Columbia	37.5	44	50	Montana	1.0	42	50	Maine	1.5
40	51	Hawaii	36.7	27	51	Oregon	0.9	38	50	West Virginia	1.5

1. May be of any race.

States and the District of Columbia, Selected Rankings

Percent high school graduates or more,[1] 2014				Percent college graduates (bachelor's degree or more),[1] 2014				Median household income, 2014			
Population rank	Percent high school graduates rank	State	Percent high school graduates [col 115]	Population rank	Percent college graduates rank	State	Percent college graduates [col 116]	Population rank	Median income rank	State	Median income (dollars) [col 123]
		United States	86.9			United States	30.1			United States	53 657
48	1	Alaska	92.9	49	1	District of Columbia	55.0	19	1	Maryland	73 971
21	2	Minnesota	92.6	15	2	Massachusetts	41.2	11	2	New Jersey	71 919
44	2	Montana	92.6	22	3	Colorado	38.3	49	3	District of Columbia	71 648
51	2	Wyoming	92.6	19	4	Maryland	38.2	48	4	Alaska	71 583
41	5	New Hampshire	92.2	29	5	Connecticut	38.0	29	5	Connecticut	70 048
47	5	North Dakota	92.2	11	6	New Jersey	37.4	40	6	Hawaii	69 592
30	7	Iowa	92.1	12	7	Virginia	36.7	15	7	Massachusetts	69 160
50	8	Vermont	92.0	41	8	New Hampshire	35.0	41	8	New Hampshire	66 532
40	9	Hawaii	91.7	50	9	Vermont	34.9	12	9	Virginia	64 902
42	9	Maine	91.7	4	10	New York	34.5	1	10	California	61 933
46	9	South Dakota	91.7	21	11	Minnesota	34.3	21	11	Minnesota	61 481
31	12	Utah	91.4	13	12	Washington	33.1	13	12	Washington	61 366
20	12	Wisconsin	91.4	5	13	Illinois	32.8	22	13	Colorado	61 303
22	14	Colorado	90.5	1	14	California	31.7	31	14	Utah	60 922
13	15	Washington	90.4	34	15	Kansas	31.5	45	15	Delaware	59 716
34	16	Kansas	90.3	31	16	Utah	31.1	47	16	North Dakota	59 029
37	16	Nebraska	90.3	40	17	Hawaii	31.0	4	17	New York	58 878
49	18	District of Columbia	90.2	27	18	Oregon	30.8	5	18	Illinois	57 444
29	19	Connecticut	90.1	45	19	Delaware	30.6	51	19	Wyoming	57 055
39	19	Idaho	90.1	43	20	Rhode Island	30.4	43	20	Rhode Island	54 891
10	21	Michigan	89.9	37	21	Nebraska	29.5	50	21	Vermont	54 166
15	22	Massachusetts	89.7	42	22	Maine	29.4	30	22	Iowa	53 712
27	22	Oregon	89.7	44	23	Montana	29.3	6	23	Pennsylvania	53 234
19	24	Maryland	89.6	8	24	Georgia	29.1	2	24	Texas	53 035
7	25	Ohio	89.4	6	25	Pennsylvania	29.0	37	25	Nebraska	52 686
6	25	Pennsylvania	89.4	9	26	North Carolina	28.7	20	26	Wisconsin	52 622
11	27	New Jersey	89.1	20	27	Wisconsin	28.4	34	27	Kansas	52 504
45	28	Delaware	89.0	48	28	Alaska	28.0	35	28	Nevada	51 450
18	29	Missouri	88.9	46	29	South Dakota	27.8	27	29	Oregon	51 075
12	30	Virginia	88.5	2	29	Texas	27.8	46	30	South Dakota	50 979
16	31	Indiana	88.4	30	31	Iowa	27.7	14	31	Arizona	50 068
5	32	Illinois	88.2	14	32	Arizona	27.6	10	32	Michigan	49 847
28	33	Oklahoma	87.3	18	33	Missouri	27.5	42	33	Maine	49 462
3	34	Florida	87.2	10	34	Michigan	27.4	16	34	Indiana	49 446
9	35	North Carolina	86.4	47	34	North Dakota	27.4	8	35	Georgia	49 321
14	36	Arizona	86.1	3	36	Florida	27.3	7	36	Ohio	49 308
23	36	South Carolina	86.1	7	37	Ohio	26.6	18	37	Missouri	48 363
43	38	Rhode Island	85.8	51	37	Wyoming	26.6	39	38	Idaho	47 861
17	38	Tennessee	85.8	36	39	New Mexico	26.4	28	39	Oklahoma	47 529
4	40	New York	85.7	23	40	South Carolina	26.3	3	40	Florida	47 463
8	41	Georgia	85.6	17	41	Tennessee	25.3	9	41	North Carolina	46 556
33	42	Arkansas	85.3	39	42	Idaho	25.0	44	42	Montana	46 328
38	43	West Virginia	85.2	16	43	Indiana	24.7	23	43	South Carolina	45 238
35	44	Nevada	85.1	28	44	Oklahoma	24.2	36	44	New Mexico	44 803
24	45	Alabama	84.7	24	45	Alabama	23.5	25	45	Louisiana	44 555
26	46	Kentucky	84.5	35	46	Nevada	23.1	17	46	Tennessee	44 361
36	47	New Mexico	84.2	25	47	Louisiana	22.9	26	47	Kentucky	42 958
25	48	Louisiana	83.6	26	48	Kentucky	22.2	24	48	Alabama	42 830
32	49	Mississippi	82.8	33	49	Arkansas	21.4	33	49	Arkansas	41 262
2	50	Texas	82.2	32	50	Mississippi	21.1	38	50	West Virginia	41 059
1	51	California	82.1	38	51	West Virginia	19.2	32	51	Mississippi	39 680

1. Persons 25 years old and over

States and the District of Columbia, Selected Rankings

	Unemployment rate, 2015				Per capita state taxes, 2013				Exports of goods by state of origin, 2015		
Population rank	Unemployment rate rank	State	Unemployment rate [col 171]	Population rank	State taxes rank	State	State taxes per capita (dollars) [col 337]	Population rank	Exports rank	State	Exports (milions of dollars) [col 119]
		United States	5.3			United States	X			United States	1 504 914
49	1	District of Columbia	6.9	47	1	North Dakota	7 325	2	1	Texas	251 087
35	2	Nevada	6.7	48	2	Alaska	6 982	1	2	California	165 367
38	2	West Virginia	6.7	50	3	Vermont	4 594	13	3	Washington	86 353
36	4	New Mexico	6.6	29	4	Connecticut	4 502	4	4	New York	80 060
48	5	Alaska	6.5	40	5	Hawaii	4 340	5	5	Illinois	63 402
32	5	Mississippi	6.5	21	6	Minnesota	3 880	3	6	Florida	53 844
25	7	Louisiana	6.3	51	7	Wyoming	3 752	10	7	Michigan	53 171
1	8	California	6.2	4	8	New York	3 749	7	8	Ohio	50 694
24	9	Alabama	6.1	45	9	Delaware	3 615	25	9	Louisiana	49 183
14	9	Arizona	6.1	15	10	Massachusetts	3 571	6	10	Pennsylvania	39 403
43	11	Rhode Island	6.0	1	11	California	3 474	8	11	Georgia	38 548
23	11	South Carolina	6.0	11	12	New Jersey	3 267	16	12	Indiana	33 652
8	13	Georgia	5.9	19	13	Maryland	3 056	17	13	Tennessee	32 431
5	13	Illinois	5.9	5	14	Illinois	3 006	11	14	New Jersey	32 076
17	15	Tennessee	5.8	42	15	Maine	2 924	23	15	South Carolina	30 861
9	16	North Carolina	5.7	33	16	Arkansas	2 901	9	16	North Carolina	30 018
27	16	Oregon	5.7	38	17	West Virginia	2 900	26	17	Kentucky	28 052
13	16	Washington	5.7	20	18	Wisconsin	2 876	15	18	Massachusetts	25 206
29	19	Connecticut	5.6	43	19	Rhode Island	2 796	14	19	Arizona	22 563
11	19	New Jersey	5.6	30	20	Iowa	2 710	20	20	Wisconsin	22 445
3	21	Florida	5.4	13	21	Washington	2 678	27	21	Oregon	20 084
26	21	Kentucky	5.4	6	22	Pennsylvania	2 659	21	22	Minnesota	19 988
10	21	Michigan	5.4	34	23	Kansas	2 633	24	23	Alabama	19 370
4	24	New York	5.3	44	24	Montana	2 605	12	24	Virginia	18 137
33	25	Arkansas	5.2	16	25	Indiana	2 577	29	25	Connecticut	15 256
19	25	Maryland	5.2	37	26	Nebraska	2 526	18	26	Missouri	13 617
6	27	Pennsylvania	5.1	10	27	Michigan	2 520	31	27	Utah	13 282
15	28	Massachusetts	5.0	35	28	Nevada	2 518	30	28	Iowa	13 114
18	28	Missouri	5.0	36	29	New Mexico	2 494	32	29	Mississippi	10 786
45	30	Delaware	4.9	32	30	Mississippi	2 475	34	30	Kansas	10 686
7	30	Ohio	4.9	26	31	Kentucky	2 461	19	31	Maryland	10 030
16	32	Indiana	4.8	9	32	North Carolina	2 414	35	32	Nevada	8 658
20	33	Wisconsin	4.6	7	33	Ohio	2 378	22	33	Colorado	7 978
2	34	Texas	4.5	27	34	Oregon	2 331	37	34	Nebraska	6 556
42	35	Maine	4.4	12	35	Virginia	2 323	33	35	Arkansas	5 874
12	35	Virginia	4.4	28	36	Oklahoma	2 309	38	36	West Virginia	5 722
34	37	Kansas	4.2	39	37	Idaho	2 220	45	37	Delaware	5 403
28	37	Oklahoma	4.2	31	38	Utah	2 180	28	38	Oklahoma	5 258
51	37	Wyoming	4.2	22	39	Colorado	2 135	48	39	Alaska	4 675
39	40	Idaho	4.1	14	40	Arizona	2 033	39	40	Idaho	4 296
44	40	Montana	4.1	25	41	Louisiana	1 994	41	41	New Hampshire	4 007
22	42	Colorado	3.9	2	42	Texas	1 955	47	42	North Dakota	3 863
30	43	Iowa	3.7	24	43	Alabama	1 917	36	43	New Mexico	3 772
21	43	Minnesota	3.7	17	44	Tennessee	1 904	50	44	Vermont	3 176
50	43	Vermont	3.7	18	45	Missouri	1 843	42	45	Maine	2 724
40	46	Hawaii	3.6	23	46	South Carolina	1 827	43	46	Rhode Island	2 125
31	47	Utah	3.5	46	47	South Dakota	1 815	40	47	Hawaii	1 896
41	48	New Hampshire	3.4	3	48	Florida	1 809	44	48	South Dakota	1 404
46	49	South Dakota	3.1	8	49	Georgia	1 781	46	49	Montana	1 386
37	50	Nebraska	3.0	41	50	New Hampshire	1 775	51	50	Wyoming	1 174
47	51	North Dakota	2.7	49	X	District of Columbia	X	49	51	District of Columbia	1 089

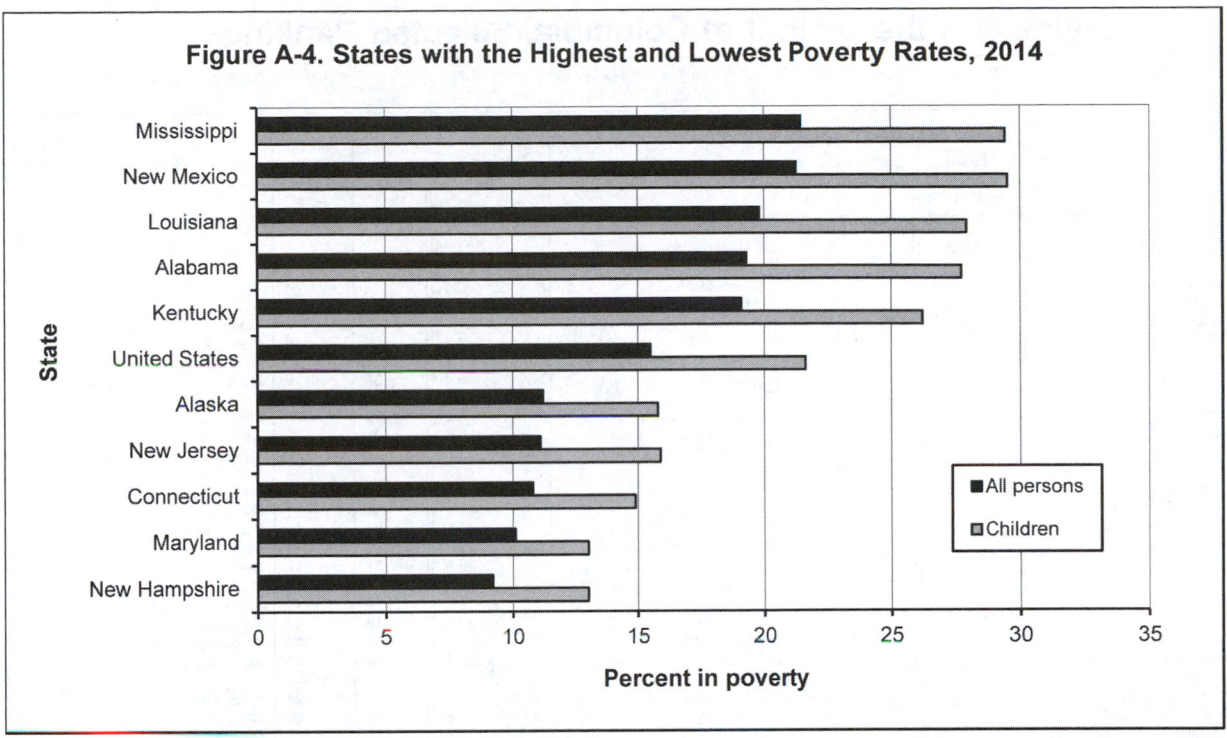

Figure A-4. States with the Highest and Lowest Poverty Rates, 2014

Nationally, 86.9 percent of the population 25 years old and over had graduated from high school. Twenty states had high school attainment levels of 90 percent or more, led by Alaska with 92.9 percent. States in the Midwest and the West tended to have above average high school attainment rates although California had the lowest rate at 82.1 percent, followed by Texas at at 82.2 percent. States with above average high school attainment levels do not necessarily have high proportions of college graduates. Nationally, 30.1 percent of the population held bachelor's degrees. In the District of Columbia, 55.0 percent of the population had graduated from college. Even when compared with other large cities, the District of Columbia had among the 10 highest proportions of college graduates in the nation. Of the 50 states, Massachusetts, Colorado, Maryland, Connecticut, New Jersey, Virginia, and New Hampshire each had 35 percent or more of their populations holding bachelor's degrees or more. States in the Northeast tended to have above average college attainment levels, while states in the South had below average rates.

Median household income ranged from $39,680 in Mississippi to $73,971 in Maryland. Nationally, the median household income was $53,657. In five states—Mississippi, West Virginia, Arkansas, Louisiana, and Alabama—30 percent or more of households had incomes below $25,000. The District of Columbia and Maryland had the highest proportions of households earning $100,000 or more, at 36.7 percent and 36.1 percent respectively, followed by New Jersey at 36.0 percent.

The poverty threshold for an individual was $11,360 in 2014. Mississippi had the highest poverty rate in the nation, with 21.5 percent of its population living in poverty. New Mexico, Louisiana, Alabama, and Kentucky all had poverty rates of 19 percent or higher. The poverty threshold for a four-person family was $24,230. Among children under 18 years old, 21.7 percent were living in poverty. Nearly 30 percent of children in Mississippi and New Mexico lived in poverty. Wyoming had the lowest proportion of children in poverty, at 12.8 percent. The District of Columbia had the highest proportion of residents 65 years and over living in poverty 14.5 percent followed by Mississippi at 13.2 percent.

The United States labor force increased by 0.8 percent between 2014 and 2015. From 2000 to 2008, it grew about an average of 1 percent a year but then declined from 2009 to 2011 followed by small increases in recent years. Fourteen states experienced a decline in their labor force between 2014 and 2015. Kentucky experienced the largest decline, dropping 2.6 percent. Meanwhile, the labor force in Delaware, District of Columbia, Oklahoma, and Utah grew by more than 2 percent in the same period. In 2015, the unemployment rate was 5.3 percent, down from 6.2 percent in 2014. Ten states had an unemployment rate over six percent. The District of Columbia, had the the highest unemployment rate in the nation at 6.9 percent followed by Nevada and West Virginia at 6.7 percent. North Dakota, had the lowest unemployment rate in 2015, at 2.7 percent—the only state with an unemployment rate below 3.0 percent.

States and the District of Columbia, Selected Rankings

Percent of persons below the poverty level, 2014				Percent of children under 18 years old below the poverty level, 2014				Percent of persons lacking health insurance, 2014			
Population rank	Poverty rate rank	State	Poverty rate [col 127]	Population rank	Poverty rate rank	State	Poverty rate [col 128]	Population rank	Percent lacking health insurance rank	State	Percent lacking health insurance [col 104]
		United States	15.5			United States	21.7			United States	11.7
32	1	Mississippi	21.5	36	1	New Mexico	29.5	2	1	Texas	19.1
36	2	New Mexico	21.3	32	2	Mississippi	29.4	48	2	Alaska	17.2
25	3	Louisiana	19.8	25	3	Louisiana	27.9	3	3	Florida	16.6
24	4	Alabama	19.3	24	4	Alabama	27.7	8	4	Georgia	15.8
26	5	Kentucky	19.1	23	5	South Carolina	27.1	28	5	Oklahoma	15.4
33	6	Arkansas	18.9	33	6	Arkansas	26.4	35	6	Nevada	15.2
8	7	Georgia	18.3	8	7	Georgia	26.3	25	7	Louisiana	14.8
17	7	Tennessee	18.3	26	8	Kentucky	26.2	32	8	Mississippu	14.5
38	7	West Virginia	18.3	17	8	Tennessee	26.2	36	8	New Mexico	14.5
14	10	Arizona	18.2	49	10	District of Columbia	26.0	44	10	Montana	14.2
23	11	South Carolina	18.0	14	11	Arizona	25.6	14	11	Arizona	13.6
49	12	District of Columbia	17.7	38	12	West Virginia	24.7	39	11	Idaho	13.6
9	13	North Carolina	17.2	2	13	Texas	24.6	23	11	South Carolina	13.6
2	13	Texas	17.2	9	14	North Carolina	24.3	9	14	North Carolina	13.1
28	15	Oklahoma	16.6	3	15	Florida	23.8	31	15	Utah	12.5
27	15	Oregon	16.6	7	16	Ohio	22.9	1	16	California	12.4
3	17	Florida	16.5	1	17	California	22.7	24	17	Alabama	12.1
1	18	California	16.4	10	18	Michigan	22.6	17	18	Tennessee	12.0
10	19	Michigan	16.2	4	18	New York	22.6	51	18	Wyoming	12.0
4	20	New York	15.9	28	20	Oklahoma	22.4	16	20	Indiana	11.9
7	21	Ohio	15.8	35	21	Nevada	22.0	33	21	Arkansas	11.8
18	22	Missouri	15.5	27	22	Oregon	21.6	18	22	Missouri	11.7
44	23	Montana	15.4	16	23	Indiana	21.5	11	23	New Jersey	10.9
16	24	Indiana	15.2	18	24	Missouri	21.1	12	23	Virginia	10.9
35	24	Nevada	15.2	5	25	Illinois	20.2	22	25	Colorado	10.3
39	26	Idaho	14.8	43	26	Rhode Island	19.8	34	26	Kansas	10.2
5	27	Illinois	14.4	6	27	Pennsylvania	19.4	42	27	Maine	10.1
43	28	Rhode Island	14.3	42	28	Maine	19.1	46	28	South Dakota	9.8
46	29	South Dakota	14.2	39	29	Idaho	18.8	5	29	Illinois	9.7
42	30	Maine	14.1	44	30	Montana	18.5	37	29	Nebraska	9.7
34	31	Kansas	13.6	20	31	Wisconsin	18.4	27	29	Oregon	9.7
6	31	Pennsylvania	13.6	46	32	South Dakota	18.0	41	32	New Hampshire	9.2
13	33	Washington	13.2	45	33	Delaware	17.7	13	32	Washington	9.2
20	33	Wisconsin	13.2	34	33	Kansas	17.7	4	34	New York	8.7
45	35	Delaware	12.5	13	35	Washington	17.5	38	35	West Virginia	8.6
37	36	Nebraska	12.4	37	36	Nebraska	16.2	26	36	Kentucky	8.5
30	37	Iowa	12.2	11	37	New Jersey	15.9	10	36	Michigan	8.5
50	37	Vermont	12.2	48	38	Alaska	15.8	6	36	Pennsylvania	8.5
22	39	Colorado	12.0	50	38	Vermont	15.8	7	39	Ohio	8.4
12	40	Virginia	11.8	12	38	Virginia	15.8	19	40	Maryland	7.9
31	41	Utah	11.7	22	41	Colorado	15.4	47	40	North Dakota	7.9
15	42	Massachusetts	11.6	30	42	Iowa	15.3	45	42	Delaware	7.8
21	43	Minnesota	11.5	15	43	Massachusetts	15.2	43	43	Rhode Island	7.4
47	43	North Dakota	11.5	29	44	Connecticut	14.9	20	44	Wisconsin	7.3
40	45	Hawaii	11.4	21	44	Minnesota	14.9	29	45	Connecticut	6.9
48	46	Alaska	11.2	47	46	North Dakota	14.8	30	46	Iowa	6.2
51	46	Wyoming	11.2	40	47	Hawaii	14.7	21	47	Minnesota	5.9
11	48	New Jersey	11.1	31	48	Utah	13.3	49	48	District of Columbia	5.3
29	49	Connecticut	10.8	19	49	Maryland	13.0	40	48	Hawaii	5.3
19	50	Maryland	10.1	41	49	New Hampshire	13.0	50	50	Vermont	5.0
41	51	New Hampshire	9.2	51	51	Wyoming	12.8	15	51	Massachusetts	3.3

States and the District of Columbia, Selected Rankings

State government employment, 2014				Value of agricultural products sold, 2012				Violent crime rate, 2014			
Popu-rank	State government employment rank	State	State government employment [col 312]	Popu-lation rank	Agricultural sales rank	State	Value of sales (millions of dollars) [col 197]	Popu-lation rank	Violent crime rate rank	State	Violent crime rate (per 100,000 population) [col 108]
		United States	4 341 163			United States	394 644			United States	376
1	1	California	406 842	1	1	California	42 627	49	1	District of Columbia	1 244
2	2	Texas	313 284	30	2	Iowa	30 822	48	2	Alaska	636
4	3	New York	240 744	2	3	Texas	25 376	35	3	Nevada	636
3	4	Florida	176 990	37	4	Nebraska	23 069	17	4	Tennessee	608
6	5	Pennsylvania	161 369	21	5	Minnesota	21 280	36	5	New Mexico	597
9	6	North Carolina	145 187	34	6	Kansas	18 461	3	6	Florida	540
11	7	New Jersey	143 707	5	7	Illinois	17 187	25	7	Louisiana	515
10	8	Michigan	142 057	9	8	North Carolina	12 588	23	8	South Carolina	498
7	9	Ohio	136 486	20	9	Wisconsin	11 744	45	9	Delaware	489
8	10	Georgia	131 916	16	10	Indiana	11 211	33	10	Arkansas	480
12	11	Virginia	127 408	47	11	North Dakota	10 951	19	11	Maryland	446
5	12	Illinois	123 001	46	12	South Dakota	10 170	18	12	Missouri	443
13	13	Washington	120 091	7	13	Ohio	10 064	24	13	Alabama	427
15	14	Massachusetts	98 985	33	14	Arkansas	9 776	10	14	Michigan	427
24	15	Alabama	88 687	8	15	Georgia	9 255	28	15	Oklahoma	406
18	16	Missouri	88 133	18	16	Missouri	9 165	2	16	Texas	406
16	17	Indiana	87 692	13	17	Washington	9 121	14	17	Arizona	400
19	18	Maryland	86 771	10	18	Michigan	8 678	1	18	California	396
26	19	Kentucky	83 409	39	19	Idaho	7 801	15	19	Massachusetts	391
21	20	Minnesota	82 223	22	20	Colorado	7 781	4	20	New York	382
22	21	Colorado	79 518	3	21	Florida	7 702	8	21	Georgia	377
17	22	Tennessee	79 258	6	22	Pennsylvania	7 401	5	22	Illinois	370
23	23	South Carolina	78 690	28	23	Oklahoma	7 130	16	23	Indiana	365
14	24	Arizona	78 689	32	24	Mississippi	6 441	34	24	Kansas	349
25	25	Louisiana	76 207	24	25	Alabama	5 571	9	25	North Carolina	330
20	26	Wisconsin	72 960	4	26	New York	5 415	46	26	South Dakota	326
27	27	Oregon	66 966	26	27	Kentucky	5 067	44	27	Montana	324
28	28	Oklahoma	66 939	27	28	Oregon	4 884	6	28	Pennsylvania	314
29	29	Connecticut	63 013	44	29	Montana	4 230	22	29	Colorado	309
33	30	Arkansas	62 079	25	30	Louisiana	3 809	38	30	West Virginia	302
40	31	Hawaii	58 409	12	31	Virginia	3 753	20	31	Wisconsin	290
32	32	Mississippi	56 884	14	32	Arizona	3 732	13	32	Washington	285
31	33	Utah	54 038	17	33	Tennessee	3 611	7	33	Ohio	285
30	34	Iowa	49 888	23	34	South Carolina	3 040	37	34	Nebraska	280
34	35	Kansas	49 469	36	35	New Mexico	2 550	32	35	Mississippi	278
36	36	New Mexico	46 114	19	36	Maryland	2 271	30	36	Iowa	274
38	37	West Virginia	40 281	31	37	Utah	1 816	47	37	North Dakota	265
37	38	Nebraska	32 101	51	38	Wyoming	1 689	11	38	New Jersey	261
35	39	Nevada	27 236	45	39	Delaware	1 274	40	39	Hawaii	259
48	40	Alaska	27 049	11	40	New Jersey	1 007	29	40	Connecticut	237
45	41	Delaware	26 135	38	41	West Virginia	807	27	41	Oregon	232
39	42	Idaho	23 814	50	42	Vermont	776	21	42	Minnesota	229
42	43	Maine	20 990	35	43	Nevada	764	43	43	Rhode Island	219
44	44	Montana	20 721	42	44	Maine	763	31	44	Utah	216
47	45	North Dakota	18 752	40	45	Hawaii	661	39	45	Idaho	212
41	46	New Hampshire	18 698	29	46	Connecticut	551	26	46	Kentucky	212
43	47	Rhode Island	18 691	15	47	Massachusetts	492	12	47	Virginia	196
46	48	South Dakota	14 625	41	48	New Hampshire	191	41	48	New Hampshire	196
50	49	Vermont	14 483	43	49	Rhode Island	60	51	49	Wyoming	196
51	50	Wyoming	13 484	48	50	Alaska	59	42	50	Maine	128
49	X	District of Columbia	X	49	X	District of Columbia	X	50	51	Vermont	99

Table A. States — Land Area and Population Characteristics

State code	STATE	Land area,[1] 2010 (sq km)	Population, 2015			Population characteristics, 2014										
			Total persons, 2015	Rank	Per square kilometer	Race alone or in combination, not Hispanic or Latino (percent)				Hispanic or Latino[2] (percent)	Age (percent)					
						White	Black	American Indian, Alaska Native	Asian and Pacific Islander		Under 5 years	5 to 17 years	18 to 24 years	25 to 34 years	35 to 44 years	45 to 54 years
		1	2	3	4	5	6	7	8	9	10	11	12	13	14	15

1. Dry land or land partially or temporarily covered by water.   2. May be of any race.

Table A. States — Population Characteristics, Immigration, and Households

STATE	Population characteristics, 2014 (cont.)									Households, 2014					
	Age (percent) (cont.)												Household type		
	55 to 64 years	65 to 74 years	75 to 84 years	85 years and over	Median age	Percent female	Percent foreign born	Percent born in state of residence	Immigrants admitted to legal status, 2014	Number	Percent change, 2013–2014	Persons per house-hold	Married couple family	Female house-holder family[1]	House-holder living alone
	16	17	18	19	20	21	22	23	24	25	26	27	28	29	30

1. No spouse present.

Table A. States — Population Change

STATE	Population, 1990–2010			Population change, 1990–2015								Population, 2020–2030		
	Census counts			Percent change			Components of change, 2010–2015					Projections		
									Migration					
	1990	2000	2010	1990–2000	2000–2010	2010–2015	Births	Deaths	Net migration	Inter-national	Net internal	2020	2025	2030
	31	32	33	34	35	36	37	38	39	40	41	42	43	44

Table A. States — Population Characteristics

STATE	Population characteristics, 2010																		
	Race (percent)						Age (percent)												
	White alone	Black alone	American Indian, Alaska Native alone	Asian and Pacific Islander alone	Some other race or two or more races	Percent Hispanic or Latino[1]	Percent foreign born	Under 5 years	5 to 17 years	18 to 24 years	25 to 34 years	35 to 44 years	45 to 54 years	55 to 64 years	65 to 74 years	75 to 84 years	85 years and over	Median age	Percent female
	45	46	47	48	49	50	51	52	53	54	55	56	57	58	59	60	61	62	63

1. May be of any race.

Table A. States — Households and Housing Units

STATE	Households, 2010					Housing units, 2010									
				Percent				Occupied units							
									Owner-occupied			Renter-occupied			
										Median owner cost					
	Number	Percent change, 2000–2010	Persons per house-hold	Female family house-holder[1]	One person house-holds	Total	Percent change, 2000–2010	Total	Percent	Median value[2] (dollars)	With a mort-gage	Without a mort-gage[3]	Median gross rent[4] (dollars)	Median rent as a percent of income	Sub-standard units[5] (percent)
	64	65	66	67	68	69	70	71	72	73	74	75	76	77	78

1. No spouse present. 2. Specified owner-occupied units. 3. Median monthly costs is often in the minimum category—10.0 percent or less, which is indicated as 10.0 percent.
4. Specified renter-occupied units. 5. Overcrowded or lacking complete plumbing facilities.

Table A. States — Housing Units

STATE	Housing units, 2014													
			Occupied units											
					Percent who pay 30 percent or more of income for housing expenses[1]		Median owner cost as a percent of income							
	Total	Percent change, 2013–2014	Total	Percent owner-occupied	Owners with a mort-gage	Renter	With a mort-gage	Without a mort-gage[2]	Median monthly housing costs (dollars)	Median value of units[3] (dollars)	Percent valued over $500,000	Median gross rent[4] (dollars)	Sub-standard units[5] (percent)	Percent living in a different house than 1 year ago
	79	80	81	82	83	84	85	86	87	88	89	90	91	92

1. Excludes units where owner costs or gross rent as a percentage of households income cannot be calculated. 2. Median monthly costs is often in the minimum category—10.0 percent or less, which is indicated as 10.0 percent. 3. Specified owner-occupied units. 4. Specified renter-occupied units. 5. Overcrowded or lacking complete plumbing facilities.

Table A. States — Residential Construction, Vital Statistics, and Health

STATE	Value of residential construction authorized by building permits, 2014				Births, 2014		Deaths, 2013					Percent lacking health insurance, 2014		
							Number		Rate					
									Total					
	New con-struction ($1,000)	Number of housing units	Percent single family	Average sales price of new manu-factured housing units put in place, 2014	Total	Rate[1]	Total	Infant[2]	Crude[1]	Age-adjusted[1]	Infant[3]	All persons	Children under 18 years	Medicare beneficiaries 65 years and older, 2014
	93	94	95	96	97	98	99	100	101	102	103	104	105	106

1. Per 1,000 resident population. 2. Deaths of infants under 1 year old. 3. Deaths of infants under 1 year old per 1,000 live births.

Table A. States — Crime and Education

STATE	Serious crime known to police,[1] 2014				Public elementary and secondary school enrollment, 2013–2014		Educational attainment[3] (percent)				Local government expenditures for education, 2012–2013	
	Violent Crime		Property Crime				2010		2014			
	Number	Rate[2]	Number	Rate[2]	Total	Student/teacher ratio	High school graduate or more	Bachelor's degree or more	High school graduate or more	Bachelor's degree or more	Total current expenditures (mil dol)	Current expenditures per student (dollars)
	107	108	109	110	111	112	113	114	115	116	117	118

1. Data for serious crimes have not been adjusted for underreporting; this may affect comparability between geographic areas and over time. 2. Per 100,000 population estimated by the FBI. 3. Persons 25 years old and over.

Table A. States — **Exports, Income, and Poverty**

STATE	Exports of goods by state of origin, 2015 (mil dol)			Income, 2014						Percent below poverty level, 2014						
				Per capita income (dollars)	Households			Median income of family of four	All persons	Children under 18 years	Persons 65 years and over	All families	Families with related children under 18		
	Total	Manu-factured	Non-manu-factured		Median income (dollars)	Percent with income of $25,000 or less	Percent with income of $100,000 or more						Married-couple families	Male house-holder[1] families	Female house-holder[1] families
	119	120	121	122	123	124	125	126	127	128	129	130	131	132	133

1. No spouse present.

Table A. States — **Personal Income**

STATE	Personal income, 2014													
			Per capita[1]		Sources of personal income (mil dol)									
										Transfer payments				
											Government payments to individuals			
	Total (mil dol)	Percent change, 2013–2014	Dollars	Rank	Wages and salaries[2]	Proprietors' income	Dividends, interest, and rent	Total	Total	Social Security	Medical payments	Income main-tenance	Unemploy-ment insurance
	134	135	136	137	138	139	140	141	142	143	144	145	146

1. Based on the resident population estimated as of July 1 of the year shown.   2. Includes supplements to wages and salaries.

Table A. States — **Personal Income and Earnings**

STATE	Personal tax payments, 2014 (mil dol)	Disposable personal income, 2014		Earnings, 2014										Gross state product, 2014 (mil dol)
								Percent by selected industries						
						Goods-related[2]		Service-related and other[3]						
		Total (mil dol)	Per capita[1] (dollars)	Total (mil dol)	Farm	Total	Manu-facturing	Total	Retail trade	Finance, insurance, real estate, rental and leasing	Health care and social assist-ance	Government	
	147	148	149	150	151	152	153	154	155	156	157	158	159

1. Based on the resident population estimated as of July 1 of the year shown.   2. Total includes mining, construction, and manufacturing.   3. Includes private sector earnings in forestry, fishing, related activities, and other; utilities; wholesale trade; transportation and warehousing; and information.

Table A. States — **Social Security, Employment, and Labor Force**

STATE	Social Security beneficiaries, December 2014		Supple-mental Security Income recipients, December 2013	Civilian employment and selected occupations,[2] 2014				Civilian labor force (annual average), 2015				
					Percent						Unemployed	
	Number	Rate[1]		Total	Management, business, science and art occupations	Services, sales, and office occupations	Construction and production occupations	Total (1,000)	Percent change, 2014–2015	Employed (1,000)	Total (1,000)	Rate[3]
	160	161	162	163	164	165	166	167	168	169	170	171

1. Per 1,000 resident population estimated as of July 1 of the year shown.   2. Persons 16 years old and over.   3. Percent of civilian labor force.

Table A. States — **Nonfarm Employment and Earnings**

STATE	Private nonfarm employment and earnings, 2015											
	Employed		Manufacturing			Employment (1,000)						
				Average earnings of production workers								
	Total (1,000)	Percent change, 2014–2015	Employment (1,000)	Hourly	Weekly	Construction	Transportation and public utilities	Wholesale trade	Retail trade	Information	Financial activities	Services[1]
	172	173	174	175	176	177	178	179	180	181	182	183

1. Includes professional and business services, educational and health services, leisure and hospitality, and other services.

Table A. States — **Agriculture**

STATE	Agriculture, 2012											
	Farms					Land in farms					Value of land and buildings (dollars)	
		Percent with:						Acres				
	Number	Fewer than 50 acres	500 acres or more	Farm operators whose principal occupation is farming (percent)	Government payments, average per farm (dollars)	Acreage (1,000)	Percent change, 2007–2012	Average size of farm	Total irrigated (1,000)	Total cropland (1,000)	Average per farm	Average per acre
	184	185	186	187	188	189	190	191	192	193	194	195

Table A. States — **Agriculture, Land, and Water**

STATE	Agriculture, 2012 (cont.)							Land, 2012			
		Value of products sold				Percent of farms with sales of:					
				Percent from:							
	Value of machinery and equipment, average per farm (dollars)	Total (mil dol)	Average per farm (dollars)	Crops	Livestock and poultry products	$10,000 or more	$100,000 or more	Cropland (percent)	Owned by the federal government (percent)	Developed (percent)	Water consumption, 2010 (mil gal per day)
	196	197	198	199	200	201	202	203	204	205	206

Table A. States — **Manufactures and Construction**

STATE	Manufactures, 2014										Construction, 2012			
	All employees			Production workers								Employees		
						Wages								
	Number (1,000)	Percent change, 2013–2014	Annual payroll (mil dol)	Number (1,000)	Work hours (millions)	Total (mil dol)	Average per worker (dollars)	Value added by manufacture (mil dol)	Value of shipments (mil dol)	Total cost of materials (mil dol)	Number of establishments	Number	Percent change, 2007–2012	Value (mil dol)	Annual payroll (mil dol)
	207	208	209	210	211	212	213	214	215	216	217	218	219	220	221

Table A. States — **Wholesale Trade and Retail Trade**

STATE	Wholesale trade, 2012					Retail trade,[1] 2012								
	Number of estab-lishments	Employees		Sales (mil dol)	Annual payroll (mil dol)	Number of estab-lishments	Employees						Sales (mil dol)	Annual payroll (mil dol)
		Number	Percent change, 2007–2012				Total	Percent change, 2007–2012	Motor vehicle and parts dealers	Food and beverage stores	Clothing and clothing accessory stores	General merchan-dise stores		
	222	223	224	225	226	227	228	229	230	231	232	233	234	235

1. Establishments with payroll.

Table A. States — **Information**

STATE	Information, 2012										
	Number of establishments	Employees		Publishing, except Internet	Motion picture and sound recording	Broadcasting, except Internet	Internet publishing and broad-casting and web search portals	Telecom-munications	Data processing, hosting, and related services	Receipts (mil dol)	Annual payroll (mil dol)
		Number	Percent change, 2007–2012								
	236	237	238	239	240	241	242	243	244	245	246

Table A. States — **Utilities, Transportation and Warehousing, and Finance and Insurance**

STATE	Utilities, 2012					Transportation and warehousing, 2012					Finance and insurance, 2012				
	Number of estab-lishments	Employees		Receipts (mil dol)	Annual payroll (mil dol)	Number of estab-lishments	Employees		Receipts (mil dol)	Annual payroll (mil dol)	Number of estab-lishments	Employees		Receipts (mil dol)	Annual payroll (mil dol)
		Number	Percent change, 2007–2012				Number	Percent change, 2007–2012				Number	Percent change, 2007–2012		
	247	248	249	250	251	252	253	254	255	256	257	258	259	260	261

Table A. States — **Real Estate and Rental and Leasing and Professional, Scientific, and Technical Services**

STATE	Real estate and rental and leasing, 2012					Professional, scientific, and technical services, 2012								
	Number of estab-lishments	Employees		Receipts (mil dol)	Annual payroll (mil dol)	Number of estab-lishments	Employees						Receipts (mil dol)	Annual payroll (mil dol)
		Number	Percent change, 2007–2012				Total	Percent change, 2007–2012	Legal services	Accounting tax preparation, book-keeping, and payroll services	Architectural, engineering, and related services	Computer systems design and related services		
	262	263	264	265	266	267	268	269	270	271	272	273	274	275

Table A. States — Health Care and Social Assistance

	Health care and social assistance, 2012												
	Subject to federal tax						Tax-exempt						
		Employees							Employees					
STATE	Number of establishments	Total	Percent change, 2007–2012	Ambulatory health care services	Hospitals	Receipts (mil dol)	Annual payroll (mil dol)	Number of establishments	Total	Percent change, 2007–2012	Ambulatory health care services	Hospitals	Receipts (mil dol)	Annual payroll (mil dol)
	276	277	278	279	280	281	282	283	284	285	286	287	288	289

Table A. States — Arts, Entertainment, and Recreation and Accommodation and Food Services

| | Arts, entertainment, and recreation, 2012 | | | | | Accommodation and food services, 2012 | | | | | |
| | | Employees | | | | | Employees | | | | |
STATE	Number of establishments	Number	Percent change, 2007–2012	Receipts (mil dol)	Annual payroll (mil dol)	Number of establishments	Total	Percent change, 2007–2012	Food services and drinking places	Receipts (mil dol)	Annual payroll (mil dol)
	290	291	292	293	294	295	296	297	298	299	300

Table A. States — Other Services, Except Public Administration, and Government Employment

| | Other services, except public administration, 2012 | | | | | | | | Government employment, 2014 | | |
| | | Employees | | | | | | | | | |
STATE	Number of establishments	Total	Percent change, 2007–2012	Repair and maintenance	Personal and laundry services	Religious, civic, and similar services	Receipts (mil dol)	Annual payroll (mil dol)	Federal civilian	Federal military	State and local
	301	302	303	304	305	306	307	308	309	310	311

Table A. States — State Government Employment and Payroll

	State government employment and payroll, 2014											
	State government employment, 2014			State government payroll, 2012			Full-time equivalent payroll (1,000 dollars)					
								Percent of total for:				
STATE	Full-time equivalent employees	Full-time employees	Part-time employees	Full-time March payroll (1,000 dollars)	Part-time March payroll (1,000 dollars)	Total March payroll (1,000 dollars)[1]	Administration	Judicial and legal	Police	Corrections	Highways and transportation	Public Welfare
	312	313	314	315	316	317	318	319	320	321	322	323

1. Includes program categories not shown separately.

Table A. States — **State Government Employment and Payroll and State Government Finances**

STATE	State government employment and payroll, 2012 (cont.)							State government finances, 2013							
	Full-time equivalent payroll (1,000 dollars) (cont.)							General revenue (mil dol)							
	Percent of total for:								From federal government		From own sources				
												Taxes		Taxes per capita[1] (dollars)	
	Health	Hospitals	Social Insurance administration	Natural resources and parks	Utilities, sewerage, and waste management	Elementary and secondary education and libraries	Higher education	Total	Total	Per capita (dollars)	Total	Total	Sales and gross receipts	Total	Sales and gross receipts
	324	325	326	327	328	329	330	331	332	333	334	335	336	337	338

1. Based on resident population estimated as of July 1 of the year shown.

Table A. States — **State Government Finances and Voting**

STATE	State government finances, 2013 (cont.)										Voting and registration, November 2014		Presidential election,[2] 2012 (percent of vote cast)		
	General expenditures (mil dol)														
			Direct general expenditures		By selected function						Debt outstanding				
	Total	To local governments	Total	Per capita[1] (dollars)	Education	Health and hospitals	Highways	Public safety	Public welfare	Natural resources, parks, and recreation	Total (mil dol)	Per capita[1]	Percent registered	Percent voted	Demo-cratic	Repub-lican	All other
	339	340	341	342	343	344	345	346	347	348	349	350	351	352	353	354	355

1. Based on resident population estimated as of July 1 of the year shown.   2. © 2013 Election Data Services, Inc. All rights reserved.

Table A. States — Land Area and Population Characteristics

State code	STATE	Land area,[1] 2010 (sq km)	Total persons, 2015	Rank	Per square kilometer	White	Black	American Indian, Alaska Native	Asian and Pacific Islander	Hispanic or Latino[2] (percent)	Under 5 years	5 to 17 years	18 to 24 years	25 to 34 years	35 to 44 years	45 to 54 years
		1	2	3	4	5	6	7	8	9	10	11	12	13	14	15
0	UNITED STATES...............	9 147 593	321 418 820	X	35.1	63.8	13.3	1.3	6.4	17.4	6.2	16.8	9.9	13.6	12.7	13.6
1	ALABAMA	131 171	4 858 979	24	37.0	67.5	27.1	1.2	1.7	4.1	6.1	16.8	9.9	12.9	12.5	13.5
2	ALASKA	1 477 953	738 432	48	0.5	67.7	4.8	18.4	9.3	6.8	7.4	17.9	11.1	16.1	12.2	13.2
4	ARIZONA	294 207	6 828 065	14	23.2	58.0	4.9	4.6	4.1	30.6	6.4	17.7	10.0	13.3	12.4	12.5
5	ARKANSAS	134 771	2 978 204	33	22.1	75.0	16.1	1.6	2.1	7.0	6.5	17.4	9.7	13.0	12.3	13.0
6	CALIFORNIA..................	403 466	39 144 818	1	97.0	40.7	6.5	1.0	16.0	38.6	6.5	17.1	10.3	14.8	13.3	13.5
8	COLORADO..................	268 431	5 456 574	22	20.3	70.9	4.8	1.3	4.1	21.2	6.3	17.0	9.8	14.9	13.5	13.3
9	CONNECTICUT..............	12 542	3 590 886	29	286.3	70.3	10.8	0.6	5.0	15.1	5.3	16.3	9.7	12.3	12.2	15.2
10	DELAWARE	5 047	945 934	45	187.4	65.5	22.6	0.9	4.3	8.9	6.0	15.8	9.6	13.2	11.8	13.9
11	DISTRICT OF COLUMBIA..	158	672 228	49	4 254.6	37.5	48.7	0.8	5.0	10.4	6.5	11.0	12.2	22.8	14.1	11.6
12	FLORIDA.......................	138 887	20 271 272	3	146.0	57.1	16.4	0.6	3.4	24.1	5.5	14.9	9.0	12.7	12.2	13.8
13	GEORGIA......................	148 959	10 214 860	8	68.6	55.8	31.7	0.7	4.4	9.3	6.6	18.1	10.1	13.7	13.6	13.9
15	HAWAII.........................	16 635	1 431 603	40	86.1	36.7	3.2	1.7	74.0	10.1	6.4	15.3	9.7	14.9	12.4	12.6
16	IDAHO..........................	214 045	1 654 930	39	7.7	84.6	1.1	1.9	2.4	12.0	7.0	19.4	9.5	13.2	12.2	12.2
17	ILLINOIS.......................	143 793	12 859 995	5	89.4	63.6	14.9	0.5	5.8	16.7	6.1	17.1	9.7	13.8	13.0	13.8
18	INDIANA.......................	92 789	6 619 680	16	71.3	81.9	10.2	0.7	2.4	6.6	6.4	17.6	10.1	12.8	12.5	13.5
19	IOWA...........................	144 669	3 123 899	30	21.6	88.5	4.1	0.7	2.7	5.6	6.3	17.1	10.3	12.6	11.7	13.1
20	KANSAS.......................	211 754	2 911 641	34	13.8	79.0	7.0	1.8	3.4	11.4	6.9	18.0	10.4	13.4	11.9	12.7
21	KENTUCKY	102 269	4 425 092	26	43.3	86.9	9.0	0.7	1.8	3.4	6.3	16.7	9.7	12.8	12.7	13.8
22	LOUISIANA	111 898	4 670 724	25	41.7	60.5	32.8	1.1	2.2	4.8	6.6	17.3	10.0	14.4	12.2	13.2
23	MAINE..........................	79 883	1 329 328	42	16.6	95.2	1.8	1.4	1.6	1.5	4.9	14.6	8.5	11.5	11.7	15.1
24	MARYLAND	25 142	6 006 401	19	238.9	54.5	30.6	0.8	7.2	9.3	6.2	16.4	9.4	13.9	12.9	14.7
25	MASSACHUSETTS	20 202	6 794 422	15	336.3	75.7	7.6	0.6	7.0	10.8	5.4	15.2	10.4	13.8	12.4	14.6
26	MICHIGAN	146 435	9 922 576	10	67.8	77.6	15.0	1.3	3.4	4.8	5.8	16.7	10.1	12.1	12.0	14.1
27	MINNESOTA..................	206 232	5 489 594	21	26.6	83.4	6.7	1.7	5.4	5.1	6.4	17.1	9.3	13.7	12.3	13.9
28	MISSISSIPPI..................	121 531	2 992 333	32	24.6	58.2	37.8	0.8	1.3	3.0	6.5	17.9	10.4	13.1	12.3	13.0
29	MISSOURI.....................	178 040	6 083 672	18	34.2	81.9	12.5	1.1	2.5	4.0	6.2	16.8	9.8	13.2	12.1	13.5
30	MONTANA.....................	376 962	1 032 949	44	2.7	89.0	1.0	7.7	1.4	3.5	6.0	16.0	9.9	12.6	11.3	12.8
31	NEBRASKA	198 974	1 896 190	37	9.5	82.0	5.5	1.3	2.7	10.2	6.9	17.9	10.2	13.5	12.0	12.7
32	NEVADA.......................	284 332	2 890 845	35	10.2	54.1	9.4	1.5	10.6	27.8	6.2	17.1	9.0	14.3	13.5	13.5
33	NEW HAMPSHIRE	23 187	1 330 608	41	57.4	92.6	1.7	0.7	3.1	3.3	4.9	15.3	9.7	11.6	11.9	15.8
34	NEW JERSEY................	19 047	8 958 013	11	470.3	58.0	13.6	0.5	10.0	19.3	6.0	16.6	8.9	12.8	13.1	15.0
35	NEW MEXICO................	314 161	2 085 109	36	6.6	40.2	2.3	9.3	2.1	47.7	6.6	17.5	10.0	13.4	11.7	12.7
36	NEW YORK....................	122 057	19 795 791	4	162.2	57.8	15.5	0.7	9.1	18.6	6.0	15.4	10.0	14.4	12.7	14.1
37	NORTH CAROLINA..........	125 920	10 042 802	9	79.8	65.6	22.4	1.7	3.2	9.0	6.1	16.9	9.9	13.0	13.1	13.8
38	NORTH DAKOTA.............	178 711	756 927	47	4.2	88.2	2.5	6.1	1.8	3.2	6.9	15.9	12.7	14.6	11.1	12.1
39	OHIO............................	105 829	11 613 423	7	109.7	81.9	13.5	0.7	2.5	3.5	6.0	16.8	9.5	12.7	12.1	13.8
40	OKLAHOMA	177 660	3 911 338	28	22.0	71.9	2.9	4.1	2.8	9.8	6.8	17.7	10.1	13.7	12.2	12.6
41	OREGON	248 608	4 028 977	27	16.2	79.9	0.9	1.9	6.0	12.5	5.8	15.8	9.2	13.7	13.0	12.9
42	PENNSYLVANIA..............	115 883	12 802 503	6	110.5	79.2	12.8	0.6	3.7	6.6	5.6	15.5	10.5	12.8	11.8	14.1
44	RHODE ISLAND	2 678	1 056 298	43	394.4	76.2	6.8	1.0	4.1	14.0	5.2	15.0	11.1	13.2	11.9	14.5
45	SOUTH CAROLINA	77 857	4 896 146	23	62.9	65.2	28.2	0.8	2.0	5.4	6.0	16.4	10.0	13.0	12.3	13.4
46	SOUTH DAKOTA.............	196 350	858 469	46	4.4	84.9	2.4	9.5	1.7	3.6	7.1	17.6	10.0	13.1	11.2	12.6
47	TENNESSEE..................	106 798	6 600 299	17	61.8	76.1	17.6	0.8	2.1	5.0	6.1	16.7	9.6	13.1	12.8	13.7
48	TEXAS..........................	676 587	27 469 114	2	40.6	44.7	12.3	0.7	5.0	38.6	7.3	19.1	10.2	14.6	13.5	12.9
49	UTAH...........................	212 818	2 995 919	31	14.1	81.1	1.5	1.4	4.4	13.5	8.6	22.2	11.3	15.0	13.1	10.4
50	VERMONT.....................	23 871	626 042	50	26.2	95.1	1.7	1.1	2.1	1.8	4.9	14.6	10.8	11.5	11.4	14.6
51	VIRGINIA.......................	102 279	8 382 993	12	82.0	65.3	20.2	0.8	7.4	8.9	6.2	16.3	10.0	14.1	13.1	14.1
53	WASHINGTON................	172 119	7 170 351	13	41.7	73.8	4.9	2.5	10.8	12.2	6.3	16.4	9.5	14.5	13.0	13.4
54	WEST VIRGINIA	62 259	1 844 128	38	29.6	94.0	4.4	0.7	1.1	1.5	5.5	15.0	9.2	11.8	12.4	13.6
55	WISCONSIN...................	140 268	5 771 337	20	41.1	83.6	7.1	1.4	3.1	6.5	5.9	16.7	9.8	12.7	12.0	14.2
56	WYOMING	251 470	586 107	51	2.3	85.6	1.8	2.9	1.5	9.8	6.5	17.1	9.8	14.1	12.0	12.6

Population, 2015 (columns 1–4) · Population characteristics, 2014 · Race alone or in combination, not Hispanic or Latino (percent) (columns 5–9) · Age (percent) (columns 10–15)

1. Dry land or land partially or temporarily covered by water.   2. May be of any race.

| | Population characteristics, 2014 (cont.) | | | | | | | | Households, 2014 | | | | | | |
| | Age (percent) (cont.) | | | | | | | | | | | | Household type | | |
STATE	55 to 64 years	65 to 74 years	75 to 84 years	85 years and over	Median age	Percent female	Percent foreign born	Percent born in state of residence	Immigrants admitted to legal status, 2014	Number	Percent change, 2013–2014	Persons per house-hold	Married couple family	Female house-holder family[1]	House-holder living alone
	16	17	18	19	20	21	22	23	24	25	26	27	28	29	30
UNITED STATES	12.6	8.3	4.3	1.9	37.7	50.8	13.3	58.7	1 016 518	117 259 427	0.8	2.65	47.9	13.0	27.8
ALABAMA	13.0	9.0	4.6	1.7	38.6	51.6	3.2	70.3	3 685	1 841 217	1.0	2.57	47.3	15.5	28.8
ALASKA	12.6	6.3	2.3	0.8	33.3	47.7	7.4	41.3	1 505	249 659	1.5	2.84	49.7	10.5	25.6
ARIZONA	11.8	9.2	4.8	1.9	37.1	50.3	13.7	39.0	16 908	2 428 743	1.2	2.71	47.0	12.5	27.6
ARKANSAS	12.5	9.1	4.8	1.9	37.8	50.9	4.7	61.1	2 793	1 131 288	0.5	2.55	48.3	13.4	28.6
CALIFORNIA	11.6	7.3	3.8	1.8	36	50.4	27.1	55.0	198 379	12 758 648	0.9	2.98	48.9	13.7	24.0
COLORADO	12.5	7.7	3.5	1.5	36.5	49.7	10.0	42.9	10 872	2 039 592	1.8	2.57	49.3	10.3	27.5
CONNECTICUT	13.5	8.5	4.5	2.5	40.6	51.2	13.7	55.4	11 252	1 355 817	1.2	2.57	48.0	12.7	28.9
DELAWARE	13.3	9.7	4.8	1.9	39.7	51.5	8.6	45.6	2 085	349 743	3.1	2.6	47.3	14.1	27.5
DISTRICT OF COLUMBIA	10.5	6.4	3.2	1.7	33.8	52.6	14.0	36.2	3 169	277 378	2.1	2.23	23.9	15.2	44.6
FLORIDA	12.9	10.5	6.0	2.6	41.8	51.1	20.0	36.1	109 310	7 328 046	1.6	2.66	46.1	13.1	29.1
GEORGIA	11.7	7.6	3.5	1.3	36.1	51.3	9.9	55.6	23 792	3 587 521	1.1	2.74	47.2	15.7	26.9
HAWAII	12.7	8.9	4.5	2.6	37.9	49.5	17.6	53.1	5 741	450 769	0.1	3.05	51.5	12.4	23.6
IDAHO	12.2	8.5	4.1	1.7	35.7	50.0	6.0	48.5	2 202	591 587	0.5	2.71	54.9	9.3	25.6
ILLINOIS	12.6	7.8	4.1	2.0	37.5	50.9	13.9	67.3	36 535	4 772 421	-0.2	2.64	47.6	12.6	28.9
INDIANA	12.8	8.1	4.2	1.9	37.5	50.8	4.8	68.3	8 008	2 502 739	0.2	2.56	48.7	12.7	27.7
IOWA	13.1	8.4	4.9	2.5	38.1	50.3	4.9	71.2	4 225	1 241 471	0.4	2.42	51.3	8.9	28.7
KANSAS	12.5	7.8	4.3	2.2	36.1	50.2	7.0	58.6	4 861	1 109 280	-0.4	2.55	50.9	10.1	28.9
KENTUCKY	13.1	8.7	4.4	1.7	38.6	50.7	3.7	69.6	5 634	1 712 094	0.4	2.5	48.4	12.6	28.5
LOUISIANA	12.6	8.0	4.0	1.6	36.3	51.1	4.2	77.7	4 382	1 718 194	-0.6	2.63	43.2	16.2	29.7
MAINE	15.5	10.6	5.4	2.4	44.2	51.3	3.7	63.3	1 382	549 841	0.4	2.35	48	10.0	29.4
MARYLAND	12.8	8.0	3.9	1.9	38.2	51.5	14.9	47.5	24 787	2 165 438	0.2	2.7	47.2	14.7	26.9
MASSACHUSETTS	13.1	8.3	4.4	2.3	39.4	51.5	15.7	61.8	29 776	2 549 336	0.5	2.55	46.4	12.5	29.0
MICHIGAN	13.8	8.8	4.5	2.1	39.6	50.9	6.4	76.7	18 185	3 834 574	0.1	2.53	47.3	12.7	29.1
MINNESOTA	13.0	7.9	4.2	2.1	37.8	50.3	7.8	68.2	13 764	2 129 195	0.4	2.5	50.5	9.6	28.7
MISSISSIPPI	12.5	8.3	4.3	1.7	36.7	51.3	2.2	71.5	1 587	1 095 823	0.4	2.64	44	18.3	28.6
MISSOURI	13.0	8.7	4.6	2.1	38.3	51.0	3.7	66.1	6 419	2 354 809	-0.3	2.5	47.8	11.9	29.8
MONTANA	14.7	9.7	4.8	2.1	39.8	49.8	2.3	54.3	451	410 962	1.2	2.42	48.5	8.2	31.2
NEBRASKA	12.5	7.7	4.5	2.2	36.2	50.2	6.7	65.2	4 442	740 765	1.4	2.47	50.2	10.5	28.6
NEVADA	12.2	8.8	4.0	1.3	37.5	49.7	19.4	25.8	10 089	1 021 519	1.9	2.74	43.8	12.5	29.2
NEW HAMPSHIRE	14.9	9.3	4.5	2.1	42.6	50.6	6.0	42.7	2 103	519 756	0.1	2.47	52.1	9.8	25.4
NEW JERSEY	12.9	8.1	4.4	2.2	39.5	51.2	21.9	52.7	51 609	3 194 844	0.6	2.74	50.3	13.8	25.9
NEW MEXICO	12.9	9.0	4.5	1.8	37.1	50.5	9.9	52.9	3 359	760 916	1.0	2.68	44.8	14.0	29.9
NEW YORK	12.7	8.1	4.4	2.2	38.3	51.5	22.6	63.3	141 406	7 282 398	0.9	2.63	43.6	14.8	29.7
NORTH CAROLINA	12.5	8.7	4.3	1.7	38.2	51.3	7.7	57.5	17 152	3 790 620	0.9	2.56	47.6	13.6	28.4
NORTH DAKOTA	12.5	7.3	4.4	2.4	34.9	49.1	3.3	65.0	1 351	305 431	2.4	2.33	48.8	8.1	30.8
OHIO	13.6	8.7	4.7	2.2	39.3	51.0	4.2	75.1	14 641	4 593 172	0.6	2.46	45.8	13.2	30.4
OKLAHOMA	12.3	8.3	4.4	1.8	36.2	50.5	5.8	60.8	4 441	1 459 759	0.9	2.58	48.7	12.5	28.2
OREGON	13.6	9.4	4.4	2.1	39.2	50.5	9.9	46.0	7 379	1 535 511	0.8	2.53	47.6	10.7	28.1
PENNSYLVANIA	13.8	9.0	5.1	2.6	40.7	51.1	6.4	73.4	23 944	4 945 972	0.1	2.5	47.8	12.0	29.6
RHODE ISLAND	13.5	8.5	4.6	2.7	39.9	51.5	13.4	58.3	3 297	409 654	0.8	2.47	43.7	14.1	29.7
SOUTH CAROLINA	13.1	9.6	4.5	1.7	38.8	51.3	4.7	57.7	4 233	1 826 914	1.8	2.57	46.4	14.8	28.8
SOUTH DAKOTA	13.1	8.1	4.7	2.4	36.8	49.9	2.9	65.1	1 108	334 475	0.9	2.45	49.5	9.3	30.7
TENNESSEE	12.9	9.0	4.4	1.7	38.6	51.3	4.9	60.9	8 507	2 509 665	0.8	2.55	47.9	13.6	28.3
TEXAS	11.0	6.8	3.4	1.3	34.2	50.3	16.8	60.1	95 295	9 277 197	1.8	2.84	49.6	14.3	25.3
UTAH	9.4	5.9	3.0	1.2	30.5	49.7	8.5	62.2	6 166	918 370	2.1	3.16	61.7	9.5	19.3
VERMONT	15.4	9.9	4.8	2.3	42.6	50.8	4.1	52.3	791	257 229	1.6	2.34	48.9	9.6	28.6
VIRGINIA	12.5	8.2	4.0	1.7	37.7	50.8	12.1	49.2	28 477	3 083 820	0.9	2.62	50.1	12.4	27.0
WASHINGTON	12.9	8.4	3.9	1.8	37.5	50.0	13.4	47.7	22 710	2 679 601	1.3	2.58	49.6	10.3	27.7
WEST VIRGINIA	14.6	10.3	5.4	2.1	42.0	50.6	1.4	70.2	783	735 375	-0.4	2.45	48.4	11.4	29.6
WISCONSIN	13.6	8.4	4.6	2.2	39.2	50.4	4.9	71.2	5 997	2 307 685	0.8	2.43	49.1	10.3	28.5
WYOMING	13.8	8.3	4.0	1.7	36.8	49.1	3.8	41.0	414	232 594	3.8	2.45	50.3	8.5	28.8

1. No spouse present.

Table A. States — Population Change

STATE	Population, 1990–2010 — Census counts			Population change, 1990–2015 — Percent change			Components of change, 2010–2015		Migration			Population, 2020–2030 — Projections		
	1990	2000	2010	1990–2000	2000–2010	2010–2015	Births	Deaths	Net migration	International	Net internal	2020	2025	2030
	31	32	33	34	35	36	37	38	39	40	41	42	43	44
UNITED STATES	248 709 873	281 421 906	308 745 538	13.2	9.7	4.1	20 782 904	13 457 078	5 334 889	5 334 889	(X)	335 804 546	349 439 199	363 584 435
ALABAMA	4 040 587	4 447 100	4 779 736	10.1	7.5	1.7	307 554	259 658	29 281	27 276	2 005	4 728 915	4 800 092	4 874 243
ALASKA	550 043	626 932	710 231	14	13.3	4.0	60 037	21 274	-10 193	12 072	-22 265	774 421	820 881	867 674
ARIZONA	3 665 228	5 130 632	6 392 017	40.0	24.6	6.8	452 651	264 373	237 810	77 464	160 346	8 456 448	9 531 537	10 712 397
ARKANSAS	2 350 725	2 673 400	2 915 918	13.7	9.1	2.1	200 199	155 691	18 004	17 755	249	3 060 219	3 151 005	3 240 208
CALIFORNIA	29 760 021	33 871 648	37 253 956	13.8	10.0	5.1	2 633 571	1 301 177	568 884	834 999	-266 115	42 206 743	44 305 177	46 444 861
COLORADO	3 294 394	4 301 261	5 029 196	30.6	16.9	8.5	345 402	175 867	251 594	59 257	192 337	5 278 867	5 522 803	5 792 357
CONNECTICUT	3 287 116	3 405 565	3 574 097	3.6	4.9	0.5	192 515	154 371	-16 342	88 195	-104 537	3 675 650	3 691 016	3 688 630
DELAWARE	666 168	783 600	897 934	17.6	14.6	5.3	58 154	42 185	31 753	13 715	18 038	963 209	990 694	1 012 658
DISTRICT OF COLUMBIA	606 900	572 059	601 723	-5.7	5.2	11.7	49 128	25 445	46 433	20 837	25 596	480 540	455 108	433 414
FLORIDA	12 937 926	15 982 378	18 801 310	23.5	17.6	7.8	1 129 845	950 117	1 261 155	610 495	650 660	23 406 525	25 912 458	28 685 769
GEORGIA	6 478 216	8 186 453	9 687 653	26.4	18.3	5.4	685 978	386 638	217 464	134 971	82 493	10 843 753	11 438 622	12 017 838
HAWAII	1 108 229	1 211 537	1 360 301	9.3	12.3	5.2	100 046	56 486	28 359	46 782	-18 423	1 412 373	1 438 720	1 466 046
IDAHO	1 006 749	1 293 953	1 567 582	28.5	21.1	5.6	119 233	62 520	29 477	9 689	19 788	1 741 333	1 852 627	1 969 624
ILLINOIS	11 430 602	12 419 293	12 830 632	8.6	3.3	0.2	835 266	539 346	-255 588	170 366	-425 954	13 236 720	13 340 507	13 432 892
INDIANA	5 544 159	6 080 485	6 483 802	9.7	6.6	2.1	437 934	308 845	10 163	57 474	-47 311	6 627 008	6 721 322	6 810 108
IOWA	2 776 755	2 926 324	3 046 355	5.4	4.1	2.5	203 935	147 916	22 110	29 280	-7 170	3 020 496	2 993 222	2 955 172
KANSAS	2 477 574	2 688 418	2 853 118	8.5	6.1	2.1	207 325	130 240	-18 749	33 848	-52 597	2 890 566	2 919 002	2 940 084
KENTUCKY	3 685 296	4 041 769	4 339 367	9.7	7.4	2.0	291 435	226 513	22 163	34 455	-12 292	4 424 431	4 489 662	4 554 998
LOUISIANA	4 219 973	4 468 976	4 533 372	5.9	1.4	3.0	328 781	220 859	28 906	39 473	-10 567	4 719 160	4 762 398	4 802 633
MAINE	1 227 928	1 274 923	1 328 361	3.8	4.2	0.1	67 308	68 954	2 898	7 041	-4 143	1 408 665	1 414 402	1 411 097
MARYLAND	4 781 468	5 296 486	5 773 552	10.8	9	4	382 151	238 493	92 461	148 515	-56 054	6 497 626	6 762 732	7 022 251
MASSACHUSETTS	6 016 425	6 349 097	6 547 629	5.5	3.1	3.8	381 739	283 898	155 501	202 434	-46 933	6 855 546	6 938 636	7 012 009
MICHIGAN	9 295 297	9 938 444	9 883 640	6.9	-0.6	0.4	597 843	475 710	-80 039	111 091	-191 130	10 695 993	10 713 730	10 694 172
MINNESOTA	4 375 099	4 919 479	5 303 925	12.4	7.8	3.5	362 433	210 398	35 651	72 374	-36 723	5 900 769	6 108 787	6 306 130
MISSISSIPPI	2 573 216	2 844 658	2 967 297	10.5	4.3	0.8	204 190	155 161	-25 547	12 952	-38 499	3 044 812	3 069 420	3 092 410
MISSOURI	5 117 073	5 595 211	5 988 927	9.3	7	1.6	397 057	295 287	-4 445	47 373	-51 818	6 199 882	6 315 366	6 430 173
MONTANA	799 065	902 195	989 415	12.9	9.7	4.4	64 424	48 198	26 503	3 692	22 811	1 022 735	1 037 387	1 044 898
NEBRASKA	1 578 385	1 711 263	1 826 341	8.4	6.7	3.8	136 434	80 032	14 162	21 893	-7 731	1 802 678	1 812 787	1 820 247
NEVADA	1 201 833	1 998 257	2 700 551	66.3	35.1	7	185 956	111 222	111 180	41 949	69 231	3 452 283	3 863 298	4 282 102
NEW HAMPSHIRE	1 109 252	1 235 786	1 316 470	11.4	6.5	1.1	66 109	56 574	4 853	10 377	-5 524	1 524 751	1 586 348	1 646 471
NEW JERSEY	7 730 188	8 414 350	8 791 894	8.9	4.5	1.9	546 887	373 269	1 112	270 306	-269 194	9 461 635	9 636 644	9 802 440
NEW MEXICO	1 515 069	1 819 046	2 059 179	20.1	13.2	1.3	140 807	87 604	-27 115	15 926	-43 041	2 084 341	2 106 584	2 099 708
NEW YORK	17 990 455	18 976 457	19 378 102	5.5	2.1	2.2	1 260 125	792 242	-22 308	630 763	-653 071	19 576 920	19 540 179	19 477 429
NORTH CAROLINA	6 628 637	8 049 313	9 535 483	21.4	18.5	5.3	630 511	432 400	297 064	116 875	180 189	10 709 289	11 449 153	12 227 739
NORTH DAKOTA	638 800	642 200	672 591	0.5	4.7	12.5	53 765	31 480	61 105	8 057	53 048	630 112	620 777	606 566
OHIO	10 847 115	11 353 140	11 536 504	4.7	1.6	0.7	728 569	586 523	-57 852	95 444	-153 296	11 644 058	11 605 738	11 550 528
OKLAHOMA	3 145 585	3 450 654	3 751 351	4.7	8.7	4.3	278 907	197 438	76 903	33 359	43 544	3 735 690	3 820 994	3 913 251
OREGON	2 842 321	3 421 399	3 831 074	20.4	12	5.2	238 882	174 286	129 687	36 279	93 408	4 260 393	4 536 418	4 833 918
PENNSYLVANIA	11 881 643	12 281 054	12 702 379	3.4	3.4	0.8	746 467	671 050	32 402	164 475	-132 073	12 787 354	12 801 945	12 768 184
RHODE ISLAND	1 003 464	1 048 319	1 052 567	4.5	0.4	0.4	57 570	50 264	-3 445	22 298	-25 743	1 154 230	1 157 855	1 152 941
SOUTH CAROLINA	3 486 703	4 012 012	4 625 364	15.1	15.3	5.9	301 101	228 566	190 997	31 974	159 023	4 822 577	4 989 550	5 148 569
SOUTH DAKOTA	696 004	754 844	814 180	8.5	7.9	5.4	63 534	37 773	18 191	7 924	10 267	801 939	801 845	800 462
TENNESSEE	4 877 185	5 689 283	6 346 105	16.7	11.5	4	420 465	324 079	154 490	49 546	104 944	6 780 670	7 073 125	7 380 634
TEXAS	16 986 510	20 851 820	25 145 561	22.8	20.6	9.2	2 028 029	920 595	1 199 941	463 449	736 492	28 634 896	30 865 134	33 317 744
UTAH	1 722 850	2 233 169	2 763 885	29.6	23.8	8.4	270 428	81 869	43 920	29 344	14 576	2 990 094	3 225 680	3 485 367
VERMONT	562 758	608 827	625 741	8.2	2.8	0	31 716	28 538	-2 432	4 050	-6 482	690 686	703 288	711 867
VIRGINIA	6 187 358	7 078 515	8 001 024	14.4	13	4.8	539 449	324 842	164 981	182 418	-17 437	8 917 395	9 364 304	9 825 019
WASHINGTON	4 866 692	5 894 121	6 724 540	21.1	14.1	6.6	459 178	268 172	251 442	127 116	124 326	7 432 136	7 996 400	8 624 801
WEST VIRGINIA	1 793 477	1 808 344	1 852 994	0.8	2.5	-0.5	108 647	114 205	-1 907	6 259	-8 166	1 801 112	1 766 435	1 719 959
WISCONSIN	4 891 769	5 363 675	5 686 986	9.6	6	1.5	353 372	254 683	-14 210	38 001	-52 211	6 004 954	6 088 374	6 150 764
WYOMING	453 588	493 782	563 626	8.9	14.1	4	39 862	23 752	6 061	2 932	3 129	530 948	529 031	522 979

Table A. States — **Population Characteristics**

STATE	Population characteristics, 2010																		
	Race (percent)							Age (percent)											
	White alone	Black alone	American Indian, Alaska Native alone	Asian and Pacific Islander alone	Some other race or two or more races	Percent Hispanic or Latino[1]	Percent foreign born	Under 5 years	5 to 17 years	18 to 24 years	25 to 34 years	35 to 44 years	45 to 54 years	55 to 64 years	65 to 74 years	75 to 84 years	85 years and over	Median age	Percent female
	45	46	47	48	49	50	51	52	53	54	55	56	57	58	59	60	61	62	63
UNITED STATES	72.4	12.6	0.9	5.0	9.1	16.3	12.9	6.5	17.5	9.9	13.3	13.3	14.6	11.8	7.0	4.2	1.8	37.2	50.8
ALABAMA	68.5	26.2	0.6	1.2	3.5	3.9	3.5	6.4	17.3	10.0	12.6	13	14.5	12.3	7.8	4.4	1.6	37.9	51.5
ALASKA	66.7	3.3	14.8	6.4	8.9	5.5	6.9	7.6	18.8	10.5	14.5	13.1	15.6	12.1	5.0	2.1	0.6	33.8	48.0
ARIZONA	73.0	4.1	4.6	3.0	15.3	29.6	13.4	7.1	18.4	9.9	13.4	12.9	13.2	11.4	7.8	4.4	1.6	35.9	50.3
ARKANSAS	77.0	15.4	0.8	1.4	5.4	6.4	4.5	6.8	17.6	9.7	12.6	12.6	14.0	12.0	8.0	4.6	1.8	37.4	50.9
CALIFORNIA	57.6	6.2	1.0	13.4	21.9	37.6	27.2	6.8	18.2	10.5	14.2	13.9	14.1	10.8	6.1	3.7	1.6	35.2	50.3
COLORADO	81.3	4.0	1.1	2.9	10.6	20.7	9.8	6.8	17.5	9.7	14.4	13.9	14.8	11.9	6.2	3.4	1.4	36.1	49.9
CONNECTICUT	77.6	10.1	0.3	3.8	8.2	13.4	13.6	5.7	17.2	9.1	11.8	13.6	16.1	12.4	7.1	4.6	2.4	40.0	51.3
DELAWARE	68.9	21.4	0.5	3.2	6.1	8.2	8.0	6.2	16.7	10.1	12.3	12.9	14.9	12.4	8.1	4.5	1.8	38.8	51.6
DISTRICT OF COLUMBIA	38.5	50.7	0.3	3.6	7.0	9.1	13.5	5.4	11.3	14.5	20.9	13.4	12.6	10.6	6.1	3.5	1.8	33.8	52.8
FLORIDA	75.0	16.0	0.4	2.5	6.1	22.5	19.4	5.7	15.6	9.3	12.1	12.9	14.6	12.4	9.2	5.7	2.4	40.7	51.1
GEORGIA	59.7	30.5	0.3	3.3	6.1	8.8	9.7	7.1	18.6	10.0	13.6	14.4	14.4	11.0	6.3	3.1	1.2	35.3	51.2
HAWAII	24.7	1.6	0.3	48.6	24.8	8.9	18.2	6.4	15.9	9.6	13.3	13.0	14.2	12.9	7.4	4.7	2.3	38.6	49.9
IDAHO	89.1	0.6	1.4	1.3	7.6	11.2	5.5	7.8	19.6	9.9	13.3	12.2	13.3	11.5	7.0	3.8	1.7	34.6	49.9
ILLINOIS	71.5	14.5	0.3	4.6	9.0	15.8	13.7	6.5	17.9	9.7	13.9	13.5	14.6	11.5	6.6	4.0	1.9	36.6	51.0
INDIANA	84.3	9.1	0.3	1.6	4.7	6.0	4.6	6.7	18.1	10.0	12.7	13.0	14.6	11.9	7.0	4.3	1.7	37.0	50.8
IOWA	91.3	2.9	0.4	1.8	3.6	5.0	4.6	6.6	17.3	10.0	12.6	12.0	14.4	12.2	7.4	5.0	2.5	38.1	50.5
KANSAS	83.8	5.9	1	2.5	6.9	10.5	6.5	7.2	18.3	10.1	13.0	12.2	14.2	11.6	6.7	4.3	2.1	36.0	50.4
KENTUCKY	87.8	7.8	0.2	1.2	3.0	3.1	3.2	6.5	17.1	9.5	13.0	13.3	14.8	12.4	7.5	4.2	1.6	38.1	50.8
LOUISIANA	62.6	32.0	0.7	1.5	3.1	4.2	3.8	6.9	17.7	10.5	13.7	12.5	14.4	11.8	6.9	3.9	1.5	35.8	51.0
MAINE	95.2	1.2	0.6	1.0	1.9	1.3	3.4	5.2	15.4	8.7	10.9	12.9	16.5	14.5	8.5	5.3	2.1	42.7	51.1
MARYLAND	58.2	29.4	0.4	5.6	6.5	8.2	13.9	6.3	17.1	9.7	13.2	13.8	15.6	12.1	6.7	3.9	1.7	38.0	51.6
MASSACHUSETTS	80.4	6.6	0.3	5.3	7.3	9.6	15	5.6	16.1	10.4	12.9	13.5	15.5	12.3	7.0	4.6	2.2	39.1	51.6
MICHIGAN	78.9	14.2	0.6	2.4	3.8	4.4	6.0	6.0	17.7	9.9	11.7	12.9	15.3	12.7	7.3	4.5	1.9	38.9	50.9
MINNESOTA	85.3	5.2	1.1	4.0	4.3	4.7	7.1	6.7	17.5	9.5	13.5	12.8	15.2	11.9	6.7	4.2	2.0	37.4	50.4
MISSISSIPPI	59.1	37.0	0.5	0.9	2.4	2.7	2.1	7.1	18.4	10.3	12.6	12.6	14.1	11.7	7.2	4.1	1.5	36.0	51.4
MISSOURI	82.8	11.6	0.5	1.7	3.4	3.5	3.9	6.5	17.3	9.8	12.9	12.5	14.8	12.1	7.5	4.5	2.0	37.9	51.0
MONTANA	89.4	0.4	6.3	0.7	3.1	2.9	2.0	6.3	16.3	9.6	12.3	11.4	15.1	14.0	8.2	4.7	2.0	39.8	49.8
NEBRASKA	86.1	4.5	1	1.9	6.5	9.2	6.1	7.2	17.9	10.0	13.2	12.1	14.2	11.7	6.7	4.7	2.2	36.2	50.4
NEVADA	66.2	8.1	1.2	7.8	16.7	26.5	18.8	6.9	17.7	9.2	14.3	14.2	13.9	11.7	7.3	3.6	1.1	36.3	49.5
NEW HAMPSHIRE	93.9	1.1	0.2	2.2	2.5	2.8	5.3	5.3	16.5	9.4	11.0	13.6	17.2	13.5	7.4	4.4	1.8	41.1	50.7
NEW JERSEY	68.6	13.7	0.3	8.3	9.1	17.7	21.0	6.2	17.3	8.7	12.6	14.1	15.7	11.9	7.0	4.5	2.0	39.0	51.3
NEW MEXICO	68.4	2.1	9.4	1.5	18.7	46.3	9.9	7.0	18.1	9.9	12.8	12.1	14.2	12.5	7.5	4.3	1.5	36.7	50.6
NEW YORK	65.7	15.9	0.6	7.3	10.4	17.6	22.2	6.0	16.4	10.2	13.7	13.5	14.9	11.9	7.0	4.5	2.0	38.0	51.6
NORTH CAROLINA	68.5	21.5	1.3	2.3	6.5	8.4	7.5	6.6	17.3	9.8	13.0	13.9	14.4	11.9	7.3	4.1	1.6	37.4	51.3
NORTH DAKOTA	90.0	1.2	5.4	1.0	2.3	2.0	2.5	6.6	15.7	12.0	13.1	11.2	14.4	12.2	7.0	5.1	2.5	37.0	49.5
OHIO	82.7	12.2	0.2	1.7	3.2	3.1	4.1	6.2	17.4	9.5	12.4	12.8	15.1	12.6	7.4	4.7	2.0	38.8	51.2
OKLAHOMA	72.2	7.4	8.6	1.8	10.0	8.9	5.5	7.0	17.7	10.2	13.5	12.3	14.0	11.7	7.5	4.4	1.6	36.2	50.5
OREGON	83.6	1.8	1.4	4.0	9.1	11.7	9.8	6.2	16.4	9.4	13.7	13.0	14.1	13.3	7.6	4.3	2.0	38.4	50.5
PENNSYLVANIA	81.9	10.8	0.2	2.7	4.3	5.7	5.8	5.7	16.2	9.9	11.9	12.7	15.3	12.8	7.7	5.3	2.5	40.1	51.3
RHODE ISLAND	81.4	5.7	0.6	3.0	9.3	12.4	12.8	5.5	15.8	11.4	12.0	13.0	15.4	12.4	7.0	4.9	2.5	39.4	51.7
SOUTH CAROLINA	66.2	27.9	0.4	1.4	4.2	5.1	4.7	6.5	16.8	10.3	12.7	13.0	14.3	12.6	8.0	4.1	1.6	37.9	51.4
SOUTH DAKOTA	85.9	1.3	8.8	0.9	3.0	2.7	2.7	7.3	17.6	10.0	12.8	11.4	14.4	12.0	7.1	4.8	2.4	36.9	50.0
TENNESSEE	77.6	16.7	0.3	1.5	3.9	4.6	4.5	6.4	17.1	9.6	12.8	13.5	14.6	12.4	7.7	4.2	1.6	38.0	51.3
TEXAS	70.4	11.8	0.7	3.9	13.2	37.6	16.4	7.7	19.6	10.2	14.3	13.8	13.7	10.3	5.9	3.3	1.2	33.6	50.4
UTAH	86.1	1.1	1.2	2.9	8.7	13.0	8.0	9.5	22.0	11.5	16.2	12.0	11.1	8.7	5.0	2.9	1.1	29.2	49.8
VERMONT	95.3	1.0	0.4	1.3	2.0	1.5	4.4	5.1	15.5	10.4	11.2	12.5	16.4	14.4	7.9	4.5	2.1	41.5	50.7
VIRGINIA	68.6	19.4	0.4	5.6	6.1	7.9	11.4	6.4	16.8	10.0	13.6	13.9	15.2	11.9	6.9	3.8	1.5	37.5	50.9
WASHINGTON	77.3	3.6	1.5	7.8	9.9	11.2	13.1	6.5	17.0	9.7	13.9	13.5	14.7	12.4	6.8	3.7	1.8	37.3	50.2
WEST VIRGINIA	93.9	3.4	0.2	0.7	1.8	1.2	1.2	5.6	15.3	9.1	11.7	12.8	14.9	14.3	8.8	5.2	2.0	41.3	50.7
WISCONSIN	86.2	6.3	1.0	2.3	4.2	5.9	4.5	6.3	17.3	9.7	12.6	12.8	15.4	12.3	7.0	4.6	2.1	38.5	50.4
WYOMING	90.7	0.8	2.4	0.9	5.2	8.9	2.8	7.1	16.9	10.0	13.6	11.9	14.8	13.0	7.0	3.8	1.6	36.8	49.0

1. May be of any race.

Table A. States — Households and Housing Units

	Households, 2010					Housing units, 2010									
STATE				Percent				Occupied units							
										Owner-occupied			Renter-occupied		
											Median owner cost				
	Number	Percent change, 2000–2010	Persons per house-hold	Female family house-holder[1]	One person house-holds	Total	Percent change, 2000–2010	Total	Percent	Median value[2] (dollars)	With a mort-gage	Without a mort-gage[3]	Median gross rent[4] (dollars)	Median rent as a percent of income	Sub-standard units[5] (percent)
	64	65	66	67	68	69	70	71	72	73	74	75	76	77	78
UNITED STATES	116 716 292	10.7	2.58	13.1	26.7	131 791 065	13.7	114 567 419	65.4	179 900	25.1	12.8	855	31.6	3.9
ALABAMA	1 883 791	8.4	2.48	15.3	27.4	2 174 428	10.7	1 815 152	70.1	123 900	23.0	12.3	667	32.2	2.4
ALASKA	258 058	16.5	2.65	10.7	25.6	307 065	17.7	254 610	63.9	241 400	23.3	10.8	981	29.0	10.2
ARIZONA	2 380 990	25.2	2.63	12.4	26.1	2 846 738	30.0	2 334 050	65.2	168 800	26.5	11.3	844	31.6	5.1
ARKANSAS	1 147 084	10.0	2.47	13.4	27.1	1 317 818	12.3	1 114 902	67.4	106 300	21.5	10.9	638	29.9	3.2
CALIFORNIA	12 577 498	9.3	2.9	13.3	23.3	13 682 976	12.0	12 406 475	55.6	370 900	30.6	11.4	1 163	33.8	9.1
COLORADO	1 972 868	19.0	2.49	10.1	27.9	2 214 262	22.5	1 960 585	65.9	236 600	25.2	10.7	863	31.2	3.2
CONNECTICUT	1 371 087	5.3	2.52	12.9	27.3	1 488 215	7.4	1 358 809	68.0	288 800	26.8	17.6	992	32.1	2.4
DELAWARE	342 297	14.6	2.55	14.2	25.6	406 489	18.5	328 765	73.0	243 600	24.8	11.8	952	32.3	2.9
DISTRICT OF COLUMBIA	266 707	7.4	2.11	16.4	44.0	296 836	8.0	252 388	42.5	426 900	24.8	11.0	1 198	30.4	3.5
FLORIDA	7 420 802	17.1	2.48	13.5	27.2	8 994 091	23.2	7 035 068	68.1	164 200	29.5	14.4	947	35.5	3.1
GEORGIA	3 585 584	19.3	2.63	15.8	25.4	4 091 482	24.7	3 482 420	66.2	156 200	25.2	12.3	819	32.4	3.2
HAWAII	455 338	12.9	2.89	12.6	23.3	519 992	12.9	445 812	58.0	525 400	30.1	10.1	1 291	33.5	9.1
IDAHO	579 408	23.4	2.66	9.6	23.8	668 634	26.7	576 709	69.6	165 100	24.7	10.6	683	30.5	3.6
ILLINOIS	4 836 972	5.3	2.59	12.9	27.8	5 297 077	8.4	4 752 857	67.7	191 800	25.9	13.8	848	31.5	3.1
INDIANA	2 502 154	7.1	2.52	12.4	26.9	2 797 172	10.5	2 470 905	70.3	123 300	21.6	11.0	683	30.8	2.2
IOWA	1 221 576	6.3	2.41	9.3	28.4	1 337 563	8.5	1 223 439	72.4	123 400	21.3	11.5	629	28.1	1.7
KANSAS	1 112 096	7.1	2.49	10.4	27.8	1 234 037	9.1	1 101 658	68.1	127 300	21.8	11.8	682	28.1	2.2
KENTUCKY	1 719 965	8.1	2.45	12.7	27.5	1 928 617	10.1	1 684 348	68.6	121 600	22.2	11.3	613	29.8	2.5
LOUISIANA	1 728 360	4.4	2.55	17.2	26.9	1 967 947	6.5	1 689 822	67.6	137 500	21.6	10.5	736	31.7	3.7
MAINE	557 219	7.5	2.32	10.0	28.6	722 217	10.8	545 417	72.7	179 100	24.1	13.9	707	29.8	2.5
MARYLAND	2 156 411	8.9	2.61	14.6	26.1	2 380 605	11.0	2 127 439	67.0	301 400	25.4	12.9	1 131	30.8	2.4
MASSACHUSETTS	2 547 075	4.2	2.48	12.5	28.7	2 808 727	7.1	2 520 419	62.2	334 100	26.1	15.3	1 009	30.4	2.0
MICHIGAN	3 872 508	2.3	2.49	13.2	27.9	4 531 231	7.0	3 806 621	72.8	123 300	24.6	13.9	730	33.3	2.1
MINNESOTA	2 087 227	10.1	2.48	9.5	28.0	2 348 242	13.7	2 091 548	73.0	194 300	24.1	11.9	764	30.2	2.3
MISSISSIPPI	1 115 768	6.6	2.58	18.5	26.3	1 276 441	9.9	1 079 999	69.8	100 100	23.5	12.0	672	33.2	4.0
MISSOURI	2 375 611	8.2	2.45	12.3	28.3	2 714 017	11.1	2 350 628	69.0	139 000	22.6	11.7	682	30.1	2.2
MONTANA	409 607	14.2	2.35	9.0	29.7	483 006	17.1	402 747	69.7	181 200	24.1	11.3	642	28.3	2.8
NEBRASKA	721 130	8.2	2.46	9.8	28.7	797 677	10.4	719 304	67.4	127 600	21.4	12.6	669	27.7	2.2
NEVADA	1 006 250	34.0	2.65	12.7	25.7	1 175 070	42.0	989 811	57.2	174 800	28.1	12.2	952	31.6	5.0
NEW HAMPSHIRE	518 973	9.3	2.46	9.7	25.6	614 996	12.4	515 431	71.7	243 000	26.5	16.5	951	30.3	1.9
NEW JERSEY	3 214 360	4.9	2.68	13.3	25.2	3 554 909	7.4	3 172 421	66.4	339 200	28.7	18.9	1 114	32.4	4.1
NEW MEXICO	791 395	16.7	2.55	14.0	28.0	902 242	15.6	765 183	67.9	161 200	24.3	10.0	699	29.3	4.7
NEW YORK	7 317 755	3.7	2.57	14.9	29.1	8 108 211	5.6	7 196 427	54.3	296 500	26.3	15.5	1 020	31.7	5.5
NORTH CAROLINA	3 745 155	19.6	2.48	13.7	27.0	4 333 479	23.0	3 670 859	67.2	154 200	24.0	12.5	731	31.3	2.8
NORTH DAKOTA	281 192	9.3	2.3	8.2	31.5	318 099	9.8	280 412	66.9	123 000	19.6	10.0	583	25.8	1.3
OHIO	4 603 435	3.5	2.44	13.1	28.9	5 128 113	7.2	4 525 066	68.4	134 400	23.4	13.1	685	31.1	1.8
OKLAHOMA	1 460 450	8.8	2.49	12.3	27.5	1 666 205	10.0	1 432 959	67.8	111 400	21.9	11.2	659	28.9	3.0
OREGON	1 518 938	13.9	2.47	10.5	27.4	1 676 476	15.4	1 507 137	62.5	244 500	27.3	12.9	816	32.7	3.4
PENNSYLVANIA	5 018 904	5.1	2.45	12.2	28.6	5 568 820	6.1	4 936 030	70.1	165 500	23.8	13.7	763	30.4	1.6
RHODE ISLAND	413 600	1.3	2.44	13.5	29.6	463 416	5.4	402 295	60.8	254 500	27.7	15.4	868	30.9	2.6
SOUTH CAROLINA	1 801 181	17.4	2.49	15.6	26.5	2 140 337	22.0	1 761 393	68.7	138 100	23.5	12.0	728	32.2	2.7
SOUTH DAKOTA	322 282	11.0	2.42	9.7	29.4	364 031	12.6	318 955	68.0	129 700	21.9	10.9	591	26.9	2.7
TENNESSEE	2 493 552	11.7	2.48	13.9	26.9	2 815 087	15.4	2 440 663	68.1	139 000	23.7	11.4	697	31.4	2.5
TEXAS	8 922 933	20.7	2.75	14.1	24.2	9 996 209	22.5	8 738 664	63.6	128 100	23.4	12.5	801	30.2	5.8
UTAH	877 692	25.2	3.1	9.7	18.7	981 821	27.7	880 025	69.9	217 200	24.8	10.0	796	29.5	4.6
VERMONT	256 442	6.6	2.34	9.6	28.2	322 698	9.6	256 922	70.4	216 800	26.0	16.3	823	31.8	2.2
VIRGINIA	3 056 058	13.2	2.54	12.4	26.0	3 368 674	16.0	2 992 732	67.7	249 100	24.7	11.4	1 019	30.2	2.6
WASHINGTON	2 620 076	15.4	2.51	10.5	27.2	2 888 594	17.9	2 606 863	63.1	271 800	26.7	12.1	908	30.6	3.4
WEST VIRGINIA	763 831	3.7	2.36	11.2	28.4	882 213	4.5	741 940	74.6	95 100	20.1	10.0	571	29.7	1.8
WISCONSIN	2 279 768	9.4	2.43	10.3	28.2	2 625 477	13.1	2 279 532	68.7	169 400	24.5	14.0	715	29.8	2.2
WYOMING	226 879	17.2	2.42	8.9	28.0	262 286	17.2	222 803	69.7	180 100	22.0	10.0	693	25.3	2.8

1. No spouse present.   2. Specified owner-occupied units.   3. Median monthly costs is often in the minimum category—10.0 percent or less, which is indicated as 10.0 percent.
4. Specified renter-occupied units.   5. Overcrowded or lacking complete plumbing facilities.

Table A. States — **Housing Units**

STATE	Total	Percent change, 2013–2014	Total	Percent owner-occupied	Owners with a mort-gage	Renter	With a mort-gage	Without a mort-gage[2]	Median monthly housing costs (dollars)	Median value of units[3] (dollars)	Percent valued over $500,000	Median gross rent[4] (dollars)	Sub-standard units[5] (percent)	Percent living in a different house than 1 year ago
	79	80	81	82	83	84	85	86	87	88	89	90	91	92
UNITED STATES	133 962 970	0.9	117 259 427	63.1	30.7	47.9	22.5	12.0	987	181 200	11.2	934	3.7	14.9
ALABAMA	2 208 030	0.8	1 841 217	67.7	28.0	44.7	21.0	10.9	726	125 600	3.1	717	2.1	14.8
ALASKA	308 571	0.4	249 659	62.5	26.9	46.8	21.9	10.2	1 258	254 500	7.1	1 183	9.6	19.2
ARIZONA	2 909 336	0.6	2 428 743	61.1	29.1	45.6	21.7	10.2	923	176 700	7.8	916	4.9	18.4
ARKANSAS	1 341 081	0.9	1 131 288	65.8	24.4	41.8	19.7	10.7	673	112 500	2.3	683	2.8	15.9
CALIFORNIA	13 901 594	0.8	12 758 648	53.7	40.3	53.8	26.2	11.0	1 399	412 700	38.9	1 268	8.6	14.3
COLORADO	2 276 280	1.3	2 039 592	63.9	28.9	48.1	22.1	10.0	1 141	255 200	13.6	1 020	2.9	19.5
CONNECTICUT	1 493 632	0.4	1 355 817	66.4	34.0	49.7	23.9	15.8	1 371	267 200	16.1	1 076	2.1	12.6
DELAWARE	417 413	1.3	349 743	70.3	31.1	46.3	22.3	11.3	1093	230 500	6.9	1 024	1.6	12.3
DISTRICT OF COLUMBIA	306 184	1.1	277 378	40.6	26.4	45.5	21.0	11.9	1 513	486 900	48.3	1 360	3.8	20.8
FLORIDA	9 144 650	1.1	7 328 046	64.1	36.9	53.6	24.4	12.6	972	162 700	7.2	1 003	3.2	16.1
GEORGIA	4 151 387	1.0	3 587 521	62.2	29.4	47.5	21.6	11.1	931	147 900	5.6	882	2.8	15.7
HAWAII	530 118	0.7	450 769	56.7	40.3	52.6	26.7	10.0	1 489	528 000	53.2	1 448	9.0	14.4
IDAHO	685 098	1.3	591 587	68.0	27.1	41.9	21.6	10.0	807	165 300	4.7	755	3.4	17.2
ILLINOIS	5 307 508	0.3	4 772 421	65.5	31.4	46.3	22.6	13.2	1 031	171 900	7.8	905	2.9	13.4
INDIANA	2 829 630	0.7	2 502 739	68.6	22.6	45.4	19.5	10.8	799	124 300	2.4	753	2.3	15
IOWA	1 362 034	0.9	1 241 491	70.9	20.8	40.2	19.4	11.7	783	133 100	2.4	711	1.9	15.4
KANSAS	1 248 861	0.7	1 109 280	66.6	23.5	42.0	20.2	11.8	831	132 100	2.9	773	2.4	17
KENTUCKY	1 950 504	0.7	1 712 094	66.1	25.7	43.2	20.3	11.0	712	123 800	2.7	678	2.5	15.9
LOUISIANA	2 011 037	1.0	1 718 194	64.4	28.1	45.4	20.4	10.0	755	143 600	3.3	801	2.9	13.6
MAINE	727 693	0.6	549 841	71.3	31.4	46.6	23.0	14.1	865	174 800	6.0	776	2.3	13.6
MARYLAND	2 422 317	0.8	2 165 438	65.9	30.9	48.8	22.9	11.2	1 405	288 500	18.1	1 242	2.6	13.9
MASSACHUSETTS	2 828 592	0.5	2 549 336	61.6	32.5	47.8	23.3	14.3	1 342	338 900	23.4	1 107	2.5	13.3
MICHIGAN	4 540 088	0.3	3 834 574	70.2	26.4	48.0	20.9	12.9	843	125 700	3.0	788	1.9	14.9
MINNESOTA	2 385 261	0.7	2 129 195	71.7	24.8	45.5	21.0	11.3	994	188 300	5.9	859	2.4	14.3
MISSISSIPPI	1 294 738	0.9	1 095 823	67.7	30.4	43.5	21.9	12.0	678	104 000	1.7	711	3.3	13.6
MISSOURI	2 735 803	0.6	2 354 809	66.9	25.2	43.6	20.7	11.7	806	138 500	3.5	754	2.0	15.9
MONTANA	491 515	1.2	410 962	66.4	30.5	41.1	22.8	10.9	744	196 800	7.1	711	2.6	16.5
NEBRASKA	814 957	1.0	740 765	65.9	22.9	38.8	20.3	12.1	825	133 800	2.7	742	2.2	16.9
NEVADA	1 198 969	1.0	1 021 519	53.6	32.0	46.9	23.1	10.0	994	192 100	6.3	955	4.4	20.3
NEW HAMPSHIRE	619 865	0.5	519 756	70.2	32.5	46.9	23.9	16.1	1 229	236 400	6.9	994	2.0	13.7
NEW JERSEY	3 591 847	0.4	3 194 844	63.3	39.3	50.0	25.7	17.3	1 482	313 200	20.1	1 202	3.2	9.9
NEW MEXICO	912 910	0.9	760 916	66.9	32.1	45.8	22.4	10.0	771	158 400	5.4	777	4.6	14.1
NEW YORK	8 191 528	0.8	7 282 398	53.0	37.1	51.4	24.5	14.6	1 230	279 100	23.4	1 148	5.4	10.8
NORTH CAROLINA	4 452 464	1.3	3 790 620	64.2	28.3	46.3	21.5	11.8	851	155 000	5.2	803	2.8	15.3
NORTH DAKOTA	350 534	3.3	305 431	63.8	16.3	36.4	18.1	10.0	733	161 800	3.6	728	2.7	17.5
OHIO	5 147 282	0.5	4 593 172	65.3	24.7	44.3	20.5	12.3	817	129 100	2.5	735	1.7	15
OKLAHOMA	1 699 556	1.0	1 459 759	65.1	24.6	39.9	20.0	10.6	744	119 800	2.8	737	3.2	17.7
OREGON	1 700 611	1.0	1 535 511	60.7	32.7	51.9	23.8	12.2	1 006	239 800	10.5	924	3.7	18.6
PENNSYLVANIA	5 590 712	0.5	4 945 972	68.8	28.5	46.6	21.8	13.2	912	165 400	5.5	848	1.7	12.2
RHODE ISLAND	462 630	0.2	409 654	58.8	36.8	49.3	24.5	15.4	1 124	236 000	8.7	934	2.1	13.3
SOUTH CAROLINA	2 188 258	1.4	1 826 914	68.0	29.3	46.3	21.6	11.0	789	140 000	5.4	791	2.2	15.4
SOUTH DAKOTA	376 347	1.7	334 475	68.2	22.5	35.9	20.2	11.1	713	142 300	2.9	647	2.8	16.7
TENNESSEE	2 869 419	1.0	2 509 665	66.1	29.0	45.6	21.8	10.8	789	142 900	4.8	770	2.6	15.6
TEXAS	10 426 760	1.7	9 277 197	61.2	27.0	45.3	21.4	11.7	933	139 600	4.9	896	5.3	16.7
UTAH	1 022 593	1.6	918 370	69.2	27.3	43.7	22.2	10.0	1 024	223 200	7.7	886	3.5	16.8
VERMONT	325 774	0.6	257 229	70.0	35.4	47.2	24.4	16.8	1 058	214 600	6.4	917	2.2	13.5
VIRGINIA	3 446 585	1.0	3 083 820	65.3	28.5	46.6	22.1	10.3	1 184	247 800	17.3	1 116	2.4	16.2
WASHINGTON	2 963 293	1.2	2 679 601	61.7	31.5	47.1	23.4	11.4	1 156	266 200	16.0	1 032	3.5	17.5
WEST VIRGINIA	884 574	0.6	735 375	72.2	22.7	37.9	18.8	10.0	565	103 900	1.5	656	2.2	11.7
WISCONSIN	2 648 342	0.6	2 307 685	66.6	27.9	44.6	22.1	13.5	901	164 700	3.6	782	2.1	14.5
WYOMING	268 205	1.0	232 594	66.9	23.6	36.2	20.4	10.0	831	201 000	7.2	792	2.5	17.7

1. Excludes units where owner costs or gross rent as a percentage of households income cannot be calculated. 2. Median monthly costs is often in the minimum category—10.0 percent or less, which is indicated as 10.0 percent. 3. Specified owner-occupied units. 4. Specified renter-occupied units. 5. Overcrowded or lacking complete plumbing facilities.

Table A. States — Residential Construction, Vital Statistics, and Health

STATE	Value of residential construction authorized by building permits, 2014 — New construction ($1,000)	Number of housing units	Percent single family	Average sales price of new manufactured housing units put in place, 2014	Births, 2014 — Total	Rate[1]	Deaths, 2013 — Number Total	Infant[2]	Rate Crude[1]	Age-adjusted[1]	Infant[3]	Percent lacking health insurance, 2014 — All persons	Children under 18 years	Medicare beneficiaries 65 years and older, 2014
	93	94	95	96	97	98	99	100	101	102	103	104	105	106
UNITED STATES	223 611 322	1 182 582	58.9	$65 300	3 988 076	12.5	2 596 993	23 440	8.2	7.3	6.0	11.7	6.0	43 117 839
ALABAMA	2 416 774	14 054	73.0	$62 100	59 422	12.3	50 189	501	10.4	9.3	8.6	12.1	3.8	706 624
ALASKA	324 596	1 298	76.4	D	11 392	15.5	3 997	64	5.4	7.2	5.6	17.2	11.4	61 652
ARIZONA	6 985 714	28 910	77.2	$74 100	86 887	12.9	50 534	451	7.6	6.7	5.3	13.6	10.0	903 776
ARKANSAS	1 380 106	8 500	67.2	$65 400	38 511	13.0	30 437	288	10.3	8.9	7.6	11.8	4.8	443 367
CALIFORNIA	22 637 174	98 188	46.5	$97 000	502 879	13.0	248 359	2 353	6.5	6.3	4.8	12.4	5.4	4 418 863
COLORADO	7 532 619	31 871	62.8	$60 200	65 830	12.3	33 712	331	6.4	6.6	5.1	10.3	5.6	617 153
CONNECTICUT	1 282 308	6 077	40.1	$56 500	36 285	10.1	29 632	169	8.2	6.5	4.7	6.9	3.7	504 849
DELAWARE	641 676	5 221	81.2	$74 800	10 972	11.7	7 967	68	8.6	7.3	6.3	7.8	5.7	143 365
DISTRICT OF COLUMBIA	495 021	4 956	5.1	X	9 509	14.4	4 719	63	7.3	7.5	6.8	5.3	2.1	57 988
FLORIDA	23 439 129	109 924	61.6	$70 100	219 991	11.1	181 112	1 326	9.3	6.6	6.2	16.6	9.3	3 301 597
GEORGIA	7 955 101	45 549	71.6	$68 000	130 946	13.0	75 088	894	7.5	8.1	6.9	15.8	7.6	1 152 963
HAWAII	1 582 395	5 422	43.5	D	18 550	13.1	10 505	124	7.5	5.9	6.5	5.3	3.1	196 749
IDAHO	1 934 066	9 954	78.2	$72 500	22 876	14.0	12 434	126	7.7	7.3	5.6	13.6	7.8	225 262
ILLINOIS	4 136 596	19 571	51.5	$59 900	158 556	12.3	103 401	942	8.0	7.2	6.0	9.7	3.3	1 641 832
INDIANA	3 737 044	18 483	68.4	$52 800	84 080	12.7	60 716	600	9.2	8.3	7.2	11.9	7.2	910 531
IOWA	2 243 252	12 097	61.4	$59 600	39 687	12.8	28 948	162	9.4	7.2	4.1	6.2	3.2	477 462
KANSAS	1 646 377	8 644	58.6	$67 300	39 223	13.5	25 414	250	8.8	7.6	6.4	10.2	5.5	393 036
KENTUCKY	1 467 802	10 566	62.5	$61 200	56 170	12.7	43 759	355	10.0	9.0	6.4	8.5	4.3	627 434
LOUISIANA	2 777 014	13 830	89.1	$64 100	64 497	13.9	43 270	547	9.4	9.0	8.7	14.8	5.2	591 175
MAINE	683 014	3 699	77.1	$69 700	12 698	9.5	13 547	90	10.2	7.5	7.0	10.1	6.3	233 972
MARYLAND	3 080 620	17 057	65.1	$59 800	73 921	12.4	45 689	477	7.7	7.1	6.6	7.9	3.2	710 924
MASSACHUSETTS	3 980 521	17 424	39.7	$96 400	71 908	10.7	54 567	298	8.2	6.6	4.2	3.3	1.5	920 639
MICHIGAN	3 850 470	18 226	73.5	$59 600	114 375	11.5	92 408	799	9.3	7.8	7.0	8.5	3.8	1 500 400
MINNESOTA	4 135 089	19 545	55.8	$62 900	69 904	12.8	40 987	349	7.6	6.5	5.1	5.9	3.8	745 121
MISSISSIPPI	1 078 138	6 845	81.9	$55 800	38 736	12.9	30 703	373	10.3	9.6	9.7	14.5	5.3	413 375
MISSOURI	3 146 410	18 344	56.4	$60 900	75 360	12.4	57 444	491	9.5	8.1	6.5	11.7	7.2	881 117
MONTANA	827 389	4 826	62.0	$71 100	12 432	12.1	9 511	70	9.4	7.6	5.7	14.2	8.2	163 227
NEBRASKA	1 317 315	8 096	64.2	$63 300	26 794	14.2	15 754	139	8.4	7.1	5.3	9.7	5.3	256 020
NEVADA	2 141 757	14 083	74.0	$77 800	35 861	12.6	21 468	191	7.7	7.7	5.5	15.2	9.6	351 756
NEW HAMPSHIRE	736 931	3 763	64.4	$81 800	12 302	9.3	10 897	70	8.2	6.8	5.7	9.2	4.4	200 224
NEW JERSEY	4 051 996	30 560	34.4	$68 000	103 305	11.6	71 403	460	8.0	6.8	4.5	10.9	4.6	1 183 136
NEW MEXICO	872 141	4 599	85.3	$71 000	26 052	12.5	16 805	144	8.1	7.3	5.5	14.5	7.3	282 171
NEW YORK	10 826 337	74 611	13.5	$64 900	238 773	12.1	150 919	1 167	7.7	6.5	4.9	8.7	3.3	2 602 198
NORTH CAROLINA	9 707 931	54 757	71.1	$61 200	120 975	12.2	83 329	832	8.5	7.8	7.0	13.1	5.2	1 388 433
NORTH DAKOTA	953 024	6 256	55.0	$64 500	11 359	15.4	6 233	65	8.6	7.1	6.1	7.9	6.9	99 006
OHIO	3 982 890	20 047	67.5	$55 100	139 467	12.0	113 258	1 018	9.8	8.1	7.3	8.4	4.8	1 705 599
OKLAHOMA	2 216 234	11 545	82.9	$62 100	53 339	13.8	38 384	364	10.0	9.1	6.8	15.4	8.7	526 653
OREGON	3 591 958	17 510	58.6	$76 100	45 556	11.5	33 939	224	8.6	7.2	5.0	9.7	4.6	604 443
PENNSYLVANIA	4 406 389	22 854	67.5	$65 100	142 268	11.1	129 123	938	10.1	7.6	6.7	8.5	5.2	2 018 431
RHODE ISLAND	211 614	998	84.3	X	10 823	10.3	9 792	70	9.3	7.1	6.5	7.4	3.3	151 842
SOUTH CAROLINA	102 723 153	31 030	78.4	$64 400	57 627	11.9	44 582	389	9.3	8.4	6.9	13.6	5.5	725 877
SOUTH DAKOTA	6 242 696	4 482	64.0	$72 100	12 283	14.4	7 099	80	8.4	6.8	6.5	9.8	5.7	129 616
TENNESSEE	740 741	32 219	67.2	$62 000	81 602	12.5	63 406	544	9.8	8.8	6.8	12.0	5.2	942 920
TEXAS	5 596 464	175 443	60.1	$61 800	399 766	14.8	179 183	2 264	6.8	7.5	5.8	19.1	11.0	2 833 707
UTAH	29 086 961	18 297	68.4	$76 300	51 154	17.4	16 366	263	5.6	7.1	5.2	12.5	9.4	268 782
VERMONT	3 851 184	1 998	46.8	$65 400	6 130	9.8	5 639	26	9.0	7.1	4.4	5.0	2.2	102 242
VIRGINIA	333 954	28 469	69.8	$64 800	103 300	12.4	62 716	634	7.6	7.2	6.2	10.9	5.7	1 045 595
WASHINGTON	4 724 305	40 374	49.0	$90 400	88 585	12.5	51 264	388	7.4	6.8	4.5	9.2	4.7	931 846
WEST VIRGINIA	417 183	2 814	72.1	$66 300	20 301	11.0	21 843	158	11.8	9.2	7.6	8.6	3.0	314 518
WISCONSIN	3 078 382	16 793	58.3	$62 800	67 161	11.7	50 026	416	8.7	7.2	6.2	7.3	4.4	858 428
WYOMING	607 666	1 903	88.3	$75 400	7 696	13.2	4 516	35	7.8	7.3	4.6	12.0	5.9	77 532

1. Per 1,000 resident population.   2. Deaths of infants under 1 year old.   3. Deaths of infants under 1 year old per 1,000 live births.

Table A. States — **Crime and Education**

STATE	Serious crime known to police,[1] 2014				Public elementary and secondary school enrollment, 2013–2014		Educational attainment[3] (percent)				Local government expenditures for education, 2012–2013	
	Violent Crime		Property Crime				2010		2014			
	Number	Rate[2]	Number	Rate[2]	Total	Student/ teacher ratio	High school graduate or more	Bachelor's degree or more	High school graduate or more	Bachelor's degree or more	Total current expenditures (mil dol)	Current expenditures per student (dollars)
	107	108	109	110	111	112	113	114	115	116	117	118
UNITED STATES...............	1 197 987	375.7	8 277 829	2 596.1	50 044 522	16.1	85.6	28.2	86.9	30.1	535 665	10 763
ALABAMA.......................	20 727	427.4	154 094	3 177.6	746 204	15.8	82.1	21.9	84.7	23.5	6 532	8 773
ALASKA.........................	4 684	635.8	20 334	2 760.0	130 944	16.6	91.0	27.9	92.9	28.0	2 395	18 217
ARIZONA.......................	26 916	399.9	215 240	3 197.5	1 102 445	22.8	85.6	25.9	86.1	27.6	81 645	74 957
ARKANSAS.....................	14 243	480.1	99 018	3 338.0	489 979	14.0	82.9	19.5	85.3	21.4	46 372	95 387
CALIFORNIA....................	153 709	396.1	947 192	2 441.1	6 312 623	24.3	80.7	30.1	82.1	31.7	583 235	92 587
COLORADO.....................	16 554	309.1	135 510	2 530.1	876 999	17.5	89.7	36.4	90.5	38.3	7 507	8 693
CONNECTICUT.................	8 522	236.9	69 070	1 920.4	546 200	12.6	88.6	35.5	90.1	38.0	95 430	17 321
DELAWARE.....................	4 576	489.1	27 900	2 982.0	131 687	14.0	87.7	27.8	89.0	30.6	1 762	13 653
DISTRICT OF COLUMBIA ...	8 199	1 244.4	34 147	5 182.5	78 153	13.0	87.4	50.1	90.2	55.0	1 563	20 530
FLORIDA........................	107 521	540.5	679 446	3 415.5	2 720 744	15.3	85.5	25.8	87.2	27.3	232 146	86 237
GEORGIA.......................	38 097	377.3	331 316	3 281.2	1 723 909	15.8	84.3	27.3	85.6	29.1	155 367	91 217
HAWAII.........................	3 680	259.2	43 297	3 050.0	186 825	15.9	89.9	29.5	91.7	31.0	2 170	11 743
IDAHO..........................	3 468	212.2	30 316	1 854.8	296 476	19.8	88.3	24.4	90.1	25.0	19 257	67 617
ILLINOIS........................	47 663	370	267 385	2 075.9	2 066 990	15.2	86.9	30.8	88.2	32.8	257 839	12 443
INDIANA........................	24 099	365.3	174 776	2 649.4	1 047 385	17.5	87.0	22.7	88.4	24.7	98 112	94 217
IOWA...........................	8 497	273.5	65 056	2 093.8	502 964	14.2	90.6	24.9	92.1	27.7	5 144	10 291
KANSAS........................	10 123	348.6	79 431	2 735.2	496 440	13.0	89.2	29.8	90.3	31.5	4 896	10 011
KENTUCKY.....................	9 340	211.6	99 166	2 246.9	677 389	16.2	81.9	20.5	84.5	22.2	6 354	9 274
LOUISIANA.....................	23 934	514.7	160 824	3 458.8	711 491	15.3	81.9	21.4	83.6	22.9	74 921	10 539
MAINE..........................	1 700	127.8	26 421	1 986.4	183 995	11.9	90.3	26.8	91.7	29.4	23 505	12 655
MARYLAND.....................	26 661	446.1	149 859	2 507.5	866 169	14.8	88.1	36.1	89.6	38.2	121 085	14 086
MASSACHUSETTS	26 399	391.4	125 267	1 857.1	955 739	13.6	89.1	39.0	89.7	41.2	14 628	15 321
MICHIGAN......................	42 348	427.3	202 547	2 043.9	1 548 841	18.1	88.7	25.2	89.9	27.4	16 355	10 515
MINNESOTA....................	12 505	229.1	125 377	2 297.5	850 973	15.6	91.8	31.8	92.6	34.3	93 544	11 065
MISSISSIPPI....................	8 338	278.5	87 462	2 921.2	492 586	15.3	81.0	19.5	82.8	21.1	4 007	8 117
MISSOURI	26 856	442.9	176 237	2 906.5	918 288	13.8	86.9	25.6	88.9	27.5	89 058	97 027
MONTANA......................	3 313	323.7	25 312	2 472.9	144 129	14.0	91.7	28.8	92.6	29.3	1 524	10 662
NEBRASKA.....................	5 275	280.4	47 479	2 523.5	307 677	13.7	90.4	28.6	90.3	29.5	3 564	11 743
NEVADA	18 045	635.6	74 538	2 625.4	451 831	20.6	84.7	21.7	85.1	23.1	3 577	8 026
NEW HAMPSHIRE	2 602	196.1	26 041	1 962.7	186 310	12.6	91.5	32.8	92.2	35.0	2 655	14 050
NEW JERSEY	23 346	261.2	154 993	1 734.1	1 370 295	12.0	88.0	35.4	89.1	37.4	25 417	18 523
NEW MEXICO	12 459	597.4	73 877	3 542.3	339 244	15.3	83.3	25.0	84.2	26.4	3 099	9 164
NEW YORK	75 398	381.8	339 282	1 718.2	2 732 770	13.2	84.9	32.5	85.7	34.5	529 386	19 529
NORTH CAROLINA.............	32 767	329.5	285 697	2 873.1	1 530 857	15.4	84.7	26.5	86.4	28.7	12 667	8 342
NORTH DAKOTA	1 960	265.1	15 605	2 110.3	103 947	11.8	90.3	27.6	92.2	27.4	1 174	11 615
OHIO............................	33 030	284.9	324 528	2 799.1	1 724 111	16.3	88.1	24.6	89.4	26.6	19 506	11 276
OKLAHOMA....................	15 744	406	115 982	2 990.7	681 848	16.2	86.2	22.9	87.3	24.2	5 330	7 914
OREGON	9 224	232.3	114 305	2 879.0	593 000	22.2	88.8	28.8	89.7	30.8	5 396	9 183
PENNSYLVANIA................	40 164	314.1	247 016	1 931.7	1 755 236	14.5	88.4	27.1	89.4	29.0	23 713	13 445
RHODE ISLAND	2 313	219.2	22 935	2 173.6	142 008	14.5	83.5	30.2	85.8	30.4	2 121	14 889
SOUTH CAROLINA	24 052	497.7	167 217	3 460.3	745 657	15.5	84.1	24.5	86.1	26.3	6 950	9 444
SOUTH DAKOTA	2 786	326.5	15 902	1 863.9	130 890	13.8	89.6	26.3	91.7	27.8	1 126	8 630
TENNESSEE	39 848	608.4	200 447	3 060.6	993 556	15.1	83.6	23.1	85.8	25.3	8 532	8 588
TEXAS..........................	109 414	405.9	813 934	3 019.4	5 153 702	15.4	80.7	25.9	82.2	27.8	41 948	8 261
UTAH	6 346	215.6	84 711	2 878.5	625 461	23.0	90.6	29.3	91.4	31.1	3 945	6 432
VERMONT	622	99.3	9 551	1 524.4	88 690	10.6	91.0	33.6	92.0	34.9	1 549	17 286
VIRGINIA	16 340	196.2	160 720	1 930.3	1 273 825	14.1	86.5	34.2	88.5	36.7	13 869	10 960
WASHINGTON	20 136	285.2	261 706	3 706.1	1 058 936	19.3	89.8	31.1	90.4	33.1	10 217	9 714
WEST VIRGINIA................	5 588	302.0	37 648	2 034.7	280 958	14.1	83.2	17.5	85.2	19.2	31 861	11 257
WISCONSIN	16 714	290.3	120 238	2 088.3	874 414	15.1	90.1	26.3	91.4	28.4	97 587	11 186
WYOMING	1 142	195.5	11 477	1 964.7	92 732	12.3	92.3	24.1	92.6	26.6	1 439	15 815

1. Data for serious crimes have not been adjusted for underreporting; this may affect comparability between geographic areas and over time.   2. Per 100,000 population estimated by the FBI.   3. Persons 25 years old and over.

Table A. States — Exports, Income, and Poverty

STATE	Exports of goods by state of origin, 2015 (mil dol)			Income, 2014					Percent below poverty level, 2014				Families with related children under 18		
	Total	Manu-factured	Non-manu-factured	Per capita income (dollars)	Median income (dollars)	Percent with income of $25,000 or less	Percent with income of $100,000 or more	Median income of family of four	All persons	Children under 18 years	Persons 65 years and over	All families	Married-couple families	Male house-holder[1] families	Female house-holder[1] families
	119	120	121	122	123	124	125	126	127	128	129	130	131	132	133
UNITED STATES	1 504 914	1 112 350	150 765	28 889	53 657	23.1	23.6	80 545	15.5	21.7	9.5	11.3	8.2	21.6	40.6
ALABAMA	19 370	17 403	1 314	23 606	42 830	30.3	16.2	67 412	19.3	27.7	11.2	15.0	9.2	26.1	51.0
ALASKA	4 675	369	4 258	33 062	71 583	14.7	33.9	105 542	11.2	15.8	4.3	7.9	5.7	18.5	29.0
ARIZONA	22 563	13 378	4 022	25 715	50 068	24.2	19.9	71 195	18.2	25.6	9.4	13.2	12.1	25.2	40.3
ARKANSAS	5 874	4 355	555	22 883	41 262	30.0	14.0	60 477	18.9	26.4	10.6	13.8	10.2	23.0	46.7
CALIFORNIA	165 367	106 500	19 988	30 441	61 933	20.4	30.1	81 740	16.4	22.7	10.6	12.2	10.6	21.9	38.5
COLORADO	7 978	6 567	440	32 357	61 303	18.4	27.3	88 796	12.0	15.4	7.1	8.0	6.2	14.2	31.7
CONNECTICUT	15 256	13 380	616	39 373	70 048	18.1	34.1	109 688	10.8	14.9	7.8	7.5	4.1	20.2	31.3
DELAWARE	5 403	3 905	132	30 488	59 716	18.8	26.3	91 790	12.5	17.7	7.5	8.5	5.7	19.0	30.6
DISTRICT OF COLUMBIA	1 089	981	69	45 877	71 648	22.9	36.7	84 299	17.7	26.0	14.5	14.2	5.4	20.1	38.5
FLORIDA	53 844	39 800	3 583	26 582	47 463	25.5	18.7	66 509	16.5	23.8	10.5	12.0	9.6	23.1	39.7
GEORGIA	38 548	32 299	2 877	25 615	49 321	25.5	20.1	70 242	18.3	26.3	10.4	14.1	9.8	26.7	43.2
HAWAII	1 896	1 710	135	29 736	69 592	16.4	31.5	91 096	11.4	14.7	8.2	7.8	6.6	13.8	26.8
IDAHO	4 296	2 524	482	23 938	47 861	24.2	16.5	67 189	14.8	18.8	9.5	10.2	8.8	19.9	41.7
ILLINOIS	63 402	48 080	5 023	30 417	57 444	21.7	25.8	86 818	14.4	20.2	8.8	10.5	7.0	20.3	41.0
INDIANA	33 652	30 470	540	25 140	49 446	23.7	17.4	74 584	15.2	21.5	7.0	10.9	7.0	22.3	42.7
IOWA	13 114	10 763	1 870	28 361	53 712	21.8	20.1	81 600	12.2	15.3	7.4	7.9	5.2	17.5	38.7
KANSAS	10 686	8 158	1 807	27 870	52 504	22.0	20.5	80 639	13.6	17.7	7.9	9.2	6.3	18.9	39.2
KENTUCKY	28 053	22 706	462	23 684	42 958	30.0	15.6	69 593	19.1	26.2	11.3	14.5	10.4	31.4	49.1
LOUISIANA	49 183	32 463	16 161	24 800	44 555	29.8	19.0	74 184	19.8	27.9	12.8	14.9	7.7	21.9	47.6
MAINE	2 724	1 712	892	27 978	49 462	24.9	18.1	78 177	14.1	19.1	8.9	9.7	6.3	26.0	42.1
MARYLAND	10 030	7 378	811	36 338	73 971	15.2	36.1	107 081	10.1	13.0	7.4	7.1	4.1	13.9	25.4
MASSACHUSETTS	25 206	19 601	1 925	37 288	69 160	19.9	34.4	111 463	11.6	15.2	9.3	8.3	4.0	17.8	35.6
MICHIGAN	53 171	44 768	2 914	26 613	49 847	24.6	19.4	80 093	16.2	22.6	8.1	11.4	7.8	23.6	43.7
MINNESOTA	19 988	17 213	1 068	32 638	61 481	18.5	26.9	98 447	11.5	14.9	7.5	7.5	4.9	15.6	36.1
MISSISSIPPI	10 786	9 103	377	21 036	39 680	32.6	13.6	62 400	21.5	29.4	13.2	16.5	9.7	25.6	48
MISSOURI	13 617	11 659	1 021	26 126	48 363	25.1	18.0	74 298	15.5	21.1	9.0	10.7	7.1	23.0	41.8
MONTANA	1 386	906	332	25 989	46 328	25.7	17.0	71 261	15.4	18.5	8.3	9.5	7.5	19.0	45.1
NEBRASKA	6 556	5 367	895	27 446	52 686	21.5	20.1	82 330	12.4	16.2	7.9	8.7	5.6	15.8	37.7
NEVADA	8 658	6 864	447	25 773	51 450	22.3	18.9	67 807	15.2	22.0	8.3	11.0	9.1	19.0	34.3
NEW HAMPSHIRE	4 007	3 089	169	34 691	66 532	16.1	30.4	100 952	9.2	13.0	5.1	6.0	3.6	13.4	32.7
NEW JERSEY	32 076	23 019	2 865	36 593	71 919	17.5	36.0	110 956	11.1	15.9	8.6	8.3	5.3	18.8	31.8
NEW MEXICO	3 772	2 118	118	23 683	44 803	29.7	17.0	61 046	21.3	29.5	13.2	16.5	14.0	25.3	46.6
NEW YORK	80 059	41 085	12 249	33 095	58 878	23.1	28.1	88 642	15.9	22.6	11.7	12.2	9.3	21.5	39.2
NORTH CAROLINA	30 018	25 521	1 850	25 774	46 556	26.2	17.8	69 727	17.2	24.3	9.7	12.8	9.0	25.8	42.9
NORTH DAKOTA	3 863	1 849	1 902	33 071	59 029	19.5	24.4	84 506	11.5	14.8	8.7	7.4	3.1	19.6	41.5
OHIO	50 694	42 777	3 095	26 937	49 308	25.4	19.1	78 889	15.8	22.9	8.1	11.6	6.6	22.0	45.4
OKLAHOMA	5 258	4 456	244	25 229	47 529	25.9	17.5	67 219	16.6	22.4	8.5	12.2	8.6	21.7	43.2
OREGON	20 084	15 946	1 955	27 646	51 075	23.6	20.2	76 240	16.6	21.6	8.8	11.0	9.2	23.4	40.8
PENNSYLVANIA	39 403	30 695	3 066	29 220	53 234	23.0	22.4	86 010	13.6	19.4	8.1	9.4	5.8	22.2	39.7
RHODE ISLAND	2 125	1 393	540	30 830	54 891	23.6	25.3	87 352	14.3	19.8	9.7	10.0	5.0	25.0	40.2
SOUTH CAROLINA	30 861	28 746	697	24 596	45 238	27.7	16.6	66 807	18.0	27.1	9.3	13.2	8.2	25.0	46.6
SOUTH DAKOTA	1 405	1 277	91	26 959	50 979	22.7	17.7	80 150	14.2	18.0	10.6	9.4	6.0	20.5	39.3
TENNESSEE	32 431	23 927	1 201	24 922	44 361	28.4	16.5	67 438	18.3	26.2	10.1	13.7	10.0	25.2	48.7
TEXAS	251 087	185 124	20 916	27 125	53 035	23.3	23.6	72 612	17.2	24.6	10.9	13.4	10.8	21.2	41.8
UTAH	13 282	12 012	628	24 877	60 922	17.0	23.8	75 687	11.7	13.3	6.7	8.5	6.2	16.3	36.9
VERMONT	3 176	2 201	79	29 178	54 166	21.8	20.8	82 930	12.2	15.8	7.1	8.7	4.2	13.0	40.0
VIRGINIA	18 137	13 652	2 735	34 052	64 902	18.5	30.9	92 623	11.8	15.8	7.8	8.3	4.9	15.9	36.6
WASHINGTON	86 353	70 445	12 550	31 841	61 366	19.0	27.3	86 782	13.2	17.5	8.4	8.8	6.1	19.8	37.1
WEST VIRGINIA	5 722	3 719	1 796	22 714	41 059	31.2	13.3	67 036	18.3	24.7	9.3	13.1	9.3	27.4	52.3
WISCONSIN	22 445	19 482	1 220	28 213	52 622	21.7	20.1	85 859	13.2	18.4	7.2	9.0	5.4	20.7	42.1
WYOMING	1 174	1 088	55	29 698	57 055	20.6	23.9	84 067	11.2	12.8	6.2	7.4	4.2	13.9	39.0

1. No spouse present.

Table A. States — **Personal Income**

STATE	Total (mil dol)	Percent change, 2013–2014	Dollars	Rank	Wages and salaries[2]	Proprietors' income	Dividends, interest, and rent	Transfer payments Total	Government payments to individuals Total	Social Security	Medical payments	Income main-tenance	Unemploy-ment insurance
	134	135	136	137	138	139	140	141	142	143	144	145	146
UNITED STATES.................	14 683 147	4.4	46 049	X	7 469 374	1 350 318	2 723 288	2 529 139	2 464 527	834 640	1 111 605	267 763	36 067
ALABAMA	181 909	4.0	37 512	45	85 189	15 932	30 267	41 265	40 278	15 319	15 979	4 780	271
ALASKA	39 793	5.3	54 012	9	20 683	3 238	6 644	6 454	6 306	1 215	2 472	839	117
ARIZONA	255 093	4.7	37 895	42	127 815	18 683	46 310	52 107	50 740	17 727	22 548	4 854	397
ARKANSAS	112 076	3.7	37 782	43	50 513	9 629	22 819	26 201	25 601	9 116	11 220	2 561	281
CALIFORNIA......................	1 939 528	4.9	49 985	12	991 163	180 424	389 198	293 656	285 763	78 820	136 367	34 985	6 134
COLORADO.......................	261 735	6.2	48 869	15	138 654	27 435	52 895	34 042	32 953	11 453	14 318	2 910	528
CONNECTICUT	233 293	4.4	64 864	2	109 036	22 313	48 208	30 527	29 804	10 420	14 446	2 499	738
DELAWARE	43 392	4.6	46 378	21	23 632	4 236	7 255	8 427	8 237	2 974	3 839	668	96
DISTRICT OF COLUMBIA ...	46 016	3.3	69 838	1	64 668	6 077	8 544	5 976	5 848	1 058	3 446	943	67
FLORIDA...........................	850 178	5.0	42 737	29	379 080	51 780	221 757	171 152	167 095	60 690	72 833	17 303	967
GEORGIA	393 594	4.7	38 980	41	212 661	29 658	64 737	69 530	67 486	23 710	26 632	9 342	562
HAWAII	65 348	4.7	46 034	22	32 856	4 394	13 562	10 467	10 181	3 614	4 250	1 310	186
IDAHO	60 041	4.4	36 734	48	26 704	7 154	12 429	11 209	10 875	4 286	4 184	1 042	139
ILLINOIS	613 672	2.4	47 643	18	333 471	47 228	113 222	94 498	91 884	32 197	40 281	11 061	2 040
INDIANA...........................	261 092	3.8	39 578	39	132 382	21 705	39 364	51 618	50 286	19 344	21 251	5 012	442
IOWA...............................	139 625	3.2	44 937	25	67 196	17 802	24 638	23 254	22 629	8 974	9 675	1 948	417
KANSAS...........................	130 364	1.6	44 891	26	64 465	14 508	25 057	20 277	19 690	7 744	8 051	1 887	296
KENTUCKY.......................	165 044	4.3	37 396	46	81 576	11 941	25 586	40 001	39 111	13 059	17 941	4 193	403
LOUISIANA.......................	195 426	3.4	42 030	31	95 498	21 887	33 142	36 644	35 697	11 504	16 623	4 576	213
MAINE	54 195	3.1	40 745	34	25 794	3 907	9 323	12 351	12 082	4 363	5 424	1 065	157
MARYLAND	323 778	3.8	54 176	8	155 117	24 657	61 473	44 799	43 586	14 138	20 955	4 298	799
MASSACHUSETTS	396 206	4.4	58 737	3	221 843	32 005	74 156	58 939	57 589	17 913	29 377	5 934	1 607
MICHIGAN	403 726	4.1	40 740	36	204 476	28 330	67 245	86 899	84 887	32 602	36 472	9 042	1 099
MINNESOTA......................	267 389	4.0	48 998	14	145 926	23 157	47 508	42 753	41 647	14 321	19 619	3 861	789
MISSISSIPPI......................	103 091	2.4	34 431	51	45 443	10 084	15 214	26 367	25 762	8 586	11 669	3 310	169
MISSOURI	252 482	3.6	41 639	32	128 795	23 066	45 678	49 233	48 010	17 732	21 407	4 358	454
MONTANA	40 844	3.5	39 903	38	18 365	3 990	9 360	7 696	7 489	2 931	2 887	621	117
NEBRASKA.......................	89 479	3.5	47 557	19	43 427	14 205	16 457	12 800	12 420	4 701	5 088	1 119	107
NEVADA...........................	115 672	5.6	40 742	35	57 653	8 114	25 604	18 890	18 308	6 854	7 503	1 926	420
NEW HAMPSHIRE	70 020	4.8	52 773	10	33 048	5 935	13 175	10 162	9 895	4 257	3 956	805	107
NEW JERSEY.....................	515 020	4.7	57 620	4	240 628	43 312	90 987	73 415	71 596	25 149	32 527	6 740	2 261
NEW MEXICO	77 356	5.1	37 091	47	36 645	5 694	14 089	17 685	17 261	5 368	7 983	2 085	209
NEW YORK	1 098 103	4.0	55 611	6	600 733	103 802	208 669	190 197	186 215	52 300	98 146	21 803	2 568
NORTH CAROLINA.............	389 513	4.7	39 171	40	201 553	28 486	66 458	77 962	75 948	27 943	32 005	8 407	495
NORTH DAKOTA	41 265	4.8	55 802	5	24 022	4 275	8 070	5 055	4 907	1 727	2 005	413	81
OHIO...............................	489 695	3.8	42 236	30	255 254	39 285	74 485	98 057	95 713	32 681	44 766	9 858	1 012
OKLAHOMA	169 228	4.7	43 637	28	75 618	27 855	28 651	30 196	29 413	10 498	12 402	2 990	244
OREGON...........................	163 653	5.7	41 220	33	85 068	12 431	31 399	33 524	32 717	11 599	14 400	3 188	611
PENNSYLVANIA.................	609 679	3.6	47 679	17	296 487	55 611	103 602	116 997	114 430	40 819	52 961	10 628	2 390
RHODE ISLAND	51 027	5.0	48 359	16	24 528	4 055	8 966	10 285	10 074	3 147	4 819	1 094	193
SOUTH CAROLINA	177 242	4.7	36 677	49	85 576	11 748	29 557	40 138	39 162	14 966	15 570	4 198	232
SOUTH DAKOTA................	38 631	2.0	45 279	24	17 030	6 092	8 381	5 827	5 656	2 266	2 260	531	32
TENNESSEE	264 965	3.7	40 457	37	129 859	35 161	37 563	54 826	53 497	19 407	22 934	6 418	379
TEXAS	1 231 085	6.0	45 669	23	633 344	186 179	196 117	178 115	172 636	53 547	79 014	21 438	2 348
UTAH	110 842	4.5	37 664	44	60 628	10 395	19 749	15 113	14 511	5 291	5 357	1 862	196
VERMONT	29 090	3.5	46 428	20	13 653	2 368	5 517	6 030	5 905	2 010	2 828	573	78
VIRGINIA	419 185	3.5	50 345	11	215 572	27 798	84 059	55 799	54 119	20 686	21 284	5 241	515
WASHINGTON	350 322	5.8	49 610	13	181 978	25 979	72 149	55 427	53 989	18 397	22 321	5 342	1 124
WEST VIRGINIA.................	66 857	2.6	36 132	50	30 081	4 564	9 493	18 371	17 997	6 611	7 807	1 685	225
WISCONSIN	254 405	3.7	44 186	27	129 574	18 560	45 104	44 028	42 863	17 124	18 079	3 980	689
WYOMING	31 885	5.6	54 584	7	14 413	3 193	9 397	3 900	3 781	1 481	1 423	245	64

1. Based on the resident population estimated as of July 1 of the year shown.   2. Includes supplements to wages and salaries.

Table A. States — Personal Income and Earnings

STATE	Disposable personal income, 2014 Personal tax payments, 2014 (mil dol)	Total (mil dol)	Per capita[1] (dollars)	Earnings, 2014 Total (mil dol)	Farm	Goods-related[2] Total	Manu-facturing	Service-related and other[3] Total	Retail trade	Finance, insurance, real estate, rental and leasing	Health care and social assist-ance	Government	Gross state product, 2014 (mil dol)
	147	148	149	150	151	152	153	154	155	156	157	158	159
UNITED STATES	1 778 556	12 904 591	40 471	10 584 038	1.1	17.0	9.6	65.2	5.9	9.2	10.8	16.8	17 232 618
ALABAMA	16 903	165 006	34 026	122 159	1.5	21.2	14.3	57.1	6.8	6.6	10.5	20.2	200 414
ALASKA	3 568	36 225	49 170	30 059	0.0	20.0	3.0	49.9	5.4	4.2	10.7	30.1	56 647
ARIZONA	25 269	229 824	34 142	175 367	0.7	14.6	8.0	67.6	7.6	9.9	12.3	17.1	286 554
ARKANSAS	10 816	101 260	34 136	71 897	3.9	19.3	12.5	59.5	7.0	5.5	11.8	17.4	120 035
CALIFORNIA	271 296	1 668 232	42 993	1 406 611	1.3	14.6	9.4	66.7	5.6	8.6	9.4	17.4	2 305 921
COLORADO	32 552	229 183	42 791	194 861	0.7	17.7	6.1	65.7	5.4	7.9	8.8	15.9	305 871
CONNECTICUT	38 391	194 903	54 190	156 511	0.1	16.2	11.1	70.2	5.6	17.2	11.6	13.5	250 569
DELAWARE	4 797	38 595	41 251	33 712	1.6	11.4	6.1	71.4	5.9	16.2	12.7	15.4	63 404
DISTRICT OF COLUMBIA	6 747	39 269	59 599	88 173	0	1.7	0.2	58.8	1.0	4.9	5.6	39.5	116 378
FLORIDA	88 540	761 638	38 286	513 850	0.5	10.2	4.8	73.3	7.9	9.7	12.8	16.0	838 939
GEORGIA	43 337	350 256	34 688	292 802	0.9	14.5	9.3	67.3	6.2	8.0	9.7	17.4	474 696
HAWAII	6 708	58 640	41 309	46 744	0.6	9.1	1.8	58.9	6.0	6.4	9.6	31.3	76 171
IDAHO	5 861	54 180	33 148	40 297	6.4	18.3	11.2	57.9	8.1	6.1	11.4	17.4	63 235
ILLINOIS	81 260	532 412	41 334	457 157	0.9	16.5	11.2	68.2	5.2	10.0	10.1	14.4	736 285
INDIANA	27 606	233 486	35 394	186 498	2.0	27.9	21.4	57.3	6.2	6.1	12.3	12.9	318 085
IOWA	14 604	125 021	40 237	101 882	7.2	23.8	16.8	53.5	6.0	9.2	9.7	15.4	169 707
KANSAS	14 173	116 191	40 010	94 165	3.2	21.6	13.4	57.6	5.6	7.2	10.4	17.7	144 407
KENTUCKY	16 837	148 207	33 581	115 016	1.1	21.6	14.5	57	6.2	6.5	12.1	20.3	187 788
LOUISIANA	18 899	176 527	37 965	139 668	0.7	25.2	9.8	57.8	6.2	6.7	10.8	16.3	251 672
MAINE	5 618	48 577	36 521	35 953	0.6	16.3	10.0	65.1	8.2	7.3	16.3	18.0	54 324
MARYLAND	43 483	280 295	46 900	218 825	0.3	11.5	4.3	63.4	5.4	7.9	11.0	24.8	346 857
MASSACHUSETTS	62 159	334 047	49 522	301 712	0.1	13.8	8.6	73.3	4.7	12.2	13.5	12.8	455 732
MICHIGAN	45 491	358 235	36 149	281 051	0.7	22.3	17.1	62.1	6.0	6.6	12.3	14.9	448 243
MINNESOTA	36 276	231 113	42 350	201 540	2.2	18.4	12.7	66.3	5.4	10.2	12.4	13.1	317 237
MISSISSIPPI	8 496	94 594	31 594	66 466	3.1	21.4	12.9	53.5	7.4	5.4	10.7	21.9	104 753
MISSOURI	26 907	225 575	37 202	182 780	2.1	16.6	10.6	65.5	6.2	8.0	11.8	15.8	279 835
MONTANA	4 502	36 341	35 504	27 045	3.1	16.6	4.3	60.1	8.1	5.9	13.4	20.2	44 135
NEBRASKA	9 394	80 084	42 564	68 271	9.3	16.5	10.0	58.8	5.5	7.9	10.1	15.4	111 007
NEVADA	12 196	103 476	36 447	80 042	0.3	12.4	3.8	70.5	7.2	5.9	9.0	16.8	135 038
NEW HAMPSHIRE	7 061	62 959	47 452	46 322	0.1	18.6	12	68.4	8.6	9.3	12.5	12.9	70 358
NEW JERSEY	70 033	444 988	49 785	341 803	0.1	13.2	7.6	71.1	6.2	9.6	11.3	15.6	551 828
NEW MEXICO	7 002	70 354	33 734	51 684	2.5	16.2	4.1	54.5	6.7	5.0	11.2	26.9	91 885
NEW YORK	184 528	913 574	46 266	855 482	0.3	8.8	4.4	74.2	4.9	18.9	10.6	16.7	1 395 488
NORTH CAROLINA	42 199	347 313	34 927	279 194	1.5	17.4	11.9	61.7	6.4	8.2	10.3	19.4	481 876
NORTH DAKOTA	5 031	36 234	48 999	33 214	4.1	26.5	5.0	54.6	5.9	7.0	9.8	14.8	55 978
OHIO	54 246	435 449	37 558	358 460	0.6	20.5	14.6	63.6	6.0	8.0	12.9	15.3	576 056
OKLAHOMA	16 549	152 679	39 370	121 809	1.9	29.0	8.9	51.4	6.2	5.7	9.4	17.8	183 174
OREGON	20 901	142 752	35 956	117 285	1.5	18.8	12.7	62.6	6.6	6.2	12.3	17.1	212 807
PENNSYLVANIA	70 896	538 783	42 135	428 659	0.6	17.3	10.2	68.4	5.5	8.5	13.8	13.7	658 290
RHODE ISLAND	5 749	45 278	42 910	34 549	0.1	13.9	8.8	69.1	5.7	10.2	14.6	16.8	54 492
SOUTH CAROLINA	17 491	159 751	33 058	118 138	0.3	20.1	14.4	59.1	7.3	7.1	9.5	20.5	189 278
SOUTH DAKOTA	3 526	35 105	41 147	27 317	9.8	17.1	10.6	56.7	7.2	8.5	13.6	16.4	46 169
TENNESSEE	21 783	243 182	37 131	194 640	0.4	18.4	12.1	67.0	6.8	7.7	15.5	14.2	297 159
TEXAS	126 163	1 104 922	40 988	949 051	0.6	25.9	8.9	59.9	5.6	8.0	8.7	13.7	1 641 044
UTAH	12 002	98 840	33 586	85 811	0.7	19.2	10.1	63.0	7.6	8.8	8.6	17.1	140 031
VERMONT	3 030	26 060	41 593	19 608	1.6	18.6	11.2	60.4	7.6	5.8	14.2	19.5	29 312
VIRGINIA	51 651	367 534	44 141	293 622	0.2	11.6	5.9	64.4	5.2	7.1	8.8	23.7	462 861
WASHINGTON	36 702	313 620	44 412	249 711	1.3	17.2	11.1	62.8	6.9	6.1	10	18.8	422 877
WEST VIRGINIA	6 376	60 481	32 686	42 461	0	23.3	8.5	55.8	6.9	4.6	15	20.9	74 296
WISCONSIN	29 260	225 144	39 104	182 687	2.0	24.3	18.7	58.6	6.0	7.4	12.3	15.1	289 616
WYOMING	3 692	28 193	48 264	21 415	1.6	30.7	3.9	44.0	5.5	5.1	6.8	23.7	43 800

1. Based on the resident population estimated as of July 1 of the year shown.   2. Total includes mining, construction, and manufacturing.   3. Includes private sector earnings in forestry, fishing, related activities, and other; utilities; wholesale trade; transportation and warehousing; and information.

Table A. States — Social Security, Employment, and Labor Force

STATE	Social Security beneficiaries, December 2014		Supplemental Security Income recipients, December 2013	Civilian employment and selected occupations,[2] 2014				Civilian labor force (annual average), 2015				
					Percent						Unemployed	
	Number	Rate[1]		Total	Management, business, science and art occupations	Services, sales, and office occupations	Construction and production occupations	Total (1,000)	Percent change, 2014–2015	Employed (1,000)	Total (1,000)	Rate[3]
	160	161	162	163	164	165	166	167	168	169	170	171
UNITED STATES	57 499 952	180.3	8 334 413	148 019 908	36.9	41.9	21.2	157 130	0.8	148 834	8 296	5.3
ALABAMA	1 095 925	226.0	174 524	2 030 482	32.9	41.2	26.0	2 146	-0.7	2 015	131	6.1
ALASKA	89 047	120.9	12 399	352 531	35.8	39.7	24.6	364	-0.5	340	24	6.5
ARIZONA	1 207 102	179.3	119 510	2 866 629	35.1	45.9	19.0	3 153	1.8	2 960	193	6.1
ARKANSAS	673 193	226.9	111 482	1 269 092	32.4	41.4	26.3	1 330	2.0	1 261	69	5.2
CALIFORNIA	5 538 810	142.7	1 304 400	17 638 152	37.6	42.1	20.3	18 982	0.8	17 799	1 183	6.2
COLORADO	794 937	148.4	72 872	2 699 282	40.3	40.9	18.9	2 829	0.5	2 719	110	3.9
CONNECTICUT	654 533	182.0	63 259	1 798 758	42.5	40.4	17.1	1 888	0.1	1 782	106	5.6
DELAWARE	192 187	205.4	16 687	441 144	38.8	41.7	19.4	467	2.9	445	23	4.9
DISTRICT OF COLUMBIA	79 716	121.0	26 782	345 592	60.0	33.2	6.7	388	2.6	362	27	6.9
FLORIDA	4 223 274	212.3	561 125	8 738 970	34.2	47.6	18.3	9 675	0.7	9 153	522	5.4
GEORGIA	1 676 778	166.1	256 314	4 466 307	36.1	41.7	22.2	4 771	0.4	4 491	280	5.9
HAWAII	251 591	177.2	25 235	664 180	34.2	47.9	17.9	677	1.3	653	25	3.6
IDAHO	306 264	187.4	30 493	726 768	33.4	41.8	24.8	797	2.0	764	33	4.1
ILLINOIS	2 155 290	167.3	275 671	6 143 429	37.1	41.7	21.2	6 512	0.0	6 126	386	5.9
INDIANA	1 286 099	195.0	127 957	3 087 270	32.9	39.9	27.2	3 266	1.2	3 109	157	4.8
IOWA	616 301	198.4	51 227	1 593 590	35.1	39.4	25.5	1 701	0.2	1 639	62	3.7
KANSAS	521 955	179.7	48 920	1 397 854	36.9	39.2	23.8	1 499	0.3	1 436	63	4.2
KENTUCKY	954 284	216.2	188 401	1 909 704	32.9	40.4	26.7	1 953	-2.6	1 848	105	5.4
LOUISIANA	854 211	183.7	181 279	2 018 024	32.3	43.3	24.4	2 160	0.1	2 025	135	6.3
MAINE	325 496	244.7	37 591	653 189	35.8	42.3	21.8	680	-2.4	650	30	4.4
MARYLAND	936 372	156.7	118 184	2 994 301	44.7	39.1	16.2	3 152	0.8	2 988	164	5.2
MASSACHUSETTS	1 224 469	181.5	188 726	3 470 655	44.7	39.7	15.7	3 570	0.4	3 392	178	5.0
MICHIGAN	2 121 776	214.1	277 309	4 448 034	35.2	41	23.8	4 751	-0.1	4 493	258	5.4
MINNESOTA	965 018	176.8	94 207	2 864 517	40.4	38.9	20.7	3 010	0.9	2 899	112	3.7
MISSISSIPPI	640 772	214.0	125 595	1 208 586	31.1	41.4	27.6	1 273	1.9	1 190	83	6.5
MISSOURI	1 246 269	205.5	142 768	2 805 646	36.0	42.6	21.4	3 114	2.0	2 958	156	5
MONTANA	212 535	207.6	18 248	494 622	36.1	41.1	22.8	523	1.4	501	22	4.1
NEBRASKA	326 078	173.3	27 719	981 449	36.0	40.5	23.4	1 013	-0.1	983	30	3
NEVADA	475 811	167.6	50 919	1 298 821	27.6	54.4	18.0	1 426	1.7	1 330	96	6.7
NEW HAMPSHIRE	283 983	214.0	19 671	704 847	39.4	40.4	20.2	741	0.0	716	25	3.4
NEW JERSEY	1 568 016	175.4	181 606	4 369 952	41.2	41.1	17.7	4 544	0.7	4 289	255	5.6
NEW MEXICO	399 987	191.8	64 059	874 753	35.2	44.2	20.6	920	-0.1	859	61	6.6
NEW YORK	3 482 978	176.4	653 601	9 354 155	39.6	43.6	16.8	9 679	0.9	9 166	513	5.3
NORTH CAROLINA	1 948 531	196.0	235 300	4 444 989	36.1	41.3	22.5	4 769	1.7	4 495	274	5.7
NORTH DAKOTA	124 372	168.2	8 224	391 644	35.9	38.7	25.4	414	-0.2	403	11	2.7
OHIO	2 267 508	195.6	313 259	5 437 533	35.6	40.9	23.5	5 700	-0.1	5 423	277	4.9
OKLAHOMA	749 794	193.3	96 975	1 735 761	34.1	40.9	25.1	1 842	2.4	1 764	78	4.2
OREGON	798 156	201.0	85 136	1 818 085	37.1	41.9	21.0	1 969	1.5	1 857	112	5.7
PENNSYLVANIA	2 722 892	212.9	374 111	6 045 924	36.9	41.3	21.8	6 424	0.5	6 094	330	5.1
RHODE ISLAND	216 029	204.7	33 280	517 864	36.3	44.6	19.1	555	-0.2	521	33	6.0
SOUTH CAROLINA	1 040 971	215.4	118 354	2 126 949	33.0	43.4	23.6	2 257	1.8	2 123	135	6.0
SOUTH DAKOTA	165 499	194.0	14 905	442 489	36.4	40.2	23.4	452	0.7	438	14	3.1
TENNESSEE	1 371 562	209.4	183 890	2 910 656	33.3	41.9	24.8	3 063	0.5	2 886	177	5.8
TEXAS	3 842 249	142.5	666 301	1 241 1 323	35.3	41.8	22.8	13 078	0.4	12 494	584	4.5
UTAH	365 730	124.3	31 212	1 364 392	36.9	41.5	21.6	1 464	2.2	1 412	52	3.5
VERMONT	140 634	224.5	15 783	325 211	40.2	38.4	21.4	344	-1.1	332	13	3.7
VIRGINIA	1 415 661	170.0	155 501	4 039 684	42.9	39.1	18.0	4 240	-0.4	4 052	189	4.4
WASHINGTON	1 230 039	174.2	151 262	3 331 888	39.4	39.5	21.0	3 544	1.5	3 344	200	5.7
WEST VIRGINIA	464 823	251.2	77 715	748 143	31.8	43.7	24.4	785	-0.6	732	53	6.7
WISCONSIN	1 153 149	200.3	117 679	2 916 863	35.0	39.6	25.4	3 095	0.3	2 953	143	4.6
WYOMING	101 296	173.4	6 786	299 225	32.7	39.0	28.2	306	-0.3	293	13	4.2

1. Per 1,000 resident population estimated as of July 1 of the year shown. 2. Persons 16 years old and over. 3. Percent of civilian labor force.

35

Table A. States — Nonfarm Employment and Earnings

STATE	Private nonfarm employment and earnings, 2015											
	Employed		Manufacturing			Employment (1,000)						
				Average earnings of production workers								
	Total (1,000)	Percent change, 2014–2015	Employment (1,000)	Hourly	Weekly	Construction	Transportation and public utilities	Wholesale trade	Retail trade	Information	Financial activities	Services¹
	172	173	174	175	176	177	178	179	180	181	182	183
UNITED STATES	141 865	2.1	12 323	19.91	856.48	6 507	5 403.6	5 907.7	16 303.2	2 768	8 201	62 480
ALABAMA	1 947	1.3	258	18.79	781.66	80.9	73.3	73.8	230.9	21.5	95.4	725.6
ALASKA	339	0.5	14	22.58	593.85	17.6	21.8	6.5	37.7	6.3	12.2	123.8
ARIZONA	2 636	2.6	158	17.96	720.20	127.6	90.9	93.5	322.2	45.3	194.7	1 182.7
ARKANSAS	1 209	1.8	155	16.18	661.76	49.0	64.2	47.2	140.7	13.4	49.3	468.7
CALIFORNIA	16 052	3.0	1 292	21.35	881.76	727.4	554.0	721.2	1 663.1	483.0	797.4	7 325.7
COLORADO	2 541	3.1	141	26.54	1 058.95	149.5	79.8	102.9	262.6	70.7	159.5	1 127.0
CONNECTICUT	1 674	0.8	159	25.65	1 038.83	57.4	49.9	62.6	184.3	32.5	130.0	758.6
DELAWARE	449	2.3	27	17.25	707.25	21.1	16.7	11.8	52.7	4.7	46.6	202.5
DISTRICT OF COLUMBIA	766	1.7	1	–	–	14.3	4.8	4.9	22.5	17.0	30.3	433.6
FLORIDA	8 093	3.4	343	20.03	833.25	429.3	265.7	334.6	1 079.6	135.9	534.8	3 884.1
GEORGIA	4 267	2.9	379	18.02	774.86	166.5	204	216.5	484.9	106.1	235.3	1 786.6
HAWAII	637	1.5	14	20.13	819.29	34.9	30.8	18.0	70.3	8.5	28.1	305.7
IDAHO	674	3.0	62	22.18	902.73	38.5	23.5	29.0	83.6	9.3	33.4	271.2
ILLINOIS	5 961	1.4	581	19.78	836.69	213	283.7	301.6	615.2	100.8	379.8	2 645.4
INDIANA	3 034	1.8	519	18.90	801.36	127.2	139.8	118.6	324.4	33.6	130.6	1 207.9
IOWA	1 562	1.0	216	19.00	799.90	78.6	67.8	67.8	180.3	24.8	105.7	564.2
KANSAS	1 400	0.6	161	18.88	785.41	60.9	56.9	60.2	148.3	20.9	79.4	546.6
KENTUCKY	1 885	1.5	241	20.33	908.75	75.8	102.3	74.7	209.8	25.2	92.5	730.8
LOUISIANA	1 989	0.2	144	22.07	986.53	140.9	87.9	72.5	232.3	25.4	91.4	819.6
MAINE	610	0.8	51	20.89	877.38	26.3	18.1	19.8	81.5	7.5	30.6	273.4
MARYLAND	2 659	1.5	104	18.86	750.63	154.1	86.9	85.8	290.7	38.4	146.3	1 248.6
MASSACHUSETTS	3 493	1.7	250	21.78	892.98	138.5	92.6	123.6	351.6	87.7	219.7	1 776.8
MICHIGAN	4 244	1.5	587	20.80	919.36	147.9	134.3	170.4	465.9	56.7	207.1	1 872
MINNESOTA	2 856	1.5	317	20.22	820.93	115.3	98.6	132.3	292.9	51.7	181.4	1 239.4
MISSISSIPPI	1 134	1.2	142	18.30	757.62	46.6	52.4	34.5	138.1	13.5	43.6	411.3
MISSOURI	2 785	1.7	261	19.62	820.12	114.4	100.2	120.2	310.7	54	166	1 220.6
MONTANA	461	1.7	19	18.01	671.77	26.5	18.4	17.4	58.7	6.4	23.8	191.9
NEBRASKA	1 006	1.3	97	17.73	744.66	48.8	54.6	42.2	109.9	17.5	71.8	391.9
NEVADA	1 258	3.3	42	17.47	711.03	69.6	60.7	34.6	143.4	13.8	59.5	664.9
NEW HAMPSHIRE	656	1.5	67	19.74	821.18	24.4	15.4	27.6	94.8	12.3	35.5	288.2
NEW JERSEY	4 022	1.4	238	20.04	797.59	148	176.6	216.8	462.3	74.4	250.8	1 839.2
NEW MEXICO	826	0.8	28	16.56	664.06	43.5	24.2	21.4	93.7	12.7	33.2	353.8
NEW YORK	9 247	1.7	455	19.40	783.76	360.5	284.8	340.7	945.1	265.8	705	4 446.0
NORTH CAROLINA	4 240	2.4	460	16.98	718.25	189.4	133.8	178.0	484.3	75.8	218.4	1 773.6
NORTH DAKOTA	454	-1.6	26	19.95	798.40	34.4	26.5	26.8	50.8	6.6	24.2	154.6
OHIO	5 421	1.4	687	19.85	835.69	200.2	206.5	235.6	570.8	71.6	292.3	2 375
OKLAHOMA	1 669	0.7	137	18.47	748.04	77.8	63.3	60.2	183.4	20.9	80.0	640.0
OREGON	1 779	3.3	186	19.67	796.64	82.7	58.8	73.9	202.9	33.3	94.9	738.2
PENNSYLVANIA	5 836	0.8	568	18.96	777.36	233.6	264.6	225.2	633.3	85.2	316.3	2 770.1
RHODE ISLAND	485	1.2	41	17.69	688.14	17.0	11.5	16.9	47.8	8.6	32.9	248.1
SOUTH CAROLINA	2 004	2.7	236	18.86	792.12	86.6	72.6	70.6	241.3	26.8	97.0	809.1
SOUTH DAKOTA	428	1.0	43	18.01	745.61	22.2	13.5	21.2	52.9	5.9	29.6	161.6
TENNESSEE	2 892	2.5	333	17.48	732.41	113.2	156.0	121.6	325.4	43.8	148.1	1 222.7
TEXAS	11 838	2.4	879	21.67	929.64	684.1	498.1	597.1	1 295.4	200.6	720.2	4 837.0
UTAH	1 378	3.8	124	19.06	745.25	84.5	55.1	50.0	158.1	34.1	79.2	548.5
VERMONT	313	0.9	31	18.92	730.70	15.3	8.3	9.3	37.8	4.6	12.1	137.4
VIRGINIA	3 851	1.8	233	19.97	854.72	183.7	126.9	110.9	417.3	69.7	197.7	1 791.4
WASHINGTON	3 154	2.9	291	25.52	1 053.98	172.9	100.7	132.8	355.7	114.4	147.6	1 271.0
WEST VIRGINIA	764	-0.7	48	19.19	765.68	32.5	25.9	22.3	86.8	9.5	36.5	325.3
WISCONSIN	2 889	1.3	469	19.32	807.58	109.6	104.9	122.3	305.0	48.8	151.0	1 164.5
WYOMING	290	-0.9	10	21.58	839.46	23.2	15.7	9.5	30.7	3.8	11.1	91.2

1. Includes professional and business services, educational and health services, leisure and hospitality, and other services.

Table A. States — **Agriculture**

STATE	Number	Fewer than 50 acres	500 acres or more	Farm operators whose principal occupation is farming (percent)	Government payments, average per farm (dollars)	Acreage (1,000)	Percent change, 2007–2012	Average size of farm	Total irrigated (1,000)	Total cropland (1,000)	Average per farm	Average per acre
	184	185	186	187	188	189	190	191	192	193	194	195
UNITED STATES...............	2 109 303	38.6	15.0	47.8	9 925	914 528	-0.8	434	55 822	389 690	1 075 491	2 481
ALABAMA........................	43 223	37.4	8.6	44.2	6 802	8 903	-1.4	206	113	2 759	547 524	2 658
ALASKA..........................	762	56.2	11.3	54.1	12 473	834	-5.4	1 094	2	84	681 479	623
ARIZONA.........................	20 005	79.9	8.1	66.1	10 245	26 249	0.5	1 312	881	1 151	844 065	643
ARKANSAS......................	45 071	30.8	13.0	47.3	20 013	13 811	-0.4	306	4 804	7 931	807 965	2 637
CALIFORNIA.....................	77 857	64.8	9.9	54.5	19 349	25 569	0.8	328	7 862	9 592	2 061 792	6 278
COLORADO......................	36 180	39.4	24.3	49.6	14 897	31 887	0.9	881	2 517	10 650	1 128 277	1 280
CONNECTICUT	5 977	69.8	1.8	46.3	9 328	437	7.6	73	9	151	809 375	11 082
DELAWARE	2 451	56.5	9.8	63.9	10 553	509	-0.3	208	127	439	1 694 584	8 166
DISTRICT OF COLUMBIA ...	X	X	X	X	X	X	X	X	X	X	X	X
FLORIDA..........................	47 740	68.6	5.6	48.0	10 158	9 548	3.4	200	1 493	2 744	1 040 259	5 201
GEORGIA	42 257	39.9	10.4	47.0	9 793	9 621	-5.2	228	1 125	4 191	702 282	3 085
HAWAII	7 000	88.1	2.6	52.0	8 325	1 129	0.7	161	82	174	1 461 342	9 058
IDAHO.............................	24 816	47.9	17.1	49.8	10 673	11 497	2.3	474	3 365	5 793	1 052 941	2 222
ILLINOIS..........................	75 087	34.1	20.4	50.4	9 829	26 775	0.6	359	522	23 753	2 261 778	6 305
INDIANA..........................	58 695	46.6	12.8	43.7	8 331	14 773	-0.4	251	437	12 591	1 342 826	5 354
IOWA..............................	88 637	30.9	22.4	54.1	11 262	30 748	-0.4	345	172	26 256	2 207 220	6 389
KANSAS..........................	61 773	19.0	31.6	48.3	10 426	46 346	-0.4	747	2 881	28 503	1 218 662	1 632
KENTUCKY.......................	77 064	36.5	6.2	41.7	5 087	13 993	-6.7	169	74	6 336	512 033	3 024
LOUISIANA	28 093	43.7	11.6	43.2	14 625	8 110	-2.6	281	1 093	4 276	718 179	2 554
MAINE.............................	8 173	43.0	6.7	48.5	7 629	1 348	7.9	178	31	477	410 633	2 308
MARYLAND	12 256	49.2	7.6	48.9	7 784	2 052	-1.0	166	105	1 396	1 148 268	6 930
MASSACHUSETTS	7 755	67.5	1.5	50.0	10 416	518	1.1	68	23	161	704 071	10 430
MICHIGAN	52 194	43.9	8.6	48.4	7 567	10 032	-0.8	191	592	7 669	766 148	4 020
MINNESOTA	74 542	25.2	18.2	52.9	8 962	26 918	-3.3	349	524	21 597	1 474 057	4 220
MISSISSIPPI	38 076	28.1	11.8	43.0	10 983	11 456	-4.6	287	1 652	5 076	652 593	2 273
MISSOURI	99 171	25.5	13.7	44.2	7 834	29 027	-2.6	285	1 181	15 259	795 444	2 791
MONTANA	28 008	28.1	42.2	55.1	16 865	61 388	-2.7	2 134	1 903	17 022	1 674 568	785
NEBRASKA	49 969	23.3	37.7	59.7	11 436	45 480	-0.3	907	8 297	21 597	2 159 268	2 380
NEVADA	4 137	53.2	18.9	53.0	9 566	5 865	0.8	1 429	688	757	1 324 673	927
NEW HAMPSHIRE	4 391	55.5	3.5	48.0	7 434	472	0.5	108	3	98	449 848	4 167
NEW JERSEY....................	9 071	71.2	3.1	49.5	7 332	733	-2.5	79	88	457	1 008 402	12 792
NEW MEXICO	24 721	51.3	25.3	50.1	12 829	43 238	-0.1	1 748	680	1 977	755 185	432
NEW YORK	35 537	32.6	8.4	57.4	7 955	7 175	0.1	202	60	4 217	525 587	2 600
NORTH CAROLINA.............	50 218	48.1	6.8	48.9	8 332	8 475	-0.7	168	175	4 745	726 944	4 338
NORTH DAKOTA	30 961	11.0	48.8	56.6	15 398	39 675	-1.0	1 268	218	27 147	1 808 801	1 426
OHIO...............................	75 462	41.1	8.3	43.9	6 603	13 957	0.0	185	47	10 749	894 933	4 837
OKLAHOMA	80 245	25.0	19.0	42.1	8 634	35 087	-2.1	428	480	11 279	573 858	1 340
OREGON	35 439	61.5	10.6	49.9	16 054	16 400	-0.6	460	1 630	4 690	865 613	1 882
PENNSYLVANIA	59 309	39.3	4.1	51.7	5 395	7 809	-1.3	130	39	4 546	704 712	5 425
RHODE ISLAND	1 243	71.1	0.9	49.8	12 344	68	2.6	56	4	23	786 093	14 041
SOUTH CAROLINA	25 266	44.1	8.1	41.0	6 867	4 889	1.7	197	159	1 967	586 518	2 981
SOUTH DAKOTA	31 989	19.6	43.6	58.9	12 451	43 666	-0.9	1 352	379	19 147	2 281 026	1 687
TENNESSEE	68 050	39.4	5.5	41.8	4 184	10 970	-0.9	160	146	5 330	569 416	3 565
TEXAS	248 809	37.7	15.8	42.1	12 293	130 399	-0.2	523	4 489	29 148	876 614	1 676
UTAH..............................	18 027	57.9	12.3	38.5	8 584	11 095	-1.1	609	1 104	1 646	888 886	1 460
VERMONT	7 338	39.2	7.3	51.5	8 929	1 233	1.5	171	4	488	546 627	3 205
VIRGINIA	46 030	38.6	7.7	45.1	7 719	8 104	2.4	180	69	2 991	776 719	4 306
WASHINGTON	37 249	63.2	11.0	47.4	22 014	14 973	-1.5	396	1 634	7 527	910 249	2 299
WEST VIRGINIA	21 489	28.3	5.8	42.6	3 203	3 698	-2.5	168	2	804	413 407	2 463
WISCONSIN	69 754	32.2	8.8	49.8	6 093	15 191	-4.1	209	422	9 911	819 551	3 924
WYOMING	11 736	28.8	36.3	49.8	10 027	30 170	0.6	2 587	1 436	2 419	1 759 200	680

Table A. States — Agriculture, Land, and Water

	Agriculture, 2012 (cont.)							Land, 2012			
STATE	Value of machinery and equipment, average per farm (dollars)	Value of products sold				Percent of farms with sales of:					Water consumption, 2010 (mil gal per day)
		Total (mil dol)	Average per farm (dollars)	Percent from:		$10,000 or more	$100,000 or more	Cropland (percent)	Owned by the federal government (percent)	Developed (percent)	
				Crops	Livestock and poultry products						
	196	197	198	199	200	201	202	203	204	205	206
UNITED STATES............	115 706	394 644	187 097	53.8	46.2	43.4	18.4	18.7	20.9	5.8	351 417.1
ALABAMA....................	71 211	5 571	128 894	23.6	76.4	33.8	11.2	6.9	2.8	8.6	9 960.0
ALASKA......................	87 445	59	77 329	42.2	57.8	42.3	11.4		41.5	2.9	1 094.5
ARIZONA....................	63 624	3 732	186 559	55.6	44.4	20.3	7.3	1.2	41.5	2.9	6 088.2
ARKANSAS.................	115 438	9 776	216 897	49.5	50.5	44.0	16.7	21.0	9.6	5.4	11 327.0
CALIFORNIA..............	124 720	42 627	547 510	71.2	28.8	57.0	26.4	9.0	46.7	6.2	37 962.2
COLORADO................	110 134	7 781	215 060	31.3	68.7	37.7	15.6	11.9	36.1	2.9	10 994.2
CONNECTICUT..........	58 958	551	92 123	70.7	29.3	30.0	7.7	5.4	0.5	33.9	3 311.0
DELAWARE................	161 559	1 274	519 794	33.7	66.3	64.6	41.7	26.8	1.6	19.0	717.5
DISTRICT OF COLUMBIA ...	X	X	X	X	X	X	X				0.1
FLORIDA....................	60 845	7 702	161 322	77.5	22.5	34.3	11	7.6	10.3	14.6	14 936.0
GEORGIA..................	93 146	9 255	219 020	39.7	60.3	37.4	17.3	11.1	5.5	12.3	4 718.8
HAWAII.....................	43 999	661	94 478	81.5	18.5	41.6	7.2	2.1	14.8	5.9	1 273.8
IDAHO......................	143 835	7 801	314 372	44.1	55.9	44.3	20.5	10.1	62.5	1.7	17 230.5
ILLINOIS...................	203 192	17 187	228 895	82.3	17.7	54.5	33.0	66.3	1.4	9.5	13 091.3
INDIANA....................	143 252	11 211	191 001	67.2	32.8	48.3	24.4	57.5	2.1	10.9	8 643.0
IOWA........................	213 856	30 822	347 728	56.3	43.7	62.8	41.0	72.1	0.6	5.4	3 070.5
KANSAS....................	156 740	18 461	298 845	37.8	62.2	56	25.5	49.1	0.9	4.0	4 004.8
KENTUCKY................	70 190	5 067	65 755	45.0	55.0	36.5	8.2	21.1	4.9	8.2	4 326.5
LOUISIANA...............	104 418	3 809	135 600	73.1	26.9	33.0	11.7	15.8	4.0	6.1	8 540.3
MAINE......................	69 780	763	93 364	62.1	37.9	34.6	9.5	1.7	1.0	4.1	449.3
MARYLAND...............	115 879	2 271	185 329	46.3	53.7	43.1	20.6	17.6	2.1	19.2	7 382.0
MASSACHUSETTS............	53 948	492	63 470	77.8	22.2	32.7	9.8	4.1	1.4	33.1	2 995.9
MICHIGAN.................	122 533	8 678	166 265	63.5	36.5	44.0	18.0	21.4	8.6	11.3	10 837.2
MINNESOTA..............	197 715	21 280	285 479	65.2	34.8	60.0	33.5	39.0	6.4	4.5	3 821.2
MISSISSIPPI..............	91 917	6 441	169 162	46.2	53.8	33.0	12.4	15.6	5.5	6.1	3 933.0
MISSOURI..................	88 960	9 165	92 415	49.8	50.2	46.8	12.5	31.3	4.5	6.7	8 568.5
MONTANA.................	137 625	4 230	151 031	53.3	46.7	50.4	26.2	15.4	28.7	1.1	7 645.2
NEBRASKA...............	230 222	23 069	461 661	49.3	50.7	68.5	43.0	40.4	1.2	2.4	8 036.3
NEVADA...................	134 658	764	184 710	47.9	52.1	42.0	21.2	0.9	84.1	0.8	2 623.1
NEW HAMPSHIRE	56 439	191	43 477	52.8	47.2	26.6	6.0	2.0	13.5	12.3	1 214.6
NEW JERSEY.............	81 470	1 007	111 006	88.5	11.5	36.1	12.3	9.3	3.4	35.4	5 670.7
NEW MEXICO	60 610	2 550	103 157	24.2	75.8	24.4	7.0	2.0	33.9	1.7	3 161.0
NEW YORK...............	117 163	5 415	152 380	41.5	58.5	49.2	20.0	16.3	0.7	12.2	10 574.5
NORTH CAROLINA.............	92 887	12 588	250 670	34.2	65.8	37.3	16.6	15.3	7.1	14.2	12 420.1
NORTH DAKOTA	300 334	10 951	353 693	88.3	11.7	59.0	40.6	54.7	3.9	2.2	1 147.1
OHIO........................	116 899	10 064	133 366	65.6	34.4	47.4	20.3	42	1.4	15.8	9 442.8
OKLAHOMA..............	74 212	7 130	88 848	26.3	73.7	40.8	10.0	19.6	2.7	4.9	3 168.2
OREGON...................	90 222	4 884	137 805	66.5	33.5	35.6	13.1	5.6	51.7	2.3	6 734.5
PENNSYLVANIA..........	89 735	7 401	124 783	37.6	62.4	48.1	19.9	17.4	2.3	15.2	8 134.9
RHODE ISLAND	56 065	60	47 990	82.1	17.9	35.7	8.7	2.1	0.5	28.4	375.5
SOUTH CAROLINA............	72 400	3 040	120 323	42.6	57.4	27.0	8.6	11.0	5.3	13.5	6 782.2
SOUTH DAKOTA.............	241 388	10 170	317 929	59.7	40.3	65.0	40.7	35.7	5.6	1.9	625.8
TENNESSEE	69 248	3 611	53 064	57.8	42.2	30.2	6.1	16.8	5.2	11.6	7 696.6
TEXAS	72 185	25 376	101 988	29.0	71.0	29.7	7.0	14.0	1.8	5.2	24 796.7
UTAH.......................	84 537	1 816	100 746	31.6	68.4	37.2	11.0	2.7	64.1	1.6	4 463.8
VERMONT	86 947	776	105 765	22.9	77.1	40.6	15.1	8.6	7.4	6.5	430.5
VIRGINIA	72 561	3 753	81 540	36.2	63.8	37.9	9.6	10.3	8.7	11.7	7 648.0
WASHINGTON	98 588	9 121	244 859	71.2	28.8	34.2	16.4	13.2	28.5	5.8	4 955.8
WEST VIRGINIA................	50 027	807	37 544	17.2	82.8	25.3	4.0	4.6	8.2	7.4	3 533.0
WISCONSIN	129 561	11 744	168 370	39.2	60.8	52.3	24.6	28.9	5.1	7.7	6 157.6
WYOMING	114 212	1 689	143 952	26.0	74.0	48.8	23.5	3.4	47.2	1.2	4 701.5

Table A. States — **Manufactures and Construction**

STATE	Manufactures, 2014										Construction, 2012				
	All employees			Production workers								Employees			
						Wages		Value added by manufacture (mil dol)	Value of shipments (mil dol)	Total cost of materials (mil dol)	Number of establishments			Value (mil dol)	Annual payroll (mil dol)
	Number (1,000)	Percent change, 2013–2014	Annual payroll (mil dol)	Number (1,000)	Work hours (millions)	Total (mil dol)	Average per worker (dollars)					Number	Percent change, 2007–2012		
	207	208	209	210	211	212	213	214	215	216	217	218	219	220	221
UNITED STATES	11 021	-0.6	618 871	7 742	15 842	350 929	45 330	2 400 063	5 880 890	3 486 762	598 065	5 669 623	-22.5	1 366 427	272 546
ALABAMA	235	0.4	11 760	177	368	7 589	42 761	46 819	135 669	88 921	6 865	78 615	-26.6	17 914	3 312
ALASKA	13	9.9	552	10	21	379	36 261	1 856	6 899	4 968	2 156	23 219	5.1	6 431	1 539
ARIZONA	135	-1.3	8 956	81	165	3 894	47 880	27 583	53 234	25 685	10 540	123 478	-44.3	26 211	5 560
ARKANSAS	149	-1.6	6 544	120	245	4 671	39 082	26 507	62 224	36 010	4 739	42 539	-15.6	8 874	1 666
CALIFORNIA	1 112	-1.8	69 487	704	1 420	31 623	44 939	245 681	530 915	283 594	60 222	597 083	-31.7	148 808	30 402
COLORADO	117	4.9	6 815	78	157	3 504	45 195	24 928	54 856	30 136	13 976	123 296	-29.0	29 762	5 868
CONNECTICUT	157	-3.3	10 586	94	191	4 720	50 223	33 090	59 076	24 314	7 173	54 595	-23.8	14 952	2 949
DELAWARE	26	-3.0	1 449	18	37	793	44 823	6 288	21 641	15 661	1 997	17 708	-31.0	3 821	868
DISTRICT OF COLUMBIA	1	-11.1	57	1	2	32	39 171	183	315	132	390	8 986	14.7	2 643	476
FLORIDA	264	-2.3	14 368	176	355	7 502	42 527	50 297	101 687	51 385	39 536	294 308	-37.9	66 489	11 621
GEORGIA	334	-0.1	16 539	253	523	10 426	41 163	67 176	165 108	98 627	13 790	144 936	-35.2	36 691	6 376
HAWAII	12	6.9	534	8	14	310	40 622	1 014	6 296	5 030	2 378	27 541	-22.5	7 939	1 564
IDAHO	51	-3.3	2 889	39	78	1 767	45 684	8 613	21 116	12 518	5 165	32 033	-36.4	6 573	1 116
ILLINOIS	537	-1.3	30 992	376	771	16 907	44 997	112 051	283 277	171 688	25 046	204 819	-24.9	54 281	11 446
INDIANA	465	1.8	25 109	349	724	16 127	46 154	108 573	262 998	155 608	12 195	123 888	-16.0	27 325	6 178
IOWA	207	1.8	10 617	151	304	6 420	42 493	46 534	123 226	76 679	7 703	65 860	-6.4	15 586	2 939
KANSAS	162	1.6	8 771	117	238	5 507	47 009	32 572	95 472	63 279	6 070	58 461	-13.7	13 644	2 681
KENTUCKY	220	1.5	11 223	171	351	7 813	45 663	45 705	137 215	91 924	6 675	63 974	-23.1	13 949	2 760
LOUISIANA	127	-2.4	8 330	91	193	5 203	57 320	49 666	242 379	190 985	7 318	136 439	0.5	26 212	7 317
MAINE	47	-2.3	2 478	35	71	1 636	47 198	8 170	16 415	8 315	4 547	25 178	-15.8	4 546	1 011
MARYLAND	92	-5.9	5 832	57	114	2 598	45 923	21 804	40 171	18 306	12 987	144 715	-24.3	37 372	7 421
MASSACHUSETTS	224	-3.2	14 965	135	274	6 658	49 438	45 744	84 537	39 357	15 689	120 685	-10.9	34 227	6 857
MICHIGAN	523	-0.4	29 442	382	794	18 383	48 179	98 692	253 890	156 166	16 123	131 609	-17.8	32 535	6 370
MINNESOTA	289	-2.7	16 119	193	393	8 557	44 244	55 604	127 119	71 647	14 615	113 633	-15.6	32 923	6 061
MISSISSIPPI	131	-1.5	6 050	103	210	4 116	40 083	22 444	65 462	43 251	3 736	41 520	-25.8	8 858	1 703
MISSOURI	242	1.8	12 982	181	361	8 316	45 930	51 610	116 645	65 701	12 435	110 274	-32.9	25 678	5 306
MONTANA	16	-4.0	794	11	21	483	45 358	2 971	11 282	8 190	4 307	23 981	-21.0	5 149	970
NEBRASKA	92	0.9	4 260	71	145	2 868	40 428	20 402	60 589	40 259	5 676	40 562	-9.1	8 728	1 683
NEVADA	39	-0.4	2 112	27	54	1 149	43 080	8 777	16 499	7 734	4 335	54 321	-55.8	12 254	2 463
NEW HAMPSHIRE	65	-0.9	4 020	40	81	1 776	44 804	10 194	19 633	9 115	3 710	24 409	-18.8	5 202	1 210
NEW JERSEY	217	-2.8	13 790	140	284	6 565	46 743	50 096	101 148	51 250	18 806	146 521	-18.7	39 872	8 053
NEW MEXICO	23	-6.8	1 253	16	31	716	45 429	4 208	12 174	16 591	4 084	37 806	-31.3	6 997	1 520
NEW YORK	402	-2.4	22 339	271	543	12 025	44 338	78 309	151 673	73 806	41 016	333 187	-4.6	87 292	18 169
NORTH CAROLINA	397	-0.4	19 002	299	604	11 706	39 163	103 729	210 398	106 178	18 294	180 433	-25.6	35 964	6 683
NORTH DAKOTA	23	0.2	1 129	17	35	736	42 221	5 093	16 045	10 890	2 729	25 882	33.6	6 557	1 240
OHIO	637	1.0	35 099	457	947	21 304	46 574	133 101	333 026	201 256	18 439	180 735	-19.4	42 772	8 582
OKLAHOMA	130	1.1	6 874	96	200	4 332	45 134	24 962	77 165	51 693	7 541	69 691	-0.2	16 229	3 004
OREGON	155	1.3	9 034	106	215	4 898	46 405	27 281	56 573	29 334	10 051	69 771	-32.2	16 562	3 296
PENNSYLVANIA	523	-2.1	28 637	368	752	16 846	45 801	106 865	231 309	125 010	24 874	237 969	-10.5	55 120	11 763
RHODE ISLAND	38	-0.2	2 177	25	50	1 145	45 053	6 108	11 915	5 814	2 868	17 418	-19.6	4 760	850
SOUTH CAROLINA	207	-0.7	10 967	157	330	7 111	45 159	42 790	111 108	68 707	8 136	68 679	-36.5	15 219	2 669
SOUTH DAKOTA	43	2.6	1 981	32	66	1 254	38 997	7 520	17 920	10 428	2 916	19 737	-4.2	4 189	757
TENNESSEE	290	-0.6	14 839	213	432	9 082	42 614	62 392	146 817	84 492	8 627	103 474	-16.9	23 078	4 505
TEXAS	759	-0.2	45 235	527	1 109	25 791	48 930	217 667	698 652	479 487	34 641	572 922	-4.0	146 299	27 831
UTAH	109	1.6	6 045	73	146	3 281	45 117	21 972	51 087	29 086	7 294	64 534	-27.4	16 329	2 716
VERMONT	28	-3.6	1 545	19	39	834	43 687	3 874	9 100	5 151	2 596	15 667	-10.3	3 012	648
VIRGINIA	226	1.4	12 428	162	330	7 328	45 358	57 324	101 147	44 142	17 108	177 074	-24.7	42 371	8 067
WASHINGTON	249	-0.1	16 060	166	341	8 958	53 917	68 578	146 224	81 833	17 741	138 649	-30.3	33 760	7 086
WEST VIRGINIA	47	-0.5	2 678	35	71	1 709	49 458	11 172	25 312	14 129	3 017	26 670	-16.6	4 975	1 116
WISCONSIN	429	-0.6	22 486	308	628	13 138	42 603	83 030	181 898	99 381	12 207	102 542	-18.8	25 625	5 063
WYOMING	9	-3.2	638	7	15	443	62 461	2 439	9 937	7 336	2 610	20 067	-10.9	3 966	877

Table A. States — Wholesale Trade and Retail Trade

STATE	Wholesale trade, 2012					Retail trade,[1] 2012								
	Number of establishments	Employees Number	Percent change, 2007–2012	Sales (mil dol)	Annual payroll (mil dol)	Number of establishments	Total	Percent change, 2007–2012	Motor vehicle and parts dealers	Food and beverage stores	Clothing and clothing accessory stores	General merchandise stores	Sales (mil dol)	Annual payroll (mil dol)
	222	223	224	225	226	227	228	229	230	231	232	233	234	235
UNITED STATES	419 464	5 881 913	-5.5	7 899 979	362 121	1 062 083	14 703 529	-5.2	1 709 998	2 864 650	1 664 114	2 772 612	4 219 822	369 001
ALABAMA	5 408	73 312	-9.6	75 845	3 669	18 211	218 531	-8.5	28 975	29 631	21 550	53 855	58 565	5 123
ALASKA	743	8 740	-3.6	9 615	517	2 508	33 721	-3.6	3 772	7 386	2 228	8 225	10 474	977
ARIZONA	6 647	88 916	-13.0	96 619	5 159	17 479	286 184	-15.2	37 592	50 041	29 030	60 429	84 717	7 368
ARKANSAS	3 462	41 577	-13.3	61 692	2 068	10 923	135 448	-3.3	17 615	18 725	10 562	37 096	36 815	3 062
CALIFORNIA	59 293	842 343	-5.1	969 250	58 755	106 419	1 540 055	-8.5	165 764	332 177	215 230	250 267	481 800	43 361
COLORADO	7 224	92 714	-12.0	118 605	6 155	18 474	245 704	-6.2	29 189	47 396	24 058	45 245	67 815	6 509
CONNECTICUT	4 324	75 460	-0.7	216 166	5 321	12 597	182 528	-6.9	20 097	43 566	24 279	23 858	51 632	4 975
DELAWARE	1 029	14 465	-25.6	20 474	1 106	3 616	51 711	-6.7	6 594	9 121	6 215	9 474	14 456	1 270
DISTRICT OF COLUMBIA	430	4 259	-17.8	4 103	341	1 710	19 780	3.5	D	6 619	9 303	D	4 440	525
FLORIDA	31 657	296 207	-9.4	342 238	15 394	71 189	947 877	-6.7	109 996	180 849	133 935	173 836	273 867	24 034
GEORGIA	13 151	184 561	-13.4	246 067	11 191	33 426	433 840	-8.7	D	83 727	48 250	D	119 801	10 290
HAWAII	1 751	18 761	-7.4	13 466	845	4 643	68 360	-3.3	5 981	13 474	13 170	12 784	18 902	1 835
IDAHO	2 012	26 221	-1.1	24 397	1 233	5 815	72 980	-9.3	10 373	11 524	5 115	16 057	20 444	1 794
ILLINOIS	19 302	314 389	-2.0	549 200	20 596	39 947	592 942	-7.2	65 978	111 600	68 011	118 814	166 635	14 576
INDIANA	7 823	110 761	-4.4	127 024	5 791	21 601	309 552	-7.1	39 062	48 662	25 910	69 169	85 858	7 079
IOWA	4 992	67 124	3.4	76 728	3 263	12 046	174 556	-1.5	21 506	36 192	12 346	33 369	44 906	3 865
KANSAS	4 565	65 118	13.1	103 968	3 701	10 548	145 480	-2.8	17 830	27 677	12 656	29 608	38 276	3 325
KENTUCKY	4 324	67 581	-4.7	100 077	3 679	15 224	202 615	-5.7	24 909	34 136	16 129	47 191	54 870	4 619
LOUISIANA	5 610	76 773	1.6	86 301	4 008	16 743	220 257	-4.8	27 024	33 458	21 780	50 414	61 396	5 335
MAINE	1 550	16 759	-10.5	16 370	818	6 351	80 155	-3.8	9 746	18 108	5 918	11 905	21 522	1 885
MARYLAND	5 698	85 955	-13.7	84 734	5 379	18 179	281 678	-4.5	35 373	63 344	34 220	48 063	76 380	7 168
MASSACHUSETTS	8 061	139 520	-8.5	182 173	10 304	24 311	351 598	-2.4	32 685	99 593	45 747	40 988	92 915	9 162
MICHIGAN	11 489	166 238	-3.5	254 319	9 800	34 858	441 190	-6.3	52 989	72 592	42 860	101 906	119 302	10 527
MINNESOTA	8 298	134 596	-3.0	167 376	9 335	19 109	288 888	-5.9	30 830	52 671	25 578	58 637	78 898	6 858
MISSISSIPPI	2 858	34 757	-6.6	35 523	1 583	11 594	136 032	-3.8	15 581	18 984	12 603	36 906	37 053	2 968
MISSOURI	7 955	126 328	-2.2	135 013	6 203	21 456	302 568	-4.6	37 602	47 881	26 145	64 255	90 547	7 278
MONTANA	1 530	14 443	1.8	15 764	650	4 831	55 418	-5.9	7 496	9 917	3 205	10 123	15 624	1 347
NEBRASKA	3 160	40 832	5.4	58 624	2 111	7 279	105 953	-2.1	12 622	19 100	7 872	19 657	30 471	2 440
NEVADA	2 970	33 250	-20.2	28 436	1 890	8 135	129 977	-7.0	13 417	21 310	23 568	24 118	38 234	3 454
NEW HAMPSHIRE	1 865	24 558	-1.6	22 683	1 588	6 127	95 660	-2.7	11 462	23 302	8 438	14 559	26 018	2 404
NEW JERSEY	14 661	263 316	-7.1	406 845	21 240	31 722	436 299	-5.3	42 776	104 425	63 756	61 632	133 666	12 676
NEW MEXICO	1 937	21 929	-4.4	17 405	1 211	6 590	90 792	-6.8	12 096	13 431	7 112	21 333	25 179	2 215
NEW YORK	32 704	368 966	-10.7	434 354	23 106	77 463	905 325	1.4	71 441	211 095	149 390	124 135	251 168	23 641
NORTH CAROLINA	11 830	172 760	-4.4	175 657	10 376	34 288	446 373	-4.3	57 916	83 490	44 074	91 034	120 691	10 421
NORTH DAKOTA	1 618	21 533	22.4	32 269	1 223	4 467	47 186	7.1	6 651	7 231	3 332	8 654	15 520	1 204
OHIO	14 266	229 244	-5.9	252 195	12 812	36 531	549 152	-7.1	69 278	100 346	48 156	110 859	153 554	13 099
OKLAHOMA	4 660	60 195	-1.7	102 935	3 251	13 051	168 839	-1.3	23 146	21 534	14 904	40 799	50 256	4 055
OREGON	5 395 (r)	7 244 6(r)	-6.6	70 111	4 163	13 879	187 402	-8.5	21 349	38 829	17 457	38 684	49 481	4 832
PENNSYLVANIA	15 053	242 365	-1.6	295 599	14 996	43 952	643 903	-4.2	75 264	144 969	66 135	106 485	178 795	15 331
RHODE ISLAND	1 367	20 235	-5.9	27 840	1 322	3 795	47 688	-6.2	4 992	12 033	5 213	6 112	12 064	1 207
SOUTH CAROLINA	5 027	64 418	-5.6	59 732	3 368	17 586	220 438	-4.9	26 447	42 487	23 822	45 385	58 094	4 955
SOUTH DAKOTA	1 487	17 702	13.1	25 292	827	3 843	49 867	-1.9	6 834	9 249	2 958	9 057	13 792	1 127
TENNESSEE	6 902	112 664	-8.8	169 781	6 170	22 615	306 078	-4.6	36 861	50 721	29 518	65 515	91 642	7 420
TEXAS	32 656	496 603	0.3	1 129 151	31 454	78 281	1 150 148	1.0	147 197	209 508	138 335	228 562	356 116	28 835
UTAH	3 664	50 741	-4.1	43 854	2 791	9 095	133 535	-6.1	16 109	21 609	13 300	26 428	38 024	3 335
VERMONT	809	10 742	1.1	12 850	566	3 509	38 910	-3.7	4 793	10 689	2 739	2 555	9 934	967
VIRGINIA	7 381	106 428	-11.4	120 174	6 064	27 415	410 918	-4.8	51 166	78 937	44 208	78 638	110 002	10 008
WASHINGTON	9 361	121 805	-7.8	143 082	7 084	21 588	307 089	-6.4	37 871	60 125	30 279	60 723	118 924	8 723
WEST VIRGINIA	1 553	19 901	-3.6	19 749	918	6 393	85 305	-7.5	11 506	13 183	5 563	19 982	22 638	1 908
WISCONSIN	7 113	113 112	-3.9	111 021	6 250	19 272	296 956	-7.2	36 012	52 527	21 622	59 092	78 202	6 835
WYOMING	839	8 290	8.4	7 238	477	2 681	30 088	-6.1	4 324	5 469	1 717	5 745	9 446	796

1. Establishments with payroll.

Table A. States — Information

STATE	Number of establishments	Number	Percent change, 2007–2012	Publishing, except Internet	Motion picture and sound recording	Broadcasting, except Internet	Internet publishing and broadcasting and web search portals	Telecommunications	Data processing, hosting, and related services	Receipts (mil dol)	Annual payroll (mil dol)
	236	237	238	239	240	241	242	243	244	245	246
UNITED STATES..............	138 341	3 321 226	-5.0	876 286	304 497	278 168	183 436	1 134 466	497 300	1 238 463	269 070
ALABAMA	1 574	35 102	-12.4	9 500	1 978	D	224	16 043	3 940	NA	1 898
ALASKA	399	6 523	-3.4	680	637	839	29	4 025	D	NA	395
ARIZONA............................	2 117	48 994	-6.8	12 950	4 561	D	684	16 008	11 055	NA	2 983
ARKANSAS.........................	1 020	23 729	-9.0	5 710	D	D	61	7 958	6 554	NA	1 362
CALIFORNIA........................	21 925	561 399	0.9	140 978	113 899	48 593	63 536	112 158	78 236	NA	70 662
COLORADO.........................	3 023	81 953	-3.1	16 527	4 294	3 720	2 938	39 441	14 723	NA	5 851
CONNECTICUT	1 675	37 338	-7.5	8 690	2 609	4 887	2 386	12 652	4 534	NA	2 712
DELAWARE	417	6 964	-18.7	1 390	365	252	183	3 535	1 077	NA	403
DISTRICT OF COLUMBIA ...	741	22 144	-9.6	7 781	1 035	4 712	2 189	4 136	1 084	NA	2 215
FLORIDA.............................	8 030	152 775	-12.9	36 131	11 716	14 729	3 032	67 240	18 959	NA	10 280
GEORGIA	4 155	123 145	0.5	20 111	6 875	12 686	5 706	58 004	19 011	NA	9 197
HAWAII	543	8 329	-17.4	1 510	1 034	D	99	4 051	771	NA	495
IDAHO................................	654	12 264	-19.1	2 654	793	1 055	D	6 084	1 040	NA	557
ILLINOIS	5 404	124 859	-8.6	35 176	9 134	8 037	9 424	42 171	19 375	NA	8 942
INDIANA.............................	2 183	42 361	-7.5	10 541	D	D	1 475	15 471	7 241	NA	2 299
IOWA.................................	1 545	30 342	-11.8	9 799	D	D	405	9 876	5 668	NA	1 400
KANSAS.............................	1 406	34 052	-35.4	6 968	1 792	2 219	D	17 537	4 665	NA	2 026
KENTUCKY.........................	1 552	33 009	-2.9	6 069	1 974	2 813	625	11 151	9 665	NA	1 393
LOUISIANA.........................	1 426	24 743	-19.0	4 191	1 957	3 079	170	12 950	2 235	NA	1 274
MAINE................................	845	11 952	-11.6	3 040	705	977	100	4 735	1 711	NA	538
MARYLAND	2 381	56 781	-10.0	12 898	3 321	5 392	1 057	22 691	9 865	NA	4 256
MASSACHUSETTS	3 673	115 614	5.1	46 869	4 771	4 691	8 714	26 157	22 905	NA	10 521
MICHIGAN..........................	3 294	67 232	-13.4	22 993	D	D	1 619	23 596	D	NA	4 349
MINNESOTA.......................	2 655	63 187	-10.1	23 085	4 282	4 234	D	15 939	9 328	NA	4 534
MISSISSIPPI.......................	926	13 879	-12.7	2 504	742	D	64	8 017	809	NA	605
MISSOURI..........................	2 422	59 607	-18.4	15 435	D	D	1 318	22 894	11 355	NA	3 805
MONTANA	615	9 160	-3.6	2 657	653	D	116	3 897	879	NA	427
NEBRASKA.........................	954	20 647	2.1	7 278	D	D	1 052	5 882	3 361	NA	1 180
NEVADA	1 234	17 216	-3.9	3 444	D	D	568	7 165	2 095	NA	931
NEW HAMPSHIRE	802	13 731	-11.3	5 780	768	596	98	4 947	1 300	NA	1 050
NEW JERSEY......................	3 705	119 179	-11.3	24 725	5 521	3 545	18 231	50 376	15 450	NA	9 815
NEW MEXICO......................	764	12 516	-10.5	2 155	1 175	1 270	109	7 057	601	NA	536
NEW YORK.........................	11 335	286 744	-4.8	71 481	32 463	43 156	20 452	73 996	32 436	NA	25 032
NORTH CAROLINA..............	3 570	79 833	4.5	20 995	4 995	5 165	1 085	32 220	14 630	NA	5 181
NORTH DAKOTA	361	7 052	-1.0	2 788	358	D	32	2 134	413	NA	391
OHIO..................................	3 956	90 083	-7.5	29 098	5 242	6 759	4 857	32 372	11 193	NA	5 607
OKLAHOMA........................	1 497	28 890	-11.1	4 770	2 001	2 628	130	15 990	2 903	NA	1 377
OREGON............................	2 010	38 799	-1.2	12 409	3 040	2 874	1 459	11 826	7 031	NA	2 312
PENNSYLVANIA..................	5 109	130 606	-4.7	38 947	6 549	8 123	2 309	51 934	17 445	NA	8 997
RHODE ISLAND	435	7 236	-10.2	1 918	D	D	D	3 154	508	NA	445
SOUTH CAROLINA.............	1 436	34 056	3.0	8 022	D	D	214	17 331	3 208	NA	1 796
SOUTH DAKOTA................	446	6 750	-7.5	1 829	D	1 108	D	2 577	600	NA	286
TENNESSEE	2 489	48 231	-5.0	9 733	5 219	5 435	653	20 647	6 336	NA	2 674
TEXAS	9 221	230 781	-7.8	42 166	17 247	16 362	4 957	99 015	48 907	NA	16 243
UTAH.................................	1 414	37 498	12.6	11 709	3 447	1 556	2 276	8 780	9 481	NA	2 241
VERMONT	507	6 775	12.0	2 188	433	576	285	1 483	1 510	NA	370
VIRGINIA	3 916	101 402	-2.6	24 116	5 102	6 648	4 123	41 053	19 447	NA	8 080
WASHINGTON....................	3 281	128 014	14.5	62 052	6 497	3 911	5 719	32 449	15 415	NA	15 482
WEST VIRGINIA.................	673	10 945	6.4	2 082	592	1 385	D	5 914	843	NA	509
WISCONSIN	2 295	52 807	-2.5	18 801	3 544	5 519	1 088	15 998	7 721	NA	2 982
WYOMING	331	3 998	-3.9	963	386	453	D	1 749	320	NA	173

Table A. States — Utilities, Transportation and Warehousing, and Finance and Insurance

STATE	Utilities, 2012					Transportation and warehousing, 2012					Finance and insurance, 2012				
	Number of establishments	Employees Number	Employees Percent change, 2007–2012	Receipts (mil dol)	Annual payroll (mil dol)	Number of establishments	Employees Number	Employees Percent change, 2007–2012	Receipts (mil dol)	Annual payroll (mil dol)	Number of establishments	Employees Number	Employees Percent change, 2007–2012	Receipts (mil dol)	Annual payroll (mil dol)
	247	248	249	250	251	252	253	254	255	256	257	258	259	260	261
UNITED STATES	17 595	651 234	2.2	531 891	58 922 951	213 809	4 305 464	-3.3	730 541	183 841	468 183	6 040 880	-8.6	3 636 114	523 553
ALABAMA	424	15 454	7.3	NA	1 361 953	2 836	57 835	-6.4	8 422	2 460	7 294	72 763	1.0	NA	4 466
ALASKA	86	2 025	17.0	NA	184 291	1 091	18 957	-5.9	5 176	1 183	740	7 215	-7.2	NA	433
ARIZONA	265	12 185	1.9	NA	1 096 751	3 110	80 725	-3.6	13 864	3 442	9 196	128 762	-12.9	NA	7 847
ARKANSAS	320	7 065	-0.9	NA	528 383	2 356	50 798	-15.5	7 945	2 047	4 319	35 504	-6.1	NA	1 924
CALIFORNIA	1 143	66 836	4.5	NA	7 009 835	21 218	441 734	-2.3	78 926	19 716	48 523	601 858	-16.4	NA	57 898
COLORADO	365	8 498	0.4	NA	736 022	3 443	61 976	-4.3	13 963	2 851	9 828	98 761	-7.8	NA	7 418
CONNECTICUT	153	10 545	3.3	NA	922 836	1 595	44 003	-0.3	5 114	1 681	6 108	119 326	-13.1	NA	16 627
DELAWARE	48	2 622	0.3	NA	246 949	612	11 938	2.6	1 056	418	1 920	36 438	-14.1	NA	3 034
DISTRICT OF COLUMBIA	47	D	NA	NA	D	193	8 483	-3.7	1 968	342	999	18 080	-7.2	NA	2 666
FLORIDA	699	27 343	-11.6	NA	2 356 891	13 280	209 381	-4.0	49 159	8 958	30 653	338 872	-8.8	NA	22 758
GEORGIA	599	22 615	-7.7	NA	1 991 441	5 972	154 248	-9.0	26 825	6 840	14 434	164 422	-8.2	NA	12 272
HAWAII	54	3 379	14.4	NA	289 114	847	26 839	-17.1	4 599	1 150	1 401	18 686	-9.9	NA	1 145
IDAHO	204	3 709	11.4	NA	287 206	1 736	17 195	1.2	2 390	588	2 793	21 698	-3.9	NA	1 035
ILLINOIS	492	29 968	8.4	NA	3 044 699	13 251	230 695	-3.0	39 888	10 023	22 230	296 035	-15.0	NA	28 201
INDIANA	538	15 558	3.8	NA	1 293 728	5 096	118 242	0.1	16 995	4 438	9 692	96 927	-12.0	NA	5 866
IOWA	272	7 656	-0.8	NA	570 315	3 499	55 762	2.4	7 641	2 111	6 071	91 750	0.7	NA	5 780
KANSAS	230	7 263	-20.7	NA	607 926	2 510	50 019	6.7	6 561	1 968	5 976	59 099	-4.1	NA	3 717
KENTUCKY	340	8 685	4.9	NA	699 968	2 910	84 757	7.4	12 816	3 859	6 346	67 888	1.6	NA	3 838
LOUISIANA	517	11 132	2.5	NA	884 069	3 764	70 059	-2.8	15 110	3 779	7 716	64 813	0.8	NA	3 643
MAINE	99	2 363	-6.0	NA	169 783	1 175	14 908	-2.0	1 729	557	1 899	25 688	-4.8	NA	1 574
MARYLAND	130	9 484	-5.7	NA	1 049 972	3 348	64 906	-3.6	8 719	2 701	7 583	100 204	-20.0	NA	8 630
MASSACHUSETTS	274	13 305	0.6	NA	1 324 451	3 558	77 843	-2.1	10 653	3 173 044	9 384	202 811	-8.8	NA	22 940
MICHIGAN	389	23 036	3.7	NA	2 030 234	5 699	106 324	-0.5	20 033	4 525 164	13 181	151 712	-13.5	NA	9 757
MINNESOTA	320	12 802	8.7	NA	1 218 248	4 617	82 311	2.5	14 948	3 334 532	9 266	157 494	0.6	NA	13 450
MISSISSIPPI	592	8 803	1.5	NA	607 227	2 019	33 100	-9.1	4 273	1 303 347	4 692	34 472	-4.0	NA	1 634
MISSOURI	361	16 131	0.6	NA	1 381 461	4 543	82 336	-7.5	13 788	3 202 496	10 876	132 479	-3.5	NA	8 884
MONTANA	204	2 925	5.9	NA	232 408	1 475	11 861	1.7	1 972	449 841	1 944	16 206	-4.7	NA	800
NEBRASKA	115	930	-28.2	NA	77 087	2 283	26 879	-43.8	5 980	1 071 756	4 201	62 434	-3.2	NA	3 811
NEVADA	123	4 991	-6.3	NA	466 381	1 409	43 720	-9.6	5 570	1 631 242	4 053	34 396	-18.2	NA	1 982
NEW HAMPSHIRE	120	3 329	4.8	NA	294 495	804	13 787	8.5	1 244	441 785	1 889	24 252	-13.7	NA	1 760
NEW JERSEY	406	20 304	10.7	NA	2 131 755	7 004	160 321	-11.7	26 485	7 078 122	11 927	198 724	-6.9	NA	20 350
NEW MEXICO	234	4 880	-2.6	NA	376 693	1 384	17 510	1.8	2 678	703 942	2 674	22 709	-10.9	NA	1 228
NEW YORK	616	42 612	11.2	NA	3 882 982	12 312	240 587	-0.6	43 409	9 676 996	27 518	539 761	-8.6	NA	98 776
NORTH CAROLINA	478	20 114	-1.8	NA	1 849 812	5 393	108 760	-7.0	14 744	4 277 276	13 088	168 278	-12.5	NA	13 115
NORTH DAKOTA	124	D	NA	NA	D	1 641	18 847	83.7	4 639	962 681	1 755	17 199	6.0	NA	919
OHIO	627	26 222	-1.1	NA	2 370 045	6 966	158 891	-10.5	23 709	6 649 313	17 443	241 719	-9.2	NA	16 209
OKLAHOMA	345	8 202	-16.5	NA	617 887	2 641	44 502	-7.4	9 571	2 144 251	6 691	57 760	-4.4	NA	3 078
OREGON	286	8 069	1.1	NA	697 565	2 991	52 351	-8.6	7 897	2 156 783	5 812	57 422	-13.9	NA	3 638
PENNSYLVANIA	757	30 687	5.2	NA	3 061 256	8 175	209 798	1.5	25 255	7 843 461	17 733	266 764	-4.5	NA	20 439
RHODE ISLAND	39	1 217	-5.1	NA	108 147	610	11 271	5.5	1 153	363 060	1 311	25 216	-19.7	NA	2 006
SOUTH CAROLINA	333	11 956	-1.5	NA	955 667	2 497	48 696	-13.1	5 443	1 859 027	7 204	66 331	-0.2	NA	3 510
SOUTH DAKOTA	158	2 216	4.4	NA	162 748	1 146	9 549	4.2	1 526	370 640	1 958	26 472	-11.2	NA	1 254
TENNESSEE	144	3 256	0.2	NA	201 896	4 047	132 825	0.6	18 040	5 168 090	9 726	112 241	-3.5	NA	7 171
TEXAS	1 953	52 894	14.6	NA	4 467 197	16 998	386 767	3.6	79 794	1 920 6 695	39 037	481 749	3.5	NA	33 436
UTAH	214	4 319	-6.9	NA	374 644	2 177	45 945	-6.9	8 848	1 957 105	4 865	52 959	-9.7	NA	3 344
VERMONT	65	D	NA	NA	D	486	5 731	-8.2	677	200 358	990	9 039	-4.1	NA	570
VIRGINIA	314	15 065	-9.4	NA	1 398 172	4 779	90 068	-5.2	14 858	3 926 070	11 190	153 274	-9.0	NA	11 430
WASHINGTON	297	9 213	58.3	NA	759 825	4 840	87 862	0.9	16 791	4 274 033	9 737	97 245	-18.4	NA	7 005
WEST VIRGINIA	221	5 849	-9.3	NA	453 649	1 234	15 705	-5.3	2 797	602 177	2 148	17 875	-10.5	NA	807
WISCONSIN	323	14 046	-10.7	NA	1 247 335	5 251	97 724	-6.7	13 100	3 707 470	9 177	140 391	-2.9	NA	9 149
WYOMING	138	2 435	8.9	NA	203 277	988	10 133	16.9	1 801	466 688	992	6 707	-2.1	NA	330

Table A. States — Real Estate and Rental and Leasing and Professional, Scientific, and Technical Services

STATE	Real estate and rental and leasing, 2012					Professional, scientific, and technical services, 2012								
		Employees					Employees							
	Number of estab-lishments	Number	Percent change, 2007–2012	Receipts (mil dol)	Annual payroll (mil dol)	Number of estab-lishments	Total	Percent change, 2007–2012	Legal services	Accounting tax preparation, book-keeping, and payroll services	Architectural, engineering, and related services	Computer systems design and related services	Receipts (mil dol)	Annual payroll (mil dol)
	262	263	264	265	266	267	268	269	270	271	272	273	274	275
UNITED STATES...............	354 106	1 923 770	-12.1	487 655	85 326	856 463	8 203 735	4.2	1 148 683	1 443 462	1 354 603	1 473 241	1 480 277	581 406
ALABAMA	3 858	22 852	-15.7	3 919	820	9 109	89 988	-4.3	13 755	12 456	24 527	18 294	16 320	5 725
ALASKA	872	4 212	-3.6	1 023	188	1 898	17 648	37.4	D	1 917	8 171	1 253	3 175	1 178
ARIZONA	8 089	40 479	-23.1	9 330	1 693	16 198	121 381	-6.2	17 690	20 352	21 731	22 873	19 268	7 379
ARKANSAS	2 802	12 867	-8.8	1 923	410	5 678	32 210	-0.5	D	6 889	5 762	2 813	4 528	1 567
CALIFORNIA....................	49 276	273 511	-12.5	78 740	13 467	114 321	1 303 232	3.4	141 018	384 308	162 594	200 809	234 371	90 437
COLORADO.....................	9 295	38 706	-18.6	8 482	1 570	23 872	180 064	12.1	19 729	20 420	39 432	41 352	33 741	12 932
CONNECTICUT	3 219	19 778	-11.9	5 349	958	9 220	97 578	-4.4	12 910	14 369	12 982	16 920	17 994	8 364
DELAWARE	1 111	5 402	-7.0	5 471	265	2 543	D	D	D	3 109	2 585	5 393	D	D
DISTRICT OF COLUMBIA ...	1 112	10 103	4.6	3 214	674	5 061	97 555	9.6	31 675	4 829	8 003	14 685	31 866	11 196
FLORIDA.........................	29 845	139 955	-18.1	30 560	5 337	70 785	440 858	2.5	93 530	73 188	60 374	76 034	70 176	27 100
GEORGIA	10 484	55 551	-15.7	14 232	2 704	28 112	D	D	31 571	42 729	33 823	56 588	D	D
HAWAII	1 919	11 369	-32.2	3 411	484	3 226	21 629	-3.7	D	3 385	5 251	2 847	3 334	1 266
IDAHO...........................	2 033	6 268	-25.1	1 040	184	4 198	32 076	1.3	D	3 702	7 951	2 623	4 274	1 728
ILLINOIS.........................	12 035	76 794	-12.2	23 649	3 816	38 673	364 336	-1.3	57 212	62 779	44 413	62 613	70 263	28 315
INDIANA	5 729	31 715	-7.5	6 548	1 172	12 829	99 962	3.9	14 668	19 194	18 906	12 437	14 702	5 491
IOWA............................	2 742	12 031	-18.0	2 268	426	6 204	48 521	14.5	7 489	9 878	5 908	7 957	6 421	2 467
KANSAS	2 999	14 256	-6.0	2 743	508	7 110	60 989	8.3	7 462	12 290	12 765	8 129	8 716	3 596
KENTUCKY	3 534	18 250	-9.4	4 846	637	8 101	62 851	1.5	10 848	15 446	9 866	8 447	7 782	2 817
LOUISIANA	4 500	31 298	1.2	7 486	1 461	11 728	88 093	3.1	19 363	16 839	26 874	6 092	13 546	5 023
MAINE...........................	1 580	6 242	-10.1	1 100	221	3 492	22 943	3.2	4 025	3 317	4 866	2 813	3 353	1 238
MARYLAND	6 001	42 838	-13.9	13 410	2 253	19 714	244 710	-2.8	D	20 872	44 204	67 825	50 025	20 161
MASSACHUSETTS	6 485	42 788	-11.9	13 628	2 358	21 422	255 022	0.8	29 271	25 343	38 428	51 240	60 370	23 827
MICHIGAN	7 826	48 706	-11.2	11 974	1 807	21 650	D	D	26 862	38 730	59 343	32 723	D	D
MINNESOTA	6 300	34 499	-12.5	7 828	1 396	16 348	140 927	-0.6	D	18 988	17 814	24 040	23 449	9 739
MISSISSIPPI	2 374	10 235	0.6	1 709	334	4 747	30 205	-2.6	D	6 904	5 529	3 438	4 023	1 450
MISSOURI	6 165	33 447	-15.6	6 730	1 298	13 279	137 981	4.3	21 063	22 228	18 976	30 349	24 293	8 615
MONTANA	1 726	5 207	-18.8	835	162	3 545	16 660	-1.4	2 972	3 236	4 129	1 185	2 192	799
NEBRASKA	2 001	10 068	0.9	1 732	389	4 448	74 514	82.5	D	42 825	5 660	8 215	5 727	3 639
NEVADA	3 866	22 412	-29.1	4 981	815	8 102	47 934	-17.5	9 894	7 385	8 885	4 681	7 759	2 832
NEW HAMPSHIRE	1 338	7 044	-3.1	1 593	310	3 825	30 159	2.4	6 571	4 357	5 756	3 948	1 697
NEW JERSEY	8 749	53 751	-16.0	17 328	2 813	29 390	307 549	-7.3	38 055	44 203	39 728	88 570	58 738	24 013
NEW MEXICO	2 369	9 754	-16.5	1 960	369	4 687	44 175	-0.3	5 449	4 647	8 101	4 058	7 619	2 772
NEW YORK	32 033	166 315	-3.1	56 410	8 654	59 302	588 820	4.2	121 085	97 246	59 318	77 105	133 639	49 200
NORTH CAROLINA............	10 140	47 155	-12.0	9 302	1 943	22 855	196 287	6.1	23 399	29 415	28 778	36 677	31 948	12 940
NORTH DAKOTA	912	5 157	37.6	1 445	248	1 722	13 715	40.0	1 902	1 821	3 213	2 586	1 847	736
OHIO.............................	9 932	60 966	-9.1	16 133	2 442	23 961	233 876	2.3	34 707	36 624	40 381	39 420	35 971	14 220
OKLAHOMA	4 000	21 261	-14.6	4 270	898	9 470	71 997	9.3	12 250	11 842	21 414	7 113	10 991	4 115
OREGON	5 644	26 016	-16.0	4 650	903	11 663	84 493	-0.9	11 773	11 963	12 941	11 952	11 386	5 841
PENNSYLVANIA................	9 438	58 585	-15.0	13 364	2 618	29 297	316 658	6.0	51 348	50 126	58 713	42 585	54 834	22 622
RHODE ISLAND................	1 058	5 615	-13.5	1 120	219	2 997	21 165	-7.5	4 086	3 091	3 470	4 696	3 338	1 310
SOUTH CAROLINA............	4 692	23 189	-23.8	4 334	826	9 721	79 824	6.5	13 690	11 165	20 796	10 923	12 722	4 817
SOUTH DAKOTA	962	3 526	-8.3	583	106	1 822	11 144	9.3	1 820	2 570	2 277	1 305	1 315	482
TENNESSEE	5 470	30 593	-18.9	6 178	1 220	10 863	104 552	3.7	D	22 269	18 445	11 327	14 200	6 129
TEXAS	26 639	169 941	-2.2	38 757	7 752	62 322	639 561	18.3	81 308	90 410	171 740	110 640	122 086	47 256
UTAH	4 446	16 197	-20.7	3 226	605	9 009	76 345	11.5	9 137	16 734	11 239	10 085	10 555	3 909
VERMONT	741	3 092	-8.9	510	104	2 113	15 948	-3.5	D	5 838	2 056	1 874	1 782	740
VIRGINIA	8 862	54 246	-10.3	11 759	2 378	29 368	429 690	11.0	27 122	35 371	73 172	162 320	92 776	36 365
WASHINGTON	9 913	45 209	-11.7	9 695	1 895	20 047	167 512	4.9	D	20 084	30 768	32 431	28 284	11 977
WEST VIRGINIA	1 405	6 011	-14.8	1 256	204	2 974	24 816	11.6	6 084	4 068	4 320	2 733	3 105	1 143
WISCONSIN	4 509	23 762	-12.7	4 359	801	11 301	99 162	1.1	14 704	18 173	17 021	13 998	15 135	5 738
WYOMING	1 076	4 546	-2.3	1 259	216	2 141	9 134	3.5	D	1 324	2 603	419	1 297	467

Table A. States — Health Care and Social Assistance

STATE	Health care and social assistance, 2012													
	Subject to federal tax							Tax-exempt						
	Number of establishments	Employees				Receipts (mil dol)	Annual payroll (mil dol)	Number of establishments	Employees				Receipts (mil dol)	Annual payroll (mil dol)
		Total	Percent change, 2007–2012	Ambulatory health care services	Hospitals				Total	Percent change, 2007–2012	Ambulatory health care services	Hospitals		
	276	277	278	279	280	281	282	283	284	285	286	287	288	289
UNITED STATES	690 525	9 542 138	14.7	5 687 621	677 114	1 008 745	409 812	140 778	8 872 619	4.8	787 378	5 074 227	1 031 697	391 428
ALABAMA	8 489	142 386	5.5	76 205	20 349	14 628	5 995	1 816	100 808	-2.3	8 624	67 461	11 412	4 244
ALASKA	1 851	21 389	38.7	12 315	1 849	2 810	1 098	581	27 312	8.4	4 359	12 617	3 565	1 336
ARIZONA	15 041	184 186	19.6	106 247	15 871	20 221	7 975	1 831	130 921	4.9	13 850	79 719	16 835	6 261
ARKANSAS	5 936	86 999	12.7	42 556	12 408	8 541	3 496	1 549	79 456	5.0	6 689	42 744	7 252	2 823
CALIFORNIA	89 999	1 005 201	13.8	630 526	66 982	127 356	48 373	13 208	771 239	8.8	72 024	466 701	121 598	42 767
COLORADO	12 701	140 738	10.8	82 675	7 852	14 693	6 167	2 168	117 160	4.7	18 826	64 999	14 795	5 710
CONNECTICUT	7 876	131 732	7.6	73 550	D	13 333	6 059	2 420	139 540	6.6	13 781	D	16 240	6 475
DELAWARE	1 964	30 400	20.1	18 888	D	3 174	1 435	560	31 497	7.1	2 618	D	3 830	1 561
DISTRICT OF COLUMBIA	1 353	24 356	23.6	13 997	3 244	2 871	1 203	712	43 386	4.9	2 717	23 473	6 093	2 393
FLORIDA	51 567	614 004	14.1	360 507	77 106	76 786	27 914	5 092	377 250	3.1	34 574	224 905	47 276	16 521
GEORGIA	20 166	256 945	12.2	158 607	D	28 196	11 171	2 568	191 515	0.7	11 486	134 809	23 604	8 344
HAWAII	2 794	26 788	-7.7	20 436	D	3 180	1 347	765	39 984	15.5	4 777	21 720	4 957	1 943
IDAHO	4 271	49 613	11.5	26 127	2 924	4 281	1 636	594	33 892	15.1	1 393	25 236	3 614	1 535
ILLINOIS	27 624	383 980	18.1	240 920	15 441	39 270	16 151	5 431	386 504	1.3	22 524	230 249	44 161	16 423
INDIANA	12 360	206 531	13.8	113 641	15 020	21 191	8 626	2 796	190 392	1.0	12 842	119 354	17 028	5 804
IOWA	5 582	78 961	12.4	43 888	D	7 151	3 357	2 549	127 945	-0.1	7 799	D	D	D
KANSAS	5 977	93 121	11.5	52 953	6 761	9 678	3 955	1 957	99 151	4.4	6 359	51 968	6 152	2 429
KENTUCKY	9 449	127 446	10.2	69 066	8 611	11 985	5 178	1 976	124 432	4.0	11 499	80 486	11 418	3 868
LOUISIANA	10 240	167 792	15.6	88 911	19 565	15 870	6 157	1 759	117 187	5.7	4 258	77 104	9 939	3 613
MAINE	3 071	41 700	4.9	23 055	D	3 487	1 613	1 659	67 531	4.9	7 036	D	D	D
MARYLAND	13 217	168 241	17.1	105 879	D	18 823	7 785	2 783	191 493	11.3	9 804	D	D	D
MASSACHUSETTS	13 136	237 631	17.2	138 145	18 506	26 639	12 209	5 250	349 854	13.5	32 003	169 964	25 847	10 415
MICHIGAN	21 447	270 655	18.4	173 860	14 278	27 435	11 944	4 784	314 875	-1.8	31 655	191 187	27 028	10 346
MINNESOTA	11 233	189 308	20.6	108 030		15 774	7 259	3 874	250 887	9.5	23 077	D	D	D
MISSISSIPPI	5 149	84 441	16.3	43 908	11 822	8 731	3 451	1 062	73 179	-1.5	3 226	54 427	6 833	2 684
MISSOURI	14 644	184 918	15.9	95 013	14 471	17 917	7 525	3 122	215 022	6.0	18 417	129 225	17 263	6 202
MONTANA	2 545	24 420	12.2	15 400	D	2 508	1 041	967	41 237	14.2	2 978	D	D	D
NEBRASKA	4 282	57 239	16.0	31 302	2 328	5 707	2 398	1 128	68 230	4.0	3 575	40 591	5 495	1 806
NEVADA	5 766	77 665	6.8	42 411	14 806	9 937	3 598	542	30 920	29.3	2 120	20 737	3 216	1 223
NEW HAMPSHIRE	2 775	35 400	8.2	21 181	2 347	444	1 770	803	51 699	1.4	9 014	25 218	5 615	2 317
NEW JERSEY	23 088	297 847	17.7	198 143	10 677	1 468	13 028	3 847	243 028	-2.9	20 746	136 380	27 740	11 297
NEW MEXICO	3 970	67 477	17.5	34 002	8 324	1 176	2 450	997	49 080	2.1	5 093	26 723	5 166	2 138
NEW YORK	43 548	540 067	17.4	397 708	3 366	237	22 401	13 186	928 920	7.3	102 840	443 108	100 067	42 779
NORTH CAROLINA	19 152	292 709	2.0	168 931	7 693	1 090	11 432	3 825	236 861	0.2	16 895	151 084	27 922	10 325
NORTH DAKOTA	1 235	15 038	6.4	9 934	D	D	776	621	41 601	9.3	1 630	D	3 609	1 638
OHIO	22 945	393 909	13.7	231 564	12 043	1 530	15 471	5 292	404 861	2.5	32 022	254 046	46 278	17 670
OKLAHOMA	8 868	128 437	6.0	63 736	19 773	3 626	4 996	1 786	84 789	6.5	5 726	49 730	9 413	3 293
OREGON	9 829	105 341	14.7	65 396	D	D	4 534	2 646	112 243	11.8	11 445	D	13 940	5 156
PENNSYLVANIA	27 983	433 818	17.7	266 329	28 531	3 968	19 364	8 569	521 661	3.1	48 929	245 857	52 550	19 962
RHODE ISLAND	2 470	35 597	2.4	20 571	D	D	1 536	766	48 470	2.7	4 687	D	4 756	2 020
SOUTH CAROLINA	8 346	132 360	14.4	70 689	16 924	2 886	5 385	1 502	80 084	-5.3	3 855	51 861	9 119	3 302
SOUTH DAKOTA	1 544	20 514	17.9	11 889	D	D	830	754	42 980	10.0	3 975	D	4 189	1 729
TENNESSEE	12 286	220 313	18.7	123 165	30 315	4 700	9 564	2 611	160 140	5.2	13 454	100 602	17 842	6 664
TEXAS	55 176	945 659	21.2	552 817	118 155	20 879	36 493	6 166	400 005	3.6	30 342	268 014	51 047	18 077
UTAH	6 601	77 036	14.9	44 035	7 957	8 254	3 017	684	49 139	7.8	5 381	32 987	5 109	1 573
VERMONT	1 370	14 976	-2.6	8 847	D	1 297	578	726	29 222	10.1	6 615	D	D	D
VIRGINIA	16 070	236 459	15.9	139 138	17 223	25 556	10 868	2 704	174 649	4.5	13 334	102 848	15 825	5 535
WASHINGTON	16 888	194 136	12.9	115 714	D	20 414	8 703	2 945	180 091	4.0	23 965	D	D	D
WEST VIRGINIA	3 734	57 400	10.8	27 271	5 215	5 125	2 108	1 205	71 675	14.0	8 152	43 463	5 810	2 094
WISCONSIN	11 460	175 153	6.1	99 434	1 679	16 357	7 785	3 199	210 988	3.3	23 362	112 126	17 578	5 514
WYOMING	1 457	13 706	17.3	8 109	1 159	1 486	608	441	17 634	0.4	1 026	9 743	1 408	561

Table A. States — Arts, Entertainment, and Recreation and Accommodation and Food Services

STATE	Arts, entertainment, and recreation, 2012					Accommodation and food services, 2012					
	Number of establishments	Employees		Receipts (mil dol)	Annual payroll (mil dol)	Number of establishments	Employees		Food services and drinking places	Receipts (mil dol)	Annual payroll (mil dol)
		Number	Percent change, 2007–2012				Total	Percent change, 2007–2012			
	290	291	292	293	294	295	296	297	298	299	300
UNITED STATES...............	124 591	2 081 668	1.0	201 193	64 052	662 489	12 007 689	3.5	10 057 608	708 139	196 103
ALABAMA	1 086	17 170	-4.5	1 194	297	8 339	157 337	4.3	142 339	7 576	2 071
ALASKA	545	5 055	13.4	407	91	2 126	26 836	4.7	20 057	2 221	626
ARIZONA	1 764	42 407	-8.8	3 810	1 263	11 669	251 455	0.3	203 083	13 997	4 030
ARKANSAS	781	8 881	-3.6	704	160	5 473	95 854	6.6	85 388	4 307	1 183
CALIFORNIA.....................	21 191	303 838	0.6	39 179	13 419	78 560	1 394 984	2.1	1 160 464	90 830	25 148
COLORADO......................	2 433	51 235	3.1	3 783	1 323	12 744	240 484	3.8	194 749	13 618	3 995
CONNECTICUT	1 610	26 476	5.2	2 298	715	8 263	134 546	1.9	107 171	9 542	2 591
DELAWARE......................	409	8 102	18.2	651	208	1 987	35 609	10.6	31 519	2 148	567
DISTRICT OF COLUMBIA ...	301	7 510	2.6	1 021	412	2 371	60 370	13.9	45 949	5 102	1 505
FLORIDA..........................	7 562	169 796	1.8	16 453	4 904	37 118	786 082	5.3	621 439	49 818	13 598
GEORGIA.........................	2 733	42 851	-4.9	3 780	1 262	18 815	353 638	-0.5	313 419	18 977	5 173
HAWAII	495	10 623	-11.4	844	249	3 518	98 364	0.0	59 938	9 537	2 536
IDAHO.............................	712	8 944	-0.8	455	138	3 564	54 257	-4.2	43 787	2 680	726
ILLINOIS..........................	4 520	77 153	-3.1	7 401	2 348	27 117	469 870	0.2	415 659	27 937	7 707
INDIANA..........................	2 069	33 726	-6.0	3 652	941	13 057	255 223	0.4	224 519	13 077	3 433
IOWA..............................	1 466	21 233	-2.0	1 626	364	7 047	115 134	-1.5	96 648	5 469	1 467
KANSAS..........................	1 000	14 341	-8.3	884	252	5 943	106 850	2.0	95 624	4 873	1 343
KENTUCKY.......................	1 242	17 360	-6.4	1 207	349	7 678	156 965	3.6	143 432	7 500	2 084
LOUISIANA.......................	1 376	23 386	-5.6	2 661	720	9 019	193 928	7.6	157 059	11 698	3 111
MAINE.............................	849	7 305	-6.3	527	155	3 958	49 672	0.6	40 538	2 901	851
MARYLAND	1 960	35 932	-4.2	3 391	1 062	11 344	204 222	6.0	181 041	12 517	3 411
MASSACHUSETTS	3 130	55 585	5.4	5 012	1 788	16 898	273 185	6.2	243 840	17 509	5 020
MICHIGAN........................	3 369	46 255	-16.1	3 709	1 416	19 491	347 337	2.4	302 053	17 962	4 872
MINNESOTA.....................	2 714	42 320	0.6	3 127	1 191	11 345	221 859	0.4	184 868	11 723	3 238
MISSISSIPPI.....................	656	8 840	8.1	587	161	5 177	116 238	-2.8	82 085	6 999	1 765
MISSOURI........................	2 095	38 190	1.8	3 716	1 341	12 459	239 264	-0.9	206 309	12 430	3 409
MONTANA........................	1 126	10 903	5.9	785	170	3 458	46 251	0.2	35 921	2 420	650
NEBRASKA......................	842	13 090	15.2	780	206	4 326	70 128	1.4	62 732	3 094	855
NEVADA..........................	1 290	26 705	-11.8	3 645	772	5 815	296 762	-8.8	102 621	27 482	8 556
NEW HAMPSHIRE	724	12 946	11.7	793	235	3 606	54 047	-2.2	44 957	2 942	891
NEW JERSEY....................	3 421	56 427	10.5	4 632	1 606	20 127	291 933	0.2	233 932	19 674	5 387
NEW MEXICO....................	652	12 259	-14.5	1 353	268	4 177	82 601	2.7	64 280	4 350	1 250
NEW YORK.......................	11 615	162 729	2.8	21 929	6 900	49 731	679 146	14.8	584 408	49 286	13 734
NORTH CAROLINA.............	3 471	58 185	5.2	4 774	1 535	19 496	358 602	4.5	318 217	18 622	5 041
NORTH DAKOTA	421	4 901	7.0	242	64	1 935	35 698	17.8	26 990	2 045	521
OHIO...............................	3 810	60 704	-7.1	5 432	1 977	23 432	437 293	0.2	403 421	20 653	5 743
OKLAHOMA......................	1 052	26 375	0.5	2 791	672	7 403	143 561	11.2	125 756	7 121	1 908
OREGON..........................	1 636	24 031	-1.2	1 607	570	10 610	150 482	0.0	126 327	8 467	2 438
PENNSYLVANIA.................	4 402	99 568	19.1	8 748	2 742	27 646	439 159	4.5	386 349	23 504	6 377
RHODE ISLAND	537	8 798	-0.4	780	216	2 973	44 063	-0.8	40 040	2 481	706
SOUTH CAROLINA.............	1 525	24 918	-1.5	1 813	432	9 828	185 282	1.3	158 300	9 764	2 650
SOUTH DAKOTA................	668	6 204	-3.6	437	103	2 363	37 974	3.4	29 328	1 874	514
TENNESSEE.....................	2 326	32 490	0.2	3 355	1 150	12 004	241 348	0.8	211 928	12 499	3 546
TEXAS	6 304	119 132	8.6	10 287	3 309	48 721	976 390	12.7	868 360	54 481	14 744
UTAH	923	20 749	12.2	1 181	401	5 108	95 933	4.5	78 587	4 789	1 363
VERMONT	451	7 147	-10.8	352	116	1 920	31 365	0.6	18 803	1 564	494
VIRGINIA..........................	2 744	54 248	6.0	4 244	1 268	16 832	320 514	6.0	273 558	17 796	4 909
WASHINGTON	2 744	58 770	2.0	5 093	1 553	16 333	234 145	0.4	198 551	14 297	4 160
WEST VIRGINIA	756	8 349	-22.7	632	128	3 629	66 302	7.4	52 982	4 036	976
WISCONSIN	2 655	43 555	1.8	3 182	1 053	14 137	221 567	-2.6	189 520	10 303	2 764
WYOMING	428	3 971	-1.8	248	79	1 799	27 580	2.2	18 763	1 645	469

Table A. States — Other Services, Except Public Administration, and Government Employment

STATE	Other services, except public administration, 2012								Government employment, 2014		
		Employees									
	Number of establishments	Total	Percent change, 2007–2012	Repair and maintenance	Personal and laundry services	Religious, civic, and similar services	Receipts (mil dol)	Annual payroll (mil dol)	Federal civilian	Federal military	State and local
	301	302	303	304	305	306	307	308	309	310	311
UNITED STATES..................	529 691	3 430 711	-1.4	1 194 122	1 349 371	887 218	426 694	108 186	2 790 000	1 982 000	19 258 000
ALABAMA	6 087	37 291	-7.9	17 145	14 117	6 029	4 378	1 117	53 539	30 107	316 155
ALASKA	1 355	7 238	-4.3	2 579	2 228	2 431	905	236	14 921	26 347	64 470
ARIZONA	8 503	62 073	-9.2	23 444	23 403	15 226	6 232	1 736	54 659	32 719	357 431
ARKANSAS	3 961	21 830	-5.9	8 514	8 577	4 739	2 339	586	20 202	18 073	193 716
CALIFORNIA	57 009	395 836	-0.9	143 971	155 062	96 803	50 439	12 251	243 381	208 077	2 165 170
COLORADO	10 246	64 398	2.6	22 061	23 944	18 393	8 519	2 100	52 768	54 316	364 289
CONNECTICUT	7 282	43 384	-9.6	13 274	20 799	9 311	4 904	1 382	17 469	13 925	230 417
DELAWARE	1 513	9 841	-1.7	2 963	4 705	2 173	975	290	5 538	8 922	60 176
DISTRICT OF COLUMBIA ...	3 357	58 982	18.3	638	7 081	51 263	19 773	4 239	198 136	14 855	38 615
FLORIDA	34 843	195 176	-3.2	60 133	84 877	50 166	20 799	5 415	131 781	95 866	930 241
GEORGIA	13 828	89 302	-8.9	35 769	36 220	17 313	10 617	2 703	98 768	95 631	569 871
HAWAII	2 808	19 348	-3.8	3 202	7 812	8 334	2 005	539	33 132	57 346	93 022
IDAHO	2 553	12 188	-10.9	5 569	4 257	2 362	1 118	311	12 350	9 235	105 730
ILLINOIS	23 334	165 366	-1.4	58 058	59 330	47 978	21 356	5 827	79 975	41 893	748 670
INDIANA	10 777	72 937	-3.1	28 900	25 835	18 202	8 910	2 107	36 322	21 488	384 808
IOWA	5 866	30 672	-3.8	11 925	11 612	7 135	3 343	848	17 574	12 211	237 692
KANSAS..............................	5 147	29 521	-6.8	10 781	10 367	8 373	3 433	849	24 903	35 922	234 658
KENTUCKY..........................	5 849	38 364	-6.3	16 863	14 589	6 912	4 071	1 090	37 701	50 331	275 235
LOUISIANA	6 293	43 500	3.0	21 958	14 140	7 402	5 409	1 479	30 032	37 750	299 463
MAINE	2 786	13 755	3.4	4 907	4 517	4 331	1 463	376	14 060	7 071	85 464
MARYLAND	9 978	79 391	2.6	25 219	31 858	22 314	10 880	2 929	172 141	49 160	345 414
MASSACHUSETTS	14 008	93 489	3.6	25 127	42 404	25 958	10 455	2 931	45 758	20 037	397 242
MICHIGAN	15 919	96 150	-5.3	37 715	37 999	20 436	10 408	2 720	51 120	18 537	536 943
MINNESOTA	10 832	72 715	-11.1	22 221	29 525	20 969	7 877	2 017	31 246	20 284	368 543
MISSISSIPPI	3 540	19 232	-5.8	8 304	6 723	4 205	1 952	549	25 391	28 329	220 852
MISSOURI	10 357	62 825	-6.9	25 284	24 124	13 417	6 980	1 835	56 981	35 375	381 156
MONTANA	2 278	10 917	5.8	4 644	2 731	3 542	1 222	303	12 998	8 104	74 061
NEBRASKA	3 989	21 832	-3.2	9 171	7 747	4 914	2 841	612	16 693	12 624	144 987
NEVADA	3 538	25 386	-6.8	8 561	12 023	4 802	2 609	706	18 121	18 550	131 509
NEW HAMPSHIRE	2 879	16 603	2.8	5 699	6 736	4 168	1 555	473	7 413	4 613	82 921
NEW JERSEY	18 327	108 216	2.4	32 991	56 552	18 673	11 608	3 150	48 999	25 070	545 412
NEW MEXICO	2 962	17 464	-3.3	7 474	5 336	4 654	1 799	501	29 538	17 563	161 766
NEW YORK	45 646	271 689	8.9	56 633	111 369	103 687	39 709	9 395	114 773	58 273	1 282 136
NORTH CAROLINA	13 716	80 710	-5.4	32 784	31 859	16 067	9 141	2 321	69 014	132 343	652 309
NORTH DAKOTA	1 716	9 232	-0.3	3 515	3 137	2 580	1 064	254	9 104	11 615	66 852
OHIO	18 851	127 366	-5.8	44 260	55 364	27 742	13 221	3 491	76 023	36 046	683 874
OKLAHOMA	5 411	32 388	2.3	13 280	12 874	6 234	4 037	940	46 348	33 988	289 059
OREGON	6 894	37 941	-3.0	14 717	13 486	9 738	4 435	1 149	27 503	11 927	238 169
PENNSYLVANIA...................	25 231	154 319	0.0	51 110	63 740	39 469	17 737	4 367	95 728	36 262	648 716
RHODE ISLAND	2 276	13 046	-9.3	4 172	5 690	3 184	1 445	391	10 246	7 303	54 254
SOUTH CAROLINA	6 666	44 374	-2.5	19 017	15 909	9 448	4 465	1 302	32 167	53 136	315 623
SOUTH DAKOTA	1 805	8 371	-1.7	3 569	2 586	2 216	939	214	11 107	8 210	65 160
TENNESSEE	8 117	55 990	-10.3	20 581	23 773	11 636	6 526	1 711	48 894	22 021	374 601
TEXAS	34 116	259 128	2.2	120 606	95 613	42 909	30 172	8 454	193 961	172 297	1 617 690
UTAH	4 259	26 026	-0.8	11 864	9 841	4 321	2 544	723	34 332	16 316	194 177
VERMONT	1 588	7 211	-0.8	2 223	2 032	2 956	755	199	6 700	4 537	47 122
VIRGINIA	14 726	112 430	1.2	34 521	41 520	36 389	17 079	4 471	189 487	139 176	535 675
WASHINGTON	12 425	69 976	-1.7	24 072	29 997	15 907	13 185	2 203	71 470	76 552	470 808
WEST VIRGINIA....................	2 661	16 583	0.3	6 969	5 759	3 855	1 773	444	23 430	9 192	124 136
WISCONSIN	10 210	62 054	-6.5	21 698	25 964	14 392	6 407	1 732	28 740	16 403	389 488
WYOMING	1 373	6 655	2.0	3 467	1 628	1 560	885	215	7 363	6 072	62 052

Table A. States — **State Government Employment and Payroll**

STATE	State government employment and payroll, 2014											
	State government employment, 2014			State government payroll, 2012		Full-time equivalent payroll (1,000 dollars)						
							Percent of total for:					
	Full-time equivalent employees	Full-time employees	Part-time employees	Full-time March payroll (1,000 dollars)	Part-time March payroll (1,000 dollars)	Total March payroll (1,000 dollars)[1]	Administration	Judicial and legal	Police	Corrections	Highways and transportation	Public Welfare
	312	313	314	315	316	317	318	319	320	321	322	323
UNITED STATES	4 341 163	3 751 771	1 591 917	18 929 609	2 225 244	21 154 853	5.3	4.9	3.1	10.2	6.3	4.8
ALABAMA	88 687	78 120	30 725	343 734	31 729	375 462	3.8	4.1	1.5	4.6	4.2	4.0
ALASKA	27 049	25 068	4 899	141 573	6 135	147 708	7.6	6.7	3.3	8.9	13.1	6.4
ARIZONA	78 689	65 846	30 516	309 324	36 471	345 796	4.1	3.2	3.1	11.2	4.2	6.1
ARKANSAS	62 079	57 095	15 944	229 879	15 280	245 159	4.6	2.2	2.0	7.6	5.8	5.4
CALIFORNIA	406 842	333 083	166 320	2 227 859	373 891	2 601 750	6.5	1.8	4.0	17.4	6.5	0.8
COLORADO	79 518	57 780	46 793	310 949	82 487	393 436	3.5	7.6	2.2	9.7	4.5	3.1
CONNECTICUT	63 013	53 662	24 468	349 454	42 086	391 540	6.6	12.0	4.0	10.6	5.1	9.4
DELAWARE	26 135	23 249	7 569	104 965	10 516	115 480	4.2	7.9	6.5	11.1	8.7	5.2
DISTRICT OF COLUMBIA	X	X	X	X	X	X	X	X	X	X	X	X
FLORIDA	176 990	159 008	46 153	676 050	56 392	732 442	4.6	11.6	2.4	10.8	4.5	4.2
GEORGIA	131 916	116 251	55 275	456 822	52 899	509 721	3.5	3.4	2.2	8.5	3.1	5.1
HAWAII	58 409	52 434	20 353	235 981	20 089	256 070	2.6	5.0	-	4.7	1.7	0.7
IDAHO	23 814	20 270	10 013	92 386	10 630	103 016	7.6	4.4	2.5	9.5	5.9	6.8
ILLINOIS	123 001	102 078	51 710	586 811	87 520	674 331	6.3	3.9	3.7	11.3	6.4	9.1
INDIANA	87 692	74 507	42 118	319 170	34 497	353 667	3.1	2.8	2.5	5.3	3.8	5.0
IOWA	49 888	40 053	28 654	247 633	23 972	271 606	2.8	5.0	2.2	5.7	4.9	5.3
KANSAS	49 469	44 041	17 293	198 639	18 428	217 067	4.2	4.5	2.3	5.5	5.4	3.7
KENTUCKY	83 409	74 615	24 919	312 910	26 455	339 364	4.2	5.8	2.5	3.6	4.6	7.7
LOUISIANA	76 207	68 801	20 786	305 281	20 729	326 009	6.1	2.5	2.9	7.7	6.1	6.3
MAINE	20 990	18 602	8 269	79 693	8 099	87 792	7.8	4.1	3.4	5.5	10.3	12.7
MARYLAND	86 771	78 023	13 723	390 743	39 432	430 175	5.6	7.0	3.2	14.2	6.9	6.9
MASSACHUSETTS	98 985	88 601	35 060	495 759	48 457	544 215	6.4	10.4	5.2	12.9	3.7	7.4
MICHIGAN	142 057	113 140	71 749	636 558	113 555	750 113	4.7	1.6	2.2	9.7	2.0	8.5
MINNESOTA	82 223	68 042	35 533	380 787	50 990	431 776	8.7	4.7	1.2	4.9	9.4	2.0
MISSISSIPPI	56 884	51 670	13 950	197 365	13 904	211 269	3.8	2.3	2.0	4.2	5.0	5.3
MISSOURI	88 133	78 298	29 622	294 591	26 124	320 715	4.4	5.4	3.4	11.2	6.2	6.7
MONTANA	20 721	16 877	10 196	72 980	11 868	84 848	7.8	4.4	3.0	5.9	12.7	8.1
NEBRASKA	32 101	26 733	10 188	112 087	11 878	123 965	3.7	3.2	3.7	9.2	7.1	6.3
NEVADA	27 236	24 524	9 711	119 577	10 979	130 557	8.0	4.2	4.3	12.7	6.2	6.2
NEW HAMPSHIRE	18 698	14 694	11 170	73 393	13 346	86 739	6.8	4.5	3.5	6.7	9.0	10.0
NEW JERSEY	143 707	130 261	30 454	798 630	49 975	848 605	4.3	9.9	3.6	6.6	11.8	6.2
NEW MEXICO	46 114	41 263	13 697	181 904	17 428	199 332	3.2	7.6	1.2	7.1	4.2	3.4
NEW YORK	240 744	222 965	46 118	1 340 751	78 717	1 419 468	8.2	9.9	3.7	13.2	12.6	1.6
NORTH CAROLINA	145 187	126 735	44 338	587 297	61 447	648 744	3.2	5.1	2.9	12.7	7.1	0.7
NORTH DAKOTA	18 752	15 747	9 760	72 319	10 287	82 606	5.3	4.4	1.5	4.5	7.6	2.2
OHIO	136 486	109 085	79 991	569 075	88 767	657 842	6.7	2.9	2.3	10.2	4.8	2.9
OKLAHOMA	66 939	59 310	24 781	243 598	23 144	266 741	5.0	5.2	3.5	5.9	4.4	9.3
OREGON	66 966	57 826	24 455	286 563	40 008	326 571	7.8	5.1	2.5	8.5	6.3	9.7
PENNSYLVANIA	161 369	140 760	64 995	689 205	108 618	797 823	5.8	3.8	5.8	11.9	7.2	5.8
RHODE ISLAND	18 691	17 073	7 053	95 526	6 850	102 376	9.1	7.3	2.6	10.2	7.9	8.0
SOUTH CAROLINA	78 690	70 754	21 553	281 930	23 452	305 382	4.9	1.4	2.7	8.2	5.0	4.8
SOUTH DAKOTA	14 625	12 774	6 262	52 245	5 351	57 596	6.7	5.3	2.6	5.5	7.2	11.3
TENNESSEE	79 258	70 425	26 794	291 925	24 791	316 715	6.0	4.7	2.7	7.2	4.2	8.9
TEXAS	313 284	278 324	90 437	1 334 437	129 062	1 463 499	3.3	2.2	2.6	9.2	4.1	5.7
UTAH	54 038	46 059	25 597	215 838	28 729	244 567	5.8	3.4	1.6	5.1	3.1	4.3
VERMONT	14 483	13 289	4 150	65 704	6 853	72 558	7.7	5.1	5.4	7.3	7.8	10.4
VIRGINIA	127 408	107 885	59 879	521 899	67 938	589 837	4.1	3.5	2.9	8.9	6.8	2.3
WASHINGTON	120 091	99 079	52 538	512 041	91 934	603 976	3.5	2.0	2.1	6.0	6.7	8.2
WEST VIRGINIA	40 281	36 579	12 091	134 872	11 144	146 016	4.9	5.5	3.1	6.2	11.4	6.7
WISCONSIN	72 960	58 052	49 880	297 532	48 867	346 400	4.5	4.4	1.5	13.1	2.6	2.8
WYOMING	13 484	12 361	3 415	53 365	3 045	56 411	8.4	5.4	2.4	8.8	12.6	4.1

1. Includes program categories not shown separately.

Table A. States — State Government Employment and Payroll and State Government Finances

STATE	State government employment and payroll, 2012 (cont.) Full-time equivalent payroll (1,000 dollars) (cont.) Percent of total for:							State government finances, 2013 General revenue (mil dol)							
									From federal government		From own sources				
												Taxes		Taxes per capita[1] (dollars)	
	Health	Hospitals	Social Insurance administration	Natural resources and parks	Utilities, sewerage, and waste management	Elementary and secondary education and libraries	Higher education	Total	Total	Per capita (dollars)	Total	Total	Sales and gross receipts	Total	Sales and gross receipts
	324	325	326	327	328	329	330	331	332	333	334	335	336	337	338
UNITED STATES	4.4	8.9	1.7	3.5	0.1	1.1	38.7	X	X	X	X	X	X	X	X
ALABAMA	5.1	13.7	1.0	2.4	-	-	48.7	22 760	8 227	1 702	14 422	9 268	4 709	1 917	974
ALASKA	3.0	0.9	1.1	9.9	-	8.0	18.2	12 280	2 747	3 737	9 526	5 133	250	6 982	340
ARIZONA	3.2	9.6	1.8	2.2	-	-	43.4	29 176	10 166	1 534	18 596	13 472	8 207	2 033	1 238
ARKANSAS	6.1	10.3	2.1	3.8	-	-	43.8	17 310	5 689	1 922	11 585	8 586	4 019	2 901	1 358
CALIFORNIA	3.7	10.3	3.0	4.4	0.2	-	34.9	219 693	54 828	1 430	161 596	133 184	48 075	3 474	1 254
COLORADO	2.2	6.5	1.5	3.1	-	-	50.2	23 129	6 428	1 220	16 620	11 246	4 280	2 135	812
CONNECTICUT	6.3	9.7	1.3	1.4	0.1	-	23.8	25 446	5 949	1 654	19 484	16 190	6 776	4 502	1 884
DELAWARE	7.4	4.4	1.0	2.5	0.5	-	30.9	7 794	1 929	2 084	5 798	3 346	487	3 615	526
DISTRICT OF COLUMBIA	X	X	X	X	X	X	X	X	X	X	X	X	X	X	X
FLORIDA	8.4	1.9	1.3	4.4	0	-	41.1	74 726	23 506	1 202	50 846	35 378	29 316	1 809	1 499
GEORGIA	3.6	6.6	0.9	4.8	-	-	52.6	38 392	14 323	1 433	23 773	17 794	7 408	1 781	741
HAWAII	4.0	9.4	0.4	1.7	-	40.2	20.3	10 825	2 327	1 657	8 494	6 093	3 932	4 340	2 801
IDAHO	7.9	2.0	3.0	8.9	-	-	32.4	7 340	2 523	1 565	4 799	3 579	1 773	2 220	1 100
ILLINOIS	2.7	8.8	1.6	2.2	-	-	36.5	65 562	16 974	1 318	48 249	38 729	14 720	3 006	1 143
INDIANA	2.0	1.8	1.1	2.6	-	-	66.4	33 499	11 192	1 703	22 231	16 931	10 298	2 577	1 567
IOWA	1.0	16.7	1.2	3.6	-	-	44.0	18 534	5 915	1 914	12 542	8 374	3 609	2 710	1 168
KANSAS	2.1	15.8	0.2	2.4	-	-	46.8	15 246	3 789	1 309	11 401	7 620	2 633	2 633	1 293
KENTUCKY	3.9	8.2	1.2	3.9	-	-	48.2	22 927	8 047	1 831	14 843	10 816	5 110	2 461	1 163
LOUISIANA	4.9	11.8	1.4	6.5	-	0.8	35.4	25 255	10 593	2 290	14 595	9 224	4 975	1 994	1 075
MAINE	5.4	2.2	1.8	6.1	-	0.1	32.0	7 991	2 821	2 124	5 161	3 884	1 780	2 924	1 340
MARYLAND	6.6	4.0	1.0	2.9	-	-	30.8	34 779	9 953	1 679	24 454	18 118	7 347	3 056	1 239
MASSACHUSETTS	6.7	4.5	1.6	2.3	0	2.1	26.9	46 180	13 233	1 977	32 474	23 901	7 455	3 571	1 114
MICHIGAN	3.5	9.9	0.6	2.5	-	-	51.0	54 343	17 830	1 802	36 336	24 936	12 298	2 520	1 243
MINNESOTA	4.0	4.3	1.2	4.3	0	-	45.1	34 651	9 142	1 687	25 336	21 032	8 290	3 880	1 529
MISSISSIPPI	5.4	18.8	1.0	5.0	-	-	39.0	17 511	7 510	2 511	9 861	7 403	4 571	2 475	1 528
MISSOURI	3.3	11.2	0.5	2.9	-	-	39.1	26 662	10 188	1 686	16 165	11 139	4 791	1 843	793
MONTANA	4.6	2.6	3.9	8.1	-	-	29.9	5 768	2 158	2 126	3 606	2 645	559	2 605	551
NEBRASKA	2.4	10.9	0.8	5.8	-	-	38.4	9 819	3 155	1 688	6 607	4 719	2 198	2 526	1 176
NEVADA	4.9	5.0	1.7	3.8	-	-	34.1	11 402	2 845	1 020	8 322	7 027	5 468	2 518	1 960
NEW HAMPSHIRE	5.0	3.0	1.4	2.9	-	-	35.8	6 132	1 660	1 254	4 249	2 350	945	1 775	714
NEW JERSEY	2.8	9.4	1.0	1.9	0.4	11.6	24.0	53 864	13 756	1 546	39 392	29 077	12 198	3 267	1 371
NEW MEXICO	5.0	16.5	0.6	3.7	-	-	41.1	14 295	5 228	2 507	8 879	5 202	2 652	2 494	1 272
NEW YORK	3.5	16.2	3.1	2.0	-	-	19.1	165 201	46 273	2 355	93 518	73 667	23 217	3 749	1 181
NORTH CAROLINA	1.8	12.5	1.1	3.3	0.2	-	42.4	47 575	15 471	1 571	31 805	23 769	9 714	2 414	986
NORTH DAKOTA	8.3	3.5	1.8	6.3	-	-	42.9	8 060	1 529	2 114	6 487	5 299	1 763	7 325	2 438
OHIO	3.0	10.8	1.5	2.0	-	-	46.9	60 946	20 483	1 770	39 832	27 517	13 822	2 378	1 195
OKLAHOMA	8.4	2.5	1.8	2.9	0.2	-	43.0	20 800	7 029	1 825	13 640	8 893	3 848	2 309	999
OREGON	3.3	8.9	4.3	4.4	-	-	35.0	22 833	7 987	2 032	14 830	9 161	1 369	2 331	348
PENNSYLVANIA	1.2	5.3	2.3	4.5	-	-	38.0	69 756	21 219	1 661	48 343	33 966	17 106	2 659	1 339
RHODE ISLAND	5.4	4.4	2.1	2.5	0.6	2.1	21.8	6 933	2 331	2 217	4 564	2 940	1 516	2 796	1 442
SOUTH CAROLINA	6.2	6.5	1.3	2.9	-	0	45.2	22 161	6 699	1 403	14 958	8 721	4 477	1 827	938
SOUTH DAKOTA	4.4	2.0	1.4	6.3	-	-	38.5	4 036	1 575	1 864	2 430	1 534	1 228	1 815	1 454
TENNESSEE	6.1	4.5	1.3	5.6	-	-	43.1	27 402	10 820	1 666	16 501	12 367	9 128	1 904	1 405
TEXAS	9.3	7.7	1.1	3.8	-	0	46.9	112 936	36 845	1 393	75 356	51 714	39 278	1 955	1 485
UTAH	3.4	16.0	1.7	2.6	-	-	47.0	14 811	4 299	1 482	10 507	6 325	2 740	2 180	945
VERMONT	3.6	1.4	1.7	5.4	-	-	32.0	5 635	1 870	2 984	3 763	2 879	983	4 594	1 569
VIRGINIA	4.0	11.5	0.9	2.7	-	0	45.9	41 140	9 412	1 139	31 181	19 187	6 193	2 323	750
WASHINGTON	4.7	9.3	3.0	4.3	0.5	-	44.4	35 670	9 737	1 397	25 639	18 667	14 647	2 678	2 101
WEST VIRGINIA	2.0	3.2	1.2	5.5	0	-	40.9	12 391	4 231	2 282	8 066	5 378	2 579	2 900	1 391
WISCONSIN	2.5	4.5	1.3	3.1	-	-	49.7	32 281	8 952	1 559	23 052	16 514	7 088	2 876	1 234
WYOMING	7.6	4.6	0.9	9.5	-	-	26.3	5 929	2 086	3 580	3 610	2 186	826	3 752	1 418

1. Based on resident population estimated as of July 1 of the year shown.

Table A. States — State Government Finances and Voting

STATE	State government finances, 2013 (cont.) General expenditures (mil dol) Direct general expenditures — Total	To local govern-ments	Total	Per capita[1] (dollars)	By selected function — Educa-tion	Health and hospitals	High-ways	Public safety	Public welfare	Natural resources, parks, and recreation	Debt outstanding Total (mil dol)	Per capita[1]	Voting and registration, November 2014 Percent registered	Percent voted	Presidential election,[2] 2012 (percent of vote cast) Demo-cratic	Repub-lican	All other
	339	340	341	342	343	344	345	346	347	348	349	350	351	352	353	354	355
UNITED STATES	X	X	X	X	X	X	X	X	X	X	X	X	59.3	38.5	51.1	47.2	3.6
ALABAMA	24 602	6 476	18 126	3 750	10 617	2 691	1 753	694	6 387	296	9 055	1 873	64.7	40.9	38.4	60.5	1.1
ALASKA	10 707	2 032	8 675	11 801	2 807	429	1 153	502	2 084	361	6 218	8 459	64.6	49.0	40.8	54.8	4.4
ARIZONA	27 751	8 210	19 541	2 949	9 423	2 608	1 972	1 061	8 495	341	13 723	2 071	54.8	35.7	44.6	53.7	1.8
ARKANSAS	17 560	4 938	12 622	4 265	7 518	1 234	1 219	513	5 140	307	3 947	1 334	59.0	36.5	36.9	60.6	2.6
CALIFORNIA	233 454	95 069	138 385	3 610	80 196	17 893	13 193	9 446	80 014	4 626	152 186	3 970	48.6	30.8	60.2	37.1	2.6
COLORADO	23 189	6 291	16 898	3 207	9 479	1 766	1 449	1 148	5 840	404	16 309	3 096	66.2	55.2	51.5	46.1	2.4
CONNECTICUT	23 719	4 909	18 811	5 231	7 019	2 239	1 056	902	7 319	226	32 357	8 998	59.9	43.0	58.1	40.7	1.2
DELAWARE	7 783	1 271	6 512	7 034	2 745	497	595	408	1 971	117	5 755	6 216	62.0	42.0	58.6	40.0	1.4
DISTRICT OF COLUMBIA	X	X	X	X	X	X	X	X	X	X	X	X	65.6	45.8	90.9	7.3	1.8
FLORIDA	71 098	17 810	53 288	2 725	23 904	4 584	5 869	2 660	22 528	1 205	37 892	1 938	56.4	40.4	50.0	49.1	0.9
GEORGIA	38 702	10 361	28 341	2 836	17 338	2 153	2 171	1 807	11 518	651	13 293	1 330	58.9	40.0	45.5	53.3	1.2
HAWAII	10 098	221	9 877	7 035	3 404	1 295	409	235	2 099	209	8 318	5 925	47.4	38.6	70.5	27.8	1.6
IDAHO	7 378	1 982	5 397	3 347	2 659	231	692	306	2 191	256	3 648	2 263	56.8	39.1	32.6	64.5	2.8
ILLINOIS	61 222	15 549	45 673	3 545	17 272	3 586	4 969	1 795	20 425	500	63 660	4 942	58.6	38.3	57.6	40.7	1.7
INDIANA	33 450	9 292	24 158	3 676	14 613	657	2 530	926	10 748	412	22 564	3 434	62.0	33.5	43.9	54.1	1.9
IOWA	17 902	4 754	13 148	4 254	6 469	1 777	1 658	431	5 265	326	6 648	2 151	67.8	51.5	52.0	46.2	1.8
KANSAS	14 516	4 058	10 458	3 614	6 057	1 913	1 182	452	3 387	271	6 825	2 358	63.7	45.3	38.0	59.7	2.3
KENTUCKY	24 458	4 803	19 655	4 472	9 453	1 824	2 366	730	7 084	433	14 984	3 409	69.2	45.9	37.8	60.5	1.7
LOUISIANA	27 800	6 241	21 559	4 661	8 881	2 455	1 716	1 058	7 165	1 160	18 589	4 019	69.5	48.6	40.6	57.8	1.6
MAINE	7 877	1 239	6 638	4 998	2 019	596	615	212	2 892	197	5 375	4 046	75.4	60.5	56.3	41.0	2.7
MARYLAND	34 171	8 641	25 530	4 306	11 398	2 667	1 949	1 947	10 045	609	26 067	4 397	65.9	44.7	62.0	35.9	2.1
MASSACHUSETTS	46 360	9 401	36 959	5 522	13 010	1 642	2 005	1 926	15 560	626	76 161	11 379	61.6	42.8	60.7	37.5	1.8
MICHIGAN	53 550	19 250	34 300	3 466	22 972	4 410	2 419	2 259	14 986	432	30 377	3 070	68.1	45.1	54.2	44.7	1.1
MINNESOTA	35 059	12 976	22 083	4 074	15 026	697	2 464	898	11 324	857	13 573	2 504	68.8	49.9	52.7	45.0	2.4
MISSISSIPPI	17 387	5 053	12 334	4 123	5 456	1 535	1 377	489	5 817	381	7 113	2 378	74.6	41.6	43.8	55.3	0.9
MISSOURI	26 039	5 772	20 267	3 353	8 952	3 269	1 595	951	7 988	381	19 308	3 194	70.9	38.0	44.4	53.8	1.9
MONTANA	6 061	1 373	4 688	4 618	1 857	225	683	242	1 421	340	3 558	3 505	64.3	49.7	41.7	55.4	2.9
NEBRASKA	9 184	2 171	7 014	3 754	3 367	738	754	333	2 517	296	1 847	988	62.4	41.4	38.0	59.8	2.2
NEVADA	10 639	4 215	6 425	2 303	4 365	541	722	386	2 400	135	3 610	1 294	51.1	32.6	52.4	45.7	2.0
NEW HAMPSHIRE	6 207	1 301	4 907	3 707	2 068	190	558	169	1 682	100	8 763	6 622	66.3	48.6	52.0	46.4	1.6
NEW JERSEY	50 052	11 102	38 950	4 377	16 426	3 366	3 192	2 255	14 701	772	64 264	7 221	57.5	31.5	58.3	40.6	1.0
NEW MEXICO	15 015	4 501	10 515	5 042	5 406	1 445	756	535	3 946	234	7 233	3 469	59.9	42.1	53.0	42.8	4.2
NEW YORK	147 156	56 237	90 920	4 627	41 152	13 966	4 239	4 434	58 010	974	136 014	6 921	52.9	30.6	63.4	35.2	1.3
NORTH CAROLINA	46 103	13 173	32 930	3 344	19 251	3 389	3 688	1 913	12 977	683	19 055	1 935	64.5	42.8	48.3	50.4	1.3
NORTH DAKOTA	5 786	1 632	4 154	5 743	1 931	215	1 052	132	943	369	1 834	2 536	64.1	49.2	38.7	58.3	3.0
OHIO	59 502	16 517	42 984	3 715	21 607	5 619	3 678	1 862	19 187	474	33 133	2 863	64.5	38.5	50.7	47.7	1.6
OKLAHOMA	19 579	4 213	15 366	3 991	7 322	1 120	1 803	803	6 258	313	9 514	2 471	57.7	32.3	33.2	66.8	0
OREGON	21 465	5 495	15 970	4 064	7 172	2 341	1 313	914	6 575	531	13 598	3 460	65.2	51.8	54.2	42.1	3.6
PENNSYLVANIA	72 244	18 834	53 410	4 181	22 629	6 870	7 601	3 031	23 079	970	47 021	3 681	61.7	38.3	52.1	46.7	1.2
RHODE ISLAND	6 563	1 170	5 392	5 128	1 987	225	319	255	2 395	88	9 568	9 100	59.4	40.4	62.7	35.3	2.1
SOUTH CAROLINA	22 331	5 454	16 877	3 535	8 352	2 456	924	674	6 051	283	14 724	3 084	67.0	41.3	44.1	54.6	1.4
SOUTH DAKOTA	4 011	740	3 271	3 872	1 266	200	653	155	972	224	3 425	4 054	64.2	43.7	39.9	57.9	2.2
TENNESSEE	27 831	7 075	20 757	3 195	9 811	1 078	1 752	1 123	10 960	377	6 192	953	62.1	35.4	39.1	59.5	1.4
TEXAS	108 025	27 590	80 435	3 041	47 479	8 012	7 536	4 502	30 781	1 208	39 625	1 498	51.4	30.2	41.4	57.2	1.4
UTAH	14 956	3 069	11 887	4 098	6 875	1 572	962	454	3 018	210	7 050	2 430	54.3	34.7	24.7	72.8	2.5
VERMONT	5 608	1 502	4 106	6 553	2 407	236	455	226	1 629	96	3 330	5 315	65.7	41.6	66.6	31.0	2.5
VIRGINIA	42 530	11 256	31 274	3 786	15 214	4 942	3 913	2 266	9 855	367	28 023	3 392	63.1	39.4	51.2	47.3	1.6
WASHINGTON	37 865	9 778	28 087	4 029	15 582	4 346	3 184	1 312	8 389	986	30 474	4 371	61.5	44.8	56.2	41.3	2.5
WEST VIRGINIA	11 709	2 470	9 239	4 983	4 334	472	1 103	376	3 527	277	7 356	3 967	61.8	33.4	35.5	62.3	2.2
WISCONSIN	31 878	9 637	22 241	3 873	10 878	2 193	2 409	1 214	8 849	693	23 188	4 038	69.0	53.8	52.8	45.9	1.3
WYOMING	5 037	1 681	3 356	5 759	1 724	279	548	194	783	423	1 021	1 752	54.7	39.1	27.8	68.6	3.5

1. Based on resident population estimated as of July 1 of the year shown. 2. © 2013 Election Data Services, Inc. All rights reserved.

States and Counties

(For explanation of symbols, see page viii)

Page

53	County Highlights and Rankings
69	State and County Column Headings
73	Table B
73	**AL**(Autauga)—**AL**(Walker)
87	**AL**(Washington)—**AR**(Cleburne)
101	**AR**(Cleveland)—**AR**(Yell)
115	**CA**(Alameda)—**CO**(Bent)
129	**CO**(Boulder)—**CT**(New London)
143	**CT**(Tolland)—**FL**(Polk)
157	**FL**(Putnam)—**GA**(Echols)
171	**GA**(Effingham)—**GA**(Pulaski)
185	**GA**(Putnam)—**ID**(Canyon)
199	**ID**(Caribou)—**IL**(Hancock)
213	**IL**(Hardin)—**IL**(Williamson)
227	**IL**(Winnebago)—**IN**(Perry)
241	**IN**(Pike)—**IA**(Floyd)
255	**IA**(Franklin)—**IA**(Wright)
269	**KS**(Allen)—**KS**(Nemaha)
283	**KS**(Neosho)—**KY**(Clark)
297	**KY**(Clay)—**KY**(Nicholas)
311	**KY**(Ohio)—**LA**(Natchitoches)
325	**LA**(Orleans)—**MD**(Queen Anne's)
339	**MD**(St. Mary's)—**MI**(Kent)
353	**MI**(Keweenaw)—**MN**(Faribault)
367	**MN**(Fillmore)—**MN**(Yellow Medicine)
381	**MS**(Adams)—**MS**(Stone)
395	**MS**(Sunflower)—**MO**(Jackson)
409	**MO**(Jasper)—**MO**(Wright)
423	**MO**(St. Louis city)—**NE**(Banner)
437	**NE**(Blaine)—**NE**(Pierce)
451	**NE**(Platte)—**NJ**(Hunterdon)
465	**NJ**(Mercer)—**NY**(Fulton)
479	**NY**(Genesee)—**NC**(Cherokee)
493	**NC**(Chowan)—**NC**(Surry)
507	**NC**(Swain)—**ND**(Walsh)
521	**ND**(Ward)—**OH**(Noble)
535	**OH**(Ottawa)—**OK**(Kingfisher)
549	**OK**(Kiowa)—**OR**(Marion)
563	**OR**(Morrow)—**PA**(Pike)
577	**PA**(Potter)—**SC**(Spartanburg)
591	**SC**(Sumter)—**SD**(Todd)
605	**SD**(Tripp)—**TN**(Marion)
619	**TN**(Marshall)—**TX**(Burnet)
633	**TX**(Caldwell)—**TX**(Grimes)
647	**TX**(Guadalupe)—**TX**(Martin)
661	**TX**(Mason)—**TX**(Titus)
675	**TX**(Tom Green)—**VT**(Caledonia)
689	**VT**(Chittenden)—**VA**(Loudoun)
703	**VA**(Louisa)—**VA**(Manassas city)
717	**VA**(Manassas Park city)—**WV**(Braxton)
731	**WV**(Brooke)—**WI**(Dane)
745	**WI**(Dodge)—**WY**(Converse)
759	**WY**(Crook)—**WY**(Weston)

Part B—States and Counties

County Highlights and Rankings

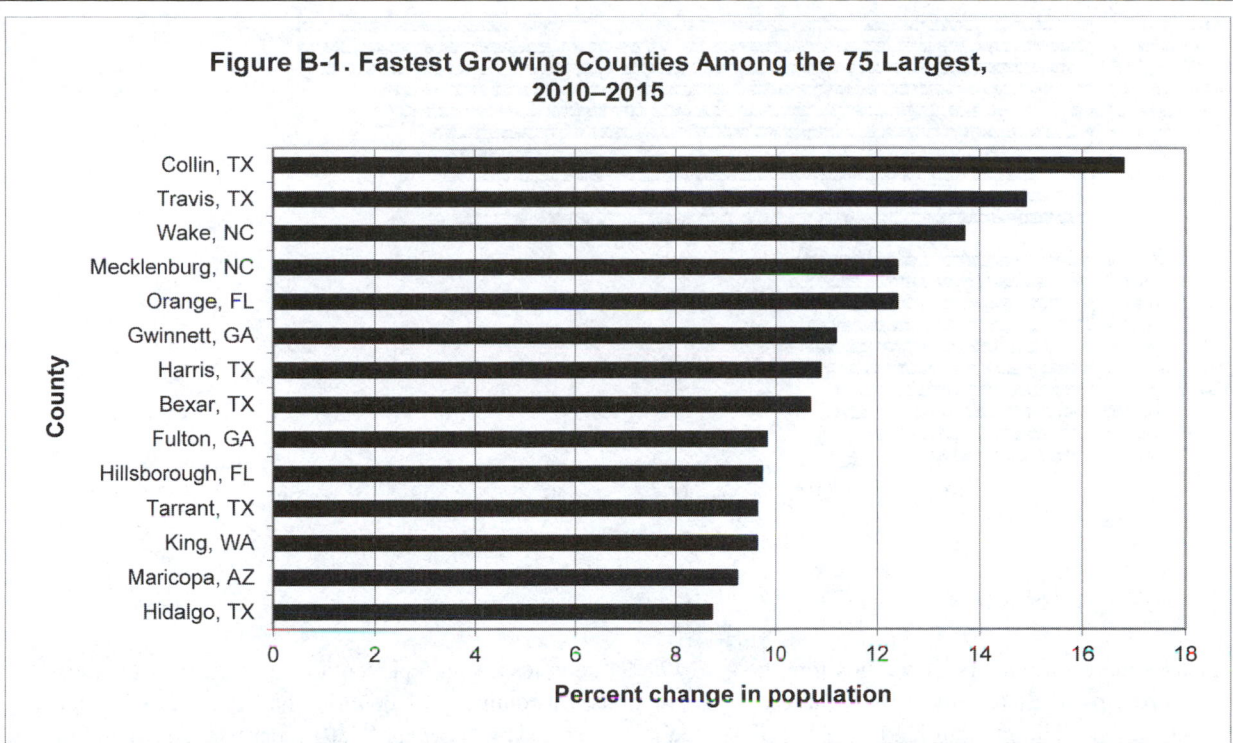

Figure B-1. Fastest Growing Counties Among the 75 Largest, 2010–2015

Five years after the 2010 census, the 2015 population estimates show that Los Angeles County, CA, remains, by far, the most populous county, with nearly 10.2 million residents. Next is Cook County, IL, which includes Chicago, with over 5.2 million people. Its population declined 3.4 percent from 2000 to 2010 but increased 0.8 percent from 2010 to 2015. New York City consists of five counties (the five boroughs), with Kings (Brooklyn) and Queens each with over 2 million residents. Queens county moved out of the top 10 in 2014 but Brooklyn's 5.3 percent growth keeps Kings the 8th most populous county in the nation.

Among the 75 most populous counties, the highest growth rates from 2010 to 2015 were found in the South. From 2010 to 2015, the fastest-growing of these large counties was Collin, TX, in the Dallas metropolitan area. During the past five years, Collin County's population increased by 16.8 percent followed by Travis County, TX (Austin) at 14.9 percent. In 2015, Collin County ranked 57th among the most populous counties. Two other counties in Texas also had growth rates over 10 percent—Harris County (Houston) and Bexar County (San Antonio) (Other large counties that experienced more than 10 percent growth in the five-year period were in North Carolina, Florida, and Georgia. More than 1,600 counties lost population during this period. The largest proportional losses were in counties with very small populations. Among the largest counties, only New Haven County, CT, Cuyahoga County, OH (Cleveland), and Wayne County, MI (Detroit), declined in

population between 2010 and 2015. One-hundred and forty-three counties had population growth rates at or above 10 percent from 2010 to 2015. Ninety-four of these fast-growing counties had more than 50,000 residents and 76 counties had more than 100,000 residents.

Within states, the number and physical size of counties varied considerably: Delaware had three counties while Texas had 254 counties. For the 3,143 counties (and county equivalents—see Appendix A) in the United States, population in 2015 ranged from 10.2 million in Los Angeles, CA, to 89 in Kalawao County, HI. Other particularly large counties in terms of population are Cook County, IL (over 5.2 million people), encompassing Chicago and its suburbs, Harris County, TX (containing Houston) with 45 million people, and Maricopa County, AZ (containing Phoenix), with nearly 4.2 million people. There were 45 counties with a population of 1,000,000 or more; these counties combined contain more than one-fourth of the U.S. population. Over half of the U.S. population lived in the 150 largest counties, those with a population of 450,000 or more. At the other extreme, there were 35 counties with fewer than 1,000 people in 2015. The median county population size was 25,699.

In terms of land area, counties range from the nearly 377,000 square kilometers of Yukon-Koyukuk Census Area, AK; to Kalawao County, HI, with 31 square kilometers; New York County, NY (Manhattan), with 59 square kilometers; Bristol County, RI, with 63 square kilometers; and Arlington

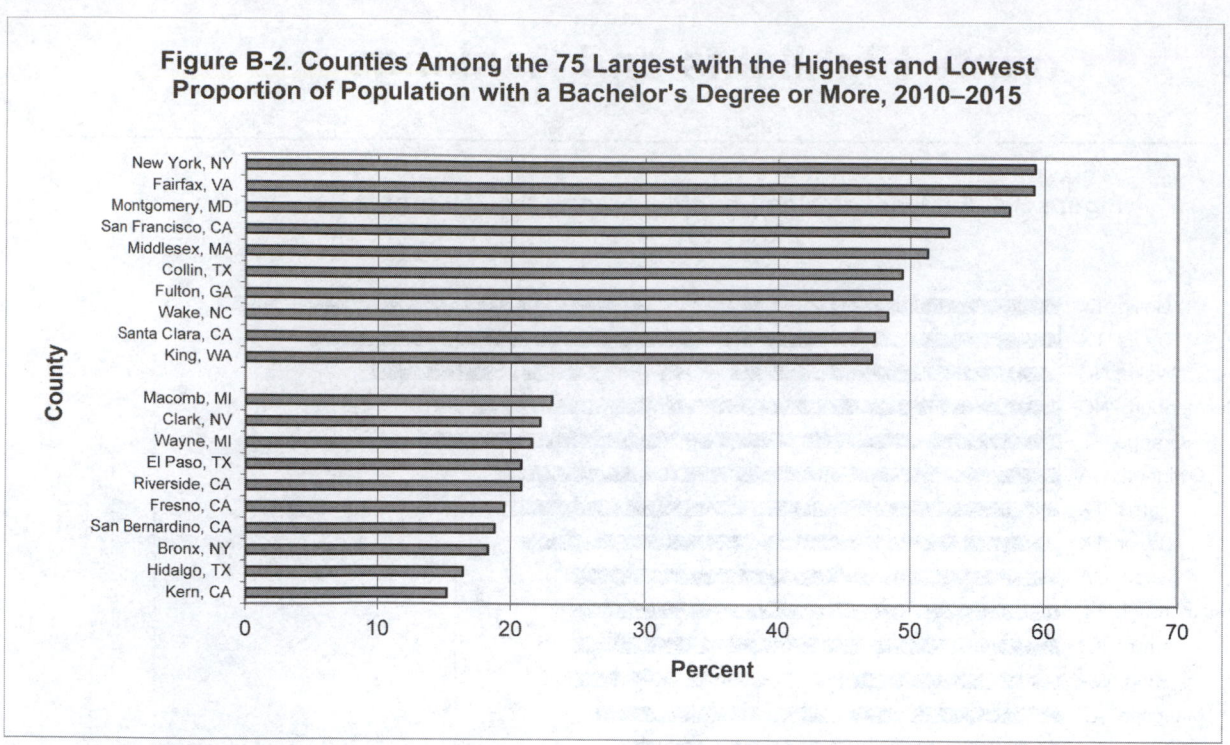

Figure B-2. Counties Among the 75 Largest with the Highest and Lowest Proportion of Population with a Bachelor's Degree or More, 2010–2015

County, VA, with 67 square kilometers.[1] Counties tend to be larger in the western United States (most of the largest 50 in size are in that region). The median land area for all U.S. counties was about 1,600 square kilometers in 2010.

While New York County, NY, had one of the smallest land areas, it had by far the highest population density among U.S. counties in 2015, with nearly 28,000 persons per square kilometer. No other county approached that density (although three other New York City boroughs were among the top five counties in population density). San Francisco had the highest population density outside of New York City, with Suffolk County, MA (Boston); Philadelphia County, PA; and Washington, DC, also among the top 10 counties. The median county only had about 17 persons per square kilometer, with only 117 counties having more than 500 persons per square kilometer. The nation's largest county in terms of population (Los Angeles) had a population density of 967.7 persons per square kilometer. This density ranked 21st among the 75 most populous U.S. counties.

Proportionally large year-to-year labor force changes are not unusual for counties with small populations. The 2015 annual averages reflect a national labor force that increased by 0.6 percent. Among the 75 most populous counties, 9 counties' labor forces grew by 2.0 percent or more between 2014 and 2015. Wake County, NC, and San Francisco, CA, experienced the largest increase among the 75 most populous counties, both over 3 percent. Mecklenburg, NC followed with an increase of 2.8 percent. Nearly 1,400 counties experienced declines in their labor forces from 2014 to 2015,

with 94 counties losing 5 percent or more. Among the most populous 75 counties, 14 counties had decreases in their labor forces, led by Wayne, MI at 1.5 percent, and including the two most populous counties—Los Angeles and Cook (Chicago)—with labor force declines of .3 and .1 percent respectively.

The national annual average unemployment rate was 5.3 percent in 2015—the lowest it has been since 2007. The unemployment rate was down from 6.2 in 2014 and 7.4 in 2013. Over 1,500 counties had unemployment rates above the national average of 5.3 percent in 2015 and 82 counties had unemployment rates greater than 10 percent, down from 1,100 counties in 2010 and 169 counties in 2014. Of the 10 counties with the highest unemployment rates, only Imperial County, CA, and Yuma County, AZ, had populations over 100,000. Among the 75 most populous counties, 28 exceeded the national unemployment rate of 5.3 percent, with the highest in two California counties—10.2 percent in Fresno and Kern counties. Hennepin, MN; Salt Lake, UT; and Travis TX had the lowest unemployment rate at 3.3 percent each. Among smaller counties in 2015, six counties in North Dakota and three in Nebraska had unemployment rates of less than 2 percent.

Among the 75 largest counties, the two counties with the highest unemployment rates, Fresno and Kern counties in CA, ranked among the top counties for agricultural sales. Meanwhile, Wayne County, MI which ranked second highest in manufacturing employment had the fifth highest unemployment rate among the 75 most populous counties. Three

---

[1]Several independent cities in Virginia, which are treated as counties for tabulation purposes, were excluded here.

of the ten lowest unemployment rates were in the three counties that topped the rankings for employment in professional, scientific, and technical occupations (Fairfax County, VA, Montgomery County, MD, and San Francisco County, CA,) These three counties were also at the top of the rankings for median household income and educational attainment, with more than 50 percent of residents holding bachelor's, master's, doctoral or professional degrees. Five large counties had college-educated proportions of less than 20 percent and four out of the five were among the 10 counties with the highest unemployment rates. Nationally, 30.1 percent of the population held bachelor's degrees or higher in 2014.

75 Largest Counties by 2015 Population
Selected Rankings

Population, 2015			Land area, 2010				Population density, 2015			
Population rank		Population [col 2]	Population rank	Land area rank	County	Land area (Square kilometers) [col 1]	Population rank	Density rank	County	Density (per square kilometer) [col 4]
1	Los Angeles, CA	10 116 705	12	1	San Bernardino, CA	51 947	20	1	New York, NY	27 733.4
2	Cook, IL	5 238 216	4	2	Maricopa, AZ	23 828	8	2	Kings, NY	14 408.4
3	Harris, TX	4 538 028	44	3	Pima, AZ	23 794	26	3	Bronx, NY	13 352.7
4	Maricopa, AZ	4 167 947	62	4	Kern, CA	21 062	11	4	Queens, NY	8 324.4
5	San Diego, CA	3 299 521	14	5	Clark, NV	20 439	64	5	San Francisco, CA	7 147.2
6	Orange, CA	3 169 776	10	6	Riverside, CA	18 665	23	6	Philadelphia, PA	4 517.1
7	Miami-Dade, FL	2 693 117	48	7	Fresno, CA	15 431	75	7	Essex, NJ	2 438.6
8	Kings, NY	2 636 735	5	8	San Diego, CA	10 895	2	8	Cook, IL	2 139.8
9	Dallas, TX	2 553 385	1	9	Los Angeles, CA	10 510	28	9	Nassau, NY	1 847.2
10	Riverside, CA	2 361 026	13	10	King, WA	5 479	53	10	Bergen, NJ	1 556.4
11	Queens, NY	2 339 150	27	11	Palm Beach, FL	5 102	6	11	Orange, CA	1 547.7
12	San Bernardino, CA	2 128 133	7	12	Miami-Dade, FL	4 915	49	12	Milwaukee, WI	1 532.4
13	King, WA	2 117 125	66	13	Ventura, CA	4 774	50	13	Pinellas, FL	1 339.7
14	Clark, NV	2 114 801	3	14	Harris, TX	4 412	9	14	Dallas, TX	1 131.3
15	Tarrant, TX	1 982 498	67	15	Pierce, WA	4 324	37	15	Fairfax, VA	1 127.6
16	Santa Clara, CA	1 918 044	68	16	Hidalgo, TX	4 069	19	16	Wayne, MI	1 110.0
17	Bexar, TX	1 897 753	73	17	Worcester, MA	3 913	55	17	DuPage, IL	1 101.1
18	Broward, FL	1 896 425	16	18	Santa Clara, CA	3 341	31	18	Cuyahoga, OH	1 060.7
19	Wayne, MI	1 759 335	17	19	Bexar, TX	3 211	69	19	Middlesex, NJ	1 051.1
20	New York, NY	1 644 518	18	20	Broward, FL	3 133	3	20	Harris, TX	1 028.6
21	Alameda, CA	1 638 215	56	21	Erie, NY	2 701	1	21	Los Angeles, CA	967.7
22	Middlesex, MA	1 585 139	29	22	Hillsborough, FL	2 642	52	22	Marion, IN	915.2
23	Philadelphia, PA	1 567 442	70	23	El Paso, TX	2 623	32	23	Franklin, OH	908.4
24	Suffolk, NY	1 501 587	36	24	Travis, TX	2 565	15	24	Tarrant, TX	886.2
25	Sacramento, CA	1 501 335	25	25	Sacramento, CA	2 498	47	25	Westchester, NY	875.7
26	Bronx, NY	1 455 444	2	26	Cook, IL	2 448	21	26	Alameda, CA	855.9
27	Palm Beach, FL	1 422 789	24	27	Suffolk, NY	2 362	35	27	Hennepin, MN	853.0
28	Nassau, NY	1 361 500	30	28	Orange, FL	2 340	40	28	Montgomery, MD	817.7
29	Hillsborough, FL	1 349 050	9	29	Dallas, TX	2 257	61	29	Gwinnett, GA	803.4
30	Orange, FL	1 288 126	33	30	Oakland, MI	2 247	74	30	Hamilton, OH	768.4
31	Cuyahoga, OH	1 255 921	15	31	Tarrant, TX	2 237	45	31	St. Louis, MO	763.0
32	Franklin, OH	1 251 722	57	32	Collin, TX	2 179	41	32	Mecklenburg, NC	762.0
33	Oakland, MI	1 242 304	42	33	Wake, NC	2 163	22	33	Middlesex, MA	748.4
34	Allegheny, PA	1 230 459	22	34	Middlesex, MA	2 118	43	34	Fulton, GA	740.9
35	Hennepin, MN	1 223 149	6	35	Orange, CA	2 048	59	35	Prince George's, MD	727.6
36	Travis, TX	1 176 558	54	36	Shelby, TN	1 977	63	36	Macomb, MI	696.9
37	Fairfax, VA	1 142 234	58	37	Duval, FL	1 974	72	37	Montgomery, PA	654.9
38	Contra Costa, CA	1 126 745	39	38	Salt Lake, UT	1 923	34	38	Allegheny, PA	650.7
39	Salt Lake, UT	1 107 314	21	39	Alameda, CA	1 914	46	39	Honolulu, HI	641.8
40	Montgomery, MD	1 040 116	60	40	Hartford, CT	1 904	24	40	Suffolk, NY	635.7
41	Mecklenburg, NC	1 034 070	34	41	Allegheny, PA	1 891	38	41	Contra Costa, CA	607.7
42	Wake, NC	1 024 198	38	42	Contra Costa, CA	1 854	18	42	Broward, FL	605.3
43	Fulton, GA	1 010 562	51	43	Fairfield, CT	1 618	25	43	Sacramento, CA	601.0
44	Pima, AZ	1 010 025	19	44	Wayne, MI	1 585	17	44	Bexar, TX	591.0
45	St. Louis, MO	1 003 362	65	45	New Haven, CT	1 566	51	45	Fairfield, CT	585.9
46	Honolulu, HI	998 714	46	46	Honolulu, HI	1 556	39	46	Salt Lake, UT	575.8
47	Westchester, NY	976 396	71	47	Baltimore, MD	1 550	16	47	Santa Clara, CA	574.1
48	Fresno, CA	974 861	35	48	Hennepin, MN	1 434	33	48	Oakland, MI	552.9
49	Milwaukee, WI	957 735	32	49	Franklin, OH	1 378	30	49	Orange, FL	550.5
50	Pinellas, FL	949 827	43	50	Fulton, GA	1 364	65	50	New Haven, CT	548.8
51	Fairfield, CT	948 053	41	51	Mecklenburg, NC	1 357	7	51	Miami-Dade, FL	547.9
52	Marion, IN	939 020	45	52	St. Louis, MO	1 315	71	52	Baltimore, MD	536.2
53	Bergen, NJ	938 506	40	53	Montgomery, MD	1 272	29	53	Hillsborough, FL	510.6
54	Shelby, TN	938 069	72	54	Montgomery, PA	1 251	54	54	Shelby, TN	474.5
55	DuPage, IL	933 736	59	55	Prince George's, MD	1 250	42	55	Wake, NC	473.5
56	Erie, NY	922 578	63	56	Macomb, MI	1 241	60	56	Hartford, CT	470.5
57	Collin, TX	914 127	31	57	Cuyahoga, OH	1 184	58	57	Duval, FL	462.5
58	Duval, FL	913 010	47	58	Westchester, NY	1 115	36	58	Travis, TX	458.7
59	Prince George's, MD	909 535	61	59	Gwinnett, GA	1 115	57	59	Collin, TX	419.5
60	Hartford, CT	895 841	74	60	Hamilton, OH	1 051	13	60	King, WA	386.4
61	Gwinnett, GA	895 823	52	61	Marion, IN	1 026	56	61	Erie, NY	341.6
62	Kern, CA	882 176	37	62	Fairfax, VA	1 013	70	62	El Paso, TX	318.6
63	Macomb, MI	864 840	55	63	DuPage, IL	848	5	63	San Diego, CA	302.8
64	San Francisco, CA	864 816	69	64	Middlesex, NJ	800	27	64	Palm Beach, FL	278.9
65	New Haven, CT	859 470	28	65	Nassau, NY	737	73	65	Worcester, MA	209.3
66	Ventura, CA	850 536	50	66	Pinellas, FL	709	68	66	Hidalgo, TX	207.0
67	Pierce, WA	843 954	49	67	Milwaukee, WI	625	67	67	Pierce, WA	195.2
68	Hidalgo, TX	842 304	53	68	Bergen, NJ	603	66	68	Ventura, CA	178.2
69	Middlesex, NJ	840 900	23	69	Philadelphia, PA	347	4	69	Maricopa, AZ	174.9
70	El Paso, TX	835 593	75	70	Essex, NJ	327	10	70	Riverside, CA	126.5
71	Baltimore, MD	831 128	11	71	Queens, NY	281	14	71	Clark, NV	103.5
72	Montgomery, PA	819 264	8	72	Kings, NY	183	48	72	Fresno, CA	63.2
73	Worcester, MA	818 963	64	73	San Francisco, CA	121	44	73	Pima, AZ	42.4
74	Hamilton, OH	807 598	26	74	Bronx, NY	109	62	74	Kern, CA	41.9
75	Essex, NJ	797 434	20	75	New York, NY	59	12	75	San Bernardino, CA	41.0

75 Largest Counties by 2015 Population
Selected Rankings

	Percent population change, 2010-2015				Employment/residence ratio, 2010-2014				Percent White, not Hispanic or Latino, alone or in combination, 2014		
Population rank	Percent change rank	County	Percent change [col 23]	Population rank	Number of employees per resident rank	County	Number of employees per resident [col 34]	Population rank	White rank	County	Percent white [col 5]
57	1	Collin, TX	16.8	20	1	New York, NY	2.79	63	1	Macomb, MI	82.5
36	2	Travis, TX	14.9	43	2	Fulton, GA	1.81	34	2	Allegheny, PA	81.1
42	3	Wake, NC	13.7	64	3	San Francisco, CA	1.39	73	3	Worcester, MA	80.2
30	4	Orange, FL	12.4	35	4	Hennepin, MN	1.36	72	4	Montgomery, PA	78.7
41	4	Mecklenburg, NC	12.4	74	5	Hamilton, OH	1.33	56	5	Erie, NY	77.8
61	6	Gwinnett, GA	11.2	52	6	Marion, IN	1.30	50	6	Pinellas, FL	76.9
3	7	Harris, TX	10.9	9	7	Dallas, TX	1.28	22	7	Middlesex, MA	76.2
17	8	Bexar, TX	10.7	41	7	Mecklenburg, NC	1.28	33	8	Oakland, MI	74.9
43	9	Fulton, GA	9.8	30	9	Orange, FL	1.26	39	9	Salt Lake, UT	74.4
29	10	Hillsborough, FL	9.7	31	10	Cuyahoga, OH	1.24	67	10	Pierce, WA	73.6
13	11	King, WA	9.6	55	11	DuPage, IL	1.20	35	11	Hennepin, MN	72.7
15	11	Tarrant, TX	9.6	32	12	Franklin, OH	1.19	24	12	Suffolk, NY	70.4
4	13	Maricopa, AZ	9.2	36	12	Travis, TX	1.19	55	13	DuPage, IL	69.4
68	14	Hidalgo, TX	8.7	45	12	St. Louis, MO	1.19	45	14	St. Louis, MO	69.2
18	15	Broward, FL	8.5	58	12	Duval, FL	1.19	74	15	Hamilton, OH	68.6
21	15	Alameda, CA	8.5	23	16	Philadelphia, PA	1.18	32	16	Franklin, OH	68.0
14	17	Clark, NV	8.4	54	16	Shelby, TN	1.18	65	17	New Haven, CT	66.4
7	18	Miami-Dade, FL	7.8	60	18	Hartford, CT	1.17	13	18	King, WA	66.1
9	18	Dallas, TX	7.8	13	19	King, WA	1.16	51	19	Fairfield, CT	64.9
10	18	Riverside, CA	7.8	3	20	Harris, TX	1.15	60	19	Hartford, CT	64.9
27	18	Palm Beach, FL	7.8	34	20	Allegheny, PA	1.15	28	21	Nassau, NY	63.3
16	22	Santa Clara, CA	7.7	39	20	Salt Lake, UT	1.15	42	22	Wake, NC	62.7
32	23	Franklin, OH	7.6	72	20	Montgomery, PA	1.15	57	23	Collin, TX	62.3
39	24	Salt Lake, UT	7.5	16	24	Santa Clara, CA	1.13	31	24	Cuyahoga, OH	61.7
38	25	Contra Costa, CA	7.4	33	24	Oakland, MI	1.13	71	25	Baltimore, MD	61.3
64	25	San Francisco, CA	7.4	29	26	Hillsborough, FL	1.10	52	26	Marion, IN	60.0
40	27	Montgomery, MD	7.0	19	27	Wayne, MI	1.09	53	27	Bergen, NJ	59.7
5	28	San Diego, CA	6.6	22	27	Middlesex, MA	1.09	4	28	Maricopa, AZ	58.8
35	29	Hennepin, MN	6.1	49	29	Milwaukee, WI	1.08	27	29	Palm Beach, FL	58.3
67	29	Pierce, WA	6.1	2	30	Cook, IL	1.07	58	30	Duval, FL	56.9
25	31	Sacramento, CA	5.8	56	30	Erie, NY	1.07	47	31	Westchester, NY	56.3
37	32	Fairfax, VA	5.6	7	32	Miami-Dade, FL	1.06	44	32	Pima, AZ	55.0
58	32	Duval, FL	5.6	17	32	Bexar, TX	1.06	37	33	Fairfax, VA	54.8
22	34	Middlesex, MA	5.5	75	32	Essex, NJ	1.06	49	33	Milwaukee, WI	54.8
6	35	Orange, CA	5.3	6	35	Orange, CA	1.05	29	35	Hillsborough, FL	53.2
8	35	Kings, NY	5.3	42	35	Wake, NC	1.05	19	36	Wayne, MI	51.8
59	35	Prince George's, MD	5.3	51	37	Fairfield, CT	1.04	36	37	Travis, TX	51.3
26	38	Bronx, NY	5.1	1	38	Los Angeles, CA	1.03	15	38	Tarrant, TX	50.9
62	38	Kern, CA	5.1	27	38	Palm Beach, FL	1.03	41	39	Mecklenburg, NC	50.3
11	40	Queens, NY	4.9	50	38	Pinellas, FL	1.03	25	40	Sacramento, CA	50.2
46	41	Honolulu, HI	4.8	4	41	Maricopa, AZ	1.02	5	41	San Diego, CA	49.4
48	41	Fresno, CA	4.8	5	41	San Diego, CA	1.02	38	42	Contra Costa, CA	49.0
12	43	San Bernardino, CA	4.6	25	41	Sacramento, CA	1.02	20	43	New York, NY	48.7
70	44	El Paso, TX	4.4	37	41	Fairfax, VA	1.02	66	43	Ventura, CA	48.7
52	45	Marion, IN	3.9	14	45	Clark, NV	1.01	40	45	Montgomery, MD	48.2
69	46	Middlesex, NJ	3.8	62	45	Kern, CA	1.01	14	46	Clark, NV	48.1
20	47	New York, NY	3.7	44	47	Pima, AZ	1.00	69	47	Middlesex, NJ	46.4
53	47	Bergen, NJ	3.7	46	47	Honolulu, HI	1.00	30	48	Orange, FL	44.6
1	49	Los Angeles, CA	3.6	48	47	Fresno, CA	1.00	6	49	Orange, CA	44.2
50	49	Pinellas, FL	3.6	21	50	Alameda, CA	0.99	2	50	Cook, IL	44.1
51	51	Fairfield, CT	3.4	70	50	El Paso, TX	0.99	64	51	San Francisco, CA	44.0
33	52	Oakland, MI	3.3	15	52	Tarrant, TX	0.98	61	52	Gwinnett, GA	42.3
66	52	Ventura, CA	3.3	53	53	Bergen, NJ	0.96	43	53	Fulton, GA	41.8
71	52	Baltimore, MD	3.3	68	53	Hidalgo, TX	0.96	18	54	Broward, FL	40.9
44	55	Pima, AZ	3.0	47	55	Westchester, NY	0.95	10	55	Riverside, CA	39.3
47	56	Westchester, NY	2.9	69	55	Middlesex, NJ	0.95	54	56	Shelby, TN	38.3
63	57	Macomb, MI	2.8	65	57	New Haven, CT	0.94	62	57	Kern, CA	37.8
23	58	Philadelphia, PA	2.7	40	58	Montgomery, MD	0.93	23	58	Philadelphia, PA	37.2
73	59	Worcester, MA	2.6	18	59	Broward, FL	0.92	8	59	Kings, NY	37.0
72	60	Montgomery, PA	2.4	12	60	San Bernardino, CA	0.91	21	60	Alameda, CA	36.1
55	61	DuPage, IL	1.8	57	61	Collin, TX	0.89	16	61	Santa Clara, CA	35.9
75	62	Essex, NJ	1.7	66	61	Ventura, CA	0.89	75	62	Essex, NJ	33.3
28	63	Nassau, NY	1.6	24	63	Suffolk, NY	0.88	46	63	Honolulu, HI	32.7
49	64	Milwaukee, WI	1.1	28	63	Nassau, NY	0.88	3	64	Harris, TX	32.5
54	64	Shelby, TN	1.1	61	63	Gwinnett, GA	0.88	48	64	Fresno, CA	32.5
2	66	Cook, IL	0.8	67	63	Pierce, WA	0.88	12	66	San Bernardino, CA	32.4
74	67	Hamilton, OH	0.7	71	67	Baltimore, MD	0.87	9	67	Dallas, TX	32.1
24	68	Suffolk, NY	0.6	73	67	Worcester, MA	0.87	17	68	Bexar, TX	30.3
34	68	Allegheny, PA	0.6	63	69	Macomb, MI	0.84	1	69	Los Angeles, CA	28.5
45	70	St. Louis, MO	0.4	10	70	Riverside, CA	0.80	11	70	Queens, NY	27.3
56	70	Erie, NY	0.4	38	71	Contra Costa, CA	0.76	59	71	Prince George's, MD	15.6
60	72	Hartford, CT	0.2	8	72	Kings, NY	0.74	7	72	Miami-Dade, FL	15.3
65	73	New Haven, CT	-0.3	59	73	Prince George's, MD	0.73	70	73	El Paso, TX	14.0
31	74	Cuyahoga, OH	-1.9	26	74	Bronx, NY	0.70	26	74	Bronx, NY	10.9
19	75	Wayne, MI	-3.4	11	75	Queens, NY	0.66	68	75	Hidalgo, TX	7.3

75 Largest Counties by 2015 Population
Selected Rankings

Percent Black, not Hispanic or Latino, alone or in combination, 2014				Percent American Indian, Alaska Native, not Hispanic or Latino, alone or in combination, 2014				Percent Asian or Pacific Islander, not Hispanic or Latino, alone or in combination, 2014			
Population rank	Black rank	County	Percent black [col 6]	Population rank	American Indian Alaska native rank	County	Percent American Indian, Alaska native [col 7]	Population rank	Asian or Pacific Islander rank	County	Percent Asian or Pacific Islander [col 8]
59	1	Prince George's, MD	63.8	44	1	Pima, AZ	3.1	46	1	Honolulu, HI	76.8
54	2	Shelby, TN	53.6	67	2	Pierce, WA	2.6	64	2	San Francisco, CA	37.3
43	3	Fulton, GA	44.4	4	3	Maricopa, AZ	2.2	16	3	Santa Clara, CA	37.0
23	4	Philadelphia, PA	42.6	13	4	King, WA	1.7	21	4	Alameda, CA	32.2
19	5	Wayne, MI	40.0	25	5	Sacramento, CA	1.5	11	5	Queens, NY	26.9
75	6	Essex, NJ	39.8	35	5	Hennepin, MN	1.5	69	6	Middlesex, NJ	24.6
41	7	Mecklenburg, NC	32.2	46	5	Honolulu, HI	1.5	6	7	Orange, CA	21.4
8	8	Kings, NY	31.9	62	8	Kern, CA	1.3	37	8	Fairfax, VA	21.1
31	9	Cuyahoga, OH	30.7	48	9	Fresno, CA	1.2	13	9	King, WA	19.7
26	10	Bronx, NY	30.4	49	9	Milwaukee, WI	1.2	38	10	Contra Costa, CA	19.1
58	11	Duval, FL	30.3	39	11	Salt Lake, UT	1.1	25	11	Sacramento, CA	19.0
52	12	Marion, IN	28.8	5	12	San Diego, CA	1.0	53	12	Bergen, NJ	17.1
71	13	Baltimore, MD	28.4	10	12	Riverside, CA	1.0	40	13	Montgomery, MD	16.5
18	14	Broward, FL	28.3	12	12	San Bernardino, CA	1.0	1	14	Los Angeles, CA	15.8
49	15	Milwaukee, WI	27.6	14	12	Clark, NV	1.0	5	15	San Diego, CA	14.1
74	16	Hamilton, OH	27.2	19	12	Wayne, MI	1.0	57	16	Collin, TX	14.0
61	17	Gwinnett, GA	26.6	38	12	Contra Costa, CA	1.0	20	17	New York, NY	13.3
45	18	St. Louis, MO	24.7	15	18	Tarrant, TX	0.9	8	18	Kings, NY	12.8
2	19	Cook, IL	24.2	21	18	Alameda, CA	0.9	14	19	Clark, NV	12.5
32	20	Franklin, OH	23.5	32	18	Franklin, OH	0.9	61	20	Gwinnett, GA	12.3
9	21	Dallas, TX	22.9	41	18	Mecklenburg, NC	0.9	55	21	DuPage, IL	12.2
42	22	Wake, NC	21.5	56	18	Erie, NY	0.9	22	22	Middlesex, MA	12.1
30	23	Orange, FL	21.0	57	18	Collin, TX	0.9	48	23	Fresno, CA	11.0
3	24	Harris, TX	19.1	59	18	Prince George's, MD	0.9	67	23	Pierce, WA	11.0
11	24	Queens, NY	19.1	63	18	Macomb, MI	0.9	28	25	Nassau, NY	9.7
40	26	Montgomery, MD	18.7	66	18	Ventura, CA	0.9	66	26	Ventura, CA	8.8
27	27	Palm Beach, FL	18.5	11	27	Queens, NY	0.8	12	27	San Bernardino, CA	8.1
7	28	Miami-Dade, FL	17.0	23	27	Philadelphia, PA	0.8	35	27	Hennepin, MN	8.1
29	29	Hillsborough, FL	16.8	33	27	Oakland, MI	0.8	72	27	Montgomery, PA	8.1
15	30	Tarrant, TX	16.2	42	27	Wake, NC	0.8	10	30	Riverside, CA	7.8
33	31	Oakland, MI	15.1	52	27	Marion, IN	0.8	2	31	Cook, IL	7.7
34	32	Allegheny, PA	14.4	58	27	Duval, FL	0.8	23	31	Philadelphia, PA	7.7
47	32	Westchester, NY	14.4	64	27	San Francisco, CA	0.8	3	33	Harris, TX	7.4
56	34	Erie, NY	14.1	71	27	Baltimore, MD	0.8	43	33	Fulton, GA	7.4
35	35	Hennepin, MN	13.9	9	35	Dallas, TX	0.7	33	35	Oakland, MI	7.3
60	35	Hartford, CT	13.9	16	35	Santa Clara, CA	0.7	36	36	Travis, TX	7.2
20	37	New York, NY	13.6	31	35	Cuyahoga, OH	0.7	42	36	Wake, NC	7.2
65	38	New Haven, CT	13.3	36	35	Travis, TX	0.7	47	38	Westchester, NY	6.8
21	39	Alameda, CA	12.5	43	35	Fulton, GA	0.7	71	39	Baltimore, MD	6.7
14	40	Clark, NV	11.9	50	35	Pinellas, FL	0.7	39	40	Salt Lake, UT	6.6
28	41	Nassau, NY	11.8	61	35	Gwinnett, GA	0.7	30	41	Orange, FL	6.4
63	42	Macomb, MI	11.7	1	42	Los Angeles, CA	0.6	9	42	Dallas, TX	6.3
25	43	Sacramento, CA	11.6	6	42	Orange, CA	0.6	51	43	Fairfield, CT	6.1
50	44	Pinellas, FL	11.3	8	42	Kings, NY	0.6	15	44	Tarrant, TX	6.0
51	44	Fairfield, CT	11.3	17	42	Bexar, TX	0.6	41	44	Mecklenburg, NC	6.0
37	46	Fairfax, VA	10.2	26	42	Bronx, NY	0.6	75	46	Essex, NJ	5.8
38	47	Contra Costa, CA	10.0	29	42	Hillsborough, FL	0.6	58	47	Duval, FL	5.7
69	47	Middlesex, NJ	10.0	30	42	Orange, FL	0.6	60	48	Hartford, CT	5.5
72	47	Montgomery, PA	10.0	37	42	Fairfax, VA	0.6	62	49	Kern, CA	5.4
57	50	Collin, TX	9.9	40	42	Montgomery, MD	0.6	32	50	Franklin, OH	5.3
12	51	San Bernardino, CA	9.2	45	42	St. Louis, MO	0.6	73	50	Worcester, MA	5.3
67	51	Pierce, WA	9.2	54	42	Shelby, TN	0.6	59	52	Prince George's, MD	5.2
1	53	Los Angeles, CA	8.8	60	42	Hartford, CT	0.6	4	53	Maricopa, AZ	5.0
36	54	Travis, TX	8.7	65	42	New Haven, CT	0.6	29	54	Hillsborough, FL	4.7
17	55	Bexar, TX	7.8	73	42	Worcester, MA	0.6	45	54	St. Louis, MO	4.7
24	55	Suffolk, NY	7.8	74	42	Hamilton, OH	0.6	65	56	New Haven, CT	4.6
13	57	King, WA	7.7	75	42	Essex, NJ	0.6	18	57	Broward, FL	4.5
10	58	Riverside, CA	6.9	2	58	Cook, IL	0.5	24	57	Suffolk, NY	4.5
64	59	San Francisco, CA	6.2	3	58	Harris, TX	0.5	49	59	Milwaukee, WI	4.4
4	60	Maricopa, AZ	5.9	18	58	Broward, FL	0.5	63	60	Macomb, MI	4.3
53	60	Bergen, NJ	5.9	20	58	New York, NY	0.5	26	61	Bronx, NY	4.2
62	60	Kern, CA	5.9	24	58	Suffolk, NY	0.5	50	62	Pinellas, FL	4.1
5	63	San Diego, CA	5.7	34	58	Allegheny, PA	0.5	34	63	Allegheny, PA	4.0
22	64	Middlesex, MA	5.6	47	58	Westchester, NY	0.5	44	64	Pima, AZ	3.8
55	65	DuPage, IL	5.4	69	58	Middlesex, NJ	0.5	19	65	Wayne, MI	3.7
48	66	Fresno, CA	5.3	70	58	El Paso, TX	0.5	56	65	Erie, NY	3.7
73	67	Worcester, MA	5.0	22	67	Middlesex, MA	0.4	31	67	Cuyahoga, OH	3.5
44	68	Pima, AZ	4.1	27	67	Palm Beach, FL	0.4	17	68	Bexar, TX	3.4
46	69	Honolulu, HI	3.9	28	67	Nassau, NY	0.4	27	69	Palm Beach, FL	3.3
70	70	El Paso, TX	3.5	51	67	Fairfield, CT	0.4	52	70	Marion, IN	3.2
16	71	Santa Clara, CA	3.0	55	67	DuPage, IL	0.4	54	71	Shelby, TN	3.0
66	72	Ventura, CA	2.2	72	67	Montgomery, PA	0.4	74	72	Hamilton, OH	2.9
39	73	Salt Lake, UT	2.1	53	73	Bergen, NJ	0.3	7	73	Miami-Dade, FL	2.0
6	74	Orange, CA	2.0	7	74	Miami-Dade, FL	0.2	70	74	El Paso, TX	1.6
68	75	Hidalgo, TX	0.5	68	75	Hidalgo, TX	0.1	68	75	Hidalgo, TX	1.1

75 Largest Counties by 2015 Population
Selected Rankings

	Percent Hispanic or Latino,[1] 2014				Percent under 18 years old, 2014				Percent 65 years old and over, 2014		
Population rank	Hispanic or Latino rank	County	Percent Hispanic or Latino [col 9]	Population rank	Under 18 years old rank	County	Percent under 18 years old [cols 10 and 11]	Population rank	65 years old and over rank	County	Percent 65 years old and over [cols 17 and 18]
68	1	Hidalgo, TX	91.1	68	1	Hidalgo, TX	33.6	50	1	Pinellas, FL	23.0
70	2	El Paso, TX	81.0	62	2	Kern, CA	29.5	27	2	Palm Beach, FL	22.7
7	3	Miami-Dade, FL	66.0	48	3	Fresno, CA	28.9	44	3	Pima, AZ	17.7
17	4	Bexar, TX	59.1	39	4	Salt Lake, UT	28.3	34	4	Allegheny, PA	17.3
26	5	Bronx, NY	54.7	70	5	El Paso, TX	28.2	56	5	Erie, NY	16.6
48	6	Fresno, CA	52.0	61	6	Gwinnett, GA	27.8	45	6	St. Louis, MO	16.5
12	7	San Bernardino, CA	51.7	12	7	San Bernardino, CA	27.2	28	7	Nassau, NY	16.4
62	8	Kern, CA	51.6	57	7	Collin, TX	27.2	31	7	Cuyahoga, OH	16.4
1	9	Los Angeles, CA	48.4	3	9	Harris, TX	27.1	72	7	Montgomery, PA	16.4
10	10	Riverside, CA	47.5	15	9	Tarrant, TX	27.1	53	10	Bergen, NJ	16.0
66	11	Ventura, CA	42.0	9	11	Dallas, TX	26.9	46	11	Honolulu, HI	15.8
3	12	Harris, TX	41.7	10	12	Riverside, CA	26.4	71	11	Baltimore, MD	15.8
9	13	Dallas, TX	39.3	17	13	Bexar, TX	26.2	47	13	Westchester, NY	15.7
44	14	Pima, AZ	36.1	26	14	Bronx, NY	25.5	60	13	Hartford, CT	15.7
6	15	Orange, CA	34.4	54	14	Shelby, TN	25.5	63	15	Macomb, MI	15.6
36	16	Travis, TX	33.9	4	16	Maricopa, AZ	25.1	65	15	New Haven, CT	15.6
5	17	San Diego, CA	33.2	42	17	Wake, NC	25.0	18	17	Broward, FL	15.3
4	18	Maricopa, AZ	30.3	52	17	Marion, IN	25.0	24	17	Suffolk, NY	15.3
14	18	Clark, NV	30.3	41	19	Mecklenburg, NC	24.6	7	19	Miami-Dade, FL	15.2
30	20	Orange, FL	29.1	25	20	Sacramento, CA	24.4	33	20	Oakland, MI	15.1
11	21	Queens, NY	28.0	49	20	Milwaukee, WI	24.4	64	21	San Francisco, CA	14.4
15	22	Tarrant, TX	27.8	66	22	Ventura, CA	24.2	20	22	New York, NY	14.3
18	23	Broward, FL	27.5	19	23	Wayne, MI	24.1	38	22	Contra Costa, CA	14.3
16	24	Santa Clara, CA	26.5	75	23	Essex, NJ	24.1	51	22	Fairfield, CT	14.3
29	24	Hillsborough, FL	26.5	67	25	Pierce, WA	24.0	73	25	Worcester, MA	14.1
20	26	New York, NY	25.9	14	26	Clark, NV	23.8	74	25	Hamilton, OH	14.1
38	27	Contra Costa, CA	25.1	37	26	Fairfax, VA	23.8	22	27	Middlesex, MA	14.0
2	28	Cook, IL	25.0	32	28	Franklin, OH	23.7	4	28	Maricopa, AZ	13.8
47	29	Westchester, NY	23.7	51	29	Fairfield, CT	23.6	19	28	Wayne, MI	13.8
21	30	Alameda, CA	22.6	40	30	Montgomery, MD	23.5	11	30	Queens, NY	13.6
25	31	Sacramento, CA	22.5	55	30	DuPage, IL	23.5	40	30	Montgomery, MD	13.6
75	32	Essex, NJ	22.2	38	32	Contra Costa, CA	23.4	66	30	Ventura, CA	13.6
27	33	Palm Beach, FL	20.7	8	33	Kings, NY	23.3	55	33	DuPage, IL	13.4
61	34	Gwinnett, GA	20.5	29	34	Hillsborough, FL	23.2	69	33	Middlesex, NJ	13.4
69	35	Middlesex, NJ	19.9	43	34	Fulton, GA	23.2	14	35	Clark, NV	13.3
8	36	Kings, NY	19.5	74	34	Hamilton, OH	23.2	6	36	Orange, CA	13.2
40	37	Montgomery, MD	18.7	16	37	Santa Clara, CA	23.1	10	36	Riverside, CA	13.2
51	37	Fairfield, CT	18.7	36	37	Travis, TX	23.1	29	36	Hillsborough, FL	13.2
53	39	Bergen, NJ	18.5	6	39	Orange, CA	22.9	2	39	Cook, IL	12.9
24	40	Suffolk, NY	18.2	47	39	Westchester, NY	22.9	25	40	Sacramento, CA	12.8
39	41	Salt Lake, UT	17.8	58	39	Duval, FL	22.9	58	40	Duval, FL	12.8
60	42	Hartford, CT	17.0	1	42	Los Angeles, CA	22.8	5	42	San Diego, CA	12.7
59	43	Prince George's, MD	16.9	2	43	Cook, IL	22.7	67	43	Pierce, WA	12.6
65	44	New Haven, CT	16.8	30	43	Orange, FL	22.7	21	44	Alameda, CA	12.5
37	45	Fairfax, VA	16.4	59	43	Prince George's, MD	22.7	23	44	Philadelphia, PA	12.5
28	46	Nassau, NY	16.1	5	46	San Diego, CA	22.4	35	44	Hennepin, MN	12.5
64	47	San Francisco, CA	15.3	24	47	Suffolk, NY	22.3	75	47	Essex, NJ	12.3
57	48	Collin, TX	15.1	45	47	St. Louis, MO	22.3	1	48	Los Angeles, CA	12.2
49	49	Milwaukee, WI	14.2	23	49	Philadelphia, PA	22.2	8	48	Kings, NY	12.2
55	50	DuPage, IL	14.1	35	49	Hennepin, MN	22.2	13	48	King, WA	12.2
23	51	Philadelphia, PA	13.6	28	51	Nassau, NY	22.1	16	48	Santa Clara, CA	12.2
41	52	Mecklenburg, NC	12.7	33	51	Oakland, MI	22.1	49	48	Milwaukee, WI	12.2
73	53	Worcester, MA	10.5	69	53	Middlesex, NJ	22.0	54	53	Shelby, TN	11.6
67	54	Pierce, WA	10.2	72	53	Montgomery, PA	22.0	37	54	Fairfax, VA	11.5
42	55	Wake, NC	10.0	73	53	Worcester, MA	22.0	52	55	Marion, IN	11.3
52	56	Marion, IN	9.8	63	56	Macomb, MI	21.9	70	55	El Paso, TX	11.3
46	57	Honolulu, HI	9.5	44	57	Pima, AZ	21.8	17	57	Bexar, TX	11.2
13	58	King, WA	9.4	60	58	Hartford, CT	21.7	26	57	Bronx, NY	11.2
50	59	Pinellas, FL	8.8	31	59	Cuyahoga, OH	21.6	48	57	Fresno, CA	11.2
58	60	Duval, FL	8.6	53	59	Bergen, NJ	21.6	59	57	Prince George's, MD	11.2
43	61	Fulton, GA	7.6	71	59	Baltimore, MD	21.6	32	61	Franklin, OH	10.9
22	62	Middlesex, MA	7.5	18	62	Broward, FL	21.5	30	62	Orange, FL	10.7
35	63	Hennepin, MN	6.8	46	62	Honolulu, HI	21.5	43	63	Fulton, GA	10.5
54	64	Shelby, TN	6.0	21	64	Alameda, CA	21.4	68	64	Hidalgo, TX	10.4
19	65	Wayne, MI	5.7	65	65	New Haven, CT	21.1	12	65	San Bernardino, CA	10.3
31	66	Cuyahoga, OH	5.4	13	66	King, WA	21.0	15	65	Tarrant, TX	10.3
32	67	Franklin, OH	5.1	56	67	Erie, NY	20.7	41	67	Mecklenburg, NC	10.1
56	67	Erie, NY	5.1	7	68	Miami-Dade, FL	20.6	42	68	Wake, NC	10.0
71	69	Baltimore, MD	5.0	22	68	Middlesex, MA	20.6	62	69	Kern, CA	9.9
72	70	Montgomery, PA	4.8	11	70	Queens, NY	20.4	57	70	Collin, TX	9.7
33	71	Oakland, MI	3.7	27	71	Palm Beach, FL	19.5	9	71	Dallas, TX	9.6
74	72	Hamilton, OH	2.9	34	72	Allegheny, PA	19.1	39	71	Salt Lake, UT	9.6
45	73	St. Louis, MO	2.7	50	73	Pinellas, FL	17.0	3	73	Harris, TX	9.2
63	74	Macomb, MI	2.5	20	74	New York, NY	14.7	61	74	Gwinnett, GA	8.6
34	75	Allegheny, PA	1.9	64	75	San Francisco, CA	13.4	36	75	Travis, TX	8.4

1. May be of any race.

75 Largest Counties by 2015 Population
Selected Rankings

Percent female-headed family households, 2010-2014				Birth rate, 2015				Percent under 65 who have no health insurance, 2014			
Population rank	Female households rank	County	Percent female households [col 30]	Population rank	Live birth rate rank	County	Birth rate [col 36]	Population rank	No health insurance rank	County	Percent with no health insurance [col 40]
26	1	Bronx, NY	31.5	68	1	Hidalgo, TX	19.5	68	1	Hidalgo, TX	33.8
54	2	Shelby, TN	20.8	39	2	Salt Lake, UT	16.5	7	2	Miami-Dade, FL	25.5
59	2	Prince George's, MD	20.8	48	2	Fresno, CA	16.5	9	3	Dallas, TX	25.0
23	4	Philadelphia, PA	20.6	62	4	Kern, CA	16.4	70	3	El Paso, TX	25.0
68	5	Hidalgo, TX	20.3	70	5	El Paso, TX	16.3	3	5	Harris, TX	23.9
70	6	El Paso, TX	20.1	8	6	Kings, NY	15.9	27	6	Palm Beach, FL	21.2
75	6	Essex, NJ	20.1	3	7	Harris, TX	15.7	18	7	Broward, FL	20.8
8	8	Kings, NY	20.0	9	8	Dallas, TX	15.6	30	8	Orange, FL	20.2
19	9	Wayne, MI	19.5	52	9	Marion, IN	15.5	61	8	Gwinnett, GA	20.2
7	10	Miami-Dade, FL	18.1	32	10	Franklin, OH	15.4	15	10	Tarrant, TX	19.8
48	11	Fresno, CA	17.5	26	11	Bronx, NY	15.0	17	11	Bexar, TX	18.7
49	12	Milwaukee, WI	17.0	17	12	Bexar, TX	14.7	36	12	Travis, TX	18.5
52	13	Marion, IN	16.9	54	13	Shelby, TN	14.6	14	13	Clark, NV	17.8
12	14	San Bernardino, CA	16.7	12	14	San Bernardino, CA	14.5	29	13	Hillsborough, FL	17.8
62	15	Kern, CA	16.6	15	14	Tarrant, TX	14.5	50	15	Pinellas, FL	17.7
17	16	Bexar, TX	16.5	49	14	Milwaukee, WI	14.5	1	16	Los Angeles, CA	17.4
9	17	Dallas, TX	16.3	23	17	Philadelphia, PA	14.3	10	17	Riverside, CA	17.0
11	18	Queens, NY	16.2	36	18	Travis, TX	14.0	43	18	Fulton, GA	16.5
31	19	Cuyahoga, OH	16.1	41	18	Mecklenburg, NC	14.0	75	18	Essex, NJ	16.5
1	20	Los Angeles, CA	15.8	58	18	Duval, FL	14.0	52	20	Marion, IN	16.1
58	20	Duval, FL	15.8	35	21	Hennepin, MN	13.9	44	21	Pima, AZ	16.0
18	22	Broward, FL	15.6	46	21	Honolulu, HI	13.9	11	22	Queens, NY	15.9
3	23	Harris, TX	15.5	67	23	Pierce, WA	13.8	4	23	Maricopa, AZ	15.6
2	24	Cook, IL	15.2	5	24	San Diego, CA	13.6	58	23	Duval, FL	15.6
43	24	Fulton, GA	15.2	74	24	Hamilton, OH	13.6	48	25	Fresno, CA	15.4
25	26	Sacramento, CA	15.1	4	26	Maricopa, AZ	13.5	54	26	Shelby, TN	15.0
30	26	Orange, FL	15.1	19	27	Wayne, MI	13.4	41	27	Mecklenburg, NC	14.9
74	26	Hamilton, OH	15.1	25	28	Sacramento, CA	13.3	39	28	Salt Lake, UT	14.8
60	29	Hartford, CT	15.0	59	28	Prince George's, MD	13.3	12	29	San Bernardino, CA	14.7
41	30	Mecklenburg, NC	14.6	2	30	Cook, IL	13.1	62	30	Kern, CA	14.5
71	31	Baltimore, MD	14.4	10	30	Riverside, CA	13.1	23	31	Philadelphia, PA	14.4
15	32	Tarrant, TX	14.3	11	30	Queens, NY	13.1	2	32	Cook, IL	14.1
32	32	Franklin, OH	14.3	43	30	Fulton, GA	13.1	26	33	Bronx, NY	13.9
61	32	Gwinnett, GA	14.3	61	30	Gwinnett, GA	13.1	59	34	Prince George's, MD	13.6
65	32	New Haven, CT	14.3	30	35	Orange, FL	12.9	5	35	San Diego, CA	13.4
29	36	Hillsborough, FL	14.2	75	35	Essex, NJ	12.9	6	35	Orange, CA	13.4
45	37	St. Louis, MO	14.1	1	37	Los Angeles, CA	12.8	66	37	Ventura, CA	13.1
14	38	Clark, NV	14.0	14	37	Clark, NV	12.8	57	38	Collin, TX	12.7
56	39	Erie, NY	13.8	29	39	Hillsborough, FL	12.7	8	39	Kings, NY	12.4
10	40	Riverside, CA	13.5	37	39	Fairfax, VA	12.7	19	40	Wayne, MI	12.2
63	41	Macomb, MI	13.1	40	39	Montgomery, MD	12.7	42	41	Wake, NC	12.0
47	42	Westchester, NY	13.0	42	42	Wake, NC	12.6	53	41	Bergen, NJ	12.0
4	43	Maricopa, AZ	12.8	66	43	Ventura, CA	12.5	69	43	Middlesex, NJ	11.9
44	43	Pima, AZ	12.8	16	44	Santa Clara, CA	12.4	25	44	Sacramento, CA	11.5
21	45	Alameda, CA	12.5	21	45	Alameda, CA	12.3	32	45	Franklin, OH	11.2
46	46	Honolulu, HI	12.4	13	46	King, WA	12.2	49	46	Milwaukee, WI	11.1
66	46	Ventura, CA	12.4	57	46	Collin, TX	12.2	37	47	Fairfax, VA	10.9
24	48	Suffolk, NY	12.3	6	48	Orange, CA	12.0	45	47	St. Louis, MO	10.9
69	48	Middlesex, NJ	12.3	31	48	Cuyahoga, OH	12.0	67	49	Pierce, WA	10.8
5	50	San Diego, CA	12.2	44	48	Pima, AZ	12.0	51	50	Fairfield, CT	10.5
51	50	Fairfield, CT	12.2	7	51	Miami-Dade, FL	11.8	47	51	Westchester, NY	10.3
73	50	Worcester, MA	12.2	18	51	Broward, FL	11.8	74	52	Hamilton, OH	10.1
6	53	Orange, CA	12.1	71	51	Baltimore, MD	11.8	31	53	Cuyahoga, OH	10.0
27	53	Palm Beach, FL	12.1	45	54	St. Louis, MO	11.6	40	53	Montgomery, MD	10.0
38	53	Contra Costa, CA	12.1	20	55	New York, NY	11.4	63	53	Macomb, MI	10.0
28	56	Nassau, NY	12.0	55	55	DuPage, IL	11.4	38	56	Contra Costa, CA	9.8
67	56	Pierce, WA	12.0	22	57	Middlesex, MA	11.3	21	57	Alameda, CA	9.6
34	58	Allegheny, PA	11.8	38	58	Contra Costa, CA	11.2	64	58	San Francisco, CA	9.3
42	59	Wake, NC	11.6	69	58	Middlesex, NJ	11.2	20	59	New York, NY	8.9
20	60	New York, NY	11.5	63	60	Macomb, MI	11.1	13	60	King, WA	8.7
36	60	Travis, TX	11.5	33	61	Oakland, MI	11.0	24	60	Suffolk, NY	8.7
40	62	Montgomery, MD	11.4	34	61	Allegheny, PA	11.0	55	62	DuPage, IL	8.6
50	63	Pinellas, FL	11.3	47	61	Westchester, NY	11.0	33	63	Oakland, MI	8.5
53	64	Bergen, NJ	11.2	56	64	Erie, NY	10.9	16	64	Santa Clara, CA	8.4
33	65	Oakland, MI	10.9	72	65	Montgomery, PA	10.8	71	64	Baltimore, MD	8.4
39	66	Salt Lake, UT	10.8	73	66	Worcester, MA	10.7	34	66	Allegheny, PA	8.0
16	67	Santa Clara, CA	10.6	51	67	Fairfield, CT	10.6	65	66	New Haven, CT	8.0
35	68	Hennepin, MN	10.3	60	68	Hartford, CT	10.5	35	68	Hennepin, MN	7.3
57	69	Collin, TX	10.1	64	68	San Francisco, CA	10.5	28	69	Nassau, NY	7.2
22	70	Middlesex, MA	9.8	24	70	Suffolk, NY	10.4	56	70	Erie, NY	6.9
72	71	Montgomery, PA	9.4	27	70	Palm Beach, FL	10.4	60	71	Hartford, CT	6.8
37	72	Fairfax, VA	9.3	28	70	Nassau, NY	10.4	72	72	Montgomery, PA	6.5
55	72	DuPage, IL	9.3	65	70	New Haven, CT	10.4	46	73	Honolulu, HI	5.5
13	74	King, WA	9.0	53	74	Bergen, NJ	10.0	73	74	Worcester, MA	3.5
64	75	San Francisco, CA	8.6	50	75	Pinellas, FL	9.2	22	75	Middlesex, MA	3.2

75 Largest Counties by 2015 Population
Selected Rankings

Percent college graduates (bachelor's degree or more), 2010–2014				Expenditures per student, 2012–2013				Per capita personal income, 2014			
Population rank	College graduates rank	County	Percent college graduates [col 51]	Population rank	Expenditures rank	County	Expenditures per student (dollars) [col 53]	Population rank	Per capita income rank	County	Per capita income (dollars) [col 64]
20	1	New York, NY	59.3	28	1	Nassau, NY	24 744	20	1	New York, NY	148.002
37	2	Fairfax, VA	59.2	47	2	Westchester, NY	23 561	51	2	Fairfield, CT	98 688
40	3	Montgomery, MD	57.4	75	3	Essex, NJ	23 340	64	3	San Francisco, CA	90 600
64	4	San Francisco, CA	52.9	20	4	New York, NY	22 518	47	4	Westchester, NY	87 777
22	5	Middlesex, MA	51.3	8	4	Kings, NY	22 518	72	5	Montgomery, PA	75 835
57	6	Collin, TX	49.4	11	4	Queens, NY	22 518	37	6	Fairfax, VA	75 007
43	7	Fulton, GA	48.6	26	4	Bronx, NY	22 518	16	7	Santa Clara, CA	74 883
42	8	Wake, NC	48.3	24	8	Suffolk, NY	21 944	28	8	Nassau, NY	73 618
16	9	Santa Clara, CA	47.3	23	9	Philadelphia, PA	20 194	53	9	Bergen, NJ	73 536
13	10	King, WA	47.1	53	10	Bergen, NJ	18 298	40	10	Montgomery, MD	73 483
55	11	DuPage, IL	46.7	56	11	Erie, NY	17 775	22	11	Middlesex, MA	69 337
35	12	Hennepin, MN	46.4	51	12	Fairfield, CT	17 442	13	12	King, WA	68 877
72	13	Montgomery, PA	46.2	60	13	Hartford, CT	17 118	27	13	Palm Beach, FL	66 914
53	14	Bergen, NJ	46.1	69	14	Middlesex, NJ	16 984	43	14	Fulton, GA	64 174
47	15	Westchester, NY	46.0	72	15	Montgomery, PA	16 934	35	15	Hennepin, MN	63 901
51	16	Fairfield, CT	45.4	65	16	New Haven, CT	16 895	38	16	Contra Costa, CA	63 752
36	17	Travis, TX	45.2	22	17	Middlesex, MA	16 245	55	17	DuPage, IL	60 684
33	18	Oakland, MI	43.7	34	18	Allegheny, PA	15 859	45	18	St. Louis, MO	60 540
28	19	Nassau, NY	42.3	40	19	Montgomery, MD	15 097	33	19	Oakland, MI	59 759
21	20	Alameda, CA	42.1	31	20	Cuyahoga, OH	14 915	57	20	Collin, TX	59 146
41	21	Mecklenburg, NC	41.5	59	21	Prince George's, MD	14 120	75	21	Essex, NJ	58 319
45	22	St. Louis, MO	41.4	55	22	DuPage, IL	14 074	3	22	Harris, TX	56 896
69	23	Middlesex, NJ	40.7	73	23	Worcester, MA	14 064	24	23	Suffolk, NY	56 725
38	24	Contra Costa, CA	39.4	37	24	Fairfax, VA	13 756	60	24	Hartford, CT	56 640
6	25	Orange, CA	37.3	2	25	Cook, IL	13 671	21	25	Alameda, CA	56 261
34	26	Allegheny, PA	36.9	32	26	Franklin, OH	13 463	6	26	Orange, CA	55 096
32	27	Franklin, OH	36.7	45	27	St. Louis, MO	13 436	36	27	Travis, TX	54 145
71	28	Baltimore, MD	36.0	74	28	Hamilton, OH	13 313	34	28	Allegheny, PA	53 976
60	29	Hartford, CT	35.6	71	29	Baltimore, MD	13 209	71	29	Baltimore, MD	53 949
2	30	Cook, IL	35.3	35	30	Hennepin, MN	13 139	69	30	Middlesex, NJ	52 486
5	31	San Diego, CA	35.1	49	31	Milwaukee, WI	12 389	9	31	Dallas, TX	52 406
61	32	Gwinnett, GA	34.4	64	32	San Francisco, CA	12 109	5	32	San Diego, CA	51 459
74	33	Hamilton, OH	34.3	46	33	Honolulu, HI	11 903	2	33	Cook, IL	51 280
73	34	Worcester, MA	34.1	33	34	Oakland, MI	11 726	74	34	Hamilton, OH	51 229
24	35	Suffolk, NY	33.5	19	35	Wayne, MI	11 693	66	35	Ventura, CA	50 405
65	36	New Haven, CT	33.4	43	36	Fulton, GA	11 224	65	36	New Haven, CT	50 261
27	37	Palm Beach, FL	32.8	52	37	Marion, IN	10 927	46	37	Honolulu, HI	49 722
46	38	Honolulu, HI	32.5	63	38	Macomb, MI	10 692	42	38	Wake, NC	49 695
75	39	Essex, NJ	32.3	1	39	Los Angeles, CA	10 053	1	39	Los Angeles, CA	49 400
8	40	Kings, NY	31.6	13	40	King, WA	10 005	41	40	Mecklenburg, NC	49 099
66	40	Ventura, CA	31.6	67	41	Pierce, WA	9 826	31	41	Cuyahoga, OH	48 521
39	42	Salt Lake, UT	31.3	62	42	Kern, CA	9 682	73	42	Worcester, MA	48 151
56	43	Erie, NY	31.2	16	43	Santa Clara, CA	9 510	15	43	Tarrant, TX	46 169
30	44	Orange, FL	30.6	54	44	Shelby, TN	9 480	50	44	Pinellas, FL	45 925
59	45	Prince George's, MD	30.4	27	45	Palm Beach, FL	9 429	32	45	Franklin, OH	45 158
31	46	Cuyahoga, OH	30.3	48	46	Fresno, CA	9 403	56	46	Erie, NY	44 740
11	47	Queens, NY	30.2	36	47	Travis, TX	9 261	54	47	Shelby, TN	44 705
18	47	Broward, FL	30.2	21	48	Alameda, CA	9 173	59	48	Prince George's, MD	44 465
44	49	Pima, AZ	30.1	68	49	Hidalgo, TX	9 112	25	49	Sacramento, CA	43 944
4	50	Maricopa, AZ	30.0	5	50	San Diego, CA	9 033	67	50	Pierce, WA	43 613
1	51	Los Angeles, CA	29.9	7	51	Miami-Dade, FL	8 986	18	51	Broward, FL	43 283
29	52	Hillsborough, FL	29.8	25	52	Sacramento, CA	8 976	23	52	Philadelphia, PA	42 617
54	52	Shelby, TN	29.8	38	53	Contra Costa, CA	8 969	39	53	Salt Lake, UT	42 535
15	54	Tarrant, TX	29.7	61	54	Gwinnett, GA	8 891	29	54	Hillsborough, FL	41 902
3	55	Harris, TX	29.0	66	55	Ventura, CA	8 813	7	55	Miami-Dade, FL	41 883
9	56	Dallas, TX	28.7	29	56	Hillsborough, FL	8 766	49	56	Milwaukee, WI	41 507
49	56	Milwaukee, WI	28.7	50	56	Pinellas, FL	8 766	58	57	Duval, FL	41 316
50	58	Pinellas, FL	28.3	6	58	Orange, CA	8 692	4	58	Maricopa, AZ	41 222
25	59	Sacramento, CA	28.2	10	59	Riverside, CA	8 583	17	59	Bexar, TX	40 857
52	60	Marion, IN	27.7	70	60	El Paso, TX	8 554	52	60	Marion, IN	40 074
17	61	Bexar, TX	26.5	12	61	San Bernardino, CA	8 544	8	61	Kings, NY	39 898
58	61	Duval, FL	26.5	58	62	Duval, FL	8 414	63	62	Macomb, MI	39 886
7	63	Miami-Dade, FL	26.4	18	63	Broward, FL	8 390	14	63	Clark, NV	39 533
23	64	Philadelphia, PA	24.5	30	64	Orange, FL	8 338	11	64	Queens, NY	39 507
67	65	Pierce, WA	24.2	17	65	Bexar, TX	8 334	30	65	Orange, FL	38 007
63	66	Macomb, MI	23.1	41	66	Mecklenburg, NC	8 224	44	66	Pima, AZ	37 031
14	67	Clark, NV	22.2	9	67	Dallas, TX	8 157	19	67	Wayne, MI	36 844
19	68	Wayne, MI	21.6	44	68	Pima, AZ	8 133	62	68	Kern, CA	36 165
10	69	Riverside, CA	20.8	3	69	Harris, TX	8 132	48	69	Fresno, CA	35 785
70	69	El Paso, TX	20.8	14	70	Clark, NV	8 066	61	70	Gwinnett, GA	35 374
48	71	Fresno, CA	19.5	57	71	Collin, TX	7 958	10	71	Riverside, CA	33 590
12	72	San Bernardino, CA	18.8	15	72	Tarrant, TX	7 941	12	72	San Bernardino, CA	32 892
26	73	Bronx, NY	18.3	42	73	Wake, NC	7 788	26	73	Bronx, NY	32 238
68	74	Hidalgo, TX	16.4	4	74	Maricopa, AZ	7 248	70	74	El Paso, TX	31 816
62	75	Kern, CA	15.2	39	75	Salt Lake, UT	6 906	68	75	Hidalgo, TX	23 753

75 Largest Counties by 2015 Population
Selected Rankings

Median household income, 2014				Median value of owner-occupied housing units, 2010–2014				Median gross rent of renter-occupied housing units, 2010–2014			
Population rank	Median income rank	County	Median income (dollars) [col 58]	Population rank	Median value rank	County	Median value (dollars) [col 91]	Population rank	Median rent rank	County	Median rent (dollars) [col 94]
37	1	Fairfax, VA	110 507	20	1	New York, NY	838 400	37	1	Fairfax, VA	1 724
28	2	Nassau, NY	98 312	64	2	San Francisco, CA	765 700	16	2	Santa Clara, CA	1 637
40	3	Montgomery, MD	97 279	16	3	Santa Clara, CA	664 100	40	3	Montgomery, MD	1 611
16	4	Santa Clara, CA	97 219	46	4	Honolulu, HI	564 400	28	4	Nassau, NY	1 559
57	5	Collin, TX	86 634	8	5	Kings, NY	557 500	64	5	San Francisco, CA	1 533
24	6	Suffolk, NY	85 886	6	6	Orange, CA	532 300	46	6	Honolulu, HI	1 528
51	7	Fairfield, CT	85 336	21	7	Alameda, CA	509 300	6	7	Orange, CA	1 522
53	8	Bergen, NJ	84 309	47	8	Westchester, NY	509 200	24	8	Suffolk, NY	1 519
22	9	Middlesex, MA	84 026	37	9	Fairfax, VA	486 900	66	9	Ventura, CA	1 494
64	10	San Francisco, CA	83 788	40	10	Montgomery, MD	448 700	20	10	New York, NY	1 480
47	11	Westchester, NY	83 152	28	11	Nassau, NY	447 700	38	11	Contra Costa, CA	1 395
38	12	Contra Costa, CA	80 338	11	12	Queens, NY	446 800	47	12	Westchester, NY	1 354
55	13	DuPage, IL	80 037	66	13	Ventura, CA	444 800	11	13	Queens, NY	1 350
72	14	Montgomery, PA	79 576	53	14	Bergen, NJ	443 500	53	14	Bergen, NJ	1 340
69	15	Middlesex, NJ	77 330	1	15	Los Angeles, CA	425 100	5	15	San Diego, CA	1 328
21	16	Alameda, CA	76 996	51	16	Fairfield, CT	422 400	51	16	Fairfield, CT	1 327
6	17	Orange, CA	76 061	38	17	Contra Costa, CA	417 400	21	17	Alameda, CA	1 325
13	18	King, WA	75 738	5	18	San Diego, CA	412 800	22	18	Middlesex, MA	1 320
20	19	New York, NY	75 459	22	19	Middlesex, MA	404 600	69	19	Middlesex, NJ	1 292
66	20	Ventura, CA	74 967	24	20	Suffolk, NY	376 800	59	20	Prince George's, MD	1 276
46	21	Honolulu, HI	73 985	13	21	King, WA	376 200	1	21	Los Angeles, CA	1 221
59	22	Prince George's, MD	71 904	26	22	Bronx, NY	366 400	8	22	Kings, NY	1 189
33	23	Oakland, MI	69 378	75	23	Essex, NJ	358 100	10	23	Riverside, CA	1 182
71	24	Baltimore, MD	67 766	69	24	Middlesex, NJ	325 000	18	24	Broward, FL	1 179
42	25	Wake, NC	66 950	72	25	Montgomery, PA	290 800	13	25	King, WA	1 161
5	26	San Diego, CA	66 034	55	26	Du Page, IL	279 700	27	26	Palm Beach, FL	1 158
60	27	Hartford, CT	65 809	59	27	Prince George's, MD	258 800	71	27	Baltimore, MD	1 155
73	28	Worcester, MA	65 217	73	28	Worcester, MA	255 600	72	28	Montgomery, PA	1 146
35	29	Hennepin, MN	64 490	65	29	New Haven, CT	250 400	55	29	DuPage, IL	1 127
39	30	Salt Lake, UT	62 536	71	30	Baltimore, MD	248 700	12	30	San Bernardino, CA	1 113
36	31	Travis, TX	61 779	60	31	Hartford, CT	238 600	7	31	Miami-Dade, FL	1 098
67	32	Pierce, WA	60 397	43	32	Fulton, GA	237 600	57	32	Collin, TX	1 086
65	33	New Haven, CT	60 387	25	33	Sacramento, CA	236 500	75	33	Essex, NJ	1 069
45	34	St. Louis, MO	60 093	10	34	Riverside, CA	236 400	65	34	New Haven, CT	1 064
61	35	Gwinnett, GA	59 858	67	35	Pierce, WA	233 800	26	35	Bronx, NY	1 060
41	36	Mecklenburg, NC	59 049	39	36	Salt Lake, UT	231 200	30	36	Orange, FL	1 036
15	37	Tarrant, TX	58 127	42	37	Wake, NC	229 200	25	37	Sacramento, CA	1 035
10	38	Riverside, CA	56 877	35	38	Hennepin, MN	227 400	61	38	Gwinnett, GA	1 029
11	39	Queens, NY	56 866	12	39	San Bernardino, CA	225 400	36	39	Travis, TX	1 022
25	40	Sacramento, CA	55 803	36	40	Travis, TX	224 600	67	40	Pierce, WA	1 021
1	41	Los Angeles, CA	55 686	2	41	Cook, IL	222 200	14	41	Clark, NV	1 009
43	42	Fulton, GA	55 516	57	42	Collin, TX	211 900	43	42	Fulton, GA	992
2	43	Cook, IL	55 058	27	43	Palm Beach, FL	194 600	60	43	Hartford, CT	983
63	44	Macomb, MI	54 865	7	44	Miami-Dade, FL	194 100	2	44	Cook, IL	976
75	45	Essex, NJ	54 603	48	45	Fresno, CA	191 700	29	45	Hillsborough, FL	960
3	46	Harris, TX	54 230	41	46	Mecklenburg, NC	181 800	50	46	Pinellas, FL	955
4	47	Maricopa, AZ	53 929	18	47	Broward, FL	177 300	4	47	Maricopa, AZ	952
32	48	Franklin, OH	53 164	4	48	Maricopa, AZ	175 600	58	48	Duval, FL	941
34	49	Allegheny, PA	52 385	45	49	St. Louis, MO	173 000	42	49	Wake, NC	935
27	50	Palm Beach, FL	52 225	33	50	Oakland, MI	170 600	33	50	Oakland, MI	934
12	51	San Bernardino, CA	51 951	61	51	Gwinnett, GA	167 700	35	50	Hennepin, MN	934
18	52	Broward, FL	51 485	14	52	Clark, NV	163 100	73	52	Worcester, MA	927
14	53	Clark, NV	51 241	30	53	Orange, FL	161 900	39	53	Salt Lake, UT	922
29	54	Hillsborough, FL	50 758	62	54	Kern, CA	161 800	23	54	Philadelphia, PA	915
17	55	Bexar, TX	50 699	44	55	Pima, AZ	161 700	41	55	Mecklenburg, NC	913
56	56	Erie, NY	50 134	29	56	Hillsborough, FL	156 700	15	56	Tarrant, TX	899
9	57	Dallas, TX	50 118	49	57	Milwaukee, WI	154 400	3	57	Harris, TX	895
74	58	Hamilton, OH	48 973	32	58	Franklin, OH	150 000	9	57	Dallas, TX	895
8	59	Kings, NY	47 547	50	59	Pinellas, FL	146 500	62	59	Kern, CA	887
62	60	Kern, CA	47 451	58	60	Duval, FL	144 000	48	60	Fresno, CA	884
30	61	Orange, FL	47 069	23	61	Philadelphia, PA	143 200	45	61	St. Louis, MO	873
58	62	Duval, FL	46 013	74	62	Hamilton, OH	143 000	17	62	Bexar, TX	862
44	63	Pima, AZ	45 871	15	63	Tarrant, TX	137 700	54	63	Shelby, TN	861
50	64	Pinellas, FL	45 162	3	64	Harris, TX	133 400	63	64	Macomb, MI	852
31	65	Cuyahoga, OH	44 138	54	65	Shelby, TN	131 700	32	65	Franklin, OH	834
54	66	Shelby, TN	44 015	9	66	Dallas, TX	129 200	44	66	Pima, AZ	813
48	67	Fresno, CA	43 338	56	67	Erie, NY	126 700	49	67	Milwaukee, WI	802
49	68	Milwaukee, WI	42 946	17	68	Bexar, TX	126 100	19	68	Wayne, MI	797
7	69	Miami-Dade, FL	42 754	34	69	Allegheny, PA	124 800	52	69	Marion, IN	781
52	70	Marion, IN	42 700	31	70	Cuyahoga, OH	123 300	34	70	Allegheny, PA	771
19	71	Wayne, MI	41 434	63	71	Macomb, MI	121 300	70	71	El Paso, TX	741
70	72	El Paso, TX	40 081	52	72	Marion, IN	117 400	56	72	Erie, NY	738
23	73	Philadelphia, PA	39 037	70	73	El Paso, TX	112 800	31	73	Cuyahoga, OH	736
68	74	Hidalgo, TX	34 368	19	74	Wayne, MI	83 200	74	74	Hamilton, OH	708
26	75	Bronx, NY	33 687	68	75	Hidalgo, TX	78 900	68	75	Hidalgo, TX	658

75 Largest Counties by 2015 Population
Selected Rankings

Percent of population below the poverty level, 2014				Percent under 18 years old below the poverty level, 2014				Unemployment rate, 2015			
Population rank	Poverty rate rank	County	Poverty rate [col 59]	Population rank	Poverty rate for children rank	County	Poverty rate for children under 18 years [col 60]	Population rank	Unemployment rate rank	County	Unemployment rate [col 100]
68	1	Hidalgo, TX	33.5	68	1	Hidalgo, TX	45.5	48	1	Fresno, CA	10.2
26	2	Bronx, NY	31.5	26	2	Bronx, NY	43.0	62	1	Kern, CA	10.2
48	3	Fresno, CA	27.5	48	3	Fresno, CA	38.0	68	3	Hidalgo, TX	7.9
23	4	Philadelphia, PA	25.8	23	4	Philadelphia, PA	36.9	26	4	Bronx, NY	7.7
62	5	Kern, CA	24.5	19	5	Wayne, MI	35.2	19	5	Wayne, MI	7.3
19	6	Wayne, MI	24.1	54	6	Shelby, TN	34.5	23	6	Philadelphia, PA	6.9
8	7	Kings, NY	23.4	8	7	Kings, NY	33.1	14	7	Clark, NV	6.8
70	7	El Paso, TX	23.4	62	8	Kern, CA	32.9	1	8	Los Angeles, CA	6.7
54	9	Shelby, TN	23.0	49	9	Milwaukee, WI	32.2	10	8	Riverside, CA	6.7
49	10	Milwaukee, WI	22.0	70	10	El Paso, TX	31.7	75	8	Essex, NJ	6.7
52	11	Marion, IN	21.3	52	11	Marion, IN	31.4	54	11	Shelby, TN	6.6
7	12	Miami-Dade, FL	20.4	31	12	Cuyahoga, OH	30.0	12	12	San Bernardino, CA	6.5
12	12	San Bernardino, CA	20.4	9	13	Dallas, TX	29.0	67	13	Pierce, WA	6.3
31	14	Cuyahoga, OH	19.6	12	14	San Bernardino, CA	28.2	2	14	Cook, IL	6.1
9	15	Dallas, TX	19.3	7	15	Miami-Dade, FL	27.7	7	14	Miami-Dade, FL	6.1
1	16	Los Angeles, CA	18.7	1	16	Los Angeles, CA	26.7	63	14	Macomb, MI	6.1
44	16	Pima, AZ	18.7	58	16	Duval, FL	26.7	65	14	New Haven, CT	6.1
17	18	Bexar, TX	18.3	17	18	Bexar, TX	26.4	25	18	Sacramento, CA	6.0
30	19	Orange, FL	18.2	44	19	Pima, AZ	25.9	8	19	Kings, NY	5.9
58	19	Duval, FL	18.2	30	20	Orange, FL	25.4	60	19	Hartford, CT	5.9
25	21	Sacramento, CA	18.1	2	21	Cook, IL	25.3	43	21	Fulton, GA	5.8
20	22	New York, NY	17.7	43	22	Fulton, GA	25.2	49	21	Milwaukee, WI	5.8
74	23	Hamilton, OH	17.6	3	23	Harris, TX	25.1	58	23	Duval, FL	5.7
43	24	Fulton, GA	17.4	32	24	Franklin, OH	24.6	66	23	Ventura, CA	5.7
3	25	Harris, TX	17.3	74	25	Hamilton, OH	24.4	44	25	Pima, AZ	5.6
32	25	Franklin, OH	17.3	4	26	Maricopa, AZ	24.3	41	26	Mecklenburg, NC	5.4
2	27	Cook, IL	17.1	25	27	Sacramento, CA	23.8	56	26	Erie, NY	5.4
4	27	Maricopa, AZ	17.1	10	28	Riverside, CA	23.5	71	26	Baltimore, MD	5.4
10	27	Riverside, CA	17.1	20	28	New York, NY	23.5	51	29	Fairfield, CT	5.3
29	30	Hillsborough, FL	16.8	75	30	Essex, NJ	23.4	59	29	Prince George's, MD	5.3
36	31	Travis, TX	16.7	29	31	Hillsborough, FL	23.3	73	29	Worcester, MA	5.3
75	31	Essex, NJ	16.7	14	32	Clark, NV	23.1	4	32	Maricopa, AZ	5.2
14	33	Clark, NV	15.6	36	32	Travis, TX	23.1	5	32	San Diego, CA	5.2
11	34	Queens, NY	15.4	56	34	Erie, NY	22.9	70	32	El Paso, TX	5.2
15	35	Tarrant, TX	15.2	50	35	Pinellas, FL	22.2	61	35	Gwinnett, GA	5.1
41	35	Mecklenburg, NC	15.2	27	36	Palm Beach, FL	21.9	11	36	Queens, NY	5.0
50	35	Pinellas, FL	15.2	15	37	Tarrant, TX	21.7	18	36	Broward, FL	5.0
56	35	Erie, NY	15.2	41	38	Mecklenburg, NC	21.1	27	36	Palm Beach, FL	5.0
27	39	Palm Beach, FL	14.9	11	39	Queens, NY	21.0	29	36	Hillsborough, FL	5.0
5	40	San Diego, CA	14.7	18	40	Broward, FL	20.1	31	36	Cuyahoga, OH	5.0
18	41	Broward, FL	14.5	61	41	Gwinnett, GA	19.9	33	36	Oakland, MI	5.0
61	42	Gwinnett, GA	13.4	5	42	San Diego, CA	18.9	38	36	Contra Costa, CA	5.0
34	43	Allegheny, PA	13.1	34	43	Allegheny, PA	18.5	52	36	Marion, IN	5.0
67	43	Pierce, WA	13.1	65	44	New Haven, CT	18.4	69	36	Middlesex, NJ	5.0
35	45	Hennepin, MN	13.0	63	45	Macomb, MI	18.3	30	45	Orange, FL	4.9
65	45	New Haven, CT	13.0	6	46	Orange, CA	17.9	50	45	Pinellas, FL	4.9
6	47	Orange, CA	12.9	60	47	Hartford, CT	17.6	20	47	New York, NY	4.8
21	48	Alameda, CA	12.5	67	48	Pierce, WA	17.5	24	47	Suffolk, NY	4.8
63	49	Macomb, MI	12.3	35	49	Hennepin, MN	17.1	34	47	Allegheny, PA	4.8
60	50	Hartford, CT	12.2	66	50	Ventura, CA	15.8	21	50	Alameda, CA	4.7
64	51	San Francisco, CA	12.1	39	51	Salt Lake, UT	15.1	42	50	Wake, NC	4.7
39	52	Salt Lake, UT	11.9	73	52	Worcester, MA	15.0	55	50	DuPage, IL	4.7
42	53	Wake, NC	11.5	59	53	Prince George's, MD	14.6	3	53	Harris, TX	4.6
66	53	Ventura, CA	11.5	21	54	Alameda, CA	14.3	45	53	St. Louis, MO	4.6
73	53	Worcester, MA	11.5	42	54	Wake, NC	14.3	47	53	Westchester, NY	4.6
13	56	King, WA	11.3	38	56	Contra Costa, CA	13.8	53	53	Bergen, NJ	4.6
38	57	Contra Costa, CA	10.5	45	57	St. Louis, MO	13.7	6	57	Orange, CA	4.5
47	58	Westchester, NY	10.4	13	58	King, WA	13.6	74	57	Hamilton, OH	4.5
59	59	Prince George's, MD	10.3	64	58	San Francisco, CA	13.6	13	59	King, WA	4.4
33	60	Oakland, MI	10.0	47	60	Westchester, NY	13.3	9	60	Dallas, TX	4.3
46	61	Honolulu, HI	9.8	71	61	Baltimore, MD	13.0	28	60	Nassau, NY	4.3
71	61	Baltimore, MD	9.8	46	62	Honolulu, HI	12.8	15	62	Tarrant, TX	4.2
45	63	St. Louis, MO	9.6	33	63	Oakland, MI	12.4	16	62	Santa Clara, CA	4.2
51	64	Fairfield, CT	9.0	51	64	Fairfield, CT	11.8	32	64	Franklin, OH	4.1
22	65	Middlesex, MA	8.9	69	65	Middlesex, NJ	10.8	22	65	Middlesex, MA	4.0
16	66	Santa Clara, CA	8.5	55	66	DuPage, IL	10.5	40	65	Montgomery, MD	4.0
69	67	Middlesex, NJ	8.3	24	67	Suffolk, NY	10.4	72	65	Montgomery, PA	4.0
55	68	DuPage, IL	7.9	22	68	Middlesex, MA	9.6	17	68	Bexar, TX	3.8
24	69	Suffolk, NY	7.7	16	69	Santa Clara, CA	9.3	37	69	Fairfax, VA	3.6
53	70	Bergen, NJ	7.6	28	69	Nassau, NY	9.3	57	69	Collin, TX	3.6
40	71	Montgomery, MD	7.2	57	71	Collin, TX	9.0	64	69	San Francisco, CA	3.6
72	72	Montgomery, PA	7.1	40	72	Montgomery, MD	8.9	46	72	Honolulu, HI	3.4
57	73	Collin, TX	7.0	53	72	Bergen, NJ	8.9	35	73	Hennepin, MN	3.3
28	74	Nassau, NY	6.7	72	72	Montgomery, PA	8.9	36	73	Travis, TX	3.3
37	74	Fairfax, VA	6.7	37	75	Fairfax, VA	8.7	39	73	Salt Lake, UT	3.3

75 Largest Counties by 2015 Population
Selected Rankings

Manufacturing employment as a percent of total nonfarm employment, 2014				Professional, scientific, and technical employment as a percent of total nonfarm employment, 2014				Per capita local government taxes, 2012			
Population rank	Manufacturing rank	County	Percent employed in manufacturing [col 107/col 105]	Population rank	Professional services rank	County	Percent employed in professional services [col 110/col 105]	Population rank	Local taxes rank	County	Per capita local taxes (dollars) [col 183]
63	1	Macomb, MI	22.7	37	1	Fairfax, VA	32.8	28	1	Nassau, NY	5 254
19	2	Wayne, MI	12.5	40	2	Montgomery, MD	19.3	47	2	Westchester, NY	5 135
73	3	Worcester, MA	11.1	64	3	San Francisco, CA	16.8	20	3	New York, NY	5 096
56	4	Erie, NY	10.8	69	4	Middlesex, NJ	14.1	8	3	Kings, NY	5 096
31	5	Cuyahoga, OH	10.5	20	5	New York, NY	13.9	11	3	Queens, NY	5 096
6	6	Orange, CA	10.4	33	5	Oakland, MI	13.9	26	3	Bronx, NY	5 096
21	6	Alameda, CA	10.4	59	5	Prince George's, MD	13.9	24	7	Suffolk, NY	4 295
49	8	Milwaukee, WI	10.3	16	8	Santa Clara, CA	13.7	64	8	San Francisco, CA	4 001
15	8	Tarrant, TX	10.3	22	9	Middlesex, MA	12.9	53	9	Bergen, NJ	3 788
60	10	Hartford, CT	10.2	43	10	Fulton, GA	12.7	51	10	Fairfield, CT	3 419
66	11	Ventura, CA	9.7	36	11	Travis, TX	11.9	40	11	Montgomery, MD	3 168
65	12	New Haven, CT	9.6	42	12	Wake, NC	11.5	55	12	DuPage, IL	3 002
48	13	Fresno, CA	9.5	5	13	San Diego, CA	11.1	75	13	Essex, NJ	2 846
24	14	Suffolk, NY	9.4	57	14	Collin, TX	10.7	37	14	Fairfax, VA	2 810
12	15	San Bernardino, CA	9.2	1	15	Los Angeles, CA	10.0	43	15	Fulton, GA	2 802
55	16	DuPage, IL	9.0	21	15	Alameda, CA	10.0	2	16	Cook, IL	2 765
1	16	Los Angeles, CA	9.0	63	17	Macomb, MI	9.9	31	16	Cuyahoga, OH	2 765
16	18	Santa Clara, CA	8.9	29	18	Hillsborough, FL	9.8	69	18	Middlesex, NJ	2 730
39	19	Salt Lake, UT	8.6	9	19	Dallas, TX	9.7	32	19	Franklin, OH	2 717
3	20	Harris, TX	8.4	2	20	Cook, IL	9.3	23	20	Philadelphia, PA	2 636
74	20	Hamilton, OH	8.4	35	20	Hennepin, MN	9.3	16	21	Santa Clara, CA	2 621
10	22	Riverside, CA	8.3	72	20	Montgomery, PA	9.3	60	22	Hartford, CT	2 571
35	23	Hennepin, MN	8.2	13	23	King, WA	9.2	13	23	King, WA	2 543
51	24	Fairfield, CT	8.1	3	24	Harris, TX	9.1	27	24	Palm Beach, FL	2 542
5	24	San Diego, CA	8.1	51	25	Fairfield, CT	8.8	72	25	Montgomery, PA	2 541
72	24	Montgomery, PA	8.1	66	25	Ventura, CA	8.8	22	26	Middlesex, MA	2 471
52	27	Marion, IN	7.9	27	27	Palm Beach, FL	8.7	36	27	Travis, TX	2 455
50	27	Pinellas, FL	7.9	6	28	Orange, CA	8.5	74	28	Hamilton, OH	2 403
13	29	King, WA	7.7	74	28	Hamilton, OH	8.5	57	29	Collin, TX	2 390
2	29	Cook, IL	7.7	75	28	Essex, NJ	8.5	56	30	Erie, NY	2 368
44	31	Pima, AZ	7.5	24	31	Suffolk, NY	8.4	21	31	Alameda, CA	2 358
33	32	Oakland, MI	7.4	39	32	Salt Lake, UT	8.2	65	31	New Haven, CT	2 358
53	32	Bergen, NJ	7.4	41	32	Mecklenburg, NC	8.2	9	33	Dallas, TX	2 338
67	32	Pierce, WA	7.4	45	32	St. Louis, MO	8.2	34	34	Allegheny, PA	2 228
69	35	Middlesex, NJ	7.3	71	32	Baltimore, MD	8.2	3	35	Harris, TX	2 171
9	36	Dallas, TX	7.2	23	36	Philadelphia, PA	8.0	45	36	St. Louis, MO	2 133
61	37	Gwinnett, GA	6.8	28	37	Nassau, NY	7.9	7	37	Miami-Dade, FL	2 132
22	38	Middlesex, MA	6.6	34	37	Allegheny, PA	7.9	15	38	Tarrant, TX	2 029
45	39	St. Louis, MO	6.4	50	37	Pinellas, FL	7.9	41	39	Mecklenburg, NC	1 923
4	39	Maricopa, AZ	6.4	61	37	Gwinnett, GA	7.9	71	40	Baltimore, MD	1 917
54	41	Shelby, TN	6.3	53	41	Bergen, NJ	7.8	35	41	Hennepin, MN	1 910
75	42	Essex, NJ	6.2	18	42	Broward, FL	7.7	1	42	Los Angeles, CA	1 891
70	42	El Paso, TX	6.2	25	42	Sacramento, CA	7.7	49	43	Milwaukee, WI	1 888
62	44	Kern, CA	6.1	38	42	Contra Costa, CA	7.7	38	44	Contra Costa, CA	1 861
57	45	Collin, TX	5.3	52	45	Marion, IN	7.4	54	45	Shelby, TN	1 828
36	46	Travis, TX	5.2	55	45	DuPage, IL	7.4	30	46	Orange, FL	1 815
32	47	Franklin, OH	5.1	60	47	Hartford, CT	7.3	6	47	Orange, CA	1 806
34	48	Allegheny, PA	5.0	4	48	Maricopa, AZ	7.1	5	48	San Diego, CA	1 791
58	48	Duval, FL	5.0	30	49	Orange, FL	6.9	59	49	Prince George's, MD	1 761
38	50	Contra Costa, CA	4.9	56	49	Erie, NY	6.9	18	50	Broward, FL	1 742
71	51	Baltimore, MD	4.8	7	51	Miami-Dade, FL	6.8	17	51	Bexar, TX	1 675
17	52	Bexar, TX	4.6	47	51	Westchester, NY	6.8	66	52	Ventura, CA	1 650
41	52	Mecklenburg, NC	4.6	62	53	Kern, CA	6.7	73	53	Worcester, MA	1 630
25	54	Sacramento, CA	4.5	32	54	Franklin, OH	6.6	50	54	Pinellas, FL	1 597
11	55	Queens, NY	4.0	19	55	Wayne, MI	6.4	58	55	Duval, FL	1 536
30	56	Orange, FL	3.9	58	56	Duval, FL	6.3	61	56	Gwinnett, GA	1 529
8	57	Kings, NY	3.8	17	57	Bexar, TX	6.2	67	57	Pierce, WA	1 521
29	58	Hillsborough, FL	3.7	31	58	Cuyahoga, OH	6.1	33	58	Oakland, MI	1 515
23	59	Philadelphia, PA	3.6	73	58	Worcester, MA	6.1	4	59	Maricopa, AZ	1 506
18	60	Broward, FL	3.5	44	60	Pima, AZ	5.5	19	60	Wayne, MI	1 499
7	60	Miami-Dade, FL	3.5	14	61	Clark, NV	5.3	52	61	Marion, IN	1 447
68	62	Hidalgo, TX	3.3	46	61	Honolulu, HI	5.3	44	62	Pima, AZ	1 438
42	63	Wake, NC	3.1	49	63	Milwaukee, WI	5.0	42	63	Wake, NC	1 436
28	64	Nassau, NY	3.0	15	64	Tarrant, TX	4.8	39	64	Salt Lake, UT	1 428
47	65	Westchester, NY	2.8	48	65	Fresno, CA	4.5	14	65	Clark, NV	1 367
59	66	Prince George's, MD	2.7	65	65	New Haven, CT	4.5	62	66	Kern, CA	1 365
46	67	Honolulu, HI	2.6	70	67	El Paso, TX	4.3	10	67	Riverside, CA	1 362
27	68	Palm Beach, FL	2.5	54	68	Shelby, TN	3.9	29	68	Hillsborough, FL	1 359
43	68	Fulton, GA	2.5	67	68	Pierce, WA	3.9	25	69	Sacramento, CA	1 357
14	70	Clark, NV	2.4	8	70	Kings, NY	3.5	46	70	Honolulu, HI	1 348
26	71	Bronx, NY	2.3	10	70	Riverside, CA	3.5	70	71	El Paso, TX	1 318
40	72	Montgomery, MD	1.8	12	72	San Bernardino, CA	3.2	12	72	San Bernardino, CA	1 287
64	73	San Francisco, CA	1.3	68	72	Hidalgo, TX	3.2	48	73	Fresno, CA	1 131
37	74	Fairfax, VA	1.1	11	74	Queens, NY	2.7	63	74	Macomb, MI	1 112
20	75	New York, NY	0.9	26	75	Bronx, NY	1.6	68	75	Hidalgo, TX	1 071

75 Largest Counties by 2015 Population
Selected Rankings

	Violent crime rate, 2014				Military as a percent of all federal employment, 2014				Percent of votes for Barack Obama, 2012		
Population rank	Violent crime rate rank	County	Violent crime rate per 100,000 population [col 46]	Population rank	Military employment rank	County	Percent military federal employment [col 195/col 194+195]	Population rank	Vote for Obama rank	County	Percent of votes for Obama [col 197]
54	1	Shelby, TN	1 306	67	1	Pierce, WA	74.5	59	1	Prince George's, MD	88.9
52	2	Marion, IN	1 226	70	2	El Paso, TX	69.3	26	2	Bronx, NY	88.7
23	3	Philadelphia, PA	1 022	5	3	San Diego, CA	68.3	20	3	New York, NY	85.7
49	4	Milwaukee, WI	1 002	46	4	Honolulu, HI	64.1	64	4	San Francisco, CA	84.2
19	5	Wayne, MI	995	12	5	San Bernardino, CA	58.0	23	5	Philadelphia, PA	83.1
64	6	San Francisco, CA	802	14	6	Clark, NV	56.0	8	6	Kings, NY	79.4
43	7	Fulton, GA	791	57	7	Collin, TX	55.6	21	7	Alameda, CA	78.8
14	8	Clark, NV	743	61	8	Gwinnett, GA	52.2	2	8	Cook, IL	76.2
3	9	Harris, TX	718	17	9	Bexar, TX	49.2	75	9	Essex, NJ	76.0
58	10	Duval, FL	687	58	10	Duval, FL	47.3	11	10	Queens, NY	75.1
30	11	Orange, FL	682	72	11	Montgomery, PA	47.2	19	11	Wayne, MI	74.1
75	12	Essex, NJ	648	69	12	Middlesex, NJ	45.5	40	12	Montgomery, MD	71.6
21	13	Alameda, CA	645	53	13	Bergen, NJ	42.3	13	13	King, WA	70.3
7	14	Miami-Dade, FL	633	66	14	Ventura, CA	42.2	46	14	Honolulu, HI	69.8
20	15	New York, NY	598	73	15	Worcester, MA	40.5	16	15	Santa Clara, CA	69.4
8	15	Kings, NY	598	51	16	Fairfield, CT	40.4	1	16	Los Angeles, CA	69.2
11	15	Queens, NY	598	44	17	Pima, AZ	40.3	68	17	Hidalgo, TX	69.0
26	15	Bronx, NY	598	4	18	Maricopa, AZ	39.5	31	18	Cuyahoga, OH	68.9
31	19	Cuyahoga, OH	561	45	19	St. Louis, MO	37.5	38	19	Contra Costa, CA	68.0
2	20	Cook, IL	558	8	20	Kings, NY	37.1	49	20	Milwaukee, WI	67.3
41	21	Mecklenburg, NC	522	42	21	Wake, NC	36.6	43	21	Fulton, GA	67.2
62	22	Kern, CA	510	29	22	Hillsborough, FL	36.4	18	22	Broward, FL	67.1
50	23	Pinellas, FL	506	10	23	Riverside, CA	36.2	70	23	El Paso, TX	65.9
25	24	Sacramento, CA	503	18	23	Broward, FL	36.2	60	24	Hartford, CT	65.2
48	25	Fresno, CA	471	26	25	Bronx, NY	35.6	22	25	Middlesex, MA	64.2
59	26	Prince George's, MD	460	28	26	Nassau, NY	33.3	36	26	Travis, TX	63.9
74	27	Hamilton, OH	457	6	27	Orange, FL	32.7	52	27	Marion, IN	63.8
17	28	Bexar, TX	454	33	28	Oakland, MI	32.3	35	28	Hennepin, MN	63.4
27	29	Palm Beach, FL	452	39	29	Salt Lake, UT	32.0	47	28	Westchester, NY	63.4
71	30	Baltimore, MD	448	41	30	Mecklenburg, NC	31.7	54	28	Shelby, TN	63.4
9	31	Dallas, TX	443	68	31	Hidalgo, TX	31.0	41	31	Mecklenburg, NC	61.8
44	31	Pima, AZ	443	22	32	Middlesex, MA	30.6	27	32	Palm Beach, FL	61.2
56	33	Erie, NY	441	21	33	Alameda, CA	29.7	65	33	New Haven, CT	61.0
67	34	Pierce, WA	432	27	34	Palm Beach, FL	29.4	69	34	Middlesex, NJ	60.4
73	35	Worcester, MA	431	50	35	Pinellas, FL	29.2	37	35	Fairfax, VA	60.1
35	36	Hennepin, MN	427	3	36	Harris, TX	28.9	72	36	Montgomery, PA	60.0
1	37	Los Angeles, CA	422	62	37	Kern, CA	28.6	32	37	Franklin, OH	59.7
32	37	Franklin, OH	422	38	38	Contra Costa, CA	28.1	45	38	St. Louis, MO	59.5
18	39	Broward, FL	409	55	39	DuPage, IL	27.8	30	39	Orange, FL	59.0
34	40	Allegheny, PA	401	1	40	Los Angeles, CA	27.3	51	40	Fairfield, CT	58.6
15	41	Tarrant, TX	400	7	41	Miami-Dade, FL	27.2	14	41	Clark, NV	58.5
12	42	San Bernardino, CA	392	35	42	Hennepin, MN	27.1	25	41	Sacramento, CA	58.5
4	43	Maricopa, AZ	383	15	43	Tarrant, TX	27.0	56	43	Erie, NY	58.0
70	44	El Paso, TX	364	65	44	New Haven, CT	26.5	7	44	Miami-Dade, FL	57.9
36	45	Travis, TX	355	25	45	Sacramento, CA	25.6	9	45	Dallas, TX	57.3
39	46	Salt Lake, UT	350	47	45	Westchester, NY	25.6	34	45	Allegheny, PA	57.3
13	47	King, WA	334	13	47	King, WA	25.5	42	47	Wake, NC	56.7
65	48	New Haven, CT	333	16	48	Santa Clara, CA	25.0	33	48	Oakland, MI	56.5
38	49	Contra Costa, CA	329	60	49	Hartford, CT	24.7	71	49	Baltimore, MD	56.2
68	49	Hidalgo, TX	329	49	50	Milwaukee, WI	23.8	73	50	Worcester, MA	55.8
5	51	San Diego, CA	325	59	51	Prince George's, MD	22.5	66	51	Ventura, CA	55.2
29	51	Hillsborough, FL	325	2	52	Cook, IL	22.3	67	51	Pierce, WA	55.2
45	53	St. Louis, MO	307	34	53	Allegheny, PA	22.2	55	53	DuPage, IL	54.7
63	54	Macomb, MI	288	32	54	Franklin, OH	22.1	53	54	Bergen, NJ	54.3
60	55	Hartford, CT	276	54	55	Shelby, TN	21.9	5	55	San Diego, CA	54.1
10	56	Riverside, CA	269	11	56	Queens, NY	21.3	28	56	Nassau, NY	53.8
16	57	Santa Clara, CA	247	30	57	Orange, FL	19.8	50	57	Pinellas, FL	53.6
51	58	Fairfield, CT	246	74	57	Hamilton, OH	19.8	63	58	Macomb, MI	53.4
47	59	Westchester, NY	226	19	59	Wayne, MI	19.6	29	59	Hillsborough, FL	53.2
66	60	Ventura, CA	223	36	60	Travis, TX	19.2	74	60	Hamilton, OH	53.0
6	61	Orange, CA	198	9	61	Dallas, TX	18.9	24	61	Suffolk, NY	52.6
61	62	Gwinnett, GA	195	24	61	Suffolk, NY	18.9	17	62	Bexar, TX	52.4
22	63	Middlesex, MA	190	31	63	Cuyahoga, OH	18.6	44	62	Pima, AZ	52.4
33	64	Oakland, MI	174	63	63	Macomb, MI	18.6	12	64	San Bernardino, CA	52.1
40	65	Montgomery, MD	169	52	65	Marion, IN	18.1	3	65	Harris, TX	50.4
57	66	Collin, TX	159	37	66	Fairfax, VA	17.9	10	66	Riverside, CA	50.2
69	67	Middlesex, NJ	155	56	67	Erie, NY	17.4	48	66	Fresno, CA	50.2
28	68	Nassau, NY	153	75	68	Essex, NJ	15.4	39	68	Salt Lake, UT	48.7
72	69	Montgomery, PA	148	23	69	Philadelphia, PA	14.8	58	68	Duval, FL	48.7
42	70	Wake, NC	126	40	70	Montgomery, MD	14.6	6	70	Orange, CA	47.6
24	71	Suffolk, NY	122	71	71	Baltimore, MD	14.4	61	71	Gwinnett, GA	44.5
37	72	Fairfax, VA	91	48	72	Fresno, CA	14.1	4	72	Maricopa, AZ	44.1
55	73	DuPage, IL	83	20	73	New York, NY	10.9	15	73	Tarrant, TX	43.7
53	74	Bergen, NJ	81	43	74	Fulton, GA	10.6	62	74	Kern, CA	40.1
46	75	Honolulu, HI	72	64	75	San Francisco, CA	10.2	57	75	Collin, TX	36.8

75 Largest Counties by 2015 Population
Selected Rankings

	Nonemployer businesses, 2014			Value of residential construction authorized by building permits, 2015				Full-time equivalent government employees, 2012			
Population rank	Nonemployer Businesses rank	County	Nonemployer businesses [col 167]	Population rank	Value ($1,000) rank	County	Value ($1,000) [col 169]	Population rank	Government Employment rank	County	Government employees [col 172]
1	1	Los Angeles, CA	991 091	4	1	Maricopa, AZ	5 171 419	20	1	New York, NY	411 393
2	2	Cook, IL	464 097	1	2	Los Angeles, CA	5 120 116	8	1	Kings, NY (included in New York, NY)	NA
7	3	Miami-Dade, FL	435 368	3	3	Harris, TX	4 793 594	11	1	Queens, NY (included in New York, NY)	NA
3	4	Harris, TX	387 455	13	4	King, WA	3 766 558	26	1	Bronx, NY (included in New York, NY)	NA
6	5	Orange, CA	291 516	8	5	Kings, NY	3 219 703	1	5	Los Angeles, CA	386 456
4	6	Maricopa, AZ	288 019	57	6	Collin, TX	2 875 678	2	6	Cook, IL	198 590
8	7	Kings, NY	260 250	9	7	Dallas, TX	2 830 893	3	7	Harris, TX	166 045
5	8	San Diego, CA	258 892	29	8	Hillsborough, FL	2 432 798	4	8	Maricopa, AZ	129 919
11	9	Queens, NY	240 308	7	9	Miami-Dade, FL	2 331 082	9	9	Dallas, TX	105 099
18	10	Broward, FL	239 667	6	10	Orange, CA	2 227 919	7	10	Miami-Dade, FL	102 308
20	11	New York, NY	225 724	36	11	Travis, TX	2 102 535	5	11	San Diego, CA	97 178
9	12	Dallas, TX	221 267	5	12	San Diego, CA	2 100 214	6	12	Orange, CA	85 251
27	13	Palm Beach, FL	162 115	15	13	Tarrant, TX	1 963 388	17	13	Bexar, TX	76 821
13	14	King, WA	159 920	42	14	Wake, NC	1 764 682	15	14	Tarrant, TX	76 274
15	15	Tarrant, TX	158 872	43	15	Fulton, GA	1 687 542	18	15	Broward, FL	73 864
10	16	Riverside, CA	158 405	2	16	Cook, IL	1 650 541	10	16	Riverside, CA	68 997
14	17	Clark, NV	148 576	11	17	Queens, NY	1 586 010	12	17	San Bernardino, CA	68 989
12	18	San Bernardino, CA	139 403	20	18	New York, NY	1 503 732	13	18	King, WA	65 821
28	19	Nassau, NY	135 574	14	19	Clark, NV	1 407 544	24	19	Suffolk, NY	63 444
16	20	Santa Clara, CA	135 043	27	20	Palm Beach, FL	1 359 567	31	20	Cuyahoga, OH	62 490
21	21	Alameda, CA	132 693	10	21	Riverside, CA	1 348 829	23	21	Philadelphia, PA	60 937
22	22	Middlesex, MA	131 892	41	22	Mecklenburg, NC	1 345 474	41	22	Mecklenburg, NC	60 489
17	23	Bexar, TX	127 915	30	23	Orange, FL	1 324 172	28	23	Nassau, NY	60 368
19	24	Wayne, MI	126 525	16	24	Santa Clara, CA	1 322 181	16	24	Santa Clara, CA	59 919
24	25	Suffolk, NY	126 453	21	25	Alameda, CA	1 186 660	21	25	Alameda, CA	56 184
30	26	Orange, FL	117 912	39	26	Salt Lake, UT	1 153 510	19	26	Wayne, MI	52 078
26	27	Bronx, NY	116 145	35	27	Hennepin, MN	1 139 582	14	27	Clark, NV	51 796
33	28	Oakland, MI	111 980	64	28	San Francisco, CA	1 041 273	22	28	Middlesex, MA	51 015
29	29	Hillsborough, FL	111 522	22	29	Middlesex, MA	935 385	25	29	Sacramento, CA	50 509
36	30	Travis, TX	110 302	46	30	Honolulu, HI	914 918	27	30	Palm Beach, FL	46 198
40	31	Montgomery, MD	108 358	32	31	Franklin, OH	843 224	29	31	Hillsborough, FL	45 811
43	32	Fulton, GA	103 193	17	32	Bexar, TX	808 959	30	32	Orange, FL	45 111
37	33	Fairfax, VA	102 475	18	33	Broward, FL	807 553	36	33	Travis, TX	45 034
35	34	Hennepin, MN	101 629	12	34	San Bernardino, CA	801 801	34	34	Allegheny, PA	43 945
25	35	Sacramento, CA	98 805	58	35	Duval, FL	781 026	32	35	Franklin, OH	43 936
61	36	Gwinnett, GA	95 618	38	36	Contra Costa, CA	743 452	43	36	Fulton, GA	43 801
64	37	San Francisco, CA	95 601	67	37	Pierce, WA	731 311	37	37	Fairfax, VA	43 275
47	38	Westchester, NY	94 864	51	38	Fairfield, CT	726 201	47	38	Westchester, NY	42 755
32	39	Franklin, OH	91 486	25	39	Sacramento, CA	711 956	54	39	Shelby, TN	39 378
51	40	Fairfield, CT	90 880	23	40	Philadelphia, PA	690 914	68	40	Hidalgo, TX	39 042
31	41	Cuyahoga, OH	90 292	24	41	Suffolk, NY	690 849	64	41	San Francisco, CA	38 712
53	42	Bergen, NJ	89 950	33	42	Oakland, MI	685 279	40	42	Montgomery, MD	38 590
41	43	Mecklenburg, NC	87 844	44	43	Pima, AZ	659 557	70	43	El Paso, TX	38 262
38	44	Contra Costa, CA	87 297	50	44	Pinellas, FL	642 613	35	44	Hennepin, MN	35 312
23	45	Philadelphia, PA	84 805	68	45	Hidalgo, TX	620 741	56	45	Erie, NY	35 259
57	46	Collin, TX	81 518	70	46	El Paso, TX	603 056	45	46	St. Louis, MO	35 141
55	47	DuPage, IL	80 582	48	47	Fresno, CA	581 775	48	47	Fresno, CA	34 954
42	48	Wake, NC	80 548	45	48	St. Louis, MO	576 373	55	48	Du Page, IL	34 627
50	49	Pinellas, FL	79 799	26	49	Bronx, NY	570 944	39	49	Salt Lake, UT	34 230
39	50	Salt Lake, UT	79 310	52	50	Marion, IN	558 371	52	50	Marion, IN	34 223
54	51	Shelby, TN	79 157	34	51	Allegheny, PA	533 473	49	51	Milwaukee, WI	34 086
34	52	Allegheny, PA	77 932	61	52	Gwinnett, GA	522 550	53	52	Bergen, NJ	32 531
59	53	Prince George's, MD	73 755	55	53	DuPage, IL	521 472	62	53	Kern, CA	32 191
45	54	St. Louis, MO	72 816	53	54	Bergen, NJ	486 319	50	54	Pinellas, FL	32 162
68	55	Hidalgo, TX	68 931	62	55	Kern, CA	473 930	33	55	Oakland, MI	32 137
72	56	Montgomery, PA	68 190	40	56	Montgomery, MD	445 838	51	56	Fairfield, CT	32 029
66	57	Ventura, CA	66 566	63	57	Macomb, MI	412 595	60	57	Hartford, CT	31 675
58	58	Duval, FL	65 791	28	58	Nassau, NY	393 115	44	58	Pima, AZ	31 634
71	59	Baltimore, MD	64 480	69	59	Middlesex, NJ	387 679	42	59	Wake, NC	31 235
75	60	Essex, NJ	63 431	19	60	Wayne, MI	353 058	38	60	Contra Costa, CA	31 030
44	61	Pima, AZ	63 004	66	61	Ventura, CA	350 485	74	61	Hamilton, OH	30 330
46	62	Honolulu, HI	62 867	59	62	Prince George's, MD	347 065	65	62	New Haven, CT	28 448
63	63	Macomb, MI	61 384	54	63	Shelby, TN	322 598	57	63	Collin, TX	28 433
52	64	Marion, IN	61 137	37	64	Fairfax, VA	292 418	73	64	Worcester, MA	28 380
65	65	New Haven, CT	58 579	56	65	Erie, NY	285 488	75	65	Essex, NJ	27 848
60	66	Hartford, CT	57 906	75	66	Essex, NJ	281 585	61	66	Gwinnett, GA	27 778
74	67	Hamilton, OH	56 359	47	67	Westchester, NY	269 569	66	67	Ventura, CA	27 714
70	68	El Paso, TX	55 159	72	68	Montgomery, PA	257 643	59	68	Prince George's, MD	27 062
69	69	Middlesex, NJ	53 731	73	69	Worcester, MA	250 894	58	69	Duval, FL	26 681
73	70	Worcester, MA	50 732	71	70	Baltimore, MD	221 603	69	70	Middlesex, NJ	26 592
48	71	Fresno, CA	50 231	31	71	Cuyahoga, OH	203 527	71	71	Baltimore, MD	26 532
49	72	Milwaukee, WI	47 239	74	72	Hamilton, OH	186 896	67	72	Pierce, WA	23 934
56	73	Erie, NY	46 740	49	73	Milwaukee, WI	184 362	72	73	Montgomery, PA	23 690
62	74	Kern, CA	44 623	65	74	New Haven, CT	146 364	63	74	Macomb, MI	20 477
67	75	Pierce, WA	40 709	60	75	Hartford, CT	129 546	46	75	Honolulu, HI	9 304

75 Countries with Highest Agricultural Sales
Selected Rankings

Value of agricultural sales, 2012			Average agricultural sales per farm, 2012				Number of farms, 2012			
Value of sales rank	County	Value of sales (millions of dollars) [col 125]	Value of sales rank	Average sales rank	County	Average sales per farm (dollars) [col 126]	Value of sales rank	Number of farms rank	County	Number of farms [col 113]
1	Fresno, CA	4 973	28	1	Haskell, KS	5 400 412	50	1	San Diego, CA	5 732
2	Tulare, CA	4 017	22	2	Hartley, TX	4 630 969	1	2	Fresno, CA	5 683
3	Kern, CA	3 999	8	3	Imperial, CA	4 486 078	15	3	Lancaster, PA	5 657
4	Monterey, CA	2 980	32	4	Scott, KS	3 642 543	2	4	Tulare, CA	4 931
5	Merced, CA	2 968	46	5	Hansford, TX	2 977 973	7	5	Stanislaus, CA	4 143
6	San Joaquin, CA	2 250	40	6	Grant, KS	2 790 860	6	6	San Joaquin, CA	3 580
7	Stanislaus, CA	2 228	4	7	Monterey, CA	2 527 341	33	7	Sonoma, CA	3 579
8	Imperial, CA	1 889	19	8	Castro, TX	2 466 429	9	8	Weld, CO	3 525
9	Weld, CO	1 861	62	9	Wichita, KS	2 357 736	45	9	Stearns, MN	3 501
10	Kings, CA	1 829	18	10	Parmer, TX	2 332 523	12	10	Yakima, WA	3 143
11	Grant, WA	1 762	66	11	Moore, TX	2 318 107	67	11	Miami-Dade, FL	2 954
12	Yakima, WA	1 646	36	12	Gray, KS	2 247 407	26	12	Riverside, CA	2 949
13	Sioux, IA	1 613	17	13	Deaf Smith, TX	2 220 734	53	13	San Luis Obispo, CA	2 666
14	Madera, CA	1 603	3	14	Kern, CA	2 063 462	71	14	Marion, OR	2 567
15	Lancaster, PA	1 475	72	15	Sherman, TX	1 886 121	5	15	Merced, CA	2 486
16	Ventura, CA	1 440	49	16	Phelps, NE	1 824 185	29	16	Maricopa, AZ	2 479
17	Deaf Smith, TX	1 379	41	17	Finney, KS	1 822 062	16	17	Ventura, CA	2 150
18	Parmer, TX	1 330	58	18	Dallam, TX	1 756 642	3	18	Kern, CA	1 938
19	Castro, TX	1 312	31	19	Yuma, AZ	1 752 685	55	19	Rockingham, VA	1 902
20	Duplin, NC	1 276	10	20	Kings, CA	1 732 231	54	20	Chester, PA	1 730
21	Sampson, NC	1 259	35	21	Gooding, ID	1 581 904	13	21	Sioux, IA	1 618
22	Hartley, TX	1 181	34	22	Cassia, ID	1 427 737	23	22	Santa Barbara, CA	1 597
23	Santa Barbara, CA	1 178	24	23	Yuma, CO	1 379 309	11	23	Grant, WA	1 552
24	Yuma, CO	1 150	20	24	Duplin, NC	1 357 895	38	24	Benton, WA	1 509
25	Cuming, NE	1 081	5	25	Merced, CA	1 193 694	14	25	Madera, CA	1 507
26	Riverside, CA	1 039	21	26	Sampson, NC	1 179 750	30	26	Palm Beach, FL	1 409
27	Texas, OK	1 014	25	27	Cuming, NE	1 177 889	75	27	Allegan, MI	1 396
28	Haskell, KS	1 010	11	28	Grant, WA	1 135 499	42	28	Custer, NE	1 352
29	Maricopa, AZ	1 004	64	29	Jerome, ID	1 101 943	51	29	Kossuth, IA	1 349
30	Palm Beach, FL	999	14	30	Madera, CA	1 063 547	59	30	Plymouth, IA	1 331
31	Yuma, AZ	985	73	31	Swisher, TX	1 038 602	70	31	Polk, MN	1 322
32	Scott, KS	980	44	32	Dawson, NE	1 025 163	60	32	Glenn, CA	1 311
33	Sonoma, CA	974	13	33	Sioux, IA	996 964	68	33	Twin Falls, ID	1 294
34	Cassia, ID	954	27	34	Texas, OK	990 157	61	34	Holt, NE	1 279
35	Gooding, ID	943	37	35	Pinal, AZ	989 059	74	35	San Bernardino, CA	1 249
36	Gray, KS	939	1	36	Fresno, CA	875 073	69	36	Sussex, DE	1 214
37	Pinal, AZ	928	48	37	Franklin, WA	838 068	56	37	Mercer, OH	1 208
38	Benton, WA	923	65	38	Morgan, CO	816 073	47	38	Huron, MI	1 205
39	Sussex, DE	921	2	39	Tulare, CA	814 657	20	39	Monterey, CA	1 179
40	Grant, KS	918	39	40	Sussex, DE	758 755	43	40	Lincoln, NE	1 168
41	Finney, KS	909	23	41	Santa Barbara, CA	737 581	21	41	Lyon, IA	1 139
42	Custer, NE	845	43	42	Lyon, IA	734 068	21	42	Sampson, NC	1 067
43	Lyon, IA	836	30	43	Palm Beach, FL	709 041	52	43	Renville, MN	1 061
44	Dawson, NE	826	57	44	Platte, NE	692 256	10	44	Kings, CA	1 056
45	Stearns, MN	808	63	45	Martin, MN	690 708	27	45	Texas, OK	1 024
46	Hansford, TX	783	47	46	Lincoln, NE	670 087	57	46	Platte, NE	942
47	Lincoln, NE	783	16	47	Ventura, CA	669 829	20	47	Duplin, NC	940
48	Franklin, WA	740	52	48	Renville, MN	669 506	37	48	Pinal, AZ	938
49	Phelps, NE	739	6	49	San Joaquin, CA	628 536	25	49	Cuming, NE	918
50	San Diego, CA	726	42	50	Custer, NE	625 226	63	50	Martin, MN	897
51	Kossuth, IA	722	38	51	Benton, WA	611 771	48	51	Franklin, WA	883
52	Renville, MN	710	56	52	Huron, MI	543 207	24	52	Yuma, CO	834
53	San Luis Obispo, CA	665	7	53	Stanislaus, CA	537 807	44	53	Dawson, NE	806
54	Chester, PA	661	51	54	Kossuth, IA	535 440	65	54	Morgan, CO	754
55	Rockingham, VA	659	9	55	Weld, CO	527 863	34	55	Cassia, ID	668
56	Huron, MI	655	12	56	Yakima, WA	523 548	17	56	Deaf Smith, TX	621
57	Platte, NE	652	61	57	Holt, NE	497 540	35	57	Gooding, ID	596
58	Dallam, TX	652	69	58	Mercer, OH	493 681	18	58	Parmer, TX	570
59	Plymouth, IA	643	60	59	Glenn, CA	486 166	73	59	Swisher, TX	565
60	Glenn, CA	637	59	60	Plymouth, IA	483 173	31	60	Yuma, AZ	562
61	Holt, NE	636	74	61	San Bernardino, CA	466 156	64	61	Jerome, ID	560
62	Wichita, KS	625	68	62	Twin Falls, ID	463 355	19	62	Castro, TX	532
63	Martin, MN	620	70	63	Polk, MN	449 722	41	63	Finney, KS	499
64	Jerome, ID	617	75	64	Allegan, MI	416 071	8	64	Imperial, CA	421
65	Morgan, CO	615	29	65	Maricopa, AZ	404 790	36	65	Gray, KS	418
66	Moore, TX	605	54	66	Chester, PA	381 933	49	66	Phelps, NE	405
67	Miami-Dade, FL	604	26	67	Riverside, CA	352 306	58	67	Dallam, TX	371
68	Twin Falls, ID	600	55	68	Rockingham, VA	346 475	40	68	Grant, KS	329
69	Mercer, OH	596	33	69	Sonoma, CA	272 253	72	69	Sherman, TX	313
70	Polk, MN	594	15	70	Lancaster, PA	260 731	32	70	Scott, KS	269
71	Marion, OR	593	53	71	San Luis Obispo, CA	249 431	62	71	Wichita, KS	265
72	Sherman, TX	590	71	72	Marion, OR	230 953	46	72	Hansford, TX	263
73	Swisher, TX	587	45	73	Stearns, MN	230 933	66	73	Moore, TX	261
74	San Bernardino, CA	582	67	74	Miami-Dade, FL	204 549	22	74	Hartley, TX	255
75	Allegan, MI	581	50	75	San Diego, CA	126 657	28	75	Haskell, KS	187

75 Countries with Highest Agricultural Sales
Selected Rankings

Average size of farm, 2012				Average value of land and buildings per farm, 2012				Average value of land and buildings per acre, 2012			
Value of sales rank	Size of farm rank	County	Average size of farm (acres) [col 119]	Value of sales rank	Value of land and buildings per farm rank	County	Average value per farm (dollars) [col 122]	Value of sales rank	Value of land and buildings per acre rank	County	Average value per acre (dollars) [col 123]
22	1	Hartley, TX	3 541	8	1	Imperial	8 577 865	67	1	Miami-Dade, FL	25 423
58	2	Dallam, TX	2 296	3	2	Kern, CA	5 332 548	50	2	San Diego, CA	17 964
46	3	Hansford, TX	2 155	4	3	Monterey	5 263 068	16	3	Ventura, CA	15 621
66	4	Moore, TX	2 006	10	4	Kings	3 847 243	33	4	Sonoma	14 620
28	5	Haskell, KS	1 944	49	5	Phelps	3 684 978	74	5	San Bernardino, CA	13 455
72	6	Sherman, TX	1 863	22	6	Hartley	3 557 855	54	6	Chester	13 070
62	7	Wichita, KS	1 750	52	7	Renville	3 547 517	15	7	Lancaster	12 529
32	8	Scott, KS	1 686	51	8	Kossuth	3 380 844	26	8	Riverside, CA	10 212
41	9	Finney, KS	1 635	14	9	Madera	3 302 033	6	9	San Joaquin	10 090
24	10	Yuma, CO	1 623	23	10	Santa Barbara	3 233 061	7	10	Stanislaus	9 636
17	11	Deaf Smith, TX	1 487	5	11	Merced	3 045 778	13	11	Sioux	9 105
36	12	Gray, KS	1 309	59	12	Plymouth	2 992 740	1	12	Fresno, CA	8 286
27	13	Texas, OK	1 257	37	13	Pinal	2 979 541	43	13	Lyon	8 245
37	14	Pinal, AZ	1 252	63	14	Martin	2 931 235	71	14	Marion	7 942
8	15	Imperial, CA	1 225	31	15	Yuma	2 758 098	69	15	Mercer	7 854
47	16	Lincoln, NE	1 219	13	16	Sioux	2 726 452	39	16	Sussex	7 853
3	17	Kern, CA	1 202	43	17	Lyon	2 677 244	5	17	Merced	7 737
42	18	Custer, NE	1 112	28	18	Haskell	2 676 770	14	18	Madera	7 614
61	19	Holt, NE	1 106	30	19	Palm Beach, FL	2 586 187	51	19	Kossuth	7 608
40	20	Grant, KS	1 105	32	20	Scott	2 556 929	2	20	Tulare	7 535
4	21	Monterey, CA	1 076	1	21	Fresno, CA	2 509 484	23	21	Santa Barbara	7 365
19	22	Castro, TX	1 030	44	22	Dawson	2 429 274	59	22	Plymouth	7 352
18	23	Parmer, TX	971	33	23	Sonoma	2 409 158	31	23	Yuma	7 220
73	24	Swisher, TX	966	70	24	Polk	2 403 190	30	24	Palm Beach, FL	7 090
34	25	Cassia, ID	915	62	25	Wichita	2 375 008	55	25	Rockingham	7 055
65	26	Morgan, CO	858	41	26	Finney	2 353 291	8	26	Imperial	7 002
70	27	Polk, MN	828	60	27	Glenn	2 342 959	63	27	Martin	6 134
49	28	Phelps, NE	818	61	28	Holt	2 314 973	52	28	Renville	6 055
44	29	Dawson, NE	782	57	29	Platte	2 302 510	10	29	Kings	6 031
48	30	Franklin, WA	708	24	30	Yuma	2 223 818	29	30	Maricopa, AZ	5 663
10	31	Kings, CA	638	6	31	San Joaquin	2 218 140	25	31	Cuming	5 364
11	32	Grant, WA	621	58	32	Dallam	2 164 833	56	32	Huron	5 202
52	33	Renville, MN	586	34	33	Cassia	2 143 115	57	33	Platte	5 088
12	34	Yakima, WA	566	11	34	Grant	2 128 600	4	34	Monterey	4 893
9	35	Weld, CO	555	25	35	Cuming	2 120 511	75	35	Allegan	4 790
60	36	Glenn, CA	510	53	36	San Luis Obispo	2 115 410	60	36	Glenn	4 593
53	37	San Luis Obispo, CA	502	42	37	Custer	2 110 533	49	37	Phelps	4 504
63	38	Martin, MN	478	48	38	Franklin	2 071 813	3	38	Kern, CA	4 435
38	39	Benton, WA	466	16	39	Ventura, CA	2 041 990	53	39	San Luis Obispo	4 212
57	40	Platte, NE	453	72	40	Sherman	2 006 652	20	40	Duplin	4 076
51	41	Kossuth, IA	444	46	41	Hansford	1 994 289	21	41	Sampson	3 975
23	42	Santa Barbara, CA	439	56	42	Huron	1 952 800	45	42	Stearns	3 901
14	43	Madera, CA	434	2	43	Tulare	1 893 271	64	43	Jerome	3 840
59	44	Plymouth, IA	407	66	44	Moore	1 884 521	35	44	Gooding	3 830
35	45	Gooding, ID	402	7	45	Stanislaus	1 786 289	11	45	Grant	3 428
25	46	Cuming, NE	395	69	46	Mercer	1 775 939	44	46	Dawson	3 106
5	47	Merced, CA	394	39	47	Sussex	1 761 092	68	47	Twin Falls	3 090
31	48	Yuma, AZ	382	47	48	Lincoln	1 749 910	48	48	Franklin	2 927
56	49	Huron, MI	375	36	49	Gray	1 747 136	70	49	Polk	2 902
68	50	Twin Falls, ID	374	35	50	Gooding	1 539 908	38	50	Benton	2 738
30	51	Palm Beach, FL	365	40	51	Grant	1 471 553	37	51	Pinal	2 379
64	52	Jerome, ID	336	17	52	Deaf Smith	1 470 176	34	52	Cassia	2 343
43	53	Lyon, IA	325	64	53	Jerome	1 289 525	61	53	Holt	2 093
1	54	Fresno, CA	303	38	54	Benton	1 276 306	9	54	Weld	1 979
13	55	Sioux, IA	299	54	55	Chester	1 242 743	42	55	Custer	1 898
21	56	Sampson, NC	273	65	56	Morgan	1 224 219	12	56	Yakima	1 803
2	57	Tulare, CA	251	26	57	Riverside, CA	1 191 416	32	57	Scott	1 517
20	58	Duplin, NC	246	68	58	Twin Falls	1 155 801	41	58	Finney	1 439
69	59	Mercer, OH	226	19	59	Castro	1 131 530	47	59	Lincoln	1 436
39	60	Sussex, DE	224	9	60	Weld	1 098 289	65	60	Morgan	1 426
6	61	San Joaquin, CA	220	29	61	Maricopa, AZ	1 087 145	28	61	Haskell	1 377
45	62	Stearns, MN	216	21	62	Sampson	1 086 479	24	62	Yuma	1 370
75	63	Allegan, MI	194	12	63	Yakima	1 021 212	62	63	Wichita	1 357
29	64	Maricopa, AZ	192	18	64	Parmer	1 010 667	36	64	Gray	1 335
7	65	Stanislaus, CA	185	27	65	Texas	1 005 370	40	65	Grant	1 332
33	66	Sonoma, CA	165	20	66	Duplin	1 001 313	19	66	Castro	1 098
16	67	Ventura, CA	131	15	67	Lancaster	973 388	72	67	Sherman	1 077
26	68	Riverside, CA	117	75	68	Allegan	927 485	18	68	Parmer	1 040
55	68	Rockingham, VA	117	73	69	Swisher	888 986	22	69	Hartley	1 005
71	70	Marion, OR	111	71	70	Marion	885 406	17	70	Deaf Smith	989
54	71	Chester, PA	95	45	71	Stearns	844 095	58	71	Dallam	943
15	72	Lancaster, PA	78	74	72	San Bernardino, CA	831 612	66	72	Moore	939
74	73	San Bernardino, CA	62	55	73	Rockingham	823 606	46	73	Hansford	925
50	74	San Diego, CA	39	67	74	Miami-Dade, FL	699 727	73	74	Swisher	921
67	75	Miami-Dade, FL	28	50	75	San Diego, CA	694 313	27	75	Texas	800

Table B. States and Counties — **Land Area and Population**

STATE/County code	CBSA code[1]	County type[2]	STATE County	Land area,[3] (sq km) 2010	Population, 2015			Population and population characteristics, 2014										
								Race alone or in combination, not Hispanic or Latino (percent)					Age (percent)					
					Total persons 2015	Rank	Per square kilometer	White	Black	American Indian, Alaska Native	Asian and Pacific Islander	Percent Hispanic or Latino[4]	Under 5 years	5 to 17 years	18 to 24 years	25 to 34 years	35 to 44 years	45 to 54 years
				1	2	3	4	5	6	7	8	9	10	11	12	13	14	15

1. CBSA = Core Based Statistical Area. See Appendix A for explanation. See Appendix B for list of metropolitan areas with component counties. 2. County type code from the Economic Research Service of USDA Rural-Urban Continuum Codes. See Appendix A for definition. 3. Dry land or land partially or temporarily covered by water. 4. May be of any race.

Table B. States and Counties — **Population and Households**

STATE County	Population, 2014 (cont.)				Population change and components of change, 2000–2015							Households, 2010–2014				
	Age (percent) (cont.)				Total persons		Percent change		Components of change, 2010–2015					Percent		
	55 to 64 years	65 to 74 years	75 years and over	Percent female	2000	2010	2000–2010	2010–2015	Births	Deaths	Net migration	Number	Persons per house-hold	Family house-holds	Female family house-holder[1]	One per-son
	16	17	18	19	20	21	22	23	24	25	26	27	28	29	30	31

1. No spouse present.

Table B. States and Counties — **Population, Vital Statistics, Medicare, and Crime**

STATE County	Daytime population, 2010–2014			Births, 2015		Deaths, 2015		Persons under 65 with no health insurance, 2014		Medicare, 2015			Serious crimes known to police,[2] 2014	
													Total	
	Persons in group quarters, 2015	Number	Employ-ment/resi-dence ratio	Total	Rate[1]	Number	Rate[1]	Number	Percent	Total Beneficiaries	Enrolled in Original Medicare	Enrolled in Medicare Advantage	Number	Rate[3]
	32	33	34	35	36	37	38	39	40	41	42	43	44	45

1. Per 1,000 estimated resident population. 2. Data for serious crimes have not been adjusted for underreporting; this may affect comparability between geographic areas and over time.
3. Per 100,000 population estimated by the FBI.

Table B. States and Counties — **Crime, Education, Money Income, and Poverty**

STATE County	Serious crimes known to police, 2014 (cont.)[1]		Education						Money income, 2010–2014				Income and poverty, 2014			
	Rate[2]		School enrollment and attainment, 2010–2014				Local government expenditures,[5] 2012–2013			Households				Percent below poverty level		
			Enrollment[3]		Attainment[4] (percent)											
	Violent	Property	Total	Per-cent private	High school grad-uate or less	Bach-elor's degree or more	Total current spending (mil dol)	Current spend-ing per student (dollars)	Per capita income[6] (dollars)	Median income (dollars)	Mean income (dollars)	Percent with income of $200,000 or more	Median house-hold income (dollars)	All per-sons	Children under 18 years	Children 5 to 17 years in families
	46	47	48	49	50	51	52	53	54	55	56	57	58	59	60	61

1. Data for serious crimes have not been adjusted for underreporting; this may affect comparability between geographic areas and over time. 2. Per 100,000 population estimated by the FBI.
3. All persons 3 years old and over enrolled in nursery school through college. 4. Persons 25 years old and over. 5. Elementary and secondary education expenditures.
6. Based on population estimated by the American Community Survey, 2010–2014.

Table B. States and Counties — **Personal Income**

STATE County	Personal income, 2014										Earnings, 2014		
	Total (mil dol)	Percent change, 2013–2014	Per capita[1]		Wages and salaries (mil dol)	Supplements to wages and salaries; employer contributions (mil dol)		Proprietors' income (mil dol)	Dividends, interest, and rent (mil dol)	Personal transfer receipts (mil dol)	Total (mil dol)	Contributions for government social insurance (mil dol)	
			Dollars	Rank		Pension and insurance	Government social insurance					From employee and self-employed	From employer
	62	63	64	65	66	67	68	69	70	71	72	73	74

1. Based on the resident population estimated as of July 1 of the year shown.

Table B. States and Counties — **Earnings, Social Security, and Housing**

STATE County	Earnings, 2014 (cont.)									Social Security beneficiaries, December 2014		Housing units, 2015	
	Percent by selected industries											Supplemental Security Income recipients, December 2014	
	Farm	Mining	Construction	Manufacturing	Information: professional, scientific, technical services	Retail trade	Finance, insurance, real estate and leasing	Health care and social assistance	Government	Number	Rate[1]		Total	Percent change, 2010–2014
	75	76	77	78	79	80	81	82	83	84	85	86	87	88

1. Per 1,000 resident population estimated as of July 1 of the year shown.

Table B. States and Counties — **Housing, Labor Force, and Employment**

STATE County	Housing units, 2010–2014								Civilian labor force, 2015				Civilian employment,[6] 2010–2014		
	Occupied units										Unemployment		Percent		
			Owner-occupied			Renter-occupied									
				Median owner cost as a percent of income											
	Total	Percent	Median value[1]	With a mortgage	Without a mortgage[2]	Median rent[3]	Median rent as a percent of income[2]	Sub-standard units[4] (percent)	Total	Percent change, 2014–2015	Total	Rate[5]	Total	Management, business, science and arts	Construction, production, and maintenance occupations
	89	90	91	92	93	94	95	96	97	98	99	100	101	102	103

1. Specified owner-occupied units. 2. A value of 10.0 represents 10 percent or less; a value of 50.0 represents 50 percent or more. 3. Specified renter-occupied units.
4. Overcrowded or lacking complete plumbing facilities. 5. Percent of civilian labor force. 6. Persons 16 years old and over.

Table B. States and Counties — **Nonfarm Employment and Agriculture**

STATE County	Private nonfarm establishments, employment and payroll, 2014								Agriculture, 2012			
	Number of establishments	Employment						Annual payroll	Farms			
		Total	Health care and social assistance	Manufacturing	Retail trade	Finance and insurance	Professional, scientific, and technical services	Total (mil dol)	Average per employee (dollars)	Number	Percent with:		Farm operators whose principal occupation is farming (percent)
											Fewer than 50 acres	500 acres or more	
	104	105	106	107	108	109	110	111	112	113	114	115	116

Table B. States and Counties — **Agriculture**

STATE County	Agriculture, 2012 (cont.)															
	Land in farms					Value of land and buildings (dollars)			Value of products sold					Percent of farms with sales of:		Government payments	
			Acres								Percent from:						
	Acreage (1,000)	Percent change, 2007–2012	Average size of farm	Total irrigated (1,000)	Total cropland (1,000)	Average per farm	Average per acre	Value of machinery and equipment, average per farm (dollars)	Total (mil dol)	Average per farm (dollars)	Crops	Live-stock and poultry products	$10,000 or more	$100,000 or more	Total ($1,000)	Percent of farms
	117	118	119	120	121	122	123	124	125	126	127	128	129	130	131	132

Table B. States and Counties — **Water Use, Wholesale Trade, Retail Trade, and Real Estate**

| STATE County | Water use, 2010 | | Wholesale trade,[1] 2012 | | | | Retail trade,[2] 2012 | | | | Real estate and rental and leasing,[2] 2012 | | | |
	Total water withdrawn (mil gal/day)	Gallons withdrawn per person per day	Number of establish-ments	Number of employees	Sales (mil dol)	Annual payroll (mil dol)	Number of establish-ments	Number of employees	Sales (mil dol)	Annual payroll (mil dol)	Number of establish-ments	Number of employees	Receipts (mil dol)	Annual payroll (mil dol)
	133	134	135	136	137	138	139	140	141	142	143	144	145	146

1. Merchant wholesalers, except manufacturers' sales branches and offices.   2. Employer establishments.

Table B. States and Counties — **Professional Services, Manufacturing, and Accommodation and Food Services**

| STATE County | Professional, scientific, and technical services, 2012 | | | | Manufacturing, 2012 | | | | Accommodation and food services, 2012 | | | |
	Number of establish-ments	Number of employees	Receipts (mil dol)	Annual payroll (mil dol)	Number of establish-ments	Number of employees	Receipts (mil dol)	Annual payroll (mil dol)	Number of establish-ments	Number of employees	Sales (mil dol)	Annual payroll (mil dol)
	147	148	149	150	151	152	153	154	155	156	157	158

Table B. States and Counties — **Health Care and Social Assistance, Other Services, Nonemployer Businesses, and Residential Construction**

| STATE County | Health care and social assistance, 2012 | | | | Other services, 2012 | | | | Nonemployer businesses, 2014 | | Value of residential construction authorized by building permits, 2015 | |
	Number of establish-ments	Number of employees	Receipts (mil dol)	Annual payroll (mil dol)	Number of establish-ments	Number of employees	Receipts (mil dol)	Annual payroll (mil dol)	Number	Receipts (mil dol)	New Construction ($1,000)	Number of housing units
	159	160	161	162	163	164	165	166	167	168	169	170

Table B. States and Counties — **Government Employment and Payroll, and Local Government Finances**

	Government employment and payroll, 2012									Local government finances, 2012				
												General revenue			
														Taxes	
STATE County															Per capita[1] (dollars)
	Full-time equivalent employees	March payroll (dollars)	Administration, judicial, and legal	Police and Corrections	Fire Protection	Highways and transportation	Health and Welfare	Natural resources and utilities	Education and libraries	Total (mil dol)	Inter-governmental (mil dol)	Total (mil dol)	Total	Property
					March payroll (percent of total)										
	171	172	173	174	175	176	177	178	179	180	181	182	183	184

1. Based on the resident population estimated as of July 1 of the year shown.

Table B. States and Counties — **Local Government Finances, Government Employment, and Voting**

	Local government finances, 2012 (cont.)									Government employment, 2014			Presidential election,[2] 2012		
	Direct general expenditure							Debt outstanding					Percent of vote cast:		
STATE County			Percent of total for:												
	Total (mil dol)	Per capita[1] (dollars)	Education	Health and hospitals	Police protection	Public welfare	Highways	Total (mil dol)	Per capita[1] (dollars)	Federal civilian	Federal military	State and local	Democratic	Republican	All other
	185	186	187	188	189	190	191	192	193	194	195	196	197	198	199

1. Based on the resident population estimated as of July 1 of the year shown.   2. © 2013 Election Data Services, Inc. All rights reserved.

Table B. States and Counties — Land Area and Population

STATE/ County code	CBSA code[1]	County type[2]	STATE County	Land area[3] (sq km) 2010	Total persons 2015	Rank	Per square kilometer	White	Black	American Indian, Alaska Native	Asian and Pacific Islander	Percent Hispanic or Latino[4]	Under 5 years	5 to 17 years	18 to 24 years	25 to 34 years	35 to 44 years	45 to 54 years
				1	2	3	4	5	6	7	8	9	10	11	12	13	14	15
00 000	...	X	UNITED STATES	9 147 593	321 418 820	X	35.1	63.8	13.3	1.3	6.4	17.4	6.2	16.8	9.9	13.6	12.7	13.6
01 000	...	X	ALABAMA...........................	131 171	4 858 979	X	37.0	67.5	27.1	1.2	1.7	4.1	6.1	16.8	9.9	12.9	12.5	13.5
01 001	33860	2	Autauga	1 540	55 347	913	35.9	77.2	19.3	1.0	1.6	2.7	6.0	19.2	9.0	12.2	13.8	14.5
01 003	19300	4	Baldwin	4 118	203 709	320	49.5	84.5	10.0	1.4	1.3	4.6	5.6	16.6	7.7	11.4	12.5	13.8
01 005	...	6	Barbour..............................	2 292	26 489	1 548	11.6	47.4	47.9	0.6	0.7	4.5	5.7	15.5	8.9	14.3	12.5	13.8
01 007	13820	1	Bibb...................................	1 612	22 583	1 705	14.0	75.1	22.3	0.8	0.4	2.1	5.3	15.7	8.6	14.2	14.2	14.8
01 009	13820	1	Blount................................	1 670	57 673	889	34.5	88.8	2.0	1.1	0.5	8.7	6.1	17.5	8.2	11.5	12.9	14.0
01 011	...	6	Bullock	1 613	10 696	2 380	6.6	22.7	69.1	0.5	0.5	7.4	6.3	15.1	9.3	14.7	12.9	13.5
01 013	...	6	Butler	2 012	20 154	1 824	10.0	53.8	44.1	0.6	1.1	1.2	6.1	17.5	8.1	12.0	11.6	12.4
01 015	11500	3	Calhoun	1 569	115 620	531	73.7	74.2	21.6	1.0	1.3	3.5	5.7	16.4	9.8	12.9	12.1	13.4
01 017	46740	6	Chambers	1 545	34 123	1 325	22.1	57.8	39.8	0.5	0.9	2.0	5.9	15.4	8.7	11.5	11.8	14.1
01 019	...	8	Cherokee	1 434	25 859	1 562	18.0	93.2	5.3	1.3	0.5	1.5	4.8	15.6	7.5	9.8	11.8	14.4
01 021	13820	1	Chilton	1 794	43 943	1 091	24.5	81.3	10.8	0.7	0.6	7.7	6.4	17.8	8.5	12.3	13.2	13.6
01 023	...	9	Choctaw	2 366	13 170	2 223	5.6	56.6	42.6	0.4	0.4	0.8	4.9	15.6	8.0	10.1	11.3	14.5
01 025	...	7	Clarke	3 208	24 675	1 621	7.7	54.0	44.6	0.6	0.7	1.3	5.6	17.0	9.1	10.5	12.1	14.2
01 027	...	9	Clay...................................	1 564	13 555	2 199	8.7	81.4	15.4	1.2	0.5	3.4	5.3	16.3	7.7	10.7	12.0	14.7
01 029	...	8	Cleburne	1 451	15 018	2 097	10.4	93.4	4.2	0.7	0.4	2.5	5.7	17.6	7.8	11.1	12.6	13.9
01 031	21460	6	Coffee	1 759	51 211	971	29.1	73.4	18.2	2.1	2.3	6.4	6.1	17.6	8.3	12.9	13.2	13.7
01 033	22520	3	Colbert	1 535	54 354	923	35.4	80.4	16.9	1.2	0.7	2.6	5.7	16.0	8.2	11.7	12.0	13.8
01 035	...	9	Conecuh	2 202	12 672	2 252	5.8	52.0	46.1	0.8	0.4	1.8	5.5	15.9	8.6	9.9	11.0	13.7
01 037	45180	8	Coosa	1 686	10 724	2 376	6.4	66.2	32.0	0.9	0.3	2.3	4.8	13.5	7.7	10.1	12.3	15.8
01 039	...	7	Covington...........................	2 669	37 835	1 229	14.2	84.5	13.6	1.2	0.6	1.6	5.9	16.2	7.9	11.3	11.4	13.4
01 041	...	8	Crenshaw	1 577	13 963	2 169	8.9	72.2	24.9	1.0	2.0	1.7	6.1	16.5	8.6	10.8	12.2	13.8
01 043	18980	6	Cullman..............................	1 903	82 005	683	43.1	93.2	1.7	1.2	0.7	4.4	5.9	16.6	8.4	12.1	12.6	13.6
01 045	37120	4	Dale	1 453	49 565	987	34.1	72.4	20.3	1.5	2.1	6.1	6.3	17.3	9.0	14.7	12.1	12.7
01 047	42820	4	Dallas	2 535	41 131	1 147	16.2	29.2	69.7	0.4	0.6	1.0	6.7	18.5	9.5	11.6	11.0	13.2
01 049	...	6	DeKalb...............................	2 013	71 130	759	35.3	82.5	2.2	2.6	0.5	14.2	6.2	18.5	8.6	11.7	13.2	13.5
01 051	33860	2	Elmore	1 602	81 468	685	50.9	75.0	21.7	0.9	1.2	2.7	5.9	17.0	9.5	13.2	13.8	14.2
01 053	...	6	Escambia	2 448	37 789	1 231	15.4	62.0	32.9	4.1	0.5	2.1	6.1	16.0	8.6	13.1	13.2	13.5
01 055	23460	3	Etowah...............................	1 386	103 057	579	74.4	79.8	16.0	1.0	1.0	3.7	5.7	16.3	8.7	11.7	12.7	13.7
01 057	...	6	Fayette...............................	1 626	16 759	1 994	10.3	86.2	12.5	0.7	0.4	1.4	5.4	16.3	8.7	10.0	11.9	13.8
01 059	...	6	Franklin	1 642	31 696	1 390	19.3	79.1	4.5	1.0	0.5	16.1	6.6	17.7	8.9	12.5	13.1	12.9
01 061	20020	3	Geneva	1 488	26 777	1 540	18.0	85.6	10.4	1.5	0.6	3.6	5.8	16.4	7.7	11.0	11.9	14.0
01 063	...	6	Greene	1 676	8 479	2 558	5.1	18.4	80.5	0.4	0.3	1.0	5.9	17.4	8.8	11.0	9.7	12.7
01 065	46220	3	Hale	1 668	15 068	2 093	9.0	40.6	58.3	0.4	0.4	1.3	6.2	17.1	9.1	11.1	10.8	14.1
01 067	20020	3	Henry	1 455	17 221	1 968	11.8	69.5	27.6	0.7	0.8	2.6	5.5	15.7	7.2	10.4	12.3	13.3
01 069	20020	3	Houston	1 502	104 173	573	69.4	68.8	27.3	1.0	1.3	3.3	6.2	17.5	8.3	12.9	12.8	13.4
01 071	42460	6	Jackson..............................	2 792	52 419	955	18.8	91.8	4.1	3.1	0.7	2.9	5.4	16.3	8.0	10.8	12.6	13.9
01 073	13820	1	Jefferson............................	2 878	660 367	100	229.5	51.8	43.1	0.6	1.9	3.8	6.6	16.5	9.2	14.4	12.7	13.1
01 075	...	9	Lamar................................	1 567	13 886	2 175	8.9	87.3	11.9	0.7	0.3	1.5	5.0	16.7	6.8	10.4	12.1	13.9
01 077	22520	3	Lauderdale..........................	1 729	92 596	630	53.6	86.0	11.0	0.9	1.0	2.4	5.2	15.3	12.0	11.3	11.3	13.1
01 079	19460	3	Lawrence	1 789	33 115	1 353	18.5	80.7	12.0	9.1	0.5	2.2	5.3	16.4	8.3	11.4	12.2	15.6
01 081	12220	3	Lee	1 574	156 993	409	99.7	68.9	24.0	0.7	3.8	3.9	5.8	15.8	19.4	14.6	12.3	11.8
01 083	26620	2	Limestone	1 450	91 663	635	63.2	79.0	14.0	1.3	1.8	5.8	5.9	17.5	7.8	13.3	14.0	15.3
01 085	33860	2	Lowndes.............................	1 854	10 458	2 398	5.6	26.0	72.8	0.5	0.4	1.2	6.7	16.4	9.4	11.7	10.5	14.2
01 087	...	6	Macon	1 577	19 105	1 869	12.1	17.1	81.6	0.6	0.6	1.5	4.7	13.6	19.3	10.3	9.4	11.9
01 089	26620	2	Madison	2 076	353 089	195	170.1	67.6	25.2	1.6	3.5	4.7	5.8	16.6	9.8	13.7	12.4	15.3
01 091	...	7	Marengo.............................	2 530	20 028	1 833	7.9	46.3	51.0	0.6	0.5	2.4	6.0	17.0	9.0	10.7	11.9	13.0
01 093	...	8	Marion	1 923	30 168	1 427	15.7	92.8	4.6	0.9	0.4	2.5	5.4	15.8	7.6	10.9	12.2	14.4
01 095	10700	4	Marshall	1 466	94 725	619	64.6	83.8	2.7	1.3	0.9	13.0	6.6	18.0	8.6	12.3	12.4	13.4
01 097	33660	2	Mobile	3 184	415 395	165	130.5	59.1	35.8	1.4	2.4	2.8	6.7	17.4	9.7	13.5	12.1	13.2
01 099	...	7	Monroe	2 656	21 673	1 746	8.2	56.3	41.7	2.0	0.7	1.2	5.5	17.9	8.8	10.0	11.8	13.7
01 101	33860	2	Montgomery........................	2 031	226 519	286	111.5	37.2	56.9	0.6	3.1	3.4	6.8	17.2	10.6	14.6	12.6	12.6
01 103	19460	3	Morgan...............................	1 500	119 565	517	79.7	78.2	13.0	1.7	1.0	7.9	6.0	17.1	8.3	12.3	12.6	14.5
01 105	...	8	Perry	1 864	9 652	2 461	5.2	30.7	67.3	0.4	0.6	1.3	5.5	16.9	14.6	10.3	10.3	11.4
01 107	46220	8	Pickens	2 283	20 864	1 781	9.1	55.5	40.5	0.5	0.4	4.1	5.2	15.3	9.0	12.5	11.5	15.0
01 109	45980	6	Pike	1 741	33 046	1 356	19.0	58.8	37.5	1.2	2.6	2.2	5.7	13.7	23.1	11.7	10.0	10.7
01 111	...	6	Randolph	1 504	22 696	1 701	15.1	76.3	20.9	0.9	0.5	2.9	5.7	16.4	8.5	10.4	11.4	13.9
01 113	17980	2	Russell...............................	1 661	59 660	872	35.9	51.3	43.2	1.1	1.6	5.0	7.6	17.7	9.6	15.6	12.5	12.9
01 115	13820	1	St. Clair..............................	1 637	87 074	661	53.2	87.2	10.0	0.9	1.0	2.3	6.1	16.9	7.7	13.2	13.5	14.3
01 117	13820	1	Shelby	2 033	208 713	312	102.7	79.8	12.5	0.7	2.6	6.0	6.0	18.4	8.1	12.9	14.6	14.4
01 119	...	8	Sumter	2 341	13 103	2 226	5.6	25.0	73.0	0.4	0.5	1.1	4.8	15.0	18.2	9.5	9.6	12.4
01 121	45180	4	Talladega	1 908	80 862	691	42.4	64.7	33.0	0.9	0.7	2.3	5.5	16.8	8.8	12.1	12.6	13.9
01 123	...	6	Tallapoosa	1 856	40 844	1 159	22.0	69.9	27.5	0.7	0.7	2.3	5.8	15.3	8.6	10.6	11.3	13.8
01 125	46220	3	Tuscaloosa	3 423	203 976	317	59.6	64.1	31.3	0.6	1.9	3.3	6.0	15.1	18.9	14.1	11.6	11.2
01 127	13820	1	Walker...............................	2 049	65 294	809	31.9	90.4	6.9	1.0	0.5	2.3	5.8	16.3	8.3	11.2	12.2	13.8

1. CBSA = Core Based Statistical Area. See Appendix A for explanation. See Appendix B for list of metropolitan areas with component counties. 2. County type code from the Economic Research Service of USDA Rural-Urban Continuum Codes. See Appendix A for definition. 3. Dry land or land partially or temporarily covered by water. 4. May be of any race.

STATE County	Age (percent) (cont.) 55 to 64 years	65 to 74 years	75 years and over	Percent female	Total persons 2000	2010	Percent change 2000–2010	2010–2015	Components of change, 2010–2015 Births	Deaths	Net migration	Households, 2010–2014 Number	Persons per household	Percent Family households	Female family householder[1]	One person
	16	17	18	19	20	21	22	23	24	25	26	27	28	29	30	31
UNITED STATES	12.6	8.3	6.2	50.8	281 421 906	308 758 105	9.7	4.1	20 782 904	13 457 078	5 334 889	116 211 092	2.63	66.2	13.0	27.6
ALABAMA	13.0	9.0	6.4	51.5	4 447 100	4 780 127	7.5	1.6	307 554	259 658	29 281	1 842 174	2.55	67.3	15.3	28.5
Autauga	11.5	8.2	5.6	51.4	43 671	54 571	25.0	1.4	3 199	2 771	227	20 304	2.69	70.3	11.8	25.9
Baldwin	13.8	11.2	7.4	51.2	140 415	182 265	29.8	11.8	11 382	10 174	19 436	73 058	2.58	69.3	10.5	26.9
Barbour	12.7	9.9	6.6	46.6	29 038	27 457	-5.4	-3.5	1 517	1 651	-850	9 145	2.65	65.6	19.0	31.7
Bibb	12.4	8.8	5.9	45.9	20 826	22 919	10.0	-1.5	1 314	1 264	-362	7 078	2.98	75.5	15.1	22.3
Blount	12.8	10.3	6.7	50.5	51 024	57 322	12.3	0.6	3 504	3 059	-163	20 934	2.73	74.9	10.2	22.7
Bullock	13.4	8.6	6.3	45.3	11 714	10 915	-6.8	-2.0	703	628	-299	3 746	2.70	60.5	26.3	34.0
Butler	14.4	9.5	8.4	53.6	21 399	20 946	-2.1	-3.8	1 346	1 354	-752	8 253	2.45	65.2	20.2	31.0
Calhoun	13.6	9.3	6.6	51.8	112 249	118 586	5.6	-2.5	7 055	7 209	-2 686	45 348	2.52	67.5	16.0	27.7
Chambers	14.2	10.6	7.7	52.3	36 583	34 170	-6.6	-0.1	2 129	2 396	196	13 901	2.42	63.4	17.9	33.5
Cherokee	15.2	13.2	7.7	50.2	23 988	25 986	8.3	-0.5	1 264	1 737	331	11 726	2.19	72.9	12.8	25.5
Chilton	13.0	9.1	6.1	50.8	39 593	43 631	10.2	0.7	2 938	2 546	-85	16 281	2.67	74.3	13.7	23.0
Choctaw	14.8	12.1	8.7	52.5	15 922	13 858	-13.0	-5.0	637	871	-450	5 526	2.42	65.5	15.6	32.0
Clarke	13.6	10.1	7.8	52.8	27 867	25 840	-7.3	-4.5	1 365	1 532	-1 030	9 791	2.56	64.8	16.2	32.6
Clay	13.9	10.9	8.5	50.6	14 254	13 932	-2.3	-2.7	761	975	-166	5 572	2.39	68.8	13.7	28.8
Cleburne	13.0	11.0	7.4	50.4	14 123	14 972	6.0	0.3	956	918	-24	5 639	2.63	71.0	12.1	26.6
Coffee	12.4	9.2	6.7	50.5	43 615	49 948	14.5	2.5	3 314	2 591	536	19 086	2.63	68.0	13.9	28.5
Colbert	14.0	10.5	8.0	51.8	54 984	54 428	-1.0	-0.1	3 139	3 518	456	22 442	2.41	68.7	14.3	27.9
Conecuh	14.9	12.0	8.4	51.6	14 089	13 228	-6.1	-4.2	774	905	-431	5 030	2.57	65.9	16.3	32.4
Coosa	17.3	11.3	7.2	49.5	12 202	11 758	-3.6	-8.8	496	661	-875	4 446	2.46	64.7	14.7	31.2
Covington	14.1	11.0	8.8	51.6	37 631	37 765	0.4	0.2	2 343	2 576	272	14 979	2.49	68.6	15.3	28.6
Crenshaw	13.9	10.6	7.4	51.1	13 665	13 906	1.8	0.4	766	874	175	5 424	2.54	66.7	16.2	31.0
Cullman	13.2	10.5	7.1	50.5	77 483	80 410	3.8	2.0	5 060	5 007	1 415	31 160	2.55	70.6	11.9	26.4
Dale	12.5	9.0	6.3	50.5	49 129	50 251	2.3	-1.4	3 536	2 519	-1 706	19 470	2.51	66.6	14.4	28.7
Dallas	13.9	9.2	6.4	53.7	46 365	43 820	-5.5	-6.1	2 965	2 742	-2 956	16 259	2.59	60.0	24.8	36.6
DeKalb	12.6	9.4	6.3	50.7	64 452	71 115	10.3	0.0	4 472	3 930	-487	24 743	2.84	72.2	10.3	25.5
Elmore	12.3	8.7	5.4	51.5	65 874	79 296	20.4	2.7	5 030	3 822	863	28 617	2.62	72.2	13.9	24.8
Escambia	12.9	9.7	7.0	48.8	38 440	38 319	-0.3	-1.4	2 358	2 328	-511	13 737	2.58	68.9	18.4	30.0
Etowah	13.8	10.2	7.1	51.6	103 459	104 427	0.9	-1.3	6 162	7 291	-210	40 001	2.56	68.9	14.2	28.0
Fayette	14.3	11.3	8.2	50.5	18 495	17 241	-6.8	-2.8	962	1 226	-218	6 967	2.40	69.1	13.6	29.2
Franklin	12.3	9.2	6.7	50.3	31 223	31 709	1.6	0.0	2 240	2 015	-249	12 247	2.56	68.9	13.0	27.7
Geneva	14.0	11.2	8.0	50.8	25 764	26 790	4.0	0.0	1 612	1 830	191	10 898	2.44	71.7	16.0	24.1
Greene	16.7	9.7	8.2	52.5	9 974	9 045	-9.3	-6.3	553	540	-571	3 282	2.66	60.5	20.8	37.7
Hale	14.3	9.8	7.5	52.8	17 185	15 760	-8.3	-4.4	1 021	933	-791	5 931	2.54	66.3	22.0	31.6
Henry	14.8	12.5	8.2	51.8	16 310	17 302	6.1	-0.5	916	1 121	115	6 900	2.47	68.2	12.7	29.5
Houston	12.9	9.3	6.8	52.1	88 787	101 547	14.4	2.6	6 718	5 435	1 359	39 464	2.59	66.8	16.5	29.2
Jackson	14.4	11.2	7.3	50.7	53 926	53 226	-1.3	-1.5	2 993	3 451	-342	20 425	2.56	70.7	10.4	26.9
Jefferson	13.2	8.0	6.3	52.8	662 047	658 350	-0.6	0.3	46 045	36 289	-6 754	259 397	2.48	63.9	18.1	31.2
Lamar	14.7	11.3	9.2	51.2	15 904	14 564	-8.4	-4.7	717	1 049	-344	6 147	2.28	73.2	11.8	25.3
Lauderdale	13.6	10.4	7.9	52.1	87 966	92 709	5.4	-0.1	4 918	5 628	614	38 691	2.35	65.4	11.8	29.9
Lawrence	13.8	10.5	6.3	51.3	34 803	34 339	-1.3	-3.6	1 840	2 039	-997	13 312	2.52	71.8	13.3	25.3
Lee	10.0	6.4	3.9	50.7	115 092	140 296	21.9	11.9	9 295	4 979	12 044	56 637	2.51	61.4	13.2	27.8
Limestone	12.4	8.4	5.4	49.7	65 676	82 782	26.0	10.7	5 220	3 690	7 088	32 156	2.59	72.1	11.3	25.3
Lowndes	13.7	10.5	6.9	52.3	13 473	11 299	-16.1	-7.4	708	697	-876	4 287	2.53	65.7	25.5	32.6
Macon	13.9	9.8	7.1	54.2	24 105	21 448	-11.0	-10.9	1 051	1 247	-2 171	8 039	2.28	61.2	24.8	35.3
Madison	12.7	7.8	5.9	51.2	276 700	334 811	21.0	5.5	21 562	14 470	10 687	135 409	2.48	65.2	12.4	30.5
Marengo	13.8	10.4	8.2	53.2	22 539	21 029	-6.7	-4.8	1 283	1 343	-985	8 477	2.39	65.5	17.6	32.7
Marion	13.6	11.6	8.6	50.4	31 214	30 777	-1.4	-2.0	1 600	2 091	-110	12 602	2.36	71.6	12.1	24.9
Marshall	12.5	9.6	6.7	50.9	82 231	93 019	13.1	1.8	6 573	5 652	678	34 524	2.70	71.4	12.7	25.8
Mobile	12.9	8.6	6.0	52.2	399 843	413 143	3.3	0.5	29 262	22 178	-4 688	154 400	2.62	67.1	18.4	28.6
Monroe	14.4	10.2	7.7	52.6	24 324	23 070	-5.2	-6.1	1 184	1 331	-1 207	8 390	2.66	66.3	15.1	32.1
Montgomery	12.2	7.6	5.8	52.6	223 510	229 363	2.6	-1.2	16 335	10 662	-8 446	89 143	2.48	64.0	21.3	31.0
Morgan	13.2	9.4	6.5	50.8	111 064	119 486	7.6	0.1	7 493	6 419	-928	45 856	2.57	68.7	13.3	28.0
Perry	13.1	9.9	8.0	53.4	11 861	10 581	-10.8	-8.8	583	708	-808	3 263	2.90	71.5	32.6	26.3
Pickens	13.7	10.1	7.7	50.6	20 949	19 746	-5.7	5.7	1 150	1 279	1 154	7 741	2.49	66.8	18.2	31.8
Pike	11.1	8.2	5.8	51.9	29 605	32 899	11.1	0.4	1 987	1 727	-160	12 909	2.42	61.9	15.6	28.3
Randolph	14.3	11.4	8.2	51.4	22 380	22 914	2.4	-1.0	1 242	1 414	-110	9 016	2.47	68.9	14.1	28.2
Russell	11.5	7.3	5.2	51.3	49 756	52 951	6.4	12.7	4 556	2 973	5 061	21 568	2.61	64.6	19.7	30.4
St. Clair	13.0	9.6	5.7	50.1	64 742	83 593	29.1	4.2	5 473	4 449	2 270	31 673	2.63	72.6	11.9	23.2
Shelby	12.6	8.1	4.9	51.2	143 293	195 218	36.2	6.9	12 556	7 016	7 684	74 790	2.65	71.4	10.0	24.5
Sumter	14.2	8.7	7.7	55.0	14 798	13 763	-7.0	-4.8	707	834	-556	4 962	2.57	61.2	25.3	32.5
Talladega	13.9	9.8	6.3	51.4	80 321	82 291	2.5	-1.7	4 564	5 144	-778	31 277	2.51	70.8	18.7	26.2
Tallapoosa	15.1	11.7	7.9	51.4	41 475	41 618	0.3	-1.9	2 481	2 792	-477	16 437	2.47	69.5	17.4	27.1
Tuscaloosa	11.3	6.9	4.9	51.7	164 875	194 653	18.1	4.8	12 721	8 713	5 284	68 103	2.77	66.1	15.0	27.8
Walker	14.1	10.8	7.4	51.4	70 713	67 023	-5.2	-2.6	4 147	5 053	-872	25 571	2.55	71.3	15.7	25.6

1. No spouse present.

Table B. States and Counties — Population, Vital Statistics, Medicare, and Crime

STATE County	Persons in group quarters, 2015	Daytime population, 2010–2014		Births, 2015		Deaths, 2015		Persons under 65 with no health insurance, 2014		Medicare, 2015			Serious crimes known to police,[2] 2014 Total	
		Number	Employment/ residence ratio	Total	Rate[1]	Number	Rate[1]	Number	Percent	Total Beneficiaries	Enrolled in Original Medicare	Enrolled in Medicare Advantage	Number	Rate[3]
	32	33	34	35	36	37	38	39	40	41	42	43	44	45
UNITED STATES	8 070 896	314 107 084	1.00	3 985 924	12.4	2 625 033	8.2	36 013 970	13.5	51 627 310	34 096 898	17 530 412	9 443 212	2 962
ALABAMA...........................	119 599	4 773 908	0.98	58 305	12.0	50 330	10.4	567 439	14.2	930 162	685 949	244 213	174 821	3 605
Autauga..............................	455	44 312	0.55	600	10.8	467	8.4	5 225	11.0	8 889	5 865	3 024	1 769	3 241
Baldwin..............................	2 309	175 863	0.81	2 240	11.1	1 992	9.9	25 892	16.1	42 444	28 071	14 373	4 227	2 189
Barbour..............................	3 352	26 936	0.98	269	10.1	309	11.6	2 942	15.3	5 325	4 419	906	728	2 894
Bibb....................................	2 236	19 304	0.57	253	11.2	223	9.9	2 323	13.6	4 540	2 778	1 762	248	1 171
Blount................................	489	45 060	0.43	603	10.5	590	10.2	7 861	16.5	9 100	5 199	3 901	1 379	2 376
Bullock...............................	1 757	10 119	0.85	123	11.4	109	10.1	1 319	17.3	1 410	1 047	363	190	1 795
Butler.................................	333	19 630	0.88	257	12.7	236	11.7	2 388	14.4	4 440	3 931	509	746	3 709
Calhoun.............................	2 804	118 892	1.04	1 335	11.5	1 395	12.0	13 543	14.2	26 839	22 473	4 366	4 615	3 965
Chambers..........................	458	29 259	0.63	429	12.6	457	13.4	4 122	14.9	8 554	6 994	1 560	1 394	4 077
Cherokee...........................	290	22 188	0.62	250	9.6	315	12.1	2 988	14.6	5 679	4 265	1 414	842	3 204
Chilton...............................	393	36 760	0.60	561	12.8	462	10.5	6 565	17.7	7 711	4 167	3 544	1 397	3 180
Choctaw.............................	129	12 894	0.86	127	9.6	168	12.7	1 509	14.3	3 476	3 129	347	96	757
Clarke................................	280	25 291	1.00	247	10.0	313	12.6	3 072	15.1	6 425	4 944	1 481	337	1 362
Clay....................................	255	12 666	0.81	149	11.0	194	14.3	1 924	17.8	3 221	2 774	447	148	1 105
Cleburne............................	178	11 891	0.46	185	12.3	189	12.6	1 741	14.3	3 204	2 753	451	299	1 992
Coffee................................	600	47 890	0.87	616	12.1	519	10.2	6 351	15.0	9 270	8 352	918	1 457	2 848
Colbert...............................	474	56 179	1.08	573	10.5	649	11.9	5 765	13.0	12 583	10 956	1 627	2 353	4 313
Conecuh............................	45	12 627	0.90	146	11.5	183	14.4	1 670	16.6	3 251	2 826	425	333	2 720
Coosa................................	266	9 029	0.41	91	8.5	106	9.8	1 331	15.5	2 683	2 271	412	233	2 263
Covington..........................	575	36 777	0.92	449	11.9	508	13.4	4 659	15.4	9 597	8 664	933	592	1 581
Crenshaw..........................	132	12 287	0.70	138	9.9	184	13.2	1 868	16.3	3 255	2 572	683	279	2 067
Cullman.............................	1 032	76 053	0.86	960	11.8	964	11.8	10 882	16.4	18 088	13 806	4 282	1 951	2 410
Dale...................................	917	52 153	1.10	653	13.2	519	10.5	5 670	13.8	10 758	9 478	1 280	1 627	3 267
Dallas................................	857	42 447	0.98	572	13.8	530	12.8	4 978	14.3	10 470	8 016	2 454	2 867	6 896
DeKalb...............................	782	67 219	0.86	833	11.7	749	10.5	12 476	20.9	13 638	10 720	2 918	1 396	2 454
Elmore...............................	5 413	64 591	0.53	948	11.7	758	9.3	7 395	11.5	14 875	10 572	4 303	2 397	2 948
Escambia...........................	3 282	38 802	1.06	438	11.6	446	11.8	4 832	17.0	8 046	7 044	1 002	919	2 423
Etowah..............................	2 085	99 819	0.89	1 168	11.3	1 449	14.0	12 311	14.6	24 259	17 947	6 312	4 647	4 475
Fayette..............................	291	15 131	0.68	186	11.3	229	13.6	1 961	14.6	3 845	3 301	544	172	1 022
Franklin.............................	272	30 149	0.88	434	13.7	366	11.6	5 248	19.9	6 797	6 151	646	871	2 766
Geneva..............................	229	22 115	0.56	299	11.2	342	12.8	3 692	17.2	6 421	5 706	715	627	2 346
Greene...............................	45	8 337	0.81	99	11.6	88	10.3	1 060	15.1	2 014	1 843	171	262	3 244
Hale..................................	221	13 019	0.54	187	12.4	186	12.3	1 735	14.0	4 157	3 805	352	176	1 364
Henry................................	199	14 785	0.61	167	9.7	201	11.7	2 040	15.1	4 180	3 327	853	318	1 895
Houston.............................	1 417	109 432	1.14	1 248	12.0	1 075	10.3	11 653	13.5	20 498	17 499	2 999	2 668	2 560
Jackson.............................	597	50 028	0.85	549	10.5	645	12.3	6 685	15.7	12 758	10 756	2 002	1 427	2 775
Jefferson...........................	16 019	727 113	1.24	8 639	13.1	7 033	10.7	70 057	12.6	131 036	73 943	57 093	32 365	5 144
Lamar................................	217	13 154	0.80	128	9.2	195	14.0	1 555	14.0	3 905	3 537	368	124	875
Lauderdale.........................	2 073	87 688	0.87	958	10.3	1 065	11.5	10 209	13.7	21 130	18 384	2 746	2 208	2 385
Lawrence...........................	229	28 408	0.57	339	10.2	387	11.6	4 471	16.1	5 849	5 101	748	606	1 881
Lee....................................	4 940	137 372	0.84	1 900	12.2	989	6.4	17 961	13.4	17 786	15 044	2 742	4 155	2 704
Limestone..........................	2 801	75 218	0.67	1 015	11.1	744	8.2	10 845	14.4	12 999	10 491	2 508	1 645	1 820
Lowndes............................	96	10 017	0.74	118	11.2	146	13.9	1 248	14.4	2 233	1 339	894	NA	NA
Macon................................	1 740	18 876	0.78	194	10.1	263	13.7	1 876	13.0	4 315	3 187	1 128	988	5 129
Madison.............................	7 793	377 644	1.21	4 185	11.9	2 900	8.2	36 806	12.5	56 071	46 796	9 275	14 404	4 117
Marengo............................	254	20 137	0.95	257	12.8	252	12.5	2 161	13.3	4 315	3 838	477	634	3 234
Marion................................	868	30 017	0.95	301	10.0	385	12.7	3 641	15.4	6 824	5 989	835	674	2 233
Marshall............................	1 066	94 463	1.01	1 214	12.8	1 086	11.5	14 751	18.8	20 534	17 785	2 749	3 046	3 199
Mobile...............................	7 507	423 808	1.06	5 585	13.5	4 343	10.5	52 191	14.9	74 616	41 524	33 092	18 673	4 505
Monroe..............................	230	22 110	0.94	197	9.0	253	11.6	3 169	17.7	4 685	3 981	704	690	3 273
Montgomery.......................	9 246	266 024	1.38	3 099	13.7	2 097	9.3	26 002	13.9	38 913	27 217	11 696	10 314	4 563
Morgan..............................	2 127	118 905	0.98	1 406	11.8	1 199	10.0	15 946	16.1	25 239	21 824	3 415	3 186	2 673
Perry..................................	790	9 674	0.79	89	9.1	134	13.7	1 135	15.3	2 107	1 971	136	NA	NA
Pickens..............................	2 197	16 909	0.58	227	11.0	245	11.9	2 180	14.3	4 635	4 275	360	NA	NA
Pike....................................	1 840	35 164	1.14	368	11.1	337	10.2	4 050	15.2	5 897	4 532	1 365	1 374	4 107
Randolph............................	407	19 647	0.63	239	10.6	265	11.7	2 998	16.8	5 130	4 393	737	358	1 578
Russell...............................	574	47 685	0.60	900	15.1	623	10.4	7 676	14.8	11 385	8 749	2 636	2 678	4 411
St. Clair.............................	1 883	68 768	0.54	1 000	11.5	878	10.1	9 585	13.4	14 231	7 916	6 315	1 386	1 603
Shelby...............................	2 634	180 641	0.79	2 331	11.2	1 422	6.9	18 670	10.6	20 389	11 685	8 704	NA	NA
Sumter...............................	840	12 712	0.84	142	10.8	147	11.2	1 721	16.7	2 807	2 564	243	249	1 902
Talladega...........................	2 949	81 159	0.98	868	10.7	1 015	12.5	8 812	13.5	17 934	13 070	4 864	3 576	4 420
Tallapoosa.........................	576	39 205	0.87	472	11.5	529	12.9	4 693	14.3	10 292	8 847	1 445	1 263	3 085
Tuscaloosa.........................	10 847	205 972	1.09	2 463	12.1	1 727	8.5	20 571	12.2	30 776	26 766	4 010	7 891	3 898
Walker...............................	851	63 624	0.89	762	11.6	918	14.0	8 065	15.2	18 716	11 765	6 951	2 722	4 186

1. Per 1,000 estimated resident population.   2. Data for serious crimes have not been adjusted for underreporting; this may affect comparability between geographic areas and over time.
3. Per 100,000 population estimated by the FBI.

Table B. States and Counties — Crime, Education, Money Income, and Poverty

STATE County	Serious crimes known to police, 2014 (cont.)[1] Rate[2] Violent	Property	Education — School enrollment and attainment, 2010–2014 Enrollment[3] Total	Percent private	Attainment[4] (percent) High school graduate or less	Bachelor's degree or more	Local government expenditures,[5] 2012–2013 Total current spending (mil dol)	Current spending per student (dollars)	Money income, 2010–2014 Per capita income[6] (dollars)	Households Median income (dollars)	Mean income (dollars)	Percent with income of $200,000 or more	Income and poverty, 2014 Median household income (dollars)	Percent below poverty level All persons	Children under 18 years	Children 5 to 17 years in families
	46	47	48	49	50	51	52	53	54	55	56	57	58	59	60	61
UNITED STATES............	366	2 596	82 735 509	16.3	41.6	29.3	530 552.8	10 700	28 555	53 482	74 596	5.0	53 657	15.5	21.7	20.4
ALABAMA	427	3 178	1 215 753	14.1	47.4	23.1	6 642.0	8 755	23 936	43 511	60 205	2.6	42 917	19.2	27.4	25.9
Autauga..........................	264	2 977	14 765	22.9	47.3	21.9	71.0	7 303	24 644	52 475	64 414	1.9	54 366	13.1	18.1	17.4
Baldwin..........................	189	2 000	42 835	15.0	39.8	28.6	243.6	8 279	26 851	50 183	67 238	3.7	49 626	13.0	19.8	18.7
Barbour..........................	374	2 520	6 051	12.4	58.9	13.6	33.8	8 742	17 350	35 634	46 592	0.7	34 971	25.4	38.1	37.0
Bibb................................	109	1 063	4 875	8.8	62.2	10.2	28.7	8 260	18 110	37 984	50 508	0.6	39 546	18.1	26.8	25.2
Blount............................	215	2 161	12 999	7.6	56.4	12.3	75.6	7 711	20 501	44 409	54 689	0.9	45 567	17.5	24.1	22.5
Bullock..........................	293	1 502	2 102	9.9	66.8	14.1	16.8	11 000	17 706	34 804	43 910	0.8	26 580	35.1	43.1	40.4
Butler............................	567	3 143	4 614	10.1	60.6	14.3	28.9	8 904	18 115	31 571	43 157	0.5	32 512	25.0	36.7	35.3
Calhoun..........................	618	3 348	29 676	10.1	52.3	16.9	164.3	9 010	21 306	40 919	53 011	1.6	41 123	20.5	28.1	25.4
Chambers......................	497	3 579	7 394	10.2	59.8	12.2	39.7	8 386	21 240	32 835	49 088	1.6	34 116	21.3	31.6	30.2
Cherokee........................	293	2 911	5 096	8.3	56.4	13.7	36.4	8 819	22 234	34 983	50 191	1.3	38 013	18.6	27.9	25.4
Chilton..........................	314	2 866	9 854	11.1	62.5	13.5	59.7	7 792	21 718	41 785	56 882	1.5	41 450	18.1	27.6	26.9
Choctaw........................	134	623	2 939	26.6	61.2	12.8	15.9	9 250	21 268	34 325	49 678	1.5	35 049	25.0	31.9	28.7
Clarke............................	388	974	5 683	10.8	63.8	11.9	41.1	8 712	20 022	30 951	48 394	1.7	36 620	24.9	33.7	31.6
Clay................................	314	791	2 842	6.2	61.4	8.6	17.3	8 414	18 957	35 286	45 287	0.5	35 940	19.5	28.9	26.7
Cleburne........................	87	1 906	3 478	9.3	63.3	10.6	22.6	8 466	19 736	37 008	49 832	1.6	40 418	17.0	24.8	23.1
Coffee............................	289	2 559	12 036	8.7	46.7	23.2	81.4	8 795	24 204	45 558	60 597	1.7	46 931	16.8	25.0	24.1
Colbert..........................	453	3 860	12 397	5.9	50.2	17.6	79.9	9 728	21 763	39 914	51 466	0.9	43 057	16.7	25.3	24.9
Conecuh........................	425	2 295	2 657	10.9	66.8	8.3	18.0	10 922	15 441	24 433	37 602	0.6	29 101	30.6	41.2	37.8
Coosa............................	185	2 079	2 169	4.5	63.6	9.1	12.1	10 513	17 749	32 340	42 392	0.6	34 679	18.8	29.0	27.8
Covington......................	171	1 410	8 139	8.4	54.1	14.6	52.9	8 493	20 941	36 256	50 674	1.5	36 149	20.8	30.2	29.1
Crenshaw........................	496	1 571	3 000	14.0	61.8	12.5	19.4	8 660	20 366	37 349	49 419	2.0	34 445	21.2	28.0	26.8
Cullman..........................	147	2 263	18 524	10.0	51.6	15.1	108.6	8 542	21 105	39 415	52 597	1.7	39 922	17.2	23.5	21.9
Dale................................	309	2 958	12 579	10.2	46.4	16.9	56.6	8 697	22 368	44 473	54 652	1.4	41 940	22.4	33.5	31.4
Dallas............................	806	6 090	11 307	12.2	57.7	14.5	71.0	9 144	17 614	26 494	42 895	2.0	26 602	35.2	49.5	44.8
DeKalb..........................	290	2 164	16 422	7.0	61.7	11.3	98.1	8 315	18 416	37 977	49 069	1.3	36 241	24.0	36.5	36.4
Elmore............................	229	2 719	19 986	19.9	48.0	21.4	101.9	7 724	24 185	54 159	65 767	2.2	54 298	14.4	20.7	19.4
Escambia........................	422	2 001	8 081	12.3	61.7	12.5	54.1	9 386	16 673	31 422	43 344	0.9	37 077	25.1	31.6	31.4
Etowah..........................	490	3 985	23 802	9.3	50.2	15.4	132.2	8 058	20 445	38 467	51 007	1.4	39 904	19.0	29.5	27.2
Fayette..........................	154	867	3 752	9.8	62.0	13.8	22.0	9 046	19 040	33 144	44 881	1.6	35 664	20.6	29.2	27.1
Franklin..........................	222	2 543	6 729	6.2	62.0	10.9	52.4	9 163	18 559	35 450	46 795	1.3	33 881	23.1	35.5	35.6
Geneva............................	397	1 949	5 358	4.0	60.5	11.2	31.9	7 946	20 027	36 268	48 370	0.8	34 425	23.9	36.4	34.9
Greene............................	718	2 526	2 157	5.0	61.6	11.5	13.3	10 626	13 956	22 170	34 290	0.5	26 504	33.2	45.7	42.9
Hale................................	139	1 224	3 919	10.7	61.3	14.0	24.8	8 679	18 774	30 839	45 620	1.4	33 315	28.1	36.8	35.3
Henry..............................	179	1 716	3 797	19.5	56.3	16.8	21.5	8 061	22 682	42 926	54 401	0.7	39 930	17.3	27.4	26.3
Houston..........................	282	2 278	24 664	15.5	49.6	20.1	133.1	8 492	23 492	41 077	57 985	2.6	40 124	20.1	31.1	29.8
Jackson..........................	311	2 464	11 870	7.5	62.1	12.9	76.8	9 160	20 055	36 874	48 964	1.4	36 923	22.0	28.8	27.8
Jefferson........................	813	4 331	168 336	16.5	38.9	30.3	1 025.5	9 862	26 896	45 239	66 254	3.8	44 852	19.5	29.4	28.9
Lamar............................	155	719	2 836	8.0	60.3	11.4	19.4	8 144	19 094	36 021	45 088	1.4	34 553	20.6	28.3	25.7
Lauderdale	270	2 115	23 592	11.5	49.5	22.1	119.5	9 100	23 975	42 703	55 864	1.9	41 324	18.7	26.3	23.0
Lawrence........................	245	1 636	7 683	6.7	61.3	11.3	45.6	8 956	21 093	40 356	52 335	0.7	41 574	16.6	23.2	21.5
Lee................................	241	2 463	54 380	9.4	38.5	33.2	193.4	8 989	24 126	43 641	60 778	2.6	41 256	25.2	26.4	24.9
Limestone......................	129	1 691	20 588	13.5	48.7	23.1	108.5	8 926	25 089	49 461	67 420	2.9	51 175	13.6	18.9	17.3
Lowndes........................	NA	NA	2 572	19.6	61.2	13.2	25.4	14 501	18 046	25 678	43 689	1.7	30 675	31.4	42.7	40.2
Macon............................	706	4 423	6 538	45.2	49.0	19.4	24.5	10 375	17 113	30 254	42 000	0.5	28 518	32.1	44.4	43.5
Madison..........................	565	3 552	92 098	16.1	31.1	38.6	486.2	9 248	32 307	58 203	79 837	5.5	58 833	14.2	20.3	18.4
Marengo........................	469	2 765	5 027	13.1	57.3	16.0	39.0	9 580	22 529	33 714	53 387	2.1	32 977	25.6	32.7	31.5
Marion............................	295	1 938	6 407	10.6	59.2	11.1	40.2	8 473	20 125	33 819	48 407	2.1	37 707	20.2	26.4	24.6
Marshall........................	218	2 981	21 337	6.9	55.4	16.1	148.3	8 802	20 975	39 473	55 108	2.3	36 536	22.0	33.3	29.8
Mobile............................	510	3 994	107 347	20.6	47.9	21.4	563.8	8 881	23 009	43 844	59 046	2.5	42 943	19.6	29.8	29.0
Monroe..........................	507	2 765	4 970	8.7	62.3	12.5	33.0	8 855	16 273	30 569	41 264	0.5	34 733	25.3	33.3	31.0
Montgomery..................	472	4 092	64 100	23.0	41.3	31.3	266.5	8 499	25 089	44 830	62 568	3.2	43 054	22.5	32.2	29.5
Morgan..........................	132	2 541	29 110	10.6	50.1	19.9	183.0	9 487	24 222	45 341	60 617	2.0	45 082	15.0	23.4	23.3
Perry..............................	NA	NA	2 647	20.1	69.1	9.1	16.7	9 580	12 988	25 528	36 433	1.0	27 403	46.9	65.9	58.1
Pickens..........................	NA	NA	4 504	13.1	63.9	9.6	25.1	9 201	17 310	29 839	41 278	0.7	31 933	25.0	34.5	33.0
Pike................................	442	3 665	11 631	5.4	53.7	23.6	41.3	9 354	19 424	32 798	48 586	1.3	31 844	26.4	34.0	34.1
Randolph........................	79	1 499	5 012	8.8	63.7	12.4	32.4	8 559	19 324	36 498	46 236	1.0	36 939	20.4	29.8	28.6
Russell..........................	428	3 982	15 650	12.1	51.2	15.5	85.0	8 189	19 652	36 066	49 195	0.9	35 585	20.9	30.3	30.3
St. Clair........................	146	1 457	19 235	14.1	53.2	15.5	102.7	7 909	23 863	51 317	62 367	2.3	50 571	14.3	18.5	17.6
Shelby............................	NA	NA	54 023	20.9	30.1	40.2	242.8	8 473	33 135	69 723	86 720	5.8	69 432	9.6	11.7	10.7
Sumter............................	374	1 528	4 467	4.4	63.1	15.0	18.6	9 875	14 042	22 865	34 992	0.1	25 413	38.1	51.1	45.2
Talladega........................	396	4 024	18 629	9.4	58.1	12.5	111.6	9 088	19 134	35 896	47 801	1.0	39 999	22.5	32.7	30.3
Tallapoosa......................	393	2 692	8 696	9.2	55.2	17.6	52.5	8 538	21 034	38 644	50 781	1.4	36 779	21.3	34.1	31.1
Tuscaloosa......................	409	3 490	60 031	9.3	43.9	27.7	249.3	8 935	23 124	46 448	62 616	2.6	46 892	18.0	23.2	22.9
Walker............................	401	3 785	13 945	7.6	58.2	10.7	99.1	9 109	20 580	36 712	50 901	1.5	37 245	23.5	32.9	28.2

1. Data for serious crimes have not been adjusted for underreporting; this may affect comparability between geographic areas and over time.   2. Per 100,000 population estimated by the FBI.
3. All persons 3 years old and over enrolled in nursery school through college.   4. Persons 25 years old and over.   5. Elementary and secondary education expenditures.
6. Based on population estimated by the American Community Survey, 2010–2014.

Table B. States and Counties — **Personal Income**

STATE County	Personal income, 2014										Earnings, 2014		
	Total (mil dol)	Percent change, 2013–2014	Per capita[1] Dollars	Per capita[1] Rank	Wages and salaries (mil dol)	Supplements to wages and salaries; employer contributions (mil dol) Pension and insurance	Supplements to wages and salaries; employer contributions (mil dol) Government social insurance	Proprietors' income (mil dol)	Dividends, interest, and rent (mil dol)	Personal transfer receipts (mil dol)	Total (mil dol)	Contributions for government social insurance (mil dol) From employee and self-employed	Contributions for government social insurance (mil dol) From employer
	62	63	64	65	66	67	68	69	70	71	72	73	74
UNITED STATES	14 683 147	4.4	46 049	X	7 469 374	1 218 072	546 274	1 350 318	2 723 288	2 529 139	10 584 038	610 864	546 274
ALABAMA..................	181 909	4.0	37 512	X	85 189	14 629	6 409	15 932	30 267	41 265	122 159	7 738	6 409
Autauga...................	2 017	3.9	36 419	1 702	406	72	30	115	278	425	623	45	30
Baldwin....................	7 812	5.4	39 040	1 316	2 364	375	181	527	1 519	1 669	3 446	242	181
Barbour....................	819	-0.3	30 449	2 658	298	61	23	89	119	253	471	30	23
Bibb........................	637	3.2	28 314	2 896	178	33	13	35	66	191	259	20	13
Blount......................	1 816	4.9	31 464	2 531	299	57	23	166	203	463	546	42	23
Bullock....................	290	1.4	26 934	2 987	94	22	7	31	39	94	153	9	7
Butler......................	669	4.8	32 954	2 288	235	45	19	60	96	208	359	24	19
Calhoun...................	3 797	3.2	32 753	2 324	1 739	362	133	237	670	1 082	2 472	160	133
Chambers.................	1 079	3.9	31 657	2 501	297	55	23	69	132	346	443	34	23
Cherokee.................	834	3.5	32 034	2 433	182	37	14	76	115	253	309	24	14
Chilton....................	1 315	4.1	29 941	2 724	337	63	26	56	153	370	482	37	26
Choctaw..................	403	2.0	30 263	2 682	179	29	12	44	51	154	265	19	12
Clarke.....................	802	4.2	32 149	2 424	335	61	24	74	114	251	494	35	24
Clay.......................	434	5.0	32 028	2 434	123	25	10	46	56	132	204	14	10
Cleburne..................	467	3.7	30 954	2 592	108	19	8	50	52	130	186	13	8
Coffee.....................	1 982	2.8	38 941	1 326	517	98	40	229	352	441	884	54	40
Colbert....................	1 888	3.7	34 616	1 996	1 043	189	81	113	277	541	1 426	94	81
Conecuh...................	380	0.0	30 009	2 715	126	26	10	44	55	143	206	15	10
Coosa.....................	295	1.2	27 057	2 977	51	10	4	7	43	95	73	7	4
Covington.................	1 197	3.2	31 568	2 519	445	92	36	98	176	378	671	46	36
Crenshaw.................	482	3.8	34 461	2 035	140	26	11	99	56	135	276	16	11
Cullman...................	2 890	4.6	35 548	1 846	1 034	178	79	326	394	744	1 616	106	79
Dale.......................	1 647	2.1	33 274	2 232	1 189	293	101	107	310	429	1 690	90	101
Dallas.....................	1 297	1.6	31 103	2 569	488	92	39	113	184	482	733	50	39
DeKalb....................	2 112	4.1	29 724	2 757	743	142	59	262	276	596	1 206	78	59
Elmore....................	2 958	3.4	36 528	1 683	672	129	52	137	447	655	990	71	52
Escambia.................	1 160	3.7	30 755	2 621	509	97	38	90	192	354	733	50	38
Etowah....................	3 455	4.3	33 374	2 217	1 299	227	100	272	484	1 056	1 898	134	100
Fayette....................	504	3.2	29 890	2 732	133	29	10	45	70	178	217	17	10
Franklin...................	964	5.0	30 509	2 650	347	72	27	70	122	278	516	34	27
Geneva....................	847	3.0	31 722	2 487	162	34	12	103	116	259	311	21	12
Greene....................	272	-4.4	31 745	2 480	60	14	5	31	47	98	111	7	5
Hale.......................	531	1.2	34 953	1 945	101	21	7	73	71	164	202	13	7
Henry......................	606	1.9	35 273	1 896	135	24	10	48	94	173	218	16	10
Houston...................	3 888	3.4	37 316	1 554	1 900	334	143	281	667	937	2 657	170	143
Jackson...................	1 767	2.9	33 550	2 186	587	116	47	153	293	480	904	62	47
Jefferson..................	32 103	4.4	48 582	453	18 805	2 849	1 371	4 917	5 905	5 665	27 942	1 694	1 371
Lamar.....................	425	2.0	30 143	2 699	128	24	9	30	58	151	191	15	9
Lauderdale...............	3 159	4.5	33 933	2 125	1 046	191	80	222	570	793	1 539	108	80
Lawrence.................	1 060	1.9	31 667	2 498	249	41	15	93	110	302	399	29	15
Lee........................	5 100	5.5	33 064	2 268	2 047	396	154	333	864	899	2 930	179	154
Limestone................	3 399	4.1	37 435	1 534	1 049	202	81	333	426	658	1 666	106	81
Lowndes..................	382	-0.1	36 082	1 769	110	24	8	58	43	113	199	12	8
Macon.....................	599	2.1	30 828	2 611	215	55	17	22	98	196	308	20	17
Madison...................	15 594	4.1	44 517	714	10 882	1 795	836	677	3 065	2 432	14 190	840	836
Marengo...................	749	3.5	37 235	1 564	286	55	21	95	108	223	457	30	21
Marion.....................	871	4.6	28 783	2 850	322	61	25	102	127	281	511	35	25
Marshall...................	3 009	3.6	31 796	2 471	1 194	232	91	210	480	819	1 727	114	91
Mobile.....................	14 542	4.1	35 031	1 933	7 903	1 291	593	1 243	2 352	3 557	11 029	701	593
Monroe....................	676	1.7	30 799	2 617	267	47	20	58	102	217	392	28	20
Montgomery..............	9 275	3.5	41 008	1 059	6 153	1 151	471	911	1 890	1 934	8 686	505	471
Morgan....................	4 209	3.3	35 188	1 906	2 050	365	154	264	675	999	2 833	183	154
Perry......................	291	-3.8	29 647	2 770	70	16	6	47	39	109	139	9	6
Pickens....................	616	1.6	30 233	2 685	140	31	11	53	83	203	235	17	11
Pike.......................	1 173	4.7	35 125	1 913	542	103	41	157	181	294	844	50	41
Randolph..................	713	5.2	31 626	2 506	158	33	12	71	91	225	274	20	12
Russell....................	1 733	3.7	29 080	2 819	506	93	38	70	239	520	708	51	38
St. Clair...................	2 838	5.0	32 737	2 328	695	119	53	125	311	659	992	74	53
Shelby.....................	9 481	5.3	45 879	608	4 267	604	304	323	1 541	1 256	5 498	348	304
Sumter....................	410	0.2	31 164	2 561	127	26	9	65	48	135	228	13	9
Talladega..................	2 540	3.8	31 233	2 551	1 341	222	102	137	324	769	1 802	123	102
Tallapoosa................	1 456	4.5	35 369	1 886	446	81	35	62	265	450	625	47	35
Tuscaloosa...............	7 175	4.5	35 482	1 859	4 066	715	300	552	1 253	1 511	5 634	345	300
Walker....................	2 428	3.5	37 085	1 588	696	130	52	207	407	726	1 086	80	52

1. Based on the resident population estimated as of July 1 of the year shown.

Table B. States and Counties — Earnings, Social Security, and Housing

STATE County	Earnings, 2014 (cont.) Percent by selected industries									Social Security beneficiaries, December 2014		Supplemental Security Income recipients, December 2014	Housing units, 2015	
	Farm	Mining	Construction	Manu-facturing	Information: professional, scientific, technical services	Retail trade	Finance, insurance, real estate and leasing	Health care and social assistance	Govern-ment	Number	Rate[1]		Total	Percent change, 2010–2014
	75	76	77	78	79	80	81	82	83	84	85	86	87	88
UNITED STATES............	1.1	1.7	5.6	9.6	13.3	5.9	9.2	10.8	16.8	57 499 952	180	8 334 413	134 789 944	2.3
ALABAMA	1.5	0.7	6.2	14.3	9.2	6.8	6.6	10.5	20.2	1 095 925	226	174 524	2 218 287	2.1
Autauga...............	1.5	0.7	7.2	16.8	3.1	9.9	5.9	9.4	18.5	11 260	204	1 508	22 847	3.2
Baldwin................	0.6	0.2	8.4	6.9	5.4	13.9	7.2	12.4	14.4	48 780	244	3 462	108 564	4.3
Barbour................	9.7	2.8	2.7	23.1	D	6.5	2.9	D	18.4	6 830	255	1 544	11 789	-0.3
Bibb.....................	1.3	D	24.0	7.9	D	6.0	2.4	D	24.7	5 450	242	1 003	8 986	0.0
Blount.................	8.3	D	8.3	11.3	4.1	8.1	3.2	9.6	18.6	14 230	247	1 607	23 817	-0.3
Bullock................	16.3	0.0	D	D	2.3	4.0	2.0	11.9	23.6	2 215	205	638	4 456	-0.8
Butler..................	7.4	0.0	5.3	19.1	D	8.3	2.4	12.2	13.4	5 850	289	1 412	9 905	-0.6
Calhoun...............	1.1	D	2.8	15.0	4.5	8.2	3.2	10.2	31.9	29 195	252	4 829	53 326	0.1
Chambers............	4.2	D	3.9	17.6	D	9.1	2.4	D	15.6	9 895	291	1 604	16 879	-0.7
Cherokee.............	9.6	0.0	3.9	17.6	D	11.1	4.1	6.8	20.3	7 845	302	912	16 230	-0.2
Chilton................	1.0	D	10.6	21.8	D	10.7	3.1	D	18.8	10 245	233	1 484	19 279	0.0
Choctaw..............	1.6	D	D	D	D	8.5	2.3	D	8.8	4 285	322	848	7 225	-0.6
Clarke.................	1.0	1.1	2.4	27.8	D	10.6	5.1	D	19.3	7 080	285	1 543	12 578	-0.5
Clay....................	9.3	0.0	4.4	33.7	1.6	5.1	2.9	D	20.7	3 980	294	531	6 729	-0.7
Cleburne.............	13.9	0.0	D	10.9	1.2	7.8	2.3	1.8	21.2	3 970	263	540	6 684	-0.5
Coffee.................	9.5	0.0	4.3	15.7	D	9.8	4.3	10.4	15.3	11 210	221	1 498	22 883	2.5
Colbert................	1.2	0.5	8.3	26.2	1.9	7.5	3.6	8.1	23.0	15 090	277	2 130	26 307	2.1
Conecuh..............	7.7	D	2.7	13.6	1.5	4.7	D	D	19.2	3 835	303	787	7 050	-0.6
Coosa.................	1.8	0.0	2.8	40.7	D	D	D	4.2	23.0	2 555	236	401	6 453	-0.6
Covington............	5.3	D	5.6	16.9	2.6	9.5	4.0	D	15.6	10 715	283	1 513	18 763	-0.4
Crenshaw............	19.4	0.0	4.0	21.3	1.5	3.9	2.6	D	10.6	3 670	263	640	6 703	-0.5
Cullman..............	7.2	D	6.9	18.6	4.9	8.4	3.7	12.0	13.1	21 215	261	2 676	37 184	0.3
Dale....................	1.8	D	2.6	21.3	3.1	2.3	1.5	2.1	48.7	10 960	221	1 795	22 828	0.7
Dallas.................	5.4	D	3.7	25.8	D	7.9	3.1	12.8	18.4	11 110	267	4 408	20 226	0.1
DeKalb................	8.3	D	5.9	27.5	3.0	7.2	2.8	8.8	13.7	16 725	236	2 269	31 036	-0.2
Elmore................	0.7	D	7.5	16.2	5.0	11.4	4.4	9.1	23.6	17 250	213	2 404	33 570	2.8
Escambia............	0.7	2.9	4.8	21.9	2.1	7.8	4.0	6.7	28.7	9 920	263	1 537	16 406	-0.5
Etowah...............	0.8	0.2	5.0	15.7	3.8	8.4	4.8	21.8	14.7	28 785	278	4 865	47 510	0.1
Fayette................	5.8	1.4	5.5	18.5	2.4	10.1	3.3	D	26.0	5 165	307	799	8 397	-0.5
Franklin..............	5.9	D	3.2	37.4	2.1	5.5	3.8	D	18.5	7 775	246	1 199	14 048	0.2
Geneva...............	19.9	0.0	4.9	9.4	D	8.0	3.8	4.2	20.6	7 425	278	1 252	12 640	-0.4
Greene................	20.1	0.0	3.2	18.7	D	D	D	D	27.2	2 525	295	807	4 987	-0.4
Hale...................	25.2	D	6.1	14.8	1.6	5.7	2.6	D	21.4	4 575	302	1 152	7 636	-0.2
Henry.................	9.1	0.0	7.9	13.1	D	5.3	3.0	D	16.0	4 870	284	653	8 967	0.9
Houston..............	0.6	D	6.3	7.5	4.8	10.7	4.4	17.4	18.6	24 985	240	4 188	46 691	3.0
Jackson...............	4.6	D	4.0	28.7	3.3	8.4	3.0	5.7	21.8	14 255	271	1 775	24 771	-0.1
Jefferson.............	0.0	0.9	8.5	7.2	11.0	5.4	11.0	14.2	14.5	138 565	210	24 744	306 664	2.0
Lamar.................	1.5	D	3.8	31.3	D	6.8	4.3	7.7	15.3	4 310	307	612	7 321	-0.4
Lauderdale..........	1.5	D	6.7	12.3	4.9	12.5	5.9	15.8	18.1	23 455	252	2 789	44 377	1.3
Lawrence............	12.1	D	5.9	23.8	D	8.1	3.0	D	18.1	9 105	272	1 531	15 163	-0.4
Lee.....................	0.4	0.1	5.2	12.5	5.1	7.3	4.4	6.6	34.5	23 600	153	3 419	66 382	6.4
Limestone...........	2.4	D	14.4	12.1	4.8	9.9	2.9	4.7	31.1	17 900	198	2 148	35 602	1.8
Lowndes.............	19.0	D	4.7	36.8	D	3.3	D	2.2	14.5	2 805	266	607	5 085	-1.1
Macon.................	2.6	D	D	D	D	3.5	1.2	D	63.5	4 745	245	1 158	10 207	-0.5
Madison..............	0.1	D	2.8	12.2	25.9	5.0	3.0	7.0	29.1	61 370	175	6 888	156 856	7.1
Marengo..............	5.0	0.0	5.5	21.4	D	6.2	3.9	D	16.7	6 115	304	1 561	10 194	-0.4
Marion................	6.1	D	3.1	29.3	1.8	7.8	4.6	D	14.9	8 545	283	1 150	14 695	-0.3
Marshall..............	3.7	D	4.0	27.8	4.6	9.5	4.4	6.5	18.1	22 580	239	3 143	40 323	0.0
Mobile................	0.3	0.8	7.0	14.8	8.8	6.7	6.4	11.6	15.2	88 830	214	15 331	182 025	2.1
Monroe...............	1.7	0.1	2.8	24.2	D	7.1	3.5	D	17.5	5 970	273	998	11 263	-0.6
Montgomery.........	0.8	0.0	5.6	11.1	9.1	5.5	6.6	10.6	29.5	44 515	197	10 167	103 995	2.3
Morgan................	1.0	0.1	7.5	32.9	4.5	6.6	4.0	7.1	13.8	27 490	230	3 341	51 580	0.8
Perry..................	16.1	0.0	2.4	12.9	D	4.3	2.2	6.7	19.9	2 675	271	1 105	4 683	-1.1
Pickens...............	11.2	D	2.9	17.7	D	5.8	1.9	D	31.8	5 600	275	1 287	9 434	-0.5
Pike....................	5.4	0.0	3.7	23.5	2.3	5.7	4.0	7.9	20.4	6 825	206	1 664	15 825	3.7
Randolph.............	12.6	D	3.6	17.8	2.2	8.9	3.5	D	20.3	6 215	276	899	11 916	-0.6
Russell...............	1.5	0.1	7.0	25.5	D	9.2	5.6	10.1	20.5	12 135	203	2 016	26 962	9.6
St. Clair..............	2.1	D	7.5	17.3	5.1	9.2	3.5	8.4	16.2	19 350	224	2 112	35 904	1.0
Shelby................	0.1	0.7	7.0	6.4	10.5	7.0	20.0	7.2	8.6	35 120	170	2 616	84 365	4.1
Sumter................	21.6	0.0	5.1	9.9	D	4.2	2.1	D	29.1	3 350	253	1 192	6 740	-0.7
Talladega............	0.6	1.7	3.6	43.7	1.8	4.7	1.9	7.7	14.9	21 600	266	4 300	37 202	0.3
Tallapoosa..........	0.7	D	5.4	18.4	3.8	8.3	3.7	D	17.3	12 945	315	1 783	22 070	-0.2
Tuscaloosa..........	0.2	4.8	4.9	18.8	5.9	6.1	4.2	9.1	26.4	38 795	192	6 890	89 065	4.9
Walker................	0.9	3.4	5.7	10.2	4.5	11.4	4.2	16.8	14.9	20 390	311	3 521	30 649	-0.5

1. Per 1,000 resident population estimated as of July 1 of the year shown.

Table B. States and Counties — **Housing, Labor Force, and Employment**

STATE County	Housing units, 2010–2014								Civilian labor force, 2015				Civilian employment,[6] 2010–2014		
	Occupied units										Unemployment			Percent	
			Owner-occupied			Renter-occupied									
				Median owner cost as a percent of income											
	Total	Percent	Median value[1]	With a mortgage	Without a mortgage[2]	Median rent[3]	Median rent as a percent of income[2]	Sub-standard units[4] (percent)	Total	Percent change, 2014–2015	Total	Rate[5]	Total	Management, business, science and arts	Construction, production, and maintenance occupations
	89	90	91	92	93	94	95	96	97	98	99	100	101	102	103
UNITED STATES..........	116 211 092	64.4	175 700	23.7	12.3	920	31.3	3.7	157 259 320	0.6	8 303 325	5.3	143 435 233	36.4	21.1
ALABAMA	1 842 174	69.2	123 800	21.7	11.4	715	30.9	2.2	2 146 171	-0.7	130 974	6.1	2 010 453	32.9	25.8
Autauga.....................	20 304	75.1	136 600	21.2	10.0	876	31.0	2.9	25 308	-1.1	1 327	5.2	24 143	32.3	25.5
Baldwin......................	73 058	71.5	168 800	23.2	11.1	882	31.2	1.8	87 316	1.1	4 791	5.5	83 530	33.3	22.8
Barbour......................	9 145	67.6	89 500	20.6	12.8	608	29.8	2.1	8 625	-2.5	771	8.9	9 237	27.0	31.2
Bibb...........................	7 078	77.0	96 300	24.2	11.8	610	26.6	0.5	8 490	-0.8	561	6.6	7 954	21.4	41.9
Blount........................	20 934	78.4	117 700	22.1	11.3	609	26.2	1.8	24 352	-0.7	1 316	5.4	22 432	27.5	34.8
Bullock......................	3 746	72.8	68 900	23.5	13.0	570	28.5	3.3	4 773	0.8	371	7.8	3 845	20.5	43.2
Butler........................	8 253	69.9	76 000	23.5	13.4	581	32.9	2.4	9 142	-1.4	690	7.5	7 748	27.0	34.7
Calhoun.....................	45 348	68.5	103 300	21.1	10.3	634	30.8	1.5	46 051	-2.5	3 214	7.0	46 310	27.2	30.2
Chambers...................	13 901	67.1	82 400	23.0	13.8	664	33.7	4.2	15 100	-1.3	908	6.0	13 210	25.7	35.2
Cherokee....................	11 726	77.3	98 500	23.9	14.1	619	31.4	2.4	11 197	-1.7	609	5.4	10 440	29.8	35.9
Chilton.......................	16 281	75.4	98 800	22.3	11.5	629	29.2	3.8	19 021	-0.4	1 078	5.7	17 682	27.0	33.6
Choctaw....................	5 526	82.1	59 100	21.5	12.3	573	30.2	2.1	4 378	-2.6	399	9.1	4 694	27.3	38.0
Clarke........................	9 791	70.1	84 700	20.4	13.8	557	31.6	1.9	7 994	-2.0	940	11.8	8 288	23.2	35.8
Clay...........................	5 572	73.3	82 200	24.2	10.0	451	27.4	5.3	5 526	0.2	340	6.2	5 102	23.4	40.9
Cleburne....................	5 639	77.6	101 000	22.5	12.4	604	24.8	3.9	5 665	-3.2	341	6.0	5 849	26.8	36.7
Coffee........................	19 086	69.3	137 000	20.4	10.2	676	28.1	1.8	20 310	0.4	1 201	5.9	20 114	31.9	25.7
Colbert......................	22 442	71.2	99 900	21.4	12.3	655	31.5	1.5	23 586	-1.8	1 864	7.9	21 271	26.7	32.2
Conecuh....................	5 030	77.2	65 800	25.7	12.8	521	43.7	5.3	4 674	-0.9	429	9.2	3 587	19.7	34.4
Coosa........................	4 446	81.2	73 100	25.4	14.1	612	26.7	3.4	4 431	-0.8	298	6.7	3 893	20.0	39.4
Covington..................	14 979	75.6	90 600	22.0	12.5	585	29.0	2.5	15 456	-2.9	1 101	7.1	14 718	25.3	35.6
Crenshaw...................	5 424	72.3	68 100	20.5	12.8	507	23.7	1.3	6 352	0.9	382	6.0	5 590	27.0	35.8
Cullman......................	31 160	75.4	107 000	23.0	12.1	621	31.7	2.4	36 181	0.7	1 908	5.3	32 471	28.4	31.8
Dale...........................	19 470	61.4	103 300	19.6	10.0	621	27.9	2.1	19 758	-2.8	1 255	6.4	19 212	27.1	31.0
Dallas........................	16 259	60.8	79 200	23.9	14.8	564	36.7	8.0	15 566	-2.8	1 502	9.6	13 978	25.9	34.8
DeKalb.......................	24 743	75.1	95 300	22.7	12.4	528	24.5	3.9	28 858	-0.3	1 740	6.0	27 498	24.0	38.1
Elmore.......................	28 617	75.6	143 800	21.2	10.6	792	27.6	1.8	36 075	-1.3	1 839	5.1	34 119	32.1	24.6
Escambia...................	13 737	70.4	88 000	21.0	13.8	579	33.5	3.0	14 575	1.4	1 020	7.0	12 287	24.2	30.3
Etowah......................	40 001	70.8	100 400	22.3	12.7	627	31.3	2.1	43 203	-1.2	2 644	6.1	40 153	28.3	31.1
Fayette......................	6 967	72.6	72 700	19.2	11.5	474	31.9	1.1	6 396	0.7	448	7.0	6 056	25.4	38.8
Franklin.....................	12 247	68.3	86 300	20.9	14.0	546	26.4	5.2	13 615	-0.8	871	6.4	12 450	19.7	46.7
Geneva......................	10 898	73.2	78 100	20.0	11.0	572	29.0	3.4	10 806	0.1	633	5.9	10 730	23.0	37.1
Greene	3 282	71.4	69 100	30.6	16.9	434	33.3	4.1	2 895	-3.1	319	11.0	2 456	16.9	36.9
Hale...........................	5 931	76.8	86 800	25.3	14.3	442	29.7	3.5	6 102	1.1	478	7.8	5 210	25.5	36.7
Henry.........................	6 900	77.8	93 900	21.1	11.4	570	25.3	1.1	6 735	-0.6	456	6.8	6 635	34.2	28.9
Houston.....................	39 464	64.7	121 600	20.7	10.1	682	29.3	1.5	44 743	-0.9	2 765	6.2	44 436	30.2	24.3
Jackson......................	20 425	74.5	93 800	20.4	11.0	550	27.5	2.2	23 512	0.3	1 549	6.6	20 934	26.1	37.8
Jefferson....................	259 397	63.9	141 300	22.8	12.0	811	32.5	1.7	309 229	-1.0	17 926	5.8	290 448	38.4	19.0
Lamar........................	6 147	73.7	66 800	19.7	11.2	473	27.7	2.9	5 633	0.1	355	6.3	5 526	25.6	41.4
Lauderdale	38 691	69.7	115 300	20.8	10.2	587	30.4	1.0	42 714	-1.8	2 964	6.9	40 047	29.9	25.9
Lawrence...................	13 312	81.2	92 400	21.4	12.0	564	24.8	1.2	13 864	-1.1	1 062	7.7	12 876	25.0	39.4
Lee.............................	56 637	60.4	150 100	21.8	10.7	777	36.5	2.0	71 548	0.2	3 660	5.1	66 893	39.3	21.5
Limestone..................	32 156	76.0	138 100	20.3	10.0	626	28.1	2.4	39 607	0.1	2 162	5.5	36 895	34.8	27.9
Lowndes....................	4 287	74.1	69 100	27.0	21.2	566	30.7	4.8	3 824	-1.3	443	11.6	3 586	21.5	41.7
Macon........................	8 039	65.7	73 400	25.7	13.3	595	33.0	2.4	7 978	-3.2	644	8.1	7 627	25.3	26.3
Madison.....................	135 409	69.0	166 500	18.9	10.0	751	28.7	1.7	169 738	-0.2	9 303	5.5	162 126	44.5	17.0
Marengo....................	8 477	71.5	89 600	21.7	13.0	517	29.9	2.5	7 357	-3.5	570	7.7	7 179	28.6	34.4
Marion.......................	12 602	75.4	77 700	20.4	12.1	482	28.9	2.3	12 439	1.2	870	7.0	11 517	27.9	33.7
Marshall.....................	34 524	71.7	114 600	21.8	11.4	593	27.3	3.8	40 348	1.1	2 329	5.8	37 953	28.3	34.8
Mobile........................	154 400	66.7	124 500	22.6	11.9	773	33.7	2.5	183 097	-1.2	12 811	7.0	169 695	31.3	23.9
Monroe......................	8 390	71.9	78 800	23.7	12.1	529	29.7	2.0	7 301	-4.2	736	10.1	7 229	25.0	37.1
Montgomery	89 143	60.0	123 100	22.0	10.2	816	32.3	2.1	103 579	-1.4	6 385	6.2	99 057	35.9	19.9
Morgan.......................	45 856	71.1	121 900	20.3	10.0	609	26.9	2.6	55 106	-1.7	3 218	5.8	52 294	28.6	31.1
Perry..........................	3 263	67.5	61 700	24.3	18.5	478	32.7	9.9	3 501	0.3	349	10.0	2 596	23.8	33.6
Pickens......................	7 741	72.0	85 600	21.2	12.9	454	33.2	2.5	7 820	0.8	529	6.8	6 499	19.4	38.0
Pike...........................	12 909	58.2	101 900	20.8	10.0	592	35.3	1.8	14 929	-0.1	1 006	6.7	14 821	29.2	29.4
Randolph....................	9 016	71.3	89 700	22.8	11.4	633	32.5	5.3	9 443	1.8	555	5.9	8 515	26.3	40.6
Russell.......................	21 568	58.6	108 600	24.5	12.9	724	30.9	2.5	24 283	-2.0	1 460	6.0	22 168	25.3	27.4
St. Clair.....................	31 673	80.6	135 200	21.2	11.6	732	26.1	1.9	38 172	-0.9	2 001	5.2	36 138	29.0	28.5
Shelby........................	74 790	78.8	192 200	21.2	10.0	948	27.4	1.4	106 491	-0.7	4 510	4.2	100 194	42.1	15.6
Sumter.......................	4 962	70.2	72 500	27.2	15.8	569	41.8	2.9	5 109	-4.9	407	8.0	4 686	25.2	26.7
Talladega...................	31 277	71.4	93 100	22.6	13.0	599	30.4	2.8	35 169	-0.6	2 310	6.6	30 462	26.1	33.7
Tallapoosa.................	16 437	70.7	101 200	21.8	11.2	581	32.3	5.4	18 717	1.6	1 147	6.1	16 236	29.0	34.3
Tuscaloosa................	68 103	64.6	154 500	22.1	10.6	782	32.6	2.0	98 051	1.0	5 347	5.5	87 331	34.4	25.4
Walker.......................	25 571	74.1	81 600	21.2	11.6	598	29.6	1.9	25 476	-1.1	1 839	7.2	24 045	25.9	31.8

1. Specified owner-occupied units.   2. A value of 10.0 represents 10 percent or less; a value of 50.0 represents 50 percent or more.   3. Specified renter-occupied units.
4. Overcrowded or lacking complete plumbing facilities.   5. Percent of civilian labor force.   6. Persons 16 years old and over.

Table B. States and Counties — Nonfarm Employment and Agriculture

STATE County	Private nonfarm establishments, employment and payroll, 2014									Agriculture, 2012			
	Number of establish-ments	Employment						Annual payroll		Farms			
		Total	Health care and social assistance	Manufac-turing	Retail trade	Finance and insurance	Professional, scientific, and technical services	Total (mil dol)	Average per employee (dollars)	Number	Percent with:		Farm operators whose principal occu-pation is farming (percent)
											Fewer than 50 acres	500 acres or more	
	104	105	106	107	108	109	110	111	112	113	114	115	116
UNITED STATES	7 563 085	121 079 879	18 861 973	11 424 251	15 372 632	6 078 713	8 619 574	5 940 443	49 062	2 109 303	38.6	15.0	47.8
ALABAMA	97 714	1 604 016	236 675	243 899	227 977	70 052	93 495	64 292	40 082	43 223	37.4	8.6	44.2
Autauga	817	10 202	1 614	D	2 525	374	285	301	29 519	389	31.6	14.4	51.2
Baldwin	4 969	56 531	6 953	4 052	13 471	1 596	1 856	1 749	30 943	989	52.6	8.1	45.8
Barbour	464	6 481	644	D	870	189	110	205	31 637	571	13.8	17.3	46.1
Bibb	274	3 424	645	344	521	82	48	120	35 006	189	29.6	13.8	38.6
Blount	656	6 446	968	D	1 259	210	218	190	29 543	1 241	40.6	3.1	48.8
Bullock	108	D	D	D	226	D	D	D	D	273	17.2	30.4	40.7
Butler	408	5 920	D	1 327	926	140	56	181	30 632	407	25.1	8.6	45.2
Calhoun	2 309	35 096	6 106	5 854	6 129	912	1 013	1 137	32 401	592	45.4	3.5	46.1
Chambers	536	5 989	767	1 491	1 123	D	160	183	30 561	301	22.6	15.6	38.9
Cherokee	357	3 714	435	D	838	125	D	114	30 794	561	32.1	11.6	45.6
Chilton	721	7 259	677	1 774	1 455	230	100	226	31 088	543	37.9	7.0	41.1
Choctaw	248	2 918	D	D	377	69	48	141	48 398	248	37.1	14.5	40.3
Clarke	602	6 999	943	1 807	1 511	D	77	242	34 537	263	38.8	9.9	35.4
Clay	187	3 125	493	1 615	292	89	55	90	28 953	401	24.7	7.7	39.7
Cleburne	161	1 750	75	323	262	58	22	73	41 551	341	36.7	5.3	47.8
Coffee	966	12 900	1 957	3 179	2 273	484	431	395	30 658	899	27.9	9.1	50.5
Colbert	1 223	20 152	2 595	6 052	2 875	639	306	766	38 015	687	39.6	9.0	36.7
Conecuh	192	2 381	276	501	296	D	30	77	32 539	346	19.1	8.4	44.8
Coosa	94	1 127	D	512	154	11	D	35	31 243	152	23.7	11.8	52.6
Covington	812	10 727	1 664	2 286	1 801	D	296	328	30 615	1 051	31.4	6.8	40.3
Crenshaw	206	3 144	476	1 243	241	98	29	106	33 769	575	21.6	12.3	40.2
Cullman	1 698	22 880	3 430	4 874	3 598	793	431	800	34 954	2 007	47.6	2.1	48.6
Dale	758	10 973	1 241	476	1 253	242	1 018	503	45 819	487	27.9	12.7	30.8
Dallas	743	10 056	1 880	2 741	1 674	D	204	334	33 263	506	22.9	25.7	45.7
DeKalb	1 065	17 391	2 493	6 909	2 311	459	363	554	31 884	2 035	44.9	3.4	50.7
Elmore	1 142	14 684	2 126	2 787	2 868	406	373	467	31 789	552	46.4	7.8	40.9
Escambia	727	9 942	1 143	2 025	1 829	443	159	339	34 087	454	44.1	13.9	39.6
Etowah	1 995	28 573	7 134	4 750	4 465	1 027	602	935	32 723	853	51.1	2.9	40.3
Fayette	309	3 045	726	786	579	82	D	92	30 210	414	24.6	8.0	38.9
Franklin	509	10 094	1 034	D	936	392	D	315	31 251	825	25.7	7.8	47.5
Geneva	402	3 667	583	D	777	139	124	106	28 866	1 017	31.6	9.8	43.1
Greene	100	1 470	D	444	179	28	8	40	27 332	304	26.0	24.0	50.3
Hale	198	1 833	401	484	273	67	D	63	34 183	456	27.0	16.0	49.8
Henry	290	2 584	189	362	339	96	123	90	34 791	498	19.5	17.1	43.0
Houston	2 702	42 566	9 546	4 265	7 919	1 172	1 071	1 545	36 307	816	38.8	12.3	44.5
Jackson	859	12 741	1 832	5 355	1 924	D	D	397	31 149	1 376	40.1	6.0	37.4
Jefferson	16 213	318 416	52 905	24 155	39 878	22 931	15 566	15 515	48 725	394	59.9	3.0	46.7
Lamar	241	2 861	D	D	308	D	56	107	37 291	353	31.7	8.5	33.4
Lauderdale	1 974	26 459	4 672	D	5 490	987	806	749	28 305	1 466	45.9	5.2	44.8
Lawrence	395	3 544	703	418	795	104	D	108	30 508	1 551	41.5	4.3	43.2
Lee	2 576	39 528	5 721	6 520	6 702	1 012	1 363	1 224	30 971	315	32.7	7.6	37.1
Limestone	1 301	16 004	2 052	D	2 908	D	786	542	33 837	1 230	40.6	6.9	46.6
Lowndes	100	2 135	D	1 177	173	27	D	123	57 612	441	24.5	21.8	48.5
Macon	206	5 280	D	D	395	D	D	211	40 009	352	26.4	15.9	48.3
Madison	8 150	154 403	22 646	15 946	19 507	3 689	33 782	7 461	48 319	1 033	48.4	8.0	49.5
Marengo	466	6 103	1 064	1 432	907	233	80	214	35 133	499	27.3	16.8	33.9
Marion	538	7 384	1 205	2 458	1 031	404	75	230	31 168	715	32.3	3.8	37.5
Marshall	1 804	30 052	3 828	10 349	4 748	765	595	932	31 004	1 505	53.2	3.1	41.9
Mobile	8 492	142 481	19 403	16 571	20 370	5 400	8 911	5 650	39 654	698	60.9	4.4	48.6
Monroe	395	5 282	615	D	890	203	D	208	39 382	480	37.1	12.1	44.6
Montgomery	5 567	103 313	16 446	12 884	12 616	4 132	5 987	4 127	39 946	603	28.0	19.2	50.4
Morgan	2 568	42 524	5 731	11 511	5 592	1 398	1 484	1 739	40 903	1 237	44.2	3.7	42.1
Perry	116	1 657	151	640	198	61	18	49	29 452	389	26.2	19.0	39.8
Pickens	271	2 746	556	575	405	150	97	84	30 515	433	28.4	9.9	46.9
Pike	635	11 058	1 067	1 619	1 465	358	D	382	34 571	600	21.5	14.7	39.5
Randolph	332	3 557	572	1 032	712	154	47	96	26 887	611	27.8	8.3	52.2
Russell	780	11 097	1 491	D	1 945	356	194	361	32 508	280	28.9	21.8	35.4
St. Clair	1 257	15 609	1 842	2 953	2 799	481	613	504	32 295	540	44.3	3.3	51.1
Shelby	4 891	79 232	7 003	5 568	8 515	9 816	5 122	3 778	47 679	401	45.4	6.7	44.6
Sumter	206	3 056	393	D	285	66	D	111	36 427	428	22.7	22.9	46.0
Talladega	1 256	24 299	2 797	8 736	2 635	484	440	1 052	43 277	519	38.2	8.5	50.3
Tallapoosa	720	10 666	2 226	2 164	1 482	261	214	325	30 448	345	35.1	5.5	42.0
Tuscaloosa	3 985	73 786	11 823	13 183	10 158	1 788	2 261	2 962	40 143	497	43.7	9.5	37.0
Walker	1 248	14 947	3 198	1 894	3 349	491	353	522	34 919	482	46.9	3.7	33.8

Table B. States and Counties — Agriculture

STATE County	Acreage (1,000) 117	Percent change, 2007–2012 118	Average size of farm 119	Total irrigated (1,000) 120	Total cropland (1,000) 121	Average per farm 122	Average per acre 123	Value of machinery and equipment, average per farm (dollars) 124	Total (mil dol) 125	Average per farm (dollars) 126	Crops 127	Live-stock and poultry products 128	$10,000 or more 129	$100,000 or more 130	Total ($1,000) 131	Percent of farms 132
UNITED STATES............	914 528	-0.8	434	55 822.2	389 690.4	1 075 491	2 481	115 662	394 644.5	187 097	53.8	46.2	43.4	18.4	8 053 346	38.5
ALABAMA	8 903	-1.4	206	113.0	2 758.5	547 524	2 658	71 210	5 571.2	128 894	23.6	76.4	33.8	11.2	88 145	30.0
Autauga................................	112	0.9	287	1.6	41.3	655 057	2 285	73 658	19.8	50 928	D	D	33.7	6.9	1 245	31.9
Baldwin................................	192	1.3	194	7.7	100.9	773 980	3 980	107 905	135.6	137 070	85.3	14.7	35.2	11.7	2 649	26.7
Barbour................................	204	2.6	358	2.3	41.3	808 758	2 261	80 371	104.4	182 760	14.1	85.9	32.7	9.6	1 806	62.5
Bibb	56	47.7	298	0.1	12.6	624 810	2 098	66 159	D	D	D	D	23.8	1.6	138	14.3
Blount	146	-3.4	118	0.5	37.1	427 880	3 632	58 512	178.2	143 587	7.0	93.0	37.4	12.7	897	19.1
Bullock.................................	165	22.9	603	1.4	26.1	1 312 890	2 178	107 813	54.5	199 813	62.0	38.0	38.8	13.6	721	31.5
Butler	88	-4.5	217	0.0	21.3	527 472	2 429	65 489	110.1	270 634	D	D	28.7	10.8	355	26.3
Calhoun................................	81	6.6	137	0.9	21.4	418 128	3 046	61 630	92.4	156 052	11.8	88.2	30.1	7.3	406	17.4
Chambers.............................	96	-8.2	320	0.1	15.3	832 784	2 602	61 761	8.3	27 708	24.3	75.7	35.2	5.3	397	15.6
Cherokee..............................	124	-6.5	221	1.3	58.8	757 134	3 419	84 629	120.0	213 913	30.0	70.0	36.4	17.3	1 985	38.1
Chilton	91	-8.8	168	0.5	23.7	493 578	2 933	55 048	16.0	29 538	63.8	36.2	36.8	5.3	296	10.3
Choctaw...............................	68	24.5	276	0.0	8.0	517 085	1 872	53 851	D	D	D	D	18.5	2.0	194	11.3
Clarke	47	-35.6	181	0.0	7.7	369 251	2 045	38 399	2.6	9 863	49.1	50.9	24.3	0.8	153	17.5
Clay	78	4.6	194	0.0	13.0	480 421	2 474	54 217	58.1	144 850	1.8	98.2	38.4	8.7	585	19.5
Cleburne	50	1.4	147	0.3	7.7	404 111	2 745	60 522	84.3	247 170	3.9	96.1	45.2	18.5	106	12.6
Coffee	202	-4.2	225	3.3	85.5	593 148	2 636	90 236	258.2	287 171	14.3	85.7	37.9	19.7	3 459	57.7
Colbert	153	18.5	222	3.7	65.7	626 991	2 820	80 017	67.0	97 531	54.3	45.7	32.3	8.7	1 996	31.4
Conecuh	94	8.6	271	0.1	20.1	539 208	1 991	72 494	16.4	47 436	44.6	55.4	35.0	6.4	770	41.0
Coosa	36	-20.8	236	D	4.3	489 967	2 072	52 934	2.1	13 763	D	D	30.3	2.0	39	5.9
Covington	209	4.2	198	1.4	65.5	447 436	2 255	67 858	119.8	114 025	26.0	74.0	30.9	12.9	2 582	43.8
Crenshaw	130	-1.9	226	0.9	29.0	458 381	2 029	80 572	143.8	250 132	3.5	96.5	36.2	17.0	919	51.0
Cullman	194	-15.5	97	0.5	58.4	403 876	4 176	64 375	417.1	207 820	3.8	96.2	43.3	21.1	567	12.0
Dale	130	-6.1	267	2.6	49.6	668 934	2 510	86 197	118.0	242 400	21.6	78.4	32.6	15.8	1 495	55.6
Dallas	255	-0.7	504	2.0	76.8	925 310	1 835	106 532	70.2	138 800	39.5	60.5	32.6	12.3	2 616	45.8
DeKalb	229	-2.5	113	0.3	72.3	427 088	3 790	70 291	461.7	226 882	5.3	94.7	37.4	17.5	2 652	24.1
Elmore	90	-12.1	164	3.1	30.2	519 685	3 175	64 795	26.5	47 986	65.6	34.4	29.3	4.3	959	15.9
Escambia..............................	107	-4.8	236	0.8	47.7	537 068	2 271	93 018	40.9	89 991	88.5	11.5	28.4	11.5	2 602	48.9
Etowah	86	-8.6	101	0.1	19.5	359 368	3 559	51 635	83.7	98 161	6.5	93.5	27.8	8.2	450	11.8
Fayette	81	2.9	196	D	27.6	415 915	2 124	83 215	36.3	87 751	D	D	30.2	7.0	903	37.4
Franklin................................	150	6.8	182	0.8	35.0	383 861	2 104	57 796	132.7	160 807	5.6	94.4	39.3	13.8	782	21.8
Geneva	219	-0.8	215	2.7	93.1	465 026	2 161	89 514	178.5	175 499	26.4	73.6	36.0	15.6	4 741	59.2
Greene	120	-11.3	396	0.3	21.8	803 934	2 030	58 648	22.4	73 658	7.7	92.3	28.0	9.2	790	35.5
Hale	161	-5.2	352	D	29.9	735 855	2 091	81 908	65.2	142 934	D	D	39.9	11.4	797	32.0
Henry	170	2.5	341	8.1	72.9	762 197	2 235	108 992	75.0	150 647	53.5	46.5	38.4	15.5	3 315	64.3
Houston	198	-3.3	243	9.1	97.4	631 875	2 604	89 566	89.2	109 336	71.7	28.3	31.1	14.8	5 065	59.3
Jackson	232	-4.5	168	0.4	89.4	440 304	2 613	65 429	117.2	85 181	30.5	69.5	35.0	8.6	1 849	34.4
Jefferson..............................	39	-3.6	99	0.2	9.1	446 142	4 507	49 924	10.4	26 277	10.5	89.5	20.6	1.3	98	8.1
Lamar	82	-2.8	233	D	13.9	344 326	1 477	42 527	7.5	21 337	20.7	79.3	21.5	2.0	203	27.5
Lauderdale............................	212	-7.1	144	0.4	100.0	428 690	2 970	56 675	72.4	49 385	55.6	44.4	30.7	6.8	2 973	34.7
Lawrence	244	9.6	157	4.7	114.7	480 849	3 059	81 876	192.1	123 829	29.4	70.6	32.0	13.9	4 764	40.4
Lee	59	-6.6	187	0.9	12.2	707 330	3 775	71 403	D	D	D	D	32.4	4.8	692	19.0
Limestone	247	4.0	201	13.1	146.1	815 963	4 068	103 711	132.7	107 913	64.2	35.8	36.3	10.7	3 605	34.6
Lowndes...............................	218	16.6	494	3.8	40.0	852 254	1 726	73 297	76.3	173 052	D	D	41.0	10.0	880	34.7
Macon..................................	103	-11.5	294	1.9	20.1	721 324	2 458	81 386	15.2	43 230	80.5	19.5	31.5	4.0	622	33.2
Madison	209	5.0	203	5.1	125.4	752 873	3 715	88 137	74.2	71 833	86.2	13.8	31.0	8.3	3 156	34.1
Marengo	165	-7.1	332	0.4	32.8	591 148	1 783	59 990	19.4	38 964	27.5	72.5	34.7	5.6	912	28.9
Marion	114	-2.9	159	0.0	21.8	353 441	2 221	47 490	100.1	139 948	3.2	96.8	27.6	11.2	599	29.0
Marshall...............................	163	5.5	108	0.2	46.7	410 550	3 791	61 688	256.5	170 433	2.9	97.1	34.2	12.3	2 102	23.7
Mobile	89	-21.9	127	2.8	36.6	516 701	4 062	78 354	84.7	121 289	90.7	9.3	33.2	8.5	796	12.2
Monroe	141	18.3	293	0.2	53.9	576 181	1 967	103 242	44.5	92 663	72.1	27.9	34.6	10.0	2 925	59.2
Montgomery	220	-1.4	365	1.7	61.2	957 657	2 624	76 778	77.4	128 421	21.5	78.5	40.6	11.8	927	23.7
Morgan	153	-5.5	123	0.3	52.6	460 337	3 732	52 647	109.3	88 335	12.7	87.3	32.7	9.1	1 462	19.6
Perry	157	-5.1	404	0.3	39.5	709 424	1 755	68 270	29.6	76 177	32.6	67.4	31.1	11.8	1 428	53.5
Pickens.................................	103	-21.5	237	D	24.6	490 279	2 068	68 935	110.6	255 370	6.0	94.0	39.5	20.6	511	20.1
Pike	167	-6.6	279	3.2	35.2	635 038	2 278	66 467	130.4	217 322	8.9	91.1	42.5	16.0	1 573	54.2
Randolph..............................	114	-0.7	186	0.1	14.4	523 882	2 810	66 257	111.5	182 509	1.9	98.1	40.4	13.9	831	21.1
Russell.................................	117	24.6	419	3.4	29.4	947 768	2 261	83 646	28.9	103 057	56.0	44.0	29.6	8.6	738	34.6
St. Clair	67	-5.8	125	0.3	13.6	479 537	3 839	55 039	64.8	120 028	15.2	84.8	30.4	9.1	119	6.1
Shelby	58	6.6	146	1.1	18.7	612 140	4 199	68 581	12.2	30 347	80.4	19.6	25.9	6.2	659	10.5
Sumter	240	32.5	560	1.5	33.3	797 215	1 423	58 586	30.5	71 199	D	D	33.2	10.0	1 057	36.4
Talladega..............................	100	-16.1	192	4.8	39.7	559 618	2 909	63 229	40.7	78 428	41.8	58.2	28.3	5.8	717	17.1
Tallapoosa	61	-4.9	177	1.1	8.4	426 409	2 414	53 971	10.6	30 635	32.2	67.8	24.6	3.2	266	10.4
Tuscaloosa	86	-22.2	173	1.1	25.3	512 952	2 965	60 022	27.7	55 682	33.8	66.2	27.0	6.0	493	17.1
Walker	55	-22.5	113	0.0	13.1	291 614	2 578	51 429	33.1	68 683	11.4	88.6	24.3	5.6	105	4.8

Table B. States and Counties — **Water Use, Wholesale Trade, Retail Trade, and Real Estate**

STATE County	Water use, 2010		Wholesale trade,[1] 2012				Retail trade,[2] 2012				Real estate and rental and leasing,[2] 2012			
	Total water withdrawn (mil gal/day)	Gallons withdrawn per person per day	Number of establishments	Number of employees	Sales (mil dol)	Annual payroll (mil dol)	Number of establishments	Number of employees	Sales (mil dol)	Annual payroll (mil dol)	Number of establishments	Number of employees	Receipts (mil dol)	Annual payroll (mil dol)
	133	134	135	136	137	138	139	140	141	142	143	144	145	146
UNITED STATES	351 417.1	1 138	355 983	4 880 666	5 208 023.5	287 549.6	1 062 083	14 703 529	4 219 821.9	369 001.4	354 106	1 923 770	487 655.2	85 326.0
ALABAMA	9 960.0	2 084	4 600	60 332	57 746.6	2 894.7	18 211	218 531	58 565.0	5 123.1	3 858	22 852	3 919.4	819.6
Autauga	55.6	1 018	22	D	D	D	166	2 385	607.9	54.6	31	D	D	D
Baldwin	64.4	353	175	1 868	1 118.2	84.1	950	12 072	3 145.8	280.0	292	1 760	250.3	53.8
Barbour	11.1	402	16	181	114.0	4.0	94	868	206.5	18.2	15	20	3.3	0.6
Bibb	7.6	332	14	52	41.0	2.3	58	474	118.9	11.3	6	8	1.9	0.3
Blount	57.1	996	36	290	153.7	10.5	135	1 255	298.7	28.6	11	19	3.3	0.5
Bullock	3.2	292	5	D	D	D	23	244	92.6	5.3	4	12	0.9	0.1
Butler	4.5	216	13	44	63.5	2.0	97	914	209.0	19.5	13	18	2.8	0.5
Calhoun	29.3	247	97	1 792	1 808.8	73.6	477	5 954	1 463.5	134.1	73	299	48.9	8.0
Chambers	5.4	158	13	104	32.6	4.2	120	1 172	282.0	23.6	14	50	5.1	0.9
Cherokee	5.5	213	12	48	55.2	2.0	88	859	200.2	17.9	12	49	5.7	1.8
Chilton	7.3	168	20	320	260.5	12.6	152	1 397	442.8	32.0	19	52	6.4	1.2
Choctaw	42.9	3 095	9	D	D	D	54	337	100.0	7.1	6	D	D	D
Clarke	24.3	941	13	126	75.2	3.8	138	1 311	341.0	28.4	13	48	6.6	1.2
Clay	2.5	180	6	D	D	D	34	291	67.7	5.4	6	9	0.6	0.1
Cleburne	1.8	120	5	49	6.6	0.8	36	275	64.0	6.9	3	4	0.5	0.2
Coffee	14.7	294	29	250	213.2	10.5	195	2 129	610.1	55.5	47	212	21.5	4.4
Colbert	1 344.3	24 699	78	853	657.4	32.1	228	2 829	1 011.5	76.5	31	144	17.8	3.5
Conecuh	2.4	181	5	236	103.9	8.8	41	280	136.4	5.6	3	3	0.2	0.1
Coosa	0.9	81	5	D	D	D	22	161	37.9	3.5	3	1	0.6	0.1
Covington	10.3	273	34	445	470.5	17.9	202	1 834	452.0	40.3	27	97	12.3	3.1
Crenshaw	3.2	227	12	405	309.0	15.2	38	301	72.7	5.9	6	20	1.6	0.4
Cullman	37.9	471	93	896	1 068.8	37.9	332	3 264	896.4	76.1	47	195	21.6	5.6
Dale	10.3	204	18	169	41.0	4.3	138	1 170	323.5	26.4	30	199	33.7	7.4
Dallas	49.1	1 121	28	215	107.1	8.5	179	1 630	413.1	37.0	30	88	13.5	2.2
DeKalb	11.9	168	37	415	161.0	13.7	246	2 173	579.7	53.2	24	140	9.3	3.3
Elmore	16.0	202	37	282	136.1	9.7	224	2 649	711.6	61.0	48	D	D	D
Escambia	45.2	1 180	22	129	134.1	6.1	176	1 542	374.9	30.3	15	63	6.2	1.2
Etowah	146.3	1 401	82	837	549.9	31.2	392	4 675	1 236.5	96.1	62	367	57.2	10.5
Fayette	4.7	270	7	24	34.8	0.6	62	562	131.2	12.2	4	D	D	D
Franklin	6.4	203	19	92	44.3	3.5	100	1 116	277.7	28.0	13	33	4.7	0.6
Geneva	7.5	278	20	D	D	D	91	713	160.8	14.6	7	14	1.4	0.4
Greene	366.4	40 504	2	D	D	D	23	164	40.3	2.8	1	D	D	D
Hale	20.3	1 285	7	24	29.4	0.9	43	317	76.5	6.4	8	D	D	D
Henry	6.5	375	8	101	40.6	3.9	55	364	100.3	7.9	3	3	0.3	0.0
Houston	118.0	1 162	168	D	D	D	570	7 598	2 164.9	182.5	100	423	73.0	16.0
Jackson	1 067.5	20 055	27	D	D	D	185	1 873	454.9	40.1	25	D	D	D
Jefferson	81.3	124	977	15 345	15 668.5	816.2	2 806	38 691	10 154.0	961.4	681	6 526	1 138.7	283.7
Lamar	2.1	143	7	D	D	D	51	344	80.9	7.1	3	D	D	D
Lauderdale	17.5	189	76	1 244	577.6	39.2	419	4 920	1 190.8	104.5	96	378	52.2	10.5
Lawrence	72.8	2 120	12	64	38.9	2.2	85	793	218.0	17.0	5	11	2.6	0.3
Lee	18.2	130	75	613	504.3	28.3	477	6 450	1 632.1	141.6	113	544	81.0	16.0
Limestone	2 744.2	33 150	45	447	332.7	17.3	261	2 804	777.1	64.3	52	166	30.7	5.5
Lowndes	4.5	394	2	D	D	D	21	177	100.8	3.2	2	D	D	D
Macon	7.1	333	6	D	D	D	45	392	93.2	7.1	5	18	1.1	0.3
Madison	79.1	236	331	4 111	3 768.8	222.9	1 316	18 653	4 958.0	450.2	409	1 706	339.9	60.9
Marengo	25.1	1 191	19	151	105.9	5.3	102	883	199.7	17.8	10	72	20.9	2.9
Marion	7.0	227	23	176	222.1	8.0	102	976	229.0	19.9	14	28	4.7	0.7
Marshall	30.5	327	81	1 253	1 177.7	47.8	419	4 559	1 280.0	102.0	58	591	34.1	9.6
Mobile	1 096.7	2 656	499	6 116	3 680.0	283.8	1 454	19 204	5 102.6	454.7	410	2 125	419.1	83.2
Monroe	50.6	2 194	16	151	101.0	7.0	89	863	211.0	17.6	13	39	4.8	1.2
Montgomery	37.6	164	299	5 401	4 140.8	257.0	911	12 148	3 258.7	302.9	228	1 907	342.5	65.5
Morgan	123.6	1 035	152	2 080	1 417.0	89.2	498	5 507	1 673.5	127.6	82	340	76.2	12.4
Perry	10.8	1 023	5	59	14.7	1.5	32	174	34.7	3.6	4	D	D	D
Pickens	6.2	312	10	69	29.8	2.2	59	427	100.6	9.0	2	D	D	D
Pike	7.8	237	29	D	D	D	143	1 465	373.6	31.3	26	91	17.8	2.0
Randolph	2.9	125	5	D	D	D	70	704	158.3	15.0	10	27	3.2	0.6
Russell	40.7	768	13	D	D	D	155	1 810	499.7	40.7	39	D	D	D
St. Clair	18.1	216	69	1 160	476.4	49.2	223	2 613	704.4	56.9	36	101	22.6	3.3
Shelby	688.6	3 530	353	4 260	4 651.3	272.0	610	8 195	2 567.4	210.9	205	1 318	396.0	59.9
Sumter	8.6	628	11	105	60.2	3.5	46	283	62.1	4.4	7	16	1.9	0.3
Talladega	46.0	559	52	D	D	D	275	2 748	743.4	60.8	37	210	22.2	4.6
Tallapoosa	12.1	290	20	D	D	D	169	1 503	361.8	32.3	27	92	20.9	3.6
Tuscaloosa	39.2	202	143	1 681	1 180.8	83.5	733	9 622	2 619.3	218.3	182	1 485	164.6	44.3
Walker	955.0	14 248	44	406	279.4	18.2	297	3 216	963.5	78.7	38	158	28.5	5.5

1. Merchant wholesalers, except manufacturers' sales branches and offices. 2. Employer establishments.

STATE County	Professional, scientific, and technical services, 2012				Manufacturing, 2012				Accommodation and food services, 2012			
	Number of establish-ments	Number of employees	Receipts (mil dol)	Annual payroll (mil dol)	Number of establish-ments	Number of employees	Receipts (mil dol)	Annual payroll (mil dol)	Number of establish-ments	Number of employees	Sales (mil dol)	Annual payroll (mil dol)
	147	148	149	150	151	152	153	154	155	156	157	158
UNITED STATES............	856 463	8 203 735	1 480 277.1	581 406.1	297 191	11 214 165	5 696 729.6	593 397.0	662 489	12 007 689	708 138.6	196 103.3
ALABAMA	9 109	89 988	16 319.9	5 724.6	4 283	232 650	124 809.8	11 099.5	8 339	157 337	7 576.5	2 071.1
Autauga........................	58	D	D	D	24	941	665.9	57.5	84	1 954	93.4	24.8
Baldwin........................	450	1 899	211.5	86.2	146	3 780	1 438.8	166.8	462	10 726	560.6	161.1
Barbour........................	39	105	16.6	3.9	25	2 837	735.1	103.3	49	596	26.2	6.4
Bibb.............................	16	44	3.6	1.1	15	283	117.5	10.8	11	170	10.1	2.2
Blount..........................	48	223	20.1	7.5	40	1 247	343.0	40.9	43	576	27.1	7.1
Bullock.........................	5	D	D	D	4	D	D	D	7	D	D	D
Butler...........................	20	58	4.8	1.7	19	1 029	811.3	42.2	40	754	32.2	8.5
Calhoun........................	167	1 140	137.1	43.1	114	5 957	2 713.2	256.9	212	4 673	199.1	53.0
Chambers.....................	32	134	15.4	4.3	21	1 513	474.0	58.3	49	566	30.3	7.5
Cherokee......................	18	52	7.1	1.7	16	949	368.0	33.0	36	369	17.2	4.5
Chilton.........................	38	94	9.6	2.9	40	1 884	287.2	56.7	52	767	35.4	9.3
Choctaw.......................	21	50	3.4	1.2	5	D	D	D	22	139	7.6	1.7
Clarke..........................	29	88	12.0	2.3	31	1 724	681.3	88.5	45	641	28.0	6.6
Clay.............................	11	56	3.5	1.6	10	1 161	D	40.9	10	117	4.8	1.2
Cleburne.......................	8	25	1.5	0.5	12	608	269.2	23.2	12	D	D	D
Coffee..........................	64	459	77.8	21.7	36	3 344	1 089.9	93.2	87	1 281	61.3	15.2
Colbert.........................	87	305	34.9	11.5	98	4 638	2 547.0	220.1	101	1 624	72.8	19.1
Conecuh.......................	12	28	4.6	1.4	11	357	79.7	11.5	11	156	6.2	1.6
Coosa..........................	5	17	2.2	0.7	6	430	D	17.4	4	D	D	D
Covington.....................	72	279	24.1	8.8	32	2 141	671.9	74.9	55	836	33.1	7.8
Crenshaw......................	12	32	2.9	0.8	9	1 082	D	38.7	12	D	D	D
Cullman........................	110	455	40.2	13.4	105	4 041	1 880.8	175.9	131	2 298	111.2	29.7
Dale.............................	98	783	126.5	46.0	31	412	110.2	14.0	83	1 131	54.6	13.5
Dallas	49	193	14.1	5.4	41	3 065	1 309.9	131.0	52	873	36.1	8.7
DeKalb.........................	72	361	32.6	11.2	106	6 814	1 551.9	243.9	98	1 545	79.0	20.9
Elmore.........................	85	440	82.4	18.2	55	2 610	800.2	140.1	93	1 517	66.9	18.7
Escambia......................	39	157	18.6	5.8	36	2 097	758.9	102.1	59	816	37.2	8.9
Etowah.........................	130	1 250	82.2	35.5	96	4 715	1 355.8	194.1	172	3 231	153.0	40.0
Fayette.........................	13	36	2.9	1.0	20	675	143.3	23.9	20	470	23.8	D
Franklin........................	27	158	15.0	6.1	47	3 830	981.2	135.9	41	470	23.8	5.9
Geneva.........................	31	123	8.3	2.5	20	581	D	19.6	24	D	D	D
Greene.........................	3	D	D	D	7	379	102.2	12.5	2	D	D	D
Hale.............................	6	21	2.0	0.5	14	537	D	20.9	11	D	D	D
Henry...........................	22	106	13.6	4.4	14	268	D	11.3	22	D	D	D
Houston........................	208	1 130	140.6	52.7	98	3 985	1 390.8	151.8	234	4 602	213.0	57.0
Jackson........................	60	243	23.4	8.7	69	5 196	1 540.4	196.5	75	1 151	49.0	12.7
Jefferson......................	1 833	16 087	2 933.8	1 064.3	582	23 463	10 951.8	1 260.0	1 352	27 207	1 461.1	422.6
Lamar...........................	15	50	3.7	1.7	16	1 035	334.2	48.5	18	D	D	D
Lauderdale	159	766	75.5	29.0	83	3 123	778.2	102.7	167	3 831	159.1	47.0
Lawrence	32	122	15.7	6.6	20	1 039	D	D	41	D	D	D
Lee..............................	202	1 474	138.0	55.1	111	5 903	2 386.1	248.4	323	5 947	271.6	70.4
Limestone	114	706	114.5	42.7	61	3 537	841.4	161.6	108	1 691	81.4	21.9
Lowndes.......................	7	D	D	D	11	1 231	2 375.0	83.6	3	46	1.7	0.6
Macon..........................	13	D	D	D	9	728	D	25.3	29	509	29.0	8.0
Madison........................	1 328	32 575	7 651.1	2 648.8	283	16 571	7 992.2	959.7	720	14 659	728.7	202.7
Marengo	17	80	10.0	2.9	23	1 356	557.0	63.5	41	466	20.3	5.1
Marion	30	82	4.9	1.8	40	2 594	686.6	92.7	48	561	25.4	6.6
Marshall.......................	124	558	50.7	18.8	107	10 666	3 234.5	327.5	180	2 936	124.4	33.9
Mobile..........................	850	9 039	1 175.1	474.0	343	16 063	10 562.7	886.3	671	13 684	617.9	167.9
Monroe.........................	17	41	4.8	1.3	17	975	423.0	67.1	30	361	15.3	3.8
Montgomery..................	606	6 178	1 307.8	403.9	197	12 585	10 786.6	615.4	491	9 986	474.5	130.9
Morgan.........................	198	1 361	152.1	62.7	182	11 009	D	166.0	202	D	D	D
Perry............................	8	14	1.0	0.3	7	D	166.0	17.8	11	D	D	D
Pickens........................	14	75	3.9	2.1	22	552	D	17.0	17	D	D	D
Pike.............................	30	645	60.9	28.4	24	1 303	611.7	57.5	72	1 349	57.8	14.8
Randolph	17	46	3.9	1.1	21	690	251.6	27.7	24	316	15.6	3.6
Russell.........................	51	215	17.5	5.1	42	2 697	1 209.2	130.6	77	1 440	70.2	16.7
St. Clair	98	648	63.4	17.4	77	2 884	931.3	134.8	120	1 969	89.8	24.7
Shelby..........................	564	4 724	845.2	269.3	152	5 062	1 700.0	259.0	337	6 640	334.4	93.6
Sumter.........................	8	D	D	D	7	156	D	D	25	262	10.7	2.8
Talladega......................	76	455	34.0	15.5	88	8 419	D	473.1	110	D	D	D
Tallapoosa....................	52	216	26.2	9.2	30	2 239	456.3	79.3	57	863	37.0	10.6
Tuscaloosa....................	337	2 167	322.9	99.7	136	11 487	14 291.1	707.2	390	D	D	D
Walker..........................	93	445	39.1	20.9	44	1 710	505.7	65.0	95	1 468	75.3	18.9

Health Care and Social Assistance, Other Services, Nonemployer Businesses, and Residential Construction

STATE County	Health care and social assistance, 2012				Other services, 2012				Nonemployer businesses, 2014		Value of residential construction authorized by building permits, 2015	
	Number of establish-ments	Number of employees	Receipts (mil dol)	Annual payroll (mil dol)	Number of establish-ments	Number of employees	Receipts (mil dol)	Annual payroll (mil dol)	Number	Receipts (mil dol)	New Construction ($1,000)	Number of housing units
	159	160	161	162	163	164	165	166	167	168	169	170
UNITED STATES............	831 303	18 414 757	2 040 441.2	801 239.5	529 691	3 430 711	426 693.7	108 185.7	23 836 937	1 115 921.4	223 611 322	1 182 582
ALABAMA	10 305	243 194	26 039.6	10 238.9	6 087	37 291	4 378.0	1 117.1	318 136	13 067.0	2 416 774	14 054
Autauga...........................	95	1 580	119.4	46.2	58	D	D	D	3 072	109.4	39 749	158
Baldwin...........................	444	7 029	622.5	265.3	269	1 203	110.5	31.9	17 301	835.2	361 390	2 203
Barbour...........................	45	791	66.7	24.1	21	72	6.5	1.6	1 510	51.0	3 292	10
Bibb................................	29	D	D	D	20	D	D	D	1 140	43.6	2 222	9
Blount.............................	48	D	D	D	64	D	D	D	3 661	137.8	5 404	49
Bullock............................	14	413	30.3	11.2	6	D	D	D	498	16.6	0	0
Butler..............................	40	948	89.0	32.4	17	71	6.7	2.0	1 073	42.3	990	3
Calhoun...........................	273	5 785	573.5	221.0	177	785	80.2	23.3	6 546	233.9	9 098	61
Chambers........................	59	1 247	99.1	40.9	33	141	12.2	3.7	2 362	55.7	680	4
Cherokee.........................	41	406	35.7	14.7	19	73	5.9	1.7	1 499	70.5	509	5
Chilton............................	56	822	66.4	25.4	36	D	D	D	2 877	102.0	2 086	19
Choctaw..........................	28	356	30.9	12.0	22	D	D	D	808	23.4	0	0
Clarke.............................	53	882	68.2	29.3	36	126	11.5	3.0	1 574	55.7	633	4
Clay................................	21	D	D	D	11	D	D	D	757	31.9	0	0
Cleburne.........................	10	D	D	D	9	45	4.8	1.3	918	32.0	170	1
Coffee.............................	101	1 798	174.3	68.3	67	310	26.6	8.2	2 619	99.1	9 738	57
Colbert............................	128	2 620	281.6	110.9	71	D	D	D	3 584	132.5	14 846	124
Conecuh..........................	16	336	31.6	12.9	14	D	D	D	688	25.2	688	4
Coosa.............................	5	D	D	D	8	D	D	D	384	12.7	0	0
Covington........................	93	1 727	139.0	55.2	49	229	21.7	6.1	2 205	80.2	1 485	8
Crenshaw........................	14	489	28.7	14.4	13	D	D	D	871	29.1	90	1
Cullman...........................	182	2 533	242.2	101.0	101	499	56.3	15.0	5 644	250.1	8 741	73
Dale................................	60	1 134	86.7	35.8	50	217	13.1	3.9	2 382	80.4	1 245	11
Dallas.............................	102	2 011	173.5	65.6	51	375	30.0	8.3	2 279	73.5	2 369	18
DeKalb............................	123	2 294	189.2	73.9	51	181	16.8	5.0	4 643	196.0	3 297	24
Elmore............................	109	1 981	156.9	59.2	78	392	38.7	9.0	5 112	205.7	12 017	165
Escambia.........................	67	1 265	105.7	42.7	46	198	17.7	4.3	2 066	65.2	174	2
Etowah............................	316	7 433	701.9	303.4	125	632	98.9	19.0	7 162	317.8	11 147	83
Fayette...........................	50	801	54.1	23.5	22	D	D	D	1 024	38.5	650	2
Franklin...........................	63	1 112	96.4	36.0	36	D	D	D	1 867	69.3	1 884	40
Geneva............................	33	632	42.9	19.4	20	D	D	D	1 616	59.0	858	6
Greene............................	13	290	16.8	7.9	5	D	D	D	525	14.1	417	4
Hale................................	17	445	28.1	11.0	7	10	1.2	0.2	750	24.7	0	0
Henry..............................	28	466	22.4	10.9	16	D	D	D	1 044	36.1	2 240	17
Houston...........................	314	9 145	1 061.9	455.9	185	1 056	115.5	27.6	7 091	314.1	68 891	304
Jackson...........................	116	D	D	D	42	175	15.8	5.0	3 046	114.0	8 914	40
Jefferson.........................	1 688	57 068	7 766.2	2 830.6	1 042	9 351	1 262.3	306.0	46 666	2 048.3	465 830	2 477
Lamar..............................	22	346	18.6	8.5	11	D	D	D	936	36.7	0	0
Lauderdale.......................	254	4 337	449.8	158.9	115	D	D	D	6 492	290.0	16 693	214
Lawrence.........................	36	736	44.1	20.3	30	80	9.0	2.3	1 984	63.0	0	0
Lee.................................	235	5 923	541.5	218.4	172	787	72.8	18.6	9 606	420.9	240 681	838
Limestone........................	121	2 163	170.1	74.9	82	512	46.6	13.8	5 606	200.7	21 556	111
Lowndes..........................	5	90	5.5	2.3	4	D	D	D	649	20.5	0	0
Macon.............................	24	D	D	D	15	D	D	D	1 059	23.6	255	1
Madison...........................	932	21 762	2 475.1	985.4	474	3 503	570.6	126.8	23 379	951.3	337 274	2 496
Marengo..........................	61	984	75.7	30.7	30	89	6.3	1.7	1 012	33.5	893	8
Marion.............................	79	1 355	125.9	46.5	27	D	D	D	1 874	74.4	0	0
Marshall..........................	191	3 727	336.0	124.7	84	370	26.4	7.4	7 028	312.1	5 539	28
Mobile.............................	734	21 863	2 397.2	927.8	570	3 577	334.8	96.2	29 747	1 106.6	144 552	907
Monroe............................	30	709	50.6	21.3	18	D	D	D	1 283	46.2	743	5
Montgomery	666	16 589	1 780.7	762.2	429	3 172	404.6	113.9	15 717	682.4	125 533	776
Morgan............................	340	5 733	497.1	187.4	150	980	94.0	27.2	7 615	307.0	20 930	139
Perry...............................	8	142	7.1	3.2	7	9	0.7	0.2	499	18.3	0	0
Pickens...........................	25	705	44.7	20.6	17	D	D	D	1 046	36.9	656	5
Pike	63	1 156	91.7	39.4	39	139	10.2	2.8	1 849	67.8	4 670	34
Randolph.........................	35	634	49.3	21.1	23	D	D	D	1 385	53.2	0	0
Russell............................	65	D	D	D	61	275	22.2	7.3	3 398	97.9	50 042	470
St. Clair	93	1 907	133.5	54.5	81	265	26.8	7.0	5 318	205.0	19 781	128
Shelby.............................	439	6 297	583.4	240.5	281	1 792	215.0	56.1	16 209	828.1	205 624	1 038
Sumter............................	24	415	26.9	10.7	5	21	2.0	0.5	805	27.7	2 120	7
Talladega.........................	160	D	D	D	66	D	D	D	3 994	144.1	3 550	24
Tallapoosa.......................	88	2 181	186.3	78.2	44	169	14.8	3.9	2 460	106.9	16 875	77
Tuscaloosa.......................	437	13 201	1 413.0	613.0	235	D	D	D	11 441	524.6	153 276	742
Walker.............................	171	3 178	311.7	114.6	83	D	D	D	3 613	136.9	3 090	13

Table B. States and Counties — Government Employment and Payroll, and Local Government Finances

	Government employment and payroll, 2012									Local government finances, 2012				
STATE County			March payroll (percent of total)							General revenue		Taxes		
													Per capita[1] (dollars)	
	Full-time equivalent employees	March payroll (dollars)	Administration, judicial, and legal	Police and Corrections	Fire Protection	Highways and transportation	Health and Welfare	Natural resources and utilities	Education and libraries	Total (mil dol)	Inter-governmental (mil dol)	Total (mil dol)	Total	Property
	171	172	173	174	175	176	177	178	179	180	181	182	183	184
UNITED STATES......	X	X	X	X	X	X	X	X	X	X	X	X	X	X
ALABAMA	X	X	X	X	X	X	X	X	X	X	X	X	X	X
Autauga..........................	1 582	5 202 816	4.0	9.6	6.8	2.7	1.7	5.0	67.1	125.4	65.8	41.7	751	262
Baldwin..........................	7 374	22 581 577	7.4	8.0	2.9	4.3	20.7	5.6	47.7	640.7	189.9	231.1	1 211	537
Barbour..........................	1 162	3 226 895	2.8	6.5	3.7	2.8	22.4	6.2	54.3	79.4	44.6	19.5	719	241
Bibb...............................	837	2 413 468	3.7	5.9	0.0	3.6	26.0	2.1	58.0	59.5	31.7	7.9	351	147
Blount............................	1 539	4 659 233	4.8	7.3	1.6	3.1	0.9	5.3	75.6	107.3	70.3	23.0	398	220
Bullock...........................	552	1 468 315	4.4	5.2	0.0	4.7	37.7	0.1	46.6	28.4	20.9	4.8	454	337
Butler.............................	934	2 423 650	4.8	7.9	2.9	6.4	14.6	5.7	55.8	65.7	35.4	23.2	1 142	306
Calhoun..........................	5 708	17 129 463	3.6	6.8	2.8	2.8	32.2	7.0	43.2	507.7	169.3	112.4	958	366
Chambers.......................	1 193	3 265 131	6.9	10.3	3.6	6.5	3.3	9.0	58.5	79.2	43.1	21.6	634	304
Cherokee.......................	997	3 526 515	5.0	5.1	0.1	2.9	16.9	6.0	63.4	50.9	29.6	16.6	640	293
Chilton..........................	1 218	3 862 506	5.9	8.9	0.5	4.3	1.4	6.0	72.4	95.1	55.9	25.1	572	321
Choctaw.........................	383	970 992	9.1	5.8	0.0	6.4	0.0	1.9	74.4	27.8	15.9	7.3	536	470
Clarke............................	1 107	3 358 366	4.7	9.6	0.0	3.2	12.7	8.4	59.5	70.9	38.1	25.5	1 015	336
Clay...............................	699	1 916 771	2.1	5.9	0.1	5.2	39.3	5.7	40.5	52.0	20.5	9.5	704	493
Cleburne........................	633	2 123 561	3.8	6.3	0.1	3.4	9.9	5.1	70.2	36.9	24.6	7.3	490	274
Coffee............................	2 026	5 912 313	3.1	6.9	2.2	3.8	13.7	5.8	63.9	136.4	72.2	40.1	782	349
Colbert...........................	3 178	10 303 212	2.2	5.5	2.5	2.4	36.7	11.6	37.7	258.1	88.3	46.3	850	424
Conecuh.........................	486	1 319 565	6.8	10.8	0.0	6.5	1.3	10.9	62.6	33.3	20.8	7.6	588	279
Coosa............................	265	695 770	2.4	13.6	0.0	6.3	0.6	1.2	75.2	21.9	15.4	4.4	397	290
Covington	1 587	4 552 054	7.2	6.3	1.6	5.3	1.1	22.2	53.7	120.6	57.2	30.6	805	249
Crenshaw.......................	472	1 600 404	4.4	5.5	0.0	6.3	0.9	7.4	75.5	27.8	16.6	6.6	471	206
Cullman..........................	3 911	11 764 023	3.0	6.7	1.9	3.3	31.4	8.4	43.9	194.4	96.2	54.4	676	276
Dale...............................	1 600	4 956 908	3.8	7.4	2.7	2.6	26.4	5.1	50.9	131.8	55.8	34.7	688	250
Dallas.............................	1 746	4 733 521	4.8	9.2	3.2	2.5	1.5	6.4	67.0	113.7	68.6	33.9	791	371
DeKalb...........................	2 193	6 908 865	4.2	8.4	2.2	3.5	4.3	10.3	66.0	169.1	97.9	42.8	602	293
Elmore...........................	2 265	6 703 799	3.5	10.3	1.2	3.1	0.8	4.6	75.0	153.6	86.5	43.7	541	251
Escambia........................	1 604	4 378 782	4.5	9.0	2.3	4.4	15.2	2.8	58.4	116.3	47.9	27.6	726	330
Etowah..........................	3 980	11 900 349	4.3	10.5	6.2	3.7	6.9	8.4	56.6	284.1	137.1	99.7	955	293
Fayette...........................	541	1 471 267	6.2	6.8	1.8	7.2	2.2	10.0	65.4	50.8	33.7	12.6	742	260
Franklin..........................	1 331	3 838 038	4.8	7.1	2.1	3.7	3.3	12.5	65.2	84.8	50.1	15.5	488	176
Geneva..........................	1 102	3 351 087	3.2	5.0	0.1	3.9	27.3	3.4	56.6	106.8	34.4	20.2	751	302
Greene	456	1 298 955	3.6	6.0	0.0	5.0	31.6	4.7	48.5	30.5	13.4	5.5	620	359
Hale...............................	605	1 537 609	4.7	7.4	0.0	3.8	23.7	1.0	59.3	51.7	27.1	9.4	613	301
Henry.............................	549	1 493 829	6.9	8.0	2.0	5.6	2.8	4.3	68.4	33.3	19.9	9.4	546	269
Houston.........................	5 714	19 682 365	3.7	6.6	3.6	2.3	45.1	5.9	30.9	590.6	124.8	126.4	1 222	429
Jackson..........................	2 490	8 016 220	3.3	6.6	1.8	3.9	29.0	8.0	46.4	205.9	91.7	40.1	756	359
Jefferson	27 700	103 543 070	5.4	12.8	7.2	3.5	7.3	9.3	49.8	2 895.7	935.7	1 334.8	2 022	856
Lamar............................	454	1 337 464	7.1	9.0	0.8	4.9	2.6	9.6	64.8	31.4	20.5	6.5	457	274
Lauderdale	2 704	9 293 198	4.1	8.4	4.2	4.1	2.8	16.3	57.5	230.1	103.9	91.1	984	414
Lawrence........................	1 156	3 399 543	4.4	7.8	0.4	3.4	14.2	4.4	64.8	74.9	46.2	11.0	324	217
Lee................................	6 506	23 295 526	2.9	5.8	2.5	1.6	40.7	4.1	41.4	640.1	158.1	164.2	1 115	594
Limestone......................	2 694	10 450 795	2.4	6.2	1.4	1.9	21.8	7.7	57.3	213.7	86.7	39.0	445	236
Lowndes.........................	502	1 360 565	8.1	8.4	0.0	4.3	0.5	2.4	75.6	38.0	25.6	9.0	830	443
Macon	731	2 048 937	7.8	7.7	2.4	4.5	1.6	16.0	58.1	49.6	28.9	15.3	746	268
Madison..........................	17 330	64 421 407	3.9	6.3	3.3	2.9	40.3	7.4	32.3	1 978.9	813.4	389.2	1 134	579
Marengo.........................	1 007	2 884 299	5.2	7.8	3.8	5.1	8.0	6.1	61.8	87.7	38.7	15.2	746	331
Marion	992	2 975 248	4.1	7.5	1.3	5.2	1.2	15.9	64.8	75.9	39.2	22.6	745	282
Marshall.........................	4 582	15 491 666	2.4	5.3	2.4	1.7	30.3	11.3	46.0	395.1	144.9	75.8	799	378
Mobile...........................	15 334	47 151 677	5.5	11.5	5.1	4.9	9.2	7.3	53.7	1 405.0	626.1	561.4	1 356	491
Monroe	1 069	3 209 902	3.2	6.5	1.2	3.7	34.3	2.7	48.2	82.1	40.2	13.0	573	337
Montgomery	8 484	27 145 960	5.0	15.4	6.4	3.3	4.4	9.5	49.6	1 098.6	290.3	265.5	1 154	360
Morgan..........................	4 927	17 209 848	3.0	7.3	3.3	2.5	22.7	9.2	50.8	514.7	208.9	123.2	1 023	501
Perry..............................	634	1 533 195	4.2	5.7	0.1	9.3	22.6	2.7	54.6	35.7	28.0	5.6	546	240
Pickens..........................	699	1 770 074	5.4	8.5	0.0	6.6	2.9	6.6	68.1	65.0	32.5	7.6	389	243
Pike...............................	1 061	3 438 644	6.1	11.4	3.5	4.1	4.1	13.7	55.5	103.3	44.5	21.4	644	263
Randolph........................	771	2 493 832	3.6	8.3	0.1	4.4	13.3	1.8	67.8	67.1	30.1	11.3	500	257
Russell	2 491	7 257 682	19.9	8.4	3.1	2.7	1.7	7.6	53.3	148.3	81.2	49.2	851	413
St. Clair	2 191	7 157 617	7.3	9.7	4.9	3.2	0.1	3.1	71.1	184.8	107.5	55.3	649	287
Shelby	5 778	16 879 679	6.7	14.3	5.9	3.1	2.9	4.8	60.5	441.4	172.8	191.6	954	567
Sumter...........................	560	1 553 057	5.4	7.7	1.9	5.9	1.9	7.7	67.6	34.6	20.5	8.9	664	293
Talladega	3 476	9 539 423	3.6	6.8	2.5	2.7	19.3	8.7	54.0	201.6	106.6	60.5	740	379
Tallapoosa......................	1 698	5 118 158	4.4	8.1	3.8	2.6	22.1	9.3	47.3	118.2	65.1	34.0	826	434
Tuscaloosa.....................	10 215	37 068 838	3.6	7.2	3.6	3.5	48.2	3.7	29.3	991.4	234.1	212.4	1 070	420
Walker...........................	2 414	6 546 224	3.1	8.7	1.3	3.2	3.4	7.9	70.5	157.6	87.1	48.0	726	246

1. Based on the resident population estimated as of July 1 of the year shown.

Table B. States and Counties — Local Government Finances, Government Employment, and Voting

STATE County	Total (mil dol)	Per capita[1] (dollars)	Education	Health and hospitals	Police protection	Public welfare	Highways	Total (mil dol)	Per capita[1] (dollars)	Federal civilian	Federal military	State and local	Democratic	Republican	All other
	185	186	187	188	189	190	191	192	193	194	195	196	197	198	199
UNITED STATES............	X	X	X	X	X	X	X	X	X	2 790 000	1 982 000	19 258 000	51.1	47.2	1.7
ALABAMA	X	X	X	X	X	X	X	X	X	53 539	30 107	316 155	38.7	60.3	0.9
Autauga..................	119.9	2 161	60.8	0.1	7.0	0.5	2.9	149.8	2 699	84	253	2 152	25.8	73.6	0.6
Baldwin..................	700.0	3 669	34.5	19.2	6.1	0.1	7.7	911.0	4 775	327	906	8 660	23.8	75.3	0.9
Barbour..................	74.3	2 732	47.4	18.7	6.4	0.0	3.9	37.2	1 369	53	118	1 629	49.0	50.4	0.6
Bibb.......................	57.9	2 564	51.4	26.2	4.4	0.0	4.1	55.2	2 445	81	93	1 181	26.6	72.4	1.0
Blount....................	108.1	1 870	72.0	0.8	5.8	0.3	6.1	48.6	841	93	262	1 805	14.5	84.0	1.5
Bullock..................	30.6	2 921	53.3	22.5	3.6	0.7	8.6	14.8	1 416	34	41	694	74.1	25.7	0.2
Butler....................	60.7	2 987	47.3	9.6	5.4	0.5	9.3	65.0	3 202	41	91	905	43.1	56.5	0.4
Calhoun.................	517.7	4 414	32.7	36.2	5.9	0.0	3.9	358.0	3 052	3 912	575	8 286	33.2	65.7	1.1
Chambers...............	78.6	2 308	50.4	1.2	8.3	0.3	7.0	72.0	2 112	49	154	1 347	45.5	53.9	0.6
Cherokee...............	48.3	1 856	75.1	0.1	4.8	0.0	4.5	60.1	2 309	47	118	1 274	23.7	74.9	1.4
Chilton..................	96.3	2 198	62.9	0.6	7.0	0.4	5.7	23.3	533	64	199	1 737	20.7	78.5	0.8
Choctaw................	28.4	2 080	53.7	0.0	6.0	0.1	13.4	22.9	1 681	28	60	467	46.1	53.5	0.4
Clarke...................	67.0	2 664	60.9	0.3	7.8	0.2	6.2	111.3	4 422	80	113	1 741	44.0	55.6	0.4
Clay......................	70.4	5 240	51.0	26.2	4.1	0.1	4.4	26.5	1 971	54	61	885	25.8	73.1	1.1
Cleburne................	41.7	2 813	52.6	0.1	4.4	17.0	6.0	35.4	2 387	42	68	741	18.0	80.3	1.7
Coffee...................	144.1	2 812	62.6	0.4	4.8	0.2	4.8	136.0	2 654	209	230	2 350	25.2	74.1	0.6
Colbert..................	259.3	4 762	32.1	37.0	3.6	0.2	3.5	178.7	3 282	798	247	4 205	39.1	59.3	1.6
Conecuh................	37.1	2 859	59.4	0.0	8.0	0.6	6.4	64.7	4 982	27	58	731	49.4	50.0	0.6
Coosa...................	22.3	2 029	59.1	0.1	7.7	0.2	19.6	8.9	810	19	48	351	40.9	58.4	0.8
Covington..............	141.5	3 727	42.0	0.3	6.6	0.1	12.6	930.5	24 517	116	171	1 996	20.5	78.8	0.7
Crenshaw...............	29.8	2 119	65.1	6.8	9.7	0.0	3.3	16.9	1 199	35	63	565	30.8	68.7	0.5
Cullman.................	206.4	2 566	52.3	2.1	7.2	1.1	7.3	191.6	2 381	211	367	4 231	16.6	81.8	1.5
Dale......................	146.4	2 902	56.7	19.7	4.5	0.2	2.5	62.7	1 242	3 092	3 816	2 123	27.3	71.9	0.8
Dallas...................	143.5	3 347	61.4	0.1	8.3	0.4	3.2	105.2	2 455	171	187	2 657	67.1	32.6	0.3
DeKalb..................	174.9	2 461	64.2	3.0	8.3	0.4	7.1	113.8	1 602	159	321	3 168	23.6	74.8	1.7
Elmore..................	159.9	1 983	65.0	0.8	7.4	0.0	7.2	169.3	2 100	141	345	4 426	24.2	75.1	0.7
Escambia...............	124.2	3 269	45.2	24.5	6.3	0.4	4.3	40.7	1 071	58	158	4 139	35.4	63.9	0.8
Etowah..................	278.9	2 672	46.7	1.9	11.2	0.2	4.8	218.9	2 097	303	464	5 117	30.2	68.4	1.4
Fayette..................	33.4	1 968	66.1	1.2	2.5	0.0	10.0	12.4	731	35	76	1 218	25.1	73.9	1.0
Franklin.................	94.1	2 961	58.5	0.1	4.4	0.0	6.5	55.6	1 752	91	143	1 824	29.7	68.8	1.5
Geneva..................	79.5	2 953	44.2	28.4	5.0	0.2	5.9	34.0	1 262	57	121	1 416	18.3	80.8	0.9
Greene..................	31.5	3 551	49.2	28.3	3.2	0.5	3.8	17.4	1 960	25	39	655	83.1	16.5	0.4
Hale.....................	48.8	3 170	51.5	17.8	6.3	0.0	12.3	13.5	876	48	68	861	60.7	39.0	0.4
Henry....................	34.2	1 979	64.6	0.0	6.7	0.7	13.2	44.3	2 565	43	78	648	34.9	64.6	0.5
Houston.................	591.0	5 716	25.3	46.6	3.9	0.1	3.3	407.2	3 938	301	501	8 191	29.3	70.1	0.6
Jackson.................	209.8	3 957	51.6	23.7	4.0	0.3	4.2	118.1	2 227	352	238	3 077	30.5	67.5	2.0
Jefferson...............	2 885.7	4 372	40.1	5.3	6.6	0.0	4.0	7 596.1	11 509	7 903	3 326	50 693	52.2	47.1	0.8
Lamar...................	32.3	2 262	61.7	0.0	6.4	0.4	4.7	29.7	2 081	36	63	562	22.8	76.6	0.6
Lauderdale.............	225.0	2 431	58.9	0.1	6.2	0.1	6.7	265.7	2 871	276	420	4 739	35.0	63.2	1.9
Lawrence...............	78.1	2 309	60.0	13.5	6.3	0.5	6.4	41.6	1 229	89	152	1 317	35.2	63.2	1.6
Lee.......................	638.8	4 338	33.9	39.7	4.1	0.0	2.6	782.4	5 313	285	727	17 024	39.6	59.3	1.1
Limestone..............	276.5	3 155	51.2	23.1	4.8	0.2	3.7	282.8	3 227	1 627	402	5 225	28.4	70.3	1.2
Lowndes................	39.8	3 667	69.6	0.0	5.6	0.0	9.7	34.2	3 148	30	48	522	74.9	24.9	0.3
Macon...................	52.1	2 539	58.2	0.3	5.4	0.0	2.5	68.8	3 349	853	90	2 155	86.9	12.8	0.3
Madison................	1 830.4	5 335	30.6	39.1	3.7	0.0	2.5	1 931.7	5 631	18 285	2 363	24 185	41.9	56.9	1.2
Marengo................	94.5	4 633	40.6	31.0	3.2	0.0	2.7	33.7	1 651	56	106	1 514	51.7	48.1	0.3
Marion..................	72.1	2 379	61.7	0.0	6.4	0.0	5.4	62.6	2 065	73	134	1 468	21.0	77.2	1.8
Marshall................	395.8	4 177	40.0	33.4	5.5	0.2	1.9	306.5	3 234	264	428	5 856	21.2	77.6	1.2
Mobile..................	1 433.8	3 464	41.2	6.0	6.8	0.5	8.3	1 386.2	3 349	2 589	2 748	23 477	45.3	54.0	0.7
Monroe.................	83.9	3 713	40.0	33.9	5.1	0.1	8.3	7.6	334	55	99	1 386	44.7	54.9	0.5
Montgomery...........	1 084.1	4 711	25.4	43.2	5.2	0.3	2.1	1 050.3	4 564	6 025	3 593	26 664	59.4	40.1	0.5
Morgan..................	592.0	4 917	54.2	17.4	4.2	0.3	2.9	883.2	7 336	318	539	6 774	27.5	71.3	1.3
Perry....................	37.4	3 675	46.2	24.5	3.6	0.4	7.2	37.3	3 663	27	76	536	72.4	27.3	0.4
Pickens.................	72.8	3 752	37.4	29.1	3.2	0.1	5.3	52.7	2 716	302	86	936	45.6	54.0	0.4
Pike......................	119.3	3 594	39.5	22.5	7.4	0.0	3.2	140.0	4 218	94	146	3 045	42.1	57.4	0.5
Randolph...............	70.0	3 087	46.0	32.1	4.6	0.0	1.9	57.2	2 521	56	101	1 091	29.5	69.1	1.4
Russell..................	149.9	2 593	59.3	0.1	5.7	0.1	3.0	302.5	5 233	94	270	2 806	53.3	46.0	0.7
St. Clair................	188.6	2 213	57.2	6.9	10.0	0.1	4.2	290.2	3 404	109	388	2 802	17.9	81.1	1.0
Shelby...................	463.8	2 308	61.2	1.7	10.9	0.2	3.8	773.4	3 849	305	933	8 085	22.8	76.2	1.1
Sumter..................	37.0	2 754	54.6	0.8	7.3	0.1	13.6	25.2	1 879	36	56	1 306	75.0	24.7	0.4
Talladega...............	213.4	2 610	55.2	4.8	7.5	0.4	5.6	225.8	2 762	481	357	4 652	40.3	58.8	0.9
Tallapoosa.............	123.8	3 008	45.4	17.8	6.1	0.0	4.1	118.8	2 886	86	186	2 002	31.4	67.9	0.7
Tuscaloosa.............	994.6	5 008	29.0	43.5	4.8	0.0	4.7	615.9	3 101	1 547	889	22 057	41.6	57.5	0.9
Walker..................	158.5	2 394	61.5	0.1	5.4	0.0	8.0	116.9	1 765	185	295	3 090	25.9	72.3	1.8

1. Based on the resident population estimated as of July 1 of the year shown.   2. © 2013 Election Data Services, Inc. All rights reserved.

Table B. States and Counties — **Land Area and Population**

STATE/ County code	CBSA code[1]	County type[2]	STATE County	Population, 2015				Population and population characteristics, 2014										
								Race alone or in combination, not Hispanic or Latino (percent)					Age (percent)					
				Land area,[3] (sq km) 2010	Total persons 2015	Rank	Per square kilometer	White	Black	American Indian, Alaska Native	Asian and Pacific Islander	Percent Hispanic or Latino[4]	Under 5 years	5 to 17 years	18 to 24 years	25 to 34 years	35 to 44 years	45 to 54 years
				1	2	3	4	5	6	7	8	9	10	11	12	13	14	15
			ALABAMA—Cont'd															
01 129	...	8	Washington	2 798	16 804	1 990	6.0	66.0	24.9	8.3	0.4	1.4	4.9	17.6	9.0	11.0	11.5	14.6
01 131	...	8	Wilcox	2 301	11 059	2 351	4.8	28.3	71.1	0.4	0.3	1.0	5.7	19.1	9.1	10.3	11.2	12.6
01 133	...	6	Winston	1 588	23 877	1 648	15.0	95.4	1.3	1.4	0.5	2.9	5.0	15.9	7.5	10.4	12.1	14.8
02 000	...	X	ALASKA	1 477 953	738 432	X	0.5	67.7	4.8	18.4	9.3	6.8	7.4	17.9	11.1	16.1	12.2	13.2
02 013	...	9	Aleutians East	18 083	3 341	2 951	0.2	14.3	12.3	22.0	42.6	13.4	2.8	7.4	12.5	16.3	18.2	22.6
02 016	...	7	Aleutians West	11 371	5 702	2 782	0.5	30.2	8.0	14.2	37.9	14.0	3.6	8.7	9.4	17.1	18.9	21.5
02 020	11260	2	Anchorage	4 415	298 695	228	67.7	65.9	7.6	11.4	14.1	8.9	7.4	17.5	11.7	17.4	12.5	12.9
02 050	...	7	Bethel	105 076	17 946	1 919	0.2	14.7	1.2	83.9	2.0	1.8	11.1	24.9	11.0	14.9	10.2	11.7
02 060	...	9	Bristol Bay	1 305	892	3 112	0.7	59.5	2.5	46.1	5.4	4.3	5.2	14.8	9.5	13.1	11.9	18.8
02 068	...	8	Denali	33 026	1 919	3 057	0.1	87.7	2.9	6.3	4.8	3.8	4.7	14.2	6.9	14.7	14.5	20.2
02 070	...	9	Dillingham	48 093	4 997	2 836	0.1	25.6	1.7	76.0	2.2	3.1	11.0	20.9	11.5	13.6	9.6	12.7
02 090	21820	3	Fairbanks North Star	19 006	99 631	594	5.2	76.5	6.3	10.3	5.3	7.7	7.7	16.4	14.8	18.7	11.8	11.4
02 100	...	9	Haines	6 005	2 534	3 004	0.4	85.2	1.5	16.6	2.7	2.5	3.7	15.4	6.1	10.0	11.6	16.6
02 105	...		Hoonah-Angoon	19 489	2 133	3 038	0.1	55.9	1.7	44.3	2.2	5.1	5.2	14.1	7.0	10.7	10.2	15.7
02 110	27940	5	Juneau	6 998	32 756	1 365	4.7	72.1	2.3	17.6	10.4	6.5	5.9	16.2	9.4	15.4	12.9	15.0
02 122	...	7	Kenai Peninsula	41 635	58 059	886	1.4	86.1	1.2	11.2	2.9	4.0	6.4	16.6	8.9	12.3	11.4	13.7
02 130	28540	7	Ketchikan Gateway	12 583	13 709	2 188	1.1	73.0	1.5	19.8	9.8	4.9	6.5	16.3	9.0	13.7	11.9	14.9
02 150	...	7	Kodiak Island	16 963	13 889	2 174	0.8	56.0	1.9	16.7	23.0	8.7	8.0	18.0	10.4	16.2	12.6	13.9
02 158	...	9	Kusilvak	44 241	8 119	2 592	0.2	7.1	0.6	92.5	1.0	1.1	13.7	28.3	12.1	14.5	8.4	10.2
02 164	...	9	Lake and Peninsula	61 258	1 563	3 077	0.0	32.2	2.3	70.2	2.1	3.2	9.3	18.9	10.9	15.5	11.2	13.5
02 170	11260	2	Matanuska-Susitna	63 734	101 095	591	1.6	85.7	2.0	10.5	3.5	4.7	7.2	20.2	9.4	14.1	12.8	13.7
02 180	...	7	Nome	59 471	9 846	2 447	0.2	22.1	1.0	78.9	2.1	2.0	11.1	23.8	10.6	14.6	11.0	11.3
02 185	...	7	North Slope	229 720	9 687	2 459	0.0	36.1	2.1	54.4	8.8	3.9	8.6	17.2	9.1	16.2	12.6	17.3
02 188	...	7	Northwest Arctic	92 133	7 752	2 614	0.1	17.4	1.3	82.7	2.2	2.1	11.5	24.7	11.3	15.4	9.8	11.8
02 195	...		Petersburg	8 500	3 177	2 960	0.4	79.0	2.4	14.1	5.3	5.6	6.7	15.6	8.3	12.7	12.2	14.7
02 198	...		Prince of Wales-Hyder	10 160	6 341	2 730	0.6	53.2	1.3	48.4	3.3	3.3	6.5	17.6	7.9	12.0	11.9	16.0
02 220	...	7	Sitka	7 434	8 863	2 523	1.2	71.2	1.7	21.2	8.9	6.0	6.1	16.1	8.4	14.2	13.3	13.6
02 230	...		Skagway	1 172	1 057	3 107	0.9	89.5	1.2	7.1	1.4	4.3	5.2	7.9	7.3	19.4	17.0	15.0
02 240	...	8	Southeast Fairbanks	64 151	6 839	2 690	0.1	80.0	2.0	14.8	2.5	4.9	7.7	17.8	9.0	13.2	11.9	13.9
02 261	...	9	Valdez-Cordova	88 681	9 362	2 482	0.1	76.5	1.4	18.2	5.8	4.7	7.1	17.3	8.3	14.0	11.3	15.3
02 275	...		Wrangell	6 582	2 382	3 016	0.4	78.3	1.6	24.4	4.2	2.2	4.8	15.6	8.3	10.6	8.3	14.7
02 282	...	9	Yakutat	19 812	613	3 133	0.0	50.9	5.8	45.6	9.6	3.3	5.7	13.5	10.2	12.4	12.3	16.9
02 290	...	8	Yukon-Koyukuk	376 856	5 533	2 801	0.0	26.5	1.2	73.8	1.3	2.0	8.3	19.5	9.1	13.0	9.7	12.2
04 000	...	X	ARIZONA	294 207	6 828 065	X	23.2	58.0	4.9	4.6	4.1	30.6	6.4	17.7	10.0	13.3	12.4	12.5
04 001	...	6	Apache	29 001	71 474	756	2.5	20.2	1.4	72.8	0.8	6.4	7.6	21.6	10.3	11.8	10.8	12.6
04 003	43420	4	Cochise	15 969	126 427	494	7.9	58.3	4.8	1.6	3.5	34.6	6.5	15.9	8.8	12.8	10.6	12.0
04 005	22380	3	Coconino	48 223	139 097	458	2.9	56.9	2.0	26.9	2.8	13.9	6.1	15.8	19.7	13.4	10.8	11.4
04 007	37740	4	Gila	12 323	53 159	939	4.3	64.2	0.9	16.1	1.1	18.8	5.7	14.7	7.2	9.3	8.5	12.0
04 009	40940	6	Graham	11 972	37 666	1 235	3.1	52.4	2.2	13.3	1.2	32.1	7.7	20.6	11.1	14.8	12.4	10.9
04 011	...	7	Greenlee	4 774	9 529	2 468	2.0	49.2	2.0	2.8	1.0	46.7	6.8	21.3	8.9	14.6	12.4	12.5
04 012	...	6	La Paz	11 654	20 152	1 825	1.7	60.9	1.4	12.8	1.0	25.6	4.6	12.9	6.3	8.2	7.5	10.4
04 013	38060	1	Maricopa	23 828	4 167 947	4	174.9	58.8	5.9	2.2	5.0	30.3	6.7	18.4	9.6	14.2	13.3	12.9
04 015	29420	4	Mohave	34 476	204 737	315	5.9	79.6	1.6	2.9	1.9	15.8	4.6	14.1	6.8	9.8	9.4	12.5
04 017	43320	4	Navajo	25 771	108 277	553	4.2	43.5	1.6	44.2	1.1	11.1	7.3	20.7	9.4	11.5	10.5	12.1
04 019	46060	2	Pima	23 794	1 010 025	44	42.4	55.0	4.1	3.1	3.8	36.1	5.9	15.9	12.2	12.3	11.4	11.9
04 021	38060	1	Pinal	13 897	406 584	171	29.3	60.3	5.2	5.5	2.8	29.6	6.0	18.3	7.9	13.4	13.2	11.4
04 023	35700	4	Santa Cruz	3 204	46 461	1 038	14.5	15.9	0.5	0.5	0.6	82.9	7.3	21.1	9.7	10.3	11.0	12.5
04 025	39140	3	Yavapai	21 040	222 255	294	10.6	82.4	1.2	2.4	1.7	14.2	4.1	13.3	6.8	9.0	9.0	12.1
04 027	49740	3	Yuma	14 281	204 275	316	14.3	33.9	2.3	1.4	1.9	61.6	7.5	18.7	11.8	13.1	10.9	11.0
05 000	...	X	ARKANSAS	134 771	2 978 204	X	22.1	75.0	16.1	1.6	2.1	7.0	6.5	17.4	9.7	13.0	12.3	13.0
05 001	...	6	Arkansas	2 561	18 433	1 894	7.2	71.6	25.0	0.8	1.2	3.0	6.8	16.3	8.4	11.3	12.1	13.0
05 003	...	7	Ashley	2 397	20 838	1 784	8.7	68.9	25.9	0.9	0.4	5.2	6.5	17.1	8.1	10.6	12.1	13.8
05 005	34260	7	Baxter	1 436	41 053	1 150	28.6	96.5	0.5	1.6	0.9	2.0	4.4	13.4	6.0	9.1	9.3	12.4
05 007	22220	2	Benton	2 195	249 672	269	113.7	76.7	2.2	2.7	4.3	16.1	7.2	19.8	8.0	14.6	14.2	12.8
05 009	25460	7	Boone	1 529	37 222	1 245	24.3	96.1	0.7	2.0	0.9	2.3	6.0	16.6	8.0	11.2	11.8	13.4
05 011	...	6	Bradley	1 682	11 094	2 349	6.6	58.0	28.1	1.2	0.6	14.4	6.9	16.5	7.7	11.9	11.9	13.2
05 013	15780	9	Calhoun	1 628	5 229	2 816	3.2	73.8	22.6	0.8	0.7	3.9	5.0	13.1	9.7	10.3	11.0	16.1
05 015	...	6	Carroll	1 632	27 704	1 503	17.0	82.8	0.9	2.2	1.4	14.6	5.5	16.6	7.1	10.5	10.8	12.8
05 017	...	7	Chicot	1 669	11 027	2 354	6.6	39.8	53.9	0.6	0.7	5.6	6.7	16.5	8.1	11.0	10.9	12.9
05 019	11660	7	Clark	2 243	22 633	1 704	10.1	70.4	24.2	0.9	0.9	4.4	4.9	14.2	21.6	10.7	10.0	11.1
05 021	...	7	Clay	1 656	15 109	2 090	9.1	96.5	1.1	1.1	0.4	1.8	4.3	16.1	8.3	10.2	11.7	14.1
05 023	...	6	Cleburne	1 434	25 467	1 588	17.8	95.9	0.7	1.5	0.5	2.6	4.8	15.0	6.5	10.0	10.2	13.7

1. CBSA = Core Based Statistical Area. See Appendix A for explanation. See Appendix B for list of metropolitan areas with component counties. 2. County type code from the Economic Research Service of USDA Rural-Urban Continuum Codes. See Appendix A for definition. 3. Dry land or land partially or temporarily covered by water. 4. May be of any race.

Table B. States and Counties — Population and Households

STATE County	Age (percent) (cont.) 55 to 64 years	65 to 74 years	75 years and over	Percent female	Total persons 2000	2010	Percent change 2000–2010	2010–2015	Components of change, 2010–2015 Births	Deaths	Net migration	Households, 2010–2014 Number	Persons per household	Percent Family households	Female family householder[1]	One person
	16	17	18	19	20	21	22	23	24	25	26	27	28	29	30	31
ALABAMA—Cont'd																
Washington	14.3	10.3	6.8	51.2	18 097	17 583	-2.8	-4.4	820	1 021	-569	6 218	2.73	74.0	10.9	23.8
Wilcox	14.3	10.1	7.6	52.4	13 183	11 665	-11.5	-5.2	699	756	-559	3 843	2.89	66.3	25.6	31.8
Winston	14.2	12.0	8.1	50.9	24 843	24 483	-1.4	-2.5	1 282	1 615	-246	9 526	2.50	68.7	10.5	29.5
ALASKA	12.6	6.3	3.1	47.4	626 932	710 249	13.3	4.0	60 037	21 274	-10 193	251 678	2.79	67.0	11.2	25.5
Aleutians East	13.6	4.3	2.3	30.9	2 697	3 141	16.5	6.4	82	30	148	577	2.43	60.3	16.6	29.1
Aleutians West	15.3	4.4	1.0	32.4	5 465	5 561	1.8	2.5	162	50	30	1 105	3.56	58.4	9.3	31.1
Anchorage	11.7	5.9	3.0	48.6	260 283	291 826	12.1	2.4	24 840	8 353	-9 365	105 164	2.76	66.6	12.0	25.0
Bethel	9.5	4.5	2.2	48.3	16 006	17 013	6.3	5.5	2 291	627	-707	4 441	3.88	74.9	17.2	17.5
Bristol Bay	16.9	6.3	3.4	44.3	1 258	997	-20.7	-10.5	57	39	-123	398	2.48	65.3	7.0	24.9
Denali	16.2	6.4	2.1	45.6	1 893	1 826	-3.5	5.1	113	40	16	722	2.24	56.1	4.8	36.4
Dillingham	12.8	5.1	2.9	48.6	4 922	4 847	-1.5	3.1	535	196	-182	1 353	3.57	67.6	16.9	28.5
Fairbanks North Star	11.2	5.4	2.5	45.9	82 840	97 581	17.8	2.1	8 969	2 411	-4 546	35 844	2.66	64.3	9.5	27.4
Haines	19.9	11.5	5.3	51.0	2 392	2 508	4.8	1.0	102	93	25	1 144	2.18	58.0	10.1	34.2
Hoonah-Angoon	20.5	11.0	5.6	46.5	NA	2 147	NA	-0.7	114	62	-74	909	2.24	61.3	9.7	32.6
Juneau	14.5	7.2	3.4	48.8	30 711	31 275	1.8	4.7	2 108	902	375	12 081	2.60	65.3	11.0	25.7
Kenai Peninsula	16.4	9.6	4.6	47.6	49 691	55 400	11.5	4.8	3 750	2 065	1 049	21 559	2.54	65.5	8.5	28.7
Ketchikan Gateway	15.4	8.3	4.2	47.9	14 070	13 479	-4.2	1.7	939	467	-224	5 305	2.52	60.5	11.0	30.3
Kodiak Island	12.3	6.0	2.6	46.2	13 913	13 606	-2.2	2.1	1 200	300	-613	4 560	2.97	76.6	10.8	20.2
Kusilvak	7.5	3.5	1.7	47.5	7 028	7 459	6.1	8.8	1 223	349	-209	1 690	4.59	84.9	24.4	12.9
Lake and Peninsula	11.9	6.1	2.9	47.1	1 823	1 635	-10.3	-4.4	157	66	-156	510	2.87	71.6	19.4	23.5
Matanuska-Susitna	13.1	6.6	3.0	47.5	59 322	88 995	50.0	13.6	7 128	2 747	7 607	31 104	2.96	71.6	9.3	22.1
Nome	10.3	5.0	2.4	47.6	9 196	9 492	3.2	3.7	1 210	416	-466	2 839	3.35	74.2	20.0	22.0
North Slope	14.1	3.4	1.4	37.5	7 385	9 430	27.7	2.7	926	228	-405	1 977	3.33	76.3	25.9	18.8
Northwest Arctic	8.7	4.2	2.7	45.8	7 208	7 523	4.4	3.0	981	255	-484	1 886	3.95	78.6	20.9	15.7
Petersburg	16.6	9.3	3.9	48.2	NA	3 207	NA	-0.9	221	82	-175	1 367	2.23	61.1	7.6	28.5
Prince of Wales-Hyder	16.5	8.1	3.4	45.3	NA	6 172	NA	2.7	419	224	22	2 377	2.63	63.2	10.8	30.6
Sitka	15.1	7.6	5.6	48.7	8 835	8 881	0.5	-0.2	527	319	-231	3 513	2.45	61.5	8.7	32.7
Skagway	17.6	7.3	3.3	47.6	NA	968	NA	9.2	52	20	60	387	2.21	53.7	5.7	32.0
Southeast Fairbanks	14.5	8.3	3.7	44.4	6 174	7 029	13.8	-2.7	615	226	-560	2 156	3.05	68.0	6.3	28.4
Valdez-Cordova	16.6	7.5	2.6	47.3	10 195	9 636	-5.5	-2.8	673	275	-656	3 225	2.91	70.2	10.1	24.2
Wrangell	20.0	11.1	6.7	48.2	NA	2 365	NA	0.7	136	92	-31	1 163	2.01	54.7	5.8	36.4
Yakutat	16.2	7.9	4.9	44.6	808	662	-18.1	-7.4	43	13	-76	265	2.17	60.4	12.1	37.0
Yukon-Koyukuk	15.0	8.1	5.2	46.3	6 551	5 588	-14.7	-1.0	464	327	-242	2 057	2.72	61.4	16.8	32.4
ARIZONA	11.8	9.2	6.7	50.3	5 130 632	6 392 307	24.6	6.8	452 651	264 373	237 810	2 387 246	2.69	65.7	12.7	27.2
Apache	11.8	8.1	5.4	50.6	69 423	71 518	3.0	-0.1	5 393	3 014	-2 312	19 046	3.71	68.1	21.4	27.9
Cochise	13.5	11.6	8.3	49.2	117 755	131 357	11.6	-3.8	8 722	6 416	-7 351	48 846	2.47	66.3	12.0	28.8
Coconino	11.8	7.0	4.0	50.6	116 320	134 437	15.6	3.5	8 997	3 933	-477	46 391	2.72	64.8	14.1	23.8
Gila	16.0	15.9	10.8	50.4	51 335	53 597	4.4	-0.8	3 277	3 814	22	20 824	2.51	65.3	11.6	29.5
Graham	10.2	7.0	5.2	46.5	33 489	37 220	11.1	1.2	3 026	1 442	-1 163	10 975	3.01	73.0	14.0	23.4
Greenlee	11.8	6.5	5.0	47.7	8 547	8 437	-1.3	12.9	646	285	739	3 446	2.53	72.2	13.9	21.0
La Paz	14.0	19.6	16.5	48.9	19 715	20 489	3.9	-1.6	1 041	1 176	-218	9 707	2.07	60.9	9.4	32.6
Maricopa	11.1	8.0	5.8	50.6	3 072 149	3 817 357	24.3	9.2	286 150	142 823	201 223	1 424 244	2.74	65.7	12.8	27.0
Mohave	15.9	15.9	11.0	49.7	155 032	200 186	29.1	2.3	9 767	13 594	7 699	80 529	2.43	63.8	10.6	28.6
Navajo	12.7	9.8	6.0	49.8	97 470	107 491	10.3	0.7	8 600	4 936	-2 931	34 018	3.09	71.7	19.3	25.0
Pima	12.6	10.0	7.7	50.8	843 746	980 263	16.2	3.0	62 878	46 603	12 769	386 155	2.50	61.8	12.8	30.8
Pinal	11.6	11.5	6.6	47.8	179 727	375 770	109.1	8.2	24 465	13 425	18 888	126 128	2.90	72.1	11.7	23.1
Santa Cruz	12.4	9.4	6.4	52.0	38 381	47 420	23.6	-2.0	3 482	1 478	-3 054	15 514	3.03	75.6	17.4	20.6
Yavapai	17.6	16.7	11.4	51.1	167 517	211 015	26.0	5.3	9 717	14 129	15 180	91 508	2.30	63.1	9.3	30.3
Yuma	9.7	9.2	8.2	48.8	160 026	195 750	22.3	4.4	16 490	7 305	-1 204	69 915	2.77	77.4	12.9	18.1
ARKANSAS	12.5	9.1	6.6	50.9	2 673 400	2 915 958	9.1	2.1	200 199	155 691	18 004	1 132 488	2.53	67.2	13.4	27.9
Arkansas	14.6	9.6	7.9	51.6	20 749	19 018	-8.3	-3.1	1 314	1 222	-635	7 787	2.39	63.3	11.6	33.4
Ashley	13.5	10.8	7.5	51.8	24 209	21 853	-9.7	-4.6	1 385	1 306	-1 087	8 518	2.49	70.7	14.3	27.2
Baxter	15.3	16.6	13.5	51.8	38 386	41 513	8.1	-1.1	1 794	3 457	1 159	18 237	2.23	64.9	9.1	30.5
Benton	10.4	7.5	5.5	50.5	153 406	221 344	44.3	12.8	17 461	8 496	18 791	83 191	2.76	74.4	9.9	20.7
Boone	13.3	11.1	8.7	50.8	33 948	36 903	8.7	0.9	2 345	2 212	177	14 855	2.47	69.7	11.0	27.0
Bradley	13.5	10.2	8.2	51.1	12 600	11 508	-8.7	-3.6	726	802	-333	4 720	2.35	69.0	15.1	28.5
Calhoun	15.1	10.9	8.9	49.2	5 744	5 368	-6.5	-2.6	250	276	-133	2 062	2.50	70.6	12.0	28.4
Carroll	15.5	12.8	8.3	50.7	25 357	27 446	8.2	0.9	1 598	1 527	321	11 069	2.47	67.5	9.0	26.9
Chicot	14.7	10.0	9.2	50.8	14 117	11 800	-16.4	-6.6	755	791	-733	4 495	2.39	66.7	18.9	31.8
Clark	11.3	8.8	7.3	52.1	23 546	22 995	-2.3	-1.6	1 281	1 339	-319	8 467	2.35	63.4	14.5	32.6
Clay	13.9	11.9	9.5	51.1	17 609	16 083	-8.7	-6.1	683	1 226	-388	6 729	2.30	65.3	11.4	30.8
Cleburne	14.4	14.2	11.2	50.7	24 046	25 969	8.0	-1.9	1 283	1 887	102	10 292	2.47	66.9	9.3	30.0

1. No spouse present.

STATE County	Daytime population, 2010–2014 — Persons in group quarters, 2015	Number	Employ-ment/resi-dence ratio	Births, 2015 — Total	Rate[1]	Deaths, 2015 — Number	Rate[1]	Persons under 65 with no health insurance, 2014 — Number	Percent	Medicare, 2015 — Total Beneficiaries	Enrolled in Original Medicare	Enrolled in Medicare Advantage	Serious crimes known to police,[2] 2014 — Total Number	Rate[3]
	32	33	34	35	36	37	38	39	40	41	42	43	44	45
ALABAMA—Cont'd														
Washington	147	16 540	0.89	147	8.7	202	12.0	2 093	15.1	3 754	3 211	543	163	975
Wilcox	108	11 471	1.04	130	11.8	126	11.4	1 482	16.3	2 949	2 628	321	214	1 903
Winston	301	23 849	0.95	250	10.4	310	12.9	3 143	16.3	6 010	5 176	834	197	984
ALASKA	27 941	736 253	1.02	11 498	15.6	4 282	5.8	123 604	19.0	73 772	72 863	909	25 018	3 396
Aleutians East	1 726	3 454	1.06	14	4.2	7	2.1	1 222	39.3	NA	NA	NA	NA	NA
Aleutians West	2 515	6 494	1.22	27	4.7	5	0.9	1 320	25.2	NA	NA	NA	NA	NA
Anchorage	8 190	307 455	1.06	4 796	16.0	1 700	5.7	44 636	16.7	30 001	29 615	386	14 136	4 692
Bethel	353	17 716	1.02	428	23.9	140	7.8	4 256	26.0	D	738	D	NA	NA
Bristol Bay	16	1 264	1.51	8	8.7	5	5.4	183	21.7	D	646	D	12	1 270
Denali	43	2 534	1.42	25	13.1	6	3.1	358	20.9	D	D	D	NA	NA
Dillingham	52	5 026	1.04	100	20.0	35	7.0	1 162	25.4	D	443	D	NA	NA
Fairbanks North Star	4 777	98 427	0.98	1 707	17.2	463	4.7	14 472	16.6	7 955	7 856	99	NA	NA
Haines	0	2 498	0.96	16	6.3	11	4.3	523	24.5	D	468	D	47	1 808
Hoonah-Angoon	0	2 115	0.99	20	9.5	17	8.0	515	29.7	D	D	D	NA	NA
Juneau	1 070	32 596	1.02	416	12.7	152	4.6	4 923	17.4	4 231	4 191	40	1 061	3 216
Kenai Peninsula	1 737	55 445	0.95	713	12.3	447	7.7	10 080	20.9	8 886	8 779	107	NA	NA
Ketchikan Gateway	273	14 057	1.06	166	12.1	87	6.3	2 502	21.1	2 007	1 980	27	NA	NA
Kodiak Island	389	14 197	1.04	232	16.6	51	3.7	3 111	24.8	819	806	13	NA	NA
Kusilvak	31	7 945	1.00	230	28.4	64	10.4	1 939	25.6	D	449	D	NA	NA
Lake and Peninsula	37	1 628	1.23	29	18.2	17	10.7	442	30.0	NA	NA	NA	NA	NA
Matanuska-Susitna	2 495	81 108	0.67	1 415	14.2	528	5.3	16 021	18.5	9 261	9 128	133	NA	NA
Nome	187	9 880	1.03	212	21.5	91	9.2	2 440	27.4	D	620	D	NA	NA
North Slope	2 650	17 661	2.51	176	18.1	53	5.5	2 123	23.3	D	377	D	185	1 909
Northwest Arctic	381	8 036	1.15	175	22.6	76	9.8	1 967	27.8	D	421	D	NA	NA
Petersburg	43	3 262	1.03	45	14.1	21	6.6	560	20.4	1 031	1 017	14	NA	NA
Prince of Wales-Hyder	50	6 414	1.02	78	12.3	48	7.5	1 563	27.7	D	634	D	NA	NA
Sitka	259	8 999	1.01	86	9.7	45	5.1	1 840	24.2	D	1 130	D	245	2 707
Skagway	32	1 015	1.03	9	8.6	15	14.3	181	19.5	D	513	D	18	1 804
Southeast Fairbanks	369	7 648	1.20	116	16.8	34	4.9	1 482	24.4	D	590	D	NA	NA
Valdez-Cordova	201	10 584	1.20	139	14.7	43	4.6	1 713	20.3	1 406	1 387	19	NA	NA
Wrangell	16	2 385	1.00	28	11.8	26	11.0	399	20.5	NA	NA	NA	29	1 204
Yakutat	18	670	1.10	10	16.0	1	1.6	169	30.7	NA	NA	NA	NA	NA
Yukon-Koyukuk	31	5 740	1.05	82	14.8	74	13.3	1 502	31.4	997	986	11	NA	NA
ARIZONA	154 682	6 537 777	0.99	87 385	12.9	53 233	7.9	886 514	16.1	1 049 840	614 171	435 669	242 156	3 597
Apache	968	71 047	0.94	1 089	15.2	642	9.0	12 883	21.0	8 911	8 168	743	510	703
Cochise	5 052	131 877	1.02	1 580	12.5	1 203	9.5	13 788	14.2	26 770	17 935	8 835	2 473	2 314
Coconino	11 174	135 936	1.00	1 691	12.2	812	5.9	21 211	18.8	19 750	16 583	3 167	4 877	3 529
Gila	919	53 988	1.04	620	11.7	777	14.6	6 740	17.6	14 696	12 485	2 211	1 414	2 702
Graham	3 237	35 721	0.86	608	16.1	270	7.1	4 339	14.5	5 142	3 336	1 806	NA	NA
Greenlee	35	10 725	1.59	143	15.2	37	3.9	894	10.9	1 148	976	172	110	1 183
La Paz	399	21 002	1.10	210	10.4	249	12.3	3 003	24.0	4 849	3 927	922	579	3 335
Maricopa	61 732	3 986 778	1.02	55 671	13.5	28 981	7.0	539 347	15.6	559 206	302 891	256 315	140 504	3 438
Mohave	4 832	192 145	0.84	1 854	9.1	2 789	13.7	28 091	19.5	54 715	38 928	15 787	6 743	3 364
Navajo	2 248	108 673	1.04	1 597	14.8	963	8.9	16 533	18.6	18 706	14 495	4 211	2 206	2 042
Pima	25 522	992 065	1.00	12 048	12.0	9 251	9.2	129 021	16.0	183 450	94 188	89 262	49 303	4 894
Pinal	25 298	340 317	0.62	4 625	11.5	2 739	6.8	43 511	14.3	54 344	31 302	23 042	8 316	2 131
Santa Cruz	407	47 617	1.02	628	13.5	301	6.5	8 064	20.7	7 802	3 668	4 134	845	1 798
Yavapai	3 777	210 034	0.95	1 914	8.7	2 726	12.4	28 098	18.1	61 698	43 516	18 182	NA	NA
Yuma	9 082	199 852	0.98	3 107	15.2	1 493	7.3	30 961	19.4	28 653	21 773	6 880	6 006	2 946
ARKANSAS	84 027	2 945 746	1.00	37 820	12.7	29 401	9.9	336 619	13.8	576 027	451 864	124 163	113 261	3 818
Arkansas	247	20 201	1.16	240	13.0	229	12.4	1 961	12.9	4 051	3 516	535	774	4 139
Ashley	191	21 372	0.99	251	12.0	259	12.4	1 983	11.7	4 959	4 228	731	749	3 545
Baxter	595	42 027	1.06	346	8.4	647	15.8	3 831	13.5	14 426	10 474	3 952	1 270	3 115
Benton	2 109	238 384	1.05	3 416	13.9	1 642	6.7	29 671	14.2	33 347	22 333	11 014	4 731	2 023
Boone	465	38 516	1.09	458	12.3	436	11.7	3 776	12.7	10 184	7 786	2 398	1 178	3 143
Bradley	223	11 190	0.97	133	12.0	128	11.6	1 628	18.1	2 490	2 165	325	158	1 413
Calhoun	175	4 825	0.81	48	9.2	43	8.3	513	12.9	981	850	131	57	1 093
Carroll	230	27 501	0.99	311	11.2	297	10.7	4 127	19.0	6 183	4 368	1 815	684	2 457
Chicot	728	11 491	1.00	121	10.9	153	13.8	1 200	14.3	2 733	2 314	419	448	3 996
Clark	2 757	22 982	1.02	245	10.8	239	10.5	2 009	12.2	4 569	3 634	935	572	2 523
Clay	125	14 161	0.77	174	11.5	198	13.1	1 716	14.6	4 007	3 478	529	179	1 175
Cleburne	339	24 973	0.91	233	9.1	352	13.8	2 635	13.9	7 293	6 292	1 001	910	3 557

1. Per 1,000 estimated resident population.   2. Data for serious crimes have not been adjusted for underreporting; this may affect comparability between geographic areas and over time.
3. Per 100,000 population estimated by the FBI.

STATE County	Serious crimes known to police, 2014 (cont.)[1] Rate[2] Violent	Property	Education School enrollment and attainment, 2010–2014 Enrollment[3] Total	Percent private	Attainment[4] (percent) High school graduate or less	Bachelor's degree or more	Local government expenditures,[5] 2012–2013 Total current spending (mil dol)	Current spending per student (dollars)	Money income, 2010–2014 Per capita income[6] (dollars)	Households Median income (dollars)	Mean income (dollars)	Percent with income of $200,000 or more	Income and poverty, 2014 Median household income (dollars)	Percent below poverty level All persons	Children under 18 years	Children 5 to 17 years in families
	46	47	48	49	50	51	52	53	54	55	56	57	58	59	60	61
ALABAMA—Cont'd																
Washington	180	796	4 015	5.8	66.5	10.3	27.8	8 681	20 737	44 731	54 921	0.7	41 321	18.5	26.7	24.2
Wilcox	578	1 325	2 564	12.9	63.5	11.5	18.6	9 760	13 881	23 406	37 286	0.3	24 035	33.7	47.1	43.8
Winston	90	894	5 235	4.9	59.5	11.1	39.5	9 109	19 078	34 064	45 931	1.3	35 528	20.1	32.0	28.4
ALASKA	636	2 760	195 548	12.3	35.7	27.7	2 394.3	18 175	33 129	71 829	88 583	5.9	70 898	11.4	15.5	14.1
Aleutians East	NA	NA	368	9.2	60.9	12.6	9.4	36 588	27 122	59 886	69 467	2.3	55 462	16.2	15.6	13.6
Aleutians West	NA	NA	937	15.4	51.2	15.4	14.1	26 956	32 700	82 284	93 892	6.2	68 387	9.9	9.7	8.6
Anchorage	865	3 827	81 836	14.0	30.8	32.9	764.2	15 555	36 508	78 121	98 317	8.0	75 200	10.0	14.2	12.7
Bethel	NA	NA	5 426	0.8	61.5	11.4	153.8	30 987	18 875	51 930	69 476	3.0	45 808	23.8	31.7	31.9
Bristol Bay	0	1 270	284	7.4	37.4	20.2	20.9	38 998	37 012	82 500	93 101	5.3	75 364	9.5	12.2	10.9
Denali	NA	NA	344	13.4	35.2	29.5	9.7	11 282	36 828	79 167	91 421	4.6	69 692	7.1	8.9	7.7
Dillingham	NA	NA	1 442	3.5	51.5	16.6	33.3	29 748	21 774	54 846	70 185	3.4	51 082	17.5	25.0	24.6
Fairbanks North Star	NA	NA	28 694	11.8	30.9	30.5	275.6	17 384	32 906	70 408	84 580	4.1	67 801	9.5	10.6	9.6
Haines	154	1 654	556	5.6	35.8	31.3	6.8	23 873	32 312	57 551	71 240	3.8	67 260	9.8	15.4	12.9
Hoonah-Angoon	NA	NA	361	10.0	40.2	29.3	9.8	35 466	30 811	50 268	66 937	4.0	51 687	19.1	31.0	28.1
Juneau	573	2 643	8 148	12.1	26.8	37.8	88.5	17 468	38 057	84 750	97 588	7.4	80 835	7.9	9.6	8.0
Kenai Peninsula	NA	NA	12 943	11.8	39.1	23.3	160.9	17 855	31 611	63 099	78 020	3.7	62 532	11.5	14.5	12.6
Ketchikan Gateway	NA	NA	3 001	11.5	40.7	24.6	39.5	17 574	31 494	61 712	78 169	4.1	57 776	12.4	17.6	15.6
Kodiak Island	NA	NA	3 761	11.7	34.7	21.6	51.0	20 007	29 993	70 529	82 756	4.6	67 972	8.3	11.0	9.7
Kusilvak	NA	NA	2 592	1.1	71.5	4.5	70.7	28 443	11 257	40 943	49 546	0.9	30 877	35.7	43.7	42.0
Lake and Peninsula	NA	NA	495	2.4	55.2	13.7	NA	NA	21 581	47 143	61 099	2.2	45 570	17.7	22.4	21.5
Matanuska-Susitna	NA	NA	26 247	16.2	39.6	20.9	267.1	15 274	30 013	72 134	84 838	5.0	73 981	10.7	13.1	11.9
Nome	NA	NA	2 875	2.1	57.8	14.7	79.7	31 129	19 651	47 579	65 042	2.0	47 160	26.1	34.0	31.8
North Slope	764	1 145	2 152	2.6	48.4	13.4	72.7	37 481	50 267	74 609	88 173	6.1	75 682	11.5	16.5	15.4
Northwest Arctic	NA	NA	2 163	2.8	62.5	12.0	61.2	30 582	21 543	63 971	77 506	3.2	65 192	23.2	28.9	26.7
Petersburg	NA	NA	748	9.4	37.7	25.2	12.8	22 590	36 307	61 492	83 202	4.5	56 655	8.8	11.4	10.5
Prince of Wales-Hyder	NA	NA	1 395	8.0	50.9	16.3	30.9	23 553	24 737	46 387	61 163	1.9	43 245	17.4	25.9	23.2
Sitka	66	2 641	2 201	7.5	29.6	32.9	26.6	20 141	33 920	69 635	81 059	5.2	65 765	8.6	10.3	9.1
Skagway	0	1 804	181	8.3	32.3	34.6	2.4	25 880	40 986	72 868	88 351	7.5	69 170	3.6	5.2	6.1
Southeast Fairbanks	NA	NA	1 843	18.2	39.4	20.7	27.0	22 153	30 402	65 481	75 871	3.7	59 641	13.8	20.6	19.3
Valdez-Cordova	NA	NA	2 494	14.0	35.0	24.1	34.0	23 316	32 610	81 736	86 613	6.0	73 998	9.9	11.4	10.2
Wrangell	208	996	407	3.2	46.3	18.7	8.0	20 420	30 671	48 324	62 806	1.7	52 201	11.9	15.6	13.1
Yakutat	NA	NA	149	0.7	47.3	20.3	3.2	34 699	33 475	69 306	73 804	2.3	52 595	14.8	24.8	23.8
Yukon-Koyukuk	NA	NA	1 505	5.1	56.3	10.1	60.6	11 024	20 149	37 796	51 010	0.8	36 708	25.7	32.9	29.4
ARIZONA	400	3 198	1 751 801	10.8	38.6	27.1	6 836.6	7 208	25 537	49 928	67 557	3.6	50 036	18.2	25.6	24.0
Apache	119	585	21 010	4.4	57.0	10.1	84.5	7 250	12 828	32 396	41 631	0.4	32 366	33.1	39.5	38.0
Cochise	283	2 032	32 983	9.3	37.4	23.1	125.5	7 181	23 552	45 974	59 813	2.5	45 025	18.7	27.5	26.4
Coconino	346	3 183	46 313	6.5	33.9	32.8	134.3	7 962	23 459	48 540	65 952	3.3	48 653	21.3	24.8	22.6
Gila	336	2 366	10 238	9.7	46.6	17.1	51.8	7 122	20 857	40 042	50 268	0.9	37 677	24.4	39.2	35.3
Graham	NA	NA	10 276	6.5	48.8	13.6	41.3	6 402	17 687	46 965	56 553	1.3	46 046	20.0	24.1	22.2
Greenlee	462	720	2 557	7.9	51.8	11.8	11.9	6 958	22 334	50 818	58 894	1.1	59 416	10.3	11.5	10.2
La Paz	202	3 133	3 085	1.3	58.8	10.2	19.7	8 013	21 772	37 009	45 868	0.6	32 533	22.8	35.1	33.7
Maricopa	383	3 055	1 080 221	11.5	36.7	30.0	4 361.4	7 248	27 477	53 689	73 344	4.6	53 929	17.1	24.3	22.8
Mohave	202	3 162	40 397	13.0	50.7	12.2	131.8	6 291	20 709	38 456	50 106	1.4	37 704	20.8	32.0	30.6
Navajo	313	1 729	29 663	6.2	48.0	14.5	132.0	7 305	16 355	36 591	48 651	1.4	35 457	28.5	35.4	33.4
Pima	443	4 451	268 443	11.1	35.3	30.1	1 033.5	8 133	25 524	46 233	63 627	3.1	45 871	18.7	25.9	25.1
Pinal	226	1 905	95 171	10.5	45.0	17.8	299.1	6 692	20 983	50 248	60 597	1.8	49 876	17.6	25.4	21.3
Santa Cruz	132	1 666	13 358	5.3	52.8	22.0	63.3	6 530	17 900	38 802	52 629	1.4	37 465	23.6	34.6	32.0
Yavapai	NA	NA	43 239	13.2	36.0	24.9	139.2	6 708	25 068	44 000	57 110	2.0	44 145	15.6	23.6	20.5
Yuma	370	2 576	54 847	6.8	53.6	14.0	207.3	5 941	18 887	41 380	54 066	1.6	39 700	22.6	30.0	30.0
ARKANSAS	480	3 338	752 073	10.7	50.7	20.6	4 521.6	9 394	22 595	41 264	56 824	2.2	41 335	18.7	26.3	24.5
Arkansas	460	3 679	4 063	6.2	60.8	13.9	27.4	8 799	23 237	37 813	54 129	1.8	36 409	20.4	28.6	27.6
Ashley	327	3 219	5 162	4.7	58.7	12.7	36.6	9 245	19 739	35 136	48 379	0.8	36 176	22.7	33.1	33.7
Baxter	140	2 975	7 576	10.0	48.7	17.4	44.8	8 710	21 693	35 594	47 730	1.2	37 873	14.9	25.6	23.4
Benton	235	1 788	59 379	13.5	44.3	29.6	353.7	8 996	27 522	56 325	75 336	4.5	57 408	11.9	16.2	15.1
Boone	413	2 729	8 403	7.2	51.6	15.1	53.7	8 462	21 348	38 705	51 523	1.7	39 779	16.9	25.5	23.3
Bradley	215	1 199	2 520	7.1	63.6	11.2	21.7	10 555	20 243	33 745	48 111	2.8	32 734	27.4	39.1	36.7
Calhoun	173	921	1 040	3.9	67.1	10.6	5.6	10 290	19 755	35 000	47 742	0.8	39 493	18.0	23.9	22.5
Carroll	312	2 144	5 210	12.1	52.5	17.0	35.3	8 946	20 604	36 897	49 115	0.9	36 964	17.9	29.7	28.5
Chicot	392	3 603	2 697	9.8	65.0	11.3	18.9	11 842	19 311	28 086	48 265	2.2	29 541	32.1	43.1	41.4
Clark	260	2 263	7 651	18.4	49.6	22.3	41.5	14 627	18 709	34 109	48 042	1.6	38 504	21.5	28.2	26.6
Clay	138	1 038	3 137	4.0	67.2	9.8	22.4	8 686	18 434	32 057	41 575	0.4	33 826	19.9	28.3	24.7
Cleburne	274	3 283	4 824	7.1	52.8	17.2	30.7	8 955	24 297	40 768	56 349	2.1	40 555	15.2	24.1	22.3

1. Data for serious crimes have not been adjusted for underreporting; this may affect comparability between geographic areas and over time.   2. Per 100,000 population estimated by the FBI.
3. All persons 3 years old and over enrolled in nursery school through college.   4. Persons 25 years old and over.   5. Elementary and secondary education expenditures.
6. Based on population estimated by the American Community Survey, 2010–2014.

Table B. States and Counties — **Personal Income**

STATE County	Personal income, 2014 Total (mil dol)	Percent change, 2013–2014	Per capita[1] Dollars	Per capita[1] Rank	Wages and salaries (mil dol)	Supplements to wages and salaries; employer contributions (mil dol) Pension and insurance	Government social insurance	Proprietors' income (mil dol)	Dividends, interest, and rent (mil dol)	Personal transfer receipts (mil dol)	Earnings, 2014 Total (mil dol)	Contributions for government social insurance (mil dol) From employee and self-employed	From employer
	62	63	64	65	66	67	68	69	70	71	72	73	74
ALABAMA—Cont'd													
Washington	564	3.9	33 496	2 197	206	45	15	40	65	159	306	21	15
Wilcox	309	-4.3	27 815	2 931	119	23	8	27	47	135	177	13	8
Winston	716	4.3	29 657	2 766	249	48	20	47	111	237	363	26	20
ALASKA	39 793	5.3	54 012	X	20 683	4 566	1 572	3 238	6 644	6 454	30 059	1 562	1 572
Aleutians East	124	5.0	36 946	1 608	82	23	7	3	12	11	114	6	7
Aleutians West	305	6.9	53 010	265	219	49	18	20	26	22	305	15	18
Anchorage	18 402	5.2	61 134	115	10 109	2 041	797	1 803	3 162	2 619	14 750	782	797
Bethel	662	5.6	37 075	1 590	300	95	20	17	61	222	432	19	20
Bristol Bay	57	5.5	59 603	139	66	17	6	5	13	9	94	5	6
Denali	124	12.5	64 631	89	109	21	10	1	19	35	141	8	10
Dillingham	250	7.0	50 212	377	121	33	10	17	40	50	181	9	10
Fairbanks North Star	5 146	4.0	51 792	303	2 520	648	203	270	944	806	3 641	175	203
Haines	200	4.4	78 115	31	38	10	3	105	30	27	156	9	3
Hoonah-Angoon	103	5.5	49 585	407	28	10	2	9	21	26	50	3	2
Juneau	1 848	3.3	57 033	171	1 007	285	66	41	365	242	1 399	62	66
Kenai Peninsula	2 918	6.5	50 760	344	1 086	257	80	235	497	549	1 657	92	80
Ketchikan Gateway	798	4.5	57 876	160	371	97	28	91	140	141	587	30	28
Kodiak Island	752	5.1	53 792	244	371	96	31	73	144	109	571	28	31
Kusilvak	230	9.4	28 762	2 852	70	35	4	2	19	108	112	4	4
Lake and Peninsula	76	4.1	46 787	538	33	11	2	1	18	18	48	2	2
Matanuska-Susitna	4 387	7.2	44 820	694	1 028	248	79	293	561	690	1 648	94	79
Nome	436	6.1	44 413	724	196	58	13	15	45	133	283	13	13
North Slope	330	5.0	34 061	2 109	1 713	213	110	5	62	60	2 042	113	110
Northwest Arctic	347	7.3	44 965	680	199	45	13	9	29	110	267	13	13
Petersburg	185	4.0	58 426	150	63	19	5	31	47	38	118	6	5
Prince of Wales-Hyder	241	4.8	37 684	1 499	90	29	6	21	43	61	146	7	6
Sitka	545	5.6	61 204	114	231	59	18	68	121	75	376	19	18
Skagway	81	7.4	77 937	34	38	8	3	10	15	9	59	3	3
Southeast Fairbanks	275	4.5	39 605	1 234	166	37	12	18	49	72	233	13	12
Valdez-Cordova	537	4.5	56 571	183	277	70	20	44	91	77	411	21	20
Wrangell	102	6.7	43 230	823	38	11	3	8	19	27	60	3	3
Yakutat	29	1.2	45 364	646	13	4	1	1	5	7	19	1	1
Yukon-Koyukuk	301	1.8	54 323	222	99	36	6	22	44	101	163	7	6
ARIZONA	255 093	4.7	37 895	X	127 815	19 635	9 234	18 683	46 310	52 107	175 367	10 822	9 234
Apache	2 049	4.5	28 521	2 880	759	197	56	59	283	871	1 071	67	56
Cochise	4 680	1.9	36 720	1 642	1 849	437	150	185	941	1 426	2 621	157	150
Coconino	5 400	5.3	39 220	1 293	2 571	548	190	315	1 108	1 026	3 623	207	190
Gila	1 831	3.0	34 463	2 034	636	123	47	62	358	718	868	64	47
Graham	1 101	5.6	29 000	2 828	373	76	27	37	134	364	513	32	27
Greenlee	350	7.9	37 431	1 535	383	52	26	12	31	79	472	27	26
La Paz	591	2.9	29 219	2 805	201	43	15	37	112	215	296	20	15
Maricopa	168 483	4.9	41 222	1 033	93 384	12 998	6 670	14 223	29 683	28 284	127 275	7 708	6 670
Mohave	5 634	4.4	27 704	2 938	1 755	309	133	306	936	1 995	2 503	203	133
Navajo	2 966	5.0	27 434	2 956	1 110	231	89	117	470	1 194	1 547	106	89
Pima	37 199	4.0	37 031	1 596	16 863	3 047	1 229	1 950	7 946	8 849	23 090	1 458	1 229
Pinal	10 388	7.1	25 846	3 037	2 435	497	175	498	1 219	2 976	3 605	254	175
Santa Cruz	1 408	3.4	30 164	2 695	620	129	48	112	278	360	910	57	48
Yavapai	7 172	5.3	32 774	2 319	2 257	398	167	282	1 884	2 309	3 103	247	167
Yuma	5 842	0.1	28 742	2 858	2 617	551	213	488	928	1 441	3 869	212	213
ARKANSAS	112 076	3.7	37 782	X	50 513	7 820	3 935	9 629	22 819	26 201	71 897	4 642	3 935
Arkansas	792	-1.6	42 602	889	415	65	35	160	96	176	675	39	35
Ashley	682	-2.9	32 540	2 365	308	48	26	61	74	235	443	31	26
Baxter	1 368	3.9	33 472	2 201	525	88	43	72	280	497	727	59	43
Benton	16 665	4.2	68 773	66	6 216	719	445	652	8 069	1 532	8 033	506	445
Boone	1 209	4.8	32 498	2 371	537	89	42	115	189	362	782	54	42
Bradley	363	7.1	32 578	2 355	118	21	10	53	44	136	202	13	10
Calhoun	151	2.0	29 043	2 823	126	18	10	6	17	43	159	10	10
Carroll	877	10.9	31 599	2 512	319	59	27	110	160	248	515	33	27
Chicot	376	-6.4	33 652	2 168	114	18	9	66	45	139	208	13	9
Clark	700	4.5	30 985	2 587	329	60	26	43	101	219	458	30	26
Clay	506	-6.1	33 496	2 197	123	21	10	71	64	160	225	15	10
Cleburne	870	4.0	33 949	2 121	237	41	20	93	181	269	391	31	20

1. Based on the resident population estimated as of July 1 of the year shown.

Table B. States and Counties — Earnings, Social Security, and Housing

STATE County	Farm	Mining	Construction	Manu-facturing	Information: professional, scientific, technical services	Retail trade	Finance, insurance, real estate and leasing	Health care and social assistance	Govern-ment	Number	Rate[1]	Supplemental Security Income recipients, December 2014	Total	Percent change, 2010–2014
	75	76	77	78	79	80	81	82	83	84	85	86	87	88
ALABAMA—Cont'd														
Washington	4.7	D	5.3	39.8	D	3.5	D	D	14.1	4 725	280	751	8 375	-0.4
Wilcox	6.8	0.0	3.1	32.7	2.6	5.0	2.8	D	20.5	3 725	337	1 523	5 612	-0.6
Winston	5.4	D	3.1	33.4	1.8	8.1	3.2	D	15.5	6 850	284	1 065	13 403	-0.5
ALASKA	0.0	9.5	7.5	3.0	8.3	5.4	4.2	10.7	30.1	89 047	121	12 399	309 448	0.8
Aleutians East	0.0	0.0	D	D	D	1.4	D	D	17.2	175	53	11	747	0.0
Aleutians West	0.9	D	2.8	43.9	1.6	3.7	D	D	14.3	235	41	24	1 932	0.2
Anchorage	0.0	5.8	7.5	1.0	12.8	5.6	5.4	12.2	26.7	33 805	113	5 823	114 908	1.7
Bethel	0.0	D	D	0.9	D	5.7	D	D	45.3	1 650	92	397	5 925	0.1
Bristol Bay	0.0	0.0	D	44.7	D	D	D	D	22.4	120	127	7	965	-0.4
Denali	0.0	D	D	0.0	D	1.1	D	D	23.2	235	123	10	1 758	-0.7
Dillingham	0.0	D	1.2	D	D	3.9	D	25.7	28.2	525	105	109	2 424	-0.1
Fairbanks North Star	0.1	4.7	8.7	1.4	4.2	5.7	D	9.6	45.8	10 010	101	1 081	41 616	-0.4
Haines	0.0	D	10.4	5.1	9.6	9.5	D	12.3	9.1	555	216	46	1 642	0.7
Hoonah-Angoon	0.0	0.0	4.1	D	D	4.6	D	D	48.9	450	215	49	1 759	-0.1
Juneau	-0.2	D	5.0	1.4	5.0	5.5	2.6	7.4	50.6	4 265	131	522	13 380	2.5
Kenai Peninsula	0.0	10.7	8.3	5.0	4.3	6.6	4.8	11.9	26.4	10 580	184	1 045	30 769	0.6
Ketchikan Gateway	0.0	D	8.3	5.2	2.8	7.9	4.4	10.5	34.1	2 225	161	234	6 263	1.5
Kodiak Island	0.0	0.0	5.0	18.2	1.5	3.4	2.9	9.0	34.8	1 550	111	160	5 329	0.5
Kusilvak	0.0	0.0	0.0	D	D	6.9	0.0	D	0.0	785	97	196	2 183	0.0
Lake and Peninsula	0.0	D	D	7.3	D	D	D	D	48.2	185	114	18	1 500	-0.3
Matanuska-Susitna	0.3	0.6	15.0	2.2	7.3	9.9	4.8	15.0	25.8	12 435	127	1 576	41 370	0.1
Nome	0.0	D	3.5	D	1.5	5.0	2.8	D	44.0	1 040	106	221	4 051	1.1
North Slope	0.0	66.8	D	D	D	0.7	D	D	9.3	630	65	13	2 598	3.9
Northwest Arctic	0.0	D	D	0.0	D	D	D	D	29.5	725	94	112	2 721	0.5
Petersburg	0.0	D	3.9	14.2	2.6	5.7	D	2.0	36.1	685	215	44	1 650	0.4
Prince of Wales-Hyder	0.0	D	3.8	4.7	D	7.1	2.8	4.1	48.5	940	147	108	3 311	-1.4
Sitka	0.0	0.0	9.2	14.7	D	4.8	2.4	11.3	32.6	1 235	139	94	4 128	0.6
Skagway	0.0	0.0	18.7	2.7	0.5	16.6	D	0.5	25.4	105	101	5	662	4.1
Southeast Fairbanks	0.0	D	4.1	0.8	6.0	4.8	1.1	D	33.1	1 140	163	153	3 884	-0.8
Valdez-Cordova	0.0	D	4.7	7.1	3.9	4.1	D	5.3	30.0	1 360	143	108	6 076	-0.4
Wrangell	0.0	0.0	5.0	8.5	D	6.5	D	D	43.3	460	195	37	1 424	0.3
Yakutat	0.0	0.0	D	D	D	D	D	0.5	53.1	110	174	0	452	0.4
Yukon-Koyukuk	0.0	0.9	10.3	D	D	4.6	D	13.0	54.0	830	149	189	4 021	-0.4
ARIZONA	0.7	0.8	5.7	8.0	10.1	7.6	9.9	12.3	17.1	1 207 102	179	119 510	2 929 030	3.0
Apache	-0.8	0.9	2.1	0.7	1.8	4.0	2.2	12.2	61.3	12 220	170	4 426	32 757	0.7
Cochise	1.7	0.2	3.0	1.1	9.1	6.4	2.6	7.4	51.6	30 525	240	3 085	60 620	2.7
Coconino	0.2	0.3	3.8	10.4	3.4	6.9	3.3	16.5	33.2	18 765	136	2 667	64 446	1.8
Gila	-0.6	11.7	4.1	15.3	D	7.0	2.3	11.1	31.0	15 720	296	1 170	33 054	1.1
Graham	5.0	D	4.5	1.9	15.4	9.2	1.9	11.4	34.5	6 655	175	1 080	13 291	2.4
Greenlee	1.2	D	D	0.0	0.0	1.5	0.2	D	6.3	1 445	155	116	4 426	1.2
La Paz	8.0	0.5	D	2.6	D	11.5	2.3	D	43.1	5 505	271	479	16 156	0.7
Maricopa	0.3	0.3	6.2	8.2	11.2	7.7	12.0	11.9	12.3	640 470	157	61 734	1 693 581	3.3
Mohave	0.4	1.5	5.0	6.3	4.6	12.6	5.3	21.0	18.8	62 965	310	4 685	112 867	1.8
Navajo	1.0	3.7	5.4	0.6	7.2	8.1	2.7	12.9	36.3	21 705	201	4 798	57 646	1.2
Pima	0.2	1.3	4.5	10.0	9.7	6.8	5.5	14.7	25.6	202 670	202	20 237	452 040	2.5
Pinal	7.4	3.0	3.6	6.4	3.4	7.2	3.0	6.8	36.4	73 070	184	5 628	166 415	4.5
Santa Cruz	0.7	0.1	1.8	2.4	4.7	9.7	2.6	4.4	38.8	8 895	191	1 392	18 163	0.8
Yavapai	0.3	D	6.8	6.5	4.6	10.0	4.8	16.0	21.7	72 670	332	3 733	113 083	2.4
Yuma	9.0	0.1	3.8	2.8	5.3	7.2	3.2	11.0	33.1	33 820	166	4 280	90 485	3.0
ARKANSAS	3.9	1.4	5.4	12.5	6.3	7.0	5.5	11.8	17.4	673 193	227	111 482	1 347 528	2.4
Arkansas	11.1	0.0	2.8	29.7	1.8	6.6	2.9	6.5	8.6	4 795	258	799	9 446	0.1
Ashley	3.9	0.0	8.9	34.6	D	5.7	3.0	D	11.8	5 825	278	1 001	10 095	-0.4
Baxter	0.6	D	4.8	17.4	6.2	9.7	7.7	25.3	11.6	16 000	392	1 026	22 629	0.2
Benton	1.7	0.3	4.1	7.3	7.4	5.2	3.4	6.1	6.8	41 765	172	3 500	99 875	7.3
Boone	4.0	D	4.5	11.8	3.6	9.0	4.2	8.0	20.8	10 795	291	1 103	16 907	0.5
Bradley	11.7	D	6.3	15.6	D	5.2	3.6	11.9	19.1	2 900	262	540	5 808	-0.9
Calhoun	0.9	D	2.8	73.1	D	D	D	1.6	7.6	1 180	227	177	2 883	-0.5
Carroll	14.8	D	5.3	26.7	2.3	6.7	4.5	8.7	11.3	7 735	279	648	13 570	0.1
Chicot	23.7	0.0	6.3	1.2	1.8	5.7	4.9	D	21.3	3 070	274	958	5 402	-0.4
Clark	2.1	0.0	1.5	20.2	3.8	8.5	5.1	D	23.9	4 965	219	793	10 426	0.4
Clay	21.8	0.0	4.7	7.0	1.9	6.8	3.4	7.6	17.3	4 755	313	709	8 030	0.0
Cleburne	4.1	5.6	9.7	12.8	3.7	9.8	4.4	D	11.8	8 510	332	826	15 868	0.3

1. Per 1,000 resident population estimated as of July 1 of the year shown.

Table B. States and Counties — Housing, Labor Force, and Employment

STATE County	Housing units, 2010–2014								Civilian labor force, 2015				Civilian employment,[6] 2010–2014		
	Occupied units										Unemployment			Percent	
			Owner-occupied			Renter-occupied									
				Median owner cost as a percent of income											
	Total	Percent	Median value[1]	With a mortgage	Without a mortgage[2]	Median rent[3]	Median rent as a percent of income[2]	Sub-stand-ard units[4] (percent)	Total	Percent change, 2014–2015	Total	Rate[5]	Total	Manage-ment, business, science and arts	Con-struction, produc-tion, and mainte-nance occu-pations
	89	90	91	92	93	94	95	96	97	98	99	100	101	102	103
ALABAMA—Cont'd															
Washington	6 218	86.7	86 200	19.7	11.3	579	30.2	2.4	6 702	0.7	594	8.9	5 791	21.8	48.4
Wilcox	3 843	73.7	72 500	20.6	17.2	470	33.1	2.2	2 812	-1.9	412	14.7	2 743	25.1	35.9
Winston	9 526	75.6	84 200	22.2	13.2	499	30.3	1.4	9 367	-2.8	712	7.6	9 018	24.4	38.1
ALASKA	251 678	63.3	246 300	22.8	10.8	1 131	28.3	9.8	363 818	-0.6	23 591	6.5	347 983	35.9	23.7
Aleutians East	577	56.2	122 400	21.3	10.2	922	21.5	6.1	2 469	10.8	80	3.2	2 607	10.8	73.6
Aleutians West	1 105	35.1	213 600	19.1	15.2	1 272	19.5	12.7	4 095	-8.6	157	3.8	3 918	15.4	56.9
Anchorage	105 164	59.8	286 600	22.8	10.9	1 172	28.9	4.7	158 216	-0.1	7 915	5.0	151 197	39.1	18.7
Bethel	4 441	63.5	185 100	20.4	12.8	1 212	23.1	53.1	7 315	0.0	1 055	14.4	6 200	36.3	19.8
Bristol Bay	398	54.3	186 500	18.1	10.0	1 043	20.6	8.8	390	-21.7	36	9.2	532	34.4	27.6
Denali	722	72.2	196 100	20.7	10.0	1 200	14.0	18.0	1 064	-0.9	93	8.7	1 171	26.7	32.5
Dillingham	1 353	58.8	198 000	21.4	12.4	997	24.5	29.8	2 036	-4.1	197	9.7	1 779	39.2	22.2
Fairbanks North Star	35 844	58.5	215 000	24.6	11.8	1 221	30.6	10.3	46 486	-0.8	2 527	5.4	46 475	36.7	23.8
Haines	1 144	69.1	188 700	23.4	10.0	824	25.9	13.4	1 098	-1.4	107	9.7	1 418	28.3	28.2
Hoonah-Angoon	909	62.0	219 400	24.4	10.0	731	24.4	13.6	1 135	-0.6	170	15.0	1 031	38.6	23.2
Juneau	12 081	63.7	318 000	23.1	11.0	1 169	26.2	6.5	17 308	-1.0	800	4.6	17 351	46.0	16.6
Kenai Peninsula	21 559	73.1	210 400	22.1	10.0	938	26.1	9.0	27 486	-1.8	2 155	7.8	25 678	29.9	29.0
Ketchikan Gateway	5 305	56.3	261 600	23.4	12.5	1 054	28.6	4.1	7 023	-1.2	477	6.8	6 648	30.6	27.8
Kodiak Island	4 560	59.7	241 200	25.8	10.9	972	29.3	9.7	6 540	-0.8	319	4.9	6 905	25.4	34.3
Kusilvak	1 690	75.3	119 800	15.3	11.8	711	23.3	67.4	2 788	-1.6	646	23.2	2 004	29.9	26.7
Lake and Peninsula	510	64.7	146 100	18.8	11.0	710	14.7	24.3	637	-1.2	81	12.7	634	37.7	30.3
Matanuska-Susitna	31 104	76.2	220 100	22.6	10.5	1 073	29.1	9.5	44 865	-0.2	3 505	7.8	40 010	32.9	27.4
Nome	2 839	55.7	132 700	18.5	15.4	1 168	25.5	39.9	4 159	0.7	485	11.7	3 646	35.1	21.1
North Slope	1 977	49.1	152 700	13.5	10.0	1 109	18.2	35.1	4 424	1.6	246	5.6	5 401	25.7	41.7
Northwest Arctic	1 886	54.6	121 900	21.1	14.1	1 126	17.7	48.2	2 978	-1.1	463	15.5	2 565	34.7	27.3
Petersburg	1 367	66.6	225 000	16.4	11.3	898	25.7	2.9	1 524	-3.9	135	8.9	1 775	26.6	36.9
Prince of Wales-Hyder	2 377	69.9	162 600	21.6	11.0	789	22.6	12.9	2 792	-1.7	348	12.5	2 817	28.0	35.7
Sitka	3 513	57.6	335 800	24.1	10.7	1 101	29.5	4.0	4 638	-1.1	211	4.5	4 664	37.0	24.8
Skagway	387	56.8	323 100	27.2	10.6	1 038	19.8	5.2	810	0.5	93	11.5	657	29.5	36.1
Southeast Fairbanks	2 156	68.0	203 500	20.9	10.0	1 165	21.4	17.7	2 963	1.3	321	10.8	3 001	33.9	30.3
Valdez-Cordova	3 225	72.7	193 200	18.4	10.0	861	19.6	9.6	4 820	-1.4	424	8.8	4 456	28.9	26.1
Wrangell	1 163	72.0	167 100	22.8	10.0	692	28.6	5.3	1 042	-2.0	81	7.8	1 051	32.3	27.1
Yakutat	265	47.2	156 800	17.6	10.0	1 000	23.4	9.1	266	-2.9	22	8.3	371	31.3	34.8
Yukon-Koyukuk	2 057	70.1	100 500	20.6	12.2	658	22.4	48.0	2 451	-5.3	442	18.0	2 021	35.5	27.6
ARIZONA	2 387 246	63.4	162 900	23.9	10.8	905	30.5	5.0	3 152 706	1.8	193 188	6.1	2 754 982	35.2	18.7
Apache	19 046	76.7	81 900	22.6	10.0	539	19.3	27.3	20 686	-2.3	2 773	13.4	18 492	28.5	25.0
Cochise	48 846	68.0	141 300	21.9	10.0	792	28.3	3.7	50 040	-1.6	3 715	7.4	45 415	35.0	18.0
Coconino	46 391	59.6	217 200	24.5	10.0	990	33.0	10.4	73 041	1.4	4 786	6.6	64 141	33.8	19.2
Gila	20 824	72.4	134 100	24.9	11.5	735	30.5	5.1	21 243	-0.6	1 691	8.0	18 172	29.2	24.3
Graham	10 975	72.4	123 700	22.3	10.2	732	25.6	7.1	14 649	1.5	1 086	7.4	11 934	31.6	29.2
Greenlee	3 446	46.1	83 200	19.5	10.0	415	10.0	9.3	4 037	-14.3	320	7.9	3 418	28.3	46.3
La Paz	9 707	77.1	81 800	25.0	10.0	588	26.0	7.4	8 164	2.7	622	7.6	6 426	27.7	29.5
Maricopa	1 424 244	61.3	175 600	23.6	10.9	952	30.4	4.6	2 007 847	2.5	103 927	5.2	1 765 058	36.7	17.7
Mohave	80 529	68.2	124 600	26.4	11.5	799	29.8	3.8	79 310	1.2	6 363	8.0	67 341	25.6	22.0
Navajo	34 018	70.8	106 500	23.1	10.0	667	27.9	14.9	40 995	-1.5	3 972	9.7	32 043	28.7	22.7
Pima	386 155	61.8	161 700	23.9	11.4	813	32.0	4.3	464 150	0.4	25 787	5.6	418 055	36.3	17.1
Pinal	126 128	73.0	122 500	24.3	11.0	979	29.8	4.3	157 284	2.4	9 963	6.3	135 058	30.0	23.2
Santa Cruz	15 514	65.1	137 800	23.8	10.7	616	30.1	6.4	20 013	-1.3	2 303	11.5	17 658	27.2	22.5
Yavapai	91 508	70.0	181 100	27.5	11.8	850	32.5	3.6	97 545	2.1	5 434	5.6	81 263	31.5	20.9
Yuma	69 915	69.3	113 500	24.8	10.9	847	30.3	7.3	93 702	0.4	20 446	21.8	70 508	25.2	27.0
ARKANSAS	1 132 488	66.5	108 700	20.4	10.6	675	29.6	3.0	1 330 102	2.0	69 486	5.2	1 251 717	31.6	27.1
Arkansas	7 787	67.9	74 800	20.9	10.8	639	28.0	0.6	9 441	0.7	414	4.4	8 489	27.6	35.7
Ashley	8 518	75.0	63 800	19.8	11.5	577	30.0	2.6	8 216	-2.2	655	8.0	8 154	26.2	37.5
Baxter	18 237	76.3	119 700	23.6	12.2	611	30.8	1.4	16 272	2.8	923	5.7	14 936	30.2	25.1
Benton	83 191	67.9	148 500	19.6	10.0	787	24.4	3.2	120 331	5.3	4 667	3.9	106 489	35.3	24.5
Boone	14 855	72.2	109 000	21.3	10.7	596	28.5	3.2	15 787	1.8	802	5.1	15 068	29.1	26.0
Bradley	4 720	70.3	64 400	23.2	10.1	611	39.8	6.6	4 435	7.7	276	6.2	4 340	25.1	39.1
Calhoun	2 062	80.0	67 800	19.3	14.6	598	32.0	0.1	2 360	0.7	137	5.8	2 355	21.7	43.7
Carroll	11 069	73.9	114 300	24.5	10.2	638	27.0	3.8	12 576	1.2	598	4.8	11 569	28.0	36.3
Chicot	4 495	68.0	55 200	21.8	15.4	566	31.3	4.5	3 734	-2.2	350	9.4	3 710	29.6	24.8
Clark	8 467	63.5	84 300	19.2	11.1	604	30.8	1.3	9 463	0.3	541	5.7	9 513	34.6	22.5
Clay	6 729	74.1	64 100	19.6	12.2	513	31.5	2.8	6 315	-0.6	433	6.9	6 361	22.5	39.7
Cleburne	10 292	77.2	121 700	21.4	11.5	650	29.8	1.8	9 607	-0.5	691	7.2	9 549	24.2	34.4

1. Specified owner-occupied units.   2. A value of 10.0 represents 10 percent or less; a value of 50.0 represents 50 percent or more.   3. Specified renter-occupied units.
4. Overcrowded or lacking complete plumbing facilities.   5. Percent of civilian labor force.   6. Persons 16 years old and over.

Table B. States and Counties — Nonfarm Employment and Agriculture

STATE County		Private nonfarm establishments, employment and payroll, 2014								Agriculture, 2012			
		Employment						Annual payroll		Farms			
											Percent with:		
	Number of establishments	Total	Health care and social assistance	Manufacturing	Retail trade	Finance and insurance	Professional, scientific, and technical services	Total (mil dol)	Average per employee (dollars)	Number	Fewer than 50 acres	500 acres or more	Farm operators whose principal occupation is farming (percent)
	104	105	106	107	108	109	110	111	112	113	114	115	116
ALABAMA—Cont'd													
Washington	209	5 408	284	3 811	277	62	D	350	64 767	371	31.3	6.2	43.4
Wilcox	182	1 743	260	D	270	90	20	72	41 415	316	30.7	24.1	44.9
Winston	449	6 769	712	3 094	822	D	83	195	28 771	520	32.3	3.3	51.0
ALASKA	20 752	266 886	47 152	12 846	33 677	7 512	18 959	15 275	57 235	762	56.2	11.3	54.1
Aleutians East	58	D	D	D	D	D	NA	D	D	NA	NA	NA	NA
Aleutians West	116	4 738	108	3 444	D	D	D	159	33 466	NA	NA	NA	NA
Anchorage	8 710	147 597	24 497	1 825	15 441	4 911	14 718	9 123	61 811	291	56.7	5.8	56.4
Bethel	230	3 201	D	D	830	34	19	145	45 170	NA	NA	NA	NA
Bristol Bay	70	327	D	47	D	D	D	42	127 994	NA	NA	NA	NA
Denali	100	459	D	NA	17	D	D	48	104 405	NA	NA	NA	NA
Dillingham	98	1 291	616	D	216	D	D	70	54 012	NA	NA	NA	NA
Fairbanks North Star	2 471	27 435	5 399	626	4 952	750	1 181	1 399	50 978	217	39.2	20.7	47.9
Haines	140	607	117	D	115	D	D	28	46 288	NA	NA	NA	NA
Hoonah-Angoon	75	209	D	D	47	NA	D	10	45 502	NA	NA	NA	NA
Juneau	1 157	11 223	2 338	D	1 780	347	543	550	48 962	52	92.3	0.0	63.5
Kenai Peninsula	2 074	15 294	3 697	703	2 542	317	496	786	51 379	162	67.9	4.9	57.4
Ketchikan Gateway	595	4 973	807	327	770	208	D	260	52 241	NA	NA	NA	NA
Kodiak Island	483	4 818	D	1 826	463	79	65	199	41 235	NA	NA	NA	NA
Kusilvak	72	647	D	D	306	D	NA	18	27 182	NA	NA	NA	NA
Lake and Peninsula	50	129	NA	D	D	D	NA	15	116 891	NA	NA	NA	NA
Matanuska-Susitna	2 089	17 200	3 755	212	3 395	481	879	827	48 087	NA	NA	NA	NA
Nome	173	1 998	D	D	377	33	D	101	50 800	NA	NA	NA	NA
North Slope	162	6 323	D	D	252	D	D	465	73 599	NA	NA	NA	NA
Northwest Arctic	74	1 745	D	NA	142	D	D	143	82 220	NA	NA	NA	NA
Petersburg	172	1 090	D	D	228	D	D	50	45 728	NA	NA	NA	NA
Prince of Wales-Hyder	138	891	194	D	220	D	NA	32	35 637	NA	NA	NA	NA
Sitka	382	2 854	838	374	423	68	D	127	44 639	NA	NA	NA	NA
Skagway	109	372	4	D	82	D	NA	24	65 003	NA	NA	NA	NA
Southeast Fairbanks	170	1 223	106	22	180	D	61	84	68 713	NA	NA	NA	NA
Valdez-Cordova	488	2 982	454	D	361	38	106	183	61 495	NA	NA	NA	NA
Wrangell	82	556	D	D	120	D	D	21	38 140	NA	NA	NA	NA
Yakutat	27	143	D	D	40	NA	NA	6	41 657	NA	NA	NA	NA
Yukon-Koyukuk	100	301	D	D	100	NA	D	14	47 512	NA	NA	NA	NA
ARIZONA	134 434	2 241 077	325 753	140 517	306 601	136 738	142 438	96 796	43 192	20 005	79.9	8.1	66.1
Apache	460	6 723	2 785	100	1 183	D	128	253	37 685	5 591	85.6	4.2	73.3
Cochise	2 222	26 487	4 766	342	5 419	548	3 616	889	33 577	1 093	43.8	22.4	56.1
Coconino	3 522	47 538	7 822	D	7 735	783	1 607	1 762	37 071	2 239	92.0	3.8	72.5
Gila	1 028	11 296	2 185	150	2 095	214	244	482	42 655	195	65.6	13.3	58.5
Graham	482	6 636	1 562	224	1 592	109	D	231	34 736	412	61.4	15.8	45.4
Greenlee	95	6 753	133	NA	189	D	D	303	44 903	159	52.8	15.1	57.9
La Paz	346	3 823	625	D	934	71	D	107	28 083	125	35.2	28.8	73.6
Maricopa	87 501	1 527 799	209 056	98 125	198 887	113 966	108 781	70 754	46 311	2 479	84.6	5.7	50.9
Mohave	3 630	40 695	8 585	2 853	9 255	1 009	945	1 336	32 841	335	59.1	23.9	51.3
Navajo	1 687	17 975	4 018	327	4 086	381	313	636	35 374	3 846	91.3	3.4	75.5
Pima	19 931	303 841	56 150	22 642	46 061	12 657	16 638	11 769	38 734	855	79.4	9.4	49.0
Pinal	3 348	46 208	7 572	3 647	8 297	995	886	1 574	34 063	938	56.5	22.8	62.8
Santa Cruz	1 142	11 139	1 183	346	2 414	220	182	334	30 000	236	53.0	19.5	58.9
Yavapai	5 647	55 932	12 415	3 227	10 259	1 315	1 752	1 871	33 444	940	69.9	13.1	64.1
Yuma	2 907	41 082	6 544	3 453	8 194	1 149	1 373	1 274	31 011	562	64.4	14.4	54.8
ARKANSAS	64 670	992 201	170 306	153 715	141 256	36 294	37 324	38 335	38 636	45 071	30.8	13.0	47.3
Arkansas	524	8 270	1 012	3 290	1 205	D	79	307	37 136	492	17.9	41.7	53.7
Ashley	401	6 442	922	D	793	182	D	258	40 085	376	47.9	12.2	40.4
Baxter	1 027	12 535	3 534	2 312	2 133	536	415	417	33 253	561	38.5	6.4	44.9
Benton	5 624	103 273	8 784	9 722	11 630	2 729	7 092	5 920	57 324	2 157	43.2	5.1	47.8
Boone	872	12 177	2 591	1 674	2 011	415	252	405	33 251	1 282	32.2	9.2	52.7
Bradley	259	2 713	483	559	324	118	37	77	28 372	185	39.5	2.7	36.8
Calhoun	59	413	D	D	58	D	D	16	38 625	92	20.7	5.4	28.3
Carroll	692	8 155	691	3 329	1 149	229	131	227	27 816	1 126	27.5	10.7	49.4
Chicot	218	2 194	879	D	319	86	35	63	28 902	313	17.6	41.5	57.5
Clark	490	6 552	1 018	D	1 217	234	175	204	31 065	381	26.0	10.0	44.1
Clay	298	2 685	D	338	515	100	39	80	29 672	610	24.6	26.6	52.5
Cleburne	587	5 947	858	1 190	1 103	D	147	179	30 058	797	32.4	7.0	40.0

Table B. States and Counties — **Agriculture**

STATE County	Land in farms					Value of land and buildings (dollars)		Value of machinery and equipment, average per farm (dollars)	Value of products sold				Percent of farms with sales of:		Government payments	
			Acres								Percent from:					
	Acreage (1,000)	Percent change, 2007–2012	Average size of farm	Total irrigated (1,000)	Total cropland (1,000)	Average per farm	Average per acre		Total (mil dol)	Average per farm (dollars)	Crops	Live-stock and poultry products	$10,000 or more	$100,000 or more	Total ($1,000)	Percent of farms
	117	118	119	120	121	122	123	124	125	126	127	128	129	130	131	132
ALABAMA—Cont'd																
Washington	96	14.3	258	0.0	12.6	435 148	1 689	62 544	31.7	85 329	15.3	84.7	26.7	7.0	373	17.5
Wilcox	120	-29.2	379	D	22.3	636 839	1 682	51 880	D	D	D	D	25.9	3.2	1 142	44.9
Winston	58	-10.2	111	D	13.5	289 904	2 601	51 921	57.6	110 785	1.4	98.6	36.7	13.8	135	7.3
ALASKA	834	-5.4	1 094	2.5	84.1	681 479	623	87 445	58.9	77 329	42.2	57.8	42.3	11.4	2 432	25.6
Aleutians East	NA	NA	NA	NA	NA	NA	NA	NA	NA	NA	NA	NA	NA	NA	NA	NA
Aleutians West	NA	NA	NA	NA	NA	NA	NA	NA	NA	NA	NA	NA	NA	NA	NA	NA
Anchorage	36	-5.2	125	1.3	17.1	879 979	7 039	92 491	30.0	103 158	47.3	52.7	46.0	14.8	354	17.5
Bethel	NA	NA	NA	NA	NA	NA	NA	NA	NA	NA	NA	NA	NA	NA	NA	NA
Bristol Bay	NA	NA	NA	NA	NA	NA	NA	NA	NA	NA	NA	NA	NA	NA	NA	NA
Denali	NA	NA	NA	NA	NA	NA	NA	NA	NA	NA	NA	NA	NA	NA	NA	NA
Dillingham	NA	NA	NA	NA	NA	NA	NA	NA	NA	NA	NA	NA	NA	NA	NA	NA
Fairbanks North Star	100	-10.1	459	1.0	61.4	580 382	1 264	94 359	9.1	42 120	84.8	15.2	42.4	10.6	1 354	30.9
Haines	NA	NA	NA	NA	NA	NA	NA	NA	NA	NA	NA	NA	NA	NA	NA	NA
Hoonah-Angoon	NA	NA	NA	NA	NA	NA	NA	NA	NA	NA	NA	NA	NA	NA	NA	NA
Juneau	1	37.5	14	0.0	0.1	740 712	54 479	152 173	12.4	238 692	7.4	92.6	51.9	23.1	25	13.5
Kenai Peninsula	29	-23.9	180	0.1	4.5	435 877	2 423	46 315	D	D	D	D	30.9	3.7	353	33.3
Ketchikan Gateway	NA	NA	NA	NA	NA	NA	NA	NA	NA	NA	NA	NA	NA	NA	NA	NA
Kodiak Island	NA	NA	NA	NA	NA	NA	NA	NA	NA	NA	NA	NA	NA	NA	NA	NA
Kusilvak	NA	NA	NA	NA	NA	NA	NA	NA	NA	NA	NA	NA	NA	NA	NA	NA
Lake and Peninsula	NA	NA	NA	NA	NA	NA	NA	NA	NA	NA	NA	NA	NA	NA	NA	NA
Matanuska-Susitna	NA	NA	NA	NA	NA	NA	NA	NA	NA	NA	NA	NA	NA	NA	NA	NA
Nome	NA	NA	NA	NA	NA	NA	NA	NA	NA	NA	NA	NA	NA	NA	NA	NA
North Slope	NA	NA	NA	NA	NA	NA	NA	NA	NA	NA	NA	NA	NA	NA	NA	NA
Northwest Arctic	NA	NA	NA	NA	NA	NA	NA	NA	NA	NA	NA	NA	NA	NA	NA	NA
Petersburg	NA	NA	NA	NA	NA	NA	NA	NA	NA	NA	NA	NA	NA	NA	NA	NA
Prince of Wales-Hyder	NA	NA	NA	NA	NA	NA	NA	NA	NA	NA	NA	NA	NA	NA	NA	NA
Sitka	NA	NA	NA	NA	NA	NA	NA	NA	NA	NA	NA	NA	NA	NA	NA	NA
Skagway	NA	NA	NA	NA	NA	NA	NA	NA	NA	NA	NA	NA	NA	NA	NA	NA
Southeast Fairbanks	NA	NA	NA	NA	NA	NA	NA	NA	NA	NA	NA	NA	NA	NA	NA	NA
Valdez-Cordova	NA	NA	NA	NA	NA	NA	NA	NA	NA	NA	NA	NA	NA	NA	NA	NA
Wrangell	NA	NA	NA	NA	NA	NA	NA	NA	NA	NA	NA	NA	NA	NA	NA	NA
Yakutat	NA	NA	NA	NA	NA	NA	NA	NA	NA	NA	NA	NA	NA	NA	NA	NA
Yukon-Koyukuk	NA	NA	NA	NA	NA	NA	NA	NA	NA	NA	NA	NA	NA	NA	NA	NA
ARIZONA	26 249	0.5	1 312	880.6	1 150.8	844 064	643	62 708	3 732.1	186 559	55.6	44.4	20.3	7.3	31 329	15.3
Apache	5 598	D	1 001	9.8	26.5	192 667	192	18 893	24.2	4 327	54.5	45.5	7.5	0.6	973	14.9
Cochise	917	11.2	839	65.5	123.3	1 175 308	1 401	81 234	150.0	137 235	D	D	37.6	13.3	2 594	16.9
Coconino	5 816	-4.7	2 597	1.9	8.3	543 406	209	23 731	25.8	11 528	9.1	90.9	9.6	1.4	987	23.0
Gila	1 189	1.9	6 098	0.8	2.8	1 993 174	327	55 646	3.8	19 241	9.1	90.9	33.8	4.6	323	10.8
Graham	1 251	-7.0	3 037	36.9	41.7	1 752 109	577	143 189	170.9	414 769	97.1	2.9	33.5	15.8	3 056	38.3
Greenlee	52	48.5	329	5.4	5.2	514 126	1 561	70 818	9.7	61 239	24.8	75.2	32.7	15.1	337	32.7
La Paz	D	D	D	93.2	120.0	2 513 648	D	345 968	183.2	1 465 944	D	D	64.8	45.6	2 011	34.4
Maricopa	476	-2.0	192	192.9	222.5	1 087 145	5 663	113 576	1 003.5	404 790	44.5	55.5	32.2	14.1	5 379	9.7
Mohave	1 244	45.0	3 714	20.8	29.1	1 792 487	483	75 743	30.2	90 102	68.9	31.1	33.7	11.9	1 242	11.3
Navajo	4 323	-4.0	1 124	6.5	20.1	291 214	259	20 164	64.5	16 775	9.0	91.0	7.6	0.6	832	13.1
Pima	D	D	D	32.4	36.7	1 651 870	D	64 622	97.3	113 786	76.8	23.2	31.2	10.3	1 085	5.3
Pinal	1 175	12.2	1 252	223.6	302.6	2 979 541	2 379	188 860	927.7	989 059	34.0	66.0	49.7	30.0	9 558	27.8
Santa Cruz	215	65.9	911	1.8	1.2	1 390 784	1 527	35 631	14.7	62 110	4.7	95.3	43.6	12.7	996	15.7
Yavapai	825	29.0	877	7.6	10.7	1 382 518	1 576	51 250	41.6	44 285	25.5	74.5	32.2	12.0	141	3.2
Yuma	215	2.0	382	181.4	200.1	2 758 098	7 220	372 064	985.0	1 752 685	D	D	61.7	28.5	1 815	17.1
ARKANSAS	13 811	-0.4	306	4 803.9	7 931.1	807 965	2 637	115 436	9 775.8	216 897	49.5	50.5	44.0	16.7	262 967	29.2
Arkansas	402	-0.7	817	314.6	360.2	2 168 250	2 653	320 372	298.2	606 043	99.7	0.3	55.5	46.5	17 373	83.9
Ashley	112	-27.7	297	70.8	83.7	861 694	2 905	127 370	72.8	193 734	91.6	8.4	31.4	15.2	3 123	31.1
Baxter	92	-5.4	164	0.1	12.8	436 902	2 668	46 217	20.4	36 305	3.0	97.0	29.8	4.1	948	16.8
Benton	305	19.7	141	0.6	88.0	626 853	4 435	68 418	529.1	245 307	1.0	99.0	46.5	17.8	1 832	13.7
Boone	257	6.2	201	0.4	38.7	515 837	2 572	54 509	124.1	96 775	1.1	98.9	45.1	10.8	3 730	34.8
Bradley	20	-21.7	107	D	5.5	372 924	3 492	57 232	43.6	235 854	D	D	41.1	16.2	133	13.0
Calhoun	14	-15.4	151	0.1	3.4	370 859	2 459	57 957	6.0	64 761	6.5	93.5	28.3	7.6	32	21.7
Carroll	256	5.7	228	0.1	48.2	579 130	2 543	70 987	307.0	272 652	0.6	99.4	56.6	20.4	2 464	25.3
Chicot	290	1.4	925	197.1	254.9	2 465 096	2 665	340 051	204.7	654 054	96.4	3.6	60.4	44.7	7 640	83.7
Clark	90	10.3	237	D	26.5	437 554	1 848	53 113	15.1	39 588	13.9	86.1	34.6	5.0	342	22.8
Clay	331	0.3	543	235.6	298.0	1 737 748	3 198	263 780	246.2	403 561	98.6	1.4	48.9	32.0	9 792	77.2
Cleburne	157	21.3	198	0.8	37.0	540 846	2 738	62 587	47.9	60 064	2.5	97.5	33.9	6.9	1 013	23.5

STATE County	Water use, 2010		Wholesale trade,[1] 2012				Retail trade,[2] 2012				Real estate and rental and leasing,[2] 2012			
	Total water withdrawn (mil gal/day)	Gallons withdrawn per person per day	Number of establish-ments	Number of employees	Sales (mil dol)	Annual payroll (mil dol)	Number of establish-ments	Number of employees	Sales (mil dol)	Annual payroll (mil dol)	Number of establish-ments	Number of employees	Receipts (mil dol)	Annual payroll (mil dol)
	133	134	135	136	137	138	139	140	141	142	143	144	145	146
ALABAMA—Cont'd														
Washington	89.6	5 098	3	D	D	D	34	232	75.7	5.5	1	D	D	D
Wilcox	22.2	1 905	7	D	D	D	47	269	72.8	5.5	3	D	D	D
Winston	2.2	89	22	171	207.7	6.8	98	754	165.0	16.3	8	22	3.5	0.6
ALASKA	1 094.5	1 541	638	7 734	5 216.3	440.9	2 508	33 721	10 474.3	977.4	872	4 212	1 022.7	187.6
Aleutians East	3.7	1 172	1	D	D	D	8	D	D	D	3	7	1.3	0.2
Aleutians West	5.0	892	13	111	145.9	7.8	11	148	53.4	4.7	4	34	11.9	1.9
Anchorage	46.2	158	336	5 228	3 147.7	296.6	860	15 253	4 966.8	462.2	383	2 403	631.3	112.1
Bethel	0.5	28	5	28	6.9	0.6	54	855	162.8	15.4	7	D	D	D
Bristol Bay	0.2	191	4	D	D	D	9	52	15.8	1.6	1	D	D	D
Denali	24.2	13 237	NA	NA	NA	NA	13	99	13.4	1.1	NA	NA	NA	NA
Dillingham	0.4	80	2	D	D	D	18	214	58.4	4.6	6	D	D	D
Fairbanks North Star	53.6	549	69	666	413.5	36.5	301	4 758	1 732.5	153.1	144	661	159.6	33.2
Haines	44.4	17 699	1	D	D	D	19	115	21.6	3.5	5	3	0.8	0.1
Hoonah-Angoon	141.1	65 623	NA	NA	NA	NA	14	48	11.4	1.0	2	D	D	D
Juneau	58.8	1 880	36	265	196.9	12.8	142	1 821	491.4	53.0	61	249	42.2	7.0
Kenai Peninsula	28.0	506	44	383	262.4	18.2	266	2 482	804.2	69.7	66	238	68.9	12.7
Ketchikan Gateway	29.9	2 220	10	D	D	D	121	856	235.9	28.1	28	103	17.5	3.3
Kodiak Island	6.1	449	22	93	78.1	4.1	41	463	115.9	12.2	13	71	6.2	1.6
Kusilvak	0.5	68	2	D	D	D	25	339	46.6	4.6	2	D	D	D
Lake and Peninsula	0.5	294	1	D	D	D	4	D	D	D	4	8	1.0	0.1
Matanuska-Susitna	33.8	379	40	298	134.9	14.8	244	3 415	1 039.1	89.3	75	181	38.3	6.2
Nome	0.7	78	4	D	D	D	34	360	78.7	7.9	5	18	4.0	0.5
North Slope	221.2	23 453	9	234	354.0	19.2	20	240	94.9	6.8	8	49	10.9	2.5
Northwest Arctic	9.8	1 307	1	D	D	D	12	D	D	D	4	6	0.7	0.0
Petersburg	62.3	16 338	8	33	22.2	1.8	28	231	44.2	6.0	5	D	D	D
Prince of Wales-Hyder	73.7	13 254	2	D	D	D	25	204	48.2	5.1	3	D	D	D
Sitka	55.3	6 221	9	48	38.3	1.9	57	424	98.5	12.4	16	47	4.3	1.2
Skagway	8.7	8 988	2	D	D	D	38	118	32.2	4.3	2	D	D	D
Southeast Fairbanks	1.0	135	4	D	D	D	34	248	78.6	6.3	8	11	0.7	0.1
Valdez-Cordova	42.7	4 431	8	44	62.7	4.9	52	372	114.0	9.5	10	21	3.0	0.9
Wrangell	48.1	20 283	2	D	D	D	20	180	27.7	4.7	3	2	0.5	0.0
Yakutat	92.6	139 849	1	D	D	D	5	41	5.2	0.9	1	D	D	D
Yukon-Koyukuk	1.8	317	2	D	D	D	33	130	32.9	2.4	3	3	1.1	0.1
ARIZONA	6 088.2	952	5 570	73 496	69 437.3	4 144.3	17 479	286 184	84 716.5	7 367.8	8 089	40 479	9 329.7	1 693.2
Apache	49.0	685	15	D	D	D	105	1 133	324.3	22.2	12	D	D	D
Cochise	238.4	1 815	47	269	133.9	10.1	408	5 266	1 267.3	115.2	113	424	57.1	11.4
Coconino	52.2	388	95	738	439.3	33.8	590	7 337	1 896.5	164.8	188	667	137.3	28.1
Gila	34.7	647	23	169	68.5	8.6	169	2 005	486.0	46.0	61	149	27.0	4.1
Graham	176.2	4 734	15	D	D	D	93	1 524	381.8	33.6	25	80	17.4	2.6
Greenlee	25.9	3 069	3	D	D	D	16	143	44.2	3.1	3	D	D	D
La Paz	668.8	32 644	11	94	64.2	4.2	81	924	436.0	19.8	21	72	10.7	1.5
Maricopa	1 953.6	512	3 957	57 945	60 841.1	3 426.0	10 415	183 609	57 296.7	4 930.7	5 398	29 825	7 607.5	1 352.0
Mohave	121.2	605	114	816	391.1	30.5	593	8 918	2 712.7	211.4	199	628	83.2	15.6
Navajo	61.7	574	36	291	170.0	12.1	300	3 935	1 120.3	89.1	94	211	36.0	7.0
Pima	305.4	312	703	6 172	3 099.3	269.6	2 770	43 642	11 377.2	1 094.8	1 250	6 042	973.5	205.5
Pinal	1 130.1	3 007	101	1 633	785.6	123.5	484	8 142	2 375.2	184.3	180	574	105.4	15.6
Santa Cruz	17.4	368	150	D	D	D	219	2 344	498.3	47.8	45	192	23.9	3.2
Yavapai	92.3	437	163	1 385	880.4	59.1	787	9 854	2 504.3	233.3	341	941	153.0	27.7
Yuma	1 161.4	5 933	137	2 433	1 439.8	102.5	449	7 408	1 996.0	171.9	159	639	91.9	18.0
ARKANSAS	11 327.0	3 885	2 884	34 492	31 256.1	1 630.8	10 923	135 448	36 815.3	3 061.5	2 802	12 867	1 922.7	409.8
Arkansas	939.7	49 410	36	428	300.4	19.8	99	1 066	336.0	26.0	22	67	10.0	1.7
Ashley	205.2	9 388	12	136	198.7	6.8	85	863	185.2	17.2	12	26	3.1	0.8
Baxter	4.8	117	21	D	D	D	210	2 105	476.6	43.4	36	150	43.7	13.8
Benton	402.5	1 818	237	2 550	2 366.0	150.5	660	10 143	2 906.0	241.3	245	897	173.2	35.7
Boone	2.8	76	36	D	D	D	143	1 739	493.3	42.2	37	D	D	D
Bradley	2.1	180	10	96	54.9	3.0	39	338	98.9	7.6	7	14	0.8	0.2
Calhoun	0.7	121	2	D	D	D	17	78	17.8	1.5	1	D	D	D
Carroll	10.7	390	9	94	33.5	3.9	147	1 142	230.2	24.0	26	72	4.3	1.0
Chicot	273.1	23 140	12	109	169.1	6.4	49	379	75.9	7.6	11	D	D	D
Clark	11.6	505	10	D	D	D	96	1 158	273.7	27.0	29	94	10.9	1.5
Clay	407.5	25 337	15	258	192.9	8.3	55	485	179.4	11.4	6	D	D	D
Cleburne	26.0	999	21	D	D	D	108	1 052	313.1	23.4	21	D	D	D

1. Merchant wholesalers, except manufacturers' sales branches and offices.   2. Employer establishments.

Table B. States and Counties — Professional Services, Manufacturing, and Accommodation and Food Services

STATE County	Professional, scientific, and technical services, 2012				Manufacturing, 2012				Accommodation and food services, 2012			
	Number of establishments	Number of employees	Receipts (mil dol)	Annual payroll (mil dol)	Number of establishments	Number of employees	Receipts (mil dol)	Annual payroll (mil dol)	Number of establishments	Number of employees	Sales (mil dol)	Annual payroll (mil dol)
	147	148	149	150	151	152	153	154	155	156	157	158
ALABAMA—Cont'd												
Washington	13	50	6.4	3.5	14	3 022	D	236.0	11	D	D	D
Wilcox	10	D	D	D	8	471	32.9	D	12	D	D	D
Winston	28	78	8.5	2.4	53	2 624	608.2	79.4	36	D	D	D
ALASKA	1 898	17 648	3 175.2	1 178.3	527	12 450	D	514.5	2 126	26 836	2 221.3	626.0
Aleutians East	NA	NA	NA	NA	5	D	D	D	11	D	D	D
Aleutians West	1	D	D	D	15	2 120	598.5	81.6	7	118	14.2	4.1
Anchorage	1 141	13 516	2 523.8	958.8	182	2 049	479.8	95.7	788	14 957	1 106.2	338.1
Bethel	6	D	D	D	4	10	D	0.4	18	D	D	D
Bristol Bay	1	D	D	D	6	509	D	17.1	19	57	15.7	4.0
Denali	6	5	1.2	0.3	NA	NA	NA	NA	34	106	63.9	17.3
Dillingham	3	D	D	D	4	267	D	8.5	12	49	4.7	0.9
Fairbanks North Star	237	1 683	293.4	86.5	67	641	1 941.2	36.2	213	3 092	255.3	66.4
Haines	5	8	0.9	0.2	8	44	26.3	3.3	20	94	5.7	1.6
Hoonah-Angoon	NA	NA	NA	NA	NA	NA	NA	NA	16	48	8.4	1.8
Juneau	89	514	79.7	31.4	26	236	75.4	11.7	119	1 329	81.5	24.1
Kenai Peninsula	122	541	65.0	27.6	63	758	D	49.6	265	1 646	149.4	37.4
Ketchikan Gateway	28	93	12.7	4.6	11	648	152.4	27.0	66	560	45.7	11.8
Kodiak Island	24	72	26.5	5.7	22	1 744	D	59.6	47	453	31.5	8.7
Kusilvak	NA	NA	NA	NA	NA	NA	NA	NA	NA	NA	NA	NA
Lake and Peninsula	NA	NA	NA	NA	4	237	57.1	6.7	11	11	9.8	2.6
Matanuska-Susitna	165	915	122.7	45.4	45	222	53.8	9.1	200	1 782	135.5	35.3
Nome	6	7	1.4	0.5	3	D	D	D	18	176	14.8	3.4
North Slope	6	46	12.7	5.9	NA	NA	NA	NA	33	783	132.9	31.7
Northwest Arctic	3	D	D	D	NA	NA	NA	NA	7	99	6.1	2.1
Petersburg	5	10	0.5	0.2	8	D	104.9	9.8	16	63	5.2	1.1
Prince of Wales-Hyder	1	D	D	D	8	161	D	5.6	26	108	10.6	2.6
Sitka	18	74	5.5	2.0	14	325	D	11.8	39	358	30.3	7.9
Skagway	2	D	D	D	3	6	D	D	22	69	13.0	3.7
Southeast Fairbanks	8	25	4.0	2.0	6	23	D	0.8	24	212	16.5	4.8
Valdez-Cordova	17	90	17.6	5.0	14	385	D	14.7	72	462	41.4	10.1
Wrangell	3	D	D	D	4	59	D	D	6	31	2.9	0.7
Yakutat	NA	NA	NA	NA	NA	NA	NA	NA	6	14	3.7	0.9
Yukon-Koyukuk	1	D	D	D	NA	NA	NA	NA	11	54	5.1	1.1
ARIZONA	16 198	121 381	19 268.1	7 378.7	4 269	131 941	51 243.5	8 193.2	11 669	251 455	13 996.6	4 030.3
Apache	27	D	D	D	10	86	D	D	70	816	47.1	12.6
Cochise	217	4 592	586.7	254.7	43	279	141.0	14.2	277	3 875	173.4	48.4
Coconino	331	1 584	178.5	65.3	90	4 025	2 181.3	312.0	545	11 436	765.7	191.8
Gila	81	354	44.5	15.4	18	723	D	32.2	130	1 673	94.6	26.5
Graham	24	227	7.3	16.4	13	167	D	5.4	57	866	36.2	9.0
Greenlee	3	D	D	D	NA	NA	NA	NA	16	D	D	D
La Paz	13	D	D	D	12	199	D	D	79	D	D	D
Maricopa	11 557	90 488	15 557.1	5 822.6	2 889	91 348	34 583.4	5 426.8	6 776	159 029	9 105.9	2 655.2
Mohave	239	931	72.4	30.8	133	2 566	D	109.5	382	5 787	256.7	74.3
Navajo	113	364	30.7	9.8	31	402	179.8	22.1	225	3 197	186.6	48.1
Pima	2 531	16 514	2 241.1	940.0	640	24 297	8 686.6	1 906.7	1 787	42 311	2 154.7	637.4
Pinal	255	1 430	101.7	42.7	111	2 713	2 244.1	133.8	345	6 125	350.5	90.1
Santa Cruz	64	167	20.6	6.8	27	289	211.0	10.2	103	1 413	58.6	17.4
Yavapai	522	1 748	190.9	74.3	184	2 765	706.9	130.8	548	8 223	407.5	130.8
Yuma	221	1 364	132.3	68.0	68	2 084	884.3	79.8	329	5 736	307.5	76.2
ARKANSAS	5 678	32 210	4 528.0	1 567.0	2 688	153 706	62 712.9	6 290.8	5 473	95 854	4 307.3	1 182.5
Arkansas	23	78	9.6	2.4	27	3 628	1 927.2	126.1	39	D	D	D
Ashley	27	71	10.0	2.4	29	2 172	1 339.9	135.4	27	425	17.3	4.4
Baxter	75	401	30.1	12.1	50	2 201	574.4	86.7	99	1 372	61.6	16.1
Benton	619	6 232	1 062.7	402.1	160	9 219	D	363.0	401	8 290	366.8	105.1
Boone	61	D	D	D	54	1 700	493.7	69.0	68	D	D	D
Bradley	11	31	2.7	0.8	8	459	127.9	18.9	11	D	D	D
Calhoun	2	D	D	D	NA	NA	NA	NA	6	17	1.0	0.2
Carroll	36	130	9.7	3.4	32	3 546	741.9	102.5	133	1 185	56.7	17.0
Chicot	13	35	3.6	1.4	6	81	D	1.7	17	187	7.5	1.9
Clark	28	463	74.8	23.9	23	1 186	392.7	53.9	55	1 025	41.5	12.1
Clay	17	39	3.0	0.9	16	341	D	12.0	19	D	D	D
Cleburne	43	167	13.8	4.9	31	1 183	190.3	42.6	59	766	33.9	8.6

1. Establishment subject to federal tax.

STATE County	Health care and social assistance, 2012				Other services, 2012				Nonemployer businesses, 2014		Value of residential construction authorized by building permits, 2015	
	Number of establishments	Number of employees	Receipts (mil dol)	Annual payroll (mil dol)	Number of establishments	Number of employees	Receipts (mil dol)	Annual payroll (mil dol)	Number	Receipts (mil dol)	New Construction ($1,000)	Number of housing units
	159	160	161	162	163	164	165	166	167	168	169	170
ALABAMA—Cont'd												
Washington	19	D	D	D	9	D	D	D	1 071	27.9	0	0
Wilcox	18	262	16.0	6.7	8	31	3.1	0.8	593	20.0	123	3
Winston	36	684	57.9	21.4	20	D	D	D	1 604	76.3	571	4
ALASKA	2 432	48 701	6 375.5	2 434.2	1 355	7 238	904.6	235.8	55 818	2 659.8	324 596	1 298
Aleutians East	10	D	D	D	4	D	D	D	248	22.1	293	2
Aleutians West	14	D	D	D	6	D	D	D	255	13.4	294	3
Anchorage	1 165	25 616	3 656.2	1 347.8	580	3 863	514.2	136.0	20 446	1 048.7	232 790	834
Bethel	47	D	D	D	14	56	8.4	1.1	1 048	20.2	2 000	10
Bristol Bay	2	D	D	D	2	D	D	D	225	12.3	402	3
Denali	3	12	1.0	0.6	3	D	D	D	176	5.4	NA	NA
Dillingham	8	D	D	D	6	17	1.5	0.6	868	25.8	875	3
Fairbanks North Star	290	5 748	746.9	305.5	185	842	88.8	25.6	5 461	242.6	2 189	7
Haines	10	134	9.2	4.0	7	D	D	D	418	16.1	2 218	8
Hoonah-Angoon	7	44	3.6	1.5	3	D	D	D	282	11.3	492	2
Juneau	144	2 458	275.5	112.4	82	406	46.5	12.9	2 692	131.6	18 824	94
Kenai Peninsula	226	3 651	352.9	144.4	138	648	78.5	19.9	6 543	297.2	22 331	117
Ketchikan Gateway	36	799	90.1	39.3	42	142	14.1	3.8	1 361	77.0	5 888	24
Kodiak Island	39	733	79.7	35.4	30	150	19.1	4.4	1 601	91.5	3 740	22
Kusilvak	19	D	D	D	4	D	D	D	593	5.6	0	0
Lake and Peninsula	NA	NA	NA	NA	1	D	D	D	276	13.2	NA	NA
Matanuska-Susitna	267	3 621	411.5	161.6	123	572	64.4	16.7	6 813	314.8	17 402	99
Nome	27	D	D	D	13	D	D	D	523	17.5	815	7
North Slope	9	D	D	D	7	D	D	D	251	6.7	2 118	8
Northwest Arctic	4	D	D	D	9	D	D	D	255	9.3	1 421	4
Petersburg	11	176	17.5	6.4	13	D	D	D	782	58.7	904	10
Prince of Wales-Hyder	10	197	13.4	6.4	7	D	D	D	561	26.5	355	2
Sitka	25	937	111.5	47.7	25	100	8.3	2.3	1 326	76.4	6 543	20
Skagway	4	4	0.3	0.1	5	22	1.3	0.4	137	7.5	1 305	7
Southeast Fairbanks	11	D	D	D	7	D	D	D	536	16.3	NA	NA
Valdez-Cordova	24	455	46.1	18.7	28	109	10.7	3.4	1 269	56.9	712	7
Wrangell	7	D	D	D	7	D	D	D	370	19.1	686	5
Yakutat	3	D	D	D	NA	NA	NA	NA	119	5.6	0	0
Yukon-Koyukuk	10	32	2.3	1.2	4	D	D	D	383	10.5	0	0
ARIZONA	16 872	315 107	37 055.9	14 236.1	8 503	62 073	6 231.7	1 736.0	438 353	19 882.9	6 985 714	28 910
Apache	64	3 300	412.8	148.1	19	75	7.7	1.6	2 692	55.7	5 308	29
Cochise	273	4 896	408.9	167.4	150	684	53.1	16.1	6 582	195.1	30 980	215
Coconino	381	6 995	1 040.7	354.3	230	1 307	105.8	32.7	8 753	353.5	91 572	566
Gila	133	2 479	259.1	97.6	57	225	18.2	5.3	3 353	118.7	25 217	108
Graham	78	822	61.3	25.1	33	219	31.2	8.0	1 361	49.2	18 839	100
Greenlee	7	D	D	D	2	D	D	D	235	5.5	397	7
La Paz	21	D	D	D	15	D	D	D	828	31.3	4 624	31
Maricopa	10 811	199 139	23 736.9	9 260.4	5 265	42 665	4 489.1	1 246.0	288 019	14 146.8	5 171 259	20 251
Mohave	478	8 222	995.0	364.2	290	1 394	110.3	29.4	10 449	450.3	128 018	636
Navajo	241	3 832	439.1	177.5	117	525	46.0	11.4	5 359	169.6	31 666	177
Pima	2 777	56 539	6 617.5	2 441.8	1 483	10 691	1 008.6	281.2	63 004	2 471.7	659 557	2 428
Pinal	420	8 118	786.3	313.8	240	1 249	120.5	33.1	16 604	588.0	394 226	2 151
Santa Cruz	70	1 135	146.0	41.0	44	154	13.4	3.7	4 123	164.2	14 636	66
Yavapai	759	11 555	1 245.1	517.8	364	1 717	142.9	41.0	18 322	751.4	292 110	1 377
Yuma	359	7 092	794.1	282.4	194	1 099	77.8	25.0	8 669	331.9	117 304	768
ARKANSAS	7 485	166 455	15 792.6	6 318.7	3 961	21 830	2 339.4	586.3	196 593	8 268.7	1 380 106	8 500
Arkansas	46	988	63.6	27.6	30	112	7.6	3.0	1 319	67.5	1 863	12
Ashley	46	931	64.3	26.8	25	100	9.3	2.6	1 084	30.9	0	0
Baxter	170	3 490	337.5	133.3	80	326	25.4	6.5	3 060	120.3	4 338	39
Benton	472	8 091	751.6	281.5	256	1 613	145.1	44.1	16 453	722.2	516 688	2 392
Boone	126	2 336	195.6	74.3	48	227	24.5	6.5	2 793	111.7	3 539	22
Bradley	25	530	38.6	14.9	21	69	6.7	1.8	514	20.3	30	1
Calhoun	4	D	D	D	2	D	D	D	199	6.4	0	0
Carroll	50	752	57.9	24.0	39	114	10.7	2.8	2 491	82.0	1 838	31
Chicot	36	900	51.2	26.7	10	58	6.5	1.6	576	24.2	170	2
Clark	59	934	65.9	26.4	27	92	10.7	2.4	1 295	46.2	844	3
Clay	33	695	42.1	19.8	29	D	D	D	820	34.7	116	2
Cleburne	45	828	54.1	21.5	33	121	10.7	2.4	2 160	84.0	100	1

Table B. States and Counties — Government Employment and Payroll, and Local Government Finances

STATE County	Government employment and payroll, 2012									Local government finances, 2012				
			March payroll (percent of total)							General revenue				
												Taxes		
													Per capita[1] (dollars)	
	Full-time equivalent employees	March payroll (dollars)	Administration, judicial, and legal	Police and Corrections	Fire Protection	Highways and transportation	Health and Welfare	Natural resources and utilities	Education and libraries	Total (mil dol)	Inter-governmental (mil dol)	Total (mil dol)	Total	Property
	171	172	173	174	175	176	177	178	179	180	181	182	183	184
ALABAMA—Cont'd														
Washington	673	2 075 254	4.0	4.1	0.0	2.0	21.7	3.3	64.7	40.9	25.0	11.8	691	514
Wilcox	583	1 459 476	6.1	7.4	0.0	6.3	11.1	6.3	60.3	29.0	18.4	7.7	674	358
Winston	1 387	3 355 200	3.1	5.2	0.8	2.7	29.1	3.2	54.4	62.5	36.3	16.1	667	283
ALASKA	X	X	X	X	X	X	X	X	X	X	X	X	X	X
Aleutians East	184	728 454	19.1	7.1	0.2	11.9	2.3	7.0	41.2	34.8	17.1	10.2	3 215	0
Aleutians West	278	1 422 298	17.8	11.2	3.2	9.9	3.0	15.4	24.7	56.1	18.9	21.5	3 872	853
Anchorage	10 003	52 917 485	4.5	7.7	6.5	5.4	2.3	9.8	62.6	1 313.0	582.8	546.6	1 831	1 623
Bethel	302	1 160 315	19.0	13.8	3.3	7.0	2.2	43.9	0.1	65.9	43.9	9.6	543	0
Bristol Bay	78	333 504	12.5	13.6	0.7	18.6	2.8	5.7	46.1	16.8	7.9	5.5	5 590	3 083
Denali	82	322 133	9.4	0.0	0.0	0.0	4.0	0.0	85.9	11.0	7.8	2.8	1 472	0
Dillingham	293	1 115 865	13.8	10.5	0.7	3.7	2.6	29.8	35.5	40.8	28.5	5.7	1 140	460
Fairbanks North Star	2 949	14 833 210	7.9	3.4	2.6	2.4	1.8	5.3	75.9	380.0	201.2	148.5	1 481	1 335
Haines	105	554 027	8.6	6.3	0.8	5.6	0.6	5.8	68.5	20.5	12.5	5.3	2 089	1 020
Hoonah-Angoon	90	310 388	14.5	8.3	2.0	8.6	2.0	9.8	54.0	12.4	8.3	1.7	814	39
Juneau	2 061	10 714 562	5.3	5.1	2.9	7.0	24.9	13.7	41.0	338.0	110.1	83.0	2 549	1 125
Kenai Peninsula	2 080	9 477 210	10.6	5.1	7.7	3.9	1.5	4.4	61.5	445.9	125.4	111.8	1 965	1 014
Ketchikan Gateway	699	3 359 138	10.3	7.2	4.6	11.2	1.5	15.2	47.8	123.4	42.9	28.8	2 087	994
Kodiak Island	637	2 986 849	7.4	6.7	2.5	6.1	0.9	9.3	64.9	102.4	55.1	27.0	1 893	1 004
Kusilvak	286	832 391	24.5	17.3	0.7	6.1	0.8	19.3	17.7	58.3	48.1	1.6	208	0
Lake and Peninsula	163	640 681	11.6	0.0	0.1	1.6	1.2	2.7	78.9	24.1	18.4	2.8	1 706	0
Matanuska-Susitna	2 847	12 057 275	8.3	3.7	1.6	2.4	3.8	2.2	76.5	386.7	229.3	136.9	1 458	1 165
Nome	378	1 484 923	12.5	9.6	0.1	4.9	2.6	23.5	37.5	50.2	28.5	9.5	963	231
North Slope	1 749	8 359 644	27.7	5.0	3.3	11.1	11.6	11.4	26.8	503.2	75.9	366.0	37 957	37 888
Northwest Arctic	630	2 686 215	7.5	8.0	1.7	3.7	1.1	9.5	61.6	100.8	72.5	4.2	541	0
Petersburg	512	2 386 453	4.4	6.0	0.8	10.0	32.9	10.6	32.3	82.3	42.5	9.6	2 490	1 229
Prince of Wales-Hyder	289	1 128 652	6.7	2.6	1.0	2.1	2.2	19.6	61.2	30.3	21.8	3.3	576	89
Sitka	525	2 686 315	6.2	5.6	2.0	2.6	30.9	12.2	35.9	89.4	30.2	15.4	1 705	671
Skagway	66	277 303	9.2	10.8	6.1	7.0	16.4	6.9	36.1	19.8	9.1	8.4	8 710	2 132
Southeast Fairbanks	12	40 359	51.1	0.0	0.0	7.5	18.3	0.0	17.1	1.8	1.3	0.0	0	0
Valdez-Cordova	506	2 285 718	8.9	9.3	3.5	9.2	14.4	12.9	38.6	103.7	27.4	50.7	5 213	4 747
Wrangell	NA	NA	NA	NA	NA	NA	NA	NA	NA	NA	NA	NA	NA	NA
Yakutat	56	174 101	20.5	10.7	0.0	9.9	2.5	2.0	50.3	6.3	4.3	1.3	1 936	647
Yukon-Koyukuk	365	1 481 198	10.8	1.7	0.6	2.6	1.1	7.6	73.3	41.9	35.8	0.9	148	52
ARIZONA	X	X	X	X	X	X	X	X	X	X	X	X	X	X
Apache	2 657	8 600 597	5.6	5.3	1.9	2.9	2.7	1.1	79.6	168.2	116.4	31.5	431	379
Cochise	4 879	16 984 358	11.7	10.2	5.2	2.9	3.0	3.3	61.1	397.9	175.5	144.2	1 092	821
Coconino	4 575	17 536 070	11.8	13.5	9.2	3.5	4.5	6.4	48.1	469.7	159.1	223.4	1 643	979
Gila	2 222	7 331 024	14.5	15.3	7.8	3.9	2.3	5.8	48.1	194.4	80.9	87.8	1 652	1 207
Graham	2 165	7 913 958	6.9	8.1	0.2	2.5	26.5	4.9	50.0	137.7	81.5	29.0	774	382
Greenlee	376	1 216 994	14.2	15.2	0.0	7.6	5.4	1.1	53.9	32.1	12.7	13.6	1 545	1 283
La Paz	799	2 443 896	12.2	19.6	6.3	4.6	4.4	6.2	44.6	60.9	26.7	21.8	1 075	779
Maricopa	129 919	553 767 788	8.2	13.2	5.3	2.8	6.3	12.4	50.5	14 121.0	4 763.7	5 936.1	1 506	958
Mohave	5 613	20 393 845	13.0	13.4	11.7	4.5	2.0	5.6	47.4	538.5	183.2	229.9	1 131	849
Navajo	4 056	13 281 721	8.7	9.6	5.1	2.8	1.5	3.5	67.5	523.9	174.9	109.2	1 020	745
Pima	31 634	115 785 276	10.5	14.5	6.6	3.5	2.2	7.1	52.9	3 257.1	1 214.5	1 427.3	1 438	1 057
Pinal	9 793	33 904 548	13.3	15.5	5.5	3.5	3.8	5.1	52.2	961.4	426.5	329.1	850	624
Santa Cruz	2 004	6 229 659	10.5	13.1	10.4	3.9	2.5	1.8	56.6	161.7	83.6	52.4	1 108	737
Yavapai	6 155	23 081 009	10.4	13.4	9.4	4.0	2.1	5.5	45.2	648.3	201.2	335.8	1 579	1 029
Yuma	7 924	25 609 990	12.0	12.1	3.1	2.2	2.4	7.3	59.9	638.9	314.0	221.6	1 108	716
ARKANSAS	X	X	X	X	X	X	X	X	X	X	X	X	X	X
Arkansas	988	2 636 492	5.7	8.3	2.3	3.4	19.7	5.4	51.8	59.0	32.8	17.1	906	316
Ashley	866	2 414 339	4.8	9.8	2.9	4.1	2.0	4.2	71.6	63.9	38.0	15.5	719	291
Baxter	1 228	3 503 816	4.6	8.5	3.2	6.2	1.3	7.6	68.0	81.3	46.3	22.7	553	251
Benton	7 214	24 863 912	5.8	8.5	5.2	2.0	0.5	6.6	70.3	624.9	346.9	196.3	845	405
Boone	1 391	3 599 052	4.9	7.8	2.9	3.4	0.3	7.1	72.7	96.8	61.2	19.7	527	210
Bradley	467	1 184 067	4.0	5.4	0.9	4.3	3.1	2.7	79.4	35.7	24.9	6.9	603	215
Calhoun	169	422 712	9.1	11.0	0.0	8.6	4.4	3.4	61.8	17.3	7.1	2.7	511	302
Carroll	1 012	2 598 555	4.9	8.8	2.4	5.9	2.4	9.3	64.4	71.0	38.3	16.2	585	295
Chicot	716	2 139 884	6.2	8.0	0.0	2.0	31.0	4.0	48.8	35.1	21.3	8.7	762	307
Clark	763	2 247 437	7.0	17.2	2.0	3.9	2.5	9.0	58.1	67.1	41.9	13.1	572	219
Clay	859	3 044 204	5.9	15.6	0.0	4.6	23.1	14.3	35.5	49.8	25.0	7.5	478	259
Cleburne	801	2 107 158	6.7	9.2	0.5	4.7	1.5	7.6	69.0	57.0	31.3	15.0	583	313

1. Based on the resident population estimated as of July 1 of the year shown.

STATE County	Direct general expenditure — Total (mil dol)	Per capita[1] (dollars)	Education	Health and hospitals	Police protection	Public welfare	Highways	Debt outstanding — Total (mil dol)	Per capita[1] (dollars)	Federal civilian	Federal military	State and local	Democratic	Republican	All other
	185	186	187	188	189	190	191	192	193	194	195	196	197	198	199
ALABAMA—Cont'd															
Washington	42.8	2 504	67.0	3.3	3.6	0.1	11.2	186.5	10 900	37	76	925	35.0	64.4	0.6
Wilcox	31.8	2 786	61.3	2.7	5.4	0.0	7.4	45.1	3 945	64	50	716	71.0	28.8	0.2
Winston	67.7	2 809	62.8	0.9	3.3	0.0	6.0	53.1	2 204	72	109	1 092	17.5	80.8	1.7
ALASKA	X	X	X	X	X	X	X	X	X	14 921	26 347	64 470	37.9	59.4	2.7
Aleutians East	35.1	11 095	24.9	0.3	3.1	0.0	6.3	40.2	12 717	22	12	268	NA	NA	NA
Aleutians West	55.3	9 975	16.7	0.1	7.8	0.0	12.5	41.9	7 550	14	30	471	NA	NA	NA
Anchorage	1 268.0	4 246	52.5	2.1	9.8	0.0	5.8	1 857.9	6 222	8 477	13 895	20 239	NA	NA	NA
Bethel	70.7	3 986	0.0	0.1	6.7	0.0	3.2	4.8	476	69	127	2 829	NA	NA	NA
Bristol Bay	15.8	15 960	28.3	4.7	6.6	0.0	2.4	1.0	993	53	0	189	NA	NA	NA
Denali	10.7	5 696	75.8	0.1	0.0	0.0	0.0	0.0	0	206	25	151	NA	NA	NA
Dillingham	39.6	7 872	29.2	2.5	8.2	2.1	5.2	15.1	2 990	47	36	690	NA	NA	NA
Fairbanks North Star	342.4	3 415	63.0	1.6	2.3	0.0	6.2	170.2	1 698	2 879	8 350	8 452	NA	NA	NA
Haines	15.3	5 980	38.0	1.6	3.3	0.0	6.3	16.4	6 424	0	19	189	NA	NA	NA
Hoonah-Angoon	11.8	5 536	49.2	1.1	4.3	0.0	4.8	3.0	1 396	98	15	270			
Juneau	318.0	9 768	26.7	30.7	5.4	0.0	4.2	225.5	6 927	712	467	6 124	NA	NA	NA
Kenai Peninsula	437.7	7 692	32.5	38.4	2.0	0.0	2.4	171.8	3 019	350	496	4 509	NA	NA	NA
Ketchikan Gateway	133.0	9 654	26.9	0.8	3.6	0.0	4.1	145.8	10 581	235	249	1 811	NA	NA	NA
Kodiak Island	95.8	6 729	46.7	0.6	5.3	0.0	3.3	62.8	4 413	300	1 007	1 107	NA	NA	NA
Kusilvak	70.2	8 985	80.8	0.2	1.6	0.0	1.3	3.8	489	21	58	1 553	NA	NA	NA
Lake and Peninsula	20.2	12 184	72.3	0.1	0.5	0.0	0.8	3.8	2 267	38	12	374	NA	NA	NA
Matanuska-Susitna	393.6	4 190	61.3	2.3	2.6	0.0	6.9	404.7	4 309	205	696	4 855	NA	NA	NA
Nome	44.7	4 511	29.0	1.0	4.3	0.0	6.8	12.3	1 244	47	70	1 617	NA	NA	NA
North Slope	459.1	47 609	17.7	2.7	3.1	1.5	3.7	510.2	52 913	20	51	1 901	NA	NA	NA
Northwest Arctic	89.1	11 410	62.5	0.1	1.7	0.0	2.2	72.5	9 289	46	53	1 068	NA	NA	NA
Petersburg	85.2	22 155	24.0	26.0	3.2	1.2	7.1	28.2	7 342	98	51	378			
Prince of Wales-Hyder	28.0	4 867	53.2	1.1	4.5	0.0	2.7	4.0	704	85	46	926			
Sitka	79.2	8 752	28.6	27.3	5.4	0.0	1.8	117.1	12 949	126	243	1 057	NA	NA	NA
Skagway	17.6	18 327	12.7	9.9	7.3	0.1	9.4	6.5	6 776	52	0	125			
Southeast Fairbanks	1.9	262	0.2	0.1	0.0	0.0	8.6	0.9	119	412	48	413	NA	NA	NA
Valdez-Cordova	84.7	8 716	25.8	23.7	2.1	0.0	3.8	37.8	3 895	139	216	1 174	NA	NA	NA
Wrangell	NA	NA	NA	NA	NA	NA	NA	NA	NA	48	17	276			
Yakutat	6.6	9 847	45.8	2.9	9.1	0.0	7.6	1.0	1 548	24	0	108	NA	NA	NA
Yukon-Koyukuk	46.4	8 035	79.2	0.3	1.0	0.0	1.2	6.9	1 200	89	40	1 346	NA	NA	NA
ARIZONA	X	X	X	X	X	X	X	X	X	54 659	32 719	357 431	45.1	53.6	1.2
Apache	161.6	2 208	65.6	3.6	3.3	0.0	6.5	280.9	3 837	2 622	158	8 160	63.4	35.2	1.3
Cochise	407.1	3 082	44.0	3.5	12.3	4.9	7.3	161.6	1 223	5 260	4 453	6 441	38.8	59.5	1.7
Coconino	457.2	3 361	35.9	3.4	6.5	1.6	7.6	377.9	2 779	2 738	296	16 059	57.8	40.8	1.3
Gila	163.2	3 071	37.4	1.4	11.8	2.5	6.1	46.8	881	452	116	4 840	35.3	63.1	1.6
Graham	132.6	3 543	64.5	0.4	8.6	1.6	4.9	28.1	752	414	77	2 305	29.0	69.8	1.2
Greenlee	31.0	3 517	44.5	5.9	11.6	0.0	6.8	16.8	1 911	30	21	519	40.0	58.8	1.2
La Paz	82.5	4 069	27.8	3.1	9.7	0.6	7.2	44.7	2 204	310	44	2 042	34.7	63.2	2.1
Maricopa	13 916.1	3 530	41.6	5.1	8.2	1.5	4.1	27 988.0	7 100	19 747	12 886	192 776	44.1	54.7	1.2
Mohave	555.1	2 730	33.9	2.7	6.9	0.1	8.7	627.7	3 087	463	444	7 370	32.7	65.6	1.7
Navajo	397.5	3 712	44.4	24.0	5.0	0.8	4.3	156.9	1 465	1 676	236	8 019	43.5	55.2	1.3
Pima	3 531.8	3 559	37.0	3.1	9.1	2.7	5.3	5 788.9	5 833	12 480	8 418	68 064	52.4	46.4	1.2
Pinal	1 130.4	2 918	46.7	4.4	9.1	1.6	3.8	1 030.3	2 660	1 722	838	18 438	42.2	56.7	1.2
Santa Cruz	148.9	3 149	48.5	3.1	10.0	0.0	3.8	161.3	3 410	1 734	103	2 096	65.3	34.0	0.8
Yavapai	653.7	3 074	36.5	2.1	7.2	1.8	9.0	725.7	3 413	1 410	491	9 187	37.0	61.4	1.6
Yuma	616.3	3 081	47.8	2.1	6.0	2.5	4.6	668.5	3 342	3 601	4 138	11 115	42.6	56.3	1.1
ARKANSAS	X	X	X	X	X	X	X	X	X	20 202	18 073	193 716	38.9	58.7	2.4
Arkansas	54.5	2 887	54.8	0.8	6.7	0.0	6.5	53.2	2 814	187	82	980	37.5	60.0	2.5
Ashley	63.4	2 945	60.9	0.2	5.8	0.0	6.5	95.2	4 425	65	93	1 098	34.4	62.6	3.0
Baxter	82.1	2 001	58.9	0.0	7.5	0.1	8.6	143.9	3 507	131	181	1 545	32.7	64.3	3.0
Benton	620.5	2 672	61.2	0.2	5.6	0.0	5.6	1 204.1	5 184	449	1 080	9 168	30.7	67.2	2.1
Boone	94.8	2 540	65.0	0.1	4.7	0.0	4.2	59.7	1 600	154	165	3 109	28.7	68.3	3.0
Bradley	34.0	2 985	65.5	0.0	5.4	0.1	7.3	14.7	1 294	33	49	862	41.6	56.0	2.4
Calhoun	20.8	3 913	57.2	1.1	3.3	0.5	6.0	106.6	20 089	12	23	268	31.2	65.9	2.9
Carroll	75.8	2 746	55.7	0.1	5.3	0.0	7.5	76.9	2 784	81	124	1 123	39.4	57.5	3.1
Chicot	34.4	3 008	57.3	2.8	6.4	0.1	7.0	15.4	1 344	41	47	957	58.4	40.7	0.9
Clark	65.6	2 861	64.3	0.1	4.3	0.0	5.6	101.8	4 437	82	90	2 544	46.9	50.7	2.4
Clay	49.7	3 171	48.6	25.1	4.0	0.0	5.7	31.5	2 010	53	67	840	40.7	55.0	4.3
Cleburne	54.0	2 093	60.3	0.2	4.9	0.1	9.9	57.4	2 225	86	114	860	26.0	70.2	3.7

1. Based on the resident population estimated as of July 1 of the year shown.   2. © 2013 Election Data Services, Inc. All rights reserved.

Table B. States and Counties — **Land Area and Population**

STATE/ County code	CBSA code[1]	County type[2]	STATE County	Land area,[3] (sq km) 2010	Total persons 2015	Rank	Per square kilometer	White	Black	American Indian, Alaska Native	Asian and Pacific Islander[4]	Percent Hispanic or Latino[4]	Under 5 years	5 to 17 years	18 to 24 years	25 to 34 years	35 to 44 years	45 to 54 years
				1	2	3	4	5	6	7	8	9	10	11	12	13	14	15
			ARKANSAS—Cont'd															
05 025	38220	3	Cleveland	1 548	8 311	2 573	5.4	86.2	12.1	0.7	0.4	2.2	5.1	18.2	7.4	10.8	12.1	13.9
05 027	31620	7	Columbia	1 984	24 114	1 641	12.2	60.0	35.9	0.8	1.1	2.7	5.8	15.8	16.4	10.9	10.4	12.0
05 029	...	6	Conway	1 430	21 019	1 772	14.7	83.5	12.2	1.7	0.9	4.0	5.9	17.2	8.1	11.6	11.3	13.8
05 031	27860	3	Craighead	1 832	104 354	568	57.0	79.3	15.1	0.8	1.4	4.7	6.9	18.0	11.5	15.2	12.6	12.0
05 033	22900	2	Crawford	1 536	61 703	850	40.2	88.1	2.0	3.8	2.0	6.7	6.0	19.1	8.1	12.2	12.4	14.0
05 035	32820	1	Crittenden	1 579	48 963	998	31.0	45.1	52.1	0.7	1.0	2.3	7.7	20.2	9.6	13.0	12.2	13.2
05 037	...	6	Cross	1 596	17 284	1 964	10.8	74.6	23.5	0.8	0.7	1.9	6.9	17.2	8.3	11.2	12.2	13.7
05 039	...	6	Dallas	1 729	7 604	2 626	4.4	55.4	42.0	0.9	0.4	2.7	5.5	16.8	7.1	11.3	10.7	12.8
05 041	...	6	Desha	1 990	11 965	2 299	6.0	47.6	47.6	0.7	0.6	4.8	6.8	18.8	8.2	11.4	10.6	12.5
05 043	...	7	Drew	2 145	18 778	1 881	8.8	67.6	28.4	0.6	1.0	2.9	6.3	16.1	13.9	11.6	11.0	12.5
05 045	30780	2	Faulkner	1 678	121 552	512	72.4	82.7	12.0	1.2	1.9	4.1	6.6	17.3	15.4	14.7	12.5	12.1
05 047	...	2	Franklin	1 577	17 702	1 933	11.2	94.1	1.3	2.1	1.2	3.0	5.9	17.7	8.8	10.9	11.9	13.5
05 049	...	9	Fulton	1 601	12 204	2 285	7.6	97.2	1.1	1.6	0.5	1.2	4.8	15.6	6.4	8.7	10.0	13.4
05 051	26300	3	Garland	1 755	97 177	606	55.4	84.9	9.3	1.5	1.2	5.3	5.7	15.2	7.7	11.2	11.2	12.9
05 053	30780	2	Grant	1 636	18 102	1 913	11.1	93.9	3.1	1.1	0.6	2.6	5.7	17.9	7.7	12.3	12.8	14.6
05 055	37500	6	Greene	1 496	44 196	1 087	29.5	95.6	1.1	1.1	0.5	2.7	6.6	18.1	8.8	12.6	13.3	13.6
05 057	...	6	Hempstead	1 884	22 084	1 728	11.7	56.8	30.4	1.0	0.8	12.7	7.3	19.2	8.1	11.3	11.6	13.3
05 059	31680	6	Hot Spring	1 593	33 426	1 341	21.0	84.3	12.2	1.3	0.7	3.3	5.3	16.3	8.5	12.4	12.4	13.9
05 061	...	7	Howard	1 524	13 300	2 216	8.7	67.1	21.1	1.4	0.9	11.1	6.9	19.2	8.0	11.7	11.3	13.7
05 063	12900	7	Independence	1 979	37 052	1 253	18.7	90.4	2.8	1.1	1.1	5.8	6.4	17.6	8.6	11.8	12.4	13.1
05 065	...	9	Izard	1 504	13 445	2 204	8.9	95.0	2.2	1.8	0.6	1.9	4.5	13.8	6.8	10.0	11.1	14.0
05 067	...	6	Jackson	1 642	17 338	1 958	10.6	78.6	18.2	1.3	0.7	2.9	5.6	14.8	7.9	14.3	13.3	14.0
05 069	38220	3	Jefferson	2 255	71 565	755	31.7	41.3	55.9	0.9	1.2	1.9	6.2	17.1	10.2	12.8	11.4	13.3
05 071	...	6	Johnson	1 709	26 141	1 556	15.3	82.7	2.2	2.0	1.4	13.5	7.1	17.7	9.8	12.7	11.5	13.3
05 073	...	8	Lafayette	1 368	6 996	2 676	5.1	60.3	37.1	0.7	0.6	2.0	4.7	15.5	8.1	9.9	10.3	14.9
05 075	...	6	Lawrence	1 522	16 779	1 991	11.0	96.8	1.3	1.2	0.4	1.2	5.6	17.0	9.8	10.8	11.4	13.3
05 077	...	6	Lee	1 561	9 650	2 462	6.2	42.6	55.0	1.2	0.7	2.7	5.4	14.2	9.2	14.8	13.2	13.3
05 079	38220	3	Lincoln	1 454	13 820	2 180	9.5	65.7	30.5	0.9	0.3	3.6	4.4	13.4	11.0	16.5	14.7	15.1
05 081	45500	6	Little River	1 379	12 472	2 261	9.0	75.2	20.3	2.8	0.6	3.1	5.3	16.9	7.6	10.7	12.3	13.5
05 083	...	6	Logan	1 834	21 714	1 744	11.8	93.0	2.0	2.0	2.1	2.7	5.6	16.9	8.3	10.4	11.6	14.6
05 085	30780	2	Lonoke	1 996	71 645	754	35.9	88.4	6.7	1.2	1.5	4.0	6.7	19.7	8.5	13.9	13.8	13.5
05 087	22220	2	Madison	2 161	15 767	2 057	7.3	92.0	0.6	2.4	1.2	5.4	6.2	17.3	7.7	10.8	11.8	14.2
05 089	...	9	Marion	1 546	16 185	2 032	10.5	96.0	0.7	1.9	0.5	2.3	4.4	12.9	6.2	8.6	9.2	13.8
05 091	45500	3	Miller	1 620	43 908	1 093	27.1	70.7	25.4	1.4	0.9	3.1	7.0	17.1	8.5	13.6	12.4	13.4
05 093	14180	4	Mississippi	2 332	43 738	1 097	18.8	60.5	35.3	0.7	0.7	4.0	7.0	19.7	9.4	13.0	11.8	13.2
05 095	...	7	Monroe	1 572	7 399	2 641	4.7	56.4	40.5	1.4	0.8	2.2	5.8	15.4	8.7	9.6	10.3	13.8
05 097	...	8	Montgomery	2 020	8 970	2 515	4.4	94.2	0.8	2.5	0.9	3.6	4.3	14.9	6.4	8.2	10.1	14.9
05 099	...	7	Nevada	1 600	8 558	2 551	5.3	65.7	31.3	0.9	0.6	3.3	6.4	16.2	7.9	10.7	11.1	13.7
05 101	25460	9	Newton	2 126	7 913	2 602	3.7	96.2	0.6	3.2	0.6	1.8	4.8	14.7	6.5	10.0	10.2	13.3
05 103	15780	7	Ouachita	1 898	24 358	1 631	12.8	57.0	41.0	1.0	0.7	2.2	6.2	16.7	7.8	11.2	10.8	13.6
05 105	30780	2	Perry	1 428	10 189	2 419	7.1	94.2	2.7	1.8	0.5	2.8	5.2	16.9	8.1	10.3	12.4	14.9
05 107	25760	7	Phillips	1 802	19 513	1 851	10.8	36.6	61.7	0.6	0.6	1.7	8.0	19.2	9.3	10.9	10.4	12.4
05 109	...	9	Pike	1 556	10 824	2 371	7.0	89.1	3.8	1.5	0.7	6.6	5.8	17.0	8.0	10.8	12.3	13.9
05 111	27860	3	Poinsett	1 964	24 040	1 642	12.2	89.2	8.7	0.8	0.5	2.7	6.4	17.3	8.9	11.6	12.1	13.7
05 113	...	7	Polk	2 221	20 216	1 820	9.1	90.6	0.8	3.5	0.9	6.4	5.9	17.5	7.5	9.8	10.6	12.9
05 115	40780	5	Pope	2 104	63 390	833	30.1	86.8	3.6	1.7	1.6	8.4	6.2	16.6	13.9	13.1	11.5	12.7
05 117	...	8	Prairie	1 678	8 291	2 576	4.9	86.4	12.1	0.9	0.2	1.2	5.0	15.1	7.3	10.2	11.1	14.4
05 119	30780	2	Pulaski	1 968	392 664	175	199.5	55.6	36.7	1.0	2.8	6.0	7.0	16.8	9.1	15.2	12.8	12.9
05 121	...	7	Randolph	1 689	17 469	1 950	10.3	96.4	1.2	1.3	0.5	1.9	5.7	16.8	7.8	11.8	11.3	13.4
05 123	22620	6	St. Francis	1 644	26 589	1 543	16.2	42.1	52.7	1.0	0.9	4.4	6.4	16.1	8.7	14.4	14.3	13.2
05 125	30780	2	Saline	1 874	117 460	526	62.7	87.8	6.9	1.1	1.4	4.2	6.0	17.8	7.3	12.9	13.5	13.3
05 127	...	6	Scott	2 311	10 513	2 395	4.5	86.2	1.2	3.2	3.9	7.6	5.7	18.0	8.5	10.6	10.8	14.6
05 129	...	9	Searcy	1 725	7 869	2 606	4.6	96.2	0.7	3.2	0.5	2.1	5.0	15.3	6.4	9.8	10.4	13.7
05 131	22900	2	Sebastian	1 378	127 780	489	92.7	73.7	7.6	3.3	5.0	13.3	6.8	17.7	9.3	13.2	12.4	13.5
05 133	...	7	Sevier	1 464	17 290	1 963	11.8	60.6	4.7	3.1	0.9	32.8	7.7	21.1	9.2	12.2	12.9	12.6
05 135	...	7	Sharp	1 565	16 912	1 984	10.8	95.6	1.2	2.2	0.6	2.1	5.2	15.2	6.9	9.3	10.0	13.0
05 137	...	9	Stone	1 571	12 456	2 263	7.9	96.9	0.7	1.9	0.6	1.8	4.9	15.2	6.6	8.8	9.9	13.0
05 139	20980	5	Union	2 692	40 144	1 170	14.9	62.8	33.1	1.0	0.9	3.6	6.5	17.4	8.1	11.8	12.1	13.7
05 141	...	8	Van Buren	1 834	16 771	1 993	9.1	95.0	0.9	2.1	0.6	3.1	4.9	14.9	6.7	9.8	10.4	13.6
05 143	22220	2	Washington	2 440	225 477	288	92.4	74.4	4.0	2.3	5.6	16.2	7.4	17.9	14.7	15.3	12.8	11.4
05 145	42620	4	White	2 681	79 161	703	29.5	90.0	5.3	1.3	0.9	4.2	6.5	17.3	12.2	12.5	11.9	13.0
05 147	...	9	Woodruff	1 520	6 741	2 701	4.4	71.4	27.8	0.9	0.5	1.5	5.7	16.2	7.6	9.9	11.1	12.8
05 149	40780	6	Yell	2 409	21 713	1 745	9.0	77.4	2.1	1.4	1.7	18.9	6.5	18.6	8.0	11.4	12.3	13.7

1. CBSA = Core Based Statistical Area. See Appendix A for explanation. See Appendix B for list of metropolitan areas with component counties. 2. County type code from the Economic Research Service of USDA Rural-Urban Continuum Codes. See Appendix A for definition. 3. Dry land or land partially or temporarily covered by water. 4. May be of any race.

Table B. States and Counties — **Population and Households**

STATE County	55 to 64 years (16)	65 to 74 years (17)	75 years and over (18)	Percent female (19)	Total persons 2000 (20)	Total persons 2010 (21)	Percent change 2000–2010 (22)	Percent change 2010–2015 (23)	Births (24)	Deaths (25)	Net migration (26)	Number (27)	Persons per household (28)	Family households (29)	Female family householder[1] (30)	One person (31)
ARKANSAS—Cont'd																
Cleveland	13.4	10.9	8.2	51.1	8 571	8 689	1.4	-4.4	451	486	-327	3 270	2.61	74.6	11.7	23.3
Columbia	12.0	8.7	7.9	52.0	25 603	24 552	-4.1	-1.8	1 529	1 606	-349	9 509	2.40	68.9	16.1	25.1
Conway	13.8	10.2	8.1	50.9	20 336	21 271	4.6	-1.2	1 371	1 287	-302	8 370	2.49	71.2	15.1	25.5
Craighead	10.8	7.5	5.4	51.3	82 148	96 443	17.4	8.2	7 432	4 592	4 923	38 081	2.53	67.6	15.1	25.1
Crawford	12.8	9.3	6.1	50.7	53 247	61 948	16.3	-0.4	4 008	3 131	-1 085	23 490	2.61	75.7	13.2	22.1
Crittenden	12.0	7.3	4.8	52.6	50 866	50 902	0.1	-3.8	4 150	2 434	-3 616	18 253	2.71	69.8	25.0	25.8
Cross	12.9	10.4	7.2	51.4	19 526	17 866	-8.5	-3.3	1 174	1 114	-618	6 882	2.52	70.1	14.7	26.2
Dallas	15.3	11.2	9.3	51.7	9 210	8 116	-11.9	-6.3	430	545	-389	3 322	2.25	65.1	13.2	32.4
Desha	14.6	10.0	7.1	53.2	15 341	13 008	-15.2	-8.0	896	807	-1 156	5 166	2.42	62.1	19.6	35.1
Drew	12.3	8.7	7.4	51.2	18 723	18 509	-1.1	1.5	1 237	990	15	7 344	2.42	67.1	15.0	25.2
Faulkner	10.2	6.8	4.4	51.1	86 014	113 237	31.6	7.3	8 171	4 499	4 479	42 964	2.63	67.3	11.6	24.8
Franklin	13.3	10.1	7.9	50.5	17 771	18 125	2.0	-2.3	1 030	1 158	-300	6 783	2.59	69.3	10.3	27.3
Fulton	15.6	14.9	10.5	50.5	11 642	12 245	5.2	-0.3	576	890	258	5 312	2.27	68.8	8.8	25.9
Garland	14.4	12.2	9.5	51.7	88 068	96 000	9.0	1.2	5 784	7 056	2 640	39 876	2.37	64.3	12.7	29.2
Grant	12.9	9.8	6.3	50.3	16 464	17 853	8.4	1.4	1 033	951	159	6 798	2.63	74.4	10.8	23.7
Greene	11.9	8.9	6.1	50.8	37 331	42 090	12.7	5.0	2 912	2 399	1 615	16 610	2.55	69.4	11.4	26.2
Hempstead	13.0	9.4	6.9	51.6	23 587	22 609	-4.1	-2.3	1 727	1 241	-974	8 115	2.72	66.5	17.0	30.8
Hot Spring	14.0	10.4	6.9	48.1	30 353	32 923	8.5	1.5	1 855	1 927	612	12 027	2.62	71.2	12.9	24.1
Howard	12.4	9.5	7.3	51.3	14 300	13 789	-3.6	-3.5	966	800	-630	5 085	2.65	70.2	17.8	25.6
Independence	13.0	9.5	7.6	51.3	34 233	36 647	7.1	1.1	2 411	2 166	239	14 405	2.49	68.8	11.6	25.6
Izard	14.9	14.0	11.0	47.6	13 249	13 696	3.4	-1.8	617	955	129	5 656	2.25	65.9	8.4	31.9
Jackson	13.4	9.9	6.8	50.3	18 418	17 998	-2.3	-3.7	1 027	1 174	-489	6 402	2.26	61.9	13.7	33.8
Jefferson	13.8	8.7	6.3	50.8	84 278	77 435	-8.1	-7.6	4 995	4 398	-6 412	28 488	2.42	63.0	19.4	33.7
Johnson	12.1	9.1	6.7	50.3	22 781	25 540	12.1	2.4	1 822	1 337	159	10 023	2.51	69.4	11.3	26.6
Lafayette	15.1	12.3	9.2	51.7	8 559	7 645	-10.7	-8.5	368	507	-493	2 827	2.57	62.9	17.8	32.7
Lawrence	12.9	10.7	8.6	50.5	17 774	17 411	-2.0	-3.6	992	1 222	-422	6 630	2.49	65.9	10.8	30.6
Lee	13.2	9.3	7.3	44.0	12 580	10 424	-17.1	-7.4	541	602	-719	3 488	2.51	64.2	18.7	33.0
Lincoln	11.3	7.5	6.1	38.9	14 492	14 134	-2.5	-2.2	631	624	-323	4 195	2.48	73.1	17.9	23.0
Little River	14.2	12.0	7.5	50.9	13 628	13 168	-3.4	-5.3	732	806	-627	5 241	2.42	68.3	16.0	28.9
Logan	13.6	11.0	8.2	50.2	22 486	22 353	-0.6	-2.9	1 324	1 453	-496	8 439	2.55	69.7	12.2	26.8
Lonoke	11.2	7.6	4.9	50.5	52 828	68 354	29.4	4.8	5 044	3 149	1 351	25 572	2.72	74.7	13.0	20.6
Madison	14.4	10.4	7.0	49.9	14 243	15 720	10.4	0.3	1 021	886	-93	6 152	2.54	73.7	9.6	23.8
Marion	18.1	16.6	10.2	50.3	16 140	16 653	3.2	-2.8	796	1 257	69	6 912	2.37	68.1	7.1	26.9
Miller	12.8	9.0	6.1	50.8	40 443	43 462	7.5	1.0	3 204	2 204	-454	16 946	2.49	66.0	16.7	30.3
Mississippi	12.4	7.7	5.7	51.3	51 979	46 480	-10.6	-5.9	3 377	2 595	-3 425	17 188	2.59	69.9	20.1	26.1
Monroe	16.1	10.9	9.4	52.5	10 254	8 150	-20.5	-9.2	505	567	-638	3 374	2.30	61.3	14.8	35.3
Montgomery	15.7	14.1	11.3	50.1	9 245	9 487	2.6	-5.4	445	638	-304	3 813	2.40	66.6	7.3	28.3
Nevada	14.5	10.8	8.5	50.6	9 955	8 997	-9.6	-4.9	559	579	-415	3 596	2.41	61.1	11.6	37.4
Newton	16.3	14.8	9.5	49.5	8 608	8 330	-3.2	-5.0	375	491	-295	3 346	2.41	69.1	7.3	28.2
Ouachita	15.2	10.2	8.1	52.6	28 790	26 121	-9.3	-6.7	1 571	1 888	-1 413	10 502	2.38	66.3	16.5	31.8
Perry	14.3	10.5	7.4	50.3	10 209	10 441	2.3	-2.4	560	644	-184	3 926	2.58	70.7	7.3	26.7
Phillips	13.6	9.4	6.9	53.0	26 445	21 757	-17.7	-10.3	1 591	1 396	-2 425	8 291	2.49	64.2	25.5	32.2
Pike	13.5	10.8	7.8	50.2	11 303	11 291	-0.1	-4.1	594	735	-303	4 352	2.52	71.9	14.2	26.4
Poinsett	13.0	10.1	7.0	51.4	25 614	24 583	-4.0	-2.2	1 580	1 756	-387	9 314	2.57	68.5	15.7	29.0
Polk	14.1	12.9	8.8	50.8	20 229	20 662	2.1	-2.2	1 258	1 385	-286	7 994	2.54	67.6	12.2	29.0
Pope	11.6	8.4	6.0	50.1	54 469	61 754	13.4	2.6	4 097	2 980	596	22 776	2.61	68.8	11.6	26.8
Prairie	14.8	12.4	9.6	50.6	9 539	8 715	-8.6	-4.9	473	534	-386	3 776	2.21	68.5	13.3	26.6
Pulaski	12.8	7.9	5.6	52.0	361 474	382 789	5.9	2.6	29 546	18 457	-974	153 323	2.49	60.9	16.0	33.7
Randolph	13.3	11.2	8.8	50.9	18 195	17 970	-1.2	-2.8	1 019	1 208	-282	7 293	2.39	70.5	10.8	26.8
St. Francis	13.1	8.4	5.5	45.1	29 329	28 258	-3.7	-5.9	1 861	1 418	-2 059	9 351	2.55	65.6	20.7	30.8
Saline	12.2	10.4	6.7	51.0	83 529	107 149	28.3	9.6	7 030	5 200	8 367	41 702	2.65	72.1	11.7	23.6
Scott	13.1	11.2	7.6	49.6	10 996	11 233	2.2	-6.4	640	630	-708	4 125	2.65	73.1	11.6	22.6
Searcy	15.7	13.6	10.1	49.6	8 261	8 195	-0.8	-4.0	412	594	-128	3 179	2.50	63.4	5.3	32.7
Sebastian	12.6	8.4	6.1	51.0	115 071	125 744	9.3	1.6	8 892	6 463	-407	49 424	2.53	65.6	13.0	30.0
Sevier	10.7	7.7	5.9	50.3	15 757	17 058	8.3	1.4	1 435	803	-359	5 918	2.88	72.2	15.5	25.1
Sharp	14.7	14.8	11.0	50.6	17 119	17 267	0.9	-2.1	893	1 313	132	7 053	2.39	65.2	8.8	29.9
Stone	16.1	15.1	10.3	50.4	11 499	12 394	7.8	0.5	637	887	274	5 267	2.35	63.1	5.7	33.1
Union	14.0	9.2	7.4	51.4	45 629	41 639	-8.7	-3.6	2 669	2 750	-1 453	16 689	2.42	68.3	16.2	28.2
Van Buren	15.2	13.7	10.8	50.3	16 192	17 294	6.8	-3.0	911	1 172	-212	7 077	2.38	66.8	12.2	29.1
Washington	9.7	6.3	4.4	49.9	157 715	203 060	28.8	11.0	16 992	7 393	12 577	80 457	2.54	62.6	10.8	27.9
White	11.4	8.8	6.3	51.1	67 165	77 076	14.8	2.7	5 235	4 184	931	29 447	2.53	71.7	11.8	24.4
Woodruff	15.5	12.2	9.0	52.0	8 741	7 264	-16.9	-7.2	403	529	-400	3 055	2.28	60.2	17.1	36.8
Yell	12.4	9.6	7.5	50.2	21 139	22 185	4.9	-2.1	1 507	1 308	-726	7 825	2.76	67.3	9.5	27.9

1. No spouse present.

Table B. States and Counties — Population, Vital Statistics, Medicare, and Crime

STATE County	Persons in group quarters, 2015	Daytime population, 2010–2014 Number	Employ-ment/resi-dence ratio	Births, 2015 Total	Rate[1]	Deaths, 2015 Number	Rate[1]	Persons under 65 with no health insurance, 2014 Number	Percent	Medicare, 2015 Total Beneficiaries	Enrolled in Original Medicare	Enrolled in Medicare Advantage	Serious crimes known to police,[2] 2014 Total Number	Rate[3]
	32	33	34	35	36	37	38	39	40	41	42	43	44	45
ARKANSAS—Cont'd														
Cleveland	52	6 701	0.41	77	9.2	79	9.4	807	11.8	1 802	1 549	253	105	1 226
Columbia	1 751	24 113	0.97	288	11.9	277	11.5	2 506	13.5	5 047	4 305	742	539	2 246
Conway	286	20 382	0.90	251	11.9	214	10.2	2 289	13.4	5 142	4 030	1 112	691	3 256
Craighead	3 853	104 427	1.10	1 435	13.9	919	8.9	11 468	13.3	17 689	14 779	2 910	4 106	4 001
Crawford	540	55 006	0.73	785	12.7	591	9.6	7 778	15.0	12 085	7 273	4 812	1 747	2 841
Crittenden	701	46 457	0.81	776	15.8	472	9.6	5 109	11.9	8 050	6 523	1 527	2 969	6 010
Cross	225	16 393	0.83	210	12.2	204	11.8	1 745	12.4	3 699	2 968	731	843	4 829
Dallas	401	8 431	1.15	72	9.4	81	10.5	791	13.5	1 824	1 412	412	254	3 218
Desha	56	13 079	1.10	155	12.8	173	14.3	1 311	13.0	2 666	2 309	357	NA	NA
Drew	1 001	18 110	0.92	249	13.3	200	10.7	1 855	12.5	3 392	2 967	425	624	3 320
Faulkner	4 450	108 723	0.84	1 567	12.9	854	7.0	12 870	12.5	16 581	14 710	1 871	4 917	4 068
Franklin	448	16 874	0.84	191	10.8	206	11.6	1 963	13.5	3 891	2 713	1 178	390	2 168
Fulton	165	10 746	0.67	115	9.4	181	14.9	1 324	14.7	3 385	2 654	731	165	1 340
Garland	2 173	98 000	1.03	1 059	10.9	1 285	13.2	11 458	15.2	30 753	24 021	6 732	NA	NA
Grant	143	14 627	0.55	190	10.5	174	9.6	1 686	11.1	3 233	2 703	530	392	2 174
Greene	602	42 486	0.97	567	12.9	447	10.2	4 118	11.2	8 519	6 744	1 775	2 344	5 415
Hempstead	301	23 036	1.07	316	14.2	218	9.8	2 997	16.2	3 856	3 073	783	903	4 026
Hot Spring	2 271	29 698	0.73	358	10.7	363	10.9	3 314	12.9	6 704	5 501	1 203	NA	NA
Howard	181	15 543	1.33	174	13.0	143	10.7	1 972	17.7	3 130	2 568	562	308	2 280
Independence	1 030	38 613	1.12	441	11.9	418	11.3	4 018	13.4	8 305	7 307	998	1 494	4 037
Izard	992	13 177	0.92	111	8.2	182	13.5	1 549	16.6	3 740	3 022	718	357	2 688
Jackson	2 219	17 864	1.02	191	11.0	210	12.1	1 754	13.9	3 827	3 327	500	917	5 243
Jefferson	4 986	76 934	1.08	936	13.0	824	11.4	6 387	11.2	15 053	11 420	3 633	3 921	5 436
Johnson	555	25 946	1.02	327	12.5	238	9.1	3 537	16.6	4 911	3 646	1 265	645	2 490
Lafayette	113	6 606	0.68	80	11.3	95	13.5	892	16.2	1 563	1 321	242	133	1 859
Lawrence	684	16 150	0.84	196	11.6	246	14.6	1 655	12.5	4 704	3 862	842	212	1 256
Lee	1 750	9 635	0.83	98	10.1	104	10.7	879	13.5	1 817	1 299	518	184	1 856
Lincoln	3 789	13 244	0.77	117	8.4	128	9.2	1 234	14.6	2 069	1 708	361	140	999
Little River	123	11 876	0.81	141	11.3	154	12.3	1 322	13.2	2 918	2 476	442	338	2 678
Logan	578	20 394	0.79	247	11.3	282	12.9	2 473	14.1	5 359	3 897	1 462	NA	NA
Lonoke	572	54 571	0.52	957	13.4	604	8.4	6 712	10.8	11 127	9 187	1 940	1 925	2 703
Madison	79	13 084	0.60	203	12.9	145	9.2	2 254	17.4	4 104	2 775	1 329	185	1 179
Marion	141	15 232	0.77	151	9.3	259	15.9	1 725	14.5	4 552	3 287	1 265	391	2 390
Miller	1 473	39 398	0.77	591	13.5	431	9.9	4 566	12.8	8 067	6 414	1 653	2 358	5 442
Mississippi	800	48 780	1.21	636	14.5	480	10.9	4 471	11.9	8 277	6 567	1 710	2 571	5 800
Monroe	84	7 857	1.00	102	13.6	122	16.3	837	14.0	1 936	1 534	402	137	1 810
Montgomery	121	8 098	0.65	84	9.3	132	14.6	1 158	17.2	2 234	1 840	394	132	1 442
Nevada	157	8 015	0.75	88	10.2	99	11.5	856	12.3	2 067	1 587	480	185	2 115
Newton	51	6 704	0.55	67	8.5	94	11.9	951	15.9	2 094	1 548	546	98	1 226
Ouachita	352	24 226	0.88	288	11.7	341	13.9	2 265	11.3	6 168	4 465	1 703	NA	NA
Perry	152	7 969	0.43	104	10.2	115	11.3	1 126	13.5	2 469	1 959	510	302	2 929
Phillips	246	20 286	0.92	294	14.9	254	12.9	2 073	12.6	4 192	3 191	1 001	NA	NA
Pike	196	10 633	0.87	102	9.3	129	11.8	1 723	19.5	2 503	2 047	456	186	1 670
Poinsett	341	21 631	0.70	292	12.1	330	13.7	2 801	14.1	5 665	4 544	1 121	820	3 811
Polk	155	20 331	0.98	254	12.6	275	13.6	2 546	16.2	5 130	4 433	697	533	2 623
Pope	3 806	63 427	1.03	786	12.4	543	8.6	7 485	14.8	11 806	9 263	2 543	2 162	3 454
Prairie	131	7 280	0.65	91	11.0	109	13.1	943	14.7	2 026	1 757	269	121	1 460
Pulaski	8 756	455 927	1.37	5 514	14.0	3 545	9.0	42 041	12.6	73 497	59 055	14 442	26 679	6 791
Randolph	349	16 440	0.80	190	10.9	229	13.1	1 897	13.6	4 147	3 058	1 089	574	3 259
St. Francis	4 090	27 998	1.04	347	13.0	279	10.4	2 352	12.3	5 471	4 235	1 236	NA	NA
Saline	1 422	86 993	0.52	1 376	11.8	1 015	8.7	10 117	10.6	10 335	8 623	1 712	2 554	2 201
Scott	79	10 794	0.95	104	9.8	109	10.3	1 526	17.7	2 605	1 831	774	262	2 506
Searcy	71	7 406	0.77	86	10.9	108	13.7	1 111	18.5	2 433	1 872	561	32	401
Sebastian	2 398	141 538	1.27	1 640	12.9	1 210	9.5	16 822	15.8	23 523	16 208	7 315	5 896	4 647
Sevier	173	16 154	0.84	271	15.6	143	8.2	3 182	21.4	2 739	2 389	350	402	2 309
Sharp	189	16 048	0.81	171	10.1	238	14.1	2 000	16.0	5 734	4 459	1 275	NA	NA
Stone	151	12 170	0.92	117	9.4	154	12.4	1 574	17.0	3 581	3 047	534	297	2 355
Union	524	42 990	1.13	498	12.4	543	13.5	4 655	14.0	9 620	8 142	1 478	1 491	3 687
Van Buren	189	16 635	0.91	166	9.9	231	13.7	1 980	15.7	4 611	3 662	949	452	2 686
Washington	8 214	214 535	1.02	3 225	14.5	1 437	6.4	31 959	16.9	29 750	22 540	7 210	NA	NA
White	3 533	75 076	0.90	996	12.6	779	9.9	8 587	13.5	16 160	13 523	2 637	NA	NA
Woodruff	106	6 715	0.84	68	10.0	103	15.1	788	14.6	1 820	1 579	241	137	1 951
Yell	323	19 911	0.76	265	12.1	231	10.6	3 425	19.0	4 647	3 718	929	511	2 343

1. Per 1,000 estimated resident population.   2. Data for serious crimes have not been adjusted for underreporting; this may affect comparability between geographic areas and over time.
3. Per 100,000 population estimated by the FBI.

Table B. States and Counties — Crime, Education, Money Income, and Poverty

STATE County	Serious crimes known to police, 2014 (cont.)[1] Rate[2] Violent	Rate[2] Property	Education School enrollment and attainment, 2010–2014 Enrollment[3] Total	Enrollment[3] Per-cent private	Attainment[4] (percent) High school grad-uate or less	Attainment[4] Bach-elor's degree or more	Local government expenditures,[5] 2012–2013 Total current spending (mil dol)	Current spend-ing per student (dollars)	Per capita income[6] (dollars)	Money income, 2010–2014 Households Median income (dollars)	Mean income (dollars)	Percent with income of $200,000 or more	Income and poverty, 2014 Median house-hold income (dollars)	Percent below poverty level All per-sons	Children under 18 years	Children 5 to 17 years in families
	46	47	48	49	50	51	52	53	54	55	56	57	58	59	60	61
ARKANSAS—Cont'd																
Cleveland	35	1 191	2 331	4.9	58.6	14.6	12.7	9 142	21 666	41 586	55 419	1.3	43 201	16.6	24.3	21.6
Columbia	292	1 954	7 243	5.9	51.2	21.3	31.6	9 119	19 893	37 509	50 463	0.8	37 495	24.1	30.9	29.5
Conway	226	3 030	4 778	11.7	56.9	16.5	41.8	12 743	21 742	37 314	53 548	2.0	42 348	18.3	27.0	23.9
Craighead	429	3 573	28 668	5.9	46.1	24.8	145.7	8 292	23 244	42 085	59 763	2.9	42 851	22.3	30.9	29.0
Crawford	289	2 551	15 610	7.8	55.2	14.3	99.1	8 744	20 104	40 712	52 167	1.5	43 466	16.6	24.1	22.4
Crittenden	1 073	4 937	14 634	5.7	55.9	14.6	95.6	9 057	19 732	37 781	51 746	1.5	35 455	27.3	41.0	39.2
Cross	773	4 055	4 197	3.0	67.2	12.4	31.2	8 958	18 919	37 725	48 023	1.1	38 597	22.3	32.7	32.2
Dallas	570	2 648	1 597	7.8	69.2	11.8	10.2	11 530	18 261	32 554	45 243	0.9	34 018	21.0	31.5	29.8
Desha	NA	NA	3 283	7.5	64.2	11.6	26.3	9 549	19 300	28 457	46 196	1.7	33 028	27.3	38.3	37.4
Drew	388	2 932	5 221	8.5	54.3	20.4	41.9	13 279	17 433	32 351	43 536	0.4	36 801	24.0	28.1	26.0
Faulkner	330	3 738	36 072	14.7	42.0	27.3	158.5	8 522	24 703	51 095	65 110	2.5	51 436	14.7	16.5	13.9
Franklin	361	1 806	4 485	7.5	57.4	12.6	27.3	9 696	20 021	39 879	50 956	1.9	40 404	17.5	25.8	23.8
Fulton	195	1 145	2 372	8.3	59.7	10.7	14.9	8 967	19 216	36 244	44 456	0.0	33 347	22.6	33.8	30.0
Garland	NA	NA	20 844	7.4	45.6	21.0	141.5	9 550	23 514	39 558	55 257	2.5	40 621	18.7	27.8	26.4
Grant	166	2 007	4 316	7.9	56.1	15.3	39.1	8 063	22 065	46 074	56 941	1.0	46 067	13.3	18.7	17.5
Greene	328	5 087	10 816	5.9	59.0	14.9	62.8	8 495	20 188	39 500	50 266	0.9	42 572	16.3	23.0	21.7
Hempstead	566	3 460	5 773	9.8	56.0	14.0	38.4	10 324	17 866	32 587	45 568	0.8	33 136	24.4	33.6	32.7
Hot Spring	NA	NA	7 710	6.6	56.9	14.1	47.7	8 715	19 819	41 353	52 253	1.1	37 831	18.7	28.6	25.7
Howard	104	2 176	3 449	4.4	58.2	14.4	27.5	8 705	20 341	38 050	50 724	2.0	37 336	18.8	28.9	27.7
Independence	497	3 540	8 872	8.8	57.0	14.8	58.5	9 335	20 222	36 186	50 219	1.6	41 085	18.6	25.7	24.3
Izard	188	2 500	2 538	7.8	57.8	12.3	20.6	11 371	18 650	31 219	43 460	1.3	32 744	22.0	28.5	27.1
Jackson	755	4 488	3 646	2.5	69.7	7.9	28.2	9 416	15 860	31 512	41 244	0.9	32 427	25.1	33.6	31.5
Jefferson	882	4 555	20 647	8.7	53.2	17.1	123.4	10 180	19 847	36 799	50 958	1.4	35 927	26.8	39.8	36.2
Johnson	220	2 270	5 742	12.9	62.9	16.3	38.5	8 624	18 993	32 553	47 965	2.0	34 923	19.7	29.1	25.8
Lafayette	224	1 636	1 594	9.8	65.9	12.4	11.1	10 028	17 707	31 215	42 150	1.1	32 225	27.5	37.3	32.9
Lawrence	213	1 043	4 294	13.4	62.9	11.8	33.9	10 456	17 064	33 481	42 107	0.3	34 916	23.0	30.8	28.6
Lee	232	1 624	2 106	11.8	72.3	6.4	11.6	11 326	13 297	26 986	37 550	0.9	28 006	39.3	46.5	43.1
Lincoln	128	871	2 669	10.6	70.8	8.5	16.1	9 597	14 501	32 615	48 956	2.5	37 644	29.0	30.4	26.6
Little River	143	2 536	3 029	9.2	54.6	11.8	18.4	9 241	20 073	39 494	48 330	0.3	37 691	18.2	25.5	23.3
Logan	NA	NA	5 008	8.1	60.2	11.8	36.0	8 973	20 114	36 062	50 706	2.1	36 391	21.1	30.1	27.1
Lonoke	312	2 392	19 124	11.0	47.6	18.7	115.4	8 364	23 339	52 805	62 603	0.8	54 459	12.3	17.6	16.1
Madison	236	943	3 360	7.9	68.7	9.7	21.3	9 242	19 930	37 351	49 853	1.5	39 158	18.0	28.2	26.5
Marion	336	2 054	2 945	4.5	56.6	12.8	20.9	12 576	17 429	33 293	40 307	0.3	33 181	20.3	33.3	31.5
Miller	600	4 842	9 787	11.2	56.4	12.7	64.2	9 584	20 853	40 829	51 085	1.0	40 877	20.8	31.0	30.6
Mississippi	970	4 830	11 749	5.4	58.1	13.1	79.7	9 630	18 732	34 424	48 382	1.4	33 577	27.1	37.2	33.6
Monroe	264	1 546	1 747	3.8	62.4	12.1	12.2	10 127	17 571	27 571	40 767	1.5	30 682	28.1	38.7	36.2
Montgomery	219	1 224	1 600	6.1	55.8	13.6	10.7	9 510	18 698	32 293	44 226	0.3	34 597	20.1	34.2	31.1
Nevada	194	1 920	2 049	7.4	58.0	14.2	13.0	8 865	18 254	31 614	42 727	1.3	30 935	25.1	33.5	32.3
Newton	275	951	1 738	3.2	63.8	11.3	14.5	10 812	18 127	32 500	43 407	0.8	35 895	20.1	35.1	32.5
Ouachita	NA	NA	6 089	4.6	56.6	15.9	46.3	10 238	19 358	32 220	44 707	1.0	34 971	23.0	32.0	29.5
Perry	514	2 415	2 346	6.6	58.8	14.4	13.5	8 258	22 534	42 030	57 347	0.9	40 556	17.3	26.7	24.7
Phillips	NA	NA	5 927	5.7	55.0	12.9	39.7	13 123	17 848	27 183	44 707	1.7	28 171	35.3	50.9	50.5
Pike	180	1 490	2 434	3.0	56.1	12.8	19.4	9 389	18 695	32 045	46 471	0.9	36 893	20.0	29.8	28.1
Poinsett	330	3 481	5 645	7.6	66.9	8.0	44.6	10 274	17 110	33 238	42 101	0.3	35 851	21.9	33.9	32.8
Polk	281	2 343	4 706	5.8	52.7	12.6	33.7	8 967	19 412	33 558	47 010	1.3	33 127	22.0	32.9	30.4
Pope	275	3 179	17 998	5.8	50.5	21.1	91.7	9 150	20 465	40 818	53 514	1.7	39 909	18.3	25.3	22.7
Prairie	193	1 267	1 884	7.1	64.5	10.4	11.9	9 278	18 977	36 904	42 863	0.0	39 896	18.7	26.7	25.1
Pulaski	1 010	5 781	101 618	19.5	37.9	32.0	586.2	11 235	27 506	46 410	66 107	3.7	45 698	16.1	23.8	22.2
Randolph	267	2 992	4 573	7.1	56.5	14.4	20.1	8 386	19 528	36 487	47 141	0.7	37 761	18.3	27.9	26.8
St. Francis	NA	NA	7 019	7.1	60.0	11.8	44.6	10 407	16 076	31 336	42 100	0.9	30 489	33.4	45.8	43.3
Saline	296	1 904	26 811	10.0	45.5	23.0	124.3	7 676	26 179	55 697	67 037	1.7	55 915	8.7	13.4	13.4
Scott	335	2 171	2 666	4.6	61.0	12.2	23.0	8 880	18 525	36 754	47 280	1.4	33 202	23.7	37.0	33.4
Searcy	113	288	1 715	15.5	60.1	13.9	18.1	11 406	17 590	33 610	41 077	1.1	31 765	23.3	38.1	36.3
Sebastian	625	4 022	32 299	9.0	49.6	19.7	183.5	9 191	23 768	39 208	59 002	3.1	39 907	22.1	31.9	30.8
Sevier	138	2 172	4 488	4.5	64.9	8.3	38.9	11 851	16 266	36 218	45 077	0.6	37 014	20.4	30.7	29.3
Sharp	NA	NA	3 548	7.5	61.4	10.6	25.6	8 687	16 906	30 826	40 017	0.6	32 101	21.6	33.5	31.6
Stone	151	2 205	2 501	11.0	57.2	16.3	14.7	8 400	19 985	29 982	45 379	0.9	30 010	24.4	38.6	35.7
Union	556	3 131	10 235	6.8	53.6	17.4	65.6	8 736	21 911	38 762	53 948	2.3	40 841	23.1	33.5	29.8
Van Buren	285	2 401	3 228	4.6	60.5	12.2	24.6	10 660	18 727	31 030	42 643	0.8	32 975	22.0	33.0	29.0
Washington	NA	NA	66 367	7.8	45.2	29.3	354.6	9 228	24 018	41 983	62 592	3.4	45 589	19.3	22.0	20.1
White	NA	NA	21 871	26.9	53.8	19.0	117.3	9 006	22 132	42 852	57 539	2.1	42 044	19.4	25.0	23.8
Woodruff	128	1 823	1 445	3.1	72.0	9.0	7.3	13 708	17 296	27 165	38 146	1.0	29 969	25.1	35.9	31.7
Yell	326	2 018	5 355	2.7	66.6	11.9	38.3	8 916	18 170	37 378	47 805	0.7	37 080	17.4	27.2	26.1

1. Data for serious crimes have not been adjusted for underreporting; this may affect comparability between geographic areas and over time.   2. Per 100,000 population estimated by the FBI.
3. All persons 3 years old and over enrolled in nursery school through college.   4. Persons 25 years old and over.   5. Elementary and secondary education expenditures.
6. Based on population estimated by the American Community Survey, 2010–2014.

Table B. States and Counties — **Personal Income**

STATE County	Personal income, 2014										Earnings, 2014		
			Per capita[1]			Supplements to wages and salaries; employer contributions (mil dol)						Contributions for government social insurance (mil dol)	
	Total (mil dol)	Percent change, 2013–2014	Dollars	Rank	Wages and salaries (mil dol)	Pension and insurance	Government social insurance	Proprietors' income (mil dol)	Dividends, interest, and rent (mil dol)	Personal transfer receipts (mil dol)	Total (mil dol)	From employee and self-employed	From employer
	62	63	64	65	66	67	68	69	70	71	72	73	74
ARKANSAS—Cont'd													
Cleveland	292	6.0	34 592	2 001	35	7	3	44	29	81	89	5	3
Columbia	837	5.6	34 990	1 938	351	59	27	95	137	239	533	36	27
Conway	763	6.0	36 170	1 751	272	44	21	108	106	213	445	28	21
Craighead	3 450	3.4	33 649	2 169	1 834	289	146	374	447	862	2 643	167	146
Crawford	1 876	4.6	30 399	2 664	735	113	61	127	210	538	1 037	74	61
Crittenden	1 652	1.7	33 335	2 221	615	98	53	159	187	474	925	60	53
Cross	613	1.1	35 560	1 843	183	30	15	78	71	173	306	20	15
Dallas	232	3.3	29 925	2 727	89	14	8	12	29	93	124	9	8
Desha	466	-1.4	38 024	1 450	167	27	14	96	60	138	303	16	14
Drew	638	0.7	34 243	2 074	225	42	17	79	84	186	363	23	17
Faulkner	4 028	4.3	33 350	2 220	1 774	255	138	184	495	895	2 351	154	138
Franklin	540	7.9	30 317	2 674	166	36	13	65	79	166	279	18	13
Fulton	327	6.2	26 991	2 983	61	13	5	45	50	132	123	10	5
Garland	3 525	4.3	36 218	1 742	1 331	203	107	213	716	1 072	1 854	138	107
Grant	615	3.6	33 876	2 135	152	24	12	47	70	147	235	17	12
Greene	1 335	2.4	30 549	2 644	576	97	50	113	172	391	836	55	50
Hempstead	676	6.4	30 298	2 677	286	51	22	88	79	207	447	27	22
Hot Spring	952	4.2	28 524	2 879	321	55	26	38	133	313	441	33	26
Howard	435	8.6	32 232	2 412	237	44	20	84	49	127	386	22	20
Independence	1 198	3.7	32 403	2 387	542	93	45	128	158	363	808	53	45
Izard	383	4.7	28 371	2 886	105	20	8	37	55	148	170	13	8
Jackson	521	0.4	29 730	2 756	206	35	16	90	67	180	347	22	16
Jefferson	2 291	0.1	31 684	2 495	1 237	227	101	140	313	721	1 705	110	101
Johnson	683	6.1	26 275	3 020	286	50	24	71	83	213	430	29	24
Lafayette	254	5.2	35 706	1 825	48	8	4	55	34	76	116	6	4
Lawrence	502	1.0	29 623	2 773	141	26	12	69	69	177	247	17	12
Lee	277	-10.4	28 088	2 908	77	14	6	54	39	97	150	9	6
Lincoln	352	-0.6	25 195	3 058	111	23	8	54	36	103	197	11	8
Little River	403	4.2	32 148	2 425	183	27	14	45	47	125	268	17	14
Logan	749	8.4	34 126	2 095	188	34	15	99	86	246	336	21	15
Lonoke	2 497	2.2	34 897	1 953	494	74	39	138	314	558	744	53	39
Madison	514	10.9	32 671	2 342	110	21	9	104	64	130	244	14	9
Marion	459	4.6	28 069	2 911	121	26	11	27	82	184	185	16	11
Miller	1 358	3.5	31 279	2 547	525	78	41	134	193	365	778	55	41
Mississippi	1 450	1.9	32 786	2 315	856	130	68	127	169	427	1 183	73	68
Monroe	270	3.6	35 577	1 842	76	12	6	50	35	87	145	9	6
Montgomery	252	3.1	27 765	2 935	47	9	4	39	37	90	98	8	4
Nevada	285	3.8	32 620	2 349	91	14	8	31	37	92	144	10	8
Newton	205	4.7	25 991	3 031	31	7	2	19	34	77	60	6	2
Ouachita	820	3.8	33 007	2 278	260	49	20	54	108	265	384	29	20
Perry	325	1.8	31 679	2 496	42	8	4	25	44	95	78	7	4
Phillips	655	1.5	32 874	2 301	209	37	17	96	76	232	360	21	17
Pike	328	6.9	29 770	2 746	76	14	6	78	58	104	134	10	6
Poinsett	737	-2.0	30 383	2 667	195	31	15	113	80	262	355	24	15
Polk	588	6.8	29 061	2 820	192	37	16	84	87	202	329	22	16
Pope	2 020	4.7	31 962	2 443	1 075	181	88	124	264	521	1 469	93	88
Prairie	281	-1.5	33 892	2 130	63	10	5	47	35	83	124	7	5
Pulaski	18 201	3.1	46 349	570	12 756	1 987	985	1 683	3 666	3 427	17 410	1 057	985
Randolph	515	2.9	29 328	2 795	147	27	12	49	68	198	235	18	12
St. Francis	682	-2.3	25 369	3 054	294	58	24	58	88	255	434	28	24
Saline	4 175	3.9	36 076	1 771	829	124	66	179	511	982	1 198	95	66
Scott	307	5.6	28 670	2 869	95	20	8	54	38	93	176	11	8
Searcy	220	4.8	27 775	2 933	48	10	4	23	37	88	84	8	4
Sebastian	4 774	4.4	37 658	1 502	2 821	429	222	503	876	1 082	3 975	254	222
Sevier	462	8.9	26 515	3 007	171	31	15	70	50	133	287	17	15
Sharp	490	6.1	29 009	2 827	116	20	9	26	73	225	171	16	9
Stone	346	7.0	27 678	2 941	74	14	6	41	72	147	135	12	6
Union	1 885	5.4	46 862	532	884	141	66	299	345	411	1 390	92	66
Van Buren	500	6.3	29 698	2 762	181	28	13	25	88	184	247	20	13
Washington	7 638	5.7	34 592	2 001	4 458	682	334	695	1 218	1 335	6 170	376	334
White	2 500	3.3	31 813	2 465	997	149	79	149	358	671	1 374	96	79
Woodruff	236	-1.8	34 082	2 104	69	13	5	38	30	78	124	7	5
Yell	679	7.4	30 915	2 600	208	42	17	94	81	201	360	22	17

1. Based on the resident population estimated as of July 1 of the year shown.

Table B. States and Counties — Earnings, Social Security, and Housing

STATE County	Earnings, 2014 (cont.) Percent by selected industries									Social Security beneficiaries, December 2014		Supplemental Security Income recipients, December 2014	Housing units, 2015	
	Farm	Mining	Construction	Manu-facturing	Information: professional, scientific, technical services	Retail trade	Finance, insur-ance, real estate and leasing	Health care and social assistance	Govern-ment	Number	Rate[1]		Total	Percent change, 2010–2014
	75	76	77	78	79	80	81	82	83	84	85	86	87	88
ARKANSAS—Cont'd														
Cleveland	40.2	0.0	2.5	4.5	D	2.6	D	4.3	17.5	2 115	251	277	4 045	-0.5
Columbia	3.2	14.1	4.4	25.7	2.9	5.5	4.5	D	17.5	5 940	246	1 325	11 598	0.0
Conway	14.7	3.2	9.5	13.7	2.3	6.7	2.7	D	14.9	5 680	270	930	9 727	0.1
Craighead	2.5	D	6.9	13.1	4.1	7.9	4.7	22.1	15.7	19 755	192	4 037	43 976	8.5
Crawford	2.5	3.2	6.5	21.3	D	6.4	3.5	6.6	11.4	14 845	241	2 086	26 484	1.4
Crittenden	5.9	D	5.6	10.9	2.3	6.7	3.3	11.7	15.5	10 080	203	3 550	21 686	0.9
Cross	15.9	0.0	2.8	9.3	2.3	10.3	5.8	D	18.6	4 455	259	844	7 896	0.6
Dallas	0.8	0.0	4.2	21.5	D	9.0	3.5	D	12.4	2 255	291	438	4 284	-0.5
Desha	27.4	0.0	2.9	18.1	1.6	5.1	3.6	D	14.4	3 215	263	742	6 303	0.7
Drew	10.0	0.0	4.3	10.6	2.4	8.3	4.0	D	26.9	4 280	229	819	8 475	0.8
Faulkner	0.2	5.4	8.3	8.9	13.7	8.0	4.6	11.4	17.3	19 915	165	2 761	49 143	5.4
Franklin	15.3	7.9	4.1	15.3	1.9	7.4	4.6	D	19.4	4 790	270	562	8 018	0.0
Fulton	16.7	D	D	3.3	2.7	6.1	4.9	12.1	23.3	3 865	318	448	6 761	-0.3
Garland	0.4	0.8	6.3	7.4	6.2	11.2	7.0	22.6	14.4	29 430	303	3 924	50 538	0.0
Grant	4.4	D	8.9	26.0	4.7	6.5	2.7	D	18.0	4 010	221	410	7 840	1.1
Greene	6.3	D	3.6	37.2	D	7.3	3.3	9.8	13.0	10 555	241	1 797	18 610	4.0
Hempstead	13.3	D	3.6	23.7	1.5	6.9	3.0	D	19.2	5 155	231	1 053	10 417	0.0
Hot Spring	0.7	D	6.0	19.0	D	5.9	3.5	D	22.2	8 780	263	1 214	14 273	-0.4
Howard	15.8	D	3.3	39.4	D	5.4	2.0	7.0	10.6	3 405	253	540	6 233	-0.1
Independence	5.6	1.0	4.1	18.7	D	8.1	4.5	19.1	13.0	9 470	256	1 288	16 299	0.7
Izard	12.1	D	5.1	7.6	1.4	7.6	4.6	14.2	27.5	4 295	318	609	7 213	-0.3
Jackson	12.9	D	2.8	21.9	2.0	6.9	2.9	D	19.5	4 745	271	959	7 588	-0.2
Jefferson	3.4	0.0	3.3	19.3	2.3	6.9	4.2	13.9	27.9	16 310	225	4 538	33 252	0.7
Johnson	9.2	D	3.7	26.9	D	6.7	2.5	D	14.3	6 085	234	957	11 346	0.3
Lafayette	40.3	9.2	6.2	1.7	D	D	1.9	D	14.2	2 040	286	460	4 340	-0.3
Lawrence	17.7	0.8	5.2	8.5	D	7.4	3.0	D	22.8	4 750	280	882	7 973	-0.3
Lee	22.0	0.0	D	D	D	5.6	2.4	D	25.0	2 220	227	783	4 360	0.1
Lincoln	24.8	D	3.2	7.6	D	2.9	1.9	D	33.6	2 455	176	542	4 852	-0.2
Little River	11.3	D	4.9	46.0	1.3	4.7	1.6	2.5	14.6	3 450	275	438	6 442	-0.3
Logan	22.6	2.8	4.9	16.4	2.8	6.6	3.2	8.5	18.9	6 440	294	907	10 124	0.2
Lonoke	7.0	D	8.7	14.0	3.7	9.0	6.0	9.0	18.9	13 790	193	1 992	28 850	5.9
Madison	31.7	D	5.3	20.2	2.7	6.1	1.7	4.0	12.6	4 180	266	454	7 483	0.0
Marion	3.9	D	4.2	40.0	D	7.6	5.7	6.3	14.5	5 630	343	561	9 319	-0.4
Miller	0.5	1.0	8.7	22.5	D	6.7	3.8	D	14.5	9 335	214	2 143	19 426	0.8
Mississippi	6.3	0.0	5.5	39.8	5.2	4.4	2.0	D	11.1	10 200	230	3 334	20 508	0.2
Monroe	25.8	0.0	2.6	3.9	D	7.4	4.6	D	14.1	2 195	289	597	4 426	-0.7
Montgomery	21.8	D	7.4	0.7	D	6.0	4.4	2.6	25.2	2 785	306	313	5 745	-0.3
Nevada	13.2	0.1	D	D	D	5.6	2.1	10.0	13.5	2 335	268	491	4 537	-0.6
Newton	12.9	0.0	4.3	2.7	D	D	D	D	35.1	2 540	321	382	4 669	0.1
Ouachita	1.2	8.9	3.8	10.5	D	8.2	4.0	D	23.5	7 025	283	1 521	13 056	-0.5
Perry	13.4	D	13.3	2.2	D	6.4	D	D	23.0	2 670	261	371	4 899	-0.1
Phillips	21.6	0.0	1.9	5.6	D	7.1	3.2	12.4	19.1	5 025	252	2 013	10 187	0.6
Pike	18.1	D	2.8	6.1	2.1	8.3	7.5	D	21.1	3 010	274	375	5 568	-0.2
Poinsett	19.0	D	3.6	10.1	1.7	5.8	4.0	6.7	16.6	6 695	277	1 605	10 932	0.1
Polk	13.7	0.9	4.7	19.0	2.6	7.4	3.7	14.3	15.3	6 105	301	688	10 028	0.3
Pope	3.9	0.9	7.6	16.1	3.8	6.7	4.4	9.7	15.5	13 745	218	2 013	25 947	1.5
Prairie	34.2	0.0	12.0	D	D	4.9	2.4	7.4	14.6	2 265	272	344	4 498	-0.1
Pulaski	0.1	0.4	5.2	5.0	11.2	6.7	9.1	12.6	24.4	76 935	196	16 599	182 285	3.8
Randolph	11.5	D	3.8	10.1	D	7.5	2.9	D	20.6	5 425	309	795	8 530	0.2
St. Francis	7.5	D	D	D	D	7.9	3.1	D	32.2	5 710	212	2 067	10 915	0.1
Saline	0.1	D	10.5	7.1	4.3	16.7	4.9	12.4	20.9	25 895	224	2 623	46 994	4.8
Scott	23.0	0.1	2.9	23.8	D	5.0	1.8	D	17.5	2 490	233	360	5 220	0.5
Searcy	6.1	0.0	6.2	8.9	D	8.1	3.8	12.9	23.2	2 710	342	453	4 893	-0.1
Sebastian	0.9	3.9	4.3	18.6	7.1	6.4	5.7	16.7	11.5	27 920	220	4 495	56 372	3.1
Sevier	18.1	D	D	D	1.4	7.0	4.0	D	18.1	3 210	185	446	6 883	-0.1
Sharp	13.8	D	3.3	3.1	D	10.1	5.8	D	20.2	6 820	403	895	9 823	0.0
Stone	13.8	1.3	5.5	4.5	D	13.8	3.7	D	20.1	4 520	363	565	6 762	0.7
Union	0.4	15.7	8.3	18.4	1.9	5.6	3.3	8.3	9.0	10 900	271	1 936	19 732	0.4
Van Buren	2.3	16.7	5.1	1.5	D	7.7	3.1	11.4	14.5	5 470	324	640	10 339	-0.1
Washington	2.0	0.2	5.2	10.4	5.4	6.9	6.4	12.7	18.9	33 555	152	4 489	90 776	3.4
White	1.2	5.6	7.7	9.6	3.1	9.0	4.4	15.9	13.1	17 610	224	2 442	33 286	2.5
Woodruff	29.8	D	2.1	8.2	D	3.8	3.2	7.1	19.0	1 950	283	453	3 878	-0.4
Yell	18.0	D	5.2	25.2	D	4.3	3.4	D	18.9	5 465	249	827	9 727	-0.3

1. Per 1,000 resident population estimated as of July 1 of the year shown.

Table B. States and Counties — Housing, Labor Force, and Employment

STATE County	Housing units, 2010–2014 Occupied units Owner-occupied Total	Percent	Median value[1]	Median owner cost as a percent of income With a mortgage	Without a mortgage[2]	Renter-occupied Median rent[3]	Median rent as a percent of income[2]	Sub-stand-ard units[4] (percent)	Civilian labor force, 2015 Total	Percent change, 2014–2015	Unemployment Total	Rate[5]	Civilian employment,[6] 2010–2014 Total	Percent Management, business, science and arts	Construction, production, and maintenance occupations
	89	90	91	92	93	94	95	96	97	98	99	100	101	102	103
ARKANSAS—Cont'd															
Cleveland	3 270	78.7	81 300	18.8	10.0	644	23.7	1.1	3 416	-0.2	197	5.8	3 349	31.9	32.3
Columbia	9 509	68.1	78 500	19.0	10.0	604	31.9	2.3	9 522	0.8	643	6.8	10 182	29.7	29.0
Conway	8 370	75.2	88 100	20.9	10.0	628	38.5	4.1	8 635	1.4	545	6.3	8 390	26.0	37.4
Craighead	38 081	58.9	127 400	18.9	10.0	670	31.3	2.3	50 611	3.3	2 322	4.6	44 529	33.6	26.4
Crawford	23 490	75.4	107 600	22.3	10.9	615	27.7	3.7	26 897	1.3	1 445	5.4	25 519	27.3	30.0
Crittenden	18 253	57.2	101 100	21.3	10.7	681	33.7	5.3	21 593	1.7	1 373	6.4	19 983	29.4	27.6
Cross	6 882	63.5	81 000	19.7	12.2	644	30.0	1.3	8 091	0.9	456	5.6	7 093	23.1	34.1
Dallas	3 322	66.1	59 700	17.9	10.1	504	28.2	3.0	2 886	1.2	215	7.4	3 168	20.2	41.2
Desha	5 166	57.3	56 900	18.0	12.1	551	34.5	2.3	5 569	1.2	422	7.6	4 668	27.7	34.6
Drew	7 344	61.4	87 400	19.8	12.5	600	39.5	2.7	7 940	0.3	567	7.1	7 370	36.4	26.9
Faulkner	42 964	63.5	141 700	19.7	10.0	726	29.0	1.9	59 655	2.0	2 888	4.8	56 291	34.4	22.8
Franklin	6 783	75.7	91 900	19.2	10.0	568	25.6	1.8	7 415	2.7	382	5.2	6 872	25.8	34.2
Fulton	5 312	76.6	88 000	21.3	10.6	493	30.6	4.3	4 798	0.9	257	5.4	4 593	29.0	32.8
Garland	39 876	67.8	130 200	22.2	10.1	709	31.3	3.0	40 046	0.2	2 268	5.7	38 861	31.7	23.6
Grant	6 798	77.0	101 600	18.8	11.0	700	24.3	2.5	8 291	1.8	389	4.7	7 730	29.2	33.4
Greene	16 610	65.0	101 700	20.1	11.9	662	29.2	1.3	19 986	2.8	1 069	5.3	17 507	27.9	35.6
Hempstead	8 115	68.6	74 900	21.5	10.3	571	34.3	3.4	9 834	0.0	508	5.2	8 816	26.7	38.4
Hot Spring	12 027	71.2	83 300	19.6	10.2	677	29.4	1.6	14 210	2.6	739	5.2	13 801	28.3	31.2
Howard	5 085	65.1	79 000	21.0	10.0	553	26.6	4.2	6 050	-1.4	266	4.4	5 776	27.1	39.7
Independence	14 405	70.0	91 300	21.5	10.8	590	31.8	3.3	15 600	1.7	1 046	6.7	15 505	27.7	33.4
Izard	5 656	79.9	74 000	23.1	12.1	547	35.4	3.8	4 988	2.4	342	6.9	4 481	32.2	25.8
Jackson	6 402	67.7	58 200	20.4	11.9	537	28.8	3.6	6 199	1.0	484	7.8	5 715	22.2	37.7
Jefferson	28 488	63.8	81 400	19.8	12.1	663	31.6	2.0	29 115	-0.4	2 110	7.2	28 556	28.3	26.9
Johnson	10 023	70.1	86 800	21.2	10.0	615	33.4	4.1	10 378	1.7	620	6.0	10 331	23.1	39.9
Lafayette	2 827	72.6	56 800	21.7	12.2	467	28.7	1.4	2 634	-0.2	208	7.9	2 530	25.7	36.5
Lawrence	6 630	70.4	62 700	19.6	11.6	526	27.7	1.9	7 034	0.2	440	6.3	6 579	25.8	32.9
Lee	3 488	55.6	56 800	24.8	12.8	501	34.1	1.3	3 209	-0.5	222	6.9	3 121	22.3	31.0
Lincoln	4 195	69.7	57 300	18.9	10.7	598	31.9	3.7	4 178	0.1	265	6.3	3 963	27.6	35.9
Little River	5 241	77.4	74 400	18.9	10.3	524	33.8	1.5	5 626	2.5	318	5.7	5 082	22.9	37.0
Logan	8 439	73.6	80 000	19.0	10.0	530	28.4	2.4	9 204	2.3	547	5.9	8 590	28.8	32.5
Lonoke	25 572	72.2	121 900	19.4	10.0	715	27.4	3.0	33 019	1.8	1 436	4.3	31 806	34.1	25.1
Madison	6 152	77.9	89 600	20.6	10.0	597	33.2	4.3	7 176	4.0	282	3.9	6 652	25.0	41.3
Marion	6 912	79.2	95 300	23.4	12.5	564	30.1	4.6	6 533	0.9	356	5.4	5 725	19.4	35.2
Miller	16 946	65.5	92 400	20.0	10.3	692	30.3	3.1	19 710	2.7	1 026	5.2	18 468	25.4	31.2
Mississippi	17 188	58.6	78 000	18.3	12.6	617	32.1	3.3	18 418	-2.6	1 717	9.3	17 116	25.4	36.5
Monroe	3 374	63.2	54 100	18.9	12.6	514	37.0	2.2	2 993	-2.3	188	6.3	2 746	24.2	33.9
Montgomery	3 813	81.4	76 600	20.9	11.8	582	30.5	2.5	3 261	-1.7	228	7.0	3 502	27.2	38.7
Nevada	3 596	72.8	64 300	21.9	11.0	545	31.6	2.9	3 653	0.1	190	5.2	3 506	21.7	33.9
Newton	3 346	85.2	72 400	23.2	10.0	351	26.1	7.2	3 383	1.6	171	5.1	3 327	19.0	40.5
Ouachita	10 502	68.2	67 800	19.5	11.9	570	31.9	1.8	9 902	0.4	656	6.6	10 026	25.7	34.2
Perry	3 926	84.3	77 200	19.0	10.0	575	27.1	5.9	4 233	1.0	267	6.3	4 281	28.2	36.3
Phillips	8 291	52.1	63 500	23.2	11.3	586	35.9	4.4	6 986	-2.5	553	7.9	7 312	31.7	22.8
Pike	4 352	73.8	74 700	21.4	11.0	468	27.2	1.9	4 180	0.3	259	6.2	4 440	24.4	39.3
Poinsett	9 314	61.6	71 300	20.5	11.9	522	30.1	5.1	10 241	2.3	584	5.7	9 275	23.7	34.5
Polk	7 994	76.0	85 100	23.8	10.0	493	28.5	4.4	8 326	-0.6	499	6.0	7 867	27.9	32.2
Pope	22 776	69.0	115 900	21.3	10.0	634	29.2	3.3	29 554	0.7	1 626	5.5	27 936	28.0	30.0
Prairie	3 776	71.8	71 300	20.6	12.6	485	27.1	3.6	3 751	-0.7	181	4.8	3 541	26.7	33.4
Pulaski	153 323	60.3	141 600	21.1	11.0	779	29.9	1.8	186 455	2.0	8 826	4.7	180 593	39.6	16.5
Randolph	7 293	74.9	70 000	19.0	10.0	491	32.0	2.3	6 183	-4.7	458	7.4	6 926	30.6	31.8
St. Francis	9 351	57.3	65 600	19.0	13.7	585	29.7	3.1	8 952	0.6	670	7.5	9 412	24.9	29.6
Saline	41 702	77.7	139 300	20.3	10.0	791	27.3	2.0	55 273	2.2	2 342	4.2	52 131	33.6	23.2
Scott	4 125	75.4	78 600	19.1	10.9	525	27.9	4.3	4 512	0.3	225	5.0	4 437	27.1	40.2
Searcy	3 179	78.9	85 400	24.9	10.0	421	35.0	3.6	3 056	3.0	178	5.8	2 766	26.5	34.0
Sebastian	49 424	62.0	113 800	20.5	10.2	635	29.4	2.8	57 390	1.3	2 868	5.0	54 954	30.9	28.0
Sevier	5 918	70.9	68 200	21.0	10.0	534	27.6	5.9	5 631	-1.9	358	6.4	6 936	19.6	47.5
Sharp	7 053	77.6	73 600	21.6	11.6	581	33.6	3.8	6 004	1.5	429	7.1	5 789	28.1	32.4
Stone	5 267	77.0	91 200	28.4	11.0	489	26.6	4.7	4 681	0.5	305	6.5	4 596	32.2	31.3
Union	16 689	69.5	72 800	18.3	11.3	646	27.7	4.7	16 780	2.2	1 073	6.4	16 468	30.5	28.8
Van Buren	7 077	74.7	86 000	23.5	12.5	593	32.1	3.9	6 458	1.0	449	7.0	5 412	22.7	37.7
Washington	80 457	55.5	149 400	20.5	10.3	708	30.4	5.5	114 790	5.2	4 141	3.6	100 820	35.0	23.3
White	29 447	68.7	103 200	19.1	10.0	635	29.7	3.3	34 405	0.7	2 225	6.5	32 353	29.2	28.5
Woodruff	3 055	62.3	57 600	19.6	12.9	456	32.5	3.5	3 042	-3.1	204	6.7	2 490	29.4	35.0
Yell	7 825	67.4	94 300	21.0	10.7	539	25.6	5.3	9 024	0.8	476	5.3	8 624	22.4	41.2

1. Specified owner-occupied units. 2. A value of 10.0 represents 10 percent or less; a value of 50.0 represents 50 percent or more. 3. Specified renter-occupied units.
4. Overcrowded or lacking complete plumbing facilities. 5. Percent of civilian labor force. 6. Persons 16 years old and over.

Table B. States and Counties — Nonfarm Employment and Agriculture

	Private nonfarm establishments, employment and payroll, 2014								Agriculture, 2012			
		Employment						Annual payroll	Farms			
											Percent with:	
STATE County	Number of establish-ments	Total	Health care and social assistance	Manufac-turing	Retail trade	Finance and insurance	Professional, scientific, and technical services	Total (mil dol)	Average per employee (dollars)	Number	Fewer than 50 acres	500 acres or more	Farm operators whose principal occu-pation is farming (percent)
	104	105	106	107	108	109	110	111	112	113	114	115	116
ARKANSAS—Cont'd													
Cleveland	79	644	D	D	D	D	D	19	29 489	211	39.8	2.8	58.8
Columbia	589	7 711	1 253	2 123	1 055	270	202	281	36 504	278	28.4	5.8	42.1
Conway	427	4 925	549	D	855	130	83	174	35 274	816	29.7	7.7	51.0
Craighead	2 431	39 394	9 576	5 633	6 799	1 069	904	1 372	34 817	583	38.6	29.5	52.0
Crawford	1 041	19 684	1 688	4 340	1 954	367	288	642	32 594	886	45.4	5.3	44.2
Crittenden	844	13 528	2 195	1 421	2 136	225	264	421	31 145	263	17.5	44.1	66.9
Cross	356	3 914	781	566	797	D	80	116	29 654	325	16.0	41.2	59.1
Dallas	194	2 415	701	D	375	66	D	66	27 251	90	18.9	11.1	51.1
Desha	311	3 606	630	D	615	D	53	116	32 292	244	20.5	43.4	64.8
Drew	401	4 446	D	630	1 040	169	109	131	29 429	308	27.3	17.2	42.9
Faulkner	2 452	36 081	5 302	3 916	5 694	1 186	1 380	1 459	40 431	1 288	40.7	6.2	33.8
Franklin	292	3 531	549	1 078	556	209	90	111	31 348	829	28.1	8.6	43.9
Fulton	156	1 467	577	145	230	79	46	33	22 686	753	20.5	13.9	47.4
Garland	2 648	32 870	7 991	2 294	6 076	967	1 549	1 015	30 879	361	49.3	2.5	55.4
Grant	272	2 990	306	1 104	478	79	93	95	31 913	257	37.4	5.8	44.4
Greene	766	18 273	1 595	5 048	1 914	588	670	500	27 375	711	37.6	15.3	40.6
Hempstead	387	6 135	1 014	2 095	915	178	100	189	30 726	748	25.1	15.2	54.4
Hot Spring	475	6 362	1 390	1 133	844	230	86	195	30 701	536	43.1	3.2	41.6
Howard	292	6 047	695	3 502	592	101	D	173	28 558	552	26.8	8.0	50.5
Independence	776	13 655	3 135	3 621	1 792	D	212	470	34 400	1 003	28.9	11.3	37.9
Izard	215	1 956	547	221	414	97	D	54	27 618	633	21.2	15.0	41.7
Jackson	325	3 988	882	1 072	815	D	96	124	31 197	437	18.5	31.8	51.0
Jefferson	1 358	20 829	4 118	4 975	3 376	842	381	723	34 690	444	35.4	26.8	52.3
Johnson	397	7 043	933	2 470	949	144	87	192	27 232	624	28.0	6.9	46.2
Lafayette	112	768	164	55	129	54	12	25	32 043	263	17.9	22.1	60.5
Lawrence	275	3 048	766	388	583	D	39	85	27 856	559	22.7	22.4	46.7
Lee	122	885	261	D	189	D	28	30	34 101	220	13.6	40.0	81.4
Lincoln	153	1 462	317	D	197	D	D	49	33 558	377	23.6	20.4	56.0
Little River	163	2 704	315	D	395	72	D	132	48 791	448	21.9	16.7	48.0
Logan	375	4 020	713	D	672	272	84	119	29 536	969	27.0	7.0	48.1
Lonoke	995	10 072	1 354	D	2 186	443	369	308	30 592	767	31.8	19.0	55.8
Madison	188	2 461	239	967	442	87	49	70	28 286	1 250	22.0	8.9	49.3
Marion	203	3 221	284	D	462	121	49	81	25 274	485	21.0	14.0	42.9
Miller	725	11 550	1 025	D	1 635	373	199	420	36 321	525	35.6	12.0	45.0
Mississippi	815	18 714	1 756	5 507	1 803	271	119	660	35 244	347	17.6	55.0	74.1
Monroe	191	1 726	305	111	338	64	D	47	27 481	230	20.0	51.3	64.8
Montgomery	141	841	67	D	132	44	D	25	29 911	449	24.1	5.3	50.1
Nevada	124	1 960	D	D	249	41	D	65	33 210	351	23.6	5.7	47.6
Newton	86	744	251	D	111	D	13	18	23 950	648	28.2	6.5	42.6
Ouachita	521	8 193	1 359	2 572	977	198	872	330	40 235	182	39.0	6.6	33.0
Perry	107	802	D	D	107	21	D	22	27 776	419	31.7	6.2	43.2
Phillips	410	4 127	1 003	D	959	D	89	129	31 295	282	13.5	50.7	68.8
Pike	200	1 766	D	245	317	85	40	46	25 893	346	24.0	8.7	55.8
Poinsett	366	3 654	692	680	779	136	43	106	29 141	397	22.2	53.4	66.2
Polk	449	5 001	1 069	1 269	910	157	D	140	28 046	893	38.4	4.4	42.6
Pope	1 545	23 370	3 343	5 119	3 619	929	476	785	33 580	977	36.6	6.3	48.2
Prairie	151	977	303	D	D	D	D	25	25 386	445	20.9	29.7	50.8
Pulaski	11 993	204 699	42 528	13 032	26 043	12 801	11 984	8 884	43 398	417	50.6	7.4	42.7
Randolph	327	3 569	1 026	615	715	110	69	97	27 283	667	21.0	15.4	39.7
St. Francis	444	5 157	1 203	D	1 052	183	122	147	28 542	326	21.2	37.1	65.3
Saline	1 813	19 715	4 356	1 351	3 976	523	576	594	30 143	386	52.8	4.9	46.9
Scott	143	1 925	250	D	293	48	11	53	27 580	602	25.6	5.3	49.8
Searcy	113	1 042	273	190	244	32	25	22	20 636	592	18.6	15.2	50.3
Sebastian	3 392	61 320	11 559	13 114	7 988	1 610	1 602	2 389	38 953	770	36.8	5.5	43.4
Sevier	268	4 134	589	D	739	132	62	125	30 286	543	28.4	6.4	44.8
Sharp	304	2 441	592	D	695	176	42	57	23 182	648	20.4	12.7	39.4
Stone	225	1 939	508	140	491	112	D	46	23 681	523	19.9	13.4	49.9
Union	1 109	17 449	2 213	2 867	2 199	439	256	799	45 814	280	34.3	5.7	48.6
Van Buren	336	3 416	731	D	546	D	46	128	37 491	587	21.8	7.7	47.5
Washington	5 017	82 559	13 723	12 574	11 775	2 253	3 519	3 181	38 528	2 502	43.2	4.1	42.3
White	1 533	22 282	4 291	D	3 522	612	511	723	32 429	1 836	35.6	7.3	35.9
Woodruff	131	1 216	152	D	271	44	D	44	36 543	217	14.7	48.8	60.8
Yell	301	4 834	995	D	553	170	69	140	29 055	794	29.7	8.3	47.9

Table B. States and Counties — **Agriculture**

STATE County	Land in farms					Value of land and buildings (dollars)		Value of machinery and equipment, average per farm (dollars)	Value of products sold				Percent of farms with sales of:		Government payments	
	Acreage (1,000)	Percent change, 2007–2012	Acres			Average per farm	Average per acre		Total (mil dol)	Average per farm (dollars)	Percent from:		$10,000 or more	$100,000 or more	Total ($1,000)	Percent of farms
			Average size of farm	Total irrigated (1,000)	Total cropland (1,000)						Crops	Live-stock and poultry products				
	117	118	119	120	121	122	123	124	125	126	127	128	129	130	131	132
ARKANSAS—Cont'd																
Cleveland	27	-12.5	129	D	6.0	502 071	3 895	83 725	105.8	501 427	0.4	99.6	48.8	36.0	237	10.4
Columbia	46	-3.1	164	0.3	12.5	353 727	2 157	65 011	41.7	150 032	12.2	87.8	38.5	11.5	84	8.6
Conway	179	-4.2	220	14.8	76.4	568 464	2 587	77 902	161.6	198 098	10.3	89.7	44.6	16.9	1 554	17.4
Craighead	338	0.2	579	271.6	314.2	1 857 806	3 208	276 847	261.6	448 714	98.9	1.1	55.1	36.5	10 157	57.8
Crawford	125	5.1	141	4.5	48.6	424 447	3 001	59 635	67.4	76 081	33.4	66.6	32.6	7.8	342	8.7
Crittenden	338	7.7	1 285	173.3	306.5	3 568 985	2 778	506 837	215.0	817 551	99.8	0.2	71.9	52.5	6 850	76.4
Cross	279	-1.4	858	214.7	255.2	2 181 258	2 542	375 991	188.8	580 855	99.8	0.2	56.9	44.9	11 662	84.9
Dallas	21	6.7	236	D	3.2	377 989	1 600	49 933	1.3	14 500	59.5	40.5	31.1	1.1	54	26.7
Desha	267	-12.9	1 095	202.1	243.9	3 053 189	2 789	683 840	212.9	872 512	97.0	3.0	68.0	49.2	7 594	87.3
Drew	130	4.4	422	66.9	86.8	1 062 338	2 520	147 227	88.3	286 841	72.0	28.0	44.8	19.5	2 580	44.8
Faulkner	185	-2.7	144	6.8	54.5	470 804	3 279	52 585	26.3	20 386	38.3	61.7	30.4	2.6	1 254	13.8
Franklin	160	4.6	193	0.6	44.8	439 010	2 277	64 706	158.2	190 806	2.7	97.3	50.5	13.9	542	10.0
Fulton	204	15.3	271	0.0	25.9	434 740	1 601	44 228	27.7	36 819	4.0	96.0	42.0	5.8	1 708	21.9
Garland	36	-9.6	99	0.3	8.4	364 504	3 688	43 119	24.1	66 756	18.6	81.4	24.7	5.3	93	8.9
Grant	65	86.9	252	0.1	10.3	567 051	2 253	61 296	20.9	81 183	2.6	97.4	26.5	6.6	55	9.7
Greene	260	-2.6	366	166.0	216.6	1 251 740	3 418	167 745	177.3	249 404	94.3	5.7	37.1	18.3	8 391	53.4
Hempstead	196	-6.7	263	D	48.9	537 639	2 047	76 608	198.5	265 362	2.3	97.7	52.1	19.5	814	24.5
Hot Spring	69	-4.7	128	0.1	19.3	329 142	2 567	48 366	23.9	44 675	4.8	95.2	30.2	3.9	202	13.1
Howard	147	32.6	266	0.5	23.2	627 100	2 357	72 839	179.1	324 422	0.8	99.2	60.3	31.5	99	15.0
Independence	248	-0.7	247	32.7	87.2	517 500	2 094	76 524	131.9	131 473	25.7	74.3	44.5	8.5	1 541	17.0
Izard	173	1.3	273	0.3	28.3	481 487	1 766	56 648	49.4	78 044	D	D	41.7	6.2	2 095	30.8
Jackson	307	1.6	703	206.5	271.7	1 768 018	2 516	289 577	186.8	427 545	98.3	1.7	54.0	37.1	12 642	70.9
Jefferson	292	-3.8	657	207.5	257.5	1 905 205	2 900	305 345	215.3	484 831	91.2	8.8	45.0	30.9	10 681	71.2
Johnson	118	11.9	190	1.0	38.7	456 329	2 405	59 563	141.0	226 029	3.1	96.9	48.7	14.6	348	12.2
Lafayette	115	18.1	438	21.7	60.8	886 065	2 022	177 734	127.9	486 259	24.7	75.3	61.2	38.0	1 817	41.4
Lawrence	253	-4.1	452	130.3	179.2	1 208 589	2 673	190 691	149.1	266 798	84.6	15.4	50.4	24.7	7 345	49.0
Lee	261	-13.8	1 185	158.0	245.9	3 313 277	2 796	452 068	171.9	781 227	99.9	0.1	76.4	47.7	6 373	82.7
Lincoln	200	7.4	530	135.0	157.5	1 481 042	2 795	274 745	219.5	582 101	53.6	46.4	54.1	35.5	7 190	55.7
Little River	172	23.2	383	10.0	59.9	643 661	1 681	86 491	76.5	170 781	23.4	76.6	45.1	16.5	833	28.8
Logan	198	23.2	204	0.9	66.8	458 086	2 246	64 342	188.0	193 997	3.4	96.6	49.0	16.4	229	9.8
Lonoke	339	-8.8	442	199.6	274.6	1 228 919	2 781	204 691	223.4	291 236	85.6	14.4	39.5	19.0	12 927	51.4
Madison	269	3.8	216	0.5	57.5	585 871	2 718	63 058	208.2	166 530	1.5	98.5	48.3	14.0	2 670	24.7
Marion	137	4.8	282	D	19.3	567 852	2 014	58 499	39.7	81 788	1.4	98.6	39.8	7.4	1 159	26.6
Miller	164	-6.3	312	5.5	85.3	620 006	1 986	71 606	45.5	86 739	53.8	46.2	39.2	8.4	1 229	18.3
Mississippi	476	3.1	1 371	286.9	462.6	3 905 478	2 849	614 256	314.6	906 764	99.9	0.1	80.7	62.8	9 887	83.3
Monroe	268	10.8	1 167	199.5	248.9	2 804 648	2 404	458 365	194.4	845 100	D	D	64.8	54.3	8 137	84.3
Montgomery	74	1.0	166	0.3	20.8	415 392	2 506	56 347	42.1	93 871	2.1	97.9	40.5	12.0	464	16.7
Nevada	67	2.2	190	0.1	16.1	360 188	1 897	66 954	47.9	136 519	2.4	97.6	45.0	13.7	178	21.7
Newton	114	1.1	176	0.1	17.2	388 836	2 206	44 318	28.7	44 221	3.5	96.5	35.2	2.2	784	29.6
Ouachita	26	-20.0	143	0.0	6.9	318 632	2 228	55 341	16.5	90 467	2.5	97.5	26.4	4.4	113	19.8
Perry	70	-3.2	168	4.7	25.4	409 379	2 438	65 847	33.1	78 955	14.8	85.2	43.7	9.1	602	17.4
Phillips	352	-19.4	1 250	231.9	345.6	3 260 908	2 610	512 504	248.0	879 426	99.9	0.1	77.7	61.3	10 328	87.2
Pike	70	-16.2	202	1.0	14.9	431 405	2 132	65 754	82.3	237 962	0.7	99.3	52.0	22.0	201	21.1
Poinsett	385	13.1	970	310.0	369.8	2 978 222	3 069	481 224	287.4	723 980	99.8	0.2	67.3	57.2	15 715	83.1
Polk	119	-10.9	133	0.4	31.9	352 879	2 651	54 186	117.8	131 885	1.4	98.6	37.0	11.3	185	14.4
Pope	154	0.1	157	6.2	51.3	432 140	2 745	67 052	150.1	153 636	6.9	93.1	39.4	11.3	828	9.7
Prairie	275	-17.1	618	179.1	214.1	1 546 649	2 501	236 348	165.1	370 933	96.7	3.3	43.6	30.6	10 031	76.4
Pulaski	84	-11.4	202	21.5	47.9	692 978	3 438	77 942	40.0	95 851	75.4	24.6	30.5	8.4	1 439	18.9
Randolph	211	-16.6	316	56.9	89.9	636 148	2 015	92 799	79.6	119 318	72.1	27.9	41.1	10.3	3 472	29.4
St. Francis	300	17.5	919	209.3	273.3	2 175 083	2 366	355 064	189.9	582 448	99.5	0.5	60.1	42.0	7 971	72.1
Saline	45	0.1	116	0.4	12.1	408 819	3 519	61 011	4.5	11 645	40.6	59.4	26.7	1.6	55	8.0
Scott	100	4.0	167	0.0	30.1	365 899	2 197	57 341	132.0	219 276	1.0	99.0	54.7	16.3	283	11.0
Searcy	169	-13.4	285	D	25.0	475 546	1 668	49 813	13.0	22 024	7.8	92.2	42.1	3.9	2 000	27.7
Sebastian	119	13.8	154	0.0	35.0	411 097	2 663	53 995	97.4	126 507	2.5	97.5	37.7	11.2	374	6.1
Sevier	129	10.9	238	D	27.4	555 635	2 335	70 293	137.4	253 066	0.6	99.4	46.8	20.1	224	24.9
Sharp	158	-14.0	244	0.1	28.8	444 068	1 818	58 008	75.6	116 607	1.4	98.6	40.7	8.5	1 522	24.1
Stone	135	-5.1	259	0.2	22.1	504 455	1 951	69 801	53.7	102 608	1.6	98.4	44.6	10.7	1 122	32.5
Union	43	12.1	152	0.0	7.8	384 639	2 534	58 164	28.0	99 829	2.0	98.0	26.4	6.4	91	15.0
Van Buren	123	7.5	209	0.3	29.5	519 421	2 481	59 424	19.9	33 981	5.3	94.7	43.3	3.4	648	17.9
Washington	312	-4.7	125	0.6	83.5	512 264	4 111	57 567	443.0	177 068	1.6	98.4	41.4	11.6	1 611	14.1
White	356	-13.5	194	39.4	138.3	498 108	2 571	61 275	100.4	54 669	39.0	61.0	27.0	5.3	4 909	26.6
Woodruff	274	-0.1	1 263	197.0	246.0	3 152 682	2 495	489 051	167.6	772 295	D	D	60.4	48.4	6 684	88.9
Yell	160	-8.5	202	3.1	56.5	458 194	2 271	73 649	196.4	247 331	3.2	96.8	49.5	18.8	1 339	22.9

Table B. States and Counties — Water Use, Wholesale Trade, Retail Trade, and Real Estate

STATE County	Water use, 2010		Wholesale trade,[1] 2012				Retail trade,[2] 2012				Real estate and rental and leasing,[2] 2012			
	Total water withdrawn (mil gal/day)	Gallons withdrawn per person per day	Number of establishments	Number of employees	Sales (mil dol)	Annual payroll (mil dol)	Number of establishments	Number of employees	Sales (mil dol)	Annual payroll (mil dol)	Number of establishments	Number of employees	Receipts (mil dol)	Annual payroll (mil dol)
	133	134	135	136	137	138	139	140	141	142	143	144	145	146
ARKANSAS—Cont'd														
Cleveland	1.4	165	2	D	D	D	12	63	13.4	0.8	1	D	D	D
Columbia	11.3	458	22	D	D	D	103	1 010	197.0	20.1	28	139	20.1	5.4
Conway	29.2	1 371	15	212	150.8	6.7	78	903	287.6	19.8	8	43	5.0	1.7
Craighead	422.7	4 383	131	1 509	1 430.1	68.3	455	6 391	1 680.9	142.6	113	473	79.2	12.8
Crawford	34.7	561	62	775	380.8	29.6	153	1 922	525.4	42.0	40	198	32.4	7.6
Crittenden	219.7	4 317	57	987	1 938.0	42.7	144	2 158	813.3	44.7	38	180	22.0	5.3
Cross	561.7	31 433	17	268	265.7	11.4	70	789	180.8	16.5	19	101	9.5	2.3
Dallas	0.8	99	4	14	6.8	0.5	46	375	71.8	7.7	5	15	3.6	0.3
Desha	484.0	37 207	19	223	389.0	10.3	67	595	153.6	11.0	8	67	3.5	1.1
Drew	37.3	2 013	10	87	147.1	4.5	91	1 000	260.7	20.0	26	102	14.6	2.9
Faulkner	8.8	78	88	818	551.7	35.0	377	5 538	1 435.8	116.8	120	447	111.9	19.5
Franklin	11.1	615	6	14	3.8	0.4	51	450	163.0	11.3	6	12	0.9	0.2
Fulton	84.4	6 894	7	39	9.3	1.0	37	208	59.3	4.1	4	13	0.8	0.1
Garland	17.6	183	79	D	D	D	513	5 877	1 564.0	133.8	133	439	65.0	13.0
Grant	5.3	298	14	D	D	D	46	450	128.9	9.5	8	D	D	D
Greene	367.0	8 719	39	573	1 067.7	23.5	154	1 799	503.5	40.2	31	52	8.1	1.1
Hempstead	4.7	206	14	96	52.0	3.3	79	893	197.6	18.2	16	52	6.4	1.2
Hot Spring	125.0	3 797	11	D	D	D	89	903	254.2	19.9	16	44	4.1	1.0
Howard	4.4	321	11	63	34.2	3.1	66	619	162.5	13.4	11	23	2.2	0.3
Independence	156.7	4 276	26	D	D	D	164	1 703	441.1	37.3	23	88	10.8	2.3
Izard	4.6	339	5	D	D	D	50	401	108.7	8.2	6	50	5.6	0.7
Jackson	442.0	24 559	16	148	106.9	7.2	66	681	177.7	15.8	14	29	3.2	0.5
Jefferson	350.6	4 528	57	463	443.9	20.2	291	3 447	843.9	77.9	63	221	38.6	6.3
Johnson	5.6	218	5	D	D	D	72	903	237.3	19.6	18	32	5.1	0.8
Lafayette	25.1	3 286	NA	NA	NA	NA	21	142	30.5	2.3	2	D	D	D
Lawrence	198.5	11 401	18	162	159.1	5.8	58	615	196.3	14.4	10	28	3.0	0.6
Lee	307.0	29 451	9	109	123.5	4.6	19	166	43.8	3.7	10	28	4.6	0.8
Lincoln	224.2	15 862	6	D	D	D	26	209	57.5	3.7	6	D	D	D
Little River	105.2	7 986	4	D	D	D	39	383	104.2	8.7	2	D	D	D
Logan	4.2	187	8	43	7.4	0.7	66	658	152.8	13.9	11	18	1.7	0.4
Lonoke	489.5	7 161	36	291	217.9	12.2	171	2 265	613.4	49.6	49	127	16.7	3.9
Madison	1.8	113	3	D	D	D	32	402	130.2	9.5	6	11	1.2	0.2
Marion	2.0	122	8	18	16.5	0.8	36	444	94.8	8.7	11	13	1.6	0.3
Miller	15.5	357	38	579	308.2	31.3	125	1 393	435.7	30.7	27	D	D	D
Mississippi	381.2	8 201	48	D	D	D	166	1 748	437.8	40.1	36	137	30.5	3.3
Monroe	297.5	36 509	14	201	126.2	9.0	39	311	90.6	6.9	4	10	0.8	0.2
Montgomery	1.0	105	4	D	D	D	18	119	28.8	3.0	8	30	1.5	0.4
Nevada	1.4	150	5	15	8.6	0.4	25	277	159.1	5.3	5	11	0.6	0.2
Newton	1.4	163	3	D	D	D	17	86	17.0	1.5	1	D	D	D
Ouachita	43.4	1 663	22	D	D	D	108	1 104	222.0	21.2	21	D	D	D
Perry	2.0	193	2	D	D	D	18	153	30.5	2.5	2	D	D	D
Phillips	266.7	12 256	33	328	594.1	14.3	85	956	223.2	21.6	17	50	5.6	0.9
Pike	1.8	163	12	146	89.8	3.3	43	331	70.0	6.3	4	85	6.8	3.1
Poinsett	937.3	38 126	22	390	424.6	25.8	69	751	178.0	13.6	11	36	4.0	1.1
Polk	4.0	191	15	D	D	D	83	966	193.5	17.5	13	130	10.5	3.1
Pope	987.2	15 985	67	469	322.4	19.3	272	3 180	869.4	67.4	69	191	29.7	5.7
Prairie	334.2	38 344	8	65	67.2	2.9	33	206	54.3	3.3	3	D	D	D
Pulaski	82.1	215	659	11 024	8 414.5	576.5	1 715	25 070	7 234.4	622.7	592	3 397	606.5	119.4
Randolph	156.2	8 692	11	83	33.8	2.1	59	600	170.7	13.5	16	32	2.6	0.6
St. Francis	363.1	12 848	22	D	D	D	113	1 104	316.2	22.0	26	63	7.1	1.1
Saline	31.9	298	69	723	351.3	30.3	278	3 995	1 404.8	100.1	65	119	24.2	3.3
Scott	1.9	170	6	D	D	D	22	293	50.4	6.1	4	12	1.1	0.3
Searcy	1.8	221	2	D	D	D	34	265	49.8	4.7	5	D	D	D
Sebastian	3.7	30	194	2 362	1 713.4	105.7	574	7 899	1 944.5	174.1	170	888	133.9	28.2
Sevier	4.6	268	5	49	19.4	2.5	67	673	190.5	14.0	7	22	3.1	0.6
Sharp	3.5	203	6	D	D	D	58	650	152.6	12.1	10	20	1.7	0.5
Stone	2.8	225	7	59	34.1	1.2	46	526	107.5	12.1	6	6	0.6	0.1
Union	20.4	490	50	D	D	D	208	2 152	511.1	46.8	39	210	37.4	8.6
Van Buren	4.4	252	10	38	35.6	1.3	57	546	168.4	12.3	6	7	0.9	0.1
Washington	3.1	15	234	2 487	1 740.0	118.1	765	11 098	2 925.8	254.6	239	2 359	191.1	64.1
White	88.0	1 142	61	575	432.9	27.9	294	3 358	911.7	72.6	65	183	29.6	5.7
Woodruff	246.3	33 928	15	157	118.1	7.7	27	240	74.2	5.3	6	7	0.8	0.1
Yell	4.1	186	10	86	15.2	2.5	55	488	121.4	9.6	10	19	1.7	0.4

1. Merchant wholesalers, except manufacturers' sales branches and offices.   2. Employer establishments.

Table B. States and Counties — Professional Services, Manufacturing, and Accommodation and Food Services

STATE County	Professional, scientific, and technical services, 2012				Manufacturing, 2012				Accommodation and food services, 2012			
	Number of establish-ments	Number of employees	Receipts (mil dol)	Annual payroll (mil dol)	Number of establish-ments	Number of employees	Receipts (mil dol)	Annual payroll (mil dol)	Number of establish-ments	Number of employees	Sales (mil dol)	Annual payroll (mil dol)
	147	148	149	150	151	152	153	154	155	156	157	158
ARKANSAS—Cont'd												
Cleveland	1	D	D	D	3	72	D	2.0	3	11	0.6	0.1
Columbia	33	218	22.7	8.0	32	2 118	602.8	97.6	41	674	30.8	6.9
Conway	31	86	8.6	2.8	24	904	384.4	45.9	25	333	13.9	3.6
Craighead	173	876	125.8	46.0	99	5 254	2 101.7	221.2	212	D	D	D
Crawford	87	283	27.6	8.3	63	4 126	1 207.8	127.1	82	1 502	64.8	18.1
Crittenden	55	264	23.5	8.4	40	1 484	849.0	60.9	89	1 565	82.8	19.8
Cross	24	70	5.4	1.8	10	588	238.8	17.3	24	322	14.3	3.5
Dallas	6	16	1.2	0.3	7	504	194.2	18.4	8	121	4.7	1.2
Desha	21	51	11.6	1.6	10	724	407.0	34.9	34	305	12.9	3.4
Drew	26	108	11.7	4.3	20	550	D	23.1	36	D	D	D
Faulkner	223	D	D	D	89	3 707	1 203.0	175.9	212	4 745	198.7	53.7
Franklin	19	94	7.0	2.0	19	1 049	D	36.1	23	255	11.3	3.0
Fulton	10	36	2.8	1.1	12	137	10.7	3.3	17	149	5.7	1.7
Garland	217	1 160	91.1	40.4	90	2 180	476.9	95.1	274	5 162	218.0	63.4
Grant	18	81	21.6	3.6	13	1 180	603.2	D	19	D	D	D
Greene	52	430	39.4	18.8	53	4 743	1 840.7	189.6	64	1 114	49.1	13.3
Hempstead	14	70	4.9	2.1	26	2 086	786.9	71.0	32	483	22.7	5.8
Hot Spring	29	93	6.6	2.1	34	1 409	728.0	61.1	34	476	21.5	5.3
Howard	14	36	2.8	1.0	19	3 455	1 022.9	93.8	19	D	D	D
Independence	59	223	20.7	6.2	34	3 891	1 211.4	137.6	66	1 173	48.8	12.2
Izard	7	22	2.7	1.0	6	215	D	8.2	13	D	D	D
Jackson	23	85	7.0	2.9	20	989	425.0	42.9	28	308	14.9	3.5
Jefferson	79	577	65.1	27.8	61	5 118	2 113.6	225.4	120	D	D	D
Johnson	29	87	9.3	2.9	32	2 791	657.3	77.5	35	439	20.4	5.3
Lafayette	5	12	1.3	0.3	5	42	D	1.4	5	55	3.1	0.7
Lawrence	14	40	4.9	1.0	20	328	73.2	10.8	19	242	9.2	2.3
Lee	10	33	3.0	0.9	3	14	5.2	0.8	6	56	3.1	0.7
Lincoln	7	D	D	D	6	343	D	16.1	11	D	D	D
Little River	9	54	6.5	1.7	14	1 239	D	87.5	11	D	D	D
Logan	31	71	9.7	2.7	16	1 138	D	52.3	26	242	9.3	2.5
Lonoke	88	313	31.8	9.7	32	D	628.5	59.1	91	1 369	60.0	15.9
Madison	15	39	2.7	1.0	22	1 066	D	32.2	13	182	7.4	1.9
Marion	17	45	3.7	1.4	16	1 539	244.8	42.5	30	166	8.5	1.9
Miller	43	226	25.7	7.8	29	2 331	D	142.1	75	D	D	D
Mississippi	40	135	10.7	3.7	46	5 306	5 231.1	340.9	77	1 178	51.5	12.4
Monroe	9	22	1.2	0.5	6	132	48.5	4.7	18	246	9.9	2.6
Montgomery	6	10	0.8	0.3	8	143	D	3.4	17	204	23.2	5.7
Nevada	7	41	1.8	0.9	7	D	D	D	7	D	D	D
Newton	4	D	D	D	9	32	5.3	1.3	11	500	19.1	5.1
Ouachita	24	D	D	D	32	2 566	D	128.1	31	D	D	D
Perry	8	D	D	D	NA	NA	NA	NA	8	D	D	D
Phillips	26	68	9.4	2.1	12	D	D	D	22	345	13.6	3.2
Pike	4	37	1.4	0.5	14	192	39.5	6.1	14	189	7.0	1.8
Poinsett	15	40	3.3	1.0	21	656	224.0	24.2	36	D	D	D
Polk	27	83	5.4	2.1	32	1 195	D	40.0	39	499	18.1	5.2
Pope	145	468	50.0	15.3	60	4 626	1 506.7	164.4	115	D	D	D
Prairie	8	30	2.9	0.8	NA	NA	NA	NA	12	84	4.0	0.7
Pulaski	1 529	10 113	1 616.1	552.9	327	13 328	6 515.9	655.6	985	19 810	961.9	281.2
Randolph	23	71	7.2	2.5	27	594	115.0	16.4	23	329	14.7	3.5
St. Francis	31	120	18.9	4.0	6	754	D	21.1	39	590	27.8	6.9
Saline	146	558	77.6	22.2	77	1 403	D	58.4	146	2 825	128.3	33.0
Scott	9	12	1.2	0.3	14	1 193	297.8	32.5	12	130	4.7	1.6
Searcy	8	28	1.4	0.3	11	96	D	2.8	9	D	D	D
Sebastian	320	1 452	244.6	61.5	183	13 713	5 156.5	560.3	270	5 467	242.1	70.0
Sevier	14	46	3.4	1.0	6	D	D	D	24	251	10.3	2.6
Sharp	17	41	2.7	0.8	13	77	D	2.3	32	288	13.1	3.4
Stone	13	43	2.7	0.9	14	88	10.5	2.8	34	395	14.8	4.1
Union	68	250	28.6	9.5	45	2 961	4 719.2	161.3	74	970	45.4	11.6
Van Buren	16	45	4.6	1.6	10	44	D	1.8	23	371	15.8	4.1
Washington	579	3 044	345.7	137.8	204	12 207	3 487.0	440.2	503	9 220	399.4	113.7
White	109	515	45.5	16.9	60	2 300	1 031.0	98.1	133	2 543	113.6	27.8
Woodruff	10	12	1.5	0.4	7	342	D	9.2	8	D	D	D
Yell	19	54	3.5	1.2	18	1 962	571.0	55.5	20	D	D	D

1. Establishment subject to federal tax.

Table B. States and Counties — Health Care and Social Assistance, Other Services, Nonemployer Businesses, and Residential Construction

STATE County	Health care and social assistance, 2012				Other services, 2012				Nonemployer businesses, 2014		Value of residential construction authorized by building permits, 2015	
	Number of establishments	Number of employees	Receipts (mil dol)	Annual payroll (mil dol)	Number of establishments	Number of employees	Receipts (mil dol)	Annual payroll (mil dol)	Number	Receipts (mil dol)	New Construction ($1,000)	Number of housing units
	159	160	161	162	163	164	165	166	167	168	169	170
ARKANSAS—Cont'd												
Cleveland	6	120	3.6	2.7	6	D	D	D	395	15.1	0	0
Columbia	77	1 212	77.7	32.7	44	178	11.9	3.4	1 243	51.8	0	0
Conway	46	649	31.4	16.2	22	78	11.1	2.4	1 331	53.2	1 455	16
Craighead	359	8 701	921.0	362.1	125	805	83.9	23.2	7 333	350.2	63 257	470
Crawford	97	1 665	140.4	59.4	65	327	32.3	8.7	3 707	144.6	9 796	76
Crittenden	117	2 181	170.6	69.4	59	379	33.3	8.9	3 640	124.1	9 055	58
Cross	46	810	42.0	21.0	19	D	D	D	1 413	55.6	2 807	14
Dallas	24	785	34.3	15.0	14	43	3.4	1.0	376	14.2	227	3
Desha	28	589	43.5	18.4	14	34	2.9	0.7	742	32.8	475	2
Drew	46	1 054	72.6	30.5	20	53	5.6	1.2	1 036	47.8	1 661	17
Faulkner	291	5 108	450.6	173.8	157	783	69.2	16.7	7 948	315.7	41 033	206
Franklin	32	623	47.9	19.3	14	40	3.8	1.0	1 028	39.5	220	1
Fulton	29	561	38.8	14.7	9	D	D	D	805	29.8	0	0
Garland	319	7 374	717.5	275.4	161	766	53.3	16.2	7 836	319.5	9 869	59
Grant	22	D	D	D	20	D	D	D	1 165	45.2	1 338	11
Greene	96	1 558	140.5	50.2	42	175	14.5	3.9	2 815	135.5	14 727	148
Hempstead	51	1 119	62.9	27.6	34	133	17.9	4.5	1 057	38.0	5 281	50
Hot Spring	46	1 334	85.6	38.7	23	D	D	D	1 781	70.9	0	0
Howard	33	D	D	D	25	86	9.4	2.3	729	36.1	145	2
Independence	98	3 010	282.1	111.5	53	276	17.8	6.0	2 490	102.8	5 185	38
Izard	28	593	32.7	15.4	11	34	3.1	0.7	851	32.8	573	2
Jackson	52	825	76.1	29.6	18	63	4.8	1.3	831	32.2	648	6
Jefferson	215	4 384	399.6	161.6	84	D	D	D	3 812	123.7	3 726	31
Johnson	40	996	65.7	28.5	28	112	5.6	2.5	1 396	52.1	4 910	55
Lafayette	9	177	8.1	4.3	4	30	2.0	0.7	337	11.1	0	0
Lawrence	32	623	40.4	19.8	15	D	D	D	1 158	49.0	2 167	12
Lee	17	323	31.4	11.0	6	18	1.0	0.3	659	27.3	0	0
Lincoln	16	323	26.6	9.4	15	D	D	D	551	22.1	0	0
Little River	14	D	D	D	13	36	3.6	0.9	582	24.3	410	5
Logan	43	613	44.4	17.4	23	81	6.6	1.9	1 242	43.1	340	4
Lonoke	98	1 274	78.5	32.0	62	235	18.1	5.6	4 329	182.3	30 264	339
Madison	18	279	13.5	6.0	15	D	D	D	1 218	43.7	193	1
Marion	18	D	D	D	15	39	3.9	0.6	1 159	35.9	7 116	50
Miller	67	D	D	D	45	238	20.1	5.6	2 504	109.4	5 817	43
Mississippi	125	1 895	131.4	53.5	43	190	15.8	4.4	2 090	75.2	5 189	50
Monroe	20	313	18.0	7.5	12	D	D	D	501	25.0	158	2
Montgomery	11	D	D	D	8	25	1.5	0.4	754	28.2	NA	NA
Nevada	15	443	19.8	9.7	9	41	2.9	0.7	453	17.2	0	0
Newton	13	216	7.8	3.8	3	D	D	D	648	23.1	0	0
Ouachita	62	D	D	D	30	D	D	D	1 300	47.0	892	4
Perry	13	D	D	D	5	D	D	D	685	27.8	68	2
Phillips	64	1 045	73.4	30.4	29	100	10.8	3.0	1 465	48.9	887	40
Pike	13	296	14.5	6.6	9	18	2.0	0.5	875	38.5	NA	NA
Poinsett	46	648	37.7	16.3	26	D	D	D	1 441	54.5	1 025	12
Polk	46	983	67.9	28.5	31	104	6.1	1.6	1 486	56.5	115	2
Pope	165	3 073	218.2	80.0	91	513	35.0	11.5	3 722	136.8	8 075	85
Prairie	11	D	D	D	10	27	2.0	0.5	471	20.5	639	4
Pulaski	1 446	41 716	5 078.9	2 013.0	807	6 109	823.4	190.7	28 279	1 314.1	180 707	1 234
Randolph	46	867	57.9	25.9	19	D	D	D	1 243	51.8	4 013	39
St. Francis	58	1 106	82.6	35.6	20	130	9.5	4.5	1 778	60.3	0	0
Saline	197	4 120	277.2	129.7	127	D	D	D	7 858	323.3	75 995	907
Scott	16	239	15.2	8.0	11	46	2.3	1.7	625	22.6	228	2
Searcy	14	D	D	D	2	D	D	D	790	30.2	200	1
Sebastian	410	11 295	1 192.7	466.3	203	963	80.5	22.8	8 488	461.8	49 951	254
Sevier	31	506	42.7	14.6	24	D	D	D	771	33.0	250	5
Sharp	46	540	29.7	13.4	22	108	7.5	1.8	1 246	45.1	75	1
Stone	23	509	31.9	15.1	15	D	D	D	1 196	44.3	599	7
Union	127	2 169	213.7	80.2	81	387	51.6	12.0	2 763	118.6	5 418	83
Van Buren	36	731	44.0	18.0	19	D	D	D	1 286	43.9	1 320	5
Washington	568	14 228	1 525.8	614.1	308	1 955	320.9	52.9	15 208	682.6	279 077	1 399
White	164	4 429	360.8	146.6	98	514	45.4	14.1	5 353	217.2	10 395	82
Woodruff	15	D	D	D	6	D	D	D	402	17.7	40	1
Yell	42	934	52.6	24.9	13	55	4.6	1.1	1 153	41.3	2 570	55

Table B. States and Counties — Government Employment and Payroll, and Local Government Finances

	Government employment and payroll, 2012									Local government finances, 2012				
			March payroll (percent of total)							General revenue				
													Taxes	
														Per capita[1] (dollars)
STATE County	Full-time equivalent employees	March payroll (dollars)	Administration, judicial, and legal	Police and Corrections	Fire Protection	Highways and transportation	Health and Welfare	Natural resources and utilities	Education and libraries	Total (mil dol)	Inter-governmental (mil dol)	Total (mil dol)	Total	Property
	171	172	173	174	175	176	177	178	179	180	181	182	183	184
ARKANSAS—Cont'd														
Cleveland	330	806 962	9.0	5.0	0.0	5.3	0.7	2.9	76.0	20.0	15.3	2.4	280	186
Columbia	810	2 122 431	5.9	8.7	1.9	4.1	0.6	7.5	70.9	84.2	34.7	16.8	686	216
Conway	751	2 035 580	5.2	11.1	0.6	3.9	0.8	8.1	70.0	72.1	44.8	15.9	748	377
Craighead	3 565	10 924 637	4.8	9.2	2.9	3.7	1.2	10.0	67.7	285.0	164.7	77.8	780	344
Crawford	2 079	8 936 720	9.1	2.8	0.0	1.4	5.5	24.0	57.1	156.8	108.4	28.6	461	213
Crittenden	2 243	7 239 687	5.6	10.1	4.1	1.8	1.6	6.1	67.6	182.3	109.3	39.6	792	258
Cross	603	1 548 890	10.4	9.4	1.4	3.4	1.1	2.8	71.5	51.1	33.6	9.9	562	280
Dallas	261	612 066	9.1	13.5	0.3	5.1	2.7	7.1	61.9	19.8	11.6	4.3	544	186
Desha	795	2 143 489	5.0	5.6	0.5	2.7	22.4	3.6	59.5	57.2	28.7	12.9	1 031	405
Drew	969	2 684 507	3.1	4.7	1.1	2.3	30.7	2.1	55.8	79.4	41.6	12.6	671	211
Faulkner	3 393	11 696 206	5.6	8.1	3.7	2.3	1.7	2.7	75.5	324.2	171.2	77.9	656	297
Franklin	616	1 780 777	6.6	4.8	0.5	3.5	2.3	1.9	77.8	48.5	35.0	9.5	525	268
Fulton	446	1 158 320	4.4	3.4	0.7	4.9	23.0	2.8	60.2	31.9	18.9	3.9	319	163
Garland	2 929	9 379 603	4.7	8.8	4.0	3.5	3.4	5.5	68.3	270.5	155.0	62.1	640	262
Grant	736	2 167 090	4.0	5.7	0.2	2.7	0.5	2.6	83.3	54.6	40.7	8.6	480	234
Greene	1 593	4 613 388	4.1	5.9	2.2	3.0	2.1	8.3	68.5	112.0	67.4	19.6	455	189
Hempstead	991	2 866 901	6.3	9.8	1.5	3.8	2.3	7.5	64.3	63.0	40.8	14.1	629	190
Hot Spring	1 020	3 135 235	4.3	4.3	1.6	3.0	1.9	5.9	78.5	75.0	50.6	15.7	471	242
Howard	721	2 467 138	7.2	17.5	1.7	5.0	3.5	21.0	42.7	46.1	28.6	9.7	704	226
Independence	1 442	3 864 054	4.6	7.4	0.9	3.5	2.2	8.2	72.6	113.1	69.9	22.7	614	314
Izard	479	1 132 741	7.6	7.8	0.2	5.9	1.2	5.3	71.6	32.9	23.1	5.4	399	259
Jackson	623	1 641 667	7.2	8.7	4.1	4.3	2.8	5.1	65.5	43.2	27.4	9.3	528	229
Jefferson	2 803	8 103 678	6.2	13.3	4.7	3.4	1.8	1.9	66.2	217.6	136.9	51.2	686	285
Johnson	832	2 711 188	3.4	5.5	0.7	2.3	0.4	12.2	75.6	63.8	42.9	12.1	466	209
Lafayette	324	1 024 900	6.7	6.5	0.5	5.3	1.6	2.4	77.1	19.1	12.6	3.8	516	258
Lawrence	1 057	2 598 077	3.2	3.6	0.8	2.1	33.0	2.4	54.7	79.8	45.0	7.8	459	210
Lee	422	1 112 758	5.2	7.2	1.9	5.4	2.5	8.4	68.7	24.4	17.7	4.1	401	201
Lincoln	362	919 481	6.2	5.9	0.1	3.6	0.2	2.7	80.4	24.4	16.8	4.2	297	152
Little River	689	1 796 446	3.9	4.0	0.1	2.7	34.8	3.7	50.8	44.7	19.0	7.9	615	273
Logan	771	2 027 835	5.6	7.0	0.2	4.0	2.6	4.4	76.0	49.8	33.4	9.6	437	237
Lonoke	2 693	7 148 935	4.2	6.7	2.0	2.1	0.5	4.6	79.3	189.2	129.4	38.9	558	260
Madison	571	1 449 917	5.1	4.6	0.0	6.7	5.3	2.7	75.2	31.5	20.9	6.6	420	180
Marion	420	1 177 227	8.0	10.7	0.3	8.0	1.6	5.5	65.4	26.6	17.6	6.1	370	207
Miller	1 370	3 792 335	7.1	17.4	7.1	4.8	0.8	2.2	58.3	120.6	70.4	29.4	674	250
Mississippi	2 048	5 872 177	5.4	9.7	2.9	3.6	2.1	9.0	65.1	191.6	104.8	32.2	707	241
Monroe	360	1 055 919	8.0	11.9	0.8	5.2	0.9	10.4	61.7	25.7	17.8	4.5	571	283
Montgomery	294	752 749	7.1	6.2	0.0	6.4	2.9	4.0	72.7	19.1	14.5	3.0	317	201
Nevada	405	978 364	8.6	11.3	0.0	8.2	3.9	6.8	59.4	20.3	14.7	3.3	374	180
Newton	434	1 232 173	2.8	2.8	0.0	2.9	1.0	1.0	89.0	59.7	55.7	2.4	298	215
Ouachita	1 097	3 081 016	5.9	8.9	2.9	5.3	2.7	5.6	68.4	75.4	51.1	15.8	623	202
Perry	344	973 732	8.1	7.6	0.0	4.4	0.3	3.1	72.6	20.7	15.2	3.5	334	164
Phillips	872	2 319 840	6.4	8.7	2.9	4.6	0.0	7.6	68.3	70.5	48.6	14.3	689	239
Pike	507	1 198 447	2.9	2.6	0.0	2.3	0.6	3.0	88.0	32.5	23.2	6.0	533	207
Poinsett	959	2 599 342	5.4	11.1	1.0	3.7	0.5	5.4	72.6	69.5	51.1	10.0	411	173
Polk	1 139	3 233 326	3.5	4.4	0.5	3.3	0.1	3.1	84.0	84.7	45.1	10.6	516	173
Pope	2 245	7 108 185	4.8	9.2	3.2	2.4	3.2	4.5	71.3	165.6	100.1	42.3	674	270
Prairie	351	1 159 649	15.7	11.7	0.5	12.8	1.1	5.2	52.5	20.8	12.8	4.0	470	235
Pulaski	15 078	52 069 152	6.0	12.7	6.6	4.5	3.5	11.7	52.8	1 476.7	724.3	418.1	1 075	551
Randolph	552	1 387 909	7.5	7.1	2.0	4.5	1.7	6.7	68.7	37.2	24.0	9.9	551	358
St. Francis	1 036	3 954 323	5.7	6.9	1.6	2.0	2.7	7.1	73.4	75.8	52.5	14.7	527	164
Saline	2 671	8 478 497	6.2	7.9	4.2	2.4	0.6	6.1	71.0	238.1	147.9	54.6	489	267
Scott	364	909 428	4.1	3.6	0.0	5.1	1.8	4.7	79.2	25.0	18.3	4.3	391	127
Searcy	296	714 402	4.4	5.2	0.0	5.9	1.5	2.7	80.0	16.3	12.2	2.5	308	178
Sebastian	4 285	15 121 933	5.9	9.8	4.3	4.0	2.6	7.8	65.5	399.0	208.5	123.0	966	364
Sevier	764	2 036 880	4.0	5.6	0.4	2.6	1.5	12.6	72.8	59.3	43.9	8.4	490	157
Sharp	745	1 804 388	5.9	6.5	3.5	5.1	0.2	6.1	71.2	44.2	31.2	7.0	408	175
Stone	424	1 109 650	6.3	5.7	0.0	5.5	1.2	9.6	70.0	26.1	18.0	5.4	423	148
Union	1 719	4 970 357	4.4	7.3	3.6	3.5	2.6	4.4	72.2	125.7	71.2	35.1	859	292
Van Buren	757	1 902 959	7.4	21.6	1.0	6.7	1.1	2.5	58.5	49.1	26.5	14.0	822	502
Washington	7 560	23 284 035	5.1	10.7	3.9	4.1	1.3	4.1	69.5	691.8	396.1	183.9	870	333
White	2 609	7 296 125	4.8	6.2	2.5	2.4	2.0	5.5	75.7	192.0	122.5	42.8	545	227
Woodruff	367	874 741	9.7	5.0	0.3	4.3	1.5	8.7	68.2	25.9	19.0	3.7	521	309
Yell	877	2 241 720	3.8	7.4	0.3	4.0	0.5	4.0	79.4	58.7	42.0	10.7	489	268

1. Based on the resident population estimated as of July 1 of the year shown.

Table B. States and Counties — Local Government Finances, Government Employment, and Voting

STATE County	Local government finances, 2012 (cont.) Direct general expenditure							Debt outstanding		Government employment, 2014			Presidential election,[2] 2012 Percent of vote cast:		
	Total (mil dol)	Per capita[1] (dollars)	Education	Health and hospitals	Police protection	Public welfare	Highways	Total (mil dol)	Per capita[1] (dollars)	Federal civilian	Federal military	State and local	Democratic	Republican	All other
	185	186	187	188	189	190	191	192	193	194	195	196	197	198	199
ARKANSAS—Cont'd															
Cleveland	19.8	2 299	72.2	0.7	3.3	0.2	9.2	7.9	916	13	38	354	26.0	69.9	4.1
Columbia	85.3	3 484	43.3	28.4	3.6	0.1	3.9	107.4	4 388	42	100	1 951	37.2	61.3	1.5
Conway	70.4	3 308	65.7	1.5	5.0	0.2	8.3	39.8	1 868	56	94	1 464	38.7	57.6	3.7
Craighead	279.3	2 800	56.9	0.3	5.7	0.1	5.4	482.8	4 841	314	448	7 663	36.5	61.0	2.6
Crawford	160.3	2 588	67.2	0.0	5.0	0.0	7.4	203.0	3 277	96	275	2 101	25.5	71.5	3.0
Crittenden	177.1	3 540	57.7	0.2	7.9	0.0	4.9	305.8	6 114	92	220	2 737	56.6	41.9	1.5
Cross	50.3	2 847	65.6	4.4	4.9	0.2	5.5	15.3	867	55	76	1 092	36.2	61.6	2.2
Dallas	18.2	2 276	53.5	0.2	7.1	0.0	9.3	15.1	1 887	20	33	385	44.3	53.0	2.7
Desha	54.8	4 365	49.1	21.1	6.0	0.1	3.4	43.6	3 478	60	55	926	54.9	42.7	2.4
Drew	81.1	4 329	53.9	22.7	3.7	0.2	6.4	39.5	2 108	57	80	2 017	39.3	58.4	2.3
Faulkner	340.2	2 866	58.3	0.1	4.3	0.0	5.9	686.1	5 780	197	534	7 576	36.3	61.6	2.1
Franklin	46.2	2 558	73.0	3.3	3.8	0.3	6.5	43.4	2 406	152	78	865	28.9	68.1	3.0
Fulton	30.6	2 485	53.3	24.1	3.1	0.1	8.4	14.3	1 159	26	54	636	38.9	57.8	3.3
Garland	268.9	2 775	57.5	0.3	5.6	0.0	3.6	344.1	3 551	490	429	4 128	36.4	61.4	2.3
Grant	54.3	3 022	74.8	0.6	4.5	0.1	4.4	31.4	1 747	28	81	817	23.0	73.9	3.1
Greene	119.5	2 769	59.8	0.2	3.6	0.1	4.4	136.1	3 152	88	194	2 027	33.4	63.0	3.6
Hempstead	64.4	2 877	60.7	0.2	4.3	0.1	5.2	53.7	2 402	80	99	1 702	39.0	58.1	2.8
Hot Spring	76.2	2 283	72.0	1.7	3.4	0.1	4.0	94.3	2 823	64	140	1 972	35.9	60.3	3.8
Howard	46.0	3 350	63.9	0.8	4.9	0.1	4.2	74.9	5 451	58	60	849	36.0	61.0	3.0
Independence	118.5	3 202	52.8	0.2	3.5	0.1	6.2	274.1	7 403	115	162	2 210	30.0	67.1	2.9
Izard	33.6	2 497	65.3	1.3	4.8	0.2	6.9	26.2	1 942	27	56	1 045	34.3	61.2	4.5
Jackson	41.6	2 363	54.0	1.4	7.4	0.1	6.9	23.9	1 457	42	69	1 478	39.5	55.9	4.6
Jefferson	217.7	2 914	59.7	0.1	7.5	0.1	4.0	226.1	3 025	1 522	327	6 831	62.2	35.9	1.9
Johnson	65.1	2 514	63.3	0.2	4.4	0.0	7.2	48.8	1 883	90	114	1 115	37.1	60.2	2.7
Lafayette	20.9	2 805	68.4	0.2	6.4	0.1	6.3	10.0	1 344	23	31	326	39.0	58.1	2.9
Lawrence	75.1	4 412	56.5	22.2	3.3	4.3	3.1	40.2	2 361	56	73	1 208	36.7	57.6	5.7
Lee	21.6	2 110	53.3	0.4	9.2	0.2	10.8	5.6	551	39	37	763	60.1	38.6	1.2
Lincoln	25.2	1 788	68.0	0.1	4.2	0.0	7.9	12.9	913	21	46	1 323	38.8	57.0	4.2
Little River	45.4	3 511	41.4	20.9	4.1	6.7	4.1	77.9	6 027	45	56	839	34.0	63.0	3.0
Logan	50.5	2 295	64.1	5.2	5.3	0.1	5.4	41.6	1 893	100	96	1 385	28.9	67.7	3.4
Lonoke	184.1	2 636	69.9	0.2	4.3	0.0	2.8	172.0	2 463	108	319	2 725	25.1	72.6	2.2
Madison	31.6	2 021	66.4	3.3	5.6	0.0	11.6	24.7	1 576	42	70	567	33.9	62.8	3.4
Marion	28.0	1 688	60.5	0.2	8.4	0.2	11.9	19.4	1 172	31	73	555	33.3	63.2	3.5
Miller	112.1	2 568	56.8	0.3	9.6	0.0	4.3	109.3	2 504	62	189	2 059	32.3	65.8	1.9
Mississippi	189.3	4 154	49.4	0.5	5.1	0.1	2.9	796.0	17 471	103	195	2 815	47.6	49.8	2.6
Monroe	25.5	3 252	52.9	1.3	5.1	0.2	10.3	10.9	1 390	26	34	440	46.8	50.9	2.3
Montgomery	18.0	1 926	60.2	0.1	3.4	0.0	10.6	13.6	1 457	55	40	503	30.1	65.3	4.6
Nevada	20.5	2 300	61.8	0.3	6.5	0.2	8.5	12.4	1 394	26	39	454	40.6	56.7	2.7
Newton	30.3	3 746	81.8	0.1	1.5	0.1	7.3	72.1	8 919	54	35	468	29.8	65.4	4.8
Ouachita	71.1	2 801	66.5	0.1	4.9	0.0	5.4	60.6	2 386	92	110	1 924	43.6	54.5	1.9
Perry	19.2	1 861	72.5	0.1	5.9	0.3	7.5	14.0	1 359	20	45	407	31.6	64.1	4.3
Phillips	71.5	3 442	65.5	0.1	5.3	0.1	3.5	34.7	1 670	64	89	1 490	63.5	34.5	2.0
Pike	30.8	2 738	73.7	0.4	3.3	0.2	7.6	17.3	1 541	61	49	590	27.5	68.8	3.8
Poinsett	65.0	2 676	70.6	0.2	6.9	0.1	4.4	35.9	1 479	63	107	1 160	34.6	61.8	3.6
Polk	82.4	4 025	54.6	28.8	2.5	0.0	3.6	60.1	2 937	87	90	1 088	25.5	71.3	3.3
Pope	163.1	2 599	67.0	1.6	6.5	0.1	6.0	190.1	3 029	258	269	4 274	27.2	70.5	2.3
Prairie	19.8	2 343	62.2	2.0	6.4	0.0	9.5	17.3	2 050	40	37	337	31.0	65.7	3.3
Pulaski	1 448.1	3 723	46.0	4.2	6.9	0.0	3.8	1 780.8	4 578	9 112	6 733	45 044	55.1	43.5	1.4
Randolph	35.5	1 979	57.5	0.0	7.8	0.0	9.3	8.9	498	30	77	1 167	39.1	57.2	3.7
St. Francis	73.2	2 628	65.4	0.5	5.9	0.1	4.9	21.2	759	663	103	1 535	57.7	41.2	1.1
Saline	246.7	2 206	68.6	0.3	4.4	0.0	5.3	376.7	3 368	76	514	4 647	28.4	69.4	2.2
Scott	25.5	2 315	68.6	0.5	4.5	0.0	7.8	31.9	2 901	72	48	601	26.4	69.9	3.8
Searcy	16.1	2 010	62.9	0.2	4.8	0.2	10.4	2.8	353	42	35	443	25.0	70.9	4.2
Sebastian	398.6	3 131	51.6	0.2	5.7	0.1	6.2	717.8	5 639	939	599	6 669	31.6	66.3	2.1
Sevier	59.7	3 477	77.9	0.0	3.5	0.1	3.6	19.8	1 151	65	78	1 125	28.2	68.2	3.6
Sharp	43.7	2 563	62.6	0.1	5.0	0.0	10.0	23.8	1 398	45	75	792	33.6	62.5	3.9
Stone	24.5	1 931	63.3	0.1	5.7	0.2	9.7	8.6	681	59	55	561	30.0	66.4	3.6
Union	124.9	3 056	60.5	0.1	5.9	0.0	7.4	143.9	3 521	145	180	2 542	36.0	62.2	1.8
Van Buren	45.8	2 692	53.0	4.9	8.6	0.2	14.4	61.6	3 616	33	75	738	32.1	63.8	4.1
Washington	690.9	3 268	59.8	0.3	5.5	0.0	3.8	886.2	4 192	1 972	975	17 549	42.4	55.5	2.0
White	187.6	2 389	67.8	0.2	5.9	0.1	5.3	228.1	2 907	160	338	3 552	25.0	72.2	2.8
Woodruff	27.6	3 888	46.7	0.3	3.9	20.3	8.1	12.6	1 776	40	31	518	51.1	43.7	5.2
Yell	56.6	2 581	70.7	0.1	6.1	0.0	5.0	53.5	2 439	115	97	1 238	33.2	63.1	3.7

1. Based on the resident population estimated as of July 1 of the year shown.   2. © 2013 Election Data Services, Inc. All rights reserved.

Table B. States and Counties — **Land Area and Population**

STATE/ County code	CBSA code[1]	County type[2]	STATE County	Land area,[3] (sq km) 2010	Total persons 2015	Rank	Per square kilometer	White	Black	American Indian, Alaska Native	Asian and Pacific Islander	Percent Hispanic or Latino[4]	Under 5 years	5 to 17 years	18 to 24 years	25 to 34 years	35 to 44 years	45 to 54 years
				1	2	3	4	5	6	7	8	9	10	11	12	13	14	15
06 000	...	X	CALIFORNIA	403 466	39 144 818	X	97.0	40.7	6.5	1.0	16.0	38.6	6.5	17.1	10.3	14.8	13.3	13.5
06 001	41860	1	Alameda	1 914	1 638 215	21	855.9	36.1	12.5	0.9	32.2	22.6	6.1	15.3	9.2	15.9	14.8	14.1
06 003	...	8	Alpine	1 912	1 110	3 104	0.6	67.6	1.3	22.7	2.3	9.7	3.3	16.7	6.7	8.2	10.6	15.2
06 005	...	6	Amador	1 540	37 001	1 256	24.0	81.9	2.6	2.8	2.3	13.0	3.7	11.6	6.6	9.9	10.8	14.6
06 007	17020	3	Butte	4 238	225 411	289	53.2	76.7	2.4	3.0	6.2	15.5	5.4	14.8	15.8	12.0	10.3	11.4
06 009	...	6	Calaveras	2 642	44 828	1 077	17.0	84.8	1.4	2.7	2.7	11.5	3.9	13.8	6.6	8.6	9.1	13.9
06 011	...	6	Colusa	2 980	21 482	1 757	7.2	38.0	1.4	1.7	2.3	58.3	7.4	20.6	9.7	13.0	11.8	12.6
06 013	41860	1	Contra Costa	1 854	1 126 745	38	607.7	49.0	10.0	1.0	19.1	25.1	5.8	17.6	8.6	12.6	13.4	14.9
06 015	18860	7	Del Norte	2 606	27 254	1 520	10.5	66.9	4.0	9.1	4.9	19.1	5.8	15.5	8.1	14.5	12.7	13.6
06 017	40900	1	El Dorado	4 423	184 452	351	41.7	81.5	1.4	1.9	5.8	12.7	4.4	16.5	7.8	9.9	11.1	15.4
06 019	23420	2	Fresno	15 431	974 861	48	63.2	32.5	5.3	1.2	11.0	52.0	8.3	20.6	11.0	14.8	12.1	11.8
06 021	...	6	Glenn	3 403	28 017	1 484	8.2	54.4	1.2	2.4	3.1	40.3	7.0	19.7	9.2	12.7	11.5	12.5
06 023	21700	5	Humboldt	9 241	135 727	468	14.7	79.7	2.2	7.5	4.6	10.8	5.4	14.1	13.2	13.7	12.0	11.7
06 025	20940	3	Imperial	10 817	180 191	357	16.7	12.8	2.7	1.0	1.7	82.2	8.3	20.2	11.0	14.1	12.1	12.0
06 027	...	7	Inyo	26 368	18 260	1 905	0.7	66.4	1.4	11.5	2.2	20.9	6.0	14.6	7.0	10.9	10.6	13.2
06 029	12540	2	Kern	21 062	882 176	62	41.9	37.8	5.9	1.3	5.4	51.6	8.4	21.1	11.1	15.0	12.5	12.1
06 031	25260	3	Kings	3 599	150 965	431	41.9	35.6	6.9	1.4	5.2	53.2	7.9	19.6	11.5	16.7	13.6	12.4
06 033	17340	4	Lake	3 254	64 591	815	19.8	74.9	2.8	4.1	2.6	19.1	5.8	14.6	7.5	10.8	10.2	13.5
06 035	45000	6	Lassen	11 762	31 345	1 400	2.7	68.3	9.2	4.2	2.5	18.5	4.5	12.5	10.5	18.2	14.9	14.5
06 037	31080	1	Los Angeles	10 510	10 170 292	1	967.7	28.5	8.8	0.6	15.8	48.4	6.4	16.4	10.5	15.6	13.9	13.7
06 039	31460	3	Madera	5 535	154 998	417	28.0	37.1	3.7	1.9	2.7	56.1	7.5	20.1	10.2	13.8	12.5	12.1
06 041	41860	1	Marin	1 348	261 221	257	193.8	75.0	3.3	0.8	8.2	16.0	4.8	15.6	6.4	9.1	13.0	16.1
06 043	...	8	Mariposa	3 752	17 531	1 944	4.7	84.5	1.7	4.5	2.3	10.4	4.4	12.3	7.0	9.8	8.9	14.1
06 045	46380	4	Mendocino	9 081	87 649	658	9.7	69.0	1.4	5.5	3.1	24.1	6.2	15.7	7.8	11.7	11.6	12.4
06 047	32900	3	Merced	5 012	268 455	253	53.6	31.1	3.8	0.9	8.6	57.6	8.1	21.9	11.9	14.1	12.3	11.8
06 049	...	6	Modoc	10 147	8 965	2 516	0.9	79.8	1.7	4.3	1.8	14.8	4.7	15.4	6.9	9.8	10.5	13.3
06 051	...	7	Mono	7 897	13 909	2 172	1.8	67.2	1.2	2.4	2.9	27.7	5.0	14.5	9.5	16.2	12.8	14.8
06 053	41500	2	Monterey	8 497	433 898	162	51.1	33.0	3.2	0.9	7.9	57.4	7.7	18.7	10.6	14.8	13.0	12.2
06 055	34900	3	Napa	1 938	142 456	449	73.5	55.8	2.5	1.1	9.4	33.7	5.4	16.4	9.1	12.4	12.7	13.8
06 057	46020	4	Nevada	2 481	98 877	598	39.9	88.0	0.9	2.0	2.6	9.2	4.2	13.5	6.8	9.9	10.4	13.3
06 059	31080	1	Orange	2 048	3 169 776	6	1 547.7	44.2	2.0	0.6	21.4	34.4	6.1	16.8	10.0	14.1	13.6	14.6
06 061	40900	1	Placer	3 644	375 391	182	103.0	77.3	2.2	1.4	9.3	13.5	5.4	17.5	7.9	11.1	12.7	14.3
06 063	...	7	Plumas	6 612	18 409	1 895	2.8	86.9	1.9	4.0	1.9	8.4	4.4	12.8	7.1	8.9	9.1	13.0
06 065	40140	1	Riverside	18 665	2 361 026	10	126.5	39.3	6.9	1.0	7.8	47.5	6.8	19.6	10.4	13.5	12.8	13.0
06 067	40900	1	Sacramento	2 498	1 501 335	25	601.0	50.2	11.6	1.5	19.0	22.5	6.7	17.7	9.5	15.1	13.0	13.3
06 069	41940	1	San Benito	3 597	58 792	878	16.3	37.4	1.1	1.0	3.7	58.3	6.7	20.1	9.7	13.1	12.9	14.2
06 071	40140	1	San Bernardino	51 947	2 128 133	12	41.0	32.4	9.2	1.0	8.1	51.7	7.3	19.9	11.3	14.6	12.9	12.9
06 073	41740	1	San Diego	10 895	3 299 521	5	302.8	49.4	5.7	1.0	14.1	33.2	6.6	15.8	11.2	16.1	13.2	13.1
06 075	41860	1	San Francisco	121	864 816	64	7 147.2	44.0	6.2	0.8	37.3	15.3	4.6	8.8	7.7	22.7	16.0	13.6
06 077	44700	2	San Joaquin	3 604	726 106	87	201.5	36.7	8.0	1.2	17.3	40.5	7.3	20.5	10.3	13.5	12.8	12.9
06 079	42020	3	San Luis Obispo	8 543	281 401	242	32.9	71.8	2.4	1.3	5.1	22.0	4.8	13.3	15.7	11.7	10.6	12.2
06 081	41860	1	San Mateo	1 161	765 135	82	659.0	43.4	3.1	0.6	31.3	25.3	6.1	15.4	7.6	14.1	14.6	14.7
06 083	42200	2	Santa Barbara	7 084	444 769	157	62.8	47.8	2.3	1.0	6.7	44.4	6.4	16.0	16.1	13.2	11.4	11.8
06 085	41940	1	Santa Clara	3 341	1 918 044	16	574.1	35.9	3.0	0.7	37.0	26.5	6.5	16.6	8.8	15.1	15.0	14.5
06 087	42100	2	Santa Cruz	1 153	274 146	247	237.8	60.9	1.6	1.2	6.3	33.3	5.6	14.5	15.4	12.0	11.9	13.1
06 089	39820	3	Shasta	9 778	179 533	360	18.4	84.2	1.8	4.1	4.3	9.4	5.8	15.8	8.4	12.3	10.6	13.1
06 091	...	8	Sierra	2 469	2 967	2 978	1.2	88.4	0.9	2.2	1.1	9.8	3.3	12.4	6.2	7.2	9.0	14.2
06 093	...	7	Siskiyou	16 260	43 554	1 102	2.7	81.5	2.2	6.3	2.7	12.0	5.4	15.0	7.2	10.2	9.6	12.4
06 095	46700	2	Solano	2 128	436 092	160	204.9	43.7	15.8	1.4	19.3	25.7	6.0	16.9	9.8	14.2	12.3	14.0
06 097	42220	2	Sonoma	4 081	502 146	137	123.0	67.2	2.2	1.6	5.9	26.1	5.3	15.3	8.9	13.0	12.1	13.9
06 099	33700	2	Stanislaus	3 872	538 388	122	139.0	46.6	3.3	1.3	7.6	44.1	7.3	20.1	10.2	14.0	12.5	12.8
06 101	49700	3	Sutter	1 560	96 463	612	61.8	50.7	2.8	2.0	18.2	30.0	6.7	19.6	9.6	13.5	12.1	12.8
06 103	39780	4	Tehama	7 640	63 308	836	8.3	71.9	1.3	3.4	2.1	24.1	6.2	17.8	8.5	11.4	11.0	13.6
06 105	...	8	Trinity	8 234	13 069	2 229	1.6	87.0	1.2	7.3	2.1	7.3	4.9	12.0	6.4	9.1	9.6	13.8
06 107	47300	2	Tulare	12 495	459 863	148	36.8	31.6	1.7	1.2	4.2	63.1	8.9	22.7	10.7	14.0	12.3	11.4
06 109	43760	4	Tuolumne	5 752	53 709	932	9.3	83.4	2.5	2.9	2.3	11.5	4.2	12.6	7.6	11.6	10.4	12.8
06 111	37100	2	Ventura	4 774	850 536	66	178.2	48.7	2.2	0.9	8.8	42.0	6.4	17.8	10.0	13.0	12.6	14.2
06 113	40900	1	Yolo	2 628	213 016	304	81.1	51.1	3.2	1.3	16.3	31.2	5.8	15.9	19.1	13.8	11.6	11.7
06 115	49700	3	Yuba	1 636	74 492	739	45.5	60.6	4.6	3.5	9.1	27.2	8.1	19.7	10.4	15.5	11.7	11.8
08 000	...	X	COLORADO	268 431	5 456 574	X	20.3	70.9	4.8	1.3	4.1	21.2	6.3	17.0	9.8	14.9	13.5	13.3
08 001	19740	1	Adams	3 024	491 337	141	162.5	53.5	3.7	1.1	4.8	38.8	7.6	20.1	9.1	16.1	14.6	12.8
08 003	...	7	Alamosa	1 872	16 496	2 007	8.8	50.5	1.8	1.9	1.6	45.1	7.7	16.2	17.8	13.4	9.9	10.8
08 005	19740	1	Arapahoe	2 067	631 096	105	305.3	64.7	11.6	1.1	6.9	18.7	6.5	18.0	8.7	15.0	14.2	13.5
08 007	...	7	Archuleta	3 497	12 352	2 273	3.5	78.7	0.8	2.4	1.6	18.6	4.9	13.5	6.4	9.5	9.7	13.3
08 009	...	9	Baca	6 617	3 615	2 934	0.5	87.3	1.4	1.8	1.0	10.5	6.6	14.7	7.3	9.5	9.0	11.9
08 011	...	7	Bent	3 918	5 830	2 770	1.5	57.3	7.0	1.7	1.4	31.0	3.7	12.4	8.9	16.0	14.7	14.2

1. CBSA = Core Based Statistical Area. See Appendix A for explanation. See Appendix B for list of metropolitan areas with component counties.   2. County type code from the Economic Research Service of USDA Rural-Urban Continuum Codes. See Appendix A for definition.   3. Dry land or land partially or temporarily covered by water.   4. May be of any race.

STATE County	55 to 64 years	65 to 74 years	75 years and over	Percent female	2000	2010	2000–2010	2010–2015	Births	Deaths	Net migration	Number	Persons per house-hold	Family house-holds	Female family householder[1]	One per-son
	16	17	18	19	20	21	22	23	24	25	26	27	28	29	30	31
CALIFORNIA	11.6	7.3	5.6	50.3	33 871 648	37 254 503	10.0	5.1	2 633 571	1 301 177	568 884	12 617 280	2.95	68.7	13.6	24.1
Alameda	12.1	7.2	5.3	51.0	1 443 741	1 510 261	4.6	8.5	102 184	50 257	78 349	551 734	2.77	65.6	12.5	26.1
Alpine	18.3	14.2	6.9	48.0	1 208	1 175	-2.7	-5.5	31	39	-62	377	3.11	69.5	11.1	27.9
Amador	17.7	15.1	10.0	46.9	35 100	38 091	8.5	-2.9	1 423	2 169	-323	13 939	2.36	65.5	8.4	28.7
Butte	13.2	9.5	7.5	50.5	203 171	220 000	8.3	2.5	12 767	11 856	4 237	85 215	2.54	59.9	11.7	29.3
Calaveras	18.9	15.7	9.4	50.0	40 554	45 578	12.4	-1.6	1 783	2 516	84	18 608	2.38	67.8	7.7	26.1
Colusa	11.8	7.6	5.6	48.6	18 804	21 419	13.9	0.3	1 650	696	-849	6 912	3.06	74.5	10.6	21.3
Contra Costa	12.8	8.3	6.0	51.3	948 816	1 049 197	10.6	7.4	64 258	38 805	51 776	380 183	2.82	70.9	12.1	23.1
Del Norte	14.3	9.2	6.4	45.2	27 507	28 610	4.0	-4.7	1 678	1 454	-1 571	9 527	2.57	61.4	14.2	33.2
El Dorado	16.9	11.0	7.0	49.9	156 299	181 057	15.8	1.9	8 233	7 381	2 543	67 220	2.67	70.8	8.4	23.1
Fresno	10.2	6.4	4.8	50.1	799 407	930 452	16.4	4.8	83 845	33 956	-5 826	292 550	3.18	73.3	17.5	21.1
Glenn	12.6	8.3	6.6	49.6	26 453	28 122	6.3	-0.4	2 099	1 164	-1 014	9 561	2.89	69.0	10.7	25.8
Humboldt	14.5	9.4	6.1	50.0	126 518	134 623	6.4	0.8	7 964	6 682	-40	53 130	2.46	57.0	12.1	32.4
Imperial	10.2	6.5	5.5	48.9	142 361	174 528	22.6	3.2	16 150	5 040	-5 747	46 952	3.55	78.1	19.5	18.7
Inyo	16.5	11.6	9.8	49.9	17 945	18 546	3.3	-1.5	1 140	1 022	-433	7 891	2.27	55.1	10.1	39.7
Kern	10.0	5.9	4.0	48.7	661 645	839 631	26.9	5.1	75 269	29 397	-2 440	257 737	3.20	75.5	16.6	19.5
Kings	9.2	5.3	3.8	44.8	129 461	152 982	18.2	-1.3	12 779	4 234	-10 754	41 108	3.24	77.8	17.2	17.4
Lake	17.0	12.6	8.0	50.0	58 309	64 665	10.9	-0.1	3 909	4 225	246	26 771	2.36	60.7	13.0	30.4
Lassen	12.4	7.6	4.9	36.3	33 828	34 895	3.2	-10.2	1 553	1 225	-3 877	9 821	2.30	64.1	8.5	27.8
Los Angeles	11.3	6.8	5.4	50.7	9 519 338	9 818 700	3.1	3.6	683 731	316 911	-3 965	3 242 391	3.02	67.1	15.8	25.6
Madera	11.0	7.6	5.2	51.9	123 109	150 865	22.5	2.7	12 400	5 396	-2 625	42 723	3.37	77.9	15.5	18.4
Marin	15.5	11.3	8.1	51.2	247 289	252 409	2.1	3.5	12 221	9 820	7 044	103 034	2.41	62.3	8.8	30.7
Mariposa	19.1	14.5	10.0	49.2	17 130	18 250	6.5	-3.9	742	862	-477	7 289	2.33	67.3	8.5	25.7
Mendocino	15.6	11.8	7.1	50.2	86 265	87 840	1.8	-0.2	5 568	4 359	-1 256	33 693	2.53	59.8	11.9	33.0
Merced	9.6	6.0	4.4	49.5	210 554	255 798	21.5	4.9	22 292	8 441	-893	76 516	3.35	77.1	18.2	18.4
Modoc	16.3	14.2	9.0	49.5	9 449	9 686	2.5	-7.4	413	558	-548	3 893	2.25	60.3	6.7	34.6
Mono	15.4	7.6	4.2	46.7	12 853	14 202	10.5	-2.1	758	243	-821	5 160	2.70	57.7	5.5	34.2
Monterey	11.0	6.7	5.2	49.0	401 762	415 057	3.3	4.5	35 039	12 593	-3 146	125 115	3.24	72.8	13.4	21.4
Napa	13.4	9.4	7.4	50.3	124 279	136 530	9.9	4.3	7 810	6 354	4 354	49 631	2.71	69.4	10.7	24.4
Nevada	18.4	14.0	9.0	50.8	92 033	98 748	7.3	0.1	4 268	4 834	936	40 838	2.39	64.4	8.1	28.3
Orange	11.7	7.4	5.8	50.6	2 846 289	3 010 266	5.8	5.3	198 487	97 434	58 490	1 002 285	3.04	72.0	12.1	21.3
Placer	13.2	10.1	7.8	51.2	248 399	348 494	40.3	7.7	19 619	15 263	22 003	134 111	2.67	70.3	9.6	23.7
Plumas	20.0	15.6	9.1	49.8	20 824	20 007	-3.9	-8.0	826	1 210	-1 146	8 529	2.21	59.9	8.4	33.9
Riverside	10.7	7.5	5.7	50.3	1 545 387	2 189 760	41.7	7.8	159 625	79 392	88 257	690 388	3.24	74.0	13.5	20.3
Sacramento	11.9	7.3	5.5	51.1	1 223 499	1 418 742	16.0	5.8	103 635	55 852	33 248	519 460	2.74	65.9	15.1	27.0
San Benito	11.9	6.7	4.6	49.8	53 234	55 269	3.8	6.4	3 937	1 518	1 137	17 121	3.30	79.7	13.8	16.3
San Bernardino	10.7	6.2	4.1	50.2	1 709 434	2 035 212	19.1	4.6	160 947	67 594	-1 556	607 604	3.34	75.8	16.7	19.5
San Diego	11.4	7.1	5.6	49.8	2 813 833	3 095 308	10.0	6.6	231 748	107 677	78 523	1 083 811	2.85	66.7	12.2	24.6
San Francisco	12.1	7.6	6.8	49.1	776 733	805 195	3.7	7.4	46 805	30 377	44 345	348 832	2.32	45.8	8.6	38.2
San Joaquin	10.9	6.4	4.9	50.2	563 598	685 308	21.6	6.0	53 135	26 076	13 029	217 343	3.15	74.7	16.0	19.8
San Luis Obispo	14.1	10.0	7.5	49.1	246 681	269 593	9.3	4.4	14 003	11 754	9 089	102 350	2.52	63.6	9.0	26.2
San Mateo	12.9	8.1	6.5	50.8	707 161	718 498	1.6	6.5	47 437	24 922	26 055	258 683	2.82	67.8	10.3	25.2
Santa Barbara	11.2	7.4	6.6	49.9	399 347	423 939	6.2	4.9	30 292	15 534	5 940	142 028	2.91	65.5	11.6	24.7
Santa Clara	11.3	6.8	5.4	49.7	1 682 585	1 781 672	5.9	7.7	124 479	50 753	65 892	614 714	2.94	71.7	10.6	21.5
Santa Cruz	14.0	8.3	5.2	50.4	255 602	262 362	2.6	4.5	16 009	9 215	4 827	94 219	2.72	62.7	10.8	26.5
Shasta	14.7	11.2	8.0	51.0	163 256	177 223	8.6	1.3	11 128	10 984	1 787	68 961	2.54	64.6	12.3	28.7
Sierra	20.9	17.1	9.7	50.0	3 555	3 240	-8.9	-8.4	86	200	-159	1 291	2.31	65.1	7.9	30.1
Siskiyou	17.7	13.9	8.8	50.3	44 301	44 900	1.4	-3.0	2 425	2 830	-888	19 380	2.25	62.2	9.6	30.7
Solano	13.2	8.1	5.5	50.3	394 542	413 344	4.8	5.5	27 379	15 911	10 833	142 521	2.87	71.6	15.7	22.4
Sonoma	14.7	9.9	6.8	51.0	458 614	483 880	5.5	3.8	27 027	20 958	11 478	186 935	2.58	63.0	10.4	28.2
Stanislaus	11.0	6.9	5.2	50.5	446 997	514 451	15.1	4.7	40 301	20 041	3 253	168 090	3.07	74.3	15.7	20.4
Sutter	11.3	8.0	6.5	50.3	78 930	94 737	20.0	1.8	6 820	3 918	-1 351	31 723	2.96	72.9	13.2	22.0
Tehama	13.6	10.4	7.4	50.2	56 039	63 461	13.2	-0.2	3 925	3 134	-899	23 480	2.65	69.2	12.7	25.1
Trinity	20.2	14.9	9.0	49.0	13 022	13 786	5.9	-5.2	577	842	-371	5 521	2.39	61.5	6.9	31.0
Tulare	9.6	6.0	4.4	49.9	368 021	442 182	20.2	4.0	41 223	14 923	-8 155	132 706	3.36	78.4	16.7	17.2
Tuolumne	17.5	13.6	9.8	47.8	54 501	55 365	1.6	-3.0	2 455	3 118	-882	22 181	2.28	66.3	10.3	28.2
Ventura	12.5	7.7	5.9	50.5	753 197	823 387	9.3	3.3	55 951	28 088	-1 072	267 829	3.07	73.6	12.4	20.6
Yolo	10.6	6.5	5.0	51.3	168 660	200 850	19.1	6.1	12 926	6 392	5 470	70 953	2.76	62.0	10.2	24.4
Yuba	11.3	6.9	4.5	49.2	60 219	72 155	19.8	3.2	6 407	2 777	-1 195	24 712	2.90	72.5	14.8	20.8
COLORADO	12.5	7.7	5.0	49.8	4 301 261	5 029 324	16.9	8.5	345 402	175 867	251 594	1 998 314	2.54	64.2	10.3	28.0
Adams	10.3	5.9	3.7	49.6	348 618	441 687	26.7	11.2	37 336	14 314	25 815	155 047	2.95	71.1	13.6	22.8
Alamosa	11.6	7.4	5.2	49.6	14 966	15 445	3.2	6.8	1 211	626	441	5 993	2.50	59.9	12.0	32.4
Arapahoe	12.2	7.2	4.7	50.7	487 967	572 155	17.3	10.3	41 308	18 701	35 686	228 267	2.59	66.2	12.2	27.7
Archuleta	19.8	15.3	7.6	49.9	9 898	12 084	22.1	2.2	595	442	158	5 343	2.24	70.0	10.1	27.1
Baca	15.4	12.2	13.5	50.1	4 517	3 788	-16.1	-4.6	225	291	-105	1 637	2.21	66.4	6.6	30.6
Bent	13.2	9.2	7.7	35.6	5 998	6 499	8.4	-10.3	210	279	-603	1 788	2.13	67.6	13.8	28.9

1. No spouse present.

Table B. States and Counties — **Population, Vital Statistics, Medicare, and Crime**

STATE County	Persons in group quarters, 2015	Daytime population, 2010–2014		Births, 2015		Deaths, 2015		Persons under 65 with no health insurance, 2014		Medicare, 2015			Serious crimes known to police,[2] 2014 Total	
		Number	Employment/residence ratio	Total	Rate[1]	Number	Rate[1]	Number	Percent	Total Beneficiaries	Enrolled in Original Medicare	Enrolled in Medicare Advantage	Number	Rate[3]
	32	33	34	35	36	37	38	39	40	41	42	43	44	45
CALIFORNIA	820 994	38 064 008	1.00	503 849	12.9	260 624	6.7	4 655 102	14.1	5 111 078	2 759 046	2 352 032	1 100 901	2 837
Alameda	36 752	1 549 038	0.99	19 996	12.3	10 261	6.3	132 685	9.6	193 891	97 068	96 823	67 976	4 236
Alpine	24	1 519	1.65	4	3.6	7	6.3	133	15.1	213	194	19	28	2 401
Amador	3 286	37 271	1.01	268	7.3	397	10.8	2 555	10.4	9 653	7 555	2 098	710	1 951
Butte	5 420	221 720	1.00	2 485	11.1	2 296	10.2	23 914	13.1	45 377	44 306	1 071	7 309	3 265
Calaveras	491	39 590	0.68	349	7.8	495	11.1	3 521	10.6	11 433	9 725	1 708	1 102	2 475
Colusa	261	21 621	1.02	316	14.8	113	5.3	3 105	16.9	3 266	2 998	268	390	1 818
Contra Costa	10 784	964 650	0.76	12 534	11.2	7 902	7.1	92 661	9.8	160 805	78 699	82 106	35 882	3 230
Del Norte	3 113	28 715	1.08	308	11.3	248	9.1	2 546	12.7	5 493	4 989	504	814	2 922
El Dorado	1 692	159 794	0.72	1 575	8.6	1 518	8.3	13 794	9.3	34 841	23 047	11 794	3 547	1 939
Fresno	17 885	950 450	1.00	16 002	16.5	6 807	7.0	129 986	15.4	114 896	76 689	38 207	37 082	3 837
Glenn	317	26 780	0.88	411	14.7	214	7.6	4 223	18.0	4 857	4 763	94	652	2 324
Humboldt	5 488	135 121	1.00	1 543	11.4	1 286	9.5	16 582	14.9	25 066	24 011	1 055	5 272	3 902
Imperial	8 914	177 028	1.00	3 127	17.4	967	5.4	23 763	16.0	24 351	20 676	3 675	6 119	3 577
Inyo	429	19 312	1.11	228	12.4	186	10.1	1 912	13.4	2 965	2 873	92	409	2 204
Kern	32 500	860 350	1.01	14 429	16.4	5 830	6.6	109 766	14.5	98 896	60 031	38 865	32 748	3 744
Kings	16 752	151 259	1.00	2 420	16.1	823	5.5	17 130	14.3	14 529	12 533	1 996	4 171	2 754
Lake	1 195	60 600	0.83	776	12.1	785	12.2	8 002	15.9	15 711	14 837	874	2 139	3 343
Lassen	8 287	34 404	1.11	281	8.9	211	6.7	1 798	9.3	4 395	4 270	125	661	2 085
Los Angeles	178 627	10 124 404	1.03	130 070	12.8	64 212	6.3	1 518 890	17.4	1 214 085	529 583	684 502	260 218	2 571
Madera	7 810	152 542	1.00	2 412	15.6	980	6.3	22 004	17.4	21 597	14 319	7 278	4 268	2 780
Marin	8 347	259 658	1.02	2 290	8.8	1 862	7.1	17 699	8.7	49 332	29 849	19 483	5 019	1 922
Mariposa	725	16 828	0.84	139	7.9	162	9.2	1 658	12.6	4 023	3 817	206	347	1 957
Mendocino	1 975	88 431	1.02	1 025	11.7	839	9.6	11 161	15.8	19 680	18 029	1 651	2 058	2 351
Merced	6 438	248 204	0.85	4 219	15.8	1 658	6.2	34 486	14.9	30 478	27 717	2 761	8 611	3 233
Modoc	356	9 099	0.93	67	7.5	107	11.9	1 034	15.3	2 175	1 987	188	215	2 372
Mono	338	14 699	1.07	145	10.4	41	2.9	1 996	16.5	2 385	2 304	81	220	1 560
Monterey	17 453	422 426	0.99	6 618	15.3	2 484	5.7	63 127	17.4	52 792	51 449	1 343	12 410	2 857
Napa	5 043	145 347	1.09	1 495	10.5	1 251	8.8	14 365	12.5	25 269	14 797	10 472	2 919	2 055
Nevada	1 220	94 806	0.91	853	8.6	893	9.0	8 818	11.7	22 983	19 222	3 761	1 899	1 926
Orange	43 952	3 164 479	1.05	37 776	12.0	19 480	6.2	360 533	13.4	411 226	200 569	210 657	61 011	1 933
Placer	3 882	356 187	0.97	3 735	10.0	3 010	8.1	26 594	8.8	69 898	37 099	32 799	7 239	1 937
Plumas	277	19 401	1.02	154	8.3	211	11.4	1 638	11.9	5 426	4 987	439	403	2 154
Riverside	33 280	2 096 294	0.80	30 828	13.1	16 108	6.9	337 395	17.0	302 539	116 482	186 057	67 694	2 907
Sacramento	23 132	1 461 376	1.02	19 781	13.3	11 188	7.5	146 521	11.5	203 376	99 427	103 949	47 698	3 222
San Benito	400	49 890	0.71	769	13.1	303	5.2	6 898	13.5	6 608	6 233	375	932	1 594
San Bernardino	39 184	2 009 160	0.91	30 817	14.5	13 769	6.5	272 822	14.7	237 231	83 097	154 134	63 059	2 986
San Diego	106 429	3 214 695	1.02	44 561	13.6	21 580	6.6	370 758	13.4	422 056	197 811	224 245	69 635	2 138
San Francisco	23 578	1 007 698	1.39	9 059	10.5	6 079	7.1	66 584	9.3	123 900	69 218	54 682	52 758	6 205
San Joaquin	14 857	672 961	0.89	10 044	13.9	5 171	7.2	81 653	13.2	91 477	55 998	35 479	30 438	4 271
San Luis Obispo	15 751	271 574	0.98	2 734	9.8	2 249	8.0	29 235	13.6	52 415	45 873	6 542	6 860	2 453
San Mateo	8 855	743 369	1.01	9 034	11.9	4 976	6.5	58 692	9.1	106 333	54 247	52 086	15 747	2 076
Santa Barbara	19 094	444 917	1.07	5 883	13.3	3 045	6.9	56 050	15.5	65 551	55 232	10 319	10 382	2 354
Santa Clara	30 891	1 955 143	1.13	23 625	12.4	10 470	5.5	137 886	8.4	220 836	126 101	94 735	47 760	2 524
Santa Cruz	13 426	256 173	0.91	2 934	10.8	1 836	6.7	29 000	12.9	39 658	35 826	3 832	9 260	3 398
Shasta	2 764	179 483	1.01	2 162	12.0	2 085	11.6	19 409	13.5	42 520	39 831	2 689	6 980	3 869
Sierra	33	2 638	0.68	10	3.4	39	13.1	329	15.0	794	757	37	40	1 324
Siskiyou	563	44 963	1.04	464	10.7	543	12.5	4 884	14.6	11 957	10 911	1 046	861	1 968
Solano	11 109	379 341	0.77	5 450	12.6	3 270	7.5	37 143	10.3	61 654	30 448	31 206	15 562	3 620
Sonoma	10 424	471 863	0.91	5 116	10.2	4 174	8.3	52 536	12.8	87 780	50 364	37 416	10 404	2 079
Stanislaus	6 477	506 769	0.92	7 736	14.5	3 826	7.1	59 158	12.8	74 092	40 342	33 750	21 385	4 027
Sutter	839	87 780	0.80	1 302	13.6	744	7.7	11 882	14.6	15 409	14 913	496	2 680	2 791
Tehama	844	60 458	0.87	754	11.9	597	9.5	6 815	13.3	11 566	11 305	261	1 910	3 019
Trinity	385	13 764	1.06	100	7.6	162	12.4	1 255	12.7	6 377	6 021	356	208	1 547
Tulare	4 956	442 832	0.95	7 751	16.9	2 908	6.3	67 762	16.7	52 948	45 628	7 320	13 301	2 895
Tuolumne	3 511	54 509	1.01	481	8.9	545	10.1	4 365	11.5	14 119	13 385	734	1 308	2 429
Ventura	11 129	793 641	0.89	10 605	12.5	5 682	6.7	94 627	13.1	121 707	81 912	39 795	18 702	2 206
Yolo	7 812	216 275	1.14	2 579	12.2	1 246	5.9	20 179	11.3	25 772	13 017	12 755	6 264	3 032
Yuba	1 238	70 709	0.91	1 220	16.4	493	6.6	9 185	14.3	10 416	9 675	741	2 431	3 286
COLORADO	115 746	5 184 031	0.99	67 057	12.4	35 126	6.5	535 569	11.7	717 109	430 766	286 343	152 064	2 839
Adams	4 094	414 219	0.78	7 015	14.4	2 815	5.8	65 957	15.3	48 196	20 814	27 382	15 449	3 228
Alamosa	1 273	18 327	1.35	233	14.2	104	6.3	2 044	15.8	2 580	1 897	683	NA	NA
Arapahoe	4 671	584 735	0.96	7 952	12.7	3 812	6.1	65 761	12.2	82 905	43 054	39 851	17 313	2 797
Archuleta	129	11 878	0.95	107	8.7	89	7.2	1 550	16.6	2 858	2 430	428	231	1 879
Baca	82	3 708	0.98	37	10.2	52	14.3	462	17.3	D	957	D	33	897
Bent	1 871	6 130	1.09	31	5.3	41	7.1	387	12.6	860	804	56	81	1 464

1. Per 1,000 estimated resident population.　2. Data for serious crimes have not been adjusted for underreporting; this may affect comparability between geographic areas and over time.
3. Per 100,000 population estimated by the FBI.

STATE County	Serious crimes known to police, 2014 (cont.)[1] Rate[2] Violent	Property	Education School enrollment and attainment, 2010–2014 Enrollment[3] Total	Percent private	Attainment[4] (percent) High school graduate or less	Bachelor's degree or more	Local government expenditures,[5] 2012–2013 Total current spending (mil dol)	Current spending per student (dollars)	Money income, 2010–2014 Per capita income[6] (dollars)	Households Median income (dollars)	Mean income (dollars)	Percent with income of $200,000 or more	Income and poverty, 2014 Median household income (dollars)	Percent below poverty level All persons	Children under 18 years	Children 5 to 17 years in families
	46	47	48	49	50	51	52	53	54	55	56	57	58	59	60	61
CALIFORNIA	396	2 441	10 602 974	14.1	39.2	31.0	58 252.1	9 220	29 906	61 489	86 704	7.6	61 927	16.4	22.6	21.9
Alameda	645	3 591	415 781	15.4	32.2	42.1	2 002.1	9 173	36 439	73 775	99 356	10.8	76 996	12.5	14.3	13.8
Alpine	343	2 058	311	14.5	37.9	30.5	3.7	35 067	24 375	61 343	70 985	1.9	53 003	19.0	28.2	21.7
Amador	223	1 728	7 125	13.3	39.2	20.5	37.2	8 886	27 373	52 964	70 485	3.6	54 610	12.9	18.6	16.8
Butte	303	2 962	63 913	7.8	35.6	25.0	306.8	9 812	24 430	43 165	60 620	2.8	42 302	21.9	24.3	24.2
Calaveras	254	2 221	8 472	12.9	34.5	21.1	63.0	10 578	29 296	54 936	70 238	3.5	53 321	13.7	20.6	18.5
Colusa	186	1 632	5 854	8.1	55.9	14.3	49.0	10 463	22 211	50 503	66 008	2.6	48 006	14.3	19.9	18.7
Contra Costa	329	2 901	292 764	16.7	29.9	39.4	1 536.7	8 969	38 770	79 799	107 920	12.0	80 338	10.5	13.8	13.3
Del Norte	592	2 330	6 474	14.1	49.6	16.0	43.0	10 243	19 424	39 302	53 193	2.0	41 419	22.4	31.0	28.9
El Dorado	224	1 716	44 629	11.5	29.3	32.1	252.9	9 301	35 128	68 507	91 565	8.6	70 235	11.4	13.1	11.5
Fresno	471	3 367	289 899	7.6	49.4	19.5	1 841.6	9 403	20 231	45 201	63 045	3.0	43 338	27.5	38.0	36.3
Glenn	446	1 878	7 828	11.5	52.4	15.7	61.1	11 492	21 698	40 106	61 237	3.1	43 755	17.1	23.7	23.3
Humboldt	359	3 543	36 216	8.3	35.5	27.5	184.6	11 006	23 516	42 153	56 409	2.1	40 581	21.0	23.9	23.1
Imperial	341	3 236	54 023	5.4	56.7	13.4	354.7	9 692	16 409	41 772	56 972	2.0	38 737	23.6	31.3	31.2
Inyo	571	1 633	3 860	9.5	44.7	21.4	52.0	11 672	27 028	45 625	60 501	2.5	49 267	14.0	20.2	18.6
Kern	510	3 234	253 077	8.7	53.4	15.2	1 708.5	9 682	20 467	48 574	65 412	3.1	47 451	24.5	32.9	31.9
Kings	460	2 295	43 279	8.8	54.2	12.5	255.8	8 888	18 518	47 341	63 381	2.5	44 490	24.9	33.8	32.4
Lake	480	2 863	13 667	9.8	43.5	16.2	89.2	9 752	21 310	35 997	50 526	1.6	36 333	24.3	32.3	32.8
Lassen	442	1 643	6 722	17.9	47.9	12.9	40.7	9 551	19 847	53 351	64 277	1.8	49 995	19.4	20.3	18.7
Los Angeles	422	2 149	2 779 216	15.5	43.7	29.9	15 689.0	10 053	27 987	55 870	82 109	6.8	55 686	18.7	26.7	26.4
Madera	578	2 201	41 640	6.2	54.2	13.5	269.6	8 845	17 797	45 490	60 120	2.1	43 171	22.3	30.7	28.4
Marin	174	1 748	60 873	25.0	19.7	54.8	377.6	11 849	58 004	91 529	141 535	19.6	94 549	8.8	10.1	8.6
Mariposa	400	1 557	3 264	6.9	39.1	22.4	21.3	11 108	28 327	50 560	65 817	2.5	47 781	16.2	25.0	24.3
Mendocino	585	1 766	20 090	10.0	40.5	22.5	146.7	11 197	23 712	43 290	58 831	2.4	42 840	18.8	26.2	24.5
Merced	558	2 675	83 534	5.1	57.2	13.0	540.7	9 596	18 464	43 066	59 868	2.8	43 818	24.8	35.9	31.8
Modoc	541	1 832	1 864	14.4	40.3	18.5	16.2	16 665	21 830	38 560	51 004	1.0	39 172	20.2	31.3	28.3
Mono	255	1 304	3 528	4.3	33.1	33.3	27.0	13 247	29 578	61 814	69 594	2.2	59 181	11.3	16.2	15.3
Monterey	422	2 435	119 905	9.3	49.8	23.1	734.8	9 999	25 048	58 582	80 474	5.7	57 428	17.0	25.2	24.1
Napa	376	1 679	34 868	15.7	36.4	31.9	216.5	10 447	35 092	70 925	95 454	8.8	71 063	9.0	12.0	11.2
Nevada	312	1 614	20 604	12.1	26.5	32.8	168.1	10 232	32 117	56 949	75 742	4.4	57 118	11.4	17.6	16.6
Orange	198	1 735	868 845	14.9	33.8	37.3	4 361.7	8 692	34 416	75 998	102 520	10.6	76 061	12.9	17.9	17.3
Placer	159	1 777	97 397	13.7	25.8	35.7	511.4	7 823	35 711	73 747	93 596	7.7	75 689	8.3	9.7	8.0
Plumas	486	1 668	3 600	8.0	33.6	22.7	25.6	11 854	29 167	48 032	62 348	3.4	47 964	14.0	21.6	20.2
Riverside	269	2 638	659 758	11.6	45.8	20.8	3 649.3	8 583	23 660	56 592	74 062	4.1	56 877	17.1	23.5	22.5
Sacramento	503	2 718	412 674	12.8	36.0	28.2	2 112.8	8 976	27 071	55 615	73 456	4.1	55 803	18.1	23.8	22.2
San Benito	335	1 259	16 574	11.1	45.7	19.0	97.0	8 661	26 317	67 874	83 170	5.6	68 166	14.1	19.8	17.8
San Bernardino	392	2 594	630 419	11.1	48.0	18.8	3 521.5	8 544	21 384	54 100	69 373	3.4	51 951	20.4	28.2	27.4
San Diego	325	1 813	869 778	14.4	33.2	35.1	4 493.3	9 033	31 043	63 996	86 416	7.2	66 034	14.7	18.9	18.6
San Francisco	802	5 402	173 252	31.1	26.4	52.9	697.6	12 109	49 986	78 378	113 933	15.0	83 788	12.1	13.6	15.2
San Joaquin	750	3 521	206 577	12.4	48.5	18.1	1 189.0	8 545	22 642	53 253	70 572	3.5	51 527	20.7	27.5	26.5
San Luis Obispo	421	2 032	75 801	9.1	30.6	32.1	324.7	9 366	30 392	59 454	78 731	5.1	61 775	14.5	15.6	14.5
San Mateo	206	1 870	187 041	22.6	28.3	45.0	980.8	10 484	47 198	91 421	131 058	17.6	100 806	7.5	9.8	9.5
Santa Barbara	293	2 060	133 587	10.4	38.5	31.4	640.6	9 585	30 526	63 409	89 545	7.6	62 116	17.4	22.6	21.7
Santa Clara	247	2 277	504 304	20.2	28.7	47.3	2 598.2	9 510	42 666	93 854	124 513	17.2	97 219	8.5	9.3	8.9
Santa Cruz	418	2 980	79 358	11.4	30.1	37.5	399.3	9 881	33 050	66 923	90 870	8.6	64 257	16.1	19.1	18.6
Shasta	707	3 162	44 208	16.2	37.1	19.1	276.2	10 161	23 763	44 556	59 056	2.5	43 661	14.7	20.3	19.7
Sierra	364	960	468	6.2	42.7	19.6	6.5	17 126	28 030	43 107	62 469	3.7	47 293	13.8	19.0	16.7
Siskiyou	313	1 655	9 507	12.6	37.3	24.0	76.2	11 968	22 482	37 495	50 453	1.5	38 641	21.1	30.3	28.4
Solano	491	3 129	111 869	13.3	36.5	24.3	544.6	8 255	29 132	67 341	83 471	5.5	67 106	12.3	16.5	15.0
Sonoma	364	1 715	123 277	12.2	33.3	32.6	674.3	9 575	33 361	63 799	85 285	6.5	66 949	11.3	13.6	12.7
Stanislaus	532	3 495	150 616	8.9	51.4	16.4	996.5	9 467	21 729	49 573	65 348	2.9	50 917	18.1	23.8	22.0
Sutter	329	2 462	26 967	10.4	46.1	18.5	166.5	7 876	23 828	51 527	69 606	3.1	51 827	15.2	20.8	19.3
Tehama	507	2 512	14 995	7.7	48.2	14.1	109.0	10 382	21 002	42 369	55 092	2.3	40 782	18.2	26.7	24.8
Trinity	253	1 294	2 562	11.1	37.0	22.0	23.2	14 298	23 145	36 862	52 729	2.1	34 961	19.9	31.7	30.8
Tulare	414	2 481	138 644	6.3	56.9	13.3	974.8	9 752	17 888	42 863	58 798	2.3	42 360	28.1	36.7	36.1
Tuolumne	280	2 148	11 047	12.9	39.1	19.8	64.4	10 312	26 063	48 493	62 446	3.0	49 476	14.3	20.5	18.9
Ventura	223	1 983	230 557	15.0	36.0	31.6	1 248.7	8 813	33 308	77 335	100 397	9.9	74 967	11.5	15.8	14.5
Yolo	366	2 665	74 802	8.6	34.4	38.3	261.6	8 942	28 080	55 508	78 494	5.9	54 509	19.5	17.5	16.4
Yuba	400	2 886	21 210	8.0	45.9	14.2	137.0	9 926	19 586	45 470	56 357	1.2	41 403	21.6	28.6	26.6
COLORADO	309	2 530	1 388 718	13.4	31.6	37.5	7 431.8	8 647	31 674	59 448	79 990	5.5	61 324	12.1	15.6	14.9
Adams	342	2 886	124 736	10.7	47.6	21.6	712.4	8 178	24 667	57 421	70 642	2.9	59 316	12.9	17.7	17.1
Alamosa	NA	NA	5 636	8.6	41.4	24.1	24.7	10 361	19 481	31 400	49 705	2.6	38 140	22.5	28.6	29.6
Arapahoe	292	2 506	160 335	14.4	28.9	39.4	1 023.3	8 951	33 574	62 213	85 655	6.4	65 359	11.2	15.6	15.4
Archuleta	179	1 700	2 092	17.6	34.7	35.3	13.7	9 993	28 506	48 186	64 034	3.5	44 508	14.7	26.7	26.3
Baca	136	761	740	6.9	46.9	16.1	8.7	11 183	22 558	38 625	50 493	2.3	36 294	20.0	29.6	30.2
Bent	145	1 319	863	5.6	63.1	7.5	7.1	8 872	15 402	39 053	51 036	1.8	35 424	32.3	34.4	30.7

1. Data for serious crimes have not been adjusted for underreporting; this may affect comparability between geographic areas and over time. 2. Per 100,000 population estimated by the FBI.
3. All persons 3 years old and over enrolled in nursery school through college. 4. Persons 25 years old and over. 5. Elementary and secondary education expenditures.
6. Based on population estimated by the American Community Survey, 2010–2014.

Table B. States and Counties — **Personal Income**

STATE County	Personal income, 2014 Total (mil dol)	Percent change, 2013–2014	Per capita[1] Dollars	Per capita[1] Rank	Wages and salaries (mil dol)	Supplements to wages and salaries; employer contributions (mil dol) Pension and insurance	Government social insurance	Proprietors' income (mil dol)	Dividends, interest, and rent (mil dol)	Personal transfer receipts (mil dol)	Earnings, 2014 Total (mil dol)	Contributions for government social insurance (mil dol) From employee and self-employed	From employer
	62	63	64	65	66	67	68	69	70	71	72	73	74
CALIFORNIA	1 939 528	4.9	49 985	X	991 163	168 421	66 603	180 424	389 198	293 656	1 406 611	81 042	66 603
Alameda	90 631	6.4	56 261	191	49 697	8 124	3 418	6 010	16 002	12 009	67 249	3 832	3 418
Alpine	70	3.2	62 410	107	41	8	2	5	17	14	57	3	2
Amador	1 451	3.7	39 504	1 248	504	150	32	116	317	362	801	51	32
Butte	8 298	3.0	37 005	1 600	3 104	724	224	795	1 568	2 217	4 847	303	224
Calaveras	1 923	4.6	43 099	836	322	93	22	159	452	472	595	48	22
Colusa	939	-6.0	43 840	775	358	84	25	251	148	157	718	29	25
Contra Costa	70 850	6.2	63 752	96	23 197	3 889	1 596	5 082	14 100	8 052	33 764	2 068	1 596
Del Norte	828	2.1	30 437	2 659	298	109	18	57	146	296	482	29	18
El Dorado	10 430	4.1	56 965	174	2 426	492	172	948	1 855	1 457	4 039	267	172
Fresno	34 568	3.6	35 785	1 810	15 198	3 455	1 119	3 638	5 438	8 271	23 410	1 292	1 119
Glenn	1 070	-1.8	38 278	1 424	319	82	23	244	180	247	669	31	23
Humboldt	5 093	3.9	37 783	1 485	1 832	490	127	515	1 096	1 296	2 963	180	127
Imperial	5 802	3.8	32 398	2 388	2 382	712	171	872	710	1 475	4 137	196	171
Inyo	821	2.7	44 602	709	325	105	20	106	167	184	555	31	20
Kern	31 629	3.8	35 443	1 753	15 468	3 367	1 087	3 911	4 333	5 945	23 833	1 275	1 087
Kings	4 864	7.3	32 371	2 391	2 119	612	155	661	763	1 001	3 547	158	155
Lake	2 263	3.8	35 259	1 897	574	156	40	187	412	745	957	70	40
Lassen	1 061	2.0	33 432	2 210	455	177	29	69	191	249	730	38	29
Los Angeles	499 768	4.5	49 400	418	257 162	43 387	17 770	56 164	102 545	84 027	374 483	21 888	17 770
Madera	5 107	2.7	33 042	2 272	1 951	487	139	979	740	1 115	3 556	171	139
Marin	25 717	5.4	98 626	7	7 482	1 173	500	2 564	8 619	1 937	11 718	702	500
Mariposa	741	4.9	41 893	962	193	56	14	56	147	192	319	22	14
Mendocino	3 475	3.7	39 545	1 241	1 187	296	85	361	837	947	1 930	125	85
Merced	9 020	4.5	33 865	2 138	2 949	790	209	1 579	1 222	2 216	5 526	257	209
Modoc	366	6.0	40 541	1 117	96	33	7	48	79	115	184	11	7
Mono	607	3.8	43 398	805	264	66	19	73	181	67	423	22	19
Monterey	19 889	3.7	46 109	592	8 549	1 877	644	2 587	4 542	2 947	13 656	682	644
Napa	7 735	4.5	54 596	218	3 779	774	278	773	1 911	1 084	5 604	315	278
Nevada	4 976	4.0	50 312	366	1 298	281	94	525	1 236	941	2 197	152	94
Orange	173 306	4.5	55 096	211	91 763	13 918	6 559	18 496	36 152	19 856	130 736	7 681	6 559
Placer	20 229	4.2	54 423	221	7 856	1 268	581	1 372	3 632	2 765	11 077	687	581
Plumas	848	5.1	45 554	635	262	80	19	71	229	237	432	29	19
Riverside	78 239	4.8	33 590	2 177	27 940	6 186	2 014	5 695	12 308	15 570	41 835	2 573	2 014
Sacramento	65 126	4.3	43 944	766	36 854	9 259	2 341	4 578	10 699	12 896	53 033	2 751	2 341
San Benito	2 417	6.1	41 486	1 011	704	162	52	245	376	356	1 163	66	52
San Bernardino	69 488	4.8	32 892	2 298	31 457	6 706	2 349	4 119	10 194	15 030	44 631	2 664	2 349
San Diego	167 931	4.4	51 459	315	87 582	16 051	6 296	13 690	36 218	23 539	123 619	6 979	6 296
San Francisco	77 233	6.0	90 600	12	63 194	8 290	3 697	9 524	18 258	6 661	84 707	4 687	3 697
San Joaquin	25 859	5.7	36 136	1 759	9 918	2 136	734	2 318	3 741	6 129	15 107	877	734
San Luis Obispo	12 823	3.9	45 947	600	4 994	1 163	353	1 321	3 192	1 993	7 830	460	353
San Mateo	68 014	5.8	89 659	14	40 287	4 200	2 151	4 826	18 087	4 476	51 463	3 043	2 151
Santa Barbara	22 264	4.0	50 523	357	10 086	2 007	716	2 220	6 702	2 890	15 029	832	716
Santa Clara	141 874	6.1	74 883	42	109 017	10 917	6 037	7 762	28 309	11 604	133 732	7 804	6 037
Santa Cruz	14 210	5.6	52 280	284	4 744	985	332	1 424	3 242	1 885	7 485	430	332
Shasta	6 815	4.6	37 905	1 467	2 608	603	191	546	1 282	2 108	3 948	263	191
Sierra	112	7.4	37 239	1 563	27	10	2	7	29	31	45	3	2
Siskiyou	1 614	3.8	37 002	1 601	502	139	38	136	375	541	815	57	38
Solano	18 139	6.2	42 073	945	7 579	1 603	536	856	3 020	3 277	10 574	630	536
Sonoma	24 607	5.7	49 185	431	9 739	1 842	711	2 404	5 800	3 747	14 696	895	711
Stanislaus	19 341	5.1	36 356	1 712	7 793	1 636	575	1 943	2 845	4 272	11 947	683	575
Sutter	3 726	2.4	38 871	1 335	1 134	243	83	501	598	779	1 960	115	83
Tehama	2 060	4.0	32 666	2 343	670	155	49	162	400	621	1 036	69	49
Trinity	425	3.5	32 261	2 407	99	36	7	22	114	161	164	14	7
Tulare	16 147	6.3	35 240	1 899	5 670	1 450	410	2 811	2 159	3 749	10 340	491	410
Tuolumne	2 080	5.4	38 639	1 372	708	196	48	135	513	589	1 087	74	48
Ventura	42 651	4.2	50 405	363	17 921	3 235	1 258	3 068	8 575	5 714	25 482	1 478	1 258
Yolo	9 369	3.3	45 132	668	5 457	1 558	341	702	1 799	1 365	8 058	377	341
Yuba	2 588	3.4	34 989	1 939	1 068	340	82	138	395	778	1 629	83	82
COLORADO	261 735	6.2	48 869	X	138 654	18 876	9 896	27 435	52 895	34 042	194 861	10 804	9 896
Adams	17 010	7.2	35 385	1 881	9 719	1 389	689	1 168	1 976	2 814	12 965	692	689
Alamosa	538	3.8	33 250	2 238	294	53	21	52	94	135	420	22	21
Arapahoe	34 836	6.4	56 294	189	19 969	2 360	1 401	6 027	6 602	3 695	29 757	1 666	1 401
Archuleta	449	6.3	36 679	1 653	128	21	9	70	125	103	228	14	9
Baca	144	-11.9	39 405	1 264	42	9	2	22	33	39	75	4	2
Bent	169	4.3	30 019	2 713	41	8	3	26	34	46	78	3	3

1. Based on the resident population estimated as of July 1 of the year shown.

Table B. States and Counties — Earnings, Social Security, and Housing

STATE County	Earnings, 2014 (cont.) Percent by selected industries									Social Security beneficiaries, December 2014		Housing units, 2015		
	Farm	Mining	Construction	Manu-facturing	Infor-mation: professional, scientific, technical services	Retail trade	Finance, insur-ance, real estate and leasing	Health care and social assistance	Govern-ment	Number	Rate[1]	Supple-mental Security Income recipients, December 2014	Total	Percent change, 2010–2014
	75	76	77	78	79	80	81	82	83	84	85	86	87	88
CALIFORNIA	1.3	0.5	4.7	9.4	18.2	5.6	8.6	9.4	17.4	5 538 810	143	1 304 400	13 987 625	2.2
Alameda	0.1	0.1	6.0	10.5	17.9	5.5	4.6	10.9	17.4	205 915	128	52 820	595 822	2.3
Alpine	0.0	0.0	4.2	0.0	27.9	0.8	3.4	1.0	33.7	215	194	37	1 766	0.3
Amador	2.1	0.8	6.7	6.3	6.1	7.2	3.7	D	40.5	10 825	295	753	18 248	1.2
Butte	5.9	0.1	5.6	5.0	6.7	8.7	5.2	19.4	22.3	49 965	223	11 615	98 035	2.3
Calaveras	1.3	D	12.2	2.6	D	8.4	4.9	7.1	31.1	12 965	291	1 127	28 131	0.7
Colusa	30.6	D	1.6	12.3	1.1	3.3	3.4	D	20.1	3 630	170	568	7 984	1.3
Contra Costa	0.1	1.4	7.1	7.4	14.6	5.9	11.1	13.3	13.0	174 230	157	26 658	408 748	2.1
Del Norte	2.8	0.0	3.1	1.1	2.7	7.4	2.5	13.7	52.8	6 025	222	1 982	11 339	1.4
El Dorado	0.1	0.3	9.2	3.0	11.9	6.3	15.7	11.4	19.8	39 580	216	3 122	89 010	1.0
Fresno	6.7	0.2	4.9	6.2	6.1	6.5	6.4	13.6	22.6	130 440	135	43 366	325 996	3.3
Glenn	32.8	D	3.6	6.3	D	4.6	2.3	D	21.4	5 545	198	1 163	10 949	1.6
Humboldt	3.3	D	5.9	4.2	5.6	9.6	5.7	13.2	30.8	27 740	206	6 629	62 577	1.7
Imperial	17.4	D	3.2	2.5	2.1	7.2	2.4	5.4	37.2	29 695	166	10 510	57 216	2.0
Inyo	1.7	1.7	6.2	12.2	2.7	7.0	2.0	D	44.1	4 230	230	458	9 529	0.5
Kern	7.4	9.8	6.4	5.0	5.4	5.6	3.7	7.9	22.7	114 465	131	34 191	293 574	3.2
Kings	16.8	0.0	2.1	8.6	2.3	4.5	2.1	8.5	41.6	17 225	115	4 612	45 253	3.2
Lake	4.7	0.4	4.9	1.9	4.0	9.2	3.2	18.0	27.0	18 090	282	3 874	35 695	0.6
Lassen	4.0	D	2.6	0.1	1.9	4.8	2.2	7.2	66.0	4 650	147	809	12 742	0.3
Los Angeles	0.0	0.7	3.2	8.0	20.6	5.5	9.2	9.8	15.1	1 274 380	126	423 398	3 504 139	1.7
Madera	21.7	D	3.4	9.9	2.7	4.7	1.9	13.3	21.8	24 215	157	4 804	50 084	1.9
Marin	0.3	D	5.7	4.0	18.5	7.0	13.6	10.8	13.6	49 940	192	3 624	112 692	1.3
Mariposa	1.9	D	5.9	1.9	3.5	6.3	D	3.6	41.2	5 050	286	537	10 373	1.8
Mendocino	3.0	0.2	6.5	9.0	4.4	10.1	4.1	13.3	24.2	20 960	239	3 526	40 829	1.3
Merced	22.6	D	3.4	10.9	2.2	5.6	2.6	8.3	24.5	35 880	135	11 320	84 322	0.7
Modoc	18.9	0.0	4.8	D	D	5.5	2.1	D	42.3	2 875	319	562	5 255	1.2
Mono	3.5	D	6.6	0.7	D	5.4	5.7	1.9	36.1	1 615	115	105	14 036	0.9
Monterey	12.5	0.3	3.5	2.6	5.6	5.4	4.1	7.5	25.3	59 520	138	9 256	140 470	1.0
Napa	2.4	D	6.9	19.5	6.2	5.2	6.0	10.2	16.3	26 435	187	2 387	55 472	1.3
Nevada	-0.1	D	13.4	5.0	9.1	8.0	8.4	13.4	20.7	26 335	267	1 949	53 404	1.6
Orange	0.0	0.3	6.5	11.6	14.8	5.8	13.8	8.5	10.8	423 770	135	74 855	1 080 987	3.1
Placer	-0.1	0.1	9.2	6.0	9.0	10.0	12.7	16.1	13.4	73 660	198	5 680	159 406	4.4
Plumas	1.0	D	7.8	7.7	3.5	5.6	3.1	7.3	38.0	6 410	345	856	15 731	1.1
Riverside	0.8	0.3	9.2	7.0	5.5	9.1	5.7	10.8	25.0	346 485	149	62 010	826 790	3.3
Sacramento	0.1	0.1	4.8	4.1	11.7	4.9	6.9	10.9	38.0	229 750	155	67 711	563 656	1.4
San Benito	8.5	D	6.0	19.6	D	12.2	3.6	4.4	21.2	8 220	141	956	18 217	1.9
San Bernardino	0.3	0.2	5.7	7.6	5.3	7.7	4.6	12.6	25.1	277 215	131	73 663	711 660	1.7
San Diego	0.3	0.1	4.9	8.3	17.5	5.2	8.7	8.4	24.2	464 905	142	85 337	1 194 415	2.5
San Francisco	0.0	0.1	2.5	1.5	32.5	3.6	17.0	4.9	14.8	119 495	140	44 827	390 204	3.5
San Joaquin	6.0	0.1	5.4	8.6	4.1	7.1	5.4	12.2	21.0	104 650	146	29 669	238 571	2.1
San Luis Obispo	3.2	0.2	8.3	6.2	8.3	7.9	6.2	10.7	22.6	55 820	200	4 951	120 137	2.4
San Mateo	0.1	0.0	5.1	9.4	37.1	3.8	10.5	6.0	6.2	110 960	146	11 407	274 837	1.4
Santa Barbara	4.8	1.7	4.6	7.4	13.5	6.1	5.7	10.3	21.9	70 420	160	9 306	155 163	1.5
Santa Clara	0.1	0.0	3.1	22.9	33.5	3.9	4.8	6.6	7.0	225 900	119	48 159	660 627	4.5
Santa Cruz	5.0	D	8.9	7.7	8.1	6.8	5.1	13.1	21.3	43 020	159	6 107	105 530	1.0
Shasta	0.9	D	6.1	3.8	6.4	9.7	5.7	18.7	24.9	48 200	268	10 178	78 101	1.0
Sierra	6.4	D	8.8	D	D	1.6	D	13.5	48.3	1 005	337	110	2 347	0.8
Siskiyou	4.5	D	4.7	4.9	4.8	7.3	2.9	12.9	32.7	12 720	293	2 503	23 985	0.3
Solano	1.0	0.3	7.8	14.3	4.0	6.8	5.5	15.9	26.0	71 210	165	12 762	155 625	1.9
Sonoma	2.2	0.2	7.7	12.4	9.5	7.6	6.6	13.6	15.5	94 015	188	9 652	207 891	1.6
Stanislaus	8.7	0.0	4.8	13.4	4.0	7.4	4.5	16.0	18.1	83 850	158	22 345	180 704	0.7
Sutter	10.2	0.6	5.1	5.0	4.3	9.2	5.7	13.5	18.0	16 935	177	4 160	34 176	0.9
Tehama	9.2	0.0	6.6	10.6	2.2	7.8	3.0	11.6	23.8	15 515	246	3 317	27 347	1.3
Trinity	-2.0	D	4.6	7.3	4.0	9.9	D	D	52.6	3 795	289	728	8 822	1.6
Tulare	20.1	0.1	3.6	8.0	3.2	6.6	3.5	6.3	23.0	62 080	136	19 398	146 520	3.4
Tuolumne	0.2	0.5	5.5	4.9	5.6	8.0	4.1	16.5	36.7	15 575	289	1 737	31 439	0.6
Ventura	3.9	1.8	4.7	15.6	9.6	6.7	9.0	9.0	17.2	130 995	155	16 583	285 880	1.5
Yolo	3.2	0.2	3.4	6.7	6.5	4.4	2.9	6.4	45.2	26 935	129	5 550	76 950	2.5
Yuba	3.4	0.4	3.7	2.6	3.0	3.5	1.5	10.0	58.8	12 660	171	4 121	28 217	2.1
COLORADO	0.7	4.9	6.7	6.1	17.8	5.4	7.9	8.8	15.9	794 937	148	72 872	2 309 228	4.4
Adams	0.4	0.7	12.1	7.9	6.6	6.4	3.0	8.7	22.1	58 460	121	7 126	167 043	2.4
Alamosa	4.5	D	4.9	1.5	6.6	9.3	5.7	D	26.4	2 725	167	591	6 811	3.9
Arapahoe	0.0	3.3	6.7	2.3	27.6	5.5	12.6	9.6	8.4	81 380	131	7 312	244 501	2.6
Archuleta	2.5	1.2	11.6	1.5	8.6	10.7	8.0	D	18.8	3 290	269	138	9 030	3.1
Baca	22.7	1.3	D	D	D	7.5	D	D	35.0	1 005	276	75	2 229	-0.8
Bent	35.1	0.0	D	D	D	4.6	D	2.3	25.8	1 000	173	221	2 211	-1.4

1. Per 1,000 resident population estimated as of July 1 of the year shown.

Table B. States and Counties — **Housing, Labor Force, and Employment**

STATE County	Housing units, 2010–2014								Civilian labor force, 2015				Civilian employment,[6] 2010–2014		
	Occupied units							Sub-stand-ard units[4] (percent)			Unemployment			Percent	
			Owner-occupied			Renter-occupied									
			Median value[1]	Median owner cost as a percent of income		Median rent[3]	Median rent as a percent of income[2]		Total	Percent change, 2014–2015			Total	Manage-ment, business, science and arts	Con-struction, produc-tion, and mainte-nance occu-pations
	Total	Percent		With a mort-gage	Without a mort-gage[2]						Total	Rate[5]			
	89	90	91	92	93	94	95	96	97	98	99	100	101	102	103
CALIFORNIA	12 617 280	54.8	371 400	28.3	11.3	1 243	33.8	8.6	18 981 771	0.8	1 183 155	6.2	16 890 442	37.1	20.1
Alameda	551 734	52.9	509 300	26.9	10.1	1 325	31.4	6.5	824 809	1.5	39 133	4.7	749 786	46.0	15.7
Alpine	377	81.7	313 800	34.4	11.3	775	35.9	2.1	520	1.4	41	7.9	505	39.0	19.4
Amador	13 939	75.7	251 800	28.3	13.9	1 029	36.9	1.5	14 404	-0.2	956	6.6	12 402	30.5	22.1
Butte	85 215	59.4	220 100	26.4	12.3	899	36.5	3.6	101 731	-0.1	7 334	7.2	88 274	33.9	18.6
Calaveras	18 608	79.0	242 600	29.9	14.3	1 072	30.2	2.2	20 614	1.2	1 330	6.5	17 212	35.2	23.9
Colusa	6 912	63.6	174 500	27.1	10.0	864	29.3	8.2	11 193	0.4	1 718	15.3	8 755	23.9	38.0
Contra Costa	380 183	65.0	417 400	27.5	11.3	1 395	32.7	4.8	549 948	1.3	27 530	5.0	499 984	42.9	15.7
Del Norte	9 527	59.6	180 100	26.8	13.3	843	33.4	4.6	9 915	-0.7	853	8.6	8 668	33.1	15.0
El Dorado	67 220	74.1	356 900	28.1	13.6	1 073	32.6	2.6	89 121	0.8	5 051	5.7	79 965	39.7	15.7
Fresno	292 550	53.1	191 700	26.3	11.1	884	35.0	10.4	444 168	0.8	45 262	10.2	367 392	28.4	28.8
Glenn	9 561	61.6	214 600	28.6	12.2	716	28.2	5.7	13 110	1.8	1 145	8.7	10 534	23.1	35.9
Humboldt	53 130	54.8	281 300	29.1	11.3	899	36.3	4.5	62 633	-0.2	3 525	5.6	58 838	32.9	20.3
Imperial	46 952	55.7	145 200	26.3	12.1	772	33.2	10.0	78 910	0.3	18 945	24.0	57 838	23.0	28.4
Inyo	7 891	63.5	235 200	25.8	12.9	835	31.5	3.7	9 181	-0.9	535	5.8	8 336	30.1	20.6
Kern	257 737	57.2	161 800	25.0	11.2	887	33.0	9.4	393 764	-0.3	40 212	10.2	321 221	26.1	33.4
Kings	41 108	52.0	170 000	25.6	10.0	875	30.7	10.0	58 354	1.0	6 120	10.5	50 951	24.5	33.5
Lake	26 771	62.7	167 900	31.9	15.3	921	39.5	3.5	29 140	-1.1	2 235	7.7	22 288	26.8	23.2
Lassen	9 821	63.6	176 500	24.0	11.4	901	30.0	3.9	10 891	0.1	792	7.3	9 411	31.0	19.7
Los Angeles	3 242 391	46.4	425 100	30.3	11.4	1 221	35.4	12.5	5 011 707	-0.3	336 860	6.7	4 548 646	35.5	20.6
Madera	42 723	60.7	179 100	29.0	11.5	937	32.6	10.3	60 566	-2.6	6 357	10.5	52 544	25.0	37.1
Marin	103 034	62.6	785 100	27.8	12.0	1 659	33.3	3.6	141 123	1.1	4 999	3.5	126 429	51.6	10.2
Mariposa	7 289	72.8	240 300	28.5	11.2	838	28.3	3.0	8 084	-0.6	583	7.2	7 454	29.7	19.8
Mendocino	33 693	56.8	310 300	31.5	12.8	972	36.3	6.1	40 207	-1.0	2 354	5.9	36 957	29.8	23.4
Merced	76 516	52.7	152 600	25.9	11.2	870	33.1	9.6	115 086	0.1	13 063	11.4	94 994	22.5	37.5
Modoc	3 893	72.4	157 300	22.4	11.5	671	34.7	2.1	3 276	-3.2	287	8.8	3 517	40.0	24.2
Mono	5 160	55.3	324 600	33.9	13.3	1 061	25.8	3.9	8 336	0.6	512	6.1	7 520	43.9	13.9
Monterey	125 115	49.6	362 100	29.4	10.7	1 228	33.7	12.7	221 383	1.1	17 875	8.1	175 455	27.7	30.3
Napa	49 631	60.4	439 000	28.0	12.0	1 376	32.5	6.6	74 752	1.2	3 442	4.6	67 312	35.1	21.9
Nevada	40 838	72.5	344 800	30.9	14.2	1 190	36.8	2.6	48 444	0.7	2 644	5.5	41 788	38.8	16.1
Orange	1 002 285	58.2	532 300	28.2	10.3	1 522	34.0	9.4	1 597 071	1.2	71 507	4.5	1 478 643	39.8	16.7
Placer	134 111	70.5	345 900	27.3	13.1	1 277	32.2	2.6	178 176	0.9	8 988	5.0	159 811	41.4	14.7
Plumas	8 529	71.5	231 400	30.0	13.6	824	30.7	3.1	7 946	-2.5	823	10.4	7 259	34.2	24.3
Riverside	690 388	65.7	236 400	29.2	13.4	1 182	35.8	7.7	1 035 178	1.8	69 645	6.7	895 237	29.0	24.1
Sacramento	519 460	55.9	236 500	26.7	10.3	1 035	33.8	5.2	688 999	0.9	41 375	6.0	619 316	37.5	16.6
San Benito	17 121	62.0	357 200	29.6	12.2	1 265	33.7	8.6	29 763	1.4	2 270	7.6	25 260	28.3	29.1
San Bernardino	607 604	60.9	225 400	28.1	11.7	1 113	35.7	9.2	926 641	1.8	59 848	6.5	812 707	28.6	26.8
San Diego	1 083 811	53.4	412 800	28.6	11.0	1 328	33.9	6.4	1 563 836	0.9	81 308	5.2	1 421 325	40.5	16.1
San Francisco	348 832	36.6	765 700	28.4	10.4	1 533	28.1	8.2	548 004	3.1	19 930	3.6	466 640	52.3	9.2
San Joaquin	217 343	56.9	211 300	27.3	11.5	1 033	34.5	7.9	316 903	1.0	28 127	8.9	275 581	28.4	28.8
San Luis Obispo	102 350	58.0	426 200	29.1	11.5	1 226	34.7	3.6	143 293	1.6	6 648	4.6	122 252	36.1	18.6
San Mateo	258 683	59.3	736 800	27.9	10.7	1 664	30.2	7.6	441 966	2.9	15 002	3.4	379 767	45.0	13.9
Santa Barbara	142 028	52.3	446 500	27.9	11.4	1 357	33.9	9.8	220 001	0.4	11 608	5.3	198 675	34.8	21.8
Santa Clara	614 714	57.0	664 100	26.7	10.0	1 637	29.1	8.1	1 018 407	2.3	42 316	4.2	888 761	50.3	14.7
Santa Cruz	94 219	58.1	559 500	29.6	11.9	1 427	35.8	6.7	144 248	0.8	10 816	7.5	129 416	40.5	19.0
Shasta	68 961	63.4	213 700	27.3	13.4	932	36.8	3.1	74 858	-0.6	5 842	7.8	67 871	32.4	19.2
Sierra	1 291	75.8	195 700	25.0	14.6	1 010	34.1	0.0	1 351	-4.9	121	9.0	1 203	35.2	28.3
Siskiyou	19 380	63.1	185 400	29.2	13.1	799	36.8	4.9	18 064	-0.2	1 694	9.4	16 225	33.5	21.3
Solano	142 521	60.2	263 600	26.9	10.0	1 290	33.2	4.9	206 604	1.3	12 650	6.1	183 876	33.0	21.6
Sonoma	186 935	59.6	414 500	28.4	12.0	1 302	33.9	5.4	260 344	1.1	11 680	4.5	235 040	35.8	19.7
Stanislaus	168 090	57.2	175 400	27.2	11.8	993	34.9	7.3	242 710	0.3	23 073	9.5	205 219	26.4	31.3
Sutter	31 723	59.1	189 600	25.4	11.1	898	31.5	7.9	44 824	0.6	4 824	10.8	37 377	29.5	27.6
Tehama	23 480	68.4	170 300	28.0	11.8	833	31.3	5.8	25 190	-0.2	2 004	8.0	22 521	25.6	29.3
Trinity	5 521	70.5	258 500	27.0	12.1	802	32.9	6.8	5 216	0.3	407	7.8	4 668	34.1	19.0
Tulare	132 706	57.2	161 000	26.9	11.3	826	33.0	11.3	203 392	2.1	23 721	11.7	170 819	23.2	37.1
Tuolumne	22 181	69.3	262 600	28.5	14.0	924	33.8	3.5	21 627	-0.3	1 541	7.1	19 455	32.6	19.0
Ventura	267 829	64.5	444 800	27.8	10.5	1 494	34.1	7.0	429 784	-0.7	24 435	5.7	394 105	37.4	20.9
Yolo	70 953	52.4	317 700	25.0	10.0	1 096	35.5	5.5	103 868	1.0	6 659	6.4	91 643	44.6	17.4
Yuba	24 712	58.1	170 800	27.2	12.6	884	34.5	8.2	28 137	0.3	2 600	9.2	24 794	26.8	26.3
COLORADO	1 998 314	64.8	239 400	23.5	10.1	969	30.8	2.9	2 828 535	0.5	109 834	3.9	2 560 703	40.1	18.4
Adams	155 047	64.5	189 400	24.6	11.0	1 003	30.9	5.1	247 538	0.5	10 721	4.3	220 941	29.1	27.4
Alamosa	5 993	58.8	142 100	24.5	10.6	622	33.1	3.1	7 639	1.2	394	5.2	6 359	29.0	24.7
Arapahoe	228 267	62.4	235 600	23.2	10.0	1 029	31.6	3.2	334 800	0.6	12 448	3.7	303 135	40.5	16.6
Archuleta	5 343	70.1	264 300	26.4	12.1	914	31.2	5.1	6 065	5.5	245	4.0	5 538	38.6	23.3
Baca	1 637	71.9	71 500	22.8	11.9	526	23.8	1.6	1 986	2.7	42	2.1	1 774	36.6	27.7
Bent	1 788	66.3	69 800	23.3	11.2	706	31.8	3.2	1 720	3.7	67	3.9	1 471	32.6	23.8

1. Specified owner-occupied units. 2. A value of 10.0 represents 10 percent or less; a value of 50.0 represents 50 percent or more. 3. Specified renter-occupied units.
4. Overcrowded or lacking complete plumbing facilities. 5. Percent of civilian labor force. 6. Persons 16 years old and over.

Table B. States and Counties — Nonfarm Employment and Agriculture

STATE County	Private nonfarm establishments, employment and payroll, 2014									Agriculture, 2012			
	Number of establishments	Employment						Annual payroll		Farms			
		Total	Health care and social assistance	Manufacturing	Retail trade	Finance and insurance	Professional, scientific, and technical services	Total (mil dol)	Average per employee (dollars)	Number	Percent with:		Farm operators whose principal occupation is farming (percent)
											Fewer than 50 acres	500 acres or more	
	104	105	106	107	108	109	110	111	112	113	114	115	116
CALIFORNIA	889 646	13 838 702	1 818 568	1 149 707	1 638 332	585 304	1 226 321	797 046	57 595	77 857	64.8	9.9	54.5
Alameda	37 901	622 942	88 265	64 573	66 392	17 552	62 352	39 513	63 430	452	60.2	12.2	48.7
Alpine	43	223	D	D	D	D	D	5	22 126	3	0.0	33.3	0.0
Amador	802	7 712	1 282	779	1 527	191	280	268	34 790	461	47.7	11.3	49.2
Butte	4 637	57 562	13 656	4 477	10 411	2 300	2 557	2 018	35 059	2 056	66.8	7.0	59.4
Calaveras	894	5 863	949	386	1 177	133	D	184	31 362	663	60.0	10.0	46.6
Colusa	370	4 027	454	663	429	108	45	150	37 267	782	27.5	23.0	61.6
Contra Costa	22 729	306 882	50 857	14 908	43 416	22 331	23 774	19 453	63 390	602	73.3	8.0	52.0
Del Norte	420	3 937	1 185	D	937	96	119	119	30 298	121	59.5	6.6	57.9
El Dorado	4 317	42 457	6 317	2 441	5 901	3 431	2 291	1 757	41 379	1 358	78.4	3.0	52.1
Fresno	16 119	244 494	41 610	23 173	35 917	8 706	11 094	9 626	39 371	5 683	59.7	11.2	59.6
Glenn	452	4 589	521	714	709	129	D	222	48 353	1 311	51.3	15.3	62.9
Humboldt	3 137	32 620	6 924	2 093	6 540	977	1 631	1 088	33 364	930	54.0	15.5	56.1
Imperial	2 465	32 849	4 764	3 647	8 461	D	780	1 003	30 535	421	29.7	40.6	69.4
Inyo	526	5 309	1 153	D	953	D	114	184	34 635	125	50.4	31.2	63.2
Kern	12 480	192 765	29 321	11 663	30 011	5 985	12 845	8 555	44 382	1 938	40.6	26.6	63.2
Kings	1 589	23 624	4 752	4 186	4 129	505	487	842	35 626	1 056	51.2	18.6	66.0
Lake	1 060	9 604	2 470	254	2 186	D	244	339	35 300	838	68.7	5.1	43.9
Lassen	404	3 706	835	D	841	95	119	122	32 987	448	40.6	25.2	51.8
Los Angeles	258 982	3 932 904	510 223	353 716	411 962	153 681	393 437	203 277	51 686	1 294	88.9	2.9	60.6
Madera	1 918	25 722	5 811	3 725	3 598	454	482	1 001	38 910	1 507	44.8	14.3	57.9
Marin	9 801	99 584	15 262	2 041	14 368	5 836	8 824	5 816	58 405	323	43.9	34.1	58.5
Mariposa	348	2 912	384	D	405	32	45	92	31 590	364	37.9	23.6	51.9
Mendocino	2 450	22 383	4 296	2 637	4 509	D	659	771	34 430	1 220	48.8	14.3	49.8
Merced	2 903	42 083	6 738	9 390	8 069	992	795	1 520	36 124	2 486	56.7	12.8	64.5
Modoc	150	1 213	446	D	200	31	36	40	33 101	437	22.4	37.8	60.4
Mono	559	5 863	D	49	628	30	103	159	27 114	72	31.9	27.8	58.3
Monterey	8 420	102 790	15 249	6 750	16 669	2 851	6 981	4 397	42 780	1 179	42.0	26.4	61.7
Napa	4 075	60 882	10 383	11 304	6 861	1 412	1 829	2 933	48 174	1 685	71.9	5.3	34.9
Nevada	2 915	26 220	4 411	2 278	4 038	907	1 396	1 043	39 781	742	79.0	2.0	46.6
Orange	90 956	1 421 125	155 183	147 609	153 007	89 430	120 389	76 941	54 141	312	85.3	4.8	58.7
Placer	9 880	131 786	20 097	4 378	22 027	9 066	10 049	6 545	49 662	1 355	82.2	2.4	45.5
Plumas	584	3 595	923	D	562	134	114	145	40 431	141	37.6	34.0	44.0
Riverside	35 595	514 885	70 739	42 645	90 373	10 760	17 890	18 944	36 793	2 949	86.0	3.5	49.1
Sacramento	27 976	435 440	77 946	19 708	59 446	25 889	33 630	21 793	50 049	1 352	72.3	7.6	48.2
San Benito	932	10 868	1 373	2 554	1 293	245	241	436	40 152	628	51.6	23.2	58.3
San Bernardino	32 930	554 359	83 068	50 767	84 014	14 048	17 794	22 164	39 981	1 249	85.9	2.1	57.0
San Diego	79 958	1 202 583	155 350	97 352	150 619	51 279	133 602	61 752	51 349	5 732	91.6	0.9	47.6
San Francisco	33 189	573 297	61 231	7 436	45 704	47 869	96 371	52 933	92 332	6	100.0	0.0	83.3
San Joaquin	10 825	168 367	26 839	18 597	25 495	6 303	4 459	6 916	41 079	3 580	63.5	8.3	59.0
San Luis Obispo	8 028	89 509	15 590	6 081	14 744	2 309	4 788	3 510	39 213	2 666	55.8	12.2	47.0
San Mateo	20 653	367 148	33 472	D	34 575	21 130	37 190	39 192	106 747	334	61.7	6.3	56.0
Santa Barbara	11 296	141 785	20 431	13 874	20 023	4 146	9 657	6 827	48 152	1 597	63.9	11.3	51.7
Santa Clara	47 019	963 099	102 405	85 253	83 843	25 331	132 254	101 283	105 163	1 003	76.4	5.6	56.0
Santa Cruz	6 830	72 301	12 651	4 671	11 946	2 105	4 001	3 144	43 481	667	73.8	4.6	62.1
Shasta	4 114	47 366	9 875	1 986	9 230	2 029	2 292	1 748	36 912	1 544	72.9	6.1	44.9
Sierra	68	211	D	D	33	D	D	7	34 664	48	14.6	27.1	56.3
Siskiyou	1 069	8 076	1 630	740	1 480	221	344	263	32 546	929	35.5	22.5	58.2
Solano	6 745	105 212	22 806	9 915	18 994	4 207	3 353	4 979	47 326	860	62.9	11.7	53.7
Sonoma	13 523	158 918	24 148	18 874	24 838	5 600	9 335	7 389	46 494	3 579	71.3	6.0	51.3
Stanislaus	8 544	132 417	23 286	19 300	22 628	3 314	5 416	5 466	41 277	4 143	68.8	5.9	59.1
Sutter	1 692	20 096	3 726	1 447	4 263	756	638	768	38 199	1 358	51.8	14.1	64.4
Tehama	958	11 723	1 943	D	1 858	228	199	446	38 007	1 743	61.6	10.7	52.3
Trinity	252	1 489	307	202	404	42	68	48	32 147	247	55.5	8.1	48.6
Tulare	6 165	90 454	15 643	12 427	15 856	2 939	2 553	3 313	36 632	4 931	61.2	8.4	58.3
Tuolumne	1 291	12 200	2 750	808	2 240	313	471	450	36 845	391	53.5	9.7	40.7
Ventura	20 251	251 566	34 844	24 280	38 761	12 799	22 262	12 826	50 984	2 150	78.0	5.2	48.7
Yolo	3 904	59 766	6 496	6 414	7 305	1 335	3 319	2 696	45 114	1 011	47.5	14.7	59.1
Yuba	806	9 237	2 042	513	1 473	196	578	335	36 248	795	61.4	10.4	44.2
COLORADO	158 064	2 181 455	279 544	120 963	262 395	103 532	193 812	112 194	51 431	36 180	39.4	24.3	49.6
Adams	8 833	147 456	19 969	11 468	17 879	2 740	4 829	6 817	46 234	841	50.4	20.6	43.0
Alamosa	491	5 409	1 659	D	1 045	381	149	180	33 342	322	22.4	24.5	51.2
Arapahoe	17 628	267 580	33 654	6 927	33 008	21 459	24 697	15 504	57 940	755	65.4	10.9	39.3
Archuleta	485	2 974	286	D	610	94	116	81	27 259	372	34.9	22.3	54.0
Baca	90	507	D	D	113	20	8	15	30 292	737	3.4	62.0	48.4
Bent	57	535	68	D	71	D	D	18	32 714	277	15.9	46.6	53.4

Table B. States and Counties — **Agriculture**

Agriculture, 2012 (cont.)

STATE County	Acreage (1,000)	Percent change, 2007–2012	Average size of farm	Total irrigated (1,000)	Total cropland (1,000)	Average per farm	Average per acre	Value of machinery and equipment, average per farm (dollars)	Total (mil dol)	Average per farm (dollars)	Crops	Live-stock and poultry products	$10,000 or more	$100,000 or more	Total ($1,000)	Percent of farms
	117	118	119	120	121	122	123	124	125	126	127	128	129	130	131	132
CALIFORNIA	25 569	0.8	328	7 862.0	9 591.8	2 061 792	6 278	124 710	42 627.5	547 510	71.2	28.8	57.0	26.4	146 919	9.8
Alameda	178	-13.1	393	8.9	20.3	2 170 265	5 517	47 292	57.5	127 261	82.7	17.3	42.7	9.7	49	3.5
Alpine	D	D	D	0.2	0.6	1 800 000	D	20 333	0.3	88 333	D	D	100.0	33.3	0	0.0
Amador	155	-5.1	337	11.3	16.0	1 324 401	3 934	51 321	32.0	69 345	68.1	31.9	49.7	15.4	37	2.8
Butte	381	1.9	185	199.7	227.3	1 408 199	7 599	135 591	541.3	263 266	97.3	2.7	59.7	26.2	9 386	13.7
Calaveras	212	5.5	320	4.5	6.1	1 043 833	3 262	40 736	26.0	39 222	45.5	54.5	36.2	7.7	8	0.6
Colusa	453	-4.4	579	260.9	285.7	3 146 341	5 431	300 276	577.3	738 252	98.7	1.3	80.7	59.1	13 629	48.5
Contra Costa	128	-13.1	212	27.3	46.5	1 786 847	8 425	80 620	89.4	148 435	84.7	15.3	43.2	13.1	232	5.6
Del Norte	D	D	D	9.2	8.6	1 481 355	D	115 661	35.7	294 636	46.5	53.5	34.7	11.6	96	12.4
El Dorado	128	19.9	95	6.8	11.1	777 782	8 228	30 537	30.5	22 465	79.8	20.2	32.3	5.7	237	3.0
Fresno	1 721	5.2	303	968.7	1 153.4	2 509 484	8 286	161 509	4 973.0	875 073	74.4	25.6	71.9	41.9	10 149	9.0
Glenn	669	36.7	510	242.9	274.3	2 342 959	4 593	192 225	637.4	486 166	79.9	20.1	68.6	38.0	13 136	35.5
Humboldt	594	-0.6	638	17.1	20.9	1 649 520	2 584	57 685	203.3	218 559	D	D	45.4	16.8	1 242	8.8
Imperial	516	20.7	1 225	455.0	487.9	8 577 865	7 002	745 304	1 888.6	4 486 078	69.4	30.6	84.3	66.7	2 788	29.5
Inyo	331	13.1	2 647	23.8	18.7	2 062 976	779	86 688	19.6	156 904	34.6	65.4	40.8	16.0	D	1.6
Kern	2 330	-1.3	1 202	730.0	899.4	5 332 548	4 435	332 960	3 999.0	2 063 462	80.8	19.2	62.0	43.8	5 306	15.5
Kings	674	-1.0	638	407.4	501.5	3 847 243	6 031	340 454	1 829.2	1 732 231	46.7	53.3	68.3	45.1	7 901	36.4
Lake	151	21.4	180	13.5	29.1	1 095 199	6 089	55 516	99.5	118 691	98.0	2.0	52.6	13.6	100	4.8
Lassen	483	5.1	1 077	66.0	70.9	2 075 935	1 927	113 085	72.7	162 212	D	D	42.0	16.3	186	9.6
Los Angeles	92	-15.5	71	39.7	59.6	882 832	12 459	45 905	193.1	149 225	90.1	9.9	34.2	11.6	247	3.1
Madera	654	-3.8	434	292.3	304.2	3 302 033	7 614	182 022	1 602.8	1 063 547	77.4	22.6	70.2	46.8	2 400	11.4
Marin	171	28.2	529	3.7	14.4	3 295 415	6 229	69 226	91.8	284 238	9.3	90.7	64.1	34.1	1 283	16.4
Mariposa	284	33.4	779	1.8	12.6	1 638 973	2 104	44 742	22.3	61 321	11.7	88.3	37.1	8.8	515	7.4
Mendocino	770	26.5	631	25.7	49.3	2 533 399	4 013	51 877	148.9	122 047	92.1	7.9	50.2	16.9	426	2.3
Merced	979	-6.0	394	468.2	522.6	3 045 778	7 737	236 454	2 967.5	1 193 694	42.9	57.1	76.0	45.7	9 528	20.2
Modoc	524	-12.4	1 198	128.4	154.7	2 061 595	1 721	125 055	106.6	243 950	66.0	34.0	60.4	37.1	701	24.7
Mono	56	26.4	783	21.5	11.4	2 205 819	2 817	144 722	18.0	249 667	49.0	51.0	48.6	40.3	D	1.4
Monterey	1 268	-4.5	1 076	263.8	358.3	5 263 068	4 893	396 806	2 979.7	2 527 341	98.5	1.5	59.6	35.4	635	7.0
Napa	253	13.5	150	54.6	63.0	3 278 130	21 801	85 134	536.1	318 188	97.8	2.2	74.5	34.1	85	1.1
Nevada	42	-40.0	57	5.3	3.3	614 920	10 834	31 177	9.1	12 256	63.9	36.1	27.9	2.4	126	2.2
Orange	60	-30.8	194	8.1	15.2	4 237 538	21 854	70 968	158.5	508 055	99.0	1.0	41.3	18.3	43	4.8
Placer	91	-30.9	67	20.7	33.6	719 330	10 664	35 897	43.4	32 057	D	D	27.2	5.0	1 305	2.8
Plumas	174	44.9	1 236	19.1	26.0	2 194 518	1 776	95 652	22.6	160 404	19.7	80.3	51.8	22.0	0	0.0
Riverside	344	-3.0	117	146.0	227.2	1 191 416	10 212	76 009	1 038.9	352 306	71.7	28.3	50.2	13.9	2 189	4.7
Sacramento	247	-24.9	183	86.0	105.7	1 302 636	7 135	85 653	326.6	241 559	63.9	36.1	43.2	18.6	2 474	10.3
San Benito	604	4.2	962	19.2	38.5	2 737 111	2 844	93 435	164.0	261 198	76.9	23.1	50.2	18.9	174	7.5
San Bernardino	77	-85.0	62	21.8	29.8	831 612	13 455	83 151	582.2	466 156	11.5	88.5	42.4	16.7	849	4.1
San Diego	222	-27.1	39	45.2	68.2	694 313	17 964	34 672	726.0	126 657	89.3	10.7	42.9	9.1	451	1.7
San Francisco	0	71.4	2	0	0	252 167	126 083	52 000	D	D	D	D	0.0	0.0	0	0.0
San Joaquin	787	6.7	220	485.4	517.9	2 218 140	10 090	145 302	2 250.2	628 536	73.7	26.3	73.5	39.3	5 508	9.4
San Luis Obispo	1 339	-2.2	502	81.6	255.4	2 115 410	4 212	92 222	665.0	249 431	92.9	7.1	52.2	19.1	3 488	9.0
San Mateo	48	-15.6	144	2.8	8.5	1 629 243	11 299	69 497	75.9	227 213	96.4	3.6	49.1	14.7	182	4.2
Santa Barbara	701	-3.6	439	96.7	132.3	3 233 061	7 365	125 663	1 177.9	737 581	95.8	4.2	58.8	29.4	554	1.5
Santa Clara	230	-23.3	229	17.8	38.4	1 538 866	6 713	69 246	243.8	243 100	95.7	4.3	45.3	12.8	20	1.2
Santa Cruz	100	110.5	150	28.9	41.1	1 857 240	12 390	113 943	565.8	848 328	96.9	3.1	59.2	28.0	D	0.1
Shasta	376	-3.7	244	38.2	36.9	682 565	2 801	36 550	65.6	42 501	36.6	63.4	26.2	4.8	420	4.6
Sierra	39	36.0	815	9.7	4.0	1 226 333	1 504	92 896	D	D	D	D	62.5	22.9	D	2.1
Siskiyou	723	21.0	778	160.0	194.8	1 586 712	2 039	121 981	223.1	240 146	85.4	14.6	42.2	18.0	2 029	19.7
Solano	407	13.6	473	130.9	169.6	2 631 010	5 558	146 770	307.4	357 463	79.0	21.0	53.1	22.7	1 911	15.7
Sonoma	590	11.1	165	75.0	130.6	2 409 158	14 620	78 965	974.4	272 253	62.2	37.8	60.3	24.3	2 615	4.1
Stanislaus	768	-2.7	185	320.8	340.9	1 786 289	9 636	117 810	2 228.1	537 807	47.7	52.3	66.5	33.9	7 049	10.7
Sutter	375	4.3	276	244.3	275.8	1 828 515	6 619	179 143	508.2	374 208	98.8	1.2	71.1	40.8	11 326	27.1
Tehama	617	15.8	354	84.9	89.3	1 053 199	2 978	71 962	240.8	138 163	70.6	29.4	46.2	13.8	1 627	9.0
Trinity	176	40.8	712	1.6	2.1	811 870	1 140	29 838	5.2	20 895	D	D	23.1	2.0	247	12.1
Tulare	1 239	6.0	251	557.4	677.5	1 893 271	7 535	144 666	4 017.1	814 657	41.6	58.4	70.2	36.6	12 174	13.5
Tuolumne	88	-25.0	225	2.3	2.8	1 039 974	4 631	59 552	27.7	70 721	9.4	90.6	25.6	3.1	D	0.5
Ventura	281	8.5	131	87.1	101.1	2 041 990	15 621	94 136	1 440.1	669 829	99.3	0.7	65.1	24.7	154	2.0
Yolo	461	-4.0	456	229.9	306.9	2 571 454	5 642	218 361	561.2	555 135	93.6	6.4	61.7	34.2	6 240	28.1
Yuba	188	16.6	236	82.5	89.8	1 367 039	5 792	149 175	193.4	243 332	79.8	20.2	47.0	25.4	3 341	15.3
COLORADO	31 887	0.9	881	2 516.8	10 649.7	1 128 277	1 280	109 260	7 780.9	215 060	31.3	68.7	37.7	15.6	165 576	30.7
Adams	691	-1.6	821	17.6	550.3	1 179 177	1 436	121 985	116.5	138 483	88.0	12.0	31.6	15.2	5 479	40.7
Alamosa	182	3.3	567	68.6	71.5	825 866	1 458	154 025	92.5	287 354	87.5	12.5	46.0	23.0	821	29.8
Arapahoe	283	12.5	375	2.5	137.2	632 109	1 685	62 514	31.7	41 933	D	D	20.9	4.6	1 635	23.2
Archuleta	210	40.5	565	24.2	13.2	1 213 137	2 147	55 333	15.5	41 653	8.3	91.7	31.7	7.3	329	4.6
Baca	1 503	15.6	2 040	62.6	872.6	1 133 718	556	153 448	125.3	170 012	63.0	37.0	48.3	28.9	15 510	87.9
Bent	726	-17.3	2 620	31.5	107.1	1 219 368	465	156 993	70.8	255 574	17.9	82.1	55.6	27.8	2 945	58.8

Table B. States and Counties — **Water Use, Wholesale Trade, Retail Trade, and Real Estate**

STATE County	Water use, 2010 Total water withdrawn (mil gal/day)	Gallons withdrawn per person per day	Wholesale trade,[1] 2012 Number of establishments	Number of employees	Sales (mil dol)	Annual payroll (mil dol)	Retail trade,[2] 2012 Number of establishments	Number of employees	Sales (mil dol)	Annual payroll (mil dol)	Real estate and rental and leasing,[2] 2012 Number of establishments	Number of employees	Receipts (mil dol)	Annual payroll (mil dol)
	133	134	135	136	137	138	139	140	141	142	143	144	145	146
CALIFORNIA	37 962.2	1 019	52 664	723 526	666 652.2	48 408.7	106 419	1 540 055	481 800.5	43 361.0	49 276	273 511	78 740.2	13 467.5
Alameda	254.9	169	2 366	44 934	37 580.6	3 133.2	4 213	61 372	20 901.0	1 826.9	1 920	9 602	2 575.5	460.9
Alpine	4.5	3 804	NA	NA	NA	NA	4	8	0.6	0.1	2	D	D	D
Amador	32.4	850	20	D	D	D	121	1 489	321.5	35.7	38	100	17.3	3.5
Butte	715.3	3 252	148	D	D	D	725	9 231	2 576.9	240.4	234	1 160	147.6	28.3
Calaveras	23.4	513	18	D	D	D	133	1 044	252.3	27.2	44	170	23.2	3.5
Colusa	835.0	38 985	27	338	428.7	18.7	59	434	127.9	10.6	19	40	7.8	1.2
Contra Costa	302.7	289	753	6 570	6 887.2	417.8	2 490	41 494	11 847.9	1 181.4	1 306	6 491	1 779.2	334.1
Del Norte	13.7	478	6	D	D	D	60	1 012	192.8	22.5	33	96	14.7	2.8
El Dorado	55.7	308	107	553	316.7	28.7	530	5 841	1 597.8	155.8	242	856	176.1	27.6
Fresno	2 813.2	3 024	819	12 981	9 266.3	663.0	2 421	32 954	9 117.8	836.0	769	4 299	715.1	139.6
Glenn	606.6	21 571	17	224	160.1	11.8	73	688	191.2	16.3	20	41	5.4	1.4
Humboldt	114.0	847	105	1 028	361.9	41.5	578	6 600	1 759.2	170.3	174	536	89.9	15.2
Imperial	1 169.2	6 699	197	1 801	1 599.1	72.5	446	7 322	1 676.9	160.3	119	574	92.6	15.9
Inyo	111.6	6 016	20	D	D	D	87	836	229.0	22.4	23	82	6.7	1.7
Kern	2 159.9	2 572	582	7 990	6 987.9	447.4	1 867	27 918	8 640.6	700.7	634	3 492	733.6	141.3
Kings	1 298.9	8 490	69	684	746.6	36.3	285	3 961	1 032.0	92.2	97	371	71.0	9.9
Lake	50.9	786	24	D	D	D	167	2 041	522.3	49.8	59	160	24.5	4.1
Lassen	202.6	5 806	9	D	D	D	79	784	215.8	19.7	23	44	19.3	3.2
Los Angeles	3 064.0	312	21 270	237 644	199 804.8	12 881.4	28 427	385 441	121 389.4	10 699.7	13 874	82 043	29 586.3	4 476.1
Madera	748.7	4 963	76	815	508.9	37.8	326	3 455	1 012.9	84.3	75	336	38.4	8.5
Marin	42.9	170	359	2 780	1 864.6	180.8	1 053	14 698	5 087.5	544.8	589	2 455	1 458.6	168.7
Mariposa	5.3	291	6	22	18.9	0.7	64	419	102.5	9.7	26	82	8.3	2.7
Mendocino	81.5	928	67	679	407.6	28.3	462	4 551	1 095.2	117.1	130	494	61.6	12.8
Merced	1 494.7	5 843	112	1 635	2 260.2	71.2	528	7 497	1 959.5	173.3	152	532	79.1	14.6
Modoc	261.5	27 001	7	D	D	D	30	203	45.7	4.9	7	15	1.3	0.2
Mono	229.7	16 174	7	D	D	D	72	653	139.8	15.2	62	312	31.1	8.0
Monterey	545.5	1 314	346	4 574	5 775.2	278.9	1 316	16 335	4 457.4	437.2	444	1 873	436.3	69.6
Napa	96.9	710	167	D	D	D	524	6 318	1 699.0	184.2	207	1 026	160.4	38.2
Nevada	48.7	493	75	D	D	D	400	3 965	1 012.3	110.2	157	747	204.6	36.7
Orange	765.4	254	6 434	79 685	97 796.0	5 200.7	9 390	143 012	45 193.6	4 135.3	5 320	38 952	9 259.7	1 921.2
Placer	191.2	549	311	4 317	4 474.4	239.9	1 231	20 999	6 437.9	592.9	661	3 544	620.1	146.9
Plumas	118.7	5 934	7	D	D	D	86	577	139.3	13.6	34	83	14.4	2.6
Riverside	1 099.3	502	1 568	21 800	18 716.8	1 071.9	4 996	81 017	25 058.9	2 128.9	2 038	8 466	1 684.9	303.8
Sacramento	681.1	480	1 096	14 448	18 746.3	816.5	3 512	55 910	15 227.3	1 484.7	1 650	8 879	1 621.2	364.9
San Benito	85.4	1 546	39	638	275.4	41.6	105	1 276	345.2	34.9	53	116	25.7	4.1
San Bernardino	659.4	324	2 493	33 768	30 996.2	1 574.6	4 748	79 792	24 380.5	2 013.4	1 570	7 788	1 622.3	316.3
San Diego	2 818.2	910	3 883	59 227	35 937.4	4 055.0	9 219	138 929	39 786.1	3 787.5	5 401	28 321	7 895.7	1 308.8
San Francisco	93.5	116	1 066	12 056	11 121.7	850.7	3 573	43 378	14 632.7	1 455.0	1 828	15 000	6 000.9	1 071.1
San Joaquin	1 753.4	2 559	515	9 279	11 713.5	495.7	1 602	24 097	7 059.5	616.4	572	2 655	464.7	97.2
San Luis Obispo	2 579.1	9 565	289	D	D	D	1 177	13 992	3 624.0	361.5	430	1 552	278.4	52.2
San Mateo	93.1	130	1 050	15 030	15 969.7	1 249.1	2 041	34 069	11 330.6	1 062.8	1 142	7 018	2 227.1	348.4
Santa Barbara	264.3	623	406	5 325	3 475.6	397.1	1 509	18 781	4 853.8	501.5	691	3 047	570.7	113.7
Santa Clara	298.2	167	2 310	84 304	91 859.0	10 822.2	4 927	84 158	40 336.7	3 212.4	2 426	12 827	4 458.9	763.7
Santa Cruz	66.4	253	266	5 614	5 898.2	297.2	887	11 120	4 368.0	294.7	363	1 271	264.1	41.8
Shasta	239.0	1 349	158	1 437	1 023.9	59.8	647	8 980	2 507.1	241.4	207	765	121.4	22.1
Sierra	39.0	12 046	1	D	D	D	9	31	5.1	0.6	1	D	D	D
Siskiyou	411.1	9 155	28	266	165.2	9.0	179	1 563	426.7	36.0	53	114	10.8	2.4
Solano	452.8	1 095	249	4 165	2 803.7	215.6	1 060	17 610	5 106.6	469.9	381	1 629	389.2	59.2
Sonoma	259.5	536	593	8 047	4 443.2	557.8	1 768	23 032	6 016.3	655.8	679	2 824	631.1	103.4
Stanislaus	1 642.7	3 193	405	6 087	5 295.1	313.6	1 374	20 970	5 933.6	527.1	433	2 141	387.9	73.2
Sutter	722.0	7 621	70	1 658	1 197.3	99.6	287	4 188	1 069.5	101.8	89	436	50.5	11.1
Tehama	825.6	13 009	25	190	88.8	6.4	151	1 696	654.6	45.5	48	152	25.7	4.6
Trinity	22.5	1 634	2	D	D	D	53	333	72.7	7.3	7	D	D	D
Tulare	2 600.3	5 881	325	4 564	3 890.5	191.8	1 044	14 210	3 903.5	340.6	306	1 421	249.0	40.9
Tuolumne	35.8	646	31	D	D	D	173	2 219	573.3	54.5	82	174	32.6	4.4
Ventura	719.5	874	985	D	D	D	2 562	37 012	11 194.2	1 011.0	1 008	4 568	983.6	196.5
Yolo	780.2	3 885	254	4 938	6 762.1	269.9	442	7 111	1 968.8	190.3	279	1 604	265.1	59.4
Yuba	261.7	3 627	26	D	D	D	127	1 369	390.2	34.7	45	123	18.0	3.3
COLORADO	10 994.2	2 186	5 733	75 717	77 035.0	4 762.1	18 474	245 704	67 815.2	6 508.6	9 295	38 706	8 482.5	1 569.6
Adams	230.9	523	608	13 547	12 918.6	760.9	1 044	16 769	5 548.7	487.2	434	2 611	522.7	91.5
Alamosa	152.4	9 868	18	166	78.8	6.0	85	1 091	280.7	27.7	18	83	11.1	2.6
Arapahoe	187.0	327	668	8 515	17 863.9	604.2	1 866	30 885	9 404.7	875.8	1 073	4 537	1 313.9	204.3
Archuleta	59.3	4 905	6	32	9.3	0.8	88	506	130.8	12.6	34	97	11.7	2.2
Baca	98.5	26 006	23	57	86.1	2.0	16	128	38.4	3.1	3	D	D	D
Bent	152.4	23 454	NA	NA	NA	NA	12	73	17.4	1.3	NA	NA	NA	NA

1. Merchant wholesalers, except manufacturers' sales branches and offices. 2. Employer establishments.

Table B. States and Counties — Professional Services, Manufacturing, and Accommodation and Food Services

STATE County	Professional, scientific, and technical services, 2012				Manufacturing, 2012				Accommodation and food services, 2012			
	Number of establishments	Number of employees	Receipts (mil dol)	Annual payroll (mil dol)	Number of establishments	Number of employees	Receipts (mil dol)	Annual payroll (mil dol)	Number of establishments	Number of employees	Sales (mil dol)	Annual payroll (mil dol)
	147	148	149	150	151	152	153	154	155	156	157	158
CALIFORNIA	114 321	1 303 232	234 371.2	90 437.3	38 741	1 163 341	512 303.2	69 316.8	78 560	1 394 984	90 830.4	25 147.8
Alameda	5 387	60 272	13 550.3	5 414.1	1 846	63 679	D	4 502.1	3 631	51 283	3 192.4	884.9
Alpine	3	D	D	D	NA	NA	NA	NA	9	D	D	D
Amador	80	277	29.1	9.8	38	599	139.6	31.6	100	2 088	242.0	53.1
Butte	424	2 394	388.0	97.2	177	4 126	1 341.1	168.3	397	7 091	350.5	96.4
Calaveras	63	187	18.1	7.1	33	358	D	11.7	99	1 105	69.6	16.6
Colusa	18	51	4.0	1.4	25	716	474.5	33.3	41	931	97.8	21.5
Contra Costa	3 347	27 079	5 926.1	2 112.6	540	15 118	33 681.2	1 090.7	1 805	27 719	1 660.0	455.8
Del Norte	30	D	D	D	9	D	D	41.2	68	611	32.3	7.8
El Dorado	515	D	D	D	162	2 415	517.4	130.9	424	5 565	319.8	86.7
Fresno	1 522	10 531	1 367.8	474.3	585	25 269	8 658.3	1 052.9	1 450	24 100	1 226.2	333.9
Glenn	33	278	45.0	21.2	26	636	D	24.4	55	598	33.2	8.4
Humboldt	244	1 996	164.6	62.4	134	2 149	D	80.9	374	4 746	257.5	70.0
Imperial	179	787	79.1	30.4	50	2 218	1 466.0	95.4	258	3 516	182.6	47.9
Inyo	35	D	D	D	13	161	D	7.4	91	1 525	99.6	26.7
Kern	1 204	11 757	1 641.3	637.3	391	12 257	6 890.7	558.2	1 278	19 829	1 092.2	284.0
Kings	85	461	51.0	18.4	60	4 380	2 904.0	180.5	172	2 824	378.6	42.6
Lake	66	243	22.2	7.6	32	265	80.5	11.1	130	1 460	88.8	24.9
Lassen	26	121	13.5	6.4	NA	NA	NA	NA	46	619	36.0	10.6
Los Angeles	31 324	521 067	66 261.5	26 244.3	12 760	359 532	163 829.6	19 852.8	20 298	355 736	22 965.1	6 390.6
Madera	116	493	66.9	21.6	92	3 298	1 441.1	168.0	193	2 461	150.1	37.1
Marin	1 744	9 095	2 037.3	698.0	219	1 935	D	92.7	751	11 578	729.7	225.6
Mariposa	19	D	D	D	14	78	D	3.5	56	1 473	157.9	32.3
Mendocino	206	729	68.1	22.9	123	2 066	453.4	82.1	339	3 369	182.6	50.8
Merced	142	791	67.1	26.2	116	9 973	4 435.6	405.4	298	4 585	232.9	60.2
Modoc	12	60	5.3	1.5	3	D	D	D	21	149	8.3	1.9
Mono	23	80	10.5	3.4	7	39	D	1.2	141	3 450	246.9	67.4
Monterey	806	7 448	847.3	338.0	263	6 078	2 258.9	252.3	979	17 786	1 328.8	378.0
Napa	395	1 801	280.5	101.5	431	10 837	4 623.5	622.5	375	10 466	774.1	247.7
Nevada	346	1 415	227.0	89.1	140	1 381	319.7	72.4	245	5 007	231.2	69.9
Orange	14 120	112 581	24 110.2	8 899.6	4 701	150 020	47 299.4	8 879.0	7 141	143 519	9 050.6	2 599.9
Placer	1 180	D	D	D	261	4 246	932.9	216.9	823	18 063	1 452.0	327.3
Plumas	51	D	D	D	17	444	D	19.8	100	D	D	D
Riverside	3 182	16 261	2 149.0	811.3	1 447	41 519	15 137.0	1 930.4	3 350	75 061	5 230.9	1 376.8
Sacramento	3 754	32 572	5 743.4	2 153.4	758	19 902	6 960.7	1 161.8	2 560	44 722	2 422.7	671.9
San Benito	70	213	26.4	8.9	62	2 222	591.1	95.6	80	925	49.9	13.5
San Bernardino	2 489	16 890	2 201.9	776.5	1 814	46 822	17 591.6	2 112.8	3 126	53 047	2 858.0	773.6
San Diego	12 528	134 334	24 111.3	9 099.2	2 891	97 346	33 320.5	6 196.1	6 880	147 457	10 403.8	2 857.4
San Francisco	6 295	84 841	29 389.5	9 033.5	693	7 506	D	327.6	4 059	73 417	6 142.7	1 841.6
San Joaquin	780	4 463	491.1	190.0	517	18 703	9 212.4	879.0	997	15 422	808.6	211.0
San Luis Obispo	868	4 914	673.1	269.5	382	6 107	2 854.0	285.7	865	14 254	824.8	229.5
San Mateo	2 999	32 982	8 831.3	3 659.8	633	22 708	D	2 299.6	1 910	33 203	2 552.9	710.9
Santa Barbara	1 347	9 785	1 751.7	654.0	458	13 896	4 157.6	851.5	1 087	20 623	1 428.9	400.1
Santa Clara	8 395	125 395	30 138.9	13 549.8	2 385	100 981	41 450.6	9 169.2	4 407	72 491	4 809.2	1 336.2
Santa Cruz	880	4 268	603.0	249.2	293	4 479	1 213.4	219.2	678	10 032	586.0	168.6
Shasta	358	D	D	D	147	1 990	511.9	93.7	376	5 421	285.5	76.7
Sierra	1	D	D	D	3	D	D	D	14	D	D	D
Siskiyou	96	362	38.8	12.0	31	667	203.4	28.2	135	1 317	71.5	19.7
Solano	547	3 258	415.3	150.6	259	9 266	11 412.2	558.9	711	11 129	625.6	163.2
Sonoma	1 514	9 140	1 244.4	524.0	821	19 324	6 131.7	1 085.2	1 192	17 606	1 058.7	301.8
Stanislaus	649	5 111	507.5	196.0	395	19 963	11 703.6	1 007.8	813	13 611	705.7	192.6
Sutter	120	568	57.8	22.1	61	1 551	543.5	78.0	142	2 263	116.6	30.1
Tehama	61	211	27.9	8.6	38	1 648	449.5	70.1	121	1 367	65.1	16.6
Trinity	19	74	7.0	2.5	14	194	D	7.9	46	205	13.4	3.3
Tulare	407	D	D	D	237	11 412	8 362.4	538.0	568	8 540	451.9	118.1
Tuolumne	88	456	57.6	23.1	59	818	173.1	38.4	161	1 611	92.8	25.9
Ventura	2 634	22 377	3 185.4	2 063.2	867	23 166	8 334.0	1 295.4	1 598	27 725	1 597.4	442.6
Yolo	411	3 207	484.6	184.3	167	6 236	2 538.4	311.3	414	8 216	656.6	177.5
Yuba	84	410	60.6	24.1	39	540	107.2	20.9	82	1 111	54.8	14.8
COLORADO	23 872	180 064	33 740.7	12 932.1	4 898	114 632	50 447.1	6 230.1	12 744	240 484	13 617.7	3 994.6
Adams	740	4 696	984.2	266.5	375	9 555	7 311.4	481.8	695	12 606	705.8	189.3
Alamosa	43	169	16.8	6.4	14	108	13.8	3.5	44	790	35.4	9.7
Arapahoe	2 748	21 416	3 778.7	1 553.6	392	7 527	1 672.6	412.7	1 226	22 577	1 235.6	366.0
Archuleta	45	120	13.1	4.2	11	63	5.0	1.6	58	744	64.9	15.8
Baca	5	D	D	D	NA	NA	NA	NA	7	D	D	D
Bent	3	5	0.7	0.1	NA	NA	NA	NA	6	50	1.9	0.5

1. Establishment subject to federal tax.

STATE County	Health care and social assistance, 2012				Other services, 2012				Nonemployer businesses, 2014		Value of residential construction authorized by building permits, 2015	
	Number of establish-ments	Number of employees	Receipts (mil dol)	Annual payroll (mil dol)	Number of establish-ments	Number of employees	Receipts (mil dol)	Annual payroll (mil dol)	Number	Receipts (mil dol)	New Construction ($1,000)	Number of housing units
	159	160	161	162	163	164	165	166	167	168	169	170
CALIFORNIA	103 207	1 776 440	248 953.6	91 139.9	57 009	395 836	50 439.2	12 251.2	3 117 591	162 457.2	22 637 174	98 188
Alameda	4 273	82 510	12 949.1	4 762.2	2 761	19 955	2 642.5	739.4	132 693	6 488.1	1 186 660	5 101
Alpine	4	D	D	D	2	D	D	D	103	3.6	1 953	4
Amador	99	1 353	147.7	55.2	51	169	19.4	5.1	2 766	116.7	5 772	27
Butte	716	12 868	1 434.5	560.2	321	2 158	190.0	56.0	13 232	620.0	124 758	621
Calaveras	97	985	108.9	41.7	60	265	20.4	5.6	3 571	152.1	30 427	102
Colusa	28	448	41.2	16.6	20	D	D	D	1 023	55.2	9 909	41
Contra Costa	2 877	50 689	8 262.6	3 051.1	1 515	10 368	1 238.8	338.4	87 297	4 997.5	743 452	2 610
Del Norte	68	1 214	121.3	44.7	21	D	D	D	1 211	51.3	4 451	20
El Dorado	461	6 504	680.9	276.7	289	1 393	129.6	38.2	15 989	777.9	186 074	584
Fresno	2 204	42 281	5 325.6	1 997.0	1 000	7 367	747.6	200.1	50 231	2 465.3	581 775	2 322
Glenn	42	546	52.0	22.2	24	70	12.7	1.8	1 376	61.8	4 582	20
Humboldt	442	7 111	695.5	263.6	225	1 257	136.4	34.1	11 450	444.8	29 581	215
Imperial	268	4 536	511.1	182.9	142	608	53.4	16.5	9 772	319.7	44 451	293
Inyo	55	1 106	121.6	44.8	40	172	17.1	4.6	1 296	46.5	2 280	8
Kern	1 550	27 833	3 675.0	1 265.4	835	5 099	567.8	153.6	44 623	2 196.1	473 930	2 200
Kings	231	4 770	587.8	203.5	94	382	37.4	9.9	4 370	193.0	100 953	591
Lake	154	2 345	256.6	98.1	67	213	22.2	5.6	3 868	140.0	11 607	71
Lassen	59	838	84.1	31.0	29	D	D	D	1 077	36.4	1 320	7
Los Angeles	29 822	498 944	67 261.3	24 116.1	15 843	110 674	13 562.1	3 278.3	991 091	51 788.7	5 120 116	23 263
Madera	204	5 871	761.0	321.0	112	489	45.2	11.8	7 108	330.4	57 569	211
Marin	1 117	15 860	2 102.3	848.3	643	4 539	583.8	160.1	37 862	2 759.7	115 112	390
Mariposa	33	D	D	D	18	D	D	D	1 320	51.9	6 782	26
Mendocino	265	4 296	427.2	174.9	158	642	78.5	17.9	8 409	328.4	16 574	107
Merced	427	6 718	788.1	302.8	183	895	72.4	26.3	10 703	513.2	50 806	232
Modoc	17	477	33.9	13.4	12	D	D	D	562	21.8	1 621	9
Mono	27	386	69.4	23.7	54	230	19.5	5.2	1 395	78.5	12 085	40
Monterey	994	14 898	2 151.0	838.2	560	3 765	457.6	111.7	24 494	1 355.6	120 923	587
Napa	404	10 222	1 360.7	553.3	241	1 359	127.7	40.0	11 740	722.3	56 035	172
Nevada	339	4 649	525.9	214.7	177	888	101.8	27.9	12 041	568.6	50 427	216
Orange	10 873	152 659	20 682.2	7 379.9	4 980	35 537	3 782.2	1 039.3	291 516	16 869.7	2 227 919	10 771
Placer	1 089	18 349	3 125.4	1 093.3	575	4 671	529.7	133.6	30 863	1 714.1	697 713	2 236
Plumas	49	900	85.2	32.9	39	124	12.9	3.3	1 558	71.7	5 198	31
Riverside	4 199	66 036	8 412.1	3 037.7	2 444	14 761	1 331.7	372.9	158 405	6 935.6	1 348 829	6 158
Sacramento	3 303	77 506	12 358.7	4 694.3	2 163	16 184	1 973.8	553.2	98 805	4 581.6	711 956	3 010
San Benito	96	1 309	143.2	61.4	68	249	22.4	5.3	3 381	172.7	62 991	218
San Bernardino	3 784	81 285	11 199.3	4 102.6	2 244	15 260	1 344.6	415.7	139 403	5 815.6	801 801	3 768
San Diego	8 522	151 783	21 337.8	7 872.6	5 193	41 437	4 080.6	1 179.4	258 892	13 057.6	2 100 214	9 883
San Francisco	3 119	62 075	10 175.8	3 926.9	2 411	20 361	4 964.1	840.0	95 601	5 806.7	1 041 273	3 665
San Joaquin	1 361	27 052	3 447.7	1 264.8	841	5 038	445.0	135.0	35 974	1 848.6	550 282	2 431
San Luis Obispo	1 010	14 086	1 580.5	650.0	430	2 668	216.9	60.5	24 487	1 264.6	239 542	821
San Mateo	2 279	33 776	5 167.0	1 928.7	1 390	11 134	3 296.9	458.0	67 479	4 307.9	555 611	1 620
Santa Barbara	1 360	20 279	2 637.3	949.2	725	4 544	933.5	142.1	33 354	1 904.0	299 793	1 082
Santa Clara	5 410	99 127	17 021.0	6 095.5	3 008	20 859	3 493.8	728.5	135 043	7 973.9	1 322 181	5 570
Santa Cruz	893	12 989	1 689.9	622.3	451	2 973	328.1	98.5	24 427	1 233.0	60 519	335
Shasta	634	10 525	1 324.6	469.3	296	1 658	162.7	48.2	11 727	536.3	72 774	375
Sierra	8	D	D	D	NA	NA	NA	NA	228	6.7	190	1
Siskiyou	115	1 630	174.1	72.8	72	242	17.3	5.0	3 338	127.1	17 562	77
Solano	861	21 490	3 241.8	1 204.0	552	3 228	326.8	102.6	22 666	922.5	314 903	1 434
Sonoma	1 462	23 222	3 156.2	1 198.4	853	4 845	494.1	146.9	45 205	2 326.8	146 363	621
Stanislaus	1 075	24 257	3 635.0	1 274.8	604	3 817	371.6	118.9	26 685	1 347.0	93 426	413
Sutter	249	3 369	392.4	147.2	108	571	53.1	16.5	5 418	350.7	31 251	165
Tehama	141	1 951	179.5	73.0	68	436	43.9	13.8	3 224	139.0	15 391	73
Trinity	24	315	27.9	11.8	12	34	3.4	0.9	985	37.9	3 873	23
Tulare	836	15 488	1 610.2	632.1	383	2 114	219.4	60.0	20 036	946.7	257 548	1 275
Tuolumne	170	2 692	345.6	131.5	79	355	35.5	11.3	4 129	172.6	10 956	49
Ventura	2 557	32 438	3 987.6	1 434.5	1 176	7 150	763.3	188.6	66 566	3 590.0	350 485	1 433
Yolo	371	6 923	847.0	333.6	300	2 124	256.0	72.3	12 266	591.4	103 678	354
Yuba	80	2 197	396.9	106.0	47	153	14.0	4.3	3 257	120.3	40 966	206
COLORADO	14 869	257 898	29 488.2	11 877.0	10 246	64 398	8 519.0	2 100.1	468 729	22 480.7	7 532 619	31 871
Adams	659	14 707	1 732.1	715.9	651	4 571	456.1	138.6	30 333	1 342.4	475 652	2 101
Alamosa	64	D	D	D	39	178	11.8	3.2	1 076	42.0	2 732	26
Arapahoe	1 885	27 029	2 888.9	1 245.0	1 114	7 534	1 008.0	267.0	53 145	2 717.6	562 026	2 830
Archuleta	35	248	15.8	6.6	18	102	8.6	2.8	1 907	84.2	28 821	113
Baca	6	D	D	D	8	D	D	D	366	15.6	0	0
Bent	7	43	2.8	1.4	3	D	D	D	224	10.1	875	2

Government Employment and Payroll, and Local Government Finances

STATE County	Government employment and payroll, 2012									Local government finances, 2012				
			March payroll (percent of total)							General revenue				
													Taxes	
														Per capita[1] (dollars)
	Full-time equivalent employees	March payroll (dollars)	Adminis- tration, judicial, and legal	Police and Corrections	Fire Protection	Highways and transpor- tation	Health and Welfare	Natural resources and utilities	Education and libraries	Total (mil dol)	Inter- govern- mental (mil dol)	Total (mil dol)	Total	Property
	171	172	173	174	175	176	177	178	179	180	181	182	183	184
CALIFORNIA...............	X	X	X	X	X	X	X	X	X	X	X	X	X	X
Alameda.....................	56 184	365 163 607	5.7	11.5	5.1	11.1	17.4	11.1	35.4	11 581.0	4 300.9	3 665.4	2 358	1 599
Alpine........................	214	872 045	11.7	13.5	1.0	7.4	8.2	7.0	43.1	24.5	12.2	8.3	7 356	6 651
Amador......................	1 266	6 168 436	11.2	19.0	1.9	5.8	6.8	6.0	39.5	128.1	55.8	50.2	1 356	1 204
Butte.........................	8 734	37 694 370	6.4	9.6	2.6	2.0	12.6	5.9	58.9	1 079.1	643.7	243.0	1 097	878
Calaveras..................	1 448	6 209 937	7.6	9.6	4.4	4.6	11.0	10.4	49.5	186.0	75.8	74.1	1 657	1 522
Colusa.......................	1 069	4 506 211	9.2	12.0	1.8	3.7	9.6	7.3	55.3	146.1	73.1	36.5	1 707	1 430
Contra Costa..............	31 030	175 288 765	5.0	11.0	4.7	3.1	16.5	6.7	49.7	5 884.2	1 770.2	2 008.9	1 861	1 450
Del Norte...................	840	3 504 433	11.7	12.1	0.5	4.3	15.7	4.5	48.9	153.3	93.2	23.2	819	669
El Dorado..................	6 061	31 562 790	7.6	11.3	7.2	4.8	7.4	6.9	49.3	878.4	352.8	300.6	1 665	1 450
Fresno.......................	34 954	165 436 346	4.1	10.3	2.1	3.3	9.7	4.5	65.0	5 127.4	3 047.2	1 071.6	1 131	789
Glenn........................	1 427	5 989 936	3.6	9.7	0.6	3.0	13.1	9.7	56.4	178.6	102.2	29.6	1 057	878
Humboldt...................	5 913	25 492 898	6.6	10.3	1.9	3.5	17.6	6.2	50.4	699.2	403.7	159.8	1 185	901
Imperial	10 122	49 143 599	4.2	6.0	1.7	1.1	19.5	16.2	45.5	1 293.3	740.8	180.2	1 019	733
Inyo..........................	1 429	7 084 588	6.7	10.0	0.3	4.1	40.9	3.3	30.9	203.7	66.4	52.2	2 825	2 089
Kern.........................	32 191	158 787 344	5.1	10.1	4.5	2.2	16.0	4.2	56.8	6 098.2	2 797.6	1 169.0	1 365	1 151
Kings........................	4 882	22 137 016	6.6	11.1	2.5	1.2	11.7	3.6	60.7	623.0	383.4	130.2	860	727
Lake.........................	2 729	12 022 755	11.2	10.5	3.8	2.4	16.8	9.3	43.1	271.7	144.5	78.7	1 231	1 043
Lassen......................	1 280	5 212 652	7.9	9.0	1.2	3.2	10.4	8.7	58.1	128.4	89.5	24.8	738	648
Los Angeles	386 456	2 230 095 495	9.6	12.3	4.7	5.7	13.7	9.3	42.7	62 878.6	29 034.6	18 834.7	1 891	1 234
Madera.....................	4 578	20 019 402	8.1	8.1	0.2	2.2	10.1	5.2	64.4	627.3	366.3	154.2	1 013	706
Marin.......................	8 544	51 753 682	10.8	11.2	8.5	4.2	8.9	10.4	44.3	1 521.9	327.6	825.0	3 222	2 533
Mariposa..................	919	3 214 468	8.2	10.8	0.6	5.1	32.1	3.0	35.0	106.5	45.5	33.4	1 867	1 123
Mendocino................	3 596	16 441 501	8.4	10.8	1.7	3.8	21.2	5.0	47.9	1 037.3	251.8	144.5	1 653	1 355
Merced.....................	10 959	49 202 192	6.5	7.6	1.6	1.1	10.0	6.7	63.4	1 305.5	840.8	219.3	836	680
Modoc......................	586	2 160 529	8.3	8.7	1.4	11.9	22.7	4.7	40.8	67.3	46.4	10.6	1 140	1 021
Mono........................	1 012	5 526 104	7.8	11.4	5.1	6.0	35.5	9.2	22.9	195.2	38.3	79.1	5 511	4 023
Monterey	16 674	95 953 296	5.6	9.2	2.7	3.8	28.8	5.1	41.4	3 062.0	1 376.2	682.3	1 599	1 199
Napa.........................	5 012	27 819 123	11.8	13.2	3.0	2.1	9.4	6.0	49.6	811.6	274.6	367.8	2 645	2 138
Nevada.....................	3 125	16 593 333	8.7	9.9	4.8	4.6	26.3	10.1	30.7	498.3	165.7	159.3	1 620	1 417
Orange......................	85 251	527 595 855	5.4	11.0	4.8	3.1	7.4	5.7	58.4	14 543.9	5 867.6	5 580.4	1 806	1 406
Placer.......................	12 015	67 291 627	7.1	9.6	4.2	2.3	5.5	9.5	58.5	1 867.4	613.0	730.0	2 018	1 673
Plumas......................	1 484	5 779 631	5.2	6.8	2.3	4.1	39.9	3.6	35.0	189.6	75.9	44.6	2 300	2 099
Riverside...................	68 997	380 597 495	8.6	11.0	1.9	2.3	12.6	7.6	54.4	10 975.4	5 598.2	3 090.1	1 362	1 054
Sacramento...............	50 509	274 337 834	5.2	13.3	5.5	4.2	8.8	13.3	46.1	7 904.0	3 980.4	1 968.0	1 357	948
San Benito................	2 079	11 695 733	4.3	7.2	1.9	1.9	29.7	5.0	47.9	317.3	147.3	81.2	1 428	1 245
San Bernardino..........	68 989	370 218 367	5.5	10.6	4.1	2.1	13.3	5.1	56.9	11 897.3	6 945.9	2 679.6	1 287	987
San Diego.................	97 178	529 647 292	9.3	10.8	3.9	3.4	11.1	7.0	52.0	16 495.7	6 780.5	5 691.2	1 791	1 381
San Francisco............	38 712	274 384 267	11.0	13.8	5.8	19.9	21.2	9.0	18.6	8 696.0	2 927.1	3 303.9	4 001	2 234
San Joaquin..............	23 911	123 453 125	6.5	12.7	3.3	2.6	14.7	5.0	53.3	3 894.7	2 276.8	855.2	1 217	851
San Luis Obispo	8 194	48 094 004	7.2	11.4	2.8	2.5	6.9	6.4	57.6	1 189.7	435.4	547.8	1 994	1 615
San Mateo.................	20 873	132 351 507	8.3	12.6	5.3	5.4	14.1	7.1	44.7	4 326.2	1 099.6	2 039.6	2 759	2 118
Santa Barbara............	15 712	89 085 924	7.3	11.4	5.3	3.7	14.4	7.2	48.4	2 761.9	960.5	877.6	2 035	1 531
Santa Clara................	59 919	402 121 133	7.6	10.2	5.0	5.0	20.4	6.5	42.7	12 701.2	3 946.9	4 816.5	2 621	1 963
Santa Cruz.................	9 292	50 504 116	8.1	10.1	3.9	7.3	13.5	7.9	47.1	1 432.9	632.4	483.8	1 813	1 441
Shasta.......................	6 528	30 533 939	6.7	8.7	2.8	3.4	15.6	9.0	52.2	922.9	498.8	217.9	1 220	1 000
Sierra........................	204	851 638	16.3	12.9	0.1	11.6	17.0	3.1	35.4	28.6	16.9	7.5	2 443	2 207
Siskiyou.....................	2 067	8 289 776	11.3	10.4	0.5	6.1	10.7	5.7	53.1	242.6	147.2	54.2	1 228	1 028
Solano.......................	14 386	72 410 858	7.6	13.9	3.4	2.8	9.9	7.1	53.4	1 896.3	937.5	594.6	1 413	1 051
Sonoma.....................	16 072	90 178 192	9.5	12.6	3.9	2.6	12.9	7.2	47.9	2 545.8	918.8	972.6	1 978	1 555
Stanislaus..................	19 446	94 702 481	5.9	8.3	2.5	1.6	11.8	9.4	58.2	2 696.4	1 547.9	554.1	1 062	825
Sutter........................	3 010	14 970 086	9.1	8.0	3.7	3.1	14.1	4.9	55.0	556.7	302.3	112.6	1 185	908
Tehama......................	2 320	9 999 317	7.1	9.2	1.1	3.3	13.4	2.6	61.2	246.2	160.2	57.2	902	755
Trinity	1 131	4 471 095	2.7	3.4	0.7	7.0	27.1	7.4	48.8	140.6	56.9	13.9	1 024	919
Tulare.......................	21 502	97 324 423	4.7	7.2	1.7	1.1	30.4	3.5	50.1	3 132.9	1 499.7	450.9	998	665
Tuolumne	1 609	7 837 540	9.3	11.4	1.9	4.0	9.2	5.7	53.0	206.6	92.6	69.5	1 287	1 105
Ventura.....................	27 714	159 457 912	10.1	10.8	4.6	3.0	13.0	7.6	49.2	4 630.9	2 005.3	1 379.1	1 650	1 378
Yolo.........................	6 203	32 178 923	11.0	12.7	5.3	1.8	9.0	7.7	48.4	954.1	449.2	304.9	1 494	1 014
Yuba........................	3 659	17 894 536	5.9	8.6	0.7	1.5	7.2	2.0	71.6	385.0	230.2	77.0	1 056	932
COLORADO...............	X	X	X	X	X	X	X	X	X	X	X	X	X	X
Adams.......................	14 341	67 598 280	8.2	13.6	4.3	2.6	4.0	12.3	52.8	1 856.9	785.2	806.6	1 755	1 137
Alamosa....................	647	1 959 302	10.3	10.3	0.7	4.6	18.5	7.3	47.7	73.8	42.5	23.1	1 428	843
Arapahoe...................	21 249	96 139 327	5.9	11.9	9.5	2.0	4.3	8.1	56.7	2 508.7	756.4	1 211.5	2 034	1 426
Archuleta...................	516	2 016 002	9.3	6.9	2.2	5.2	24.8	8.6	30.1	79.3	24.7	31.1	2 580	1 862
Baca.........................	511	1 703 710	8.5	7.0	0.0	11.1	42.4	7.3	21.4	31.5	11.2	5.7	1 519	1 381
Bent.........................	294	918 613	7.0	10.4	0.0	4.8	21.4	18.4	36.0	56.2	15.6	20.3	3 509	2 068

1. Based on the resident population estimated as of July 1 of the year shown.

Table B. States and Counties — **Local Government Finances, Government Employment, and Voting**

STATE County	Direct general expenditure Total (mil dol)	Per capita[1] (dollars)	Percent of total for: Education	Health and hospitals	Police protection	Public welfare	Highways	Debt outstanding Total (mil dol)	Per capita[1] (dollars)	Government employment, 2014 Federal civilian	Federal military	State and local	Presidential election,[2] 2012 Percent of vote cast: Democratic	Republican	All other
	185	186	187	188	189	190	191	192	193	194	195	196	197	198	199
CALIFORNIA	X	X	X	X	X	X	X	X	X	243 381	208 077	2 165 170	61.0	37.0	2.0
Alameda	12 422.0	7 990	22.9	13.4	5.2	5.4	2.3	24 528.0	15 776	9 378	3 956	99 616	78.8	19.3	2.0
Alpine	26.0	23 015	19.6	7.3	10.1	5.8	8.6	23.6	20 861	11	0	253	61.0	36.4	2.6
Amador	133.4	3 602	30.1	6.7	9.8	7.2	5.6	61.9	1 670	91	52	4 114	41.5	56.1	2.3
Butte	1 098.2	4 957	46.2	6.8	4.4	11.8	3.6	480.5	2 169	542	342	14 609	49.8	47.5	2.7
Calaveras	179.1	4 002	37.4	6.3	5.0	8.1	5.2	135.0	3 017	125	68	2 105	42.1	55.1	2.8
Colusa	142.2	6 642	35.7	6.2	5.7	4.9	6.5	51.5	2 404	76	33	2 060	40.0	58.1	2.0
Contra Costa	6 294.4	5 830	33.6	19.1	6.3	5.7	4.7	7 234.2	6 701	4 557	1 785	41 650	68.0	30.2	1.8
Del Norte	142.9	5 052	31.7	5.8	3.7	12.4	2.6	70.4	2 488	147	49	3 464	45.4	52.1	2.5
El Dorado	940.2	5 207	36.4	3.7	4.8	5.2	6.4	905.2	5 013	714	281	9 318	43.6	54.1	2.2
Fresno	5 031.5	5 308	44.7	7.0	5.6	10.3	3.4	3 847.5	4 059	9 875	1 617	56 254	50.2	48.1	1.7
Glenn	186.6	6 665	40.1	6.9	4.5	11.9	5.2	33.9	1 212	233	43	1 760	37.8	59.8	2.4
Humboldt	731.8	5 428	44.2	7.8	4.7	10.6	4.7	396.3	2 939	716	374	12 193	62.3	34.1	3.6
Imperial	1 172.3	6 625	40.7	23.6	4.1	7.5	2.9	1 408.8	7 962	2 356	412	15 111	62.2	36.1	1.7
Inyo	199.3	10 776	23.8	41.6	4.6	3.3	3.2	72.4	3 915	346	28	2 703	43.9	53.0	3.1
Kern	5 683.5	6 638	55.4	8.5	3.6	6.7	3.0	3 571.0	4 171	9 728	3 889	48 902	40.1	57.9	2.0
Kings	602.9	3 983	45.9	6.6	4.9	9.6	2.9	261.9	1 730	1 102	5 123	12 294	42.0	56.1	1.9
Lake	267.3	4 177	39.4	7.1	5.3	13.9	3.9	107.2	1 675	144	98	3 784	58.2	38.9	2.9
Lassen	133.2	3 956	45.5	7.1	5.0	10.9	6.5	58.3	1 734	1 842	38	4 238	31.5	65.7	2.8
Los Angeles	60 312.8	6 054	35.0	11.1	7.8	8.7	3.1	84 320.3	8 464	47 215	17 747	509 744	69.2	28.8	2.0
Madera	649.2	4 265	45.6	3.7	3.9	8.8	6.2	475.5	3 124	322	227	9 642	42.4	55.7	1.9
Marin	1 569.1	6 127	34.5	6.9	6.2	4.1	3.1	2 304.2	8 998	754	591	14 261	78.0	20.2	1.8
Mariposa	101.6	5 675	21.1	24.5	6.6	10.1	6.4	22.6	1 262	712	26	1 056	42.5	54.9	2.6
Mendocino	1 025.1	11 725	70.9	7.3	2.3	5.1	2.4	577.0	6 600	261	160	6 311	69.6	26.8	3.6
Merced	1 403.1	5 349	48.6	3.6	4.1	10.0	2.7	901.0	3 435	757	403	16 796	53.3	45.0	1.7
Modoc	67.1	7 198	38.4	16.9	4.0	6.8	8.8	4.6	497	236	13	938	29.7	67.4	2.9
Mono	192.0	13 383	15.1	34.5	6.6	4.9	8.7	76.3	5 321	227	243	1 278	55.5	42.3	2.2
Monterey	2 904.3	6 806	36.5	22.7	4.6	5.4	2.6	1 444.4	3 385	5 284	6 040	25 259	68.2	29.9	2.0
Napa	821.7	5 909	37.5	5.9	7.5	4.2	4.0	746.0	5 365	215	212	9 716	65.1	32.7	2.2
Nevada	537.0	5 464	23.8	31.3	4.9	5.6	4.7	392.6	3 994	356	152	5 001	51.4	46.1	2.5
Orange	13 915.7	4 503	41.4	2.9	7.7	7.3	4.5	22 316.3	7 222	11 042	5 359	136 230	47.6	50.2	2.2
Placer	1 896.3	5 243	41.7	2.8	5.8	5.9	6.0	2 500.4	6 913	674	589	16 459	43.4	54.7	1.9
Plumas	177.2	9 133	26.8	34.8	4.1	4.9	5.8	57.6	2 967	405	28	1 821	42.8	54.7	2.5
Riverside	11 682.2	5 149	39.3	8.1	6.7	7.1	4.3	13 164.6	5 802	6 849	3 892	115 494	50.2	47.9	1.9
Sacramento	7 966.3	5 494	34.4	6.0	4.9	8.6	5.8	16 350.5	11 275	8 742	3 009	174 336	58.5	39.5	2.0
San Benito	327.5	5 757	32.1	32.0	3.9	5.6	3.2	125.8	2 211	137	90	2 561	60.5	37.7	1.8
San Bernardino	11 798.5	5 669	38.7	15.6	6.0	7.5	5.5	11 574.3	5 561	13 540	18 704	100 772	52.1	45.8	2.2
San Diego	16 846.0	5 302	37.0	9.8	5.3	6.9	2.9	27 732.0	8 729	46 225	99 789	182 955	54.1	43.9	1.9
San Francisco	7 412.4	8 975	16.3	24.7	5.1	6.5	3.4	17 985.0	21 777	13 994	1 595	87 726	84.2	13.7	2.2
San Joaquin	3 717.2	5 291	40.5	9.2	5.9	8.8	3.5	3 309.2	4 710	3 143	1 160	33 472	54.4	43.8	1.8
San Luis Obispo	1 206.8	4 391	38.5	5.9	6.2	8.2	3.9	850.7	3 096	543	544	20 187	51.4	46.0	2.6
San Mateo	4 256.2	5 757	34.0	11.6	7.7	4.4	3.8	4 651.4	6 292	3 680	1 357	27 141	73.5	24.7	1.8
Santa Barbara	2 786.6	6 462	32.4	18.7	5.7	6.7	3.0	1 346.9	3 123	3 704	3 333	30 922	60.4	37.5	2.1
Santa Clara	11 865.9	6 458	32.5	21.8	5.2	5.2	2.2	17 898.2	9 740	9 916	3 312	76 989	69.4	28.6	2.0
Santa Cruz	1 415.2	5 305	36.6	6.6	6.3	8.5	2.3	1 074.8	4 029	535	404	17 817	77.5	19.8	2.7
Shasta	906.1	5 074	43.3	8.1	5.8	10.6	4.0	544.3	3 048	1 300	317	11 334	35.9	61.7	2.4
Sierra	29.0	9 401	28.7	10.0	10.3	10.1	12.9	6.1	1 986	48	0	302	37.3	58.2	4.5
Siskiyou	251.0	5 684	48.4	6.3	5.8	7.4	5.5	80.4	1 822	746	67	3 109	43.3	53.7	3.1
Solano	1 873.8	4 454	35.1	6.1	9.3	7.8	4.2	1 624.0	3 860	3 726	7 106	20 051	63.4	34.8	1.8
Sonoma	2 601.9	5 290	35.4	10.3	6.3	6.4	5.0	2 547.1	5 179	1 394	1 401	26 595	73.6	24.0	2.3
Stanislaus	2 792.3	5 352	50.1	6.9	4.9	10.2	3.4	4 496.8	8 619	818	819	25 891	49.9	48.1	2.0
Sutter	526.6	5 542	44.9	7.7	4.4	6.1	1.8	241.8	2 545	94	149	4 338	40.7	57.4	1.9
Tehama	244.9	3 862	49.8	6.6	5.9	14.9	4.0	28.9	456	225	97	3 399	36.6	60.7	2.7
Trinity	128.3	9 486	22.7	15.7	2.1	6.0	7.0	47.2	3 487	247	20	945	50.7	46.1	3.2
Tulare	3 186.6	7 050	39.0	24.4	3.2	8.0	4.7	1 380.8	3 055	1 051	705	29 899	41.5	56.8	1.7
Tuolumne	214.2	3 966	35.6	9.8	6.8	8.2	4.3	66.5	1 230	521	78	5 000	42.4	55.1	2.4
Ventura	4 471.8	5 349	38.6	13.1	7.5	4.6	3.5	3 011.8	3 603	6 917	5 055	35 902	55.2	42.9	1.9
Yolo	951.1	4 659	30.3	3.8	6.2	8.0	5.9	944.3	4 626	3 497	328	33 594	67.1	30.8	2.1
Yuba	436.2	5 982	54.3	2.1	4.1	10.8	4.0	399.0	5 472	1 346	4 761	5 499	41.4	56.1	2.5
COLORADO	X	X	X	X	X	X	X	X	X	52 768	54 316	364 289	53.7	44.7	1.6
Adams	1 860.3	4 048	42.2	0.3	5.7	9.9	5.6	2 579.2	5 612	1 352	1 625	37 420	58.2	39.9	1.9
Alamosa	68.0	4 210	38.8	5.3	7.5	20.9	5.9	38.4	2 379	141	40	2 202	56.0	41.9	2.1
Arapahoe	2 593.0	4 354	41.7	1.1	7.2	3.0	5.0	6 000.2	10 075	3 417	3 246	33 553	55.7	42.8	1.5
Archuleta	68.6	5 681	20.6	27.4	2.8	7.3	11.0	57.7	4 780	46	32	701	42.8	54.9	2.3
Baca	31.8	8 484	29.7	35.6	3.0	11.3	8.9	2.1	559	37	0	653	24.6	72.3	3.1
Bent	42.9	7 437	18.7	2.0	8.7	5.5	17.8	8.1	1 402	40	10	459	41.6	56.1	2.3

1. Based on the resident population estimated as of July 1 of the year shown.   2. © 2013 Election Data Services, Inc. All rights reserved.

Table B. States and Counties — **Land Area and Population**

STATE/ County code	CBSA code[1]	County type[2]	STATE County	Land area,[3] (sq km) 2010	Population, 2015			Population and population characteristics, 2014										
								Race alone or in combination, not Hispanic or Latino (percent)					Age (percent)					
					Total persons 2015	Rank	Per square kilometer	White	Black	Amer- ican Indian, Alaska Native	Asian and Pacific Islander	Percent Hispanic or Latino[4]	Under 5 years	5 to 17 years	18 to 24 years	25 to 34 years	35 to 44 years	45 to 54 years
				1	2	3	4	5	6	7	8	9	10	11	12	13	14	15
			COLORADO—Cont'd															
08 013	14500	2	Boulder	1 881	319 372	212	169.8	80.2	1.4	0.9	5.8	13.8	5.0	15.2	15.2	13.2	13.0	13.5
08 014	19740	1	Broomfield	86	65 065	810	756.6	80.3	1.7	0.9	7.6	12.0	6.0	18.6	7.9	13.7	15.4	14.3
08 015	...	7	Chaffee	2 625	18 658	1 886	7.1	86.0	1.9	1.5	1.1	10.1	4.0	11.8	6.8	11.9	11.3	13.5
08 017	...	9	Cheyenne	4 606	1 829	3 067	0.4	85.8	1.0	1.2	0.9	12.8	8.3	16.7	6.3	12.1	10.6	13.5
08 019	19740	1	Clear Creek	1 024	9 303	2 486	9.1	92.0	1.2	1.4	1.2	5.6	3.8	11.6	5.8	9.7	13.6	16.7
08 021	...	9	Conejos	3 334	8 130	2 591	2.4	44.5	0.5	1.3	0.6	54.1	6.5	20.7	8.7	10.5	9.9	12.6
08 023	...	9	Costilla	3 178	3 584	2 936	1.1	33.1	0.8	1.4	1.5	64.6	3.9	14.3	8.6	8.5	8.1	12.5
08 025	...	8	Crowley	2 039	5 562	2 797	2.7	55.0	9.1	1.9	1.6	29.0	4.3	10.0	9.7	19.1	16.0	16.2
08 027	...	8	Custer	1 913	4 445	2 868	2.3	92.7	1.5	1.3	0.8	5.3	2.5	12.1	5.5	6.1	8.4	13.5
08 029	...	6	Delta	2 958	29 979	1 432	10.1	83.1	0.8	1.4	1.1	14.6	5.1	15.8	6.9	9.7	10.1	12.6
08 031	19740	1	Denver	396	682 545	94	1 723.6	55.3	10.3	1.3	4.7	30.8	6.8	14.0	8.7	22.0	15.5	11.6
08 033	...	9	Dolores	2 764	1 978	3 050	0.7	91.2	1.1	4.6	0.7	5.1	4.9	15.5	6.0	8.8	11.5	14.0
08 035	19740	1	Douglas	2 176	322 387	210	148.2	85.8	1.8	0.7	5.6	8.3	6.3	22.1	7.0	10.6	16.1	16.4
08 037	20780	5	Eagle	4 363	53 605	933	12.3	67.7	0.8	0.7	1.5	30.0	6.1	17.1	7.6	17.1	16.6	14.9
08 039	19740	1	Elbert	4 794	24 735	1 618	5.2	91.4	1.2	1.3	1.6	6.4	3.9	18.6	7.4	7.7	11.7	18.6
08 041	17820	2	El Paso	5 508	674 471	98	122.5	73.6	7.8	1.5	4.9	16.3	6.9	18.1	11.5	15.1	12.4	13.0
08 043	15860	4	Fremont	3 971	46 692	1 035	11.8	80.9	4.2	2.3	1.2	13.1	4.0	12.5	7.2	14.0	13.0	14.5
08 045	24060	5	Garfield	7 634	58 095	885	7.6	70.0	0.9	1.2	1.2	28.1	7.1	18.8	8.2	14.0	14.1	13.9
08 047	19740	1	Gilpin	388	5 828	2 771	15.0	91.2	2.2	2.1	2.3	6.6	3.8	15.0	5.0	9.9	14.4	18.2
08 049	...	8	Grand	4 782	14 615	2 129	3.1	90.6	0.9	1.1	1.5	8.0	4.2	14.3	7.2	13.4	13.3	15.1
08 051	...	7	Gunnison	8 389	16 067	2 035	1.9	88.8	0.9	1.3	1.1	9.3	4.8	13.1	18.3	14.2	13.1	12.0
08 053	...	9	Hinsdale	2 894	774	3 121	0.3	94.9	1.0	1.5	1.3	3.7	6.2	12.5	5.9	9.5	8.8	13.6
08 055	...	6	Huerfano	4 121	6 492	2 716	1.6	63.3	0.9	2.0	1.2	34.6	3.8	11.8	6.2	7.9	8.0	13.2
08 057	...	9	Jackson	4 180	1 356	3 090	0.3	87.5	0.6	1.5	0.6	11.0	3.4	14.4	6.6	10.6	12.0	14.3
08 059	19740	1	Jefferson	1 979	565 524	114	285.8	80.3	1.5	1.1	3.6	15.2	5.3	15.6	8.4	13.8	12.8	14.8
08 061	...	9	Kiowa	4 578	1 423	3 084	0.3	91.8	1.2	0.9	0.3	6.2	6.4	14.1	8.6	8.6	9.4	12.9
08 063	...	7	Kit Carson	5 597	7 758	2 613	1.4	79.5	2.8	1.3	0.9	20.0	6.2	16.3	8.0	13.8	12.2	13.3
08 065	...	7	Lake	976	7 485	2 637	7.7	60.1	0.8	1.6	0.8	37.8	6.5	16.6	9.2	15.1	14.0	13.1
08 067	20420	6	La Plata	4 382	54 688	917	12.5	81.1	0.8	6.3	1.3	12.7	5.1	14.2	10.5	14.2	12.6	13.3
08 069	22660	2	Larimer	6 724	333 577	203	49.6	85.1	1.4	1.1	3.1	11.1	5.4	15.1	14.7	13.9	12.1	11.9
08 071	...	7	Las Animas	12 361	14 058	2 160	1.1	53.6	1.8	1.9	1.2	42.5	5.1	13.9	8.6	10.9	10.1	12.8
08 073	...	8	Lincoln	6 676	5 557	2 798	0.8	79.5	5.6	1.5	1.4	13.4	5.6	14.1	8.6	15.6	12.0	14.5
08 075	44540	7	Logan	4 762	22 036	1 730	4.6	80.0	4.6	1.5	1.2	16.6	5.0	13.8	12.3	14.9	12.4	13.0
08 077	24300	3	Mesa	8 622	148 513	439	17.2	83.7	1.2	1.4	1.5	14.1	6.3	16.1	10.2	13.3	11.2	12.2
08 079	...	9	Mineral	2 268	726	3 126	0.3	94.2	1.0	1.2	0.6	4.5	4.7	7.9	5.2	9.7	9.3	13.0
08 081	18780	7	Moffat	12 285	12 937	2 234	1.1	83.5	0.9	1.4	1.3	14.3	6.9	19.1	7.9	13.1	11.6	13.6
08 083	...	6	Montezuma	5 256	26 168	1 555	5.0	75.0	0.7	12.7	1.4	12.1	6.2	16.5	7.3	10.8	10.8	13.1
08 085	33940	7	Montrose	5 803	40 946	1 154	7.1	77.8	0.7	1.3	1.3	20.3	5.6	17.0	7.0	10.4	11.9	12.9
08 087	22820	6	Morgan	3 316	28 360	1 476	8.6	61.1	2.9	0.9	0.9	35.4	7.6	18.9	9.1	12.6	11.4	13.0
08 089	...	6	Otero	3 268	18 343	1 899	5.6	56.8	1.1	1.4	1.2	41.2	6.5	17.8	9.3	10.9	10.7	12.2
08 091	...	9	Ouray	1 403	4 691	2 855	3.3	93.3	0.6	0.9	1.1	5.5	3.4	13.7	5.1	7.0	10.0	14.7
08 093	19740	1	Park	5 682	16 510	2 005	2.9	91.8	1.0	1.8	1.7	6.2	3.7	12.9	5.5	8.3	11.4	18.2
08 095	...	9	Phillips	1 782	4 349	2 875	2.4	77.1	1.1	0.8	1.0	20.5	6.1	17.9	8.3	10.3	10.1	12.8
08 097	24060	7	Pitkin	2 514	17 787	1 930	7.1	87.8	1.0	0.7	2.0	9.9	3.7	12.6	6.7	15.1	13.9	15.7
08 099	...	7	Prowers	4 243	11 954	2 301	2.8	61.9	0.9	1.1	0.6	36.3	6.9	19.3	9.8	11.1	11.4	11.8
08 101	39380	3	Pueblo	6 180	163 591	393	26.5	54.1	2.2	1.3	1.3	42.5	6.0	17.2	9.6	12.3	11.6	12.7
08 103	...	9	Rio Blanco	8 342	6 571	2 712	0.8	86.3	1.5	2.1	1.4	11.1	6.8	17.8	10.7	13.3	11.3	12.7
08 105	...	7	Rio Grande	2 362	11 543	2 321	4.9	53.9	0.7	1.5	0.8	44.2	6.3	17.5	8.2	11.4	10.6	12.3
08 107	44460	7	Routt	6 118	24 130	1 640	3.9	90.9	0.8	0.8	1.4	7.0	4.4	14.8	8.3	14.6	14.6	14.6
08 109	...	9	Saguache	8 206	6 251	2 738	0.8	59.1	1.0	2.3	1.3	38.2	6.4	16.1	6.3	9.1	9.9	13.9
08 111	...	9	San Juan	1 004	701	3 127	0.7	83.7	0.6	1.7	2.1	14.2	2.1	11.5	5.0	13.8	14.4	13.8
08 113	...	9	San Miguel	3 332	7 879	2 605	2.4	89.0	0.8	1.1	1.6	9.6	4.7	14.2	6.1	16.5	15.5	16.1
08 115	...	9	Sedgwick	1 419	2 399	3 014	1.7	83.6	0.9	1.1	1.0	15.2	5.2	15.1	6.5	10.5	9.8	11.6
08 117	14720	7	Summit	1 576	30 257	1 426	19.2	83.0	1.0	0.6	1.5	14.7	4.6	11.7	8.5	19.9	16.1	14.1
08 119	17820	2	Teller	1 443	23 385	1 662	16.2	91.4	1.1	1.7	1.6	6.2	3.8	14.7	6.7	8.3	10.4	17.1
08 121	...	9	Washington	6 522	4 864	2 843	0.7	88.9	1.1	0.9	0.6	9.5	5.1	16.9	8.0	11.1	9.6	13.4
08 123	24540	3	Weld	10 327	285 174	240	27.6	68.3	1.4	1.2	2.1	29.0	7.3	19.7	10.0	14.3	13.4	12.8
08 125	...	7	Yuma	6 124	10 146	2 426	1.7	76.7	0.5	0.6	0.5	21.8	7.5	19.0	7.9	11.9	11.1	12.8
09 000	...	X	CONNECTICUT	12 542	3 590 886	X	286.3	70.3	10.8	0.6	5.0	15.1	5.3	16.3	9.7	12.3	12.2	15.2
09 001	14860	2	Fairfield	1 618	948 053	51	585.9	64.9	11.3	0.4	6.1	18.7	5.7	17.9	8.8	11.7	13.0	14.8
09 003	25540	1	Hartford	1 904	895 841	60	470.5	64.9	13.9	0.6	5.5	17.0	5.4	16.3	9.2	13.0	12.3	14.8
09 005	45860	4	Litchfield	2 384	183 603	352	77.0	91.2	2.0	0.6	2.2	5.5	4.2	15.2	7.5	9.8	11.2	16.9
09 007	25540	1	Middlesex	956	164 063	391	171.6	86.2	5.6	0.6	3.7	5.8	4.5	14.9	8.6	11.0	11.5	16.4
09 009	35300	2	New Haven	1 566	859 470	65	548.8	66.4	13.3	0.6	4.6	16.8	5.3	15.8	10.2	13.1	12.1	14.7
09 011	35980	2	New London	1 722	271 863	250	157.9	79.0	7.3	1.8	5.4	10.0	5.1	15.2	10.5	12.7	11.6	14.9

1. CBSA = Core Based Statistical Area. See Appendix A for explanation. See Appendix B for list of metropolitan areas with component counties.   2. County type code from the Economic Research Service of USDA Rural-Urban Continuum Codes. See Appendix A for definition.   3. Dry land or land partially or temporarily covered by water.   4. May be of any race.

STATE County	Population, 2014 (cont.) Age (percent) (cont.)				Population change and components of change, 2000–2015							Households, 2010–2014				
					Total persons		Percent change		Components of change, 2010–2015					Percent		
	55 to 64 years	65 to 74 years	75 years and over	Percent female	2000	2010	2000–2010	2010–2015	Births	Deaths	Net migration	Number	Persons per household	Family households	Female family householder[1]	One person
	16	17	18	19	20	21	22	23	24	25	26	27	28	29	30	31
COLORADO—Cont'd																
Boulder	12.6	7.4	4.9	49.8	269 814	294 571	9.2	8.4	15 535	8 580	17 624	121 526	2.43	59.1	8.3	27.9
Broomfield	11.9	7.2	5.0	50.4	38 272	55 866	46.0	16.5	3 644	1 744	7 253	22 651	2.59	68.5	7.6	25.8
Chaffee	17.7	14.0	9.0	47.2	16 242	17 809	9.6	4.8	728	835	1 004	7 735	2.19	64.8	8.3	28.6
Cheyenne	14.4	8.9	9.2	48.5	2 231	1 836	-17.7	-0.4	140	93	-37	788	2.67	64.8	3.0	30.6
Clear Creek	20.9	12.7	5.2	48.0	9 322	9 075	-2.6	2.5	349	287	165	4 103	2.19	61.0	5.4	30.1
Conejos	13.9	9.7	7.6	50.2	8 400	8 256	-1.7	-1.5	623	407	-372	3 023	2.71	72.7	13.1	26.6
Costilla	18.3	16.3	9.5	47.6	3 663	3 524	-3.8	1.7	154	181	94	1 396	2.56	60.7	8.4	37.5
Crowley	11.7	7.8	5.2	30.2	5 518	5 823	5.5	-4.5	197	179	-318	1 173	3.44	65.6	13.6	23.8
Custer	23.0	20.4	8.5	49.1	3 503	4 255	21.5	4.5	123	165	266	2 125	2.00	62.9	2.6	33.9
Delta	16.4	13.5	10.0	50.1	27 834	30 952	11.2	-3.1	1 663	1 840	-818	12 527	2.33	66.9	9.3	27.9
Denver	10.5	6.3	4.6	50.0	554 636	599 860	8.2	13.8	50 069	22 480	54 114	271 054	2.28	48.1	10.4	40.1
Dolores	17.3	13.2	8.7	48.0	1 844	2 064	11.9	-4.2	94	77	-109	759	2.28	60.1	9.7	36.1
Douglas	11.6	6.6	3.3	50.3	175 766	285 465	62.4	12.9	18 472	5 530	23 508	105 404	2.84	77.9	7.5	17.3
Eagle	12.4	6.2	2.0	47.0	41 659	52 197	25.3	2.7	3 450	511	-1 502	18 038	2.89	64.7	7.9	23.8
Elbert	18.2	9.8	4.1	49.8	19 872	23 086	16.2	7.1	892	638	1 326	8 259	2.84	74.6	4.3	20.2
El Paso	11.4	6.9	4.6	49.6	516 929	622 261	20.4	8.4	48 480	20 647	23 574	240 154	2.62	68.1	11.5	25.9
Fremont	14.6	11.8	8.4	42.3	46 145	46 824	1.5	-0.3	1 909	2 768	633	16 600	2.16	64.3	9.1	30.0
Garfield	13.1	6.7	4.0	48.9	43 791	56 389	28.8	3.0	4 289	1 521	-1 090	20 330	2.74	71.5	9.4	22.5
Gilpin	20.7	9.9	3.3	47.3	4 757	5 441	14.4	7.1	224	120	293	2 463	2.22	56.6	5.0	35.6
Grand	18.7	10.0	3.9	47.0	12 442	14 843	19.3	-1.5	597	290	-513	5 208	2.72	62.6	6.0	28.3
Gunnison	13.2	7.9	3.3	45.9	13 956	15 324	9.8	4.8	773	342	321	6 336	2.28	56.9	7.6	29.2
Hinsdale	17.8	18.2	7.5	48.2	790	843	6.7	-8.2	35	18	-86	418	2.06	67.2	1.0	25.9
Huerfano	19.4	17.6	12.1	49.6	7 862	6 711	-14.6	-3.3	244	487	31	2 864	2.15	59.6	7.7	37.4
Jackson	17.8	11.5	9.4	46.7	1 577	1 394	-11.6	-2.7	54	48	-46	644	2.12	60.4	3.9	35.9
Jefferson	14.6	8.7	5.9	50.3	525 507	534 764	1.8	5.8	30 168	21 044	21 351	220 814	2.44	64.8	9.7	28.0
Kiowa	15.9	11.7	12.4	50.8	1 622	1 398	-13.8	1.8	85	96	17	559	2.46	65.3	7.0	33.8
Kit Carson	13.1	8.8	8.3	44.8	8 011	8 270	3.2	-6.2	492	396	-618	3 053	2.39	67.5	9.3	31.2
Lake	14.4	7.2	3.9	46.7	7 812	7 310	-6.4	2.4	440	184	-81	3 106	2.30	56.8	7.5	37.7
La Plata	15.7	9.2	5.0	49.2	43 941	51 334	16.8	6.5	2 863	1 638	2 120	21 124	2.39	60.5	8.4	29.2
Larimer	12.9	8.4	5.6	50.2	251 494	299 630	19.1	11.3	17 937	10 268	25 303	122 743	2.46	63.2	8.2	25.1
Las Animas	16.3	13.4	8.9	48.4	15 207	15 507	2.0	-9.3	712	871	-1 291	5 890	2.41	65.9	11.7	30.1
Lincoln	12.2	8.7	8.7	40.9	6 087	5 469	-10.2	1.6	304	249	42	1 757	2.17	65.9	10.2	31.6
Logan	12.9	8.1	7.6	43.5	20 504	22 709	10.8	-3.0	1 223	1 018	-933	7 825	2.75	63.0	10.8	32.1
Mesa	13.7	9.4	7.5	50.3	116 255	146 723	26.2	1.2	9 653	7 148	-856	58 966	2.44	65.1	10.6	27.4
Mineral	23.6	18.2	8.3	47.6	831	712	-14.3	2.0	25	22	15	375	1.79	58.7	0.5	38.9
Moffat	14.9	8.1	4.7	48.1	13 184	13 795	4.6	-6.2	951	493	-1 324	4 890	2.67	64.2	5.2	31.0
Montezuma	16.2	11.5	7.6	50.3	23 830	25 535	7.2	2.5	1 650	1 363	355	10 659	2.37	65.4	9.8	28.8
Montrose	14.9	12.1	9.2	50.8	33 432	41 278	23.5	-0.8	2 402	2 122	-627	16 815	2.40	68.2	8.6	27.0
Morgan	12.0	7.8	7.6	50.2	27 171	28 159	3.6	0.7	2 280	1 289	-887	10 443	2.66	67.2	13.6	23.8
Otero	13.6	10.0	9.0	50.4	20 311	18 831	-7.3	-2.6	1 161	1 207	-432	7 381	2.46	67.2	12.5	29.5
Ouray	21.5	17.7	7.6	50.9	3 742	4 434	18.5	5.8	167	153	243	1 969	2.30	64.6	4.7	25.3
Park	23.7	12.5	3.8	47.3	14 523	16 201	11.6	1.9	557	416	312	7 184	2.23	65.5	6.1	28.9
Phillips	13.8	9.2	11.6	50.4	4 480	4 442	-0.8	-2.1	281	252	-126	1 656	2.61	68.7	6.8	28.6
Pitkin	16.7	11.0	4.5	47.6	14 872	17 148	15.3	3.7	699	241	249	7 357	2.33	50.0	4.5	36.7
Prowers	13.5	8.9	7.3	49.9	14 483	12 551	-13.3	-4.8	840	594	-838	4 925	2.43	69.0	11.4	26.8
Pueblo	13.5	9.5	7.6	50.7	141 472	159 063	12.4	2.8	9 975	8 609	3 038	62 829	2.48	63.7	14.2	30.7
Rio Blanco	13.8	8.1	5.6	48.1	5 986	6 669	11.4	-1.5	420	252	-246	2 644	2.28	69.0	6.9	27.8
Rio Grande	14.9	11.0	7.6	50.1	12 413	11 982	-3.5	-3.7	750	617	-589	4 741	2.44	65.4	11.8	28.5
Routt	16.4	8.7	3.6	47.6	19 690	23 506	19.4	2.7	1 126	500	2	9 573	2.40	62.2	7.0	28.6
Saguache	19.3	13.1	5.8	49.5	5 917	6 108	3.2	2.3	375	191	-37	2 598	2.37	56.7	10.4	37.6
San Juan	19.0	16.3	4.2	43.1	558	699	25.3	0.3	20	22	4	338	1.93	44.7	8.6	49.4
San Miguel	16.4	8.0	2.5	46.9	6 594	7 359	11.6	7.1	368	113	261	3 330	2.27	53.2	6.5	33.7
Sedgwick	16.8	11.8	12.6	50.0	2 747	2 379	-13.4	0.8	127	180	75	932	2.49	64.6	9.3	29.7
Summit	14.3	8.4	2.5	45.9	23 548	27 994	18.9	8.1	1 460	269	1 134	10 386	2.70	57.2	5.3	30.7
Teller	21.0	13.4	4.6	49.1	20 555	23 350	13.6	0.1	980	776	-74	9 611	2.41	71.5	8.2	24.9
Washington	15.1	10.8	10.0	48.5	4 926	4 814	-2.3	1.0	215	237	47	1 986	2.28	69.2	7.4	28.7
Weld	11.5	6.8	4.3	49.6	180 926	252 831	39.7	12.8	20 309	8 092	19 457	92 369	2.80	71.9	10.3	21.9
Yuma	12.5	9.1	8.4	50.0	9 841	10 043	2.1	1.0	764	504	-179	3 833	2.61	56.5	5.6	39.4
CONNECTICUT	13.5	8.5	7.0	51.2	3 405 565	3 574 118	4.9	0.5	192 515	154 371	-16 342	1 356 206	2.56	66.3	13.0	27.9
Fairfield	12.9	7.7	6.6	51.2	882 567	916 850	3.9	3.4	53 486	34 170	13 815	333 502	2.74	69.5	12.2	25.5
Hartford	13.4	8.4	7.3	51.5	857 183	894 029	4.3	0.2	49 880	41 172	-5 716	348 204	2.50	65.4	15.0	28.9
Litchfield	16.7	10.6	7.8	50.7	182 193	189 927	4.2	-3.3	7 708	9 138	-4 588	75 229	2.45	67.3	9.1	27.1
Middlesex	15.4	10.0	7.7	51.2	155 071	165 676	6.8	-1.0	7 505	7 583	-1 262	66 372	2.40	65.6	9.3	27.9
New Haven	13.3	8.5	7.1	51.8	824 008	862 474	4.7	-0.3	47 416	39 802	-9 854	327 086	2.55	64.0	14.3	30.3
New London	13.9	9.1	6.9	49.9	259 088	274 046	5.8	-0.8	14 404	12 229	-4 063	106 882	2.44	65.0	11.6	28.5

1. No spouse present.

Table B. States and Counties — **Population, Vital Statistics, Medicare, and Crime**

STATE County	Persons in group quarters, 2015	Daytime population, 2010–2014 Number	Employ- ment/ resi- dence ratio	Births, 2015 Total	Rate[1]	Deaths, 2015 Number	Rate[1]	Persons under 65 with no health insurance, 2014 Number	Percent	Medicare, 2015 Total Beneficiaries	Enrolled in Original Medicare	Enrolled in Medicare Advantage	Serious crimes known to police,[2] 2014 Total Number	Rate[3]
	32	33	34	35	36	37	38	39	40	41	42	43	44	45
COLORADO—Cont'd														
Boulder	10 887	332 794	1.17	2 933	9.3	1 755	5.5	26 315	9.9	44 977	26 021	18 956	6 581	2 617
Broomfield	282	65 078	1.20	714	11.2	339	5.3	3 688	6.8	8 932	4 265	4 667	1 071	1 765
Chaffee	1 472	18 329	1.03	141	7.6	148	8.0	1 600	12.4	4 475	3 610	865	286	1 522
Cheyenne	42	2 404	1.23	22	11.9	12	6.5	270	18.0	299	281	18	2	104
Clear Creek	84	7 522	0.68	64	6.9	55	6.0	570	7.6	903	600	303	201	2 287
Conejos	36	7 165	0.63	126	15.4	73	8.9	980	14.5	1 525	1 014	511	14	168
Costilla	0	3 349	0.82	27	7.6	26	7.3	541	20.7	1 061	741	320	28	792
Crowley	2 534	5 638	1.06	37	6.6	29	5.2	309	12.7	713	593	120	7	134
Custer	150	3 980	0.79	28	6.4	33	7.5	459	15.6	1 247	1 008	239	40	928
Delta	697	29 273	0.90	294	9.8	357	11.9	3 614	16.1	7 717	5 645	2 072	577	2 036
Denver	16 189	781 605	1.45	10 104	15.0	4 648	6.9	80 847	14.0	78 384	36 336	42 048	26 648	4 005
Dolores	0	1 608	0.82	15	7.6	9	4.6	245	15.9	462	406	56	20	984
Douglas	612	257 107	0.72	3 560	11.2	1 179	3.7	14 448	5.1	19 131	11 018	8 113	3 617	1 157
Eagle	75	50 526	0.94	633	11.9	98	1.8	8 214	17.0	3 769	3 454	315	1 007	1 905
Elbert	73	16 826	0.43	185	7.6	127	5.2	1 914	9.2	3 433	2 330	1 103	20	85
El Paso	17 887	646 307	1.00	9 437	14.1	4 208	6.3	58 348	10.2	84 190	57 430	26 760	22 224	3 336
Fremont	8 243	46 615	0.98	361	7.8	532	11.4	3 544	12.2	10 607	7 344	3 263	907	1 946
Garfield	884	55 424	0.96	792	13.7	318	5.5	9 144	18.1	6 886	6 024	862	1 082	1 867
Gilpin	49	7 920	1.79	43	7.4	21	3.6	325	6.5	616	354	262	360	6 353
Grand	223	14 207	0.97	121	8.3	56	3.8	1 727	13.8	1 948	1 657	291	140	1 088
Gunnison	931	16 333	1.10	139	8.7	60	3.8	1 962	15.0	1 723	1 607	116	231	1 478
Hinsdale	56	829	0.90	6	7.7	1	1.3	90	15.4	191	175	16	4	494
Huerfano	165	6 442	0.95	44	6.8	81	12.5	627	14.0	1 918	1 538	380	139	2 132
Jackson	2	1 425	1.05	10	7.3	6	4.4	193	17.5	309	293	16	2	146
Jefferson	7 738	496 015	0.82	6 064	10.8	4 224	7.5	43 240	9.2	84 401	35 412	48 989	16 525	2 955
Kiowa	14	1 404	1.00	20	14.1	15	10.6	132	12.4	D	305	D	NA	NA
Kit Carson	546	8 444	1.09	93	11.9	80	10.3	989	16.8	1 384	1 317	67	127	1 724
Lake	146	6 291	0.74	82	11.0	24	3.2	1 100	17.2	802	728	74	95	1 291
La Plata	1 824	53 252	1.03	557	10.3	343	6.3	6 124	13.8	8 242	7 240	1 002	833	1 541
Larimer	8 933	303 156	0.95	3 543	10.8	2 016	6.1	27 958	10.3	47 105	33 356	13 749	7 548	2 345
Las Animas	862	15 002	1.03	119	8.5	150	10.7	1 378	13.5	3 500	2 842	658	388	2 714
Lincoln	1 029	6 018	1.34	59	10.7	44	8.0	423	11.9	903	848	55	26	477
Logan	3 334	22 213	0.96	246	11.2	199	9.0	2 006	13.2	3 647	3 195	452	604	2 685
Mesa	4 209	144 849	0.96	1 816	12.3	1 379	9.3	15 547	13.0	27 273	16 415	10 858	4 393	2 955
Mineral	0	738	1.10	4	5.6	3	4.2	62	12.0	213	188	25	2	274
Moffat	102	12 452	0.87	172	13.3	79	6.1	1 387	12.4	1 850	1 695	155	246	1 891
Montezuma	237	24 709	0.92	337	13.0	257	9.9	3 618	17.5	5 180	4 516	664	530	2 053
Montrose	542	39 462	0.92	458	11.2	421	10.3	5 030	15.8	9 351	7 094	2 257	1 058	2 711
Morgan	564	28 434	1.01	418	14.8	234	8.3	3 708	15.8	4 285	3 853	432	487	1 756
Otero	457	18 507	0.97	205	11.1	218	11.9	2 040	14.0	4 372	3 629	743	428	2 335
Ouray	0	4 386	0.93	31	6.7	28	6.0	428	12.3	897	752	145	15	408
Park	92	11 285	0.45	107	6.5	93	5.7	1 600	11.8	2 397	1 702	695	67	414
Phillips	59	4 516	1.06	59	13.5	50	11.4	554	16.1	937	914	23	34	781
Pitkin	72	24 186	1.69	119	6.7	37	2.1	2 042	13.7	1 950	1 860	90	396	2 258
Prowers	342	12 197	0.97	158	13.2	102	8.5	1 700	17.4	2 178	2 102	76	234	1 904
Pueblo	4 482	159 220	0.98	1 911	11.7	1 694	10.4	15 017	11.5	32 217	20 467	11 750	9 275	5 695
Rio Blanco	302	7 046	1.09	69	10.4	40	6.0	679	12.3	895	727	168	79	1 147
Rio Grande	198	11 325	0.89	145	12.5	123	10.6	1 434	15.4	2 467	1 833	634	200	1 692
Routt	362	24 544	1.08	208	8.7	104	4.3	2 405	11.6	2 783	2 510	273	421	1 847
Saguache	18	5 758	0.82	64	10.3	54	8.7	1 110	22.4	1 234	901	333	84	1 341
San Juan	0	671	1.05	4	5.6	5	7.0	76	13.1	138	123	15	18	2 601
San Miguel	9	8 537	1.22	68	8.7	13	1.7	936	13.4	739	650	89	100	1 281
Sedgwick	35	2 281	0.92	23	9.7	30	12.7	254	14.4	601	567	34	30	1 266
Summit	273	30 425	1.11	269	9.0	50	1.7	3 400	13.0	2 584	2 271	313	777	2 683
Teller	132	20 566	0.75	194	8.3	168	7.2	1 938	10.2	4 622	3 022	1 600	360	1 541
Washington	185	4 140	0.70	43	8.9	45	9.3	482	13.4	880	848	32	47	973
Weld	4 692	243 909	0.83	4 041	14.4	1 634	5.8	29 259	12.1	31 275	21 516	9 759	6 203	2 261
Yuma	263	10 390	1.05	140	13.7	86	8.4	1 378	16.7	1 716	1 668	48	45	439
CONNECTICUT	116 932	3 578 399	0.99	36 225	10.1	29 594	8.2	236 861	8.0	582 779	423 781	158 998	77 592	2 157
Fairfield	20 233	952 092	1.04	10 078	10.6	6 604	7.0	83 782	10.5	133 598	100 888	32 710	17 221	1 857
Hartford	26 881	971 085	1.17	9 425	10.5	7 945	8.9	50 548	6.8	151 241	104 336	46 905	22 951	2 621
Litchfield	2 693	160 791	0.72	1 419	7.7	1 728	9.4	10 457	7.0	35 813	28 176	7 637	NA	NA
Middlesex	4 823	149 738	0.82	1 384	8.4	1 413	8.6	7 290	5.5	29 990	22 201	7 789	NA	NA
New Haven	29 707	840 567	0.94	8 968	10.4	7 596	8.8	56 146	8.0	142 496	98 806	43 690	24 314	3 009
New London	12 059	276 142	1.02	2 715	10.0	2 387	8.8	15 152	6.9	47 759	38 563	9 196	NA	NA

1. Per 1,000 estimated resident population.   2. Data for serious crimes have not been adjusted for underreporting; this may affect comparability between geographic areas and over time.
3. Per 100,000 population estimated by the FBI.

Table B. States and Counties — Crime, Education, Money Income, and Poverty

| STATE County | Serious crimes known to police, 2014 (cont.)[1] Rate[2] | | Education — School enrollment and attainment, 2010–2014 | | | | Local government expenditures,[5] 2012–2013 | | Money income, 2010–2014 | | | | Income and poverty, 2014 | | | |
| | | | Enrollment[3] | | Attainment[4] (percent) | | | | | Households | | | | Percent below poverty level | | |
	Violent	Property	Total	Percent private	High school graduate or less	Bachelor's degree or more	Total current spending (mil dol)	Current spending per student (dollars)	Per capita income[6] (dollars)	Median income (dollars)	Mean income (dollars)	Percent with income of $200,000 or more	Median household income (dollars)	All persons	Children under 18 years	Children 5 to 17 years in families
	46	47	48	49	50	51	52	53	54	55	56	57	58	59	60	61
COLORADO—Cont'd																
Boulder	246	2 372	95 081	12.5	18.9	58.2	[7]521.1	[7]8 769	38 524	69 407	94 871	9.2	71 546	13.3	13.6	12.4
Broomfield	51	1 714	17 011	17.8	20.4	49.5	[7]	[7]	38 706	80 430	99 462	8.6	85 885	4.0	6.3	5.8
Chaffee	80	1 442	2 998	11.0	37.4	34.2	21.0	9 786	27 467	48 528	62 146	2.5	48 840	12.4	18.7	17.5
Cheyenne	104	0	563	9.6	44.1	21.8	4.9	15 665	23 415	53 900	62 111	3.2	52 273	13.4	19.8	21.3
Clear Creek	569	1 718	1 647	16.1	25.5	40.8	10.4	10 869	42 446	68 531	93 440	5.3	69 115	8.5	13.7	12.4
Conejos	12	156	2 179	3.5	49.8	20.2	15.0	9 394	18 247	37 357	47 751	0.1	33 998	22.9	29.8	27.8
Costilla	226	566	766	6.1	52.3	18.2	5.8	12 539	20 592	33 594	46 762	1.6	27 882	28.5	40.2	36.4
Crowley	38	96	1 108	9.1	61.4	10.5	4.4	9 930	11 726	31 534	42 370	1.6	32 570	40.5	38.0	38.0
Custer	93	835	661	18.2	27.0	34.8	3.9	9 309	25 842	32 261	51 552	2.5	48 368	14.9	30.6	26.1
Delta	67	1 969	6 117	11.7	48.2	18.9	41.7	7 796	24 590	42 389	59 629	2.5	45 283	15.6	22.9	20.7
Denver	601	3 404	152 164	20.4	32.6	43.7	881.5	10 572	34 423	51 800	77 658	6.4	54 872	15.9	22.7	23.6
Dolores	98	886	299	1.7	46.9	21.7	3.0	10 399	21 543	32 578	46 210	1.8	44 235	15.4	19.5	18.5
Douglas	85	1 072	90 958	16.4	16.2	55.9	505.8	7 824	44 105	102 626	123 768	13.9	107 250	3.7	4.1	3.5
Eagle	163	1 743	13 129	15.4	28.4	47.3	62.3	9 717	39 355	73 774	104 924	9.7	76 661	7.8	11.8	11.0
Elbert	4	81	5 983	17.9	32.4	29.5	28.5	7 917	36 421	82 154	100 199	8.9	83 603	5.9	8.9	7.4
El Paso	385	2 951	189 209	13.8	27.6	35.2	907.8	8 136	29 314	57 487	76 178	4.4	59 286	12.2	15.4	14.5
Fremont	225	1 721	8 659	14.5	52.1	15.9	43.4	8 061	19 161	44 690	52 361	1.6	41 385	19.1	23.5	22.4
Garfield	171	1 697	14 960	12.0	39.0	29.3	97.2	8 606	27 022	57 214	72 499	3.4	62 529	10.2	14.2	13.6
Gilpin	335	6 017	1 171	3.8	27.3	29.5	4.8	12 788	37 375	65 851	82 103	4.6	64 752	7.9	11.6	8.5
Grand	101	987	2 797	10.9	31.5	36.3	17.4	10 368	31 713	64 109	76 866	4.3	59 379	10.4	14.5	13.3
Gunnison	186	1 293	4 880	11.3	22.4	54.4	15.7	8 483	27 070	51 371	64 592	2.7	48 940	14.9	16.7	15.4
Hinsdale	0	494	85	38.8	24.0	41.3	1.5	17 963	36 046	55 682	74 667	3.6	51 241	10.1	25.4	26.1
Huerfano	353	1 779	1 201	7.8	43.6	28.9	7.6	10 143	23 440	32 932	52 497	2.7	32 750	22.0	37.9	35.2
Jackson	0	146	280	3.6	51.4	17.5	2.6	12 515	25 818	45 606	53 925	0.9	45 073	16.6	26.9	23.9
Jefferson	233	2 723	135 420	13.9	27.6	41.1	728.8	8 520	36 427	69 698	88 241	6.5	70 687	8.3	10.7	9.7
Kiowa	NA	NA	421	7.1	39.1	19.4	3.3	12 588	22 173	39 375	53 598	1.6	42 310	13.5	19.6	19.5
Kit Carson	204	1 520	1 817	9.4	49.9	13.9	13.6	9 442	21 330	41 495	54 332	1.6	46 394	14.9	20.2	20.1
Lake	245	1 046	1 571	11.1	37.5	30.3	15.0	12 853	25 998	46 174	58 030	0.5	46 765	16.0	25.7	24.7
La Plata	165	1 376	13 190	11.5	24.0	43.4	68.6	10 229	31 016	58 456	73 871	3.9	60 658	10.7	13.0	12.5
Larimer	190	2 156	93 757	9.5	23.6	44.1	379.0	8 405	31 082	58 844	77 012	4.5	57 659	12.8	12.1	11.9
Las Animas	147	2 567	3 348	7.3	42.9	18.0	21.6	9 062	23 365	45 707	55 852	1.5	39 625	17.4	26.4	25.8
Lincoln	73	404	947	14.1	61.8	16.1	13.0	17 489	17 594	43 701	59 597	3.1	41 248	18.3	23.7	23.9
Logan	307	2 379	5 196	5.6	46.2	15.9	27.5	9 077	23 533	41 749	58 237	3.2	45 439	17.7	21.4	19.3
Mesa	346	2 609	37 108	10.5	40.4	25.2	174.7	7 802	26 518	48 610	65 297	2.6	50 106	15.4	19.5	17.8
Mineral	137	137	42	26.2	26.5	39.4	1.6	20 885	34 305	47 986	61 179	1.9	51 257	8.9	12.6	15.1
Moffat	146	1 745	3 303	7.9	49.1	14.2	19.5	8 561	24 623	50 123	61 398	0.9	56 193	11.2	16.1	14.4
Montezuma	186	1 867	5 615	8.2	39.3	26.4	32.0	8 142	23 611	43 431	55 308	1.9	44 163	16.3	26.7	25.2
Montrose	164	2 547	8 869	15.6	44.7	24.6	51.8	8 002	23 408	44 885	55 569	1.5	46 336	15.5	23.4	21.4
Morgan	216	1 540	7 284	4.2	52.2	13.9	44.3	8 105	21 297	46 223	56 967	1.4	47 631	13.4	18.6	17.9
Otero	125	2 209	5 082	5.8	44.9	15.5	32.7	10 103	18 868	32 594	46 298	0.7	33 043	26.0	34.7	32.4
Ouray	82	327	760	15.0	21.7	50.0	7.6	14 531	32 562	60 701	72 378	4.0	57 242	9.6	14.7	12.9
Park	117	297	3 046	10.3	29.9	31.6	15.7	9 416	31 838	60 800	69 977	1.5	58 487	9.4	15.0	13.0
Phillips	161	620	1 111	10.0	46.0	18.2	12.0	12 473	22 996	44 390	58 971	2.8	47 006	11.5	16.9	16.2
Pitkin	63	2 195	3 304	21.5	16.0	56.4	24.3	14 046	54 441	71 060	117 574	10.3	73 274	7.0	9.2	8.5
Prowers	57	1 847	3 383	3.4	47.9	13.9	21.0	8 660	19 039	35 408	48 933	0.7	39 184	20.9	29.9	27.7
Pueblo	577	5 119	42 656	8.7	41.0	21.4	210.6	7 852	22 229	41 974	54 865	1.4	41 382	19.0	25.3	24.2
Rio Blanco	102	1 045	1 614	11.8	43.1	20.8	13.1	10 430	27 776	63 910	70 278	2.6	63 184	10.9	15.9	16.8
Rio Grande	152	1 540	2 925	7.9	46.4	20.9	17.2	8 351	21 104	38 673	51 247	1.6	40 593	18.3	30.7	29.8
Routt	140	1 707	4 995	10.4	21.9	48.7	36.9	11 744	35 019	61 095	80 908	5.4	66 846	8.4	10.6	9.8
Saguache	128	1 213	1 393	4.4	46.5	25.7	12.2	12 751	20 569	33 398	47 817	1.6	31 227	29.9	40.4	37.2
San Juan	145	2 457	51	0.0	35.2	27.1	1.6	25 129	25 926	37 679	47 278	0.0	40 006	15.5	31.9	27.3
San Miguel	115	1 166	1 290	17.1	20.9	54.4	12.6	11 673	40 993	59 490	90 990	7.4	59 603	9.9	14.9	14.0
Sedgwick	338	928	498	3.4	46.0	18.6	8.5	6 725	22 124	43 864	52 623	1.9	44 562	13.9	21.7	21.1
Summit	135	2 548	5 279	11.3	21.6	48.1	33.1	10 477	34 842	64 521	83 812	6.3	68 352	9.7	12.5	11.6
Teller	304	1 237	4 615	12.9	32.8	30.9	27.1	9 054	31 732	62 559	74 184	2.2	62 380	9.5	14.8	13.4
Washington	124	849	1 092	9.1	45.0	17.6	11.1	12 710	24 326	44 271	57 365	2.8	45 784	11.4	17.4	15.7
Weld	285	1 976	76 820	9.6	40.7	25.9	325.5	8 426	25 959	58 100	72 491	3.2	61 501	10.5	12.8	12.3
Yuma	10	430	2 608	6.0	44.9	18.6	17.6	9 658	22 902	43 279	56 827	1.8	46 838	14.0	19.7	18.3
CONNECTICUT	237	1 920	947 192	20.6	38.1	37.0	8 888.7	16 631	38 480	69 899	99 110	9.4	70 007	10.8	14.9	13.7
Fairfield	246	1 611	254 087	24.3	33.3	45.4	2 503.2	17 442	49 688	83 163	135 743	17.7	85 336	9.0	11.8	10.9
Hartford	276	2 345	235 279	17.5	38.9	35.6	2 281.9	17 118	35 307	65 499	88 644	7.4	65 809	12.2	17.6	16.1
Litchfield	NA	NA	42 740	18.2	38.2	33.7	424.0	17 647	37 696	72 068	92 075	6.3	73 413	7.7	9.1	8.2
Middlesex	NA	NA	40 670	22.7	33.9	39.7	380.6	17 229	40 589	77 931	99 490	9.4	76 365	7.9	9.1	7.7
New Haven	333	2 676	227 911	23.9	41.6	33.4	2 073.6	16 895	32 794	61 646	83 146	6.4	60 387	13.0	18.4	17.4
New London	NA	NA	66 741	17.6	40.3	31.5	618.5	17 545	34 241	66 693	85 484	5.8	65 813	11.1	16.7	15.5

1. Data for serious crimes have not been adjusted for underreporting; this may affect comparability between geographic areas and over time.   2. Per 100,000 population estimated by the FBI.
3. All persons 3 years old and over enrolled in nursery school through college.   4. Persons 25 years old and over.   5. Elementary and secondary education expenditures.
6. Based on population estimated by the American Community Survey, 2010–2014.   7. Broomfield county is included with Boulder county.

Table B. States and Counties — **Personal Income**

STATE County	Personal income, 2014										Earnings, 2014		
	Total (mil dol)	Percent change, 2013–2014	Per capita[1] Dollars	Per capita[1] Rank	Wages and salaries (mil dol)	Supplements to wages and salaries; employer contributions (mil dol) Pension and insurance	Supplements to wages and salaries; employer contributions (mil dol) Government social insurance	Proprietors' income (mil dol)	Dividends, interest, and rent (mil dol)	Personal transfer receipts (mil dol)	Total (mil dol)	Contributions for government social insurance (mil dol) From employee and self-employed	Contributions for government social insurance (mil dol) From employer
	62	63	64	65	66	67	68	69	70	71	72	73	74
COLORADO—Cont'd													
Boulder	18 370	5.6	58 627	147	10 852	1 386	747	1 448	4 920	1 644	14 432	794	747
Broomfield	4 787	7.8	77 030	36	2 706	292	178	313	523	310	3 488	204	178
Chaffee	650	5.8	35 391	1 879	257	43	18	40	197	154	357	22	18
Cheyenne	95	-8.4	50 823	339	33	6	2	28	22	13	69	3	2
Clear Creek	533	5.6	57 988	157	165	23	12	102	104	54	301	17	12
Conejos	243	7.5	29 402	2 791	49	10	3	32	36	75	94	6	3
Costilla	102	6.8	28 725	2 861	25	5	2	8	18	39	40	3	2
Crowley	126	7.6	23 574	3 091	45	8	3	15	19	36	71	3	3
Custer	172	6.3	39 355	1 273	29	5	2	19	58	41	55	4	2
Delta	1 014	2.5	33 937	2 123	318	56	22	150	215	258	547	34	22
Denver	41 743	6.8	62 880	102	31 351	3 950	2 167	9 016	8 817	4 280	46 484	2 532	2 167
Dolores	82	41.2	41 652	992	43	6	4	4	14	17	57	3	4
Douglas	19 137	7.4	60 821	120	6 820	748	462	506	3 051	1 353	8 535	501	462
Eagle	3 066	5.5	57 927	159	1 382	148	108	325	1 067	178	1 962	108	108
Elbert	1 146	7.1	47 361	507	139	21	10	43	171	132	214	14	10
El Paso	27 831	4.7	41 945	955	14 553	2 561	1 153	1 261	5 752	4 645	19 529	1 028	1 153
Fremont	1 361	5.4	29 266	2 800	521	108	36	66	273	422	730	45	36
Garfield	2 725	5.7	47 429	503	1 260	175	93	209	954	300	1 737	94	93
Gilpin	259	7.7	44 308	732	225	19	17	43	44	30	304	17	17
Grand	562	6.4	38 643	1 371	252	37	19	60	159	75	367	20	19
Gunnison	607	6.0	38 618	1 375	294	48	21	37	205	74	399	21	21
Hinsdale	32	6.5	40 774	1 090	8	2	1	2	15	7	12	1	1
Huerfano	224	5.0	34 598	1 999	56	11	4	11	52	88	82	6	4
Jackson	57	11.1	40 638	1 105	20	4	2	6	15	11	32	2	2
Jefferson	28 631	6.1	51 264	321	12 250	1 716	896	1 249	5 684	3 731	16 111	950	896
Kiowa	73	-4.2	52 221	287	24	4	2	18	17	13	47	1	2
Kit Carson	296	0.0	36 626	1 663	123	20	9	56	59	57	207	10	9
Lake	222	5.6	30 177	2 694	86	16	6	10	46	42	118	6	6
La Plata	2 580	5.7	47 784	488	1 205	166	84	351	718	307	1 806	98	84
Larimer	14 127	6.7	43 584	794	7 027	1 041	487	914	3 016	1 967	9 469	523	487
Las Animas	525	4.7	37 365	1 543	216	37	16	34	93	170	303	18	16
Lincoln	184	13.9	33 434	2 209	84	16	5	16	39	40	122	5	5
Logan	921	3.5	40 888	1 074	340	58	24	217	164	160	640	33	24
Mesa	5 645	5.0	38 074	1 445	2 669	390	201	444	1 054	1 113	3 703	222	201
Mineral	37	3.5	52 974	268	16	2	1	3	17	7	23	1	1
Moffat	547	3.7	42 306	926	235	42	17	81	78	90	374	20	17
Montezuma	924	5.8	35 870	1 797	345	61	24	54	195	218	484	29	24
Montrose	1 381	4.7	33 784	2 150	550	93	40	146	287	332	829	51	40
Morgan	1 132	9.1	39 956	1 183	518	86	38	165	149	205	807	41	38
Otero	612	2.7	33 091	2 264	226	42	17	54	103	203	339	20	17
Ouray	213	4.6	46 108	593	62	10	5	17	82	33	94	6	5
Park	603	6.5	36 899	1 617	84	15	6	28	129	103	133	9	6
Phillips	171	-4.3	39 290	1 283	66	12	4	24	36	36	107	5	4
Pitkin	1 988	4.8	112 796	5	834	83	62	186	1 138	84	1 165	63	62
Prowers	459	1.7	38 129	1 437	157	29	11	90	91	111	286	13	11
Pueblo	5 450	5.5	33 666	2 164	2 490	394	190	284	876	1 591	3 359	208	190
Rio Blanco	276	3.7	41 185	1 039	173	28	12	25	47	43	238	12	12
Rio Grande	438	2.9	37 721	1 495	143	26	11	68	86	120	249	14	11
Routt	1 518	4.9	63 613	97	689	85	50	176	556	113	1 001	55	50
Saguache	184	6.5	29 745	2 752	59	11	4	14	37	44	89	4	4
San Juan	23	6.9	31 900	2 448	8	1	1	2	7	4	12	1	1
San Miguel	474	7.2	60 426	128	202	25	16	55	219	27	297	16	16
Sedgwick	111	6.0	47 321	510	30	6	2	34	20	23	71	2	2
Summit	1 490	6.7	50 685	347	753	89	57	135	539	105	1 035	56	57
Teller	999	4.4	42 705	880	267	39	19	39	207	187	363	24	19
Washington	222	13.1	46 459	562	55	11	4	74	33	35	144	5	4
Weld	10 736	7.7	38 664	1 368	4 895	680	358	1 134	1 424	1 587	7 067	385	358
Yuma	474	-2.4	46 491	558	178	29	12	131	83	75	351	13	12
CONNECTICUT	233 293	4.4	64 864	X	109 036	17 672	7 489	22 313	48 208	30 527	156 511	8 651	7 489
Fairfield	93 304	4.9	98 688	6	37 394	4 977	2 256	11 213	24 371	7 248	55 840	3 101	2 256
Hartford	50 862	4.0	56 640	181	34 238	5 521	2 409	4 518	8 009	8 176	46 686	2 546	2 409
Litchfield	10 099	3.8	54 593	219	2 816	556	223	936	2 147	1 452	4 531	268	223
Middlesex	9 726	3.8	58 963	146	3 645	685	272	773	1 682	1 263	5 375	300	272
New Haven	43 288	4.2	50 261	370	20 391	3 584	1 562	3 384	7 490	8 070	28 921	1 621	1 562
New London	13 758	3.6	50 271	369	6 899	1 451	500	791	2 647	2 317	9 641	508	500

1. Based on the resident population estimated as of July 1 of the year shown.

STATE County	Farm	Mining	Construction	Manufacturing	Information: professional, scientific, technical services	Retail trade	Finance, insurance, real estate and leasing	Health care and social assistance	Government	Social Security beneficiaries, December 2014 Number	Rate[1]	Supplemental Security Income recipients, December 2014	Housing units, 2015 Total	Percent change, 2010–2014
	75	76	77	78	79	80	81	82	83	84	85	86	87	88
COLORADO—Cont'd														
Boulder	0.1	0.5	3.8	12.2	31.1	4.9	5.4	9.3	14.6	41 290	132	2 528	132 457	4.2
Broomfield	0.0	D	4.3	16.6	37.6	4.7	4.3	3.3	2.4	8 255	133	424	26 680	17.9
Chaffee	0.7	1.4	12.1	2.8	6.8	10.4	6.8	6.7	27.8	4 820	261	224	10 443	4.2
Cheyenne	29.6	17.1	D	D	D	3.8	D	D	17.6	325	175	9	975	0.0
Clear Creek	0.0	D	8.3	D	D	3.6	D	D	12.8	1 660	181	77	5 683	0.1
Conejos	18.4	D	9.9	1.3	D	7.5	D	10.7	25.2	1 870	226	351	4 299	0.3
Costilla	22.7	D	D	D	D	D	D	5.0	31.6	1 150	324	232	2 710	3.7
Crowley	22.8	0.0	D	0.0	0.7	4.6	D	3.9	41.5	850	151	145	1 552	-0.4
Custer	3.2	0.9	28.2	4.9	7.4	9.3	D	D	19.0	1 415	326	40	4 203	6.2
Delta	3.7	25.9	5.1	4.7	3.6	7.5	3.5	7.8	22.1	8 385	280	523	14 510	-0.4
Denver	0.0	11.6	3.9	3.4	18.7	2.8	10.7	6.7	11.8	83 340	126	14 872	304 037	6.4
Dolores	4.0	D	D	D	D	3.4	D	D	15.0	550	278	22	1 462	-0.4
Douglas	0.0	2.3	6.5	2.0	24.7	7.1	10.9	8.5	8.3	34 965	111	965	121 665	13.9
Eagle	0.2	1.3	12.3	1.2	7.3	8.4	9.9	10.1	9.7	4 395	83	100	31 730	1.3
Elbert	0.2	D	26.6	3.5	D	7.0	D	2.6	19.1	3 885	161	97	9 184	2.7
El Paso	0.0	0.2	5.5	4.8	16.0	6.3	6.2	9.1	33.8	96 555	146	8 653	268 981	6.4
Fremont	0.4	1.2	6.5	5.1	2.8	7.6	2.6	12.7	46.8	11 835	255	1 113	19 309	0.3
Garfield	0.1	13.2	14.6	1.2	6.7	7.5	5.7	9.9	16.9	7 310	127	360	23 423	0.5
Gilpin	0.0	0.0	1.6	D	D	0.2	D	D	9.3	855	149	23	3 589	0.8
Grand	1.7	0.7	13.4	1.6	D	7.2	6.4	2.1	20.7	2 125	147	67	16 305	1.5
Gunnison	0.6	11.3	9.6	1.2	7.8	7.7	4.8	3.9	25.9	1 995	127	80	11 614	1.8
Hinsdale	2.2	D	11.4	0.0	D	D	D	D	30.2	210	269	0	1 405	1.2
Huerfano	0.3	D	9.5	2.1	D	9.8	1.9	D	24.2	2 225	346	264	5 140	1.3
Jackson	11.7	0.0	D	D	D	6.9	D	1.4	26.8	320	229	12	1 287	0.1
Jefferson	0.0	0.8	6.6	12.3	16.7	6.6	5.5	11.5	16.1	92 590	166	5 570	235 607	2.4
Kiowa	48.6	D	D	0.0	D	2.4	0.0	D	20.7	325	230	18	809	0.5
Kit Carson	20.4	D	7.8	3.0	2.2	5.0	4.0	3.1	15.6	1 505	193	94	3 508	-0.5
Lake	0.0	D	8.2	D	2.1	4.8	1.3	9.0	29.1	915	124	73	4 262	-0.2
La Plata	-0.1	8.0	11.0	1.9	11.2	6.6	9.1	11.6	19.8	8 875	165	419	26 826	3.7
Larimer	0.5	0.7	8.7	13.4	13.1	6.6	4.8	8.9	22.2	51 960	160	2 617	140 892	6.2
Las Animas	3.5	17.7	6.2	1.1	3.9	6.5	3.8	D	24.9	3 760	267	582	8 228	0.1
Lincoln	10.7	0.0	3.7	D	D	8.3	3.7	5.4	44.2	1 060	192	81	2 429	0.3
Logan	8.6	13.2	4.4	7.2	1.6	8.4	2.6	9.5	19.4	3 865	176	384	8 951	-0.3
Mesa	0.7	10.3	8.2	4.5	6.5	7.7	5.8	14.3	16.4	30 075	203	2 453	64 247	2.6
Mineral	3.8	D	7.6	D	D	8.2	D	D	16.0	250	360	0	1 229	2.3
Moffat	2.2	26.6	4.9	1.1	2.2	7.4	2.9	D	16.4	2 180	169	177	6 157	-0.6
Montezuma	0.7	5.9	8.9	3.4	4.7	10.2	3.4	13.5	26.8	5 970	231	469	11 998	-0.8
Montrose	2.1	3.2	10.2	7.9	5.9	9.5	4.4	12.3	21.5	10 105	247	615	18 377	0.7
Morgan	12.7	7.1	6.3	21.1	3.5	4.3	2.9	D	12.6	4 750	168	414	11 480	-0.1
Otero	9.6	0.0	5.0	8.2	3.8	7.1	4.0	D	23.8	4 320	234	811	8 897	-0.8
Ouray	1.5	11.3	14.1	3.2	10.1	8.0	4.7	D	19.4	1 125	243	26	3 162	2.6
Park	-2.0	D	15.7	2.4	11.0	7.4	3.0	2.0	28.3	3 140	193	132	14 239	2.1
Phillips	18.2	D	6.6	1.1	D	5.2	2.8	D	25.3	940	214	54	2 093	0.3
Pitkin	0.0	D	6.6	0.5	8.8	6.5	12.1	3.1	13.0	2 315	132	22	13 114	1.2
Prowers	23.1	2.6	5.8	5.3	3.5	8.0	5.0	6.4	22.7	2 395	199	341	5 874	-1.1
Pueblo	0.3	0.2	7.6	11.4	6.1	8.1	3.1	19.8	21.1	34 920	216	6 287	70 142	0.9
Rio Blanco	2.8	29.4	13.1	0.7	1.6	3.8	1.6	0.7	26.1	1 045	156	41	3 356	1.4
Rio Grande	10.7	0.0	5.2	2.2	2.0	4.7	3.1	7.9	19.0	2 765	238	360	6 604	-0.4
Routt	0.8	6.4	16.6	D	9.2	6.3	10.6	8.9	10.0	3 065	128	80	16 492	1.2
Saguache	22.8	D	3.6	2.7	D	4.9	0.6	3.0	25.4	1 435	231	184	3 952	2.8
San Juan	0.0	0.0	D	D	D	10.8	D	D	29.9	140	195	0	755	-0.1
San Miguel	0.4	D	14.0	3.2	8.8	6.0	8.6	4.1	14.7	885	114	25	6 748	1.7
Sedgwick	48.5	0.0	D	1.5	D	3.7	D	D	20.0	640	274	45	1 407	-0.6
Summit	0.1	D	8.8	0.7	9.7	9.9	8.6	8.0	13.1	2 775	94	28	30 584	2.5
Teller	-0.6	D	5.2	D	9.7	8.2	3.9	5.3	17.8	5 455	233	214	12 881	1.9
Washington	47.1	D	2.3	1.3	D	4.5	2.8	0.7	13.9	970	203	64	2 412	-0.9
Weld	5.4	12.7	13.0	10.2	3.8	5.6	4.7	7.1	11.8	38 130	138	3 431	102 603	6.6
Yuma	36.2	7.1	3.4	3.9	1.7	4.4	3.8	D	14.1	1 845	180	101	4 445	-0.5
CONNECTICUT	0.1	0.1	5.0	11.1	11.9	5.6	17.2	11.6	13.5	654 533	182	63 259	1 495 953	0.5
Fairfield	0.0	0.1	4.2	9.2	14.2	5.2	26.9	8.5	7.5	148 140	157	12 136	366 122	1.4
Hartford	0.1	0.0	4.4	11.6	12.4	4.9	19.6	11.9	14.1	169 330	189	20 816	374 933	0.2
Litchfield	0.2	0.2	D	16.1	6.5	9.0	D	12.6	14.4	40 305	218	1 738	87 407	-0.2
Middlesex	0.4	D	7.2	16.8	8.3	7.0	4.9	14.8	17.7	33 605	204	1 568	75 365	0.7
New Haven	0.1	0.1	5.7	9.3	10.5	6.2	6.5	15.9	15.0	160 930	187	19 800	362 679	0.2
New London	0.6	0.1	5.0	18.3	8.0	5.9	2.8	11.5	28.3	53 905	198	4 082	121 637	0.5

1. Per 1,000 resident population estimated as of July 1 of the year shown.

Table B. States and Counties — Housing, Labor Force, and Employment

STATE County	Housing units, 2010–2014 Occupied units Owner-occupied Total	Percent	Median value[1]	Median owner cost as a percent of income With a mortgage	Without a mortgage[2]	Renter-occupied Median rent[3]	Median rent as a percent of income[2]	Sub-standard units[4] (percent)	Civilian labor force, 2015 Total	Percent change, 2014–2015	Unemployment Total	Rate[5]	Civilian employment,[6] 2010–2014 Total	Percent Management, business, science and arts	Construction, production, and maintenance occupations
	89	90	91	92	93	94	95	96	97	98	99	100	101	102	103
COLORADO—Cont'd															
Boulder	121 526	62.5	358 000	22.1	10.0	1 149	34.8	2.3	176 726	-0.2	5 599	3.2	162 646	52.6	11.7
Broomfield	22 651	69.6	284 100	21.7	10.0	1 248	27.9	2.2	34 673	1.0	1 157	3.3	30 607	49.3	13.1
Chaffee	7 735	75.7	265 700	26.5	10.5	817	27.8	1.4	8 502	0.9	290	3.4	8 290	36.0	18.9
Cheyenne	788	76.9	84 200	21.1	10.0	600	16.3	2.5	1 026	5.1	28	2.7	1 078	41.3	28.5
Clear Creek	4 103	80.4	273 400	23.3	10.0	795	22.3	1.6	5 591	0.9	205	3.7	5 140	37.3	24.1
Conejos	3 023	79.4	111 000	24.1	10.5	538	29.0	4.2	3 720	2.6	209	5.6	3 085	33.7	26.7
Costilla	1 396	77.4	101 200	27.7	10.3	614	41.3	5.2	1 630	0.8	106	6.5	1 251	23.2	29.1
Crowley	1 173	78.9	73 700	27.1	13.0	600	27.5	3.7	1 311	-0.8	59	4.5	1 384	30.8	24.9
Custer	2 125	79.7	215 400	31.7	10.2	692	32.9	4.7	2 004	0.8	71	3.5	1 433	27.6	30.9
Delta	12 527	71.8	190 500	25.8	13.0	810	32.9	3.4	13 603	-0.4	774	5.7	11 737	32.8	27.1
Denver	271 054	49.7	257 500	22.9	10.4	913	29.9	3.8	373 109	0.7	13 818	3.7	334 730	43.8	15.4
Dolores	759	81.0	117 400	29.4	12.6	643	27.5	5.1	1 371	2.7	42	3.1	714	34.6	23.9
Douglas	105 404	80.7	340 300	22.2	10.0	1 353	26.8	1.0	171 569	0.9	5 301	3.1	154 549	53.5	9.4
Eagle	18 038	67.4	435 600	27.3	11.5	1 231	28.4	3.8	32 910	1.1	1 027	3.1	31 604	35.6	17.5
Elbert	8 259	88.9	327 300	26.6	10.0	1 109	28.5	2.6	13 242	1.7	416	3.1	11 999	38.8	20.1
El Paso	240 154	63.2	214 300	23.5	10.0	941	30.3	2.8	307 936	-0.1	14 200	4.6	284 443	40.3	17.0
Fremont	16 600	72.0	157 400	25.5	11.1	697	30.6	1.4	14 636	0.2	903	6.2	14 114	28.3	19.5
Garfield	20 330	65.4	290 600	30.0	11.0	1 111	31.5	5.5	30 581	-2.3	1 265	4.1	28 904	28.6	28.8
Gilpin	2 463	74.2	260 000	26.6	10.0	1 043	28.8	4.1	3 483	0.5	108	3.1	2 993	37.9	18.8
Grand	5 208	75.7	292 700	26.9	10.5	982	22.6	3.2	9 175	2.2	292	3.2	8 151	31.1	28.7
Gunnison	6 336	58.9	325 800	27.1	10.0	882	31.4	3.7	9 835	1.2	288	2.9	8 867	33.3	25.0
Hinsdale	418	79.2	264 800	26.4	10.0	722	25.0	1.9	440	0.9	13	3.0	413	41.2	20.1
Huerfano	2 864	73.5	154 700	27.8	11.9	682	33.9	4.3	2 383	-1.7	184	7.7	2 253	38.5	22.5
Jackson	644	68.8	124 800	20.6	11.8	708	30.0	4.7	840	0.1	31	3.7	786	30.5	39.3
Jefferson	220 814	70.1	267 200	22.7	10.0	1 008	30.1	1.7	311 470	0.8	10 957	3.5	286 794	43.7	15.9
Kiowa	559	73.0	76 400	21.1	11.3	683	23.8	2.0	793	4.9	21	2.6	700	41.1	20.0
Kit Carson	3 053	66.4	121 600	23.1	13.7	644	27.3	2.0	4 404	1.6	107	2.4	3 558	29.2	29.5
Lake	3 106	60.4	168 800	23.8	10.8	917	26.5	3.1	4 606	1.7	176	3.8	4 022	31.2	25.2
La Plata	21 124	66.7	333 100	24.2	10.0	1 026	30.7	2.0	30 068	0.0	1 039	3.5	27 219	39.4	18.1
Larimer	122 743	65.0	251 600	23.2	10.0	1 001	33.7	1.8	180 306	1.3	5 942	3.3	159 635	42.7	16.4
Las Animas	5 890	71.6	151 200	26.7	10.3	761	31.9	1.9	6 203	-3.9	348	5.6	6 287	27.1	29.7
Lincoln	1 757	66.1	124 300	23.2	11.3	677	29.4	1.7	2 178	1.6	74	3.4	1 654	33.5	18.4
Logan	7 825	67.6	122 300	21.5	11.8	634	26.9	2.8	11 047	0.0	343	3.1	10 603	24.2	27.7
Mesa	58 966	69.7	203 200	24.2	10.0	841	33.5	2.5	72 039	-2.0	3 997	5.5	67 168	31.7	24.5
Mineral	375	85.3	280 200	28.8	10.0	663	31.6	0.0	437	2.6	16	3.7	340	36.8	27.6
Moffat	4 890	73.8	177 700	22.2	12.2	739	32.1	2.1	7 169	-2.3	324	4.5	6 593	23.9	33.7
Montezuma	10 659	69.7	184 300	26.3	10.4	713	31.2	4.9	12 483	-1.8	702	5.6	11 126	33.4	22.6
Montrose	16 815	70.1	194 600	26.9	11.8	829	31.1	2.4	19 514	0.8	989	5.1	17 539	30.4	29.2
Morgan	10 443	63.1	135 000	23.2	12.7	736	26.7	5.5	14 800	-0.5	562	3.8	13 137	23.9	38.8
Otero	7 381	65.0	93 200	22.6	12.5	646	34.0	3.5	7 988	-0.2	462	5.8	7 331	31.9	22.8
Ouray	1 969	72.8	389 600	32.0	10.0	1 053	29.7	1.8	2 179	1.7	93	4.3	2 172	46.4	16.3
Park	7 184	87.4	244 300	27.7	10.4	1 087	34.3	2.0	9 470	0.7	325	3.4	8 936	34.1	25.1
Phillips	1 656	68.1	132 900	22.1	12.0	615	29.4	5.1	2 392	5.7	57	2.4	2 027	33.0	30.5
Pitkin	7 357	67.2	570 700	27.4	13.3	1 242	26.3	1.9	10 799	-2.5	415	3.8	10 217	38.6	10.5
Prowers	4 925	66.6	86 200	19.8	13.1	548	28.6	2.8	5 854	1.7	239	4.1	5 290	31.2	25.0
Pueblo	62 829	64.9	137 600	24.2	12.2	761	33.2	2.1	71 996	-0.9	4 069	5.7	65 240	29.9	21.2
Rio Blanco	2 644	67.1	199 800	20.8	10.0	736	19.0	3.9	2 839	-3.9	150	5.3	3 384	25.1	36.1
Rio Grande	4 741	66.1	126 300	24.1	12.1	569	23.7	3.8	4 922	1.6	309	6.3	4 943	31.1	29.4
Routt	9 573	71.1	378 100	29.1	10.9	1 150	30.9	1.7	14 356	-0.7	464	3.2	13 738	35.8	19.9
Saguache	2 598	68.6	142 200	28.5	10.9	639	31.5	5.3	3 110	3.0	190	6.1	2 592	30.5	37.2
San Juan	338	61.5	230 300	34.0	11.2	833	35.0	3.3	482	1.0	20	4.1	366	33.3	26.8
San Miguel	3 330	61.9	511 800	33.8	11.1	1 113	30.7	4.4	5 149	4.1	192	3.7	4 571	38.6	18.0
Sedgwick	932	69.6	84 500	21.7	10.0	559	22.5	1.5	1 156	6.0	39	3.4	1 053	29.8	25.9
Summit	10 386	67.5	461 100	29.2	10.0	1 143	29.3	3.8	20 692	2.6	518	2.5	17 827	32.1	19.5
Teller	9 611	81.5	232 300	23.6	10.0	961	35.0	2.0	11 599	-0.3	513	4.4	11 454	37.5	17.5
Washington	1 986	73.6	111 500	21.7	11.5	580	25.1	1.6	2 797	5.2	71	2.5	2 200	37.7	29.2
Weld	92 369	70.0	196 500	23.6	10.2	868	31.0	4.3	147 984	1.3	5 670	3.8	125 738	32.6	26.5
Yuma	3 833	64.8	137 200	24.4	10.0	626	24.5	1.0	5 202	4.4	138	2.7	4 856	25.6	36.2
CONNECTICUT	1 356 206	67.3	274 500	25.3	16.7	1 069	31.9	2.2	1 888 003	0.1	106 484	5.6	1 766 934	41.3	17.0
Fairfield	333 502	68.5	422 400	26.7	18.0	1 327	32.6	2.9	479 044	0.5	25 273	5.3	455 515	43.4	14.5
Hartford	348 204	65.1	238 600	24.2	15.8	983	30.9	2.3	472 790	0.0	27 682	5.9	436 608	42.1	16.5
Litchfield	75 229	77.3	259 800	25.6	16.7	946	29.4	1.3	105 479	0.1	5 301	5.0	98 661	40.2	20.2
Middlesex	66 372	75.3	288 300	24.4	16.2	1 069	29.4	0.9	92 074	0.2	4 410	4.8	87 351	45.7	16.0
New Haven	327 086	63.2	250 400	26.1	17.9	1 064	34.0	2.3	454 396	-0.2	27 907	6.1	416 917	39.7	18.1
New London	106 882	67.2	247 700	24.5	14.9	1 024	29.3	1.8	136 630	-0.3	7 939	5.8	133 363	38.2	17.3

1. Specified owner-occupied units.   2. A value of 10.0 represents 10 percent or less; a value of 50.0 represents 50 percent or more.   3. Specified renter-occupied units.
4. Overcrowded or lacking complete plumbing facilities.   5. Percent of civilian labor force.   6. Persons 16 years old and over.

STATE County	Number of establishments	Total	Health care and social assistance	Manufacturing	Retail trade	Finance and insurance	Professional, scientific, and technical services	Total (mil dol)	Average per employee (dollars)	Number	Fewer than 50 acres	500 acres or more	Farm operators whose principal occupation is farming (percent)
	104	105	106	107	108	109	110	111	112	113	114	115	116
COLORADO—Cont'd													
Boulder	11 932	145 558	19 729	14 554	17 389	3 414	27 024	8 918	61 265	855	72.0	4.3	44.9
Broomfield	1 861	39 556	2 191	2 825	4 755	3 471	4 092	2 652	67 049	25	60.0	20.0	44.0
Chaffee	851	5 502	802	180	1 032	250	217	173	31 362	223	33.2	17.0	52.9
Cheyenne	57	743	D	NA	60	D	D	45	60 366	345	5.5	70.4	67.5
Clear Creek	329	2 624	77	36	247	D	78	107	40 782	25	60.0	12.0	24.0
Conejos	102	588	130	D	187	D	11	18	30 218	605	26.1	19.8	47.4
Costilla	40	238	45	D	42	D	NA	6	24 311	251	34.3	15.1	65.3
Crowley	30	483	D	NA	79	D	D	16	33 157	228	11.8	50.4	58.3
Custer	138	557	D	D	172	D	21	17	29 811	198	20.7	27.8	47.0
Delta	828	6 738	1 413	579	1 194	225	172	223	33 064	1 250	58.9	5.9	56.4
Denver	23 558	414 818	51 910	16 602	29 740	24 129	40 894	24 567	59 225	10	100.0	0.0	40.0
Dolores	48	216	35	D	D	D	D	7	31 204	283	21.9	27.2	48.8
Douglas	8 355	99 978	11 282	2 210	18 570	7 052	9 515	5 521	55 225	1 116	64.3	6.3	51.1
Eagle	3 306	29 837	1 958	274	3 933	800	1 267	1 089	36 511	165	38.2	21.2	41.2
Elbert	581	2 400	151	135	443	69	168	93	38 643	1 330	32.6	21.3	42.3
El Paso	16 292	224 066	33 431	11 113	30 451	10 451	20 962	9 721	43 386	1 206	45.4	17.2	49.5
Fremont	827	7 638	1 951	444	1 693	249	171	222	29 098	809	68.0	12.0	40.8
Garfield	2 403	18 937	2 526	211	3 087	647	994	885	46 723	625	52.2	13.8	48.3
Gilpin	119	4 658	46	D	D	D	39	164	35 125	24	33.3	4.2	45.8
Grand	798	7 640	344	152	634	D	732	230	30 071	205	29.3	30.7	52.2
Gunnison	1 059	6 171	491	83	902	D	D	197	31 843	244	32.4	20.9	47.5
Hinsdale	72	139	D	NA	32	D	D	4	30 784	26	3.8	30.8	38.5
Huerfano	151	1 099	436	D	208	25	57	32	28 901	407	22.9	34.6	54.8
Jackson	68	251	D	D	D	D	13	8	31 355	105	14.3	63.8	63.8
Jefferson	16 436	193 767	26 193	15 993	29 073	10 368	24 931	9 258	47 781	521	72.6	5.6	41.8
Kiowa	37	242	D	D	D	D	D	9	38 992	395	2.5	64.8	58.0
Kit Carson	267	2 021	261	183	303	103	43	64	31 592	704	8.9	57.4	55.5
Lake	203	1 264	196	D	176	25	D	31	24 704	23	17.4	30.4	52.2
La Plata	2 300	20 938	3 028	566	3 354	1 033	1 153	958	45 732	1 124	44.3	11.3	45.7
Larimer	10 031	116 753	18 786	11 069	17 918	3 915	10 941	5 209	44 612	1 625	60.7	8.5	46.5
Las Animas	358	3 226	763	D	629	141	80	100	30 844	602	17.6	49.5	47.3
Lincoln	134	1 215	D	D	308	64	D	39	32 104	464	8.2	69.8	57.3
Logan	570	5 462	1 072	336	1 178	187	84	180	33 043	891	12.3	47.3	53.6
Mesa	4 427	50 695	9 581	2 539	8 288	1 797	2 313	2 142	42 259	2 264	75.4	5.4	48.6
Mineral	66	187	D	D	D	D	D	8	41 610	14	21.4	14.3	57.1
Moffat	420	3 486	506	54	731	D	85	147	42 301	492	29.1	31.9	37.2
Montezuma	744	6 653	1 451	282	1 220	159	295	226	33 895	1 138	49.4	9.6	45.3
Montrose	1 256	11 560	2 575	1 237	2 158	339	583	410	35 499	1 128	52.7	10.6	48.4
Morgan	681	9 001	1 307	2 733	1 028	D	148	333	36 969	754	20.2	34.9	56.5
Otero	426	4 140	1 135	482	729	166	107	125	30 080	541	29.6	25.0	48.6
Ouray	274	1 041	D	58	140	D	81	33	32 090	108	38.0	15.7	73.1
Park	426	1 219	117	59	190	D	D	40	32 692	209	23.4	26.3	41.6
Phillips	140	1 004	D	26	171	47	D	33	33 298	319	11.0	60.5	69.0
Pitkin	1 576	16 880	731	132	1 544	234	669	611	36 176	82	36.6	18.3	46.3
Prowers	349	2 840	593	173	703	181	87	85	29 755	553	19.5	46.5	52.8
Pueblo	3 014	47 148	12 634	4 136	7 914	1 154	1 595	1 757	37 269	894	38.9	21.3	52.3
Rio Blanco	230	2 062	D	D	226	147	35	121	58 872	313	31.0	36.7	53.7
Rio Grande	336	2 528	374	65	423	101	75	74	29 411	377	27.1	24.9	54.1
Routt	1 616	16 659	1 346	104	1 562	239	504	665	39 899	799	43.7	20.9	41.3
Saguache	113	790	81	D	124	D	D	24	30 100	277	14.1	44.4	59.6
San Juan	68	197	D	D	26	NA	D	4	22 472	0	0.0	0.0	0.0
San Miguel	611	4 688	159	98	481	D	149	136	29 005	135	40.0	23.7	48.9
Sedgwick	74	477	D	D	98	D	D	14	29 398	226	13.7	51.3	72.1
Summit	2 170	19 662	1 092	172	3 286	249	691	545	27 716	38	26.3	21.1	26.3
Teller	673	5 278	417	61	851	175	258	172	32 649	123	45.5	21.1	39.0
Washington	111	570	44	9	91	D	D	19	32 784	824	11.5	47.7	48.4
Weld	5 637	77 367	8 424	11 820	9 238	3 634	2 571	3 647	47 142	3 525	35.5	19.6	49.8
Yuma	369	2 631	623	84	453	148	81	92	34 880	834	12.8	56.7	61.4
CONNECTICUT	88 555	1 485 426	276 251	151 363	186 153	113 514	103 077	87 867	59 152	5 977	69.8	1.8	46.3
Fairfield	27 022	408 854	65 138	33 195	50 234	39 358	35 959	31 864	77 935	439	82.2	1.6	57.9
Hartford	22 531	442 655	83 232	45 353	50 872	49 963	32 359	25 957	58 639	899	71.2	1.3	49.6
Litchfield	4 781	52 087	9 597	8 910	8 790	1 417	1 730	2 116	40 621	1 207	67.9	2.5	41.5
Middlesex	4 161	61 384	13 798	9 756	8 964	1 812	2 748	2 867	46 713	518	78.2	1.2	48.6
New Haven	19 467	338 587	73 535	32 597	42 717	12 527	15 224	16 614	49 068	695	77.3	1.2	43.0
New London	5 732	102 281	17 339	D	14 579	2 066	7 461	4 882	47 734	949	64.0	1.3	48.6

Table B. States and Counties — **Agriculture**

STATE County	Land in farms — Acreage (1,000)	Percent change, 2007–2012	Average size of farm (Acres)	Total irrigated (1,000)	Total cropland (1,000)	Value of land and buildings — Average per farm	Average per acre	Value of machinery and equipment, average per farm (dollars)	Value of products sold — Total (mil dol)	Average per farm (dollars)	Crops	Live-stock and poultry products	Percent of farms with sales of: $10,000 or more	$100,000 or more	Government payments — Total ($1,000)	Percent of farms
	117	118	119	120	121	122	123	124	125	126	127	128	129	130	131	132
COLORADO—Cont'd																
Boulder	133	-3.4	155	30.1	39.2	888 591	5 715	49 384	33.9	39 629	D	D	22.8	5.8	474	12.0
Broomfield	11	78.5	446	1.1	11.1	874 920	1 960	90 840	1.5	61 480	90.9	9.1	28.0	20.0	37	24.0
Chaffee	78	-2.2	348	13.5	15.9	1 053 157	3 024	75 278	9.6	43 130	30.5	69.5	30.9	9.9	74	7.6
Cheyenne	977	8.6	2 832	26.6	536.6	2 203 649	778	216 333	87.1	252 417	68.1	31.9	64.3	40.6	6 203	78.3
Clear Creek	8	-33.4	332	D	0.3	910 680	2 744	41 080	0.3	13 720	D	D	32.0	0.0	0	0.0
Conejos	258	12.7	426	100.1	112.6	646 739	1 518	97 661	42.7	70 650	61.8	38.2	47.8	16.0	1 240	28.9
Costilla	376	-6.2	1 499	34.3	49.9	1 646 637	1 099	126 490	29.0	115 398	84.7	15.3	39.8	11.2	475	28.3
Crowley	500	10.8	2 193	5.9	45.3	750 031	342	73 939	161.5	708 268	1.0	99.0	47.4	23.2	2 044	61.4
Custer	189	37.0	953	12.3	20.3	1 451 495	1 523	76 455	8.2	41 379	27.2	72.8	38.9	13.1	301	23.7
Delta	251	-0.7	201	59.2	60.7	665 865	3 319	63 422	55.6	44 511	42.4	57.6	36.3	8.2	728	9.5
Denver	0	-76.5	14	0.0	0.0	775 500	54 231	93 200	D	D	D	D	60.0	20.0	0	0.0
Dolores	160	-8.0	565	7.4	73.1	815 583	1 443	71 901	10.1	35 629	62.9	37.1	28.6	9.9	1 153	63.3
Douglas	200	5.7	179	1.7	23.3	900 148	5 022	53 598	13.7	12 234	33.5	66.5	19.5	1.3	502	4.4
Eagle	129	4.4	785	12.7	14.9	3 090 273	3 939	91 448	7.9	48 109	42.2	57.8	30.9	8.5	68	4.8
Elbert	1 043	-8.0	784	8.4	180.5	879 390	1 121	60 820	45.0	33 805	19.9	80.1	28.9	8.1	2 328	17.4
El Paso	649	5.3	538	7.9	53.7	650 029	1 208	45 053	43.9	36 403	47.1	52.9	24.5	5.1	1 232	10.3
Fremont	290	-1.8	359	8.4	17.7	839 582	2 339	42 611	21.2	26 214	20.2	79.8	19.0	2.8	313	7.0
Garfield	311	-7.3	497	32.3	46.2	1 380 994	2 777	72 635	22.7	36 272	24.9	75.1	30.2	8.8	604	12.6
Gilpin	6	-56.7	240	D	0.4	679 792	2 832	30 250	0.2	6 875	D	D	25.0	0.0	D	20.8
Grand	227	8.8	1 107	27.5	34.9	2 530 395	2 286	94 561	13.5	65 883	15.6	84.4	40.5	13.2	91	6.8
Gunnison	190	9.5	780	42.2	41.6	2 197 246	2 818	95 365	13.0	53 221	13.8	86.2	37.7	13.5	52	4.9
Hinsdale	10	73.5	394	2.4	1.1	2 083 538	5 293	91 308	0.7	27 385	15.4	84.6	38.5	3.8	0	0.0
Huerfano	581	12.0	1 427	11.7	25.1	1 233 226	864	48 887	11.3	27 656	13.1	86.9	26.8	4.7	675	13.0
Jackson	342	-11.5	3 261	59.6	65.5	3 397 571	1 042	187 457	23.6	224 771	19.8	80.1	61.9	35.2	34	11.4
Jefferson	68	-26.8	131	2.3	10.1	719 981	5 493	39 426	9.1	17 465	81.0	19.0	15.7	3.5	41	4.0
Kiowa	1 113	16.2	2 818	3.1	713.3	1 924 033	683	177 504	96.1	243 205	38.5	61.5	54.4	28.6	7 743	86.8
Kit Carson	1 377	1.8	1 956	110.2	872.3	2 214 455	1 132	320 912	499.8	709 908	28.1	71.9	58.8	37.5	12 129	75.6
Lake	12	-17.9	530	3.6	0.8	1 544 261	2 916	26 957	0.9	37 478	8.9	91.0	43.5	13.0	0	0.0
La Plata	590	3.6	525	61.7	85.9	975 981	1 858	66 034	25.0	22 234	33.4	66.6	29.5	4.3	752	9.8
Larimer	450	-8.0	277	52.5	106.4	854 599	3 083	72 401	128.6	79 167	44.6	55.4	28.8	7.6	1 061	11.2
Las Animas	2 141	-1.8	3 556	11.3	71.1	1 441 724	405	60 860	28.4	47 228	11.1	88.9	39.4	14.1	3 371	28.1
Lincoln	1 473	5.2	3 175	4.8	581.6	1 514 664	477	163 039	75.6	162 860	53.5	46.5	61.6	33.4	7 741	70.0
Logan	1 099	-2.9	1 234	94.0	516.0	1 071 964	869	167 899	566.9	636 255	20.8	79.2	63.0	34.9	9 526	76.1
Mesa	387	3.9	171	75.3	71.4	575 360	3 367	51 431	84.6	37 360	48.1	51.9	25.7	6.1	821	7.1
Mineral	7	-25.2	473	D	0.5	2 055 643	4 342	34 286	0.1	6 357	16.9	83.1	14.3	0.0	0	0.0
Moffat	930	11.2	1 890	23.5	119.6	1 380 283	730	77 575	27.0	54 866	13.0	87.0	28.9	10.6	1 866	33.9
Montezuma	691	-1.9	607	62.6	97.4	672 749	1 108	67 594	46.4	40 748	64.7	35.3	30.8	6.6	1 387	15.6
Montrose	330	2.7	292	70.4	70.0	838 902	2 871	74 786	103.2	91 508	32.6	67.4	39.5	12.9	930	17.7
Morgan	647	-11.1	858	100.9	303.6	1 224 219	1 426	198 156	615.3	816 073	17.3	82.7	59.7	32.9	6 315	66.7
Otero	707	13.2	1 306	43.6	74.3	852 516	653	124 166	144.2	266 608	20.8	79.2	53.6	22.7	2 473	54.5
Ouray	81	-13.3	753	9.8	10.1	2 138 602	2 840	88 769	4.3	39 574	16.5	83.5	40.7	13.0	24	6.5
Park	180	-44.4	861	3.8	10.2	1 146 282	1 331	64 617	7.7	37 057	9.2	90.8	22.5	2.9	140	7.7
Phillips	436	1.2	1 368	72.9	370.8	2 477 361	1 810	329 323	208.0	652 056	56.5	43.5	70.5	51.7	6 831	82.8
Pitkin	32	12.5	391	7.5	4.8	2 190 561	5 597	95 427	3.0	36 122	13.3	86.7	28.0	7.3	149	12.2
Prowers	1 022	-1.5	1 848	79.9	480.5	1 270 078	687	180 617	318.2	575 496	20.4	79.6	53.2	27.8	6 892	62.6
Pueblo	895	-1.7	1 001	18.6	88.5	735 098	734	62 169	51.1	57 149	35.4	64.6	27.2	8.1	2 223	20.6
Rio Blanco	507	31.2	1 621	25.6	42.7	2 154 358	1 329	101 540	24.4	77 994	16.2	83.8	39.3	18.8	786	15.0
Rio Grande	185	3.7	492	93.6	105.4	1 163 151	2 364	237 934	106.5	282 470	88.9	11.1	57.8	37.7	1 003	29.2
Routt	613	14.9	767	46.6	117.3	1 700 572	2 218	75 899	46.5	58 148	16.8	83.2	29.8	10.1	847	14.1
Saguache	311	8.4	1 124	90.5	115.3	1 670 177	1 486	284 354	110.0	397 069	84.2	15.8	54.5	32.9	1 298	31.0
San Juan	0	0.0	0	0.0	0.0	0	0	0	0.0	0	0.0	0.0	0.0	0.0	0	0.0
San Miguel	127	-16.2	937	12.7	14.6	1 366 578	1 458	66 570	4.7	35 089	11.3	88.7	30.4	9.6	209	14.8
Sedgwick	336	13.2	1 487	38.1	207.2	1 889 363	1 271	249 558	101.3	448 066	56.8	43.2	70.8	46.0	3 427	80.5
Summit	25	-47.0	668	4.2	5.8	2 218 579	3 324	63 553	D	D	D	D	23.7	10.5	D	2.6
Teller	71	-3.2	577	0.4	3.4	1 156 211	2 006	33 358	1.3	10 195	12.6	87.4	17.9	2.4	102	8.9
Washington	1 216	-11.6	1 476	47.0	699.7	1 441 458	977	177 691	220.7	267 856	44.6	55.4	54.0	29.2	11 607	76.5
Weld	1 956	-6.3	555	299.9	850.2	1 098 289	1 979	146 652	1 860.7	527 863	20.1	79.9	42.8	20.2	15 649	39.7
Yuma	1 353	1.4	1 623	233.0	607.2	2 223 818	1 370	298 933	1 150.3	1 379 309	27.1	72.9	60.0	43.5	12 866	73.5
CONNECTICUT	437	7.6	73	9.3	151.1	809 375	11 082	58 958	550.6	92 123	70.7	29.3	30.0	7.7	4 841	8.7
Fairfield	54	36.4	123	0.3	5.0	1 492 513	12 145	68 132	34.8	79 317	60.1	39.9	35.3	7.5	160	5.5
Hartford	54	1.0	60	4.9	25.7	760 429	12 645	63 402	113.9	126 692	94.1	5.9	36.9	12.0	583	8.8
Litchfield	91	4.1	75	0.4	37.2	859 063	11 399	52 797	46.3	38 344	60.5	39.5	26.3	5.3	1 209	10.8
Middlesex	24	44.8	46	0.6	7.7	654 002	14 074	59 284	53.5	103 257	94.5	5.5	27.0	4.6	167	5.4
New Haven	42	-7.4	61	1.3	14.1	764 679	12 561	56 881	84.6	121 755	91.7	8.3	31.9	10.1	383	7.3
New London	65	2.8	69	0.8	22.8	709 299	10 330	47 891	118.3	124 690	43.2	56.8	26.9	6.7	537	9.2

Table B. States and Counties — Water Use, Wholesale Trade, Retail Trade, and Real Estate

STATE County	Water use, 2010		Wholesale trade,[1] 2012				Retail trade,[2] 2012				Real estate and rental and leasing,[2] 2012			
	Total water withdrawn (mil gal/day)	Gallons withdrawn per person per day	Number of establishments	Number of employees	Sales (mil dol)	Annual payroll (mil dol)	Number of establishments	Number of employees	Sales (mil dol)	Annual payroll (mil dol)	Number of establishments	Number of employees	Receipts (mil dol)	Annual payroll (mil dol)
	133	134	135	136	137	138	139	140	141	142	143	144	145	146
COLORADO—Cont'd														
Boulder	231.6	786	392	D	D	D	1 174	16 623	4 498.3	478.9	648	1 954	434.3	74.5
Broomfield	6.4	115	52	D	D	D	261	4 606	1 000.2	101.7	96	313	77.1	11.4
Chaffee	101.9	5 719	19	95	41.4	2.9	134	1 049	249.3	25.4	78	132	17.4	3.2
Cheyenne	37.9	20 632	3	D	D	D	13	73	18.5	1.3	2	D	D	D
Clear Creek	1.8	200	12	D	D	D	46	265	75.3	5.1	17	24	3.1	0.6
Conejos	382.5	46 330	4	19	4.6	0.9	18	203	35.9	4.3	4	11	0.4	0.1
Costilla	139.9	39 702	1	D	D	D	10	33	11.7	0.6	NA	NA	NA	NA
Crowley	13.7	2 358	1	D	D	D	8	89	17.0	2.3	1	D	D	D
Custer	27.2	6 402	3	2	0.4	0.0	25	164	48.6	3.4	10	9	1.9	0.3
Delta	359.5	11 615	28	174	47.2	6.7	116	1 158	309.8	27.6	36	254	16.5	4.6
Denver	150.5	251	1 175	17 997	14 625.8	1 090.1	2 282	26 469	7 111.4	725.7	1 451	9 373	2 723.8	488.3
Dolores	5.6	2 708	5	D	D	D	5	39	10.0	0.7	NA	NA	NA	NA
Douglas	51.6	181	241	2 398	2 701.7	205.2	851	15 688	4 308.8	398.1	476	1 154	283.5	48.3
Eagle	137.9	2 642	68	D	D	D	455	3 621	806.0	102.1	362	1 880	280.9	63.5
Elbert	13.8	598	14	D	D	D	38	406	105.7	8.7	16	19	3.7	0.7
El Paso	116.1	187	430	4 395	2 563.3	247.4	1 955	28 743	7 929.3	757.3	1 031	3 344	657.4	119.9
Fremont	146.2	3 123	27	D	D	D	130	1 594	334.9	34.9	39	159	15.9	3.2
Garfield	261.5	4 637	62	D	D	D	285	2 982	950.0	92.1	158	794	213.2	38.1
Gilpin	3.4	618	2	D	D	D	8	20	6.4	0.6	4	7	0.5	0.2
Grand	186.5	12 567	7	17	4.7	0.5	107	628	156.1	15.7	68	583	45.0	13.3
Gunnison	562.7	36 723	9	15	3.5	0.4	133	907	190.0	20.4	89	189	23.8	5.2
Hinsdale	30.4	36 074	NA	NA	NA	NA	17	27	9.0	0.9	4	3	1.2	0.1
Huerfano	38.3	5 701	4	D	D	D	31	215	62.9	4.7	7	15	2.3	0.3
Jackson	347.9	249 541	2	D	D	D	10	63	16.5	1.6	NA	NA	NA	NA
Jefferson	78.3	146	529	4 575	3 082.1	289.5	1 866	28 060	7 465.0	724.2	866	2 800	527.7	113.3
Kiowa	5.6	3 977	8	30	20.1	0.8	6	35	10.2	0.6	NA	NA	NA	NA
Kit Carson	130.5	15 780	20	184	271.9	8.5	41	312	115.0	7.6	7	24	2.9	0.7
Lake	14.7	2 005	4	D	D	D	30	199	37.4	4.5	13	51	2.9	0.9
La Plata	336.6	6 558	55	508	222.3	22.8	314	3 128	756.9	83.4	139	454	69.9	14.9
Larimer	412.9	1 378	295	4 294	5 143.6	368.5	1 244	17 307	4 341.3	414.2	526	2 112	307.0	71.4
Las Animas	73.7	4 755	9	D	D	D	60	679	178.9	16.7	22	66	8.6	2.5
Lincoln	4.5	821	1	D	D	D	31	330	183.9	7.1	3	5	0.3	0.0
Logan	164.4	7 239	24	D	D	D	100	1 124	320.0	26.3	15	40	7.1	1.3
Mesa	754.7	5 144	219	2 076	876.5	96.2	604	7 966	2 173.3	202.6	263	889	170.7	33.7
Mineral	18.5	25 955	NA	NA	NA	NA	13	60	13.5	1.4	3	3	0.4	0.1
Moffat	170.1	12 332	23	D	D	D	72	714	201.9	21.3	9	13	3.3	0.3
Montezuma	255.1	9 989	19	164	72.6	7.2	99	1 159	349.9	32.3	29	91	20.4	3.2
Montrose	702.9	17 028	47	313	156.2	11.7	180	2 152	583.8	55.9	53	125	18.0	3.6
Morgan	186.0	6 606	32	D	D	D	92	953	256.9	21.8	26	49	5.5	1.2
Otero	436.8	23 195	24	158	94.8	5.5	75	775	213.8	17.1	14	82	8.2	1.8
Ouray	111.0	25 020	1	D	D	D	38	145	22.6	2.5	9	16	1.8	0.5
Park	24.4	1 506	10	D	D	D	40	170	49.7	4.1	22	26	5.2	1.1
Phillips	58.9	13 267	10	D	D	D	21	158	46.1	4.0	3	3	0.1	0.2
Pitkin	123.4	7 194	11	D	D	D	235	1 504	344.4	46.4	203	959	167.3	38.7
Prowers	152.3	12 131	16	115	97.5	4.0	56	656	162.3	13.1	15	D	D	D
Pueblo	288.9	1 816	85	D	D	D	508	7 551	1 952.8	183.4	143	585	105.1	17.7
Rio Blanco	267.2	40 078	4	D	D	D	35	246	54.8	4.6	9	24	7.0	1.6
Rio Grande	579.2	48 339	25	313	238.4	13.2	48	369	99.8	9.5	18	52	4.8	1.2
Routt	204.0	8 678	35	250	131.2	12.7	215	1 616	360.9	41.4	131	530	57.0	14.3
Saguache	270.9	44 355	10	265	108.1	9.8	16	118	23.3	2.1	1	D	D	D
San Juan	1.6	2 232	NA	NA	NA	NA	14	29	6.8	0.6	2	D	D	D
San Miguel	37.9	5 156	5	15	4.0	0.9	72	478	79.7	10.5	78	196	32.5	7.1
Sedgwick	61.4	25 818	4	27	20.6	1.1	13	92	28.1	2.1	1	D	D	D
Summit	68.7	2 454	30	D	D	D	346	3 041	627.2	68.0	245	932	117.6	26.3
Teller	7.6	325	12	36	13.3	1.2	70	762	207.8	17.6	43	83	11.7	2.3
Washington	73.4	15 247	7	62	209.8	4.7	14	89	31.6	1.9	1	D	D	D
Weld	462.1	1 828	246	3 166	5 349.2	157.4	620	8 154	2 707.6	228.7	212	870	149.0	31.5
Yuma	220.8	21 986	29	215	855.5	10.0	63	456	125.6	9.6	12	17	1.9	0.4
CONNECTICUT	3 311.0	926	3 675	58 814	161 962.2	3 934.4	12 597	182 528	51 632.5	4 974.5	3 219	19 778	5 349.5	958.4
Fairfield	494.3	539	1 190	18 611	130 674.8	1 622.4	3 459	49 401	15 166.5	1 553.9	1 077	6 971	1 808.6	418.1
Hartford	200.7	225	970	19 033	15 797.2	1 086.7	3 134	49 862	13 762.4	1 257.3	868	5 027	1 087.0	230.9
Litchfield	68.4	360	162	D	D	D	692	8 669	2 655.0	241.2	137	388	60.3	13.6
Middlesex	133.6	807	167	2 288	1 537.6	146.7	659	8 548	2 202.6	215.5	124	809	126.4	30.3
New Haven	113.5	132	922	14 185	11 237.2	821.2	2 901	41 925	11 567.5	1 100.7	673	5 378	2 008.0	220.2
New London	2 249.8	8 209	150	D	D	D	1 023	14 372	3 679.3	364.3	204	765	182.6	32.0

1. Merchant wholesalers, except manufacturers' sales branches and offices.   2. Employer establishments.

STATE County	Professional, scientific, and technical services, 2012				Manufacturing, 2012				Accommodation and food services, 2012			
	Number of establish-ments	Number of employees	Receipts (mil dol)	Annual payroll (mil dol)	Number of establish-ments	Number of employees	Receipts (mil dol)	Annual payroll (mil dol)	Number of establish-ments	Number of employees	Sales (mil dol)	Annual payroll (mil dol)
	147	148	149	150	151	152	153	154	155	156	157	158
COLORADO—Cont'd												
Boulder	2 679	27 395	4 767.9	2 011.5	536	14 305	5 061.5	998.4	866	15 855	842.2	252.2
Broomfield	325	6 060	1 252.4	496.8	82	3 087	3 918.4	188.5	143	2 944	169.6	54.7
Chaffee	96	223	24.1	7.6	29	199	25.3	6.0	108	1 172	58.9	19.7
Cheyenne	4	5	0.3	0.1	NA	NA	NA	NA	4	28	1.1	0.2
Clear Creek	48	78	11.7	3.9	8	D	D	D	42	540	30.3	8.8
Conejos	5	9	0.8	0.2	5	53	D	2.6	11	38	3.9	1.0
Costilla	NA	NA	NA	NA	NA	NA	NA	NA	6	D	D	D
Crowley	3	D	D	D	NA	NA	NA	NA	3	12	0.8	0.0
Custer	16	21	3.8	0.8	7	32	D	1.3	12	56	3.2	0.7
Delta	76	D	D	D	50	619	168.1	27.4	76	623	27.2	8.0
Denver	4 291	42 123	9 140.6	3 409.8	759	17 032	5 343.9	761.4	1 982	42 906	2 884.9	823.2
Dolores	4	2	0.3	0.1	NA	NA	NA	NA	8	39	2.5	1.0
Douglas	1 623	10 273	2 561.7	798.6	133	2 169	460.4	119.3	522	10 295	541.8	167.0
Eagle	401	1 289	183.9	65.7	50	238	73.8	11.2	259	7 998	477.8	175.3
Elbert	87	176	22.0	8.5	21	143	D	6.5	26	190	9.3	2.5
El Paso	2 417	19 740	2 983.8	1 258.0	465	10 425	3 375.9	560.5	1 300	26 734	1 443.2	389.2
Fremont	64	178	14.1	4.3	34	409	116.8	20.5	85	878	39.2	11.2
Garfield	300	1 004	137.6	55.1	46	246	41.1	9.4	201	2 727	161.3	49.1
Gilpin	23	34	5.7	1.8	4	D	D	D	10	2 408	404.7	81.0
Grand	81	247	75.4	42.1	14	136	18.6	3.7	136	1 826	84.3	29.4
Gunnison	125	312	28.7	10.0	25	80	9.5	2.2	121	1 339	87.0	16.1
Hinsdale	1	D	D	D	NA	NA	NA	NA	17	75	4.1	1.3
Huerfano	14	35	2.7	1.2	3	26	D	1.4	26	172	9.0	2.4
Jackson	5	10	0.6	0.1	NA	NA	NA	NA	11	51	2.9	0.7
Jefferson	2 985	23 587	4 908.0	1 823.0	448	12 913	6 119.0	907.3	1 160	20 616	1 069.2	318.1
Kiowa	2	D	D	D	NA	NA	NA	NA	2	D	D	D
Kit Carson	18	41	3.8	1.2	8	165	D	4.6	23	261	12.8	3.4
Lake	11	40	3.6	1.6	4	36	D	D	37	268	13.1	3.7
La Plata	326	1 100	139.8	55.3	57	518	84.9	21.1	206	4 226	209.2	68.4
Larimer	1 493	8 727	1 031.1	450.9	403	10 163	4 275.7	642.6	847	14 821	756.5	218.0
Las Animas	24	93	7.2	2.8	6	56	9.0	2.6	50	656	30.9	8.4
Lincoln	10	25	2.2	0.6	NA	NA	NA	NA	19	222	9.6	2.3
Logan	30	101	10.9	3.4	20	308	213.0	11.9	46	595	26.2	7.5
Mesa	561	2 529	289.0	119.8	159	2 388	520.6	95.1	300	6 052	282.6	88.8
Mineral	3	4	0.3	0.1	NA	NA	NA	NA	19	66	7.9	2.5
Moffat	31	129	10.1	4.0	11	50	D	1.6	33	454	20.7	5.9
Montezuma	80	281	30.1	11.8	32	264	49.9	9.2	85	1 263	83.2	22.8
Montrose	110	438	46.3	20.6	66	1 167	210.7	39.2	78	1 007	49.6	15.4
Morgan	36	120	10.4	3.1	42	3 147	2 444.1	105.4	57	693	29.5	8.4
Otero	32	105	7.3	2.4	15	465	75.9	18.2	52	603	22.9	6.4
Ouray	47	78	10.4	3.7	11	36	4.9	1.2	47	280	21.5	6.3
Park	57	86	10.2	3.3	15	55	D	1.7	40	230	18.4	3.8
Phillips	10	18	2.2	0.5	3	16	4.1	0.7	15	76	2.6	0.8
Pitkin	224	636	154.3	43.7	17	104	16.7	4.5	160	5 089	305.3	118.2
Prowers	28	95	11.2	3.5	14	150	31.5	5.4	35	414	17.6	4.2
Pueblo	238	1 744	435.3	157.3	90	4 221	2 333.3	216.8	356	5 698	236.0	67.8
Rio Blanco	15	51	4.8	1.6	3	10	D	D	30	200	11.5	3.1
Rio Grande	28	72	6.1	2.1	10	59	10.5	2.4	32	278	12.8	3.9
Routt	193	531	81.9	25.5	24	118	17.4	4.8	146	5 159	241.4	80.0
Saguache	9	13	1.1	0.5	5	45	D	2.0	5	30	1.1	0.3
San Juan	6	D	D	D	3	8	D	0.4	24	86	6.2	1.5
San Miguel	75	129	19.7	5.6	14	84	10.9	4.9	72	1 439	77.2	29.2
Sedgwick	5	17	1.0	0.3	3	29	D	0.7	4	53	1.4	0.5
Summit	258	575	89.3	30.4	26	166	40.6	7.9	250	6 201	311.3	101.3
Teller	88	411	57.8	22.6	14	46	6.5	1.7	71	1 649	110.8	38.1
Washington	7	18	1.7	0.4	6	100	D	D	6	27	1.0	0.3
Weld	533	2 362	311.5	113.7	284	11 102	5 991.4	485.8	400	5 794	273.9	76.2
Yuma	27	62	6.6	2.0	11	78	164.8	2.8	26	231	8.5	2.5
CONNECTICUT	9 220	97 578	17 993.7	8 364.1	4 350	163 847	55 160.1	10 546.2	8 263	134 546	9 542.1	2 590.8
Fairfield	3 481	40 694	8 738.6	3 975.9	837	35 507	13 412.5	2 338.2	2 266	30 574	2 153.3	604.6
Hartford	2 238	26 427	5 239.4	1 968.7	1 261	57 332	16 965.5	3 899.3	2 043	32 877	1 905.3	549.8
Litchfield	372	D	D	D	382	9 062	2 615.3	463.3	411	4 426	265.2	75.3
Middlesex	374	2 735	425.1	166.9	243	8 920	3 605.4	543.1	421	5 434	329.5	99.3
New Haven	1 907	16 222	2 461.1	1 216.8	1 151	31 792	10 818.1	1 879.2	1 969	26 342	1 487.2	411.3
New London	529	8 100	666.1	862.0	172	12 435	4 693.7	950.2	698	28 347	3 023.8	748.7

1. Establishment subject to federal tax.

STATE County	Health care and social assistance, 2012				Other services, 2012				Nonemployer businesses, 2014		Value of residential construction authorized by building permits, 2015	
	Number of establishments	Number of employees	Receipts (mil dol)	Annual payroll (mil dol)	Number of establishments	Number of employees	Receipts (mil dol)	Annual payroll (mil dol)	Number	Receipts (mil dol)	New Construction ($1,000)	Number of housing units
	159	160	161	162	163	164	165	166	167	168	169	170
COLORADO—Cont'd												
Boulder	1 332	18 386	2 129.6	841.9	717	4 415	670.1	176.7	37 760	1 966.9	354 113	1 249
Broomfield	145	1 611	172.9	64.4	109	704	141.8	23.7	5 385	228.3	145 059	447
Chaffee	66	791	76.3	31.3	40	175	11.7	3.7	2 251	90.8	30 691	121
Cheyenne	1	D	D	D	4	6	1.0	0.2	194	9.2	1 239	6
Clear Creek	19	67	5.8	2.2	10	27	1.8	0.5	959	50.3	4 217	18
Conejos	11	254	17.1	6.9	4	D	D	D	595	28.2	3 161	21
Costilla	7	37	1.7	0.9	3	D	D	D	259	9.0	7 942	35
Crowley	3	D	D	D	1	D	D	D	163	5.8	515	5
Custer	2	D	D	D	10	120	5.3	2.6	645	24.3	11 216	43
Delta	89	1 716	115.7	48.9	50	185	15.2	4.1	2 727	101.0	1 179	7
Denver	2 093	54 161	7 316.9	3 008.8	1 607	13 247	1 868.2	472.2	63 584	3 447.3	1 265 944	7 901
Dolores	5	D	D	D	NA	NA	NA	NA	173	5.8	0	0
Douglas	743	8 339	1 137.4	412.4	508	3 075	270.0	80.6	29 962	1 548.4	741 294	2 889
Eagle	168	2 052	384.1	115.8	189	1 278	119.3	37.3	7 105	427.7	149 675	188
Elbert	25	132	8.2	3.9	42	118	11.9	3.2	2 719	128.7	35 613	149
El Paso	1 897	D	D	D	1 086	8 419	1 805.3	323.0	47 068	1 890.3	1 150 952	3 580
Fremont	93	1 982	128.3	60.6	46	214	13.1	4.4	2 750	101.1	11 136	54
Garfield	161	D	D	D	152	692	91.3	20.8	6 097	312.5	35 913	138
Gilpin	6	43	4.0	1.5	3	7	0.4	0.1	516	18.2	7 000	16
Grand	36	324	35.9	13.3	46	103	12.0	2.6	1 826	86.0	41 470	128
Gunnison	64	494	50.3	18.0	64	221	27.3	5.7	2 291	95.0	27 919	98
Hinsdale	1	D	D	D	6	D	D	D	142	4.6	1 852	6
Huerfano	18	424	31.2	15.3	7	D	D	D	596	21.3	5 369	32
Jackson	3	7	0.5	0.2	1	D	D	D	168	5.8	949	4
Jefferson	1 565	24 678	2 717.4	1 084.2	1 121	6 073	628.1	172.8	52 896	2 384.2	482 567	1 852
Kiowa	2	D	D	D	4	4	0.5	0.1	140	5.0	0	0
Kit Carson	26	284	22.2	9.0	13	D	D	D	662	30.2	0	0
Lake	14	195	18.3	6.8	12	32	2.1	0.5	659	24.6	6 566	39
La Plata	237	2 737	335.0	125.2	143	612	53.9	16.6	6 235	297.8	91 763	336
Larimer	1 021	18 142	1 988.2	783.2	658	3 536	374.1	96.2	29 905	1 342.9	569 560	2 434
Las Animas	36	D	D	D	36	129	11.0	3.0	927	34.2	663	3
Lincoln	7	245	21.3	8.4	11	41	3.4	0.9	371	13.6	1 466	15
Logan	65	1 027	88.3	33.5	53	203	21.5	5.2	1 243	61.3	5 725	27
Mesa	426	10 176	1 029.0	427.2	293	1 883	182.6	47.8	11 180	513.3	115 142	486
Mineral	2	D	D	D	3	D	D	D	160	8.7	976	12
Moffat	40	440	50.3	19.1	37	219	18.5	6.7	973	39.5	842	7
Montezuma	90	1 422	109.3	45.2	47	173	15.7	3.6	2 289	88.8	4 255	23
Montrose	172	2 338	221.5	83.5	86	368	36.5	9.4	3 652	158.6	19 305	124
Morgan	57	1 186	118.5	46.1	40	139	14.1	3.2	1 794	85.7	13 234	78
Otero	57	921	50.8	24.8	27	81	7.1	1.8	1 035	37.4	652	4
Ouray	18	52	3.9	1.6	8	35	2.6	0.8	907	50.3	12 847	35
Park	23	96	4.6	2.1	24	76	9.1	2.4	1 795	73.6	21 095	123
Phillips	9	298	21.2	8.8	12	24	3.2	0.7	382	21.4	2 322	9
Pitkin	74	D	D	D	115	913	122.3	36.8	3 648	278.4	98 991	103
Prowers	30	625	48.8	20.7	23	87	10.5	2.1	835	40.9	1 466	6
Pueblo	419	11 404	1 063.1	458.0	238	1 222	93.1	28.2	8 095	305.1	46 258	282
Rio Blanco	10	176	19.0	8.8	12	25	3.0	0.8	540	24.2	3 141	11
Rio Grande	34	420	28.7	11.9	24	94	12.6	2.9	1 027	33.6	3 118	14
Routt	118	1 170	141.6	51.0	86	438	37.7	10.9	3 651	178.4	57 289	102
Saguache	6	D	D	D	8	D	D	D	589	21.8	1 945	29
San Juan	3	D	D	D	3	17	0.7	0.4	111	5.1	650	6
San Miguel	28	132	10.0	4.2	44	270	29.1	7.8	1 718	98.5	58 213	32
Sedgwick	5	D	D	D	5	10	1.6	0.2	191	8.6	0	0
Summit	104	852	134.8	39.9	121	420	60.5	12.3	4 315	266.7	104 295	195
Teller	58	D	D	D	42	129	11.5	3.1	2 475	99.6	21 732	85
Washington	8	32	1.7	0.5	8	D	D	D	360	15.5	923	5
Weld	435	7 951	893.1	325.4	329	1 537	175.9	44.5	20 025	972.0	680 955	3 186
Yuma	26	584	53.7	22.6	22	D	D	D	958	42.9	140	1
CONNECTICUT	10 296	271 272	29 573.1	12 533.5	7 282	43 384	4 904.0	1 382.4	269 845	15 819.6	1 282 308	6 077
Fairfield	2 827	63 963	8 087.6	3 291.8	2 103	13 041	1 654.3	420.8	90 880	6 355.3	726 201	2 598
Hartford	2 771	79 917	8 536.4	3 723.3	1 935	12 855	1 454.4	450.4	57 906	3 189.0	129 546	892
Litchfield	515	9 500	929.2	374.9	359	1 621	163.1	46.6	17 010	950.4	33 621	112
Middlesex	470	13 869	1 411.2	645.8	339	1 650	163.1	49.9	13 410	745.3	60 770	302
New Haven	2 408	73 162	7 788.2	3 238.4	1 717	9 881	977.8	297.8	58 579	3 051.3	146 364	1 161
New London	734	17 357	1 728.0	751.2	459	2 498	274.7	61.9	16 099	780.0	108 515	531

Table B. States and Counties — Government Employment and Payroll, and Local Government Finances

STATE County	Full-time equivalent employees	March payroll (dollars)	Administration, judicial, and legal	Police and Corrections	Fire Protection	Highways and transportation	Health and Welfare	Natural resources and utilities	Education and libraries	General revenue Total (mil dol)	Inter-governmental (mil dol)	Taxes Total (mil dol)	Per capita[1] (dollars) Total	Property
	171	172	173	174	175	176	177	178	179	180	181	182	183	184
COLORADO—Cont'd														
Boulder	11 666	48 102 144	8.2	10.8	5.0	2.7	5.3	10.3	53.3	1 374.3	334.5	816.3	2 674	1 840
Broomfield	687	3 465 698	16.4	35.0	0.0	2.4	10.3	27.3	3.9	167.6	16.5	123.6	2 120	775
Chaffee	981	3 205 729	12.3	6.1	0.6	3.3	43.6	2.3	30.5	122.6	43.2	31.0	1 707	1 041
Cheyenne	186	506 783	7.0	5.9	0.0	7.9	25.6	3.5	46.1	11.6	3.9	4.8	2 562	2 163
Clear Creek	426	1 607 157	17.1	24.4	1.0	10.4	10.2	4.5	29.9	55.5	7.7	41.0	4 539	4 152
Conejos	417	1 165 848	8.0	8.9	0.0	4.9	9.9	3.0	62.1	35.4	24.9	8.0	965	500
Costilla	216	594 990	12.8	7.1	0.6	14.3	13.6	6.0	39.9	21.5	11.8	7.4	2 049	1 959
Crowley	149	372 979	13.1	7.4	0.2	7.6	12.0	7.9	49.2	13.0	9.3	3.0	554	412
Custer	188	561 207	16.3	10.1	0.7	9.8	17.6	3.0	41.1	14.0	3.5	7.4	1 741	1 402
Delta	1 667	6 363 576	6.3	7.6	0.1	3.4	39.9	9.2	32.0	159.9	41.2	32.5	1 067	738
Denver	31 444	153 513 001	5.5	11.6	4.4	12.7	23.1	10.5	30.8	5 569.5	1 334.4	2 071.4	3 266	1 406
Dolores	125	332 266	21.5	7.7	0.0	17.4	6.7	1.6	42.7	5.7	2.5	2.8	1 418	1 324
Douglas	8 978	36 551 403	6.0	11.8	1.8	3.0	0.7	5.6	68.6	1 187.6	326.8	623.8	2 092	1 621
Eagle	1 753	9 241 964	10.1	13.6	8.4	9.4	9.0	14.1	30.0	388.1	36.2	240.3	4 632	3 109
Elbert	793	2 420 569	5.3	13.3	4.8	6.6	3.6	3.3	61.8	68.8	28.9	26.5	1 132	853
El Paso	24 223	94 407 600	4.8	9.4	3.9	2.0	15.6	15.5	46.2	2 544.0	807.4	804.8	1 248	728
Fremont	1 361	4 257 494	6.5	12.3	3.9	5.6	7.8	6.9	53.3	113.3	43.1	39.2	837	567
Garfield	2 715	10 773 217	7.9	10.4	4.9	3.5	18.8	8.7	43.3	377.7	79.3	217.3	3 815	3 060
Gilpin	323	1 493 439	17.4	31.0	11.0	10.9	2.8	6.6	15.7	64.3	18.7	33.2	6 047	1 928
Grand	899	3 399 937	11.0	8.9	1.9	8.6	29.9	12.4	25.0	112.4	11.3	66.9	4 715	3 643
Gunnison	938	4 262 174	12.1	9.1	1.5	9.8	23.1	10.8	16.9	118.1	21.2	51.6	3 335	2 295
Hinsdale	78	213 518	22.4	6.9	0.0	16.9	17.4	4.9	28.8	6.8	1.9	3.5	4 346	3 385
Huerfano	683	2 657 574	9.1	15.2	0.3	8.0	42.0	6.2	18.4	59.2	16.3	13.5	2 049	1 649
Jackson	109	283 034	16.2	7.4	0.3	12.1	6.1	7.8	43.4	7.5	4.3	2.3	1 700	1 447
Jefferson	16 292	67 925 819	8.0	14.5	6.3	2.7	4.7	8.0	53.4	1 796.8	529.1	959.0	1 758	1 296
Kiowa	195	518 331	6.2	3.4	0.1	6.2	53.7	0.0	26.7	13.7	4.6	3.5	2 400	2 321
Kit Carson	599	1 765 320	8.1	7.1	2.1	6.4	30.3	7.6	36.2	45.5	15.1	12.7	1 565	1 397
Lake	1 036	3 786 124	2.2	2.4	4.0	1.7	9.4	2.1	76.3	123.9	28.5	61.1	8 331	7 915
La Plata	2 067	7 718 347	12.2	16.8	4.4	5.9	9.2	7.1	41.1	215.9	60.0	121.8	2 324	1 552
Larimer	10 782	47 317 101	8.8	11.5	1.1	2.8	7.5	18.4	46.2	1 178.8	292.6	577.8	1 861	1 211
Las Animas	790	3 154 143	13.1	10.3	5.0	7.2	4.0	23.0	36.5	67.9	34.0	24.1	1 610	1 155
Lincoln	433	1 393 504	11.8	4.7	0.0	8.0	44.9	2.8	25.9	42.3	17.3	9.6	1 763	1 199
Logan	1 057	3 288 524	7.3	7.7	3.0	24.9	6.5	4.7	43.0	98.6	25.5	33.4	1 475	969
Mesa	5 197	18 735 519	8.2	13.3	5.0	4.1	7.0	9.6	48.8	498.4	180.8	228.0	1 542	966
Mineral	54	178 882	27.1	10.8	0.0	16.4	3.6	2.1	40.0	2.9	0.6	1.5	2 123	1 523
Moffat	596	2 538 838	9.9	13.4	0.2	10.3	6.2	10.3	44.2	92.8	17.6	36.4	2 760	2 173
Montezuma	1 215	5 805 045	11.6	22.2	1.0	7.2	7.7	14.6	27.4	95.8	39.0	40.1	1 577	1 113
Montrose	2 104	7 665 788	7.4	9.0	2.9	5.0	34.2	6.0	34.1	212.1	63.1	64.1	1 574	943
Morgan	1 340	3 811 946	7.6	9.5	0.4	4.0	9.8	9.7	57.0	108.9	39.6	44.8	1 573	1 252
Otero	1 005	2 762 692	7.5	7.2	2.0	3.8	7.9	18.7	51.8	77.3	47.6	18.6	995	589
Ouray	217	778 899	20.7	8.6	4.2	8.7	4.3	7.5	43.5	24.2	6.0	13.1	2 889	2 250
Park	565	1 709 266	7.9	11.7	9.4	8.8	7.9	2.6	45.3	79.9	43.2	27.9	1 739	1 620
Phillips	387	1 231 524	5.8	2.8	0.0	4.9	50.9	5.0	28.5	41.2	11.7	7.9	1 819	1 329
Pitkin	1 617	8 457 732	10.5	7.7	1.5	20.9	24.6	13.9	14.7	334.3	32.9	154.4	8 946	4 437
Prowers	976	3 070 921	6.7	5.7	0.9	3.5	37.0	8.6	32.8	89.1	35.2	16.6	1 340	781
Pueblo	5 698	21 434 409	5.8	12.3	11.0	3.0	6.6	9.0	49.7	552.8	247.0	223.3	1 388	895
Rio Blanco	743	2 764 159	6.3	7.4	0.2	5.5	52.7	8.3	15.4	118.7	16.4	59.8	8 716	7 064
Rio Grande	594	2 555 313	11.1	23.0	0.0	5.2	6.7	1.8	52.0	64.6	42.5	16.8	1 408	981
Routt	1 184	5 565 786	14.7	11.9	5.9	17.1	2.2	12.5	30.0	144.8	31.4	79.2	3 394	2 136
Saguache	347	1 034 643	14.8	8.6	0.3	8.8	6.1	10.3	48.3	55.6	45.0	6.6	1 042	909
San Juan	40	161 715	24.7	12.1	0.0	15.7	7.6	8.1	30.7	9.6	6.5	2.6	3 820	2 945
San Miguel	502	2 269 390	18.4	15.3	2.9	13.4	5.4	10.0	33.5	93.6	14.2	55.2	7 283	5 078
Sedgwick	255	812 165	5.4	2.7	1.9	4.4	48.8	7.8	27.6	22.9	7.9	4.8	2 001	1 581
Summit	1 631	6 095 822	12.4	10.1	11.6	10.3	3.7	14.3	28.7	206.4	13.5	141.5	5 044	2 991
Teller	955	3 818 256	16.1	19.9	2.6	7.0	8.6	7.5	33.5	87.9	28.6	45.4	1 942	1 236
Washington	385	1 126 606	13.3	11.8	0.0	8.2	7.0	2.5	56.0	43.4	28.9	10.2	2 145	1 945
Weld	8 663	35 763 495	8.2	17.4	4.0	5.2	6.6	11.0	45.5	919.9	308.8	411.9	1 562	1 194
Yuma	749	2 253 233	4.4	5.3	0.0	6.1	43.0	5.1	34.4	88.3	21.8	23.8	2 349	2 036
CONNECTICUT	X	X	X	X	X	X	X	X	X	X	X	X	X	X
Fairfield	32 029	179 963 079	3.5	9.1	5.1	3.1	3.2	3.7	70.6	4 597.7	963.2	3 193.1	3 419	3 370
Hartford	31 675	164 755 032	3.0	8.6	3.8	2.4	3.4	4.9	72.4	4 279.2	1 571.4	2 306.6	2 571	2 541
Litchfield	5 578	26 405 841	4.3	6.4	1.8	5.2	1.9	2.5	76.6	698.9	167.1	476.8	2 542	2 521
Middlesex	5 503	26 698 181	4.2	7.4	4.5	3.5	3.5	3.2	71.4	656.2	154.4	441.0	2 663	2 643
New Haven	28 448	140 929 161	3.5	10.1	6.3	2.6	2.7	5.4	68.7	3 790.8	1 443.5	2 034.2	2 358	2 333
New London	8 967	42 369 410	4.4	7.7	3.8	3.8	2.3	8.0	68.3	1 101.6	386.5	598.5	2 183	2 159

1. Based on the resident population estimated as of July 1 of the year shown.

	Local government finances, 2012 (cont.)									Government employment, 2014			Presidential election,[2] 2012		
	Direct general expenditure							Debt outstanding					Percent of vote cast:		
			Percent of total for:												
STATE County	Total (mil dol)	Per capita[1] (dollars)	Education	Health and hospitals	Police protection	Public welfare	Highways	Total (mil dol)	Per capita[1] (dollars)	Federal civilian	Federal military	State and local	Democratic	Republican	All other
	185	186	187	188	189	190	191	192	193	194	195	196	197	198	199
COLORADO—Cont'd															
Boulder	1 414.6	4 633	43.6	2.5	8.2	2.3	4.6	1 940.0	6 354	1 977	887	30 712	72.3	26.1	1.6
Broomfield	144.5	2 479	0.0	1.3	11.0	7.9	6.3	650.9	11 165	139	165	1 178	54.9	43.3	1.8
Chaffee	126.2	6 953	33.9	30.5	2.8	4.5	3.0	96.2	5 298	79	45	1 767	49.0	49.1	1.9
Cheyenne	10.0	5 359	50.3	1.1	4.3	21.9	4.7	4.3	2 284	12	0	272	17.8	80.1	2.1
Clear Creek	50.3	5 569	22.6	4.4	10.8	5.5	14.8	19.7	2 186	38	24	653	57.8	39.9	2.3
Conejos	32.7	3 950	48.7	4.8	3.1	18.2	5.7	7.1	857	44	22	523	55.6	42.7	1.7
Costilla	19.3	5 383	36.1	8.6	3.1	5.2	18.0	10.6	2 962	10	10	354	73.4	24.5	2.2
Crowley	12.3	2 296	34.8	0.9	4.5	16.8	7.5	5.3	989	11	0	511	35.4	62.6	1.9
Custer	14.0	3 302	29.4	21.6	5.5	3.1	12.9	5.3	1 249	16	11	231	34.7	63.6	1.7
Delta	164.5	5 405	28.7	38.1	3.5	2.1	6.4	79.3	2 607	166	78	2 146	32.9	65.2	1.8
Denver	4 720.3	7 442	20.3	15.1	4.8	3.6	3.3	12 146.9	19 151	13 886	2 391	53 171	75.5	23.0	1.5
Dolores	8.4	4 230	38.7	1.5	9.3	1.7	28.9	3.1	1 535	10	0	212	30.3	67.2	2.5
Douglas	1 073.0	3 598	46.7	0.7	5.5	1.9	8.1	1 832.6	6 145	382	838	11 659	40.8	58.0	1.2
Eagle	360.2	6 944	19.9	3.1	5.6	0.9	7.0	691.4	13 329	128	142	3 014	60.9	37.8	1.3
Elbert	66.6	2 849	52.4	1.1	2.8	6.7	8.4	163.8	7 006	31	64	891	28.9	69.0	2.1
El Paso	2 502.2	3 880	37.1	21.9	6.0	2.0	8.1	4 398.1	6 819	12 577	39 241	36 037	39.9	58.7	1.4
Fremont	111.0	2 373	42.2	0.5	8.6	5.0	5.7	106.8	2 282	1 085	102	4 014	34.4	63.6	2.0
Garfield	343.8	6 036	29.4	12.6	5.3	5.4	6.2	453.7	7 965	267	151	5 016	49.2	49.2	1.6
Gilpin	50.9	9 270	11.0	2.3	12.0	3.9	11.8	57.5	10 467	10	15	435	59.2	38.0	2.8
Grand	101.5	7 151	19.1	14.0	6.2	1.0	9.3	159.5	11 235	138	38	1 224	48.6	49.7	1.7
Gunnison	122.5	7 917	13.3	24.8	4.1	3.0	11.9	140.6	9 086	167	39	1 840	62.6	35.3	2.1
Hinsdale	7.9	9 716	19.4	25.6	3.8	0.3	8.5	0.7	895	0	0	86	40.1	57.4	2.5
Huerfano	56.4	8 549	15.8	41.7	1.6	2.4	10.2	12.0	1 821	12	17	459	54.6	43.4	2.0
Jackson	7.0	5 173	38.5	4.4	6.1	2.3	23.7	0.7	487	41	0	140	30.3	68.3	1.3
Jefferson	1 793.4	3 289	42.8	1.2	9.3	2.3	4.8	1 397.5	2 563	8 555	1 530	27 449	53.6	44.6	1.8
Kiowa	14.6	10 098	23.1	43.2	3.7	4.8	11.6	4.6	3 195	21	0	218	20.9	76.3	2.8
Kit Carson	45.0	5 561	31.8	27.5	3.7	5.2	8.8	19.9	2 455	38	19	738	26.5	71.3	2.2
Lake	135.4	18 454	79.4	5.5	1.1	1.4	2.2	36.4	4 957	55	19	698	61.9	35.9	2.2
La Plata	202.8	3 869	35.0	1.1	7.0	2.7	5.9	291.6	5 566	343	139	5 243	57.4	41.1	1.5
Larimer	1 080.2	3 479	37.9	4.5	6.4	3.0	9.0	1 388.6	4 472	2 429	868	32 314	54.0	44.3	1.7
Las Animas	67.0	4 482	36.8	3.7	4.8	14.4	8.4	26.1	1 744	68	35	1 603	52.7	45.6	1.7
Lincoln	47.4	8 698	36.7	27.0	2.8	5.8	9.1	9.7	1 786	24	12	984	23.7	74.5	1.8
Logan	73.2	3 236	40.5	1.4	5.0	4.8	10.0	99.6	4 400	66	50	2 385	31.7	66.9	1.4
Mesa	517.8	3 502	35.4	1.7	13.1	5.6	9.4	476.5	3 223	1 459	398	8 275	34.5	64.0	1.5
Mineral	2.9	4 056	57.4	0.8	5.3	0.0	15.9	1.2	1 746	0	0	85	43.3	53.6	3.0
Moffat	93.2	7 060	24.3	30.6	5.6	6.2	10.7	40.3	3 050	145	34	988	26.9	70.4	2.6
Montezuma	95.7	3 762	36.0	3.0	10.1	11.6	6.2	60.5	2 379	335	68	2 397	39.4	58.9	1.7
Montrose	215.1	5 283	25.1	29.4	6.1	3.0	9.2	127.2	3 123	301	107	2 680	33.9	63.7	2.4
Morgan	102.1	3 585	44.8	1.5	4.7	4.6	7.3	72.8	2 556	116	74	2 164	37.3	61.3	1.5
Otero	73.8	3 949	48.8	9.4	2.9	2.4	5.4	37.0	1 981	113	48	1 727	44.0	54.5	1.6
Ouray	18.2	4 027	38.4	1.5	6.2	7.7	14.2	11.3	2 485	12	12	367	53.5	44.7	1.9
Park	79.6	4 968	50.7	2.8	3.8	4.7	6.8	28.9	1 800	53	43	775	45.3	52.2	2.5
Phillips	43.4	9 946	35.1	40.0	2.6	1.2	5.0	19.5	4 468	21	11	573	27.5	71.3	1.2
Pitkin	271.6	15 734	9.3	32.7	4.0	1.8	4.6	380.2	22 024	91	47	2 087	73.7	24.9	1.3
Prowers	85.2	6 880	36.9	27.3	5.4	4.4	4.5	184.4	14 887	37	31	1 345	32.2	65.9	1.8
Pueblo	566.4	3 521	40.3	1.5	6.6	5.3	3.7	456.3	2 837	1 034	438	11 451	56.7	41.8	1.5
Rio Blanco	94.0	13 703	15.7	31.1	5.7	2.8	9.7	113.7	16 584	69	17	1 119	20.8	77.4	1.7
Rio Grande	62.5	5 236	64.5	2.5	4.3	3.9	5.0	22.1	1 851	105	30	824	45.0	53.8	1.2
Routt	151.7	6 501	26.1	0.5	3.9	3.9	7.2	168.4	7 217	106	63	1 802	62.7	35.8	1.5
Saguache	54.4	8 636	66.9	1.8	1.8	8.1	6.5	14.0	2 225	48	16	486	63.0	34.7	2.3
San Juan	9.9	14 307	73.7	1.8	5.2	0.9	5.5	1.8	2 645	0	0	74	53.2	44.0	2.8
San Miguel	78.7	10 376	17.1	8.1	5.4	1.7	11.2	104.6	13 797	43	21	730	77.0	21.4	1.6
Sedgwick	21.9	9 187	35.7	36.4	2.6	2.8	4.4	1.7	700	18	0	337	34.6	63.4	1.9
Summit	193.3	6 894	18.6	1.3	5.5	1.0	7.9	128.1	4 569	48	78	2 502	65.8	32.8	1.4
Teller	84.7	3 621	35.6	6.2	7.8	2.8	8.5	55.5	2 371	58	62	1 298	35.0	63.1	1.9
Washington	40.7	8 539	68.2	2.8	2.6	6.4	6.5	14.9	3 135	50	12	447	21.1	77.6	1.4
Weld	839.9	3 185	42.6	1.2	7.3	4.0	6.6	868.6	3 294	591	727	15 640	44.7	53.4	1.9
Yuma	77.9	7 698	25.5	39.3	3.2	4.7	6.7	65.7	6 497	46	27	951	24.9	73.3	1.8
CONNECTICUT	X	X	X	X	X	X	X	X	X	17 469	13 925	230 417	60.7	38.1	1.1
Fairfield	4 616.9	4 944	50.9	1.2	6.6	1.0	3.1	4 013.1	4 297	2 809	1 902	45 058	58.6	40.6	0.7
Hartford	4 219.6	4 703	56.1	0.9	6.3	0.8	4.1	2 673.7	2 980	5 507	1 807	68 506	65.2	33.7	1.1
Litchfield	765.4	4 081	66.1	1.3	3.5	0.2	6.7	390.3	2 081	418	371	8 105	51.6	46.7	1.7
Middlesex	673.0	4 064	63.2	0.8	4.2	0.4	4.0	355.1	2 144	362	326	10 458	60.8	37.8	1.5
New Haven	4 427.8	5 132	58.4	0.6	4.3	0.3	2.5	3 649.0	4 229	5 335	1 921	44 838	61.0	37.8	1.2
New London	1 142.0	4 165	60.1	0.7	5.5	0.6	6.1	911.5	3 324	2 510	7 050	29 671	59.9	38.8	1.3

1. Based on the resident population estimated as of July 1 of the year shown.   2. © 2013 Election Data Services, Inc. All rights reserved.

Table B. States and Counties — **Land Area and Population**

STATE/County code	CBSA code[1]	County type[2]	STATE County	Land area,[3] (sq km) 2010	Total persons 2015	Rank	Per square kilometer	White	Black	American Indian, Alaska Native	Asian and Pacific Islander	Percent Hispanic or Latino[4]	Under 5 years	5 to 17 years	18 to 24 years	25 to 34 years	35 to 44 years	45 to 54 years
				1	2	3	4	5	6	7	8	9	10	11	12	13	14	15
			CONNECTICUT—Cont'd															
09 013	25540	1	Tolland	1 062	151 420	428	142.6	87.4	3.8	0.6	4.7	5.0	4.0	14.5	18.3	10.4	10.7	14.7
09 015	49340	4	Windham	1 328	116 573	528	87.8	85.5	2.7	1.1	1.9	10.9	5.2	15.6	10.2	12.4	12.4	15.5
10 000	...	X	DELAWARE	5 047	945 934	X	187.4	65.5	22.6	0.9	4.3	8.9	6.0	15.8	9.6	13.2	11.8	13.9
10 001	20100	3	Kent	1 518	173 533	369	114.3	65.9	26.1	1.3	3.2	6.9	6.5	17.1	10.8	13.4	11.5	13.3
10 003	37980	1	New Castle	1 104	556 779	117	504.3	61.1	25.1	0.7	5.8	9.4	6.1	16.1	10.2	14.2	14.3	14.3
10 005	41540	4	Sussex	2 424	215 622	299	89.0	76.6	13.4	1.1	1.6	9.3	5.6	14.0	7.0	10.5	10.1	13.0
11 000	...	X	DISTRICT OF COLUMBIA	158	672 228	X	4 254.6	37.5	48.7	0.8	5.0	10.4	6.5	11.0	12.2	22.8	14.1	11.6
11 001	47900	1	District of Columbia	158	672 228	99	4 254.6	37.5	48.7	0.8	5.0	10.4	6.5	11.0	12.2	22.8	14.1	11.6
12 000	...	X	FLORIDA	138 887	20 271 272	X	146.0	57.1	16.4	0.6	3.4	24.1	5.5	14.9	9.0	12.7	12.2	13.8
12 001	23540	3	Alachua	2 266	259 964	260	114.7	64.7	21.1	0.7	6.9	9.1	5.6	12.5	22.3	15.1	10.3	10.5
12 003	27260	1	Baker	1 516	27 420	1 514	18.1	83.2	13.9	1.0	1.0	2.4	6.3	18.5	8.6	13.9	13.3	14.3
12 005	37460	3	Bay	1 964	181 635	356	92.5	80.3	12.1	1.5	3.5	5.7	6.1	15.4	9.0	14.0	12.0	14.2
12 007	...	6	Bradford	761	26 928	1 538	35.4	76.4	19.7	0.8	1.0	3.8	5.8	14.4	8.2	14.2	12.3	13.9
12 009	37340	2	Brevard	2 631	568 088	113	215.9	77.7	11.1	0.9	3.3	9.3	4.6	14.0	7.8	10.7	10.3	14.7
12 011	33100	1	Broward	3 133	1 896 425	18	605.3	40.9	28.3	0.5	4.5	27.5	5.8	15.7	8.5	13.5	13.4	15.0
12 013	...	6	Calhoun	1 469	14 462	2 134	9.8	78.9	14.3	2.1	1.2	5.8	5.5	15.3	7.6	14.0	13.4	14.2
12 015	39460	3	Charlotte	1 762	173 115	372	98.2	85.9	6.3	0.7	1.9	6.7	3.1	9.9	5.5	7.3	7.9	11.8
12 017	26140	4	Citrus	1 507	141 058	454	93.6	90.0	3.5	0.9	1.9	5.2	3.8	11.2	5.7	7.6	8.1	12.2
12 019	27260	1	Clay	1 565	203 967	318	130.3	77.0	11.2	1.0	4.3	9.2	5.5	18.8	8.7	12.0	13.1	15.0
12 021	34940	2	Collier	5 176	357 305	193	69.0	65.1	7.1	0.4	1.8	26.8	4.8	13.5	7.0	9.9	10.2	12.2
12 023	29380	6	Columbia	2 066	68 348	781	33.1	74.5	19.0	1.0	1.5	5.6	5.9	15.9	9.3	12.7	11.8	13.3
12 027	11580	6	DeSoto	1 650	35 458	1 291	21.5	55.7	13.0	0.5	0.8	30.4	5.5	15.5	9.8	13.7	12.0	12.3
12 029	...	6	Dixie	1 826	16 203	2 030	8.9	86.6	9.6	1.1	0.7	3.7	5.6	13.5	6.9	11.2	11.2	14.4
12 031	27260	1	Duval	1 974	913 010	58	462.5	56.9	30.3	0.8	5.7	8.6	6.8	16.1	9.8	15.9	12.7	13.6
12 033	37860	2	Escambia	1 700	311 003	217	182.9	68.3	23.7	1.7	4.5	5.5	6.0	14.8	13.2	14.0	10.7	12.7
12 035	19660	4	Flagler	1 257	105 392	564	83.8	76.6	11.6	0.7	2.9	9.7	4.2	13.9	6.6	8.9	10.2	12.5
12 037	...	6	Franklin	1 385	11 761	2 308	8.5	80.2	15.3	0.9	1.0	5.2	4.3	12.3	7.4	16.2	12.5	13.0
12 039	45220	2	Gadsden	1 337	46 036	1 047	34.4	34.0	55.2	0.6	0.9	10.5	6.1	16.1	8.3	12.3	12.8	14.2
12 041	23540	3	Gilchrist	906	17 199	1 969	19.0	88.3	6.1	1.0	0.7	5.2	5.3	15.1	12.0	10.0	10.7	13.3
12 043	...	6	Glades	2 088	13 670	2 191	6.5	61.8	12.6	4.7	0.9	21.9	4.0	13.1	6.8	13.1	12.0	12.1
12 045	37460	6	Gulf	1 461	15 871	2 047	10.9	75.1	19.7	1.2	0.9	5.0	4.3	11.2	7.5	15.2	14.1	15.7
12 047	...	6	Hamilton	1 331	14 295	2 148	10.7	56.3	33.5	1.1	1.1	9.5	5.4	13.9	12.1	13.2	13.2	13.2
12 049	48100	6	Hardee	1 652	27 502	1 511	16.6	48.4	7.5	0.7	1.4	43.1	7.2	19.5	10.5	13.7	12.1	12.0
12 051	17500	6	Hendry	2 986	39 119	1 200	13.1	34.6	12.3	1.7	1.3	50.9	7.7	20.4	9.6	14.3	12.4	12.5
12 053	45300	1	Hernando	1 224	178 439	362	145.8	81.7	5.8	0.8	1.9	11.6	4.4	14.3	7.0	9.3	10.2	13.0
12 055	42700	4	Highlands	2 633	99 491	595	37.8	70.0	10.3	0.9	1.8	18.5	4.7	13.1	6.5	9.2	8.7	10.7
12 057	45300	1	Hillsborough	2 642	1 349 050	29	510.6	53.2	16.8	0.6	4.7	26.5	6.4	16.8	9.6	14.8	13.6	13.9
12 059	...	6	Holmes	1 240	19 324	1 858	15.6	88.9	7.5	2.0	1.0	2.7	5.0	15.3	8.8	12.5	12.2	13.8
12 061	42680	3	Indian River	1 302	147 919	441	113.6	77.3	9.5	0.6	1.9	11.9	4.4	13.2	6.8	9.0	9.2	12.6
12 063	...	6	Jackson	2 377	48 599	1 007	20.4	67.2	27.5	1.2	1.0	4.8	4.9	13.9	8.9	13.0	14.0	13.9
12 065	45220	2	Jefferson	1 549	14 081	2 158	9.1	60.2	35.6	0.9	0.8	4.1	4.9	12.6	6.7	11.7	12.3	15.2
12 067	...	8	Lafayette	1 407	8 663	2 540	6.2	71.9	15.4	0.8	0.4	12.5	5.1	15.0	11.4	15.0	15.1	13.4
12 069	36740	1	Lake	2 430	325 875	206	134.1	73.7	10.5	0.8	2.7	13.8	5.0	14.8	7.0	10.2	11.0	12.3
12 071	15980	2	Lee	2 032	701 982	90	345.5	70.3	8.8	0.5	2.1	19.6	4.9	13.8	7.4	10.7	10.6	12.3
12 073	45220	2	Leon	1 727	286 272	238	165.8	59.1	31.9	0.8	4.0	6.1	5.2	13.8	23.1	14.1	10.5	10.9
12 075	...	8	Levy	2 896	39 832	1 177	13.8	81.7	9.8	1.2	0.9	8.2	5.0	14.8	7.3	10.3	10.3	13.8
12 077	...	8	Liberty	2 164	8 331	2 569	3.8	72.8	20.2	1.3	0.5	6.6	4.8	14.2	8.6	17.1	16.2	15.4
12 079	...	6	Madison	1 802	18 408	1 896	10.2	55.6	39.2	0.9	0.6	5.0	5.5	14.6	8.7	13.1	12.0	14.0
12 081	35840	2	Manatee	1 924	363 369	187	188.9	73.4	9.4	0.6	2.4	15.7	5.0	14.4	7.1	10.3	10.6	12.9
12 083	36100	2	Marion	4 104	343 254	198	83.6	73.6	13.2	0.8	2.0	12.0	4.9	13.9	7.2	10.2	9.9	12.3
12 085	38940	2	Martin	1 408	156 283	412	111.0	80.2	5.8	0.5	1.6	12.9	4.1	12.7	6.7	9.0	9.5	13.7
12 086	33100	1	Miami-Dade	4 915	2 693 117	7	547.9	15.3	17.0	0.2	2.0	66.0	5.8	14.8	9.3	14.2	14.2	14.9
12 087	28580	4	Monroe	2 547	77 482	714	30.4	70.1	6.5	0.9	1.8	22.5	4.6	10.6	6.7	12.5	12.2	15.8
12 089	27260	1	Nassau	1 680	78 444	709	46.7	88.5	6.8	0.8	1.5	3.8	5.1	15.3	7.4	10.9	11.6	14.4
12 091	18880	3	Okaloosa	2 409	198 664	331	82.5	78.1	11.0	1.3	5.2	8.5	6.7	15.5	10.0	15.8	11.3	13.3
12 093	36380	4	Okeechobee	1 991	39 469	1 188	19.8	64.5	8.9	1.2	1.2	25.3	6.2	16.5	8.8	12.8	12.3	13.3
12 095	36740	1	Orange	2 340	1 288 126	30	550.5	44.6	21.0	0.6	6.4	29.1	6.2	16.5	11.5	16.4	14.0	13.7
12 097	36740	1	Osceola	3 438	323 993	208	94.2	37.1	10.4	0.5	3.4	49.4	6.4	18.7	9.8	14.0	14.2	13.5
12 099	33100	1	Palm Beach	5 102	1 422 789	27	278.9	58.3	18.5	0.4	3.3	20.7	5.1	14.4	8.0	11.7	11.7	13.7
12 101	45300	1	Pasco	1 934	497 909	139	257.5	78.8	5.7	0.7	3.0	13.4	5.0	15.4	7.3	10.7	12.2	13.8
12 103	45300	1	Pinellas	709	949 827	50	1 339.7	76.9	11.3	0.7	4.1	8.8	4.5	12.5	7.2	11.4	11.2	14.8
12 105	29460	2	Polk	4 656	650 092	101	139.6	63.4	15.5	0.7	2.3	19.6	5.9	17.0	8.7	12.3	11.7	12.6

1. CBSA = Core Based Statistical Area. See Appendix A for explanation. See Appendix B for list of metropolitan areas with component counties. 2. County type code from the Economic Research Service of USDA Rural-Urban Continuum Codes. See Appendix A for definition. 3. Dry land or land partially or temporarily covered by water. 4. May be of any race.

STATE County	55 to 64 years	65 to 74 years	75 years and over	Percent female	Total persons 2000	Total persons 2010	2000–2010	2010–2015	Births	Deaths	Net migration	Number	Persons per household	Family households	Female family householder[1]	One person
	16	17	18	19	20	21	22	23	24	25	26	27	28	29	30	31
CONNECTICUT—Cont'd																
Tolland	13.4	8.3	5.7	49.8	136 364	152 682	12.0	-0.8	6 013	5 169	-1 822	54 444	2.50	68.4	9.8	24.5
Windham	14.1	8.5	6.2	50.4	109 091	118 434	8.6	-1.6	6 103	5 108	-2 852	44 487	2.53	67.5	12.2	26.1
DELAWARE	13.3	9.7	6.7	51.6	783 600	897 936	14.6	5.3	58 154	42 185	31 753	339 046	2.63	67.2	13.9	26.6
Kent	11.9	9.3	6.3	51.8	126 697	162 349	28.1	6.9	11 447	7 682	7 173	59 142	2.74	70.1	15.2	24.3
New Castle	12.8	7.8	5.9	51.6	500 265	538 477	7.6	3.4	34 969	22 878	6 555	201 543	2.62	65.9	14.0	27.5
Sussex	15.7	14.9	9.3	51.5	156 638	197 110	25.8	9.4	11 738	11 625	18 025	78 361	2.56	68.4	12.5	25.8
DISTRICT OF COLUMBIA	10.5	6.4	4.9	52.6	572 059	601 767	5.2	11.7	49 128	25 445	46 433	267 415	2.22	42.5	15.5	45.1
District of Columbia	10.5	6.4	4.9	52.6	572 059	601 767	5.2	11.7	49 128	25 445	46 433	267 415	2.22	42.5	15.5	45.1
FLORIDA	12.9	10.5	8.6	51.1	15 982 378	18 804 623	17.7	7.8	1 129 845	950 117	1 261 155	7 217 508	2.62	64.4	13.2	29.0
Alachua	11.3	7.3	5.2	51.7	217 955	247 335	13.5	5.1	15 115	9 333	6 638	96 137	2.45	53.0	11.6	32.7
Baker	12.3	7.9	5.0	47.9	22 259	27 115	21.8	1.1	1 826	1 200	-318	8 351	2.95	76.6	14.2	18.2
Bay	13.1	9.3	6.8	50.2	148 217	168 852	13.9	7.6	11 790	9 117	9 591	67 388	2.52	64.9	11.7	28.4
Bradford	13.5	10.0	7.6	45.6	26 088	28 520	9.3	-5.6	1 626	1 508	-1 776	8 824	2.71	67.9	15.5	27.7
Brevard	15.2	12.1	10.5	51.2	476 230	543 378	14.1	4.5	26 746	33 680	30 354	221 582	2.45	64.0	11.8	30.0
Broward	12.7	8.3	7.0	51.4	1 623 018	1 748 148	7.7	8.5	112 725	76 811	112 114	667 578	2.69	63.3	15.6	29.9
Calhoun	12.7	9.8	7.5	45.5	13 017	14 625	12.4	-1.1	740	784	-149	4 756	2.66	67.7	15.3	27.9
Charlotte	16.7	20.4	17.3	51.3	141 627	159 991	13.0	8.2	5 336	12 323	19 957	70 948	2.25	64.9	8.2	29.7
Citrus	16.1	19.2	16.0	51.6	118 085	141 236	19.6	-0.1	5 440	12 586	6 775	60 670	2.27	63.8	8.6	30.6
Clay	12.8	8.9	5.4	50.8	140 814	190 865	35.5	6.9	11 005	8 095	10 003	68 016	2.84	75.2	13.8	19.9
Collier	13.1	15.4	14.0	50.8	251 377	321 520	27.9	11.1	16 903	15 853	34 572	126 331	2.61	67.0	9.2	28.1
Columbia	13.9	10.3	7.0	48.2	56 513	67 532	19.5	1.2	4 188	4 035	689	23 714	2.67	63.5	14.2	32.3
DeSoto	11.7	10.9	8.8	43.7	32 209	34 862	8.2	1.7	2 012	1 483	91	10 964	2.82	68.7	15.1	26.7
Dixie	15.2	13.6	8.4	46.0	13 827	16 422	18.8	-1.3	815	1 071	81	6 020	2.47	64.0	9.3	30.1
Duval	12.4	7.6	5.2	51.6	778 879	864 263	11.0	5.6	65 702	39 539	21 868	334 721	2.58	62.4	15.8	31.0
Escambia	12.9	9.0	6.7	50.1	294 410	297 619	1.1	4.5	20 331	16 591	9 318	112 395	2.53	60.7	13.9	32.4
Flagler	15.3	16.7	11.7	52.0	49 832	95 696	92.0	10.1	4 275	5 953	11 110	35 939	2.74	71.8	8.6	23.2
Franklin	14.2	12.9	7.2	42.2	11 057	11 549	4.4	1.8	558	663	323	4 253	2.28	65.0	12.1	29.5
Gadsden	14.7	9.1	6.3	49.5	45 087	47 746	5.9	-3.6	2 953	2 402	-2 233	16 986	2.56	66.6	20.3	29.8
Gilchrist	14.1	11.3	8.1	48.0	14 437	16 939	17.3	1.5	986	921	175	6 274	2.50	70.6	11.5	24.2
Glades	12.4	14.7	11.8	43.7	10 576	12 884	21.8	6.1	358	527	761	3 846	3.08	63.6	11.4	30.2
Gulf	13.8	10.8	7.2	39.8	13 332	15 863	19.0	0.1	658	866	147	5 381	2.51	68.9	12.2	26.4
Hamilton	14.1	9.9	6.0	42.9	13 327	14 799	11.0	-3.4	814	665	-679	4 704	2.37	65.9	19.5	29.8
Hardee	10.3	8.3	6.5	46.5	26 938	27 731	2.9	-0.8	2 074	1 040	-1 289	7 534	3.37	76.7	15.1	19.3
Hendry	10.4	7.3	5.4	48.0	36 210	39 140	8.1	-0.1	3 102	1 438	-1 792	11 156	3.20	72.6	18.6	21.5
Hernando	14.3	14.9	12.6	52.1	130 802	172 775	32.1	3.3	7 779	13 190	10 646	70 183	2.45	67.9	12.1	27.6
Highlands	13.4	16.9	16.9	51.5	87 366	98 786	13.1	0.7	4 716	7 621	3 525	39 882	2.42	63.7	9.5	31.3
Hillsborough	11.7	7.6	5.6	51.3	998 948	1 229 224	23.1	9.7	86 922	51 160	81 846	477 472	2.64	63.5	14.2	29.0
Holmes	13.5	10.8	8.1	46.6	18 564	19 927	7.3	-3.0	995	1 313	-243	6 758	2.64	68.9	11.4	28.5
Indian River	14.8	15.3	14.8	52.0	112 947	138 028	22.2	7.2	6 624	9 673	12 758	57 342	2.43	63.3	9.9	31.3
Jackson	13.5	10.1	7.9	44.8	46 755	49 761	6.4	-2.3	2 573	2 922	-685	15 961	2.58	65.8	14.3	31.2
Jefferson	16.4	12.3	7.8	47.7	12 902	14 761	14.4	-4.6	685	769	-599	5 372	2.27	68.6	15.3	28.5
Lafayette	10.9	7.8	6.2	40.0	7 022	8 870	26.3	-2.3	416	363	-249	2 706	2.69	68.0	15.6	25.7
Lake	13.1	14.3	11.8	51.6	210 528	297 046	41.1	9.7	16 185	18 637	30 914	117 657	2.56	69.5	9.7	25.2
Lee	14.0	15.0	11.3	51.0	440 888	618 754	40.3	13.5	33 534	33 097	81 946	246 061	2.59	65.7	10.7	28.2
Leon	10.9	6.9	4.5	52.5	239 452	275 480	15.0	3.9	15 927	9 103	3 723	110 669	2.41	55.2	13.0	29.9
Levy	15.6	14.0	9.0	50.8	34 450	40 801	18.4	-2.4	2 065	2 704	-358	15 638	2.52	65.6	13.9	29.0
Liberty	11.9	7.2	4.6	37.6	7 021	8 365	19.1	-0.4	421	323	-127	2 362	2.83	66.0	11.1	27.6
Madison	14.3	10.5	7.4	47.2	18 733	19 226	2.6	-4.3	1 091	1 142	-813	6 651	2.53	67.5	13.9	30.3
Manatee	14.2	13.9	11.6	51.6	264 002	322 833	22.3	12.6	17 942	18 627	40 209	133 445	2.48	65.3	10.6	28.3
Marion	13.7	15.6	12.3	52.0	258 916	331 304	28.0	3.6	17 540	23 794	17 207	133 137	2.45	65.9	11.8	28.4
Martin	15.0	14.7	14.7	50.4	126 731	146 850	15.9	6.4	6 252	9 416	12 402	60 828	2.40	62.6	7.7	32.4
Miami-Dade	11.6	8.1	7.1	51.4	2 253 362	2 498 017	10.9	7.8	163 446	99 443	128 596	833 541	3.06	68.2	18.1	26.2
Monroe	17.0	12.8	7.7	47.5	79 589	73 090	-8.2	6.0	3 807	3 484	4 055	28 418	2.57	57.3	6.8	32.4
Nassau	15.3	12.7	7.3	50.8	57 663	73 314	27.1	7.0	3 949	3 776	4 843	28 068	2.65	72.9	10.8	23.0
Okaloosa	12.3	8.5	6.5	49.2	170 498	180 822	6.1	9.9	14 168	8 347	11 676	73 655	2.50	66.5	12.8	27.7
Okeechobee	12.3	10.1	7.7	46.2	35 910	39 996	11.4	-1.3	2 796	2 095	-1 422	13 213	2.77	68.7	14.6	25.8
Orange	10.8	6.3	4.4	50.9	896 344	1 145 954	27.8	12.4	82 612	37 593	96 360	423 609	2.76	64.3	15.1	27.1
Osceola	10.8	7.7	5.0	51.0	172 493	268 687	55.8	20.6	20 562	9 796	43 819	90 414	3.17	74.4	17.4	20.1
Palm Beach	12.7	10.9	11.8	51.6	1 131 184	1 320 134	16.7	7.8	73 992	71 629	97 586	529 729	2.53	61.9	12.1	31.4
Pasco	13.1	12.5	10.0	51.4	344 765	464 703	34.8	7.1	25 097	29 399	36 385	184 806	2.52	66.0	10.7	28.0
Pinellas	15.4	12.1	10.9	52.1	921 482	916 812	-0.5	3.6	44 437	60 438	47 867	402 536	2.25	55.3	11.3	37.3
Polk	12.4	11.1	8.4	51.0	483 924	602 095	24.4	8.0	38 488	32 068	40 367	220 556	2.73	69.0	13.7	25.8

1. No spouse present.

Table B. States and Counties — **Population, Vital Statistics, Medicare, and Crime**

STATE County	Persons in group quarters, 2015	Daytime population, 2010–2014 Number	Employment/residence ratio	Births, 2015 Total	Rate[1]	Deaths, 2015 Number	Rate[1]	Persons under 65 with no health insurance, 2014 Number	Percent	Medicare, 2015 Total Beneficiaries	Enrolled in Original Medicare	Enrolled in Medicare Advantage	Serious crimes known to police,[2] 2014 Total Number	Rate[3]
	32	33	34	35	36	37	38	39	40	41	42	43	44	45
CONNECTICUT—Cont'd														
Tolland	15 718	124 793	0.65	1 104	7.3	963	6.4	6 407	5.6	21 534	15 411	6 123	NA	NA
Windham	4 818	103 191	0.74	1 132	9.7	958	8.2	7 079	7.4	20 348	15 400	4 948	NA	NA
DELAWARE	25 583	918 069	1.00	11 033	11.7	8 445	9.0	70 640	9.3	169 207	153 646	15 561	32 476	3 471
Kent	4 665	159 244	0.89	2 196	12.7	1 585	9.2	13 073	9.2	29 976	27 486	2 490	5 424	3 160
New Castle	18 106	562 597	1.06	6 585	11.9	4 454	8.0	39 410	8.6	83 374	73 811	9 563	19 718	3 557
Sussex	2 812	196 228	0.91	2 252	10.6	2 406	11.3	18 157	11.5	55 857	52 349	3 508	7 334	3 499
DISTRICT OF COLUMBIA	40 209	1 118 142	2.50	9 593	14.4	5 218	7.8	32 799	5.9	72 721	61 159	11 562	42 346	6 427
District of Columbia	40 209	1 118 142	2.50	9 593	14.4	5 218	7.8	32 799	5.9	72 721	61 159	11 562	42 346	6 427
FLORIDA	430 649	19 316 128	0.99	220 628	11.0	190 735	9.5	3 176 171	20.2	3 824 025	2 243 409	1 580 616	786 967	3 956
Alachua	13 362	266 682	1.13	2 904	11.2	1 875	7.3	35 351	16.6	38 155	30 963	7 192	9 091	3 552
Baker	2 417	23 564	0.64	354	13.0	219	8.0	3 301	15.4	4 121	3 052	1 069	454	1 668
Bay	3 850	174 879	1.02	2 325	12.9	1 847	10.3	27 551	18.7	35 548	28 882	6 666	8 060	4 532
Bradford	3 295	24 925	0.71	293	10.9	310	11.6	3 249	17.1	4 484	3 504	980	425	1 623
Brevard	6 874	540 857	0.96	5 232	9.3	6 653	11.8	75 213	17.7	134 101	84 910	49 191	17 253	3 098
Broward	16 179	1 743 289	0.92	22 161	11.8	15 213	8.1	326 737	20.8	271 704	117 911	153 793	64 848	3 457
Calhoun	1 887	13 247	0.69	130	9.0	154	10.6	2 027	19.8	2 589	1 880	709	139	938
Charlotte	3 190	158 672	0.92	1 027	6.0	2 478	14.5	21 264	20.7	52 587	36 303	16 284	3 208	1 918
Citrus	2 247	133 811	0.86	1 031	7.4	2 497	17.8	16 556	18.6	46 663	32 012	14 651	2 868	2 096
Clay	1 251	158 630	0.57	2 123	10.5	1 614	8.0	24 341	14.3	29 134	22 245	6 889	4 649	2 333
Collier	4 546	342 628	1.06	3 293	9.3	3 276	9.3	64 436	26.5	81 936	64 638	17 298	5 985	1 726
Columbia	5 103	67 928	1.01	826	12.1	781	11.5	8 792	17.0	14 019	11 173	2 846	2 513	3 692
DeSoto	3 766	34 621	0.99	381	10.8	275	7.8	7 685	30.8	6 203	4 667	1 536	1 109	3 197
Dixie	1 634	15 213	0.81	155	9.7	202	12.6	2 083	18.9	3 619	2 781	838	479	3 003
Duval	20 751	958 872	1.19	12 714	14.0	7 960	8.8	119 045	15.6	137 046	94 199	42 847	41 884	4 664
Escambia	19 335	318 141	1.10	3 885	12.5	3 314	10.7	38 355	15.8	61 106	43 920	17 186	14 468	4 663
Flagler	684	88 188	0.69	817	7.9	1 171	11.3	13 520	18.6	29 288	17 906	11 382	2 053	2 017
Franklin	1 853	11 684	1.01	103	8.8	110	9.4	1 432	18.9	2 411	1 791	620	212	1 811
Gadsden	3 490	42 259	0.72	538	11.7	467	10.1	7 274	20.0	8 783	4 395	4 388	1 127	2 474
Gilchrist	953	14 779	0.63	183	10.7	176	10.3	2 819	22.1	3 461	2 645	816	222	1 302
Glades	1 482	12 158	0.73	67	4.9	106	7.8	2 406	28.2	1 296	976	320	165	1 217
Gulf	3 380	14 809	0.82	128	8.0	172	10.8	1 812	18.9	3 453	2 825	628	341	2 137
Hamilton	2 670	14 075	0.90	156	11.0	117	8.3	1 672	17.8	2 682	2 099	583	466	3 238
Hardee	1 965	27 131	0.95	395	14.4	183	6.7	5 872	27.2	3 910	2 965	945	730	2 626
Hendry	696	38 318	1.00	589	15.2	291	7.5	9 540	28.9	5 188	3 811	1 377	1 477	3 950
Hernando	1 827	160 412	0.76	1 518	8.6	2 569	14.5	23 745	18.8	54 485	26 421	28 064	4 456	2 529
Highlands	1 733	97 283	0.97	893	9.0	1 419	14.4	16 123	25.1	30 160	21 543	8 617	2 841	3 182
Hillsborough	22 974	1 336 917	1.10	16 995	12.7	10 572	7.9	200 532	17.8	195 626	100 806	94 820	31 923	2 424
Holmes	1 791	17 292	0.60	183	9.4	227	11.6	2 695	18.9	4 334	3 613	721	341	1 719
Indian River	1 322	141 478	1.01	1 264	8.6	1 989	13.6	22 887	22.8	42 698	32 838	9 860	3 579	2 484
Jackson	8 315	48 952	0.99	495	10.2	589	12.1	5 164	16.0	11 213	9 251	1 962	956	2 057
Jefferson	1 289	12 184	0.57	127	9.0	146	10.4	1 731	17.3	2 936	1 627	1 309	321	2 265
Lafayette	1 724	8 133	0.77	77	8.8	61	7.0	1 408	24.2	974	824	150	70	784
Lake	3 951	277 135	0.76	3 230	10.1	3 834	12.0	46 253	20.0	130 890	89 873	41 017	7 955	2 624
Lee	8 479	633 779	0.94	6 583	9.5	6 808	9.9	115 883	23.5	155 944	105 636	50 308	15 855	2 342
Leon	14 925	299 885	1.14	3 052	10.7	1 764	6.2	32 733	13.8	33 842	18 152	15 690	14 204	4 974
Levy	336	35 548	0.66	396	10.0	517	13.0	6 839	22.6	9 224	6 899	2 325	NA	NA
Liberty	2 071	7 891	0.85	87	10.4	67	8.0	969	18.4	1 225	757	468	54	641
Madison	1 970	17 526	0.77	201	10.9	223	12.1	2 462	18.4	3 868	2 823	1 045	556	2 966
Manatee	4 816	315 854	0.85	3 543	9.9	3 742	10.5	54 145	20.9	73 781	47 562	26 219	11 798	3 374
Marion	9 329	326 457	0.93	3 405	10.0	4 560	13.4	50 481	21.4	100 704	60 910	39 794	8 346	2 444
Martin	4 080	151 412	1.03	1 229	7.9	1 885	12.2	20 945	19.9	40 160	30 143	10 017	3 025	1 968
Miami-Dade	41 107	2 670 763	1.06	31 534	11.8	20 313	7.6	566 562	25.5	407 629	142 187	265 442	122 865	4 606
Monroe	2 015	78 016	1.07	749	9.7	708	9.2	13 561	22.5	14 743	12 966	1 777	3 140	4 037
Nassau	543	63 972	0.65	750	9.7	806	10.4	8 971	14.7	16 166	11 950	4 216	1 321	1 718
Okaloosa	4 362	197 842	1.10	2 836	14.4	1 718	8.7	26 759	16.5	35 320	30 475	4 845	5 536	2 796
Okeechobee	2 628	38 576	0.94	534	13.6	392	10.0	8 046	27.1	8 325	5 354	2 971	1 369	3 469
Orange	35 191	1 346 658	1.26	16 381	12.9	7 645	6.0	220 714	20.2	154 612	83 463	71 149	57 567	4 586
Osceola	3 284	255 784	0.73	4 176	13.1	2 029	6.4	58 223	21.8	51 990	22 823	29 167	9 492	3 075
Palm Beach	20 798	1 376 049	1.03	14 637	10.4	14 434	10.2	225 149	21.2	283 767	174 330	109 437	47 324	3 391
Pasco	5 890	413 902	0.67	4 930	10.0	5 742	11.7	67 552	18.1	109 421	51 554	57 867	12 892	2 676
Pinellas	19 753	936 691	1.03	8 671	9.2	12 029	12.7	126 650	17.7	214 985	112 453	102 532	39 202	4 172
Polk	12 617	592 742	0.90	7 596	11.8	6 409	10.0	97 953	19.6	123 864	64 669	59 195	19 500	3 080

1. Per 1,000 estimated resident population.   2. Data for serious crimes have not been adjusted for underreporting; this may affect comparability between geographic areas and over time.
3. Per 100,000 population estimated by the FBI.

Table B. States and Counties — Crime, Education, Money Income, and Poverty

STATE County	Serious crimes known to police, 2014 (cont.)[1] Rate[2] Violent	Property	Education — School enrollment and attainment, 2010–2014 Enrollment[3] Total	Percent private	Attainment[4] (percent) High school graduate or less	Bachelor's degree or more	Local government expenditures,[5] 2012–2013 Total current spending (mil dol)	Current spending per student (dollars)	Money income, 2010–2014 Per capita income[6] (dollars)	Households Median income (dollars)	Mean income (dollars)	Percent with income of $200,000 or more	Income and poverty, 2014 Median house-hold income (dollars)	Percent below poverty level All persons	Children under 18 years	Children 5 to 17 years in families
	46	47	48	49	50	51	52	53	54	55	56	57	58	59	60	61
CONNECTICUT—Cont'd																
Tolland	NA	NA	49 529	11.2	34.4	36.8	340.0	15 804	35 022	79 988	95 669	7.2	78 653	7.5	7.3	6.3
Windham	NA	NA	30 235	11.0	47.7	22.9	266.9	17 361	28 044	59 218	72 054	2.7	57 547	10.3	15.5	14.3
DELAWARE	489	2 982	234 668	19.8	43.5	29.4	1 689.5	13 833	30 191	60 231	78 589	4.9	59 853	13.0	19.2	17.8
Kent	422	2 737	46 496	17.1	47.4	22.7	306.6	13 046	25 259	55 169	67 230	2.3	54 271	14.1	21.2	20.6
New Castle	532	3 025	148 457	22.6	39.1	34.5	984.7	14 721	32 616	64 857	85 814	6.3	64 632	12.3	16.8	15.7
Sussex	426	3 073	39 715	12.6	51.4	21.9	398.2	14 075	27 748	53 505	68 578	3.4	53 316	13.9	24.3	21.4
DISTRICT OF COLUMBIA	1 244	5 182	160 085	43.5	29.7	53.4	883.2	17 953	46 502	69 235	104 615	12.8	69 992	18.4	28.9	28.6
District of Columbia	1 244	5 182	160 085	43.5	29.7	53.4	883.2	19 990	46 502	69 235	104 615	12.8	69 992	18.4	28.9	28.6
FLORIDA	540	3 415	4 665 703	17.5	43.2	26.8	23 144.9	8 433	26 499	47 212	67 143	3.9	47 439	16.6	24.2	22.9
Alachua	567	2 985	92 572	9.7	29.9	40.8	243.3	8 744	25 020	42 045	62 557	4.0	44 325	21.6	22.1	20.6
Baker	503	1 165	6 805	12.8	65.1	10.9	40.0	8 036	20 346	46 865	62 283	2.7	47 121	19.6	25.7	23.5
Bay	508	4 024	40 037	12.3	43.4	21.6	209.8	7 876	24 937	47 274	61 335	2.5	44 800	15.6	23.4	22.1
Bradford	420	1 203	5 327	15.0	60.2	10.4	30.7	9 378	18 540	40 481	51 987	2.0	39 980	22.6	28.2	27.9
Brevard	493	2 605	120 193	17.9	39.1	26.7	568.2	7 977	27 360	48 483	64 613	3.0	47 973	14.5	22.0	20.2
Broward	409	3 048	470 845	21.4	39.9	30.2	2 183.4	8 390	28 329	51 574	72 726	4.7	51 485	14.5	20.1	19.4
Calhoun	135	803	3 135	5.6	65.5	9.2	19.8	8 730	15 463	34 053	45 209	0.9	35 256	22.3	30.5	28.3
Charlotte	176	1 741	24 499	16.2	45.2	20.9	146.4	8 952	26 374	44 265	57 511	1.7	43 242	11.9	21.8	20.7
Citrus	355	1 741	22 801	13.7	51.4	16.8	136.2	8 895	23 495	38 109	51 970	1.7	36 383	20.1	34.1	34.0
Clay	269	2 064	54 452	14.0	39.7	23.6	278.4	7 900	26 489	59 103	72 966	3.3	58 539	10.9	15.5	14.0
Collier	260	1 466	62 925	14.6	41.2	32.3	445.8	10 182	37 236	56 250	92 954	8.5	58 403	14.3	26.1	23.6
Columbia	598	3 094	15 575	13.2	51.6	14.1	80.5	8 212	19 884	39 194	52 497	1.8	38 484	21.7	31.1	29.3
DeSoto	424	2 773	6 932	7.5	68.7	9.9	44.2	9 298	15 596	36 114	43 964	0.8	36 945	29.7	41.1	37.9
Dixie	451	2 551	3 005	9.0	62.0	7.5	17.8	8 696	16 954	35 000	43 191	0.4	32 121	27.1	36.3	36.8
Duval	687	3 977	228 960	20.7	40.5	26.5	1 057.5	8 414	26 267	47 582	65 638	3.3	46 013	18.2	26.7	25.4
Escambia	690	3 974	76 480	21.5	40.4	23.9	338.9	8 334	24 014	44 883	59 869	2.3	46 139	15.3	23.8	23.5
Flagler	246	1 772	19 926	14.1	43.7	23.4	109.4	8 468	24 393	47 733	62 379	2.5	51 556	11.6	21.1	20.2
Franklin	299	1 512	1 897	8.5	57.6	16.0	13.1	10 655	20 287	37 815	54 491	2.7	36 788	25.3	37.1	35.3
Gadsden	439	2 035	11 212	15.0	57.6	16.3	61.8	10 174	18 101	36 146	47 519	0.6	35 849	25.6	39.7	37.9
Gilchrist	323	979	3 362	9.2	57.1	11.0	24.3	9 445	20 536	40 984	54 028	1.2	40 788	19.8	26.4	24.6
Glades	258	959	2 260	13.1	68.1	10.3	13.6	8 987	16 799	33 609	42 248	0.9	38 783	21.1	29.1	25.1
Gulf	407	1 729	2 954	11.1	55.8	14.7	18.0	9 344	19 411	40 964	52 127	2.0	38 419	23.1	30.0	28.4
Hamilton	410	2 828	2 529	13.9	62.7	10.8	17.9	10 769	15 012	35 629	45 772	0.7	31 734	31.7	39.9	39.3
Hardee	245	2 381	6 342	4.7	71.9	10.0	45.2	8 927	15 783	36 094	52 450	1.6	35 371	29.9	38.8	36.5
Hendry	735	3 215	10 340	7.3	69.1	10.6	58.8	8 603	16 381	36 504	51 976	1.5	38 494	25.3	35.6	33.9
Hernando	255	2 274	36 298	13.5	50.9	15.7	176.6	7 950	21 245	40 457	50 848	1.3	40 094	15.3	24.4	23.1
Highlands	308	2 874	17 094	11.8	54.1	15.9	103.3	8 558	20 455	35 911	47 817	1.3	35 787	19.5	32.1	31.4
Hillsborough	325	2 099	344 677	16.5	40.7	29.8	1 757.4	8 766	27 532	50 122	70 619	4.6	50 758	16.8	23.3	21.6
Holmes	292	1 427	4 322	6.2	60.8	10.9	27.7	8 331	16 946	36 236	46 000	0.8	35 651	26.7	34.5	32.5
Indian River	282	2 202	27 582	14.7	42.2	26.7	144.9	8 047	31 089	44 645	72 695	5.3	47 548	14.7	25.0	23.6
Jackson	385	1 672	10 964	12.9	56.8	14.2	61.9	8 938	17 611	36 310	47 957	1.3	36 876	24.3	31.7	29.7
Jefferson	981	1 284	2 791	20.8	51.0	17.8	11.7	11 210	20 972	42 866	55 784	1.6	40 205	18.0	28.3	27.4
Lafayette	246	538	1 799	7.3	59.0	11.6	10.1	8 448	18 125	35 720	55 600	1.8	38 071	25.6	30.8	27.6
Lake	308	2 316	62 692	15.6	46.8	21.0	320.6	7 727	24 103	45 465	59 945	2.0	46 895	13.8	23.2	22.0
Lee	340	2 002	134 209	12.4	45.1	25.3	756.4	8 819	27 578	47 908	67 710	4.0	49 147	16.0	26.1	24.5
Leon	747	4 226	107 929	10.7	27.4	44.3	290.1	8 677	26 486	46 620	65 643	3.8	45 463	23.3	22.8	20.9
Levy	NA	NA	8 666	11.5	59.7	10.5	48.0	8 486	19 655	35 483	47 092	0.8	37 433	21.2	36.0	33.8
Liberty	83	558	1 615	3.5	67.0	13.1	14.7	9 966	16 928	38 990	52 721	1.6	38 473	24.7	28.9	27.6
Madison	800	2 166	4 012	9.2	58.8	10.4	25.0	9 443	15 664	33 520	43 556	0.7	33 017	27.7	35.5	34.0
Manatee	563	2 810	68 049	15.7	43.3	27.5	396.2	8 583	27 948	49 228	67 259	3.9	51 673	14.1	22.5	21.1
Marion	415	2 028	65 763	17.1	51.2	17.2	350.4	8 344	21 752	39 339	52 111	1.7	39 860	17.8	29.7	28.5
Martin	247	1 721	29 395	16.7	37.4	31.2	164.2	8 789	35 183	51 703	82 461	7.0	55 472	12.1	20.7	19.2
Miami-Dade	633	3 973	658 830	21.0	48.9	26.4	3 183.4	8 986	23 433	43 099	66 582	4.5	42 754	20.4	27.7	27.4
Monroe	505	3 532	12 541	14.4	38.3	29.7	87.1	10 425	34 424	55 449	81 727	6.6	57 411	14.0	20.5	20.7
Nassau	116	1 603	16 589	12.4	45.1	23.0	89.7	8 099	29 321	55 256	75 511	3.7	56 728	11.7	18.1	17.5
Okaloosa	394	2 402	46 249	12.1	36.0	28.1	249.9	8 388	29 082	55 768	71 527	3.9	55 952	12.4	20.2	19.4
Okeechobee	385	3 084	9 083	11.5	66.1	10.7	55.9	8 598	18 087	35 490	50 362	1.8	37 065	25.9	35.3	34.3
Orange	682	3 905	349 929	18.9	39.2	30.6	1 526.4	8 338	25 052	47 556	67 285	3.9	47 069	18.2	25.4	23.5
Osceola	411	2 664	78 722	14.1	50.1	17.8	455.4	8 073	18 996	44 551	55 682	1.6	42 945	19.3	27.5	27.2
Palm Beach	452	2 939	310 363	19.3	38.5	32.8	1 692.7	9 429	33 072	52 878	80 961	6.4	52 225	14.9	21.9	21.0
Pasco	280	2 395	103 961	15.3	46.6	21.1	535.8	7 978	24 076	44 518	58 913	2.2	45 219	14.7	20.2	19.2
Pinellas	506	3 666	185 090	18.0	40.4	28.3	908.1	8 766	29 617	45 574	64 834	3.6	45 162	15.2	22.2	22.0
Polk	349	2 732	148 005	15.8	53.1	18.6	888.4	9 165	21 157	43 063	56 063	1.8	42 768	18.1	27.3	24.4

1. Data for serious crimes have not been adjusted for underreporting; this may affect comparability between geographic areas and over time.   2. Per 100,000 population estimated by the FBI.
3. All persons 3 years old and over enrolled in nursery school through college.   4. Persons 25 years old and over.   5. Elementary and secondary education expenditures.
6. Based on population estimated by the American Community Survey, 2010–2014.

STATE County	Personal income, 2014										Earnings, 2014		
			Per capita[1]			Supplements to wages and salaries; employer contributions (mil dol)						Contributions for government social insurance (mil dol)	
	Total (mil dol)	Percent change, 2013–2014	Dollars	Rank	Wages and salaries (mil dol)	Pension and insurance	Government social insurance	Proprietors' income (mil dol)	Dividends, interest, and rent (mil dol)	Personal transfer receipts (mil dol)	Total (mil dol)	From employee and self-employed	From employer
	62	63	64	65	66	67	68	69	70	71	72	73	74
CONNECTICUT—Cont'd													
Tolland	7 507	3.9	49 598	405	1 961	514	134	465	1 120	992	3 074	165	134
Windham	4 749	3.6	40 590	1 111	1 692	384	132	235	743	1 008	2 443	141	132
DELAWARE	43 392	4.6	46 378	X	23 632	4 090	1 754	4 236	7 255	8 427	33 712	1 915	1 754
Kent	6 555	4.8	38 114	1 440	2 936	699	234	588	979	1 558	4 458	244	234
New Castle	28 037	4.2	50 720	346	17 876	2 834	1 294	2 783	4 631	4 503	24 788	1 397	1 294
Sussex	8 800	5.9	41 737	976	2 819	557	227	864	1 645	2 366	4 467	274	227
DISTRICT OF COLUM- BIA	46 016	3.3	69 838	X	64 668	12 623	4 805	6 077	8 544	5 976	88 173	4 472	4 805
District of Columbia	46 016	3.3	69 838	59	64 668	12 623	4 805	6 077	8 544	5 976	88 173	4 472	4 805
FLORIDA	850 178	5.0	42 737	X	379 080	55 789	27 201	51 780	221 757	171 152	513 850	32 758	27 201
Alachua	9 974	4.9	38 903	1 332	5 744	1 217	410	394	1 996	1 830	7 765	438	410
Baker	734	3.8	27 097	2 974	241	56	18	28	89	205	343	22	18
Bay	6 889	6.0	38 487	1 396	3 287	590	256	342	1 471	1 572	4 474	272	256
Bradford	731	2.0	27 386	2 959	245	50	18	30	109	234	343	24	18
Brevard	21 647	3.5	38 872	1 334	9 555	1 471	700	855	4 598	5 457	12 581	840	700
Broward	80 906	5.2	43 283	817	39 465	5 347	2 811	5 350	18 032	13 275	52 974	3 276	2 811
Calhoun	339	3.4	23 321	3 093	95	23	7	12	48	121	137	10	7
Charlotte	6 124	5.6	36 350	1 714	1 697	266	126	309	1 756	2 063	2 398	203	126
Citrus	4 766	3.2	34 194	2 082	1 249	214	92	177	1 211	1 814	1 731	160	92
Clay	7 453	5.0	37 302	1 555	1 847	302	136	196	1 291	1 580	2 482	171	136
Collier	25 764	4.9	73 869	45	6 389	802	445	1 272	14 236	3 010	8 908	596	445
Columbia	2 069	4.9	30 494	2 652	874	183	66	86	301	628	1 210	77	66
DeSoto	760	4.8	21 696	3 105	336	63	25	54	147	270	478	30	25
Dixie	395	5.0	24 836	3 063	90	22	6	23	68	163	141	12	6
Duval	37 089	4.6	41 316	1 025	26 331	3 761	1 935	2 675	7 243	7 073	34 702	2 049	1 935
Escambia	11 380	3.5	36 632	1 662	6 236	1 167	484	412	2 484	2 773	8 299	490	484
Flagler	3 763	6.0	36 748	1 638	739	136	55	22	1 013	1 097	952	89	55
Franklin	383	3.3	32 430	2 382	115	25	8	22	111	101	170	12	8
Gadsden	1 341	4.0	28 979	2 831	462	107	33	54	213	404	657	43	33
Gilchrist	541	7.5	31 808	2 466	108	25	8	86	64	148	227	13	8
Glades	289	2.9	21 210	3 107	77	16	6	38	55	82	137	9	6
Gulf	440	4.3	27 599	2 946	136	30	10	18	94	130	194	14	10
Hamilton	339	3.5	24 160	3 077	145	34	10	7	43	121	196	13	10
Hardee	664	2.7	24 176	3 076	264	57	19	73	109	191	413	23	19
Hendry	1 076	-1.7	27 941	2 923	493	89	37	138	139	284	756	35	37
Hernando	5 684	4.5	32 324	2 402	1 426	246	107	221	1 022	2 059	2 000	178	107
Highlands	3 011	3.2	30 650	2 634	942	169	71	145	644	1 151	1 327	104	71
Hillsborough	55 156	5.1	41 902	960	34 525	4 909	2 470	4 330	9 244	9 941	46 233	2 758	2 470
Holmes	519	2.8	26 427	3 011	111	29	8	46	76	189	194	15	8
Indian River	9 140	5.1	63 140	100	2 099	299	153	332	4 310	1 547	2 884	209	153
Jackson	1 389	2.4	28 459	2 881	517	122	38	49	227	484	726	49	38
Jefferson	498	5.0	35 446	1 869	88	20	6	34	103	132	149	10	6
Lafayette	197	7.5	22 286	3 101	50	14	4	34	28	50	102	5	4
Lake	11 297	5.9	35 786	1 809	3 308	552	245	394	2 117	3 288	4 499	348	245
Lee	28 705	5.9	42 243	931	10 145	1 572	735	2 008	10 022	6 275	14 460	992	735
Leon	10 878	4.8	38 305	1 421	6 482	1 372	459	604	2 066	1 772	8 917	500	459
Levy	1 209	4.0	30 514	2 646	279	58	21	49	204	408	407	33	21
Liberty	208	2.1	24 822	3 065	74	18	6	5	31	56	102	7	6
Madison	522	5.4	28 176	2 904	152	37	11	32	92	174	232	16	11
Manatee	14 385	5.5	40 895	1 073	4 720	696	344	911	4 157	3 215	6 671	464	344
Marion	11 047	4.2	32 571	2 356	3 729	622	275	410	2 494	3 815	5 036	402	275
Martin	10 055	4.6	65 551	83	2 615	375	188	470	4 542	1 487	3 649	249	188
Miami-Dade	111 529	5.0	41 883	963	57 785	8 094	4 066	11 094	24 748	22 515	81 039	5 033	4 066
Monroe	5 368	4.8	69 593	61	1 723	265	126	260	2 669	591	2 375	145	126
Nassau	3 611	4.8	47 127	518	893	139	64	102	1 002	676	1 199	85	64
Okaloosa	8 783	3.9	44 695	705	4 701	976	389	404	2 499	1 607	6 470	349	389
Okeechobee	1 118	7.9	28 554	2 875	410	73	31	124	158	364	638	39	31
Orange	47 623	5.8	38 007	1 453	36 830	4 735	2 595	3 161	7 734	8 349	47 321	2 781	2 595
Osceola	8 713	7.6	28 088	2 908	3 222	489	237	253	1 001	2 257	4 201	283	237
Palm Beach	93 526	4.9	66 914	73	30 640	3 916	2 101	6 001	41 039	12 204	42 657	2 739	2 101
Pasco	16 478	5.5	33 953	2 119	4 170	692	308	304	2 490	4 671	5 473	441	308
Pinellas	43 082	4.4	45 925	603	20 134	2 879	1 436	2 253	10 209	9 346	26 702	1 736	1 436
Polk	20 722	4.8	32 652	2 346	8 705	1 385	630	1 098	3 888	5 672	11 818	804	630

1. Based on the resident population estimated as of July 1 of the year shown.

Table B. States and Counties — Earnings, Social Security, and Housing

STATE County	Earnings, 2014 (cont.)									Social Security beneficiaries, December 2014			Housing units, 2015	
	Percent by selected industries											Supplemental Security Income recipients, December 2014		Percent change, 2010–2014
	Farm	Mining	Construction	Manufacturing	Information: professional, scientific, technical services	Retail trade	Finance, insurance, real estate and leasing	Health care and social assistance	Government	Number	Rate[1]		Total	
	75	76	77	78	79	80	81	82	83	84	85	86	87	88
CONNECTICUT—Cont'd														
Tolland	0.6	D	8.3	7.1	6.1	7.0	3.1	11.4	38.3	25 400	168	1 037	58 632	1.2
Windham	0.5	D	D	18.8	4.9	8.3	D	15.3	21.5	22 920	196	2 082	49 178	0.2
DELAWARE	1.6	D	5.4	6.1	15.3	5.9	16.2	12.7	15.4	192 187	205	16 687	421 747	3.9
Kent	3.3	D	5.4	D	4.8	7.9	6.0	11.9	36.8	36 125	210	3 769	68 692	5.1
New Castle	0.1	D	4.8	D	19.0	4.8	19.7	12.4	12.0	96 305	174	10 091	221 637	1.9
Sussex	8.1	0.0	8.3	11.8	5.0	9.7	7.1	15.3	12.7	59 755	283	2 827	131 418	6.8
DISTRICT OF COLUMBIA	0.0	0.0	1.6	0.2	26.2	1.0	4.9	5.6	39.5	79 716	121	26 782	309 574	4.3
District of Columbia	0.0	0.0	1.6	0.2	26.2	1.0	4.9	5.6	39.5	79 716	121	26 782	309 574	4.3
FLORIDA	0.5	0.1	5.2	4.8	12.3	7.9	9.7	12.8	16.0	4 223 274	212	561 125	9 209 857	2.5
Alachua	0.3	D	3.1	4.4	7.5	5.6	5.8	17.5	39.7	41 140	160	6 359	114 596	1.6
Baker	3.4	0.0	4.2	1.7	2.8	8.1	1.7	D	42.1	5 000	184	638	9 623	-0.7
Bay	0.0	0.1	5.4	5.7	8.0	8.9	6.3	13.2	27.1	38 485	215	4 849	100 697	1.1
Bradford	1.4	D	2.8	3.9	2.6	9.2	2.9	14.9	31.0	5 985	224	840	10 870	-1.3
Brevard	0.1	0.0	4.6	15.8	11.7	7.5	4.3	14.0	17.9	150 235	270	11 594	273 096	1.2
Broward	0.0	0.1	5.6	3.7	14.1	8.4	9.6	10.1	14.6	302 775	162	44 368	818 623	1.0
Calhoun	0.9	D	D	D	D	8.3	3.0	20.1	37.8	3 095	213	557	5 910	-1.5
Charlotte	2.1	0.2	6.8	1.5	7.0	12.7	5.8	23.9	15.8	62 695	372	2 698	101 775	1.1
Citrus	0.1	0.2	7.7	1.1	6.5	12.5	4.1	23.4	14.8	56 635	407	3 228	77 726	-0.4
Clay	0.1	D	8.4	3.6	11.2	10.5	5.0	18.0	18.5	38 125	191	2 790	78 179	3.6
Collier	1.3	0.5	9.8	2.6	9.4	9.4	11.2	14.2	10.6	85 895	247	3 982	206 375	4.6
Columbia	2.8	D	3.2	9.5	3.4	10.2	3.7	13.6	30.4	15 875	234	2 633	28 273	-1.3
DeSoto	11.7	D	3.7	4.1	1.7	6.2	2.5	D	22.2	7 110	202	1 015	14 788	1.4
Dixie	4.9	0.0	3.3	15.3	D	6.1	2.2	4.0	36.1	4 475	281	771	9 130	-2.0
Duval	0.0	0.1	4.7	5.5	12.4	5.9	14.5	12.9	14.8	152 940	170	24 498	398 541	2.6
Escambia	0.0	0.1	4.7	5.0	8.5	6.9	7.5	15.5	30.3	69 235	224	10 171	139 055	1.7
Flagler	0.4	D	5.0	5.2	9.5	11.3	5.0	13.5	22.7	34 085	332	1 711	50 044	3.0
Franklin	0.0	0.0	D	D	6.2	8.9	7.9	D	32.2	2 795	239	350	8 554	-1.2
Gadsden	5.5	2.0	8.4	8.2	2.5	6.3	1.7	3.5	37.7	10 460	227	2 637	19 383	-0.6
Gilchrist	23.7	0.0	8.9	0.9	1.6	2.8	1.5	D	25.5	4 030	237	509	7 227	-1.1
Glades	18.2	0.0	3.6	5.8	1.5	D	1.3	D	20.4	2 530	188	172	6 803	-2.5
Gulf	0.0	0.0	5.5	1.7	6.2	8.2	7.8	D	34.9	3 665	230	383	9 245	1.6
Hamilton	2.6	0.0	D	D	D	4.3	D	D	30.8	3 050	217	630	5 687	-1.6
Hardee	17.9	6.4	2.1	2.9	1.7	5.9	3.8	D	23.2	4 605	168	834	9 600	-1.3
Hendry	26.4	D	3.5	3.5	6.5	5.0	2.4	4.4	17.0	5 835	152	1 487	14 339	-1.5
Hernando	0.2	0.1	6.2	5.1	4.9	11.8	3.8	22.9	18.9	59 335	338	4 093	84 801	0.4
Highlands	7.6	0.0	3.2	2.5	4.8	10.8	3.8	22.3	17.8	32 655	333	2 729	54 822	-1.0
Hillsborough	0.4	0.1	4.7	4.1	16.5	7.0	13.1	11.2	14.3	221 945	168	40 578	560 454	4.5
Holmes	4.6	D	6.5	5.7	D	8.4	2.7	D	38.6	4 825	246	794	8 558	-1.0
Indian River	1.8	0.2	6.0	4.9	9.9	10.4	8.4	17.7	11.9	46 020	318	2 387	77 900	2.0
Jackson	1.9	0.5	7.3	4.7	D	8.4	2.8	D	41.8	12 150	249	2 046	20 774	-1.1
Jefferson	15.7	0.0	5.4	0.2	D	5.7	2.1	D	27.0	3 515	250	622	6 580	-0.8
Lafayette	32.0	D	2.5	3.2	D	4.3	D	D	34.7	1 500	169	140	3 297	-0.9
Lake	1.1	0.3	8.5	4.2	6.2	11.8	5.4	20.0	17.4	94 245	298	6 858	148 706	2.6
Lee	0.3	0.2	8.2	3.1	10.2	9.8	6.4	12.1	19.4	172 795	254	12 730	379 018	2.1
Leon	0.0	D	3.4	1.2	14.4	6.1	6.1	12.9	39.5	40 375	142	6 042	127 601	2.8
Levy	6.4	0.4	9.6	7.7	3.3	10.4	4.2	7.5	23.6	11 950	302	1 352	19 810	-1.6
Liberty	-0.7	0.0	1.8	18.1	D	2.3	D	16.7	41.0	1 450	173	296	3 317	-1.2
Madison	7.0	D	1.9	11.1	2.4	6.7	2.6	10.0	32.4	4 525	244	978	8 421	-0.7
Manatee	2.0	0.1	7.7	8.0	9.4	9.8	6.8	14.3	12.6	89 280	254	6 020	182 119	5.5
Marion	-0.3	0.1	6.2	8.9	6.5	11.1	5.4	19.1	17.2	110 610	327	9 350	163 808	-0.1
Martin	1.2	D	7.0	6.2	11.2	10.6	7.6	17.7	10.5	43 245	282	1 626	79 239	1.1
Miami-Dade	0.3	0.1	4.1	3.0	13.8	7.5	11.0	11.6	14.2	407 735	153	159 102	1 010 556	2.1
Monroe	0.0	0.3	5.7	0.8	6.5	10.2	6.1	6.8	23.7	16 490	215	1 323	52 985	0.4
Nassau	0.3	0.1	3.5	8.8	12.5	7.7	4.6	8.8	22.0	18 665	244	1 119	36 450	4.1
Okaloosa	0.0	0.1	3.8	3.8	11.2	6.1	5.8	7.1	44.7	38 345	196	3 126	95 494	3.3
Okeechobee	14.8	D	4.7	6.1	D	8.2	3.2	D	19.9	8 620	220	1 053	18 155	-1.9
Orange	0.2	0.0	4.6	5.1	13.8	6.4	9.6	10.6	11.0	177 195	141	34 358	516 477	5.9
Osceola	1.0	0.0	5.6	1.8	4.3	10.2	6.4	15.4	19.2	55 125	177	10 054	137 090	7.0
Palm Beach	0.5	0.3	5.0	3.7	13.7	7.2	13.2	13.2	11.4	303 240	217	23 434	679 026	2.2
Pasco	0.5	0.1	6.8	3.6	6.4	12.5	4.5	22.1	18.5	127 465	262	11 475	234 450	2.4
Pinellas	0.0	0.1	4.2	8.8	13.7	8.0	10.2	15.5	12.1	236 695	252	21 394	505 353	0.3
Polk	0.9	0.7	5.4	9.3	5.4	8.9	8.0	14.0	14.1	148 405	234	20 892	284 342	1.1

1. Per 1,000 resident population estimated as of July 1 of the year shown.

Table B. States and Counties — Housing, Labor Force, and Employment

STATE County	Housing units, 2010–2014								Civilian labor force, 2015				Civilian employment,[6] 2010–2014		
	Occupied units							Sub-standard units[4] (percent)	Total	Percent change, 2014–2015	Unemployment		Total	Percent	
	Owner-occupied					Renter-occupied								Management, business, science and arts	Construction, production, and maintenance occupations
	Total	Percent	Median value[1]	Median owner cost as a percent of income		Median rent[3]	Median rent as a percent of income[2]				Total	Rate[5]			
				With a mortgage	Without a mortgage[2]										
	89	90	91	92	93	94	95	96	97	98	99	100	101	102	103
CONNECTICUT—Cont'd															
Tolland	54 444	74.0	252 400	23.6	13.9	1 041	30.0	1.2	84 579	0.3	4 061	4.8	80 191	41.8	19.2
Windham	44 487	70.5	203 200	25.3	16.0	863	32.0	1.9	63 011	0.3	3 911	6.2	58 328	32.1	24.2
DELAWARE	339 046	71.6	232 900	23.5	11.1	1 012	30.6	2.2	467 472	3.1	22 894	4.9	426 103	38.1	19.3
Kent	59 142	70.9	200 200	24.3	11.5	985	31.9	1.9	76 887	2.2	4 149	5.4	73 692	32.7	24.2
New Castle	201 543	69.3	243 400	22.9	10.7	1 030	30.2	2.1	292 754	3.3	13 889	4.7	264 630	42.4	16.3
Sussex	78 361	78.1	231 400	24.8	11.5	965	30.5	2.6	97 831	3.1	4 856	5.0	87 781	30.0	24.6
DISTRICT OF COLUMBIA	267 415	41.6	454 500	22.9	10.9	1 302	29.6	3.6	388 388	2.7	26 844	6.9	325 838	60.5	7.0
District of Columbia	267 415	41.6	454 500	22.9	10.9	1 302	29.6	3.6	388 388	2.7	26 844	6.9	325 838	60.5	7.0
FLORIDA	7 217 508	66.1	156 200	26.9	13.3	998	34.7	3.1	9 675 326	0.7	522 065	5.4	8 335 023	33.8	18.0
Alachua	96 137	53.5	164 600	23.0	11.5	883	36.9	2.2	130 067	0.2	5 910	4.5	114 660	45.6	10.8
Baker	8 351	76.9	118 100	22.8	10.7	727	32.3	3.8	11 335	0.9	607	5.4	10 041	29.3	25.3
Bay	67 388	61.4	156 500	24.8	11.6	932	31.9	2.1	87 575	-0.2	4 737	5.4	76 336	32.2	20.1
Bradford	8 824	75.8	93 000	22.3	11.2	704	34.8	2.9	10 750	-0.3	514	4.8	9 100	29.9	22.1
Brevard	221 582	72.4	138 500	24.8	12.1	904	32.5	1.7	257 684	-0.3	15 122	5.9	226 562	36.9	17.7
Broward	667 578	64.5	177 300	29.5	16.5	1 179	36.1	4.0	992 392	0.3	49 980	5.0	867 834	35.0	16.0
Calhoun	4 756	78.5	76 200	25.7	10.2	609	37.9	6.3	4 913	-0.9	301	6.1	4 592	24.5	26.4
Charlotte	70 948	78.7	140 900	29.5	13.1	900	33.5	1.5	67 559	0.8	3 967	5.9	54 891	30.2	17.3
Citrus	60 670	81.5	113 500	24.5	12.4	780	35.3	1.9	47 739	-1.3	3 552	7.4	43 783	28.0	20.6
Clay	68 016	75.3	153 700	23.1	10.0	1 025	28.8	1.9	99 182	1.1	4 853	4.9	84 417	34.9	20.7
Collier	126 331	72.9	258 400	29.1	13.4	1 027	33.4	4.1	162 124	1.0	8 447	5.2	135 857	29.5	19.6
Columbia	23 714	71.6	106 600	24.3	11.0	776	28.8	3.4	28 998	2.0	1 562	5.4	24 555	30.7	23.5
DeSoto	10 964	72.2	83 800	24.9	11.2	686	28.6	7.2	12 814	-2.9	768	6.0	12 253	15.8	42.4
Dixie	6 020	78.4	79 000	27.5	11.8	604	28.4	2.1	5 588	0.3	341	6.1	5 179	23.7	31.7
Duval	334 721	60.3	144 000	25.0	12.2	941	33.3	2.2	465 537	0.9	26 386	5.7	399 633	34.8	18.2
Escambia	112 395	62.4	123 000	23.9	11.6	890	31.8	1.6	139 644	0.0	7 760	5.6	126 273	32.5	18.3
Flagler	35 939	79.7	163 800	28.4	12.8	1 046	31.5	2.0	43 502	0.4	2 685	6.2	34 989	30.8	17.3
Franklin	4 253	73.0	128 700	27.3	13.4	720	29.7	3.5	4 796	-3.2	223	4.6	4 191	27.9	27.9
Gadsden	16 986	71.2	107 900	25.5	11.7	685	36.9	6.6	18 463	-2.1	1 293	7.0	16 636	29.9	24.5
Gilchrist	6 274	80.5	105 300	23.7	12.8	719	30.0	3.4	6 565	-0.1	363	5.5	5 993	26.1	27.9
Glades	3 846	73.9	84 100	26.4	11.6	711	32.4	2.8	4 698	-4.8	332	7.1	3 893	21.8	25.9
Gulf	5 381	71.9	119 900	28.1	11.7	842	35.8	5.2	6 127	-0.2	310	5.1	5 590	25.3	27.1
Hamilton	4 704	74.2	69 400	22.9	10.1	565	33.0	2.8	5 668	22.7	289	5.1	4 098	28.6	26.7
Hardee	7 534	71.7	84 200	27.1	12.1	648	30.9	10.1	10 307	-0.6	693	6.7	9 287	19.3	44.4
Hendry	11 156	70.2	72 400	24.6	11.4	764	30.7	8.2	15 317	-3.5	1 574	10.3	14 129	24.0	42.5
Hernando	70 183	78.5	111 800	27.1	12.6	894	35.4	2.3	66 609	0.3	4 520	6.8	56 925	29.3	20.9
Highlands	39 882	76.9	87 700	25.8	12.0	722	33.9	3.0	35 272	-1.8	2 602	7.4	30 546	26.4	23.7
Hillsborough	477 472	59.3	156 700	24.5	11.9	960	32.8	3.2	689 463	0.7	34 139	5.0	592 692	36.9	17.2
Holmes	6 758	80.2	83 200	24.0	10.9	595	32.5	1.6	6 721	-2.3	415	6.2	6 249	27.7	26.9
Indian River	57 342	74.2	156 300	25.8	13.0	861	36.2	1.7	61 307	-1.0	4 140	6.8	52 784	31.7	19.1
Jackson	15 961	74.9	86 900	23.6	13.1	624	33.1	2.7	17 258	-1.4	1 006	5.8	15 747	28.1	20.3
Jefferson	5 372	74.7	127 100	22.5	13.3	665	33.9	1.0	5 424	-1.5	315	5.8	5 099	41.6	17.5
Lafayette	2 706	79.4	106 000	28.3	11.3	565	27.4	2.4	3 244	-3.5	147	4.5	3 026	26.1	32.3
Lake	117 657	74.5	137 900	25.0	12.9	950	34.7	2.6	140 471	1.3	7 565	5.4	119 459	30.5	20.5
Lee	246 061	69.3	150 000	26.7	13.6	939	32.3	2.9	319 967	2.8	16 084	5.0	253 789	30.0	18.4
Leon	110 669	53.1	180 600	23.3	10.9	930	37.5	2.8	148 346	-1.3	7 373	5.0	137 022	44.5	11.1
Levy	15 638	76.5	89 800	25.2	12.0	674	33.0	3.2	16 505	1.0	948	5.7	13 788	24.8	29.0
Liberty	2 362	78.4	73 200	21.7	10.0	584	23.2	7.2	2 661	-3.6	152	5.7	2 717	32.7	26.5
Madison	6 651	77.6	77 500	25.7	14.3	683	40.7	4.7	7 545	-2.8	465	6.2	6 188	25.1	33.3
Manatee	133 445	70.4	163 700	26.2	13.1	936	33.8	2.9	164 480	2.2	8 162	5.0	137 068	33.1	18.6
Marion	133 137	75.9	111 500	26.6	12.7	819	33.6	2.3	131 147	-0.6	8 358	6.4	116 660	27.1	20.3
Martin	60 828	76.1	191 500	27.1	13.5	958	33.2	1.9	69 915	1.5	3 670	5.2	59 938	36.9	16.6
Miami-Dade	833 541	55.0	194 100	31.8	15.4	1 098	39.5	6.1	1 334 402	0.8	81 983	6.1	1 168 256	31.3	19.4
Monroe	28 418	60.5	379 700	34.3	14.9	1 400	37.3	4.1	46 046	2.0	1 600	3.5	37 217	31.0	18.8
Nassau	28 068	77.6	176 200	25.0	10.4	1 026	31.3	1.9	36 696	0.9	1 840	5.0	31 476	32.7	24.8
Okaloosa	73 655	64.6	181 800	24.4	10.5	1 015	31.3	2.1	92 220	-0.1	4 138	4.5	83 892	33.4	18.6
Okeechobee	13 213	72.2	100 900	26.5	11.7	699	30.6	6.3	17 346	-2.1	1 068	6.2	13 285	22.2	32.1
Orange	423 609	56.0	161 900	27.2	12.8	1 036	35.3	2.8	688 018	1.4	33 714	4.9	583 214	34.8	15.8
Osceola	90 414	62.5	124 500	29.5	13.9	1 035	36.2	3.3	155 082	1.3	8 768	5.7	125 760	24.6	20.7
Palm Beach	529 729	70.2	194 600	28.6	15.5	1 158	36.1	3.2	693 635	1.0	34 867	5.0	601 783	35.4	16.1
Pasco	184 806	75.2	115 700	26.3	12.5	919	33.0	2.2	214 802	0.6	12 388	5.8	183 333	34.9	17.3
Pinellas	402 536	65.5	146 500	26.6	14.9	955	33.5	1.8	476 203	0.6	23 111	4.9	416 202	37.1	16.0
Polk	220 556	69.6	107 100	24.9	12.5	870	32.7	3.6	279 903	0.2	17 349	6.2	241 628	29.7	24.4

1. Specified owner-occupied units.   2. A value of 10.0 represents 10 percent or less; a value of 50.0 represents 50 percent or more.   3. Specified renter-occupied units.
4. Overcrowded or lacking complete plumbing facilities.   5. Percent of civilian labor force.   6. Persons 16 years old and over.

Table B. States and Counties — Nonfarm Employment and Agriculture

	Private nonfarm establishments, employment and payroll, 2014									Agriculture, 2012			
		Employment						Annual payroll		Farms			
												Percent with:	
STATE County	Number of establishments	Total	Health care and social assistance	Manufacturing	Retail trade	Finance and insurance	Professional, scientific, and technical services	Total (mil dol)	Average per employee (dollars)	Number	Fewer than 50 acres	500 acres or more	Farm operators whose principal occupation is farming (percent)
	104	105	106	107	108	109	110	111	112	113	114	115	116
CONNECTICUT—Cont'd													
Tolland	2 418	32 223	6 077	3 323	4 892	643	1 173	1 170	36 317	578	64.5	2.4	34.3
Windham	2 052	30 180	7 293	5 655	5 078	694	537	1 176	38 952	692	62.0	3.0	51.3
DELAWARE	24 312	391 636	64 183	25 665	54 479	39 140	33 125	20 919	53 414	2 451	56.5	9.8	63.9
Kent	3 263	49 311	9 676	4 449	9 130	1 675	2 271	1 903	38 583	863	54.5	9.0	56.8
New Castle	15 504	274 816	42 921	12 000	32 443	34 862	27 782	16 521	60 116	374	64.7	9.4	57.8
Sussex	5 340	63 078	11 504	9 216	12 905	1 892	1 844	2 180	34 561	1 214	55.4	10.5	70.8
DISTRICT OF COLUMBIA..	22 210	495 453	66 564	940	21 074	17 363	99 978	36 953	74 585	NA	NA	NA	NA
District of Columbia	22 210	495 453	66 564	940	21 074	17 363	99 978	36 953	74 585	NA	NA	NA	NA
FLORIDA	519 875	7 441 584	1 026 665	290 647	1 026 295	343 371	469 687	312 960	42 056	47 740	68.6	5.6	48.0
Alachua	5 938	85 536	22 726	3 013	13 344	4 078	5 035	3 283	38 377	1 662	69.7	4.9	42.3
Baker	395	5 252	1 767	D	860	126	D	168	31 904	381	74.8	3.4	35.7
Bay	4 461	60 513	9 899	4 744	10 865	1 567	3 383	1 986	32 822	115	71.3	2.6	42.6
Bradford	428	4 076	867	169	927	127	86	118	28 976	470	68.3	1.9	46.0
Brevard	13 348	166 056	29 270	17 305	27 329	5 656	11 772	6 804	40 976	513	80.3	5.1	38.8
Broward	58 549	647 907	87 022	22 542	105 651	31 187	49 794	28 847	44 523	615	93.7	1.3	50.1
Calhoun	192	1 768	637	41	D	76	D	46	26 149	218	51.8	8.3	31.2
Charlotte	3 704	35 818	8 475	492	8 669	1 074	1 380	1 119	31 235	284	61.3	12.0	51.1
Citrus	2 632	26 262	8 364	236	5 452	D	830	871	33 183	559	73.9	3.4	49.7
Clay	3 657	37 630	7 930	1 080	8 518	1 023	2 869	1 179	31 341	403	75.9	2.0	44.7
Collier	11 003	114 225	16 666	2 900	20 412	3 854	4 907	4 690	41 057	319	74.0	10.3	43.9
Columbia	1 316	17 849	4 414	741	3 067	532	469	655	36 695	945	65.4	4.6	46.5
DeSoto	430	5 068	1 145	D	1 046	168	127	167	33 044	836	63.0	9.4	48.4
Dixie	181	1 499	D	454	268	38	25	42	27 825	204	60.3	6.4	30.9
Duval	23 987	417 182	59 384	20 995	49 281	45 699	26 326	20 054	48 071	352	76.4	3.1	59.9
Escambia	6 657	99 633	20 619	4 755	15 434	6 401	6 459	3 750	37 639	729	68.2	4.5	43.2
Flagler	1 928	17 207	2 924	850	3 445	592	553	506	29 406	118	46.6	14.4	54.2
Franklin	313	2 310	281	D	436	58	66	59	25 331	20	65.0	0.0	40.0
Gadsden	636	8 523	2 474	966	1 235	147	116	306	35 848	402	56.5	5.2	39.6
Gilchrist	217	1 453	526	D	179	48	46	46	31 509	581	66.3	5.3	44.8
Glades	111	754	103	D	36	17	D	21	27 369	331	53.5	15.7	39.3
Gulf	283	2 214	499	D	391	D	D	74	33 319	34	41.2	5.9	52.9
Hamilton	174	1 941	204	D	374	D	D	84	43 234	292	36.0	9.6	64.4
Hardee	375	4 377	1 191	308	742	259	D	143	32 738	982	57.3	9.4	50.2
Hendry	548	5 528	1 069	D	1 132	184	215	185	33 411	406	49.8	22.7	51.2
Hernando	3 004	30 578	7 606	1 601	7 248	757	1 173	932	30 465	799	76.0	3.3	51.2
Highlands	1 833	19 520	5 582	720	4 351	568	596	580	29 723	969	64.3	11.0	49.3
Hillsborough	34 020	557 545	74 431	20 768	66 699	47 652	54 540	25 873	46 405	2 466	80.3	2.1	51.7
Holmes	264	1 944	557	103	379	48	81	53	27 025	801	41.7	4.2	52.6
Indian River	4 058	40 165	8 151	1 773	8 704	1 275	1 649	1 453	36 170	461	73.1	7.2	49.0
Jackson	774	8 674	1 781	536	1 908	324	236	257	29 662	1 160	39.0	8.7	42.1
Jefferson	245	1 574	D	D	351	D	58	45	28 686	617	56.1	6.6	37.0
Lafayette	93	746	119	59	153	D	D	17	22 995	221	29.9	13.6	59.7
Lake	6 649	73 167	16 179	2 981	14 800	1 851	2 443	2 340	31 987	1 784	76.7	3.3	43.9
Lee	16 857	193 523	34 032	4 649	37 239	5 488	10 246	7 063	36 496	844	79.5	4.5	48.1
Leon	7 471	95 086	17 252	1 568	16 317	4 434	11 014	3 703	38 945	284	63.4	4.6	38.4
Levy	687	5 199	581	494	1 411	209	160	144	27 729	1 053	64.7	4.4	49.9
Liberty	79	1 289	528	D	D	D	D	36	28 216	80	30.0	5.0	30.0
Madison	315	2 892	649	441	533	75	58	82	28 385	669	36.2	10.3	38.6
Manatee	8 244	89 428	15 424	7 344	17 688	2 669	3 535	3 156	35 296	689	62.6	9.6	43.4
Marion	6 842	76 032	15 900	6 089	15 479	2 020	3 665	2 586	34 011	3 870	76.7	2.2	49.5
Martin	5 201	51 673	9 403	2 848	9 844	1 839	3 128	1 980	38 319	587	74.3	9.7	54.7
Miami-Dade	80 197	919 859	138 427	31 808	135 886	46 786	62 775	41 687	45 318	2 954	92.8	1.2	56.5
Monroe	3 689	30 871	2 501	187	5 658	680	1 024	993	32 175	28	92.9	0.0	25.0
Nassau	1 689	16 169	2 328	1 360	2 939	377	578	563	34 835	444	74.1	2.9	45.0
Okaloosa	5 146	57 515	9 054	D	12 091	2 309	5 977	2 065	35 905	477	62.0	4.8	37.9
Okeechobee	764	6 700	1 379	D	1 571	187	162	209	31 169	678	47.9	25.1	56.6
Orange	34 229	659 812	68 298	25 973	83 151	21 450	45 708	27 855	42 217	662	80.5	4.1	51.8
Osceola	5 340	69 236	10 849	1 627	14 145	1 254	1 629	2 082	30 078	365	58.1	15.9	58.9
Palm Beach	45 323	484 794	77 461	12 290	76 030	22 185	42 286	22 386	46 177	1 409	90.0	3.5	56.7
Pasco	8 884	87 322	18 869	2 990	20 765	2 476	4 212	2 875	32 924	1 065	75.1	5.3	52.1
Pinellas	27 023	363 063	67 654	28 515	50 288	24 339	28 669	15 268	42 054	118	91.5	0.0	45.8
Polk	11 021	171 305	27 107	14 418	24 889	11 348	5 774	6 558	38 285	2 415	64.4	7.2	45.3

Table B. States and Counties — Agriculture

STATE County	Acreage (1,000) [117]	Percent change, 2007–2012 [118]	Average size of farm [119]	Total irrigated (1,000) [120]	Total cropland (1,000) [121]	Average per farm [122]	Average per acre [123]	Value of machinery and equipment, average per farm (dollars) [124]	Total (mil dol) [125]	Average per farm (dollars) [126]	Crops [127]	Live-stock and poultry products [128]	$10,000 or more [129]	$100,000 or more [130]	Total ($1,000) [131]	Percent of farms [132]
CONNECTICUT—Cont'd																
Tolland	48	21.4	83	0.5	18.5	820 254	9 926	78 550	55.0	95 107	64.9	35.1	26.8	8.0	544	7.8
Windham	58	-3.1	84	0.5	20.1	642 272	7 628	58 766	44.2	63 890	40.8	59.2	31.8	7.1	1 259	10.8
DELAWARE	509	-0.3	208	127.3	439.2	1 694 584	8 166	161 559	1 274.0	519 794	33.7	66.3	64.6	41.7	9 677	37.4
Kent	172	-0.9	200	31.8	147.4	1 596 656	7 999	121 074	277.7	321 816	D	D	53.3	29.8	2 550	37.2
New Castle	64	-4.2	172	4.6	56.1	1 704 668	9 935	138 596	75.2	200 957	D	D	51.6	18.7	1 802	31.0
Sussex	272	1.0	224	90.8	235.7	1 761 092	7 853	197 414	921.1	758 755	27.1	72.9	76.7	57.2	5 325	39.5
DISTRICT OF COLUMBIA	NA	NA	NA	NA	NA	NA	NA	NA	NA	NA	NA	NA	NA	NA	NA	NA
District of Columbia	NA	NA	NA	NA	NA	NA	NA	NA	NA	NA	NA	NA	NA	NA	NA	NA
FLORIDA	9 548	3.4	200	1 493.3	2 744.1	1 040 259	5 201	60 838	7 701.5	161 322	77.5	22.5	34.3	10.9	40 164	8.3
Alachua	188	8.8	113	10.7	58.7	608 861	5 383	50 010	101.2	60 865	68.5	31.5	31.5	6.3	654	6.2
Baker	33	23.2	86	0.3	4.4	560 165	6 483	29 995	15.8	41 491	14.9	85.1	20.7	2.1	103	4.2
Bay	10	-15.9	91	D	2.7	473 730	5 193	36 009	2.7	23 635	83.6	16.4	20.0	0.9	65	7.0
Bradford	35	18.4	75	0.7	9.2	312 011	4 181	34 200	13.1	27 962	18.7	81.3	19.1	2.6	52	4.5
Brevard	146	-12.3	286	13.4	19.3	1 545 698	5 414	45 433	46.0	89 651	77.2	22.8	36.8	6.6	142	2.1
Broward	14	65.9	24	1.8	4.3	540 185	22 916	31 886	47.4	77 099	91.2	8.8	41.0	8.6	246	2.9
Calhoun	43	9.6	197	1.6	18.9	417 583	2 124	60 647	19.9	91 096	83.4	16.6	38.0	7.8	332	22.9
Charlotte	217	30.8	765	13.7	18.4	3 875 556	5 067	65 965	103.4	364 088	91.8	8.2	38.0	13.0	92	1.8
Citrus	41	1.3	73	0.7	7.3	480 195	6 621	29 451	14.1	25 190	54.9	45.1	17.7	3.4	146	3.6
Clay	52	24.2	128	0.6	5.2	450 531	3 520	28 380	9.3	22 970	62.8	37.2	17.1	2.2	24	3.2
Collier	124	12.4	387	26.4	66.9	1 736 727	4 482	151 806	202.8	635 583	98.1	1.9	36.4	14.7	207	2.8
Columbia	101	18.0	107	6.1	33.4	486 956	4 536	73 098	108.6	114 893	17.4	82.6	18.0	5.0	709	10.4
DeSoto	303	16.4	362	47.7	62.4	1 701 201	4 696	60 083	198.3	237 166	82.2	17.8	39.4	14.4	196	1.3
Dixie	45	7.6	222	3.4	10.6	873 338	3 943	72 917	19.1	93 686	D	D	20.6	2.9	124	5.4
Duval	28	5.6	80	1.1	5.5	557 054	6 935	32 875	16.2	45 903	75.9	24.1	21.3	2.6	141	5.1
Escambia	75	-9.0	102	4.6	40.1	499 244	4 880	59 298	42.6	58 375	89.4	10.6	18.7	6.0	1 426	24.1
Flagler	44	-25.3	369	3.9	5.5	1 566 102	4 239	60 636	16.9	143 602	91.9	8.1	33.1	11.0	D	2.5
Franklin	2	251.6	90	0.0	0.8	174 150	1 943	48 400	0.6	28 500	44.7	55.4	40.0	10.0	63	30.0
Gadsden	51	7.9	126	2.7	13.1	559 923	4 430	38 505	54.4	135 388	97.7	2.3	23.1	4.5	255	18.2
Gilchrist	84	18.0	144	12.6	43.7	481 217	3 332	62 892	88.7	152 732	31.6	68.4	27.4	7.4	746	12.0
Glades	443	10.0	1 338	88.5	56.5	4 087 441	3 056	84 066	106.5	321 807	73.2	26.8	32.3	14.8	383	7.9
Gulf	5	-3.1	135	D	0.5	565 500	4 184	39 588	0.9	27 147	4.8	95.2	14.7	5.9	D	8.8
Hamilton	72	11.0	246	9.5	28.4	710 452	2 886	87 274	45.5	155 771	80.2	19.8	31.8	9.2	234	31.8
Hardee	274	-2.1	279	36.0	51.8	1 150 569	4 125	52 140	218.4	222 378	66.4	33.6	48.1	20.0	345	2.4
Hendry	496	6.6	1 221	193.1	262.4	4 953 187	4 057	206 352	499.9	1 231 345	95.8	4.2	53.4	31.8	527	5.9
Hernando	62	10.1	78	2.7	15.5	650 753	8 394	38 645	28.4	35 492	56.1	43.9	24.8	6.1	441	1.8
Highlands	490	2.9	506	61.8	84.0	1 484 852	2 937	82 911	273.4	282 121	72.6	27.4	41.4	21.4	609	2.2
Hillsborough	215	-2.2	87	26.1	75.8	788 988	9 052	54 052	378.1	153 316	84.2	15.8	32.5	10.5	865	2.5
Holmes	106	-30.5	132	1.1	34.4	371 996	2 823	42 097	28.9	36 105	46.0	54.0	25.1	7.7	754	26.7
Indian River	162	3.3	352	57.6	54.8	1 359 020	3 856	54 672	144.9	314 419	92.2	7.8	49.7	18.4	809	4.1
Jackson	262	-15.8	226	21.5	117.6	761 272	3 367	65 673	92.7	79 907	81.4	18.6	34.0	11.0	3 805	41.3
Jefferson	130	-12.1	210	2.4	24.6	884 258	4 212	53 783	48.3	78 292	43.6	56.4	25.6	4.7	425	19.0
Lafayette	91	12.3	413	10.7	22.3	1 703 208	4 124	114 973	87.6	396 217	13.0	87.0	39.8	24.0	914	32.6
Lake	152	25.3	85	15.2	36.0	642 919	7 539	34 263	142.1	79 631	94.0	6.0	32.7	9.9	255	1.2
Lee	87	1.6	103	13.6	22.8	979 161	9 485	53 895	105.9	125 478	95.8	4.2	32.8	7.3	61	1.7
Leon	81	-10.4	286	2.0	6.6	1 574 884	5 501	37 673	3.8	13 493	72.7	27.3	22.5	3.5	42	5.6
Levy	167	-3.9	159	13.7	59.8	949 232	5 972	62 627	80.4	76 335	52.4	47.6	32.5	10.8	1 244	8.0
Liberty	14	-40.0	177	D	1.2	479 600	2 705	34 450	1.5	18 750	2.9	97.1	22.5	5.0	39	8.8
Madison	143	-4.0	214	8.1	38.5	719 737	3 367	49 706	51.8	77 463	30.4	69.6	28.4	8.4	520	26.3
Manatee	186	-17.2	271	50.1	70.4	1 512 093	5 590	115 546	298.4	433 160	91.4	8.6	42.4	13.2	11	0.9
Marion	321	20.6	83	13.2	69.8	776 909	9 353	37 481	188.2	48 624	23.3	76.7	27.8	8.2	483	2.1
Martin	139	7.7	237	34.8	43.8	1 561 876	6 581	64 925	165.5	281 862	68.1	31.9	39.0	11.6	398	4.8
Miami-Dade	81	21.3	28	45.2	64.9	699 727	25 423	47 644	604.2	204 549	98.0	2.0	58.5	16.0	6 944	8.5
Monroe	0	154.5	17	0.0	0.1	322 607	18 977	60 036	10.8	386 964	6.0	94.0	50.0	21.4	0	0.0
Nassau	39	25.8	89	0.1	4.9	424 045	4 786	37 444	6.5	14 739	18.7	81.3	14.6	1.1	D	0.9
Okaloosa	61	-6.7	129	0.2	18.6	467 688	3 628	51 556	10.3	21 562	81.1	18.9	21.0	4.4	983	30.8
Okeechobee	442	30.6	652	19.4	52.1	2 992 147	4 592	82 420	256.9	378 876	19.7	80.3	45.0	21.4	2 120	18.1
Orange	132	-2.7	200	9.5	13.8	1 673 992	8 365	56 754	261.6	395 193	96.2	3.8	51.5	26.1	11	0.6
Osceola	547	-15.4	1 499	29.2	29.7	5 917 241	3 948	89 249	108.6	297 660	63.4	36.6	38.9	16.4	326	4.4
Palm Beach	514	-2.2	365	362.7	440.7	2 586 187	7 090	182 476	999.0	709 041	98.3	1.7	43.2	16.2	1 536	6.0
Pasco	171	14.1	161	6.6	24.7	1 086 574	6 763	41 420	73.9	69 351	40.4	59.6	31.2	7.1	355	2.4
Pinellas	1	1.6	13	0.1	0.6	377 805	30 143	43 763	2.6	22 415	72.9	27.1	39.0	4.2	9	5.1
Polk	521	-5.1	216	79.9	125.1	1 182 091	5 480	64 954	350.3	145 042	90.2	9.8	48.1	18.3	419	1.4

STATE County	Water use, 2010		Wholesale trade,[1] 2012				Retail trade,[2] 2012				Real estate and rental and leasing,[2] 2012			
	Total water withdrawn (mil gal/day)	Gallons withdrawn per person per day	Number of establishments	Number of employees	Sales (mil dol)	Annual payroll (mil dol)	Number of establishments	Number of employees	Sales (mil dol)	Annual payroll (mil dol)	Number of establishments	Number of employees	Receipts (mil dol)	Annual payroll (mil dol)
	133	134	135	136	137	138	139	140	141	142	143	144	145	146
CONNECTICUT—Cont'd														
Tolland	15.9	104	55	516	230.0	27.9	373	4 932	1 303.1	120.4	90	312	55.7	9.5
Windham	34.6	292	59	1 048	289.3	48.4	356	4 819	1 296.2	121.2	46	128	20.9	3.7
DELAWARE	717.5	799	835	7 653	5 628.9	385.9	3 616	51 711	14 456.0	1 270.1	1 111	5 402	5 471.2	264.9
Kent	43.3	267	94	D	D	D	561	8 856	2 690.8	214.1	127	459	92.2	17.0
New Castle	404.7	752	589	D	D	D	1 948	30 756	8 623.2	768.5	717	3 548	5 144.4	199.0
Sussex	269.5	1 367	152	1 203	783.4	52.6	1 107	12 099	3 142.1	287.6	267	1 395	234.6	48.9
DISTRICT OF COLUMBIA	0.1	0	335	3 415	2 591.9	260.6	1 710	19 780	4 439.9	525.2	1 112	10 103	3 213.9	673.7
District of Columbia	0.1	0	335	3 415	2 591.9	260.6	1 710	19 780	4 439.9	525.2	1 112	10 103	3 213.9	673.7
FLORIDA	14 936.0	794	27 109	252 418	252 626.6	12 867.6	71 189	947 877	273 867.1	24 033.5	29 845	139 955	30 560.1	5 337.4
Alachua	53.8	218	197	1 852	1 297.5	90.7	929	13 067	3 208.7	283.3	319	1 714	231.1	51.9
Baker	5.2	191	12	D	D	D	69	764	217.3	16.7	12	D	D	D
Bay	301.4	1 785	157	1 460	514.8	63.4	818	10 295	2 728.2	249.7	276	1 402	207.0	39.1
Bradford	4.3	151	15	D	D	D	82	830	241.2	20.2	22	155	9.8	2.1
Brevard	251.4	463	451	3 962	1 846.5	195.7	1 955	24 885	6 527.5	606.1	642	2 056	340.7	66.7
Broward	1 279.1	732	3 902	33 141	33 606.6	1 781.8	7 070	97 344	32 042.9	2 675.4	3 237	17 682	3 934.9	701.7
Calhoun	4.1	281	6	19	4.7	0.6	39	318	70.1	6.7	4	7	0.8	0.1
Charlotte	58.8	367	94	D	D	D	558	8 000	2 091.3	185.9	232	680	113.1	19.1
Citrus	1 201.2	8 505	80	D	D	D	455	5 122	1 421.0	121.8	172	415	54.4	10.4
Clay	23.3	122	105	897	329.7	35.0	580	8 009	1 909.5	182.3	181	584	117.2	18.1
Collier	256.9	799	306	2 417	2 306.5	163.1	1 418	18 924	5 304.1	511.0	907	2 610	546.6	109.8
Columbia	13.7	203	60	760	508.6	33.0	250	2 791	815.9	69.0	51	262	32.0	6.9
DeSoto	97.4	2 793	17	D	D	D	72	1 003	255.4	23.8	22	95	11.8	2.2
Dixie	4.6	280	3	7	0.6	0.1	39	251	56.9	6.0	4	3	0.4	0.0
Duval	758.1	877	1 126	19 090	19 018.9	1 081.3	3 231	45 707	12 985.3	1 164.5	1 204	7 127	1 839.1	321.6
Escambia	311.7	1 047	273	2 534	1 396.3	108.7	1 120	14 671	4 096.3	360.1	339	1 445	287.0	47.8
Flagler	23.4	245	54	239	70.5	10.0	235	3 094	773.3	73.3	137	355	75.7	13.2
Franklin	2.3	198	11	D	D	D	67	403	97.9	8.6	17	117	12.0	4.2
Gadsden	17.8	383	34	787	404.7	27.4	132	1 114	347.3	25.6	19	46	6.6	1.2
Gilchrist	9.1	538	8	44	58.4	2.0	29	178	52.5	3.5	6	13	1.4	0.4
Glades	162.3	12 599	3	D	D	D	13	38	11.7	0.7	2	D	D	D
Gulf	2.3	142	6	12	7.3	0.5	39	341	76.9	7.2	15	58	6.3	1.7
Hamilton	37.5	2 533	4	D	D	D	38	280	78.3	5.0	3	22	0.9	0.3
Hardee	52.4	1 891	19	282	176.8	9.6	76	667	172.1	14.3	21	58	6.1	1.4
Hendry	424.1	10 834	25	D	D	D	101	991	258.1	23.2	24	70	13.0	2.7
Hernando	38.8	225	92	367	149.2	14.4	431	6 620	1 749.4	155.2	138	394	50.4	9.1
Highlands	107.8	1 091	57	D	D	D	316	4 292	1 112.5	100.2	87	264	51.2	7.5
Hillsborough	1 960.7	1 595	1 727	25 316	21 082.8	1 237.1	4 389	63 643	18 274.2	1 670.9	1 848	9 476	2 483.5	414.7
Holmes	4.5	226	11	D	D	D	54	384	104.1	7.7	5	12	0.9	0.2
Indian River	154.5	1 119	125	D	D	D	659	7 958	1 881.3	189.1	231	1 213	162.3	36.9
Jackson	62.8	1 263	22	D	D	D	170	1 799	574.0	40.6	32	82	10.7	1.9
Jefferson	7.3	495	11	D	D	D	42	284	67.3	5.9	8	17	1.3	0.4
Lafayette	6.4	722	7	D	D	D	17	125	46.6	3.3	2	D	D	D
Lake	104.9	353	217	1 208	498.0	42.8	978	13 430	3 761.0	329.6	391	1 476	262.5	45.2
Lee	746.6	1 207	585	5 144	2 481.0	232.6	2 517	34 453	9 445.3	850.6	1 218	3 992	856.4	135.9
Leon	37.6	136	230	2 339	1 763.1	169.7	991	15 309	3 482.4	334.4	395	2 024	283.9	60.1
Levy	32.5	797	30	D	D	D	141	1 342	360.8	31.4	29	67	7.5	1.3
Liberty	1.5	181	2	D	D	D	15	111	30.2	2.3	1	D	D	D
Madison	14.0	730	8	D	D	D	62	447	171.2	9.5	11	19	2.3	0.5
Manatee	126.5	392	304	2 479	1 628.8	122.9	1 136	15 943	4 191.1	378.1	487	1 935	402.6	63.6
Marion	65.4	197	277	3 157	1 719.3	143.3	1 152	14 430	4 263.6	353.9	338	1 382	211.8	41.3
Martin	101.1	691	167	D	D	D	748	9 540	2 553.3	239.1	259	1 581	252.2	57.7
Miami-Dade	461.0	185	8 242	61 377	78 985.4	3 003.6	10 389	123 883	38 361.2	3 252.7	4 776	19 563	4 936.4	811.9
Monroe	1.2	16	88	276	259.4	12.3	639	5 576	1 467.1	149.1	317	948	193.1	30.5
Nassau	50.3	686	41	D	D	D	249	2 663	703.8	63.2	88	D	D	D
Okaloosa	26.3	145	137	1 029	429.7	52.2	850	11 135	2 886.5	266.9	342	1 385	252.9	54.9
Okeechobee	61.9	1 548	29	D	D	D	157	1 518	508.1	38.7	36	94	15.3	2.9
Orange	238.3	208	1 614	19 479	18 498.9	1 016.9	4 677	74 266	23 076.7	1 791.8	2 147	18 232	5 603.4	750.0
Osceola	97.6	363	134	1 288	2 461.0	57.6	845	12 399	3 236.2	272.3	448	4 095	433.7	119.5
Palm Beach	706.5	535	1 933	15 255	12 157.3	888.7	5 236	69 625	19 700.1	1 904.6	2 462	11 445	2 133.8	482.9
Pasco	1 658.8	3 570	303	1 725	709.2	72.5	1 385	18 940	5 278.2	450.4	438	1 432	234.6	41.9
Pinellas	493.0	538	1 122	13 166	12 411.5	703.1	3 562	47 381	14 578.2	1 253.7	1 517	5 979	1 035.5	206.6
Polk	298.7	496	544	8 056	10 601.3	394.0	1 756	22 988	6 495.3	558.8	651	2 928	510.6	93.1

1. Merchant wholesalers, except manufacturers' sales branches and offices. 2. Employer establishments.

Table B. States and Counties — Professional Services, Manufacturing, and Accommodation and Food Services

STATE County	Professional, scientific, and technical services, 2012				Manufacturing, 2012				Accommodation and food services, 2012			
	Number of establishments	Number of employees	Receipts (mil dol)	Annual payroll (mil dol)	Number of establishments	Number of employees	Receipts (mil dol)	Annual payroll (mil dol)	Number of establishments	Number of employees	Sales (mil dol)	Annual payroll (mil dol)
	147	148	149	150	151	152	153	154	155	156	157	158
CONNECTICUT—Cont'd												
Tolland	189	1 152	166.2	65.5	134	3 251	903.6	179.2	221	3 719	219.1	57.1
Windham	130	D	D	D	170	5 549	2 146.1	293.6	234	2 827	158.6	44.6
DELAWARE	2 543	D	D	D	573	26 355	22 597.4	1 393.2	1 987	35 609	2 148.4	566.7
Kent	278	D	D	D	74	4 797	1 930.8	218.9	272	6 183	475.8	101.1
New Castle	1 912	D	D	D	364	12 721	17 046.7	856.3	1 102	20 628	1 128.3	312.6
Sussex	353	D	D	D	135	8 837	3 619.9	318.0	613	8 798	544.3	152.9
DISTRICT OF COLUMBIA	5 061	97 555	31 866.3	11 196.4	113	1 361	309.8	61.5	2 371	60 370	5 101.6	1 504.8
District of Columbia	5 061	97 555	31 866.3	11 196.4	113	1 361	309.8	61.5	2 371	60 370	5 101.6	1 504.8
FLORIDA	70 785	440 858	70 175.6	27 100.4	12 890	277 089	96 924.1	14 270.0	37 118	786 082	49 817.9	13 598.2
Alachua	819	4 648	547.7	219.4	149	3 166	D	167.8	569	D	D	D
Baker	20	100	8.6	3.1	4	126	D	D	35	581	23.7	6.4
Bay	407	3 335	466.0	177.0	100	3 840	1 473.8	195.3	465	9 994	565.2	161.3
Bradford	32	94	7.1	2.6	11	137	5.5	5.5	38	531	28.1	6.7
Brevard	1 669	13 893	2 433.6	981.2	407	19 152	5 441.9	1 311.3	1 042	18 994	902.6	257.7
Broward	9 583	46 815	8 286.6	2 833.0	1 454	21 057	6 010.6	1 054.7	3 685	72 428	5 129.2	1 322.2
Calhoun	8	32	2.1	1.3	7	51	D	1.6	14	D	D	D
Charlotte	381	1 295	138.5	50.5	69	402	90.4	14.6	261	4 804	219.2	61.7
Citrus	254	891	106.3	35.8	44	203	35.8	7.2	191	2 362	114.6	32.2
Clay	394	D	D	D	73	927	D	D	271	5 095	238.5	67.4
Collier	1 342	4 810	784.7	270.4	197	2 722	607.5	130.0	763	19 624	1 406.5	404.2
Columbia	113	433	43.7	14.4	42	608	249.0	26.7	116	2 331	106.6	29.5
DeSoto	32	114	15.1	3.7	8	235	D	11.4	31	402	19.6	5.2
Dixie	9	D	D	D	7	418	D	14.9	18	145	7.3	1.7
Duval	3 166	29 737	5 572.2	2 176.5	598	21 699	10 158.2	1 256.0	1 930	37 804	2 016.5	558.9
Escambia	774	7 159	939.6	359.4	174	4 026	2 427.8	242.5	558	11 548	598.4	162.5
Flagler	206	462	74.0	20.1	45	591	D	26.7	155	4 248	238.7	80.8
Franklin	27	52	7.8	2.3	NA	NA	NA	NA	45	555	28.8	9.0
Gadsden	36	D	D	D	31	840	178.6	31.9	53	559	28.8	7.7
Gilchrist	22	65	5.5	1.7	9	104	D	2.0	9	D	D	D
Glades	7	D	D	D	5	103	D	5.6	10	103	4.7	1.1
Gulf	27	130	27.8	7.2	10	64	8.6	2.2	32	324	16.5	4.4
Hamilton	9	22	1.9	0.5	5	D	D	D	16	165	6.1	1.7
Hardee	24	71	4.4	1.5	8	253	D	7.6	28	364	17.2	4.2
Hendry	40	D	D	D	20	887	D	44.0	65	760	37.4	9.3
Hernando	280	1 144	102.8	34.6	85	1 490	326.4	59.4	248	3 936	193.1	54.7
Highlands	132	602	57.5	18.4	44	570	214.0	22.7	147	2 331	110.6	30.7
Hillsborough	5 216	52 511	8 442.1	3 624.5	786	19 144	9 341.8	914.9	2 329	49 344	3 410.9	839.4
Holmes	17	87	14.8	3.3	14	103	14.6	3.9	16	203	9.4	2.4
Indian River	454	1 601	229.1	84.3	84	1 487	D	68.7	250	4 351	225.1	66.2
Jackson	43	233	22.7	9.5	16	459	D	18.0	70	1 044	52.2	11.9
Jefferson	17	49	5.4	1.6	4	D	D	D	17	D	D	D
Lafayette	8	D	D	D	4	62	D	2.1	7	D	D	D
Lake	622	2 090	238.2	87.7	145	2 439	D	99.3	451	8 045	394.9	109.9
Lee	1 893	12 312	2 202.7	844.3	366	4 010	812.8	165.1	1 189	25 851	1 346.6	402.6
Leon	1 363	11 176	1 519.5	766.3	97	1 462	400.0	72.0	644	13 783	629.0	170.3
Levy	42	149	15.8	4.8	20	385	D	13.9	66	661	28.8	7.9
Liberty	5	D	D	D	4	271	138.7	11.8	4	47	2.0	0.5
Madison	19	65	5.8	2.4	12	367	181.0	16.6	22	276	13.9	4.3
Manatee	928	12 131	728.3	402.2	283	8 121	2 338.0	403.9	593	9 987	532.9	155.6
Marion	669	3 676	415.5	157.2	178	4 806	1 471.2	212.9	437	7 369	375.2	102.5
Martin	697	3 071	403.4	149.0	162	2 869	1 103.3	151.9	334	6 215	312.7	91.6
Miami-Dade	12 008	58 711	11 734.8	4 018.8	2 070	30 387	7 192.9	1 318.2	5 052	104 467	7 696.6	2 078.4
Monroe	360	1 064	165.2	53.0	49	177	26.5	6.2	511	11 414	1 002.8	275.8
Nassau	184	559	80.2	28.5	37	1 239	929.1	80.9	158	3 378	203.3	71.5
Okaloosa	613	6 033	918.6	391.1	86	2 719	D	135.1	462	10 900	566.3	167.5
Okeechobee	45	164	15.4	4.9	17	197	D	6.8	56	912	40.1	10.3
Orange	4 882	44 689	6 856.9	3 044.6	747	23 702	8 280.9	1 531.7	2 715	102 733	8 326.4	2 131.0
Osceola	428	1 862	237.0	82.6	87	1 078	D	41.5	542	13 348	866.9	237.9
Palm Beach	7 364	36 924	6 189.1	2 368.7	928	11 731	3 550.4	614.2	2 665	57 739	3 467.3	1 044.3
Pasco	978	4 249	511.1	176.0	223	2 839	743.9	130.7	608	10 473	503.4	145.1
Pinellas	3 973	27 841	3 846.9	1 490.2	1 027	28 305	8 411.6	1 478.1	2 090	36 887	2 193.1	607.3
Polk	1 036	6 724	768.7	300.4	401	14 200	9 822.2	681.0	788	15 188	797.9	220.1

1. Establishment subject to federal tax.

STATE County	Health care and social assistance, 2012				Other services, 2012				Nonemployer businesses, 2014		Value of residential construction authorized by building permits, 2015	
	Number of establishments	Number of employees	Receipts (mil dol)	Annual payroll (mil dol)	Number of establishments	Number of employees	Receipts (mil dol)	Annual payroll (mil dol)	Number	Receipts (mil dol)	New Construction ($1,000)	Number of housing units
	159	160	161	162	163	164	165	166	167	168	169	170
CONNECTICUT—Cont'd												
Tolland	302	5 920	501.9	227.1	188	1 110	141.8	37.2	9 330	450.1	62 835	388
Windham	269	7 584	590.7	280.9	182	728	74.7	17.8	6 631	298.4	14 456	93
DELAWARE	2 524	61 897	7 003.3	2 995.9	1 513	9 841	974.7	290.1	59 078	3 531.5	641 676	5 221
Kent	398	9 405	990.6	379.5	233	1 325	105.5	32.0	9 359	536.4	144 720	1 061
New Castle	1 603	41 861	4 843.5	2 154.2	931	6 651	703.0	207.5	34 393	2 215.0	146 268	1 713
Sussex	523	10 631	1 169.2	462.2	349	1 865	166.2	50.6	15 326	780.1	350 688	2 447
DISTRICT OF COLUMBIA	2 065	67 742	8 964.0	3 596.5	3 357	58 982	19 773.5	4 238.6	55 013	2 676.8	495 021	4 956
District of Columbia	2 065	67 742	8 964.0	3 596.5	3 357	58 982	19 773.5	4 238.6	55 013	2 676.8	495 021	4 956
FLORIDA	56 659	991 254	124 061.4	44 435.6	34 843	195 176	20 798.9	5 414.5	1 948 357	84 606.9	23 439 129	109 924
Alachua	736	21 940	2 707.5	1 027.7	384	2 650	463.7	92.8	17 251	665.7	143 709	1 171
Baker	38	1 783	117.8	66.7	32	D	D	D	1 209	39.6	6 141	39
Bay	490	9 575	1 034.4	396.1	305	1 892	157.5	42.5	13 265	633.6	223 172	884
Bradford	39	831	80.0	25.6	24	86	7.2	2.0	1 198	46.8	0	0
Brevard	1 522	31 218	3 727.6	1 387.7	958	4 563	372.7	117.7	41 106	1 616.9	557 448	1 918
Broward	6 273	89 756	12 193.7	4 272.6	4 124	21 448	2 245.9	602.5	239 667	10 096.9	807 553	5 452
Calhoun	29	475	40.6	14.1	7	37	3.6	0.8	759	26.5	869	8
Charlotte	485	8 927	1 119.6	401.0	297	1 326	113.0	33.0	12 454	571.3	246 218	1 129
Citrus	390	7 932	819.7	307.1	212	744	53.2	15.5	8 882	345.3	86 746	378
Clay	448	7 152	825.0	300.2	280	D	D	D	12 351	480.4	185 840	982
Collier	995	16 310	2 089.4	772.0	850	5 209	474.4	138.1	36 864	2 165.4	1 275 698	4 060
Columbia	175	4 387	567.3	215.6	70	299	27.1	6.3	3 851	167.6	11 990	80
DeSoto	44	1 009	96.8	38.3	25	78	4.4	1.5	1 584	61.3	17 800	118
Dixie	14	136	9.1	3.4	14	46	4.9	0.8	787	29.6	3 348	26
Duval	2 513	55 950	7 324.9	2 580.2	1 612	D	D	D	65 791	2 563.7	781 026	4 514
Escambia	758	20 561	2 476.2	948.2	439	2 685	260.9	73.5	20 404	838.7	192 801	1 392
Flagler	196	2 629	336.2	106.8	136	533	40.6	10.7	8 564	400.8	185 562	587
Franklin	21	303	22.2	8.1	15	59	4.1	1.4	1 296	53.8	12 047	55
Gadsden	54	2 437	155.6	99.5	32	111	9.1	2.6	2 949	91.2	8 781	38
Gilchrist	21	497	45.1	15.8	8	14	1.5	0.4	914	34.2	5 309	43
Glades	7	D	D	D	6	D	D	D	547	18.9	1 757	15
Gulf	25	476	43.8	16.4	16	44	3.0	0.9	1 133	54.4	23 196	104
Hamilton	17	D	D	D	13	41	3.8	1.1	576	21.2	2 212	22
Hardee	57	1 123	82.0	35.7	29	60	4.3	1.1	1 286	58.6	2 709	17
Hendry	69	1 081	85.1	35.8	46	172	13.0	3.7	2 786	92.0	7 909	87
Hernando	507	7 744	984.0	302.9	212	1 008	71.4	21.5	10 359	402.0	75 760	431
Highlands	325	5 021	576.5	194.8	134	504	37.4	9.1	5 835	232.1	33 229	162
Hillsborough	3 703	72 572	10 416.0	3 584.0	2 080	14 640	1 646.3	432.3	111 522	4 951.0	2 432 798	9 486
Holmes	33	511	36.0	12.2	14	49	3.1	1.1	1 087	36.7	3 009	19
Indian River	466	7 828	886.2	333.8	280	1 395	124.5	34.6	12 995	734.4	339 050	873
Jackson	83	1 796	157.4	64.3	53	225	22.9	6.0	2 748	84.8	6 088	35
Jefferson	26	238	12.0	5.1	12	31	2.0	0.5	1 049	33.6	4 554	27
Lafayette	11	135	7.7	3.4	3	D	D	D	327	12.1	2 009	10
Lake	825	15 150	1 648.7	639.5	449	2 246	194.7	57.9	23 544	914.3	727 651	2 778
Lee	1 488	26 009	3 362.1	1 226.1	1 209	6 696	580.1	164.2	61 657	2 964.1	1 380 982	6 879
Leon	745	16 817	1 893.7	744.3	615	4 445	666.4	170.7	20 054	804.9	118 914	695
Levy	62	566	35.3	14.5	48	111	13.2	2.3	2 715	120.0	7 433	49
Liberty	10	D	D	D	3	13	2.2	0.5	391	10.3	1 768	15
Madison	39	648	42.5	17.2	17	D	D	D	999	39.4	4 390	35
Manatee	877	14 956	1 512.5	582.0	534	2 743	196.5	59.5	28 247	1 322.6	707 131	3 619
Marion	878	15 494	1 874.0	674.9	455	2 315	196.6	54.0	23 622	978.3	195 638	1 055
Martin	536	8 591	946.3	388.8	399	2 032	181.9	54.8	15 261	820.4	184 772	412
Miami-Dade	9 030	132 886	17 547.4	6 100.1	4 903	28 561	3 116.7	758.0	435 368	18 064.5	2 331 082	12 617
Monroe	225	2 464	323.1	109.9	252	1 060	106.9	32.0	12 157	723.3	81 864	262
Nassau	168	2 337	230.5	89.6	123	D	D	D	5 627	266.9	257 768	1 110
Okaloosa	545	8 715	1 111.1	373.8	348	1 683	146.0	44.2	15 010	755.6	200 292	702
Okeechobee	99	1 305	162.4	52.9	54	225	17.6	5.0	2 201	83.0	20 547	69
Orange	3 056	66 554	8 920.9	3 080.9	2 033	15 498	1 676.9	435.9	117 912	4 731.0	1 324 172	9 606
Osceola	540	10 184	1 301.7	460.0	330	1 364	155.8	30.6	27 895	941.4	1 251 496	6 760
Palm Beach	5 319	75 097	9 756.7	3 371.0	3 204	18 011	1 831.0	493.9	162 115	8 251.7	1 359 567	5 381
Pasco	1 160	17 932	2 142.5	771.5	640	2 765	231.7	66.4	33 127	1 319.5	474 357	2 639
Pinellas	3 215	64 140	7 744.4	2 913.0	1 924	10 377	1 033.2	292.6	79 799	3 657.2	642 613	3 097
Polk	1 048	27 066	3 015.2	1 109.8	673	3 366	328.5	94.6	40 327	1 524.1	584 385	3 039

Table B. States and Counties — Government Employment and Payroll, and Local Government Finances

STATE County	Full-time equivalent employees	March payroll (dollars)	Administration, judicial, and legal	Police and Corrections	Fire Protection	Highways and transportation	Health and Welfare	Natural resources and utilities	Education and libraries	Total (mil dol)	Inter-governmental (mil dol)	Taxes Total (mil dol)	Taxes Per capita Total	Taxes Per capita Property
	171	172	173	174	175	176	177	178	179	180	181	182	183	184
CONNECTICUT—Cont'd														
Tolland	4 711	21 137 708	4.8	2.7	1.1	3.4	2.1	2.9	81.0	531.4	189.3	302.4	1 996	1 971
Windham	3 899	15 623 446	4.2	2.5	1.2	4.0	0.5	3.9	82.0	430.6	207.6	189.4	1 611	1 586
DELAWARE	X	X	X	X	X	X	X	X	X	X	X	X	X	X
Kent	4 210	17 226 252	4.7	6.0	0.1	0.6	1.6	5.6	79.4	494.8	323.1	88.0	525	459
New Castle	13 350	61 131 759	5.7	9.5	1.4	3.2	2.2	5.4	70.9	1 685.7	768.1	591.4	1 083	883
Sussex	5 143	20 898 662	5.1	4.6	0.0	1.2	3.3	4.3	80.0	633.4	356.0	169.5	833	671
DISTRICT OF COLUMBIA	X	X	X	X	X	X	X	X	X	X	X	X	X	X
District of Columbia	44 423	263 772 974	11.1	14.2	4.3	27.8	12.5	5.9	19.0	11 142.1	3 474.2	5 933.8	9 384	2 970
FLORIDA	X	X	X	X	X	X	X	X	X	X	X	X	X	X
Alachua	9 411	34 346 743	10.1	15.9	4.6	4.8	3.1	12.0	45.8	854.0	266.5	363.0	1 444	1 113
Baker	867	2 564 944	5.5	3.7	1.2	2.9	5.4	3.6	77.0	73.2	44.3	18.9	699	507
Bay	8 014	30 150 146	3.2	6.0	2.6	3.8	35.9	4.9	42.5	823.2	190.5	261.0	1 518	1 060
Bradford	881	2 067 161	5.4	1.3	0.4	2.7	7.1	1.3	75.8	71.8	37.9	23.1	853	598
Brevard	19 755	66 076 682	7.5	12.3	7.0	4.4	7.8	7.9	52.0	1 764.4	557.0	634.8	1 160	923
Broward	73 864	331 154 408	5.1	13.2	6.2	3.7	29.6	6.0	33.6	9 918.0	2 186.8	3 161.3	1 742	1 392
Calhoun	510	1 309 655	4.9	3.6	0.2	5.5	0.9	3.7	80.8	46.1	34.0	8.6	581	443
Charlotte	4 654	16 650 878	13.2	15.5	8.9	5.6	2.0	7.8	45.5	559.2	101.1	264.1	1 626	1 290
Citrus	3 890	11 674 757	8.6	11.3	0.1	3.6	5.4	3.4	65.1	322.4	98.7	162.1	1 163	1 064
Clay	6 995	21 858 185	5.6	10.0	3.5	1.9	1.2	5.5	71.3	556.6	210.2	185.3	953	696
Collier	9 918	41 162 175	6.9	15.7	6.7	3.5	4.2	9.1	52.0	1 300.6	231.7	737.4	2 218	2 006
Columbia	2 446	7 323 140	6.4	8.1	2.5	3.8	3.8	3.8	69.3	195.9	99.6	58.8	865	641
DeSoto	1 506	4 657 631	3.9	13.7	4.7	2.2	25.3	4.7	44.3	123.0	39.7	31.6	911	665
Dixie	584	1 731 414	9.6	25.5	0.3	3.8	8.6	2.7	49.0	42.4	22.0	12.7	789	669
Duval	26 681	104 173 723	5.7	15.6	6.2	2.1	1.2	7.3	52.4	3 353.2	1 044.0	1 351.0	1 536	1 039
Escambia	10 348	32 971 310	5.4	14.5	2.6	2.7	4.7	8.0	59.2	937.6	348.0	338.3	1 118	772
Flagler	2 869	10 004 315	13.0	9.5	8.0	1.8	3.2	8.7	53.9	286.1	72.0	141.3	1 437	1 235
Franklin	399	1 124 749	9.6	10.0	1.7	7.1	5.5	9.5	54.3	60.6	21.8	24.9	2 130	1 812
Gadsden	1 850	4 901 351	12.9	12.9	1.7	6.4	3.2	4.9	56.6	109.5	61.3	33.5	721	528
Gilchrist	624	1 705 173	8.0	8.7	0.9	3.7	4.8	1.4	69.5	43.8	24.4	13.1	781	660
Glades	401	1 250 845	13.0	0.2	0.5	3.3	5.2	7.6	67.4	65.1	17.5	12.8	974	884
Gulf	661	1 888 717	10.9	17.7	0.2	5.5	8.9	6.1	46.3	58.3	19.3	27.3	1 735	1 504
Hamilton	602	1 883 338	4.3	14.6	0.6	4.0	4.1	19.8	50.0	60.4	31.4	21.4	1 452	1 298
Hardee	1 238	3 660 532	9.3	12.4	2.4	3.4	4.4	4.8	59.9	83.9	40.3	30.3	1 103	950
Hendry	1 671	5 341 045	10.9	8.7	1.0	3.6	17.8	12.2	43.4	156.7	60.3	45.0	1 201	842
Hernando	5 261	17 523 253	4.9	11.1	6.5	1.8	0.9	20.4	52.8	557.9	169.7	301.2	1 737	1 597
Highlands	3 358	10 445 615	8.2	12.8	2.4	5.5	3.7	6.4	56.9	264.2	111.3	100.2	1 021	799
Hillsborough	45 811	168 419 971	6.8	14.7	5.5	5.2	2.8	7.1	56.0	4 882.0	2 046.8	1 736.7	1 359	996
Holmes	889	2 422 344	5.2	5.1	0.0	3.5	20.9	5.0	58.1	71.8	52.9	10.8	548	332
Indian River	4 188	14 858 891	4.7	16.3	4.8	5.0	5.1	12.6	48.7	445.1	88.8	266.5	1 896	1 553
Jackson	2 760	8 398 373	4.9	6.0	2.2	2.8	34.8	2.6	46.1	203.4	76.8	40.3	823	456
Jefferson	365	927 774	7.8	2.9	2.0	7.8	9.8	3.9	63.2	30.2	13.1	12.4	871	675
Lafayette	373	1 167 432	11.8	22.1	0.0	1.9	8.3	6.2	48.5	18.5	10.9	4.9	555	451
Lake	10 347	30 892 756	6.4	14.3	6.8	2.9	1.5	7.4	57.3	851.0	286.9	352.0	1 161	905
Lee	29 739	118 190 826	4.0	7.9	5.4	3.4	39.4	4.7	33.6	3 672.5	586.2	1 065.4	1 651	1 448
Leon	11 335	40 616 545	8.8	12.0	3.5	5.4	3.6	15.1	47.5	1 138.8	359.2	388.1	1 368	952
Levy	1 489	4 220 044	6.6	13.3	0.6	4.8	6.8	4.6	61.2	107.5	52.0	38.2	954	772
Liberty	390	1 120 616	1.3	0.1	28.3	3.3	4.3	2.5	59.6	26.9	19.5	5.1	613	482
Madison	949	2 696 175	4.6	8.3	1.1	3.0	18.6	2.7	58.5	73.1	37.0	16.5	874	617
Manatee	11 893	40 190 709	10.2	12.9	5.6	2.7	2.6	5.6	58.7	1 162.4	346.0	503.0	1 507	1 276
Marion	10 760	33 096 942	6.2	11.8	9.0	0.5	2.5	5.9	63.0	875.9	312.2	296.0	883	746
Martin	4 603	17 106 522	8.9	17.9	12.8	2.6	1.6	5.7	48.8	500.0	104.9	304.6	2 047	1 811
Miami-Dade	102 308	498 941 928	4.9	14.9	6.0	5.9	20.8	6.6	32.3	14 058.6	3 695.7	5 524.1	2 132	1 564
Monroe	3 585	14 624 150	5.7	22.6	8.9	2.9	3.9	19.5	34.7	567.8	118.5	263.2	3 519	2 437
Nassau	1 980	6 570 847	4.2	2.9	11.2	4.6	1.0	4.9	66.5	222.9	55.5	123.9	1 660	1 424
Okaloosa	6 391	22 546 268	5.1	9.5	4.5	3.0	2.3	7.4	65.4	596.0	213.5	239.6	1 260	1 023
Okeechobee	1 527	4 441 541	4.9	15.8	5.3	1.7	1.2	7.3	62.2	123.6	58.3	42.0	1 065	682
Orange	45 111	168 174 502	6.0	14.3	7.4	5.4	6.3	9.8	48.0	5 410.1	1 451.5	2 181.6	1 815	1 273
Osceola	10 876	36 955 599	7.4	13.0	6.2	2.3	1.1	9.5	58.0	1 052.2	358.1	406.0	1 412	1 006
Palm Beach	46 198	195 497 482	7.6	16.4	10.2	2.6	5.1	13.1	41.6	6 353.4	1 180.9	3 449.0	2 542	2 211
Pasco	14 918	46 238 730	6.6	11.6	5.0	1.2	1.2	4.8	67.1	1 276.0	533.4	417.6	888	715
Pinellas	32 162	118 407 394	7.7	19.5	5.8	3.8	3.8	10.1	45.5	3 227.6	836.8	1 470.9	1 597	1 224
Polk	22 910	75 047 946	7.9	12.5	4.2	2.1	2.6	10.6	56.6	1 844.2	710.5	644.8	1 047	726

1. Based on the resident population estimated as of July 1 of the year shown.

Table B. States and Counties — Local Government Finances, Government Employment, and Voting

	Local government finances, 2012 (cont.)									Government employment, 2014			Presidential election,[2] 2012		
	Direct general expenditure							Debt outstanding					Percent of vote cast:		
			Percent of total for:												
STATE County	Total (mil dol)	Per capita[1] (dollars)	Education	Health and hospitals	Police protection	Public welfare	Highways	Total (mil dol)	Per capita[1] (dollars)	Federal civilian	Federal military	State and local	Democratic	Republican	All other
	185	186	187	188	189	190	191	192	193	194	195	196	197	198	199
CONNECTICUT—Cont'd															
Tolland	554.3	3 658	66.0	0.7	2.3	0.3	5.5	321.3	2 121	258	320	15 787	59.6	38.8	1.6
Windham	416.8	3 544	69.2	0.6	2.8	0.4	4.7	176.2	1 498	270	228	7 994	60.7	37.7	1.6
DELAWARE	X	X	X	X	X	X	X	X	X	5 538	8 922	60 176	61.9	36.9	1.1
Kent	527.3	3 145	73.4	1.1	4.4	0.0	1.5	478.7	2 856	1 728	4 389	17 564	54.4	44.6	1.1
New Castle	1 812.2	3 319	59.7	0.8	7.5	0.0	2.5	1 735.3	3 178	3 289	3 245	34 494	69.7	29.1	1.2
Sussex	613.0	3 014	69.2	2.1	4.3	0.1	1.7	515.0	2 532	521	1 288	8 118	45.2	53.8	0.9
DISTRICT OF COLUMBIA..	X	X	X	X	X	X	X	X	X	198 136	14 855	38 615	92.5	6.5	1.0
District of Columbia	10 765.0	17 025	22.0	6.3	5.2	26.6	4.9	13 246.6	20 949	198 136	14 855	38 615	92.5	6.5	1.0
FLORIDA	X	X	X	X	X	X	X	X	X	131 781	95 866	930 241	51.0	48.2	0.8
Alachua	900.5	3 582	38.5	3.8	8.3	1.7	4.6	1 948.7	7 751	4 476	551	37 977	60.2	38.6	1.1
Baker	88.4	3 262	47.4	4.9	5.7	1.3	10.3	18.5	682	58	47	2 497	21.0	78.4	0.5
Bay	927.6	5 396	32.4	24.5	6.6	0.0	4.4	885.7	5 152	3 607	4 176	8 660	29.2	69.9	1.0
Bradford	72.8	2 691	44.9	6.1	6.5	0.0	6.2	13.5	501	33	44	1 941	29.4	69.7	0.9
Brevard	1 830.9	3 345	36.4	11.6	7.9	0.4	4.3	1 872.2	3 421	6 157	2 836	22 388	44.3	54.7	0.9
Broward	10 214.0	5 627	24.6	26.3	10.2	1.2	1.4	8 639.5	4 760	6 967	3 957	93 722	67.1	32.4	0.5
Calhoun	49.3	3 348	43.9	2.4	5.2	0.1	28.4	3.8	256	23	24	938	29.2	69.6	1.2
Charlotte	563.6	3 470	33.1	3.8	11.0	1.5	11.1	628.4	3 868	323	314	5 408	45.8	53.1	1.1
Citrus	362.7	2 602	47.4	5.5	9.1	2.5	6.6	493.5	3 541	213	280	4 171	41.3	57.4	1.3
Clay	560.4	2 884	52.3	0.7	8.2	0.5	6.0	488.9	2 515	332	393	6 753	28.2	71.1	0.7
Collier	1 313.8	3 952	37.5	3.0	12.1	0.6	6.0	2 257.5	6 791	628	651	12 032	38.3	60.8	0.8
Columbia	210.8	3 101	53.8	3.7	6.1	0.1	6.0	94.4	1 389	1 333	120	4 283	32.6	66.4	1.0
DeSoto	129.0	3 717	35.1	28.2	5.2	0.4	2.7	71.9	2 070	49	59	1 710	43.3	55.6	1.1
Dixie	42.5	2 637	45.4	10.3	7.8	0.0	6.5	11.2	694	11	27	942	26.5	71.5	2.0
Duval	3 336.4	3 793	39.0	1.9	9.4	1.4	4.4	11 704.3	13 306	15 425	13 869	36 825	48.7	50.6	0.6
Escambia	1 097.8	3 627	40.4	3.3	6.7	0.2	4.3	1 910.8	6 312	5 797	12 253	15 309	39.9	59.2	0.9
Flagler	307.1	3 122	38.2	1.4	7.1	0.2	6.7	437.4	4 447	131	192	3 437	50.4	48.8	0.7
Franklin	62.9	5 386	27.2	14.8	10.5	0.2	5.5	56.4	4 826	15	19	1 002	35.4	63.3	1.3
Gadsden	120.4	2 588	50.5	4.7	7.8	0.8	7.5	55.7	1 197	93	81	4 464	69.2	30.3	0.5
Gilchrist	44.2	2 629	55.7	5.0	6.8	0.4	8.4	4.7	282	31	30	1 073	25.5	72.3	2.1
Glades	69.5	5 305	21.6	4.0	6.8	0.1	6.4	202.1	15 417	17	23	467	41.1	57.7	1.2
Gulf	59.6	3 791	32.4	9.7	5.8	0.4	7.6	52.0	3 310	13	23	1 195	29.8	69.1	1.1
Hamilton	59.7	4 061	31.9	3.6	5.9	0.1	5.3	3.7	253	27	22	1 088	42.3	56.9	0.8
Hardee	86.6	3 149	54.2	4.1	11.3	0.2	5.3	9.9	360	45	48	1 622	34.6	64.3	1.1
Hendry	180.1	4 810	32.7	25.6	7.7	0.4	3.5	74.6	1 991	73	71	2 045	45.9	53.1	0.9
Hernando	566.7	3 268	33.0	2.6	5.9	0.1	3.9	365.6	2 108	300	330	5 624	47.7	51.2	1.1
Highlands	276.6	2 818	46.6	3.7	7.8	0.6	6.0	143.0	1 457	252	182	3 745	40.5	58.6	1.0
Hillsborough	5 230.4	4 093	38.8	3.2	7.5	2.6	3.9	6 006.8	4 701	14 314	8 202	65 972	53.2	46.0	0.8
Holmes	71.5	3 610	38.8	22.5	3.3	0.1	8.7	33.4	1 686	60	35	1 340	16.8	81.9	1.3
Indian River	470.0	3 343	38.2	4.8	9.4	0.8	8.2	436.2	3 103	336	271	4 684	42.1	56.9	1.0
Jackson	226.5	4 626	38.1	33.8	3.4	0.0	8.3	82.2	1 680	483	76	4 753	35.6	63.6	0.8
Jefferson	31.4	2 204	37.8	7.2	14.4	0.5	9.5	3.9	274	35	24	710	51.4	47.7	0.9
Lafayette	19.1	2 172	55.0	7.9	4.8	0.6	8.7	1.7	189	15	13	628	19.1	79.8	1.1
Lake	925.8	3 054	40.3	3.7	8.1	0.5	5.1	1 090.4	3 596	553	590	12 362	42.8	56.4	0.8
Lee	3 730.8	5 782	25.4	32.3	4.8	0.5	3.9	5 119.6	7 934	2 526	1 334	36 328	44.5	54.8	0.7
Leon	1 138.4	4 012	38.2	0.6	7.6	0.0	7.4	4 257.0	15 002	1 742	600	52 043	61.7	37.5	0.8
Levy	112.3	2 806	46.8	5.0	8.6	0.8	9.0	30.9	772	67	101	1 755	35.8	62.8	1.4
Liberty	27.8	3 361	51.9	8.1	3.7	0.3	10.1	4.7	568	36	12	752	27.3	71.4	1.3
Madison	78.8	4 166	46.8	15.6	5.2	0.4	9.1	16.3	861	39	31	1 369	47.9	51.0	1.0
Manatee	1 227.1	3 675	40.6	2.5	8.5	0.7	4.4	1 359.0	4 070	899	685	10 930	46.1	53.1	0.8
Marion	879.1	2 623	48.9	2.0	7.6	0.7	6.3	732.6	2 186	673	626	13 955	43.7	55.3	1.0
Martin	526.0	3 534	36.8	8.1	9.7	2.3	3.4	296.9	1 995	264	283	5 459	42.8	56.4	0.8
Miami-Dade	14 468.1	5 584	25.8	12.2	7.5	3.5	2.2	23 549.3	9 089	19 667	7 330	118 785	57.9	41.8	0.4
Monroe	536.4	7 170	22.9	4.6	11.0	0.5	2.3	1 453.0	19 423	1 173	1 440	4 454	51.9	47.0	1.1
Nassau	230.5	3 089	41.0	5.2	7.0	0.2	6.7	231.3	3 100	564	144	2 741	27.7	71.5	0.7
Okaloosa	687.4	3 616	51.5	2.4	6.6	0.3	2.9	368.2	1 937	8 164	16 647	7 900	27.1	72.0	0.9
Okeechobee	121.9	3 087	49.3	2.5	8.0	0.7	4.0	78.4	1 987	68	69	2 057	39.9	59.1	0.9
Orange	5 320.5	4 426	36.8	4.6	7.1	0.7	4.0	9 996.1	8 315	10 699	2 644	61 828	59.0	40.4	0.6
Osceola	1 153.9	4 015	42.2	1.2	7.2	1.7	8.7	2 678.5	9 319	366	581	11 799	59.6	39.8	0.6
Palm Beach	6 575.2	4 847	27.6	4.7	9.3	2.5	2.5	7 440.3	5 485	6 611	2 756	54 621	61.2	38.3	0.5
Pasco	1 277.5	2 716	49.4	2.0	7.9	0.8	5.8	1 324.5	2 816	735	907	15 722	47.7	51.2	1.1
Pinellas	3 402.6	3 693	34.6	4.2	11.2	3.0	4.2	3 555.7	3 859	6 881	2 836	36 841	53.6	45.3	1.1
Polk	1 992.7	3 234	48.6	3.2	8.2	1.6	5.5	2 776.3	4 506	1 017	1 242	26 220	46.5	52.6	0.9

1. Based on the resident population estimated as of July 1 of the year shown.   2. © 2013 Election Data Services, Inc. All rights reserved.

Table B. States and Counties — **Land Area and Population**

STATE/ County code	CBSA code[1]	County type[2]	STATE County	Land area,[3] (sq km) 2010	Total persons 2015	Rank	Per square kilometer	White	Black	American Indian, Alaska Native	Asian and Pacific Islander	Percent Hispanic or Latino[4]	Under 5 years	5 to 17 years	18 to 24 years	25 to 34 years	35 to 44 years	45 to 54 years
				1	2	3	4	5	6	7	8	9	10	11	12	13	14	15
			FLORIDA—Cont'd															
12 107	37260	4	Putnam	1 885	72 023	750	38.2	73.2	16.8	1.0	1.0	9.6	5.7	15.9	7.9	10.7	10.3	13.3
12 109	27260	1	St. Johns	1 556	226 640	285	145.7	85.4	6.0	0.7	3.4	6.1	4.8	17.2	7.7	10.3	12.7	15.0
12 111	38940	2	St. Lucie	1 481	298 563	230	201.6	60.9	20.3	0.7	2.4	17.6	5.2	15.6	7.7	11.0	11.3	13.4
12 113	37860	2	Santa Rosa	2 620	167 040	383	63.8	85.5	7.2	1.6	3.6	5.2	5.7	16.9	8.5	13.6	12.9	15.1
12 115	35840	2	Sarasota	1 440	405 549	172	281.6	84.8	5.2	0.6	2.1	8.7	3.7	11.2	6.1	8.3	9.0	12.4
12 117	36740	1	Seminole	801	449 144	154	560.7	65.3	11.9	0.7	4.9	19.2	5.2	16.3	9.1	14.0	13.3	14.8
12 119	45540	4	Sumter	1 417	118 891	519	83.9	85.6	8.2	0.7	1.0	5.7	2.0	5.4	3.4	5.9	6.5	7.5
12 121	...	6	Suwannee	1 783	43 760	1 096	24.5	76.9	13.9	0.9	1.0	9.1	5.8	15.6	8.3	13.1	11.2	13.0
12 123	...	6	Taylor	2 702	22 493	1 707	8.3	73.8	21.1	1.6	1.2	4.0	5.3	13.7	8.3	14.4	12.7	14.0
12 125	...	6	Union	631	15 234	2 085	24.1	71.6	23.1	0.8	0.7	5.3	5.3	14.0	8.9	15.8	13.6	15.0
12 127	19660	2	Volusia	2 852	517 887	129	181.6	75.2	11.2	0.8	2.3	12.2	4.7	13.4	8.6	11.0	10.6	13.6
12 129	45220	2	Wakulla	1 571	31 535	1 395	20.1	79.9	15.8	1.3	1.0	3.8	5.3	15.5	7.6	14.4	15.0	15.7
12 131	18880	6	Walton	2 687	63 508	830	23.6	86.2	6.3	1.8	1.7	6.1	5.4	14.7	7.1	12.4	12.4	14.4
12 133	...	6	Washington	1 509	24 687	1 620	16.4	79.0	16.4	2.1	1.2	3.5	4.9	14.9	9.0	13.1	13.2	14.6
13 000	...	X	**GEORGIA**	148 959	10 214 860	X	68.6	55.8	31.7	0.7	4.4	9.3	6.6	18.1	10.1	13.7	13.6	13.9
13 001	...	7	Appling	1 313	18 454	1 892	14.1	70.9	19.7	0.4	0.9	9.3	6.9	18.5	8.5	11.7	12.3	13.3
13 003	...	9	Atkinson	879	8 398	2 563	9.6	58.1	17.9	0.7	0.7	24.0	8.4	19.7	9.3	12.0	13.4	13.5
13 005	...	7	Bacon	670	11 299	2 339	16.9	75.5	17.1	0.3	0.7	8.0	6.9	19.1	8.7	12.1	13.9	12.5
13 007	10500	3	Baker	886	3 180	2 959	3.6	48.7	45.2	0.6	1.3	4.8	5.1	15.5	8.0	11.3	11.0	14.3
13 009	33300	4	Baldwin	668	45 459	1 063	68.1	54.5	42.1	0.5	2.1	2.2	5.2	14.1	19.3	12.0	10.2	12.8
13 011	...	8	Banks	601	18 495	1 890	30.8	89.2	3.2	0.8	1.5	6.5	5.3	18.0	8.3	10.9	13.4	15.0
13 013	12060	1	Barrow	415	75 370	734	181.6	75.1	12.3	0.7	4.2	9.6	7.2	20.2	8.3	14.7	14.5	13.3
13 015	12060	1	Bartow	1 190	102 747	582	86.3	80.1	11.3	0.8	1.3	8.0	6.4	18.8	8.8	12.8	13.6	14.7
13 017	22340	7	Ben Hill	648	17 403	1 954	26.9	57.7	35.9	0.6	1.0	6.3	7.7	17.7	8.4	12.6	11.9	13.0
13 019	...	6	Berrien	1 170	18 963	1 876	16.2	83.2	11.3	0.5	0.9	5.0	6.1	17.4	8.1	11.8	12.7	14.5
13 021	31420	3	Bibb	647	153 721	421	237.6	41.2	54.0	0.5	2.3	3.2	7.2	18.0	10.6	13.2	11.8	12.6
13 023	...	6	Bleckley	559	12 243	2 280	21.9	69.8	27.1	0.4	1.2	2.6	5.4	16.1	14.6	11.2	10.9	13.7
13 025	15260	3	Brantley	1 146	18 455	1 891	16.1	93.9	4.0	1.0	0.5	2.1	5.7	19.3	8.1	11.5	13.0	14.4
13 027	46660	3	Brooks	1 277	15 658	2 066	12.3	58.5	35.3	0.8	0.9	5.6	6.7	15.2	7.8	12.0	11.3	14.4
13 029	42340	2	Bryan	1 129	35 137	1 298	31.1	76.1	16.2	0.9	2.9	6.3	7.3	21.7	8.1	14.0	15.2	13.2
13 031	44340	4	Bulloch	1 743	72 651	747	41.7	65.4	29.4	0.6	2.3	3.7	5.6	14.8	25.8	13.5	10.3	10.3
13 033	12260	2	Burke	2 142	22 745	1 698	10.6	48.2	48.6	0.7	0.8	3.0	7.0	19.3	9.3	12.2	11.3	13.4
13 035	12060	1	Butts	478	23 593	1 655	49.4	68.6	27.9	0.6	0.8	3.1	5.8	16.2	9.4	14.0	13.2	14.4
13 037	...	8	Calhoun	726	6 479	2 717	8.9	34.1	61.5	0.5	0.8	4.7	4.8	14.3	9.5	15.6	15.7	14.9
13 039	41220	4	Camden	1 588	52 102	957	32.8	72.4	20.4	1.1	2.7	6.2	7.6	17.6	13.3	15.9	11.2	12.5
13 043	...	7	Candler	629	10 886	2 367	17.3	63.9	24.7	0.4	1.0	11.2	6.3	19.4	8.4	12.0	12.0	12.2
13 045	12060	1	Carroll	1 293	114 545	536	88.6	73.6	20.0	0.7	1.3	6.5	6.4	17.8	14.1	12.9	12.5	12.7
13 047	16860	2	Catoosa	420	66 050	801	157.3	92.9	3.3	0.9	1.8	2.8	5.7	18.8	8.2	11.9	13.6	14.3
13 049	...	6	Charlton	2 004	12 965	2 232	6.5	63.7	32.7	0.9	1.0	3.5	5.6	13.4	9.9	16.3	14.7	15.2
13 051	42340	2	Chatham	1 104	286 956	237	259.9	51.4	40.5	0.7	3.6	6.0	6.9	15.3	12.0	16.7	11.9	12.0
13 053	17980	2	Chattahoochee	644	11 368	2 332	17.7	62.2	19.4	1.4	4.5	15.0	9.5	13.1	32.3	24.3	9.0	4.7
13 055	44900	6	Chattooga	812	24 922	1 610	30.7	84.3	11.1	0.7	0.8	4.8	5.6	16.9	8.8	12.6	12.7	13.6
13 057	12060	1	Cherokee	1 092	235 900	278	216.0	81.7	6.9	0.7	2.5	10.1	6.2	19.8	8.2	11.9	15.0	15.3
13 059	12020	3	Clarke	309	123 912	504	401.0	57.5	27.9	0.5	5.2	10.8	5.8	11.8	27.6	16.7	11.0	8.8
13 061	...	9	Clay	506	3 141	2 961	6.2	38.6	60.2	0.6	0.7	1.1	6.6	15.2	7.6	10.6	8.8	11.3
13 063	12060	1	Clayton	367	273 955	248	746.5	14.7	67.5	0.7	5.6	13.1	7.2	20.5	10.5	14.8	14.0	13.5
13 065	...	6	Clinch	2 073	6 893	2 683	3.3	67.3	28.8	1.0	0.5	4.2	7.6	18.3	9.4	12.3	12.1	12.2
13 067	12060	1	Cobb	879	741 334	85	843.4	55.6	27.4	0.7	5.8	12.7	6.6	18.0	9.4	14.3	14.9	14.7
13 069	20060	7	Coffee	1 489	43 108	1 108	29.0	60.4	28.3	0.5	1.1	10.9	6.7	18.0	10.9	14.0	13.2	13.6
13 071	34220	6	Colquitt	1 409	45 844	1 052	32.5	58.0	23.2	0.6	1.1	18.3	7.8	19.1	9.2	13.3	12.6	12.8
13 073	12260	2	Columbia	751	144 052	446	191.8	72.7	17.4	0.8	5.4	6.2	6.3	19.6	8.7	13.4	13.9	14.2
13 075	...	6	Cook	588	17 124	1 972	29.1	65.4	28.1	0.6	1.0	6.1	6.7	19.9	8.1	12.6	12.7	13.3
13 077	12060	1	Coweta	1 142	138 427	460	121.2	73.6	18.5	0.7	2.5	6.7	6.2	19.5	8.4	12.2	14.2	15.2
13 079	31420	3	Crawford	841	12 388	2 271	14.7	74.5	21.6	0.9	0.6	3.1	5.0	16.3	8.0	11.1	11.5	16.7
13 081	18380	6	Crisp	706	22 881	1 687	32.4	52.2	43.8	0.4	1.4	3.2	6.8	18.1	8.9	12.1	11.3	13.0
13 083	16860	2	Dade	451	16 264	2 026	36.1	95.1	1.8	1.0	1.5	2.1	5.4	14.4	12.8	11.1	11.6	13.4
13 085	12060	1	Dawson	546	23 312	1 669	42.7	94.3	1.3	0.9	1.0	4.0	5.1	16.7	7.6	11.2	12.4	14.9
13 087	12460	6	Decatur	1 547	27 174	1 525	17.6	52.4	41.5	0.6	0.8	5.6	6.9	17.8	9.5	12.0	12.1	13.7
13 089	12060	1	DeKalb	693	734 871	86	1 060.4	31.1	54.4	0.7	6.5	8.9	7.3	16.4	9.2	16.6	15.0	13.7
13 091	...	7	Dodge	1 284	20 882	1 778	16.3	66.4	30.0	0.5	0.6	3.4	6.1	14.8	9.9	12.8	13.2	14.8
13 093	...	6	Dooly	1 015	14 035	2 163	13.8	42.9	49.3	0.4	0.8	7.3	4.7	15.0	8.6	13.2	13.5	14.5
13 095	10500	3	Dougherty	851	91 332	638	107.3	28.1	68.5	0.5	1.3	2.6	7.4	17.5	12.3	13.6	11.4	12.0
13 097	12060	1	Douglas	518	140 733	455	271.7	46.7	43.7	0.8	2.3	8.9	6.6	20.3	9.3	12.3	15.1	14.9
13 099	...	6	Early	1 328	10 575	2 388	8.0	47.4	50.2	0.6	0.8	2.2	6.6	18.6	8.7	10.2	11.6	13.2
13 101	46660	3	Echols	1 075	4 040	2 900	3.8	64.3	5.3	2.3	0.8	27.8	8.8	18.9	8.5	14.2	14.2	12.9

1. CBSA = Core Based Statistical Area. See Appendix A for explanation. See Appendix B for list of metropolitan areas with component counties.
Service of USDA Rural-Urban Continuum Codes. See Appendix A for definition. 3. Dry land or land partially or temporarily covered by water. 2. County type code from the Economic Research
4. May be of any race.

Table B. States and Counties — **Population and Households**

STATE County	55 to 64 years	65 to 74 years	75 years and over	Percent female	2000	2010	2000–2010	2010–2015	Births	Deaths	Net migration	Number	Persons per household	Family households	Female family householder[1]	One person
	16	17	18	19	20	21	22	23	24	25	26	27	28	29	30	31
FLORIDA—Cont'd																
Putnam	15.1	12.3	8.8	50.7	70 423	74 364	5.6	-3.1	4 419	4 962	-1 611	27 842	2.57	64.8	14.3	29.9
St. Johns	14.2	11.0	7.2	51.3	123 135	190 039	54.3	19.3	10 295	8 479	34 043	77 443	2.59	68.9	8.8	24.5
St. Lucie	13.3	12.3	10.3	51.2	192 695	277 257	43.9	7.7	15 750	15 130	20 211	107 104	2.62	67.5	13.4	26.9
Santa Rosa	12.8	9.0	5.6	48.9	117 743	151 372	28.6	10.4	9 576	6 675	12 390	57 583	2.67	72.5	10.9	21.0
Sarasota	15.3	17.3	16.6	52.2	325 957	379 435	16.4	6.9	15 146	27 009	37 611	172 720	2.21	60.9	8.6	32.7
Seminole	12.9	8.3	6.0	51.6	365 196	422 718	15.8	6.3	23 362	16 160	18 261	147 932	2.90	66.5	12.3	27.5
Sumter	16.4	33.9	19.0	49.3	53 345	93 420	75.1	27.3	2 414	7 193	30 145	45 868	2.05	69.6	5.0	25.8
Suwannee	13.4	11.2	8.4	47.8	34 844	41 551	19.2	5.3	2 469	2 752	2 437	15 583	2.69	70.3	14.3	25.5
Taylor	13.6	10.7	7.3	43.6	19 256	22 568	17.2	-0.3	1 243	1 181	-151	7 464	2.55	68.5	14.1	25.8
Union	15.0	8.1	4.3	35.4	13 442	15 535	15.6	-1.9	910	1 019	-203	3 816	2.71	71.9	16.9	24.8
Volusia	14.9	12.7	10.5	51.2	443 343	494 597	11.6	4.7	24 613	33 551	31 689	197 092	2.47	61.9	11.0	31.5
Wakulla	13.3	8.6	4.5	44.7	22 863	30 783	34.6	2.4	1 666	1 264	325	10 905	2.51	72.9	14.1	23.3
Walton	14.9	11.6	7.1	49.1	40 601	55 043	35.6	15.4	3 626	2 908	7 487	22 638	2.46	65.3	9.8	29.9
Washington	13.0	10.5	6.8	45.2	20 973	24 896	18.7	-0.8	1 257	1 428	-44	8 381	2.65	66.0	10.2	29.9
GEORGIA	11.7	7.6	4.8	51.2	8 186 453	9 688 681	18.4	5.4	685 978	386 638	217 464	3 540 690	2.72	68.0	15.4	26.7
Appling	13.2	9.6	6.1	49.9	17 419	18 236	4.7	1.2	1 355	982	-153	6 878	2.61	67.1	14.7	29.1
Atkinson	12.0	7.3	4.5	49.6	7 609	8 382	10.2	0.2	676	326	-345	2 713	3.04	68.7	14.0	27.8
Bacon	12.7	8.5	5.7	50.8	10 103	11 096	9.8	1.8	774	639	89	3 953	2.71	68.6	10.5	26.3
Baker	17.0	10.2	7.6	52.1	4 074	3 451	-15.3	-7.9	172	106	-303	1 362	2.45	65.3	16.9	30.9
Baldwin	12.2	8.5	5.7	49.6	44 700	45 835	2.5	-0.8	2 463	2 106	-740	16 194	2.60	59.6	17.5	30.6
Banks	13.2	10.5	5.4	49.3	14 422	18 395	27.5	0.5	992	725	-207	6 703	2.73	76.3	10.7	19.5
Barrow	10.7	7.2	4.0	50.7	46 144	69 367	50.3	8.7	5 509	2 742	3 163	23 064	3.06	76.8	13.7	18.4
Bartow	12.1	8.2	4.6	50.7	76 019	100 157	31.8	2.6	6 802	4 410	90	35 293	2.83	73.1	12.7	21.4
Ben Hill	13.4	9.2	6.2	52.5	17 484	17 634	0.9	-1.3	1 235	1 083	-377	6 349	2.72	68.3	21.7	28.8
Berrien	12.8	9.8	6.7	50.7	16 235	19 286	18.8	-1.7	1 197	988	-539	7 102	2.66	70.4	15.1	26.4
Bibb	12.6	8.0	6.0	53.0	153 887	155 512	1.1	-1.2	11 857	8 519	-5 140	56 660	2.62	63.3	21.2	31.8
Bleckley	11.3	9.2	7.5	52.2	11 666	13 063	12.0	-6.3	703	704	-854	4 019	2.82	67.3	15.8	28.1
Brantley	13.3	9.4	5.3	50.6	14 629	18 410	25.8	0.2	1 072	930	-68	6 523	2.82	74.8	12.9	22.2
Brooks	14.1	11.3	7.3	51.2	16 450	16 324	-0.8	-4.1	1 061	985	-765	6 550	2.39	62.2	14.3	33.2
Bryan	10.4	6.4	3.7	50.2	23 417	30 238	29.1	16.2	2 601	1 155	3 418	11 231	2.86	78.4	11.7	17.3
Bulloch	9.5	6.3	4.0	50.6	55 983	70 217	25.4	3.5	4 401	2 559	438	25 803	2.57	59.5	14.8	23.9
Burke	13.5	8.7	5.4	52.0	22 243	23 316	4.8	-2.4	1 658	1 282	-995	7 970	2.87	69.7	21.7	26.0
Butts	12.7	9.1	5.1	47.1	19 522	23 655	21.2	-0.3	1 467	1 286	-238	7 781	2.72	72.9	12.9	24.4
Calhoun	12.7	6.9	5.7	40.0	6 320	6 694	5.9	-3.2	300	299	-261	1 787	2.19	63.3	18.1	33.7
Camden	10.5	7.6	3.7	48.6	43 664	50 513	15.7	3.1	4 246	1 594	-1 142	18 560	2.68	75.3	12.4	19.0
Candler	13.1	10.5	6.2	50.4	9 577	10 998	14.8	-1.0	764	612	-297	3 944	2.73	68.6	17.8	25.8
Carroll	11.0	7.6	4.8	50.9	87 268	110 591	26.7	3.6	7 740	5 029	1 190	39 610	2.73	69.0	14.6	25.0
Catoosa	12.4	9.5	6.4	51.3	53 282	63 940	20.0	3.3	3 879	2 786	856	23 813	2.71	73.4	10.8	23.6
Charlton	11.5	8.1	5.2	39.7	10 282	12 171	18.4	6.5	666	499	527	3 552	3.28	73.1	13.7	23.1
Chatham	11.6	8.0	5.6	51.8	232 048	265 133	14.3	8.2	20 577	11 947	12 678	103 807	2.55	60.5	16.5	31.9
Chattahoochee	3.0	2.4	1.7	32.7	14 882	11 267	-24.3	0.9	1 300	157	-1 097	2 602	3.35	77.1	9.6	16.3
Chattooga	13.4	9.7	6.7	48.8	25 470	26 015	2.1	-4.2	1 457	1 619	-894	9 347	2.52	68.0	14.5	28.0
Cherokee	11.7	7.9	4.0	50.7	141 903	214 346	51.1	10.1	14 687	6 566	13 261	77 654	2.84	75.6	11.8	20.1
Clarke	8.6	5.6	4.1	52.3	101 489	116 707	15.0	6.2	7 375	3 616	3 242	42 107	2.59	49.1	12.9	33.9
Clay	16.6	13.9	9.4	53.1	3 357	3 183	-5.2	-1.3	189	193	-28	1 170	2.61	61.0	24.0	34.4
Clayton	10.6	5.5	2.8	52.6	236 517	259 470	9.7	5.6	21 793	7 937	531	87 490	2.98	65.1	23.2	29.9
Clinch	13.1	9.9	5.1	51.0	6 878	6 798	-1.2	1.4	529	361	-74	2 579	2.52	63.4	17.6	32.2
Cobb	11.6	6.7	3.9	51.4	607 751	688 076	13.2	7.7	49 603	20 516	24 183	264 805	2.64	67.9	13.3	25.3
Coffee	11.3	7.7	4.6	48.7	37 413	42 356	13.2	1.8	3 139	1 957	-476	14 597	2.70	68.0	15.9	28.4
Colquitt	11.4	8.3	5.6	50.4	42 053	45 498	8.2	0.8	3 665	2 384	-901	15 893	2.83	72.5	16.8	24.2
Columbia	12.1	7.4	4.4	51.1	89 288	124 059	38.9	16.1	8 510	4 259	15 365	44 764	2.94	78.3	12.4	18.8
Cook	11.9	8.8	5.9	51.6	15 771	17 212	9.1	-0.5	1 185	964	-316	6 255	2.70	75.7	16.1	20.3
Coweta	11.9	8.0	4.5	51.2	89 215	127 317	42.7	8.7	8 650	4 713	6 905	47 666	2.75	74.2	12.2	21.8
Crawford	14.6	11.0	5.8	49.4	12 495	12 630	1.1	-1.9	687	621	-325	4 655	2.66	74.2	17.8	23.3
Crisp	13.8	9.1	6.9	52.4	21 996	23 439	6.6	-2.4	1 564	1 265	-835	8 574	2.68	72.8	22.8	23.6
Dade	14.4	10.1	6.9	50.8	15 154	16 633	9.8	-2.2	877	855	-375	6 175	2.48	74.8	8.7	21.7
Dawson	14.2	12.3	5.6	49.9	15 999	22 339	39.6	4.4	1 229	878	555	8 277	2.70	76.2	9.1	18.7
Decatur	12.6	8.7	6.7	51.4	28 240	27 842	-1.4	-2.4	1 881	1 619	-938	10 473	2.51	66.6	19.8	30.9
DeKalb	11.5	6.4	4.0	52.5	665 865	691 891	3.9	6.2	57 396	22 618	8 736	264 120	2.62	58.6	17.5	33.8
Dodge	13.2	8.9	6.3	47.8	19 171	21 797	13.7	-4.2	1 277	1 165	-1 052	8 056	2.38	68.7	15.7	28.9
Dooly	14.7	10.0	5.7	46.0	11 525	14 918	29.4	-5.9	606	616	-883	4 957	2.50	62.1	18.1	35.0
Dougherty	12.2	7.8	5.8	53.5	96 065	94 565	-1.6	-3.4	7 364	4 637	-5 953	35 585	2.53	63.1	24.9	31.8
Douglas	11.2	6.8	3.5	52.1	92 174	132 339	43.6	6.3	9 152	4 532	3 640	46 708	2.86	73.8	18.2	22.1
Early	12.7	10.7	7.7	52.8	12 354	11 004	-10.9	-3.9	739	706	-452	4 096	2.55	69.1	20.7	29.5
Echols	11.2	6.3	5.0	50.7	3 754	4 034	7.5	0.1	334	138	-206	1 434	2.80	75.3	15.1	18.8

1. No spouse present.

Table B. States and Counties — Population, Vital Statistics, Medicare, and Crime

STATE County	Persons in group quarters, 2015	Daytime population, 2010–2014 Number	Daytime population, 2010–2014 Employment/residence ratio	Births, 2015 Total	Births, 2015 Rate[1]	Deaths, 2015 Number	Deaths, 2015 Rate[1]	Persons under 65 with no health insurance, 2014 Number	Persons under 65 with no health insurance, 2014 Percent	Medicare, 2015 Total Beneficiaries	Medicare, 2015 Enrolled in Original Medicare	Medicare, 2015 Enrolled in Medicare Advantage	Serious crimes known to police,[2] 2014 Total Number	Serious crimes known to police,[2] 2014 Total Rate[3]
	32	33	34	35	36	37	38	39	40	41	42	43	44	45
FLORIDA—Cont'd														
Putnam	1 430	68 234	0.79	827	11.5	934	13.0	12 024	21.6	16 727	12 101	4 626	2 566	3 527
St. Johns	2 890	180 572	0.75	2 163	9.7	1 759	7.9	23 226	13.2	43 150	33 141	10 009	4 419	2 044
St. Lucie	3 051	259 815	0.78	3 029	10.3	3 104	10.5	46 859	21.0	63 297	39 464	23 833	7 045	2 419
Santa Rosa	6 675	131 595	0.61	1 831	11.1	1 347	8.2	20 223	15.1	27 724	20 067	7 657	2 072	1 259
Sarasota	5 623	401 865	1.10	2 929	7.3	5 434	13.5	51 416	19.8	134 972	100 535	34 437	10 018	2 528
Seminole	3 517	402 123	0.85	4 536	10.2	3 340	7.5	58 322	15.5	60 311	36 004	24 307	11 502	2 597
Sumter	8 431	107 386	1.17	484	4.2	1 560	13.4	7 378	16.1	17 306	11 202	6 104	1 302	1 178
Suwannee	3 424	41 928	0.90	468	10.7	551	12.6	6 756	21.0	9 764	7 845	1 919	883	1 987
Taylor	3 242	22 926	1.03	225	10.0	226	10.0	2 661	17.5	4 255	3 412	843	503	2 176
Union	4 846	16 041	1.19	172	11.3	202	13.3	1 304	14.8	1 932	1 541	391	161	1 062
Volusia	13 402	478 646	0.89	4 766	9.3	6 560	12.8	81 258	21.4	128 163	69 285	58 878	17 894	3 546
Wakulla	3 431	24 297	0.47	316	10.0	230	7.3	3 498	14.8	5 464	2 668	2 796	697	2 226
Walton	1 962	58 844	1.04	755	12.1	558	8.9	10 455	21.7	9 880	7 892	1 988	1 734	2 820
Washington	2 745	23 363	0.85	245	10.0	272	11.1	3 323	19.0	4 707	3 897	810	411	1 658
GEORGIA	260 364	9 905 281	1.00	130 592	12.9	77 052	7.6	1 549 301	18.0	1 424 933	963 248	461 685	369 413	3 659
Appling	410	18 995	1.08	249	13.5	204	11.0	3 197	20.9	3 237	2 331	906	211	1 139
Atkinson	20	7 313	0.69	138	16.6	41	4.9	2 008	27.9	1 398	990	408	NA	NA
Bacon	325	10 996	0.96	138	12.2	102	9.0	2 077	22.0	1 761	1 255	506	NA	NA
Baker	0	2 774	0.56	34	10.5	20	6.2	511	19.1	104	76	28	31	932
Baldwin	5 698	46 191	1.02	451	9.9	439	9.6	5 605	16.4	7 949	4 411	3 538	1 649	3 561
Banks	0	15 115	0.59	197	10.7	126	6.8	3 097	20.1	2 238	1 584	654	450	2 524
Barrow	287	57 452	0.57	1 036	13.9	549	7.4	11 992	18.4	11 228	7 604	3 624	2 253	3 123
Bartow	981	93 482	0.83	1 326	13.0	862	8.4	16 574	18.8	15 420	11 002	4 418	5 407	5 342
Ben Hill	315	17 698	1.03	221	12.7	200	11.5	2 612	17.9	3 581	2 432	1 149	757	4 316
Berrien	182	16 257	0.57	243	12.9	201	10.7	3 375	21.7	3 535	2 525	1 010	472	2 479
Bibb	6 357	177 779	1.39	2 279	14.8	1 669	10.9	21 577	17.0	31 843	21 044	10 799	NA	NA
Blockley	596	11 665	0.69	138	11.0	108	8.6	1 643	17.3	1 015	833	182	504	3 955
Brantley	63	14 741	0.42	217	11.8	187	10.1	3 281	20.9	2 778	2 043	735	597	3 261
Brooks	171	13 638	0.61	175	11.3	195	12.5	2 803	22.5	2 693	1 885	808	479	3 252
Bryan	101	23 960	0.45	534	15.5	211	6.1	4 200	13.8	4 641	3 201	1 440	567	1 668
Bulloch	5 314	69 909	0.93	854	11.8	491	6.8	11 291	19.1	8 741	6 489	2 252	1 964	2 766
Burke	276	23 447	1.04	301	13.2	233	10.3	3 558	18.4	3 571	2 167	1 404	936	4 147
Butts	2 662	21 793	0.80	288	12.3	245	10.4	3 147	17.6	4 734	2 975	1 759	492	2 108
Calhoun	1 705	6 539	1.00	49	7.6	44	6.8	905	22.5	1 549	1 031	518	730	12 352
Camden	1 898	48 369	0.88	818	15.7	310	6.0	6 043	13.6	6 614	5 150	1 464	1 551	3 071
Candler	233	10 137	0.78	134	12.3	117	10.8	2 026	22.8	1 880	1 303	577	NA	NA
Carroll	3 922	106 243	0.88	1 486	13.0	991	8.7	17 587	18.4	20 641	13 999	6 642	4 057	3 586
Catoosa	570	51 788	0.55	716	10.9	565	8.6	8 790	16.0	8 464	5 978	2 486	2 528	3 839
Charlton	2 978	11 398	0.59	111	8.6	74	5.7	1 466	17.4	1 867	1 430	437	203	1 513
Chatham	13 961	301 692	1.21	4 001	14.0	2 392	8.4	43 189	18.6	43 161	28 346	14 815	11 517	4 076
Chattahoochee	3 273	19 210	2.15	220	18.9	27	2.3	1 156	14.3	536	369	167	8	60
Chattooga	1 370	23 874	0.81	278	11.2	298	12.0	3 768	19.3	5 730	3 927	1 803	614	2 507
Cherokee	1 178	179 530	0.59	2 839	12.2	1 300	5.6	31 663	15.7	18 018	11 969	6 049	3 420	1 497
Clarke	11 706	137 987	1.36	1 354	11.1	724	5.9	19 631	19.9	15 975	11 677	4 298	4 702	3 833
Clay	116	2 791	0.61	36	11.5	34	10.9	462	19.7	586	371	215	NA	NA
Clayton	4 523	252 844	0.89	3 886	14.3	1 593	5.9	54 818	22.8	36 016	21 437	14 579	13 362	5 020
Clinch	146	6 800	1.01	103	15.0	57	8.3	1 244	21.5	1 321	910	411	279	4 091
Cobb	7 842	686 033	0.93	9 650	13.1	4 209	5.7	111 408	17.3	100 995	67 141	33 854	19 613	2 699
Coffee	3 079	43 904	1.06	619	14.4	382	8.9	7 717	22.4	6 629	4 663	1 966	2 151	5 086
Colquitt	941	44 690	0.93	650	14.1	437	9.5	10 142	26.0	7 806	5 487	2 319	NA	NA
Columbia	762	103 609	0.52	1 565	11.0	863	6.1	14 528	11.9	14 881	10 766	4 115	2 221	1 602
Cook	142	15 168	0.73	236	13.7	185	10.8	3 314	22.7	3 038	2 132	906	411	2 533
Coweta	650	109 739	0.63	1 700	12.4	936	6.8	16 659	14.1	18 532	12 325	6 207	2 832	2 098
Crawford	150	9 331	0.36	101	8.1	124	10.0	1 950	19.0	1 092	658	434	325	2 822
Crisp	491	24 061	1.08	275	12.0	262	11.4	3 272	17.3	4 359	2 771	1 588	1 140	4 873
Dade	963	13 693	0.61	169	10.4	166	10.2	2 164	17.0	3 504	2 416	1 088	252	1 524
Dawson	137	20 989	0.84	244	10.6	168	7.3	3 448	18.5	4 399	3 224	1 175	460	2 013
Decatur	1 135	26 931	0.94	339	12.5	330	12.1	4 598	20.8	5 005	3 595	1 410	2 247	8 221
DeKalb	11 832	682 446	0.92	10 871	14.9	4 464	6.1	123 206	19.4	80 479	47 919	32 560	45 768	6 348
Dodge	1 813	19 288	0.73	221	10.6	229	10.9	3 097	19.2	4 855	3 484	1 371	861	4 562
Dooly	1 870	13 843	0.87	108	7.6	106	7.5	2 362	23.3	1 942	1 243	699	NA	NA
Dougherty	3 958	107 455	1.41	1 342	14.6	886	9.6	14 253	18.6	17 389	12 367	5 022	5 512	5 936
Douglas	1 161	118 670	0.72	1 745	12.5	949	6.8	21 242	17.2	15 961	10 461	5 500	4 384	3 182
Early	213	10 576	0.98	121	11.5	140	13.3	1 564	18.5	2 207	1 469	738	506	4 944
Echols	0	2 639	0.21	45	11.1	23	5.7	1 076	30.5	155	128	27	30	736

1. Per 1,000 estimated resident population.   2. Data for serious crimes have not been adjusted for underreporting; this may affect comparability between geographic areas and over time.
3. Per 100,000 population estimated by the FBI.

Table B. States and Counties — Crime, Education, Money Income, and Poverty

STATE County	Serious crimes known to police, 2014 (cont.)[1] Rate[2] Violent	Property	Education — School enrollment and attainment, 2010–2014 Enrollment[3] Total	Percent private	Attainment[4] (percent) High school graduate or less	Bachelor's degree or more	Local government expenditures,[5] 2012–2013 Total current spending (mil dol)	Current spending per student (dollars)	Money income, 2010–2014 Per capita income[6] (dollars)	Households Median income (dollars)	Mean income (dollars)	Percent with income of $200,000 or more	Income and poverty, 2014 Median household income (dollars)	Percent below poverty level All persons	Children under 18 years	Children 5 to 17 years in families
	46	47	48	49	50	51	52	53	54	55	56	57	58	59	60	61
FLORIDA—Cont'd																
Putnam	561	2 967	14 885	10.9	61.9	11.6	98.0	8 853	18 587	32 714	45 678	1.0	32 054	28.5	44.3	40.9
St. Johns	258	1 786	52 653	21.5	27.7	41.4	259.0	7 982	37 147	65 575	94 434	8.4	66 560	8.2	11.0	9.9
St. Lucie	327	2 093	67 424	13.8	48.5	19.0	330.8	8 344	23 422	42 665	58 811	2.3	42 722	17.3	26.6	24.1
Santa Rosa	151	1 109	40 685	12.8	38.1	26.5	204.5	7 903	27 478	58 199	73 525	3.7	58 587	11.2	16.3	15.9
Sarasota	260	2 269	66 322	14.9	38.4	31.1	423.7	10 310	33 300	50 304	72 327	4.8	52 109	10.8	19.1	16.7
Seminole	341	2 256	122 329	17.1	32.3	35.0	492.4	7 639	28 870	57 875	77 779	4.8	56 443	11.8	16.1	15.1
Sumter	188	990	9 427	12.6	42.8	26.4	68.5	8 569	28 875	49 874	62 711	2.5	51 907	10.9	30.5	29.9
Suwannee	481	1 505	8 837	13.1	63.1	11.9	51.0	8 512	18 966	37 879	48 275	1.4	38 177	23.7	33.2	32.0
Taylor	679	1 497	4 201	18.9	63.2	10.0	26.7	9 585	16 748	36 907	49 035	0.6	36 374	23.4	30.9	29.9
Union	303	759	2 782	9.0	62.5	8.6	19.4	8 474	13 467	41 476	49 170	0.6	40 207	24.3	26.1	24.7
Volusia	434	3 112	109 495	18.1	45.3	21.3	484.6	7 935	23 844	41 714	56 364	2.2	40 881	17.7	27.2	25.0
Wakulla	275	1 951	6 800	9.2	51.0	17.2	39.8	7 928	21 738	53 143	61 310	1.4	51 642	15.1	20.8	19.3
Walton	382	2 438	11 772	11.0	43.5	25.1	75.1	9 611	25 854	44 468	63 419	4.1	46 867	15.8	26.8	25.5
Washington	202	1 456	5 504	11.4	59.8	11.4	36.6	10 646	17 950	38 563	48 649	1.0	36 482	20.0	28.9	27.6
GEORGIA	377	3 281	2 769 628	14.7	43.5	28.3	15 444.1	9 099	25 427	49 342	68 317	4.1	49 240	18.4	26.3	24.8
Appling	65	1 074	4 015	4.7	66.9	12.9	33.4	9 364	19 440	38 461	49 025	0.5	36 642	24.9	36.5	34.2
Atkinson	NA	NA	2 308	3.9	72.0	7.7	15.7	8 941	16 228	30 403	44 164	0.7	31 740	26.5	37.7	37.3
Bacon	NA	NA	2 583	3.8	65.8	12.1	18.1	8 932	18 109	37 668	48 499	0.6	34 201	25.9	39.4	35.6
Baker	120	812	772	3.9	63.3	11.0	3.8	11 418	22 136	45 526	53 673	1.8	43 115	27.3	41.3	37.9
Baldwin	562	3 000	13 789	12.6	55.8	18.3	49.5	8 856	18 582	31 758	49 524	0.9	37 008	29.5	34.8	34.5
Banks	76	2 360	4 417	7.0	65.5	11.8	25.1	8 854	20 433	42 826	53 533	1.5	46 018	16.9	27.4	25.0
Barrow	466	2 657	19 529	12.2	52.7	16.6	105.4	8 091	21 185	53 256	62 193	1.0	49 698	13.0	19.3	18.3
Bartow	506	4 836	25 255	9.7	56.4	17.3	170.0	9 241	21 715	48 306	59 635	1.6	51 440	14.3	20.6	20.4
Ben Hill	319	3 997	4 358	4.5	60.3	10.8	30.2	9 176	15 497	30 643	40 165	0.9	31 081	28.5	40.4	39.9
Berrien	215	2 264	4 964	5.7	57.0	13.0	27.1	8 386	16 660	31 812	42 042	0.1	35 078	26.7	36.2	33.8
Bibb	NA	NA	43 069	20.4	50.0	23.4	239.7	9 782	21 276	36 614	55 718	2.8	36 014	28.2	42.6	40.8
Bleckley	369	3 586	4 224	9.1	61.6	15.2	22.5	9 219	19 191	35 507	55 168	2.1	40 454	23.2	31.8	29.4
Brantley	180	3 080	4 654	6.1	67.2	6.9	30.5	8 583	16 774	36 301	44 492	0.0	36 865	21.7	32.1	28.6
Brooks	455	2 797	3 849	6.2	59.9	11.1	23.6	10 366	19 473	31 686	45 980	1.6	32 903	28.8	42.0	40.5
Bryan	174	1 494	9 779	14.2	37.7	32.4	58.7	7 341	27 941	65 123	78 511	3.7	66 556	11.9	16.8	16.1
Bulloch	180	2 586	29 893	6.4	44.1	28.0	92.1	9 311	18 546	35 642	51 364	1.7	36 315	31.4	34.8	32.7
Burke	611	3 535	6 439	14.6	62.8	10.0	55.2	12 364	16 663	33 299	44 853	0.3	35 055	31.1	42.4	40.3
Butts	197	1 911	5 079	11.9	66.0	9.7	29.8	8 829	20 165	47 385	57 728	1.5	41 505	21.3	31.0	30.3
Calhoun	2 809	9 543	1 522	12.6	68.7	9.4	8.1	12 287	15 410	26 309	51 213	2.9	30 760	38.5	44.7	42.3
Camden	400	2 671	13 701	12.9	39.8	21.2	80.4	8 688	23 833	52 799	63 090	2.2	51 793	12.0	18.0	18.2
Candler	NA	NA	2 837	7.0	62.8	15.1	19.2	8 880	16 943	30 518	44 993	1.2	31 829	29.1	43.6	39.5
Carroll	293	3 294	33 928	8.8	51.5	18.3	168.4	8 761	21 384	45 009	58 918	2.0	43 442	22.9	32.8	31.3
Catoosa	284	3 555	15 968	15.3	47.6	18.5	103.1	9 423	22 415	50 180	58 918	0.9	50 728	12.6	18.9	17.8
Charlton	194	1 320	2 800	5.9	65.1	11.4	15.0	8 922	17 586	41 059	52 687	1.0	34 312	29.5	34.0	33.4
Chatham	412	3 664	77 426	24.2	37.6	32.3	344.1	9 400	25 636	46 987	64 240	3.8	50 154	17.9	27.5	28.0
Chattahoochee	0	60	3 654	10.0	33.1	31.5	10.1	10 902	19 538	48 488	55 779	0.7	45 933	18.8	22.4	27.6
Chattooga	155	2 352	5 365	8.7	70.2	8.5	34.3	8 101	15 932	32 496	42 234	1.1	34 830	21.1	28.2	26.4
Cherokee	90	1 407	60 929	16.8	35.3	34.3	323.2	8 230	30 299	67 371	85 060	5.7	71 168	9.3	12.6	11.6
Clarke	368	3 465	50 056	7.8	36.6	39.3	150.8	11 892	19 333	33 430	51 153	2.8	31 487	37.8	39.0	40.1
Clay	NA	NA	642	8.9	66.1	6.9	3.7	10 802	12 446	21 300	31 555	0.0	27 512	37.3	56.4	53.0
Clayton	588	4 432	79 485	13.6	49.6	18.1	410.5	7 931	18 074	40 314	50 244	0.8	42 985	22.9	36.4	34.6
Clinch	543	3 548	1 586	3.5	65.8	14.1	13.3	9 416	18 256	29 125	45 170	1.5	31 577	28.5	40.6	35.9
Cobb	255	2 445	201 713	17.9	28.5	43.8	1 075.2	9 196	33 418	64 657	88 016	7.6	66 970	13.0	17.8	16.8
Coffee	392	4 693	11 019	5.1	62.6	12.3	70.9	9 032	16 796	34 523	47 685	1.7	33 125	28.1	38.5	38.6
Colquitt	NA	NA	12 030	3.0	65.3	12.9	84.2	8 817	16 972	32 233	46 715	1.6	33 509	26.5	39.9	37.6
Columbia	51	1 551	37 419	13.1	33.8	34.2	193.7	7 928	30 411	68 516	86 415	5.8	68 067	9.5	13.0	11.7
Cook	160	2 372	4 491	4.2	62.0	13.4	29.6	8 892	18 858	34 230	50 600	1.8	32 408	26.1	33.7	32.3
Coweta	224	1 875	34 106	13.5	43.8	26.6	197.2	8 692	27 462	61 662	74 681	2.9	60 809	12.5	17.2	15.0
Crawford	104	2 718	3 036	10.2	60.7	11.1	16.5	8 920	21 128	41 910	52 250	0.9	43 111	19.9	31.0	28.7
Crisp	351	4 523	6 411	7.5	56.8	14.7	38.8	9 035	19 455	36 280	50 359	2.1	31 176	32.5	45.9	43.2
Dade	659	865	4 398	34.4	54.9	16.2	20.4	8 957	21 760	44 992	57 821	1.3	42 953	16.4	21.5	21.0
Dawson	92	1 921	5 297	9.6	44.0	26.3	35.4	10 139	28 138	54 457	75 837	5.7	57 491	11.8	18.2	16.8
Decatur	955	7 266	6 877	7.3	55.8	15.1	47.9	8 590	18 387	31 090	47 287	2.1	33 968	27.7	40.6	39.4
DeKalb	679	5 669	193 751	24.2	32.9	40.3	909.6	8 868	28 971	50 799	73 744	5.6	50 597	20.4	33.0	31.8
Dodge	419	4 143	4 354	5.9	63.1	14.4	33.9	10 156	17 771	34 812	46 429	0.4	32 293	25.9	36.9	37.3
Dooly	NA	NA	3 115	10.9	69.9	9.0	15.0	10 214	14 411	28 251	39 362	0.8	31 103	30.4	39.5	34.9
Dougherty	867	5 069	30 911	8.1	48.5	17.8	149.3	9 437	18 770	31 458	47 407	1.9	32 150	31.7	47.4	47.4
Douglas	288	2 894	41 087	15.8	44.2	24.5	230.8	9 168	23 356	52 997	65 679	2.7	54 581	14.2	20.0	18.6
Early	1 036	3 908	2 975	7.6	58.9	14.8	21.2	9 495	19 302	35 000	47 678	1.4	34 906	29.9	40.6	37.8
Echols	98	638	1 176	7.9	66.9	7.5	7.6	9 621	17 350	32 667	47 709	2.3	34 444	27.1	37.1	37.8

1. Data for serious crimes have not been adjusted for underreporting; this may affect comparability between geographic areas and over time.   2. Per 100,000 population estimated by the FBI.
3. All persons 3 years old and over enrolled in nursery school through college.   4. Persons 25 years old and over.   5. Elementary and secondary education expenditures.
6. Based on population estimated by the American Community Survey, 2010–2014.

STATE County	Personal income, 2014										Earnings, 2014		
			Per capita[1]			Supplements to wages and salaries; employer contributions (mil dol)							Contributions for government social insurance (mil dol)	
	Total (mil dol)	Percent change, 2013–2014	Dollars	Rank	Wages and salaries (mil dol)	Pension and insurance	Government social insurance	Proprietors' income (mil dol)	Dividends, interest, and rent (mil dol)	Personal transfer receipts (mil dol)	Total (mil dol)	From employee and self-employed	From employer
	62	63	64	65	66	67	68	69	70	71	72	73	74

STATE County	62	63	64	65	66	67	68	69	70	71	72	73	74
FLORIDA—Cont'd													
Putnam	1 950	3.1	27 031	2 978	635	130	46	39	313	776	851	65	46
St. Johns	12 722	6.2	58 379	151	2 802	414	201	262	3 401	1 629	3 679	249	201
St. Lucie	9 932	5.7	34 129	2 092	2 862	501	211	313	2 118	2 776	3 887	290	211
Santa Rosa	6 146	4.0	37 610	1 508	1 408	264	108	137	1 145	1 239	1 916	131	108
Sarasota	21 494	5.0	54 147	229	7 170	971	510	1 275	9 115	4 290	9 926	704	510
Seminole	18 500	5.2	41 806	971	8 072	1 104	584	928	3 185	2 966	10 689	668	584
Sumter	4 295	8.5	37 558	1 517	1 063	189	78	93	1 140	1 842	1 422	150	78
Suwannee	1 256	5.4	28 536	2 877	383	82	28	145	184	421	639	41	28
Taylor	631	2.1	27 944	2 922	283	55	21	26	90	194	385	25	21
Union	271	1.3	17 811	3 112	132	39	9	10	44	91	191	11	9
Volusia	18 298	5.0	36 052	1 776	6 349	1 009	471	556	4 175	5 099	8 385	613	471
Wakulla	929	4.8	29 568	2 776	190	46	14	29	125	203	278	20	14
Walton	2 816	5.6	45 764	615	832	127	61	146	895	480	1 167	77	61
Washington	629	3.6	25 727	3 039	205	48	15	19	88	225	287	21	15
GEORGIA	393 594	4.7	38 980	X	212 661	35 512	14 971	29 658	64 737	69 530	292 802	16 898	14 971
Appling	540	0.6	29 115	2 814	290	76	20	57	65	154	443	24	20
Atkinson	217	1.6	26 384	3 013	67	15	5	27	25	63	115	6	5
Bacon	330	3.9	29 225	2 804	131	31	9	49	35	98	220	12	9
Baker	95	-22.7	29 192	2 809	21	4	1	12	17	26	39	2	1
Baldwin	1 325	4.5	28 857	2 841	557	149	38	62	201	430	805	48	38
Banks	602	4.9	32 904	2 295	111	26	8	106	68	137	251	14	8
Barrow	2 284	6.7	31 181	2 558	668	130	47	136	247	471	981	62	47
Bartow	3 406	4.8	33 483	2 199	1 461	278	107	335	422	733	2 180	130	107
Ben Hill	483	3.7	27 647	2 944	199	43	16	33	77	174	292	19	16
Berrien	521	-1.8	27 855	2 930	127	32	9	19	82	159	188	14	9
Bibb	5 725	3.3	37 199	1 569	3 683	632	263	408	1 068	1 444	4 985	297	263
Bleckley	407	1.3	31 785	2 475	81	26	6	16	75	121	129	9	6
Brantley	426	3.1	23 153	3 097	70	20	5	18	45	145	113	9	5
Brooks	484	-2.5	31 408	2 538	109	24	7	37	77	148	177	12	7
Bryan	1 548	4.2	45 657	624	258	56	18	78	206	226	410	26	18
Bulloch	2 023	1.8	28 062	2 914	870	217	61	93	328	462	1 242	69	61
Burke	691	0.0	30 433	2 660	389	95	27	55	85	206	565	32	27
Butts	679	4.9	29 046	2 822	221	51	15	29	90	190	316	21	15
Calhoun	163	-1.0	25 182	3 059	36	12	2	24	24	52	74	4	2
Camden	1 651	4.3	31 725	2 485	976	232	81	39	351	338	1 328	69	81
Candler	302	3.2	27 750	2 936	96	23	7	21	40	102	147	10	7
Carroll	3 709	4.5	32 508	2 369	1 677	330	119	198	559	856	2 324	138	119
Catoosa	2 069	4.7	31 531	2 522	510	101	37	164	227	487	812	56	37
Charlton	306	4.5	23 746	3 087	79	16	6	14	33	90	115	8	6
Chatham	11 582	3.7	40 872	1 077	7 015	1 233	516	672	2 335	2 152	9 436	535	516
Chattahoochee	379	0.2	32 020	2 436	1 072	320	108	4	219	36	1 505	52	108
Chattooga	691	4.0	27 704	2 938	212	53	16	40	88	232	320	22	16
Cherokee	9 545	6.8	41 322	1 024	2 152	365	152	391	1 127	1 280	3 059	196	152
Clarke	3 483	4.4	28 803	2 845	2 960	719	199	216	762	724	4 094	211	199
Clay	87	-3.0	27 998	2 920	5	1	1	-1	16	33	24	2	1
Clayton	7 018	5.1	26 232	3 022	6 041	1 116	421	405	847	1 770	7 983	446	421
Clinch	190	4.2	27 798	2 932	81	19	6	21	20	70	127	7	6
Cobb	36 193	5.7	49 513	413	19 844	2 629	1 368	3 455	5 494	3 953	27 297	1 573	1 368
Coffee	1 199	1.6	28 016	2 916	572	118	43	83	179	345	816	48	43
Colquitt	1 336	1.0	28 971	2 832	486	116	34	105	195	390	740	43	34
Columbia	5 976	5.1	42 916	857	1 220	227	88	250	911	876	1 784	112	88
Cook	447	-0.5	25 986	3 032	119	32	8	20	64	148	179	12	8
Coweta	5 310	5.6	39 169	1 301	1 503	277	108	187	686	824	2 075	130	108
Crawford	403	3.6	32 550	2 362	50	12	4	61	43	101	126	8	4
Crisp	604	2.4	26 351	3 016	298	57	21	29	98	204	406	26	21
Dade	469	3.9	28 643	2 871	118	24	9	35	65	126	185	13	9
Dawson	845	5.5	36 801	1 632	226	44	16	80	134	156	365	23	16
Decatur	900	-2.2	33 052	2 270	293	73	20	104	151	250	489	28	20
DeKalb	31 964	5.1	44 261	735	16 349	2 517	1 163	3 084	5 573	4 551	23 113	1 333	1 163
Dodge	559	2.1	26 643	3 004	169	50	11	27	83	170	257	16	11
Dooly	296	-4.9	20 853	3 108	100	28	7	17	48	99	152	9	7
Dougherty	2 947	2.5	31 889	2 453	2 018	414	145	148	525	893	2 724	156	145
Douglas	4 412	5.8	31 791	2 473	1 542	278	111	168	461	873	2 099	129	111
Early	366	-4.6	34 862	1 959	197	42	13	29	51	109	281	16	13
Echols	99	2.4	24 828	3 064	20	5	1	12	11	23	39	2	1

1. Based on the resident population estimated as of July 1 of the year shown.

Table B. States and Counties — Earnings, Social Security, and Housing

STATE County	Farm	Mining	Construction	Manufacturing	Information: professional, scientific, technical services	Retail trade	Finance, insurance, real estate and leasing	Health care and social assistance	Government	Number	Rate[1]	Supplemental Security Income recipients, December 2014	Total	Percent change, 2010–2014
	75	76	77	78	79	80	81	82	83	84	85	86	87	88
FLORIDA—Cont'd														
Putnam	1.7	0.4	3.4	13.9	D	9.3	2.7	13.7	29.9	19 940	277	3 004	36 528	-2.2
St. Johns	0.5	D	6.3	6.1	7.8	9.4	8.4	12.4	16.0	46 005	211	2 447	99 469	10.7
St. Lucie	0.7	0.1	5.2	4.3	6.6	9.8	3.9	22.1	22.1	73 760	254	6 782	138 071	0.9
Santa Rosa	0.3	0.7	6.6	2.3	9.8	9.2	4.3	12.6	29.0	32 285	198	2 445	68 574	5.9
Sarasota	0.1	0.2	7.9	4.8	12.2	9.6	9.3	17.8	10.4	128 735	324	4 698	232 623	1.8
Seminole	0.0	0.0	8.6	4.0	15.2	9.8	11.8	10.1	10.2	76 050	172	7 075	186 619	2.9
Sumter	1.4	0.6	11.1	5.5	D	8.8	5.1	14.2	22.9	61 425	539	1 588	66 850	26.1
Suwannee	16.2	0.2	4.3	11.7	D	8.8	3.2	8.4	22.6	11 240	257	1 435	18 801	-1.9
Taylor	0.6	D	8.7	30.5	D	8.3	2.3	D	21.4	5 145	228	762	10 852	-1.4
Union	0.7	D	3.9	4.5	D	D	0.9	D	60.5	2 305	152	387	4 459	-1.1
Volusia	0.4	0.0	5.7	8.1	7.1	10.0	5.6	18.6	15.7	141 410	279	12 095	256 967	1.1
Wakulla	-0.1	0.0	6.3	16.7	6.9	8.3	2.2	5.5	34.9	5 755	183	601	12 892	0.7
Walton	1.1	0.1	9.4	2.0	6.3	11.8	6.4	10.6	16.5	13 985	227	1 206	48 751	8.0
Washington	1.0	D	6.6	3.2	5.3	7.1	2.6	D	40.7	6 080	249	925	10 659	-1.3
GEORGIA	0.9	0.2	5.0	9.3	14.0	6.2	8.0	9.7	17.4	1 676 778	166	256 314	4 182 110	2.3
Appling	8.9	0.0	5.0	8.4	1.6	6.8	1.8	D	16.6	4 035	218	716	8 396	-1.4
Atkinson	16.1	D	D	36.9	D	4.1	2.3	D	18.1	1 550	189	358	3 445	-2.3
Bacon	16.7	0.0	1.8	16.5	D	4.4	D	D	14.2	2 325	207	412	4 726	-1.6
Baker	38.4	0.0	D	D	D	2.1	D	3.9	14.0	550	168	149	1 623	-1.8
Baldwin	0.0	0.0	D	15.6	D	9.1	3.4	D	36.4	9 115	199	1 477	20 196	0.1
Banks	22.3	0.0	7.2	6.5	D	7.4	1.3	D	17.1	3 690	201	183	7 528	-0.9
Barrow	2.1	D	9.8	12.6	D	11.1	3.9	7.5	18.2	12 465	170	1 761	27 241	3.2
Bartow	2.1	0.4	8.2	27.0	5.0	6.1	3.4	7.2	14.0	18 790	185	2 254	39 945	0.3
Ben Hill	1.4	0.0	2.0	24.4	D	7.8	3.4	D	18.9	4 065	233	912	7 876	-0.8
Berrien	-1.0	D	4.6	24.4	D	10.8	4.8	D	26.8	3 895	208	804	8 618	-1.0
Bibb	0.1	D	3.3	7.2	8.5	8.2	13.4	20.8	12.6	32 025	208	8 019	70 267	0.9
Bleckley	0.1	0.0	4.8	1.2	0.0	11.3	D	4.8	46.8	2 675	209	420	5 274	-0.6
Brantley	0.1	D	9.8	10.3	D	5.0	1.9	5.0	38.0	3 650	198	505	7 888	-2.4
Brooks	17.5	0.0	3.1	6.1	D	5.3	3.2	8.7	20.4	4 005	260	716	7 642	-0.8
Bryan	1.2	0.0	9.1	6.2	D	9.0	6.5	6.6	26.6	5 165	152	606	13 278	12.1
Bulloch	0.7	0.0	5.9	7.1	4.2	8.0	4.3	12.3	35.3	10 260	142	1 680	30 197	4.9
Burke	4.6	0.0	1.9	7.1	4.2	4.6	1.5	D	15.3	4 995	220	1 233	9 835	-0.3
Butts	0.6	0.0	D	13.2	D	8.9	3.9	D	28.2	4 870	208	710	9 269	-0.9
Calhoun	26.4	0.0	D	D	D	4.0	D	D	34.4	1 415	220	337	2 376	-1.4
Camden	0.2	0.0	D	5.0	17.1	5.7	2.6	4.3	51.5	8 090	156	831	21 467	1.7
Candler	3.1	0.0	6.5	7.3	9.9	9.7	D	D	27.8	2 295	211	477	4 683	-1.6
Carroll	2.8	D	6.9	16.4	D	8.2	2.7	15.2	19.0	22 015	193	3 355	44 735	0.2
Catoosa	1.9	0.0	7.6	9.2	2.8	12.5	4.8	14.4	18.4	14 010	214	885	26 882	1.0
Charlton	5.8	D	3.0	12.4	D	5.3	D	3.5	22.5	2 235	173	362	4 401	-1.7
Chatham	0.0	0.0	4.0	16.9	5.3	6.6	4.7	13.0	18.8	48 210	170	6 913	123 669	3.6
Chattahoochee	0.1	0.0	0.4	D	D	0.3	D	D	90.6	705	59	159	3 336	-1.2
Chattooga	3.7	0.0	3.8	37.7	D	7.8	2.4	D	22.5	6 260	251	1 024	10 863	-1.0
Cherokee	0.5	0.1	10.8	8.1	9.2	10.0	6.1	10.1	16.9	34 990	152	2 182	87 486	6.2
Clarke	0.1	D	2.9	11.0	3.8	6.4	6.3	16.0	36.3	16 050	133	2 878	52 221	2.3
Clay	-3.9	D	D	0.0	0.0	5.6	D	11.7	48.3	790	255	170	2 078	-1.1
Clayton	0.0	D	2.7	4.0	2.1	5.3	2.2	6.1	12.4	35 465	132	7 247	104 719	0.0
Clinch	10.3	0.0	2.8	34.2	2.3	3.2	D	3.5	19.8	1 575	231	439	2 959	-1.6
Cobb	0.0	0.2	9.2	6.5	16.8	6.7	8.6	8.9	8.6	94 800	130	9 323	295 622	3.2
Coffee	4.6	0.0	3.9	16.0	2.9	9.8	3.0	D	17.5	7 860	184	1 685	16 890	-1.0
Colquitt	9.2	0.0	3.9	14.9	D	8.7	4.7	D	25.9	9 145	199	1 968	18 308	0.0
Columbia	0.2	D	8.5	10.7	8.2	11.1	7.0	10.6	18.8	20 785	149	1 539	54 554	12.2
Cook	5.9	D	9.1	12.5	3.2	7.2	3.2	D	34.3	3 675	214	718	7 241	-0.6
Coweta	0.2	D	5.0	14.0	6.1	9.3	3.5	15.5	16.2	21 765	161	1 947	52 660	5.0
Crawford	19.4	D	11.4	1.5	D	7.5	1.7	D	17.5	2 755	221	306	5 246	-0.9
Crisp	0.9	0.0	2.8	12.4	D	8.4	4.9	D	18.2	4 775	208	1 114	10 690	-0.4
Dade	5.2	0.0	D	17.3	4.0	7.5	D	7.1	15.9	3 830	234	414	7 252	-0.7
Dawson	5.2	0.1	7.6	7.8	3.7	23.6	4.7	4.3	16.2	4 560	199	428	10 747	3.0
Decatur	11.4	D	4.2	6.9	3.5	11.2	4.7	D	28.2	6 090	224	1 361	12 114	-0.1
DeKalb	0.0	D	5.2	4.4	15.3	5.6	7.4	12.5	13.9	98 150	136	18 820	308 118	1.0
Dodge	2.9	D	2.6	10.4	2.8	7.9	3.6	D	40.1	4 295	205	856	9 715	-1.5
Dooly	7.1	0.0	1.2	28.0	0.8	6.4	D	D	28.5	2 335	164	508	6 202	-2.0
Dougherty	0.6	0.0	4.1	9.7	7.4	6.5	4.1	18.4	26.6	18 510	200	5 234	40 701	-0.2
Douglas	0.0	D	7.4	10.8	3.9	10.8	4.7	11.5	17.2	20 725	150	2 846	52 012	0.7
Early	7.9	0.0	3.4	24.5	D	5.7	D	D	24.0	2 565	245	650	4 907	-1.3
Echols	7.1	0.0	9.6	0.0	0.9	1.5	D	D	24.7	565	139	45	1 529	-1.9

1. Per 1,000 resident population estimated as of July 1 of the year shown.

Table B. States and Counties — Housing, Labor Force, and Employment

	Housing units, 2010–2014								Civilian labor force, 2015				Civilian employment,[6] 2010–2014		
	Occupied units										Unemployment			Percent	
			Owner-occupied			Renter-occupied									
				Median owner cost as a percent of income											
STATE County	Total	Percent	Median value[1]	With a mortgage	Without a mortgage[2]	Median rent[3]	Median rent as a percent of income[2]	Substandard units[4] (percent)	Total	Percent change, 2014–2015	Total	Rate[5]	Total	Management, business, science and arts	Construction, production, and maintenance occupations
	89	90	91	92	93	94	95	96	97	98	99	100	101	102	103

STATE County	89	90	91	92	93	94	95	96	97	98	99	100	101	102	103
FLORIDA—Cont'd															
Putnam	27 842	75.2	86 600	26.6	11.2	655	34.6	2.9	28 630	0.2	2 072	7.2	24 583	22.7	31.5
St. Johns	77 443	75.6	240 400	24.9	10.9	1 105	31.8	1.3	112 131	1.1	4 335	3.9	93 963	44.3	12.9
St. Lucie	107 104	73.3	120 700	28.3	13.8	990	38.9	2.1	131 333	0.4	8 191	6.2	110 761	28.2	20.6
Santa Rosa	57 583	73.3	160 200	23.4	11.1	1 014	30.0	2.1	73 537	0.3	3 499	4.8	65 969	36.4	19.7
Sarasota	172 720	73.5	172 800	27.1	13.3	1 008	32.1	1.3	178 877	2.0	8 880	5.0	152 040	33.4	15.8
Seminole	147 932	69.6	175 100	25.6	11.8	1 059	32.5	1.4	239 943	1.4	11 493	4.8	205 887	42.2	13.2
Sumter	45 868	90.3	199 500	24.8	11.5	780	30.8	1.5	28 583	0.9	2 130	7.5	21 880	27.9	20.7
Suwannee	15 583	70.2	93 800	24.3	10.4	674	31.3	3.3	17 818	-0.5	978	5.5	15 679	25.4	31.4
Taylor	7 464	76.3	84 000	22.6	11.2	545	26.2	1.1	9 061	-3.7	601	6.6	7 301	26.3	26.4
Union	3 816	67.5	87 000	25.2	10.0	646	24.7	3.5	4 755	0.2	227	4.8	4 268	23.0	20.1
Volusia	197 092	71.0	133 100	27.4	13.4	918	36.4	2.2	239 320	0.4	13 715	5.7	195 513	30.2	20.4
Wakulla	10 905	76.0	129 900	23.4	10.4	854	29.5	2.2	14 061	-1.6	643	4.6	12 915	32.2	20.0
Walton	22 638	72.5	161 500	28.1	11.2	993	33.5	4.3	27 646	0.5	1 281	4.6	24 836	32.5	19.5
Washington	8 381	77.2	84 500	23.3	11.8	608	31.1	3.0	9 599	-1.4	564	5.9	8 448	29.9	22.3
GEORGIA	3 540 690	64.2	148 000	23.4	11.6	874	31.8	2.8	4 770 895	0.4	279 952	5.9	4 300 074	35.8	22.2
Appling	6 878	65.8	69 500	21.8	10.0	534	21.1	2.3	8 754	1.0	621	7.1	7 469	22.5	42.6
Atkinson	2 713	71.7	74 000	20.6	13.3	457	28.8	3.9	3 872	7.0	216	5.6	3 204	19.6	45.3
Bacon	3 953	69.7	74 400	17.5	11.3	606	29.4	1.8	5 033	3.9	275	5.5	4 501	28.4	39.2
Baker	1 362	74.4	76 500	22.5	10.3	414	37.7	5.1	1 143	2.4	83	7.3	1 327	30.4	29.5
Baldwin	16 194	55.3	104 300	24.3	11.8	705	40.7	2.4	17 454	-5.6	1 355	7.8	16 672	32.8	23.0
Banks	6 703	76.8	130 700	24.9	11.8	721	32.6	2.8	8 162	0.2	444	5.4	8 018	26.3	39.8
Barrow	23 064	76.5	122 600	23.5	10.8	904	30.9	2.6	35 577	1.1	1 833	5.2	31 412	28.3	27.2
Bartow	35 293	66.9	123 900	23.3	10.7	796	30.0	3.4	47 007	0.8	2 701	5.7	43 679	29.0	29.9
Ben Hill	6 349	66.3	80 400	24.9	13.3	609	32.7	3.2	5 318	-5.0	481	9.0	5 865	27.4	33.5
Berrien	7 102	72.7	80 900	25.8	11.8	533	33.1	2.8	7 010	-3.2	489	7.0	6 560	26.5	34.5
Bibb	56 660	53.8	122 000	24.0	12.0	742	36.9	2.3	68 327	-1.0	4 484	6.6	59 479	34.6	17.4
Bleckley	4 019	70.2	85 500	19.7	16.1	636	32.7	1.6	4 413	-4.7	402	9.1	4 189	28.3	23.2
Brantley	6 523	78.2	66 900	25.5	11.8	523	26.9	0.7	6 918	0.4	503	7.3	6 539	24.4	33.2
Brooks	6 550	69.6	91 800	27.5	14.5	577	32.7	5.7	6 740	1.6	401	5.9	5 872	26.0	34.8
Bryan	11 231	69.7	184 800	22.1	10.0	1 075	29.4	2.1	15 784	1.5	817	5.2	14 167	34.4	24.2
Bulloch	25 803	50.3	128 200	22.1	10.4	760	38.3	2.4	34 855	0.9	2 077	6.0	30 465	32.7	22.0
Burke	7 970	72.1	79 700	22.3	14.9	579	32.0	3.6	9 131	-0.5	735	8.0	8 481	26.2	33.5
Butts	7 781	74.3	122 300	25.4	11.3	783	30.6	3.1	10 154	1.2	654	6.4	8 778	22.5	33.1
Calhoun	1 787	65.5	52 400	29.0	16.4	563	34.1	0.7	2 135	-0.3	130	6.1	2 323	17.4	35.1
Camden	18 560	61.3	151 800	25.4	10.0	910	28.5	1.8	22 416	2.1	1 227	5.5	20 223	32.8	21.8
Candler	3 944	65.0	83 400	25.2	10.0	550	32.6	3.0	5 006	-1.4	280	5.6	4 289	27.1	33.4
Carroll	39 610	64.6	115 600	22.4	11.2	789	33.1	2.7	52 274	0.6	3 451	6.6	46 828	27.7	32.4
Catoosa	23 813	74.3	129 300	21.3	10.3	737	27.9	2.1	31 304	0.8	1 606	5.1	29 802	33.1	24.9
Charlton	3 552	78.5	85 000	23.6	10.0	667	32.5	1.1	4 789	-0.3	299	6.2	4 329	24.6	39.5
Chatham	103 807	56.0	171 100	24.9	12.6	935	33.0	2.0	133 265	1.2	7 640	5.7	121 745	34.9	20.5
Chattahoochee	2 602	28.1	83 100	16.9	17.1	1 262	31.5	4.0	2 199	-1.6	193	8.8	2 165	26.2	26.6
Chattooga	9 347	68.7	66 700	24.0	13.0	581	27.9	7.4	10 393	-1.2	644	6.2	8 736	23.6	42.9
Cherokee	77 654	78.3	186 900	22.7	10.0	997	28.8	2.3	119 452	1.2	5 463	4.6	106 790	38.2	17.5
Clarke	42 107	42.6	152 700	22.9	11.4	790	38.1	2.7	56 558	0.6	3 317	5.9	52 092	40.0	16.7
Clay	1 170	56.9	63 700	25.8	16.0	401	33.4	6.2	869	-5.0	98	11.3	822	21.2	42.2
Clayton	87 490	53.9	89 100	25.4	12.0	886	35.7	4.9	125 051	0.3	9 343	7.5	111 507	23.9	28.7
Clinch	2 579	66.8	66 500	22.7	13.0	467	23.9	1.3	2 843	0.5	193	6.8	2 287	28.3	36.6
Cobb	264 805	65.0	194 500	21.8	10.0	988	30.1	2.5	398 123	1.2	19 802	5.0	357 838	44.3	15.3
Coffee	14 597	67.3	79 700	25.7	10.7	564	29.9	3.4	17 395	-1.4	1 142	6.6	15 513	29.4	31.1
Colquitt	15 893	64.6	79 300	23.9	11.9	582	33.1	6.3	19 707	-1.9	1 266	6.4	18 160	25.8	37.7
Columbia	44 764	78.8	170 100	21.5	10.0	1 052	27.4	1.1	66 525	0.1	3 332	5.0	58 728	42.0	18.5
Cook	6 255	70.2	83 200	25.1	11.8	674	30.6	2.5	7 252	-2.0	479	6.6	7 053	27.1	32.9
Coweta	47 666	74.1	178 800	22.9	11.4	925	29.5	1.9	67 350	1.3	3 497	5.2	60 166	33.6	25.7
Crawford	4 655	80.6	86 100	26.8	13.7	699	30.4	3.1	5 597	-0.2	344	6.1	5 027	28.8	32.5
Crisp	8 574	60.7	89 100	20.4	13.3	589	38.3	4.3	9 314	-1.5	641	6.9	8 797	29.7	26.2
Dade	6 175	79.2	116 800	22.5	10.8	649	29.8	2.9	7 948	0.8	426	5.4	7 639	26.4	28.7
Dawson	8 277	75.3	174 400	26.6	10.0	984	31.4	1.3	10 918	1.1	542	5.0	9 728	31.2	27.4
Decatur	10 473	63.3	99 800	23.4	12.9	630	34.0	8.0	11 344	-0.3	759	6.7	10 065	29.2	29.1
DeKalb	264 120	56.0	163 600	24.5	12.0	977	32.9	3.1	371 671	0.8	22 052	5.9	334 438	42.3	16.6
Dodge	8 056	63.6	70 700	21.1	10.3	544	31.0	3.0	6 992	-6.0	578	8.3	7 920	32.2	30.2
Dooly	4 957	68.0	63 600	24.1	13.0	528	32.9	3.9	4 785	3.1	359	7.5	4 677	20.4	39.8
Dougherty	35 585	46.3	100 800	23.2	13.5	697	35.4	3.6	37 924	-1.9	2 906	7.7	33 905	29.3	25.5
Douglas	46 708	68.8	125 500	24.4	10.6	945	33.1	2.4	68 274	0.9	4 224	6.2	60 173	32.4	23.3
Early	4 096	66.4	83 900	22.8	13.1	576	29.1	3.7	4 359	0.4	296	6.8	3 834	28.6	27.0
Echols	1 434	64.0	71 500	19.6	11.1	656	22.7	5.4	1 840	3.2	86	4.7	1 764	17.7	50.5

1. Specified owner-occupied units.　　2. A value of 10.0 represents 10 percent or less; a value of 50.0 represents 50 percent or more.　　3. Specified renter-occupied units.
4. Overcrowded or lacking complete plumbing facilities.　　5. Percent of civilian labor force.　　6. Persons 16 years old and over.

STATE County		Private nonfarm establishments, employment and payroll, 2014								Agriculture, 2012			
			Employment						Annual payroll	Farms			
												Percent with:	
	Number of establishments	Total	Health care and social assistance	Manufacturing	Retail trade	Finance and insurance	Professional, scientific, and technical services	Total (mil dol)	Average per employee (dollars)	Number	Fewer than 50 acres	500 acres or more	Farm operators whose principal occupation is farming (percent)
	104	105	106	107	108	109	110	111	112	113	114	115	116
FLORIDA—Cont'd													
Putnam	1 231	12 036	2 426	1 837	2 659	323	306	383	31 799	430	64.0	7.9	44.7
St. Johns	5 499	51 842	7 280	1 664	9 644	1 730	3 235	1 867	36 013	188	67.0	12.2	47.3
St. Lucie	5 123	56 108	10 909	2 624	13 146	1 141	2 354	1 895	33 770	406	50.7	18.0	53.0
Santa Rosa	2 528	22 879	3 533	488	4 851	612	2 011	767	33 519	666	59.6	6.9	41.3
Sarasota	13 062	132 202	26 782	6 818	22 889	5 338	9 459	5 141	38 890	283	72.1	7.1	44.5
Seminole	12 766	157 172	17 378	5 819	26 288	13 348	11 227	6 432	40 926	312	84.6	2.2	49.4
Sumter	1 334	18 994	3 773	1 168	3 179	657	595	697	36 689	1 367	70.1	4.0	34.7
Suwannee	683	7 742	1 428	1 818	1 549	128	159	224	28 992	1 266	50.6	5.5	54.2
Taylor	392	4 591	621	1 517	993	D	78	170	37 093	181	44.8	7.2	57.5
Union	128	1 838	D	D	164	D	D	60	32 888	291	58.4	4.1	41.2
Volusia	12 143	136 213	27 489	8 291	24 959	4 595	6 558	4 601	33 777	1 363	81.6	2.5	55.1
Wakulla	419	3 233	154	D	876	74	145	91	28 270	171	70.2	5.3	49.7
Walton	1 925	18 202	1 976	176	4 249	253	513	580	31 859	670	43.0	6.4	44.8
Washington	380	3 915	779	D	732	D	272	114	29 020	406	41.9	5.7	36.0
GEORGIA	220 605	3 551 163	462 968	352 455	453 396	167 775	247 331	163 852	46 140	42 257	39.9	10.4	47.0
Appling	348	5 442	914	606	864	142	D	251	46 051	475	38.5	13.9	43.2
Atkinson	87	1 189	D	610	136	54	D	40	33 800	194	28.4	20.6	70.1
Bacon	214	2 536	D	664	278	149	D	83	32 666	268	35.1	12.7	48.1
Baker	25	217	D	NA	28	D	D	8	38 894	150	17.3	32.7	72.7
Baldwin	792	12 986	3 924	1 529	2 283	382	D	421	32 422	124	38.7	7.3	42.7
Banks	271	2 919	174	D	D	46	D	76	25 976	519	40.7	1.9	59.5
Barrow	1 105	14 973	1 434	2 417	2 417	309	920	478	31 936	304	52.3	3.3	35.9
Bartow	1 884	29 469	2 859	7 630	3 917	659	494	1 168	39 633	458	53.1	5.0	50.7
Ben Hill	320	4 792	634	1 601	721	154	55	149	31 101	209	38.8	13.9	44.0
Berrien	259	2 509	321	D	461	146	D	76	30 361	380	28.4	25.3	64.2
Bibb	4 116	72 701	15 286	4 685	10 330	8 843	2 794	2 687	36 965	113	38.1	1.8	50.4
Bleckley	164	1 395	D	D	338	79	43	36	26 064	219	31.5	15.5	39.3
Brantley	180	1 240	D	D	289	D	D	36	29 205	215	49.3	2.8	49.8
Brooks	201	1 999	551	D	341	72	D	63	31 612	364	39.3	19.5	51.9
Bryan	622	5 550	597	D	1 182	129	278	160	28 778	60	65.0	11.7	58.3
Bulloch	1 387	16 743	2 957	1 482	3 325	514	538	475	28 376	544	28.9	18.6	42.1
Burke	291	5 189	345	738	746	147	D	308	59 415	393	29.3	20.4	43.3
Butts	358	4 014	624	732	697	D	79	126	31 278	140	44.3	5.0	58.6
Calhoun	73	596	D	D	93	29	D	21	35 181	151	25.2	37.1	48.3
Camden	792	8 038	957	143	1 956	302	D	214	26 575	69	60.9	10.1	44.9
Candler	207	2 173	556	163	381	98	D	62	28 379	238	29.4	11.3	47.5
Carroll	1 978	32 496	4 783	7 130	4 931	661	594	1 217	37 452	909	45.5	1.8	50.8
Catoosa	886	11 670	1 813	1 697	2 540	409	D	366	31 351	269	50.2	1.1	43.9
Charlton	146	1 798	269	D	216	40	47	59	32 798	84	48.8	8.3	51.2
Chatham	7 416	126 850	19 239	14 979	17 146	2 792	5 158	5 227	41 205	35	37.1	5.7	57.1
Chattahoochee	100	1 444	68	D	134	D	181	57	39 691	13	15.4	15.4	30.8
Chattooga	305	4 501	330	D	680	137	D	130	28 818	292	31.8	7.5	39.0
Cherokee	4 971	45 667	5 800	3 746	9 479	1 393	2 811	1 548	33 905	430	69.5	1.9	49.1
Clarke	2 940	45 676	9 879	5 379	7 084	1 122	1 465	1 623	35 532	90	64.4	3.3	23.3
Clay	36	D	46	NA	62	D	D	D	D	70	17.1	21.4	45.7
Clayton	3 757	70 883	7 885	3 740	10 742	1 617	863	2 563	36 160	23	87.0	0.0	69.6
Clinch	128	1 843	D	D	157	D	28	52	28 159	80	35.0	16.3	55.0
Cobb	19 336	318 225	29 234	19 172	37 456	16 627	28 439	17 147	53 882	110	81.8	0.0	55.5
Coffee	837	12 260	1 941	2 791	1 884	311	202	404	32 964	587	29.1	15.2	43.8
Colquitt	887	11 169	2 189	3 022	1 812	326	175	332	29 746	484	30.2	19.2	60.5
Columbia	2 143	26 600	3 158	3 136	5 309	744	1 306	888	33 377	145	57.2	2.8	45.5
Cook	307	2 922	D	754	520	126	D	83	28 483	234	41.0	18.4	41.0
Coweta	2 193	30 700	4 271	4 685	5 570	667	866	1 074	34 990	357	52.1	4.5	44.5
Crawford	100	549	D	D	111	D	8	18	33 124	155	38.7	8.4	53.5
Crisp	500	6 674	1 142	1 012	1 419	230	D	219	32 808	244	30.3	23.4	51.2
Dade	203	2 681	217	493	474	96	D	88	32 891	192	38.5	3.1	38.5
Dawson	603	6 241	337	D	2 764	119	126	147	23 490	182	64.3	1.6	41.2
Decatur	579	6 493	984	1 365	1 359	262	171	214	32 972	358	27.7	25.7	55.0
DeKalb	16 300	262 339	39 228	10 892	31 300	8 657	19 811	13 350	50 888	25	84.0	4.0	36.0
Dodge	340	3 178	807	346	718	139	103	86	27 148	401	26.4	8.7	53.4
Dooly	156	2 028	52	884	300	D	D	59	28 937	290	27.2	21.0	58.6
Dougherty	2 337	37 973	8 313	2 964	6 571	1 137	1 812	1 350	35 558	121	45.5	18.2	51.2
Douglas	2 438	34 833	4 820	2 948	7 557	684	912	1 101	31 599	117	67.5	2.6	43.6
Early	216	2 806	D	831	363	122	63	133	47 574	334	25.1	27.8	47.3
Echols	26	108	D	D	D	D	NA	4	36 204	40	17.5	17.5	40.0

Table B. States and Counties — **Agriculture**

STATE County	Land in farms — Acreage (1,000) [117]	Acres — Percent change, 2007–2012 [118]	Acres — Average size of farm [119]	Acres — Total irrigated (1,000) [120]	Acres — Total cropland (1,000) [121]	Value of land and buildings (dollars) — Average per farm [122]	Value of land and buildings (dollars) — Average per acre [123]	Value of machinery and equipment, average per farm (dollars) [124]	Value of products sold — Total (mil dol) [125]	Value of products sold — Average per farm (dollars) [126]	Percent from: Crops [127]	Percent from: Live-stock and poultry products [128]	Percent of farms with sales of: $10,000 or more [129]	Percent of farms with sales of: $100,000 or more [130]	Government payments — Total ($1,000) [131]	Government payments — Percent of farms [132]
FLORIDA—Cont'd																
Putnam	70	-5.5	164	5.5	10.3	904 658	5 529	50 742	44.2	102 761	85.0	15.0	31.9	9.5	153	5.3
St. Johns	34	0.3	179	11.7	18.5	1 172 793	6 556	259 819	69.7	370 527	98.7	1.3	38.8	16.5	162	5.9
St. Lucie	195	27.1	481	59.2	66.6	2 287 172	4 758	82 488	168.1	413 975	87.5	12.5	48.3	25.1	872	6.7
Santa Rosa	98	39.1	147	2.4	69.6	518 886	3 539	87 569	62.8	94 249	94.9	5.1	31.7	13.2	2 545	31.5
Sarasota	80	31.3	283	2.0	4.7	1 363 223	4 814	44 753	25.0	88 456	60.0	40.0	28.6	10.6	384	2.5
Seminole	22	-39.0	70	1.2	2.4	547 465	7 872	35 391	27.5	88 042	95.1	4.9	34.0	9.3	40	2.2
Sumter	183	14.7	134	3.1	20.7	717 143	5 350	45 931	42.1	30 773	58.9	41.1	19.3	5.3	164	2.9
Suwannee	193	15.5	153	27.8	84.1	613 355	4 014	92 742	296.3	234 060	29.2	70.8	35.8	13.3	1 332	12.1
Taylor	37	11.7	207	D	2.3	787 271	3 805	39 011	5.8	32 160	58.7	41.3	26.0	4.4	19	5.5
Union	46	-0.7	159	1.0	7.3	567 890	3 574	39 282	7.4	25 495	75.8	24.2	25.4	3.4	111	4.8
Volusia	106	27.3	78	9.0	23.4	477 479	6 137	44 275	111.5	81 802	89.7	10.3	35.2	9.5	1 427	8.0
Wakulla	31	9.1	181	0.2	2.0	632 977	3 502	31 655	2.3	13 322	D	D	31.0	2.3	39	7.6
Walton	148	16.6	221	1.3	30.7	634 997	2 876	47 294	28.6	42 633	37.5	62.5	22.8	6.0	819	25.2
Washington	58	-21.1	144	1.1	18.4	412 480	2 874	59 667	13.5	33 370	69.3	30.7	25.9	4.4	450	30.0
GEORGIA	9 621	-5.2	228	1 125.4	4 190.9	702 282	3 085	93 143	9 255.1	219 020	39.7	60.3	37.4	17.3	142 322	34.4
Appling	123	21.0	259	7.5	73.8	605 707	2 341	143 872	139.6	293 888	45.8	54.2	48.8	28.8	2 049	44.8
Atkinson	87	12.5	448	6.6	35.1	1 195 005	2 669	136 820	70.0	360 840	43.0	57.0	60.3	36.6	961	49.5
Bacon	58	-8.7	215	4.4	30.3	624 134	2 896	108 507	65.2	243 127	48.6	51.4	56.0	23.5	624	34.3
Baker	146	8.4	977	30.5	60.6	2 680 720	2 745	266 427	84.4	562 620	74.0	26.0	56.7	38.7	3 011	74.7
Baldwin	19	-37.7	151	0.0	4.5	368 589	2 448	60 427	1.2	9 936	42.4	57.6	26.6	0.8	10	7.3
Banks	60	27.8	115	0.1	14.3	631 780	5 494	70 378	179.5	345 890	1.0	99.0	56.1	40.1	247	16.8
Barrow	30	-12.0	98	0.1	6.5	538 576	5 493	46 885	39.9	131 306	1.4	98.6	29.9	10.9	123	10.5
Bartow	64	-1.9	140	2.2	25.6	618 074	4 430	68 517	95.4	208 210	15.5	84.5	35.2	17.0	1 141	21.2
Ben Hill	57	-23.3	274	6.9	26.5	695 507	2 536	93 340	27.0	129 029	86.7	13.3	32.5	13.4	762	58.9
Berrien	143	20.7	377	21.6	76.4	1 001 384	2 653	184 247	101.6	267 384	80.0	20.0	55.3	29.7	2 653	56.6
Bibb	15	2.2	130	0.3	6.2	425 690	3 267	48 389	11.4	100 770	11.3	88.7	28.3	10.6	86	17.7
Bleckley	66	-25.1	301	13.0	33.3	701 356	2 328	91 685	24.6	112 502	93.9	6.1	32.0	16.9	1 049	66.7
Brantley	23	-7.6	109	0.8	7.5	315 219	2 893	50 674	7.7	35 967	52.0	48.0	37.2	5.1	143	22.3
Brooks	148	-21.6	407	19.7	77.0	1 344 739	3 303	144 365	112.1	308 014	66.7	33.3	38.7	17.9	3 095	53.8
Bryan	15	-25.0	254	D	4.4	743 867	2 932	105 567	D	D	D	D	20.0	6.7	D	25.0
Bulloch	180	-8.5	331	7.8	108.9	802 399	2 421	124 037	105.3	193 612	84.7	15.3	40.1	14.0	3 610	68.4
Burke	161	-15.9	411	27.5	88.7	924 547	2 252	159 715	106.4	270 817	67.0	33.0	39.2	19.3	3 146	52.2
Butts	21	-16.9	151	0.0	4.9	526 171	3 484	47 029	2.4	17 143	51.2	48.9	35.0	3.6	21	14.3
Calhoun	108	-12.3	712	21.1	61.4	1 560 185	2 191	279 291	93.2	617 053	72.4	27.6	53.6	32.5	2 817	78.8
Camden	16	17.4	228	0.1	1.0	497 348	2 180	32 899	0.5	6 594	71.0	29.0	14.5	1.4	102	15.9
Candler	54	-27.6	225	3.0	23.4	536 151	2 383	64 819	22.4	94 277	60.6	39.4	34.0	14.3	832	49.2
Carroll	86	-10.7	95	D	19.4	419 188	4 435	51 799	192.1	211 382	4.7	95.3	29.9	13.0	513	9.9
Catoosa	21	0.3	77	0.3	7.3	434 822	5 669	62 424	43.4	161 260	10.1	89.9	31.6	14.5	77	9.7
Charlton	13	-34.5	159	0.1	1.5	324 679	2 040	56 214	8.8	105 214	6.2	93.8	23.8	4.8	25	10.7
Chatham	4	-10.8	110	0.0	1.5	565 600	5 162	52 943	4.1	118 029	93.1	6.9	31.4	11.4	4	11.4
Chattahoochee	4	-4.3	314	0.0	0.3	652 846	2 080	42 462	0.0	3 154	D	D	7.7	0.0	13	46.2
Chattooga	50	-5.6	172	0.2	13.0	528 260	3 079	54 678	23.8	81 565	7.7	92.3	34.2	6.5	152	23.3
Cherokee	25	7.5	59	0.1	5.0	555 347	9 486	39 460	44.0	102 426	14.6	85.4	27.7	9.8	16	3.0
Clarke	9	-15.0	99	0.1	2.1	557 689	5 648	38 556	41.1	457 111	D	D	34.4	6.7	68	25.6
Clay	40	-10.2	571	6.8	18.7	945 343	1 654	150 500	17.8	254 800	96.3	3.7	27.1	22.9	718	81.4
Clayton	1	-50.9	36	D	0.2	202 348	5 574	23 609	0.1	4 130	34.7	65.3	13.0	0.0	0	0.0
Clinch	27	41.0	333	2.9	5.4	903 375	2 710	152 763	23.5	293 513	91.7	8.3	67.5	41.3	68	25.0
Cobb	5	-39.5	47	0.0	1.4	572 027	12 235	30 482	3.4	31 227	88.6	11.4	20.0	3.6	20	14.5
Coffee	168	-9.2	286	22.8	87.0	753 704	2 633	133 838	200.2	341 043	44.3	55.7	47.2	29.8	3 049	56.0
Colquitt	189	-4.1	390	47.5	106.6	1 144 308	2 938	154 525	251.6	519 804	65.2	34.8	50.8	28.3	4 920	60.5
Columbia	13	-30.5	90	0.1	2.0	443 579	4 910	51 034	3.0	20 538	65.0	35.0	23.4	3.4	10	2.8
Cook	68	5.1	293	14.8	44.2	804 987	2 751	158 726	87.0	371 714	64.5	35.5	50.4	23.9	1 661	55.6
Coweta	55	-25.8	155	0.4	11.4	766 835	4 942	50 751	11.5	32 140	51.9	48.1	19.6	3.1	161	7.6
Crawford	34	-9.9	219	4.7	14.0	675 006	3 084	92 968	52.2	336 626	50.9	49.1	38.7	20.0	125	24.5
Crisp	117	40.8	481	22.3	81.9	1 004 480	2 090	216 049	77.1	315 783	90.0	10.0	42.2	27.0	2 312	62.7
Dade	32	-7.9	169	0.0	7.2	535 115	3 163	50 755	29.4	153 193	1.8	98.2	27.1	8.9	195	9.9
Dawson	13	-24.8	70	0.0	2.3	543 434	7 782	82 945	54.3	298 418	1.2	98.8	32.4	20.9	21	6.6
Decatur	199	10.6	556	54.7	123.6	1 545 198	2 780	229 341	209.4	584 919	90.7	9.3	40.2	29.1	4 158	72.9
DeKalb	3	205.2	118	0.0	0.3	335 920	2 857	32 920	0.6	25 800	84.5	15.5	44.0	12.0	22	20.0
Dodge	90	-29.3	225	7.9	27.7	494 833	2 202	61 095	35.6	88 838	52.9	47.1	26.2	6.7	1 142	61.3
Dooly	127	-18.5	437	28.0	86.6	1 025 624	2 345	215 472	80.9	279 052	86.4	13.6	41.0	24.1	3 688	77.9
Dougherty	65	-25.5	541	13.0	19.7	1 771 504	3 277	134 256	33.6	277 562	94.2	5.8	24.8	12.4	408	42.1
Douglas	8	17.3	71	D	2.2	469 940	6 591	30 325	1.2	9 974	69.8	30.2	17.1	2.6	55	9.4
Early	169	-4.6	507	32.7	93.8	1 089 147	2 148	143 674	86.5	258 934	91.2	8.8	43.1	26.3	4 347	72.8
Echols	13	-7.1	333	2.3	4.8	878 025	2 638	152 050	8.3	208 125	88.8	11.2	42.5	20.0	80	47.5

STATE County	Water use, 2010		Wholesale trade,[1] 2012				Retail trade,[2] 2012				Real estate and rental and leasing,[2] 2012			
	Total water withdrawn (mil gal/day)	Gallons withdrawn per person per day	Number of establishments	Number of employees	Sales (mil dol)	Annual payroll (mil dol)	Number of establishments	Number of employees	Sales (mil dol)	Annual payroll (mil dol)	Number of establishments	Number of employees	Receipts (mil dol)	Annual payroll (mil dol)
	133	134	135	136	137	138	139	140	141	142	143	144	145	146
FLORIDA—Cont'd														
Putnam	74.7	1 004	24	D	D	D	239	2 429	633.5	56.8	52	136	16.2	3.3
St. Johns	43.9	231	163	1 429	1 426.3	81.2	760	9 003	2 502.6	205.6	302	1 076	199.0	34.0
St. Lucie	1 201.3	4 325	185	1 473	686.0	61.8	690	12 368	3 709.5	361.3	260	752	134.5	22.9
Santa Rosa	26.2	173	57	419	323.2	16.0	357	4 644	1 259.9	108.4	150	336	53.3	9.0
Sarasota	31.3	82	447	3 613	1 868.1	160.1	1 696	21 356	5 751.7	548.8	814	2 753	666.0	116.9
Seminole	69.1	164	617	6 435	2 813.7	295.8	1 666	24 591	6 972.0	608.4	705	3 850	609.2	131.7
Sumter	32.0	342	45	D	D	D	217	2 840	908.8	62.1	79	176	25.6	5.7
Suwannee	138.2	3 325	31	D	D	D	128	1 347	343.1	32.5	28	106	10.8	2.4
Taylor	42.9	1 901	20	D	D	D	87	816	205.2	17.5	12	27	2.8	0.7
Union	2.7	172	5	D	D	D	29	158	44.8	3.8	4	8	1.0	0.2
Volusia	228.3	462	420	2 983	1 655.1	144.8	1 869	23 642	6 168.3	569.3	655	2 511	402.4	75.0
Wakulla	5.3	173	10	D	D	D	62	738	176.1	16.1	16	25	3.3	0.5
Walton	13.9	252	47	595	454.1	27.0	344	3 638	817.4	79.6	186	915	151.9	31.4
Washington	3.7	148	11	D	D	D	67	736	174.7	15.7	12	22	2.7	0.6
GEORGIA	4 718.8	487	10 637	150 168	143 645.3	8 476.3	33 426	433 840	119 801.5	10 290.1	10 484	55 551	14 232.4	2 703.7
Appling	60.9	3 341	23	137	86.1	4.7	76	699	211.3	15.4	10	31	2.9	0.6
Atkinson	2.6	313	5	94	46.5	2.6	29	141	43.8	3.1	1	D	D	D
Bacon	2.3	203	16	230	160.9	6.9	40	280	72.7	5.4	2	D	D	D
Baker	36.5	10 568	2	D	D	D	5	25	4.7	0.4	2	D	D	D
Baldwin	6.9	151	23	D	D	D	182	2 187	554.5	46.6	34	D	D	D
Banks	3.7	200	13	158	110.3	7.1	58	795	213.7	16.9	5	D	D	D
Barrow	6.5	94	61	732	1 189.7	34.5	181	2 350	671.6	56.5	36	90	10.1	1.8
Bartow	109.2	1 090	103	995	861.5	44.9	302	3 590	1 264.9	87.7	92	301	40.0	8.2
Ben Hill	6.0	339	10	D	D	D	78	724	200.3	14.6	10	31	3.2	0.6
Berrien	4.9	256	18	68	58.5	2.8	67	465	127.1	10.8	6	8	2.0	0.2
Bibb	41.9	270	192	2 433	1 522.4	117.0	815	10 199	2 597.5	232.7	194	906	170.4	30.8
Bleckley	8.3	634	5	33	22.8	1.9	45	340	88.4	7.1	5	D	D	D
Brantley	1.7	95	4	D	D	D	40	299	74.0	5.2	3	6	0.3	0.1
Brooks	8.7	536	8	D	D	D	46	309	83.9	6.9	3	D	D	D
Bryan	3.3	107	20	D	D	D	96	1 051	352.3	23.8	28	D	D	D
Bulloch	9.0	128	44	273	311.2	11.2	266	3 203	796.8	67.6	72	304	48.8	7.7
Burke	74.6	3 201	18	248	210.7	9.2	54	712	196.7	17.2	8	D	D	D
Butts	3.0	127	10	187	534.9	8.1	79	681	333.8	13.9	16	28	3.7	0.6
Calhoun	27.8	4 154	8	70	26.4	2.2	15	100	19.6	2.0	1	D	D	D
Camden	6.4	127	10	D	D	D	158	2 314	600.1	50.2	43	173	23.1	3.7
Candler	2.2	200	7	D	D	D	51	401	120.0	9.2	6	13	0.7	0.2
Carroll	15.0	136	79	601	436.0	24.4	364	4 474	1 310.4	104.7	80	304	46.7	7.9
Catoosa	6.9	109	41	470	244.2	19.8	174	2 500	687.4	56.9	39	139	23.6	4.3
Charlton	1.3	104	9	97	51.5	2.7	32	224	58.8	3.8	3	D	D	D
Chatham	278.2	1 049	317	3 925	5 812.9	197.6	1 204	15 767	4 256.4	375.3	388	1 837	383.3	60.4
Chattahoochee	0.9	78	1	D	D	D	18	126	22.7	1.9	NA	NA	NA	NA
Chattooga	10.8	416	10	D	D	D	74	657	158.0	13.5	6	19	2.8	0.5
Cherokee	24.4	114	220	1 639	711.9	83.8	544	8 254	2 271.6	196.1	207	527	95.8	18.0
Clarke	15.1	130	99	1 801	1 947.0	85.0	516	6 963	1 684.2	145.6	190	926	140.6	27.0
Clay	4.8	1 508	2	D	D	D	13	76	12.5	1.1	1	D	D	D
Clayton	7.7	30	240	6 102	4 341.7	257.4	733	10 921	3 229.6	270.5	199	900	210.0	34.9
Clinch	3.4	496	5	67	13.1	1.8	22	176	44.7	3.3	3	D	D	D
Cobb	55.0	80	1 090	16 264	18 591.4	968.9	2 222	35 733	10 368.7	905.9	1 045	5 639	1 390.1	303.0
Coffee	9.4	223	45	447	487.9	19.7	191	1 784	487.5	38.7	29	99	11.4	2.4
Colquitt	24.2	531	48	501	513.5	19.9	184	1 784	460.0	40.0	37	89	14.1	2.4
Columbia	19.1	154	64	882	382.2	44.6	298	5 383	1 580.6	140.9	95	409	71.7	12.3
Cook	8.6	501	16	139	40.3	5.2	60	486	136.6	9.7	8	27	4.6	0.6
Coweta	53.1	417	73	830	1 518.7	38.1	329	5 166	1 479.5	120.0	120	300	61.3	11.3
Crawford	3.5	276	1	D	D	D	24	115	23.1	2.3	NA	NA	NA	NA
Crisp	21.0	897	32	D	D	D	119	1 365	303.5	24.7	27	188	13.4	3.8
Dade	2.3	137	3	D	D	D	61	455	184.6	8.5	3	7	0.5	0.1
Dawson	2.5	110	18	87	23.5	3.3	191	2 520	523.9	47.5	18	60	28.4	1.9
Decatur	73.5	2 641	29	D	D	D	136	1 333	324.7	28.8	22	D	D	D
DeKalb	2.7	4	756	9 390	5 554.7	488.9	2 217	30 430	7 956.5	738.7	890	6 039	1 710.5	263.3
Dodge	13.5	620	12	41	24.9	1.0	72	713	152.3	12.6	15	57	6.7	1.4
Dooly	29.3	1 962	11	79	67.5	3.1	39	250	147.1	6.1	1	D	D	D
Dougherty	82.3	871	120	1 451	841.3	65.1	494	6 397	1 529.9	135.0	141	537	98.4	17.1
Douglas	23.0	174	97	1 387	1 224.2	64.3	427	7 174	1 955.8	171.8	114	560	107.1	17.3
Early	146.4	13 299	12	58	85.6	2.5	51	388	86.1	6.8	5	21	2.9	0.8
Echols	1.5	374	1	D	D	D	3	D	D	D	1	D	D	D

1. Merchant wholesalers, except manufacturers' sales branches and offices. 2. Employer establishments.

Table B. States and Counties — Professional Services, Manufacturing, and Accommodation and Food Services

STATE County	Professional, scientific, and technical services, 2012				Manufacturing, 2012				Accommodation and food services, 2012			
	Number of establishments	Number of employees	Receipts (mil dol)	Annual payroll (mil dol)	Number of establishments	Number of employees	Receipts (mil dol)	Annual payroll (mil dol)	Number of establishments	Number of employees	Sales (mil dol)	Annual payroll (mil dol)
	147	148	149	150	151	152	153	154	155	156	157	158
FLORIDA—Cont'd												
Putnam	101	286	25.2	8.2	35	1 678	865.8	89.8	94	1 218	56.9	15.1
St. Johns	759	D	D	D	91	1 449	409.8	59.3	455	8 680	517.9	149.3
St. Lucie	514	2 173	281.6	97.3	134	2 015	605.7	85.4	390	6 652	329.3	91.3
Santa Rosa	289	1 851	295.2	126.7	55	407	124.1	19.7	189	3 219	145.7	41.4
Sarasota	1 775	8 573	1 216.7	439.1	308	5 559	1 200.1	267.0	853	16 450	896.2	263.7
Seminole	1 884	10 221	1 479.7	542.0	358	5 741	1 567.5	244.9	776	14 747	761.1	216.2
Sumter	128	500	53.9	21.0	36	942	461.9	40.7	106	2 464	117.2	35.9
Suwannee	49	204	18.8	5.3	19	D	D	46.9	53	679	34.1	8.2
Taylor	29	109	8.1	3.1	18	1 458	691.7	84.2	38	427	19.9	5.3
Union	8	D	D	D	4	D	D	D	9	82	3.6	0.9
Volusia	1 304	6 854	812.3	281.4	335	7 633	D	340.7	1 001	18 628	895.8	260.7
Wakulla	38	D	D	D	9	D	D	D	41	429	19.7	5.2
Walton	198	452	57.3	16.6	27	113	D	4.5	204	5 140	373.8	110.8
Washington	32	214	27.1	10.2	6	D	D	12.5	38	434	21.9	5.1
GEORGIA	28 112	D	D	D	7 456	333 837	155 836.8	15 316.6	18 815	353 638	18 976.6	5 173.4
Appling	20	55	5.7	1.7	25	529	407.3	23.1	29	410	18.8	5.0
Atkinson	2	D	D	D	10	468	144.8	15.3	7	52	2.4	0.5
Bacon	12	46	3.8	1.4	12	496	D	16.2	16	181	9.0	2.2
Baker	2	D	D	D	NA	NA	NA	NA	NA	NA	NA	NA
Baldwin	51	D	D	D	20	D	D	D	92	D	D	D
Banks	12	D	D	D	9	208	D	8.3	43	912	47.5	13.0
Barrow	101	3 525	137.7	87.7	69	1 940	889.2	76.1	81	D	D	D
Bartow	141	486	78.1	20.2	106	7 133	4 341.9	348.0	163	2 977	140.6	40.7
Ben Hill	12	66	5.1	1.4	28	1 408	512.4	51.6	35	361	17.7	3.9
Berrien	13	15	1.3	0.5	14	1 583	453.4	63.1	21	270	10.2	3.0
Bibb	382	2 581	340.7	118.9	119	4 441	1 573.5	213.4	403	7 905	352.5	98.9
Bleckley	11	52	2.7	1.7	8	303	D	12.3	14	202	10.2	2.5
Brantley	7	19	2.5	0.8	10	110	D	4.0	10	138	4.2	1.2
Brooks	12	53	5.8	2.1	10	187	D	7.4	16	D	D	D
Bryan	66	230	30.2	12.1	13	291	D	14.8	74	968	36.7	9.4
Bulloch	116	497	57.1	19.0	39	1 442	416.8	52.4	136	2 757	114.0	30.9
Burke	16	D	D	D	14	677	197.0	25.9	26	D	D	D
Butts	22	78	6.1	2.1	11	589	259.6	19.7	34	536	24.2	7.0
Calhoun	2	D	D	D	NA	NA	NA	NA	5	18	0.8	0.3
Camden	66	D	D	D	7	111	D	6.3	107	1 950	80.5	23.4
Candler	20	63	7.4	2.2	10	156	D	6.5	24	D	D	D
Carroll	147	716	74.8	23.5	112	7 174	6 237.8	299.1	198	3 261	157.7	42.4
Catoosa	64	300	26.4	10.4	43	1 537	D	71.1	89	1 733	87.5	23.4
Charlton	9	44	1.8	0.8	5	237	D	6.9	15	178	7.3	1.9
Chatham	708	5 871	640.2	253.4	175	13 829	D	1 015.1	897	18 046	1 024.7	277.3
Chattahoochee	28	232	26.4	11.4	NA	NA	NA	NA	9	42	2.0	0.5
Chattooga	13	58	7.1	2.2	14	2 156	403.9	56.9	31	318	17.4	3.8
Cherokee	740	2 735	421.6	133.0	144	3 813	1 027.8	145.6	323	6 256	281.7	81.2
Clarke	303	1 697	190.6	68.5	78	5 115	2 004.8	229.5	342	6 927	307.6	83.9
Clay	1	D	D	D	NA	NA	NA	NA	2	D	D	D
Clayton	221	982	119.9	39.9	100	3 676	1 873.4	165.7	388	8 178	450.9	129.9
Clinch	11	D	D	D	9	D	D	D	11	D	D	D
Cobb	3 387	33 011	5 509.8	2 097.4	460	19 738	8 587.2	1 180.3	1 451	27 543	1 516.1	418.6
Coffee	60	219	22.1	8.2	35	2 338	670.4	79.8	61	1 178	54.7	14.4
Colquitt	57	173	17.8	4.9	42	2 811	760.1	78.7	59	D	D	D
Columbia	208	1 348	626.9	70.9	55	2 978	2 023.7	168.7	182	3 389	153.2	41.0
Cook	15	44	3.7	1.9	25	517	201.8	17.9	29	D	D	D
Coweta	195	894	89.1	35.1	86	4 315	1 908.9	192.7	166	3 647	168.5	48.2
Crawford	3	D	D	D	7	D	D	D	4	33	1.4	0.3
Crisp	24	76	4.8	2.1	22	1 024	426.9	45.7	44	D	D	D
Dade	7	D	D	D	13	538	D	22.0	22	D	D	D
Dawson	54	135	19.6	5.4	21	1 161	263.5	37.0	40	697	39.9	10.9
Decatur	38	147	15.4	5.5	32	1 260	D	54.0	41	D	D	D
DeKalb	2 872	17 884	3 291.8	1 107.2	412	10 958	3 630.8	511.5	1 413	23 641	1 358.1	362.0
Dodge	21	90	6.7	2.3	18	639	193.9	27.3	25	360	15.3	4.4
Dooly	10	17	2.6	0.8	9	877	176.9	25.4	17	123	5.7	1.5
Dougherty	220	D	D	D	65	3 262	3 184.1	185.6	217	4 149	185.3	48.8
Douglas	226	1 000	102.4	37.2	88	2 512	690.3	101.7	202	4 276	210.1	56.6
Early	15	77	6.0	1.9	9	776	D	57.4	21	156	7.6	2.0
Echols	NA	NA	NA	NA	NA	NA	NA	NA	1	D	D	D

1. Establishment subject to federal tax.

Table B. States and Counties — **Health Care and Social Assistance, Other Services, Nonemployer Businesses, and Residential Construction**

STATE County	Health care and social assistance, 2012				Other services, 2012				Nonemployer businesses, 2014		Value of residential construction authorized by building permits, 2015	
	Number of establish-ments	Number of employees	Receipts (mil dol)	Annual payroll (mil dol)	Number of establish-ments	Number of employees	Receipts (mil dol)	Annual payroll (mil dol)	Number	Receipts (mil dol)	New Construction ($1,000)	Number of housing units
	159	160	161	162	163	164	165	166	167	168	169	170
FLORIDA—Cont'd												
Putnam	170	2 503	234.6	77.7	86	401	28.2	8.4	3 964	123.3	4 360	15
St. Johns	518	7 502	740.5	278.5	322	2 269	1 094.9	119.1	19 164	913.8	826 334	3 026
St. Lucie	655	10 230	1 342.1	441.1	362	1 779	148.2	42.0	22 748	859.0	196 774	1 189
Santa Rosa	261	3 479	429.1	143.2	155	732	46.8	15.0	10 920	450.6	185 741	1 242
Sarasota	1 516	25 814	2 976.0	1 087.1	914	4 738	451.7	117.4	40 002	2 095.9	894 622	3 522
Seminole	1 305	16 947	1 937.9	704.4	780	4 186	378.4	110.8	40 361	1 648.6	364 660	1 330
Sumter	146	2 956	381.2	123.8	64	304	22.2	6.7	5 834	225.8	451 041	1 568
Suwannee	65	1 342	104.8	38.7	37	186	20.1	5.5	2 420	93.1	7 679	40
Taylor	41	838	70.7	29.0	25	131	8.9	2.3	929	33.6	3 853	41
Union	15	D	D	D	5	D	D	D	529	20.9	250	23
Volusia	1 346	25 561	2 776.3	1 051.0	1 014	4 984	543.9	175.7	39 439	1 622.0	433 659	1 460
Wakulla	26	164	13.1	4.1	33	114	9.9	2.1	2 047	71.7	18 442	136
Walton	113	2 560	266.9	100.3	87	462	52.0	12.3	7 099	447.6	504 314	1 325
Washington	47	796	65.8	25.3	24	172	7.4	2.7	1 477	47.7	4 242	26
GEORGIA	22 734	448 460	51 800.6	19 515.2	13 828	89 302	10 617.1	2 703.1	848 952	33 492.6	7 955 101	45 549
Appling	36	D	D	D	28	99	8.6	2.2	1 100	39.8	333	3
Atkinson	3	D	D	D	2	D	D	D	530	19.2	0	0
Bacon	18	D	D	D	16	D	D	D	592	22.9	0	0
Baker	3	D	D	D	2	D	D	D	202	5.3	0	0
Baldwin	111	D	D	D	50	283	19.2	6.0	2 965	87.8	18 445	144
Banks	13	113	12.5	3.7	13	D	D	D	1 235	48.7	3 343	24
Barrow	91	1 292	117.4	44.6	79	322	34.7	9.0	5 641	224.0	52 910	389
Bartow	177	2 803	324.2	123.9	120	805	108.5	25.0	7 821	323.5	68 921	348
Ben Hill	31	698	49.9	18.9	22	D	D	D	1 126	34.8	748	9
Berrien	32	316	19.3	8.2	10	22	2.8	0.5	1 120	43.1	3 150	20
Bibb	540	14 875	1 757.6	642.6	256	1 605	183.0	51.2	12 674	408.3	19 148	113
Bleckley	20	291	19.7	8.0	10	33	3.8	0.9	822	22.0	0	0
Brantley	15	121	7.8	3.3	15	24	2.8	0.5	1 037	35.2	3 613	28
Brooks	17	D	D	D	18	D	D	D	839	32.0	3 680	26
Bryan	52	D	D	D	43	D	D	D	2 385	100.6	81 779	407
Bulloch	183	2 747	318.0	109.8	96	446	39.7	9.9	4 481	176.4	40 646	274
Burke	30	D	D	D	18	D	D	D	1 462	52.3	7 650	44
Butts	29	529	39.8	14.2	27	D	D	D	1 512	51.3	5 360	34
Calhoun	8	252	17.0	6.8	2	D	D	D	303	9.5	450	1
Camden	103	672	63.9	24.5	59	219	19.7	5.1	2 451	72.6	37 548	140
Candler	15	545	35.7	14.5	7	34	2.2	0.6	817	29.6	360	2
Carroll	214	4 784	634.3	238.3	122	D	D	D	8 212	298.0	26 190	168
Catoosa	100	D	D	D	40	272	18.5	5.2	4 159	171.8	38 968	254
Charlton	11	260	17.6	7.2	5	13	1.5	0.4	512	15.5	2 147	11
Chatham	721	18 354	2 327.4	860.8	414	D	D	D	20 015	885.7	202 517	959
Chattahoochee	5	20	2.6	1.0	5	D	D	D	229	6.4	0	0
Chattooga	28	382	27.7	10.9	17	65	11.5	2.0	1 421	68.8	60	1
Cherokee	447	5 141	471.4	208.8	324	1 402	118.2	35.1	22 054	972.5	469 549	2 000
Clarke	439	8 443	1 124.3	446.3	192	1 261	184.9	38.6	8 113	288.5	72 380	642
Clay	5	D	D	D	2	D	D	D	180	4.2	800	5
Clayton	400	7 024	810.1	306.3	270	1 349	144.9	36.5	26 532	623.9	97 727	427
Clinch	12	159	13.9	4.7	6	11	1.0	0.2	518	14.7	480	0
Cobb	1 803	28 679	3 519.7	1 393.8	1 237	9 389	847.7	295.9	74 241	3 264.7	545 343	2 129
Coffee	103	1 877	210.2	72.2	49	218	17.0	5.3	2 937	107.7	5 451	32
Colquitt	92	2 148	192.2	73.9	48	193	17.9	4.3	2 933	112.3	6 400	39
Columbia	215	3 078	254.4	102.3	134	794	69.6	22.5	9 066	390.9	239 955	1 464
Cook	31	D	D	D	12	50	3.7	1.1	1 069	42.5	4 591	38
Coweta	228	3 415	373.4	152.0	144	653	57.4	16.3	10 589	372.5	278 036	981
Crawford	7	D	D	D	7	51	5.0	1.9	808	26.3	4 288	19
Crisp	73	1 235	130.4	39.5	30	148	20.9	4.5	1 670	54.4	2 314	18
Dade	18	D	D	D	18	87	6.9	2.1	1 080	40.2	85	1
Dawson	41	D	D	D	35	161	11.0	2.9	2 147	114.6	35 109	173
Decatur	56	D	D	D	42	157	12.4	3.2	1 936	70.5	2 495	24
DeKalb	1 782	39 802	4 808.8	1 748.3	1 075	6 406	806.5	217.5	74 278	2 448.9	358 294	2 167
Dodge	51	893	65.8	27.5	17	124	6.0	1.7	1 451	41.7	1 734	9
Dooly	11	123	6.3	3.1	11	D	D	D	697	33.6	0	0
Dougherty	306	8 924	875.1	336.1	152	994	90.1	24.5	7 204	205.8	7 853	86
Douglas	266	4 639	498.1	185.7	183	796	87.3	22.3	11 884	378.1	34 897	249
Early	16	346	32.1	11.7	14	35	2.7	0.8	633	26.8	1 475	9
Echols	4	D	D	D	1	D	D	D	183	7.5	1 090	7

Table B. States and Counties — Government Employment and Payroll, and Local Government Finances

	Government employment and payroll, 2012									Local government finances, 2012				
STATE County			March payroll (percent of total)							General revenue				
													Taxes	
														Per capita[1] (dollars)
	Full-time equivalent employees	March payroll (dollars)	Administration, judicial, and legal	Police and Corrections	Fire Protection	Highways and transportation	Health and Welfare	Natural resources and utilities	Education and libraries	Total (mil dol)	Inter-governmental (mil dol)	Total (mil dol)	Total	Property
	171	172	173	174	175	176	177	178	179	180	181	182	183	184
FLORIDA—Cont'd														
Putnam	3 846	14 358 652	7.4	13.9	0.8	1.5	2.5	26.1	46.6	395.8	157.9	190.3	2 597	2 417
St. Johns	6 382	21 674 061	7.3	12.2	6.8	2.0	1.9	5.0	59.5	671.6	162.3	311.6	1 541	1 380
St. Lucie	10 618	40 360 120	6.2	13.8	7.0	2.1	1.9	6.5	59.0	1 062.2	343.2	409.9	1 444	1 184
Santa Rosa	4 424	14 124 230	11.2	10.2	1.2	2.6	1.4	3.0	69.2	350.7	153.5	129.3	816	709
Sarasota	15 008	61 458 391	6.0	10.2	6.3	3.8	31.5	5.2	34.0	2 009.8	280.1	709.8	1 838	1 447
Seminole	13 257	48 666 111	6.8	14.5	7.5	2.5	1.1	6.0	60.1	1 274.8	440.7	579.9	1 346	977
Sumter	1 509	4 669 736	4.3	3.1	1.1	6.4	1.4	4.3	72.3	251.5	43.7	105.9	1 042	834
Suwannee	1 250	3 665 519	1.8	2.1	4.9	6.0	1.5	1.5	76.2	111.4	59.1	33.8	773	579
Taylor	786	2 148 026	10.9	14.9	3.3	3.6	2.4	3.5	59.2	67.3	33.3	26.1	1 148	904
Union	487	1 232 008	5.4	0.2	0.0	3.3	7.6	4.3	78.2	32.6	21.2	6.6	433	280
Volusia	20 784	73 359 257	5.4	11.5	4.2	2.1	24.3	6.2	44.1	2 117.9	503.9	753.8	1 517	1 158
Wakulla	827	2 245 238	3.1	0.4	1.1	0.0	4.2	3.1	87.4	79.8	43.2	24.2	784	664
Walton	2 328	7 662 784	10.7	15.8	12.5	4.9	2.3	2.2	47.4	217.6	48.3	141.1	2 450	1 824
Washington	925	2 765 292	6.8	13.6	0.1	3.5	2.8	2.9	69.5	77.2	44.1	22.4	901	681
GEORGIA	X	X	X	X	X	X	X	X	X	X	X	X	X	X
Appling	1 166	3 357 745	5.4	4.9	0.2	3.4	40.2	2.3	42.9	101.3	23.2	31.5	1 717	1 055
Atkinson	477	2 010 541	3.8	3.1	0.0	1.5	3.3	1.4	85.2	27.4	15.3	7.7	927	571
Bacon	457	1 275 084	6.8	7.3	3.9	3.1	3.3	3.9	70.6	31.3	15.9	11.6	1 032	637
Baker	109	265 135	10.3	11.8	0.0	4.2	6.9	0.3	66.0	7.6	2.8	4.1	1 214	935
Baldwin	2 074	6 857 034	4.5	7.7	2.8	1.2	39.8	4.6	38.7	195.7	44.2	53.0	1 143	638
Banks	669	1 937 141	7.1	10.1	4.9	1.5	0.8	3.5	69.3	49.3	16.9	23.2	1 267	661
Barrow	2 271	8 023 913	5.3	11.2	6.0	1.9	0.4	3.2	70.8	183.6	75.3	79.2	1 129	694
Bartow	3 986	13 981 683	6.0	7.9	4.2	1.8	11.2	5.6	61.8	329.5	108.9	176.5	1 753	972
Ben Hill	1 147	3 286 219	4.4	6.3	2.0	2.8	28.8	5.8	44.8	73.5	21.8	20.5	1 168	664
Berrien	719	2 060 957	6.9	9.8	0.2	4.4	3.1	4.2	71.1	50.3	26.7	17.3	911	561
Bibb	6 298	22 932 839	6.6	10.3	5.2	2.3	5.6	6.2	62.4	582.3	249.1	239.3	1 530	1 004
Bleckley	611	1 809 213	5.2	7.5	1.5	2.9	15.6	2.6	64.0	43.0	19.1	12.4	960	647
Brantley	674	1 858 203	5.0	7.6	1.1	3.5	4.4	0.6	76.4	47.4	24.7	17.9	963	714
Brooks	547	1 728 938	6.4	10.4	2.7	2.7	0.2	3.5	70.4	39.5	17.4	16.6	1 079	809
Bryan	1 408	4 117 520	6.2	9.0	3.9	3.1	0.9	1.8	72.5	105.5	39.0	54.1	1 679	990
Bulloch	2 932	8 670 844	4.4	9.3	1.3	2.3	13.2	5.4	62.9	203.4	80.5	82.0	1 128	580
Burke	1 329	4 107 904	4.5	7.8	10.8	4.1	1.0	2.7	66.7	98.4	35.0	53.8	2 324	1 816
Butts	841	2 814 107	8.3	12.6	6.9	3.6	1.8	7.2	58.7	67.2	18.6	39.3	1 671	1 021
Calhoun	366	979 335	10.2	7.4	0.7	2.9	40.9	1.9	35.5	30.9	10.8	7.0	1 076	732
Camden	2 030	7 548 391	6.8	8.0	6.1	2.8	1.4	3.1	70.2	151.8	54.9	73.4	1 428	963
Candler	567	1 831 024	5.7	4.7	0.3	2.6	32.8	2.7	50.3	45.3	16.5	11.4	1 029	561
Carroll	4 120	14 298 798	4.5	9.2	3.6	1.3	0.9	5.5	74.6	321.7	126.8	135.2	1 212	693
Catoosa	521	1 425 530	21.0	30.9	13.0	7.3	4.0	13.5	1.6	366.0	65.6	70.0	1 077	575
Charlton	616	1 655 066	4.2	6.4	0.0	3.2	24.8	3.3	57.2	42.4	11.9	18.8	1 412	1 079
Chatham	10 068	34 099 398	11.9	16.1	3.9	3.9	4.3	8.5	48.0	1 650.2	303.7	617.1	2 233	1 331
Chattahoochee	245	688 357	6.1	3.3	0.0	3.3	1.1	3.7	81.0	12.5	8.2	2.8	217	112
Chattooga	892	2 643 680	6.6	8.6	0.4	3.0	1.5	9.6	68.8	64.8	29.2	23.2	901	517
Cherokee	7 029	24 643 064	5.0	7.9	5.8	1.4	0.4	4.0	73.8	584.3	192.5	290.4	1 312	942
Clarke	4 598	14 811 444	7.4	13.2	5.1	3.9	6.5	8.9	52.4	786.3	118.3	156.8	1 304	951
Clay	153	338 738	12.0	11.6	0.0	5.9	10.5	4.9	53.7	11.6	5.8	4.5	1 443	1 081
Clayton	10 173	35 407 764	8.8	11.0	2.0	2.2	3.2	6.1	63.2	920.8	359.2	426.5	1 604	962
Clinch	408	1 264 709	7.4	6.1	2.4	2.4	26.1	1.7	53.7	37.6	11.7	10.4	1 552	1 170
Cobb	21 811	86 644 451	7.5	8.4	4.5	1.1	2.0	6.1	69.0	2 213.0	659.3	1 157.2	1 636	1 103
Coffee	1 488	4 411 069	6.7	9.4	3.0	2.6	0.9	5.5	70.9	107.8	47.8	44.0	1 020	537
Colquitt	2 449	7 687 804	4.2	6.3	1.7	2.0	30.8	3.3	49.7	222.7	74.9	47.4	1 028	553
Columbia	3 933	13 876 194	6.0	9.6	0.3	1.7	1.1	3.8	75.8	345.5	122.6	173.7	1 319	749
Cook	873	2 387 884	12.7	9.3	2.3	3.3	2.5	4.1	61.5	46.6	20.7	17.3	1 025	578
Coweta	4 492	16 492 046	4.9	10.2	4.8	1.9	0.7	3.7	71.5	348.5	120.9	183.0	1 397	887
Crawford	409	1 190 596	12.1	7.9	0.3	4.3	0.0	2.2	71.6	30.1	16.0	10.8	855	645
Crisp	1 725	5 432 319	3.5	6.3	2.7	2.0	36.6	9.1	38.4	77.9	34.1	32.8	1 391	767
Dade	530	1 479 400	6.8	9.6	0.2	3.2	0.6	3.0	72.4	34.2	13.9	16.9	1 027	529
Dawson	883	2 870 993	9.9	10.6	5.7	1.7	1.3	5.5	64.0	77.9	18.2	53.2	2 374	1 408
Decatur	1 769	5 577 746	4.6	10.6	0.9	2.4	30.0	3.0	47.3	136.5	40.7	37.7	1 372	723
DeKalb	26 888	103 868 526	7.1	8.8	3.1	0.8	23.2	3.6	52.3	2 945.3	639.0	1 074.5	1 520	1 096
Dodge	906	3 199 644	3.3	4.7	0.8	1.5	30.4	2.0	56.5	119.4	31.6	18.8	881	486
Dooly	464	1 464 602	8.7	18.6	0.6	3.5	5.3	4.9	57.6	43.0	17.6	16.5	1 150	731
Dougherty	4 532	14 341 822	8.6	11.0	5.2	3.2	6.8	9.3	52.1	390.9	181.4	135.1	1 429	878
Douglas	4 786	16 883 097	6.3	9.7	3.9	1.7	1.1	5.1	70.7	416.9	160.6	203.6	1 520	907
Early	569	1 743 416	4.9	3.4	2.7	3.8	5.9	5.5	72.8	41.8	16.7	18.3	1 726	1 066
Echols	193	553 759	4.6	9.7	0.0	4.1	4.2	1.7	75.0	10.7	5.7	4.4	1 110	953

1. Based on the resident population estimated as of July 1 of the year shown.

STATE County	Local government finances, 2012 (cont.)									Government employment, 2014			Presidential election,[2] 2012		
	Direct general expenditure							Debt outstanding					Percent of vote cast:		
			Percent of total for:												
	Total (mil dol)	Per capita[1] (dollars)	Educa-tion	Health and hospitals	Police protec-tion	Public welfare	High-ways	Total (mil dol)	Per capita[1] (dollars)	Federal civilian	Federal military	State and local	Demo-cratic	Republi-can	All other
	185	186	187	188	189	190	191	192	193	194	195	196	197	198	199
FLORIDA—Cont'd															
Putnam	399.5	5 452	34.5	1.8	5.6	0.6	3.0	210.9	2 879	109	134	3 952	39.9	59.2	0.9
St. Johns	735.8	3 639	40.2	2.2	9.5	1.0	5.3	1 504.0	7 439	607	411	8 472	33.8	65.4	0.8
St. Lucie	1 134.8	3 998	41.4	1.0	7.9	0.9	6.3	2 450.5	8 632	736	618	11 940	55.7	43.5	0.8
Santa Rosa	415.0	2 618	54.4	1.5	8.3	0.0	4.4	1 574.0	9 930	761	1 411	5 589	25.6	73.5	1.0
Sarasota	2 019.2	5 229	26.3	30.5	5.5	0.1	4.4	1 927.4	4 991	1 016	795	13 398	49.5	49.6	0.9
Seminole	1 294.2	3 004	46.2	1.0	8.8	0.8	9.2	890.7	2 067	975	830	15 872	48.2	51.0	0.7
Sumter	263.4	2 592	27.3	1.6	6.0	0.5	7.8	594.1	5 846	1 603	200	2 951	36.1	63.2	0.7
Suwannee	116.7	2 674	46.6	3.1	7.6	0.8	7.6	34.0	778	100	77	2 389	27.8	71.0	1.2
Taylor	68.5	3 013	44.4	2.4	9.4	0.2	11.3	16.9	741	31	36	1 547	29.9	68.9	1.1
Union	34.6	2 273	56.6	4.9	7.0	1.2	3.9	2.9	192	16	20	2 108	24.6	74.4	1.0
Volusia	2 177.8	4 382	29.7	25.3	7.3	0.4	3.5	2 589.6	5 211	1 148	998	18 115	52.4	46.7	0.9
Wakulla	81.9	2 657	52.0	3.7	9.6	0.2	3.4	16.7	542	82	52	1 673	36.9	61.7	1.3
Walton	219.9	3 819	35.9	5.8	9.3	0.1	9.2	133.4	2 316	145	142	2 963	26.5	72.3	1.1
Washington	78.4	3 150	61.0	1.7	5.4	0.1	8.3	30.5	1 226	36	41	1 946	25.7	73.5	0.8
GEORGIA	X	X	X	X	X	X	X	X	X	98 768	95 631	569 871	47.0	52.2	0.8
Appling	103.6	5 642	37.2	40.4	3.0	1.1	5.8	23.1	1 257	46	52	1 345	26.4	72.7	0.9
Atkinson	26.9	3 242	60.6	0.2	3.6	0.4	3.5	11.0	1 324	18	24	403	32.3	66.8	0.9
Bacon	33.2	2 969	55.2	3.2	4.9	1.2	7.9	46.1	4 115	23	32	600	20.7	78.4	0.8
Baker	7.5	2 220	56.9	5.0	7.4	0.6	8.6	0.8	252	0	0	117	50.1	49.1	0.8
Baldwin	184.3	3 974	29.8	43.5	4.6	0.1	2.8	85.5	1 843	67	132	5 413	51.9	47.3	0.8
Banks	40.1	2 192	68.6	0.3	5.3	0.4	2.2	21.8	1 192	14	53	838	16.5	82.1	1.5
Barrow	186.4	2 607	60.5	0.7	6.9	0.3	2.8	222.6	3 172	171	210	2 739	27.1	71.7	1.2
Bartow	347.5	3 452	58.9	1.4	8.8	0.2	4.1	306.7	3 047	181	290	4 720	26.8	72.0	1.3
Ben Hill	81.8	4 663	37.3	32.7	4.5	0.4	3.3	18.0	1 027	26	49	1 048	42.9	56.6	0.5
Berrien	45.9	2 409	60.4	2.4	5.6	0.4	7.6	17.9	939	31	53	981	22.8	76.0	1.2
Bibb	601.4	3 844	44.1	7.1	6.5	0.3	1.9	510.5	3 262	1 041	443	9 106	58.7	40.7	0.5
Bleckley	45.7	3 536	52.6	19.3	4.9	1.0	4.6	14.9	1 152	27	33	1 251	27.2	72.1	0.7
Brantley	50.2	2 701	61.4	2.5	3.2	0.6	11.1	13.3	715	26	76	814	17.8	80.9	1.2
Brooks	42.2	2 737	55.7	1.6	6.5	0.4	4.6	12.1	786	24	44	660	43.0	56.6	0.4
Bryan	99.9	3 100	63.6	2.1	7.7	0.9	3.7	45.2	1 404	193	97	1 590	28.3	70.9	0.8
Bulloch	216.1	2 973	48.2	11.2	5.7	0.0	4.0	302.9	4 167	139	202	7 784	40.1	59.3	0.7
Burke	98.6	4 264	55.4	3.2	4.7	0.4	6.1	14.9	643	37	65	1 452	54.4	45.1	0.5
Butts	62.8	2 668	49.4	2.9	7.3	0.3	5.2	43.9	1 866	45	61	1 574	33.7	65.4	0.9
Calhoun	30.5	4 684	35.5	34.1	3.8	0.3	3.0	4.2	644	21	14	534	60.7	39.0	0.3
Camden	144.7	2 816	55.4	4.1	7.1	0.2	4.1	84.7	1 648	2 198	4 148	2 266	37.9	61.5	0.6
Candler	48.2	4 334	45.1	28.6	3.5	0.0	4.0	21.3	1 913	19	31	737	34.4	65.0	0.7
Carroll	329.8	2 956	58.0	0.6	6.4	0.2	2.6	335.3	3 005	200	316	7 415	33.0	65.9	1.2
Catoosa	277.3	4 263	51.2	31.2	2.8	0.4	2.1	143.9	2 212	76	188	2 524	24.6	74.4	1.0
Charlton	40.5	3 046	38.8	25.3	5.1	0.3	7.6	12.6	947	40	29	441	32.5	66.9	0.6
Chatham	1 559.0	5 640	26.6	30.7	10.1	0.3	2.2	741.4	2 682	2 560	5 875	15 772	56.9	42.5	0.6
Chattahoochee	16.1	1 234	73.5	1.4	3.7	4.7	3.0	4.9	376	108	16 959	273	50.2	49.1	0.7
Chattooga	68.3	2 655	56.6	0.3	5.8	0.3	4.1	31.8	1 237	33	68	1 311	31.3	67.1	1.7
Cherokee	581.9	2 629	63.6	3.8	4.8	0.4	2.5	701.9	3 172	290	661	7 362	23.8	74.9	1.2
Clarke	854.7	7 107	20.1	50.3	3.2	0.1	1.3	564.4	4 693	1 067	389	22 771	65.0	33.7	1.3
Clay	11.5	3 685	36.6	23.2	6.0	0.7	6.5	1.6	517	44	0	165	61.0	38.8	0.2
Clayton	908.8	3 418	54.3	3.7	8.1	0.7	2.7	457.9	1 722	1 449	808	14 098	83.0	16.6	0.4
Clinch	33.2	4 943	44.6	27.7	3.7	0.3	5.5	16.1	2 403	15	19	512	36.7	62.2	1.1
Cobb	2 261.5	3 197	56.3	1.0	7.2	0.7	7.3	3 722.8	5 262	2 398	2 445	32 850	44.8	54.2	1.0
Coffee	114.8	2 659	57.4	0.3	6.5	0.2	5.8	18.7	434	107	114	2 624	35.0	64.5	0.5
Colquitt	216.3	4 688	39.4	34.4	3.5	0.1	4.0	54.2	1 175	115	130	3 382	30.8	68.4	0.8
Columbia	330.5	2 511	64.3	0.9	6.4	0.3	6.0	242.1	1 840	273	399	4 845	28.4	71.0	0.6
Cook	49.1	2 900	54.5	1.3	8.1	0.5	6.5	18.8	1 112	27	49	1 242	35.2	64.1	0.8
Coweta	343.0	2 620	61.2	1.1	6.1	0.1	4.2	213.3	1 629	218	389	4 938	29.0	70.2	0.9
Crawford	30.2	2 394	59.2	1.1	4.7	0.3	5.5	12.0	952	0	35	448	35.0	64.1	1.0
Crisp	83.6	3 542	57.8	1.1	7.1	0.3	5.0	31.7	1 343	53	65	1 269	40.9	58.6	0.5
Dade	36.5	2 215	63.4	1.1	8.9	0.2	6.0	9.7	586	21	44	565	25.2	73.4	1.5
Dawson	84.8	3 783	48.5	2.7	4.7	0.9	3.3	124.1	5 535	47	66	1 063	16.4	82.6	1.0
Decatur	143.5	5 218	34.0	27.4	5.0	0.1	3.7	45.5	1 655	48	75	2 632	42.6	56.8	0.6
DeKalb	2 937.7	4 155	37.1	33.5	4.6	0.5	1.6	2 476.3	3 502	10 464	2 185	31 200	79.0	20.3	0.7
Dodge	77.8	3 646	46.0	31.2	3.4	1.0	3.8	21.4	1 005	41	55	1 950	31.6	67.5	0.9
Dooly	37.4	2 615	43.0	10.8	9.8	0.5	6.6	10.1	704	53	35	791	51.4	47.9	0.7
Dougherty	400.6	4 239	40.5	13.1	5.7	0.1	2.1	219.4	2 322	2 772	584	7 219	67.3	32.3	0.4
Douglas	492.1	3 674	53.7	0.9	4.5	0.4	2.1	632.2	4 719	160	397	5 502	50.5	48.7	0.8
Early	43.1	4 068	53.5	7.9	10.2	0.0	3.3	13.2	1 250	34	30	1 244	48.8	50.8	0.4
Echols	10.8	2 706	74.2	0.3	4.4	0.4	3.7	19.9	4 981	0	12	212	16.9	82.6	0.4

1. Based on the resident population estimated as of July 1 of the year shown.   2. © 2013 Election Data Services, Inc. All rights reserved.

Table B. States and Counties — **Land Area and Population**

STATE/County code	CBSA code[1]	County type[2]	STATE County	Land area[3] (sq km) 2010	Total persons 2015	Rank	Per square kilometer	White	Black	American Indian, Alaska Native	Asian and Pacific Islander	Percent Hispanic or Latino[4]	Under 5 years	5 to 17 years	18 to 24 years	25 to 34 years	35 to 44 years	45 to 54 years
				1	2	3	4	5	6	7	8	9	10	11	12	13	14	15
			GEORGIA—Cont'd															
13 103	42340	2	Effingham	1 237	57 106	894	46.2	81.1	14.6	0.9	1.4	3.7	6.6	20.3	8.9	12.8	14.2	14.6
13 105	...	6	Elbert	909	19 364	1 856	21.3	64.7	29.4	0.6	1.0	5.5	6.0	16.1	8.5	11.5	11.1	14.1
13 107	...	7	Emanuel	1 763	22 708	1 699	12.9	60.7	34.5	0.5	0.8	4.6	6.9	18.1	9.2	13.2	11.6	12.8
13 109	...	6	Evans	474	10 787	2 373	22.8	57.3	30.3	0.5	1.1	12.1	7.7	19.1	8.4	13.4	11.9	13.0
13 111	...	8	Fannin	1 002	24 303	1 632	24.3	96.5	1.1	1.1	0.7	2.0	4.5	13.3	6.4	8.7	10.2	13.4
13 113	12060	1	Fayette	503	110 714	548	220.1	66.5	22.5	0.7	5.2	7.1	4.1	19.8	9.0	7.9	11.5	16.6
13 115	40660	3	Floyd	1 321	96 504	611	73.1	73.6	15.2	0.6	1.7	10.3	6.1	17.3	10.5	12.4	12.4	13.2
13 117	12060	1	Forsyth	580	212 438	307	366.3	77.7	3.7	0.6	9.8	9.7	6.2	22.6	6.9	10.0	16.6	16.4
13 119	...	8	Franklin	677	22 311	1 715	33.0	85.3	10.2	0.7	1.1	4.3	5.7	16.2	9.9	11.1	11.5	13.5
13 121	12060	1	Fulton	1 364	1 010 562	43	740.9	41.8	44.4	0.7	7.4	7.6	6.4	16.8	10.5	16.4	14.9	13.9
13 123	...	6	Gilmer	1 105	29 400	1 445	26.6	87.5	1.0	0.9	0.6	10.9	5.3	15.2	7.0	10.3	11.2	13.5
13 125	...	9	Glascock	372	3 065	2 968	8.2	88.1	10.5	1.0	0.6	1.5	4.8	19.2	8.0	9.8	13.9	13.8
13 127	15260	3	Glynn	1 087	83 579	675	76.9	65.4	27.0	0.7	2.0	6.5	6.2	16.9	8.3	12.1	11.8	13.5
13 129	15660	6	Gordon	922	56 574	901	61.4	79.5	4.7	0.6	1.3	15.3	6.5	19.1	8.8	12.7	13.4	14.4
13 131	...	6	Grady	1 177	25 205	1 602	21.4	59.7	28.9	1.0	0.7	10.9	6.8	18.9	8.1	12.6	11.6	13.3
13 133	...	6	Greene	1 003	16 710	1 996	16.7	57.1	36.3	0.7	0.8	6.3	5.4	13.7	6.9	9.9	9.9	11.9
13 135	12060	1	Gwinnett	1 115	895 823	61	803.4	42.3	26.6	0.7	12.3	20.5	6.9	20.9	9.2	13.5	15.3	15.0
13 137	18460	6	Habersham	717	43 996	1 090	61.4	79.8	4.4	0.8	2.7	13.6	5.9	17.3	9.3	12.2	12.6	12.9
13 139	23580	3	Hall	1 017	193 535	338	190.3	63.0	8.0	0.6	2.2	27.5	6.9	19.6	9.4	13.0	13.2	13.4
13 141	33300	7	Hancock	1 222	8 551	2 552	7.0	25.0	72.6	0.5	0.8	1.7	4.5	11.7	9.2	13.0	11.1	14.4
13 143	12060	1	Haralson	731	28 854	1 460	39.5	92.6	5.8	1.0	0.9	1.4	5.9	18.6	8.3	12.0	12.6	14.5
13 145	17980	2	Harris	1 201	33 381	1 344	27.8	78.5	17.4	0.8	1.5	3.3	4.7	17.4	8.0	9.5	12.9	15.7
13 147	...	6	Hart	602	25 534	1 583	42.4	76.5	19.6	0.4	1.1	3.6	5.5	15.9	8.2	10.7	11.2	13.9
13 149	12060	1	Heard	767	11 539	2 323	15.0	85.9	11.6	0.9	0.8	2.5	5.7	17.8	8.7	10.9	12.6	14.9
13 151	12060	1	Henry	834	217 739	298	261.1	50.2	40.8	0.8	4.1	6.4	6.9	21.2	9.5	11.6	14.8	15.6
13 153	47580	3	Houston	973	150 033	433	154.2	60.3	31.0	0.9	3.8	6.6	6.9	18.7	9.7	14.8	12.8	14.1
13 155	...	7	Irwin	918	9 245	2 492	10.1	69.3	27.0	0.3	0.9	3.6	5.7	16.5	8.9	12.4	12.7	13.7
13 157	27600	6	Jackson	880	63 360	834	72.0	84.0	7.8	0.7	2.3	6.7	6.6	19.1	8.0	12.2	14.1	14.5
13 159	12060	1	Jasper	954	13 635	2 195	14.3	73.7	22.1	0.8	0.6	4.2	6.0	18.0	7.8	11.8	12.2	14.6
13 161	...	7	Jeff Davis	857	14 920	2 104	17.4	72.7	15.7	0.5	0.7	11.3	7.4	20.1	8.0	12.4	12.6	13.1
13 163	...	6	Jefferson	1 364	16 106	2 034	11.8	42.7	53.8	0.5	0.7	3.3	6.3	17.9	8.7	11.7	11.5	13.5
13 165	...	6	Jenkins	899	8 957	2 518	10.0	52.1	42.6	0.6	0.6	5.1	5.7	16.9	9.9	13.3	13.0	13.7
13 167	20140	9	Johnson	785	9 656	2 460	12.3	62.5	35.0	0.5	0.5	2.2	4.5	15.2	8.1	13.6	14.2	15.3
13 169	31420	3	Jones	1 020	28 494	1 471	27.9	72.7	25.3	0.6	1.0	1.5	5.2	19.3	8.3	11.3	12.8	14.5
13 171	12060	1	Lamar	475	18 201	1 907	38.3	65.5	32.4	0.8	0.8	2.2	5.5	15.2	15.1	11.2	11.2	12.7
13 173	46660	3	Lanier	480	10 312	2 408	21.5	69.9	23.6	1.2	2.1	5.5	7.8	17.8	8.6	16.6	13.1	12.9
13 175	20140	6	Laurens	2 091	47 731	1 023	22.8	60.3	36.6	0.6	1.3	2.5	6.7	18.1	8.8	11.7	12.2	13.4
13 177	10500	3	Lee	921	29 202	1 449	31.7	74.1	21.2	0.7	2.9	2.6	6.4	20.4	8.4	12.8	15.1	13.9
13 179	25980	3	Liberty	1 269	62 467	843	49.2	45.3	41.4	1.2	4.0	12.1	11.1	17.6	15.4	19.6	10.6	9.9
13 181	12260	8	Lincoln	545	7 673	2 620	14.1	66.5	31.8	0.8	0.7	1.3	4.6	14.5	7.5	10.2	10.3	14.7
13 183	25980	3	Long	1 037	17 731	1 932	17.1	61.4	25.7	1.3	2.7	11.8	8.2	20.5	9.5	17.0	14.5	12.4
13 185	46660	3	Lowndes	1 285	112 865	540	87.8	56.3	36.9	0.7	2.4	5.5	7.1	17.7	18.4	14.3	11.0	10.9
13 187	...	6	Lumpkin	733	31 408	1 399	42.8	92.1	2.3	1.4	1.3	4.9	5.0	13.9	18.1	11.1	10.7	12.3
13 189	12260	2	McDuffie	667	21 540	1 753	32.3	55.5	40.9	0.7	0.8	2.8	6.2	19.1	8.6	11.6	11.5	13.8
13 191	15260	3	McIntosh	1 099	13 969	2 167	12.7	63.3	35.9	0.8	0.7	2.0	5.4	13.6	8.0	9.3	10.8	14.2
13 193	...	6	Macon	1 038	13 632	2 196	13.1	34.6	59.6	0.5	1.9	4.1	4.9	15.1	10.2	14.3	12.2	14.0
13 195	12020	3	Madison	731	28 441	1 474	38.9	84.5	9.8	0.6	1.5	4.7	5.4	17.8	8.5	11.6	12.6	14.8
13 197	17980	2	Marion	948	8 761	2 532	9.2	60.7	30.8	1.2	1.4	7.7	6.1	15.7	8.5	10.7	11.7	15.3
13 199	12060	1	Meriwether	1 298	21 190	1 765	16.3	57.5	39.8	0.7	0.8	2.2	5.4	17.0	8.5	11.3	10.9	14.1
13 201	...	8	Miller	731	5 854	2 767	8.0	69.7	28.4	0.8	0.9	2.0	6.2	17.2	7.8	10.9	11.7	13.6
13 205	...	6	Mitchell	1 326	22 574	1 706	17.0	47.1	48.1	0.5	0.9	4.3	6.0	17.6	9.0	13.2	13.1	13.6
13 207	31420	3	Monroe	1 025	27 103	1 528	26.4	72.9	24.1	0.6	1.2	2.3	5.1	15.9	8.8	11.3	12.1	14.9
13 209	47080	9	Montgomery	620	8 951	2 519	14.4	67.7	26.5	0.4	0.7	6.0	5.7	16.6	12.0	11.3	12.3	13.6
13 211	12060	6	Morgan	900	18 046	1 915	20.1	72.7	23.6	0.7	1.0	3.0	5.2	17.8	8.1	9.8	12.0	14.6
13 213	19140	3	Murray	892	39 565	1 185	44.4	84.3	1.5	0.6	0.6	14.0	6.4	18.8	9.0	12.4	13.8	14.5
13 215	17980	2	Muscogee	560	200 579	327	358.2	44.3	46.3	0.9	3.5	7.5	7.6	16.7	11.6	16.4	12.5	12.1
13 217	12060	1	Newton	705	105 473	563	149.6	51.3	43.2	0.7	1.5	4.9	6.7	20.5	9.7	12.0	14.1	14.2
13 219	12020	3	Oconee	477	35 965	1 274	75.4	85.9	5.7	0.4	4.5	4.6	5.3	21.5	8.1	9.0	14.0	15.3
13 221	12020	3	Oglethorpe	1 137	14 871	2 111	13.1	77.7	18.5	0.7	1.0	3.9	5.3	16.3	8.2	11.1	12.4	15.0
13 223	12060	1	Paulding	809	152 238	426	188.2	75.5	18.5	0.8	1.6	5.7	6.5	21.3	8.7	12.7	15.9	15.2
13 225	47580	6	Peach	389	26 720	1 541	68.7	46.8	45.7	0.8	1.5	7.3	6.0	16.3	15.8	12.1	10.7	13.3
13 227	12060	1	Pickens	601	30 309	1 425	50.4	94.1	1.9	1.0	1.0	3.1	4.9	16.0	7.4	10.4	11.8	14.1
13 229	48180	6	Pierce	820	19 103	1 870	23.3	84.6	9.7	0.8	1.0	5.1	6.6	18.8	8.0	11.7	13.3	13.7
13 231	12060	1	Pike	560	17 941	1 920	32.0	87.4	11.1	0.8	0.8	1.6	5.0	19.9	8.2	10.5	13.7	15.4
13 233	16340	6	Polk	804	41 524	1 135	51.6	73.6	13.6	0.6	1.0	13.0	6.8	19.2	8.6	13.3	12.1	13.1
13 235	47580	6	Pulaski	645	11 396	2 330	17.7	63.6	32.2	0.5	1.2	3.5	4.5	15.2	8.3	12.1	12.6	14.4

1. CBSA = Core Based Statistical Area. See Appendix A for explanation. See Appendix B for list of metropolitan areas with component counties.   2. County type code from the Economic Research Service of USDA Rural-Urban Continuum Codes. See Appendix A for definition.   3. Dry land or land partially or temporarily covered by water.   4. May be of any race.

Table B. States and Counties — **Population and Households**

STATE County	55 to 64 years	65 to 74 years	75 years and over	Percent female	Total persons 2000	Total persons 2010	2000–2010	2010–2015	Births	Deaths	Net migration	Number	Persons per household	Family house-holds	Female family house-holder[1]	One per-son
	16	17	18	19	20	21	22	23	24	25	26	27	28	29	30	31
GEORGIA—Cont'd																
Effingham	11.7	7.1	3.7	50.1	37 535	52 250	39.2	9.3	3 682	1 953	3 035	17 942	2.98	75.8	11.4	19.9
Elbert	13.7	10.8	8.2	52.1	20 511	20 166	-1.7	-4.0	1 218	1 318	-715	7 786	2.50	70.0	16.9	27.1
Emanuel	12.3	9.4	6.4	51.1	21 837	22 594	3.5	0.5	1 708	1 441	-220	8 003	2.73	68.8	18.9	26.9
Evans	11.5	8.5	6.6	51.7	10 495	11 001	4.8	-1.9	878	556	-560	3 936	2.64	67.5	16.6	28.9
Fannin	18.0	15.7	9.9	51.1	19 798	23 693	19.7	2.6	1 036	1 544	1 085	9 684	2.42	68.0	11.5	28.1
Fayette	14.9	10.0	6.2	51.6	91 263	106 566	16.8	3.9	4 335	4 067	3 686	38 231	2.81	77.9	9.5	20.3
Floyd	12.4	8.9	6.8	51.5	90 565	96 317	6.4	0.2	6 228	5 308	-673	34 794	2.65	67.1	13.5	27.4
Forsyth	10.1	7.1	4.0	50.3	98 407	175 511	78.4	21.0	11 663	5 003	29 646	59 633	3.16	80.7	8.2	16.1
Franklin	13.3	10.8	7.9	51.2	20 285	22 084	8.9	1.0	1 401	1 434	258	8 527	2.50	68.0	11.8	26.6
Fulton	10.7	6.3	4.2	51.4	816 006	920 579	12.8	9.8	67 084	31 738	53 339	373 005	2.50	55.5	15.2	37.2
Gilmer	15.6	14.0	8.1	50.1	23 456	28 281	20.6	4.0	1 617	1 306	689	10 959	2.57	70.4	8.4	25.1
Glascock	13.2	9.8	7.5	51.1	2 556	3 082	20.6	-0.6	151	200	21	1 155	2.59	70.6	11.2	25.7
Glynn	13.6	10.8	6.9	52.7	67 568	79 626	17.8	5.0	5 221	4 205	2 755	31 743	2.51	68.2	16.7	27.9
Gordon	11.7	8.3	5.1	50.4	44 104	55 186	25.1	2.5	3 662	2 488	256	19 320	2.85	72.9	13.0	21.9
Grady	12.7	9.5	6.5	51.3	23 659	25 012	5.7	0.8	1 868	1 294	-391	9 378	2.67	71.0	14.6	24.8
Greene	16.0	17.5	8.7	51.2	14 406	15 994	11.0	4.5	867	997	830	6 491	2.46	71.4	17.2	24.7
Gwinnett	10.6	5.6	3.0	51.0	588 448	805 324	36.9	11.2	60 396	19 623	49 180	270 773	3.09	76.4	14.3	19.2
Habersham	12.3	10.2	7.2	52.6	35 902	43 041	19.9	2.2	2 638	2 129	374	14 613	2.78	71.3	9.6	25.2
Hall	10.9	8.1	5.5	50.1	139 277	179 684	29.0	7.7	13 258	6 894	7 160	61 361	2.97	73.9	12.1	21.6
Hancock	16.2	12.2	7.7	46.0	10 076	9 402	-6.7	-9.1	421	450	-838	2 787	2.62	59.5	21.3	36.8
Haralson	12.3	9.7	6.3	51.6	25 690	28 780	12.0	0.3	1 797	1 771	23	10 688	2.63	72.6	12.9	24.3
Harris	15.1	10.9	5.8	50.2	23 695	32 026	35.2	4.2	1 507	1 246	1 047	11 554	2.78	78.7	10.1	19.5
Hart	14.0	12.1	8.5	50.4	22 997	25 213	9.6	1.3	1 416	1 424	259	10 050	2.45	67.2	13.6	28.4
Heard	13.6	10.0	5.7	50.1	11 012	11 834	7.5	-2.5	672	632	-310	4 358	2.65	68.1	11.0	25.9
Henry	11.0	6.8	3.6	52.2	119 341	203 879	70.8	6.8	12 766	6 735	7 669	69 717	2.99	75.8	17.0	20.8
Houston	11.2	6.9	4.9	51.3	110 765	139 912	26.3	7.2	10 667	5 516	4 660	52 564	2.74	70.2	14.3	25.9
Irwin	11.9	10.3	7.9	49.2	9 931	9 538	-4.0	-3.1	529	494	-365	3 325	2.66	70.5	12.2	25.4
Jackson	11.9	8.7	4.8	50.4	41 589	60 485	45.4	4.8	4 060	2 709	1 325	20 927	2.88	76.1	12.4	19.0
Jasper	14.2	9.8	5.7	51.3	11 426	13 900	21.7	-1.9	904	681	-517	5 142	2.63	74.0	14.5	22.1
Jeff Davis	12.2	8.7	5.5	50.5	12 684	15 068	18.8	-1.0	1 082	765	-429	5 383	2.77	71.2	10.7	23.4
Jefferson	13.4	10.0	7.0	51.4	17 266	16 930	-1.9	-4.9	1 116	1 159	-816	6 100	2.61	67.8	20.2	30.1
Jenkins	12.2	9.4	5.9	46.8	8 575	8 340	-2.7	7.4	542	518	527	3 411	2.55	66.8	24.0	28.1
Johnson	13.6	9.4	6.2	43.5	8 560	9 984	16.6	-3.3	457	475	-316	3 253	2.78	70.2	14.7	27.5
Jones	13.2	9.4	5.9	51.6	23 639	28 669	21.3	-0.6	1 559	1 359	-453	10 329	2.76	74.7	14.9	21.6
Lamar	13.0	9.8	6.2	52.3	15 912	18 317	15.1	-0.6	1 003	1 049	-117	6 427	2.62	70.1	14.7	26.8
Lanier	11.2	7.4	4.7	49.6	7 241	10 074	39.1	2.4	686	425	-44	3 737	2.68	70.5	15.1	27.8
Laurens	12.7	9.4	6.9	52.4	44 874	48 434	7.9	-1.5	3 399	2 850	-1 320	17 614	2.66	68.1	18.3	28.7
Lee	12.3	7.2	3.6	49.8	24 757	28 298	14.3	3.2	1 889	1 010	-21	10 060	2.73	77.2	12.0	19.0
Liberty	8.4	5.1	2.4	48.8	61 610	63 472	3.0	-1.6	7 591	1 656	-7 244	22 863	2.73	74.6	17.2	20.0
Lincoln	17.5	12.7	7.9	50.7	8 348	7 996	-4.2	-4.0	359	430	-229	3 397	2.27	66.6	16.7	31.8
Long	10.1	4.7	3.0	49.7	10 304	14 445	40.2	22.7	1 187	427	2 461	5 078	3.10	73.7	17.7	23.7
Lowndes	9.5	6.5	4.5	51.1	92 115	109 233	18.6	3.3	8 748	4 375	-1 051	39 718	2.73	64.0	16.9	26.1
Lumpkin	13.3	10.2	5.5	50.2	21 016	29 966	42.6	4.8	1 628	1 237	954	11 096	2.63	64.1	9.6	26.9
McDuffie	13.3	9.9	6.0	53.1	21 231	21 869	3.0	-1.5	1 575	1 230	-688	8 177	2.60	73.6	19.2	23.4
McIntosh	17.0	13.6	8.1	50.8	10 847	14 332	32.1	-2.5	647	590	-414	4 991	2.82	67.3	13.7	28.4
Macon	14.5	9.8	5.1	45.9	14 074	14 740	4.7	-7.5	732	787	-1 025	4 655	2.70	64.1	20.4	32.5
Madison	13.8	9.7	5.8	50.7	25 730	28 120	9.3	1.1	1 783	1 481	28	9 819	2.84	70.5	11.4	24.9
Marion	14.9	11.0	6.0	50.1	7 144	8 742	22.4	0.2	483	394	-79	3 114	2.78	62.9	13.0	33.6
Meriwether	14.2	11.6	7.0	52.0	22 534	21 992	-2.4	-3.6	1 297	1 308	-769	8 083	2.61	71.0	20.0	27.2
Miller	13.0	10.3	9.2	51.6	6 383	6 129	-4.0	-4.5	369	379	-269	2 396	2.44	68.3	17.8	28.3
Mitchell	12.5	8.7	6.2	47.7	23 932	23 498	-1.8	-3.9	1 471	1 219	-1 238	8 159	2.57	63.0	20.4	33.8
Monroe	15.2	10.2	6.6	49.6	21 757	26 459	21.6	2.4	1 408	1 356	503	9 626	2.65	74.5	14.4	23.1
Montgomery	13.1	9.4	6.1	48.3	8 270	9 123	10.3	-1.9	546	415	-316	3 166	2.60	66.0	14.6	30.3
Morgan	14.4	10.7	7.5	51.5	15 457	17 868	15.6	1.0	974	883	103	6 408	2.76	75.2	13.6	21.6
Murray	11.8	8.6	4.7	50.3	36 506	39 628	8.6	-0.2	2 622	1 879	-887	14 020	2.79	75.1	13.7	21.3
Muscogee	11.1	6.7	5.3	50.8	186 291	190 545	2.3	5.3	16 593	9 395	2 552	72 556	2.58	64.7	21.1	30.4
Newton	10.9	7.5	4.4	52.3	62 001	99 958	61.2	5.5	7 023	4 159	2 569	34 516	2.90	73.8	19.1	22.6
Oconee	13.2	8.6	4.9	51.1	26 225	32 815	25.1	9.6	1 691	1 105	2 493	11 621	2.89	80.1	9.8	17.3
Oglethorpe	13.7	11.2	6.8	50.7	12 635	14 899	17.9	-0.2	807	675	-217	5 428	2.68	74.0	11.3	21.5
Paulding	10.2	6.3	3.2	51.2	81 678	142 324	74.3	7.0	9 795	4 189	4 172	48 472	2.99	80.1	13.6	16.3
Peach	12.5	8.1	5.2	51.7	23 668	27 694	17.0	-3.5	1 660	1 210	-1 484	9 677	2.60	67.9	18.1	27.2
Pickens	15.2	13.3	7.0	50.7	22 983	29 422	28.0	3.0	1 571	1 576	824	11 019	2.65	77.4	8.2	19.1
Pierce	12.3	9.6	5.9	50.4	15 636	18 758	20.0	1.8	1 231	985	129	6 857	2.73	74.3	14.8	22.1
Pike	12.7	9.1	5.5	50.5	13 688	17 869	30.5	0.4	839	791	-14	6 096	2.88	80.0	13.2	17.9
Polk	12.0	9.1	5.8	50.9	38 127	41 475	8.8	0.1	2 998	2 413	-537	14 778	2.76	73.6	12.5	24.7
Pulaski	14.0	11.3	7.6	56.8	9 588	11 999	25.1	-5.0	491	525	-598	4 148	2.45	70.9	20.5	25.9

1. No spouse present.

Table B. States and Counties — **Population, Vital Statistics, Medicare, and Crime**

STATE County	Persons in group quarters, 2015	Daytime population, 2010–2014 Number	Employment/ residence ratio	Births, 2015 Total	Births Rate[1]	Deaths, 2015 Number	Deaths Rate[1]	Persons under 65 with no health insurance, 2014 Number	Percent	Medicare, 2015 Total Beneficiaries	Enrolled in Original Medicare	Enrolled in Medicare Advantage	Serious crimes known to police,[2] 2014 Total Number	Rate[3]
	32	33	34	35	36	37	38	39	40	41	42	43	44	45
GEORGIA—Cont'd														
Effingham	549	40 915	0.47	706	12.5	409	7.3	7 157	14.6	6 469	4 616	1 853	505	916
Elbert	310	19 218	0.93	228	11.8	254	13.1	3 271	21.0	4 754	3 273	1 481	734	3 757
Emanuel	942	21 929	0.90	321	14.1	263	11.6	3 575	19.4	4 552	3 072	1 480	642	2 917
Evans	387	11 294	1.11	164	15.1	119	11.0	1 869	21.2	1 981	1 331	650	119	1 208
Fannin	154	22 822	0.90	195	8.1	278	11.6	3 951	22.5	6 744	5 183	1 561	427	1 790
Fayette	543	103 627	0.91	893	8.1	794	7.2	10 746	11.8	17 939	12 823	5 116	1 663	1 525
Floyd	3 990	100 896	1.12	1 158	12.0	1 032	10.7	14 824	19.1	19 066	14 454	4 612	4 392	4 576
Forsyth	582	172 294	0.80	2 250	10.8	1 087	5.2	21 185	11.7	17 132	11 244	5 888	2 020	1 005
Franklin	810	22 761	1.09	258	11.6	270	12.1	3 464	19.8	5 404	4 078	1 326	341	1 692
Fulton	34 190	1 332 214	1.81	13 096	13.1	6 877	6.9	142 085	16.5	101 356	62 423	38 933	55 136	5 499
Gilmer	187	26 404	0.80	304	10.4	299	10.3	5 768	25.8	6 564	5 005	1 559	599	2 084
Glascock	84	2 278	0.37	28	9.2	35	11.5	379	15.1	649	466	183	9	368
Glynn	1 255	86 700	1.17	978	11.8	817	9.8	12 295	18.4	16 206	12 065	4 141	4 247	5 166
Gordon	775	55 690	1.00	679	12.1	501	8.9	10 817	22.5	9 161	7 177	1 984	1 547	2 797
Grady	193	21 911	0.62	335	13.3	249	9.9	5 153	24.5	4 275	2 894	1 381	739	2 907
Greene	167	16 979	1.14	158	9.5	195	11.8	2 526	21.0	4 548	3 298	1 250	368	2 236
Gwinnett	5 138	796 791	0.88	11 576	13.1	4 070	4.6	160 436	20.2	71 593	45 344	26 249	21 401	2 445
Habersham	2 518	42 340	0.94	505	11.5	413	9.4	7 635	22.5	8 811	6 315	2 496	1 088	2 502
Hall	2 908	186 873	1.02	2 535	13.2	1 480	7.7	35 062	21.6	28 640	20 414	8 226	4 071	2 139
Hancock	1 246	8 185	0.61	69	8.1	108	12.7	981	17.1	1 899	995	904	119	1 355
Haralson	335	26 917	0.85	332	11.6	329	11.4	4 029	16.8	5 662	3 851	1 811	1 249	4 380
Harris	610	23 150	0.37	273	8.2	284	8.6	3 380	12.5	4 555	3 169	1 386	357	1 120
Hart	665	23 077	0.76	262	10.3	269	10.6	3 672	18.7	4 392	3 309	1 083	866	3 473
Heard	126	9 616	0.53	117	10.1	118	10.2	1 738	17.9	1 677	1 086	591	155	1 345
Henry	987	177 548	0.65	2 551	11.8	1 398	6.5	27 695	14.5	25 311	15 987	9 324	6 209	2 911
Houston	1 575	146 974	1.02	1 965	13.1	1 134	7.6	19 067	14.6	20 319	16 645	3 674	6 774	4 518
Irwin	744	8 585	0.71	93	10.1	92	10.0	1 219	17.7	1 463	1 021	442	260	2 761
Jackson	824	55 869	0.80	771	12.3	514	8.2	8 669	16.3	13 264	9 372	3 892	1 163	1 956
Jasper	93	10 428	0.43	149	11.0	129	9.5	2 156	19.1	2 078	1 365	713	241	1 776
Jeff Davis	111	14 138	0.84	198	13.3	141	9.5	2 658	21.1	2 519	1 927	592	462	3 074
Jefferson	692	16 356	0.96	207	12.8	219	13.5	2 566	19.6	3 503	2 341	1 162	606	3 898
Jenkins	1 200	7 769	0.67	95	10.5	84	9.3	1 330	20.2	1 508	960	548	NA	NA
Johnson	1 791	8 158	0.56	77	8.0	92	9.5	1 196	18.1	1 656	1 129	527	175	1 868
Jones	318	21 280	0.36	233	8.1	275	9.6	3 611	14.9	2 972	1 775	1 197	1 190	4 224
Lamar	1 223	15 742	0.66	185	10.2	217	11.9	2 379	16.8	3 343	2 036	1 307	1 583	9 124
Lanier	227	8 481	0.46	132	12.8	88	8.5	1 751	19.6	1 128	835	293	243	2 309
Laurens	1 061	49 624	1.09	617	12.9	523	11.0	6 812	17.3	9 796	6 767	3 029	1 566	3 430
Lee	910	20 644	0.37	345	11.8	205	7.0	3 477	13.8	3 220	2 414	806	841	3 265
Liberty	2 468	71 427	1.25	1 466	23.0	321	5.0	8 676	15.0	5 567	4 114	1 453	2 127	3 286
Lincoln	48	6 110	0.47	72	9.4	83	10.9	1 103	18.4	1 695	1 158	537	221	2 864
Long	327	11 035	0.22	229	13.1	84	4.8	2 933	18.9	975	754	221	286	1 661
Lowndes	5 374	120 183	1.16	1 675	14.8	881	7.8	18 119	19.1	16 491	12 574	3 917	4 790	4 198
Lumpkin	2 560	25 641	0.63	275	8.8	260	8.3	4 510	18.9	4 520	3 403	1 117	351	1 126
McDuffie	275	20 977	0.93	293	13.6	238	11.1	3 171	17.8	4 054	2 370	1 684	NA	NA
McIntosh	71	12 003	0.57	127	9.1	119	8.5	2 160	19.5	2 607	1 755	852	307	2 533
Macon	1 903	13 856	0.91	131	9.5	154	11.2	2 266	22.8	2 148	1 293	855	456	3 394
Madison	242	21 264	0.41	362	12.7	266	9.4	4 753	20.0	5 491	3 864	1 627	657	2 435
Marion	76	7 805	0.71	87	9.9	84	9.6	1 592	22.0	964	621	343	NA	NA
Meriwether	245	19 229	0.71	241	11.4	238	11.2	3 234	18.9	4 165	2 445	1 720	740	3 641
Miller	132	5 422	0.74	63	10.7	66	11.2	874	18.5	1 216	843	373	167	2 832
Mitchell	2 162	23 964	1.10	262	11.6	225	9.9	3 169	18.3	3 956	2 617	1 339	616	2 721
Monroe	1 189	23 814	0.72	238	8.8	284	10.5	3 462	16.1	3 869	2 717	1 152	737	2 709
Montgomery	695	7 612	0.57	92	10.3	76	8.5	1 400	20.2	1 537	1 068	469	NA	NA
Morgan	145	19 053	1.16	189	10.5	151	8.4	2 438	16.7	3 681	2 459	1 222	450	2 642
Murray	263	34 577	0.68	495	12.5	369	9.3	7 707	22.7	6 293	5 188	1 105	926	2 355
Muscogee	8 388	225 371	1.32	3 102	15.4	1 822	9.1	30 900	18.2	33 028	22 974	10 054	14 548	7 038
Newton	1 609	86 749	0.65	1 369	13.1	817	7.8	15 126	16.8	16 421	10 593	5 828	3 006	2 908
Oconee	117	29 710	0.74	314	8.8	201	5.7	3 732	12.3	4 915	3 575	1 340	546	1 587
Oglethorpe	175	10 699	0.36	154	10.4	131	8.9	2 251	18.8	1 718	1 257	461	399	2 750
Paulding	364	105 401	0.40	1 809	12.0	887	5.9	19 138	14.2	11 546	7 778	3 768	3 470	2 337
Peach	953	25 421	0.83	352	13.1	244	9.1	4 277	19.3	5 941	4 244	1 697	951	3 534
Pickens	337	27 323	0.82	295	9.8	320	10.6	4 471	18.8	7 266	5 352	1 914	530	2 039
Pierce	187	16 053	0.61	233	12.2	181	9.5	3 360	21.1	3 862	2 899	963	262	1 377
Pike	212	13 395	0.40	158	8.9	145	8.1	2 383	15.9	3 127	2 049	1 078	235	1 346
Polk	408	37 732	0.77	570	13.8	476	11.5	7 098	20.4	8 667	6 236	2 431	4 409	10 694
Pulaski	1 208	11 406	0.93	97	8.5	107	9.4	1 549	18.9	2 031	1 552	479	NA	NA

1. Per 1,000 estimated resident population.   2. Data for serious crimes have not been adjusted for underreporting; this may affect comparability between geographic areas and over time.
3. Per 100,000 population estimated by the FBI.

Table B. States and Counties — Crime, Education, Money Income, and Poverty

STATE County	Serious crimes known to police, 2014 (cont.)[1] Rate[2] Violent	Property	School enrollment and attainment, 2010–2014 Enrollment[3] Total	Per cent private	Attainment[4] (percent) High school grad- uate or less	Bach- elor's degree or more	Local government expenditures,[5] 2012–2013 Total current spending (mil dol)	Current spend- ing per student (dollars)	Money income, 2010–2014 Per capita income[6] (dollars)	Households Median income (dollars)	Mean income (dollars)	Percent with income of $200,000 or more	Income and poverty, 2014 Median house- hold income (dollars)	Percent below poverty level All per- sons	Children under 18 years	Children 5 to 17 years in families
	46	47	48	49	50	51	52	53	54	55	56	57	58	59	60	61
GEORGIA—Cont'd																
Effingham	76	839	15 087	11.7	51.4	17.9	95.0	8 242	25 481	63 903	73 272	2.5	61 195	11.0	16.7	15.6
Elbert	312	3 445	4 346	9.4	69.9	10.7	32.3	10 249	19 709	35 170	48 630	1.7	35 351	21.4	31.9	30.5
Emanuel	227	2 690	5 540	4.9	63.6	10.0	37.4	8 572	16 960	33 142	46 597	1.6	30 119	32.7	45.0	43.3
Evans	122	1 086	2 830	14.2	62.2	14.5	16.8	9 003	19 177	37 804	51 636	1.7	33 293	26.6	38.5	37.2
Fannin	126	1 664	4 641	9.1	59.1	14.7	32.1	10 561	19 520	35 441	45 987	0.7	37 813	19.6	32.3	30.2
Fayette	76	1 449	31 232	17.7	27.4	43.3	183.0	9 014	35 987	79 993	99 744	8.9	79 069	6.9	9.7	8.5
Floyd	349	4 227	25 081	20.5	52.8	18.6	163.8	10 091	20 863	41 046	55 584	2.1	41 814	21.1	29.2	27.4
Forsyth	56	949	56 953	16.8	29.0	44.6	306.6	7 891	35 118	87 657	107 055	10.5	86 413	6.3	8.0	7.0
Franklin	114	1 578	4 897	15.3	64.0	12.0	29.7	8 096	18 242	35 878	45 910	0.2	38 055	24.4	31.1	30.0
Fulton	791	4 707	279 328	22.0	27.5	48.6	1 610.2	11 224	36 827	56 642	91 439	10.0	55 516	17.4	25.2	23.9
Gilmer	292	1 792	5 774	9.3	55.5	16.9	41.5	9 625	21 260	39 581	53 481	2.4	40 010	19.7	33.0	30.1
Glascock	41	327	779	6.3	60.9	11.4	6.2	9 630	19 134	40 089	50 560	0.3	39 643	19.4	24.6	21.4
Glynn	522	4 645	19 178	10.9	42.0	26.4	118.4	9 266	26 667	45 588	66 379	4.1	46 737	19.3	30.0	28.5
Gordon	284	2 513	14 027	7.9	60.8	13.9	92.0	8 701	19 595	42 414	54 109	1.7	43 880	17.8	26.0	26.1
Grady	209	2 699	6 448	5.1	63.8	12.7	37.8	8 100	16 286	31 653	43 178	1.1	35 237	26.2	38.0	36.4
Greene	201	2 035	3 238	12.8	54.2	24.4	29.8	13 463	28 179	41 390	68 584	6.2	42 823	24.4	39.3	38.4
Gwinnett	195	2 250	255 386	13.0	36.0	34.4	1 500.4	8 891	26 060	60 329	77 816	4.4	59 858	13.4	19.9	18.4
Habersham	189	2 313	10 605	11.7	56.8	16.5	66.3	9 594	18 816	40 689	52 630	1.5	40 994	15.3	22.3	21.6
Hall	173	1 965	49 282	10.5	51.0	22.8	290.9	8 521	23 551	51 036	68 110	3.6	52 238	16.8	24.9	25.5
Hancock	125	1 230	1 713	6.3	67.5	10.6	15.8	14 483	12 661	24 552	35 568	0.8	26 309	35.3	43.9	43.1
Haralson	698	3 682	7 164	6.0	61.5	13.8	51.6	9 042	20 468	41 482	54 164	1.1	40 387	18.8	27.6	25.3
Harris	72	1 048	8 432	9.9	38.8	27.8	45.6	8 775	32 002	69 060	85 918	6.1	66 249	9.5	14.4	13.1
Hart	329	3 144	5 494	12.0	57.2	14.6	32.0	9 138	20 881	36 867	51 340	1.0	38 564	21.4	30.3	28.4
Heard	191	1 154	2 861	9.4	64.2	10.4	19.6	9 599	19 360	41 354	50 466	0.2	41 348	19.0	27.5	25.7
Henry	175	2 736	66 707	17.1	41.1	26.2	346.6	8 626	25 123	60 269	72 319	2.5	60 388	13.7	19.0	17.0
Houston	289	4 229	43 568	11.1	41.2	23.2	258.1	9 349	24 613	55 170	65 798	2.5	53 027	17.2	23.6	22.4
Irwin	276	2 485	2 181	2.2	57.7	10.7	16.1	9 271	18 614	36 729	49 823	2.5	35 955	25.3	35.3	34.0
Jackson	153	1 803	15 935	8.3	53.4	18.6	106.3	9 133	23 076	52 857	66 498	2.1	51 931	13.5	18.5	16.8
Jasper	302	1 474	3 202	17.6	59.8	14.0	18.9	8 297	21 526	42 099	56 285	1.8	41 818	18.2	29.2	28.1
Jeff Davis	413	2 662	3 962	2.3	63.8	9.0	24.2	7 796	17 898	36 707	47 220	1.0	35 235	24.8	38.9	35.4
Jefferson	592	3 306	3 940	6.9	70.4	9.2	27.0	9 363	14 795	26 796	38 007	0.8	30 835	26.4	37.5	35.5
Jenkins	NA	NA	2 705	11.2	62.2	12.3	14.2	10 141	18 351	28 910	45 125	1.6	30 678	34.6	45.0	41.4
Johnson	374	1 495	2 129	6.1	64.0	9.6	11.4	9 520	17 078	36 466	46 144	0.7	29 818	30.4	36.9	33.3
Jones	99	4 125	7 199	8.1	51.3	18.5	47.9	8 669	25 526	54 512	67 609	3.1	51 749	14.5	20.5	18.5
Lamar	697	8 427	5 261	10.6	54.0	16.6	24.5	9 396	19 137	41 038	51 817	1.1	40 339	21.3	30.7	27.7
Lanier	333	1 977	2 861	7.1	51.7	12.4	15.3	8 624	16 860	36 904	44 784	0.3	37 113	23.9	37.1	35.6
Laurens	263	3 167	11 699	6.7	63.1	14.5	81.6	8 392	19 002	33 487	49 105	1.5	35 807	25.4	36.8	35.5
Lee	198	3 067	8 684	11.7	43.6	22.3	48.6	7 703	26 886	60 667	75 837	3.4	64 533	11.8	17.4	15.2
Liberty	399	2 888	18 504	10.8	40.9	19.5	97.6	9 576	20 308	43 209	54 436	1.3	41 682	17.2	27.8	31.9
Lincoln	389	2 475	1 598	3.7	60.8	10.8	12.0	10 218	21 579	34 596	49 088	0.7	39 484	17.9	29.6	28.0
Long	99	1 562	4 613	8.8	54.1	13.9	22.8	7 897	18 206	49 317	53 199	0.2	43 193	21.9	31.3	29.9
Lowndes	278	3 920	37 080	7.8	45.6	23.0	154.5	8 430	19 353	37 248	52 624	1.8	38 887	24.5	32.9	29.9
Lumpkin	42	1 084	9 425	8.7	44.1	27.5	35.1	9 241	20 333	42 764	52 682	1.2	44 653	18.6	23.2	22.3
McDuffie	NA	NA	5 533	5.2	61.2	15.3	40.1	9 406	18 743	37 899	48 510	1.0	37 413	27.6	42.1	38.8
McIntosh	91	2 443	3 027	6.2	58.6	14.2	15.8	9 477	23 286	45 216	59 365	1.2	37 603	23.3	36.1	34.5
Macon	365	3 030	3 309	8.7	68.4	8.7	18.6	10 633	13 546	29 295	37 615	0.6	29 430	34.1	40.8	36.5
Madison	174	2 261	6 712	10.8	59.0	14.8	47.5	10 009	20 661	43 746	55 172	1.4	45 557	19.7	29.4	25.9
Marion	NA	NA	2 032	7.4	61.0	13.4	12.8	9 706	19 420	36 271	50 363	1.6	36 055	25.9	39.5	37.6
Meriwether	276	3 365	4 638	10.0	66.2	9.3	31.5	9 842	18 441	36 606	48 218	1.3	37 243	23.6	33.9	31.1
Miller	271	2 561	1 438	9.2	58.5	12.3	9.8	8 753	20 641	33 224	48 170	2.2	35 276	25.1	37.2	35.2
Mitchell	278	2 443	5 723	12.0	66.4	11.1	41.1	10 247	15 547	31 101	41 549	1.2	32 711	32.6	39.2	36.1
Monroe	217	2 492	6 205	18.6	54.6	19.8	40.3	9 863	23 196	47 815	61 853	2.2	53 542	14.8	20.9	19.5
Montgomery	NA	NA	2 231	17.7	62.5	14.4	9.3	9 393	17 378	34 653	46 468	1.3	36 436	22.4	31.3	28.4
Morgan	176	2 466	4 516	12.3	52.1	22.3	31.1	9 330	25 012	49 746	67 080	3.3	50 295	15.0	24.1	21.6
Murray	221	2 134	9 596	6.5	68.1	8.6	59.7	7 876	16 481	34 478	44 648	0.5	40 976	18.7	27.3	24.3
Muscogee	533	6 505	57 610	11.7	42.2	23.7	322.7	10 031	23 209	41 362	59 695	2.9	41 783	21.9	31.7	30.5
Newton	370	2 537	30 271	13.2	48.5	19.4	167.2	8 715	21 811	49 208	61 951	1.7	48 058	19.4	28.9	29.3
Oconee	110	1 476	10 035	17.3	27.7	44.6	58.5	8 756	34 086	75 057	96 523	7.7	80 631	7.9	10.3	8.7
Oglethorpe	407	2 344	3 564	12.1	55.8	18.2	21.5	9 523	21 764	46 901	57 008	1.3	46 840	15.8	24.8	23.5
Paulding	153	2 184	44 354	13.1	46.5	23.3	222.1	7 817	24 868	61 153	72 573	2.3	63 964	10.7	15.6	14.4
Peach	524	3 010	9 062	10.8	48.2	19.5	37.4	9 923	20 256	39 085	55 190	1.3	40 550	21.7	32.5	31.2
Pickens	215	1 823	6 217	11.1	49.6	23.7	46.0	10 509	26 444	50 452	68 330	3.6	51 047	12.3	22.3	20.2
Pierce	173	1 203	4 533	6.0	60.6	12.7	28.9	7 703	21 601	41 685	57 152	1.0	40 526	18.9	27.8	26.2
Pike	120	1 226	5 251	14.2	50.2	17.3	26.3	7 630	23 670	51 985	67 588	1.6	50 395	13.7	18.2	16.4
Polk	832	9 862	10 286	13.3	62.9	12.7	64.7	8 476	18 773	39 121	50 685	1.3	38 847	20.6	30.6	29.2
Pulaski	NA	NA	2 291	12.1	65.9	11.0	14.2	9 992	17 379	35 430	47 324	0.6	36 128	23.9	32.7	29.4

1. Data for serious crimes have not been adjusted for underreporting; this may affect comparability between geographic areas and over time. 2. Per 100,000 population estimated by the FBI.
3. All persons 3 years old and over enrolled in nursery school through college. 4. Persons 25 years old and over. 5. Elementary and secondary education expenditures.
6. Based on population estimated by the American Community Survey, 2010–2014.

Table B. States and Counties — **Personal Income**

STATE County	Personal income, 2014										Earnings, 2014		
	Total (mil dol)	Percent change, 2013–2014	Per capita[1] Dollars	Per capita[1] Rank	Wages and salaries (mil dol)	Supplements to wages and salaries; employer contributions (mil dol) Pension and insurance	Supplements to wages and salaries; employer contributions (mil dol) Government social insurance	Proprietors' income (mil dol)	Dividends, interest, and rent (mil dol)	Personal transfer receipts (mil dol)	Total (mil dol)	Contributions for government social insurance (mil dol) From employee and self-employed	Contributions for government social insurance (mil dol) From employer
	62	63	64	65	66	67	68	69	70	71	72	73	74
GEORGIA—Cont'd													
Effingham	2 001	3.7	36 108	1 762	402	91	27	50	182	335	569	37	27
Elbert	617	3.9	31 716	2 490	205	49	15	66	103	195	334	22	15
Emanuel	624	0.5	27 430	2 957	225	59	16	31	83	229	331	22	16
Evans	326	4.3	29 906	2 730	149	34	10	25	48	91	218	13	10
Fannin	713	5.1	30 036	2 709	179	37	13	67	134	251	296	23	13
Fayette	5 872	5.4	53 548	253	1 778	286	126	345	991	740	2 535	156	126
Floyd	3 238	3.9	33 705	2 159	1 634	306	118	220	511	874	2 278	140	118
Forsyth	9 977	8.7	48 837	445	3 515	496	245	37	1 212	889	4 293	254	245
Franklin	757	5.5	33 990	2 115	245	48	18	160	102	203	471	25	18
Fulton	63 938	5.1	64 174	91	58 886	7 501	3 949	8 443	13 722	5 854	78 779	4 415	3 949
Gilmer	873	6.8	30 288	2 679	240	54	17	126	141	271	438	27	17
Glascock	82	3.5	27 016	2 981	11	4	1	3	11	27	19	2	1
Glynn	3 151	3.0	38 341	1 413	1 516	308	108	137	826	677	2 070	123	108
Gordon	1 730	4.5	30 872	2 606	855	160	63	168	195	406	1 246	72	63
Grady	755	1.8	29 754	2 750	210	45	15	81	108	202	351	22	15
Greene	735	5.2	44 552	712	202	37	14	64	247	186	317	21	14
Gwinnett	31 056	6.2	35 374	1 885	18 424	2 559	1 269	1 555	3 858	4 033	23 806	1 373	1 269
Habersham	1 275	5.3	29 133	2 812	507	126	36	98	222	348	767	46	36
Hall	6 770	5.1	35 491	1 858	3 551	615	236	519	1 062	1 283	4 920	292	236
Hancock	225	3.0	26 399	3 012	59	18	4	14	32	86	95	7	4
Haralson	888	4.4	31 007	2 582	264	55	19	59	110	259	398	27	19
Harris	1 474	5.2	44 842	691	140	36	10	169	246	242	356	25	10
Hart	800	6.0	31 508	2 525	237	50	18	86	134	232	390	24	18
Heard	315	5.2	27 145	2 970	107	27	8	21	32	94	162	10	8
Henry	7 224	5.7	33 779	2 151	2 079	400	151	310	772	1 274	2 940	183	151
Houston	5 793	4.1	38 852	1 342	2 898	772	227	226	1 069	1 069	4 122	218	227
Irwin	248	-9.7	27 286	2 963	68	18	5	9	43	87	100	7	5
Jackson	2 164	5.7	34 982	1 940	848	155	60	157	252	447	1 221	73	60
Jasper	428	5.4	31 851	2 456	67	18	5	31	57	115	121	9	5
Jeff Davis	453	3.3	30 501	2 651	162	36	12	61	59	124	271	17	12
Jefferson	482	0.8	29 652	2 768	171	39	12	41	64	167	263	17	12
Jenkins	224	-3.0	24 598	3 072	48	13	3	11	34	80	76	6	3
Johnson	222	2.0	22 915	3 100	56	16	4	9	29	85	86	6	4
Jones	948	3.3	32 923	2 292	159	36	11	35	114	220	242	18	11
Lamar	532	4.6	29 204	2 807	129	34	9	42	65	161	215	14	9
Lanier	245	3.5	23 625	3 089	44	12	3	11	31	76	70	5	3
Laurens	1 525	2.5	31 860	2 455	678	150	50	86	237	439	964	61	50
Lee	1 191	2.9	40 795	1 088	235	46	17	51	148	185	349	21	17
Liberty	2 116	3.0	32 448	2 380	1 770	527	163	42	563	406	2 502	103	163
Lincoln	250	3.2	32 755	2 323	43	11	3	17	41	74	75	6	3
Long	380	4.2	22 221	3 102	33	12	2	9	58	93	57	4	2
Lowndes	3 754	4.1	33 067	2 267	2 017	475	153	224	695	823	2 869	153	153
Lumpkin	948	5.5	30 397	2 665	257	68	18	50	159	243	393	25	18
McDuffie	686	4.1	32 120	2 428	241	52	18	39	96	200	350	21	18
McIntosh	349	2.5	24 529	3 073	62	17	4	19	61	109	103	8	4
Macon	396	4.6	28 745	2 856	110	26	7	81	61	112	224	10	7
Madison	912	5.1	32 201	2 418	109	30	8	98	115	236	245	16	8
Marion	218	4.1	24 768	3 067	47	12	3	21	32	66	83	5	3
Meriwether	654	4.5	30 836	2 609	159	42	12	31	90	209	244	18	12
Miller	200	-5.2	33 510	2 195	58	17	4	6	35	60	85	5	4
Mitchell	688	-2.2	30 209	2 688	245	62	17	86	102	199	408	22	17
Monroe	1 026	3.6	37 942	1 465	288	76	20	48	152	212	432	26	20
Montgomery	230	-0.4	25 577	3 043	53	13	4	6	32	67	75	6	4
Morgan	753	5.7	41 919	957	237	44	17	90	147	153	388	23	17
Murray	1 027	4.4	26 057	3 028	359	75	28	55	105	297	517	33	28
Muscogee	7 714	2.9	38 400	1 406	4 582	922	334	354	1 888	1 737	6 192	345	334
Newton	2 998	5.1	28 920	2 838	925	196	66	65	327	717	1 252	82	66
Oconee	1 778	6.6	50 679	348	394	73	27	87	348	201	580	35	27
Oglethorpe	476	6.2	32 459	2 378	61	16	4	76	62	114	156	8	4
Paulding	4 725	5.7	31 713	2 491	797	162	56	194	414	772	1 210	80	56
Peach	882	2.4	32 760	2 322	359	75	27	33	138	238	494	29	27
Pickens	1 192	5.3	39 730	1 218	316	57	23	67	228	290	462	33	23
Pierce	584	1.9	30 771	2 619	144	31	10	32	78	175	218	15	10
Pike	584	4.0	32 819	2 310	96	23	7	33	72	129	158	12	7
Polk	1 167	4.3	28 366	2 888	425	88	31	54	138	370	599	40	31
Pulaski	294	-0.3	25 591	3 042	107	24	7	12	57	84	150	9	7

1. Based on the resident population estimated as of July 1 of the year shown.

Table B. States and Counties — Earnings, Social Security, and Housing

STATE County	Earnings, 2014 (cont.) Percent by selected industries									Social Security beneficiaries, December 2014		Supplemental Security Income recipients, December 2014	Housing units, 2015	
	Farm	Mining	Construction	Manufacturing	Information: professional, scientific, technical services	Retail trade	Finance, insurance, real estate and leasing	Health care and social assistance	Government	Number	Rate[1]		Total	Percent change, 2010–2014
	75	76	77	78	79	80	81	82	83	84	85	86	87	88

GEORGIA—Cont'd

STATE County	75	76	77	78	79	80	81	82	83	84	85	86	87	88
Effingham	0.1	D	5.0	23.1	5.4	7.4	2.8	D	29.7	8 685	157	849	20 955	5.4
Elbert	6.9	5.4	2.6	28.8	D	5.6	4.0	5.0	21.5	5 385	277	847	9 490	-1.0
Emanuel	0.2	D	3.0	21.2	3.0	7.5	4.0	D	32.0	5 075	223	1 125	9 852	-1.2
Evans	6.6	0.0	6.7	37.0	D	6.6	D	D	16.3	2 345	216	458	4 635	-0.6
Fannin	1.8	0.0	D	3.4	4.8	11.5	6.6	D	17.8	7 845	331	720	16 716	3.1
Fayette	0.1	D	9.3	9.7	7.9	8.3	5.0	14.4	13.8	20 665	188	999	41 613	2.0
Floyd	1.1	D	2.4	17.3	D	7.5	4.0	23.7	14.9	21 700	226	3 362	40 410	-0.3
Forsyth	0.3	0.2	8.4	13.6	15.4	6.1	4.2	9.7	10.7	25 605	126	871	74 095	15.7
Franklin	22.8	0.0	3.6	17.6	1.7	6.4	2.6	D	12.2	5 675	255	744	10 446	-1.0
Fulton	0.0	0.1	2.8	4.2	27.2	3.6	13.4	7.9	11.1	123 905	124	26 695	455 996	4.3
Gilmer	16.5	D	5.2	14.1	D	8.2	4.7	9.0	15.8	7 960	276	637	16 706	0.9
Glascock	5.0	D	D	0.0	D	D	D	D	42.4	705	231	92	1 498	-1.4
Glynn	0.0	D	4.6	7.1	5.2	8.1	4.3	8.2	33.1	18 215	221	1 950	42 053	3.3
Gordon	5.5	0.0	4.2	39.1	2.3	5.7	2.4	7.8	13.3	10 950	196	1 493	22 265	-0.1
Grady	7.9	0.0	5.6	10.5	2.9	7.8	D	D	19.7	5 635	223	1 102	10 673	-0.8
Greene	7.7	0.3	13.4	8.1	4.3	7.8	6.9	10.8	14.4	5 330	324	601	9 181	5.7
Gwinnett	0.0	D	6.3	9.4	15.7	8.5	9.0	6.9	9.8	93 810	107	11 182	301 824	3.5
Habersham	6.1	D	3.5	28.8	3.2	7.6	2.9	4.4	21.6	9 965	228	919	18 089	-0.3
Hall	0.6	D	5.5	20.9	4.2	6.7	4.7	15.4	12.4	32 355	170	3 029	70 107	1.9
Hancock	1.8	D	D	D	D	4.5	D	D	40.7	2 350	276	478	5 271	-1.3
Haralson	3.8	0.0	6.5	24.7	3.3	7.5	2.8	8.2	22.4	6 720	235	941	12 232	-0.4
Harris	0.1	0.0	12.6	D	D	3.3	10.7	D	18.0	6 995	213	460	13 772	2.8
Hart	16.2	0.0	4.7	24.2	4.3	6.2	2.7	D	16.3	6 850	270	753	12 936	-0.5
Heard	6.2	D	13.8	19.7	D	1.5	1.0	1.9	20.9	2 590	223	420	5 097	-1.0
Henry	0.0	0.2	5.3	7.8	4.4	10.7	4.6	12.1	21.5	32 340	151	4 691	78 469	2.6
Houston	-0.1	D	2.5	7.0	7.2	5.9	2.3	5.5	57.7	23 410	157	3 534	61 023	4.6
Irwin	2.1	0.0	5.2	11.9	D	7.7	2.5	4.2	35.6	2 145	236	401	4 016	-0.4
Jackson	5.0	D	4.3	29.4	D	6.8	3.0	3.5	13.0	12 610	204	1 920	23 930	0.7
Jasper	8.4	0.0	6.0	15.7	2.2	6.5	3.0	D	25.6	3 280	244	422	6 264	1.8
Jeff Davis	3.4	0.0	1.1	24.1	1.2	9.5	1.9	2.8	15.9	3 030	204	503	6 396	-1.4
Jefferson	8.4	D	4.4	16.5	D	7.3	3.1	D	20.9	4 155	256	940	7 224	-1.0
Jenkins	6.5	0.0	2.8	0.6	D	5.4	2.3	5.7	37.3	1 875	205	471	4 166	-1.3
Johnson	1.5	0.0	4.8	6.0	0.0	4.8	D	15.5	36.1	2 345	242	599	4 055	-1.6
Jones	1.4	D	13.4	1.2	D	5.4	4.0	D	26.6	5 935	206	396	11 562	-1.1
Lamar	10.3	D	3.3	17.6	2.0	6.7	3.1	4.4	30.8	4 190	230	535	7 500	0.3
Lanier	4.4	0.0	7.4	7.2	D	6.3	D	5.8	34.5	1 785	172	339	4 291	1.0
Laurens	-0.5	0.0	5.4	13.0	D	9.0	3.7	D	29.9	11 310	237	2 166	21 247	-0.6
Lee	6.9	0.0	12.3	3.3	D	6.8	3.0	D	23.0	4 705	161	461	10 848	5.6
Liberty	0.1	0.0	D	6.6	D	2.4	1.5	1.7	76.9	7 150	110	1 210	27 365	2.3
Lincoln	2.1	0.0	21.4	D	1.6	7.7	4.9	2.0	26.7	2 135	281	251	4 775	-0.2
Long	7.7	D	4.7	D	D	2.5	1.5	1.7	59.5	1 645	96	239	6 347	5.3
Lowndes	0.4	D	6.2	8.0	5.9	8.4	4.8	9.6	37.0	18 220	160	3 772	45 933	4.6
Lumpkin	2.5	D	6.1	9.0	D	7.4	2.8	8.8	38.2	6 390	205	579	13 126	1.6
McDuffie	6.7	0.2	5.7	23.7	3.9	8.9	3.2	D	21.6	5 025	233	971	9 233	-0.9
McIntosh	3.2	D	4.8	D	D	8.3	1.7	1.6	34.0	3 065	219	428	9 281	0.7
Macon	30.9	D	3.3	19.0	D	3.7	1.6	D	19.8	2 665	193	721	6 032	-1.7
Madison	26.7	1.1	7.9	4.2	D	5.3	2.4	D	26.8	6 495	229	905	11 749	-0.3
Marion	10.7	D	5.1	24.5	D	5.4	D	4.9	23.1	1 790	204	304	4 099	-1.4
Meriwether	3.3	0.0	7.2	15.0	1.5	5.8	D	D	32.4	5 595	264	1 051	9 902	-0.6
Miller	1.4	0.0	4.9	0.8	D	9.0	8.8	D	47.4	1 600	270	316	2 743	-1.8
Mitchell	16.7	0.0	1.2	28.5	D	5.6	2.8	D	19.7	4 990	219	1 252	8 915	-0.9
Monroe	4.8	D	5.7	2.3	D	5.0	1.8	D	33.8	5 800	214	546	10 993	2.5
Montgomery	-0.4	0.0	4.4	9.2	0.6	5.9	8.0	D	26.1	1 690	188	256	3 882	-1.0
Morgan	10.6	0.0	6.2	16.5	7.5	6.9	5.0	3.3	15.1	4 340	241	425	7 526	0.7
Murray	5.4	D	2.0	43.0	D	6.4	2.4	D	15.6	8 365	212	1 181	15 732	-1.5
Muscogee	0.0	D	4.2	7.4	7.4	6.1	16.6	13.1	27.2	35 870	178	7 349	84 274	1.9
Newton	0.2	D	6.3	26.5	D	7.3	2.5	8.7	22.0	18 145	175	2 837	38 467	0.3
Oconee	5.7	D	5.7	4.3	7.7	7.5	10.1	10.2	15.4	5 985	170	370	13 418	8.3
Oglethorpe	46.8	2.7	7.2	3.9	D	2.3	2.0	D	18.7	3 555	242	535	6 490	0.1
Paulding	0.4	D	12.7	4.5	5.2	11.4	3.9	9.4	25.7	20 050	135	1 471	53 948	3.5
Peach	4.3	0.1	5.1	34.4	1.6	7.0	1.9	5.3	24.5	5 355	200	1 173	11 401	3.2
Pickens	3.9	3.4	7.0	9.7	4.5	7.7	6.6	21.2	16.4	8 550	285	606	13 705	0.2
Pierce	4.5	0.0	8.8	9.4	D	7.5	2.8	D	20.9	4 125	217	739	7 967	-0.2
Pike	2.0	D	14.1	10.9	D	6.4	2.9	D	24.2	3 550	200	301	6 828	0.1
Polk	1.8	D	4.3	32.1	D	8.5	2.4	6.8	16.7	9 445	230	1 614	16 907	0.0
Pulaski	10.6	0.0	D	D	D	5.8	4.0	D	23.7	2 195	191	393	5 138	-0.2

1. Per 1,000 resident population estimated as of July 1 of the year shown.

Table B. States and Counties — Housing, Labor Force, and Employment

STATE County	Housing units, 2010–2014								Civilian labor force, 2015		Unemployment		Civilian employment,[6] 2010–2014		
	Occupied units													Percent	
		Owner-occupied				Renter-occupied									
				Median owner cost as a percent of income			Median rent as a percent of income[2]	Sub-standard units[4] (percent)		Percent change, 2014–2015				Management, business, science and arts	Con-struction, produc-tion, and mainte-nance occu-pations
	Total	Percent	Median value[1]	With a mort-gage	Without a mort-gage[2]	Median rent[3]			Total		Total	Rate[5]	Total		
	89	90	91	92	93	94	95	96	97	98	99	100	101	102	103
GEORGIA—Cont'd															
Effingham	17 942	77.3	153 700	21.7	10.6	937	28.4	3.2	26 706	1.7	1 338	5.0	24 376	30.0	30.9
Elbert	7 786	67.8	81 800	22.6	11.8	602	31.5	3.9	7 613	-5.6	566	7.4	7 287	21.5	41.7
Emanuel	8 003	67.4	69 400	23.8	13.3	585	32.5	5.4	8 400	-2.1	715	8.5	8 212	22.2	34.3
Evans	3 936	63.2	88 000	21.8	13.7	617	27.2	4.6	4 685	-1.1	258	5.5	3 901	33.5	34.8
Fannin	9 684	77.0	159 400	28.0	12.8	653	34.0	1.6	10 094	2.4	610	6.0	8 354	26.9	27.5
Fayette	38 231	81.5	229 400	22.3	10.0	1 097	28.2	1.6	54 393	1.2	2 774	5.1	49 163	42.8	18.2
Floyd	34 794	61.7	117 500	22.9	12.5	702	31.1	3.1	42 787	-1.1	2 812	6.6	38 760	28.4	28.1
Forsyth	59 633	85.1	260 200	21.8	10.0	1 157	29.5	1.4	101 774	1.4	4 501	4.4	88 124	47.0	14.0
Franklin	8 527	69.3	109 600	25.2	13.2	628	29.4	2.7	9 203	-0.6	579	6.3	8 288	27.3	33.9
Fulton	373 005	52.6	237 600	23.5	11.9	992	30.9	2.6	514 221	0.9	30 075	5.8	456 634	49.0	11.6
Gilmer	10 959	74.8	144 700	26.5	10.9	711	34.0	4.2	11 694	-2.2	684	5.8	10 592	26.1	27.7
Glascock	1 155	75.8	63 800	24.7	10.0	459	21.0	3.2	1 234	-2.7	81	6.6	1 298	27.3	41.5
Glynn	31 743	61.2	157 200	24.4	10.4	829	29.8	3.6	37 236	0.4	2 232	6.0	35 596	31.0	19.1
Gordon	19 320	66.6	113 100	23.4	10.5	671	30.3	3.4	26 223	0.6	1 506	5.7	23 272	25.1	38.5
Grady	9 378	58.2	107 100	24.2	14.3	716	35.8	2.9	10 412	-0.4	625	6.0	8 784	30.3	31.2
Greene	6 491	74.2	164 300	26.2	14.4	657	35.2	3.1	6 362	-1.0	445	7.0	5 681	25.5	26.0
Gwinnett	270 773	67.5	167 700	24.0	10.6	1 029	32.3	3.1	449 411	1.1	22 807	5.1	399 320	37.7	19.6
Habersham	14 613	75.5	129 800	23.7	12.8	675	30.5	4.4	18 844	-0.7	1 059	5.6	16 694	24.2	31.1
Hall	61 361	67.3	162 200	24.2	10.8	853	30.5	5.3	92 277	2.4	4 383	4.7	81 685	29.0	31.8
Hancock	2 787	78.6	66 800	38.2	21.0	641	33.1	2.1	2 423	-3.9	243	10.0	2 278	26.6	26.8
Haralson	10 688	70.3	105 000	22.0	13.7	701	28.9	3.8	11 926	0.5	753	6.3	11 113	28.2	32.2
Harris	11 554	85.5	201 000	22.3	13.0	912	30.8	1.9	15 480	-1.6	808	5.2	15 120	40.3	21.9
Hart	10 050	75.3	114 800	26.2	11.6	572	29.4	1.7	10 304	-0.8	630	6.1	9 818	28.1	36.2
Heard	4 358	75.1	86 900	24.4	13.1	763	33.7	2.3	4 999	0.7	310	6.2	4 493	24.7	38.3
Henry	69 717	73.9	142 300	23.9	10.6	1 071	30.2	1.7	104 569	1.0	6 319	6.0	92 428	33.1	22.8
Houston	52 564	66.0	132 300	19.6	10.1	857	29.3	3.0	65 143	-1.2	3 781	5.8	62 644	35.9	23.3
Irwin	3 325	72.7	76 900	19.8	13.0	595	32.7	1.7	3 058	-2.7	249	8.1	3 168	31.4	33.0
Jackson	20 927	77.5	156 700	24.4	12.5	782	29.2	1.9	30 402	1.9	1 449	4.8	26 168	31.0	28.0
Jasper	5 142	74.6	113 100	24.5	13.6	832	39.9	3.1	6 431	1.2	348	5.4	5 741	24.4	35.1
Jeff Davis	5 383	75.4	80 600	21.0	11.3	481	26.6	3.2	6 383	-0.2	411	6.4	5 768	22.1	36.2
Jefferson	6 100	63.1	66 800	26.3	16.6	546	34.3	4.7	6 350	-4.5	567	8.9	5 216	23.7	34.5
Jenkins	3 411	68.9	61 900	24.9	14.2	564	36.7	5.7	3 140	-3.8	259	8.2	3 193	23.3	32.5
Johnson	3 253	74.8	66 500	22.6	14.0	496	34.4	3.5	3 847	-2.3	268	7.0	3 882	22.2	41.3
Jones	10 329	79.4	131 900	22.6	12.7	833	27.8	1.0	13 666	-0.2	730	5.3	12 048	30.6	26.3
Lamar	6 427	71.4	120 900	23.2	13.5	649	29.2	1.6	7 787	0.0	590	7.6	7 081	27.7	24.8
Lanier	3 737	63.6	102 500	24.5	10.9	640	31.8	4.7	3 783	-0.2	251	6.6	3 454	24.5	26.7
Laurens	17 614	63.9	85 700	22.2	12.0	603	30.8	2.1	18 486	-2.9	1 393	7.5	17 071	29.2	26.3
Lee	10 060	72.7	156 400	20.3	12.3	959	29.8	1.1	13 986	-1.1	742	5.3	13 003	37.3	20.9
Liberty	22 863	49.0	124 300	24.4	12.0	960	31.0	1.1	25 338	-1.2	1 597	6.3	22 756	30.9	24.9
Lincoln	3 397	76.6	99 100	25.1	18.4	569	27.7	1.7	3 347	0.3	222	6.6	3 231	18.1	34.1
Long	5 078	66.5	97 900	21.5	10.0	681	29.8	3.3	6 668	-0.4	395	5.9	5 675	27.5	32.4
Lowndes	39 718	52.5	133 100	23.9	10.4	776	33.1	3.0	50 355	-0.4	2 996	5.9	45 306	28.8	21.2
Lumpkin	11 096	64.5	169 700	26.4	11.4	863	36.8	2.2	15 170	-0.6	810	5.3	13 999	32.8	22.1
McDuffie	8 177	65.3	106 300	24.8	12.2	590	35.1	2.3	8 727	-0.9	718	8.2	8 105	28.2	34.0
McIntosh	4 991	80.0	120 800	25.4	12.4	598	27.4	1.4	5 947	1.3	379	6.4	5 551	26.6	31.4
Macon	4 655	65.3	69 200	25.5	15.0	543	35.6	3.0	4 689	-1.0	418	8.9	4 482	21.5	39.2
Madison	9 819	73.7	118 800	22.1	10.0	679	29.3	3.6	12 752	0.4	686	5.4	11 771	29.0	30.2
Marion	3 114	69.9	103 300	23.1	15.6	502	29.6	3.8	3 454	-0.1	282	8.2	3 366	25.9	42.0
Meriwether	8 083	66.9	88 400	23.6	16.2	723	36.9	5.3	8 781	0.4	687	7.8	7 687	19.7	42.7
Miller	2 396	72.9	90 700	21.7	13.9	602	30.8	5.0	2 694	0.7	144	5.3	2 365	28.8	27.0
Mitchell	8 159	64.1	80 400	26.5	13.4	547	33.7	3.7	8 790	0.3	577	6.6	7 827	26.5	33.7
Monroe	9 626	75.0	150 000	23.9	10.4	748	35.3	2.8	12 692	-0.2	714	5.6	10 941	32.5	25.7
Montgomery	3 166	72.7	73 400	26.1	12.3	534	29.2	3.6	3 766	-2.3	316	8.4	3 306	26.4	35.5
Morgan	6 408	79.0	175 600	27.1	12.8	912	27.7	1.4	8 486	1.5	455	5.4	7 653	31.6	27.2
Murray	14 020	67.1	86 200	23.5	11.4	654	31.3	6.1	15 810	-0.4	1 171	7.4	15 549	19.8	43.7
Muscogee	72 556	50.8	134 200	23.5	11.6	826	31.2	2.4	79 038	-2.2	5 827	7.4	77 476	33.8	18.5
Newton	34 516	72.5	118 500	25.4	11.0	945	35.3	2.4	48 245	0.6	3 200	6.6	42 748	30.9	27.1
Oconee	11 621	79.0	235 000	21.0	10.0	884	25.4	1.2	17 430	1.0	756	4.3	15 790	51.1	15.9
Oglethorpe	5 428	78.0	125 100	23.0	12.1	740	32.2	1.6	6 731	1.1	360	5.3	6 328	33.0	32.2
Paulding	48 472	80.1	131 800	22.8	11.6	1 019	30.0	2.0	75 712	1.2	3 848	5.1	68 178	33.8	23.8
Peach	9 677	65.0	123 300	23.0	10.0	680	32.3	1.8	11 354	-1.1	897	7.9	11 411	27.8	29.3
Pickens	11 019	77.3	167 500	24.4	12.3	837	30.1	1.6	13 920	0.7	728	5.2	12 285	30.1	26.0
Pierce	6 857	75.0	86 200	21.4	12.4	602	28.3	2.6	8 106	0.2	492	6.1	7 330	29.0	31.6
Pike	6 096	83.1	155 800	23.4	13.5	814	38.4	2.1	8 260	0.8	459	5.6	7 534	33.0	28.9
Polk	14 778	68.9	102 000	25.3	12.7	669	29.5	4.1	17 991	-1.9	1 172	6.5	15 981	23.1	36.9
Pulaski	4 148	63.2	87 800	23.5	10.4	584	28.5	5.3	4 036	-0.7	263	6.5	4 113	30.4	30.6

1. Specified owner-occupied units.   2. A value of 10.0 represents 10 percent or less; a value of 50.0 represents 50 percent or more.   3. Specified renter-occupied units.
4. Overcrowded or lacking complete plumbing facilities.   5. Percent of civilian labor force.   6. Persons 16 years old and over.

Table B. States and Counties — Nonfarm Employment and Agriculture

STATE County	Number of establishments	Total	Health care and social assistance	Manufacturing	Retail trade	Finance and insurance	Professional, scientific, and technical services	Total (mil dol)	Average per employee (dollars)	Number	Fewer than 50 acres	500 acres or more	Farm operators whose principal occupation is farming (percent)
	104	105	106	107	108	109	110	111	112	113	114	115	116
GEORGIA—Cont'd													
Effingham	679	7 398	905	D	1 300	152	247	280	37 842	186	48.9	9.1	35.5
Elbert	423	4 475	508	1 879	621	D	D	142	31 724	411	35.3	4.6	55.2
Emanuel	380	4 854	848	1 740	747	169	121	141	28 949	438	24.9	19.6	39.3
Evans	213	3 873	445	D	496	86	56	121	31 163	202	32.2	8.4	45.5
Fannin	561	4 776	1 006	400	1 039	156	231	127	26 655	198	62.6	1.0	41.4
Fayette	3 235	38 978	6 050	2 405	6 843	991	2 243	1 438	36 901	126	50.8	3.2	52.4
Floyd	1 942	33 947	7 575	5 951	4 565	815	722	1 236	36 412	559	44.4	3.6	36.5
Forsyth	5 796	66 853	7 169	7 165	9 875	1 897	5 820	3 030	45 329	311	68.8	0.0	53.7
Franklin	411	6 303	962	1 522	778	147	119	190	30 084	775	44.6	1.8	52.3
Fulton	34 622	739 045	77 430	18 474	50 868	57 257	93 785	49 309	66 720	187	66.3	2.1	56.7
Gilmer	512	5 748	643	D	1 110	137	148	154	26 848	296	43.9	0.7	66.2
Glascock	24	D	D	D	21	D	D	D	D	96	30.2	17.7	47.9
Glynn	2 452	30 438	4 709	2 180	4 994	737	890	1 027	33 745	53	77.4	1.9	45.3
Gordon	977	19 713	1 655	7 921	2 324	375	218	724	36 737	671	47.5	4.2	53.1
Grady	399	4 284	426	1 006	745	162	108	130	30 272	471	34.2	13.2	35.2
Greene	408	4 509	546	559	698	198	D	160	35 466	193	34.7	11.9	58.5
Gwinnett	22 012	311 031	26 590	21 242	43 990	14 857	24 714	14 579	46 874	179	67.6	1.1	37.4
Habersham	793	11 518	1 276	D	1 872	410	225	363	31 528	422	58.5	2.4	53.8
Hall	4 040	66 547	10 260	17 916	7 902	2 000	1 688	2 833	42 564	622	59.0	2.3	51.3
Hancock	68	595	D	D	91	D	D	19	31 326	133	30.8	11.3	40.6
Haralson	433	5 050	809	1 442	924	103	108	189	37 510	299	48.5	1.7	38.5
Harris	399	4 475	399	1 333	275	D	73	111	24 777	252	42.5	4.0	50.0
Hart	386	5 366	336	2 201	923	106	117	201	37 401	584	42.8	4.1	58.9
Heard	123	1 188	D	D	88	D	28	53	44 227	168	38.1	6.0	39.9
Henry	3 411	48 299	7 066	3 004	9 669	1 203	1 413	1 548	32 049	254	56.7	2.8	47.6
Houston	2 391	35 678	6 098	3 547	7 096	1 016	4 016	1 151	32 248	226	52.7	13.3	38.9
Irwin	121	1 622	665	D	155	38	D	51	31 237	373	23.6	22.3	50.7
Jackson	1 175	17 278	1 074	5 434	2 997	258	672	646	37 378	774	53.0	3.2	47.5
Jasper	148	1 394	D	398	209	D	D	38	27 369	239	39.3	7.1	51.0
Jeff Davis	239	3 322	307	1 250	619	82	35	108	32 366	192	32.8	24.0	46.4
Jefferson	302	4 079	524	917	732	160	32	139	33 964	358	23.7	20.7	40.5
Jenkins	101	1 009	266	D	142	D	D	33	32 344	224	24.6	23.2	41.5
Johnson	116	988	231	118	158	D	D	29	29 691	255	22.0	10.2	31.8
Jones	324	2 529	427	66	500	62	75	78	30 715	175	37.1	2.9	41.1
Lamar	217	2 591	307	538	359	D	D	78	30 175	252	44.4	4.4	33.3
Lanier	98	817	242	99	130	D	20	17	21 411	86	38.4	26.7	41.9
Laurens	1 057	15 051	2 991	2 441	2 637	500	224	502	33 346	694	26.2	12.1	32.1
Lee	371	3 930	272	D	655	182	469	142	36 213	192	28.1	19.3	46.4
Liberty	820	12 182	2 051	1 977	1 954	353	662	462	37 912	46	47.8	10.9	34.8
Lincoln	130	839	D	D	154	D	D	23	26 820	150	44.0	6.7	37.3
Long	66	262	24	D	75	D	D	6	22 260	67	34.3	4.5	46.3
Lowndes	2 700	39 742	7 440	3 318	6 607	978	1 156	1 209	30 417	411	50.6	5.4	46.0
Lumpkin	510	4 681	700	786	977	100	152	134	28 659	220	63.6	0.9	53.6
McDuffie	432	6 094	847	1 843	1 024	129	148	191	31 296	208	44.2	11.1	35.1
McIntosh	175	1 327	35	D	317	D	D	30	22 265	56	62.5	8.9	42.9
Macon	182	2 183	433	697	234	49	D	77	35 221	279	26.5	17.2	60.2
Madison	359	2 009	240	174	441	53	71	55	27 303	745	46.3	0.9	46.4
Marion	76	1 397	D	D	107	16	D	35	25 299	203	24.1	12.3	42.4
Meriwether	296	3 380	946	718	544	152	44	108	32 031	295	32.9	8.1	44.7
Miller	127	1 081	329	D	D	D	23	33	30 106	183	20.8	30.1	56.3
Mitchell	369	5 818	520	D	741	152	D	151	25 980	443	30.5	25.5	47.9
Monroe	511	6 678	993	D	D	116	209	202	30 292	183	41.0	8.7	38.8
Montgomery	110	977	D	153	174	25	D	29	29 447	229	30.6	13.1	36.2
Morgan	451	5 355	474	1 258	871	170	277	186	34 675	572	35.1	6.1	45.5
Murray	374	7 314	411	4 107	750	D	53	240	32 839	320	48.4	3.8	39.1
Muscogee	4 266	79 475	15 815	6 237	11 538	D	2 426	2 959	37 234	22	40.9	13.6	45.5
Newton	1 299	17 441	2 226	3 796	2 941	492	482	640	36 690	285	50.2	6.0	53.3
Oconee	1 010	9 792	1 513	583	1 858	393	756	346	35 349	375	44.8	5.1	43.2
Oglethorpe	166	1 131	116	59	D	D	D	30	26 328	406	34.7	8.1	50.2
Paulding	1 758	16 510	2 379	793	4 393	356	584	476	28 854	142	66.2	0.7	35.2
Peach	456	6 114	743	D	839	120	109	227	37 147	190	58.9	8.9	36.8
Pickens	645	6 017	1 169	706	1 173	257	175	204	33 970	262	63.0	1.1	48.5
Pierce	324	3 152	242	378	430	89	68	94	29 938	356	46.3	11.8	52.8
Pike	241	1 552	240	D	D	D	D	48	30 974	296	44.6	5.7	35.1
Polk	585	9 759	920	3 313	1 522	D	107	327	33 556	353	45.0	2.8	41.4
Pulaski	167	2 119	937	D	353	D	48	70	33 104	176	37.5	18.2	52.8

Table B. States and Counties — Agriculture

STATE County	Land in farms Acreage (1,000)	Percent change, 2007–2012	Average size of farm	Total irrigated (1,000)	Total cropland (1,000)	Value of land and buildings (dollars) Average per farm	Average per acre	Value of machinery and equipment, average per farm (dollars)	Value of products sold Total (mil dol)	Average per farm (dollars)	Percent from: Crops	Live-stock and poultry products	Percent of farms with sales of: $10,000 or more	$100,000 or more	Government payments Total ($1,000)	Percent of farms
	117	118	119	120	121	122	123	124	125	126	127	128	129	130	131	132
GEORGIA—Cont'd																
Effingham	40	0.0	217	1.1	17.4	604 253	2 779	106 022	13.8	74 038	90.5	9.5	36.0	10.2	255	28.5
Elbert	57	-9.4	139	0.1	13.6	490 494	3 537	53 966	79.2	192 749	3.7	96.3	37.2	17.3	362	32.6
Emanuel	152	9.5	346	3.7	65.1	738 584	2 132	92 105	57.3	130 845	92.8	7.2	37.4	17.1	2 136	58.2
Evans	36	-31.7	178	3.0	14.7	461 465	2 587	75 366	39.8	197 055	40.8	59.2	39.1	17.8	429	33.7
Fannin	14	-26.3	70	0.2	3.7	455 722	6 505	47 121	16.1	81 293	8.0	92.0	23.7	7.1	16	5.6
Fayette	11	-6.8	91	0.1	2.7	557 341	6 110	48 786	4.0	31 635	90.4	9.6	21.4	4.0	9	6.3
Floyd	70	-17.1	126	0.8	19.6	489 283	3 898	54 420	77.0	137 828	6.9	93.1	29.3	8.6	616	19.7
Forsyth	16	-18.8	52	0.1	3.3	568 206	10 995	41 273	31.7	101 897	8.2	91.8	24.8	10.9	30	4.5
Franklin	77	-5.0	100	0.3	19.7	539 779	5 412	76 230	367.1	473 618	1.2	98.8	52.8	36.4	328	14.3
Fulton	14	-9.3	75	0.8	3.0	511 385	6 780	35 460	4.6	24 460	71.8	28.2	29.4	3.2	44	9.6
Gilmer	26	-30.1	86	0.1	5.3	530 159	6 141	88 270	213.9	722 466	1.0	99.0	56.1	44.3	140	8.4
Glascock	24	13.1	250	0.3	6.4	461 958	1 847	50 208	3.4	35 135	77.8	22.2	33.3	5.2	160	25.0
Glynn	4	-38.3	68	0.0	0.3	266 472	3 923	116 453	0.4	6 943	60.3	39.7	22.6	0.0	16	15.1
Gordon	85	7.3	127	1.8	32.8	607 225	4 797	66 523	261.2	389 270	4.9	95.1	45.5	23.1	1 200	16.5
Grady	130	9.5	277	9.2	54.4	850 864	3 077	104 682	99.2	210 690	64.1	35.9	43.1	17.4	2 083	52.4
Greene	49	-12.2	252	0.2	8.3	811 705	3 225	67 798	47.8	247 829	4.5	95.5	43.0	16.1	215	13.5
Gwinnett	10	25.4	58	0.1	2.1	604 374	10 335	53 011	12.1	67 425	92.5	7.5	27.4	4.5	33	10.1
Habersham	38	29.5	90	0.0	9.6	516 374	5 746	66 038	125.8	298 085	1.3	98.7	48.1	31.3	142	9.2
Hall	52	-9.3	84	0.1	12.3	686 416	8 212	68 188	166.3	267 434	2.1	97.9	34.9	19.8	115	8.2
Hancock	32	-15.9	240	0.2	4.8	822 805	3 424	61 669	4.5	34 008	35.8	64.2	33.1	6.8	165	18.0
Haralson	27	-22.0	90	0.0	5.4	377 763	4 212	46 033	42.6	142 539	0.8	99.2	23.4	7.7	172	9.7
Harris	32	-46.7	129	0.2	6.9	618 067	4 802	39 357	2.3	9 183	62.8	37.2	18.7	0.8	42	5.2
Hart	68	-3.0	117	1.6	21.7	605 507	5 181	79 663	208.1	356 355	3.7	96.3	46.9	26.2	793	22.8
Heard	27	14.7	161	D	3.4	559 560	3 473	58 190	36.1	215 137	2.4	97.6	38.7	17.3	70	6.5
Henry	22	-7.9	85	0.1	5.6	489 512	5 735	26 445	3.3	12 917	58.6	41.4	24.0	2.0	70	9.8
Houston	47	1.7	210	9.0	23.1	650 288	3 097	94 969	22.5	99 668	69.3	30.7	31.0	10.2	756	25.7
Irwin	148	2.1	398	31.6	95.7	1 012 070	2 542	182 375	117.5	314 944	86.3	13.7	52.5	33.0	4 677	71.0
Jackson	77	-8.8	100	0.3	17.7	553 712	5 539	69 008	189.4	244 758	2.9	97.1	39.7	20.8	502	14.7
Jasper	44	-22.3	183	0.4	8.1	634 649	3 462	64 134	25.2	105 586	13.7	86.3	28.0	4.2	114	9.2
Jeff Davis	79	35.7	411	9.8	44.5	1 364 479	3 321	119 953	51.9	270 260	78.6	21.4	43.8	26.0	1 115	49.0
Jefferson	146	33.7	407	22.3	74.7	812 567	1 998	116 911	72.9	203 567	72.7	27.3	43.0	22.6	2 695	65.4
Jenkins	91	7.9	408	14.2	44.1	766 795	1 879	141 826	37.5	167 295	90.5	9.5	37.5	20.5	1 808	68.3
Johnson	57	-14.2	224	1.7	15.1	401 690	1 796	53 239	6.7	26 443	78.9	21.2	28.2	3.9	405	45.9
Jones	23	-28.9	132	0.0	6.3	417 766	3 176	68 857	10.4	59 269	5.3	94.7	23.4	5.1	156	9.1
Lamar	35	-0.6	141	1.7	12.0	540 194	3 837	77 290	54.4	215 821	19.7	80.3	34.9	14.3	268	21.4
Lanier	42	-21.7	484	6.9	19.7	1 649 140	3 408	207 430	21.2	246 209	98.1	1.9	39.5	25.6	824	58.1
Laurens	184	11.7	265	10.3	60.7	544 447	2 051	74 219	35.9	51 713	84.5	15.5	31.0	7.8	2 023	61.1
Lee	105	-16.5	549	16.9	52.7	1 579 948	2 877	164 563	72.5	377 734	D	D	39.6	19.3	1 529	59.9
Liberty	6	-33.7	135	0.0	0.6	285 370	2 111	33 000	0.3	6 761	47.9	52.1	28.3	0.0	23	17.4
Lincoln	24	-14.5	157	0.0	3.6	436 273	2 772	62 560	4.1	27 020	12.9	87.1	22.7	3.3	127	20.7
Long	10	-21.9	153	D	2.8	377 328	2 463	58 806	11.5	172 179	6.1	93.9	35.8	11.9	120	40.3
Lowndes	65	-4.4	158	8.0	25.4	559 107	3 538	72 920	31.1	75 786	79.1	20.9	30.4	7.8	464	40.1
Lumpkin	17	-21.1	79	0.1	3.0	710 636	8 994	47 768	52.5	238 436	3.8	96.2	37.7	18.6	71	6.8
McDuffie	38	5.2	183	0.3	8.2	523 361	2 866	40 394	27.8	133 582	D	D	26.0	4.3	251	14.4
McIntosh	17	87.3	305	0.3	1.0	786 375	2 581	88 643	3.5	62 732	63.5	36.5	37.5	12.5	5	5.4
Macon	101	-17.4	362	29.3	53.9	928 871	2 563	145 670	172.5	618 305	21.0	79.0	51.3	33.7	2 301	58.4
Madison	71	-6.9	96	0.2	19.5	536 699	5 616	54 460	213.3	286 311	1.4	98.6	43.4	21.9	611	16.8
Marion	47	1.6	233	2.1	13.2	524 025	2 246	69 227	27.4	134 818	20.9	79.1	33.5	9.9	367	41.9
Meriwether	62	-23.8	210	0.9	16.0	666 929	3 171	63 573	12.4	42 003	46.0	54.0	28.1	5.8	287	16.6
Miller	96	-5.9	523	31.7	61.0	1 289 738	2 465	233 066	69.8	381 339	91.7	8.3	63.4	36.6	2 746	67.2
Mitchell	191	-6.5	431	67.2	117.4	1 233 991	2 860	189 664	277.8	627 196	51.4	48.6	54.2	34.5	4 902	57.8
Monroe	34	-12.2	189	0.0	5.3	642 836	3 410	79 377	37.3	203 885	2.2	97.8	27.9	9.8	354	18.0
Montgomery	58	11.9	252	5.0	18.1	435 651	1 728	75 183	14.3	62 358	85.3	14.7	25.8	8.7	795	61.6
Morgan	95	2.3	165	1.4	30.0	722 206	4 371	118 593	103.0	180 004	6.9	93.1	37.6	16.1	858	32.9
Murray	47	17.6	147	0.6	18.8	629 225	4 288	81 572	78.7	246 072	14.2	85.8	40.0	17.5	273	16.6
Muscogee	4	-44.5	194	0.0	2.0	997 818	5 137	43 500	0.1	2 273	34.0	66.0	0.0	0.0	6	22.7
Newton	41	5.7	143	0.1	8.8	603 568	4 224	46 418	D	D	D	D	27.4	2.5	81	12.3
Oconee	45	-7.2	121	2.1	12.7	872 227	7 223	56 709	73.7	196 496	32.0	68.0	34.7	13.9	336	30.4
Oglethorpe	81	-6.7	199	0.7	17.2	644 724	3 239	78 283	180.7	445 118	4.6	95.4	43.3	27.3	697	24.4
Paulding	8	-26.7	59	0.0	2.4	385 641	6 544	37 458	13.9	97 789	3.6	96.4	23.9	4.9	8	8.5
Peach	35	-11.7	186	4.7	22.2	743 532	3 999	102 589	31.0	163 116	94.4	5.6	26.3	8.9	307	19.5
Pickens	17	-29.1	64	0.0	4.0	431 542	6 715	42 969	72.6	277 233	1.4	98.6	29.4	15.6	22	2.3
Pierce	78	9.0	220	10.8	44.9	523 298	2 381	125 357	64.4	180 787	61.1	38.9	42.7	16.9	2 363	46.3
Pike	38	-17.4	129	0.6	9.0	469 351	3 650	40 432	11.1	37 419	22.3	77.7	22.0	2.7	248	22.0
Polk	45	2.5	127	0.0	13.7	459 448	3 606	51 759	35.1	99 442	8.6	91.4	27.8	6.8	437	18.7
Pulaski	63	9.8	355	19.5	43.7	929 739	2 617	236 636	76.2	433 119	64.8	35.2	35.2	27.3	1 512	60.8

Table B. States and Counties — Water Use, Wholesale Trade, Retail Trade, and Real Estate

STATE County	Water use, 2010		Wholesale trade,[1] 2012				Retail trade,[2] 2012				Real estate and rental and leasing,[2] 2012			
	Total water withdrawn (mil gal/day)	Gallons withdrawn per person per day	Number of establishments	Number of employees	Sales (mil dol)	Annual payroll (mil dol)	Number of establishments	Number of employees	Sales (mil dol)	Annual payroll (mil dol)	Number of establishments	Number of employees	Receipts (mil dol)	Annual payroll (mil dol)
	133	134	135	136	137	138	139	140	141	142	143	144	145	146
GEORGIA—Cont'd														
Effingham	122.8	2 350	11	D	D	D	107	1 290	358.5	28.6	29	D	D	D
Elbert	3.5	172	41	309	61.8	8.3	79	611	142.0	13.1	3	D	D	D
Emanuel	6.6	292	18	143	89.1	4.2	82	778	203.3	16.4	15	D	D	D
Evans	5.0	455	5	33	4.4	0.6	56	453	178.8	12.5	3	11	1.6	0.2
Fannin	9.3	391	18	73	21.1	2.5	104	943	256.6	20.3	29	55	11.2	1.4
Fayette	12.9	121	168	1 664	1 205.2	90.0	407	6 588	1 453.7	139.4	176	565	79.3	17.3
Floyd	474.7	4 928	74	812	691.5	33.8	386	3 986	1 022.4	89.3	76	252	41.7	8.2
Forsyth	27.4	156	384	5 014	3 722.6	349.7	581	8 463	2 366.8	230.9	232	507	105.3	21.6
Franklin	4.7	214	23	257	105.8	7.1	91	881	270.7	17.3	9	12	2.0	0.3
Fulton	208.5	227	1 496	27 530	29 149.1	1 970.4	3 368	49 050	13 382.7	1 292.8	2 068	17 597	5 968.3	1 241.3
Gilmer	6.8	240	23	134	63.5	4.3	91	1 103	291.8	23.6	32	53	8.6	1.4
Glascock	0.4	130	NA	NA	NA	NA	5	14	5.7	0.3	NA	NA	NA	NA
Glynn	64.6	811	66	446	270.0	19.9	452	4 567	1 407.1	111.2	143	512	70.6	16.4
Gordon	13.5	245	65	D	D	D	240	2 311	627.5	48.5	42	125	26.5	3.5
Grady	9.8	392	27	408	364.4	16.8	79	754	184.7	16.0	20	46	4.4	1.2
Greene	4.5	280	15	65	38.6	3.8	72	695	206.0	16.1	21	42	5.5	1.7
Gwinnett	10.6	13	1 718	30 603	30 301.0	2 002.5	2 759	41 508	12 673.4	1 068.5	976	4 554	1 286.3	214.0
Habersham	12.2	283	35	179	99.2	6.3	158	1 795	462.1	41.2	22	50	6.8	0.9
Hall	100.2	558	235	3 265	9 022.6	173.1	579	7 640	2 231.9	193.5	164	450	116.5	17.1
Hancock	2.3	246	1	D	D	D	21	99	24.8	2.1	2	D	D	D
Haralson	3.9	136	20	142	52.6	7.4	84	851	321.2	23.5	8	D	D	D
Harris	7.1	222	9	D	D	D	43	260	70.2	4.9	13	D	D	D
Hart	4.2	168	15	154	33.9	6.0	75	849	173.6	15.9	10	D	D	D
Heard	50.5	4 267	NA	NA	NA	NA	18	84	22.8	2.3	4	D	D	D
Henry	43.0	211	98	1 182	833.8	74.2	550	9 005	2 402.5	200.7	164	590	112.3	19.0
Houston	34.2	245	48	377	220.6	13.3	442	6 625	1 762.8	150.4	124	447	68.8	12.0
Irwin	8.8	924	9	136	79.6	4.1	30	149	32.3	2.9	2	D	D	D
Jackson	13.5	224	53	953	574.8	36.2	232	2 594	1 482.5	54.3	44	75	15.9	2.1
Jasper	2.9	208	2	D	D	D	26	213	47.6	4.0	4	2	0.3	0.0
Jeff Davis	4.7	309	10	131	64.4	4.3	67	726	251.9	17.8	5	D	D	D
Jefferson	17.1	1 007	16	259	217.8	6.3	70	640	142.8	12.3	8	42	1.9	1.0
Jenkins	2.7	320	3	D	D	D	23	154	40.5	2.9	1	D	D	D
Johnson	2.0	196	6	29	19.2	0.9	24	148	37.1	3.0	NA	NA	NA	NA
Jones	10.3	358	7	D	D	D	51	423	97.0	8.4	13	D	D	D
Lamar	3.8	209	5	84	20.6	2.6	43	421	107.2	9.1	4	D	D	D
Lanier	2.0	199	4	D	D	D	21	D	D	D	1	D	D	D
Laurens	27.7	571	36	396	306.0	16.5	248	2 647	700.5	53.5	38	129	15.0	3.2
Lee	43.1	1 523	15	259	566.2	30.7	61	589	155.0	13.8	17	45	8.8	1.7
Liberty	16.6	262	11	D	D	D	171	1 938	564.1	40.9	48	183	24.6	5.5
Lincoln	1.8	229	7	33	11.1	0.8	22	160	38.8	3.2	4	D	D	D
Long	2.2	149	1	D	D	D	12	52	16.2	1.1	3	4	0.4	0.1
Lowndes	29.1	266	115	1 069	1 227.0	41.2	493	5 974	1 748.5	132.2	137	1 447	104.7	26.2
Lumpkin	3.3	110	6	38	12.7	1.1	81	767	192.3	18.3	24	D	D	D
McDuffie	7.0	318	9	29	21.9	1.3	103	1 027	295.0	23.9	15	54	5.4	1.3
McIntosh	1.6	110	4	D	D	D	58	433	98.1	7.4	5	8	1.0	0.1
Macon	30.8	2 088	12	76	265.1	4.4	43	227	43.5	4.6	3	4	0.6	0.1
Madison	3.3	116	13	D	D	D	57	403	135.7	8.7	13	D	D	D
Marion	3.0	347	2	D	D	D	22	104	35.3	2.2	NA	NA	NA	NA
Meriwether	1.7	79	6	19	16.8	0.8	90	622	116.1	11.8	5	D	D	D
Miller	46.8	7 639	5	63	54.6	2.4	33	237	77.4	5.0	5	7	0.3	0.1
Mitchell	67.4	2 870	22	394	172.9	10.2	96	735	156.8	14.6	9	21	1.6	0.5
Monroe	68.9	2 607	21	198	112.6	8.8	74	783	186.9	16.4	17	43	6.8	1.3
Montgomery	2.5	270	6	49	17.9	1.8	28	190	46.7	3.6	3	4	0.5	0.1
Morgan	5.4	299	15	190	117.0	6.6	69	893	309.2	19.5	18	31	4.2	1.0
Murray	3.9	97	26	399	123.5	17.1	90	711	198.1	16.0	12	D	D	D
Muscogee	44.1	232	157	1 843	1 550.1	80.6	796	11 371	2 847.8	250.2	237	1 461	258.1	55.7
Newton	14.3	143	53	518	278.2	20.9	210	2 778	747.3	60.7	52	182	36.8	6.6
Oconee	7.3	222	28	257	90.7	11.6	103	1 630	397.2	38.2	58	246	79.0	14.1
Oglethorpe	2.2	148	8	D	D	D	22	145	40.6	3.1	1	D	D	D
Paulding	2.1	15	62	254	161.7	12.2	253	4 075	1 174.4	96.7	51	284	55.7	15.5
Peach	10.4	376	23	D	D	D	102	806	296.1	19.0	21	60	11.6	2.3
Pickens	4.1	138	18	87	56.6	2.7	97	1 177	327.4	26.9	34	D	D	D
Pierce	4.1	219	16	D	D	D	65	414	114.4	8.9	9	17	7.9	0.6
Pike	8.1	453	11	D	D	D	31	165	36.2	3.1	5	D	D	D
Polk	7.8	187	15	D	D	D	131	1 399	326.5	30.8	18	85	8.2	1.9
Pulaski	18.0	1 495	2	D	D	D	37	358	87.6	9.6	6	12	0.7	0.2

1. Merchant wholesalers, except manufacturers' sales branches and offices.   2. Employer establishments.

STATE County	Professional, scientific, and technical services, 2012				Manufacturing, 2012				Accommodation and food services, 2012			
	Number of establishments	Number of employees	Receipts (mil dol)	Annual payroll (mil dol)	Number of establishments	Number of employees	Receipts (mil dol)	Annual payroll (mil dol)	Number of establishments	Number of employees	Sales (mil dol)	Annual payroll (mil dol)
	147	148	149	150	151	152	153	154	155	156	157	158
GEORGIA—Cont'd												
Effingham	59	259	22.0	9.3	20	1 743	D	108.9	62	727	36.5	9.6
Elbert	21	50	4.1	1.2	89	2 028	379.6	70.7	24	325	13.7	4.0
Emanuel	26	D	D	D	29	1 694	706.3	50.5	32	416	17.4	4.2
Evans	11	54	3.9	1.6	14	1 769	D	45.0	14	D	D	D
Fannin	47	201	17.0	5.8	23	311	39.8	9.4	57	683	40.8	9.4
Fayette	422	2 127	275.0	130.8	92	2 230	853.7	112.5	217	4 857	211.5	64.6
Floyd	186	809	104.1	35.0	100	5 567	3 615.6	265.3	183	3 593	163.4	46.9
Forsyth	1 066	4 442	841.2	307.1	223	6 998	2 364.3	311.6	297	5 679	257.6	74.5
Franklin	25	109	8.1	2.7	30	1 204	434.5	49.5	43	643	29.4	7.9
Fulton	6 943	93 363	19 604.0	7 831.0	590	17 925	8 987.2	929.6	2 941	70 043	4 627.8	1 273.8
Gilmer	46	168	14.0	5.0	28	1 507	369.4	40.2	52	712	33.5	8.7
Glascock	2	D	D	D	NA	NA	NA	NA	1	D	D	D
Glynn	267	870	116.3	39.6	52	2 059	975.6	126.1	259	6 502	387.5	119.8
Gordon	62	337	66.0	23.5	104	6 492	2 499.1	260.5	92	1 371	70.9	18.0
Grady	19	61	7.3	1.9	19	511	141.2	21.4	28	310	14.2	3.2
Greene	39	92	12.0	4.0	11	414	557.6	19.3	29	887	56.7	19.0
Gwinnett	3 177	D	D	D	700	19 358	6 847.7	984.4	1 597	25 387	1 355.5	366.5
Habersham	63	257	36.1	8.6	52	4 122	1 219.0	137.8	75	1 145	53.5	13.7
Hall	402	D	D	D	225	17 020	7 629.2	647.1	283	4 742	298.3	67.4
Hancock	1	D	D	D	4	D	D	D	9	D	D	D
Haralson	33	86	8.3	2.2	33	1 364	834.1	55.2	38	D	D	D
Harris	30	D	D	D	18	D	D	D	28	523	25.0	6.7
Hart	38	104	11.9	3.6	28	2 115	602.1	91.1	29	D	D	D
Heard	4	D	D	D	10	419	D	17.4	8	D	D	D
Henry	294	1 380	198.3	57.5	69	2 872	2 035.1	137.2	340	5 783	281.5	73.1
Houston	271	3 288	437.6	169.5	54	3 105	2 051.0	129.1	270	5 726	259.0	69.1
Irwin	9	106	5.4	2.2	5	106	D	4.6	6	28	2.1	0.5
Jackson	99	468	75.5	21.3	70	4 420	1 924.1	183.9	68	1 015	46.9	13.3
Jasper	11	D	D	D	15	308	84.0	13.1	12	103	5.8	1.4
Jeff Davis	15	43	3.5	1.6	23	994	304.0	35.4	16	269	10.8	2.8
Jefferson	10	38	2.4	0.8	27	981	251.4	39.3	22	258	11.4	2.7
Jenkins	2	D	D	D	5	12	D	0.4	10	D	D	D
Johnson	6	16	0.8	0.2	5	167	14.9	3.5	9	54	2.7	0.6
Jones	20	68	5.1	1.8	12	68	D	3.2	20	D	D	D
Lamar	16	54	3.8	1.2	12	436	230.4	19.4	24	324	13.2	3.3
Lanier	4	17	0.8	0.2	4	124	D	3.4	12	103	4.6	1.4
Laurens	65	293	30.2	12.4	41	2 533	640.0	99.0	99	1 727	77.8	20.3
Lee	28	102	10.4	3.3	12	203	D	5.7	21	279	11.9	3.3
Liberty	74	D	D	D	18	D	D	D	99	D	D	D
Lincoln	10	D	D	D	4	93	10.7	2.8	15	D	D	D
Long	2	D	D	D	NA	NA	NA	NA	6	D	D	D
Lowndes	223	1 165	137.6	49.0	89	2 953	2 600.3	131.5	293	5 705	245.8	66.0
Lumpkin	59	159	15.4	5.5	25	569	100.0	22.3	59	974	46.7	12.3
McDuffie	24	D	D	D	32	1 627	554.4	63.2	38	515	24.7	5.9
McIntosh	18	23	2.6	0.7	7	28	D	0.9	29	402	17.9	4.3
Macon	6	13	1.1	0.3	16	547	478.5	31.9	14	D	D	D
Madison	25	75	5.9	1.9	24	210	21.4	7.3	20	D	D	D
Marion	4	D	D	D	3	D	D	D	6	16	1.3	0.2
Meriwether	13	43	3.6	1.3	14	688	320.5	27.6	29	D	D	D
Miller	8	22	1.7	0.6	NA	NA	NA	NA	10	78	3.1	0.7
Mitchell	20	253	17.4	7.8	16	2 928	D	80.3	29	354	18.6	5.1
Monroe	57	176	17.0	7.2	15	489	116.2	15.8	40	590	25.2	6.5
Montgomery	4	12	1.1	0.3	6	61	D	2.8	8	52	2.5	0.6
Morgan	44	479	56.9	19.3	26	1 097	314.1	50.0	52	830	35.4	10.3
Murray	19	D	D	D	65	3 656	1 306.6	122.5	41	D	D	D
Muscogee	350	2 520	301.3	113.9	122	6 977	1 937.2	297.0	442	10 453	519.3	149.2
Newton	103	392	43.9	12.8	77	3 759	1 854.8	186.1	108	1 718	112.9	23.6
Oconee	147	738	93.8	31.6	25	566	D	20.3	57	D	D	D
Oglethorpe	15	D	D	D	11	58	D	2.2	4	D	D	D
Paulding	165	565	65.6	22.3	48	775	191.0	31.9	129	2 645	121.1	33.8
Peach	27	101	7.6	2.7	28	D	D	D	55	764	40.8	9.4
Pickens	81	328	20.7	7.3	40	757	144.6	28.4	45	672	33.5	9.4
Pierce	15	73	4.7	1.6	14	380	D	13.6	21	239	11.2	2.9
Pike	18	D	D	D	8	160	D	6.0	9	D	D	D
Polk	36	113	9.5	2.8	31	3 234	D	132.0	65	903	40.6	10.9
Pulaski	14	56	4.9	2.1	3	D	D	D	18	229	10.5	2.3

1. Establishment subject to federal tax.

Table B. States and Counties — Health Care and Social Assistance, Other Services, Nonemployer Businesses, and Residential Construction

STATE County	Health care and social assistance, 2012				Other services, 2012				Nonemployer businesses, 2014		Value of residential construction authorized by building permits, 2015	
	Number of establishments	Number of employees	Receipts (mil dol)	Annual payroll (mil dol)	Number of establishments	Number of employees	Receipts (mil dol)	Annual payroll (mil dol)	Number	Receipts (mil dol)	New Construction ($1,000)	Number of housing units
	159	160	161	162	163	164	165	166	167	168	169	170
GEORGIA—Cont'd												
Effingham	57	D	D	D	41	D	D	D	3 414	133.1	195 684	1 041
Elbert	33	D	D	D	19	55	6.1	1.2	1 443	54.9	1 954	15
Emanuel	50	875	69.5	26.3	26	87	9.5	2.1	1 855	67.7	478	7
Evans	19	482	38.8	14.8	14	69	5.6	2.0	714	23.1	1 601	21
Fannin	66	1 039	115.7	39.3	29	106	9.7	2.4	2 721	119.5	41 068	206
Fayette	369	5 006	692.1	256.5	226	1 441	123.1	37.0	10 242	452.5	96 469	546
Floyd	281	8 058	1 049.2	412.6	104	831	64.9	19.5	6 910	237.4	18 298	93
Forsyth	463	6 830	704.5	283.8	307	1 541	188.7	50.8	18 918	922.3	447 884	3 502
Franklin	42	711	67.5	27.8	27	172	41.0	5.3	1 593	63.7	8 650	39
Fulton	3 542	71 584	9 875.8	3 610.7	2 108	21 451	3 833.9	763.1	103 193	5 297.5	1 687 542	9 705
Gilmer	46	577	46.2	20.2	37	169	16.4	4.8	2 620	101.1	15 683	99
Glascock	5	D	D	D	3	4	0.3	0.0	180	5.7	NA	NA
Glynn	262	5 031	645.8	235.5	141	746	84.3	17.9	6 573	285.2	122 392	464
Gordon	66	1 518	207.6	64.2	44	D	D	D	3 514	155.9	12 879	87
Grady	33	447	43.4	12.9	25	81	10.3	2.1	1 467	51.3	5 280	25
Greene	49	568	48.2	19.2	23	105	8.9	3.3	1 513	67.2	65 778	225
Gwinnett	1 834	25 079	2 700.3	1 067.6	1 382	8 424	840.6	245.4	95 618	3 901.4	522 550	3 918
Habersham	85	1 360	108.1	48.2	47	187	13.7	4.2	3 020	109.9	2 861	17
Hall	443	9 275	1 297.8	493.4	246	1 193	123.8	32.4	14 384	637.9	158 694	946
Hancock	6	D	D	D	7	D	D	D	516	10.9	2 129	16
Haralson	39	699	64.2	24.3	36	D	D	D	2 025	81.5	6 093	27
Harris	24	231	16.5	6.2	14	D	D	D	2 390	103.3	38 882	146
Hart	33	567	45.5	17.4	27	115	10.4	2.2	1 870	62.5	7 915	38
Heard	5	D	D	D	8	D	D	D	741	25.1	2 363	19
Henry	396	6 223	782.2	239.1	226	996	79.7	23.1	18 505	631.5	261 486	1 269
Houston	289	5 917	553.9	220.3	143	799	63.9	18.2	9 319	288.4	154 204	988
Irwin	20	758	42.8	20.1	7	25	3.5	0.8	571	17.2	1 538	8
Jackson	84	1 182	80.2	34.7	74	521	48.8	19.4	4 887	195.9	132 369	612
Jasper	14	D	D	D	7	29	1.5	0.5	1 085	41.5	7 369	55
Jeff Davis	18	316	24.0	9.5	10	19	1.6	0.3	863	36.1	300	3
Jefferson	22	430	32.2	16.4	14	D	D	D	1 185	40.1	0	0
Jenkins	8	393	14.6	9.7	6	14	1.8	0.4	570	19.4	1 100	11
Johnson	11	314	21.2	8.9	8	D	D	D	575	20.4	0	0
Jones	33	D	D	D	20	71	16.5	2.2	1 904	67.3	12 339	102
Lamar	22	D	D	D	13	216	14.4	7.2	1 202	37.4	4 745	40
Lanier	10	D	D	D	4	D	D	D	529	22.8	4 098	35
Laurens	142	4 233	600.0	214.6	64	D	D	D	3 934	146.9	778	11
Lee	32	360	21.7	10.8	27	D	D	D	2 106	74.7	12 145	99
Liberty	76	2 026	249.2	101.0	66	D	D	D	2 928	89.2	60 274	285
Lincoln	6	D	D	D	10	D	D	D	519	19.5	4 894	23
Long	5	29	1.9	0.6	2	D	D	D	591	19.1	3 000	260
Lowndes	369	D	D	D	151	881	60.2	17.1	6 968	344.9	90 637	559
Lumpkin	52	612	54.6	23.0	28	75	7.0	1.7	2 332	91.0	29 655	215
McDuffie	51	970	76.8	24.9	28	114	16.0	3.6	1 462	48.9	4 243	24
McIntosh	14	54	3.6	1.6	13	36	2.5	0.7	920	37.7	10 358	43
Macon	18	425	33.8	11.5	8	D	D	D	830	20.0	574	3
Madison	25	D	D	D	15	D	D	D	2 098	68.8	17 032	79
Marion	7	D	D	D	2	D	D	D	399	13.8	1 076	12
Meriwether	28	948	63.0	29.4	16	39	3.6	0.7	1 545	47.9	6 488	31
Miller	12	318	24.5	10.7	6	23	2.4	0.5	371	11.1	550	1
Mitchell	25	472	36.4	14.8	29	117	8.3	2.5	1 400	45.0	5 880	3
Monroe	55	D	D	D	29	D	D	D	1 973	84.9	18 121	82
Montgomery	4	24	1.2	0.5	3	4	0.2	0.1	554	18.1	1 672	11
Morgan	34	456	33.1	13.9	32	128	13.4	3.2	1 886	86.9	11 233	57
Murray	33	469	42.8	17.3	24	103	8.5	2.9	1 855	76.6	8 575	38
Muscogee	590	14 823	1 454.8	578.6	322	2 293	223.3	62.4	13 015	421.0	90 085	616
Newton	122	2 039	189.0	77.1	79	336	25.9	7.4	8 984	270.6	50 100	251
Oconee	126	1 525	127.0	56.1	53	380	44.3	11.8	3 709	183.5	93 464	403
Oglethorpe	12	D	D	D	11	D	D	D	1 004	33.0	525	35
Paulding	143	2 000	184.6	69.1	124	455	38.3	11.0	11 376	393.0	108 948	981
Peach	42	618	39.3	16.8	30	171	14.6	4.4	1 839	70.6	7 595	47
Pickens	64	1 186	118.7	48.4	39	D	D	D	3 013	130.9	15 703	67
Pierce	22	263	13.8	6.6	24	66	4.7	1.2	1 213	41.2	4 374	48
Pike	17	D	D	D	17	D	D	D	1 469	57.4	5 974	40
Polk	52	781	57.6	25.9	40	395	40.3	10.9	2 673	78.6	5 420	32
Pulaski	20	715	60.9	27.3	8	13	1.0	0.3	672	19.2	1 015	13

Table B. States and Counties — Government Employment and Payroll, and Local Government Finances

		Government employment and payroll, 2012								Local government finances, 2012				
			March payroll (percent of total)								General revenue			
													Taxes	
														Per capita[1] (dollars)
STATE County	Full-time equivalent employees	March payroll (dollars)	Adminis- tration, judicial, and legal	Police and Corrections	Fire Protection	Highways and transpor- tation	Health and Welfare	Natural resources and utilities	Education and libraries	Total (mil dol)	Inter- govern- mental (mil dol)	Total (mil dol)	Total	Property
	171	172	173	174	175	176	177	178	179	180	181	182	183	184

GEORGIA—Cont'd

Effingham	2 486	7 934 109	4.0	6.9	1.7	0.8	16.1	2.9	65.1	191.3	66.5	72.8	1 366	843
Elbert	1 023	2 910 130	6.0	7.4	1.7	2.3	20.0	5.2	54.4	74.4	24.4	21.3	1 084	728
Emanuel	1 380	4 099 290	4.7	6.6	1.2	3.3	32.4	1.6	49.5	134.4	38.4	25.2	1 102	650
Evans	411	1 161 088	7.5	7.5	1.2	2.3	0.9	7.4	72.6	32.8	16.8	10.9	1 022	548
Fannin	760	2 415 781	6.9	7.2	1.6	5.7	4.3	5.2	68.0	63.1	21.3	34.9	1 484	927
Fayette	4 677	16 227 469	6.0	9.6	6.9	2.0	0.0	3.4	70.7	331.0	78.7	204.0	1 897	1 391
Floyd	3 631	12 476 709	5.7	9.3	4.2	4.2	1.7	5.5	67.7	620.3	284.0	151.4	1 574	957
Forsyth	5 440	15 768 647	8.4	9.3	5.1	2.1	0.8	5.4	66.7	548.8	158.2	323.5	1 721	1 160
Franklin	907	2 573 274	6.9	12.5	0.0	2.6	4.2	5.9	64.4	64.2	24.6	29.2	1 334	759
Fulton	43 801	165 333 873	9.4	12.0	4.7	15.4	3.4	6.1	47.6	5 335.6	1 131.9	2 739.7	2 802	1 941
Gilmer	920	2 851 278	9.0	12.0	2.0	3.3	4.8	1.4	67.0	76.9	24.5	43.0	1 524	1 036
Glascock	129	342 830	4.9	4.2	0.0	3.5	1.7	4.2	80.7	8.3	4.5	3.0	970	705
Glynn	4 919	18 972 711	4.6	6.1	2.8	0.9	46.3	3.8	35.3	515.4	78.5	158.8	1 960	1 234
Gordon	2 032	7 129 189	6.2	7.7	4.0	2.9	0.3	5.2	71.1	172.1	62.6	78.3	1 404	810
Grady	1 132	2 874 976	6.5	7.8	2.0	1.9	2.7	6.1	69.6	66.6	29.6	25.7	1 009	623
Greene	269	680 713	19.0	33.4	1.8	17.6	6.5	14.2	0.0	58.7	12.0	38.3	2 379	1 693
Gwinnett	27 778	103 170 776	5.7	8.0	3.3	0.8	1.5	3.8	75.9	2 774.6	950.1	1 287.6	1 529	1 100
Habersham	3 305	10 231 305	4.4	3.6	1.2	1.1	19.8	2.2	67.1	181.0	64.5	53.3	1 225	714
Hall	6 523	22 620 107	6.4	9.1	7.3	1.6	4.4	4.9	65.4	563.5	217.3	266.2	1 436	890
Hancock	382	962 206	6.0	11.2	0.0	2.9	5.0	4.4	68.0	28.6	10.2	16.3	1 811	1 568
Haralson	1 277	3 955 709	6.4	9.3	4.8	2.9	2.1	6.3	67.7	88.2	38.2	39.1	1 375	852
Harris	1 034	3 285 198	4.4	8.8	0.1	2.2	4.9	3.4	74.7	80.5	24.1	43.3	1 331	974
Hart	900	2 651 269	5.4	6.4	1.0	2.6	1.4	3.1	73.5	59.3	20.8	30.8	1 208	771
Heard	504	1 507 476	3.9	8.3	9.3	3.8	1.5	6.9	62.5	42.2	12.2	27.6	2 376	938
Henry	7 960	25 579 364	7.4	7.5	4.5	1.4	1.0	5.6	71.5	718.9	328.0	305.3	1 460	969
Houston	5 500	18 181 428	5.3	9.1	2.9	2.2	2.3	3.3	73.1	461.3	189.3	203.0	1 389	803
Irwin	623	2 698 793	4.3	21.9	4.3	7.8	23.1	6.2	32.3	40.3	14.0	9.7	1 013	702
Jackson	2 530	7 918 962	6.3	11.0	0.4	1.4	3.5	4.7	71.2	198.5	64.2	107.0	1 767	1 201
Jasper	596	1 714 273	5.5	6.8	0.6	0.7	23.1	3.8	56.7	44.3	14.2	16.0	1 176	880
Jeff Davis	671	2 209 748	5.1	5.1	1.9	1.6	22.2	2.5	60.6	64.7	22.7	14.5	959	451
Jefferson	926	2 709 948	7.4	10.5	1.1	0.9	22.0	2.9	53.3	61.2	24.1	20.9	1 273	787
Jenkins	429	1 431 503	7.7	9.7	1.7	6.7	21.4	3.0	48.9	28.0	15.0	8.5	923	581
Johnson	327	789 670	7.1	8.8	1.3	2.1	5.8	3.8	70.5	20.2	10.3	7.8	788	516
Jones	1 142	2 976 385	4.8	7.6	0.3	3.1	1.4	2.8	79.5	77.2	38.1	33.3	1 165	839
Lamar	637	1 432 522	7.9	19.7	2.3	3.0	3.1	7.3	55.8	44.4	15.3	19.3	1 069	698
Lanier	309	907 306	5.1	6.3	0.4	4.9	0.6	0.8	81.4	22.8	12.3	8.7	840	599
Laurens	2 333	6 680 665	4.4	7.5	2.2	2.2	14.7	4.0	62.8	168.6	86.7	55.3	1 151	626
Lee	1 281	3 572 458	6.0	9.8	3.1	2.1	3.3	1.7	73.1	83.1	33.8	38.4	1 337	897
Liberty	2 620	8 517 567	5.5	9.7	1.7	0.8	17.6	1.9	58.9	231.2	86.6	70.0	1 070	640
Lincoln	343	943 673	7.0	8.3	0.1	4.6	4.7	4.1	70.2	24.9	9.7	11.6	1 495	1 126
Long	484	1 237 309	6.2	6.7	0.0	3.9	0.5	1.1	81.0	41.0	26.8	10.9	678	497
Lowndes	6 045	19 639 563	3.1	7.2	1.9	1.4	42.6	2.7	39.9	581.5	129.5	139.2	1 215	637
Lumpkin	914	2 710 822	6.9	9.8	4.9	4.4	1.3	4.6	66.2	65.6	21.0	35.6	1 164	771
McDuffie	1 115	3 376 988	4.5	5.8	1.9	1.8	17.5	5.3	60.7	89.6	43.8	29.4	1 357	750
McIntosh	543	1 451 916	10.8	16.2	0.3	3.5	4.5	2.5	58.6	37.8	12.8	19.7	1 422	1 061
Macon	468	1 330 912	6.2	9.8	1.1	3.9	3.2	8.0	66.6	35.4	15.4	15.7	1 103	778
Madison	1 012	3 107 942	5.4	7.1	0.0	1.8	4.3	1.4	78.7	69.1	34.5	27.9	998	714
Marion	276	887 260	6.5	7.1	0.0	4.2	3.2	3.5	74.6	27.1	16.3	8.1	933	664
Meriwether	1 203	3 245 971	5.5	9.3	0.8	1.8	22.0	3.1	55.0	84.2	30.1	25.7	1 210	867
Miller	558	1 697 352	5.4	6.0	0.2	1.6	45.2	3.2	35.5	39.7	21.9	7.8	1 308	873
Mitchell	1 021	2 901 088	6.0	10.9	2.5	2.8	3.0	6.3	61.9	77.9	28.7	31.6	1 366	899
Monroe	1 172	3 579 175	4.2	11.4	1.2	4.4	12.1	3.3	61.1	93.8	21.4	53.1	1 992	1 362
Montgomery	230	587 331	8.4	7.4	0.5	6.6	3.1	1.4	72.5	17.7	8.0	7.4	835	546
Morgan	953	3 020 860	6.6	5.9	0.9	3.0	17.7	3.8	59.5	58.7	20.9	31.5	1 763	1 132
Murray	1 247	3 919 836	4.1	6.6	2.6	2.5	1.1	1.8	77.8	92.6	46.9	36.7	932	519
Muscogee	9 038	29 241 738	4.1	12.0	4.8	2.6	7.5	7.2	60.0	741.6	293.1	273.0	1 376	1 010
Newton	4 446	13 949 576	4.8	7.6	3.4	1.7	14.6	4.6	61.7	372.2	178.8	121.8	1 200	823
Oconee	1 252	3 915 501	7.1	6.7	0.4	2.2	1.3	3.9	74.9	100.2	32.7	57.1	1 698	1 106
Oglethorpe	532	1 614 557	5.6	5.6	0.8	1.8	3.5	1.4	81.2	31.8	13.7	15.1	1 034	808
Paulding	5 393	14 332 833	3.2	7.3	2.8	1.5	0.5	2.6	80.1	356.7	171.7	150.3	1 038	665
Peach	1 087	3 443 843	6.7	12.0	3.0	1.1	15.5	2.4	56.5	102.9	28.0	38.7	1 399	851
Pickens	1 155	3 419 594	7.3	9.4	3.0	2.8	3.9	5.3	64.6	83.1	24.1	47.4	1 618	1 120
Pierce	624	2 237 998	1.9	4.1	0.0	2.0	2.7	2.2	84.6	46.0	24.2	18.2	963	622
Pike	638	1 686 429	6.9	9.0	0.0	3.2	0.0	2.0	78.9	39.8	18.6	17.9	1 005	826
Polk	1 548	4 904 910	5.6	10.2	2.6	2.4	1.4	4.0	66.8	116.2	53.1	48.3	1 172	717
Pulaski	358	909 842	9.2	11.0	3.6	4.3	1.3	4.5	64.6	27.3	12.1	11.6	990	649

1. Based on the resident population estimated as of July 1 of the year shown.

| | Local government finances, 2012 (cont.) | | | | | | | | | Government employment, 2014 | | | Presidential election,[2] 2012 | | |
| | Direct general expenditure | | | | | | | Debt outstanding | | | | | Percent of vote cast: | | |
STATE County	Total (mil dol)	Per capita[1] (dollars)	Educa-tion	Health and hospitals	Police protec-tion	Public welfare	High-ways	Total (mil dol)	Per capita[1] (dollars)	Federal civilian	Federal military	State and local	Demo-cratic	Republi-can	All other
	185	186	187	188	189	190	191	192	193	194	195	196	197	198	199
GEORGIA—Cont'd															
Effingham	215.1	4 037	47.5	28.2	3.7	0.3	2.7	102.6	1 925	63	158	2 851	24.3	75.0	0.7
Elbert	78.1	3 967	39.3	26.1	4.2	0.7	4.5	17.7	901	127	55	1 138	40.5	58.5	1.0
Emanuel	128.4	5 609	29.9	50.2	2.4	0.2	2.9	34.5	1 507	65	63	2 003	37.2	62.0	0.8
Evans	39.2	3 664	67.4	1.1	4.4	0.0	3.4	8.1	760	36	30	649	35.6	63.9	0.5
Fannin	65.9	2 803	54.6	3.5	4.0	0.5	11.3	12.3	524	47	68	885	24.7	73.8	1.6
Fayette	360.7	3 354	57.2	1.1	6.8	0.2	4.4	279.1	2 596	484	353	4 367	34.2	64.9	0.9
Floyd	658.4	6 846	27.4	47.2	2.2	0.1	2.6	238.0	2 474	206	267	5 577	31.2	67.6	1.1
Forsyth	529.3	2 816	59.8	0.4	6.1	0.5	4.9	349.8	1 861	177	587	6 623	20.4	78.5	1.1
Franklin	58.5	2 670	56.1	3.0	9.3	0.4	6.3	19.6	730	48	62	1 050	23.7	75.2	1.1
Fulton	4 905.9	5 017	36.2	1.9	6.5	2.3	2.4	20 181.5	20 640	24 368	2 893	77 158	67.2	32.1	0.7
Gilmer	71.0	2 520	60.5	0.4	6.0	0.2	2.7	75.3	2 672	82	83	1 152	23.4	75.4	1.1
Glascock	8.8	2 789	73.4	1.9	3.4	1.5	6.9	0.4	113	0	0	188	14.7	84.2	1.1
Glynn	522.7	6 452	28.7	45.8	4.4	0.1	1.6	353.6	4 364	1 671	273	6 897	38.0	61.4	0.6
Gordon	172.7	3 096	59.5	1.2	6.0	0.4	3.7	114.7	2 057	90	160	2 662	24.2	74.5	1.3
Grady	73.3	2 881	53.7	1.8	4.8	0.0	6.5	41.6	1 635	77	73	1 128	37.8	61.7	0.5
Greene	66.3	4 122	48.1	0.3	8.8	1.2	6.7	33.3	2 068	41	47	788	42.2	57.2	0.6
Gwinnett	2 810.6	3 338	58.1	1.5	5.7	0.1	4.5	3 709.8	4 406	2 378	2 594	32 709	44.5	54.7	0.8
Habersham	168.2	3 865	41.0	30.6	3.5	0.3	3.1	147.2	3 382	103	119	2 860	19.6	79.5	1.0
Hall	566.0	3 053	55.8	6.1	4.5	0.8	2.5	1 522.9	8 213	458	542	9 917	24.1	75.0	0.8
Hancock	25.7	2 852	59.1	3.1	5.4	1.7	5.0	11.1	1 235	14	21	778	81.4	18.3	0.3
Haralson	90.4	3 182	64.8	1.4	5.5	0.3	2.9	42.6	1 502	45	82	1 555	20.3	78.0	1.7
Harris	77.2	2 371	65.4	3.4	5.0	0.0	4.2	45.3	1 392	56	93	1 159	28.1	71.4	0.5
Hart	58.4	2 289	53.1	3.2	5.6	0.4	4.4	16.0	628	85	71	1 095	33.6	65.4	1.0
Heard	36.5	3 133	56.5	4.4	5.1	2.9	4.3	21.9	1 878	14	33	662	24.7	74.2	1.2
Henry	565.4	2 705	60.8	0.4	5.5	0.9	6.1	704.9	3 372	920	615	7 722	45.9	53.4	0.7
Houston	446.8	3 057	57.5	4.7	6.4	0.0	5.5	209.8	1 435	15 126	4 028	9 358	39.5	59.7	0.8
Irwin	42.7	4 450	40.9	35.7	4.1	0.2	7.1	10.1	1 048	23	24	694	31.3	68.1	0.7
Jackson	211.8	3 497	53.3	2.4	5.8	0.3	7.5	505.9	8 352	138	176	2 782	21.6	77.4	1.0
Jasper	43.8	3 215	45.0	24.5	4.1	0.6	6.1	15.0	1 099	19	38	619	32.8	66.3	0.9
Jeff Davis	60.0	3 960	38.1	36.0	3.5	0.2	7.6	20.3	1 337	29	42	786	25.7	73.3	1.0
Jefferson	64.9	3 950	43.6	21.7	4.9	1.0	3.6	24.3	1 480	43	45	1 053	57.4	42.3	0.3
Jenkins	26.9	2 917	51.4	4.2	4.4	0.8	9.3	4.9	533	20	23	542	43.1	56.3	0.6
Johnson	19.4	1 960	61.3	3.0	5.3	0.3	6.1	0.9	88	17	23	635	32.8	66.5	0.6
Jones	72.0	2 520	65.4	0.6	5.4	0.6	6.1	11.5	403	32	82	1 144	36.8	62.6	0.7
Lamar	47.0	2 605	52.2	0.8	7.4	0.7	3.3	56.0	3 100	39	49	1 103	35.8	63.4	0.8
Lanier	22.1	2 125	69.1	0.5	7.1	0.4	6.2	11.4	1 096	16	29	481	37.0	62.2	0.8
Laurens	182.6	3 801	47.1	15.1	4.8	0.3	4.0	54.7	1 138	1 395	136	2 766	39.0	60.5	0.6
Lee	84.5	2 939	66.3	3.3	5.2	0.0	3.2	70.7	2 459	45	81	1 512	23.7	75.8	0.5
Liberty	250.0	3 818	53.4	19.3	4.8	0.0	2.3	82.6	1 262	3 910	16 721	3 175	64.0	35.6	0.5
Lincoln	23.8	3 082	54.0	3.7	3.6	2.7	6.6	35.4	4 577	14	22	403	37.4	61.8	0.8
Long	36.7	2 284	68.5	0.5	5.4	1.5	8.2	6.7	417	10	48	690	37.3	61.4	1.2
Lowndes	649.1	5 667	24.9	53.1	3.9	0.7	2.3	369.8	3 228	1 104	4 732	10 385	45.0	54.3	0.7
Lumpkin	67.2	2 197	60.3	1.9	7.6	0.1	3.6	75.2	2 455	69	198	2 461	23.3	75.2	1.5
McDuffie	90.0	4 153	49.0	21.0	4.1	1.3	2.2	31.7	1 464	29	138	1 270	42.3	57.2	0.5
McIntosh	35.7	2 581	47.5	2.9	9.5	0.0	4.1	3.4	246	24	41	641	46.6	52.7	0.7
Macon	36.4	2 549	51.7	1.7	6.1	0.5	5.1	4.5	314	22	34	873	65.3	34.4	0.4
Madison	72.1	2 583	67.3	2.6	3.1	0.5	4.4	51.6	1 850	41	81	1 194	26.2	72.6	1.3
Marion	31.7	3 643	77.5	1.8	2.4	2.2	1.7	21.1	2 425	31	25	343	43.4	55.7	0.9
Meriwether	85.0	3 997	44.3	21.9	5.5	0.2	2.8	60.8	2 859	46	60	1 460	47.0	52.4	0.6
Miller	38.7	6 487	24.8	50.2	3.2	0.1	3.5	25.7	4 303	19	17	736	29.9	69.4	0.8
Mitchell	87.6	3 783	42.9	4.0	5.8	0.0	7.0	58.1	2 509	78	59	1 474	47.7	51.7	0.6
Monroe	92.6	3 477	43.8	14.7	6.5	0.1	5.1	33.5	1 257	34	74	2 584	33.8	65.4	0.8
Montgomery	17.6	1 979	59.5	3.0	4.8	1.0	4.3	1.9	217	18	24	371	29.1	70.2	0.7
Morgan	72.8	4 070	44.7	20.5	4.7	0.9	5.4	29.9	1 674	36	51	1 087	33.8	65.4	0.8
Murray	90.2	2 289	67.5	2.4	4.0	0.9	5.5	39.4	1 001	99	113	1 341	26.6	71.9	1.5
Muscogee	832.5	4 196	45.9	7.7	5.9	2.3	4.4	677.3	3 413	6 562	4 947	13 166	59.6	39.9	0.5
Newton	383.8	3 782	52.5	20.5	4.2	0.0	2.1	387.3	3 816	218	294	4 302	50.3	49.1	0.7
Oconee	98.9	2 943	63.3	1.2	4.1	0.6	5.9	108.6	3 230	115	101	1 392	28.2	70.7	1.1
Oglethorpe	32.9	2 254	68.3	2.8	3.0	1.0	3.7	24.2	1 653	15	42	567	34.6	64.3	1.1
Paulding	341.1	2 355	68.6	0.9	5.0	0.1	7.3	260.6	1 800	123	428	4 798	30.2	68.8	1.0
Peach	89.7	3 247	45.2	13.6	6.8	0.2	2.5	47.6	1 722	104	80	2 007	53.1	46.3	0.6
Pickens	82.3	2 812	55.3	3.3	6.4	0.2	4.6	22.2	758	55	85	1 251	20.3	78.2	1.5
Pierce	44.8	2 375	64.8	2.3	3.1	0.8	6.5	18.5	982	46	54	722	18.5	81.0	0.6
Pike	37.6	2 114	69.3	2.4	7.0	0.2	3.7	11.8	662	27	51	723	19.2	79.8	1.0
Polk	111.7	2 712	59.9	1.2	7.3	0.3	4.7	44.4	1 079	68	117	1 580	28.7	69.8	1.5
Pulaski	35.2	3 007	42.6	2.6	5.9	0.2	5.4	5.9	508	19	30	692	34.8	64.6	0.6

1. Based on the resident population estimated as of July 1 of the year shown.   2. © 2013 Election Data Services, Inc. All rights reserved.

Table B. States and Counties — **Land Area and Population**

STATE/ County code	CBSA code[1]	County type[2]	STATE County	Land area[3] (sq km) 2010	Total persons 2015	Rank	Per square kilometer	White	Black	American Indian, Alaska Native	Asian and Pacific Islander	Percent Hispanic or Latino[4]	Under 5 years	5 to 17 years	18 to 24 years	25 to 34 years	35 to 44 years	45 to 54 years
				1	2	3	4	5	6	7	8	9	10	11	12	13	14	15
			GEORGIA—Cont'd															
13 237	...	6	Putnam	893	21 353	1 761	23.9	65.9	27.2	0.4	0.8	6.6	5.9	15.4	6.9	11.0	10.6	13.2
13 239	...	9	Quitman	392	2 302	3 025	5.9	51.4	47.7	0.5	0.3	1.4	4.5	13.0	6.0	8.6	9.5	13.0
13 241	...	9	Rabun	958	16 281	2 023	17.0	89.0	1.9	1.0	1.2	8.4	4.2	14.2	7.2	9.6	11.1	12.9
13 243	...	6	Randolph	1 109	7 193	2 658	6.5	37.0	60.9	0.3	0.6	2.1	5.7	14.9	10.7	10.6	9.0	12.8
13 245	12260	2	Richmond	840	201 793	324	240.2	38.3	56.0	0.9	2.9	4.6	7.2	16.5	12.1	15.9	11.3	12.2
13 247	12060	1	Rockdale	336	88 856	646	264.5	37.8	51.0	0.7	2.4	10.0	6.0	19.6	9.5	11.4	12.9	14.9
13 249	11140	8	Schley	432	5 168	2 825	12.0	73.9	21.6	0.3	0.9	4.4	5.1	22.5	8.2	9.9	13.1	15.2
13 251	...	6	Screven	1 671	14 162	2 156	8.5	56.1	41.9	0.7	0.7	1.7	6.6	16.1	9.2	11.3	11.4	13.8
13 253	...	6	Seminole	609	8 647	2 541	14.2	63.8	33.4	0.6	1.0	3.0	5.6	16.3	8.2	9.4	10.8	13.6
13 255	12060	1	Spalding	509	64 051	819	125.8	61.5	33.8	0.7	1.3	4.5	6.6	17.8	8.8	12.6	12.3	13.1
13 257	45740	7	Stephens	464	25 586	1 579	55.1	84.7	12.5	0.8	1.3	3.0	5.8	16.5	10.1	11.2	11.0	13.1
13 259	...	8	Stewart	1 188	5 851	2 768	4.9	28.1	45.9	0.6	1.3	24.2	4.4	11.0	11.7	19.3	13.8	12.4
13 261	11140	6	Sumter	1 250	30 779	1 416	24.6	40.8	52.7	0.6	1.6	5.3	6.5	17.5	13.9	12.3	10.6	12.5
13 263	...	8	Talbot	1 014	6 337	2 731	6.2	41.5	56.9	0.8	0.5	2.1	4.5	14.2	8.6	9.4	10.3	15.4
13 265	...	8	Taliaferro	504	1 639	3 075	3.3	38.8	57.5	0.5	0.8	4.0	6.5	12.0	8.0	10.2	10.1	14.2
13 267	...	6	Tattnall	1 242	25 229	1 601	20.3	59.8	29.6	0.5	0.7	10.6	5.9	15.3	10.1	15.8	14.6	13.4
13 269	...	8	Taylor	976	8 330	2 570	8.5	59.2	38.1	0.4	1.0	2.3	5.1	15.9	9.6	10.2	12.1	14.4
13 271	...	7	Telfair	1 133	16 400	2 015	14.5	50.0	35.0	0.3	0.9	14.7	4.2	13.5	8.1	15.7	16.0	14.3
13 273	10500	3	Terrell	869	9 113	2 505	10.5	36.5	60.8	0.6	0.7	2.6	6.9	16.7	9.3	12.0	9.6	13.8
13 275	45620	4	Thomas	1 410	45 063	1 070	32.0	58.8	37.0	0.8	1.1	3.4	6.5	17.6	8.1	11.9	11.9	13.9
13 277	45700	4	Tift	671	40 764	1 160	60.8	57.6	30.2	0.5	1.7	11.3	6.6	18.5	11.8	13.1	12.2	12.3
13 279	47080	7	Toombs	943	27 241	1 522	28.9	62.6	26.3	0.4	1.2	11.2	7.7	19.5	8.6	12.8	11.9	12.4
13 281	...	9	Towns	431	11 182	2 345	25.9	95.4	1.4	0.6	0.8	2.6	3.7	10.2	13.1	7.3	8.5	10.9
13 283	...	7	Treutlen	517	6 785	2 695	13.1	64.3	32.3	0.5	0.4	2.9	6.3	18.3	9.3	13.6	12.0	12.2
13 285	29300	4	Troup	1 072	69 763	769	65.1	59.0	36.0	0.6	2.1	3.7	6.7	18.6	10.6	13.0	12.2	13.1
13 287	...	6	Turner	739	8 214	2 582	11.1	55.8	39.1	0.6	1.1	4.6	6.0	20.2	8.5	11.7	10.5	12.2
13 289	31420	3	Twiggs	928	8 390	2 564	9.0	56.6	40.9	0.8	0.6	1.9	5.5	13.6	7.7	11.1	10.1	15.8
13 291	...	9	Union	834	22 267	1 716	26.7	95.2	1.2	1.0	0.9	3.1	3.3	13.5	6.2	7.9	9.0	12.5
13 293	45580	6	Upson	838	26 368	1 550	31.5	68.9	28.2	0.7	1.0	2.5	6.4	16.0	8.6	11.0	12.1	14.3
13 295	16860	2	Walker	1 156	68 066	783	58.9	92.6	5.2	0.8	0.8	2.0	5.5	17.1	8.0	11.8	13.3	14.0
13 297	12060	1	Walton	844	88 399	650	104.7	77.8	17.4	0.7	1.8	3.9	6.2	19.7	8.5	11.7	13.2	14.7
13 299	48180	4	Ware	2 311	35 370	1 293	15.3	65.7	29.9	0.8	1.4	3.7	6.9	16.9	9.1	13.3	11.9	12.9
13 301	...	8	Warren	736	5 460	2 804	7.4	38.6	60.2	0.7	0.5	1.1	5.8	15.7	8.1	9.9	9.6	14.5
13 303	...	7	Washington	1 757	20 816	1 788	11.8	44.8	53.0	0.4	0.7	2.2	6.1	16.2	9.2	12.6	11.6	14.7
13 305	27700	6	Wayne	1 662	29 534	1 440	17.8	72.5	21.1	0.9	0.9	6.3	6.8	17.6	8.4	13.3	13.3	13.7
13 307	...	8	Webster	542	2 648	2 996	4.9	53.8	42.5	0.5	0.5	3.7	3.5	17.7	7.7	9.2	11.4	14.9
13 309	...	9	Wheeler	765	7 903	2 604	10.3	56.8	38.1	0.5	0.4	5.4	4.3	12.6	10.1	17.7	15.8	15.2
13 311	...	8	White	623	28 319	1 477	45.5	93.7	3.0	1.2	0.8	2.9	4.8	16.4	9.0	9.7	11.4	13.7
13 313	19140	3	Whitfield	752	104 216	572	138.6	61.2	4.3	0.6	1.7	33.3	7.1	19.9	9.7	13.2	13.2	13.4
13 315	...	9	Wilcox	978	8 857	2 525	9.1	59.5	36.0	0.8	0.8	4.1	5.1	13.6	9.1	15.3	14.0	14.3
13 317	...	6	Wilkes	1 216	9 867	2 446	8.1	53.3	43.2	0.5	0.8	3.9	5.8	15.9	7.7	10.2	10.6	13.9
13 319	...	8	Wilkinson	1 159	9 155	2 497	7.9	58.0	39.2	0.5	0.7	2.7	6.3	16.4	8.1	11.6	10.7	14.4
13 321	10500	3	Worth	1 478	20 699	1 794	14.0	68.4	29.1	0.6	0.7	2.1	6.0	16.7	8.7	12.2	11.3	14.1
15 000	...	X	HAWAII	16 635	1 431 603	X	86.1	36.7	3.2	1.7	74.0	10.1	6.4	15.3	9.7	14.9	12.4	12.6
15 001	25900	5	Hawaii	10 434	196 428	334	18.8	47.8	1.8	2.5	67.9	12.4	6.2	15.8	8.2	12.7	11.4	12.3
15 003	46520	2	Honolulu	1 556	998 714	46	641.8	32.7	3.9	1.5	76.8	9.5	6.5	15.0	10.5	15.7	12.5	12.3
15 005	27980	9	Kalawao	31	89	3 142	2.9	40.4	6.7	3.4	64.0	1.1	0.0	0.0	0.0	12.4	10.1	18.0
15 007	28180	5	Kauai	1 606	71 735	753	44.7	44.7	1.4	1.8	67.4	10.7	6.4	15.9	7.5	12.6	12.1	13.2
15 009	27980	5	Maui	3 008	164 637	388	54.7	44.6	1.6	1.8	66.5	10.9	6.2	16.1	7.6	13.5	13.1	14.1
16 000	...	X	IDAHO	214 045	1 654 930	X	7.7	84.6	1.1	1.9	2.4	12.0	7.0	19.4	9.5	13.2	12.2	12.2
16 001	14260	2	Ada	2 726	434 211	161	159.3	87.6	1.7	1.2	4.2	7.7	6.2	18.9	8.6	14.7	13.9	13.2
16 003	...	8	Adams	3 530	3 843	2 914	1.1	95.4	0.6	1.7	1.0	3.2	4.2	12.8	5.6	8.2	8.9	13.0
16 005	38540	3	Bannock	2 880	83 744	673	29.1	86.6	1.2	3.6	2.4	8.0	7.3	19.4	10.6	15.5	11.8	10.8
16 007	...	7	Bear Lake	2 525	5 922	2 760	2.3	94.6	0.5	1.0	0.7	4.2	7.3	20.3	7.2	10.2	10.8	10.8
16 009	...	6	Benewah	2 011	9 052	2 509	4.5	88.6	0.7	10.5	1.1	3.3	5.7	16.5	7.0	9.3	10.0	13.4
16 011	13940	6	Bingham	5 423	44 990	1 072	8.3	75.7	0.5	6.2	1.2	17.8	8.6	23.1	8.6	12.0	11.7	11.6
16 013	25200	7	Blaine	6 847	21 592	1 748	3.2	77.9	0.4	0.6	1.5	20.7	5.2	17.9	6.7	11.1	13.1	14.5
16 015	14260	2	Boise	4 919	7 058	2 669	1.4	94.1	0.8	2.0	1.4	3.6	3.2	15.4	5.4	6.8	10.0	15.6
16 017	41760	6	Bonner	4 493	41 859	1 129	9.3	95.4	0.5	2.0	1.3	2.9	4.9	15.4	6.4	9.5	10.9	14.2
16 019	26820	3	Bonneville	4 833	110 089	549	22.8	85.3	1.0	1.2	1.6	12.6	8.9	22.5	8.4	14.1	12.1	11.2
16 021	...	7	Boundary	3 286	11 318	2 337	3.4	92.7	0.9	2.9	1.2	4.2	5.1	17.8	6.9	9.3	11.0	12.8
16 023	26820	8	Butte	5 780	2 501	3 007	0.4	93.1	0.8	2.0	0.9	5.9	4.9	20.7	7.2	9.2	10.0	12.0
16 025	25200	9	Camas	2 783	1 066	3 106	0.4	90.2	1.3	3.0	1.1	7.5	5.7	18.7	4.4	9.3	14.0	13.9
16 027	14260	2	Canyon	1 521	207 478	314	136.4	73.1	0.9	1.5	1.8	24.7	7.9	22.0	9.5	13.2	12.8	11.6

1. CBSA = Core Based Statistical Area. See Appendix A for explanation. See Appendix B for list of metropolitan areas with component counties. 2. County type code from the Economic Research Service of USDA Rural-Urban Continuum Codes. See Appendix A for definition. 3. Dry land or land partially or temporarily covered by water. 4. May be of any race.

Table B. States and Counties — Population and Households

STATE County	Age (percent) (cont.) 55 to 64 years	65 to 74 years	75 years and over	Percent female	Total persons 2000	2010	Percent change 2000–2010	2010–2015	Components of change, 2010–2015 Births	Deaths	Net migration	Households, 2010–2014 Number	Persons per household	Percent Family households	Female family householder[1]	One person
	16	17	18	19	20	21	22	23	24	25	26	27	28	29	30	31
GEORGIA—Cont'd																
Putnam	15.5	13.8	7.7	51.5	18 812	21 218	12.8	0.6	1 250	1 201	98	8 457	2.49	73.5	15.8	18.8
Quitman	17.5	17.1	10.6	50.6	2 598	2 513	-3.3	-8.4	119	150	-180	1 001	2.40	65.8	13.9	31.5
Rabun	15.3	15.5	9.9	50.6	15 050	16 276	8.1	0.0	780	983	206	6 966	2.29	64.6	8.6	29.3
Randolph	15.3	11.4	9.4	53.4	7 791	7 719	-0.9	-6.8	461	460	-508	2 868	2.49	69.9	28.8	25.7
Richmond	12.3	7.4	5.2	51.6	199 775	200 549	0.4	0.6	15 826	9 981	-4 515	71 776	2.68	60.7	21.9	34.0
Rockdale	12.9	8.1	4.7	52.7	70 111	85 215	21.5	4.3	5 207	3 211	1 625	29 284	2.92	73.5	19.5	22.3
Schley	11.2	9.3	5.4	52.6	3 766	5 010	33.0	3.2	266	164	60	1 967	2.56	70.8	13.5	25.8
Screven	14.7	10.2	6.7	51.2	15 374	14 593	-5.1	-3.0	995	920	-529	5 252	2.64	64.0	16.1	32.5
Seminole	14.4	12.8	9.0	52.0	9 369	8 729	-6.8	-0.9	547	566	-38	3 310	2.63	72.5	15.6	24.6
Spalding	12.6	10.0	6.2	51.7	58 417	64 073	9.7	0.0	4 438	3 741	-799	23 013	2.73	71.6	20.6	24.9
Stephens	13.9	11.1	7.2	51.8	25 435	26 172	2.9	-2.2	1 623	1 733	-518	9 260	2.69	71.4	11.0	26.3
Stewart	12.0	8.6	6.7	38.9	5 252	6 058	15.3	-3.4	256	357	-122	1 791	2.62	53.1	24.4	42.5
Sumter	12.0	8.8	6.1	52.6	33 200	32 817	-1.2	-6.2	2 130	1 752	-2 477	11 574	2.58	65.4	21.4	31.8
Talbot	18.4	12.1	7.0	52.3	6 498	6 863	5.6	-7.7	312	368	-473	2 688	2.44	71.4	22.5	25.6
Taliaferro	16.5	12.6	9.8	51.1	2 077	1 717	-17.3	-4.5	85	114	-43	682	2.48	59.5	14.8	35.2
Tattnall	11.4	7.6	4.9	42.3	22 305	25 519	14.4	-1.1	1 604	1 156	-745	8 036	2.49	68.4	16.2	26.7
Taylor	14.3	11.0	7.2	52.5	8 815	8 906	1.0	-6.5	475	509	-600	3 584	2.28	70.6	22.6	27.1
Telfair	12.8	8.5	6.8	40.7	11 794	16 500	39.9	-0.6	708	743	-101	5 428	2.34	67.2	17.2	29.8
Terrell	14.0	10.5	7.2	52.5	10 970	9 507	-13.3	-4.1	671	506	-561	3 227	2.77	69.1	22.7	27.0
Thomas	13.3	9.6	7.2	52.6	42 737	44 719	4.6	0.8	3 117	2 620	-155	17 352	2.52	64.5	16.6	31.8
Tift	11.4	8.2	5.8	51.9	38 407	40 122	4.5	1.6	2 978	2 009	-405	13 966	2.79	65.7	17.9	29.3
Toombs	11.9	8.9	6.3	52.6	26 067	27 223	4.4	0.1	2 114	1 540	-555	10 579	2.53	65.0	14.2	31.7
Towns	14.1	17.8	14.5	52.2	9 319	10 471	12.4	6.8	418	818	1 096	4 299	2.29	64.2	5.9	32.5
Treutlen	13.4	9.0	6.0	49.7	6 854	6 885	0.5	-1.5	419	335	-163	2 596	2.42	66.1	18.4	30.9
Troup	12.1	8.0	5.7	51.8	58 779	67 044	14.1	4.1	4 767	3 468	1 403	24 597	2.71	70.3	20.7	25.5
Turner	12.2	10.7	7.9	50.9	9 504	8 930	-6.0	-8.0	598	548	-807	3 086	2.63	70.1	24.7	26.5
Twiggs	16.7	12.7	6.9	51.1	10 590	9 023	-14.8	-7.0	483	558	-520	3 033	2.81	73.7	17.0	24.9
Union	16.3	18.7	12.5	51.6	17 289	21 359	23.5	4.3	834	1 499	1 495	8 447	2.50	68.0	7.1	29.5
Upson	13.9	10.7	7.1	52.3	27 597	27 153	-1.6	-2.9	1 690	1 892	-550	10 363	2.52	70.5	16.0	26.4
Walker	13.6	9.9	6.7	50.7	61 053	68 756	12.6	-1.0	3 846	3 652	-772	26 123	2.57	70.6	13.7	25.3
Walton	11.8	8.9	5.3	51.3	60 687	83 768	38.0	5.5	5 695	3 880	2 685	29 490	2.87	78.3	13.3	18.6
Ware	12.9	9.0	7.1	50.5	35 483	36 306	2.3	-2.6	2 566	2 298	-1 269	13 702	2.44	66.4	15.4	29.6
Warren	16.1	11.8	8.5	53.1	6 336	5 834	-7.9	-6.4	312	374	-321	2 126	2.61	60.2	19.3	38.1
Washington	13.5	9.4	6.6	49.6	21 176	21 187	0.1	-1.8	1 268	1 130	-552	7 122	2.68	70.8	21.7	27.2
Wayne	12.1	8.9	5.8	48.1	26 565	30 099	13.3	-1.9	2 104	1 647	-1 049	10 226	2.74	71.3	14.6	25.0
Webster	15.8	11.0	8.7	50.0	2 390	2 801	17.2	-5.5	97	82	-188	1 175	2.33	63.7	15.1	34.4
Wheeler	11.5	8.0	4.8	34.8	6 179	7 421	20.1	6.5	327	296	410	1 877	2.01	67.9	14.7	30.7
White	14.2	12.9	7.7	51.0	19 944	27 144	36.1	4.3	1 360	1 331	1 081	11 507	2.36	70.4	9.3	25.1
Whitfield	10.8	7.5	5.2	50.3	83 525	102 599	22.8	1.6	7 376	4 027	-1 720	34 734	2.94	73.7	13.0	21.3
Wilcox	12.7	8.9	7.1	41.1	8 577	9 255	7.9	-4.3	495	568	-350	2 735	2.56	65.4	13.9	32.4
Wilkes	14.4	12.6	8.9	52.2	10 687	10 593	-0.9	-6.9	581	702	-625	4 078	2.44	60.7	16.5	35.9
Wilkinson	14.7	10.3	7.6	51.9	10 220	9 563	-6.4	-4.3	607	593	-424	3 343	2.80	69.5	18.4	27.9
Worth	14.1	10.2	6.6	52.0	21 967	21 679	-1.3	-4.5	1 316	1 136	-1 147	8 016	2.65	72.2	16.6	25.5
HAWAII	12.7	8.9	7.1	49.4	1 211 537	1 360 301	12.3	5.2	100 046	56 486	28 359	450 299	3.00	69.2	12.3	23.9
Hawaii	15.9	10.7	6.8	50.0	148 677	185 079	24.5	6.1	12 889	8 275	6 519	64 586	2.88	66.1	12.5	26.5
Honolulu	11.6	8.4	7.4	49.2	876 156	953 207	8.8	4.8	71 809	39 221	13 834	310 141	3.03	70.1	12.4	23.5
Kalawao	30.3	3.4	25.8	52.8	147	90	-38.8	-1.1	0	1	0	46	1.39	23.9	0.0	60.9
Kauai	14.9	10.3	7.2	49.9	58 463	67 090	14.8	6.9	4 641	2 995	2 946	22 395	3.03	69.2	10.6	22.9
Maui	14.2	9.2	5.9	49.7	128 094	154 835	20.9	6.3	10 707	5 994	5 060	53 131	2.94	68.1	12.4	23.9
IDAHO	12.2	8.5	5.8	49.9	1 293 953	1 567 652	21.2	5.6	119 233	62 520	29 477	585 259	2.68	69.5	9.6	24.4
Ada	11.8	7.6	5.0	49.9	300 904	392 365	30.4	10.7	26 710	13 399	27 996	154 408	2.60	67.5	9.3	25.2
Adams	22.4	16.3	8.6	48.5	3 476	3 976	14.4	-3.3	144	149	-80	1 643	2.34	67.5	8.7	27.8
Bannock	11.7	7.5	5.3	50.2	75 565	82 839	9.6	1.1	6 906	3 441	-2 544	30 277	2.68	66.3	11.0	27.2
Bear Lake	13.8	11.3	8.3	50.3	6 411	5 986	-6.6	-1.1	430	340	-155	2 437	2.42	71.0	7.9	26.4
Benewah	16.9	13.3	7.9	49.5	9 171	9 285	1.2	-2.5	575	582	-228	3 703	2.44	65.9	9.8	27.9
Bingham	11.6	7.3	5.5	49.8	41 735	45 607	9.3	-1.4	3 891	1 681	-2 752	14 840	3.05	76.4	9.5	20.5
Blaine	15.7	10.6	5.2	49.2	18 991	21 378	12.6	1.0	1 179	518	-468	9 258	2.26	66.6	8.9	26.8
Boise	22.4	15.5	5.7	48.4	6 670	7 028	5.4	0.4	204	267	122	3 038	2.24	60.9	5.5	34.6
Bonner	18.4	13.6	7.8	50.0	36 835	40 877	11.0	2.4	2 090	2 061	791	17 388	2.33	64.6	8.4	28.6
Bonneville	10.8	6.9	5.2	50.4	82 522	104 304	26.4	5.5	10 065	3 994	-367	36 402	2.89	74.4	11.3	21.6
Boundary	16.5	12.8	7.7	49.4	9 871	10 972	11.2	3.2	661	578	251	4 101	2.63	68.9	7.2	25.7
Butte	16.4	11.4	8.2	49.5	2 899	2 893	-0.2	-13.5	158	123	-430	1 028	2.61	65.7	6.8	30.0
Camas	15.5	11.9	6.6	48.8	991	1 117	12.7	-4.6	55	25	-96	465	2.48	62.8	5.6	32.9
Canyon	10.4	7.6	4.8	50.6	131 441	188 923	43.7	9.8	16 421	6 807	8 593	64 514	2.98	73.4	12.0	22.0

1. No spouse present.

STATE County	Persons in group quarters, 2015	Daytime population, 2010–2014 Number	Employment/residence ratio	Births, 2015 Total	Rate[1]	Deaths, 2015 Number	Rate[1]	Persons under 65 with no health insurance, 2014 Number	Percent	Medicare, 2015 Total Beneficiaries	Enrolled in Original Medicare	Enrolled in Medicare Advantage	Serious crimes known to police,[2] 2014 Total Number	Rate[3]
	32	33	34	35	36	37	38	39	40	41	42	43	44	45
GEORGIA—Cont'd														
Putnam	172	19 021	0.75	217	10.2	239	11.2	3 274	19.8	4 579	3 259	1 320	814	3 789
Quitman	0	2 050	0.49	15	6.5	27	11.7	347	20.7	186	125	61	4	171
Rabun	391	16 720	1.07	155	9.5	200	12.3	2 982	24.9	4 377	3 467	910	401	2 463
Randolph	413	7 320	0.96	89	12.3	76	10.5	997	18.4	1 483	951	532	135	1 900
Richmond	10 970	239 916	1.48	3 138	15.6	1 918	9.5	28 078	16.9	35 905	22 871	13 034	3 478	1 714
Rockdale	791	85 024	0.97	989	11.2	632	7.2	13 957	18.4	12 081	7 485	4 596	2 955	3 374
Schley	0	4 166	0.54	50	9.7	31	6.0	858	19.5	700	451	249	52	1 015
Screven	438	13 115	0.78	179	12.7	179	12.7	2 101	18.4	2 808	1 882	926	349	2 556
Seminole	75	8 501	0.90	104	12.0	106	12.3	1 296	19.2	2 124	1 532	592	163	1 806
Spalding	1 186	62 139	0.92	823	12.9	761	11.9	9 441	17.9	12 989	8 318	4 671	3 354	5 243
Stephens	573	25 246	0.95	328	12.9	304	11.9	3 491	17.2	7 359	5 561	1 798	876	3 416
Stewart	1 664	5 700	0.87	45	7.7	69	11.8	680	19.9	996	603	393	6	136
Sumter	1 673	32 658	1.07	380	12.3	328	10.6	4 710	18.8	5 629	3 660	1 969	1 824	6 003
Talbot	17	4 913	0.29	56	8.8	71	11.2	1 017	19.7	1 411	859	552	84	1 396
Taliaferro	7	1 433	0.52	15	9.0	25	15.0	296	22.5	441	261	180	NA	NA
Tattnall	4 573	24 013	0.82	274	10.9	221	8.8	3 845	21.7	3 799	2 525	1 274	379	1 694
Taylor	147	7 759	0.74	95	11.3	86	10.3	1 298	19.1	1 915	1 215	700	117	1 390
Telfair	3 710	16 952	1.11	131	8.0	155	9.4	1 920	18.6	2 488	1 713	775	NA	NA
Terrell	267	8 556	0.76	127	13.9	97	10.6	1 424	19.5	1 980	1 233	747	214	2 384
Thomas	882	46 825	1.13	616	13.7	499	11.1	6 982	18.9	10 720	7 359	3 361	2 014	4 494
Tift	1 561	45 428	1.31	585	14.4	392	9.6	7 066	21.1	7 664	5 239	2 425	1 953	4 831
Toombs	398	28 833	1.15	412	15.1	306	11.2	4 645	20.2	5 949	4 403	1 546	1 007	4 385
Towns	1 033	10 494	0.95	82	7.4	152	13.7	1 483	22.5	4 137	2 990	1 147	178	1 638
Treutlen	432	5 644	0.54	89	13.1	61	9.0	970	17.7	1 202	770	432	NA	NA
Troup	2 281	77 313	1.33	943	13.5	692	9.9	9 693	16.7	12 257	8 598	3 659	2 914	4 177
Turner	391	7 693	0.71	120	14.7	104	12.7	1 324	20.9	2 007	1 263	744	1 266	17 319
Twiggs	178	7 593	0.59	83	9.9	123	14.7	1 276	19.2	1 666	1 043	623	154	1 835
Union	247	21 542	1.00	161	7.3	266	12.0	3 039	20.3	6 883	5 146	1 737	336	1 549
Upson	490	25 416	0.87	311	11.8	369	14.0	3 672	17.1	5 536	3 409	2 127	881	3 321
Walker	1 493	56 551	0.56	739	10.8	719	10.5	10 100	18.0	15 196	10 462	4 734	5 661	8 295
Walton	635	70 755	0.60	1 149	13.1	769	8.7	11 926	16.0	16 413	10 957	5 456	3 590	4 152
Ware	2 128	39 925	1.31	476	13.4	410	11.6	5 141	18.4	8 831	6 599	2 232	1 849	5 185
Warren	89	5 091	0.72	51	9.3	64	11.7	828	18.9	1 202	744	458	96	1 739
Washington	1 887	21 088	1.03	251	12.1	223	10.8	2 698	17.0	3 817	2 177	1 640	566	2 777
Wayne	1 543	29 395	0.93	379	12.7	315	10.6	4 277	18.2	5 265	3 772	1 493	1 737	5 759
Webster	0	2 220	0.55	19	7.2	11	4.2	423	19.9	375	227	148	14	516
Wheeler	2 511	8 068	1.10	64	8.1	64	8.1	860	19.4	1 011	693	318	51	639
White	604	25 439	0.81	270	9.6	267	9.5	4 134	19.1	5 833	4 209	1 624	778	2 776
Whitfield	1 106	114 868	1.27	1 386	13.3	770	7.4	21 681	24.2	16 062	13 275	2 787	3 185	3 157
Wilcox	1 974	8 587	0.80	95	10.7	106	12.0	1 001	17.8	1 689	1 122	567	81	962
Wilkes	114	9 735	0.90	104	10.5	135	13.6	1 529	19.8	2 543	1 757	786	105	1 058
Wilkinson	108	9 355	0.97	121	13.1	132	14.3	1 284	16.9	2 278	1 509	769	99	1 252
Worth	183	17 040	0.48	237	11.4	219	10.5	3 525	20.4	3 234	2 350	884	595	2 797
HAWAII	44 033	1 393 312	1.00	19 298	13.5	11 684	8.2	69 936	6.0	219 570	104 303	115 267	46 977	3 309
Hawaii	3 711	189 030	1.00	2 506	12.8	1 780	9.1	11 752	7.3	34 363	18 330	16 033	7 182	3 722
Honolulu	36 280	976 692	1.00	13 789	13.9	8 010	8.0	44 203	5.5	150 496	69 069	81 427	11 193	1 126
Kalawao	3	87	1.25	0	0.0	NA	NA	0	0.0	NA	NA	NA	NA	NA
Kauai	1 252	68 841	1.00	912	12.8	624	8.8	3 781	6.5	11 894	6 601	5 293	1 120	1 592
Maui	2 787	158 662	1.00	2 091	12.7	1 270	7.7	10 200	7.4	22 817	10 303	12 514	6 309	3 889
IDAHO	30 374	1 577 368	0.97	22 751	13.8	11 826	7.2	216 276	15.7	266 209	175 708	90 501	33 784	2 067
Ada	10 834	427 588	1.10	5 128	11.9	2 636	6.1	42 686	11.6	60 530	31 384	29 146	7 989	1 878
Adams	21	3 698	0.86	29	7.5	18	4.7	515	18.0	1 032	827	205	24	628
Bannock	2 006	81 704	0.95	1 266	15.1	638	7.6	9 638	13.6	13 298	8 684	4 614	2 131	2 540
Bear Lake	31	5 479	0.81	84	14.1	58	9.8	635	13.3	1 280	1 219	61	103	1 723
Benewah	70	9 474	1.09	107	11.8	112	12.4	1 262	17.8	2 365	1 886	479	141	1 558
Bingham	323	42 643	0.84	704	15.6	324	7.2	7 641	19.7	6 450	4 924	1 526	655	1 440
Blaine	258	22 414	1.10	219	10.2	102	4.7	3 765	20.8	3 437	2 518	919	221	1 028
Boise	34	6 317	0.79	43	6.2	47	6.8	908	17.0	1 183	634	549	102	1 610
Bonner	353	39 776	0.93	417	10.0	393	9.4	5 480	16.9	9 260	6 489	2 771	878	2 145
Bonneville	1 242	111 657	1.11	1 860	17.0	762	7.0	13 053	13.8	15 650	12 029	3 621	2 449	2 247
Boundary	73	10 678	0.94	139	12.5	121	10.9	1 816	21.1	2 549	1 759	790	129	1 184
Butte	18	4 532	2.75	31	12.1	18	7.0	324	15.5	592	581	11	10	385
Camas	0	1 056	0.80	8	7.6	4	3.8	199	23.8	177	141	36	2	194
Canyon	3 439	177 244	0.77	3 211	15.6	1 303	6.3	34 360	19.8	30 121	14 472	15 649	5 051	2 491

1. Per 1,000 estimated resident population. 2. Data for serious crimes have not been adjusted for underreporting; this may affect comparability between geographic areas and over time.
3. Per 100,000 population estimated by the FBI.

Table B. States and Counties — Crime, Education, Money Income, and Poverty

	Serious crimes known to police, 2014 (cont.)[1] Rate[2]		Education School enrollment and attainment, 2010–2014 Enrollment[3]		Attainment[4] (percent)		Local government expenditures,[5] 2012–2013		Money income, 2010–2014	Households			Income and poverty, 2014	Percent below poverty level		
STATE County	Violent	Property	Total	Percent private	High school graduate or less	Bachelor's degree or more	Total current spending (mil dol)	Current spending per student (dollars)	Per capita income[6] (dollars)	Median income (dollars)	Mean income (dollars)	Percent with income of $200,000 or more	Median household income (dollars)	All persons	Children under 18 years	Children 5 to 17 years in families
	46	47	48	49	50	51	52	53	54	55	56	57	58	59	60	61

STATE County	46	47	48	49	50	51	52	53	54	55	56	57	58	59	60	61
GEORGIA—Cont'd																
Putnam	582	3 207	4 582	21.5	52.8	18.1	31.2	11 126	24 807	44 058	62 207	3.3	42 125	18.9	33.8	32.6
Quitman	85	85	512	7.0	66.7	7.2	3.8	11 119	15 644	30 313	36 760	0.4	29 477	29.5	48.4	46.7
Rabun	129	2 334	3 059	16.5	48.6	25.8	27.4	11 962	22 848	34 043	51 664	2.6	38 449	20.6	33.1	31.7
Randolph	239	1 660	1 640	19.3	62.2	14.8	11.9	10 861	24 084	26 837	56 262	1.5	25 807	36.3	51.4	48.3
Richmond	127	1 587	55 150	14.4	47.8	20.4	296.7	9 257	20 549	37 704	51 724	1.7	36 012	26.0	37.9	36.8
Rockdale	282	3 092	24 515	14.3	44.1	25.4	152.7	9 624	23 409	52 341	65 501	2.6	48 287	17.3	27.4	24.6
Schley	195	820	1 551	3.5	59.5	14.1	13.2	9 521	20 650	38 537	51 656	1.4	39 601	20.1	27.0	23.2
Screven	425	2 131	3 610	7.8	62.0	13.0	22.4	9 316	18 650	34 097	47 005	1.4	34 012	26.2	40.2	40.4
Seminole	144	1 662	2 106	6.0	57.3	15.1	15.2	9 136	18 939	34 894	48 386	0.9	37 672	26.4	42.7	38.6
Spalding	583	4 660	15 251	9.7	58.1	15.2	97.6	9 220	19 656	40 243	52 638	2.2	35 555	27.4	41.4	40.1
Stephens	281	3 135	6 424	17.1	57.2	15.7	36.1	8 897	19 624	40 103	52 008	1.4	36 870	20.9	30.3	28.2
Stewart	45	90	893	9.0	76.1	9.7	6.9	12 286	13 354	21 880	32 528	0.5	27 635	39.4	44.7	43.9
Sumter	698	5 305	9 802	9.2	55.8	19.4	47.9	9 751	17 838	33 694	46 027	1.2	34 017	33.9	47.6	47.6
Talbot	66	1 330	1 438	19.5	64.1	13.2	6.3	12 194	18 545	34 073	44 819	0.8	33 370	23.8	37.2	36.4
Taliaferro	NA	NA	306	8.5	77.2	8.3	2.9	14 640	13 742	24 783	32 308	0.0	28 716	32.3	49.0	53.7
Tattnall	49	1 645	5 251	9.4	64.0	11.2	32.4	8 796	14 777	35 346	46 964	1.7	34 010	28.2	37.8	37.5
Taylor	226	1 164	2 013	13.9	61.7	10.1	15.3	9 886	17 311	30 288	42 407	1.1	32 815	25.4	35.4	32.8
Telfair	NA	NA	2 816	0.8	74.7	10.8	15.5	8 825	12 156	27 760	36 284	0.7	29 244	33.7	41.6	38.0
Terrell	379	2 006	2 196	11.2	66.6	10.1	14.8	9 980	16 592	32 602	44 265	0.7	34 604	29.8	46.1	45.7
Thomas	290	4 204	11 368	13.5	52.9	17.6	77.8	9 143	19 636	35 515	48 351	1.9	36 973	24.5	35.5	34.7
Tift	552	4 279	11 974	9.0	53.9	16.6	73.4	9 280	19 560	34 830	52 755	2.6	36 303	28.6	40.4	40.7
Toombs	414	3 972	7 442	6.4	60.4	15.3	47.1	8 283	18 663	31 291	46 938	1.6	34 008	24.5	37.9	37.0
Towns	285	1 353	2 498	29.6	47.3	22.2	12.7	11 252	20 620	37 425	49 007	1.1	39 453	18.1	28.4	28.4
Treutlen	NA	NA	1 625	6.3	67.1	14.1	10.1	8 274	20 643	40 143	52 426	1.8	32 536	27.1	39.8	36.8
Troup	308	3 869	17 840	11.9	53.2	18.6	113.8	8 955	21 386	41 906	57 823	2.8	41 141	19.5	27.5	25.8
Turner	2 066	15 253	2 264	16.7	64.1	10.4	15.7	10 035	17 215	29 763	44 939	0.6	32 171	31.7	46.6	41.7
Twiggs	226	1 609	1 631	11.0	72.7	9.6	9.7	10 613	17 629	31 285	47 198	0.1	36 886	28.1	39.4	39.2
Union	230	1 318	4 029	18.8	47.9	20.6	27.4	10 497	21 345	39 179	50 791	0.5	40 667	15.1	29.1	25.8
Upson	381	2 940	6 386	7.3	58.5	11.4	38.9	8 878	17 728	34 614	44 939	0.7	34 867	25.9	41.0	38.4
Walker	816	7 479	15 573	13.2	57.3	14.3	94.6	9 075	20 466	39 688	52 361	1.7	39 078	20.0	27.8	25.7
Walton	365	3 787	22 637	14.3	50.5	17.2	127.9	8 487	22 987	53 454	65 041	2.4	52 082	15.6	23.8	22.9
Ware	477	4 708	8 558	5.6	60.0	13.1	60.1	9 988	18 341	35 247	47 462	1.3	34 288	28.8	40.5	38.3
Warren	217	1 522	1 134	19.6	75.6	8.0	7.4	10 452	17 344	28 929	41 703	0.8	31 623	28.9	42.8	41.5
Washington	299	2 478	4 772	9.6	66.3	11.3	31.3	10 081	17 330	34 877	48 363	1.3	36 137	30.2	44.2	40.7
Wayne	491	5 268	7 259	10.8	60.3	12.2	44.5	8 152	18 139	37 970	49 998	1.3	41 093	25.5	35.1	33.5
Webster	221	295	645	10.9	72.0	6.0	4.5	10 092	17 740	31 809	40 660	0.3	33 893	22.8	35.6	29.7
Wheeler	25	614	739	1.4	78.7	8.1	9.8	9 796	8 200	27 629	37 283	0.0	30 264	38.9	37.4	33.7
White	153	2 622	6 276	15.8	48.8	19.4	46.6	11 959	22 016	40 547	52 397	1.3	42 126	16.9	27.0	24.6
Whitfield	216	2 941	27 731	6.4	60.8	14.3	186.2	8 923	20 124	40 081	57 264	2.7	43 731	20.7	28.4	26.3
Wilcox	285	677	1 712	9.2	72.0	8.7	13.1	10 336	12 919	32 545	40 371	0.5	32 722	30.7	39.8	38.2
Wilkes	282	776	2 196	10.2	65.0	15.3	17.2	10 393	17 753	30 729	41 371	1.1	32 042	26.7	40.9	37.9
Wilkinson	164	1 088	2 024	7.3	69.6	8.2	17.7	11 032	18 048	37 258	47 162	0.4	34 512	23.2	34.9	34.4
Worth	338	2 458	5 156	9.6	66.4	7.8	30.3	8 873	19 048	38 339	48 744	0.8	40 382	22.6	34.7	34.5
HAWAII	259	3 050	339 184	23.3	37.4	30.5	2 199.3	11 823	29 552	68 201	85 972	6.1	69 549	11.5	15.2	14.9
Hawaii	237	3 486	43 287	17.8	41.8	25.9	(7)	(7)	24 395	51 213	65 521	2.9	51 887	18.1	25.3	25.5
Honolulu	72	1 054	245 014	25.4	35.8	32.5	(7)2 199.3	(7)11 903	30 735	73 581	91 139	6.9	73 985	9.8	12.8	12.5
Kalawao	NA	NA	2	0.0	46.3	43.3	(7)	(7)	43 771	61 250	64 680	0.0	NA	NA	NA	NA
Kauai	128	1 464	14 440	15.8	38.9	26.9	(7)	(7)	27 079	62 946	78 042	4.7	58 883	12.3	15.1	14.1
Maui	314	3 575	36 441	19.1	40.9	25.6	(7)	(7)	29 499	64 567	84 035	5.7	64 916	13.1	17.3	16.0
IDAHO	212	1 855	446 143	13.3	38.6	25.4	1 852.2	6 791	23 087	47 334	61 544	2.4	47 572	14.8	19.0	17.3
Ada	226	1 651	117 694	11.8	27.8	36.4	453.2	6 700	28 318	55 805	73 523	4.1	57 908	11.6	13.1	11.8
Adams	131	497	796	11.9	44.8	20.8	4.1	10 554	21 275	38 583	51 154	1.0	40 777	14.9	27.3	25.5
Bannock	223	2 317	25 701	7.6	35.3	27.3	89.6	6 374	21 891	43 953	58 312	1.5	44 324	17.4	20.3	17.9
Bear Lake	268	1 455	1 433	10.2	47.8	17.6	7.6	6 913	21 867	44 974	54 511	1.3	45 504	13.4	19.6	18.2
Benewah	276	1 282	1 893	13.6	55.9	13.3	13.1	9 610	21 131	38 963	50 054	0.9	46 277	15.7	24.0	20.9
Bingham	101	1 338	13 523	6.4	46.0	17.1	61.2	6 317	19 647	48 088	58 824	1.7	47 292	15.0	20.4	18.9
Blaine	144	884	4 411	15.1	25.3	44.8	53.7	16 157	34 517	62 489	80 436	5.8	63 490	10.6	15.6	14.0
Boise	110	1 500	1 379	12.1	37.0	24.8	8.0	9 373	25 562	41 194	56 155	1.0	50 874	15.6	25.0	21.0
Bonner	122	2 023	8 117	15.8	39.2	21.7	41.7	8 090	24 333	41 879	56 564	2.4	45 193	16.2	24.7	21.9
Bonneville	183	2 063	30 849	11.8	37.0	26.4	126.4	5 986	23 160	50 897	66 407	2.9	51 440	15.5	20.1	18.8
Boundary	73	1 111	2 142	14.4	49.7	14.1	10.6	7 199	20 049	39 204	50 383	1.9	42 720	16.7	24.7	22.3
Butte	269	115	639	8.6	47.2	15.0	3.5	8 280	21 444	41 000	53 684	1.9	42 907	14.8	18.7	15.1
Camas	0	194	253	2.8	43.2	22.0	1.9	13 397	22 073	41 250	52 469	5.2	49 569	12.8	20.6	17.4
Canyon	258	2 233	56 365	14.1	48.4	17.4	213.0	5 949	17 954	43 108	52 293	1.0	43 489	18.0	24.0	21.1

1. Data for serious crimes have not been adjusted for underreporting; this may affect comparability between geographic areas and over time.   2. Per 100,000 population estimated by the FBI.
3. All persons 3 years old and over enrolled in nursery school through college.   4. Persons 25 years old and over.   5. Elementary and secondary education expenditures.
6. Based on population estimated by the American Community Survey, 2010–2014.   7. Hawaii, Kalawao, Kauai, and Maui counties are included with Honolulu county.

Table B. States and Counties — **Personal Income**

STATE County	Personal income, 2014										Earnings, 2014		
			Per capita[1]			Supplements to wages and salaries; employer contributions (mil dol)						Contributions for government social insurance (mil dol)	
	Total (mil dol)	Percent change, 2013–2014	Dollars	Rank	Wages and salaries (mil dol)	Pension and insurance	Government social insurance	Proprietors' income (mil dol)	Dividends, interest, and rent (mil dol)	Personal transfer receipts (mil dol)	Total (mil dol)	From employee and self-employed	From employer
	62	63	64	65	66	67	68	69	70	71	72	73	74
GEORGIA—Cont'd													
Putnam	720	4.9	33 978	2 116	195	50	14	56	161	199	315	21	14
Quitman	60	1.6	25 888	3 034	13	4	1	3	8	27	21	2	1
Rabun	546	2.9	33 638	2 170	148	31	11	37	155	166	228	17	11
Randolph	237	-2.0	32 429	2 383	66	17	5	52	30	71	140	8	5
Richmond	6 554	2.9	32 549	2 363	5 473	1 274	418	257	1 348	1 804	7 421	387	418
Rockdale	2 759	4.9	31 440	2 535	1 517	264	109	121	370	621	2 010	120	109
Schley	134	4.4	25 887	3 035	38	11	3	14	18	31	65	4	3
Screven	394	2.0	28 003	2 919	118	29	8	29	67	132	183	12	8
Seminole	269	-4.3	31 016	2 581	85	18	6	35	42	94	144	10	6
Spalding	1 937	4.1	30 264	2 681	775	171	56	91	291	606	1 094	71	56
Stephens	869	5.0	34 121	2 097	368	74	27	103	122	248	572	35	27
Stewart	133	1.2	23 070	3 099	47	11	3	7	23	48	69	5	3
Sumter	929	0.8	29 745	2 752	369	92	26	61	162	284	548	33	26
Talbot	190	3.5	29 746	2 751	29	8	2	3	31	65	42	4	2
Taliaferro	44	9.4	26 127	3 025	6	2	0	7	8	18	15	1	0
Tattnall	716	2.3	28 371	2 886	210	57	14	96	96	181	378	18	14
Taylor	214	3.1	25 385	3 053	59	14	4	15	34	77	93	7	4
Telfair	305	4.0	18 443	3 111	111	29	9	15	43	115	165	11	9
Terrell	350	-1.1	38 307	1 420	88	21	6	33	66	95	148	9	6
Thomas	1 663	2.1	36 983	1 603	885	157	62	81	311	430	1 186	73	62
Tift	1 342	4.9	32 964	2 286	743	171	50	95	209	340	1 059	59	50
Toombs	868	1.5	31 801	2 470	428	85	32	54	120	257	598	36	32
Towns	341	4.8	30 739	2 622	104	26	8	21	92	142	159	13	8
Treutlen	171	3.6	25 226	3 056	35	9	2	14	21	59	60	4	2
Troup	2 311	4.5	33 267	2 233	1 695	281	126	106	361	557	2 208	130	126
Turner	258	-2.8	31 630	2 504	73	17	5	16	39	90	111	8	5
Twiggs	259	1.4	31 104	2 568	44	10	3	8	29	95	65	6	3
Union	726	5.4	33 044	2 271	223	54	15	42	149	244	334	25	15
Upson	809	3.7	30 815	2 613	245	52	17	44	120	264	358	25	17
Walker	1 928	3.6	28 266	2 898	456	116	35	101	253	575	708	51	35
Walton	2 871	6.2	32 767	2 320	795	154	58	63	399	633	1 069	71	58
Ware	1 060	2.9	29 851	2 737	574	118	48	57	156	378	796	52	48
Warren	157	2.3	28 434	2 882	60	12	5	7	22	55	84	6	5
Washington	622	2.0	30 159	2 696	266	66	18	33	124	189	384	24	18
Wayne	903	1.2	30 144	2 698	337	80	24	46	111	271	486	31	24
Webster	70	-0.3	26 571	3 006	21	5	1	8	14	17	35	2	1
Wheeler	126	0.6	15 787	3 113	47	11	3	10	19	48	71	4	3
White	818	5.0	29 232	2 802	236	47	17	68	125	231	368	25	17
Whitfield	3 358	3.7	32 435	2 381	2 408	404	181	405	559	707	3 398	196	181
Wilcox	220	-4.8	24 861	3 062	42	13	3	25	34	74	82	5	3
Wilkes	295	5.7	29 628	2 772	99	25	7	42	56	104	173	10	7
Wilkinson	283	5.0	30 335	2 671	165	29	12	14	36	93	219	14	12
Worth	637	-2.0	30 433	2 660	127	30	9	40	93	169	206	14	9
HAWAII	65 348	4.7	46 034	X	32 856	6 783	2 711	4 394	13 562	10 467	46 744	2 714	2 711
Hawaii	6 771	5.4	34 870	1 957	2 771	555	222	508	1 470	1 713	4 057	258	222
Honolulu	49 313	4.4	49 722	397	25 610	5 464	2 135	3 134	10 130	7 063	36 344	2 065	2 135
Kalawao	(3)	(3)	(3)	(3)	(3)	(3)	(3)	(3)	(3)	(3)	(3)	(3)	(3)
Kauai	2 831	6.0	40 163	1 149	1 310	231	105	217	604	581	1 863	116	105
Maui	(3)6 433	(3)5.7	(3)39 439	(3)1 255	(3)3 165	(3)532	(3)248	(3)535	(3)1 357	(3)1 110	(3)4 480	(3)274	(3)248
IDAHO	60 041	4.4	36 734	X	26 704	4 080	2 359	7 154	12 429	11 209	40 297	2 487	2 359
Ada	18 643	5.5	43 738	783	10 219	1 375	858	2 270	3 862	2 613	14 723	926	858
Adams	131	4.5	33 999	2 113	39	8	4	13	41	34	64	4	4
Bannock	2 672	3.6	32 063	2 431	1 210	222	114	152	428	629	1 698	112	114
Bear Lake	214	4.3	35 842	1 800	57	13	6	20	37	50	96	6	6
Benewah	290	3.2	31 805	2 468	133	25	12	30	58	86	200	14	12
Bingham	1 456	-1.3	32 166	2 422	535	93	48	210	245	299	887	52	48
Blaine	1 795	4.8	83 573	23	523	63	48	146	1 003	123	780	49	48
Boise	239	5.0	35 044	1 927	41	9	4	9	57	57	63	5	4
Bonner	1 405	4.3	33 786	2 149	477	80	45	111	411	338	712	52	45
Bonneville	4 184	2.7	38 518	1 388	1 674	243	152	653	845	702	2 722	172	152
Boundary	327	2.5	29 769	2 747	122	23	12	35	75	90	192	13	12
Butte	89	-1.7	34 119	2 098	611	42	47	13	17	23	713	44	47
Camas	33	-2.4	31 448	2 534	21	3	2	2	10	7	27	2	2
Canyon	5 478	4.8	26 968	2 985	2 046	323	190	375	816	1 382	2 935	198	190

1. Based on the resident population estimated as of July 1 of the year shown. 3. Kalawao county is included with Maui county.

Table B. States and Counties — Earnings, Social Security, and Housing

| | Earnings, 2014 (cont.) | | | | | | | | | Social Security beneficiaries, December 2014 | | | Housing units, 2015 | |
| | Percent by selected industries | | | | | | | | | | | | | |
STATE County	Farm	Mining	Construction	Manu-facturing	Infor-mation: professional, scientific, technical services	Retail trade	Finance, insur-ance, real estate and leasing	Health care and social assistance	Govern-ment	Number	Rate[1]	Supple-mental Security Income recipients, December 2014	Total	Percent change, 2010–2014
	75	76	77	78	79	80	81	82	83	84	85	86	87	88
GEORGIA—Cont'd														
Putnam	4.1	0.0	11.8	7.2	3.4	6.7	4.8	D	26.3	5 620	265	494	12 720	-0.7
Quitman	13.7	0.0	D	D	D	D	D	D	34.9	780	339	160	2 001	-2.3
Rabun	2.7	D	9.2	7.1	3.0	13.6	5.5	D	20.7	5 040	311	421	12 478	1.3
Randolph	8.5	0.0	D	D	D	10.7	3.4	D	21.7	1 745	239	424	4 087	-1.6
Richmond	0.0	D	4.2	7.7	7.1	5.0	3.0	13.5	42.4	38 210	190	8 206	87 612	1.5
Rockdale	0.0	D	10.3	22.0	9.9	7.7	4.9	10.7	13.0	15 215	174	1 929	33 375	0.3
Schley	10.0	0.0	D	26.3	D	D	D	D	27.3	875	170	133	2 154	-2.4
Screven	10.2	0.0	3.5	26.6	3.8	6.6	3.3	D	27.5	3 405	242	724	6 631	-1.6
Seminole	7.9	0.0	1.6	15.0	D	6.1	3.2	14.6	16.9	2 380	275	451	4 770	-0.6
Spalding	-0.1	D	3.2	18.8	D	7.8	3.6	15.2	23.4	14 970	234	2 610	27 063	1.1
Stephens	4.9	D	19.5	2.9	7.2	2.8	D	17.7	7 055	277	1 187	12 489	-1.4
Stewart	2.4	0.0	D	D	D	1.9	D	19.4	33.7	1 145	197	278	2 327	-2.3
Sumter	4.4	D	2.6	8.7	D	8.0	3.0	D	27.4	6 555	210	1 371	13 818	-0.6
Talbot	-0.3	12.2	23.6	0.0	D	2.2	D	D	28.7	1 685	264	368	3 359	-1.1
Taliaferro	38.9	0.0	D	D	0.0	D	D	D	38.6	515	304	111	1 002	-1.3
Tattnall	25.9	0.0	3.5	1.9	2.0	4.2	3.1	D	28.6	4 380	174	960	9 837	-1.3
Taylor	7.0	D	3.3	2.8	D	7.4	2.8	15.3	24.2	1 940	230	433	4 491	-1.6
Telfair	4.0	0.0	D	D	1.8	4.9	4.2	D	24.9	2 855	173	637	7 189	-1.5
Terrell	13.9	0.0	2.6	14.4	2.6	6.9	5.2	D	22.0	2 410	264	594	4 147	-0.3
Thomas	0.4	D	4.3	17.0	3.5	6.4	5.7	D	15.9	10 450	232	2 188	20 359	0.9
Tift	1.1	0.0	3.2	6.3	4.8	9.2	3.3	7.6	37.5	8 080	199	1 638	16 403	-0.2
Toombs	3.3	0.0	5.0	10.4	D	9.9	2.7	D	14.2	6 350	234	1 405	12 077	-0.6
Towns	0.6	D	7.1	3.4	5.2	10.3	6.3	D	16.7	4 490	405	247	7 968	3.1
Treutlen	11.7	0.0	D	D	D	8.9	D	D	29.0	1 405	206	331	2 974	-0.6
Troup	0.1	D	4.7	34.9	4.1	7.9	3.6	8.8	10.3	13 650	196	2 373	28 314	1.0
Turner	8.1	0.0	1.8	11.0	D	7.1	4.1	4.2	27.9	2 250	277	492	3 857	0.4
Twiggs	6.3	D	D	D	D	D	D	D	24.9	2 435	291	416	4 173	-1.5
Union	2.4	D	5.8	4.1	D	9.6	5.1	D	26.1	8 030	366	479	14 315	1.9
Upson	5.3	0.0	6.3	18.0	D	7.9	5.1	17.2	20.9	7 235	276	1 247	12 088	-0.6
Walker	5.3	D	3.8	32.2	2.6	5.8	4.5	5.1	24.2	15 890	233	2 195	30 097	0.0
Walton	1.2	0.1	13.3	14.3	4.2	12.0	2.9	7.8	21.0	17 015	195	2 463	32 736	0.9
Ware	0.4	0.0	3.8	9.7	D	10.3	3.6	19.0	21.1	8 025	226	1 799	16 447	0.8
Warren	4.3	D	0.8	23.9	D	4.4	2.7	D	15.5	1 460	265	289	2 938	-1.6
Washington	1.1	3.7	5.5	8.0	4.8	6.2	4.1	D	30.0	4 750	230	919	9 087	0.4
Wayne	2.0	0.0	9.0	19.8	D	7.5	3.0	D	32.5	6 385	213	1 101	12 097	-0.8
Webster	18.9	D	D	D	0.0	6.2	0.9	0.0	19.2	460	174	79	1 501	-1.5
Wheeler	14.6	0.0	1.6	0.0	D	2.5	D	8.9	20.6	1 085	136	233	2 588	-1.4
White	7.8	D	12.8	14.3	D	9.8	3.5	D	17.5	7 115	255	611	15 986	-0.5
Whitfield	0.7	0.2	2.5	37.3	8.4	6.9	2.0	8.8	9.7	17 915	173	2 519	39 637	-0.7
Wilcox	23.0	0.0	D	D	D	4.4	D	D	36.0	1 805	204	377	3 474	-1.0
Wilkes	16.8	0.0	3.2	15.1	D	6.5	4.4	5.8	24.8	2 920	294	481	5 140	-0.3
Wilkinson	1.0	44.2	6.8	13.3	D	2.1	D	2.4	11.8	2 505	268	380	4 428	-1.3
Worth	11.8	0.0	6.0	8.3	3.0	6.6	3.1	D	24.5	4 665	223	725	9 170	-0.9
HAWAII	0.6	0.1	7.2	1.8	7.2	6.0	6.4	9.6	31.3	251 591	177	25 235	532 455	2.5
Hawaii	2.2	D	8.4	1.7	D	8.6	6.2	D	24.8	41 180	212	5 481	86 009	4.5
Honolulu	0.2	0.1	7.0	1.9	8.0	5.3	6.5	9.9	34.2	168 315	170	16 642	344 108	2.1
Kalawao	(3)	(3)	(3)	(3)	(3)	(3)	(3)	(3)	(3)	10	112	0	113	0.0
Kauai	1.4	D	7.4	0.9	D	8.1	7.6	D	20.8	14 305	202	1 019	30 503	2.4
Maui	(3)2.2	(3)D	(3)7.9	(3)1.5	(3)4.2	(3)8.4	(3)5.9	(3)7.0	(3)17.9	27 780	170	2 093	71 722	1.9
IDAHO	6.4	0.8	6.3	11.2	8.5	8.1	6.1	11.4	17.4	306 264	187	30 493	692 493	3.7
Ada	0.4	0.6	6.7	12.9	9.7	8.3	8.7	13.5	14.7	69 260	162	6 522	170 868	7.1
Adams	9.4	0.0	5.0	12.7	4.2	6.5	3.4	D	27.3	1 170	304	50	2 633	-0.1
Bannock	1.0	D	4.9	7.7	5.6	8.2	6.8	15.9	26.1	13 960	167	1 867	33 457	0.8
Bear Lake	12.1	D	3.4	2.4	D	8.5	D	D	33.3	1 435	241	106	4 013	2.5
Benewah	2.5	D	2.6	16.4	2.7	10.5	1.6	D	33.8	2 625	289	253	4 612	-0.4
Bingham	13.3	D	7.1	14.1	2.3	4.6	3.3	8.8	20.8	7 930	175	906	16 263	0.8
Blaine	1.6	D	12.7	4.1	12.8	7.8	11.0	9.8	12.1	3 815	178	107	15 187	0.9
Boise	1.6	0.0	7.4	2.4	D	5.8	D	3.2	38.4	1 940	284	104	5 358	1.2
Bonner	0.4	1.4	7.6	16.8	5.9	13.3	5.2	7.4	19.0	11 290	272	834	24 572	-0.4
Bonneville	1.6	0.1	6.9	5.8	9.2	10.5	5.5	16.5	12.6	17 945	165	2 196	41 026	3.3
Boundary	4.3	0.0	6.4	18.9	3.9	7.3	2.6	7.4	29.9	2 990	272	259	5 281	2.0
Butte	1.5	0.0	0.4	0.4	92.7	0.3	0.4	0.6	2.2	675	258	59	1 351	-0.3
Camas	12.6	0.0	D	D	D	1.3	D	D	21.7	220	212	11	837	0.7
Canyon	5.4	0.1	8.7	15.7	4.6	9.2	4.2	9.5	16.5	35 130	173	4 757	72 278	4.1

1. Per 1,000 resident population estimated as of July 1 of the year shown. 3. Kalawao county is included with Maui county.

Table B. States and Counties — Housing, Labor Force, and Employment

STATE County	Housing units, 2010–2014								Civilian labor force, 2015				Civilian employment,[6] 2010–2014		
	Occupied units							Substandard units[4] (percent)			Unemployment			Percent	
	Owner-occupied					Renter-occupied									Construction, production, and maintenance occupations
				Median owner cost as a percent of income										Management, business, science and arts	
	Total	Percent	Median value[1]	With a mortgage	Without a mortgage[2]	Median rent[3]	Median rent as a percent of income[2]		Total	Percent change, 2014–2015	Total	Rate[5]	Total		
	89	90	91	92	93	94	95	96	97	98	99	100	101	102	103
GEORGIA—Cont'd															
Putnam	8 457	74.8	140 400	24.7	12.3	688	30.0	1.1	7 701	-4.8	614	8.0	8 989	29.4	22.3
Quitman	1 001	77.7	63 600	25.9	13.9	628	35.2	2.6	833	-6.5	56	6.7	721	10.4	30.9
Rabun	6 966	72.7	160 200	29.0	13.3	723	37.3	1.8	6 529	-0.4	433	6.6	6 319	27.7	25.7
Randolph	2 868	64.4	73 400	30.0	14.3	613	34.0	5.2	2 439	-10.3	219	9.0	2 357	23.9	32.2
Richmond	71 776	53.3	100 400	23.0	12.3	785	33.2	2.8	84 209	-0.5	6 146	7.3	77 153	29.9	21.8
Rockdale	29 284	69.8	143 900	24.0	10.0	933	34.1	3.5	42 292	0.6	2 694	6.4	37 108	33.2	24.7
Schley	1 967	64.2	91 200	21.4	15.7	642	24.2	3.3	2 094	-3.7	138	6.6	1 997	26.3	34.8
Screven	5 252	70.9	78 200	25.5	11.7	521	34.6	1.2	5 097	-4.9	413	8.1	5 321	27.2	32.2
Seminole	3 310	80.3	76 300	27.3	13.2	637	27.2	3.7	3 126	0.1	250	8.0	3 088	30.0	25.7
Spalding	23 013	62.0	114 600	24.8	13.0	785	36.8	3.0	27 415	0.5	2 142	7.8	23 574	25.0	30.4
Stephens	9 260	74.7	99 500	22.8	12.2	591	28.9	3.6	10 720	-4.3	695	6.5	10 374	26.0	27.9
Stewart	1 791	63.4	46 100	19.4	15.1	486	37.3	2.3	2 120	-3.2	141	6.7	1 560	22.8	33.1
Sumter	11 574	59.5	85 000	24.6	12.3	609	30.4	2.7	12 924	-3.8	1 060	8.2	11 949	30.9	28.2
Talbot	2 688	77.5	76 900	27.5	16.7	574	26.5	4.0	2 708	-3.5	205	7.6	2 423	23.6	33.8
Taliaferro	682	70.4	57 800	26.0	19.7	608	32.4	4.8	579	-2.2	47	8.1	538	15.4	38.1
Tattnall	8 036	68.9	90 100	26.3	12.5	564	24.8	3.7	9 348	-1.9	560	6.0	7 742	28.8	27.6
Taylor	3 584	69.3	61 600	23.9	17.1	553	20.9	4.0	2 741	-3.7	255	9.3	3 001	24.2	36.4
Telfair	5 428	59.4	58 200	27.5	14.1	540	25.1	4.1	4 877	-7.1	414	8.5	4 355	29.8	25.6
Terrell	3 227	59.5	81 600	25.2	13.9	602	35.9	3.9	3 600	-0.5	265	7.4	3 215	23.3	37.1
Thomas	17 352	57.9	124 200	25.0	13.8	693	34.7	2.1	16 798	-2.0	1 190	7.1	16 612	33.5	22.7
Tift	13 966	59.9	116 200	22.9	11.0	602	28.8	3.5	18 001	-1.4	1 109	6.2	15 534	30.4	28.0
Toombs	10 579	62.0	89 400	23.2	12.0	557	33.7	3.8	12 014	-1.9	1 022	8.5	10 637	26.1	31.7
Towns	4 299	82.3	162 700	31.8	13.0	693	34.3	1.3	3 900	-5.8	304	7.8	3 590	30.2	24.2
Treutlen	2 596	67.1	73 200	23.3	10.5	486	23.7	1.3	2 730	-2.3	224	8.2	2 479	19.4	32.8
Troup	24 597	60.3	118 300	23.1	12.2	767	32.4	3.6	35 946	-0.4	2 142	6.0	27 787	28.6	32.0
Turner	3 086	64.3	74 600	21.4	17.4	594	36.4	6.1	3 243	-0.5	212	6.5	2 820	32.3	29.3
Twiggs	3 033	78.1	55 400	21.2	13.9	536	30.6	1.4	2 957	-1.4	270	9.1	2 545	26.0	36.4
Union	8 447	80.4	181 400	25.0	13.4	576	29.0	0.9	9 786	2.9	508	5.2	7 270	27.0	22.5
Upson	10 363	64.1	82 600	23.9	13.2	675	32.9	3.4	11 126	-1.6	791	7.1	9 865	24.5	33.6
Walker	26 123	71.9	100 100	21.9	12.0	642	29.2	4.4	29 580	0.6	1 729	5.8	27 846	27.8	33.2
Walton	29 490	74.3	153 500	23.7	11.5	821	32.8	1.8	41 853	1.1	2 206	5.3	37 224	29.6	25.4
Ware	13 702	62.9	79 700	22.0	12.7	641	30.1	4.3	14 747	-0.1	937	6.4	13 114	30.8	29.2
Warren	2 126	67.9	67 700	25.0	16.0	563	33.6	1.4	2 650	-2.4	203	7.7	1 953	17.7	44.1
Washington	7 122	70.8	82 300	22.4	12.6	568	35.3	2.3	7 268	-3.8	498	6.9	7 284	29.3	27.7
Wayne	10 226	68.9	85 300	22.3	11.9	633	29.0	1.5	11 373	-3.9	835	7.3	10 857	27.6	34.7
Webster	1 175	77.6	43 500	28.1	10.0	567	19.0	2.3	984	-3.1	88	8.9	1 181	30.7	31.4
Wheeler	1 877	65.7	61 100	26.0	11.6	460	28.2	0.4	1 719	-7.9	184	10.7	1 376	24.6	31.9
White	11 507	71.3	161 700	25.9	12.9	758	35.0	2.0	13 740	-0.7	698	5.1	11 455	27.5	25.9
Whitfield	34 734	64.4	120 800	23.0	10.4	678	30.3	6.3	44 695	-0.1	2 832	6.3	44 469	21.8	41.2
Wilcox	2 735	72.5	70 000	25.7	12.2	478	33.0	5.3	2 742	-3.5	208	7.6	2 448	30.1	27.8
Wilkes	4 078	69.4	92 800	30.3	16.4	574	34.0	1.3	3 709	-0.7	278	7.5	3 810	24.5	35.5
Wilkinson	3 343	79.2	71 800	21.4	12.2	571	31.6	1.8	3 582	-3.7	266	7.4	3 174	21.0	37.7
Worth	8 016	76.1	69 200	22.4	12.3	612	32.3	2.0	8 855	-0.9	565	6.4	8 468	24.1	34.6
HAWAII	450 299	57.1	504 500	28.7	10.0	1 417	33.5	9.4	677 439	1.4	24 500	3.6	645 571	33.9	18.3
Hawaii	64 586	65.8	301 500	28.9	10.0	1 039	34.6	9.4	89 065	1.3	3 973	4.5	81 197	31.1	19.5
Honolulu	310 141	54.9	564 400	28.0	10.0	1 528	33.9	9.0	468 885	1.3	15 920	3.4	452 324	35.8	17.7
Kalawao	46	4.3	NA	NA	NA	830	16.3	0.0	NA	NA	NA	NA	53	41.5	18.9
Kauai	22 395	62.7	483 800	32.8	11.3	1 265	29.9	9.1	35 256	1.1	1 443	4.1	32 633	29.1	19.1
Maui	53 131	57.3	510 300	31.4	10.0	1 281	31.8	12.4	84 233	1.9	3 164	3.8	79 364	28.1	19.8
IDAHO	585 259	69.2	160 500	23.4	10.0	738	29.7	3.5	797 478	2.1	33 011	4.1	703 410	33.3	24.4
Ada	154 408	67.3	183 300	22.3	10.0	844	29.6	2.1	217 281	2.4	7 798	3.6	195 104	41.6	15.6
Adams	1 643	79.9	142 800	23.8	11.7	554	23.9	3.5	1 731	3.0	132	7.6	1 534	26.3	28.9
Bannock	30 277	68.9	143 800	22.0	10.1	627	30.4	2.9	42 141	1.3	1 673	4.0	37 810	34.3	22.0
Bear Lake	2 437	81.4	127 200	19.2	10.5	568	26.0	2.3	2 841	-0.9	124	4.4	2 492	26.3	31.9
Benewah	3 703	72.3	135 600	23.8	11.6	654	26.3	6.7	4 072	2.4	267	6.6	3 673	25.6	38.3
Bingham	14 840	73.7	136 300	21.5	10.0	617	24.3	5.4	22 159	0.2	907	4.1	19 103	29.6	31.1
Blaine	9 258	67.0	373 000	27.3	11.8	934	26.8	3.5	11 879	3.5	416	3.5	11 845	34.3	18.6
Boise	3 038	80.4	187 700	24.0	11.5	553	32.7	4.4	3 006	2.8	187	6.2	2 780	37.1	23.4
Bonner	17 388	72.1	215 600	29.4	10.6	734	29.0	4.3	18 525	1.4	1 094	5.9	16 119	29.1	26.9
Bonneville	36 402	73.2	154 000	21.7	10.0	706	29.5	2.5	51 227	3.1	1 765	3.4	46 872	34.5	22.8
Boundary	4 101	73.1	173 500	26.2	11.3	719	33.5	3.1	5 075	3.2	272	5.4	3 731	30.3	29.8
Butte	1 028	80.7	111 400	24.1	11.8	539	35.0	1.3	1 335	2.3	58	4.3	1 036	36.7	29.6
Camas	465	66.7	154 200	28.2	10.0	664	34.0	1.5	644	1.7	23	3.6	515	28.2	35.0
Canyon	64 514	68.8	120 200	24.7	10.8	748	30.5	4.9	90 816	1.8	4 483	4.9	79 002	26.1	30.4

1. Specified owner-occupied units. 2. A value of 10.0 represents 10 percent or less; a value of 50.0 represents 50 percent or more. 3. Specified renter-occupied units.
4. Overcrowded or lacking complete plumbing facilities. 5. Percent of civilian labor force. 6. Persons 16 years old and over.

Table B. States and Counties — Nonfarm Employment and Agriculture

STATE County	Private nonfarm establishments, employment and payroll, 2014									Agriculture, 2012			
		Employment						Annual payroll		Farms			
												Percent with:	
	Number of establishments	Total	Health care and social assistance	Manufacturing	Retail trade	Finance and insurance	Professional, scientific, and technical services	Total (mil dol)	Average per employee (dollars)	Number	Fewer than 50 acres	500 acres or more	Farm operators whose principal occupation is farming (percent)
	104	105	106	107	108	109	110	111	112	113	114	115	116
GEORGIA—Cont'd													
Putnam	408	4 896	528	583	1 005	166	57	141	28 824	165	37.0	6.7	41.2
Quitman	35	248	D	D	61	D	D	6	23 540	21	19.0	23.8	23.8
Rabun	446	4 064	532	342	D	140	D	114	28 031	114	57.0	0.9	62.3
Randolph	129	1 346	D	D	171	D	26	44	32 863	197	11.2	27.4	45.7
Richmond	4 322	87 631	24 086	7 485	10 941	2 260	4 702	3 521	40 182	123	59.3	5.7	40.7
Rockdale	1 939	31 313	3 801	6 267	4 455	805	880	1 330	42 469	103	77.7	1.0	58.3
Schley	66	640	D	300	74	D	D	26	41 138	92	17.4	19.6	41.3
Screven	205	2 296	256	D	361	102	D	72	31 474	344	14.8	26.2	48.5
Seminole	182	1 540	388	19	386	D	32	45	29 312	149	28.2	27.5	67.1
Spalding	1 120	16 898	4 251	2 888	2 620	457	392	557	32 963	258	63.6	1.9	49.2
Stephens	523	7 999	1 273	2 098	1 120	177	277	293	36 616	218	45.0	0.9	53.7
Stewart	62	697	115	D	56	20	D	21	30 334	108	7.4	36.1	36.1
Sumter	615	8 907	2 548	1 106	1 397	238	D	303	34 071	369	19.2	19.0	38.2
Talbot	64	558	D	D	D	30	D	19	33 618	90	22.2	23.3	43.3
Taliaferro	17	64	D	D	D	D	NA	2	24 734	55	16.4	10.9	43.6
Tattnall	294	3 123	763	73	424	119	D	100	31 961	565	35.6	8.3	59.1
Taylor	124	908	207	61	117	D	D	30	33 401	224	21.0	15.2	46.9
Telfair	179	3 516	374	D	302	93	29	70	19 840	300	29.3	9.0	36.7
Terrell	163	1 758	154	D	299	D	28	54	30 863	248	21.4	24.2	42.3
Thomas	1 078	15 105	D	2 781	2 341	608	316	615	40 736	407	35.4	21.1	54.3
Tift	1 021	14 944	2 458	1 308	2 588	428	543	497	33 242	285	39.6	15.4	43.2
Toombs	668	9 649	2 240	1 274	1 650	290	574	314	32 535	268	36.9	12.7	29.9
Towns	270	2 843	479	51	302	78	229	72	25 209	109	58.7	0.0	49.5
Treutlen	87	621	147	D	141	27	D	15	24 256	149	31.5	11.4	27.5
Troup	1 406	32 282	3 070	10 953	3 090	1 042	490	1 353	41 902	212	48.1	7.1	50.5
Turner	148	1 341	158	331	172	70	D	40	30 073	262	34.7	20.2	40.8
Twiggs	71	D	137	NA	55	D	D	D	D	108	36.1	12.0	37.0
Union	542	4 997	1 124	286	1 112	D	165	159	31 795	249	51.8	2.8	42.6
Upson	448	5 698	1 293	1 053	1 113	D	158	184	32 252	296	43.6	5.1	39.9
Walker	679	10 408	991	D	1 362	317	157	326	31 298	528	40.3	6.3	53.4
Walton	1 543	15 843	1 816	1 744	2 421	438	511	545	34 372	477	50.3	3.4	54.3
Ware	853	11 679	2 934	1 340	2 514	337	234	369	31 604	280	44.3	8.9	43.9
Warren	65	738	144	287	85	D	D	25	34 453	134	26.1	13.4	38.1
Washington	341	5 446	953	512	745	160	175	217	39 805	408	22.5	13.0	36.8
Wayne	531	5 701	D	D	1 208	171	D	192	33 717	287	37.3	13.9	41.5
Webster	28	D	D	D	47	D	NA	D	D	102	19.6	22.5	39.2
Wheeler	67	879	D	NA	63	D	D	28	31 911	136	15.4	17.6	25.7
White	595	5 517	502	926	995	141	119	160	28 951	299	64.2	2.7	53.8
Whitfield	2 167	46 761	4 354	15 882	4 753	718	1 878	1 821	38 937	378	45.2	2.6	49.2
Wilcox	89	543	169	D	D	53	D	16	28 610	365	21.6	23.6	47.9
Wilkes	198	2 102	448	D	326	76	30	62	29 357	317	24.0	13.2	47.0
Wilkinson	144	2 172	189	D	176	38	D	106	48 811	114	29.8	4.4	39.5
Worth	273	2 515	545	441	413	D	58	73	29 087	487	27.3	28.5	51.1
HAWAII	31 801	519 130	68 461	11 958	70 860	19 244	23 499	20 847	40 158	7 000	88.1	2.6	52.0
Hawaii	3 962	52 063	8 370	1 276	9 423	1 175	1 533	1 818	34 929	4 282	87.6	2.3	48.2
Honolulu	21 195	354 302	50 939	9 191	47 643	16 519	18 858	14 993	42 317	999	90.6	2.1	66.3
Kalawao	1	D	NA	NA	D	NA	NA	D	D	NA	NA	NA	NA
Kauai	1 988	25 824	3 117	293	4 118	378	856	926	35 846	591	85.3	4.2	52.3
Maui	4 499	63 429	6 018	1 198	9 672	935	1 497	2 300	36 254	1 128	89.0	3.5	54.0
IDAHO	43 816	530 490	87 810	55 281	79 518	22 628	34 193	20 015	37 730	24 816	47.9	17.1	49.8
Ada	12 507	182 706	31 308	D	23 153	9 673	15 506	8 328	45 580	1 233	80.0	3.1	43.6
Adams	107	486	D	D	95	D	D	14	28 541	234	35.5	20.1	53.4
Bannock	1 943	25 273	4 970	1 693	4 580	2 754	1 389	765	30 274	819	46.6	16.1	42.6
Bear Lake	122	955	D	D	243	D	9	26	27 324	493	25.2	24.7	46.9
Benewah	225	2 123	402	D	280	62	45	75	35 277	274	35.0	16.8	45.6
Bingham	833	9 860	1 902	2 146	1 208	285	265	332	33 698	1 265	56.4	17.1	58.5
Blaine	1 376	10 327	828	356	1 366	280	703	397	38 484	186	39.2	30.1	58.6
Boise	149	549	D	D	91	D	D	12	22 761	105	43.8	12.4	57.1
Bonner	1 416	11 388	1 649	1 784	2 016	271	498	396	34 804	686	51.0	3.4	42.9
Bonneville	3 314	44 285	7 920	2 722	7 631	1 200	D	1 722	38 874	893	53.1	18.6	39.0
Boundary	358	2 327	592	387	393	58	79	65	28 120	370	44.3	12.2	41.4
Butte	63	D	D	D	88	D	D	D	D	214	21.5	31.3	71.0
Camas	29	169	D	D	D	D	NA	5	28 000	114	24.6	36.8	56.1
Canyon	3 723	47 157	6 832	8 279	7 676	1 099	1 426	1 476	31 291	2 331	71.3	6.0	45.6

Table B. States and Counties — **Agriculture**

STATE County	\	Land in farms — Acres			Value of land and buildings (dollars)		Value of machinery and equipment, average per farm (dollars)	Value of products sold		Percent from:		Percent of farms with sales of:		Government payments	
	Acreage (1,000)	Percent change, 2007–2012	Average size of farm	Total irrigated (1,000)	Total cropland (1,000)	Average per farm	Average per acre		Total (mil dol)	Average per farm (dollars)	Crops	Live-stock and poultry products	$10,000 or more	$100,000 or more	Total ($1,000)	Percent of farms
	117	118	119	120	121	122	123	124	125	126	127	128	129	130	131	132
GEORGIA—Cont'd																
Putnam	28	-24.5	173	0.8	9.6	656 891	3 803	91 436	38.0	230 521	3.8	96.2	35.8	13.3	567	20.0
Quitman	9	-20.0	433	0.0	2.4	924 667	2 133	66 762	D	D	D	D	14.3	9.5	D	57.1
Rabun	8	1.7	71	D	3.6	500 658	7 078	73 737	21.3	186 719	20.8	79.2	50.9	21.9	138	11.4
Randolph	119	32.4	605	22.0	64.7	1 171 264	1 935	185 523	50.3	255 442	95.8	4.2	40.1	22.3	2 025	79.7
Richmond	14	11.1	113	0.1	3.9	299 699	2 650	58 967	2.0	16 276	45.6	54.4	28.5	6.5	42	12.2
Rockdale	5	-13.6	53	0.0	0.9	370 515	6 982	38 777	0.5	4 660	56.5	43.5	11.7	1.0	4	6.8
Schley	35	-2.3	385	0.8	7.1	875 543	2 273	56 413	18.1	196 239	11.2	88.8	34.8	15.2	284	58.7
Screven	180	1.0	525	17.9	103.0	1 119 872	2 134	170 779	66.6	193 669	92.3	7.7	37.5	18.3	2 076	75.0
Seminole	88	-14.8	592	38.9	62.0	1 600 074	2 703	268 034	74.7	501 631	90.7	9.3	63.1	35.6	1 883	65.1
Spalding	19	-28.8	73	0.0	5.1	381 438	5 229	37 888	5.2	20 298	19.2	80.8	17.4	3.9	60	12.8
Stephens	18	19.7	84	0.0	4.8	445 170	5 272	96 917	79.7	365 583	0.6	99.4	50.5	25.7	189	12.4
Stewart	59	28.6	549	4.4	19.7	1 076 824	1 963	127 593	14.6	135 417	80.6	19.4	30.6	17.6	917	68.5
Sumter	160	4.8	435	44.3	90.4	983 650	2 264	167 710	123.3	334 236	68.4	31.6	36.3	18.4	3 044	68.6
Talbot	34	-18.7	377	D	4.9	784 578	2 084	42 133	0.7	8 200	37.0	63.1	18.9	2.2	266	21.1
Taliaferro	14	-2.1	251	0.1	3.6	552 345	2 202	66 745	8.5	153 709	5.0	95.0	40.0	18.2	75	23.6
Tattnall	108	-20.7	190	13.8	49.2	528 524	2 778	97 715	236.2	418 099	36.7	63.3	49.4	27.1	1 594	36.5
Taylor	62	-29.0	275	6.0	21.7	556 027	2 025	65 634	22.7	101 505	55.5	44.5	29.0	6.7	510	51.3
Telfair	67	7.9	222	4.0	13.8	422 643	1 903	46 887	6.1	20 390	78.8	21.2	25.7	4.7	581	57.3
Terrell	121	-11.6	487	25.8	73.2	1 150 536	2 364	163 758	68.2	274 843	96.7	3.3	33.9	26.2	3 795	81.5
Thomas	173	-15.2	426	11.5	81.6	1 423 002	3 344	159 329	83.5	205 061	77.8	22.2	43.7	22.6	2 676	56.3
Tift	84	-36.4	296	20.6	50.0	941 074	3 176	135 681	70.6	247 653	94.0	6.0	43.5	23.5	1 695	50.5
Toombs	73	-18.5	273	9.9	30.6	647 821	2 371	84 123	58.9	219 746	78.3	21.7	31.3	11.2	745	48.5
Towns	8	12.3	77	0.0	2.1	456 587	5 913	50 862	3.2	29 367	36.6	63.4	30.3	8.3	35	4.6
Treutlen	35	16.7	236	D	9.7	423 060	1 794	64 107	8.3	55 376	95.0	5.0	20.1	3.4	259	60.4
Troup	32	-14.4	153	0.2	5.2	608 769	3 981	52 245	4.2	19 660	23.6	76.3	25.9	2.4	94	8.0
Turner	87	-25.0	332	19.1	47.5	791 313	2 384	141 511	58.4	223 050	86.8	13.2	39.7	19.8	2 000	72.1
Twiggs	39	-13.9	358	5.1	14.3	895 907	2 501	93 389	9.3	85 685	93.5	6.5	23.1	7.4	738	30.6
Union	21	-1.2	83	0.0	6.1	500 076	6 015	65 426	19.4	77 751	23.5	76.5	39.8	5.6	221	15.7
Upson	45	-6.1	151	D	8.2	478 044	3 160	51 111	23.0	77 770	8.5	91.5	20.9	5.7	193	14.5
Walker	80	12.0	151	0.3	28.5	589 797	3 907	71 972	108.2	204 932	8.1	91.9	42.8	13.6	1 049	16.3
Walton	52	-2.3	110	0.9	14.3	590 239	5 367	39 698	29.4	61 660	21.2	78.8	32.1	7.5	371	21.0
Ware	57	12.8	203	4.9	18.5	499 896	2 468	72 825	30.6	109 114	65.6	34.4	40.4	10.4	339	32.9
Warren	34	-7.5	257	0.1	9.2	518 627	2 019	54 731	5.6	41 694	58.0	42.0	27.6	8.2	225	23.1
Washington	100	-9.3	245	7.8	42.8	506 213	2 067	88 184	27.5	67 507	73.8	26.2	32.8	9.8	1 104	52.0
Wayne	62	9.6	217	6.6	35.6	595 854	2 746	115 289	44.3	154 456	59.8	40.2	42.5	19.5	748	42.5
Webster	48	-12.1	471	4.8	22.2	834 667	1 772	59 471	17.2	168 471	88.7	11.3	32.4	16.7	619	74.5
Wheeler	51	-11.4	372	2.5	11.6	556 206	1 493	60 529	8.1	59 706	95.5	4.5	28.7	6.6	473	66.9
White	23	11.8	79	0.1	5.9	539 097	6 866	50 181	77.4	258 957	2.9	97.1	45.2	27.1	129	9.7
Whitfield	39	-8.5	103	0.0	10.6	501 405	4 846	66 577	144.2	381 362	1.2	98.8	36.0	17.2	85	7.4
Wilcox	115	14.5	316	28.4	75.2	771 348	2 439	146 175	104.9	287 512	64.5	35.5	41.9	26.3	2 491	80.3
Wilkes	94	4.4	296	0.1	19.7	820 962	2 777	62 407	58.7	185 306	5.6	94.4	45.1	16.7	662	33.1
Wilkinson	16	-46.8	140	0.5	4.8	297 851	2 134	40 939	4.5	39 614	29.3	70.7	24.6	8.8	42	23.7
Worth	229	19.1	471	47.2	137.4	1 216 889	2 584	177 600	153.5	315 187	90.6	9.4	42.5	28.7	5 342	67.8
HAWAII	1 129	0.7	161	81.8	174.0	1 461 342	9 058	43 999	661.3	94 478	81.5	18.5	41.6	7.2	5 228	9.0
Hawaii	687	0.4	160	7.0	72.0	1 280 898	7 985	36 698	247.2	57 741	63.3	36.7	40.6	6.1	4 153	8.2
Honolulu	69	14.5	69	10.8	22.2	1 396 597	20 171	56 908	161.5	161 650	90.0	10.0	54.6	12.7	283	6.1
Kalawao	NA	NA	NA	NA	NA	NA	NA	NA	NA	NA	NA	NA	NA	NA	NA	NA
Kauai	144	-4.9	244	22.5	30.2	1 853 486	7 600	57 464	64.5	109 161	86.3	13.7	35.2	6.6	234	16.2
Maui	229	1.6	203	41.5	49.6	1 998 207	9 836	53 229	188.1	166 755	96.5	3.5	37.1	7.1	558	10.5
IDAHO	11 760	2.3	474	3 365.3	5 793.3	1 052 941	2 222	143 835	7 801.4	314 372	44.1	55.9	44.3	20.5	99 789	37.7
Ada	144	-24.8	117	55.3	53.4	616 596	5 278	70 942	221.0	179 229	20.2	79.8	26.8	7.9	704	10.2
Adams	136	-8.6	582	19.0	19.8	885 517	1 521	67 226	13.5	57 902	25.1	74.9	41.9	11.5	104	16.7
Bannock	295	-8.3	360	52.6	164.1	651 077	1 807	83 179	54.3	66 267	66.6	33.4	29.4	9.2	3 067	37.0
Bear Lake	258	10.6	523	54.5	112.5	743 225	1 421	101 310	29.5	59 850	35.4	64.6	52.7	15.8	1 316	47.1
Benewah	147	-4.5	535	0.9	81.7	849 000	1 587	106 938	23.9	87 058	96.9	3.1	29.6	10.9	1 516	45.6
Bingham	870	-4.7	687	333.4	369.5	1 536 482	2 235	194 538	453.3	358 314	82.7	17.3	46.5	23.7	5 568	33.9
Blaine	179	-6.7	963	41.9	47.6	2 752 371	2 858	165 301	38.6	207 376	72.2	27.8	62.9	32.8	415	40.3
Boise	D	D	D	2.4	3.0	667 895	D	34 914	3.1	29 133	39.8	60.3	29.5	6.7	D	6.7
Bonner	81	-14.6	118	1.2	26.1	513 108	4 366	43 496	10.2	14 940	60.1	39.9	24.2	1.9	96	4.7
Bonneville	409	-9.7	458	133.6	278.8	1 061 908	2 317	134 569	204.2	228 641	71.8	28.2	39.9	17.9	5 044	43.2
Boundary	75	2.3	203	2.1	46.7	694 997	3 420	72 922	27.8	75 203	84.1	15.8	41.1	15.7	785	23.5
Butte	125	3.3	585	58.7	68.6	901 136	1 540	148 860	39.3	183 640	82.4	17.6	71.0	38.8	1 539	67.3
Camas	168	21.1	1 471	20.4	82.7	2 182 649	1 484	176 982	21.6	189 500	83.5	16.5	51.8	26.3	406	55.3
Canyon	304	16.7	130	225.3	217.8	694 984	5 332	109 214	513.7	220 387	53.0	47.0	38.9	15.6	2 241	20.6

Table B. States and Counties — Water Use, Wholesale Trade, Retail Trade, and Real Estate

STATE County	Water use, 2010		Wholesale trade,[1] 2012				Retail trade,[2] 2012				Real estate and rental and leasing,[2] 2012			
	Total water withdrawn (mil gal/day)	Gallons withdrawn per person per day	Number of establishments	Number of employees	Sales (mil dol)	Annual payroll (mil dol)	Number of establishments	Number of employees	Sales (mil dol)	Annual payroll (mil dol)	Number of establishments	Number of employees	Receipts (mil dol)	Annual payroll (mil dol)
	133	134	135	136	137	138	139	140	141	142	143	144	145	146
GEORGIA—Cont'd														
Putnam	957.6	45 130	16	68	57.9	2.7	75	668	157.4	14.1	12	225	9.7	3.9
Quitman	0.5	183	1	D	D	D	10	55	12.1	0.9	1	D	D	D
Rabun	3.2	194	4	6	0.5	0.1	76	902	247.7	22.3	19	D	D	D
Randolph	25.2	3 263	5	40	70.8	1.7	27	191	47.6	4.2	5	5	1.8	0.1
Richmond	114.4	571	182	1 856	864.7	81.5	812	10 830	2 627.3	229.5	201	1 069	248.9	37.9
Rockdale	13.6	160	80	636	525.7	34.1	293	4 625	1 239.6	116.2	77	327	83.0	14.9
Schley	1.0	202	4	56	44.4	2.1	14	76	19.3	1.6	NA	NA	NA	NA
Screven	7.1	488	8	D	D	D	49	360	74.5	6.9	4	7	0.7	0.2
Seminole	45.6	5 224	13	76	109.1	4.2	52	331	73.0	6.4	4	7	1.4	0.1
Spalding	6.3	98	39	428	467.1	17.9	224	2 669	638.8	59.4	48	185	29.9	5.7
Stephens	5.9	225	19	D	D	D	99	1 113	262.5	24.5	14	46	6.2	1.2
Stewart	1.6	262	2	D	D	D	15	42	17.1	1.0	1	D	D	D
Sumter	42.1	1 282	35	425	305.9	13.2	137	1 382	311.0	29.1	22	57	8.1	1.3
Talbot	2.9	415	3	11	8.8	0.2	12	65	11.7	0.8	NA	NA	NA	NA
Taliaferro	0.1	76	NA	NA	NA	NA	5	10	2.3	0.1	1	D	D	D
Tattnall	9.0	351	21	459	212.9	18.1	64	444	103.0	8.0	6	17	2.0	0.3
Taylor	6.0	671	4	D	D	D	29	152	36.9	2.6	3	8	0.7	0.1
Telfair	6.2	378	11	48	35.7	1.4	43	290	59.8	4.8	1	D	D	D
Terrell	26.1	2 798	7	162	250.1	4.0	45	316	68.0	6.0	4	D	D	D
Thomas	11.1	249	60	441	406.8	18.4	218	2 154	564.6	48.0	42	123	82.2	4.6
Tift	17.3	432	67	1 041	634.1	42.8	221	2 405	805.6	54.4	36	136	21.8	4.5
Toombs	10.8	396	28	566	996.3	20.8	149	1 640	406.4	35.5	24	59	7.6	1.3
Towns	4.5	429	8	19	2.9	0.4	57	344	87.1	6.9	15	22	7.0	0.8
Treutlen	2.2	312	2	D	D	D	22	140	29.9	2.6	1	D	D	D
Troup	12.0	179	58	D	D	D	258	3 072	911.1	73.7	61	272	41.3	7.5
Turner	9.4	1 053	13	148	81.6	5.3	32	179	66.7	4.0	2	D	D	D
Twiggs	6.6	729	3	D	D	D	16	68	27.9	1.1	1	D	D	D
Union	8.0	375	9	57	26.8	1.9	93	1 007	242.9	22.0	32	71	9.9	2.1
Upson	6.3	231	7	D	D	D	93	970	207.9	20.6	11	26	3.4	0.6
Walker	8.6	125	34	D	D	D	151	1 441	355.1	28.1	16	29	4.4	1.0
Walton	6.8	81	74	620	295.0	28.5	196	2 403	744.5	57.9	65	149	23.0	5.0
Ware	5.8	159	33	D	D	D	204	2 356	627.4	52.4	26	85	10.2	2.2
Warren	1.8	300	1	D	D	D	14	86	14.5	1.7	3	10	0.5	0.2
Washington	24.4	1 151	12	105	133.5	4.1	72	766	187.0	17.3	14	117	9.2	3.2
Wayne	62.0	2 059	12	99	71.0	2.9	120	1 201	293.1	25.4	16	57	5.3	1.3
Webster	9.3	3 323	3	D	D	D	5	38	9.0	1.1	NA	NA	NA	NA
Wheeler	2.9	385	3	5	6.5	0.3	14	70	21.2	1.2	2	D	D	D
White	2.9	106	15	79	30.7	2.1	119	1 097	279.7	23.0	18	59	6.1	1.0
Whitfield	22.6	220	191	2 604	1 196.6	103.0	435	4 690	1 302.4	107.7	63	D	D	D
Wilcox	8.9	966	7	38	34.3	1.5	19	90	23.4	1.6	NA	NA	NA	NA
Wilkes	1.9	180	9	81	24.1	3.2	48	406	70.4	7.4	4	11	0.9	0.3
Wilkinson	15.1	1 578	8	35	8.4	1.1	24	150	32.5	2.4	1	D	D	D
Worth	19.0	876	22	D	D	D	56	430	117.1	10.9	9	D	D	D
HAWAII	1 273.8	936	1 561	16 686	9 608.0	724.5	4 643	68 360	18 901.7	1 835.0	1 919	11 369	3 411.2	483.9
Hawaii	134.7	728	178	D	D	D	648	9 084	2 390.8	241.3	245	1 172	226.5	39.1
Honolulu	799.2	838	1 167	13 446	8 052.8	596.9	2 889	46 165	13 036.4	1 233.1	1 219	7 213	2 553.5	340.7
Kalawao	0.0	111	NA	NA	NA	NA	1	D	D	D	NA	NA	NA	NA
Kauai	61.8	921	76	D	D	D	347	3 937	1 013.5	102.4	149	962	176.9	33.3
Maui	278.1	1 796	140	1 141	714.6	50.4	758	D	D	D	306	2 022	454.4	70.8
IDAHO	17 230.5	10 992	1 739	21 470	17 906.0	960.8	5 815	72 980	20 444.3	1 794.0	2 033	6 268	1 039.9	184.2
Ada	832.2	2 121	550	8 141	7 352.5	419.6	1 410	20 428	5 766.7	538.7	712	2 578	456.9	85.2
Adams	78.2	19 663	1	D	D	D	12	D	D	D	7	4	0.4	0.1
Bannock	168.1	2 029	80	D	D	D	299	4 330	1 155.3	95.7	80	221	31.5	5.2
Bear Lake	177.0	29 571	5	54	13.8	1.4	26	232	58.8	4.0	5	14	1.1	0.2
Benewah	2.5	265	4	D	D	D	34	286	76.5	7.3	6	9	1.2	0.2
Bingham	956.8	20 979	50	1 047	635.9	33.6	111	1 132	256.2	23.6	19	37	5.7	1.1
Blaine	109.2	5 107	31	D	D	D	183	1 348	298.6	38.7	92	D	D	D
Boise	6.8	966	1	D	D	D	15	107	20.0	1.5	5	11	1.4	0.2
Bonner	20.1	491	28	157	45.5	5.5	199	1 960	438.0	45.4	68	220	30.9	6.9
Bonneville	716.8	6 877	169	2 021	3 049.6	90.5	477	6 757	1 956.5	157.1	134	460	80.6	13.8
Boundary	100.8	9 191	7	D	D	D	47	386	100.1	9.0	7	5	0.8	0.1
Butte	160.7	55 597	3	D	D	D	13	86	21.8	1.6	2	D	D	D
Camas	164.7	147 449	NA	NA	NA	NA	3	D	D	D	NA	NA	NA	NA
Canyon	746.5	3 951	148	1 600	1 089.0	71.7	485	7 102	2 149.4	182.5	149	434	49.0	10.6

1. Merchant wholesalers, except manufacturers' sales branches and offices. 2. Employer establishments.

194 GA(Putnam)—ID(Canyon)   Items 133—146

STATE County	Professional, scientific, and technical services, 2012				Manufacturing, 2012				Accommodation and food services, 2012			
	Number of establish-ments	Number of employees	Receipts (mil dol)	Annual payroll (mil dol)	Number of establish-ments	Number of employees	Receipts (mil dol)	Annual payroll (mil dol)	Number of establish-ments	Number of employees	Sales (mil dol)	Annual payroll (mil dol)
	147	148	149	150	151	152	153	154	155	156	157	158
GEORGIA—Cont'd												
Putnam	32	66	8.6	1.7	21	612	127.2	18.6	23	399	16.4	4.7
Quitman	1	D	D	D	NA	NA	NA	NA	1	D	D	D
Rabun	36	122	10.2	3.7	21	336	D	11.8	62	736	47.2	12.7
Randolph	8	28	2.5	0.6	4	D	D	D	11	66	2.7	0.7
Richmond	478	4 251	569.6	213.8	111	7 884	5 452.2	451.0	424	9 448	447.0	125.6
Rockdale	181	952	100.6	43.4	84	4 746	2 292.2	252.3	175	3 708	179.0	51.3
Schley	2	D	D	D	7	416	123.7	18.7	4	15	0.9	0.2
Screven	13	37	2.3	0.8	13	829	173.4	36.5	17	D	D	D
Seminole	8	D	D	D	3	6	D	D	15	D	D	D
Spalding	85	374	47.2	14.5	56	3 005	2 404.7	152.9	111	1 718	86.9	23.9
Stephens	39	205	28.1	15.2	54	1 807	511.6	73.5	42	595	24.9	6.4
Stewart	2	D	D	D	NA	NA	NA	NA	6	25	1.3	0.2
Sumter	39	D	D	D	25	1 103	492.5	37.8	59	882	37.2	10.2
Talbot	3	7	0.3	0.1	3	9	D	D	2	D	D	D
Taliaferro	NA	NA	NA	NA	NA	NA	NA	NA	1	D	D	D
Tattnall	20	76	5.4	1.7	9	59	7.3	1.5	15	D	D	D
Taylor	3	D	D	D	6	74	D	2.1	6	20	1.2	0.3
Telfair	10	37	2.7	1.0	8	D	D	D	15	D	D	D
Terrell	9	D	D	D	6	493	D	13.4	13	D	D	D
Thomas	74	331	41.1	12.2	41	2 677	674.9	109.0	82	1 240	59.3	15.0
Tift	81	533	47.6	23.0	39	1 289	528.1	51.5	98	2 175	100.8	26.9
Toombs	48	402	26.4	10.4	34	1 558	D	44.8	63	1 032	49.5	12.1
Towns	19	61	6.4	2.3	9	41	D	1.3	30	621	32.4	9.2
Treutlen	2	D	D	D	4	79	D	1.4	3	37	1.4	0.6
Troup	96	965	66.2	29.0	88	10 356	12 011.1	522.6	122	2 187	96.7	26.8
Turner	8	29	2.9	0.9	10	300	92.8	11.5	19	208	8.8	1.9
Twiggs	5	D	D	D	NA	NA	NA	NA	3	D	D	D
Union	43	165	15.3	5.5	27	260	54.0	10.2	46	547	28.4	7.1
Upson	30	126	15.3	3.8	19	1 252	D	51.1	39	512	25.3	6.6
Walker	51	497	16.1	7.1	55	3 652	1 753.7	129.3	49	D	D	D
Walton	158	516	65.3	18.8	56	1 800	777.9	84.4	103	1 603	72.9	19.9
Ware	61	252	23.2	6.9	31	1 118	D	35.1	66	1 317	59.3	14.8
Warren	4	6	0.7	0.2	NA	NA	NA	NA	3	7	0.4	0.1
Washington	24	170	14.2	7.8	17	565	157.5	21.4	27	409	18.3	5.0
Wayne	32	141	9.7	8.2	20	1 161	D	69.7	51	690	34.5	8.2
Webster	NA	NA	NA	NA	NA	NA	NA	NA	NA	NA	NA	NA
Wheeler	1	D	D	D	NA	NA	NA	NA	5	17	1.0	0.1
White	41	95	11.9	3.4	29	715	122.9	31.9	88	956	63.9	14.4
Whitfield	169	D	D	D	265	14 310	5 805.3	546.3	172	D	D	D
Wilcox	1	D	D	D	NA	NA	NA	NA	4	11	0.6	0.2
Wilkes	11	30	2.3	0.7	16	549	175.7	21.1	16	184	6.7	1.8
Wilkinson	5	38	2.9	0.9	12	763	D	52.9	6	25	1.0	0.2
Worth	16	55	5.4	1.7	11	256	D	10.2	14	D	D	D
HAWAII	3 226	21 629	3 334.1	1 265.6	796	11 440	D	465.0	3 518	98 364	9 536.7	2 536.0
Hawaii	294	1 502	193.3	72.1	112	1 182	283.3	46.4	430	12 297	1 124.5	324.7
Honolulu	2 399	18 234	2 895.1	1 105.4	544	9 076	D	370.8	2 355	57 486	5 273.2	1 333.0
Kalawao	NA	NA	NA	NA	NA	NA	NA	NA	NA	NA	NA	NA
Kauai	143	512	59.3	21.1	41	185	D	6.8	234	8 638	831.5	252.5
Maui	390	1 381	186.4	67.0	99	997	D	41.1	499	19 943	2 307.5	625.7
IDAHO	4 198	32 076	4 273.6	1 728.0	1 759	52 084	20 201.4	2 445.5	3 564	54 257	2 680.2	726.1
Ada	1 634	12 378	1 827.8	721.2	373	14 538	D	931.7	947	16 660	763.1	220.7
Adams	8	D	D	D	7	98	D	3.4	14	D	D	D
Bannock	165	1 277	84.2	40.3	44	1 633	916.3	67.7	197	3 199	135.5	37.2
Bear Lake	5	5	0.7	0.2	3	25	6.7	1.2	14	117	4.9	1.4
Benewah	9	D	D	D	11	548	D	D	23	D	D	D
Bingham	51	197	16.3	5.7	41	2 384	768.9	91.5	46	D	D	D
Blaine	154	652	91.7	45.5	45	298	57.8	12.8	111	2 628	138.2	49.2
Boise	9	8	0.6	0.1	4	13	4.2	0.7	23	D	D	D
Bonner	139	D	D	D	79	1 647	369.4	77.9	113	1 816	65.0	20.2
Bonneville	377	8 397	1 371.6	583.9	134	2 447	631.0	90.6	235	4 462	198.3	57.1
Boundary	23	90	6.0	2.2	24	293	D	11.6	23	D	D	D
Butte	2	D	D	D	NA	NA	NA	NA	11	D	D	D
Camas	NA	NA	NA	NA	NA	NA	NA	NA	7	32	1.4	0.2
Canyon	255	1 212	113.0	48.5	189	7 267	D	273.4	254	4 257	180.1	49.5

1. Establishment subject to federal tax.

Table B. States and Counties — Health Care and Social Assistance, Other Services, Nonemployer Businesses, and Residential Construction

STATE County	Health care and social assistance, 2012				Other services, 2012				Nonemployer businesses, 2014		Value of residential construction authorized by building permits, 2015	
	Number of establishments	Number of employees	Receipts (mil dol)	Annual payroll (mil dol)	Number of establishments	Number of employees	Receipts (mil dol)	Annual payroll (mil dol)	Number	Receipts (mil dol)	New Construction ($1,000)	Number of housing units
	159	160	161	162	163	164	165	166	167	168	169	170
GEORGIA—Cont'd												
Putnam	30	476	36.2	14.9	21	165	5.9	5.1	1 796	74.9	22 369	122
Quitman	3	D	D	D	2	D	D	D	142	4.5	84	1
Rabun	34	532	41.8	18.5	36	113	13.3	3.2	1 778	66.1	19 458	52
Randolph	8	D	D	D	8	18	2.8	0.4	402	10.8	500	2
Richmond	645	24 184	3 260.4	1 241.3	275	1 816	196.3	53.1	12 474	385.0	88 432	721
Rockdale	242	3 648	392.9	138.9	135	804	89.1	22.6	8 223	260.7	31 014	138
Schley	4	D	D	D	5	D	D	D	310	9.5	1 277	6
Screven	14	222	11.5	5.2	23	91	7.3	1.5	951	36.0	3 218	19
Seminole	22	D	D	D	11	D	D	D	654	25.9	645	4
Spalding	132	4 459	351.5	122.9	76	415	32.4	9.5	4 855	148.7	23 938	190
Stephens	52	1 390	110.8	47.2	29	222	12.1	3.9	1 662	64.0	5 390	26
Stewart	9	171	13.0	4.4	7	54	3.3	0.9	266	5.3	0	0
Sumter	80	D	D	D	45	D	D	D	1 898	54.9	1 408	10
Talbot	3	D	D	D	6	13	1.1	0.3	495	14.0	792	6
Taliaferro	1	D	D	D	4	D	D	D	95	3.6	NA	NA
Tattnall	27	720	99.8	26.5	15	D	D	D	1 295	43.0	2 543	20
Taylor	16	198	10.2	4.2	7	D	D	D	575	17.7	1 533	20
Telfair	18	476	25.2	12.3	14	51	6.4	1.4	694	25.8	0	0
Terrell	15	D	D	D	14	D	D	D	764	22.6	507	4
Thomas	146	3 668	404.9	149.3	63	483	52.9	11.5	3 206	140.5	28 039	79
Tift	110	3 122	399.3	149.5	56	290	26.7	7.8	3 110	125.9	6 856	71
Toombs	106	1 982	197.9	78.5	40	215	22.9	6.1	2 001	75.6	978	15
Towns	25	548	34.2	14.7	10	17	1.5	0.4	1 123	49.0	22 606	115
Treutlen	9	131	7.3	3.1	7	25	1.5	0.5	428	13.2	390	2
Troup	131	3 139	300.6	128.6	81	636	66.4	18.2	5 318	153.8	23 622	106
Turner	8	170	7.2	3.3	7	D	D	D	649	21.5	6 954	63
Twiggs	7	D	D	D	6	D	D	D	567	15.1	205	1
Union	66	1 110	97.3	39.7	28	168	20.5	4.3	2 118	76.9	32 970	129
Upson	65	1 433	130.3	53.2	40	D	D	D	1 698	51.3	2 111	14
Walker	53	957	64.0	26.6	39	258	22.2	7.7	4 195	159.1	16 281	104
Walton	133	1 554	176.9	57.5	113	346	33.7	8.0	7 813	292.1	56 598	441
Ware	119	2 883	284.9	112.7	53	261	25.1	7.1	1 854	62.9	12 129	98
Warren	5	134	6.5	3.2	4	D	D	D	330	11.5	0	0
Washington	33	1 001	56.1	27.1	29	71	6.4	1.7	1 243	37.7	6 090	56
Wayne	65	1 036	102.4	35.3	31	160	16.3	3.7	1 785	61.6	3 251	21
Webster	1	D	D	D	1	D	D	D	142	5.7	415	5
Wheeler	5	D	D	D	3	3	0.4	0.1	347	11.8	0	0
White	34	418	26.6	11.1	41	168	13.5	3.4	2 499	97.0	9 572	55
Whitfield	192	4 275	482.4	180.7	117	855	76.7	25.8	5 989	292.4	17 688	121
Wilcox	12	D	D	D	7	D	D	D	528	17.2	NA	NA
Wilkes	24	547	32.2	13.1	10	37	3.5	0.7	648	23.2	396	5
Wilkinson	15	D	D	D	10	29	2.2	0.6	626	16.0	571	5
Worth	26	D	D	D	27	64	7.4	1.8	1 273	48.3	2 900	14
HAWAII	3 559	66 772	8 136.9	3 290.6	2 808	19 348	2 004.8	538.7	102 544	4 857.8	1 582 395	5 422
Hawaii	469	7 503	781.2	356.4	288	1 387	166.1	41.0	17 101	726.3	399 961	882
Honolulu	2 520	50 049	6 302.6	2 481.0	2 012	14 967	1 522.4	411.8	62 867	3 082.6	914 918	3 833
Kalawao	NA	NA	NA	NA	NA	NA	NA	NA	NA	NA	NA	NA
Kauai	177	3 082	311.6	145.0	125	809	78.2	23.9	6 709	288.9	127 851	205
Maui	393	6 138	741.5	308.2	383	2 185	238.1	62.0	15 867	759.9	139 665	502
IDAHO	4 865	83 505	7 895.6	3 171.2	2 553	12 188	1 118.2	311.4	118 885	5 070.0	1 934 066	9 954
Ada	1 387	29 953	3 174.3	1 355.9	768	4 121	377.4	112.2	34 722	1 600.4	905 705	4 241
Adams	5	D	D	D	3	D	D	D	372	16.1	3 566	4
Bannock	335	3 819	314.1	115.4	120	591	61.6	15.7	5 008	188.0	23 503	190
Bear Lake	13	314	24.7	10.4	5	D	D	D	436	13.6	8 374	26
Benewah	16	391	28.2	12.2	14	D	D	D	539	22.0	2 089	15
Bingham	96	1 817	155.9	67.8	51	279	33.8	8.4	2 750	127.4	10 195	99
Blaine	72	687	73.4	31.9	89	299	46.6	11.2	3 384	195.2	59 926	62
Boise	5	18	1.3	0.5	8	D	D	D	605	18.5	10 255	51
Bonner	141	1 640	130.6	53.4	79	322	22.6	6.5	3 906	142.6	8 773	58
Bonneville	537	7 680	846.0	289.1	174	852	87.1	22.0	8 020	358.3	85 315	724
Boundary	28	536	30.2	14.8	18	40	3.4	0.9	903	40.6	12 370	51
Butte	7	D	D	D	6	D	D	D	192	5.3	488	2
Camas	4	13	0.4	0.2	NA	NA	NA	NA	89	2.6	330	3
Canyon	374	6 754	530.8	216.1	206	1 039	93.0	26.7	11 906	473.7	184 323	1 148

Table B. States and Counties — Government Employment and Payroll, and Local Government Finances

	Government employment and payroll, 2012									Local government finances, 2012				
			March payroll (percent of total)							General revenue				
												Taxes		
													Per capita[1] (dollars)	
STATE County	Full-time equivalent employees	March payroll (dollars)	Administration, judicial, and legal	Police and Corrections	Fire Protection	Highways and transportation	Health and Welfare	Natural resources and utilities	Education and libraries	Total (mil dol)	Intergovernmental (mil dol)	Total (mil dol)	Total	Property
	171	172	173	174	175	176	177	178	179	180	181	182	183	184
GEORGIA—Cont'd														
Putnam	984	3 113 107	7.0	8.5	2.1	1.9	21.4	3.9	53.4	77.1	16.7	40.8	1 927	1 196
Quitman	121	315 487	9.9	7.4	0.2	4.3	8.7	2.9	65.7	8.3	4.1	3.2	1 332	1 155
Rabun	712	2 242 761	6.8	10.9	2.2	4.4	7.2	5.6	61.5	63.4	12.6	43.0	2 638	1 882
Randolph	534	1 324 386	4.1	6.0	1.2	2.8	42.1	4.5	38.3	42.9	11.1	14.3	1 951	1 486
Richmond	7 950	24 545 151	7.9	10.6	4.4	2.7	3.5	7.3	62.0	723.6	324.4	222.4	1 098	673
Rockdale	3 955	12 355 812	6.2	9.9	4.2	1.3	0.7	4.5	71.2	266.8	93.9	129.0	1 503	1 071
Schley	221	708 164	2.4	6.6	0.0	3.3	4.8	4.1	78.8	16.0	8.4	5.0	1 011	733
Screven	656	1 803 310	6.3	10.5	2.8	3.9	4.8	5.5	64.2	45.6	23.1	16.0	1 128	780
Seminole	372	1 424 704	4.2	9.3	2.0	3.8	4.4	1.3	74.5	27.2	10.7	13.1	1 463	928
Spalding	2 703	8 758 007	4.7	13.1	5.5	2.0	7.8	7.1	56.8	223.0	90.1	90.6	1 418	906
Stephens	894	2 549 588	7.6	10.7	2.8	2.5	1.9	9.9	61.7	120.9	28.0	31.7	1 223	823
Stewart	231	632 898	9.4	19.7	2.8	4.9	5.1	4.7	52.5	14.0	5.9	5.5	915	668
Sumter	1 492	4 667 090	4.8	12.0	4.4	1.8	14.0	4.3	55.3	123.8	56.0	47.3	1 498	959
Talbot	263	648 950	15.0	7.1	0.0	6.9	4.5	5.3	60.1	16.0	5.2	8.8	1 350	1 039
Taliaferro	95	252 316	11.8	15.2	0.0	6.8	1.6	0.9	60.8	6.4	2.1	3.2	1 880	1 613
Tattnall	764	2 267 688	6.8	7.3	0.0	4.7	3.0	3.2	73.4	51.7	24.6	20.6	810	496
Taylor	402	1 087 805	6.6	7.8	0.7	2.6	1.3	2.5	76.3	24.2	12.5	8.6	1 017	618
Telfair	434	1 158 142	7.7	9.9	4.9	3.3	2.8	4.0	66.4	30.4	12.8	13.3	813	533
Terrell	443	1 230 523	6.4	14.1	3.6	2.3	4.9	4.0	64.2	29.7	13.0	12.4	1 376	912
Thomas	2 420	7 648 981	5.7	7.9	3.2	3.4	8.3	6.5	59.1	194.9	58.8	64.1	1 432	870
Tift	3 242	12 909 421	2.9	4.3	0.8	1.6	59.8	2.1	26.8	404.4	50.3	64.4	1 568	788
Toombs	1 085	3 290 743	4.9	9.0	1.7	1.4	3.9	3.2	74.9	191.8	42.5	32.2	1 177	561
Towns	518	1 438 233	4.8	7.4	0.8	3.1	0.3	24.8	49.8	26.3	6.4	15.9	1 518	962
Treutlen	241	645 937	7.5	7.8	0.4	3.2	1.3	4.5	74.0	28.8	21.1	5.0	740	446
Troup	3 339	10 586 640	4.7	11.9	4.4	1.8	9.1	6.2	59.3	240.0	99.8	101.3	1 480	879
Turner	509	1 317 091	10.3	7.4	1.7	4.5	3.8	5.8	62.7	31.0	13.3	10.2	1 209	826
Twiggs	296	826 420	11.0	20.1	0.5	4.9	0.4	1.5	60.0	20.2	6.9	10.5	1 247	910
Union	1 493	4 119 774	3.0	5.1	1.6	1.3	48.9	4.1	35.5	56.7	15.8	34.2	1 593	1 016
Upson	965	2 830 552	6.4	11.2	2.1	2.0	0.7	3.7	72.7	154.8	37.1	28.6	1 073	730
Walker	2 622	7 660 154	5.8	5.5	2.5	2.1	10.7	4.8	66.0	172.5	90.6	54.3	798	474
Walton	3 007	10 183 150	6.0	8.9	3.5	2.6	2.5	5.6	68.5	253.5	88.7	125.8	1 487	1 043
Ware	1 747	5 214 214	5.1	10.2	4.2	3.4	17.2	1.0	56.2	150.2	74.1	48.2	1 345	705
Warren	197	551 517	8.8	6.8	0.0	4.0	6.1	5.3	64.2	16.7	6.7	7.4	1 320	928
Washington	1 131	3 414 908	4.5	6.7	0.9	3.9	35.1	4.5	42.2	125.1	24.7	31.9	1 530	951
Wayne	1 486	4 440 469	3.8	6.1	0.9	3.2	35.1	2.4	45.9	139.5	38.9	37.7	1 243	759
Webster	104	294 610	7.7	5.3	0.0	3.0	2.2	1.0	80.8	9.5	3.7	4.2	1 493	1 310
Wheeler	259	643 558	10.3	8.6	0.0	6.2	1.6	4.0	68.1	17.9	10.2	6.1	772	542
White	868	2 678 650	6.8	11.0	0.9	2.2	1.2	3.4	72.6	77.2	27.9	40.3	1 464	942
Whitfield	4 096	14 180 499	3.9	6.7	4.0	3.4	7.2	11.9	61.8	347.4	152.6	112.5	1 088	733
Wilcox	281	825 846	7.4	8.9	0.0	5.0	0.3	1.5	76.4	20.6	10.9	7.4	819	578
Wilkes	700	2 101 724	4.1	4.7	2.3	3.1	36.0	3.8	45.3	48.7	11.7	15.5	1 540	1 102
Wilkinson	479	1 156 738	10.2	14.5	0.0	4.8	0.4	1.9	66.2	39.7	18.0	19.1	1 997	1 336
Worth	797	2 247 660	7.4	8.5	3.1	4.5	0.1	4.6	69.5	50.7	23.4	19.6	900	588
HAWAII	X	X	X	X	X	X	X	X	X	X	X	X	X	X
Hawaii	2 415	11 250 002	15.2	26.6	22.6	11.1	5.5	17.0	0.0	375.6	91.7	253.3	1 339	1 101
Honolulu	9 304	47 881 176	14.1	35.4	14.0	2.6	6.8	20.8	0.0	2 232.4	331.8	1 316.4	1 348	833
Kalawao	NA	NA	NA	NA	NA	NA	NA	NA	NA	NA	NA	NA	NA	NA
Kauai	1 232	5 830 608	20.2	19.2	15.5	10.5	6.2	20.4	0.0	188.8	66.9	100.2	1 465	1 179
Maui	2 328	11 762 934	19.0	23.7	16.4	6.9	6.2	25.4	0.0	252.6	23.1	224.7	1 420	1 317
IDAHO	X	X	X	X	X	X	X	X	X	X	X	X	X	X
Ada	12 112	39 983 613	9.7	14.3	6.3	4.1	3.0	5.8	55.5	1 138.5	454.6	413.3	1 010	956
Adams	147	443 031	15.8	17.4	0.0	11.4	1.6	4.6	45.7	11.9	6.2	4.4	1 132	952
Bannock	2 618	8 746 568	9.9	14.1	5.7	4.5	6.0	6.6	51.4	238.0	114.9	73.0	871	828
Bear Lake	229	654 192	13.1	9.9	0.2	7.8	3.3	5.5	57.6	22.6	13.4	2.6	441	419
Benewah	501	1 444 872	5.0	6.6	1.0	3.3	36.5	3.9	43.4	44.1	19.2	5.9	652	616
Bingham	1 565	4 338 272	6.4	11.2	2.5	4.1	0.9	3.8	70.0	101.5	63.5	23.4	514	501
Blaine	959	4 228 217	10.2	10.1	5.2	3.3	0.5	6.4	61.6	114.6	26.2	66.7	3 152	3 047
Boise	251	737 278	24.2	12.1	0.6	8.0	2.0	2.2	50.8	23.1	11.0	7.0	1 022	1 015
Bonner	1 368	4 223 862	11.1	13.5	5.6	4.8	4.5	6.4	51.1	107.8	42.8	46.9	1 158	1 112
Bonneville	3 464	10 839 917	6.9	10.9	5.5	3.6	4.1	8.8	57.9	271.5	135.2	82.8	776	747
Boundary	529	1 491 650	6.9	7.2	0.6	4.2	37.3	5.6	37.2	38.9	14.5	7.6	707	698
Butte	218	969 719	3.5	4.5	0.0	4.1	61.6	0.6	25.3	15.1	4.0	3.5	1 273	1 204
Camas	63	187 878	16.7	9.7	0.0	19.8	0.0	1.9	52.0	4.7	2.8	1.5	1 353	1 312
Canyon	5 895	18 424 410	6.4	13.6	4.1	2.0	2.4	5.1	63.5	487.9	253.1	149.0	768	705

1. Based on the resident population estimated as of July 1 of the year shown.

Table B. States and Counties — Local Government Finances, Government Employment, and Voting

STATE County	Direct general expenditure — Total (mil dol)	Per capita[1] (dollars)	Education	Health and hospitals	Police protection	Public welfare	Highways	Debt outstanding — Total (mil dol)	Per capita[1] (dollars)	Government employment, 2014 — Federal civilian	Federal military	State and local	Presidential election,[2] 2012 — Democratic	Republican	All other
	185	186	187	188	189	190	191	192	193	194	195	196	197	198	199
GEORGIA—Cont'd															
Putnam	72.9	3 441	44.6	23.5	6.0	0.8	3.3	32.9	1 552	60	61	1 485	34.0	65.3	0.7
Quitman	8.2	3 406	52.3	7.2	6.2	1.8	4.5	6.3	2 614	0	0	146	53.6	45.7	0.7
Rabun	76.9	4 718	60.5	4.4	4.4	0.2	5.2	64.1	3 932	52	46	729	26.3	72.2	1.5
Randolph	40.0	5 457	32.6	34.8	3.1	0.0	2.6	8.5	1 166	20	20	616	57.0	42.6	0.4
Richmond	773.0	3 816	44.0	5.8	5.2	0.1	2.9	1 078.9	5 326	7 388	11 340	23 087	65.7	33.8	0.5
Rockdale	265.4	3 093	63.2	1.2	6.2	0.4	1.5	131.0	1 526	100	251	4 157	54.4	44.9	0.7
Schley	15.2	3 050	68.7	0.6	3.4	0.2	3.0	10.5	2 102	0	15	317	27.6	72.0	0.4
Screven	51.6	3 634	47.5	4.3	4.4	0.5	7.2	16.6	1 168	38	40	968	46.7	52.8	0.5
Seminole	28.0	3 127	58.5	3.1	7.8	0.0	6.4	2.0	222	22	25	461	41.5	57.9	0.5
Spalding	220.8	3 457	49.2	9.1	6.7	0.1	2.5	97.8	1 531	128	181	4 609	40.2	58.9	0.9
Stephens	131.2	5 068	39.4	38.7	2.9	0.3	1.2	65.0	2 510	66	72	1 791	25.7	73.1	1.2
Stewart	14.4	2 389	48.8	0.7	7.9	0.1	8.9	2.2	358	88	12	267	62.0	37.2	0.8
Sumter	189.6	6 009	27.5	40.2	3.7	0.1	1.5	43.4	1 374	125	85	2 762	52.8	46.7	0.5
Talbot	16.6	2 545	46.5	5.7	6.5	0.7	8.6	6.3	967	14	18	245	64.0	35.2	0.8
Taliaferro	6.4	3 816	48.9	2.7	14.8	2.5	5.5	0.7	438	0	0	131	64.9	34.2	0.8
Tattnall	52.9	2 082	60.1	2.7	5.1	0.1	7.0	17.8	701	47	60	2 133	28.8	70.4	0.8
Taylor	23.7	2 820	66.0	2.8	6.0	0.4	4.5	3.3	389	19	24	426	42.9	56.4	0.7
Telfair	30.5	1 866	55.4	3.3	8.2	0.4	6.3	11.0	675	30	37	818	42.6	56.8	0.6
Terrell	29.3	3 236	51.1	4.8	7.0	0.1	4.1	9.0	992	67	26	541	56.6	42.8	0.6
Thomas	190.8	4 266	41.2	9.8	5.5	0.1	5.3	245.9	5 499	190	128	3 094	41.8	57.7	0.5
Tift	381.3	9 285	20.1	64.4	1.5	0.1	1.9	195.8	4 767	201	113	5 378	33.3	66.1	0.5
Toombs	186.3	6 822	31.2	50.6	2.8	0.0	1.5	76.6	2 805	64	77	1 573	30.6	68.7	0.7
Towns	27.3	2 598	47.1	4.4	6.0	2.9	4.7	28.4	2 702	26	29	501	24.2	74.8	1.0
Treutlen	32.8	4 842	80.8	1.3	2.9	0.7	1.9	13.3	1 965	14	18	353	37.6	61.8	0.5
Troup	264.2	3 858	45.4	7.1	6.4	0.4	8.6	84.1	1 228	138	193	3 843	40.2	59.1	0.7
Turner	30.7	3 654	53.3	4.1	8.0	0.8	7.1	13.4	1 596	30	22	578	40.2	59.0	0.8
Twiggs	20.6	2 444	54.2	2.1	10.0	1.2	8.4	10.3	1 223	0	24	324	53.2	46.2	0.7
Union	54.6	2 546	54.2	3.2	5.7	0.9	3.8	28.4	1 326	48	62	1 621	23.4	75.4	1.3
Upson	143.4	5 384	30.0	51.3	2.2	0.0	1.4	37.4	1 403	37	74	1 323	35.6	63.8	0.6
Walker	177.3	2 604	57.4	15.8	4.9	0.8	3.6	84.0	1 233	102	193	3 267	25.9	72.7	1.4
Walton	248.4	2 937	56.6	1.1	6.4	1.4	4.9	295.1	3 490	142	250	3 523	23.5	75.6	0.8
Ware	150.8	4 210	40.9	26.4	5.2	0.2	4.1	43.3	1 209	99	97	2 959	32.5	66.9	0.6
Warren	15.9	2 855	53.9	0.2	11.9	1.1	8.2	9.0	1 620	20	16	271	58.4	40.9	0.7
Washington	93.4	4 474	37.1	33.1	4.7	0.1	6.2	65.8	3 153	49	55	2 330	52.0	47.6	0.5
Wayne	133.6	4 408	40.5	35.6	3.7	0.5	4.6	47.0	1 550	395	80	2 197	27.1	72.0	1.0
Webster	9.9	3 552	48.2	4.4	3.0	0.6	5.2	2.9	1 037	0	0	134	46.4	52.9	0.7
Wheeler	20.1	2 548	57.2	2.6	5.1	0.0	4.0	7.1	901	11	16	290	35.9	63.7	0.4
White	82.8	3 003	62.2	1.4	5.2	0.4	3.1	24.2	879	48	79	1 065	20.2	78.7	1.1
Whitfield	397.4	3 845	52.0	10.1	3.9	0.2	4.6	103.9	1 005	136	295	5 452	29.5	69.5	1.0
Wilcox	20.2	2 223	65.8	2.8	6.4	1.0	7.1	1.1	120	23	20	603	30.9	68.3	0.8
Wilkes	56.9	5 644	29.5	36.5	4.0	0.5	3.2	51.2	5 077	36	28	798	45.8	53.5	0.6
Wilkinson	52.8	5 509	73.3	2.0	4.8	0.6	3.6	25.9	2 707	21	27	511	49.2	50.3	0.6
Worth	55.0	2 532	54.0	1.3	8.3	0.1	10.1	14.9	684	38	60	866	30.4	69.1	0.6
HAWAII	X	X	X	X	X	X	X	X	X	33 132	57 346	93 022	71.8	26.6	1.6
Hawaii	354.9	1 876	0.0	0.0	13.4	1.9	13.5	415.5	2 196	1 373	1 362	11 366	75.9	22.2	1.8
Honolulu	1 596.7	1 635	0.0	1.5	15.2	0.0	7.8	5 300.0	5 428	30 393	54 206	68 530	69.8	28.7	1.4
Kalawao	NA	NA	NA	NA	NA	NA	NA	NA	NA	(3)	(3)	(3)	NA	NA	NA
Kauai	196.1	2 865	0.0	0.0	13.7	5.8	8.0	246.2	3 598	540	618	4 133	75.0	22.9	2.1
Maui	264.1	1 669	0.0	0.0	15.8	6.0	2.7	281.6	1 780	(3)826	(3)1 160	(3)8 993	76.7	21.5	1.8
IDAHO	X	X	X	X	X	X	X	X	X	12 350	9 235	105 730	36.1	61.5	2.4
Ada	1 060.4	2 592	40.6	0.3	10.7	0.9	7.6	516.6	1 263	5 367	1 591	27 518	45.8	52.0	2.1
Adams	10.4	2 645	37.6	0.0	12.3	0.0	13.2	4.7	1 205	111	14	206	31.4	65.4	3.2
Bannock	221.0	2 637	41.2	2.7	8.1	1.0	5.5	54.8	654	529	296	7 682	42.1	55.1	2.7
Bear Lake	24.3	4 106	33.5	22.5	2.2	0.4	1.3	2.5	424	46	22	622	17.1	80.8	2.2
Benewah	38.9	4 264	35.2	40.0	2.3	0.7	4.2	11.6	1 277	50	33	1 258	33.8	63.5	2.7
Bingham	100.2	2 204	61.5	0.3	7.5	0.7	6.2	46.6	1 024	219	163	3 765	25.8	71.3	2.9
Blaine	113.0	5 346	53.5	2.2	8.7	3.0	3.7	69.4	3 281	99	77	1 383	65.7	32.5	1.8
Boise	17.6	2 582	45.9	0.8	0.9	0.9	9.6	15.5	2 261	138	25	320	32.9	64.5	2.7
Bonner	109.1	2 696	37.9	3.6	6.5	0.6	9.0	31.1	769	181	150	2 188	40.1	57.0	2.9
Bonneville	269.6	2 527	46.0	1.3	7.4	0.3	4.9	252.9	2 370	734	393	5 180	27.4	70.3	2.3
Boundary	40.5	3 751	26.8	27.6	9.8	1.0	7.6	14.5	1 345	161	40	929	31.4	65.0	3.6
Butte	12.7	4 635	28.6	45.0	2.1	0.8	3.4	2.7	1 003	72	27	150	22.6	74.9	2.6
Camas	4.6	4 281	41.0	0.3	12.3	0.2	19.9	3.6	3 301	27	0	91	30.3	68.3	1.5
Canyon	467.4	2 411	45.9	1.7	8.3	1.0	4.9	465.5	2 401	337	727	8 653	31.4	66.5	2.1

1. Based on the resident population estimated as of July 1 of the year shown. 2. © 2013 Election Data Services, Inc. All rights reserved. 3. Kalawao county is included with Maui county.

Table B. States and Counties — **Land Area and Population**

STATE/ County code	CBSA code[1]	County type[2]	STATE County	Population, 2015				Population and population characteristics, 2014										
								Race alone or in combination, not Hispanic or Latino (percent)					Age (percent)					
				Land area,[3] (sq km) 2010	Total persons 2015	Rank	Per square kilometer	White	Black	American Indian, Alaska Native	Asian and Pacific Islander	Percent Hispanic or Latino[4]	Under 5 years	5 to 17 years	18 to 24 years	25 to 34 years	35 to 44 years	45 to 54 years
				1	2	3	4	5	6	7	8	9	10	11	12	13	14	15
			IDAHO—Cont'd															
16 029	...	6	Caribou	4 569	6 770	2 697	1.5	93.7	0.5	1.1	1.0	5.3	7.4	21.2	7.4	10.9	11.6	11.2
16 031	15420	7	Cassia	6 644	23 506	1 658	3.5	72.0	0.4	1.1	1.0	26.6	8.3	24.0	9.0	12.0	11.4	10.9
16 033	...	8	Clark	4 569	880	3 113	0.2	55.1	1.0	1.7	1.0	42.2	5.9	22.1	8.4	13.3	11.1	12.6
16 035	...	6	Clearwater	6 364	8 496	2 556	1.3	93.8	0.9	3.2	1.2	3.6	4.0	12.3	6.4	9.5	10.4	15.1
16 037	...	9	Custer	12 745	4 087	2 894	0.3	94.5	0.4	1.6	0.7	4.1	4.3	13.1	5.8	9.2	10.1	13.8
16 039	34300	4	Elmore	7 964	25 876	1 561	3.2	76.4	3.5	1.9	4.4	16.1	8.0	18.4	13.5	15.8	10.9	11.3
16 041	30860	3	Franklin	1 719	13 074	2 228	7.6	92.4	0.5	1.1	0.5	6.9	8.0	26.0	8.0	10.5	12.5	10.7
16 043	39940	6	Fremont	4 827	12 819	2 242	2.7	86.1	0.5	1.3	0.7	12.4	6.9	21.5	8.3	11.0	11.9	12.0
16 045	14260	2	Gem	1 453	16 852	1 988	11.6	90.0	0.5	1.8	2.0	8.3	5.7	17.9	7.3	9.5	9.9	13.8
16 047	...	7	Gooding	1 888	15 284	2 081	8.1	69.6	0.4	1.5	1.1	28.5	6.9	21.4	8.6	11.3	11.7	12.1
16 049	...	6	Idaho	21 956	16 272	2 024	0.7	93.4	0.6	4.0	0.9	3.1	5.2	14.8	7.0	9.0	9.3	12.8
16 051	26820	3	Jefferson	2 832	27 157	1 527	9.6	88.3	0.5	1.1	1.1	10.3	8.8	26.0	8.0	12.5	12.2	11.1
16 053	46300	7	Jerome	1 547	22 814	1 691	14.7	64.6	0.5	1.4	0.8	34.0	9.2	21.6	9.2	13.7	11.2	11.8
16 055	17660	3	Kootenai	3 222	150 346	432	46.7	93.2	0.7	2.2	1.8	4.3	6.1	17.6	8.3	12.4	11.9	13.1
16 057	34140	4	Latah	2 787	38 778	1 208	13.9	91.7	1.3	1.6	3.2	4.1	5.8	12.7	25.6	14.0	9.7	9.8
16 059	...	7	Lemhi	11 819	7 735	2 616	0.7	95.0	0.8	1.9	0.9	3.1	4.0	14.2	5.5	9.2	8.8	12.7
16 061	...	8	Lewis	1 240	3 789	2 920	3.1	89.7	1.0	7.0	1.2	4.1	5.3	17.8	5.7	9.8	8.2	12.8
16 063	25200	9	Lincoln	3 112	5 297	2 813	1.7	68.1	0.9	1.5	0.7	30.3	7.0	24.0	8.8	12.2	12.6	11.5
16 065	39940	6	Madison	1 215	38 273	1 215	31.5	90.6	0.8	0.8	2.3	7.0	10.0	17.0	30.7	16.2	7.6	6.4
16 067	15420	7	Minidoka	1 962	20 461	1 809	10.4	64.9	0.5	1.5	0.9	33.7	8.2	20.7	8.8	11.6	11.2	11.7
16 069	30300	3	Nez Perce	2 197	40 048	1 173	18.2	89.7	0.8	6.6	1.8	3.7	6.2	15.5	9.2	12.5	11.0	12.9
16 071	...	8	Oneida	3 108	4 281	2 880	1.4	94.1	0.5	0.9	0.9	4.0	6.7	21.3	6.8	9.3	10.8	11.3
16 073	14260	2	Owyhee	19 854	11 310	2 338	0.6	69.9	0.5	3.9	1.0	26.6	6.4	20.2	8.9	10.4	11.9	12.6
16 075	36620	6	Payette	1 054	22 896	1 686	21.7	81.1	0.5	2.0	1.6	16.7	6.9	20.2	8.4	10.9	11.4	13.2
16 077	...	3	Power	3 637	7 648	2 623	2.1	65.3	0.5	3.0	1.0	30.9	9.9	20.6	8.7	11.5	10.4	12.0
16 079	...	6	Shoshone	6 811	12 432	2 268	1.8	94.1	0.5	3.1	1.0	3.4	5.2	14.6	7.0	9.8	10.6	14.1
16 081	27220	9	Teton	1 164	10 564	2 390	9.1	81.4	0.4	0.7	0.9	17.8	7.8	19.9	6.5	13.2	18.2	14.0
16 083	46300	5	Twin Falls	4 976	82 375	680	16.6	81.9	0.8	1.3	2.0	15.2	7.7	19.9	9.0	13.7	12.0	11.4
16 085	...	8	Valley	9 491	10 103	2 429	1.1	94.4	0.4	1.4	0.9	4.4	4.3	14.0	5.3	9.7	12.0	12.8
16 087	...	6	Washington	3 763	9 984	2 435	2.7	80.8	0.6	2.0	1.2	17.2	5.0	18.4	7.7	8.6	10.7	12.5
17 000	...	X	ILLINOIS	143 793	12 859 995	X	89.4	63.6	14.9	0.5	5.8	16.7	6.1	17.1	9.7	13.8	13.0	13.8
17 001	39500	5	Adams	2 215	67 013	792	30.3	93.9	4.8	0.4	1.0	1.4	6.2	16.3	8.7	12.1	11.0	13.5
17 003	16020	7	Alexander	610	6 780	2 696	11.1	64.3	39.8	0.9	0.6	2.3	6.4	16.5	8.3	11.3	11.1	13.7
17 005	41180	1	Bond	985	16 950	1 981	17.2	89.6	7.1	0.8	1.1	3.5	4.5	14.9	9.7	13.1	13.4	14.2
17 007	40420	2	Boone	727	53 585	934	73.7	75.8	2.8	0.6	1.7	20.6	5.7	20.4	9.1	10.5	13.5	14.8
17 009	...	7	Brown	792	6 829	2 692	8.6	74.3	19.0	0.4	0.4	6.2	3.8	11.3	12.2	18.5	16.0	14.2
17 011	36860	6	Bureau	2 251	33 587	1 338	14.9	89.4	1.2	0.5	1.0	8.6	5.0	16.7	7.8	10.5	11.4	13.9
17 013	41180	1	Calhoun	657	4 899	2 841	7.5	98.0	0.6	0.3	0.3	1.1	5.2	15.2	7.1	9.6	10.9	14.7
17 015	...	7	Carroll	1 152	14 616	2 128	12.7	94.1	1.6	0.5	1.0	3.4	4.5	14.6	7.4	9.9	10.6	13.4
17 017	...	6	Cass	973	12 847	2 237	13.2	77.7	3.4	0.5	0.7	19.0	6.4	18.0	8.2	12.0	12.1	14.0
17 019	16580	3	Champaign	2 580	208 861	311	81.0	71.3	13.7	0.5	11.3	5.6	5.5	13.6	23.2	15.0	10.7	10.3
17 021	45380	6	Christian	1 837	33 642	1 337	18.3	95.9	2.1	0.4	0.9	1.6	5.5	15.7	8.1	12.1	11.9	14.2
17 023	...	6	Clark	1 299	15 979	2 043	12.3	97.8	0.8	0.5	0.6	1.4	5.8	16.9	7.8	11.3	11.5	14.2
17 025	...	7	Clay	1 213	13 428	2 208	11.1	97.6	0.9	0.5	0.9	1.5	6.5	16.4	8.0	10.8	11.4	13.8
17 027	41180	1	Clinton	1 228	37 786	1 232	30.8	92.7	4.0	0.5	0.9	3.1	5.5	16.0	8.3	13.3	12.5	15.0
17 029	16660	5	Coles	1 316	52 521	952	39.9	93.5	4.8	0.5	1.5	2.4	4.9	13.1	20.5	13.0	10.2	11.2
17 031	16980	1	Cook	2 448	5 238 216	2	2 139.8	44.1	24.2	0.5	7.7	25.0	6.5	16.2	9.5	16.3	13.6	13.1
17 033	...	6	Crawford	1 149	19 414	1 854	16.9	92.2	5.3	0.5	0.9	2.2	5.4	14.4	8.3	12.9	12.5	14.3
17 035	16660	9	Cumberland	896	10 898	2 364	12.2	97.0	0.9	0.5	0.9	1.0	5.4	17.4	7.6	11.3	11.8	13.9
17 037	16980	1	DeKalb	1 635	104 352	569	63.8	79.6	8.1	0.5	3.3	11.0	5.8	16.0	21.0	13.4	10.9	11.5
17 039	14010	6	De Witt	1 030	16 247	2 028	15.8	96.4	1.3	0.5	0.9	2.3	5.5	16.2	7.4	11.2	12.3	14.5
17 041	...	6	Douglas	1 079	19 823	1 843	18.4	91.5	1.0	0.5	0.8	7.3	6.7	18.9	7.8	12.3	11.7	12.9
17 043	16980	1	DuPage	848	933 736	55	1 101.1	69.4	5.4	0.4	12.2	14.1	5.9	17.6	8.8	12.7	13.0	15.0
17 045	...	6	Edgar	1 615	17 664	1 935	10.9	98.3	0.8	0.5	0.4	1.0	5.0	16.1	7.3	11.1	11.9	13.3
17 047	...	9	Edwards	576	6 534	2 714	11.3	97.6	1.0	0.4	0.6	1.2	5.7	17.3	7.7	10.0	12.0	13.6
17 049	20820	7	Effingham	1 240	34 371	1 319	27.7	97.1	0.8	0.4	0.7	1.9	6.5	17.2	8.7	12.3	10.9	14.0
17 051	...	6	Fayette	1 856	22 043	1 729	11.9	92.6	5.1	0.5	0.6	1.7	5.2	16.5	8.9	12.8	12.6	14.1
17 053	16580	3	Ford	1 258	13 736	2 186	10.9	95.3	1.3	0.6	0.7	2.9	5.4	17.4	7.7	10.3	11.6	13.6
17 055	...	5	Franklin	1 059	39 485	1 187	37.3	96.9	1.0	0.7	0.7	1.6	5.8	16.3	7.7	11.1	12.2	13.6
17 057	15900	6	Fulton	2 242	35 699	1 282	15.9	93.0	4.1	0.6	0.5	2.7	5.1	15.1	8.0	12.3	12.9	13.8
17 059	...	8	Gallatin	837	5 265	2 815	6.3	96.4	1.4	0.9	0.5	1.9	4.6	15.3	7.3	10.6	12.2	13.4
17 061	...	6	Greene	1 406	13 241	2 220	9.4	98.5	1.4	0.4	0.3	1.1	5.8	16.2	7.8	11.1	12.1	14.3
17 063	16980	1	Grundy	1 083	50 541	979	46.7	88.4	1.8	0.4	1.2	9.3	6.3	19.5	8.3	12.6	13.9	14.4
17 065	...	7	Hamilton	1 126	8 200	2 585	7.3	97.4	1.0	0.5	0.5	1.6	5.5	16.8	7.4	10.8	11.4	13.2
17 067	22800	7	Hancock	2 056	18 543	1 889	9.0	97.2	0.8	0.5	0.6	1.5	5.0	15.5	6.9	9.9	10.6	13.7

1. CBSA = Core Based Statistical Area. See Appendix A for explanation. See Appendix B for list of metropolitan areas with component counties.
Service of USDA Rural-Urban Continuum Codes. See Appendix A for definition.　3. Dry land or land partially or temporarily covered by water.　2. County type code from the Economic Research
4. May be of any race.

Table B. States and Counties — Population and Households

STATE County	Age (percent) (cont.) 55 to 64 years	65 to 74 years	75 years and over	Percent female	Total persons 2000	2010	Percent change 2000-2010	2010-2015	Components of change, 2010-2015 Births	Deaths	Net migration	Households Number	Persons per household	Percent Family households	Female family householder[1]	One person
	16	17	18	19	20	21	22	23	24	25	26	27	28	29	30	31
IDAHO—Cont'd																
Caribou	13.5	9.4	7.3	49.8	7 304	6 963	-4.7	-2.8	485	323	-352	2 683	2.52	72.2	2.7	25.4
Cassia	10.9	7.4	6.2	49.3	21 416	22 958	7.2	2.4	2 038	991	-453	7 744	2.95	71.7	6.5	25.3
Clark	11.9	7.7	7.0	47.3	1 022	982	-3.9	-10.4	54	41	-110	282	2.85	77.0	19.1	20.6
Clearwater	17.0	15.3	10.1	45.2	8 930	8 761	-1.9	-3.0	338	555	-18	3 560	2.14	65.6	6.0	27.0
Custer	19.8	14.9	8.9	48.7	4 342	4 366	0.6	-6.4	204	193	-296	1 783	2.34	66.4	6.1	29.2
Elmore	10.3	7.0	4.8	47.8	29 130	27 038	-7.2	-4.3	2 516	872	-2 894	9 682	2.64	71.1	8.8	23.9
Franklin	10.8	7.5	6.1	49.3	11 329	12 786	12.9	2.3	1 053	504	-250	4 241	3.01	76.6	5.7	21.1
Fremont	12.4	9.4	6.6	47.8	11 819	13 242	12.0	-3.2	1 022	527	-900	4 539	2.74	75.0	5.3	22.7
Gem	14.6	12.3	9.0	50.3	15 181	16 719	10.1	0.8	1 014	985	92	6 400	2.59	69.2	12.3	26.2
Gooding	11.6	9.1	7.4	48.7	14 155	15 464	9.2	-1.2	1 085	752	-504	5 433	2.78	71.6	7.8	21.4
Idaho	18.0	14.3	9.7	47.8	15 511	16 267	4.9	0.0	805	904	137	6 523	2.41	67.4	8.1	28.0
Jefferson	10.3	6.6	4.5	49.7	19 155	26 140	36.5	3.9	2 544	724	-772	8 175	3.24	82.2	8.1	15.6
Jerome	11.2	7.1	5.0	49.3	18 342	22 374	22.0	2.0	2 119	801	-839	7 686	2.92	75.9	9.9	21.4
Kootenai	13.7	10.2	6.8	50.6	108 685	138 494	27.4	8.6	9 076	6 502	9 123	55 807	2.53	69.6	11.0	23.3
Latah	10.7	7.0	4.9	48.5	34 935	37 244	6.6	4.1	2 334	1 188	406	15 069	2.31	54.8	6.1	26.9
Lemhi	18.4	16.4	10.9	49.3	7 806	7 936	1.7	-2.5	357	494	-64	3 868	1.97	58.8	4.5	37.5
Lewis	16.3	13.4	10.7	49.8	3 747	3 821	2.0	-0.8	206	182	-54	1 657	2.26	62.9	7.2	31.6
Lincoln	11.7	7.0	5.3	48.5	4 044	5 206	28.7	1.7	391	191	-116	1 608	3.24	74.9	7.0	18.9
Madison	6.1	3.4	2.6	49.7	27 467	37 536	36.7	2.0	5 698	655	-4 369	10 376	3.55	79.1	5.6	11.7
Minidoka	12.3	8.6	6.9	49.4	20 174	20 063	-0.6	2.0	1 742	900	-452	7 104	2.83	76.2	8.1	21.1
Nez Perce	13.7	10.0	8.9	50.5	37 410	39 265	5.0	2.0	2 497	2 530	851	16 159	2.39	63.2	11.0	29.7
Oneida	14.5	9.9	9.4	50.4	4 125	4 286	3.9	-0.1	255	189	-72	1 657	2.54	74.8	7.5	24.3
Owyhee	13.2	9.8	6.5	49.1	10 644	11 526	8.3	-1.9	707	469	-450	3 888	2.90	71.3	9.1	24.3
Payette	12.1	9.8	7.2	50.5	20 578	22 623	9.9	1.2	1 633	999	-336	8 218	2.74	72.0	10.3	23.7
Power	13.1	8.3	5.6	49.1	7 538	7 817	3.7	-2.2	713	307	-564	2 543	3.02	77.9	12.2	17.4
Shoshone	17.0	12.8	8.9	49.5	13 771	12 765	-7.3	-2.6	666	948	-57	5 796	2.12	60.6	6.2	34.8
Teton	11.8	5.7	2.8	48.2	5 999	10 170	69.5	3.9	793	178	-197	3 558	2.87	68.9	7.1	24.8
Twin Falls	11.4	8.1	6.6	50.7	64 284	77 230	20.1	6.7	6 383	3 733	2 455	28 581	2.71	71.0	11.6	23.1
Valley	20.3	14.5	7.1	48.1	7 651	9 862	28.9	2.4	456	308	69	3 240	2.93	65.5	5.4	30.7
Washington	14.5	13.0	9.7	50.1	9 977	10 198	2.2	-2.1	560	610	-170	3 897	2.54	63.6	9.3	31.3
ILLINOIS	12.6	7.8	6.1	50.9	12 419 293	12 831 549	3.3	0.2	835 266	539 346	-255 588	4 778 633	2.63	65.5	12.7	28.7
Adams	13.4	9.6	9.2	51.1	68 277	67 103	-1.7	-0.1	4 310	4 087	-422	26 866	2.44	64.9	10.3	30.2
Alexander	14.5	10.1	8.1	49.7	9 590	8 238	-14.1	-17.7	552	511	-1 471	2 826	2.62	66.1	24.2	32.0
Bond	13.7	8.9	7.6	47.3	17 633	17 768	0.8	-4.6	869	867	-818	6 230	2.57	67.9	9.0	29.0
Boone	12.0	8.5	5.5	50.2	41 786	54 167	29.6	-1.1	3 043	1 924	-1 665	18 162	2.96	76.8	11.4	19.0
Brown	11.0	6.9	6.2	35.6	6 950	6 937	-0.2	-1.6	287	290	-92	2 124	2.47	63.1	7.4	32.6
Bureau	14.7	10.3	9.7	51.0	35 503	34 978	-1.5	-4.0	1 893	1 948	-1 307	14 111	2.40	66.2	9.4	28.7
Calhoun	14.6	12.4	10.4	49.9	5 084	5 089	0.1	-3.7	263	285	-176	2 052	2.40	71.7	5.9	25.3
Carroll	16.0	13.2	10.3	50.0	16 674	15 388	-7.7	-5.0	740	975	-472	6 531	2.26	65.2	9.3	30.2
Cass	12.9	8.5	7.9	49.3	13 695	13 638	-0.4	-5.8	861	727	-917	5 205	2.54	66.3	10.6	28.6
Champaign	10.6	6.1	5.0	50.1	179 669	201 081	11.9	3.9	12 534	6 453	1 771	79 624	2.36	53.6	10.3	33.2
Christian	13.9	9.7	8.9	49.1	35 372	34 800	-1.6	-3.3	1 890	2 083	-979	14 089	2.31	64.1	10.7	30.6
Clark	13.7	10.0	8.7	50.8	17 008	16 335	-4.0	-2.2	1 048	1 081	-316	6 689	2.39	67.5	10.5	28.1
Clay	14.3	10.1	8.7	50.7	14 560	13 815	-5.1	-2.8	817	902	-277	5 410	2.46	67.6	9.6	29.0
Clinton	13.3	8.5	7.5	48.2	35 535	37 762	6.3	0.1	2 151	1 785	-391	13 944	2.57	69.2	8.8	26.7
Coles	12.3	7.9	7.1	51.7	53 196	53 873	1.3	-2.5	2 624	2 623	-1 294	21 017	2.34	57.5	11.6	31.7
Cook	12.0	7.2	5.7	51.5	5 376 741	5 195 022	-3.4	0.8	368 207	208 640	-106 395	1 937 060	2.65	61.2	15.2	32.1
Crawford	14.0	9.7	8.6	48.4	20 452	19 817	-3.1	-2.0	1 081	1 237	-259	7 644	2.40	66.4	7.9	30.1
Cumberland	14.9	9.6	8.1	49.9	11 253	11 048	-1.8	-1.4	661	571	-244	4 230	2.55	67.1	7.9	30.1
DeKalb	10.3	6.3	4.9	50.5	88 969	105 160	18.2	-0.8	6 372	3 625	-3 664	37 374	2.64	60.6	10.7	27.9
De Witt	14.8	10.3	7.8	50.1	16 798	16 561	-1.4	-1.9	904	941	-268	6 746	2.39	65.7	8.7	30.2
Douglas	13.4	8.3	8.0	50.4	19 922	19 982	0.3	-0.8	1 367	974	-494	7 534	2.61	70.2	10.0	24.6
DuPage	13.5	7.8	5.6	51.0	904 161	916 892	1.4	1.8	55 964	31 349	-6 440	337 003	2.71	71.0	9.3	24.5
Edgar	14.9	11.0	9.3	51.5	19 704	18 576	-5.7	-4.9	1 009	1 256	-657	7 912	2.26	68.7	12.0	28.0
Edwards	14.5	10.2	9.0	51.1	6 971	6 721	-3.6	-2.8	407	367	-212	2 747	2.41	64.7	8.3	31.4
Effingham	13.5	9.0	7.9	50.2	34 264	34 242	-0.1	0.4	2 288	1 821	-384	13 386	2.53	68.5	9.2	26.6
Fayette	12.9	9.0	8.0	46.9	21 802	22 142	1.6	-0.4	1 272	1 125	-250	7 981	2.58	68.3	8.3	28.0
Ford	14.2	9.6	10.2	50.5	14 241	14 081	-1.1	-2.5	765	1 016	-123	5 611	2.40	62.8	9.1	32.7
Franklin	13.8	11.0	8.4	50.9	39 018	39 989	2.5	-1.3	2 484	2 767	-157	16 243	2.42	63.8	12.1	32.2
Fulton	13.9	10.0	8.9	47.8	38 250	37 069	-3.1	-3.7	1 754	2 303	-847	14 501	2.37	65.5	10.1	28.5
Gallatin	13.8	13.5	9.3	51.5	6 445	5 589	-13.3	-5.8	295	431	-172	2 351	2.31	68.7	12.5	27.6
Greene	14.4	9.9	8.5	49.7	14 761	13 886	-5.9	-4.6	749	768	-614	5 689	2.36	67.6	9.7	26.8
Grundy	12.2	7.7	5.2	50.1	37 535	50 063	33.4	1.0	3 278	1 972	-862	18 408	2.71	71.6	11.9	23.4
Hamilton	14.7	10.7	9.5	51.0	8 621	8 457	-1.9	-3.0	445	597	-70	3 499	2.35	65.7	7.9	29.7
Hancock	15.1	12.4	10.7	50.6	20 121	19 104	-5.1	-2.9	987	1 071	-560	7 983	2.32	68.3	8.1	27.8

1. No spouse present.

Table B. States and Counties — **Population, Vital Statistics, Medicare, and Crime**

STATE County	Persons in group quarters, 2015	Daytime population, 2010–2014 Number	Employ-ment/resi-dence ratio	Births, 2015 Total	Rate[1]	Deaths, 2015 Number	Rate[1]	Persons under 65 with no health insurance, 2014 Number	Percent	Medicare, 2015 Total Beneficiaries	Enrolled in Original Medicare	Enrolled in Medicare Advantage	Serious crimes known to police,[2] 2014 Total Number	Rate[3]
	32	33	34	35	36	37	38	39	40	41	42	43	44	45
IDAHO—Cont'd														
Caribou	79	7 323	1.15	92	13.5	61	9.0	745	13.2	1 250	1 048	202	48	704
Cassia	286	24 458	1.13	386	16.4	179	7.6	4 343	21.8	3 446	2 684	762	530	2 249
Clark	2	811	0.97	12	13.7	5	5.7	242	33.5	121	93	28	13	1 535
Clearwater	628	8 906	1.11	65	7.6	89	10.5	944	16.4	2 259	2 215	44	205	2 377
Custer	21	4 211	0.95	41	10.0	30	7.3	564	18.0	976	944	32	29	682
Elmore	636	25 910	0.96	488	18.7	168	6.4	3 755	16.9	3 524	2 876	648	371	1 420
Franklin	102	11 218	0.68	195	15.0	86	6.6	1 765	15.9	1 923	1 878	45	142	1 095
Fremont	455	11 184	0.66	178	13.9	86	6.7	1 965	19.1	2 151	1 727	424	118	912
Gem	151	14 422	0.62	195	11.6	189	11.2	2 143	16.4	3 819	2 058	1 761	131	779
Gooding	52	14 857	0.94	206	13.6	117	7.7	3 078	24.9	2 630	1 992	638	194	1 286
Idaho	523	15 692	0.90	143	8.8	173	10.7	2 226	18.9	3 592	3 485	107	198	1 223
Jefferson	111	22 567	0.63	458	16.9	128	4.7	3 698	15.5	3 327	2 545	782	208	762
Jerome	106	21 704	0.90	406	17.8	159	7.0	4 883	24.8	3 093	2 035	1 058	434	1 913
Kootenai	1 488	135 421	0.88	1 781	12.0	1 284	8.6	19 135	15.8	30 012	20 592	9 420	4 328	2 951
Latah	3 264	35 018	0.83	437	11.3	212	5.5	3 620	11.7	5 101	4 208	893	926	2 402
Lemhi	80	7 739	0.97	62	8.0	100	12.9	923	16.6	2 255	2 197	58	87	1 128
Lewis	74	3 860	1.02	38	10.0	30	7.9	509	17.8	1 711	1 663	48	73	1 848
Lincoln	37	4 468	0.65	67	12.6	23	4.3	1 086	23.6	697	553	144	28	520
Madison	833	38 955	1.08	1 128	29.6	112	2.9	4 579	13.2	2 487	1 900	587	353	937
Minidoka	82	19 229	0.89	324	15.9	158	7.8	3 543	20.9	3 514	2 543	971	393	1 918
Nez Perce	966	42 279	1.14	483	12.1	443	11.1	4 372	13.7	9 572	7 320	2 252	1 295	3 209
Oneida	50	3 762	0.74	41	9.7	40	9.4	517	15.5	886	722	164	26	605
Owyhee	160	10 462	0.77	127	11.2	82	7.3	2 610	28.2	1 759	1 032	727	178	1 541
Payette	94	19 931	0.70	311	13.6	194	8.5	3 288	17.6	4 341	2 612	1 729	358	1 573
Power	47	8 177	1.14	137	17.9	64	8.4	1 373	21.3	1 018	796	222	110	1 421
Shoshone	160	12 837	1.05	132	10.6	167	13.5	1 539	16.1	3 225	2 583	642	397	3 108
Teton	7	8 635	0.67	134	12.8	28	2.7	2 150	22.9	979	887	92	53	511
Twin Falls	993	79 947	1.03	1 231	15.1	734	9.0	11 498	16.9	14 050	9 852	4 198	1 993	2 456
Valley	66	9 905	1.06	91	9.1	60	6.0	1 318	17.2	2 104	1 511	593	206	2 139
Washington	119	9 220	0.77	116	11.6	89	8.9	1 583	20.8	2 463	1 610	853	165	1 658
ILLINOIS	299 694	12 857 526	1.00	156 440	12.2	104 233	8.1	1 211 871	11.2	1 926 604	1 476 750	449 854	315 048	2 446
Adams	2 216	70 314	1.10	837	12.5	792	11.8	4 347	8.1	14 266	12 479	1 787	1 769	2 666
Alexander	132	7 259	0.77	102	14.7	99	14.3	599	10.5	1 722	1 552	170	315	4 209
Bond	1 889	16 034	0.79	162	9.5	157	9.2	1 154	9.2	3 274	2 830	444	148	876
Boone	310	46 914	0.70	574	10.7	339	6.3	4 935	10.7	7 766	5 766	2 000	772	1 433
Brown	2 110	8 276	1.51	61	8.9	64	9.4	272	7.0	930	774	156	NA	NA
Bureau	456	31 717	0.83	388	11.5	373	11.1	2 581	9.6	7 273	6 255	1 018	415	1 304
Calhoun	90	3 914	0.49	49	9.9	61	12.4	328	8.6	1 142	1 007	135	NA	NA
Carroll	223	13 286	0.75	133	9.0	186	12.7	1 097	9.8	3 997	3 152	845	132	1 074
Cass	184	13 326	0.98	140	10.8	131	10.1	1 317	12.0	2 461	2 073	388	175	1 322
Champaign	16 225	213 589	1.09	2 410	11.6	1 276	6.1	15 866	9.4	24 900	12 702	12 198	6 201	3 034
Christian	1 610	30 753	0.76	358	10.6	373	11.0	2 265	8.6	7 204	5 438	1 766	417	1 266
Clark	221	14 311	0.74	201	12.5	204	12.7	1 115	8.5	3 510	2 851	659	83	679
Clay	305	13 263	0.93	143	10.6	179	13.3	958	8.8	2 932	2 741	191	168	1 245
Clinton	2 082	31 566	0.66	400	10.6	366	9.7	2 270	7.6	5 748	5 131	617	375	1 097
Coles	3 944	55 307	1.07	499	9.5	472	9.0	3 681	8.9	8 718	6 715	2 003	729	1 360
Cook	90 944	5 405 948	1.07	68 855	13.1	40 987	7.8	631 967	14.1	691 609	512 861	178 748	163 003	3 158
Crawford	1 495	19 715	1.01	199	10.3	241	12.4	1 274	8.7	3 991	3 638	353	NA	NA
Cumberland	117	8 639	0.52	137	12.6	101	9.3	730	8.2	2 017	1 652	365	82	752
DeKalb	6 062	96 377	0.83	1 202	11.5	689	6.6	8 014	9.2	13 797	11 087	2 710	2 192	2 127
De Witt	249	14 622	0.77	155	9.5	207	12.7	1 030	7.8	3 247	2 405	842	182	1 269
Douglas	168	18 593	0.86	267	13.5	169	8.5	2 058	12.4	2 991	1 832	1 159	137	831
DuPage	12 866	1 021 828	1.20	10 623	11.4	6 194	6.6	68 724	8.6	129 922	107 099	22 823	12 508	1 338
Edgar	249	17 725	0.94	200	11.3	223	12.6	1 275	9.0	3 838	3 244	594	307	1 858
Edwards	52	6 465	0.92	79	12.0	63	9.6	480	9.0	1 349	1 253	96	32	555
Effingham	440	38 757	1.26	414	12.1	328	9.5	2 171	7.6	7 269	6 576	693	629	1 834
Fayette	1 894	20 280	0.80	239	10.9	200	9.1	1 745	10.5	4 028	3 522	506	299	1 424
Ford	410	13 162	0.88	154	11.2	189	13.8	970	8.9	2 616	1 957	659	229	1 767
Franklin	517	35 200	0.69	488	12.4	503	12.7	3 185	10.1	9 640	7 806	1 834	605	1 732
Fulton	2 742	31 020	0.62	307	8.6	449	12.5	2 635	9.8	7 899	5 798	2 101	471	1 506
Gallatin	25	5 007	0.80	54	10.2	76	14.4	417	10.2	1 383	1 199	184	63	1 390
Greene	173	11 142	0.57	132	9.9	165	12.4	994	9.2	3 004	2 694	310	130	959
Grundy	254	45 138	0.78	607	12.0	383	7.6	3 335	7.6	7 664	6 963	701	720	1 463
Hamilton	117	7 260	0.67	80	9.7	109	13.2	619	9.4	1 824	1 598	226	NA	NA
Hancock	223	15 305	0.59	184	9.9	207	11.1	1 245	8.8	4 415	3 875	540	NA	NA

1. Per 1,000 estimated resident population.   2. Data for serious crimes have not been adjusted for underreporting; this may affect comparability between geographic areas and over time.
3. Per 100,000 population estimated by the FBI.

Table B. States and Counties — **Crime, Education, Money Income, and Poverty**

STATE County	Serious crimes known to police, 2014 (cont.)[1] Rate[2]		Education School enrollment and attainment, 2010–2014				Local government expenditures,[5] 2012–2013		Money income, 2010–2014	Households			Income and poverty, 2014	Percent below poverty level		
			Enrollment[3]		Attainment[4] (percent)											
	Violent	Property	Total	Percent private	High school graduate or less	Bachelor's degree or more	Total current spending (mil dol)	Current spending per student (dollars)	Per capita income[6] (dollars)	Median income (dollars)	Mean income (dollars)	Percent with income of $200,000 or more	Median household income (dollars)	All persons	Children under 18 years	Children 5 to 17 years in families
	46	47	48	49	50	51	52	53	54	55	56	57	58	59	60	61

STATE County																
IDAHO—Cont'd																
Caribou	15	690	1 750	9.3	45.9	17.8	11.5	7 748	24 279	54 481	62 206	2.2	55 770	11.5	14.9	13.8
Cassia	170	2 079	6 479	5.4	48.1	16.9	31.9	6 202	17 942	44 847	52 924	1.1	45 078	15.6	20.6	19.4
Clark	118	1 417	171	0.0	55.3	15.9	2.2	13 393	15 734	32 770	41 315	0.0	45 979	17.3	20.2	16.4
Clearwater	244	2 134	1 410	15.7	49.8	15.8	9.6	9 637	20 154	39 750	49 230	1.3	41 304	16.6	23.6	20.9
Custer	47	635	834	10.9	44.2	26.2	5.6	8 691	22 537	39 432	52 592	0.3	42 704	15.7	21.2	19.4
Elmore	222	1 198	6 910	10.4	45.1	17.0	28.9	6 797	21 016	43 516	55 241	1.6	45 049	14.4	21.7	21.2
Franklin	31	1 064	3 827	7.2	44.0	18.2	16.7	5 374	17 694	45 542	53 858	0.1	50 545	10.8	14.9	13.4
Fremont	77	834	3 581	12.0	44.1	19.7	15.0	6 540	19 348	44 991	55 082	0.7	45 578	15.1	23.5	21.6
Gem	107	672	3 973	12.6	49.5	16.9	18.1	7 159	20 623	41 969	51 849	1.0	41 688	15.9	24.9	22.6
Gooding	172	1 113	3 942	9.6	56.9	11.8	19.8	6 903	18 965	38 447	52 502	1.7	44 669	17.1	25.2	22.8
Idaho	105	1 118	3 230	20.2	50.3	16.8	17.5	10 416	19 527	38 320	45 774	0.4	39 551	16.3	23.3	22.2
Jefferson	26	737	8 250	12.7	42.0	21.0	34.7	5 528	19 515	52 495	62 195	1.5	52 428	11.5	15.3	14.1
Jerome	238	1 675	6 182	7.9	58.0	13.3	24.4	5 875	17 474	40 718	50 363	1.4	46 513	15.7	22.6	21.8
Kootenai	279	2 672	35 128	13.2	36.7	23.1	136.4	6 501	25 190	49 292	63 629	2.8	49 061	12.9	18.0	16.5
Latah	83	2 319	14 906	9.7	24.9	44.0	42.6	8 996	22 575	41 944	56 196	1.6	43 482	19.9	16.2	15.5
Lemhi	259	869	1 242	18.3	40.7	22.9	8.2	8 557	24 178	34 457	49 134	1.4	37 869	18.2	26.9	24.0
Lewis	101	1 746	770	16.1	46.0	16.5	9.0	10 168	21 542	36 159	48 392	0.7	39 918	13.7	25.6	23.4
Lincoln	242	279	1 464	4.5	58.9	11.3	8.5	8 843	16 328	41 088	49 255	0.0	44 046	14.1	21.6	19.6
Madison	45	892	19 468	56.6	21.2	34.4	39.1	5 895	15 406	32 052	52 234	1.8	36 065	27.1	20.5	20.7
Minidoka	156	1 762	5 302	7.0	55.5	11.8	25.8	6 335	20 238	44 220	56 096	2.1	46 332	16.8	23.2	22.4
Nez Perce	156	3 053	9 379	10.9	40.7	22.1	48.3	8 785	24 570	46 608	58 145	1.2	46 214	14.6	18.4	16.3
Oneida	23	581	1 103	6.2	47.9	12.7	5.9	6 660	21 286	43 078	53 994	1.4	46 503	13.9	19.4	17.6
Owyhee	138	1 402	2 904	12.8	63.0	9.0	16.5	6 827	16 733	32 589	46 381	1.2	38 478	23.6	30.0	27.3
Payette	228	1 344	5 780	8.9	49.1	15.0	25.0	5 908	20 332	44 326	54 861	1.1	45 533	14.2	20.6	20.1
Power	90	1 331	2 087	10.2	62.5	12.5	14.1	8 705	18 184	45 010	54 710	0.6	48 048	15.7	23.3	24.7
Shoshone	344	2 764	2 350	8.0	50.8	13.7	19.5	10 196	20 803	38 006	46 775	0.4	36 577	18.9	27.2	24.3
Teton	116	395	2 337	9.7	32.4	38.2	12.4	7 416	23 409	52 316	60 814	2.4	57 644	11.6	18.2	17.4
Twin Falls	242	2 214	21 560	7.8	44.7	16.9	89.3	6 630	21 167	44 138	56 693	2.1	44 236	14.5	19.4	18.3
Valley	374	1 765	2 247	19.4	33.8	34.0	14.5	11 953	23 880	49 722	57 495	1.2	49 380	11.7	19.8	18.2
Washington	60	1 597	2 382	9.8	50.6	14.4	13.6	7 552	19 342	36 483	47 940	2.3	35 955	17.8	24.6	21.1
ILLINOIS	370	2 076	3 467 696	18.7	39.4	31.9	25 785.0	12 288	30 019	57 166	78 521	5.6	57 458	14.3	20.1	18.8
Adams	335	2 331	15 635	18.1	45.7	20.8	92.5	9 504	24 247	45 472	58 150	1.9	46 061	14.2	20.0	18.5
Alexander	1 416	2 793	1 825	5.7	59.5	7.7	13.2	12 087	14 052	25 895	35 104	0.4	30 699	35.6	52.0	47.2
Bond	41	835	4 355	16.3	51.5	17.4	22.2	9 062	23 232	48 120	61 447	2.6	49 886	16.2	20.9	18.7
Boone	154	1 279	14 869	17.8	49.8	19.4	103.2	10 101	25 950	60 166	75 015	4.1	58 792	10.2	15.2	13.3
Brown	NA	NA	1 431	6.1	57.3	12.8	7.5	9 866	20 518	45 463	60 385	1.9	50 225	14.2	15.4	14.6
Bureau	129	1 175	8 018	8.9	49.2	17.5	62.5	11 448	26 587	49 921	63 520	2.4	52 138	13.1	19.9	17.7
Calhoun	NA	NA	1 095	29.7	52.2	14.4	6.6	11 522	26 446	52 661	63 890	3.2	49 689	12.1	16.0	14.7
Carroll	16	1 057	3 064	8.4	53.4	15.5	27.2	10 946	26 918	49 629	61 513	2.3	50 750	12.6	20.0	18.1
Cass	484	839	3 256	9.3	60.5	13.2	22.6	9 269	23 423	47 443	58 370	1.7	46 289	13.2	18.6	17.3
Champaign	480	2 554	80 886	7.1	28.8	42.5	292.7	12 063	26 087	46 680	64 924	4.1	47 966	22.6	23.5	22.7
Christian	206	1 059	7 467	9.5	55.6	13.9	53.1	11 344	24 016	45 727	59 204	2.1	46 870	14.4	20.2	18.4
Clark	204	474	3 770	7.3	47.3	18.4	24.5	8 841	25 061	50 412	60 358	2.1	50 645	13.9	20.4	19.6
Clay	44	1 201	3 026	4.3	52.7	13.5	21.6	8 815	22 160	43 189	52 873	1.0	45 709	13.6	19.7	19.2
Clinton	111	986	8 868	16.5	43.9	20.1	49.6	9 318	28 255	62 407	74 249	3.4	60 556	9.9	13.0	12.0
Coles	220	1 140	18 518	5.4	42.9	24.0	79.7	12 255	22 464	38 174	54 841	2.0	41 319	22.9	24.8	22.7
Cook	558	2 600	1 384 976	23.4	39.3	35.3	10 615.4	13 671	30 468	54 828	79 147	6.2	55 058	17.1	25.3	24.4
Crawford	NA	NA	4 312	7.0	45.4	17.7	30.7	10 293	25 613	46 057	63 873	3.1	45 889	15.2	21.0	20.0
Cumberland	147	605	2 410	5.3	51.1	13.9	16.2	8 892	22 631	43 825	55 919	1.6	49 567	12.2	16.2	14.4
DeKalb	250	1 877	39 042	9.3	34.8	29.9	218.9	12 809	23 903	53 771	64 799	2.1	56 536	14.7	15.7	14.0
De Witt	188	1 081	3 702	6.6	48.6	17.4	28.3	10 090	27 575	53 129	66 562	2.2	55 193	10.9	17.3	15.4
Douglas	200	631	4 553	14.4	53.6	17.1	32.1	9 714	24 330	51 701	62 683	2.1	52 526	10.0	15.0	13.8
DuPage	83	1 255	251 373	22.0	27.0	46.7	2 227.0	14 074	38 931	79 016	105 253	10.6	80 037	7.9	10.5	9.9
Edgar	327	1 531	3 832	4.4	53.0	16.9	30.2	8 247	25 018	43 075	57 095	1.6	45 485	15.1	23.2	21.1
Edwards	104	451	1 473	6.4	48.4	10.2	8.9	9 148	21 896	42 573	52 147	1.0	46 894	11.6	16.7	15.3
Effingham	201	1 633	8 154	12.4	44.4	20.2	51.6	9 526	26 774	52 374	67 528	3.6	52 578	11.8	17.2	15.2
Fayette	129	1 296	4 795	12.2	57.9	13.4	29.8	10 117	21 845	44 603	56 185	1.5	41 268	17.5	24.9	22.7
Ford	216	1 551	3 178	7.6	50.6	16.1	33.2	11 146	25 495	48 908	61 469	3.3	50 877	12.1	19.3	17.0
Franklin	166	1 566	8 948	7.4	48.6	12.7	72.7	11 154	20 591	37 333	48 618	0.8	37 758	19.9	29.7	27.7
Fulton	131	1 375	8 044	5.7	49.5	15.5	53.1	9 935	22 478	45 938	55 170	1.0	44 435	16.5	22.1	19.8
Gallatin	132	1 257	1 091	3.1	54.6	10.7	7.9	9 852	22 890	40 721	53 835	0.9	41 045	17.5	27.9	24.5
Greene	170	789	3 061	13.2	54.3	12.8	20.5	10 101	22 483	43 178	53 916	1.0	39 738	16.2	21.8	20.1
Grundy	89	1 374	13 247	12.3	44.1	21.4	142.2	11 032	29 439	65 197	78 323	3.4	70 092	8.5	10.5	9.6
Hamilton	NA	NA	1 757	6.4	48.6	14.5	12.6	9 839	23 160	41 801	54 899	1.1	49 790	14.0	20.5	18.8
Hancock	NA	NA	3 817	6.4	48.7	18.6	32.5	10 326	24 418	45 741	56 749	1.7	48 767	11.6	18.2	16.7

1. Data for serious crimes have not been adjusted for underreporting; this may affect comparability between geographic areas and over time. 2. Per 100,000 population estimated by the FBI.
3. All persons 3 years old and over enrolled in nursery school through college. 4. Persons 25 years old and over. 5. Elementary and secondary education expenditures.
6. Based on population estimated by the American Community Survey, 2010–2014.

Table B. States and Counties — **Personal Income**

STATE County	Personal income, 2014										Earnings, 2014		
			Per capita[1]			Supplements to wages and salaries; employer contributions (mil dol)						Contributions for government social insurance (mil dol)	
	Total (mil dol)	Percent change, 2013–2014	Dollars	Rank	Wages and salaries (mil dol)	Pension and insurance	Government social insurance	Proprietors' income (mil dol)	Dividends, interest, and rent (mil dol)	Personal transfer receipts (mil dol)	Total (mil dol)	From employee and self-employed	From employer
	62	63	64	65	66	67	68	69	70	71	72	73	74

IDAHO—Cont'd

STATE County	62	63	64	65	66	67	68	69	70	71	72	73	74
Caribou	263	3.0	38 507	1 392	181	31	15	27	48	46	254	15	15
Cassia	977	4.0	41 492	1 010	375	58	34	330	138	145	797	32	34
Clark	21	-21.9	23 832	3 084	17	3	1	1	5	4	23	1	1
Clearwater	278	2.4	32 487	2 374	105	23	10	21	58	87	158	12	10
Custer	179	3.3	43 158	829	65	12	6	20	50	33	103	6	6
Elmore	885	4.5	33 907	2 128	433	111	42	82	242	173	668	30	42
Franklin	390	6.4	29 941	2 724	102	21	9	49	58	73	182	10	9
Fremont	411	-1.1	31 964	2 441	107	22	10	74	87	84	213	11	10
Gem	522	4.4	30 937	2 595	108	20	11	22	124	147	161	14	11
Gooding	861	19.0	57 168	168	222	35	19	395	97	108	671	16	19
Idaho	516	4.3	31 804	2 469	167	33	15	61	128	136	277	19	15
Jefferson	814	3.0	30 142	2 700	196	36	18	125	118	144	375	21	18
Jerome	849	9.5	37 198	1 571	324	47	29	278	103	136	679	27	29
Kootenai	5 400	5.0	36 656	1 656	2 060	332	191	367	1 135	1 143	2 950	204	191
Latah	1 315	2.2	34 244	2 072	494	125	44	81	296	211	743	45	44
Lemhi	280	5.2	36 210	1 743	79	17	7	27	87	75	131	9	7
Lewis	162	-7.3	42 219	932	54	10	5	20	29	56	89	6	5
Lincoln	201	10.6	37 734	1 492	58	11	5	70	24	32	145	5	5
Madison	828	1.8	21 779	3 104	459	77	42	90	133	200	668	40	42
Minidoka	687	0.8	33 795	2 147	269	43	24	99	122	136	435	23	24
Nez Perce	1 470	2.7	36 744	1 639	849	131	74	101	290	351	1 155	78	74
Oneida	129	0.7	30 802	2 615	33	8	3	12	23	32	55	4	3
Owyhee	360	8.8	31 741	2 482	97	17	8	79	68	77	201	8	8
Payette	772	4.8	33 802	2 146	231	37	22	112	133	175	402	24	22
Power	249	-6.6	32 654	2 345	153	26	13	37	42	50	229	11	13
Shoshone	417	0.3	33 665	2 165	197	29	17	18	76	129	261	19	17
Teton	297	3.4	28 763	2 851	101	15	9	33	81	43	158	10	9
Twin Falls	2 795	5.0	34 545	2 015	1 227	185	113	412	508	588	1 936	115	113
Valley	417	5.0	42 397	913	140	25	13	34	153	73	212	14	13
Washington	339	1.5	33 870	2 136	90	18	9	37	68	88	155	10	9
ILLINOIS	613 672	2.4	47 643	X	333 471	53 031	23 427	47 228	113 222	94 498	457 157	25 523	23 427
Adams	2 632	0.6	39 285	1 284	1 389	255	102	173	479	560	1 918	111	102
Alexander	215	1.0	28 746	2 855	76	21	5	15	29	91	117	6	5
Bond	569	3.1	32 967	2 285	189	47	14	51	100	137	301	18	14
Boone	2 121	1.9	39 377	1 267	798	138	66	71	290	345	1 074	64	66
Brown	182	-8.0	26 648	3 002	171	31	12	13	33	39	226	12	12
Bureau	1 305	-5.5	38 576	1 381	497	96	37	97	238	275	728	43	37
Calhoun	177	1.8	35 708	1 824	26	7	2	10	32	43	45	3	2
Carroll	582	-4.7	39 543	1 242	157	35	12	33	122	144	236	16	12
Cass	486	-3.1	36 951	1 606	223	49	17	61	69	102	350	18	17
Champaign	7 878	3.5	38 035	1 448	4 589	1 135	288	424	1 573	1 076	6 436	297	288
Christian	1 238	-4.1	36 538	1 681	420	88	31	118	221	307	658	38	31
Clark	637	0.4	39 340	1 275	176	40	13	98	102	137	328	18	13
Clay	492	-4.6	36 386	1 707	196	45	15	48	78	142	304	18	15
Clinton	1 572	2.0	41 527	1 005	409	90	30	180	250	274	708	37	30
Coles	1 819	-0.2	34 122	2 096	1 009	236	71	98	348	393	1 413	72	71
Cook	269 036	3.2	51 280	320	164 129	23 782	11 387	26 842	53 133	41 626	226 140	12 658	11 387
Crawford	760	0.8	39 166	1 303	372	107	26	81	131	156	586	31	26
Cumberland	426	-5.2	39 324	1 280	93	20	7	55	59	85	174	10	7
DeKalb	3 657	1.0	34 679	1 986	1 626	404	109	161	644	605	2 300	115	109
De Witt	679	-5.9	41 688	983	288	60	19	73	103	135	440	24	19
Douglas	864	-1.2	43 450	800	344	65	26	129	138	143	565	31	26
DuPage	56 601	3.5	60 684	122	38 780	5 142	2 790	4 109	10 698	5 467	50 821	2 838	2 790
Edgar	697	-6.1	39 045	1 314	266	55	21	71	110	166	413	23	21
Edwards	217	-8.5	32 867	2 305	94	19	7	16	45	52	136	9	7
Effingham	1 492	3.5	43 462	799	819	142	63	157	298	256	1 181	65	63
Fayette	653	-6.2	29 836	2 739	183	43	13	71	114	173	310	18	13
Ford	651	-4.2	47 595	493	186	40	13	151	93	113	390	18	13
Franklin	1 289	0.4	32 715	2 330	325	73	25	81	196	405	504	35	25
Fulton	1 195	-2.3	33 186	2 246	294	75	20	56	191	318	444	29	20
Gallatin	226	-12.4	42 743	877	46	10	3	49	39	56	108	5	3
Greene	464	-4.6	34 521	2 021	92	22	6	55	67	116	174	10	6
Grundy	2 162	0.3	42 868	862	1 010	194	71	152	288	301	1 426	78	71
Hamilton	339	-7.8	40 904	1 072	92	18	6	52	57	79	169	9	6
Hancock	767	0.9	41 294	1 028	143	36	10	123	118	164	312	16	10

1. Based on the resident population estimated as of July 1 of the year shown.

Table B. States and Counties — Earnings, Social Security, and Housing

STATE County	Earnings, 2014 (cont.) Percent by selected industries									Social Security beneficiaries, December 2014		Supplemental Security Income recipients, December 2014	Housing units, 2015	
	Farm	Mining	Construction	Manufacturing	Information: professional, scientific, technical services	Retail trade	Finance, insurance, real estate and leasing	Health care and social assistance	Government	Number	Rate[1]		Total	Percent change, 2010–2014
	75	76	77	78	79	80	81	82	83	84	85	86	87	88
IDAHO—Cont'd														
Caribou	9.4	D	10.1	33.2	D	3.0	D	1.3	13.4	1 390	204	70	3 216	-0.3
Cassia	39.8	1.0	3.7	9.0	D	6.1	2.2	7.1	9.3	3 905	166	412	8 454	1.0
Clark	14.3	0.0	D	D	D	D	3.7	D	27.1	135	154	10	533	0.4
Clearwater	1.5	D	6.1	3.7	3.3	5.8	2.5	D	34.6	2 735	321	247	4 482	0.7
Custer	13.1	D	4.4	D	4.7	5.1	1.4	D	22.3	1 130	273	61	3 081	-0.7
Elmore	11.7	0.0	1.9	3.1	1.6	4.8	1.8	6.3	57.8	4 235	161	511	12 218	0.5
Franklin	22.8	D	7.7	5.7	D	8.8	2.4	D	22.3	2 235	172	167	4 676	3.3
Fremont	31.1	D	9.5	0.6	1.5	4.8	1.9	2.6	25.4	2 455	191	169	8 692	1.9
Gem	4.3	D	8.3	3.3	2.8	9.1	3.5	17.2	26.2	4 605	275	461	7 118	0.3
Gooding	67.2	0.0	1.6	6.9	D	1.7	D	D	7.6	3 040	201	288	6 053	-0.7
Idaho	8.1	1.6	8.9	7.0	2.7	9.2	4.9	8.5	27.3	4 680	289	372	8 624	-1.4
Jefferson	18.9	0.1	10.3	14.2	1.7	8.2	2.7	D	14.6	4 045	150	292	8 931	2.4
Jerome	39.7	0.0	2.7	12.0	2.2	5.6	1.3	3.7	7.3	3 595	158	391	8 270	2.1
Kootenai	0.1	1.0	8.1	8.9	6.8	10.8	6.8	12.6	21.8	34 135	232	2 647	67 028	6.1
Latah	1.8	D	4.2	2.7	6.7	7.5	2.9	9.3	46.9	5 465	142	455	16 421	2.7
Lemhi	10.0	D	10.5	2.5	D	8.8	2.1	D	36.1	2 570	333	199	4 743	0.3
Lewis	18.7	D	3.1	15.9	3.4	5.3	3.1	4.8	23.0	1 490	390	244	1 872	-0.4
Lincoln	55.0	0.0	D	D	D	2.1	D	3.8	16.4	850	160	75	1 954	-1.1
Madison	2.2	D	4.8	5.6	6.5	8.4	3.6	D	15.2	2 935	77	273	13 306	18.0
Minidoka	24.5	0.0	4.6	16.4	3.0	4.0	1.7	2.5	15.3	4 120	203	388	7 796	1.7
Nez Perce	-0.2	D	4.6	21.3	4.2	7.8	8.3	17.0	19.3	10 510	263	1 051	17 427	-0.1
Oneida	8.9	D	D	1.6	2.5	D	6.8	3.0	30.3	1 010	240	57	1 948	2.2
Owyhee	49.4	2.5	3.4	4.3	D	3.1	D	D	14.5	2 190	194	258	4 768	-0.3
Payette	20.3	D	3.9	13.2	D	4.0	5.5	D	12.5	5 360	235	552	9 151	2.3
Power	24.0	0.0	1.5	32.7	D	2.3	D	D	13.0	1 370	178	109	2 934	-0.3
Shoshone	-0.1	28.0	6.2	2.2	4.8	19.0	2.1	5.3	18.6	3 795	306	456	6 962	-1.4
Teton	3.7	0.0	16.9	2.6	10.2	7.3	6.0	8.3	15.2	1 165	113	55	5 520	0.8
Twin Falls	12.0	D	3.7	13.9	6.2	8.9	4.3	14.8	12.0	15 445	190	1 813	32 052	3.2
Valley	1.2	D	10.1	0.6	4.9	10.5	8.9	11.2	27.9	2 465	251	117	11 981	1.6
Washington	21.7	0.0	3.4	13.6	6.0	5.8	2.2	D	23.1	2 820	282	262	4 546	0.4
ILLINOIS	0.9	0.3	4.9	11.2	13.7	5.2	10.0	10.1	14.4	2 155 290	167	275 671	5 317 383	0.4
Adams	2.7	1.0	4.7	18.1	4.2	8.1	7.7	17.2	12.4	15 305	228	1 363	29 994	0.5
Alexander	9.1	D	D	6.5	D	2.6	1.0	D	43.9	1 925	271	494	3 945	-1.5
Bond	7.3	1.3	4.2	18.2	3.0	3.3	3.0	D	24.8	3 790	221	335	7 087	0.0
Boone	0.7	D	7.1	49.1	2.8	4.6	2.6	3.8	12.4	9 765	182	510	19 949	-0.1
Brown	3.2	0.1	5.8	0.2	D	D	D	D	13.8	1 100	161	96	2 439	-0.9
Bureau	5.4	0.5	6.1	14.1	D	4.9	3.3	D	18.5	8 055	238	413	15 634	-0.5
Calhoun	11.9	D	5.4	1.4	D	7.6	D	D	32.6	1 255	253	81	2 839	0.1
Carroll	5.7	D	6.4	20.0	D	6.3	5.1	4.2	20.3	4 170	282	235	8 408	-0.3
Cass	13.5	0.0	3.0	D	D	4.1	4.0	D	14.3	2 595	198	251	5 770	-1.1
Champaign	1.8	D	4.0	7.0	8.5	4.7	4.5	13.3	40.3	26 460	128	3 053	90 478	3.3
Christian	9.8	0.5	4.5	15.6	4.8	7.1	3.8	D	16.6	8 400	248	695	15 520	-0.3
Clark	18.5	3.6	7.2	23.7	D	5.0	2.7	4.5	14.2	3 860	239	286	7 735	-0.5
Clay	4.2	5.5	2.5	32.9	D	5.1	3.6	D	18.6	3 510	261	340	6 348	-0.9
Clinton	15.0	D	11.7	6.2	3.1	8.0	D	10.0	20.9	7 105	188	285	15 588	1.8
Coles	2.7	0.4	4.1	12.0	D	5.6	3.6	16.1	29.4	9 940	189	1 119	23 408	-0.1
Cook	0.0	0.1	4.4	7.2	18.6	4.1	13.7	9.6	12.5	786 215	150	156 435	2 178 274	-0.1
Crawford	4.2	4.7	5.5	40.6	D	4.5	2.9	D	17.7	4 535	234	323	8 627	-0.4
Cumberland	18.1	D	4.0	15.2	D	9.0	D	8.0	16.9	2 535	232	174	4 832	-0.9
DeKalb	0.7	D	6.5	11.2	3.3	6.9	3.7	12.7	34.9	14 510	139	916	40 976	-0.3
De Witt	10.2	D	7.0	11.5	D	5.4	2.1	D	13.4	3 635	224	256	7 506	-0.2
Douglas	10.6	D	6.4	41.4	1.7	5.0	2.5	3.3	10.5	3 725	188	219	8 375	-0.2
DuPage	0.0	0.1	5.2	9.5	15.9	5.3	9.1	9.0	8.1	138 455	148	8 224	358 144	0.6
Edgar	11.6	D	3.5	30.7	2.5	4.5	7.7	D	15.3	4 510	253	427	8 772	-0.4
Edwards	1.1	4.2	D	D	D	3.9	D	2.1	11.2	1 645	248	81	3 152	-1.1
Effingham	4.8	D	7.4	17.9	D	8.7	3.6	17.2	9.9	7 610	222	505	14 724	1.1
Fayette	12.1	2.6	5.2	6.7	3.3	8.0	4.1	D	22.2	4 280	195	421	9 206	-1.0
Ford	23.9	D	3.1	9.0	2.0	7.7	2.2	D	11.6	3 025	221	198	6 330	0.8
Franklin	4.2	2.2	8.5	6.8	D	9.2	3.4	9.8	26.2	10 450	264	1 367	18 503	-1.1
Fulton	2.9	D	5.8	3.3	3.0	8.5	5.4	18.8	31.9	8 580	239	730	16 176	-0.1
Gallatin	33.6	D	5.6	0.8	D	5.1	D	D	13.0	1 540	290	216	2 722	-0.9
Greene	23.8	D	4.7	2.2	2.4	6.5	D	D	21.4	3 100	233	380	6 360	-0.5
Grundy	2.1	D	11.8	11.3	3.1	7.1	2.7	9.1	12.4	8 545	169	334	20 487	2.5
Hamilton	19.7	D	6.3	2.8	D	4.0	2.5	4.1	18.7	1 900	229	194	4 060	-1.1
Hancock	28.2	D	5.4	5.9	5.9	4.4	3.7	D	18.5	4 805	258	314	9 215	-0.6

1. Per 1,000 resident population estimated as of July 1 of the year shown.

Table B. States and Counties — Housing, Labor Force, and Employment

STATE County	Housing units, 2010–2014								Civilian labor force, 2015				Civilian employment,[6] 2010–2014		
	Occupied units										Unemployment			Percent	
			Owner-occupied			Renter-occupied									
				Median owner cost as a percent of income											
	Total	Percent	Median value[1]	With a mortgage	Without a mortgage[2]	Median rent[3]	Median rent as a percent of income[2]	Sub-standard units[4] (percent)	Total	Percent change, 2014–2015	Total	Rate[5]	Total	Management, business, science and arts	Construction, production, and maintenance occupations
	89	90	91	92	93	94	95	96	97	98	99	100	101	102	103
IDAHO—Cont'd															
Caribou	2 683	82.4	124 800	18.6	10.0	528	15.3	1.2	3 757	-2.6	157	4.2	3 070	31.7	34.8
Cassia	7 744	69.6	128 200	22.6	10.0	564	28.3	4.4	11 546	2.5	385	3.3	9 406	28.5	35.9
Clark	282	62.1	100 400	29.3	10.0	478	19.6	14.2	406	-8.6	15	3.7	385	19.2	42.3
Clearwater	3 560	78.6	131 200	24.7	11.9	629	24.2	1.4	3 108	-0.9	250	8.0	2 916	31.0	32.8
Custer	1 783	77.4	154 500	21.3	10.0	539	29.0	1.7	2 161	0.9	143	6.6	1 752	31.8	33.0
Elmore	9 682	61.0	131 200	23.2	10.7	732	26.0	4.2	10 918	-1.0	510	4.7	10 248	28.2	33.8
Franklin	4 241	80.3	159 200	25.5	12.4	636	24.2	3.3	6 556	2.2	202	3.1	5 247	23.9	37.2
Fremont	4 539	81.0	150 100	23.2	10.8	649	30.1	5.2	7 237	3.5	257	3.6	5 477	28.4	31.7
Gem	6 400	72.8	141 900	23.1	11.0	775	32.6	1.8	7 661	1.8	391	5.1	6 240	30.9	23.8
Gooding	5 433	68.9	119 000	24.4	10.0	735	33.2	8.1	8 038	0.6	273	3.4	6 488	26.3	44.3
Idaho	6 523	79.8	151 600	26.1	11.1	602	24.4	3.2	6 407	-1.4	391	6.1	6 410	27.3	32.9
Jefferson	8 175	84.1	155 700	23.7	10.0	673	24.1	3.4	12 610	2.7	425	3.4	11 154	32.3	30.9
Jerome	7 686	63.5	138 300	25.2	11.1	681	28.2	7.4	11 613	4.3	378	3.3	9 419	24.8	40.6
Kootenai	55 807	70.2	184 200	24.5	10.5	823	30.5	3.5	71 896	1.8	3 582	5.0	62 920	30.9	23.1
Latah	15 069	54.5	189 100	21.1	10.0	655	35.8	2.1	19 481	0.8	676	3.5	18 422	40.9	17.5
Lemhi	3 868	70.3	174 800	23.9	10.0	541	35.2	3.1	3 381	0.4	235	7.0	3 382	31.5	27.0
Lewis	1 657	73.3	114 800	21.9	12.2	573	29.6	3.1	1 619	1.3	97	6.0	1 561	32.0	26.5
Lincoln	1 608	73.0	112 100	22.6	13.0	716	26.4	7.2	2 663	2.1	118	4.4	2 200	19.7	39.6
Madison	10 376	48.4	174 400	23.4	10.0	640	42.1	8.9	19 805	3.9	538	2.7	16 029	37.8	17.5
Minidoka	7 104	72.8	109 000	19.5	10.0	561	23.1	5.2	10 709	2.7	392	3.7	8 944	21.6	41.6
Nez Perce	16 159	69.3	166 000	22.8	11.5	667	27.1	2.2	20 746	1.8	765	3.7	18 919	29.8	25.9
Oneida	1 657	83.6	130 600	27.4	12.8	529	25.6	3.4	2 132	0.5	75	3.5	1 834	26.9	36.2
Owyhee	3 888	65.4	123 200	26.3	10.3	587	25.9	8.1	5 304	5.4	246	4.6	4 176	23.8	46.9
Payette	8 218	75.4	128 200	25.9	11.1	687	28.9	2.7	11 160	1.6	551	4.9	9 122	25.8	29.1
Power	2 543	66.8	130 300	25.7	10.0	722	20.1	6.8	3 906	-2.0	180	4.6	3 190	24.0	43.2
Shoshone	5 796	67.8	117 500	22.1	11.6	604	27.9	3.5	5 169	-0.9	399	7.7	4 640	26.9	30.2
Teton	3 558	71.2	220 700	29.4	11.1	852	28.9	3.2	5 805	3.1	199	3.4	4 980	34.0	25.8
Twin Falls	28 581	66.5	150 400	24.2	10.0	703	29.0	3.9	39 617	3.4	1 429	3.6	35 163	27.8	29.7
Valley	3 240	76.8	207 200	26.8	11.0	692	28.7	2.7	4 773	4.5	291	6.1	4 398	32.2	23.0
Washington	3 897	73.0	132 200	26.7	10.3	619	35.7	4.1	4 562	-0.7	262	5.7	3 702	25.6	35.8
ILLINOIS	4 778 633	66.9	175 700	24.2	13.5	903	30.7	3.0	6 512 400	0.0	386 083	5.9	6 032 031	36.5	21.2
Adams	26 866	71.1	106 500	19.9	10.4	588	29.7	1.2	32 588	-0.4	1 641	5.0	32 337	28.7	26.9
Alexander	2 826	65.7	52 800	24.4	14.7	367	25.9	3.9	2 516	-1.7	216	8.6	2 488	19.5	25.5
Bond	6 230	75.8	106 500	21.8	12.4	631	26.7	2.0	7 944	0.4	423	5.3	7 329	28.4	27.2
Boone	18 162	82.6	150 900	24.1	12.8	720	28.5	2.9	26 362	-0.1	1 740	6.6	24 354	29.7	31.2
Brown	2 124	75.0	85 200	19.1	12.2	600	22.8	2.8	2 753	0.4	102	3.7	2 787	27.8	33.6
Bureau	14 111	75.1	102 000	20.7	12.6	635	26.5	1.2	17 113	-2.3	1 116	6.5	16 231	25.5	31.9
Calhoun	2 052	80.4	111 300	24.6	12.2	593	26.3	3.2	2 375	0.0	162	6.8	2 220	27.4	32.6
Carroll	6 531	77.7	97 000	20.7	11.8	560	28.6	1.6	7 973	1.3	439	5.5	7 013	28.3	34.9
Cass	5 205	72.1	75 700	19.3	10.7	602	25.6	2.7	6 522	1.1	372	5.7	6 067	24.2	39.4
Champaign	79 624	54.9	149 200	20.6	11.1	807	35.5	1.4	104 416	0.7	5 445	5.2	101 486	44.3	14.8
Christian	14 089	74.0	84 100	19.5	11.5	606	27.4	2.3	15 522	-1.9	1 031	6.6	15 414	27.1	28.1
Clark	6 689	74.9	88 100	19.3	13.2	607	25.1	1.6	8 119	1.7	508	6.3	7 586	31.9	30.6
Clay	5 410	80.0	76 000	20.1	12.2	508	21.9	2.9	6 662	3.2	472	7.1	6 201	25.3	37.2
Clinton	13 944	82.7	130 700	19.7	11.7	735	23.9	1.5	20 159	0.8	914	4.5	19 096	31.5	27.5
Coles	21 017	61.5	90 400	20.5	12.4	627	35.1	1.1	24 298	-0.2	1 506	6.2	24 804	28.3	24.7
Cook	1 937 060	57.6	222 200	27.2	15.6	976	31.7	4.2	2 649 758	-0.1	161 588	6.1	2 433 661	37.9	19.2
Crawford	7 644	80.1	79 100	18.1	10.2	573	25.6	2.0	9 687	-0.8	577	6.0	8 438	26.7	35.4
Cumberland	4 230	80.7	87 100	19.7	11.7	510	23.5	2.6	5 900	0.4	316	5.4	4 935	27.5	35.0
DeKalb	37 374	59.6	169 100	25.0	14.5	846	34.3	2.5	55 407	0.6	3 111	5.6	52 099	33.0	21.9
De Witt	6 746	78.5	107 000	19.5	11.3	580	25.8	0.9	7 926	-0.3	441	5.6	8 028	26.0	26.8
Douglas	7 534	76.4	99 100	21.2	10.6	677	25.1	2.8	10 051	1.7	500	5.0	9 535	26.9	32.6
DuPage	337 003	73.8	279 700	25.0	14.3	1 127	29.0	2.6	511 043	0.2	23 840	4.7	474 601	44.3	15.9
Edgar	7 912	74.0	75 700	19.0	11.4	601	31.2	1.0	9 400	2.7	601	6.4	7 795	26.0	34.1
Edwards	2 747	82.5	64 300	20.4	10.0	477	26.6	0.9	2 940	2.9	176	6.0	2 841	21.2	41.3
Effingham	13 386	79.2	118 400	20.0	11.0	579	22.0	1.1	18 519	0.5	899	4.9	17 280	28.0	28.8
Fayette	7 981	80.4	81 700	19.7	10.4	549	24.7	2.2	9 763	0.0	633	6.5	9 163	25.0	32.6
Ford	5 611	75.3	91 000	19.3	12.3	581	23.8	1.9	6 521	0.8	355	5.4	6 197	29.0	30.9
Franklin	16 243	74.5	65 300	20.1	11.9	578	27.9	2.0	16 459	-1.3	1 349	8.2	15 316	25.3	31.3
Fulton	14 501	75.4	81 300	19.0	12.5	613	29.2	1.2	15 816	0.1	1 218	7.7	15 161	29.0	29.6
Gallatin	2 351	78.5	63 800	18.5	11.2	424	27.4	2.3	2 466	-0.3	169	6.9	2 248	31.7	30.2
Greene	5 689	76.6	74 600	19.4	11.7	583	24.5	2.4	6 102	-1.5	378	6.2	6 136	27.9	34.6
Grundy	18 408	75.0	178 800	24.1	12.8	941	29.8	2.6	25 400	-0.6	1 735	6.8	23 505	30.0	28.8
Hamilton	3 499	78.3	77 000	17.9	11.5	546	28.6	1.8	4 543	4.7	241	5.3	3 529	25.8	33.0
Hancock	7 983	78.8	84 000	19.3	11.5	547	22.8	1.6	8 812	-1.1	564	6.4	8 701	27.5	30.9

1. Specified owner-occupied units. 2. A value of 10.0 represents 10 percent or less; a value of 50.0 represents 50 percent or more. 3. Specified renter-occupied units.
4. Overcrowded or lacking complete plumbing facilities. 5. Percent of civilian labor force. 6. Persons 16 years old and over.

Table B. States and Counties — Nonfarm Employment and Agriculture

	Private nonfarm establishments, employment and payroll, 2014								Agriculture, 2012			
		Employment					Annual payroll		Farms			
										Percent with:		
STATE County	Number of establishments	Total	Health care and social assistance	Manufacturing	Retail trade	Finance and insurance	Professional, scientific, and technical services	Total (mil dol)	Average per employee (dollars)	Number	Fewer than 50 acres	500 acres or more	Farm operators whose principal occupation is farming (percent)
	104	105	106	107	108	109	110	111	112	113	114	115	116
IDAHO—Cont'd													
Caribou	190	2 687	235	837	230	D	D	173	64 311	436	19.3	40.4	55.3
Cassia	639	7 469	1 256	1 268	1 495	232	175	233	31 148	668	42.7	27.1	56.1
Clark	14	82	NA	D	35	D	D	2	27 573	72	12.5	41.7	61.1
Clearwater	226	1 864	519	309	D	43	41	64	34 490	256	35.5	11.7	34.8
Custer	162	880	D	D	171	23	D	40	45 582	272	36.4	23.9	52.9
Elmore	435	4 291	776	D	1 096	161	D	108	25 180	349	53.9	21.2	47.6
Franklin	271	1 980	D	306	502	74	48	56	28 484	834	40.0	19.2	43.5
Fremont	278	1 494	173	54	253	D	D	48	32 284	601	33.8	22.1	52.2
Gem	351	2 299	787	93	455	D	63	62	27 180	830	68.1	7.3	48.3
Gooding	348	2 613	510	475	364	75	69	85	32 348	596	53.4	14.1	52.0
Idaho	473	3 370	671	D	464	187	167	121	35 907	731	24.5	33.0	51.8
Jefferson	453	3 930	333	D	476	78	D	119	30 279	776	53.5	16.8	43.9
Jerome	545	5 871	489	1 282	857	101	107	227	38 670	560	46.3	15.4	63.2
Kootenai	4 366	46 988	9 025	4 980	8 612	2 091	2 914	1 660	35 334	824	58.4	6.7	48.1
Latah	895	8 294	1 309	311	1 865	254	501	233	28 147	1 053	30.6	15.9	43.3
Lemhi	295	1 681	504	D	348	34	60	46	27 475	350	46.6	20.0	48.6
Lewis	117	764	D	D	165	26	D	21	27 619	216	13.9	44.9	54.6
Lincoln	86	563	89	D	D	D	D	20	35 837	310	27.1	23.5	57.7
Madison	776	14 737	1 370	971	1 959	D	426	344	23 313	472	48.3	19.7	46.2
Minidoka	398	4 406	491	926	481	83	95	169	38 305	622	51.1	14.0	56.6
Nez Perce	1 106	16 724	2 975	3 698	2 540	1 227	544	620	37 077	430	41.4	30.0	52.1
Oneida	84	712	D	D	153	D	D	20	27 758	503	28.2	27.8	45.5
Owyhee	184	1 525	194	149	185	D	D	49	32 396	578	41.0	26.6	67.6
Payette	496	4 642	639	1 257	479	214	141	146	31 535	655	65.8	6.6	52.1
Power	155	2 217	175	D	D	D	D	82	36 811	308	24.4	50.3	63.3
Shoshone	345	3 993	494	144	D	73	171	181	45 209	36	61.1	0.0	33.3
Teton	442	2 065	D	D	282	55	107	80	38 669	291	30.2	21.3	42.3
Twin Falls	2 497	29 530	6 120	3 503	5 008	933	1 451	889	30 113	1 294	42.9	13.4	55.3
Valley	563	3 081	443	67	465	85	D	90	29 216	117	35.9	22.2	47.0
Washington	215	1 804	D	464	285	45	57	50	27 849	559	42.4	20.9	54.4
ILLINOIS	316 120	5 312 290	787 928	544 488	605 655	328 292	419 062	273 438	51 473	75 087	34.1	20.4	50.4
Adams	1 795	30 389	5 509	5 119	4 902	1 753	745	1 170	38 488	1 298	28.2	18.3	44.5
Alexander	96	1 075	230	D	118	D	D	38	35 695	144	25.0	19.4	56.9
Bond	304	3 749	541	D	356	117	86	119	31 662	661	39.2	16.5	46.1
Boone	838	14 682	910	8 198	1 351	246	473	647	44 061	479	49.9	15.7	53.0
Brown	121	3 126	D	D	139	D	D	131	41 765	413	23.2	16.7	41.2
Bureau	756	9 639	2 147	1 652	1 066	328	D	373	38 709	1 056	26.1	26.1	55.8
Calhoun	87	590	108	D	94	70	D	13	21 997	478	30.5	10.0	39.3
Carroll	403	3 434	464	891	467	186	56	118	34 439	643	26.7	22.4	56.9
Cass	239	4 391	364	D	468	D	73	156	35 565	446	29.6	24.2	48.2
Champaign	4 135	68 541	D	7 149	10 584	2 934	2 881	2 626	38 320	1 312	29.3	30.6	57.7
Christian	723	8 930	1 750	999	1 375	333	561	291	32 612	816	34.1	27.2	51.6
Clark	333	4 039	335	D	454	156	D	155	38 489	677	34.0	21.4	47.6
Clay	362	4 685	592	1 981	463	156	94	168	35 815	774	35.4	18.7	49.6
Clinton	855	8 652	1 741	762	1 611	298	180	263	30 349	915	29.0	16.3	47.9
Coles	1 175	17 592	4 376	2 657	2 670	561	405	620	35 226	704	37.2	23.2	56.7
Cook	130 833	2 335 270	368 366	179 201	230 565	182 350	217 854	134 276	57 499	127	81.1	3.9	44.1
Crawford	424	6 568	843	1 772	672	229	D	282	42 882	599	32.4	18.9	51.3
Cumberland	180	2 063	578	D	174	D	23	54	26 047	733	40.5	13.5	38.5
DeKalb	1 921	25 404	5 057	3 426	4 342	928	645	951	37 434	880	32.7	26.9	61.1
De Witt	382	4 459	555	529	693	D	91	217	48 563	511	42.3	24.7	55.4
Douglas	588	6 504	D	2 452	1 221	193	D	250	38 372	735	40.7	21.1	54.8
DuPage	33 668	595 352	66 403	53 722	60 072	31 908	44 270	33 552	56 356	74	82.4	2.7	35.1
Edgar	347	5 957	825	2 490	625	252	D	236	39 638	673	27.3	31.1	54.4
Edwards	140	1 880	101	D	208	66	D	72	38 488	365	41.4	16.4	39.7
Effingham	1 193	23 157	2 689	3 229	2 826	461	331	846	36 554	1 302	37.6	12.5	47.2
Fayette	469	4 654	927	324	871	218	134	125	26 895	1 240	39.2	12.6	42.7
Ford	378	4 270	1 107	681	518	D	129	142	33 157	546	26.4	35.7	53.5
Franklin	743	6 907	1 276	553	1 487	269	245	221	31 992	711	42.9	10.4	38.8
Fulton	647	6 162	1 812	172	1 357	344	191	183	29 746	970	29.7	20.2	53.1
Gallatin	101	896	103	14	67	D	D	43	47 895	203	24.1	36.0	56.2
Greene	251	1 735	364	93	410	143	D	54	31 282	689	30.2	22.9	52.8
Grundy	1 060	14 994	2 148	1 275	1 834	415	380	841	56 058	431	23.2	29.5	63.8
Hamilton	202	1 509	414	77	164	47	36	65	43 097	695	37.6	12.5	25.6
Hancock	392	2 906	517	D	446	D	154	101	34 811	1 090	28.4	21.5	50.0

Table B. States and Counties — **Agriculture**

STATE County	Acreage (1,000) [117]	Percent change, 2007–2012 [118]	Average size of farm [119]	Total irrigated (1,000) [120]	Total cropland (1,000) [121]	Average per farm [122]	Average per acre [123]	Value of machinery and equipment, average per farm (dollars) [124]	Total (mil dol) [125]	Average per farm (dollars) [126]	Crops [127]	Live-stock and poultry products [128]	$10,000 or more [129]	$100,000 or more [130]	Total ($1,000) [131]	Percent of farms [132]
IDAHO—Cont'd																
Caribou	395	-6.4	905	66.0	215.4	1 267 638	1 401	196 009	88.0	201 934	76.8	23.2	51.6	27.3	4 068	62.8
Cassia	611	-5.2	915	237.8	333.8	2 143 115	2 343	350 045	953.7	1 427 737	27.0	73.0	58.5	37.3	5 934	43.9
Clark	151	-4.2	2 101	29.2	52.5	3 059 583	1 456	304 333	35.2	488 792	75.1	24.9	66.7	38.9	572	56.9
Clearwater	73	4.4	284	0.2	28.9	534 063	1 883	59 699	9.7	38 078	74.6	25.4	25.8	6.3	797	43.0
Custer	143	15.0	525	51.6	44.4	1 208 224	2 302	107 033	26.2	96 471	33.6	66.4	50.4	22.8	588	23.2
Elmore	345	-0.5	988	89.9	117.9	2 021 562	2 046	204 605	350.6	1 004 536	26.9	73.1	41.0	21.5	838	20.9
Franklin	263	16.8	315	61.2	140.8	632 061	2 007	117 307	106.1	127 228	23.1	76.9	45.1	18.5	3 420	48.7
Fremont	316	9.8	526	124.8	207.8	1 175 121	2 233	216 087	158.6	263 942	89.5	10.5	47.4	24.0	3 473	52.1
Gem	179	-6.2	216	34.2	31.7	595 434	2 761	57 441	42.4	51 031	39.1	60.9	34.5	9.3	517	19.9
Gooding	240	7.4	402	142.0	150.7	1 539 908	3 830	272 973	942.8	1 581 904	10.7	89.3	59.9	33.7	1 873	29.0
Idaho	639	8.2	874	5.0	209.8	1 219 897	1 395	99 766	80.8	110 564	77.4	22.6	47.2	23.1	5 658	50.5
Jefferson	323	-0.8	416	175.3	191.1	1 089 749	2 620	162 642	257.2	331 387	57.8	42.2	51.3	25.4	2 332	41.0
Jerome	188	-0.4	336	149.0	148.9	1 289 525	3 840	304 766	617.1	1 101 943	23.5	76.5	65.9	36.4	1 880	47.3
Kootenai	124	-5.1	151	13.8	64.3	624 138	4 139	57 726	23.7	28 750	83.8	16.2	19.5	4.1	1 075	20.1
Latah	416	20.9	396	0.5	254.2	713 039	1 803	102 611	87.9	83 435	94.5	5.5	26.7	12.6	8 001	69.0
Lemhi	187	-1.2	535	56.7	49.7	1 189 800	2 222	89 217	32.2	91 863	15.1	84.9	44.6	20.0	533	12.6
Lewis	221	-10.0	1 024	D	158.7	1 437 389	1 403	201 764	62.5	289 292	95.4	4.6	57.4	40.7	3 763	80.6
Lincoln	130	10.5	418	71.4	72.6	1 098 352	2 625	208 332	175.6	566 510	21.8	78.2	64.2	33.2	1 703	44.2
Madison	201	-4.4	427	122.3	167.4	1 413 886	3 314	232 362	131.1	277 694	94.2	5.8	54.0	26.9	2 678	49.4
Minidoka	244	7.9	392	204.5	217.4	1 360 826	3 468	253 349	368.9	593 125	72.6	27.4	57.2	33.9	2 782	52.6
Nez Perce	322	-8.8	749	0.8	181.4	1 261 165	1 683	150 307	81.2	188 777	89.0	11.0	46.0	26.3	5 030	56.0
Oneida	329	4.7	653	34.1	175.7	775 891	1 187	106 209	32.5	64 545	58.1	41.9	42.5	12.1	3 972	66.4
Owyhee	749	31.5	1 295	133.5	140.7	1 590 689	1 228	183 332	291.6	504 424	32.2	67.8	66.8	36.7	2 041	40.1
Payette	157	-5.5	240	56.9	51.6	724 612	3 021	117 252	236.2	360 676	21.3	78.7	43.4	16.9	652	22.1
Power	467	3.5	1 517	120.9	361.7	2 293 497	1 512	378 549	238.3	773 747	85.4	14.6	48.7	31.5	6 836	67.9
Shoshone	D	D	D	D	0.8	387 167	D	43 778	0.1	3 944	32.4	66.9	11.1	0.0	D	2.8
Teton	133	8.8	458	56.4	87.6	1 506 742	3 292	137 058	35.8	123 086	83.9	16.1	44.0	18.6	1 206	44.0
Twin Falls	484	10.1	374	257.0	275.1	1 155 801	3 090	159 620	599.6	463 355	36.0	64.0	63.3	36.9	3 657	48.1
Valley	61	-1.3	524	26.2	8.8	1 294 667	2 473	72 564	6.6	56 675	18.2	81.8	36.8	11.1	62	12.8
Washington	426	2.3	763	42.7	79.5	762 163	999	96 005	75.3	134 664	49.1	50.9	48.3	20.4	1 036	39.9
ILLINOIS	26 938	0.6	359	522.5	23 752.8	2 261 778	6 305	203 184	17 187.1	228 895	82.3	17.7	54.5	33.0	553 300	75.0
Adams	389	3.9	299	2.3	294.2	1 479 562	4 940	147 340	174.0	134 044	74.9	25.1	55.5	27.4	7 898	73.2
Alexander	62	31.1	434	5.0	51.8	1 433 333	3 306	145 569	25.7	178 771	97.9	2.1	39.6	20.8	778	66.0
Bond	198	-11.8	300	0.0	176.7	1 941 345	6 470	174 467	66.0	99 800	82.0	18.0	46.3	24.5	3 940	74.7
Boone	135	-1.8	281	0.9	126.9	1 926 883	6 849	204 127	99.0	206 676	89.1	10.9	56.8	35.5	3 391	51.4
Brown	138	-9.0	333	0.4	85.5	1 327 644	3 987	105 603	42.0	101 717	79.4	20.6	40.2	20.1	3 102	87.9
Bureau	450	-5.9	426	10.6	410.8	3 125 461	7 332	246 925	420.2	397 908	89.9	10.1	68.7	49.0	8 943	80.8
Calhoun	88	-0.2	184	0.0	48.5	697 808	3 801	80 816	23.7	49 513	83.1	16.9	35.8	11.1	2 053	76.4
Carroll	256	-3.4	398	11.3	218.8	2 723 677	6 838	250 918	270.7	421 009	69.6	30.4	57.5	43.7	6 884	81.3
Cass	183	5.3	410	21.3	151.1	2 290 363	5 592	209 209	123.7	277 296	77.8	22.2	53.1	29.8	3 866	80.5
Champaign	616	12.0	470	17.9	591.1	3 740 816	7 961	294 914	424.2	323 295	94.5	5.5	73.5	50.7	11 068	84.7
Christian	374	-16.9	458	D	352.7	3 469 135	7 576	240 299	288.7	353 750	90.6	9.4	60.2	44.2	5 962	79.0
Clark	267	11.8	394	6.6	230.3	1 935 795	4 912	234 895	130.8	193 163	69.9	30.1	47.1	25.1	6 033	79.8
Clay	270	28.8	349	0.1	235.2	1 663 978	4 764	148 499	66.7	86 142	81.2	18.8	38.6	19.3	6 246	85.5
Clinton	285	6.4	312	1.9	259.6	1 824 631	5 848	228 694	206.0	225 184	42.9	57.1	62.4	33.1	5 669	81.5
Coles	267	4.7	379	0.0	245.9	2 671 436	7 050	235 723	136.0	193 229	96.3	3.7	54.5	34.8	4 927	77.6
Cook	8	3.7	67	0.4	7.5	700 701	10 471	76 598	10.7	84 150	79.4	20.6	51.2	18.1	104	15.0
Crawford	215	4.7	359	8.3	186.7	1 793 496	4 997	228 519	65.9	110 018	86.3	13.7	43.4	22.7	6 248	85.1
Cumberland	170	17.4	232	0.1	143.5	1 262 847	5 440	150 681	89.1	121 583	68.5	31.5	41.9	21.4	4 423	84.2
DeKalb	398	7.3	452	3.3	383.5	3 549 751	7 853	289 255	474.9	539 677	70.8	29.2	70.2	55.3	11 835	76.1
De Witt	196	-1.6	383	0.1	182.6	2 749 990	7 188	228 883	154.9	303 139	89.0	11.0	53.8	36.6	3 265	73.6
Douglas	263	0.5	358	0.3	247.8	2 721 101	7 609	214 850	166.7	226 789	85.4	14.6	61.6	40.5	4 948	63.8
DuPage	7	-8.8	98	0.1	5.9	680 851	6 947	82 162	10.0	135 514	95.3	4.7	37.8	14.9	80	14.9
Edgar	352	-0.2	523	D	326.3	3 432 028	6 568	287 382	205.1	304 807	D	D	62.3	42.9	6 450	83.2
Edwards	107	-8.5	292	D	88.1	1 176 600	4 024	173 096	33.7	92 282	85.7	14.3	39.7	18.4	2 276	80.8
Effingham	287	18.6	220	1.7	241.9	1 277 618	5 796	157 144	165.8	127 337	50.5	49.5	49.9	27.3	6 722	80.2
Fayette	303	0.0	244	0.3	248.2	1 089 291	4 456	131 927	97.4	78 521	86.1	13.9	40.0	18.8	5 615	73.7
Ford	308	13.8	564	0.8	298.0	4 278 846	7 581	312 397	191.7	351 125	82.5	17.5	74.4	50.0	5 740	85.3
Franklin	181	-12.8	255	0.1	152.7	946 098	3 709	113 533	55.8	78 457	73.0	27.0	27.3	12.8	3 330	66.5
Fulton	355	-7.9	366	2.1	266.4	1 921 065	5 249	166 037	212.1	218 637	71.7	28.3	53.8	28.9	6 943	67.1
Gallatin	186	0.3	917	25.9	170.3	4 030 990	4 394	455 074	90.1	443 606	98.8	1.2	69.5	40.9	2 545	83.3
Greene	290	6.2	421	8.8	233.4	2 373 734	5 637	220 164	186.2	270 305	77.0	23.0	55.7	32.4	6 005	74.0
Grundy	217	0.7	504	0.0	206.0	3 835 093	7 617	315 223	128.9	298 993	96.7	3.3	74.9	54.1	3 667	80.0
Hamilton	223	1.6	321	0.0	195.3	1 163 304	3 620	146 839	55.7	80 098	98.0	2.0	26.9	14.5	4 621	84.7
Hancock	386	-1.7	354	2.6	315.7	2 029 171	5 726	194 508	317.2	290 977	66.7	33.3	57.7	35.0	8 365	78.3

Table B. States and Counties — Water Use, Wholesale Trade, Retail Trade, and Real Estate

STATE County	Water use, 2010		Wholesale trade,[1] 2012				Retail trade,[2] 2012				Real estate and rental and leasing,[2] 2012			
	Total water withdrawn (mil gal/day)	Gallons withdrawn per person per day	Number of establishments	Number of employees	Sales (mil dol)	Annual payroll (mil dol)	Number of establishments	Number of employees	Sales (mil dol)	Annual payroll (mil dol)	Number of establishments	Number of employees	Receipts (mil dol)	Annual payroll (mil dol)
	133	134	135	136	137	138	139	140	141	142	143	144	145	146
IDAHO—Cont'd														
Caribou	307.9	44 221	12	88	134.6	3.5	33	279	79.2	7.4	4	5	0.7	0.1
Cassia	812.7	35 410	30	360	702.9	15.6	116	1 301	323.9	29.8	23	38	6.0	0.8
Clark	96.9	98 625	1	D	D	D	4	D	D	D	1	D	D	D
Clearwater	68.9	7 859	4	94	54.1	5.5	36	279	55.5	6.4	6	10	0.5	0.1
Custer	678.7	155 389	NA	NA	NA	NA	29	212	39.4	3.5	6	D	D	D
Elmore	362.8	13 418	13	83	36.5	3.0	76	974	256.3	22.2	13	28	3.7	0.5
Franklin	224.1	17 523	10	D	D	D	45	511	116.4	9.7	9	D	D	D
Fremont	358.7	27 087	8	195	114.5	5.8	33	241	73.4	6.8	6	7	1.2	0.2
Gem	468.3	28 011	12	D	D	D	43	412	93.6	8.8	9	23	2.6	0.4
Gooding	1 284.6	83 072	21	178	217.6	6.4	44	355	91.5	7.1	7	D	D	D
Idaho	24.4	1 500	11	101	54.1	4.0	57	455	94.8	11.1	10	17	2.1	0.4
Jefferson	1 405.3	53 760	25	D	D	D	44	464	116.4	10.0	11	D	D	D
Jerome	1 437.6	64 252	36	308	217.3	14.1	71	845	277.0	20.3	22	73	8.0	1.9
Kootenai	56.5	408	132	D	D	D	574	7 996	2 501.7	207.0	201	623	122.6	19.1
Latah	10.5	282	21	D	D	D	139	1 874	356.1	37.2	44	159	19.3	3.5
Lemhi	268.8	33 875	5	D	D	D	42	335	98.4	8.0	16	33	2.5	0.7
Lewis	1.5	390	5	D	D	D	23	133	26.5	2.5	5	13	1.2	0.2
Lincoln	281.4	54 038	NA	NA	NA	NA	12	D	D	D	3	D	D	D
Madison	481.2	12 820	37	533	221.2	15.5	118	1 607	370.7	34.2	56	174	25.1	3.2
Minidoka	629.2	31 352	46	661	430.9	27.8	62	418	157.9	9.3	12	37	6.1	1.2
Nez Perce	128.3	3 268	42	D	D	D	200	2 249	682.9	56.9	39	137	25.5	4.5
Oneida	177.0	41 295	1	D	D	D	18	142	30.4	2.3	4	15	1.0	0.1
Owyhee	811.3	70 386	6	D	D	D	24	169	42.6	3.9	4	9	0.2	0.0
Payette	242.0	10 697	21	203	113.5	6.0	61	483	136.4	10.7	21	26	3.8	0.6
Power	452.0	57 827	13	212	221.7	7.3	16	164	29.6	3.1	7	D	D	D
Shoshone	3.0	231	11	D	D	D	61	846	518.2	31.2	13	35	4.4	0.4
Teton	180.3	17 731	9	D	D	D	38	299	66.1	6.3	34	51	7.6	1.5
Twin Falls	1 462.0	18 930	111	1 096	492.8	42.6	380	4 789	1 233.5	112.8	112	313	49.7	8.5
Valley	71.3	7 228	10	65	20.0	2.2	69	462	105.9	10.3	38	58	10.0	1.4
Washington	203.2	19 924	9	194	26.4	3.6	33	276	83.7	6.5	11	27	2.3	0.4
ILLINOIS	13 091.3	1 020	16 036	255 531	295 457.0	15 973.3	39 947	592 942	166 634.5	14 576.1	12 035	76 794	23 649.1	3 816.1
Adams	19.4	289	120	D	D	D	299	4 790	1 066.5	101.4	61	D	D	D
Alexander	2.2	271	5	16	8.0	0.5	23	135	24.2	2.3	3	8	0.8	0.2
Bond	2.0	113	21	247	182.4	11.2	46	363	124.2	6.5	8	D	D	D
Boone	6.0	110	31	239	202.6	12.4	108	1 369	395.4	31.6	24	61	9.9	1.6
Brown	0.5	75	10	D	D	D	20	149	32.8	3.0	NA	NA	NA	NA
Bureau	6.0	173	53	896	1 472.5	39.3	97	1 166	299.8	23.2	16	D	D	D
Calhoun	0.5	104	5	D	D	D	15	116	27.3	2.5	1	D	D	D
Carroll	6.5	422	28	243	285.8	9.1	50	427	95.5	8.8	7	21	1.5	0.2
Cass	5.6	411	18	179	501.0	8.7	48	491	119.6	10.3	5	16	2.0	0.4
Champaign	32.3	161	176	2 872	2 589.6	126.5	626	10 256	2 472.7	220.2	201	2 986	557.4	117.9
Christian	838.9	24 107	45	605	845.6	30.5	111	1 377	410.3	31.4	20	94	12.9	2.7
Clark	5.6	345	19	191	257.9	6.0	51	445	141.7	10.9	5	22	4.4	0.7
Clay	1.3	94	26	196	172.8	6.8	46	464	113.3	8.9	7	49	3.9	0.9
Clinton	11.9	315	48	541	451.0	20.9	141	1 561	425.9	40.3	21	181	14.7	8.9
Coles	5.0	94	50	553	627.4	25.3	198	2 645	701.3	59.5	50	166	29.4	4.8
Cook	1 672.7	322	6 130	94 754	100 829.6	6 169.4	15 225	222 918	62 767.4	5 733.8	5 629	40 439	12 377.8	2 244.4
Crawford	69.2	3 493	19	181	179.3	6.2	61	796	187.1	16.2	14	D	D	D
Cumberland	1.4	125	16	153	188.2	5.0	24	188	38.6	2.9	1	D	D	D
DeKalb	10.4	99	60	586	353.2	27.1	280	4 404	1 052.7	91.7	69	447	100.2	14.2
De Witt	767.1	46 317	30	352	603.6	23.8	52	677	220.6	17.3	9	30	2.5	0.4
Douglas	3.0	150	30	329	478.1	16.6	120	1 173	218.7	19.1	12	38	8.3	1.0
DuPage	16.6	18	2 322	45 595	65 510.4	3 110.6	3 336	59 068	17 758.8	1 543.7	1 310	11 880	6 433.2	673.0
Edgar	4.3	232	13	148	227.4	9.4	51	623	157.0	13.6	9	30	4.6	0.9
Edwards	0.7	103	15	D	D	D	28	202	55.0	3.9	2	D	D	D
Effingham	4.5	130	62	D	D	D	203	2 977	934.7	66.1	43	214	32.0	7.0
Fayette	3.9	176	25	321	398.4	13.1	85	929	256.4	19.5	12	25	3.1	0.7
Ford	3.9	280	34	354	566.7	19.9	51	537	119.1	10.1	8	D	D	D
Franklin	15.3	388	34	265	126.3	13.3	143	1 549	408.1	35.0	15	69	6.4	1.6
Fulton	283.6	7 650	22	247	184.1	11.7	115	1 378	316.6	27.8	15	49	6.7	1.1
Gallatin	28.2	5 038	4	43	25.0	1.5	13	76	16.1	1.7	1	D	D	D
Greene	1.9	136	18	152	321.5	5.9	49	408	125.6	9.1	3	2	0.1	0.0
Grundy	501.9	10 026	47	490	738.0	27.1	144	1 744	524.7	38.1	28	71	15.7	2.4
Hamilton	0.7	84	8	81	64.5	3.2	34	161	45.4	3.4	7	15	1.3	0.3
Hancock	2.9	152	31	233	361.4	9.8	67	474	97.0	9.0	4	10	1.2	0.2

1. Merchant wholesalers, except manufacturers' sales branches and offices.   2. Employer establishments.

Professional Services, Manufacturing, and Accommodation and Food Services

STATE County	Professional, scientific, and technical services, 2012				Manufacturing, 2012				Accommodation and food services, 2012			
	Number of establishments	Number of employees	Receipts (mil dol)	Annual payroll (mil dol)	Number of establishments	Number of employees	Receipts (mil dol)	Annual payroll (mil dol)	Number of establishments	Number of employees	Sales (mil dol)	Annual payroll (mil dol)
	147	148	149	150	151	152	153	154	155	156	157	158
IDAHO—Cont'd												
Caribou	10	D	D	D	9	761	D	52.8	18	119	3.9	1.1
Cassia	49	146	12.1	4.1	31	1 345	917.1	53.3	51	D	D	D
Clark	2	D	D	D	3	D	D	0.3	1	D	D	D
Clearwater	11	46	2.4	1.1	21	251	D	8.5	27	175	6.5	2.1
Custer	8	D	D	D	5	D	D	D	31	D	D	D
Elmore	19	82	8.1	2.6	11	343	D	9.7	54	613	28.9	7.6
Franklin	17	51	6.2	1.5	19	247	39.9	8.7	16	204	5.6	1.6
Fremont	14	41	3.9	0.9	13	33	5.7	0.8	30	140	10.7	2.3
Gem	23	50	4.4	1.4	16	68	D	1.7	28	D	D	D
Gooding	21	D	D	D	23	405	D	20.5	30	183	7.3	1.9
Idaho	24	D	D	D	37	519	161.3	21.5	51	273	12.0	3.3
Jefferson	27	D	D	D	22	D	214.8	26.5	34	D	D	D
Jerome	25	113	13.4	3.8	24	1 301	D	52.9	30	329	16.7	4.0
Kootenai	442	D	D	D	241	4 011	D	170.2	362	D	D	D
Latah	80	D	D	D	26	277	D	12.3	121	D	D	D
Lemhi	19	62	3.1	1.2	9	60	12.2	1.5	35	223	10.3	2.5
Lewis	2	D	D	D	5	142	45.8	4.8	15	114	4.9	1.4
Lincoln	5	12	1.1	0.6	3	D	D	D	4	28	1.2	0.3
Madison	67	734	44.6	20.0	29	878	184.6	26.1	52	901	32.3	9.1
Minidoka	26	D	D	D	23	935	649.7	42.3	29	D	D	D
Nez Perce	80	D	D	D	35	2 791	1 124.5	133.9	99	2 096	108.5	30.1
Oneida	3	D	D	D	5	32	D	1.9	10	90	2.8	0.7
Owyhee	7	25	1.7	0.7	7	146	D	4.7	25	D	D	D
Payette	34	124	12.7	3.6	28	1 101	D	30.8	34	237	8.0	2.1
Power	8	D	D	D	7	D	D	D	12	52	2.2	0.5
Shoshone	27	D	D	D	16	182	D	7.4	42	D	D	D
Teton	39	103	11.1	3.8	9	76	D	2.6	37	257	15.0	5.0
Twin Falls	223	1 079	99.4	37.2	96	2 876	D	113.3	173	2 721	132.5	34.7
Valley	36	89	9.5	3.3	16	36	4.0	1.0	76	774	40.1	13.7
Washington	19	56	4.1	1.5	12	453	D	12.6	19	138	5.4	1.5
ILLINOIS	38 673	364 336	70 263.2	28 314.9	13 868	542 004	281 037.8	28 413.7	27 117	469 870	27 937.4	7 707.1
Adams	132	D	D	D	88	4 749	D	242.0	147	2 278	103.2	29.2
Alexander	7	37	1.7	0.8	4	145	D	6.2	14	61	2.2	0.7
Bond	25	D	D	D	16	838	419.8	37.4	33	332	14.9	3.8
Boone	59	639	57.0	29.4	78	7 619	5 906.2	404.0	69	796	41.8	10.6
Brown	6	26	2.0	0.7	5	138	36.3	5.9	11	D	D	D
Bureau	48	330	20.4	6.9	37	1 358	D	62.2	81	818	33.4	9.0
Calhoun	4	D	D	D	4	13	2.0	0.5	19	D	D	D
Carroll	24	62	6.6	1.6	26	784	293.1	31.4	39	317	15.0	3.7
Cass	11	54	6.0	1.7	13	2 297	D	83.4	28	D	D	D
Champaign	439	2 767	362.4	137.4	132	7 063	3 024.6	313.9	517	9 809	437.5	120.4
Christian	47	471	20.8	8.3	21	1 059	D	49.1	68	887	34.0	9.9
Clark	16	90	11.9	5.6	16	1 004	539.2	46.5	43	446	19.9	5.3
Clay	16	127	7.0	2.7	17	1 772	763.1	74.3	29	292	12.5	3.2
Clinton	46	208	18.6	7.1	33	732	D	26.3	98	1 090	41.4	10.8
Coles	67	405	40.7	13.1	40	2 615	D	109.0	130	2 232	84.7	24.1
Cook	19 017	217 861	48 255.4	18 955.5	5 120	181 315	79 527.0	9 622.8	11 329	207 364	14 553.1	4 023.7
Crawford	29	165	18.2	7.5	16	1 878	D	131.4	34	367	17.2	4.7
Cumberland	7	32	2.2	0.8	12	443	D	11.8	7	D	D	D
DeKalb	151	683	64.4	24.5	110	3 499	1 339.4	154.6	214	3 161	135.9	35.7
De Witt	23	90	9.1	2.7	14	513	181.4	20.7	38	489	19.8	5.7
Douglas	28	89	6.4	2.0	82	2 146	841.3	106.5	50	656	28.1	7.2
DuPage	5 117	46 480	8 120.0	3 347.2	1 680	53 913	18 896.7	2 921.6	2 132	40 549	2 424.3	690.5
Edgar	25	99	8.3	2.5	20	1 751	714.8	76.0	30	D	D	D
Edwards	7	22	1.7	0.5	9	D	D	D	11	103	2.8	0.8
Effingham	56	310	39.4	11.9	60	2 913	697.9	123.5	106	2 111	97.5	26.7
Fayette	21	134	9.9	4.2	13	439	113.9	15.6	45	506	21.0	6.0
Ford	18	104	10.2	3.1	17	562	D	24.7	31	D	D	D
Franklin	43	253	25.3	8.1	39	783	199.1	31.3	77	972	38.2	10.5
Fulton	38	187	17.6	7.7	19	218	47.5	6.8	72	856	28.7	8.1
Gallatin	7	22	1.5	0.7	4	7	1.0	0.2	8	29	1.4	0.3
Greene	16	65	6.6	2.6	12	167	D	6.0	28	D	D	D
Grundy	94	781	86.9	37.0	47	1 306	2 113.8	97.8	100	1 380	59.7	15.8
Hamilton	12	40	2.9	1.1	7	72	D	2.4	12	123	4.6	1.3
Hancock	21	173	32.3	7.4	24	1 217	D	D	32	227	10.5	2.8

1. Establishment subject to federal tax.

Health Care and Social Assistance, Other Services, Nonemployer Businesses, and Residential Construction

STATE County	Health care and social assistance, 2012				Other services, 2012				Nonemployer businesses, 2014		Value of residential construction authorized by building permits, 2015	
	Number of establishments	Number of employees	Receipts (mil dol)	Annual payroll (mil dol)	Number of establishments	Number of employees	Receipts (mil dol)	Annual payroll (mil dol)	Number	Receipts (mil dol)	New Construction ($1,000)	Number of housing units
	159	160	161	162	163	164	165	166	167	168	169	170
IDAHO—Cont'd												
Caribou	21	226	18.2	6.9	15	D	D	D	448	17.1	2 115	10
Cassia	83	1 246	95.1	34.2	37	D	D	D	1 490	75.6	17 438	102
Clark	1	D	D	D	NA	NA	NA	NA	52	1.3	763	7
Clearwater	24	515	40.4	19.1	14	D	D	D	496	17.6	2 120	18
Custer	8	D	D	D	5	6	0.5	0.1	425	14.0	837	3
Elmore	51	723	56.4	22.1	34	125	7.0	2.2	1 251	43.5	11 388	52
Franklin	25	325	25.1	9.1	19	D	D	D	1 005	38.1	10 233	52
Fremont	17	222	12.8	5.2	16	D	D	D	1 077	47.4	9 967	62
Gem	46	733	46.0	18.8	23	D	D	D	1 202	41.2	5 318	38
Gooding	35	496	39.5	15.0	23	D	D	D	871	31.9	2 422	15
Idaho	32	700	48.8	23.3	21	D	D	D	1 208	45.6	111	1
Jefferson	33	D	D	D	14	D	D	D	2 063	97.1	26 796	136
Jerome	36	502	35.3	17.7	48	162	17.0	4.1	1 120	52.9	9 662	65
Kootenai	509	8 630	806.2	308.4	236	D	D	D	11 422	484.2	278 541	1 414
Latah	85	1 360	115.0	49.3	52	D	D	D	2 529	88.5	18 427	99
Lemhi	27	366	28.2	10.7	22	75	7.7	1.5	718	22.3	2 838	23
Lewis	13	D	D	D	3	D	D	D	305	10.1	994	8
Lincoln	8	99	4.7	2.1	3	6	0.7	0.1	279	8.4	224	2
Madison	92	1 390	131.8	42.0	33	D	D	D	2 586	102.4	49 480	279
Minidoka	40	519	34.4	15.2	26	D	D	D	1 184	43.6	11 550	68
Nez Perce	138	3 029	341.2	123.0	85	D	D	D	2 134	81.7	17 199	108
Oneida	8	D	D	D	3	D	D	D	331	12.0	2 252	17
Owyhee	17	142	6.9	3.0	5	D	D	D	660	26.6	3 978	21
Payette	42	535	34.8	15.2	27	80	6.8	2.1	1 415	57.0	7 506	44
Power	12	190	11.5	5.4	11	58	6.6	1.4	358	15.0	198	1
Shoshone	33	488	35.7	13.6	17	58	5.0	1.6	810	23.9	4 467	19
Teton	29	250	21.1	9.0	20	61	6.0	1.8	1 365	50.1	21 407	93
Twin Falls	325	5 626	497.8	192.1	155	850	75.4	21.4	5 369	240.3	75 311	413
Valley	29	393	32.7	16.6	31	186	12.1	3.8	1 247	56.4	23 484	93
Washington	26	401	28.2	11.1	14	72	5.0	1.3	633	20.2	1 829	17
ILLINOIS	33 055	770 484	83 431.8	32 574.0	23 334	165 366	21 355.5	5 826.6	955 153	41 274.9	4 136 596	19 571
Adams	142	5 586	691.3	238.4	158	D	D	D	3 963	140.8	10 314	67
Alexander	8	237	12.2	6.6	6	10	0.8	0.2	381	8.2	0	0
Bond	30	593	47.3	21.9	21	99	8.8	2.6	1 017	27.9	9 311	113
Boone	73	1 077	80.1	30.0	67	372	30.0	9.4	3 076	124.4	3 077	12
Brown	9	D	D	D	12	D	D	D	326	9.1	0	0
Bureau	80	2 114	171.6	75.8	78	D	D	D	1 930	74.1	9 380	52
Calhoun	5	D	D	D	5	14	1.1	0.3	326	13.7	900	8
Carroll	26	616	23.8	9.5	32	191	13.4	4.0	1 040	34.9	4 555	16
Cass	17	379	15.7	7.3	25	D	D	D	717	20.6	1 855	7
Champaign	364	D	D	D	271	2 173	403.7	66.3	11 813	438.1	157 983	1 202
Christian	64	1 721	119.7	48.2	62	292	19.8	5.1	1 965	69.3	4 471	27
Clark	22	375	20.4	8.9	20	63	5.4	1.2	1 118	40.8	430	12
Clay	41	650	42.4	18.8	31	95	8.6	1.7	1 018	38.0	605	5
Clinton	84	1 624	128.7	52.6	66	284	25.0	6.1	2 313	84.0	20 609	89
Coles	155	3 981	367.2	149.0	96	465	35.2	11.2	2 696	91.5	2 318	13
Cook	14 637	358 374	39 639.9	15 523.6	9 887	78 562	12 262.7	3 166.7	464 097	20 265.3	1 650 541	7 855
Crawford	42	975	73.2	28.7	41	170	15.7	3.5	1 221	46.8	2 750	14
Cumberland	14	260	14.4	6.1	16	100	7.4	3.3	768	25.3	100	2
DeKalb	229	4 786	503.1	179.1	147	994	67.3	17.8	6 042	230.3	24 886	118
De Witt	28	581	38.5	17.1	27	98	9.5	2.5	867	27.9	4 913	28
Douglas	30	356	20.6	8.8	31	111	8.8	2.5	1 528	60.8	3 681	27
DuPage	3 215	62 644	7 846.5	3 116.4	2 047	17 768	2 184.8	676.0	80 582	4 374.4	521 472	1 592
Edgar	30	752	65.5	25.4	24	96	9.9	2.4	979	33.3	7 464	45
Edwards	14	120	5.9	3.2	14	D	D	D	485	16.9	NA	NA
Effingham	124	2 778	320.0	109.8	94	989	65.7	28.0	2 774	116.9	9 841	55
Fayette	42	987	48.3	20.2	33	157	14.7	3.6	1 404	49.9	201	1
Ford	35	1 053	88.1	37.9	28	D	D	D	956	35.5	1 405	7
Franklin	73	1 229	75.4	28.5	55	186	24.0	3.9	2 229	72.0	1 021	13
Fulton	70	2 037	171.7	66.2	50	260	14.2	4.2	1 764	54.8	7 109	55
Gallatin	7	109	5.3	2.0	11	D	D	D	303	12.3	NA	NA
Greene	22	378	22.9	11.7	15	D	D	D	805	29.6	2 940	28
Grundy	124	D	D	D	85	487	55.3	13.1	2 815	121.9	22 536	188
Hamilton	19	447	25.3	10.1	17	55	5.8	1.4	545	17.5	NA	NA
Hancock	28	493	34.1	15.0	29	70	5.7	1.5	1 303	44.4	1 063	5

Table B. States and Counties — Government Employment and Payroll, and Local Government Finances

| | | | | | | | | | Government employment and payroll, 2012 | | Local government finances, 2012 | | | |
STATE County	Full-time equivalent employees	March payroll (dollars)	Administration, judicial, and legal	Police and Corrections	Fire Protection	Highways and transportation	Health and Welfare	Natural resources and utilities	Education and libraries	General revenue — Total (mil dol)	Intergovernmental (mil dol)	Taxes — Total (mil dol)	Per capita[1] (dollars) — Total	Per capita[1] (dollars) — Property
	171	172	173	174	175	176	177	178	179	180	181	182	183	184
IDAHO—Cont'd														
Caribou	536	1 743 847	5.7	7.1	0.0	5.1	23.6	2.6	54.8	30.0	15.1	9.8	1 451	1 424
Cassia	841	2 609 053	6.9	10.2	1.3	4.4	1.0	7.7	66.0	72.2	36.8	15.3	658	460
Clark	64	182 907	15.4	10.5	0.0	12.5	0.0	3.3	58.1	5.0	3.3	1.2	1 353	1 265
Clearwater	338	951 830	12.2	14.7	0.3	8.5	5.3	6.8	50.6	26.1	13.8	8.4	974	934
Custer	193	546 688	12.5	6.7	0.1	16.9	1.2	5.5	56.7	15.9	9.6	3.8	876	845
Elmore	1 019	3 030 975	6.9	10.0	0.6	5.4	25.3	5.0	45.8	85.0	33.0	18.8	717	631
Franklin	560	1 720 585	5.4	4.8	0.0	3.4	34.4	1.8	50.0	29.4	21.3	5.3	417	394
Fremont	515	1 419 098	11.6	16.1	2.7	6.1	2.9	5.3	54.6	35.8	16.2	14.1	1 086	1 034
Gem	557	1 566 566	7.1	9.6	1.2	2.9	21.3	5.1	50.7	48.1	18.9	14.1	844	831
Gooding	579	1 442 650	8.1	9.0	1.3	5.5	3.6	3.7	66.2	56.3	24.7	15.8	1 036	1 004
Idaho	626	1 781 949	5.1	6.7	0.0	7.5	28.5	2.9	44.8	45.1	21.7	8.0	491	490
Jefferson	872	2 231 238	5.7	8.4	1.8	4.0	1.4	0.9	76.4	54.6	35.5	14.4	541	538
Jerome	672	1 876 675	11.2	10.1	3.4	5.6	0.5	5.4	62.3	54.6	29.4	15.7	697	673
Kootenai	6 580	25 436 541	6.0	8.3	3.6	2.4	37.6	3.3	38.1	678.7	158.8	148.1	1 040	972
Latah	1 001	3 595 367	11.4	10.5	0.8	5.9	0.5	6.2	63.7	82.9	35.0	31.3	819	745
Lemhi	403	1 235 515	7.2	7.5	0.2	3.9	46.4	3.5	30.0	38.3	15.0	4.0	511	478
Lewis	228	620 176	8.8	8.6	0.0	7.6	0.3	4.4	69.1	19.4	10.6	6.1	1 560	1 538
Lincoln	225	639 708	10.8	7.0	0.8	6.1	0.7	4.7	69.2	12.7	7.9	3.6	675	614
Madison	1 018	2 964 631	10.1	13.1	1.9	4.4	1.9	2.7	63.6	142.6	48.3	21.2	565	517
Minidoka	971	2 994 496	5.6	6.8	1.4	1.2	25.7	9.8	49.0	70.9	29.8	11.3	562	530
Nez Perce	1 348	5 048 001	7.1	13.3	6.7	5.6	4.0	8.5	50.0	119.0	49.4	44.7	1 132	1 075
Oneida	180	488 815	12.4	9.4	0.2	6.7	2.2	3.2	65.1	13.7	7.2	3.0	709	690
Owyhee	420	1 130 203	5.4	8.3	0.9	4.7	0.4	2.7	73.7	36.6	20.4	12.9	1 130	780
Payette	742	2 179 486	8.8	11.0	1.4	4.1	2.9	4.4	66.6	54.2	28.9	16.9	747	643
Power	430	1 383 820	5.4	5.9	0.3	7.0	26.0	3.4	51.1	39.7	13.4	10.9	1 398	1 360
Shoshone	609	1 865 396	6.7	7.4	2.8	7.1	21.4	5.7	48.1	52.0	20.0	14.5	1 140	1 102
Teton	450	1 567 917	7.7	3.7	5.3	2.4	33.2	1.8	43.6	55.4	16.6	14.5	1 445	1 299
Twin Falls	3 114	9 543 688	6.8	11.2	2.7	2.8	5.5	3.6	66.3	357.5	212.6	68.8	876	846
Valley	517	1 760 075	11.5	14.1	6.6	9.0	7.9	8.9	39.9	49.2	15.8	24.3	2 542	2 475
Washington	545	1 653 304	6.7	8.4	0.8	4.2	28.1	6.1	43.6	48.8	16.8	12.1	1 202	1 131
ILLINOIS	X	X	X	X	X	X	X	X	X	X	X	X	X	X
Adams	2 703	8 715 868	5.5	10.4	4.2	4.1	5.0	6.1	62.7	223.4	108.4	76.6	1 140	966
Alexander	313	970 447	7.7	9.2	0.0	10.6	2.3	10.0	57.2	30.3	20.7	4.6	595	522
Bond	553	1 740 375	8.4	8.6	0.2	5.4	9.2	6.9	61.0	47.8	21.7	14.3	811	782
Boone	1 665	6 568 081	5.5	11.2	2.8	2.0	1.2	4.1	72.4	168.6	64.4	88.0	1 632	1 512
Brown	202	635 285	9.5	7.4	0.4	13.0	4.1	3.1	62.1	17.3	8.3	5.3	772	738
Bureau	1 639	5 498 491	7.7	6.6	1.2	2.6	22.0	6.1	53.1	152.9	48.9	47.1	1 371	1 315
Calhoun	170	503 707	8.6	7.8	0.2	10.3	6.6	2.8	63.7	12.8	6.7	4.6	917	910
Carroll	571	1 922 747	6.7	10.1	1.2	4.6	1.4	4.6	70.2	50.2	17.9	26.2	1 744	1 700
Cass	549	1 630 366	5.5	5.1	0.7	5.7	1.6	4.6	73.9	47.1	27.4	13.9	1 039	967
Champaign	7 295	27 910 700	5.6	8.8	3.9	7.8	5.7	5.8	60.6	779.8	297.9	355.6	1 749	1 502
Christian	1 070	3 699 842	8.2	9.1	2.1	5.7	2.0	6.3	66.0	97.0	49.7	35.0	1 009	963
Clark	656	1 941 162	6.3	7.0	1.4	5.2	2.5	7.5	65.2	49.9	25.6	16.5	1 017	965
Clay	731	2 318 318	7.1	5.7	0.1	3.7	25.1	6.3	51.0	65.8	22.2	11.1	807	758
Clinton	1 065	3 651 290	8.0	9.9	0.0	4.7	3.6	5.9	67.0	83.0	32.3	37.3	980	957
Coles	2 055	7 515 260	6.6	9.1	4.4	3.1	2.6	3.4	70.1	193.9	95.6	62.8	1 170	1 079
Cook	198 590	1 055 085 174	5.5	19.7	3.8	8.4	5.0	6.1	49.9	30 214.0	10 506.2	14 465.1	2 765	2 126
Crawford	1 004	3 546 258	3.9	4.8	1.2	4.9	40.2	1.7	42.6	92.3	22.6	23.8	1 214	1 192
Cumberland	489	1 701 831	5.1	5.3	0.6	4.4	1.3	6.8	75.7	24.9	13.2	8.4	765	749
DeKalb	3 677	13 579 842	6.4	11.5	5.3	3.7	5.7	4.9	61.7	427.7	136.1	235.3	2 247	1 839
De Witt	856	2 898 838	6.6	7.9	0.9	3.4	26.5	4.6	49.0	74.5	16.6	32.1	1 956	1 907
Douglas	604	1 931 336	13.2	8.9	0.8	4.9	0.1	2.9	68.4	57.7	23.4	26.8	1 352	1 325
DuPage	34 627	161 978 004	4.8	10.0	5.2	2.3	1.4	8.6	66.4	4 380.5	931.7	2 785.7	3 002	2 700
Edgar	762	2 449 135	5.9	7.4	2.5	12.8	1.9	5.1	63.4	53.8	26.7	21.4	1 175	1 081
Edwards	230	593 869	6.7	6.9	0.5	3.2	1.4	6.8	74.3	13.3	7.7	3.8	573	568
Effingham	1 139	4 092 064	7.6	10.0	2.5	4.1	2.3	4.6	67.2	103.7	48.7	39.5	1 151	1 088
Fayette	798	2 298 002	8.1	12.9	0.0	4.6	5.0	3.9	65.2	56.1	29.6	16.6	754	737
Ford	495	1 697 539	6.4	9.3	0.0	5.1	0.0	3.3	75.1	45.2	18.3	21.4	1 530	1 465
Franklin	1 582	5 056 096	5.7	8.6	1.7	3.6	12.7	9.1	58.0	140.8	72.3	25.5	646	571
Fulton	1 688	5 342 718	6.0	7.3	2.2	3.1	5.4	5.4	70.1	131.1	60.0	46.1	1 259	1 214
Gallatin	190	667 273	12.7	6.1	0.2	4.8	0.2	7.6	67.8	16.8	10.0	3.8	699	636
Greene	546	1 577 821	8.0	6.8	0.3	8.5	4.3	8.2	63.4	36.4	17.9	12.3	908	861
Grundy	1 993	7 671 944	5.9	9.9	3.1	2.7	1.3	1.8	74.1	223.4	53.5	147.8	2 939	2 877
Hamilton	413	1 340 057	6.2	3.3	0.0	3.7	34.5	5.5	46.3	33.7	13.2	5.1	604	603
Hancock	809	2 296 267	7.2	7.5	0.4	6.0	1.8	4.7	71.8	55.0	25.2	21.7	1 147	1 101

1. Based on the resident population estimated as of July 1 of the year shown.

STATE County	Total (mil dol)	Per capita[1] (dollars)	Educa-tion	Health and hospitals	Police protec-tion	Public welfare	High-ways	Total (mil dol)	Per capita[1] (dollars)	Federal civilian	Federal military	State and local	Demo-cratic	Republi-can	All other
	185	186	187	188	189	190	191	192	193	194	195	196	197	198	199
IDAHO—Cont'd															
Caribou	29.0	4 268	41.5	0.2	10.7	0.5	13.5	1.0	151	47	25	624	16.7	80.4	2.8
Cassia	58.1	2 497	57.1	0.4	5.3	0.8	5.6	30.3	1 303	125	84	1 495	17.0	80.5	2.6
Clark	5.2	6 037	40.8	0.2	6.5	0.5	26.7	4.2	4 807	30	0	97	17.1	81.3	1.6
Clearwater	26.0	3 028	39.9	2.2	7.1	1.3	13.0	2.0	229	170	29	814	31.0	65.8	3.2
Custer	16.4	3 790	37.4	7.3	4.7	0.5	14.1	0.2	42	152	15	291	26.0	72.0	2.0
Elmore	76.8	2 930	37.5	27.0	6.8	0.0	7.2	27.5	1 049	808	3 373	1 049	30.7	67.2	2.1
Franklin	28.7	2 243	61.1	1.8	7.2	0.4	7.4	5.0	394	33	47	961	11.8	83.7	4.5
Fremont	39.0	3 014	39.0	1.3	7.0	0.8	11.9	29.5	2 277	75	45	923	18.1	79.9	2.0
Gem	41.4	2 481	43.1	21.4	5.8	0.6	5.5	23.5	1 409	77	61	790	27.3	70.3	2.5
Gooding	85.0	5 557	26.2	51.3	2.6	0.7	3.7	49.5	3 236	63	54	1 117	27.6	69.8	2.5
Idaho	41.4	2 537	44.3	2.9	4.7	1.4	20.3	6.4	391	340	57	897	24.6	71.8	3.6
Jefferson	64.3	2 411	54.0	0.0	6.7	0.2	4.6	89.0	3 335	50	98	1 276	15.7	81.8	2.5
Jerome	53.8	2 393	44.7	0.3	5.9	1.1	9.0	39.2	1 743	45	82	980	26.2	71.5	2.3
Kootenai	637.0	4 475	29.8	40.2	5.8	0.4	3.9	121.1	851	561	529	9 849	35.7	62.0	2.3
Latah	87.4	2 290	48.2	0.3	11.6	1.1	4.1	40.7	1 065	166	149	6 274	51.9	45.1	3.0
Lemhi	34.8	4 485	25.3	39.2	3.9	0.7	4.9	15.4	1 987	206	28	586	25.8	71.6	2.6
Lewis	21.4	5 498	42.3	0.7	5.0	0.7	11.4	4.3	1 109	46	14	392	26.6	70.7	2.8
Lincoln	12.3	2 332	69.2	0.0	4.6	0.1	9.2	6.3	1 194	78	19	373	29.1	65.9	5.0
Madison	144.7	3 862	27.9	37.4	3.3	0.2	4.1	137.2	3 662	56	135	1 959	12.5	85.2	2.3
Minidoka	75.3	3 760	38.1	24.8	4.2	0.5	5.7	46.9	2 341	84	73	1 332	23.7	73.8	2.5
Nez Perce	119.5	3 023	41.4	0.7	8.3	0.2	7.5	25.2	637	201	143	3 978	40.0	58.1	1.9
Oneida	14.2	3 368	42.9	22.5	6.2	0.3	7.9	2.7	633	18	15	418	17.6	79.7	2.6
Owyhee	32.2	2 814	58.3	0.0	6.5	0.9	6.7	21.0	1 836	43	41	631	23.3	74.5	2.2
Payette	52.4	2 315	48.3	3.5	7.4	1.5	7.7	25.3	1 117	30	83	1 038	28.0	69.5	2.4
Power	34.2	4 401	40.1	20.7	3.4	0.6	11.8	11.5	1 480	21	27	629	36.1	61.7	2.1
Shoshone	52.1	4 102	38.6	21.3	5.0	0.8	10.7	38.7	3 043	70	44	907	44.5	52.1	3.4
Teton	51.0	5 069	26.2	24.7	2.1	0.1	4.7	22.8	2 269	39	38	393	49.4	48.6	2.0
Twin Falls	356.9	4 541	65.8	1.8	3.6	0.9	4.2	190.1	2 418	358	291	4 284	30.4	67.1	2.4
Valley	50.0	5 243	33.1	0.0	8.0	0.2	14.2	52.4	5 495	238	35	733	45.4	52.3	2.2
Washington	43.6	4 322	34.4	33.0	5.6	1.2	5.7	9.6	952	49	36	695	27.5	70.3	2.2
ILLINOIS	X	X	X	X	X	X	X	X	X	79 975	41 893	748 670	61.9	36.8	1.3
Adams	201.0	2 991	56.5	3.5	5.7	0.2	5.8	99.6	1 482	237	131	3 967	38.3	60.7	1.0
Alexander	30.3	3 916	49.2	1.4	5.2	0.5	5.8	3.3	426	25	14	585	55.6	43.0	1.4
Bond	45.6	2 583	46.2	7.7	7.5	0.1	9.0	52.0	2 948	333	31	748	48.5	49.8	1.7
Boone	156.0	2 893	62.0	1.2	6.0	0.1	5.4	126.3	2 341	69	108	2 055	51.1	47.0	1.9
Brown	16.0	2 312	46.9	4.0	5.1	0.0	14.3	5.3	774	40	10	381	38.4	60.1	1.5
Bureau	156.2	4 551	37.8	25.0	3.8	0.0	9.0	77.1	2 245	122	68	2 201	51.9	46.2	1.8
Calhoun	11.5	2 294	52.1	0.5	3.8	0.1	22.6	8.5	1 693	24	10	243	52.7	45.2	2.0
Carroll	49.2	3 280	55.2	1.4	4.9	0.0	10.6	31.3	2 088	66	29	795	51.7	46.9	1.5
Cass	48.5	3 633	48.0	10.6	5.0	0.1	5.9	32.3	2 418	53	26	858	49.7	48.4	1.9
Champaign	826.4	4 066	48.3	2.5	5.1	1.9	5.6	670.9	3 301	1 233	420	35 228	57.8	40.3	2.0
Christian	110.2	3 182	62.3	1.4	5.2	0.2	6.9	48.6	1 404	74	65	1 778	45.8	52.1	2.1
Clark	50.6	3 123	49.6	1.9	5.8	0.2	12.5	27.6	1 705	50	32	844	45.1	53.2	1.7
Clay	65.1	4 732	32.8	32.8	3.4	0.1	5.2	24.2	1 756	45	27	899	37.6	60.8	1.6
Clinton	81.6	2 145	54.7	2.6	8.5	0.0	9.4	57.5	1 510	102	72	2 218	44.2	54.0	1.7
Coles	224.0	4 175	60.6	1.0	4.9	0.1	7.5	97.1	1 809	139	102	6 106	50.8	47.6	1.7
Cook	29 791.5	5 695	39.4	4.1	7.7	1.3	4.1	59 701.4	11 412	37 945	10 882	281 608	76.2	22.8	1.0
Crawford	103.4	5 277	28.7	46.8	2.5	0.1	5.6	46.4	2 366	55	36	1 812	42.5	55.5	1.9
Cumberland	25.4	2 316	59.2	2.1	4.8	0.2	11.9	9.6	878	29	22	489	38.6	59.3	2.1
DeKalb	465.9	4 450	45.9	1.7	5.4	3.0	4.9	394.6	3 769	181	203	12 982	57.5	40.8	1.7
De Witt	72.0	4 384	38.0	25.7	5.5	0.1	7.2	34.3	2 088	47	32	1 002	42.4	55.7	1.9
Douglas	56.1	2 825	47.8	1.8	6.3	0.3	11.0	34.9	1 760	56	40	1 057	38.6	59.9	1.5
DuPage	4 276.8	4 609	55.0	0.8	6.9	1.6	4.5	4 424.5	4 768	4 981	1 915	46 632	54.7	43.9	1.4
Edgar	59.4	3 263	54.0	3.0	5.0	0.0	11.2	50.5	2 777	53	36	958	45.3	53.3	1.4
Edwards	13.2	1 968	61.7	1.1	4.8	0.1	7.8	6.7	1 005	24	13	291	34.0	63.8	2.2
Effingham	107.8	3 137	47.2	2.6	6.9	0.7	10.6	58.0	1 688	146	70	1 673	31.3	67.3	1.5
Fayette	56.3	2 557	53.8	6.6	7.2	0.0	7.1	24.9	1 130	58	41	1 067	41.0	56.8	2.2
Ford	49.5	3 535	64.3	0.7	5.7	0.0	8.3	21.0	1 501	48	27	815	34.9	63.9	1.3
Franklin	143.4	3 639	47.5	12.4	7.3	0.3	5.1	32.0	811	196	79	1 877	47.6	50.4	1.9
Fulton	132.3	3 611	54.8	3.6	4.8	2.2	7.8	85.5	2 332	91	67	2 209	59.6	38.3	2.1
Gallatin	16.0	2 938	50.0	0.8	2.9	0.3	11.8	8.2	1 509	28	11	230	55.5	42.4	2.1
Greene	37.1	2 735	54.1	5.0	5.5	0.4	12.8	12.2	901	44	27	669	45.1	52.6	2.3
Grundy	239.2	4 757	60.5	1.0	4.2	0.0	7.5	311.7	6 199	105	102	2 660	49.9	48.2	1.9
Hamilton	35.0	4 183	33.6	40.5	2.7	0.1	8.6	25.1	3 002	35	17	505	42.1	55.2	2.7
Hancock	59.2	3 132	56.6	5.9	3.8	1.1	11.6	21.0	1 109	77	37	1 139	43.7	54.5	1.8

1. Based on the resident population estimated as of July 1 of the year shown.   2. © 2013 Election Data Services, Inc. All rights reserved.

Table B. States and Counties — Land Area and Population

STATE/ County code	CBSA code[1]	County type[2]	STATE County	Land area,[3] (sq km) 2010	Total persons 2015	Rank	Per square kilometer	White	Black	American Indian, Alaska Native	Asian and Pacific Islander	Percent Hispanic or Latino[4]	Under 5 years	5 to 17 years	18 to 24 years	25 to 34 years	35 to 44 years	45 to 54 years
				1	2	3	4	5	6	7	8	9	10	11	12	13	14	15
			ILLINOIS—Cont'd															
17 069	...	9	Hardin	460	4 135	2 892	9.0	94.1	1.1	1.1	1.0	1.6	4.7	15.3	6.3	8.5	11.6	14.5
17 071	15460	9	Henderson	981	6 995	2 677	7.1	96.3	0.9	0.6	0.6	1.5	3.5	14.8	7.1	9.6	9.6	14.7
17 073	19340	2	Henry	2 132	49 489	988	23.2	92.1	2.4	0.5	0.8	5.4	5.4	17.2	7.9	10.6	11.9	13.8
17 075	...	6	Iroquois	2 894	28 672	1 468	9.9	91.8	1.6	0.5	0.8	6.5	5.5	16.8	7.6	10.5	11.0	13.7
17 077	16060	5	Jackson	1 513	59 362	874	39.2	77.2	16.0	1.0	4.8	4.2	5.0	13.0	24.0	14.1	9.7	10.3
17 079	...	7	Jasper	1 281	9 607	2 464	7.5	97.9	0.6	0.4	0.5	1.4	6.1	16.8	7.2	11.4	11.0	15.0
17 081	34500	7	Jefferson	1 479	38 353	1 211	25.9	87.9	9.6	0.6	1.4	2.3	6.3	15.5	8.5	12.5	12.3	13.5
17 083	41180	1	Jersey	956	22 372	1 711	23.4	97.4	1.0	0.7	0.7	1.3	5.0	16.6	9.6	11.0	11.4	14.9
17 085	...	6	Jo Daviess	1 557	22 086	1 727	14.2	95.2	0.9	0.5	0.7	3.1	4.3	15.0	6.6	9.3	10.4	13.4
17 087	...	7	Johnson	891	12 762	2 246	14.3	86.8	8.5	0.6	0.4	3.2	4.8	13.7	9.2	12.6	12.4	14.4
17 089	16980	1	Kane	1 347	530 847	127	394.1	59.2	6.0	0.4	4.4	31.3	6.7	20.4	8.9	12.2	14.0	14.4
17 091	28100	3	Kankakee	1 752	110 879	547	63.3	73.7	16.0	0.5	1.4	9.8	6.0	18.1	10.4	12.0	12.1	13.5
17 093	16980	1	Kendall	830	123 355	505	148.6	73.1	6.9	0.3	4.0	16.9	7.3	22.6	7.8	13.4	16.9	13.7
17 095	23660	4	Knox	1 855	51 441	970	27.7	85.8	9.1	0.6	1.2	5.6	5.0	15.0	10.0	11.7	11.5	13.0
17 097	16980	1	Lake	1 149	703 910	89	612.6	64.8	7.6	0.5	8.0	21.0	5.9	19.5	10.2	11.0	13.0	15.4
17 099	36860	4	LaSalle	2 940	111 333	544	37.9	87.3	2.7	0.5	1.1	8.8	5.4	16.7	8.3	11.8	11.5	14.4
17 101	...	7	Lawrence	964	16 491	2 008	17.1	85.5	10.2	0.5	0.5	3.7	5.1	13.7	9.6	14.5	14.1	13.4
17 103	19940	4	Lee	1 877	34 584	1 315	18.4	87.7	5.6	0.5	1.1	5.8	5.1	15.2	8.3	12.2	12.1	15.0
17 105	38700	4	Livingston	2 705	36 671	1 261	13.6	91.4	6.2	0.5	0.9	4.6	5.6	16.0	8.8	12.4	12.0	14.3
17 107	30660	6	Logan	1 601	29 494	1 441	18.4	87.8	8.5	0.5	1.1	3.4	4.7	14.3	11.1	13.7	12.6	13.4
17 109	31380	5	McDonough	1 527	31 333	1 401	20.5	90.5	6.1	0.6	2.7	2.7	4.8	11.8	25.6	12.2	9.1	10.1
17 111	16980	1	McHenry	1 562	307 343	221	196.8	83.4	1.7	0.4	3.4	12.4	5.5	19.4	8.7	10.8	13.4	16.8
17 113	14010	3	McLean	3 065	173 166	371	56.5	82.2	8.7	0.5	5.9	4.8	6.1	16.0	18.2	12.9	11.5	12.3
17 115	19500	5	Macon	1 504	107 303	557	71.3	79.4	18.7	0.6	1.7	2.1	6.2	16.2	9.3	11.7	11.5	12.8
17 117	41180	1	Macoupin	2 235	46 045	1 046	20.6	97.4	1.5	0.7	0.6	1.0	5.1	16.5	8.1	11.0	11.8	14.1
17 119	41180	1	Madison	1 853	266 209	255	143.7	87.4	9.3	0.6	1.5	3.1	5.9	16.4	8.9	13.3	12.2	14.0
17 121	16460	4	Marion	1 482	38 339	1 214	25.9	93.5	5.0	0.5	0.9	1.8	6.3	16.7	8.4	11.2	11.5	13.4
17 123	37900	2	Marshall	1 002	11 982	2 298	12.0	95.4	0.7	0.5	0.9	3.3	4.9	15.0	7.6	10.1	11.1	14.0
17 125	...	6	Mason	1 397	13 701	2 189	9.8	97.6	1.1	0.7	0.6	1.0	4.8	16.3	7.8	10.4	11.6	14.5
17 127	37140	7	Massac	614	14 766	2 120	24.0	91.1	7.0	0.8	0.7	2.6	5.8	16.1	7.2	10.8	11.9	13.9
17 129	44100	3	Menard	814	12 444	2 266	15.3	96.9	1.6	0.7	0.6	1.4	5.3	17.1	7.7	10.4	11.5	14.9
17 131	19340	2	Mercer	1 454	15 858	2 048	10.9	96.7	1.0	0.4	0.5	2.1	4.9	16.9	7.1	9.7	11.4	14.6
17 133	41180	1	Monroe	997	33 879	1 331	34.0	97.4	0.6	0.5	0.8	1.6	5.2	17.6	7.5	10.8	12.4	15.8
17 135	...	6	Montgomery	1 823	28 898	1 458	15.9	95.3	3.8	0.4	0.6	1.7	5.1	15.4	8.3	12.5	12.0	14.5
17 137	27300	5	Morgan	1 473	34 828	1 309	23.6	90.5	7.4	0.5	0.8	2.3	5.2	14.9	10.3	12.6	11.3	13.6
17 139	...	6	Moultrie	870	14 931	2 103	17.2	97.5	0.8	0.5	0.4	1.3	6.1	18.4	7.6	11.8	11.3	13.0
17 141	40300	4	Ogle	1 965	51 659	965	26.3	88.8	1.6	0.5	0.8	9.6	5.2	18.0	8.3	10.5	11.9	15.1
17 143	37900	1	Peoria	1 604	186 221	347	116.1	73.6	19.7	0.6	4.3	4.6	7.0	16.8	9.7	13.9	12.1	12.6
17 145	...	7	Perry	1 144	21 543	1 752	18.8	87.8	9.6	0.5	0.7	3.1	4.9	14.6	10.2	13.0	13.4	13.5
17 147	16580	3	Piatt	1 138	16 387	2 019	14.4	97.5	1.0	0.5	0.9	1.1	5.2	17.0	7.4	10.5	11.9	14.9
17 149	...	7	Pike	2 153	15 989	2 041	7.4	96.7	2.3	0.5	0.5	1.2	5.6	16.4	7.7	11.4	11.6	13.3
17 151	...	9	Pope	955	4 226	2 885	4.4	90.7	7.1	0.9	0.5	1.9	3.4	12.2	11.8	8.9	10.1	14.4
17 153	...	9	Pulaski	516	5 678	2 785	11.0	65.6	32.9	1.1	0.6	1.9	5.1	16.7	7.6	10.7	10.8	13.0
17 155	36860	8	Putnam	415	5 644	2 791	13.6	94.3	1.4	0.4	0.5	4.7	4.7	15.6	7.6	10.0	10.7	14.2
17 157	...	6	Randolph	1 491	32 852	1 362	22.0	86.2	10.4	0.4	0.6	2.8	5.0	14.5	7.9	14.0	13.1	14.4
17 159	...	7	Richland	932	16 029	2 037	17.2	96.6	1.0	0.5	1.1	1.5	5.8	16.2	7.9	11.2	11.3	13.6
17 161	19340	2	Rock Island	1 108	146 133	442	131.9	75.3	10.6	0.6	2.7	12.4	6.1	16.0	8.9	12.6	11.7	13.0
17 163	41180	1	St. Clair	1 704	264 052	256	155.0	64.4	31.2	0.6	2.2	3.8	6.4	17.7	9.1	13.1	12.6	14.1
17 165	...	5	Saline	984	24 548	1 623	24.9	93.4	5.0	0.9	0.9	1.7	6.0	15.7	8.6	11.7	11.4	13.6
17 167	44100	3	Sangamon	2 249	198 712	330	88.4	83.4	13.7	0.6	2.4	2.2	6.0	17.0	8.5	12.8	12.2	14.0
17 169	...	7	Schuyler	1 133	7 032	2 673	6.2	95.6	3.6	0.4	0.4	1.8	4.9	15.3	7.0	10.6	12.6	14.6
17 171	27300	9	Scott	650	5 092	2 829	7.8	98.6	0.9	0.6	0.5	1.2	5.1	17.2	7.4	10.0	12.3	15.3
17 173	...	6	Shelby	1 965	21 751	1 738	11.1	97.9	0.7	0.5	0.5	1.0	5.3	16.1	7.7	10.6	11.4	13.8
17 175	37900	2	Stark	746	5 788	2 776	7.8	97.2	1.1	0.6	0.8	1.1	4.9	15.5	7.4	9.0	10.9	13.2
17 177	23300	4	Stephenson	1 462	45 749	1 054	31.3	86.3	11.2	0.5	1.1	3.5	5.6	16.2	7.9	10.3	10.4	14.1
17 179	37900	2	Tazewell	1 681	134 880	469	80.2	95.5	1.8	0.6	1.3	2.2	6.0	17.0	7.6	12.5	12.9	13.5
17 181	...	7	Union	1 071	17 408	1 953	16.3	92.9	1.7	0.9	0.6	5.1	5.3	15.7	7.7	11.1	11.7	14.1
17 183	19180	3	Vermilion	2 327	79 282	702	34.1	81.0	14.5	0.6	1.2	4.7	6.7	17.3	8.5	11.6	11.7	13.1
17 185	...	6	Wabash	578	11 542	2 322	20.0	96.5	1.4	0.7	1.1	1.5	5.8	16.1	8.6	11.2	10.9	13.3
17 187	...	7	Warren	1 405	17 527	1 945	12.5	86.8	3.0	0.5	2.1	9.4	6.0	15.6	12.4	10.5	10.9	12.2
17 189	...	7	Washington	1 457	14 270	2 150	9.8	96.7	1.3	0.4	0.6	1.6	4.5	16.3	7.7	11.7	11.4	14.7
17 191	...	7	Wayne	1 849	16 423	2 012	8.9	97.4	0.9	0.5	0.9	1.3	5.7	16.8	7.5	11.1	11.6	13.4
17 193	...	6	White	1 281	14 327	2 146	11.2	97.8	0.8	0.5	0.5	1.3	6.5	15.3	6.8	11.3	10.4	13.8
17 195	44580	4	Whiteside	1 772	57 079	895	32.2	85.8	2.2	0.5	0.8	11.7	5.4	16.9	8.2	10.7	11.5	13.8
17 197	16980	1	Will	2 168	687 263	93	317.0	66.6	12.0	0.4	5.9	16.5	6.1	20.6	9.2	11.5	14.5	15.4
17 199	16060	5	Williamson	1 088	67 466	787	62.0	91.7	5.0	0.7	1.3	2.4	5.9	16.0	7.8	13.3	12.8	13.5

1. CBSA = Core Based Statistical Area. See Appendix A for explanation. See Appendix B for list of metropolitan areas with component counties. 2. County type code from the Economic Research Service of USDA Rural-Urban Continuum Codes. See Appendix A for definition. 3. Dry land or land partially or temporarily covered by water. 4. May be of any race.

Table B. States and Counties — Population and Households

STATE County	55 to 64 years (16)	65 to 74 years (17)	75 years and over (18)	Percent female (19)	2000 (20)	2010 (21)	2000–2010 (22)	2010–2015 (23)	Births (24)	Deaths (25)	Net migration (26)	Number (27)	Persons per house-hold (28)	Family house-holds (29)	Female family house-holder[1] (30)	One per-son (31)
ILLINOIS—Cont'd																
Hardin	15.9	14.1	9.1	49.4	4 800	4 320	-10.0	-4.3	189	305	-47	1 731	2.40	63.4	7.9	33.4
Henderson	17.2	13.2	10.5	51.0	8 213	7 328	-10.8	-4.5	361	432	-252	3 116	2.25	68.2	9.8	27.5
Henry	14.6	10.2	8.3	50.2	51 020	50 485	-1.0	-2.0	2 872	2 743	-1 061	20 237	2.43	67.2	9.9	28.3
Iroquois	14.6	10.7	9.7	51.1	31 334	29 718	-5.2	-3.5	1 575	1 877	-721	11 804	2.43	67.3	9.3	27.7
Jackson	10.9	7.2	5.8	49.8	59 612	60 218	1.0	-1.4	3 505	2 398	-2 006	23 471	2.36	50.5	10.0	37.1
Jasper	14.3	9.5	8.7	50.0	10 117	9 698	-4.1	-0.9	615	515	-161	3 796	2.52	71.5	8.1	24.3
Jefferson	13.8	9.9	7.7	48.6	40 045	38 825	-3.0	-1.2	2 404	2 342	-510	15 289	2.40	64.4	11.0	30.8
Jersey	14.0	9.5	8.1	51.3	21 668	22 985	6.1	-2.7	1 159	1 222	-542	8 873	2.46	73.4	10.8	23.5
Jo Daviess	16.5	14.1	10.5	49.8	22 289	22 677	1.7	-2.6	965	1 254	-230	9 555	2.33	67.0	7.8	27.6
Johnson	13.8	11.8	7.5	44.3	12 878	12 582	-2.3	1.4	573	631	287	4 380	2.45	68.0	8.8	29.3
Kane	11.7	7.0	4.7	50.2	404 119	515 306	27.5	3.0	36 135	15 697	-5 733	171 316	3.01	75.1	11.1	20.5
Kankakee	12.9	8.3	6.6	50.9	103 833	113 449	9.3	-2.3	7 110	5 627	-4 105	41 430	2.60	68.2	15.2	26.2
Kendall	9.3	5.7	3.3	50.6	54 544	114 721	110.3	7.5	8 965	2 674	2 367	38 453	3.07	78.2	8.9	17.5
Knox	14.3	10.4	9.2	49.7	55 836	52 919	-5.2	-2.8	2 843	3 459	-784	21 438	2.25	58.9	11.4	34.7
Lake	12.9	7.1	5.1	50.1	644 356	703 409	9.2	0.1	42 125	22 390	-19 195	241 846	2.83	74.2	10.7	21.9
LaSalle	14.3	9.2	8.4	49.8	111 509	113 922	2.2	-2.3	6 064	6 584	-2 045	43 891	2.50	66.3	11.5	28.6
Lawrence	12.6	8.7	8.3	44.0	15 452	16 903	9.4	-2.4	893	1 076	-225	4 981	2.23	66.5	12.3	31.0
Lee	14.7	9.5	8.0	47.2	36 062	36 031	-0.1	-4.0	1 895	1 848	-1 415	13 468	2.42	66.2	8.9	28.1
Livingston	14.0	8.8	8.2	49.6	39 678	38 950	-1.8	-5.9	2 198	2 160	-2 346	14 515	2.35	66.7	9.9	28.7
Logan	13.0	8.8	8.3	49.4	31 183	30 305	-2.8	-2.7	1 572	1 641	-749	10 908	2.14	65.8	10.8	28.8
McDonough	11.5	7.9	7.0	50.5	32 913	32 612	-0.9	-3.9	1 545	1 510	-1 337	12 553	2.20	55.9	10.5	33.3
McHenry	13.3	7.5	4.6	50.1	260 077	308 826	18.7	-0.5	17 091	10 092	-8 702	109 221	2.80	75.7	9.4	19.8
McLean	10.9	6.4	5.1	51.3	150 433	169 572	12.7	2.1	11 128	5 896	-1 603	64 415	2.55	61.9	9.2	28.0
Macon	14.4	9.6	8.3	52.2	114 706	110 768	-3.4	-3.1	7 082	6 141	-4 207	45 153	2.35	61.6	12.1	33.0
Macoupin	14.7	10.1	8.6	50.6	49 019	47 765	-2.6	-3.6	2 342	2 942	-1 188	19 098	2.42	68.4	10.0	26.2
Madison	13.6	8.6	7.1	51.1	258 941	269 328	4.0	-1.2	16 453	14 189	-5 118	107 298	2.45	66.0	12.0	27.5
Marion	14.1	10.0	8.4	51.1	41 691	39 437	-5.4	-2.8	2 556	2 568	-1 095	15 835	2.41	65.7	13.3	29.4
Marshall	15.5	11.5	10.3	50.7	13 180	12 640	-4.1	-5.2	625	799	-464	4 926	2.44	65.2	6.2	29.5
Mason	14.8	10.6	9.3	50.4	16 038	14 666	-8.6	-6.6	750	978	-836	6 155	2.29	64.7	10.2	30.2
Massac	14.0	10.7	9.6	52.4	15 161	15 429	1.8	-4.3	848	1 083	-449	6 013	2.47	64.0	11.3	31.0
Menard	15.0	10.3	7.8	51.3	12 486	12 705	1.8	-2.1	643	674	-211	5 119	2.44	69.2	7.8	26.0
Mercer	14.9	11.5	9.0	50.6	16 957	16 434	-3.1	-3.5	800	945	-436	6 662	2.40	70.9	10.0	25.1
Monroe	14.7	8.2	7.8	50.3	27 619	32 957	19.3	2.8	1 686	1 478	650	12 557	2.63	76.7	7.7	20.5
Montgomery	13.8	9.3	9.2	47.7	30 652	30 104	-1.8	-4.0	1 601	1 848	-988	10 923	2.22	68.3	11.8	27.8
Morgan	13.9	9.7	8.5	49.4	36 616	35 551	-2.9	-2.0	1 977	2 004	-662	13 961	2.30	64.0	12.2	30.9
Moultrie	13.0	9.6	9.4	51.0	14 287	14 846	3.9	0.6	974	948	42	5 669	2.56	70.6	10.3	24.4
Ogle	13.9	9.5	7.7	50.3	51 032	53 497	4.8	-3.4	2 757	2 530	-2 042	20 759	2.51	66.8	8.5	27.4
Peoria	12.8	8.4	6.7	51.6	183 433	186 494	1.7	-0.1	13 824	9 275	-4 500	76 019	2.39	62.5	14.2	31.3
Perry	13.1	9.7	7.5	45.6	23 094	22 350	-3.2	-3.6	1 137	1 214	-724	8 048	2.48	62.1	10.1	34.1
Piatt	14.9	9.9	8.3	50.3	16 365	16 727	2.2	-2.0	904	905	-334	6 623	2.48	71.9	6.9	23.7
Pike	14.2	10.2	9.6	49.9	17 384	16 430	-5.5	-2.7	903	1 028	-318	6 675	2.35	65.6	9.1	29.3
Pope	17.9	12.1	9.2	47.1	4 413	4 470	1.3	-5.5	142	222	-131	1 672	2.41	66.1	8.6	32.1
Pulaski	15.8	10.7	9.4	51.9	7 348	6 161	-16.2	-7.8	319	397	-396	2 337	2.52	60.6	12.8	37.1
Putnam	17.4	11.8	8.0	49.1	6 086	6 006	-1.3	-6.0	252	276	-296	2 427	2.43	68.5	6.3	26.1
Randolph	13.9	9.2	8.0	45.0	33 893	33 476	-1.2	-1.9	1 802	1 907	-554	12 050	2.46	67.3	11.4	29.0
Richland	13.9	9.7	10.3	50.6	16 149	16 233	0.5	-1.3	1 041	1 009	-198	6 576	2.41	63.5	7.7	31.5
Rock Island	14.0	9.6	8.0	50.8	149 374	147 546	-1.2	-1.0	9 633	7 849	-2 972	60 367	2.36	61.9	12.7	33.6
St. Clair	13.2	7.6	6.3	51.8	256 082	270 063	5.5	-2.2	17 809	13 070	-10 729	102 404	2.58	66.5	17.3	29.4
Saline	13.8	10.5	8.7	50.7	26 733	24 913	-6.8	-1.5	1 611	1 823	-124	10 070	2.41	64.5	13.0	31.5
Sangamon	14.0	8.7	6.8	52.0	188 951	197 465	4.5	0.6	12 283	10 031	-879	83 102	2.34	61.6	12.3	32.0
Schuyler	15.2	10.5	9.2	47.3	7 189	7 544	4.9	-6.8	312	439	-330	3 042	2.26	71.3	6.2	25.8
Scott	14.2	9.5	9.1	51.9	5 537	5 355	-3.3	-4.9	227	304	-168	2 074	2.51	68.1	10.3	25.8
Shelby	14.6	11.2	9.4	50.6	22 893	22 363	-2.3	-2.6	1 250	1 220	-549	8 941	2.46	71.0	7.8	25.3
Stark	14.7	12.8	11.6	50.7	6 332	5 994	-5.3	-3.4	334	417	-99	2 403	2.41	67.2	5.0	29.3
Stephenson	14.9	10.5	10.0	51.6	48 979	47 711	-2.6	-4.1	2 568	2 803	-1 732	19 311	2.39	63.9	12.2	30.8
Tazewell	13.5	9.2	7.8	50.6	128 485	135 394	5.4	-0.4	8 438	7 200	-1 902	54 330	2.45	68.7	10.2	26.7
Union	14.5	11.2	8.7	50.1	18 293	17 808	-2.7	-2.2	980	1 179	-219	6 815	2.49	66.5	10.7	31.4
Vermilion	13.7	9.6	7.8	50.3	83 919	81 625	-2.7	-2.9	5 629	4 863	-2 968	31 601	2.48	64.3	14.3	31.1
Wabash	15.2	9.6	9.2	50.6	12 937	11 947	-7.7	-3.4	708	717	-347	4 806	2.42	68.4	8.6	28.5
Warren	13.9	9.9	8.5	51.2	18 735	17 710	-5.5	-1.0	1 146	954	-384	6 817	2.43	65.3	10.2	29.8
Washington	14.9	9.5	8.9	49.9	15 148	14 716	-2.9	-3.0	810	767	-483	5 788	2.46	68.3	7.6	28.8
Wayne	14.0	10.6	9.2	50.7	17 151	16 760	-2.3	-2.0	1 048	1 103	-233	7 047	2.34	69.6	9.2	28.4
White	14.2	11.0	10.8	51.4	15 371	14 665	-4.6	-2.3	838	1 144	-41	6 300	2.25	67.4	9.4	28.5
Whiteside	14.6	10.0	8.9	50.7	60 653	58 498	-3.6	-2.4	3 414	3 323	-1 448	23 328	2.43	66.4	10.0	29.2
Will	11.6	6.8	4.4	50.4	502 266	677 574	34.9	1.4	41 583	21 035	-11 247	223 379	3.02	76.6	10.9	19.7
Williamson	13.2	10.2	7.5	50.3	61 296	66 362	8.3	1.7	4 074	3 915	966	26 758	2.42	67.6	12.3	28.0

1. No spouse present.

Table B. States and Counties — Population, Vital Statistics, Medicare, and Crime

STATE County	Persons in group quarters, 2015	Daytime population, 2010–2014 Number	Employ-ment/ resi-dence ratio	Births, 2015 Total	Rate[1]	Deaths, 2015 Number	Rate[1]	Persons under 65 with no health insurance, 2014 Number	Percent	Medicare, 2015 Total Beneficiaries	Enrolled in Original Medicare	Enrolled in Medicare Advantage	Serious crimes known to police,[2] 2014 Total Number	Rate[3]
	32	33	34	35	36	37	38	39	40	41	42	43	44	45
ILLINOIS—Cont'd														
Hardin	112	3 863	0.74	35	8.4	59	14.1	312	9.9	1 054	909	145	56	1 350
Henderson	51	5 268	0.46	86	12.3	87	12.4	519	9.8	1 562	1 338	224	NA	NA
Henry	726	42 131	0.66	550	11.1	524	10.6	3 059	7.7	9 831	8 151	1 680	758	1 702
Iroquois	468	26 304	0.78	286	10.0	330	11.5	2 312	10.1	6 750	5 781	969	465	1 652
Jackson	3 847	64 274	1.16	678	11.4	438	7.4	5 543	11.4	9 616	7 516	2 100	1 967	3 332
Jasper	54	8 317	0.71	117	12.2	82	8.5	690	8.8	1 870	1 663	207	87	911
Jefferson	2 238	43 282	1.28	459	12.0	425	11.1	2 419	8.1	8 050	7 022	1 028	1 400	3 630
Jersey	814	18 470	0.58	221	9.8	196	8.7	1 485	8.2	3 788	3 234	554	397	1 762
Jo Daviess	167	20 154	0.79	168	7.6	244	11.0	1 593	9.5	5 625	3 428	2 197	221	1 006
Johnson	1 764	11 433	0.70	98	7.7	125	9.8	744	8.6	2 924	2 290	634	111	957
Kane	6 797	487 877	0.86	6 763	12.8	3 179	6.0	55 759	12.1	68 161	52 209	15 952	7 563	1 475
Kankakee	5 161	108 987	0.92	1 329	12.0	1 099	9.9	8 749	9.6	19 764	15 918	3 846	2 999	3 053
Kendall	208	91 205	0.54	1 659	13.5	508	4.1	7 500	6.8	8 832	7 068	1 764	1 536	1 277
Knox	3 960	52 221	0.99	555	10.7	575	11.1	3 625	9.4	11 795	7 868	3 927	1 392	3 137
Lake	17 974	719 018	1.05	7 896	11.2	4 419	6.3	59 635	9.9	89 208	76 902	12 306	12 035	1 722
LaSalle	3 578	107 758	0.90	1 119	10.0	1 199	10.7	8 021	8.9	22 151	19 365	2 786	2 067	1 904
Lawrence	2 589	17 203	1.12	170	10.3	219	13.2	1 010	8.9	3 116	2 860	256	133	951
Lee	3 052	34 163	0.93	371	10.7	375	10.8	2 224	8.5	7 017	5 855	1 162	385	1 145
Livingston	2 605	38 040	0.97	383	10.4	361	9.8	2 192	7.7	6 549	5 158	1 391	617	1 624
Logan	4 309	28 767	0.88	306	10.3	306	10.3	1 541	7.4	5 474	3 945	1 529	590	2 094
McDonough	3 830	33 625	1.09	277	8.8	274	8.7	2 148	9.2	5 328	3 945	1 383	546	1 685
McHenry	1 647	260 889	0.69	3 177	10.3	1 899	6.2	23 404	8.7	47 426	42 136	5 290	3 510	1 166
McLean	10 593	177 921	1.06	2 070	11.9	1 143	6.6	9 396	6.5	22 752	15 666	7 086	3 598	2 072
Macon	4 130	115 572	1.12	1 316	12.2	1 143	10.6	7 108	8.2	22 944	18 097	4 847	3 039	2 793
Macoupin	835	38 621	0.59	415	9.0	566	12.3	3 062	8.2	10 652	9 249	1 403	666	1 521
Madison	3 826	250 435	0.86	3 057	11.5	2 716	10.2	17 320	7.8	49 791	34 624	15 167	5 136	1 930
Marion	758	37 891	0.94	480	12.5	403	10.5	2 916	9.4	9 869	8 793	1 076	1 041	2 802
Marshall	255	10 780	0.72	129	10.8	139	11.6	786	8.4	2 626	2 140	486	110	1 036
Mason	206	12 780	0.74	141	10.2	168	12.2	1 065	9.6	3 671	3 066	605	NA	NA
Massac	292	13 570	0.73	153	10.3	171	11.5	1 071	9.0	3 291	2 817	474	374	2 497
Menard	154	8 964	0.40	118	9.4	136	10.9	758	7.4	2 420	1 689	731	50	483
Mercer	185	12 391	0.50	154	9.7	174	10.9	906	7.2	3 320	2 569	751	NA	NA
Monroe	343	25 390	0.52	325	9.6	306	9.1	1 690	6.0	5 533	3 661	1 872	193	575
Montgomery	2 070	29 304	0.96	306	10.6	375	12.9	1 763	8.0	6 642	5 813	829	395	1 355
Morgan	3 074	35 821	1.03	388	11.1	358	10.3	2 281	8.7	6 989	5 618	1 371	653	1 960
Moultrie	395	14 065	0.87	199	13.3	153	10.3	1 203	10.1	3 349	2 805	544	NA	NA
Ogle	525	46 269	0.73	516	10.0	469	9.0	3 922	9.2	9 376	7 109	2 267	297	747
Peoria	4 882	209 736	1.27	2 629	14.1	1 720	9.2	13 886	8.9	33 314	21 880	11 434	6 989	3 702
Perry	2 406	20 138	0.77	228	10.6	216	10.0	1 365	8.7	4 209	3 324	885	185	875
Piatt	72	12 673	0.53	186	11.3	165	10.1	921	6.9	3 497	2 147	1 350	124	827
Pike	627	14 714	0.78	168	10.5	178	11.1	1 350	10.9	3 614	3 188	426	178	1 108
Pope	408	3 979	0.74	22	5.2	22	5.2	342	10.7	955	795	160	NA	NA
Pulaski	21	6 214	1.12	60	10.4	65	11.3	472	10.2	1 355	1 168	187	50	1 033
Putnam	2	5 089	0.69	41	7.2	62	10.8	382	8.2	1 296	1 101	195	28	637
Randolph	4 504	33 596	1.04	337	10.2	373	11.3	1 949	8.3	6 654	5 323	1 331	357	1 177
Richland	364	15 787	0.95	198	12.3	182	11.3	1 054	8.3	3 768	3 392	376	384	2 376
Rock Island	4 631	158 973	1.18	1 767	12.1	1 425	9.7	12 269	10.5	29 111	22 493	6 618	3 955	2 702
St. Clair	4 653	255 755	0.89	3 308	12.5	2 578	9.7	20 376	9.0	43 145	29 461	13 684	7 551	2 930
Saline	884	25 455	1.06	304	12.4	324	13.2	1 982	10.2	6 273	5 347	926	502	2 158
Sangamon	3 912	213 225	1.15	2 285	11.5	2 040	10.3	12 682	7.7	36 400	22 397	14 003	8 784	4 600
Schuyler	463	6 401	0.66	49	6.9	73	10.2	593	10.1	1 457	1 219	238	70	944
Scott	43	4 321	0.59	34	6.6	46	9.0	391	9.2	997	834	163	NA	NA
Shelby	205	18 629	0.63	244	11.1	252	11.5	1 518	8.7	4 786	4 349	437	86	495
Stark	92	5 113	0.70	68	11.7	85	14.6	395	9.0	1 375	1 033	342	NA	NA
Stephenson	835	45 984	0.95	478	10.4	530	11.5	3 002	8.2	11 142	7 281	3 861	856	1 871
Tazewell	2 733	128 429	0.88	1 567	11.6	1 387	10.3	7 015	6.3	26 484	19 139	7 345	2 370	1 846
Union	582	15 656	0.72	194	11.1	219	12.6	1 475	10.6	4 008	3 143	865	343	1 958
Vermilion	2 979	79 651	0.97	1 063	13.4	911	11.5	5 617	8.8	17 093	10 132	6 961	3 240	4 120
Wabash	88	10 337	0.74	129	11.2	119	10.3	803	8.6	2 429	2 214	215	201	1 735
Warren	1 010	16 873	0.89	233	13.2	180	10.2	1 369	10.1	3 428	2 703	725	296	1 671
Washington	246	14 994	1.06	167	11.7	134	9.3	845	7.3	2 676	2 324	352	246	1 712
Wayne	76	15 392	0.84	200	12.1	202	12.3	1 237	9.3	3 614	3 319	295	242	1 557
White	391	13 708	0.86	154	10.7	209	14.6	1 024	9.2	3 744	3 310	434	NA	NA
Whiteside	1 010	53 615	0.84	649	11.4	597	10.5	3 942	8.6	13 364	11 255	2 109	986	1 765
Will	9 114	602 828	0.75	7 638	11.4	4 230	6.2	55 299	9.2	77 078	62 523	14 555	9 998	1 478
Williamson	2 138	65 943	0.97	769	11.4	754	11.2	4 842	9.0	12 900	10 667	2 233	950	1 497

1. Per 1,000 estimated resident population.   2. Data for serious crimes have not been adjusted for underreporting; this may affect comparability between geographic areas and over time.
3. Per 100,000 population estimated by the FBI.

Table B. States and Counties — Crime, Education, Money Income, and Poverty

STATE County	Serious crimes known to police, 2014 (cont.)[1] Rate[2] Violent	Property	Education — School enrollment and attainment, 2010–2014 — Enrollment[3] Total	Percent private	Attainment[4] (percent) High school graduate or less	Bachelor's degree or more	Local government expenditures,[5] 2012–2013 Total current spending (mil dol)	Current spending per student (dollars)	Money income, 2010–2014 — Households Per capita income[6] (dollars)	Median income (dollars)	Mean income (dollars)	Percent with income of $200,000 or more	Income and poverty, 2014 Median household income (dollars)	Percent below poverty level All persons	Children under 18 years	Children 5 to 17 years in families
	46	47	48	49	50	51	52	53	54	55	56	57	58	59	60	61
ILLINOIS—Cont'd																
Hardin	265	1 085	930	5.6	54.7	10.8	5.5	8 671	21 901	38 170	50 410	2.7	37 331	20.6	32.5	29.5
Henderson	NA	NA	1 382	9.8	54.1	14.1	9.4	10 084	27 132	48 438	61 712	0.8	50 999	11.7	19.1	17.1
Henry	128	1 574	11 668	8.9	47.7	19.6	86.6	9 943	26 845	52 518	65 639	2.2	51 025	11.3	14.8	13.3
Iroquois	121	1 531	6 650	11.0	53.2	14.7	55.4	11 742	25 234	47 184	61 808	2.9	46 895	15.8	22.3	19.7
Jackson	425	2 907	24 365	5.5	34.3	33.8	90.3	12 079	20 729	32 681	50 407	1.8	34 395	30.4	32.9	31.1
Jasper	42	869	2 125	14.9	47.5	18.4	19.6	13 880	25 063	54 133	62 243	1.1	52 919	11.0	17.5	16.7
Jefferson	570	3 059	8 887	9.8	47.7	15.9	63.0	10 260	22 849	43 173	57 040	2.1	43 073	19.5	28.2	28.5
Jersey	102	1 659	5 925	25.8	45.6	16.2	26.7	9 808	26 154	54 391	66 070	2.1	52 493	11.6	16.5	14.7
Jo Daviess	109	897	4 626	12.9	46.8	23.5	39.6	11 720	29 477	52 065	67 996	2.7	51 282	10.7	15.6	14.5
Johnson	233	724	2 595	4.9	48.3	15.8	19.4	9 850	19 684	41 414	54 704	1.8	45 773	15.9	19.7	17.9
Kane	159	1 316	150 034	16.1	40.8	31.8	1 350.7	11 026	30 645	70 514	91 016	7.3	72 131	10.7	15.6	14.8
Kankakee	329	2 724	30 749	19.7	47.3	17.6	204.9	10 598	24 117	51 000	63 556	1.8	56 326	14.7	21.0	20.3
Kendall	95	1 182	36 455	13.6	32.2	34.3	284.0	10 312	31 110	83 844	93 969	5.7	90 640	5.4	7.4	6.8
Knox	338	2 799	12 292	18.0	50.6	17.6	87.4	11 680	22 273	39 800	52 327	1.2	38 992	19.3	27.2	25.9
Lake	148	1 574	200 830	16.6	32.1	42.7	1 963.5	14 339	38 459	77 873	109 622	12.2	78 001	9.5	12.6	11.2
LaSalle	118	1 786	26 977	11.1	49.1	16.3	210.5	12 311	25 668	51 232	63 458	2.1	51 205	13.6	19.5	17.5
Lawrence	93	858	3 702	15.5	57.2	9.3	21.4	9 061	14 208	39 569	50 450	1.3	41 759	18.1	24.1	22.3
Lee	92	1 053	7 801	12.7	49.2	16.5	48.9	10 937	24 943	52 004	63 092	2.4	54 472	10.9	16.2	15.4
Livingston	190	1 435	8 938	8.8	52.6	16.0	76.5	11 956	25 831	54 723	67 649	2.5	53 918	11.9	16.7	15.6
Logan	302	1 792	7 504	14.8	48.7	16.4	38.4	11 397	21 986	49 882	60 948	2.1	54 353	12.6	18.1	16.4
McDonough	231	1 454	12 842	6.4	37.7	33.5	47.5	13 364	20 592	37 959	51 619	1.5	42 684	23.6	23.2	22.2
McHenry	91	1 075	87 462	15.8	34.4	32.2	597.9	11 522	33 118	76 345	92 090	6.5	76 856	6.9	8.9	8.1
McLean	279	1 794	57 902	12.6	30.7	43.4	276.7	10 992	30 728	61 955	80 056	5.1	60 460	14.3	12.6	11.8
Macon	364	2 429	26 691	20.7	45.6	23.1	211.2	12 747	26 259	46 696	62 486	2.6	47 575	16.3	26.3	24.0
Macoupin	144	1 377	11 277	12.3	48.8	17.0	77.9	8 710	25 402	50 911	61 928	1.8	48 544	12.9	19.7	17.8
Madison	196	2 050	69 815	15.9	41.6	24.8	424.2	10 110	28 093	53 912	68 807	3.2	54 375	13.1	17.6	16.2
Marion	280	2 522	8 814	11.0	49.2	13.8	80.9	11 485	22 398	41 783	53 816	1.1	44 289	18.6	29.9	28.4
Marshall	188	848	2 591	10.6	48.8	17.7	15.3	11 136	26 399	53 914	64 015	2.0	53 732	10.7	15.8	14.3
Mason	NA	NA	3 063	6.2	55.1	13.3	29.8	10 150	23 937	42 476	54 657	1.1	46 878	14.8	20.3	18.5
Massac	307	2 190	3 547	5.0	49.9	15.3	23.4	9 432	23 190	43 092	55 628	1.9	40 590	20.7	30.0	27.9
Menard	77	406	2 998	9.7	45.5	21.2	22.6	8 981	29 391	59 989	72 090	3.1	61 388	10.1	15.3	13.6
Mercer	NA	NA	3 676	8.4	50.4	15.5	26.7	9 189	26 739	51 259	64 008	2.4	54 916	9.6	13.2	10.9
Monroe	39	536	8 280	17.9	41.3	26.2	49.2	9 239	33 059	69 592	86 386	5.9	73 684	5.1	6.0	5.0
Montgomery	158	1 197	6 355	7.7	57.3	12.7	41.3	8 963	20 067	45 158	56 958	1.6	45 288	17.0	23.4	20.1
Morgan	93	1 867	8 870	29.4	51.1	22.1	57.4	11 568	24 822	46 524	61 350	2.3	46 406	15.1	21.4	20.0
Moultrie	NA	NA	3 486	12.1	53.5	15.5	15.9	9 344	23 801	47 438	59 868	1.5	52 790	11.8	17.9	15.9
Ogle	78	669	13 669	11.4	45.6	20.0	115.8	12 191	27 337	55 894	68 441	2.3	57 126	11.4	15.7	13.5
Peoria	472	3 229	48 792	24.9	39.1	29.3	327.2	11 127	28 414	51 454	68 769	3.6	52 448	16.7	23.8	22.7
Perry	109	766	4 802	7.4	51.7	13.3	27.0	9 639	19 999	40 532	51 364	0.7	42 032	16.7	21.7	20.1
Piatt	147	680	4 056	9.8	41.5	26.6	31.0	9 546	31 750	63 002	78 986	4.8	65 971	7.4	9.9	9.0
Pike	93	1 014	3 789	10.0	56.1	14.7	26.2	9 637	20 925	38 740	50 047	1.0	39 005	15.2	22.6	21.1
Pope	NA	NA	840	5.2	48.6	14.7	5.2	9 014	21 431	39 395	51 808	1.3	40 722	19.7	30.8	29.3
Pulaski	351	682	1 504	8.6	53.6	11.2	14.1	13 790	19 575	33 946	47 616	1.7	33 943	23.0	35.9	32.7
Putnam	0	637	1 291	6.2	50.2	13.7	9.9	10 935	28 158	55 360	68 137	3.7	62 024	8.9	14.7	12.8
Randolph	115	1 062	6 718	12.4	58.4	12.3	47.6	11 339	22 771	48 901	59 100	1.3	47 862	13.8	19.1	17.5
Richland	278	2 098	3 787	13.9	43.3	21.3	23.2	9 245	23 996	44 514	56 923	2.2	43 396	14.6	21.6	19.9
Rock Island	327	2 376	36 078	19.5	43.7	21.7	243.3	11 043	26 459	48 226	62 093	2.7	48 024	16.3	25.1	21.3
St. Clair	618	2 313	75 611	14.4	38.5	25.6	483.6	11 350	26 459	50 728	66 745	3.0	50 155	19.1	27.4	25.1
Saline	288	1 870	5 400	3.8	47.1	14.0	41.0	9 628	21 295	38 772	50 808	1.3	38 329	21.0	31.9	29.7
Sangamon	835	3 764	50 553	16.3	36.1	33.0	356.0	11 926	30 594	55 565	72 162	3.9	55 371	15.3	22.6	21.1
Schuyler	135	809	1 486	4.8	50.1	17.8	12.9	10 538	23 852	48 575	59 850	0.9	47 092	13.2	17.2	15.7
Scott	NA	NA	1 285	8.2	58.5	12.1	9.1	9 608	24 395	48 500	59 995	2.1	51 584	12.0	18.0	16.0
Shelby	52	444	4 878	8.4	53.0	14.3	22.8	9 374	23 279	47 411	56 380	1.0	48 994	11.7	17.6	16.4
Stark	NA	NA	1 292	10.4	49.9	17.6	10.4	10 169	27 104	52 956	64 362	4.2	50 219	11.9	15.8	14.7
Stephenson	116	1 756	11 229	12.2	47.1	18.0	81.0	11 837	23 686	44 631	55 988	1.1	48 569	14.1	22.2	21.5
Tazewell	188	1 659	33 215	16.6	40.9	24.6	206.6	10 159	28 953	57 052	71 394	2.9	60 490	9.1	12.9	11.5
Union	205	1 752	4 045	8.9	46.3	21.3	27.3	9 346	22 430	41 849	54 800	2.1	40 957	17.9	24.5	22.3
Vermilion	598	3 523	18 153	8.3	54.1	13.8	146.8	10 877	21 924	42 548	54 076	1.4	42 036	19.0	27.7	26.3
Wabash	181	1 553	2 841	14.3	43.3	17.4	15.6	8 680	24 493	48 679	58 787	1.5	49 385	14.8	21.2	19.1
Warren	209	1 462	5 055	27.5	47.8	20.5	23.9	8 633	22 923	43 683	57 996	1.9	44 180	13.5	19.0	17.4
Washington	397	1 315	3 148	16.8	42.4	21.5	18.3	9 520	27 996	52 761	67 166	2.1	54 683	10.2	13.1	11.8
Wayne	283	1 274	3 764	10.8	48.5	12.5	25.0	9 743	23 897	44 535	56 154	1.9	46 839	14.9	22.9	21.3
White	NA	NA	2 973	3.2	47.6	13.5	35.0	13 985	26 388	45 347	60 675	2.1	46 927	14.1	22.1	21.7
Whiteside	175	1 589	13 650	13.3	48.6	16.6	104.5	10 918	24 815	48 343	59 887	1.4	49 895	12.2	18.0	16.6
Will	162	1 316	203 973	16.9	36.5	32.6	1 321.6	11 250	30 791	76 142	91 602	6.5	75 176	8.1	11.8	10.7
Williamson	63	1 434	15 176	7.5	40.8	22.1	103.8	10 093	24 096	43 855	58 366	1.8	46 322	15.8	23.2	21.2

1. Data for serious crimes have not been adjusted for underreporting; this may affect comparability between geographic areas and over time.   2. Per 100,000 population estimated by the FBI.
3. All persons 3 years old and over enrolled in nursery school through college.   4. Persons 25 years old and over.   5. Elementary and secondary education expenditures.
6. Based on population estimated by the American Community Survey, 2010–2014.

Table B. States and Counties — **Personal Income**

| STATE County | Personal income, 2014 | | | | | | | | | | Earnings, 2014 | | |
	Total (mil dol)	Percent change, 2013–2014	Per capita¹ Dollars	Per capita¹ Rank	Wages and salaries (mil dol)	Supplements to wages and salaries; employer contributions (mil dol) Pension and insurance	Government social insurance	Proprietors' income (mil dol)	Dividends, interest, and rent (mil dol)	Personal transfer receipts (mil dol)	Total (mil dol)	Contributions for government social insurance (mil dol) From employee and self-employed	From employer
	62	63	64	65	66	67	68	69	70	71	72	73	74
ILLINOIS—Cont'd													
Hardin	138	0.8	33 435	2 208	37	8	3	8	20	50	56	4	3
Henderson	265	-8.3	38 335	1 416	40	11	3	32	45	58	86	5	3
Henry	2 085	-1.4	42 008	949	551	122	39	195	364	374	907	54	39
Iroquois	1 164	-7.2	40 307	1 138	288	63	21	167	199	259	540	29	21
Jackson	1 950	0.9	32 675	2 340	1 149	325	70	141	384	427	1 685	78	70
Jasper	405	-4.6	42 100	943	83	21	6	99	72	76	209	9	6
Jefferson	1 421	2.8	36 878	1 620	862	155	65	117	237	341	1 200	67	65
Jersey	803	-1.4	35 586	1 841	179	41	13	34	120	185	266	18	13
Jo Daviess	983	-1.5	44 164	747	295	62	22	81	253	183	460	29	22
Johnson	338	2.3	26 824	2 991	87	25	5	23	56	105	140	9	5
Kane	22 604	3.7	42 868	862	10 061	1 788	734	1 040	3 245	2 889	13 622	747	734
Kankakee	3 971	0.7	35 657	1 830	1 821	361	135	168	535	940	2 485	142	135
Kendall	4 970	3.7	40 957	1 067	1 139	228	80	108	484	503	1 554	87	80
Knox	1 889	-1.2	36 280	1 727	813	161	72	96	322	522	1 142	72	72
Lake	46 069	3.5	65 329	85	25 120	3 745	1 648	2 113	11 145	4 035	32 626	1 789	1 648
LaSalle	4 285	-0.3	38 524	1 386	1 943	372	143	47	694	890	2 714	159	143
Lawrence	548	-1.8	33 163	2 253	180	41	14	47	100	144	282	17	14
Lee	1 330	-2.1	38 301	1 422	538	104	39	109	213	282	790	47	39
Livingston	1 466	-8.3	38 685	1 367	632	127	44	227	223	287	1 030	51	44
Logan	1 015	-7.3	34 127	2 094	365	74	26	124	162	235	589	31	26
McDonough	1 082	-2.4	33 945	2 122	520	150	31	67	208	231	768	35	31
McHenry	14 356	3.2	46 720	543	4 485	814	332	312	2 149	1 702	5 943	340	332
McLean	7 518	-1.0	43 192	826	4 851	806	318	532	1 134	921	6 507	347	318
Macon	4 704	1.5	43 413	802	2 666	456	193	409	775	990	3 724	216	193
Macoupin	1 647	-2.6	35 451	1 866	393	87	28	81	278	401	589	39	28
Madison	10 647	2.7	39 942	1 187	4 429	859	328	482	1 705	2 169	6 098	359	328
Marion	1 421	0.3	36 846	1 626	545	112	44	88	226	426	789	48	44
Marshall	484	-7.6	40 311	1 137	134	28	10	40	84	106	211	13	10
Mason	510	-6.3	36 705	1 644	127	33	8	61	85	131	230	12	8
Massac	506	0.8	33 923	2 127	174	37	12	30	79	152	252	16	12
Menard	502	-4.2	39 944	1 186	68	18	4	38	83	92	129	8	4
Mercer	662	-3.2	41 513	1 007	114	27	8	60	114	135	209	13	8
Monroe	1 692	4.0	50 171	378	309	62	22	126	278	224	519	31	22
Montgomery	976	-6.0	33 234	2 241	353	75	26	111	179	257	565	31	26
Morgan	1 237	-1.7	35 422	1 873	585	120	43	107	230	300	854	48	43
Moultrie	620	-3.0	41 805	972	157	30	11	104	89	111	302	17	11
Ogle	2 077	-1.6	39 870	1 197	762	160	53	107	330	392	1 083	64	53
Peoria	8 537	1.4	45 572	634	5 246	832	390	401	1 466	1 452	6 870	390	390
Perry	668	-0.2	30 801	2 616	191	50	13	54	112	178	307	18	13
Piatt	779	0.7	47 430	502	129	31	9	72	119	127	241	13	9
Pike	599	-4.2	37 363	1 544	157	35	11	109	97	141	312	15	11
Pope	128	2.1	29 850	2 738	24	7	2	10	20	35	42	3	2
Pulaski	199	-5.1	34 197	2 081	75	21	5	13	27	73	114	6	5
Putnam	243	-1.1	41 732	977	76	14	5	21	47	44	116	6	5
Randolph	1 052	2.0	32 011	2 437	452	110	32	56	193	264	650	35	32
Richland	603	-0.2	37 540	1 518	233	48	17	79	106	151	376	21	17
Rock Island	5 823	1.8	39 868	1 198	4 340	757	300	297	1 155	1 152	5 694	324	300
St. Clair	10 288	2.5	38 717	1 361	4 548	981	358	419	1 837	2 247	6 306	351	358
Saline	901	-1.3	36 588	1 670	394	82	29	70	141	270	576	34	29
Sangamon	8 423	2.2	42 326	921	4 786	948	329	566	1 574	1 495	6 629	352	329
Schuyler	327	-2.1	44 588	710	111	24	7	48	44	56	190	9	7
Scott	182	-4.6	35 034	1 932	40	10	3	24	27	39	78	4	3
Shelby	784	-6.7	35 557	1 844	172	38	13	101	128	173	324	18	13
Stark	213	-15.6	36 633	1 661	53	12	4	23	39	48	91	5	4
Stephenson	1 735	-1.7	37 359	1 545	780	144	58	120	326	407	1 101	67	58
Tazewell	5 658	1.2	41 690	982	3 720	542	255	285	907	1 016	4 802	278	255
Union	590	-1.3	33 805	2 145	161	41	11	26	99	189	239	16	11
Vermilion	2 791	-1.0	35 009	1 935	1 223	263	92	227	417	729	1 805	105	92
Wabash	478	-1.3	41 393	1 022	130	32	9	42	90	100	213	12	9
Warren	617	-4.1	34 522	2 020	225	47	16	57	106	138	345	20	16
Washington	671	-1.1	46 771	539	270	56	20	114	114	112	461	23	20
Wayne	643	-2.4	38 863	1 339	166	38	12	144	106	142	359	18	12
White	658	-3.2	45 748	616	190	38	14	133	112	145	375	21	14
Whiteside	2 228	-0.4	39 174	1 299	865	198	61	141	396	519	1 265	73	61
Will	30 065	3.5	43 864	772	10 760	1 912	798	828	3 664	3 850	14 298	804	798
Williamson	2 610	1.9	38 946	1 325	1 140	251	85	132	402	582	1 608	93	85

1. Based on the resident population estimated as of July 1 of the year shown.

Table B. States and Counties — Earnings, Social Security, and Housing

STATE County	Earnings, 2014 (cont.) Percent by selected industries									Social Security beneficiaries, December 2014		Supplemental Security Income recipients, December 2014	Housing units, 2015	
	Farm	Mining	Construction	Manufacturing	Information: professional, scientific, technical services	Retail trade	Finance, insurance, real estate and leasing	Health care and social assistance	Government	Number	Rate[1]		Total	Percent change, 2010–2014
	75	76	77	78	79	80	81	82	83	84	85	86	87	88

ILLINOIS—Cont'd

Hardin	0.9	14.5	D	D	D	4.8	D	21.5	23.0	1 235	293	176	2 454	-1.4
Henderson	23.8	D	5.3	D	D	4.2	D	5.4	22.1	1 710	244	105	3 819	-0.2
Henry	5.2	D	9.0	16.0	D	7.6	5.0	6.9	22.1	11 245	226	629	22 101	-0.3
Iroquois	22.6	0.1	7.2	6.4	2.2	6.9	3.7	D	15.4	7 160	249	479	13 431	-0.2
Jackson	1.5	D	4.7	2.5	4.4	6.2	3.1	15.7	45.3	9 140	154	1 475	28 692	0.4
Jasper	37.6	4.3	2.8	4.7	D	5.3	D	D	14.4	2 185	227	136	4 326	-0.4
Jefferson	4.0	1.7	2.6	23.3	4.2	6.2	4.7	D	14.2	8 650	225	1 008	16 795	-0.9
Jersey	1.8	0.0	9.0	1.8	D	10.3	3.5	D	26.9	5 335	237	370	10 037	1.9
Jo Daviess	8.4	D	7.5	15.6	4.2	6.8	4.1	D	17.7	6 145	275	186	13 594	0.2
Johnson	1.2	D	6.2	1.0	4.1	4.5	D	D	49.0	3 235	253	275	5 544	-1.0
Kane	0.2	0.2	7.3	17.0	8.9	5.9	5.4	11.0	17.8	71 410	135	5 180	184 940	1.6
Kankakee	2.7	D	4.0	19.5	D	7.4	4.7	17.2	16.7	22 205	199	2 723	45 185	-0.1
Kendall	1.1	D	7.4	17.0	5.6	8.8	3.8	6.4	24.9	14 140	116	548	41 442	2.8
Knox	4.1	D	3.2	6.2	D	9.2	3.2	D	18.9	12 075	232	1 283	23 858	-0.9
Lake	0.0	D	3.5	22.2	10.1	7.1	6.6	6.7	13.4	100 285	142	7 888	262 331	0.8
LaSalle	1.5	3.4	5.2	20.9	4.1	7.5	4.4	9.7	15.4	24 940	223	1 599	49 892	-0.2
Lawrence	5.4	15.7	4.4	18.7	1.7	4.5	8.8	8.3	19.5	3 480	210	294	6 975	0.6
Lee	3.1	0.9	3.0	24.3	2.7	6.0	3.5	16.3	16.8	7 835	225	528	15 019	-0.2
Livingston	15.0	D	5.0	18.2	D	6.0	3.1	8.1	17.2	8 140	220	505	15 815	-0.5
Logan	16.0	D	2.5	15.9	2.9	6.6	4.1	10.0	16.4	6 200	209	412	12 015	-0.8
McDonough	5.2	D	3.1	12.2	2.6	5.8	3.1	D	49.7	5 600	177	558	14 376	-0.3
McHenry	0.5	0.1	9.6	19.0	5.8	7.7	3.5	10.8	17.5	47 885	156	2 011	117 351	1.1
McLean	1.9	D	3.4	4.6	D	4.8	22.4	9.1	15.5	24 805	142	1 744	71 527	2.7
Macon	2.1	0.1	6.5	31.7	4.9	5.0	3.7	11.9	10.5	24 855	229	3 257	50 298	-0.4
Macoupin	5.6	D	6.1	8.4	2.7	7.3	4.2	D	22.3	11 440	247	1 017	21 529	-0.3
Madison	0.9	0.3	7.8	18.2	7.1	7.0	4.4	11.1	17.7	54 975	206	5 863	118 471	1.2
Marion	5.2	2.8	5.4	18.8	D	5.2	3.6	14.7	17.5	9 550	248	1 203	18 085	-1.2
Marshall	10.4	0.5	6.7	32.9	2.3	3.3	3.7	7.4	13.8	3 005	250	119	5 886	-0.5
Mason	20.5	D	3.5	1.4	1.8	5.1	3.4	5.3	30.0	3 530	254	253	7 013	-0.9
Massac	5.5	0.0	D	11.9	D	4.7	2.6	6.7	24.6	3 995	269	487	7 060	-0.7
Menard	20.6	D	8.1	0.9	4.6	5.7	5.7	D	27.4	2 750	219	155	5 670	0.3
Mercer	19.6	0.0	6.9	13.2	2.0	5.8	4.6	9.0	21.0	4 000	250	182	7 356	0.0
Monroe	6.9	0.2	8.5	4.1	15.9	8.3	7.2	6.2	16.5	6 300	187	161	13 857	3.5
Montgomery	13.5	6.6	4.4	6.5	3.2	7.7	4.8	D	18.5	7 015	241	681	13 048	-0.2
Morgan	5.1	0.0	3.7	17.1	4.2	7.5	7.5	11.1	20.0	7 940	227	874	15 383	-0.9
Moultrie	11.9	D	9.0	32.8	4.5	4.2	3.6	D	10.0	2 815	189	160	6 381	1.9
Ogle	1.6	D	6.6	22.3	D	5.5	4.9	5.8	17.1	10 945	210	570	22 536	-0.1
Peoria	0.4	D	5.2	11.4	15.4	5.1	5.6	22.6	11.8	36 555	195	4 916	83 560	0.6
Perry	7.9	D	4.5	10.7	D	6.4	3.6	D	32.7	4 820	223	429	9 490	0.7
Piatt	20.5	D	4.2	4.6	D	5.9	5.2	11.6	22.2	3 775	230	141	7 344	1.0
Pike	27.3	D	5.3	1.5	2.0	8.1	5.5	8.8	17.2	3 855	241	353	7 933	-0.2
Pope	13.1	D	5.9	D	D	D	D	D	41.6	945	221	88	2 464	-1.1
Pulaski	4.9	0.0	D	3.5	D	3.8	D	1.1	48.3	1 570	270	286	3 124	-1.0
Putnam	15.9	0.0	D	20.7	2.0	3.1	3.3	D	13.4	1 440	248	42	3 123	1.6
Randolph	5.5	D	5.0	21.5	D	7.3	2.9	D	27.3	7 060	214	531	13 797	0.7
Richland	13.3	6.2	2.2	7.2	2.6	5.7	5.2	13.7	16.0	3 950	245	436	7 470	-0.6
Rock Island	0.2	0.1	4.0	13.1	6.8	5.0	5.5	9.5	20.0	31 050	211	2 779	65 864	0.2
St. Clair	0.6	D	4.9	6.1	8.9	6.7	3.9	12.4	32.9	48 300	182	8 256	118 841	2.2
Saline	3.3	D	7.2	3.7	4.2	6.8	4.2	12.8	21.0	6 620	269	1 105	11 594	-0.9
Sangamon	1.2	D	4.7	3.1	8.6	5.9	8.4	21.4	26.0	40 820	205	4 627	90 785	1.0
Schuyler	21.3	D	4.0	1.3	0.9	3.5	1.7	3.0	23.1	1 670	231	99	3 431	-0.8
Scott	25.4	0.0	D	D	D	3.4	D	D	20.9	1 165	226	64	2 439	-0.8
Shelby	24.0	D	3.3	13.8	D	5.4	6.9	8.2	14.0	4 990	226	348	10 467	0.7
Stark	14.1	0.0	7.5	15.2	D	8.2	D	4.7	20.2	1 425	244	84	2 660	-0.5
Stephenson	3.3	0.0	10.6	24.0	3.7	5.1	8.0	14.0	14.7	11 735	253	1 121	21 883	-0.9
Tazewell	1.1	0.0	5.5	46.7	2.8	4.8	3.9	4.8	9.8	28 785	212	1 887	58 581	1.9
Union	3.2	D	4.3	6.2	2.8	9.8	3.4	D	32.8	4 605	264	652	7 908	-0.2
Vermilion	5.3	D	2.7	20.4	2.1	6.4	5.0	9.4	21.5	18 700	234	2 819	35 940	-1.0
Wabash	5.1	16.0	8.9	6.8	4.1	5.5	3.5	D	29.5	2 740	237	201	5 518	-1.2
Warren	10.8	D	2.3	28.4	D	4.9	D	D	12.0	3 860	217	287	7 660	-0.3
Washington	14.0	2.6	4.2	18.1	2.0	8.3	2.6	D	10.7	3 110	216	142	6 569	0.5
Wayne	27.6	9.9	2.9	7.4	2.0	5.2	2.3	D	14.2	3 930	238	274	7 873	-1.3
White	13.1	29.1	3.5	4.5	1.7	7.1	2.9	D	12.7	3 940	275	415	7 115	-0.9
Whiteside	2.9	D	3.3	26.6	3.5	6.0	3.4	5.4	25.9	14 235	249	1 125	25 737	-0.1
Will	0.2	0.2	8.4	12.0	7.0	6.8	3.8	10.8	17.0	97 685	142	6 602	240 823	1.4
Williamson	0.6	D	5.2	9.4	4.2	7.5	7.0	16.8	27.3	15 285	227	1 692	30 858	1.6

1. Per 1,000 resident population estimated as of July 1 of the year shown.

Table B. States and Counties — Housing, Labor Force, and Employment

STATE County	Housing units, 2010–2014								Civilian labor force, 2015		Unemployment		Civilian employment,[6] 2010–2014	Percent	
	Occupied units														
			Owner-occupied			Renter-occupied									
				Median owner cost as a percent of income											
	Total	Percent	Median value[1]	With a mortgage	Without a mortgage[2]	Median rent[3]	Median rent as a percent of income[2]	Substandard units[4] (percent)	Total	Percent change, 2014–2015	Total	Rate[5]	Total	Management, business, science and arts	Construction, production, and maintenance occupations
	89	90	91	92	93	94	95	96	97	98	99	100	101	102	103
ILLINOIS—Cont'd															
Hardin	1 731	82.7	68 100	18.5	12.5	303	30.5	2.1	1 549	-5.8	127	8.2	1 421	25.7	32.4
Henderson	3 116	79.6	86 300	19.2	10.0	589	22.8	1.1	3 767	0.6	223	5.9	3 390	28.4	33.2
Henry	20 237	77.5	110 100	19.4	12.4	620	24.3	1.0	25 147	-0.6	1 564	6.2	23 572	31.0	28.9
Iroquois	11 804	75.6	96 000	22.3	11.9	621	29.4	3.2	14 822	-1.4	850	5.7	13 463	27.6	31.2
Jackson	23 471	52.9	100 400	20.7	12.1	667	42.0	1.7	28 905	1.3	1 629	5.6	25 779	35.3	17.3
Jasper	3 796	86.3	91 800	18.9	10.1	531	24.0	0.7	4 678	0.4	297	6.3	4 833	28.8	32.6
Jefferson	15 289	72.6	85 400	19.7	12.4	588	28.1	2.3	17 323	-1.9	1 174	6.8	16 551	25.4	29.4
Jersey	8 873	80.2	121 700	20.3	11.8	653	27.9	1.1	11 195	0.8	708	6.3	10 592	31.6	25.8
Jo Daviess	9 555	78.2	137 200	22.7	13.0	659	23.1	1.0	11 515	-0.7	639	5.5	11 179	28.9	29.7
Johnson	4 380	81.4	88 700	20.1	13.6	636	27.1	1.6	4 144	-0.7	355	8.6	4 153	27.8	23.7
Kane	171 316	74.5	216 000	25.7	14.2	1 002	32.1	4.7	266 855	0.5	15 514	5.8	250 660	33.8	23.9
Kankakee	41 430	68.6	143 100	23.8	13.4	808	29.4	1.7	55 211	-1.0	3 763	6.8	49 729	29.2	28.0
Kendall	38 453	83.1	204 100	25.8	14.7	1 206	28.2	2.2	65 148	0.0	3 333	5.1	59 481	39.9	19.7
Knox	21 438	66.8	80 800	19.5	12.2	589	29.1	1.9	23 252	-1.7	1 440	6.2	21 563	29.8	27.0
Lake	241 846	75.1	247 300	25.4	14.7	1 055	30.5	2.8	368 107	0.3	20 072	5.5	335 183	42.0	17.1
LaSalle	43 891	74.4	123 400	22.2	12.4	688	28.3	1.2	57 537	0.3	4 042	7.0	51 263	26.7	29.9
Lawrence	4 981	76.0	66 200	17.8	10.6	530	25.7	2.3	6 144	-3.3	438	7.1	4 262	29.9	27.4
Lee	13 468	74.2	110 700	21.3	11.9	670	25.6	0.7	17 833	-2.0	971	5.4	15 893	29.6	27.4
Livingston	14 515	72.9	109 200	20.4	12.3	629	24.5	1.2	17 472	-0.2	961	5.5	16 082	27.4	32.7
Logan	10 908	69.3	97 500	18.0	11.8	610	27.2	0.7	13 077	0.1	720	5.5	11 108	31.3	22.2
McDonough	12 553	61.8	87 100	18.6	10.0	656	42.4	1.5	14 040	-2.0	882	6.3	14 462	33.1	20.2
McHenry	109 221	81.6	213 400	25.6	14.9	1 064	30.8	1.9	165 699	0.0	8 771	5.3	155 400	37.2	21.0
McLean	64 415	66.5	158 800	19.8	11.5	768	28.4	1.8	91 110	0.1	4 432	4.9	89 808	41.7	14.7
Macon	45 153	69.2	94 000	19.0	12.0	665	29.5	1.8	50 593	-0.7	3 588	7.1	48 675	31.7	24.5
Macoupin	19 098	76.2	96 000	18.0	10.9	617	28.5	2.3	23 302	0.5	1 477	6.3	21 598	28.1	29.6
Madison	107 298	71.4	125 100	21.1	11.9	782	30.5	1.2	133 510	0.7	8 080	6.1	125 122	33.9	23.7
Marion	15 835	75.2	68 500	19.9	12.4	626	33.2	2.7	18 083	0.0	1 242	6.9	16 981	26.3	31.9
Marshall	4 926	83.3	103 200	20.0	11.8	628	26.5	0.9	5 742	-0.4	382	6.7	5 641	27.8	32.6
Mason	6 155	76.0	80 800	20.4	12.1	582	29.7	1.2	6 649	-0.1	479	7.2	6 061	26.9	33.6
Massac	6 013	74.2	83 200	21.8	11.8	681	31.3	1.9	6 152	-2.9	453	7.4	5 930	27.9	27.1
Menard	5 119	80.5	119 900	19.1	10.9	653	23.1	2.0	6 767	0.0	323	4.8	6 319	32.3	23.5
Mercer	6 662	78.1	93 700	19.2	11.9	587	23.0	1.1	8 228	-0.9	514	6.2	7 632	30.5	33.5
Monroe	12 557	82.0	192 400	22.0	12.7	833	25.3	1.0	18 055	0.7	798	4.4	17 109	36.0	20.8
Montgomery	10 923	77.1	81 100	19.5	12.3	606	26.3	1.8	12 073	-0.8	927	7.7	9 999	31.9	24.5
Morgan	13 961	69.1	94 600	19.1	10.2	615	28.5	1.2	17 099	-1.0	865	5.1	16 403	32.0	25.8
Moultrie	5 669	77.6	96 700	19.8	11.0	622	25.7	2.7	7 362	4.2	324	4.4	6 624	28.4	33.1
Ogle	20 759	75.8	143 600	21.5	14.3	693	25.3	1.9	26 063	0.2	1 621	6.2	25 051	30.3	32.4
Peoria	76 019	65.1	124 700	20.2	11.7	712	28.6	2.1	90 864	-1.1	6 276	6.9	84 967	38.5	19.1
Perry	8 048	75.2	77 100	21.0	11.7	512	30.8	2.2	8 863	-0.5	642	7.2	8 445	24.6	35.5
Piatt	6 623	82.8	118 700	18.5	11.3	739	22.9	0.5	8 420	0.9	429	5.1	8 325	35.4	25.2
Pike	6 675	78.7	72 700	20.1	12.0	507	25.7	1.6	7 633	-1.8	395	5.2	7 189	25.0	33.1
Pope	1 672	83.3	107 600	20.1	15.0	501	23.1	1.5	1 781	-1.0	124	7.0	1 535	22.1	34.0
Pulaski	2 337	77.9	56 200	20.6	13.2	489	33.3	2.3	2 089	-2.4	187	9.0	2 116	25.1	29.6
Putnam	2 427	81.0	123 800	21.5	11.2	600	23.8	1.7	3 038	-0.2	193	6.4	2 707	27.4	32.9
Randolph	12 050	77.0	93 600	19.3	11.0	634	24.6	1.1	14 269	0.5	786	5.5	14 104	24.6	36.9
Richland	6 576	73.8	79 300	19.1	10.6	558	26.7	3.2	7 401	2.1	446	6.0	7 131	28.1	34.2
Rock Island	60 367	69.9	113 200	21.3	12.2	672	29.1	2.3	72 188	-0.8	4 670	6.5	67 927	30.0	26.4
St. Clair	102 404	66.5	121 300	21.6	12.8	802	31.5	1.6	127 292	0.4	8 444	6.6	117 313	34.1	20.6
Saline	10 070	71.6	71 100	20.1	12.2	590	29.4	1.9	10 565	-2.5	814	7.7	9 367	26.0	28.5
Sangamon	83 102	69.8	127 500	19.5	10.8	738	30.6	1.6	104 942	0.3	5 534	5.3	96 915	40.4	15.2
Schuyler	3 042	81.5	78 700	19.8	11.3	566	26.2	1.4	3 535	2.0	208	5.9	3 171	26.7	29.3
Scott	2 074	76.7	83 300	18.4	10.9	549	24.8	1.9	2 571	0.4	150	5.8	2 409	27.3	32.5
Shelby	8 941	80.7	86 100	19.8	10.7	622	23.7	1.3	10 211	0.4	617	6.0	9 888	28.2	34.5
Stark	2 403	81.8	87 800	18.8	10.9	600	22.4	1.6	2 781	-1.1	184	6.6	2 668	33.5	27.7
Stephenson	19 311	71.5	100 300	21.4	13.1	608	31.8	1.0	21 608	-3.1	1 445	6.7	21 476	29.1	30.5
Tazewell	54 330	76.2	133 300	20.0	11.3	680	26.5	1.2	67 541	-0.7	4 260	6.3	64 120	35.1	23.9
Union	6 815	76.1	88 400	19.9	13.4	519	29.2	1.6	7 354	0.6	571	7.8	7 042	32.2	27.0
Vermilion	31 601	70.1	75 200	19.8	11.5	634	29.3	1.6	35 642	0.0	2 542	7.1	32 612	25.9	31.6
Wabash	4 806	75.6	82 400	19.2	10.8	567	25.8	2.0	5 619	0.7	318	5.7	5 459	27.4	36.0
Warren	6 817	74.1	82 000	21.3	11.5	613	25.9	3.2	8 556	-2.3	465	5.4	8 065	27.7	28.1
Washington	5 788	79.9	107 500	21.6	11.9	629	26.1	1.8	9 320	3.0	363	3.9	7 401	31.6	33.0
Wayne	7 047	79.5	76 800	19.4	10.2	522	27.2	1.8	7 524	-2.1	524	7.0	7 629	26.0	36.5
White	6 300	75.7	71 700	18.4	10.5	533	22.9	1.8	7 010	-1.2	408	5.8	6 350	25.7	35.4
Whiteside	23 328	75.4	99 200	20.3	12.5	636	29.1	1.3	28 408	-0.9	1 786	6.3	26 434	27.5	30.8
Will	223 379	81.9	212 700	25.5	14.1	1 025	31.2	2.3	355 617	-0.3	21 485	6.0	327 270	36.1	22.4
Williamson	26 758	72.2	98 000	19.3	12.6	627	29.0	1.2	31 842	1.2	1 990	6.2	29 048	31.4	20.7

1. Specified owner-occupied units.   2. A value of 10.0 represents 10 percent or less; a value of 50.0 represents 50 percent or more.   3. Specified renter-occupied units.
4. Overcrowded or lacking complete plumbing facilities.   5. Percent of civilian labor force.   6. Persons 16 years old and over.

Table B. States and Counties — **Nonfarm Employment and Agriculture**

STATE County	Number of establishments	Total	Health care and social assistance	Manufacturing	Retail trade	Finance and insurance	Professional, scientific, and technical services	Total (mil dol)	Average per employee (dollars)	Number	Fewer than 50 acres	500 acres or more	Farm operators whose principal occupation is farming (percent)
	104	105	106	107	108	109	110	111	112	113	114	115	116
ILLINOIS—Cont'd													
Hardin	67	742	331	D	82	D	D	24	32 524	150	22.0	6.7	34.0
Henderson	114	707	D	D	128	D	36	18	26 079	396	24.2	28.8	68.7
Henry	1 075	13 146	1 573	4 204	1 793	538	291	463	35 197	1 373	30.6	21.5	56.6
Iroquois	691	6 421	D	699	1 044	329	99	204	31 733	1 470	25.4	29.2	55.0
Jackson	1 312	16 534	3 496	869	3 780	611	665	529	32 017	783	34.7	10.9	42.1
Jasper	209	1 456	125	251	277	101	D	49	33 941	910	34.5	19.6	41.2
Jefferson	956	18 300	3 362	4 061	2 344	415	639	682	37 246	1 063	38.4	33.1	33.1
Jersey	423	4 673	1 139	93	907	192	126	123	26 370	509	37.9	17.5	47.0
Jo Daviess	717	6 803	687	1 071	927	245	196	232	34 078	935	26.4	13.6	50.6
Johnson	162	1 150	214	D	190	58	D	25	21 903	558	33.0	5.7	30.1
Kane	12 345	184 016	21 685	30 780	23 446	9 605	9 207	7 697	41 826	590	51.4	16.1	66.3
Kankakee	2 360	36 792	7 355	5 599	5 724	1 495	761	1 328	36 103	818	33.7	24.4	56.8
Kendall	2 063	22 115	1 853	2 272	5 054	578	745	724	32 720	364	35.2	21.2	61.5
Knox	1 053	15 525	3 053	1 164	3 738	436	284	466	29 990	856	29.7	22.1	56.9
Lake	19 623	330 815	33 957	41 551	37 237	14 260	34 400	22 942	69 349	349	79.7	4.3	56.2
LaSalle	2 687	38 778	6 291	4 788	6 273	1 327	999	1 523	39 275	1 583	29.1	24.1	58.8
Lawrence	274	3 542	545	915	361	271	47	133	37 552	379	36.4	26.4	58.8
Lee	698	10 663	2 269	3 166	1 316	336	246	407	38 196	835	28.0	26.7	55.2
Livingston	866	11 228	1 708	3 202	1 624	390	225	429	38 235	1 349	25.2	31.9	62.9
Logan	599	7 453	1 541	1 030	1 080	292	175	238	31 944	779	32.6	31.2	54.8
McDonough	667	8 877	1 750	1 439	1 615	335	242	276	31 038	740	26.9	23.9	58.4
McHenry	7 827	84 791	10 916	15 088	15 269	2 310	3 232	3 550	41 865	911	52.3	13.0	62.5
McLean	3 653	76 679	8 628	3 920	9 367	21 126	2 667	3 887	50 688	1 489	30.2	29.0	55.6
Macon	2 434	46 164	7 916	7 130	5 672	1 637	1 214	1 902	41 208	674	35.9	29.5	59.1
Macoupin	886	8 498	1 682	573	1 299	451	141	270	31 755	1 190	29.9	19.6	48.7
Madison	5 806	83 211	13 641	11 999	12 270	2 971	3 393	3 436	41 292	1 110	45.2	15.1	41.9
Marion	931	11 072	2 841	2 717	1 305	386	288	387	34 998	1 152	36.4	11.8	44.1
Marshall	270	2 914	481	975	310	107	D	105	36 160	440	20.9	29.3	58.0
Mason	282	2 272	D	D	422	139	D	84	37 149	490	25.5	33.9	58.4
Massac	221	3 220	776	D	301	104	32	135	41 867	412	39.8	11.7	40.5
Menard	209	1 230	67	30	291	D	D	39	32 093	369	37.4	26.8	56.9
Mercer	274	2 391	D	592	366	124	34	79	32 903	715	32.2	21.1	59.3
Monroe	796	8 227	922	326	1 435	328	630	271	32 882	563	39.6	20.2	43.9
Montgomery	689	6 756	1 336	647	1 415	386	174	226	33 406	1 021	31.5	22.8	48.1
Morgan	847	12 832	2 667	1 576	1 832	1 074	633	427	33 244	757	31.0	26.0	62.1
Moultrie	321	4 912	724	D	370	146	117	179	36 539	553	45.8	20.3	55.3
Ogle	1 051	13 045	1 531	3 776	1 411	499	212	555	42 521	1 148	36.8	19.5	52.3
Peoria	4 519	104 510	22 039	5 843	10 889	3 818	4 953	5 819	55 678	917	35.2	16.5	49.9
Perry	407	4 221	804	D	761	178	D	141	33 520	560	30.7	19.5	43.0
Piatt	331	2 297	D	D	416	165	107	77	33 625	426	28.6	35.2	58.2
Pike	370	3 000	540	196	605	D	69	93	30 879	970	24.8	23.1	55.6
Pope	47	193	76	D	46	D	5	4	22 834	349	20.9	9.7	35.5
Pulaski	92	609	D	D	120	41	D	17	28 263	230	30.4	20.0	34.8
Putnam	136	1 143	D	392	134	D	D	59	51 806	183	25.7	16.4	46.4
Randolph	665	10 493	2 130	2 894	1 345	306	236	366	34 884	793	27.9	17.7	47.7
Richland	458	5 250	987	497	652	191	D	177	33 723	554	41.5	19.3	37.9
Rock Island	3 258	62 827	9 127	8 919	7 787	2 750	3 052	3 189	50 761	666	41.3	11.9	50.3
St. Clair	5 217	76 601	14 800	4 605	13 245	2 329	5 271	2 804	36 607	732	38.4	21.2	47.4
Saline	569	7 079	1 633	408	1 257	339	167	288	40 703	483	40.4	14.9	37.5
Sangamon	5 024	83 211	21 002	2 715	12 315	6 347	4 336	3 324	39 946	1 092	41.4	20.0	50.5
Schuyler	151	1 139	D	51	228	D	D	36	31 928	542	24.0	16.6	35.2
Scott	82	567	D	D	81	57	9	24	41 531	356	29.5	23.0	43.8
Shelby	433	4 105	678	1 027	634	D	231	136	33 056	1 282	32.9	19.9	51.6
Stark	118	982	D	244	162	78	D	38	38 701	348	29.0	33.0	62.4
Stephenson	1 060	14 588	2 374	2 993	2 025	1 100	452	587	40 232	1 087	36.0	17.7	56.9
Tazewell	2 803	44 318	5 367	7 942	7 295	1 880	1 127	1 752	39 540	942	36.5	22.7	49.8
Union	348	3 527	1 373	212	652	141	D	95	27 041	623	35.8	6.9	37.4
Vermilion	1 451	24 259	5 288	4 771	3 765	1 232	429	941	38 805	956	36.6	29.5	54.5
Wabash	269	2 831	818	166	325	96	D	104	36 824	213	29.6	25.4	52.1
Warren	349	4 994	D	1 334	587	195	D	162	32 342	605	25.8	32.2	59.2
Washington	383	4 811	D	D	768	166	92	183	38 009	777	27.0	26.9	50.7
Wayne	378	3 326	804	D	653	132	D	105	31 515	1 187	34.5	13.6	34.5
White	385	3 615	629	D	489	D	D	134	36 991	582	35.6	19.6	38.3
Whiteside	1 218	16 807	3 042	3 576	2 695	553	320	609	36 237	1 110	33.4	20.4	50.5
Will	14 565	206 073	26 586	18 804	29 172	5 030	9 206	8 666	42 053	882	55.8	15.4	54.8
Williamson	1 611	22 491	5 817	2 489	3 799	1 313	626	813	36 154	702	44.7	6.1	39.6

Table B. States and Counties — **Agriculture**

STATE County	Acreage (1,000) 117	Percent change, 2007-2012 118	Average size of farm 119	Total irrigated (1,000) 120	Total cropland (1,000) 121	Average per farm (dollars) 122	Average per acre 123	Value of machinery and equipment, average per farm (dollars) 124	Total (mil dol) 125	Average per farm (dollars) 126	Crops 127	Live-stock and poultry products 128	$10,000 or more 129	$100,000 or more 130	Total ($1,000) 131	Percent of farms 132
ILLINOIS—Cont'd																
Hardin	33	-4.4	221	0.0	16.8	782 720	3 536	68 840	4.0	26 513	D	D	27.3	5.3	288	48.7
Henderson	172	0.7	433	10.9	141.7	2 681 811	6 190	237 106	138.4	349 467	84.8	15.2	70.2	51.5	3 974	81.8
Henry	479	-2.2	349	8.7	436.8	2 384 519	6 831	226 993	397.9	289 824	79.6	20.4	62.6	42.4	11 930	78.6
Iroquois	669	-1.3	455	3.1	638.2	3 096 555	6 801	256 896	493.5	335 710	86.4	13.6	72.0	50.5	15 428	87.8
Jackson	214	-4.6	274	1.5	172.9	1 077 216	3 938	144 249	67.4	86 087	87.9	12.1	34.6	13.9	2 883	59.9
Jasper	251	3.0	276	D	218.2	1 396 085	5 066	154 589	159.3	175 074	46.9	53.1	51.3	27.3	11 040	87.4
Jefferson	214	-8.0	201	0.3	172.5	725 120	3 604	102 292	60.2	56 591	81.3	18.7	34.2	11.9	3 775	69.3
Jersey	155	-17.9	305	0.0	126.1	1 800 929	5 896	165 061	69.2	135 959	94.7	5.3	50.5	27.7	2 589	73.5
Jo Daviess	272	-3.4	291	0.1	190.2	1 411 296	4 855	151 134	154.1	164 857	54.0	46.0	50.8	27.4	8 935	79.9
Johnson	90	-10.7	161	0.1	48.2	485 810	3 022	71 670	12.1	21 685	70.6	29.4	23.8	4.3	1 747	52.7
Kane	169	-12.4	286	1.8	154.3	2 535 083	8 874	199 881	196.2	332 464	84.1	15.9	60.7	37.1	4 322	45.3
Kankakee	343	-11.2	419	14.6	327.9	2 769 373	6 612	264 800	287.5	351 460	90.2	9.8	71.8	48.5	5 827	76.5
Kendall	130	-22.3	356	D	123.6	3 094 407	8 682	229 712	103.0	283 091	83.8	16.2	70.6	42.0	1 986	69.2
Knox	348	-4.2	406	0.0	288.7	2 788 956	6 868	193 379	293.1	342 459	80.2	19.8	56.2	34.7	8 091	74.6
Lake	30	-13.0	86	0.5	22.0	894 759	10 396	88 287	35.4	101 544	72.6	27.4	43.0	14.6	272	9.2
LaSalle	602	-6.4	380	5.0	569.0	3 001 877	7 890	247 122	459.3	290 132	94.7	5.3	71.4	48.3	10 769	78.8
Lawrence	184	-5.1	486	13.6	169.3	2 378 997	4 897	257 005	101.5	267 902	71.6	28.4	53.3	34.3	4 542	76.5
Lee	369	-6.7	442	25.4	348.9	3 344 959	7 568	293 399	361.0	432 352	86.7	13.3	67.9	51.7	8 885	81.8
Livingston	656	4.4	486	0.4	632.1	3 496 319	7 187	280 713	409.6	303 664	81.4	18.6	76.6	52.2	11 676	85.5
Logan	363	13.4	466	1.1	343.0	3 349 367	7 182	250 374	240.0	308 109	91.0	9.0	62.3	43.9	8 215	85.5
McDonough	292	-5.1	395	0.1	253.5	2 773 084	7 027	210 159	209.2	282 639	88.7	11.3	60.7	38.9	6 739	76.5
McHenry	234	8.6	257	11.2	212.6	2 074 731	8 070	177 105	182.4	200 256	83.6	16.4	51.0	27.6	4 732	38.1
McLean	692	2.4	465	1.6	653.9	3 803 046	8 180	297 883	501.0	336 465	88.6	11.4	69.4	47.8	13 140	81.7
Macon	337	15.8	499	0.0	321.7	3 911 432	7 833	294 921	211.3	313 540	95.7	4.3	66.0	42.7	5 762	80.1
Macoupin	439	11.3	369	0.0	371.0	2 291 757	6 218	186 864	221.8	186 369	81.3	18.7	53.4	31.9	8 416	79.0
Madison	307	-1.9	277	2.4	276.5	1 765 512	6 381	184 861	141.7	127 692	87.3	12.7	54.8	23.8	4 518	60.8
Marion	267	2.4	232	0.2	216.9	972 948	4 201	103 237	68.8	59 693	75.6	24.4	28.0	12.7	5 884	82.6
Marshall	209	2.2	475	2.2	183.7	3 290 455	6 924	274 420	136.1	309 418	96.2	3.8	71.8	51.4	4 416	85.7
Mason	290	6.0	592	102.3	265.5	3 458 004	5 846	344 157	201.2	410 545	88.7	11.3	63.9	43.9	5 881	84.1
Massac	102	14.0	248	6.1	83.3	887 687	3 577	115 689	39.5	95 782	81.8	18.2	37.6	15.3	2 256	66.7
Menard	158	-6.4	428	4.3	139.9	2 703 653	6 324	240 477	84.6	229 138	94.3	5.7	52.0	35.2	2 978	77.8
Mercer	252	-17.7	352	7.9	212.3	2 139 906	6 072	196 516	216.9	303 290	82.2	17.8	55.5	38.0	6 391	78.2
Monroe	193	8.5	343	3.8	167.7	1 777 323	5 179	209 716	111.7	198 455	81.0	19.0	50.1	31.3	2 792	68.0
Montgomery	382	10.0	375	D	346.7	2 230 784	5 956	197 314	227.3	222 582	78.6	21.4	54.9	34.3	7 252	80.6
Morgan	309	-3.5	408	3.8	272.3	2 729 232	6 683	232 711	201.9	266 663	86.0	14.0	60.2	38.8	5 870	78.1
Moultrie	205	22.2	371	0.0	194.2	2 849 613	7 687	206 665	130.7	236 318	94.8	5.2	58.8	34.7	3 550	59.1
Ogle	376	2.7	328	1.1	335.9	2 273 063	6 932	209 389	323.7	281 925	76.4	23.6	58.5	37.7	9 746	69.3
Peoria	250	-3.4	273	3.2	211.1	1 888 508	6 920	163 937	187.4	204 315	87.3	12.7	60.5	32.5	4 738	64.6
Perry	181	-9.8	323	0.2	143.9	1 313 157	4 071	168 170	45.4	81 054	88.6	11.4	43.6	22.5	2 310	78.9
Piatt	259	-3.1	608	1.0	251.4	2 262 390	8 654	359 110	187.0	438 925	98.2	1.8	70.9	50.9	4 294	81.9
Pike	411	5.6	424	1.7	310.2	2 085 246	4 916	160 991	232.2	239 381	65.5	34.5	51.5	26.9	9 067	79.0
Pope	78	28.3	223	0.3	43.6	582 077	2 605	67 040	12.7	36 364	81.0	19.0	25.5	8.0	1 251	66.2
Pulaski	82	-18.8	357	1.2	64.7	1 436 774	4 022	155 809	28.3	123 191	95.4	4.6	30.9	17.0	1 604	72.2
Putnam	60	-4.1	329	1.0	52.3	2 068 290	6 294	239 754	81.7	446 224	97.1	2.9	61.2	41.5	1 727	84.7
Randolph	279	10.1	351	1.1	228.0	1 566 426	4 459	174 168	104.4	131 629	89.1	10.9	53.0	26.6	4 034	73.4
Richland	189	-6.9	341	D	167.3	1 498 597	4 395	160 653	81.4	146 910	53.9	46.1	42.8	20.0	5 909	82.1
Rock Island	149	-16.5	224	4.0	119.6	1 396 574	6 235	141 845	101.4	152 303	88.7	11.3	50.6	28.4	3 369	66.8
St. Clair	252	-17.8	344	0.5	227.4	2 173 104	6 314	225 559	119.2	162 816	89.3	10.7	56.8	33.1	4 174	69.4
Saline	140	19.3	290	0.0	117.7	1 221 402	4 218	137 004	58.7	121 449	65.7	34.3	35.0	17.8	1 878	68.1
Sangamon	514	-0.8	471	1.0	475.8	3 468 062	7 367	270 515	358.4	328 162	93.9	6.1	50.6	34.0	9 359	72.4
Schuyler	182	-12.2	336	1.7	124.6	1 470 393	4 377	119 697	78.4	144 705	67.2	32.8	43.4	19.2	3 899	85.2
Scott	148	8.7	414	7.0	122.8	2 412 295	5 821	232 750	89.2	250 511	85.6	14.4	57.0	30.9	2 904	79.5
Shelby	406	4.8	317	0.0	362.7	1 910 895	6 037	175 446	214.3	167 165	82.0	18.0	54.7	29.4	8 301	76.5
Stark	168	-1.0	483	D	159.5	3 592 802	7 437	309 853	133.0	382 089	94.4	5.6	68.1	53.2	3 634	85.1
Stephenson	352	4.3	324	0.0	315.8	2 205 409	6 801	208 247	313.2	288 094	57.7	42.3	58.5	36.4	9 449	73.2
Tazewell	337	2.5	358	38.5	304.0	2 664 259	7 439	207 022	263.7	279 942	88.7	11.3	59.3	41.7	6 853	77.5
Union	121	-1.0	194	0.8	79.3	689 525	3 545	81 409	33.9	54 413	91.2	8.8	30.2	6.3	2 516	58.4
Vermilion	434	-5.0	454	0.2	409.5	3 200 276	7 043	259 283	283.6	296 653	95.7	4.3	60.4	41.8	7 122	76.2
Wabash	106	-6.9	500	1.1	94.4	2 653 826	5 311	244 742	43.5	204 188	95.3	4.7	49.3	33.3	1 690	77.9
Warren	338	14.8	559	8.0	306.0	3 871 392	6 921	290 898	274.6	453 820	87.1	12.9	74.9	51.7	6 194	77.4
Washington	355	0.3	457	0.6	325.7	2 366 162	5 180	263 172	144.8	186 342	65.5	34.5	62.9	35.8	6 187	85.5
Wayne	369	10.6	310	2.9	318.7	1 387 644	4 470	115 500	150.3	126 600	70.1	29.9	32.3	17.0	7 260	85.2
White	311	4.7	534	15.2	275.1	2 394 223	4 482	260 127	130.9	224 912	94.5	5.5	41.4	23.9	4 491	79.7
Whiteside	403	-0.5	363	57.4	370.0	2 485 254	6 841	238 705	435.7	392 487	77.4	22.6	62.8	42.4	11 400	78.3
Will	234	6.1	266	1.5	221.2	2 080 146	7 832	185 451	169.1	191 723	94.2	5.8	54.6	29.3	3 639	53.4
Williamson	103	9.9	147	0.0	72.1	649 405	4 408	74 148	22.5	32 031	74.2	25.8	24.6	6.1	1 392	46.7

Table B. States and Counties — Water Use, Wholesale Trade, Retail Trade, and Real Estate

STATE County	Water use, 2010		Wholesale trade,[1] 2012				Retail trade,[2] 2012				Real estate and rental and leasing,[2] 2012			
	Total water withdrawn (mil gal/day)	Gallons withdrawn per person per day	Number of establishments	Number of employees	Sales (mil dol)	Annual payroll (mil dol)	Number of establishments	Number of employees	Sales (mil dol)	Annual payroll (mil dol)	Number of establishments	Number of employees	Receipts (mil dol)	Annual payroll (mil dol)
	133	134	135	136	137	138	139	140	141	142	143	144	145	146
ILLINOIS—Cont'd														
Hardin	1.3	306	NA	NA	NA	NA	8	57	14.5	1.0	2	D	D	D
Henderson	9.1	1 240	12	61	303.0	3.4	15	105	39.4	2.2	1	D	D	D
Henry	7.8	155	64	656	1 229.5	29.1	156	1 792	500.1	41.6	20	31	5.5	0.7
Iroquois	5.7	191	56	590	822.4	26.8	87	1 074	287.4	21.3	18	50	7.9	1.3
Jackson	70.3	1 167	26	239	187.6	9.7	225	3 684	1 008.3	76.4	77	350	49.9	7.4
Jasper	660.1	68 062	18	108	211.5	4.6	31	288	73.3	6.0	2	D	D	D
Jefferson	1.3	34	56	D	D	D	180	2 295	709.5	55.0	21	68	12.1	2.0
Jersey	4.0	174	24	D	D	D	69	909	230.6	21.3	10	16	3.0	0.5
Jo Daviess	7.7	341	21	135	94.8	5.3	118	880	293.7	21.2	18	27	6.7	1.3
Johnson	1.6	130	4	7	3.1	0.3	27	240	88.6	5.6	4	1	0.1	0.0
Kane	65.8	128	741	9 371	9 628.8	571.7	1 487	22 836	5 681.1	508.2	439	2 045	583.8	83.7
Kankakee	26.8	236	119	2 196	1 443.3	95.0	370	5 548	1 463.3	120.0	95	371	70.9	10.6
Kendall	12.5	109	75	1 327	2 125.6	64.4	237	4 777	1 151.5	106.6	60	139	21.8	4.0
Knox	1.9	36	48	680	502.4	29.0	193	3 463	791.3	75.6	35	123	18.6	2.7
Lake	657.3	934	1 106	27 371	26 255.5	2 227.7	2 309	37 702	14 900.5	1 112.0	745	3 386	994.6	193.0
LaSalle	110.6	971	124	1 719	2 344.1	78.3	420	6 168	1 689.5	142.3	86	533	63.6	16.9
Lawrence	16.9	1 003	14	233	113.8	7.5	38	406	117.3	9.0	7	14	1.4	0.3
Lee	15.8	439	28	D	D	D	100	1 264	379.9	30.1	21	112	13.8	2.6
Livingston	7.6	196	60	692	1 011.2	36.9	135	1 610	479.4	36.9	16	69	6.9	1.9
Logan	13.5	446	45	552	858.7	32.1	88	1 082	292.3	24.7	25	86	9.9	2.1
McDonough	3.9	120	29	D	D	D	121	1 554	340.8	32.9	26	110	16.3	2.1
McHenry	35.2	114	411	5 284	2 932.5	264.5	941	15 021	3 664.4	337.2	219	745	113.4	24.1
McLean	14.5	85	166	2 515	9 130.9	161.3	580	9 434	2 441.6	201.1	143	718	149.0	22.7
Macon	39.4	356	112	D	D	D	395	5 724	1 494.2	133.7	88	471	105.2	13.8
Macoupin	6.2	129	47	680	885.2	29.6	133	1 375	392.0	30.0	21	54	5.9	1.5
Madison	404.8	1 503	226	2 822	2 764.2	147.4	832	12 506	3 230.2	292.4	230	974	171.4	31.4
Marion	4.1	104	39	336	334.8	11.8	150	1 349	353.7	30.6	23	101	10.3	2.6
Marshall	3.3	259	16	D	D	D	42	384	85.7	6.7	6	D	D	D
Mason	98.6	6 722	27	306	664.8	14.7	45	445	130.5	8.9	5	11	1.2	0.2
Massac	665.5	43 134	8	D	D	D	37	319	84.9	7.5	5	36	3.0	0.6
Menard	2.0	158	10	87	153.4	4.7	31	319	76.8	5.9	4	7	0.9	0.2
Mercer	3.2	195	14	148	435.0	6.5	41	351	72.6	6.7	6	10	1.1	0.2
Monroe	3.3	100	21	284	182.7	13.4	96	1 393	481.7	41.7	28	151	18.8	5.4
Montgomery	478.7	15 901	47	314	372.9	13.3	128	1 518	432.5	34.1	15	53	6.5	1.2
Morgan	109.6	3 084	42	D	D	D	151	1 845	454.5	37.9	27	D	D	D
Moultrie	1.8	119	11	95	245.4	4.4	42	363	109.4	7.3	5	15	0.7	0.1
Ogle	66.2	1 237	53	D	D	D	138	1 466	408.1	29.2	36	104	11.3	1.9
Peoria	535.9	2 873	202	3 235	1 782.0	153.6	726	10 839	2 576.7	249.2	198	987	181.7	33.1
Perry	2.1	93	13	D	D	D	59	718	189.5	16.1	5	11	1.3	0.4
Piatt	5.8	344	25	275	429.7	15.4	47	446	143.4	10.6	4	D	D	D
Pike	14.6	890	24	193	340.6	9.4	53	566	174.3	12.2	7	16	7.6	0.3
Pope	0.1	16	NA	NA	NA	NA	11	52	11.5	0.8	2	D	D	D
Pulaski	0.7	117	6	D	D	D	18	85	35.0	2.2	NA	NA	NA	NA
Putnam	200.4	33 370	9	59	224.7	2.2	16	135	29.2	2.5	1	D	D	D
Randolph	37.1	1 109	33	429	406.4	20.0	100	1 440	373.4	32.9	9	21	3.8	0.6
Richland	3.0	184	25	329	566.0	12.1	62	720	176.4	15.2	6	20	1.6	0.4
Rock Island	1 140.0	7 726	152	2 826	3 164.9	182.9	479	7 931	1 859.1	186.9	119	526	108.1	14.3
St. Clair	20.7	77	177	1 846	2 643.8	85.8	910	13 296	3 234.2	305.3	230	1 005	171.6	31.4
Saline	2.6	103	14	104	51.3	3.5	111	1 245	353.6	31.5	9	39	10.1	1.3
Sangamon	323.6	1 639	196	3 346	3 372.0	151.3	754	11 950	3 128.6	277.1	211	842	153.5	25.5
Schuyler	1.5	192	7	67	68.6	3.1	28	207	39.0	4.6	3	D	D	D
Scott	7.9	1 466	3	D	D	D	9	98	39.1	2.4	1	D	D	D
Shelby	4.0	177	26	226	239.8	7.8	71	603	155.0	11.4	9	D	D	D
Stark	0.8	140	8	D	D	D	21	168	68.1	5.4	3	D	D	D
Stephenson	8.3	174	49	D	D	D	157	2 026	521.6	45.8	29	92	10.8	2.5
Tazewell	98.9	731	131	2 089	1 929.2	98.6	406	6 864	1 942.3	169.6	88	306	78.9	9.8
Union	4.0	224	12	130	40.2	3.8	64	649	167.1	15.3	11	34	3.8	0.8
Vermilion	14.0	171	77	1 788	3 136.5	84.3	255	3 401	850.3	74.3	45	158	28.7	4.5
Wabash	4.5	379	13	D	D	D	42	345	81.1	8.3	11	18	2.7	0.5
Warren	3.4	189	29	240	516.2	10.2	54	552	143.2	11.1	9	18	2.0	0.3
Washington	4.0	273	30	586	415.7	25.9	64	584	200.8	15.3	14	24	1.7	0.2
Wayne	7.0	415	22	196	214.0	8.6	68	602	157.6	13.7	7	13	1.5	0.4
White	23.4	1 594	25	218	161.9	7.4	58	510	142.9	11.2	10	52	14.2	2.1
Whiteside	24.3	415	61	597	689.1	24.7	190	2 676	578.0	57.9	38	111	15.1	2.5
Will	2 363.1	3 488	735	11 420	14 925.1	680.5	1 606	27 615	7 862.1	657.3	467	2 311	458.3	97.1
Williamson	216.9	3 269	60	723	255.2	28.5	271	3 783	1 116.3	93.8	51	187	29.2	5.3

1. Merchant wholesalers, except manufacturers' sales branches and offices. 2. Employer establishments.

Table B. States and Counties — Professional Services, Manufacturing, and Accommodation and Food Services

STATE County	Professional, scientific, and technical services, 2012				Manufacturing, 2012				Accommodation and food services, 2012			
	Number of establishments	Number of employees	Receipts (mil dol)	Annual payroll (mil dol)	Number of establishments	Number of employees	Receipts (mil dol)	Annual payroll (mil dol)	Number of establishments	Number of employees	Sales (mil dol)	Annual payroll (mil dol)
	147	148	149	150	151	152	153	154	155	156	157	158
ILLINOIS—Cont'd												
Hardin	4	D	D	D	NA	NA	NA	NA	9	D	D	D
Henderson	6	29	2.3	0.7	NA	NA	NA	NA	11	D	D	D
Henry	69	289	21.2	7.2	55	4 230	D	155.3	85	D	D	D
Iroquois	33	206	12.6	4.4	30	642	515.2	21.9	60	537	22.5	6.6
Jackson	108	689	68.5	27.1	39	673	178.3	25.8	140	2 927	111.5	31.4
Jasper	10	22	1.9	0.5	12	288	101.6	10.7	15	122	4.4	1.2
Jefferson	76	523	48.4	20.2	32	2 998	D	144.3	81	1 647	71.1	20.9
Jersey	20	146	13.5	6.7	14	62	D	2.2	44	644	26.3	7.4
Jo Daviess	56	250	36.1	12.2	37	1 018	480.2	45.1	108	1 656	73.6	22.5
Johnson	13	259	5.4	2.5	9	36	D	1.7	17	D	D	D
Kane	1 539	9 323	1 603.3	573.6	799	30 327	10 338.7	1 548.3	850	15 058	720.3	207.4
Kankakee	152	735	64.1	24.5	100	4 889	4 842.8	269.7	219	3 675	160.3	47.4
Kendall	199	D	D	D	79	2 298	719.2	108.9	163	2 865	139.4	38.1
Knox	64	307	27.7	11.0	38	D	321.4	36.3	124	1 715	76.3	21.3
Lake	3 052	26 120	3 483.8	2 220.4	846	35 174	12 046.0	1 950.0	1 498	24 702	1 399.2	405.5
LaSalle	166	1 098	120.8	43.7	143	4 665	2 345.6	246.9	318	4 213	188.6	52.3
Lawrence	13	45	4.8	1.2	11	541	D	20.7	22	D	D	D
Lee	38	256	32.0	13.0	36	2 775	1 193.6	117.0	82	722	38.9	8.8
Livingston	55	229	27.4	9.1	60	3 376	1 210.5	166.3	76	855	36.2	9.2
Logan	34	180	16.6	6.4	18	1 034	555.3	46.3	63	853	31.0	9.5
McDonough	44	258	20.2	8.5	20	1 538	420.9	68.9	96	1 599	71.6	17.9
McHenry	898	D	D	D	491	15 508	5 163.2	820.7	558	9 074	435.7	125.5
McLean	363	2 852	280.7	125.2	92	3 881	1 590.2	199.5	379	8 136	393.0	108.7
Macon	157	1 216	142.7	54.0	109	8 240	13 379.3	435.3	225	4 331	189.8	55.6
Macoupin	40	149	15.3	4.3	33	567	D	24.6	89	D	D	D
Madison	549	3 711	748.1	216.0	193	12 308	19 140.5	841.4	582	9 920	431.2	124.6
Marion	60	250	18.1	8.2	42	2 567	710.6	101.5	77	848	38.2	11.1
Marshall	12	24	2.2	0.7	12	888	D	37.1	30	281	7.4	2.4
Mason	9	23	2.5	0.7	12	80	24.6	3.5	41	D	D	D
Massac	9	D	D	D	10	522	D	29.5	28	D	D	D
Menard	15	79	7.2	2.5	5	24	D	1.1	21	231	5.5	1.5
Mercer	11	28	2.5	0.7	12	669	D	25.8	22	D	D	D
Monroe	81	596	89.9	40.9	23	264	D	11.3	63	1 134	43.0	12.7
Montgomery	35	198	17.2	6.6	23	679	313.6	29.4	63	875	37.3	10.8
Morgan	39	642	60.3	29.9	30	1 867	D	82.1	90	1 353	63.7	15.9
Moultrie	16	67	5.9	3.1	36	1 621	533.4	65.0	26	D	D	D
Ogle	68	210	16.0	7.5	62	3 356	1 530.9	146.0	110	1 063	52.9	12.0
Peoria	429	5 236	719.2	311.0	157	7 747	6 197.5	466.3	470	8 372	383.5	109.8
Perry	19	52	4.9	1.4	19	412	D	19.0	37	492	15.5	4.8
Piatt	28	96	8.5	3.7	13	183	D	7.0	31	D	D	D
Pike	17	73	8.0	2.2	19	143	62.4	6.2	37	350	14.0	3.6
Pope	5	D	D	D	NA	NA	NA	NA	5	9	0.6	0.1
Pulaski	1	D	D	D	NA	NA	NA	NA	6	D	D	D
Putnam	5	20	1.7	0.6	8	440	D	16.8	14	69	2.5	0.5
Randolph	36	227	24.2	8.3	28	2 902	609.3	77.6	64	806	29.6	8.5
Richland	25	135	50.1	9.9	28	438	143.5	17.2	36	D	D	D
Rock Island	291	2 847	667.4	163.6	153	8 245	6 845.4	451.8	342	5 592	344.4	75.6
St. Clair	511	5 662	870.2	364.7	158	4 922	2 779.9	241.6	561	10 416	589.3	155.9
Saline	39	160	16.3	5.5	24	348	D	11.5	47	776	37.2	8.3
Sangamon	527	4 381	549.2	224.9	109	2 834	D	139.1	523	9 447	439.2	129.0
Schuyler	7	23	2.4	0.7	6	95	D	2.4	12	D	D	D
Scott	3	9	1.1	0.3	4	163	D	6.8	11	56	2.7	0.6
Shelby	21	184	21.6	8.5	21	1 042	D	45.2	41	375	14.2	4.0
Stark	8	66	5.0	1.9	7	248	D	11.5	3	6	0.3	0.1
Stephenson	81	454	55.4	19.6	62	3 037	1 145.2	155.4	89	1 033	47.6	12.0
Tazewell	180	1 187	118.5	52.8	110	8 215	5 850.3	443.8	306	6 143	358.5	92.3
Union	19	80	6.7	2.9	12	164	D	5.4	30	D	D	D
Vermilion	84	428	46.7	16.6	96	5 168	2 353.2	256.1	143	2 161	86.0	25.4
Wabash	22	140	14.2	5.7	9	188	43.3	8.9	21	296	11.8	3.5
Warren	20	85	8.1	2.2	17	1 803	632.7	71.2	36	481	20.6	5.4
Washington	22	105	12.2	3.9	14	D	445.6	D	30	D	D	D
Wayne	21	58	4.2	1.4	16	607	D	24.6	22	D	D	D
White	19	71	6.0	1.8	12	304	D	10.6	26	D	D	D
Whiteside	81	341	36.1	12.6	88	3 955	1 453.2	198.3	124	1 589	66.5	18.6
Will	1 586	D	D	D	588	20 377	20 627.2	1 191.0	1 108	20 582	1 313.5	320.8
Williamson	121	636	65.4	21.4	42	1 748	793.0	78.5	148	2 724	123.7	35.4

1. Establishment subject to federal tax.

STATE County	Health care and social assistance, 2012				Other services, 2012				Nonemployer businesses, 2014		Value of residential construction authorized by building permits, 2015	
	Number of establishments	Number of employees	Receipts (mil dol)	Annual payroll (mil dol)	Number of establishments	Number of employees	Receipts (mil dol)	Annual payroll (mil dol)	Number	Receipts (mil dol)	New Construction ($1,000)	Number of housing units
	159	160	161	162	163	164	165	166	167	168	169	170
ILLINOIS—Cont'd												
Hardin	12	252	18.3	7.9	3	3	0.3	0.1	232	7.0	0	0
Henderson	8	153	7.3	3.4	7	D	D	D	399	14.3	1 161	9
Henry	88	1 640	123.4	49.0	97	380	31.0	8.7	2 848	94.1	7 921	36
Iroquois	66	1 588	105.2	44.6	48	148	19.7	3.2	2 060	72.0	3 709	22
Jackson	167	3 463	517.9	159.6	93	396	41.7	8.4	3 190	107.1	1 775	38
Jasper	14	143	6.6	2.2	19	61	5.6	1.0	804	30.3	0	0
Jefferson	146	3 518	391.1	145.4	82	416	43.0	11.2	2 318	95.2	2 113	14
Jersey	48	D	D	D	35	109	8.5	2.3	1 273	39.1	3 928	30
Jo Daviess	41	656	43.1	17.8	57	247	22.8	6.0	1 976	79.8	9 851	34
Johnson	19	209	12.6	4.7	10	D	D	D	753	23.1	0	0
Kane	1 153	21 559	2 406.9	968.7	821	5 885	596.9	169.7	32 747	1 432.3	286 108	1 471
Kankakee	311	7 349	753.9	294.5	180	956	100.3	25.1	6 215	210.1	16 974	89
Kendall	177	D	D	D	164	795	73.6	21.5	7 656	300.3	34 873	178
Knox	122	3 696	338.7	125.8	77	562	125.9	15.1	2 325	71.2	4 445	19
Lake	1 949	33 669	4 026.3	1 549.4	1 276	7 626	728.2	224.2	53 642	2 988.5	217 412	643
LaSalle	284	5 993	448.1	188.7	237	1 205	109.6	31.7	5 956	204.7	14 689	71
Lawrence	23	617	30.3	13.5	22	111	11.0	3.5	811	30.1	8 108	47
Lee	80	2 137	166.8	72.1	60	345	33.1	9.5	1 873	65.6	4 780	29
Livingston	74	2 090	144.5	62.4	66	334	29.3	8.3	1 951	58.4	3 750	18
Logan	58	1 330	111.3	41.5	54	206	15.9	4.2	1 424	46.3	1 573	8
McDonough	71	1 768	138.8	58.5	65	D	D	D	1 555	51.3	800	4
McHenry	718	D	D	D	634	3 300	260.3	77.6	22 321	1 009.7	88 394	583
McLean	371	8 547	969.7	368.4	259	2 311	212.2	74.8	9 422	387.6	45 790	368
Macon	291	8 193	886.2	332.1	176	1 170	239.1	37.3	5 940	184.8	11 023	47
Macoupin	91	1 920	115.8	48.0	85	318	25.5	6.3	2 566	86.1	16 596	85
Madison	677	13 914	1 194.9	486.2	456	2 888	272.1	79.6	14 154	532.6	89 604	389
Marion	113	3 009	249.3	94.0	73	268	21.7	5.6	2 181	75.8	125	1
Marshall	19	468	22.1	9.5	15	D	D	D	638	22.6	2 736	10
Mason	26	506	36.7	16.5	27	90	6.8	1.6	721	28.3	1 209	6
Massac	26	755	53.8	24.4	21	65	7.9	1.8	838	23.4	135	4
Menard	12	75	6.3	2.1	16	64	5.6	1.3	809	23.2	5 645	26
Mercer	24	344	23.5	9.3	16	64	5.9	1.6	924	32.5	9 075	49
Monroe	79	846	57.1	24.2	71	407	25.0	9.6	2 085	82.9	32 729	135
Montgomery	73	D	D	D	57	233	20.8	5.6	1 641	50.6	5 440	27
Morgan	121	D	D	D	64	260	18.4	4.8	1 977	74.7	1 241	11
Moultrie	32	735	36.2	16.8	17	D	D	D	1 027	38.4	4 237	49
Ogle	82	1 505	103.9	41.0	75	343	36.6	10.3	3 327	120.5	11 963	55
Peoria	516	22 518	2 665.0	1 057.0	304	4 714	449.2	206.3	9 561	359.8	31 406	116
Perry	45	890	63.7	25.9	46	161	11.9	3.1	1 066	31.9	6 649	33
Piatt	21	D	D	D	18	D	D	D	1 115	39.2	7 452	26
Pike	25	586	49.0	18.0	26	109	12.8	3.2	1 072	38.5	1 010	14
Pope	11	D	D	D	3	D	D	D	207	5.8	0	0
Pulaski	14	151	6.8	2.6	14	43	3.6	0.9	315	9.5	1 007	5
Putnam	4	18	1.5	0.6	4	D	D	D	362	14.9	2 168	15
Randolph	73	2 170	260.4	123.7	61	266	28.4	8.6	1 495	46.1	4 619	21
Richland	50	1 014	71.7	31.3	40	162	17.2	4.0	1 161	47.0	2 238	10
Rock Island	416	8 883	802.3	345.0	265	1 600	138.9	43.0	6 841	249.4	23 526	190
St. Clair	595	15 933	1 363.8	594.9	387	2 528	213.0	73.6	14 092	451.1	116 876	585
Saline	78	1 808	143.9	60.3	47	172	22.0	4.0	1 590	65.9	0	0
Sangamon	445	20 510	2 559.6	892.3	474	3 319	416.7	124.8	12 369	466.6	67 668	357
Schuyler	14	323	28.2	10.7	12	D	D	D	477	15.4	0	0
Scott	4	D	D	D	4	10	1.4	0.3	316	8.7	NA	NA
Shelby	33	674	42.3	18.7	32	93	11.9	2.5	1 350	43.1	6 801	38
Stark	8	167	8.9	3.7	4	D	D	D	347	13.2	910	3
Stephenson	104	2 545	329.3	92.9	95	642	46.2	16.0	2 952	97.0	1 811	11
Tazewell	246	5 435	388.8	155.2	242	1 270	113.7	37.2	6 466	244.6	60 919	289
Union	52	1 215	72.6	30.4	22	80	7.1	2.1	1 094	40.6	1 761	17
Vermilion	143	4 736	514.4	235.4	121	540	47.4	13.3	4 329	139.3	1 340	10
Wabash	26	832	62.0	22.6	22	94	6.5	1.5	839	32.4	1 530	3
Warren	37	694	48.6	19.5	31	115	11.8	2.2	899	32.5	2 296	9
Washington	26	616	39.9	15.4	27	61	7.0	1.3	968	34.6	3 828	19
Wayne	32	799	53.9	22.2	27	113	14.4	3.2	1 252	49.3	85	2
White	43	638	36.5	14.9	33	160	16.2	4.7	1 170	48.1	987	5
Whiteside	99	3 068	261.2	99.1	109	608	54.1	13.5	2 861	103.0	4 455	27
Will	1 406	24 364	2 467.6	967.5	1 053	6 884	681.5	195.1	45 713	2 007.4	299 445	1 200
Williamson	204	5 977	677.0	251.1	93	519	52.4	14.1	4 273	148.4	12 077	99

Table B. States and Counties — Government Employment and Payroll, and Local Government Finances

STATE County	Government employment and payroll, 2012									Local government finances, 2012				
			March payroll (percent of total)							General revenue				
													Taxes	
														Per capita¹ (dollars)
	Full-time equivalent employees	March payroll (dollars)	Administration, judicial, and legal	Police and Corrections	Fire Protection	Highways and transportation	Health and Welfare	Natural resources and utilities	Education and libraries	Total (mil dol)	Inter-governmental (mil dol)	Total (mil dol)	Total	Property
	171	172	173	174	175	176	177	178	179	180	181	182	183	184
ILLINOIS—Cont'd														
Hardin	285	791 768	2.8	3.0	0.0	56.6	0.9	4.7	31.7	16.6	13.4	1.6	384	331
Henderson	266	806 748	8.3	7.3	0.3	7.4	10.9	2.4	62.8	21.4	9.7	7.4	1 047	1 030
Henry	1 997	6 801 070	4.9	8.8	1.9	3.9	16.2	5.8	57.8	199.6	66.8	68.8	1 372	1 289
Iroquois	1 017	3 877 441	5.9	6.3	0.5	4.2	0.4	1.9	79.8	90.3	38.3	39.1	1 337	1 242
Jackson	2 101	6 263 626	8.2	10.9	3.5	4.0	8.7	8.4	55.9	187.5	83.7	70.9	1 181	879
Jasper	379	1 198 050	10.1	7.5	0.4	7.8	10.7	3.7	59.8	34.3	16.7	13.8	1 437	1 424
Jefferson	1 638	5 345 187	5.0	7.6	2.9	4.0	1.2	3.6	74.9	147.2	83.4	43.3	1 119	882
Jersey	837	3 076 248	4.5	7.9	0.3	2.8	30.8	3.6	48.9	78.3	24.9	21.1	926	828
Jo Daviess	997	3 300 597	8.1	8.4	0.0	5.4	17.9	2.0	56.6	94.9	21.9	52.5	2 329	2 191
Johnson	372	1 081 737	6.4	5.0	0.0	5.0	0.2	4.9	77.4	26.5	15.8	7.0	547	545
Kane	21 805	101 252 430	5.2	10.1	5.2	2.0	0.9	6.8	68.3	2 745.0	798.1	1 591.7	3 046	2 837
Kankakee	4 413	16 356 166	7.8	13.5	3.6	3.7	1.5	3.4	65.4	441.9	208.0	169.2	1 496	1 433
Kendall	3 451	14 665 867	5.1	10.4	5.3	1.3	0.8	4.9	71.6	446.4	125.8	268.8	2 276	2 192
Knox	2 362	8 240 583	5.2	9.0	3.0	3.3	7.4	6.1	64.9	191.6	87.1	68.2	1 306	1 155
Lake	27 930	134 406 176	5.8	8.4	4.0	2.3	3.7	6.6	68.5	3 687.1	912.8	2 300.4	3 276	3 089
LaSalle	4 146	16 025 437	6.1	10.7	2.6	3.3	2.5	3.9	69.6	433.1	147.6	217.8	1 928	1 756
Lawrence	525	1 443 702	5.9	7.2	0.3	7.5	2.8	3.7	71.9	44.1	29.2	8.7	523	515
Lee	1 249	4 093 940	7.1	9.2	4.8	4.5	2.0	3.9	68.0	116.7	37.8	58.8	1 677	1 531
Livingston	1 564	5 591 107	6.4	8.8	1.4	4.2	3.1	3.6	72.0	146.1	52.6	67.2	1 738	1 641
Logan	897	2 996 965	7.7	10.0	3.8	5.0	4.3	2.9	65.3	74.1	29.9	31.4	1 045	1 003
McDonough	1 625	5 796 187	4.2	7.7	1.7	2.8	51.0	3.4	28.6	163.5	47.6	32.0	983	944
McHenry	11 260	47 454 823	5.9	10.6	5.0	2.9	2.6	5.6	65.8	1 313.1	295.8	821.5	2 666	2 473
McLean	6 296	24 583 518	6.5	10.3	4.7	4.3	5.2	5.3	61.6	657.7	182.2	354.7	2 059	1 702
Macon	4 204	17 133 160	5.9	11.8	4.5	3.0	2.0	8.2	63.3	407.1	180.7	163.9	1 488	1 260
Macoupin	1 579	5 464 855	7.7	8.5	0.5	3.9	2.1	5.6	71.2	159.2	103.8	40.1	850	818
Madison	8 550	34 777 691	7.6	11.4	3.9	3.8	1.5	6.9	63.4	966.9	418.8	400.7	1 496	1 338
Marion	1 941	6 738 024	6.0	6.5	2.0	6.9	1.1	4.0	73.0	188.6	94.3	42.9	1 104	1 038
Marshall	389	1 147 988	11.1	7.9	0.1	5.9	0.0	3.3	70.7	32.3	9.0	19.1	1 547	1 484
Mason	923	2 905 218	5.6	6.6	1.1	4.1	31.2	2.1	49.0	70.8	24.6	21.1	1 473	1 402
Massac	642	2 312 058	4.9	5.8	3.7	5.1	27.2	5.6	47.5	66.0	26.3	12.5	822	786
Menard	629	1 816 714	5.1	6.6	0.0	3.4	18.6	6.4	58.9	48.9	20.5	18.4	1 447	1 400
Mercer	808	2 500 408	4.4	7.5	0.1	4.2	27.9	2.7	52.0	60.4	20.7	22.0	1 356	1 324
Monroe	1 183	4 219 452	6.0	6.8	0.1	3.0	9.8	5.0	68.2	102.0	27.3	50.1	1 503	1 423
Montgomery	1 039	3 506 922	6.9	10.8	2.5	5.7	5.0	6.3	61.4	82.3	39.4	28.5	963	919
Morgan	1 212	4 876 454	5.8	9.2	2.8	3.7	1.9	5.1	70.1	101.9	48.0	40.0	1 135	1 038
Moultrie	521	1 796 777	7.8	7.6	2.7	4.3	1.3	9.1	66.3	36.7	14.6	17.0	1 135	1 079
Ogle	2 397	8 623 161	5.6	8.6	3.0	3.7	0.9	6.5	71.3	242.2	66.1	126.2	2 388	2 325
Peoria	6 795	26 829 973	7.0	12.3	5.0	5.9	4.2	8.9	54.4	819.7	356.0	319.4	1 706	1 383
Perry	777	2 700 659	4.7	8.5	1.5	3.8	27.6	5.4	47.3	84.4	42.3	13.8	627	594
Piatt	763	2 418 221	6.8	10.0	0.5	5.3	14.9	3.4	57.7	66.5	26.6	26.9	1 631	1 599
Pike	558	1 854 503	4.9	7.2	0.0	8.0	4.7	8.8	66.1	46.6	23.4	15.2	932	910
Pope	138	448 003	20.0	12.1	0.0	2.4	0.2	11.1	54.2	9.3	5.8	2.3	545	536
Pulaski	327	899 884	7.1	8.9	0.0	20.1	0.0	3.3	59.6	25.7	17.3	2.4	395	366
Putnam	225	602 290	16.8	7.7	4.2	6.1	0.0	5.9	58.5	21.9	11.9	8.0	1 357	1 315
Randolph	1 307	4 546 917	4.9	6.9	0.2	2.7	38.8	4.6	41.3	133.8	44.5	27.5	833	774
Richland	975	3 144 076	4.3	4.3	0.6	2.4	0.2	3.1	84.3	57.1	27.3	13.0	807	742
Rock Island	5 596	23 551 782	5.9	9.4	3.6	6.1	4.6	7.6	61.4	620.9	245.3	250.9	1 701	1 489
St. Clair	9 810	39 541 919	4.8	9.2	1.9	2.6	2.2	3.8	73.7	1 194.0	627.0	382.0	1 421	1 216
Saline	1 108	4 428 993	4.7	6.7	0.9	2.6	0.3	6.0	77.8	90.8	50.3	23.2	930	837
Sangamon	8 380	36 468 884	5.0	9.4	3.8	4.6	1.2	19.7	56.0	774.9	316.2	329.5	1 654	1 429
Schuyler	476	1 475 450	5.3	4.7	0.2	4.4	42.6	3.1	38.9	44.3	11.9	8.0	1 069	1 046
Scott	279	678 856	8.7	3.5	0.5	4.1	18.9	5.6	57.3	16.8	8.0	4.6	873	829
Shelby	598	1 947 657	9.5	8.9	1.8	7.6	2.8	6.4	62.1	47.8	23.5	17.9	808	790
Stark	247	745 997	7.9	3.6	5.2	4.9	5.8	1.4	71.0	24.8	11.5	10.9	1 837	1 825
Stephenson	2 084	7 077 197	4.5	9.2	3.6	2.9	5.4	4.5	68.9	190.4	85.0	73.4	1 563	1 449
Tazewell	4 864	18 067 473	5.1	9.0	3.1	2.4	2.6	4.8	70.8	521.3	190.4	225.1	1 655	1 450
Union	758	2 771 148	9.5	6.1	0.8	5.1	0.0	5.2	72.8	60.0	30.9	17.9	1 015	992
Vermilion	3 642	12 242 579	7.0	7.8	2.7	3.5	3.6	4.2	67.9	289.5	151.8	91.4	1 132	940
Wabash	629	2 227 140	2.9	4.6	1.3	1.8	48.4	3.1	37.5	63.3	16.1	9.7	830	795
Warren	522	1 914 920	7.4	10.5	4.1	3.6	0.2	4.0	69.9	49.1	22.4	18.5	1 044	1 001
Washington	568	1 952 729	6.8	5.6	0.6	5.3	31.1	4.1	46.3	61.8	13.6	15.4	1 056	1 044
Wayne	680	1 956 742	7.1	7.6	1.1	3.6	2.2	8.9	66.5	46.0	28.5	12.0	724	652
White	705	2 274 585	7.3	7.6	0.6	4.7	1.6	8.1	69.3	49.9	30.9	10.9	747	707
Whiteside	3 387	13 850 341	3.2	4.6	1.2	1.9	52.6	3.0	32.7	404.5	88.0	74.4	1 287	1 222
Will	22 376	101 738 743	4.7	11.4	5.8	2.2	2.7	5.6	66.5	2 654.5	767.6	1 489.2	2 182	2 004
Williamson	2 123	8 108 041	5.1	8.0	3.0	3.7	0.5	5.2	72.9	224.1	117.2	75.8	1 137	974

1. Based on the resident population estimated as of July 1 of the year shown.

Table B. States and Counties — **Local Government Finances, Government Employment, and Voting**

STATE County	Local government finances, 2012 (cont.)									Government employment, 2014			Presidential election,[2] 2012		
	Direct general expenditure							Debt outstanding					Percent of vote cast:		
			Percent of total for:												
	Total (mil dol)	Per capita[1] (dollars)	Education	Health and hospitals	Police protection	Public welfare	Highways	Total (mil dol)	Per capita[1] (dollars)	Federal civilian	Federal military	State and local	Democratic	Republican	All other
	185	186	187	188	189	190	191	192	193	194	195	196	197	198	199
ILLINOIS—Cont'd															
Hardin	9.4	2 219	53.6	4.3	2.9	0.3	6.9	3.9	917	0	0	216	39.6	59.0	1.5
Henderson	23.7	3 370	36.9	8.9	3.5	0.0	12.3	3.3	465	40	14	387	58.1	40.4	1.5
Henry	218.5	4 357	39.3	20.6	5.2	2.4	5.6	98.2	1 957	119	99	3 561	53.2	45.4	1.4
Iroquois	91.6	3 132	53.4	3.1	3.5	0.1	7.9	32.1	1 098	97	57	1 650	34.1	64.0	1.9
Jackson	186.2	3 100	49.6	4.1	7.0	4.9	4.5	96.1	1 600	167	123	12 047	59.7	37.9	2.3
Jasper	35.9	3 739	55.0	4.2	2.9	0.1	13.9	9.9	1 031	39	19	537	40.2	57.8	2.0
Jefferson	141.2	3 647	60.3	0.7	5.4	0.0	6.2	65.0	1 679	145	75	2 474	43.5	54.3	2.2
Jersey	88.3	3 885	32.7	37.7	3.8	0.1	7.5	73.1	3 212	39	44	1 083	47.6	50.4	2.0
Jo Daviess	84.9	3 767	44.0	15.8	6.1	0.0	11.0	34.5	1 528	62	45	1 346	54.5	44.0	1.5
Johnson	27.3	2 141	60.1	1.3	4.1	0.1	8.6	19.6	1 535	71	22	803	31.7	66.3	2.0
Kane	2 646.1	5 064	55.1	0.4	6.5	0.1	5.6	4 427.4	8 474	1 610	1 054	29 078	55.2	43.4	1.3
Kankakee	442.3	3 912	52.1	0.7	6.1	0.1	5.9	327.2	2 894	229	215	6 017	51.5	46.9	1.5
Kendall	434.1	3 676	60.8	0.5	5.2	0.9	3.7	902.1	7 638	113	245	5 672	53.1	45.8	1.1
Knox	198.6	3 801	51.6	1.5	5.0	4.2	8.6	156.9	3 002	171	97	3 304	59.2	39.3	1.6
Lake	3 519.2	5 012	56.6	2.1	5.9	0.6	4.2	3 079.5	4 386	5 505	12 065	36 584	59.3	39.6	1.1
LaSalle	473.9	4 195	57.8	1.3	5.1	1.1	6.6	284.6	2 520	344	220	6 063	54.7	43.6	1.7
Lawrence	51.2	3 083	63.6	1.4	3.9	0.1	9.0	34.7	2 091	44	28	826	46.1	52.1	1.8
Lee	113.4	3 238	58.0	1.7	5.2	0.1	7.1	71.5	2 040	80	65	1 912	47.6	50.6	1.8
Livingston	169.3	4 381	47.9	3.0	3.8	0.2	5.0	65.3	1 689	103	70	2 376	39.6	58.8	1.6
Logan	71.3	2 376	51.1	5.0	5.4	0.1	7.6	26.9	895	97	51	1 334	40.7	57.6	1.7
McDonough	169.8	5 218	27.4	39.5	3.7	3.4	9.6	21.4	657	95	60	5 623	52.0	46.4	1.6
McHenry	1 256.5	4 078	49.3	2.2	6.5	1.2	7.2	1 209.9	3 926	460	618	14 974	51.9	46.6	1.5
McLean	663.9	3 853	46.3	1.2	4.8	1.3	5.4	781.5	4 536	490	336	14 704	49.8	48.5	1.7
Macon	452.8	4 112	52.8	2.0	7.8	0.1	8.1	462.5	4 200	318	219	5 467	49.8	48.7	1.5
Macoupin	129.5	2 741	63.8	2.0	7.1	0.2	7.8	66.0	1 397	119	92	2 233	54.0	44.2	1.8
Madison	939.6	3 507	50.9	0.8	6.8	1.6	6.8	839.9	3 135	551	537	15 965	53.7	44.6	1.7
Marion	186.5	4 794	59.6	11.4	3.2	0.2	3.5	110.6	2 844	113	77	2 097	48.1	50.1	1.9
Marshall	33.3	2 698	45.3	2.0	5.5	0.1	16.2	9.4	759	35	24	495	48.6	49.7	1.7
Mason	72.0	5 027	41.2	33.1	3.0	0.0	4.5	27.4	1 914	56	28	1 082	52.0	46.1	1.8
Massac	63.9	4 197	33.1	34.0	4.6	0.0	6.8	35.3	2 315	51	30	930	37.5	60.8	1.7
Menard	46.5	3 652	52.7	4.5	4.3	13.7	7.4	27.0	2 121	29	25	674	41.9	56.8	1.3
Mercer	59.7	3 679	42.8	21.8	3.5	0.1	6.2	15.9	978	58	32	772	55.2	43.3	1.4
Monroe	99.7	2 990	44.6	3.1	5.8	10.1	10.9	136.3	4 085	70	68	1 434	44.0	54.6	1.4
Montgomery	84.4	2 851	51.5	3.4	7.1	0.1	10.4	52.7	1 779	99	55	1 537	50.4	47.8	1.8
Morgan	103.7	2 940	52.8	1.6	5.8	3.3	9.0	36.7	1 040	77	64	2 311	48.6	49.4	1.9
Moultrie	39.7	2 658	46.1	1.8	4.8	0.0	9.9	11.4	763	27	29	503	42.6	55.4	1.9
Ogle	280.5	5 307	64.6	0.8	3.1	0.0	5.5	269.6	5 101	116	104	2 871	45.3	52.9	1.8
Peoria	776.9	4 149	41.7	1.1	6.6	3.2	6.5	850.1	4 540	1 603	441	9 543	56.2	42.3	1.5
Perry	91.6	4 151	51.3	22.3	3.7	0.2	4.4	32.0	1 453	50	39	1 295	47.0	50.9	2.1
Piatt	65.0	3 940	47.2	2.6	3.6	12.4	9.9	36.4	2 205	37	33	994	42.9	55.5	1.7
Pike	48.7	2 986	53.6	6.0	6.0	0.3	9.7	27.7	1 701	61	31	896	39.7	58.5	1.8
Pope	9.6	2 241	48.1	0.0	2.7	0.0	16.4	0.3	64	69	0	193	37.9	60.2	1.9
Pulaski	23.9	3 981	59.8	1.8	6.4	0.3	6.2	12.7	2 118	65	12	765	50.1	48.7	1.2
Putnam	21.7	3 688	43.8	2.5	4.8	0.3	13.3	3.0	508	18	12	313	56.9	41.3	1.8
Randolph	140.7	4 269	35.0	36.0	4.5	2.8	6.9	54.6	1 657	87	58	2 471	48.6	49.6	1.8
Richland	75.7	4 677	78.3	0.4	3.6	0.1	5.2	28.2	1 746	47	32	928	41.6	56.6	1.8
Rock Island	636.7	4 318	45.3	1.1	6.6	3.0	5.2	418.1	2 835	5 010	717	7 743	61.7	37.1	1.2
St. Clair	1 159.8	4 314	54.3	1.3	5.1	0.1	4.2	908.3	3 378	6 155	5 127	13 079	60.6	38.1	1.3
Saline	95.1	3 814	54.7	1.0	5.6	0.6	5.5	54.8	2 197	97	48	1 835	44.5	53.4	2.2
Sangamon	823.4	4 132	52.9	1.4	7.6	0.2	4.4	2 513.3	12 612	1 761	440	18 660	51.4	47.0	1.6
Schuyler	47.2	6 325	29.5	48.7	2.2	0.1	10.2	10.5	1 403	24	14	672	49.7	47.9	2.4
Scott	17.4	3 281	46.2	2.2	3.3	13.9	8.8	6.2	1 174	15	10	306	41.9	56.0	2.1
Shelby	50.5	2 273	53.6	3.0	5.5	0.1	12.8	14.9	670	99	44	790	39.1	58.9	2.1
Stark	18.9	3 183	55.8	0.5	5.0	0.5	11.8	11.4	1 922	22	12	323	46.7	52.0	1.3
Stephenson	184.9	3 937	57.2	2.4	4.7	3.3	6.3	98.3	2 092	130	92	2 741	52.5	45.9	1.6
Tazewell	547.5	4 028	52.3	1.6	5.5	0.1	6.4	349.0	2 567	511	269	7 333	46.0	52.1	1.9
Union	60.8	3 445	72.9	2.7	4.1	0.0	5.3	53.7	3 042	55	34	1 149	43.0	54.9	2.1
Vermilion	308.3	3 819	56.4	0.7	6.4	3.5	6.3	102.1	1 265	1 488	155	4 309	49.4	48.8	1.7
Wabash	60.5	5 156	29.5	47.7	4.0	0.5	5.0	14.7	1 254	25	23	1 040	42.6	56.3	1.1
Warren	53.0	2 987	53.6	0.4	5.3	0.0	6.7	45.8	2 584	65	34	819	53.4	45.3	1.3
Washington	72.8	4 985	42.5	34.2	2.5	0.1	6.1	55.0	3 766	50	29	881	42.1	56.4	1.5
Wayne	47.3	2 854	59.1	1.9	4.8	0.1	9.4	21.3	1 285	59	33	885	31.6	66.8	1.7
White	56.9	3 908	63.4	1.7	4.0	0.1	9.2	23.5	1 610	47	28	849	44.5	53.5	2.0
Whiteside	392.0	6 777	27.5	52.5	2.6	0.2	2.3	129.8	2 244	154	113	4 913	58.0	40.4	1.5
Will	2 568.4	3 763	52.2	1.6	6.9	0.8	5.1	3 781.8	5 541	940	1 380	33 399	56.0	42.8	1.2
Williamson	279.8	4 196	65.4	0.0	3.9	0.1	4.9	229.8	3 447	1 673	132	4 057	41.9	56.4	1.7

1. Based on the resident population estimated as of July 1 of the year shown.   2. © 2013 Election Data Services, Inc. All rights reserved.

Table B. States and Counties — **Land Area and Population**

					Population, 2015			Population and population characteristics, 2014									
								Race alone or in combination, not Hispanic or Latino (percent)					Age (percent)					
STATE/ County code	CBSA code[1]	County type[2]	STATE County	Land area,[3] (sq km) 2010	Total persons 2015	Rank	Per square kilometer	White	Black	American Indian, Alaska Native	Asian and Pacific Islander	Percent Hispanic or Latino[4]	Under 5 years	5 to 17 years	18 to 24 years	25 to 34 years	35 to 44 years	45 to 54 years
				1	2	3	4	5	6	7	8	9	10	11	12	13	14	15
			ILLINOIS—Cont'd															
17 201	40420	2	Winnebago	1 330	287 078	236	215.8	72.7	13.7	0.6	3.1	12.0	6.2	17.6	8.7	12.2	12.3	14.0
17 203	37900	2	Woodford	1 367	39 227	1 194	28.7	96.5	1.2	0.5	1.0	1.8	6.1	18.5	8.8	10.6	11.8	13.9
18 000	...	X	INDIANA	92 789	6 619 680	X	71.3	81.9	10.2	0.7	2.4	6.6	6.4	17.6	10.1	12.8	12.5	13.5
18 001	19540	6	Adams	878	34 980	1 305	39.8	94.8	0.8	0.4	0.4	4.4	9.4	21.9	8.6	11.2	10.9	11.9
18 003	23060	2	Allen	1 702	368 450	186	216.5	77.3	13.5	0.8	4.0	7.2	7.2	19.1	9.4	13.3	12.6	12.9
18 005	18020	3	Bartholomew	1 054	81 162	688	77.0	85.9	2.8	0.6	5.7	6.4	6.6	17.7	8.4	13.5	13.2	13.3
18 007	29200	3	Benton	1 053	8 681	2 538	8.2	93.5	1.3	0.4	0.4	5.4	6.1	19.2	7.8	10.9	11.9	14.4
18 009	...	6	Blackford	428	12 298	2 277	28.7	97.2	1.3	0.8	0.6	1.6	6.1	16.2	7.9	10.3	11.5	13.9
18 011	26900	1	Boone	1 095	63 344	835	57.8	93.5	2.0	0.6	2.9	2.6	6.6	20.4	7.7	11.2	13.9	15.3
18 013	26900	1	Brown	808	14 977	2 099	18.5	97.2	0.9	1.0	0.6	1.6	4.1	15.4	6.9	8.5	11.0	14.6
18 015	29200	3	Carroll	964	19 856	1 840	20.6	95.2	0.9	0.5	0.3	4.1	5.3	17.9	7.9	10.4	12.2	14.0
18 017	30900	4	Cass	1 067	37 979	1 222	35.6	83.1	2.1	0.6	1.8	13.9	6.5	17.6	8.5	11.3	12.7	13.8
18 019	31140	1	Clark	966	115 371	533	119.4	86.3	8.5	0.7	1.4	5.2	6.3	16.8	8.1	13.8	13.8	13.8
18 021	45460	3	Clay	926	26 503	1 547	28.6	97.7	1.0	0.6	0.6	1.3	6.1	17.0	8.1	11.8	12.4	13.8
18 023	23140	6	Clinton	1 049	32 609	1 368	31.1	84.5	0.9	0.4	0.4	14.9	6.9	19.4	8.1	11.6	12.1	13.3
18 025	...	8	Crawford	792	10 483	2 396	13.2	97.8	0.8	0.8	0.5	1.4	5.3	17.1	7.8	10.1	12.4	14.8
18 027	47780	7	Daviess	1 112	32 906	1 360	29.6	93.5	1.4	0.4	0.8	4.6	8.2	21.0	9.0	12.0	11.2	12.3
18 029	17140	1	Dearborn	790	49 455	989	62.6	97.5	1.2	0.5	0.7	1.2	5.5	18.1	7.9	10.7	12.5	15.5
18 031	24700	6	Decatur	965	26 521	1 544	27.5	96.3	0.8	0.5	1.5	1.8	6.0	18.9	8.4	11.8	12.5	13.9
18 033	12140	4	DeKalb	940	42 589	1 117	45.3	95.7	0.9	0.5	0.8	2.6	6.0	18.7	8.5	11.5	12.6	14.4
18 035	34620	3	Delaware	1 016	116 852	527	115.0	89.2	8.2	0.7	1.8	2.1	5.1	13.8	20.1	11.0	10.4	11.9
18 037	27540	7	Dubois	1 107	42 461	1 122	38.4	92.3	0.7	0.3	0.7	6.2	6.1	17.9	8.0	11.4	11.8	14.9
18 039	21140	3	Elkhart	1 200	203 474	321	169.6	77.8	7.0	0.7	1.5	15.1	7.5	20.4	9.0	12.6	12.5	12.9
18 041	18220	7	Fayette	557	23 434	1 660	42.1	97.0	2.0	0.5	0.5	0.9	5.3	17.3	7.6	10.3	12.9	13.6
18 043	31140	1	Floyd	383	76 778	718	200.5	90.4	6.5	0.6	1.5	2.9	5.8	17.4	8.7	12.2	12.7	14.8
18 045	...	6	Fountain	1 025	16 591	2 002	16.2	96.0	0.8	0.8	0.6	2.6	5.8	16.8	8.0	10.5	11.7	14.5
18 047	...	1	Franklin	996	22 872	1 688	23.0	97.9	0.4	0.5	0.7	1.1	5.7	19.0	8.1	9.9	12.5	14.8
18 049	...	7	Fulton	954	20 315	1 817	21.3	93.3	1.3	0.8	0.8	5.1	6.1	17.8	8.1	11.0	12.0	13.4
18 051	...	2	Gibson	1 263	33 775	1 332	26.7	95.4	3.0	0.6	0.7	1.6	6.0	17.2	8.6	11.7	12.0	14.0
18 053	31980	4	Grant	1 072	67 979	784	63.4	87.6	8.5	0.8	1.2	4.0	5.5	15.2	13.5	10.3	10.8	13.1
18 055	...	3	Greene	1 405	32 441	1 375	23.1	97.6	0.6	0.8	0.6	1.3	5.4	17.2	7.7	10.9	11.9	14.7
18 057	26900	1	Hamilton	1 021	309 697	218	303.3	86.3	4.6	0.4	6.5	3.8	6.8	21.7	7.1	12.3	15.6	15.1
18 059	26900	1	Hancock	793	72 520	749	91.5	94.5	2.7	0.6	1.3	2.1	5.5	18.7	7.9	11.3	13.1	15.3
18 061	31140	1	Harrison	1 255	39 578	1 184	31.5	97.1	1.0	0.6	0.7	1.8	5.4	17.2	7.6	11.8	12.6	15.1
18 063	26900	1	Hendricks	1 054	158 192	407	150.1	87.8	6.7	0.5	3.1	3.5	6.0	19.9	7.9	12.7	14.7	14.5
18 065	35220	4	Henry	1 015	48 985	997	48.3	95.0	3.2	0.6	0.7	1.6	4.9	16.0	8.3	11.4	12.9	14.8
18 067	29020	3	Howard	759	82 556	678	108.8	88.6	8.6	0.9	1.6	3.1	6.1	16.9	8.4	11.3	11.8	13.9
18 069	26540	6	Huntington	991	36 630	1 262	37.0	96.4	1.0	0.7	0.9	2.1	5.8	16.6	10.2	11.7	11.9	14.1
18 071	42980	4	Jackson	1 319	44 069	1 089	33.4	90.9	1.3	0.7	1.6	6.4	6.9	17.3	8.3	12.5	13.0	13.9
18 073	16980	1	Jasper	1 449	33 470	1 340	23.1	92.6	1.3	0.5	0.6	5.9	5.9	18.6	9.7	10.7	12.4	13.9
18 075	...	6	Jay	994	21 121	1 768	21.2	96.1	0.7	0.5	0.6	3.0	7.0	19.1	8.2	10.9	11.7	13.7
18 077	31500	6	Jefferson	934	32 416	1 376	34.7	94.5	2.6	0.6	1.0	2.5	5.4	15.8	10.3	11.5	12.4	14.4
18 079	35860	6	Jennings	975	27 897	1 492	28.6	96.4	1.4	0.7	0.4	2.3	6.2	18.0	9.1	10.9	12.9	15.1
18 081	26900	1	Johnson	830	149 633	434	180.3	92.2	2.4	0.6	2.9	3.4	6.5	19.0	8.7	12.9	13.6	13.9
18 083	47180	4	Knox	1 337	37 927	1 225	28.4	94.2	3.7	0.6	1.1	1.8	6.2	15.0	13.7	11.6	10.6	12.9
18 085	47700	1	Kosciusko	1 376	78 620	705	57.1	89.7	1.4	0.6	1.5	8.0	6.5	18.2	9.3	12.4	11.9	13.4
18 087	...	6	LaGrange	983	38 809	1 206	39.5	95.1	0.6	0.5	0.6	3.9	9.6	24.0	9.0	11.9	11.0	11.2
18 089	16980	1	Lake	1 292	487 865	143	377.6	55.9	25.1	0.6	1.8	18.0	6.3	18.2	9.1	12.3	12.5	13.5
18 091	33140	3	LaPorte	1 550	110 884	548	71.5	81.7	12.3	0.7	0.9	6.1	5.9	16.1	8.6	13.0	12.6	14.0
18 093	13260	4	Lawrence	1 163	45 495	1 061	39.1	97.1	0.8	0.9	0.9	1.6	5.6	16.8	7.6	10.9	12.1	14.5
18 095	26900	3	Madison	1 170	129 723	483	110.9	87.1	9.4	0.6	0.9	3.7	5.7	16.4	8.9	12.4	12.7	13.8
18 097	26900	1	Marion	1 026	939 020	52	915.2	60.0	28.8	0.8	3.2	9.8	7.6	17.4	9.8	16.4	12.9	12.9
18 099	38500	6	Marshall	1 149	46 857	1 034	40.8	89.3	1.0	0.6	0.8	9.4	6.3	19.2	8.6	10.9	11.9	13.6
18 101	...	6	Martin	870	10 226	2 416	11.8	98.2	0.6	0.7	0.5	0.8	6.1	17.1	7.6	10.8	11.7	14.5
18 103	37940	6	Miami	968	35 862	1 277	37.0	91.1	5.5	1.6	0.7	2.8	5.1	16.5	8.6	12.5	13.7	14.5
18 105	14020	3	Monroe	1 022	144 705	443	141.6	86.5	4.2	0.7	7.4	3.3	4.5	11.6	27.8	14.7	10.0	10.0
18 107	18820	6	Montgomery	1 307	38 227	1 216	29.2	93.9	1.6	0.7	0.9	4.5	6.3	17.0	9.7	11.0	11.9	14.1
18 109	26900	1	Morgan	1 046	69 648	771	66.6	97.4	0.9	0.7	0.8	1.4	5.6	18.0	8.2	10.9	12.5	15.5
18 111	16980	1	Newton	1 041	14 008	2 164	13.5	93.5	0.8	0.7	0.4	5.9	5.1	17.1	7.7	10.9	11.8	14.6
18 113	28340	6	Noble	1 064	47 733	1 022	44.9	88.6	1.0	0.6	0.7	10.1	6.4	19.3	8.4	11.5	12.6	13.9
18 115	17140	1	Ohio	223	5 938	2 758	26.6	98.2	0.7	0.5	0.6	1.2	4.7	15.3	6.6	10.6	11.4	16.1
18 117	...	6	Orange	1 032	19 605	1 848	19.0	96.6	1.5	0.9	0.6	1.3	5.5	17.9	8.2	10.7	12.0	14.0
18 119	14020	3	Owen	998	20 872	1 779	20.9	97.1	0.8	0.9	0.4	1.3	4.7	17.1	7.6	10.2	11.6	15.6
18 121	...	6	Parke	1 152	16 901	1 986	14.7	95.5	3.0	0.6	0.4	1.3	6.0	15.5	8.3	12.8	11.9	14.4
18 123	...	6	Perry	989	19 347	1 857	19.6	95.4	3.3	0.5	0.7	1.3	5.5	15.4	8.5	13.3	12.7	14.1

1. CBSA = Core Based Statistical Area. See Appendix A for explanation. See Appendix B for list of metropolitan areas with component counties.   2. County type code from the Economic Research Service of USDA Rural-Urban Continuum Codes. See Appendix A for definition.   3. Dry land or land partially or temporarily covered by water.   4. May be of any race.

STATE County	Population, 2014 (cont.) Age (percent) (cont.) 55 to 64 years	65 to 74 years	75 years and over	Percent female	Population change and components of change, 2000–2015 Total persons 2000	2010	Percent change 2000–2010	2010–2015	Components of change, 2010–2015 Births	Deaths	Net migration	Households, 2010–2014 Number	Persons per house-hold	Percent Family house-holds	Female family house-holder[1]	One per-son
	16	17	18	19	20	21	22	23	24	25	26	27	28	29	30	31
ILLINOIS—Cont'd																
Winnebago	13.3	8.8	6.8	51.2	278 418	295 264	6.1	-2.8	18 807	14 168	-12 669	113 553	2.53	65.9	14.6	28.9
Woodford	14.0	8.5	7.8	50.4	35 469	38 664	9.0	1.5	2 393	1 917	37	14 373	2.64	75.9	7.7	21.9
INDIANA	12.8	8.1	6.1	50.7	6 080 485	6 484 229	6.6	2.1	437 934	308 845	10 163	2 492 183	2.55	66.5	12.4	27.8
Adams	11.6	7.5	7.0	50.5	33 625	34 387	2.3	1.7	3 520	1 542	-1 349	12 164	2.80	70.8	9.0	25.9
Allen	12.3	7.4	5.6	51.2	331 849	355 327	7.1	3.7	27 233	15 387	1 540	139 384	2.55	65.2	13.1	29.2
Bartholomew	12.4	8.5	6.4	50.1	71 435	76 786	7.5	5.7	5 551	3 700	2 604	30 516	2.54	68.2	10.7	27.4
Benton	13.5	9.1	7.1	50.3	9 421	8 836	-6.2	-1.8	549	432	-223	3 464	2.51	65.7	10.7	29.3
Blackford	14.3	11.0	8.8	50.4	14 048	12 766	-9.1	-3.7	755	783	-445	5 236	2.37	69.5	12.5	26.6
Boone	12.3	7.2	5.5	50.5	46 107	56 638	22.8	11.8	3 809	2 466	5 215	22 248	2.64	74.3	9.2	21.6
Brown	18.5	13.7	7.4	50.2	14 957	15 242	1.9	-1.7	639	787	-67	5 926	2.52	70.2	11.4	25.1
Carroll	14.6	10.1	7.6	50.3	20 165	20 159	0.0	-1.5	1 128	922	-438	7 828	2.55	69.2	7.4	26.6
Cass	13.4	8.7	7.5	50.0	40 930	38 966	-4.8	-2.5	2 553	2 005	-1 496	14 759	2.55	66.5	10.6	28.6
Clark	13.1	8.6	5.7	50.9	96 472	110 234	14.3	4.7	7 854	5 673	2 897	42 774	2.59	66.8	12.6	27.5
Clay	14.2	9.3	7.3	50.8	26 556	26 887	1.2	-1.4	1 630	1 520	-499	10 221	2.59	71.8	11.0	24.0
Clinton	12.8	8.2	7.6	50.5	33 866	33 219	-1.9	-1.8	2 274	1 793	-1 090	11 853	2.73	70.0	11.0	24.6
Crawford	15.4	10.7	6.5	49.3	10 743	10 713	-0.3	-2.1	574	600	-189	4 166	2.53	68.7	11.9	27.1
Daviess	11.9	8.0	6.5	50.2	29 820	31 654	6.2	4.0	2 826	1 736	221	11 462	2.76	70.9	8.5	26.5
Dearborn	14.5	9.2	6.1	50.2	46 109	50 047	8.5	-1.2	2 683	2 267	-923	18 648	2.64	71.7	9.0	23.9
Decatur	13.3	8.4	7.0	50.6	24 555	25 740	4.8	3.0	1 796	1 338	322	9 809	2.63	70.4	11.9	25.7
DeKalb	13.4	8.6	6.3	50.2	40 285	42 223	4.8	0.9	2 753	1 996	-362	16 235	2.58	70.9	11.8	25.1
Delaware	11.6	8.8	7.1	51.9	118 769	117 671	-0.9	-0.7	6 640	6 220	-1 119	46 239	2.37	59.9	12.6	29.5
Dubois	13.9	8.6	7.3	50.6	39 674	41 889	5.6	1.4	2 760	2 049	-206	15 926	2.59	71.0	8.0	25.7
Elkhart	11.7	7.4	5.9	50.5	182 791	197 561	8.1	3.0	15 789	8 279	-1 498	70 427	2.78	72.1	13.0	23.4
Fayette	14.6	10.4	8.1	50.5	25 588	24 302	-5.0	-3.6	1 271	1 606	-504	9 336	2.52	66.8	12.6	28.7
Floyd	13.9	8.5	6.0	51.4	70 823	74 578	5.3	2.9	4 646	3 753	1 286	29 017	2.56	68.5	13.4	27.1
Fountain	13.4	10.4	8.9	50.2	17 954	17 238	-4.0	-3.8	1 044	1 002	-643	6 912	2.43	68.8	11.6	25.7
Franklin	14.4	8.9	6.7	49.8	22 151	23 087	4.2	-0.9	1 287	1 088	-395	8 726	2.61	75.6	7.5	20.2
Fulton	14.2	9.9	7.7	50.0	20 511	20 836	1.6	-2.5	1 325	1 234	-534	8 208	2.49	68.2	8.4	28.1
Gibson	13.9	9.0	7.5	50.1	32 500	33 503	3.1	0.8	2 217	1 831	-80	12 987	2.53	69.4	8.8	26.3
Grant	13.7	9.8	8.0	52.2	73 403	70 063	-4.6	-3.0	4 152	4 196	-1 923	26 829	2.38	65.0	13.7	30.3
Greene	14.2	10.3	7.6	50.1	33 157	33 164	0.0	-2.2	1 781	2 007	-491	12 879	2.53	69.1	9.3	28.1
Hamilton	10.9	6.4	4.0	51.2	182 740	274 569	50.3	12.8	20 271	7 495	21 966	105 578	2.73	73.9	8.4	21.9
Hancock	13.1	9.3	5.9	50.9	55 391	70 045	26.5	3.5	4 057	3 101	1 517	26 142	2.69	73.7	10.2	21.6
Harrison	14.3	9.6	6.3	50.1	34 325	39 364	14.7	0.5	2 153	1 947	17	14 678	2.65	71.7	9.5	24.0
Hendricks	11.9	7.4	5.0	50.2	104 093	145 412	39.7	8.8	9 112	5 220	8 588	53 959	2.74	74.6	9.7	21.3
Henry	13.7	10.1	7.8	48.3	48 508	49 462	2.0	-1.0	2 550	2 940	-140	18 214	2.52	67.0	11.3	28.9
Howard	13.7	10.2	7.8	51.7	84 964	82 752	-2.6	-0.2	5 182	4 782	-590	34 386	2.38	63.5	11.8	31.9
Huntington	13.9	8.5	7.4	50.8	38 075	37 124	-2.5	-1.3	2 221	2 094	-672	14 413	2.46	68.1	8.3	25.5
Jackson	12.8	8.6	6.7	50.2	41 335	42 380	2.5	4.0	3 031	2 293	937	16 657	2.55	70.1	10.4	25.2
Jasper	13.0	9.2	6.6	50.2	30 043	33 478	11.4	0.0	1 994	1 656	-311	11 988	2.71	75.7	8.2	21.2
Jay	12.9	9.2	7.3	50.7	21 806	21 253	-2.5	-0.6	1 564	1 198	-442	8 196	2.56	68.7	10.4	26.7
Jefferson	13.9	9.7	6.5	51.8	31 705	32 428	2.3	0.0	1 816	1 873	90	12 746	2.36	69.6	13.3	26.6
Jennings	13.1	9.4	5.4	49.8	27 554	28 525	3.5	-2.2	1 808	1 449	-959	10 585	2.63	68.3	12.9	25.1
Johnson	11.8	8.1	5.8	50.7	115 209	139 867	21.4	7.0	9 640	6 339	6 234	52 873	2.67	72.6	10.7	22.5
Knox	13.3	9.2	7.5	49.3	39 256	38 440	-2.1	-1.3	2 450	2 256	-649	14 705	2.41	63.5	10.4	31.7
Kosciusko	13.2	8.8	6.3	50.1	74 057	77 356	4.5	1.6	5 378	3 535	-420	29 414	2.59	71.2	8.4	24.3
LaGrange	10.7	7.6	5.0	49.6	34 909	37 130	6.4	4.5	4 055	1 347	-993	11 735	3.19	78.2	8.5	19.4
Lake	13.5	8.1	6.4	51.6	484 564	496 069	2.4	-1.7	31 867	24 460	-15 012	182 919	2.66	67.3	17.0	28.1
LaPorte	14.0	9.3	6.5	48.2	110 106	111 467	1.2	-0.5	6 913	5 989	-1 367	42 756	2.39	66.1	12.6	28.1
Lawrence	14.4	10.6	7.6	50.5	45 922	46 129	0.5	-1.4	2 473	2 856	-209	18 561	2.44	70.9	11.0	25.2
Madison	13.1	9.6	7.3	50.1	133 358	131 636	-1.3	-1.5	8 050	7 712	-2 041	51 232	2.42	64.9	12.9	29.8
Marion	11.8	6.4	4.9	51.8	860 454	903 389	5.0	3.9	75 950	40 075	1 288	361 648	2.50	58.8	16.9	33.9
Marshall	13.4	8.8	7.3	50.5	45 128	47 047	4.3	-0.4	3 037	2 328	-917	17 468	2.65	68.6	9.1	27.4
Martin	15.2	10.0	7.1	49.4	10 369	10 378	0.1	-1.5	711	540	-286	4 199	2.43	64.8	8.3	31.3
Miami	13.3	9.3	6.6	46.3	36 082	36 903	2.3	-2.8	1 931	1 817	-1 107	13 246	2.60	69.2	11.0	26.2
Monroe	10.1	6.4	4.9	50.2	120 563	137 959	14.4	4.9	6 765	4 545	4 521	53 778	2.35	51.2	9.5	34.1
Montgomery	13.3	9.2	7.5	49.6	37 629	38 126	1.3	0.3	2 437	1 982	-313	14 574	2.53	69.1	9.3	25.5
Morgan	14.3	9.2	5.8	50.4	66 689	68 939	3.4	1.0	3 954	3 323	92	25 456	2.70	74.1	10.7	20.2
Newton	15.1	10.3	7.4	49.0	14 566	14 244	-2.2	-1.7	712	800	-123	5 327	2.62	69.9	10.4	25.1
Noble	13.3	8.6	6.0	50.1	46 275	47 536	2.7	0.4	3 049	2 331	-578	17 703	2.64	72.6	11.2	23.9
Ohio	15.7	11.9	7.7	50.2	5 623	6 128	9.0	-3.1	281	316	-169	2 445	2.46	65.3	6.7	28.0
Orange	14.2	10.3	7.2	50.2	19 306	19 840	2.8	-1.2	1 256	1 098	-349	7 618	2.56	66.6	9.5	28.2
Owen	15.9	11.0	6.3	49.7	21 786	21 583	-0.9	-3.3	1 214	1 176	-734	8 539	2.47	70.8	10.2	24.2
Parke	13.9	10.4	6.7	53.1	17 241	17 354	0.7	-2.6	1 014	864	-562	6 128	2.55	69.5	7.8	24.2
Perry	14.0	9.2	7.4	46.2	18 899	19 338	2.3	0.0	1 031	1 025	3	7 356	2.41	68.1	8.7	28.2

1. No spouse present.

Table B. States and Counties — Population, Vital Statistics, Medicare, and Crime

STATE County	Persons in group quarters, 2015	Daytime population, 2010–2014 Number	Daytime population Employment/residence ratio	Births, 2015 Total	Births Rate[1]	Deaths, 2015 Number	Deaths Rate[1]	Persons under 65 with no health insurance, 2014 Number	Percent	Medicare, 2015 Total Beneficiaries	Enrolled in Original Medicare	Enrolled in Medicare Advantage	Serious crimes known to police,[2] 2014 Total Number	Rate[3]
	32	33	34	35	36	37	38	39	40	41	42	43	44	45
ILLINOIS—Cont'd														
Winnebago	4 716	297 421	1.04	3 492	12.1	2 660	9.2	26 100	10.8	53 027	37 730	15 297	11 199	3 890
Woodford	1 021	31 862	0.62	476	12.1	397	10.1	1 990	6.2	5 949	4 757	1 192	327	946
INDIANA	188 505	6 488 969	0.98	83 796	12.7	58 536	8.9	768 504	14.0	1 106 547	836 438	270 109	198 875	3 015
Adams	421	33 852	0.95	664	19.0	252	7.2	4 945	16.7	5 313	3 271	2 042	NA	NA
Allen	6 112	374 594	1.08	5 129	14.0	2 983	8.1	45 469	14.5	56 779	31 371	25 408	10 470	2 868
Bartholomew	1 147	87 010	1.22	1 102	13.7	674	8.4	9 160	13.6	15 152	12 312	2 840	2 664	3 316
Benton	92	7 249	0.61	110	12.7	82	9.4	1 137	15.7	1 749	1 489	260	NA	NA
Blackford	163	11 272	0.74	147	11.9	162	13.1	1 372	14.0	2 977	2 377	600	250	2 036
Boone	574	53 151	0.79	773	12.4	457	7.3	5 175	9.7	8 143	6 144	1 999	NA	NA
Brown	163	11 316	0.46	133	8.9	135	9.0	1 970	16.8	1 944	1 453	491	122	814
Carroll	106	16 528	0.61	211	10.6	182	9.2	2 524	15.5	3 096	2 469	627	NA	NA
Cass	1 034	37 552	0.93	467	12.2	397	10.4	5 542	17.5	7 094	5 690	1 404	1 044	2 722
Clark	1 466	105 664	0.88	1 592	13.9	1 093	9.5	13 536	14.0	20 515	15 846	4 669	4 415	3 886
Clay	341	22 865	0.66	304	11.5	275	10.4	3 122	14.2	5 889	4 966	923	NA	NA
Clinton	830	30 210	0.81	418	12.8	309	9.5	4 166	15.3	5 982	4 946	1 036	1 067	3 246
Crawford	62	8 647	0.54	107	10.1	107	10.1	1 378	15.7	2 463	2 032	431	115	1 084
Daviess	581	30 776	0.90	548	16.7	318	9.7	5 228	18.9	4 921	4 470	451	762	2 337
Dearborn	530	41 114	0.63	483	9.8	423	8.6	4 729	11.4	8 929	6 749	2 180	NA	NA
Decatur	377	27 585	1.12	381	14.4	255	9.6	2 829	12.7	4 842	3 687	1 155	NA	NA
DeKalb	615	43 563	1.07	538	12.6	387	9.1	4 879	13.6	8 164	4 429	3 735	NA	NA
Delaware	9 138	119 257	1.04	1 277	10.9	1 160	9.9	13 378	14.8	22 915	19 059	3 856	3 820	3 250
Dubois	893	47 355	1.24	551	13.0	381	9.0	4 230	12.1	7 308	6 597	711	NA	NA
Elkhart	3 758	221 462	1.25	3 028	14.9	1 557	7.7	33 286	19.3	30 909	22 017	8 892	5 051	2 507
Fayette	392	22 421	0.83	242	10.3	275	11.7	2 878	15.2	5 679	4 768	911	NA	NA
Floyd	1 329	70 206	0.85	870	11.4	712	9.3	7 762	12.1	14 111	11 418	2 693	2 640	3 590
Fountain	172	15 179	0.75	214	12.8	183	11.0	1 831	13.7	4 161	3 533	628	NA	NA
Franklin	187	17 106	0.44	240	10.5	189	8.3	2 663	13.8	3 412	2 343	1 069	134	630
Fulton	224	18 843	0.80	268	13.1	197	9.7	2 952	17.6	4 015	2 431	1 584	NA	NA
Gibson	738	37 478	1.25	433	12.8	377	11.2	3 029	10.9	6 370	4 731	1 639	NA	NA
Grant	5 032	71 167	1.07	825	12.1	789	11.6	7 068	13.6	15 359	12 150	3 209	1 967	2 852
Greene	281	27 015	0.57	326	10.0	406	12.5	3 827	14.4	6 539	5 802	737	467	1 530
Hamilton	1 631	265 828	0.84	3 936	12.8	1 536	5.0	21 030	7.8	30 599	22 196	8 403	NA	NA
Hancock	649	57 544	0.61	783	10.8	576	8.0	6 179	10.2	11 872	8 393	3 479	750	1 042
Harrison	461	32 329	0.62	425	10.8	336	8.5	4 359	13.3	7 310	5 910	1 400	446	1 139
Hendricks	4 108	133 395	0.76	1 761	11.2	986	6.3	12 830	9.7	19 364	13 823	5 541	3 164	2 027
Henry	3 631	44 096	0.73	516	10.5	548	11.2	4 854	13.1	10 307	8 142	2 165	NA	NA
Howard	1 280	87 356	1.13	977	11.8	918	11.1	8 728	13.0	18 969	16 445	2 524	2 466	3 017
Huntington	1 333	34 826	0.88	426	11.6	380	10.4	3 673	12.3	8 034	4 309	3 725	NA	NA
Jackson	595	44 495	1.07	607	13.8	419	9.5	5 897	16.1	8 396	5 918	2 478	1 514	3 463
Jasper	926	31 326	0.86	361	10.8	310	9.3	3 727	13.6	6 409	5 537	872	NA	NA
Jay	243	20 383	0.90	293	13.9	219	10.4	2 650	15.1	4 261	3 093	1 168	263	1 373
Jefferson	2 021	31 752	0.95	334	10.3	336	10.3	3 568	14.0	7 313	6 343	970	NA	NA
Jennings	298	24 317	0.67	345	12.3	280	10.0	3 330	14.1	4 964	3 858	1 106	470	1 666
Johnson	2 537	124 278	0.72	1 841	12.4	1 223	8.2	13 726	11.0	23 453	17 140	6 313	4 371	3 000
Knox	2 533	39 253	1.06	454	12.0	390	10.3	4 017	13.7	8 204	7 493	711	NA	NA
Kosciusko	1 594	77 781	1.00	1 057	13.5	658	8.4	10 440	15.9	12 558	7 372	5 186	1 157	1 480
LaGrange	325	36 535	0.92	815	21.1	236	6.1	8 415	25.2	5 094	3 278	1 816	218	570
Lake	6 424	481 703	0.94	5 956	12.2	4 749	9.7	60 789	14.7	83 520	70 418	13 102	16 973	3 689
LaPorte	6 521	107 495	0.92	1 320	11.9	1 169	10.5	11 814	13.5	20 421	17 893	2 528	2 473	2 427
Lawrence	653	41 096	0.75	457	10.0	529	11.6	5 155	13.9	9 783	8 078	1 705	884	2 130
Madison	6 051	119 869	0.80	1 526	11.8	1 394	10.7	13 915	13.6	28 914	22 002	6 912	3 375	2 641
Marion	16 991	1 046 240	1.30	14 487	15.5	7 724	8.2	130 640	16.1	132 589	95 504	37 085	54 433	6 133
Marshall	670	45 623	0.93	574	12.2	448	9.5	6 997	17.8	8 227	5 215	3 012	NA	NA
Martin	133	14 004	1.80	150	14.7	89	8.7	1 204	14.4	2 213	2 008	205	NA	NA
Miami	3 326	31 805	0.68	364	10.1	348	9.7	4 099	15.2	6 829	5 595	1 234	627	1 741
Monroe	15 146	150 184	1.14	1 279	8.9	858	6.0	15 616	13.9	18 433	15 016	3 417	4 166	2 916
Montgomery	1 174	37 611	0.97	463	12.1	371	9.7	4 587	14.9	7 884	6 086	1 798	1 111	2 906
Morgan	592	54 565	0.54	728	10.5	624	9.0	8 010	13.6	12 495	9 552	2 943	NA	NA
Newton	168	11 729	0.61	129	9.2	139	9.9	1 691	14.6	2 245	1 944	301	99	704
Noble	820	45 511	0.91	584	12.3	434	9.1	6 567	16.3	7 531	4 198	3 333	488	1 077
Ohio	52	4 806	0.55	53	8.9	70	11.7	609	12.6	1 119	886	233	NA	NA
Orange	258	19 079	0.92	263	13.4	206	10.5	2 391	14.9	4 058	3 262	796	NA	NA
Owen	197	17 422	0.57	240	11.5	223	10.6	2 717	15.8	3 778	2 952	826	NA	NA
Parke	1 615	14 582	0.61	197	11.5	171	10.0	2 247	17.7	3 041	2 560	481	64	372
Perry	1 612	18 752	0.91	180	9.3	169	8.7	1 911	13.0	3 677	3 313	364	NA	NA

1. Per 1,000 estimated resident population.   2. Data for serious crimes have not been adjusted for underreporting; this may affect comparability between geographic areas and over time.
3. Per 100,000 population estimated by the FBI.

Table B. States and Counties — Crime, Education, Money Income, and Poverty

STATE County	Violent (46)	Property (47)	Total (48)	Per-cent private (49)	High school graduate or less (50)	Bach-elor's degree or more (51)	Total current spending (mil dol) (52)	Current spend-ing per student (dollars) (53)	Per capita income (dollars) (54)	Median income (dollars) (55)	Mean income (dollars) (56)	Percent with income of $200,000 or more (57)	Median house-hold income (dollars) (58)	All per-sons (59)	Children under 18 years (60)	Children 5 to 17 years in families (61)
ILLINOIS—Cont'd																
Winnebago	764	3 127	74 164	20.3	46.8	21.7	541.9	11 618	24 802	47 523	61 963	2.6	47 708	16.9	25.2	21.6
Woodford	78	868	10 527	16.5	39.4	27.9	85.3	10 690	30 300	68 119	80 269	4.0	70 127	6.3	8.5	7.8
INDIANA	365	2 649	1 745 318	16.2	47.3	23.6	9 658.7	9 566	24 953	48 737	63 736	2.7	49 384	15.2	21.2	19.3
Adams	NA	NA	8 738	31.0	59.2	14.9	45.9	10 451	21 161	47 964	59 883	1.9	50 172	15.4	28.5	28.2
Allen	257	2 610	102 032	21.4	40.7	26.6	495.5	9 289	25 485	49 124	64 683	2.8	48 651	15.2	21.7	19.0
Bartholomew	110	3 206	19 622	14.8	45.1	27.9	112.6	9 142	27 623	54 488	69 198	3.3	54 101	11.8	16.4	15.8
Benton	NA	NA	2 063	12.4	57.2	16.4	18.6	10 064	22 591	46 909	56 562	0.5	46 196	12.8	18.0	16.0
Blackford	41	1 995	2 602	5.5	63.4	10.5	16.8	9 299	20 754	39 370	50 477	0.9	39 563	15.0	23.8	22.2
Boone	NA	NA	15 913	12.6	34.1	42.5	105.1	9 347	38 024	67 416	101 236	10.2	68 352	7.2	8.4	7.3
Brown	67	747	3 180	6.6	49.9	21.2	23.6	11 569	27 664	53 107	67 463	2.3	52 582	12.9	20.6	18.8
Carroll	NA	NA	4 665	13.4	54.2	16.7	21.9	8 032	25 040	52 806	63 015	2.0	55 318	10.9	15.6	14.5
Cass	70	2 651	9 677	8.3	58.7	13.6	69.8	10 648	21 609	41 356	54 793	1.6	44 430	13.8	21.2	19.2
Clark	393	3 492	26 774	14.8	46.9	19.7	151.9	9 217	25 057	51 182	62 668	2.1	52 050	10.6	16.4	15.3
Clay	NA	NA	6 276	11.9	57.9	14.2	38.9	8 824	21 520	46 228	55 530	1.2	44 385	14.5	21.3	19.8
Clinton	113	3 134	7 929	8.0	60.8	14.3	58.3	9 435	22 205	49 669	58 961	1.4	49 945	12.6	19.6	17.7
Crawford	236	849	2 409	6.0	65.7	10.7	17.2	11 164	19 002	40 905	46 613	0.0	40 657	18.0	29.8	26.8
Daviess	175	2 162	7 445	21.7	62.7	12.9	42.4	9 825	21 532	47 104	59 111	1.5	47 670	13.8	21.7	20.9
Dearborn	NA	NA	12 632	15.9	50.3	18.2	78.3	8 806	27 746	58 000	72 480	3.1	59 280	11.7	17.3	14.5
Decatur	NA	NA	6 474	11.3	59.5	14.5	40.1	9 102	22 609	49 631	58 072	1.3	50 258	13.1	19.4	17.8
DeKalb	NA	NA	11 124	16.4	52.3	17.0	88.9	12 062	23 768	49 561	60 758	1.7	51 911	10.1	14.8	13.3
Delaware	281	2 970	38 416	5.2	47.4	23.3	148.2	9 741	21 360	37 900	52 729	1.7	39 449	22.2	26.1	23.5
Dubois	NA	NA	10 222	9.8	54.0	17.9	67.8	9 147	25 841	54 186	66 123	1.9	53 211	8.0	9.9	9.1
Elkhart	357	2 149	51 734	14.8	56.6	17.9	347.2	9 626	21 403	46 983	58 860	1.8	50 192	13.9	19.8	18.8
Fayette	NA	NA	5 736	6.5	63.3	10.1	41.9	10 710	19 633	37 833	47 735	1.2	40 122	16.4	23.4	21.3
Floyd	126	3 464	19 337	16.7	45.0	24.3	107.3	9 502	27 449	53 431	68 681	3.4	53 186	11.6	17.2	15.0
Fountain	NA	NA	3 786	6.7	59.0	12.5	26.3	8 660	23 153	45 660	56 926	0.8	45 168	14.6	19.8	18.5
Franklin	33	597	5 607	17.0	57.4	17.7	41.4	8 259	23 741	50 262	62 169	2.2	54 086	11.1	15.4	12.9
Fulton	NA	NA	4 756	10.6	58.5	12.5	23.5	8 939	21 523	42 585	52 930	1.0	44 762	13.0	21.6	20.5
Gibson	NA	NA	7 978	13.7	49.6	15.0	47.8	9 648	24 256	48 176	61 339	1.6	46 466	11.8	16.9	15.5
Grant	218	2 635	18 697	31.2	55.7	17.2	107.5	9 774	20 442	39 885	51 076	1.3	40 234	20.0	30.7	29.1
Greene	36	1 494	7 093	7.5	55.8	13.2	51.7	9 771	22 491	43 470	55 638	1.3	41 077	15.5	21.9	19.6
Hamilton	NA	NA	85 789	18.0	19.9	55.6	483.9	8 733	40 012	84 635	108 833	10.4	89 861	4.9	5.7	5.3
Hancock	78	964	18 788	14.4	40.8	26.7	92.0	7 356	28 722	65 517	75 616	3.5	68 334	6.9	9.4	8.1
Harrison	77	1 063	8 964	12.8	54.6	15.5	55.8	9 363	24 469	53 483	62 896	1.2	56 787	10.0	15.9	14.0
Hendricks	210	1 818	40 102	15.1	36.5	32.1	223.5	8 128	30 018	68 342	82 231	4.1	70 358	6.4	7.9	7.5
Henry	NA	NA	11 756	9.8	58.6	15.0	75.5	9 920	20 165	40 247	51 915	1.3	41 955	15.5	21.8	18.3
Howard	225	2 792	20 799	10.1	48.9	19.5	128.0	9 608	23 897	42 078	56 450	1.6	47 433	16.8	24.0	20.7
Huntington	NA	NA	9 234	23.8	53.3	18.0	49.3	8 734	22 875	47 356	57 172	1.1	49 832	10.7	16.6	15.8
Jackson	208	3 255	10 249	18.4	59.9	14.4	59.5	8 831	22 556	47 758	56 747	0.8	48 308	14.9	19.8	18.8
Jasper	NA	NA	8 600	16.6	56.4	15.3	41.9	8 025	24 501	56 214	65 769	1.7	55 190	10.3	13.9	13.0
Jay	99	1 274	5 169	8.0	63.9	10.2	36.5	10 409	19 812	40 761	50 357	0.9	38 663	19.9	35.2	29.5
Jefferson	NA	NA	7 486	23.6	54.1	17.2	45.3	10 471	22 218	45 306	55 752	0.8	45 964	16.2	25.4	20.7
Jennings	298	1 368	7 083	13.3	62.6	10.8	53.2	11 134	20 812	44 758	54 368	1.1	43 783	17.5	22.2	20.2
Johnson	256	2 744	38 416	15.5	42.5	27.3	226.5	8 954	28 500	60 644	76 126	3.9	58 833	10.2	13.2	11.6
Knox	NA	NA	10 415	8.8	50.7	14.5	49.5	9 397	21 801	42 997	53 868	1.6	44 077	17.4	24.3	23.5
Kosciusko	133	1 347	18 826	16.5	52.1	21.4	129.3	9 362	25 531	52 706	66 812	3.1	54 068	12.0	16.7	15.3
LaGrange	97	473	8 691	32.5	68.5	10.8	55.7	9 335	19 863	49 112	62 183	1.9	52 003	10.9	16.6	16.7
Lake	447	3 241	131 789	15.8	48.8	20.0	788.0	10 095	24 294	49 617	63 224	2.2	50 774	17.6	27.3	24.4
LaPorte	143	2 283	26 737	14.3	52.4	17.1	178.6	10 209	23 074	47 117	60 207	2.1	46 243	17.9	28.9	26.2
Lawrence	275	1 855	10 387	13.3	56.4	14.6	68.1	9 778	23 046	44 553	55 927	1.8	45 232	12.5	19.3	18.1
Madison	181	2 460	30 368	17.7	51.9	17.1	162.2	9 467	22 049	43 440	54 590	1.3	44 730	16.7	23.4	22.3
Marion	1 226	4 907	244 857	19.6	44.1	27.7	1 403.5	10 927	24 145	42 378	58 912	2.5	42 700	21.3	31.4	29.2
Marshall	NA	NA	11 691	15.7	56.1	17.3	72.2	9 438	22 580	47 219	59 585	1.6	52 508	10.9	15.8	14.5
Martin	NA	NA	2 420	13.7	59.3	11.8	14.2	9 212	23 038	45 113	55 553	0.7	48 381	13.5	18.8	17.3
Miami	164	1 577	9 138	5.1	58.3	10.7	48.8	9 497	21 209	43 862	54 906	1.0	41 065	17.1	23.3	20.5
Monroe	281	2 636	60 487	7.8	31.2	44.2	130.9	9 712	23 837	41 857	59 778	3.4	43 841	24.0	19.0	16.4
Montgomery	837	2 069	9 300	16.7	55.9	16.8	59.1	9 766	22 392	46 286	57 001	1.3	46 945	12.3	18.5	17.6
Morgan	NA	NA	16 675	12.8	53.9	15.5	99.9	8 649	25 245	54 986	67 098	1.8	54 849	11.5	17.6	15.8
Newton	64	640	3 298	11.2	64.0	9.1	23.3	9 929	24 389	49 769	60 626	2.0	51 285	11.5	17.9	15.8
Noble	97	980	11 867	14.2	56.5	14.2	67.5	8 956	22 821	49 102	60 355	1.5	50 997	11.1	16.5	15.0
Ohio	NA	NA	1 262	10.1	63.6	12.8	8.5	9 998	23 906	47 208	57 318	0.0	51 403	11.1	16.9	15.0
Orange	NA	NA	4 367	9.3	63.1	12.1	41.1	12 062	19 023	38 556	47 344	0.2	39 572	18.0	28.1	25.9
Owen	NA	NA	4 550	14.1	60.7	10.7	26.2	9 586	21 636	44 684	53 440	1.2	46 001	15.4	23.9	21.5
Parke	64	308	3 836	10.9	57.1	14.3	16.1	7 075	22 131	43 214	59 654	1.6	42 056	17.5	25.9	24.8
Perry	NA	NA	3 826	7.4	64.8	10.4	27.6	9 383	21 050	47 309	54 703	1.0	44 623	15.5	19.5	18.3

1. Data for serious crimes have not been adjusted for underreporting; this may affect comparability between geographic areas and over time.　　2. Per 100,000 population estimated by the FBI.
3. All persons 3 years old and over enrolled in nursery school through college.　　4. Persons 25 years old and over.　　5. Elementary and secondary education expenditures.
6. Based on population estimated by the American Community Survey, 2010–2014.

Table B. States and Counties — **Personal Income**

STATE County	Personal income, 2014										Earnings, 2014		
	Total (mil dol)	Percent change, 2013–2014	Per capita[1] Dollars	Per capita[1] Rank	Wages and salaries (mil dol)	Supplements to wages and salaries; employer contributions (mil dol) — Pension and insurance	Supplements — Government social insurance	Proprietors' income (mil dol)	Dividends, interest, and rent (mil dol)	Personal transfer receipts (mil dol)	Total (mil dol)	Contributions for government social insurance (mil dol) — From employee and self-employed	Contributions — From employer
	62	63	64	65	66	67	68	69	70	71	72	73	74
ILLINOIS—Cont'd													
Winnebago	10 970	2.3	38 020	1 451	5 998	1 049	447	601	1 647	2 365	8 096	474	447
Woodford	1 788	-0.7	45 631	626	461	87	34	101	318	253	683	39	34
INDIANA	261 092	3.8	39 578	X	132 382	22 380	10 031	21 705	39 364	51 618	186 498	11 491	10 031
Adams	1 163	5.3	33 424	2 211	497	95	39	214	164	229	845	49	39
Allen	14 531	4.9	39 712	1 223	8 105	1 328	624	1 246	2 363	2 755	11 303	701	624
Bartholomew	3 540	3.5	44 129	751	2 565	395	189	297	552	593	3 447	208	189
Benton	370	-4.6	42 582	891	93	18	7	101	51	65	219	11	7
Blackford	432	0.2	34 809	1 967	114	23	9	34	59	131	180	13	9
Boone	3 917	3.5	63 269	98	1 098	168	86	475	640	357	1 827	109	86
Brown	592	3.0	39 598	1 236	86	18	7	50	97	135	160	13	7
Carroll	789	0.1	39 616	1 233	194	40	14	124	107	149	372	21	14
Cass	1 316	1.4	34 249	2 071	541	108	41	93	187	359	782	49	41
Clark	4 297	4.7	37 610	1 508	2 030	368	157	276	526	934	2 832	179	157
Clay	912	1.2	34 329	2 057	255	53	20	87	123	233	416	27	20
Clinton	1 118	2.5	34 116	2 099	445	84	34	76	160	256	639	39	34
Crawford	326	6.5	30 623	2 636	65	14	5	22	37	102	106	8	5
Daviess	1 208	1.8	36 914	1 614	410	76	31	182	190	251	699	40	31
Dearborn	2 080	3.4	42 008	949	550	104	42	179	275	385	875	59	42
Decatur	1 021	2.9	38 480	1 398	581	98	44	122	141	210	844	50	44
DeKalb	1 569	3.9	37 014	1 598	970	156	77	120	225	327	1 323	83	77
Delaware	3 739	2.8	31 933	2 444	1 818	349	140	236	595	1 071	2 543	166	140
Dubois	2 121	5.8	50 087	382	1 176	182	90	329	457	303	1 777	103	90
Elkhart	7 542	6.0	37 344	1 548	5 494	914	435	711	1 138	1 403	7 553	450	435
Fayette	798	2.6	34 016	2 112	238	45	19	44	110	271	345	26	19
Floyd	3 459	4.2	45 404	642	1 179	211	90	201	644	631	1 680	108	90
Fountain	614	-1.9	36 844	1 627	174	37	14	71	85	146	296	18	14
Franklin	897	1.2	39 129	1 307	153	34	12	51	148	181	249	19	12
Fulton	736	-1.3	35 903	1 791	246	46	19	65	116	172	376	25	19
Gibson	1 418	2.2	41 992	952	1 025	162	77	228	188	272	1 492	87	77
Grant	2 437	2.2	35 547	1 847	1 107	204	88	184	337	737	1 584	104	88
Greene	1 147	3.5	35 035	1 931	236	48	18	82	169	296	384	26	18
Hamilton	19 108	4.9	63 141	99	6 926	957	505	1 879	3 150	1 402	10 268	619	505
Hancock	3 157	3.4	43 860	773	953	153	72	289	414	506	1 468	96	72
Harrison	1 418	3.5	36 090	1 766	374	68	29	62	197	307	532	38	29
Hendricks	6 702	3.9	42 945	851	2 228	371	172	534	741	867	3 305	207	172
Henry	1 607	1.5	32 800	2 312	447	85	34	100	223	470	666	48	34
Howard	2 965	3.4	35 728	1 816	1 888	295	146	137	427	813	2 466	161	146
Huntington	1 340	2.1	36 507	1 686	538	104	42	83	214	302	767	49	42
Jackson	1 693	4.1	38 733	1 360	860	159	66	143	212	343	1 228	74	66
Jasper	1 343	0.8	40 130	1 154	464	85	36	186	168	251	771	44	36
Jay	808	5.4	38 169	1 430	278	56	22	185	83	175	542	28	22
Jefferson	1 196	4.6	36 794	1 634	498	100	38	81	174	304	717	46	38
Jennings	912	2.8	32 563	2 358	284	51	22	38	95	290	396	28	22
Johnson	6 182	4.0	41 899	961	1 879	310	147	450	830	981	2 786	181	147
Knox	1 575	2.9	41 512	1 008	711	142	52	177	230	391	1 083	63	52
Kosciusko	3 179	4.8	40 469	1 122	1 867	377	138	207	501	550	2 590	152	138
LaGrange	1 195	6.8	31 081	2 575	534	98	43	187	159	201	862	48	43
Lake	18 818	3.5	38 386	1 407	9 210	1 512	687	1 063	2 510	4 265	12 473	796	687
LaPorte	3 999	3.3	35 882	1 795	1 698	298	133	251	585	925	2 379	153	133
Lawrence	1 573	4.3	34 424	2 043	488	87	38	85	223	425	698	49	38
Madison	4 235	3.0	32 563	2 358	1 489	259	115	220	561	1 257	2 082	150	115
Marion	37 439	4.1	40 074	1 166	32 531	5 090	2 405	3 500	5 906	7 585	43 526	2 581	2 405
Marshall	1 685	3.1	35 767	1 813	724	131	57	110	255	355	1 023	65	57
Martin	391	9.1	38 333	1 417	478	130	39	51	63	84	699	35	39
Miami	1 091	3.1	30 334	2 672	361	81	30	66	168	294	537	35	30
Monroe	4 867	4.5	33 953	2 119	2 649	588	196	236	1 053	830	3 669	214	196
Montgomery	1 337	-1.4	35 039	1 928	649	114	50	104	186	304	917	57	50
Morgan	2 577	3.0	36 975	1 604	570	103	44	91	316	559	808	59	44
Newton	529	1.6	37 390	1 540	137	24	11	63	63	116	234	12	11
Noble	1 576	4.1	33 107	2 261	728	134	58	104	199	333	1 024	64	58
Ohio	208	8.0	34 505	2 026	45	8	4	14	24	49	71	5	4
Orange	646	3.8	32 893	2 296	255	42	21	50	88	188	368	25	21
Owen	666	2.2	31 772	2 477	184	46	14	30	90	191	274	20	14
Parke	519	-2.7	30 092	2 706	102	23	8	52	81	148	185	13	8
Perry	657	7.7	33 752	2 153	265	50	19	45	96	158	379	24	19

1. Based on the resident population estimated as of July 1 of the year shown.

Table B. States and Counties — Earnings, Social Security, and Housing

STATE County	Farm	Mining	Construction	Manu-facturing	Information: professional, scientific, technical services	Retail trade	Finance, insurance, real estate and leasing	Health care and social assistance	Govern-ment	Number	Rate[1]	Supplemental Security Income recipients, December 2014	Total	Percent change, 2010–2014
										Social Security beneficiaries, December 2014			Housing units, 2015	
	75	76	77	78	79	80	81	82	83	84	85	86	87	88
ILLINOIS—Cont'd														
Winnebago	0.1	0.0	4.7	23.4	4.8	7.1	5.8	16.9	13.0	60 030	208	7 235	125 446	-0.4
Woodford	8.7	D	12.1	21.6	3.5	6.1	2.7	7.9	16.0	7 650	195	271	15 411	1.8
INDIANA	2.0	0.6	5.9	21.4	7.0	6.2	6.1	12.3	12.9	1 286 099	195	127 957	2 841 373	1.6
Adams	10.3	D	8.7	33.8	D	6.3	3.0	4.6	12.0	6 150	177	362	13 146	1.0
Allen	0.5	0.1	5.8	18.5	7.4	6.3	8.3	17.5	9.5	66 565	182	7 846	155 295	2.0
Bartholomew	1.2	D	3.3	47.0	4.9	5.2	4.0	6.4	9.1	15 990	199	1 245	33 727	1.9
Benton	26.8	D	2.8	11.1	D	3.6	4.4	D	12.4	1 970	227	147	3 907	-0.5
Blackford	5.8	D	1.8	33.1	D	9.1	3.3	D	13.8	3 595	290	270	5 982	-1.1
Boone	3.1	D	8.9	8.0	D	15.5	D	5.9	10.6	9 980	161	463	25 684	12.9
Brown	1.4	0.0	12.1	3.9	8.4	7.7	3.8	11.7	22.7	4 030	270	97	8 538	3.1
Carroll	21.0	D	6.9	D	2.3	4.4	2.6	D	10.2	4 570	230	173	9 433	-0.4
Cass	5.9	D	5.1	28.1	2.3	7.7	3.2	D	21.5	8 435	220	787	16 304	-1.0
Clark	0.5	D	6.5	17.5	4.0	9.8	6.7	9.2	15.3	24 240	212	2 413	49 410	3.4
Clay	7.6	0.7	4.6	34.9	D	7.2	2.6	D	14.0	6 080	230	668	11 684	-0.1
Clinton	9.4	0.0	4.9	37.5	D	4.5	2.7	7.7	12.7	6 800	208	534	13 234	-0.6
Crawford	1.6	D	D	D	0.0	5.5	D	5.7	21.9	2 840	267	354	5 443	-1.4
Daviess	10.8	1.5	16.7	15.2	3.7	7.8	3.0	D	13.7	5 805	177	535	12 465	-0.1
Dearborn	0.4	D	8.1	14.6	3.4	8.1	3.4	7.5	19.5	10 630	215	620	20 262	0.5
Decatur	6.8	D	2.8	44.0	D	4.3	2.6	3.6	10.3	5 785	218	456	11 252	0.4
DeKalb	2.2	0.2	3.3	45.7	3.6	3.9	2.2	6.1	8.0	9 080	214	698	17 668	0.6
Delaware	0.8	D	4.1	10.7	7.1	8.2	6.0	19.0	22.8	25 775	220	3 061	52 489	0.3
Dubois	5.3	D	3.5	35.5	2.6	6.5	2.3	10.8	6.1	8 555	202	388	17 653	1.5
Elkhart	1.5	D	3.2	49.1	2.8	4.4	2.6	8.1	6.1	35 190	174	3 150	78 030	0.3
Fayette	4.7	D	2.7	23.6	4.0	8.7	3.2	19.0	15.4	6 775	289	895	10 803	-0.9
Floyd	0.1	D	7.6	22.7	6.6	5.8	5.4	11.5	20.7	15 515	204	1 533	32 407	1.4
Fountain	14.1	0.0	3.9	35.5	2.1	7.5	3.3	D	12.9	4 330	259	330	7 791	-0.9
Franklin	7.8	0.2	8.0	21.5	D	8.9	D	8.9	18.3	5 050	221	316	9 579	0.4
Fulton	5.5	D	9.3	27.7	3.0	7.7	3.9	4.6	19.0	4 910	240	354	9 642	-0.7
Gibson	4.7	8.6	2.0	48.2	1.7	3.4	1.0	D	4.6	7 265	215	513	14 812	1.1
Grant	2.4	D	2.9	23.2	2.7	6.2	3.4	17.6	14.1	17 325	252	2 053	30 283	-0.5
Greene	11.7	2.4	8.8	6.7	4.5	8.4	3.3	D	23.5	7 800	238	730	15 025	-1.2
Hamilton	0.3	0.2	7.6	4.8	14.2	6.5	20.0	9.9	7.4	38 325	126	1 453	119 799	12.2
Hancock	2.2	0.0	9.8	15.1	17.4	5.9	3.7	8.1	14.1	14 080	196	635	29 207	3.8
Harrison	2.8	1.2	4.6	16.4	2.5	7.9	3.9	D	20.1	8 675	221	620	16 708	1.1
Hendricks	1.2	D	6.8	8.5	4.8	10.9	3.9	8.9	14.6	24 385	156	830	59 371	7.1
Henry	5.5	D	6.5	19.0	2.6	8.4	4.3	8.4	23.8	12 315	251	1 049	21 107	-0.9
Howard	0.9	D	3.1	45.3	3.2	6.1	3.2	12.6	10.0	20 995	254	2 242	38 747	0.2
Huntington	5.2	D	4.7	31.3	D	5.6	4.8	8.7	10.0	8 305	226	552	15 890	0.5
Jackson	5.6	D	3.5	36.8	1.7	6.8	2.6	4.6	13.6	9 740	222	861	18 655	2.5
Jasper	13.4	D	8.0	14.0	2.6	7.4	2.4	4.7	12.0	7 050	211	426	13 371	1.5
Jay	22.7	D	3.5	38.5	1.7	3.4	2.0	3.4	11.9	4 925	233	385	9 193	-0.3
Jefferson	2.3	0.0	3.8	26.9	D	8.3	2.3	14.0	15.9	7 500	231	782	14 315	0.0
Jennings	5.6	D	11.3	26.7	1.5	5.8	2.3	7.7	16.4	6 555	234	714	12 072	0.0
Johnson	1.0	D	7.3	13.8	5.0	9.8	5.3	12.4	14.3	26 925	183	1 501	59 309	4.7
Knox	7.8	8.7	3.1	10.5	3.4	5.7	4.1	11.4	23.3	8 615	228	994	16 963	-0.4
Kosciusko	3.9	D	2.6	49.5	2.4	5.1	2.6	6.2	6.1	15 730	201	903	37 723	1.9
LaGrange	11.9	D	3.7	50.1	1.5	4.4	2.0	D	7.8	5 885	153	312	14 463	2.6
Lake	0.1	0.1	9.1	22.6	4.6	7.4	3.6	15.7	11.1	96 420	197	12 964	210 868	1.0
LaPorte	2.5	D	8.3	21.2	3.1	6.9	3.8	13.9	15.0	24 165	216	2 201	48 782	0.7
Lawrence	3.0	1.4	4.9	22.7	6.5	9.3	4.6	15.2	14.3	11 275	247	1 012	20 926	-0.7
Madison	2.3	D	5.2	14.9	4.0	7.1	4.5	16.3	15.7	31 905	245	3 385	58 735	-0.6
Marion	0.0	0.1	5.6	14.4	11.8	4.8	8.7	14.3	12.6	151 935	163	26 057	419 801	0.5
Marshall	3.6	D	3.7	38.3	D	6.7	5.1	7.6	10.2	9 785	208	658	19 994	0.8
Martin	6.7	0.0	0.8	3.6	11.3	1.2	0.5	0.6	71.6	2 410	236	234	4 739	-1.0
Miami	7.3	0.5	4.8	19.7	1.8	5.1	3.6	D	28.7	7 805	217	792	15 278	-1.3
Monroe	0.2	0.4	4.5	12.4	6.2	5.7	4.3	15.1	32.7	20 595	143	1 809	60 523	2.4
Montgomery	4.8	D	3.4	39.8	D	6.2	2.7	D	10.4	8 465	222	599	16 546	0.1
Morgan	4.6	0.4	8.5	18.0	D	9.6	4.4	10.9	15.9	15 570	224	1 010	28 025	0.9
Newton	28.6	D	3.6	14.6	D	3.3	3.1	4.4	14.0	3 405	242	203	6 035	0.1
Noble	3.9	D	3.8	51.7	D	4.8	2.1	5.3	9.3	9 520	200	669	20 231	0.6
Ohio	9.5	0.0	4.1	D	D	2.5	D	4.5	21.7	1 470	245	82	2 805	0.8
Orange	5.2	D	15.3	16.0	D	5.4	1.6	D	12.2	4 990	253	514	9 077	-1.1
Owen	1.6	0.0	5.4	45.6	D	5.2	2.9	D	13.1	5 255	250	404	9 970	-1.2
Parke	11.5	D	8.2	13.1	D	6.7	4.3	D	25.8	3 885	226	250	8 064	-0.3
Perry	4.7	D	3.9	40.5	2.4	5.4	3.2	D	20.1	4 485	231	322	8 547	0.6

1. Per 1,000 resident population estimated as of July 1 of the year shown.

Table B. States and Counties — Housing, Labor Force, and Employment

STATE County	Total [89]	Percent [90]	Median value[1] [91]	With a mortgage [92]	Without a mortgage[2] [93]	Median rent[3] [94]	Median rent as a percent of income[2] [95]	Sub-standard units[4] (percent) [96]	Total [97]	Percent change, 2014–2015 [98]	Total [99]	Rate[5] [100]	Total [101]	Manage-ment, business, science and arts [102]	Con-struction, produc-tion, and mainte-nance occu-pations [103]
ILLINOIS—Cont'd															
Winnebago	113 553	66.5	119 400	23.0	13.3	750	30.2	2.2	142 254	-0.1	10 073	7.1	130 643	30.2	27.6
Woodford	14 373	81.2	158 000	20.6	10.5	733	26.3	1.5	19 619	-0.7	998	5.1	18 751	38.1	23.2
INDIANA	2 492 183	69.5	122 700	20.4	10.9	741	30.1	2.2	3 265 767	1.2	156 547	4.8	2 994 736	32.2	27.0
Adams	12 164	78.3	118 400	20.7	10.0	550	28.3	9.7	16 918	3.0	639	3.8	14 871	25.8	38.9
Allen	139 384	69.4	112 600	19.4	10.0	673	27.7	2.1	178 779	1.7	8 123	4.5	166 902	34.1	24.4
Bartholomew	30 516	69.8	135 900	19.8	11.9	807	26.4	2.1	43 649	2.4	1 559	3.6	37 887	39.0	25.6
Benton	3 464	71.5	84 300	19.0	10.2	697	26.4	1.9	4 627	3.4	205	4.4	4 063	26.5	36.5
Blackford	5 236	76.1	67 600	19.7	11.4	599	30.1	1.0	5 276	0.2	318	6.0	5 137	22.3	39.1
Boone	22 248	76.4	183 900	19.7	11.5	800	28.0	1.6	32 959	2.4	1 212	3.7	29 331	45.0	19.3
Brown	5 926	80.9	156 300	21.9	15.7	941	37.8	2.5	7 482	1.7	354	4.7	7 102	31.8	28.6
Carroll	7 828	80.0	107 100	19.8	10.1	645	26.9	2.5	10 141	2.6	432	4.3	9 271	26.6	34.5
Cass	14 759	74.6	81 100	21.1	10.9	629	29.1	3.7	17 699	-0.2	816	4.6	17 230	24.8	37.9
Clark	42 774	71.6	127 800	21.1	11.3	741	28.3	1.9	58 764	2.0	2 623	4.5	53 871	29.3	26.2
Clay	10 221	75.6	91 400	19.4	11.8	674	30.1	1.7	12 370	-0.6	652	5.3	11 775	25.7	32.3
Clinton	11 853	71.8	96 600	19.7	10.8	686	26.5	2.6	16 991	2.0	677	4.0	15 116	21.8	44.1
Crawford	4 166	81.3	88 100	20.7	13.6	551	27.4	2.1	4 929	0.7	296	6.0	4 341	21.5	41.1
Daviess	11 462	74.3	103 400	19.2	10.0	595	24.9	2.3	15 687	3.3	592	3.8	14 214	23.4	42.1
Dearborn	18 648	78.8	158 700	20.8	12.4	734	29.3	1.3	25 302	0.7	1 284	5.1	24 184	28.8	29.1
Decatur	9 809	71.2	112 300	22.2	10.7	750	25.0	2.0	14 369	1.3	576	4.0	12 025	27.6	38.2
DeKalb	16 235	79.1	108 400	20.8	10.0	648	26.1	1.3	21 792	2.5	888	4.1	19 262	27.5	36.8
Delaware	46 239	63.4	88 300	19.6	11.6	690	36.7	1.2	54 475	1.6	3 087	5.7	51 063	31.9	21.7
Dubois	15 926	78.0	132 900	19.5	10.4	614	25.2	2.2	22 556	2.3	766	3.4	21 665	28.6	34.8
Elkhart	70 427	70.3	122 600	20.6	10.7	715	29.3	3.0	104 616	2.4	4 021	3.8	90 640	24.2	37.9
Fayette	9 336	69.8	80 900	21.7	13.4	634	33.8	1.7	8 950	-1.6	585	6.5	9 149	25.0	30.6
Floyd	29 017	72.1	152 800	20.8	10.9	728	29.9	1.9	39 918	2.1	1 694	4.2	36 457	34.0	22.7
Fountain	6 912	75.4	86 400	18.5	11.0	650	24.8	2.2	8 084	-1.4	479	5.9	7 376	24.7	42.0
Franklin	8 726	79.6	144 900	22.0	10.5	665	26.4	2.9	11 369	4.5	576	5.1	10 751	30.5	34.6
Fulton	8 208	76.1	93 800	19.9	12.8	612	30.0	1.3	9 916	1.2	474	4.8	9 019	27.0	41.6
Gibson	12 987	78.5	103 500	18.6	10.9	649	26.9	1.9	18 864	2.3	716	3.8	15 908	25.5	39.3
Grant	26 829	70.0	80 200	20.2	10.9	628	28.3	1.8	32 446	-0.7	1 771	5.5	28 981	27.8	26.4
Greene	12 879	79.0	88 700	18.8	12.1	569	27.6	4.1	13 791	-0.5	942	6.8	14 192	28.0	33.8
Hamilton	105 578	78.8	218 000	19.7	10.0	985	24.8	0.7	164 518	2.1	5 528	3.4	148 848	52.3	10.7
Hancock	26 142	78.6	157 600	20.3	10.2	851	27.5	0.7	37 332	1.9	1 562	4.2	34 357	37.5	22.2
Harrison	14 678	82.0	123 900	20.0	10.0	668	27.3	1.4	19 418	2.0	878	4.5	18 375	29.0	31.8
Hendricks	53 959	80.8	160 700	19.7	10.8	940	27.7	1.6	82 290	2.0	3 128	3.8	73 771	39.2	21.1
Henry	18 214	73.4	92 100	21.2	11.5	633	28.5	1.2	21 597	0.6	1 148	5.3	19 170	28.5	30.5
Howard	34 386	68.6	96 200	19.1	10.0	647	31.5	0.9	36 934	0.0	1 844	5.0	35 084	29.2	28.2
Huntington	14 413	76.4	97 100	20.0	11.5	667	28.0	2.1	18 788	1.3	812	4.3	17 750	28.2	34.9
Jackson	16 657	74.5	112 900	19.6	10.5	696	27.1	2.6	21 830	2.4	865	4.0	19 670	26.6	36.2
Jasper	11 988	78.6	148 700	19.7	10.0	698	27.3	1.7	16 311	1.0	941	5.8	14 963	26.9	36.7
Jay	8 196	75.1	80 000	19.8	11.6	571	26.8	2.7	9 931	-1.7	494	5.0	9 507	22.3	44.6
Jefferson	12 746	71.3	112 500	22.0	10.1	679	28.8	3.1	15 251	1.2	738	4.8	14 125	26.3	35.4
Jennings	10 585	75.9	91 100	21.9	12.8	720	27.3	2.9	13 187	0.7	674	5.1	12 092	25.3	37.1
Johnson	52 873	72.5	142 600	20.1	10.3	841	30.6	2.5	77 004	1.9	3 114	4.0	69 551	36.1	22.6
Knox	14 705	66.2	83 100	18.3	11.0	628	29.2	1.8	19 039	1.0	867	4.6	17 414	26.4	32.5
Kosciusko	29 414	77.1	132 000	19.7	10.0	698	24.7	2.2	40 808	1.2	1 649	4.0	37 195	27.9	37.9
LaGrange	11 735	80.8	161 000	25.0	10.2	693	24.4	5.0	18 886	3.6	683	3.6	15 369	20.9	51.2
Lake	182 919	68.9	135 900	22.1	11.8	811	32.3	2.6	230 072	-0.2	15 603	6.8	211 279	29.9	27.1
LaPorte	42 756	71.2	124 000	20.3	10.8	698	31.1	2.3	48 522	-0.8	3 033	6.3	46 747	27.5	30.4
Lawrence	18 561	78.5	103 000	21.1	12.1	621	28.0	2.5	20 295	-0.4	1 324	6.5	19 892	29.5	30.6
Madison	51 232	69.1	91 200	19.9	11.8	700	31.4	2.1	58 737	1.4	3 292	5.6	53 997	28.7	25.3
Marion	361 648	55.3	117 400	21.1	11.5	781	32.5	2.6	472 929	1.2	23 713	5.0	428 929	33.5	21.8
Marshall	17 468	76.7	124 100	21.4	11.4	653	27.6	3.6	24 078	1.5	998	4.1	21 326	27.5	37.9
Martin	4 199	81.6	88 500	20.0	10.0	529	26.8	2.1	5 032	1.5	212	4.2	4 656	30.9	34.0
Miami	13 246	74.4	85 100	19.1	12.1	646	26.4	2.4	15 686	0.0	821	5.2	14 569	25.0	36.0
Monroe	53 778	54.1	158 700	20.3	10.0	819	39.4	1.3	67 158	-0.5	3 267	4.9	68 119	43.0	16.2
Montgomery	14 574	71.4	108 200	19.9	10.0	672	28.6	1.8	19 285	3.1	767	4.0	17 261	24.9	34.5
Morgan	25 456	76.3	139 900	20.8	10.2	763	27.6	1.8	35 614	1.7	1 656	4.6	32 505	29.0	31.1
Newton	5 327	76.2	109 800	19.8	10.9	708	24.7	0.8	7 013	0.9	402	5.7	6 186	19.6	42.3
Noble	17 703	75.6	111 500	20.5	10.0	641	26.8	4.0	23 701	2.4	1 001	4.2	21 520	24.2	42.6
Ohio	2 445	75.3	135 500	21.4	13.6	733	27.9	1.8	3 236	0.5	175	5.4	2 914	22.4	37.5
Orange	7 618	75.9	88 100	21.7	11.9	574	28.2	4.3	8 772	2.7	523	6.0	8 119	23.3	35.0
Owen	8 539	78.3	110 400	22.8	12.6	693	25.6	3.6	9 382	-1.1	583	6.2	9 292	24.7	39.9
Parke	6 128	82.1	89 000	20.9	10.4	579	28.4	3.1	7 080	1.8	401	5.7	6 834	23.4	36.7
Perry	7 356	79.5	98 400	19.7	10.8	578	26.5	1.7	9 226	0.5	434	4.7	8 334	18.0	44.8

1. Specified owner-occupied units. 2. A value of 10.0 represents 10 percent or less; a value of 50.0 represents 50 percent or more. 3. Specified renter-occupied units.
4. Overcrowded or lacking complete plumbing facilities. 5. Percent of civilian labor force. 6. Persons 16 years old and over.

Table B. States and Counties — Nonfarm Employment and Agriculture

STATE County	Private nonfarm establishments, employment and payroll, 2014									Agriculture, 2012			
	Number of establishments	Employment						Annual payroll		Farms			
		Total	Health care and social assistance	Manufacturing	Retail trade	Finance and insurance	Professional, scientific, and technical services	Total (mil dol)	Average per employee (dollars)	Number	Percent with:		Farm operators whose principal occupation is farming (percent)
											Fewer than 50 acres	500 acres or more	
	104	105	106	107	108	109	110	111	112	113	114	115	116
ILLINOIS—Cont'd													
Winnebago	6 471	117 702	20 602	24 708	14 793	3 810	4 437	4 806	40 833	807	46.0	12.4	44.2
Woodford	755	8 817	1 419	2 075	1 000	220	D	335	38 004	958	32.7	20.5	52.8
INDIANA	143 826	2 602 895	403 393	475 831	314 603	98 648	110 540	107 452	41 282	58 695	46.6	12.8	43.7
Adams	724	11 917	1 421	4 798	1 477	D	197	398	33 399	1 476	61.9	6.8	32.4
Allen	9 070	166 360	31 884	25 204	20 877	8 621	5 572	6 666	40 070	1 725	57.7	7.8	43.4
Bartholomew	1 796	44 983	4 598	11 771	4 762	988	3 401	2 094	46 552	623	44.1	14.4	44.8
Benton	184	1 391	D	346	171	95	52	48	34 463	381	26.0	36.7	63.5
Blackford	231	2 599	365	935	303	90	113	91	35 189	263	43.7	16.3	46.8
Boone	1 445	20 809	2 292	1 825	2 550	374	795	727	34 922	607	49.6	21.4	47.3
Brown	353	2 081	356	135	373	43	D	48	23 258	173	54.9	2.3	24.9
Carroll	376	4 379	136	D	375	87	97	150	34 215	491	35.6	23.2	50.7
Cass	731	12 922	2 354	4 247	1 563	298	208	439	33 960	688	42.7	16.9	42.9
Clark	2 400	45 829	6 488	7 239	6 935	1 912	1 105	1 622	35 400	515	49.3	7.4	41.6
Clay	468	5 864	649	2 220	945	138	78	173	29 549	579	44.9	16.1	39.4
Clinton	588	9 365	1 307	3 725	1 026	D	140	335	35 752	597	43.4	22.8	50.9
Crawford	123	1 379	D	380	185	D	12	41	29 666	338	27.8	3.6	29.9
Daviess	866	10 250	1 373	1 970	1 461	252	577	359	35 037	1 325	60.1	7.0	28.6
Dearborn	911	12 459	2 481	1 627	1 886	458	251	427	34 291	561	39.9	1.6	39.8
Decatur	615	11 813	1 095	D	1 263	D	108	435	36 795	610	31.1	19.0	49.0
DeKalb	986	19 053	1 821	8 546	1 462	351	496	794	41 685	924	49.9	8.5	28.2
Delaware	2 322	38 419	8 997	4 306	6 157	3 020	1 472	1 314	34 199	610	49.5	13.3	54.8
Dubois	1 288	26 215	D	10 403	3 132	554	D	1 066	40 646	720	34.2	12.4	40.3
Elkhart	4 825	117 990	10 537	60 478	9 119	1 960	1 964	4 917	41 671	1 724	62.8	3.9	38.3
Fayette	445	5 634	1 733	1 111	973	151	201	191	33 889	347	40.9	12.4	44.4
Floyd	1 761	25 577	5 483	5 884	3 218	747	1 108	956	37 363	277	67.9	2.9	48.0
Fountain	313	3 944	D	1 885	582	D	75	130	32 920	460	34.6	22.8	48.0
Franklin	413	5 380	666	642	657	D	41	204	37 842	727	32.2	7.7	47.9
Fulton	467	5 347	761	1 955	892	177	129	181	33 941	653	40.9	13.9	49.0
Gibson	708	17 822	1 642	7 173	1 609	173	312	801	44 920	589	36.8	23.6	52.3
Grant	1 308	29 791	6 118	4 660	3 120	620	350	959	32 200	500	37.6	22.2	53.6
Greene	580	4 917	897	D	1 039	D	253	144	29 379	810	41.0	8.5	42.0
Hamilton	8 274	122 263	17 544	5 891	16 100	13 892	10 236	6 189	50 621	598	62.2	11.5	40.1
Hancock	1 369	19 717	2 365	3 244	2 083	330	3 926	761	38 581	604	60.1	15.1	41.6
Harrison	651	9 053	1 558	1 499	1 296	267	159	268	29 574	967	48.5	4.7	43.3
Hendricks	3 027	52 733	7 682	3 091	9 268	862	1 247	1 837	34 839	694	55.9	15.6	54.3
Henry	820	10 517	2 894	1 894	1 525	365	164	334	31 791	702	50.4	13.0	42.3
Howard	1 742	31 758	5 413	9 768	4 963	690	685	1 340	42 203	476	40.8	15.5	57.4
Huntington	875	12 710	1 782	3 813	1 325	341	180	389	30 570	695	47.5	16.3	44.9
Jackson	1 004	18 875	2 105	6 384	2 353	410	288	707	37 469	744	37.0	13.2	39.5
Jasper	736	8 881	1 245	1 478	1 429	309	191	305	34 378	615	38.7	24.7	47.2
Jay	395	6 520	802	3 069	607	148	95	202	31 010	836	50.6	11.2	38.9
Jefferson	660	11 519	2 003	3 101	1 642	205	224	409	35 488	615	42.4	5.9	38.2
Jennings	413	6 530	1 020	1 951	805	D	D	232	35 547	528	47.2	11.0	39.2
Johnson	3 065	43 929	7 505	5 420	8 977	1 093	1 277	1 555	35 408	562	57.8	14.9	45.0
Knox	913	13 423	D	D	1 944	315	218	474	35 299	496	30.2	31.5	61.3
Kosciusko	1 899	36 425	3 900	14 344	4 093	856	496	1 886	51 780	1 247	54.2	10.2	39.9
LaGrange	801	12 460	951	6 869	1 188	D	185	486	39 014	2 419	58.7	2.3	43.3
Lake	9 852	167 974	32 660	23 187	24 055	4 095	5 881	7 158	42 616	430	57.2	15.1	47.0
LaPorte	2 290	33 509	5 349	7 092	5 824	794	930	1 206	35 998	731	43.8	17.1	51.4
Lawrence	857	10 935	2 554	1 942	1 936	376	688	362	33 063	800	42.0	6.5	39.5
Madison	2 242	34 727	6 618	2 704	4 799	908	1 354	1 145	32 958	737	52.6	16.1	54.5
Marion	22 808	520 458	83 016	40 953	47 359	24 221	38 491	25 856	49 679	231	79.7	4.8	36.4
Marshall	1 049	17 041	1 869	6 288	2 029	484	356	604	35 442	878	46.8	12.3	40.7
Martin	181	2 490	141	386	314	47	947	102	41 052	283	44.9	9.5	35.3
Miami	569	6 800	1 000	1 786	885	347	121	211	31 094	666	45.0	14.6	44.4
Monroe	2 892	48 821	8 960	D	7 197	1 449	1 996	1 816	37 194	462	48.3	3.7	37.7
Montgomery	843	13 479	1 146	5 251	1 681	277	160	521	38 648	732	44.3	20.8	48.9
Morgan	1 158	12 464	1 879	1 966	2 313	D	332	409	32 841	583	55.6	11.1	42.5
Newton	255	2 312	274	547	261	112	74	76	32 878	348	29.6	32.2	54.9
Noble	867	15 698	1 513	8 296	1 558	257	179	571	36 378	1 163	52.8	8.0	38.5
Ohio	86	1 146	94	D	83	D	16	28	24 040	171	38.0	2.9	33.9
Orange	382	5 976	873	1 355	731	93	67	174	29 080	478	33.7	9.4	36.8
Owen	281	2 931	347	1 000	416	113	74	86	29 290	549	39.5	7.1	40.3
Parke	255	2 069	211	495	294	64	D	62	29 770	574	38.0	13.4	43.4
Perry	363	6 010	847	2 730	719	94	96	210	34 896	413	26.6	5.1	39.2

STATE County	Land in farms Acreage (1,000)	Percent change, 2007–2012	Acres Average size of farm	Total irrigated (1,000)	Total cropland (1,000)	Value of land and buildings (dollars) Average per farm	Average per acre	Value of machinery and equipment, average per farm (dollars)	Value of products sold Total (mil dol)	Average per farm (dollars)	Percent from: Crops	Live-stock and poultry products	Percent of farms with sales of: $10,000 or more	$100,000 or more	Government payments Total ($1,000)	Percent of farms
	117	118	119	120	121	122	123	124	125	126	127	128	129	130	131	132
ILLINOIS—Cont'd																
Winnebago	183	-0.4	227	0.5	159.6	1 434 529	6 329	127 939	106.4	131 822	79.1	20.9	43.2	23.4	5 109	61.6
Woodford	323	12.0	337	0.5	291.6	2 612 922	7 750	210 760	240.6	251 196	78.5	21.5	62.3	40.6	6 107	79.2
INDIANA	14 720	-0.4	251	437.4	12 590.6	1 342 826	5 354	143 235	11 210.8	191 001	67.2	32.8	48.3	24.4	267 287	54.7
Adams	210	15.2	142	0.1	186.0	825 272	5 794	92 331	250.3	169 571	48.1	51.9	55.8	25.1	3 765	37.6
Allen	271	6.6	157	0.4	241.5	969 217	6 174	87 928	187.6	108 776	79.6	20.4	48.8	20.6	6 302	52.5
Bartholomew	172	3.2	275	13.5	153.4	1 619 191	5 878	151 406	95.6	153 387	89.5	10.5	54.9	27.1	4 647	63.7
Benton	254	-6.1	667	D	247.4	4 308 843	6 457	328 864	210.9	553 499	80.8	19.2	73.5	59.8	4 782	85.0
Blackford	88	4.0	335	D	81.2	1 414 730	4 228	176 620	71.5	271 764	D	D	56.3	28.9	1 380	66.2
Boone	222	-0.5	365	0.9	210.3	2 253 794	6 171	194 476	146.0	240 486	88.5	11.5	52.9	32.6	3 428	54.7
Brown	15	-14.0	84	0.1	6.6	337 468	4 002	37 514	4.2	24 486	D	D	16.8	2.9	156	28.3
Carroll	204	6.1	416	0.4	189.5	2 837 483	6 826	234 244	221.4	450 982	61.5	38.5	65.4	46.4	3 497	63.7
Cass	200	-12.2	291	1.9	181.6	1 575 185	5 412	185 317	158.4	230 281	78.2	21.8	55.8	30.5	4 080	73.3
Clark	79	-9.4	153	0.4	54.2	644 767	4 228	83 882	32.1	62 418	82.4	17.6	37.9	11.5	1 034	48.2
Clay	163	3.4	281	0.2	137.4	1 226 095	4 358	143 682	60.3	104 079	92.2	7.8	42.8	22.3	2 433	76.0
Clinton	223	-12.5	374	D	211.6	2 497 002	6 672	245 072	251.5	421 293	71.0	29.0	61.1	40.7	4 216	69.5
Crawford	46	2.2	137	0.0	16.2	351 639	2 561	40 038	7.2	21 323	D	D	17.2	2.4	288	29.6
Daviess	225	12.9	170	5.8	189.4	1 100 902	6 479	108 929	190.1	143 498	41.9	58.1	44.5	17.1	3 949	24.0
Dearborn	57	-14.1	101	0.1	26.8	410 578	4 071	46 287	12.4	22 191	74.9	25.1	27.3	6.1	650	33.9
Decatur	187	-8.9	306	0.0	162.6	1 627 090	5 321	166 746	159.4	261 293	58.0	42.0	62.8	37.0	3 721	74.1
DeKalb	161	0.1	174	0.8	136.8	771 247	4 429	92 135	106.9	115 738	65.5	34.5	35.8	16.6	4 689	73.6
Delaware	175	13.5	287	0.0	160.4	1 522 762	5 300	152 951	125.6	205 836	93.2	6.8	52.1	26.9	3 980	67.4
Dubois	175	-4.0	243	0.2	130.0	1 086 538	4 473	142 382	241.0	334 742	21.8	78.2	55.7	25.1	3 256	63.5
Elkhart	173	5.8	100	25.5	140.2	808 782	8 067	83 012	296.8	172 178	28.0	72.0	51.8	27.4	2 785	20.1
Fayette	78	-15.4	225	D	63.8	1 047 712	4 647	117 945	40.1	115 651	82.7	17.3	49.3	25.1	1 421	61.1
Floyd	21	-10.6	77	0.0	12.2	413 040	5 331	53 170	4.6	16 621	78.7	21.4	17.3	3.2	299	23.8
Fountain	214	13.6	466	D	190.5	2 236 072	4 797	218 709	116.7	253 644	D		52.4	30.9	3 690	68.9
Franklin	125	-1.1	172	0.1	85.1	786 644	4 577	92 254	54.0	74 304	78.8	21.2	47.3	17.6	2 101	61.9
Fulton	188	1.9	289	22.9	169.4	1 449 573	5 024	178 933	140.7	215 464	84.9	15.1	57.7	31.1	3 180	61.1
Gibson	268	16.0	455	4.8	250.3	2 426 261	5 329	255 418	146.4	248 542	87.7	12.3	63.2	35.5	4 803	70.6
Grant	183	-9.3	367	D	171.5	2 046 020	5 579	209 740	138.0	275 964	90.4	9.6	60.0	36.8	3 298	68.4
Greene	181	6.7	224	2.2	132.9	881 351	3 942	108 274	97.4	120 212	55.7	44.3	37.9	12.3	2 470	40.7
Hamilton	131	5.9	219	3.7	120.9	1 406 630	6 428	132 154	116.2	194 256	97.1	2.9	45.8	21.7	1 833	44.1
Hancock	166	-3.4	275	0.2	156.6	1 570 192	5 718	148 467	110.4	182 821	83.7	16.3	47.2	24.8	3 001	50.8
Harrison	135	-12.9	140	0.0	85.0	513 898	3 681	71 044	58.0	59 968	47.1	52.9	29.2	8.0	1 556	38.8
Hendricks	218	27.2	315	0.1	200.9	1 835 824	5 834	163 981	89.4	128 772	92.0	8.0	42.9	20.7	3 783	48.4
Henry	176	1.2	251	0.0	158.4	1 244 617	4 952	157 963	115.5	164 479	74.6	25.4	49.1	23.8	3 282	58.4
Howard	144	-11.1	303	D	134.5	1 924 391	6 353	182 880	140.4	294 874	81.1	18.9	68.1	37.2	2 993	67.0
Huntington	189	-5.1	272	0.7	172.6	1 481 458	5 452	216 573	174.8	251 550	65.7	34.3	50.5	28.2	4 185	71.7
Jackson	184	-12.1	247	2.9	139.9	1 132 552	4 582	174 212	184.4	247 907	42.2	57.8	50.8	24.5	3 876	66.7
Jasper	283	-16.9	460	21.1	256.7	2 819 873	6 132	250 876	357.4	581 142	58.3	41.7	61.3	40.0	4 736	72.8
Jay	176	-10.9	210	D	156.3	1 380 341	6 565	137 579	282.0	337 292	35.2	64.8	53.7	29.3	3 621	64.6
Jefferson	95	-6.9	155	0.0	61.7	549 182	3 540	72 820	40.4	65 737	76.7	23.3	32.4	8.8	1 907	53.3
Jennings	123	-10.8	234	0.1	87.7	910 475	3 896	126 716	79.7	150 917	57.8	42.2	37.5	16.9	3 214	57.4
Johnson	145	1.7	257	3.1	131.6	1 567 699	6 091	140 655	70.6	125 575	87.1	12.9	42.7	23.5	2 779	50.5
Knox	329	0.6	664	34.9	304.0	3 748 468	5 646	405 986	218.1	439 627	83.4	16.6	70.8	45.8	5 837	72.6
Kosciusko	255	1.4	204	18.0	219.6	1 198 890	5 866	110 144	282.1	226 226	47.0	53.0	42.4	20.8	4 140	51.7
LaGrange	204	26.2	84	25.6	147.4	628 366	7 448	56 611	262.6	108 542	26.1	73.9	55.2	23.1	2 276	12.5
Lake	133	3.6	309	8.1	124.2	1 755 500	5 673	178 735	100.8	234 374	98.1	1.9	44.4	30.0	2 419	49.1
LaPorte	228	-11.0	312	54.4	209.3	1 896 432	6 084	188 253	223.1	305 215	80.5	19.5	55.7	33.8	4 036	58.4
Lawrence	135	0.0	168	D	70.8	534 073	3 172	64 313	33.2	41 486	68.1	31.9	31.5	5.3	2 091	48.1
Madison	205	-5.6	278	0.9	191.5	1 677 897	6 028	169 689	164.4	223 026	91.7	8.3	53.5	29.0	3 565	58.8
Marion	20	16.5	87	0.2	16.0	558 134	6 422	60 861	27.3	117 991	D	D	29.4	10.8	220	16.5
Marshall	206	15.2	235	13.4	181.8	1 222 325	5 202	140 648	147.6	168 141	73.5	26.5	49.7	26.9	3 430	49.2
Martin	63	2.0	221	0.4	39.0	892 177	4 037	105 095	54.3	191 735	24.9	75.1	36.7	13.4	701	33.2
Miami	175	-1.5	263	3.1	158.1	1 333 943	5 069	145 643	156.9	235 605	67.1	32.9	55.0	32.6	3 696	68.8
Monroe	53	-1.4	114	0.1	27.6	551 762	4 831	55 294	13.0	28 134	66.7	33.3	28.4	5.6	754	29.0
Montgomery	287	-4.8	392	1.0	264.6	2 189 187	5 585	199 959	175.4	239 638	83.9	16.1	53.4	30.6	6 178	68.6
Morgan	137	20.2	235	0.0	114.2	1 158 144	4 922	130 446	51.8	88 768	87.9	12.1	36.4	14.8	2 146	46.0
Newton	192	0.8	552	6.3	174.3	3 131 055	5 674	315 417	242.6	697 187	53.1	46.9	66.1	46.3	3 086	79.6
Noble	181	13.5	156	13.7	150.1	754 298	4 834	95 800	143.7	123 588	57.4	42.6	44.3	18.4	4 236	52.5
Ohio	21	-0.2	126	0.2	10.5	446 731	3 560	57 649	4.2	24 462	74.7	25.3	28.7	4.1	368	34.5
Orange	98	0.9	206	0.0	56.9	717 036	3 488	102 278	64.0	133 902	22.4	77.6	30.3	8.6	1 599	47.9
Owen	96	8.8	174	0.1	62.5	590 885	3 396	76 073	23.5	42 805	82.7	17.3	29.0	8.0	1 537	49.7
Parke	177	-0.4	308	2.7	120.9	1 282 422	4 169	131 817	64.2	111 779	81.9	18.1	43.7	22.1	2 785	50.7
Perry	66	-5.9	160	0.0	30.7	481 276	2 999	62 182	20.3	49 208	47.4	52.6	35.1	7.5	605	42.4

Table B. States and Counties — Water Use, Wholesale Trade, Retail Trade, and Real Estate

STATE County	Water use, 2010 Total water withdrawn (mil gal/day)	Gallons withdrawn per person per day	Wholesale trade,[1] 2012 Number of establishments	Number of employees	Sales (mil dol)	Annual payroll (mil dol)	Retail trade,[2] 2012 Number of establishments	Number of employees	Sales (mil dol)	Annual payroll (mil dol)	Real estate and rental and leasing,[2] 2012 Number of establishments	Number of employees	Receipts (mil dol)	Annual payroll (mil dol)
	133	134	135	136	137	138	139	140	141	142	143	144	145	146
ILLINOIS—Cont'd														
Winnebago	35.6	120	333	4 123	2 700.4	207.0	986	14 298	3 752.1	326.5	212	1 512	169.0	43.7
Woodford	9.6	248	44	578	608.0	31.7	95	956	337.8	25.6	17	30	2.6	0.5
INDIANA	8 643.0	1 333	6 460	91 474	81 173.4	4 650.5	21 601	309 552	85 858.0	7 078.7	5 729	31 715	6 547.9	1 171.7
Adams	7.8	226	35	267	240.0	9.9	133	1 500	377.2	33.3	19	D	D	D
Allen	48.6	137	506	7 683	9 187.6	368.3	1 273	19 912	5 197.7	467.2	382	1 863	361.6	66.5
Bartholomew	18.2	237	77	998	774.4	52.7	306	4 701	1 113.1	99.4	72	303	57.0	9.4
Benton	0.9	101	15	201	203.4	8.0	31	199	53.3	3.8	3	2	0.3	0.1
Blackford	2.0	155	10	D	D	D	38	406	96.7	9.0	12	33	3.5	0.5
Boone	4.4	78	58	901	1 684.0	45.1	160	2 238	1 137.9	72.0	52	170	35.1	5.4
Brown	0.3	21	5	46	2.6	0.6	77	343	58.4	6.4	11	76	5.4	1.5
Carroll	5.1	255	18	161	302.4	7.1	51	395	99.8	8.0	11	38	5.1	1.3
Cass	28.8	738	39	434	570.0	19.0	118	1 502	341.6	33.5	17	59	8.2	1.3
Clark	25.7	233	95	1 011	1 024.5	52.3	426	6 966	1 814.3	158.5	79	502	87.5	17.1
Clay	1.2	43	13	D	D	D	84	878	312.7	19.0	15	24	5.2	0.6
Clinton	6.2	185	24	D	D	D	102	992	239.1	21.3	11	38	4.8	0.8
Crawford	2.8	262	5	80	42.5	2.5	24	201	89.9	3.8	3	D	D	D
Daviess	8.6	271	31	336	227.3	14.3	122	1 502	485.9	37.9	18	58	6.9	1.1
Dearborn	601.2	12 013	31	207	311.2	9.3	140	1 962	576.5	48.7	36	103	14.2	2.7
Decatur	5.3	204	32	391	455.7	17.2	110	1 259	357.2	27.8	17	45	8.1	1.2
DeKalb	8.8	208	41	D	D	D	125	1 469	383.3	32.2	25	118	14.5	4.9
Delaware	15.6	132	92	894	805.8	32.1	428	6 189	1 519.9	131.9	95	447	90.7	16.5
Dubois	7.6	182	74	1 053	637.0	50.3	217	3 332	919.2	79.8	31	D	D	D
Elkhart	33.0	167	340	5 803	3 329.9	249.5	678	8 754	2 440.4	206.9	157	768	134.5	25.4
Fayette	2.9	117	14	114	110.9	5.5	75	1 070	234.4	23.6	20	68	7.1	1.3
Floyd	254.6	3 414	69	579	323.3	23.3	206	3 146	772.3	69.6	69	205	34.4	5.9
Fountain	2.2	129	12	77	127.3	3.6	64	572	148.3	10.8	5	12	1.1	0.3
Franklin	3.9	169	7	33	14.8	1.3	68	662	170.2	13.4	8	14	1.6	0.3
Fulton	7.7	368	18	141	98.2	5.6	79	913	214.0	19.3	15	39	4.3	0.9
Gibson	59.8	1 785	20	267	188.5	11.3	120	1 643	557.6	37.8	17	47	11.8	1.4
Grant	11.8	169	37	367	251.0	15.6	244	3 113	793.3	65.7	43	154	17.7	3.8
Greene	5.5	166	17	130	107.2	4.5	103	1 054	252.4	20.2	19	59	5.2	1.3
Hamilton	72.7	265	357	4 138	3 403.7	291.1	865	15 746	4 338.4	397.7	395	2 349	1 394.5	144.2
Hancock	7.0	100	42	624	737.6	27.2	162	2 102	600.8	48.3	45	167	32.4	4.6
Harrison	3.7	95	20	D	D	D	114	1 423	470.2	30.7	18	36	5.8	0.8
Hendricks	8.6	59	101	2 980	2 723.4	141.5	441	8 760	2 561.4	201.3	108	506	82.6	16.7
Henry	5.1	103	31	D	D	D	152	1 551	466.2	33.1	25	73	7.5	1.7
Howard	17.5	212	62	559	512.7	31.6	328	4 927	1 193.3	104.0	71	311	50.4	8.9
Huntington	4.7	125	36	D	D	D	135	1 347	318.1	26.9	30	73	12.2	1.6
Jackson	9.9	233	35	D	D	D	183	2 225	592.7	49.9	45	115	17.7	2.5
Jasper	55.6	1 662	33	251	529.3	14.7	123	1 449	572.1	31.3	20	89	23.1	2.2
Jay	4.2	195	15	185	230.3	7.3	66	650	136.9	14.1	6	9	2.2	0.3
Jefferson	1 249.1	38 519	19	D	D	D	128	1 550	390.9	35.3	30	70	11.6	2.1
Jennings	3.1	107	15	D	D	D	66	751	196.9	16.9	10	32	3.2	0.8
Johnson	13.6	97	103	1 981	1 174.7	114.6	494	8 639	2 324.6	192.1	117	356	84.5	10.3
Knox	47.1	1 224	54	588	463.0	23.6	161	2 062	459.1	40.1	38	197	21.5	4.2
Kosciusko	24.4	315	89	D	D	D	298	3 566	921.5	82.7	72	162	24.7	3.8
LaGrange	19.9	536	33	313	182.4	10.4	151	1 127	284.4	24.7	26	47	7.4	1.2
Lake	1 696.0	3 419	413	4 472	4 599.1	219.2	1 513	23 986	7 495.3	551.0	373	2 090	371.9	74.3
LaPorte	44.0	395	100	1 161	694.9	46.8	457	5 845	1 367.8	116.2	84	367	95.2	10.6
Lawrence	8.2	177	22	D	D	D	160	1 897	519.2	42.6	21	68	8.1	1.8
Madison	19.1	145	73	974	1 301.2	50.0	346	4 944	1 378.7	107.9	81	348	58.2	10.3
Marion	283.5	314	1 295	23 766	18 700.3	1 359.0	2 952	46 739	14 421.7	1 155.9	1 244	11 355	2 105.2	465.9
Marshall	7.3	154	53	523	430.5	21.5	172	1 993	568.6	45.0	30	86	10.9	2.1
Martin	1.5	149	4	D	D	D	34	350	150.1	7.8	3	10	0.2	0.1
Miami	21.2	575	29	D	D	D	94	900	226.2	18.1	17	44	4.9	0.8
Monroe	18.3	133	82	D	D	D	458	7 390	1 661.3	145.2	163	865	152.5	27.7
Montgomery	6.1	160	41	343	365.7	16.0	129	1 651	446.6	34.4	29	63	12.0	1.9
Morgan	183.8	2 668	33	275	139.3	13.8	196	2 374	638.0	49.7	44	97	15.6	2.8
Newton	6.0	422	19	178	214.9	7.2	40	336	88.0	6.4	5	13	0.6	0.2
Noble	11.2	235	39	507	450.7	22.7	139	1 543	392.9	33.4	34	87	12.2	2.2
Ohio	1.0	162	4	D	D	D	13	88	15.3	1.3	3	D	D	D
Orange	1.5	77	12	74	63.7	2.9	61	668	156.0	13.6	11	35	2.3	0.6
Owen	2.5	115	10	D	D	D	38	424	111.9	9.3	7	7	1.5	0.2
Parke	2.8	163	7	97	47.6	2.8	43	304	70.1	5.7	11	66	6.2	2.2
Perry	2.5	131	9	66	13.3	1.9	65	718	157.2	13.2	11	33	4.3	0.7

1. Merchant wholesalers, except manufacturers' sales branches and offices. 2. Employer establishments.

Table B. States and Counties — Professional Services, Manufacturing, and Accommodation and Food Services

STATE County	Professional, scientific, and technical services, 2012				Manufacturing, 2012				Accommodation and food services, 2012			
	Number of establishments	Number of employees	Receipts (mil dol)	Annual payroll (mil dol)	Number of establishments	Number of employees	Receipts (mil dol)	Annual payroll (mil dol)	Number of establishments	Number of employees	Sales (mil dol)	Annual payroll (mil dol)
	147	148	149	150	151	152	153	154	155	156	157	158
ILLINOIS—Cont'd												
Winnebago	608	3 779	660.0	191.5	600	25 024	8 145.6	1 491.8	566	10 168	490.0	137.0
Woodford	47	205	20.5	8.5	45	2 464	1 363.6	122.9	61	830	28.5	8.2
INDIANA	12 829	99 962	14 702.0	5 490.6	8 141	452 513	242 763.8	23 041.3	13 057	255 223	13 076.6	3 432.7
Adams	45	215	19.0	8.0	63	4 246	2 200.6	172.8	55	800	27.7	7.3
Allen	874	5 326	720.8	254.0	501	24 975	16 200.1	1 336.5	712	15 250	643.1	190.1
Bartholomew	159	3 550	299.0	234.7	142	11 663	5 636.4	553.6	201	4 243	198.6	54.2
Benton	8	31	3.5	0.8	15	341	D	13.3	9	51	1.8	0.4
Blackford	11	97	13.3	3.5	24	1 056	255.6	43.8	20	221	7.7	2.2
Boone	166	645	120.2	33.5	69	1 759	D	70.7	117	1 686	71.4	20.3
Brown	32	80	9.5	4.0	15	111	D	2.7	33	D	D	D
Carroll	23	90	7.0	2.2	25	1 963	D	76.1	32	407	19.4	5.6
Cass	44	224	17.7	5.9	50	4 197	1 768.1	144.2	79	1 062	40.8	11.0
Clark	177	1 021	126.2	37.9	143	7 708	2 376.6	340.7	219	D	D	D
Clay	23	D	D	D	33	2 198	520.4	82.3	45	531	21.4	5.7
Clinton	44	144	12.6	4.1	37	3 035	3 192.7	143.0	52	680	27.5	7.9
Crawford	4	12	0.4	0.1	5	D	D	D	21	D	D	D
Daviess	42	554	125.3	42.0	73	1 726	848.1	56.0	56	981	35.3	9.4
Dearborn	69	320	24.6	9.3	46	1 460	385.1	64.9	69	D	D	D
Decatur	31	131	12.6	4.2	56	4 722	4 663.4	208.9	51	953	38.1	10.8
DeKalb	71	449	40.5	14.5	111	8 128	4 742.1	414.3	81	1 387	53.1	14.7
Delaware	163	1 522	240.5	63.4	130	4 205	1 591.3	191.2	211	4 417	172.7	49.6
Dubois	83	355	34.8	12.1	103	9 834	D	363.1	100	1 727	65.8	18.1
Elkhart	313	2 004	220.2	81.0	795	53 705	14 833.3	2 288.0	348	6 500	280.7	75.8
Fayette	28	214	10.5	4.1	30	1 195	489.7	60.2	43	D	D	D
Floyd	195	1 068	151.9	45.7	108	5 421	1 726.9	264.2	130	D	D	D
Fountain	17	75	4.8	1.5	21	2 368	615.1	96.6	38	370	13.0	3.7
Franklin	17	52	9.1	1.3	18	551	258.0	26.2	40	589	27.1	7.3
Fulton	32	142	43.4	4.5	43	1 751	513.9	75.7	45	488	18.9	4.8
Gibson	48	281	29.9	16.3	41	6 144	6 041.4	368.0	68	1 192	45.9	13.2
Grant	75	359	31.6	10.8	68	4 770	2 013.0	278.8	129	2 061	89.8	24.7
Greene	47	253	25.7	9.6	23	449	118.7	23.9	54	702	22.1	6.5
Hamilton	1 260	6 790	1 168.3	472.1	196	5 171	1 641.7	242.7	579	11 974	588.2	166.1
Hancock	124	4 210	274.6	186.2	56	2 998	1 183.9	124.7	98	1 872	80.7	23.3
Harrison	40	159	11.1	4.6	41	1 613	473.0	64.4	61	2 442	349.8	49.6
Hendricks	285	1 105	127.4	44.7	96	3 336	2 660.1	148.1	298	6 387	292.8	82.5
Henry	50	209	17.5	5.4	42	1 845	579.9	78.3	64	921	42.8	11.5
Howard	114	631	61.2	22.6	70	7 671	D	593.4	186	3 866	159.9	46.1
Huntington	43	180	15.6	5.4	64	3 417	1 740.6	170.7	87	1 207	47.3	13.3
Jackson	54	294	25.9	8.4	64	5 395	2 307.5	268.1	86	1 536	65.4	18.3
Jasper	49	203	16.0	4.9	35	1 426	650.4	65.8	64	868	34.5	9.5
Jay	22	83	4.7	1.7	34	3 042	1 059.2	119.1	33	545	19.9	5.4
Jefferson	42	242	15.3	7.4	43	2 754	1 548.4	132.8	83	1 408	50.6	14.6
Jennings	19	88	11.1	3.3	37	1 712	425.6	68.3	31	453	17.8	4.9
Johnson	270	1 332	166.6	51.7	123	4 932	2 024.1	237.4	282	6 135	263.6	75.4
Knox	46	216	18.9	6.1	40	1 789	464.0	66.8	84	1 508	63.5	16.8
Kosciusko	138	475	44.8	14.4	173	13 247	7 235.4	750.6	167	2 452	113.3	31.3
LaGrange	39	178	10.8	4.3	134	5 141	1 416.3	234.2	68	907	39.6	11.2
Lake	886	6 003	709.3	261.6	349	23 122	30 831.9	1 746.0	983	18 097	1 167.0	265.5
LaPorte	158	1 069	85.0	40.4	172	7 589	2 644.0	350.5	235	4 992	357.0	78.7
Lawrence	66	784	87.5	34.2	60	2 008	437.3	100.3	69	1 177	52.2	13.6
Madison	182	769	70.8	23.0	94	2 701	1 391.1	129.3	229	3 885	165.5	47.6
Marion	2 747	32 947	5 954.4	2 344.4	881	42 808	28 049.4	2 579.2	2 130	47 455	2 645.5	734.8
Marshall	62	334	24.4	8.9	130	5 712	1 816.5	240.3	90	1 343	56.6	16.7
Martin	20	1 107	163.2	64.4	10	324	64.2	15.9	25	243	8.8	2.7
Miami	31	111	8.6	3.1	38	1 542	D	68.7	55	796	31.2	8.7
Monroe	289	2 014	240.8	98.8	94	6 578	1 548.5	283.0	368	7 805	335.9	92.3
Montgomery	53	187	15.3	5.1	64	4 658	2 719.5	230.0	91	1 150	49.5	12.6
Morgan	94	323	31.4	10.1	64	1 847	649.4	86.0	71	D	D	D
Newton	17	61	5.8	1.9	24	663	156.2	24.9	28	209	8.7	2.2
Noble	46	165	16.6	5.0	123	8 351	2 937.7	337.5	74	1 046	38.5	10.5
Ohio	4	D	D	D	4	16	D	D	12	D	D	D
Orange	18	75	4.5	1.8	24	1 216	208.9	43.5	39	1 921	148.8	37.4
Owen	22	68	5.3	1.9	27	1 117	169.4	48.8	18	363	12.3	3.4
Parke	10	62	4.0	1.4	13	402	D	20.2	24	211	9.1	2.3
Perry	24	78	10.4	2.9	29	1 883	945.5	102.1	40	500	23.7	6.1

1. Establishment subject to federal tax.

Table B. States and Counties — **Health Care and Social Assistance, Other Services, Nonemployer Businesses, and Residential Construction**

STATE County	Health care and social assistance, 2012				Other services, 2012				Nonemployer businesses, 2014		Value of residential construction authorized by building permits, 2015	
	Number of establish-ments	Number of employees	Receipts (mil dol)	Annual payroll (mil dol)	Number of establish-ments	Number of employees	Receipts (mil dol)	Annual payroll (mil dol)	Number	Receipts (mil dol)	New Construction ($1,000)	Number of housing units
	159	160	161	162	163	164	165	166	167	168	169	170
ILLINOIS—Cont'd												
Winnebago	665	19 871	2 398.9	923.1	534	3 186	306.6	82.3	18 325	651.7	15 990	122
Woodford	51	2 063	112.3	60.6	48	213	24.0	6.6	2 531	94.4	20 100	84
INDIANA	15 156	396 923	42 493.1	16 208.7	10 777	72 937	8 909.7	2 106.7	399 201	16 105.7	3 737 044	18 483
Adams	53	1 475	100.3	47.7	76	392	31.2	7.6	3 061	153.3	10 653	69
Allen	947	28 368	2 803.4	1 195.5	661	4 571	441.6	133.1	23 075	915.4	243 649	1 232
Bartholomew	221	4 824	512.8	203.1	111	692	82.5	19.7	4 229	166.8	52 630	233
Benton	13	67	4.0	2.2	10	29	3.5	0.8	624	22.1	1 866	10
Blackford	22	385	27.6	10.6	21	65	7.0	1.5	629	20.5	1 151	7
Boone	120	2 318	207.4	87.6	98	606	44.7	11.8	5 077	237.5	125 560	451
Brown	22	311	18.8	8.2	18	97	7.2	2.5	1 456	55.7	9 189	48
Carroll	26	255	18.4	7.9	26	85	6.8	1.8	1 254	51.6	11 247	87
Cass	65	2 332	180.8	88.4	59	328	22.5	5.1	1 813	64.8	1 598	12
Clark	239	5 916	591.2	239.0	173	1 192	138.5	33.2	6 614	285.5	78 881	456
Clay	44	574	59.5	17.3	40	360	23.0	6.4	1 449	52.9	0	0
Clinton	50	1 162	79.5	34.0	48	303	26.9	7.6	1 620	56.8	2 692	33
Crawford	14	D	D	D	8	D	D	D	666	23.6	0	0
Daviess	75	1 452	99.5	42.3	69	325	81.7	12.4	2 160	90.0	600	6
Dearborn	117	D	D	D	71	328	29.3	8.1	2 915	118.8	17 185	79
Decatur	59	1 064	99.7	42.2	40	242	22.8	4.7	1 550	65.6	7 958	50
DeKalb	87	1 613	126.8	53.2	70	353	26.5	6.2	2 553	99.7	19 333	98
Delaware	313	9 158	873.1	318.7	174	1 043	105.9	26.2	5 510	206.6	10 089	46
Dubois	124	3 358	314.6	124.1	82	462	58.1	13.4	2 745	105.3	20 954	93
Elkhart	362	10 105	1 160.8	413.6	336	2 069	261.0	61.1	12 645	545.5	65 196	309
Fayette	61	1 773	127.7	57.0	39	171	13.6	3.8	1 121	40.9	1 156	11
Floyd	238	5 715	577.4	218.7	127	864	81.9	18.4	5 171	212.6	47 329	187
Fountain	24	511	36.2	11.8	33	82	7.4	1.7	962	33.5	454	3
Franklin	52	833	55.8	19.3	38	107	10.4	2.6	1 611	67.2	6 890	36
Fulton	45	847	78.6	26.9	38	126	14.1	3.0	1 329	51.9	3 353	16
Gibson	77	1 923	150.9	61.2	53	246	21.9	6.2	1 677	57.0	21 460	143
Grant	192	5 281	508.2	211.7	106	475	50.7	13.4	3 238	114.4	14 342	80
Greene	66	1 049	75.4	27.6	50	176	14.2	3.2	1 798	58.2	NA	NA
Hamilton	897	16 978	2 311.3	740.4	498	3 201	249.8	74.1	26 268	1 359.2	765 598	4 047
Hancock	136	2 511	256.0	93.5	94	391	36.8	9.4	4 937	195.6	61 859	365
Harrison	68	1 346	103.6	39.4	39	127	13.8	3.4	2 574	93.5	18 843	94
Hendricks	296	7 036	763.3	293.4	206	1 574	114.9	37.1	10 450	442.5	180 123	999
Henry	90	2 718	194.9	82.2	66	323	31.9	6.7	2 438	89.3	4 823	31
Howard	221	5 417	456.4	182.6	129	922	68.2	18.9	4 247	148.9	48 462	441
Huntington	66	1 812	141.2	53.9	75	369	23.1	6.4	1 895	65.5	11 200	55
Jackson	106	2 528	237.0	87.4	75	435	38.5	9.3	2 178	77.7	21 761	188
Jasper	47	1 400	85.1	40.8	55	D	D	D	1 815	74.0	15 293	66
Jay	28	819	62.4	25.5	35	99	10.6	1.8	1 303	55.2	3 050	16
Jefferson	74	1 963	187.1	80.7	53	257	19.9	4.8	1 698	73.0	7 573	46
Jennings	74	933	70.5	30.0	24	84	6.5	1.7	1 501	58.0	4 865	34
Johnson	331	7 291	632.2	272.9	222	1 587	160.0	49.9	9 683	455.2	138 914	624
Knox	110	3 345	327.7	129.2	69	347	36.4	9.9	1 888	72.3	6 762	43
Kosciusko	149	3 711	321.4	118.8	145	934	108.8	24.1	4 944	182.8	46 038	265
LaGrange	46	807	69.7	25.4	44	197	20.3	5.8	3 418	151.6	16 202	132
Lake	1 254	31 946	3 812.7	1 353.0	876	6 336	638.4	185.0	27 982	1 056.9	222 033	1 008
LaPorte	228	5 626	611.2	208.3	194	1 090	79.0	22.5	5 826	204.4	39 741	159
Lawrence	94	2 646	202.8	80.1	73	361	30.7	8.6	2 506	85.1	737	8
Madison	251	6 498	697.3	262.5	199	1 088	77.1	21.6	6 597	218.4	20 625	101
Marion	2 414	83 226	10 235.0	4 151.7	1 625	17 182	3 477.5	665.9	61 137	2 390.0	558 371	1 846
Marshall	72	1 809	156.9	50.9	84	501	50.6	14.3	2 908	114.8	17 547	74
Martin	9	D	D	D	12	63	6.2	2.2	611	20.4	720	5
Miami	40	1 148	98.7	36.7	44	349	34.5	9.2	1 667	61.3	4 849	20
Monroe	329	8 906	927.6	356.4	204	1 905	265.5	55.8	9 022	359.7	73 848	372
Montgomery	84	1 332	106.2	43.3	83	304	24.1	5.8	2 153	76.4	6 063	32
Morgan	109	2 069	235.0	74.2	97	452	42.8	11.5	4 527	188.0	20 805	112
Newton	13	253	13.1	6.2	18	D	D	D	731	31.3	4 070	18
Noble	73	1 347	132.7	43.6	81	280	42.4	7.7	2 509	97.6	16 333	92
Ohio	8	D	D	D	6	D	D	D	326	10.8	1 371	8
Orange	42	862	69.7	25.6	31	138	11.1	2.3	1 181	43.2	202	1
Owen	23	422	22.9	10.0	27	68	4.8	1.1	1 381	49.8	2 920	23
Parke	19	D	D	D	29	71	8.0	1.6	1 046	51.4	5 270	39
Perry	36	846	80.3	26.4	26	83	6.8	1.8	883	38.4	11 877	74

Table B. States and Counties — Government Employment and Payroll, and Local Government Finances

	Government employment and payroll, 2012									Local government finances, 2012				
			March payroll (percent of total)							General revenue				
												Taxes		
													Per capita[1] (dollars)	
STATE County	Full-time equivalent employees	March payroll (dollars)	Administration, judicial, and legal	Police and Corrections	Fire Protection	Highways and transportation	Health and Welfare	Natural resources and utilities	Education and libraries	Total (mil dol)	Inter-governmental (mil dol)	Total (mil dol)	Total	Property
	171	172	173	174	175	176	177	178	179	180	181	182	183	184
ILLINOIS—Cont'd														
Winnebago	10 237	41 731 581	5.0	11.9	6.0	3.7	3.9	7.5	61.2	1 183.6	493.6	527.0	1 804	1 627
Woodford	1 508	5 339 422	4.9	6.4	1.3	4.5	0.9	2.8	78.6	119.7	45.6	61.2	1 570	1 555
INDIANA	X	X	X	X	X	X	X	X	X	X	X	X	X	X
Adams	1 561	4 888 145	4.7	5.9	0.8	2.1	44.7	3.1	37.8	145.4	46.1	31.4	914	779
Allen	10 511	40 339 187	6.4	12.9	4.3	4.7	1.4	5.9	62.8	1 115.0	515.1	426.4	1 183	960
Bartholomew	4 371	15 688 309	3.2	6.6	2.9	1.3	44.5	3.1	37.7	469.7	111.3	106.7	1 348	1 076
Benton	555	1 313 464	8.3	7.4	0.0	6.3	5.5	2.3	69.0	40.6	19.2	16.2	1 838	1 489
Blackford	419	1 328 279	7.1	13.0	1.8	3.7	2.2	4.2	65.8	39.7	21.9	11.2	898	707
Boone	2 618	9 699 681	4.3	6.4	4.6	1.8	30.1	1.6	50.8	311.1	88.4	80.6	1 367	1 089
Brown	487	1 429 248	8.6	9.6	0.0	3.1	3.6	3.8	70.3	49.6	24.3	20.7	1 373	893
Carroll	613	1 723 537	7.5	7.8	0.0	5.1	6.1	5.3	66.8	54.7	26.6	20.7	1 030	776
Cass	2 403	7 224 020	3.1	5.7	1.4	1.6	31.7	7.4	48.9	182.8	62.7	46.0	1 192	797
Clark	4 732	18 084 071	3.7	7.9	2.7	2.4	38.3	3.7	41.0	466.1	142.4	134.5	1 201	884
Clay	1 049	2 619 145	6.8	6.9	1.9	3.0	1.0	5.5	72.4	75.7	42.8	22.3	831	529
Clinton	1 323	4 321 114	6.4	5.1	2.9	2.8	0.7	8.5	67.5	112.5	54.4	40.9	1 238	878
Crawford	416	1 229 568	6.6	5.4	0.0	4.7	3.2	1.7	77.0	32.3	18.4	8.3	783	640
Daviess	1 354	4 234 993	5.9	7.5	1.3	3.1	36.1	7.1	38.5	148.6	57.8	30.0	937	730
Dearborn	2 410	9 132 488	4.4	7.5	0.7	1.6	40.1	3.6	41.5	318.7	143.7	50.2	1 007	864
Decatur	1 237	4 252 343	4.4	5.2	2.3	2.0	40.2	2.9	42.7	119.2	37.5	26.3	1 009	794
DeKalb	1 614	5 058 353	9.1	8.5	2.6	3.0	1.3	8.0	66.9	153.8	68.7	51.5	1 216	955
Delaware	3 335	10 832 587	6.2	9.0	3.6	4.7	3.7	4.2	64.9	345.4	171.1	109.1	930	778
Dubois	1 643	4 804 962	7.3	8.1	0.8	5.6	2.5	16.6	59.1	155.2	64.9	49.7	1 180	905
Elkhart	6 985	24 411 992	5.4	8.4	4.1	2.5	1.6	3.6	73.6	630.5	315.1	218.4	1 094	907
Fayette	815	2 807 530	4.2	10.7	4.2	2.9	3.8	5.1	67.2	77.2	42.2	24.8	1 032	701
Floyd	4 128	15 144 305	3.0	3.9	2.2	0.8	54.1	2.1	33.3	467.4	119.9	81.4	1 081	846
Fountain	702	1 835 852	6.6	8.5	1.6	5.5	6.2	3.5	67.3	53.7	31.0	15.9	930	767
Franklin	568	1 607 664	8.0	8.8	0.0	4.5	1.5	2.6	73.5	47.8	26.1	16.2	704	477
Fulton	976	3 541 251	3.8	5.5	1.3	2.2	47.4	1.8	37.3	96.4	27.9	20.7	1 000	751
Gibson	1 093	3 390 759	8.4	7.1	3.0	3.7	4.8	4.6	68.3	107.6	54.3	38.1	1 140	1 012
Grant	2 226	7 247 230	7.6	13.8	3.6	3.3	0.8	2.9	67.7	198.6	103.6	70.9	1 023	759
Greene	1 299	4 191 866	4.9	6.2	1.0	2.4	23.5	4.2	56.9	123.7	53.8	24.9	756	573
Hamilton	9 749	38 707 131	4.7	8.4	7.3	2.0	14.0	2.7	59.9	1 219.3	387.4	488.6	1 688	1 330
Hancock	2 896	9 851 360	4.6	8.2	3.9	1.7	31.8	2.5	45.9	327.9	103.5	93.6	1 319	977
Harrison	1 349	4 713 395	5.2	4.9	0.0	2.6	36.7	2.0	47.0	155.4	72.7	26.9	689	469
Hendricks	6 025	22 075 204	3.7	5.6	5.8	1.4	30.4	2.6	50.1	681.2	209.2	213.8	1 421	1 074
Henry	2 369	7 555 604	4.3	5.2	1.2	2.3	32.1	3.4	50.6	241.5	75.8	42.1	853	643
Howard	4 091	15 459 399	5.0	6.2	3.5	2.0	35.8	3.0	42.2	435.8	136.7	118.7	1 433	1 170
Huntington	1 237	3 734 687	5.5	8.0	4.3	3.5	1.1	5.4	69.0	101.2	49.3	39.0	1 055	770
Jackson	2 118	8 012 413	3.8	6.5	2.3	1.6	47.5	1.4	36.3	212.1	54.8	30.5	707	506
Jasper	1 433	4 507 418	5.5	8.1	0.3	2.6	29.7	5.3	47.8	131.9	42.0	40.9	1 224	719
Jay	1 099	3 415 778	5.2	6.1	1.4	1.7	36.1	3.1	45.2	123.7	55.6	25.5	1 196	860
Jefferson	902	3 038 763	7.5	7.5	0.7	2.5	2.6	4.5	74.2	89.4	47.0	26.9	826	757
Jennings	908	2 922 410	4.4	7.4	0.6	3.0	2.6	5.4	75.0	78.7	47.6	22.3	793	611
Johnson	4 964	16 948 881	4.8	8.7	2.9	1.9	18.6	2.7	59.4	506.1	198.1	162.0	1 131	885
Knox	2 489	8 335 443	2.7	4.6	1.9	1.6	60.2	2.8	25.4	286.7	52.9	33.9	890	737
Kosciusko	2 569	8 158 465	6.1	8.0	0.4	2.3	0.9	3.7	77.8	243.0	119.1	85.5	1 101	909
LaGrange	1 149	3 367 799	4.8	6.5	0.3	3.1	0.6	2.5	80.6	95.5	51.4	32.4	865	663
Lake	18 892	64 877 066	9.2	9.9	4.1	4.4	2.1	8.2	60.1	2 367.0	1 042.1	989.0	2 003	1 956
LaPorte	4 264	12 639 630	5.9	11.9	4.3	3.5	3.5	6.6	63.1	369.8	180.5	137.0	1 231	1 055
Lawrence	1 833	6 258 969	4.2	7.1	2.2	2.7	24.3	3.4	55.6	143.8	73.1	50.7	1 100	799
Madison	3 695	12 894 572	8.1	13.7	4.5	3.9	1.5	11.3	55.4	411.1	191.4	142.7	1 095	811
Marion	34 223	145 267 021	3.8	7.6	6.1	1.6	14.0	18.4	48.0	4 321.3	1 815.1	1 329.5	1 447	1 014
Marshall	1 390	4 686 571	6.2	10.5	1.5	4.0	1.4	5.1	69.8	140.9	76.1	48.0	1 020	856
Martin	313	962 585	8.0	8.2	0.0	3.8	2.8	1.5	67.8	29.8	16.1	7.1	689	541
Miami	1 311	4 091 188	4.5	6.1	2.6	3.8	0.7	6.7	70.0	119.6	65.2	34.0	931	637
Monroe	3 589	12 483 781	10.4	10.4	5.5	5.0	2.7	8.7	56.9	339.2	139.6	147.6	1 046	827
Montgomery	1 366	4 441 185	3.7	7.5	4.2	3.9	1.0	10.2	68.9	131.4	58.1	56.2	1 468	1 078
Morgan	2 356	7 692 514	4.7	7.9	3.4	3.0	18.5	1.3	60.5	238.5	98.7	72.4	1 044	538
Newton	607	1 789 217	10.0	9.0	0.0	3.9	4.7	2.6	67.9	61.2	25.8	18.1	1 291	1 109
Noble	1 526	4 688 687	7.9	9.1	1.0	3.1	0.3	4.9	73.3	132.6	63.7	46.2	972	770
Ohio	248	804 741	9.9	6.7	0.0	5.5	3.4	20.4	52.3	29.4	20.3	4.8	786	579
Orange	656	2 087 602	7.2	6.3	0.2	4.7	1.4	5.5	73.3	74.2	49.7	16.5	838	620
Owen	478	1 467 231	7.6	11.8	0.0	5.3	4.5	1.2	68.4	51.9	27.2	15.9	742	538
Parke	550	1 469 526	6.3	9.1	0.8	4.5	3.5	4.2	69.9	47.3	28.5	14.7	862	531
Perry	892	2 938 269	4.0	4.8	0.4	4.2	35.8	7.7	42.5	92.9	30.5	18.1	929	744

1. Based on the resident population estimated as of July 1 of the year shown.

Table B. States and Counties — Local Government Finances, Government Employment, and Voting

	Local government finances, 2012 (cont.)									Government employment, 2014			Presidential election,[2] 2012		
	Direct general expenditure							Debt outstanding					Percent of vote cast:		
				Percent of total for:											
STATE County	Total (mil dol)	Per capita[1] (dollars)	Education	Health and hospitals	Police protection	Public welfare	Highways	Total (mil dol)	Per capita[1] (dollars)	Federal civilian	Federal military	State and local	Democratic	Republican	All other
	185	186	187	188	189	190	191	192	193	194	195	196	197	198	199
ILLINOIS—Cont'd															
Winnebago	1 135.0	3 886	50.2	1.7	8.1	3.0	5.4	750.7	2 570	830	600	14 113	55.6	42.8	1.7
Woodford	116.2	2 982	68.7	1.1	3.9	0.0	7.1	40.0	1 026	69	77	1 853	35.9	62.6	1.5
INDIANA	X	X	X	X	X	X	X	X	X	36 322	21 488	384 808	49.9	48.9	1.1
Adams	133.8	3 893	35.3	41.5	1.9	0.6	3.0	120.4	3 505	58	111	2 074	36.5	62.2	1.3
Allen	969.6	2 690	50.6	0.7	6.5	0.4	3.3	1 061.3	2 945	1 851	1 193	17 041	47.4	51.8	0.8
Bartholomew	465.6	5 883	32.7	40.9	1.8	0.5	0.9	364.3	4 603	162	256	6 073	43.7	55.0	1.3
Benton	35.9	4 079	50.7	2.9	2.6	0.5	7.6	27.8	3 163	26	28	608	41.0	57.2	1.8
Blackford	31.6	2 526	55.3	0.6	5.0	0.9	4.4	22.9	1 830	21	39	564	49.2	49.4	1.4
Boone	254.2	4 312	38.4	34.0	3.4	0.2	3.0	422.2	7 162	88	198	3 279	36.6	62.4	1.0
Brown	46.1	3 056	59.2	0.2	2.0	0.2	4.2	23.3	1 545	15	48	826	47.8	50.4	1.8
Carroll	44.9	2 233	56.6	1.7	3.2	1.1	6.3	15.9	791	63	64	802	42.8	55.6	1.6
Cass	169.3	4 387	43.5	32.2	4.5	0.2	2.9	80.8	2 094	83	121	3 108	44.8	53.3	1.9
Clark	456.8	4 081	34.1	34.1	3.8	0.2	1.1	411.3	3 674	1 496	365	6 162	46.0	53.1	0.9
Clay	70.5	2 627	57.4	1.1	2.7	0.5	3.4	38.3	1 426	76	85	1 230	43.5	55.0	1.5
Clinton	106.0	3 210	57.5	0.5	2.8	0.7	3.5	96.4	2 919	59	103	1 635	42.8	55.8	1.3
Crawford	28.5	2 676	60.9	2.8	2.1	0.1	4.3	20.9	1 955	23	34	569	48.2	50.4	1.4
Daviess	136.7	4 263	34.6	34.7	1.9	0.2	4.2	136.4	4 253	69	104	1 727	31.8	67.1	1.1
Dearborn	292.4	5 869	28.3	29.1	2.1	0.0	1.6	199.3	3 999	101	158	2 930	32.1	67.0	0.9
Decatur	123.9	4 759	32.1	32.1	1.8	0.1	1.8	144.4	5 545	62	84	1 468	37.1	61.5	1.4
DeKalb	141.5	3 344	61.2	0.3	3.3	0.3	3.6	92.5	2 185	81	135	1 960	41.8	57.0	1.1
Delaware	323.3	2 755	48.4	0.8	3.9	0.5	2.7	191.9	1 635	281	352	10 587	56.9	41.9	1.1
Dubois	122.5	2 913	62.4	0.6	3.1	0.1	4.8	195.3	4 641	104	134	2 092	47.1	51.3	1.6
Elkhart	609.8	3 055	58.2	1.0	3.9	0.2	3.5	758.8	3 801	248	640	8 430	43.9	55.1	0.9
Fayette	72.1	3 001	59.5	1.8	4.9	0.2	5.4	37.9	1 577	44	74	1 036	46.4	52.0	1.6
Floyd	441.6	5 865	25.8	49.3	1.8	0.0	1.1	309.6	4 113	212	241	5 978	44.5	54.6	0.9
Fountain	45.0	2 632	61.9	2.3	2.9	0.3	7.1	40.9	2 387	61	53	774	41.8	56.1	2.1
Franklin	38.8	1 688	69.0	0.1	2.0	0.3	4.9	26.8	1 166	41	73	958	32.1	66.1	1.8
Fulton	83.1	4 008	31.5	45.7	2.8	0.1	2.5	22.8	1 097	41	65	1 330	41.1	57.2	1.7
Gibson	99.3	2 969	54.6	1.5	3.1	0.1	6.2	186.7	5 581	85	106	1 319	42.8	56.0	1.3
Grant	175.3	2 529	54.4	0.3	7.8	0.2	3.4	108.6	1 566	997	205	2 946	42.9	56.0	1.0
Greene	110.5	3 356	48.9	22.9	1.7	0.1	3.4	52.3	1 587	72	105	1 741	41.9	56.4	1.7
Hamilton	1 098.2	3 794	43.5	16.9	3.8	0.1	2.9	2 131.8	7 364	362	971	12 571	38.5	60.7	0.7
Hancock	259.1	3 652	38.3	36.3	2.5	0.1	3.7	430.2	6 065	106	230	3 667	34.7	64.3	1.1
Harrison	142.1	3 631	38.8	32.2	0.5	0.1	1.6	105.0	2 682	98	125	1 998	40.3	58.3	1.4
Hendricks	586.7	3 900	37.8	29.3	2.6	0.1	1.7	985.7	6 552	273	490	8 115	37.8	61.2	1.0
Henry	226.4	4 588	34.1	40.7	1.5	0.1	1.6	118.3	2 397	90	146	2 898	47.2	51.1	1.7
Howard	406.5	4 907	32.7	36.7	3.9	0.3	1.8	200.3	2 417	220	264	5 037	46.3	52.4	1.3
Huntington	90.3	2 442	58.2	0.3	3.7	0.1	4.3	59.5	1 608	84	114	1 410	35.8	63.0	1.2
Jackson	185.0	4 294	31.0	55.4	1.0	0.1	1.1	103.4	2 400	85	139	2 850	42.3	56.0	1.7
Jasper	124.9	3 732	37.4	35.2	2.1	0.1	2.1	207.7	6 207	89	105	1 877	39.2	59.6	1.3
Jay	94.3	4 414	38.3	35.4	2.3	0.6	3.7	67.3	3 148	42	67	1 293	45.1	52.9	2.0
Jefferson	77.9	2 394	64.1	1.2	3.5	0.2	4.5	52.1	1 600	80	98	2 382	46.4	52.3	1.3
Jennings	82.7	2 935	66.8	0.7	2.7	0.2	2.8	49.5	1 758	70	89	1 193	44.9	52.9	2.2
Johnson	466.1	3 255	49.3	17.5	3.5	0.1	2.7	489.4	3 417	405	695	6 407	36.8	62.2	1.0
Knox	274.0	7 186	18.6	63.3	1.2	0.1	2.8	128.9	3 381	170	114	4 775	46.1	52.6	1.3
Kosciusko	216.4	2 788	61.0	1.0	3.8	0.1	4.8	226.2	2 915	164	248	3 011	30.6	68.0	1.4
LaGrange	85.5	2 278	67.1	0.1	1.4	0.1	3.8	71.2	1 896	60	123	1 320	38.6	60.1	1.3
Lake	1 850.2	3 748	45.8	0.6	5.4	1.1	1.8	1 929.7	3 909	1 335	1 562	24 767	66.7	32.5	0.8
LaPorte	330.9	2 974	53.0	1.0	4.1	0.3	2.3	311.4	2 799	172	355	6 671	60.2	38.2	1.6
Lawrence	114.9	2 494	59.2	0.4	4.2	0.2	6.0	97.1	2 107	122	145	1 996	38.9	59.4	1.7
Madison	322.0	2 470	48.2	0.7	5.0	0.2	3.7	497.2	3 814	245	400	5 909	52.6	46.0	1.4
Marion	4 896.8	5 329	31.1	23.0	4.5	0.2	0.9	11 765.5	12 803	14 630	3 238	65 422	63.8	35.4	0.8
Marshall	129.3	2 749	63.4	1.7	4.8	0.2	5.4	98.6	2 098	93	150	2 025	42.5	56.1	1.4
Martin	26.7	2 598	58.5	0.8	2.4	0.3	8.0	14.6	1 421	4 042	75	414	34.8	63.7	1.5
Miami	111.4	3 054	57.5	0.2	2.1	0.2	4.7	101.3	2 777	648	119	1 975	39.4	58.9	1.7
Monroe	289.9	2 055	45.2	1.2	4.9	0.4	4.3	383.5	2 719	282	453	21 354	65.6	33.4	1.0
Montgomery	110.0	2 875	52.3	0.3	3.9	0.5	5.8	103.4	2 703	83	119	1 822	39.3	59.3	1.4
Morgan	210.4	3 033	48.5	21.5	2.5	0.1	2.6	96.0	1 385	92	223	2 518	35.9	62.9	1.2
Newton	55.2	3 932	46.4	2.3	2.3	0.2	6.4	34.2	2 435	26	45	719	43.4	54.6	2.0
Noble	113.5	2 385	60.5	0.3	5.9	0.1	4.5	94.3	1 982	79	151	1 846	41.6	57.0	1.4
Ohio	23.6	3 888	36.5	0.1	3.4	0.1	3.1	15.6	2 573	14	19	344	39.7	58.7	1.6
Orange	63.7	3 235	54.0	0.2	0.9	0.1	3.8	72.0	3 654	41	62	916	41.9	56.1	2.0
Owen	40.1	1 878	63.7	0.0	2.5	0.2	4.4	41.4	1 939	34	67	756	43.7	54.0	2.3
Parke	44.2	2 588	55.1	0.9	2.6	0.1	6.9	39.4	2 308	46	50	1 051	42.0	56.1	1.9
Perry	80.3	4 126	33.1	41.5	1.7	0.0	3.6	65.0	3 340	71	57	1 423	60.6	37.7	1.7

1. Based on the resident population estimated as of July 1 of the year shown.   2. © 2013 Election Data Services, Inc. All rights reserved.

Table B. States and Counties — **Land Area and Population**

STATE/ County code	CBSA code[1]	County type[2]	STATE County	Land area[3] (sq km) 2010	Total persons 2015	Rank	Per square kilometer	White	Black	American Indian, Alaska Native	Asian and Pacific Islander	Percent Hispanic or Latino[4]	Under 5 years	5 to 17 years	18 to 24 years	25 to 34 years	35 to 44 years	45 to 54 years
				1	2	3	4	5	6	7	8	9	10	11	12	13	14	15
			INDIANA—Cont'd															
18 125	27540	6	Pike	866	12 594	2 256	14.5	97.5	0.8	0.6	0.5	1.3	5.4	16.4	7.1	10.6	11.8	14.5
18 127	16980	1	Porter	1 083	167 688	381	154.8	85.2	4.0	0.6	1.9	9.5	5.5	17.3	9.2	12.4	13.1	13.9
18 129	21780	2	Posey	1 061	25 512	1 585	24.0	97.4	1.7	0.5	0.6	1.1	5.8	17.0	8.0	10.9	11.8	14.6
18 131	...	6	Pulaski	1 123	12 889	2 236	11.5	95.4	1.3	0.9	0.5	2.9	5.4	17.4	7.9	10.7	11.8	14.5
18 133	26900	1	Putnam	1 245	37 585	1 236	30.2	92.6	4.6	0.6	1.3	1.9	4.7	15.0	14.3	11.9	11.9	14.3
18 135	...	6	Randolph	1 172	25 172	1 603	21.5	95.7	1.2	0.7	0.6	3.2	5.9	17.7	7.8	10.2	12.2	13.9
18 137	...	6	Ripley	1 156	28 701	1 466	24.8	96.8	0.7	0.6	0.9	1.7	6.0	18.3	8.3	10.6	12.2	14.3
18 139	...	6	Rush	1 057	16 672	2 000	15.8	97.4	1.4	0.5	0.6	1.4	5.6	17.7	8.2	10.5	12.0	14.6
18 141	43780	2	St. Joseph	1 186	268 441	254	226.3	76.4	14.2	0.9	2.9	8.2	6.5	17.5	11.1	13.0	11.9	12.8
18 143	31140	6	Scott	493	23 744	1 652	48.2	97.2	0.7	0.5	0.8	1.8	5.9	17.0	8.1	11.6	13.0	15.0
18 145	26900	1	Shelby	1 065	44 478	1 084	41.8	94.0	1.5	0.5	1.1	3.9	5.8	17.2	8.3	11.5	12.4	15.1
18 147	...	8	Spencer	1 028	20 715	1 792	20.2	95.9	1.1	0.5	0.5	2.8	5.5	17.1	7.6	10.3	11.8	15.0
18 149	...	8	Starke	801	22 958	1 683	28.7	95.6	0.8	0.9	0.5	3.4	5.8	17.4	8.3	11.1	11.9	13.9
18 151	11420	7	Steuben	800	34 372	1 318	43.0	94.9	1.1	0.5	0.8	3.2	4.9	16.2	10.8	10.4	11.3	14.2
18 153	45460	3	Sullivan	1 158	20 928	1 777	18.1	93.3	5.1	0.8	0.5	1.8	5.1	15.1	8.7	13.6	13.7	14.2
18 155	...	8	Switzerland	571	10 524	2 393	18.4	96.7	1.1	0.6	0.4	1.7	6.1	18.7	7.7	11.0	12.0	15.1
18 157	29200	3	Tippecanoe	1 294	185 826	348	143.6	79.6	5.5	0.6	7.9	8.0	6.2	14.6	24.0	14.3	10.6	10.3
18 159	...	3	Tipton	675	15 267	2 082	22.6	96.2	0.7	0.4	0.7	2.6	4.3	17.1	8.0	9.9	11.9	14.9
18 161	17140	8	Union	418	7 182	2 660	17.2	97.5	1.2	0.8	0.7	1.5	4.5	18.2	8.4	10.0	12.1	15.6
18 163	21780	2	Vanderburgh	605	181 877	355	300.6	86.6	10.8	0.6	1.8	2.5	6.4	15.6	10.5	14.4	11.3	13.1
18 165	45460	3	Vermillion	665	15 692	2 063	23.6	98.0	0.8	0.6	0.5	1.1	5.3	16.9	7.4	10.7	12.4	13.7
18 167	45460	3	Vigo	1 045	107 896	554	103.2	87.9	8.4	0.6	0.8	2.5	5.9	14.9	15.6	12.6	11.7	12.4
18 169	47340	6	Wabash	1 068	32 138	1 381	30.1	95.6	1.1	1.2	0.7	2.4	5.2	16.4	10.3	10.4	11.3	13.2
18 171	...	8	Warren	945	8 269	2 577	8.8	97.9	0.5	0.5	0.7	1.4	5.7	16.8	7.5	9.9	11.4	15.5
18 173	21780	2	Warrick	997	61 897	847	62.1	94.4	2.2	0.5	2.4	1.7	5.7	19.0	7.6	10.5	13.1	14.3
18 175	31140	1	Washington	1 331	27 827	1 496	20.9	97.6	0.7	0.6	0.5	1.4	5.7	17.9	8.1	11.2	12.7	15.0
18 177	39980	5	Wayne	1 041	67 000	793	64.4	91.4	6.6	0.8	1.5	2.7	6.2	16.3	9.0	11.4	11.9	13.7
18 179	23060	2	Wells	953	27 964	1 488	29.3	96.3	0.9	0.6	0.6	2.5	6.5	17.7	8.1	11.4	11.2	13.8
18 181	...	6	White	1 308	24 293	1 633	18.6	91.3	0.8	0.8	0.6	7.7	6.2	17.2	7.9	10.0	11.8	13.5
18 183	23060	2	Whitley	869	33 406	1 342	38.4	96.8	0.9	0.7	0.7	2.0	5.8	17.6	7.9	11.3	12.4	14.2
19 000	...	X	IOWA	144 669	3 123 899	X	21.6	88.5	4.1	0.7	2.7	5.6	6.3	17.1	10.3	12.6	11.7	13.1
19 001	...	8	Adair	1 474	7 228	2 654	4.9	97.9	0.6	0.4	0.6	1.7	4.8	17.3	6.9	10.0	10.4	14.1
19 003	...	9	Adams	1 097	3 796	2 918	3.5	97.7	0.7	0.6	0.9	1.1	6.5	15.0	6.5	11.1	9.8	14.0
19 005	...	6	Allamakee	1 655	13 886	2 175	8.4	92.0	1.6	0.5	0.7	5.7	6.1	16.3	7.2	10.1	9.9	13.6
19 007	...	7	Appanoose	1 288	12 529	2 222	9.7	97.5	1.1	0.7	0.6	1.5	6.0	16.4	7.3	10.6	10.3	13.1
19 009	...	8	Audubon	1 147	5 773	2 777	5.0	98.0	0.6	0.4	0.7	1.1	4.6	15.7	6.9	8.8	9.5	14.8
19 011	16300	3	Benton	1 855	25 658	1 575	13.8	97.7	1.0	0.4	0.5	1.3	5.7	18.1	7.7	10.1	12.0	15.6
19 013	47940	3	Black Hawk	1 465	133 455	474	91.1	84.6	10.1	0.5	2.7	4.1	6.1	15.3	15.9	13.1	10.8	11.4
19 015	14340	6	Boone	1 480	26 643	1 542	18.0	95.7	1.7	0.6	0.8	2.4	5.6	17.1	7.7	12.1	11.8	13.7
19 017	47940	3	Bremer	1 128	24 722	1 619	21.9	97.2	1.4	0.3	1.2	1.4	5.1	16.7	12.4	11.0	11.2	12.6
19 019	...	6	Buchanan	1 479	21 062	1 770	14.2	97.4	1.0	0.4	0.7	1.4	6.8	19.9	7.3	11.8	12.3	13.6
19 021	44740	7	Buena Vista	1 489	20 493	1 805	13.8	63.2	2.9	0.4	9.4	24.7	7.3	18.0	12.5	12.1	10.3	12.2
19 023	...	8	Butler	1 503	14 915	2 105	9.9	98.3	0.8	0.4	0.7	1.1	6.1	17.5	6.6	10.5	10.9	12.7
19 025	...	9	Calhoun	1 476	9 818	2 449	6.7	95.5	2.4	0.6	0.5	2.0	5.6	15.0	7.7	10.6	10.3	12.9
19 027	...	7	Carroll	1 475	20 498	1 804	13.9	96.3	1.2	0.4	0.7	2.3	6.5	17.6	7.6	10.5	10.7	13.5
19 029	...	6	Cass	1 461	13 427	2 209	9.2	96.6	0.7	0.6	0.8	2.4	5.7	16.9	7.0	10.2	10.5	13.3
19 031	...	6	Cedar	1 501	18 340	1 900	12.2	97.0	0.9	0.5	1.0	1.8	5.1	17.7	6.9	10.6	11.8	14.8
19 033	32380	5	Cerro Gordo	1 472	43 017	1 112	29.2	93.1	2.1	0.5	1.5	4.4	5.6	14.9	8.5	11.2	10.6	13.9
19 035	...	6	Cherokee	1 494	11 574	2 318	7.7	95.2	1.4	0.4	0.9	3.2	6.0	15.0	7.0	10.3	9.9	13.6
19 037	...	6	Chickasaw	1 306	12 097	2 293	9.3	97.4	0.8	0.3	0.5	2.3	6.1	17.7	7.7	9.8	9.9	13.9
19 039	...	6	Clarke	1 117	9 259	2 490	8.3	86.2	1.2	0.5	1.0	12.1	6.5	17.8	7.9	11.5	10.8	13.6
19 041	43980	7	Clay	1 469	16 507	2 006	11.2	95.2	1.2	0.5	0.9	3.2	5.7	17.1	7.6	11.1	11.4	12.9
19 043	...	8	Clayton	2 016	17 644	1 937	8.8	96.9	1.0	0.4	0.6	1.9	5.7	16.6	7.1	9.5	10.2	13.8
19 045	17540	4	Clinton	1 800	47 768	1 021	26.5	93.3	4.1	0.6	0.9	3.0	6.1	16.6	8.4	10.9	11.3	14.2
19 047	...	6	Crawford	1 850	17 094	1 976	9.2	69.1	2.2	0.4	1.7	27.4	7.2	18.3	9.2	11.2	11.6	12.8
19 049	19780	2	Dallas	1 524	80 133	695	52.6	88.0	2.2	0.5	4.1	6.3	8.2	20.4	6.2	15.5	15.5	12.8
19 051	36900	9	Davis	1 301	8 769	2 530	6.7	98.3	0.6	0.6	0.6	1.2	8.0	20.9	7.7	10.2	10.5	12.3
19 053	...	9	Decatur	1 378	8 220	2 581	6.0	94.1	2.3	0.8	1.5	2.6	5.1	16.7	17.6	9.4	9.4	10.8
19 055	...	6	Delaware	1 496	17 403	1 954	11.6	97.9	0.7	0.3	0.5	1.1	5.7	18.2	7.8	9.7	10.8	14.9
19 057	15460	5	Des Moines	1 078	40 055	1 172	37.2	90.2	7.1	0.7	1.4	2.9	6.0	17.0	7.6	11.7	11.3	13.4
19 059	44020	7	Dickinson	986	17 111	1 973	17.4	97.2	0.7	0.4	0.9	1.7	4.9	14.2	6.4	9.9	10.6	13.0
19 061	20220	3	Dubuque	1 576	97 125	607	61.6	92.9	3.6	0.5	2.0	2.2	6.1	17.0	10.2	12.8	10.8	13.5
19 063	...	7	Emmet	1 025	9 769	2 453	9.5	88.7	1.2	0.9	0.8	10.5	5.6	16.1	9.7	11.7	10.5	12.0
19 065	...	6	Fayette	1 893	20 257	1 818	10.7	95.5	1.8	0.4	1.0	2.2	5.8	15.4	10.0	10.2	9.9	13.7
19 067	...	7	Floyd	1 297	15 960	2 046	12.3	94.2	2.5	0.4	1.8	2.3	5.7	17.4	8.1	10.1	10.8	13.3

1. CBSA = Core Based Statistical Area. See Appendix A for explanation. See Appendix B for list of metropolitan areas with component counties. 2. County type code from the Economic Research Service of USDA Rural-Urban Continuum Codes. See Appendix A for definition. 3. Dry land or land partially or temporarily covered by water. 4. May be of any race.

STATE County	55 to 64 years	65 to 74 years	75 years and over	Percent female	Total persons 2000	2010	2000–2010	2010–2015	Births	Deaths	Net migration	Number	Persons per household	Family households	Female family householder[1]	One person
	16	17	18	19	20	21	22	23	24	25	26	27	28	29	30	31
INDIANA—Cont'd																
Pike	15.0	10.6	8.4	49.6	12 837	12 844	0.1	-1.9	765	716	-273	5 093	2.45	71.3	8.4	25.3
Porter	14.2	8.5	5.9	50.9	146 798	164 347	12.0	2.0	9 284	7 354	1 412	61 693	2.63	70.9	11.9	24.3
Posey	15.8	9.3	6.9	50.3	27 061	25 910	-4.3	-1.5	1 466	1 234	-578	10 178	2.49	73.1	9.1	23.7
Pulaski	14.5	10.0	7.8	49.3	13 755	13 402	-2.6	-3.8	724	786	-452	5 134	2.52	70.7	7.6	26.0
Putnam	12.8	8.4	6.7	47.0	36 019	37 952	5.4	-1.0	1 886	1 748	-508	12 557	2.56	72.3	11.4	23.3
Randolph	13.8	10.1	8.4	50.8	27 401	26 171	-4.5	-3.8	1 596	1 476	-1 111	10 514	2.42	65.8	9.0	29.0
Ripley	13.4	9.5	7.4	50.7	26 523	28 818	8.7	-0.4	1 751	1 574	-309	10 871	2.59	73.2	10.3	23.3
Rush	14.0	9.5	7.9	50.6	18 261	17 392	-4.8	-4.1	900	990	-607	6 920	2.44	72.0	11.3	23.8
St. Joseph	12.9	7.7	6.6	51.5	265 559	266 929	0.5	0.6	18 601	13 051	-3 690	101 759	2.50	64.1	13.7	29.8
Scott	13.6	9.7	6.1	50.8	22 960	24 181	5.3	-1.8	1 488	1 562	-400	8 973	2.63	69.0	11.8	27.0
Shelby	14.1	8.8	6.8	50.6	43 445	44 393	2.2	0.2	2 651	2 304	-247	17 315	2.53	67.8	12.0	26.3
Spencer	14.7	10.7	7.3	49.3	20 391	20 952	2.8	-1.1	1 191	1 050	-448	7 917	2.60	73.0	7.0	22.7
Starke	14.9	10.0	6.8	50.4	23 556	23 363	-0.8	-1.7	1 368	1 410	-369	9 009	2.57	71.3	12.4	25.4
Steuben	14.9	10.3	6.9	49.3	33 214	34 183	2.9	0.6	2 011	1 570	-179	13 409	2.45	69.7	9.7	24.8
Sullivan	13.2	9.5	6.8	45.7	21 751	21 475	-1.3	-2.5	1 237	1 202	-555	7 720	2.46	71.3	11.2	23.6
Switzerland	13.1	9.9	6.4	48.9	9 065	10 613	17.1	-0.8	670	520	-219	4 065	2.56	71.6	11.3	23.9
Tippecanoe	9.7	5.8	4.5	48.9	148 955	172 803	16.0	7.5	11 719	5 765	7 168	66 921	2.45	57.2	10.3	29.4
Tipton	14.6	11.1	8.3	50.1	16 577	15 936	-3.9	-4.2	742	889	-477	6 479	2.39	72.4	10.2	24.7
Union	14.2	10.3	6.6	50.7	7 349	7 516	2.3	-4.4	374	352	-368	2 949	2.47	66.8	8.7	29.6
Vanderburgh	13.5	8.1	7.1	51.6	171 922	179 703	4.5	1.2	12 071	9 839	184	74 365	2.34	60.7	13.2	32.9
Vermillion	14.9	10.7	7.9	50.6	16 788	16 212	-3.4	-3.2	872	1 099	-297	6 491	2.42	64.3	10.7	30.9
Vigo	12.4	8.2	6.3	49.3	105 848	107 848	1.9	0.0	6 764	5 992	-777	39 769	2.48	62.4	12.3	30.4
Wabash	13.8	9.9	9.5	51.4	34 960	32 888	-5.9	-2.3	1 856	2 145	-530	12 777	2.39	70.8	10.0	26.0
Warren	14.6	10.3	8.3	50.3	8 419	8 508	1.1	-2.8	474	378	-347	3 325	2.50	72.5	6.8	24.2
Warrick	13.7	9.7	6.4	50.6	52 383	59 689	13.9	3.7	3 356	2 786	1 560	22 675	2.64	74.2	7.8	21.7
Washington	13.9	9.3	6.1	50.1	27 223	28 262	3.8	-1.5	1 661	1 507	-584	10 512	2.64	70.6	12.9	25.4
Wayne	13.6	9.7	8.1	51.5	71 097	69 003	-2.9	-2.9	4 159	4 303	-1 816	27 891	2.36	65.5	14.2	29.4
Wells	14.3	9.1	7.9	50.7	27 600	27 636	0.1	1.2	1 789	1 350	-138	10 952	2.48	71.2	10.2	26.8
White	14.6	10.3	8.5	50.3	25 267	24 643	-2.5	-1.4	1 545	1 384	-526	9 458	2.55	70.7	8.4	25.4
Whitley	14.8	9.1	6.9	50.1	30 707	33 291	8.4	0.3	1 997	1 535	-277	13 091	2.51	71.4	10.0	24.9
IOWA	13.1	8.4	7.4	50.3	2 926 324	3 046 869	4.1	2.5	203 935	147 916	22 110	1 232 228	2.42	64.7	9.3	28.8
Adair	14.4	9.9	12.2	50.9	8 243	7 682	-6.8	-5.9	362	550	-269	3 252	2.27	63.4	6.1	30.4
Adams	15.1	11.4	10.6	49.9	4 482	4 029	-10.1	-5.8	259	257	-212	1 735	2.19	68.4	4.7	26.9
Allamakee	15.4	11.4	9.9	48.8	14 675	14 328	-2.4	-3.1	925	841	-522	5 899	2.34	66.8	5.9	27.4
Appanoose	14.8	11.5	10.0	50.6	13 721	12 887	-6.1	-2.8	771	871	-241	5 447	2.31	62.4	7.4	33.2
Audubon	15.3	11.2	13.1	51.6	6 830	6 119	-10.4	-5.7	322	416	-256	2 703	2.14	63.3	7.4	32.3
Benton	13.9	9.0	7.9	50.3	25 308	26 076	3.0	-1.6	1 488	1 187	-707	10 137	2.52	72.3	7.9	23.6
Black Hawk	12.6	7.9	6.9	51.1	128 012	131 090	2.4	1.8	8 933	6 210	-257	52 438	2.40	59.2	10.5	31.8
Boone	15.0	8.9	8.1	49.7	26 224	26 306	0.3	1.3	1 586	1 529	255	10 619	2.40	64.7	7.8	29.3
Bremer	12.6	9.7	8.7	50.8	23 325	24 276	4.1	1.8	1 297	1 054	203	9 296	2.46	70.5	6.7	26.1
Buchanan	13.2	8.8	7.5	50.2	21 093	20 958	-0.6	0.5	1 496	1 066	-300	8 298	2.48	69.6	7.4	25.4
Buena Vista	12.9	6.7	7.9	49.4	20 411	20 260	-0.7	1.2	1 724	966	-485	7 635	2.54	65.0	6.8	30.2
Butler	14.6	10.7	10.3	50.5	15 305	14 867	-2.9	0.3	842	932	155	6 222	2.37	70.1	6.2	25.4
Calhoun	15.6	10.2	12.1	48.6	11 115	10 177	-8.4	-3.5	570	728	-184	4 310	2.18	64.9	7.4	31.7
Carroll	14.4	8.5	10.7	51.4	21 421	20 816	-2.8	-1.5	1 369	1 264	-439	8 557	2.36	63.8	8.8	33.5
Cass	14.9	10.6	11.0	50.7	14 684	13 956	-5.0	-3.8	772	1 016	-278	6 074	2.20	64.2	8.5	32.4
Cedar	14.5	9.5	8.9	50.5	18 187	18 495	1.7	-0.8	955	916	-153	7 639	2.37	68.8	7.1	26.1
Cerro Gordo	15.6	10.0	9.8	51.0	46 447	44 151	-4.9	-2.6	2 482	2 557	-1 049	19 864	2.14	58.4	8.2	35.4
Cherokee	15.9	10.2	12.1	50.4	13 035	12 072	-7.4	-4.1	670	818	-343	5 384	2.15	62.6	8.9	32.9
Chickasaw	15.4	9.9	9.5	50.0	13 095	12 439	-5.0	-2.7	742	712	-282	5 330	2.28	67.8	6.8	28.3
Clarke	14.2	9.5	8.1	49.8	9 133	9 286	1.7	-0.3	650	544	-145	3 686	2.47	62.8	8.3	31.1
Clay	14.6	9.5	10.0	50.9	17 372	16 667	-4.1	-1.0	1 065	1 002	-196	7 269	2.24	63.3	8.0	29.3
Clayton	16.3	10.7	10.2	49.7	18 678	18 129	-2.9	-2.7	1 014	1 005	-461	7 698	2.28	67.1	7.7	27.3
Clinton	14.3	9.6	8.8	50.9	50 149	49 116	-2.1	-2.7	2 989	2 815	-1 511	19 977	2.39	64.2	9.4	30.0
Crawford	12.9	8.8	8.1	49.0	16 942	17 096	0.9	0.0	1 266	824	-396	6 371	2.63	69.6	9.3	27.5
Dallas	10.2	6.4	4.8	51.0	40 750	66 137	62.3	21.2	6 125	1 980	9 500	26 819	2.67	71.3	8.4	22.5
Davis	13.0	9.0	8.5	50.0	8 541	8 753	2.5	0.2	705	420	-290	3 085	2.80	72.3	7.8	24.4
Decatur	12.7	9.1	9.2	49.8	8 689	8 457	-2.7	-2.8	484	507	-230	3 085	2.44	67.6	9.3	28.5
Delaware	14.9	9.1	9.0	50.0	18 404	17 764	-3.5	-2.0	1 067	903	-516	7 115	2.44	70.4	7.3	26.0
Des Moines	14.1	10.1	8.8	50.9	42 351	40 325	-4.8	-0.7	2 436	2 406	-278	16 881	2.34	64.4	12.9	31.2
Dickinson	16.9	12.7	11.5	50.2	16 424	16 667	1.5	2.7	861	1 027	621	7 831	2.12	65.4	5.4	29.9
Dubuque	13.4	8.4	7.8	50.6	89 143	93 653	5.1	3.7	6 293	4 598	1 744	37 720	2.41	65.2	9.0	29.2
Emmet	15.2	9.2	10.0	49.3	11 027	10 302	-6.6	-5.2	586	645	-483	4 150	2.27	66.5	10.4	29.5
Fayette	14.6	10.2	10.2	49.9	22 008	20 880	-5.1	-3.0	1 100	1 267	-419	8 470	2.34	62.8	7.0	31.3
Floyd	13.9	10.6	10.1	50.9	16 900	16 303	-3.5	-2.1	993	1 014	-335	6 923	2.29	66.8	10.6	29.5

1. No spouse present.

Table B. States and Counties — **Population, Vital Statistics, Medicare, and Crime**

STATE County	Persons in group quarters, 2015	Daytime population, 2010–2014 Number	Employment/residence ratio	Births, 2015 Total	Rate[1]	Deaths, 2015 Number	Rate[1]	Persons under 65 with no health insurance, 2014 Number	Percent	Medicare, 2015 Total Beneficiaries	Enrolled in Original Medicare	Enrolled in Medicare Advantage	Serious crimes known to police,[2] 2014 Total Number	Rate[3]
	32	33	34	35	36	37	38	39	40	41	42	43	44	45
INDIANA—Cont'd														
Pike	213	10 948	0.68	149	11.8	141	11.2	1 290	12.7	2 583	2 060	523	125	1 214
Porter	3 409	150 413	0.80	1 784	10.7	1 510	9.0	15 218	10.9	26 340	21 973	4 367	2 330	1 456
Posey	242	23 064	0.79	281	11.0	239	9.4	1 936	9.1	4 252	3 184	1 068	591	2 326
Pulaski	193	12 527	0.89	140	10.8	132	10.2	1 596	15.2	2 777	2 323	454	NA	NA
Putnam	5 194	36 033	0.89	387	10.3	322	8.6	3 650	13.6	6 011	4 367	1 644	NA	NA
Randolph	329	22 588	0.71	298	11.8	256	10.1	3 227	15.8	5 582	4 685	897	NA	NA
Ripley	449	27 448	0.91	331	11.6	289	10.1	2 899	12.3	6 150	4 803	1 347	289	1 230
Rush	178	14 872	0.70	164	9.8	189	11.3	2 044	14.8	3 207	2 613	594	NA	NA
St. Joseph	11 231	271 021	1.03	3 589	13.4	2 411	9.0	31 772	14.5	45 838	31 582	14 256	9 184	3 449
Scott	312	21 228	0.72	281	11.9	293	12.4	2 798	14.2	5 418	4 358	1 060	520	2 636
Shelby	683	41 686	0.87	492	11.1	422	9.5	4 683	12.6	7 436	5 739	1 697	1 102	2 457
Spencer	368	18 811	0.78	233	11.2	222	10.7	2 166	12.8	3 921	3 250	671	NA	NA
Starke	16	19 148	0.56	252	11.0	266	11.6	2 861	14.9	4 703	3 941	762	149	763
Steuben	1 303	32 893	0.92	418	12.2	302	8.8	3 866	14.2	6 945	3 994	2 951	801	2 326
Sullivan	2 185	19 931	0.84	238	11.4	199	9.5	2 191	14.2	3 989	3 528	461	166	978
Switzerland	107	8 719	0.58	130	12.4	105	10.0	1 359	15.7	1 643	1 408	235	NA	NA
Tippecanoe	14 488	189 023	1.13	2 244	12.1	1 085	5.9	21 455	14.2	21 735	17 702	4 033	5 132	2 852
Tipton	205	14 140	0.79	134	8.7	156	10.2	1 513	12.2	2 962	2 489	473	123	788
Union	67	5 472	0.45	69	9.6	61	8.5	810	13.5	1 487	1 197	290	NA	NA
Vanderburgh	7 424	202 078	1.25	2 282	12.5	1 833	10.1	18 509	12.4	35 183	25 509	9 674	8 382	4 607
Vermillion	209	14 387	0.77	170	10.8	193	12.3	1 673	13.1	3 342	2 935	407	NA	NA
Vigo	9 570	117 410	1.20	1 280	11.8	1 124	10.4	12 267	14.6	19 999	17 433	2 566	4 424	4 164
Wabash	1 837	31 633	0.94	360	11.2	390	12.1	3 327	13.5	7 260	4 289	2 971	NA	NA
Warren	84	6 731	0.57	80	9.6	83	10.0	832	12.3	1 173	1 062	111	NA	NA
Warrick	726	48 681	0.59	633	10.3	579	9.4	5 037	9.9	10 402	7 729	2 673	945	1 539
Washington	261	22 657	0.54	338	12.1	279	10.0	3 772	16.1	5 076	3 716	1 360	NA	NA
Wayne	2 681	69 790	1.05	758	11.3	868	12.9	8 210	15.3	15 479	13 550	1 929	NA	NA
Wells	472	25 631	0.84	329	11.8	237	8.5	2 858	12.5	4 845	2 890	1 955	478	1 715
White	307	22 801	0.85	304	12.5	284	11.7	2 910	14.8	5 679	4 732	947	37	151
Whitley	436	29 198	0.74	386	11.6	283	8.5	3 328	12.0	6 536	3 115	3 421	NA	NA
IOWA	100 975	3 081 639	1.00	39 470	12.7	27 728	8.9	185 413	7.3	552 763	466 113	86 650	73 553	2 367
Adair	163	6 783	0.80	70	9.6	92	12.6	450	7.8	1 436	1 322	114	60	807
Adams	104	3 455	0.76	53	13.8	47	12.3	301	10.0	915	883	32	42	1 085
Allamakee	298	12 774	0.80	182	13.0	176	12.6	1 137	10.4	3 194	2 834	360	7	49
Appanoose	126	12 491	0.95	137	10.9	159	12.6	887	9.0	3 106	2 669	437	358	2 825
Audubon	137	5 194	0.75	68	11.8	68	11.8	359	8.2	1 419	1 360	59	35	601
Benton	289	19 351	0.49	302	11.8	220	8.6	1 300	6.1	4 425	3 569	856	64	276
Black Hawk	5 585	141 989	1.15	1 730	13.0	1 172	8.8	8 159	7.5	23 716	20 343	3 373	4 559	3 424
Boone	765	23 721	0.80	290	10.9	285	10.7	1 425	6.6	4 720	4 076	644	406	1 536
Bremer	1 644	23 559	0.93	252	10.2	200	8.1	987	5.3	4 941	4 493	448	241	973
Buchanan	330	18 485	0.76	289	13.7	197	9.3	1 228	7.1	4 014	3 436	578	41	195
Buena Vista	1 080	21 666	1.12	343	16.7	163	7.9	2 035	12.2	3 398	3 212	186	322	1 558
Butler	201	12 101	0.60	158	10.6	176	11.8	763	6.5	3 491	3 143	348	13	86
Calhoun	737	8 769	0.73	114	11.6	129	13.1	526	7.4	2 331	2 225	106	74	748
Carroll	462	21 915	1.11	264	12.9	253	12.3	1 007	6.1	4 755	4 388	367	144	700
Cass	307	13 601	0.99	139	10.4	185	13.8	853	8.2	3 360	3 052	308	206	1 521
Cedar	319	14 579	0.60	184	10.0	182	9.9	855	5.7	3 214	2 613	601	170	924
Cerro Gordo	1 070	46 332	1.12	471	10.9	495	11.5	2 323	6.8	10 347	10 062	285	1 350	3 101
Cherokee	370	11 662	0.95	134	11.5	164	14.0	651	7.2	2 710	2 349	361	109	914
Chickasaw	106	11 252	0.82	133	10.9	117	9.6	852	8.7	2 426	2 356	70	76	617
Clarke	151	9 308	1.01	124	13.4	90	9.7	671	8.9	1 650	1 498	152	160	1 711
Clay	253	17 370	1.10	213	12.9	172	10.4	843	6.4	3 880	3 838	42	325	1 971
Clayton	282	16 677	0.86	191	10.8	185	10.5	1 156	8.3	4 103	3 371	732	48	271
Clinton	806	49 040	1.02	547	11.4	511	10.7	2 471	6.4	9 869	8 392	1 477	1 673	3 460
Crawford	578	16 865	0.95	229	13.4	148	8.6	1 681	11.8	3 119	2 832	287	62	353
Dallas	500	61 790	0.73	1 257	15.9	408	5.2	3 579	5.2	6 764	5 626	1 138	1 262	1 640
Davis	86	7 834	0.75	135	15.4	77	8.8	897	12.5	1 609	1 454	155	25	284
Decatur	765	7 809	0.87	98	11.9	85	10.3	588	9.8	1 640	1 460	180	2	25
Delaware	222	15 685	0.80	219	12.6	179	10.3	989	7.0	3 078	2 514	564	204	1 165
Des Moines	701	43 671	1.19	449	11.2	421	10.5	2 274	7.1	9 232	8 484	748	1 493	3 676
Dickinson	202	17 151	1.03	167	9.8	176	10.3	823	6.4	4 357	4 140	217	144	844
Dubuque	4 349	103 091	1.16	1 240	12.8	878	9.1	4 763	6.1	18 614	10 728	7 886	1 908	1 980
Emmet	446	9 620	0.91	112	11.4	104	10.6	778	10.0	2 164	2 094	70	155	1 558
Fayette	928	19 771	0.91	197	9.7	221	10.9	1 181	7.6	4 351	3 879	472	263	1 286
Floyd	294	14 738	0.82	196	12.3	193	12.1	991	7.9	3 478	3 380	98	161	1 002

1. Per 1,000 estimated resident population.   2. Data for serious crimes have not been adjusted for underreporting; this may affect comparability between geographic areas and over time.
3. Per 100,000 population estimated by the FBI.

| STATE County | Serious crimes known to police, 2014 (cont.)[1] Rate[2] | | Education — School enrollment and attainment, 2010–2014 | | | | Local government expenditures,[5] 2012–2013 | | Money income, 2010–2014 — Households | | | | Income and poverty, 2014 | | | |
	Violent	Property	Enrollment[3] Total	Percent private	Attainment[4] (percent) High school graduate or less	Bachelor's degree or more	Total current spending (mil dol)	Current spending per student (dollars)	Per capita income[6] (dollars)	Median income (dollars)	Mean income (dollars)	Percent with income of $200,000 or more	Median household income (dollars)	Percent below poverty level — All persons	Children under 18 years	Children 5 to 17 years in families
	46	47	48	49	50	51	52	53	54	55	56	57	58	59	60	61
INDIANA—Cont'd																
Pike	58	1 156	2 699	6.4	61.5	12.0	23.2	11 719	22 974	43 065	56 384	0.8	47 217	11.3	16.9	15.2
Porter	96	1 360	44 194	18.9	43.1	26.4	230.9	8 502	29 043	62 818	76 165	3.3	63 030	10.0	13.2	11.8
Posey	232	2 094	6 165	16.5	45.7	21.3	37.4	10 243	29 426	59 969	73 167	3.0	59 975	10.7	13.6	12.5
Pulaski	NA	NA	3 054	9.8	60.3	12.0	23.1	11 098	21 725	42 910	54 122	1.3	43 770	14.2	21.7	20.6
Putnam	NA	NA	9 895	30.6	55.0	15.5	60.2	9 835	21 541	49 914	62 269	1.1	49 467	13.5	17.9	16.1
Randolph	NA	NA	6 310	4.9	59.1	12.6	42.6	9 776	22 386	41 537	54 500	1.1	41 577	16.1	23.7	21.7
Ripley	30	1 200	7 058	13.6	58.1	14.7	36.6	11 410	23 206	50 364	60 624	1.2	52 491	10.7	16.0	15.1
Rush	NA	NA	3 916	8.2	63.4	14.7	23.4	9 388	23 872	46 021	58 443	1.7	47 418	14.4	20.8	18.7
St. Joseph	344	3 106	77 275	30.4	43.6	27.2	385.8	10 137	24 039	45 012	61 263	2.9	46 388	17.2	26.5	24.6
Scott	243	2 393	5 777	10.7	60.1	13.2	36.8	8 918	21 575	43 739	54 137	0.7	41 649	17.6	27.0	25.7
Shelby	499	1 958	10 422	9.2	56.8	15.0	65.9	9 077	24 200	52 341	60 356	1.5	54 831	11.8	16.5	15.1
Spencer	NA	NA	4 737	7.4	56.0	15.4	33.0	9 841	24 346	53 073	61 800	1.3	54 468	9.3	12.8	11.6
Starke	97	666	5 433	12.1	60.9	11.2	38.3	10 098	20 292	40 357	51 221	0.9	43 740	15.5	23.6	22.2
Steuben	46	2 279	8 721	20.4	49.3	20.1	38.1	9 279	24 345	48 750	61 045	2.3	50 078	12.8	19.3	16.6
Sullivan	147	830	4 037	10.0	55.4	13.0	29.1	9 513	20 193	45 176	54 235	1.3	43 933	16.9	21.8	20.0
Switzerland	NA	NA	2 324	11.3	65.0	8.7	15.1	10 265	19 255	44 447	49 113	0.8	47 606	17.4	28.2	26.1
Tippecanoe	228	2 623	69 837	8.8	36.9	35.2	202.8	9 426	23 337	44 474	60 264	2.7	46 276	22.1	20.3	18.0
Tipton	90	698	3 472	11.4	52.2	17.3	21.6	8 228	26 350	53 340	64 095	2.1	55 008	9.5	13.3	11.5
Union	NA	NA	1 819	5.4	52.2	19.3	16.9	11 313	21 805	47 083	53 052	0.0	47 410	13.8	21.7	18.0
Vanderburgh	368	4 239	43 497	17.4	44.6	23.5	234.9	10 202	24 426	43 067	58 080	2.1	42 622	17.7	25.4	22.4
Vermillion	NA	NA	3 773	5.6	57.7	13.2	24.8	9 576	23 475	44 088	55 731	1.6	44 388	13.9	20.1	17.8
Vigo	264	3 900	31 437	13.1	47.5	21.6	147.4	9 569	21 766	41 175	55 965	2.1	41 260	20.2	28.0	28.8
Wabash	NA	NA	8 252	20.8	55.9	17.1	53.6	10 147	21 943	45 657	54 746	1.1	45 151	15.2	21.3	18.9
Warren	NA	NA	1 899	17.0	55.6	17.2	11.2	9 671	28 574	56 642	71 424	4.9	55 925	9.9	16.3	14.8
Warrick	192	1 347	15 553	17.5	39.9	26.8	85.3	8 559	30 197	62 747	79 095	4.0	65 793	8.2	11.1	10.0
Washington	NA	NA	6 596	12.1	64.3	12.2	40.6	9 382	20 317	42 424	52 201	1.0	43 573	16.2	25.0	22.2
Wayne	NA	NA	16 686	15.6	54.6	17.7	95.9	9 302	21 130	37 932	51 023	1.3	40 929	17.8	26.3	24.8
Wells	14	1 701	6 637	16.2	52.0	16.6	40.4	8 536	24 126	49 050	60 034	1.3	51 182	10.7	15.8	14.9
White	16	135	5 289	5.9	54.4	15.1	44.2	9 068	24 116	51 250	61 213	1.1	50 731	11.2	17.9	17.8
Whitley	NA	NA	8 415	16.8	51.3	18.1	41.8	8 738	26 120	54 023	65 243	2.0	59 266	9.4	13.2	12.6
IOWA	273	2 094	812 470	16.2	41.2	26.4	5 177.7	10 313	27 621	52 716	67 621	3.0	53 816	12.3	15.5	14.5
Adair	67	740	1 608	4.3	51.3	15.2	9.5	10 642	25 657	47 264	57 994	1.5	48 216	10.3	15.5	13.5
Adams	129	956	790	10.1	51.2	14.7	5.9	10 846	25 169	47 335	56 825	1.9	51 929	12.2	18.9	19.9
Allamakee	0	49	2 927	13.6	55.3	15.9	21.2	9 326	25 622	47 886	60 995	2.1	45 229	12.4	19.1	18.8
Appanoose	221	2 604	2 594	10.9	48.8	18.4	18.9	9 148	22 744	41 525	52 615	1.7	40 422	17.5	25.4	24.0
Audubon	34	566	1 308	7.3	52.3	16.4	7.8	9 635	30 714	47 556	67 251	4.0	50 014	11.1	16.9	14.9
Benton	17	259	6 461	15.9	45.5	20.0	35.1	8 949	28 177	59 186	70 982	2.2	61 931	8.8	11.7	10.2
Black Hawk	558	2 866	38 570	10.5	43.7	26.2	233.5	12 526	24 771	47 002	60 230	2.0	51 331	14.5	17.4	16.4
Boone	310	1 225	6 427	14.4	42.5	22.5	36.8	9 325	27 160	52 714	65 973	2.3	54 186	10.4	13.1	12.1
Bremer	250	723	7 105	28.3	39.5	28.2	47.0	9 314	29 632	61 619	75 627	3.5	62 438	7.6	6.8	5.7
Buchanan	10	185	5 136	15.4	50.9	17.3	28.6	9 540	28 193	56 393	72 508	3.1	55 781	10.7	15.7	15.0
Buena Vista	295	1 263	5 475	19.4	51.5	19.7	40.8	10 034	23 707	48 010	61 910	2.2	50 719	12.4	17.6	17.4
Butler	7	80	3 327	6.3	50.0	15.5	18.2	9 223	26 327	51 701	63 226	1.6	52 273	9.9	12.5	11.7
Calhoun	40	708	2 070	5.7	45.7	18.9	17.6	10 119	26 486	44 934	60 175	2.8	49 456	13.7	16.7	15.6
Carroll	87	612	4 848	29.0	49.6	18.2	25.0	9 737	26 479	48 998	62 242	2.2	52 367	9.9	11.8	11.1
Cass	222	1 299	2 901	7.3	51.6	20.0	28.7	10 912	25 555	43 960	56 600	2.3	46 159	13.1	18.7	17.7
Cedar	60	864	4 375	5.3	45.5	20.8	33.2	9 607	27 566	59 672	66 413	2.5	61 423	7.9	9.8	8.5
Cerro Gordo	115	2 986	9 580	13.1	39.9	22.0	55.1	9 835	27 605	45 012	60 366	2.7	49 569	12.0	15.1	14.0
Cherokee	143	772	2 555	5.1	44.4	20.5	16.5	9 336	28 150	50 828	62 988	3.1	52 894	9.6	14.2	13.8
Chickasaw	195	422	2 997	15.8	54.7	14.5	20.0	9 729	25 137	46 020	58 044	2.1	50 788	9.8	14.2	13.0
Clarke	128	1 583	2 118	6.5	55.5	15.7	16.1	8 742	23 743	42 430	57 495	0.8	45 413	14.4	20.5	19.1
Clay	164	1 807	3 878	12.8	44.6	18.5	23.1	9 478	29 138	49 438	67 828	2.1	51 514	11.5	16.1	14.3
Clayton	79	192	3 754	7.9	53.2	16.2	46.1	18 843	25 853	47 725	60 154	2.0	49 018	10.8	16.8	15.4
Clinton	416	3 045	12 031	13.1	45.6	19.2	81.1	10 105	26 751	49 849	63 562	2.2	48 528	12.9	18.3	16.4
Crawford	51	302	4 255	7.1	58.8	14.3	37.3	9 625	23 066	47 437	60 148	2.0	50 370	11.6	16.4	16.2
Dallas	187	1 453	19 348	21.6	27.5	43.7	133.8	8 938	36 677	74 876	96 495	8.3	79 173	6.2	7.1	6.8
Davis	114	170	2 033	23.8	51.2	16.8	11.6	9 265	23 046	46 048	61 687	3.6	46 750	15.4	24.7	25.8
Decatur	0	25	2 386	33.5	50.8	19.2	11.5	10 672	19 321	38 275	49 592	1.5	36 742	21.3	26.6	24.7
Delaware	154	1 011	4 180	17.1	54.1	14.9	21.9	9 390	26 776	54 801	65 059	1.8	55 958	8.9	12.3	11.3
Des Moines	460	3 215	9 172	11.1	43.6	20.2	62.6	9 420	23 724	42 146	55 470	1.9	45 292	15.7	24.0	21.1
Dickinson	70	774	3 266	7.1	36.7	25.2	25.4	9 826	32 869	56 086	71 561	4.1	56 551	7.4	10.4	9.3
Dubuque	177	1 803	25 444	33.9	44.0	27.8	144.7	9 945	26 791	53 410	66 517	2.6	55 320	11.5	13.6	12.4
Emmet	392	1 166	2 603	5.2	46.4	14.8	17.3	9 830	28 293	48 545	68 839	2.9	47 342	11.3	17.4	16.8
Fayette	308	978	4 979	21.1	50.7	18.4	36.1	9 740	24 236	45 443	57 480	1.4	45 522	14.4	18.4	17.7
Floyd	180	822	3 496	13.5	48.3	17.0	21.0	10 033	25 142	43 169	57 925	1.7	48 292	12.7	18.2	16.5

1. Data for serious crimes have not been adjusted for underreporting; this may affect comparability between geographic areas and over time.   2. Per 100,000 population estimated by the FBI.
3. All persons 3 years old and over enrolled in nursery school through college.   4. Persons 25 years old and over.   5. Elementary and secondary education expenditures.
6. Based on population estimated by the American Community Survey, 2010–2014.

Table B. States and Counties — **Personal Income**

STATE County	Total (mil dol)	Percent change, 2013–2014	Per capita¹ Dollars	Per capita¹ Rank	Wages and salaries (mil dol)	Pension and insurance	Government social insurance	Proprietors' income (mil dol)	Dividends, interest, and rent (mil dol)	Personal transfer receipts (mil dol)	Earnings Total (mil dol)	From employee and self-employed	From employer
	62	63	64	65	66	67	68	69	70	71	72	73	74
INDIANA—Cont'd													
Pike................	462	1.8	36 597	1 669	182	35	13	51	56	115	281	18	13
Porter.............	7 430	4.0	44 472	716	2 700	429	205	408	1 015	1 218	3 742	243	205
Posey.............	1 144	1.3	44 806	695	459	101	32	152	170	203	744	43	32
Pulaski...........	499	-2.7	38 488	1 395	180	34	13	60	87	113	287	16	13
Putnam...........	1 187	-0.7	31 565	2 520	455	82	37	78	161	266	652	42	37
Randolph........	967	1.1	38 103	1 443	279	54	22	167	121	237	522	32	22
Ripley.............	1 115	4.6	39 137	1 305	565	102	42	49	163	218	758	46	42
Rush...............	655	-2.3	38 764	1 355	193	37	15	94	89	147	339	19	15
St. Joseph......	10 821	5.4	40 433	1 126	5 323	893	412	1 146	1 761	2 076	7 773	483	412
Scott..............	750	3.5	31 623	2 507	264	51	21	24	86	230	359	26	21
Shelby............	1 673	0.5	37 528	1 522	745	126	57	129	225	363	1 058	65	57
Spencer..........	827	1.4	39 772	1 211	275	53	21	64	108	158	412	26	21
Starke............	700	0.5	30 354	2 670	144	30	11	64	83	229	249	18	11
Steuben..........	1 235	5.5	36 000	1 780	540	103	43	65	221	270	750	49	43
Sullivan..........	663	-1.8	31 501	2 526	264	54	19	45	91	185	382	24	19
Switzerland.....	282	4.0	26 959	2 986	75	12	6	13	33	75	106	8	6
Tippecanoe	6 090	4.6	33 266	2 234	3 813	727	283	369	1 034	1 009	5 192	303	283
Tipton............	617	2.6	40 049	1 168	175	31	13	48	102	136	267	17	13
Union.............	239	-3.9	32 933	2 290	45	10	3	26	32	60	84	6	3
Vanderburgh....	7 305	5.1	40 135	1 153	4 785	781	369	720	1 277	1 561	6 655	411	369
Vermillion.......	557	0.0	35 496	1 857	215	40	16	48	74	151	318	20	16
Vigo...............	3 631	2.6	33 567	2 181	2 005	379	158	220	603	973	2 762	174	158
Wabash...........	1 290	3.5	40 011	1 173	456	86	35	183	201	325	760	47	35
Warren............	348	-3.9	41 703	980	74	13	6	64	43	68	157	8	6
Warrick...........	2 788	4.6	45 596	629	736	122	54	156	417	452	1 068	72	54
Washington......	930	4.7	33 352	2 219	214	41	17	97	109	239	369	23	17
Wayne............	2 355	3.5	34 801	1 968	1 162	211	90	143	337	692	1 606	105	90
Wells..............	1 093	2.6	39 244	1 290	475	79	34	133	174	216	720	44	34
White.............	916	-0.4	37 473	1 528	358	65	28	73	143	212	524	31	28
Whitley...........	1 239	2.4	37 099	1 585	491	91	37	39	179	246	658	43	37
IOWA	139 625	3.2	44 937	X	67 196	11 692	5 192	17 802	24 638	23 254	101 882	5 970	5 192
Adair..............	345	2.9	46 276	576	101	19	8	72	58	61	200	10	8
Adams............	236	1.1	60 829	119	46	10	3	101	33	39	160	8	3
Allamakee	584	2.5	41 568	1 003	171	38	14	124	104	115	347	19	14
Appanoose	452	4.5	35 713	1 820	156	32	13	56	74	123	256	17	13
Audubon..........	322	-3.6	55 516	205	63	13	5	100	57	52	180	8	5
Benton............	1 192	0.2	46 422	564	213	44	16	163	192	186	436	27	16
Black Hawk......	5 285	3.0	39 769	1 213	3 379	568	258	337	907	1 047	4 543	282	258
Boone.............	1 175	1.3	44 461	719	390	78	32	102	202	250	602	37	32
Bremer	1 096	2.1	44 316	731	407	77	31	97	200	179	611	37	31
Buchanan........	885	0.3	42 070	946	239	48	18	101	178	155	407	23	18
Buena Vista	1 023	3.1	49 724	396	384	78	29	335	151	141	826	40	29
Butler.............	704	-2.6	46 884	531	144	29	11	157	113	128	341	17	11
Calhoun..........	490	5.2	49 693	401	102	21	8	142	83	87	273	11	8
Carroll............	1 044	2.9	50 782	342	426	76	32	273	179	171	806	42	32
Cass...............	600	1.4	44 620	708	215	44	17	103	125	131	379	22	17
Cedar.............	849	0.5	46 138	587	201	37	16	107	162	124	360	22	16
Cerro Gordo.....	2 007	2.9	46 395	566	967	160	77	296	381	394	1 500	95	77
Cherokee	623	-2.3	52 647	278	188	37	14	214	100	100	452	24	14
Chickasaw.......	666	0.4	54 289	224	186	34	15	213	109	99	449	25	15
Clarke............	346	6.4	37 563	1 515	149	29	11	58	48	85	248	14	11
Clay...............	762	2.3	46 111	591	351	63	27	150	146	132	591	33	27
Clayton...........	795	-0.1	44 955	682	242	48	20	139	165	151	449	25	20
Clinton...........	1 884	-1.2	39 208	1 294	860	159	70	127	311	443	1 215	79	70
Crawford.........	730	-1.9	42 393	915	290	57	21	170	121	121	539	28	21
Dallas............	4 323	6.8	55 851	202	1 980	264	145	175	740	364	2 564	155	145
Davis..............	310	4.2	35 320	1 890	66	14	5	74	43	61	159	10	5
Decatur...........	273	5.2	33 039	2 273	74	17	6	40	41	68	137	8	6
Delaware.........	838	4.0	48 169	470	265	52	21	209	155	121	548	27	21
Des Moines......	1 963	4.4	48 755	448	915	156	77	448	312	380	1 596	101	77
Dickinson	857	3.1	50 606	352	325	63	27	102	233	148	517	33	27
Dubuque..........	4 160	4.1	43 167	828	2 439	388	191	327	822	720	3 345	212	191
Emmet............	417	0.3	41 714	978	151	30	12	75	63	87	268	15	12
Fayette...........	801	1.3	39 372	1 269	249	48	20	130	146	196	447	25	20
Floyd..............	677	2.5	42 131	939	218	45	17	112	125	151	392	22	17

1. Based on the resident population estimated as of July 1 of the year shown.

STATE County	Farm	Mining	Construction	Manu-facturing	Information: professional, scientific, technical services	Retail trade	Finance, insurance, real estate and leasing	Health care and social assistance	Govern-ment	Number	Rate[1]	Supple-mental Security Income recipients, December 2014	Total	Percent change, 2010–2014
	75	76	77	78	79	80	81	82	83	84	85	86	87	88
INDIANA—Cont'd														
Pike	9.1	20.3	12.0	4.2	D	2.4	D	3.7	10.2	3 160	250	256	5 753	0.3
Porter	0.3	D	9.6	25.4	5.3	6.4	3.8	12.7	9.5	32 385	194	1 923	67 383	1.8
Posey	7.9	0.7	5.4	40.4	D	8.2	2.3	D	7.7	5 635	221	355	11 358	1.3
Pulaski	17.6	D	3.5	28.3	D	5.1	3.6	D	18.0	3 195	246	247	6 039	-0.3
Putnam	6.9	0.6	3.8	22.2	D	5.4	3.0	6.9	17.6	7 525	200	434	14 857	1.0
Randolph	12.3	D	5.6	32.6	2.3	3.9	1.7	D	10.5	6 380	252	489	11 623	-1.0
Ripley	4.0	0.2	3.6	17.5	4.1	3.9	6.9	D	8.5	6 265	219	439	12 158	1.7
Rush	21.7	D	5.7	20.8	2.6	5.8	2.4	4.2	16.2	3 945	234	312	7 459	-0.7
St. Joseph	0.2	D	4.6	15.5	8.9	6.2	5.8	15.5	9.3	50 565	189	5 913	115 778	0.8
Scott	1.6	D	2.7	34.1	2.5	8.3	3.0	D	15.9	6 305	266	926	10 441	0.0
Shelby	6.0	0.4	6.1	31.6	2.5	5.0	2.1	D	12.9	9 335	210	689	19 106	0.2
Spencer	7.8	0.2	5.1	19.0	D	3.9	2.0	4.7	10.9	4 605	221	271	8 947	0.8
Starke	17.0	0.0	3.0	21.0	2.1	7.8	1.8	D	19.3	6 170	268	554	11 007	0.4
Steuben	2.4	0.0	4.3	37.4	3.3	7.7	2.4	D	9.3	7 910	230	447	19 571	1.0
Sullivan	5.7	D	2.9	10.5	3.6	5.8	2.1	3.5	23.4	4 740	226	386	8 846	-1.0
Switzerland	4.7	D	D	D	D	4.2	1.3	D	21.3	2 185	208	195	5 120	3.0
Tippecanoe	0.8	D	3.9	22.8	5.6	5.6	4.8	13.0	27.0	24 730	135	2 161	74 822	5.2
Tipton	11.9	D	9.5	23.3	4.9	9.2	2.8	D	13.4	3 760	244	152	6 956	-0.6
Union	12.4	0.0	6.3	15.3	0.0	7.1	D	D	23.3	1 775	246	127	3 218	-0.6
Vanderburgh	0.2	3.3	10.0	15.9	6.6	6.3	3.7	16.9	8.9	38 635	212	4 627	83 545	0.7
Vermillion	8.6	D	17.7	22.2	2.9	6.2	D	8.6	10.1	4 015	256	326	7 459	-0.4
Vigo	0.1	0.8	5.5	18.1	3.9	7.1	5.1	18.4	18.2	22 540	208	3 180	46 649	1.4
Wabash	10.2	D	5.9	31.0	D	6.5	3.6	D	12.7	8 495	263	597	14 084	-0.6
Warren	33.6	D	4.4	17.5	D	4.0	D	9.0	10.8	1 985	238	79	3 690	0.3
Warrick	1.2	4.1	8.0	21.2	5.4	5.4	4.7	21.8	10.5	12 460	203	654	25 191	4.1
Washington	19.4	D	5.4	23.4	3.2	7.4	3.4	8.5	15.8	6 575	236	658	12 187	-0.3
Wayne	2.3	0.1	3.0	21.7	D	8.5	4.2	19.5	14.0	17 120	254	2 137	31 152	-0.3
Wells	9.0	D	3.6	26.0	D	4.4	7.5	10.5	8.4	6 195	223	296	11 712	0.5
White	13.9	D	7.9	27.1	D	8.0	2.5	D	11.5	5 985	245	344	12 963	-0.1
Whitley	3.7	0.1	5.4	46.2	D	5.3	2.3	6.7	10.8	7 145	214	368	14 512	1.6
IOWA	7.2	0.2	6.8	16.8	6.2	6.0	9.2	9.7	15.4	616 301	198	51 227	1 369 359	2.5
Adair	27.1	D	8.4	13.4	1.6	5.5	4.1	D	12.0	1 905	257	111	3 671	-0.7
Adams	29.0	D	2.7	33.5	D	2.6	D	D	7.6	1 050	271	67	2 007	-0.1
Allamakee	20.4	0.2	7.5	16.7	2.0	6.2	3.4	6.9	15.5	3 545	252	185	7 667	0.7
Appanoose	8.4	D	5.3	20.1	2.9	8.3	2.8	11.1	14.4	3 425	271	440	6 567	-1.0
Audubon	43.4	0.0	5.2	5.6	D	4.0	D	D	12.4	1 605	277	77	2 995	0.8
Benton	14.2	D	9.5	15.6	2.8	7.7	3.9	D	19.2	5 380	210	293	11 085	-0.1
Black Hawk	0.7	D	4.8	27.1	4.8	6.3	6.4	12.4	15.3	26 120	196	3 231	57 069	2.1
Boone	10.3	D	7.8	5.6	D	5.9	D	8.4	24.5	5 720	217	337	11 806	0.4
Bremer	8.0	D	5.5	19.7	3.1	5.8	13.1	D	17.6	5 255	214	212	10 200	2.9
Buchanan	17.4	D	8.1	17.6	2.4	6.7	4.5	D	19.9	4 250	202	290	9 005	0.4
Buena Vista	22.7	0.0	3.1	20.3	D	4.4	2.9	D	11.6	3 500	169	266	8 293	0.7
Butler	35.3	D	6.9	15.7	2.2	4.1	3.0	4.9	11.5	3 740	250	172	6 737	0.8
Calhoun	44.2	0.0	4.5	1.6	1.4	4.2	3.0	D	13.2	2 575	261	141	5 088	-0.4
Carroll	20.1	D	5.3	14.5	2.9	6.2	7.2	D	8.0	4 755	231	272	9 427	0.5
Cass	15.9	D	7.8	10.6	D	7.0	4.2	7.9	21.3	3 700	276	345	6 562	-0.4
Cedar	13.9	0.0	8.3	10.0	6.2	5.7	2.6	D	15.0	3 910	213	154	8 124	0.8
Cerro Gordo	2.4	D	5.4	20.6	5.7	7.4	5.4	21.9	11.0	10 915	253	843	22 281	0.5
Cherokee	20.7	D	5.1	29.4	1.8	4.7	2.3	D	12.3	3 040	257	134	5 780	0.1
Chickasaw	14.4	D	7.0	39.2	1.4	4.4	2.7	D	7.7	2 885	237	133	5 660	-0.3
Clarke	15.8	D	2.4	27.8	1.5	6.4	2.3	6.0	17.1	2 055	223	136	4 129	1.1
Clay	14.5	D	5.2	10.1	D	11.8	3.9	9.8	16.7	3 980	241	240	8 117	0.7
Clayton	22.3	D	11.5	11.6	D	5.7	3.7	D	16.1	4 665	264	236	9 036	0.4
Clinton	1.8	D	5.4	28.5	3.3	7.4	4.5	13.9	11.5	11 045	230	1 182	21 836	0.5
Crawford	19.5	0.0	4.4	30.7	2.0	5.0	2.8	4.8	14.7	3 535	205	186	6 984	0.6
Dallas	2.1	D	4.6	4.4	4.5	6.9	44.0	7.7	8.1	10 275	133	428	31 144	14.2
Davis	13.7	D	10.4	8.6	11.4	6.3	3.0	D	19.1	1 785	204	127	3 576	-0.7
Decatur	20.2	D	5.9	2.4	D	4.6	D	D	20.8	1 820	220	191	3 845	0.3
Delaware	24.0	D	6.8	25.8	D	4.1	2.8	D	13.3	3 590	206	195	8 027	0.0
Des Moines	1.3	D	5.4	40.7	3.2	6.0	3.1	12.5	9.3	9 655	240	1 049	18 456	-0.4
Dickinson	4.6	D	9.3	24.1	3.8	9.3	5.7	6.8	12.8	4 895	289	203	13 300	3.5
Dubuque	2.2	D	5.7	19.9	8.4	6.6	8.7	14.1	8.2	20 045	208	1 576	40 588	4.2
Emmet	18.3	0.0	6.4	17.0	3.6	5.9	3.0	D	15.5	2 390	242	117	4 786	0.6
Fayette	24.1	D	5.3	6.5	2.3	5.9	3.0	D	13.5	5 075	249	506	9 538	-0.2
Floyd	18.9	0.0	7.8	22.5	2.7	5.5	5.3	D	13.5	4 110	256	322	7 523	0.0

1. Per 1,000 resident population estimated as of July 1 of the year shown.

Table B. States and Counties — Housing, Labor Force, and Employment

STATE County	Housing units, 2010–2014 — Occupied units — Owner-occupied					Renter-occupied		Sub-standard units⁴ (percent)	Civilian labor force, 2015		Unemployment		Civilian employment,⁶ 2010–2014 Percent		
	Total	Percent	Median value¹	Median owner cost as a percent of income — With a mortgage	Median owner cost as a percent of income — Without a mortgage²	Median rent³	Median rent as a percent of income²		Total	Percent change, 2014–2015	Total	Rate⁵	Total	Management, business, science and arts	Construction, production, and maintenance occupations
	89	90	91	92	93	94	95	96	97	98	99	100	101	102	103
INDIANA—Cont'd															
Pike	5 093	82.4	87 900	18.9	12.0	608	26.9	1.5	6 149	-3.2	269	4.4	5 747	22.1	45.6
Porter	61 693	77.4	165 000	19.9	10.7	858	28.3	1.8	84 161	0.1	4 524	5.4	77 588	34.9	26.3
Posey	10 178	83.1	129 000	18.7	10.5	656	28.5	2.3	13 326	1.3	526	3.9	12 227	30.7	32.4
Pulaski	5 134	77.4	92 300	21.2	11.4	657	27.3	0.8	6 293	1.6	283	4.5	5 686	25.9	40.1
Putnam	12 557	76.4	120 500	22.4	11.8	683	24.3	1.9	16 520	1.5	836	5.1	15 359	27.7	31.7
Randolph	10 514	73.9	77 300	20.3	11.3	606	27.6	1.6	12 697	1.6	629	5.0	11 376	26.5	36.9
Ripley	10 871	76.7	132 000	20.3	11.8	678	24.0	1.9	13 541	-0.8	728	5.4	12 967	28.1	33.6
Rush	6 920	71.1	102 800	20.0	11.1	624	25.7	0.5	8 855	3.8	385	4.3	7 764	29.4	37.0
St. Joseph	101 759	68.4	113 400	19.9	10.0	723	30.0	1.5	130 912	1.6	6 538	5.0	122 074	33.9	22.7
Scott	8 973	71.7	98 900	22.8	12.1	711	29.1	1.3	10 344	1.5	554	5.4	9 523	22.6	38.3
Shelby	17 315	71.2	122 600	20.6	11.5	718	27.0	2.3	22 820	1.7	1 003	4.4	21 105	26.0	37.0
Spencer	7 917	81.6	112 700	19.6	10.7	588	24.2	1.8	10 997	2.3	455	4.1	9 871	26.3	36.6
Starke	9 009	80.2	96 400	24.1	11.3	672	24.9	2.1	10 526	2.8	626	5.9	9 330	25.2	37.1
Steuben	13 409	77.7	124 300	21.7	11.0	650	27.2	1.6	20 007	0.9	782	3.9	16 115	26.7	32.9
Sullivan	7 720	73.5	78 000	18.3	11.2	659	34.0	3.8	8 688	0.4	538	6.2	8 056	25.8	35.6
Switzerland	4 065	72.4	116 200	26.1	13.9	768	27.7	4.2	4 830	0.5	238	4.9	4 419	15.9	38.3
Tippecanoe	66 921	53.7	132 100	19.5	10.0	800	35.2	2.4	92 613	1.4	3 880	4.2	84 136	38.7	21.7
Tipton	6 479	77.2	107 900	19.0	10.6	668	27.8	0.8	8 386	2.6	335	4.0	7 267	28.7	32.6
Union	2 949	75.5	105 700	22.8	11.3	640	31.7	1.2	3 603	1.6	160	4.4	3 499	29.5	23.5
Vanderburgh	74 365	63.4	114 700	21.1	11.6	723	30.5	2.4	92 371	0.3	3 921	4.2	85 907	30.2	24.8
Vermillion	6 491	79.0	75 300	19.7	11.8	545	23.8	2.1	7 211	-0.2	511	7.1	6 834	22.2	35.2
Vigo	39 769	62.2	91 200	19.0	11.5	683	31.9	2.2	49 008	-1.0	2 996	6.1	47 262	32.0	24.7
Wabash	12 777	75.8	95 100	19.4	10.0	636	29.9	2.0	15 448	-0.2	736	4.8	14 786	28.0	31.7
Warren	3 325	78.0	106 200	17.6	10.2	711	23.5	2.5	4 113	0.4	202	4.9	3 997	27.9	38.9
Warrick	22 675	83.4	144 400	20.7	10.9	796	31.0	1.8	31 398	0.6	1 273	4.1	29 521	34.9	23.9
Washington	10 512	78.9	101 100	22.9	10.8	629	28.3	2.0	13 645	2.4	701	5.1	11 872	24.5	40.2
Wayne	27 891	67.2	92 200	21.6	12.0	632	31.7	2.0	30 684	-0.8	1 629	5.3	28 004	30.2	27.3
Wells	10 952	79.4	114 000	18.7	10.0	596	29.4	1.8	14 140	2.7	550	3.9	13 327	26.3	33.0
White	9 458	76.7	106 400	18.6	11.1	689	27.3	2.1	13 613	1.1	553	4.1	11 367	24.1	35.2
Whitley	13 091	81.4	129 600	21.4	10.0	615	26.7	1.5	17 207	2.1	699	4.1	16 247	26.1	37.2
IOWA	1 232 228	71.8	126 300	20.0	11.5	689	27.7	1.8	1 701 327	0.2	62 460	3.7	1 562 492	34.3	25.5
Adair	3 252	76.3	88 900	21.7	11.5	552	21.7	1.9	4 266	2.8	135	3.2	3 932	25.6	35.3
Adams	1 735	75.5	86 600	20.7	12.9	525	20.0	1.3	2 300	4.0	63	2.7	2 023	35.2	32.1
Allamakee	5 899	77.5	111 100	20.0	12.9	544	23.0	2.4	7 727	0.3	373	4.8	7 028	30.8	33.5
Appanoose	5 447	72.5	77 600	18.7	13.1	554	27.3	2.0	6 255	1.8	301	4.8	5 689	30.2	34.9
Audubon	2 703	82.5	69 800	18.9	10.7	561	20.4	0.4	3 251	-0.2	126	3.9	3 035	34.2	27.0
Benton	10 137	80.7	137 100	20.5	11.3	604	24.9	1.1	13 868	0.1	527	3.8	13 098	31.7	29.2
Black Hawk	52 438	67.3	125 700	19.5	10.9	694	31.8	1.8	70 499	-2.3	3 168	4.5	66 181	31.1	25.9
Boone	10 619	75.7	119 800	20.8	12.5	642	26.9	2.5	15 361	1.1	453	2.9	13 299	32.4	28.0
Bremer	9 296	80.7	146 000	19.4	10.1	601	24.3	0.8	14 029	-1.0	484	3.4	12 630	35.9	25.0
Buchanan	8 298	79.1	123 600	19.9	10.8	633	23.6	3.0	11 302	-1.4	473	4.2	10 371	30.3	33.9
Buena Vista	7 635	70.2	100 300	20.6	10.0	581	23.6	6.0	11 630	1.3	415	3.6	10 511	26.3	38.2
Butler	6 222	79.7	104 000	18.2	11.4	581	20.3	1.2	8 304	-0.9	357	4.3	7 333	28.7	32.6
Calhoun	4 310	77.9	74 600	18.4	10.1	507	26.3	0.5	4 469	1.2	190	4.3	4 618	32.6	26.2
Carroll	8 557	75.5	110 100	18.7	10.0	541	29.7	0.7	11 300	0.7	291	2.6	10 945	28.0	29.4
Cass	6 074	70.7	88 900	20.2	11.5	566	24.4	0.9	7 467	1.2	266	3.6	6 706	29.3	29.5
Cedar	7 639	79.3	134 200	20.3	12.2	697	24.4	1.4	11 001	0.7	371	3.4	9 824	32.1	28.7
Cerro Gordo	19 864	71.7	112 400	19.9	12.3	610	26.5	1.0	23 063	-0.7	896	3.9	22 647	29.5	27.7
Cherokee	5 384	74.6	81 500	17.3	10.0	507	19.6	0.9	6 395	-3.5	325	5.1	6 223	29.9	32.5
Chickasaw	5 330	78.9	99 000	18.9	10.8	519	26.8	1.1	6 498	0.3	288	4.4	6 005	28.2	36.5
Clarke	3 686	69.5	86 500	20.9	15.4	657	31.9	2.1	4 766	1.9	191	4.0	4 367	25.6	32.9
Clay	7 269	73.9	106 400	19.0	11.4	568	24.5	2.0	8 803	-1.5	315	3.6	8 511	29.0	31.3
Clayton	7 698	78.9	104 900	21.8	12.3	558	24.9	2.1	10 325	1.4	419	4.1	9 089	27.9	32.9
Clinton	19 977	74.1	110 100	19.6	12.8	610	28.0	1.2	24 498	-1.0	1 201	4.9	23 619	27.8	30.9
Crawford	6 371	75.7	87 300	18.7	10.0	500	24.4	3.5	8 841	1.3	360	4.1	8 217	24.8	39.4
Dallas	26 819	76.2	184 400	20.0	11.3	905	25.1	1.6	42 930	0.5	1 206	2.8	39 094	47.2	15.3
Davis	3 085	78.0	98 700	22.7	11.0	582	28.0	4.9	4 173	1.6	183	4.4	3 763	29.3	34.9
Decatur	3 085	67.0	81 700	22.1	14.5	482	28.0	4.1	4 444	0.1	143	3.2	3 622	35.1	26.0
Delaware	7 115	79.0	123 000	21.7	10.0	558	26.2	0.6	10 737	2.0	355	3.3	9 489	26.4	37.3
Des Moines	16 881	72.7	94 300	21.8	13.4	638	28.7	1.7	20 855	0.1	953	4.6	18 306	28.5	29.6
Dickinson	7 831	74.4	165 800	22.3	10.1	641	25.3	0.9	10 220	5.3	388	3.8	8 812	32.9	28.7
Dubuque	37 720	72.6	146 500	20.2	11.6	690	30.3	1.3	55 729	0.3	1 997	3.6	49 877	33.2	24.0
Emmet	4 150	78.4	82 400	18.3	10.6	603	24.8	0.8	5 715	-0.3	209	3.7	5 118	24.6	37.1
Fayette	8 470	76.2	85 000	19.4	12.2	537	25.9	1.2	10 831	0.4	483	4.5	10 024	32.5	32.5
Floyd	6 923	71.6	96 700	19.0	10.8	551	26.6	1.7	8 745	4.0	324	3.7	8 037	31.3	31.4

1. Specified owner-occupied units. 2. A value of 10.0 represents 10 percent or less; a value of 50.0 represents 50 percent or more. 3. Specified renter-occupied units.
4. Overcrowded or lacking complete plumbing facilities. 5. Percent of civilian labor force. 6. Persons 16 years old and over.

Table B. States and Counties — Nonfarm Employment and Agriculture

| | Private nonfarm establishments, employment and payroll, 2014 | | | | | | | | Agriculture, 2012 | | | |
| | Employment | | | | | | Annual payroll | | Farms | | | |
STATE County	Number of establishments	Total	Health care and social assistance	Manufacturing	Retail trade	Finance and insurance	Professional, scientific, and technical services	Total (mil dol)	Average per employee (dollars)	Number	Percent with: Fewer than 50 acres	Percent with: 500 acres or more	Farm operators whose principal occupation is farming (percent)
	104	105	106	107	108	109	110	111	112	113	114	115	116
INDIANA—Cont'd													
Pike	193	2 376	281	D	274	D	24	116	48 923	321	34.0	11.2	32.1
Porter	3 476	51 981	8 111	9 834	7 383	1 094	1 851	2 254	43 360	481	53.4	15.2	48.0
Posey	480	8 296	426	2 722	682	105	314	465	56 068	408	31.6	31.6	60.5
Pulaski	318	3 449	559	1 206	436	D	57	128	37 071	536	38.6	20.7	46.6
Putnam	691	10 900	1 589	2 342	1 265	258	189	335	30 701	847	49.6	11.9	41.0
Randolph	499	6 325	714	D	571	D	107	221	34 922	772	40.7	18.3	52.7
Ripley	636	10 085	1 208	2 281	825	247	D	464	46 048	876	41.3	10.0	43.8
Rush	363	3 742	519	D	375	94	130	125	33 360	601	32.6	20.6	54.2
St. Joseph	5 740	116 701	19 035	14 645	15 072	3 840	4 915	4 405	37 750	691	54.7	11.7	45.0
Scott	407	5 839	948	1 779	839	102	162	188	32 264	321	51.4	5.9	35.5
Shelby	918	14 780	D	5 040	1 489	198	232	609	41 196	569	39.4	24.4	56.8
Spencer	402	5 258	290	1 307	1 019	145	D	201	38 160	597	32.8	15.1	38.5
Starke	301	2 699	289	779	606	65	D	80	29 738	511	50.7	13.3	33.9
Steuben	951	14 163	1 378	4 731	2 142	221	185	443	31 276	562	39.0	8.5	38.3
Sullivan	343	4 421	D	523	525	D	108	194	43 988	433	32.3	23.8	55.2
Switzerland	127	1 722	160	66	157	D	13	47	27 535	383	41.0	3.1	39.9
Tippecanoe	3 415	63 735	9 595	14 608	9 018	2 693	2 413	2 521	39 549	702	56.7	15.2	39.3
Tipton	306	3 110	D	618	484	D	89	117	37 726	377	35.3	23.3	53.8
Union	108	899	D	316	204	26	30	26	28 788	242	31.0	19.8	49.6
Vanderburgh	4 938	101 712	19 507	10 897	12 785	4 564	3 751	4 093	40 239	275	46.5	16.4	42.5
Vermillion	265	3 119	514	D	582	58	44	158	50 552	270	37.8	23.7	48.1
Vigo	2 487	45 722	9 014	8 508	6 728	1 174	1 104	1 619	35 405	450	56.2	14.2	44.7
Wabash	741	10 835	2 086	2 908	1 232	290	D	359	33 119	745	44.8	13.4	44.4
Warren	117	1 401	D	528	112	34	D	49	34 946	413	43.1	22.0	46.2
Warrick	1 116	13 640	3 313	D	1 591	539	404	581	42 589	379	47.8	16.1	44.9
Washington	437	4 546	797	1 534	700	125	D	136	29 896	831	40.7	9.7	49.8
Wayne	1 501	25 090	4 958	5 398	3 783	815	447	904	36 031	805	41.5	8.9	44.7
Wells	632	10 268	1 676	2 894	993	182	201	353	34 405	636	40.1	17.5	49.2
White	601	6 879	701	2 517	1 137	191	113	243	35 274	631	39.9	25.0	53.2
Whitley	680	10 508	1 020	4 513	1 408	229	199	402	38 250	710	51.7	8.5	34.4
IOWA	80 466	1 316 447	216 134	209 256	180 421	90 882	51 433	52 563	39 928	88 637	30.9	22.4	54.1
Adair	186	1 749	347	D	D	77	63	56	31 768	726	25.5	28.5	55.2
Adams	112	924	D	D	92	37	D	32	34 826	467	24.4	27.4	53.3
Allamakee	394	4 206	919	1 194	554	180	D	127	30 299	1 011	25.4	17.5	41.5
Appanoose	308	3 754	737	1 094	675	106	58	113	30 056	744	30.1	13.4	46.1
Audubon	185	1 164	299	193	177	54	24	37	31 602	622	33.1	28.1	61.1
Benton	564	4 477	801	660	766	192	D	151	33 665	1 215	30.1	24.1	54.3
Black Hawk	3 209	69 526	14 718	13 991	8 861	2 514	3 726	2 580	37 110	924	33.0	21.4	55.6
Boone	560	6 835	D	D	1 035	188	148	237	34 674	938	42.6	19.9	49.7
Bremer	603	9 090	1 864	1 672	1 198	897	198	358	39 433	982	34.7	16.6	49.1
Buchanan	482	5 376	1 356	1 020	864	222	D	186	34 533	1 075	30.6	19.7	57.6
Buena Vista	549	9 103	1 372	3 369	1 166	484	194	314	34 489	858	27.9	32.5	65.3
Butler	327	2 623	493	833	356	D	66	96	36 780	1 096	37.2	19.9	51.3
Calhoun	279	2 134	670	D	323	107	46	65	30 227	826	29.5	31.1	52.7
Carroll	877	9 626	2 183	1 279	1 553	768	191	318	33 009	1 065	29.1	21.6	57.0
Cass	478	4 814	1 220	D	912	208	115	152	31 581	703	25.3	29.2	50.2
Cedar	474	4 349	622	572	641	151	D	135	31 062	955	37.6	21.3	51.8
Cerro Gordo	1 388	21 100	5 300	2 742	3 655	1 065	580	791	37 478	780	35.1	27.4	59.0
Cherokee	346	4 209	929	838	630	176	D	133	31 504	805	22.0	28.6	64.0
Chickasaw	417	3 967	604	1 335	439	161	59	145	36 600	1 036	34.0	18.8	55.5
Clarke	188	3 168	611	D	547	86	32	97	30 721	627	27.1	15.3	35.9
Clay	610	7 365	1 552	787	1 441	266	167	251	34 139	720	26.1	32.1	57.6
Clayton	528	4 944	1 153	866	668	180	87	166	33 512	1 577	29.2	13.9	50.3
Clinton	1 139	27 126	3 613	4 303	2 671	676	305	927	34 182	1 244	30.9	23.4	63.1
Crawford	444	5 803	1 000	1 895	832	212	95	217	37 384	900	26.6	30.6	61.7
Dallas	1 762	35 151	3 647	1 820	5 849	1 502	1 684	47 896	1 001	43.6	17.5	43.7
Davis	172	1 439	397	146	268	60	49	45	31 098	917	28.9	10.9	44.1
Decatur	137	1 741	320	D	198	36	D	38	21 633	711	27.3	18.3	44.6
Delaware	490	5 727	1 123	1 846	658	269	113	213	37 119	1 382	29.7	16.2	60.2
Des Moines	1 102	19 774	3 623	4 643	3 128	514	352	739	37 366	663	37.4	17.3	46.5
Dickinson	769	7 085	963	1 661	1 095	240	148	263	37 107	441	29.5	32.0	58.0
Dubuque	2 779	53 990	7 804	9 073	7 241	3 527	2 856	2 129	39 439	1 462	28.3	10.3	52.5
Emmet	318	3 329	727	911	503	128	85	108	32 381	475	25.9	37.3	64.0
Fayette	554	6 308	1 306	644	866	D	D	181	28 688	1 286	30.4	18.2	56.2
Floyd	402	4 505	974	D	747	192	D	169	37 473	944	35.1	22.9	51.8

Table B. States and Counties — **Agriculture**

STATE County	\[Land in farms\] Acreage (1,000)	Percent change, 2007–2012	Acres Average size of farm	Total irrigated (1,000)	Total cropland (1,000)	Value of land and buildings (dollars) Average per farm	Average per acre	Value of machinery and equipment, average per farm (dollars)	Value of products sold Total (mil dol)	Average per farm (dollars)	Percent from: Crops	Live-stock and poultry products	Percent of farms with sales of: $10,000 or more	$100,000 or more	Government payments Total ($1,000)	Percent of farms
	117	118	119	120	121	122	123	124	125	126	127	128	129	130	131	132
INDIANA—Cont'd																
Pike	80	8.7	249	D	65.0	1 064 710	4 271	115 533	50.8	158 343	57.1	42.9	39.6	20.9	1 395	71.3
Porter	121	4.8	251	10.0	109.4	1 502 112	5 993	176 526	106.8	222 133	93.2	6.8	48.6	31.0	2 268	55.5
Posey	229	12.1	561	16.4	215.7	2 689 417	4 797	375 517	139.7	342 500	87.5	12.5	69.4	44.4	3 332	75.2
Pulaski	217	-6.8	404	18.5	197.1	2 080 849	5 152	192 328	185.3	345 784	67.9	32.1	53.9	34.9	4 080	79.7
Putnam	198	17.3	233	0.1	156.0	979 574	4 198	116 544	76.1	89 791	80.9	19.1	33.6	14.0	3 467	50.6
Randolph	241	4.0	312	0.2	216.6	1 588 816	5 088	181 580	227.0	294 035	56.6	43.4	60.4	34.7	4 656	66.8
Ripley	167	4.8	190	0.1	124.1	776 272	4 079	98 368	94.0	107 283	80.6	19.4	47.7	20.2	2 604	66.4
Rush	208	-4.3	345	0.5	188.7	2 103 171	6 089	216 255	162.5	270 401	60.6	39.4	68.1	42.1	4 158	67.1
St. Joseph	152	-14.9	220	27.6	136.3	1 350 298	6 140	142 120	123.5	178 734	86.6	13.4	48.3	24.6	2 468	54.7
Scott	51	-17.0	160	D	38.4	575 841	3 591	96 140	24.0	74 903	97.3	2.7	25.5	9.0	877	45.5
Shelby	233	13.4	410	4.3	220.6	2 508 759	6 125	238 496	128.9	226 522	86.5	13.5	65.7	38.7	4 519	63.4
Spencer	170	13.4	285	0.2	132.5	1 104 744	3 870	158 107	91.9	153 982	65.6	34.4	52.8	22.9	2 593	66.3
Starke	133	-13.1	261	25.6	115.4	1 144 699	4 383	156 188	69.8	136 528	95.0	5.0	32.9	19.0	3 463	82.0
Steuben	105	-1.7	186	2.1	84.6	834 635	4 486	109 486	61.8	109 888	65.9	34.1	36.7	14.6	1 868	72.6
Sullivan	170	-4.0	393	6.0	150.0	1 642 543	4 178	216 111	91.5	211 358	79.0	21.0	56.4	31.2	2 788	71.6
Switzerland	51	6.4	132	0.1	25.9	465 300	3 528	56 084	12.3	32 180	D	D	28.2	5.2	940	50.7
Tippecanoe	220	0.9	314	4.3	201.7	2 111 205	6 731	195 491	150.6	214 583	88.0	12.0	43.2	24.2	4 159	53.1
Tipton	145	-12.5	385	1.2	138.7	2 812 836	7 304	249 233	159.9	424 141	82.5	17.5	74.5	46.9	2 774	80.9
Union	74	1.7	308	D	63.9	1 525 157	4 955	172 099	41.7	172 190	88.3	11.7	61.6	33.1	1 200	69.4
Vanderburgh	77	6.4	278	D	70.6	1 177 945	4 231	157 189	36.1	131 247	90.2	9.8	52.4	28.4	1 078	64.0
Vermillion	118	-10.5	438	D	100.3	2 083 200	4 751	218 111	62.2	230 389	74.1	25.9	45.6	28.9	2 502	67.8
Vigo	114	-3.2	261	1.1	101.3	1 012 440	3 876	123 420	47.4	105 222	97.7	2.3	40.2	17.8	1 437	55.1
Wabash	198	-1.5	265	2.1	172.9	1 370 395	5 167	177 270	227.2	305 032	51.3	48.7	52.5	29.9	4 325	67.8
Warren	176	-10.2	426	2.1	156.5	2 509 559	5 890	222 634	111.7	270 574	94.8	5.2	43.3	29.3	3 349	66.3
Warrick	100	-9.4	263	D	88.6	1 276 810	4 856	164 979	39.7	104 873	93.1	6.9	37.7	22.4	2 192	63.6
Washington	200	-0.2	240	0.1	142.8	797 445	3 321	105 395	129.2	155 489	43.2	56.8	40.7	17.1	3 448	42.5
Wayne	156	-5.0	194	0.7	124.6	1 002 708	5 177	111 768	91.9	114 170	73.6	26.4	49.6	23.7	3 828	59.6
Wells	200	2.9	315	0.0	189.0	1 993 800	6 330	195 305	210.2	330 434	67.1	32.9	64.6	39.5	3 322	73.6
White	288	-9.4	457	4.2	267.7	3 122 778	6 837	265 100	297.4	471 342	57.0	43.0	59.1	40.1	4 960	71.2
Whitley	140	2.2	197	2.2	120.3	1 013 832	5 138	132 938	100.2	141 182	75.9	24.1	48.6	21.3	2 465	60.7
IOWA	30 623	-0.4	345	171.7	26 256.3	2 207 220	6 389	213 849	30 821.5	347 728	56.3	43.7	62.8	41.0	782 290	78.4
Adair	324	3.8	446	0.0	251.5	2 085 185	4 679	214 081	188.2	259 185	65.6	34.4	64.0	38.0	5 695	76.0
Adams	229	1.9	491	D	165.9	2 107 058	4 292	208 206	120.3	257 557	64.8	35.2	61.2	36.2	4 107	79.4
Allamakee	289	5.2	286	0.0	185.8	1 217 119	4 255	144 265	220.6	218 199	41.4	58.6	51.8	29.8	7 526	82.7
Appanoose	188	-5.1	252	D	111.8	749 059	2 969	84 641	38.4	51 620	55.5	44.5	43.5	10.2	3 704	82.0
Audubon	280	0.5	451	0.0	251.9	3 003 379	6 663	236 170	287.9	462 814	48.9	51.1	62.7	43.4	7 006	82.0
Benton	422	5.3	347	0.1	381.8	2 508 267	7 219	235 523	381.4	313 927	72.2	27.8	67.1	47.0	10 826	78.0
Black Hawk	297	5.2	321	0.1	273.8	2 559 448	7 969	245 895	287.2	310 850	65.4	34.6	68.2	44.2	7 606	81.4
Boone	313	-5.6	334	0.1	283.3	2 520 885	7 546	180 946	301.8	321 707	74.9	25.1	54.6	34.2	6 378	75.8
Bremer	272	11.7	276	0.7	242.5	2 132 518	7 713	222 672	271.7	276 729	63.2	36.8	62.9	41.1	7 929	81.6
Buchanan	342	-5.1	318	0.0	318.5	2 331 990	7 332	246 866	390.7	363 461	63.2	36.8	71.5	47.6	10 788	71.9
Buena Vista	361	-0.5	421	0.7	334.0	3 070 632	7 301	290 162	577.1	672 564	44.5	55.5	73.5	60.1	8 715	83.4
Butler	363	-3.5	331	0.4	330.9	2 260 181	6 829	206 931	358.2	326 838	55.1	44.9	59.7	38.0	9 333	81.2
Calhoun	358	-0.3	434	0.3	337.4	3 332 812	7 685	276 166	366.3	443 500	57.8	42.2	68.3	51.9	7 928	88.7
Carroll	359	0.2	337	D	328.1	2 535 277	7 524	243 800	540.6	507 578	35.6	64.4	75.6	53.0	8 377	81.3
Cass	290	-8.8	412	0.3	240.7	2 253 533	5 464	220 265	228.3	324 761	57.7	42.3	63.4	41.8	5 974	78.1
Cedar	312	-7.3	327	0.4	275.6	2 346 182	7 171	250 577	315.9	330 800	69.4	30.6	58.2	42.2	8 363	75.2
Cerro Gordo	327	-2.9	419	D	306.3	2 778 794	6 631	282 482	245.0	314 089	80.4	19.6	60.1	42.3	8 384	82.3
Cherokee	337	7.1	419	0.0	290.4	3 110 383	7 422	272 880	407.5	506 183	56.5	43.5	84.8	65.0	6 226	82.7
Chickasaw	299	3.5	289	0.3	271.3	2 067 023	7 158	208 558	336.2	324 558	52.2	47.8	64.0	41.3	11 550	82.2
Clarke	169	-11.4	269	0.0	98.9	910 281	3 378	87 847	93.4	148 973	29.5	70.5	43.7	15.3	4 294	67.3
Clay	319	-2.9	443	0.3	292.5	3 269 768	7 385	292 085	403.5	560 428	58.5	41.5	71.5	54.6	7 683	83.6
Clayton	398	-2.7	252	0.2	291.7	1 207 906	4 786	149 960	402.6	255 286	47.8	52.2	54.4	32.4	15 965	80.9
Clinton	417	5.5	335	0.0	372.1	2 381 902	7 103	228 046	381.3	306 518	70.4	29.6	68.2	46.8	10 432	78.9
Crawford	451	4.3	501	1.0	404.7	3 465 877	6 918	324 907	417.6	463 991	63.3	36.7	74.3	49.4	7 985	77.0
Dallas	306	3.1	306	0.4	270.7	2 059 497	6 728	168 490	237.2	236 924	73.6	26.4	51.0	29.8	6 668	65.7
Davis	214	-2.1	233	0.1	135.2	686 799	2 943	94 828	90.8	99 061	32.3	67.7	49.8	15.2	4 670	59.2
Decatur	232	1.3	326	D	127.0	972 918	2 988	121 181	92.4	130 018	34.7	65.3	47.5	19.3	5 905	66.4
Delaware	366	9.5	265	0.1	321.2	1 906 151	7 206	228 110	495.1	358 221	41.9	58.1	70.2	49.6	14 190	85.2
Des Moines	173	-6.6	260	3.1	137.6	1 451 878	5 574	166 958	118.7	179 054	82.3	17.7	54.1	30.6	4 631	82.8
Dickinson	187	-17.2	425	0.9	173.6	2 999 796	7 061	278 673	192.3	435 941	67.6	32.4	67.1	52.6	3 868	80.7
Dubuque	291	-6.2	199	0.0	224.3	1 214 544	6 093	172 274	387.8	265 260	31.0	69.0	67.5	39.7	11 080	81.2
Emmet	219	-12.3	461	0.4	201.9	3 356 078	7 280	322 318	292.2	615 097	53.7	46.3	71.8	57.3	4 456	82.3
Fayette	388	-6.9	302	0.3	333.3	2 077 995	6 879	214 755	432.2	336 045	54.0	46.0	61.5	44.3	13 738	87.1
Floyd	318	6.4	337	2.1	291.1	2 154 441	6 401	225 738	280.4	297 050	65.8	34.2	58.3	41.2	8 273	80.8

Water Use, Wholesale Trade, Retail Trade, and Real Estate

STATE County	Water use, 2010		Wholesale trade,[1] 2012				Retail trade,[2] 2012				Real estate and rental and leasing,[2] 2012			
	Total water withdrawn (mil gal/day)	Gallons withdrawn per person per day	Number of establish-ments	Number of employees	Sales (mil dol)	Annual payroll (mil dol)	Number of establish-ments	Number of employees	Sales (mil dol)	Annual payroll (mil dol)	Number of establish-ments	Number of employees	Receipts (mil dol)	Annual payroll (mil dol)
	133	134	135	136	137	138	139	140	141	142	143	144	145	146
INDIANA—Cont'd														
Pike	595.1	46 329	7	D	D	D	31	266	72.5	4.8	6	D	D	D
Porter	599.5	3 648	147	1 860	1 574.9	94.2	449	6 931	2 035.4	159.7	150	648	101.3	19.6
Posey	18.9	731	22	329	506.8	15.8	67	692	307.6	18.3	10	27	3.2	0.6
Pulaski	9.2	687	25	272	480.8	10.8	60	438	134.3	9.4	5	7	0.8	0.1
Putnam	8.7	228	16	141	48.5	6.3	106	1 211	349.0	25.4	24	69	7.4	1.5
Randolph	5.1	193	15	161	127.5	6.4	71	600	443.4	12.9	10	26	2.1	0.4
Ripley	3.3	116	17	D	D	D	102	844	222.9	19.9	19	D	D	D
Rush	2.8	163	23	516	527.1	32.5	49	420	108.1	9.0	12	15	2.6	0.3
St. Joseph	45.6	171	307	4 366	3 131.0	213.3	911	14 702	3 775.3	343.9	218	1 233	205.3	41.5
Scott	3.6	147	10	D	D	D	79	828	240.2	18.1	19	41	6.3	1.0
Shelby	9.3	210	37	676	370.9	25.8	118	1 392	502.4	37.0	41	126	18.5	3.6
Spencer	33.5	1 600	17	D	D	D	66	708	130.1	19.2	12	22	1.5	0.2
Starke	6.1	262	14	83	95.9	3.6	59	625	170.7	14.8	13	24	2.5	0.4
Steuben	4.9	144	37	279	185.1	10.7	185	2 028	613.8	41.1	44	102	16.9	3.0
Sullivan	423.9	19 741	18	162	164.4	6.9	54	553	138.2	11.7	8	16	1.2	0.4
Switzerland	2.2	209	3	7	2.3	0.4	15	108	20.2	1.6	2	D	D	D
Tippecanoe	33.9	196	109	1 275	751.1	54.5	529	8 815	2 225.7	189.2	167	852	142.9	28.6
Tipton	1.9	116	13	126	108.6	5.7	57	499	180.6	12.8	9	17	1.1	0.3
Union	0.7	96	4	D	D	D	21	191	32.9	3.4	1	D	D	D
Vanderburgh	31.3	174	259	4 815	2 679.5	295.9	791	12 637	3 141.7	290.9	208	1 500	247.1	45.5
Vermillion	623.2	38 441	13	D	D	D	52	591	194.1	12.8	4	6	0.7	0.2
Vigo	334.3	3 100	91	1 163	506.6	48.6	445	6 676	1 588.3	137.4	89	524	86.4	17.7
Wabash	7.0	212	31	275	348.5	12.0	130	1 332	324.5	29.8	15	95	8.9	2.7
Warren	1.5	181	9	146	206.2	6.7	14	86	22.1	1.5	2	D	D	D
Warrick	761.3	12 754	40	D	D	D	126	1 630	391.1	33.7	27	152	23.5	3.4
Washington	4.7	166	12	36	9.2	1.2	79	691	215.4	14.6	9	29	3.3	0.6
Wayne	11.1	160	55	678	868.2	27.3	267	3 664	950.8	80.7	53	190	37.5	5.9
Wells	7.2	259	26	D	D	D	84	982	231.5	21.6	23	66	6.8	1.5
White	5.9	239	34	324	339.4	16.7	97	1 099	302.9	25.5	17	53	5.9	0.9
Whitley	4.4	132	24	D	D	D	108	1 415	343.4	31.4	23	76	16.8	2.5
IOWA	3 070.5	1 008	4 302	58 872	62 318.3	2 841.8	12 046	174 556	44 905.6	3 865.3	2 742	12 031	2 268.3	425.9
Adair	2.3	301	10	132	183.2	5.2	30	252	63.0	4.3	5	D	D	D
Adams	1.8	454	5	46	36.3	1.5	19	101	21.3	2.1	2	D	D	D
Allamakee	123.3	8 602	33	443	275.9	16.0	59	563	144.6	11.2	13	36	2.5	0.5
Appanoose	11.1	864	9	64	40.4	1.9	58	636	138.8	13.0	8	D	D	D
Audubon	2.1	346	16	125	203.5	5.1	18	186	40.3	2.9	1	D	D	D
Benton	3.3	126	30	319	295.3	11.4	87	744	197.2	15.7	11	D	D	D
Black Hawk	37.0	282	151	2 687	1 980.4	126.8	509	8 793	2 110.5	191.0	138	617	118.1	17.5
Boone	3.6	136	23	D	D	D	69	978	217.2	22.9	15	26	2.3	0.6
Bremer	3.9	162	27	283	299.5	14.3	86	1 246	361.8	27.1	18	D	D	D
Buchanan	4.3	207	29	329	337.0	15.6	79	901	247.4	19.5	11	D	D	D
Buena Vista	8.2	402	25	256	514.6	12.7	94	1 149	281.0	24.8	18	71	8.9	2.6
Butler	5.9	397	29	225	407.7	8.6	58	372	104.9	7.0	7	4	1.0	0.1
Calhoun	2.9	295	20	235	353.0	11.6	48	340	127.0	8.3	4	23	3.1	0.9
Carroll	6.8	326	55	1 543	1 888.5	69.9	144	1 596	360.0	36.7	20	121	25.2	4.6
Cass	3.0	212	24	207	260.4	9.1	75	875	195.9	18.0	14	55	10.9	2.3
Cedar	4.8	261	28	384	387.3	15.0	59	611	208.1	12.2	13	18	2.7	0.4
Cerro Gordo	9.9	224	83	932	1 320.8	45.1	226	3 784	956.5	81.2	60	146	27.0	4.1
Cherokee	6.6	544	19	137	201.0	5.8	59	658	145.6	13.3	4	D	D	D
Chickasaw	4.0	318	33	292	469.7	14.8	51	437	116.9	9.3	5	9	1.2	0.2
Clarke	2.2	235	4	29	30.9	1.2	36	560	151.1	10.8	6	7	0.6	0.1
Clay	4.2	254	49	D	D	D	111	1 460	313.0	34.6	25	98	16.8	2.9
Clayton	6.5	360	26	310	917.2	15.2	82	654	211.6	13.4	9	16	2.8	0.5
Clinton	106.9	2 176	47	391	396.2	18.0	193	2 708	652.1	56.4	35	119	22.5	3.6
Crawford	7.0	408	19	208	318.8	10.4	72	853	184.4	15.8	7	8	1.1	0.2
Dallas	5.3	80	52	501	412.8	28.7	256	5 292	1 270.5	105.0	68	519	111.8	35.0
Davis	1.6	184	6	51	31.3	1.5	31	274	62.2	5.3	3	D	D	D
Decatur	1.6	184	7	82	34.8	1.6	24	210	35.6	3.1	4	6	0.7	0.1
Delaware	8.4	472	29	327	360.6	14.0	62	674	188.1	15.0	9	21	3.9	0.6
Des Moines	77.3	1 916	48	621	1 096.2	27.7	203	3 064	684.2	66.2	37	654	117.8	25.6
Dickinson	7.3	440	20	D	D	D	111	1 083	292.9	26.0	44	87	15.0	2.2
Dubuque	40.5	432	158	2 353	2 083.1	107.4	442	7 157	1 659.1	149.1	110	381	72.4	12.2
Emmet	3.3	320	17	107	222.5	4.1	50	467	90.0	8.6	6	13	0.7	0.1
Fayette	4.5	217	40	415	696.5	19.9	88	760	178.0	16.2	12	36	8.3	0.9
Floyd	4.1	252	20	380	295.8	20.4	62	723	188.8	14.0	10	35	3.3	0.7

1. Merchant wholesalers, except manufacturers' sales branches and offices.   2. Employer establishments.

Table B. States and Counties — Professional Services, Manufacturing, and Accommodation and Food Services

STATE County	Professional, scientific, and technical services, 2012				Manufacturing, 2012				Accommodation and food services, 2012			
	Number of establishments	Number of employees	Receipts (mil dol)	Annual payroll (mil dol)	Number of establishments	Number of employees	Receipts (mil dol)	Annual payroll (mil dol)	Number of establishments	Number of employees	Sales (mil dol)	Annual payroll (mil dol)
	147	148	149	150	151	152	153	154	155	156	157	158
INDIANA—Cont'd												
Pike	9	28	2.1	0.7	7	247	D	11.7	17	138	5.2	1.4
Porter	350	2 035	273.7	101.0	137	9 239	9 469.9	695.2	319	5 925	270.6	72.2
Posey	37	518	44.5	21.6	26	2 689	6 454.3	235.2	35	463	18.8	5.8
Pulaski	24	58	4.9	1.1	21	1 274	498.6	65.4	21	166	8.0	2.0
Putnam	50	187	13.9	5.4	30	2 001	745.6	82.7	69	1 216	51.4	13.3
Randolph	34	100	10.5	2.8	49	2 045	847.6	93.2	40	512	18.8	5.2
Ripley	37	145	8.6	4.7	43	2 444	864.9	98.9	41	D	D	D
Rush	34	136	17.0	4.0	28	616	D	21.5	23	328	14.7	3.8
St. Joseph	516	4 882	1 359.4	273.9	365	13 831	6 508.6	733.1	559	10 899	485.6	139.1
Scott	28	178	14.5	5.3	21	1 594	866.1	72.8	39	D	D	D
Shelby	66	225	23.3	8.3	80	4 770	2 700.7	235.3	77	1 495	62.6	17.6
Spencer	20	84	7.2	2.0	24	1 399	1 634.2	64.3	27	335	19.4	4.4
Starke	19	51	4.4	1.3	20	853	253.1	30.2	30	326	14.2	3.7
Steuben	55	171	13.0	4.1	95	4 044	1 279.2	161.0	93	1 397	60.1	16.8
Sullivan	21	103	6.6	2.5	14	712	D	29.5	31	409	15.4	4.3
Switzerland	10	15	0.8	0.3	8	D	D	D	16	D	D	D
Tippecanoe	300	2 297	334.4	105.9	121	14 295	11 875.0	846.1	405	8 035	362.1	98.9
Tipton	19	56	4.4	1.4	17	777	236.3	33.9	26	295	12.9	3.3
Union	8	D	D	D	5	36	D	D	8	86	3.8	1.0
Vanderburgh	434	3 727	471.4	178.0	248	10 623	3 972.5	494.1	465	11 293	566.5	150.0
Vermillion	13	D	D	D	15	676	D	54.3	33	443	24.5	5.8
Vigo	200	1 162	120.3	44.0	112	8 872	3 512.9	438.4	276	5 439	230.1	66.6
Wabash	52	375	30.8	8.2	62	2 623	1 312.0	121.0	68	1 049	40.2	11.5
Warren	6	15	2.0	0.3	13	635	165.3	20.9	8	D	D	D
Warrick	98	389	44.3	14.7	48	2 631	1 853.2	174.2	71	1 087	44.1	13.0
Washington	27	111	11.9	3.2	36	1 395	339.0	55.5	30	D	D	D
Wayne	90	433	30.5	12.2	105	4 875	2 155.1	214.3	154	2 812	120.3	34.6
Wells	39	216	22.3	7.4	51	2 536	1 126.5	101.9	41	587	20.5	5.8
White	31	102	7.5	2.5	35	2 144	926.4	91.2	61	540	23.2	6.3
Whitley	37	179	14.4	4.7	69	4 541	2 199.7	220.0	64	851	39.5	8.7
IOWA	6 204	48 521	6 420.6	2 466.8	3 598	203 722	116 668.8	10 021.2	7 047	115 134	5 468.7	1 466.6
Adair	13	36	2.9	0.9	3	D	D	D	14	D	D	D
Adams	9	25	2.9	0.7	8	155	D	6.7	6	D	D	D
Allamakee	19	102	11.5	3.0	27	1 208	262.1	36.0	33	235	9.7	2.3
Appanoose	22	64	5.6	1.9	17	599	303.3	24.6	29	422	16.5	5.4
Audubon	9	16	1.9	0.3	7	172	D	8.0	6	D	D	D
Benton	30	76	7.2	2.4	29	717	166.5	24.6	33	D	D	D
Black Hawk	232	3 781	288.1	203.8	164	13 067	9 665.5	655.2	304	6 630	318.4	84.6
Boone	38	145	15.4	5.5	28	416	97.7	19.6	46	499	16.9	4.2
Bremer	36	180	17.7	5.5	36	1 714	883.7	86.3	46	562	20.0	5.5
Buchanan	22	83	10.3	2.9	41	1 124	677.4	45.2	33	399	12.2	3.1
Buena Vista	36	182	20.3	8.5	30	3 507	2 233.5	121.1	45	738	23.2	6.9
Butler	19	68	5.5	1.4	28	836	463.6	35.4	16	D	D	D
Calhoun	16	43	3.6	0.9	14	82	D	2.9	15	D	D	D
Carroll	46	197	27.4	6.9	38	1 286	904.3	60.2	59	687	22.5	6.4
Cass	27	115	12.3	4.8	21	513	157.5	20.5	36	371	14.4	3.8
Cedar	23	93	10.1	2.9	34	643	255.0	27.8	38	D	D	D
Cerro Gordo	95	613	73.7	29.9	52	2 687	1 361.7	122.5	129	D	D	D
Cherokee	18	77	10.4	2.0	23	1 109	653.3	38.9	28	344	11.6	3.3
Chickasaw	18	59	6.2	1.5	48	1 242	712.4	52.0	24	284	8.5	2.1
Clarke	13	45	3.3	1.0	13	887	D	34.8	22	571	67.5	8.7
Clay	39	179	18.9	6.4	27	999	320.1	44.5	55	645	24.9	6.4
Clayton	26	149	21.0	5.7	31	899	217.8	33.5	58	D	D	D
Clinton	60	295	35.6	10.2	53	4 405	4 731.1	228.3	108	1 664	103.5	22.7
Crawford	21	92	8.7	2.9	21	2 471	1 657.9	98.6	44	419	14.9	4.3
Dallas	184	1 361	229.7	70.2	39	2 067	740.2	77.8	149	2 911	148.0	44.0
Davis	14	52	5.3	1.5	8	145	D	5.5	15	100	3.2	0.9
Decatur	6	20	1.6	0.3	5	76	D	2.9	12	D	D	D
Delaware	27	105	11.2	4.6	37	1 831	872.7	78.1	29	246	8.4	2.3
Des Moines	60	317	31.9	11.6	52	4 367	1 626.7	194.1	97	D	D	D
Dickinson	46	148	15.2	5.2	37	1 491	719.8	55.8	94	978	56.8	16.6
Dubuque	166	2 956	450.9	147.7	144	8 498	6 036.4	434.6	242	4 456	169.5	49.8
Emmet	19	80	8.5	3.1	21	931	357.0	38.9	22	291	9.6	2.9
Fayette	34	112	8.6	3.4	25	530	D	21.5	45	570	18.4	4.8
Floyd	26	90	5.2	2.0	20	947	593.4	51.9	36	344	13.3	3.1

1. Establishment subject to federal tax.

Table B. States and Counties — Health Care and Social Assistance, Other Services, Nonemployer Businesses, and Residential Construction

STATE County	Health care and social assistance, 2012				Other services, 2012				Nonemployer businesses, 2014		Value of residential construction authorized by building permits, 2015	
	Number of establish-ments	Number of employees	Receipts (mil dol)	Annual payroll (mil dol)	Number of establish-ments	Number of employees	Receipts (mil dol)	Annual payroll (mil dol)	Number	Receipts (mil dol)	New Construction ($1,000)	Number of housing units
	159	160	161	162	163	164	165	166	167	168	169	170
INDIANA—Cont'd												
Pike	17	376	19.0	7.3	21	70	8.5	2.9	578	17.1	2 975	20
Porter	377	7 837	775.3	316.8	282	2 002	150.3	49.5	9 454	415.1	130 167	605
Posey	36	550	29.4	11.7	40	134	14.7	3.4	1 408	49.9	11 639	58
Pulaski	25	573	40.6	18.2	21	80	7.5	1.7	782	30.0	2 178	15
Putnam	71	1 649	110.7	46.2	66	278	18.9	5.5	2 035	77.3	11 167	53
Randolph	38	645	51.8	19.6	43	169	13.7	2.9	1 389	51.9	3 629	21
Ripley	67	1 404	130.5	53.0	49	178	17.3	4.0	1 732	69.0	12 740	80
Rush	31	555	50.8	17.7	28	88	8.9	1.7	1 127	45.3	1 668	12
St. Joseph	644	17 762	2 160.5	722.0	459	D	D	D	15 762	607.9	77 558	435
Scott	53	865	65.9	25.4	23	105	8.1	2.2	1 136	39.9	5 087	45
Shelby	77	2 008	194.2	70.0	69	452	41.0	10.7	2 818	123.2	14 789	89
Spencer	24	D	D	D	32	86	7.5	1.9	1 193	39.0	7 398	42
Starke	23	460	35.9	12.3	31	131	10.8	2.5	1 218	44.7	7 221	38
Steuben	84	1 384	97.2	36.3	76	424	53.0	12.3	2 147	100.9	33 710	121
Sullivan	31	647	50.7	20.5	21	113	6.9	1.7	988	30.9	215	2
Switzerland	15	D	D	D	13	39	4.1	0.9	582	23.3	3 321	57
Tippecanoe	385	10 859	1 194.7	423.0	240	1 793	208.1	46.8	8 912	377.1	94 026	430
Tipton	26	614	63.4	26.0	20	102	10.4	2.4	964	39.1	1 284	7
Union	11	D	D	D	12	D	D	D	505	21.3	675	3
Vanderburgh	554	18 044	2 025.2	775.4	360	2 889	300.6	86.0	9 521	387.1	45 555	343
Vermillion	23	534	61.6	19.5	23	54	5.4	0.9	733	24.3	70	1
Vigo	360	8 910	1 138.1	352.1	178	1 150	109.0	30.3	4 912	184.2	27 126	212
Wabash	76	2 143	141.7	52.9	60	303	25.0	5.5	1 698	54.6	3 901	20
Warren	10	D	D	D	6	D	D	D	536	20.0	3 022	15
Warrick	125	3 119	369.6	124.9	86	431	49.5	12.6	3 730	159.1	48 872	233
Washington	45	765	52.8	21.0	25	148	10.2	3.5	1 671	60.1	4 698	34
Wayne	205	5 350	523.3	204.3	117	509	47.0	10.5	3 628	146.7	13 238	104
Wells	57	1 641	128.3	51.5	61	280	21.2	5.7	1 653	61.0	11 070	51
White	36	852	63.3	25.2	33	121	12.6	2.7	1 482	63.6	9 217	32
Whitley	65	1 120	103.5	35.8	69	344	28.9	8.4	2 125	76.1	14 667	72
IOWA	8 131	206 906	18 583.8	7 894.4	5 866	30 672	3 343.2	847.7	205 908	9 021.3	2 243 252	12 097
Adair	16	336	21.7	8.4	15	D	D	D	645	26.2	955	7
Adams	17	327	27.3	9.5	9	32	1.9	0.5	339	14.3	1 000	4
Allamakee	48	1 022	51.1	24.2	33	90	12.2	2.5	1 166	55.3	4 991	35
Appanoose	37	714	52.5	21.7	25	71	7.5	1.5	912	39.2	483	5
Audubon	15	321	21.6	8.8	18	52	5.2	1.4	487	21.4	1 524	24
Benton	45	775	50.7	21.4	51	148	15.6	3.9	1 834	63.4	5 620	28
Black Hawk	362	10 530	990.2	416.7	225	1 484	137.5	36.7	7 238	340.0	50 259	300
Boone	53	1 623	110.8	48.8	48	171	19.1	5.0	1 736	67.9	10 953	61
Bremer	58	1 672	119.4	51.6	64	D	D	D	1 639	70.2	21 245	94
Buchanan	41	1 025	71.1	32.3	20	D	D	D	1 443	63.3	3 683	27
Buena Vista	46	1 341	90.4	41.8	32	129	13.0	2.9	1 296	60.9	1 985	7
Butler	28	513	24.4	11.6	22	D	D	D	1 079	39.7	4 154	24
Calhoun	33	685	51.2	20.8	14	D	D	D	704	30.3	4 865	19
Carroll	110	2 188	172.5	68.7	58	200	19.7	4.2	1 923	93.5	7 501	35
Cass	46	1 154	80.9	34.9	39	154	20.8	3.7	1 196	44.1	4 832	16
Cedar	51	617	29.3	13.6	33	D	D	D	1 293	50.7	7 793	34
Cerro Gordo	141	4 853	541.7	217.7	110	D	D	D	3 029	120.5	14 285	48
Cherokee	36	915	64.1	31.7	27	78	9.6	2.2	822	33.9	2 665	9
Chickasaw	36	561	50.0	16.7	31	98	14.3	1.9	995	35.8	1 934	9
Clarke	28	617	39.3	15.4	18	D	D	D	565	21.2	3 300	52
Clay	60	1 480	139.3	60.9	37	202	18.3	4.7	1 312	60.4	11 713	68
Clayton	57	999	54.8	24.3	35	D	D	D	1 382	49.7	5 615	25
Clinton	131	3 554	248.0	107.2	92	331	28.8	7.8	2 699	99.0	12 046	56
Crawford	37	1 008	67.8	28.2	38	D	D	D	909	40.5	5 982	62
Dallas	169	3 175	271.9	123.9	88	731	72.0	35.2	5 805	291.8	218 043	918
Davis	21	418	33.6	14.2	11	31	2.9	0.6	755	52.2	523	4
Decatur	20	335	21.0	10.2	5	D	D	D	619	24.5	120	1
Delaware	38	969	65.8	30.0	42	149	14.3	2.8	1 308	57.5	1 903	9
Des Moines	143	3 273	323.7	123.0	93	447	37.9	10.8	2 362	82.6	7 468	44
Dickinson	56	647	34.5	15.1	39	169	14.2	3.8	1 722	79.3	35 589	162
Dubuque	271	7 806	702.0	318.7	201	1 157	109.4	28.1	6 251	277.6	55 045	255
Emmet	35	941	72.2	28.6	26	76	6.4	1.7	701	30.8	3 545	17
Fayette	56	1 290	80.7	36.4	49	197	22.5	5.3	1 444	54.4	3 951	21
Floyd	49	969	62.3	28.7	36	119	8.8	2.2	1 185	41.6	5 026	46

Table B. States and Counties — Government Employment and Payroll, and Local Government Finances

	Government employment and payroll, 2012									Local government finances, 2012				
			March payroll (percent of total)							General revenue				
												Taxes		
													Per capita[1] (dollars)	
STATE County	Full-time equivalent employees	March payroll (dollars)	Administration, judicial, and legal	Police and Corrections	Fire Protection	Highways and transportation	Health and Welfare	Natural resources and utilities	Education and libraries	Total (mil dol)	Intergovernmental (mil dol)	Total (mil dol)	Total	Property
	171	172	173	174	175	176	177	178	179	180	181	182	183	184
INDIANA—Cont'd														
Pike	517	1 538 013	6.0	5.7	0.0	2.8	2.9	3.1	78.9	37.9	19.2	13.1	1 029	1 017
Porter	4 682	15 472 739	6.2	11.3	4.3	3.7	2.1	4.6	66.6	488.1	210.9	195.5	1 180	1 059
Posey	911	2 762 902	6.5	6.5	1.9	5.2	4.2	4.8	69.9	91.5	46.7	35.1	1 370	1 173
Pulaski	708	2 273 852	6.2	7.1	0.1	2.4	37.6	1.9	44.1	67.8	28.8	13.4	1 019	724
Putnam	1 642	4 711 936	4.0	5.6	1.1	2.5	24.9	2.7	57.3	152.8	52.1	46.2	1 223	1 010
Randolph	1 040	2 903 572	6.2	8.7	2.2	3.1	2.3	2.6	74.3	87.0	51.7	23.2	898	698
Ripley	1 010	3 272 378	6.6	6.7	0.8	3.3	2.0	5.4	74.4	92.3	48.8	27.6	967	752
Rush	863	2 783 719	5.3	5.5	1.8	3.6	34.1	2.2	47.2	62.7	23.4	13.5	788	596
St. Joseph	9 537	31 853 965	4.7	12.0	7.2	4.2	1.2	7.1	62.0	1 039.1	434.1	391.0	1 468	1 064
Scott	984	3 352 561	6.3	6.5	0.1	1.7	23.7	3.5	56.0	87.7	37.4	20.6	865	696
Shelby	1 997	6 919 558	3.0	7.4	2.7	1.5	36.5	2.1	46.2	272.2	100.9	54.8	1 233	968
Spencer	769	2 237 381	7.1	8.1	0.1	3.7	2.1	4.2	74.1	70.8	38.9	21.7	1 042	882
Starke	708	2 237 301	6.6	4.8	2.5	3.1	0.7	1.7	75.9	73.3	44.3	20.2	868	715
Steuben	1 096	3 394 672	9.6	9.3	2.3	3.8	4.4	6.2	63.6	108.5	47.5	40.3	1 182	873
Sullivan	911	2 516 743	6.1	5.1	1.0	4.1	30.7	3.5	49.0	93.6	35.3	20.1	951	859
Switzerland	398	1 091 343	11.4	6.6	0.0	5.1	2.6	5.1	68.7	40.0	28.0	6.9	658	486
Tippecanoe	4 468	15 188 885	7.3	12.7	5.8	5.8	2.2	5.7	59.5	457.5	213.5	170.7	962	767
Tipton	903	3 143 238	4.0	4.5	1.9	2.0	42.8	4.2	38.9	44.9	22.7	15.5	989	726
Union	448	1 183 280	9.6	3.8	1.0	2.9	1.2	2.3	78.6	26.8	13.9	8.2	1 116	890
Vanderburgh	5 583	20 513 638	6.9	13.0	6.2	3.9	1.5	8.7	57.8	578.5	275.8	204.6	1 131	901
Vermillion	614	1 596 357	7.0	7.2	0.5	4.5	1.0	2.1	76.9	49.4	28.3	15.4	963	931
Vigo	3 145	11 398 778	8.5	10.1	5.8	4.8	0.9	6.3	62.4	343.5	178.1	110.8	1 022	808
Wabash	1 443	4 610 578	4.1	7.2	4.2	2.4	29.9	2.5	49.7	143.9	51.1	32.9	1 017	612
Warren	295	823 372	8.8	8.6	0.0	7.3	2.3	2.0	70.9	26.8	11.8	11.6	1 393	1 027
Warrick	1 757	5 629 245	7.9	6.7	0.8	2.6	1.7	3.6	76.2	168.5	76.5	59.4	982	827
Washington	845	2 699 186	6.9	6.0	1.0	3.5	1.8	2.8	76.4	72.6	43.4	21.5	769	601
Wayne	2 355	8 196 624	6.3	10.4	3.9	3.3	3.6	11.9	58.9	225.2	109.7	75.5	1 104	906
Wells	917	2 758 659	6.4	11.3	1.0	3.1	1.4	4.9	70.3	82.1	43.3	25.6	927	656
White	1 059	3 072 979	5.9	7.0	4.5	4.1	1.4	4.8	71.6	119.7	51.9	36.9	1 509	1 286
Whitley	1 054	3 089 365	6.7	13.1	0.0	4.8	0.9	1.6	71.8	89.8	43.2	27.3	820	609
IOWA	X	X	X	X	X	X	X	X	X	X	X	X	X	X
Adair	361	1 122 671	8.0	6.1	0.0	8.8	28.8	3.4	44.3	37.5	13.2	12.9	1 725	1 407
Adams	179	522 990	8.9	6.5	0.0	10.7	6.7	3.3	62.4	16.9	7.2	7.4	1 901	1 634
Allamakee	647	2 079 591	5.0	5.7	0.1	6.8	25.3	3.2	53.2	65.4	22.8	22.7	1 596	1 243
Appanoose	443	1 437 537	5.8	7.1	0.8	6.8	1.1	3.0	74.6	41.7	21.0	16.6	1 308	1 005
Audubon	328	1 089 236	5.8	5.2	0.0	7.5	33.7	1.3	45.9	32.8	8.6	11.6	1 971	1 623
Benton	846	2 776 401	7.0	6.1	0.1	7.7	1.3	7.5	70.0	87.3	37.6	37.9	1 468	1 188
Black Hawk	4 471	16 944 268	4.8	10.2	4.6	4.7	6.0	11.4	55.6	566.6	249.4	219.9	1 668	1 325
Boone	1 271	4 353 230	3.6	5.2	1.3	4.7	29.4	4.3	50.3	126.6	35.0	39.6	1 510	1 205
Bremer	952	3 191 387	7.1	7.5	0.0	5.7	7.0	3.2	66.5	149.1	41.3	41.6	1 698	1 343
Buchanan	834	2 711 732	5.2	6.6	0.5	5.4	22.7	8.0	51.3	79.4	27.4	29.1	1 389	1 115
Buena Vista	1 236	4 037 429	5.3	5.7	0.3	4.3	36.7	2.1	45.6	128.8	34.8	37.1	1 802	1 417
Butler	352	1 075 176	10.9	10.2	0.1	14.2	6.9	7.8	48.7	80.8	53.4	20.5	1 365	1 136
Calhoun	506	1 374 475	7.1	6.8	0.0	9.4	7.0	3.4	64.2	42.3	15.6	21.9	2 208	1 889
Carroll	828	2 504 489	5.6	6.3	0.2	7.0	5.5	7.6	66.7	87.4	32.6	36.2	1 753	1 373
Cass	903	2 917 219	3.3	2.3	0.2	3.9	43.1	0.9	45.0	91.1	26.3	27.8	2 024	1 557
Cedar	668	1 997 014	6.7	9.8	0.1	8.4	4.5	4.8	63.2	67.2	27.0	32.7	1 774	1 427
Cerro Gordo	1 766	6 541 728	4.4	8.2	2.8	8.5	5.2	5.1	64.4	203.2	74.2	86.1	1 967	1 505
Cherokee	418	1 242 156	8.2	6.7	0.6	9.2	1.4	5.2	66.5	40.1	14.5	20.3	1 703	1 336
Chickasaw	502	1 552 970	6.1	5.4	0.0	7.3	4.9	6.3	69.5	40.9	17.9	18.5	1 511	1 176
Clarke	529	1 675 579	5.4	5.8	0.0	5.3	31.8	3.4	47.7	54.9	15.5	16.8	1 795	1 452
Clay	1 187	4 281 441	3.5	4.2	0.5	6.0	45.8	8.0	29.0	143.1	24.9	30.2	1 822	1 405
Clayton	718	2 326 866	6.3	6.5	0.1	7.1	14.8	3.5	61.2	88.3	36.5	28.8	1 614	1 312
Clinton	1 731	6 177 764	5.4	9.5	3.6	5.4	2.6	5.5	66.4	199.4	80.5	85.7	1 760	1 345
Crawford	917	3 208 303	4.3	4.0	0.1	5.6	29.6	4.8	49.8	89.7	30.6	26.4	1 524	1 243
Dallas	2 341	8 457 626	5.2	4.5	0.6	2.8	6.9	2.8	76.8	257.1	92.3	126.9	1 764	1 534
Davis	419	1 521 730	4.6	4.0	0.1	5.6	40.7	2.5	42.4	45.3	13.6	10.3	1 184	967
Decatur	476	1 395 435	5.0	5.3	0.0	7.8	24.8	1.6	54.5	38.0	14.7	12.4	1 498	1 205
Delaware	974	3 412 646	4.0	3.6	0.0	4.3	41.3	2.0	44.6	99.6	31.6	29.8	1 695	1 409
Des Moines	1 756	6 340 038	4.4	7.5	3.3	4.2	1.8	4.4	73.0	171.7	72.6	68.2	1 691	1 253
Dickinson	844	3 005 898	7.0	6.0	0.0	4.6	29.5	6.9	45.5	102.7	15.7	50.1	2 950	2 520
Dubuque	3 261	12 486 456	6.7	9.6	3.9	7.2	5.0	6.0	60.6	400.9	169.8	165.8	1 743	1 320
Emmet	840	2 701 635	4.3	4.2	0.0	4.0	1.6	3.9	81.5	71.8	26.5	22.1	2 185	1 847
Fayette	775	2 536 072	6.6	8.5	0.5	8.6	2.3	3.9	69.1	78.2	37.2	31.6	1 519	1 194
Floyd	655	2 381 344	4.8	5.4	1.3	6.9	31.5	3.8	44.8	76.5	22.6	24.9	1 552	1 207

1. Based on the resident population estimated as of July 1 of the year shown.

Table B. States and Counties — **Local Government Finances, Government Employment, and Voting**

STATE County	Local government finances, 2012 (cont.)									Government employment, 2014			Presidential election,[2] 2012		
	Direct general expenditure							Debt outstanding					Percent of vote cast:		
			Percent of total for:												
	Total (mil dol)	Per capita[1] (dollars)	Educa-tion	Health and hospitals	Police protec-tion	Public welfare	High-ways	Total (mil dol)	Per capita[1] (dollars)	Federal civilian	Federal military	State and local	Demo-cratic	Republi-can	All other
	185	186	187	188	189	190	191	192	193	194	195	196	197	198	199
INDIANA—Cont'd															
Pike	34.3	2 684	63.8	1.9	2.6	0.2	4.1	28.8	2 253	31	40	578	44.8	53.4	1.8
Porter	434.6	2 623	59.0	1.1	3.4	0.2	3.6	510.5	3 081	420	529	6 447	53.0	45.8	1.2
Posey	70.6	2 759	61.6	1.8	2.5	0.3	4.9	54.0	2 108	65	82	1 114	45.6	53.3	1.1
Pulaski	61.0	4 646	39.3	31.3	2.5	0.3	4.3	30.0	2 286	38	41	1 011	41.3	56.8	1.8
Putnam	123.0	3 258	52.6	25.9	2.2	0.1	3.9	99.5	2 636	77	104	2 395	43.2	55.2	1.5
Randolph	72.4	2 803	61.3	1.1	3.3	0.3	5.5	45.1	1 749	65	81	1 189	44.8	53.6	1.7
Ripley	77.1	2 698	69.6	0.9	2.4	0.1	3.5	73.8	2 582	73	90	1 292	34.4	63.9	1.7
Rush	60.9	3 561	39.7	33.6	2.8	0.2	6.5	41.7	2 438	43	54	1 074	42.3	56.0	1.7
St. Joseph	848.7	3 186	49.9	0.6	4.9	0.4	3.0	856.7	3 216	888	922	12 596	58.0	41.0	1.0
Scott	82.2	3 453	49.0	26.1	3.2	0.1	2.3	53.4	2 245	73	75	1 056	48.1	50.1	1.8
Shelby	217.7	4 896	31.6	43.4	3.2	0.1	2.2	156.3	3 515	134	141	2 359	39.8	58.8	1.4
Spencer	60.9	2 923	50.0	0.5	2.5	0.2	3.3	52.3	2 510	68	66	950	49.5	49.1	1.4
Starke	57.6	2 481	62.7	1.4	2.4	0.1	5.1	49.3	2 124	42	74	1 000	50.5	47.3	2.3
Steuben	88.6	2 597	53.3	1.0	3.4	0.2	3.8	103.6	3 037	62	106	1 479	44.4	54.2	1.3
Sullivan	83.4	3 936	37.2	35.1	0.9	0.2	3.7	81.5	3 848	48	61	1 779	48.8	49.5	1.8
Switzerland	38.7	3 712	40.1	0.3	1.1	0.2	3.1	17.5	1 683	22	33	446	45.0	53.3	1.7
Tippecanoe	406.1	2 288	50.8	0.2	6.3	0.6	5.9	369.7	2 083	459	587	23 152	55.2	43.6	1.2
Tipton	40.8	2 597	56.2	0.2	3.5	0.2	6.7	38.3	2 442	36	49	768	41.5	56.9	1.6
Union	23.2	3 150	73.7	0.1	2.6	0.0	4.3	25.2	3 429	15	23	428	36.6	61.6	1.9
Vanderburgh	605.3	3 347	39.0	0.7	7.5	0.3	2.7	673.3	3 723	957	569	9 430	50.8	48.3	0.9
Vermillion	47.0	2 933	53.2	0.4	2.5	0.4	5.1	23.9	1 493	33	50	685	56.1	42.2	1.7
Vigo	303.7	2 801	52.3	0.6	4.1	0.6	2.7	415.8	3 835	1 103	339	7 473	57.3	41.5	1.2
Wabash	128.9	3 983	46.9	29.1	2.8	0.1	3.3	49.4	1 525	74	98	1 874	39.3	59.4	1.3
Warren	25.3	3 032	48.5	1.2	1.6	1.1	6.3	5.8	698	15	27	347	43.9	54.2	1.9
Warrick	150.3	2 485	55.3	0.5	3.2	0.1	2.8	121.4	2 008	105	195	2 126	43.0	55.9	1.1
Washington	72.9	2 611	64.1	0.6	1.7	0.2	4.2	47.7	1 710	56	89	1 124	40.4	57.7	2.0
Wayne	192.9	2 822	52.8	1.7	4.5	0.3	3.0	101.7	1 489	158	209	4 724	47.1	51.0	1.9
Wells	73.2	2 646	66.0	0.6	4.1	0.1	4.5	54.7	1 977	58	88	1 185	33.7	65.1	1.3
White	92.9	3 804	53.9	0.2	2.1	0.1	3.9	122.7	5 024	60	78	1 374	44.9	53.2	1.8
Whitley	83.9	2 515	50.7	0.4	3.1	0.1	5.2	89.8	2 693	71	106	1 374	38.6	60.1	1.3
IOWA	X	X	X	X	X	X	X	X	X	17 574	12 211	237 692	53.9	44.4	1.7
Adair	35.9	4 797	29.3	28.1	3.8	0.1	14.9	30.8	4 112	25	29	446	47.5	50.8	1.7
Adams	18.9	4 842	43.4	5.1	6.6	0.8	17.5	25.1	6 408	29	15	220	50.7	47.4	1.9
Allamakee	60.7	4 262	38.8	26.8	3.5	0.2	12.3	42.3	2 969	75	55	1 068	56.2	42.0	1.8
Appanoose	38.5	3 030	55.1	4.8	8.0	0.2	13.4	8.5	670	53	50	605	48.1	49.9	2.0
Audubon	32.4	5 481	33.4	34.9	4.0	0.2	13.4	10.0	1 694	26	22	414	50.6	47.6	1.8
Benton	81.0	3 135	52.4	3.2	3.8	0.1	11.3	122.8	4 756	67	101	1 453	51.5	47.0	1.5
Black Hawk	637.5	4 836	53.7	3.2	4.6	0.3	7.4	430.8	3 268	522	529	11 487	60.5	38.1	1.5
Boone	124.1	4 739	36.1	35.5	3.3	0.4	7.7	248.4	9 484	102	102	2 358	52.8	45.2	2.0
Bremer	157.5	6 436	38.3	35.9	2.7	0.2	6.4	95.8	3 915	61	91	1 897	53.9	44.6	1.5
Buchanan	82.2	3 927	41.5	24.9	4.2	0.1	11.1	83.7	3 995	45	82	1 426	58.5	40.0	1.5
Buena Vista	124.9	6 065	34.7	32.6	3.3	0.1	7.7	93.1	4 522	106	78	1 625	48.4	50.2	1.4
Butler	80.9	5 400	24.9	40.1	2.8	0.3	13.2	30.8	2 054	42	59	784	46.9	51.6	1.4
Calhoun	44.1	4 453	58.6	8.7	3.3	0.5	11.4	14.8	1 490	39	36	657	45.1	52.8	2.2
Carroll	82.7	4 011	45.1	5.7	3.3	4.3	11.5	57.3	2 780	83	80	1 197	51.0	47.3	1.6
Cass	117.4	8 552	29.2	40.3	2.1	0.2	6.2	80.0	5 832	73	52	1 300	43.7	54.5	1.8
Cedar	69.5	3 774	57.4	5.4	4.1	0.0	10.6	54.8	2 977	83	72	990	54.0	44.4	1.6
Cerro Gordo	204.6	4 672	54.1	4.7	5.2	0.6	6.3	164.2	3 750	148	167	2 617	59.7	38.8	1.5
Cherokee	39.0	3 267	46.5	3.5	4.6	0.1	19.0	23.5	1 969	45	46	957	45.4	53.0	1.7
Chickasaw	44.7	3 641	56.0	3.0	4.0	0.2	13.2	29.3	2 390	54	48	594	59.6	38.8	1.6
Clarke	51.9	5 544	32.9	36.7	3.5	0.4	8.8	35.1	3 750	36	36	746	49.9	47.6	2.5
Clay	129.8	7 817	21.1	46.9	2.7	0.2	5.4	102.7	6 185	58	65	1 613	46.7	51.8	1.5
Clayton	98.8	5 538	51.9	15.0	3.1	0.4	9.5	56.2	3 150	79	69	1 260	57.8	40.6	1.6
Clinton	230.7	4 735	45.9	4.9	4.2	0.3	8.2	231.1	4 743	114	187	2 483	60.7	37.7	1.5
Crawford	93.1	5 378	36.5	33.2	2.6	0.1	10.1	85.1	4 916	77	66	1 273	51.7	46.5	1.8
Dallas	257.2	3 574	65.5	8.1	2.9	0.2	6.0	404.2	5 617	95	305	3 543	46.4	51.9	1.7
Davis	44.2	5 085	27.2	43.8	2.8	0.2	9.8	35.8	4 115	37	34	498	44.0	53.1	2.9
Decatur	44.9	5 439	33.8	43.0	3.1	1.0	8.7	35.6	4 310	32	30	566	48.4	49.2	2.4
Delaware	94.8	5 392	30.9	40.4	2.9	0.2	10.4	55.0	3 130	42	68	1 193	52.2	46.2	1.6
Des Moines	184.0	4 560	60.7	3.6	4.8	0.2	4.9	138.1	3 424	136	159	2 472	60.6	37.5	1.9
Dickinson	103.1	6 073	27.9	30.2	3.5	0.3	13.2	137.6	8 106	68	66	1 110	46.7	52.1	1.2
Dubuque	405.9	4 268	37.6	4.5	4.7	2.0	7.0	372.4	3 916	253	382	4 480	59.7	38.9	1.5
Emmet	70.6	6 975	75.4	3.2	3.2	0.1	6.0	24.8	2 448	40	38	748	51.2	47.3	1.4
Fayette	72.6	3 494	51.6	4.0	5.1	0.2	16.4	32.0	1 541	74	77	1 142	57.6	41.0	1.5
Floyd	71.8	4 475	33.5	31.9	2.8	0.9	9.2	26.4	1 647	44	63	934	59.6	37.7	2.7

1. Based on the resident population estimated as of July 1 of the year shown.   2. © 2013 Election Data Services, Inc. All rights reserved.

STATE/ County code	CBSA code[1]	County type[2]	STATE County	Land area,[3] (sq km) 2010	Total persons 2015	Rank	Per square kilometer	White	Black	American Indian, Alaska Native	Asian and Pacific Islander	Percent Hispanic or Latino[4]	Under 5 years	5 to 17 years	18 to 24 years	25 to 34 years	35 to 44 years	45 to 54 years
				1	2	3	4	5	6	7	8	9	10	11	12	13	14	15
			IOWA—Cont'd															
19 069	...	7	Franklin	1 507	10 295	2 411	6.8	87.1	0.8	0.5	0.8	11.8	5.7	17.1	7.7	10.3	10.7	12.9
19 071	...	8	Fremont	1 324	6 906	2 682	5.2	96.0	1.0	0.7	0.5	2.6	5.4	16.6	6.3	9.5	11.0	13.1
19 073	...	6	Greene	1 475	9 027	2 510	6.1	95.8	0.8	0.8	0.7	2.9	5.3	17.6	7.3	9.6	10.3	13.6
19 075	47940	3	Grundy	1 300	12 435	2 267	9.6	97.9	0.8	0.3	0.5	1.2	6.0	17.4	7.4	10.4	11.4	13.6
19 077	19780	2	Guthrie	1 530	10 676	2 381	7.0	96.8	0.7	0.6	0.6	2.3	5.3	16.9	6.8	9.4	10.8	13.9
19 079	...	6	Hamilton	1 494	15 190	2 086	10.2	91.3	1.0	0.6	2.5	5.4	5.6	17.3	7.1	11.2	11.0	14.2
19 081	...	7	Hancock	1 479	10 974	2 359	7.4	95.4	1.0	0.6	0.8	3.5	5.4	17.3	6.7	10.3	10.8	13.7
19 083	...	6	Hardin	1 474	17 367	1 957	11.8	93.3	1.9	0.6	0.8	4.1	5.2	15.9	9.3	10.2	10.6	12.9
19 085	36540	2	Harrison	1 805	14 265	2 151	7.9	97.5	0.7	0.7	0.6	1.4	5.5	17.1	7.5	10.0	11.3	14.5
19 087	...	7	Henry	1 125	19 950	1 838	17.7	90.7	3.3	0.7	3.4	4.8	5.9	16.4	9.9	11.9	11.6	13.5
19 089	...	7	Howard	1 226	9 410	2 476	7.7	97.4	1.2	0.4	0.5	1.4	6.8	18.4	7.0	10.7	10.3	13.4
19 091	...	7	Humboldt	1 125	9 555	2 466	8.5	95.0	0.9	0.5	0.6	4.0	5.5	17.4	7.4	11.1	10.1	13.3
19 093	...	8	Ida	1 118	7 028	2 674	6.3	97.0	0.9	0.7	0.7	2.0	7.1	16.7	6.9	10.5	9.9	12.3
19 095	...	8	Iowa	1 519	16 401	2 014	10.8	96.3	0.9	0.4	0.5	2.5	5.9	17.4	7.5	10.6	11.4	14.6
19 097	...	6	Jackson	1 647	19 444	1 852	11.8	97.0	1.1	0.6	1.3	1.3	5.4	16.9	7.5	9.7	10.7	15.0
19 099	35500	2	Jasper	1 892	36 827	1 257	19.5	95.2	2.2	0.7	0.9	1.9	5.5	17.0	7.4	11.9	12.0	14.4
19 101	21840	7	Jefferson	1 128	17 555	1 942	15.6	83.6	2.2	0.8	11.0	2.9	4.3	12.5	12.3	13.2	9.8	11.0
19 103	26980	3	Johnson	1 590	144 251	445	90.7	82.5	6.7	0.6	6.9	5.5	6.2	14.2	20.7	16.6	11.6	10.5
19 105	16300	3	Jones	1 491	20 466	1 807	13.7	95.1	2.5	0.4	0.7	1.6	5.2	16.5	7.5	11.1	11.8	14.7
19 107	...	8	Keokuk	1 500	10 163	2 422	6.8	97.6	0.8	0.5	0.3	1.6	6.3	16.9	7.2	10.3	10.8	13.6
19 109	...	7	Kossuth	2 519	15 165	2 087	6.0	96.8	0.9	0.3	0.7	2.0	5.5	16.3	7.3	9.9	9.5	13.4
19 111	22800	5	Lee	1 340	35 089	1 300	26.2	92.9	4.0	0.8	1.0	3.4	6.2	15.4	8.0	11.7	11.1	13.8
19 113	16300	3	Linn	1 857	219 916	297	118.4	90.1	5.7	0.6	2.9	2.9	6.3	17.5	9.5	13.6	12.8	13.6
19 115	...	8	Louisa	1 041	11 185	2 343	10.7	80.4	1.3	0.6	2.3	16.2	5.3	17.9	8.2	11.3	11.7	15.3
19 117	...	6	Lucas	1 115	8 682	2 537	7.8	98.3	0.4	0.5	0.5	1.3	5.6	17.7	7.6	8.9	10.1	13.9
19 119	...	8	Lyon	1 522	11 745	2 309	7.7	96.4	0.4	0.5	0.5	2.7	7.3	20.8	7.2	10.8	11.7	12.2
19 121	19780	2	Madison	1 453	15 753	2 058	10.8	97.2	0.7	0.6	0.8	1.5	5.8	20.1	6.4	10.0	13.2	14.4
19 123	36820	7	Mahaska	1 479	22 324	1 714	15.1	95.4	1.8	0.6	1.5	1.9	6.1	17.6	9.7	11.7	11.4	12.9
19 125	...	6	Marion	1 436	33 294	1 350	23.2	95.9	1.4	0.5	1.7	1.9	6.1	18.1	10.7	10.8	11.5	13.3
19 127	32260	2	Marshall	1 483	40 746	1 161	27.5	75.1	2.4	0.7	3.2	19.9	7.0	17.9	8.7	11.7	10.8	12.7
19 129	36540	2	Mills	1 133	14 844	2 113	13.1	96.1	1.0	0.9	1.1	2.7	5.7	18.5	7.0	9.6	12.4	15.0
19 131	...	7	Mitchell	1 215	10 832	2 369	8.9	97.7	0.8	0.3	0.5	1.2	5.6	18.2	7.7	9.5	9.8	14.0
19 133	...	6	Monona	1 798	8 979	2 513	5.0	96.3	0.8	1.4	0.6	2.0	5.1	16.3	7.1	8.8	9.8	13.0
19 135	...	7	Monroe	1 123	7 973	2 599	7.1	96.6	1.0	0.5	1.1	2.4	5.5	18.0	7.6	10.3	11.7	13.7
19 137	...	6	Montgomery	1 098	10 234	2 414	9.3	95.2	0.7	0.8	0.6	3.4	5.7	17.0	7.3	9.2	11.1	13.6
19 139	34700	4	Muscatine	1 133	43 011	1 113	38.0	79.5	2.4	0.6	1.4	17.2	6.7	18.7	8.6	12.1	12.0	13.6
19 141	...	7	O'Brien	1 484	13 984	2 166	9.4	93.9	0.9	0.4	1.0	4.5	6.0	17.6	7.4	10.5	10.3	13.0
19 143	...	7	Osceola	1 033	6 154	2 745	6.0	92.2	0.6	0.5	0.9	6.8	6.0	17.3	7.0	10.0	10.9	13.5
19 145	...	7	Page	1 385	15 527	2 073	11.2	92.6	2.9	1.0	1.6	2.9	5.6	14.9	7.6	11.1	12.1	12.9
19 147	...	7	Palo Alto	1 460	9 133	2 502	6.3	96.1	1.2	0.7	1.0	2.1	5.9	16.2	9.1	10.6	10.1	12.4
19 149	43580	6	Plymouth	2 235	24 800	1 612	11.1	94.6	0.9	0.5	0.9	4.1	5.9	19.2	7.5	10.1	11.7	13.8
19 151	...	9	Pocahontas	1 495	7 008	2 675	4.7	95.2	1.4	0.6	0.7	3.4	5.7	16.9	7.1	8.8	9.4	14.0
19 153	19780	2	Polk	1 486	467 711	147	314.7	81.0	7.6	0.6	4.8	8.0	7.2	18.0	9.0	15.7	13.4	13.4
19 155	36540	2	Pottawattamie	2 461	93 671	624	38.1	90.0	2.2	0.9	1.2	7.2	6.5	17.2	9.0	12.4	11.8	13.6
19 157	...	7	Poweshiek	1 515	18 550	1 888	12.2	93.3	1.8	0.6	2.5	3.0	5.2	15.2	14.4	9.7	9.8	12.8
19 159	...	9	Ringgold	1 387	5 068	2 831	3.7	97.3	0.6	0.5	0.6	2.0	5.8	17.5	6.5	9.6	9.3	12.2
19 161	...	9	Sac	1 489	10 021	2 432	6.7	96.3	0.7	0.4	0.5	2.8	5.4	16.6	7.2	9.4	10.0	13.5
19 163	19340	2	Scott	1 186	172 126	374	145.1	83.7	8.9	0.8	3.0	6.3	6.6	17.5	8.6	13.7	12.5	13.5
19 165	...	6	Shelby	1 530	11 927	2 302	7.8	96.2	0.8	0.7	0.7	2.3	5.6	17.1	7.3	8.3	10.1	14.6
19 167	...	6	Sioux	1 990	34 937	1 306	17.6	88.5	0.8	0.3	1.2	9.8	7.4	19.5	13.9	11.6	10.4	11.2
19 169	11180	4	Story	1 484	96 021	616	64.7	85.6	3.2	0.5	7.6	3.1	4.9	12.3	30.6	13.3	9.3	9.2
19 171	...	6	Tama	1 867	17 337	1 959	9.3	84.7	1.0	7.4	0.8	8.4	6.0	18.2	7.8	9.8	11.0	13.7
19 173	...	9	Taylor	1 378	6 205	2 741	4.5	91.7	0.6	0.5	0.4	7.5	6.3	16.7	6.9	11.7	9.8	13.3
19 175	...	6	Union	1 097	12 469	2 262	11.4	94.7	1.2	0.6	0.8	2.7	6.1	17.0	8.9	11.3	11.2	12.8
19 177	...	9	Van Buren	1 256	7 344	2 643	5.8	98.3	0.6	0.4	0.8	1.3	6.7	16.6	6.8	9.9	10.7	13.2
19 179	36900	5	Wapello	1 118	35 173	1 295	31.5	86.5	2.6	0.7	1.4	10.0	6.0	16.4	9.1	12.5	11.5	13.3
19 181	19780	2	Warren	1 476	48 626	1 006	32.9	95.9	1.1	0.5	1.1	2.5	6.0	19.2	9.5	10.8	12.6	14.3
19 183	26980	3	Washington	1 473	22 247	1 720	15.1	92.7	1.3	0.6	0.9	5.6	6.6	18.2	7.5	10.8	11.1	13.7
19 185	...	9	Wayne	1 361	6 385	2 725	4.7	97.3	1.0	0.7	0.5	1.7	7.0	17.2	7.3	10.3	9.2	12.8
19 187	22700	5	Webster	1 853	37 071	1 252	20.0	90.1	5.2	0.6	1.2	4.3	5.8	15.6	11.6	12.2	10.3	12.7
19 189	...	7	Winnebago	1 037	10 609	2 385	10.2	93.3	1.9	0.4	1.3	3.9	5.2	16.2	9.1	10.5	10.4	12.7
19 191	...	7	Winneshiek	1 787	20 709	1 793	11.6	95.9	1.1	0.3	1.4	2.1	4.3	14.6	16.4	9.7	9.4	13.0
19 193	43580	3	Woodbury	2 261	102 782	581	45.5	77.7	3.8	2.3	3.3	15.2	7.3	18.7	10.2	13.0	12.0	12.7
19 195	32380	9	Worth	1 036	7 569	2 631	7.3	96.0	1.2	0.5	0.8	2.7	5.1	16.6	7.9	10.0	11.0	14.4
19 197	...	7	Wright	1 503	12 773	2 245	8.5	88.3	0.9	0.6	0.6	10.2	5.7	17.4	7.0	10.0	10.8	12.7

1. CBSA = Core Based Statistical Area. See Appendix A for explanation. See Appendix B for list of metropolitan areas with component counties. 2. County type code from the Economic Research Service of USDA Rural-Urban Continuum Codes. See Appendix A for definition. 3. Dry land or land partially or temporarily covered by water. 4. May be of any race.

Table B. States and Counties — Population and Households

	Population, 2014 (cont.)				Population change and components of change, 2000–2015							Households, 2010–2014				
	Age (percent) (cont.)				Total persons		Percent change		Components of change, 2010–2015					Percent		
STATE County	55 to 64 years	65 to 74 years	75 years and over	Percent female	2000	2010	2000–2010	2010–2015	Births	Deaths	Net migration	Number	Persons per house-hold	Family house-holds	Female family house-holder[1]	One per-son
	16	17	18	19	20	21	22	23	24	25	26	27	28	29	30	31
IOWA—Cont'd																
Franklin	15.5	9.8	10.3	49.8	10 704	10 680	-0.2	-3.6	630	603	-379	4 321	2.41	70.1	8.7	24.6
Fremont	16.5	11.2	10.5	50.6	8 010	7 441	-7.1	-7.2	383	458	-416	3 003	2.34	68.0	8.5	28.8
Greene	14.9	10.1	11.3	51.1	10 366	9 337	-9.9	-3.3	548	613	-239	3 849	2.36	68.1	9.4	28.2
Grundy	14.0	9.8	10.0	50.9	12 369	12 453	0.7	-0.1	715	654	-58	5 112	2.40	68.4	6.0	26.9
Guthrie	15.2	11.1	10.6	50.2	11 353	10 954	-3.5	-2.5	561	647	-134	4 559	2.32	68.9	9.3	28.3
Hamilton	14.2	9.4	10.0	50.7	16 438	15 673	-4.7	-3.1	919	902	-529	6 354	2.39	66.7	9.3	29.7
Hancock	15.6	9.9	10.3	49.8	12 100	11 341	-6.3	-3.2	575	666	-242	4 629	2.37	67.5	6.5	28.7
Hardin	14.7	10.0	11.3	50.0	18 812	17 534	-6.8	-1.0	956	1 123	46	6 997	2.37	63.9	4.7	32.2
Harrison	14.9	10.0	9.1	50.3	15 666	14 937	-4.7	-4.5	816	937	-557	5 959	2.40	67.7	8.1	27.7
Henry	13.1	9.5	8.1	48.8	20 336	20 145	-0.9	-1.0	1 196	1 123	-277	7 512	2.51	67.6	9.6	28.0
Howard	13.7	9.6	10.1	50.2	9 932	9 566	-3.7	-1.6	616	565	-205	3 917	2.37	63.2	7.6	31.7
Humboldt	14.9	9.5	10.9	51.0	10 381	9 814	-5.5	-2.6	556	612	-196	4 200	2.29	64.8	8.6	29.1
Ida	15.0	10.0	11.5	50.1	7 837	7 089	-9.5	-0.9	417	500	16	3 124	2.22	65.5	7.7	28.9
Iowa	14.6	8.4	9.6	50.5	15 671	16 355	4.4	0.3	1 001	909	-51	6 705	2.38	70.8	6.4	24.7
Jackson	14.9	10.4	9.3	50.3	20 296	19 848	-2.2	-2.0	1 056	1 189	-291	8 494	2.29	68.2	7.6	26.8
Jasper	13.8	9.4	8.5	49.0	37 213	36 842	-1.0	0.0	2 196	1 917	-265	14 658	2.37	66.2	9.1	27.1
Jefferson	18.1	11.4	7.4	46.1	16 181	16 843	4.1	4.2	774	820	777	6 886	2.23	59.3	6.7	33.9
Johnson	10.3	5.8	4.1	50.2	111 006	130 882	17.9	10.2	9 407	3 403	7 219	54 850	2.34	54.3	8.5	30.5
Jones	14.5	9.7	8.9	48.1	20 221	20 638	2.1	-0.8	1 126	1 052	-205	8 235	2.33	69.0	8.4	24.9
Keokuk	14.9	9.9	10.1	49.8	11 400	10 511	-7.8	-3.3	662	568	-431	4 386	2.33	64.1	6.5	30.2
Kossuth	15.6	10.2	12.3	49.8	17 163	15 543	-9.4	-2.4	867	947	-259	6 628	2.27	64.1	6.3	31.8
Lee	15.1	10.5	8.2	50.1	38 052	35 862	-5.8	-2.2	2 167	2 222	-698	14 319	2.43	64.7	10.3	30.1
Linn	12.4	7.8	6.5	50.6	191 701	211 226	10.2	4.1	14 377	8 577	2 936	87 004	2.41	63.2	9.9	29.4
Louisa	13.7	9.0	7.6	49.3	12 183	11 387	-6.5	-1.8	695	529	-364	4 386	2.55	71.1	9.4	24.7
Lucas	15.2	10.6	10.4	49.6	9 422	8 898	-5.6	-2.4	517	540	-196	3 745	2.30	65.6	8.5	30.1
Lyon	13.0	7.9	9.0	49.8	11 763	11 581	-1.5	1.4	872	589	-91	4 495	2.56	71.9	5.7	25.2
Madison	13.7	8.9	7.4	50.2	14 019	15 679	11.8	0.5	859	756	-53	6 103	2.52	68.0	6.5	25.7
Mahaska	13.7	8.7	8.2	49.6	22 335	22 381	0.2	-0.3	1 469	1 166	-359	9 084	2.39	64.3	8.0	31.1
Marion	13.1	8.7	7.8	50.1	32 052	33 309	3.9	0.0	1 951	1 736	-217	12 843	2.45	70.2	5.5	27.1
Marshall	13.7	9.1	8.3	49.5	39 311	40 648	3.4	0.2	2 896	2 478	-327	15 354	2.59	68.1	9.8	27.4
Mills	16.0	9.5	6.3	49.9	14 547	15 059	3.5	-1.4	784	715	-257	5 348	2.67	73.9	6.3	23.2
Mitchell	13.7	9.6	12.0	50.5	10 874	10 772	-0.9	0.6	681	684	58	4 453	2.36	66.4	6.0	29.8
Monona	15.4	11.8	12.8	50.6	10 020	9 243	-7.8	-2.9	436	775	68	3 972	2.25	63.2	7.5	33.5
Monroe	14.1	10.0	9.0	49.8	8 016	7 970	-0.6	0.0	462	519	72	3 280	2.40	63.6	9.5	32.4
Montgomery	15.4	10.4	10.4	51.1	11 771	10 740	-8.8	-4.7	599	788	-321	4 590	2.25	68.0	13.0	28.3
Muscatine	13.2	8.5	6.6	50.2	41 722	42 749	2.5	0.6	2 898	1 976	-640	16 301	2.60	70.2	10.6	24.6
O'Brien	14.7	8.9	11.7	49.8	15 102	14 398	-4.7	-2.9	859	951	-342	6 018	2.29	65.6	5.4	30.8
Osceola	15.1	9.3	10.9	49.4	7 003	6 462	-7.7	-4.8	377	354	-336	2 697	2.29	67.2	4.7	28.1
Page	15.0	10.4	10.4	47.8	16 976	15 943	-6.1	-2.6	917	1 093	-213	6 379	2.30	64.3	6.9	30.9
Palo Alto	14.4	9.7	11.7	50.3	10 147	9 421	-7.2	-3.1	524	649	-149	4 011	2.22	62.1	7.6	32.0
Plymouth	14.3	9.1	8.6	50.3	24 849	24 981	0.5	-0.7	1 458	1 258	-318	9 899	2.48	70.6	7.7	25.0
Pocahontas	15.7	10.4	11.9	50.2	8 662	7 310	-15.6	-4.1	410	468	-226	3 222	2.18	61.1	6.2	34.6
Polk	11.5	6.7	4.9	50.8	374 601	430 635	15.0	8.6	35 317	16 731	18 305	174 759	2.50	65.1	11.3	27.8
Pottawattamie	13.8	8.7	7.0	50.9	87 704	93 149	6.2	0.6	6 376	4 671	-1 095	36 615	2.48	67.0	12.5	27.2
Poweshiek	13.8	9.7	9.4	51.1	18 815	18 914	0.5	-1.9	950	1 150	-131	7 424	2.30	61.9	7.4	33.0
Ringgold	13.8	12.0	13.3	50.8	5 469	5 131	-6.2	-1.2	276	384	54	2 078	2.36	66.6	5.8	28.8
Sac	15.6	9.8	12.5	50.9	11 529	10 350	-10.2	-3.2	592	715	-180	4 413	2.25	63.4	6.1	32.9
Scott	13.1	8.1	6.3	51.0	158 668	165 224	4.1	4.2	11 711	7 418	2 742	67 325	2.46	63.2	11.2	30.2
Shelby	14.6	10.3	12.1	50.8	13 173	12 167	-7.6	-2.0	643	729	-152	5 171	2.28	63.9	7.6	31.9
Sioux	11.5	6.9	7.6	49.8	31 589	33 704	6.7	3.7	2 706	1 318	-147	11 782	2.70	75.3	7.1	21.8
Story	9.7	5.7	5.0	48.1	79 981	89 542	12.0	7.2	5 020	2 489	4 023	35 666	2.34	53.3	5.4	27.7
Tama	14.5	9.5	9.6	50.9	18 103	17 767	-1.9	-2.4	1 142	1 069	-493	6 815	2.51	71.8	10.8	24.9
Taylor	14.3	10.4	10.7	49.3	6 958	6 317	-9.2	-1.8	400	386	-122	2 752	2.22	67.5	8.9	27.1
Union	13.8	9.9	9.0	51.3	12 309	12 534	1.8	-0.5	727	761	-28	5 293	2.31	62.2	6.7	31.9
Van Buren	15.3	10.9	9.8	49.2	7 809	7 570	-3.1	-3.0	479	465	-239	2 986	2.47	71.2	5.8	24.4
Wapello	14.2	9.0	8.0	50.6	36 051	35 625	-1.2	-1.3	2 256	2 110	-484	14 608	2.36	64.8	12.0	29.8
Warren	12.6	8.5	6.4	50.8	40 671	46 228	13.7	5.2	2 806	1 963	1 541	17 584	2.58	73.4	9.4	22.9
Washington	13.6	9.4	9.1	50.8	20 670	21 704	5.0	2.5	1 554	1 227	217	9 056	2.38	66.9	7.5	27.6
Wayne	13.9	11.0	11.3	51.6	6 730	6 403	-4.9	-0.3	463	441	-62	2 548	2.46	64.4	7.5	32.2
Webster	14.2	8.8	8.4	48.2	40 235	38 013	-5.5	-2.5	2 316	2 356	-844	15 397	2.27	58.6	11.8	35.2
Winnebago	15.5	9.5	10.9	51.4	11 723	10 866	-7.3	-2.4	632	669	-245	4 584	2.21	66.8	4.9	30.9
Winneshiek	14.4	8.9	9.2	50.5	21 310	21 058	-1.2	-1.7	893	933	-280	8 141	2.28	65.9	6.1	29.4
Woodbury	12.4	7.6	6.2	50.5	103 877	102 177	-1.6	0.6	8 125	4 786	-2 519	38 818	2.56	65.8	12.7	28.7
Worth	15.1	10.4	9.4	50.2	7 909	7 598	-3.9	-0.4	398	433	21	3 194	2.34	69.5	9.1	26.9
Wright	15.1	9.8	11.5	49.6	14 334	13 229	-7.7	-3.4	769	834	-364	5 419	2.36	60.5	7.1	34.4

1. No spouse present.

Table B. States and Counties — Population, Vital Statistics, Medicare, and Crime

STATE County	Persons in group quarters, 2015	Daytime population, 2010–2014 Number	Daytime population, Employment/residence ratio	Births, 2015 Total	Births, 2015 Rate[1]	Deaths, 2015 Number	Deaths, 2015 Rate[1]	Persons under 65 with no health insurance, 2014 Number	Persons under 65 with no health insurance, 2014 Percent	Medicare, 2015 Total Beneficiaries	Medicare, 2015 Enrolled in Original Medicare	Medicare, 2015 Enrolled in Medicare Advantage	Serious crimes known to police,[2] 2014 Total Number	Serious crimes known to police,[2] 2014 Total Rate[3]
	32	33	34	35	36	37	38	39	40	41	42	43	44	45
IOWA—Cont'd														
Franklin	190	9 971	0.88	122	11.8	100	9.7	906	10.9	1 945	1 899	46	13	123
Fremont	139	6 454	0.78	69	9.9	80	11.5	372	6.8	1 667	1 507	160	4	57
Greene	137	8 740	0.88	111	12.2	119	13.1	562	7.8	2 145	1 891	254	64	703
Grundy	150	10 423	0.67	137	11.0	120	9.7	498	5.0	2 480	2 199	281	91	739
Guthrie	159	9 237	0.70	115	10.8	129	12.1	640	7.7	2 619	2 216	403	52	488
Hamilton	190	14 669	0.91	197	13.0	170	11.2	945	7.8	3 168	2 863	305	251	1 644
Hancock	132	10 887	0.95	113	10.3	126	11.5	627	7.2	2 214	2 171	43	54	488
Hardin	867	17 243	0.98	180	10.4	213	12.3	928	7.1	4 137	3 880	257	231	1 567
Harrison	277	11 998	0.64	168	11.7	167	11.7	864	7.5	3 108	2 792	316	57	397
Henry	1 324	20 133	0.99	230	11.5	192	9.6	1 200	7.8	4 039	3 658	381	389	2 116
Howard	209	9 119	0.91	117	12.4	113	12.0	676	9.0	2 071	2 007	64	132	1 384
Humboldt	121	9 136	0.87	108	11.3	113	11.8	541	7.1	2 041	1 953	88	69	713
Ida	119	7 693	1.17	79	11.2	99	14.1	380	6.9	1 506	1 368	138	95	1 324
Iowa	289	16 432	1.01	199	12.1	179	10.9	794	5.9	3 097	2 600	497	113	690
Jackson	199	16 775	0.70	201	10.3	217	11.2	1 259	8.1	4 219	3 225	994	207	1 058
Jasper	1 822	31 836	0.71	419	11.4	359	9.7	1 860	6.5	7 085	6 095	990	881	2 402
Jefferson	1 719	17 898	1.10	159	9.1	160	9.1	1 217	9.6	3 300	2 867	433	395	2 344
Johnson	8 015	146 432	1.13	1 811	12.6	675	4.7	8 141	6.7	14 539	12 403	2 136	3 186	2 252
Jones	1 247	17 819	0.71	224	10.9	203	9.9	1 094	7.0	3 822	3 063	759	137	664
Keokuk	139	8 537	0.63	123	12.1	100	9.8	715	8.8	2 356	2 004	352	53	640
Kossuth	248	15 314	1.00	168	11.1	159	10.5	743	6.3	3 461	3 399	62	93	608
Lee	1 322	37 777	1.14	423	12.0	408	11.6	2 035	7.4	7 446	6 640	806	937	2 624
Linn	5 081	226 204	1.10	2 739	12.5	1 659	7.6	9 961	5.4	35 643	25 648	9 995	6 585	3 025
Louisa	120	9 598	0.69	138	12.3	108	9.7	877	9.5	2 002	1 722	280	67	594
Lucas	73	8 495	0.93	99	11.4	94	10.8	621	9.1	1 925	1 685	240	205	2 349
Lyon	162	10 460	0.79	162	13.8	99	8.4	707	7.3	2 031	1 864	167	113	1 234
Madison	191	12 051	0.52	154	9.8	142	9.1	824	6.3	2 630	2 189	441	155	1 006
Mahaska	686	20 591	0.83	277	12.4	222	9.9	1 249	6.9	4 029	3 518	511	465	2 070
Marion	1 471	34 353	1.06	381	11.4	322	9.7	1 467	5.5	6 164	5 584	580	NA	NA
Marshall	1 338	41 176	1.01	535	13.1	468	11.5	3 189	9.7	8 536	7 398	1 138	1 033	2 510
Mills	608	12 186	0.61	138	9.3	125	8.4	758	6.3	2 804	2 444	360	269	1 808
Mitchell	234	10 395	0.93	140	13.0	122	11.3	675	8.0	2 560	2 533	27	60	627
Monona	202	8 387	0.81	80	8.9	149	16.6	557	8.3	2 216	1 862	354	111	1 218
Monroe	120	7 668	0.90	88	11.0	89	11.2	706	11.0	1 626	1 450	176	71	884
Montgomery	209	10 559	1.00	121	11.7	133	12.9	629	7.7	2 467	2 280	187	175	1 686
Muscatine	548	44 323	1.07	559	13.0	342	8.0	2 846	7.9	7 313	5 571	1 742	782	1 821
O'Brien	371	13 772	0.94	175	12.5	187	13.3	862	7.8	3 242	3 088	154	205	1 466
Osceola	104	5 687	0.82	77	12.5	67	10.8	475	9.6	1 276	1 216	60	13	211
Page	1 454	16 186	1.06	173	11.1	196	12.6	869	7.9	3 530	3 249	281	225	1 434
Palo Alto	326	8 892	0.92	105	11.5	109	12.0	475	6.8	2 200	2 157	43	116	1 268
Plymouth	318	23 551	0.90	271	10.9	237	9.5	1 193	5.8	4 243	3 579	664	316	1 264
Pocahontas	124	6 954	0.93	86	12.2	79	11.2	388	7.1	1 776	1 696	80	38	533
Polk	9 929	487 708	1.18	6 951	15.0	3 264	7.0	27 908	7.0	64 432	51 569	12 863	14 919	3 260
Pottawattamie	2 273	86 751	0.86	1 223	13.1	932	10.0	6 087	7.9	17 508	13 307	4 201	5 184	5 589
Poweshiek	1 625	20 064	1.14	176	9.4	196	10.5	879	6.4	3 706	3 350	356	301	1 621
Ringgold	180	4 831	0.88	57	11.3	56	11.1	396	10.6	1 188	1 091	97	29	572
Sac	205	8 962	0.76	125	12.5	122	12.2	602	7.8	2 455	2 336	119	47	469
Scott	3 484	172 795	1.05	2 262	13.2	1 391	8.1	10 491	7.3	28 798	22 283	6 515	5 650	3 309
Shelby	214	12 208	1.03	123	10.3	141	11.8	626	6.8	2 781	2 559	222	NA	NA
Sioux	2 385	36 192	1.11	517	14.8	254	7.3	2 463	9.0	5 123	4 762	361	139	399
Story	11 329	93 977	1.04	968	10.1	491	5.1	5 364	7.2	11 641	10 287	1 354	1 647	1 903
Tama	302	15 207	0.71	223	12.8	189	10.9	1 266	9.1	3 614	3 102	512	199	1 350
Taylor	67	5 331	0.70	77	12.5	65	10.5	474	9.9	1 516	1 499	17	26	424
Union	449	13 578	1.17	132	10.5	139	11.1	831	8.3	3 470	3 192	278	207	1 639
Van Buren	57	6 909	0.83	85	11.5	100	13.6	586	10.0	1 844	1 609	235	86	1 159
Wapello	821	36 948	1.10	421	12.0	396	11.2	2 840	10.0	8 047	7 252	795	1 298	3 667
Warren	1 578	34 754	0.50	550	11.4	384	7.9	1 958	4.9	7 353	6 029	1 324	844	1 770
Washington	311	19 894	0.82	324	14.6	214	9.7	1 460	8.2	4 431	3 869	562	204	921
Wayne	95	6 047	0.87	91	14.2	89	13.9	530	10.8	1 485	1 287	198	46	717
Webster	2 742	39 001	1.10	435	11.7	418	11.3	2 059	7.3	7 979	7 329	650	1 604	4 345
Winnebago	416	11 344	1.13	133	12.5	124	11.7	568	7.0	2 465	2 375	90	77	733
Winneshiek	2 184	21 568	1.05	170	8.2	186	9.0	944	6.3	4 121	3 488	633	108	514
Woodbury	2 629	102 094	0.99	1 544	15.0	879	8.6	9 681	11.3	17 738	13 682	4 056	3 752	3 668
Worth	90	6 304	0.67	77	10.1	70	9.2	420	6.9	1 539	1 449	90	69	914
Wright	200	13 062	1.01	148	11.5	150	11.7	872	8.7	3 025	2 899	126	76	587

1. Per 1,000 estimated resident population.   2. Data for serious crimes have not been adjusted for underreporting; this may affect comparability between geographic areas and over time.
3. Per 100,000 population estimated by the FBI.

Table B. States and Counties — **Crime, Education, Money Income, and Poverty**

STATE County	Serious crimes known to police, 2014 (cont.)[1] Rate[2]		Education						Money income, 2010–2014				Income and poverty, 2014			
			School enrollment and attainment, 2010–2014				Local government expenditures,[5] 2012–2013		Households				Percent below poverty level			
			Enrollment[3]		Attainment[4] (percent)											
	Violent	Property	Total	Percent private	High school graduate or less	Bachelor's degree or more	Total current spending (mil dol)	Current spending per student (dollars)	Per capita income[6] (dollars)	Median income (dollars)	Mean income (dollars)	Percent with income of $200,000 or more	Median household income (dollars)	All persons	Children under 18 years	Children 5 to 17 years in families
	46	47	48	49	50	51	52	53	54	55	56	57	58	59	60	61
IOWA—Cont'd																
Franklin	9	114	2 506	4.2	50.0	16.3	22.4	9 649	25 719	48 218	62 103	2.4	51 045	12.1	18.5	17.9
Fremont	43	14	1 603	4.7	47.2	20.9	10.2	11 603	28 656	52 221	67 920	4.1	54 154	11.7	17.0	15.8
Greene	77	626	2 089	7.1	44.7	17.3	17.5	10 761	27 140	47 255	64 113	3.0	49 125	13.2	17.7	16.0
Grundy	98	642	2 878	8.0	42.3	20.5	26.1	9 397	30 701	55 896	73 315	4.2	61 215	6.7	8.7	8.2
Guthrie	66	423	2 564	5.3	47.0	18.0	23.7	8 927	28 746	50 238	67 793	3.4	49 507	12.4	14.6	13.2
Hamilton	242	1 402	3 811	7.0	43.5	19.0	27.5	9 939	25 531	47 358	60 728	1.9	53 691	9.4	15.6	14.8
Hancock	117	371	2 451	5.4	45.5	17.9	17.2	9 871	27 025	52 057	64 052	2.3	57 682	8.4	12.7	11.6
Hardin	88	1 479	4 216	13.7	44.2	19.0	32.7	10 253	25 792	50 941	62 182	2.2	53 277	11.7	18.7	17.5
Harrison	21	377	3 364	7.3	48.2	18.3	28.8	9 924	26 217	53 506	62 755	1.4	52 824	11.0	14.8	13.6
Henry	299	1 817	4 743	16.1	44.6	20.5	33.8	9 854	23 679	49 036	60 634	1.9	50 347	13.3	17.8	16.7
Howard	94	1 290	2 142	16.6	57.0	11.7	16.1	9 461	25 040	47 300	59 297	2.5	49 837	12.1	17.4	17.0
Humboldt	83	630	2 259	15.4	46.6	16.6	15.4	9 801	26 592	47 500	60 672	1.9	49 696	10.1	15.0	13.4
Ida	167	1 157	1 566	5.7	48.2	18.8	12.0	10 176	26 712	45 912	60 815	2.7	53 905	10.9	14.7	14.5
Iowa	98	593	3 946	12.0	45.0	21.7	25.7	9 524	28 249	58 553	69 302	1.8	58 234	7.5	9.4	8.7
Jackson	61	997	4 543	12.6	54.8	14.1	29.5	9 551	24 988	47 004	58 476	1.9	50 299	11.3	17.1	15.8
Jasper	248	2 154	8 534	9.7	48.6	17.7	55.4	9 385	25 825	52 430	63 518	1.4	52 750	11.2	14.1	12.8
Jefferson	59	2 285	4 766	42.4	37.3	33.0	24.1	10 143	27 408	44 688	64 325	3.1	41 094	16.9	21.1	19.7
Johnson	254	1 998	51 564	8.2	21.6	51.7	165.7	10 036	31 131	54 985	76 117	5.5	59 946	15.9	11.3	11.1
Jones	82	582	4 527	15.2	49.3	15.7	29.6	9 179	26 671	54 264	67 323	2.2	51 558	11.6	14.0	12.9
Keokuk	145	495	2 384	6.0	52.2	15.3	11.5	9 390	23 544	44 745	55 126	0.9	48 316	13.5	18.4	17.5
Kossuth	157	451	3 509	19.3	42.5	19.4	22.6	11 211	29 229	52 345	67 131	3.4	52 967	9.6	13.1	11.8
Lee	498	2 126	7 869	12.4	51.5	15.5	50.0	9 645	22 960	43 314	54 333	1.2	44 719	17.7	24.4	22.9
Linn	222	2 803	58 001	19.2	33.0	31.7	416.4	11 500	30 949	59 560	74 973	3.6	62 700	9.3	11.8	11.4
Louisa	106	488	2 674	3.2	56.2	14.2	27.0	10 107	25 411	52 750	63 795	1.1	50 924	11.1	15.0	13.1
Lucas	172	2 177	1 893	6.8	54.6	12.7	13.0	9 122	22 060	43 280	52 251	1.0	42 582	16.0	24.6	23.1
Lyon	153	1 081	2 814	21.6	47.9	19.6	18.7	8 805	25 578	54 344	66 247	2.8	61 750	7.9	9.7	9.0
Madison	117	889	3 837	7.4	45.4	21.7	29.6	8 592	27 848	56 661	70 700	3.3	62 230	8.8	10.0	8.9
Mahaska	249	1 820	6 291	28.6	47.2	22.4	28.7	9 337	24 875	48 750	59 994	1.8	48 584	12.9	16.4	14.9
Marion	NA	NA	9 035	31.5	42.2	24.0	52.0	9 248	26 161	55 419	66 373	2.4	57 046	11.1	12.6	10.9
Marshall	420	2 090	9 805	7.2	48.2	20.1	68.8	9 727	24 549	52 354	62 905	1.9	50 244	13.0	18.2	17.0
Mills	249	1 559	4 034	12.2	42.5	24.4	29.6	9 264	27 942	65 160	75 408	1.9	59 399	9.7	12.7	11.4
Mitchell	31	596	2 348	15.5	53.8	15.1	14.6	8 840	24 629	47 326	58 994	1.5	52 616	11.5	16.5	15.3
Monona	143	1 076	1 963	6.4	53.6	14.0	18.1	10 983	24 645	41 238	55 834	2.1	43 178	14.3	19.2	17.7
Monroe	50	834	1 808	5.9	55.8	17.3	11.3	9 128	23 983	47 297	57 264	0.7	44 705	11.7	18.3	16.9
Montgomery	173	1 513	2 326	4.4	48.4	15.4	18.6	10 313	23 342	43 566	53 261	1.4	42 046	19.3	29.6	21.6
Muscatine	405	1 416	10 883	7.1	49.3	18.2	72.1	9 370	25 007	52 899	63 706	1.8	54 441	11.4	16.5	15.3
O'Brien	250	1 216	3 346	18.9	47.3	19.5	23.2	9 745	30 213	52 458	70 093	4.7	55 968	10.3	14.1	12.3
Osceola	65	146	1 392	7.9	52.0	14.4	7.8	9 764	25 239	50 700	59 444	1.6	51 423	9.1	14.9	14.4
Page	134	1 300	3 486	16.1	47.5	18.3	25.2	10 548	23 630	44 786	56 343	2.0	46 927	14.6	22.9	20.9
Palo Alto	350	918	2 116	14.3	41.4	18.3	17.4	10 296	26 111	46 334	59 475	2.1	50 600	11.5	15.0	14.0
Plymouth	132	1 132	6 388	20.4	44.1	20.0	38.9	9 511	27 848	57 583	69 455	2.2	62 745	7.6	9.9	9.0
Pocahontas	98	434	1 475	12.4	46.5	18.2	33.0	30 206	26 144	45 500	57 864	2.1	49 625	12.9	18.5	17.5
Polk	361	2 900	117 158	20.3	33.8	35.4	800.4	10 808	30 863	59 844	77 252	4.4	61 028	13.1	17.6	16.9
Pottawattamie	491	5 099	23 233	11.4	45.9	19.7	182.7	11 613	26 821	51 939	66 317	2.8	51 947	12.3	17.5	16.4
Poweshiek	199	1 422	5 254	34.3	43.8	25.4	27.4	9 496	26 855	51 650	65 562	2.9	52 791	12.1	13.8	12.6
Ringgold	79	493	1 092	13.7	49.2	18.9	8.6	11 034	24 553	44 032	59 831	3.3	42 854	16.6	24.5	22.7
Sac	30	439	2 181	8.4	49.0	19.4	18.6	10 570	27 224	48 581	61 492	2.4	49 513	10.8	14.8	13.3
Scott	468	2 840	43 830	18.0	35.3	31.9	299.8	10 525	29 243	53 704	71 588	3.7	54 959	12.2	16.4	15.2
Shelby	NA	NA	2 772	12.4	47.5	19.7	17.8	10 417	27 178	49 599	62 556	2.4	55 637	9.6	12.1	11.2
Sioux	29	370	10 485	49.7	44.0	24.9	44.0	9 463	25 343	59 272	71 873	3.5	60 205	7.5	8.8	8.3
Story	127	1 776	39 830	3.9	23.0	48.5	105.8	9 640	26 113	51 270	65 323	3.3	52 128	19.5	10.3	9.1
Tama	353	997	4 250	9.7	50.0	16.2	23.3	9 629	26 247	54 325	66 084	2.2	54 957	12.9	18.0	16.6
Taylor	33	391	1 360	5.1	50.8	15.3	10.8	10 340	24 044	44 939	54 560	1.1	46 501	13.1	17.4	16.9
Union	174	1 465	3 030	12.4	45.9	16.6	19.7	9 400	23 647	44 134	55 856	1.7	44 905	12.8	18.5	17.0
Van Buren	135	1 024	1 583	16.1	53.4	14.0	10.0	9 849	23 045	45 057	56 943	1.1	42 555	14.4	23.7	23.8
Wapello	271	3 396	8 329	9.9	54.0	15.3	78.3	12 444	21 909	41 519	52 223	1.5	42 414	16.7	21.9	20.9
Warren	306	1 464	12 785	20.0	37.2	28.5	81.0	8 867	29 449	64 956	76 427	2.4	67 342	6.3	8.0	7.4
Washington	298	623	5 227	10.7	44.8	21.5	36.7	9 566	27 051	55 198	66 318	1.4	56 243	10.2	14.9	14.1
Wayne	140	577	1 384	17.8	54.9	13.8	10.7	9 814	22 433	42 083	54 843	1.6	42 006	16.7	24.8	24.1
Webster	496	3 849	9 799	16.5	42.4	19.1	50.0	9 687	24 213	42 112	56 056	2.0	43 490	16.3	19.7	18.5
Winnebago	114	619	2 567	22.6	42.4	21.3	23.9	11 050	25 387	49 208	58 608	1.0	50 703	10.4	13.3	13.3
Winneshiek	10	504	6 328	45.8	43.8	26.8	30.1	10 541	25 709	53 735	64 356	1.7	55 984	9.4	10.2	9.3
Woodbury	317	3 352	27 726	17.6	48.0	21.3	207.2	11 321	23 221	46 015	59 263	1.8	45 641	15.2	20.9	20.0
Worth	146	769	1 659	12.0	42.5	13.7	13.7	9 457	24 886	49 977	58 415	1.8	50 286	11.0	15.4	14.1
Wright	70	518	2 862	3.1	47.7	17.3	26.6	9 805	25 964	43 082	60 568	2.5	50 108	12.0	17.8	16.5

1. Data for serious crimes have not been adjusted for underreporting; this may affect comparability between geographic areas and over time. 2. Per 100,000 population estimated by the FBI.
3. All persons 3 years old and over enrolled in nursery school through college. 4. Persons 25 years old and over. 5. Elementary and secondary education expenditures.
6. Based on population estimated by the American Community Survey, 2010–2014.

Table B. States and Counties — **Personal Income**

STATE County	Personal income, 2014										Earnings, 2014		
	Total (mil dol)	Percent change, 2013–2014	Per capita[1] Dollars	Per capita[1] Rank	Wages and salaries (mil dol)	Supplements to wages and salaries; employer contributions (mil dol) Pension and insurance	Supplements to wages and salaries; employer contributions (mil dol) Government social insurance	Proprietors' income (mil dol)	Dividends, interest, and rent (mil dol)	Personal transfer receipts (mil dol)	Total (mil dol)	Contributions for government social insurance (mil dol) From employee and self-employed	Contributions for government social insurance (mil dol) From employer
	62	63	64	65	66	67	68	69	70	71	72	73	74
IOWA—Cont'd													
Franklin	564	0.4	54 037	233	169	32	13	160	112	84	373	16	13
Fremont	324	-3.8	46 159	584	124	21	10	57	50	68	212	12	10
Greene	455	3.3	49 487	415	132	28	10	104	87	83	274	13	10
Grundy	622	-0.8	50 238	372	168	30	14	87	138	94	299	16	14
Guthrie	517	3.4	48 233	467	122	25	9	98	95	94	254	13	9
Hamilton	800	7.3	52 923	270	214	41	16	240	130	128	511	24	16
Hancock	594	1.3	53 874	240	285	50	27	146	88	87	509	25	27
Hardin	838	1.3	48 404	460	271	55	21	186	180	148	533	26	21
Harrison	604	-3.6	42 191	934	155	30	12	73	93	131	270	16	12
Henry	784	3.1	38 761	1 356	362	68	29	93	147	159	552	33	29
Howard	424	3.2	44 872	687	147	30	13	101	84	72	290	14	13
Humboldt	498	0.5	51 686	305	147	30	11	142	84	79	330	18	11
Ida	345	-3.3	49 036	435	147	26	11	79	66	61	264	14	11
Iowa	847	2.4	51 695	304	359	80	30	130	189	120	599	33	30
Jackson	769	0.9	39 472	1 251	200	40	16	76	146	164	331	22	16
Jasper	1 433	3.5	38 871	1 335	426	83	34	135	242	292	679	43	34
Jefferson	673	3.7	38 852	1 342	277	58	22	79	185	132	436	26	22
Johnson	6 434	4.5	45 218	657	3 891	960	292	419	1 346	685	5 562	303	292
Jones	820	2.4	40 110	1 159	240	48	19	84	157	155	390	23	19
Keokuk	479	3.1	46 771	539	90	18	7	115	78	89	230	12	7
Kossuth	812	-4.2	53 329	259	276	48	21	233	147	124	577	29	21
Lee	1 327	6.9	37 610	1 508	740	129	64	99	228	325	1 032	66	64
Linn	10 220	4.1	46 934	525	6 495	1 001	496	636	1 801	1 519	8 629	530	496
Louisa	418	0.6	37 485	1 526	134	29	10	60	63	79	233	13	10
Lucas	340	4.5	39 045	1 314	125	22	9	45	61	77	201	12	9
Lyon	700	1.4	59 955	132	165	31	12	275	101	72	484	18	12
Madison	676	3.3	43 287	815	132	27	10	68	105	106	237	14	10
Mahaska	869	1.9	38 830	1 346	299	62	24	120	156	173	505	29	24
Marion	1 325	2.6	39 714	1 221	722	124	60	72	264	237	978	60	60
Marshall	1 567	2.7	38 339	1 414	752	140	59	114	287	364	1 064	66	59
Mills	712	-3.6	47 975	481	167	37	12	64	96	199	281	18	12
Mitchell	558	5.4	51 813	301	147	28	12	208	94	80	394	21	12
Monona	395	-6.3	43 927	768	97	19	7	84	73	84	208	11	7
Monroe	312	4.7	39 029	1 318	161	29	12	45	52	67	248	14	12
Montgomery	411	-1.3	39 429	1 259	160	33	12	39	75	107	243	15	12
Muscatine	1 965	3.1	45 801	613	1 076	170	87	335	315	328	1 668	102	87
O'Brien	756	-0.5	53 812	243	229	43	17	192	137	118	481	22	17
Osceola	313	-0.1	50 321	365	82	16	6	96	51	47	200	7	6
Page	623	0.3	40 204	1 147	223	46	17	85	121	147	371	22	17
Palo Alto	446	0.6	48 976	440	131	27	10	129	75	79	297	14	10
Plymouth	1 391	1.2	55 913	200	458	81	35	378	219	168	953	45	35
Pocahontas	370	0.1	51 876	299	121	21	10	104	58	63	256	11	10
Polk	22 296	5.7	48 484	456	15 184	2 197	1 137	2 312	3 639	2 993	20 830	1 260	1 137
Pottawattamie	3 671	1.4	39 423	1 260	1 551	264	125	305	567	799	2 246	145	125
Poweshiek	836	4.5	44 777	697	399	68	33	145	173	133	645	34	33
Ringgold	228	4.3	45 124	669	51	11	4	57	47	48	122	6	4
Sac	549	1.8	54 719	217	122	23	9	175	102	88	330	15	9
Scott	8 164	3.3	47 637	491	3 833	600	300	652	1 436	1 386	5 385	335	300
Shelby	615	-1.1	51 503	312	223	45	17	130	119	110	415	21	17
Sioux	1 637	4.0	47 192	516	746	140	57	482	271	201	1 425	65	57
Story	3 574	4.6	37 990	1 455	2 076	491	155	334	795	468	3 056	173	155
Tama	738	0.1	42 266	929	174	37	13	101	135	139	325	18	13
Taylor	265	2.3	43 193	825	67	15	5	67	40	55	154	7	5
Union	480	2.8	38 381	1 410	238	49	19	69	77	110	374	21	19
Van Buren	274	2.8	36 646	1 659	72	17	6	47	51	64	141	8	6
Wapello	1 251	2.7	35 516	1 854	631	117	51	84	184	329	883	57	51
Warren	2 030	4.2	42 326	921	389	75	31	92	308	306	586	41	31
Washington	1 050	3.3	47 578	494	298	59	23	206	194	172	586	30	23
Wayne	251	4.6	39 258	1 288	70	17	5	52	46	57	144	7	5
Webster	1 560	4.4	42 219	932	770	143	60	242	267	321	1 215	72	60
Winnebago	409	6.8	38 695	1 364	159	30	13	67	83	85	268	14	13
Winneshiek	895	1.3	43 077	838	387	76	31	146	183	147	640	36	31
Woodbury	3 892	4.4	38 055	1 446	2 074	363	166	344	598	769	2 948	182	166
Worth	301	2.3	39 443	1 254	80	16	7	49	56	56	152	8	7
Wright	615	-0.5	47 917	483	237	47	19	129	113	121	432	21	19

1. Based on the resident population estimated as of July 1 of the year shown.

Table B. States and Counties — Earnings, Social Security, and Housing

STATE County	Earnings, 2014 (cont.) Percent by selected industries									Social Security beneficiaries, December 2014		Supplemental Security Income recipients, December 2014	Housing units, 2015	
	Farm	Mining	Construction	Manufacturing	Information: professional, scientific, technical services	Retail trade	Finance, insurance, real estate and leasing	Health care and social assistance	Government	Number	Rate[1]		Total	Percent change, 2010–2014
	75	76	77	78	79	80	81	82	83	84	85	86	87	88
IOWA—Cont'd														
Franklin	36.2	D	7.1	15.1	1.7	3.0	2.8	3.3	11.1	2 530	243	120	4 850	-0.9
Fremont	18.7	0.0	2.3	29.1	D	11.8	2.8	7.3	10.5	1 880	267	137	3 446	0.4
Greene	30.3	D	3.6	16.0	3.2	4.0	4.8	4.3	18.0	2 395	260	169	4 531	-0.4
Grundy	22.3	0.0	15.5	6.7	D	5.9	5.0	D	11.6	2 900	234	80	5 555	0.5
Guthrie	34.7	0.0	9.1	5.1	3.2	2.9	D	5.4	17.9	2 705	253	122	5 749	-0.1
Hamilton	31.4	D	4.0	19.3	3.2	4.1	3.6	D	12.2	3 620	238	215	7 175	-0.6
Hancock	22.5	D	2.4	42.1	1.1	2.3	1.7	D	7.1	2 735	249	96	5 315	-0.3
Hardin	27.2	D	6.7	10.3	3.2	5.2	3.3	D	17.4	4 255	245	253	8 162	-0.8
Harrison	17.7	D	4.8	6.8	3.8	7.6	4.2	D	16.8	3 330	232	236	6 755	0.3
Henry	7.3	D	4.2	25.4	D	5.3	2.9	D	19.1	4 555	228	354	8 278	0.0
Howard	26.1	0.0	6.9	24.2	1.6	6.1	3.2	D	13.3	2 185	231	96	4 359	-0.2
Humboldt	16.2	D	5.2	31.8	2.4	4.2	2.8	D	10.7	2 315	241	145	4 696	0.3
Ida	18.7	0.0	5.6	35.0	1.1	3.6	4.6	8.3	6.9	1 680	239	58	3 433	0.2
Iowa	10.0	D	5.8	48.1	2.3	5.6	1.6	D	9.1	3 530	215	154	7 277	0.3
Jackson	13.4	0.0	6.2	13.8	3.9	9.5	6.0	8.0	16.7	4 990	256	379	9 480	0.7
Jasper	10.8	D	8.0	17.7	D	6.3	3.3	7.0	20.8	8 600	233	560	16 157	-0.1
Jefferson	8.3	D	4.1	13.4	8.3	7.3	14.1	5.8	14.6	3 900	223	328	7 539	-0.7
Johnson	0.8	D	4.3	6.7	6.7	5.3	4.2	7.0	46.0	17 300	121	1 644	59 787	6.8
Jones	14.8	D	9.5	13.5	3.2	8.5	3.4	8.6	19.7	4 565	223	257	8 902	-0.1
Keokuk	32.9	D	5.8	3.9	D	8.3	3.4	4.4	12.4	2 455	240	166	4 875	-1.1
Kossuth	26.2	D	5.4	21.7	3.6	4.6	6.3	D	9.9	3 960	260	178	7 483	0.0
Lee	3.3	D	13.3	31.1	2.3	6.0	2.7	10.6	12.8	8 635	245	1 001	16 164	-0.3
Linn	0.2	0.1	6.8	22.1	9.2	6.8	10.8	10.5	10.2	39 820	183	3 685	95 333	3.3
Louisa	19.5	D	3.6	28.9	D	3.0	2.1	D	16.6	2 330	208	178	5 004	0.0
Lucas	11.7	0.0	6.0	4.4	2.2	6.0	3.5	D	19.0	2 245	259	220	4 199	-0.9
Lyon	42.4	D	4.0	17.7	4.7	2.4	2.2	3.4	6.7	2 240	192	60	4 991	2.9
Madison	15.9	1.6	11.2	7.7	4.6	6.7	5.3	5.8	21.7	3 145	201	141	6 728	2.7
Mahaska	15.7	D	5.2	20.9	3.8	6.2	2.8	5.1	17.7	4 825	216	452	9 802	0.4
Marion	3.0	D	4.7	46.5	D	4.7	2.8	10.7	9.6	6 945	209	388	14 077	1.2
Marshall	5.5	D	5.0	29.3	D	5.6	2.7	10.7	19.1	8 875	217	700	16 708	-0.7
Mills	7.0	D	7.0	5.4	D	7.7	4.7	D	34.9	3 285	223	252	6 080	-0.5
Mitchell	18.1	D	10.5	35.9	1.2	4.1	2.6	3.6	9.5	2 650	246	130	4 939	1.9
Monona	33.6	0.0	4.3	2.1	1.8	5.5	D	15.4	13.4	2 540	283	135	4 716	0.4
Monroe	12.6	D	6.5	38.3	D	3.9	2.1	D	12.4	1 900	239	121	3 961	2.0
Montgomery	10.0	D	6.0	16.7	6.9	6.0	3.6	D	22.0	2 765	265	255	5 198	-0.8
Muscatine	1.6	0.2	4.0	45.5	5.6	4.8	2.2	5.5	9.5	8 615	201	805	18 031	0.7
O'Brien	32.3	D	6.4	9.2	D	4.3	4.0	10.5	10.8	3 460	246	200	6 647	0.4
Osceola	48.0	D	4.6	8.3	D	2.3	D	5.6	8.0	1 485	239	59	2 961	-1.0
Page	13.3	D	4.2	16.1	D	9.0	3.2	D	22.3	4 010	258	325	7 178	0.0
Palo Alto	30.7	0.0	3.5	20.0	1.7	4.0	2.9	D	16.0	2 295	252	132	4 599	-0.6
Plymouth	26.9	D	3.7	20.6	1.7	3.7	3.2	3.7	8.9	5 175	208	208	10 688	1.3
Pocahontas	38.6	D	10.8	10.1	2.2	3.5	D	D	11.6	1 915	269	105	3 765	-0.8
Polk	0.1	D	8.1	6.1	10.8	5.3	20.4	10.7	12.7	71 030	154	7 827	195 114	7.1
Pottawattamie	2.8	0.2	10.2	16.0	4.4	8.0	3.8	12.9	15.4	18 955	203	2 217	39 616	0.7
Poweshiek	17.1	D	7.7	14.4	D	4.0	9.9	D	7.4	4 100	219	206	9 053	1.2
Ringgold	37.9	D	11.2	1.1	D	4.4	D	7.1	19.1	1 295	257	101	2 602	-0.4
Sac	37.0	D	3.0	16.7	D	2.9	D	6.5	9.1	2 655	264	99	5 399	-0.6
Scott	0.7	0.0	7.5	17.4	8.1	8.9	5.8	12.9	10.3	31 900	186	3 920	73 279	2.0
Shelby	22.7	0.7	4.5	10.5	7.2	4.1	4.3	D	13.7	3 090	258	197	5 566	0.4
Sioux	26.4	0.2	5.8	25.2	3.1	3.7	3.6	5.2	8.1	5 645	163	188	12 659	3.1
Story	1.2	D	6.8	15.9	7.0	4.7	3.1	7.0	39.3	12 210	128	646	38 569	4.8
Tama	24.8	0.0	6.1	7.0	D	4.3	2.9	D	29.2	4 120	237	219	7 748	-0.2
Taylor	39.4	D	3.1	15.9	D	2.8	1.8	D	12.6	1 610	262	108	3 085	-0.7
Union	11.9	D	5.5	22.9	D	6.5	3.6	5.4	20.9	2 975	236	268	5 904	-0.6
Van Buren	27.1	D	3.7	22.3	D	4.4	3.4	2.3	21.0	1 965	265	128	3 616	-1.5
Wapello	2.8	D	7.7	27.0	2.5	7.8	3.2	13.5	16.5	8 220	233	1 121	15 999	-0.6
Warren	3.7	0.0	12.3	6.2	5.6	8.8	5.1	11.4	22.3	8 865	185	402	19 315	5.1
Washington	24.5	D	10.2	12.0	2.3	7.2	2.5	5.6	14.1	4 895	222	349	9 570	0.6
Wayne	28.5	0.0	3.2	19.5	2.5	3.8	D	4.6	23.2	1 615	253	123	3 177	-1.1
Webster	8.1	0.3	7.7	22.3	4.2	6.3	2.6	12.4	14.1	8 510	230	832	17 016	-0.1
Winnebago	23.2	D	7.2	15.4	4.1	6.7	4.3	D	14.2	2 595	245	137	5 181	-0.3
Winneshiek	12.8	D	7.1	14.8	D	7.0	3.4	D	17.0	4 420	213	201	8 838	1.3
Woodbury	2.4	D	11.6	11.8	4.8	8.3	4.1	15.5	14.8	19 005	185	1 984	41 560	0.2
Worth	22.9	0.8	5.7	13.4	1.1	3.4	D	3.6	15.3	1 735	228	79	3 518	-0.8
Wright	27.4	D	3.2	21.3	4.5	3.4	2.4	4.1	19.1	3 155	245	179	6 493	-0.6

1. Per 1,000 resident population estimated as of July 1 of the year shown.

Table B. States and Counties — Housing, Labor Force, and Employment

STATE County	Housing units, 2010–2014								Civilian labor force, 2015				Civilian employment, 2010–2014		
	Occupied units										Unemployment			Percent	
			Owner-occupied			Renter-occupied									
				Median owner cost as a percent of income											
	Total	Percent	Median value[1]	With a mortgage	Without a mortgage[2]	Median rent[3]	Median rent as a percent of income[2]	Substandard units[4] (percent)	Total	Percent change, 2014–2015	Total	Rate[5]	Total	Management, business, science and arts	Construction, production, and maintenance occupations
	89	90	91	92	93	94	95	96	97	98	99	100	101	102	103

IOWA—Cont'd

STATE County	89	90	91	92	93	94	95	96	97	98	99	100	101	102	103
Franklin	4 321	76.0	86 000	20.8	10.4	571	21.4	0.9	5 990	0.3	198	3.3	5 215	28.6	35.7
Fremont	3 003	76.1	96 300	18.3	10.9	583	26.8	1.3	4 166	0.0	136	3.3	3 506	36.2	29.0
Greene	3 849	76.3	82 600	21.6	11.1	619	25.3	0.8	5 606	6.4	193	3.4	4 386	32.8	27.0
Grundy	5 112	80.8	127 800	19.3	11.6	605	25.8	0.7	6 728	0.1	250	3.7	6 109	31.7	29.9
Guthrie	4 559	80.0	98 500	19.6	11.7	591	24.2	1.4	5 728	2.1	208	3.6	5 274	33.4	27.9
Hamilton	6 354	70.4	90 800	20.3	11.6	615	27.3	1.7	7 226	1.8	302	4.2	7 424	30.3	33.1
Hancock	4 629	82.6	90 100	19.3	10.0	536	24.7	1.4	6 393	1.5	170	2.7	5 649	30.0	37.1
Hardin	6 997	76.5	89 800	18.2	11.8	560	22.5	1.1	8 869	1.9	342	3.9	8 057	31.9	32.3
Harrison	5 959	76.7	107 500	20.9	11.7	614	25.8	1.0	7 650	1.5	253	3.3	7 328	32.2	29.7
Henry	7 512	74.1	103 900	20.1	12.5	605	25.8	2.4	9 623	0.8	374	3.9	9 050	30.2	28.3
Howard	3 917	79.7	95 500	21.0	11.0	608	32.1	2.0	5 426	2.1	190	3.5	4 821	28.7	37.5
Humboldt	4 200	74.2	85 900	18.6	11.4	582	23.1	0.3	5 353	1.8	175	3.3	4 589	29.3	32.3
Ida	3 124	74.3	78 800	17.7	10.0	426	20.0	1.8	3 959	1.8	122	3.1	3 608	31.0	34.2
Iowa	6 705	78.5	138 300	20.5	11.3	539	20.5	1.7	10 409	2.0	358	3.4	8 737	31.6	29.7
Jackson	8 494	75.2	110 500	20.6	11.8	570	27.5	1.0	11 185	1.6	464	4.1	9 706	25.6	35.6
Jasper	14 658	72.4	116 200	21.5	11.4	648	25.0	1.6	19 089	-1.2	729	3.8	17 300	29.5	30.3
Jefferson	6 886	68.8	94 600	20.6	11.9	652	26.1	1.2	9 150	0.8	343	3.7	8 245	38.7	21.9
Johnson	54 850	59.6	191 900	20.9	10.4	860	35.1	2.4	83 891	-0.1	2 177	2.6	76 464	45.7	15.1
Jones	8 235	77.1	127 300	20.7	11.7	591	24.1	0.6	10 843	0.5	443	4.1	9 906	29.0	32.9
Keokuk	4 386	79.5	76 900	19.0	12.7	564	27.3	3.0	5 462	-1.0	227	4.2	5 041	31.5	31.4
Kossuth	6 628	81.0	93 700	18.3	10.0	553	24.9	1.3	8 857	2.3	249	2.8	7 773	33.7	29.3
Lee	14 319	74.0	85 000	19.6	12.2	576	26.6	1.7	18 325	3.4	972	5.3	16 370	23.7	34.6
Linn	87 004	73.5	145 700	19.8	12.2	689	26.9	1.4	119 815	-0.9	4 456	3.7	113 222	38.1	21.4
Louisa	4 386	76.9	99 000	21.5	11.8	617	20.7	5.3	6 029	1.7	224	3.7	5 552	25.5	40.9
Lucas	3 745	78.5	80 700	21.6	12.8	481	28.4	3.9	4 425	2.7	153	3.5	3 936	23.7	29.9
Lyon	4 495	82.2	109 000	19.2	10.9	563	19.2	1.8	7 105	1.3	139	2.0	5 904	36.0	27.9
Madison	6 103	75.8	156 600	22.0	12.4	812	27.5	1.7	8 292	0.8	315	3.8	7 625	36.8	26.0
Mahaska	9 084	70.2	103 800	20.5	11.3	582	24.2	1.0	11 853	0.0	461	3.9	10 877	31.8	31.2
Marion	12 843	75.6	135 800	19.9	11.9	664	26.1	0.9	17 495	0.4	560	3.2	16 926	33.3	26.1
Marshall	15 354	73.3	104 200	20.5	12.0	654	24.3	3.1	19 478	-1.8	975	5.0	19 324	29.8	33.2
Mills	5 348	83.0	151 700	21.2	10.0	706	24.5	1.6	7 496	1.4	297	4.0	7 240	32.8	25.8
Mitchell	4 453	82.4	105 300	19.7	11.8	534	24.7	2.1	5 524	1.2	155	2.8	5 211	30.9	36.6
Monona	3 972	72.3	78 900	18.4	11.3	542	26.0	0.9	4 766	0.3	205	4.3	4 141	28.9	31.2
Monroe	3 280	76.1	96 800	19.1	13.2	542	21.8	3.4	4 087	0.3	177	4.3	3 682	33.1	30.6
Montgomery	4 590	69.2	78 100	18.5	12.0	586	25.7	1.7	5 200	0.8	182	3.5	4 736	31.9	28.4
Muscatine	16 301	74.4	126 700	20.4	12.4	736	29.8	2.2	22 125	0.1	843	3.8	20 816	28.2	33.9
O'Brien	6 018	74.4	101 100	18.3	10.0	582	23.2	1.1	8 469	2.8	235	2.8	7 245	28.8	32.9
Osceola	2 697	76.6	80 900	18.7	10.0	561	21.9	2.9	3 545	2.5	100	2.8	3 340	29.3	37.7
Page	6 379	73.6	80 700	18.3	11.6	563	24.6	2.5	6 598	0.0	267	4.0	7 294	33.2	28.3
Palo Alto	4 011	75.2	84 900	19.0	10.8	501	23.8	1.4	4 860	0.2	148	3.0	4 727	31.5	29.1
Plymouth	9 899	80.5	133 500	18.3	10.2	598	24.2	0.5	14 833	1.2	410	2.8	13 181	31.5	29.6
Pocahontas	3 222	78.5	62 500	16.7	10.8	494	20.1	1.4	4 368	1.0	130	3.0	3 544	32.8	31.2
Polk	174 759	68.6	155 400	20.5	11.7	792	28.0	2.6	255 763	0.1	9 172	3.6	234 860	39.7	17.8
Pottawattamie	36 615	70.1	124 500	21.2	11.7	758	28.5	2.2	49 267	0.2	1 757	3.6	46 677	29.4	25.1
Poweshiek	7 424	69.8	125 700	21.3	11.1	640	26.9	0.5	10 485	0.8	375	3.6	9 661	34.0	24.4
Ringgold	2 078	75.7	76 800	20.0	13.6	482	19.5	2.7	2 572	1.7	85	3.3	2 160	36.0	30.3
Sac	4 413	80.2	81 200	18.5	10.1	538	20.7	1.2	5 693	2.5	185	3.2	5 160	28.1	30.1
Scott	67 325	68.7	144 900	19.9	11.6	703	28.6	1.3	87 133	-1.5	4 025	4.6	82 617	36.0	22.9
Shelby	5 171	76.9	106 500	20.5	11.3	636	27.0	0.4	7 072	0.3	197	2.8	6 058	31.4	27.8
Sioux	11 782	78.3	137 500	19.7	10.0	607	22.5	2.5	20 799	3.3	500	2.4	18 582	32.2	28.9
Story	35 666	53.8	164 200	19.8	10.0	760	35.1	2.0	57 365	1.3	1 377	2.4	49 703	45.2	17.9
Tama	6 815	76.1	101 400	18.8	11.2	659	25.6	1.9	9 698	5.0	418	4.3	8 277	29.6	32.6
Taylor	2 752	71.9	66 200	18.7	11.3	589	25.0	2.4	3 248	0.2	100	3.1	3 052	29.8	36.3
Union	5 293	73.5	90 700	19.5	14.7	591	28.7	1.5	6 604	-3.1	269	4.1	6 235	26.4	33.4
Van Buren	2 986	85.2	75 000	21.1	12.3	523	21.9	3.5	3 862	-1.3	154	4.0	3 444	25.7	37.8
Wapello	14 608	72.9	76 900	19.9	13.1	619	31.0	2.5	17 983	-0.8	911	5.1	16 216	24.0	38.0
Warren	17 584	78.1	159 300	20.2	11.8	740	26.6	1.2	26 796	0.1	893	3.3	24 946	37.5	19.6
Washington	9 056	73.4	121 900	21.4	11.5	701	24.8	1.4	12 451	1.1	380	3.1	11 250	33.2	28.0
Wayne	2 548	80.8	66 400	19.5	13.3	481	25.9	3.0	2 857	-0.5	110	3.9	2 758	31.9	36.0
Webster	15 397	67.5	84 600	18.9	10.9	561	27.1	0.7	20 299	2.4	862	4.2	17 088	30.0	26.5
Winnebago	4 584	75.8	94 200	19.0	11.1	493	21.6	0.8	5 187	-0.7	201	3.9	5 284	29.7	31.7
Winneshiek	8 141	76.0	155 300	22.4	11.9	590	22.6	0.4	12 230	1.4	442	3.6	12 066	36.4	24.4
Woodbury	38 818	67.5	98 300	19.8	11.5	660	29.0	2.6	55 883	-0.1	2 080	3.7	51 311	27.9	29.7
Worth	3 194	79.7	98 600	19.1	11.4	531	27.2	2.1	4 240	0.9	166	3.9	3 926	24.7	35.2
Wright	5 419	75.9	72 800	17.9	10.3	544	25.6	1.6	6 952	0.1	265	3.8	6 037	30.5	33.0

1. Specified owner-occupied units.   2. A value of 10.0 represents 10 percent or less; a value of 50.0 represents 50 percent or more.   3. Specified renter-occupied units.
4. Overcrowded or lacking complete plumbing facilities.   5. Percent of civilian labor force.   6. Persons 16 years old and over.

Table B. States and Counties — Nonfarm Employment and Agriculture

STATE County	Private nonfarm establishments, employment and payroll, 2014									Agriculture, 2012			
		Employment						Annual payroll		Farms			
											Percent with:		
	Number of establishments	Total	Health care and social assistance	Manufacturing	Retail trade	Finance and insurance	Professional, scientific, and technical services	Total (mil dol)	Average per employee (dollars)	Number	Fewer than 50 acres	500 acres or more	Farm operators whose principal occupation is farming (percent)
	104	105	106	107	108	109	110	111	112	113	114	115	116
IOWA—Cont'd													
Franklin	322	3 277	569	886	320	105	67	127	38 693	853	29.9	29.3	54.3
Fremont	188	2 094	D	553	592	69	41	83	39 612	533	27.0	32.8	62.3
Greene	267	2 721	D	436	381	117	80	92	33 962	780	31.0	30.5	60.8
Grundy	314	3 319	700	527	429	D	50	139	42 010	737	33.0	27.0	56.3
Guthrie	313	2 495	458	388	394	244	61	88	35 074	829	29.2	24.2	53.3
Hamilton	383	4 307	687	620	732	186	D	152	35 384	761	36.4	27.1	56.6
Hancock	300	3 530	480	1 087	410	77	292	128	36 159	889	32.2	28.0	65.8
Hardin	562	5 439	1 061	550	874	262	156	205	37 648	819	31.3	28.0	54.1
Harrison	364	3 070	791	276	483	D	82	101	32 957	819	28.2	32.5	57.4
Henry	518	8 110	1 209	2 480	875	177	139	282	34 713	903	31.3	16.4	47.5
Howard	256	2 782	536	919	369	D	49	86	30 809	883	30.2	19.3	51.4
Humboldt	316	3 463	460	972	526	125	D	122	35 362	574	28.6	30.1	52.4
Ida	247	2 859	474	1 033	263	D	D	119	41 548	547	30.2	30.5	55.4
Iowa	489	8 102	814	D	1 383	120	D	308	38 070	1 019	32.0	17.0	48.4
Jackson	534	4 928	907	849	888	261	83	146	29 601	1 255	29.6	12.7	47.4
Jasper	726	8 946	1 551	D	1 445	242	448	273	30 493	1 098	34.9	21.8	52.8
Jefferson	678	6 848	591	966	868	832	678	245	35 813	685	29.6	15.6	46.3
Johnson	3 218	60 242	16 166	5 348	9 030	2 240	2 254	2 401	39 861	1 342	34.7	14.7	50.2
Jones	490	4 872	881	936	979	201	118	153	31 337	1 061	28.8	20.8	53.3
Keokuk	250	1 803	397	223	212	105	39	63	34 869	982	27.2	20.0	47.5
Kossuth	570	5 769	D	1 315	923	484	182	214	37 085	1 349	30.0	33.5	67.4
Lee	890	13 065	2 172	4 124	2 075	D	197	488	37 327	917	32.4	16.4	42.6
Linn	5 391	116 405	15 458	16 424	14 414	9 560	5 718	5 425	46 606	1 402	37.4	15.5	58.6
Louisa	205	2 827	371	D	210	78	D	101	35 649	612	34.3	18.1	43.0
Lucas	173	2 883	537	D	481	D	31	106	36 831	648	25.0	14.8	37.7
Lyon	395	3 344	412	D	423	164	127	118	35 169	1 139	25.2	21.3	62.6
Madison	367	2 472	565	159	461	122	86	80	32 239	961	37.3	15.7	40.9
Mahaska	568	6 784	1 091	1 347	1 160	210	148	232	34 241	1 012	30.4	22.6	48.7
Marion	813	15 671	2 381	D	1 552	293	342	631	40 271	1 024	38.3	16.0	39.9
Marshall	785	14 096	2 051	D	2 109	367	316	556	39 441	882	34.4	25.3	60.1
Mills	297	2 276	626	D	349	105	D	73	32 160	500	32.0	30.8	61.4
Mitchell	318	3 069	554	997	383	118	77	101	32 926	903	29.1	24.9	65.7
Monona	231	2 184	632	D	397	124	D	64	29 387	538	19.5	39.2	65.8
Monroe	174	2 260	444	890	284	70	34	82	36 337	592	24.2	17.1	64.3
Montgomery	311	3 198	788	490	534	124	D	102	31 863	499	21.2	34.1	62.3
Muscatine	942	20 276	1 877	6 844	2 235	417	D	920	45 350	786	34.4	18.1	51.4
O'Brien	512	5 358	1 390	571	908	207	D	155	28 881	884	24.8	25.1	61.3
Osceola	190	1 542	265	300	141	86	23	53	34 301	555	22.2	33.0	71.4
Page	414	5 384	1 488	D	621	176	124	178	33 102	739	20.7	29.1	58.9
Palo Alto	279	2 813	731	530	357	108	46	86	30 732	874	31.5	27.0	54.6
Plymouth	693	9 898	1 331	2 584	1 016	311	195	381	38 537	1 331	24.0	28.8	67.8
Pocahontas	222	1 952	253	482	260	93	D	64	32 724	742	25.6	34.9	72.0
Polk	12 078	249 489	33 899	16 726	30 376	34 716	15 249	12 121	48 583	773	51.2	16.0	51.5
Pottawattamie	1 981	31 202	5 103	5 155	6 012	771	625	1 044	33 460	1 188	29.5	30.3	66.2
Poweshiek	529	9 337	1 007	1 652	1 199	D	113	337	36 057	852	27.6	24.8	55.4
Ringgold	146	1 094	370	D	204	44	52	30	27 147	651	20.4	24.9	46.2
Sac	339	2 552	545	384	332	134	55	83	32 545	914	32.5	28.9	53.9
Scott	4 353	81 166	13 100	11 353	11 904	2 584	2 845	3 160	38 932	759	35.4	18.7	55.3
Shelby	390	5 236	889	651	574	250	145	186	35 470	869	21.7	33.1	65.0
Sioux	1 229	18 307	2 535	5 360	1 617	568	921	638	34 832	1 618	31.4	19.2	61.0
Story	2 003	31 660	5 246	5 112	5 092	732	1 249	1 213	38 315	966	42.8	20.9	49.1
Tama	336	3 545	519	366	522	D	D	116	32 581	1 132	29.7	24.1	62.4
Taylor	135	1 372	D	455	128	D	D	55	40 216	639	25.2	22.1	44.4
Union	326	4 877	839	1 490	728	186	72	161	32 914	648	33.0	16.7	44.3
Van Buren	151	1 672	313	D	198	D	18	53	31 909	753	27.2	14.1	48.2
Wapello	749	14 448	2 606	3 868	2 436	410	248	493	34 125	742	31.4	15.0	45.0
Warren	800	7 820	1 242	358	1 443	D	313	233	29 737	1 334	43.4	10.0	37.3
Washington	704	6 933	1 306	1 038	1 059	222	174	215	31 079	1 139	31.3	17.3	53.8
Wayne	151	1 411	D	392	209	37	43	47	33 544	691	27.4	21.3	43.0
Webster	1 008	15 363	2 860	1 603	2 642	402	D	593	38 630	968	29.8	29.3	64.2
Winnebago	325	6 639	595	D	515	178	128	245	36 950	642	34.0	26.2	52.5
Winneshiek	613	9 723	1 458	1 383	1 250	263	231	298	30 621	1 535	33.4	15.2	49.1
Woodbury	2 672	46 158	8 489	5 106	7 677	1 238	1 052	1 538	33 310	973	28.5	28.6	58.6
Worth	175	1 762	201	425	163	58	D	55	31 085	640	33.4	28.0	54.5
Wright	389	4 321	934	1 459	531	142	D	168	38 842	775	34.2	32.8	61.3

Table B. States and Counties — **Agriculture**

STATE County	Land in farms Acreage (1,000) [117]	Percent change, 2007–2012 [118]	Average size of farm [119]	Total irrigated (1,000) [120]	Total cropland (1,000) [121]	Value of land and buildings (dollars) Average per farm [122]	Average per acre [123]	Value of machinery and equipment, average per farm (dollars) [124]	Total (mil dol) [125]	Average per farm (dollars) [126]	Crops [127]	Live-stock and poultry products [128]	$10,000 or more [129]	$100,000 or more [130]	Government payments Total ($1,000) [131]	Percent of farms [132]
IOWA—Cont'd																
Franklin	355	-3.1	417	D	336.7	2 769 033	6 646	259 810	454.4	532 687	55.9	44.1	69.3	51.9	9 424	83.0
Fremont	287	17.2	539	8.5	253.9	3 311 917	6 141	274 623	180.4	338 409	89.6	10.4	62.7	46.5	5 009	83.1
Greene	357	0.9	458	D	325.6	3 185 444	6 962	289 094	308.1	395 058	67.7	32.3	65.3	47.9	7 356	82.3
Grundy	318	0.7	432	0.0	301.1	3 465 753	8 031	330 237	362.7	492 126	76.6	23.4	69.2	56.9	7 556	82.8
Guthrie	328	-7.7	395	D	262.2	2 291 450	5 798	193 695	257.5	310 555	52.5	47.5	55.9	31.8	8 272	81.3
Hamilton	327	-5.6	430	D	305.1	3 489 958	8 121	268 636	540.4	710 103	44.2	55.8	64.9	50.2	9 809	80.0
Hancock	353	-2.1	397	1.2	338.4	2 765 206	6 957	268 795	475.1	534 388	49.3	50.7	69.0	51.6	8 438	86.6
Hardin	332	-2.0	406	0.0	306.2	2 996 061	7 385	272 880	534.5	652 620	48.8	51.2	66.3	50.5	9 829	83.7
Harrison	394	7.8	481	29.1	343.3	2 799 425	5 824	257 150	249.2	304 277	85.9	14.1	64.2	44.1	7 528	83.9
Henry	270	12.5	299	0.0	220.7	1 471 299	4 929	145 765	171.8	190 219	70.4	29.6	45.4	27.5	8 270	82.5
Howard	300	7.6	340	0.2	273.3	2 239 316	6 593	243 708	322.3	365 058	57.3	42.7	62.7	41.0	9 932	81.9
Humboldt	235	-13.1	409	0.0	220.1	3 120 220	7 627	258 958	242.1	421 793	70.1	29.9	72.5	57.1	6 158	81.9
Ida	261	-4.3	477	D	234.1	3 237 473	6 786	276 272	272.2	497 678	60.1	39.9	72.8	53.9	7 024	83.7
Iowa	336	-2.6	330	D	275.5	1 996 335	6 053	170 894	276.9	271 734	64.8	35.2	58.5	36.3	8 803	80.0
Jackson	309	4.2	246	0.2	214.2	1 312 333	5 331	150 764	236.1	188 110	45.6	54.4	58.1	26.8	8 990	76.2
Jasper	374	-12.7	340	0.8	324.8	2 115 648	6 217	209 787	327.0	297 853	76.7	23.3	63.2	42.5	7 997	74.4
Jefferson	198	0.4	289	0.1	153.4	1 328 096	4 591	134 391	104.1	151 991	70.2	29.8	43.8	22.6	6 713	78.4
Johnson	329	2.3	245	0.2	285.1	1 682 142	6 868	154 571	258.3	192 443	67.9	32.1	58.7	34.1	8 623	67.7
Jones	314	-3.1	296	0.1	255.7	1 982 445	6 699	205 724	276.2	260 306	59.6	40.4	65.7	39.2	9 960	80.5
Keokuk	295	-7.1	301	0.0	240.6	1 499 580	4 984	164 024	230.8	234 996	57.0	43.0	54.9	33.2	12 904	85.0
Kossuth	599	-0.3	444	0.3	568.6	3 380 844	7 608	295 763	722.3	535 440	64.2	35.8	74.9	62.1	13 183	87.5
Lee	236	-0.9	257	1.1	172.3	1 098 520	4 268	114 699	130.1	141 845	70.7	29.3	49.5	23.8	5 417	72.5
Linn	339	1.2	242	0.2	292.6	1 626 668	6 722	173 044	260.8	185 998	76.1	23.9	58.3	30.0	8 202	72.7
Louisa	169	-9.4	275	9.9	139.5	1 581 547	5 743	187 708	172.5	281 889	60.8	39.2	53.8	33.5	5 560	77.8
Lucas	177	3.6	274	D	101.5	786 495	2 874	99 623	51.1	78 872	47.7	52.3	42.1	15.3	4 571	73.6
Lyon	370	14.5	325	1.5	334.0	2 677 244	8 245	275 852	836.1	734 068	30.7	69.3	87.4	65.6	7 064	79.0
Madison	276	-2.6	287	0.1	184.1	1 408 613	4 903	122 793	132.9	138 322	65.2	34.8	47.9	19.9	5 013	65.9
Mahaska	323	9.4	319	0.1	273.9	1 794 609	5 623	204 132	311.1	307 382	54.9	45.1	60.8	36.9	11 369	79.8
Marion	265	7.6	259	0.1	200.0	1 154 279	4 462	117 525	137.9	134 660	80.5	19.5	46.4	22.4	6 603	72.3
Marshall	312	-3.7	354	0.2	280.6	2 345 805	6 623	227 533	313.1	354 966	75.1	24.9	63.7	45.7	7 063	76.1
Mills	206	4.8	413	D	182.3	2 606 084	6 316	242 756	120.6	241 170	95.4	4.6	59.8	44.2	4 403	77.6
Mitchell	296	0.7	328	1.0	272.8	2 418 524	7 372	214 307	363.4	402 482	47.0	53.0	73.6	51.9	6 663	75.0
Monona	338	-14.1	629	61.1	300.6	3 451 381	5 491	370 487	221.3	411 253	86.6	13.4	73.6	51.9	5 639	82.0
Monroe	195	-3.0	330	D	111.8	1 045 139	3 171	95 220	59.0	99 581	55.3	44.7	49.3	17.2	3 873	70.9
Montgomery	245	11.1	491	0.4	207.4	2 753 371	5 610	272 595	189.4	379 615	71.3	28.7	71.1	47.9	4 831	82.8
Muscatine	215	-3.1	274	7.4	183.2	1 720 141	6 289	166 092	187.3	238 233	72.5	27.5	56.4	35.1	6 401	76.0
O'Brien	304	-11.9	344	0.9	276.5	2 940 939	8 538	244 251	533.4	603 437	43.4	56.6	84.8	66.9	5 935	81.9
Osceola	238	-5.2	429	1.3	223.3	3 021 315	7 039	277 225	410.6	739 865	42.8	57.2	81.8	66.5	5 504	86.8
Page	317	16.9	429	0.2	263.0	2 158 371	5 031	221 513	198.3	268 369	81.6	18.4	70.5	44.8	6 816	83.8
Palo Alto	359	1.5	410	4.8	340.8	3 088 190	7 523	288 436	498.6	570 531	55.0	45.0	65.7	50.2	8 245	86.1
Plymouth	542	4.7	407	2.0	479.8	2 992 740	7 352	280 373	643.1	483 173	40.8	59.2	77.9	51.8	11 860	80.5
Pocahontas	332	-8.4	448	0.6	317.5	3 416 018	7 635	309 951	406.7	548 144	64.8	35.2	76.7	61.7	9 485	90.3
Polk	198	-20.8	256	0.5	178.6	1 802 039	7 052	169 371	153.9	199 128	92.3	7.7	54.5	27.0	4 768	62.0
Pottawattamie	533	9.6	449	3.9	481.8	3 154 295	7 033	280 880	464.5	391 035	70.1	29.9	67.3	47.6	9 377	72.9
Poweshiek	334	6.9	393	0.0	286.8	2 386 670	6 080	231 304	350.4	411 247	60.1	39.9	64.9	42.3	7 393	79.3
Ringgold	270	1.8	414	D	178.8	1 417 304	3 420	149 154	116.6	179 161	41.8	58.2	58.7	26.0	6 034	76.8
Sac	357	-1.7	391	0.5	333.0	2 898 569	7 420	255 801	474.7	519 315	45.6	54.4	71.6	50.1	9 715	82.5
Scott	221	-11.3	291	0.6	201.4	2 359 184	8 118	234 090	248.2	326 949	66.5	33.5	65.9	43.1	7 134	71.5
Shelby	372	3.9	428	0.0	344.3	2 901 694	6 772	255 117	351.3	404 253	70.4	29.6	80.9	58.1	8 494	85.7
Sioux	484	1.2	299	8.5	442.4	2 726 452	9 105	277 347	1 613.1	996 964	19.7	80.3	83.9	66.1	11 514	74.1
Story	306	-13.1	317	0.4	279.4	2 482 983	7 838	205 934	292.8	303 082	79.6	20.4	60.0	37.3	6 566	73.5
Tama	403	-6.5	356	0.0	351.7	2 313 300	6 503	214 804	355.2	313 764	78.5	21.5	65.4	43.1	9 820	81.4
Taylor	279	-1.4	436	0.0	212.0	1 668 700	3 827	195 518	144.2	225 667	58.6	41.4	56.3	28.5	6 371	78.7
Union	214	-0.1	331	0.0	147.6	1 138 708	3 441	138 670	118.2	182 338	46.2	53.8	50.5	24.7	4 243	70.7
Van Buren	213	-3.7	283	0.0	140.8	984 527	3 475	101 955	110.1	146 246	52.6	47.4	43.8	17.9	5 497	68.7
Wapello	189	13.6	255	0.1	138.7	1 049 902	4 125	126 195	86.2	116 235	72.4	27.6	42.0	19.5	5 473	67.7
Warren	264	9.1	198	0.0	184.0	1 010 263	5 114	93 412	110.1	82 542	81.6	18.4	42.1	12.1	7 169	57.6
Washington	314	-3.5	276	0.2	264.6	1 685 741	6 107	175 919	526.8	462 551	31.7	68.3	59.3	39.4	12 460	75.9
Wayne	274	0.2	396	0.1	199.0	1 280 719	3 233	143 864	74.3	107 534	64.5	35.5	47.9	19.0	7 885	72.4
Webster	409	-9.9	422	D	383.6	3 106 004	7 352	252 019	353.6	365 319	82.4	17.6	65.4	48.7	11 421	85.4
Winnebago	235	-6.4	367	0.0	222.0	2 474 578	6 748	266 843	281.5	438 438	59.4	40.6	61.4	44.7	6 474	87.1
Winneshiek	376	19.9	245	0.0	305.3	1 460 745	5 959	173 344	345.9	225 362	50.0	50.0	56.7	35.2	14 181	83.2
Woodbury	446	0.0	458	5.3	384.6	2 736 038	5 974	230 038	416.5	428 025	56.6	43.4	66.9	46.5	9 174	77.6
Worth	235	1.4	367	1.1	218.4	2 255 917	6 145	240 556	188.1	293 936	86.8	13.2	60.2	43.9	6 708	86.1
Wright	360	9.8	464	0.0	344.6	3 345 938	7 209	316 590	484.9	625 738	53.0	47.0	65.5	51.7	11 670	84.3

Table B. States and Counties — Water Use, Wholesale Trade, Retail Trade, and Real Estate

STATE County	Water use, 2010		Wholesale trade,[1] 2012				Retail trade,[2] 2012				Real estate and rental and leasing,[2] 2012			
	Total water withdrawn (mil gal/day)	Gallons withdrawn per person per day	Number of establish-ments	Number of employees	Sales (mil dol)	Annual payroll (mil dol)	Number of establish-ments	Number of employees	Sales (mil dol)	Annual payroll (mil dol)	Number of establish-ments	Number of employees	Receipts (mil dol)	Annual payroll (mil dol)
	133	134	135	136	137	138	139	140	141	142	143	144	145	146
IOWA—Cont'd														
Franklin	4.1	386	23	346	697.8	14.5	40	327	79.7	6.9	11	20	3.0	0.4
Fremont	2.6	345	14	202	212.1	9.7	30	534	145.6	10.6	6	10	0.2	0.1
Greene	5.8	624	12	449	1 016.7	24.4	39	367	94.1	7.0	4	10	0.6	0.1
Grundy	2.2	178	19	240	494.8	12.9	44	406	83.4	7.0	8	D	D	D
Guthrie	3.2	294	15	119	175.2	5.1	44	378	105.7	7.1	9	D	D	D
Hamilton	4.1	264	33	828	731.6	37.2	60	660	158.6	12.3	6	D	D	D
Hancock	4.6	406	26	176	333.3	8.1	47	424	216.1	8.2	8	28	1.9	0.5
Hardin	9.2	526	38	889	2 961.5	51.1	80	819	175.9	17.3	14	30	5.1	0.8
Harrison	10.6	712	28	452	263.2	17.9	52	467	197.2	10.8	9	15	1.3	0.5
Henry	3.3	164	31	279	224.8	9.9	63	880	229.1	19.3	16	32	2.8	0.3
Howard	4.3	448	18	165	262.0	6.3	45	363	100.7	7.4	4	D	D	D
Humboldt	3.1	311	31	238	274.0	11.6	50	480	108.9	9.4	9	19	1.8	0.4
Ida	3.3	464	17	184	272.8	7.5	36	305	64.1	5.5	8	12	1.4	0.4
Iowa	3.2	196	18	139	162.0	6.4	130	1 365	234.1	20.2	4	D	D	D
Jackson	3.2	161	26	230	201.6	8.5	76	946	258.0	18.9	13	20	2.8	0.4
Jasper	7.9	213	36	342	445.1	13.7	108	1 302	355.4	27.7	24	60	6.5	1.4
Jefferson	2.2	132	38	D	D	D	86	916	171.7	18.8	26	48	6.9	1.0
Johnson	37.3	285	85	1 389	1 011.8	61.0	509	8 743	1 861.7	195.8	134	538	131.1	20.8
Jones	4.1	200	24	301	903.0	12.0	79	1 062	269.3	26.3	14	D	D	D
Keokuk	3.1	299	25	229	214.3	9.9	36	240	55.0	3.5	4	12	1.4	0.1
Kossuth	6.5	417	38	388	500.1	19.6	93	879	246.8	19.2	11	48	2.4	0.7
Lee	28.3	790	39	390	482.8	18.1	151	2 014	474.3	43.4	22	72	9.9	1.7
Linn	146.0	691	310	4 863	3 030.7	261.4	716	14 387	4 483.3	351.2	214	944	203.0	34.1
Louisa	15.7	1 378	12	175	242.2	10.7	25	210	60.7	3.9	7	8	0.7	0.1
Lucas	1.3	148	5	D	D	D	29	381	86.1	8.0	4	6	1.0	0.1
Lyon	7.4	642	26	252	461.6	10.7	52	364	106.6	7.0	8	19	1.5	0.8
Madison	2.1	135	13	227	221.0	9.5	45	493	92.5	8.4	5	D	D	D
Mahaska	4.2	189	34	D	D	D	103	1 210	242.5	24.4	10	26	4.8	0.8
Marion	4.0	121	42	459	315.8	19.2	131	1 517	363.8	33.4	26	63	10.9	1.4
Marshall	11.3	279	39	D	D	D	150	2 059	438.0	43.6	32	394	74.0	14.1
Mills	2.1	136	16	222	173.7	10.5	36	315	96.4	6.1	15	50	7.1	1.4
Mitchell	5.8	539	23	294	514.0	14.8	55	365	73.8	6.1	7	50	0.9	0.2
Monona	16.5	1 780	12	105	140.9	4.7	43	392	119.6	9.0	2	D	D	D
Monroe	2.6	324	11	173	52.0	5.8	32	302	85.9	5.7	5	4	0.7	0.1
Montgomery	2.1	198	15	119	222.4	6.2	49	529	108.4	10.1	9	46	4.4	1.2
Muscatine	235.3	5 505	50	D	D	D	141	2 070	489.0	44.1	47	199	28.1	5.7
O'Brien	6.5	451	32	358	776.7	14.7	99	930	204.5	17.5	4	18	4.4	0.5
Osceola	7.0	1 077	8	D	D	D	29	164	81.0	3.5	1	D	D	D
Page	3.3	208	18	157	146.9	6.3	72	692	153.8	12.6	8	10	1.9	0.1
Palo Alto	4.8	511	17	138	262.9	6.2	41	340	81.1	6.9	7	17	4.0	0.3
Plymouth	10.5	419	35	351	469.0	13.8	97	1 013	270.0	20.9	18	57	5.9	1.3
Pocahontas	2.2	298	12	137	303.5	5.6	33	245	50.3	4.7	1	D	D	D
Polk	58.3	135	678	11 409	9 500.5	631.6	1 518	27 663	7 616.3	689.8	549	3 095	632.1	123.1
Pottawattamie	568.5	6 102	96	1 331	1 737.8	64.7	308	5 957	1 757.6	128.5	80	351	53.4	8.8
Poweshiek	3.0	161	21	182	226.5	7.6	84	1 107	432.9	33.4	13	28	2.9	0.5
Ringgold	1.5	298	7	55	90.7	2.2	28	194	79.6	4.3	2	D	D	D
Sac	8.8	848	29	229	275.3	13.3	57	381	101.6	7.5	4	4	1.4	0.1
Scott	120.6	730	266	4 020	2 642.1	195.5	638	11 210	3 098.7	266.1	181	744	194.3	27.8
Shelby	3.5	284	28	400	255.2	13.5	56	571	175.3	10.7	5	17	1.7	0.2
Sioux	20.8	618	87	1 554	1 401.0	60.6	149	1 622	433.3	35.3	24	106	18.4	5.8
Story	12.5	140	74	D	D	D	288	4 708	1 084.2	98.5	97	465	75.5	16.1
Tama	5.8	325	22	136	204.5	5.7	64	530	122.3	11.1	5	D	D	D
Taylor	1.0	158	5	D	D	D	18	147	32.6	2.2	3	D	D	D
Union	6.1	483	18	236	552.4	10.1	49	756	174.9	16.8	11	D	D	D
Van Buren	1.2	152	8	46	39.3	1.5	29	192	40.5	3.4	3	D	D	D
Wapello	14.6	410	29	211	314.3	7.9	135	2 290	538.4	48.5	23	91	12.5	2.9
Warren	2.6	56	37	549	287.1	24.6	103	1 513	367.8	32.3	23	69	10.4	1.6
Washington	5.3	244	42	306	273.0	13.4	103	1 091	256.1	22.1	12	22	1.6	0.3
Wayne	0.8	120	5	79	55.3	2.6	31	197	70.1	4.2	1	D	D	D
Webster	16.5	433	59	D	D	D	171	2 616	595.8	54.5	39	103	20.2	2.6
Winnebago	2.8	256	22	169	280.8	7.4	56	485	131.4	9.5	5	D	D	D
Winneshiek	6.3	298	33	271	281.9	14.5	121	1 185	293.0	26.8	11	23	1.9	0.4
Woodbury	1 021.4	9 997	149	2 253	2 107.7	101.7	432	7 336	1 776.1	155.7	90	516	65.2	13.3
Worth	10.2	1 344	14	103	189.5	4.8	20	183	36.7	3.6	1	D	D	D
Wright	6.2	470	18	286	628.1	15.4	61	606	117.9	10.4	14	21	2.7	0.3

1. Merchant wholesalers, except manufacturers' sales branches and offices.   2. Employer establishments.

Table B. States and Counties — Professional Services, Manufacturing, and Accommodation and Food Services

STATE County	Professional, scientific, and technical services, 2012				Manufacturing, 2012				Accommodation and food services, 2012			
	Number of establishments	Number of employees	Receipts (mil dol)	Annual payroll (mil dol)	Number of establishments	Number of employees	Receipts (mil dol)	Annual payroll (mil dol)	Number of establishments	Number of employees	Sales (mil dol)	Annual payroll (mil dol)
	147	148	149	150	151	152	153	154	155	156	157	158
IOWA—Cont'd												
Franklin	20	76	5.6	2.2	24	719	229.3	36.4	18	154	5.6	1.6
Fremont	8	34	3.2	1.2	10	632	654.4	30.5	21	180	7.5	1.9
Greene	17	79	7.5	3.5	10	287	86.0	13.5	18	D	D	D
Grundy	12	37	4.4	1.3	13	504	153.9	20.5	20	138	4.4	1.2
Guthrie	17	68	10.2	2.5	9	354	D	15.4	18	D	D	D
Hamilton	24	99	12.1	4.1	22	639	275.3	22.3	29	286	10.1	2.7
Hancock	16	163	13.3	5.0	23	1 037	348.5	44.8	20	D	D	D
Hardin	34	164	14.1	4.7	25	535	1 272.7	24.5	34	441	14.6	3.8
Harrison	18	D	D	D	13	303	107.6	13.1	30	302	10.3	2.9
Henry	40	148	18.3	6.0	36	2 139	815.9	86.0	43	565	24.1	6.1
Howard	14	52	3.2	1.3	23	944	260.5	38.8	22	D	D	D
Humboldt	18	62	9.3	2.2	23	934	228.7	41.0	22	215	8.8	2.3
Ida	10	55	3.6	1.1	13	1 026	679.5	49.9	11	D	D	D
Iowa	26	147	26.7	15.9	27	3 254	1 475.9	168.2	41	567	21.6	6.8
Jackson	32	114	7.7	2.6	31	839	255.2	28.8	47	496	16.6	4.7
Jasper	55	469	116.8	18.6	37	1 576	306.3	53.5	59	846	33.6	9.3
Jefferson	133	697	69.8	25.1	36	1 134	266.2	50.4	46	467	19.0	5.9
Johnson	272	1 969	299.6	92.2	80	4 983	3 400.4	232.9	375	D	D	D
Jones	28	120	11.3	4.5	28	811	246.0	35.4	38	D	D	D
Keokuk	10	37	7.0	1.7	12	185	53.1	7.8	11	D	D	D
Kossuth	35	187	22.0	7.1	28	1 223	875.8	53.6	34	380	13.8	3.6
Lee	49	189	18.1	5.1	62	4 138	2 511.7	227.0	95	1 047	38.7	10.1
Linn	506	5 486	728.9	321.5	208	17 686	10 073.9	1 288.4	499	8 790	388.8	113.4
Louisa	11	33	2.6	0.8	12	1 401	D	49.0	19	99	4.1	1.0
Lucas	12	34	2.7	0.9	11	146	D	6.9	16	D	D	D
Lyon	21	120	17.2	9.7	27	589	111.8	26.8	18	D	D	D
Madison	31	102	9.7	3.3	15	162	D	6.6	23	D	D	D
Mahaska	35	136	12.5	6.2	33	1 211	969.9	60.6	38	D	D	D
Marion	58	360	32.5	11.9	43	6 128	2 031.6	378.0	68	935	30.8	8.7
Marshall	43	338	51.3	13.6	38	5 011	2 232.2	246.8	87	1 070	44.7	12.1
Mills	26	D	D	D	7	35	8.2	1.0	16	145	6.4	1.6
Mitchell	12	87	4.8	1.5	25	984	644.4	41.6	21	D	D	D
Monona	15	46	4.2	1.8	4	74	D	D	25	D	D	D
Monroe	10	40	5.0	1.2	12	426	D	14.0	21	D	D	D
Montgomery	15	68	9.5	2.5	9	417	242.8	21.1	25	254	10.0	2.9
Muscatine	59	678	71.9	36.2	63	6 623	3 982.7	339.5	88	1 129	47.1	12.6
O'Brien	27	158	21.2	5.6	25	522	D	24.1	27	D	D	D
Osceola	8	26	4.9	0.7	14	271	D	10.3	12	D	D	D
Page	19	110	6.4	2.8	17	1 355	303.3	60.0	31	369	14.4	3.9
Palo Alto	11	30	4.5	1.5	20	514	676.5	23.7	26	548	43.5	7.7
Plymouth	35	234	12.7	12.6	31	2 471	1 084.3	111.7	57	857	26.9	7.4
Pocahontas	17	52	3.2	1.2	13	342	75.3	15.3	15	D	D	D
Polk	1 398	14 140	2 345.9	878.5	337	16 660	10 472.9	834.2	1 100	20 540	1 012.6	290.6
Pottawattamie	130	686	77.2	27.1	62	4 787	3 929.2	205.4	207	5 282	412.8	90.8
Poweshiek	41	126	10.9	3.5	33	1 576	453.7	61.1	53	583	20.9	5.4
Ringgold	8	50	16.3	1.8	6	D	3.1	0.6	10	D	D	D
Sac	15	43	5.5	1.1	24	398	198.0	14.3	22	D	D	D
Scott	405	2 548	316.6	108.5	182	11 389	6 704.5	657.0	423	8 987	440.2	120.6
Shelby	20	136	13.3	4.2	19	666	176.3	27.1	25	D	D	D
Sioux	83	980	124.2	32.9	90	5 331	1 596.6	208.6	74	1 248	40.6	11.3
Story	203	1 114	118.0	53.3	77	4 821	2 787.2	256.8	229	4 269	172.6	48.0
Tama	22	61	5.2	1.5	19	280	116.9	12.7	27	D	D	D
Taylor	9	37	2.5	0.7	6	539	237.5	16.2	8	D	D	D
Union	17	63	5.0	2.1	13	1 654	284.0	61.1	28	366	14.3	3.7
Van Buren	7	25	2.1	0.7	11	901	203.7	39.9	12	D	D	D
Wapello	48	280	24.7	10.0	24	4 264	D	196.6	77	1 198	47.0	13.2
Warren	56	294	37.6	12.4	27	425	78.6	19.5	64	890	32.9	9.1
Washington	56	158	14.5	4.6	45	1 078	398.8	43.5	44	D	D	D
Wayne	8	39	4.1	1.0	9	408	102.1	14.3	11	80	2.1	0.6
Webster	71	1 053	35.7	52.8	44	1 246	1 549.8	68.0	83	1 365	61.9	16.6
Winnebago	23	168	10.4	4.7	18	2 588	734.7	109.0	23	D	D	D
Winneshiek	28	161	19.7	8.4	34	1 402	300.9	60.6	61	757	32.4	8.0
Woodbury	196	977	121.1	40.3	91	5 068	4 061.2	210.7	268	4 980	240.7	66.7
Worth	9	23	1.6	0.6	12	431	257.4	15.9	10	D	D	D
Wright	23	125	12.0	3.0	22	1 280	1 437.3	63.4	36	D	D	D

1. Establishment subject to federal tax.

STATE County	Health care and social assistance, 2012				Other services, 2012				Nonemployer businesses, 2014		Value of residential construction authorized by building permits, 2015	
	Number of establishments	Number of employees	Receipts (mil dol)	Annual payroll (mil dol)	Number of establishments	Number of employees	Receipts (mil dol)	Annual payroll (mil dol)	Number	Receipts (mil dol)	New Construction ($1,000)	Number of housing units
	159	160	161	162	163	164	165	166	167	168	169	170
IOWA—Cont'd												
Franklin	31	560	35.3	14.7	28	91	8.7	1.9	802	38.8	1 180	5
Fremont	17	415	25.6	11.0	12	D	D	D	480	18.6	1 915	6
Greene	30	588	39.3	16.5	26	88	8.6	1.7	711	30.0	1 610	6
Grundy	26	493	33.0	14.0	20	D	D	D	880	33.6	4 448	20
Guthrie	27	535	34.8	16.1	28	83	9.7	2.2	1 018	45.0	2 100	8
Hamilton	34	D	D	D	31	94	16.0	2.6	1 019	38.3	765	4
Hancock	18	463	30.9	12.8	26	253	26.4	10.1	870	38.2	1 670	8
Hardin	49	1 054	69.8	30.2	47	137	13.8	3.8	1 286	51.6	2 616	10
Harrison	33	858	59.3	23.9	25	63	5.4	1.2	1 065	43.6	4 323	23
Henry	54	1 141	85.2	39.3	43	137	9.5	3.3	1 320	43.9	5 105	28
Howard	22	547	28.3	11.9	16	46	4.0	1.0	809	38.1	450	2
Humboldt	24	472	27.1	11.1	16	49	6.1	1.2	741	32.0	4 755	15
Ida	22	503	31.8	12.6	14	D	D	D	579	28.0	750	5
Iowa	37	827	46.2	22.7	26	D	D	D	1 230	52.5	2 487	16
Jackson	41	855	51.8	23.7	49	120	17.7	2.7	1 509	57.7	5 563	35
Jasper	83	1 563	102.4	46.8	60	283	17.4	5.1	2 239	85.1	10 604	43
Jefferson	46	726	58.7	22.9	47	154	74.3	4.8	1 879	63.1	1 289	14
Johnson	383	15 739	1 967.8	768.9	217	1 519	187.4	42.4	9 097	450.7	195 486	1 248
Jones	36	842	55.1	21.8	41	108	12.6	2.4	1 412	56.8	3 137	20
Keokuk	21	374	21.0	10.5	19	D	D	D	703	34.0	0	0
Kossuth	44	829	66.4	25.6	49	126	15.2	3.0	1 436	67.3	8 160	51
Lee	108	2 268	166.4	74.7	74	232	24.8	5.6	1 897	65.9	1 620	9
Linn	582	14 939	1 451.7	615.2	377	2 610	253.6	77.3	12 979	576.1	106 087	1 025
Louisa	28	343	15.5	7.2	17	D	D	D	618	25.5	2 300	14
Lucas	25	595	33.6	15.2	13	26	3.7	0.7	609	28.3	100	1
Lyon	24	443	21.6	8.0	32	94	9.4	2.1	1 005	46.3	9 988	41
Madison	28	572	37.8	15.9	22	62	6.8	1.6	1 305	57.3	26 948	148
Mahaska	51	1 056	80.1	39.2	39	142	14.7	3.4	1 509	55.3	3 735	21
Marion	92	1 991	165.7	70.9	60	215	17.8	4.8	2 123	74.1	14 074	58
Marshall	82	1 930	155.4	70.4	61	284	25.3	6.0	1 877	69.4	6 308	27
Mills	37	740	32.8	17.2	24	62	6.4	1.6	938	35.5	1 406	6
Mitchell	33	590	37.3	15.3	33	73	6.9	1.7	897	37.1	929	5
Monona	21	698	60.5	21.2	14	49	3.4	1.1	632	23.7	2 385	12
Monroe	21	454	28.9	10.3	7	16	2.4	0.3	549	23.1	1 690	8
Montgomery	32	765	52.9	24.7	32	131	13.4	3.8	737	28.0	3 210	21
Muscatine	97	1 944	139.9	60.2	68	368	48.6	10.2	2 101	81.8	4 895	27
O'Brien	52	1 446	82.4	32.1	41	171	21.6	4.6	1 006	50.0	4 440	14
Osceola	14	260	16.5	6.5	11	D	D	D	431	20.7	1 573	7
Page	57	1 452	106.6	48.4	23	69	6.9	1.4	947	31.5	1 465	8
Palo Alto	30	705	48.2	20.4	15	D	D	D	715	32.7	1 554	6
Plymouth	56	1 139	81.9	30.9	59	277	30.5	8.1	1 705	85.8	11 725	54
Pocahontas	19	315	18.7	8.3	9	D	D	D	562	30.5	550	2
Polk	1 113	33 649	3 659.7	1 655.7	942	6 904	887.0	228.0	31 391	1 512.6	858 456	4 373
Pottawattamie	225	5 323	509.6	184.3	159	772	98.3	22.0	5 023	223.4	30 511	141
Poweshiek	55	1 098	87.2	38.0	35	112	13.2	3.0	1 289	50.5	4 320	18
Ringgold	14	399	27.5	12.2	13	40	5.3	0.9	459	20.2	0	0
Sac	28	560	32.8	15.3	16	43	4.9	1.1	869	40.7	175	1
Scott	482	12 086	1 132.3	490.6	306	2 165	188.8	52.9	10 221	458.0	82 115	476
Shelby	39	1 134	78.1	26.2	28	114	9.5	2.1	971	45.2	3 383	13
Sioux	78	2 437	149.6	62.7	83	306	36.2	7.4	2 668	123.4	28 608	139
Story	192	4 855	513.2	206.0	146	1 000	136.1	27.5	5 358	227.5	97 639	555
Tama	29	460	22.3	10.3	20	67	5.2	1.2	1 167	45.2	3 787	20
Taylor	15	D	D	D	11	D	D	D	547	23.3	1 015	5
Union	40	917	64.6	29.4	28	128	22.3	4.5	806	26.5	1 529	11
Van Buren	14	315	19.5	8.0	12	13	1.8	0.3	674	29.5	314	3
Wapello	92	2 615	214.4	90.0	50	249	19.9	6.7	1 717	64.4	2 529	24
Warren	77	1 232	73.9	33.0	63	227	17.4	4.6	3 575	187.0	64 705	260
Washington	67	1 252	78.5	34.9	53	148	20.3	4.0	1 765	66.0	11 461	79
Wayne	16	366	26.5	13.9	11	D	D	D	549	36.3	330	1
Webster	116	2 974	238.4	109.4	62	372	52.0	11.6	2 101	83.4	3 004	13
Winnebago	40	620	27.1	11.2	14	D	D	D	797	34.1	200	1
Winneshiek	61	1 422	105.8	51.0	42	D	D	D	1 858	68.2	13 995	56
Woodbury	331	8 431	820.1	310.1	181	1 331	92.1	29.0	5 686	246.1	46 603	289
Worth	12	179	8.5	3.9	12	D	D	D	548	18.2	941	6
Wright	38	924	83.8	34.0	24	57	5.3	1.1	847	33.0	1 637	6

Table B. States and Counties — Government Employment and Payroll, and Local Government Finances

STATE County	Government employment and payroll, 2012		March payroll (percent of total)							Local government finances, 2012				
										General revenue			Taxes	
														Per capita[1] (dollars)
	Full-time equivalent employees	March payroll (dollars)	Administration, judicial, and legal	Police and Corrections	Fire Protection	Highways and transportation	Health and Welfare	Natural resources and utilities	Education and libraries	Total (mil dol)	Inter-governmental (mil dol)	Total (mil dol)	Total	Property
	171	172	173	174	175	176	177	178	179	180	181	182	183	184
IOWA—Cont'd														
Franklin	668	2 088 400	4.9	4.3	0.0	6.1	28.3	1.6	54.1	66.9	22.7	23.0	2 183	1 785
Fremont	347	973 340	7.5	7.8	0.0	11.0	2.0	3.1	66.2	34.7	15.8	16.0	2 243	1 866
Greene	666	2 223 582	5.3	3.9	0.1	5.8	41.2	3.9	39.3	57.4	14.6	19.1	2 082	1 727
Grundy	563	1 970 199	5.6	4.4	0.0	5.6	33.3	4.7	45.8	64.2	18.4	21.5	1 731	1 370
Guthrie	748	2 384 845	4.1	2.8	0.0	5.3	24.8	3.4	59.0	68.4	20.6	29.3	2 716	2 276
Hamilton	889	2 941 083	5.3	6.3	0.7	5.4	28.8	4.7	47.5	85.2	24.2	29.7	1 934	1 608
Hancock	533	1 678 758	4.9	4.9	1.1	7.4	29.0	1.1	50.1	52.6	15.5	18.7	1 678	1 364
Hardin	771	2 439 397	10.0	8.8	0.3	7.6	3.2	3.8	65.7	93.9	30.1	33.2	1 921	1 546
Harrison	661	2 116 699	6.1	6.5	0.0	7.4	2.6	6.5	68.9	60.2	26.0	28.5	1 960	1 608
Henry	1 101	3 801 450	6.1	5.0	0.3	3.4	27.7	5.1	50.9	103.1	34.1	30.0	1 484	1 188
Howard	610	1 837 491	3.8	4.1	0.0	6.3	32.8	4.1	48.6	53.0	15.0	18.0	1 887	1 526
Humboldt	551	1 979 695	10.2	4.3	0.1	15.7	23.2	4.8	41.3	51.5	15.8	17.9	1 843	1 479
Ida	324	944 758	6.5	5.6	0.0	8.7	0.4	3.6	73.9	24.5	9.5	11.8	1 661	1 328
Iowa	946	2 546 590	3.6	5.9	0.1	6.6	25.6	2.5	55.1	74.3	23.2	29.8	1 838	1 381
Jackson	760	2 545 154	6.2	8.0	0.2	6.2	18.9	3.4	56.7	78.0	28.3	27.5	1 395	1 119
Jasper	1 510	5 999 123	4.8	6.2	2.0	4.5	25.8	3.5	51.2	155.2	47.6	58.5	1 597	1 284
Jefferson	662	2 186 709	5.0	7.9	0.9	5.5	30.3	6.8	43.2	74.0	18.6	24.1	1 426	1 178
Johnson	2 791	12 750 946	7.7	8.1	1.5	4.7	5.9	5.3	62.3	508.5	160.5	263.7	1 934	1 579
Jones	764	2 287 665	6.5	6.6	0.0	6.9	3.4	2.6	72.1	73.5	35.1	28.3	1 369	1 067
Keokuk	574	1 571 936	7.3	3.7	0.0	8.5	14.2	3.5	62.2	51.8	19.5	19.7	1 897	1 573
Kossuth	791	2 418 144	8.4	5.5	0.2	7.0	33.0	4.1	41.0	91.7	21.6	29.7	1 937	1 582
Lee	1 300	4 660 014	5.4	7.2	3.1	4.7	4.4	9.0	64.9	121.2	55.2	48.2	1 353	989
Linn	9 095	37 187 147	3.6	5.9	2.8	6.2	2.3	4.9	72.4	1 182.6	511.6	437.3	2 031	1 562
Louisa	609	1 866 882	4.6	6.3	0.0	4.4	2.1	2.8	79.3	56.0	27.3	22.6	2 003	1 495
Lucas	520	1 767 462	3.7	2.9	0.0	5.3	32.1	16.9	38.6	45.7	14.5	12.3	1 406	1 112
Lyon	499	1 482 179	6.0	6.8	0.0	8.4	4.9	6.3	65.1	46.7	19.3	20.2	1 715	1 324
Madison	798	2 825 675	6.6	2.7	0.0	7.8	22.7	7.6	52.2	80.3	28.9	28.9	1 848	1 518
Mahaska	1 014	3 634 697	4.3	4.7	0.9	4.1	46.1	1.9	35.8	108.1	29.6	33.7	1 503	1 164
Marion	1 252	3 936 638	5.4	7.6	0.0	6.5	4.1	9.6	65.6	122.5	47.7	49.1	1 469	1 141
Marshall	1 954	7 209 585	3.6	6.6	1.9	3.7	0.6	4.3	78.3	184.2	83.4	70.1	1 715	1 332
Mills	661	1 998 540	5.5	6.9	1.4	7.4	5.2	1.1	71.4	51.3	23.3	23.3	1 569	1 336
Mitchell	526	1 692 873	5.0	4.8	0.0	5.4	33.0	2.6	47.2	57.0	14.0	18.3	1 705	1 409
Monona	396	1 218 905	10.0	7.1	0.0	11.2	2.6	8.7	59.5	37.4	15.9	15.8	1 736	1 419
Monroe	387	1 402 370	4.4	6.0	0.1	5.9	41.4	2.3	39.4	25.8	12.4	11.4	1 418	1 109
Montgomery	722	2 440 051	4.3	3.9	1.5	5.4	42.7	3.0	37.5	72.5	19.7	21.2	2 004	1 573
Muscatine	1 797	6 903 785	4.4	8.5	3.1	3.4	2.3	23.5	51.0	179.8	71.9	69.9	1 630	1 298
O'Brien	688	2 291 194	4.3	7.0	0.0	6.3	0.5	5.0	75.2	67.6	25.7	28.4	2 007	1 628
Osceola	225	737 061	10.1	8.0	0.0	13.2	1.6	6.2	60.4	21.0	8.0	9.8	1 588	1 342
Page	735	2 422 895	5.4	5.6	0.4	5.2	28.7	4.2	50.0	75.7	24.0	22.9	1 458	1 116
Palo Alto	595	1 986 443	5.8	3.7	0.8	6.9	35.4	3.3	43.7	67.2	16.0	23.3	2 512	2 103
Plymouth	1 172	4 151 413	4.7	5.6	0.3	5.4	25.2	3.7	54.8	126.6	33.5	46.1	1 850	1 539
Pocahontas	388	1 255 236	7.6	7.3	0.0	7.9	24.8	7.4	43.9	40.0	11.0	14.7	2 054	1 718
Polk	17 358	73 983 487	5.6	9.0	3.6	4.4	8.6	5.6	61.7	2 215.8	755.8	962.0	2 168	1 882
Pottawattamie	3 555	14 074 472	5.1	12.0	3.8	3.4	3.5	4.9	66.5	469.3	187.7	200.8	2 162	1 672
Poweshiek	616	2 161 055	7.6	7.8	1.1	6.4	2.2	6.6	67.8	70.4	26.8	32.7	1 745	1 368
Ringgold	380	1 133 677	4.5	3.2	0.0	9.7	40.0	2.0	40.3	38.0	10.1	11.1	2 172	1 874
Sac	370	1 168 894	8.0	8.4	0.0	9.1	4.9	9.7	53.3	38.8	16.2	16.8	1 655	1 346
Scott	6 132	26 019 745	5.1	9.3	3.9	3.8	2.4	4.0	69.8	729.6	283.5	333.3	1 974	1 565
Shelby	746	2 472 519	5.4	3.6	0.2	6.1	48.6	4.6	28.4	74.6	17.8	20.6	1 705	1 402
Sioux	1 410	5 040 852	7.0	4.6	0.0	3.5	32.1	5.9	45.0	155.5	40.9	50.2	1 466	1 159
Story	2 892	10 932 541	7.4	7.6	2.9	7.7	10.1	9.9	52.8	476.0	102.3	138.3	1 518	1 219
Tama	838	2 616 822	5.8	6.4	0.0	7.4	4.6	3.7	70.0	73.1	34.0	30.1	1 717	1 370
Taylor	283	832 177	7.3	5.5	0.0	10.1	5.8	4.1	65.8	26.1	12.6	9.8	1 572	1 285
Union	985	3 478 275	2.6	3.0	0.6	3.4	37.5	2.3	50.1	116.7	47.2	22.5	1 788	1 421
Van Buren	420	1 439 759	4.4	3.0	0.0	5.3	38.1	2.3	46.6	36.7	12.5	10.5	1 409	1 133
Wapello	1 563	6 980 218	2.5	3.5	1.9	4.5	2.0	4.5	80.0	186.1	86.6	52.4	1 482	1 084
Warren	1 608	6 242 328	5.6	5.6	1.1	3.5	2.5	5.3	75.5	156.4	71.0	65.1	1 387	1 216
Washington	1 128	3 614 174	5.4	6.2	0.4	4.7	26.2	4.4	52.3	111.8	34.7	38.8	1 771	1 403
Wayne	428	1 412 234	4.6	3.7	0.0	5.5	52.3	1.9	31.5	45.4	11.7	10.9	1 714	1 444
Webster	1 646	5 911 455	5.2	5.8	2.4	3.6	3.2	3.1	76.3	189.7	73.6	61.4	1 648	1 262
Winnebago	563	1 699 897	5.9	5.4	0.0	5.7	4.8	5.5	71.6	53.4	20.2	24.6	2 324	1 932
Winneshiek	1 453	4 847 620	2.3	3.4	0.2	3.7	28.1	2.1	59.9	162.1	45.6	40.6	1 928	1 635
Woodbury	3 937	16 380 804	4.5	9.7	4.1	5.4	2.2	5.6	67.1	475.0	216.3	177.2	1 732	1 265
Worth	353	1 078 114	9.5	7.7	0.0	8.8	3.7	3.5	65.9	35.3	14.3	16.5	2 191	1 830
Wright	944	3 639 368	3.1	3.8	0.0	4.6	48.9	2.0	37.6	120.8	27.5	28.8	2 216	1 856

1. Based on the resident population estimated as of July 1 of the year shown.

STATE County	Direct general expenditure Total (mil dol)	Per capita¹ (dollars)	Percent of total for: Education	Health and hospitals	Police protection	Public welfare	Highways	Debt outstanding Total (mil dol)	Per capita¹ (dollars)	Government employment, 2014 Federal civilian	Federal military	State and local	Presidential election,² 2012 Percent of vote cast: Democratic	Republican	All other
	185	186	187	188	189	190	191	192	193	194	195	196	197	198	199
IOWA—Cont'd															
Franklin	74.7	7 078	38.7	27.4	2.8	0.1	7.5	53.7	5 092	40	41	782	50.0	48.6	1.4
Fremont	36.0	5 034	46.9	4.3	4.1	0.1	19.2	10.1	1 415	30	27	456	47.4	51.1	1.5
Greene	58.6	6 398	31.8	39.4	3.0	0.2	8.2	19.5	2 133	40	36	864	49.4	48.9	1.7
Grundy	60.9	4 889	35.4	29.1	3.1	0.1	12.1	34.5	2 773	42	49	673	40.9	57.8	1.4
Guthrie	64.7	6 005	45.4	24.0	2.4	0.1	9.0	71.3	6 614	56	42	861	44.9	52.6	2.6
Hamilton	89.3	5 820	41.9	27.7	3.4	0.2	7.1	95.4	6 215	46	59	1 157	49.7	48.4	1.9
Hancock	59.9	5 378	31.9	38.4	3.3	0.1	11.3	36.3	3 260	47	43	643	47.3	50.9	1.8
Hardin	98.1	5 668	39.4	22.8	3.6	0.1	10.4	60.0	3 470	72	65	1 760	49.6	48.7	1.7
Harrison	56.0	3 853	56.3	5.5	3.7	0.3	12.4	33.4	2 299	68	56	830	46.9	51.5	1.6
Henry	99.5	4 919	39.9	36.4	3.0	0.3	4.6	76.0	3 758	66	74	1 710	46.4	51.4	2.2
Howard	49.9	5 214	37.9	32.9	2.9	0.4	8.5	14.5	1 518	30	37	775	62.2	36.4	1.4
Humboldt	60.5	6 223	36.7	23.4	2.9	0.2	10.8	37.9	3 894	52	38	643	42.2	56.5	1.3
Ida	25.1	3 531	55.4	4.9	4.2	0.2	13.6	14.0	1 973	29	27	368	41.0	57.4	1.6
Iowa	74.5	4 600	48.3	23.2	3.7	0.4	9.2	69.2	4 275	47	64	985	49.2	49.0	1.8
Jackson	75.2	3 817	46.3	20.7	4.1	0.1	9.2	36.7	1 860	76	77	1 000	61.3	36.9	1.8
Jasper	146.8	4 011	39.1	28.3	4.3	0.3	6.0	102.6	2 802	88	139	2 261	52.8	45.3	1.9
Jefferson	72.9	4 323	28.0	30.9	3.6	0.2	10.0	71.8	4 254	61	62	1 025	58.7	38.5	2.8
Johnson	524.4	3 847	35.0	4.1	4.1	0.9	6.0	708.3	5 196	1 929	574	33 607	69.9	28.4	1.7
Jones	81.7	3 958	56.2	5.0	3.3	0.1	12.9	52.6	2 548	57	76	1 338	54.4	44.0	1.6
Keokuk	46.7	4 504	42.3	19.6	2.4	0.1	11.3	24.3	2 344	50	40	537	47.0	50.6	2.5
Kossuth	92.1	6 004	26.6	34.3	2.6	0.2	10.8	73.1	4 765	67	59	1 028	50.8	47.6	1.6
Lee	137.2	3 851	55.0	7.3	5.0	0.5	5.8	121.6	3 414	95	152	1 985	57.0	41.0	2.0
Linn	1 336.0	6 206	46.5	3.0	3.7	1.2	4.7	1 559.7	7 244	1 008	845	12 625	60.0	38.5	1.5
Louisa	54.0	4 790	58.9	3.9	3.7	0.1	10.4	92.9	8 237	57	44	673	51.3	47.0	1.7
Lucas	45.7	5 216	36.3	40.7	2.3	0.2	8.8	77.6	8 862	36	34	644	45.3	52.1	2.6
Lyon	43.5	3 701	45.1	4.4	4.6	0.1	20.2	26.6	2 260	37	46	651	26.9	71.9	1.2
Madison	80.3	5 130	45.0	29.6	2.4	0.1	8.2	120.8	7 718	39	61	915	44.0	54.0	2.0
Mahaska	103.0	4 588	32.3	43.1	3.7	0.2	7.0	35.6	1 584	60	86	1 432	40.8	57.4	1.8
Marion	110.4	3 302	53.4	5.1	4.5	0.3	11.9	105.0	3 142	138	127	1 685	43.6	54.3	2.1
Marshall	192.9	4 722	64.1	3.0	4.2	0.3	6.4	177.1	4 335	117	157	3 471	53.7	44.4	1.9
Mills	49.6	3 346	58.3	5.0	5.7	1.1	10.6	46.3	3 118	37	56	1 594	40.9	57.4	1.7
Mitchell	58.6	5 460	27.5	34.6	2.8	0.1	12.4	39.9	3 723	36	42	699	55.1	42.8	2.0
Monona	39.6	4 341	49.5	4.3	4.7	0.4	17.8	19.2	2 100	42	35	537	47.8	50.3	1.9
Monroe	25.6	3 175	52.7	6.3	5.3	0.3	19.1	18.5	2 294	34	31	526	46.4	51.6	2.0
Montgomery	75.5	7 150	27.3	38.4	8.7	0.2	5.5	34.3	3 246	42	41	937	44.0	54.6	1.4
Muscatine	169.3	3 949	47.2	3.6	5.1	0.4	6.8	78.4	1 828	88	168	2 644	57.1	41.5	1.4
O'Brien	67.2	4 738	61.1	4.1	3.9	0.2	8.1	45.7	3 226	45	54	1 070	31.9	66.7	1.4
Osceola	20.4	3 288	41.6	8.9	9.7	0.1	18.2	8.6	1 389	28	24	292	33.1	64.8	2.1
Page	86.1	5 483	33.4	39.4	2.8	0.1	7.4	65.9	4 192	72	56	1 331	39.4	59.1	1.5
Palo Alto	64.4	6 948	31.7	32.8	2.9	0.1	15.3	37.1	4 003	34	35	966	50.5	47.7	1.8
Plymouth	123.5	4 958	40.4	28.0	3.4	2.2	7.8	86.7	3 483	71	98	1 440	37.0	62.0	1.0
Pocahontas	41.8	5 851	31.5	27.7	4.1	0.5	11.0	23.7	3 313	33	28	533	44.9	53.3	1.8
Polk	2 428.8	5 474	46.0	7.6	4.5	1.5	5.2	2 789.0	6 286	5 939	1 929	29 348	56.4	41.8	1.8
Pottawattamie	475.8	5 121	56.9	3.4	5.2	0.3	4.5	433.2	4 662	206	363	5 239	48.3	50.2	1.5
Poweshiek	66.2	3 533	47.3	5.0	4.5	0.2	10.8	65.3	3 483	60	68	864	55.0	43.3	1.7
Ringgold	38.2	7 503	25.9	44.8	2.8	0.2	9.0	42.2	8 280	32	19	404	46.0	52.1	1.9
Sac	42.6	4 196	49.4	6.2	4.3	0.1	13.4	17.5	1 720	47	39	583	44.6	53.5	1.8
Scott	760.2	4 504	54.4	2.6	4.9	0.1	3.6	683.1	4 047	572	668	8 358	56.6	42.1	1.3
Shelby	87.3	7 233	22.6	50.5	1.7	0.1	7.8	52.5	4 348	46	47	1 034	44.4	54.0	1.6
Sioux	160.8	4 691	31.1	29.5	3.1	0.1	6.7	182.6	5 329	100	128	2 086	18.2	80.9	0.9
Story	440.2	4 830	30.3	42.8	3.2	0.5	3.7	391.5	4 295	998	356	18 839	57.0	40.8	2.2
Tama	71.1	4 056	60.3	5.1	3.5	0.1	12.6	36.6	2 088	52	68	2 019	55.3	43.2	1.5
Taylor	30.7	4 937	39.9	4.5	3.6	0.1	25.2	25.0	4 034	43	24	392	44.5	53.1	2.4
Union	122.3	9 707	35.7	41.6	1.4	0.1	4.0	91.1	7 230	58	48	1 270	50.7	47.0	2.2
Van Buren	35.9	4 821	31.7	41.5	2.3	0.1	11.2	9.2	1 230	41	29	634	42.8	55.0	2.2
Wapello	204.9	5 795	64.7	3.0	2.8	0.3	9.3	88.9	2 514	112	137	2 465	55.3	41.8	2.9
Warren	173.5	3 701	60.2	4.1	4.2	0.3	5.2	262.4	5 595	79	184	2 209	49.4	48.8	1.8
Washington	127.8	5 831	38.9	20.4	2.8	0.3	9.4	155.3	7 085	65	86	1 495	48.6	49.4	2.0
Wayne	43.2	6 809	20.6	52.3	2.4	0.2	7.7	24.6	3 877	38	25	569	45.5	52.5	2.0
Webster	231.6	6 213	65.0	3.5	2.6	0.2	5.7	235.4	6 314	193	138	2 819	53.4	44.9	1.6
Winnebago	54.8	5 168	50.8	4.8	2.4	0.1	18.2	51.9	4 900	43	40	727	53.5	44.9	1.7
Winneshiek	175.5	8 333	54.9	26.3	1.7	0.1	5.5	125.4	5 954	70	74	2 158	60.5	37.9	1.6
Woodbury	498.8	4 875	56.0	4.2	4.6	0.6	3.9	465.5	4 550	683	397	6 315	49.1	49.6	1.4
Worth	37.0	4 920	43.7	3.8	4.3	0.1	12.6	25.7	3 424	31	30	453	60.3	37.8	1.9
Wright	134.7	10 370	22.1	58.1	1.8	0.2	4.2	130.1	10 011	61	50	1 303	48.5	50.0	1.5

1. Based on the resident population estimated as of July 1 of the year shown.   2. © 2013 Election Data Services, Inc. All rights reserved.

Table B. States and Counties — **Land Area and Population**

STATE/ County code	CBSA code[1]	County type[2]	STATE County	Land area[3] (sq km) 2010	Total persons 2015	Rank	Per square kilometer	White	Black	American Indian, Alaska Native	Asian and Pacific Islander	Percent Hispanic or Latino[4]	Under 5 years	5 to 17 years	18 to 24 years	25 to 34 years	35 to 44 years	45 to 54 years
				1	2	3	4	5	6	7	8	9	10	11	12	13	14	15
20 000	...	X	KANSAS	211 754	2 911 641	X	13.8	79.0	7.0	1.8	3.4	11.4	6.9	18.0	10.4	13.4	11.9	12.7
20 001	...	7	Allen	1 296	12 717	2 248	9.8	93.1	3.2	1.8	0.9	3.3	6.0	17.3	9.4	11.0	11.1	12.5
20 003	...	6	Anderson	1 501	7 808	2 608	5.2	96.3	1.2	1.6	0.9	1.7	6.2	19.0	7.4	10.2	10.4	12.9
20 005	11860	6	Atchison	1 117	16 398	2 016	14.7	90.8	6.5	1.5	1.0	2.9	6.4	17.0	14.1	11.1	10.3	12.4
20 007	...	9	Barber	2 937	4 823	2 848	1.6	95.0	1.3	1.4	0.7	3.6	6.9	15.6	7.5	11.6	9.4	12.7
20 009	24460	7	Barton	2 319	27 103	1 528	11.7	83.8	1.9	1.1	0.6	14.4	6.9	17.6	9.2	12.0	10.2	12.8
20 011	...	6	Bourbon	1 646	14 712	2 123	8.9	92.9	4.2	1.9	1.1	2.3	6.8	18.3	9.8	11.2	10.6	11.5
20 013	...	6	Brown	1 479	9 776	2 452	6.6	86.3	2.4	9.7	0.7	3.8	7.0	18.4	7.6	10.7	10.1	12.7
20 015	48620	2	Butler	3 703	66 741	795	18.0	91.8	2.5	2.0	1.5	4.5	6.0	20.0	9.1	11.6	12.3	13.8
20 017	...	8	Chase	2 002	2 679	2 993	1.3	94.0	1.8	1.4	0.7	4.1	4.5	16.7	7.7	9.4	10.9	13.3
20 019	...	9	Chautauqua	1 655	3 402	2 943	2.1	91.3	1.8	7.7	0.8	3.1	5.5	15.1	7.0	10.4	8.8	12.7
20 021	...	6	Cherokee	1 522	20 533	1 802	13.5	92.4	1.4	6.8	1.0	2.3	5.7	18.6	7.5	11.0	11.6	14.3
20 023	...	9	Cheyenne	2 641	2 679	2 993	1.0	91.4	0.5	0.7	1.5	7.1	5.1	15.6	6.4	9.5	9.6	11.4
20 025	...	9	Clark	2 524	2 096	3 040	0.8	87.9	1.9	2.4	2.0	10.0	7.4	19.7	6.9	9.2	10.8	12.9
20 027	...	7	Clay	1 671	8 347	2 566	5.0	95.6	1.0	1.1	0.8	2.6	6.4	16.8	6.8	10.8	11.5	12.0
20 029	...	7	Cloud	1 853	9 219	2 493	5.0	95.0	1.5	1.0	1.1	3.5	6.6	16.0	10.5	11.3	9.4	12.2
20 031	...	6	Coffey	1 624	8 384	2 565	5.2	94.9	1.2	1.4	0.9	2.8	4.7	17.7	7.3	10.5	10.8	14.3
20 033	...	9	Comanche	2 042	1 843	3 065	0.9	94.2	0.9	1.1	0.6	5.0	7.6	19.0	5.2	9.5	10.7	11.0
20 035	11680	4	Cowley	2 916	35 788	1 280	12.3	83.2	3.9	3.2	2.3	10.3	6.6	17.4	10.5	11.8	11.1	12.7
20 037	38260	4	Crawford	1 527	39 217	1 195	25.7	89.7	3.1	1.9	2.3	5.1	6.2	15.8	18.2	12.4	10.3	11.2
20 039	...	9	Decatur	2 314	2 932	2 983	1.3	97.0	1.7	1.0	0.6	2.0	6.4	13.8	5.7	9.9	7.8	12.5
20 041	...	7	Dickinson	2 194	19 303	1 859	8.8	93.5	1.8	1.3	0.9	4.5	6.3	17.8	7.7	11.2	11.5	13.3
20 043	41140	3	Doniphan	1 019	7 797	2 609	7.7	92.3	4.3	2.2	0.9	2.8	5.7	16.1	12.2	11.2	11.0	12.1
20 045	29940	3	Douglas	1 181	118 053	524	100.0	82.9	5.7	3.5	5.7	5.8	5.2	13.7	24.1	15.3	11.2	10.2
20 047	...	9	Edwards	1 611	2 968	2 976	1.8	79.3	0.9	0.9	0.7	19.8	6.6	17.2	7.0	9.6	10.5	13.7
20 049	...	8	Elk	1 669	2 605	2 999	1.6	94.0	1.4	2.9	1.3	3.8	4.1	16.0	6.8	8.5	8.8	12.7
20 051	25700	5	Ellis	2 331	29 029	1 454	12.5	91.6	1.7	0.7	1.7	5.8	6.9	15.0	17.4	14.2	10.0	10.7
20 053	...	7	Ellsworth	1 854	6 343	2 729	3.4	87.9	5.7	1.3	0.7	5.9	5.0	12.9	9.0	13.6	11.2	13.6
20 055	23780	5	Finney	3 372	37 118	1 250	11.0	44.7	3.1	0.8	4.3	48.3	9.5	21.6	10.9	13.9	11.6	12.7
20 057	19980	5	Ford	2 845	34 536	1 316	12.1	42.4	2.8	0.8	2.1	52.8	9.6	20.7	10.5	14.4	12.4	12.1
20 059	36840	1	Franklin	1 481	25 609	1 577	17.3	93.5	2.2	1.9	0.8	3.9	6.3	18.6	9.2	11.7	11.3	14.1
20 061	27920	5	Geary	996	37 030	1 255	37.2	62.3	20.0	2.0	6.0	15.0	11.4	18.9	17.0	20.6	11.1	7.3
20 063	...	9	Gove	2 776	2 640	2 997	1.0	97.2	0.7	0.5	0.6	2.7	6.8	17.0	7.3	10.2	9.4	11.3
20 065	...	9	Graham	2 327	2 591	3 000	1.1	91.5	5.4	1.9	1.4	3.2	6.6	13.4	6.1	9.5	8.6	13.4
20 067	...	7	Grant	1 489	7 733	2 617	5.2	52.4	0.7	0.9	0.6	46.6	8.3	23.7	9.0	11.5	12.6	12.1
20 069	...	9	Gray	2 250	6 133	2 746	2.7	84.5	0.9	0.7	0.4	14.2	7.5	21.7	8.1	11.4	11.9	13.2
20 071	...	9	Greeley	2 016	1 330	3 093	0.7	80.9	0.6	1.1	0.5	17.5	7.7	16.9	6.4	12.0	9.0	12.6
20 073	...	6	Greenwood	2 961	6 244	2 739	2.1	94.1	1.0	2.5	0.7	4.0	5.1	16.2	6.2	9.0	10.0	13.6
20 075	...	9	Hamilton	2 581	2 474	3 008	1.0	64.8	0.8	1.3	0.8	33.9	8.4	21.5	7.5	13.0	12.3	13.5
20 077	...	8	Harper	2 075	5 817	2 772	2.8	90.8	0.9	1.7	0.6	7.0	6.9	16.9	7.2	11.0	10.2	11.6
20 079	48620	2	Harvey	1 398	35 073	1 302	25.1	85.4	2.5	1.3	1.3	11.5	6.9	18.4	9.5	11.0	11.1	12.2
20 081	...	9	Haskell	1 496	4 064	2 897	2.7	69.9	0.8	0.9	1.2	29.0	7.6	21.3	9.7	11.4	12.0	12.1
20 083	...	9	Hodgeman	2 227	1 893	3 060	0.9	92.1	1.7	0.8	0.6	6.5	7.4	15.3	7.3	9.2	8.8	13.2
20 085	45820	3	Jackson	1 700	13 338	2 215	7.8	87.3	1.4	9.2	0.8	4.8	6.5	19.3	7.6	10.5	10.3	14.2
20 087	45820	3	Jefferson	1 379	18 930	1 878	13.7	95.4	1.1	2.1	0.5	2.6	5.3	18.3	7.0	10.0	11.1	15.9
20 089	...	9	Jewell	2 356	2 970	2 975	1.3	96.5	0.7	1.0	0.6	2.4	4.6	14.9	6.1	8.9	8.1	12.2
20 091	28140	1	Johnson	1 226	580 159	110	473.2	82.8	5.7	0.9	5.5	7.4	6.7	18.6	7.8	14.0	13.9	13.9
20 093	23780	9	Kearny	2 255	3 956	2 904	1.8	67.7	1.1	1.9	0.7	29.5	8.1	21.1	9.5	12.1	10.7	12.9
20 095	48620	6	Kingman	2 236	7 687	2 618	3.4	95.1	0.6	1.6	0.8	3.1	5.4	16.4	7.6	10.5	9.8	13.8
20 097	...	9	Kiowa	1 872	2 564	3 002	1.4	90.4	1.3	1.6	0.9	6.4	6.5	14.2	13.5	9.7	10.0	12.3
20 099	37660	7	Labette	1 671	20 803	1 789	12.4	89.0	5.9	3.9	1.0	4.4	6.4	17.2	8.6	11.2	10.9	13.8
20 101	...	9	Lane	1 858	1 670	3 074	0.9	91.9	1.3	1.9	0.7	6.4	5.6	15.7	7.2	7.9	10.1	13.7
20 103	28140	1	Leavenworth	1 199	79 315	701	66.2	81.6	10.3	1.6	2.4	6.9	6.6	17.7	8.3	13.9	14.4	13.9
20 105	...	9	Lincoln	1 863	3 105	2 965	1.7	96.7	1.0	1.1	0.5	2.4	6.3	18.0	6.3	9.0	9.7	12.7
20 107	28140	1	Linn	1 539	9 536	2 467	6.2	95.9	1.1	1.9	0.7	2.3	5.0	18.3	6.5	10.0	11.3	13.8
20 109	...	9	Logan	2 779	2 825	2 986	1.0	92.4	1.6	1.4	1.6	4.9	5.9	16.4	7.7	12.4	10.2	11.6
20 111	21380	5	Lyon	2 195	33 339	1 347	15.2	73.7	3.1	1.4	3.0	20.7	6.1	16.4	17.6	12.6	10.1	11.4
20 113	32700	6	McPherson	2 327	28 941	1 456	12.4	94.0	1.9	1.1	1.2	3.8	6.2	16.9	9.1	11.4	10.7	12.7
20 115	...	6	Marion	2 446	12 103	2 292	4.9	94.7	1.5	1.6	0.7	3.2	5.0	16.9	9.9	9.1	9.2	13.3
20 117	...	7	Marshall	2 331	9 936	2 440	4.3	96.3	1.0	1.1	0.9	2.4	6.2	16.9	6.8	11.1	10.0	12.8
20 119	...	9	Meade	2 533	4 330	2 877	1.7	80.8	1.4	1.5	1.0	16.9	5.5	21.6	8.9	9.8	10.4	12.7
20 121	28140	1	Miami	1 491	32 553	1 371	21.8	94.8	1.8	1.5	0.8	3.1	6.1	19.6	7.3	10.2	12.4	15.5
20 123	...	7	Mitchell	1 818	6 282	2 735	3.5	97.4	0.5	0.9	0.6	2.0	6.1	15.7	9.9	10.0	9.4	12.0
20 125	17700	5	Montgomery	1 667	33 314	1 349	20.0	84.5	6.9	5.8	1.4	6.3	6.9	17.0	9.6	11.7	10.4	12.8
20 127	...	9	Morris	1 801	5 645	2 790	3.1	94.5	1.0	1.4	0.7	4.4	5.7	15.5	6.1	10.3	9.1	13.8
20 129	...	9	Morton	1 890	3 007	2 971	1.6	75.9	1.5	1.7	2.4	21.4	6.9	18.9	7.6	10.2	11.9	13.4
20 131	...	8	Nemaha	1 858	10 227	2 415	5.5	96.6	1.1	1.1	0.6	1.7	7.0	18.5	7.9	10.3	10.1	13.3

1. CBSA = Core Based Statistical Area. See Appendix A for explanation. See Appendix B for list of metropolitan areas with component counties. 2. County type code from the Economic Research Service of USDA Rural-Urban Continuum Codes. See Appendix A for definition. 3. Dry land or land partially or temporarily covered by water. 4. May be of any race.

Table B. States and Counties — **Population and Households**

STATE County	Population, 2014 (cont.) Age (percent) (cont.)				Population change and components of change, 2000–2015							Households, 2010–2014				
					Total persons		Percent change		Components of change, 2010–2015						Percent	
	55 to 64 years	65 to 74 years	75 years and over	Percent female	2000	2010	2000–2010	2010–2015	Births	Deaths	Net migration	Number	Persons per house-hold	Family house-holds	Female family house-holder[1]	One per-son
	16	17	18	19	20	21	22	23	24	25	26	27	28	29	30	31
KANSAS................	12.5	7.8	6.5	50.2	2 688 418	2 853 132	6.1	2.1	207 325	130 240	-18 749	1 112 335	2.52	65.7	10.4	28.5
Allen.............	13.8	9.5	9.5	51.1	14 385	13 371	-7.0	-4.9	756	947	-464	5 398	2.38	64.3	10.0	31.8
Anderson.........	13.2	10.9	9.7	50.6	8 110	8 102	-0.1	-3.6	505	497	-304	3 314	2.36	64.4	9.3	33.0
Atchison.........	12.5	8.5	7.8	51.3	16 774	16 924	0.9	-3.1	1 056	938	-631	6 180	2.49	64.2	10.8	31.7
Barber...........	15.9	11.0	9.3	48.8	5 307	4 861	-8.4	-0.8	332	288	-57	2 146	2.26	65.6	7.7	31.1
Barton...........	14.0	8.6	8.7	50.5	28 205	27 674	-1.9	-2.1	1 925	1 572	-907	11 480	2.36	65.0	10.6	30.5
Bourbon..........	13.3	9.7	8.8	50.6	15 379	15 173	-1.3	-3.0	1 096	932	-614	5 702	2.55	68.0	11.6	27.7
Brown............	14.6	10.2	8.8	51.2	10 724	9 984	-6.9	-2.1	733	674	-275	4 157	2.35	64.4	10.4	33.0
Butler...........	13.1	7.6	6.4	49.8	59 482	65 880	10.8	1.3	4 024	3 210	-22	24 062	2.65	71.2	8.9	25.1
Chase............	14.5	13.0	10.1	49.6	3 030	2 790	-7.9	-4.0	134	157	-65	1 139	2.30	61.6	6.4	33.0
Chautauqua.......	14.8	13.4	12.5	48.3	4 359	3 669	-15.8	-7.3	181	279	-159	1 584	2.20	67.6	7.9	30.9
Cherokee.........	13.7	10.3	7.4	50.4	22 605	21 603	-4.4	-5.0	1 191	1 401	-826	8 132	2.57	71.4	9.5	26.4
Cheyenne.........	15.9	12.2	14.3	50.8	3 165	2 726	-13.9	-1.7	150	205	18	1 294	2.05	62.4	7.0	35.9
Clark............	12.2	9.3	11.6	51.0	2 390	2 215	-7.3	-5.4	120	151	-98	958	2.21	65.7	7.3	31.2
Clay.............	13.8	11.1	10.8	50.3	8 822	8 535	-3.3	-2.2	550	546	-200	3 398	2.44	67.4	7.9	27.3
Cloud............	12.9	10.2	10.9	50.8	10 268	9 533	-7.2	-3.3	593	702	-185	3 972	2.23	60.3	10.1	34.8
Coffey...........	15.4	10.9	8.4	50.3	8 865	8 601	-3.0	-2.5	480	522	-159	3 578	2.33	67.5	7.9	29.0
Comanche.........	14.1	12.2	10.7	51.1	1 967	1 891	-3.9	-2.5	123	145	-24	757	2.44	67.0	5.5	30.8
Cowley...........	12.9	9.1	7.9	49.9	36 291	36 311	0.1	-1.4	2 400	2 199	-738	13 783	2.48	64.0	9.9	29.9
Crawford.........	11.2	7.8	6.9	49.9	38 242	39 134	2.3	0.2	2 562	2 065	-381	15 364	2.43	58.8	9.6	31.9
Decatur..........	16.8	11.9	15.2	49.4	3 472	2 961	-14.7	-1.0	169	243	38	1 442	1.95	55.7	6.2	41.0
Dickinson........	13.7	9.1	9.4	50.1	19 344	19 754	2.1	-2.3	1 187	1 182	-449	7 838	2.46	69.6	7.9	26.2
Doniphan.........	14.1	9.4	8.1	49.4	8 249	7 945	-3.7	-1.9	443	380	-196	3 138	2.32	68.7	10.1	26.4
Douglas..........	10.0	5.9	4.4	50.1	99 962	110 826	10.9	6.5	6 484	3 251	3 976	43 834	2.39	54.1	8.5	29.9
Edwards..........	16.1	9.4	9.8	50.3	3 449	3 037	-11.9	-2.3	185	161	-81	1 287	2.26	63.5	5.1	32.7
Elk..............	15.9	14.4	12.8	50.4	3 261	2 882	-11.6	-9.6	146	215	-211	1 276	2.10	66.8	9.1	30.5
Ellis............	12.0	6.7	7.1	49.7	27 507	28 452	3.4	2.0	1 995	1 304	-127	11 859	2.33	55.5	7.0	33.1
Ellsworth........	15.1	10.0	9.5	42.8	6 525	6 497	-0.4	-2.4	306	411	-39	2 549	2.13	63.8	8.4	32.5
Finney...........	10.4	5.5	4.0	49.0	40 523	36 776	-9.2	0.9	3 639	1 070	-2 203	12 670	2.88	72.7	12.4	22.2
Ford.............	9.9	5.4	5.0	48.3	32 458	33 848	4.3	2.0	3 554	1 240	-1 687	11 086	3.06	74.3	13.2	21.3
Franklin.........	13.5	8.8	6.6	50.3	24 784	25 996	4.9	-1.5	1 710	1 304	-798	9 933	2.55	70.5	8.3	24.6
Geary............	6.1	4.2	3.4	46.8	27 947	34 362	23.0	7.8	5 367	1 069	-1 815	12 782	2.79	69.4	11.2	24.1
Gove.............	14.7	10.3	12.9	49.0	3 068	2 695	-12.2	-2.0	158	204	-2	1 212	2.25	69.6	4.8	27.1
Graham...........	17.0	11.5	13.8	50.4	2 946	2 597	-11.8	-0.2	131	152	16	1 158	2.21	62.8	7.5	33.6
Grant............	11.6	6.2	4.9	49.1	7 909	7 829	-1.0	-1.2	627	244	-491	2 776	2.80	78.0	14.7	15.6
Gray.............	11.8	8.0	6.4	50.2	5 904	6 006	1.7	2.1	498	225	-164	2 125	2.80	76.4	7.5	20.3
Greeley..........	14.5	8.6	12.3	50.9	1 534	1 247	-18.7	6.7	114	78	43	471	2.54	73.0	3.4	24.2
Greenwood........	16.2	12.5	11.1	50.2	7 673	6 689	-12.8	-6.7	311	460	-267	2 860	2.24	64.8	9.0	32.6
Hamilton.........	11.9	6.9	5.1	48.6	2 670	2 690	0.7	-8.0	219	129	-308	1 008	2.60	71.2	9.7	24.0
Harper...........	14.5	10.9	10.9	49.6	6 536	6 034	-7.7	-3.6	398	474	-135	2 567	2.23	64.3	7.8	31.5
Harvey...........	13.1	8.6	9.4	50.9	32 869	34 684	5.5	1.1	2 331	1 925	-54	13 329	2.51	68.6	7.6	27.4
Haskell..........	13.8	6.4	5.6	50.2	4 307	4 256	-1.2	-4.5	274	122	-354	1 421	2.92	75.9	7.2	22.0
Hodgeman.........	15.6	10.0	13.2	50.6	2 085	1 916	-8.1	-1.2	117	103	-54	814	2.35	71.5	4.9	26.0
Jackson..........	13.4	9.9	7.2	49.5	12 657	13 462	6.4	-0.9	864	692	-308	5 288	2.51	73.9	10.6	22.4
Jefferson........	15.2	9.8	7.4	49.4	18 426	19 124	3.8	-1.0	1 017	889	-285	7 498	2.49	70.9	6.3	24.8
Jewell...........	17.8	13.0	14.3	48.8	3 791	3 077	-18.8	-3.5	136	213	-33	1 438	2.10	65.1	4.8	32.3
Johnson..........	12.4	7.3	5.4	51.0	451 086	544 179	20.6	6.6	38 810	18 760	15 350	217 826	2.55	67.9	9.0	26.6
Kearny...........	11.5	7.4	6.7	49.7	4 531	3 977	-12.2	-0.5	320	198	-144	1 341	2.88	73.4	8.5	23.9
Kingman..........	14.9	10.4	11.2	49.8	8 673	7 858	-9.4	-2.2	437	509	-122	3 084	2.47	67.4	8.4	29.2
Kiowa............	15.0	8.5	10.4	50.3	3 278	2 553	-22.1	0.4	183	135	-40	1 051	2.24	60.5	7.6	33.1
Labette..........	13.7	10.0	8.1	50.5	22 835	21 607	-5.4	-3.7	1 423	1 358	-855	8 495	2.43	66.6	8.2	29.5
Lane.............	16.2	11.6	11.9	50.3	2 155	1 750	-18.8	-4.6	116	120	-77	811	2.01	56.4	4.8	38.2
Leavenworth......	12.5	7.5	5.1	46.7	68 691	76 227	11.0	4.1	5 043	2 922	1 011	26 398	2.71	71.2	9.9	24.5
Lincoln..........	17.3	9.9	10.8	50.2	3 578	3 241	-9.4	-4.2	158	186	-108	1 397	2.23	63.9	8.8	31.9
Linn.............	14.3	12.5	8.4	50.5	9 570	9 656	0.9	-1.2	501	607	14	4 140	2.29	68.4	6.6	29.1
Logan............	15.0	8.8	10.9	49.2	3 046	2 756	-9.5	2.5	178	161	59	1 228	2.23	64.0	7.7	31.4
Lyon.............	12.1	7.4	6.3	51.1	35 935	33 690	-6.2	-1.0	2 207	1 443	-1 185	13 069	2.48	60.8	10.1	29.9
McPherson........	14.0	9.1	9.9	50.7	29 554	29 180	-1.3	-0.8	1 718	1 916	-61	11 726	2.39	69.5	6.9	25.8
Marion...........	14.7	11.0	11.2	50.0	13 361	12 660	-5.2	-4.4	595	810	-332	4 845	2.40	67.9	6.7	29.0
Marshall.........	15.1	9.7	11.4	50.1	10 965	10 117	-7.7	-1.8	636	643	-170	4 289	2.30	66.2	6.1	30.4
Meade............	13.6	7.6	10.0	49.0	4 631	4 575	-1.2	-5.4	330	235	-344	1 761	2.45	75.6	7.9	21.6
Miami............	13.7	8.6	6.6	50.4	28 351	32 783	15.6	-0.7	1 763	1 335	-641	12 350	2.60	71.6	9.6	24.3
Mitchell.........	14.4	10.9	11.6	48.8	6 932	6 373	-8.1	-1.4	382	500	29	2 795	2.15	65.2	6.9	32.8
Montgomery.......	13.5	9.8	8.3	50.7	36 252	35 471	-2.2	-6.1	2 332	2 209	-2 290	13 706	2.45	65.8	11.8	30.9
Morris...........	15.9	12.0	11.6	50.5	6 104	5 923	-3.0	-4.7	317	381	-201	2 437	2.35	68.1	6.6	30.3
Morton...........	12.8	8.7	9.5	49.2	3 496	3 233	-7.5	-7.0	207	180	-250	1 199	2.56	70.5	13.0	24.5
Nemaha...........	12.8	8.5	11.6	49.3	10 717	10 178	-5.0	0.5	738	631	-68	4 161	2.35	67.0	6.1	28.6

1. No spouse present.

Table B. States and Counties — Population, Vital Statistics, Medicare, and Crime

STATE County	Persons in group quarters, 2015	Daytime population, 2010–2014 Number	Daytime population, 2010–2014 Employment/residence ratio	Births, 2015 Total	Births, 2015 Rate[1]	Deaths, 2015 Number	Deaths, 2015 Rate[1]	Persons under 65 with no health insurance, 2014 Number	Persons under 65 with no health insurance, 2014 Percent	Medicare, 2015 Total Beneficiaries	Medicare, 2015 Enrolled in Original Medicare	Medicare, 2015 Enrolled in Medicare Advantage	Serious crimes known to police,[2] 2014 Total Number	Serious crimes known to police,[2] 2014 Total Rate[3]
	32	33	34	35	36	37	38	39	40	41	42	43	44	45
KANSAS	79 014	2 895 515	1.01	38 954	13.4	24 141	8.3	284 342	11.7	464 261	395 713	68 548	89 554	3 084
Allen	382	13 784	1.10	133	10.4	168	13.1	1 142	11.2	2 799	2 547	252	296	2 265
Anderson	103	6 836	0.69	98	12.5	96	12.2	859	13.8	1 700	1 609	91	144	1 834
Atchison	1 379	16 560	0.98	191	11.6	169	10.3	1 382	10.9	3 020	2 791	229	493	2 948
Barber	40	4 821	0.97	58	12.0	51	10.5	517	13.3	1 024	1 002	22	100	2 010
Barton	672	27 374	0.99	350	12.9	297	10.9	3 238	14.6	5 148	5 053	95	1 298	4 724
Bourbon	410	14 651	0.96	210	14.2	152	10.3	1 431	12.2	3 062	2 736	326	539	3 647
Brown	116	10 336	1.09	139	14.2	120	12.3	1 134	14.4	2 031	1 971	60	225	2 249
Butler	2 310	55 602	0.66	763	11.5	589	8.9	5 298	9.6	9 978	8 462	1 516	1 614	2 479
Chase	145	2 377	0.69	28	10.4	13	4.8	259	13.2	569	549	20	11	410
Chautauqua	79	3 118	0.70	35	10.2	41	11.9	485	18.9	869	839	30	20	567
Cherokee	202	18 562	0.72	215	10.4	249	12.1	2 275	13.4	4 260	3 853	407	650	3 248
Cheyenne	49	2 656	0.97	31	11.6	40	14.9	296	15.0	723	693	30	40	1 488
Clark	57	2 028	0.86	18	8.5	18	8.5	215	12.7	386	375	11	42	1 915
Clay	140	8 038	0.90	108	12.9	105	12.6	625	9.7	1 877	1 772	105	162	1 935
Cloud	498	9 369	0.99	102	11.0	139	15.0	871	12.3	2 194	2 117	77	301	3 258
Coffey	130	9 024	1.13	103	12.2	78	9.3	661	9.8	1 728	1 657	71	89	1 140
Comanche	65	1 909	1.00	22	11.6	17	9.0	214	14.5	D	476	D	NA	NA
Cowley	2 004	35 112	0.93	438	12.2	399	11.1	3 664	13.0	6 434	5 736	698	1 188	3 352
Crawford	1 771	39 761	1.03	485	12.3	356	9.1	4 264	13.3	7 391	6 933	458	1 716	4 400
Decatur	81	2 781	0.90	35	12.0	35	12.0	270	12.8	804	761	43	10	342
Dickinson	307	17 896	0.81	220	11.4	194	10.0	1 671	10.7	3 700	3 383	317	357	1 824
Doniphan	427	6 756	0.69	79	10.1	73	9.3	703	11.5	1 534	1 497	37	144	1 839
Douglas	8 793	107 443	0.89	1 247	10.6	617	5.3	10 862	11.3	14 614	12 667	1 947	2 521	2 190
Edwards	35	2 722	0.81	37	12.4	21	7.0	364	15.0	651	622	29	20	685
Elk	40	2 533	0.82	31	11.7	35	13.2	359	18.4	778	749	29	13	499
Ellis	1 033	29 689	1.05	361	12.4	250	8.6	2 565	10.6	4 783	4 678	105	659	2 255
Ellsworth	983	6 420	0.99	49	7.7	70	11.0	430	10.1	1 271	1 241	30	103	1 748
Finney	547	37 396	1.02	657	17.7	199	5.4	5 924	18.0	3 992	3 838	154	1 222	3 290
Ford	708	35 299	1.04	672	19.4	220	6.3	5 639	18.5	4 228	4 100	128	1 035	2 955
Franklin	478	23 902	0.84	325	12.7	240	9.4	2 093	9.9	4 488	4 110	378	698	2 718
Geary	847	42 498	1.35	1 012	27.4	197	5.3	3 454	10.5	3 359	3 023	336	815	2 147
Gove	56	2 893	1.08	29	10.8	39	14.6	297	14.3	672	651	21	24	860
Graham	40	2 596	1.00	22	8.6	30	11.7	236	12.4	665	632	33	31	1 197
Grant	79	8 092	1.07	119	15.3	26	3.3	1 232	17.9	951	936	15	147	1 842
Gray	78	5 813	0.93	105	17.2	38	6.2	825	15.9	984	955	29	92	1 532
Greeley	26	1 287	1.11	27	20.5	11	8.3	120	11.7	D	280	D	6	462
Greenwood	90	5 819	0.76	60	9.6	76	12.1	609	12.7	1 715	1 660	55	127	1 996
Hamilton	0	2 647	1.01	35	13.8	13	5.1	482	21.2	D	381	D	10	386
Harper	129	6 009	1.04	93	16.0	90	15.5	679	15.0	1 296	1 270	26	132	2 984
Harvey	1 311	33 720	0.93	443	12.7	326	9.3	3 111	11.3	6 883	5 626	1 257	852	2 452
Haskell	33	4 184	0.99	50	12.3	21	5.2	718	20.0	509	493	16	63	1 535
Hodgeman	14	1 837	0.90	19	10.0	28	14.7	188	12.8	D	363	D	24	1 223
Jackson	133	11 255	0.67	168	12.5	129	9.6	1 322	11.9	2 553	2 356	197	175	1 380
Jefferson	235	14 018	0.47	199	10.5	132	7.0	1 630	10.5	3 528	3 097	431	367	1 958
Jewell	27	2 706	0.75	26	8.7	33	11.0	311	14.1	857	811	46	NA	NA
Johnson	5 163	580 085	1.07	7 397	12.8	3 703	6.4	37 808	7.6	75 099	52 418	22 681	9 318	1 689
Kearny	81	3 416	0.71	64	16.2	23	5.8	585	17.5	532	519	13	71	1 817
Kingman	190	7 206	0.82	92	12.0	104	13.5	724	12.1	1 590	1 544	46	112	1 521
Kiowa	149	2 631	1.08	35	13.7	24	9.4	254	13.4	526	515	11	28	1 113
Labette	480	21 888	1.07	271	13.0	222	10.7	2 027	11.9	4 529	4 181	348	577	2 778
Lane	3	1 621	0.96	24	14.3	18	10.7	188	14.6	435	423	12	35	2 038
Leavenworth	6 515	70 573	0.79	973	12.3	562	7.1	5 004	8.0	10 133	8 731	1 402	2 008	2 554
Lincoln	50	2 895	0.81	25	8.0	31	9.9	370	14.8	687	674	13	55	1 759
Linn	63	8 431	0.71	94	9.9	117	12.3	1 005	13.5	2 134	1 623	511	74	866
Logan	41	2 867	1.06	35	12.5	19	6.8	304	13.6	626	592	34	41	1 461
Lyon	1 446	32 935	0.97	414	12.4	257	7.7	4 434	16.2	5 666	5 320	346	536	1 644
McPherson	925	30 553	1.08	306	10.5	360	12.4	2 173	9.4	5 907	5 403	504	944	3 356
Marion	723	11 164	0.78	112	9.2	140	11.5	1 048	11.6	2 778	2 649	129	171	1 411
Marshall	164	10 639	1.12	127	12.7	111	11.1	779	9.9	2 388	2 245	143	153	1 533
Meade	119	4 210	0.89	79	18.2	38	8.7	523	14.8	775	752	23	45	1 051
Miami	645	25 829	0.55	293	9.0	271	8.3	2 240	8.2	4 568	3 500	1 068	638	1 943
Mitchell	246	6 926	1.19	72	11.5	99	15.8	407	8.6	1 477	1 411	66	82	1 383
Montgomery	1 114	36 141	1.10	408	12.1	361	10.7	3 689	13.7	8 030	7 493	537	NA	NA
Morris	66	5 272	0.81	57	10.1	73	12.9	535	12.3	1 514	1 416	98	97	1 701
Morton	83	3 357	1.14	32	10.5	28	9.2	357	14.2	D	535	D	41	1 313
Nemaha	259	10 551	1.08	156	15.3	82	8.0	735	9.1	2 121	2 073	48	92	905

1. Per 1,000 estimated resident population.   2. Data for serious crimes have not been adjusted for underreporting; this may affect comparability between geographic areas and over time.
3. Per 100,000 population estimated by the FBI.

STATE County	Serious crimes known to police, 2014 (cont.)[1] Rate[2]		Education — School enrollment and attainment, 2010–2014 Enrollment[3]		Attainment[4] (percent)		Local government expenditures,[5] 2012–2013		Money income, 2010–2014	Households			Income and poverty, 2014	Percent below poverty level		
	Violent	Property	Total	Percent private	High school graduate or less	Bachelor's degree or more	Total current spending (mil dol)	Current spending per student (dollars)	Per capita income[6] (dollars)	Median income (dollars)	Mean income (dollars)	Percent with income of $200,000 or more	Median household income (dollars)	All persons	Children under 18 years	Children 5 to 17 years in families
	46	47	48	49	50	51	52	53	54	55	56	57	58	59	60	61
KANSAS	349	2 735	795 354	13.5	37.2	30.7	4 808.2	9 828	27 367	51 872	69 271	3.5	52 392	13.5	17.6	16.4
Allen	191	2 073	3 116	6.2	44.8	16.1	26.0	10 870	20 105	38 712	47 771	0.3	39 196	18.2	24.5	22.4
Anderson	293	1 541	1 674	13.8	50.4	17.5	13.6	10 413	22 122	40 567	52 176	0.5	45 368	14.3	21.2	19.3
Atchison	287	2 661	4 906	35.0	51.5	19.0	24.6	10 524	22 446	44 648	58 392	1.5	44 199	17.4	22.0	20.7
Barber	342	1 668	954	9.1	45.8	18.1	8.2	10 934	27 785	48 462	62 260	3.5	51 676	12.4	17.1	16.7
Barton	360	4 364	6 568	7.7	46.4	17.3	41.1	9 298	25 750	43 573	61 770	1.7	46 942	17.8	22.0	20.3
Bourbon	575	3 072	3 808	8.8	43.3	21.4	22.2	9 367	20 798	39 555	51 262	1.2	38 430	18.4	29.2	27.2
Brown	240	2 009	2 243	6.9	49.3	19.6	17.2	11 587	22 284	41 126	52 465	2.0	45 781	17.3	26.9	24.6
Butler	184	2 295	19 385	11.0	33.8	27.5	134.8	8 672	27 431	57 474	73 565	3.3	60 123	11.3	14.0	12.5
Chase	149	261	587	13.3	42.1	24.7	4.3	11 803	23 653	38 633	53 501	1.4	47 025	13.2	17.3	14.9
Chautauqua	57	510	654	11.9	49.7	17.7	6.3	11 877	23 325	39 444	52 457	2.0	39 120	16.4	26.0	25.4
Cherokee	305	2 943	5 017	4.8	47.5	16.1	39.8	10 579	19 849	40 920	50 251	0.7	40 686	17.4	27.4	23.8
Cheyenne	223	1 264	537	4.8	42.0	18.7	5.5	13 070	24 309	39 681	50 510	0.5	41 797	11.5	18.4	16.9
Clark	274	1 642	524	9.0	32.8	30.7	5.9	12 565	25 116	43 750	56 771	2.3	47 650	13.0	17.2	15.8
Clay	191	1 743	1 959	8.2	37.9	22.3	13.4	9 583	26 143	51 375	63 766	2.7	53 131	10.9	16.1	15.4
Cloud	465	2 793	2 318	10.3	44.3	17.2	19.1	11 559	21 265	39 509	47 568	0.6	42 697	14.0	18.8	17.4
Coffey	38	1 102	2 014	7.0	46.0	19.7	18.0	11 269	29 044	56 274	69 030	2.8	55 705	10.9	13.3	11.6
Comanche	NA	NA	450	4.4	34.6	26.0	4.1	11 284	22 107	44 417	52 317	0.5	45 353	11.4	16.4	15.4
Cowley	302	3 050	9 555	13.3	39.5	19.4	59.6	9 622	21 848	42 157	55 939	1.9	45 180	15.0	21.1	19.6
Crawford	295	4 105	12 621	11.3	38.5	28.9	63.4	10 314	20 854	37 154	51 159	1.5	38 491	20.8	25.0	23.5
Decatur	68	273	487	12.9	46.0	23.3	4.4	11 910	28 094	37 396	57 225	3.5	41 434	13.9	18.8	18.6
Dickinson	143	1 681	4 734	9.4	46.7	18.7	35.6	10 053	24 754	50 123	61 480	2.9	47 493	11.1	16.0	15.3
Doniphan	141	1 699	2 183	10.5	47.9	17.6	16.9	11 659	23 246	48 659	58 721	1.2	47 599	15.0	20.9	19.3
Douglas	203	1 986	44 052	9.1	25.0	49.4	137.2	9 243	26 790	50 732	67 135	3.4	49 246	19.4	15.3	14.1
Edwards	171	514	696	2.0	46.4	21.7	5.9	13 315	24 899	47 101	59 434	1.8	49 256	10.5	14.0	13.0
Elk	0	499	501	4.6	44.7	18.9	6.9	13 705	21 693	38 182	45 559	0.2	36 471	17.4	28.3	25.7
Ellis	263	1 991	9 283	9.7	35.0	32.3	38.6	10 084	25 310	45 127	60 217	2.1	49 508	13.0	12.3	12.3
Ellsworth	170	1 578	1 156	9.3	43.2	21.1	13.8	11 688	23 458	45 417	57 862	2.4	46 961	12.4	14.1	13.3
Finney	506	2 783	10 383	5.2	53.2	18.6	87.6	10 049	22 179	47 994	64 546	2.9	48 609	18.8	25.7	24.4
Ford	400	2 555	9 454	5.2	54.3	17.0	73.8	9 828	21 269	51 374	63 925	2.9	51 144	15.0	21.6	20.4
Franklin	280	2 438	6 555	14.1	45.4	21.0	47.1	10 293	23 980	50 415	61 530	1.3	50 745	13.3	18.9	17.2
Geary	414	1 733	10 957	9.8	39.5	19.7	79.8	9 463	21 318	45 660	58 584	1.3	41 193	13.9	20.4	22.4
Gove	107	752	558	7.9	43.9	21.7	6.8	14 079	27 571	48 276	63 510	2.5	50 886	10.4	15.4	14.8
Graham	116	1 081	515	6.2	39.4	25.6	4.3	10 135	28 290	45 192	61 681	3.5	45 341	12.0	17.6	17.3
Grant	263	1 579	1 942	7.6	58.8	18.5	15.6	8 894	26 386	54 478	74 513	4.0	60 279	10.9	16.7	15.9
Gray	216	1 315	1 529	13.7	50.8	20.2	15.2	11 342	25 585	58 656	70 144	3.0	58 543	8.3	11.4	10.1
Greeley	154	308	280	9.6	44.6	20.0	2.8	13 308	25 766	51 023	62 722	1.3	52 795	10.8	15.3	15.5
Greenwood	141	1 854	1 408	3.8	52.4	15.4	12.0	11 792	24 123	39 286	53 608	1.5	39 732	16.9	24.9	21.6
Hamilton	155	232	649	4.5	52.1	13.1	5.8	11 720	23 360	44 274	63 266	2.3	47 709	12.8	18.2	16.9
Harper	430	2 555	1 241	7.5	46.4	19.1	12.1	11 130	24 913	41 332	57 510	2.9	50 525	12.9	21.0	20.7
Harvey	391	2 061	9 723	18.6	40.7	25.8	56.6	9 174	23 846	49 576	60 544	1.4	55 074	12.4	18.5	15.6
Haskell	244	1 291	1 112	11.6	52.9	17.6	10.2	12 720	25 213	55 742	71 502	3.7	59 596	10.7	14.9	13.6
Hodgeman	102	1 121	411	6.3	37.5	21.0	3.7	11 367	30 474	53 190	72 798	4.2	52 394	8.8	9.6	9.4
Jackson	189	1 190	3 422	6.8	46.1	18.1	25.3	10 407	25 030	55 296	63 881	1.9	53 796	10.3	14.5	12.7
Jefferson	171	1 787	4 548	10.5	47.9	21.0	40.4	10 836	26 259	56 531	65 594	1.0	56 927	9.4	13.4	11.8
Jewell	NA	NA	564	6.2	46.7	14.1	3.4	10 224	23 393	41 042	49 463	1.1	44 101	13.5	18.8	16.9
Johnson	136	1 553	154 691	19.8	19.7	52.1	872.2	9 310	39 447	75 017	99 787	8.6	76 104	6.6	8.0	7.5
Kearny	281	1 535	1 061	4.7	42.6	17.8	11.0	11 763	23 719	54 732	66 175	3.1	53 484	12.2	18.8	17.6
Kingman	177	1 345	1 773	16.8	43.9	18.9	13.2	10 610	24 892	50 000	60 552	1.4	53 378	11.2	16.7	16.0
Kiowa	239	875	651	27.2	35.2	22.6	7.0	10 512	22 301	41 211	52 292	1.7	46 318	12.8	13.6	13.4
Labette	385	2 393	5 510	10.4	43.5	20.1	40.1	9 951	20 506	41 434	50 491	0.9	40 822	18.3	27.2	25.9
Lane	175	1 864	324	0.9	41.2	24.0	4.4	12 755	31 892	54 292	65 348	3.2	53 739	10.9	17.9	16.7
Leavenworth	440	2 114	21 408	16.8	39.7	29.8	117.1	8 857	26 902	64 909	75 104	3.2	65 549	10.9	14.0	12.9
Lincoln	32	1 727	659	10.9	40.0	21.1	7.3	11 571	24 509	43 487	55 526	1.1	44 896	12.7	18.6	17.5
Linn	129	737	2 083	3.0	47.3	14.3	20.6	10 835	25 525	46 448	59 715	1.7	44 520	14.8	22.1	19.4
Logan	107	1 354	650	15.1	43.8	18.5	6.1	10 777	27 296	47 073	61 486	3.3	49 852	9.7	12.6	11.9
Lyon	141	1 503	10 853	5.9	47.2	25.0	55.3	9 789	20 272	40 427	51 026	1.3	43 038	18.0	21.1	17.5
McPherson	146	3 210	7 075	16.5	40.2	26.7	48.1	9 930	27 979	55 437	69 742	2.5	57 878	8.8	10.8	9.5
Marion	116	1 296	3 012	17.2	46.3	22.6	23.3	11 215	23 152	45 964	56 015	1.0	47 723	11.9	14.8	13.4
Marshall	120	1 413	2 151	15.3	52.6	15.7	19.2	10 595	25 828	44 615	59 421	2.5	47 901	11.1	13.9	13.4
Meade	70	981	1 066	6.7	43.9	22.0	7.4	11 524	22 727	51 326	57 692	0.7	53 903	11.7	15.8	13.2
Miami	167	1 775	8 789	12.9	38.0	23.2	46.6	9 153	28 822	60 622	75 061	3.2	63 924	9.5	12.1	10.9
Mitchell	304	1 080	1 585	16.7	41.1	22.1	13.0	11 243	27 271	46 836	61 317	3.8	48 645	11.2	16.0	15.2
Montgomery	NA	NA	8 763	9.6	44.4	16.4	55.3	9 355	20 912	40 716	50 874	1.2	42 221	18.0	24.8	23.2
Morris	140	1 561	1 174	3.8	49.4	16.9	12.5	11 328	24 558	48 072	56 974	0.9	44 774	12.5	19.5	19.0
Morton	352	961	772	9.3	46.9	17.0	9.9	9 399	23 486	45 638	60 212	1.6	55 378	11.1	15.5	14.1
Nemaha	118	787	2 363	10.0	53.1	21.9	20.0	10 670	25 319	47 141	61 993	2.0	54 149	9.9	11.9	11.0

1. Data for serious crimes have not been adjusted for underreporting; this may affect comparability between geographic areas and over time.   2. Per 100,000 population estimated by the FBI.
3. All persons 3 years old and over enrolled in nursery school through college.   4. Persons 25 years old and over.   5. Elementary and secondary education expenditures.
6. Based on population estimated by the American Community Survey, 2010–2014.

Table B. States and Counties — **Personal Income**

| STATE County | Personal income, 2014 | | | | | | | | | | Earnings, 2014 | | |
| | Total (mil dol) | Percent change, 2013–2014 | Per capita¹ Dollars | Per capita¹ Rank | Wages and salaries (mil dol) | Supplements to wages and salaries; employer contributions (mil dol) Pension and insurance | Government social insurance | Proprietors' income (mil dol) | Dividends, interest, and rent (mil dol) | Personal transfer receipts (mil dol) | Total (mil dol) | Contributions for government social insurance (mil dol) From employee and self-employed | From employer |
	62	63	64	65	66	67	68	69	70	71	72	73	74
KANSAS	130 364	1.6	44 891	X	64 465	10 168	5 024	14 508	25 057	20 277	94 165	5 621	5 024
Allen	530	0.1	41 068	1 052	204	41	16	108	81	124	369	22	16
Anderson	338	-0.1	42 909	858	71	14	6	97	42	73	187	11	6
Atchison	571	0.4	34 551	2 014	235	40	19	76	88	132	371	22	19
Barber	227	0.3	46 337	571	67	13	5	61	54	41	146	9	5
Barton	1 377	4.4	50 295	367	568	87	44	327	220	225	1 026	61	44
Bourbon	518	3.0	35 067	1 921	242	41	20	51	75	129	353	23	20
Brown	419	-3.0	42 729	879	192	34	15	64	70	90	305	17	15
Butler	2 861	1.9	43 203	824	716	149	56	401	394	443	1 321	81	56
Chase	205	9.5	76 296	37	24	5	2	88	24	20	118	6	2
Chautauqua	173	3.8	49 696	399	26	6	2	47	27	36	80	5	2
Cherokee	784	1.1	37 696	1 497	229	42	19	169	88	190	460	29	19
Cheyenne	114	-3.5	42 255	930	30	5	2	31	21	26	68	3	2
Clark	109	-0.4	50 774	343	28	6	2	32	21	20	68	3	2
Clay	423	-2.3	50 808	341	105	21	8	69	74	74	203	12	8
Cloud	335	-2.1	35 643	1 833	112	21	9	52	58	86	194	12	9
Coffey	446	-1.9	52 830	274	273	54	20	90	54	76	437	24	20
Comanche	63	-20.0	32 244	2 410	20	5	2	2	16	19	29	2	2
Cowley	1 390	0.2	38 656	1 369	544	99	44	289	197	309	976	61	44
Crawford	1 241	2.0	31 582	2 515	609	119	49	25	243	326	802	51	49
Decatur	138	7.9	47 362	506	29	6	2	43	28	27	80	4	2
Dickinson	811	-1.8	41 832	967	237	48	19	32	136	155	336	22	19
Doniphan	281	-3.4	35 699	1 827	84	17	7	36	43	62	145	8	7
Douglas	4 277	3.9	36 686	1 649	1 891	366	148	223	822	624	2 628	157	148
Edwards	143	-19.0	47 343	509	39	7	3	36	21	26	84	4	3
Elk	107	5.9	39 840	1 201	20	5	1	19	18	30	44	3	1
Ellis	1 339	3.1	46 158	585	635	109	48	280	218	193	1 072	63	48
Ellsworth	268	2.2	41 905	959	120	21	9	37	43	53	186	11	9
Finney	1 460	2.0	39 259	1 287	728	121	55	275	199	207	1 179	65	55
Ford	1 158	-2.2	33 291	2 227	657	116	49	125	175	181	946	54	49
Franklin	907	0.3	35 421	1 876	382	56	30	62	127	211	530	35	30
Geary	1 592	1.8	43 353	809	1 608	467	156	45	382	215	2 277	92	156
Gove	110	-12.1	40 158	1 152	42	8	3	23	25	24	76	4	3
Graham	147	-8.6	57 421	166	42	7	3	55	21	26	107	6	3
Grant	353	-1.0	45 117	670	159	26	11	121	38	40	318	14	11
Gray	425	-1.2	69 924	58	113	19	8	208	46	33	349	10	8
Greeley	64	-29.0	49 218	427	25	4	2	16	11	11	47	2	2
Greenwood	256	2.6	40 423	1 128	60	11	5	38	43	68	114	7	5
Hamilton	169	0.9	65 111	86	40	7	3	96	15	16	146	3	3
Harper	255	-7.2	43 843	774	94	19	7	56	40	52	176	11	7
Harvey	1 531	0.7	43 956	764	558	88	46	382	186	276	1 074	68	46
Haskell	258	-21.1	62 759	103	75	12	5	113	36	22	206	5	5
Hodgeman	81	-8.9	42 446	904	20	4	1	21	17	13	46	2	1
Jackson	538	1.2	39 712	1 223	142	26	11	68	79	105	247	16	11
Jefferson	726	1.3	38 495	1 394	142	26	11	35	103	137	214	15	11
Jewell	141	-9.9	46 245	577	25	6	2	44	27	28	77	3	2
Johnson	35 608	4.2	62 005	110	18 893	2 222	1 411	3 467	7 070	3 134	25 993	1 584	1 411
Kearny	202	-9.0	51 635	306	54	11	4	72	26	25	141	4	4
Kingman	323	-5.9	41 979	953	97	17	8	53	68	63	175	12	8
Kiowa	98	-15.6	38 947	1 324	37	8	3	17	22	21	64	4	3
Labette	836	2.2	39 896	1 194	358	69	29	85	120	221	541	34	29
Lane	121	-16.7	71 963	51	29	5	2	55	20	15	91	3	2
Leavenworth	3 060	3.5	38 832	1 345	1 385	343	124	145	647	507	1 996	106	124
Lincoln	127	-9.1	40 013	1 172	30	7	2	25	22	28	64	3	2
Linn	319	4.1	33 556	2 183	96	21	7	23	49	84	148	10	7
Logan	127	-13.4	45 406	641	46	11	3	22	25	23	82	4	3
Lyon	997	1.0	30 034	2 710	515	102	40	33	175	242	690	44	40
McPherson	1 343	2.2	45 925	603	664	124	51	219	212	230	1 057	64	51
Marion	454	-7.3	37 164	1 577	119	23	9	71	67	105	223	15	9
Marshall	465	-6.7	46 479	560	202	32	18	86	86	88	338	21	18
Meade	223	-20.7	51 165	325	67	12	5	53	43	30	137	6	5
Miami	1 312	2.8	39 988	1 177	309	53	25	50	211	230	437	30	25
Mitchell	274	-7.6	43 610	793	126	23	10	47	48	58	206	12	10
Montgomery	1 269	3.0	37 244	1 562	643	112	53	132	179	316	940	59	53
Morris	233	-4.0	40 820	1 086	50	10	4	36	45	50	101	5	4
Morton	123	-16.8	39 584	1 238	50	9	4	19	22	22	82	4	4
Nemaha	546	-3.5	53 832	242	212	34	16	128	118	73	391	20	16

1. Based on the resident population estimated as of July 1 of the year shown.

Table B. States and Counties — Earnings, Social Security, and Housing

STATE County	Earnings, 2014 (cont.)									Social Security beneficiaries, December 2014		Housing units, 2015		
	Percent by selected industries													
	Farm	Mining	Construction	Manufacturing	Information: professional, scientific, technical services	Retail trade	Finance, insurance, real estate and leasing	Health care and social assistance	Government	Number	Rate[1]	Supplemental Security Income recipients, December 2014	Total	Percent change, 2010–2014
	75	76	77	78	79	80	81	82	83	84	85	86	87	88
KANSAS	3.2	2.7	5.5	13.4	9.3	5.6	7.2	10.4	17.7	521 955	180	48 920	1 253 861	1.7
Allen	8.8	D	3.1	30.7	2.0	5.5	2.6	5.9	18.7	3 260	252	363	6 254	0.4
Anderson	17.1	7.4	5.2	21.7	1.2	8.2	3.5	D	12.9	1 965	249	114	3 713	-0.2
Atchison	9.0	D	6.6	25.9	3.1	5.4	4.0	D	11.4	3 535	214	319	6 934	-0.8
Barber	7.6	32.7	6.4	7.4	D	5.5	D	D	18.6	1 180	242	60	2 739	-0.9
Barton	5.8	24.1	10.4	6.3	2.9	6.1	6.4	9.7	10.7	5 785	212	497	12 641	-0.4
Bourbon	4.2	1.4	4.4	19.5	3.7	5.5	8.4	16.4	14.4	3 440	233	381	7 089	-1.1
Brown	13.8	0.0	2.8	16.8	3.7	6.6	8.3	12.1	22.2	2 360	241	212	4 744	-0.7
Butler	4.1	7.4	7.8	14.3	D	7.1	4.1	14.2	20.3	12 080	183	810	26 476	1.6
Chase	23.5	15.3	7.9	1.8	3.7	3.8	D	D	7.9	600	224	39	1 496	-0.5
Chautauqua	15.1	D	4.7	4.6	D	4.9	D	7.8	13.0	1 085	312	120	2 135	-0.7
Cherokee	7.2	D	10.1	24.9	3.2	5.5	2.5	10.8	13.7	5 160	249	638	9 797	-0.9
Cheyenne	42.6	D	3.1	1.3	D	3.0	D	12.1	13.3	775	288	21	1 499	-1.3
Clark	41.6	D	D	D	D	3.8	2.9	D	31.2	485	229	30	1 129	-0.5
Clay	16.0	D	7.5	10.7	2.8	7.9	D	D	20.2	2 110	253	110	4 060	0.4
Cloud	13.6	D	3.7	15.1	5.1	7.8	4.3	D	18.2	2 445	262	180	4 615	-0.9
Coffey	6.7	4.5	9.8	2.5	3.6	3.0	D	1.7	12.9	2 055	243	163	4 011	1.2
Comanche	-2.3	7.5	3.1	7.0	D	7.2	D	D	35.4	515	264	37	1 034	-1.0
Cowley	3.0	3.3	3.4	41.5	2.3	5.2	3.1	8.0	17.3	7 870	219	771	15 968	-0.4
Crawford	2.0	0.5	2.5	15.6	4.0	7.1	3.5	12.9	28.7	7 710	196	1 049	17 971	1.0
Decatur	39.5	2.4	D	D	D	5.6	D	9.6	11.5	855	296	47	1 803	-0.8
Dickinson	5.1	D	4.3	23.1	3.5	6.5	3.6	D	23.3	4 355	225	291	9 112	1.6
Doniphan	16.6	D	5.5	14.1	D	2.9	3.4	5.5	26.5	1 680	214	113	3 548	-0.8
Douglas	0.8	0.6	5.4	9.1	10.0	6.6	4.3	7.1	35.3	15 545	133	1 345	48 540	3.9
Edwards	37.8	1.0	3.4	7.7	D	2.9	1.7	8.3	12.4	690	228	40	1 623	-0.8
Elk	32.1	6.7	D	D	D	2.8	2.2	D	28.4	880	327	56	1 749	-0.6
Ellis	2.5	19.0	5.0	5.5	6.3	6.9	5.3	15.8	16.0	5 005	173	288	13 103	1.8
Ellsworth	9.2	D	2.9	12.3	D	3.1	3.4	23.6	23.5	1 495	235	74	3 206	-1.0
Finney	7.9	3.6	5.9	18.3	2.8	7.3	3.4	9.1	14.1	4 605	124	671	13 309	0.2
Ford	4.3	0.4	3.9	31.3	3.9	6.4	2.6	D	15.2	4 250	122	454	12 141	1.1
Franklin	3.9	1.7	5.7	10.1	3.0	6.2	2.2	D	19.6	5 550	217	509	11 099	-0.4
Geary	0.2	0.0	1.6	1.5	D	1.8	1.5	1.1	83.0	4 210	115	566	15 224	4.9
Gove	14.0	6.4	4.8	8.1	D	9.7	3.3	3.4	22.7	705	261	17	1 410	2.7
Graham	13.4	D	D	D	D	4.1	3.5	4.0	15.1	725	284	41	1 479	-0.3
Grant	26.6	15.2	8.3	3.3	D	3.3	2.9	4.4	9.8	1 135	146	89	2 915	-1.0
Gray	53.6	D	8.9	1.1	3.7	2.2	1.6	1.4	10.4	1 010	166	36	2 415	3.2
Greeley	42.8	D	2.4	0.0	D	6.8	D	D	13.8	305	234	0	633	0.6
Greenwood	24.2	19.5	2.2	6.5	3.1	3.6	1.8	D	16.5	2 000	317	166	4 028	-1.0
Hamilton	71.4	D	D	D	D	2.0	3.6	D	10.2	445	172	29	1 222	-1.1
Harper	0.2	19.1	3.6	16.4	D	8.6	D	D	21.8	1 435	246	83	3 165	1.6
Harvey	2.1	5.2	6.0	22.7	3.5	5.7	5.4	D	9.0	7 190	207	432	14 650	0.8
Haskell	58.1	5.6	D	D	D	1.7	D	D	13.4	585	144	33	1 657	-0.5
Hodgeman	43.9	D	2.5	0.0	D	4.0	3.2	0.3	26.4	400	209	16	969	-0.4
Jackson	4.2	D	D	5.2	2.9	6.9	4.5	D	37.5	3 065	228	185	5 777	0.0
Jefferson	7.3	D	23.5	5.5	D	4.6	D	D	23.4	4 080	216	236	8 230	0.9
Jewell	44.7	0.1	D	D	D	5.0	2.3	D	18.4	935	309	47	2 021	-0.5
Johnson	0.0	0.4	4.9	6.6	20.7	5.8	14.4	10.1	7.2	83 290	145	3 888	235 548	4.0
Kearny	54.3	D	D	D	D	2.4	D	0.6	22.8	615	156	55	1 544	-0.8
Kingman	0.4	16.5	11.2	14.2	D	5.2	6.2	8.5	13.4	1 890	245	107	3 811	-0.2
Kiowa	9.6	5.2	D	D	D	D	3.0	D	22.4	575	227	53	1 226	0.5
Labette	3.5	D	2.8	22.3	2.4	5.8	3.2	12.8	25.9	5 120	245	750	10 030	-0.6
Lane	60.4	D	0.6	0.0	D	2.2	2.4	D	11.8	455	270	15	978	-1.2
Leavenworth	0.2	0.1	4.9	3.4	6.3	3.7	4.1	4.4	62.5	12 740	162	955	29 252	1.9
Lincoln	27.7	D	7.4	D	D	3.3	D	3.8	27.4	740	235	40	1 854	-0.5
Linn	5.5	4.7	11.2	3.7	D	4.9	3.3	D	22.7	2 615	275	201	5 471	0.5
Logan	18.3	D	D	D	D	5.9	4.9	D	39.9	645	231	38	1 444	0.2
Lyon	0.8	0.7	3.5	22.7	3.6	7.3	3.1	8.6	30.4	5 875	177	649	15 164	-0.5
McPherson	3.1	6.0	13.3	32.4	2.8	3.9	2.7	8.3	8.5	6 375	219	294	12 933	1.7
Marion	8.1	1.1	2.7	22.0	3.5	4.0	3.3	D	17.6	3 020	247	143	5 923	-0.4
Marshall	10.5	D	3.8	24.4	5.8	5.9	4.2	6.5	9.3	2 445	245	141	4 919	1.1
Meade	37.8	2.4	4.8	1.0	D	2.4	2.7	D	18.9	865	198	30	1 989	-0.5
Miami	4.1	1.7	9.7	8.1	3.8	10.6	5.9	12.2	24.4	6 355	194	450	13 361	1.3
Mitchell	11.5	D	5.6	15.0	D	7.8	D	D	22.5	1 565	250	87	3 291	-0.2
Montgomery	4.1	1.7	9.0	27.1	D	5.3	2.4	D	12.8	8 395	247	1 111	16 408	-1.0
Morris	32.3	0.2	4.6	6.6	D	4.0	3.5	D	20.5	1 485	262	81	3 187	-0.6
Morton	25.9	6.9	D	D	D	5.6	3.1	D	30.8	620	202	44	1 451	-1.1
Nemaha	20.6	D	4.0	27.0	2.1	3.6	5.0	D	8.6	2 225	219	98	4 582	0.4

1. Per 1,000 resident population estimated as of July 1 of the year shown.

Table B. States and Counties — Housing, Labor Force, and Employment

STATE County	Housing units, 2010–2014								Civilian labor force, 2015		Unemployment		Civilian employment,[6] 2010–2014		
	Occupied units													Percent	
		Owner-occupied				Renter-occupied									
				Median owner cost as a percent of income											
	Total	Percent	Median value[1]	With a mortgage	Without a mortgage[2]	Median rent[3]	Median rent as a percent of income[2]	Substandard units[4] (percent)	Total	Percent change, 2014–2015	Total	Rate[5]	Total	Management, business, science and arts	Construction, production, and maintenance occupations
	89	90	91	92	93	94	95	96	97	98	99	100	101	102	103
KANSAS	1 112 335	67.1	129 400	21.0	11.9	748	28.2	2.5	1 499 021	0.3	63 132	4.2	1 391 836	36.5	23.3
Allen	5 398	72.3	61 700	19.8	12.5	539	29.3	1.8	6 695	-1.8	346	5.2	5 874	29.2	33.5
Anderson	3 314	74.4	93 300	22.1	12.6	642	30.2	0.2	4 134	-1.4	205	5.0	3 691	25.8	31.3
Atchison	6 180	72.8	85 800	22.1	12.5	622	25.6	0.7	7 581	-0.8	466	6.1	7 558	33.2	29.8
Barber	2 146	73.7	66 000	17.2	10.2	550	20.6	1.7	2 679	-1.5	116	4.3	2 478	33.4	32.6
Barton	11 480	69.3	79 800	18.4	11.5	603	26.8	2.6	14 674	-5.2	631	4.3	13 384	29.9	27.6
Bourbon	5 702	70.5	80 100	18.5	13.3	580	27.5	2.4	7 159	0.8	348	4.9	6 671	31.8	27.5
Brown	4 157	68.2	81 600	21.7	11.8	513	27.0	1.7	5 384	-0.6	217	4.0	4 682	33.0	27.3
Butler	24 062	74.9	130 800	20.8	11.9	725	27.4	1.6	32 125	0.4	1 379	4.3	30 916	37.5	25.5
Chase	1 139	72.8	78 200	21.5	10.9	471	26.2	2.0	1 247	1.0	46	3.7	1 202	31.9	33.1
Chautauqua	1 584	79.9	50 700	22.0	14.8	651	25.7	1.0	1 562	-1.1	91	5.8	1 519	29.6	36.5
Cherokee	8 132	76.3	70 600	20.4	12.6	586	27.1	1.8	10 491	1.2	472	4.5	9 347	30.1	29.2
Cheyenne	1 294	77.1	83 000	21.3	13.0	564	23.6	1.0	1 362	3.5	38	2.8	1 316	34.0	24.1
Clark	958	71.0	63 500	18.2	10.0	670	23.0	3.7	1 173	2.4	29	2.5	1 031	39.7	24.1
Clay	3 398	79.7	93 100	18.4	12.3	674	23.9	0.6	4 148	-0.7	180	4.3	4 109	32.9	24.6
Cloud	3 972	73.0	69 700	17.9	12.5	558	24.3	1.6	4 345	-1.2	168	3.9	4 425	27.4	29.2
Coffey	3 578	75.2	100 000	19.1	10.8	565	26.6	2.1	4 835	-1.4	276	5.7	4 118	34.7	25.6
Comanche	757	75.7	64 100	20.9	11.7	515	18.8	0.0	1 009	3.0	35	3.5	945	40.0	23.9
Cowley	13 783	69.5	79 900	20.1	12.5	625	29.2	2.4	17 084	-1.2	795	4.7	15 700	27.3	30.7
Crawford	15 364	60.1	85 000	20.0	12.9	683	33.4	3.8	18 977	-1.0	977	5.1	18 588	32.2	23.6
Decatur	1 442	78.6	51 300	21.5	11.3	555	34.9	0.7	1 352	-0.2	51	3.8	1 339	38.1	22.7
Dickinson	7 838	73.4	107 100	20.6	12.1	608	26.7	1.0	9 553	-1.9	502	5.3	9 057	31.7	29.9
Doniphan	3 138	74.5	84 100	19.5	12.0	589	22.7	3.1	4 339	0.9	191	4.4	3 770	31.7	33.7
Douglas	43 834	51.7	181 300	22.2	12.2	860	32.8	1.8	65 273	0.8	2 411	3.7	61 189	44.4	14.6
Edwards	1 287	76.2	56 500	17.6	10.0	507	20.6	2.4	1 635	1.7	54	3.3	1 478	32.7	34.9
Elk	1 276	79.2	50 700	19.6	12.6	539	26.7	2.7	1 311	0.0	64	4.9	1 170	35.5	32.1
Ellis	11 859	62.7	143 200	21.6	12.3	625	29.8	1.4	17 592	-1.9	533	3.0	16 183	32.3	21.6
Ellsworth	2 549	74.7	78 200	19.9	11.0	567	24.8	0.7	2 949	-14.5	110	3.7	2 828	32.7	29.1
Finney	12 670	62.7	112 000	22.5	12.1	680	22.6	6.5	20 225	0.0	720	3.6	18 709	25.1	37.0
Ford	11 086	64.3	92 200	20.7	11.5	614	22.7	6.7	18 236	0.2	627	3.4	16 202	20.6	44.8
Franklin	9 933	71.6	120 000	23.0	13.2	725	28.5	2.8	14 161	0.6	655	4.6	12 465	29.2	30.8
Geary	12 782	44.6	136 900	23.1	12.7	1 002	28.1	4.9	12 246	-0.8	760	6.2	13 318	28.6	27.8
Gove	1 212	79.5	74 700	19.9	10.0	532	22.9	1.2	1 510	1.7	39	2.6	1 391	38.2	27.0
Graham	1 158	80.1	66 000	18.0	10.9	480	26.1	0.4	1 281	-2.5	51	4.0	1 255	35.9	26.6
Grant	2 776	73.5	95 100	18.8	10.0	542	26.8	3.4	3 932	-0.3	144	3.7	3 670	30.9	35.3
Gray	2 125	72.8	99 800	19.4	10.0	631	19.3	3.9	3 589	2.5	84	2.3	3 102	33.7	29.8
Greeley	471	77.5	83 000	21.5	14.3	600	14.7	1.3	925	3.0	20	2.2	621	33.3	23.7
Greenwood	2 860	77.6	57 100	18.1	12.5	496	27.6	2.6	3 280	-1.6	155	4.7	2 941	28.2	35.0
Hamilton	1 008	74.2	82 900	23.5	11.7	495	19.3	4.7	1 697	2.0	34	2.0	1 347	28.0	36.2
Harper	2 567	76.5	66 800	20.4	11.1	600	25.3	0.8	2 866	-4.0	113	3.9	2 778	37.6	26.1
Harvey	13 329	71.1	112 000	19.7	11.7	665	30.9	1.3	17 264	0.7	679	3.9	16 585	35.1	26.2
Haskell	1 421	74.0	110 400	18.2	10.0	723	20.1	2.6	2 379	0.8	61	2.6	2 100	33.4	30.9
Hodgeman	814	74.9	77 600	16.7	10.0	543	21.7	2.5	1 039	0.4	34	3.3	999	44.3	26.8
Jackson	5 288	74.6	118 900	21.3	12.9	702	25.4	1.6	7 389	-0.1	275	3.7	6 767	29.0	28.9
Jefferson	7 498	82.8	126 500	22.3	13.3	724	23.9	2.2	10 205	-0.3	432	4.2	9 317	34.9	27.1
Jewell	1 438	80.8	53 600	18.3	11.6	503	18.7	1.9	1 393	0.8	62	4.5	1 479	36.5	28.6
Johnson	217 826	69.8	212 300	20.9	10.7	932	27.2	1.5	325 010	1.2	11 116	3.4	298 342	49.1	12.3
Kearny	1 341	71.1	93 600	18.2	10.6	585	13.7	1.7	2 156	1.7	68	3.2	1 913	27.9	39.0
Kingman	3 084	73.6	88 000	21.8	11.7	623	21.4	2.3	3 688	2.2	161	4.4	3 405	28.8	35.9
Kiowa	1 051	63.2	107 700	23.1	10.9	503	25.8	0.4	1 460	8.0	44	3.0	1 258	34.4	24.7
Labette	8 495	70.6	67 700	20.4	13.2	579	27.6	4.0	10 839	0.4	630	5.8	9 550	31.0	28.4
Lane	811	76.6	62 600	13.8	10.9	505	23.6	0.0	876	1.4	30	3.4	848	39.2	28.7
Leavenworth	26 398	67.0	165 500	21.8	11.7	885	25.2	1.9	35 436	1.1	1 609	4.5	32 781	37.2	20.5
Lincoln	1 397	77.7	63 400	21.2	12.2	473	23.6	2.0	1 814	2.2	64	3.5	1 526	38.5	31.5
Linn	4 140	80.6	90 700	22.3	12.8	663	24.7	6.1	4 358	0.7	280	6.4	3 941	34.5	29.7
Logan	1 228	70.1	78 100	18.0	11.2	678	26.6	4.5	1 755	1.0	43	2.5	1 418	35.0	31.3
Lyon	13 069	59.6	92 500	21.0	12.3	594	28.6	2.6	16 672	0.8	727	4.4	16 994	26.1	32.4
McPherson	11 726	76.8	127 600	20.1	10.3	632	23.1	1.7	17 305	2.7	525	3.0	15 205	35.4	28.6
Marion	4 845	78.8	83 200	20.2	11.8	560	26.9	2.8	6 197	0.8	239	3.9	5 836	33.2	28.9
Marshall	4 289	76.7	83 300	20.0	11.2	499	26.7	3.6	5 773	-1.9	170	2.9	5 044	29.9	33.5
Meade	1 761	69.8	86 400	18.5	11.2	652	21.7	2.7	2 419	1.5	73	3.0	2 136	38.4	31.5
Miami	12 350	79.1	167 100	23.0	13.1	801	36.4	1.8	17 076	1.2	737	4.3	15 808	33.6	26.7
Mitchell	2 795	70.2	75 800	18.5	11.5	539	25.6	1.3	3 811	-0.8	128	3.4	3 228	37.3	29.2
Montgomery	13 706	70.1	72 400	19.2	12.5	601	30.1	2.0	16 777	-3.4	1 097	6.5	14 860	27.4	32.7
Morris	2 437	77.9	83 100	22.0	10.5	553	24.7	2.7	3 126	0.8	136	4.4	2 838	28.9	34.8
Morton	1 199	69.1	87 200	19.1	12.8	603	23.1	0.8	1 448	-2.8	63	4.4	1 458	29.9	32.8
Nemaha	4 161	77.4	101 300	19.3	10.7	516	24.0	1.9	5 941	1.5	155	2.6	5 178	33.7	30.0

1. Specified owner-occupied units.   2. A value of 10.0 represents 10 percent or less; a value of 50.0 represents 50 percent or more.   3. Specified renter-occupied units.
4. Overcrowded or lacking complete plumbing facilities.   5. Percent of civilian labor force.   6. Persons 16 years old and over.

STATE County	Number of establishments	Total	Health care and social assistance	Manufacturing	Retail trade	Finance and insurance	Professional, scientific, and technical services	Total (mil dol)	Average per employee (dollars)	Number	Fewer than 50 acres	500 acres or more	Farm operators whose principal occupation is farming (percent)
	104	105	106	107	108	109	110	111	112	113	114	115	116
KANSAS..........	74 055	1 178 062	195 155	164 749	150 237	62 642	63 836	49 713	42 199	61 773	19.0	31.6	48.3
Allen..........	385	4 475	435	2 128	596	112	110	141	31 556	650	20.5	19.5	46.2
Anderson..........	208	1 522	361	210	D	91	D	45	29 334	707	20.8	25.5	47.5
Atchison..........	353	5 702	802	1 245	618	D	69	180	31 654	611	19.8	17.7	50.2
Barber..........	207	1 521	263	D	216	56	48	57	37 348	378	10.1	50.3	54.2
Barton..........	975	12 674	2 523	1 247	1 541	821	347	447	35 292	694	14.4	39.2	45.7
Bourbon..........	349	4 732	990	1 227	655	207	118	136	28 686	903	18.9	18.4	45.0
Brown..........	261	3 416	797	553	393	182	D	109	31 931	510	19.8	29.2	60.6
Butler..........	1 298	13 420	3 065	1 323	2 121	476	777	443	33 038	1 353	34.3	20.8	39.8
Chase..........	71	504	D	D	63	D	D	16	32 681	252	15.9	45.6	54.8
Chautauqua..........	72	456	D	D	89	D	D	13	27 487	312	8.0	38.1	53.2
Cherokee..........	345	5 596	1 073	1 595	527	131	93	219	39 055	729	27.8	24.8	50.2
Cheyenne..........	103	556	159	D	103	30	22	16	29 185	393	9.4	51.7	47.8
Clark..........	64	D	D	D	D	40	D	D	D	283	4.9	51.9	53.0
Clay..........	260	2 424	596	D	386	86	D	73	30 018	541	15.0	37.5	53.2
Cloud..........	308	2 950	700	D	547	D	85	92	31 120	461	14.8	35.1	46.4
Coffey..........	240	D	482	D	392	103	217	D	D	667	19.2	26.7	38.5
Comanche..........	79	448	154	D	87	33	D	9	20 971	234	6.8	61.1	52.1
Cowley..........	751	11 338	2 117	3 619	1 520	D	240	369	32 577	990	19.3	24.5	48.6
Crawford..........	892	13 948	2 902	2 665	1 853	320	315	412	29 506	846	25.5	19.1	36.9
Decatur..........	102	606	D	D	96	34	D	15	25 300	293	10.6	55.6	61.1
Dickinson..........	467	4 994	877	1 116	757	176	153	150	30 133	1 011	19.8	31.2	41.5
Doniphan..........	156	1 447	186	403	D	55	D	48	33 064	422	20.4	24.9	55.2
Douglas..........	2 675	38 850	6 227	3 370	6 188	1 029	1 695	1 182	30 424	945	38.5	9.7	35.8
Edwards..........	88	619	D	152	D	D	D	21	33 981	292	7.9	45.2	61.3
Elk..........	72	343	D	D	34	27	D	8	21 918	315	14.9	42.5	53.0
Ellis..........	1 142	13 745	3 228	1 219	2 183	402	382	443	32 232	645	13.2	35.0	40.2
Ellsworth..........	163	1 627	423	263	225	D	75	56	34 497	435	11.0	34.9	48.7
Finney..........	1 003	14 921	2 042	D	2 573	382	268	513	34 411	499	11.0	60.1	65.1
Ford..........	766	15 278	1 273	6 313	1 755	295	516	516	33 784	655	12.4	43.1	51.0
Franklin..........	571	8 524	1 590	678	1 103	152	D	331	38 876	1 024	31.1	16.3	42.5
Geary..........	573	7 918	1 476	D	1 264	277	411	240	30 257	238	28.2	27.3	45.4
Gove..........	131	991	246	D	174	50	D	30	29 836	395	8.6	55.4	57.7
Graham..........	103	744	D	D	119	D	D	26	34 366	431	7.4	43.2	49.2
Grant..........	223	2 469	220	192	241	112	33	108	43 628	329	10.6	40.7	45.9
Gray..........	219	1 630	D	80	172	49	42	53	32 258	418	9.6	46.2	53.1
Greeley..........	45	339	D	NA	54	22	D	12	35 690	262	5.0	53.8	55.7
Greenwood..........	183	1 152	221	D	221	D	D	36	31 299	551	13.2	37.4	52.5
Hamilton..........	67	607	139	NA	88	D	4	20	33 033	397	4.5	54.4	53.9
Harper..........	211	1 842	318	D	256	96	D	63	34 146	482	13.5	39.6	49.8
Harvey..........	762	13 741	3 072	3 357	1 464	315	275	494	35 939	744	30.5	25.1	48.9
Haskell..........	120	815	D	58	61	27	D	28	34 785	187	10.7	61.5	74.9
Hodgeman..........	47	291	D	NA	39	D	D	10	32 928	399	3.0	56.6	57.9
Jackson..........	254	2 933	544	216	369	103	74	81	27 587	1 054	26.7	15.3	36.8
Jefferson..........	303	2 285	415	D	297	73	66	85	36 988	996	27.9	10.9	38.2
Jewell..........	83	496	D	D	60	D	D	13	26 540	453	9.1	50.1	66.2
Johnson..........	17 423	322 765	38 629	22 917	37 792	27 849	29 516	16 784	52 000	571	52.0	8.4	35.4
Kearny..........	81	651	D	D	D	D	8	24	37 014	343	4.7	50.7	53.6
Kingman..........	210	1 837	382	232	202	121	190	62	33 633	808	14.2	31.7	43.8
Kiowa..........	94	832	192	NA	68	32	D	27	32 969	403	6.5	43.7	43.4
Labette..........	462	9 128	3 983	2 107	983	259	D	262	28 692	977	20.2	17.3	46.6
Lane..........	66	332	D	D	D	D	D	11	34 503	315	8.6	52.4	48.3
Leavenworth..........	1 221	14 022	2 959	1 124	2 304	811	1 209	490	34 937	1 133	41.0	6.6	35.4
Lincoln..........	92	449	129	D	50	D	D	13	28 078	431	13.7	41.5	62.9
Linn..........	193	1 225	58	100	245	69	D	56	45 683	913	18.8	16.2	38.4
Logan..........	115	710	D	D	135	55	D	24	33 154	325	5.2	55.7	48.6
Lyon..........	810	11 250	1 910	2 684	1 857	321	260	349	31 056	946	21.7	26.5	47.5
McPherson..........	896	14 543	3 347	4 502	1 155	637	206	594	40 824	1 147	20.2	29.9	54.7
Marion..........	289	2 652	626	D	273	94	99	69	25 914	981	19.1	32.7	50.8
Marshall..........	368	4 347	593	1 488	678	221	98	158	36 419	796	14.8	34.3	55.8
Meade..........	130	906	D	D	147	50	D	32	34 776	439	7.7	51.9	52.4
Miami..........	713	6 671	2 000	456	988	253	306	237	35 478	1 305	38.4	9.7	41.5
Mitchell..........	247	2 629	D	D	372	140	D	84	32 049	415	11.1	43.4	60.5
Montgomery..........	825	12 692	2 363	3 495	1 625	362	189	431	33 985	1 012	23.9	14.4	41.3
Morris..........	138	1 251	282	222	177	59	57	37	29 822	454	13.4	35.0	53.1
Morton..........	112	898	D	D	91	D	D	37	41 220	323	3.7	49.8	50.5
Nemaha..........	370	4 700	886	1 377	518	186	111	182	38 813	903	15.2	26.7	49.3

Table B. States and Counties — **Agriculture**

STATE County	Land in farms Acreage (1,000) [117]	Percent change, 2007–2012 [118]	Average size of farm [119]	Total irrigated (1,000) [120]	Total cropland (1,000) [121]	Value of land and buildings (dollars) Average per farm [122]	Average per acre [123]	Value of machinery and equipment, average per farm (dollars) [124]	Value of products sold Total (mil dol) [125]	Average per farm (dollars) [126]	Percent from: Crops [127]	Live-stock and poultry products [128]	Percent of farms with sales of: $10,000 or more [129]	$100,000 or more [130]	Government payments Total ($1,000) [131]	Percent of farms [132]
KANSAS	46 137	-0.4	747	2 881.3	28 503.3	1 218 662	1 632	156 737	18 460.6	298 845	37.8	62.2	56.0	25.5	442 090	68.6
Allen	245	-8.3	377	D	129.5	526 683	1 396	93 555	38.2	58 702	58.5	41.5	46.9	13.1	2 652	62.9
Anderson	366	-0.3	518	1.4	224.0	806 658	1 557	132 429	73.4	103 812	55.7	44.3	57.9	21.8	4 436	66.3
Atchison	220	-13.3	361	0.5	144.4	777 051	2 154	134 581	56.5	92 530	76.6	23.4	64.2	21.8	2 999	60.9
Barber	591	-3.4	1 563	8.9	193.1	1 898 704	1 215	171 399	88.5	234 053	51.3	48.7	68.3	37.3	2 849	75.7
Barton	566	1.3	816	39.2	421.3	1 278 262	1 567	210 909	279.0	401 964	34.5	65.5	64.4	31.8	5 572	80.8
Bourbon	334	2.1	370	0.3	126.4	536 239	1 448	68 483	53.7	59 508	29.6	70.4	46.3	9.6	2 601	56.6
Brown	295	-15.0	578	5.0	232.3	1 891 461	3 271	223 178	140.5	275 506	85.4	14.6	67.5	36.1	3 416	72.9
Butler	768	-2.4	568	5.1	295.9	999 409	1 760	108 387	282.3	208 676	27.9	72.1	44.6	17.7	3 069	37.5
Chase	393	22.7	1 558	D	56.0	2 113 111	1 356	118 929	84.7	336 111	12.8	87.2	72.2	34.5	714	52.0
Chautauqua	310	0.7	995	D	39.7	1 148 269	1 155	73 324	35.2	112 805	D	D	61.5	18.3	626	34.9
Cherokee	308	-5.0	423	0.8	226.4	787 462	1 862	118 760	86.9	119 213	81.1	18.9	55.3	21.3	3 158	50.6
Cheyenne	547	-5.2	1 391	39.5	336.7	2 203 377	1 584	192 557	143.9	366 117	52.4	47.6	61.8	39.9	4 717	84.7
Clark	503	3.6	1 778	6.6	191.4	1 617 572	910	143 989	126.2	445 763	13.0	87.0	49.8	29.0	3 389	89.0
Clay	363	3.3	670	29.2	230.8	1 414 349	2 111	204 776	115.9	214 174	69.5	30.5	68.6	38.1	3 830	81.9
Cloud	322	-16.2	698	15.2	208.8	1 390 777	1 991	175 219	80.0	173 627	84.4	15.6	70.1	31.0	3 226	73.1
Coffey	329	1.4	494	1.2	183.4	753 148	1 526	94 421	61.7	92 496	53.0	47.0	46.6	18.3	3 527	76.6
Comanche	485	12.2	2 073	7.5	144.9	1 910 051	921	146 675	48.7	208 034	44.7	55.3	66.7	41.0	2 448	79.5
Cowley	575	-0.2	580	6.2	266.1	831 902	1 433	134 058	109.0	110 077	54.0	46.0	54.3	18.7	3 203	61.0
Crawford	323	-5.6	382	1.1	192.1	640 069	1 675	105 483	75.6	89 355	68.3	31.7	49.2	15.6	2 040	61.5
Decatur	462	-4.3	1 578	11.1	269.1	2 407 051	1 525	246 949	136.8	466 915	37.6	62.4	75.1	42.3	3 139	85.7
Dickinson	510	-5.0	505	4.3	335.4	1 017 926	2 017	139 688	157.1	155 342	52.5	47.5	55.2	26.0	5 935	79.7
Doniphan	180	-27.5	425	1.2	133.8	1 531 073	3 599	178 036	80.8	191 472	93.4	6.6	58.3	33.2	2 819	70.4
Douglas	211	-4.5	223	3.3	127.3	636 186	2 854	82 519	43.9	46 436	66.2	33.8	37.7	8.4	2 332	46.9
Edwards	394	-10.2	1 351	92.3	284.9	2 882 414	2 134	298 442	151.7	519 538	83.7	16.3	64.0	43.2	3 850	92.1
Elk	316	-0.1	1 004	D	51.4	1 274 378	1 269	84 156	42.1	133 556	16.0	84.0	56.5	23.5	694	41.3
Ellis	497	-5.6	770	1.9	253.4	1 025 119	1 332	130 081	99.6	154 462	32.7	67.3	59.8	19.1	3 503	78.9
Ellsworth	381	4.4	876	0.6	182.7	1 161 667	1 326	144 347	51.6	118 699	66.8	33.2	54.3	25.5	2 787	84.8
Finney	816	7.3	1 635	186.6	670.4	2 353 291	1 439	399 313	909.2	1 822 062	20.3	79.7	64.1	46.5	9 784	80.0
Ford	700	10.3	1 068	82.0	541.7	1 301 528	1 218	232 826	441.8	674 560	25.9	74.1	60.6	31.3	7 279	79.4
Franklin	362	15.4	353	2.2	200.8	820 041	2 321	103 643	101.3	98 951	54.6	45.4	43.5	10.8	3 448	52.6
Geary	146	-1.9	612	3.6	57.9	1 187 118	1 939	121 773	30.4	127 550	51.0	49.0	45.4	22.7	971	67.6
Gove	579	-2.5	1 465	21.1	368.9	1 883 304	1 286	227 359	196.1	496 537	34.9	65.1	68.1	42.3	6 300	83.5
Graham	483	-6.2	1 120	13.3	292.0	1 478 046	1 319	183 213	57.9	134 267	76.3	23.7	54.3	25.3	5 847	81.9
Grant	364	7.8	1 105	88.7	298.2	1 471 553	1 332	253 924	918.2	2 790 860	9.4	90.6	50.8	36.2	5 153	84.5
Gray	547	0.2	1 309	124.2	420.9	1 747 136	1 335	320 818	939.4	2 247 407	14.9	85.1	59.8	44.3	7 391	82.8
Greeley	497	0.9	1 898	23.2	458.2	2 823 103	1 487	306 420	123.1	470 031	47.9	52.1	64.5	42.7	5 269	90.8
Greenwood	701	15.1	1 272	0.2	104.0	1 792 824	1 409	96 279	89.6	162 530	19.8	80.2	59.9	21.4	1 382	45.6
Hamilton	635	4.0	1 600	30.9	486.4	1 617 219	1 011	198 665	367.2	925 033	15.1	84.9	47.4	29.0	6 441	88.9
Harper	506	5.1	1 050	3.8	329.0	1 592 678	1 517	176 824	109.6	227 477	58.8	41.2	60.4	35.1	5 601	85.5
Harvey	340	0.3	456	47.2	297.2	1 173 019	2 570	154 589	161.7	217 360	69.4	30.6	59.4	31.6	4 135	68.5
Haskell	364	-8.8	1 944	116.7	259.0	2 676 770	1 377	550 995	1 009.9	5 400 412	10.6	89.4	71.7	59.9	4 074	82.9
Hodgeman	543	3.2	1 360	30.7	328.1	1 461 356	1 075	227 945	182.1	456 386	29.2	70.8	65.4	36.6	6 590	87.7
Jackson	329	-3.0	312	0.8	136.1	549 724	1 760	78 991	57.9	54 893	40.3	59.7	45.7	11.4	2 322	50.4
Jefferson	244	-14.8	245	3.6	133.4	547 394	2 238	86 031	53.1	53 344	62.7	37.3	41.6	8.9	2 013	45.5
Jewell	464	-1.6	1 024	15.0	294.8	1 975 925	1 930	223 843	136.5	301 278	77.1	22.9	73.7	47.0	5 236	83.9
Johnson	99	-13.0	174	1.1	59.2	755 205	4 340	76 618	24.4	42 680	66.0	34.0	34.2	9.3	911	30.3
Kearny	547	5.3	1 594	70.9	423.6	2 067 618	1 297	238 297	337.4	983 639	23.9	76.1	56.9	38.2	6 069	86.6
Kingman	542	-0.8	671	33.7	329.3	958 710	1 429	139 131	103.2	127 708	74.0	26.0	56.7	25.0	5 868	84.2
Kiowa	455	3.4	1 130	49.9	233.2	1 391 826	1 232	141 444	80.6	199 943	79.4	20.6	56.3	26.6	3 852	88.6
Labette	371	-0.2	379	0.6	196.7	563 481	1 486	94 384	122.8	125 668	41.5	58.5	53.7	14.7	2 247	51.4
Lane	452	12.7	1 436	18.7	337.0	1 846 321	1 286	204 457	216.8	688 343	14.4	85.6	54.0	30.8	5 512	91.4
Leavenworth	184	-5.3	163	0.3	102.5	526 699	3 235	63 351	36.4	32 098	69.3	30.7	35.7	5.9	1 452	29.0
Lincoln	397	-8.2	922	1.4	204.7	1 377 181	1 494	166 234	63.5	147 355	68.1	31.9	65.7	31.8	3 280	87.9
Linn	355	33.7	388	0.0	167.8	683 687	1 760	75 490	39.5	43 245	62.7	37.3	41.9	8.1	2 608	54.3
Logan	566	0.0	1 743	11.1	329.4	2 057 326	1 180	197 542	78.8	242 551	74.3	25.7	70.8	41.2	4 297	83.4
Lyon	535	12.9	565	0.4	228.4	881 912	1 560	107 999	111.4	117 727	31.6	68.4	49.3	17.1	3 429	67.4
McPherson	572	0.9	498	42.3	409.1	1 124 564	2 257	171 576	208.5	181 763	61.5	38.5	66.4	32.3	8 021	77.6
Marion	596	-0.5	608	4.4	341.4	1 282 189	2 109	140 915	151.5	154 412	51.1	48.9	63.7	31.4	4 559	76.8
Marshall	438	-14.8	551	2.9	301.7	1 483 474	2 693	194 613	127.9	160 700	81.4	18.6	71.4	36.4	4 946	80.9
Meade	618	2.6	1 408	129.5	372.2	1 717 237	1 220	295 836	296.8	676 175	49.6	50.4	58.1	37.4	6 661	86.1
Miami	296	-3.7	227	1.3	166.5	709 454	3 131	71 108	51.0	39 090	66.4	33.6	36.9	7.4	1 946	36.2
Mitchell	439	-1.2	1 058	8.4	303.5	2 369 728	2 240	254 643	153.5	369 872	57.3	42.7	71.8	44.6	4 609	84.8
Montgomery	336	6.9	332	3.7	163.1	513 052	1 547	98 773	79.4	78 478	61.2	38.8	45.9	9.4	1 771	37.7
Morris	389	-5.9	857	0.5	153.9	1 259 154	1 469	134 231	116.8	257 302	28.1	71.9	68.3	27.1	2 296	72.9
Morton	457	3.4	1 414	59.5	389.3	1 197 084	846	156 164	169.7	525 477	34.4	65.6	47.4	30.0	6 208	86.4
Nemaha	383	-15.1	424	0.9	259.0	1 195 878	2 822	170 190	224.6	248 729	34.9	65.1	73.8	32.3	6 391	79.8

Table B. States and Counties — Water Use, Wholesale Trade, Retail Trade, and Real Estate

STATE County	Water use, 2010 Total water withdrawn (mil gal/day)	Gallons withdrawn per person per day	Wholesale trade,[1] 2012 Number of establishments	Number of employees	Sales (mil dol)	Annual payroll (mil dol)	Retail trade,[2] 2012 Number of establishments	Number of employees	Sales (mil dol)	Annual payroll (mil dol)	Real estate and rental and leasing,[2] 2012 Number of establishments	Number of employees	Receipts (mil dol)	Annual payroll (mil dol)
	133	134	135	136	137	138	139	140	141	142	143	144	145	146
KANSAS	4 004.8	1 404	3 790	52 168	60 226.3	3 055.4	10 548	145 480	38 276.5	3 325.0	2 999	14 256	2 743.1	507.6
Allen	3.8	284	17	D	D	D	57	544	152.8	12.7	22	42	2.8	0.5
Anderson	1.9	239	12	54	69.0	2.3	38	268	92.1	5.8	2	D	D	D
Atchison	5.4	321	18	382	206.5	15.1	49	640	126.9	12.7	9	D	D	D
Barber	5.9	1 220	11	94	89.0	5.5	32	222	76.4	4.5	5	8	1.0	0.1
Barton	36.8	1 328	65	542	389.6	27.0	128	1 651	420.4	38.0	29	105	16.3	3.8
Bourbon	3.1	203	13	D	D	D	48	611	132.7	12.1	9	35	4.6	0.9
Brown	2.5	246	15	128	244.4	5.7	32	365	74.8	7.1	4	8	0.6	0.1
Butler	15.6	237	54	440	317.5	23.2	184	2 053	620.1	46.4	52	103	17.3	2.6
Chase	1.4	516	3	D	D	D	9	64	16.0	0.9	2	D	D	D
Chautauqua	1.0	262	2	D	D	D	15	96	20.0	1.4	NA	NA	NA	NA
Cherokee	94.1	4 354	17	154	209.1	6.5	56	497	125.4	10.3	4	16	2.0	0.4
Cheyenne	42.9	15 719	11	115	113.2	4.8	22	79	17.2	1.4	3	3	0.7	0.1
Clark	5.2	2 348	1	D	D	D	9	53	9.1	1.0	NA	NA	NA	NA
Clay	9.1	1 060	15	169	135.3	8.2	38	425	94.2	7.8	4	D	D	D
Cloud	10.7	1 117	20	264	199.1	10.6	56	558	136.5	12.5	5	9	1.2	0.2
Coffey	21.1	2 451	12	72	63.7	2.4	50	408	111.4	7.8	3	D	D	D
Comanche	8.3	4 363	2	D	D	D	17	69	18.7	1.6	1	D	D	D
Cowley	8.4	230	26	D	D	D	121	1 445	337.1	32.9	19	39	6.6	1.1
Crawford	7.2	185	39	577	297.7	20.8	165	1 915	406.1	37.0	38	108	15.2	2.3
Decatur	9.4	3 168	10	79	83.7	2.1	19	89	23.6	1.6	4	10	1.4	0.2
Dickinson	5.8	292	24	282	231.1	12.8	70	768	187.5	17.0	14	D	D	D
Doniphan	0.6	70	11	98	90.0	4.0	21	141	30.9	2.5	2	D	D	D
Douglas	19.1	172	71	610	282.9	24.6	373	6 066	1 354.2	122.6	157	761	97.7	20.9
Edwards	99.3	32 697	9	124	150.2	5.0	13	82	54.5	1.4	1	D	D	D
Elk	0.9	316	2	D	D	D	10	56	23.1	0.7	1	D	D	D
Ellis	5.5	192	46	405	201.7	17.0	183	2 166	621.0	49.5	43	145	18.2	3.3
Ellsworth	2.6	405	9	73	80.9	2.8	29	238	53.6	4.0	1	D	D	D
Finney	281.3	7 650	79	D	D	D	174	2 393	577.0	53.7	36	132	33.5	5.1
Ford	96.5	2 850	62	750	633.9	36.1	126	1 805	499.5	40.9	23	60	15.5	2.7
Franklin	3.6	140	15	148	138.8	6.9	90	1 054	271.1	21.9	13	D	D	D
Geary	14.7	428	8	D	D	D	96	1 309	345.9	27.4	37	292	77.1	11.6
Gove	17.9	6 642	11	D	D	D	20	184	91.5	4.8	NA	NA	NA	NA
Graham	14.2	5 483	9	24	29.2	1.3	21	132	35.5	2.8	2	D	D	D
Grant	129.1	16 493	13	123	87.6	6.9	33	269	52.8	5.0	6	D	D	D
Gray	190.1	31 648	22	210	238.5	9.9	29	171	50.1	4.0	5	25	4.5	0.6
Greeley	17.7	14 226	3	D	D	D	6	44	11.8	1.1	NA	NA	NA	NA
Greenwood	1.8	271	9	D	D	D	32	193	49.5	4.0	2	D	D	D
Hamilton	43.5	16 186	6	58	89.5	2.6	11	95	19.1	1.9	NA	NA	NA	NA
Harper	3.7	617	15	98	151.1	5.6	36	233	62.7	5.3	2	D	D	D
Harvey	44.1	1 273	31	250	144.0	9.9	120	1 446	335.1	32.2	26	D	D	D
Haskell	198.6	46 668	15	124	147.5	5.5	13	63	21.1	1.1	1	D	D	D
Hodgeman	23.2	12 098	5	D	D	D	8	D	D	D	NA	NA	NA	NA
Jackson	2.2	162	13	85	45.3	3.1	40	379	83.2	7.6	6	18	1.9	0.6
Jefferson	3.7	196	6	20	5.7	0.4	48	318	74.0	5.4	1	D	D	D
Jewell	55.3	17 979	10	56	30.5	1.6	13	59	18.3	1.0	NA	NA	NA	NA
Johnson	18.1	33	915	18 267	27 613.7	1 397.4	1 868	35 648	10 481.4	897.6	914	4 765	1 271.2	217.1
Kearny	175.7	44 182	5	D	D	D	9	51	12.2	0.7	3	D	D	D
Kingman	22.2	2 824	25	145	100.4	5.8	26	202	45.7	3.8	6	6	1.2	0.1
Kiowa	58.5	22 902	10	104	115.6	6.2	16	85	28.3	1.8	NA	NA	NA	NA
Labette	4.5	209	15	D	D	D	89	931	198.6	19.8	12	34	4.0	0.8
Lane	15.4	8 811	9	54	52.5	1.8	12	50	9.6	0.8	NA	NA	NA	NA
Leavenworth	27.0	354	19	94	45.0	3.8	174	2 088	541.5	45.8	48	164	45.5	4.9
Lincoln	1.5	463	7	74	31.1	1.8	11	57	9.2	1.0	1	D	D	D
Linn	11.6	1 201	6	30	12.1	1.2	35	241	53.5	3.6	1	D	D	D
Logan	6.7	2 442	13	85	103.9	3.6	15	126	35.3	2.7	NA	NA	NA	NA
Lyon	7.7	227	21	426	287.8	17.2	162	1 814	493.9	36.5	38	152	14.8	3.4
McPherson	31.5	1 080	37	264	560.9	14.9	130	1 197	295.5	27.0	24	75	5.4	1.1
Marion	3.6	284	19	187	133.9	8.7	50	313	79.2	6.1	7	7	2.5	0.3
Marshall	3.5	348	25	159	229.5	7.3	70	687	234.9	13.9	6	12	0.5	0.1
Meade	153.3	33 510	12	104	198.5	5.1	22	221	32.2	3.6	NA	NA	NA	NA
Miami	4.9	149	21	65	97.6	3.1	87	981	262.4	22.7	28	D	D	D
Mitchell	13.0	2 045	23	191	109.5	7.9	43	426	127.7	10.4	5	26	2.2	0.4
Montgomery	11.7	330	30	D	D	D	131	1 536	350.3	35.2	29	89	8.7	1.6
Morris	1.7	285	4	13	11.1	0.6	28	185	44.0	3.8	NA	NA	NA	NA
Morton	47.7	14 748	10	89	127.7	4.1	13	97	21.5	2.1	NA	NA	NA	NA
Nemaha	3.3	327	21	142	141.0	5.9	74	616	156.5	11.4	1	D	D	D

1. Merchant wholesalers, except manufacturers' sales branches and offices.   2. Employer establishments.

Table B. States and Counties — Professional Services, Manufacturing, and Accommodation and Food Services

STATE County	Professional, scientific, and technical services, 2012				Manufacturing, 2012				Accommodation and food services, 2012			
	Number of establishments	Number of employees	Receipts (mil dol)	Annual payroll (mil dol)	Number of establishments	Number of employees	Receipts (mil dol)	Annual payroll (mil dol)	Number of establishments	Number of employees	Sales (mil dol)	Annual payroll (mil dol)
	147	148	149	150	151	152	153	154	155	156	157	158
KANSAS	7 110	60 989	8 716.1	3 596.2	2 875	152 423	86 076.3	7 578.3	5 943	106 850	4 873.4	1 342.9
Allen	27	97	7.1	2.6	25	1 875	470.9	65.1	25	315	13.2	3.2
Anderson	13	29	1.9	0.6	11	150	D	7.3	16	D	D	D
Atchison	21	D	D	D	19	1 333	635.0	79.6	34	D	D	D
Barber	13	54	4.1	1.5	7	119	39.6	5.9	14	110	5.3	1.0
Barton	58	332	38.4	13.9	47	D	337.4	D	62	934	41.1	11.1
Bourbon	28	116	9.4	3.6	27	980	174.9	35.9	32	386	15.2	4.1
Brown	12	68	8.5	3.4	17	530	248.8	20.4	22	289	7.9	2.4
Butler	104	838	49.7	17.5	46	1 306	D	84.7	102	1 590	74.7	18.0
Chase	6	D	D	D	4	88	D	3.6	5	D	D	D
Chautauqua	3	D	D	D	5	79	24.7	2.0	8	D	D	D
Cherokee	28	91	5.6	1.7	33	1 475	452.8	64.0	28	340	13.2	3.6
Cheyenne	7	20	1.7	0.6	3	11	D	D	6	D	D	D
Clark	6	30	3.7	0.9	NA	NA	NA	NA	5	34	0.5	0.1
Clay	15	63	5.6	1.6	10	339	D	13.3	18	162	6.9	1.9
Cloud	14	76	6.5	3.1	9	424	D	16.5	21	285	14.1	3.6
Coffey	14	D	D	D	6	131	D	4.4	22	176	7.2	2.0
Comanche	5	7	0.6	0.1	7	44	D	1.3	6	50	1.5	0.4
Cowley	64	218	21.6	5.6	39	3 333	2 043.9	161.6	62	1 008	48.0	11.7
Crawford	68	D	D	D	49	2 347	823.4	90.7	82	1 488	59.2	14.4
Decatur	6	26	2.6	0.7	NA	NA	NA	NA	7	D	D	D
Dickinson	31	160	14.4	4.1	15	1 146	280.6	42.1	41	442	17.8	4.9
Doniphan	10	D	D	D	13	375	110.8	16.6	8	D	D	D
Douglas	292	D	D	D	69	3 079	1 217.3	136.1	301	6 511	261.1	72.2
Edwards	6	13	0.7	0.2	6	133	D	4.6	5	22	0.9	0.2
Elk	7	15	0.9	0.3	NA	NA	NA	NA	7	D	D	D
Ellis	79	329	34.2	12.4	37	D	219.0	40.5	99	1 925	74.9	21.8
Ellsworth	6	69	6.9	2.7	10	296	52.4	13.7	12	132	4.4	1.3
Finney	58	263	28.5	9.9	26	3 711	D	124.1	76	1 412	74.5	18.5
Ford	45	488	50.8	23.1	23	6 272	5 948.2	220.2	73	1 032	56.1	14.4
Franklin	36	D	D	D	27	654	318.7	30.2	50	D	D	D
Geary	40	D	D	D	7	655	189.3	19.1	82	1 475	64.7	16.5
Gove	9	11	1.2	0.3	7	77	22.8	4.2	8	D	D	D
Graham	8	13	1.2	0.5	NA	NA	NA	NA	6	D	D	D
Grant	10	30	3.0	0.9	12	188	131.6	9.7	17	249	9.7	2.6
Gray	17	55	6.1	2.6	9	84	D	4.3	8	D	D	D
Greeley	4	5	0.7	0.3	NA	NA	NA	NA	2	D	D	D
Greenwood	9	24	2.2	0.7	6	68	D	4.2	12	107	3.4	0.9
Hamilton	3	10	0.5	0.1	NA	NA	NA	NA	5	D	D	D
Harper	12	20	2.1	0.5	21	424	154.1	16.3	17	191	10.7	2.5
Harvey	48	235	22.0	8.3	62	3 004	1 286.7	134.5	61	956	32.7	9.8
Haskell	8	29	2.9	1.0	3	D	D	2.3	8	D	D	D
Hodgeman	3	D	D	D	NA	NA	NA	NA	3	9	0.4	0.1
Jackson	21	78	5.0	1.4	6	214	D	7.6	21	D	D	D
Jefferson	23	54	9.8	1.7	10	282	D	10.5	23	D	D	D
Jewell	4	10	0.7	0.2	NA	NA	NA	NA	7	D	D	D
Johnson	2 669	29 498	4 846.6	2 133.2	478	20 164	7 140.8	1 058.6	1 158	25 214	1 225.3	365.9
Kearny	6	22	1.0	0.2	NA	NA	NA	NA	6	51	1.6	0.4
Kingman	11	47	4.1	1.3	9	403	D	18.2	13	168	7.2	1.5
Kiowa	3	D	D	D	NA	NA	NA	NA	6	D	D	D
Labette	22	105	9.9	3.4	40	1 908	415.1	80.8	36	481	18.7	4.9
Lane	6	14	1.3	0.6	NA	NA	NA	NA	2	D	D	D
Leavenworth	125	D	D	D	33	1 202	455.8	41.9	98	1 439	66.7	17.1
Lincoln	7	8	1.1	0.5	NA	NA	NA	NA	5	D	D	D
Linn	13	D	D	D	10	67	D	2.3	11	D	D	D
Logan	8	25	4.1	0.7	3	11	D	D	8	D	D	D
Lyon	45	D	D	D	37	2 723	2 034.0	119.9	88	1 358	50.0	15.1
McPherson	48	225	18.4	6.8	59	4 633	5 481.6	264.6	62	853	33.1	9.7
Marion	15	D	D	D	25	325	D	12.6	21	D	D	D
Marshall	22	93	13.3	3.3	16	1 391	341.7	67.1	25	221	10.6	2.6
Meade	6	26	1.3	0.4	NA	NA	NA	NA	9	D	D	D
Miami	67	D	D	D	25	447	D	26.7	44	D	D	D
Mitchell	16	53	4.6	1.3	13	574	144.2	22.9	14	D	D	D
Montgomery	49	182	15.5	5.2	52	3 468	6 105.5	196.5	85	1 265	46.3	13.0
Morris	10	53	5.1	1.6	7	171	D	7.4	13	D	D	D
Morton	5	16	1.3	0.3	3	D	D	D	7	D	D	D
Nemaha	22	80	11.4	3.1	26	1 307	413.2	59.7	25	282	8.2	2.0

1. Establishment subject to federal tax.

STATE County	Health care and social assistance, 2012				Other services, 2012				Nonemployer businesses, 2014		Value of residential construction authorized by building permits, 2015	
	Number of establishments	Number of employees	Receipts (mil dol)	Annual payroll (mil dol)	Number of establishments	Number of employees	Receipts (mil dol)	Annual payroll (mil dol)	Number	Receipts (mil dol)	New Construction ($1,000)	Number of housing units
	159	160	161	162	163	164	165	166	167	168	169	170
KANSAS	7 934	192 272	18 248.4	7 504.6	5 147	29 521	3 433.0	849.2	193 919	8 602.6	1 646 377	8 644
Allen	41	626	47.8	20.1	29	76	9.6	2.1	883	30.0	3 353	29
Anderson	21	359	24.2	9.8	11	17	1.7	0.3	620	21.1	0	0
Atchison	46	799	64.6	26.7	20	D	D	D	874	28.4	350	2
Barber	14	288	14.7	8.4	21	52	5.8	1.1	531	24.3	240	1
Barton	111	1 917	152.5	64.0	75	309	38.4	8.6	2 304	107.9	4 895	27
Bourbon	42	1 031	70.0	32.2	29	82	15.6	2.0	1 011	32.5	0	0
Brown	37	882	58.3	27.0	21	D	D	D	709	29.1	300	1
Butler	156	3 409	278.4	103.7	76	400	32.7	8.4	4 116	155.7	33 057	160
Chase	3	D	D	D	9	15	1.3	0.2	223	9.0	0	0
Chautauqua	7	138	8.1	4.0	2	D	D	D	305	12.9	0	0
Cherokee	40	984	70.6	25.8	22	118	5.8	1.5	1 061	42.4	170	3
Cheyenne	10	D	D	D	5	D	D	D	250	10.2	0	0
Clark	7	D	D	D	4	D	D	D	199	5.9	0	0
Clay	25	565	36.1	16.9	26	65	6.1	1.4	651	24.1	1 526	9
Cloud	35	744	38.1	19.1	25	78	5.9	1.6	659	23.0	100	1
Coffey	27	493	39.9	15.4	15	D	D	D	676	33.5	4 921	27
Comanche	7	166	7.1	3.2	6	9	0.7	0.2	166	5.5	0	0
Cowley	118	2 199	132.1	59.1	53	208	24.0	5.0	2 006	76.5	8 416	111
Crawford	129	3 042	233.8	97.9	63	261	20.0	5.5	2 151	73.7	10 456	59
Decatur	7	251	11.8	5.9	8	19	1.7	0.4	258	11.3	0	0
Dickinson	42	883	49.6	24.6	42	148	12.5	2.4	1 271	39.7	1 989	18
Doniphan	9	179	8.7	3.5	7	D	D	D	486	18.9	566	4
Douglas	289	6 580	545.8	211.1	181	1 423	230.7	37.2	7 861	317.6	126 050	839
Edwards	10	158	14.6	5.8	11	D	D	D	214	9.7	147	1
Elk	5	D	D	D	5	D	D	D	291	13.4	NA	NA
Ellis	117	3 239	319.4	128.5	85	362	40.8	8.9	2 869	126.2	14 037	64
Ellsworth	23	466	30.5	13.8	16	32	3.4	0.7	449	15.6	600	2
Finney	98	D	D	D	69	D	D	D	2 230	128.8	17 570	129
Ford	92	1 583	164.3	63.8	59	282	28.6	7.1	1 726	92.6	5 706	32
Franklin	68	1 733	93.7	42.1	43	179	14.3	4.6	1 550	64.0	3 970	21
Geary	51	1 577	153.3	58.7	55	241	18.9	5.5	1 245	39.4	4 323	32
Gove	11	237	18.0	6.9	11	D	D	D	288	17.9	1 730	20
Graham	12	237	14.1	6.1	5	D	D	D	301	12.4	175	6
Grant	17	104	7.3	2.7	15	43	5.5	1.3	511	27.9	795	6
Gray	11	149	6.5	3.1	11	D	D	D	634	33.5	984	4
Greeley	1	D	D	D	4	D	D	D	132	3.7	489	3
Greenwood	14	270	20.1	9.6	11	16	1.9	0.4	540	19.9	0	0
Hamilton	6	144	9.5	4.1	6	D	D	D	203	8.9	0	0
Harper	16	300	19.5	9.1	14	38	4.3	1.0	505	23.7	690	4
Harvey	117	2 967	251.3	102.3	56	262	26.2	7.2	2 416	78.0	8 459	45
Haskell	7	D	D	D	8	D	D	D	370	17.2	0	0
Hodgeman	7	D	D	D	5	D	D	D	178	9.4	229	2
Jackson	22	530	32.5	13.4	27	100	8.6	2.1	767	27.3	7 263	57
Jefferson	29	D	D	D	27	D	D	D	1 213	50.6	7 825	57
Jewell	4	D	D	D	6	16	1.9	0.3	261	9.4	0	0
Johnson	1 739	37 514	4 657.7	1 766.9	969	7 032	789.4	227.0	47 905	2 562.1	729 152	3 029
Kearny	5	D	D	D	4	D	D	D	310	15.1	931	12
Kingman	21	425	22.1	11.0	16	22	2.2	0.5	656	30.4	1 265	8
Kiowa	10	192	12.9	5.5	6	8	1.4	0.2	233	9.0	130	1
Labette	88	4 122	178.2	88.9	33	D	D	D	1 241	44.3	400	4
Lane	4	D	D	D	6	D	D	D	197	6.3	0	0
Leavenworth	137	2 981	288.2	114.7	99	447	36.5	11.6	3 681	132.7	39 836	220
Lincoln	7	D	D	D	7	22	0.9	0.2	242	6.9	3	1
Linn	10	D	D	D	14	71	6.7	1.4	701	21.4	3 782	29
Logan	7	D	D	D	13	23	1.9	0.4	263	10.3	0	0
Lyon	101	2 138	148.3	64.3	60	228	24.9	5.2	1 733	63.5	7 016	92
McPherson	100	2 333	128.2	58.7	84	364	36.0	9.6	2 422	101.5	20 759	189
Marion	31	608	38.3	14.8	26	88	14.9	2.3	902	27.3	4 255	28
Marshall	34	588	38.3	16.6	31	96	6.9	1.7	781	31.0	1 766	9
Meade	9	D	D	D	11	D	D	D	383	19.8	785	6
Miami	67	D	D	D	50	166	13.6	3.6	2 449	111.9	18 196	92
Mitchell	24	607	43.1	20.3	21	63	5.7	1.5	621	24.7	1 895	5
Montgomery	100	2 270	119.4	57.7	58	200	17.1	4.7	1 903	60.5	2 554	21
Morris	14	268	18.7	6.8	8	14	1.1	0.2	460	15.9	898	4
Morton	7	D	D	D	5	D	D	D	228	7.0	0	0
Nemaha	43	848	51.3	24.0	28	57	7.7	1.4	761	28.9	3 317	13

Table B. States and Counties — Government Employment and Payroll, and Local Government Finances

	Government employment and payroll, 2012								Local government finances, 2012				
			March payroll (percent of total)						General revenue				
												Taxes	
												Per capita[1] (dollars)	
STATE County	Full-time equivalent employees	March payroll (dollars)	Administration, judicial, and legal	Police and Corrections	Fire Protection	Highways and transportation	Health and Welfare	Natural resources and utilities	Education and libraries	Total (mil dol)	Intergovernmental (mil dol)	Total (mil dol)	Total	Property
	171	172	173	174	175	176	177	178	179	180	181	182	183	184
KANSAS	X	X	X	X	X	X	X	X	X	X	X	X	X	X
Allen	895	2 577 982	5.0	6.1	3.4	3.7	4.1	8.9	67.1	63.9	30.0	21.1	1 583	1 268
Anderson	497	1 619 637	6.2	5.4	1.6	4.7	1.1	6.1	73.7	23.0	11.7	7.8	980	756
Atchison	692	1 978 776	6.6	8.4	3.3	4.3	7.8	7.0	60.5	55.0	21.3	23.4	1 390	1 002
Barber	411	1 245 913	6.3	3.3	0.1	7.0	45.0	3.3	32.0	35.8	4.2	16.4	3 382	2 951
Barton	1 660	5 166 241	4.8	6.8	2.0	3.6	6.0	4.3	70.0	122.6	44.4	49.3	1 788	1 396
Bourbon	839	2 300 103	4.1	6.3	2.0	3.3	0.0	5.1	77.6	59.7	27.2	20.2	1 354	1 059
Brown	402	1 209 798	8.3	11.3	0.2	5.2	0.6	6.9	64.8	36.4	13.4	17.7	1 790	1 406
Butler	4 199	12 617 495	2.9	6.0	1.7	2.3	2.5	2.9	79.0	296.1	116.0	108.1	1 642	1 429
Chase	138	378 267	8.3	25.9	0.5	9.7	5.3	1.8	44.0	11.2	3.5	6.0	2 181	1 999
Chautauqua	172	502 746	9.7	7.9	0.0	8.5	6.3	5.4	60.4	13.8	5.5	6.9	1 943	1 619
Cherokee	874	3 187 294	11.0	10.0	0.6	9.2	3.4	2.6	61.3	64.1	33.3	21.8	1 027	758
Cheyenne	165	389 236	10.5	5.0	0.1	7.4	2.7	8.2	64.4	12.1	4.1	6.6	2 450	2 088
Clark	347	1 038 878	4.4	3.1	0.0	2.2	61.9	2.5	24.8	28.0	3.9	8.5	3 919	3 852
Clay	803	2 480 508	2.7	3.1	1.1	3.9	30.1	7.3	50.0	45.5	12.6	13.2	1 545	1 227
Cloud	581	1 796 777	3.3	5.8	1.8	7.0	2.6	3.3	72.8	44.9	18.4	15.2	1 616	1 216
Coffey	673	2 404 634	6.2	5.9	0.0	6.6	43.0	4.7	31.1	69.1	9.0	35.4	4 162	4 031
Comanche	187	510 886	10.4	5.9	0.0	8.5	34.5	11.2	28.4	18.5	6.5	6.4	3 350	3 116
Cowley	2 458	8 016 863	4.3	5.7	2.3	2.2	22.2	5.9	56.0	203.4	66.1	46.6	1 284	1 024
Crawford	1 777	5 700 396	5.1	9.6	2.5	3.3	21.7	6.6	49.1	136.9	53.7	45.9	1 166	827
Decatur	132	423 037	12.8	5.9	0.4	9.6	3.7	7.1	54.7	9.9	2.9	5.6	1 953	1 752
Dickinson	1 141	3 857 618	5.1	5.3	1.0	3.4	29.1	5.5	49.6	105.0	33.0	29.3	1 484	1 175
Doniphan	654	1 750 518	4.8	4.1	0.0	3.2	3.0	4.0	80.3	45.4	18.2	12.9	1 635	1 413
Douglas	4 535	18 551 008	5.6	11.2	5.0	2.9	33.2	7.9	33.4	537.2	114.0	188.6	1 671	1 239
Edwards	153	450 266	16.0	7.2	0.2	14.9	6.8	4.1	50.1	13.9	5.5	7.3	2 459	2 226
Elk	292	687 044	6.7	3.5	0.3	5.8	15.5	4.5	62.3	14.4	5.9	5.3	1 934	1 803
Ellis	1 003	3 461 008	7.9	9.4	2.7	5.0	5.7	5.6	61.1	88.4	23.1	51.1	1 759	1 232
Ellsworth	296	866 464	7.5	7.6	0.0	7.7	5.7	8.2	60.7	28.4	9.8	14.2	2 194	1 862
Finney	2 267	7 504 277	5.0	10.7	1.8	2.9	2.9	4.3	70.6	186.5	73.2	74.7	2 008	1 584
Ford	1 844	5 930 863	5.1	8.2	3.9	2.6	3.3	4.3	71.6	177.3	76.6	65.8	1 894	1 286
Franklin	1 501	5 023 604	6.2	8.2	1.6	2.3	29.7	5.6	44.5	115.7	36.0	39.3	1 518	1 176
Geary	2 097	7 346 708	3.8	7.7	1.7	1.2	23.2	1.3	60.2	186.7	68.2	47.0	1 236	779
Gove	329	918 512	4.3	1.7	0.0	4.8	54.5	0.9	32.9	24.5	5.7	7.8	2 849	2 457
Graham	232	804 031	8.2	3.8	0.6	8.9	44.4	4.5	28.5	22.4	4.0	9.8	3 805	3 282
Grant	403	1 281 935	6.8	7.4	0.2	7.9	5.9	5.1	65.0	41.0	11.0	26.3	3 319	3 166
Gray	309	995 915	8.2	7.4	0.0	6.0	2.2	5.2	67.3	26.3	10.8	12.0	1 998	1 829
Greeley	53	153 774	8.6	0.0	0.0	6.4	1.7	4.3	78.3	4.0	1.5	2.0	1 555	1 519
Greenwood	339	898 356	8.5	7.0	0.4	6.6	4.3	4.5	67.1	22.5	10.0	10.4	1 605	1 400
Hamilton	163	402 085	10.0	8.0	0.1	7.1	6.4	7.9	57.3	13.4	3.7	8.9	3 358	3 144
Harper	602	1 701 546	6.8	3.5	0.1	6.1	45.7	4.3	29.4	45.9	10.6	12.9	2 179	2 024
Harvey	1 517	4 865 931	8.6	8.1	5.6	3.6	3.0	5.5	65.1	120.5	49.4	44.5	1 277	900
Haskell	378	1 272 364	6.3	6.7	0.0	7.9	37.3	0.8	40.4	39.0	3.8	22.7	5 336	5 085
Hodgeman	127	312 316	11.2	6.4	0.0	12.3	7.7	10.6	49.0	11.5	3.2	6.7	3 390	3 354
Jackson	744	2 123 015	4.8	7.4	0.0	4.1	0.8	6.6	74.7	41.1	21.8	14.9	1 107	922
Jefferson	801	2 548 797	6.5	6.7	0.0	4.8	6.2	3.9	68.5	65.4	32.7	24.4	1 288	1 179
Jewell	228	595 682	6.9	3.1	0.0	12.6	38.5	5.3	30.9	15.8	4.4	6.1	2 003	1 819
Johnson	22 393	88 446 886	6.5	10.0	4.1	3.0	4.2	7.6	63.3	2 399.0	615.6	1 250.4	2 233	1 568
Kearny	501	1 624 976	4.9	5.2	1.0	3.4	47.9	3.2	32.3	40.1	5.1	19.2	4 834	4 739
Kingman	303	939 992	10.2	7.8	0.3	9.1	3.5	5.9	62.1	29.0	9.1	16.4	2 088	1 871
Kiowa	190	513 068	15.3	8.3	1.6	10.8	2.8	6.8	50.3	18.3	5.8	10.3	4 132	3 569
Labette	1 476	4 983 554	3.5	5.4	1.3	2.4	37.6	2.9	46.0	131.2	39.2	25.9	1 215	896
Lane	185	518 931	8.0	5.3	2.8	7.3	34.7	3.4	37.1	15.3	2.4	7.9	4 633	4 497
Leavenworth	2 924	9 219 623	4.7	9.0	2.4	3.1	3.7	5.2	70.5	234.3	105.0	92.8	1 194	954
Lincoln	278	791 585	5.0	2.8	0.1	6.6	36.5	5.0	42.1	16.1	5.5	7.6	2 408	2 131
Linn	469	1 414 132	7.1	7.1	0.7	5.0	2.4	6.1	70.4	38.3	14.7	20.4	2 163	2 067
Logan	328	920 118	5.1	3.8	0.2	3.2	54.6	2.9	29.9	24.5	3.1	9.2	3 298	2 915
Lyon	2 245	7 549 055	4.5	8.4	2.7	3.3	26.6	2.6	50.3	180.6	54.8	53.5	1 586	1 073
McPherson	1 486	4 467 777	5.3	7.9	1.7	5.1	4.7	13.1	58.6	102.2	34.2	49.8	1 697	1 261
Marion	702	1 972 669	7.2	6.2	0.1	6.0	17.8	6.6	54.8	54.7	18.7	20.1	1 630	1 376
Marshall	507	1 385 386	5.8	6.0	0.0	7.1	3.5	3.5	71.8	35.7	13.7	17.7	1 764	1 524
Meade	403	1 284 083	4.9	3.3	1.1	4.4	54.9	3.4	27.0	33.8	5.5	11.9	2 711	2 487
Miami	1 386	4 167 179	7.7	8.9	1.2	4.9	3.1	3.9	68.5	96.7	33.9	47.7	1 463	1 199
Mitchell	539	1 523 148	6.6	5.9	0.1	6.8	5.3	10.9	62.8	39.3	15.8	13.9	2 189	1 626
Montgomery	1 708	5 095 652	3.7	7.7	2.9	3.7	1.3	9.3	68.3	148.4	54.4	62.4	1 812	1 449
Morris	233	667 311	10.9	7.8	0.3	7.9	1.6	3.9	64.1	17.4	6.0	9.0	1 545	1 277
Morton	433	1 384 778	4.2	3.1	0.1	4.3	50.6	2.3	32.2	39.0	7.6	14.7	4 633	4 454
Nemaha	548	1 548 782	6.0	6.7	0.0	5.8	2.1	9.9	67.8	39.4	16.0	18.2	1 794	1 515

1. Based on the resident population estimated as of July 1 of the year shown.

STATE County	Direct general expenditure Total (mil dol) [185]	Per capita[1] (dollars) [186]	Percent of total for: Education [187]	Health and hospitals [188]	Police protection [189]	Public welfare [190]	Highways [191]	Debt outstanding Total (mil dol) [192]	Per capita[1] (dollars) [193]	Government employment, 2014 Federal civilian [194]	Federal military [195]	State and local [196]	Presidential election,[2] 2012 Percent of vote cast: Democratic [197]	Republican [198]	All other [199]
KANSAS	X	X	X	X	X	X	X	X	X	24 903	35 922	234 658	41.7	56.6	1.7
Allen	63.1	4 735	58.0	4.0	3.4	0.0	6.4	50.6	3 796	54	52	1 674	37.4	60.7	1.9
Anderson	40.1	5 062	61.6	2.1	2.8	0.0	8.0	28.9	3 654	38	32	545	32.4	65.1	2.5
Atchison	59.4	3 536	45.7	1.0	4.9	4.7	7.9	33.0	1 961	47	63	871	45.1	52.7	2.2
Barber	36.3	7 477	24.0	41.7	2.6	0.0	10.3	11.4	2 336	27	20	652	24.3	74.5	1.3
Barton	120.9	4 389	60.4	2.7	3.3	0.0	7.9	58.1	2 108	75	111	2 337	27.4	70.6	2.1
Bourbon	65.3	4 385	57.0	0.9	3.2	0.0	6.3	43.5	2 920	77	59	1 088	35.3	62.5	2.2
Brown	35.1	3 553	49.9	0.9	4.2	0.0	11.2	44.1	4 465	103	40	1 574	30.1	68.2	1.7
Butler	329.4	5 004	68.1	1.1	2.9	0.0	5.2	551.1	8 372	127	265	5 861	32.9	65.1	2.0
Chase	11.4	4 131	37.7	3.0	3.4	0.0	10.4	5.1	1 857	18	11	241	27.7	70.5	1.8
Chautauqua	13.5	3 787	47.9	5.7	3.6	0.0	9.6	9.2	2 578	19	14	245	21.7	76.6	1.8
Cherokee	63.8	3 007	60.9	2.7	4.3	0.0	8.9	20.0	944	55	85	1 388	37.2	60.9	1.9
Cheyenne	11.4	4 256	50.1	5.6	3.7	0.0	9.9	0.8	296	14	11	230	21.6	76.6	1.8
Clark	28.0	12 839	20.3	57.2	4.3	0.0	4.7	5.4	2 461	11	0	425	21.1	77.4	1.5
Clay	46.8	5 482	29.6	33.0	3.0	0.0	7.6	34.9	4 095	34	34	918	24.9	74.0	1.2
Cloud	46.3	4 930	66.5	3.2	3.3	0.0	6.9	13.5	1 434	43	37	814	27.7	70.1	2.2
Coffey	70.3	8 270	29.8	34.4	3.0	0.0	10.8	13.0	1 531	47	34	1 150	26.5	72.2	1.3
Comanche	19.2	10 056	20.4	23.8	2.0	0.0	6.2	6.1	3 165	0	0	254	19.9	78.5	1.5
Cowley	191.8	5 286	45.5	21.1	3.6	0.0	3.2	166.3	4 583	101	141	3 452	36.4	61.6	2.1
Crawford	135.7	3 448	45.0	17.8	5.0	0.0	3.9	114.8	2 916	87	159	4 885	49.5	48.1	2.4
Decatur	10.3	3 573	44.7	3.6	4.6	0.0	12.8	7.9	2 755	23	12	247	22.2	76.8	1.0
Dickinson	107.2	5 425	50.6	21.7	3.1	0.0	5.6	91.6	4 637	97	79	1 672	27.9	70.2	1.9
Doniphan	45.9	5 834	72.7	2.2	2.9	0.0	6.0	12.8	1 623	37	31	929	31.3	66.6	2.2
Douglas	474.7	4 206	28.6	35.1	4.9	0.0	3.3	544.9	4 828	424	479	15 168	64.4	33.6	2.0
Edwards	14.5	4 871	42.0	3.4	4.5	0.0	14.5	1.2	396	19	12	234	24.5	73.3	2.1
Elk	14.6	5 351	44.7	2.8	2.7	13.2	10.2	3.0	1 097	12	11	333	25.3	72.7	2.0
Ellis	86.9	2 990	45.4	3.2	5.5	0.0	7.4	38.7	1 332	138	116	3 340	32.2	65.9	1.8
Ellsworth	28.5	4 390	50.2	3.3	4.0	0.0	18.7	22.2	3 424	29	22	890	29.0	68.8	2.2
Finney	182.2	4 899	60.1	1.9	6.7	0.0	4.4	162.9	4 378	127	152	3 113	31.6	66.9	1.5
Ford	201.8	5 806	49.4	1.2	3.5	1.0	2.6	336.1	9 671	229	141	2 615	33.7	64.6	1.6
Franklin	118.9	4 591	39.4	30.1	1.6	0.0	5.7	81.1	3 129	68	104	1 981	37.8	60.3	1.9
Geary	176.2	4 635	47.3	25.0	6.0	0.0	2.9	273.5	7 194	3 219	17 477	2 843	43.1	55.5	1.4
Gove	24.9	9 123	26.3	51.1	1.8	0.0	8.5	1.5	532	14	11	428	18.4	80.1	1.5
Graham	21.4	8 308	22.0	38.9	2.6	0.0	9.1	0.4	152	27	10	323	22.8	74.5	2.7
Grant	35.6	4 496	41.9	5.9	4.7	0.0	7.6	27.3	3 445	18	32	708	23.9	75.0	1.2
Gray	25.6	4 246	56.7	2.7	4.4	0.0	11.9	24.2	4 013	24	25	916	20.6	77.5	1.9
Greeley	4.0	3 089	72.8	0.0	1.1	0.0	4.3	5.0	3 847	10	0	179	20.3	79.3	0.4
Greenwood	21.3	3 303	53.1	3.8	5.8	0.0	13.3	21.4	3 323	45	26	454	27.3	71.0	1.7
Hamilton	11.6	4 401	48.9	2.0	5.9	0.0	10.1	4.6	1 740	0	11	334	21.3	77.0	1.7
Harper	45.6	7 720	25.8	36.2	2.0	6.9	9.7	21.2	3 581	33	24	864	26.3	71.5	2.2
Harvey	109.6	3 145	50.9	2.7	5.6	0.1	5.4	180.9	5 190	67	139	2 034	40.5	57.7	1.9
Haskell	39.1	9 192	29.1	42.9	3.2	0.0	10.1	10.5	2 463	14	17	596	17.7	81.3	1.0
Hodgeman	10.7	5 451	37.8	5.5	4.6	0.0	12.0	11.5	5 870	15	0	285	19.3	78.9	1.8
Jackson	41.1	3 058	62.3	0.8	5.4	0.0	10.4	21.9	1 625	53	56	1 950	36.9	60.9	2.1
Jefferson	63.2	3 338	64.8	5.4	5.1	0.0	7.4	46.3	2 446	72	77	1 083	39.6	58.3	2.1
Jewell	13.7	4 485	29.6	21.3	2.8	0.0	17.3	0.8	250	30	12	344	19.8	77.7	2.5
Johnson	2 304.6	4 116	47.4	2.5	7.7	0.9	5.7	5 877.0	10 496	2 535	2 367	27 935	44.8	53.8	1.3
Kearny	42.8	10 778	27.2	45.6	2.8	0.0	6.2	5.6	1 409	15	16	704	20.9	78.2	0.9
Kingman	29.4	3 741	43.5	3.2	4.6	0.0	13.3	19.1	2 432	38	31	556	26.3	71.0	2.7
Kiowa	16.8	6 718	43.0	3.4	4.6	0.0	10.9	3.4	1 371	16	10	381	17.6	80.4	2.0
Labette	134.7	6 331	39.7	39.0	2.6	0.0	4.0	95.8	4 500	80	85	2 813	42.5	55.4	2.1
Lane	15.6	9 127	29.8	31.7	3.9	0.0	8.7	0.5	288	14	0	255	18.8	79.3	1.9
Leavenworth	188.5	2 425	61.8	0.0	5.1	0.0	3.5	316.9	4 076	4 383	3 989	4 034	43.3	54.9	1.8
Lincoln	16.5	5 197	44.3	7.0	2.8	0.0	13.6	1.8	569	32	13	407	21.9	75.9	2.2
Linn	38.3	4 053	55.6	3.0	4.7	0.0	10.2	11.7	1 244	48	39	757	30.9	66.8	2.3
Logan	27.7	9 951	22.7	51.3	2.8	0.0	4.7	6.2	2 220	19	11	759	15.6	82.4	1.9
Lyon	166.1	4 920	39.3	28.9	4.3	0.0	4.3	94.4	2 798	104	132	4 250	45.9	51.9	2.2
McPherson	101.4	3 454	45.5	2.3	4.3	0.0	12.0	90.9	3 097	82	117	1 956	31.5	66.8	1.7
Marion	54.2	4 388	42.4	18.1	3.1	0.0	9.1	43.6	3 528	68	48	973	29.7	68.6	1.6
Marshall	34.8	3 472	53.8	2.9	4.3	0.0	13.1	19.2	1 915	54	41	831	35.4	62.7	1.9
Meade	34.5	7 851	21.7	41.1	2.2	3.8	7.6	13.7	3 120	16	18	600	18.5	79.8	1.8
Miami	87.9	2 695	49.6	2.9	5.9	0.0	9.2	104.9	3 215	60	133	2 113	37.3	61.0	1.6
Mitchell	42.4	6 669	50.7	7.8	3.9	0.0	12.6	15.4	2 417	32	25	1 027	21.9	76.2	1.9
Montgomery	142.0	4 121	61.6	2.3	3.8	0.0	5.5	137.7	3 996	110	136	2 542	31.2	66.9	1.9
Morris	25.5	4 361	59.2	5.3	2.7	0.0	10.7	21.0	3 594	35	23	454	31.9	66.0	2.1
Morton	37.0	11 666	31.7	47.6	0.9	0.0	2.7	4.6	1 453	19	13	528	16.3	82.2	1.4
Nemaha	36.9	3 640	57.0	1.5	3.6	0.0	11.8	35.6	3 511	54	41	777	26.7	71.2	2.1

1. Based on the resident population estimated as of July 1 of the year shown. 2. © 2013 Election Data Services, Inc. All rights reserved.

STATE/ County code	CBSA code[1]	County type[2]	STATE County	Land area,[3] (sq km) 2010	Total persons 2015	Rank	Per square kilometer	White	Black	American Indian, Alaska Native	Asian and Pacific Islander	Percent Hispanic or Latino[4]	Under 5 years	5 to 17 years	18 to 24 years	25 to 34 years	35 to 44 years	45 to 54 years
				1	2	3	4	5	6	7	8	9	10	11	12	13	14	15
			KANSAS—Cont'd															
20 133	...	7	Neosho	1 480	16 346	2 021	11.0	92.1	1.8	1.8	1.1	5.2	7.1	17.7	8.9	10.8	10.8	12.9
20 135	...	9	Ness	2 784	3 005	2 972	1.1	89.8	1.1	0.7	0.4	9.9	5.9	17.3	5.8	9.9	8.7	13.4
20 137	...	7	Norton	2 274	5 550	2 799	2.4	90.9	3.7	1.0	1.2	5.3	5.2	13.8	8.3	13.3	12.2	14.6
20 139	45820	3	Osage	1 827	15 847	2 050	8.7	95.6	1.2	1.6	0.6	2.7	5.6	18.2	7.5	9.9	11.3	14.1
20 141	...	9	Osborne	2 312	3 683	2 928	1.6	96.8	0.7	0.9	0.7	1.8	5.4	15.0	7.4	10.1	8.3	13.3
20 143	41460	9	Ottawa	1 867	5 975	2 755	3.2	95.5	1.4	1.0	0.6	3.1	5.9	18.0	7.5	10.1	11.6	13.9
20 145	...	7	Pawnee	1 954	6 838	2 691	3.5	84.6	5.8	1.2	0.7	7.8	4.9	14.4	8.3	12.8	11.6	14.0
20 147	...	7	Phillips	2 294	5 428	2 809	2.4	96.2	0.9	0.8	1.1	3.0	6.5	17.0	7.4	10.4	9.5	12.7
20 149	31740	6	Pottawatomie	2 178	23 298	1 670	10.7	92.0	2.2	1.5	1.7	5.2	8.2	21.2	8.2	13.1	11.8	12.4
20 151	...	7	Pratt	1 904	9 691	2 458	5.1	91.3	2.0	1.4	1.1	6.9	7.2	17.2	10.4	11.5	10.0	11.5
20 153	...	9	Rawlins	2 770	2 506	3 006	0.9	95.4	0.8	0.6	0.6	4.8	5.7	14.1	6.5	9.9	8.2	11.6
20 155	26740	4	Reno	3 251	63 718	824	19.6	86.6	4.1	1.3	0.9	9.0	6.0	17.1	9.1	12.4	11.0	12.6
20 157	...	9	Republic	1 858	4 725	2 853	2.5	97.7	0.8	0.6	0.8	1.5	5.5	13.8	6.2	9.3	7.9	13.1
20 159	...	7	Rice	1 881	9 977	2 437	5.3	86.2	2.2	1.8	1.0	11.1	6.7	17.1	12.0	11.4	10.1	11.7
20 161	31740	5	Riley	1 579	75 247	735	47.7	80.4	7.9	1.3	6.1	8.2	6.9	10.7	32.5	18.9	8.8	6.8
20 163	...	9	Rooks	2 306	5 174	2 823	2.2	96.0	1.1	0.6	0.7	2.5	6.3	17.0	7.0	11.0	10.4	12.6
20 165	...	9	Rush	1 859	3 130	2 963	1.7	95.7	0.8	1.3	0.5	3.3	4.3	15.3	6.9	9.1	9.5	13.5
20 167	...	7	Russell	2 295	7 039	2 672	3.1	94.0	1.9	1.5	1.0	2.5	6.3	15.3	7.1	10.5	10.2	13.0
20 169	41460	5	Saline	1 865	55 691	910	29.9	82.9	4.8	1.1	3.2	10.9	6.8	17.4	9.3	12.7	11.5	13.5
20 171	...	7	Scott	1 858	4 964	2 839	2.7	82.5	0.7	0.7	0.7	17.9	6.4	19.4	7.9	10.4	11.5	13.2
20 173	48620	2	Sedgwick	2 584	511 574	132	198.0	71.6	10.6	2.0	5.1	13.9	7.6	18.9	9.6	14.4	12.0	12.5
20 175	30580	7	Seward	1 656	23 152	1 677	14.0	34.4	4.0	1.0	3.2	59.5	9.8	21.4	11.7	14.9	12.3	12.0
20 177	45820	3	Shawnee	1 409	178 725	361	126.8	77.7	10.1	2.1	2.0	11.6	6.7	17.6	8.6	12.9	11.4	12.9
20 179	...	9	Sheridan	2 321	2 512	3 005	1.1	95.5	0.5	0.8	0.4	3.8	4.8	18.6	6.2	9.4	10.0	12.8
20 181	...	7	Sherman	2 735	5 983	2 753	2.2	86.0	1.6	0.9	1.5	12.3	7.0	16.9	8.9	12.5	10.1	12.4
20 183	...	9	Smith	2 319	3 704	2 924	1.6	97.8	1.1	1.2	0.6	1.7	5.2	14.6	6.6	8.6	8.8	13.6
20 185	...	9	Stafford	2 051	4 236	2 883	2.1	85.3	0.9	1.4	0.6	13.1	5.3	18.7	7.3	9.7	9.4	14.3
20 187	...	9	Stanton	1 762	2 072	3 042	1.2	61.4	1.0	1.7	0.2	35.9	7.9	20.0	7.2	10.8	12.3	12.5
20 189	...	7	Stevens	1 884	5 806	2 773	3.1	62.8	1.0	1.4	0.6	34.6	7.8	22.9	8.6	11.1	11.9	12.9
20 191	48620	2	Sumner	3 061	23 535	1 657	7.7	92.3	1.7	2.4	0.6	5.3	6.6	18.3	8.0	11.1	10.7	13.3
20 193	...	7	Thomas	2 783	7 904	2 603	2.8	93.0	1.3	1.0	1.1	5.4	7.2	15.7	14.0	12.7	10.0	11.6
20 195	...	9	Trego	2 304	2 927	2 984	1.3	96.0	1.0	0.8	0.7	2.0	4.4	13.6	6.4	10.2	10.0	13.7
20 197	45820	3	Wabaunsee	2 057	6 951	2 680	3.4	95.4	1.2	1.7	0.5	3.4	7.5	17.5	6.8	10.0	11.0	14.0
20 199	...	9	Wallace	2 366	1 518	3 079	0.6	91.7	1.0	0.7	0.3	6.7	5.8	18.8	7.9	9.2	9.2	12.7
20 201	...	9	Washington	2 317	5 598	2 796	2.4	94.8	0.9	0.7	0.7	3.4	5.5	17.1	7.1	9.8	9.7	13.2
20 203	...	9	Wichita	1 861	2 157	3 035	1.2	70.6	1.0	0.5	0.3	28.4	7.7	18.7	7.6	9.8	11.4	12.1
20 205	...	7	Wilson	1 477	8 856	2 526	6.0	95.0	1.1	2.8	1.1	2.8	5.8	18.1	7.2	10.5	10.6	12.2
20 207	...	9	Woodson	1 289	3 115	2 964	2.4	95.6	1.4	2.3	0.2	2.7	4.8	16.1	6.1	11.6	8.7	13.5
20 209	28140	1	Wyandotte	393	163 369	394	415.7	44.5	25.2	1.4	4.0	27.2	8.4	20.0	9.1	15.0	12.5	12.3
21 000	...	X	**KENTUCKY**	102 269	4 425 092	X	43.3	86.9	9.0	0.7	1.8	3.4	6.3	16.7	9.7	12.8	12.7	13.8
21 001	...	7	Adair	1 050	19 027	1 873	18.1	95.7	3.7	0.6	0.4	1.9	5.5	15.5	13.3	11.2	11.1	14.0
21 003	14540	6	Allen	892	20 640	1 796	23.1	96.2	1.6	0.8	0.4	1.9	6.2	17.7	8.3	11.7	12.6	14.2
21 005	23180	6	Anderson	523	21 979	1 733	42.0	95.5	2.9	0.6	0.8	1.5	5.7	18.2	7.8	11.2	14.1	15.5
21 007	37140	9	Ballard	639	8 212	2 583	12.9	95.4	4.1	0.9	0.6	1.3	5.2	16.7	7.5	10.5	12.6	13.4
21 009	23980	6	Barren	1 263	43 570	1 101	34.5	92.3	4.9	0.6	0.8	3.0	6.2	17.4	7.9	11.8	12.3	14.2
21 011	34460	8	Bath	722	12 228	2 284	16.9	97.2	2.1	0.5	0.4	1.3	6.6	18.7	7.9	10.3	13.0	14.0
21 013	33180	7	Bell	930	27 337	1 517	29.4	96.2	3.1	1.1	0.6	1.0	6.4	15.1	8.8	11.7	12.7	14.2
21 015	17140	1	Boone	638	127 712	490	200.2	90.2	3.8	0.5	3.3	4.0	7.2	20.1	7.9	12.7	14.3	14.7
21 017	30460	2	Bourbon	750	20 116	1 828	26.8	86.4	7.1	0.5	0.5	6.8	5.7	17.0	8.2	10.6	12.6	14.7
21 019	26580	2	Boyd	414	48 325	1 014	116.7	94.8	3.7	0.7	0.8	1.6	5.8	15.5	7.5	12.1	12.9	14.0
21 021	19220	7	Boyle	467	29 809	1 435	63.8	87.9	8.9	0.7	1.3	3.0	5.2	15.1	12.2	11.2	12.2	13.5
21 023	17140	1	Bracken	533	8 321	2 572	15.6	97.6	1.2	0.7	0.3	1.6	6.4	17.9	7.6	11.4	12.3	15.1
21 025	...	7	Breathitt	1 275	13 484	2 203	10.6	97.6	0.7	0.4	0.9	0.8	5.8	15.3	8.7	11.6	13.3	15.0
21 027	...	8	Breckinridge	1 469	20 018	1 835	13.6	95.8	2.8	0.8	0.4	1.3	5.6	17.3	7.6	10.4	11.5	14.9
21 029	31140	1	Bullitt	769	78 702	704	102.3	96.1	1.4	0.8	0.9	1.7	5.2	17.9	8.5	12.4	13.8	15.4
21 031	14540	8	Butler	1 104	12 938	2 233	11.7	94.8	1.0	0.6	0.4	4.0	5.8	17.0	7.1	12.7	12.5	13.6
21 033	...	6	Caldwell	893	12 681	2 251	14.2	92.2	6.2	0.6	0.6	1.5	5.9	16.4	7.8	10.4	12.5	13.3
21 035	34660	7	Calloway	997	38 343	1 213	38.5	90.9	4.8	0.6	2.6	2.7	5.1	13.0	21.1	11.8	10.1	11.5
21 037	17140	1	Campbell	392	92 066	632	234.9	94.1	4.0	0.5	1.3	1.8	6.1	15.9	10.6	14.3	11.9	13.9
21 039	...	9	Carlisle	491	4 874	2 842	9.9	95.3	2.1	0.9	0.6	2.4	5.7	16.5	7.4	11.6	11.8	13.5
21 041	...	6	Carroll	333	10 699	2 379	32.1	91.0	2.8	0.8	0.8	7.0	7.9	17.7	8.7	12.5	12.1	13.7
21 043	...	6	Carter	1 061	27 158	1 526	25.6	97.5	0.9	0.7	0.4	1.2	6.1	16.4	9.7	11.3	12.4	14.0
21 045	...	9	Casey	1 151	15 808	2 054	13.7	96.2	1.1	0.6	0.4	2.9	6.5	16.1	7.8	11.3	12.4	13.5
21 047	17300	3	Christian	1 858	73 309	744	39.5	69.6	22.3	1.1	2.7	7.6	9.8	17.9	15.5	17.0	10.4	9.4
21 049	30460	2	Clark	654	35 757	1 281	54.7	91.6	5.7	0.6	0.7	2.8	5.8	17.0	7.9	11.4	13.4	14.5

1. CBSA = Core Based Statistical Area. See Appendix A for explanation. See Appendix B for list of metropolitan areas with component counties. 2. County type code from the Economic Research Service of USDA Rural-Urban Continuum Codes. See Appendix A for definition. 3. Dry land or land partially or temporarily covered by water. 4. May be of any race.

Table B. States and Counties — Population and Households

STATE County	55 to 64 years	65 to 74 years	75 years and over	Percent female	Total persons 2000	2010	Percent change 2000–2010	2010–2015	Births	Deaths	Net migration	Number	Persons per household	Family households	Female family householder[1]	One person
	16	17	18	19	20	21	22	23	24	25	26	27	28	29	30	31
KANSAS—Cont'd																
Neosho	13.4	9.4	8.9	50.3	16 997	16 512	-2.9	-1.0	1 138	1 014	-262	6 503	2.45	67.5	11.5	27.6
Ness	15.2	10.4	13.4	50.8	3 454	3 107	-10.0	-3.3	177	223	-48	1 403	2.17	68.1	8.4	30.2
Norton	13.1	9.5	9.9	44.4	5 953	5 671	-4.7	-2.1	266	307	-73	2 212	2.16	63.1	10.6	34.2
Osage	15.0	10.5	8.0	50.0	16 712	16 295	-2.5	-2.7	844	979	-315	6 544	2.44	69.5	9.2	27.4
Osborne	15.6	10.8	14.0	49.6	4 452	3 858	-13.3	-4.5	232	270	-133	1 767	2.09	60.6	6.5	36.7
Ottawa	14.9	9.4	8.6	47.9	6 163	6 091	-1.2	-1.9	321	329	-91	2 479	2.41	70.5	6.3	24.7
Pawnee	15.1	9.7	9.3	44.4	7 233	6 973	-3.6	-1.9	355	367	-135	2 525	2.36	57.9	9.1	36.3
Phillips	15.1	11.0	10.4	50.7	6 001	5 642	-6.0	-3.8	333	366	-172	2 414	2.26	66.1	6.7	32.4
Pottawatomie	12.0	7.2	5.9	50.2	18 209	21 604	18.6	7.8	1 907	836	620	8 109	2.71	70.6	6.6	25.3
Pratt	14.3	8.2	9.6	50.1	9 647	9 656	0.1	0.4	700	585	-74	4 071	2.30	65.7	10.4	31.5
Rawlins	17.3	12.2	14.4	48.8	2 966	2 519	-15.1	-0.5	116	181	49	1 211	2.07	63.0	6.1	32.5
Reno	13.7	9.1	8.9	49.6	64 790	64 511	-0.4	-1.2	3 915	3 840	-830	25 335	2.42	66.1	11.2	29.5
Republic	16.9	12.2	15.1	51.0	5 835	4 980	-14.7	-5.1	242	447	-24	2 258	2.11	57.1	5.0	39.5
Rice	13.5	8.9	8.6	49.8	10 761	10 083	-6.3	-1.1	652	606	-147	3 837	2.47	65.2	6.3	31.7
Riley	7.4	4.3	3.6	46.6	62 843	71 131	13.2	5.8	5 578	1 726	76	26 162	2.49	53.6	7.9	29.6
Rooks	15.1	9.8	10.8	50.9	5 685	5 181	-8.9	-0.1	329	332	2	2 310	2.17	63.2	7.9	34.1
Rush	17.2	11.2	13.0	50.4	3 551	3 307	-6.9	-5.4	151	235	-75	1 535	2.05	57.8	5.9	35.4
Russell	15.2	11.0	11.4	49.9	7 370	6 970	-5.4	1.0	475	474	98	3 317	2.06	61.4	9.3	32.4
Saline	13.1	8.4	7.4	50.3	53 597	55 606	3.7	0.2	4 066	2 675	-1 221	22 497	2.41	64.2	12.8	29.4
Scott	13.4	8.7	9.1	49.5	5 120	4 936	-3.6	0.6	328	310	6	2 157	2.26	71.2	2.0	26.9
Sedgwick	12.2	7.2	5.6	50.4	452 869	498 365	10.0	2.7	40 602	21 727	-5 635	192 303	2.59	65.0	12.3	29.9
Seward	9.0	4.9	4.0	48.5	22 510	22 952	2.0	0.9	2 359	666	-1 460	7 442	3.07	74.6	15.0	19.7
Shawnee	13.8	8.8	7.3	51.5	169 871	177 934	4.7	0.4	12 700	8 969	-2 881	72 069	2.42	63.1	11.9	30.8
Sheridan	15.5	10.0	12.7	48.8	2 813	2 556	-9.1	-1.7	149	146	-48	1 130	2.22	61.8	8.8	36.0
Sherman	14.0	9.1	9.2	50.0	6 760	6 010	-11.1	-0.4	417	384	-54	2 738	2.17	59.0	8.1	34.6
Smith	16.3	11.4	14.8	50.1	4 536	3 853	-15.1	-3.9	162	285	-21	1 690	2.20	64.5	5.9	32.9
Stafford	14.8	9.6	10.8	49.1	4 789	4 437	-7.4	-4.5	232	282	-128	1 877	2.27	67.5	6.3	29.3
Stanton	12.6	7.2	3.9	49.7	2 406	2 235	-7.1	-7.3	167	89	-226	833	2.58	69.5	11.3	26.7
Stevens	11.6	6.6	6.7	50.0	5 463	5 724	4.8	1.4	472	198	-166	1 939	2.92	78.5	5.8	20.4
Sumner	14.9	9.1	8.0	50.1	25 946	24 132	-7.0	-2.5	1 451	1 368	-727	9 053	2.58	68.2	8.1	28.7
Thomas	13.2	7.6	7.9	50.8	8 180	7 900	-3.4	0.1	549	373	-176	3 167	2.40	61.2	5.8	34.1
Trego	17.5	11.4	12.7	50.6	3 319	3 001	-9.6	-2.5	155	229	-10	1 250	2.30	68.5	7.0	28.4
Wabaunsee	15.7	9.9	7.6	49.3	6 885	7 053	2.4	-1.4	486	318	-242	2 701	2.57	72.3	6.5	25.8
Wallace	14.9	9.0	12.4	50.8	1 749	1 485	-15.1	2.2	100	88	20	614	2.53	65.8	2.3	31.4
Washington	13.9	11.3	12.3	49.6	6 483	5 799	-10.6	-3.5	365	377	-187	2 458	2.26	65.6	6.0	31.0
Wichita	14.7	8.3	9.7	48.2	2 531	2 234	-11.7	-3.4	144	125	-93	867	2.52	71.7	12.5	27.3
Wilson	15.5	11.2	9.0	50.6	10 332	9 409	-8.9	-5.9	597	666	-444	3 836	2.36	66.5	9.5	28.7
Woodson	16.7	11.7	11.0	50.4	3 788	3 309	-12.6	-5.9	162	263	-73	1 499	2.13	61.0	7.6	33.6
Wyandotte	11.4	6.5	4.7	50.7	157 882	157 505	-0.2	3.7	14 246	7 176	-945	58 057	2.72	64.7	18.8	29.3
KENTUCKY	13.1	8.7	6.1	50.8	4 041 769	4 339 349	7.4	2.0	291 435	226 513	22 163	1 702 235	2.50	66.6	12.8	28.1
Adair	13.0	9.6	6.8	50.6	17 244	18 656	8.2	2.0	1 054	1 020	352	7 124	2.51	68.4	9.7	28.2
Allen	13.2	9.8	6.3	50.6	17 800	19 967	12.2	3.4	1 357	1 115	477	8 057	2.48	69.4	9.9	26.2
Anderson	13.1	8.6	5.6	51.1	19 111	21 421	12.1	2.6	1 312	1 010	247	8 353	2.58	71.9	11.1	22.4
Ballard	14.7	11.3	8.3	50.7	8 286	8 247	-0.5	-0.4	421	535	84	3 279	2.49	66.3	8.2	28.7
Barren	13.3	9.6	7.2	51.5	38 033	42 173	10.9	3.3	2 720	2 441	1 078	16 789	2.50	69.0	12.0	28.7
Bath	13.5	9.4	6.6	50.5	11 085	11 591	4.6	5.5	812	715	525	4 361	2.70	69.2	12.8	24.7
Bell	13.8	10.5	6.8	51.3	30 060	28 691	-4.6	-4.7	1 845	1 941	-1 188	11 181	2.44	66.2	15.9	29.7
Boone	11.9	7.1	4.1	50.4	85 991	118 811	38.2	7.5	8 982	4 032	3 970	43 903	2.78	74.2	11.1	21.2
Bourbon	13.6	10.3	7.3	51.2	19 360	19 985	3.2	0.7	1 198	1 088	45	7 782	2.53	68.2	14.7	26.5
Boyd	14.4	10.0	7.8	50.3	49 752	49 538	-0.4	-2.4	2 968	3 062	-993	19 533	2.40	68.0	11.4	28.0
Boyle	13.0	9.8	7.8	50.0	27 697	28 420	2.6	4.9	1 619	1 567	1 277	10 981	2.43	67.8	13.1	28.2
Bracken	13.9	9.2	6.2	50.2	8 279	8 488	2.5	-2.0	545	473	-230	3 303	2.55	66.8	10.1	28.2
Breathitt	14.8	9.6	5.8	50.0	16 100	13 876	-13.8	-2.8	911	988	-326	5 434	2.44	67.1	16.0	29.9
Breckinridge	15.0	10.8	6.8	50.0	18 648	20 042	7.5	-0.1	1 154	1 164	28	7 325	2.70	71.2	9.7	24.6
Bullitt	13.2	8.8	4.8	50.5	61 236	74 321	21.4	5.9	4 072	2 752	2 912	28 282	2.68	74.8	13.1	20.3
Butler	13.8	10.2	7.2	50.6	13 010	12 690	-2.5	2.0	837	702	113	5 107	2.47	67.5	11.9	29.9
Caldwell	14.5	11.2	8.1	51.6	13 060	12 984	-0.6	-2.3	771	854	-142	5 320	2.39	67.7	14.7	29.0
Calloway	11.5	9.4	6.6	51.9	34 177	37 191	8.8	3.1	2 002	2 032	1 191	14 854	2.32	58.7	8.2	33.6
Campbell	13.4	7.9	5.9	50.9	88 616	90 336	1.9	1.9	5 858	4 334	309	35 478	2.49	63.6	12.1	29.9
Carlisle	13.7	10.2	9.7	51.2	5 351	5 104	-4.6	-4.5	314	336	-216	2 075	2.40	71.0	10.7	27.1
Carroll	12.7	8.6	6.1	50.0	10 155	10 811	6.5	-1.0	785	627	-284	4 108	2.55	66.8	11.6	28.7
Carter	13.6	10.0	6.5	50.7	26 889	27 718	3.1	-2.0	1 833	1 597	-886	10 525	2.54	69.6	10.2	26.1
Casey	13.6	11.4	7.4	51.3	15 447	15 952	3.3	-0.9	1 002	1 006	-163	6 186	2.53	68.1	7.3	29.1
Christian	8.9	6.2	5.0	47.3	72 265	73 939	2.3	-0.9	7 902	3 137	-5 586	25 734	2.67	70.5	15.0	25.7
Clark	13.8	9.7	6.6	51.5	33 144	35 613	7.4	0.4	2 184	2 022	26	14 368	2.45	68.7	11.5	25.4

1. No spouse present.

Table B. States and Counties — Population, Vital Statistics, Medicare, and Crime

STATE County	Persons in group quarters, 2015	Daytime population, 2010–2014 Number	Employment/residence ratio	Births, 2015 Total	Rate[1]	Deaths, 2015 Number	Rate[1]	Persons under 65 with no health insurance, 2014 Number	Percent	Medicare, 2015 Total Beneficiaries	Enrolled in Original Medicare	Enrolled in Medicare Advantage	Serious crimes known to police,[2] 2014 Total Number	Rate[3]
	32	33	34	35	36	37	38	39	40	41	42	43	44	45
KANSAS—Cont'd														
Neosho	450	16 110	0.95	209	12.8	167	10.2	1 556	11.9	3 337	3 171	166	204	1 242
Ness	70	3 445	1.22	33	10.8	42	13.8	311	13.2	776	755	21	39	1 272
Norton	822	5 672	1.02	53	9.6	62	11.2	408	10.9	1 115	1 060	55	62	1 104
Osage	194	12 326	0.46	150	9.4	203	12.8	1 397	10.8	3 316	3 146	170	186	1 183
Osborne	100	3 661	0.92	49	13.2	39	10.5	369	13.2	945	920	25	49	1 285
Ottawa	98	4 815	0.57	59	9.8	53	8.8	557	11.3	1 136	1 049	87	92	1 525
Pawnee	1 026	7 604	1.21	67	9.8	71	10.3	500	10.7	785	772	13	180	2 583
Phillips	68	5 635	1.03	71	13.0	64	11.7	536	12.4	1 316	1 279	37	11	199
Pottawatomie	299	21 367	0.91	368	15.9	178	7.7	1 802	9.1	2 994	2 736	258	332	1 447
Pratt	380	10 076	1.07	125	12.8	90	9.2	902	11.5	1 781	1 755	26	305	3 068
Rawlins	40	2 483	0.94	20	7.9	24	9.5	251	13.3	683	657	26	23	881
Reno	3 121	63 631	0.98	734	11.5	683	10.7	5 629	11.3	13 405	12 478	927	2 254	3 515
Republic	103	4 781	0.96	51	10.7	68	14.3	430	12.4	1 332	1 290	42	108	2 255
Rice	648	9 745	0.94	133	13.3	95	9.5	1 017	13.2	1 966	1 901	65	NA	NA
Riley	9 075	73 858	0.98	967	12.9	332	4.4	6 197	10.2	7 008	6 493	515	1 375	1 799
Rooks	72	4 970	0.92	61	11.8	72	13.9	513	12.6	1 181	1 147	34	34	654
Rush	66	2 974	0.84	29	9.2	28	8.9	280	11.6	845	820	25	95	3 011
Russell	89	6 562	0.89	92	13.1	88	12.5	729	13.6	1 753	1 724	29	143	2 066
Saline	1 465	57 535	1.06	766	13.8	466	8.4	5 610	12.2	10 505	9 349	1 156	2 169	3 890
Scott	105	4 861	0.96	65	13.1	63	12.7	588	14.2	D	531	D	76	1 502
Sedgwick	7 293	521 121	1.07	7 575	14.8	4 244	8.3	57 454	13.2	75 518	60 757	14 761	23 243	4 583
Seward	476	24 627	1.12	441	19.0	110	4.7	4 204	20.2	2 073	2 039	34	693	2 949
Shawnee	4 398	191 589	1.16	2 357	13.2	1 741	9.7	16 906	11.6	34 748	31 259	3 489	7 867	4 430
Sheridan	33	2 491	0.96	31	12.3	20	7.9	273	13.9	515	503	12	21	822
Sherman	102	5 990	0.97	80	13.3	82	13.6	716	14.6	1 239	1 216	23	135	2 197
Smith	56	3 728	0.97	30	8.1	45	12.1	360	13.0	1 099	1 061	38	NA	NA
Stafford	69	4 000	0.82	45	10.5	45	10.5	575	16.9	1 382	1 350	32	61	1 404
Stanton	47	2 218	1.03	35	16.7	16	7.6	355	20.5	D	329	D	NA	NA
Stevens	72	5 329	0.85	94	16.1	26	4.5	888	17.8	740	723	17	NA	NA
Sumner	409	20 662	0.71	273	11.6	243	10.3	2 239	11.6	4 915	4 291	624	556	2 544
Thomas	353	8 257	1.07	102	12.9	60	7.6	689	10.7	1 303	1 257	46	211	2 653
Trego	64	2 812	0.90	32	11.0	44	15.1	244	11.2	681	668	13	31	1 041
Wabaunsee	90	5 378	0.51	97	13.9	42	6.0	509	8.9	1 273	1 221	52	92	1 304
Wallace	19	1 527	0.95	20	13.2	13	8.6	179	15.2	349	338	11	1	63
Washington	114	5 064	0.77	80	14.3	81	14.4	586	13.7	1 426	1 370	56	25	447
Wichita	26	2 387	1.16	26	12.0	20	9.2	319	18.0	D	372	D	31	1 421
Wilson	121	8 931	0.94	101	11.3	118	13.2	1 055	14.8	2 078	1 994	84	202	2 235
Woodson	39	2 825	0.71	28	8.9	43	13.7	353	14.5	803	754	49	97	3 029
Wyandotte	1 335	175 149	1.23	2 692	16.5	1 377	8.5	26 743	18.9	23 095	15 810	7 285	9 074	5 633
KENTUCKY	128 838	4 405 133	1.01	55 691	12.6	43 086	9.8	360 275	9.9	827 848	605 896	221 952	108 506	2 459
Adair	1 162	16 787	0.69	208	10.9	212	11.2	1 790	12.2	3 659	2 895	764	106	564
Allen	197	17 611	0.67	274	13.3	236	11.5	1 930	11.4	3 887	3 074	813	204	1 000
Anderson	108	16 433	0.49	264	12.0	190	8.7	1 552	8.3	3 767	2 346	1 421	141	643
Ballard	127	7 766	0.85	72	8.8	99	12.1	633	9.7	2 329	1 921	408	119	1 423
Barren	701	42 934	1.01	514	11.9	497	11.5	3 669	10.3	8 551	6 600	1 951	653	1 508
Bath	103	10 147	0.56	155	12.7	147	12.1	1 210	11.8	2 325	1 585	740	9	75
Bell	952	29 189	1.12	334	12.1	348	12.6	2 407	10.8	6 814	5 469	1 345	869	3 135
Boone	835	140 952	1.30	1 735	13.7	865	6.8	7 684	6.9	18 393	11 433	6 960	2 803	2 226
Bourbon	236	19 087	0.90	237	11.8	214	10.7	2 122	13.1	3 810	2 495	1 315	359	1 792
Boyd	2 272	57 741	1.47	556	11.5	567	11.7	3 401	8.9	10 832	8 365	2 467	1 286	2 638
Boyle	3 205	32 621	1.30	322	9.9	295	9.9	1 995	9.3	6 672	5 114	1 558	513	1 759
Bracken	41	6 543	0.45	98	11.7	97	11.6	651	9.2	1 842	1 285	557	94	1 210
Breathitt	322	12 976	0.84	185	13.7	184	13.7	1 174	10.5	3 306	2 591	715	33	245
Breckinridge	300	17 194	0.60	228	11.4	200	10.0	1 879	11.6	3 942	3 311	631	43	214
Bullitt	340	61 207	0.59	826	10.5	587	7.5	5 271	7.9	10 446	7 248	3 198	1 099	1 417
Butler	203	11 263	0.69	182	14.1	114	8.8	1 297	12.4	2 404	1 721	683	126	982
Caldwell	148	12 144	0.86	154	12.1	154	12.1	955	9.4	3 079	2 461	618	241	1 883
Calloway	3 353	38 730	1.04	366	9.6	385	10.1	3 137	10.8	7 004	5 202	1 802	928	2 455
Campbell	3 291	76 510	0.67	1 070	11.6	847	9.2	6 421	8.4	14 139	8 587	5 552	2 422	2 655
Carlisle	60	4 057	0.54	59	12.0	58	11.8	438	11.0	1 185	958	227	32	642
Carroll	325	13 923	1.74	130	12.1	121	11.3	984	10.9	2 185	1 686	499	102	927
Carter	650	24 270	0.68	351	11.9	324	11.9	2 293	10.4	4 569	3 455	1 114	182	671
Casey	479	14 505	0.73	187	11.8	207	13.1	1 654	13.2	3 174	2 608	566	88	546
Christian	5 393	96 276	1.74	1 467	19.9	596	8.1	6 397	10.5	10 463	8 255	2 208	1 790	2 435
Clark	458	33 141	0.84	416	11.6	343	9.6	2 856	9.7	7 029	4 914	2 115	1 120	3 141

1. Per 1,000 estimated resident population. 2. Data for serious crimes have not been adjusted for underreporting; this may affect comparability between geographic areas and over time.
3. Per 100,000 population estimated by the FBI.

Table B. States and Counties — Crime, Education, Money Income, and Poverty

STATE County	Violent	Property	Total	Percent private	High school graduate or less	Bachelor's degree or more	Total current spending (mil dol)	Current spending per student (dollars)	Per capita income (dollars)	Median income (dollars)	Mean income (dollars)	Percent with income of $200,000 or more	Median household income (dollars)	All persons	Children under 18 years	Children 5 to 17 years in families
	46	47	48	49	50	51	52	53	54	55	56	57	58	59	60	61
KANSAS—Cont'd																
Neosho	152	1 090	3 849	8.1	41.5	18.4	25.3	10 423	22 474	44 879	55 139	1.6	41 527	17.7	25.7	25.8
Ness	261	1 011	609	13.0	47.5	19.1	5.6	11 341	29 713	48 021	65 901	3.2	51 923	10.0	14.1	13.1
Norton	107	997	1 180	4.5	46.8	16.0	10.7	11 283	23 323	45 484	56 085	1.9	44 846	13.5	16.4	15.6
Osage	64	1 119	3 734	7.3	49.1	20.7	30.4	10 790	24 199	49 716	59 065	1.4	52 749	12.9	16.7	15.1
Osborne	131	1 154	792	16.7	46.7	19.7	6.4	13 374	27 104	38 686	58 184	3.2	38 848	12.9	20.8	20.0
Ottawa	83	1 443	1 430	9.6	41.2	19.9	13.6	10 897	27 899	60 098	68 792	2.8	52 744	10.4	13.0	11.7
Pawnee	258	2 325	1 586	7.5	40.9	22.4	12.0	10 415	22 191	40 791	57 277	2.3	47 351	13.9	16.9	15.1
Phillips	72	127	1 297	6.2	43.5	20.4	9.5	11 626	25 146	44 292	57 187	1.8	45 856	11.4	19.2	18.7
Pottawatomie	214	1 233	6 034	17.9	35.4	32.2	38.8	9 559	25 469	60 479	69 585	2.3	65 373	10.0	11.7	11.0
Pratt	191	2 877	2 357	6.5	37.8	24.4	15.9	9 358	26 807	49 519	64 545	2.4	54 701	10.3	15.7	15.1
Rawlins	191	689	448	4.9	38.4	23.8	3.9	12 192	27 719	43 555	58 825	1.3	44 932	11.8	16.6	16.2
Reno	363	3 152	15 643	12.2	40.3	19.7	97.7	9 589	23 378	44 673	57 680	1.8	46 533	15.8	21.1	19.5
Republic	230	2 025	941	11.5	44.0	21.0	8.1	11 230	25 642	40 538	53 046	1.2	42 381	12.7	18.2	17.8
Rice	NA	NA	2 548	16.0	43.2	21.4	21.0	11 369	23 633	46 342	59 707	0.8	49 152	14.7	19.9	18.7
Riley	242	1 557	30 302	5.6	22.3	45.5	73.8	10 053	23 872	44 522	62 265	3.0	46 468	20.2	16.5	16.4
Rooks	135	520	1 043	8.9	44.0	21.6	10.8	13 095	23 829	43 816	53 526	1.7	48 383	12.0	16.3	15.9
Rush	158	2 853	561	2.7	44.3	20.8	6.1	12 399	24 642	40 746	51 497	0.8	43 083	12.1	19.2	17.3
Russell	361	1 704	1 338	4.6	42.8	23.9	8.6	10 591	26 641	40 369	54 993	1.8	45 443	13.3	19.8	19.2
Saline	373	3 517	14 506	11.4	44.1	24.5	89.0	10 424	25 577	47 745	62 329	2.7	48 460	13.0	18.6	17.8
Scott	376	1 127	986	5.1	53.3	20.0	10.0	10 396	26 991	47 079	62 643	1.1	56 032	8.3	12.5	11.7
Sedgwick	604	3 979	142 729	16.5	38.0	29.4	816.9	9 782	25 897	50 326	65 954	3.1	51 175	14.7	19.4	18.9
Seward	370	2 579	6 794	5.1	60.8	12.6	55.0	9 675	19 872	48 621	60 276	2.1	47 381	15.7	21.5	20.6
Shawnee	425	4 005	46 967	14.2	40.7	28.9	283.1	9 992	26 682	49 695	65 250	2.4	52 795	15.0	20.8	18.4
Sheridan	117	705	539	2.4	42.5	21.4	6.4	10 410	27 102	48 750	59 569	2.1	52 300	10.9	15.9	13.9
Sherman	293	1 904	1 328	2.9	44.2	15.2	10.0	9 340	20 944	38 528	46 848	1.1	43 100	16.2	23.0	22.1
Smith	NA	NA	742	3.4	44.7	18.9	8.2	12 455	26 964	42 174	58 724	3.0	41 303	13.5	18.2	17.9
Stafford	184	1 220	975	3.2	41.2	20.3	11.5	13 228	24 169	44 180	56 325	2.3	45 945	14.1	19.6	16.8
Stanton	NA	NA	582	9.8	45.6	17.9	5.5	11 724	22 623	42 146	57 935	1.0	56 591	11.5	17.4	16.8
Stevens	NA	NA	1 568	6.8	51.6	16.3	14.4	10 748	25 126	57 614	71 257	3.8	59 773	9.7	13.7	12.5
Sumner	224	2 320	5 986	9.9	46.1	18.4	41.5	10 368	23 670	50 310	60 355	1.4	52 476	13.3	19.0	16.8
Thomas	390	2 263	2 103	9.6	32.5	30.5	10.4	9 519	28 364	48 649	69 550	6.5	50 639	11.3	13.4	12.7
Trego	67	973	693	13.0	41.7	23.2	4.4	11 171	24 860	50 670	58 683	1.3	46 859	9.9	12.1	11.4
Wabaunsee	340	964	1 666	16.0	44.7	22.3	11.5	11 838	24 980	55 018	62 031	1.2	59 160	9.4	14.3	13.8
Wallace	63	0	363	11.0	44.2	21.2	4.1	13 468	28 254	48 125	71 030	4.6	49 109	12.0	12.7	11.3
Washington	72	376	1 228	9.0	49.7	15.5	9.8	11 310	22 910	42 738	52 461	0.9	43 264	10.8	14.7	13.5
Wichita	504	917	579	2.6	48.0	18.9	5.2	12 248	25 191	57 266	64 379	2.3	53 447	11.5	15.3	14.4
Wilson	266	1 970	1 967	5.0	53.7	12.5	18.4	10 852	20 235	38 811	48 592	0.9	39 764	16.7	25.8	24.2
Woodson	312	2 717	626	7.2	50.3	18.4	5.8	12 085	22 912	36 863	49 919	1.9	35 502	18.4	26.2	22.4
Wyandotte	703	4 930	43 089	10.5	54.2	15.8	288.5	9 786	18 753	39 326	49 432	0.8	37 087	24.4	34.5	31.8
KENTUCKY	212	2 247	1 101 178	14.9	50.3	21.8	6 444.5	9 316	23 741	43 342	59 312	2.5	42 914	19.0	25.9	24.0
Adair	27	538	4 826	26.3	62.9	15.6	24.2	9 018	17 772	34 490	45 204	0.9	31 558	26.3	38.3	36.0
Allen	44	956	4 755	11.7	60.0	13.3	25.5	8 431	19 651	40 273	49 152	1.1	39 801	19.0	29.3	26.9
Anderson	59	584	5 224	9.6	53.3	18.4	31.7	8 092	23 566	53 410	59 872	0.8	54 331	11.3	17.2	15.7
Ballard	24	1 399	1 856	7.7	57.0	12.4	12.7	8 752	23 417	42 852	57 517	2.3	44 732	16.8	24.0	21.6
Barren	83	1 425	10 060	6.6	61.6	14.7	73.9	9 406	19 907	38 885	49 495	1.2	37 666	19.5	29.2	27.5
Bath	8	66	2 731	8.5	63.8	11.5	18.4	8 596	17 137	33 091	44 662	1.0	34 126	22.7	33.8	31.8
Bell	137	2 998	6 089	11.1	68.3	10.2	48.3	9 606	14 657	24 976	35 361	0.6	24 868	33.5	45.1	42.9
Boone	108	2 118	34 336	19.3	36.3	30.8	181.4	8 484	29 656	67 286	81 417	4.5	66 939	8.0	11.3	10.5
Bourbon	115	1 677	4 481	12.3	55.8	15.7	33.7	9 033	23 267	43 521	57 831	2.1	42 812	19.2	28.5	27.2
Boyd	121	2 517	10 881	9.7	48.4	16.7	70.1	9 289	24 446	41 739	60 484	2.5	40 224	23.1	34.7	29.2
Boyle	154	1 605	7 650	25.0	49.9	22.2	43.0	9 353	22 394	40 853	56 929	2.6	41 538	17.5	24.2	22.4
Bracken	39	1 171	1 867	8.6	60.0	14.6	13.0	8 356	21 742	40 194	54 760	1.4	41 910	18.6	25.7	23.5
Breathitt	15	230	2 977	8.3	66.4	11.5	27.3	10 403	15 574	26 094	37 757	0.4	28 647	33.0	44.1	42.5
Breckinridge	30	184	4 524	12.6	66.7	9.4	29.8	9 225	18 151	40 039	48 162	0.5	41 547	19.2	27.3	25.7
Bullitt	86	1 331	18 861	16.4	55.3	13.4	101.5	7 755	24 364	56 199	64 185	1.1	54 924	12.3	17.4	15.4
Butler	86	896	2 666	15.7	68.5	8.7	17.7	8 156	18 747	34 581	44 170	0.4	35 219	20.6	31.0	27.9
Caldwell	172	1 711	2 656	3.4	55.4	17.3	16.9	8 001	21 194	40 135	51 288	1.3	42 640	18.2	28.4	27.5
Calloway	119	2 336	12 803	4.7	44.5	27.5	44.3	8 988	21 093	38 589	51 436	1.4	37 705	20.2	24.7	23.1
Campbell	172	2 483	24 829	20.2	42.4	28.1	112.5	9 511	27 479	54 482	68 553	3.0	52 349	13.2	17.7	17.1
Carlisle	20	622	1 070	12.5	56.0	13.1	8.1	9 423	21 959	39 125	52 516	0.3	40 701	17.0	27.6	25.2
Carroll	82	845	2 359	6.7	68.0	11.1	21.7	10 794	19 711	39 668	51 138	0.2	43 615	20.4	28.2	28.3
Carter	30	642	6 474	13.4	64.2	11.1	42.6	8 781	17 139	37 139	48 829	0.8	34 991	23.9	32.6	29.0
Casey	25	521	3 254	7.3	66.5	9.3	22.2	9 542	15 949	30 051	39 851	0.4	29 344	30.6	42.6	40.9
Christian	200	2 235	19 929	12.7	48.0	15.7	85.4	9 086	19 704	38 720	51 724	1.7	36 736	21.6	30.4	31.5
Clark	140	3 000	8 183	15.5	52.1	19.9	48.5	8 411	24 787	46 554	61 091	1.7	49 012	16.0	25.3	24.2

1. Data for serious crimes have not been adjusted for underreporting; this may affect comparability between geographic areas and over time.   2. Per 100,000 population estimated by the FBI.
3. All persons 3 years old and over enrolled in nursery school through college.   4. Persons 25 years old and over.   5. Elementary and secondary education expenditures.
6. Based on population estimated by the American Community Survey, 2010–2014.

Table B. States and Counties — **Personal Income**

STATE County	Personal income, 2014					Supplements to wages and salaries; employer contributions (mil dol)		Proprietors' income (mil dol)	Dividends, interest, and rent (mil dol)	Personal transfer receipts (mil dol)	Earnings, 2014	Contributions for government social insurance (mil dol)	
	Total (mil dol)	Percent change, 2013–2014	Per capita[1] Dollars	Per capita[1] Rank	Wages and salaries (mil dol)	Pension and insurance	Government social insurance				Total (mil dol)	From employee and self-employed	From employer
	62	63	64	65	66	67	68	69	70	71	72	73	74
KANSAS—Cont'd													
Neosho	522	1.1	31 795	2 472	232	42	18	56	82	153	349	22	18
Ness	174	-1.8	56 175	194	58	10	4	52	38	28	124	7	4
Norton	223	-2.1	40 037	1 169	98	19	8	46	44	40	170	9	8
Osage	580	-0.6	36 392	1 705	89	20	7	22	87	137	138	11	7
Osborne	164	-9.9	43 761	781	45	8	3	43	30	34	100	6	3
Ottawa	211	-9.9	34 834	1 963	46	9	4	16	32	46	75	5	4
Pawnee	270	-10.0	38 988	1 320	123	27	9	55	47	56	214	11	9
Phillips	273	-0.6	49 273	423	89	20	7	66	53	52	182	10	7
Pottawatomie	1 083	1.9	47 301	511	379	63	30	104	144	136	576	35	30
Pratt	420	-8.0	42 653	884	195	31	15	74	78	74	315	18	15
Rawlins	139	-10.4	53 967	236	35	6	3	49	28	27	93	6	3
Reno	2 290	0.4	35 898	1 792	1 030	171	80	153	432	527	1 433	94	80
Republic	204	-7.9	42 439	905	63	13	5	50	34	44	131	6	5
Rice	383	-2.0	38 240	1 426	148	27	11	55	65	79	241	14	11
Riley	2 712	1.6	36 070	1 773	1 174	250	89	83	670	330	1 597	91	89
Rooks	195	-3.5	37 896	1 469	79	15	6	13	41	47	112	7	6
Rush	133	-6.9	41 451	1 013	43	9	3	12	26	31	68	4	3
Russell	283	3.5	40 721	1 096	113	23	9	24	62	66	168	10	9
Saline	2 302	1.3	41 294	1 028	1 154	190	91	344	414	419	1 780	111	91
Scott	260	-11.5	51 120	328	85	13	6	85	47	38	189	7	6
Sedgwick	23 516	2.8	46 219	579	12 193	1 840	947	2 388	6 063	3 470	17 367	1 060	947
Seward	820	0.7	34 936	1 948	492	86	37	135	88	118	748	42	37
Shawnee	7 362	2.6	41 263	1 031	4 544	739	355	378	1 242	1 549	6 016	377	355
Sheridan	129	-23.7	50 951	334	41	7	3	40	23	19	91	4	3
Sherman	227	-10.1	37 199	1 569	90	17	7	33	41	58	146	8	7
Smith	153	-9.7	40 646	1 103	43	8	3	32	37	36	87	5	3
Stafford	158	-18.1	36 663	1 655	44	10	3	19	36	35	76	4	3
Stanton	102	-27.3	48 209	468	34	6	2	14	28	14	57	3	2
Stevens	242	-18.4	41 680	984	112	18	9	39	41	29	178	9	9
Sumner	807	-5.2	34 310	2 061	265	46	23	49	126	178	382	26	23
Thomas	274	-17.3	34 703	1 983	147	24	11	12	57	54	194	12	11
Trego	124	-3.5	42 856	864	47	10	4	22	22	29	83	4	4
Wabaunsee	314	2.4	44 665	706	43	9	3	16	83	52	72	5	3
Wallace	68	-35.1	45 224	656	22	4	2	18	11	13	45	2	2
Washington	230	-10.0	41 167	1 042	61	13	5	42	43	50	120	6	5
Wichita	146	-17.8	66 867	74	32	6	2	68	25	16	108	2	2
Wilson	331	5.0	36 652	1 657	136	27	11	34	56	91	209	13	11
Woodson	115	2.4	36 427	1 700	22	5	2	20	19	31	48	3	2
Wyandotte	4 707	3.1	29 119	2 813	4 574	675	372	346	540	1 233	5 968	366	372
KENTUCKY	165 044	4.3	37 396	X	81 576	15 093	6 405	11 941	25 586	40 001	115 016	7 122	6 405
Adair	500	5.4	26 038	3 029	150	35	12	32	64	195	229	16	12
Allen	688	6.5	33 737	2 155	145	30	11	162	66	180	349	23	11
Anderson	776	4.4	35 476	1 861	164	37	13	22	94	165	235	17	13
Ballard	305	-2.2	37 031	1 596	130	20	10	38	39	80	198	12	10
Barren	1 426	4.8	33 054	2 269	582	111	47	143	189	404	882	57	47
Bath	343	6.5	28 128	2 906	62	15	5	12	38	125	94	8	5
Bell	776	6.2	27 927	2 925	287	67	23	25	90	369	402	30	23
Boone	5 268	5.2	41 674	988	3 612	529	284	290	573	738	4 714	285	284
Bourbon	712	3.3	35 662	1 829	288	48	22	25	136	174	384	25	22
Boyd	1 726	3.4	35 347	1 888	1 268	232	98	100	224	538	1 697	107	98
Boyle	985	4.2	33 163	2 253	545	100	46	52	180	267	743	48	46
Bracken	274	4.5	32 616	2 350	54	12	4	11	31	76	82	6	4
Breathitt	406	9.1	30 257	2 684	116	29	9	11	38	213	165	13	9
Breckinridge	652	4.1	32 780	2 316	122	29	9	72	109	188	232	15	9
Bullitt	2 768	5.3	35 508	1 855	762	129	62	149	256	571	1 101	78	62
Butler	402	2.7	31 251	2 549	97	23	8	34	43	130	161	11	8
Caldwell	429	0.8	33 707	2 158	136	28	11	42	58	133	218	15	11
Calloway	1 267	2.5	33 100	2 262	555	150	42	111	193	304	857	49	42
Campbell	3 789	4.7	41 262	1 032	1 198	234	91	176	569	691	1 698	108	91
Carlisle	198	-7.1	39 822	1 203	32	7	2	45	26	51	86	4	2
Carroll	374	3.5	34 539	2 016	329	51	26	25	43	102	431	27	26
Carter	788	4.7	28 953	2 836	185	42	15	31	76	298	273	22	15
Casey	431	4.8	27 126	2 972	114	27	9	30	55	179	181	14	9
Christian	2 625	-1.0	35 355	1 887	3 201	881	309	147	606	560	4 539	195	309
Clark	1 446	4.9	40 425	1 127	562	101	45	231	188	326	940	61	45

1. Based on the resident population estimated as of July 1 of the year shown.

Table B. States and Counties — Earnings, Social Security, and Housing

STATE County	Earnings, 2014 (cont.) Percent by selected industries									Social Security beneficiaries, December 2014		Supplemental Security Income recipients, December 2014	Housing units, 2015	
	Farm	Mining	Construction	Manufacturing	Information: professional, scientific, technical services	Retail trade	Finance, insurance, real estate and leasing	Health care and social assistance	Government	Number	Rate[1]		Total	Percent change, 2010–2014
	75	76	77	78	79	80	81	82	83	84	85	86	87	88
KANSAS—Cont'd														
Neosho	5.3	8.7	3.6	16.9	2.7	7.7	4.4	D	26.0	3 780	231	386	7 718	2.7
Ness	17.6	30.6	4.3	1.3	D	D	D	0.5	15.6	825	268	22	1 730	-0.6
Norton	17.8	5.2	3.5	7.9	4.7	5.7	D	9.0	24.2	1 255	227	59	2 529	-0.5
Osage	8.5	D	5.8	4.1	D	8.2	5.5	8.9	35.4	3 910	245	368	7 484	-0.3
Osborne	19.0	11.5	2.8	D	D	8.3	4.3	6.0	14.9	1 050	279	48	2 183	-1.0
Ottawa	13.8	D	4.9	10.9	D	4.5	6.1	12.6	25.3	1 365	225	77	2 773	-0.2
Pawnee	17.8	D	8.7	0.9	1.5	3.2	3.0	5.5	41.8	1 450	211	91	3 158	0.2
Phillips	10.9	7.1	4.8	20.8	1.9	3.9	D	5.2	16.8	1 465	267	57	3 063	0.5
Pottawatomie	3.6	0.1	11.0	24.0	5.6	8.8	4.2	D	9.9	3 895	170	197	9 236	7.1
Pratt	9.2	16.9	7.4	2.6	3.2	7.8	4.3	D	16.1	2 050	210	129	4 476	-0.8
Rawlins	8.9	0.3	7.4	7.7	D	5.5	D	4.4	14.5	725	284	34	1 457	-0.1
Reno	2.7	2.4	5.9	13.6	5.9	7.1	5.0	15.3	17.7	14 580	229	1 345	28 300	0.1
Republic	34.6	D	4.3	7.8	2.2	5.8	D	D	14.8	1 405	294	63	2 894	0.6
Rice	16.3	9.9	5.0	10.9	3.6	4.0	D	D	18.8	2 190	219	141	4 555	0.2
Riley	1.2	0.6	5.1	2.2	6.1	6.5	5.5	10.2	44.8	7 225	97	540	30 135	6.8
Rooks	8.2	13.8	2.8	2.8	3.1	5.3	3.4	3.6	25.6	1 350	261	69	2 759	-0.3
Rush	18.5	D	2.9	23.6	5.8	2.7	2.9	3.4	21.4	905	284	62	1 859	-0.5
Russell	11.8	18.5	3.3	17.0	3.7	4.0	3.9	D	15.6	1 905	272	131	3 881	-0.7
Saline	0.7	D	5.7	17.1	5.8	7.5	3.7	14.8	12.1	11 365	204	1 082	24 232	0.5
Scott	45.3	D	3.0	0.8	D	3.9	D	D	8.9	1 035	208	40	2 194	0.0
Sedgwick	0.1	4.2	5.6	23.8	6.5	5.9	4.4	11.3	12.7	87 205	171	10 967	215 200	1.7
Seward	3.6	10.4	D	D	D	6.4	2.8	D	16.3	2 615	112	355	8 139	1.0
Shawnee	0.2	0.5	5.6	7.1	8.1	4.9	11.2	15.2	23.7	37 665	211	4 936	79 547	0.5
Sheridan	31.1	2.9	D	D	D	4.0	6.9	D	15.3	535	211	15	1 260	-0.4
Sherman	17.0	D	3.8	4.4	3.5	9.0	5.3	D	25.7	1 385	228	125	3 117	-1.0
Smith	31.5	D	D	D	1.9	5.9	3.0	10.1	16.7	1 170	313	56	2 248	0.7
Stafford	23.9	D	2.1	3.2	D	2.2	4.3	D	31.1	980	228	55	2 304	-0.6
Stanton	27.2	0.6	1.4	0.6	D	2.9	D	D	26.6	355	167	17	977	-1.3
Stevens	12.9	D	23.7	9.8	D	4.0	2.9	D	19.7	715	122	39	2 293	-0.6
Sumner	6.4	2.1	2.3	18.5	3.4	6.6	5.0	D	21.8	4 975	212	380	10 863	0.0
Thomas	3.5	D	5.8	2.5	4.6	12.5	5.2	D	18.7	1 485	189	75	3 576	1.1
Trego	26.1	D	1.7	2.4	D	4.3	D	D	25.7	740	254	36	1 674	-0.5
Wabaunsee	12.3	D	10.9	11.0	D	3.1	D	D	26.3	1 515	217	84	3 259	1.0
Wallace	38.0	0.0	D	D	D	2.6	D	D	14.4	320	211	16	777	-0.5
Washington	37.7	D	3.0	7.5	D	3.4	D	4.3	22.0	1 510	268	67	2 949	-0.2
Wichita	67.1	1.0	1.7	2.8	D	1.6	D	0.6	12.3	430	198	22	1 042	-1.1
Wilson	10.0	1.8	8.8	28.8	1.9	3.9	2.9	8.1	20.6	2 420	269	248	4 643	-0.8
Woodson	19.0	31.9	D	D	D	5.1	D	3.5	20.9	910	288	74	2 003	-0.9
Wyandotte	0.0	0.1	5.8	17.2	2.8	4.8	1.9	16.8	18.3	25 835	159	5 397	67 675	1.4
KENTUCKY	1.1	1.5	5.5	14.5	7.3	6.2	6.5	12.1	20.3	954 284	216	188 401	1 957 037	1.6
Adair	4.8	0.9	5.4	6.8	D	8.8	5.6	D	22.3	4 565	241	1 020	8 500	-0.8
Allen	6.0	0.0	D	15.7	D	29.7	3.1	D	12.5	4 810	235	905	9 325	0.2
Anderson	-2.2	D	8.2	29.4	2.9	9.3	4.4	5.5	21.2	4 645	212	433	9 278	1.7
Ballard	11.6	0.0	D	27.8	7.9	3.7	1.3	2.8	11.0	2 270	276	297	3 884	0.0
Barren	4.6	0.1	5.7	22.3	D	8.7	3.0	15.2	14.4	10 625	247	1 791	19 477	1.5
Bath	3.4	0.0	12.5	D	D	5.2	4.0	8.9	30.6	3 185	262	912	5 380	-0.5
Bell	-0.1	10.9	2.1	11.4	D	10.6	4.7	16.3	23.7	7 875	284	3 133	13 087	-0.5
Boone	-0.1	D	4.5	17.6	4.9	6.3	5.8	5.6	9.3	19 315	153	1 580	48 239	4.5
Bourbon	6.2	D	4.9	22.1	2.5	8.4	4.6	D	14.3	4 700	235	653	9 025	1.1
Boyd	-0.1	D	9.9	17.2	6.8	6.4	2.7	21.7	12.2	12 685	260	2 521	21 666	-0.6
Boyle	0.0	D	3.0	16.0	D	7.9	4.0	23.7	13.9	7 045	237	1 225	12 417	0.9
Bracken	-0.7	0.0	11.3	D	D	3.9	D	5.7	25.7	2 065	246	287	3 825	-0.4
Breathitt	0.2	D	D	1.0	2.1	9.3	4.3	26.6	35.0	4 735	352	2 979	6 201	-0.5
Breckinridge	18.3	0.5	10.4	6.7	3.3	8.1	4.8	D	20.1	4 980	250	857	10 608	-0.1
Bullitt	-0.4	D	11.6	16.0	4.4	5.1	3.3	4.4	14.6	15 770	202	1 388	30 650	4.5
Butler	12.0	D	5.6	28.2	1.3	4.1	3.7	D	20.0	3 150	245	528	5 858	-0.3
Caldwell	7.7	D	4.8	22.1	3.2	10.6	3.5	D	15.8	3 545	278	563	6 271	-0.3
Calloway	4.6	D	5.4	16.1	4.4	7.4	3.1	5.0	32.5	8 100	212	832	18 538	2.6
Campbell	-0.1	0.0	D	13.1	7.9	7.3	5.1	11.4	24.9	16 445	179	2 045	39 942	1.1
Carlisle	35.9	0.0	7.2	7.5	1.8	5.3	10.0	5.2	14.5	1 390	279	215	2 436	-0.2
Carroll	-0.3	0.0	D	48.5	9.2	4.7	1.5	D	9.3	2 500	233	475	4 683	-0.3
Carter	-1.1	1.8	7.5	11.7	4.2	12.1	4.6	D	25.2	7 540	277	1 794	12 273	-0.3
Casey	0.8	D	5.6	22.3	D	7.0	D	12.5	19.2	4 180	264	1 032	7 401	-1.1
Christian	0.7	D	1.7	7.4	2.9	2.2	1.4	4.2	71.0	11 820	160	2 395	29 763	1.0
Clark	0.3	D	9.2	18.8	7.4	7.0	4.0	9.3	9.8	8 330	233	1 411	15 749	0.3

1. Per 1,000 resident population estimated as of July 1 of the year shown.

Table B. States and Counties — Housing, Labor Force, and Employment

STATE County	Housing units, 2010–2014								Civilian labor force, 2015				Civilian employment,[6] 2010–2014		
	Occupied units							Sub-stand-ard units[4] (percent)			Unemployment			Percent	
	Owner-occupied					Renter-occupied									
				Median owner cost as a percent of income											
	Total	Percent	Median value[1]	With a mortgage	Without a mortgage[2]	Median rent[3]	Median rent as a percent of income[2]		Total	Percent change, 2014–2015	Total	Rate[5]	Total	Management, business, science and arts	Construction, production, and maintenance occupations
	89	90	91	92	93	94	95	96	97	98	99	100	101	102	103
KANSAS—Cont'd															
Neosho	6 503	73.3	70 300	19.0	10.9	576	25.5	2.3	6 289	-1.8	472	7.5	7 689	31.0	30.4
Ness	1 403	81.2	64 200	17.6	10.0	562	20.4	1.9	1 563	-3.2	51	3.3	1 580	32.7	30.4
Norton	2 212	74.3	66 700	16.4	12.9	630	20.5	4.0	2 961	-2.7	75	2.5	2 755	29.6	29.8
Osage	6 544	76.0	99 100	20.9	12.8	661	27.5	1.9	8 147	0.0	408	5.0	7 290	32.1	29.3
Osborne	1 767	76.2	54 300	19.0	10.2	485	22.5	1.5	2 113	2.6	75	3.5	1 896	39.3	26.0
Ottawa	2 479	81.1	91 400	20.0	11.5	619	25.3	0.6	3 244	-0.1	125	3.9	3 053	35.1	31.3
Pawnee	2 525	70.7	73 800	23.1	10.7	478	26.6	0.0	3 331	-1.9	124	3.7	3 134	36.3	26.0
Phillips	2 414	77.0	66 100	20.6	11.9	494	20.3	1.6	2 981	2.4	98	3.3	2 811	36.6	26.2
Pottawatomie	8 109	77.5	154 800	19.7	11.9	731	23.8	2.6	12 407	3.0	439	3.5	10 739	36.9	24.4
Pratt	4 071	68.4	84 300	18.7	11.5	617	21.8	1.3	5 344	-3.0	220	4.1	4 648	35.9	28.0
Rawlins	1 211	69.0	72 000	22.8	10.0	590	22.9	0.9	1 567	3.2	37	2.4	1 314	39.3	21.0
Reno	25 335	68.3	92 500	20.8	12.3	666	26.4	1.7	30 981	-0.8	1 347	4.3	29 489	29.4	25.9
Republic	2 258	78.3	47 900	19.3	10.3	505	20.9	1.8	2 621	1.9	74	2.8	2 412	34.3	28.3
Rice	3 837	73.7	77 400	18.1	11.4	527	26.0	3.3	5 503	0.9	211	3.8	4 839	29.5	32.0
Riley	26 162	42.3	174 800	21.4	10.8	878	32.7	8.7	37 682	2.9	1 236	3.3	33 853	41.4	17.1
Rooks	2 310	74.3	67 500	20.4	10.0	514	26.5	2.6	2 828	-0.9	131	4.6	2 535	34.8	28.5
Rush	1 535	76.2	60 400	17.8	11.1	543	31.1	2.2	1 821	0.6	65	3.6	1 619	38.4	25.4
Russell	3 317	73.1	76 500	19.9	12.0	584	27.5	2.2	3 728	-3.0	141	3.8	3 514	32.1	28.7
Saline	22 497	66.8	120 400	21.8	12.0	679	29.7	2.1	31 008	0.9	1 184	3.8	28 058	30.4	29.7
Scott	2 157	75.2	109 000	25.4	10.0	683	24.0	3.9	2 923	2.3	82	2.8	2 543	33.6	36.6
Sedgwick	192 303	64.6	125 400	21.1	11.5	725	28.8	2.4	248 120	0.3	11 938	4.8	236 631	34.7	24.0
Seward	7 442	65.8	88 900	20.3	10.5	661	23.4	6.2	10 739	-3.9	469	4.4	10 811	19.8	48.9
Shawnee	72 069	64.5	120 100	20.2	12.0	727	30.1	2.5	91 606	-0.4	3 927	4.3	84 110	35.8	19.2
Sheridan	1 130	78.0	85 100	16.9	12.2	464	18.8	0.6	1 499	2.6	35	2.3	1 262	38.8	27.4
Sherman	2 738	56.0	71 600	19.3	12.3	662	27.5	0.0	3 129	1.1	93	3.0	2 938	33.3	25.8
Smith	1 690	78.8	65 400	21.7	11.0	405	28.3	0.8	2 109	-0.5	83	3.9	1 837	39.9	26.2
Stafford	1 877	82.4	58 500	17.4	13.0	552	22.5	3.1	2 207	1.9	89	4.0	2 132	39.9	24.2
Stanton	833	75.2	79 200	23.1	12.2	560	22.7	1.8	1 056	2.8	32	3.0	1 117	26.4	32.5
Stevens	1 939	77.8	88 600	18.4	10.8	674	27.5	0.5	3 223	-4.4	121	3.8	2 783	28.5	36.9
Sumner	9 053	77.7	84 000	21.3	12.5	626	24.6	2.4	11 189	1.0	501	4.5	10 913	31.3	32.7
Thomas	3 167	72.6	103 700	19.7	11.7	452	23.1	0.7	4 437	1.2	119	2.7	4 352	37.3	22.2
Trego	1 250	74.2	75 400	17.2	10.0	584	22.7	1.7	1 509	1.3	54	3.6	1 551	31.2	27.1
Wabaunsee	2 701	84.6	113 300	20.9	12.9	745	24.1	2.3	3 788	0.6	146	3.9	3 392	37.3	26.8
Wallace	614	75.9	67 700	18.9	10.0	409	16.0	0.3	885	0.9	24	2.7	765	36.6	22.2
Washington	2 458	80.4	58 300	17.8	11.1	470	19.2	1.0	3 139	1.0	100	3.2	2 923	28.1	35.6
Wichita	867	74.5	75 300	17.8	11.2	658	18.8	5.8	1 259	1.9	38	3.0	1 120	36.3	35.2
Wilson	3 836	73.7	62 700	20.6	11.7	565	25.7	3.3	4 013	-3.8	267	6.7	4 051	29.0	34.0
Woodson	1 499	80.9	49 400	19.0	13.8	535	27.9	3.6	1 614	-0.9	83	5.1	1 529	26.7	38.2
Wyandotte	58 057	59.4	91 400	24.6	16.1	766	32.7	4.5	76 236	0.7	4 647	6.1	68 667	23.0	31.5
KENTUCKY	1 702 235	67.7	121 600	21.2	10.9	667	29.5	2.3	1 953 399	-2.6	105 458	5.4	1 870 879	32.7	26.3
Adair	7 124	74.3	80 100	20.5	10.8	498	26.8	1.7	6 930	-4.0	527	7.6	7 451	27.6	34.6
Allen	8 057	71.4	93 000	21.4	10.1	606	25.7	4.1	8 472	-2.2	423	5.0	8 143	24.5	38.0
Anderson	8 353	75.2	133 500	22.0	10.2	732	25.9	2.2	11 163	-2.3	474	4.2	10 318	26.9	31.2
Ballard	3 279	81.9	94 600	18.9	10.5	573	32.9	1.7	3 534	-3.9	252	7.1	3 454	26.9	33.3
Barren	16 789	68.2	101 900	20.5	12.0	586	31.0	2.1	18 050	-3.6	953	5.3	18 435	28.4	35.2
Bath	4 361	76.2	69 700	26.4	11.8	575	35.2	4.7	4 658	-1.3	363	7.8	3 913	24.8	37.8
Bell	11 181	67.1	62 600	23.9	10.6	486	33.7	3.9	8 917	-4.2	757	8.5	8 416	24.8	31.0
Boone	43 903	74.2	174 200	20.9	10.6	892	26.9	2.2	63 598	-2.5	2 664	4.2	61 454	38.9	20.2
Bourbon	7 782	60.3	139 300	20.5	10.0	657	29.2	1.5	9 552	-1.0	464	4.9	8 751	30.8	30.2
Boyd	19 533	69.1	96 700	19.1	10.7	602	30.0	1.2	18 211	-4.5	1 268	7.0	18 343	33.8	23.6
Boyle	10 981	64.9	133 000	21.9	10.7	630	28.5	0.5	11 870	-3.4	674	5.7	12 126	32.7	24.9
Bracken	3 303	77.9	93 400	21.8	11.3	536	32.9	2.5	3 686	-2.9	237	6.4	3 520	28.1	35.7
Breathitt	5 434	76.4	49 300	23.3	12.7	488	30.3	3.8	3 940	-5.7	376	9.5	4 337	27.2	26.4
Breckinridge	7 325	79.1	84 600	20.1	10.0	520	25.9	4.8	7 824	-3.2	474	6.1	7 412	23.9	40.1
Bullitt	28 282	81.4	145 700	22.1	11.1	776	25.1	1.6	38 493	-1.8	1 795	4.7	36 809	25.1	33.5
Butler	5 107	73.9	89 300	19.9	11.1	550	28.5	2.2	5 016	-3.3	300	6.0	4 970	25.9	37.2
Caldwell	5 320	71.4	93 700	19.0	11.5	540	27.7	1.4	5 304	-2.7	299	5.6	5 454	30.8	30.8
Calloway	14 854	65.1	119 500	20.9	11.5	541	34.1	1.4	18 037	-3.6	866	4.8	16 855	33.3	23.6
Campbell	35 478	68.8	147 700	20.5	11.4	741	28.3	1.7	46 674	-2.5	1 983	4.2	45 481	36.9	19.2
Carlisle	2 075	79.0	72 500	20.2	10.2	557	23.5	2.7	2 298	-3.5	133	5.8	2 170	23.8	33.8
Carroll	4 108	62.4	97 900	21.3	10.5	642	29.0	6.9	4 842	-0.5	281	5.8	4 184	20.6	41.2
Carter	10 525	77.5	76 000	19.9	11.3	559	29.3	3.0	10 118	-3.5	1 012	10.0	10 173	24.3	35.8
Casey	6 186	79.5	68 900	25.5	12.9	484	24.8	1.4	6 570	-0.7	377	5.7	5 636	26.1	35.0
Christian	25 734	49.6	106 800	21.3	10.0	756	30.7	3.4	24 962	-1.8	1 601	6.4	23 768	29.1	30.7
Clark	14 368	64.0	144 800	20.6	11.0	690	29.2	2.5	16 684	-1.7	882	5.3	15 815	33.7	26.4

1. Specified owner-occupied units. 2. A value of 10.0 represents 10 percent or less; a value of 50.0 represents 50 percent or more. 3. Specified renter-occupied units.
4. Overcrowded or lacking complete plumbing facilities. 5. Percent of civilian labor force. 6. Persons 16 years old and over.

Table B. States and Counties — Nonfarm Employment and Agriculture

	Private nonfarm establishments, employment and payroll, 2014									Agriculture, 2012			
	Employment						Annual payroll		Farms			
											Percent with:		
STATE County	Number of establishments	Total	Health care and social assistance	Manufacturing	Retail trade	Finance and insurance	Professional, scientific, and technical services	Total (mil dol)	Average per employee (dollars)	Number	Fewer than 50 acres	500 acres or more	Farm operators whose principal occupation is farming (percent)
	104	105	106	107	108	109	110	111	112	113	114	115	116
KANSAS—Cont'd													
Neosho	447	5 161	1 166	1 020	804	221	145	178	34 442	702	23.4	19.8	43.2
Ness	154	1 081	D	D	89	50	D	43	39 531	557	8.3	45.6	44.0
Norton	176	1 838	454	D	207	102	50	61	33 235	367	12.3	48.2	59.7
Osage	265	2 686	D	D	387	123	66	54	20 023	1 014	22.9	21.0	43.0
Osborne	152	1 103	284	D	205	69	D	35	31 532	343	10.2	50.1	65.0
Ottawa	133	858	253	D	104	70	D	24	28 029	525	12.0	35.4	49.9
Pawnee	157	1 905	1 005	D	214	D	D	68	35 874	401	13.7	45.4	53.1
Phillips	241	1 738	342	180	201	163	106	65	37 613	441	17.7	46.3	58.3
Pottawatomie	568	8 314	1 318	1 462	D	210	192	310	37 287	890	22.5	23.7	42.9
Pratt	390	3 699	662	118	730	157	120	136	36 815	543	7.6	37.9	45.1
Rawlins	105	641	185	41	96	32	D	21	32 733	307	6.2	67.1	63.2
Reno	1 631	22 803	4 372	3 990	3 407	822	628	790	34 625	1 633	20.6	23.6	49.0
Republic	192	1 395	313	184	207	65	33	37	26 753	575	13.0	34.6	60.7
Rice	267	2 760	389	440	266	140	D	85	30 907	532	15.0	38.9	54.5
Riley	1 608	20 662	3 392	599	4 333	873	1 059	592	28 651	493	24.3	22.7	44.6
Rooks	198	1 603	D	119	D	78	D	56	34 784	440	10.9	50.0	48.2
Rush	101	1 100	D	D	67	39	D	39	35 681	528	12.3	40.7	47.0
Russell	272	1 993	D	D	268	82	D	63	31 840	504	11.1	36.5	48.2
Saline	1 537	27 229	4 511	5 372	3 975	821	1 200	921	33 837	674	19.7	30.1	46.7
Scott	199	1 387	373	37	281	103	45	42	30 472	269	14.5	51.7	64.3
Sedgwick	11 852	227 564	34 059	46 433	28 883	9 324	9 971	10 241	45 001	1 344	36.5	19.0	46.1
Seward	556	10 036	1 155	D	1 261	210	155	382	38 044	363	8.8	39.7	44.6
Shawnee	4 218	76 525	17 831	6 340	9 715	5 491	4 515	3 146	41 108	826	39.8	11.3	39.3
Sheridan	103	652	D	D	D	D	D	24	36 299	384	6.0	60.4	67.7
Sherman	258	2 284	676	D	395	98	70	60	26 189	416	6.3	51.2	58.7
Smith	138	894	D	D	172	72	D	23	26 021	497	12.3	47.3	62.2
Stafford	130	646	D	D	D	62	12	20	30 995	536	9.0	45.0	51.3
Stanton	64	464	D	D	61	51	24	18	39 800	278	0.7	54.0	52.5
Stevens	140	2 144	D	129	168	D	D	77	36 036	315	6.0	41.0	38.4
Sumner	483	4 481	931	903	618	215	73	146	32 645	1 096	17.5	33.2	51.8
Thomas	338	2 841	384	84	686	132	66	91	32 145	460	10.0	51.5	58.5
Trego	132	954	D	42	154	35	D	32	33 612	384	9.9	47.9	50.3
Wabaunsee	126	882	134	136	106	50	8	23	26 541	617	18.2	27.9	43.9
Wallace	58	305	D	D	D	D	D	10	32 551	294	6.1	57.5	54.1
Washington	213	1 504	382	178	222	70	26	38	25 223	732	15.6	37.6	52.3
Wichita	89	541	D	D	D	29	D	19	35 055	265	7.9	60.0	62.6
Wilson	240	3 522	700	976	268	102	48	142	40 364	423	13.0	33.1	52.2
Woodson	85	458	130	D	62	D	8	12	26 972	315	14.0	41.9	53.0
Wyandotte	3 072	68 001	13 947	9 948	7 425	1 030	2 408	3 105	45 659	164	70.7	1.8	39.6
KENTUCKY	91 418	1 535 417	247 078	226 808	203 584	71 574	71 029	60 162	39 183	77 064	36.5	6.2	41.7
Adair	316	4 139	706	360	687	D	56	102	24 546	1 243	33.8	3.8	38.5
Allen	241	3 375	D	D	391	D	D	96	28 451	1 080	35.7	4.6	48.0
Anderson	324	3 327	343	947	720	D	83	109	32 700	676	38.2	3.4	40.4
Ballard	127	1 708	D	D	159	D	D	92	53 902	408	36.5	11.3	46.1
Barren	869	14 665	2 492	3 813	2 318	387	280	448	30 532	1 869	39.5	4.4	51.1
Bath	147	1 170	221	D	184	D	35	35	29 839	690	23.9	8.4	47.4
Bell	487	6 760	1 453	1 057	1 488	266	98	204	30 123	81	56.8	3.7	48.1
Boone	3 014	74 617	4 523	13 630	8 932	3 783	1 898	3 129	41 934	608	53.5	3.5	40.3
Bourbon	389	5 111	709	1 455	849	D	245	213	41 690	907	38.4	11.4	53.3
Boyd	1 365	22 464	2 614	3 969	608	629	977	43 502	214	37.9	1.4	35.5
Boyle	742	14 756	3 095	2 128	1 690	337	303	442	29 979	620	38.7	8.5	39.0
Bracken	94	877	84	D	128	D	22	27	30 715	587	28.4	3.7	42.2
Breathitt	242	2 886	836	45	489	D	89	85	29 584	120	34.2	10.0	26.7
Breckinridge	300	2 420	554	257	543	138	68	69	28 654	1 304	27.2	7.6	37.3
Bullitt	1 073	17 185	1 188	2 717	1 609	303	359	549	31 922	488	54.5	1.8	43.9
Butler	196	1 991	319	D	239	D	D	60	30 273	697	23.4	8.3	36.4
Caldwell	284	3 781	D	D	670	123	52	110	29 164	538	32.5	8.0	34.6
Calloway	845	13 774	2 298	2 622	1 808	401	333	396	28 715	821	40.4	9.4	38.4
Campbell	1 646	23 641	3 130	2 294	4 193	484	988	822	34 760	504	48.0	1.6	42.1
Carlisle	84	622	D	93	106	D	D	16	26 018	325	41.2	14.2	39.7
Carroll	235	5 810	D	2 653	616	77	93	316	54 460	278	20.1	5.4	37.4
Carter	416	4 985	528	D	882	D	D	123	24 699	786	30.8	3.7	31.3
Casey	237	2 988	506	D	378	D	D	79	26 282	1 118	27.4	4.1	52.6
Christian	1 318	22 984	3 086	5 652	3 144	682	687	796	34 653	1 179	27.1	10.7	45.9
Clark	735	11 725	1 505	2 402	1 558	291	357	412	35 158	883	42.7	7.1	39.2

Table B. States and Counties — **Agriculture**

STATE County	Land in farms — Acreage (1,000) [117]	Percent change, 2007–2012 [118]	Average size of farm [119]	Total irrigated (1,000) [120]	Total cropland (1,000) [121]	Value of land and buildings — Average per farm (dollars) [122]	Average per acre [123]	Value of machinery and equipment, average per farm (dollars) [124]	Value of products sold — Total (mil dol) [125]	Average per farm (dollars) [126]	Percent from: Crops [127]	Livestock and poultry products [128]	Percent of farms with sales of: $10,000 or more [129]	$100,000 or more [130]	Government payments — Total ($1,000) [131]	Percent of farms [132]
KANSAS—Cont'd																
Neosho	308	-4.2	439	0.1	175.4	657 053	1 497	105 855	68.0	96 806	60.8	39.2	50.1	15.1	2 284	57.0
Ness	678	9.4	1 218	4.8	412.3	1 267 795	1 041	143 088	63.5	114 077	71.7	28.3	55.1	28.4	7 435	90.7
Norton	502	-5.5	1 368	14.5	270.6	1 812 496	1 325	210 428	146.1	397 976	34.9	65.1	66.5	32.7	3 716	85.3
Osage	442	16.3	436	0.0	251.4	709 350	1 626	105 941	71.0	70 021	52.4	47.6	43.3	14.9	4 728	64.1
Osborne	440	4.7	1 283	6.7	232.5	1 758 099	1 370	162 679	69.6	202 854	67.6	32.4	70.0	42.3	3 509	85.1
Ottawa	420	-4.0	800	4.2	239.0	1 505 440	1 883	167 135	99.0	188 631	60.6	39.4	64.4	28.0	3 509	82.3
Pawnee	480	-1.4	1 198	78.5	398.5	2 184 032	1 823	247 526	362.3	903 614	25.4	74.6	61.3	35.4	5 993	90.3
Phillips	495	0.0	1 123	7.5	232.2	1 404 333	1 251	170 676	100.4	227 633	48.7	51.3	63.7	34.9	3 275	76.9
Pottawatomie	410	-4.4	460	21.9	164.9	878 335	1 908	101 524	117.0	131 421	44.8	55.2	53.9	17.9	2 860	57.2
Pratt	465	-3.3	855	86.2	356.8	1 368 877	1 600	188 613	273.4	503 547	46.0	54.0	53.6	33.0	7 049	86.6
Rawlins	609	3.1	1 984	17.7	354.9	3 461 316	1 744	266 081	91.4	297 700	75.7	24.3	85.7	54.1	4 191	87.9
Reno	790	1.1	483	58.4	591.7	868 492	1 796	138 632	267.3	163 698	56.7	43.3	50.6	22.3	9 785	73.1
Republic	361	-11.2	628	46.5	258.5	1 664 640	2 651	228 520	197.3	343 073	58.8	41.2	71.7	37.7	4 144	78.6
Rice	458	6.8	860	28.6	360.9	1 373 859	1 597	238 983	258.2	485 303	38.3	61.7	62.8	37.8	5 201	79.3
Riley	218	-5.9	443	4.1	99.4	809 619	1 829	107 047	54.4	110 404	66.7	33.3	54.6	22.7	1 265	64.9
Rooks	551	-1.8	1 253	6.9	316.9	1 644 650	1 312	187 098	85.3	193 841	66.6	33.4	58.2	35.7	3 975	85.2
Rush	453	11.6	858	13.2	321.9	1 112 680	1 297	166 716	66.8	126 566	71.4	28.6	55.7	25.9	5 200	86.7
Russell	436	-1.8	864	0.5	234.9	986 889	1 142	129 329	56.8	112 649	64.6	35.4	56.0	22.8	4 283	83.9
Saline	364	-15.5	541	4.8	236.2	1 068 445	1 976	155 677	84.4	125 258	70.5	29.5	58.6	25.4	3 461	77.0
Scott	453	0.0	1 686	36.5	363.4	2 556 929	1 517	344 584	979.8	3 642 543	6.6	93.4	71.7	46.5	4 947	76.6
Sedgwick	487	-4.6	362	45.4	396.0	860 281	2 376	133 063	148.5	110 479	87.7	12.3	52.8	20.4	4 973	58.3
Seward	402	1.5	1 107	101.0	307.7	1 274 033	1 151	214 950	465.3	1 281 838	20.6	79.4	46.3	26.4	4 481	77.4
Shawnee	194	-5.8	235	19.0	117.7	585 475	2 489	78 510	50.3	60 844	83.0	17.0	39.5	10.4	2 350	40.8
Sheridan	562	7.6	1 463	79.3	363.5	2 808 255	1 919	288 505	328.7	855 951	33.3	66.7	79.7	51.0	5 406	83.6
Sherman	595	-9.6	1 430	87.0	498.7	2 441 558	1 707	280 512	170.2	409 043	77.2	22.8	63.5	41.8	7 341	86.8
Smith	500	9.4	1 007	7.3	334.4	1 633 296	1 622	212 620	111.0	223 270	67.2	32.8	71.6	38.6	5 354	84.3
Stafford	499	-0.7	931	103.4	396.5	1 644 125	1 767	234 315	197.6	368 696	60.8	39.2	55.6	36.4	6 769	85.6
Stanton	429	3.6	1 544	76.7	390.6	1 708 899	1 107	304 309	163.7	588 986	48.6	51.4	54.7	36.3	6 864	91.4
Stevens	456	-9.5	1 446	145.2	354.3	1 982 368	1 371	373 492	328.5	1 042 711	44.0	56.0	47.3	31.4	5 414	84.4
Sumner	720	1.4	657	16.1	592.9	1 177 329	1 793	178 303	168.7	153 935	88.8	11.2	62.9	28.2	7 384	77.0
Thomas	675	2.7	1 468	90.0	576.5	3 128 313	2 132	332 954	253.4	550 976	57.6	42.4	73.3	47.0	8 819	80.7
Trego	447	4.0	1 163	6.7	258.7	1 525 997	1 312	157 602	58.9	153 425	60.8	39.2	62.8	28.4	3 651	89.6
Wabaunsee	396	-15.8	642	7.0	107.6	944 000	1 470	92 042	58.3	94 561	36.9	63.1	53.3	21.1	1 959	56.7
Wallace	488	13.6	1 660	58.0	353.3	2 093 398	1 261	233 490	97.2	330 708	66.2	33.8	64.3	40.5	6 452	85.0
Washington	490	-10.6	669	9.7	298.2	1 562 583	2 334	197 657	187.1	255 668	53.2	46.8	69.5	36.9	5 492	79.5
Wichita	464	-10.8	1 750	67.5	351.2	2 375 008	1 357	320 019	624.8	2 357 736	D	D	72.1	49.1	5 701	87.2
Wilson	255	-23.6	602	2.2	142.4	865 076	1 437	129 043	55.4	131 021	84.4	15.6	62.4	23.6	1 636	65.0
Woodson	295	12.6	935	0.0	153.9	1 286 667	1 376	140 746	54.6	173 343	49.5	50.5	60.0	28.9	1 856	69.5
Wyandotte	12	-33.7	73	D	7.3	352 140	4 809	42 561	3.3	20 067	82.2	17.8	22.6	3.0	106	9.8
KENTUCKY	13 049	-6.7	169	73.6	6 336.2	512 033	3 024	70 188	5 067.3	65 755	45.0	55.0	36.5	8.2	169 821	43.3
Adair	170	-9.5	137	0.1	66.6	350 537	2 560	49 813	53.4	42 936	25.9	74.1	37.4	7.1	2 392	54.9
Allen	146	-12.6	135	0.3	52.3	398 629	2 955	51 991	53.2	49 291	26.5	73.5	39.4	6.9	2 086	44.4
Anderson	81	-7.5	120	0.2	29.4	373 490	3 116	48 127	12.7	18 857	33.7	66.3	29.6	3.3	625	22.9
Ballard	107	-2.7	263	0.4	85.2	893 627	3 402	150 120	57.6	141 206	54.7	45.3	42.6	14.7	1 937	65.9
Barren	249	-6.1	133	0.2	130.0	391 780	2 945	68 049	113.0	60 474	33.4	66.6	45.2	8.2	4 232	40.6
Bath	142	10.2	206	0.0	47.9	402 174	1 951	58 223	19.3	27 915	46.7	53.3	42.6	5.8	1 041	41.6
Bell	8	-20.9	100	0.0	1.8	193 704	1 945	25 827	0.5	6 037	D	D	21.0	0.0	7	7.4
Boone	67	-10.1	111	0.2	28.3	682 016	6 170	64 265	12.4	20 467	66.2	33.8	26.3	4.6	450	26.2
Bourbon	184	-0.3	203	0.4	74.8	862 352	4 256	90 714	108.4	119 568	34.5	65.5	50.3	13.2	1 916	39.6
Boyd	22	-24.1	102	0.0	4.8	237 617	2 333	53 234	1.9	8 813	27.0	73.0	13.6	0.9	22	6.5
Boyle	102	7.8	164	0.2	41.9	557 629	3 405	64 198	31.0	49 953	22.9	77.1	41.5	9.8	687	33.5
Bracken	87	-13.8	148	0.2	29.0	309 826	2 095	53 532	10.9	18 547	62.5	37.5	31.9	3.4	837	39.0
Breathitt	22	-49.0	185	0.0	4.8	264 842	1 430	58 558	1.7	14 267	43.0	57.0	14.2	3.3	192	39.2
Breckinridge	260	-5.4	199	0.0	116.6	477 849	2 399	64 376	79.5	60 995	42.8	57.2	40.3	8.2	3 246	58.2
Bullitt	46	-9.8	95	D	20.2	344 717	3 645	48 629	7.7	15 873	59.6	40.4	21.5	2.7	369	23.0
Butler	153	-12.3	219	0.2	62.8	442 750	2 023	59 912	42.4	60 822	54.7	45.3	29.6	7.9	2 052	48.6
Caldwell	133	-6.5	248	D	85.5	678 645	2 735	83 006	38.5	71 561	86.7	13.3	33.1	7.4	2 270	60.4
Calloway	176	11.6	214	3.8	131.9	636 456	2 968	109 851	109.7	133 619	57.3	42.7	35.8	16.2	5 573	68.7
Campbell	42	-10.9	84	0.1	15.0	367 524	4 393	49 331	6.9	13 718	45.7	54.3	24.4	3.2	179	16.3
Carlisle	99	3.0	303	0.6	79.6	858 588	2 829	151 486	73.1	224 939	46.6	53.4	38.2	20.0	2 245	74.2
Carroll	54	-15.9	193	0.1	21.7	508 050	2 637	55 694	6.4	23 169	69.9	30.1	36.0	2.5	354	41.7
Carter	106	-15.7	135	0.1	22.6	236 774	1 758	40 621	9.5	12 080	32.7	67.3	21.5	1.7	400	23.9
Casey	179	-6.5	160	0.1	60.6	325 356	2 031	49 997	29.6	26 471	47.1	52.9	38.2	5.1	1 559	47.5
Christian	360	4.0	306	3.3	252.3	1 055 497	3 454	121 645	185.8	157 625	80.2	19.8	48.3	20.6	7 302	56.4
Clark	137	-7.9	156	0.2	50.5	510 663	3 282	63 019	34.8	39 361	31.7	68.3	40.1	8.3	790	25.3

STATE County	Water use, 2010		Wholesale trade,[1] 2012				Retail trade,[2] 2012				Real estate and rental and leasing,[2] 2012			
	Total water withdrawn (mil gal/day)	Gallons withdrawn per person per day	Number of establish-ments	Number of employees	Sales (mil dol)	Annual payroll (mil dol)	Number of establish-ments	Number of employees	Sales (mil dol)	Annual payroll (mil dol)	Number of establish-ments	Number of employees	Receipts (mil dol)	Annual payroll (mil dol)
	133	134	135	136	137	138	139	140	141	142	143	144	145	146
KANSAS—Cont'd														
Neosho	2.8	170	28	223	96.2	8.2	86	800	197.7	18.8	11	18	2.0	0.4
Ness	4.1	1 304	16	D	D	D	19	98	15.4	1.6	1	D	D	D
Norton	13.8	2 437	8	68	38.3	2.5	27	183	51.2	3.9	1	D	D	D
Osage	2.3	144	15	73	48.6	2.9	42	360	74.0	5.8	5	D	D	D
Osborne	2.0	513	14	136	157.7	5.9	31	212	46.6	3.2	NA	NA	NA	NA
Ottawa	2.8	458	10	D	D	D	14	79	16.2	1.3	3	2	1.3	0.1
Pawnee	71.5	10 260	9	100	130.3	5.0	28	224	50.1	4.7	4	16	1.9	0.3
Phillips	18.3	3 251	13	63	69.7	2.8	35	227	51.5	4.1	1	D	D	D
Pottawatomie	40.7	1 883	30	549	224.8	23.5	81	1 819	338.9	48.4	18	D	D	D
Pratt	89.1	9 225	25	190	230.6	9.2	54	734	173.3	16.4	13	36	2.7	0.6
Rawlins	14.1	5 613	9	109	108.6	6.4	15	103	25.1	1.8	1	D	D	D
Reno	70.9	1 098	84	D	D	D	265	3 345	818.1	74.6	67	167	26.8	4.6
Republic	17.7	3 544	15	120	181.0	3.9	39	237	48.2	4.2	2	D	D	D
Rice	24.3	2 409	18	113	113.7	4.9	39	280	50.0	4.7	3	5	0.5	0.1
Riley	5.3	75	26	176	82.3	7.3	272	4 389	903.9	81.6	111	D	D	D
Rooks	11.1	2 142	17	159	178.2	6.9	28	200	69.2	3.8	2	D	D	D
Rush	8.9	2 703	14	74	58.6	2.9	10	65	29.1	1.8	NA	NA	NA	NA
Russell	1.3	182	14	114	101.2	4.3	39	267	76.5	4.7	8	25	3.1	0.6
Saline	10.4	188	95	1 195	996.5	54.7	250	3 989	1 120.4	87.4	64	208	52.5	6.4
Scott	43.7	8 857	19	126	192.1	6.1	33	223	56.8	3.9	4	3	0.5	0.1
Sedgwick	94.0	189	589	8 367	8 308.4	478.6	1 720	27 362	7 201.5	646.4	554	3 997	582.4	133.0
Seward	157.4	6 857	36	407	264.4	19.7	91	1 262	371.0	28.5	20	54	10.3	2.1
Shawnee	36.0	202	154	1 992	1 376.1	100.0	653	9 678	2 364.3	212.6	202	903	134.7	26.3
Sheridan	72.3	28 290	14	124	160.6	7.1	19	89	21.0	1.6	NA	NA	NA	NA
Sherman	99.1	16 491	23	225	341.0	9.3	34	409	132.3	8.9	4	D	D	D
Smith	2.2	563	10	134	128.2	4.8	24	169	67.4	3.4	2	D	D	D
Stafford	88.5	19 950	8	D	D	D	17	125	34.8	2.3	1	D	D	D
Stanton	113.5	50 774	9	D	D	D	5	D	D	D	1	D	D	D
Stevens	197.6	34 521	11	95	128.0	4.2	14	144	37.0	3.3	2	D	D	D
Sumner	9.4	391	28	167	157.4	7.0	65	592	159.8	11.1	12	D	D	D
Thomas	82.4	10 433	28	296	388.2	16.2	63	666	233.5	14.3	8	34	8.5	0.8
Trego	6.1	2 029	11	78	104.2	2.7	24	154	47.7	3.1	3	D	D	D
Wabaunsee	3.7	519	4	34	20.5	1.5	18	88	36.7	1.7	4	D	D	D
Wallace	45.3	30 478	5	D	D	D	7	42	7.6	1.0	2	D	D	D
Washington	5.7	988	21	183	264.8	6.3	36	215	45.6	4.1	6	9	0.4	0.0
Wichita	53.9	24 105	11	93	111.4	3.8	14	70	19.8	1.5	NA	NA	NA	NA
Wilson	2.6	281	5	20	31.7	0.7	43	234	57.7	4.5	3	3	0.2	0.0
Woodson	1.2	369	5	44	25.9	1.7	17	69	22.0	1.7	3	D	D	D
Wyandotte	287.0	1 822	225	5 758	5 611.1	302.2	452	6 929	1 769.4	172.6	136	593	112.2	20.2
KENTUCKY	4 326.5	997	3 690	57 630	71 745.9	3 090.3	15 224	202 615	54 870.0	4 619.2	3 534	18 250	4 845.5	637.3
Adair	3.4	184	15	72	42.1	1.6	64	691	204.3	16.2	5	D	D	D
Allen	2.3	114	9	D	D	D	59	410	111.3	8.4	9	23	2.4	0.6
Anderson	4.1	190	6	33	10.1	1.4	51	738	188.9	15.4	14	49	4.3	1.0
Ballard	31.7	3 837	4	D	D	D	26	162	57.6	3.6	3	D	D	D
Barren	10.4	246	39	D	D	D	188	2 193	562.8	49.5	23	71	9.9	1.6
Bath	6.0	515	3	D	D	D	31	182	47.8	3.8	8	D	D	D
Bell	4.4	152	18	189	212.9	5.9	128	1 515	365.1	31.2	19	71	9.2	1.6
Boone	11.1	94	170	6 614	21 688.2	542.7	470	9 132	2 564.6	208.6	102	719	175.3	25.2
Bourbon	3.2	162	4	D	D	D	65	876	248.2	21.8	10	16	4.0	0.5
Boyd	44.1	890	65	904	1 288.6	39.3	239	3 719	1 010.4	78.8	45	408	52.6	14.6
Boyle	6.8	240	20	140	114.1	5.7	134	1 717	431.4	39.6	23	66	8.7	1.5
Bracken	1.7	203	2	D	D	D	18	131	25.6	2.2	2	D	D	D
Breathitt	10.3	744	1	D	D	D	45	499	118.3	10.4	8	21	2.6	0.5
Breckinridge	2.6	132	8	72	36.0	2.3	55	543	148.2	12.2	9	23	2.2	0.8
Bullitt	6.9	92	28	564	519.7	22.0	144	1 550	586.4	36.0	31	118	19.6	4.0
Butler	1.7	134	6	D	D	D	33	232	49.9	4.3	4	5	0.3	0.1
Caldwell	1.4	108	9	D	D	D	57	687	159.9	15.0	6	9	1.7	0.3
Calloway	6.4	172	39	D	D	D	153	1 987	523.8	41.4	37	188	20.8	4.5
Campbell	29.9	330	60	1 036	835.3	60.6	265	4 285	1 105.2	94.3	62	544	93.9	26.4
Carlisle	0.7	141	4	20	4.2	0.5	12	81	19.9	1.6	7	8	2.3	0.2
Carroll	42.9	3 965	8	53	17.0	1.8	49	629	187.8	13.7	3	D	D	D
Carter	5.1	184	11	289	209.6	7.6	96	881	272.8	17.6	13	D	D	D
Casey	1.8	115	12	136	33.7	3.1	56	375	83.1	6.7	4	11	0.5	0.1
Christian	17.4	235	67	886	1 060.4	33.1	249	3 239	1 019.9	77.6	58	D	D	D
Clark	94.0	2 638	34	623	873.0	27.9	127	1 623	471.5	37.0	28	71	12.0	1.7

1. Merchant wholesalers, except manufacturers' sales branches and offices. 2. Employer establishments.

Table B. States and Counties — Professional Services, Manufacturing, and Accommodation and Food Services

STATE County	Professional, scientific, and technical services, 2012				Manufacturing, 2012				Accommodation and food services, 2012			
	Number of establish-ments	Number of employees	Receipts (mil dol)	Annual payroll (mil dol)	Number of establish-ments	Number of employees	Receipts (mil dol)	Annual payroll (mil dol)	Number of establish-ments	Number of employees	Sales (mil dol)	Annual payroll (mil dol)
	147	148	149	150	151	152	153	154	155	156	157	158
KANSAS—Cont'd												
Neosho	33	123	42.9	5.5	31	922	223.1	39.6	27	D	D	D
Ness	5	20	1.7	0.5	4	23	7.5	1.0	7	D	D	D
Norton	14	46	3.8	0.8	5	D	D	D	13	140	6.1	1.8
Osage	17	54	6.0	1.6	3	D	D	D	20	D	D	D
Osborne	7	42	12.6	1.6	6	113	D	4.5	12	D	D	D
Ottawa	14	D	D	D	8	84	D	2.2	10	41	1.2	0.3
Pawnee	16	74	8.1	2.2	NA	NA	NA	NA	16	153	5.5	1.5
Phillips	16	97	11.6	4.0	10	178	D	11.1	14	140	4.3	1.0
Pottawatomie	52	198	15.5	5.8	30	1 368	377.5	74.6	35	422	17.7	4.5
Pratt	28	115	11.7	4.7	9	78	42.6	3.4	32	438	25.0	5.1
Rawlins	11	16	1.3	0.3	7	31	9.4	1.2	5	25	0.5	0.1
Reno	102	642	61.8	24.5	87	3 752	1 232.8	168.4	117	2 141	91.6	26.3
Republic	13	25	3.4	0.6	10	168	D	6.3	11	D	D	D
Rice	16	143	9.4	2.6	14	328	291.2	14.9	22	D	D	D
Riley	146	D	D	D	30	480	94.5	18.9	166	3 903	146.8	42.1
Rooks	13	43	4.9	1.9	6	130	D	4.1	17	88	3.1	0.8
Rush	6	14	1.4	0.7	6	320	D	11.3	7	36	1.5	0.3
Russell	12	44	4.7	1.2	7	114	D	5.1	18	283	11.6	3.3
Saline	112	D	D	D	75	5 497	D	237.2	137	3 047	119.6	31.8
Scott	19	52	7.7	1.6	6	20	D	1.0	14	D	D	D
Sedgwick	1 155	10 100	1 586.7	570.9	533	40 629	15 547.1	2 316.4	1 102	22 151	1 029.8	287.6
Seward	22	139	12.0	5.0	7	D	D	D	45	789	40.4	10.4
Shawnee	449	D	D	D	105	5 291	2 588.3	244.4	362	D	D	D
Sheridan	3	16	1.0	0.3	3	6	D	D	6	D	D	D
Sherman	22	79	6.6	1.9	5	46	D	2.1	25	D	D	D
Smith	8	21	2.6	0.4	6	107	D	3.3	8	D	D	D
Stafford	6	11	2.0	0.7	NA	NA	NA	NA	10	D	D	D
Stanton	5	16	1.2	0.4	NA	NA	NA	NA	4	D	D	D
Stevens	11	40	3.3	0.9	4	22	D	1.9	12	144	5.0	1.3
Sumner	32	114	13.9	5.6	37	827	D	35.6	42	458	19.3	5.0
Thomas	28	65	7.2	2.1	9	45	D	1.8	31	464	21.8	6.2
Trego	8	24	1.4	0.4	6	41	D	1.4	11	119	4.8	1.2
Wabaunsee	7	8	1.2	0.3	7	D	D	D	8	30	1.3	0.2
Wallace	3	D	D	D	NA	NA	NA	NA	3	D	D	D
Washington	10	24	3.4	0.8	8	174	35.1	5.4	12	110	3.2	0.8
Wichita	4	6	0.3	0.1	4	62	D	2.3	4	D	D	D
Wilson	13	34	4.1	1.1	19	888	181.5	35.0	20	D	D	D
Woodson	5	D	D	D	3	13	D	0.5	8	D	D	D
Wyandotte	191	2 703	305.9	93.5	174	10 537	11 105.9	666.4	265	5 206	284.6	75.1
KENTUCKY	8 101	62 851	7 782.5	2 816.7	3 782	213 545	129 284.4	10 140.1	7 678	156 965	7 500.1	2 083.5
Adair	17	D	D	D	25	323	153.1	10.9	19	D	D	D
Allen	7	84	3.4	1.7	10	D	D	D	16	D	D	D
Anderson	29	96	11.1	3.1	26	1 130	746.5	70.8	30	403	20.4	5.5
Ballard	10	D	D	D	11	678	D	49.0	10	D	D	D
Barren	47	265	22.5	7.9	45	3 480	929.5	139.8	86	1 554	71.9	18.6
Bath	10	D	D	D	8	D	D	4.8	12	D	D	D
Bell	29	104	9.2	3.3	19	1 075	304.4	34.6	44	855	36.7	9.5
Boone	224	2 184	228.4	72.6	188	12 910	5 069.7	653.0	286	D	D	D
Bourbon	32	321	35.0	14.7	24	1 731	1 066.6	78.2	27	D	D	D
Boyd	96	720	73.9	33.4	34	2 798	D	218.5	120	2 704	129.4	35.0
Boyle	55	275	34.6	10.2	22	1 881	673.6	77.7	61	1 325	59.6	17.2
Bracken	4	12	0.6	0.3	NA	NA	NA	NA	8	D	D	D
Breathitt	10	D	D	D	5	25	D	1.0	10	D	D	D
Breckinridge	19	77	6.0	2.0	13	248	29.7	9.4	15	195	8.7	2.4
Bullitt	77	336	31.4	11.4	42	2 117	811.5	85.7	90	1 930	82.9	22.4
Butler	10	31	1.6	0.7	13	573	185.8	24.0	13	D	D	D
Caldwell	18	45	3.5	0.8	12	864	391.2	31.8	25	393	13.2	3.5
Calloway	65	357	29.6	12.5	30	2 548	828.7	93.4	87	1 679	60.4	16.1
Campbell	146	950	125.1	41.8	78	2 651	994.7	123.9	208	D	D	D
Carlisle	2	D	D	D	4	80	10.4	1.8	6	31	1.3	0.3
Carroll	16	93	10.0	4.6	13	2 452	D	177.2	28	D	D	D
Carter	28	111	6.9	2.6	15	791	253.5	23.6	32	636	28.1	7.3
Casey	10	D	D	D	31	1 266	237.7	28.4	12	192	7.6	2.6
Christian	111	958	100.0	41.0	72	4 647	1 894.8	207.8	113	D	D	D
Clark	55	293	31.4	13.5	40	2 378	1 016.0	108.4	58	1 148	56.5	15.6

1. Establishment subject to federal tax.

STATE County	Health care and social assistance, 2012				Other services, 2012				Nonemployer businesses, 2014		Value of residential construction authorized by building permits, 2015	
	Number of establishments	Number of employees	Receipts (mil dol)	Annual payroll (mil dol)	Number of establishments	Number of employees	Receipts (mil dol)	Annual payroll (mil dol)	Number	Receipts (mil dol)	New Construction ($1,000)	Number of housing units
	159	160	161	162	163	164	165	166	167	168	169	170
KANSAS—Cont'd												
Neosho	52	1 148	94.8	36.3	31	102	8.7	1.7	1 098	38.5	810	5
Ness	9	257	15.5	7.4	14	D	D	D	301	10.5	0	0
Norton	22	497	26.3	13.1	11	D	D	D	417	15.7	900	8
Osage	27	1 648	40.6	25.0	18	D	D	D	1 083	42.1	3 406	24
Osborne	13	334	16.2	8.1	10	33	4.5	0.9	350	11.2	0	0
Ottawa	12	D	D	D	11	D	D	D	485	18.2	221	3
Pawnee	16	1 210	87.4	43.8	14	30	2.7	0.5	409	21.3	80	1
Phillips	19	346	21.3	10.5	25	84	11.0	1.6	521	18.0	4 050	23
Pottawatomie	50	1 048	78.1	29.6	53	152	14.6	3.8	1 726	74.7	43 326	197
Pratt	36	713	64.2	27.4	34	107	9.5	2.3	792	41.6	549	3
Rawlins	9	210	12.3	5.8	7	11	1.2	0.2	245	8.2	518	4
Reno	176	4 895	441.4	176.7	115	514	46.5	12.0	3 854	133.1	15 408	147
Republic	15	296	16.8	8.1	15	42	4.0	0.8	388	14.4	135	1
Rice	20	400	22.1	11.7	19	62	8.2	1.7	644	19.8	2 963	16
Riley	180	3 201	313.2	112.9	119	1 100	208.7	44.9	3 212	135.7	54 357	299
Rooks	12	245	17.8	7.2	10	39	3.5	0.7	595	23.7	325	0
Rush	7	163	9.1	3.7	5	D	D	D	296	10.1	0	0
Russell	13	132	8.1	3.6	18	71	7.4	1.7	837	46.5	955	3
Saline	181	D	D	D	113	D	D	D	3 510	135.9	14 364	82
Scott	11	341	19.6	10.4	17	42	6.5	1.0	449	18.4	627	4
Sedgwick	1 358	34 266	3 501.4	1 450.6	796	5 733	677.1	172.7	31 141	1 442.2	302 583	1 785
Seward	74	1 079	91.4	35.5	44	166	23.0	4.5	1 267	74.0	1 604	10
Shawnee	523	16 404	1 706.2	740.6	371	3 580	322.3	102.6	9 697	404.1	46 932	232
Sheridan	7	D	D	D	10	58	1.8	0.3	280	12.4	NA	NA
Sherman	38	353	23.9	11.7	20	71	7.4	1.7	455	18.0	0	0
Smith	7	D	D	D	13	D	D	D	315	9.0	0	0
Stafford	15	168	10.1	4.7	13	21	1.7	0.3	373	15.6	1 635	9
Stanton	3	D	D	D	5	D	D	D	206	9.6	0	0
Stevens	6	D	D	D	8	D	D	D	366	18.0	711	4
Sumner	58	947	58.2	25.4	39	116	9.9	2.6	1 459	54.5	2 228	23
Thomas	34	407	33.1	13.4	29	121	10.8	2.9	804	26.7	3 086	18
Trego	6	D	D	D	9	22	1.7	0.5	338	13.3	0	0
Wabaunsee	8	D	D	D	6	D	D	D	510	18.7	4 140	18
Wallace	4	D	D	D	6	D	D	D	163	5.9	0	0
Washington	25	317	16.3	7.6	19	D	D	D	443	17.0	0	0
Wichita	6	D	D	D	8	D	D	D	191	9.4	0	0
Wilson	33	695	46.6	18.8	17	35	3.8	0.8	588	21.6	0	0
Woodson	10	126	5.7	2.1	5	D	D	D	281	14.6	265	4
Wyandotte	320	13 552	1 568.6	707.1	222	1 320	270.7	42.0	7 594	287.5	31 876	179
KENTUCKY	11 425	251 878	26 264.7	10 184.1	5 849	38 364	4 071.4	1 090.0	277 731	11 596.1	1 467 802	10 566
Adair	36	739	48.8	20.2	14	D	D	D	1 542	58.1	0	0
Allen	23	D	D	D	17	D	D	D	1 419	56.1	900	10
Anderson	34	329	19.1	8.4	30	84	8.6	2.3	1 378	44.6	10 182	50
Ballard	6	D	D	D	5	D	D	D	458	13.2	NA	NA
Barren	105	D	D	D	59	223	14.9	4.7	3 202	114.1	12 907	84
Bath	9	296	10.1	4.3	8	D	D	D	799	22.6	250	1
Bell	78	D	D	D	35	154	11.2	2.9	1 463	40.3	1 995	20
Boone	243	4 772	446.2	181.8	180	D	D	D	7 348	314.3	73 464	589
Bourbon	47	714	59.3	22.2	21	D	D	D	1 301	52.8	7 370	26
Boyd	245	7 292	993.0	372.3	96	D	D	D	2 547	102.1	0	0
Boyle	132	2 917	297.4	130.9	53	208	16.8	4.2	1 980	70.4	9 432	95
Bracken	8	D	D	D	5	D	D	D	596	16.5	NA	NA
Breathitt	48	1 277	97.7	42.7	10	34	5.2	1.3	563	15.6	90	1
Breckinridge	31	589	39.9	13.5	19	38	3.7	0.8	1 211	54.0	534	6
Bullitt	108	1 386	95.1	39.7	90	1 584	46.3	42.7	4 382	172.1	69 631	342
Butler	20	352	19.9	9.7	18	D	D	D	820	29.7	0	0
Caldwell	34	570	44.7	16.4	17	D	D	D	729	27.0	365	7
Calloway	110	2 119	190.7	73.4	47	182	13.1	3.8	2 427	108.4	7 328	101
Campbell	158	3 490	334.3	130.9	126	D	D	D	5 378	209.1	57 945	319
Carlisle	6	D	D	D	5	10	1.1	0.2	413	14.9	NA	NA
Carroll	20	373	32.0	13.9	14	D	D	D	541	21.0	60	1
Carter	44	519	38.8	14.9	30	D	D	D	1 730	66.2	295	3
Casey	21	527	35.4	16.0	8	34	3.0	0.7	1 181	52.5	0	0
Christian	157	3 130	300.4	106.2	87	D	D	D	3 234	136.4	7 342	79
Clark	126	1 518	139.2	51.2	45	181	15.1	4.4	2 167	78.6	7 211	39

STATE County	Full-time equivalent employees	March payroll (dollars)	Adminis- tration, judicial, and legal	Police and Corrections	Fire Protection	Highways and transpor- tation	Health and Welfare	Natural resources and utilities	Education and libraries	Total (mil dol)	Inter- govern- mental (mil dol)	Total (mil dol)	Per capita[1] (dollars) Total	Property
	171	172	173	174	175	176	177	178	179	180	181	182	183	184
KANSAS—Cont'd														
Neosho	1 176	4 053 546	4.7	4.8	1.4	3.1	33.7	7.7	43.8	111.1	29.1	28.8	1 755	1 392
Ness	342	928 162	3.6	3.8	0.3	7.5	55.5	2.1	25.8	27.2	3.0	10.5	3 412	3 238
Norton	415	1 296 107	5.9	8.5	0.2	5.3	36.1	4.9	38.5	21.8	9.5	8.3	1 476	1 235
Osage	664	1 848 318	7.4	9.1	0.0	4.8	2.0	8.1	66.8	51.8	25.1	19.9	1 231	1 069
Osborne	160	407 550	12.5	11.0	0.0	10.3	6.0	16.5	39.9	12.2	3.9	6.3	1 668	1 374
Ottawa	333	902 710	6.3	6.6	0.0	8.3	3.0	8.5	63.2	26.0	12.4	11.0	1 813	1 494
Pawnee	440	1 250 370	6.8	9.0	0.2	6.2	4.7	6.2	62.4	27.5	10.2	13.2	1 900	1 520
Phillips	269	733 417	9.3	5.4	0.0	11.5	9.3	7.3	56.3	24.1	8.0	10.9	1 969	1 705
Pottawatomie	900	2 555 697	7.0	7.4	0.4	6.4	5.6	4.0	68.4	81.2	25.0	45.4	2 033	1 711
Pratt	620	2 089 279	5.5	7.1	0.6	5.9	5.9	8.3	64.6	48.5	14.6	24.6	2 526	2 145
Rawlins	120	323 307	14.0	8.7	0.1	13.4	2.7	5.2	54.9	9.2	3.2	4.8	1 855	1 554
Reno	3 036	10 310 558	4.2	9.4	4.3	3.9	2.4	5.3	68.8	260.0	97.6	109.2	1 695	1 318
Republic	280	743 094	10.6	6.2	0.0	10.1	3.1	14.2	51.3	22.0	7.1	12.0	2 465	2 116
Rice	740	2 211 947	5.2	5.5	0.1	4.7	28.7	3.7	50.7	54.4	18.2	18.8	1 885	1 542
Riley	2 188	7 227 365	9.0	12.5	5.2	5.3	2.9	8.2	55.4	194.7	54.3	101.1	1 339	930
Rooks	433	1 169 894	7.0	5.2	0.1	6.4	36.2	3.6	40.2	44.1	11.5	14.8	2 837	2 597
Rush	240	677 611	5.6	5.2	0.0	9.2	28.1	6.5	42.1	19.8	4.2	7.4	2 306	2 203
Russell	400	1 117 489	12.4	9.0	1.7	7.9	3.8	13.6	49.3	31.8	7.8	19.4	2 790	2 354
Saline	2 537	8 460 384	4.0	12.5	4.8	4.8	1.1	5.4	63.9	204.8	71.4	88.3	1 578	1 104
Scott	243	604 532	5.5	5.8	0.4	5.4	1.4	5.5	73.4	23.7	6.5	15.0	3 033	2 531
Sedgwick	17 666	64 762 573	6.4	12.0	4.9	3.5	5.0	4.5	61.8	1 873.6	724.4	682.0	1 354	1 041
Seward	1 811	5 549 695	5.2	6.6	1.4	2.3	29.2	3.6	49.3	146.4	48.8	38.4	1 629	1 116
Shawnee	8 380	28 121 726	3.6	11.0	4.3	2.8	2.6	4.9	70.3	768.6	263.0	299.3	1 672	1 189
Sheridan	256	590 482	3.7	3.2	0.0	5.6	53.2	2.1	27.9	10.1	2.5	6.2	2 430	2 074
Sherman	464	1 377 731	5.7	6.0	0.9	6.3	39.8	6.9	32.6	30.8	10.9	12.2	1 999	1 467
Smith	252	661 334	7.3	6.7	0.0	9.5	8.4	7.9	57.9	20.6	8.5	9.3	2 464	2 115
Stafford	276	853 136	9.9	5.7	0.8	9.4	3.5	6.5	62.0	24.1	7.5	12.6	2 881	2 680
Stanton	212	627 118	5.8	6.3	0.0	9.1	35.1	3.1	40.4	19.3	3.0	11.2	5 142	4 980
Stevens	518	1 610 255	4.2	4.8	0.3	4.7	38.6	4.1	41.0	50.0	6.3	27.4	4 762	4 526
Sumner	1 279	3 843 881	5.5	7.0	2.2	5.1	19.6	5.9	51.4	100.9	37.4	33.6	1 421	1 151
Thomas	600	1 667 889	4.5	6.5	1.4	4.8	3.5	6.7	70.3	44.9	12.3	19.0	2 396	1 891
Trego	344	1 000 545	5.7	4.2	0.2	6.3	56.4	2.5	22.3	13.1	3.4	7.5	2 518	2 196
Wabaunsee	308	821 494	10.9	7.3	0.0	6.3	2.4	6.6	65.2	27.8	12.1	10.7	1 521	1 395
Wallace	110	277 969	12.4	3.3	0.0	9.0	2.3	2.0	66.6	8.8	2.7	5.1	3 337	3 267
Washington	376	1 063 217	7.0	4.3	0.0	6.6	18.3	6.1	55.7	29.9	10.0	12.3	2 144	1 966
Wichita	216	654 420	4.5	3.3	0.1	4.9	41.8	2.5	39.5	16.5	3.9	5.9	2 609	2 207
Wilson	601	1 662 978	4.6	6.7	0.8	4.2	19.9	9.3	49.8	43.5	17.0	11.6	1 274	1 131
Woodson	181	419 389	10.5	9.6	3.3	11.4	2.2	8.1	52.8	13.3	5.4	6.7	2 052	1 782
Wyandotte	8 144	34 012 450	5.6	11.1	6.6	2.6	2.4	14.3	54.4	766.0	289.0	302.6	1 901	1 204
KENTUCKY	X	X	X	X	X	X	X	X	X	X	X	X	X	X
Adair	919	2 441 497	2.9	3.7	0.0	1.1	35.9	4.2	51.1	55.9	21.6	8.0	427	308
Allen	767	1 841 667	2.0	8.2	0.2	1.6	4.0	4.1	78.7	41.3	23.7	11.2	555	342
Anderson	809	2 162 986	6.1	5.8	0.3	3.2	5.0	4.0	75.1	51.0	24.5	18.4	846	649
Ballard	248	590 155	9.9	12.4	0.0	2.7	9.1	4.7	61.1	23.3	12.4	8.2	986	597
Barren	1 664	5 001 627	2.5	3.2	0.0	0.8	0.2	25.7	67.1	124.1	60.3	35.4	831	508
Bath	406	1 111 046	4.3	4.3	0.9	1.2	4.3	5.5	79.0	26.0	18.6	5.0	425	253
Bell	1 171	3 090 979	2.7	6.2	2.6	2.0	1.9	1.6	81.4	75.8	50.5	15.0	534	291
Boone	3 843	13 434 279	1.9	8.5	6.9	1.7	0.4	3.4	75.6	360.0	112.7	201.9	1 637	990
Bourbon	965	3 068 260	6.3	8.4	5.9	2.9	15.6	4.1	55.9	56.7	29.4	20.5	1 028	562
Boyd	2 063	6 328 157	3.3	7.1	4.8	2.9	12.1	6.5	61.5	147.1	62.5	56.2	1 143	583
Boyle	1 287	4 095 739	3.9	9.0	16.6	1.6	5.9	2.0	59.3	83.9	32.8	34.1	1 190	651
Bracken	356	894 119	6.9	4.0	0.0	2.5	7.4	5.6	73.1	19.7	12.1	5.3	621	450
Breathitt	629	1 632 815	3.0	3.4	0.6	2.7	1.6	1.3	86.6	44.7	30.3	8.4	615	272
Breckinridge	636	1 726 384	4.2	7.6	0.0	2.7	3.3	0.7	81.4	49.9	26.8	10.3	513	381
Bullitt	2 379	7 126 688	1.5	7.4	2.5	1.5	4.1	1.8	80.6	162.7	71.4	70.4	927	693
Butler	426	1 274 899	3.6	4.6	0.0	4.2	0.0	5.4	82.2	27.2	19.3	5.9	459	211
Caldwell	534	1 550 863	4.7	6.1	2.3	3.5	12.5	10.7	58.9	23.5	15.7	6.2	481	274
Calloway	2 147	6 749 443	2.1	4.3	1.7	1.6	54.4	1.7	34.0	317.2	34.5	23.7	628	447
Campbell	2 562	8 812 479	5.0	13.2	6.5	2.9	0.4	2.0	69.5	232.7	71.5	119.3	1 312	806
Carlisle	229	547 363	15.5	2.7	0.0	3.0	7.2	0.5	71.2	13.3	8.5	2.9	573	399
Carroll	523	1 513 204	6.2	11.6	1.6	2.3	2.6	4.1	71.1	176.6	16.1	13.1	1 202	549
Carter	1 152	2 867 307	1.7	3.7	0.0	1.6	9.7	2.9	78.0	60.6	42.8	11.2	410	234
Casey	760	1 971 527	2.7	6.8	0.5	1.5	27.9	2.2	58.2	51.9	25.0	6.6	412	269
Christian	1 972	5 973 027	3.9	11.1	5.4	1.2	2.6	9.3	61.0	153.9	80.7	50.3	666	318
Clark	1 289	3 897 749	3.3	8.0	8.0	1.8	7.1	3.9	65.0	104.2	43.5	36.8	1 029	594

1. Based on the resident population estimated as of July 1 of the year shown.

Table B. States and Counties — Local Government Finances, Government Employment, and Voting

STATE County	Total (mil dol)	Per capita[1] (dollars)	Education	Health and hospitals	Police protection	Public welfare	Highways	Total (mil dol)	Per capita[1] (dollars)	Federal civilian	Federal military	State and local	Democratic	Republican	All other
	185	186	187	188	189	190	191	192	193	194	195	196	197	198	199
KANSAS—Cont'd															
Neosho	113.5	6 916	38.0	33.2	2.1	0.0	7.7	154.6	9 423	59	66	1 736	35.6	62.2	2.2
Ness	25.4	8 281	22.4	50.3	3.1	0.0	8.6	2.1	688	26	13	435	19.0	79.1	1.9
Norton	22.4	3 997	48.1	6.0	4.3	0.0	6.6	10.5	1 866	26	20	848	20.6	77.8	1.7
Osage	52.1	3 229	56.9	1.1	5.3	0.0	9.4	54.0	3 346	76	65	1 156	33.6	63.9	2.5
Osborne	12.6	3 304	32.2	8.6	8.0	0.0	13.4	3.3	875	28	15	327	20.9	77.2	1.9
Ottawa	26.4	4 347	50.1	4.7	3.2	0.0	13.3	17.8	2 933	26	25	457	22.8	75.3	1.9
Pawnee	26.1	3 762	43.8	6.6	5.2	0.0	13.5	27.5	3 968	38	24	1 781	30.6	67.6	1.8
Phillips	25.4	4 596	38.5	5.1	3.7	0.0	12.6	4.9	881	41	23	776	19.7	78.9	1.4
Pottawatomie	89.9	4 029	54.4	5.8	3.3	0.0	7.9	77.1	3 455	55	95	1 242	26.4	70.4	3.1
Pratt	49.1	5 044	57.5	3.6	5.0	0.0	9.2	35.4	3 643	31	39	1 159	30.9	67.4	1.8
Rawlins	10.8	4 225	35.7	5.3	4.3	0.0	11.1	4.4	1 700	18	11	315	17.6	80.5	1.9
Reno	245.7	3 812	58.1	2.1	5.1	0.0	4.6	208.5	3 236	166	251	5 267	37.4	60.8	1.8
Republic	23.3	4 788	35.1	4.3	3.0	0.0	14.7	7.7	1 591	31	19	491	24.0	74.1	2.0
Rice	56.5	5 654	43.4	25.1	2.5	0.0	7.7	50.8	5 088	43	39	1 063	28.9	69.1	1.9
Riley	230.8	3 057	51.3	0.7	7.0	0.0	6.1	524.1	6 941	445	308	11 295	45.6	52.7	1.7
Rooks	50.5	9 668	22.1	22.3	3.3	5.5	5.9	39.4	7 551	30	21	655	18.1	79.9	2.0
Rush	21.5	6 668	27.9	26.9	0.9	0.0	10.6	8.4	2 621	27	13	329	28.3	68.8	2.9
Russell	31.0	4 458	38.8	4.9	4.7	0.0	12.1	17.1	2 459	35	28	699	22.4	76.2	1.5
Saline	211.2	3 772	45.1	1.4	5.3	0.0	7.8	251.6	4 493	266	226	4 097	35.9	62.2	1.9
Scott	22.4	4 533	43.6	4.5	6.5	2.3	7.7	37.8	7 650	22	21	354	14.7	83.7	1.6
Sedgwick	1 940.5	3 851	46.8	4.2	5.7	0.1	5.3	5 893.5	11 696	4 623	4 925	26 213	42.7	55.4	1.8
Seward	172.9	7 343	40.9	33.7	2.9	0.0	2.5	86.1	3 658	92	95	2 294	28.0	71.0	1.0
Shawnee	739.9	4 134	52.9	2.2	6.5	0.2	2.7	1 291.7	7 217	3 422	991	19 359	49.0	49.3	1.7
Sheridan	9.9	3 891	38.8	11.7	2.2	0.0	16.8	0.6	238	14	10	328	18.5	80.5	1.0
Sherman	28.9	4 724	57.7	3.1	3.6	0.0	7.8	18.3	2 989	51	25	725	25.4	72.4	2.1
Smith	21.3	5 645	40.2	5.3	2.0	0.0	17.3	2.0	535	31	15	342	20.2	78.0	1.8
Stafford	24.7	5 668	48.8	4.4	4.1	0.0	14.9	2.2	513	40	18	600	26.1	72.1	1.8
Stanton	28.2	12 976	20.1	52.9	1.2	0.0	8.9	15.2	6 985	0	0	326	22.7	75.9	1.3
Stevens	55.6	9 664	30.0	27.7	3.3	0.0	8.1	24.5	4 259	23	24	751	13.3	85.3	1.4
Sumner	97.3	4 110	41.6	20.7	4.1	0.0	7.7	85.1	3 595	73	96	1 785	32.4	65.2	2.4
Thomas	47.7	6 010	55.4	1.6	2.9	0.0	9.6	33.5	4 224	29	31	891	21.4	77.2	1.3
Trego	13.1	4 381	37.4	4.9	2.1	0.6	14.1	16.4	5 487	15	12	461	25.1	73.3	1.6
Wabaunsee	25.0	3 546	48.3	1.1	3.9	0.0	12.8	27.4	3 889	26	29	481	29.4	68.0	2.6
Wallace	9.8	6 453	40.5	2.8	3.1	2.3	13.0	5.2	3 412	14	0	160	11.9	85.8	2.2
Washington	29.5	5 125	44.0	14.4	0.8	0.0	17.0	3.2	559	49	23	683	22.1	75.4	2.4
Wichita	16.8	7 467	32.0	38.6	3.0	0.0	8.8	7.0	3 099	16	0	288	16.0	82.4	1.6
Wilson	43.9	4 825	41.2	25.8	5.1	0.0	6.6	43.5	4 772	37	37	907	28.4	69.2	2.5
Woodson	12.5	3 824	43.4	1.9	6.1	0.0	13.6	2.8	845	15	13	276	32.0	66.0	2.0
Wyandotte	733.0	4 606	51.2	1.5	7.1	0.0	1.3	2 162.3	13 588	1 187	663	16 187	69.7	28.9	1.4
KENTUCKY	X	X	X	X	X	X	X	X	X	37 701	50 331	275 235	41.2	57.4	1.4
Adair	60.0	3 213	34.8	41.3	2.1	0.0	3.2	137.2	7 348	41	57	894	22.9	75.5	1.6
Allen	49.2	2 435	63.1	7.8	3.4	0.1	4.2	71.1	3 516	38	65	782	27.4	71.2	1.5
Anderson	51.5	2 370	63.4	5.7	3.7	0.0	3.5	69.4	3 192	38	70	911	32.8	65.2	1.9
Ballard	29.1	3 486	40.4	3.5	3.4	0.0	6.5	122.6	14 712	29	26	392	35.1	62.5	2.4
Barren	120.1	2 816	69.4	1.0	3.9	0.7	2.6	241.8	5 673	105	136	2 193	32.3	66.2	1.4
Bath	23.4	1 987	68.5	4.7	2.1	0.0	5.2	23.4	1 980	27	39	506	48.6	49.2	2.2
Bell	70.9	2 517	61.7	2.1	3.4	0.0	2.6	42.0	1 492	131	86	1 687	29.0	69.6	1.4
Boone	317.2	2 573	54.9	0.6	4.8	1.9	8.0	852.8	6 915	1 223	403	5 083	32.1	66.6	1.3
Bourbon	58.2	2 912	60.5	5.7	3.8	0.1	3.2	52.5	2 629	41	63	976	40.6	57.9	1.5
Boyd	151.0	3 072	52.9	5.0	3.7	0.0	4.0	303.6	6 176	421	149	3 173	43.0	55.3	1.7
Boyle	80.8	2 820	48.5	3.9	4.6	0.3	3.0	210.1	7 332	65	85	1 801	37.7	60.9	1.3
Bracken	19.5	2 296	59.4	6.5	3.2	0.0	7.7	14.9	1 758	19	27	418	36.5	60.8	2.7
Breathitt	41.9	3 073	57.4	8.4	3.1	0.0	7.9	24.9	1 827	57	42	920	43.8	53.1	3.1
Breckinridge	54.2	2 698	52.5	2.3	2.2	0.1	4.0	265.6	13 235	60	63	792	36.5	62.0	1.5
Bullitt	164.4	2 166	55.3	3.4	4.5	0.0	2.2	188.8	2 488	66	249	2 565	33.1	65.4	1.5
Butler	27.0	2 105	61.6	0.3	3.5	0.1	7.5	53.2	4 145	28	41	596	29.3	69.6	1.1
Caldwell	28.0	2 163	70.3	2.5	2.0	0.1	6.9	20.0	1 544	35	40	648	35.7	62.4	2.0
Calloway	176.1	4 676	22.2	62.3	2.8	0.0	1.6	108.2	2 874	72	112	5 161	40.0	58.4	1.6
Campbell	217.1	2 389	52.4	0.5	8.0	0.4	4.4	506.2	5 568	364	284	5 944	38.8	59.7	1.6
Carlisle	16.7	3 315	59.4	5.5	1.6	0.0	10.4	23.2	4 601	15	16	240	33.6	64.9	1.5
Carroll	170.1	15 605	12.4	0.6	0.8	0.0	1.2	3 066.5	281 328	34	34	694	44.8	53.0	2.3
Carter	66.1	2 418	70.9	4.9	3.9	0.0	3.5	99.7	3 647	60	85	1 255	44.0	53.5	2.5
Casey	49.1	3 053	40.2	33.9	1.5	0.0	4.4	63.3	3 935	28	49	683	20.5	78.5	1.0
Christian	164.3	2 178	52.4	3.1	7.2	0.2	3.3	420.2	5 571	4 509	29 878	3 638	39.0	60.1	0.9
Clark	108.6	3 033	59.0	5.7	3.5	0.1	2.7	125.2	3 499	95	113	1 488	36.8	61.8	1.4

1. Based on the resident population estimated as of July 1 of the year shown.   2. © 2013 Election Data Services, Inc. All rights reserved.

Table B. States and Counties — **Land Area and Population**

STATE/ County code	CBSA code[1]	County type[2]	STATE County	Land area[3] (sq km) 2010	Total persons 2015	Rank	Per square kilometer	White	Black	American Indian, Alaska Native	Asian and Pacific Islander	Percent Hispanic or Latino[4]	Under 5 years	5 to 17 years	18 to 24 years	25 to 34 years	35 to 44 years	45 to 54 years
				1	2	3	4	5	6	7	8	9	10	11	12	13	14	15
			KENTUCKY—Cont'd															
21 051	...	7	Clay	1 215	21 013	1 774	17.3	93.5	4.6	0.6	0.3	2.0	6.2	15.0	8.6	14.7	14.7	14.8
21 053	...	9	Clinton	511	10 174	2 420	19.9	95.8	1.0	0.7	0.5	2.8	5.6	17.2	7.6	10.8	11.8	14.6
21 055	...	6	Crittenden	932	9 183	2 496	9.9	97.8	1.4	0.8	0.4	0.9	5.7	17.0	7.2	11.0	12.0	13.8
21 057	...	9	Cumberland	790	6 759	2 698	8.6	95.8	3.6	0.4	0.4	1.1	5.6	15.8	8.0	9.7	11.0	14.2
21 059	36980	3	Daviess	1 187	99 259	596	83.6	91.2	6.3	0.3	1.2	2.8	6.6	17.6	8.5	12.3	12.0	13.6
21 061	14540	3	Edmonson	784	12 007	2 297	15.3	96.5	2.2	0.7	0.4	1.0	4.6	14.8	9.2	11.2	12.5	14.0
21 063	...	9	Elliott	607	7 648	2 623	12.6	95.4	3.7	0.4	0.3	1.0	4.4	14.4	7.7	13.5	14.3	13.6
21 065	...	6	Estill	655	14 375	2 142	21.9	98.6	0.5	0.6	0.2	0.9	5.4	16.5	7.7	11.0	12.8	15.6
21 067	30460	2	Fayette	735	314 488	215	427.9	74.2	16.0	0.7	4.5	6.8	6.2	14.8	14.5	15.6	13.2	12.5
21 069	...	7	Fleming	903	14 637	2 126	16.2	97.1	2.0	0.4	0.4	1.3	6.9	17.4	7.9	11.0	12.6	14.4
21 071	...	7	Floyd	1 019	37 756	1 233	37.1	97.9	1.2	0.4	0.4	0.7	6.6	15.4	8.4	11.8	13.0	14.0
21 073	23180	4	Franklin	538	50 375	981	93.6	83.8	12.3	0.7	2.1	3.0	5.5	15.4	9.8	12.2	12.6	14.1
21 075	46460	7	Fulton	532	6 238	2 740	11.7	73.5	25.4	0.9	1.0	1.5	6.4	14.6	8.1	12.9	10.4	13.5
21 077	17140	1	Gallatin	262	8 636	2 542	33.0	92.5	2.3	0.6	0.7	5.1	6.5	19.1	8.7	11.5	12.7	15.9
21 079	...	6	Garrard	596	17 237	1 967	28.9	94.7	2.6	0.5	0.5	2.3	5.1	17.0	7.0	10.9	12.8	16.0
21 081	17140	1	Grant	668	24 757	1 615	37.1	95.8	1.6	0.6	0.8	2.6	7.0	20.3	8.6	12.1	13.3	14.2
21 083	32460	7	Graves	1 429	37 421	1 242	26.2	88.6	5.7	0.7	0.7	6.0	6.5	17.9	8.2	11.5	12.2	13.5
21 085	...	6	Grayson	1 286	26 221	1 554	20.4	97.1	1.6	0.7	0.5	1.4	6.3	17.5	8.3	11.5	12.7	13.5
21 087	...	6	Green	741	11 010	2 355	14.9	95.8	2.8	0.9	0.4	1.4	5.0	16.0	7.4	10.4	12.3	14.8
21 089	26580	2	Greenup	892	36 068	1 272	40.4	97.2	1.4	0.8	0.7	1.1	5.4	16.5	7.5	10.6	12.6	14.0
21 091	36980	3	Hancock	486	8 692	2 536	17.9	97.2	1.8	0.5	0.4	1.4	6.4	19.2	8.0	10.0	13.0	14.4
21 093	21060	3	Hardin	1 614	106 439	560	65.9	78.9	14.0	1.1	3.6	5.6	6.8	18.3	10.3	13.6	12.9	14.0
21 095	...	7	Harlan	1 206	27 703	1 504	23.0	96.5	2.9	0.6	0.7	0.8	7.0	15.7	8.2	11.9	12.0	13.8
21 097	...	6	Harrison	793	18 763	1 883	23.7	94.7	3.1	0.6	0.5	2.1	5.8	17.5	8.1	10.2	12.5	15.1
21 099	...	8	Hart	1 067	18 454	1 892	17.3	93.4	5.6	0.6	0.4	1.7	6.1	18.2	8.5	10.8	11.5	15.1
21 101	21780	2	Henderson	1 131	46 407	1 041	41.0	89.3	9.1	0.5	0.7	2.3	6.3	17.1	7.9	12.6	12.2	13.9
21 103	31140	1	Henry	741	15 620	2 068	21.1	93.4	3.8	1.0	0.5	3.2	5.8	18.1	7.8	10.9	12.3	14.6
21 105	...	9	Hickman	627	4 612	2 857	7.4	89.4	10.1	0.8	0.5	1.2	4.1	15.7	7.1	9.7	11.2	14.5
21 107	31580	4	Hopkins	1 404	46 222	1 044	32.9	90.8	7.9	0.7	0.9	1.8	5.9	16.9	7.8	11.8	12.4	13.7
21 109	...	9	Jackson	894	13 352	2 214	14.9	98.5	0.5	0.6	0.2	0.7	5.7	16.6	8.0	11.7	13.8	14.4
21 111	31140	1	Jefferson	985	763 623	83	775.3	71.1	22.5	0.7	3.1	4.8	6.5	16.2	8.9	14.4	12.7	13.5
21 113	30460	2	Jessamine	446	51 961	961	116.5	91.9	4.4	0.8	1.5	2.9	6.7	18.0	10.1	12.6	13.0	13.8
21 115	...	7	Johnson	678	23 175	1 675	34.2	98.4	0.8	0.6	0.6	0.7	6.5	16.1	8.1	11.7	13.0	14.2
21 117	17140	1	Kenton	415	165 012	386	397.6	90.8	5.9	0.5	1.6	2.9	7.1	17.4	8.4	14.7	12.9	14.0
21 119	...	9	Knott	910	15 693	2 062	17.2	98.1	1.1	0.5	0.2	0.8	5.7	14.7	10.8	10.6	12.3	15.0
21 121	30940	7	Knox	1 001	31 730	1 388	31.7	97.2	1.6	0.8	0.5	1.1	6.7	17.1	9.3	11.8	12.3	13.6
21 123	21060	3	Larue	677	14 241	2 152	21.0	93.2	4.0	0.9	0.4	3.1	5.3	17.1	8.0	12.5	11.6	14.7
21 125	30940	7	Laurel	1 124	60 094	866	53.5	96.9	1.2	0.8	0.7	1.4	6.1	17.4	8.1	12.7	13.3	14.2
21 127	...	6	Lawrence	1 076	15 745	2 059	14.6	98.7	0.7	0.6	0.3	0.7	6.5	16.6	8.0	11.3	12.6	14.5
21 129	...	9	Lee	541	6 752	2 700	12.5	107.3	3.1	1.0	0.4	1.2	4.8	14.2	7.6	14.4	13.3	16.7
21 131	...	9	Leslie	1 038	10 711	2 377	10.3	99.2	0.7	0.5	0.3	0.5	6.4	15.3	7.8	12.0	12.7	15.1
21 133	...	9	Letcher	875	23 123	1 680	26.4	98.4	0.8	0.5	0.3	0.7	5.9	15.6	7.2	12.0	12.6	14.3
21 135	...	8	Lewis	1 251	13 682	2 190	10.9	98.9	0.7	0.6	0.1	0.7	6.3	16.6	7.8	11.2	12.6	14.9
21 137	19220	7	Lincoln	865	24 463	1 627	28.3	95.6	3.0	0.8	0.3	1.5	6.2	17.5	7.8	11.3	12.6	14.5
21 139	37140	9	Livingston	811	9 316	2 484	11.5	97.1	0.9	1.0	0.7	1.5	5.6	14.9	7.2	9.9	11.3	15.1
21 141	...	6	Logan	1 430	26 910	1 539	18.8	90.0	7.7	0.7	0.5	2.8	6.4	17.8	7.7	11.7	11.7	14.1
21 143	...	8	Lyon	554	8 306	2 574	15.0	92.7	6.2	0.8	0.5	1.6	4.0	11.4	6.7	11.5	12.3	14.7
21 145	37140	3	McCracken	644	65 018	811	101.0	85.6	12.1	0.8	1.3	2.4	5.9	16.0	7.8	11.9	12.1	13.7
21 147	...	9	McCreary	1 105	17 878	1 926	16.2	91.0	6.0	1.5	0.5	2.4	6.3	15.9	8.9	13.6	14.6	14.4
21 149	36980	3	McLean	654	9 512	2 470	14.5	97.7	1.2	0.7	0.3	1.3	6.5	17.2	7.5	10.4	12.1	14.2
21 151	40080	4	Madison	1 133	87 824	656	77.5	92.4	5.5	0.9	1.6	2.3	5.7	15.4	17.9	12.0	12.5	12.6
21 153	...	9	Magoffin	799	12 808	2 243	16.0	98.3	0.5	0.6	0.2	0.8	5.6	17.3	8.2	11.0	13.5	15.3
21 155	...	6	Marion	888	19 365	1 855	21.8	92.0	9.7	0.5	1.1	2.5	6.2	17.5	8.5	13.1	13.1	14.5
21 157	...	7	Marshall	780	31 101	1 408	39.9	97.4	0.6	0.7	0.6	1.4	5.1	15.0	7.3	10.5	11.9	14.4
21 159	...	8	Martin	595	12 307	2 275	20.7	89.2	7.4	0.6	0.3	3.2	5.4	15.2	8.3	16.4	14.8	13.8
21 161	32500	6	Mason	622	17 099	1 975	27.5	91.4	7.6	0.7	0.8	1.5	6.5	17.1	8.2	10.9	12.0	14.2
21 163	21060	1	Meade	791	27 924	1 490	35.3	90.0	4.6	1.3	1.7	4.3	5.7	18.9	9.0	14.0	13.5	14.3
21 165	34460	9	Menifee	527	6 358	2 726	12.1	95.7	3.1	0.7	0.4	1.0	5.3	15.0	9.3	10.7	11.7	14.6
21 167	...	2	Mercer	644	21 407	1 759	33.2	92.6	4.7	0.8	0.9	2.5	6.0	16.1	7.8	10.7	11.8	15.0
21 169	23980	9	Metcalfe	750	9 909	2 441	13.2	96.2	2.2	0.5	0.4	1.6	6.7	16.9	7.9	11.1	11.4	14.5
21 171	...	9	Monroe	853	10 667	2 382	12.5	94.4	2.7	0.6	0.3	3.1	5.8	16.6	8.1	10.9	11.5	14.6
21 173	34460	6	Montgomery	511	27 608	1 506	54.0	94.5	3.4	0.5	0.5	2.6	6.8	17.4	8.2	12.1	14.1	14.0
21 175	...	7	Morgan	987	13 275	2 217	13.4	94.1	4.6	0.6	0.4	0.8	4.6	14.2	8.4	15.0	14.7	14.1
21 177	...	6	Muhlenberg	1 210	31 183	1 407	25.8	93.1	5.4	0.6	0.4	1.4	5.3	15.6	9.2	11.8	12.8	14.0
21 179	12680	9	Nelson	1 081	45 126	1 069	41.7	92.0	6.1	0.5	0.8	2.1	6.7	18.3	8.4	12.3	12.9	14.2
21 181	...	8	Nicholas	505	7 131	2 663	14.1	96.1	1.0	0.5	0.3	2.1	5.7	17.0	7.8	11.1	12.5	15.3

1. CBSA = Core Based Statistical Area. See Appendix A for explanation. See Appendix B for list of metropolitan areas with component counties.   2. County type code from the Economic Research Service of USDA Rural-Urban Continuum Codes. See Appendix A for definition.   3. Dry land or land partially or temporarily covered by water.   4. May be of any race.

STATE County	55 to 64 years	65 to 74 years	75 years and over	Percent female	2000	2010	2000–2010	2010–2015	Births	Deaths	Net migration	Number	Persons per household	Family households	Female family householder[1]	One person
	16	17	18	19	20	21	22	23	24	25	26	27	28	29	30	31
KENTUCKY—Cont'd																
Clay	12.5	8.3	5.2	47.0	24 556	21 730	-11.5	-3.3	1 518	1 372	-878	7 652	2.56	69.0	15.1	28.3
Clinton	14.2	10.9	7.2	50.3	9 634	10 272	6.6	-1.0	619	649	-35	3 878	2.59	66.1	9.8	32.5
Crittenden	14.1	11.5	7.8	49.5	9 384	9 315	-0.7	-1.4	520	622	2	3 812	2.38	65.1	6.8	31.6
Cumberland	15.1	11.7	9.1	51.2	7 147	6 856	-4.1	-1.4	428	531	14	2 684	2.51	67.4	11.7	30.6
Daviess	13.3	8.8	7.2	51.5	91 545	96 658	5.6	2.7	6 887	5 175	877	38 000	2.50	67.6	12.0	27.9
Edmonson	14.5	11.7	7.6	49.8	11 644	12 161	4.4	-1.3	535	678	-38	4 734	2.48	73.4	8.8	23.2
Elliott	13.7	11.0	7.4	43.5	6 748	7 852	16.4	-2.6	318	373	-173	2 790	2.43	70.0	13.5	25.4
Estill	13.9	10.8	6.3	50.7	15 307	14 672	-4.1	-2.0	838	933	-178	5 706	2.53	70.6	15.5	25.6
Fayette	11.5	6.8	4.9	50.9	260 512	295 803	13.5	6.3	21 173	11 077	8 822	124 101	2.35	57.3	12.4	32.6
Fleming	13.6	10.0	6.2	50.8	13 792	14 355	4.1	2.0	1 034	886	136	5 542	2.61	71.7	12.2	25.5
Floyd	14.7	9.8	6.2	51.2	42 441	39 451	-7.0	-4.3	2 719	2 772	-1 751	15 438	2.47	69.5	13.3	26.7
Franklin	14.1	9.7	6.6	51.8	47 687	49 285	3.4	2.2	3 034	2 615	612	21 065	2.26	61.3	13.0	32.8
Fulton	14.8	10.7	8.7	50.6	7 752	6 813	-12.1	-8.4	406	565	-431	2 662	2.31	65.8	12.8	32.0
Gallatin	13.3	8.4	3.9	49.5	7 870	8 589	9.1	0.5	599	435	-110	3 024	2.79	66.8	12.5	27.6
Garrard	14.8	9.9	6.5	50.8	14 792	16 912	14.3	1.9	939	815	208	6 567	2.55	75.3	12.4	22.6
Grant	11.9	8.0	4.5	50.1	22 384	24 662	10.2	0.4	1 839	1 097	-673	8 301	2.93	75.8	12.0	18.7
Graves	13.1	9.8	7.4	50.9	37 028	37 121	0.3	0.8	2 609	2 268	-6	14 284	2.58	69.3	10.7	28.4
Grayson	13.9	9.8	6.5	49.7	24 053	25 746	7.0	1.8	1 764	1 627	381	9 839	2.60	69.7	8.1	26.8
Green	14.6	11.3	8.3	50.5	11 518	11 260	-2.2	-2.2	569	689	-136	4 474	2.47	69.9	11.0	26.8
Greenup	14.4	11.0	8.0	51.5	36 891	36 914	0.1	-2.3	2 074	2 352	-531	14 230	2.55	71.9	11.6	25.4
Hancock	12.8	10.3	5.9	48.8	8 392	8 565	2.1	1.5	559	438	15	3 367	2.54	75.8	14.8	21.8
Hardin	11.9	7.2	5.1	50.1	94 174	105 537	12.1	0.9	8 506	4 547	-3 281	39 955	2.60	70.3	13.5	25.4
Harlan	15.0	9.8	6.5	51.3	33 202	29 278	-11.8	-5.4	2 016	2 193	-1 427	11 251	2.50	69.9	15.6	27.2
Harrison	14.3	9.6	6.9	51.0	17 983	18 849	4.8	-0.5	1 098	1 128	-67	7 257	2.52	63.6	12.3	30.0
Hart	13.5	9.7	6.6	50.6	17 445	18 199	4.3	1.4	1 231	1 046	68	7 135	2.55	72.0	12.8	24.1
Henderson	14.4	9.2	6.4	51.5	44 829	46 250	3.2	0.3	2 979	2 595	-149	18 875	2.39	65.8	12.9	30.9
Henry	14.4	10.0	6.1	50.6	15 060	15 414	2.4	1.3	948	869	158	5 984	2.56	72.0	13.4	23.3
Hickman	14.0	12.6	11.0	52.6	5 262	4 902	-6.8	-5.9	189	335	-133	1 992	2.30	63.6	12.4	31.5
Hopkins	14.4	9.8	7.3	51.2	46 519	46 920	0.9	-1.5	2 820	2 979	-512	18 533	2.47	67.1	13.0	29.2
Jackson	14.2	9.9	5.7	50.0	13 495	13 494	0.0	-1.1	833	855	-120	5 670	2.34	74.4	15.8	23.1
Jefferson	13.3	8.1	6.4	51.8	693 604	741 085	6.8	3.0	52 537	38 166	9 365	306 511	2.40	60.6	14.7	33.0
Jessamine	12.3	7.7	5.7	51.4	39 041	48 586	24.4	6.9	3 533	1 998	1 776	18 120	2.63	75.3	13.4	19.9
Johnson	14.3	10.0	6.1	50.8	23 445	23 358	-0.4	-0.8	1 572	1 548	-190	9 134	2.51	72.7	10.8	24.3
Kenton	12.8	7.5	5.2	50.6	151 464	159 721	5.5	3.3	12 249	7 270	453	61 962	2.57	64.6	13.4	29.0
Knott	15.1	9.8	6.0	50.3	17 649	16 346	-7.4	-4.0	958	1 051	-524	5 776	2.67	68.3	12.1	27.7
Knox	12.5	10.3	6.6	51.5	31 795	31 883	0.3	-0.5	2 192	2 046	-357	12 524	2.49	65.7	14.6	30.9
Larue	13.8	9.2	7.8	50.5	13 373	14 193	6.1	0.3	818	840	66	5 294	2.62	73.1	13.7	23.9
Laurel	13.2	9.2	5.8	51.0	52 715	58 849	11.6	2.1	3 792	3 025	437	23 184	2.53	71.2	14.1	24.5
Lawrence	14.5	10.0	5.9	50.1	15 569	15 858	1.9	-0.7	1 010	1 070	-79	5 940	2.65	71.8	10.3	25.2
Lee	13.9	9.3	5.7	44.6	7 916	7 889	-0.3	-14.4	369	524	-1 000	2 957	2.31	58.9	11.8	36.8
Leslie	14.5	9.6	6.6	50.5	12 401	11 310	-8.8	-5.3	721	876	-483	4 212	2.59	69.6	13.2	27.4
Letcher	15.6	10.2	6.5	50.6	25 277	24 519	-3.0	-5.7	1 462	1 670	-1 182	9 391	2.53	70.1	11.7	26.7
Lewis	14.1	10.2	6.4	50.2	14 092	13 872	-1.6	-1.4	865	794	-227	5 222	2.62	70.9	11.2	25.4
Lincoln	13.3	9.8	7.0	51.0	23 361	24 754	6.0	-1.2	1 731	1 412	-604	9 693	2.51	71.4	14.5	25.6
Livingston	16.0	12.2	7.7	50.9	9 804	9 519	-2.9	-2.1	539	653	-93	3 708	2.52	73.1	9.3	25.0
Logan	13.4	10.2	7.0	51.1	26 573	26 835	1.0	0.3	1 974	1 522	-334	10 862	2.44	65.2	11.3	30.6
Lyon	16.2	14.3	9.1	44.4	8 080	8 319	3.0	-0.2	293	571	273	3 263	2.17	58.6	7.8	35.9
McCracken	14.5	10.2	8.0	51.9	65 514	65 565	0.1	-0.8	4 093	4 218	-422	27 409	2.35	63.8	13.6	32.4
McCreary	12.3	8.9	5.1	45.6	17 080	18 306	7.2	-2.3	1 232	996	-636	6 210	2.60	72.4	13.0	25.9
McLean	13.6	10.9	7.6	50.2	9 938	9 531	-4.1	-0.2	622	628	-24	3 744	2.52	70.8	8.6	25.7
Madison	11.2	7.6	5.1	51.5	70 872	82 916	17.0	5.9	5 177	3 568	3 174	31 752	2.50	63.9	11.8	27.2
Magoffin	14.2	9.1	5.7	49.8	13 332	13 333	0.0	-3.9	838	765	-594	4 928	2.62	70.4	12.0	27.7
Marion	12.4	8.5	6.3	48.2	18 212	19 820	8.8	-2.3	1 230	1 059	-689	7 385	2.53	66.3	11.4	29.6
Marshall	14.7	12.3	8.8	51.1	30 125	31 448	4.4	-1.1	1 639	2 134	211	12 426	2.47	72.9	10.6	23.6
Martin	12.7	8.1	5.3	44.2	12 578	12 929	2.8	-4.8	727	747	-613	4 381	2.57	73.1	12.5	22.8
Mason	14.3	9.8	7.0	51.6	16 800	17 490	4.1	-2.2	1 120	1 015	-479	6 636	2.57	71.0	14.5	25.9
Meade	12.3	7.5	4.7	49.9	26 349	28 621	8.6	-2.4	1 432	1 130	-1 041	10 557	2.75	77.2	10.5	18.7
Menifee	15.1	11.2	7.1	49.5	6 556	6 306	-3.8	0.8	379	369	38	2 404	2.57	71.4	14.3	25.2
Mercer	14.4	10.7	7.4	51.0	20 817	21 331	2.5	0.4	1 300	1 318	119	8 770	2.41	68.0	12.6	27.7
Metcalfe	13.9	9.7	7.9	50.3	10 037	10 099	0.6	-1.9	687	671	-223	3 918	2.53	67.8	7.8	27.9
Monroe	14.1	11.0	7.4	50.2	11 756	10 963	-6.7	-2.7	672	792	-172	4 436	2.41	67.0	12.5	27.2
Montgomery	12.5	8.9	5.9	51.3	22 554	26 499	17.5	4.2	2 006	1 354	433	10 288	2.58	67.4	15.1	26.7
Morgan	14.4	8.5	6.1	43.8	13 948	13 923	-0.2	-4.7	696	769	-564	4 841	2.44	74.1	12.7	21.6
Muhlenberg	13.4	10.4	7.4	49.2	31 839	31 499	-1.1	-1.0	1 800	2 010	-78	11 619	2.57	72.8	12.7	25.2
Nelson	13.3	8.3	5.2	50.8	37 477	43 437	15.9	3.9	3 108	1 913	483	16 660	2.62	74.7	13.6	21.5
Nicholas	13.5	9.9	7.2	50.7	6 813	7 128	4.6	0.0	496	536	32	2 861	2.43	70.8	12.3	24.9

1. No spouse present.

Table B. States and Counties — **Population, Vital Statistics, Medicare, and Crime**

STATE County	Persons in group quarters, 2015	Daytime population, 2010–2014 Number	Employ-ment/resi-dence ratio	Births, 2015 Total	Rate[1]	Deaths, 2015 Number	Rate[1]	Persons under 65 with no health insurance, 2014 Number	Percent	Medicare, 2015 Total Beneficiaries	Enrolled in Original Medicare	Enrolled in Medicare Advantage	Serious crimes known to police,[2] 2014 Total Number	Rate[3]
	32	33	34	35	36	37	38	39	40	41	42	43	44	45
KENTUCKY—Cont'd														
Clay	2 031	20 301	0.79	279	13.2	234	11.1	1 965	12.0	4 359	3 566	793	113	530
Clinton	136	10 999	1.24	119	11.7	103	10.1	971	11.8	2 454	2 023	431	6	59
Crittenden	210	8 263	0.71	97	10.6	96	10.4	773	10.6	1 983	1 591	392	74	800
Cumberland	86	6 500	0.87	82	12.1	115	17.0	649	12.2	1 652	1 284	368	38	560
Daviess	2 611	99 457	1.04	1 312	13.3	995	10.1	6 033	7.5	20 610	16 410	4 200	2 874	2 911
Edmonson	352	9 288	0.37	101	8.4	140	11.6	1 153	11.9	1 944	1 487	457	62	515
Elliott	1 038	7 024	0.63	58	7.6	68	8.9	604	11.4	2 731	1 890	841	1	13
Estill	118	12 365	0.52	158	11.0	171	11.9	1 305	11.0	3 412	2 599	813	56	387
Fayette	12 967	335 043	1.20	4 093	13.1	2 130	6.8	28 937	11.0	41 219	27 908	13 311	13 919	4 463
Fleming	22	12 718	0.69	207	14.2	165	11.3	1 632	13.4	3 199	2 371	828	65	447
Floyd	671	38 551	0.96	498	13.1	538	14.2	3 677	11.5	10 431	7 735	2 696	117	306
Franklin	1 917	60 611	1.52	607	12.1	484	9.6	3 720	9.3	13 187	8 355	4 832	1 431	2 873
Fulton	445	6 797	1.11	71	11.4	98	15.7	456	9.8	1 910	1 631	279	NA	NA
Gallatin	85	7 043	0.59	115	13.3	65	7.5	853	11.4	1 327	932	395	76	899
Garrard	109	12 421	0.36	181	10.6	166	9.7	1 678	12.0	3 377	2 467	910	158	933
Grant	457	20 465	0.57	344	13.9	210	8.5	1 991	9.3	4 763	3 115	1 648	243	980
Graves	463	34 685	0.82	496	13.2	400	10.7	3 908	12.7	8 684	6 554	2 130	548	1 484
Grayson	768	24 524	0.86	347	13.3	281	10.7	2 395	11.3	5 903	4 816	1 087	390	1 531
Green	113	9 044	0.53	102	9.2	123	11.2	1 084	12.2	2 396	1 902	494	37	331
Greenup	454	32 058	0.65	405	11.2	453	12.5	2 782	9.6	10 260	7 666	2 594	161	441
Hancock	90	9 634	1.27	107	12.3	78	9.0	534	7.3	1 721	1 422	299	24	275
Hardin	3 261	113 163	1.11	1 589	14.8	893	8.3	7 738	8.5	18 785	15 867	2 918	1 948	1 793
Harlan	627	29 128	1.05	356	12.8	387	13.9	2 694	11.6	7 088	5 616	1 472	150	529
Harrison	275	16 211	0.68	227	12.1	193	10.3	1 532	9.9	3 792	2 766	1 026	427	2 312
Hart	227	17 124	0.81	223	12.1	189	10.2	2 025	13.1	3 555	2 850	705	53	284
Henderson	1 165	45 677	0.96	560	12.1	514	11.1	3 141	8.2	9 260	6 653	2 607	1 292	2 783
Henry	80	12 027	0.49	191	12.2	157	10.1	1 336	10.3	3 377	2 214	1 163	35	252
Hickman	212	4 616	0.90	31	6.7	72	15.5	373	10.7	915	762	153	37	784
Hopkins	1 086	46 358	0.98	529	11.4	524	11.3	3 623	9.6	10 363	7 716	2 647	802	1 720
Jackson	110	11 659	0.58	164	12.3	144	10.8	1 246	11.2	2 809	2 242	567	59	439
Jefferson	15 195	832 045	1.23	10 000	13.1	7 220	9.5	60 297	9.5	133 840	92 877	40 963	35 527	4 670
Jessamine	1 765	45 494	0.82	684	13.3	374	7.3	4 286	10.1	7 459	5 149	2 310	1 458	2 880
Johnson	531	22 289	0.84	287	12.4	290	12.5	1 957	10.2	5 579	4 192	1 387	144	613
Kenton	2 506	148 693	0.83	2 275	13.8	1 396	8.5	11 985	8.5	23 169	14 761	8 408	3 954	2 408
Knott	791	14 757	0.70	184	11.6	180	11.4	1 359	10.6	3 092	2 245	847	22	150
Knox	685	31 580	0.97	423	13.3	430	13.6	2 883	11.1	5 476	4 471	1 005	198	622
Larue	313	11 879	0.59	175	12.3	152	10.7	1 236	10.7	2 910	2 289	621	43	306
Laurel	698	62 134	1.12	734	12.2	618	10.3	5 305	10.5	10 771	8 470	2 301	651	1 089
Lawrence	108	14 535	0.75	178	11.3	203	12.9	1 373	10.4	3 708	3 001	707	83	523
Lee	180	7 479	0.90	70	10.3	108	16.0	540	9.9	1 582	1 217	365	10	140
Leslie	227	9 999	0.63	125	11.6	169	15.7	1 017	11.3	2 538	1 971	567	11	104
Letcher	243	22 696	0.82	260	11.2	286	12.3	1 976	10.2	5 711	4 307	1 404	82	350
Lewis	139	11 968	0.57	168	12.2	141	10.2	1 282	11.2	2 806	2 213	593	45	326
Lincoln	219	20 358	0.54	349	14.3	266	10.9	2 360	11.7	5 730	4 297	1 433	52	226
Livingston	69	8 239	0.67	106	11.4	114	12.2	759	10.2	2 426	1 994	432	78	836
Logan	277	25 196	0.84	401	14.9	275	10.2	2 401	10.9	5 767	4 604	1 163	408	1 516
Lyon	1 216	7 691	0.73	49	5.9	121	14.5	527	9.9	2 119	1 550	569	61	718
McCracken	1 189	76 503	1.39	799	12.3	820	12.6	4 499	8.6	14 636	11 766	2 870	1 849	2 827
McCreary	2 144	16 812	0.71	216	12.1	164	9.2	1 628	11.9	3 561	2 848	713	85	474
McLean	82	7 827	0.57	115	12.1	113	11.9	766	10.0	2 282	1 640	642	58	610
Madison	5 757	83 269	0.94	996	11.4	675	7.7	6 346	9.1	14 291	9 843	4 448	2 177	2 522
Magoffin	127	11 990	0.69	166	12.9	149	11.6	1 357	12.4	2 815	2 154	661	19	148
Marion	502	20 587	1.08	228	11.8	184	9.5	1 591	10.0	3 778	2 993	785	168	847
Marshall	464	29 684	0.88	330	10.6	415	13.4	2 134	8.8	7 759	6 146	1 613	421	1 355
Martin	1 622	13 016	1.11	123	9.9	153	12.3	954	10.3	2 537	1 925	612	100	793
Mason	298	18 875	1.20	211	12.3	190	11.1	1 354	9.6	3 875	2 916	959	447	2 592
Meade	212	22 803	0.46	278	9.7	209	7.3	2 254	8.9	3 646	2 920	726	182	619
Menifee	272	5 477	0.58	71	11.2	85	13.4	655	12.8	1 842	1 170	672	45	717
Mercer	128	19 477	0.79	244	11.4	258	12.1	1 605	9.3	4 668	3 331	1 337	336	1 646
Metcalfe	121	8 915	0.72	129	13.0	137	13.8	927	11.3	2 405	1 653	752	60	602
Monroe	143	10 119	0.82	139	13.0	148	13.8	1 111	12.8	2 724	2 156	568	1	10
Montgomery	357	27 437	1.04	357	13.0	265	9.6	2 436	10.5	5 205	3 574	1 631	832	3 029
Morgan	1 788	12 928	0.84	135	10.1	151	11.4	1 082	11.2	2 588	1 768	820	NA	NA
Muhlenberg	2 098	29 568	0.84	355	11.4	423	13.6	2 700	11.1	7 040	5 266	1 774	163	524
Nelson	496	40 942	0.83	594	13.2	380	8.5	3 471	9.0	8 287	6 508	1 779	545	1 216
Nicholas	95	5 571	0.51	111	15.6	113	15.9	667	11.5	1 544	1 178	366	47	669

1. Per 1,000 estimated resident population.   2. Data for serious crimes have not been adjusted for underreporting; this may affect comparability between geographic areas and over time.
3. Per 100,000 population estimated by the FBI.

Table B. States and Counties — **Crime, Education, Money Income, and Poverty**

STATE County	Serious crimes known to police, 2014 (cont.)[1] Rate[2]		Education School enrollment and attainment, 2010–2014				Local government expenditures,[5] 2012–2013		Money income, 2010–2014	Households			Income and poverty, 2014 Percent below poverty level		
			Enrollment[3]		Attainment[4] (percent)										
	Violent	Property	Total	Percent private	High school graduate or less	Bachelor's degree or more	Total current spending (mil dol)	Current spending per student (dollars)	Per capita income[6] (dollars)	Median income (dollars)	Mean income (dollars)	Percent with income of $200,000 or more	Median house-hold income (dollars)	All persons	Children under 18 years	Children 5 to 17 years in families
	46	47	48	49	50	51	52	53	54	55	56	57	58	59	60	61

KENTUCKY—Cont'd

STATE County	46	47	48	49	50	51	52	53	54	55	56	57	58	59	60	61
Clay	47	483	4 447	6.7	72.0	9.5	34.6	10 026	14 574	22 626	36 715	0.5	25 215	38.2	46.8	43.9
Clinton	10	49	2 379	7.5	68.6	9.0	18.4	10 117	17 171	27 285	41 626	2.4	28 341	25.7	37.5	35.1
Crittenden	65	735	1 701	7.6	58.7	11.3	11.7	8 670	20 548	33 356	49 656	1.3	38 338	20.3	31.2	28.3
Cumberland	0	560	1 481	15.0	63.6	12.2	10.0	9 690	17 245	30 813	40 436	1.4	29 067	27.8	37.8	36.4
Daviess	147	2 764	25 318	16.9	50.3	19.9	150.3	9 248	23 140	45 760	57 957	2.3	43 390	15.0	21.5	19.9
Edmonson	83	432	2 623	4.7	65.7	11.6	17.7	8 761	20 652	42 404	51 861	1.3	38 544	19.9	28.4	26.1
Elliott	0	13	1 415	7.6	66.5	6.4	10.0	9 417	15 159	28 363	37 800	0.6	30 556	32.4	40.2	36.1
Estill	28	360	3 017	4.6	73.4	8.4	23.2	9 050	16 449	29 905	40 080	0.2	30 333	29.8	38.0	33.4
Fayette	344	4 119	91 308	14.9	31.9	40.2	465.6	10 755	29 168	48 667	69 679	4.4	48 552	19.8	23.7	20.9
Fleming	21	426	3 375	9.1	61.8	10.9	23.2	9 984	20 719	33 392	52 199	2.5	35 878	19.3	30.2	29.3
Floyd	31	274	8 060	9.7	59.7	12.8	61.4	9 547	17 958	30 190	44 330	0.9	30 127	31.1	44.3	39.9
Franklin	233	2 640	11 304	11.4	45.8	27.4	64.2	8 997	26 592	46 818	61 638	1.9	49 400	12.9	21.3	20.0
Fulton	NA	NA	1 307	7.7	61.1	13.2	11.6	11 532	18 892	32 948	44 178	0.2	30 671	31.2	44.9	43.4
Gallatin	35	864	1 926	7.9	65.1	9.9	14.9	8 857	20 507	48 917	55 931	1.2	45 483	16.7	25.5	23.4
Garrard	77	856	3 727	7.6	58.4	16.5	22.5	8 523	22 334	44 304	55 841	1.1	43 647	18.0	26.7	23.7
Grant	60	919	6 344	10.2	61.7	11.4	42.5	8 592	19 872	46 382	57 358	0.7	46 226	16.9	25.9	24.5
Graves	84	1 400	9 044	7.9	56.4	16.7	56.0	8 634	21 367	39 529	53 657	2.4	39 247	17.7	26.0	24.6
Grayson	79	1 453	6 207	10.3	66.7	9.1	36.4	8 342	19 404	33 788	48 848	1.2	35 726	21.7	30.5	29.1
Green	18	313	2 318	14.9	69.5	10.8	16.3	9 287	19 465	34 368	47 040	1.3	33 640	21.5	29.6	26.8
Greenup	25	417	8 098	7.8	53.4	15.7	53.5	8 521	22 360	44 035	56 047	1.7	42 452	16.4	22.5	19.6
Hancock	23	252	2 074	5.4	58.1	11.6	16.1	9 548	22 637	50 311	57 748	1.1	50 358	13.8	18.9	17.1
Hardin	110	1 683	29 152	13.0	43.7	22.2	149.2	8 715	24 559	49 602	63 398	2.2	50 407	14.3	21.8	20.9
Harlan	46	483	6 220	5.3	65.3	11.1	45.6	8 811	15 543	25 186	38 200	0.7	26 351	34.2	42.6	40.1
Harrison	103	2 209	4 357	7.4	59.0	13.6	26.1	8 399	21 488	35 957	52 433	1.4	41 406	18.5	24.2	23.0
Hart	21	262	4 241	14.1	69.8	9.8	22.9	9 321	18 289	34 771	46 392	0.8	38 038	23.0	33.7	32.1
Henderson	162	2 621	10 999	12.4	51.8	16.4	70.5	9 382	22 968	41 006	54 950	2.1	43 040	18.1	27.2	24.6
Henry	14	237	3 580	8.5	65.1	11.6	24.8	8 483	21 288	44 764	54 102	1.0	43 799	18.3	25.7	23.6
Hickman	64	721	1 088	8.5	55.8	11.7	8.4	10 269	20 051	42 256	45 833	0.6	41 588	18.4	29.3	25.3
Hopkins	88	1 632	10 287	8.0	56.1	13.9	69.4	8 860	22 632	42 404	54 820	1.4	42 477	16.9	24.9	22.9
Jackson	15	424	2 959	4.7	73.4	8.6	23.9	10 090	15 760	27 224	37 554	0.5	29 090	26.8	36.0	33.4
Jefferson	549	4 121	189 848	24.2	39.3	30.8	1 143.9	11 361	28 464	47 692	67 896	4.2	48 264	16.8	23.9	22.1
Jessamine	130	2 750	13 494	30.9	43.7	28.3	68.9	8 664	26 235	50 057	70 087	4.0	51 227	14.7	21.6	20.7
Johnson	51	562	5 283	6.2	64.5	10.5	44.5	9 631	18 380	35 026	46 104	1.1	34 271	25.6	31.5	29.3
Kenton	184	2 224	41 583	21.1	41.0	28.9	208.9	9 035	27 788	54 817	70 126	3.7	54 728	15.5	22.3	20.9
Knott	0	150	3 663	19.4	66.7	12.8	26.7	10 489	18 304	31 624	46 348	0.6	27 709	33.7	44.1	40.8
Knox	35	588	7 647	7.9	71.7	10.2	52.6	10 056	15 013	25 523	36 635	0.6	26 048	34.9	49.0	48.7
Larue	43	263	3 340	9.9	63.5	10.8	21.4	8 930	20 051	39 364	51 259	1.6	40 312	18.0	27.8	25.5
Laurel	54	1 035	13 686	9.0	63.0	11.9	81.9	8 170	19 375	35 746	49 240	1.4	34 678	24.7	35.0	30.6
Lawrence	50	473	3 450	7.2	63.6	11.7	22.7	8 996	19 037	36 225	48 499	0.8	32 835	25.9	33.1	30.7
Lee	0	140	1 540	5.1	70.7	7.0	10.6	9 861	15 059	23 968	34 441	0.2	25 473	35.0	45.1	41.4
Leslie	9	94	2 412	9.5	67.9	8.2	19.2	10 022	16 708	29 156	41 091	0.6	27 777	33.0	38.4	38.7
Letcher	9	342	4 986	5.9	61.7	11.9	38.0	9 846	18 163	31 630	44 317	0.3	28 574	30.1	37.1	34.7
Lewis	22	304	3 224	6.2	69.0	10.9	21.3	8 775	15 764	27 707	39 883	0.4	30 217	34.4	44.9	41.9
Lincoln	4	221	5 560	9.0	66.5	10.2	37.9	9 261	18 192	35 949	45 434	0.8	35 368	27.6	35.3	33.0
Livingston	64	772	1 977	15.4	63.6	10.0	12.4	9 626	20 700	40 580	50 455	0.6	42 892	14.1	23.0	22.1
Logan	137	1 378	6 268	5.6	62.6	13.0	41.8	8 889	19 063	36 101	46 592	0.8	41 150	16.9	25.9	24.0
Lyon	0	718	1 278	5.9	52.9	15.8	8.1	9 022	23 621	43 715	55 456	1.0	43 067	15.4	22.7	21.2
McCracken	188	2 639	15 017	14.2	43.8	22.7	90.0	8 982	26 559	43 650	61 215	2.6	41 216	17.5	26.0	24.6
McCreary	22	452	4 100	6.3	67.8	7.5	29.9	9 678	11 287	20 000	30 086	0.1	24 265	47.0	50.2	49.1
McLean	42	568	2 221	9.5	57.9	10.2	14.7	8 810	20 789	40 851	52 172	1.3	42 288	16.9	24.4	22.9
Madison	155	2 367	27 771	14.3	43.7	28.6	103.9	8 309	21 535	42 155	55 750	1.9	44 358	19.7	22.9	20.8
Magoffin	8	140	3 058	3.0	70.1	8.5	21.6	9 303	15 838	27 947	39 441	0.2	29 421	30.2	41.0	35.6
Marion	76	771	4 768	10.6	62.7	13.0	28.6	8 926	18 741	38 478	48 768	1.5	39 089	21.8	27.6	26.1
Marshall	61	1 294	6 336	10.2	53.3	16.4	42.2	8 761	23 595	44 539	57 401	1.4	45 596	13.1	19.2	17.2
Martin	56	738	2 497	3.2	63.9	7.3	22.2	9 936	15 406	28 040	41 294	0.6	27 484	40.6	42.9	40.7
Mason	128	2 465	3 877	6.8	58.0	14.4	26.4	9 004	23 694	39 783	61 204	3.2	40 260	18.6	30.2	28.9
Meade	71	548	7 763	6.6	52.1	13.4	41.7	8 141	23 229	49 379	62 324	1.4	52 377	12.6	20.9	19.2
Menifee	0	717	1 406	3.8	65.3	11.9	11.4	10 187	16 464	30 313	41 073	0.6	30 828	27.1	42.0	39.5
Mercer	83	1 563	5 089	14.1	55.2	18.3	30.1	8 616	22 614	42 658	53 839	1.3	43 945	17.6	24.7	21.3
Metcalfe	10	592	2 142	12.6	66.9	11.1	16.9	10 384	17 265	30 453	42 278	0.6	30 460	25.2	37.5	36.7
Monroe	0	10	2 457	6.3	67.9	11.7	19.7	10 197	17 571	30 378	42 894	0.5	30 172	26.2	39.1	35.6
Montgomery	109	2 920	6 360	5.1	57.9	17.3	42.0	8 797	21 057	38 373	53 067	1.9	41 139	20.8	27.8	27.6
Morgan	NA	NA	2 607	3.0	64.2	12.6	19.5	9 415	16 379	29 730	44 334	0.4	30 872	30.4	39.7	36.5
Muhlenberg	64	460	6 871	3.8	63.9	9.6	54.5	10 342	19 200	38 849	48 974	0.6	38 916	21.6	30.0	28.4
Nelson	83	1 133	10 872	16.3	55.1	16.2	65.5	8 711	23 531	45 655	61 436	2.4	54 540	12.7	19.0	17.6
Nicholas	43	626	1 512	11.0	58.4	13.7	9.4	8 022	21 276	41 996	51 839	0.9	37 061	19.4	29.5	28.2

1. Data for serious crimes have not been adjusted for underreporting; this may affect comparability between geographic areas and over time.   2. Per 100,000 population estimated by the FBI.
3. All persons 3 years old and over enrolled in nursery school through college.   4. Persons 25 years old and over.   5. Elementary and secondary education expenditures.
6. Based on population estimated by the American Community Survey, 2010–2014.

Table B. States and Counties — **Personal Income**

STATE County	Personal income, 2014										Earnings, 2014		
	Total (mil dol)	Percent change, 2013–2014	Per capita[1] Dollars	Per capita[1] Rank	Wages and salaries (mil dol)	Supplements to wages and salaries; employer contributions (mil dol) Pension and insurance	Supplements to wages and salaries; employer contributions (mil dol) Government social insurance	Proprietors' income (mil dol)	Dividends, interest, and rent (mil dol)	Personal transfer receipts (mil dol)	Total (mil dol)	Contributions for government social insurance (mil dol) From employee and self-employed	Contributions for government social insurance (mil dol) From employer
	62	63	64	65	66	67	68	69	70	71	72	73	74
KENTUCKY—Cont'd													
Clay	531	6.2	25 090	3 060	145	40	11	17	55	287	214	17	11
Clinton	288	9.0	28 327	2 892	115	29	9	24	31	132	178	12	9
Crittenden	318	-1.0	34 488	2 030	58	14	5	26	38	95	103	7	5
Cumberland	198	8.4	29 369	2 793	56	13	5	12	24	96	85	7	5
Daviess	3 868	4.1	39 362	1 271	1 766	315	137	323	640	930	2 541	159	137
Edmonson	340	4.1	28 323	2 893	52	16	4	16	40	116	89	8	4
Elliott	153	1.6	19 879	3 110	28	11	2	3	17	72	43	4	2
Estill	409	5.8	28 342	2 891	83	20	7	7	43	168	116	10	7
Fayette	13 756	4.5	44 262	734	8 738	1 676	654	1 271	2 638	2 207	12 340	697	654
Fleming	418	7.6	28 726	2 860	104	28	8	36	51	143	176	12	8
Floyd	1 237	5.0	32 459	2 378	441	91	35	136	133	533	703	51	35
Franklin	1 889	4.6	37 875	1 473	1 351	381	94	78	317	521	1 903	103	94
Fulton	205	-3.8	32 678	2 338	81	18	7	30	32	78	137	8	7
Gallatin	253	11.5	29 473	2 782	119	20	9	11	23	73	158	10	9
Garrard	502	5.9	29 802	2 742	78	19	6	38	67	147	140	11	6
Grant	774	5.1	31 126	2 567	179	38	14	33	79	216	263	20	14
Graves	1 301	1.8	34 584	2 007	389	82	30	202	161	375	703	40	30
Grayson	789	5.2	30 122	2 702	252	57	21	55	101	257	386	27	21
Green	349	4.5	31 592	2 513	57	17	4	24	43	128	103	8	4
Greenup	1 278	2.8	35 200	1 903	341	63	31	38	142	411	473	39	31
Hancock	341	2.7	38 907	1 331	294	43	21	59	32	71	417	26	21
Hardin	4 179	3.1	38 598	1 377	2 382	584	203	372	784	906	3 542	189	203
Harlan	772	3.8	27 425	2 958	270	60	21	19	88	389	370	28	21
Harrison	605	3.8	32 529	2 367	185	39	14	36	80	159	275	19	14
Hart	534	5.5	28 696	2 865	166	36	13	40	71	176	256	18	13
Henderson	1 611	2.0	34 671	1 988	789	147	62	84	223	420	1 082	68	62
Henry	528	3.8	33 903	2 129	106	25	8	26	75	135	165	12	8
Hickman	197	-7.0	41 644	994	34	8	3	70	23	57	115	4	3
Hopkins	1 654	4.0	35 657	1 830	765	142	60	102	225	450	1 070	68	60
Jackson	321	6.0	24 129	3 079	61	19	5	5	34	141	91	8	5
Jefferson	34 610	4.8	45 538	636	23 065	3 397	1 769	3 246	6 347	6 480	31 476	1 924	1 769
Jessamine	1 881	5.1	37 008	1 599	618	111	50	121	288	346	899	58	50
Johnson	725	3.7	31 162	2 562	201	46	16	28	84	283	291	22	16
Kenton	7 563	4.8	46 137	588	3 290	558	248	347	1 741	1 188	4 444	274	248
Knott	444	6.3	27 947	2 921	93	23	7	19	41	217	143	12	7
Knox	891	7.8	28 007	2 918	270	60	23	95	88	396	447	34	23
Larue	456	1.7	32 168	2 421	82	20	7	20	70	133	129	10	7
Laurel	1 855	6.3	30 916	2 598	890	159	75	114	187	592	1 238	83	75
Lawrence	436	4.8	27 611	2 945	120	26	10	14	42	193	170	14	10
Lee	188	8.5	24 691	3 069	56	13	5	6	23	98	80	6	5
Leslie	325	5.1	29 735	2 755	64	16	5	12	28	157	97	9	5
Letcher	689	4.0	29 506	2 780	172	38	13	43	59	317	265	22	13
Lewis	371	5.4	26 759	2 996	65	17	5	23	34	140	109	9	5
Lincoln	673	4.2	27 520	2 954	138	33	11	26	83	243	208	18	11
Livingston	309	2.2	33 012	2 277	140	24	11	12	40	97	187	13	11
Logan	899	-1.2	33 466	2 202	347	64	26	89	120	253	526	34	26
Lyon	241	3.9	28 587	2 872	66	21	5	9	43	85	101	7	5
McCracken	2 778	3.9	42 532	896	1 634	283	130	243	519	650	2 291	144	130
McCreary	396	7.0	22 152	3 103	96	29	8	14	49	221	147	12	8
McLean	365	-1.0	38 516	1 389	61	14	5	79	37	94	158	7	5
Madison	2 830	5.7	32 406	2 386	1 320	288	104	146	374	675	1 859	113	104
Magoffin	320	5.5	24 791	3 066	65	17	5	16	34	176	103	9	5
Marion	618	5.5	30 883	2 604	290	54	25	27	89	174	396	26	25
Marshall	1 159	3.1	37 460	1 531	538	98	42	84	180	314	762	50	42
Martin	344	2.5	27 447	2 955	123	28	9	13	43	158	174	13	9
Mason	608	3.0	35 422	1 873	392	73	32	36	104	158	532	33	32
Meade	970	2.6	33 278	2 229	158	38	12	44	159	217	252	18	12
Menifee	174	5.3	27 737	2 937	29	9	2	4	19	76	44	4	2
Mercer	714	4.0	33 504	2 196	296	51	22	38	103	198	408	28	22
Metcalfe	277	7.1	27 683	2 940	63	16	5	18	32	105	102	8	5
Monroe	330	9.5	30 798	2 618	95	22	8	42	38	127	167	11	8
Montgomery	869	5.0	31 619	2 509	406	77	34	43	108	234	560	37	34
Morgan	315	2.7	23 713	3 088	101	30	8	10	36	137	149	11	8
Muhlenberg	966	4.2	30 955	2 591	410	85	33	65	127	316	593	39	33
Nelson	1 686	4.2	37 629	1 507	578	109	46	74	213	352	807	54	46
Nicholas	225	8.0	31 908	2 447	29	8	2	14	25	79	53	4	2

1. Based on the resident population estimated as of July 1 of the year shown.

Table B. States and Counties — Earnings, Social Security, and Housing

STATE County	Farm	Mining	Construction	Manufacturing	Information: professional, scientific, technical services	Retail trade	Finance, insurance, real estate and leasing	Health care and social assistance	Government	Social Security beneficiaries, December 2014 Number	Rate[1]	Supplemental Security Income recipients, December 2014	Housing units, 2015 Total	Percent change, 2010–2014
	75	76	77	78	79	80	81	82	83	84	85	86	87	88
KENTUCKY—Cont'd														
Clay	-1.3	D	4.2	0.8	3.1	10.1	2.2	D	45.5	5 300	251	3 354	8 858	-0.2
Clinton	5.4	D	4.0	34.5	1.2	4.8	2.0	14.7	17.5	2 805	275	858	5 238	-1.4
Crittenden	13.8	D	D	14.9	4.5	6.5	4.9	D	19.4	2 590	282	337	4 549	-0.4
Cumberland	3.6	D	D	11.1	D	6.4	3.9	30.2	20.8	1 900	282	477	3 650	-1.1
Daviess	2.9	0.6	5.1	16.2	4.2	7.6	8.2	17.5	13.2	23 000	234	3 763	42 785	3.2
Edmonson	2.9	0.0	12.8	D	D	5.4	D	D	43.8	3 035	252	435	6 450	-0.3
Elliott	-0.3	0.0	3.3	0.0	D	4.1	D	10.8	64.3	1 400	183	473	3 359	-0.4
Estill	-2.3	1.9	D	D	D	8.1	3.3	17.7	31.4	3 700	256	1 315	6 843	-0.3
Fayette	0.2	1.4	6.0	8.6	11.6	6.3	5.6	11.0	25.1	45 970	148	6 861	139 842	3.5
Fleming	7.9	D	5.5	11.7	2.1	8.6	4.7	8.2	29.5	3 870	267	768	6 600	-0.4
Floyd	0.0	D	6.1	1.1	12.0	7.1	2.9	15.7	19.2	11 945	314	4 051	18 153	-0.1
Franklin	-0.1	D	3.9	8.7	5.4	4.5	3.9	D	52.0	13 940	279	1 529	23 248	0.4
Fulton	15.3	D	3.6	13.1	D	9.4	2.9	D	19.8	1 815	290	526	3 359	-0.4
Gallatin	2.6	D	2.3	D	D	3.6	1.2	4.2	15.4	1 900	221	365	3 836	1.3
Garrard	4.8	0.0	18.2	D	5.2	5.0	3.6	D	24.8	4 100	242	680	7 458	-0.1
Grant	-0.7	0.0	5.7	14.0	5.5	12.0	4.0	D	25.5	5 455	220	882	9 983	0.4
Graves	21.0	D	4.1	11.4	3.3	7.2	3.4	D	15.9	9 395	250	1 596	16 738	-0.2
Grayson	2.9	D	8.4	23.8	D	7.6	3.5	D	23.0	6 845	262	1 430	13 485	-0.6
Green	9.5	D	D	3.2	D	8.3	5.8	11.3	35.7	3 135	284	649	5 275	-0.9
Greenup	-0.7	D	3.7	10.4	D	7.2	3.0	23.6	17.5	9 260	255	1 472	16 279	-0.3
Hancock	0.8	D	12.9	69.6	0.6	1.1	0.9	1.7	5.9	2 135	245	271	3 714	-0.5
Hardin	-0.2	0.0	2.8	12.3	9.3	5.6	3.6	5.6	47.3	19 455	179	2 995	46 006	6.4
Harlan	-0.1	23.1	2.5	0.9	4.7	7.5	3.7	D	26.0	8 405	300	2 800	13 464	-0.4
Harrison	2.6	D	7.6	29.8	D	6.5	D	D	16.9	4 445	238	784	8 217	0.1
Hart	4.4	D	D	39.9	1.5	5.8	1.9	D	17.6	4 565	246	1 069	8 812	3.0
Henderson	3.1	0.3	4.9	29.4	2.7	6.3	3.2	D	14.8	10 665	230	1 754	20 467	0.7
Henry	3.5	D	6.2	18.3	D	5.2	D	D	27.4	3 555	228	523	6 679	0.6
Hickman	58.7	0.0	D	D	D	3.5	3.1	D	11.4	1 430	304	184	2 337	-0.2
Hopkins	3.2	11.0	5.2	14.4	D	6.9	3.3	16.3	17.2	11 450	247	2 077	21 294	0.5
Jackson	-5.0	D	4.5	5.5	D	5.2	3.5	D	39.4	3 475	261	1 413	6 514	-0.2
Jefferson	0.0	0.1	5.0	12.4	10.3	4.9	12.0	14.8	11.8	147 400	194	25 950	343 241	1.7
Jessamine	0.7	D	10.2	18.3	D	12.4	3.1	4.7	15.4	9 130	179	1 315	20 066	3.8
Johnson	-0.4	D	4.7	1.1	7.1	14.3	4.0	D	28.1	6 605	284	2 102	10 531	-0.9
Kenton	-0.1	D	6.3	8.9	9.3	4.5	11.5	14.9	17.4	28 035	171	3 958	69 689	1.0
Knott	-0.4	D	D	D	6.6	5.8	D	13.7	28.8	4 575	288	1 726	7 442	-0.3
Knox	-0.4	D	3.7	7.1	6.7	11.5	2.9	D	20.6	8 675	273	3 321	14 446	-0.3
Larue	-0.2	0.0	12.7	15.0	D	5.5	6.1	9.7	26.3	3 475	245	402	6 307	2.2
Laurel	-0.2	3.2	5.1	17.3	D	9.1	4.0	12.7	13.3	14 580	243	3 260	25 418	-0.1
Lawrence	-0.9	D	6.1	D	D	10.2	2.8	21.6	21.3	4 320	274	1 468	7 266	-0.3
Lee	-1.1	5.4	D	D	D	10.1	D	18.8	27.3	2 010	297	858	3 430	-0.2
Leslie	-0.1	14.6	D	D	5.2	6.6	D	D	31.3	3 270	300	1 191	5 266	-0.2
Letcher	0.0	D	2.4	3.0	4.5	16.0	2.3	D	22.7	6 875	294	2 163	11 580	-0.2
Lewis	2.2	0.0	D	12.7	2.7	5.4	3.8	10.2	29.0	3 040	220	992	6 469	-0.2
Lincoln	1.1	0.0	8.4	14.5	6.7	8.1	3.3	12.0	25.7	6 260	256	1 538	10 865	0.4
Livingston	0.8	D	33.4	2.8	D	3.4	1.2	7.1	15.8	2 645	283	267	4 816	-0.2
Logan	5.3	D	6.5	36.4	2.9	5.7	2.4	7.3	12.7	6 460	240	961	12 305	-0.3
Lyon	-0.4	0.0	7.5	D	D	5.3	D	8.9	49.0	2 430	290	157	4 807	0.3
McCracken	0.4	D	5.4	8.7	6.9	9.4	4.1	20.0	12.6	16 155	247	2 329	31 544	1.5
McCreary	-0.8	D	D	D	D	8.8	3.4	8.3	56.6	4 270	239	1 912	7 415	-1.2
McLean	44.5	D	3.7	5.5	D	5.9	D	4.0	15.9	2 595	275	362	4 250	-0.3
Madison	0.2	D	7.6	18.4	8.8	7.3	2.7	9.2	26.9	16 330	188	3 128	36 015	2.8
Magoffin	-1.6	5.9	D	D	6.8	7.0	D	11.8	31.9	3 590	277	1 687	5 927	-0.4
Marion	1.7	D	3.2	48.2	D	4.9	2.4	9.3	12.2	4 335	226	944	8 211	0.4
Marshall	2.0	D	17.2	33.9	D	6.1	3.7	D	12.5	9 010	290	841	15 984	1.5
Martin	-0.5	22.0	D	D	D	6.7	D	6.5	39.0	3 330	266	1 387	5 152	-0.2
Mason	1.4	D	17.8	16.3	D	8.3	2.5	12.6	13.3	4 205	246	793	8 138	0.4
Meade	4.6	2.7	12.7	12.4	5.7	8.6	4.8	D	23.7	5 800	198	890	12 234	3.9
Menifee	-1.4	D	D	12.1	D	4.9	3.2	D	43.9	1 845	293	567	3 749	0.1
Mercer	1.1	D	5.8	42.4	3.3	6.5	2.0	D	12.1	5 525	258	716	10 098	1.6
Metcalfe	9.7	D	D	29.9	D	5.6	D	3.6	26.1	2 690	269	662	4 670	-0.2
Monroe	16.4	0.0	5.8	14.1	1.3	7.8	3.5	11.9	18.4	3 015	282	720	5 201	-0.1
Montgomery	0.0	D	4.7	39.9	D	9.6	4.0	D	13.0	6 270	229	1 310	11 785	0.7
Morgan	-3.2	D	D	9.7	6.4	7.2	D	8.2	34.9	3 200	240	1 039	5 874	0.8
Muhlenberg	4.9	D	8.1	7.9	D	6.3	2.3	D	28.9	8 425	270	1 473	13 640	-0.4
Nelson	0.5	D	9.2	32.4	3.0	7.4	3.3	10.4	13.2	9 735	217	1 376	18 687	3.4
Nicholas	16.1	0.0	7.2	3.5	D	5.7	D	11.3	30.8	1 800	254	326	3 244	-0.4

1. Per 1,000 resident population estimated as of July 1 of the year shown.

Table B. States and Counties — Housing, Labor Force, and Employment

STATE County	Housing units, 2010–2014 Total	Percent	Median value[1]	With a mortgage	Without a mortgage[2]	Median rent[3]	Median rent as a percent of income[2]	Substandard units[4] (percent)	Civilian labor force, 2015 Total	Percent change, 2014–2015	Unemployment Total	Rate[5]	Civilian employment[6] 2010–2014 Total	Management, business, science and arts	Construction, production, and maintenance occupations
	89	90	91	92	93	94	95	96	97	98	99	100	101	102	103
KENTUCKY—Cont'd															
Clay	7 652	74.6	58 600	21.5	13.1	469	36.5	2.5	5 387	-3.0	521	9.7	5 712	27.9	30.7
Clinton	3 878	75.2	66 300	21.5	12.4	558	26.7	1.9	3 830	-4.3	318	8.3	3 437	22.3	39.5
Crittenden	3 812	77.0	71 800	19.6	10.0	489	24.3	3.7	3 749	-3.1	207	5.5	3 467	26.6	38.6
Cumberland	2 684	72.2	62 600	26.6	13.4	461	24.6	2.2	2 870	-2.7	173	6.0	2 499	35.3	31.9
Daviess	38 000	69.0	113 100	19.9	10.0	643	29.2	1.9	44 609	-2.9	2 095	4.7	43 112	29.8	27.8
Edmonson	4 734	79.8	92 700	23.7	10.0	574	28.9	0.2	4 641	-2.9	331	7.1	4 652	28.3	30.3
Elliott	2 790	81.8	64 600	24.4	13.6	422	36.9	3.4	2 104	-2.3	211	10.0	2 099	26.6	37.9
Estill	5 706	71.7	69 400	23.6	12.8	531	34.0	4.6	5 217	-3.5	323	6.2	4 774	21.2	41.4
Fayette	124 101	54.9	166 000	20.3	10.0	766	31.0	2.3	164 121	-1.7	6 433	3.9	154 890	42.5	15.5
Fleming	5 542	73.9	78 900	23.1	11.4	505	25.3	3.6	6 186	-2.9	388	6.3	5 863	30.1	35.1
Floyd	15 438	70.5	72 000	22.6	11.2	550	32.7	2.6	11 754	-5.2	1 110	9.4	12 562	30.2	25.3
Franklin	21 065	62.4	138 600	21.7	10.0	688	31.9	2.1	23 796	-2.3	1 036	4.4	21 682	36.5	23.1
Fulton	2 662	58.5	59 200	19.2	13.1	489	29.4	1.8	2 064	-7.4	159	7.7	2 352	27.2	34.7
Gallatin	3 024	70.3	98 900	21.2	12.9	682	20.9	3.0	3 745	-3.0	200	5.3	3 725	19.1	40.7
Garrard	6 567	76.7	124 300	23.2	10.4	632	33.9	3.0	7 492	-1.3	387	5.2	7 254	28.7	32.8
Grant	8 301	70.9	128 200	23.3	12.2	726	28.0	3.4	10 906	-2.6	591	5.4	10 208	22.9	33.9
Graves	14 284	74.0	89 200	20.9	10.5	577	32.4	2.5	15 136	-4.6	953	6.3	15 457	26.6	31.6
Grayson	9 839	72.7	90 400	23.0	11.5	516	29.3	2.0	10 496	-3.4	714	6.8	9 944	27.5	39.4
Green	4 474	77.1	71 400	20.4	10.2	532	33.2	1.4	4 939	-2.8	269	5.4	4 646	23.0	35.4
Greenup	14 230	76.7	93 600	20.7	10.4	626	30.5	2.7	13 626	-4.6	1 058	7.8	13 276	34.4	25.8
Hancock	3 367	78.6	96 600	16.4	10.0	550	22.8	1.6	3 868	-2.8	196	5.1	3 640	22.2	45.7
Hardin	39 955	62.8	141 200	20.1	10.0	750	26.8	1.8	45 953	-1.4	2 344	5.1	44 863	34.3	23.3
Harlan	11 251	68.9	50 300	21.3	11.3	483	28.4	4.6	7 692	-8.4	897	11.7	7 922	28.6	30.7
Harrison	7 257	66.7	110 300	22.0	12.5	589	30.3	1.3	8 268	-1.8	388	4.7	7 662	23.6	32.9
Hart	7 135	73.7	84 900	21.6	10.8	504	33.0	2.5	7 654	-2.1	399	5.2	6 950	21.2	41.8
Henderson	18 875	65.7	101 500	20.8	10.7	601	31.2	1.8	20 961	-3.2	1 041	5.0	20 438	28.7	30.4
Henry	5 984	70.8	122 000	22.1	12.1	715	31.4	3.0	7 526	-1.5	360	4.8	6 915	26.8	33.2
Hickman	1 992	80.7	64 400	20.5	10.9	594	31.5	4.7	2 080	-2.3	121	5.8	1 735	28.8	33.3
Hopkins	18 533	72.0	87 200	18.8	11.7	597	26.6	2.2	19 442	-4.8	1 112	5.7	19 539	29.3	30.0
Jackson	5 670	74.1	60 500	25.6	13.1	505	27.5	4.7	4 376	-4.5	376	8.6	4 155	25.3	43.2
Jefferson	306 511	62.2	149 900	21.2	11.5	734	29.2	1.7	370 336	-1.9	18 143	4.9	355 687	36.7	21.7
Jessamine	18 120	64.2	158 200	23.7	11.3	773	28.7	2.6	24 442	-1.9	1 054	4.3	22 946	34.2	22.9
Johnson	9 134	75.7	79 800	20.6	13.1	518	27.7	4.8	7 567	-6.0	638	8.4	7 265	27.7	28.5
Kenton	61 962	67.0	143 900	21.2	11.1	746	28.1	2.1	81 007	-2.5	3 688	4.6	78 082	35.1	22.2
Knott	5 776	79.5	61 300	20.2	10.0	498	22.6	2.4	4 882	-4.9	484	9.9	4 804	33.0	27.3
Knox	12 524	63.6	73 600	22.5	12.3	536	32.2	3.5	9 694	-4.2	800	8.3	9 350	24.5	32.1
Larue	5 294	73.8	106 000	21.1	10.5	631	31.1	2.0	5 665	-1.7	300	5.3	5 562	24.8	43.7
Laurel	23 184	69.2	91 000	22.3	11.5	566	29.2	2.9	23 216	-3.8	1 470	6.3	21 792	25.2	29.1
Lawrence	5 940	77.5	84 400	19.9	10.3	514	31.7	2.5	5 140	-2.6	481	9.4	5 508	24.3	34.2
Lee	2 957	73.9	64 600	25.4	14.7	429	41.6	4.2	2 195	-5.1	187	8.5	2 141	29.6	36.8
Leslie	4 212	75.2	46 500	21.4	10.0	478	22.6	3.9	2 989	-5.9	324	10.8	3 226	26.2	37.3
Letcher	9 391	75.1	57 900	19.9	10.0	524	36.3	2.9	6 912	-4.6	774	11.2	7 469	34.1	30.7
Lewis	5 222	78.9	62 600	22.7	11.7	376	28.7	4.2	5 029	-2.7	431	8.6	4 465	26.6	43.5
Lincoln	9 693	74.1	89 100	21.7	11.7	558	31.7	2.7	8 947	-4.1	618	6.9	9 308	25.5	36.3
Livingston	3 708	81.9	79 500	19.8	10.4	565	31.9	2.4	3 612	-3.9	267	7.4	3 776	20.3	40.7
Logan	10 862	70.8	90 700	22.1	12.3	574	32.4	1.7	11 554	-3.1	554	4.8	10 475	24.8	40.4
Lyon	3 263	81.9	116 000	25.7	10.0	402	23.5	1.2	2 881	-3.3	166	5.8	2 721	25.1	27.7
McCracken	27 409	67.3	121 500	19.4	10.0	600	28.1	1.2	28 214	-4.3	1 670	5.9	28 883	31.6	23.7
McCreary	6 210	68.8	63 100	24.6	14.0	559	39.7	2.8	4 789	-5.1	397	8.3	4 533	21.6	32.8
McLean	3 744	79.5	81 400	18.7	10.0	520	26.0	2.2	4 187	-3.0	209	5.0	4 035	31.8	35.4
Madison	31 752	59.1	144 000	21.4	10.9	640	31.1	1.9	44 277	-2.3	1 963	4.4	39 106	36.5	20.3
Magoffin	4 928	74.9	49 700	19.8	11.4	502	40.1	3.4	3 614	-3.0	530	14.7	3 674	28.6	37.2
Marion	7 385	74.1	98 700	22.7	12.3	549	30.5	2.1	9 036	-1.7	459	5.1	7 990	27.4	37.6
Marshall	12 426	79.3	105 200	21.4	10.0	596	28.3	2.1	14 668	-1.9	839	5.7	13 059	29.6	29.1
Martin	4 381	71.2	78 800	29.8	10.3	571	35.1	3.4	3 302	-3.9	316	9.6	2 581	30.1	38.2
Mason	6 636	68.8	102 600	21.8	10.0	555	27.3	1.4	7 446	-3.8	453	6.1	7 347	29.8	30.1
Meade	10 557	71.8	123 500	20.5	10.0	803	29.8	2.7	11 919	-1.7	672	5.6	11 421	29.1	33.4
Menifee	2 404	76.4	80 100	23.4	12.8	498	38.0	2.7	2 324	-1.4	203	8.7	2 076	20.6	40.4
Mercer	8 770	72.9	131 500	21.0	11.4	573	32.1	3.1	9 673	-2.3	492	5.1	9 075	29.1	31.3
Metcalfe	3 918	75.9	82 000	23.4	11.2	512	25.7	3.8	4 004	-3.1	212	5.3	3 957	22.8	40.9
Monroe	4 436	72.5	72 000	25.2	11.1	538	31.7	3.5	4 556	-1.0	200	4.4	4 090	29.4	38.3
Montgomery	10 288	65.0	111 800	22.2	11.6	638	25.9	2.0	11 620	-1.1	770	6.6	10 602	29.1	35.6
Morgan	4 841	73.4	75 600	23.0	11.7	482	33.8	2.4	4 612	-3.8	367	8.0	3 937	29.1	31.3
Muhlenberg	11 619	78.6	78 200	20.2	10.7	530	28.5	2.4	11 856	-4.1	840	7.1	11 410	24.1	38.6
Nelson	16 660	74.7	125 200	22.0	10.0	673	33.2	2.9	20 769	-2.5	1 068	5.1	19 786	26.8	35.8
Nicholas	2 861	73.5	83 200	19.6	10.0	510	26.5	2.3	3 292	-4.6	199	6.0	3 086	27.9	33.3

1. Specified owner-occupied units.   2. A value of 10.0 represents 10 percent or less; a value of 50.0 represents 50 percent or more.   3. Specified renter-occupied units.   4. Overcrowded or lacking complete plumbing facilities.   5. Percent of civilian labor force.   6. Persons 16 years old and over.

Table B. States and Counties — Nonfarm Employment and Agriculture

| | Private nonfarm establishments, employment and payroll, 2014 | | | | | | | | | Agriculture, 2012 | | | |
STATE County	Number of establishments	Total	Health care and social assistance	Manufacturing	Retail trade	Finance and insurance	Professional, scientific, and technical services	Annual payroll Total (mil dol)	Average per employee (dollars)	Farms Number	Percent with: Fewer than 50 acres	500 acres or more	Farm operators whose principal occupation is farming (percent)
	104	105	106	107	108	109	110	111	112	113	114	115	116
KENTUCKY—Cont'd													
Clay	243	2 732	912	D	634	82	54	69	25 399	243	31.7	4.5	33.3
Clinton	186	3 076	482	D	272	88	D	80	26 027	508	33.9	6.5	43.7
Crittenden	160	1 800	358	269	D	D	D	49	27 323	592	27.4	10.3	33.4
Cumberland	106	1 180	D	212	185	58	20	33	28 197	371	31.8	7.5	49.1
Daviess	2 241	41 934	8 090	4 821	6 226	3 097	1 870	1 470	35 064	837	46.5	12.7	48.7
Edmonson	131	816	221	D	166	D	D	22	27 134	638	33.1	4.2	32.0
Elliott	52	354	173	NA	65	D	NA	8	23 607	389	26.5	4.1	38.8
Estill	179	1 480	361	D	317	D	D	39	26 485	380	27.1	4.5	39.2
Fayette	8 565	154 990	29 337	8 619	20 225	5 133	13 060	6 346	40 941	718	47.4	7.4	57.0
Fleming	239	2 120	D	D	445	112	40	63	29 813	1 087	26.9	5.7	47.7
Floyd	833	8 953	2 084	159	1 469	253	298	329	36 724	87	54.0	3.4	29.9
Franklin	1 189	15 524	2 089	2 242	2 505	944	858	591	38 090	579	35.8	5.5	37.1
Fulton	130	1 532	383	D	194	D	D	55	35 966	178	33.7	23.6	51.1
Gallatin	86	764	D	D	197	28	D	18	23 147	185	34.1	5.9	47.6
Garrard	220	1 381	D	D	154	D	D	40	29 154	805	35.5	6.7	44.5
Grant	366	3 642	464	D	955	D	D	115	31 524	812	36.5	3.1	46.1
Graves	713	9 869	D	2 695	1 300	318	537	287	29 050	1 442	41.7	8.5	45.5
Grayson	503	5 968	D	1 621	1 031	224	92	176	29 542	1 407	30.9	4.3	32.8
Green	163	1 273	548	D	236	D	D	32	25 346	1 050	32.0	3.5	41.2
Greenup	522	5 039	1 223	572	668	D	167	178	35 259	604	30.6	3.6	40.2
Hancock	126	3 553	D	2 592	126	D	D	234	65 973	350	33.4	4.0	26.6
Hardin	2 313	34 714	7 521	5 441	5 703	1 402	1 352	1 203	34 643	1 357	45.8	6.1	40.8
Harlan	434	4 934	1 307	D	995	137	195	185	37 414	34	58.8	11.8	29.4
Harrison	284	3 813	819	D	577	104	D	145	38 040	1 064	29.9	6.6	44.1
Hart	277	3 948	427	2 288	451	80	55	127	32 252	1 372	35.9	3.4	38.5
Henderson	1 005	16 500	2 475	5 271	2 192	401	460	623	37 781	465	41.9	14.8	44.7
Henry	212	1 926	238	492	296	93	44	59	30 604	869	33.9	4.1	48.3
Hickman	74	976	159	D	286	D	D	31	31 336	298	32.2	16.4	53.0
Hopkins	972	14 716	D	2 237	2 429	408	524	634	43 083	731	33.2	9.8	40.5
Jackson	95	1 327	237	524	153	D	D	35	26 693	588	32.1	4.1	30.8
Jefferson	19 558	404 871	61 835	41 762	42 601	27 839	24 519	18 601	45 943	382	69.6	1.0	44.0
Jessamine	1 068	14 744	1 155	2 562	2 553	D	589	487	33 007	668	49.6	4.0	38.6
Johnson	423	4 084	767	62	1 414	186	153	127	31 139	196	31.6	1.5	31.6
Kenton	3 072	51 652	10 409	3 555	5 438	D	3 266	2 316	44 843	459	51.4	1.5	34.9
Knott	169	1 604	406	D	273	46	47	50	31 400	42	31.0	9.5	19.0
Knox	442	7 520	1 078	945	1 217	191	1 058	194	25 748	243	32.5	4.9	40.3
Larue	220	1 847	364	552	222	200	D	53	28 476	720	40.1	4.9	46.5
Laurel	1 130	23 054	2 659	3 594	3 200	885	773	734	31 851	1 006	44.3	1.6	37.0
Lawrence	219	2 437	D	D	701	114	61	81	33 185	291	26.5	5.5	35.4
Lee	100	1 296	572	D	216	D	25	29	22 679	142	38.0	3.5	30.3
Leslie	111	1 381	D	D	191	D	D	41	29 586	15	40.0	6.7	26.7
Letcher	325	4 021	1 008	D	644	124	137	159	39 634	54	57.4	0.0	24.1
Lewis	121	1 432	D	518	237	83	13	45	31 520	676	25.3	6.8	39.1
Lincoln	309	2 419	426	416	549	D	74	75	31 005	1 202	40.8	7.2	45.8
Livingston	151	1 878	356	82	171	32	D	77	40 909	403	15.9	15.9	32.0
Logan	497	6 959	765	D	943	163	170	284	40 799	1 060	29.3	9.2	43.4
Lyon	142	1 147	244	D	193	D	40	31	27 421	219	27.4	4.6	32.0
McCracken	2 099	33 747	6 852	2 593	6 167	1 230	1 340	1 322	39 168	447	51.5	5.8	31.5
McCreary	174	1 528	305	D	358	96	D	36	23 348	155	45.2	3.9	36.8
McLean	166	1 118	166	D	197	D	D	38	34 121	413	38.5	16.7	56.9
Madison	1 639	23 846	3 356	5 028	4 092	586	788	852	35 715	1 219	36.8	8.2	45.9
Magoffin	175	1 322	213	D	247	D	135	39	29 293	361	31.0	2.2	34.1
Marion	357	7 425	1 145	3 915	635	134	140	252	33 986	1 016	33.4	6.7	40.1
Marshall	658	9 009	981	2 489	1 110	310	241	399	44 271	719	46.3	4.5	27.8
Martin	160	2 022	212	D	367	75	D	88	43 305	20	40.0	15.0	45.0
Mason	439	7 079	1 242	1 142	1 372	225	92	245	34 541	634	26.7	8.4	43.7
Meade	371	3 608	349	D	594	113	D	116	32 262	754	44.6	4.9	49.3
Menifee	63	470	189	81	90	D	D	14	29 151	294	31.0	5.1	38.8
Mercer	356	5 019	623	2 152	655	128	48	205	40 771	1 067	42.3	4.6	40.9
Metcalfe	118	1 200	D	644	177	D	D	34	28 390	924	32.9	4.5	48.4
Monroe	215	2 367	511	542	506	86	D	67	28 425	858	26.8	9.0	49.3
Montgomery	554	9 980	1 069	4 065	1 520	D	161	329	32 948	609	35.1	4.9	42.0
Morgan	157	2 059	351	D	382	114	71	62	30 292	694	23.1	7.1	35.0
Muhlenberg	550	6 334	1 364	871	1 240	194	152	216	34 124	630	33.0	7.8	39.8
Nelson	948	14 434	1 409	4 096	1 798	330	284	492	34 103	1 326	47.5	5.1	43.1
Nicholas	80	542	215	D	139	24	D	12	22 642	570	23.3	6.0	49.3

Table B. States and Counties — **Agriculture**

STATE County	Acreage (1,000) 117	Percent change, 2007–2012 118	Average size of farm 119	Total irrigated (1,000) 120	Total cropland (1,000) 121	Average per farm 122	Average per acre 123	Value of machinery and equipment, average per farm (dollars) 124	Total (mil dol) 125	Average per farm (dollars) 126	Crops 127	Live-stock and poultry products 128	$10,000 or more 129	$100,000 or more 130	Total ($1,000) 131	Percent of farms 132
KENTUCKY—Cont'd																
Clay	35	-31.4	145	0.2	9.9	230 173	1 592	48 691	4.7	19 169	70.5	29.5	25.1	7.0	239	33.3
Clinton	74	-18.7	146	0.3	26.0	378 150	2 594	53 791	29.8	58 632	12.7	87.3	43.5	6.9	551	44.7
Crittenden	149	-7.1	251	1.1	83.0	541 215	2 153	75 215	31.6	53 311	63.0	37.0	34.0	5.9	2 672	50.7
Cumberland	65	-36.7	176	D	17.7	301 164	1 707	42 027	12.8	34 596	25.0	75.0	29.6	3.0	346	42.9
Daviess	237	-7.7	283	9.6	190.2	1 100 748	3 884	144 342	176.4	210 760	65.6	34.4	43.0	18.5	3 286	54.4
Edmonson	85	-12.1	133	0.0	34.9	316 882	2 379	44 666	20.2	31 699	33.5	66.5	28.4	4.5	1 960	44.8
Elliott	56	-15.7	145	0.1	13.5	196 622	1 358	39 936	3.2	8 321	42.9	57.1	26.7	0.0	479	30.3
Estill	52	-19.3	138	0.0	14.1	254 342	1 848	37 968	4.4	11 655	51.2	48.7	26.6	2.1	337	41.3
Fayette	115	-15.5	160	1.1	40.4	1 457 641	9 112	96 464	176.2	245 461	7.7	92.3	46.9	14.8	1 263	28.7
Fleming	183	0.9	169	0.2	73.1	353 267	2 096	62 407	52.7	48 516	34.1	65.9	50.6	9.1	1 630	63.6
Floyd	8	4.8	94	0.0	1.2	138 034	1 472	22 207	0.6	6 644	74.4	25.6	11.5	1.1	D	2.3
Franklin	79	2.9	136	0.3	30.1	499 653	3 684	55 269	19.4	33 463	41.9	58.1	35.4	4.7	546	31.3
Fulton	83	-8.8	468	2.5	74.3	1 635 017	3 490	183 713	46.6	261 562	72.4	27.6	48.3	31.5	2 716	77.0
Gallatin	28	-17.8	150	0.0	10.8	454 384	3 026	67 178	5.7	30 546	80.0	20.0	31.9	6.5	232	38.9
Garrard	127	4.6	158	0.2	43.7	390 569	2 471	61 070	38.5	47 794	27.2	72.8	43.4	9.2	805	37.6
Grant	98	-14.4	121	0.1	33.0	370 686	3 060	53 784	11.7	14 408	56.4	43.6	28.7	2.2	729	30.7
Graves	292	5.0	202	4.5	221.9	656 060	3 242	105 221	337.7	234 209	25.7	74.3	36.4	18.5	7 722	69.1
Grayson	201	-7.2	143	0.1	87.1	324 133	2 270	54 270	45.7	32 454	40.1	59.9	33.1	5.0	2 928	51.0
Green	153	4.8	145	0.1	67.4	329 032	2 265	59 282	39.2	37 304	56.1	43.9	42.5	6.4	2 908	61.1
Greenup	79	-14.4	130	0.1	17.5	230 462	1 770	45 828	5.0	8 333	56.1	43.9	20.0	0.3	311	33.3
Hancock	52	-17.2	149	0.5	23.4	419 334	2 812	81 900	14.0	40 037	72.6	27.4	30.9	3.7	515	50.3
Hardin	203	-8.7	150	0.7	114.4	524 307	3 505	74 682	57.9	42 704	70.2	29.8	35.9	6.9	2 030	40.5
Harlan	6	106.5	184	D	0.3	243 765	1 323	34 529	0.3	8 294	53.9	46.1	14.7	2.9	D	2.9
Harrison	164	1.7	155	2.0	64.2	422 032	2 730	61 867	36.0	33 848	54.0	46.0	39.4	7.3	1 123	34.7
Hart	182	-4.5	133	0.2	76.1	295 020	2 219	53 891	33.5	24 409	42.5	57.5	35.1	5.2	4 176	54.4
Henderson	176	-10.1	378	6.0	150.0	1 381 355	3 651	193 890	78.6	169 024	93.2	6.8	47.1	17.6	3 464	67.1
Henry	129	-12.2	148	0.8	58.2	494 348	3 343	59 478	30.7	35 292	60.0	40.0	42.8	6.6	1 549	47.6
Hickman	141	8.8	474	6.1	119.7	1 647 913	3 480	199 456	159.2	534 356	35.7	64.3	48.0	29.9	2 918	76.8
Hopkins	163	2.3	223	0.2	94.2	646 970	2 902	81 895	107.7	147 369	32.6	67.4	26.7	9.2	2 662	46.5
Jackson	78	-5.8	132	0.0	23.0	240 571	1 818	43 282	9.9	16 774	26.4	73.6	27.9	3.2	588	44.0
Jefferson	23	-28.5	60	0.2	11.0	521 759	8 633	43 777	7.8	20 343	79.4	20.6	22.8	3.9	288	18.1
Jessamine	84	4.4	125	0.2	33.6	685 317	5 473	49 979	25.0	37 446	21.1	78.9	35.9	7.0	863	36.4
Johnson	24	-12.5	124	D	4.9	216 969	1 750	44 179	1.3	6 561	35.8	64.3	15.8	0.5	81	20.9
Kenton	38	-10.3	83	0.1	15.1	362 353	4 360	48 092	5.3	11 475	43.2	56.8	20.5	3.3	324	29.4
Knott	7	-2.8	161	0.0	1.8	217 095	1 352	61 881	0.4	8 524	17.6	82.4	23.8	2.4	D	2.4
Knox	34	-34.4	138	0.1	9.6	241 292	1 749	50 700	2.3	9 358	60.6	39.4	19.3	0.8	206	21.4
Larue	112	-10.7	156	0.1	66.9	532 196	3 422	82 204	41.9	58 163	74.3	25.7	39.9	7.8	1 295	43.2
Laurel	96	-6.3	95	0.1	35.0	329 341	3 449	43 809	15.3	15 187	41.5	58.5	27.4	2.1	536	29.3
Lawrence	42	-30.8	143	0.0	6.5	202 818	1 416	41 120	1.6	5 375	53.4	46.6	15.8	0.0	31	12.4
Lee	22	-24.5	156	0.0	5.4	297 641	1 902	40 134	1.0	6 852	47.2	52.8	19.0	1.4	86	30.3
Leslie	D	D	D	0.0	0.2	412 867	D	33 533	0.0	267	D	D	0.0	0.0	3	20.0
Letcher	3	-20.5	53	D	0.4	123 185	2 313	43 722	0.1	2 463	64.7	34.6	3.7	0.0	0	0.0
Lewis	118	-19.6	174	0.0	32.8	256 246	1 469	49 519	12.8	18 944	70.8	29.2	27.4	4.0	968	49.6
Lincoln	181	1.4	150	0.3	72.6	374 358	2 489	59 559	57.4	47 729	30.6	69.4	42.3	9.7	1 680	43.5
Livingston	123	5.3	306	0.0	62.5	650 496	2 128	90 191	21.3	52 898	50.3	49.7	40.4	10.7	1 651	54.8
Logan	276	-4.9	260	2.7	192.4	871 373	3 349	105 848	134.9	127 283	71.8	28.2	42.8	15.2	6 034	59.8
Lyon	42	-23.1	190	D	23.6	384 995	2 025	67 187	6.8	30 968	78.0	22.0	37.0	6.4	561	52.5
McCracken	67	-10.8	150	0.3	49.7	462 497	3 077	66 349	22.2	49 738	73.3	26.7	28.6	8.1	947	53.0
McCreary	18	20.2	117	0.0	3.3	208 974	1 790	42 200	1.0	6 671	35.4	64.6	21.3	0.0	11	5.8
McLean	124	-13.7	301	1.2	96.5	1 132 448	3 760	162 719	179.7	435 218	32.1	67.9	55.9	32.0	2 451	71.7
Madison	233	6.7	191	0.2	73.0	576 284	3 018	65 868	60.5	49 656	14.2	85.8	43.3	9.5	783	43.3
Magoffin	44	-27.9	123	D	7.9	182 543	1 482	33 341	1.3	3 479	53.7	46.3	8.9	0.0	235	32.7
Marion	166	3.6	164	0.3	70.2	441 025	2 693	65 181	56.5	55 601	40.2	59.8	46.8	11.1	1 357	56.6
Marshall	95	-2.9	132	0.1	54.8	403 344	3 057	61 174	45.3	63 042	31.7	68.3	25.0	6.1	1 902	52.9
Martin	D	D	D	0.0	0.3	1 783 100	D	35 100	0.1	4 750	D	D	10.0	0.0	0	0.0
Mason	127	-9.4	200	0.0	57.9	515 345	2 578	69 967	30.9	48 784	59.5	40.5	48.3	12.1	1 693	52.8
Meade	119	-1.6	158	0.0	63.7	514 138	3 244	78 910	36.6	48 503	51.7	48.3	35.7	7.6	1 424	52.0
Menifee	41	-5.0	139	D	10.0	248 966	1 787	41 129	3.8	13 082	44.1	55.9	22.8	2.7	177	29.3
Mercer	144	2.0	135	0.0	59.4	456 854	3 379	67 196	50.7	47 495	18.6	81.4	42.4	9.3	1 472	31.8
Metcalfe	125	-16.2	136	0.1	49.7	305 962	2 256	56 923	35.0	37 899	30.1	69.9	43.5	8.4	2 185	45.0
Monroe	172	-2.0	201	0.1	62.0	473 586	2 359	68 647	77.2	90 021	23.5	76.5	51.6	11.2	1 603	48.0
Montgomery	99	-7.0	163	0.0	40.0	447 880	2 743	58 650	19.0	31 209	31.1	68.9	42.2	6.4	539	36.1
Morgan	119	-12.8	171	0.0	24.0	218 340	1 276	50 761	6.9	9 938	42.0	58.0	26.4	0.4	579	37.3
Muhlenberg	129	-8.6	204	0.2	67.1	474 975	2 324	78 500	68.9	109 373	35.6	64.4	31.0	9.5	2 162	44.6
Nelson	188	-4.3	142	0.7	97.2	476 235	3 363	65 611	64.4	48 597	53.3	46.7	34.9	8.1	2 129	35.2
Nicholas	102	-7.3	179	0.1	40.9	387 086	2 159	59 526	20.7	36 384	50.6	49.4	45.4	7.5	712	36.0

Table B. States and Counties — **Water Use, Wholesale Trade, Retail Trade, and Real Estate**

STATE County	Water use, 2010		Wholesale trade,[1] 2012				Retail trade,[2] 2012				Real estate and rental and leasing,[2] 2012			
	Total water withdrawn (mil gal/day)	Gallons withdrawn per person per day	Number of establishments	Number of employees	Sales (mil dol)	Annual payroll (mil dol)	Number of establishments	Number of employees	Sales (mil dol)	Annual payroll (mil dol)	Number of establishments	Number of employees	Receipts (mil dol)	Annual payroll (mil dol)
	133	134	135	136	137	138	139	140	141	142	143	144	145	146
KENTUCKY—Cont'd														
Clay	4.5	205	5	D	D	D	63	543	138.8	11.6	7	D	D	D
Clinton	4.0	393	11	64	87.1	2.3	39	296	59.4	4.4	7	19	3.0	0.4
Crittenden	1.4	151	5	118	11.8	2.5	31	273	58.8	5.1	6	13	1.7	0.3
Cumberland	1.0	144	NA	NA	NA	NA	30	181	46.0	3.4	3	7	0.3	0.1
Daviess	268.9	2 782	97	1 266	1 105.8	55.6	411	5 906	1 443.4	134.3	80	578	99.7	19.2
Edmonson	2.2	180	NA	NA	NA	NA	31	177	39.2	3.0	NA	NA	NA	NA
Elliott	0.6	74	NA	NA	NA	NA	12	D	D	D	NA	NA	NA	NA
Estill	1.6	111	3	D	D	D	42	299	75.3	5.9	5	D	D	D
Fayette	52.3	177	352	7 283	4 517.8	527.7	1 192	19 820	4 994.8	466.9	431	2 128	442.3	76.6
Fleming	2.3	162	10	D	D	D	61	455	134.8	11.2	10	15	1.9	0.2
Floyd	5.4	136	39	475	395.4	19.0	164	1 506	448.3	34.4	30	131	18.2	5.3
Franklin	10.2	206	28	282	372.8	15.5	178	2 477	654.2	54.0	38	191	22.2	4.6
Fulton	1.3	194	7	53	377.2	4.8	26	184	44.0	3.2	4	7	0.6	0.2
Gallatin	2.4	274	1	D	D	D	21	241	128.0	4.6	7	D	D	D
Garrard	2.4	141	6	23	7.4	0.8	35	167	59.1	3.3	7	10	2.0	0.2
Grant	2.3	95	8	D	D	D	74	943	284.4	21.2	17	38	4.0	1.0
Graves	10.2	273	38	613	767.9	25.6	123	1 374	403.7	32.0	34	70	10.9	1.5
Grayson	3.4	133	11	D	D	D	104	1 069	258.6	22.2	12	141	7.1	3.7
Green	2.7	239	6	29	15.1	0.9	32	246	62.1	5.2	3	D	D	D
Greenup	14.1	382	9	D	D	D	86	837	211.7	18.0	16	57	8.1	1.3
Hancock	306.8	35 820	3	D	D	D	17	138	43.5	2.6	5	13	2.5	0.3
Hardin	16.8	159	57	422	245.7	18.3	408	5 754	1 639.1	137.8	109	490	62.4	11.7
Harlan	5.4	185	25	204	177.3	9.5	101	1 043	205.4	21.2	14	46	4.8	0.9
Harrison	3.9	207	10	44	30.0	1.3	46	566	134.5	11.7	7	32	2.9	0.6
Hart	5.2	285	9	39	12.7	1.5	65	406	157.9	8.1	7	16	1.5	0.4
Henderson	14.8	320	45	D	D	D	170	2 174	729.9	53.7	44	275	23.4	5.2
Henry	1.3	84	13	D	D	D	36	342	171.4	6.3	4	D	D	D
Hickman	5.6	1 144	6	31	67.8	0.9	20	267	76.1	6.2	3	5	0.3	0.0
Hopkins	12.8	273	44	414	240.3	20.6	182	2 325	692.4	55.5	41	114	15.2	3.3
Jackson	2.1	156	NA	NA	NA	NA	25	187	45.7	2.7	5	14	1.4	0.4
Jefferson	687.0	927	1 006	15 867	13 048.4	836.7	2 659	41 294	10 964.4	1 004.0	926	7 168	2 895.1	289.1
Jessamine	7.0	144	40	D	D	D	158	2 638	920.3	71.1	31	124	14.0	3.3
Johnson	3.0	129	17	110	57.2	4.0	91	1 333	383.0	31.1	16	41	4.5	0.9
Kenton	0.5	3	119	1 888	886.0	92.5	394	5 422	1 331.7	120.4	129	656	161.3	27.0
Knott	2.2	136	NA	NA	NA	NA	39	297	72.5	5.4	3	D	D	D
Knox	1.0	31	11	70	39.9	2.0	106	1 194	343.1	26.2	11	51	4.8	1.0
Larue	1.1	80	7	D	D	D	30	255	63.9	4.6	3	3	0.1	0.1
Laurel	9.7	165	61	732	597.3	29.0	228	3 348	1 015.1	78.2	46	166	27.6	4.6
Lawrence	12.0	757	11	229	136.5	9.0	52	645	161.5	12.5	9	36	4.0	0.7
Lee	0.8	105	4	17	4.8	0.5	22	236	63.9	4.9	4	D	D	D
Leslie	1.8	156	NA	NA	NA	NA	26	220	55.6	3.7	NA	NA	NA	NA
Letcher	3.7	152	11	D	D	D	59	678	151.2	15.1	11	18	3.9	0.6
Lewis	1.6	118	3	D	D	D	32	252	70.5	4.1	2	D	D	D
Lincoln	3.3	135	14	D	D	D	61	623	145.9	10.9	6	10	1.1	0.2
Livingston	4.2	443	9	D	D	D	25	181	47.1	3.7	4	D	D	D
Logan	2.4	88	22	192	156.6	6.8	98	926	264.9	22.1	11	18	3.4	0.5
Lyon	3.1	368	3	D	D	D	20	190	65.1	4.0	3	4	0.9	0.1
McCracken	779.8	11 893	104	D	D	D	411	6 163	1 638.5	140.7	79	330	60.9	9.8
McCreary	2.1	114	2	D	D	D	42	378	81.9	7.5	8	13	0.8	0.2
McLean	1.9	200	8	D	D	D	28	185	61.0	4.1	NA	NA	NA	NA
Madison	11.9	144	38	308	262.0	9.6	299	4 171	1 080.7	85.1	68	D	D	D
Magoffin	1.3	97	2	D	D	D	34	241	61.1	4.8	2	D	D	D
Marion	5.9	298	11	68	34.4	2.1	65	649	171.0	14.0	9	19	3.1	0.8
Marshall	18.7	594	27	228	99.3	9.2	103	1 081	392.3	27.7	15	29	4.7	0.7
Martin	5.0	386	4	D	D	D	40	364	93.8	7.9	3	D	D	D
Mason	22.9	1 306	15	358	79.8	14.0	93	1 385	363.8	29.8	13	34	6.2	1.0
Meade	9.7	338	10	77	49.2	2.8	63	609	197.3	12.5	17	50	5.6	1.1
Menifee	1.3	198	NA	NA	NA	NA	15	123	23.2	1.4	3	D	D	D
Mercer	9.5	445	8	32	14.7	0.7	62	705	169.7	15.4	11	21	2.8	0.5
Metcalfe	0.8	82	2	D	D	D	27	233	49.6	4.7	3	4	0.9	0.1
Monroe	3.0	275	7	47	26.9	1.5	42	449	104.1	9.8	6	18	1.3	0.3
Montgomery	3.7	141	17	D	D	D	114	1 501	457.8	34.0	19	35	5.1	0.8
Morgan	1.7	121	NA	NA	NA	NA	45	390	93.9	7.9	2	D	D	D
Muhlenberg	1 236.8	39 263	13	151	33.9	6.2	115	1 291	304.1	27.5	15	58	6.8	1.4
Nelson	8.5	196	30	292	147.4	9.4	159	1 826	535.2	42.7	28	63	11.6	2.1
Nicholas	1.9	262	1	D	D	D	16	139	27.4	2.8	1	D	D	D

1. Merchant wholesalers, except manufacturers' sales branches and offices.   2. Employer establishments.

Table B. States and Counties — **Professional Services, Manufacturing, and Accommodation and Food Services**

STATE County	Professional, scientific, and technical services, 2012				Manufacturing, 2012				Accommodation and food services, 2012			
	Number of establishments	Number of employees	Receipts (mil dol)	Annual payroll (mil dol)	Number of establishments	Number of employees	Receipts (mil dol)	Annual payroll (mil dol)	Number of establishments	Number of employees	Sales (mil dol)	Annual payroll (mil dol)
	147	148	149	150	151	152	153	154	155	156	157	158
KENTUCKY—Cont'd												
Clay	19	62	5.1	1.4	8	236	D	4.0	20	D	D	D
Clinton	15	33	2.6	1.0	12	D	D	D	15	D	D	D
Crittenden	12	224	11.0	5.6	12	170	D	5.0	12	202	5.3	1.7
Cumberland	9	D	D	D	7	189	30.8	6.4	14	D	D	D
Daviess	155	1 499	100.4	42.9	104	5 092	3 773.5	238.6	173	D	D	D
Edmonson	5	13	1.1	0.3	3	D	D	D	13	D	D	D
Elliott	NA	NA	NA	NA	NA	NA	NA	NA	5	D	D	D
Estill	9	41	1.8	0.5	8	180	D	4.0	20	D	D	D
Fayette	1 072	10 073	1 441.2	561.1	224	8 005	2 922.0	351.1	772	17 490	939.4	270.7
Fleming	15	36	3.5	1.0	20	350	82.9	11.4	7	D	D	D
Floyd	69	D	D	D	13	145	30.7	5.0	49	851	36.3	9.1
Franklin	127	777	88.9	33.5	41	2 383	1 748.1	110.1	106	1 948	98.3	26.3
Fulton	7	19	1.3	0.5	9	366	240.7	14.0	13	170	7.2	1.9
Gallatin	10	37	10.3	1.2	4	D	D	D	10	D	D	D
Garrard	15	34	3.2	1.0	15	240	39.2	7.3	11	D	D	D
Grant	24	67	4.8	1.9	15	588	860.2	24.3	43	D	D	D
Graves	47	370	17.4	7.3	48	2 128	480.8	75.8	51	808	29.6	7.7
Grayson	27	77	5.5	1.8	28	1 507	441.0	52.9	30	D	D	D
Green	12	27	2.4	0.9	9	58	D	1.3	9	174	6.4	1.7
Greenup	31	208	13.3	5.0	17	557	D	27.2	36	676	30.4	9.1
Hancock	6	45	3.5	1.5	12	1 720	D	114.2	6	D	D	D
Hardin	217	1 492	168.9	63.4	68	4 931	2 078.1	230.9	182	4 504	192.0	54.4
Harlan	37	257	17.5	9.6	10	74	D	3.3	33	D	D	D
Harrison	16	90	6.8	3.5	19	1 182	559.7	66.4	22	334	13.1	3.3
Hart	16	62	4.2	1.5	18	2 113	D	75.1	24	D	D	D
Henderson	71	416	39.9	13.8	76	4 930	2 857.6	215.1	85	1 411	65.4	16.8
Henry	18	52	3.4	1.1	4	396	D	17.7	15	D	D	D
Hickman	4	D	D	D	3	D	D	D	4	D	D	D
Hopkins	60	380	38.7	14.3	46	2 270	964.5	127.5	73	1 415	54.3	15.0
Jackson	6	13	1.0	0.4	9	181	D	8.4	7	44	2.2	0.6
Jefferson	2 197	22 198	3 274.3	1 139.3	718	40 666	28 642.1	2 159.3	1 651	39 711	2 006.3	572.1
Jessamine	85	548	81.4	20.4	69	2 550	681.4	93.4	73	D	D	D
Johnson	30	141	23.9	6.1	6	53	D	1.4	40	D	D	D
Kenton	355	2 723	313.0	130.5	90	3 891	1 674.8	219.8	307	D	D	D
Knott	11	45	8.3	2.1	NA	NA	NA	NA	8	81	5.3	1.3
Knox	40	1 133	57.5	27.4	14	1 021	191.2	35.0	43	715	37.5	9.7
Larue	20	48	4.4	1.3	14	498	D	D	17	121	5.2	1.5
Laurel	93	467	40.0	15.7	54	3 237	924.1	129.5	94	2 181	101.9	28.3
Lawrence	12	66	5.1	2.3	3	7	D	0.3	20	D	D	D
Lee	5	17	0.9	0.4	NA	NA	NA	NA	5	D	D	D
Leslie	7	50	6.6	1.6	NA	NA	NA	NA	4	D	D	D
Letcher	19	177	10.0	5.6	8	21	D	0.7	23	D	D	D
Lewis	4	D	D	D	14	385	94.8	12.1	8	D	D	D
Lincoln	22	76	5.9	1.9	13	726	188.1	24.4	18	397	12.6	3.4
Livingston	7	D	D	D	6	73	D	3.5	10	D	D	D
Logan	29	148	11.8	5.0	39	2 271	2 571.5	118.6	34	D	D	D
Lyon	10	39	3.2	1.5	NA	NA	NA	NA	22	D	D	D
McCracken	203	1 194	219.4	56.2	58	3 077	2 308.6	164.2	213	4 111	181.7	52.4
McCreary	6	72	3.4	0.9	10	373	D	7.2	17	273	7.9	2.3
McLean	8	19	1.4	0.4	9	126	D	4.6	14	91	3.6	0.9
Madison	137	679	71.4	25.1	65	3 597	D	162.6	159	3 495	164.5	43.5
Magoffin	16	105	14.2	4.1	NA	NA	NA	NA	10	154	6.4	1.8
Marion	28	101	8.3	3.1	31	3 586	895.0	135.8	34	D	D	D
Marshall	36	197	20.6	9.3	36	2 172	3 212.2	171.1	79	1 224	45.9	12.6
Martin	11	23	2.7	0.8	3	27	D	0.6	12	152	6.3	1.6
Mason	25	110	9.3	3.5	11	1 249	D	57.1	40	774	35.6	10.1
Meade	33	269	11.2	4.4	6	250	D	3.4	30	409	23.1	5.9
Menifee	2	D	D	D	5	D	D	3.4	2	D	D	D
Mercer	23	58	4.7	1.4	12	2 096	2 130.5	131.8	38	D	D	D
Metcalfe	5	11	0.8	0.2	8	716	311.6	22.4	10	89	3.8	1.0
Monroe	8	16	0.8	0.3	18	547	85.9	17.4	16	D	D	D
Montgomery	35	149	14.0	4.5	35	3 919	1 040.4	140.0	35	D	D	D
Morgan	13	75	3.8	1.7	5	409	47.4	8.2	11	D	D	D
Muhlenberg	34	148	16.8	3.9	26	793	218.7	26.1	49	D	D	D
Nelson	68	243	18.9	5.2	53	3 434	1 820.0	164.9	59	1 198	48.3	13.3
Nicholas	6	11	1.1	0.4	4	39	4.5	1.2	6	30	1.2	0.2

1. Establishment subject to federal tax.

STATE County	Health care and social assistance, 2012				Other services, 2012				Nonemployer businesses, 2014		Value of residential construction authorized by building permits, 2015	
	Number of establishments	Number of employees	Receipts (mil dol)	Annual payroll (mil dol)	Number of establishments	Number of employees	Receipts (mil dol)	Annual payroll (mil dol)	Number	Receipts (mil dol)	New Construction ($1,000)	Number of housing units
	159	160	161	162	163	164	165	166	167	168	169	170
KENTUCKY—Cont'd												
Clay	36	943	106.1	37.7	10	34	3.9	0.9	1 118	35.9	0	0
Clinton	24	322	28.5	11.4	5	D	D	D	784	28.7	0	0
Crittenden	17	407	26.9	12.5	14	D	D	D	611	22.8	0	0
Cumberland	14	456	37.2	15.8	9	27	2.9	0.6	579	22.8	0	0
Daviess	324	7 657	744.6	296.5	150	D	D	D	5 521	238.6	32 855	241
Edmonson	18	D	D	D	8	D	D	D	849	31.5	NA	NA
Elliott	10	130	7.6	3.9	2	D	D	D	294	8.9	NA	NA
Estill	28	442	36.8	15.8	7	24	2.6	0.6	869	22.1	0	0
Fayette	1 048	29 625	3 726.0	1 437.5	553	4 405	738.6	141.8	21 737	1 064.4	137 582	1 342
Fleming	21	561	48.2	18.4	16	D	D	D	1 278	49.2	160	1
Floyd	131	1 939	198.7	75.6	43	298	34.9	9.8	2 194	91.7	1 365	16
Franklin	156	1 800	210.2	60.8	128	749	87.8	25.3	3 128	115.2	8 699	40
Fulton	15	D	D	D	6	D	D	D	288	10.0	0	0
Gallatin	9	D	D	D	5	D	D	D	388	14.5	1 236	8
Garrard	24	231	13.0	6.0	10	D	D	D	1 234	42.0	0	0
Grant	32	D	D	D	24	D	D	D	1 285	54.5	8 442	38
Graves	97	D	D	D	33	217	28.9	8.0	2 647	114.7	192	1
Grayson	58	1 131	86.6	34.8	29	D	D	D	1 905	95.5	1 952	10
Green	24	572	39.7	17.5	16	47	4.9	0.9	934	35.4	0	0
Greenup	104	D	D	D	25	D	D	D	1 854	58.0	4 444	13
Hancock	14	102	6.4	2.1	5	D	D	D	436	13.9	390	2
Hardin	341	7 473	697.5	304.9	145	D	D	D	5 384	205.0	33 282	212
Harlan	52	1 332	137.9	50.6	24	86	8.7	2.0	1 393	39.2	0	0
Harrison	46	909	84.0	30.6	21	D	D	D	1 071	41.1	3 444	19
Hart	27	470	32.1	14.9	16	46	4.4	1.1	1 594	81.3	9 567	90
Henderson	137	2 500	233.7	87.1	62	534	76.6	19.5	2 417	92.0	10 202	129
Henry	19	257	15.2	7.0	16	D	D	D	1 062	41.6	4 268	26
Hickman	10	179	12.6	5.7	2	D	D	D	316	10.1	NA	NA
Hopkins	122	3 143	289.1	117.6	68	498	56.4	15.7	2 269	85.9	12 357	78
Jackson	9	219	15.1	6.2	4	12	1.6	0.3	842	23.6	0	0
Jefferson	2 390	65 785	7 401.3	2 838.2	1 307	11 226	1 278.7	353.7	51 997	2 384.2	288 448	2 080
Jessamine	112	1 026	64.9	31.7	68	235	26.2	5.7	4 100	181.7	51 189	197
Johnson	56	828	84.6	29.5	30	D	D	D	1 371	51.0	0	0
Kenton	344	10 407	1 298.0	519.8	232	D	D	D	9 531	434.5	52 293	252
Knott	17	220	21.0	6.6	9	D	D	D	773	29.4	NA	NA
Knox	71	1 357	93.3	38.0	19	D	D	D	2 128	74.4	0	0
Larue	19	284	11.9	6.1	14	46	4.5	1.1	1 065	39.5	6 759	32
Laurel	136	2 528	320.2	128.2	67	D	D	D	3 862	171.8	1 711	15
Lawrence	30	702	69.8	25.8	18	D	D	D	780	24.4	NA	NA
Lee	19	612	21.3	10.6	1	D	D	D	414	13.8	NA	NA
Leslie	16	328	26.3	10.8	4	26	2.7	0.7	514	17.5	NA	NA
Letcher	45	937	96.7	36.6	13	D	D	D	1 213	37.5	0	0
Lewis	12	298	20.4	8.7	9	26	1.8	0.3	869	31.4	126	2
Lincoln	39	710	51.7	20.4	22	D	D	D	1 579	53.5	5 695	29
Livingston	20	D	D	D	9	D	D	D	572	17.8	NA	NA
Logan	48	677	68.6	19.4	34	105	9.5	2.9	1 760	79.5	1 482	29
Lyon	14	204	12.3	5.1	7	D	D	D	506	16.6	2 085	11
McCracken	276	6 441	782.5	281.4	129	D	D	D	4 186	175.6	45 580	487
McCreary	25	320	18.3	8.3	4	D	D	D	893	35.1	0	0
McLean	10	132	8.3	3.1	12	D	D	D	526	16.6	0	0
Madison	254	3 580	283.6	115.7	96	515	53.7	13.4	5 397	205.4	17 988	276
Magoffin	17	278	20.2	7.3	11	29	4.4	0.6	650	18.5	NA	NA
Marion	44	1 333	86.5	33.5	17	D	D	D	1 148	46.8	1 254	12
Marshall	64	986	59.3	25.8	38	174	15.1	4.3	2 154	85.9	9 074	45
Martin	23	237	18.3	6.8	7	24	2.9	0.9	457	12.5	NA	NA
Mason	65	1 200	109.4	40.9	42	160	10.7	2.9	1 138	41.3	3 928	20
Meade	38	363	19.3	8.6	23	D	D	D	1 470	60.0	9 694	64
Menifee	10	185	12.5	5.6	2	D	D	D	416	12.2	NA	NA
Mercer	42	696	60.8	24.2	29	D	D	D	1 435	60.5	7 265	61
Metcalfe	17	D	D	D	8	16	1.1	0.2	849	30.1	NA	NA
Monroe	29	494	34.3	14.7	9	44	5.3	0.9	916	35.7	NA	NA
Montgomery	73	913	83.4	30.2	29	D	D	D	1 783	65.3	4 761	25
Morgan	16	297	28.1	10.5	11	D	D	D	767	25.2	1 275	17
Muhlenberg	58	1 318	87.0	37.2	41	163	15.6	4.1	1 606	57.2	426	6
Nelson	97	1 577	126.8	49.4	46	182	15.5	4.0	2 969	114.9	24 199	161
Nicholas	13	269	15.2	7.2	4	23	1.7	0.5	465	14.1	195	1

Table B. States and Counties — Government Employment and Payroll, and Local Government Finances

	Government employment and payroll, 2012									Local government finances, 2012				
			March payroll (percent of total)							General revenue				
													Taxes	
													Per capita[1] (dollars)	
STATE County	Full-time equivalent employees	March payroll (dollars)	Administration, judicial, and legal	Police and Corrections	Fire Protection	Highways and transportation	Health and Welfare	Natural resources and utilities	Education and libraries	Total (mil dol)	Inter-governmental (mil dol)	Total (mil dol)	Total	Property
	171	172	173	174	175	176	177	178	179	180	181	182	183	184
KENTUCKY—Cont'd														
Clay	994	2 631 167	3.1	5.8	0.0	2.7	3.9	4.3	79.7	47.7	34.9	7.4	345	209
Clinton	443	1 162 284	4.8	3.5	0.0	2.1	6.0	0.7	82.6	24.4	16.8	5.6	548	258
Crittenden	318	847 790	5.5	13.8	0.0	2.2	0.0	6.6	71.2	21.9	15.1	4.5	482	288
Cumberland	454	1 348 734	2.8	4.3	0.1	1.8	42.8	3.6	43.6	42.0	9.9	4.0	592	292
Daviess	4 233	13 420 532	3.9	7.2	3.3	2.8	7.4	14.6	60.1	320.6	123.3	99.0	1 012	595
Edmonson	508	1 172 078	2.9	4.0	0.4	1.8	3.8	6.2	80.7	24.3	16.3	5.3	442	332
Elliott	264	668 556	3.5	2.6	0.0	3.1	11.5	2.5	75.8	15.4	11.7	2.1	276	169
Estill	575	2 082 079	1.7	13.1	7.0	4.2	11.0	3.5	58.3	35.1	24.2	6.6	452	275
Fayette	9 962	37 856 745	4.3	13.5	7.8	2.1	6.3	4.9	58.5	920.0	203.8	539.7	1 767	835
Fleming	697	2 194 909	3.1	2.3	0.7	1.3	36.8	2.2	53.4	87.7	20.7	8.0	553	322
Floyd	1 386	3 755 718	2.5	3.5	2.7	1.3	3.7	4.8	81.3	96.9	62.9	22.7	584	472
Franklin	1 716	6 237 758	4.5	8.7	9.2	2.6	1.1	8.1	54.8	158.6	42.6	66.3	1 332	688
Fulton	418	1 044 790	3.3	7.0	5.9	10.5	0.4	9.6	58.4	26.4	17.0	5.5	847	491
Gallatin	332	954 873	7.1	3.3	0.0	2.1	2.1	3.8	81.6	30.0	13.7	8.5	1 007	632
Garrard	526	1 692 901	3.4	1.7	0.1	1.9	5.2	1.5	86.1	39.9	19.9	12.9	761	479
Grant	998	2 854 787	5.3	7.3	1.9	1.5	0.1	5.4	77.4	59.9	37.6	15.0	611	477
Graves	1 308	3 544 113	2.9	8.2	3.0	2.3	0.0	2.8	79.5	77.1	43.4	23.1	614	366
Grayson	956	2 669 148	4.8	14.5	0.3	2.2	2.1	3.6	70.5	66.8	40.3	15.8	608	317
Green	635	2 084 431	5.8	8.4	4.2	2.1	27.5	9.5	41.8	40.4	15.6	5.1	451	288
Greenup	1 220	4 273 541	2.1	6.9	1.4	1.9	0.4	3.3	82.5	86.3	43.9	29.1	793	654
Hancock	406	1 128 193	8.8	3.1	0.0	3.6	5.5	3.0	73.5	70.5	13.2	9.1	1 052	490
Hardin	5 176	17 598 804	1.2	3.7	1.8	1.2	45.7	3.6	41.7	459.3	132.4	90.3	844	479
Harlan	1 193	3 057 085	2.8	6.7	0.2	2.7	1.0	4.6	81.1	96.7	61.1	16.0	562	404
Harrison	635	1 973 639	6.3	9.3	3.0	3.0	0.0	2.3	76.0	38.3	20.2	14.4	771	361
Hart	599	1 691 514	2.9	6.7	0.1	2.1	4.8	5.2	76.9	36.5	22.7	9.6	522	293
Henderson	2 096	5 804 471	5.3	9.5	3.7	4.2	1.2	14.4	60.1	156.8	64.1	42.2	908	550
Henry	640	1 779 003	8.8	3.5	0.0	1.4	1.9	5.1	79.3	35.5	21.0	10.1	661	488
Hickman	198	524 720	7.5	5.4	0.0	2.2	2.3	1.0	80.8	11.7	7.7	3.0	622	421
Hopkins	1 879	5 461 945	4.2	9.4	3.9	3.0	5.6	7.9	65.5	126.7	65.8	37.0	791	444
Jackson	523	1 629 435	2.4	2.5	0.0	2.9	0.5	0.3	90.4	29.9	23.5	5.0	377	231
Jefferson	25 957	96 919 915	3.8	11.0	4.8	4.5	4.7	8.9	60.3	2 308.9	694.0	1 084.7	1 445	808
Jessamine	1 836	5 035 213	4.3	7.1	3.4	1.5	7.8	4.8	68.6	116.9	46.1	57.3	1 153	712
Johnson	862	2 638 353	2.4	1.8	1.1	1.5	0.7	2.6	86.7	69.4	42.9	14.0	598	338
Kenton	5 823	21 356 962	2.4	8.9	5.6	14.3	2.9	9.7	54.0	710.4	161.7	228.8	1 415	873
Knott	613	1 519 486	4.8	3.6	0.0	2.3	3.8	6.9	78.6	39.0	27.2	8.8	546	448
Knox	1 187	3 283 773	1.7	2.6	0.1	1.9	10.4	2.7	80.2	87.2	55.9	18.9	597	369
Larue	547	1 474 160	4.8	6.4	0.0	1.7	3.2	2.6	80.9	31.5	21.6	7.0	497	357
Laurel	2 042	5 388 170	2.8	6.5	0.3	2.5	3.9	3.5	79.3	125.4	73.3	38.1	641	329
Lawrence	604	1 562 126	4.8	3.3	1.1	2.8	4.5	4.0	78.6	54.7	23.2	8.2	517	381
Lee	279	772 061	4.6	4.7	0.0	3.4	11.0	4.8	71.3	19.3	12.6	4.2	539	364
Leslie	447	1 317 537	5.5	3.0	0.0	2.8	0.0	4.1	79.4	32.5	23.5	7.5	668	472
Letcher	1 021	2 457 149	1.7	4.3	0.4	2.2	3.8	4.0	81.9	57.9	40.2	11.8	493	377
Lewis	560	1 776 699	3.4	5.5	0.0	2.3	1.5	4.2	82.9	29.1	20.7	6.3	457	316
Lincoln	879	2 396 927	2.4	4.3	0.3	1.9	3.1	3.5	84.1	50.5	35.4	11.5	471	295
Livingston	346	854 563	7.6	3.0	8.2	3.7	4.9	4.1	68.4	22.0	13.3	6.5	688	436
Logan	972	2 732 295	5.2	7.8	1.4	1.6	0.3	3.8	78.6	68.7	39.7	21.0	787	379
Lyon	237	841 257	5.7	3.3	0.2	3.5	5.4	4.3	50.3	18.0	7.4	7.1	847	615
McCracken	2 541	8 688 735	3.1	9.6	3.2	4.7	11.0	11.5	55.4	229.1	82.8	78.2	1 193	632
McCreary	751	1 960 007	1.9	4.5	0.0	1.6	6.3	4.0	80.7	47.9	30.0	16.4	907	789
McLean	404	945 835	4.5	1.7	0.0	2.1	0.7	5.7	75.6	30.6	17.9	7.4	778	382
Madison	2 628	7 891 742	2.5	5.2	3.8	2.3	9.6	4.2	68.4	199.0	81.8	79.3	935	482
Magoffin	510	1 498 254	4.1	2.3	0.8	3.5	6.7	3.0	79.4	38.5	29.7	6.1	470	216
Marion	789	2 206 926	2.6	13.7	0.3	6.2	3.0	6.0	67.3	49.3	25.1	15.3	763	452
Marshall	1 233	3 676 388	2.4	4.3	0.0	2.0	23.4	5.4	61.5	138.8	34.7	36.4	1 160	589
Martin	565	1 560 146	7.3	3.2	0.0	2.3	6.6	3.2	77.0	32.7	22.1	7.2	566	272
Mason	917	2 257 527	7.8	11.9	3.1	2.4	6.1	5.7	59.4	62.2	21.7	18.3	1 043	494
Meade	931	2 688 037	3.4	5.7	0.1	1.5	3.2	3.3	81.9	56.8	35.1	14.8	508	380
Menifee	255	589 112	3.9	0.5	0.0	2.1	3.1	2.7	87.6	17.2	10.7	4.3	691	525
Mercer	736	2 237 637	6.9	9.4	2.9	5.4	2.8	4.1	67.1	50.4	24.0	20.1	944	596
Metcalfe	377	953 969	2.6	3.0	0.0	3.1	0.6	4.9	85.9	23.2	15.8	5.4	544	294
Monroe	585	1 493 674	4.7	6.7	0.0	1.6	5.1	5.9	75.8	28.4	19.3	6.0	550	323
Montgomery	853	2 642 340	1.3	2.9	6.2	0.8	6.6	1.1	80.9	69.6	34.6	22.4	832	434
Morgan	486	1 237 685	4.6	5.7	0.0	1.9	4.7	5.7	76.6	34.6	23.0	6.2	453	241
Muhlenberg	1 235	3 174 925	4.8	7.6	1.4	3.6	3.9	4.0	74.3	72.9	47.9	14.7	471	350
Nelson	1 501	4 602 823	4.7	5.8	0.7	1.6	4.5	4.2	76.6	108.2	44.4	36.8	829	669
Nicholas	219	557 957	7.9	3.1	0.4	3.0	1.0	7.7	75.2	15.4	10.3	3.1	437	281

1. Based on the resident population estimated as of July 1 of the year shown.

STATE County	Local government finances, 2012 (cont.)									Government employment, 2014			Presidential election,[2] 2012		
	Direct general expenditure							Debt outstanding					Percent of vote cast:		
			Percent of total for:												
	Total (mil dol)	Per capita[1] (dollars)	Education	Health and hospitals	Police protection	Public welfare	Highways	Total (mil dol)	Per capita[1] (dollars)	Federal civilian	Federal military	State and local	Democratic	Republican	All other
	185	186	187	188	189	190	191	192	193	194	195	196	197	198	199
KENTUCKY—Cont'd															
Clay	48.2	2 236	66.0	2.1	3.1	0.0	7.1	33.2	1 542	371	61	1 171	21.1	77.5	1.4
Clinton	23.1	2 250	70.0	3.9	2.9	0.0	4.7	18.9	1 842	47	32	583	18.2	80.7	1.1
Crittenden	20.2	2 174	49.6	0.3	3.2	0.0	6.6	34.3	3 698	19	29	400	31.9	66.3	1.8
Cumberland	47.8	7 014	21.3	57.7	1.5	0.0	3.3	40.3	5 903	0	21	325	24.9	73.5	1.6
Daviess	344.4	3 519	39.4	6.6	4.3	0.1	2.9	1 124.1	11 488	243	326	5 516	44.2	54.3	1.5
Edmonson	23.8	1 975	69.3	5.0	2.8	0.0	5.3	36.6	3 036	217	37	505	31.3	67.6	1.1
Elliott	14.7	1 891	60.4	9.7	1.5	1.2	7.3	16.4	2 107	0	21	538	61.0	35.9	3.1
Estill	39.4	2 719	67.4	7.2	1.3	0.0	3.6	33.1	2 286	18	46	705	29.3	69.3	1.4
Fayette	871.4	2 852	47.8	1.8	5.5	1.0	1.3	1 402.6	4 591	4 127	1 010	37 307	51.7	46.9	1.3
Fleming	60.2	4 132	42.2	39.1	1.6	0.0	3.5	101.3	6 957	47	47	939	39.1	58.8	2.1
Floyd	95.8	2 460	58.7	3.2	3.0	0.0	4.7	77.1	1 979	126	120	2 408	48.1	49.4	2.5
Franklin	148.7	2 986	38.2	6.9	4.7	0.1	3.3	147.3	2 957	504	166	13 958	48.9	49.5	1.7
Fulton	26.8	4 114	37.8	0.2	5.2	0.0	5.6	13.8	2 107	26	34	503	43.8	54.2	2.0
Gallatin	31.5	3 721	44.7	3.1	3.1	0.0	2.2	306.7	36 176	33	27	424	40.0	57.6	2.3
Garrard	36.7	2 171	53.0	18.0	3.1	0.0	3.4	63.2	3 736	24	54	660	27.9	71.0	1.1
Grant	60.7	2 479	63.9	0.5	3.4	0.1	3.7	87.4	3 568	44	78	1 209	35.5	62.9	1.5
Graves	76.9	2 049	62.2	0.3	2.9	0.2	4.8	208.0	5 539	201	119	1 711	36.2	62.2	1.6
Grayson	62.1	2 391	54.7	1.0	2.5	0.6	4.1	106.8	4 113	87	81	1 584	31.8	66.7	1.5
Green	39.0	3 443	35.6	43.0	2.1	0.0	3.4	34.9	3 088	18	35	734	23.7	74.5	1.8
Greenup	85.0	2 315	62.5	3.4	4.2	0.0	4.8	61.8	1 684	58	115	1 424	41.9	56.0	2.1
Hancock	79.0	9 101	19.3	0.8	0.8	0.1	2.2	714.6	82 360	20	28	418	51.5	46.5	2.0
Hardin	430.7	4 025	34.9	44.6	2.8	0.0	2.0	304.8	2 848	5 997	6 854	7 227	39.1	59.8	1.1
Harlan	95.7	3 353	47.6	20.0	2.5	1.4	4.6	87.7	3 072	83	88	1 771	26.1	72.3	1.6
Harrison	37.7	2 026	62.3	1.1	5.4	0.2	9.1	17.8	956	42	59	802	38.4	59.6	2.0
Hart	35.3	1 923	58.3	4.8	2.9	0.1	5.4	51.6	2 807	38	59	788	33.6	64.5	1.9
Henderson	158.7	3 411	41.1	0.2	3.9	0.4	4.8	595.8	12 809	120	145	2 787	50.6	47.9	1.5
Henry	38.5	2 513	68.2	3.6	3.2	0.0	4.4	41.2	2 690	91	50	728	39.4	59.0	1.6
Hickman	12.5	2 633	61.6	0.0	3.3	0.0	8.4	15.6	3 280	21	14	237	36.1	62.5	1.4
Hopkins	127.9	2 738	50.6	2.9	4.8	0.7	5.6	336.3	7 198	167	145	3 271	36.7	61.6	1.7
Jackson	37.2	2 791	73.7	0.3	0.9	0.0	5.1	39.0	2 924	32	42	695	14.2	84.4	1.4
Jefferson	2 460.2	3 277	46.7	1.4	4.8	0.5	3.0	4 784.1	6 372	6 432	2 624	42 766	55.5	43.5	1.0
Jessamine	118.6	2 390	54.7	4.5	6.5	0.1	5.6	197.1	3 971	77	157	2 387	30.8	67.8	1.3
Johnson	63.4	2 713	62.6	7.2	2.4	0.0	4.6	48.3	2 065	41	73	1 462	28.3	69.8	1.9
Kenton	844.4	5 222	24.0	2.1	3.6	0.0	2.7	2 312.8	14 302	4 156	555	7 321	38.8	59.7	1.5
Knott	35.4	2 196	66.3	0.1	2.3	0.2	6.1	25.7	1 594	47	48	726	44.9	52.7	2.4
Knox	85.5	2 695	53.4	8.3	1.8	0.0	3.5	96.3	3 036	159	100	1 414	27.0	71.6	1.4
Larue	29.1	2 055	63.2	2.5	2.5	0.0	4.3	46.0	3 247	43	44	598	31.0	67.2	1.8
Laurel	122.8	2 066	64.1	2.4	3.8	0.9	3.4	206.4	3 470	250	190	2 553	20.5	78.5	1.0
Lawrence	56.4	3 560	42.6	2.7	1.4	0.0	5.0	323.0	20 378	32	50	673	36.0	62.0	1.9
Lee	18.2	2 364	53.5	6.3	4.4	0.1	10.1	9.1	1 180	12	21	437	27.1	71.3	1.6
Leslie	38.3	3 427	60.6	0.3	1.6	0.0	6.1	45.7	4 093	18	34	570	17.4	81.3	1.3
Letcher	57.7	2 407	65.1	0.2	2.3	0.0	4.0	48.6	2 030	54	74	1 098	31.9	65.2	3.0
Lewis	32.1	2 322	56.5	3.9	2.6	0.0	6.9	85.2	6 155	21	44	616	31.5	67.1	1.4
Lincoln	57.7	2 358	64.0	2.6	1.3	0.1	4.4	51.0	2 086	58	78	967	30.1	68.5	1.4
Livingston	21.9	2 329	53.2	2.8	2.6	0.0	6.2	29.9	3 170	88	30	457	35.3	62.9	1.8
Logan	70.1	2 633	53.7	15.9	4.9	0.0	4.2	64.5	2 421	60	85	1 218	35.0	63.6	1.4
Lyon	19.0	2 270	40.7	6.1	4.4	0.8	10.5	27.6	3 304	31	23	939	40.9	57.6	1.5
McCracken	222.0	3 387	53.7	0.1	3.1	0.1	3.3	760.9	11 608	615	233	3 893	36.7	61.9	1.4
McCreary	46.4	2 568	59.4	1.1	0.7	0.0	4.6	41.3	2 284	473	51	718	23.3	75.4	1.3
McLean	31.1	3 277	41.5	3.3	0.7	0.6	9.6	42.6	4 483	31	30	511	44.4	54.0	1.7
Madison	191.9	2 263	56.3	9.2	4.2	0.1	3.1	375.9	4 434	1 022	277	7 183	38.1	60.5	1.4
Magoffin	33.9	2 601	61.0	4.8	2.9	0.0	5.3	40.5	3 109	11	41	638	45.3	52.3	2.4
Marion	48.7	2 426	52.2	2.0	3.7	0.0	4.4	59.9	2 983	44	60	881	47.2	50.5	2.3
Marshall	146.0	4 657	26.1	18.0	3.9	0.3	2.3	483.2	15 417	84	98	1 650	36.7	61.4	1.9
Martin	33.5	2 633	63.8	9.1	1.1	0.0	5.6	13.4	1 048	390	35	585	21.9	76.5	1.6
Mason	67.9	3 879	34.1	4.5	4.5	0.0	7.5	293.2	16 743	53	54	1 540	40.6	57.6	1.8
Meade	55.3	1 892	66.3	2.2	2.1	0.0	3.0	96.2	3 291	34	93	1 084	38.8	59.7	1.5
Menifee	19.5	3 133	66.1	3.5	3.4	0.2	4.2	20.7	3 323	51	19	326	51.3	46.4	2.3
Mercer	48.2	2 267	58.2	3.7	3.9	0.0	4.4	86.2	4 054	43	68	877	31.4	67.4	1.2
Metcalfe	34.7	3 479	78.8	1.8	2.2	0.0	4.0	60.2	6 042	22	32	502	32.2	65.1	2.7
Monroe	27.3	2 526	64.8	9.0	3.4	0.0	4.9	27.3	2 518	26	34	600	22.9	75.8	1.3
Montgomery	73.1	2 716	63.0	9.0	4.6	0.0	2.4	73.0	2 713	64	87	1 219	41.0	57.6	1.5
Morgan	36.5	2 671	54.2	4.4	1.9	6.8	7.3	55.1	4 035	34	37	988	42.9	54.7	2.4
Muhlenberg	94.2	3 022	66.4	2.4	2.2	0.1	4.0	83.6	2 681	526	93	1 833	48.3	50.0	1.7
Nelson	117.2	2 645	59.2	2.1	3.0	0.2	2.8	245.4	5 537	78	142	1 791	42.2	55.9	1.9
Nicholas	15.9	2 269	62.2	1.2	3.9	0.5	10.0	17.4	2 481	14	22	307	42.8	55.0	2.2

1. Based on the resident population estimated as of July 1 of the year shown.   2. © 2013 Election Data Services, Inc. All rights reserved.

Table B. States and Counties — **Land Area and Population**

STATE/County code	CBSA code[1]	County type[2]	STATE County	Land area[3] (sq km) 2010	Total persons 2015	Rank	Per square kilometer	White	Black	American Indian, Alaska Native	Asian and Pacific Islander	Percent Hispanic or Latino[4]	Under 5 years	5 to 17 years	18 to 24 years	25 to 34 years	35 to 44 years	45 to 54 years
				1	2	3	4	5	6	7	8	9	10	11	12	13	14	15
			KENTUCKY—Cont'd															
21 183	...	6	Ohio	1 521	24 216	1 636	15.9	95.1	1.3	0.5	0.4	3.3	6.4	18.1	7.7	11.7	12.6	13.2
21 185	31140	1	Oldham	485	64 875	812	133.8	89.0	4.8	0.7	2.1	3.8	4.6	21.7	8.1	9.8	14.8	17.0
21 187	...	8	Owen	909	10 730	2 375	11.8	96.4	1.3	0.6	0.3	2.4	4.9	18.3	7.4	10.5	12.8	14.4
21 189	...	9	Owsley	511	4 461	2 867	8.7	98.0	0.8	0.6	0.2	1.0	5.7	15.3	7.5	12.0	11.5	14.6
21 191	17140	1	Pendleton	718	14 408	2 139	20.1	98.2	0.9	0.5	0.5	1.2	5.7	16.8	8.9	11.2	12.5	16.0
21 193	...	7	Perry	880	27 565	1 507	31.3	96.7	2.3	0.5	0.7	0.8	6.6	14.9	7.9	12.6	13.2	14.7
21 195	...	7	Pike	2 038	61 792	849	30.3	98.0	1.1	0.4	0.7	0.8	5.7	15.3	9.0	11.5	13.3	14.6
21 197	...	6	Powell	464	12 269	2 279	26.4	98.0	1.1	0.5	0.4	1.3	6.9	16.9	8.4	12.2	13.4	14.0
21 199	43700	5	Pulaski	1 705	63 782	822	37.4	95.7	1.6	0.7	0.7	2.4	5.7	16.9	7.8	11.3	12.6	14.2
21 201	...	8	Robertson	259	2 138	3 037	8.3	98.9	0.6	0.6	0.2	1.1	3.4	16.5	8.4	9.6	10.4	15.8
21 203	40080	7	Rockcastle	820	16 942	1 982	20.7	98.4	0.6	0.8	0.3	0.8	5.5	16.5	8.1	11.0	12.7	15.6
21 205	...	7	Rowan	725	23 892	1 646	33.0	95.6	2.4	0.6	1.1	1.5	5.6	13.7	21.5	11.9	10.7	12.0
21 207	...	9	Russell	657	17 662	1 936	26.9	95.1	1.1	0.7	0.6	3.6	6.3	16.1	7.6	10.6	12.1	14.2
21 209	30460	3	Scott	730	52 420	954	71.8	88.8	6.6	0.6	1.5	4.2	6.8	19.0	9.8	12.8	15.0	14.3
21 211	31140	1	Shelby	983	45 632	1 058	46.4	82.7	8.4	0.7	1.3	8.7	7.1	17.1	8.4	12.1	13.7	14.8
21 213	...	6	Simpson	607	18 006	1 918	29.7	87.0	10.8	0.8	1.2	2.0	6.3	17.8	8.4	11.7	12.6	14.2
21 215	31140	1	Spencer	483	17 894	1 924	37.0	95.6	2.3	0.7	0.7	1.8	5.2	18.6	7.4	10.6	14.7	17.1
21 217	15820	7	Taylor	690	25 420	1 592	36.8	92.1	6.3	0.6	1.0	2.2	6.3	15.8	12.5	11.8	10.4	13.1
21 219	...	8	Todd	970	12 531	2 258	12.9	87.2	8.9	0.7	0.5	4.1	7.3	19.9	8.2	11.6	12.1	13.4
21 221	17300	3	Trigg	1 143	14 233	2 154	12.5	89.8	8.6	0.9	0.7	1.7	5.3	16.4	7.1	9.2	11.4	14.4
21 223	31140	1	Trimble	393	8 769	2 530	22.3	95.7	1.0	0.7	0.9	3.6	5.6	18.1	7.9	11.0	13.2	15.0
21 225	...	3	Union	888	15 050	2 095	16.9	84.3	14.1	0.6	0.9	1.8	5.3	14.8	16.6	11.0	11.3	12.3
21 227	14540	3	Warren	1 403	122 851	506	87.6	82.1	10.4	0.6	3.8	5.1	6.3	16.1	16.6	13.5	12.1	12.1
21 229	...	8	Washington	770	12 063	2 294	15.7	89.4	7.2	0.5	0.6	3.8	6.0	17.0	9.8	10.1	11.7	14.9
21 231	...	7	Wayne	1 187	20 464	1 808	17.2	95.1	2.2	0.7	0.5	2.7	5.5	15.9	8.1	11.2	12.3	14.1
21 233	...	2	Webster	860	13 170	2 223	15.3	90.5	4.9	0.7	0.7	4.7	6.6	16.4	7.7	11.8	12.7	13.9
21 235	30940	7	Whitley	1 134	36 129	1 271	31.9	96.7	1.2	1.0	0.7	1.0	6.9	17.0	11.5	11.6	11.9	13.5
21 237	...	9	Wolfe	575	7 259	2 650	12.6	98.3	0.6	0.7	0.2	0.7	6.1	17.6	7.1	10.7	11.8	14.5
21 239	30460	2	Woodford	489	25 793	1 563	52.7	87.6	5.8	0.5	0.9	6.6	5.4	17.3	8.0	10.7	12.5	15.2
22 000	...	X	**LOUISIANA**	111 898	4 670 724	X	41.7	60.5	32.8	1.1	2.2	4.8	6.6	17.3	10.0	14.4	12.2	13.2
22 001	29180	4	Acadia	1 697	62 577	842	36.9	78.9	19.0	0.5	0.6	2.2	7.1	19.6	9.1	13.1	11.6	13.6
22 003	...	6	Allen	1 973	25 683	1 573	13.0	71.7	23.9	2.9	1.1	2.1	6.2	16.4	8.8	15.6	14.0	14.1
22 005	12940	2	Ascension	751	119 455	518	159.1	70.3	23.2	0.6	1.6	5.2	7.1	20.5	8.5	14.0	14.3	14.2
22 007	...	6	Assumption	877	22 842	1 690	26.0	66.8	30.1	0.8	0.6	2.6	5.7	17.2	9.1	12.4	11.7	14.7
22 009	...	6	Avoyelles	2 156	41 103	1 149	19.1	66.8	30.3	1.9	0.9	1.8	6.6	17.2	8.6	13.5	12.1	13.8
22 011	19760	6	Beauregard	2 998	36 462	1 264	12.2	81.3	14.2	1.9	1.3	3.6	6.8	18.1	8.6	13.4	13.0	13.1
22 013	...	6	Bienville	2 101	13 786	2 185	6.6	56.6	42.6	0.8	0.6	1.6	6.3	16.8	8.3	11.4	10.5	14.3
22 015	43340	2	Bossier	2 176	125 175	500	57.5	69.8	22.5	1.0	2.6	6.5	7.4	17.9	9.8	15.5	13.0	12.3
22 017	43340	2	Caddo	2 275	251 460	265	110.5	47.5	48.6	0.9	1.7	2.8	7.2	17.1	9.3	14.2	11.8	12.5
22 019	29340	3	Calcasieu	2 755	198 788	309	72.2	70.1	26.0	1.0	1.7	3.1	6.8	18.1	9.7	14.1	11.8	12.9
22 021	...	8	Caldwell	1 371	9 993	2 434	7.3	79.4	17.2	0.7	0.5	2.9	5.7	16.9	8.4	12.6	12.9	13.6
22 023	29340	3	Cameron	3 328	6 817	2 693	2.0	91.1	4.6	0.9	0.3	3.6	4.7	17.8	8.4	12.4	11.6	15.9
22 025	...	9	Catahoula	1 834	10 147	2 425	5.5	65.7	32.5	0.6	0.3	1.3	6.1	16.3	9.3	14.0	11.6	13.0
22 027	...	7	Claiborne	1 955	16 295	2 022	8.3	46.5	51.4	0.9	1.0	1.4	5.3	13.2	9.1	15.2	12.5	14.0
22 029	35020	7	Concordia	1 805	20 142	1 827	11.2	57.7	41.1	0.6	0.5	1.2	6.5	18.1	9.2	13.3	11.6	12.6
22 031	43340	2	De Soto	2 268	27 052	1 531	11.9	58.4	38.5	1.3	0.5	2.8	6.7	18.0	8.3	11.8	11.9	13.7
22 033	12940	2	East Baton Rouge	1 179	446 753	156	378.9	46.6	46.5	0.6	3.7	3.9	6.5	16.3	14.7	14.9	11.5	11.8
22 035	...	7	East Carroll	1 090	7 307	2 644	6.7	29.8	67.8	0.7	0.8	2.3	7.5	17.4	10.7	14.4	11.8	13.0
22 037	12940	2	East Feliciana	1 174	19 696	1 846	16.8	53.8	44.6	0.9	0.7	1.4	5.4	14.1	8.8	13.3	12.0	15.1
22 039	...	6	Evangeline	1 716	33 743	1 334	19.7	68.5	28.6	0.6	0.6	2.5	7.3	19.1	9.9	12.6	11.5	13.4
22 041	...	7	Franklin	1 618	20 410	1 812	12.6	66.2	32.1	0.5	0.5	1.4	7.0	18.5	8.7	12.0	10.9	12.8
22 043	10780	3	Grant	1 665	22 343	1 713	13.4	78.0	16.4	1.7	0.8	4.7	5.7	16.0	8.4	16.8	14.5	13.4
22 045	29180	4	Iberia	1 487	74 103	741	49.8	60.7	32.6	0.7	3.4	3.9	7.0	19.5	9.3	12.9	11.6	13.7
22 047	12940	6	Iberville	1 602	33 095	1 354	20.7	48.5	49.2	0.5	0.7	2.6	6.2	15.6	9.5	14.7	12.5	14.8
22 049	...	6	Jackson	1 474	15 858	2 048	10.8	68.9	29.7	0.8	0.6	1.5	5.6	16.7	8.1	13.4	11.6	13.3
22 051	35380	1	Jefferson	766	436 275	159	569.5	55.3	26.9	0.8	4.7	13.8	6.3	15.6	8.5	14.8	12.4	13.8
22 053	...	6	Jefferson Davis	1 687	31 439	1 398	18.6	79.7	18.2	1.1	0.6	2.3	7.2	18.7	8.5	12.5	11.6	13.7
22 055	29180	3	Lafayette	696	240 098	277	345.0	67.5	26.6	0.7	2.1	4.4	6.8	17.1	10.6	16.9	12.6	12.9
22 057	26380	3	Lafourche	2 767	98 325	602	35.5	78.3	14.3	3.5	1.1	4.6	6.3	17.3	9.8	14.2	12.0	14.5
22 059	...	6	La Salle	1 618	14 974	2 102	9.3	83.6	12.8	1.6	0.3	2.5	5.9	17.1	8.9	14.3	12.6	12.9
22 061	40820	4	Lincoln	1 222	47 774	1 020	39.1	54.1	42.0	0.7	2.1	2.7	6.0	14.3	26.6	12.6	9.0	9.7
22 063	12940	2	Livingston	1 679	137 788	461	82.1	89.3	6.6	0.8	0.8	3.5	6.8	19.5	8.6	14.4	14.0	13.5
22 065	...	7	Madison	1 617	11 514	2 324	7.1	36.0	62.6	0.7	0.4	1.7	7.7	16.9	10.0	16.2	11.8	12.7
22 067	12820	6	Morehouse	2 059	26 395	1 549	12.8	50.8	47.6	0.6	0.7	1.2	7.0	17.4	8.6	12.0	11.3	12.8
22 069	35060	6	Natchitoches	3 243	39 179	1 197	12.1	54.8	42.0	1.8	1.0	2.2	6.4	17.3	16.7	11.7	10.0	11.2

1. CBSA = Core Based Statistical Area. See Appendix A for explanation. See Appendix B for list of metropolitan areas with component counties. 2. County type code from the Economic Research Service of USDA Rural-Urban Continuum Codes. See Appendix A for definition. 3. Dry land or land partially or temporarily covered by water. 4. May be of any race.

Table B. States and Counties — **Population and Households**

STATE County	55 to 64 years (16)	65 to 74 years (17)	75 years and over (18)	Percent female (19)	2000 (20)	2010 (21)	2000–2010 (22)	2010–2015 (23)	Births (24)	Deaths (25)	Net migration (26)	Number (27)	Persons per household (28)	Family households (29)	Female family householder[1] (30)	One person (31)
KENTUCKY—Cont'd																
Ohio	13.3	10.0	6.9	50.1	22 916	23 842	4.0	1.6	1 551	1 390	254	8 573	2.76	73.6	12.4	22.9
Oldham	12.4	7.9	3.8	47.5	46 178	60 335	30.7	7.5	2 722	1 861	3 733	19 610	2.92	81.6	9.4	15.0
Owen	15.1	10.4	6.2	50.1	10 547	10 838	2.8	-1.0	568	537	-88	4 355	2.46	68.6	10.7	29.3
Owsley	15.6	11.0	6.8	51.2	4 858	4 755	-2.1	-6.2	247	388	-136	1 740	2.64	64.9	16.8	34.9
Pendleton	14.4	8.9	5.6	49.6	14 390	14 876	3.4	-3.1	816	759	-497	5 349	2.70	66.5	9.2	27.4
Perry	14.7	9.5	5.9	50.5	29 390	28 712	-2.3	-4.0	2 055	2 217	-1 011	11 005	2.51	70.8	14.9	24.0
Pike	14.8	9.7	6.2	51.0	68 736	65 024	-5.4	-5.0	3 875	4 254	-2 806	26 312	2.40	67.5	12.3	28.5
Powell	13.8	8.7	5.6	50.4	13 237	12 613	-4.7	-2.7	821	799	-345	4 628	2.67	63.0	13.2	31.4
Pulaski	13.8	10.5	7.2	51.2	56 217	63 063	12.2	1.1	3 839	3 983	867	26 052	2.40	67.8	13.6	27.9
Robertson	14.0	12.4	9.6	48.0	2 266	2 282	0.7	-6.3	104	166	-86	911	2.40	64.8	9.8	32.1
Rockcastle	13.9	10.2	6.5	51.0	16 582	17 056	2.9	-0.7	933	1 070	31	6 634	2.51	71.6	14.7	25.5
Rowan	11.1	7.8	5.7	51.3	22 094	23 333	5.6	2.4	1 496	1 147	221	8 407	2.45	62.0	9.8	31.3
Russell	14.2	10.9	8.0	51.1	16 315	17 568	7.7	0.5	1 150	1 144	137	7 223	2.42	64.1	11.9	31.7
Scott	11.6	6.7	4.0	50.8	33 061	47 173	42.7	11.1	3 397	1 655	3 404	18 306	2.61	72.2	12.3	23.4
Shelby	12.9	8.9	5.1	51.5	33 337	42 066	26.2	8.5	3 295	1 661	1 962	15 665	2.67	74.9	12.1	21.3
Simpson	13.3	9.5	6.3	51.1	16 405	17 327	5.6	3.9	1 205	924	438	6 660	2.59	67.5	10.8	27.2
Spencer	13.9	8.4	4.0	49.6	11 766	17 061	45.0	4.9	950	664	538	6 301	2.75	80.9	9.7	15.2
Taylor	12.9	9.8	7.5	51.5	22 927	24 512	6.9	3.7	1 736	1 533	673	9 491	2.53	67.5	14.0	28.8
Todd	11.9	9.2	6.4	50.3	11 971	12 460	4.1	0.6	972	693	-232	4 567	2.70	72.7	13.3	24.0
Trigg	15.1	13.1	8.1	51.1	12 597	14 334	13.8	-0.7	756	907	65	6 055	2.34	69.6	11.5	26.2
Trimble	13.6	9.8	5.8	49.5	8 125	8 809	8.4	-0.5	528	435	-128	3 578	2.45	70.0	9.8	25.3
Union	13.7	8.7	6.3	48.1	15 637	15 007	-4.0	0.3	927	855	-40	5 620	2.42	68.0	14.1	28.8
Warren	11.1	7.2	4.9	51.1	92 522	113 781	23.0	8.0	7 995	4 734	5 801	44 923	2.46	64.2	12.3	27.2
Washington	13.4	9.7	7.5	51.2	10 916	11 717	7.3	3.0	753	699	281	4 514	2.54	69.1	11.8	27.9
Wayne	14.7	11.0	7.1	50.5	19 923	20 813	4.5	-1.7	1 189	1 086	-347	8 004	2.55	68.1	12.5	29.1
Webster	14.5	9.2	7.1	50.0	14 120	13 621	-3.5	-3.3	824	879	-377	5 057	2.60	72.5	9.6	25.0
Whitley	12.6	9.2	5.9	50.9	35 865	35 637	-0.6	1.4	2 900	2 339	-153	12 931	2.62	72.2	13.9	23.8
Wolfe	14.5	11.0	6.8	50.5	7 065	7 355	4.1	-1.3	482	521	-64	2 826	2.53	64.3	13.6	31.2
Woodford	15.1	9.7	6.1	52.1	23 208	24 939	7.5	3.4	1 421	1 119	532	9 716	2.56	68.3	9.5	25.9
LOUISIANA	12.6	8.0	5.6	51.1	4 468 976	4 533 479	1.4	3.0	328 781	220 859	28 906	1 718 876	2.60	65.9	16.9	28.7
Acadia	12.4	7.7	5.8	51.5	58 861	61 773	4.9	1.3	4 689	3 372	-488	22 788	2.68	68.7	16.6	26.4
Allen	11.8	7.7	5.6	43.3	25 440	25 764	1.3	-0.3	1 802	1 270	-592	8 108	2.65	67.8	14.6	30.2
Ascension	11.1	6.6	3.6	50.7	76 627	107 194	39.9	11.4	8 724	3 664	7 021	39 447	2.83	76.5	13.9	19.9
Assumption	14.0	9.0	6.2	51.1	23 388	23 421	0.1	-2.5	1 387	1 146	-795	8 726	2.62	71.6	14.1	24.4
Avoyelles	12.7	8.7	6.8	49.9	41 481	42 073	1.4	-2.3	2 945	2 538	-1 381	15 107	2.51	69.0	16.7	27.4
Beauregard	12.6	8.8	5.6	48.7	32 986	35 654	8.1	2.3	2 537	1 798	80	13 095	2.67	74.2	13.0	22.4
Bienville	13.3	10.1	9.0	52.2	15 752	14 353	-8.9	-4.0	869	1 103	-361	5 888	2.34	63.9	17.3	32.9
Bossier	11.3	7.3	5.5	50.4	98 310	116 979	19.0	7.0	9 356	5 000	3 787	46 285	2.59	66.0	14.7	30.5
Caddo	13.2	8.3	6.5	52.6	252 161	254 969	1.1	-1.4	20 048	14 091	-9 270	98 427	2.54	62.7	20.3	32.9
Calcasieu	12.8	7.9	5.8	51.2	183 577	192 770	5.0	3.1	14 217	9 933	1 968	74 757	2.56	68.4	16.2	26.7
Caldwell	13.4	9.7	6.7	48.8	10 560	10 132	-4.1	-1.4	627	632	-122	3 851	2.49	66.1	12.7	30.7
Cameron	14.1	8.8	6.2	50.0	9 991	6 859	-31.3	-0.6	343	242	-159	2 577	2.60	76.3	6.5	19.9
Catahoula	14.1	8.9	6.9	46.9	10 920	10 407	-4.7	-2.5	709	680	-287	3 786	2.47	70.2	13.3	27.7
Claiborne	13.3	9.4	8.1	43.4	16 851	17 195	2.0	-5.2	883	969	-827	5 677	2.65	62.2	17.9	35.5
Concordia	13.5	8.6	6.6	49.2	20 247	20 822	2.8	-3.3	1 341	1 200	-826	7 767	2.43	69.6	22.7	28.2
De Soto	13.7	9.5	6.5	51.7	25 494	26 656	4.6	1.5	1 814	1 501	118	10 172	2.62	70.7	19.2	25.8
East Baton Rouge	11.9	7.3	5.1	52.1	412 852	440 178	6.6	1.5	31 850	19 070	-5 778	168 534	2.57	61.4	17.2	30.9
East Carroll	12.0	7.3	6.0	45.8	9 421	7 759	-17.6	-5.8	650	383	-718	2 592	2.46	64.9	26.2	32.6
East Feliciana	15.4	10.1	5.8	46.4	21 360	20 263	-5.1	-2.8	1 143	1 208	-536	6 909	2.50	71.7	17.2	26.0
Evangeline	11.9	8.4	5.9	49.3	35 434	33 984	-4.1	-0.7	2 488	1 938	-786	12 053	2.62	68.7	18.9	28.2
Franklin	13.1	9.2	7.7	51.4	21 263	20 767	-2.3	-1.7	1 482	1 383	-432	7 748	2.47	65.1	17.8	32.4
Grant	11.5	8.4	5.4	43.9	18 698	22 309	19.3	0.2	1 308	1 087	-135	7 204	2.63	66.7	13.7	28.7
Iberia	12.6	7.8	5.5	51.0	73 266	73 240	0.0	1.2	5 563	3 709	-978	26 433	2.75	71.3	19.5	24.3
Iberville	13.2	8.0	5.6	48.8	33 320	33 407	0.3	-0.9	2 095	1 551	-788	11 257	2.62	70.7	21.5	25.9
Jackson	12.9	10.3	8.0	49.0	15 397	16 274	5.7	-2.6	916	974	-325	6 166	2.48	71.1	16.5	23.5
Jefferson	13.7	8.7	6.4	51.5	455 466	432 552	-5.0	0.9	29 688	21 316	-4 247	167 840	2.57	64.0	16.4	30.6
Jefferson Davis	12.7	8.4	6.8	51.1	31 435	31 594	0.5	-0.5	2 220	1 889	-482	11 553	2.68	70.0	15.3	26.1
Lafayette	12.0	6.5	4.7	51.1	190 503	221 571	16.3	8.4	17 579	8 823	9 639	87 602	2.55	62.2	14.6	30.6
Lafourche	12.3	7.9	5.8	50.7	89 974	96 592	7.4	1.8	6 486	4 411	-246	35 329	2.69	71.5	15.2	22.4
La Salle	12.5	9.1	6.8	48.1	14 282	14 890	4.3	0.6	900	883	76	5 715	2.40	71.6	13.4	23.1
Lincoln	9.5	6.8	5.4	51.3	42 509	46 735	9.9	2.2	3 035	1 931	-77	17 060	2.56	59.2	17.6	29.1
Livingston	11.5	7.5	4.2	50.6	91 814	128 040	39.5	7.6	9 638	5 175	5 111	46 960	2.79	74.4	13.4	21.3
Madison	11.8	7.6	5.3	50.4	13 728	12 099	-11.9	-4.8	883	695	-786	4 035	2.61	61.7	22.7	34.8
Morehouse	14.1	9.2	7.7	51.8	31 021	27 979	-9.8	-5.7	1 893	1 953	-1 497	10 383	2.55	64.9	18.8	31.9
Natchitoches	11.5	8.7	6.5	52.3	39 080	39 566	1.2	-1.0	2 858	2 042	-1 231	14 598	2.63	63.7	17.7	28.9

1. No spouse present.

Table B. States and Counties — Population, Vital Statistics, Medicare, and Crime

STATE County	Daytime population, 2010–2014 Persons in group quarters, 2015	Number	Employment/residence ratio	Births, 2015 Total	Rate[1]	Deaths, 2015 Number	Rate[1]	Persons under 65 with no health insurance, 2014 Number	Percent	Medicare, 2015 Total Beneficiaries	Enrolled in Original Medicare	Enrolled in Medicare Advantage	Serious crimes known to police,[2] 2014 Total Number	Rate[3]
	32	33	34	35	36	37	38	39	40	41	42	43	44	45
KENTUCKY—Cont'd														
Ohio	307	23 103	0.90	284	11.8	252	10.4	1 891	9.6	5 044	3 627	1 417	194	806
Oldham	5 176	49 500	0.56	543	8.4	361	5.6	2 993	5.8	7 126	4 904	2 222	586	931
Owen	0	9 028	0.60	106	9.9	97	9.1	829	9.4	1 491	1 032	459	34	320
Owsley	90	4 469	0.81	49	10.9	56	12.5	413	11.2	1 112	904	208	5	110
Pendleton	215	11 158	0.46	150	10.4	146	10.1	1 227	10.0	2 641	1 735	906	121	870
Perry	611	31 676	1.37	381	13.8	421	15.3	2 476	10.7	7 248	5 767	1 481	400	1 435
Pike	1 360	67 269	1.14	747	12.0	799	12.8	5 442	10.5	15 934	12 011	3 923	666	1 056
Powell	188	11 270	0.65	153	12.4	140	11.4	1 225	11.6	2 593	1 829	764	160	1 283
Pulaski	962	65 195	1.07	703	11.0	757	11.9	5 490	10.5	16 096	11 769	4 327	1 506	2 357
Robertson	57	1 992	0.67	17	7.9	32	14.8	196	11.5	466	345	121	2	103
Rockcastle	341	14 900	0.66	177	10.5	238	14.1	1 445	10.4	3 322	2 626	696	68	440
Rowan	2 443	25 209	1.18	301	12.7	199	8.4	1 858	10.3	4 131	2 652	1 479	287	1 216
Russell	177	18 207	1.10	214	12.1	214	12.1	1 871	13.0	4 125	3 213	912	133	746
Scott	1 320	51 754	1.11	689	13.3	355	6.8	3 586	8.1	6 475	4 123	2 352	1 215	2 398
Shelby	1 808	39 465	0.79	636	14.0	300	6.6	4 410	11.8	6 423	4 438	1 985	796	1 781
Simpson	327	18 773	1.16	230	12.8	152	8.5	1 407	9.6	3 418	2 727	691	439	2 448
Spencer	113	10 890	0.22	176	9.9	145	8.2	1 251	8.2	2 576	1 839	737	115	646
Taylor	1 193	26 444	1.14	350	13.9	307	12.1	2 086	10.7	6 513	5 176	1 337	592	2 396
Todd	195	10 595	0.60	192	15.3	131	10.5	1 447	13.9	2 110	1 735	375	134	1 069
Trigg	78	12 937	0.75	148	10.4	161	11.4	1 299	11.7	3 491	2 576	915	176	1 231
Trimble	41	6 686	0.40	99	11.3	98	11.2	707	9.6	1 606	1 206	400	4	45
Union	1 658	15 716	1.09	183	12.1	173	11.5	1 424	11.1	2 920	2 149	771	155	1 035
Warren	6 316	124 698	1.14	1 590	13.1	892	7.3	11 576	11.6	19 599	15 084	4 515	3 726	3 115
Washington	425	10 272	0.68	156	13.0	127	10.6	1 028	10.7	2 287	1 766	521	46	386
Wayne	331	19 784	0.86	220	10.7	190	9.3	1 960	11.9	4 422	3 310	1 112	175	847
Webster	393	12 464	0.81	147	11.1	153	11.6	1 205	11.2	2 927	2 057	870	51	430
Whitley	1 736	35 502	1.00	593	16.5	427	11.9	3 021	10.5	11 859	9 668	2 191	509	1 420
Wolfe	132	6 799	0.74	92	12.7	102	14.1	632	10.7	1 947	1 439	508	60	830
Woodford	341	22 785	0.81	261	10.2	213	8.3	2 192	10.4	4 508	2 837	1 671	471	1 856
LOUISIANA	128 384	4 612 671	1.01	63 515	13.6	43 124	9.3	661 811	16.9	752 792	517 092	235 700	184 758	3 974
Acadia	1 050	53 700	0.66	921	14.7	636	10.2	9 541	17.8	10 127	8 897	1 230	1 715	2 818
Allen	4 180	25 782	1.01	363	14.1	231	9.0	3 251	17.7	3 912	3 444	468	NA	NA
Ascension	790	99 003	0.75	1 773	15.0	791	6.7	12 752	12.3	13 805	6 052	7 753	3 834	3 300
Assumption	199	18 045	0.42	266	11.6	220	9.6	3 452	17.8	3 888	2 772	1 116	388	1 675
Avoyelles	3 343	38 431	0.78	565	13.7	441	10.7	5 785	18.1	7 951	6 852	1 099	1 401	3 591
Beauregard	1 299	31 633	0.69	472	13.0	365	10.0	4 950	16.6	6 862	6 128	734	650	1 792
Bienville	319	13 639	0.90	130	9.4	200	14.5	1 798	16.1	3 103	2 589	514	267	1 920
Bossier	2 370	115 382	0.89	1 751	14.0	1 003	8.0	15 667	14.7	16 901	14 020	2 881	4 369	3 481
Caddo	6 256	271 187	1.14	3 725	14.8	2 647	10.5	34 736	16.5	44 740	35 664	9 076	11 618	4 625
Calcasieu	3 799	200 267	1.06	2 766	14.0	1 902	9.6	28 679	17.2	34 248	28 836	5 412	9 984	5 095
Caldwell	584	8 823	0.70	114	11.4	117	11.7	1 430	18.5	2 087	1 689	398	263	2 640
Cameron	20	7 314	1.19	66	9.8	57	8.4	906	16.1	512	422	90	150	2 227
Catahoula	866	9 351	0.74	148	14.5	116	11.4	1 562	20.2	2 185	1 883	302	216	2 227
Claiborne	2 917	15 833	0.83	166	10.2	186	11.4	2 157	20.0	2 898	2 442	456	NA	NA
Concordia	1 485	20 023	0.91	236	11.6	234	11.5	3 294	20.6	3 782	3 154	628	833	4 092
De Soto	215	25 117	0.82	333	12.3	279	10.3	3 962	17.5	5 102	4 388	714	851	3 130
East Baton Rouge	11 145	496 943	1.25	6 140	13.8	3 714	8.3	60 709	15.9	64 784	35 411	29 373	20 851	4 669
East Carroll	1 067	7 460	0.93	122	16.5	74	10.0	993	18.3	1 260	1 111	149	106	1 417
East Feliciana	2 401	17 232	0.62	226	11.4	222	11.2	2 203	15.3	3 771	2 360	1 411	208	1 060
Evangeline	1 379	30 926	0.74	463	13.7	372	11.0	4 595	16.6	6 201	5 637	564	611	2 329
Franklin	732	19 286	0.81	274	13.4	270	13.2	3 367	20.3	3 909	3 188	721	159	812
Grant	2 951	18 120	0.40	252	11.3	173	7.7	2 833	17.2	3 699	3 043	656	191	869
Iberia	944	75 139	1.05	1 082	14.6	746	10.1	11 146	17.6	12 899	11 636	1 263	1 509	2 202
Iberville	3 999	37 337	1.31	354	10.7	286	8.6	3 957	15.8	5 669	2 891	2 778	1 281	3 837
Jackson	1 038	14 562	0.70	163	10.2	201	12.6	2 106	17.3	3 500	2 809	691	NA	NA
Jefferson	3 317	427 837	0.97	5 630	12.9	4 120	9.5	67 111	18.3	77 041	32 522	44 519	17 691	4 062
Jefferson Davis	567	28 077	0.71	426	13.6	376	12.0	4 596	17.4	5 362	4 906	456	509	1 891
Lafayette	5 166	255 023	1.24	3 613	15.2	1 776	7.5	33 680	16.4	31 778	27 635	4 143	10 965	4 921
Lafourche	1 628	94 157	0.93	1 286	13.1	826	8.4	15 312	18.4	14 846	11 000	3 846	2 453	2 520
La Salle	1 243	14 337	0.90	175	11.7	166	11.1	1 802	15.9	2 640	2 238	402	70	474
Lincoln	4 931	47 188	1.00	591	12.4	396	8.3	7 662	20.6	6 628	5 440	1 188	1 512	3 556
Livingston	1 192	99 583	0.45	1 899	13.9	1 047	7.7	18 378	15.5	18 005	8 446	9 559	4 467	3 308
Madison	1 597	11 494	0.87	149	12.8	159	13.6	1 745	19.6	1 664	1 469	195	460	3 958
Morehouse	768	24 588	0.71	348	13.1	346	13.0	3 989	18.4	6 099	4 644	1 455	1 697	6 315
Natchitoches	2 205	38 698	0.96	559	14.3	383	9.8	5 745	18.4	6 796	5 859	937	2 051	5 249

1. Per 1,000 estimated resident population.   2. Data for serious crimes have not been adjusted for underreporting; this may affect comparability between geographic areas and over time.
3. Per 100,000 population estimated by the FBI.

STATE County	Serious crimes known to police, 2014 (cont.)[1] Rate[2]		Education School enrollment and attainment, 2010–2014				Local government expenditures,[5] 2012–2013		Money income, 2010–2014 Households				Income and poverty, 2014 Percent below poverty level		
			Enrollment[3]		Attainment[4] (percent)										
	Violent	Property	Total	Percent private	High school graduate or less	Bachelor's degree or more	Total current spending (mil dol)	Current spending per student (dollars)	Per capita income[6] (dollars)	Median income (dollars)	Mean income (dollars)	Percent with income of $200,000 or more	Median household income (dollars)	All persons	Children under 18 years	Children 5 to 17 years in families
	46	47	48	49	50	51	52	53	54	55	56	57	58	59	60	61
KENTUCKY—Cont'd																
Ohio	83	723	5 405	9.1	66.2	8.2	34.9	8 175	18 991	39 574	50 340	1.4	38 261	19.7	28.9	28.1
Oldham	49	882	18 351	17.3	31.1	39.8	101.4	8 404	34 113	84 447	105 608	10.8	92 097	5.5	6.8	5.6
Owen	0	320	2 387	9.2	60.9	14.0	16.5	8 669	22 346	40 995	54 302	1.4	43 626	17.4	25.4	22.6
Owsley	0	110	997	5.8	70.0	15.5	10.7	12 732	14 591	19 146	35 175	0.0	23 047	45.1	54.8	50.9
Pendleton	14	856	3 428	13.5	62.1	12.6	21.6	8 492	23 755	46 085	59 842	1.8	47 023	15.6	22.7	21.2
Perry	57	1 377	6 062	5.5	62.9	13.0	49.9	9 545	18 606	32 302	46 967	1.5	31 265	27.5	35.5	34.7
Pike	17	1 039	14 251	10.3	64.5	12.5	102.8	9 489	19 749	32 571	47 344	1.6	32 666	27.4	32.4	30.6
Powell	56	1 227	2 912	14.7	66.3	13.6	22.0	8 723	16 544	29 141	42 691	1.4	32 783	26.7	38.7	36.5
Pulaski	106	2 251	14 233	7.1	60.6	14.5	87.6	8 391	20 348	33 425	48 651	2.1	32 767	26.0	34.4	30.8
Robertson	0	103	459	5.2	62.9	14.9	4.0	11 056	17 326	30 479	41 500	0.0	37 281	23.0	35.0	29.1
Rockcastle	78	363	3 945	7.5	65.6	11.1	27.8	9 452	17 146	31 536	42 880	1.0	33 789	24.1	32.3	30.4
Rowan	25	1 190	8 176	5.3	49.1	25.5	29.3	8 776	18 168	40 697	49 125	1.2	37 287	23.4	29.6	28.3
Russell	62	684	3 582	8.5	63.3	12.0	26.9	8 794	17 181	30 773	40 419	1.0	33 623	26.3	37.4	35.0
Scott	150	2 248	13 634	24.9	43.1	28.0	70.0	8 034	27 906	62 134	73 750	3.3	61 989	10.9	15.5	14.1
Shelby	114	1 667	10 822	18.4	46.5	23.7	64.5	8 932	27 152	57 890	73 563	4.5	57 447	12.8	17.9	16.5
Simpson	139	2 309	4 036	8.4	58.5	13.8	26.2	8 756	18 840	39 055	49 091	0.6	45 269	15.0	23.7	22.7
Spencer	34	613	4 455	21.6	48.5	17.4	22.9	7 877	26 564	65 149	73 271	1.7	67 437	8.8	12.5	11.0
Taylor	125	2 271	6 421	24.2	59.7	15.0	34.4	8 999	18 430	35 521	45 885	1.0	34 633	26.7	35.4	31.6
Todd	56	1 013	2 945	14.4	63.9	10.2	19.1	8 886	18 592	41 047	49 301	0.7	40 002	19.3	29.4	27.1
Trigg	70	1 161	3 256	9.2	47.7	17.6	19.1	8 798	24 982	45 303	58 252	1.6	44 676	15.8	26.3	23.9
Trimble	0	45	2 066	15.8	59.9	13.5	13.5	9 176	22 804	47 119	55 275	0.3	46 708	16.2	23.3	21.4
Union	120	914	3 747	16.8	57.2	10.9	23.9	9 707	19 611	38 367	50 837	1.5	44 119	18.9	22.9	20.6
Warren	198	2 917	36 750	5.5	44.3	27.3	151.0	8 221	24 012	45 209	61 608	2.1	48 925	18.3	22.5	20.5
Washington	25	361	3 143	20.6	60.1	15.0	16.9	9 898	19 818	39 313	49 332	1.0	39 983	19.7	20.8	20.2
Wayne	58	789	4 394	4.8	69.7	10.0	32.1	9 249	15 935	29 295	38 890	0.5	30 619	26.2	37.7	35.2
Webster	42	388	2 876	10.3	64.7	7.9	19.1	8 328	20 983	40 852	54 575	1.3	43 024	17.3	24.3	23.8
Whitley	98	1 323	9 019	19.0	63.3	14.5	76.5	9 158	16 406	32 255	43 524	1.0	31 086	29.8	38.5	36.2
Wolfe	69	760	1 572	7.4	73.0	10.7	13.5	10 473	13 455	21 198	32 379	1.0	25 768	36.2	50.3	46.9
Woodford	55	1 801	6 194	14.7	42.0	32.4	NA	NA	29 995	58 639	75 810	4.4	57 067	11.2	16.3	14.9
LOUISIANA	515	3 459	1 185 269	19.2	51.1	22.1	7 057.3	10 490	24 775	44 991	63 565	3.4	44 680	19.9	28.0	26.3
Acadia	414	2 404	15 141	21.3	66.3	9.9	91.7	9 255	20 264	37 684	52 904	1.4	40 269	22.0	27.6	25.2
Allen	NA	NA	5 581	7.7	63.5	11.5	44.9	10 356	19 259	39 440	54 021	1.2	36 852	22.5	26.2	23.0
Ascension	334	2 966	31 263	18.6	46.4	25.8	213.4	10 161	28 834	70 207	79 850	3.9	67 299	13.7	18.3	16.0
Assumption	263	1 412	5 392	16.7	67.1	10.7	43.4	11 406	23 085	47 961	60 703	2.5	46 317	17.8	26.7	25.1
Avoyelles	643	2 948	9 101	16.0	69.3	9.3	51.7	8 639	17 899	33 781	47 923	1.4	34 022	25.5	33.8	32.9
Beauregard	116	1 676	8 286	10.3	58.5	14.9	61.0	10 026	23 451	46 420	62 717	2.4	43 918	18.9	23.1	21.0
Bienville	316	1 604	3 220	8.0	61.6	12.0	31.7	13 569	20 622	32 826	47 677	1.4	33 134	27.4	37.5	34.0
Bossier	409	3 071	31 446	11.5	42.9	25.1	205.4	9 571	27 199	52 754	68 376	3.3	51 138	14.3	21.8	19.6
Caddo	603	4 022	64 695	14.1	47.5	23.5	441.0	10 672	24 673	41 251	61 121	3.4	39 812	24.1	36.5	34.0
Calcasieu	555	4 541	50 005	15.0	50.6	20.3	324.6	10 060	24 521	44 045	62 066	3.0	45 979	18.4	26.3	22.9
Caldwell	231	2 409	2 283	10.6	70.2	9.8	17.5	10 605	22 752	36 792	54 710	2.5	36 350	23.3	31.1	27.4
Cameron	223	2 004	1 555	5.1	58.8	15.7	24.8	19 414	29 450	64 129	76 804	5.8	59 300	12.2	17.0	15.1
Catahoula	289	1 938	2 062	9.9	69.0	11.6	18.4	12 180	21 237	35 093	55 850	3.5	34 116	23.3	32.3	30.8
Claiborne	NA	NA	3 311	15.7	63.6	13.0	20.2	10 458	17 672	34 216	47 627	1.2	35 385	28.2	37.3	36.3
Concordia	845	3 247	4 781	10.2	64.6	10.5	38.5	10 081	16 931	29 824	44 053	0.5	31 835	30.9	43.4	37.7
De Soto	382	2 747	6 458	10.2	60.8	12.0	83.3	16 060	22 027	41 486	55 247	1.5	40 642	23.5	31.4	30.8
East Baton Rouge	565	4 103	132 411	19.8	37.4	34.1	609.0	11 190	27 558	48 535	69 584	4.5	46 831	18.4	24.2	24.1
East Carroll	535	882	1 956	10.7	71.2	9.4	13.9	12 071	12 129	24 947	34 957	0.8	25 402	43.0	54.3	53.8
East Feliciana	331	728	4 188	19.9	61.6	12.9	23.2	11 593	21 370	46 220	59 050	2.1	41 651	20.4	25.4	24.1
Evangeline	213	2 116	8 427	18.6	66.6	12.6	56.2	9 214	18 535	30 323	48 630	2.1	32 615	24.1	31.6	28.6
Franklin	51	761	5 030	18.4	65.5	12.0	30.1	9 316	17 816	30 607	46 518	1.1	32 318	29.0	44.2	39.3
Grant	68	801	4 728	13.5	64.0	9.4	28.7	8 715	18 415	39 729	51 619	1.5	40 668	22.8	25.7	23.5
Iberia	209	1 993	18 183	18.3	63.3	14.3	128.8	9 281	23 562	45 022	63 984	2.9	45 205	19.4	29.1	27.2
Iberville	1 072	2 765	7 647	17.1	61.7	12.7	62.8	13 595	21 576	45 692	60 501	2.5	47 377	19.9	31.0	30.2
Jackson	NA	NA	3 407	12.0	61.4	13.3	22.8	10 003	18 875	36 466	48 024	0.6	37 130	24.6	33.1	30.5
Jefferson	441	3 621	104 216	33.5	47.5	23.8	530.0	11 496	27 067	47 871	67 089	4.2	47 024	15.8	25.7	24.8
Jefferson Davis	238	1 653	8 143	12.0	61.6	14.3	62.4	10 630	21 656	40 335	56 333	2.3	37 968	21.7	27.5	25.7
Lafayette	569	4 353	62 578	22.4	43.2	29.0	307.1	9 997	29 332	51 406	73 080	5.3	51 340	15.1	19.8	18.8
Lafourche	139	2 382	24 025	17.4	65.6	15.1	142.9	9 768	25 010	50 396	66 613	2.9	47 382	17.6	25.1	25.7
La Salle	217	258	3 201	10.7	63.0	13.0	26.1	9 880	21 998	41 173	57 215	1.3	44 139	18.0	20.9	19.2
Lincoln	393	3 163	18 108	10.9	42.0	34.6	65.6	11 250	21 150	34 210	55 863	3.0	32 889	29.7	30.5	28.1
Livingston	446	2 862	34 102	10.1	56.2	17.3	214.1	8 466	25 508	57 478	69 788	2.4	58 818	12.3	16.9	14.9
Madison	585	3 373	2 771	10.8	61.7	11.4	19.2	10 170	14 526	24 028	38 402	0.9	26 732	41.4	50.9	50.5
Morehouse	554	5 761	5 879	12.8	64.4	13.3	46.7	10 717	17 969	28 304	45 363	1.4	30 636	29.4	44.7	43.5
Natchitoches	619	4 630	12 012	12.0	54.9	20.6	68.6	10 165	20 607	33 629	53 100	2.2	34 522	31.1	37.7	34.8

1. Data for serious crimes have not been adjusted for underreporting; this may affect comparability between geographic areas and over time.   2. Per 100,000 population estimated by the FBI.
3. All persons 3 years old and over enrolled in nursery school through college.   4. Persons 25 years old and over.   5. Elementary and secondary education expenditures.
6. Based on population estimated by the American Community Survey, 2010–2014.

Table B. States and Counties — **Personal Income**

STATE County	Personal income, 2014 Total (mil dol) [62]	Percent change, 2013–2014 [63]	Per capita¹ Dollars [64]	Per capita¹ Rank [65]	Wages and salaries (mil dol) [66]	Supplements — Pension and insurance [67]	Supplements — Government social insurance [68]	Proprietors' income (mil dol) [69]	Dividends, interest, and rent (mil dol) [70]	Personal transfer receipts (mil dol) [71]	Earnings Total (mil dol) [72]	Contributions — From employee and self-employed [73]	Contributions — From employer [74]
KENTUCKY—Cont'd													
Ohio	759	3.9	31 646	2 502	244	58	19	69	89	237	391	25	19
Oldham	3 210	5.4	50 558	355	614	117	46	95	532	351	872	56	46
Owen	346	3.9	32 486	2 375	65	17	5	12	37	102	99	8	5
Owsley	123	9.4	27 274	2 964	19	6	1	2	11	75	28	3	1
Pendleton	456	3.6	31 478	2 528	100	22	7	11	64	120	141	11	7
Perry	954	4.3	34 578	2 009	482	98	38	51	115	399	669	44	38
Pike	2 134	2.4	33 850	2 139	947	167	74	177	232	792	1 365	96	74
Powell	372	6.8	29 930	2 726	79	21	6	31	33	143	137	11	6
Pulaski	2 145	6.8	33 607	2 174	881	179	73	100	254	794	1 234	85	73
Robertson	63	7.3	28 745	2 856	9	3	1	1	8	24	13	1	1
Rockcastle	464	6.0	27 596	2 948	117	28	9	9	47	183	163	13	9
Rowan	665	3.8	28 114	2 907	333	91	25	23	85	224	472	28	25
Russell	532	5.2	29 910	2 729	180	42	15	61	77	202	298	21	15
Scott	1 939	5.7	37 808	1 483	1 322	181	103	69	200	302	1 675	102	103
Shelby	1 694	3.8	37 745	1 491	604	111	49	79	258	303	843	54	49
Simpson	591	-1.9	33 172	2 252	320	55	27	61	80	156	463	28	27
Spencer	651	4.9	36 866	1 622	67	16	5	12	55	122	100	9	5
Taylor	801	5.2	31 725	2 485	364	72	31	43	109	261	509	34	31
Todd	431	-3.8	34 443	2 039	81	20	6	67	55	104	174	10	6
Trigg	481	-4.0	34 044	2 111	109	24	9	20	77	139	163	13	9
Trimble	277	4.2	31 476	2 529	48	13	4	4	28	78	68	6	4
Union	534	-2.8	35 185	1 907	265	45	20	41	69	144	371	23	20
Warren	4 138	4.8	34 354	2 054	2 437	456	190	286	597	903	3 369	201	190
Washington	415	5.6	34 698	1 985	123	25	10	19	59	108	177	13	10
Wayne	535	5.8	26 113	3 026	165	39	14	24	68	229	241	18	14
Webster	484	-1.6	36 569	1 677	183	35	13	68	56	124	300	17	13
Whitley	1 077	4.8	30 324	2 673	445	90	38	19	130	462	593	43	38
Wolfe	184	9.2	25 437	3 052	37	10	3	3	17	108	55	5	3
Woodford	1 136	3.3	44 447	720	394	74	30	42	239	187	540	34	30
LOUISIANA	195 426	3.4	42 030	X	95 498	16 220	6 063	21 887	33 142	36 644	139 668	7 505	6 063
Acadia	2 501	2.9	40 023	1 170	578	110	36	475	309	498	1 200	64	36
Allen	772	2.2	30 017	2 714	305	77	16	77	93	188	476	23	16
Ascension	5 938	5.4	50 737	345	2 297	383	148	1 118	522	655	3 945	206	148
Assumption	907	4.8	39 384	1 266	201	37	12	88	100	186	338	21	12
Avoyelles	1 403	0.7	34 087	2 101	369	83	21	159	179	408	632	35	21
Beauregard	1 397	2.1	38 604	1 376	380	70	23	75	187	296	549	33	23
Bienville	479	2.8	34 496	2 027	186	39	11	56	70	151	292	17	11
Bossier	5 038	3.8	40 287	1 141	2 099	439	153	499	827	925	3 189	159	153
Caddo	11 092	2.2	43 909	769	5 328	936	351	1 684	2 365	2 197	8 299	441	351
Calcasieu	7 891	7.1	40 016	1 171	4 320	799	278	623	1 224	1 527	6 019	326	278
Caldwell	340	0.8	34 362	2 052	85	19	5	17	38	99	127	8	5
Cameron	288	6.7	43 080	837	445	60	26	17	59	37	547	29	26
Catahoula	316	-4.7	31 132	2 565	78	19	5	58	39	102	159	8	5
Claiborne	534	1.7	32 541	2 364	157	35	9	60	97	149	261	14	9
Concordia	648	-0.1	31 670	2 497	207	45	12	79	95	189	344	18	12
De Soto	1 008	2.7	37 123	1 580	378	67	22	66	191	233	533	31	22
East Baton Rouge	19 227	3.4	43 106	835	13 937	2 328	861	1 083	3 816	3 216	18 209	941	861
East Carroll	259	-12.0	34 601	1 998	67	17	4	56	41	84	143	5	4
East Feliciana	721	2.0	36 384	1 708	207	57	9	42	101	191	315	16	9
Evangeline	1 170	2.1	34 718	1 980	309	63	20	90	146	322	482	29	20
Franklin	638	-4.6	31 200	2 555	162	39	9	100	76	213	311	16	9
Grant	664	2.7	29 658	2 765	156	40	11	41	82	172	247	16	11
Iberia	2 933	2.8	39 679	1 229	1 739	247	109	292	486	606	2 388	134	109
Iberville	1 215	1.8	36 443	1 697	961	176	59	109	154	273	1 305	69	59
Jackson	547	6.2	34 188	2 084	174	35	10	60	58	150	280	16	10
Jefferson	20 023	3.5	45 954	598	9 742	1 396	631	2 406	3 791	3 412	14 175	798	631
Jefferson Davis	1 235	5.0	39 225	1 292	357	70	22	140	174	262	589	32	22
Lafayette	12 161	5.1	51 608	307	7 666	1 011	486	2 344	2 010	1 490	11 508	609	486
Lafourche	5 541	4.7	56 528	184	2 484	395	150	1 257	876	700	4 286	220	150
La Salle	548	2.5	36 939	1 609	184	39	11	35	56	127	268	15	11
Lincoln	1 623	2.6	34 077	2 107	712	142	42	242	323	330	1 139	56	42
Livingston	4 918	4.3	36 230	1 739	986	183	61	310	441	853	1 540	94	61
Madison	334	-9.0	28 210	2 902	109	27	7	54	43	105	197	9	7
Morehouse	895	-4.2	33 450	2 205	239	50	16	101	113	309	406	23	16
Natchitoches	1 387	1.9	35 422	1 873	486	112	28	212	188	343	838	42	28

1. Based on the resident population estimated as of July 1 of the year shown.

Table B. States and Counties — Earnings, Social Security, and Housing

STATE County	Earnings, 2014 (cont.) Percent by selected industries									Social Security beneficiaries, December 2014		Supplemental Security Income recipients, December 2014	Housing units, 2015	
	Farm	Mining	Construction	Manu-facturing	Infor-mation: professional, scientific, technical services	Retail trade	Finance, insur-ance, real estate and leasing	Health care and social assistance	Govern-ment	Number	Rate¹		Total	Percent change, 2010–2014
	75	76	77	78	79	80	81	82	83	84	85	86	87	88
KENTUCKY—Cont'd														
Ohio	8.5	D	4.0	32.9	D	6.6	1.6	D	21.1	6 225	259	1 113	10 252	0.3
Oldham	0.3	D	9.9	6.3	10.2	5.6	12.5	11.3	22.2	9 115	142	564	21 399	3.4
Owen	3.1	0.0	3.7	D	D	5.5	D	10.2	26.4	2 510	236	379	5 634	0.0
Owsley	-2.4	D	D	D	D	D	4.7	19.0	49.6	190	42	52	2 324	-0.2
Pendleton	-0.8	D	D	19.6	D	3.6	4.5	7.9	24.9	3 190	221	518	6 308	-0.5
Perry	0.0	D	1.9	0.3	D	9.0	3.1	D	20.2	7 785	282	2 971	12 788	0.0
Pike	-0.1	22.4	2.9	2.8	5.6	8.6	4.2	20.0	13.7	19 350	308	5 034	30 317	0.0
Powell	-1.4	D	D	8.1	D	10.0	3.5	8.3	27.8	3 470	280	1 116	5 590	-0.1
Pulaski	0.3	D	4.6	14.9	4.3	9.3	4.3	21.7	17.2	17 850	280	3 897	31 151	-0.9
Robertson	-7.0	0.0	D	0.0	1.9	D	0.0	18.6	50.2	575	263	113	1 090	-0.5
Rockcastle	-2.3	D	D	4.1	6.7	5.9	D	28.8	25.0	4 235	252	1 182	7 688	-0.2
Rowan	-0.1	D	3.2	8.8	2.0	8.5	3.4	D	37.6	4 935	208	1 258	10 134	0.3
Russell	3.2	0.0	D	30.1	D	9.0	3.7	D	18.6	4 855	273	1 238	9 928	-0.7
Scott	0.5	D	2.7	49.9	D	3.2	1.9	5.4	7.4	7 905	154	1 036	20 767	7.6
Shelby	1.8	D	4.9	30.2	D	7.3	4.4	7.1	14.9	8 230	183	773	17 171	3.4
Simpson	5.2	0.0	4.1	40.2	D	9.5	2.5	D	10.1	4 150	232	552	7 577	1.9
Spencer	0.8	0.1	8.0	D	D	7.3	6.3	D	35.0	3 335	189	329	6 994	4.3
Taylor	2.1	0.0	D	11.1	2.6	8.0	4.5	D	20.8	6 560	261	1 308	10 968	1.0
Todd	25.3	0.0	6.8	10.1	2.5	5.6	3.0	D	17.1	2 705	216	394	5 291	0.1
Trigg	1.3	D	8.3	15.7	10.1	9.1	4.5	D	25.3	3 950	279	452	7 837	0.4
Trimble	-0.9	0.0	D	3.4	D	2.5	6.1	D	28.2	2 120	243	264	3 923	-0.2
Union	3.8	36.4	2.6	9.6	2.1	4.9	3.6	D	10.8	3 465	229	446	6 218	1.3
Warren	0.9	0.4	6.7	18.1	4.7	6.9	4.8	13.4	17.0	20 420	169	3 688	50 295	6.5
Washington	2.0	0.0	10.4	34.5	D	5.2	D	D	15.4	2 755	230	446	5 112	1.3
Wayne	5.4	D	2.9	26.9	D	8.9	D	D	22.0	5 495	268	1 880	10 810	-1.2
Webster	16.5	D	11.7	5.1	D	3.3	D	4.0	11.8	3 345	253	518	5 913	-0.4
Whitley	-0.6	D	2.5	8.7	7.5	7.5	2.2	D	19.8	8 835	247	4 141	15 167	0.0
Wolfe	-2.7	D	3.0	D	D	11.7	D	D	38.7	2 265	313	1 271	3 651	-0.2
Woodford	2.7	0.0	5.2	24.3	8.6	5.7	3.5	D	17.0	5 345	209	415	11 010	2.8
LOUISIANA	0.7	6.2	9.1	9.8	8.2	6.2	6.7	10.8	16.3	854 211	184	181 279	2 024 645	3.0
Acadia	4.3	8.7	11.1	11.1	6.1	6.5	9.1	8.8	12.4	12 405	198	2 923	25 956	2.2
Allen	1.0	D	3.0	9.4	D	5.1	4.5	D	49.6	4 760	185	851	9 801	0.7
Ascension	0.1	D	14.8	21.7	5.3	7.2	13.2	7.2	8.0	16 735	143	2 292	45 024	10.4
Assumption	1.5	2.8	10.3	23.8	D	5.0	4.4	D	16.7	5 005	217	1 017	10 532	1.7
Avoyelles	7.6	3.4	9.7	2.4	4.5	8.7	5.2	D	27.3	9 370	228	2 771	18 238	1.1
Beauregard	-0.7	0.5	10.3	17.1	D	7.2	9.6	11.6	16.8	7 195	199	1 065	15 254	1.4
Bienville	0.9	7.5	5.2	19.5	D	3.9	6.4	7.0	16.3	3 445	250	818	7 726	0.1
Bossier	0.2	7.5	6.1	4.5	3.8	9.2	4.7	7.4	33.4	20 245	162	3 295	55 362	12.2
Caddo	0.1	10.7	5.7	6.5	6.3	6.4	6.3	18.0	16.6	49 425	196	13 218	112 860	0.7
Calcasieu	0.3	1.1	15.8	18.1	7.2	6.2	3.9	12.1	13.3	37 670	191	6 383	86 931	5.9
Caldwell	2.1	2.4	4.7	D	4.5	9.4	7.0	21.4	24.2	2 180	220	484	5 038	0.9
Cameron	1.5	2.8	64.7	8.4	D	D	0.9	0.9	7.8	1 185	177	59	3 875	7.8
Catahoula	22.8	4.8	D	D	D	8.4	3.6	7.5	20.6	2 510	246	751	4 914	0.8
Claiborne	11.5	15.0	6.6	4.9	D	4.6	2.1	D	26.0	3 570	218	859	7 758	0.0
Concordia	11.7	9.0	2.2	2.6	D	8.9	3.7	D	24.1	4 305	211	1 181	9 445	0.7
De Soto	-0.6	18.9	D	D	1.6	7.7	3.1	D	19.1	6 100	226	1 350	12 498	1.7
East Baton Rouge	0.0	0.3	15.1	7.3	12.3	5.5	6.5	12.4	18.4	71 265	160	15 208	192 436	2.7
East Carroll	35.2	D	0.7	5.2	D	5.5	4.2	D	24.2	1 400	188	650	2 897	-0.2
East Feliciana	1.3	1.8	4.0	7.5	1.6	4.0	3.3	D	49.9	3 810	192	882	8 216	2.5
Evangeline	7.8	0.5	4.9	13.2	2.9	7.0	4.7	D	17.3	7 200	213	2 133	14 909	1.7
Franklin	14.7	0.7	7.7	3.1	D	11.4	4.2	D	23.8	4 555	223	1 317	9 122	1.0
Grant	1.1	D	10.9	6.7	D	3.9	D	D	46.9	4 260	190	858	9 074	2.1
Iberia	0.1	18.2	9.2	15.4	5.2	6.3	9.1	6.2	10.3	14 740	199	3 237	30 169	1.6
Iberville	0.5	2.0	12.2	42.1	2.0	3.0	2.9	D	14.0	6 190	187	1 453	13 097	3.1
Jackson	2.5	D	21.1	D	2.7	6.6	2.8	D	20.6	3 525	221	614	7 768	1.1
Jefferson	0.0	3.3	9.3	5.8	10.6	7.9	8.9	12.3	10.6	84 600	194	13 545	189 161	0.0
Jefferson Davis	4.2	5.5	6.4	5.8	2.4	7.0	6.7	13.3	18.9	6 730	214	1 080	13 642	2.5
Lafayette	0.0	20.4	6.6	7.0	9.5	5.8	8.0	12.7	7.7	35 150	149	5 905	99 227	5.9
Lafourche	0.3	7.9	6.1	7.5	3.3	3.7	4.7	4.4	10.3	18 565	190	3 443	40 009	3.4
La Salle	-0.2	17.4	2.8	3.0	D	7.2	3.1	7.1	28.4	3 185	214	511	6 595	0.5
Lincoln	2.9	2.3	5.8	8.1	7.7	9.0	6.0	14.9	21.6	6 955	147	1 562	19 803	1.7
Livingston	0.0	1.3	16.4	10.8	D	10.2	7.3	6.6	20.2	22 045	162	2 858	54 438	8.5
Madison	24.1	0.0	1.2	6.9	1.1	6.3	2.9	D	23.1	2 030	172	715	4 972	3.5
Morehouse	15.1	D	6.4	6.3	D	8.0	4.1	19.6	16.8	6 900	258	1 810	12 543	1.0
Natchitoches	4.7	0.3	4.5	21.9	D	7.0	4.0	7.1	26.5	7 685	196	2 232	18 802	1.2

1. Per 1,000 resident population estimated as of July 1 of the year shown.

Table B. States and Counties — **Housing, Labor Force, and Employment**

STATE County	Housing units, 2010–2014								Civilian labor force, 2015				Civilian employment,[6] 2010–2014		
	Occupied units							Sub-stand-ard units[4] (percent)			Unemployment			Percent	
	Owner-occupied					Renter-occupied									
				Median owner cost as a percent of income											
	Total	Percent	Median value[1]	With a mortgage	Without a mortgage[2]	Median rent[3]	Median rent as a percent of income[2]		Total	Percent change, 2014–2015	Total	Rate[5]	Total	Management, business, science and arts	Construction, production, and maintenance occupations
	89	90	91	92	93	94	95	96	97	98	99	100	101	102	103
KENTUCKY—Cont'd															
Ohio	8 573	79.6	80 900	20.4	10.6	543	29.7	4.0	9 250	-2.8	593	6.4	8 979	25.1	39.4
Oldham	19 610	85.7	246 000	21.0	10.0	823	29.3	0.9	29 834	-1.4	1 192	4.0	28 394	46.2	17.1
Owen	4 355	76.5	99 100	22.5	12.5	511	24.0	4.5	5 383	-2.5	223	4.1	4 415	27.2	36.4
Owsley	1 740	76.0	70 100	30.2	16.1	278	28.0	4.4	1 139	-3.3	118	10.4	1 165	34.2	30.0
Pendleton	5 349	75.8	103 900	23.8	12.2	578	23.8	1.3	6 573	-2.8	359	5.5	6 526	27.1	39.0
Perry	11 005	71.8	69 200	22.9	10.0	535	29.6	4.1	9 034	-5.3	803	8.9	9 559	30.9	24.6
Pike	26 312	71.4	67 300	21.0	10.9	597	30.4	2.5	20 816	-5.4	1 978	9.5	20 501	27.4	30.1
Powell	4 628	70.1	78 100	21.6	12.8	545	37.5	5.5	4 820	-3.0	349	7.2	3 910	28.3	38.5
Pulaski	26 052	70.3	105 100	22.1	11.7	579	36.9	2.8	25 455	-3.1	1 515	6.0	25 443	28.9	24.3
Robertson	911	76.5	89 900	21.0	12.2	571	33.2	2.7	794	-1.9	52	6.5	746	28.4	42.2
Rockcastle	6 634	77.5	75 300	21.5	13.4	514	28.5	3.0	6 729	-2.3	442	6.6	6 176	21.5	31.2
Rowan	8 407	65.4	105 000	19.4	10.3	635	28.1	1.7	10 279	-2.6	613	6.0	9 528	32.9	23.6
Russell	7 223	73.9	84 800	24.2	12.6	500	26.6	2.8	6 097	-7.4	728	11.9	6 024	27.9	34.6
Scott	18 306	71.9	160 400	19.6	10.0	729	26.7	2.5	26 050	-1.6	1 057	4.1	24 481	36.1	29.3
Shelby	15 665	69.9	170 300	21.4	10.0	772	27.5	3.6	22 186	-1.4	917	4.1	20 404	31.9	25.9
Simpson	6 660	65.3	116 800	20.7	11.2	650	28.2	1.7	8 191	-3.5	397	4.8	7 510	24.1	30.8
Spencer	6 301	84.1	174 600	21.0	10.5	616	23.2	2.1	9 009	-1.6	395	4.4	8 515	28.2	31.6
Taylor	9 491	69.0	96 300	21.2	10.0	565	33.3	2.3	10 902	-3.3	717	6.6	10 379	24.7	32.1
Todd	4 567	72.6	86 000	22.9	10.4	584	29.4	1.6	5 359	-1.8	255	4.8	4 745	22.6	42.5
Trigg	6 055	80.3	117 000	22.6	10.0	578	30.2	3.0	5 623	-1.6	329	5.9	5 461	33.5	29.0
Trimble	3 578	76.9	106 200	21.3	10.5	709	27.0	2.6	3 794	-2.1	219	5.8	3 695	25.0	42.3
Union	5 620	71.2	80 700	19.2	12.8	515	31.4	4.3	6 142	-9.1	422	6.9	5 831	25.1	37.7
Warren	44 923	58.4	141 300	20.6	10.0	681	30.8	2.1	57 784	-2.7	2 650	4.6	55 986	32.6	24.5
Washington	4 514	80.9	100 500	22.0	11.7	536	31.5	3.4	6 003	-2.0	267	4.4	5 257	25.4	37.2
Wayne	8 004	71.1	77 200	21.2	11.2	484	34.2	4.0	7 143	-1.6	576	8.1	6 889	22.3	40.6
Webster	5 057	72.1	72 800	19.2	10.0	571	27.4	3.7	6 079	-3.3	315	5.2	5 216	25.6	41.2
Whitley	12 931	68.2	75 300	24.3	11.0	591	29.9	1.8	12 833	-4.3	893	7.0	12 560	26.7	26.7
Wolfe	2 826	69.4	51 500	30.4	11.9	497	50.0	2.2	1 917	-6.8	194	10.1	1 873	23.8	25.6
Woodford	9 716	69.6	183 300	20.5	10.0	724	26.2	0.8	14 064	-1.2	506	3.6	12 668	38.0	26.5
LOUISIANA	1 718 876	66.3	140 400	20.9	10.0	786	32.0	3.0	2 160 205	0.2	135 094	6.3	2 002 410	31.9	24.7
Acadia	22 788	69.5	88 500	19.2	10.0	536	27.5	4.6	26 186	-2.1	1 751	6.7	24 879	26.5	31.0
Allen	8 108	72.7	80 800	18.8	10.0	561	27.8	3.6	8 866	-0.7	612	6.9	8 375	25.9	31.1
Ascension	39 447	80.1	166 300	18.8	10.0	872	30.2	3.0	60 925	1.7	3 055	5.0	54 286	36.5	23.9
Assumption	8 726	80.8	104 800	17.1	10.0	600	27.8	3.6	9 865	-2.3	768	7.8	9 089	27.4	36.2
Avoyelles	15 107	70.0	89 600	21.1	10.7	607	31.7	3.2	16 077	-0.7	1 188	7.4	14 871	26.5	28.2
Beauregard	13 095	76.9	97 300	18.2	10.0	650	30.4	3.6	15 227	1.7	952	6.3	14 308	27.1	33.7
Bienville	5 888	71.9	60 900	19.0	10.2	490	31.9	2.6	5 838	-1.9	476	8.2	5 096	29.8	36.2
Bossier	46 285	65.9	147 500	20.1	10.0	888	29.6	3.7	58 126	-0.4	3 264	5.6	56 710	35.2	24.4
Caddo	98 427	61.7	123 100	20.6	10.1	741	31.4	2.4	110 757	-0.7	7 845	7.1	110 166	32.1	21.6
Calcasieu	74 757	69.6	119 100	19.5	10.0	756	30.7	2.2	98 561	3.9	5 281	5.4	84 999	29.5	26.4
Caldwell	3 851	72.5	66 800	17.7	10.0	541	32.7	2.9	4 064	-0.5	332	8.2	4 017	23.6	31.0
Cameron	2 577	90.0	104 400	16.0	10.0	715	19.0	3.3	3 599	4.2	167	4.6	3 127	28.0	38.3
Catahoula	3 786	75.5	65 600	18.4	10.0	480	21.9	3.4	3 728	-3.3	345	9.3	3 706	27.5	32.0
Claiborne	5 677	71.6	74 800	20.0	10.6	601	33.2	4.0	6 204	-2.7	453	7.3	5 744	22.1	34.5
Concordia	7 767	60.9	78 800	21.1	11.5	493	29.4	4.7	7 607	-2.3	652	8.6	6 892	25.3	28.7
De Soto	10 172	74.6	91 300	19.3	10.0	604	34.8	4.9	11 111	-0.5	880	7.9	10 688	25.9	30.6
East Baton Rouge	168 534	60.0	166 800	21.3	10.0	833	33.1	2.7	236 689	1.6	12 656	5.3	214 904	37.1	18.4
East Carroll	2 592	52.1	48 300	19.2	11.7	490	41.2	4.2	2 236	0.2	311	13.9	2 115	25.1	26.0
East Feliciana	6 909	79.1	128 000	20.7	10.0	632	29.1	2.6	8 327	1.3	486	5.8	7 438	25.0	27.2
Evangeline	12 053	66.0	79 800	16.9	10.6	514	37.0	3.5	12 997	-1.3	962	7.4	11 207	28.0	34.6
Franklin	7 748	70.7	76 800	19.3	10.0	514	31.2	3.4	7 608	-0.2	724	9.5	7 460	27.1	30.6
Grant	7 204	76.2	80 400	19.0	10.5	721	28.4	1.8	8 522	1.0	616	7.2	7 231	26.6	31.9
Iberia	26 433	69.9	99 200	18.9	10.0	666	28.4	4.3	32 226	-1.4	2 549	7.9	31 547	25.9	32.2
Iberville	11 257	75.7	105 300	19.3	10.1	623	29.8	4.8	14 610	1.3	1 040	7.1	13 010	22.2	29.9
Jackson	6 166	67.1	77 000	19.5	10.0	504	32.9	2.5	7 206	0.3	434	6.0	5 734	25.7	31.0
Jefferson	167 840	62.5	171 100	23.9	10.5	908	31.9	2.7	220 629	0.8	12 533	5.7	208 694	31.6	23.8
Jefferson Davis	11 553	74.4	91 700	18.3	10.0	545	29.2	3.8	13 589	-0.2	839	6.2	12 034	28.4	31.7
Lafayette	87 602	64.5	163 800	19.5	10.0	771	29.3	2.4	119 830	-2.5	6 687	5.6	114 065	34.8	21.6
Lafourche	35 329	76.5	131 700	18.9	10.0	717	29.1	3.3	46 863	-3.7	2 500	5.3	43 367	26.4	34.4
La Salle	5 715	82.1	70 800	16.6	10.0	466	23.2	2.2	6 685	0.5	448	6.7	5 715	32.5	28.6
Lincoln	17 060	53.7	118 400	19.6	10.0	648	36.8	3.1	20 150	2.0	1 463	7.3	20 310	36.1	20.3
Livingston	46 960	80.4	151 100	19.7	10.0	785	27.3	3.1	67 857	1.6	3 436	5.1	60 046	29.6	30.6
Madison	4 035	55.1	62 600	21.7	10.7	523	34.5	4.9	3 941	0.1	365	9.3	4 009	27.1	24.2
Morehouse	10 383	64.7	77 400	23.2	11.6	548	32.0	3.7	10 860	-3.1	1 187	10.9	9 706	24.8	30.7
Natchitoches	14 598	61.5	100 600	19.4	10.1	623	41.2	5.1	15 938	-2.5	1 249	7.8	15 503	26.5	26.0

1. Specified owner-occupied units.　2. A value of 10.0 represents 10 percent or less; a value of 50.0 represents 50 percent or more.　3. Specified renter-occupied units.
4. Overcrowded or lacking complete plumbing facilities.　5. Percent of civilian labor force.　6. Persons 16 years old and over.

Table B. States and Counties — Nonfarm Employment and Agriculture

STATE County	Number of establishments	Total	Health care and social assistance	Manufacturing	Retail trade	Finance and insurance	Professional, scientific, and technical services	Total (mil dol)	Average per employee (dollars)	Number	Fewer than 50 acres	500 acres or more	Farm operators whose principal occupation is farming (percent)
	104	105	106	107	108	109	110	111	112	113	114	115	116
KENTUCKY—Cont'd													
Ohio	359	7 958	1 096	D	739	113	100	274	34 447	944	32.1	5.1	31.0
Oldham	1 211	11 709	2 592	936	1 142	D	603	408	34 807	419	53.9	7.2	40.1
Owen	118	1 414	D	D	167	49	D	47	33 243	701	23.3	7.4	40.8
Owsley	47	363	205	D	D	D	D	8	22 741	163	22.7	6.7	47.2
Pendleton	182	1 725	D	460	200	60	51	58	33 790	810	32.1	3.3	33.2
Perry	626	9 992	2 724	D	1 892	311	218	377	37 730	49	51.0	14.3	44.9
Pike	1 346	18 512	4 227	575	3 919	768	649	708	38 226	56	26.8	14.3	42.9
Powell	179	1 509	178	D	391	D	D	43	28 803	229	41.5	3.1	39.7
Pulaski	1 456	19 774	5 135	3 760	3 246	D	441	635	32 110	1 713	38.3	3.7	50.0
Robertson	18	132	D	NA	D	D	D	3	23 326	251	21.1	5.2	48.6
Rockcastle	216	2 756	969	101	325	92	58	71	25 857	677	36.8	4.1	36.2
Rowan	503	7 366	D	1 030	1 328	227	85	220	29 810	356	35.7	3.1	29.5
Russell	369	5 017	1 012	1 441	778	135	53	137	27 389	726	45.5	4.7	39.4
Scott	895	23 284	1 597	9 748	1 601	D	318	1 141	49 018	838	44.4	7.4	50.5
Shelby	939	12 624	1 364	3 899	1 744	297	293	486	38 460	1 518	50.4	4.0	40.5
Simpson	362	7 015	419	3 074	924	134	72	242	34 539	467	50.7	8.6	50.3
Spencer	205	1 156	256	D	212	D	59	28	23 954	529	44.2	4.0	41.0
Taylor	621	8 529	D	1 139	1 408	248	91	261	30 605	874	42.9	4.3	37.8
Todd	200	1 532	226	388	D	77	D	42	27 192	603	22.4	13.8	55.9
Trigg	230	2 221	382	476	438	73	D	61	27 688	397	30.2	10.1	41.3
Trimble	78	639	D	D	78	56	D	32	50 798	439	37.1	4.3	40.1
Union	268	4 785	865	D	734	92	54	224	46 794	310	35.5	25.2	46.1
Warren	2 934	49 690	8 316	8 566	7 313	1 527	1 825	1 861	37 450	1 648	45.9	4.7	32.9
Washington	257	2 922	436	1 004	322	D	66	90	30 709	1 011	28.7	4.3	37.1
Wayne	277	3 719	565	1 456	667	183	49	104	27 991	778	35.5	5.7	49.9
Webster	213	2 393	284	256	326	95	D	109	45 473	500	26.0	13.2	40.0
Whitley	626	10 365	2 517	879	1 511	236	D	305	29 401	496	38.7	2.6	29.8
Wolfe	80	650	259	D	166	D	D	17	25 903	297	28.6	4.7	37.7
Woodford	543	6 557	586	1 785	752	212	553	264	40 286	713	44.6	7.3	38.7
LOUISIANA	104 976	1 717 797	287 898	129 832	229 419	64 362	100 652	76 731	44 668	28 093	43.7	11.6	43.2
Acadia	1 131	13 425	2 420	1 250	2 503	412	373	458	34 112	841	50.9	14.3	47.1
Allen	316	3 491	851	D	624	121	D	116	33 087	429	48.0	9.3	35.7
Ascension	2 133	36 244	3 261	5 266	6 037	1 017	1 266	1 857	51 235	250	60.8	9.6	32.8
Assumption	258	3 189	831	327	464	D	83	125	39 296	81	37.0	42.0	66.7
Avoyelles	717	9 129	2 473	236	1 495	439	232	251	27 507	937	43.1	15.0	43.0
Beauregard	602	6 687	1 192	829	1 314	D	199	260	38 926	860	36.9	5.9	37.0
Bienville	225	3 460	482	1 143	291	152	46	127	36 746	233	33.0	6.4	54.1
Bossier	2 446	37 056	4 001	1 672	7 022	1 073	1 079	1 170	31 572	472	50.8	8.3	53.0
Caddo	6 310	106 795	26 144	5 778	13 915	3 053	5 271	4 089	38 286	614	54.4	9.6	48.2
Calcasieu	4 376	72 192	13 519	9 093	10 803	2 112	4 397	3 078	42 630	902	51.3	9.3	35.9
Caldwell	188	1 716	680	39	281	118	93	51	29 567	295	39.7	10.5	40.3
Cameron	156	1 315	88	D	D	D	55	68	51 897	342	25.7	20.5	33.9
Catahoula	197	1 557	390	D	329	88	83	43	27 929	567	25.2	18.3	34.0
Claiborne	249	2 826	819	169	374	87	D	97	34 310	295	32.5	7.8	42.0
Concordia	370	4 261	977	D	900	D	206	144	33 846	461	26.2	23.4	33.8
De Soto	422	5 583	661	D	905	172	101	285	51 033	669	38.1	8.5	49.6
East Baton Rouge	12 063	249 880	36 665	10 447	28 650	12 333	19 729	12 248	49 014	432	54.4	4.9	39.8
East Carroll	121	1 168	305	101	D	35	23	47	39 836	227	18.9	46.3	61.2
East Feliciana	249	3 381	1 836	293	261	139	45	125	36 866	399	36.8	12.8	32.3
Evangeline	528	6 505	2 668	964	957	287	110	193	29 723	663	45.2	10.3	36.3
Franklin	386	3 770	1 086	170	945	213	171	102	27 131	915	33.7	12.8	38.6
Grant	171	1 801	260	D	263	65	D	60	33 473	238	35.3	10.1	29.4
Iberia	1 710	30 483	3 716	5 345	3 558	860	818	1 564	51 309	279	57.7	16.8	57.3
Iberville	523	10 289	725	3 773	1 073	267	D	677	65 800	165	38.8	24.2	61.8
Jackson	230	2 716	518	D	528	107	39	108	39 738	196	48.0	1.0	49.5
Jefferson	11 648	182 695	30 536	6 710	28 674	9 415	11 232	8 075	44 201	57	70.2	3.5	14.0
Jefferson Davis	651	7 345	1 556	D	1 413	303	314	250	34 067	656	35.5	19.1	48.6
Lafayette	8 492	131 883	22 771	7 324	16 955	3 447	9 465	6 306	47 814	632	70.1	3.0	31.0
Lafourche	1 805	28 854	3 958	1 942	4 087	873	868	1 468	50 886	407	43.0	10.8	36.6
La Salle	391	3 618	867	D	560	D	D	130	35 917	186	35.5	2.7	31.2
Lincoln	1 037	14 620	2 986	1 378	2 363	584	701	482	32 939	346	33.2	4.6	41.9
Livingston	1 694	19 878	2 068	1 873	4 731	667	616	674	33 905	405	69.6	0.7	42.2
Madison	210	2 675	1 177	D	417	59	D	70	26 055	295	13.9	42.0	54.9
Morehouse	444	5 521	1 927	589	1 009	208	88	147	26 563	434	23.5	31.3	48.2
Natchitoches	818	10 846	1 944	2 544	1 762	D	231	369	34 051	630	31.9	15.7	39.5

Table B. States and Counties — **Agriculture**

Agriculture, 2012 (cont.)

STATE County	Land in farms Acreage (1,000)	Percent change, 2007–2012	Average size of farm	Total irrigated (1,000)	Total cropland (1,000)	Value of land and buildings (dollars) Average per farm	Average per acre	Value of machinery and equipment, average per farm (dollars)	Value of products sold Total (mil dol)	Average per farm (dollars)	Crops	Live-stock and poultry products	Percent of farms with sales of: $10,000 or more	$100,000 or more	Government payments Total ($1,000)	Percent of farms
	117	118	119	120	121	122	123	124	125	126	127	128	129	130	131	132
KENTUCKY—Cont'd																
Ohio	158	-6.1	168	0.6	78.8	410 305	2 448	84 484	98.8	104 698	36.8	63.2	29.0	7.1	1 434	48.8
Oldham	60	0.5	144	0.2	24.3	899 907	6 247	68 687	14.8	35 439	61.4	38.6	41.5	5.3	296	18.4
Owen	132	-16.4	188	0.3	45.8	434 031	2 306	56 652	21.2	30 298	49.3	50.7	37.2	5.7	1 113	42.2
Owsley	28	-23.1	169	0.0	6.9	228 049	1 349	41 859	1.6	9 939	71.1	28.9	25.8	0.6	234	42.3
Pendleton	101	-19.8	125	0.9	31.7	296 179	2 368	50 151	11.5	14 167	73.6	26.4	23.6	2.5	622	26.3
Perry	11	2.7	224	D	0.9	269 490	1 206	68 408	2.1	42 082	7.3	92.7	24.5	10.2	D	2.0
Pike	13	-5.9	239	0.0	2.1	318 875	1 334	49 732	0.6	10 018	40.8	59.0	32.1	0.0	D	1.8
Powell	30	-8.3	131	0.0	7.5	208 742	1 590	42 210	2.5	10 773	63.4	36.6	22.7	1.7	133	34.9
Pulaski	228	-1.6	133	0.4	90.1	385 814	2 896	58 635	63.5	37 072	36.5	63.5	39.9	6.9	1 599	38.4
Robertson	39	-24.6	155	0.1	12.7	279 578	1 808	58 873	4.1	16 163	43.6	56.4	30.3	3.6	396	37.8
Rockcastle	91	0.5	134	0.0	30.3	272 708	2 032	49 790	12.4	18 251	53.5	46.5	29.4	3.1	557	32.6
Rowan	42	-15.4	119	0.0	15.0	253 205	2 133	47 567	5.2	14 705	48.1	51.9	18.5	2.8	262	31.2
Russell	89	-4.0	123	0.0	34.9	379 095	3 080	62 912	44.5	61 331	16.1	83.9	40.5	9.2	1 892	46.6
Scott	127	-8.3	152	0.8	48.1	695 570	4 572	63 774	38.8	46 254	34.6	65.4	36.2	10.4	1 180	31.5
Shelby	199	-2.9	131	1.3	111.3	640 994	4 881	68 175	76.8	50 596	71.4	28.6	34.1	7.6	2 489	34.3
Simpson	102	-14.8	217	0.2	78.5	905 017	4 163	107 238	73.9	158 208	60.0	40.0	43.9	12.8	2 406	57.8
Spencer	69	-5.7	131	0.4	31.2	409 495	3 134	54 915	15.6	29 516	66.0	34.0	35.9	5.3	487	42.7
Taylor	115	-3.5	131	0.1	59.5	364 644	2 782	60 556	37.9	43 362	44.5	55.5	37.4	8.1	1 458	58.7
Todd	181	-8.6	300	1.5	126.6	1 107 604	3 690	133 570	180.2	298 915	48.2	51.8	64.2	31.5	3 015	51.2
Trigg	129	-4.9	325	1.5	71.8	961 912	2 960	103 461	47.2	118 862	82.6	17.4	43.3	14.9	1 514	46.3
Trimble	56	-14.5	127	0.1	19.0	399 913	3 156	57 303	9.1	20 738	73.6	26.4	33.0	3.9	519	42.6
Union	195	-3.0	629	2.6	167.9	2 579 713	4 104	324 342	96.5	311 268	92.3	7.7	49.0	27.1	2 969	61.3
Warren	247	-6.9	150	0.4	146.2	539 892	3 606	71 369	114.7	69 603	47.9	52.1	31.9	8.1	6 190	39.2
Washington	141	-13.5	139	0.3	55.9	356 909	2 560	55 341	33.8	33 403	47.7	52.3	43.1	6.0	2 275	38.9
Wayne	129	-9.9	165	0.1	40.8	376 098	2 274	65 197	68.1	87 496	17.2	82.8	41.5	11.2	544	39.3
Webster	152	-1.7	305	0.4	107.9	973 724	3 194	135 228	102.4	204 744	43.3	56.7	33.2	16.4	4 331	73.4
Whitley	58	-20.4	118	0.0	16.9	255 401	2 168	39 494	5.4	10 851	31.4	68.6	20.6	1.6	86	14.9
Wolfe	42	-26.4	143	0.0	8.0	212 566	1 487	43 566	1.7	5 721	57.9	42.1	15.2	0.0	377	45.5
Woodford	112	-6.0	157	0.3	34.7	1 280 116	8 155	103 851	76.6	107 421	12.5	87.5	46.1	12.3	997	26.8
LOUISIANA	7 901	-2.6	281	1 092.9	4 275.6	718 179	2 554	104 418	3 809.4	135 600	73.1	26.9	33.0	11.7	138 164	33.6
Acadia	238	2.3	283	82.9	187.1	628 439	2 219	117 468	124.3	147 830	86.7	13.3	34.2	16.3	6 775	51.6
Allen	88	5.8	205	18.4	47.2	431 168	2 101	76 105	23.7	55 187	85.2	14.8	28.2	7.7	2 111	35.4
Ascension	50	11.0	202	0.0	20.3	710 252	3 519	90 016	20.5	81 968	86.4	13.6	26.4	5.6	56	3.2
Assumption	62	-2.4	768	D	56.0	2 339 247	3 048	556 259	64.8	800 235	98.6	1.4	65.4	48.1	65	8.6
Avoyelles	299	7.4	319	21.7	203.5	724 316	2 269	113 847	137.8	147 048	91.2	8.8	37.9	14.5	5 632	45.4
Beauregard	146	-18.3	170	3.1	42.6	424 519	2 497	56 241	15.7	18 269	59.7	40.3	25.1	2.7	1 523	18.3
Bienville	56	37.3	240	0.1	16.2	570 425	2 379	88 854	34.5	148 039	5.5	94.5	30.9	8.2	136	10.3
Bossier	81	-21.4	172	1.5	28.4	579 184	3 363	91 169	17.7	37 517	60.8	39.2	27.1	6.8	717	11.0
Caddo	140	-7.5	228	13.5	58.6	620 078	2 722	81 067	50.6	82 437	83.6	16.4	28.3	7.7	2 364	14.8
Calcasieu	338	-8.1	375	15.8	85.9	961 407	2 566	70 263	33.2	36 756	60.0	40.0	23.9	5.1	2 653	22.2
Caldwell	62	-7.7	211	4.1	28.8	522 678	2 476	70 064	11.5	38 929	84.1	15.9	28.5	9.2	1 762	44.4
Cameron	235	8.8	688	11.5	55.3	1 210 319	1 759	97 509	19.1	55 857	61.7	38.3	36.3	9.1	896	24.0
Catahoula	224	-3.1	395	33.7	166.2	958 256	2 427	129 684	91.9	162 157	96.0	4.0	37.0	15.7	7 435	71.4
Claiborne	57	17.8	194	D	12.5	488 681	2 518	90 197	71.2	241 434	2.7	97.3	34.2	17.6	177	15.3
Concordia	240	14.2	522	28.5	171.3	1 203 475	2 308	172 974	118.3	256 534	97.9	2.1	37.1	21.0	6 348	85.2
De Soto	164	-1.8	246	0.3	30.2	665 374	2 709	74 991	17.7	26 417	25.2	74.8	28.3	3.7	841	11.7
East Baton Rouge	58	-20.3	133	0.7	13.3	765 382	5 746	48 398	11.5	26 523	24.0	76.0	26.2	3.9	209	8.1
East Carroll	251	-3.7	1 106	125.6	214.3	3 029 084	2 739	409 366	192.3	846 934	99.6	0.4	68.3	51.1	7 976	85.5
East Feliciana	113	-12.2	282	0.2	26.0	840 722	2 981	74 306	13.5	33 802	49.6	50.4	35.8	6.3	527	15.0
Evangeline	192	11.4	289	40.1	103.9	613 686	2 121	77 027	62.6	94 450	83.6	16.4	32.0	10.6	4 088	47.7
Franklin	246	-29.1	269	88.8	162.4	613 407	2 280	106 741	143.2	156 467	96.7	3.3	35.8	17.3	7 665	80.2
Grant	48	-7.3	202	0.5	17.0	430 168	2 134	65 084	7.9	33 050	74.8	25.2	28.2	8.4	723	22.3
Iberia	107	-7.5	384	0.4	85.5	1 205 219	3 135	231 706	92.2	330 351	97.2	2.8	39.8	18.6	311	16.8
Iberville	163	90.5	990	1.0	63.0	1 785 261	1 803	395 085	67.6	409 436	96.6	3.4	52.7	20.6	223	23.6
Jackson	19	-7.3	95	0.1	3.5	268 638	2 830	49 990	30.6	155 934	1.1	98.9	27.0	9.7	48	2.6
Jefferson	8	-48.7	136	D	0.8	517 123	3 804	58 070	1.6	28 228	24.1	75.8	42.1	7.0	41	21.1
Jefferson Davis	265	-8.0	404	67.7	186.5	917 733	2 272	122 320	85.1	129 771	87.3	12.7	38.4	17.2	5 149	59.3
Lafayette	56	-17.4	88	3.2	34.8	420 315	4 770	67 704	30.5	48 180	89.2	10.8	19.0	4.0	316	11.4
Lafourche	158	49.0	389	0.4	52.4	834 602	2 148	117 747	58.0	142 462	73.7	26.3	41.0	6.6	51	2.5
La Salle	20	-3.8	105	D	4.0	269 210	2 565	56 677	1.0	5 538	34.4	65.7	13.4	0.0	186	10.8
Lincoln	56	6.4	161	0.4	9.4	536 971	3 328	65 902	101.7	293 928	1.4	98.6	37.9	18.2	387	13.6
Livingston	28	-8.1	68	0.3	5.3	391 205	5 747	46 447	4.8	11 924	25.6	74.4	20.5	1.2	103	5.7
Madison	225	-4.2	761	63.1	180.7	1 877 692	2 467	335 441	155.1	525 681	99.4	0.6	58.3	45.4	6 131	87.1
Morehouse	279	2.0	643	141.5	206.7	1 521 809	2 367	204 793	176.1	405 781	96.9	3.1	47.2	31.1	11 646	68.7
Natchitoches	201	-9.4	319	10.5	70.3	774 152	2 427	91 722	129.0	204 767	23.4	76.6	40.2	13.8	3 061	33.0

Table B. States and Counties — Water Use, Wholesale Trade, Retail Trade, and Real Estate

STATE County	Water use, 2010		Wholesale trade,[1] 2012				Retail trade,[2] 2012				Real estate and rental and leasing,[2] 2012			
	Total water withdrawn (mil gal/day)	Gallons withdrawn per person per day	Number of establishments	Number of employees	Sales (mil dol)	Annual payroll (mil dol)	Number of establishments	Number of employees	Sales (mil dol)	Annual payroll (mil dol)	Number of establishments	Number of employees	Receipts (mil dol)	Annual payroll (mil dol)
	133	134	135	136	137	138	139	140	141	142	143	144	145	146
KENTUCKY—Cont'd														
Ohio	11.3	474	7	77	22.6	2.4	67	724	190.0	14.6	11	26	2.5	0.5
Oldham	6.4	106	36	280	117.6	14.9	103	1 182	369.3	30.5	52	89	18.4	3.1
Owen	1.8	167	4	48	18.3	0.8	29	186	62.2	4.2	3	D	D	D
Owsley	0.4	90	1	D	D	D	8	100	16.1	1.6	2	D	D	D
Pendleton	2.9	198	8	D	D	D	26	202	51.5	4.1	4	D	D	D
Perry	6.7	235	29	448	254.1	24.0	146	1 950	525.1	42.1	20	96	60.5	4.0
Pike	10.9	167	50	512	483.2	26.0	281	3 734	936.2	86.0	40	164	25.7	5.2
Powell	2.2	171	5	39	10.0	1.6	41	451	100.4	7.4	5	9	1.9	0.2
Pulaski	165.0	2 616	66	D	D	D	282	3 304	864.1	76.4	51	211	22.4	5.0
Robertson	0.2	79	NA	NA	NA	NA	3	D	D	D	1	D	D	D
Rockcastle	2.9	168	9	44	13.1	1.3	50	323	95.2	6.2	3	D	D	D
Rowan	5.7	244	14	143	39.1	4.5	100	1 399	339.0	27.9	21	54	11.0	1.8
Russell	18.7	1 065	8	D	D	D	90	694	185.9	14.0	6	37	8.5	0.9
Scott	4.4	93	27	D	D	D	125	1 828	573.3	38.1	37	118	27.3	3.0
Shelby	4.4	104	33	D	D	D	126	1 654	569.1	39.3	39	155	27.2	4.3
Simpson	2.1	123	16	181	372.0	6.1	67	1 016	389.6	23.3	12	44	5.1	0.8
Spencer	0.5	30	NA	NA	NA	NA	26	233	81.1	4.8	3	D	D	D
Taylor	5.2	213	22	D	D	D	126	1 416	342.1	31.9	21	79	8.8	2.0
Todd	1.9	155	9	42	77.4	1.4	35	295	77.3	5.7	5	11	0.9	0.1
Trigg	3.2	222	3	15	5.2	0.4	46	405	95.2	7.8	8	D	D	D
Trimble	10.2	1 158	NA	NA	NA	NA	13	96	25.6	1.1	1	D	D	D
Union	4.9	327	15	214	278.4	9.9	67	703	195.9	16.7	7	D	D	D
Warren	19.8	174	131	1 800	2 822.5	83.0	489	7 103	1 692.1	154.7	125	427	84.0	12.7
Washington	2.8	237	9	D	D	D	37	285	76.0	5.4	4	D	D	D
Wayne	3.1	147	11	124	27.8	2.9	62	663	157.7	14.4	4	6	0.2	0.1
Webster	10.8	793	10	134	38.1	3.6	39	342	80.0	6.9	1	D	D	D
Whitley	6.1	170	22	351	172.0	17.7	132	1 432	442.6	32.5	23	62	9.3	1.7
Wolfe	0.5	64	2	D	D	D	29	185	58.2	3.8	2	D	D	D
Woodford	23.0	921	16	244	115.0	11.5	67	743	230.3	17.4	17	17	5.5	0.6
LOUISIANA	8 540.3	1 884	4 823	64 259	68 012.8	3 260.2	16 743	220 257	61 396.4	5 334.6	4 500	31 298	7 486.4	1 461.4
Acadia	230.9	3 738	44	709	528.8	24.4	192	2 383	602.7	55.5	34	163	20.4	5.3
Allen	24.5	951	8	24	18.8	0.6	65	623	157.6	12.2	5	14	1.3	0.3
Ascension	162.1	1 512	138	1 667	995.5	92.4	374	5 491	1 538.9	129.5	89	559	177.7	30.8
Assumption	21.2	906	11	64	79.4	1.8	42	475	121.0	10.4	5	8	3.1	0.4
Avoyelles	56.4	1 340	26	253	306.5	10.3	159	1 446	354.7	29.5	21	59	7.8	1.3
Beauregard	27.8	781	13	D	D	D	104	1 330	383.7	29.1	21	111	15.7	4.4
Bienville	13.2	918	8	68	27.6	3.1	47	344	66.5	6.0	4	D	D	D
Bossier	15.3	131	114	1 453	941.9	68.3	452	6 434	1 923.3	159.1	109	556	114.1	17.5
Caddo	147.0	576	328	5 258	5 800.1	258.1	958	13 053	4 034.9	331.3	307	2 379	445.9	94.5
Calcasieu	223.6	1 160	188	2 125	1 941.1	97.9	755	10 139	3 127.1	238.7	208	954	213.8	38.5
Caldwell	3.8	378	4	26	9.0	1.0	28	267	81.1	5.5	3	D	D	D
Cameron	26.6	3 892	11	71	29.9	4.8	17	101	28.3	2.3	8	64	21.9	2.9
Catahoula	30.0	2 883	15	89	315.8	3.5	35	268	66.6	5.4	2	D	D	D
Claiborne	2.6	152	11	152	134.7	6.4	48	362	83.7	7.9	5	D	D	D
Concordia	42.8	2 053	12	232	344.5	11.2	81	904	275.4	20.8	11	104	6.2	3.1
De Soto	36.6	1 375	11	36	13.2	1.4	68	873	251.6	20.2	13	116	25.6	5.3
East Baton Rouge	179.4	408	568	7 674	4 993.5	417.3	1 863	27 576	7 389.7	677.5	546	3 088	631.1	111.2
East Carroll	26.6	3 426	12	142	466.5	6.9	22	147	30.7	2.9	2	D	D	D
East Feliciana	3.7	183	10	D	D	D	42	276	80.3	5.9	5	12	2.8	0.4
Evangeline	203.7	5 993	15	112	72.2	3.2	108	986	213.7	18.8	24	75	9.2	1.7
Franklin	40.3	1 942	19	125	248.8	4.3	78	914	250.9	19.2	11	30	4.5	0.7
Grant	5.3	238	2	D	D	D	27	227	83.2	5.2	2	D	D	D
Iberia	31.0	423	94	1 192	560.5	57.3	285	3 524	970.7	89.3	104	2 038	915.5	192.9
Iberville	481.4	14 418	24	D	D	D	88	1 083	279.3	23.7	22	149	42.9	7.2
Jackson	4.0	245	4	D	D	D	40	547	128.1	11.2	7	12	0.7	0.2
Jefferson	816.7	1 888	719	9 641	8 453.9	518.4	1 807	27 991	8 112.3	737.5	498	3 605	896.5	141.6
Jefferson Davis	175.1	5 541	27	275	261.1	10.9	127	1 504	402.8	32.5	19	317	73.2	16.8
Lafayette	41.2	186	485	7 554	4 113.5	406.8	1 057	15 818	4 355.1	399.4	473	3 636	938.6	194.0
Lafourche	43.6	453	61	868	947.9	46.3	290	4 020	965.6	86.0	66	333	58.8	11.5
La Salle	2.4	164	10	153	257.8	5.5	51	563	142.3	11.8	10	26	3.5	0.7
Lincoln	8.2	176	34	500	197.0	15.2	166	2 243	592.6	52.9	48	235	25.7	6.2
Livingston	15.2	119	47	389	345.3	17.8	287	4 390	1 180.5	98.7	63	565	43.8	13.3
Madison	42.1	3 480	12	90	258.9	5.0	38	387	158.9	9.2	9	D	D	D
Morehouse	83.3	2 977	15	223	147.1	10.6	85	978	237.4	22.7	23	59	9.9	1.4
Natchitoches	34.3	868	24	157	77.8	5.8	145	1 676	404.8	33.6	46	223	28.7	3.6

1. Merchant wholesalers, except manufacturers' sales branches and offices.   2. Employer establishments.

Professional Services, Manufacturing, and Accommodation and Food Services

STATE County	Professional, scientific, and technical services, 2012				Manufacturing, 2012				Accommodation and food services, 2012			
	Number of establish-ments	Number of employees	Receipts (mil dol)	Annual payroll (mil dol)	Number of establish-ments	Number of employees	Receipts (mil dol)	Annual payroll (mil dol)	Number of establish-ments	Number of employees	Sales (mil dol)	Annual payroll (mil dol)
	147	148	149	150	151	152	153	154	155	156	157	158
KENTUCKY—Cont'd												
Ohio	23	78	6.5	2.3	27	2 667	576.2	73.3	22	D	D	D
Oldham	170	516	69.3	25.6	45	785	304.0	36.9	70	1 322	72.8	16.8
Owen	5	D	D	D	NA	NA	NA	NA	10	D	D	D
Owsley	3	6	0.7	0.3	NA	NA	NA	NA	1	D	D	D
Pendleton	9	42	2.3	1.1	16	D	D	D	10	D	D	D
Perry	52	248	25.4	9.4	10	143	20.0	6.8	49	977	46.4	12.7
Pike	105	886	99.6	40.6	24	616	219.0	28.8	89	1 845	91.8	24.3
Powell	7	8	0.6	0.2	10	194	D	6.2	19	D	D	D
Pulaski	97	390	41.2	12.6	74	3 470	1 411.6	132.3	100	1 837	88.2	23.8
Robertson	1	D	D	D	NA	NA	NA	NA	NA	NA	NA	NA
Rockcastle	17	47	2.9	1.2	12	98	D	4.2	21	292	12.7	3.7
Rowan	22	82	5.7	2.0	20	981	291.9	30.5	51	1 057	46.4	11.9
Russell	21	66	4.3	1.1	25	1 610	404.0	42.8	32	376	16.2	4.1
Scott	77	311	36.7	14.1	37	8 525	10 844.2	552.2	88	1 795	89.7	24.1
Shelby	94	317	35.4	10.7	55	3 562	1 484.5	149.2	61	D	D	D
Simpson	16	112	9.2	2.9	34	2 958	1 387.3	137.3	41	868	40.0	10.9
Spencer	18	49	4.6	1.7	7	D	D	D	12	187	7.0	2.2
Taylor	51	97	9.5	2.6	26	1 191	D	37.7	45	818	35.2	8.7
Todd	11	30	3.3	1.2	19	416	108.9	11.5	11	104	3.1	0.9
Trigg	9	33	2.3	0.7	15	536	136.6	18.4	19	D	D	D
Trimble	4	7	0.4	0.1	3	D	D	D	4	D	D	D
Union	10	50	4.3	1.5	14	440	142.8	16.0	18	D	D	D
Warren	212	2 075	179.7	63.0	113	7 962	5 110.1	405.4	260	5 737	264.1	70.6
Washington	17	51	4.2	1.2	12	858	248.3	39.2	13	D	D	D
Wayne	18	52	3.8	1.4	24	1 498	267.2	44.9	26	D	D	D
Webster	10	23	1.4	0.3	12	259	189.4	10.8	14	D	D	D
Whitley	55	910	51.1	23.0	21	888	228.0	32.8	67	1 109	53.0	15.3
Wolfe	3	7	0.6	0.2	3	21	D	D	5	D	D	D
Woodford	63	496	76.6	29.7	29	1 828	644.1	103.0	33	D	D	D
LOUISIANA	11 728	88 093	13 546.2	5 022.9	3 308	136 327	271 191.1	8 489.3	9 019	193 928	11 697.9	3 110.7
Acadia	125	378	43.2	15.9	43	1 138	D	45.5	74	1 185	52.7	13.3
Allen	23	64	7.2	1.6	11	584	D	29.7	28	D	D	D
Ascension	162	922	137.4	53.2	100	4 518	14 208.5	427.9	173	3 211	167.2	43.5
Assumption	37	88	12.3	3.8	9	375	D	19.7	12	67	3.9	0.8
Avoyelles	60	224	28.0	7.4	20	279	D	8.4	51	1 842	153.8	39.6
Beauregard	50	189	15.6	5.9	18	757	D	57.2	40	720	35.0	8.7
Bienville	12	52	5.3	2.8	11	1 165	D	30.0	17	D	D	D
Bossier	197	1 032	116.1	42.2	70	1 534	911.8	74.6	235	7 792	667.0	135.9
Caddo	620	4 278	613.6	214.6	182	6 230	4 965.5	347.6	493	12 976	766.3	200.0
Calcasieu	423	5 141	451.3	218.1	126	D	D	D	353	10 769	983.3	210.5
Caldwell	26	74	13.4	1.9	6	24	D	0.8	10	D	D	D
Cameron	9	71	28.0	4.8	NA	NA	NA	NA	5	48	1.4	0.3
Catahoula	30	74	8.1	3.1	NA	NA	NA	NA	8	D	D	D
Claiborne	11	35	4.4	1.0	11	185	D	8.2	16	D	D	D
Concordia	28	162	19.6	6.6	11	234	79.7	9.9	25	382	17.9	4.5
De Soto	24	93	6.1	2.1	13	707	D	D	32	416	23.0	4.9
East Baton Rouge	1 693	17 189	2 800.2	1 013.8	334	11 176	53 388.8	774.5	1 000	23 462	1 230.7	345.7
East Carroll	5	18	1.6	0.5	5	D	D	1.3	13	64	3.5	0.7
East Feliciana	22	75	12.8	3.4	12	236	D	13.0	14	D	D	D
Evangeline	43	119	10.7	3.5	18	704	D	24.7	25	D	D	D
Franklin	34	163	13.8	4.2	9	178	D	4.1	22	D	D	D
Grant	6	D	D	D	11	307	D	10.8	5	76	2.6	0.8
Iberia	149	820	123.7	42.5	135	4 659	D	254.8	94	1 685	78.9	20.1
Iberville	33	208	23.6	13.8	30	3 165	8 877.1	287.6	36	497	22.5	6.6
Jackson	16	50	5.9	1.3	8	D	D	D	17	D	D	D
Jefferson	1 336	10 711	1 848.1	687.2	317	11 438	2 996.9	626.6	1 037	19 493	1 056.5	303.1
Jefferson Davis	65	344	33.4	17.7	17	534	D	21.4	43	669	29.4	7.3
Lafayette	1 269	8 970	1 597.9	547.4	295	10 996	D	717.5	665	14 444	782.6	230.2
Lafourche	160	1 635	138.6	73.0	59	2 575	864.1	119.7	159	2 654	115.3	29.1
La Salle	100	150	27.3	7.2	6	55	D	2.5	14	D	D	D
Lincoln	91	669	97.6	38.6	35	1 084	421.6	59.2	93	2 015	91.0	23.9
Livingston	140	627	65.0	24.5	67	1 772	504.0	81.0	156	2 737	115.9	31.5
Madison	11	29	1.5	0.8	5	D	D	D	20	D	D	D
Morehouse	23	96	12.4	3.4	14	111	D	4.2	26	D	D	D
Natchitoches	64	251	33.1	8.3	16	2 340	1 162.1	97.2	81	1 647	70.0	17.6

1. Establishment subject to federal tax.

Table B. States and Counties — Health Care and Social Assistance, Other Services, Nonemployer Businesses, and Residential Construction

STATE County	Health care and social assistance, 2012				Other services, 2012				Nonemployer businesses, 2014		Value of residential construction authorized by building permits, 2015	
	Number of establishments	Number of employees	Receipts (mil dol)	Annual payroll (mil dol)	Number of establishments	Number of employees	Receipts (mil dol)	Annual payroll (mil dol)	Number	Receipts (mil dol)	New Construction ($1,000)	Number of housing units
	159	160	161	162	163	164	165	166	167	168	169	170
KENTUCKY—Cont'd												
Ohio	39	1 020	65.6	28.4	30	89	9.8	2.5	1 143	39.1	1 593	12
Oldham	142	2 410	169.5	76.5	81	D	D	D	4 899	250.4	80 401	301
Owen	10	265	23.0	8.2	10	38	2.7	0.7	722	27.6	0	4
Owsley	9	192	10.5	5.2	3	16	1.3	0.3	267	9.1	NA	NA
Pendleton	18	249	14.7	6.5	11	D	D	D	766	26.3	0	0
Perry	128	2 853	304.5	107.6	27	D	D	D	1 383	45.5	533	5
Pike	213	4 427	579.9	210.9	78	389	41.9	11.3	2 822	116.5	784	3
Powell	19	213	17.6	6.6	8	42	3.5	0.9	841	26.1	0	0
Pulaski	240	5 134	484.7	192.4	66	353	29.9	8.2	4 386	170.0	787	14
Robertson	3	D	D	D	1	D	D	D	115	2.9	NA	NA
Rockcastle	36	808	66.5	31.2	11	76	6.0	1.6	959	30.0	NA	NA
Rowan	86	1 998	198.5	79.0	24	117	6.6	1.8	1 361	47.9	1 285	17
Russell	47	1 015	86.4	30.8	17	D	D	D	1 339	55.4	1 725	24
Scott	129	1 426	119.6	46.7	68	273	24.2	6.7	3 244	126.3	59 768	502
Shelby	85	1 415	110.8	44.5	67	501	50.2	13.4	3 040	126.2	55 461	333
Simpson	35	D	D	D	23	111	10.0	2.6	1 222	58.1	7 240	65
Spencer	17	219	13.4	6.1	14	D	D	D	1 158	43.5	14 748	81
Taylor	84	D	D	D	43	D	D	D	1 756	63.0	2 550	20
Todd	17	215	14.6	5.3	9	D	D	D	845	39.3	196	2
Trigg	22	378	23.4	9.7	14	D	D	D	896	33.6	0	0
Trimble	6	108	10.6	4.2	3	D	D	D	499	16.7	NA	NA
Union	33	896	83.6	28.0	12	56	9.5	1.7	712	26.3	2 586	12
Warren	383	7 745	852.6	320.8	199	1 035	86.7	25.8	8 705	486.5	139 518	1 137
Washington	27	410	18.6	8.7	16	110	7.5	2.1	737	27.2	2 013	28
Wayne	32	546	35.4	16.0	16	D	D	D	1 128	39.6	0	0
Webster	19	266	14.3	7.2	11	46	6.5	1.3	633	19.1	40	5
Whitley	97	2 467	272.1	98.8	31	D	D	D	2 233	87.0	4 038	40
Wolfe	12	230	14.7	6.1	3	D	D	D	464	15.3	NA	NA
Woodford	62	559	45.4	18.6	37	D	D	D	2 107	89.9	19 371	100
LOUISIANA	11 999	284 979	27 951.8	10 646.9	6 293	43 500	5 408.9	1 479.2	357 815	15 879.3	2 777 014	13 830
Acadia	128	2 215	157.2	62.7	70	346	26.4	7.1	4 225	203.8	32 294	181
Allen	43	907	61.8	22.1	20	D	D	D	1 117	33.8	3 795	22
Ascension	180	3 300	255.4	105.2	150	1 260	152.0	44.6	8 222	356.3	137 043	853
Assumption	22	675	25.3	13.4	17	D	D	D	1 527	61.9	6 951	33
Avoyelles	85	2 104	131.1	49.3	42	153	13.8	3.4	2 471	95.3	6 332	39
Beauregard	64	1 086	84.1	35.7	29	121	10.8	2.7	1 918	75.4	6 788	28
Bienville	15	486	30.7	10.9	11	D	D	D	771	29.2	0	0
Bossier	216	4 289	376.0	137.9	141	846	84.5	23.3	8 424	389.5	94 829	557
Caddo	818	28 245	2 809.9	1 111.3	381	D	D	D	20 215	887.4	84 816	417
Calcasieu	519	D	D	D	240	1 605	177.0	50.8	12 847	594.1	167 029	987
Caldwell	25	651	49.7	20.7	13	37	3.4	0.8	606	22.6	3 574	15
Cameron	2	D	D	D	4	12	1.0	0.3	697	31.4	6 882	47
Catahoula	15	526	19.1	9.8	14	D	D	D	631	27.5	1 015	3
Claiborne	21	791	46.2	19.7	13	63	4.2	0.8	791	30.7	0	0
Concordia	46	882	62.5	24.8	26	D	D	D	1 127	45.7	4 654	20
De Soto	30	722	54.5	19.8	20	D	D	D	1 866	65.1	27 070	108
East Baton Rouge	1 403	38 136	4 112.4	1 527.3	876	8 742	1 008.1	367.9	37 127	1 628.2	349 922	1 475
East Carroll	11	328	22.1	8.8	6	9	0.6	0.1	444	16.3	0	0
East Feliciana	32	1 821	117.2	64.9	16	54	9.1	1.7	1 295	48.4	9 047	45
Evangeline	95	2 618	184.3	72.9	26	55	4.7	1.0	1 578	71.4	10 410	47
Franklin	52	1 157	75.5	34.1	22	73	6.8	1.4	1 421	57.5	4 438	15
Grant	17	255	14.9	5.4	11	50	3.4	0.9	1 063	43.1	9 563	49
Iberia	207	3 985	309.5	122.6	124	868	111.9	29.7	6 117	252.2	19 878	98
Iberville	48	D	D	D	30	136	15.8	4.8	2 270	72.6	18 795	105
Jackson	22	555	41.0	15.6	17	71	5.2	1.6	781	29.5	12 076	24
Jefferson	1 318	26 711	3 077.9	1 178.8	730	5 002	551.7	161.5	41 156	1 948.6	79 436	400
Jefferson Davis	75	1 553	121.3	49.7	35	116	18.2	3.3	1 786	77.6	17 327	101
Lafayette	1 018	22 618	2 452.2	909.5	421	3 607	491.3	120.7	22 447	1 237.6	354 525	1 949
Lafourche	194	4 123	476.7	177.9	110	686	71.7	19.8	6 916	337.6	88 717	450
La Salle	22	747	69.1	23.3	12	D	D	D	854	42.6	677	3
Lincoln	115	3 306	304.1	106.2	52	214	15.2	4.7	2 820	136.4	72 914	84
Livingston	150	2 060	141.1	56.9	106	487	56.7	15.2	9 173	363.6	158 223	747
Madison	36	1 145	56.4	24.7	12	26	2.1	0.4	764	20.8	8 465	52
Morehouse	76	2 087	112.7	49.9	32	137	7.3	2.0	1 694	50.4	0	0
Natchitoches	102	1 758	138.0	50.9	41	150	12.0	2.7	2 331	96.5	12 935	54

STATE County	Full-time equivalent employees	March payroll (dollars)	Administration, judicial, and legal	Police and Corrections	Fire Protection	Highways and transportation	Health and Welfare	Natural resources and utilities	Education and libraries	Total (mil dol)	Intergovernmental (mil dol)	Total (mil dol)	Total	Property
						March payroll (percent of total)				Total (mil dol)	Intergovernmental (mil dol)	Taxes Total (mil dol)	Per capita (dollars) Total	Per capita (dollars) Property
	171	172	173	174	175	176	177	178	179	180	181	182	183	184
KENTUCKY—Cont'd														
Ohio	1 248	3 369 261	2.7	2.9	0.0	1.3	36.2	2.8	52.4	62.2	36.1	14.2	590	347
Oldham	2 024	6 660 606	0.3	5.8	2.0	0.6	3.6	1.6	84.6	158.6	58.3	71.9	1 171	957
Owen	363	1 105 970	4.6	2.3	3.8	2.1	0.7	0.2	83.4	23.3	14.0	7.1	661	495
Owsley	278	620 892	6.0	3.8	0.0	3.9	0.3	2.8	81.2	13.2	10.6	1.4	301	184
Pendleton	588	1 671 881	4.1	2.6	1.6	2.8	15.0	6.1	67.8	38.5	22.7	9.2	631	467
Perry	1 406	4 111 977	3.0	3.4	1.5	2.6	18.7	2.8	66.7	100.4	52.4	23.0	814	540
Pike	2 126	6 896 536	3.5	4.4	1.3	2.8	7.1	1.3	78.6	183.6	110.6	49.7	775	500
Powell	571	1 479 612	5.5	7.2	0.0	1.0	5.3	5.1	75.7	31.1	21.3	6.1	493	235
Pulaski	2 626	7 286 813	4.1	5.1	1.6	1.7	17.0	5.8	64.1	151.6	74.3	49.2	773	465
Robertson	124	297 631	8.0	3.4	0.0	4.9	0.2	0.6	83.0	5.9	4.4	1.2	557	414
Rockcastle	758	1 967 231	6.5	9.5	0.4	2.3	2.6	2.4	74.7	38.4	26.7	7.6	448	184
Rowan	813	2 389 386	2.9	7.6	0.4	3.5	14.9	2.7	67.0	61.6	29.3	19.7	841	374
Russell	920	2 454 498	2.9	5.5	0.4	0.9	28.6	4.1	57.3	61.4	21.4	14.1	807	422
Scott	1 616	5 156 528	2.9	7.7	7.0	2.1	6.1	0.1	73.2	151.0	48.9	60.2	1 227	530
Shelby	1 282	4 061 414	3.4	9.9	2.6	1.9	6.5	0.8	73.8	102.9	42.5	43.5	997	724
Simpson	616	2 092 237	8.9	11.0	1.5	2.3	5.8	3.3	66.5	40.7	23.2	18.0	1 026	501
Spencer	523	1 426 278	5.8	4.0	0.7	1.4	3.1	2.3	81.4	34.5	19.5	12.1	693	525
Taylor	1 374	4 732 730	2.1	2.7	0.9	1.1	51.8	2.5	38.2	123.7	56.5	19.0	769	374
Todd	505	1 331 511	3.1	7.5	0.2	1.9	3.5	7.4	76.3	31.2	20.1	6.9	544	268
Trigg	587	1 746 830	2.8	3.6	0.1	2.4	28.3	5.6	56.1	27.8	15.3	10.2	708	456
Trimble	305	972 373	7.5	3.6	0.0	1.9	2.3	5.1	78.5	32.6	10.9	5.6	634	445
Union	599	1 762 787	11.1	6.4	2.1	5.7	0.5	5.2	67.9	38.7	23.0	11.5	777	532
Warren	4 084	12 459 019	3.2	8.5	4.4	1.8	4.7	10.4	63.3	304.6	116.1	128.4	1 096	529
Washington	407	1 176 342	5.5	5.0	0.0	4.1	9.6	4.1	69.1	26.8	14.5	8.5	718	377
Wayne	760	2 029 072	4.1	6.1	0.2	1.7	4.0	0.3	83.0	44.7	31.3	10.0	478	288
Webster	605	1 592 385	5.5	8.5	4.2	2.0	2.8	7.4	66.8	37.5	24.0	7.8	574	425
Whitley	1 867	5 263 187	2.4	4.6	3.4	1.6	6.6	7.3	73.7	112.5	68.5	23.7	669	308
Wolfe	313	774 203	3.3	1.9	0.0	1.4	0.4	3.3	85.8	23.7	18.4	2.4	336	190
Woodford	911	3 023 818	4.5	9.8	2.1	1.8	8.6	2.9	68.0	69.9	26.8	32.2	1 286	739
LOUISIANA	X	X	X	X	X	X	X	X	X	X	X	X	X	X
Acadia	1 914	5 479 946	5.7	5.4	2.7	4.1	2.9	4.6	73.3	180.8	90.9	63.9	1 033	388
Allen	973	2 882 412	11.1	8.9	0.4	3.1	19.2	2.8	54.4	94.4	48.2	28.5	1 114	473
Ascension	4 531	13 738 983	6.7	8.8	2.0	2.3	2.8	3.8	71.9	408.3	139.8	213.9	1 905	870
Assumption	1 463	4 579 903	6.7	5.0	0.6	13.3	13.8	10.4	49.4	74.9	42.1	25.4	1 102	571
Avoyelles	1 542	3 784 025	3.9	22.1	1.3	2.7	13.2	4.5	52.2	121.6	72.1	26.8	644	144
Beauregard	1 561	4 516 320	4.2	3.0	1.7	3.0	29.5	1.5	56.6	146.5	59.0	50.2	1 382	629
Bienville	604	1 849 545	7.1	11.8	0.0	5.8	0.4	1.9	72.9	72.4	15.3	51.7	3 673	2 477
Bossier	4 814	15 229 557	8.2	15.0	5.4	2.1	0.4	3.1	64.8	444.2	156.3	238.0	1 948	757
Caddo	11 080	37 545 778	5.6	16.6	7.2	2.8	2.9	5.7	57.7	1 117.9	399.7	540.3	2 102	1 067
Calcasieu	9 145	28 598 210	5.0	14.5	3.5	5.7	7.9	5.4	56.0	961.3	315.0	432.3	2 223	866
Caldwell	302	782 732	5.3	3.7	0.3	0.5	0.0	1.0	89.3	33.5	19.0	10.2	1 019	536
Cameron	525	1 990 275	6.0	0.0	0.3	7.0	7.7	4.9	74.1	94.4	45.2	42.7	6 367	6 281
Catahoula	616	1 309 075	8.8	22.3	0.4	5.1	2.5	3.4	57.4	54.6	21.6	8.9	869	412
Claiborne	847	2 308 077	5.0	2.0	2.4	2.3	47.8	2.4	38.2	69.3	34.1	15.8	939	530
Concordia	1 328	3 662 764	3.6	24.2	2.0	3.1	16.5	5.2	44.7	109.8	52.5	25.5	1 253	622
De Soto	1 141	3 608 492	7.4	7.4	0.8	6.3	2.6	3.1	71.2	213.8	37.7	149.7	5 553	2 010
East Baton Rouge	16 122	60 516 124	9.3	10.2	6.8	4.4	7.2	8.9	49.7	1 776.4	573.7	866.4	1 949	820
East Carroll	291	819 177	9.3	8.7	1.7	2.4	46.3	8.0	23.1	47.3	28.8	7.1	947	459
East Feliciana	631	1 666 825	14.0	19.9	0.0	2.6	1.1	4.2	58.2	44.3	27.0	13.4	671	245
Evangeline	1 334	3 509 396	4.9	9.7	2.3	4.2	2.0	5.9	70.6	136.3	68.0	37.5	1 111	500
Franklin	1 046	2 791 309	5.1	15.1	1.2	2.0	28.2	2.9	45.4	84.3	40.9	21.5	1 046	283
Grant	604	1 502 745	8.0	3.6	0.0	2.3	3.2	5.7	76.5	50.6	32.7	12.2	551	301
Iberia	3 450	9 630 156	4.1	12.3	3.2	2.7	20.2	5.1	51.6	320.8	141.9	101.3	1 368	514
Iberville	1 742	4 067 053	7.6	14.8	2.5	5.7	1.5	5.6	57.3	154.3	45.0	93.6	2 817	1 287
Jackson	824	2 175 796	2.6	14.3	1.3	2.9	30.0	2.2	46.2	80.9	29.0	33.0	2 033	1 323
Jefferson	16 179	70 416 195	8.0	11.6	2.9	2.3	31.2	6.3	36.3	2 140.2	681.5	696.5	1 606	721
Jefferson Davis	1 386	3 583 234	4.3	9.8	2.0	2.1	0.3	3.8	76.9	101.8	54.3	35.4	1 127	532
Lafayette	8 193	26 369 258	8.2	13.8	4.3	3.8	0.8	11.2	56.6	791.5	255.4	391.9	1 726	692
Lafourche	4 602	16 739 494	5.8	10.8	0.0	3.9	32.6	3.4	42.1	526.8	177.3	149.9	1 545	846
La Salle	890	2 469 446	4.0	15.2	0.4	1.6	31.7	2.8	44.0	119.2	60.2	20.7	1 388	759
Lincoln	1 655	6 428 631	8.8	13.7	9.5	6.9	3.8	12.8	43.0	139.1	54.9	66.4	1 414	645
Livingston	4 067	13 075 838	6.4	8.4	0.8	1.6	0.8	3.2	78.1	359.5	202.1	123.4	935	334
Madison	681	1 378 550	9.2	30.1	0.1	5.0	0.3	1.6	53.3	76.9	38.0	17.4	1 428	929
Morehouse	1 347	4 002 380	5.9	10.2	2.9	1.8	23.0	0.9	54.6	125.8	64.1	30.3	1 099	513
Natchitoches	2 176	6 441 570	5.4	11.8	1.9	2.7	29.9	5.7	41.6	198.4	86.0	59.1	1 498	518

1. Based on the resident population estimated as of July 1 of the year shown.

STATE County	Local government finances, 2012 (cont.) Direct general expenditure Total (mil dol)	Per capita[1] (dollars)	Education	Health and hospitals	Police protection	Public welfare	Highways	Debt outstanding Total (mil dol)	Per capita[1] (dollars)	Government employment, 2014 Federal civilian	Federal military	State and local	Presidential election,[2] 2012 Percent of vote cast: Democratic	Republican	All other
	185	186	187	188	189	190	191	192	193	194	195	196	197	198	199
KENTUCKY—Cont'd															
Ohio	54.6	2 269	56.5	1.1	4.2	0.1	4.9	203.8	8 463	83	76	1 415	40.8	57.2	1.9
Oldham	156.7	2 552	60.0	4.3	4.0	0.4	2.1	428.5	6 978	67	189	3 222	34.1	64.8	1.1
Owen	24.6	2 286	63.4	3.3	2.4	0.5	6.5	37.0	3 440	20	34	452	35.7	62.5	1.9
Owsley	13.9	2 954	73.5	0.4	2.7	0.0	7.0	5.8	1 224	0	14	295	22.6	75.9	1.5
Pendleton	38.4	2 629	51.2	14.8	3.0	0.0	6.3	59.7	4 086	29	46	638	34.9	63.4	1.7
Perry	108.4	3 839	51.5	14.3	2.9	0.0	4.1	267.3	9 465	133	86	2 658	33.2	65.2	1.6
Pike	184.3	2 872	57.9	3.3	2.1	0.2	4.9	348.9	5 437	257	197	2 942	42.1	55.9	2.0
Powell	29.2	2 335	66.0	6.6	2.1	0.0	3.4	14.4	1 150	35	39	766	41.5	57.1	1.4
Pulaski	161.3	2 537	51.9	11.8	5.1	0.1	3.7	170.4	2 679	175	201	3 982	21.7	77.1	1.2
Robertson	15.0	6 849	83.7	0.5	0.9	0.0	3.9	36.7	16 787	0	0	137	44.4	52.5	3.1
Rockcastle	38.2	2 248	63.7	4.5	2.8	0.0	4.0	25.4	1 494	34	53	744	22.5	75.8	1.7
Rowan	57.8	2 467	44.0	13.0	4.0	0.6	5.0	89.2	3 802	81	71	3 247	50.0	47.9	2.1
Russell	56.8	3 247	41.5	34.9	2.6	0.4	3.2	42.4	2 424	66	56	1 005	21.0	77.3	1.7
Scott	139.0	2 834	46.7	7.0	4.0	0.2	2.7	633.9	12 922	56	160	2 116	39.1	59.7	1.2
Shelby	102.9	2 359	54.2	6.2	3.7	0.0	2.4	238.0	5 456	67	138	2 302	37.1	61.8	1.2
Simpson	44.9	2 560	53.3	3.9	5.1	1.0	3.9	71.7	4 088	36	56	788	38.0	60.7	1.3
Spencer	29.0	1 665	65.8	2.9	4.3	0.1	5.6	48.6	2 788	24	56	594	31.3	66.8	1.9
Taylor	135.0	5 469	23.2	57.5	1.9	0.0	2.1	111.7	4 523	88	76	1 679	29.1	69.7	1.2
Todd	33.7	2 664	60.0	5.0	3.2	0.0	4.5	102.5	8 103	33	39	614	31.2	67.5	1.3
Trigg	28.2	1 952	58.5	2.4	4.6	0.1	8.2	21.2	1 469	92	45	632	34.4	64.2	1.4
Trimble	33.1	3 770	40.0	1.5	0.6	0.0	3.9	423.4	48 190	16	28	351	38.9	58.7	2.3
Union	38.1	2 567	54.2	0.6	4.9	0.4	7.4	15.5	1 046	51	43	730	46.5	51.7	1.8
Warren	300.9	2 570	45.9	4.4	6.6	0.1	3.4	970.8	8 290	363	374	9 654	40.0	58.9	1.1
Washington	29.1	2 457	61.1	3.2	3.0	0.1	7.7	78.0	6 592	29	37	494	35.8	62.7	1.5
Wayne	46.9	2 252	65.2	3.1	3.1	0.0	3.8	44.3	2 129	41	65	934	30.6	67.6	1.8
Webster	36.1	2 657	46.4	1.2	2.4	0.0	5.6	63.7	4 692	42	41	658	43.1	54.8	2.0
Whitley	116.0	3 267	65.4	7.7	3.4	0.0	3.2	141.1	3 974	79	109	2 163	25.4	73.1	1.5
Wolfe	19.1	2 667	68.4	0.1	0.9	0.0	6.6	20.2	2 819	21	23	403	50.3	47.4	2.3
Woodford	67.4	2 689	51.3	5.2	8.7	0.0	4.7	133.5	5 323	37	81	1 524	40.9	58.0	1.1
LOUISIANA	X	X	X	X	X	X	X	X	X	30 032	37 750	299 463	39.9	58.6	1.5
Acadia	174.4	2 817	55.1	8.1	6.4	0.3	4.6	40.6	656	96	279	2 522	26.3	72.0	1.7
Allen	95.8	3 750	51.3	17.0	5.7	0.0	5.7	24.4	955	652	98	3 735	30.5	66.9	2.6
Ascension	402.3	3 583	57.6	3.1	6.1	0.0	4.1	796.9	7 097	134	529	5 005	31.4	67.1	1.5
Assumption	72.6	3 151	65.4	0.1	5.9	0.8	2.8	12.4	536	28	104	999	43.4	54.6	2.0
Avoyelles	119.8	2 877	51.1	10.8	10.3	0.0	2.9	26.7	640	81	172	3 705	37.4	60.4	2.2
Beauregard	151.0	4 161	49.3	23.5	4.9	0.0	5.2	90.4	2 493	69	159	1 653	21.8	76.2	2.0
Bienville	72.3	5 139	63.9	2.2	6.1	0.2	6.3	29.9	2 123	48	62	779	48.3	50.8	0.9
Bossier	464.2	3 799	47.3	1.0	9.1	0.1	5.0	486.1	3 978	1 879	5 928	7 086	27.7	71.4	0.9
Caddo	1 081.2	4 206	48.6	1.7	7.4	0.0	2.2	1 079.9	4 201	2 854	1 154	16 391	51.1	48.1	0.8
Calcasieu	908.6	4 671	38.0	7.0	6.7	0.4	7.0	2 311.6	11 885	532	975	13 175	36.8	61.4	1.8
Caldwell	34.6	3 461	63.2	7.2	3.0	0.2	3.0	14.9	1 485	28	42	609	22.8	75.5	1.6
Cameron	87.3	13 024	42.4	9.7	4.1	0.4	4.8	20.4	3 043	17	30	739	16.2	81.4	2.4
Catahoula	65.8	6 390	33.4	42.7	3.0	0.0	2.4	37.4	3 632	47	42	638	31.8	66.7	1.5
Claiborne	68.0	4 039	33.4	28.7	3.9	0.7	3.0	18.0	1 071	43	61	1 188	44.2	54.8	1.0
Concordia	116.6	5 726	35.0	12.7	6.4	0.0	2.6	38.7	1 899	58	86	1 523	39.5	59.5	1.0
De Soto	190.9	7 081	58.1	1.3	4.0	1.7	8.4	134.5	4 987	45	122	1 548	42.8	56.2	1.1
East Baton Rouge	2 083.6	4 687	38.7	5.0	6.4	0.1	5.2	2 247.5	5 056	2 235	2 175	46 905	50.5	48.3	1.2
East Carroll	50.8	6 748	38.0	18.4	3.5	0.0	2.7	36.4	4 836	20	29	690	63.7	35.2	1.1
East Feliciana	43.2	2 161	59.7	0.7	8.1	0.0	4.6	5.3	264	25	79	2 471	44.1	54.6	1.3
Evangeline	132.8	3 939	46.5	23.7	4.1	0.0	6.4	25.6	760	50	147	1 535	36.6	61.3	2.1
Franklin	83.8	4 076	38.5	25.0	7.6	0.3	4.2	14.2	691	54	90	1 372	31.6	67.1	1.3
Grant	55.3	2 505	70.8	0.2	6.0	0.0	2.2	23.9	1 085	746	97	798	17.2	80.7	2.1
Iberia	346.8	4 686	45.5	17.9	5.9	0.2	5.6	224.6	3 035	102	331	4 109	37.7	60.7	1.7
Iberville	172.3	5 186	44.7	0.6	7.8	1.5	10.8	142.1	4 275	85	133	2 913	54.9	43.8	1.3
Jackson	80.7	4 976	35.7	20.0	10.5	0.0	5.3	72.6	4 475	29	68	1 082	31.7	67.1	1.2
Jefferson	2 141.8	4 939	30.3	30.9	4.8	2.5	3.5	1 621.8	3 740	1 405	2 451	19 383	35.9	62.5	1.6
Jefferson Davis	102.5	3 259	62.2	1.3	8.7	0.1	3.0	56.9	1 811	97	140	1 932	29.1	68.7	2.2
Lafayette	816.4	3 596	40.1	0.7	7.8	0.1	5.7	1 609.2	7 087	953	1 082	12 633	33.6	64.9	1.5
Lafourche	483.7	4 985	32.9	32.8	5.3	0.5	2.6	200.2	2 064	134	460	6 682	25.5	71.5	3.0
La Salle	118.0	7 903	25.1	37.6	3.9	0.0	1.8	23.9	1 604	53	62	1 374	13.1	85.5	1.4
Lincoln	137.7	2 933	55.0	0.5	7.2	0.6	5.1	82.8	1 764	111	203	4 345	43.2	55.7	1.1
Livingston	373.0	2 827	65.1	0.6	5.1	0.0	2.6	445.0	3 373	134	611	5 410	13.1	85.0	1.9
Madison	79.7	6 557	26.6	19.8	12.1	0.1	3.5	74.6	6 141	36	47	776	58.5	40.6	0.9
Morehouse	124.7	4 525	44.2	20.5	4.1	0.1	2.7	101.1	3 668	55	118	1 277	43.9	55.0	1.1
Natchitoches	210.4	5 335	45.1	20.9	4.9	0.5	3.0	50.5	1 281	164	172	3 760	45.7	53.0	1.2

1. Based on the resident population estimated as of July 1 of the year shown.   2. © 2013 Election Data Services, Inc. All rights reserved.

Table B. States and Counties — **Land Area and Population**

STATE/ County code	CBSA code[1]	County type[2]	STATE County	Population, 2015				Population and population characteristics, 2014										
								Race alone or in combination, not Hispanic or Latino (percent)					Age (percent)					
				Land area,[3] (sq km) 2010	Total persons 2015	Rank	Per square kilometer	White	Black	American Indian, Alaska Native	Asian and Pacific Islander	Percent Hispanic or Latino[4]	Under 5 years	5 to 17 years	18 to 24 years	25 to 34 years	35 to 44 years	45 to 54 years
				1	2	3	4	5	6	7	8	9	10	11	12	13	14	15
			LOUISIANA—Cont'd															
22 071	35380	1	Orleans	439	389 617	176	887.5	32.1	59.6	0.7	3.4	5.5	6.1	14.3	10.2	18.5	12.7	12.9
22 073	33740	3	Ouachita	1 581	156 761	411	99.2	59.5	37.8	0.6	1.3	2.2	7.0	18.5	10.4	14.1	12.2	12.4
22 075	35380	1	Plaquemines	2 020	23 495	1 659	11.6	68.2	21.2	2.4	4.4	6.5	7.3	19.4	9.0	12.9	13.2	14.2
22 077	12940	2	Pointe Coupee	1 444	22 251	1 719	15.4	61.8	36.2	0.5	0.5	2.5	6.2	16.8	8.0	11.5	10.6	13.9
22 079	10780	3	Rapides	3 414	132 141	476	38.7	63.0	32.6	1.5	1.9	2.8	6.8	18.4	9.2	13.1	11.8	13.3
22 081	...	6	Red River	1 008	8 593	2 546	8.5	58.3	39.9	0.7	0.3	1.6	7.0	17.6	8.5	11.7	11.0	14.0
22 083	...	6	Richland	1 448	20 523	1 803	14.2	62.0	35.9	0.7	0.5	2.1	7.1	18.0	8.6	12.8	12.1	13.4
22 085	...	6	Sabine	2 245	24 186	1 638	10.8	71.4	17.7	10.0	0.6	3.8	6.8	17.6	7.9	11.6	10.7	13.4
22 087	35380	1	St. Bernard	978	45 408	1 066	46.4	65.6	22.5	1.2	2.9	9.6	8.0	18.8	9.1	17.3	12.4	12.9
22 089	35380	1	St. Charles	723	52 812	945	73.0	66.5	26.6	0.8	1.3	5.9	6.2	19.2	8.9	12.7	12.8	15.4
22 091	12940	2	St. Helena	1 058	10 587	2 389	10.0	45.2	53.1	0.7	0.3	1.6	5.8	16.7	8.7	12.6	10.6	13.8
22 093	35380	6	St. James	626	21 567	1 750	34.5	48.9	49.5	0.4	0.4	1.7	6.3	17.5	9.1	12.8	10.4	14.9
22 095	35380	1	St. John the Baptist	552	43 626	1 099	79.0	38.5	55.2	0.6	1.3	5.4	6.6	18.6	9.3	13.2	12.1	14.5
22 097	36660	4	St. Landry	2 393	83 848	672	35.0	56.0	41.8	0.6	0.7	1.9	7.8	19.3	8.8	12.5	10.9	13.2
22 099	29180	3	St. Martin	1 910	53 835	930	28.2	65.9	30.9	0.8	1.2	2.5	6.6	18.3	9.0	13.4	12.2	14.1
22 101	34020	4	St. Mary	1 438	52 810	946	36.7	57.9	33.0	2.3	2.0	6.4	6.8	17.8	9.2	12.7	11.7	14.2
22 103	35380	1	St. Tammany	2 190	250 088	268	114.2	80.7	12.5	1.0	1.9	5.4	5.7	18.7	7.8	11.5	12.8	14.5
22 105	25220	4	Tangipahoa	2 049	128 755	486	62.8	65.0	30.6	0.8	1.0	3.9	7.2	17.6	11.3	14.4	11.8	12.4
22 107	...	9	Tensas	1 561	4 740	2 851	3.0	43.7	55.4	0.5	0.4	1.9	5.9	19.1	7.7	9.4	9.6	12.5
22 109	26380	3	Terrebonne	3 190	113 972	539	35.7	69.2	19.9	6.6	1.6	4.9	7.0	18.6	9.3	14.6	11.9	14.0
22 111	33740	3	Union	2 271	22 477	1 709	9.9	69.4	26.2	0.6	0.3	4.4	6.2	16.5	7.9	11.9	10.9	13.4
22 113	29180	4	Vermilion	3 039	59 875	867	19.7	79.6	15.3	0.7	2.6	3.2	6.9	19.6	8.3	13.1	12.0	13.6
22 115	22860	4	Vernon	3 439	50 803	977	14.8	72.5	15.5	2.3	3.5	9.6	8.9	17.6	13.7	17.7	12.7	9.9
22 117	14220	6	Washington	1 734	46 371	1 042	26.7	67.0	30.9	0.8	0.5	2.1	6.3	17.9	8.4	12.1	11.8	13.3
22 119	43340	6	Webster	1 536	40 021	1 174	26.1	63.6	34.5	1.0	0.7	1.8	6.2	17.1	8.3	12.3	11.4	13.4
22 121	12940	2	West Baton Rouge	498	25 490	1 587	51.2	58.1	38.8	0.5	0.8	2.7	6.7	17.4	9.1	15.9	11.8	14.2
22 123	...	9	West Carroll	931	11 293	2 340	12.1	80.1	16.6	0.7	0.5	3.1	5.8	18.5	8.6	11.5	12.2	13.3
22 125	12940	2	West Feliciana	1 044	15 385	2 079	14.7	52.4	46.2	0.5	0.4	1.6	4.2	12.3	6.1	14.0	18.0	18.2
22 127	...	6	Winn	2 461	14 568	2 132	5.9	66.2	31.2	1.3	0.7	1.9	5.5	16.3	8.3	13.3	12.8	14.2
23 000	...	X	MAINE	79 883	1 329 328	X	16.6	95.2	1.8	1.4	1.6	1.5	4.9	14.6	8.5	11.5	11.7	15.1
23 001	30340	3	Androscoggin	1 212	107 233	558	88.5	93.4	4.6	1.1	1.3	1.7	6.1	15.9	8.8	12.3	12.2	14.8
23 003	...	7	Aroostook	17 279	68 628	776	4.0	95.8	1.1	2.6	0.8	1.1	4.7	14.0	8.0	9.8	10.9	14.9
23 005	38860	2	Cumberland	2 163	289 977	234	134.1	92.7	3.4	0.9	2.9	1.9	4.9	14.6	9.0	12.8	12.4	15.2
23 007	...	6	Franklin	4 394	29 991	1 430	6.8	97.4	0.8	1.2	1.0	1.2	4.6	14.1	10.4	10.4	10.4	14.7
23 009	...	6	Hancock	4 110	54 659	918	13.3	96.3	1.0	1.1	1.5	1.3	4.3	13.1	7.7	10.4	11.0	14.7
23 011	12300	4	Kennebec	2 247	119 980	516	53.4	96.6	1.1	1.3	1.3	1.5	5.0	14.9	8.5	11.2	11.7	15.4
23 013	...	7	Knox	946	39 855	1 176	42.1	96.9	1.0	1.2	0.8	1.2	4.5	13.9	6.6	10.2	11.3	14.1
23 015	...	8	Lincoln	1 181	33 969	1 327	28.8	97.4	0.7	1.0	1.1	1.0	4.1	13.5	6.4	9.0	10.5	14.0
23 017	...	6	Oxford	5 379	57 202	893	10.6	97.1	0.8	1.3	1.1	1.2	4.5	15.1	7.0	10.2	11.3	15.8
23 019	12620	3	Penobscot	8 799	152 692	424	17.4	95.5	1.3	2.0	1.5	1.3	4.8	13.9	11.3	13.1	11.3	14.6
23 021	...	8	Piscataquis	10 259	16 931	1 983	1.7	96.6	0.8	1.3	1.1	1.3	4.2	13.5	6.2	8.4	10.6	15.3
23 023	38860	2	Sagadahoc	657	35 149	1 297	53.5	96.4	1.4	1.0	1.3	1.5	4.7	14.8	6.7	10.9	11.7	15.5
23 025	...	6	Somerset	10 164	51 113	974	5.0	97.1	0.9	1.3	0.9	1.0	4.7	15.2	7.0	10.3	12.0	15.8
23 027	...	6	Waldo	1 890	39 155	1 199	20.7	97.3	0.8	1.3	0.9	1.1	5.0	14.6	7.4	10.3	11.9	14.3
23 029	...	7	Washington	6 637	31 625	1 392	4.8	91.9	0.9	6.2	0.9	1.8	4.9	14.1	7.6	9.6	10.6	14.3
23 031	38860	2	York	2 566	201 169	326	78.4	96.2	1.1	0.9	1.6	1.7	4.8	15.0	7.7	11.3	11.8	15.6
24 000	...	X	MARYLAND	25 142	6 006 401	X	238.9	54.5	30.6	0.8	7.2	9.3	6.2	16.4	9.4	13.9	12.9	14.7
24 001	19060	3	Allegany	1 099	72 528	748	66.0	89.0	9.3	0.5	1.3	1.6	4.8	12.8	12.8	12.6	11.7	13.2
24 003	12580	1	Anne Arundel	1 075	564 195	115	524.8	72.5	17.3	0.8	5.0	7.2	6.3	16.3	9.0	14.1	13.1	15.0
24 005	12580	1	Baltimore	1 550	831 128	71	536.2	61.3	28.4	0.8	6.7	5.0	6.0	15.6	9.4	13.9	12.2	13.7
24 009	47900	1	Calvert	552	90 595	641	164.1	81.3	14.3	0.9	2.7	3.5	5.5	18.7	8.7	11.1	11.8	17.7
24 011	...	6	Caroline	827	32 579	1 370	39.4	78.5	15.0	0.6	1.2	6.4	6.0	18.0	8.3	12.1	11.9	14.9
24 013	12580	1	Carroll	1 159	167 627	382	144.6	91.7	4.1	0.5	2.3	3.0	4.9	17.6	9.0	10.6	11.6	17.2
24 015	37980	1	Cecil	897	102 382	585	114.1	87.9	7.6	0.7	1.8	4.1	5.8	17.8	8.6	12.0	12.4	15.9
24 017	47900	1	Charles	1 186	156 118	413	131.6	47.2	45.3	1.6	4.5	5.3	6.0	18.8	9.4	12.6	13.7	16.7
24 019	15700	6	Dorchester	1 401	32 384	1 377	23.1	66.2	28.8	0.8	1.5	4.6	6.2	15.2	7.6	11.5	10.6	14.2
24 021	47900	1	Frederick	1 710	245 322	274	143.5	78.0	10.1	0.7	5.5	8.4	6.0	18.0	8.9	12.3	13.2	16.1
24 023	...	6	Garrett	1 676	29 460	1 443	17.6	97.3	1.4	0.4	0.7	1.0	4.9	14.9	8.6	10.4	11.5	14.6
24 025	12580	1	Harford	1 132	250 290	267	221.1	79.5	14.2	0.7	3.9	4.2	5.5	17.4	8.5	12.3	12.3	15.7
24 027	12580	1	Howard	649	313 414	216	482.9	58.3	19.6	0.8	18.5	6.4	6.0	18.6	8.2	12.6	13.9	16.0
24 029	...	6	Kent	718	19 787	1 845	27.6	80.0	15.7	0.5	1.3	4.3	4.5	12.4	12.1	10.4	8.7	12.8
24 031	47900	1	Montgomery	1 272	1 040 116	40	817.7	48.2	18.7	0.6	16.5	18.7	6.5	17.0	7.8	13.5	13.9	14.7
24 033	47900	1	Prince George's	1 250	909 535	59	727.6	15.6	63.8	0.9	5.2	16.9	6.7	16.0	10.7	15.1	13.7	14.5
24 035	12580	1	Queen Anne's	963	48 904	999	50.8	88.6	7.6	0.6	1.6	3.4	5.3	17.0	7.6	10.0	11.4	16.9

1. CBSA = Core Based Statistical Area. See Appendix A for explanation. See Appendix B for list of metropolitan areas with component counties.   2. County type code from the Economic Research Service of USDA Rural-Urban Continuum Codes. See Appendix A for definition.   3. Dry land or land partially or temporarily covered by water.   4. May be of any race.

Table B. States and Counties — Population and Households

STATE County	55 to 64 years (16)	65 to 74 years (17)	75 years and over (18)	Percent female (19)	2000 (20)	2010 (21)	2000–2010 (22)	2010–2015 (23)	Births (24)	Deaths (25)	Net migration (26)	Number (27)	Persons per household (28)	Family households (29)	Female family householder[1] (30)	One person (31)
LOUISIANA—Cont'd																
Orleans	13.1	7.2	4.9	52.2	484 674	343 829	-29.1	13.3	25 005	16 186	36 059	150 409	2.37	51.4	19.6	40.2
Ouachita	12.0	7.5	5.8	52.1	147 250	153 720	4.4	2.0	11 862	7 863	-1 051	57 732	2.55	66.2	19.9	29.7
Plaquemines	11.8	7.2	5.0	50.1	26 757	23 042	-13.9	2.0	1 531	903	-165	8 772	2.65	73.7	15.5	21.1
Pointe Coupee	14.9	10.5	7.6	52.0	22 763	22 802	0.2	-2.4	1 441	1 231	-737	8 888	2.53	66.3	13.0	29.3
Rapides	12.5	8.5	6.4	51.7	126 337	131 613	4.2	0.4	9 382	7 256	-1 536	47 704	2.68	66.1	16.5	30.2
Red River	13.6	9.9	6.7	51.6	9 622	9 091	-5.5	-5.5	662	538	-594	3 382	2.60	68.7	17.4	28.1
Richland	13.3	8.7	6.4	51.7	20 981	20 725	-1.2	-1.0	1 466	1 240	-405	7 676	2.58	74.0	18.6	24.0
Sabine	13.5	11.1	7.4	50.5	23 459	24 233	3.3	-0.2	1 580	1 359	-153	9 174	2.60	66.5	14.6	29.7
St. Bernard	11.7	6.0	3.8	50.5	67 229	35 897	-46.6	26.5	3 401	1 650	7 486	14 051	2.90	71.9	19.5	21.7
St. Charles	13.3	6.9	4.7	50.8	48 072	52 887	10.0	-0.1	3 408	2 117	-1 378	18 421	2.83	74.4	19.1	20.9
St. Helena	14.2	10.1	7.6	51.5	10 525	11 203	6.4	-5.7	575	572	-685	4 155	2.61	70.2	23.2	28.7
St. James	13.9	8.8	6.3	51.5	21 216	22 102	4.2	-2.4	1 418	1 008	-993	7 925	2.72	76.3	23.9	22.1
St. John the Baptist	13.1	7.9	4.7	51.3	43 044	45 817	6.4	-4.8	3 032	2 100	-3 186	15 444	2.84	73.6	20.2	22.2
St. Landry	12.8	8.4	6.4	51.9	87 700	83 384	-4.9	0.6	6 792	4 875	-1 412	30 664	2.68	68.4	18.9	28.1
St. Martin	13.1	8.2	5.1	50.6	48 583	52 167	7.4	3.2	3 740	2 311	244	18 834	2.78	70.6	17.0	25.9
St. Mary	13.0	8.4	6.1	50.6	53 500	54 650	2.1	-3.4	3 957	2 862	-2 873	20 183	2.62	69.2	18.9	25.8
St. Tammany	14.0	9.1	5.8	51.4	191 268	233 737	22.2	7.0	14 567	10 755	12 310	87 975	2.70	72.8	12.7	22.3
Tangipahoa	12.4	8.0	4.9	51.5	100 588	121 101	20.4	6.3	9 982	6 051	3 574	45 027	2.68	68.1	17.4	26.2
Tensas	16.2	11.9	7.7	51.5	6 618	5 252	-20.6	-9.7	340	280	-568	1 936	2.46	60.3	19.5	36.4
Terrebonne	12.0	7.6	5.0	50.6	104 503	111 584	6.8	2.1	8 714	5 297	-1 004	39 635	2.80	71.4	15.1	23.2
Union	14.9	10.8	7.6	50.6	22 803	22 782	-0.1	-1.3	1 472	1 267	-480	8 712	2.55	69.2	15.2	27.2
Vermilion	12.5	7.8	6.2	51.4	53 807	57 999	7.8	3.2	4 111	2 840	596	21 623	2.69	71.3	15.5	23.8
Vernon	8.9	6.3	4.2	47.2	52 531	52 334	-0.4	-2.9	5 668	1 931	-5 377	18 112	2.78	73.7	13.0	22.7
Washington	14.1	9.8	6.6	50.6	43 926	47 171	7.4	-1.7	2 950	2 937	-807	17 589	2.56	66.9	18.2	30.4
Webster	13.3	10.0	8.1	51.2	41 831	41 207	-1.5	-2.9	2 608	2 711	-1 089	15 831	2.52	64.9	16.4	31.4
West Baton Rouge	12.9	7.1	5.0	51.1	21 601	23 788	10.1	7.2	1 841	979	860	9 030	2.63	71.4	17.8	23.8
West Carroll	12.5	9.8	7.7	49.8	12 314	11 604	-5.8	-2.7	737	733	-313	4 216	2.54	68.1	16.3	28.7
West Feliciana	14.4	8.1	4.5	34.1	15 111	15 625	3.4	-1.5	653	572	-317	3 976	2.93	73.3	14.0	23.0
Winn	13.4	9.8	6.4	46.7	16 894	15 313	-9.4	-4.9	920	875	-750	5 371	2.43	71.3	16.9	26.6
MAINE	15.5	10.6	7.8	51.1	1 274 923	1 328 361	4.2	0.1	67 308	68 954	2 898	553 086	2.34	62.9	9.6	29.1
Androscoggin	13.9	9.0	6.9	50.9	103 793	107 702	3.8	-0.4	6 801	5 354	-1 896	44 391	2.35	62.2	11.7	29.7
Aroostook	16.4	11.8	9.5	50.7	73 938	71 871	-2.8	-4.5	3 455	4 387	-2 122	30 571	2.24	62.4	8.7	32.5
Cumberland	14.5	9.3	7.1	51.4	265 612	281 673	6.0	2.9	14 856	13 124	6 150	117 406	2.35	61.3	9.5	29.7
Franklin	16.3	11.4	7.8	51.0	29 467	30 768	4.4	-2.5	1 392	1 592	-524	11 975	2.46	65.1	9.0	26.1
Hancock	17.3	12.9	8.6	51.2	51 791	54 420	5.1	0.4	2 483	2 992	836	24 317	2.18	61.3	7.9	31.0
Kennebec	15.7	10.1	7.5	51.3	117 114	122 151	4.3	-1.8	6 053	6 734	-825	51 242	2.30	62.6	10.5	29.2
Knox	17.0	12.7	9.6	50.6	39 618	39 736	0.3	0.3	1 908	2 220	412	17 038	2.26	62.6	9.6	31.7
Lincoln	17.1	15.0	10.3	51.0	33 616	34 457	2.5	-1.4	1 392	2 102	163	14 905	2.26	64.0	8.5	28.4
Oxford	16.8	11.2	8.1	50.4	54 755	57 831	5.6	-1.1	2 822	3 264	-123	22 392	2.53	64.0	8.9	29.3
Penobscot	14.6	9.3	7.3	50.6	144 919	153 920	6.2	-0.8	7 770	7 908	-1 202	62 215	2.36	62.0	9.4	28.0
Piscataquis	18.2	14.3	9.3	50.2	17 235	17 535	1.7	-3.4	735	1 129	-166	7 666	2.22	65.3	9.9	26.7
Sagadahoc	16.2	11.5	8.1	51.5	35 214	35 293	0.2	-0.4	1 757	1 769	-169	15 108	2.31	64.5	8.8	27.8
Somerset	16.1	11.4	7.4	50.4	50 888	52 228	2.6	-2.1	2 600	2 867	-864	21 567	2.37	64.9	10.6	28.1
Waldo	16.8	12.3	7.3	51.0	36 280	38 786	6.9	1.0	1 960	1 994	408	16 527	2.31	64.9	9.4	28.6
Washington	16.8	12.9	9.1	50.7	33 941	32 856	-3.2	-3.7	1 613	2 159	-625	14 173	2.20	62.8	9.9	31.4
York	15.7	10.4	7.6	51.3	186 742	197 134	5.6	2.0	9 711	9 359	3 445	81 593	2.40	65.0	9.6	27.0
MARYLAND	12.8	8.0	5.8	51.5	5 296 486	5 773 785	9.0	4.0	382 151	238 493	92 461	2 155 983	2.67	67.1	14.6	26.9
Allegany	12.9	10.3	8.9	47.8	74 930	75 087	0.2	-3.4	3 573	4 713	-1 290	28 490	2.32	61.3	11.4	31.9
Anne Arundel	12.7	8.2	5.3	50.5	489 656	537 654	9.8	4.9	36 242	20 996	12 212	201 429	2.66	69.2	11.3	24.7
Baltimore	13.3	8.4	7.4	52.7	754 292	804 953	6.7	3.3	51 069	41 280	16 543	313 408	2.54	65.1	14.4	28.9
Calvert	13.5	7.9	5.1	50.6	74 563	88 737	19.0	2.1	4 817	3 323	260	31 041	2.87	76.0	12.6	19.6
Caroline	13.5	9.1	6.3	51.2	29 772	33 088	11.1	-1.5	2 054	1 703	-893	11 842	2.72	71.9	12.9	23.0
Carroll	13.8	9.0	6.3	50.6	150 897	167 138	10.8	0.3	8 319	7 635	-540	59 907	2.73	74.7	9.1	21.1
Cecil	13.8	8.6	5.2	50.3	85 951	101 108	17.6	1.3	5 796	4 571	168	36 453	2.75	72.1	11.8	23.4
Charles	11.8	6.9	4.2	51.8	120 546	146 551	21.6	6.5	9 719	5 013	4 758	52 269	2.86	74.3	16.6	21.2
Dorchester	15.0	11.2	8.5	52.5	30 674	32 618	6.3	-0.7	1 985	1 911	-281	13 419	2.39	67.6	17.2	27.3
Frederick	12.7	7.6	5.3	50.7	195 277	233 385	19.5	5.1	14 581	8 518	5 790	87 259	2.69	72.5	10.1	22.2
Garrett	15.2	11.7	8.3	50.3	29 846	30 097	0.8	-2.1	1 512	1 582	-592	11 851	2.48	69.4	9.1	27.5
Harford	13.6	8.7	5.8	51.0	218 590	244 826	12.0	2.2	14 138	10 177	1 415	91 037	2.70	73.3	11.8	21.9
Howard	12.6	7.6	4.6	51.0	247 842	287 085	15.8	9.2	18 029	8 102	16 507	107 516	2.76	74.0	10.7	21.1
Kent	14.7	13.8	10.6	52.1	19 197	20 197	5.2	-2.0	912	1 270	-66	7 448	2.46	63.7	10.5	32.0
Montgomery	12.9	7.6	6.0	51.8	873 341	971 806	11.3	7.0	68 880	30 585	30 860	362 608	2.75	69.1	11.4	25.2
Prince George's	12.1	7.0	4.2	51.8	801 515	863 519	7.7	5.3	63 120	28 447	12 503	305 115	2.83	66.3	20.8	27.6
Queen Anne's	14.5	10.7	6.6	50.3	40 563	47 776	17.8	2.4	2 383	2 101	895	17 354	2.76	76.5	9.1	18.7

1. No spouse present.

Table B. States and Counties — Population, Vital Statistics, Medicare, and Crime

STATE County	Persons in group quarters, 2015	Daytime population, 2010–2014 Number	Daytime population, 2010–2014 Employment/residence ratio	Births, 2015 Total	Births, 2015 Rate[1]	Deaths, 2015 Number	Deaths, 2015 Rate[1]	Persons under 65 with no health insurance, 2014 Number	Persons under 65 with no health insurance, 2014 Percent	Medicare, 2015 Total Beneficiaries	Medicare, 2015 Enrolled in Original Medicare	Medicare, 2015 Enrolled in Medicare Advantage	Serious crimes known to police,[2] 2014 Total Number	Serious crimes known to police,[2] 2014 Total Rate[3]
	32	33	34	35	36	37	38	39	40	41	42	43	44	45
LOUISIANA—Cont'd														
Orleans	13 403	419 423	1.32	4 953	12.8	3 268	8.4	59 791	18.3	51 829	26 346	25 483	20 564	5 312
Ouachita	5 558	160 991	1.09	2 259	14.4	1 578	10.1	22 231	17.0	25 218	19 802	5 416	11 125	7 341
Plaquemines	272	32 513	1.87	281	12.0	175	7.5	3 418	16.8	3 036	1 348	1 688	298	1 259
Pointe Coupee	116	19 946	0.71	259	11.6	243	10.9	3 232	17.7	4 118	2 280	1 838	420	1 997
Rapides	4 501	137 209	1.10	1 785	13.5	1 382	10.4	17 944	16.3	25 678	21 755	3 923	7 766	6 039
Red River	164	8 638	0.90	113	13.1	108	12.5	1 260	17.7	1 528	1 248	280	183	2 065
Richland	1 039	20 171	0.92	274	13.3	241	11.7	3 135	18.7	3 804	3 089	715	659	3 673
Sabine	438	22 703	0.82	290	12.0	221	9.2	4 089	21.0	4 856	4 155	701	241	1 082
St. Bernard	293	37 324	0.78	686	15.3	351	7.8	6 948	17.5	5 252	2 473	2 779	919	2 025
St. Charles	592	54 114	1.06	682	12.9	408	7.7	6 398	13.9	7 174	3 109	4 065	1 202	2 285
St. Helena	121	8 896	0.44	99	9.3	101	9.5	1 688	19.4	1 235	821	414	199	1 969
St. James	204	22 313	1.06	267	12.4	207	9.6	2 587	14.3	3 838	2 215	1 623	656	3 587
St. John the Baptist	471	42 114	0.87	558	12.8	403	9.2	6 413	16.9	6 847	3 282	3 565	1 379	3 183
St. Landry	1 105	77 313	0.80	1 306	11.7	984	11.7	11 741	16.6	17 828	15 513	2 315	3 198	4 124
St. Martin	701	43 933	0.62	723	13.5	475	8.9	7 224	15.8	7 940	6 788	1 152	796	1 692
St. Mary	868	58 238	1.21	763	14.4	526	9.9	8 741	19.5	9 759	8 065	1 694	1 960	3 676
St. Tammany	1 276	218 558	0.80	2 930	11.8	2 159	8.7	31 117	15.0	41 585	20 349	21 236	4 211	1 722
Tangipahoa	3 654	116 278	0.85	1 965	15.4	1 224	9.6	19 394	18.0	21 532	14 770	6 762	7 591	6 096
Tensas	16	4 924	0.95	65	13.6	54	11.3	769	19.9	1 007	885	122	NA	NA
Terrebonne	1 479	120 875	1.18	1 714	15.1	1 045	9.2	18 661	19.1	19 269	16 276	2 993	4 108	3 631
Union	476	19 950	0.67	272	12.1	222	9.9	3 384	18.8	4 901	3 926	975	387	1 739
Vermilion	536	51 441	0.70	787	13.2	561	9.4	8 569	16.8	9 636	8 834	802	1 714	2 876
Vernon	2 260	54 909	1.09	1 053	20.4	358	7.0	6 521	14.7	6 804	6 273	531	1 269	2 620
Washington	1 582	45 065	0.89	571	12.3	593	12.8	7 182	19.2	9 934	7 287	2 647	1 801	3 892
Webster	1 231	38 580	0.85	485	12.1	520	13.0	5 622	17.5	9 189	7 544	1 645	779	1 989
West Baton Rouge	556	23 876	0.96	382	15.1	199	7.9	2 909	13.6	3 605	1 707	1 898	760	3 071
West Carroll	434	10 428	0.73	148	13.0	143	12.5	1 847	20.3	2 417	2 151	266	305	2 665
West Feliciana	5 316	16 010	1.11	119	7.7	113	7.4	1 166	13.9	1 690	1 106	584	208	1 350
Winn	1 760	14 421	0.88	179	12.2	184	12.6	1 979	18.3	2 629	2 218	411	423	2 876
MAINE	35 797	1 314 229	0.98	12 837	9.7	13 287	10.0	131 550	12.4	290 815	225 836	64 979	28 121	2 114
Androscoggin	2 781	105 935	0.97	1 233	11.5	1 006	9.4	10 497	12.0	22 766	16 850	5 916	2 474	2 297
Aroostook	2 017	70 144	0.98	657	9.5	808	11.7	7 996	14.9	18 595	16 262	2 333	987	1 416
Cumberland	9 157	310 018	1.17	2 951	10.2	2 546	8.8	24 273	10.4	54 243	39 488	14 755	6 562	2 288
Franklin	1 027	29 563	0.93	264	8.8	307	10.2	3 214	13.8	6 320	4 799	1 521	443	1 454
Hancock	1 190	54 199	0.99	490	9.0	609	11.1	6 348	15.1	12 581	10 430	2 151	924	1 679
Kennebec	3 647	125 410	1.07	1 090	9.0	1 285	10.7	10 271	10.6	27 548	19 778	7 770	3 092	2 554
Knox	1 374	41 343	1.09	380	9.5	427	10.7	4 199	14.2	10 187	8 192	1 995	693	1 752
Lincoln	489	31 126	0.81	250	7.3	401	11.8	3 670	14.5	9 171	6 977	2 194	491	1 442
Oxford	850	51 408	0.75	561	9.8	641	11.2	6 488	14.2	12 813	10 329	2 484	1 425	2 490
Penobscot	7 502	156 291	1.04	1 483	9.7	1 506	9.8	17 410	14.3	32 937	25 599	7 338	3 585	2 337
Piscataquis	241	17 020	0.96	137	8.1	211	12.4	1 859	14.5	4 806	4 089	717	263	1 543
Sagadahoc	264	34 027	0.94	334	9.5	379	10.8	3 060	10.9	7 557	5 478	2 079	499	1 426
Somerset	714	49 393	0.89	490	9.6	510	10.0	5 914	14.5	11 931	10 014	1 917	1 450	2 808
Waldo	501	34 388	0.74	348	8.9	398	10.2	4 258	13.8	8 815	6 761	2 054	495	1 269
Washington	827	32 123	0.98	302	9.5	388	12.2	4 275	17.8	8 408	7 492	916	490	1 528
York	3 216	171 841	0.73	1 867	9.3	1 865	9.3	17 818	11.0	42 137	33 298	8 839	4 045	2 020
MARYLAND	140 256	5 613 120	0.91	72 754	12.1	47 898	8.0	450 280	8.9	832 579	745 137	87 442	176 520	2 954
Allegany	7 597	77 637	1.13	658	9.0	894	12.3	3 954	7.5	16 990	16 124	866	2 580	3 520
Anne Arundel	14 514	543 589	0.98	6 936	12.3	4 260	7.6	30 840	6.6	77 918	71 731	6 187	15 896	2 833
Baltimore	21 439	765 357	0.87	9 752	11.8	8 295	10.0	57 092	8.4	130 476	115 279	15 197	24 582	2 966
Calvert	643	68 390	0.53	911	10.1	680	7.5	4 330	5.5	12 119	11 419	700	1 665	1 829
Caroline	441	27 088	0.62	382	11.7	330	10.1	2 885	10.5	5 794	5 697	97	888	2 719
Carroll	3 347	136 347	0.64	1 612	9.6	1 520	9.1	7 579	5.5	30 676	28 676	2 000	2 593	1 544
Cecil	1 443	86 843	0.68	1 044	10.2	906	8.9	6 326	7.2	16 140	15 003	1 137	3 388	3 312
Charles	1 406	117 168	0.55	1 863	12.0	1 018	6.6	8 235	6.1	16 908	15 676	1 232	3 597	2 326
Dorchester	501	30 448	0.86	382	11.8	385	11.9	2 588	9.9	7 436	7 287	149	1 231	3 763
Frederick	4 315	219 904	0.84	2 814	11.5	1 665	6.8	13 979	6.7	30 265	28 187	2 078	4 340	1 781
Garrett	526	29 489	0.97	293	9.9	313	10.6	2 220	9.4	5 948	5 488	460	527	1 763
Harford	2 740	218 586	0.77	2 718	10.9	2 041	8.2	12 073	5.7	38 121	34 555	3 566	4 266	1 702
Howard	1 697	295 322	0.98	3 483	11.2	1 671	5.4	14 043	5.2	28 183	25 629	2 554	6 343	2 050
Kent	1 496	20 656	1.07	177	8.9	265	13.4	1 422	10.3	5 861	5 711	150	385	1 933
Montgomery	9 208	969 749	0.93	13 106	12.7	5 950	5.7	88 472	10.0	121 309	106 240	15 069	18 475	1 795
Prince George's	20 056	761 852	0.73	12 025	13.3	6 101	6.7	106 368	13.6	100 369	83 655	16 714	30 671	3 415
Queen Anne's	436	39 760	0.65	444	9.1	392	8.0	2 685	6.7	7 366	7 148	218	863	1 769

1. Per 1,000 estimated resident population.   2. Data for serious crimes have not been adjusted for underreporting; this may affect comparability between geographic areas and over time.
3. Per 100,000 population estimated by the FBI.

Table B. States and Counties — Crime, Education, Money Income, and Poverty

STATE County	Serious crimes known to police, 2014 (cont.)[1] Rate[2] Violent	Property	Education: School enrollment and attainment, 2010–2014 Enrollment[3] Total	Percent private	Attainment[4] (percent) High school graduate or less	Bachelor's degree or more	Local government expenditures,[5] 2012–2013 Total current spending (mil dol)	Current spending per student (dollars)	Money income, 2010–2014 Per capita income[6] (dollars)	Households Median income (dollars)	Mean income (dollars)	Percent with income of $200,000 or more	Income and poverty, 2014 Median household income (dollars)	Percent below poverty level All persons	Children under 18 years	Children 5 to 17 years in families
	46	47	48	49	50	51	52	53	54	55	56	57	58	59	60	61
LOUISIANA—Cont'd																
Orleans	976	4 336	97 117	32.9	39.2	34.4	275.4	13 627	27 255	36 964	62 880	4.7	35 468	27.9	43.3	42.0
Ouachita	1 399	5 942	40 828	9.6	49.4	22.8	284.0	9 903	22 160	39 111	57 567	3.2	40 877	23.6	36.1	34.3
Plaquemines	135	1 124	6 353	16.5	57.4	15.4	62.4	16 026	26 672	54 835	70 302	3.4	51 304	16.0	19.9	18.9
Pointe Coupee	594	1 403	5 307	26.8	62.0	12.6	30.1	10 306	24 552	46 158	60 494	2.7	44 469	18.3	28.1	25.9
Rapides	952	5 087	34 064	13.5	52.7	18.2	220.5	9 163	22 106	41 305	57 558	2.0	40 406	19.8	26.7	25.3
Red River	485	1 580	2 103	18.4	68.4	11.2	20.2	13 599	21 395	37 681	54 768	2.9	33 322	25.3	34.5	32.8
Richland	485	3 188	4 876	11.4	60.4	14.7	34.3	9 927	19 440	38 708	51 922	1.9	36 666	24.9	35.7	34.5
Sabine	130	952	5 553	8.1	59.5	13.8	47.4	10 906	23 058	36 513	55 557	3.3	39 561	21.2	27.1	25.6
St. Bernard	190	1 836	10 553	12.9	60.6	12.5	80.8	12 021	21 079	44 706	57 579	1.6	45 615	17.9	27.0	26.8
St. Charles	333	1 953	14 207	17.2	50.1	20.1	148.4	15 279	26 623	57 785	72 758	2.9	60 751	12.1	18.2	16.0
St. Helena	336	1 633	2 639	7.6	64.4	8.9	9.2	11 593	19 582	35 262	50 724	1.2	35 004	24.0	36.5	34.4
St. James	552	3 034	5 406	16.8	60.5	13.4	56.4	14 980	24 757	53 259	66 886	2.9	47 477	16.1	24.8	23.2
St. John the Baptist	127	3 056	12 520	28.4	56.1	15.2	83.2	13 296	22 785	50 716	63 508	1.8	47 225	20.8	30.9	28.2
St. Landry	672	3 452	19 681	16.1	67.3	13.1	127.5	8 586	19 282	33 928	50 129	1.8	32 683	30.1	40.2	35.4
St. Martin	232	1 460	13 931	22.8	64.7	13.9	75.1	8 973	22 783	42 948	59 704	2.6	46 713	18.0	26.9	25.1
St. Mary	439	3 237	11 880	14.6	67.8	11.1	97.7	10 377	21 616	41 956	55 278	2.5	42 075	21.8	30.2	28.0
St. Tammany	157	1 565	62 862	24.5	38.8	30.4	414.3	11 044	30 948	61 942	82 675	6.3	63 441	11.2	14.9	13.6
Tangipahoa	789	5 308	34 453	13.6	55.1	19.3	176.4	8 892	21 262	40 721	56 217	1.8	39 927	22.5	31.9	30.5
Tensas	NA	NA	1 085	20.9	68.1	9.8	9.0	13 306	16 819	26 178	40 773	1.0	27 522	32.0	44.6	39.9
Terrebonne	331	3 300	26 797	16.7	64.0	12.9	163.5	8 773	23 999	49 932	65 546	3.1	49 044	20.9	27.1	24.4
Union	274	1 465	4 337	13.0	61.2	11.6	26.0	10 998	19 437	35 115	48 179	1.4	38 998	22.0	33.3	30.0
Vermilion	408	2 469	14 070	15.0	65.4	13.0	87.7	9 258	23 303	47 344	62 326	2.2	45 331	18.3	24.5	21.0
Vernon	283	2 337	13 528	10.5	48.8	18.7	96.2	9 785	21 609	46 867	57 413	1.5	46 682	13.9	20.3	21.2
Washington	573	3 319	11 671	16.1	64.3	11.0	80.8	10 707	17 459	31 750	44 959	1.4	29 749	29.1	38.2	35.5
Webster	398	1 591	9 108	9.9	61.1	14.4	61.3	9 200	20 623	35 292	50 337	1.0	36 003	22.2	31.9	30.1
West Baton Rouge	364	2 707	6 056	19.6	55.7	18.0	45.7	11 704	25 296	49 202	66 573	2.4	51 550	20.5	28.6	28.3
West Carroll	245	2 421	2 523	2.8	71.6	10.1	21.1	9 603	19 296	31 843	50 017	1.3	33 959	22.5	31.8	29.0
West Feliciana	247	1 103	2 979	10.7	60.2	19.1	28.2	13 181	21 916	53 967	73 092	4.3	53 679	24.0	20.9	19.2
Winn	530	2 346	3 190	7.5	63.6	12.3	24.9	9 915	17 508	32 608	47 654	1.5	36 644	26.8	33.6	31.2
MAINE	128	1 986	303 115	16.5	42.2	28.4	2 335.6	12 147	27 332	48 804	64 327	2.9	49 381	14.0	19.0	17.0
Androscoggin	141	2 156	26 228	18.3	49.4	19.9	196.7	11 599	24 734	45 765	58 930	1.7	46 701	15.4	22.6	20.8
Aroostook	105	1 311	15 184	9.8	52.6	17.0	125.6	13 095	21 933	37 378	49 340	1.5	36 066	20.1	27.9	24.8
Cumberland	121	2 167	68 885	19.9	30.1	42.0	500.5	13 382	33 844	59 560	80 328	5.5	61 436	10.8	13.7	12.6
Franklin	92	1 362	7 105	8.6	46.2	24.5	40.8	12 888	22 576	41 665	54 990	2.1	41 035	15.8	22.6	20.8
Hancock	65	1 614	10 707	18.1	39.9	32.6	96.1	14 592	28 077	45 747	61 913	2.6	45 807	12.9	18.6	17.0
Kennebec	184	2 370	27 432	18.1	45.0	23.9	194.9	11 827	25 636	46 559	59 980	2.2	45 556	13.8	19.4	16.8
Knox	33	1 719	7 439	11.8	42.2	30.7	87.6	14 740	28 062	50 515	63 468	2.9	50 002	13.9	19.6	17.7
Lincoln	167	1 274	5 981	19.3	39.3	32.3	51.3	11 852	28 798	50 027	65 439	3.1	47 905	11.7	19.3	15.6
Oxford	126	2 365	12 437	14.0	54.8	18.8	120.2	12 939	21 577	40 695	52 034	1.1	40 120	16.1	22.6	21.1
Penobscot	77	2 260	40 370	13.2	44.9	24.2	262.5	11 775	24 076	44 543	57 849	2.1	42 728	18.0	21.9	19.4
Piscataquis	123	1 420	3 163	17.0	51.3	18.2	18.5	9 864	22 796	37 110	50 596	1.7	36 994	20.3	29.8	26.8
Sagadahoc	29	1 397	7 415	10.6	37.8	32.3	63.0	13 233	29 879	55 046	69 026	2.6	55 630	10.5	16.3	14.7
Somerset	130	2 678	11 290	10.2	54.5	15.7	103.2	12 703	21 765	39 792	51 536	1.3	39 001	17.3	25.0	22.1
Waldo	82	1 187	8 066	21.0	43.4	29.0	55.5	13 777	23 729	43 484	54 905	1.0	46 598	15.0	22.3	19.7
Washington	125	1 403	6 511	10.4	50.8	20.2	64.5	14 363	21 450	38 239	48 328	1.0	38 057	18.5	26.2	26.1
York	153	1 867	44 902	18.9	40.4	29.1	354.8	12 080	29 741	56 701	71 453	3.5	55 482	11.2	14.1	12.0
MARYLAND	446	2 508	1 577 160	19.7	36.7	37.3	11 905.0	13 829	36 670	74 149	97 135	9.1	73 851	10.4	13.8	13.2
Allegany	274	3 246	17 428	8.5	54.8	17.0	127.8	14 316	21 653	39 794	54 526	1.6	39 808	18.5	22.9	21.2
Anne Arundel	431	2 402	144 694	20.9	34.0	37.6	1 009.8	12 984	41 315	89 031	110 059	11.2	86 654	6.7	9.2	9.0
Baltimore	448	2 517	217 304	22.1	37.1	36.0	1 412.5	13 209	34 701	66 940	87 861	6.4	67 766	9.8	13.0	12.4
Calvert	144	1 685	25 000	10.3	39.0	29.3	217.9	13 347	38 633	95 425	109 409	9.3	92 446	7.2	7.7	6.9
Caroline	321	2 397	7 735	10.3	60.0	13.9	66.3	11 871	25 193	55 605	67 163	2.9	49 573	16.0	23.7	23.1
Carroll	218	1 325	44 610	18.6	38.9	32.7	350.4	13 129	36 936	85 532	101 285	8.1	84 500	5.9	7.4	6.6
Cecil	485	2 827	24 301	18.9	49.3	21.8	195.2	12 486	29 025	65 124	78 047	4.0	62 198	10.6	14.8	13.2
Charles	353	1 973	41 876	12.2	39.7	26.8	348.8	13 090	37 223	91 910	104 847	9.5	86 703	7.2	10.3	9.9
Dorchester	434	3 329	7 283	11.7	55.6	19.3	62.2	13 178	26 755	45 628	63 245	2.4	42 279	17.5	29.4	28.7
Frederick	249	1 532	66 138	19.8	33.0	38.8	509.0	12 583	37 254	84 480	100 723	8.8	83 698	6.5	8.3	7.6
Garrett	241	1 522	6 198	17.4	56.1	18.4	57.9	14 469	24 974	46 096	61 039	2.2	47 441	12.4	19.7	18.2
Harford	244	1 458	65 522	18.2	35.6	33.4	484.5	12 793	35 763	81 016	95 858	7.9	79 403	8.0	9.8	8.8
Howard	198	1 852	86 930	18.1	19.3	60.4	781.5	15 013	48 243	110 133	132 666	18.3	106 871	6.1	7.1	6.8
Kent	231	1 702	4 476	44.3	47.7	28.0	32.2	15 099	28 411	58 201	70 961	4.8	53 288	13.8	21.0	19.7
Montgomery	169	1 626	272 511	23.4	22.9	57.4	2 246.2	15 097	48 916	98 704	132 688	17.7	97 279	7.2	8.9	8.5
Prince George's	460	2 956	248 988	17.8	41.0	30.4	1 747.2	14 120	32 637	73 856	89 867	6.5	71 904	10.3	14.6	14.7
Queen Anne's	223	1 546	11 445	13.9	38.0	34.1	90.7	11 699	38 392	86 406	103 775	9.4	80 650	7.5	10.9	9.8

1. Data for serious crimes have not been adjusted for underreporting; this may affect comparability between geographic areas and over time.   2. Per 100,000 population estimated by the FBI.
3. All persons 3 years old and over enrolled in nursery school through college.   4. Persons 25 years old and over.   5. Elementary and secondary education expenditures.
6. Based on population estimated by the American Community Survey, 2010–2014.

Table B. States and Counties — **Personal Income**

STATE County	Personal income, 2014										Earnings, 2014		
	Total (mil dol)	Percent change, 2013–2014	Per capita[1]		Wages and salaries (mil dol)	Supplements to wages and salaries; employer contributions (mil dol)		Proprietors' income (mil dol)	Dividends, interest, and rent (mil dol)	Personal transfer receipts (mil dol)	Total (mil dol)	Contributions for government social insurance (mil dol)	
			Dollars	Rank		Pension and insurance	Government social insurance					From employee and self-employed	From employer
	62	63	64	65	66	67	68	69	70	71	72	73	74
LOUISIANA—Cont'd													
Orleans	17 711	4.1	46 084	594	10 514	1 676	697	2 235	4 431	2 811	15 122	794	697
Ouachita	5 744	2.2	36 744	1 639	2 896	509	184	630	930	1 312	4 219	229	184
Plaquemines	1 086	3.7	46 297	575	1 035	185	66	219	154	148	1 505	77	66
Pointe Coupee	900	1.2	40 182	1 148	212	41	14	88	132	196	355	21	14
Rapides	5 329	1.8	40 222	1 145	2 451	471	158	488	945	1 385	3 568	194	158
Red River	291	1.1	33 534	2 192	108	22	7	29	44	82	166	9	7
Richland	694	-3.1	33 459	2 203	221	46	15	81	79	211	363	20	15
Sabine	805	1.9	33 277	2 230	205	43	12	111	132	217	372	21	12
St. Bernard	1 269	4.7	28 582	2 873	521	120	31	74	189	283	746	40	31
St. Charles	2 304	3.6	43 689	785	1 778	345	108	127	286	339	2 358	124	108
St. Helena	405	0.0	38 167	1 431	59	14	3	45	41	111	122	8	3
St. James	894	2.5	41 331	1 023	545	117	33	68	95	176	763	41	33
St. John the Baptist	1 654	3.3	37 812	1 482	821	168	51	148	180	347	1 187	65	51
St. Landry	3 037	2.1	36 285	1 725	960	194	59	144	425	846	1 356	83	59
St. Martin	1 978	3.1	37 106	1 583	645	103	41	116	279	411	905	55	41
St. Mary	2 070	1.9	38 941	1 326	1 470	226	90	151	364	450	1 937	107	90
St. Tammany	12 996	4.8	52 867	272	3 993	642	243	1 701	2 284	1 845	6 581	358	243
Tangipahoa	4 344	3.6	34 192	2 083	1 697	338	96	279	529	1 146	2 411	130	96
Tensas	181	-10.8	37 538	1 520	40	9	2	46	35	50	96	4	2
Terrebonne	4 859	3.6	42 878	861	3 251	436	208	183	651	835	4 077	233	208
Union	771	2.5	34 215	2 079	157	36	10	73	105	214	276	17	10
Vermilion	2 275	2.7	38 153	1 434	666	117	40	167	347	437	991	56	40
Vernon	2 001	1.0	38 384	1 408	1 050	296	92	78	419	377	1 516	66	92
Washington	1 429	1.9	30 882	2 605	394	88	23	79	177	494	583	38	23
Webster	1 451	1.6	35 986	1 782	509	93	32	125	232	412	759	47	32
West Baton Rouge	1 049	4.8	41 807	970	675	112	45	93	101	175	925	50	45
West Carroll	315	-1.7	27 361	2 960	80	19	5	39	36	115	143	8	5
West Feliciana	503	1.7	32 651	2 347	271	71	13	52	90	85	407	17	13
Winn	489	3.4	33 159	2 255	184	35	12	88	58	136	320	18	12
MAINE	54 195	3.1	40 745	X	25 794	4 345	1 907	3 907	9 323	12 351	35 953	2 371	1 907
Androscoggin	3 900	3.0	36 300	1 722	2 045	322	155	271	487	1 029	2 793	186	155
Aroostook	2 487	1.6	35 814	1 803	1 036	210	76	175	346	803	1 497	102	76
Cumberland	14 327	3.6	49 781	394	8 908	1 265	653	1 059	2 751	2 304	11 884	752	653
Franklin	1 008	1.7	33 256	2 236	405	76	29	79	178	288	589	41	29
Hancock	2 204	3.8	40 289	1 140	870	144	68	204	514	509	1 286	90	68
Kennebec	4 796	2.1	39 602	1 235	2 496	493	174	302	693	1 171	3 465	214	174
Knox	1 611	3.2	40 592	1 109	654	113	49	172	409	375	988	69	49
Lincoln	1 440	3.1	42 155	936	399	68	30	97	383	337	594	46	30
Oxford	1 937	2.4	33 843	2 140	631	114	47	133	304	566	925	69	47
Penobscot	5 510	2.4	35 914	1 788	2 845	519	206	387	761	1 446	3 958	256	206
Piscataquis	567	2.6	33 323	2 224	191	43	14	40	95	200	288	21	14
Sagadahoc	1 504	3.2	42 902	859	773	137	59	74	307	308	1 043	68	59
Somerset	1 818	4.2	35 534	1 850	708	125	53	165	238	545	1 050	74	53
Waldo	1 367	4.1	34 997	1 936	436	72	33	105	240	376	646	48	33
Washington	1 102	2.3	34 646	1 993	383	80	28	87	177	407	579	40	28
York	8 618	3.7	42 939	853	3 012	566	231	557	1 442	1 686	4 367	294	231
MARYLAND	323 778	3.8	54 176	X	155 117	27 387	11 665	24 657	61 473	44 799	218 825	12 676	11 665
Allegany	2 622	3.5	35 943	1 785	1 209	266	102	110	459	850	1 687	112	102
Anne Arundel	33 369	3.6	59 574	140	19 115	3 772	1 478	2 542	6 338	3 719	26 906	1 484	1 478
Baltimore	44 612	3.4	53 949	238	20 619	3 480	1 547	3 371	8 876	6 936	29 018	1 745	1 547
Calvert	4 854	3.2	53 566	251	1 059	209	80	163	853	596	1 511	94	80
Caroline	1 336	2.8	41 065	1 053	382	78	30	130	185	324	620	37	30
Carroll	8 929	3.0	53 200	262	2 519	435	194	459	1 393	1 205	3 606	227	194
Cecil	4 262	4.4	41 632	995	1 484	297	117	168	639	831	2 065	128	117
Charles	7 827	4.0	50 582	353	1 973	408	155	304	1 241	978	2 839	168	155
Dorchester	1 302	2.3	39 974	1 179	461	104	36	110	242	374	711	44	36
Frederick	12 806	3.7	52 554	279	5 241	895	401	621	2 040	1 534	7 158	420	401
Garrett	1 274	4.4	42 936	854	428	88	35	200	232	291	752	47	35
Harford	12 709	3.3	50 817	340	4 848	1 005	383	507	2 041	1 832	6 743	398	383
Howard	20 909	4.1	67 605	71	11 172	1 406	798	1 341	3 592	1 645	14 717	860	798
Kent	999	2.9	50 419	362	325	62	25	83	314	222	496	32	25
Montgomery	75 720	3.9	73 483	48	34 247	5 415	2 472	9 129	16 940	5 823	51 264	2 908	2 472
Prince George's	40 216	4.0	44 465	717	18 235	3 714	1 420	1 743	6 938	5 556	25 112	1 419	1 420
Queen Anne's	2 621	2.7	53 705	247	572	109	44	186	518	377	911	57	44

1. Based on the resident population estimated as of July 1 of the year shown.

Table B. States and Counties — Earnings, Social Security, and Housing

STATE County	Earnings, 2014 (cont.) Percent by selected industries									Social Security beneficiaries, December 2014		Supplemental Security Income recipients, December 2014	Housing units, 2015	
	Farm	Mining	Construction	Manufacturing	Information: professional, scientific, technical services	Retail trade	Finance, insurance, real estate and leasing	Health care and social assistance	Government	Number	Rate[1]		Total	Percent change, 2010–2014
	75	76	77	78	79	80	81	82	83	84	85	86	87	88
LOUISIANA—Cont'd														
Orleans	0.0	4.6	4.4	2.3	15.7	3.7	7.4	8.7	19.2	59 305	154	20 710	193 035	1.7
Ouachita	0.3	0.4	5.6	9.0	10.2	8.3	9.0	18.0	15.7	28 375	182	6 904	66 953	3.8
Plaquemines	0.4	14.2	6.7	15.1	D	1.5	6.1	D	13.3	3 500	150	580	9 954	3.7
Pointe Coupee	7.0	4.3	7.2	7.9	D	9.2	7.3	6.0	17.1	4 940	221	1 064	11 337	1.9
Rapides	1.0	0.6	9.3	8.2	6.1	8.0	4.3	18.6	22.0	27 825	210	6 993	57 328	3.0
Red River	4.6	D	6.7	10.6	3.2	4.8	3.8	D	18.6	1 715	198	503	4 131	0.1
Richland	7.8	0.6	7.4	9.4	D	10.8	4.7	D	15.9	4 515	218	1 143	8 863	2.8
Sabine	12.2	2.7	7.4	16.5	6.5	7.7	4.5	D	18.0	5 680	236	999	14 496	2.6
St. Bernard	0.2	D	9.8	27.0	2.5	6.7	2.5	D	17.7	6 510	146	1 706	16 857	0.4
St. Charles	0.0	D	13.6	29.3	6.7	3.0	1.9	2.5	10.1	8 810	167	1 172	20 372	2.1
St. Helena	3.8	D	7.3	10.1	D	7.2	D	8.1	25.4	2 365	223	480	5 163	0.3
St. James	0.4	D	3.3	51.6	D	2.5	2.8	1.8	12.2	4 410	204	743	8 756	3.6
St. John the Baptist	0.2	4.2	9.7	31.2	2.8	5.7	2.7	4.9	12.2	8 485	194	1 817	17 647	1.1
St. Landry	1.0	3.7	8.4	7.0	5.0	11.1	4.7	13.5	22.7	18 860	225	5 561	36 264	1.6
St. Martin	0.7	8.9	7.0	29.2	3.8	7.6	6.4	6.3	12.3	10 410	195	1 851	22 707	3.5
St. Mary	-0.1	15.1	5.5	21.7	3.4	4.2	6.6	D	13.7	11 015	207	2 332	23 252	1.0
St. Tammany	0.1	12.9	8.2	4.7	8.4	7.9	7.3	12.4	13.9	47 030	191	4 850	100 061	4.9
Tangipahoa	0.5	0.5	5.1	5.9	4.4	10.2	11.2	11.4	25.9	23 460	185	5 986	53 138	6.1
Tensas	43.0	D	D	2.2	D	D	D	D	17.5	1 200	250	407	3 380	0.7
Terrebonne	0.1	15.8	6.5	16.0	5.6	6.0	5.7	9.3	7.7	21 090	186	4 670	44 841	2.4
Union	13.1	0.9	6.5	19.0	D	8.8	3.2	9.2	16.5	5 250	234	954	11 457	1.0
Vermilion	5.2	19.9	8.0	8.6	4.5	7.2	5.1	5.8	17.7	11 600	195	1 941	26 043	3.2
Vernon	-0.1	0.2	2.8	2.1	4.5	3.6	2.7	4.8	68.4	8 060	154	1 253	21 819	1.8
Washington	0.9	1.9	8.8	15.4	D	7.8	4.2	D	28.5	11 175	241	2 943	21 345	1.4
Webster	0.0	9.8	8.5	14.7	2.6	9.9	4.2	D	15.6	9 710	241	2 028	19 449	0.6
West Baton Rouge	-0.2	D	25.6	24.8	D	4.2	3.5	D	10.3	4 160	165	835	10 297	10.4
West Carroll	17.7	D	D	D	D	8.7	D	7.3	29.3	2 710	235	517	5 085	0.8
West Feliciana	3.6	D	6.4	7.3	D	2.9	3.6	D	36.7	1 900	124	342	5 293	3.8
Winn	2.5	4.6	3.0	15.4	D	4.4	7.0	23.5	12.6	3 250	220	665	7 230	-0.1
MAINE	0.6	0.0	6.3	10.0	8.1	8.2	7.3	16.3	18.0	325 496	245	37 591	729 413	1.1
Androscoggin	1.3	D	6.9	11.2	6.8	8.0	6.3	21.2	11.2	25 220	235	4 103	49 105	0.0
Aroostook	3.1	0.0	4.3	11.9	3.5	9.5	4.3	17.8	24.5	20 645	298	2 691	39 448	-0.2
Cumberland	0.1	D	5.2	6.3	12.7	6.7	12.9	16.7	11.9	58 465	203	5 638	140 875	1.6
Franklin	0.6	0.0	6.7	19.3	D	10.0	4.1	D	18.6	7 880	261	933	21 983	1.3
Hancock	0.6	D	9.8	8.0	12.2	10.6	4.5	13.8	14.1	14 500	265	1 101	40 582	1.0
Kennebec	0.6	0.1	5.0	5.1	6.1	8.9	3.4	16.4	30.6	30 295	250	4 095	61 681	1.2
Knox	0.2	0.0	8.3	10.4	6.9	9.3	5.7	15.2	15.3	11 085	279	886	23 984	1.0
Lincoln	0.5	D	9.4	D	7.4	10.3	6.1	14.3	15.0	10 215	299	701	23 694	0.9
Oxford	0.5	0.1	6.7	19.3	5.4	8.5	4.1	13.1	17.8	15 480	270	1 975	36 379	0.9
Penobscot	0.4	D	5.3	5.0	5.3	9.7	4.2	22.6	20.6	35 935	234	5 489	74 331	0.6
Piscataquis	0.4	D	5.0	23.4	D	10.1	2.5	D	27.5	5 530	325	778	15 429	0.6
Sagadahoc	0.4	0.0	7.2	D	6.7	5.9	3.2	5.7	11.7	8 630	246	708	18 463	1.0
Somerset	2.3	D	14.6	22.8	3.2	7.7	2.5	13.0	13.7	14 105	275	2 110	30 811	0.8
Waldo	1.5	D	7.2	10.7	3.8	8.1	11.5	15.0	13.3	10 340	265	1 267	21 848	1.3
Washington	5.1	D	4.8	10.2	2.9	9.9	4.0	15.0	25.4	9 555	300	1 344	23 057	0.2
York	0.1	0.1	7.1	11.4	5.5	8.7	4.5	11.7	28.2	47 615	237	3 772	107 743	1.9
MARYLAND	0.3	0.1	7.1	4.3	16.9	5.4	7.9	11.0	24.8	936 372	157	118 184	2 434 307	2.3
Allegany	0.0	0.5	3.7	8.9	D	7.3	3.7	21.1	28.6	17 400	238	2 297	33 155	-0.5
Anne Arundel	0.0	D	6.3	5.5	14.2	4.7	4.1	7.2	36.1	86 860	155	7 457	220 989	4.0
Baltimore	0.1	0.0	7.3	4.6	13.6	6.7	13.2	13.7	18.2	152 825	185	15 718	337 439	0.6
Calvert	-0.2	D	10.7	2.4	7.0	7.2	4.2	14.4	22.0	14 140	156	945	34 766	2.9
Caroline	10.9	D	7.7	9.7	D	9.8	D	D	17.9	6 690	206	758	13 522	0.3
Carroll	0.7	D	12.8	8.3	9.9	8.1	4.4	13.8	16.0	30 380	181	1 554	63 403	1.6
Cecil	1.6	0.4	4.5	20.9	3.4	6.2	2.5	10.4	24.4	18 830	184	1 773	42 565	3.6
Charles	0.0	D	11.1	1.5	8.9	12.1	3.7	10.4	31.7	20 530	133	2 147	58 865	7.1
Dorchester	6.6	2.2	D	18.9	D	5.1	3.1	11.0	23.3	8 245	253	1 226	16 686	0.8
Frederick	0.6	D	D	5.9	D	6.9	D	9.9	20.2	37 065	152	2 193	94 741	5.1
Garrett	2.4	3.3	11.5	8.3	6.8	9.8	D	D	14.6	7 255	245	623	19 091	1.3
Harford	0.2	0.1	7.0	5.0	13.4	7.0	3.8	9.2	36.7	44 365	177	3 144	98 938	3.5
Howard	0.1	D	8.0	4.5	31.4	5.2	7.6	7.1	9.7	37 485	121	3 076	116 614	6.7
Kent	5.1	D	8.6	10.6	8.4	6.7	4.3	13.1	13.6	5 465	276	360	10 693	1.4
Montgomery	0.0	0.0	7.4	3.2	26.0	4.4	10.1	8.7	21.7	128 920	125	13 918	389 000	3.5
Prince George's	0.0	D	9.8	2.2	12.3	6.3	3.5	8.0	38.2	110 005	122	13 936	331 325	1.0
Queen Anne's	4.2	D	10.6	8.4	8.1	9.4	4.6	5.9	19.6	9 825	202	432	20 895	3.8

1. Per 1,000 resident population estimated as of July 1 of the year shown.

Table B. States and Counties — Housing, Labor Force, and Employment

STATE County	Total	Percent	Median value[1]	With a mortgage	Without a mortgage[2]	Median rent[3]	Median rent as a percent of income[2]	Sub-standard units[4] (percent)	Total	Percent change, 2014–2015	Total	Rate[5]	Total	Management, business, science and arts	Construction, production, and mainte-nance occu-pations
	89	90	91	92	93	94	95	96	97	98	99	100	101	102	103
LOUISIANA—Cont'd															
Orleans	150 409	46.9	184 100	26.3	14.1	927	37.2	3.2	180 778	0.6	11 680	6.5	164 119	40.9	15.6
Ouachita	57 732	60.0	122 400	19.5	10.0	694	33.0	2.7	72 395	0.2	4 745	6.6	65 202	32.2	20.7
Plaquemines	8 772	70.6	159 700	23.9	10.0	1 036	28.0	2.4	10 373	1.0	574	5.5	10 004	28.8	34.0
Pointe Coupee	8 888	77.5	115 300	19.9	10.0	567	28.1	3.6	10 276	1.3	666	6.5	9 570	24.5	32.2
Rapides	47 704	64.9	121 800	21.2	10.0	726	32.3	2.8	58 577	0.6	3 734	6.4	52 605	31.7	22.4
Red River	3 382	74.9	81 300	18.1	10.0	551	28.4	3.7	3 961	-1.1	271	6.8	3 175	29.4	33.9
Richland	7 676	65.9	81 300	19.4	10.0	551	25.2	3.0	8 714	-0.5	751	8.6	8 157	28.1	26.1
Sabine	9 174	77.4	78 100	17.5	10.5	485	28.1	3.3	9 509	3.0	672	7.1	8 975	27.1	38.4
St. Bernard	14 051	69.9	127 300	21.5	10.0	812	34.2	2.1	19 424	0.7	1 275	6.6	17 061	24.4	33.9
St. Charles	18 421	80.6	181 000	22.3	11.1	871	30.7	1.9	25 750	0.7	1 455	5.7	24 910	31.8	26.0
St. Helena	4 155	82.6	83 400	22.3	11.5	636	33.6	5.7	4 585	0.7	408	8.9	3 783	17.7	31.3
St. James	7 925	80.1	128 100	19.7	10.0	708	30.1	4.0	9 895	0.9	826	8.3	9 057	24.6	32.3
St. John the Baptist	15 444	76.8	149 200	23.1	10.1	875	31.5	3.4	20 553	0.5	1 510	7.3	19 638	27.6	28.5
St. Landry	30 664	70.3	88 700	19.9	10.0	578	34.8	3.1	33 832	-1.3	2 689	7.9	31 232	25.0	28.8
St. Martin	18 834	79.6	98 500	19.2	10.0	660	27.6	4.0	24 235	-2.1	1 633	6.7	23 811	23.5	31.1
St. Mary	20 183	68.9	89 700	20.5	10.4	671	27.1	5.0	24 523	-3.5	1 835	7.5	21 469	24.8	35.4
St. Tammany	87 975	77.5	197 500	22.9	10.1	991	32.1	1.5	116 272	0.8	6 219	5.3	109 434	37.6	19.2
Tangipahoa	45 027	67.9	135 400	21.9	10.0	748	34.0	3.2	54 029	0.2	3 870	7.2	52 234	29.0	27.1
Tensas	1 936	62.7	55 600	20.6	12.3	472	32.7	2.8	1 735	-3.2	169	9.7	1 742	22.4	26.6
Terrebonne	39 635	72.3	133 900	19.3	10.0	865	27.8	4.6	53 135	-3.1	3 132	5.9	48 382	24.7	33.3
Union	8 712	79.3	83 300	21.1	10.0	499	37.6	4.5	9 418	0.1	661	7.0	8 214	23.2	36.7
Vermilion	21 623	75.5	97 600	18.4	10.0	633	25.5	5.1	26 123	-1.9	1 764	6.8	24 848	24.8	34.1
Vernon	18 112	54.7	93 400	17.7	10.0	908	25.8	2.3	17 703	1.1	1 363	7.7	17 546	30.8	24.7
Washington	17 589	72.6	79 200	23.4	10.8	567	36.2	4.1	17 043	0.1	1 293	7.6	15 290	26.5	30.1
Webster	15 831	71.1	82 400	19.6	10.4	601	30.2	2.9	15 690	-0.3	1 367	8.7	15 345	24.6	32.7
West Baton Rouge	9 030	69.6	149 500	19.3	10.0	797	27.0	2.1	13 169	1.9	738	5.6	11 490	29.3	28.2
West Carroll	4 216	68.7	67 000	18.8	10.0	526	27.8	3.1	4 162	-2.3	555	13.3	4 136	23.5	31.0
West Feliciana	3 976	73.9	166 000	20.8	10.0	769	25.9	5.4	5 460	1.5	285	5.2	4 966	39.8	20.7
Winn	5 371	69.2	68 400	17.2	10.6	569	30.8	2.8	5 382	-1.6	448	8.3	4 967	29.9	31.4
MAINE	553 086	71.4	173 600	23.6	14.0	772	31.0	2.2	679 751	-2.4	29 895	4.4	646 438	35.3	22.4
Androscoggin	44 391	64.1	152 800	23.4	14.8	706	29.8	2.5	54 566	-2.4	2 259	4.1	51 426	31.7	23.6
Aroostook	30 571	71.1	92 500	21.2	12.9	557	29.3	2.2	31 629	-4.0	1 895	6.0	31 039	30.1	26.8
Cumberland	117 406	68.0	242 000	24.2	14.4	956	31.1	2.0	156 529	-1.6	5 300	3.4	151 278	43.7	15.6
Franklin	11 975	78.2	130 800	22.2	11.7	635	32.4	3.4	14 492	-3.4	691	4.8	14 321	29.9	27.9
Hancock	24 317	72.9	197 800	24.1	14.0	792	32.2	3.1	28 857	-3.1	1 635	5.7	27 021	35.1	25.1
Kennebec	51 242	70.2	151 400	21.9	13.2	704	30.8	1.6	61 366	-3.1	2 597	4.2	57 497	34.9	22.0
Knox	17 038	78.0	193 300	25.7	14.3	754	28.6	2.3	20 282	-1.8	831	4.1	19 483	32.0	25.2
Lincoln	14 905	81.3	209 900	25.1	13.6	809	28.7	2.5	16 678	-3.0	741	4.4	16 446	34.2	25.2
Oxford	22 392	78.2	136 100	24.2	14.6	623	33.5	2.4	26 479	-3.3	1 447	5.5	25 429	26.7	31.3
Penobscot	62 215	67.4	137 700	22.2	13.4	730	33.1	2.3	76 643	-3.0	3 649	4.8	72 696	34.5	20.5
Piscataquis	7 666	76.9	107 300	23.9	14.7	609	30.2	3.1	7 450	-3.4	429	5.8	6 954	29.5	31.7
Sagadahoc	15 108	76.3	190 800	23.2	13.4	781	35.3	1.8	18 790	-1.3	658	3.5	17 477	37.4	21.0
Somerset	21 567	78.2	110 500	22.9	14.1	674	33.5	3.1	23 453	-3.5	1 540	6.6	22 190	26.8	32.5
Waldo	16 527	77.7	156 000	24.6	14.1	724	31.0	2.5	20 354	-2.2	1 042	5.1	18 086	32.8	25.6
Washington	14 173	76.0	104 700	23.6	14.0	571	26.3	3.2	13 988	-3.2	928	6.6	13 169	28.7	30.9
York	81 593	72.7	226 700	24.7	14.8	883	30.5	1.5	108 195	-1.6	4 253	3.9	101 926	34.2	22.9
MARYLAND	2 155 983	67.1	287 500	24.0	12.1	1 218	30.9	2.4	3 151 932	0.8	163 827	5.2	2 949 440	44.5	15.7
Allegany	28 490	69.4	120 800	21.1	13.8	618	30.9	1.6	32 732	-1.7	2 311	7.1	29 719	29.7	22.6
Anne Arundel	201 429	74.2	333 100	23.6	11.5	1 479	29.2	1.8	300 068	0.8	13 543	4.5	280 719	45.6	15.0
Baltimore	313 408	66.2	248 700	23.1	12.0	1 155	30.6	2.0	444 854	0.7	24 228	5.4	409 624	43.6	15.6
Calvert	31 041	81.2	347 300	23.9	11.5	1 477	30.6	1.5	47 681	0.9	2 215	4.6	45 190	40.4	19.6
Caroline	11 842	70.8	203 900	27.2	14.2	947	32.7	3.3	17 461	0.2	975	5.6	15 184	25.5	29.6
Carroll	59 907	82.5	322 000	23.9	12.5	1 060	29.6	1.2	93 569	1.0	4 034	4.3	88 599	43.6	17.7
Cecil	36 453	73.2	244 600	24.1	14.2	996	29.7	1.7	53 245	1.5	3 203	6.0	48 288	34.8	24.7
Charles	52 269	77.9	287 000	24.4	11.4	1 505	34.1	1.4	80 945	0.9	4 096	5.1	75 526	42.0	16.3
Dorchester	13 419	65.8	188 100	26.0	15.3	842	32.8	1.8	15 849	0.3	1 166	7.4	15 270	29.4	28.3
Frederick	87 259	74.4	301 300	23.5	11.5	1 272	30.6	1.7	129 295	0.9	5 867	4.5	125 473	46.5	15.4
Garrett	11 851	75.8	165 500	24.1	11.3	657	28.7	1.7	15 564	0.1	1 012	6.5	13 898	31.1	28.2
Harford	91 037	79.1	279 300	23.4	11.9	1 139	29.7	1.2	136 343	0.7	6 847	5.0	126 658	42.3	17.7
Howard	107 516	73.3	426 300	22.8	10.0	1 548	29.2	2.0	175 167	0.9	6 872	3.9	160 742	60.2	9.0
Kent	7 448	72.3	244 600	24.4	13.5	913	29.9	2.0	10 625	2.6	579	5.4	8 915	36.3	21.3
Montgomery	362 608	66.6	448 700	23.4	10.4	1 611	30.7	3.0	549 287	0.8	21 777	4.0	533 893	56.0	10.1
Prince George's	305 115	62.3	258 800	26.9	11.8	1 276	31.3	3.9	490 697	0.8	26 048	5.3	459 978	37.4	18.1
Queen Anne's	17 354	84.6	341 100	24.7	12.9	1 211	29.9	1.4	26 694	1.2	1 228	4.6	25 061	40.1	17.7

1. Specified owner-occupied units.   2. A value of 10.0 represents 10 percent or less; a value of 50.0 represents 50 percent or more.   3. Specified renter-occupied units.
4. Overcrowded or lacking complete plumbing facilities.   5. Percent of civilian labor force.   6. Persons 16 years old and over.

	Private nonfarm establishments, employment and payroll, 2014								Agriculture, 2012			
		Employment						Annual payroll	Farms			
											Percent with:	
STATE County	Number of establish-ments	Total	Health care and social assistance	Manufac-turing	Retail trade	Finance and insurance	Professional, scientific, and technical services	Total (mil dol)	Average per employee (dollars)	Number	Fewer than 50 acres	500 acres or more	Farm operators whose principal occu-pation is farming (percent)
	104	105	106	107	108	109	110	111	112	113	114	115	116
LOUISIANA—Cont'd													
Orleans	8 853	169 860	22 509	5 860	12 637	5 948	14 132	8 217	48 374	14	100.0	0.0	64.3
Ouachita	4 220	62 579	14 467	4 735	9 666	4 038	2 790	2 225	35 553	450	48.2	9.1	41.1
Plaquemines	699	11 741	483	2 045	564	124	364	785	66 845	140	52.1	20.7	42.9
Pointe Coupee	359	4 244	D	D	906	190	95	160	37 648	393	39.4	18.1	47.1
Rapides	3 149	47 950	13 977	3 594	7 683	1 547	1 911	1 780	37 122	853	54.6	9.5	50.1
Red River	134	2 059	450	D	D	75	D	89	43 457	252	32.9	21.0	56.0
Richland	412	5 524	1 825	D	819	188	81	170	30 756	762	31.8	19.2	47.1
Sabine	492	4 165	825	670	907	D	258	148	35 616	392	37.5	4.3	51.3
St. Bernard	677	7 804	720	1 280	1 733	167	137	325	41 699	56	46.4	23.2	60.7
St. Charles	968	20 810	1 436	4 578	1 304	259	2 028	1 357	65 218	70	45.7	2.9	64.3
St. Helena	112	1 208	428	D	296	D	D	36	30 193	373	41.3	7.2	44.0
St. James	318	6 244	469	2 174	521	186	D	417	66 840	63	46.0	25.4	61.9
St. John the Baptist	695	14 825	1 070	2 480	1 620	297	394	728	49 082	23	39.1	13.0	56.5
St. Landry	1 593	22 178	5 731	1 328	3 762	760	579	819	36 946	1 338	51.0	10.6	40.3
St. Martin	970	12 576	1 667	1 891	1 651	334	321	562	44 676	340	64.1	12.1	44.4
St. Mary	1 315	22 131	1 868	3 960	2 236	528	655	1 115	50 387	128	46.9	32.0	50.8
St. Tammany	6 191	76 382	15 087	3 643	13 560	3 240	5 746	3 210	42 023	604	74.3	1.8	42.4
Tangipahoa	2 307	34 530	8 718	2 322	6 433	2 073	1 014	1 224	35 458	1 070	52.1	3.0	44.1
Tensas	79	505	70	D	82	D	D	17	33 503	251	27.1	29.1	37.8
Terrebonne	3 020	54 990	7 375	7 642	7 232	1 199	2 652	2 805	51 007	189	47.6	14.8	58.7
Union	332	4 097	761	D	579	114	54	118	28 923	413	31.0	4.1	48.2
Vermilion	1 047	10 516	1 851	414	2 071	467	336	410	38 952	1 184	43.2	10.9	53.7
Vernon	722	8 648	1 959	145	1 634	313	1 008	302	34 920	471	53.1	2.5	49.7
Washington	634	8 916	2 424	D	1 367	309	115	278	31 191	826	52.8	3.1	44.1
Webster	802	11 122	2 319	1 613	2 061	397	230	418	37 593	447	40.5	2.7	44.7
West Baton Rouge	542	10 980	423	2 171	1 073	180	170	531	48 378	106	66.0	15.1	50.9
West Carroll	186	1 702	523	D	382	78	D	47	27 397	733	28.5	9.5	25.0
West Feliciana	187	2 668	399	D	284	D	D	147	55 154	163	28.2	28.2	40.5
Winn	287	4 289	D	693	D	120	D	162	37 718	179	37.4	3.4	43.6
MAINE	40 369	492 690	107 476	48 760	81 554	26 294	23 627	19 632	39 846	8 173	43.0	6.7	48.5
Androscoggin	2 667	44 283	9 590	5 082	6 087	3 155	2 122	1 681	37 968	463	51.6	5.0	56.4
Aroostook	1 974	21 024	5 863	2 827	4 363	759	331	677	32 216	895	18.2	19.1	43.9
Cumberland	10 926	160 331	32 671	9 148	22 343	12 625	10 225	7 375	45 996	718	60.6	4.2	46.5
Franklin	814	9 147	1 688	D	1 660	D	133	286	31 213	388	43.6	3.9	34.3
Hancock	2 179	16 598	3 008	1 485	3 268	535	1 957	672	40 473	404	50.0	5.0	52.0
Kennebec	3 218	45 581	13 036	2 648	8 308	1 296	1 672	1 698	37 260	604	47.4	4.6	45.7
Knox	1 715	14 166	3 160	1 637	2 722	658	441	497	35 074	314	53.8	1.6	54.8
Lincoln	1 395	8 374	1 876	752	1 606	330	305	293	34 973	344	53.2	1.5	51.2
Oxford	1 286	14 225	2 838	2 213	2 220	329	336	474	33 314	551	44.5	6.4	44.8
Penobscot	4 138	57 531	14 011	3 445	11 094	1 902	1 773	2 025	35 192	677	36.9	7.7	51.7
Piscataquis	436	4 543	D	1 039	854	71	50	145	31 929	203	21.7	9.4	51.2
Sagadahoc	923	13 169	1 390	D	1 866	285	928	616	46 781	229	53.7	3.1	48.9
Somerset	1 173	13 870	2 677	D	2 333	265	388	543	39 126	579	32.5	11.4	50.3
Waldo	967	8 644	1 706	1 170	1 427	D	195	300	34 749	633	41.5	3.5	48.7
Washington	828	7 000	1 669	869	1 770	276	132	232	33 091	392	35.5	8.7	44.9
York	5 500	51 699	10 878	6 510	9 631	1 613	2 021	1 940	37 519	779	53.8	1.5	54.0
MARYLAND	136 501	2 216 867	360 751	96 939	291 866	99 391	280 028	114 338	51 576	12 256	49.2	7.6	48.9
Allegany	1 575	24 909	5 965	2 469	3 860	822	1 520	811	32 542	291	30.9	2.1	43.0
Anne Arundel	13 881	222 781	27 079	11 250	33 591	5 575	28 243	11 574	51 953	381	66.9	2.9	57.5
Baltimore	19 869	310 382	57 326	14 783	49 064	19 746	25 512	14 385	46 347	640	63.0	3.1	49.5
Calvert	1 671	17 579	3 362	417	3 071	347	1 221	733	41 686	269	49.4	5.9	45.0
Caroline	593	6 970	808	D	1 317	156	250	248	35 514	658	37.4	14.7	60.0
Carroll	4 215	49 797	9 944	3 404	8 543	1 055	2 506	1 835	36 852	1 092	59.3	4.9	39.7
Cecil	1 771	24 487	4 873	D	3 880	452	494	1 080	44 109	496	54.4	7.3	51.2
Charles	2 618	32 571	4 945	438	8 358	746	2 228	1 185	36 389	382	52.1	5.0	52.6
Dorchester	710	9 233	1 863	2 405	1 191	203	184	314	33 959	423	36.2	16.1	54.1
Frederick	5 975	86 414	11 460	5 870	12 641	5 829	7 814	3 989	46 165	1 308	49.5	6.0	47.6
Garrett	897	11 089	1 667	1 177	1 631	362	405	369	33 314	667	31.8	4.2	49.0
Harford	5 377	70 062	11 172	4 662	14 945	1 920	8 241	2 803	40 008	582	58.4	4.5	42.8
Howard	9 139	168 040	14 920	4 856	16 409	6 898	39 264	10 047	59 789	293	65.9	7.2	37.9
Kent	631	7 304	1 272	1 078	1 010	193	206	243	33 245	367	27.0	17.7	49.3
Montgomery	27 113	429 302	65 377	7 542	46 208	20 395	82 644	27 577	64 237	540	66.9	4.8	42.0
Prince George's	14 459	250 855	30 300	6 821	37 844	5 877	34 909	11 620	46 320	347	61.4	2.3	44.4
Queen Anne's	1 355	11 634	941	1 071	2 616	360	550	390	33 516	530	36.6	17.0	48.9

Table B. States and Counties — **Agriculture**

		Land in farms			Value of land and buildings (dollars)			Value of products sold				Percent of farms with sales of:		Government payments	
			Acres							Percent from:					
STATE County	Acreage (1,000)	Percent change, 2007–2012	Average size of farm	Total irrigated (1,000)	Total cropland (1,000)	Average per farm	Average per acre	Value of machinery and equipment, average per farm (dollars)	Total (mil dol)	Average per farm (dollars)	Crops	Live-stock and poultry products	$10,000 or more	$100,000 or more	Total ($1,000)	Percent of farms
	117	118	119	120	121	122	123	124	125	126	127	128	129	130	131	132
LOUISIANA—Cont'd																
Orleans	111	D	8	0.0	0.0	122 786	15 486	114 143	0.5	37 143	41.2	59.0	42.9	7.1	D	7.1
Ouachita	93	9.1	207	12.1	47.4	603 420	2 916	72 287	49.1	109 047	54.9	45.1	29.3	9.8	1 933	25.8
Plaquemines	89	-26.8	635	0.1	8.5	801 564	1 262	64 250	15.0	107 457	39.1	61.0	61.4	15.0	60	7.9
Pointe Coupee	182	-4.4	464	6.1	143.8	1 272 481	2 744	240 089	130.1	331 163	95.8	4.2	58.8	18.3	2 786	41.0
Rapides	211	19.0	247	21.1	132.1	628 930	2 543	99 732	132.2	154 972	88.3	11.7	42.3	16.4	3 644	22.2
Red River	135	31.0	537	3.0	34.3	1 049 234	1 954	129 516	38.6	153 024	33.5	66.5	41.3	15.5	1 506	34.9
Richland	279	-4.2	366	85.1	189.5	840 475	2 296	126 639	127.3	167 038	93.5	6.5	37.1	18.2	10 171	76.1
Sabine	52	2.5	132	0.1	12.0	420 495	3 180	71 528	142.1	362 612	0.9	99.1	37.8	14.0	441	11.5
St. Bernard	32	-0.5	569	0.0	4.3	946 804	1 663	68 750	5.8	103 482	2.7	97.3	32.1	12.5	19	14.3
St. Charles	16	D	232	D	1.9	501 871	2 166	57 929	1.2	16 571	12.8	87.3	44.3	0.0	D	8.6
St. Helena	53	1.4	142	1.4	17.0	476 399	3 346	62 539	25.6	68 542	8.3	91.7	28.4	7.5	298	18.2
St. James	40	-7.7	634	0.0	37.1	2 231 444	3 520	369 730	33.2	526 270	98.8	1.2	58.7	28.6	84	17.5
St. John the Baptist	11	-21.5	468	0.0	8.0	1 361 261	2 910	240 391	9.3	402 696	98.6	1.4	43.5	13.0	D	4.3
St. Landry	301	0.8	225	29.8	223.9	540 722	2 405	90 250	125.0	93 408	91.7	8.3	28.3	9.7	5 809	39.3
St. Martin	76	-3.8	223	6.7	58.2	552 229	2 473	154 956	52.8	155 250	91.0	9.0	37.1	14.1	506	17.6
St. Mary	76	4.6	594	0.0	63.0	1 490 961	2 508	392 164	65.8	513 867	98.4	1.6	43.8	27.3	173	21.1
St. Tammany	34	-25.0	56	0.4	7.9	413 126	7 315	44 215	11.3	18 685	61.1	38.9	22.2	4.0	38	2.5
Tangipahoa	107	-13.8	100	0.7	36.3	410 570	4 117	54 967	45.7	42 694	40.2	59.8	29.1	7.2	790	17.3
Tensas	197	-12.8	783	40.3	168.2	1 721 227	2 197	275 825	129.2	514 558	99.8	0.2	37.5	29.5	7 350	86.5
Terrebonne	93	-47.0	492	0.6	21.5	1 102 540	2 243	147 534	37.1	196 418	43.6	56.4	37.0	13.2	95	9.0
Union	63	-7.0	152	0.0	16.8	441 254	2 909	75 138	92.0	224 986	1.5	98.5	40.7	15.3	166	9.2
Vermilion	284	-2.3	240	59.2	171.9	622 631	2 599	100 574	141.1	119 207	69.7	30.3	36.7	10.3	6 832	57.3
Vernon	49	-3.2	104	0.0	8.9	328 764	3 160	43 987	3.2	6 794	29.0	70.9	14.0	0.6	89	4.0
Washington	81	-16.7	99	0.4	28.6	349 438	3 545	54 988	28.3	34 259	40.2	59.8	23.0	4.4	434	14.6
Webster	52	5.6	117	D	10.1	407 367	3 483	51 532	10.1	22 501	17.3	82.7	27.1	2.2	81	7.2
West Baton Rouge	30	17.4	286	0.1	25.6	1 071 953	3 750	222 868	31.4	295 934	88.7	11.3	39.6	17.9	181	33.0
West Carroll	166	-15.8	226	45.2	115.9	482 630	2 135	86 151	72.5	98 966	97.1	2.9	19.9	11.3	5 879	83.8
West Feliciana	101	51.9	621	0.0	28.9	1 639 712	2 639	99 767	18.7	114 497	76.8	23.2	41.1	8.0	273	30.7
Winn	25	16.7	139	0.0	4.1	337 184	2 418	59 615	18.0	100 575	4.0	96.0	24.6	4.5	118	14.0
MAINE	1 454	7.9	178	30.9	477.3	410 633	2 308	69 762	763.1	93 364	62.1	37.9	34.6	9.5	10 162	16.3
Androscoggin	59	16.9	128	0.8	22.0	329 181	2 564	72 955	53.8	116 266	22.1	77.9	32.8	8.0	445	15.6
Aroostook	351	-6.6	392	11.4	187.5	559 514	1 427	157 318	210.5	235 215	91.6	8.4	42.9	21.5	2 492	43.0
Cumberland	63	21.2	87	0.7	18.0	428 535	4 907	61 922	26.3	36 635	65.6	34.4	33.7	7.5	497	8.1
Franklin	49	21.3	127	0.1	9.6	276 724	2 172	47 778	D	D	D	D	22.4	5.4	595	17.8
Hancock	53	1.2	132	0.2	12.0	444 960	3 369	51 351	D	D	D	D	38.6	6.9	187	14.9
Kennebec	78	-5.3	129	0.4	32.8	370 354	2 866	69 992	49.8	82 505	28.9	71.1	36.8	8.8	711	12.3
Knox	29	-2.3	94	0.3	7.5	355 739	3 798	35 876	D	D	D	D	31.2	4.1	116	14.6
Lincoln	32	5.2	92	0.1	7.4	320 218	3 489	43 009	10.2	29 541	51.2	48.8	32.8	5.5	269	7.8
Oxford	75	9.5	137	0.4	15.7	347 443	2 543	48 483	19.2	34 880	75.4	24.6	27.0	5.3	488	12.5
Penobscot	113	-1.4	167	2.3	35.6	336 186	2 015	63 316	50.2	74 084	32.3	67.7	33.4	9.0	1 044	13.3
Piscataquis	47	37.1	230	0.2	12.4	394 502	1 715	49 310	D	D	D	D	29.1	9.4	405	22.2
Sagadahoc	20	7.9	88	0.2	5.2	331 555	3 779	39 664	D	D	D	D	30.1	5.7	139	7.4
Somerset	140	25.7	242	0.2	30.2	512 425	2 119	92 294	86.4	149 278	64.1	35.9	44.7	19.2	1 053	16.6
Waldo	131	91.5	206	0.2	24.8	384 874	1 865	39 363	D	D	D	D	29.1	6.5	837	16.6
Washington	149	-5.9	380	12.1	35.7	594 518	1 564	79 079	154.6	394 508	D	D	45.7	9.4	526	18.6
York	65	8.7	83	1.3	21.0	403 257	4 869	58 392	27.5	35 239	D	D	31.8	6.4	358	5.9
MARYLAND	2 031	-1.0	166	104.9	1 396.1	1 148 268	6 930	115 879	2 271.4	185 329	46.3	53.7	43.1	20.6	36 024	37.8
Allegany	36	-1.0	125	0.0	11.8	435 282	3 493	52 261	3.1	10 735	59.5	40.5	30.6	1.0	253	31.6
Anne Arundel	28	-3.9	74	0.3	14.7	854 354	11 579	71 680	19.7	51 627	84.0	16.0	25.7	5.8	160	10.0
Baltimore	70	-10.0	110	0.5	44.6	1 038 656	9 440	91 152	76.3	119 228	88.6	11.4	34.5	12.5	840	18.3
Calvert	33	24.4	122	0.2	21.2	921 743	7 536	72 149	11.1	41 416	95.3	4.7	37.2	9.7	523	23.8
Caroline	150	14.5	229	27.0	121.4	1 395 853	6 109	155 213	257.9	391 968	33.1	66.9	68.2	46.0	3 335	61.7
Carroll	133	-6.6	121	1.4	97.2	989 130	8 144	101 499	111.6	102 232	67.3	32.7	34.5	12.6	3 440	40.2
Cecil	77	-9.8	155	0.6	54.8	1 121 347	7 255	132 554	113.8	229 466	60.3	39.7	43.8	19.4	1 505	30.4
Charles	47	-10.5	122	0.5	25.3	788 220	6 453	70 134	11.9	31 272	89.8	10.2	26.4	6.5	508	22.8
Dorchester	126	-5.1	299	22.4	92.0	1 557 508	5 211	204 546	187.1	442 215	37.3	62.7	51.1	40.0	2 501	75.9
Frederick	182	-10.2	139	1.4	127.1	1 053 941	7 595	108 462	150.5	115 030	49.5	50.5	41.1	17.9	3 060	33.6
Garrett	95	-0.3	143	0.0	41.5	600 378	4 207	80 346	31.5	47 168	34.7	65.3	46.0	14.4	540	18.9
Harford	65	-12.9	112	0.5	40.4	929 613	8 264	89 722	46.0	79 041	68.1	31.9	33.8	12.9	894	28.5
Howard	37	27.6	128	0.2	20.9	1 401 898	10 961	84 051	31.9	108 816	86.9	13.1	32.4	11.9	309	20.8
Kent	133	3.9	363	8.3	104.6	2 472 676	6 813	197 866	112.3	305 858	69.8	30.2	61.3	33.2	2 931	77.9
Montgomery	63	-6.1	118	1.0	45.6	1 195 894	10 171	101 435	48.3	89 520	86.6	13.4	29.1	10.6	836	17.2
Prince George's	33	-11.9	94	0.8	14.4	741 326	7 889	56 916	18.0	51 873	91.3	8.7	30.0	5.2	157	11.5
Queen Anne's	157	6.8	296	15.8	129.9	2 204 232	7 444	181 240	166.9	314 821	61.9	38.1	53.2	35.1	4 242	73.6

Table B. States and Counties — Water Use, Wholesale Trade, Retail Trade, and Real Estate

STATE County	Water use, 2010 Total water withdrawn (mil gal/day)	Gallons withdrawn per person per day	Wholesale trade,[1] 2012 Number of establishments	Number of employees	Sales (mil dol)	Annual payroll (mil dol)	Retail trade,[2] 2012 Number of establishments	Number of employees	Sales (mil dol)	Annual payroll (mil dol)	Real estate and rental and leasing,[2] 2012 Number of establishments	Number of employees	Receipts (mil dol)	Annual payroll (mil dol)
	133	134	135	136	137	138	139	140	141	142	143	144	145	146
LOUISIANA—Cont'd														
Orleans	615.3	1 790	256	3 794	2 687.0	191.5	1 275	12 371	3 245.1	337.8	379	2 156	411.6	79.1
Ouachita	68.2	443	182	D	D	D	710	9 203	2 387.1	205.9	185	1 145	228.0	37.9
Plaquemines	85.1	3 694	54	982	2 228.3	57.5	66	499	134.1	13.3	41	364	116.3	23.0
Pointe Coupee	343.8	15 077	10	140	436.2	6.3	77	775	201.2	17.0	12	37	10.7	1.7
Rapides	547.9	4 163	123	D	D	D	584	7 769	2 211.5	188.3	137	D	D	D
Red River	4.4	484	7	70	22.9	2.3	18	154	37.3	2.6	3	D	D	D
Richland	30.6	1 474	21	234	529.8	13.8	65	715	250.4	16.9	16	113	8.1	2.0
Sabine	4.2	172	14	123	55.8	4.6	79	860	217.2	19.3	13	23	3.1	0.4
St. Bernard	260.7	7 263	26	D	D	D	137	1 432	392.2	35.7	19	60	8.9	2.2
St. Charles	2 475.5	46 903	73	1 944	4 939.9	105.6	112	1 184	402.9	31.0	35	172	49.9	9.3
St. Helena	1.1	96	2	D	D	D	29	345	80.0	4.4	2	D	D	D
St. James	192.4	8 703	10	D	D	D	50	490	128.6	10.7	6	14	1.8	0.3
St. John the Baptist	67.5	1 471	29	D	D	D	118	1 586	479.2	36.4	29	199	58.2	8.7
St. Landry	77.3	926	59	578	782.4	24.5	305	3 806	976.8	86.8	53	674	124.3	31.0
St. Martin	39.5	757	52	795	458.3	43.5	142	1 615	559.0	33.9	38	814	352.9	59.5
St. Mary	120.7	2 208	75	D	D	D	198	2 295	605.2	54.2	80	1 141	259.8	65.0
St. Tammany	28.6	122	244	2 224	5 060.2	125.1	915	12 433	3 550.7	301.2	215	1 112	250.7	55.5
Tangipahoa	20.1	166	86	1 701	1 300.4	68.5	438	6 290	1 769.7	144.7	94	498	86.5	18.5
Tensas	31.7	6 043	9	72	195.4	3.7	15	78	27.7	1.8	NA	NA	NA	NA
Terrebonne	5.9	52	196	2 102	996.0	113.8	503	7 070	1 929.4	170.2	167	1 690	471.5	101.9
Union	4.1	179	5	D	D	D	66	609	141.3	14.4	5	9	1.3	0.2
Vermilion	93.7	1 616	33	307	235.8	15.1	180	2 057	577.3	47.8	39	224	41.9	9.0
Vernon	8.5	162	18	90	57.3	3.3	134	1 537	426.7	34.7	31	268	70.5	11.3
Washington	34.6	733	20	118	128.3	3.5	138	1 152	297.0	26.5	15	41	4.0	0.8
Webster	7.3	177	34	394	204.7	15.4	163	2 193	549.4	47.2	33	155	34.4	6.7
West Baton Rouge	10.8	454	43	755	967.9	41.2	85	1 173	455.5	25.3	11	121	29.2	5.9
West Carroll	15.2	1 308	5	D	D	D	34	397	87.4	7.8	5	12	1.8	0.3
West Feliciana	41.6	2 664	3	D	D	D	28	283	86.6	5.7	6	D	D	D
Winn	2.3	152	10	108	65.2	3.8	48	543	113.9	11.3	8	29	3.3	0.8
MAINE	449.3	338	1 344	14 753	12 961.3	691.5	6 351	80 155	21 521.7	1 884.6	1 580	6 242	1 100.4	220.6
Androscoggin	15.3	142	102	1 236	473.9	54.6	439	6 018	1 818.1	138.5	111	376	62.9	11.6
Aroostook	23.0	320	72	503	308.9	21.8	346	4 186	1 119.4	90.0	76	252	50.4	6.5
Cumberland	64.1	228	456	5 956	5 925.3	308.3	1 448	21 738	5 751.4	522.3	516	2 787	519.6	109.3
Franklin	39.1	1 270	14	D	D	D	161	1 623	395.5	34.4	27	68	8.2	1.6
Hancock	31.2	573	59	464	244.5	14.7	379	3 471	852.6	86.4	80	185	27.2	5.5
Kennebec	12.9	105	96	1 990	1 613.7	96.4	526	8 111	2 179.3	201.2	99	429	65.5	14.1
Knox	5.0	126	49	256	165.9	9.6	257	2 656	632.9	60.7	69	151	22.2	5.5
Lincoln	2.5	74	30	D	D	D	210	1 648	421.7	39.6	49	114	15.2	3.2
Oxford	37.2	644	34	D	D	D	224	2 212	611.4	53.6	37	129	14.6	3.5
Penobscot	58.4	379	162	1 794	955.4	82.3	735	10 931	3 203.1	249.6	172	692	123.3	22.9
Piscataquis	2.5	141	8	D	D	D	91	823	212.2	19.0	12	27	3.3	0.6
Sagadahoc	2.6	74	22	108	43.5	3.8	141	1 864	465.5	42.8	32	60	8.7	1.9
Somerset	72.9	1 396	28	176	61.1	6.6	213	2 353	611.0	51.9	31	219	48.7	10.0
Waldo	4.0	103	23	D	D	D	163	1 479	365.7	34.4	29	59	7.1	2.1
Washington	31.4	956	45	230	125.4	5.2	150	1 670	433.1	37.1	20	46	4.1	1.2
York	47.3	240	144	1 163	818.2	55.2	868	9 372	2 448.7	223.0	220	648	119.4	21.0
MARYLAND	7 382.0	1 279	4 768	73 369	60 734.2	4 378.5	18 179	281 678	76 379.7	7 168.5	6 001	42 838	13 410.1	2 253.2
Allegany	42.2	562	45	D	D	D	288	3 854	922.8	81.5	52	199	29.3	5.6
Anne Arundel	341.2	635	492	8 187	7 606.5	484.5	2 005	33 052	8 758.8	831.2	566	4 232	1 254.5	203.5
Baltimore	673.3	836	749	10 796	5 548.5	609.6	2 745	47 973	12 645.7	1 235.1	855	6 432	3 201.7	344.6
Calvert	3 265.4	36 798	42	268	91.8	13.6	205	2 955	848.4	72.4	80	285	79.2	15.3
Caroline	19.7	594	21	186	118.9	8.3	86	980	476.2	28.7	15	D	D	D
Carroll	13.8	83	150	1 286	723.9	61.7	495	7 901	2 245.2	184.3	137	474	83.1	15.7
Cecil	8.4	83	60	D	D	D	264	3 895	1 146.3	87.9	72	191	27.7	5.5
Charles	1 282.1	8 748	56	435	950.4	21.1	495	8 729	2 245.0	207.7	107	394	97.3	13.3
Dorchester	21.0	643	32	276	234.2	12.2	100	1 133	288.7	25.4	37	92	8.3	2.6
Frederick	40.6	174	199	2 212	1 185.8	119.4	736	11 814	3 267.7	299.3	246	864	207.0	39.8
Garrett	7.7	257	23	D	D	D	136	1 714	517.9	39.1	34	D	D	D
Harford	19.1	78	170	1 865	2 420.7	99.4	723	13 420	3 792.9	342.6	215	751	192.9	27.9
Howard	4.1	14	478	11 707	9 266.7	784.1	854	15 811	4 867.7	427.7	379	3 356	1 025.9	181.9
Kent	5.2	257	24	172	127.1	6.9	99	848	185.9	18.6	25	57	18.0	2.0
Montgomery	737.9	759	676	9 113	10 456.8	672.7	2 702	46 240	13 706.2	1 333.7	1 324	12 342	4 534.5	829.3
Prince George's	745.3	863	536	11 108	7 639.8	651.0	2 217	36 414	9 358.1	907.2	640	6 216	1 186.5	281.3
Queen Anne's	14.0	294	70	778	353.0	37.8	210	2 305	547.5	49.1	47	155	36.1	4.8

1. Merchant wholesalers, except manufacturers' sales branches and offices.　2. Employer establishments.

Table B. States and Counties — Professional Services, Manufacturing, and Accommodation and Food Services

STATE County	Professional, scientific, and technical services, 2012				Manufacturing, 2012				Accommodation and food services, 2012			
	Number of establishments	Number of employees	Receipts (mil dol)	Annual payroll (mil dol)	Number of establishments	Number of employees	Receipts (mil dol)	Annual payroll (mil dol)	Number of establishments	Number of employees	Sales (mil dol)	Annual payroll (mil dol)
	147	148	149	150	151	152	153	154	155	156	157	158
LOUISIANA—Cont'd												
Orleans	1 450	13 212	2 613.2	971.7	144	6 049	4 352.7	335.6	1 300	35 510	2 765.4	764.7
Ouachita	435	2 696	373.8	123.8	126	D	D	D	294	D	D	D
Plaquemines	51	382	114.7	28.9	37	2 174	D	192.2	61	737	59.8	18.8
Pointe Coupee	30	99	15.8	5.4	8	385	D	16.0	37	344	18.5	3.8
Rapides	285	D	D	D	72	3 851	D	217.3	237	4 330	216.8	58.3
Red River	9	29	4.0	1.0	4	194	D	8.2	10	D	D	D
Richland	27	92	10.4	2.8	11	904	396.5	37.5	24	D	D	D
Sabine	50	185	19.8	7.6	16	753	D	36.1	25	D	D	D
St. Bernard	34	148	14.2	4.3	33	1 195	11 904.0	109.8	81	D	D	D
St. Charles	95	1 402	162.3	75.5	40	4 695	29 174.8	471.2	82	995	49.3	12.7
St. Helena	6	16	2.2	0.4	5	257	D	D	8	D	D	D
St. James	17	75	8.0	3.3	24	2 156	D	201.7	25	D	D	D
St. John the Baptist	57	335	46.3	15.3	24	2 788	D	234.5	75	1 235	58.5	14.4
St. Landry	142	553	78.8	25.3	57	1 353	3 421.2	60.8	99	1 594	76.6	21.0
St. Martin	100	325	50.6	13.5	69	1 911	D	86.0	75	1 321	63.2	15.5
St. Mary	104	614	97.7	34.5	81	4 170	1 901.2	249.1	107	2 823	201.1	55.7
St. Tammany	844	5 154	700.8	292.6	123	3 676	D	205.3	556	9 615	443.8	128.0
Tangipahoa	208	889	93.5	33.6	79	2 389	681.2	84.4	213	4 285	185.8	50.9
Tensas	2	D	D	D	3	13	D	D	6	D	D	D
Terrebonne	287	2 797	353.6	138.9	143	6 301	1 538.3	343.2	235	5 138	295.2	84.7
Union	14	41	5.3	1.4	10	D	D	D	16	D	D	D
Vermilion	118	291	33.0	11.6	40	636	D	24.9	61	928	49.4	11.3
Vernon	86	725	70.3	32.6	14	200	D	6.4	66	1 412	58.8	16.2
Washington	43	133	19.4	5.2	27	1 027	616.1	65.5	61	713	33.5	8.5
Webster	53	247	21.0	6.4	29	1 436	D	D	61	807	34.8	8.7
West Baton Rouge	26	238	22.2	8.1	36	2 300	7 272.3	151.5	56	878	49.1	10.9
West Carroll	11	D	D	D	3	D	D	D	11	186	6.3	1.8
West Feliciana	26	77	7.9	4.3	8	324	D	D	27	341	14.7	3.9
Winn	21	47	4.4	1.4	14	606	D	28.1	18	D	D	D
MAINE	3 492	22 943	3 352.6	1 238.0	1 650	49 238	16 044.5	2 424.3	3 958	49 672	2 901.3	850.8
Androscoggin	183	1 652	359.2	80.1	150	5 205	1 886.9	251.6	209	3 021	153.3	44.5
Aroostook	97	343	31.4	11.9	92	2 689	1 037.9	121.1	156	1 897	83.2	23.9
Cumberland	1 410	10 188	1 627.5	641.9	380	8 691	D	433.9	973	15 001	839.9	254.8
Franklin	43	D	D	D	25	1 454	D	72.7	92	1 114	41.4	12.8
Hancock	138	1 773	268.7	99.5	90	1 463	520.2	73.7	301	2 040	211.1	54.9
Kennebec	302	D	D	D	95	2 386	634.2	114.8	302	4 055	222.9	66.8
Knox	132	440	53.5	20.8	94	1 443	377.8	63.4	166	1 663	96.8	30.9
Lincoln	108	D	D	D	72	742	D	31.9	149	1 127	84.6	24.3
Oxford	75	307	32.8	10.9	61	2 434	860.6	138.6	133	2 562	103.8	32.5
Penobscot	328	1 831	179.4	84.5	134	3 749	977.7	164.0	315	5 639	313.9	86.7
Piscataquis	13	D	D	D	22	1 045	177.5	37.8	47	259	14.9	3.6
Sagadahoc	99	917	103.0	52.7	39	D	D	D	81	1 053	54.9	17.1
Somerset	59	332	37.1	13.4	72	3 330	1 607.3	177.8	92	846	43.8	12.8
Waldo	60	187	15.7	7.1	45	1 163	168.4	36.4	93	789	46.2	13.3
Washington	31	D	D	D	36	994	359.2	40.7	80	558	28.2	7.8
York	414	2 078	356.0	106.6	243	D	2 762.3	D	769	8 048	562.4	164.0
MARYLAND	19 714	244 710	50 024.9	20 161.2	3 096	100 079	39 533.0	5 908.9	11 344	204 222	12 516.8	3 410.5
Allegany	96	486	42.7	18.3	52	2 547	D	119.2	181	D	D	D
Anne Arundel	2 027	24 815	5 787.2	2 467.9	275	11 547	4 456.9	993.6	1 158	25 939	1 564.0	419.4
Baltimore	2 692	24 678	3 990.9	1 657.7	451	16 807	8 066.7	1 003.7	1 578	27 158	1 555.8	415.4
Calvert	215	1 286	162.5	54.7	38	455	84.1	18.8	146	D	D	D
Caroline	38	D	D	D	28	1 167	302.3	42.8	36	D	D	D
Carroll	494	2 471	324.9	125.6	124	3 402	1 019.4	178.4	262	5 810	246.8	73.1
Cecil	155	570	52.7	19.1	49	4 496	1 989.3	312.3	176	2 792	154.1	41.7
Charles	273	1 979	311.6	127.5	43	399	84.0	18.4	244	D	D	D
Dorchester	53	169	17.8	5.2	44	2 546	843.1	93.7	58	D	D	D
Frederick	845	6 686	1 098.7	427.9	163	6 026	3 236.1	354.3	441	8 452	449.6	130.0
Garrett	53	397	37.4	17.3	50	1 128	D	39.6	74	D	D	D
Harford	697	D	D	D	137	4 058	1 866.8	207.2	394	7 960	390.9	104.7
Howard	1 883	35 086	10 616.5	3 126.2	186	5 013	1 538.2	276.8	543	11 000	610.9	177.1
Kent	51	D	D	D	29	945	360.0	50.7	74	D	D	D
Montgomery	5 701	74 255	14 389.9	6 751.1	381	8 233	2 172.6	619.7	1 818	31 526	2 080.0	571.8
Prince George's	1 662	26 331	4 349.1	1 903.9	264	7 291	2 216.8	424.1	1 269	23 872	1 685.5	436.2
Queen Anne's	158	D	D	D	49	921	208.3	41.8	94	2 111	113.0	33.7

1. Establishment subject to federal tax.

Table B. States and Counties — Health Care and Social Assistance, Other Services, Nonemployer Businesses, and Residential Construction

STATE County	Health care and social assistance, 2012				Other services, 2012				Nonemployer businesses, 2014		Value of residential construction authorized by building permits, 2015	
	Number of establishments	Number of employees	Receipts (mil dol)	Annual payroll (mil dol)	Number of establishments	Number of employees	Receipts (mil dol)	Annual payroll (mil dol)	Number	Receipts (mil dol)	New Construction ($1,000)	Number of housing units
	159	160	161	162	163	164	165	166	167	168	169	170
LOUISIANA—Cont'd												
Orleans	861	21 761	2 667.4	964.2	578	4 297	791.8	139.5	35 533	1 470.1	72 830	496
Ouachita	629	14 085	1 354.2	483.6	229	1 533	141.0	41.4	12 755	513.2	118 726	576
Plaquemines	21	468	40.0	17.7	44	D	D	D	2 411	136.9	14 429	56
Pointe Coupee	35	709	49.3	19.3	28	D	D	D	1 499	70.2	11 609	47
Rapides	506	14 112	1 514.4	554.9	198	1 018	104.1	27.5	7 781	360.7	37 650	240
Red River	15	444	37.8	11.4	6	D	D	D	500	14.2	0	0
Richland	80	1 783	100.9	40.6	18	D	D	D	1 404	53.1	5 977	25
Sabine	44	846	53.5	20.5	22	79	19.5	2.2	1 309	60.9	10 370	55
St. Bernard	51	D	D	D	37	D	D	D	3 440	132.3	12 533	79
St. Charles	65	D	D	D	50	D	D	D	4 074	168.9	28 260	134
St. Helena	14	D	D	D	7	D	D	D	783	18.9	0	0
St. James	28	764	69.8	29.3	16	D	D	D	1 376	44.4	11 393	43
St. John the Baptist	70	D	D	D	39	367	57.3	16.1	3 175	94.6	5 103	32
St. Landry	289	6 071	433.5	172.0	77	361	31.7	8.9	5 646	230.7	31 919	146
St. Martin	79	1 675	79.2	37.7	44	126	20.5	4.3	4 397	174.8	32 798	148
St. Mary	115	2 094	164.1	64.7	89	523	65.0	19.2	3 764	166.0	8 611	57
St. Tammany	791	14 504	1 581.8	607.7	356	1 993	219.0	60.3	23 491	1 238.4	314 297	1 255
Tangipahoa	301	8 143	655.2	261.4	149	966	98.1	25.5	9 468	350.3	89 632	627
Tensas	9	66	5.1	2.1	2	D	D	D	328	11.6	791	11
Terrebonne	284	6 992	704.8	288.9	175	1 449	232.6	73.0	7 991	392.2	56 484	213
Union	32	851	53.6	20.7	14	35	3.3	0.7	1 483	57.9	4 859	29
Vermilion	101	1 764	122.8	46.2	56	252	24.6	6.2	4 386	179.3	23 210	107
Vernon	77	2 010	222.5	85.8	41	170	15.3	3.6	2 037	80.0	10 780	54
Washington	84	2 309	171.6	73.6	28	106	10.0	2.3	2 991	107.7	9 751	62
Webster	86	2 332	173.5	65.1	39	250	29.9	7.2	2 586	107.8	6 060	25
West Baton Rouge	32	443	26.4	11.3	38	263	40.4	10.7	1 603	65.5	33 118	245
West Carroll	16	549	35.9	14.9	15	60	4.2	1.1	637	26.3	1 600	8
West Feliciana	24	462	36.9	13.6	10	D	D	D	785	32.8	13 806	52
Winn	38	957	67.2	29.2	18	D	D	D	690	39.0	0	0
MAINE	4 730	109 231	10 297.0	4 393.0	2 786	13 755	1 462.8	376.3	111 777	4 921.6	683 014	3 699
Androscoggin	385	9 531	947.5	402.8	211	1 024	84.6	23.5	6 117	280.0	16 167	74
Aroostook	229	6 120	471.8	207.2	122	397	45.8	9.1	4 119	165.6	6 417	56
Cumberland	1 339	33 687	3 348.8	1 475.2	734	4 502	518.8	130.4	27 280	1 372.6	225 594	1 157
Franklin	106	1 882	156.4	74.4	44	214	19.8	4.8	2 366	80.4	10 514	51
Hancock	159	3 144	306.6	127.7	140	686	101.2	21.7	7 520	343.6	50 754	188
Kennebec	464	13 374	1 293.6	552.0	289	1 265	139.0	37.9	8 309	316.1	30 384	203
Knox	163	3 022	256.5	104.8	126	593	66.9	19.1	5 838	289.2	22 563	89
Lincoln	113	1 800	144.6	51.5	81	547	51.7	16.2	4 678	183.4	19 586	82
Oxford	125	2 777	198.2	85.1	90	335	31.1	8.4	4 333	172.4	27 248	147
Penobscot	547	14 740	1 570.2	624.9	273	1 395	142.7	36.9	9 243	363.0	74 118	555
Piscataquis	36	1 508	106.4	51.6	25	92	6.6	1.9	1 199	40.5	5 728	38
Sagadahoc	116	1 375	80.7	36.0	59	266	27.3	6.9	3 221	124.8	14 384	77
Somerset	144	2 809	208.6	96.4	88	286	26.2	6.3	3 268	122.1	5 231	48
Waldo	113	1 622	148.9	65.4	82	264	26.3	6.4	3 844	135.4	12 153	75
Washington	108	2 058	137.6	66.4	51	209	19.7	4.3	3 771	178.2	7 222	45
York	583	9 782	920.8	371.5	371	1 680	155.0	42.5	16 671	754.3	145 919	746
MARYLAND	16 000	359 734	40 821.9	16 319.9	9 978	79 391	10 879.7	2 928.5	473 516	20 213.1	3 080 620	17 057
Allegany	250	6 283	616.1	235.0	139	780	58.0	16.9	3 051	117.2	4 593	49
Anne Arundel	1 272	26 683	2 975.3	1 196.9	1 077	8 665	902.9	291.8	40 473	1 934.5	369 740	2 656
Baltimore	2 619	58 216	6 062.4	2 458.5	1 376	9 983	1 044.2	295.7	64 480	2 863.4	221 603	1 312
Calvert	181	3 475	342.2	149.7	122	773	59.6	20.1	6 239	258.3	73 782	332
Caroline	46	826	44.6	23.3	48	226	23.7	7.6	2 548	103.4	7 427	46
Carroll	459	9 821	950.3	358.3	355	2 195	180.2	57.5	12 222	519.0	69 690	319
Cecil	196	4 679	534.5	259.0	164	867	68.1	20.9	5 725	258.2	24 254	109
Charles	325	4 598	456.6	190.4	213	1 353	113.6	35.7	10 191	357.8	213 461	1 214
Dorchester	84	1 826	158.1	65.8	68	360	19.7	5.3	2 373	87.4	9 103	36
Frederick	613	11 380	1 206.1	516.3	426	2 837	348.7	93.7	17 911	827.1	245 575	1 303
Garrett	76	1 797	118.6	52.0	73	1 219	106.6	47.9	2 315	102.3	66 758	224
Harford	594	10 550	1 029.1	406.1	422	2 691	227.0	90.5	16 208	693.3	156 419	923
Howard	928	14 235	1 406.4	600.2	509	4 399	552.9	179.8	25 508	1 328.6	281 457	1 593
Kent	74	1 374	115.6	47.4	44	172	19.5	4.8	1 824	80.7	7 528	25
Montgomery	3 584	61 807	7 227.2	3 069.1	1 891	19 109	4 325.3	1 001.8	108 358	5 462.1	445 838	2 080
Prince George's	1 812	31 493	3 126.4	1 249.8	1 126	8 923	996.2	297.7	73 755	2 128.1	347 065	1 757
Queen Anne's	85	1 064	74.1	34.4	103	526	45.1	12.7	4 797	251.6	34 212	168

Table B. States and Counties — Government Employment and Payroll, and Local Government Finances

	Government employment and payroll, 2012									Local government finances, 2012				
			March payroll (percent of total)							General revenue				
													Taxes	
													Per capita[1] (dollars)	
STATE County	Full-time equivalent employees	March payroll (dollars)	Adminis-tration, judicial, and legal	Police and Corrections	Fire Protection	Highways and transpor-tation	Health and Welfare	Natural resources and utilities	Education and libraries	Total (mil dol)	Inter-govern-mental (mil dol)	Total (mil dol)	Total	Property
	171	172	173	174	175	176	177	178	179	180	181	182	183	184
LOUISIANA—Cont'd														
Orleans	7 189	28 500 562	12.7	30.3	9.1	2.5	3.8	25.1	9.9	1 968.9	669.4	766.2	2 075	1 020
Ouachita	7 210	21 316 630	7.2	10.3	3.6	2.2	3.7	5.2	67.2	636.4	302.9	268.8	1 730	618
Plaquemines	1 620	5 259 702	13.4	13.1	0.6	7.9	7.0	6.2	48.6	320.9	176.8	96.4	4 031	2 274
Pointe Coupee	1 063	2 905 856	7.3	13.8	0.0	1.6	21.6	5.3	50.2	93.0	34.1	31.6	1 391	766
Rapides	5 615	17 417 361	10.4	15.6	7.9	3.6	1.4	5.7	52.6	487.4	230.0	195.3	1 475	567
Red River	533	1 454 876	5.8	37.4	0.0	1.9	0.9	1.0	50.4	43.6	18.0	22.1	2 455	992
Richland	1 229	3 799 353	5.9	17.8	0.1	3.2	35.8	2.3	34.3	105.4	49.7	25.9	1 238	508
Sabine	818	2 028 527	9.4	18.3	0.0	4.8	3.6	7.0	55.7	96.4	47.5	40.6	1 668	405
St. Bernard	1 804	5 761 067	8.7	16.2	6.9	6.4	1.4	5.2	54.8	484.3	396.4	68.9	1 655	655
St. Charles	3 451	12 023 950	5.4	15.1	0.0	1.8	10.8	8.5	57.6	387.0	80.9	211.6	4 016	2 217
St. Helena	456	1 219 647	8.6	9.7	0.0	3.8	45.3	1.3	30.5	32.8	13.8	7.5	676	349
St. James	1 306	4 803 097	7.4	11.1	0.0	2.6	16.4	8.2	49.6	231.2	42.5	70.5	3 247	1 994
St. John the Baptist	1 701	5 496 602	10.6	10.0	0.0	8.8	0.1	9.7	60.5	229.3	53.3	82.6	1 845	913
St. Landry	4 416	14 852 877	5.9	10.1	3.0	2.4	26.6	3.1	48.4	409.3	165.3	100.0	1 196	372
St. Martin	1 824	5 579 531	5.5	14.8	0.1	2.7	7.9	2.9	65.6	147.8	80.2	54.1	1 026	489
St. Mary	3 043	9 174 661	6.1	12.3	1.5	2.5	10.9	8.1	57.1	251.5	102.3	102.4	1 907	1 061
St. Tammany	10 707	35 822 862	5.7	10.3	0.3	2.6	33.9	2.1	44.3	1 250.6	404.2	450.6	1 882	995
Tangipahoa	6 393	23 444 209	4.2	6.0	1.2	1.7	46.4	1.8	37.5	621.2	213.8	128.9	1 044	366
Tensas	264	627 291	16.3	4.0	0.0	4.9	1.7	3.9	68.6	27.3	17.2	7.3	1 474	872
Terrebonne	5 509	18 140 503	3.6	8.6	1.2	1.4	31.1	4.6	49.2	603.6	234.4	173.9	1 554	551
Union	834	2 308 579	6.3	18.6	0.2	2.1	11.0	6.9	53.9	62.9	32.1	20.7	923	359
Vermilion	2 406	8 239 940	6.2	8.3	1.8	3.2	23.4	6.7	50.2	227.6	95.5	73.9	1 258	572
Vernon	2 133	5 249 110	6.4	9.9	1.2	3.6	0.1	1.9	76.0	155.1	98.2	46.0	855	294
Washington	1 946	5 729 429	5.2	6.2	1.5	2.7	14.9	1.9	66.9	160.0	81.0	45.0	964	454
Webster	1 523	4 175 873	6.3	15.2	1.4	3.3	0.1	7.0	65.3	133.5	64.2	57.4	1 402	613
West Baton Rouge	1 000	3 133 887	7.9	4.1	2.2	2.9	2.9	12.2	62.7	112.9	36.3	55.4	2 296	1 199
West Carroll	438	1 121 168	6.5	2.8	0.0	4.1	3.9	2.4	79.0	46.7	23.8	13.0	1 133	428
West Feliciana	748	2 572 616	10.2	10.9	0.2	3.9	16.8	3.4	53.6	68.8	21.1	29.6	1 922	1 366
Winn	679	1 633 669	7.5	13.5	1.8	3.1	0.7	8.9	63.3	42.7	25.9	13.6	909	416
MAINE	X	X	X	X	X	X	X	X	X	X	X	X	X	X
Androscoggin	3 959	13 779 680	4.1	8.3	4.8	4.2	2.0	5.1	70.2	355.6	153.6	163.3	1 517	1 507
Aroostook	3 302	10 418 372	5.5	4.9	2.0	3.8	16.3	5.3	61.4	264.2	111.0	83.6	1 180	1 174
Cumberland	10 861	40 790 587	5.2	9.0	5.8	4.8	5.4	6.8	61.0	1 129.5	280.4	610.0	2 149	2 117
Franklin	1 043	3 602 511	5.4	8.2	1.3	4.4	1.5	4.1	73.6	80.5	29.1	43.4	1 418	1 414
Hancock	1 982	6 326 482	6.8	6.5	2.5	3.7	1.0	4.2	73.3	197.6	39.3	137.4	2 518	2 502
Kennebec	4 312	13 281 549	5.2	7.6	3.0	3.6	1.2	5.8	72.6	343.2	144.3	155.9	1 280	1 266
Knox	1 307	4 815 634	8.9	8.8	3.1	4.4	3.3	2.5	67.5	129.9	19.5	90.5	2 283	2 267
Lincoln	1 389	4 505 799	5.7	4.0	0.5	2.0	2.2	3.4	80.2	135.6	34.2	88.2	2 582	2 572
Oxford	2 319	7 212 500	4.7	5.3	2.5	4.9	0.8	2.5	78.4	186.7	69.4	103.9	1 807	1 800
Penobscot	5 352	18 128 721	5.6	7.8	5.2	7.6	1.3	6.1	64.9	466.9	185.2	205.7	1 338	1 324
Piscataquis	1 109	4 071 817	4.7	4.0	0.2	1.9	47.9	1.9	38.2	99.6	35.5	26.2	1 514	1 504
Sagadahoc	1 209	4 568 672	5.0	6.6	2.7	2.7	1.0	3.8	74.9	131.3	38.0	73.7	2 093	2 078
Somerset	2 667	8 560 527	3.4	6.5	1.2	2.5	0.5	1.6	82.6	185.9	90.8	84.4	1 626	1 622
Waldo	1 256	3 892 726	8.1	6.4	0.8	2.8	1.9	2.4	74.8	102.4	36.3	56.7	1 460	1 455
Washington	1 219	3 492 782	6.9	7.3	1.2	2.6	3.5	5.0	70.9	100.0	42.2	47.1	1 450	1 445
York	7 047	25 948 699	5.4	9.0	4.1	3.0	1.2	5.9	70.5	637.1	181.5	390.3	1 961	1 938
MARYLAND	X	X	X	X	X	X	X	X	X	X	X	X	X	X
Allegany	2 826	11 858 505	3.5	6.0	2.0	3.5	0.4	6.3	75.4	272.3	133.1	86.3	1 167	773
Anne Arundel	17 468	83 267 035	4.0	8.6	6.2	4.4	2.8	3.8	67.7	2 076.5	568.1	1 135.3	2 062	1 152
Baltimore	26 532	122 265 325	4.1	12.0	5.2	1.3	3.0	2.6	69.5	2 786.6	910.6	1 567.3	1 917	1 039
Calvert	3 256	15 584 064	4.8	7.8	0.1	1.9	2.8	4.8	74.3	388.6	117.7	224.0	2 500	1 684
Caroline	1 269	4 767 293	5.8	8.2	0.0	2.2	3.3	4.6	71.4	117.5	59.9	45.1	1 379	973
Carroll	5 844	23 979 765	5.5	5.5	0.7	1.6	1.0	2.9	80.6	641.8	205.1	366.2	2 190	1 331
Cecil	3 436	14 149 378	4.6	8.1	1.2	1.6	2.8	2.0	76.9	375.0	153.4	172.0	1 691	1 137
Charles	5 864	27 330 417	4.8	12.4	0.0	0.6	3.1	3.7	73.5	663.0	226.7	318.3	2 114	1 346
Dorchester	1 251	4 831 214	5.1	13.0	0.0	3.8	4.8	2.5	66.5	134.8	62.3	54.8	1 683	1 219
Frederick	10 553	47 827 090	4.3	6.4	4.0	1.9	4.9	3.7	73.1	1 033.9	315.3	529.5	2 210	1 385
Garrett	1 283	4 466 807	6.7	4.8	0.8	10.6	1.8	3.9	70.1	214.5	59.8	111.5	3 734	2 998
Harford	8 483	39 111 192	6.1	9.6	0.3	2.6	1.8	4.3	73.8	952.9	307.2	524.4	2 109	1 291
Howard	12 202	62 646 998	4.3	7.7	1.9	1.0	4.2	4.1	75.2	1 532.5	372.1	962.2	3 214	1 692
Kent	708	2 731 612	8.4	10.5	0.0	4.3	1.1	5.9	64.0	74.9	18.1	46.4	2 298	1 677
Montgomery	38 590	236 750 984	3.3	7.6	4.0	3.0	6.2	10.6	64.3	5 240.0	1 125.4	3 182.9	3 168	1 422
Prince George's	27 062	140 810 958	4.4	15.2	3.4	1.2	4.0	1.6	67.6	3 399.7	1 344.2	1 551.8	1 761	1 007
Queen Anne's	1 906	8 133 110	4.6	6.4	0.2	2.6	7.3	5.6	72.6	207.2	65.4	111.4	2 293	1 412

1. Based on the resident population estimated as of July 1 of the year shown.

STATE County	Direct general expenditure Total (mil dol) [185]	Per capita[1] (dollars) [186]	Education [187]	Health and hospitals [188]	Police protection [189]	Public welfare [190]	Highways [191]	Debt outstanding Total (mil dol) [192]	Per capita[1] (dollars) [193]	Federal civilian [194]	Federal military [195]	State and local [196]	Democratic [197]	Republican [198]	All other [199]
LOUISIANA—Cont'd															
Orleans	1 848.6	5 006	12.2	0.7	7.8	0.1	6.6	2 707.7	7 333	8 891	3 842	26 260	79.4	19.1	1.5
Ouachita	687.9	4 428	53.4	2.3	5.8	0.1	2.6	489.7	3 152	434	687	10 433	36.9	62.1	1.0
Plaquemines	321.2	13 429	37.8	2.1	4.1	0.5	1.0	163.7	6 844	660	453	1 804	32.3	66.0	1.7
Pointe Coupee	90.9	4 001	37.3	22.2	6.6	0.4	2.1	45.9	2 021	55	101	1 123	44.4	53.9	1.7
Rapides	504.4	3 810	49.3	0.1	8.4	0.1	5.3	504.4	3 811	2 253	583	9 795	35.0	63.6	1.4
Red River	47.2	5 251	59.8	0.0	3.7	0.0	1.4	5.0	560	28	39	485	44.9	53.7	1.4
Richland	109.4	5 231	36.1	29.1	3.4	0.1	5.6	51.6	2 464	79	89	1 022	36.1	62.6	1.3
Sabine	85.0	3 493	69.8	0.2	4.8	0.0	5.6	27.9	1 145	42	108	1 277	23.3	74.9	1.9
St. Bernard	516.0	12 393	31.7	3.5	2.5	0.2	1.3	186.9	4 490	45	200	2 199	25.8	71.2	3.0
St. Charles	382.3	7 256	43.1	9.6	4.8	0.3	5.3	894.4	16 978	142	237	3 572	33.6	64.8	1.6
St. Helena	32.3	2 917	31.4	38.0	4.6	0.0	8.8	5.1	457	10	48	597	57.7	40.8	1.5
St. James	156.3	7 194	43.5	11.8	3.9	0.6	2.5	1 439.8	66 281	34	97	1 390	55.7	43.2	1.1
St. John the Baptist	252.0	5 630	34.8	0.5	4.6	0.5	5.1	1 281.3	28 626	114	197	2 074	57.4	41.2	1.5
St. Landry	414.8	4 958	43.1	29.0	4.8	0.0	3.0	98.9	1 182	165	376	5 434	47.7	50.9	1.4
St. Martin	141.4	2 682	59.3	0.9	8.4	0.2	5.1	123.9	2 349	61	239	1 897	38.8	59.6	1.6
St. Mary	245.0	4 562	42.6	10.2	6.7	0.2	3.8	139.7	2 602	127	361	4 600	40.8	57.6	1.6
St. Tammany	1 244.6	5 198	37.0	28.1	5.6	0.3	4.8	977.9	4 084	473	1 111	13 236	22.5	75.8	1.7
Tangipahoa	692.4	5 610	29.5	47.0	3.7	0.0	2.7	361.5	2 929	344	561	9 980	33.8	64.7	1.5
Tensas	26.2	5 284	36.9	2.0	4.8	0.0	4.9	26.6	5 361	23	22	301	54.1	45.0	0.9
Terrebonne	620.6	5 546	29.8	28.6	4.4	0.3	2.9	301.9	2 698	259	549	5 150	28.5	69.3	2.2
Union	60.2	2 685	49.1	8.9	5.4	0.2	6.0	5.9	265	89	100	741	28.6	70.1	1.3
Vermilion	223.8	3 812	42.2	20.8	4.9	2.1	5.1	37.7	643	135	279	2 820	25.2	72.8	2.0
Vernon	159.1	2 953	69.0	0.3	5.5	0.1	5.4	78.1	1 451	2 106	8 486	2 390	22.4	75.8	1.8
Washington	160.8	3 445	54.9	14.8	4.7	0.0	5.1	63.6	1 363	97	203	2 757	32.9	65.6	1.5
Webster	135.1	3 299	55.0	0.5	6.2	0.1	4.2	123.2	3 010	104	178	2 009	36.2	62.5	1.3
West Baton Rouge	118.0	4 896	36.6	0.9	8.9	0.6	4.0	182.2	7 559	63	111	1 533	42.5	56.1	1.4
West Carroll	47.4	4 114	52.9	20.0	3.8	2.1	3.9	8.1	701	32	50	735	17.6	81.1	1.3
West Feliciana	67.9	4 410	41.6	23.6	6.1	0.1	2.4	71.0	4 612	15	46	2 336	43.0	56.0	1.0
Winn	46.7	3 110	63.7	0.5	5.9	0.0	4.7	11.5	766	53	59	771	30.2	68.4	1.4
MAINE	X	X	X	X	X	X	X	X	X	14 060	7 071	85 464	57.7	40.4	1.9
Androscoggin	348.5	3 239	53.0	0.2	4.0	0.4	5.6	353.5	3 285	257	348	5 139	56.5	41.3	2.1
Aroostook	269.7	3 805	46.4	17.9	2.8	0.3	7.2	101.0	1 426	1 160	223	5 031	53.7	44.2	2.1
Cumberland	1 113.8	3 923	43.9	0.9	4.4	2.5	5.5	1 208.5	4 257	1 907	2 326	18 188	64.1	34.2	1.7
Franklin	104.7	3 419	60.2	0.7	3.7	0.2	8.5	100.7	3 287	118	97	1 930	58.9	38.6	2.5
Hancock	188.4	3 453	54.5	0.6	3.0	0.2	9.3	154.0	2 823	325	263	2 903	58.7	39.4	1.8
Kennebec	348.6	2 861	58.7	0.5	3.4	0.3	6.1	214.9	1 764	2 082	435	14 193	56.4	41.6	1.9
Knox	129.2	3 257	48.4	1.5	4.4	0.2	9.5	77.3	1 950	104	202	2 473	59.7	38.4	1.9
Lincoln	134.0	3 920	66.7	0.7	2.9	0.4	7.8	90.9	2 659	79	133	1 612	55.1	43.0	1.9
Oxford	185.2	3 222	64.2	0.5	2.9	0.4	8.6	87.1	1 516	145	187	3 084	56.7	40.6	2.7
Penobscot	527.2	3 429	48.1	1.1	3.8	0.2	4.2	409.3	2 662	1 172	495	13 083	51.7	46.6	1.7
Piscataquis	98.3	5 686	30.4	44.3	1.9	0.2	4.5	37.9	2 194	49	56	1 389	47.0	50.7	2.3
Sagadahoc	124.2	3 528	56.8	0.2	3.5	0.3	5.7	98.8	2 807	303	141	1 474	57.0	40.9	2.0
Somerset	179.7	3 461	69.3	0.2	2.5	0.2	6.3	81.7	1 574	186	167	2 427	51.8	46.1	2.2
Waldo	97.2	2 504	58.5	1.5	3.5	0.6	10.7	48.3	1 244	92	135	1 507	54.8	43.1	2.1
Washington	103.7	3 194	54.3	2.0	2.7	0.1	8.6	31.8	979	348	160	2 331	49.5	48.5	2.0
York	629.4	3 163	57.4	0.5	5.3	0.3	6.4	355.5	1 787	5 733	1 703	8 700	59.4	38.8	1.8
MARYLAND	X	X	X	X	X	X	X	X	X	172 141	49 160	345 414	61.9	36.5	1.6
Allegany	267.9	3 619	60.6	0.8	3.3	0.6	4.9	173.8	2 348	509	208	6 140	36.0	61.9	2.2
Anne Arundel	2 207.3	4 010	54.8	2.4	5.2	1.0	4.4	1 723.1	3 130	42 151	16 790	34 655	48.2	50.0	1.9
Baltimore	3 004.9	3 676	56.3	1.7	6.9	0.4	2.5	3 573.5	4 372	15 400	2 591	40 992	56.2	41.7	2.1
Calvert	401.4	4 479	58.4	0.8	3.8	1.0	3.2	210.1	2 344	132	322	4 119	46.1	52.4	1.5
Caroline	111.8	3 416	59.2	0.3	4.3	0.1	4.2	60.3	1 842	70	102	1 598	37.6	60.6	1.8
Carroll	634.2	3 793	62.1	0.8	3.5	1.2	4.4	467.0	2 793	278	529	8 029	33.1	64.3	2.6
Cecil	362.9	3 569	58.8	0.9	5.1	1.4	5.0	330.6	3 251	1 762	322	4 479	41.6	56.1	2.3
Charles	647.7	4 301	63.4	0.9	8.5	0.6	1.8	442.9	2 941	2 171	1 051	7 439	62.2	36.7	1.1
Dorchester	119.9	3 683	50.4	0.7	6.1	0.1	5.4	66.4	2 040	181	102	2 110	45.3	53.5	1.3
Frederick	1 022.3	4 267	56.6	0.7	5.2	3.4	3.4	1 148.1	4 792	3 698	1 807	11 364	48.6	49.6	1.8
Garrett	204.6	6 852	39.8	0.8	9.6	0.1	12.7	131.5	4 404	64	93	1 623	29.0	69.2	1.8
Harford	983.7	3 957	58.8	0.5	6.5	0.7	5.0	907.9	3 652	11 510	2 437	9 751	39.4	58.2	2.4
Howard	1 583.8	5 289	57.3	0.6	5.3	0.9	2.7	1 520.4	5 078	612	1 148	16 481	60.0	38.1	1.9
Kent	68.7	3 405	43.8	1.6	9.3	1.4	5.8	56.0	2 776	61	58	1 007	49.4	49.0	1.6
Montgomery	5 475.9	5 450	50.5	1.8	5.2	3.2	3.5	5 936.8	5 909	46 800	8 005	43 219	71.6	27.0	1.4
Prince George's	3 659.3	4 153	49.8	1.7	6.7	0.8	3.4	2 724.6	3 092	26 572	7 734	63 734	88.9	10.4	0.7
Queen Anne's	220.6	4 540	56.7	1.1	3.1	1.6	2.2	152.9	3 146	83	154	2 490	35.7	62.7	1.6

1. Based on the resident population estimated as of July 1 of the year shown.   2. © 2013 Election Data Services, Inc. All rights reserved.

Table B. States and Counties — **Land Area and Population**

STATE/ County code	CBSA code[1]	County type[2]	STATE County	Population, 2015				Population and population characteristics, 2014										
								Race alone or in combination, not Hispanic or Latino (percent)					Age (percent)					
				Land area,[3] (sq km) 2010	Total persons 2015	Rank	Per square kilometer	White	Black	American Indian, Alaska Native	Asian and Pacific Islander	Percent Hispanic or Latino[4]	Under 5 years	5 to 17 years	18 to 24 years	25 to 34 years	35 to 44 years	45 to 54 years
				1	2	3	4	5	6	7	8	9	10	11	12	13	14	15
			MARYLAND—Cont'd															
24 037	15680	4	St. Mary's	925	111 413	543	120.4	77.9	15.7	0.8	4.0	4.7	6.6	18.3	9.7	13.9	12.4	15.5
24 039	41540	3	Somerset	828	25 768	1 568	31.1	53.1	43.9	0.9	1.4	3.7	5.2	11.6	19.0	12.6	11.1	12.8
24 041	20660	6	Talbot	696	37 512	1 239	53.9	79.5	13.5	0.4	1.8	6.3	4.6	13.9	6.7	9.6	9.9	13.5
24 043	25180	3	Washington	1 186	149 585	435	126.1	83.3	12.1	0.6	2.3	4.3	5.8	16.4	8.4	12.9	12.9	15.0
24 045	41540	3	Wicomico	970	102 370	586	105.5	66.6	26.0	0.6	3.6	5.2	5.9	16.0	15.6	12.0	11.0	12.7
24 047	41540	4	Worcester	1 213	51 540	968	42.5	81.4	14.5	0.6	1.8	3.5	4.5	13.4	7.3	9.9	9.9	14.2
24 510	12580	1	Baltimore city	210	621 849	108	2 961.2	29.5	63.4	0.9	3.3	4.7	6.7	14.5	10.9	18.4	12.0	13.0
25 000	...	X	**MASSACHUSETTS**	20 202	6 794 422	X	336.3	75.7	7.6	0.6	7.0	10.8	5.4	15.2	10.4	13.8	12.4	14.6
25 001	12700	3	Barnstable	1 020	214 333	301	210.1	92.9	3.1	1.2	1.9	2.7	3.9	12.0	7.1	8.7	9.1	14.2
25 003	38340	3	Berkshire	2 400	127 828	488	53.3	91.5	3.9	0.6	2.0	4.1	4.4	13.6	9.7	10.4	10.5	14.8
25 005	39300	1	Bristol	1 433	556 772	118	388.5	86.5	4.8	0.7	2.8	6.9	5.2	15.9	9.6	12.3	12.7	15.3
25 007	47240	7	Dukes	267	17 299	1 961	64.8	91.1	4.9	2.3	1.9	3.1	4.7	13.6	6.7	11.1	11.7	15.3
25 009	14460	1	Essex	1 276	776 043	80	608.2	74.4	3.7	0.4	4.1	18.6	5.7	16.3	9.4	11.9	12.2	15.2
25 011	24640	2	Franklin	1 811	70 601	766	39.0	93.0	1.8	1.0	2.1	3.8	4.5	13.7	7.7	11.8	11.5	14.9
25 013	44140	2	Hampden	1 598	470 690	145	294.5	66.2	8.7	0.6	2.7	23.2	5.9	16.6	10.9	12.6	11.5	14.0
25 015	44140	2	Hampshire	1 366	161 292	398	118.1	86.5	3.3	0.6	6.3	5.3	3.6	12.0	23.4	10.3	9.9	12.8
25 017	14460	1	Middlesex	2 118	1 585 139	22	748.4	76.2	5.6	0.4	12.1	7.5	5.6	15.0	9.7	15.2	13.3	14.7
25 019	...	7	Nantucket	116	10 925	2 363	94.2	78.3	8.5	0.5	1.8	12.8	6.4	14.5	6.2	14.7	15.3	15.9
25 021	14460	1	Norfolk	1 026	696 023	91	678.4	79.2	6.9	0.4	11.1	4.0	5.4	16.2	8.7	12.5	12.7	15.4
25 023	14460	1	Plymouth	1 707	510 393	135	299.0	85.0	10.2	0.7	2.1	3.6	5.3	17.2	8.7	10.4	12.1	15.9
25 025	14460	1	Suffolk	151	778 121	78	5 153.1	48.1	21.6	0.7	9.6	21.7	5.7	11.6	14.6	22.7	12.8	11.6
25 027	49340	2	Worcester	3 913	818 963	73	209.3	80.2	5.0	0.6	5.3	10.5	5.6	16.4	10.0	12.3	12.6	15.6
26 000	...	X	**MICHIGAN**	146 435	9 922 576	X	67.8	77.6	15.0	1.3	3.4	4.8	5.8	16.7	10.1	12.1	12.0	14.1
26 001	...	9	Alcona	1 747	10 349	2 403	5.9	97.3	0.6	1.2	0.5	1.5	3.1	10.1	5.3	6.1	7.4	13.4
26 003	...	9	Alger	2 370	9 383	2 479	4.0	87.4	7.6	5.8	0.8	1.3	3.4	11.9	6.8	11.4	11.0	13.8
26 005	26090	4	Allegan	2 137	114 625	535	53.6	90.3	1.9	1.2	1.1	7.1	6.0	18.9	8.1	11.3	11.9	14.7
26 007	10980	7	Alpena	1 481	28 803	1 461	19.4	97.2	0.9	1.1	0.9	1.3	4.6	14.8	7.6	9.9	10.8	14.4
26 009	...	9	Antrim	1 232	23 154	1 676	18.8	96.5	0.7	1.8	0.5	2.0	4.3	14.7	6.5	8.7	9.4	14.1
26 011	...	8	Arenac	941	15 261	2 083	16.2	96.3	0.8	1.8	0.7	1.9	4.1	14.4	7.0	9.5	10.1	14.7
26 013	...	9	Baraga	2 326	8 575	2 549	3.7	77.3	8.5	16.4	1.0	1.4	4.5	14.5	8.0	11.8	12.5	14.4
26 015	24340	2	Barry	1 433	59 314	875	41.4	96.0	0.9	1.0	0.7	2.6	5.3	17.6	8.0	10.5	11.7	15.0
26 017	13020	3	Bay	1 146	105 659	562	92.2	92.1	2.6	1.1	1.0	5.0	5.2	15.8	8.3	11.8	11.6	14.1
26 019	45900	9	Benzie	828	17 457	1 952	21.1	95.3	1.1	2.1	0.6	2.3	4.2	15.0	6.5	9.4	10.4	14.2
26 021	35660	3	Berrien	1 470	154 636	419	105.2	77.2	16.2	1.2	2.5	5.1	6.0	16.4	8.7	11.2	11.5	13.9
26 023	17740	6	Branch	1 311	43 664	1 098	33.3	92.3	2.5	0.9	1.1	4.3	6.2	17.5	7.9	12.0	11.9	13.9
26 025	12980	3	Calhoun	1 829	134 314	470	73.4	81.8	12.6	1.4	2.5	4.8	6.1	17.1	9.3	11.9	11.8	13.7
26 027	43780	2	Cass	1 269	51 657	966	40.7	89.1	6.8	2.1	1.2	3.5	4.6	16.7	8.0	9.9	11.4	14.6
26 029	...	7	Charlevoix	1 078	26 238	1 551	24.3	95.5	0.9	2.5	0.8	1.8	4.8	15.5	6.9	9.7	9.9	14.6
26 031	...	7	Cheboygan	1 853	25 427	1 591	13.7	94.7	1.1	4.8	0.7	1.4	4.0	13.8	6.8	8.7	10.4	14.1
26 033	42300	5	Chippewa	4 036	38 033	1 220	9.4	74.9	7.4	19.2	1.6	1.8	4.8	14.2	11.8	13.2	12.8	13.8
26 035	...	7	Clare	1 462	30 553	1 419	20.9	96.3	1.2	1.5	0.6	1.9	5.4	14.5	7.4	10.0	10.4	13.9
26 037	29620	2	Clinton	1 467	77 390	715	52.8	91.7	2.6	0.9	2.0	4.4	5.4	17.6	9.1	11.7	12.1	14.9
26 039	...	7	Crawford	1 441	13 801	2 183	9.6	96.3	1.2	1.2	0.8	1.8	4.1	13.9	6.7	9.0	9.3	15.4
26 041	21540	5	Delta	3 033	36 377	1 266	12.0	95.7	0.8	3.8	0.8	1.1	5.1	15.2	7.4	9.7	10.6	13.9
26 043	27020	5	Dickinson	1 972	25 788	1 565	13.1	96.9	0.8	1.3	0.8	1.4	5.0	15.1	7.4	10.6	10.1	14.0
26 045	29620	2	Eaton	1 490	108 801	551	73.0	85.4	7.8	1.1	2.5	5.3	5.4	16.4	9.0	12.4	11.6	14.2
26 047	...	7	Emmet	1 211	33 161	1 352	27.4	93.6	1.2	5.0	0.9	1.6	4.8	15.8	7.8	10.7	11.1	13.7
26 049	22420	2	Genesee	1 650	410 849	168	249.0	74.6	21.8	1.3	1.5	3.2	6.0	17.4	9.2	11.6	12.2	14.1
26 051	...	6	Gladwin	1 300	25 164	1 604	19.4	97.2	0.7	1.1	0.5	1.3	4.7	14.6	6.5	8.8	10.0	13.8
26 053	...	7	Gogebic	2 854	15 431	2 077	5.4	91.5	5.0	3.5	0.8	1.2	3.9	12.1	8.1	11.2	11.0	14.2
26 055	45900	5	Grand Traverse	1 203	91 636	636	76.2	94.1	1.8	1.8	1.1	2.7	5.4	15.5	8.1	12.8	12.0	14.2
26 057	10940	6	Gratiot	1 472	41 540	1 134	28.2	87.8	5.9	1.0	0.7	5.7	5.2	15.3	11.4	12.7	12.5	14.1
26 059	25880	6	Hillsdale	1 549	45 941	1 050	29.7	96.2	1.0	1.1	0.6	2.1	5.5	16.8	9.7	10.4	11.3	13.6
26 061	26340	5	Houghton	2 614	36 380	1 265	13.9	94.8	1.2	1.3	3.7	1.4	5.3	15.3	21.3	10.3	9.1	10.6
26 063	...	7	Huron	2 164	31 883	1 385	14.7	96.4	0.7	0.8	0.7	2.1	4.7	14.9	7.0	9.4	9.8	14.1
26 065	29620	2	Ingham	1 440	286 085	239	198.7	74.2	13.6	1.3	6.9	7.6	5.7	14.7	20.2	13.6	10.9	11.4
26 067	26960	2	Ionia	1 480	64 223	817	43.4	89.5	5.4	0.9	0.7	4.7	5.7	17.5	9.6	13.4	13.4	14.6
26 069	...	7	Iosco	1 422	25 345	1 596	17.8	95.9	1.1	1.6	1.0	2.1	4.5	12.5	6.2	8.7	8.8	13.5
26 071	...	7	Iron	3 020	11 348	2 333	3.8	96.8	0.8	1.8	0.6	1.7	4.2	12.3	5.9	8.1	8.6	13.4
26 073	34380	5	Isabella	1 483	70 698	765	47.7	88.2	3.5	4.3	2.5	3.7	4.7	12.7	29.6	12.3	9.2	10.2
26 075	27100	3	Jackson	1 817	159 494	404	87.8	87.3	9.7	1.0	1.2	3.4	5.5	16.6	9.4	11.8	12.2	14.5
26 077	28020	2	Kalamazoo	1 455	260 263	258	178.9	81.2	12.8	1.2	3.3	4.7	6.0	16.1	16.3	12.9	11.4	11.9
26 079	45900	7	Kalkaska	1 450	17 260	1 965	11.9	96.2	1.1	1.7	0.8	1.9	5.5	16.1	7.0	10.7	11.4	14.3
26 081	24340	2	Kent	2 194	636 369	103	290.0	77.0	11.0	1.0	3.3	10.1	7.0	18.1	9.8	15.1	12.3	13.3

1. CBSA = Core Based Statistical Area. See Appendix A for explanation. See Appendix B for list of metropolitan areas with component counties.   2. County type code from the Economic Research Service of USDA Rural-Urban Continuum Codes. See Appendix A for definition.   3. Dry land or land partially or temporarily covered by water.   4. May be of any race.

STATE County	55 to 64 years	65 to 74 years	75 years and over	Percent female	Total persons 2000	Total persons 2010	Percent change 2000–2010	Percent change 2010–2015	Births	Deaths	Net migration	Number	Persons per household	Family households	Female family householder[1]	One person
	16	17	18	19	20	21	22	23	24	25	26	27	28	29	30	31
MARYLAND—Cont'd																
St. Mary's	11.7	7.2	4.8	50.2	86 211	105 151	22.0	6.0	7 454	3 888	2 524	37 947	2.78	73.6	9.8	21.3
Somerset	12.5	8.7	6.5	45.8	24 747	26 470	7.0	-2.7	1 368	1 417	-645	8 498	2.26	59.5	14.8	31.1
Talbot	15.0	14.7	12.0	52.6	33 812	37 782	11.7	-0.7	1 764	2 266	237	16 140	2.32	67.7	12.7	28.7
Washington	12.8	8.7	7.1	49.0	131 923	147 430	11.8	1.5	9 115	7 786	676	55 769	2.52	67.4	12.9	27.0
Wicomico	12.4	8.3	6.1	52.2	84 644	98 733	16.6	3.7	6 413	4 817	1 982	36 479	2.64	66.8	15.7	25.4
Worcester	15.5	14.4	10.9	51.4	46 543	51 451	10.5	0.2	2 327	3 170	968	20 492	2.48	65.0	9.3	29.8
Baltimore city	12.2	7.0	5.3	52.9	651 154	621 143	-4.6	0.1	46 581	33 222	-11 530	242 212	2.47	52.0	22.9	39.0
MASSACHUSETTS	13.1	8.3	6.7	51.5	6 349 097	6 547 817	3.1	3.8	381 739	283 898	155 501	2 538 485	2.53	63.6	12.6	28.8
Barnstable	17.1	15.2	12.6	52.4	222 230	215 888	-2.9	-0.7	8 293	14 792	4 731	94 371	2.24	61.6	9.2	32.8
Berkshire	15.8	11.3	9.5	51.6	134 953	131 272	-2.7	-2.6	5 865	7 434	-1 754	55 369	2.23	59.4	12.1	34.6
Bristol	13.2	8.7	7.0	51.5	534 678	548 285	2.5	1.5	30 029	26 412	5 211	211 001	2.53	65.9	14.4	28.0
Dukes	17.1	12.4	7.4	50.5	14 987	16 535	10.3	4.6	857	707	631	5 839	2.86	66.2	12.3	28.7
Essex	13.7	8.6	7.0	51.8	723 419	743 175	2.7	4.4	44 596	33 083	21 775	286 896	2.58	66.7	14.0	27.7
Franklin	17.6	11.0	7.2	51.2	71 535	71 372	-0.2	-1.1	3 273	3 450	-387	30 390	2.30	60.5	10.8	29.9
Hampden	13.3	8.3	7.0	51.7	456 228	463 625	1.6	1.5	28 281	22 404	1 957	177 736	2.54	65.6	17.9	28.4
Hampshire	13.3	8.6	6.2	53.4	152 251	158 080	3.8	2.0	5 830	6 325	3 585	58 776	2.34	59.0	10.3	30.3
Middlesex	12.6	7.7	6.3	51.2	1 465 396	1 503 126	2.6	5.5	92 938	57 737	49 665	583 809	2.54	64.0	9.8	27.6
Nantucket	13.5	7.7	5.7	48.9	9 520	10 172	6.8	7.4	725	289	304	3 978	2.53	60.0	10.8	31.0
Norfolk	13.4	8.3	7.3	52.1	650 308	670 743	3.1	3.8	38 159	29 249	17 181	258 675	2.57	65.8	10.0	27.9
Plymouth	14.1	9.5	6.7	51.4	472 822	494 915	4.7	3.1	26 959	22 213	10 412	180 659	2.71	71.4	12.8	23.5
Suffolk	10.1	6.1	4.9	51.7	689 807	722 087	4.7	7.8	50 105	24 867	32 144	290 631	2.41	49.4	17.0	36.6
Worcester	13.5	7.9	6.2	50.7	750 963	798 542	6.3	2.6	45 829	34 936	10 046	300 355	2.60	67.0	12.2	26.7
MICHIGAN	13.8	8.8	6.6	50.9	9 938 444	9 884 129	-0.5	0.4	597 843	475 710	-80 039	3 827 880	2.52	65.3	12.8	28.9
Alcona	19.8	20.3	14.5	49.8	11 719	10 942	-6.6	-5.4	328	952	80	5 007	2.10	64.2	5.9	31.4
Alger	17.9	13.5	10.3	45.0	9 862	9 601	-2.6	-2.3	328	566	15	3 609	2.34	64.7	6.2	31.6
Allegan	14.0	9.0	6.1	50.1	105 665	111 408	5.4	2.9	7 056	4 714	690	41 767	2.66	73.6	9.8	21.7
Alpena	16.4	11.5	10.0	50.9	31 314	29 598	-5.5	-2.7	1 385	1 882	-245	12 860	2.23	64.9	10.3	29.4
Antrim	17.1	14.7	10.5	50.3	23 110	23 580	2.0	-1.8	1 034	1 369	-76	9 593	2.41	69.9	6.2	25.9
Arenac	17.7	13.0	9.5	49.3	17 269	15 899	-7.9	-4.0	622	1 089	-161	6 409	2.37	67.7	7.9	28.0
Baraga	15.2	11.3	7.8	45.1	8 746	8 860	1.3	-3.2	418	544	-166	3 055	2.11	61.6	10.5	35.2
Barry	15.0	10.2	6.8	49.7	56 755	59 175	4.3	0.2	3 210	2 710	-359	22 700	2.58	71.4	6.9	23.2
Bay	15.0	10.2	8.1	50.7	110 157	107 771	-2.2	-2.0	5 644	6 069	-1 626	43 712	2.42	64.8	12.2	29.3
Benzie	16.3	13.9	10.4	50.4	15 998	17 525	9.5	-0.4	804	1 085	178	7 388	2.32	65.6	9.1	28.3
Berrien	14.4	9.9	8.0	51.2	162 453	156 817	-3.5	-1.4	9 810	8 651	-3 263	60 320	2.50	66.7	13.1	29.2
Branch	14.0	9.6	7.0	48.4	45 787	45 248	-1.2	-3.5	2 817	2 210	-2 134	15 863	2.62	68.9	10.7	25.6
Calhoun	13.7	9.0	7.4	51.2	137 985	136 148	-1.3	-1.3	8 784	7 612	-2 924	52 842	2.49	64.8	14.6	29.3
Cass	15.5	12.1	7.3	50.0	51 104	52 286	2.3	-1.2	2 506	2 629	-530	19 804	2.60	69.8	10.2	26.1
Charlevoix	17.1	12.6	8.9	50.6	26 090	25 949	-0.5	1.1	1 258	1 430	435	10 518	2.45	67.4	8.9	27.7
Cheboygan	17.6	14.4	10.2	50.2	26 448	26 150	-1.1	-2.8	1 007	1 653	-68	11 250	2.27	67.0	9.3	27.9
Chippewa	13.2	9.3	6.8	44.9	38 543	38 673	0.3	-1.7	1 843	1 843	-687	14 382	2.37	62.3	9.1	30.9
Clare	16.5	13.1	8.7	50.2	31 252	30 926	-1.0	-1.2	1 657	1 999	57	13 208	2.29	65.2	11.4	29.8
Clinton	14.0	9.0	6.4	50.6	64 753	75 382	16.4	2.7	4 180	2 942	624	28 568	2.65	69.8	9.1	23.6
Crawford	17.5	14.4	9.6	49.6	14 273	14 074	-1.4	-1.9	608	843	31	5 781	2.37	67.7	8.4	27.0
Delta	16.8	11.6	9.7	50.4	38 520	37 069	-3.8	-1.9	1 883	2 216	-313	15 695	2.31	62.9	8.3	32.2
Dickinson	16.3	10.7	9.7	49.9	27 472	26 168	-4.7	-1.5	1 344	1 585	-91	11 263	2.28	66.4	10.6	29.9
Eaton	14.6	9.7	6.7	51.1	103 655	107 759	4.0	1.0	6 085	5 020	16	43 562	2.44	65.9	11.0	29.0
Emmet	16.3	11.2	8.5	50.7	31 437	32 694	4.0	1.4	1 607	1 695	550	13 612	2.38	67.6	8.5	25.7
Genesee	13.9	8.8	6.8	51.8	436 141	425 790	-2.4	-3.5	26 341	22 440	-18 632	165 962	2.49	64.9	16.8	29.8
Gladwin	16.5	14.8	10.3	49.7	26 023	25 692	-1.3	-2.1	1 250	1 771	75	10 827	2.34	67.7	8.4	28.1
Gogebic	16.5	12.2	10.7	45.6	17 370	16 427	-5.4	-6.1	645	1 146	-431	6 916	2.09	58.1	9.1	35.5
Grand Traverse	15.1	9.9	7.3	50.6	77 654	86 986	12.0	5.3	4 887	4 182	3 839	34 833	2.46	64.7	9.5	28.7
Gratiot	12.4	8.8	7.7	46.7	42 285	42 476	0.5	-2.2	2 177	2 254	-925	14 705	2.47	68.4	10.3	26.5
Hillsdale	15.0	10.4	7.3	50.1	46 527	46 688	0.3	-1.6	2 870	2 359	-1 214	17 632	2.54	68.1	9.2	27.1
Houghton	12.0	8.9	7.2	45.8	36 016	36 628	1.7	-0.7	1 997	1 821	-480	13 941	2.48	57.6	7.6	31.8
Huron	16.6	12.6	10.9	50.5	36 079	33 118	-8.2	-3.7	1 588	2 275	-498	13 965	2.29	65.1	8.8	30.9
Ingham	11.7	7.0	4.9	51.5	279 320	280 891	0.6	1.8	17 201	10 615	-1 299	109 806	2.40	56.1	12.1	32.8
Ionia	12.9	7.8	5.1	46.3	61 518	63 905	3.9	0.5	3 926	2 593	-1 018	22 140	2.70	71.5	11.3	24.0
Iosco	17.8	15.7	12.2	50.4	27 339	25 887	-5.3	-2.1	1 195	2 053	357	11 361	2.21	61.3	9.0	33.3
Iron	19.4	14.7	13.5	50.6	13 138	11 817	-10.1	-4.0	473	980	41	5 415	2.07	58.4	7.7	36.6
Isabella	10.4	6.2	4.7	51.4	63 351	70 311	11.0	0.6	3 427	2 374	-610	24 773	2.59	55.4	10.4	27.5
Jackson	14.0	9.0	7.0	48.8	158 422	160 248	1.2	-0.5	9 339	8 320	-1 677	60 485	2.50	66.4	12.9	28.3
Kalamazoo	11.9	7.6	5.9	51.0	238 603	250 327	4.9	4.0	16 483	10 643	4 117	100 042	2.46	59.9	11.5	29.9
Kalkaska	15.9	11.9	7.1	49.2	16 571	17 153	3.5	0.6	898	948	208	7 123	2.39	63.7	7.3	29.7
Kent	12.1	6.8	5.5	50.8	574 335	602 622	4.9	5.6	46 691	23 078	10 220	230 895	2.62	66.8	12.6	26.2

1. No spouse present.

Table B. States and Counties — Population, Vital Statistics, Medicare, and Crime

STATE County	Persons in group quarters, 2015	Daytime population, 2010–2014 Number	Daytime population, 2010–2014 Employment/ residence ratio	Births, 2015 Total	Births, 2015 Rate[1]	Deaths, 2015 Number	Deaths, 2015 Rate[1]	Persons under 65 with no health insurance, 2014 Number	Persons under 65 with no health insurance, 2014 Percent	Medicare, 2015 Total Beneficiaries	Medicare, 2015 Enrolled in Original Medicare	Medicare, 2015 Enrolled in Medicare Advantage	Serious crimes known to police,[2] 2014 Total Number	Serious crimes known to police,[2] 2014 Total Rate[3]
	32	33	34	35	36	37	38	39	40	41	42	43	44	45
MARYLAND—Cont'd														
St. Mary's	2 799	105 516	0.95	1 422	12.8	784	7.1	6 006	6.4	13 475	13 213	262	2 474	2 232
Somerset	5 336	25 302	0.89	257	10.0	268	10.4	1 802	10.7	4 555	4 460	95	534	2 033
Talbot	373	41 124	1.19	338	9.0	458	12.2	2 636	9.6	9 926	9 600	326	901	2 370
Washington	8 237	150 293	1.02	1 731	11.6	1 486	9.9	9 699	8.1	26 770	23 922	2 848	3 715	2 471
Wicomico	4 864	100 773	1.01	1 194	11.7	997	9.8	8 933	10.7	16 965	16 616	349	3 884	3 823
Worcester	721	53 367	1.08	438	8.5	635	12.3	3 914	10.2	13 043	12 646	397	2 422	4 680
Baltimore city	26 121	728 560	1.40	8 774	14.1	6 584	10.6	52 199	9.8	95 966	81 175	14 791	38 656	6 200
MASSACHUSETTS	252 083	6 720 500	1.02	73 104	10.8	55 291	8.2	208 262	3.8	1 118 080	849 989	268 091	151 666	2 248
Barnstable	3 962	210 919	0.96	1 526	7.1	2 801	13.1	6 234	4.1	66 532	58 903	7 629	5 243	2 434
Berkshire	6 056	132 340	1.04	1 078	8.4	1 365	10.6	3 928	4.0	30 898	29 347	1 551	2 911	2 446
Bristol	16 432	505 039	0.82	5 714	10.3	5 077	9.1	19 640	4.3	106 531	88 922	17 609	14 496	2 610
Dukes	141	17 154	1.03	168	9.7	129	7.5	653	4.7	3 744	3 657	87	NA	NA
Essex	18 946	704 447	0.86	8 626	11.2	6 467	8.4	25 423	4.0	133 215	106 170	27 045	15 926	2 088
Franklin	1 671	63 725	0.79	602	8.5	649	9.2	2 061	3.6	14 548	11 318	3 230	1 386	2 312
Hampden	16 184	459 962	0.97	5 344	11.4	4 203	8.9	16 185	4.2	90 201	58 498	31 703	15 982	3 471
Hampshire	22 613	155 372	0.94	1 099	6.8	1 214	7.5	4 452	3.8	25 614	19 633	5 981	2 819	1 815
Middlesex	56 676	1 608 594	1.09	17 850	11.3	11 343	7.2	41 504	3.2	227 092	169 230	57 862	24 908	1 587
Nantucket	57	10 661	1.04	133	12.2	52	4.8	479	5.1	1 530	1 495	35	309	2 945
Norfolk	17 850	663 859	0.94	7 368	10.6	5 700	8.2	15 531	2.7	106 342	84 219	22 123	9 607	1 462
Plymouth	12 286	446 527	0.78	5 224	10.3	4 405	8.7	14 075	3.4	89 399	75 118	14 281	9 054	1 965
Suffolk	50 201	986 384	1.63	9 620	12.4	5 071	6.6	34 170	5.3	91 043	67 246	23 797	27 101	3 540
Worcester	29 008	755 517	0.87	8 752	10.7	6 815	8.3	23 927	3.5	131 391	76 233	55 158	18 697	2 322
MICHIGAN	227 185	9 850 547	0.99	114 521	11.5	90 822	9.2	827 968	10.1	1 841 539	1 236 024	605 515	244 895	2 471
Alcona	127	9 504	0.64	58	5.6	160	15.4	905	13.4	3 977	2 974	1 003	148	1 408
Alger	1 051	9 271	0.92	74	7.9	119	12.6	735	11.6	2 430	1 838	592	90	945
Allegan	954	103 240	0.82	1 362	11.9	878	7.7	8 854	9.2	17 474	9 327	8 147	1 601	1 418
Alpena	513	30 089	1.07	268	9.3	337	11.7	2 520	11.2	8 865	7 224	1 641	547	1 886
Antrim	226	20 588	0.70	202	8.7	253	10.9	2 161	12.5	6 093	4 211	1 882	432	1 850
Arenac	207	14 928	0.88	110	7.2	197	12.9	1 472	12.5	4 882	3 629	1 253	164	1 128
Baraga	1 023	9 297	1.23	78	9.1	102	11.8	735	12.1	2 010	1 577	433	NA	NA
Barry	612	46 776	0.52	583	9.8	536	9.0	4 289	8.8	9 650	5 628	4 022	674	1 190
Bay	1 437	98 225	0.80	1 026	9.7	1 132	10.7	7 671	8.9	23 914	17 238	6 676	2 436	2 283
Benzie	252	14 969	0.67	165	9.4	198	11.3	1 668	12.6	4 465	3 007	1 458	200	1 148
Berrien	3 536	155 568	0.99	1 876	12.1	1 624	10.5	15 178	12.1	36 289	27 080	9 209	3 541	2 345
Branch	1 980	41 538	0.86	555	12.7	387	8.9	3 948	11.4	8 245	6 510	1 735	715	1 651
Calhoun	4 011	141 524	1.11	1 705	12.7	1 367	10.2	10 886	9.9	28 256	22 455	5 801	4 563	3 383
Cass	609	42 228	0.55	514	9.9	511	9.9	4 921	11.9	7 343	5 338	2 005	706	1 532
Charlevoix	279	25 299	0.93	233	8.9	273	10.4	2 255	11.1	6 554	4 576	1 978	394	1 503
Cheboygan	388	23 549	0.77	194	7.6	342	13.4	2 569	13.5	6 545	4 889	1 656	397	1 547
Chippewa	4 938	38 664	1.00	342	9.0	345	9.0	3 660	13.3	7 681	5 932	1 749	567	1 462
Clare	407	28 607	0.78	302	9.9	374	12.2	3 198	13.5	8 213	6 186	2 027	695	2 279
Clinton	680	60 541	0.55	798	10.3	543	7.0	4 426	6.8	9 941	6 708	3 233	561	727
Crawford	197	13 488	0.91	114	8.3	158	11.5	1 135	11.0	3 099	2 303	796	266	1 916
Delta	623	36 455	0.97	349	9.6	402	11.0	3 000	10.5	10 165	7 521	2 644	802	2 174
Dickinson	453	27 934	1.16	272	10.5	293	11.3	1 876	9.1	6 523	4 855	1 668	NA	NA
Eaton	1 559	104 245	0.92	1 159	10.7	946	8.7	7 129	8.0	15 502	10 737	4 765	1 932	1 823
Emmet	505	36 053	1.20	304	9.2	299	9.0	2 942	11.1	8 637	6 257	2 380	429	1 289
Genesee	5 982	405 271	0.91	4 965	12.1	4 332	10.5	30 107	8.7	86 632	56 063	30 569	13 935	3 374
Gladwin	289	22 499	0.63	243	9.6	357	14.1	2 340	12.4	7 862	5 736	2 126	380	1 493
Gogebic	1 537	15 852	0.97	118	7.6	213	13.7	1 327	12.2	4 501	3 283	1 218	204	1 290
Grand Traverse	2 698	97 137	1.19	974	10.7	792	8.7	7 090	9.7	21 245	14 307	6 938	1 190	1 310
Gratiot	5 429	41 929	0.99	402	9.7	427	10.3	2 891	9.6	8 183	6 159	2 024	657	1 568
Hillsdale	1 645	43 132	0.83	558	12.1	438	9.5	4 155	11.4	9 084	6 693	2 391	571	1 241
Houghton	3 076	36 601	0.99	363	10.0	338	9.3	2 981	10.6	6 503	4 749	1 754	462	1 278
Huron	524	32 792	1.02	306	9.6	452	14.1	2 711	11.1	8 448	6 728	1 720	373	1 251
Ingham	18 166	315 967	1.26	3 314	11.6	2 103	7.4	22 936	9.8	50 945	37 333	13 612	8 162	2 886
Ionia	5 478	56 170	0.69	756	11.8	498	7.7	4 896	9.8	9 930	6 541	3 389	1 007	1 671
Iosco	400	26 176	1.08	236	9.3	376	14.8	2 190	12.0	8 605	6 481	2 124	513	2 023
Iron	358	11 039	0.87	91	8.0	187	16.5	914	11.3	3 378	2 626	752	216	1 886
Isabella	6 548	73 526	1.10	661	9.3	436	6.2	6 652	11.7	10 082	7 336	2 746	1 340	1 900
Jackson	9 268	155 241	0.93	1 734	10.9	1 575	9.9	11 840	9.4	31 686	23 779	7 907	4 054	2 559
Kalamazoo	8 508	262 225	1.06	3 203	12.3	2 101	8.1	19 737	9.1	42 407	27 929	14 478	8 494	3 286
Kalkaska	138	15 136	0.68	165	9.5	166	9.6	1 764	12.6	3 238	2 428	810	387	2 246
Kent	11 534	665 152	1.17	9 085	14.3	4 497	7.1	58 272	10.7	95 139	46 164	48 975	14 921	2 379

1. Per 1,000 estimated resident population. 2. Data for serious crimes have not been adjusted for underreporting; this may affect comparability between geographic areas and over time.
3. Per 100,000 population estimated by the FBI.

Table B. States and Counties — Crime, Education, Money Income, and Poverty

STATE County	Serious crimes known to police, 2014 (cont.)[1] Rate[2] Violent	Property	Education School enrollment and attainment, 2010–2014 Enrollment[3] Total	Per cent private	Attainment[4] (percent) High school graduate or less	Bachelor's degree or more	Local government expenditures,[5] 2012–2013 Total current spending (mil dol)	Current spending per student (dollars)	Money income, 2010–2014 Per capita income[6] (dollars)	Households Median income (dollars)	Mean income (dollars)	Percent with income of $200,000 or more	Income and poverty, 2014 Median household income (dollars)	Percent below poverty level All persons	Children under 18 years	Children 5 to 17 years in families
	46	47	48	49	50	51	52	53	54	55	56	57	58	59	60	61
MARYLAND—Cont'd																
St. Mary's	237	1 995	30 011	15.4	40.9	29.8	217.6	12 469	36 602	88 190	100 919	8.2	84 686	8.6	12.4	11.9
Somerset	266	1 766	7 750	6.1	63.0	15.1	40.3	13 702	16 471	36 716	49 098	0.9	38 376	25.5	32.6	31.6
Talbot	266	2 104	7 808	20.9	40.1	33.4	54.5	11 934	37 661	58 495	86 583	7.3	54 836	11.7	17.9	15.8
Washington	319	2 152	35 312	13.0	51.5	19.9	281.8	12 576	26 477	56 477	70 948	3.5	54 606	13.8	19.9	17.9
Wicomico	446	3 377	30 324	10.6	45.5	27.7	188.1	12 980	26 298	52 301	68 847	3.4	51 927	16.9	23.5	22.7
Worcester	367	4 313	9 967	12.4	44.0	28.2	107.4	16 147	33 376	58 820	79 668	4.9	55 691	11.9	20.5	20.1
Baltimore city	1 355	4 845	163 549	23.8	48.8	27.7	1 275.4	15 050	25 062	41 819	60 355	3.2	41 895	23.3	32.2	32.2
MASSACHUSETTS	391	1 857	1 760 905	27.1	36.0	40.0	14 325.0	14 515	36 441	67 846	92 850	8.5	69 200	11.7	15.3	14.2
Barnstable	431	2 003	40 397	16.9	30.1	39.9	400.2	16 305	36 964	61 597	82 356	5.2	64 150	8.9	13.4	12.4
Berkshire	309	2 136	30 392	23.8	41.5	31.3	275.5	16 468	30 168	49 737	68 773	4.0	49 890	13.0	20.4	17.8
Bristol	543	2 068	137 786	17.7	48.1	25.6	1 086.4	13 970	29 173	55 957	73 844	4.1	57 732	12.4	17.4	15.8
Dukes	NA	NA	3 293	22.0	30.6	41.2	56.7	27 353	33 738	65 518	84 712	4.3	61 259	9.0	13.4	12.6
Essex	386	1 702	194 703	20.9	37.0	37.2	1 649.0	14 861	36 035	68 776	93 006	8.5	70 074	10.7	15.5	14.5
Franklin	424	1 888	15 812	14.5	35.7	34.4	160.7	16 818	29 658	54 072	68 263	2.9	53 953	12.0	16.7	15.3
Hampden	595	2 875	123 225	18.5	46.5	25.4	1 084.2	15 522	26 249	50 036	66 866	3.3	49 072	17.7	26.2	24.3
Hampshire	261	1 554	58 106	20.4	31.3	43.2	281.6	15 416	29 884	61 460	79 083	4.8	57 737	15.0	12.5	11.1
Middlesex	190	1 397	411 038	31.9	29.2	51.3	3 384.5	16 245	43 667	83 488	112 455	12.7	84 026	8.9	9.6	8.8
Nantucket	67	2 878	2 416	23.0	28.5	45.7	30.4	21 982	47 548	86 529	118 193	8.8	82 596	7.1	8.2	8.0
Norfolk	192	1 270	180 065	32.5	27.8	49.9	1 521.9	15 073	45 375	86 469	117 756	14.0	90 039	6.5	7.0	6.8
Plymouth	366	1 599	130 665	17.6	37.2	34.0	1 138.5	13 343	35 869	75 816	96 541	8.4	74 576	8.5	11.5	10.3
Suffolk	770	2 770	219 820	47.1	39.9	41.0	1 462.9	21 011	33 522	54 169	81 050	7.1	54 280	21.5	31.5	32.7
Worcester	431	1 891	213 187	20.5	39.1	34.1	1 792.5	14 064	32 072	65 453	83 806	6.2	65 217	11.5	15.0	13.4
MICHIGAN	427	2 044	2 647 203	13.1	40.9	26.4	15 409.4	10 948	26 143	49 087	65 790	3.3	49 755	16.2	22.6	20.8
Alcona	95	1 313	1 472	7.2	51.3	13.5	7.3	9 494	23 304	38 019	48 706	1.3	36 377	17.5	30.9	28.2
Alger	252	693	1 702	16.2	56.6	17.1	11.3	10 423	20 798	39 211	51 155	0.7	45 308	15.5	23.3	21.4
Allegan	213	1 205	27 695	12.8	48.8	20.8	177.5	10 008	24 599	52 472	65 101	1.9	54 232	11.4	15.2	13.9
Alpena	265	1 621	6 248	10.7	45.6	16.1	45.0	11 337	21 975	38 353	49 610	0.9	38 121	16.8	26.0	23.0
Antrim	146	1 704	4 907	9.6	42.7	24.9	33.4	9 322	25 725	46 480	61 272	3.1	45 743	13.0	22.7	19.8
Arenac	241	887	3 019	4.4	58.3	11.5	21.3	9 514	20 663	38 129	49 041	1.5	36 460	19.9	31.5	26.0
Baraga	NA	NA	1 462	13.9	62.2	12.5	12.6	10 673	17 319	40 935	50 541	1.8	41 624	15.8	21.6	19.2
Barry	136	1 054	14 200	9.9	46.2	18.5	84.2	9 003	25 264	53 730	65 153	1.5	57 235	10.2	15.0	13.4
Bay	284	1 999	25 363	12.0	46.5	18.6	155.3	11 226	24 538	45 715	58 536	1.6	46 061	16.8	24.7	20.5
Benzie	115	1 033	3 381	9.3	43.6	24.8	19.9	9 256	25 433	47 620	59 167	1.6	48 846	11.8	18.6	17.2
Berrien	390	1 955	39 230	21.6	43.2	24.8	262.7	11 019	24 304	44 701	60 787	2.5	44 145	17.7	26.2	23.4
Branch	282	1 369	9 921	10.3	54.5	13.1	74.7	12 092	20 823	42 538	55 341	1.9	46 371	15.2	23.3	21.1
Calhoun	548	2 835	34 541	11.2	45.6	18.6	239.7	12 695	23 202	43 199	57 522	1.9	45 916	15.4	23.5	22.2
Cass	215	1 317	12 609	9.2	49.1	16.9	70.3	10 377	23 222	45 166	58 664	1.6	48 030	14.8	22.1	19.3
Charlevoix	137	1 366	5 711	10.2	40.3	27.1	57.7	16 010	27 231	46 709	64 854	3.5	47 991	12.6	19.0	17.2
Cheboygan	121	1 426	4 933	9.8	51.7	16.8	37.2	12 346	23 648	39 486	52 789	1.7	41 930	16.1	28.3	25.6
Chippewa	273	1 188	9 112	10.2	48.7	19.4	55.3	12 400	20 563	40 828	52 734	1.5	38 989	19.9	24.7	22.2
Clare	321	1 958	6 470	9.0	56.2	10.5	53.8	11 999	18 572	33 264	42 983	0.5	34 655	24.5	38.8	35.1
Clinton	80	647	22 488	11.2	34.6	28.7	102.6	10 210	28 889	60 381	74 882	3.1	60 650	10.0	11.0	10.4
Crawford	259	1 657	2 722	9.3	50.2	15.8	15.3	9 388	21 964	42 666	51 644	0.2	41 101	16.5	28.4	26.1
Delta	160	2 014	8 112	8.7	45.5	18.0	51.9	10 770	22 525	42 070	51 458	0.8	43 338	14.8	20.7	18.4
Dickinson	NA	NA	5 330	8.5	47.6	21.4	43.5	11 485	24 948	44 350	57 294	1.7	45 174	14.4	18.5	16.2
Eaton	205	1 619	27 259	14.6	36.7	24.2	180.1	10 340	27 089	55 223	65 803	2.1	57 088	9.8	14.4	12.7
Emmet	201	1 087	7 922	12.1	32.9	33.3	49.6	10 194	30 861	51 113	73 464	4.6	50 191	11.6	16.4	15.1
Genesee	654	2 720	112 255	10.5	44.0	19.2	699.6	10 792	22 536	41 879	55 656	1.7	41 787	21.5	33.2	30.4
Gladwin	212	1 280	4 785	12.4	55.6	12.5	26.7	8 578	20 753	37 725	48 791	1.3	39 721	18.5	31.0	28.5
Gogebic	89	1 202	2 816	6.5	46.8	17.6	17.9	10 041	20 570	34 021	45 791	1.0	33 600	20.9	30.7	28.4
Grand Traverse	216	1 094	20 459	12.9	34.4	30.8	151.9	13 568	28 400	52 487	70 307	3.5	55 592	9.7	13.5	12.4
Gratiot	217	1 351	10 262	22.3	53.0	13.8	78.6	11 613	18 922	41 833	52 365	1.0	43 509	18.5	22.9	20.4
Hillsdale	183	1 058	11 461	23.7	53.6	15.6	63.7	10 674	20 888	42 183	53 133	1.3	44 780	16.6	25.6	22.7
Houghton	116	1 162	12 800	5.6	43.1	29.6	53.4	10 008	19 883	36 443	50 084	1.6	39 126	18.7	18.5	17.3
Huron	201	1 050	6 798	10.2	56.8	14.1	57.7	11 189	22 739	41 290	51 577	1.4	41 678	14.1	20.9	19.0
Ingham	580	2 306	103 328	8.7	29.9	36.5	449.5	12 010	25 010	45 278	62 430	3.2	45 840	20.1	23.7	22.0
Ionia	241	1 430	16 308	10.9	50.5	14.2	94.7	11 418	20 549	48 100	56 900	1.0	48 681	15.2	18.5	16.3
Iosco	213	1 810	4 368	9.8	52.6	14.5	40.4	10 180	23 262	36 928	50 404	1.3	37 122	19.0	31.4	30.7
Iron	148	1 737	1 986	7.6	52.0	19.9	12.3	9 097	22 092	35 689	46 421	1.4	35 961	17.3	25.5	23.4
Isabella	191	1 709	31 056	5.4	42.0	26.1	54.6	9 226	19 698	37 615	53 068	2.0	42 431	28.3	21.7	18.6
Jackson	414	2 145	40 319	15.8	44.9	19.0	257.0	11 350	22 879	45 452	58 582	1.9	46 670	15.4	24.0	22.7
Kalamazoo	500	2 786	82 298	10.6	31.3	34.4	367.5	11 053	25 943	46 356	64 554	3.4	46 283	18.9	20.4	18.7
Kalkaska	325	1 921	3 639	7.7	56.5	13.0	20.5	9 086	20 445	39 986	48 994	1.2	40 709	17.4	27.0	25.9
Kent	365	2 015	172 320	20.6	36.7	32.6	1 049.4	11 232	26 436	52 716	69 172	3.6	53 342	15.3	20.0	19.2

1. Data for serious crimes have not been adjusted for underreporting; this may affect comparability between geographic areas and over time. 2. Per 100,000 population estimated by the FBI.
3. All persons 3 years old and over enrolled in nursery school through college. 4. Persons 25 years old and over. 5. Elementary and secondary education expenditures.
6. Based on population estimated by the American Community Survey, 2010–2014.

Table B. States and Counties — **Personal Income**

STATE County	Personal income, 2014										Earnings, 2014		
	Total (mil dol)	Percent change, 2013–2014	Per capita[1] Dollars	Per capita[1] Rank	Wages and salaries (mil dol)	Supplements to wages and salaries; employer contributions (mil dol) Pension and insurance	Supplements Government social insurance	Proprietors' income (mil dol)	Dividends, interest, and rent (mil dol)	Personal transfer receipts (mil dol)	Total (mil dol)	Contributions for government social insurance (mil dol) From employee and self-employed	From employer
	62	63	64	65	66	67	68	69	70	71	72	73	74
MARYLAND—Cont'd													
St. Mary's	5 545	3.7	50 234	373	3 046	635	240	225	997	714	4 145	229	240
Somerset	760	2.6	29 389	2 792	301	84	23	92	133	250	499	27	23
Talbot	2 376	2.0	63 111	101	815	137	62	193	767	410	1 207	77	62
Washington	5 966	3.5	39 887	1 195	2 909	529	225	273	966	1 307	3 936	243	225
Wicomico	3 776	4.7	37 187	1 574	1 906	390	147	276	610	929	2 719	160	147
Worcester	2 563	3.4	49 592	406	848	159	71	251	721	553	1 329	85	71
Baltimore city	26 424	4.4	42 428	909	21 402	3 709	1 580	2 182	4 440	7 542	28 874	1 675	1 580
MASSACHUSETTS	396 206	4.4	58 737	X	221 843	32 657	15 208	32 005	74 156	58 939	301 712	16 472	15 208
Barnstable	12 872	4.2	59 892	133	4 274	786	324	1 046	3 570	2 490	6 430	382	324
Berkshire	6 109	3.2	47 458	501	2 732	502	203	457	1 205	1 492	3 894	225	203
Bristol	24 843	4.2	44 827	692	10 530	1 945	776	1 185	3 102	5 552	14 436	812	776
Dukes	1 190	5.3	68 574	68	411	70	32	149	462	144	662	36	32
Essex	43 263	4.6	56 252	192	17 758	2 925	1 287	2 908	7 564	6 822	24 878	1 383	1 287
Franklin	3 195	3.1	45 088	671	1 050	232	77	207	558	778	1 566	89	77
Hampden	20 321	3.3	43 407	804	9 868	1 876	714	966	2 582	5 833	13 424	739	714
Hampshire	6 838	3.0	42 490	901	2 799	702	184	393	1 324	1 083	4 077	195	184
Middlesex	108 881	4.7	69 337	62	67 753	8 400	4 638	8 621	23 144	10 703	89 412	4 925	4 638
Nantucket	981	7.1	90 326	13	374	51	31	134	436	60	590	31	31
Norfolk	51 816	4.4	74 851	43	21 101	3 023	1 524	3 465	11 865	4 871	29 113	1 601	1 524
Plymouth	28 593	4.7	56 393	187	9 300	1 700	669	2 318	4 375	4 455	13 987	768	669
Suffolk	48 136	4.8	62 737	104	56 329	7 321	3 499	8 011	8 701	7 893	75 160	3 977	3 499
Worcester	39 169	4.2	48 151	471	17 563	3 124	1 251	2 146	5 268	6 763	24 084	1 308	1 251
MICHIGAN	403 726	4.1	40 740	X	204 476	32 528	15 716	28 330	67 245	86 899	281 051	17 839	15 716
Alcona	354	2.9	33 838	2 141	60	13	5	21	78	144	99	11	5
Alger	264	3.8	27 903	2 928	94	22	7	14	50	92	137	10	7
Allegan	4 424	5.0	38 858	1 341	1 668	295	128	427	672	823	2 519	158	128
Alpena	1 023	3.5	35 286	1 893	444	93	36	71	161	356	644	44	36
Antrim	883	5.2	37 967	1 458	169	38	14	63	233	273	284	24	14
Arenac	517	4.4	33 653	2 166	154	31	13	48	77	181	245	19	13
Baraga	269	3.4	31 089	2 572	121	33	10	13	47	84	177	11	10
Barry	2 297	4.9	38 742	1 359	483	102	37	209	350	465	831	57	37
Bay	3 867	3.6	36 419	1 702	1 561	278	122	159	567	1 107	2 120	147	122
Benzie	621	5.0	35 451	1 866	138	27	12	38	151	179	215	18	12
Berrien	6 227	4.7	40 113	1 158	2 894	554	223	328	1 003	1 487	4 000	254	223
Branch	1 361	1.8	31 262	2 548	534	103	42	88	216	387	768	52	42
Calhoun	4 732	2.6	35 084	1 916	2 850	482	217	163	734	1 291	3 712	236	217
Cass	1 920	4.2	37 195	1 572	348	72	27	84	311	475	531	42	27
Charlevoix	1 130	4.3	43 251	820	421	77	35	61	310	248	594	41	35
Cheboygan	839	3.5	32 688	2 336	209	41	19	52	184	292	322	27	19
Chippewa	1 157	-4.0	30 187	2 693	475	137	38	44	198	340	694	43	38
Clare	932	3.3	30 419	2 663	267	59	21	82	138	356	428	34	21
Clinton	3 074	4.2	39 770	1 212	699	111	56	247	429	497	1 113	74	56
Crawford	409	4.8	29 737	2 754	157	31	13	33	71	148	234	17	13
Delta	1 272	3.4	34 790	1 970	552	101	46	49	209	389	748	53	46
Dickinson	1 080	4.5	41 617	997	637	122	53	28	196	271	840	52	53
Eaton	3 959	3.1	36 463	1 695	1 604	277	124	161	587	844	2 165	145	124
Emmet	1 499	3.8	45 142	666	692	118	59	92	410	328	960	62	59
Genesee	14 401	3.3	34 878	1 954	5 979	1 022	470	827	1 946	4 386	8 299	573	470
Gladwin	779	3.9	30 640	2 635	148	30	12	13	124	303	204	21	12
Gogebic	523	4.0	33 262	2 235	197	46	16	24	110	184	283	20	16
Grand Traverse	3 870	5.1	42 633	886	2 032	347	161	570	745	743	3 110	195	161
Gratiot	1 432	2.4	34 374	2 051	531	110	42	167	185	369	850	53	42
Hillsdale	1 453	1.8	31 667	2 494	534	101	42	92	206	400	769	52	42
Houghton	1 154	3.4	31 614	2 510	484	119	38	42	229	338	684	44	38
Huron	1 358	1.7	42 356	918	439	84	35	208	276	361	767	45	35
Ingham	10 213	3.7	35 888	1 794	7 258	1 452	542	677	1 664	2 162	9 929	581	542
Ionia	1 929	4.7	30 000	2 716	675	144	55	130	230	442	1 004	61	55
Iosco	813	3.0	31 971	2 439	274	57	23	31	154	339	384	31	23
Iron	404	2.8	35 497	1 856	133	30	11	13	73	159	186	14	11
Isabella	2 176	4.2	30 810	2 614	1 101	270	86	130	355	589	1 587	94	86
Jackson	5 509	2.9	34 490	2 029	2 564	478	200	248	803	1 426	3 490	227	200
Kalamazoo	10 659	3.9	41 182	1 040	5 637	959	432	611	2 067	1 979	7 640	467	432
Kalkaska	534	5.5	30 679	2 630	195	32	15	49	75	173	291	22	15
Kent	29 329	5.2	46 610	550	17 191	2 551	1 337	2 521	7 201	4 356	23 601	1 434	1 337

1. Based on the resident population estimated as of July 1 of the year shown.

Table B. States and Counties — Earnings, Social Security, and Housing

STATE County	Earnings, 2014 (cont.) — Percent by selected industries									Social Security beneficiaries, December 2014		Supplemental Security Income recipients, December 2014	Housing units, 2015	
	Farm	Mining	Construction	Manu-facturing	Infor-mation: professional, scientific, technical services	Retail trade	Finance, insurance, real estate and leasing	Health care and social assistance	Govern-ment	Number	Rate[1]		Total	Percent change, 2010–2014
	75	76	77	78	79	80	81	82	83	84	85	86	87	88
MARYLAND—Cont'd														
St. Mary's	0.0	D	4.1	0.7	25.7	3.8	1.5	6.2	45.7	14 925	135	1 586	43 625	5.7
Somerset	11.6	0.0	4.5	4.0	2.8	3.1	D	10.1	44.3	5 300	207	826	11 271	1.3
Talbot	1.7	D	7.2	5.0	12.5	8.1	7.8	19.5	11.6	10 720	285	547	20 236	3.4
Washington	1.4	0.1	5.1	12.1	4.9	10.1	11.4	15.1	15.8	30 775	206	3 409	61 344	0.9
Wicomico	2.7	D	5.2	8.3	6.2	9.1	4.4	20.0	19.2	19 730	194	2 567	42 225	2.5
Worcester	3.4	D	6.0	3.0	4.9	13.4	6.5	9.6	19.8	14 640	284	839	55 856	0.2
Baltimore city	0.0	0.0	D	3.1	11.9	2.3	10.1	19.2	21.4	103 995	167	36 853	297 063	0.1
MASSACHUSETTS	0.1	0.1	5.1	8.6	18.5	4.7	12.2	13.5	12.8	1 224 469	181	188 726	2 845 699	1.3
Barnstable	0.1	0.1	10.1	2.5	9.4	9.5	6.7	16.9	19.8	69 375	323	3 336	162 118	1.1
Berkshire	0.1	0.1	6.9	9.9	8.6	7.7	7.5	18.9	15.0	33 980	264	4 076	68 397	-0.2
Bristol	0.1	0.0	6.5	D	6.8	8.1	3.7	16.0	16.2	118 590	214	19 151	231 628	0.5
Dukes	0.1	D	19.6	D	D	9.7	5.8	9.8	17.7	4 065	235	139	17 614	2.5
Essex	0.0	D	6.0	17.3	11.4	6.3	5.9	15.9	13.8	144 875	188	23 082	309 219	0.8
Franklin	0.2	D	7.3	14.4	6.3	7.8	3.0	13.0	20.2	16 430	232	2 100	33 695	-0.2
Hampden	0.0	0.1	5.5	10.4	6.0	6.3	9.8	19.6	19.7	99 535	212	30 333	192 002	-0.1
Hampshire	0.1	0.1	4.8	4.7	D	6.5	3.8	12.5	33.7	28 705	178	2 898	63 004	0.6
Middlesex	0.1	0.2	4.7	11.2	29.3	3.5	6.6	8.6	9.1	242 715	154	25 590	621 741	1.6
Nantucket	0.0	0.0	21.2	D	D	9.3	5.7	6.6	12.6	1 620	150	34	11 951	2.9
Norfolk	0.0	0.1	7.4	7.3	15.7	6.7	13.4	12.9	10.4	119 571	172	10 399	273 949	1.3
Plymouth	0.1	0.1	9.5	6.2	9.4	7.4	7.1	14.6	18.8	100 845	199	9 234	203 357	1.6
Suffolk	0.0	D	2.3	1.2	20.7	2.1	26.6	15.5	11.4	96 325	125	35 367	326 935	3.6
Worcester	0.0	0.1	5.9	13.5	9.8	6.1	7.1	16.4	17.2	148 235	182	22 987	330 089	1.0
MICHIGAN	0.7	0.4	4.9	17.1	11.8	6.0	6.6	12.3	14.9	2 121 776	214	277 309	4 550 296	0.4
Alcona	2.1	0.0	7.8	12.9	D	10.1	4.5	17.8	19.8	4 720	452	310	11 038	-0.3
Alger	0.9	0.0	4.5	23.5	D	5.5	D	7.9	32.3	2 885	305	180	6 607	0.8
Allegan	4.2	0.8	8.0	34.7	3.0	5.4	4.1	4.8	11.9	23 725	209	1 676	50 007	1.2
Alpena	0.5	2.2	5.8	16.7	D	9.5	3.9	9.8	30.4	9 500	328	1 190	15 943	-0.7
Antrim	2.6	D	10.0	15.4	5.2	7.8	5.4	D	23.4	7 825	337	518	17 865	0.2
Arenac	5.2	D	4.6	15.2	5.2	7.4	2.0	14.5	19.0	5 190	339	635	9 739	-0.7
Baraga	0.1	D	2.5	19.1	2.4	3.2	D	D	49.5	2 350	272	192	5 251	-0.4
Barry	6.2	0.1	5.9	25.7	D	5.0	6.9	10.2	16.6	13 890	234	752	27 094	0.3
Bay	0.8	0.1	3.8	13.2	12.8	8.1	3.6	17.8	18.4	28 345	267	3 279	47 973	-0.5
Benzie	1.6	D	12.7	10.2	D	8.7	5.3	9.3	20.5	5 380	307	319	12 309	0.9
Berrien	1.3	0.2	4.0	30.2	3.9	5.5	3.9	11.2	14.3	37 255	240	5 020	76 793	-0.2
Branch	2.7	D	4.6	18.2	D	7.5	5.1	5.3	24.4	9 955	228	967	20 564	-1.3
Calhoun	0.6	D	3.6	20.9	D	5.0	2.0	13.4	21.8	31 855	236	4 941	60 602	-0.7
Cass	3.7	0.0	5.8	20.3	3.3	5.3	3.8	D	23.6	12 890	249	1 049	25 922	0.2
Charlevoix	0.4	D	D	27.4	D	5.3	4.8	13.1	18.3	7 435	284	505	17 399	0.9
Cheboygan	0.7	D	15.1	2.8	5.2	12.9	5.3	9.1	20.6	8 775	342	701	18 303	0.0
Chippewa	0.5	0.4	3.3	3.9	2.7	7.6	2.6	4.6	58.6	8 570	224	886	21 207	-0.2
Clare	1.5	D	8.4	13.8	3.6	8.7	2.6	9.0	25.3	9 960	325	1 322	23 095	-0.6
Clinton	7.8	0.4	10.4	17.5	D	7.9	5.9	6.4	13.1	14 990	194	659	31 150	1.5
Crawford	0.0	D	D	11.7	5.2	7.9	3.1	21.9	24.2	4 435	323	349	11 088	0.0
Delta	0.8	D	8.3	21.3	D	8.4	4.1	11.9	17.8	11 115	304	1 022	20 201	-0.1
Dickinson	0.1	0.0	19.1	20.6	D	7.0	2.2	6.3	25.6	7 235	279	534	13 994	0.0
Eaton	0.5	0.1	5.2	9.6	D	7.0	20.0	6.0	18.1	24 150	222	1 688	47 075	0.1
Emmet	0.2	D	7.4	8.4	D	9.9	4.8	22.2	16.5	8 505	256	537	21 382	0.4
Genesee	0.3	0.0	4.7	12.0	9.6	8.3	6.1	18.1	17.2	97 225	235	17 113	190 887	-0.7
Gladwin	1.0	D	9.2	15.9	1.8	12.8	4.1	D	23.7	9 035	355	929	17 633	-0.2
Gogebic	-0.1	0.0	4.5	13.9	2.7	7.3	4.1	13.7	32.9	4 730	302	434	10 734	-0.6
Grand Traverse	0.2	5.1	6.5	10.1	7.8	8.3	8.6	22.5	13.7	20 515	226	1 464	42 634	2.5
Gratiot	6.1	0.1	2.6	16.5	D	5.1	3.4	D	18.8	9 105	219	1 139	16 185	-0.9
Hillsdale	3.7	D	4.1	31.9	D	6.5	3.2	9.3	19.9	11 360	247	1 229	21 645	-0.5
Houghton	0.3	D	7.2	5.1	5.1	7.1	3.5	15.7	42.2	7 875	216	648	18 611	-0.1
Huron	19.8	D	5.4	12.7	D	5.9	4.7	D	13.6	9 660	301	739	21 155	-0.2
Ingham	0.2	0.4	3.7	11.7	7.8	4.6	7.9	13.6	31.3	47 830	168	7 838	122 150	0.7
Ionia	9.7	D	4.8	25.3	1.6	6.7	4.0	4.7	23.6	12 175	189	1 348	24 589	-0.8
Iosco	0.9	0.6	5.4	11.7	3.9	8.3	4.2	D	24.1	9 775	385	817	20 407	-0.2
Iron	0.6	D	5.5	9.6	D	9.7	3.8	13.8	28.5	4 075	359	305	9 261	0.7
Isabella	0.8	3.5	8.5	10.0	3.2	6.2	5.6	7.4	38.2	11 240	159	1 258	28 730	1.2
Jackson	0.2	0.2	3.9	19.9	5.1	6.7	3.5	14.5	15.6	36 200	227	4 603	69 016	-0.6
Kalamazoo	0.8	0.1	5.2	22.2	5.5	6.0	8.7	15.2	14.0	48 800	188	6 360	110 509	0.5
Kalkaska	0.5	21.4	13.5	5.9	2.3	4.7	4.7	3.3	16.7	5 045	290	479	12 113	-0.5
Kent	0.3	0.2	5.0	20.6	8.6	6.5	7.6	14.8	8.2	108 035	171	15 139	249 972	1.2

1. Per 1,000 resident population estimated as of July 1 of the year shown.

Table B. States and Counties — **Housing, Labor Force, and Employment**

STATE County	Housing units, 2010–2014 Occupied units — Total	Percent	Owner-occupied Median value[1]	With a mortgage	Without a mortgage[2]	Median rent[3]	Median rent as a percent of income[2]	Sub-standard units[4] (percent)	Civilian labor force, 2015 Total	Percent change, 2014–2015	Unemployment Total	Rate[5]	Civilian employment,[6] 2010–2014 Total	Percent Management, business, science and arts	Construction, production, and maintenance occupations
	89	90	91	92	93	94	95	96	97	98	99	100	101	102	103
MARYLAND—Cont'd															
St. Mary's	37 947	72.6	300 200	22.0	12.1	1 259	26.2	1.7	54 498	0.7	2 701	5.0	53 169	43.0	18.7
Somerset	8 498	64.6	149 700	28.4	16.1	716	40.8	1.5	9 438	1.7	779	8.3	8 198	27.2	22.7
Talbot	16 140	70.0	324 100	24.7	13.1	1 042	34.8	0.7	19 244	0.5	978	5.1	17 647	37.4	17.0
Washington	55 769	64.4	200 700	23.7	12.5	852	28.7	1.4	76 345	-0.1	4 417	5.8	67 997	32.7	24.2
Wicomico	36 479	63.1	175 500	23.2	13.4	992	33.0	3.3	50 820	1.5	3 473	6.8	47 545	34.5	21.7
Worcester	20 492	76.8	242 000	26.6	13.9	945	31.7	1.6	26 029	1.4	2 752	10.6	23 069	35.6	17.9
Baltimore city	242 212	47.2	155 000	25.3	14.9	944	32.9	2.7	295 482	0.4	22 726	7.7	269 078	39.5	16.1
MASSACHUSETTS	2 538 485	62.3	329 900	24.6	14.9	1 088	30.3	2.1	3 569 955	0.4	177 846	5.0	3 354 036	43.9	15.7
Barnstable	94 371	78.7	362 800	28.3	15.7	1 101	33.8	1.2	111 332	-0.2	7 011	6.3	100 903	37.2	18.3
Berkshire	55 369	68.5	204 100	23.5	14.5	754	30.3	1.0	65 608	-0.5	3 658	5.6	62 178	37.9	17.9
Bristol	211 001	62.5	275 400	25.2	15.1	813	30.1	1.7	288 062	0.1	18 144	6.3	265 468	33.7	21.7
Dukes	5 839	78.0	641 100	38.0	19.7	1 461	28.4	1.2	9 328	-1.1	640	6.9	8 764	41.7	19.6
Essex	286 896	63.1	349 300	25.2	15.4	1 063	31.3	2.3	405 706	0.5	20 928	5.2	377 044	40.9	17.1
Franklin	30 390	68.6	220 400	24.7	14.4	836	29.9	1.5	39 341	-0.1	1 777	4.5	37 423	39.9	20.9
Hampden	177 736	61.5	196 600	23.5	15.1	807	32.5	2.9	221 258	-0.3	14 967	6.8	207 957	33.5	20.5
Hampshire	58 776	65.7	261 700	24.0	13.7	946	31.4	1.5	86 635	0.1	3 835	4.4	83 351	45.0	15.4
Middlesex	583 809	62.5	404 600	23.9	14.4	1 320	28.7	2.0	857 671	0.6	34 731	4.0	817 053	52.8	12.3
Nantucket	3 978	64.2	912 600	31.6	16.3	1 742	27.0	4.2	6 948	0.2	383	5.5	6 145	28.5	27.9
Norfolk	258 675	69.0	393 500	24.1	14.7	1 305	29.3	1.7	368 331	0.6	16 012	4.3	351 762	51.1	12.0
Plymouth	180 659	76.4	328 200	25.6	16.0	1 120	32.4	1.4	267 574	0.4	13 992	5.2	248 411	38.3	17.5
Suffolk	290 631	35.5	365 200	26.0	15.4	1 279	31.0	3.7	416 871	0.7	19 256	4.6	388 711	44.1	12.5
Worcester	300 355	65.2	255 600	24.0	14.4	927	29.8	2.1	425 290	0.0	22 512	5.3	398 866	40.7	18.4
MICHIGAN	3 827 880	71.5	120 200	22.6	13.4	780	32.3	1.9	4 750 639	-0.1	257 643	5.4	4 293 574	34.7	22.8
Alcona	5 007	88.6	95 800	24.5	13.2	623	35.1	2.0	3 842	-0.1	296	7.7	3 294	23.6	31.9
Alger	3 609	85.5	117 200	26.1	12.5	605	32.1	1.7	3 242	-2.7	267	8.2	3 175	29.4	29.2
Allegan	41 767	81.7	137 500	22.9	12.4	754	28.0	2.3	60 922	1.5	2 410	4.0	50 406	28.4	33.8
Alpena	12 860	77.4	94 900	22.6	12.4	550	29.8	1.0	13 751	1.1	817	5.9	12 227	30.1	24.9
Antrim	9 593	85.7	136 800	25.8	12.9	692	33.6	2.8	10 052	-0.6	720	7.2	9 462	25.7	29.0
Arenac	6 409	83.6	87 800	24.8	13.5	570	30.5	1.1	6 258	-2.6	539	8.6	5 505	27.7	28.9
Baraga	3 055	83.1	86 500	23.3	14.1	529	28.0	0.9	3 306	-5.0	290	8.8	2 493	29.4	26.1
Barry	22 700	81.9	135 900	22.8	12.5	760	28.6	1.9	30 639	1.8	1 249	4.1	26 294	30.5	32.8
Bay	43 712	78.1	93 300	21.6	12.9	650	33.3	1.0	52 570	-1.5	2 902	5.5	45 845	30.2	23.5
Benzie	7 388	84.6	147 400	24.9	12.9	765	28.4	2.2	8 794	0.3	580	6.6	7 688	29.9	26.4
Berrien	60 320	71.9	130 700	21.5	12.8	665	32.3	1.7	74 150	0.5	3 694	5.0	67 637	32.3	24.8
Branch	15 863	77.7	94 800	22.6	12.2	672	30.7	3.5	19 256	-0.6	941	4.9	17 676	23.0	34.8
Calhoun	52 842	69.8	97 100	22.5	13.6	685	30.1	1.4	64 682	0.5	3 159	4.9	56 739	27.5	28.5
Cass	19 804	83.1	121 100	24.1	12.5	686	29.9	2.0	24 288	1.4	1 165	4.8	22 090	29.3	32.5
Charlevoix	10 518	81.2	149 700	24.9	13.1	654	30.3	1.0	13 207	0.4	754	5.7	11 534	29.5	26.3
Cheboygan	11 250	81.7	110 800	23.9	12.8	601	29.2	2.2	10 695	-0.2	939	8.8	9 847	24.3	27.2
Chippewa	14 382	70.3	101 500	21.2	12.7	612	32.0	1.8	16 880	-0.4	1 257	7.4	14 485	30.3	19.4
Clare	13 208	80.1	79 300	26.8	13.3	599	34.7	2.8	11 896	-0.7	880	7.4	10 289	22.4	29.8
Clinton	28 568	80.0	155 000	21.7	12.1	778	30.7	0.9	40 104	0.8	1 497	3.7	35 949	38.4	20.3
Crawford	5 781	82.0	97 000	22.6	12.6	711	32.3	2.5	5 254	-2.0	396	7.5	5 102	26.6	26.4
Delta	15 695	78.6	99 400	23.1	12.6	540	31.1	1.8	17 336	-1.1	1 123	6.5	15 480	26.6	29.7
Dickinson	11 263	82.1	86 800	21.7	14.2	653	28.2	0.8	12 802	-0.9	688	5.4	11 297	30.7	27.0
Eaton	43 562	71.5	133 400	21.8	13.1	772	28.7	1.4	56 313	0.5	2 379	4.2	50 620	33.9	22.8
Emmet	13 612	76.7	165 500	23.6	12.5	764	30.4	1.7	17 762	-1.4	1 224	6.9	15 808	34.4	18.5
Genesee	165 962	69.4	88 300	23.5	14.1	718	35.4	1.5	182 886	-1.1	10 653	5.8	157 974	30.2	24.2
Gladwin	10 827	84.5	99 000	25.3	13.6	556	33.3	2.5	10 116	0.3	700	6.9	8 490	25.9	31.4
Gogebic	6 916	76.1	66 900	21.5	13.5	527	29.9	1.1	6 625	-1.5	461	7.0	5 720	27.8	28.7
Grand Traverse	34 833	75.7	167 600	23.3	13.4	857	31.6	1.9	48 580	0.9	2 161	4.4	42 785	33.2	20.1
Gratiot	14 705	74.4	87 300	22.1	12.7	586	32.5	1.8	18 429	-0.7	999	5.4	16 135	27.7	28.0
Hillsdale	17 632	77.8	100 600	23.5	13.0	655	30.7	2.8	20 918	1.6	1 061	5.1	18 908	26.5	35.3
Houghton	13 941	69.1	89 900	20.6	13.1	620	34.0	2.4	16 743	-1.6	1 008	6.0	15 383	38.1	17.6
Huron	13 965	81.3	92 100	23.5	12.8	598	29.8	1.4	16 603	-0.1	855	5.1	13 729	27.3	34.1
Ingham	109 806	58.2	117 700	22.3	13.2	790	34.4	1.6	146 501	0.3	6 515	4.4	131 256	39.4	16.8
Ionia	22 140	78.4	109 100	23.0	13.2	679	33.9	1.9	29 544	0.5	1 293	4.4	26 013	26.4	31.6
Iosco	11 361	80.3	86 300	23.1	12.4	583	29.0	1.4	10 158	-1.8	733	7.2	8 845	23.6	30.0
Iron	5 415	84.9	75 800	24.1	15.2	535	29.3	0.7	5 265	0.7	354	6.7	4 441	26.2	27.4
Isabella	24 773	59.3	120 600	22.5	12.4	698	42.5	2.2	35 647	0.0	1 619	4.5	32 795	28.7	18.1
Jackson	60 485	72.6	110 500	22.4	12.9	731	33.1	2.0	73 043	-0.4	3 719	5.1	65 099	29.4	26.0
Kalamazoo	100 042	64.1	135 400	21.6	13.0	726	33.4	1.3	129 993	1.0	5 379	4.1	119 766	37.7	19.2
Kalkaska	7 123	80.8	95 200	24.8	13.3	702	29.1	2.9	7 761	0.2	564	7.3	6 697	22.1	32.4
Kent	230 895	69.2	136 700	21.6	12.4	762	30.1	2.1	343 743	1.7	12 314	3.6	296 289	35.6	23.0

1. Specified owner-occupied units.   2. A value of 10.0 represents 10 percent or less; a value of 50.0 represents 50 percent or more.   3. Specified renter-occupied units.
4. Overcrowded or lacking complete plumbing facilities.   5. Percent of civilian labor force.   6. Persons 16 years old and over.

Table B. States and Counties — **Nonfarm Employment and Agriculture**

STATE County	Private nonfarm establishments, employment and payroll, 2014									Agriculture, 2012			
	Number of establishments	Employment						Annual payroll		Farms			
		Total	Health care and social assistance	Manufacturing	Retail trade	Finance and insurance	Professional, scientific, and technical services	Total (mil dol)	Average per employee (dollars)	Number	Percent with:		Farm operators whose principal occupation is farming (percent)
											Fewer than 50 acres	500 acres or more	
	104	105	106	107	108	109	110	111	112	113	114	115	116
MARYLAND—Cont'd													
St. Mary's	1 925	28 959	4 224	308	4 563	482	8 638	1 436	49 587	632	48.3	3.3	53.6
Somerset	357	3 792	1 224	352	452	85	D	129	33 906	286	44.4	12.9	55.6
Talbot	1 464	17 049	3 341	1 348	2 761	621	1 002	651	38 203	328	34.8	22.9	46.0
Washington	3 435	59 656	10 467	6 061	10 172	6 652	1 758	2 163	36 263	860	46.3	5.3	49.8
Wicomico	2 534	36 723	8 628	3 012	6 558	1 171	1 355	1 393	37 941	510	52.4	8.0	60.2
Worcester	2 133	17 710	2 151	588	3 648	511	664	581	32 811	374	44.9	11.2	49.7
Baltimore city	12 377	290 404	76 521	11 700	17 530	16 424	21 486	16 888	58 155	NA	NA	NA	NA
MASSACHUSETTS	173 575	3 087 030	607 944	221 793	359 700	178 707	261 703	185 353	60 042	7 755	67.5	1.5	50.0
Barnstable	8 390	72 254	16 114	2 084	14 572	2 181	4 641	3 134	43 378	333	91.9	0.0	58.0
Berkshire	3 900	52 802	11 587	4 764	8 755	1 997	D	2 192	41 507	525	49.9	4.4	51.0
Bristol	12 703	192 140	41 180	24 131	34 019	4 980	6 128	8 241	42 889	717	74.5	0.7	49.0
Dukes	1 062	5 239	D	D	1 149	D	251	289	55 119	88	83.0	2.3	55.7
Essex	18 332	281 447	63 171	37 778	38 653	11 227	14 464	13 984	49 686	522	78.0	1.0	56.7
Franklin	1 579	19 620	3 427	3 652	2 955	516	602	765	39 010	780	49.4	3.3	56.9
Hampden	9 669	166 806	39 289	19 771	23 174	8 907	6 846	7 293	43 719	582	62.7	1.0	41.6
Hampshire	3 548	58 693	19 845	2 956	7 759	1 518	1 878	1 916	32 639	799	62.5	1.4	50.6
Middlesex	43 131	848 024	129 678	55 612	83 091	28 342	108 972	60 649	71 518	739	75.9	0.1	52.1
Nantucket	985	4 377	D	D	918	116	179	289	65 943	20	85.0	5.0	15.0
Norfolk	19 637	334 197	67 124	19 131	44 046	26 446	23 224	18 101	54 163	245	78.0	0.8	58.4
Plymouth	12 020	162 524	32 212	10 035	27 877	7 011	9 322	7 383	45 429	825	73.9	1.9	49.7
Suffolk	20 495	572 232	120 933	10 352	33 505	68 608	63 041	45 659	79 791	20	100.0	0.0	65.0
Worcester	17 661	283 752	61 772	31 399	39 223	14 706	17 194	13 250	46 696	1 560	64.4	1.0	43.4
MICHIGAN	218 282	3 620 465	603 270	538 840	457 164	152 273	249 224	165 700	45 768	52 194	43.9	8.8	48.4
Alcona	183	1 234	223	205	264	28	49	38	30 698	235	34.0	7.7	55.3
Alger	227	1 653	252	D	262	D	44	62	37 298	93	48.4	9.7	50.5
Allegan	2 279	36 129	3 609	13 028	3 507	D	1 462	1 600	44 286	1 396	51.8	7.9	48.2
Alpena	775	9 883	2 654	1 203	1 826	329	223	342	34 638	458	33.2	6.6	49.6
Antrim	534	3 462	323	626	585	125	97	108	31 301	415	41.0	5.5	56.9
Arenac	320	3 149	582	699	485	D	D	101	31 947	421	38.7	10.5	38.0
Baraga	195	1 751	300	505	267	54	D	56	32 093	57	29.8	15.8	43.9
Barry	853	9 582	1 315	2 972	1 242	712	D	361	37 638	1 031	44.5	6.7	43.5
Bay	2 234	30 512	7 125	3 480	5 474	915	1 435	1 142	37 420	766	36.9	14.6	54.4
Benzie	444	3 228	384	400	491	D	74	94	29 144	181	41.4	3.9	52.5
Berrien	3 543	53 366	9 144	8 773	6 966	1 262	1 932	2 273	42 584	1 063	57.9	7.0	51.0
Branch	820	11 010	1 611	2 438	1 720	534	372	406	36 921	1 054	41.0	10.8	46.0
Calhoun	2 617	61 843	19 006	13 013	6 127	974	2 212	2 725	44 067	1 023	35.1	10.8	45.7
Cass	725	7 112	1 002	2 318	816	191	D	226	31 821	798	43.4	10.0	49.0
Charlevoix	786	7 808	1 321	2 367	786	192	203	313	40 104	297	36.7	4.0	38.0
Cheboygan	745	4 534	824	276	1 072	211	97	144	31 707	313	39.0	4.8	40.6
Chippewa	821	8 979	2 053	536	1 800	D	271	264	29 355	409	25.4	11.7	39.1
Clare	534	5 775	1 245	951	1 008	D	159	196	33 917	460	40.7	5.0	50.2
Clinton	1 315	15 320	1 854	2 322	2 351	885	542	564	36 793	1 128	44.1	10.1	46.3
Crawford	299	3 570	D	535	505	D	76	140	39 314	49	61.2	0.0	49.0
Delta	1 048	11 647	1 936	D	2 250	689	394	408	35 051	283	23.3	16.3	58.3
Dickinson	867	12 714	D	D	1 964	323	341	539	42 410	162	27.2	8.0	35.2
Eaton	2 053	39 526	3 464	7 293	5 702	3 644	975	1 631	41 253	1 163	40.9	10.9	49.6
Emmet	1 461	14 353	3 292	1 174	2 652	337	416	547	38 131	287	33.1	3.5	44.9
Genesee	7 716	115 459	26 791	9 999	19 642	4 145	3 658	4 474	38 750	835	58.6	6.2	50.1
Gladwin	404	3 680	696	833	642	D	54	120	32 582	533	35.5	3.2	41.8
Gogebic	398	4 110	584	678	734	106	88	116	28 150	62	32.3	0.0	27.4
Grand Traverse	3 337	42 568	9 148	4 661	7 603	1 757	2 217	1 681	39 491	504	52.4	3.4	55.2
Gratiot	734	10 632	2 319	2 817	1 215	419	211	379	35 647	878	37.5	17.3	56.3
Hillsdale	762	10 299	1 286	3 951	1 349	260	187	368	35 767	1 530	44.2	7.8	38.4
Houghton	851	8 688	2 025	761	1 698	346	495	258	29 738	177	29.4	5.1	37.3
Huron	941	10 639	1 765	3 423	1 437	406	229	371	34 907	1 205	31.4	21.3	55.5
Ingham	6 118	105 370	22 407	7 742	13 436	8 245	6 100	4 487	42 587	944	55.3	8.5	51.5
Ionia	879	11 481	1 215	3 528	1 779	641	181	383	33 350	1 109	42.1	11.5	48.0
Iosco	612	6 051	927	988	1 270	239	181	197	32 485	283	40.3	5.3	45.2
Iron	366	2 562	428	354	497	D	105	80	31 063	117	30.8	6.8	49.6
Isabella	1 384	23 024	3 218	2 572	3 484	694	622	733	31 847	928	34.6	8.9	49.2
Jackson	2 905	48 179	9 518	8 773	7 310	1 292	2 724	2 109	43 784	1 073	48.7	7.7	45.4
Kalamazoo	5 511	103 748	18 184	15 810	13 267	5 702	3 802	4 690	45 202	734	56.1	8.9	48.6
Kalkaska	337	3 456	503	425	603	58	55	154	44 606	224	46.0	3.6	39.3
Kent	15 749	332 683	47 182	62 836	33 569	13 762	14 525	14 305	42 998	1 159	53.9	4.6	48.2

Table B. States and Counties — **Agriculture**

STATE County	Land in farms Acreage (1,000)	Percent change, 2007–2012	Acres Average size of farm	Total irrigated (1,000)	Total cropland (1,000)	Value of land and buildings (dollars) Average per farm	Average per acre	Value of machinery and equipment, average per farm (dollars)	Value of products sold Total (mil dol)	Average per farm (dollars)	Percent from: Crops	Live-stock and poultry products	Percent of farms with sales of: $10,000 or more	$100,000 or more	Government payments Total ($1,000)	Percent of farms
	117	118	119	120	121	122	123	124	125	126	127	128	129	130	131	132
MARYLAND—Cont'd																
St. Mary's	67	-2.3	106	0.7	41.2	700 921	6 603	80 758	21.8	34 494	87.4	12.6	42.6	6.6	783	30.1
Somerset	65	8.2	228	0.4	36.4	1 247 458	5 471	182 073	219.0	765 559	12.2	87.8	58.0	50.0	1 653	61.9
Talbot	119	9.6	364	7.6	98.2	2 408 598	6 612	177 098	89.5	272 893	71.2	28.8	58.5	34.8	2 380	69.2
Washington	130	13.6	151	0.8	85.3	901 269	5 981	117 867	107.7	125 219	42.2	57.8	47.6	24.2	1 078	26.2
Wicomico	84	-9.8	164	9.4	56.1	1 031 771	6 284	134 363	236.3	463 375	22.7	77.3	54.9	35.5	2 360	53.7
Worcester	99	-10.4	266	5.0	71.3	1 585 529	5 971	163 979	199.3	532 794	25.8	74.2	52.7	39.6	1 733	58.6
Baltimore city	NA	NA	NA	NA	NA	NA	NA	NA	NA	NA	NA	NA	NA	NA	NA	NA
MASSACHUSETTS	524	1.1	68	23.4	160.8	704 071	10 430	53 920	492.2	63 470	77.8	22.2	32.7	9.8	8 124	10.1
Barnstable	5	-10.6	14	1.2	1.5	500 691	35 657	50 009	19.1	57 438	50.8	49.2	40.5	11.4	358	7.5
Berkshire	62	-7.1	117	0.2	18.4	824 924	7 024	51 476	22.5	42 796	45.1	54.9	29.5	6.7	268	9.3
Bristol	35	-11.2	49	1.6	11.9	709 223	14 584	51 411	37.7	52 522	79.4	20.6	36.3	8.6	1 527	12.7
Dukes	13	60.6	145	0.2	D	1 416 193	9 800	84 943	3.5	39 671	71.9	28.1	34.1	6.8	D	3.4
Essex	22	-19.5	43	0.6	9.2	893 351	20 821	56 138	25.2	48 205	71.7	28.3	31.0	8.0	207	4.0
Franklin	90	13.0	115	2.1	22.5	700 144	6 083	68 964	55.1	70 585	71.0	29.0	31.9	10.3	1 987	16.4
Hampden	39	5.1	67	0.9	11.1	488 323	7 343	45 735	23.6	40 564	73.6	26.4	26.5	6.5	480	9.1
Hampshire	54	2.3	68	0.9	21.5	544 950	8 071	53 222	49.2	61 613	75.6	24.4	30.5	10.1	682	11.9
Middlesex	28	-16.7	38	1.7	10.7	730 977	19 135	50 583	76.6	103 593	89.7	10.3	35.7	10.1	482	9.3
Nantucket	1	100.3	62	D	0.6	1 642 150	26 658	20 950	1.7	82 800	84.0	15.9	55.0	15.0	0	0.0
Norfolk	9	-18.9	39	0.6	3.4	936 188	24 277	47 890	12.5	51 012	75.8	24.2	33.5	12.7	D	6.9
Plymouth	64	29.1	78	12.0	17.3	893 370	11 510	65 783	108.1	130 986	92.2	7.8	46.9	19.2	1 306	12.4
Suffolk	0	-75.8	1	D	D	246 000	205 000	7 700	0.2	8 100	96.3	4.3	40.0	0.0	0	0.0
Worcester	102	-4.3	65	1.3	32.2	609 428	9 338	47 396	57.5	36 845	68.9	31.1	25.4	7.0	690	8.1
MICHIGAN	9 949	-0.8	191	592.2	7 669.1	766 148	4 020	122 528	8 678.1	166 265	63.5	36.5	44.0	18.0	155 919	39.5
Alcona	38	-15.6	163	0.0	23.8	394 591	2 421	78 426	11.4	48 511	40.3	59.7	31.9	9.8	263	24.3
Alger	18	-3.1	191	0.0	8.7	395 710	2 070	54 075	3.0	32 527	29.4	70.6	38.7	6.5	119	29.0
Allegan	270	-1.8	194	28.1	223.3	927 485	4 790	152 066	580.8	416 071	33.4	66.6	45.1	19.7	3 286	27.1
Alpena	69	-19.4	151	0.0	44.1	367 974	2 433	82 430	23.7	51 644	40.2	59.8	37.3	11.4	694	32.8
Antrim	64	-4.7	155	3.4	33.9	554 149	3 554	77 942	21.0	50 593	73.0	27.0	29.9	8.7	1 324	31.1
Arenac	82	-13.7	194	D	63.0	539 781	2 782	114 143	51.2	121 620	70.0	30.0	33.0	17.8	1 570	72.2
Baraga	18	-4.9	311	0.0	7.9	574 842	1 848	71 667	1.5	25 825	53.2	46.9	38.6	7.0	79	26.3
Barry	165	-1.8	160	4.3	119.4	637 736	3 980	89 944	140.1	135 859	33.9	66.1	35.3	11.2	2 853	37.1
Bay	194	4.0	253	6.3	174.5	1 015 918	4 017	198 977	165.3	215 789	95.1	4.9	58.6	31.9	2 628	68.0
Benzie	21	-2.0	114	0.3	9.8	475 486	4 169	65 177	6.4	35 337	51.9	48.1	30.9	8.8	808	20.4
Berrien	156	-7.5	147	18.1	126.1	822 736	5 591	123 913	161.5	151 968	90.3	9.7	51.6	20.6	3 303	29.4
Branch	244	-2.4	232	44.5	197.7	823 531	3 554	132 288	175.3	166 362	71.5	28.5	44.0	20.3	4 329	54.2
Calhoun	225	-1.4	220	10.7	175.6	807 980	3 676	117 543	133.0	130 044	64.6	35.4	43.4	17.5	3 618	47.7
Cass	189	-0.9	236	57.6	148.0	936 370	3 960	147 259	187.2	234 535	67.1	32.9	43.1	19.9	2 666	47.9
Charlevoix	38	-9.4	126	0.2	20.8	465 684	3 684	52 899	9.9	33 391	60.3	39.7	30.6	6.4	182	14.5
Cheboygan	46	-4.2	146	0.5	21.8	361 479	2 483	51 425	9.3	29 633	60.5	39.5	25.2	3.2	221	20.1
Chippewa	93	-6.0	227	0.1	57.4	368 870	1 622	60 252	12.6	30 724	41.7	58.3	39.6	6.8	934	31.5
Clare	63	-8.6	136	D	30.7	385 265	2 835	54 583	20.4	44 263	30.3	69.7	31.1	8.3	438	24.8
Clinton	244	-10.2	216	4.2	205.7	939 155	4 345	133 106	262.6	232 828	46.7	53.3	49.6	21.5	3 797	54.2
Crawford	3	9.2	56	0.0	0.8	185 959	3 307	54 816	0.3	5 306	26.9	73.1	14.3	0.0	0	0.0
Delta	71	-8.9	250	0.6	35.0	488 406	1 951	83 208	15.0	52 883	51.0	49.0	38.5	13.1	588	35.7
Dickinson	29	15.0	177	0.3	15.5	390 512	2 211	77 451	5.6	34 759	51.6	48.4	34.0	7.4	186	30.2
Eaton	223	0.5	192	1.5	176.1	714 449	3 722	119 525	119.0	102 364	83.8	16.2	46.9	19.8	3 008	46.6
Emmet	40	0.6	139	0.3	17.9	438 456	3 161	55 383	6.7	23 429	66.1	33.9	34.1	4.9	117	12.5
Genesee	123	-4.6	148	1.5	102.6	570 910	3 867	107 984	91.3	109 389	88.7	11.3	38.4	12.9	2 131	32.2
Gladwin	67	-0.7	126	0.5	40.1	355 311	2 820	61 334	19.3	36 300	70.6	29.4	34.5	4.7	599	38.3
Gogebic	6	55.6	98	0.0	2.4	257 194	2 624	34 226	0.5	8 016	72.8	27.2	25.8	0.0	D	3.2
Grand Traverse	55	-12.8	108	3.0	36.4	577 258	5 333	79 274	18.2	36 202	76.3	23.7	40.1	9.7	1 273	28.8
Gratiot	289	0.9	330	9.5	259.5	1 486 503	4 510	209 694	345.0	392 976	57.7	42.3	56.3	31.7	4 522	68.6
Hillsdale	262	-2.8	171	9.1	207.9	590 512	3 444	101 482	161.5	105 577	71.8	28.2	35.6	14.5	6 159	57.7
Houghton	27	15.0	154	0.1	10.8	272 254	1 772	42 633	4.0	22 678	53.0	47.0	27.7	2.3	101	18.1
Huron	452	2.6	375	2.0	406.0	1 952 800	5 202	304 740	654.6	543 207	51.1	48.9	62.5	43.8	9 479	79.6
Ingham	201	7.7	212	1.7	167.4	866 715	4 079	128 773	131.3	139 131	77.4	22.6	42.2	17.2	2 925	27.2
Ionia	248	4.2	224	6.0	203.1	934 093	4 170	154 311	406.1	366 228	31.6	68.4	50.9	25.4	4 662	51.9
Iosco	38	-20.4	134	0.0	23.7	358 890	2 673	85 230	17.1	60 364	36.4	63.6	29.3	7.8	467	30.4
Iron	23	-17.3	196	0.5	9.5	390 043	1 989	50 376	3.7	31 222	87.3	12.7	25.6	6.8	25	17.9
Isabella	188	-3.9	203	3.4	148.9	772 920	3 806	104 693	119.4	128 664	65.7	34.3	46.7	19.2	2 703	52.3
Jackson	183	0.4	171	3.9	136.0	652 247	3 822	85 794	78.2	72 866	69.2	30.8	36.4	12.0	4 210	32.1
Kalamazoo	144	-0.9	196	39.1	112.9	909 857	4 653	148 903	244.0	332 383	79.7	20.3	48.5	21.5	2 473	26.7
Kalkaska	26	10.0	115	1.6	12.9	350 875	3 044	45 339	8.8	39 299	92.1	7.9	23.2	3.1	104	17.0
Kent	157	-7.4	136	10.0	120.5	795 991	5 858	111 424	231.9	200 053	77.8	22.2	42.6	16.6	2 417	22.7

Table B. States and Counties — Water Use, Wholesale Trade, Retail Trade, and Real Estate

STATE County	Water use, 2010 Total water withdrawn (mil gal/day)	Gallons withdrawn per person per day	Wholesale trade,[1] 2012 Number of establishments	Number of employees	Sales (mil dol)	Annual payroll (mil dol)	Retail trade,[2] 2012 Number of establishments	Number of employees	Sales (mil dol)	Annual payroll (mil dol)	Real estate and rental and leasing,[2] 2012 Number of establishments	Number of employees	Receipts (mil dol)	Annual payroll (mil dol)
	133	134	135	136	137	138	139	140	141	142	143	144	145	146
MARYLAND—Cont'd														
St. Mary's	7.9	75	39	397	189.5	17.6	294	4 835	1 227.0	109.5	83	312	94.7	11.4
Somerset	3.8	145	14	D	D	D	61	434	112.2	9.5	17	42	4.8	0.7
Talbot	7.2	191	56	443	277.4	19.9	222	2 635	670.2	64.6	55	179	34.7	6.3
Washington	58.8	399	137	1 917	1 804.2	89.0	612	9 244	2 457.6	207.6	141	755	216.5	29.4
Wicomico	19.9	202	108	1 122	1 231.4	49.9	390	6 375	1 608.3	145.0	126	624	86.3	20.7
Worcester	18.2	354	47	D	D	D	401	3 370	835.6	81.9	152	467	75.3	15.1
Baltimore city	25.3	41	544	8 592	7 954.3	495.2	1 839	15 747	3 647.7	379.0	596	4 055	883.7	187.6
MASSACHUSETTS	2 995.9	458	6 619	114 195	123 904.4	8 035.1	24 311	351 598	92 915.4	9 161.7	6 485	42 788	13 628.4	2 357.9
Barnstable	60.8	282	178	1 152	563.1	57.0	1 503	14 395	3 856.9	401.4	331	1 361	260.5	53.1
Berkshire	24.3	185	105	1 242	455.0	58.0	711	8 482	1 916.5	201.7	108	715	99.5	23.1
Bristol	882.1	1 609	517	10 556	9 375.8	626.2	2 192	33 806	8 403.5	813.8	418	1 382	293.7	53.1
Dukes	3.1	186	16	D	D	D	205	1 276	373.6	43.7	63	142	41.6	6.6
Essex	420.3	566	726	11 128	15 101.2	768.2	2 585	37 792	10 037.9	995.4	602	2 734	629.9	113.9
Franklin	47.1	659	64	D	D	D	262	2 903	703.7	73.3	37	110	16.9	2.9
Hampden	148.2	320	385	6 581	6 028.9	355.0	1 573	22 637	5 753.0	540.3	364	1 839	289.2	66.0
Hampshire	28.4	180	85	1 676	1 807.0	81.2	546	7 914	1 750.0	187.6	114	435	279.8	15.5
Middlesex	431.1	287	1 760	36 339	46 631.4	3 169.0	5 156	80 738	21 344.6	2 155.0	1 567	11 979	5 087.1	616.2
Nantucket	4.5	446	7	D	D	D	155	998	317.5	35.8	53	157	59.7	7.9
Norfolk	44.1	66	890	15 930	13 702.9	1 083.4	2 548	43 010	11 801.1	1 163.3	774	6 263	1 778.1	382.1
Plymouth	619.6	1 252	488	5 947	9 622.7	353.9	1 892	26 703	6 889.6	698.5	364	1 550	341.1	69.6
Suffolk	0.2	0	630	11 314	12 840.7	809.3	2 411	31 965	8 851.0	892.5	1 093	11 366	3 821.2	826.9
Worcester	282.3	353	768	11 502	7 126.8	636.8	2 572	38 979	10 916.5	959.5	597	2 755	630.2	120.8
MICHIGAN	10 837.2	1 096	9 392	132 490	115 704.9	7 474.6	34 858	441 190	119 302.0	10 527.3	7 826	48 706	11 974.5	1 806.9
Alcona	6.3	575	4	14	3.2	0.4	35	236	52.5	4.9	3	5	0.8	0.1
Alger	5.6	582	3	D	D	D	45	272	64.6	5.6	3	4	0.7	0.1
Allegan	23.6	212	106	1 354	609.4	130.1	335	3 354	949.9	76.3	69	210	38.9	8.0
Alpena	120.3	4 065	32	409	223.9	17.6	146	1 731	448.8	41.5	18	111	7.3	2.1
Antrim	58.7	2 490	9	40	15.7	1.2	88	530	169.6	13.4	22	D	D	D
Arenac	61.1	3 842	10	D	D	D	71	459	150.8	9.6	5	D	D	D
Baraga	15.5	1 752	3	9	3.3	0.2	29	275	53.1	5.3	5	D	D	D
Barry	8.2	139	26	179	122.5	7.3	124	1 198	286.0	24.0	24	68	8.1	2.8
Bay	608.3	5 644	87	D	D	D	419	5 526	1 303.0	124.5	65	212	29.3	4.7
Benzie	2.6	146	5	D	D	D	73	535	128.0	11.2	15	33	3.3	0.7
Berrien	2 019.0	12 875	133	D	D	D	587	6 783	1 681.1	147.2	152	614	78.3	19.5
Branch	13.2	292	28	265	124.3	11.3	132	1 612	435.2	39.0	31	77	15.0	2.2
Calhoun	28.1	206	94	D	D	D	488	5 858	1 702.3	133.4	87	373	53.9	10.5
Cass	22.6	432	45	321	316.2	15.8	116	876	256.9	18.9	28	48	7.9	1.0
Charlevoix	21.3	820	15	51	9.6	1.4	116	823	196.8	18.0	29	115	18.0	3.9
Cheboygan	7.6	291	13	89	37.4	3.1	147	1 161	310.2	27.3	17	D	D	D
Chippewa	8.9	232	25	295	145.4	11.0	148	1 725	454.1	36.8	26	96	8.9	1.8
Clare	3.8	122	11	D	D	D	118	1 027	261.3	22.5	9	24	2.5	0.4
Clinton	9.7	128	52	869	659.2	39.7	170	2 090	749.2	53.0	53	204	34.7	6.8
Crawford	2.3	161	4	34	21.5	1.3	60	531	214.6	12.0	13	22	3.7	0.7
Delta	67.4	1 817	45	331	157.1	12.3	183	2 160	507.1	45.0	29	64	6.8	1.2
Dickinson	25.2	963	42	D	D	D	154	1 824	431.2	40.4	28	D	D	D
Eaton	8.9	83	71	1 474	1 076.7	65.4	330	5 619	1 453.0	129.9	79	380	78.8	12.4
Emmet	6.3	193	34	217	95.8	9.4	293	2 606	627.8	63.5	41	204	24.8	3.9
Genesee	13.4	31	272	3 969	3 673.6	218.5	1 459	19 368	5 307.9	444.9	318	1 843	255.8	57.1
Gladwin	2.3	91	7	38	11.2	1.4	82	598	141.0	11.6	13	102	6.1	2.6
Gogebic	2.3	138	9	66	74.3	2.1	79	764	159.6	15.1	14	104	7.2	1.6
Grand Traverse	14.3	165	134	1 146	454.0	52.5	560	7 184	1 767.8	174.8	151	488	96.5	17.0
Gratiot	8.4	198	27	D	D	D	135	1 339	344.2	28.2	19	60	7.5	1.3
Hillsdale	9.4	201	33	301	407.9	12.7	139	1 330	370.2	32.1	25	54	12.0	1.4
Houghton	4.0	110	21	D	D	D	149	1 638	329.4	32.7	25	D	D	D
Huron	62.5	1 887	38	518	523.6	26.4	161	1 481	361.9	29.1	9	11	2.6	0.4
Ingham	220.5	785	204	2 701	5 407.9	130.9	916	13 217	3 260.5	293.0	253	1 946	236.4	68.8
Ionia	9.7	151	26	D	D	D	143	1 589	430.4	34.8	17	45	6.9	1.1
Iosco	4.3	168	5	D	D	D	115	1 302	327.2	28.8	19	37	4.3	0.6
Iron	1.4	115	10	44	11.7	1.3	61	433	101.6	9.1	17	37	3.5	0.7
Isabella	8.2	117	51	504	362.3	19.7	215	3 322	769.9	71.5	55	1 077	70.7	27.6
Jackson	20.3	127	137	D	D	D	526	7 003	1 841.7	163.5	99	567	82.0	15.5
Kalamazoo	51.8	207	234	3 668	1 553.7	197.3	863	12 708	3 129.4	284.2	210	2 328	223.7	71.6
Kalkaska	3.4	197	18	167	75.7	7.1	54	525	155.9	12.7	9	D	D	D
Kent	27.7	46	976	22 090	17 703.0	1 235.3	2 116	31 615	8 698.6	803.1	640	3 990	698.0	143.7

1. Merchant wholesalers, except manufacturers' sales branches and offices. 2. Employer establishments.

Table B. States and Counties — Professional Services, Manufacturing, and Accommodation and Food Services

STATE County	Professional, scientific, and technical services, 2012				Manufacturing, 2012				Accommodation and food services, 2012			
	Number of establishments	Number of employees	Receipts (mil dol)	Annual payroll (mil dol)	Number of establishments	Number of employees	Receipts (mil dol)	Annual payroll (mil dol)	Number of establishments	Number of employees	Sales (mil dol)	Annual payroll (mil dol)
	147	148	149	150	151	152	153	154	155	156	157	158
MARYLAND—Cont'd												
St. Mary's	309	8 327	1 654.0	640.7	28	225	D	9.6	184	3 670	166.6	48.1
Somerset	20	D	D	D	13	340	223.2	13.2	29	272	12.8	3.1
Talbot	134	1 678	260.2	97.6	41	1 465	D	57.9	133	2 476	131.4	42.1
Washington	234	1 726	190.6	72.1	127	5 612	2 735.0	307.2	290	5 083	258.7	73.8
Wicomico	227	1 661	238.8	91.0	79	3 108	1 216.8	127.2	208	3 871	187.1	48.7
Worcester	142	642	65.5	28.7	36	604	241.7	24.6	413	6 050	552.3	153.6
Baltimore city	1 555	21 994	4 747.0	1 890.5	409	11 748	5 043.3	574.0	1 541	21 832	1 607.8	435.6
MASSACHUSETTS	21 422	255 022	60 370.0	23 826.5	6 806	234 168	81 927.8	14 395.3	16 898	273 185	17 509.0	5 019.8
Barnstable	733	4 806	932.9	341.7	187	2 157	478.6	119.4	1 143	13 117	1 000.4	291.5
Berkshire	338	2 688	397.7	162.8	151	5 275	1 288.9	310.7	522	7 006	418.7	124.2
Bristol	1 045	6 050	823.3	295.3	674	26 935	8 015.0	1 552.1	1 241	19 755	969.1	276.1
Dukes	62	221	38.5	13.6	21	108	D	4.6	138	878	120.3	36.7
Essex	2 137	15 135	2 330.9	1 075.8	869	38 451	12 747.9	2 517.9	1 797	25 502	1 536.1	431.0
Franklin	132	584	153.6	27.6	105	3 615	1 682.5	171.4	147	1 864	85.5	25.4
Hampden	854	6 893	883.2	358.6	583	20 588	6 259.4	1 100.7	928	14 276	714.2	198.4
Hampshire	360	1 834	228.2	87.6	134	2 939	1 096.3	140.0	384	5 977	264.4	78.5
Middlesex	6 817	111 444	28 751.6	11 746.3	1 652	59 454	22 760.7	4 255.8	3 662	59 109	3 940.3	1 125.1
Nantucket	56	176	35.7	11.0	18	75	D	2.0	111	849	119.4	36.6
Norfolk	2 640	20 674	4 096.5	1 498.9	628	20 613	10 798.9	1 248.1	1 596	27 505	1 613.3	463.8
Plymouth	1 245	7 134	1 125.5	426.1	487	10 374	2 493.2	521.2	1 038	18 005	909.4	272.8
Suffolk	3 188	61 414	17 726.5	6 606.9	335	8 908	3 805.2	472.0	2 469	54 643	4 551.0	1 304.5
Worcester	1 815	15 969	2 846.1	1 174.2	962	34 677	10 475.8	1 979.4	1 722	24 699	1 266.9	355.4
MICHIGAN	21 650	D	D	D	12 444	514 058	238 892.4	27 611.4	19 491	347 337	17 962.4	4 871.7
Alcona	7	29	5.0	1.6	17	175	27.5	8.0	26	102	3.9	1.1
Alger	10	17	2.3	1.1	11	471	D	24.9	40	260	16.8	3.7
Allegan	161	1 387	171.6	85.8	202	13 273	5 286.6	633.9	207	2 697	131.9	37.1
Alpena	40	193	16.8	6.9	43	1 227	480.3	56.0	72	879	35.1	10.4
Antrim	36	128	9.8	3.3	40	776	175.0	29.6	59	946	42.6	15.5
Arenac	15	83	11.1	5.4	28	694	145.7	28.0	48	457	28.2	8.0
Baraga	3	11	0.9	0.3	21	440	150.3	17.1	17	D	D	D
Barry	63	308	20.7	8.9	49	2 725	1 115.7	122.9	80	982	38.5	11.3
Bay	152	1 360	111.0	57.1	123	3 650	1 149.4	190.6	233	4 039	172.0	47.6
Benzie	31	61	5.6	1.8	21	363	D	10.8	56	1 068	50.4	16.9
Berrien	284	2 149	201.0	108.3	289	8 330	1 962.8	388.9	365	5 323	241.7	69.4
Branch	45	391	114.4	18.1	72	2 604	812.7	115.1	78	1 071	47.2	12.8
Calhoun	191	1 058	93.0	55.5	148	11 179	5 445.1	599.3	280	6 023	471.2	104.3
Cass	47	191	15.4	5.8	70	2 249	721.7	96.4	65	778	30.9	8.5
Charlevoix	61	224	23.7	8.3	47	2 266	728.4	109.2	75	1 288	61.9	18.6
Cheboygan	41	112	11.2	4.2	31	248	57.1	10.2	119	689	67.4	18.0
Chippewa	42	D	D	D	27	498	90.1	22.1	111	2 157	136.3	38.3
Clare	30	144	16.5	7.9	26	811	254.0	42.7	64	812	34.7	9.1
Clinton	132	576	82.5	26.7	60	1 868	625.5	98.0	98	1 504	55.9	16.5
Crawford	17	62	10.3	2.1	21	499	184.2	24.2	43	550	22.6	5.6
Delta	78	499	57.8	12.1	68	2 364	854.3	137.4	99	1 213	45.3	12.4
Dickinson	53	358	31.3	12.4	41	2 224	983.6	109.6	73	809	31.6	8.7
Eaton	177	883	100.9	37.8	91	7 872	10 600.6	488.1	206	4 230	169.2	50.6
Emmet	110	394	61.3	22.2	54	984	281.2	40.1	139	2 280	122.4	37.5
Genesee	639	3 544	370.3	143.2	273	10 675	9 418.1	684.4	704	13 207	563.9	157.4
Gladwin	26	51	4.5	1.2	27	771	185.0	33.5	43	476	17.8	5.1
Gogebic	18	90	7.3	3.3	19	641	90.8	22.7	59	968	42.1	11.7
Grand Traverse	369	2 118	295.2	109.2	176	4 464	1 153.9	216.1	249	5 649	343.1	93.6
Gratiot	29	142	14.2	7.0	51	2 401	809.7	116.7	72	1 009	42.5	12.4
Hillsdale	46	166	17.1	5.4	77	3 673	1 445.7	149.8	68	786	31.8	8.7
Houghton	72	455	47.8	20.3	41	552	D	D	110	1 372	51.0	14.0
Huron	48	227	22.2	10.9	65	3 285	891.7	132.1	102	885	38.0	9.8
Ingham	742	5 940	1 026.8	344.1	190	7 572	4 972.9	416.5	609	11 266	483.0	134.6
Ionia	46	159	15.0	6.6	70	3 251	1 363.0	135.5	77	976	35.5	10.2
Iosco	30	218	11.9	5.5	41	869	226.7	33.2	80	677	34.0	9.1
Iron	29	105	9.9	4.2	17	395	D	16.7	33	293	12.5	3.0
Isabella	104	677	62.2	26.0	59	2 197	616.7	95.8	125	5 523	447.4	98.9
Jackson	217	2 504	367.1	180.4	268	8 414	2 621.3	409.3	275	4 788	201.5	57.3
Kalamazoo	544	3 689	576.8	203.2	311	15 557	7 385.6	911.1	546	11 663	477.9	146.3
Kalkaska	18	38	7.6	2.1	13	430	146.4	20.5	31	345	16.6	4.6
Kent	1 635	13 433	2 016.6	777.1	1 068	57 371	17 535.6	2 899.2	1 192	25 307	1 154.4	335.4

1. Establishment subject to federal tax.

Table B. States and Counties — **Health Care and Social Assistance, Other Services, Nonemployer Businesses, and Residential Construction**

STATE County	Health care and social assistance, 2012				Other services, 2012				Nonemployer businesses, 2014		Value of residential construction authorized by building permits, 2015	
	Number of establishments	Number of employees	Receipts (mil dol)	Annual payroll (mil dol)	Number of establishments	Number of employees	Receipts (mil dol)	Annual payroll (mil dol)	Number	Receipts (mil dol)	New Construction ($1,000)	Number of housing units
	159	160	161	162	163	164	165	166	167	168	169	170
MARYLAND—Cont'd												
St. Mary's	179	4 110	379.9	172.2	142	865	80.7	30.1	6 742	245.3	114 960	641
Somerset	38	1 121	74.7	35.1	30	101	11.8	2.2	1 439	50.1	24 699	181
Talbot	173	3 517	387.0	147.2	118	610	74.4	17.4	4 420	214.3	26 005	73
Washington	440	10 210	1 056.4	428.4	261	1 594	136.6	38.4	8 438	363.0	59 495	320
Wicomico	361	8 798	935.1	385.7	189	1 286	99.0	31.1	6 133	258.3	19 031	137
Worcester	140	1 956	196.1	80.4	143	868	82.8	23.4	5 039	253.6	51 945	266
Baltimore city	1 471	79 915	11 349.2	4 158.7	939	8 989	1 303.0	305.5	43 327	1 455.5	205 977	1 293
MASSACHUSETTS	18 386	587 485	63 583.1	27 696.7	14 008	93 489	10 455.1	2 931.3	502 274	26 790.8	3 980 521	17 424
Barnstable	811	15 781	1 766.8	730.5	590	3 176	320.4	95.6	25 490	1 313.5	198 776	572
Berkshire	438	11 415	1 091.4	488.4	278	1 675	144.1	39.5	10 121	445.3	58 072	214
Bristol	1 414	39 215	3 485.9	1 573.5	1 085	5 614	479.1	138.6	31 674	1 495.2	147 356	820
Dukes	61	784	91.1	42.7	54	164	25.6	6.4	3 879	212.1	81 720	123
Essex	2 080	62 430	5 324.0	2 497.2	1 449	8 386	727.3	225.5	58 468	3 030.2	264 578	1 100
Franklin	194	3 671	291.8	121.8	132	578	52.4	15.2	6 081	224.5	21 678	119
Hampden	1 161	37 660	3 822.0	1 659.5	809	5 662	497.1	138.7	23 956	1 152.8	51 332	270
Hampshire	435	18 108	875.9	459.1	301	1 627	164.1	48.9	12 853	556.7	43 952	188
Middlesex	4 489	124 041	15 136.6	6 421.7	3 397	24 727	2 984.3	890.7	131 892	7 254.4	935 385	4 645
Nantucket	35	392	53.4	23.0	44	155	39.9	8.1	2 418	185.9	125 623	144
Norfolk	2 234	66 785	5 406.8	2 524.8	1 576	10 253	1 184.0	321.8	55 172	3 453.9	346 806	1 441
Plymouth	1 213	31 032	2 904.1	1 305.7	969	5 915	500.5	163.9	36 565	1 973.1	238 493	1 183
Suffolk	1 816	116 274	16 983.3	7 058.9	1 988	17 967	2 602.9	629.2	52 973	2 990.1	1 215 855	5 313
Worcester	2 005	59 895	6 350.0	2 790.0	1 336	7 590	733.5	209.4	50 732	2 503.0	250 894	1 292
MICHIGAN	26 231	585 530	63 018.8	25 556.5	15 919	96 150	10 407.7	2 719.9	696 730	29 278.4	3 850 470	18 226
Alcona	12	D	D	D	8	D	D	D	682	26.0	2 411	24
Alger	20	299	22.2	8.6	13	37	4.0	0.9	584	18.9	3 621	23
Allegan	172	3 225	265.9	111.8	172	795	92.5	22.7	7 804	336.4	90 714	369
Alpena	83	1 724	122.6	47.4	65	258	23.5	5.3	1 938	75.4	3 322	22
Antrim	54	302	15.9	7.7	39	160	13.5	3.8	2 081	86.3	7 232	44
Arenac	34	647	58.7	20.6	24	D	D	D	885	33.1	3 627	18
Baraga	18	324	27.2	10.4	16	36	3.5	0.7	391	14.8	1 519	15
Barry	82	1 336	123.4	50.3	83	402	42.0	11.3	3 662	160.1	33 312	173
Bay	329	7 152	682.5	261.2	190	928	70.8	21.3	5 499	200.1	17 296	147
Benzie	30	D	D	D	25	86	5.6	1.7	1 729	64.5	12 050	58
Berrien	399	9 410	816.5	329.2	251	1 199	116.0	32.2	9 818	380.6	58 833	208
Branch	100	1 497	143.0	57.1	67	276	18.4	6.8	2 448	106.5	4 899	30
Calhoun	323	9 313	966.4	421.9	208	1 173	448.4	41.7	6 605	228.3	9 584	59
Cass	60	904	66.3	30.0	58	D	D	D	2 988	126.4	24 180	89
Charlevoix	74	1 187	104.5	48.7	65	247	25.4	6.3	2 574	113.4	9 555	32
Cheboygan	54	1 025	87.3	35.4	74	208	17.6	5.1	1 929	75.2	12 303	61
Chippewa	79	1 939	170.1	68.1	53	D	D	D	1 965	53.9	6 862	48
Clare	59	1 106	86.2	28.5	38	159	14.1	3.3	1 735	74.2	3 447	28
Clinton	112	1 664	140.4	50.3	94	495	37.7	11.6	5 243	213.2	41 534	214
Crawford	32	971	111.5	41.9	21	155	16.7	5.7	846	30.5	2 656	17
Delta	104	2 016	167.7	67.1	84	392	37.7	9.2	2 061	70.3	7 444	52
Dickinson	118	D	D	D	66	249	21.5	5.6	1 464	54.3	5 953	29
Eaton	236	3 506	282.4	117.2	157	1 093	136.7	45.4	6 953	250.1	22 302	107
Emmet	185	2 962	345.5	151.9	109	651	67.7	17.6	3 494	166.7	30 376	88
Genesee	1 294	25 418	2 787.5	1 148.7	562	3 406	376.2	91.1	28 368	973.6	81 603	413
Gladwin	39	611	55.8	17.0	26	154	11.1	2.9	1 514	75.1	10 880	54
Gogebic	32	661	63.0	25.8	42	131	10.2	2.6	867	27.9	2 280	13
Grand Traverse	396	8 782	995.6	397.1	199	1 327	133.2	37.5	9 236	432.6	77 243	447
Gratiot	104	2 339	236.7	82.4	46	223	35.1	6.4	2 242	90.0	4 222	23
Hillsdale	104	D	D	D	51	D	D	D	2 790	113.0	15 462	106
Houghton	92	D	D	D	67	D	D	D	1 977	59.0	8 248	44
Huron	97	1 741	159.2	59.9	60	234	24.6	5.6	2 273	97.5	10 728	47
Ingham	807	22 354	2 566.1	999.5	566	5 094	633.8	183.6	18 834	869.6	144 394	735
Ionia	103	1 226	105.2	39.0	66	271	22.9	5.7	3 295	110.6	11 922	59
Iosco	52	814	81.5	29.8	50	176	12.6	3.1	1 551	58.5	7 201	47
Iron	18	431	52.4	19.1	24	D	D	D	780	26.2	3 741	25
Isabella	202	3 040	222.1	94.7	111	601	46.0	12.3	3 565	160.9	13 943	114
Jackson	351	9 060	936.8	409.4	210	1 361	129.7	37.1	8 815	320.8	23 822	117
Kalamazoo	653	18 751	2 261.9	865.0	427	3 007	384.4	91.0	16 055	661.5	128 570	491
Kalkaska	27	475	42.9	15.0	26	136	17.2	5.2	1 193	49.9	6 722	52
Kent	1 581	50 294	5 244.9	2 133.2	1 083	8 294	765.1	220.5	44 902	2 167.8	455 038	1 838

STATE County	Government employment and payroll, 2012		March payroll (percent of total)							Local government finances, 2012		General revenue		
													Taxes	
														Per capita[1] (dollars)
	Full-time equivalent employees	March payroll (dollars)	Administration, judicial, and legal	Police and Corrections	Fire Protection	Highways and transportation	Health and Welfare	Natural resources and utilities	Education and libraries	Total (mil dol)	Inter-governmental (mil dol)	Total (mil dol)	Total	Property
	171	172	173	174	175	176	177	178	179	180	181	182	183	184
MARYLAND—Cont'd														
St. Mary's..................	3 187	14 069 480	5.9	10.5	0.0	2.3	1.5	4.3	73.2	356.5	125.4	191.8	1 760	923
Somerset..................	890	3 320 415	5.7	9.8	0.0	2.6	2.1	5.5	67.9	83.1	45.3	26.3	1 002	735
Talbot.....................	1 356	5 353 079	6.3	12.0	0.0	3.6	4.8	9.8	53.9	135.2	24.3	75.9	1 992	1 178
Washington	5 270	21 889 886	4.2	7.2	2.7	2.6	0.7	8.0	73.2	547.6	234.3	228.4	1 531	989
Wicomico...................	4 063	15 857 286	4.2	10.7	1.8	1.7	1.9	5.3	73.7	376.1	166.7	134.3	1 334	842
Worcester..................	2 609	11 789 178	8.3	14.2	2.1	3.0	6.7	9.7	51.9	340.0	56.3	227.1	4 403	3 313
Baltimore city............	27 461	126 508 297	5.8	15.9	7.5	3.3	8.2	10.7	47.4	3 714.0	1 967.9	1 238.8	1 994	1 229
MASSACHUSETTS	X	X	X	X	X	X	X	X	X	X	X	X	X	X
Barnstable.................	7 548	35 968 725	7.2	11.5	10.0	4.2	3.5	6.4	53.6	1 003.5	207.7	645.0	2 994	2 809
Berkshire..................	4 790	19 230 480	4.3	8.5	3.3	5.5	1.3	4.1	71.5	506.3	218.2	246.7	1 897	1 828
Bristol....................	17 070	76 423 100	3.0	10.6	7.2	2.1	2.0	5.3	68.1	2 032.5	942.1	830.7	1 507	1 453
Dukes......................	1 048	4 632 999	7.6	11.3	1.4	6.7	6.9	4.4	59.7	141.2	27.4	88.5	5 195	4 963
Essex......................	25 587	123 574 109	3.4	8.7	6.1	2.3	1.3	6.5	69.6	2 861.5	1 081.5	1 475.0	1 952	1 898
Franklin...................	2 963	11 147 283	5.4	6.1	2.8	5.5	1.3	4.8	71.6	305.5	144.0	135.0	1 887	1 847
Hampden....................	18 660	82 237 236	2.8	9.5	5.8	2.3	1.5	8.2	68.6	2 010.8	1 105.6	711.6	1 527	1 484
Hampshire..................	5 845	24 568 656	4.7	9.8	7.3	3.2	2.8	5.3	64.6	489.0	185.2	236.2	1 478	1 434
Middlesex..................	51 015	257 135 128	5.3	9.1	7.3	2.5	5.9	5.3	61.9	7 258.0	1 991.8	3 798.4	2 471	2 386
Nantucket..................	564	3 317 115	5.0	8.7	5.6	10.9	11.3	6.7	48.7	127.3	11.0	80.2	7 784	6 281
Norfolk....................	21 584	108 297 457	3.8	9.0	7.0	2.5	1.4	5.7	68.8	2 684.4	649.6	1 685.1	2 471	2 399
Plymouth...................	17 576	78 325 658	3.7	8.5	6.3	2.3	1.5	4.3	71.8	1 886.5	696.4	1 001.7	2 004	1 943
Suffolk....................	22 999	131 415 091	3.4	16.9	11.5	2.0	7.1	7.2	49.6	3 908.1	1 488.3	1 972.4	2 650	2 442
Worcester..................	28 380	132 203 123	3.5	8.3	5.1	3.2	1.5	4.3	73.0	3 064.8	1 424.8	1 314.3	1 630	1 589
MICHIGAN	X	X	X	X	X	X	X	X	X	X	X	X	X	X
Alcona	260	869 231	18.9	12.8	2.7	13.1	5.9	0.9	43.1	26.7	8.8	13.3	1 250	1 247
Alger	293	1 015 817	13.5	7.1	0.5	18.5	0.2	4.4	52.0	30.8	13.5	10.2	1 071	1 037
Allegan	3 023	10 951 667	9.1	7.0	1.3	3.2	8.0	2.2	67.1	353.3	194.8	109.8	980	962
Alpena	2 199	8 769 942	4.0	2.3	1.9	3.0	58.9	0.8	28.5	257.0	79.4	32.4	1 109	1 087
Antrim	795	2 618 552	12.6	9.1	1.8	7.2	4.1	3.3	59.1	89.8	22.9	43.1	1 841	1 822
Arenac	446	1 462 195	13.6	6.7	0.0	5.4	0.6	3.4	66.5	44.9	24.2	14.4	928	920
Baraga	413	1 533 081	10.5	4.7	0.2	7.7	36.0	3.8	36.1	56.1	20.1	9.9	1 142	1 141
Barry.....................	1 440	5 121 005	9.4	7.0	1.4	5.4	12.9	2.3	58.3	149.7	79.8	42.0	711	706
Bay.......................	4 027	15 471 429	6.7	5.7	2.4	4.8	13.5	5.1	61.1	536.8	284.0	123.7	1 157	1 137
Benzie....................	473	1 629 367	11.3	8.6	1.6	6.8	9.1	2.1	57.3	57.9	16.6	24.9	1 423	1 407
Berrien...................	4 813	18 604 576	9.6	10.9	2.0	2.9	2.9	4.5	64.6	601.1	301.4	200.9	1 288	1 264
Branch....................	1 691	6 939 089	6.6	5.2	1.3	3.6	38.9	3.2	38.5	226.8	88.1	39.0	889	873
Calhoun...................	4 008	16 572 500	10.0	11.0	3.1	3.3	5.9	4.4	61.4	671.0	371.6	175.1	1 296	1 142
Cass......................	1 418	4 769 730	10.8	7.3	0.6	2.9	0.9	2.2	72.4	172.3	89.2	43.1	825	808
Charlevoix................	1 150	4 194 441	10.6	5.9	1.3	5.8	28.6	3.6	42.0	158.1	43.7	73.2	2 813	2 799
Cheboygan.................	787	2 583 533	17.3	8.3	0.3	7.1	0.7	3.5	58.4	82.5	33.6	37.9	1 467	1 464
Chippewa..................	1 196	4 184 040	10.1	7.0	2.7	11.4	6.7	6.0	52.6	135.4	67.2	34.8	894	891
Clare.....................	1 104	4 192 533	8.2	5.7	0.9	5.4	0.8	1.5	74.1	127.0	64.5	31.2	1 013	1 002
Clinton...................	1 742	6 413 165	10.6	9.9	0.7	3.5	0.4	3.2	69.3	200.2	105.1	60.4	794	775
Crawford..................	409	1 431 323	13.6	11.5	1.6	16.3	4.0	2.0	47.9	39.4	16.7	15.9	1 133	1 086
Delta.....................	1 241	4 680 702	6.7	9.5	0.0	5.2	3.8	6.7	65.7	127.4	66.1	38.2	1 037	1 028
Dickinson.................	1 535	6 348 874	4.3	5.6	1.0	3.4	58.2	2.3	23.9	184.8	56.0	31.4	1 196	1 182
Eaton.....................	2 554	9 735 640	10.8	10.4	3.7	4.1	3.2	4.4	60.8	310.5	152.5	99.7	923	899
Emmet.....................	1 325	5 336 908	10.4	6.0	0.7	4.0	16.4	3.6	56.1	264.7	141.6	74.6	2 266	2 213
Genesee...................	15 234	64 330 939	5.5	5.9	1.4	3.5	24.1	3.5	55.1	2 005.4	1 056.8	353.2	844	786
Gladwin...................	706	2 311 382	11.6	6.0	5.6	5.3	0.0	6.6	61.0	64.7	29.2	22.5	882	866
Gogebic...................	622	2 249 336	12.5	6.4	0.2	9.6	0.9	8.4	60.0	90.5	45.8	17.4	1 082	1 078
Grand Traverse............	3 921	13 601 114	7.7	6.2	1.5	4.9	19.6	4.5	54.3	484.0	209.1	154.5	1 733	1 707
Gratiot...................	1 175	3 955 893	11.4	7.1	0.6	5.7	0.5	4.7	67.3	148.7	93.4	35.9	853	831
Hillsdale.................	1 203	4 074 488	12.8	8.9	1.5	5.5	0.3	8.2	59.8	131.8	71.6	31.6	684	680
Houghton..................	1 000	3 212 799	11.7	7.0	0.3	9.7	5.5	5.2	58.7	146.4	70.0	29.8	815	804
Huron.....................	1 172	3 974 661	13.7	7.4	3.0	6.1	17.1	4.5	45.7	144.4	58.3	49.0	1 508	1 483
Ingham....................	10 953	47 886 830	7.3	7.2	3.2	4.6	11.6	7.8	53.9	1 384.5	665.7	427.0	1 516	1 387
Ionia.....................	1 653	5 904 984	8.9	6.9	0.5	4.2	2.6	4.1	71.7	208.2	123.1	53.2	832	780
Iosco.....................	1 129	3 442 430	9.4	4.0	0.3	4.8	27.8	2.2	46.8	108.8	50.8	33.6	1 326	1 313
Iron......................	408	1 333 527	19.7	8.3	1.1	6.9	9.9	12.6	38.2	67.8	34.2	17.2	1 482	1 471
Isabella..................	1 686	5 798 126	10.7	6.7	1.2	7.0	29.5	4.2	39.4	236.5	148.6	46.1	653	641
Jackson...................	4 304	17 626 740	7.6	8.1	2.4	4.2	3.5	3.4	69.5	585.1	325.3	139.2	868	809
Kalamazoo	6 988	32 644 262	7.1	11.8	16.7	2.9	2.7	3.6	54.2	970.9	521.9	297.6	1 169	1 137
Kalkaska..................	695	2 106 824	12.6	6.6	0.4	8.0	43.8	2.8	23.7	84.6	15.9	18.4	1 075	1 058
Kent......................	16 442	72 374 352	7.5	10.6	3.2	4.8	1.8	4.9	66.1	2 471.0	1 223.4	763.8	1 243	1 084

1. Based on the resident population estimated as of July 1 of the year shown.

STATE County	Local government finances, 2012 (cont.)									Government employment, 2014			Presidential election,[2] 2012		
	Direct general expenditure							Debt outstanding					Percent of vote cast:		
			Percent of total for:												
	Total (mil dol)	Per capita[1] (dollars)	Educa-tion	Health and hospitals	Police protec-tion	Public welfare	High-ways	Total (mil dol)	Per capita[1] (dollars)	Federal civilian	Federal military	State and local	Demo-cratic	Republi-can	All other
	185	186	187	188	189	190	191	192	193	194	195	196	197	198	199
MARYLAND—Cont'd															
St. Mary's	331.8	3 045	62.8	2.2	6.2	0.9	2.7	197.3	1 810	8 977	2 451	4 656	42.8	55.6	1.5
Somerset	126.9	4 833	34.0	0.9	3.5	0.2	3.0	52.4	1 996	45	94	3 030	48.2	50.8	1.1
Talbot	130.3	3 419	40.1	3.0	8.2	0.8	5.1	87.8	2 304	213	135	1 655	44.4	54.1	1.5
Washington	564.3	3 783	59.9	0.7	4.0	0.4	4.5	391.3	2 623	592	461	8 451	42.6	55.5	1.9
Wicomico	357.2	3 549	57.8	1.0	6.3	3.1	2.6	203.7	2 024	290	310	7 583	46.4	52.2	1.4
Worcester	300.6	5 827	35.7	2.9	10.6	0.7	4.0	284.8	5 522	186	192	3 593	41.6	57.1	1.3
Baltimore city	4 080.5	6 567	34.4	2.9	9.1	0.0	5.1	2 807.8	4 519	9 784	2 064	57 216	87.2	11.7	1.2
MASSACHUSETTS	X	X	X	X	X	X	X	X	X	45 758	20 037	397 242	62.0	36.2	1.7
Barnstable	1 041.6	4 835	45.9	1.1	5.3	0.2	3.5	892.5	4 143	1 684	1 183	13 276	56.1	42.4	1.5
Berkshire	629.4	4 841	60.3	0.5	3.2	0.3	5.9	274.5	2 111	367	318	8 318	75.2	22.6	2.2
Bristol	1 991.8	3 614	57.9	0.9	5.0	1.0	2.5	1 318.2	2 392	1 092	1 413	27 912	60.7	37.5	1.8
Dukes	159.8	9 379	47.0	2.7	4.8	0.1	3.1	92.7	5 440	47	44	1 480	75.1	23.2	1.6
Essex	2 925.1	3 871	57.7	0.4	4.6	0.2	2.8	1 876.8	2 484	3 706	2 000	37 770	59.4	39.0	1.6
Franklin	333.5	4 661	58.8	0.4	2.7	0.4	4.8	96.2	1 344	190	177	4 900	72.7	24.9	2.4
Hampden	2 073.1	4 449	58.0	0.5	4.5	0.6	2.9	1 537.4	3 300	3 928	1 361	30 732	61.5	36.4	2.1
Hampshire	545.4	3 413	56.1	0.8	5.8	0.5	3.8	283.7	1 775	1 298	361	17 005	71.8	26.0	2.3
Middlesex	7 035.9	4 577	49.7	11.6	4.1	0.2	2.6	4 420.3	2 876	11 467	5 048	77 686	64.2	34.1	1.7
Nantucket	106.8	10 369	26.6	0.4	4.0	6.2	0.6	224.6	21 811	54	53	662	67.5	31.0	1.5
Norfolk	2 651.4	3 889	55.1	0.5	5.1	0.2	3.0	2 012.1	2 951	1 564	1 737	33 564	58.5	40.0	1.6
Plymouth	1 986.2	3 974	61.8	0.6	4.6	0.3	2.6	1 305.2	2 612	3 256	1 301	28 644	53.0	45.4	1.5
Suffolk	3 805.2	5 112	33.9	7.5	8.8	1.3	1.5	2 110.9	2 836	14 134	3 020	66 142	77.5	21.1	1.4
Worcester	3 304.7	4 099	61.5	0.4	4.0	0.2	3.4	2 495.3	3 095	2 971	2 021	49 151	55.8	42.1	2.1
MICHIGAN	X	X	X	X	X	X	X	X	X	51 120	18 537	536 943	57.4	41.0	1.6
Alcona	27.1	2 545	30.2	4.5	5.3	0.9	24.2	3.8	359	27	18	304	45.1	53.0	1.9
Alger	32.4	3 395	36.3	4.6	2.9	0.0	17.5	26.3	2 754	85	14	654	52.0	46.1	1.9
Allegan	347.7	3 103	55.1	7.4	3.5	3.5	7.8	410.3	3 662	159	192	4 838	43.7	54.4	1.9
Alpena	248.9	8 516	25.0	59.1	1.5	0.3	2.8	47.7	1 630	118	51	2 848	51.1	47.2	1.7
Antrim	88.3	3 774	40.2	3.4	4.7	14.5	8.8	44.8	1 913	61	39	1 093	43.9	54.2	1.9
Arenac	43.2	2 790	50.7	2.2	3.0	0.5	12.9	32.8	2 122	41	26	669	51.1	46.8	2.0
Baraga	72.9	8 401	19.5	53.3	1.1	0.2	10.4	63.4	7 303	28	13	1 565	47.3	50.7	2.0
Barry	150.3	2 547	48.0	5.6	3.7	9.3	7.8	79.7	1 352	80	99	2 176	44.0	53.8	2.2
Bay	521.5	4 877	44.7	20.6	3.3	4.5	4.2	246.5	2 305	245	238	5 591	56.7	41.4	1.8
Benzie	56.3	3 226	36.8	7.9	2.1	12.2	8.7	30.3	1 734	34	44	673	52.9	45.5	1.7
Berrien	618.7	3 965	53.9	7.1	5.5	1.4	5.2	398.2	2 551	312	278	9 140	52.0	46.5	1.5
Branch	225.6	5 144	34.9	36.1	2.4	5.3	5.0	73.0	1 664	75	70	2 702	46.0	52.1	1.8
Calhoun	680.5	5 037	45.5	17.6	4.3	2.6	5.4	473.1	3 502	2 906	285	7 801	53.8	44.5	1.7
Cass	179.5	3 436	58.6	7.1	3.5	4.6	5.4	185.2	3 544	74	87	1 995	51.3	47.1	1.6
Charlevoix	145.4	5 587	41.5	16.3	2.3	9.8	7.0	79.2	3 043	53	63	1 683	47.4	50.9	1.7
Cheboygan	82.0	3 173	52.2	1.5	4.4	1.1	11.7	35.0	1 356	45	110	933	48.3	49.8	1.9
Chippewa	142.9	3 672	42.0	7.3	3.4	0.4	14.8	140.9	3 620	464	225	6 031	49.0	49.5	1.5
Clare	130.5	4 244	66.9	0.3	2.7	0.5	8.1	36.5	1 188	78	51	1 621	51.5	46.6	1.9
Clinton	197.5	2 598	55.6	0.4	4.2	0.6	7.3	261.6	3 442	187	135	1 880	49.5	48.8	1.6
Crawford	38.5	2 750	41.0	1.0	4.9	1.1	14.9	20.3	1 451	128	23	680	47.9	49.6	2.5
Delta	137.3	3 722	63.6	3.6	2.1	0.2	6.5	110.1	2 984	190	61	1 844	52.3	46.0	1.7
Dickinson	190.3	7 257	25.2	50.0	2.2	0.1	4.5	120.1	4 580	845	64	2 048	45.0	53.0	2.0
Eaton	316.4	2 929	51.9	3.6	5.8	6.6	6.0	453.6	4 200	195	194	5 338	53.4	45.0	1.7
Emmet	280.3	8 515	27.0	38.8	1.4	4.8	4.5	162.6	4 941	94	56	2 412	46.9	51.3	1.8
Genesee	2 064.7	4 935	41.9	28.1	3.5	1.1	3.3	995.9	2 380	1 041	691	19 784	65.5	32.9	1.6
Gladwin	61.5	2 415	46.1	2.0	3.8	0.6	13.3	37.6	1 474	50	43	798	49.8	48.3	2.0
Gogebic	91.1	5 666	31.9	7.4	3.1	10.2	9.5	75.9	4 719	147	24	1 527	57.6	40.3	2.1
Grand Traverse	471.3	5 288	46.6	17.8	2.7	5.6	3.8	445.4	4 998	498	267	5 958	47.7	50.7	1.6
Gratiot	152.9	3 635	57.9	7.3	3.1	1.2	8.1	103.0	2 449	68	61	2 298	51.3	46.9	1.8
Hillsdale	131.8	2 850	51.6	0.9	3.3	14.1	8.6	74.2	1 605	95	75	2 357	42.9	54.9	2.3
Houghton	140.9	3 858	41.4	5.6	2.0	13.7	7.0	113.0	3 095	168	88	3 660	46.8	50.7	2.5
Huron	148.9	4 587	35.1	11.1	2.9	10.7	18.5	113.5	3 496	92	67	1 692	48.8	49.2	1.9
Ingham	1 371.5	4 868	44.9	13.6	4.2	3.1	3.5	1 588.9	5 640	1 552	604	39 831	65.9	32.6	1.6
Ionia	225.2	3 523	60.0	7.0	2.6	0.5	5.8	294.7	4 610	113	100	3 256	46.0	51.8	2.2
Iosco	108.1	4 265	39.8	17.8	2.4	6.7	7.8	52.0	2 052	110	64	1 521	51.5	46.4	2.1
Iron	59.7	5 151	21.7	4.9	2.7	29.2	9.9	46.6	4 026	34	19	924	50.0	47.8	2.2
Isabella	230.9	3 270	25.5	39.2	3.2	5.6	6.2	128.0	1 812	156	113	10 500	58.8	39.6	1.6
Jackson	586.0	3 655	54.4	10.1	2.6	3.6	6.4	539.6	3 366	325	256	7 351	50.3	47.9	1.8
Kalamazoo	958.5	3 765	47.3	14.6	7.5	1.0	4.4	1 168.8	4 591	739	429	13 753	58.9	39.4	1.7
Kalkaska	63.6	3 721	23.4	42.5	3.6	0.2	7.4	40.1	2 342	25	29	870	44.5	53.3	2.3
Kent	2 442.6	3 975	51.3	6.7	4.7	1.7	3.6	3 992.0	6 497	2 746	1 106	23 522	49.4	48.9	1.6

1. Based on the resident population estimated as of July 1 of the year shown.   2. © 2013 Election Data Services, Inc. All rights reserved.

STATE/ County code	CBSA code[1]	County type[2]	STATE County	Land area,[3] (sq km) 2010	Total persons 2015	Rank	Per square kilometer	White	Black	American Indian, Alaska Native	Asian and Pacific Islander	Percent Hispanic or Latino[4]	Under 5 years	5 to 17 years	18 to 24 years	25 to 34 years	35 to 44 years	45 to 54 years
					Population, 2015			Population and population characteristics, 2014										
								Race alone or in combination, not Hispanic or Latino (percent)					Age (percent)					
				1	2	3	4	5	6	7	8	9	10	11	12	13	14	15
			MICHIGAN—Cont'd															
26 083	26340	9	Keweenaw	1 399	2 168	3 033	1.5	98.8	0.5	0.7	0.1	1.0	3.8	13.4	5.7	6.9	9.2	11.8
26 085	...	8	Lake	1 469	11 424	2 329	7.8	87.5	10.0	1.8	0.6	2.5	3.5	13.4	5.7	8.2	9.8	14.0
26 087	19820	1	Lapeer	1 665	88 373	651	53.1	93.4	1.5	1.0	0.8	4.5	4.8	17.2	8.4	9.9	11.8	16.4
26 089	45900	9	Leelanau	899	21 981	1 732	24.5	92.0	0.8	3.8	0.9	4.1	3.8	13.7	6.6	8.1	8.4	12.7
26 091	10300	4	Lenawee	1 941	98 573	601	50.8	89.0	3.4	1.0	0.8	7.7	5.6	16.3	9.6	11.2	12.2	14.0
26 093	19820	1	Livingston	1 464	187 316	344	127.9	95.8	0.9	0.9	1.4	2.2	5.0	18.1	8.1	10.1	12.2	17.0
26 095	...	7	Luce	2 329	6 415	2 720	2.8	82.0	12.2	7.0	0.6	1.4	4.2	12.3	7.8	12.7	13.7	13.9
26 097	...	7	Mackinac	2 646	10 890	2 366	4.1	79.1	2.1	21.3	0.8	1.6	3.8	13.0	6.4	8.7	10.3	14.3
26 099	19820	1	Macomb	1 241	864 840	63	696.9	82.5	11.7	0.9	4.3	2.5	5.4	16.5	8.6	12.3	12.9	15.1
26 101	...	7	Manistee	1 404	24 461	1 628	17.4	91.2	3.9	3.1	0.7	3.0	3.8	14.0	7.5	10.0	10.1	14.0
26 103	32100	5	Marquette	4 684	67 215	790	14.3	94.4	2.2	2.9	1.0	1.5	4.9	13.2	15.6	11.9	10.6	12.3
26 105	31220	7	Mason	1 282	28 783	1 462	22.5	93.2	1.4	1.7	0.9	4.6	5.3	15.4	7.7	10.3	10.3	13.2
26 107	13660	6	Mecosta	1 438	43 067	1 109	29.9	93.3	3.8	1.5	1.3	2.1	4.8	14.1	20.0	10.8	9.2	11.4
26 109	31940	7	Menominee	2 704	23 548	1 656	8.7	95.1	1.0	3.4	0.7	1.7	4.7	14.9	6.9	9.3	10.4	14.8
26 111	33220	4	Midland	1 337	83 632	674	62.6	93.2	1.8	0.9	2.8	2.5	5.2	16.7	9.2	11.7	11.7	15.2
26 113	15620	9	Missaukee	1 463	14 903	2 107	10.2	96.2	0.9	1.3	0.7	2.6	6.1	17.1	7.6	10.8	10.2	14.0
26 115	33780	3	Monroe	1 423	149 568	436	105.1	93.3	3.0	0.9	1.0	3.4	5.4	17.1	8.4	11.0	12.1	15.3
26 117	24340	6	Montcalm	1 827	62 945	841	34.5	93.2	2.8	1.1	0.7	3.4	5.6	17.3	8.3	11.8	12.6	14.5
26 119	...	9	Montmorency	1 416	9 259	2 490	6.5	97.6	0.9	1.3	0.4	1.3	3.6	11.6	5.4	7.4	8.6	13.2
26 121	34740	3	Muskegon	1 293	172 790	373	133.6	79.1	15.6	1.6	1.0	5.3	6.1	17.6	9.0	12.5	11.9	13.9
26 123	...	2	Newaygo	2 106	47 948	1 018	22.8	91.8	1.7	1.3	0.6	5.9	5.7	17.4	8.1	10.7	10.9	14.5
26 125	19820	1	Oakland	2 247	1 242 304	33	552.9	74.9	15.1	0.8	7.3	3.7	5.5	16.6	8.2	12.3	13.0	15.2
26 127	...	8	Oceana	1 326	26 105	1 557	19.7	83.9	1.2	1.6	0.5	14.4	6.2	17.8	7.8	10.2	10.3	14.0
26 129	...	9	Ogemaw	1 459	20 937	1 776	14.4	96.6	0.7	1.6	0.6	2.0	4.7	14.1	7.1	9.1	9.8	13.2
26 131	...	9	Ontonagon	3 396	6 007	2 751	1.8	97.4	0.7	2.0	0.7	1.1	2.4	10.8	4.6	6.0	8.0	15.1
26 133	...	7	Osceola	1 467	23 058	1 682	15.7	96.8	1.4	1.4	0.5	1.6	5.7	17.8	7.6	10.4	10.9	13.6
26 135	...	9	Oscoda	1 465	8 251	2 580	5.6	97.7	0.6	1.6	0.4	1.4	4.5	14.2	6.6	8.4	8.5	13.1
26 137	...	7	Otsego	1 334	24 253	1 635	18.2	96.5	1.2	1.6	0.9	1.5	5.4	16.0	8.0	10.1	10.9	14.8
26 139	24340	3	Ottawa	1 459	279 955	243	191.9	85.8	2.2	0.7	3.4	9.4	6.3	18.6	13.6	11.8	11.7	13.1
26 141	...	7	Presque Isle	1 706	12 841	2 239	7.5	97.1	0.9	1.4	0.5	1.2	3.6	12.9	5.7	7.4	8.9	13.4
26 143	...	7	Roscommon	1 346	23 898	1 645	17.8	96.4	0.9	1.4	0.8	1.5	3.7	11.4	5.8	7.5	8.5	13.4
26 145	40980	3	Saginaw	2 072	193 307	340	93.3	71.5	19.7	0.8	1.6	8.1	5.8	16.2	10.4	11.5	11.2	13.5
26 147	19820	1	St. Clair	1 868	159 875	403	85.6	93.3	3.4	1.1	0.9	3.2	5.1	16.8	8.3	10.4	12.0	15.8
26 149	44780	4	St. Joseph	1 297	61 018	860	47.0	88.7	3.7	1.0	1.1	7.2	6.5	18.5	8.3	11.6	11.5	13.5
26 151	...	6	Sanilac	2 493	41 475	1 138	16.6	94.9	0.8	0.9	0.5	3.7	5.3	16.8	7.7	9.9	10.9	14.3
26 153	...	7	Schoolcraft	3 034	8 173	2 588	2.7	89.6	1.0	11.6	0.5	0.9	4.5	13.7	6.7	7.9	10.1	14.8
26 155	37020	4	Shiawassee	1 374	68 619	777	49.9	95.6	1.1	1.0	0.8	2.9	5.2	17.1	9.0	10.7	11.9	15.3
26 157	...	6	Tuscola	2 080	53 777	931	25.9	94.7	1.5	1.1	0.6	3.3	5.0	16.4	8.1	10.6	11.4	14.8
26 159	28020	2	Van Buren	1 573	75 077	736	47.7	83.7	5.0	1.7	0.9	11.1	6.4	17.9	8.1	10.8	11.6	14.3
26 161	11460	2	Washtenaw	1 828	358 880	191	196.3	73.8	14.1	1.0	10.0	4.4	5.3	14.5	18.1	14.1	11.7	12.6
26 163	19820	1	Wayne	1 585	1 759 335	19	1 110.0	51.8	40.0	1.0	3.7	5.7	6.5	17.6	9.8	12.7	12.5	13.8
26 165	15620	7	Wexford	1 463	33 003	1 357	22.6	96.1	1.1	1.4	1.0	1.8	6.2	17.2	7.9	11.4	11.1	14.1
27 000	...	X	MINNESOTA	206 232	5 489 594	X	26.6	83.4	6.7	1.7	5.4	5.1	6.4	17.1	9.3	13.7	12.3	13.9
27 001	...	8	Aitkin	4 718	15 702	2 061	3.3	95.9	0.9	3.3	0.7	1.2	4.1	13.4	5.5	7.5	8.4	13.0
27 003	33460	1	Anoka	1 096	344 151	197	314.0	85.7	6.4	1.4	5.1	4.0	6.2	18.2	8.1	13.3	13.4	15.9
27 005	...	6	Becker	3 406	33 386	1 343	9.8	89.8	0.9	9.8	0.9	1.8	6.3	18.3	6.9	10.7	10.6	12.8
27 007	13420	7	Beltrami	6 488	45 672	1 056	7.0	76.2	1.4	22.2	1.3	2.1	7.8	17.7	13.9	12.5	10.1	11.3
27 009	41060	3	Benton	1 057	39 710	1 182	37.6	94.1	3.3	0.9	1.6	2.0	6.8	17.9	8.6	15.9	12.3	13.5
27 011	...	9	Big Stone	1 292	5 040	2 833	3.9	97.7	0.8	0.9	0.3	1.1	6.1	14.5	6.9	9.0	8.7	13.5
27 013	31860	5	Blue Earth	1 937	65 787	804	34.0	90.6	4.1	0.6	2.9	3.2	5.6	14.1	21.1	14.4	10.1	10.6
27 015	35580	7	Brown	1 583	25 313	1 597	16.0	95.1	0.7	0.3	0.9	3.7	5.5	16.1	9.9	10.8	9.8	13.5
27 017	20260	2	Carlton	2 231	35 569	1 285	15.9	90.7	2.1	7.1	0.9	1.7	5.7	17.1	7.7	11.8	12.6	14.6
27 019	33460	1	Carver	918	98 741	599	107.6	91.2	2.0	0.5	3.7	4.1	6.5	21.5	8.0	11.3	14.2	16.7
27 021	14660	9	Cass	5 236	28 706	1 465	5.5	86.1	0.8	12.8	0.9	1.7	5.6	15.5	6.6	8.8	9.5	13.4
27 023	...	7	Chippewa	1 505	12 109	2 291	8.0	91.1	1.1	1.7	1.9	5.7	5.9	17.0	8.1	11.4	9.9	13.1
27 025	33460	1	Chisago	1 074	54 293	924	50.6	95.3	1.8	1.1	1.4	1.9	5.4	18.2	7.9	11.7	12.9	16.7
27 027	22020	3	Clay	2 707	62 324	844	23.0	91.3	2.4	2.0	2.1	4.3	6.7	16.6	16.5	14.0	11.4	11.3
27 029	...	8	Clearwater	2 587	8 803	2 529	3.4	88.2	1.1	11.2	1.0	1.6	6.0	18.7	7.2	10.1	11.2	13.0
27 031	...	9	Cook	3 761	5 194	2 822	1.4	88.3	1.3	9.9	1.4	1.9	4.0	12.3	5.7	9.6	10.2	14.1
27 033	...	7	Cottonwood	1 654	11 549	2 320	7.0	88.6	1.3	0.7	3.5	7.4	6.6	17.0	7.5	9.8	10.2	12.4
27 035	14660	5	Crow Wing	2 588	63 428	831	24.5	96.7	1.1	1.5	0.8	1.4	5.9	16.3	7.3	11.1	10.5	13.5
27 037	33460	1	Dakota	1 456	414 686	167	284.8	82.7	6.7	0.9	5.7	6.6	6.5	18.4	8.0	13.4	13.3	15.3
27 039	40340	3	Dodge	1 138	20 364	1 816	17.9	93.6	1.0	0.5	1.0	4.9	6.4	21.2	7.7	11.3	13.5	14.2
27 041	10820	7	Douglas	1 651	37 075	1 251	22.5	97.2	0.9	0.6	0.7	1.4	5.4	15.7	7.8	11.5	10.6	12.7
27 043	...	7	Faribault	1 845	14 050	2 161	7.6	92.7	0.8	0.7	0.6	6.2	5.7	16.3	6.6	10.3	10.1	12.8

1. CBSA = Core Based Statistical Area. See Appendix A for explanation. See Appendix B for list of metropolitan areas with component counties. 2. County type code from the Economic Research Service of USDA Rural-Urban Continuum Codes. See Appendix A for definition. 3. Dry land or land partially or temporarily covered by water. 4. May be of any race.

Table B. States and Counties — **Population and Households**

STATE County	Population, 2014 (cont.) Age (percent) (cont.) 55 to 64 years	65 to 74 years	75 years and over	Percent female	Population change and components of change, 2000–2015 Total persons 2000	2010	Percent change 2000–2010	2010–2015	Components of change, 2010–2015 Births	Deaths	Net migration	Households, 2010–2014 Number	Persons per house-hold	Percent Family house-holds	Female family house-holder[1]	One per-son
	16	17	18	19	20	21	22	23	24	25	26	27	28	29	30	31
MICHIGAN—Cont'd																
Keweenaw	18.4	18.9	12.0	48.7	2 301	2 156	-6.3	0.6	86	93	-8	1 021	2.11	60.9	6.0	33.8
Lake	19.3	16.2	10.0	49.2	11 333	11 539	1.8	-1.0	507	785	196	4 308	2.57	60.1	10.5	35.4
Lapeer	15.6	9.8	6.1	49.3	87 904	88 316	0.5	0.1	4 296	4 074	-192	32 510	2.66	74.6	9.0	21.9
Leelanau	19.0	15.4	12.3	50.8	21 119	21 708	2.8	1.3	911	1 191	431	9 136	2.33	69.4	6.3	25.2
Lenawee	14.3	9.8	6.9	49.4	98 890	99 892	1.0	-1.3	5 565	5 006	-1 883	37 859	2.48	66.5	11.1	28.0
Livingston	14.9	9.1	5.5	50.0	156 951	180 967	15.3	3.5	9 111	7 043	3 954	68 279	2.67	75.0	9.0	20.9
Luce	15.3	11.2	8.9	41.5	7 024	6 631	-5.6	-3.3	261	377	-96	2 345	2.31	63.2	10.1	31.5
Mackinac	18.1	14.7	10.8	48.6	11 943	11 113	-6.9	-2.0	451	686	15	5 066	2.13	62.7	7.6	31.0
Macomb	13.7	8.6	7.0	51.4	788 149	840 987	6.7	2.8	48 657	42 661	18 213	334 508	2.51	66.8	13.1	28.6
Manistee	17.3	13.5	9.9	48.3	24 527	24 733	0.8	-1.1	962	1 607	410	10 452	2.22	63.8	8.9	31.1
Marquette	14.8	9.3	7.3	49.6	64 634	67 077	3.8	0.2	3 320	3 347	194	26 693	2.36	59.3	7.4	32.2
Mason	16.5	12.2	9.0	50.4	28 274	28 705	1.5	0.3	1 489	1 691	338	12 133	2.32	67.1	10.9	29.5
Mecosta	12.9	10.1	6.8	49.9	40 553	42 798	5.5	0.6	2 180	1 911	46	15 529	2.58	64.3	8.5	26.3
Menominee	17.2	11.7	9.9	49.4	25 326	24 029	-5.1	-2.0	1 069	1 380	-106	10 668	2.20	63.3	9.4	32.3
Midland	14.0	8.7	7.7	50.8	82 874	83 629	0.9	0.0	4 467	3 662	-811	33 709	2.44	68.1	9.2	26.1
Missaukee	15.1	11.0	8.2	49.2	14 478	14 849	2.6	0.4	890	826	25	5 925	2.49	69.2	9.2	27.2
Monroe	15.0	9.1	6.6	50.6	145 945	152 021	4.2	-1.6	8 146	7 211	-3 420	58 328	2.56	70.7	10.8	24.9
Montcalm	13.8	9.3	6.8	48.5	61 266	63 342	3.4	-0.6	3 883	3 059	-1 174	23 219	2.60	69.8	11.2	26.1
Montmorency	20.8	17.1	12.4	49.0	10 315	9 765	-5.3	-5.2	328	825	-26	3 985	2.35	65.6	9.3	29.3
Muskegon	13.9	8.6	6.5	50.3	170 200	172 188	1.2	0.3	11 180	8 723	-1 960	64 889	2.54	67.9	15.3	27.0
Newaygo	14.8	10.4	7.5	49.7	47 874	48 460	1.2	-1.1	2 851	2 531	-823	18 157	2.61	70.5	10.6	24.0
Oakland	14.2	8.7	6.4	51.4	1 194 156	1 202 362	0.7	3.3	70 363	52 668	23 043	489 797	2.47	65.3	10.9	29.4
Oceana	14.5	11.3	7.8	49.6	26 873	26 570	-1.1	-1.8	1 580	1 321	-684	9 668	2.64	72.1	8.9	23.8
Ogemaw	17.6	14.3	10.0	50.4	21 645	21 699	0.2	-3.5	961	1 532	-89	9 398	2.25	64.9	10.5	30.0
Ontonagon	21.0	18.9	13.2	49.0	7 818	6 780	-13.3	-11.4	157	522	-389	3 201	1.98	58.7	5.0	35.3
Osceola	14.8	11.1	8.0	49.4	23 197	23 528	1.4	-2.0	1 412	1 229	-596	8 847	2.58	68.9	11.8	25.4
Oscoda	18.5	15.6	10.5	48.7	9 418	8 640	-8.3	-4.5	393	654	-93	3 743	2.26	64.6	7.4	30.1
Otsego	15.3	11.2	8.4	50.5	23 301	24 164	3.7	0.4	1 267	1 368	149	9 811	2.42	66.9	8.5	27.0
Ottawa	11.8	7.5	5.8	50.7	238 314	263 801	10.7	6.1	17 840	9 039	7 256	95 304	2.74	74.0	8.5	20.4
Presque Isle	19.4	15.5	13.2	50.2	14 411	13 376	-7.2	-4.0	467	991	5	6 091	2.12	64.7	6.0	31.4
Roscommon	19.7	18.0	12.0	50.1	25 469	24 449	-4.0	-2.3	929	2 018	672	11 796	2.02	60.0	10.3	33.9
Saginaw	14.1	9.6	7.7	51.5	210 039	200 169	-4.7	-3.4	12 013	10 677	-8 039	77 589	2.47	64.2	14.4	30.7
St. Clair	14.9	9.7	7.0	50.3	164 235	163 040	-0.7	-1.9	8 323	8 714	-2 748	64 182	2.48	67.7	11.2	26.4
St. Joseph	13.6	9.4	7.1	50.3	62 422	61 295	-1.8	-0.5	4 364	3 122	-1 372	22 856	2.64	69.6	11.3	26.0
Sanilac	15.6	10.9	8.6	50.4	44 547	43 114	-3.2	-3.8	2 342	2 368	-1 542	16 177	2.58	66.1	8.5	29.4
Schoolcraft	18.3	13.5	10.6	50.6	8 903	8 485	-4.7	-3.7	361	571	-109	3 495	2.34	63.3	7.2	32.0
Shiawassee	14.5	9.6	6.9	50.5	71 687	70 648	-1.4	-2.9	3 769	3 621	-2 149	27 435	2.51	70.2	11.3	24.6
Tuscola	15.3	10.6	7.7	49.9	58 266	55 729	-4.4	-3.5	2 841	2 955	-1 897	21 318	2.51	70.3	9.7	25.6
Van Buren	15.0	9.6	6.4	50.5	76 263	76 265	0.0	-1.6	4 840	3 795	-2 234	28 178	2.62	69.4	11.5	25.9
Washtenaw	11.7	7.2	4.8	50.7	322 895	345 066	6.9	4.0	19 637	11 191	5 342	136 471	2.44	57.3	9.6	31.5
Wayne	13.3	7.7	6.1	51.9	2 061 162	1 820 641	-11.7	-3.4	123 577	93 702	-89 890	667 553	2.65	62.8	19.5	32.6
Wexford	14.6	10.2	7.3	50.1	30 484	32 735	7.4	0.8	2 191	1 803	-104	12 662	2.56	68.2	10.0	26.8
MINNESOTA	13.0	7.9	6.4	50.3	4 919 479	5 303 925	7.8	3.5	362 433	210 398	35 651	2 115 337	2.48	64.9	9.6	28.2
Aitkin	18.1	18.0	12.0	49.4	15 301	16 202	5.9	-3.1	612	1 066	3	7 637	2.06	64.9	7.1	30.7
Anoka	13.0	7.4	4.5	50.0	298 084	330 844	11.0	4.0	21 756	9 539	1 337	123 446	2.70	71.6	10.5	22.7
Becker	15.2	11.0	8.3	49.9	30 000	32 504	8.3	2.7	2 206	1 769	486	13 534	2.40	67.7	9.5	26.0
Beltrami	12.4	8.0	6.4	50.1	39 650	44 442	12.1	2.8	3 687	2 126	-324	16 793	2.57	66.2	13.6	26.9
Benton	11.4	7.1	6.4	49.9	34 226	38 451	12.3	3.3	2 940	1 678	-23	15 446	2.46	65.7	10.6	26.3
Big Stone	15.6	11.4	14.3	51.1	5 820	5 269	-9.5	-4.3	293	380	-161	2 316	2.17	66.8	6.5	30.9
Blue Earth	11.2	6.7	6.2	49.6	55 941	64 013	14.4	2.8	3 910	2 418	287	24 719	2.46	58.5	6.5	27.8
Brown	14.4	9.5	10.5	50.1	26 911	25 893	-3.8	-2.2	1 410	1 565	-452	10 749	2.26	63.1	6.2	31.9
Carlton	14.2	8.8	7.4	47.9	31 671	35 386	11.7	0.5	1 941	1 899	112	13 542	2.49	66.9	7.9	27.6
Carver	11.9	5.8	4.2	50.4	70 205	91 079	29.7	8.4	5 998	2 343	3 942	33 813	2.76	75.6	7.1	20.1
Cass	16.7	14.6	9.2	49.3	27 150	28 567	5.2	0.5	1 790	1 580	-5	12 876	2.19	69.1	10.1	25.4
Chippewa	14.5	9.7	10.5	50.6	13 088	12 441	-4.9	-2.7	823	766	-371	5 050	2.37	65.7	10.4	31.0
Chisago	13.2	8.2	5.7	48.3	41 101	53 887	31.1	0.8	2 866	1 939	-582	19 757	2.63	72.0	8.0	22.1
Clay	10.9	6.5	6.2	50.6	51 229	58 999	15.2	5.6	4 235	2 354	1 411	22 545	2.49	64.8	9.7	27.9
Clearwater	14.3	10.6	8.9	49.6	8 423	8 695	3.2	1.2	571	497	48	3 539	2.44	69.2	7.5	26.6
Cook	19.8	15.3	9.0	50.5	5 168	5 176	0.2	0.3	229	234	38	2 627	1.95	63.4	8.3	28.7
Cottonwood	14.0	10.7	11.7	50.5	12 167	11 687	-3.9	-1.2	804	717	-233	4 855	2.34	67.1	7.3	28.6
Crow Wing	14.6	11.9	8.8	50.1	55 099	62 500	13.4	1.5	3 822	3 302	423	26 654	2.33	66.6	9.2	27.5
Dakota	12.9	7.1	5.0	50.8	355 904	398 552	12.0	4.0	27 336	11 955	376	155 220	2.60	69.7	10.6	24.3
Dodge	12.5	7.0	6.2	50.0	17 731	20 087	13.3	1.4	1 317	677	-333	7 491	2.68	73.5	9.6	22.8
Douglas	14.7	11.7	9.9	50.0	32 821	36 009	9.7	3.0	2 110	2 024	877	15 639	2.29	66.2	5.0	28.6
Faribault	15.7	10.8	11.7	50.5	16 181	14 553	-10.1	-3.5	745	989	-259	6 311	2.21	65.9	8.5	29.7

1. No spouse present.

Table B. States and Counties — Population, Vital Statistics, Medicare, and Crime

STATE County	Persons in group quarters, 2015	Daytime population, 2010–2014		Births, 2015		Deaths, 2015		Persons under 65 with no health insurance, 2014		Medicare, 2015			Serious crimes known to police,[2] 2014 Total	
		Number	Employment/residence ratio	Total	Rate[1]	Number	Rate[1]	Number	Percent	Total Beneficiaries	Enrolled in Original Medicare	Enrolled in Medicare Advantage	Number	Rate[3]
	32	33	34	35	36	37	38	39	40	41	42	43	44	45
MICHIGAN—Cont'd														
Keweenaw	10	1 827	0.56	15	6.9	14	6.4	158	10.4	1 002	727	275	51	2 313
Lake	357	10 479	0.69	97	8.5	139	12.2	1 072	13.3	3 131	2 371	760	261	2 296
Lapeer	1 719	75 979	0.66	799	9.1	819	9.3	6 992	9.6	15 741	10 711	5 030	1 051	1 187
Leelanau	284	19 578	0.77	183	8.3	219	10.0	1 875	11.9	4 755	3 110	1 645	114	523
Lenawee	5 426	88 363	0.74	1 083	11.0	953	9.7	7 304	9.4	21 073	15 092	5 981	1 276	1 287
Livingston	1 395	151 110	0.64	1 727	9.3	1 405	7.5	11 151	7.1	24 742	15 961	8 781	1 707	920
Luce	1 211	6 809	1.15	39	6.1	81	12.6	504	12.5	1 500	1 217	283	136	2 097
Mackinac	95	11 252	1.04	98	8.9	132	12.0	1 299	15.9	2 960	2 202	758	356	3 217
Macomb	7 521	786 688	0.84	9 541	11.1	8 123	9.4	71 670	10.0	156 551	105 862	50 689	18 157	2 114
Manistee	1 410	24 237	0.97	177	7.2	294	12.0	2 076	11.9	6 588	4 846	1 742	360	1 473
Marquette	4 595	67 895	1.01	602	8.9	646	9.6	4 715	9.0	13 626	10 092	3 534	1 074	1 581
Mason	442	28 501	0.98	275	9.6	287	10.0	2 507	11.1	7 648	5 704	1 944	693	2 423
Mecosta	3 333	42 571	0.96	391	9.1	337	7.8	3 506	10.7	8 866	5 728	3 138	877	2 029
Menominee	382	21 454	0.76	214	9.1	236	10.0	1 869	10.1	5 590	3 765	1 825	448	1 885
Midland	1 274	86 512	1.08	840	10.1	702	8.4	5 819	8.5	15 312	10 338	4 974	1 148	1 366
Missaukee	194	13 188	0.70	162	10.8	159	10.6	1 579	13.1	2 981	2 254	727	234	1 547
Monroe	1 462	129 141	0.67	1 516	10.1	1 341	9.0	9 760	7.8	27 742	19 076	8 666	2 847	1 947
Montcalm	2 839	57 054	0.74	739	11.7	572	9.1	5 608	11.2	13 663	8 935	4 728	1 148	1 889
Montmorency	175	9 233	0.90	60	6.5	156	16.8	829	12.8	3 984	3 003	981	39	421
Muskegon	6 496	164 534	0.90	2 129	12.3	1 665	9.6	14 362	10.2	35 642	21 352	14 290	6 907	4 041
Newaygo	557	43 744	0.76	535	11.2	494	10.3	4 677	12.0	9 381	5 179	4 202	931	1 955
Oakland	13 048	1 295 904	1.13	13 629	11.0	10 343	8.3	88 242	8.5	208 706	139 974	68 732	18 943	1 528
Oceana	303	24 386	0.81	267	10.2	245	9.4	3 244	15.4	6 368	4 185	2 183	564	2 395
Ogemaw	244	21 436	1.01	173	8.2	270	12.9	2 010	12.7	6 529	5 172	1 357	391	1 906
Ontonagon	83	6 138	0.85	25	4.1	105	17.3	521	12.5	2 300	1 780	520	37	594
Osceola	464	22 236	0.87	252	10.9	221	9.6	2 102	11.4	6 134	4 387	1 747	335	1 443
Oscoda	65	8 151	0.86	62	7.5	107	12.9	896	14.5	2 193	1 716	477	163	1 957
Otsego	345	25 512	1.13	231	9.5	281	11.6	2 073	10.8	5 842	4 232	1 610	415	1 719
Ottawa	8 260	255 795	0.89	3 509	12.6	1 763	6.3	18 624	8.0	43 913	18 451	25 462	4 730	1 719
Presque Isle	230	12 264	0.81	86	6.7	175	13.6	1 204	13.1	4 504	3 550	954	87	668
Roscommon	289	23 901	0.97	172	7.2	352	14.7	2 230	13.4	9 381	6 928	2 453	494	2 065
Saginaw	7 134	209 197	1.15	2 266	11.7	2 055	10.6	14 692	9.4	43 062	29 694	13 368	5 135	2 621
St. Clair	1 999	143 754	0.74	1 569	9.8	1 634	10.2	13 223	10.0	33 981	23 790	10 191	2 895	1 809
St. Joseph	765	58 817	0.91	843	13.8	552	9.0	5 881	11.7	11 548	8 755	2 793	1 240	2 114
Sanilac	564	39 167	0.81	434	10.4	471	11.3	4 291	12.9	9 310	7 074	2 236	519	1 351
Schoolcraft	140	8 298	0.98	64	7.8	105	12.8	750	12.2	2 420	1 923	497	NA	NA
Shiawassee	821	59 338	0.65	739	10.7	691	10.1	5 858	10.3	15 292	10 388	4 904	1 125	1 668
Tuscola	1 079	46 963	0.64	541	10.0	621	11.5	4 699	10.8	12 778	9 369	3 409	618	1 186
Van Buren	877	67 760	0.75	893	11.9	752	10.0	7 324	11.7	16 366	11 376	4 990	1 471	1 952
Washtenaw	17 890	387 701	1.21	3 709	10.4	2 193	6.1	22 780	7.7	47 474	33 428	14 046	7 632	2 139
Wayne	22 874	1 850 540	1.09	23 586	13.4	17 736	10.1	183 978	12.2	308 568	204 160	104 408	75 016	4 268
Wexford	389	34 715	1.15	432	13.1	312	9.5	3 078	11.4	7 771	5 832	1 939	908	2 898
MINNESOTA	133 971	5 396 510	1.00	69 852	12.8	40 142	7.3	308 991	6.7	864 841	382 176	482 665	137 882	2 527
Aitkin	274	14 600	0.79	114	7.3	200	12.7	987	9.1	5 066	2 085	2 981	377	2 409
Anoka	2 979	278 054	0.67	4 223	12.3	1 826	5.3	17 861	6.0	40 701	14 672	26 029	8 361	2 449
Becker	458	31 601	0.91	400	12.0	350	10.5	2 492	9.4	6 880	2 990	3 890	477	1 426
Beltrami	2 061	45 799	1.03	673	14.7	402	8.8	3 855	10.3	8 292	4 639	3 653	1 639	3 562
Benton	1 048	36 073	0.85	540	13.6	299	7.6	1 989	5.9	4 359	1 694	2 665	788	1 997
Big Stone	137	5 030	0.94	49	9.6	68	13.4	284	7.5	1 419	708	711	53	1 040
Blue Earth	4 080	68 470	1.11	726	11.1	450	6.9	3 373	6.3	11 314	5 667	5 647	1 770	2 682
Brown	1 124	27 298	1.13	277	10.9	294	11.6	1 137	5.9	5 770	3 105	2 665	298	1 181
Carlton	1 994	33 403	0.87	366	10.3	360	10.1	2 027	7.1	6 927	3 342	3 585	851	2 395
Carver	916	83 153	0.78	1 186	12.1	466	4.8	3 758	4.3	9 163	3 327	5 836	1 027	1 061
Cass	223	27 164	0.89	347	12.1	311	10.9	2 434	11.3	7 040	3 429	3 611	1 207	4 223
Chippewa	237	11 901	0.95	158	13.1	129	10.7	762	8.0	2 426	1 041	1 385	213	1 771
Chisago	1 673	43 014	0.60	532	9.8	372	6.9	2 701	6.0	9 177	3 348	5 829	704	1 308
Clay	3 561	49 541	0.67	830	13.4	427	6.9	2 887	5.7	8 497	4 379	4 118	1 150	1 881
Clearwater	115	8 237	0.86	116	13.2	93	10.6	697	10.0	1 971	915	1 056	148	1 666
Cook	51	5 274	1.03	42	8.1	45	8.6	368	9.4	1 392	717	675	120	2 301
Cottonwood	244	12 043	1.07	155	13.4	145	12.5	645	7.2	2 127	1 195	932	128	1 102
Crow Wing	747	64 513	1.06	708	11.2	617	9.7	3 622	7.3	15 970	7 044	8 926	1 569	2 472
Dakota	2 832	366 109	0.82	5 258	12.7	2 421	5.9	20 501	5.7	38 462	15 515	22 947	8 722	2 119
Dodge	149	15 600	0.56	242	11.9	127	6.2	921	5.2	2 884	1 434	1 450	284	1 390
Douglas	522	37 710	1.07	413	11.2	391	10.6	1 650	5.8	9 625	3 525	6 100	697	1 897
Faribault	336	13 687	0.91	145	10.3	161	11.4	855	7.9	3 562	1 591	1 971	171	1 210

1. Per 1,000 estimated resident population. 2. Data for serious crimes have not been adjusted for underreporting; this may affect comparability between geographic areas and over time.
3. Per 100,000 population estimated by the FBI.

Table B. States and Counties — Crime, Education, Money Income, and Poverty

STATE County	Serious crimes known to police, 2014 (cont.)[1] Rate[2] Violent	Property	Education — School enrollment and attainment, 2010-2014 — Enrollment[3] Total	Percent private	Attainment[4] (percent) High school graduate or less	Bachelor's degree or more	Local government expenditures,[5] 2012-2013 Total current spending (mil dol)	Current spending per student (dollars)	Money income, 2010-2014 Per capita income[6] (dollars)	Households Median income (dollars)	Mean income (dollars)	Percent with income of $200,000 or more	Income and poverty, 2014 Median household income (dollars)	Percent below poverty level All persons	Children under 18 years	Children 5 to 17 years in families
	46	47	48	49	50	51	52	53	54	55	56	57	58	59	60	61
MICHIGAN—Cont'd																
Keweenaw	227	2 086	380	8.2	40.4	24.6	0.2	46 250	25 197	39 180	52 164	2.5	40 411	12.7	21.0	18.8
Lake	369	1 926	1 970	11.2	60.0	9.2	7.5	13 897	16 275	28 872	37 299	0.4	30 990	29.2	44.4	38.6
Lapeer	155	1 033	21 317	10.4	47.6	16.8	120.2	9 560	24 102	53 016	64 255	1.6	51 510	11.1	15.9	14.6
Leelanau	83	441	4 471	16.3	29.0	39.5	26.2	12 590	32 883	56 521	77 852	5.5	60 622	8.9	14.8	13.1
Lenawee	189	1 098	25 777	16.7	47.0	19.7	169.2	10 775	22 834	48 118	58 124	1.2	48 194	14.5	20.5	19.1
Livingston	101	820	48 213	12.9	31.6	33.0	274.0	10 056	32 681	73 694	86 662	5.0	74 341	6.1	8.1	6.9
Luce	324	1 774	1 119	6.8	56.3	12.4	7.2	9 702	17 951	36 398	47 385	0.5	37 590	20.6	28.6	26.2
Mackinac	217	3 000	1 851	10.4	50.8	17.9	14.2	10 543	23 453	38 690	51 376	2.0	39 359	15.4	25.6	24.4
Macomb	288	1 826	216 214	12.3	42.3	23.1	1 319.4	10 692	27 145	54 059	67 773	2.4	54 865	12.3	18.3	17.1
Manistee	229	1 244	4 619	19.3	47.2	19.4	32.9	11 030	22 649	40 408	53 377	1.7	37 477	16.6	26.6	23.8
Marquette	155	1 427	18 530	7.3	38.7	28.8	86.0	10 705	23 760	45 066	57 569	1.7	44 735	15.4	16.5	15.6
Mason	311	2 112	6 228	10.2	43.7	20.1	53.6	13 129	23 563	42 156	54 978	1.2	42 896	16.3	27.3	24.5
Mecosta	507	1 523	15 155	8.4	45.5	22.2	66.3	12 430	19 783	40 396	52 129	1.1	41 572	23.0	30.8	27.3
Menominee	198	1 687	4 999	11.1	51.6	15.5	35.2	9 777	22 705	41 293	49 918	0.8	42 191	14.5	21.4	19.1
Midland	125	1 241	22 065	14.5	35.6	32.0	126.4	10 591	29 408	52 613	72 440	5.3	51 629	11.9	14.8	12.8
Missaukee	205	1 342	3 319	12.9	56.7	13.3	19.4	8 768	20 594	40 983	50 444	1.1	40 455	16.1	24.6	22.5
Monroe	224	1 723	37 827	11.5	45.9	18.5	245.8	10 550	26 617	54 911	67 721	2.3	57 719	10.4	15.0	13.7
Montcalm	342	1 547	15 356	11.5	52.0	13.4	96.4	10 367	19 371	40 739	50 314	0.8	41 554	20.4	30.7	28.8
Montmorency	65	357	1 589	10.5	54.7	10.3	7.8	10 091	20 209	36 448	44 898	0.6	37 961	15.7	31.2	29.5
Muskegon	443	3 597	43 429	10.3	46.6	17.6	294.0	10 921	21 037	41 842	54 191	1.4	42 588	20.0	26.7	24.3
Newaygo	326	1 630	11 460	11.2	55.3	13.0	88.9	10 994	20 713	42 640	53 593	1.5	41 588	21.0	27.5	25.2
Oakland	174	1 353	319 541	17.0	27.4	43.7	2 098.9	11 726	37 089	66 436	91 053	8.1	69 378	10.0	12.4	11.5
Oceana	221	2 174	5 927	11.9	50.6	16.1	32.5	10 204	19 459	40 969	50 920	1.1	41 166	20.1	30.7	28.3
Ogemaw	268	1 638	4 112	9.6	56.6	11.6	20.3	9 373	20 600	35 850	46 197	1.1	35 968	21.4	35.8	33.3
Ontonagon	112	482	994	4.8	50.3	15.8	10.9	17 311	21 364	35 365	43 015	0.1	35 387	17.8	30.8	25.7
Osceola	224	1 219	5 384	9.1	57.1	12.9	38.2	9 249	18 670	38 899	47 444	0.6	40 235	20.4	31.1	29.1
Oscoda	192	1 765	1 429	18.5	58.9	9.8	9.1	9 523	18 611	33 240	41 735	0.5	33 975	20.5	31.9	29.6
Otsego	157	1 561	5 278	14.4	45.4	20.5	35.0	8 744	24 695	47 693	60 536	1.8	44 693	13.2	20.6	19.0
Ottawa	233	1 486	82 310	19.1	38.3	30.5	447.8	10 816	25 919	58 160	72 360	3.0	60 577	9.1	9.7	9.1
Presque Isle	115	553	2 285	12.4	52.8	16.4	13.6	9 217	22 938	40 404	49 028	0.9	39 420	16.1	25.7	22.8
Roscommon	284	1 780	4 030	7.1	53.5	13.3	34.7	12 850	23 074	33 540	47 142	1.5	35 002	20.7	34.4	32.9
Saginaw	659	1 962	52 749	12.0	46.5	20.1	299.4	11 025	22 891	43 566	56 792	1.8	44 548	17.4	25.2	21.4
St. Clair	286	1 523	39 317	11.5	46.4	17.3	284.9	10 114	24 820	48 703	61 371	1.9	50 303	13.8	19.7	17.2
St. Joseph	303	1 810	14 558	7.7	53.9	15.0	109.3	10 144	21 122	44 145	54 249	1.5	43 687	18.5	26.6	24.2
Sanilac	266	1 086	9 650	9.8	58.6	11.6	67.7	10 036	21 298	41 578	52 878	1.5	42 081	14.7	23.4	21.2
Schoolcraft	NA	NA	1 545	14.3	59.0	13.9	8.1	9 534	21 038	35 955	48 070	1.4	39 539	17.6	27.1	24.3
Shiawassee	239	1 429	17 313	11.3	46.7	15.1	124.5	10 297	23 206	47 723	57 979	1.2	47 882	15.3	23.0	20.5
Tuscola	217	969	12 733	14.8	53.1	13.5	93.3	11 518	21 449	44 017	53 520	0.8	43 186	15.6	23.9	22.1
Van Buren	308	1 644	18 759	7.3	48.3	18.4	182.0	11 473	22 034	46 536	57 296	1.6	46 715	16.5	23.5	22.3
Washtenaw	288	1 851	124 700	10.3	21.6	51.8	462.8	12 094	34 258	60 805	84 027	7.0	62 861	14.3	14.0	12.3
Wayne	995	3 273	488 306	12.2	45.9	21.6	2 525.1	11 693	22 643	41 421	58 013	2.6	41 434	24.1	35.2	33.6
Wexford	338	2 560	7 328	11.2	50.7	16.7	63.2	12 630	20 473	40 368	51 018	1.3	39 807	19.0	29.0	28.4
MINNESOTA	229	2 297	1 413 179	17.1	34.1	33.2	9 329.7	11 089	31 642	60 828	79 106	5.0	61 473	11.4	14.8	13.5
Aitkin	128	2 281	2 663	6.5	50.4	14.8	19.8	9 992	25 378	42 036	54 050	1.3	40 676	14.9	23.9	21.1
Anoka	125	2 324	89 225	13.8	35.4	27.3	660.0	10 721	31 474	70 464	84 196	3.9	70 868	7.6	10.7	9.8
Becker	66	1 360	7 681	10.9	42.6	21.6	46.9	10 198	25 899	51 470	62 672	2.4	51 116	14.6	19.1	17.2
Beltrami	243	3 318	12 993	6.8	36.9	26.7	105.4	14 172	22 120	43 990	57 559	2.2	43 706	18.5	24.8	24.1
Benton	147	1 850	9 894	11.6	41.3	20.3	52.6	9 058	24 791	53 006	61 619	1.4	52 531	13.6	14.8	13.0
Big Stone	39	1 001	981	3.2	52.9	18.3	10.1	11 795	27 698	47 537	61 409	2.7	46 495	12.8	17.0	16.9
Blue Earth	198	2 483	22 249	9.0	34.8	30.4	105.2	10 202	26 181	50 977	66 315	2.7	49 513	17.9	16.8	15.3
Brown	67	1 113	6 214	41.5	48.1	21.5	39.5	11 794	27 801	49 527	64 951	3.1	52 272	8.9	11.7	10.4
Carlton	158	2 238	8 593	12.6	43.3	22.3	63.9	9 951	24 508	53 429	61 947	1.3	53 291	12.1	13.7	12.0
Carver	60	1 001	27 486	19.7	25.7	45.0	168.9	10 810	38 638	86 391	107 401	10.2	88 500	4.8	5.5	4.7
Cass	280	3 943	5 510	8.6	45.0	19.6	50.1	12 212	25 525	45 567	58 336	2.0	45 179	15.7	25.9	24.5
Chippewa	141	1 630	2 788	8.0	45.9	17.6	24.9	12 363	26 402	51 523	62 204	1.7	51 274	11.5	17.5	14.5
Chisago	76	1 232	13 766	8.4	40.6	21.5	74.4	9 907	29 293	70 223	78 527	2.8	75 122	6.2	7.3	6.4
Clay	137	1 743	18 491	22.3	34.9	30.5	90.7	9 730	25 398	55 582	65 794	2.3	55 560	13.3	14.7	13.5
Clearwater	259	1 407	1 993	7.5	52.6	14.2	15.6	10 703	22 773	45 105	55 690	1.5	43 674	17.8	26.8	23.7
Cook	38	2 262	757	9.9	29.4	40.6	5.3	11 267	33 598	51 913	68 183	3.3	48 593	10.4	16.2	14.4
Cottonwood	146	956	2 572	11.0	48.1	17.0	22.1	11 579	24 275	47 350	58 946	2.7	48 176	12.9	18.9	17.8
Crow Wing	192	2 280	14 420	9.9	38.5	23.0	98.5	10 531	26 974	49 186	63 155	2.5	50 162	10.9	16.3	14.4
Dakota	118	2 001	107 712	16.3	27.3	39.5	801.1	11 091	35 755	74 995	92 577	6.8	76 269	7.3	9.6	8.7
Dodge	157	1 233	5 623	8.7	39.3	24.1	36.5	8 893	29 786	68 587	78 672	2.6	68 777	7.6	10.2	8.9
Douglas	133	1 764	8 214	9.5	37.0	24.2	52.2	9 903	28 755	52 485	66 132	3.0	52 298	9.6	12.7	11.4
Faribault	78	1 132	3 030	8.9	50.2	17.0	21.4	11 199	25 834	45 601	58 209	2.3	48 163	13.5	21.1	20.3

1. Data for serious crimes have not been adjusted for underreporting; this may affect comparability between geographic areas and over time.   2. Per 100,000 population estimated by the FBI.
3. All persons 3 years old and over enrolled in nursery school through college.   4. Persons 25 years old and over.   5. Elementary and secondary education expenditures.
6. Based on population estimated by the American Community Survey, 2010–2014.

Table B. States and Counties — **Personal Income**

STATE County	Personal income, 2014 Total (mil dol)	Percent change, 2013–2014	Per capita Dollars	Per capita Rank	Wages and salaries (mil dol)	Supplements to wages and salaries; employer contributions (mil dol) Pension and insurance	Government social insurance	Proprietors' income (mil dol)	Dividends, interest, and rent (mil dol)	Personal transfer receipts (mil dol)	Earnings, 2014 Total (mil dol)	Contributions for government social insurance (mil dol) From employee and self-employed	From employer
	62	63	64	65	66	67	68	69	70	71	72	73	74
MICHIGAN—Cont'd													
Keweenaw	82	6.4	37 073	1 591	12	3	1	1	21	26	17	2	1
Lake	332	3.5	29 231	2 803	50	12	4	22	61	146	89	9	4
Lapeer	3 204	3.8	36 342	1 716	762	155	63	167	434	730	1 147	84	63
Leelanau	1 073	4.5	48 971	441	230	49	19	58	387	211	355	26	19
Lenawee	3 328	2.5	33 604	2 175	1 143	215	90	144	444	850	1 591	111	90
Livingston	8 691	4.6	46 829	534	2 355	379	187	409	1 157	1 231	3 330	224	187
Luce	177	3.3	27 582	2 951	67	19	5	8	32	69	99	7	5
Mackinac	403	1.0	36 483	1 689	146	30	14	21	95	125	211	15	14
Macomb	34 306	4.5	39 886	1 196	16 650	2 471	1 293	2 107	4 407	7 008	22 520	1 458	1 293
Manistee	819	4.1	33 549	2 187	273	67	21	38	156	288	399	29	21
Marquette	2 411	2.6	35 626	1 837	1 162	228	90	91	388	611	1 570	101	90
Mason	1 058	5.0	36 707	1 643	417	82	34	83	181	309	615	42	34
Mecosta	1 256	3.7	29 087	2 817	531	135	41	75	202	377	782	51	41
Menominee	885	4.2	37 321	1 552	258	59	21	67	158	221	405	28	21
Midland	3 850	4.0	46 151	586	2 161	335	150	163	679	683	2 810	176	150
Missaukee	470	5.6	31 248	2 550	118	24	10	65	72	133	217	14	10
Monroe	5 886	3.8	39 284	1 285	1 997	335	152	276	727	1 242	2 759	188	152
Montcalm	1 825	3.7	29 020	2 825	612	123	48	89	232	535	872	60	48
Montmorency	295	2.1	31 741	2 482	71	15	6	17	59	126	109	10	6
Muskegon	5 662	4.6	32 856	2 306	2 588	452	205	304	790	1 632	3 548	236	205
Newaygo	1 518	4.5	31 698	2 493	467	94	37	82	218	446	680	48	37
Oakland	73 973	4.4	59 759	138	42 100	5 144	3 203	7 748	13 602	9 456	58 195	3 593	3 203
Oceana	834	4.0	31 821	2 459	257	53	21	36	150	257	367	26	21
Ogemaw	632	4.1	30 022	2 712	190	39	16	42	110	256	286	23	16
Ontonagon	204	3.6	33 037	2 275	44	12	3	9	39	91	67	6	3
Osceola	668	5.4	28 847	2 842	283	49	22	30	93	223	383	27	22
Oscoda	259	7.2	30 996	2 584	54	13	4	18	45	114	90	8	4
Otsego	816	4.3	33 789	2 148	370	64	30	76	164	220	539	37	30
Ottawa	10 867	5.6	39 330	1 278	5 259	901	409	539	1 939	1 708	7 108	433	409
Presque Isle	428	3.4	32 893	2 296	118	25	10	10	80	157	162	14	10
Roscommon	750	2.5	31 292	2 546	171	38	14	22	164	346	245	25	14
Saginaw	6 640	3.4	34 050	2 110	3 623	617	287	362	958	2 006	4 889	323	287
St. Clair	6 002	3.9	37 497	1 525	1 944	361	155	324	857	1 450	2 784	194	155
St. Joseph	1 963	2.5	32 203	2 417	898	162	72	83	292	519	1 216	79	72
Sanilac	1 403	1.1	33 734	2 156	402	79	33	129	226	431	643	43	33
Schoolcraft	281	3.8	34 444	2 038	110	27	8	9	47	100	155	11	8
Shiawassee	2 260	3.2	32 787	2 314	624	128	50	64	290	621	866	65	50
Tuscola	1 700	3.4	31 487	2 527	468	99	37	93	242	548	697	52	37
Van Buren	2 563	2.2	34 078	2 105	869	188	69	88	388	683	1 213	79	69
Washtenaw	17 260	4.4	48 365	461	10 316	2 208	758	844	3 460	2 258	14 125	802	758
Wayne	65 022	3.6	36 844	1 627	41 200	5 891	3 110	4 547	9 221	18 375	54 748	3 468	3 110
Wexford	1 023	4.2	31 101	2 570	506	101	41	40	154	318	687	46	41
MINNESOTA	267 389	4.0	48 998	X	145 926	21 393	11 065	23 157	47 508	42 753	201 540	12 119	11 065
Aitkin	573	8.3	36 321	1 720	126	26	10	50	118	201	212	17	10
Anoka	14 841	5.0	43 412	803	5 973	884	478	709	1 800	2 316	8 043	505	478
Becker	1 389	2.1	41 771	974	516	92	42	157	261	336	807	52	42
Beltrami	1 600	5.2	35 037	1 929	716	140	57	113	269	471	1 026	64	57
Benton	1 622	5.1	41 053	1 054	652	106	56	252	203	294	1 066	66	56
Big Stone	247	-2.1	48 171	469	67	14	5	35	51	65	121	7	5
Blue Earth	2 665	3.6	40 756	1 093	1 573	269	124	375	463	458	2 341	135	124
Brown	1 158	2.2	45 804	612	516	99	41	162	208	235	817	46	41
Carlton	1 308	4.4	36 758	1 637	575	110	46	59	178	335	791	51	46
Carver	5 839	5.4	59 984	131	1 924	309	148	411	867	469	2 793	167	148
Cass	1 208	4.4	42 300	927	295	64	24	151	269	361	534	40	24
Chippewa	608	-4.4	50 215	376	214	42	17	150	104	117	423	23	17
Chisago	2 153	4.2	39 844	1 200	552	97	45	75	278	382	769	52	45
Clay	2 364	1.8	38 566	1 382	764	137	65	153	353	469	1 120	71	65
Clearwater	321	3.2	36 469	1 693	107	20	10	35	49	92	171	11	10
Cook	221	4.4	42 326	921	87	18	7	22	64	53	134	9	7
Cottonwood	546	-3.1	46 907	527	171	34	14	158	94	118	377	19	14
Crow Wing	2 393	5.4	37 819	1 481	1 080	188	90	133	471	656	1 492	99	90
Dakota	21 524	5.1	52 177	288	9 717	1 434	756	1 593	3 148	2 643	13 500	818	756
Dodge	891	4.7	43 761	781	241	42	19	147	117	127	450	25	19
Douglas	1 587	4.9	43 123	833	735	125	57	133	309	362	1 051	70	57
Faribault	650	-2.7	45 769	614	234	39	14	89	119	148	376	23	14

1. Based on the resident population estimated as of July 1 of the year shown.

STATE County	Earnings, 2014 (cont.) Percent by selected industries									Social Security beneficiaries, December 2014		Supplemental Security Income recipients, December 2014	Housing units, 2015	
	Farm	Mining	Construction	Manufacturing	Information: professional, scientific, technical services	Retail trade	Finance, insurance, real estate and leasing	Health care and social assistance	Government	Number	Rate[1]		Total	Percent change, 2010–2014
	75	76	77	78	79	80	81	82	83	84	85	86	87	88
MICHIGAN—Cont'd														
Keweenaw	0.0	D	4.9	D	D	4.8	D	D	35.7	830	376	32	2 475	0.3
Lake	1.2	0.4	6.5	3.9	D	6.9	D	18.7	31.0	3 995	352	561	14 945	-0.1
Lapeer	1.5	0.6	7.7	23.6	3.5	8.9	4.4	7.1	22.6	20 145	228	1 336	36 263	-0.2
Leelanau	4.4	D	10.9	4.3	D	4.3	7.1	8.1	28.1	6 870	314	138	15 310	2.5
Lenawee	2.2	D	4.1	26.5	3.1	8.1	5.3	9.2	19.5	24 035	243	2 016	43 455	0.0
Livingston	0.3	0.1	8.6	19.0	9.9	8.5	8.0	9.1	12.5	35 570	192	1 279	75 466	3.6
Luce	1.1	0.0	D	D	D	7.1	5.2	D	55.5	1 760	274	217	4 341	0.0
Mackinac	1.7	2.6	6.2	2.0	D	8.3	3.2	D	27.4	3 690	334	207	11 027	0.2
Macomb	0.1	D	5.8	29.5	6.5	7.2	4.2	10.2	13.7	178 975	208	20 354	362 513	1.6
Manistee	0.5	0.5	4.5	16.9	2.4	7.0	2.3	D	43.1	7 705	316	693	15 680	-0.1
Marquette	0.0	13.0	5.9	3.2	6.1	6.6	4.9	20.0	23.1	15 435	228	1 147	34 561	0.7
Mason	2.7	D	6.8	19.0	3.2	7.7	3.8	10.9	18.4	8 280	288	774	17 293	0.0
Mecosta	1.8	D	2.4	14.0	3.9	9.5	2.5	7.5	40.7	10 160	235	1 132	21 140	0.0
Menominee	6.0	D	3.8	31.3	D	5.2	3.0	D	23.6	6 655	282	491	14 163	-0.4
Midland	0.2	D	6.2	24.3	4.6	4.3	3.0	11.7	8.3	18 625	223	1 627	36 465	1.4
Missaukee	22.3	0.7	7.4	13.0	2.0	5.9	2.6	D	14.4	3 985	266	338	9 069	-0.5
Monroe	1.3	D	8.7	16.4	D	7.0	3.0	9.2	13.1	33 720	225	2 595	63 654	1.1
Montcalm	6.1	D	4.6	20.6	2.6	7.8	2.4	D	22.4	15 025	239	1 799	28 095	-0.4
Montmorency	2.9	D	6.3	12.5	1.9	7.0	D	D	20.6	3 720	400	259	9 530	-0.7
Muskegon	1.0	D	4.8	26.3	3.9	9.9	3.8	17.3	14.7	41 200	239	6 406	73 331	-0.3
Newaygo	5.5	D	4.3	20.8	5.7	9.4	7.9	8.1	22.3	12 650	264	1 341	24 903	-0.7
Oakland	0.0	0.1	4.6	11.2	23.1	5.8	10.6	11.0	6.3	234 900	189	22 037	535 285	1.5
Oceana	8.6	0.5	4.7	22.0	D	5.3	2.5	D	25.9	7 295	279	817	15 976	0.2
Ogemaw	5.5	2.2	5.9	4.6	2.5	15.3	3.5	D	21.9	7 330	349	771	16 038	-0.1
Ontonagon	1.0	0.0	6.7	D	D	14.4	4.8	14.1	31.2	2 725	443	158	5 637	-0.6
Osceola	4.6	2.5	25.0	22.3	3.2	3.9	D	10.3	15.8	6 510	281	904	13 562	-0.5
Oscoda	2.0	D	7.6	20.9	D	9.2	2.8	D	29.4	3 610	432	399	9 089	-0.3
Otsego	0.2	8.6	5.7	9.5	D	16.2	4.1	D	15.5	6 555	271	563	14 776	0.3
Ottawa	2.4	0.0	5.5	35.7	5.1	4.8	4.1	5.5	15.3	48 640	176	2 704	105 493	2.9
Presque Isle	2.6	D	6.0	4.2	1.5	8.2	3.5	D	21.6	5 045	388	376	10 406	-0.2
Roscommon	-0.2	1.5	5.7	10.9	D	16.4	4.4	D	30.8	10 065	419	948	24 357	-0.4
Saginaw	0.6	0.2	4.0	19.4	6.7	7.3	5.7	18.0	15.0	49 015	251	8 545	86 822	0.0
St. Clair	0.3	D	6.0	17.2	D	8.0	4.9	15.4	16.7	37 915	237	3 508	71 888	0.1
St. Joseph	2.7	D	3.3	44.4	D	6.4	2.3	8.4	13.9	13 625	223	1 327	27 609	-0.6
Sanilac	13.1	0.6	5.3	17.9	D	9.5	3.9	D	17.3	11 105	267	986	22 549	-0.8
Schoolcraft	0.3	7.2	4.8	10.1	D	8.0	D	5.2	41.0	2 710	332	292	6 326	0.2
Shiawassee	2.4	0.2	4.6	13.0	D	9.6	3.3	D	22.3	16 710	243	1 717	30 020	-1.0
Tuscola	6.0	D	4.7	17.1	D	6.6	3.2	D	25.9	14 595	270	1 335	24 225	-0.9
Van Buren	6.3	D	4.1	10.7	8.2	6.1	1.9	5.9	27.9	17 525	233	2 217	36 643	-0.4
Washtenaw	0.1	0.0	2.4	8.8	16.4	4.3	4.4	11.0	36.5	54 985	154	5 451	150 075	1.7
Wayne	0.0	0.3	4.0	14.8	D	4.4	5.7	13.6	12.8	355 660	201	85 261	814 328	-0.9
Wexford	0.4	0.5	2.1	27.6	D	8.1	3.2	12.5	19.1	8 610	262	1 178	16 681	-0.3
MINNESOTA	2.2	0.4	5.3	12.7	11.2	5.4	10.2	12.4	13.1	965 018	177	94 207	2 397 720	2.2
Aitkin	1.2	D	9.0	8.0	D	12.1	3.9	D	21.1	5 870	374	284	16 364	2.1
Anoka	0.2	0.0	8.5	27.1	4.8	6.6	4.0	12.1	12.7	53 910	158	4 504	130 080	2.7
Becker	4.8	0.4	8.2	14.8	3.5	10.6	3.8	D	20.7	8 055	242	632	19 236	2.4
Beltrami	1.6	D	8.3	5.3	5.0	9.4	3.0	17.3	30.3	9 000	197	1 310	20 930	2.0
Benton	2.5	0.0	15.0	19.3	6.6	6.3	3.5	9.2	9.0	6 665	169	410	16 580	2.7
Big Stone	18.9	D	13.9	0.8	D	5.1	2.9	D	25.8	1 495	292	97	3 129	0.4
Blue Earth	5.1	D	6.4	13.3	7.9	7.9	4.9	19.5	14.8	10 930	167	1 000	27 388	4.5
Brown	12.0	D	6.9	21.4	7.0	6.3	3.6	12.0	11.4	6 190	245	274	11 640	1.3
Carlton	0.1	D	13.3	15.0	3.2	5.8	3.6	9.8	34.4	7 680	217	593	15 819	1.0
Carver	0.7	0.0	7.8	29.0	7.3	4.6	4.2	10.9	11.0	11 785	121	504	36 901	6.8
Cass	0.9	0.0	8.0	3.5	3.8	8.6	5.6	D	33.9	9 065	317	702	25 391	2.0
Chippewa	16.0	D	6.7	24.3	7.3	4.8	3.5	D	15.9	2 810	233	166	5 697	-0.4
Chisago	0.6	D	10.2	16.5	2.2	7.2	2.4	24.9	19.0	9 440	175	433	21 518	1.6
Clay	3.8	D	5.9	6.2	4.2	7.6	3.2	10.3	23.3	9 830	160	1 057	25 452	6.2
Clearwater	6.7	0.0	16.4	18.9	D	4.3	D	D	15.8	2 240	255	220	4 754	-0.4
Cook	0.0	0.0	9.5	D	2.9	9.1	4.3	4.0	35.8	1 575	302	49	5 993	2.6
Cottonwood	25.6	D	5.1	23.4	D	4.0	2.2	D	11.9	2 955	255	222	5 403	-0.2
Crow Wing	2.9	0.0	8.3	9.1	7.7	10.1	6.9	15.7	19.5	16 735	265	1 188	41 147	2.4
Dakota	0.5	0.2	8.1	14.9	12.9	6.6	11.0	7.6	11.0	61 530	149	4 355	164 056	2.8
Dodge	13.4	D	10.8	25.4	2.7	2.7	3.7	2.4	14.4	3 345	164	177	8 068	1.5
Douglas	1.3	D	9.5	19.1	5.1	8.6	4.0	9.1	19.0	10 040	273	462	20 623	3.6
Faribault	13.6	0.0	5.2	17.9	D	4.3	4.5	D	16.1	3 825	270	260	7 037	-0.7

1. Per 1,000 resident population estimated as of July 1 of the year shown.

Table B. States and Counties — Housing, Labor Force, and Employment

STATE County	Housing units, 2010–2014 Occupied units Owner-occupied Total	Percent	Median value[1]	Median owner cost as a percent of income With a mortgage	Without a mortgage[2]	Renter-occupied Median rent[3]	Median rent as a percent of income[2]	Sub-stand-ard units[4] (percent)	Civilian labor force, 2015 Total	Percent change, 2014–2015	Unemployment Total	Rate[5]	Civilian employment,[6] 2010–2014 Total	Percent Management, business, science and arts	Construction, production, and maintenance occupations
	89	90	91	92	93	94	95	96	97	98	99	100	101	102	103
MICHIGAN—Cont'd															
Keweenaw	1 021	88.7	101 400	23.1	15.4	725	34.7	2.9	966	-2.2	84	8.7	860	33.4	23.4
Lake	4 308	80.7	74 100	28.4	14.2	571	44.2	3.6	3 694	1.7	302	8.2	3 173	19.4	30.7
Lapeer	32 510	83.1	131 100	24.4	13.0	792	31.1	2.0	39 322	-0.6	2 967	7.5	36 825	29.1	31.7
Leelanau	9 136	85.4	239 100	27.2	11.9	821	29.3	1.6	10 673	0.9	536	5.0	9 630	38.8	20.8
Lenawee	37 859	77.2	113 900	23.9	13.5	724	31.7	1.3	47 944	-0.6	2 301	4.8	43 016	28.8	26.9
Livingston	68 279	84.7	183 800	22.8	12.0	915	28.2	0.9	94 748	0.1	4 647	4.9	89 806	38.3	21.1
Luce	2 345	74.1	78 300	20.4	12.1	605	30.1	2.4	2 511	0.7	166	6.6	2 027	23.9	26.0
Mackinac	5 066	76.4	119 100	25.1	13.3	582	27.2	2.3	5 158	-3.0	479	9.3	4 447	24.4	23.6
Macomb	334 508	74.2	121 300	22.5	13.9	852	31.3	1.7	415 825	-0.4	25 253	6.1	390 546	33.5	22.4
Manistee	10 452	79.2	107 200	24.1	13.4	649	30.7	1.7	10 554	1.4	665	6.3	9 113	26.2	24.6
Marquette	26 693	69.5	127 200	19.8	12.0	618	31.5	1.5	33 597	-1.1	1 930	5.7	29 567	31.3	23.0
Mason	12 133	75.0	118 600	24.5	13.2	672	30.1	2.3	14 603	-1.0	844	5.8	12 182	29.7	28.9
Mecosta	15 529	73.8	110 700	23.1	12.0	622	35.3	3.2	19 305	0.2	1 132	5.9	16 892	28.4	26.9
Menominee	10 668	80.8	94 400	22.6	12.1	526	27.7	2.6	11 630	-1.3	597	5.1	10 299	27.2	33.6
Midland	33 709	75.1	128 000	20.4	12.0	729	30.2	1.8	41 702	-0.3	1 941	4.7	37 080	39.7	20.7
Missaukee	5 925	81.5	99 800	24.1	13.0	713	31.6	3.1	7 078	-0.3	443	6.3	6 192	24.2	37.2
Monroe	58 328	79.2	137 500	22.5	12.5	791	29.8	1.8	76 732	0.4	3 345	4.4	67 133	28.5	31.3
Montcalm	23 219	79.3	94 800	24.7	13.4	687	30.1	1.6	28 038	0.9	1 525	5.4	23 888	24.4	35.3
Montmorency	3 985	87.4	94 800	26.1	12.2	608	38.5	1.8	3 066	-3.3	295	9.6	2 802	22.8	32.1
Muskegon	64 889	74.7	98 600	22.3	12.9	669	35.3	2.1	77 763	0.3	4 319	5.6	68 439	28.7	28.3
Newaygo	18 157	83.1	100 400	23.9	14.0	688	34.0	2.8	23 184	2.0	1 215	5.2	18 375	24.7	35.9
Oakland	489 797	70.9	170 600	21.9	13.3	934	28.8	1.5	625 346	0.1	31 385	5.0	591 801	47.4	13.8
Oceana	9 668	80.5	104 200	24.1	13.4	685	31.4	4.2	12 638	-2.0	963	7.6	10 311	25.4	38.5
Ogemaw	9 398	82.2	88 100	24.9	14.5	647	36.8	1.5	8 514	-1.4	640	7.5	7 615	24.7	26.6
Ontonagon	3 201	87.1	69 300	26.4	12.9	410	30.9	1.4	2 317	-3.1	209	9.0	2 152	26.4	29.8
Osceola	8 847	78.9	89 000	23.0	13.2	571	30.5	2.5	10 243	-0.2	639	6.2	8 849	24.5	39.5
Oscoda	3 743	84.6	81 300	26.3	13.5	591	36.8	2.4	2 946	-1.5	246	8.4	2 808	20.7	30.6
Otsego	9 811	78.8	119 200	21.6	12.6	686	31.7	1.1	11 284	0.2	671	5.9	10 408	30.0	24.8
Ottawa	95 304	77.7	153 500	21.3	11.5	782	29.8	2.2	152 668	1.8	5 282	3.5	131 872	33.6	27.9
Presque Isle	6 091	87.2	93 400	22.6	13.0	575	27.4	1.8	5 407	-1.2	528	9.8	4 549	28.2	31.1
Roscommon	11 796	80.4	90 600	27.5	12.8	672	36.8	1.9	7 774	-2.7	684	8.8	7 451	21.9	27.3
Saginaw	77 589	72.8	94 800	22.5	13.0	710	32.6	1.4	89 015	-0.6	4 856	5.5	80 930	30.7	22.4
St. Clair	64 182	76.5	119 700	23.8	14.0	735	32.5	1.6	72 335	-1.0	5 166	7.1	68 560	27.1	29.4
St. Joseph	22 856	75.5	105 800	22.4	12.0	646	29.6	3.0	29 307	1.0	1 254	4.3	25 283	25.5	40.0
Sanilac	16 177	80.6	94 400	23.7	13.5	627	29.3	1.7	19 631	-0.5	1 227	6.3	16 880	25.8	34.6
Schoolcraft	3 495	82.2	87 700	22.6	12.8	568	39.8	1.6	3 455	-2.6	361	10.4	2 717	28.7	27.1
Shiawassee	27 435	76.6	104 700	23.0	13.0	675	29.4	1.2	33 392	-0.1	1 803	5.4	29 583	27.8	30.4
Tuscola	21 318	81.8	93 400	23.8	13.2	638	32.0	1.5	24 760	-2.0	1 589	6.4	22 555	26.2	30.9
Van Buren	28 178	78.1	119 200	23.6	13.3	665	29.8	2.1	35 670	0.4	2 132	6.0	32 200	28.0	31.5
Washtenaw	136 471	60.6	199 200	22.3	12.8	938	32.1	1.5	189 852	0.9	6 701	3.5	173 369	51.0	12.6
Wayne	667 553	63.9	83 200	23.4	14.9	797	36.4	3.0	750 854	-1.5	54 821	7.3	686 931	31.5	23.1
Wexford	12 662	75.9	95 000	24.6	13.5	712	31.3	1.9	14 582	-1.2	946	6.5	13 211	25.8	34.6
MINNESOTA	2 115 337	72.1	185 200	22.5	11.5	835	29.6	2.4	3 010 372	0.9	111 506	3.7	2 781 933	39.2	20.8
Aitkin	7 637	82.6	165 400	27.8	13.1	617	28.7	3.1	6 828	0.5	409	6.0	6 531	26.8	25.8
Anoka	123 446	80.9	186 800	22.6	11.3	957	31.3	2.1	191 057	0.7	6 891	3.6	178 642	36.8	22.6
Becker	13 534	79.2	173 400	23.3	12.8	677	28.2	2.1	18 468	2.4	817	4.4	15 668	32.2	29.9
Beltrami	16 793	70.0	147 200	23.3	12.5	661	30.5	3.3	23 626	1.0	1 141	4.8	20 340	30.0	21.5
Benton	15 466	69.7	155 500	23.6	11.6	658	30.1	2.4	21 867	0.4	967	4.4	19 701	28.6	30.5
Big Stone	2 316	79.6	93 900	21.2	10.8	518	25.0	1.6	2 722	4.7	121	4.4	2 453	37.0	27.3
Blue Earth	24 719	65.8	159 100	21.6	10.3	726	32.8	1.4	39 068	1.0	1 153	3.0	35 889	32.0	22.0
Brown	10 749	77.7	123 000	21.5	10.9	607	27.7	1.8	14 699	3.2	607	4.1	13 504	30.3	30.2
Carlton	13 542	78.2	158 400	22.8	12.4	692	29.4	2.9	17 511	-0.8	869	5.0	16 103	31.5	25.4
Carver	33 813	81.2	264 900	22.7	10.9	941	28.9	1.5	55 104	1.2	1 748	3.2	50 888	45.5	15.9
Cass	12 876	80.8	172 800	24.3	12.1	660	29.4	3.3	14 059	0.1	939	6.7	12 114	30.0	25.8
Chippewa	5 050	72.5	103 900	19.3	10.1	688	23.8	0.8	6 973	0.8	307	4.4	6 365	29.0	31.5
Chisago	19 757	84.6	190 300	24.4	11.0	773	30.0	1.8	28 963	1.0	1 207	4.2	27 429	33.4	26.6
Clay	22 545	69.4	155 500	21.6	11.2	713	35.3	2.0	35 850	1.6	1 102	3.1	32 598	33.6	23.5
Clearwater	3 539	79.9	115 000	23.1	12.4	531	29.6	5.6	4 641	1.8	428	9.2	3 549	27.3	35.4
Cook	2 627	73.3	243 700	25.0	10.2	656	24.6	6.3	3 184	3.8	140	4.4	2 795	36.6	17.3
Cottonwood	4 855	77.9	86 500	19.4	10.5	567	30.8	2.5	5 870	4.9	279	4.8	5 501	29.3	30.5
Crow Wing	26 654	74.9	177 400	23.7	11.8	720	29.0	1.3	31 582	0.0	1 651	5.2	28 675	31.7	22.6
Dakota	155 220	75.3	220 500	22.0	10.2	955	28.7	1.7	234 087	0.8	7 698	3.3	220 143	42.0	16.9
Dodge	7 491	84.2	160 200	21.2	11.8	675	27.9	1.3	11 481	1.7	424	3.7	10 789	36.9	26.8
Douglas	15 639	76.2	189 800	23.7	12.7	685	30.4	0.8	20 172	1.2	690	3.4	18 462	34.1	25.7
Faribault	6 311	77.2	84 500	19.9	11.9	529	24.9	1.6	7 537	1.9	328	4.4	7 067	31.0	31.5

1. Specified owner-occupied units.　　2. A value of 10.0 represents 10 percent or less; a value of 50.0 represents 50 percent or more.　　3. Specified renter-occupied units.
4. Overcrowded or lacking complete plumbing facilities.　　5. Percent of civilian labor force.　　6. Persons 16 years old and over.

Table B. States and Counties — Nonfarm Employment and Agriculture

	Private nonfarm establishments, employment and payroll, 2014									Agriculture, 2012			
	Employment							Annual payroll		Farms			
											Percent with:		
STATE County	Number of establishments	Total	Health care and social assistance	Manufacturing	Retail trade	Finance and insurance	Professional, scientific, and technical services	Total (mil dol)	Average per employee (dollars)	Number	Fewer than 50 acres	500 acres or more	Farm operators whose principal occupation is farming (percent)
	104	105	106	107	108	109	110	111	112	113	114	115	116
MICHIGAN—Cont'd													
Keweenaw	65	192	D	D	15	D	D	5	24 505	6	66.7	0.0	33.3
Lake	156	1 067	233	87	242	D	D	28	25 876	200	38.0	5.0	49.5
Lapeer	1 601	17 580	2 602	4 959	3 053	440	689	589	33 509	1 133	52.8	7.2	51.3
Leelanau	749	4 357	608	288	626	183	D	168	38 577	494	38.3	2.6	55.5
Lenawee	1 801	22 985	3 058	5 136	3 663	888	459	773	33 615	1 618	45.7	11.7	39.3
Livingston	4 173	48 727	5 253	8 882	8 948	3 562	2 646	1 828	37 521	734	58.3	4.6	54.8
Luce	163	1 535	D	D	276	59	D	50	32 276	43	44.2	16.3	44.2
Mackinac	446	2 066	392	101	343	84	35	100	48 169	103	30.1	11.7	57.3
Macomb	18 641	285 162	38 169	64 614	41 132	7 433	28 159	13 132	46 051	502	59.4	6.4	53.8
Manistee	565	5 470	872	760	1 003	161	108	189	34 623	324	35.2	2.5	43.8
Marquette	1 626	21 631	5 391	891	3 823	878	661	767	35 454	168	41.1	6.0	48.8
Mason	729	9 108	1 305	2 077	1 489	201	151	356	39 082	440	34.5	8.2	45.2
Mecosta	736	9 055	1 449	2 122	1 966	216	352	317	34 965	779	31.8	5.9	48.1
Menominee	454	5 421	259	2 029	621	137	D	175	32 266	398	25.6	9.8	47.5
Midland	1 908	34 973	6 145	6 005	4 163	1 064	891	2 304	65 880	555	47.9	7.0	46.7
Missaukee	286	2 257	D	395	372	D	70	70	30 809	433	38.6	10.6	48.3
Monroe	2 260	36 169	5 418	6 868	5 019	871	1 091	1 550	42 856	1 144	53.0	10.9	46.3
Montcalm	1 005	11 869	2 751	2 334	2 347	351	245	388	32 692	1 127	41.3	9.4	54.3
Montmorency	201	1 534	225	412	231	D	D	49	32 198	151	31.1	8.6	36.4
Muskegon	3 153	52 027	10 904	12 286	8 006	1 055	1 431	2 009	38 614	514	56.6	4.9	48.4
Newaygo	787	9 572	1 605	2 112	1 556	D	379	344	35 947	923	45.8	5.1	45.1
Oakland	38 592	661 188	102 402	49 141	73 637	35 427	91 670	37 607	56 878	537	70.9	2.0	51.6
Oceana	498	4 413	615	1 453	576	124	129	143	32 513	609	37.9	9.4	52.7
Ogemaw	560	5 698	1 433	277	1 632	D	117	170	29 916	280	24.6	11.4	49.3
Ontonagon	165	919	D	D	209	59	D	25	26 739	109	12.8	14.7	45.0
Osceola	431	6 037	905	1 999	610	104	D	245	40 655	750	34.0	4.9	35.9
Oscoda	188	1 392	158	288	228	D	29	40	28 647	145	43.4	2.1	52.4
Otsego	748	8 415	D	839	2 101	165	167	279	33 182	180	37.2	9.4	47.2
Ottawa	5 905	103 279	11 666	32 734	10 216	2 549	3 285	4 085	39 558	1 363	55.2	5.6	51.5
Presque Isle	332	2 146	D	D	360	D	34	72	33 658	323	22.9	9.9	55.1
Roscommon	539	4 581	565	616	1 309	174	58	116	25 324	58	44.8	3.4	34.5
Saginaw	4 368	77 998	17 749	10 595	13 184	2 705	2 310	2 933	37 606	1 318	41.0	12.1	48.9
St. Clair	3 056	40 685	7 702	8 178	7 268	1 232	968	1 587	39 011	1 049	46.1	7.9	56.0
St. Joseph	1 162	18 600	1 771	8 974	2 344	413	462	722	38 828	967	44.9	10.9	41.8
Sanilac	818	7 979	1 273	2 580	1 562	417	172	262	32 866	1 467	29.9	17.3	55.6
Schoolcraft	225	1 752	D	D	373	D	D	60	33 992	65	27.7	6.2	50.8
Shiawassee	1 130	12 675	2 401	1 870	2 545	377	302	404	31 838	1 033	42.1	10.6	51.2
Tuscola	849	8 653	2 213	1 352	1 594	326	233	291	33 591	1 322	40.0	12.3	48.6
Van Buren	1 272	15 994	2 562	2 883	2 369	329	D	602	37 653	1 113	49.5	4.4	53.2
Washtenaw	8 049	142 761	D	12 749	16 897	3 913	13 688	7 389	51 755	1 236	55.3	6.9	48.8
Wayne	31 877	605 093	105 213	75 732	67 617	30 463	38 667	30 862	51 004	287	77.7	1.4	59.9
Wexford	844	12 855	2 078	3 459	1 981	312	254	451	35 075	357	42.6	3.4	37.5
MINNESOTA	147 483	2 566 086	444 786	298 024	296 383	151 068	166 364	126 186	49 175	74 542	25.2	18.2	52.9
Aitkin	398	3 053	827	D	630	90	34	91	29 810	471	19.7	12.5	40.8
Anoka	7 420	113 460	15 665	20 290	15 561	2 207	3 551	6 000	52 886	396	58.3	4.5	44.7
Becker	947	11 436	2 124	1 961	1 959	259	D	387	33 799	1 107	17.3	15.4	54.9
Beltrami	1 141	15 549	3 444	874	3 116	408	416	504	32 401	573	15.5	17.6	44.9
Benton	925	16 813	3 282	3 680	2 200	192	216	593	35 290	958	29.7	7.8	51.8
Big Stone	196	1 506	579	D	201	D	D	52	34 332	400	14.8	34.0	63.0
Blue Earth	1 940	35 284	8 186	4 193	6 123	995	1 083	1 229	34 822	1 070	26.9	22.4	53.7
Brown	754	12 240	2 274	2 655	1 726	438	452	437	35 722	1 055	21.0	19.9	55.9
Carlton	701	8 171	2 063	1 359	1 341	405	195	303	37 039	501	21.6	5.8	43.7
Carver	2 485	39 102	5 355	10 467	3 679	900	1 999	1 883	48 156	789	38.3	9.6	51.3
Cass	800	6 525	1 033	290	940	192	549	182	27 962	546	20.1	12.6	54.0
Chippewa	411	5 382	1 163	1 284	665	197	88	185	34 411	674	23.7	30.4	67.1
Chisago	1 206	13 019	D	2 169	1 876	269	D	530	40 731	832	44.2	4.7	37.6
Clay	1 238	17 236	3 792	940	2 704	411	442	523	30 332	804	20.5	33.6	52.6
Clearwater	201	2 332	616	D	235	66	D	96	40 979	519	12.5	15.4	36.0
Cook	286	2 052	D	D	336	D	D	60	29 407	18	50.0	5.6	16.7
Cottonwood	350	4 106	718	1 498	530	100	69	130	31 579	813	23.1	31.1	66.8
Crow Wing	2 092	26 056	5 814	2 320	4 416	1 211	834	902	34 619	533	28.5	8.1	50.5
Dakota	10 343	178 419	24 110	16 693	22 815	11 513	9 703	8 640	48 428	892	42.2	13.6	56.8
Dodge	440	4 265	366	D	D	117	D	192	44 912	621	39.6	19.5	58.5
Douglas	1 318	17 560	3 760	3 788	3 124	440	470	661	37 652	1 091	24.6	11.2	39.4
Faribault	423	4 063	814	1 128	576	236	D	132	32 522	824	21.4	32.0	67.4

Table B. States and Counties — **Agriculture**

STATE County	Land in farms Acreage (1,000)	Percent change, 2007–2012	Acres Average size of farm	Total irrigated (1,000)	Total cropland (1,000)	Value of land and buildings (dollars) Average per farm	Average per acre	Value of machinery and equipment, average per farm (dollars)	Value of products sold Total (mil dol)	Average per farm (dollars)	Percent from: Crops	Live-stock and poultry products	Percent of farms with sales of: $10,000 or more	$100,000 or more	Government payments Total ($1,000)	Percent of farms
	117	118	119	120	121	122	123	124	125	126	127	128	129	130	131	132
MICHIGAN—Cont'd																
Keweenaw	0	-80.1	53	0.0	0.0	133 333	2 516	34 167	D	D	D	D	0.0	0.0	0	0.0
Lake	26	21.7	130	0.0	11.5	338 075	2 598	55 965	4.1	20 305	56.4	43.6	22.0	4.0	88	12.0
Lapeer	176	-0.4	155	2.1	137.1	708 546	4 572	126 049	113.4	100 049	80.6	19.4	41.8	15.3	2 214	23.1
Leelanau	59	6.7	120	2.2	33.3	810 441	6 731	96 296	20.5	41 486	86.7	13.3	43.1	9.1	2 363	31.0
Lenawee	344	-1.2	213	4.4	299.3	863 720	4 058	134 226	204.6	126 435	70.4	29.6	42.0	17.4	10 028	62.1
Livingston	86	-10.7	117	1.4	61.0	569 114	4 849	88 651	52.3	71 187	74.1	25.9	36.0	10.4	1 090	16.5
Luce	12	31.5	270	D	4.3	619 116	2 295	97 233	3.6	84 070	81.7	18.3	39.5	11.6	79	20.9
Mackinac	22	3.3	218	0.0	11.5	452 359	2 078	57 767	5.4	52 039	22.1	77.9	45.6	7.8	142	21.4
Macomb	68	9.6	135	2.5	58.4	747 673	5 523	120 797	73.2	145 900	79.7	20.3	53.4	24.7	956	23.5
Manistee	44	-3.8	137	1.3	20.1	393 093	2 875	41 111	7.6	23 543	85.1	14.9	28.4	5.9	241	13.0
Marquette	31	2.0	183	0.1	9.2	372 268	2 038	68 690	2.3	13 679	35.5	64.5	26.8	1.2	209	8.9
Mason	79	3.4	180	3.0	56.7	512 948	2 855	109 655	52.9	120 184	59.9	40.1	43.0	15.0	828	27.0
Mecosta	123	7.2	158	14.4	79.7	471 610	2 987	90 709	113.3	145 388	40.6	59.4	46.5	13.0	904	36.5
Menominee	92	-11.3	231	0.0	50.3	463 201	2 006	84 543	41.4	104 025	19.1	80.9	37.7	14.6	1 131	37.4
Midland	90	-1.2	161	1.0	69.5	580 838	3 600	98 339	70.1	126 285	67.9	32.1	39.1	14.1	2 310	44.3
Missaukee	100	12.6	230	7.5	71.7	695 275	3 025	154 582	126.0	290 998	24.8	75.2	41.6	18.7	1 568	28.6
Monroe	215	3.2	188	9.8	196.2	853 688	4 553	135 682	173.9	152 008	95.5	4.5	54.6	20.3	3 653	50.8
Montcalm	237	-2.3	211	55.9	181.1	702 214	3 336	131 319	213.9	189 831	72.1	27.9	44.1	17.9	2 577	40.6
Montmorency	24	11.6	161	D	14.6	366 252	2 272	84 497	8.1	53 854	52.8	47.2	37.7	9.9	175	25.2
Muskegon	74	-6.8	144	9.5	49.0	741 080	5 130	95 333	76.0	147 860	61.6	38.4	38.9	15.6	658	21.8
Newaygo	126	-5.8	136	7.5	83.4	484 268	3 557	91 385	113.8	123 346	39.9	60.1	39.5	13.8	1 193	20.8
Oakland	32	-2.4	59	0.7	18.8	506 358	8 572	54 261	25.9	48 244	87.5	12.5	25.1	6.9	226	6.9
Oceana	128	3.6	210	10.4	89.4	675 791	3 221	124 509	101.2	166 141	63.3	36.7	48.6	18.7	2 529	31.2
Ogemaw	68	11.8	243	0.1	40.2	645 025	2 650	129 246	46.3	165 218	29.1	70.9	42.1	18.9	927	47.1
Ontonagon	29	-5.7	267	0.0	13.9	451 716	1 694	61 257	2.2	20 220	75.1	24.9	40.4	4.6	91	12.8
Osceola	111	-9.5	147	1.4	64.7	373 809	2 536	65 007	45.7	60 912	28.5	71.5	30.0	8.5	1 124	22.8
Oscoda	17	-4.7	116	0.0	7.9	303 648	2 629	48 641	6.9	47 635	17.1	82.9	45.5	13.8	44	6.2
Otsego	32	-3.9	179	1.2	14.3	453 122	2 526	72 189	7.1	39 250	85.5	14.5	39.4	6.1	88	32.2
Ottawa	186	9.2	137	18.1	138.1	881 996	6 458	142 875	534.4	392 080	56.2	43.8	56.9	26.9	2 689	25.5
Presque Isle	82	14.7	252	1.4	45.4	541 449	2 145	82 938	22.8	70 653	76.5	23.5	39.6	10.8	684	31.0
Roscommon	7	56.2	128	0.3	2.7	336 517	2 626	56 966	D	D	D	D	24.1	0.0	D	6.9
Saginaw	310	-4.5	235	2.3	274.5	896 656	3 816	144 832	243.6	184 855	91.7	8.3	55.8	27.6	6 093	71.6
St. Clair	180	12.1	172	0.4	151.6	640 936	3 736	122 904	107.9	102 895	90.7	9.3	47.5	17.8	1 714	32.6
St. Joseph	222	2.9	229	112.4	188.2	1 090 049	4 754	158 803	238.1	246 177	80.2	19.8	48.4	25.0	4 196	46.8
Sanilac	457	9.5	311	1.8	405.5	1 365 955	4 386	217 288	421.0	286 957	66.5	33.5	61.0	36.3	7 213	60.3
Schoolcraft	19	-27.2	299	D	5.3	485 169	1 624	59 031	2.2	33 354	63.0	37.1	32.3	9.2	93	10.8
Shiawassee	223	-1.4	216	0.8	195.2	773 484	3 577	136 423	145.2	140 532	78.1	21.9	52.6	22.0	3 634	55.3
Tuscola	325	-5.1	246	5.4	284.5	1 117 802	4 542	168 867	274.4	207 599	82.4	17.6	48.9	26.2	4 778	56.9
Van Buren	175	-5.5	157	34.0	125.1	699 335	4 445	132 358	194.7	174 900	82.9	17.1	46.6	16.4	2 425	21.5
Washtenaw	170	2.0	138	3.6	133.5	701 358	5 095	92 338	87.8	71 004	77.0	23.0	42.5	14.6	3 466	31.7
Wayne	16	-9.6	55	0.3	10.9	408 840	7 442	80 902	26.5	92 456	98.2	1.8	36.9	8.4	102	9.4
Wexford	40	4.8	113	0.9	23.7	321 616	2 847	47 675	9.7	27 104	49.9	50.1	26.1	5.0	122	15.1
MINNESOTA	26 036	-3.3	349	524.0	21 597.1	1 474 057	4 220	197 702	21 280.2	285 479	65.2	34.8	60.0	33.5	467 867	70.0
Aitkin	123	-7.6	260	3.1	61.8	458 718	1 762	64 280	15.7	33 395	52.4	47.6	36.9	6.8	275	22.1
Anoka	45	-2.5	113	2.6	33.0	683 038	6 032	84 725	47.5	119 922	81.5	18.5	35.6	11.6	329	23.7
Becker	435	9.9	393	10.4	309.9	1 067 005	2 716	145 055	261.5	236 218	67.8	32.2	45.9	21.0	6 592	62.9
Beltrami	181	-14.4	315	2.6	88.2	535 471	1 699	70 642	32.4	56 518	66.0	34.0	41.2	10.3	1 146	32.6
Benton	189	1.5	197	11.5	139.9	676 684	3 435	130 284	167.5	174 846	44.1	55.9	59.5	24.5	3 168	63.9
Big Stone	249	-1.4	622	2.1	215.7	2 426 078	3 901	304 623	164.6	411 560	84.0	16.0	72.0	47.5	3 512	85.8
Blue Earth	376	-9.4	352	1.7	338.8	2 256 415	6 413	234 723	505.4	472 358	51.8	48.2	65.8	46.4	7 732	80.4
Brown	326	-8.1	309	2.4	296.4	1 705 125	5 518	216 063	382.9	362 955	57.5	42.5	76.5	51.5	7 384	88.3
Carlton	93	-5.5	185	D	42.4	345 838	1 872	55 281	11.0	21 878	49.3	50.7	39.1	2.4	D	12.2
Carver	155	-8.3	197	0.2	131.6	1 139 812	5 793	194 842	134.4	170 340	65.4	34.6	59.6	28.9	3 149	62.4
Cass	157	-7.1	288	8.8	61.3	549 962	1 910	68 947	38.2	69 877	27.5	72.5	44.3	8.1	542	23.4
Chippewa	335	-8.9	497	4.3	310.6	2 569 132	5 167	332 969	333.2	494 408	79.3	20.7	66.5	48.5	6 261	87.5
Chisago	114	-1.3	137	1.6	76.2	595 308	4 354	79 403	56.5	67 945	77.7	22.3	47.8	12.6	1 081	38.6
Clay	611	-0.5	760	9.9	555.2	2 673 295	3 519	311 899	398.1	495 118	90.3	9.7	62.3	41.3	8 241	75.7
Clearwater	167	-14.0	322	4.0	76.2	539 944	1 679	79 719	31.1	59 836	48.3	51.7	48.4	9.8	886	41.0
Cook	2	-5.4	126	0.0	0.2	598 778	4 744	28 444	0.3	14 278	90.3	9.7	27.8	5.6	D	5.6
Cottonwood	373	-2.2	459	1.4	336.4	2 519 027	5 494	312 232	374.1	460 135	62.6	37.4	70.6	53.4	7 918	83.9
Crow Wing	100	-17.9	188	2.2	44.8	485 445	2 588	75 574	24.8	46 593	58.6	41.5	36.8	8.8	546	30.6
Dakota	220	-10.6	246	50.4	192.7	1 398 640	5 675	195 370	241.0	270 188	77.8	22.2	63.9	32.5	3 892	54.4
Dodge	225	-9.2	363	D	202.5	2 231 597	6 148	237 108	288.1	463 976	61.6	38.4	63.6	40.3	4 124	68.9
Douglas	268	1.8	245	3.4	197.8	754 903	3 078	113 163	120.9	110 813	73.7	26.3	52.6	23.1	4 467	77.7
Faribault	390	-14.0	473	0.3	370.2	2 662 949	5 624	317 608	414.2	502 671	77.9	22.1	78.9	61.0	7 763	82.8

Table B. States and Counties — Water Use, Wholesale Trade, Retail Trade, and Real Estate

STATE County	Water use, 2010		Wholesale trade,[1] 2012				Retail trade,[2] 2012				Real estate and rental and leasing,[2] 2012			
	Total water withdrawn (mil gal/day)	Gallons withdrawn per person per day	Number of establishments	Number of employees	Sales (mil dol)	Annual payroll (mil dol)	Number of establishments	Number of employees	Sales (mil dol)	Annual payroll (mil dol)	Number of establishments	Number of employees	Receipts (mil dol)	Annual payroll (mil dol)
	133	134	135	136	137	138	139	140	141	142	143	144	145	146
MICHIGAN—Cont'd														
Keweenaw	0.2	93	2	D	D	D	11	39	3.9	0.5	1	D	D	D
Lake	2.0	173	4	D	D	D	30	243	60.2	4.8	4	D	D	D
Lapeer	7.9	90	50	438	282.1	20.7	239	2 859	867.1	66.0	56	219	24.5	5.2
Leelanau	3.6	167	11	D	D	D	124	568	139.3	12.4	30	D	D	D
Lenawee	13.3	133	56	D	D	D	304	3 804	961.6	86.9	57	169	30.5	8.2
Livingston	20.0	111	198	2 435	3 092.5	144.1	599	8 695	2 410.2	205.7	124	544	95.4	18.5
Luce	1.3	201	4	D	D	D	26	256	84.2	5.9	7	36	2.4	0.6
Mackinac	10.1	908	8	48	65.3	1.9	93	366	121.9	10.3	12	D	D	D
Macomb	9.2	11	787	10 277	5 776.1	580.9	2 786	40 305	11 304.2	1 006.0	617	3 018	572.1	99.2
Manistee	42.9	1 736	13	117	225.6	6.6	107	905	231.9	19.0	18	42	5.8	0.9
Marquette	271.9	4 053	47	370	203.2	15.9	275	3 741	789.3	77.2	64	266	37.8	6.3
Mason	23.7	827	19	135	190.9	5.8	113	1 428	370.3	32.4	30	560	117.8	31.7
Mecosta	15.1	353	19	D	D	D	142	1 881	488.2	40.3	38	94	15.8	2.4
Menominee	5.8	243	18	297	144.1	11.9	68	584	155.5	11.9	16	D	D	D
Midland	10.6	127	44	297	703.7	16.7	314	4 050	1 015.7	88.4	63	257	36.8	8.4
Missaukee	3.9	263	16	111	69.6	4.5	39	332	120.0	8.9	4	5	0.5	0.1
Monroe	1 830.0	12 038	89	D	D	D	377	4 977	1 471.2	110.5	78	306	43.8	7.9
Montcalm	30.0	474	39	314	144.6	12.0	214	2 231	601.8	50.2	22	64	9.5	1.4
Montmorency	1.1	110	2	D	D	D	33	224	66.7	4.9	3	D	D	D
Muskegon	271.7	1 578	121	D	D	D	552	7 597	1 919.4	171.2	91	457	71.7	14.8
Newaygo	8.3	171	29	201	105.1	8.7	149	1 423	377.1	31.9	26	65	9.0	1.7
Oakland	50.2	42	2 048	28 521	25 910.5	1 806.5	4 880	70 570	20 886.2	1 879.2	1 644	15 464	3 085.1	678.8
Oceana	6.4	241	10	65	31.2	2.7	88	606	160.5	12.8	17	43	6.2	1.2
Ogemaw	3.2	149	21	441	155.5	17.4	119	1 574	387.6	35.3	21	58	9.0	1.6
Ontonagon	5.5	807	4	9	1.9	0.3	30	242	48.4	5.2	3	5	0.3	0.2
Osceola	5.5	234	13	116	134.7	5.2	73	601	176.1	15.4	9	9	2.3	0.4
Oscoda	1.2	142	2	D	D	D	37	241	59.5	4.6	7	14	1.8	0.2
Otsego	4.1	171	42	379	167.4	15.1	148	2 025	528.6	46.1	21	66	9.7	1.8
Ottawa	944.1	3 579	295	3 659	2 645.2	190.1	764	9 714	2 666.6	230.5	196	825	143.8	27.3
Presque Isle	23.7	1 770	5	8	2.0	0.2	64	388	110.9	8.6	7	D	D	D
Roscommon	2.7	112	10	48	12.6	1.4	111	1 220	331.4	28.7	15	63	9.7	1.6
Saginaw	22.3	111	181	1 975	1 264.9	96.7	870	12 210	2 913.3	262.8	132	602	101.1	16.3
St. Clair	1 495.2	9 171	89	924	548.7	40.4	532	6 745	1 760.0	148.7	94	272	56.4	8.2
St. Joseph	35.6	580	42	D	D	D	196	2 254	631.8	51.7	40	133	18.7	2.7
Sanilac	6.1	141	33	315	248.9	16.9	156	1 502	374.2	30.7	18	41	5.3	1.0
Schoolcraft	7.7	904	6	5	2.8	0.1	46	376	124.6	7.9	1	D	D	D
Shiawassee	7.4	104	40	457	201.1	18.2	200	2 413	713.9	58.1	35	77	11.2	2.0
Tuscola	8.9	160	39	465	404.6	23.0	157	1 581	481.9	34.8	19	75	8.7	1.4
Van Buren	167.0	2 189	53	D	D	D	252	2 285	634.6	54.1	32	102	15.3	1.9
Washtenaw	34.8	101	276	3 580	4 695.9	221.8	1 106	16 577	4 461.1	411.4	306	2 409	727.2	115.9
Wayne	1 797.3	987	1 483	23 525	25 358.3	1 417.5	6 091	65 409	17 409.4	1 539.9	1 070	6 044	4 464.6	225.3
Wexford	7.6	232	25	409	162.6	19.5	163	1 922	497.4	42.8	34	105	15.6	2.9
MINNESOTA	3 821.2	720	6 569	108 467	104 485.1	7 170.1	19 109	288 888	78 898.2	6 857.5	6 300	34 499	7 827.9	1 396.0
Aitkin	3.4	212	12	114	125.1	4.8	69	647	173.3	13.3	9	9	1.4	0.2
Anoka	126.1	381	326	12 633	7 485.0	1 617.5	884	15 209	3 982.1	355.7	345	1 149	249.9	34.9
Becker	8.6	264	37	263	150.8	10.1	132	1 731	459.7	38.9	34	77	17.8	2.5
Beltrami	6.4	144	44	D	D	D	220	3 106	702.7	66.5	30	83	14.5	2.4
Benton	21.9	568	42	1 130	911.7	58.9	119	1 800	510.3	42.9	35	80	13.5	2.4
Big Stone	1.4	270	8	74	208.2	3.9	27	209	38.2	3.7	3	3	0.3	0.1
Blue Earth	34.6	540	89	1 383	953.2	65.6	321	6 061	1 413.1	128.0	83	557	66.5	13.3
Brown	4.0	155	28	376	701.3	19.2	109	1 606	347.1	32.6	18	59	7.5	1.5
Carlton	10.7	302	17	287	226.0	11.4	107	1 344	351.8	28.3	16	51	10.5	1.1
Carver	11.2	122	127	2 247	1 699.4	200.5	210	3 484	907.8	80.6	96	603	123.4	29.1
Cass	6.0	211	14	187	87.9	10.0	131	913	255.7	19.8	37	236	13.3	5.9
Chippewa	2.1	170	19	313	532.2	15.7	54	650	198.9	13.9	14	122	6.5	2.4
Chisago	4.7	86	45	435	176.2	18.3	154	1 722	469.2	37.1	44	D	D	D
Clay	6.6	112	68	900	1 175.4	47.0	160	2 682	665.1	57.7	41	160	19.2	3.7
Clearwater	5.7	660	2	D	D	D	34	245	48.8	4.1	NA	NA	NA	NA
Cook	174.8	33 773	3	D	D	D	52	337	66.7	7.8	15	43	4.3	0.9
Cottonwood	5.4	464	25	168	287.4	9.6	51	506	102.8	9.8	6	19	3.3	0.8
Crow Wing	11.4	182	67	450	265.1	18.4	365	4 518	1 125.0	101.2	89	203	46.4	6.3
Dakota	339.7	852	524	7 768	11 786.0	484.9	1 122	21 719	6 485.6	576.6	479	2 310	439.8	83.3
Dodge	2.6	131	21	521	406.7	28.5	48	452	87.9	7.1	7	D	D	D
Douglas	5.7	159	48	997	502.2	44.5	234	3 078	743.4	65.8	43	146	36.6	4.5
Faribault	3.2	218	25	227	227.0	6.6	66	618	122.3	11.8	5	10	1.0	0.2

1. Merchant wholesalers, except manufacturers' sales branches and offices.   2. Employer establishments.

Table B. States and Counties — **Professional Services, Manufacturing, and Accommodation and Food Services**

STATE County	Professional, scientific, and technical services, 2012				Manufacturing, 2012				Accommodation and food services, 2012			
	Number of establish-ments	Number of employees	Receipts (mil dol)	Annual payroll (mil dol)	Number of establish-ments	Number of employees	Receipts (mil dol)	Annual payroll (mil dol)	Number of establish-ments	Number of employees	Sales (mil dol)	Annual payroll (mil dol)
	147	148	149	150	151	152	153	154	155	156	157	158
MICHIGAN—Cont'd												
Keweenaw	NA	NA	NA	NA	4	10	D	D	19	99	5.4	1.5
Lake	4	16	1.1	0.5	8	D	D	D	30	D	D	D
Lapeer	132	623	74.6	25.7	125	4 923	1 303.5	198.8	117	1 933	80.2	22.4
Leelanau	72	223	32.2	10.0	35	240	D	8.8	72	718	46.5	17.0
Lenawee	119	613	50.9	20.1	131	4 569	2 047.2	234.5	167	2 658	105.7	30.4
Livingston	502	2 276	402.4	129.3	248	8 508	3 252.3	420.4	264	5 085	226.3	62.0
Luce	8	12	0.9	0.4	6	171	69.2	7.7	22	180	7.0	1.9
Mackinac	16	32	3.5	1.4	19	143	D	4.6	115	749	122.1	35.2
Macomb	1 581	30 331	3 348.4	2 177.3	1 593	59 114	27 017.3	3 495.8	1 565	28 350	1 263.1	347.5
Manistee	40	108	11.6	4.1	24	816	419.5	46.5	54	1 406	155.4	25.1
Marquette	113	676	66.7	28.6	49	871	275.7	45.3	174	2 806	114.4	34.9
Mason	44	156	13.1	5.0	38	1 800	432.2	86.2	88	980	50.2	13.9
Mecosta	46	281	34.3	16.4	32	1 880	677.0	77.4	78	1 178	45.7	13.5
Menominee	28	88	6.4	2.5	47	1 665	461.7	76.7	47	575	21.8	6.0
Midland	154	785	87.9	34.9	62	6 241	3 591.1	466.1	138	2 861	136.2	40.7
Missaukee	11	18	2.0	0.7	21	363	99.4	12.7	20	168	10.0	2.6
Monroe	147	828	129.9	40.6	128	6 591	2 976.5	351.3	259	4 280	179.9	49.6
Montcalm	51	220	16.1	5.6	74	2 738	528.3	121.1	82	1 003	44.9	12.2
Montmorency	10	21	1.8	0.7	15	369	74.5	12.6	22	D	D	D
Muskegon	223	1 513	182.5	65.7	259	12 483	3 727.0	608.0	335	5 450	236.1	67.6
Newaygo	54	348	52.1	17.4	40	1 897	663.4	84.6	76	906	39.9	10.5
Oakland	6 134	82 960	13 269.4	6 209.6	1 669	47 243	18 446.3	2 707.5	2 755	51 669	2 567.3	739.9
Oceana	28	123	14.4	5.5	41	1 324	473.2	46.6	57	599	29.3	8.2
Ogemaw	31	118	9.5	3.4	30	265	79.0	8.1	65	789	38.1	11.0
Ontonagon	6	9	0.8	0.2	NA	NA	NA	NA	27	156	6.2	1.4
Osceola	25	88	8.5	2.7	41	1 898	968.5	92.5	39	543	25.4	8.0
Oscoda	9	58	2.8	1.4	17	246	70.0	8.9	23	196	8.0	2.4
Otsego	55	205	31.2	9.7	37	682	141.4	25.9	60	1 037	54.4	14.7
Ottawa	466	3 228	471.5	190.5	544	31 831	11 067.3	1 529.6	381	7 573	321.8	89.8
Presque Isle	14	32	1.9	0.6	13	166	D	7.0	43	286	10.6	3.0
Roscommon	30	160	5.4	2.1	16	602	131.7	29.2	71	987	39.8	12.2
Saginaw	318	2 226	299.2	109.3	206	11 249	4 523.3	653.2	368	7 829	373.8	97.6
St. Clair	222	982	112.8	39.8	235	8 080	4 027.0	384.7	283	4 635	191.5	53.3
St. Joseph	74	4 239	44.9	63.4	132	7 683	3 542.4	350.7	104	1 368	57.9	15.8
Sanilac	51	210	15.3	5.3	74	2 385	729.7	95.7	61	567	27.8	6.9
Schoolcraft	9	45	2.9	1.2	9	185	104.4	11.4	35	261	11.6	3.1
Shiawassee	66	308	33.5	10.8	60	1 811	466.5	71.7	109	1 491	61.7	16.8
Tuscola	50	193	19.6	7.9	44	1 216	513.6	54.5	61	753	29.3	8.0
Van Buren	77	1 348	195.0	65.4	87	2 781	1 224.1	140.8	149	1 967	97.2	26.8
Washtenaw	1 284	13 390	2 329.9	928.1	332	13 232	5 419.9	725.8	766	14 879	764.9	216.3
Wayne	2 848	46 825	7 135.0	3 444.6	1 483	71 526	56 638.5	4 413.5	3 184	61 446	4 238.8	1 050.2
Wexford	60	298	28.1	13.2	49	3 890	1 119.0	173.9	78	1 064	46.6	12.8
MINNESOTA	16 348	140 927	23 449.1	9 739.3	7 313	297 884	123 076.3	15 822.6	11 345	221 859	11 722.6	3 238.0
Aitkin	14	D	D	D	27	298	62.1	11.4	51	448	18.8	5.1
Anoka	720	3 290	511.7	176.0	611	20 086	6 716.2	1 164.4	470	9 467	434.0	123.0
Becker	53	181	24.5	7.1	43	2 240	455.7	97.3	88	1 097	57.7	14.6
Beltrami	64	359	34.3	13.6	37	732	D	25.3	94	1 711	76.2	22.1
Benton	48	217	31.1	12.6	70	2 975	681.7	124.1	59	1 072	45.0	12.6
Big Stone	11	D	D	D	5	20	1.1	0.3	18	D	D	D
Blue Earth	147	1 090	127.2	52.6	88	3 896	3 938.5	189.7	156	3 584	143.6	39.2
Brown	43	405	43.4	15.9	38	2 935	1 506.6	129.7	61	955	32.5	9.4
Carlton	45	178	15.3	5.1	27	1 397	D	85.8	67	887	34.6	9.5
Carver	319	2 820	373.5	97.0	144	9 666	3 992.3	572.5	145	D	D	D
Cass	35	131	10.9	4.6	36	300	56.4	10.2	136	2 297	144.7	38.5
Chippewa	19	77	6.9	2.9	27	1 085	358.5	47.3	29	406	14.1	3.5
Chisago	72	D	D	D	80	1 952	552.9	88.0	86	D	D	D
Clay	77	D	D	D	38	832	409.3	D	81	1 824	68.8	20.2
Clearwater	11	53	3.1	1.0	13	443	D	14.1	21	D	D	D
Cook	15	D	D	D	5	43	12.5	1.9	62	637	46.8	14.0
Cottonwood	19	72	7.4	2.2	26	1 780	1 059.6	60.6	21	272	9.7	2.6
Crow Wing	143	940	125.8	50.7	104	2 480	496.6	103.9	209	3 003	169.5	45.9
Dakota	1 385	8 495	1 552.6	595.7	432	16 946	17 442.9	921.0	688	15 357	762.1	211.9
Dodge	22	D	D	D	23	1 123	719.7	57.8	27	336	12.6	3.3
Douglas	83	508	84.5	21.4	89	3 174	920.1	157.1	117	2 023	89.8	25.7
Faribault	20	79	7.9	2.8	24	1 134	326.0	46.6	34	260	11.8	2.5

1. Establishment subject to federal tax.

STATE County	Health care and social assistance, 2012				Other services, 2012				Nonemployer businesses, 2014		Value of residential construction authorized by building permits, 2015	
	Number of establish-ments	Number of employees	Receipts (mil dol)	Annual payroll (mil dol)	Number of establish-ments	Number of employees	Receipts (mil dol)	Annual payroll (mil dol)	Number	Receipts (mil dol)	New Construction ($1,000)	Number of housing units
	159	160	161	162	163	164	165	166	167	168	169	170
MICHIGAN—Cont'd												
Keweenaw	1	D	D	D	2	D	D	D	147	3.5	1 200	12
Lake	12	248	13.8	7.4	10	23	1.9	0.3	612	22.3	1 638	57
Lapeer	201	2 532	239.7	91.1	103	420	37.5	9.3	6 391	267.0	22 382	119
Leelanau	55	D	D	D	34	84	9.3	2.3	2 840	135.2	27 308	116
Lenawee	231	3 168	274.6	112.9	146	758	50.6	14.1	5 960	217.1	13 624	81
Livingston	376	5 161	522.1	191.9	281	1 853	146.9	48.3	14 731	685.2	174 915	646
Luce	16	414	37.4	15.9	10	D	D	D	341	9.0	591	3
Mackinac	19	332	47.3	13.9	15	D	D	D	927	28.9	3 904	21
Macomb	2 308	37 149	4 079.6	1 683.2	1 391	7 991	736.6	223.6	61 384	2 619.3	412 595	1 986
Manistee	65	906	93.7	35.5	44	179	13.7	4.4	1 701	56.4	1 659	8
Marquette	237	5 537	592.1	252.1	131	564	52.6	13.2	3 460	97.6	18 917	97
Mason	93	1 446	124.1	56.5	57	203	16.5	4.7	1 987	64.3	12 211	49
Mecosta	84	1 528	112.8	51.6	62	336	29.4	7.1	2 129	74.9	5 511	37
Menominee	40	334	18.5	8.2	30	161	16.5	4.0	1 327	63.0	6 723	35
Midland	239	6 268	682.2	242.8	147	882	113.0	23.2	4 922	187.4	23 111	130
Missaukee	26	326	14.1	6.6	19	50	4.8	1.2	1 094	52.4	3 206	20
Monroe	282	5 347	457.9	193.6	156	727	67.6	17.0	8 394	356.9	49 920	291
Montcalm	106	3 054	276.4	110.5	88	317	32.7	7.5	3 684	136.0	13 170	89
Montmorency	12	219	15.7	6.1	13	D	D	D	563	21.0	0	0
Muskegon	369	11 494	982.3	483.8	250	1 315	120.8	29.6	9 409	339.1	45 234	241
Newaygo	76	1 706	168.0	69.7	66	211	40.0	5.2	2 801	119.2	11 252	115
Oakland	5 120	100 125	10 835.6	4 461.3	2 371	16 548	1 962.1	474.5	111 980	6 402.8	685 279	2 645
Oceana	45	628	44.7	18.8	37	93	8.7	2.0	1 688	60.1	2 015	13
Ogemaw	66	1 321	102.6	45.5	44	152	11.1	2.9	1 288	52.5	4 062	23
Ontonagon	18	243	17.0	6.9	12	44	7.2	0.8	362	12.6	1 120	12
Osceola	50	1 106	90.0	34.5	30	109	12.4	2.8	1 387	54.9	4 417	27
Oscoda	14	164	9.9	3.6	12	50	3.3	0.8	590	22.5	1 212	14
Otsego	83	1 420	211.2	58.3	61	238	21.0	5.8	1 981	84.5	1 377	17
Ottawa	516	9 453	895.3	314.2	436	2 569	261.1	73.9	18 563	865.8	267 700	1 572
Presque Isle	26	331	22.9	9.0	23	45	5.3	0.9	898	24.5	180	1
Roscommon	45	531	38.0	15.3	56	176	14.5	3.9	1 499	53.8	4 266	18
Saginaw	582	17 262	1 766.5	712.8	328	1 943	161.3	45.2	10 952	395.1	49 680	382
St. Clair	378	7 828	696.4	292.1	201	912	87.1	20.5	10 345	411.0	27 802	134
St. Joseph	108	2 062	187.0	74.5	97	330	31.6	9.0	3 584	140.3	14 276	72
Sanilac	90	1 317	114.8	37.9	55	153	18.0	3.9	3 118	121.4	4 368	38
Schoolcraft	22	D	D	D	14	71	5.0	1.4	401	12.6	2 160	16
Shiawassee	134	2 549	217.0	87.8	97	463	37.7	9.1	4 252	163.4	6 916	27
Tuscola	107	2 444	186.7	78.4	55	168	13.0	3.2	3 484	130.2	4 244	47
Van Buren	107	2 497	195.5	81.3	89	360	30.1	6.6	4 659	186.6	19 393	132
Washtenaw	964	36 873	4 710.2	2 219.2	537	3 891	489.6	143.2	28 506	1 242.6	104 778	420
Wayne	4 091	101 848	12 420.4	4 712.3	2 645	16 865	1 763.8	497.5	126 525	3 945.3	353 058	1 774
Wexford	96	2 022	169.8	70.1	68	254	25.5	6.6	2 229	86.8	10 959	51
MINNESOTA	15 107	440 195	40 403.6	17 514.4	10 832	72 715	7 877.3	2 017.1	394 690	17 982.1	4 135 089	19 545
Aitkin	29	720	67.2	25.3	35	127	14.7	2.1	1 103	43.8	24 581	122
Anoka	625	15 314	1 631.1	710.6	535	3 642	350.2	102.1	22 317	956.5	213 097	795
Becker	78	1 800	149.8	65.9	82	371	39.4	7.1	2 848	140.6	33 639	168
Beltrami	138	3 934	434.5	151.1	90	415	49.8	12.1	2 988	115.9	18 581	193
Benton	84	3 071	116.7	56.0	79	588	48.9	15.2	2 586	110.2	24 402	165
Big Stone	20	898	56.9	24.6	15	33	3.7	0.5	388	19.5	1 326	11
Blue Earth	223	9 080	671.0	323.3	130	D	D	D	4 035	173.1	75 591	681
Brown	64	2 350	172.1	74.3	70	269	35.9	7.3	1 821	72.5	7 934	36
Carlton	88	2 058	145.3	68.3	62	243	22.2	5.8	1 974	71.4	10 344	55
Carver	201	4 828	471.1	202.5	171	1 051	84.6	24.4	7 850	400.1	187 564	729
Cass	68	1 227	65.1	27.7	59	228	18.4	3.7	2 600	118.9	48 388	224
Chippewa	39	1 100	69.6	29.2	41	156	20.1	3.9	874	38.2	1 301	7
Chisago	131	4 202	313.6	152.4	95	400	29.8	8.6	3 782	157.7	26 340	160
Clay	167	3 955	186.6	87.0	105	491	38.3	10.8	3 961	156.1	85 345	581
Clearwater	16	551	22.9	12.0	13	34	3.8	0.6	637	24.9	506	4
Cook	15	233	20.9	8.1	9	D	D	D	782	29.9	14 412	54
Cottonwood	34	818	50.1	19.9	27	89	8.0	2.0	822	39.0	2 016	9
Crow Wing	231	5 938	482.6	215.6	141	694	54.5	13.7	5 065	227.5	72 547	447
Dakota	1 012	23 031	1 679.6	745.8	729	6 034	582.8	183.3	28 468	1 274.4	311 543	1 306
Dodge	31	245	15.0	6.9	41	264	29.3	7.6	1 311	69.5	16 088	70
Douglas	129	3 480	266.1	105.0	109	464	42.6	9.5	3 283	161.3	48 046	298
Faribault	38	807	56.7	23.5	32	141	14.8	3.5	1 128	56.0	1 988	10

Table B. States and Counties — Government Employment and Payroll, and Local Government Finances

	Government employment and payroll, 2012									Local government finances, 2012				
			March payroll (percent of total)							General revenue				
												Taxes		
													Per capita[1] (dollars)	
STATE County	Full-time equivalent employees	March payroll (dollars)	Administration, judicial, and legal	Police and Corrections	Fire Protection	Highways and transportation	Health and Welfare	Natural resources and utilities	Education and libraries	Total (mil dol)	Inter-governmental (mil dol)	Total (mil dol)	Total	Property
	171	172	173	174	175	176	177	178	179	180	181	182	183	184
MICHIGAN—Cont'd														
Keweenaw	94	226 587	43.0	12.5	0.3	32.4	0.3	5.4	3.3	7.1	2.2	2.4	1 085	1 064
Lake	335	1 121 895	29.9	22.5	0.7	15.2	0.2	4.0	24.4	41.5	20.4	15.6	1 355	1 353
Lapeer	2 193	8 102 009	9.7	7.1	0.9	3.7	6.5	3.4	67.0	261.5	141.1	64.1	727	687
Leelanau	610	2 337 768	17.9	7.8	10.1	6.0	1.3	2.0	50.2	66.0	15.8	38.3	1 774	1 747
Lenawee	2 916	10 906 000	8.3	8.7	1.9	4.7	2.7	5.5	65.8	340.2	180.3	97.9	989	958
Livingston	3 683	15 206 225	8.3	7.3	2.3	3.3	1.3	2.2	69.7	518.2	264.0	170.8	934	916
Luce	511	1 851 870	3.9	1.5	0.5	3.4	68.0	1.9	19.9	52.1	10.7	6.0	924	922
Mackinac	650	2 008 291	8.8	6.7	0.6	5.6	41.9	4.0	30.0	45.0	12.9	23.1	2 077	1 972
Macomb	20 477	98 514 743	5.7	8.9	3.4	3.3	4.1	2.4	70.5	3 154.9	1 534.9	942.2	1 112	1 087
Manistee	1 223	4 900 512	8.6	4.0	2.1	5.6	46.5	1.1	31.4	89.4	31.4	32.7	1 326	1 315
Marquette	2 307	8 582 841	9.4	7.9	1.6	8.1	17.8	11.0	40.6	242.6	106.7	75.0	1 105	1 084
Mason	951	3 483 823	12.1	7.3	0.1	7.1	0.9	4.3	66.7	123.3	40.6	57.2	1 996	1 980
Mecosta	1 566	5 890 046	7.7	5.5	1.5	4.1	36.2	3.2	40.3	182.4	76.2	42.5	980	926
Menominee	588	2 056 771	19.0	9.3	2.8	9.0	0.0	3.2	55.6	62.8	33.4	19.2	806	799
Midland	2 175	9 622 686	11.4	7.8	3.3	4.0	3.3	5.7	62.5	271.7	113.5	103.5	1 235	1 220
Missaukee	422	1 353 016	12.8	7.9	0.0	5.9	3.8	2.5	64.8	51.3	27.9	11.7	775	714
Monroe	3 882	16 268 085	7.1	8.4	1.4	3.3	1.1	4.8	72.4	475.7	225.8	166.5	1 102	1 074
Montcalm	1 898	7 424 584	9.0	5.3	0.5	3.4	5.9	1.9	72.7	230.7	138.4	56.8	901	887
Montmorency	201	694 558	20.5	8.4	2.1	11.4	4.4	2.8	43.7	25.7	7.3	10.4	1 095	1 081
Muskegon	5 428	21 789 876	7.5	7.4	2.5	3.3	9.1	3.1	65.4	721.5	413.6	168.4	989	913
Newaygo	1 567	5 734 250	9.2	6.4	0.9	3.1	12.6	1.5	64.0	180.6	100.9	46.4	967	962
Oakland	32 137	148 761 141	8.1	11.5	4.0	2.5	1.6	3.0	67.0	4 845.3	2 149.8	1 849.8	1 515	1 468
Oceana	787	2 716 638	12.5	6.8	0.6	9.1	6.1	3.2	57.2	91.5	36.3	30.4	1 156	1 142
Ogemaw	842	2 976 350	8.9	6.3	0.2	5.1	44.2	1.3	31.8	88.5	51.5	18.2	849	836
Ontonagon	240	749 123	19.9	5.8	0.6	28.7	0.1	8.1	33.5	31.1	13.6	12.2	1 900	1 897
Osceola	733	2 622 547	9.4	6.1	0.6	5.1	5.4	1.4	70.9	69.7	41.4	19.9	853	849
Oscoda	244	725 038	18.2	5.2	0.5	9.3	2.2	2.3	61.4	22.2	10.6	9.0	1 046	1 036
Otsego	766	3 112 250	10.4	4.0	0.5	8.3	0.2	1.8	71.3	77.8	31.0	34.0	1 415	1 413
Ottawa	6 822	27 516 658	8.5	6.3	1.4	2.9	4.0	6.4	67.9	866.8	436.0	302.6	1 125	1 104
Presque Isle	353	1 093 950	16.9	10.3	0.0	9.1	0.4	3.7	54.2	39.4	19.9	14.6	1 112	1 107
Roscommon	871	3 202 024	11.2	10.4	2.9	8.2	2.8	1.9	61.8	97.6	32.0	44.6	1 849	1 841
Saginaw	5 686	21 466 345	8.3	8.5	2.2	2.7	9.8	4.8	61.7	786.5	475.8	154.2	777	684
St. Clair	4 714	19 193 428	9.3	10.1	2.3	4.7	2.9	4.1	64.9	638.8	345.1	182.6	1 136	1 082
St. Joseph	2 407	8 504 558	8.9	6.1	1.5	3.5	17.3	3.9	56.9	263.0	120.1	64.5	1 061	1 051
Sanilac	1 146	3 992 557	10.8	9.0	0.7	4.8	2.5	4.3	65.5	164.8	92.6	39.4	932	918
Schoolcraft	461	1 943 689	9.8	4.5	1.3	9.9	52.0	3.2	18.6	62.6	11.5	8.5	1 020	1 018
Shiawassee	2 564	9 090 340	7.2	7.6	1.3	2.6	17.5	2.4	59.3	229.5	141.1	48.8	706	694
Tuscola	1 649	6 143 983	21.0	6.5	0.2	4.3	0.6	1.4	64.0	203.6	117.9	44.3	810	798
Van Buren	2 988	10 792 044	6.7	6.5	1.0	3.0	15.9	2.4	63.8	369.9	183.5	110.9	1 470	1 455
Washtenaw	9 997	45 620 706	8.5	10.1	3.0	4.2	5.2	5.4	62.0	1 472.6	631.4	577.8	1 646	1 596
Wayne	52 078	243 918 311	7.3	16.2	6.7	6.5	2.2	6.4	52.0	9 260.6	4 384.4	2 686.6	1 499	1 195
Wexford	861	3 131 204	9.3	8.2	2.0	8.9	0.5	6.9	62.4	121.3	63.1	38.8	1 190	1 183
MINNESOTA	X	X	X	X	X	X	X	X	X	X	X	X	X	X
Aitkin	582	2 073 612	15.2	11.2	0.4	6.7	11.2	4.6	46.4	60.1	32.6	17.4	1 089	1 074
Anoka	10 501	53 828 905	6.5	8.8	1.4	2.5	5.0	3.0	71.0	1 331.2	702.4	418.5	1 244	1 193
Becker	932	4 604 178	7.8	4.6	0.0	8.2	10.4	5.5	61.2	127.6	63.7	39.1	1 185	1 161
Beltrami	1 932	6 706 796	6.4	7.1	0.7	3.3	9.3	2.1	68.3	213.6	142.5	38.4	846	783
Benton	983	5 694 288	6.7	6.0	0.2	10.1	6.5	2.2	67.4	129.9	70.8	39.7	1 023	988
Big Stone	457	1 386 890	7.6	3.9	0.1	6.3	36.5	4.2	39.3	61.1	19.6	7.4	1 429	1 407
Blue Earth	2 214	8 872 355	7.8	8.8	1.3	4.6	6.9	5.2	63.0	311.6	161.3	79.4	1 221	1 080
Brown	1 088	4 160 686	9.0	10.8	0.0	6.2	20.5	12.8	39.2	121.7	52.1	29.1	1 145	1 070
Carlton	1 862	6 624 488	5.4	5.5	3.7	4.3	24.0	2.7	53.1	175.9	81.0	37.5	1 060	1 044
Carver	2 896	13 125 660	8.3	9.1	0.5	3.7	9.7	7.6	58.3	405.9	156.2	153.3	1 636	1 556
Cass	1 234	4 242 722	11.4	8.7	0.0	4.7	8.0	7.4	56.2	139.1	77.1	36.0	1 270	1 262
Chippewa	807	3 441 530	7.9	4.1	0.2	6.5	37.5	2.9	37.6	70.5	36.6	15.5	1 281	1 255
Chisago	1 385	5 404 860	10.1	10.6	0.1	5.4	10.2	3.2	57.7	193.7	95.4	66.1	1 237	1 214
Clay	2 229	9 153 639	5.8	9.5	2.1	3.2	9.3	7.6	60.6	275.2	152.5	52.4	871	834
Clearwater	344	1 650 939	7.5	7.1	0.0	4.2	13.2	2.5	62.5	36.7	20.9	8.5	982	979
Cook	357	1 321 609	10.7	6.6	0.1	6.3	41.6	8.6	23.6	43.3	14.6	10.6	2 035	1 721
Cottonwood	572	1 944 398	8.0	7.4	0.1	6.3	7.4	9.1	58.7	74.4	30.9	14.0	1 205	1 195
Crow Wing	2 463	11 443 269	7.2	9.3	0.8	3.7	30.0	2.2	44.6	346.9	130.2	91.9	1 461	1 378
Dakota	12 238	59 978 327	5.3	8.3	1.1	2.3	5.3	4.9	70.7	1 651.5	821.5	536.9	1 325	1 284
Dodge	717	3 409 832	6.5	6.4	0.0	3.9	12.4	1.9	67.9	88.6	44.2	22.9	1 131	1 119
Douglas	1 101	6 909 728	5.8	7.2	0.1	2.6	9.8	5.5	66.7	237.1	64.8	46.8	1 286	1 248
Faribault	667	3 058 474	6.0	6.7	0.1	5.1	34.0	6.2	39.8	90.8	34.3	16.1	1 130	1 101

1. Based on the resident population estimated as of July 1 of the year shown.

STATE County	Total (mil dol)	Per capita[1] (dollars)	Education	Health and hospitals	Police protection	Public welfare	Highways	Total (mil dol)	Per capita[1] (dollars)	Federal civilian	Federal military	State and local	Democratic	Republican	All other
	185	186	187	188	189	190	191	192	193	194	195	196	197	198	199
MICHIGAN—Cont'd															
Keweenaw	6.9	3 101	2.6	1.3	7.4	0.3	34.9	4.3	1 951	22	0	107	43.3	53.6	3.1
Lake	31.5	2 738	24.3	2.6	4.3	1.0	15.0	21.8	1 898	59	19	407	55.2	42.9	2.0
Lapeer	274.0	3 108	46.0	7.1	3.5	8.9	6.8	238.6	2 706	133	147	4 096	47.3	50.3	2.4
Leelanau	61.1	2 829	43.8	4.2	3.6	0.7	9.8	51.6	2 388	129	37	1 748	50.9	48.0	1.2
Lenawee	351.5	3 551	55.5	5.5	3.4	4.6	6.5	276.7	2 796	185	159	4 576	51.6	46.6	1.8
Livingston	530.7	2 902	57.0	7.6	3.3	0.5	5.0	1 200.5	6 566	247	313	6 022	42.5	55.8	1.7
Luce	51.6	7 912	15.9	60.1	0.9	0.2	7.0	15.2	2 335	14	0	778	43.5	54.4	2.2
Mackinac	45.6	4 094	32.8	5.3	3.6	0.1	14.6	33.1	2 975	57	62	953	47.3	51.1	1.6
Macomb	3 200.9	3 777	51.2	8.3	6.2	1.5	3.9	3 701.0	4 368	7 918	1 812	28 375	53.4	44.8	1.9
Manistee	95.8	3 885	34.2	1.9	3.0	12.4	11.2	104.6	4 240	89	56	2 694	55.6	42.4	2.0
Marquette	235.2	3 464	37.8	1.8	6.5	6.4	9.7	135.1	1 989	286	124	5 422	59.2	38.9	1.9
Mason	115.8	4 037	56.0	0.9	2.9	9.4	8.9	57.5	2 005	95	63	1 871	51.3	46.9	1.7
Mecosta	174.1	4 018	38.9	30.3	3.2	0.8	5.0	74.8	1 726	88	69	4 901	48.8	49.5	1.7
Menominee	61.6	2 585	51.9	0.5	6.7	0.2	12.8	22.8	958	65	40	1 950	54.0	43.8	2.1
Midland	272.5	3 250	51.0	2.8	4.1	2.1	7.6	318.6	3 800	138	139	3 353	47.4	50.9	1.7
Missaukee	54.0	3 591	36.3	33.2	2.2	0.6	9.3	4.1	276	25	25	494	38.7	59.7	1.7
Monroe	515.6	3 414	53.6	6.7	3.7	0.2	9.1	557.6	3 691	219	252	5 304	51.3	46.9	1.8
Montcalm	236.5	3 748	58.8	7.6	2.3	0.4	7.4	191.1	3 029	123	102	2 890	48.8	49.1	2.0
Montmorency	24.1	2 539	34.8	1.0	4.8	1.0	13.9	10.5	1 103	17	15	389	44.8	53.0	2.2
Muskegon	746.4	4 386	51.2	13.2	3.2	3.6	4.5	688.6	4 046	335	306	7 308	63.9	34.6	1.5
Newaygo	194.0	4 046	57.6	5.7	2.5	6.5	7.1	159.0	3 316	139	80	2 218	46.7	51.3	2.0
Oakland	4 863.5	3 984	50.4	6.9	6.5	0.2	4.9	4 726.4	3 872	4 645	2 215	44 381	56.5	42.0	1.4
Oceana	89.5	3 401	42.0	4.4	3.7	17.2	11.9	48.9	1 859	150	44	1 354	51.2	46.8	2.0
Ogemaw	91.5	4 268	23.9	47.2	2.2	0.7	7.5	60.2	2 807	54	35	1 056	50.1	47.7	2.3
Ontonagon	29.7	4 631	39.8	1.3	2.4	0.1	24.2	24.8	3 875	41	10	341	50.6	46.9	2.5
Osceola	69.8	2 999	56.1	2.5	3.0	0.3	11.7	41.1	1 765	57	38	901	44.0	54.2	1.8
Oscoda	22.1	2 573	44.7	4.2	4.0	8.4	11.5	3.6	419	55	14	383	43.6	53.6	2.8
Otsego	81.5	3 391	48.3	3.2	2.7	0.6	12.1	42.7	1 777	135	41	1 023	44.7	53.5	1.8
Ottawa	885.8	3 292	57.1	5.1	3.6	0.9	6.5	1 000.3	3 717	396	514	15 877	37.3	61.2	1.5
Presque Isle	40.5	3 081	35.5	1.1	3.7	0.7	13.8	21.2	1 618	51	22	591	49.6	48.0	2.4
Roscommon	94.2	3 908	58.3	2.5	4.2	1.6	7.4	44.3	1 836	29	40	1 204	50.4	47.9	1.7
Saginaw	801.9	4 043	42.8	14.5	5.8	0.7	5.8	494.0	2 490	1 419	330	9 485	57.9	40.6	1.5
St. Clair	651.8	4 058	44.3	15.8	3.9	0.1	6.4	526.8	3 280	622	339	5 966	50.3	47.6	2.1
St. Joseph	268.7	4 420	49.4	24.1	3.0	0.3	4.3	102.6	3 074	98	102	2 697	47.9	50.1	1.9
Sanilac	165.3	3 911	47.1	12.6	4.3	6.0	11.0	127.3	3 011	105	70	1 735	44.9	52.9	2.2
Schoolcraft	58.9	7 054	15.2	41.3	2.0	13.4	8.4	36.7	4 402	44	14	1 050	50.5	47.6	1.9
Shiawassee	236.8	3 421	55.9	8.0	3.1	6.2	8.8	102.4	1 479	125	115	3 154	53.3	44.7	2.1
Tuscola	211.4	3 867	51.0	9.0	3.1	9.1	9.0	137.5	2 515	127	91	2 755	48.6	49.4	2.0
Van Buren	365.1	4 839	52.4	18.4	2.7	0.9	6.5	300.6	3 984	134	126	5 212	53.5	44.7	1.9
Washtenaw	1 495.8	4 262	46.0	12.6	6.5	0.9	4.9	2 033.3	5 794	3 943	622	69 842	69.8	28.8	1.4
Wayne	9 500.3	5 300	36.3	3.3	7.0	5.2	2.9	21 084.6	11 764	13 897	3 395	74 054	74.1	24.7	1.2
Wexford	112.1	3 437	54.4	1.5	4.1	1.5	9.9	59.5	1 825	127	55	1 905	47.0	51.2	1.8
MINNESOTA	X	X	X	X	X	X	X	X	X	31 246	20 284	368 543	54.1	43.8	2.1
Aitkin	64.5	4 049	33.1	1.4	4.3	8.2	22.4	16.8	1 053	45	57	801	48.8	48.8	2.4
Anoka	1 279.3	3 803	53.7	0.9	5.4	5.1	9.5	1 587.7	4 720	395	1 247	14 440	47.7	50.1	2.1
Becker	136.5	4 137	44.4	1.1	4.2	11.3	12.3	95.6	2 898	236	121	2 772	45.3	52.2	2.5
Beltrami	237.7	5 239	45.5	1.1	3.5	7.4	8.2	329.6	7 264	404	160	4 801	54.1	43.9	2.0
Benton	105.9	2 726	49.8	1.2	5.5	8.3	10.1	177.0	4 555	83	142	1 594	43.7	53.5	2.8
Big Stone	57.1	11 056	19.8	43.6	2.3	4.0	9.5	316.3	61 258	35	18	616	51.9	45.6	2.5
Blue Earth	298.5	4 586	38.2	0.6	4.8	5.4	14.5	311.4	4 785	255	263	5 192	55.1	42.1	2.7
Brown	114.6	4 507	33.1	12.3	4.8	7.0	11.5	109.7	4 315	75	89	1 602	42.7	54.7	2.6
Carlton	170.7	4 830	39.9	19.7	3.8	7.4	8.0	194.2	5 495	68	123	5 227	62.3	35.5	2.2
Carver	420.3	4 485	43.0	0.6	4.3	4.9	9.0	930.8	9 933	210	354	4 509	41.6	56.7	1.8
Cass	150.7	5 316	45.3	1.8	4.4	6.4	12.0	129.6	4 571	252	104	3 815	44.6	53.1	2.3
Chippewa	70.8	5 832	38.1	1.0	3.7	12.0	12.1	81.7	6 730	67	44	1 162	51.6	45.7	2.7
Chisago	182.5	3 415	43.9	1.5	4.9	4.7	15.5	291.7	5 458	93	192	2 401	43.6	53.9	2.5
Clay	286.2	4 758	32.4	1.9	4.5	6.9	10.4	437.1	7 267	124	212	4 229	57.0	40.9	2.1
Clearwater	40.3	4 626	44.8	0.2	5.1	9.0	18.1	19.0	2 179	35	32	496	44.1	53.8	2.2
Cook	44.8	8 644	13.1	30.8	6.2	4.2	13.3	40.0	7 721	132	19	760	60.3	37.0	2.7
Cottonwood	74.7	6 441	31.9	19.0	3.8	5.3	14.2	80.5	6 940	57	42	791	45.7	52.3	2.0
Crow Wing	333.5	5 303	34.0	22.0	4.7	6.2	6.0	491.9	7 822	192	271	4 466	45.1	52.8	2.1
Dakota	1 670.9	4 125	51.3	0.8	5.2	4.3	6.8	2 383.8	5 885	2 249	1 521	17 639	51.8	46.3	1.9
Dodge	88.6	4 380	46.8	2.3	6.2	13.6	9.3	114.3	5 648	36	74	1 189	43.7	53.5	2.8
Douglas	244.5	6 713	25.3	35.9	2.8	3.2	7.4	374.7	10 290	137	133	3 232	44.2	53.7	2.0
Faribault	106.3	7 456	21.6	34.8	2.4	1.7	14.0	77.3	5 420	56	51	1 139	45.8	51.5	2.7

1. Based on the resident population estimated as of July 1 of the year shown. 2. © 2013 Election Data Services, Inc. All rights reserved.

Items 185.—199

Table B. States and Counties — Land Area and Population

STATE/ County code	CBSA code[1]	County type[2]	STATE County	Land area,[3] (sq km) 2010	Total persons 2015	Rank	Per square kilometer	White	Black	American Indian, Alaska Native	Asian and Pacific Islander	Percent Hispanic or Latino[4]	Under 5 years	5 to 17 years	18 to 24 years	25 to 34 years	35 to 44 years	45 to 54 years
				1	2	3	4	5	6	7	8	9	10	11	12	13	14	15
			MINNESOTA—Cont'd															
27 045	40340	8	Fillmore	2 231	20 834	1 785	9.3	97.6	0.6	0.4	0.7	1.2	6.2	17.5	7.1	10.3	11.0	13.0
27 047	10660	7	Freeborn	1 831	30 613	1 418	16.7	88.1	1.3	0.6	1.7	9.5	5.8	16.1	7.0	11.0	10.5	13.6
27 049	39860	4	Goodhue	1 960	46 435	1 039	23.7	93.9	1.7	1.6	1.2	3.1	5.8	17.1	7.3	11.0	11.2	14.4
27 051	...	9	Grant	1 420	5 903	2 761	4.2	96.8	0.9	0.8	0.7	1.9	5.7	16.0	6.5	10.4	10.4	12.5
27 053	33460	1	Hennepin	1 434	1 223 149	35	853.0	72.7	13.9	1.5	8.1	6.8	6.6	15.6	8.9	17.1	13.1	13.6
27 055	29100	3	Houston	1 430	18 773	1 882	13.1	97.8	1.2	0.6	0.8	0.8	5.0	16.4	7.5	10.2	11.0	14.5
27 057	...	7	Hubbard	2 397	20 655	1 795	8.6	95.1	0.9	3.1	0.7	1.8	5.7	15.3	5.9	9.1	9.9	14.0
27 059	33460	1	Isanti	1 129	38 429	1 210	34.0	96.0	1.2	1.2	1.4	1.8	6.0	18.5	7.8	12.5	12.3	15.4
27 061	...	6	Itasca	6 909	45 435	1 065	6.6	94.3	0.9	5.1	0.8	1.3	5.4	15.9	7.1	9.8	10.7	13.3
27 063	...	7	Jackson	1 821	10 079	2 431	5.5	94.3	1.0	0.6	2.1	3.3	6.0	16.5	7.6	10.9	10.9	13.4
27 065	...	6	Kanabec	1 351	15 837	2 052	11.7	96.5	1.0	1.5	0.8	1.7	4.9	16.9	7.3	10.3	11.8	14.1
27 067	48820	4	Kandiyohi	2 064	42 542	1 119	20.6	83.9	3.6	0.6	0.9	11.4	6.4	17.2	8.8	12.1	10.7	12.6
27 069	...	9	Kittson	2 846	4 424	2 870	1.6	96.8	0.7	0.5	0.4	2.0	5.2	16.4	7.1	8.1	9.7	14.0
27 071	...	7	Koochiching	8 040	12 841	2 239	1.6	95.0	1.1	3.4	0.7	1.3	4.0	15.0	7.4	9.2	10.3	14.1
27 073	...	9	Lac qui Parle	1 981	6 856	2 687	3.5	96.6	0.7	0.6	1.0	2.0	5.2	15.2	6.7	8.4	8.9	13.3
27 075	...	6	Lake	5 463	10 631	2 384	1.9	97.0	0.9	1.3	0.6	1.5	5.0	13.8	6.0	9.9	9.6	13.6
27 077	...	9	Lake of the Woods	3 361	3 923	2 908	1.2	96.1	1.1	1.9	1.7	1.5	4.5	13.9	6.2	8.4	9.5	15.2
27 079	33460	6	Le Sueur	1 162	27 663	1 505	23.8	92.8	1.0	0.8	1.0	5.7	5.7	18.8	7.4	11.3	12.2	14.8
27 081	...	9	Lincoln	1 390	5 771	2 778	4.2	97.0	0.5	0.5	0.6	1.9	5.5	16.8	6.0	9.9	10.6	11.9
27 083	32140	7	Lyon	1 851	25 673	1 574	13.9	87.3	3.1	0.8	3.6	6.4	7.2	17.6	10.8	13.9	11.4	12.2
27 085	26780	6	McLeod	1 273	35 932	1 275	28.2	93.0	0.9	0.6	1.0	5.3	6.1	17.7	7.8	11.6	11.9	14.3
27 087	...	8	Mahnomen	1 445	5 457	2 805	3.8	56.1	1.5	46.9	0.6	3.1	10.2	20.4	7.9	10.4	10.1	11.4
27 089	...	8	Marshall	4 597	9 423	2 475	2.0	94.5	0.6	1.1	0.4	4.1	6.1	16.9	7.3	10.8	10.6	13.6
27 091	...	7	Martin	1 845	20 022	1 834	10.9	94.7	0.8	0.6	0.9	3.9	5.4	16.2	7.3	10.6	10.0	13.1
27 093	...	6	Meeker	1 575	23 102	1 681	14.7	95.3	0.8	0.5	0.5	3.4	6.2	18.4	7.2	10.5	11.2	13.7
27 095	33460	6	Mille Lacs	1 482	25 788	1 565	17.4	91.8	1.0	6.6	0.8	1.8	6.4	18.0	7.2	11.4	11.6	14.1
27 097	...	6	Morrison	2 914	32 775	1 364	11.2	97.1	0.8	0.8	0.7	1.5	6.0	17.5	7.4	11.4	11.3	14.2
27 099	12380	4	Mower	1 842	39 116	1 201	21.2	83.2	3.9	0.5	2.8	11.2	6.9	18.0	8.1	11.8	11.6	13.0
27 101	...	9	Murray	1 825	8 413	2 562	4.6	94.7	0.7	0.5	1.6	3.6	5.8	15.9	6.8	9.3	9.8	13.0
27 103	31860	5	Nicollet	1 162	33 347	1 345	28.7	91.2	2.9	0.6	1.9	4.2	5.6	16.3	13.4	14.2	11.4	12.5
27 105	49380	7	Nobles	1 852	21 770	1 739	11.8	62.9	4.4	0.7	6.5	26.2	8.1	18.3	9.2	12.9	11.2	12.2
27 107	...	8	Norman	2 261	6 678	2 705	3.0	94.1	1.1	3.5	0.9	4.9	5.3	17.9	7.4	8.9	10.8	13.6
27 109	40340	3	Olmsted	1 692	151 436	427	89.5	83.5	6.4	0.6	7.1	4.5	7.1	17.6	7.8	14.9	12.6	13.5
27 111	22260	6	Otter Tail	5 108	57 716	887	11.3	94.7	1.4	1.1	1.0	3.1	5.8	15.6	7.2	9.8	9.5	13.6
27 113	...	6	Pennington	1 597	14 219	2 155	8.9	92.7	1.7	2.4	1.3	3.4	6.7	16.4	8.5	13.7	11.8	12.9
27 115	...	6	Pine	3 655	29 069	1 453	8.0	91.3	2.6	3.9	1.0	2.9	4.9	15.7	6.9	12.1	11.9	15.2
27 117	...	6	Pipestone	1 204	9 271	2 489	7.7	91.9	1.5	1.9	1.1	5.0	6.4	18.1	7.4	10.4	10.4	13.2
27 119	24220	3	Polk	5 105	31 533	1 396	6.2	90.9	1.7	2.4	1.5	5.9	6.4	17.0	10.2	12.2	10.6	13.2
27 121	...	8	Pope	1 735	11 041	2 353	6.4	97.8	0.9	0.6	0.7	1.2	5.8	15.4	6.6	10.8	10.3	12.5
27 123	33460	1	Ramsey	394	538 133	123	1 365.8	66.7	12.9	1.5	14.6	7.3	7.1	16.3	10.8	16.4	11.7	12.5
27 125	...	8	Red Lake	1 120	4 055	2 898	3.6	94.8	1.4	2.3	0.5	3.0	7.4	17.5	6.0	10.7	11.2	13.1
27 127	...	7	Redwood	2 275	15 471	2 075	6.8	89.0	1.0	5.5	3.4	2.9	6.4	17.9	7.4	10.3	10.2	13.4
27 129	...	9	Renville	2 546	14 892	2 108	5.8	90.4	1.0	1.4	0.9	7.8	5.8	16.8	7.2	10.4	10.4	13.9
27 131	22060	4	Rice	1 284	65 400	807	50.9	85.5	4.5	0.7	2.9	7.8	5.8	16.6	14.7	11.4	11.7	13.4
27 133	...	6	Rock	1 250	9 600	2 465	7.7	96.0	1.3	0.8	1.1	2.5	6.4	18.5	7.3	9.7	11.8	12.2
27 135	...	7	Roseau	4 329	15 770	2 056	3.6	93.8	0.9	2.2	3.2	1.1	6.0	18.6	7.9	10.1	11.8	15.9
27 137	20260	2	St. Louis	16 181	200 431	328	12.4	93.6	2.4	3.3	1.6	1.5	5.2	14.1	12.7	11.9	10.7	12.9
27 139	33460	1	Scott	923	141 660	451	153.5	84.9	4.2	1.3	7.0	4.8	7.4	21.5	7.3	12.8	15.5	15.8
27 141	33460	1	Sherburne	1 121	91 705	634	81.8	93.7	2.7	0.9	1.7	2.5	6.8	20.6	8.3	13.5	14.4	15.3
27 143	33460	8	Sibley	1 525	14 875	2 110	9.8	90.4	0.9	0.5	0.9	8.5	6.0	18.5	7.3	10.8	11.7	14.7
27 145	41060	3	Stearns	3 479	154 708	418	44.5	90.5	4.5	0.6	2.7	3.1	6.1	16.6	15.6	12.6	11.0	12.8
27 147	36940	5	Steele	1 113	36 755	1 259	33.0	88.7	3.2	0.5	1.2	7.5	6.7	18.5	7.9	12.0	11.6	14.3
27 149	...	7	Stevens	1 460	9 796	2 451	6.7	91.3	1.7	2.2	2.3	4.2	5.3	15.6	20.3	11.5	8.9	10.2
27 151	...	7	Swift	1 922	9 340	2 483	4.9	94.4	1.2	0.7	0.7	3.9	6.0	15.6	7.4	10.5	10.3	13.9
27 153	...	6	Todd	2 447	24 257	1 634	9.9	92.9	0.8	1.0	1.1	5.5	6.9	17.1	7.7	9.9	10.1	13.8
27 155	...	9	Traverse	1 486	3 401	2 945	2.3	92.8	1.3	5.2	0.6	1.9	4.8	15.9	7.1	9.2	9.3	13.0
27 157	40340	3	Wabasha	1 355	21 239	1 764	15.7	95.9	0.8	0.5	0.8	3.1	6.0	16.4	7.3	10.5	11.3	14.9
27 159	...	7	Wadena	1 389	13 875	2 177	10.0	96.4	1.6	1.3	0.8	1.7	6.2	17.9	8.0	9.9	10.4	12.6
27 161	...	7	Waseca	1 096	18 989	1 874	17.3	90.6	3.0	1.2	1.1	5.7	6.0	17.3	7.4	13.2	12.8	13.4
27 163	33460	1	Washington	995	251 597	264	252.9	85.9	5.1	0.9	6.3	3.8	6.1	19.1	8.0	11.9	13.0	15.8
27 165	...	7	Watonwan	1 127	10 952	2 362	9.7	75.7	1.0	0.5	1.2	23.2	6.8	17.8	8.0	10.7	10.9	12.4
27 167	47420	6	Wilkin	1 945	6 396	2 724	3.3	95.6	0.8	1.7	0.7	2.4	5.8	17.2	7.7	10.6	10.9	15.2
27 169	49100	4	Winona	1 622	50 885	976	31.4	92.9	1.9	0.6	2.9	2.7	4.4	13.9	21.4	11.2	9.6	11.7
27 171	33460	1	Wright	1 713	131 311	478	76.7	94.4	1.8	0.7	1.8	2.7	7.4	21.4	7.2	12.5	14.4	14.9
27 173	...	9	Yellow Medicine	1 966	9 875	2 444	5.0	92.5	0.8	3.7	0.8	4.2	6.4	16.9	7.5	11.0	10.1	13.2

1. CBSA = Core Based Statistical Area. See Appendix A for explanation. See Appendix B for list of metropolitan areas with component counties. 2. County type code from the Economic Research Service of USDA Rural-Urban Continuum Codes. See Appendix A for definition. 3. Dry land or land partially or temporarily covered by water. 4. May be of any race.

Table B. States and Counties — **Population and Households**

STATE County	Age (percent) 55 to 64 years	Age (percent) 65 to 74 years	Age (percent) 75 years and over	Percent female	Total persons 2000	Total persons 2010	Percent change 2000–2010	Percent change 2010–2015	Components of change, 2010–2015 Births	Deaths	Net migration	Households Number	Persons per house-hold	Family house-holds	Female family house-holder[1]	One per-son
	16	17	18	19	20	21	22	23	24	25	26	27	28	29	30	31
MINNESOTA—Cont'd																
Fillmore	14.5	10.2	10.1	50.0	21 122	20 866	-1.2	-0.2	1 326	1 204	-180	8 424	2.43	67.6	6.7	28.1
Freeborn	14.5	10.8	10.7	50.4	32 584	31 255	-4.1	-2.1	1 835	1 868	-562	13 077	2.33	62.9	9.5	31.8
Goodhue	14.7	9.8	8.7	50.2	44 127	46 183	4.7	0.5	2 712	2 477	-108	18 743	2.42	67.2	8.7	27.7
Grant	15.2	12.0	11.3	50.4	6 289	6 018	-4.3	-1.9	368	372	-88	2 576	2.28	68.2	7.2	26.6
Hennepin	12.5	7.0	5.5	50.8	1 116 200	1 152 388	3.2	6.1	86 095	41 923	28 081	484 868	2.39	57.9	10.3	32.8
Houston	16.0	10.0	9.4	50.2	19 718	19 027	-3.5	-1.3	995	882	-386	7 862	2.36	67.9	7.1	27.6
Hubbard	16.5	13.9	9.7	49.7	18 376	20 428	11.2	1.1	1 159	1 033	136	8 740	2.33	68.4	6.2	26.4
Isanti	13.1	8.4	6.1	49.6	31 287	37 816	20.9	1.6	2 371	1 528	-304	13 958	2.69	72.5	10.3	22.8
Itasca	16.8	12.0	9.0	49.4	43 992	45 058	2.4	0.8	2 424	2 657	700	18 821	2.35	68.6	8.7	26.1
Jackson	14.7	9.2	10.6	49.1	11 268	10 266	-8.9	-1.8	585	563	-197	4 442	2.27	66.7	6.9	29.1
Kanabec	16.1	10.9	7.7	49.2	14 996	16 239	8.3	-2.5	791	761	-386	6 256	2.53	68.3	8.8	25.8
Kandiyohi	14.6	9.0	8.5	50.0	41 203	42 239	2.5	0.7	3 019	1 993	-683	16 885	2.45	68.5	9.3	26.3
Kittson	16.9	10.9	11.7	49.5	5 285	4 552	-13.9	-2.8	266	350	-32	1 917	2.28	62.2	8.6	34.0
Koochiching	18.4	11.8	9.9	50.2	14 355	13 311	-7.3	-3.5	579	778	-256	6 006	2.14	59.9	7.2	35.4
Lac qui Parle	17.3	11.3	13.5	49.9	8 067	7 259	-10.0	-5.6	354	470	-293	3 094	2.25	67.5	7.2	28.7
Lake	17.6	12.5	12.0	49.1	11 058	10 866	-1.7	-2.2	570	723	-81	5 010	2.10	64.7	6.4	29.2
Lake of the Woods	20.2	12.5	9.5	49.1	4 522	4 045	-10.5	-3.0	175	241	-46	1 700	2.30	65.5	5.2	30.4
Le Sueur	13.9	9.1	6.9	49.6	25 426	27 703	9.0	-0.1	1 641	1 092	-526	11 007	2.49	69.9	6.9	25.1
Lincoln	14.4	10.8	14.1	49.7	6 429	5 896	-8.3	-2.1	358	406	-104	2 469	2.28	65.3	5.3	31.2
Lyon	12.5	7.1	7.3	50.4	25 425	25 857	1.7	-0.7	1 892	1 117	-970	10 076	2.43	63.4	8.6	30.4
McLeod	13.1	9.2	8.2	50.4	34 898	36 651	5.0	-2.0	2 231	1 706	-1 334	14 727	2.42	68.7	7.5	26.8
Mahnomen	12.9	9.4	7.4	49.8	5 190	5 413	4.3	0.8	555	294	-240	2 018	2.68	69.5	17.3	26.2
Marshall	14.8	10.0	10.0	49.3	10 155	9 439	-7.1	-0.2	570	393	-156	4 072	2.29	64.7	6.0	30.2
Martin	15.7	10.3	11.3	50.8	21 802	20 840	-4.4	-3.9	1 151	1 290	-628	8 780	2.30	64.1	8.1	31.9
Meeker	14.9	9.5	8.5	49.1	22 644	23 300	2.9	-0.8	1 457	1 113	-549	9 279	2.46	69.8	6.2	26.3
Mille Lacs	13.3	9.8	8.2	50.0	22 330	26 097	16.9	-1.2	1 705	1 484	-529	10 249	2.47	67.2	11.4	27.4
Morrison	14.7	9.3	8.2	49.6	31 712	33 198	4.7	-1.3	1 999	1 635	-736	13 494	2.41	67.1	7.8	28.0
Mower	12.9	8.4	9.3	50.0	38 603	39 163	1.5	-0.1	2 631	1 919	-762	15 511	2.50	63.9	9.1	32.0
Murray	15.7	12.1	11.8	49.8	9 165	8 725	-4.8	-3.6	436	524	-241	3 768	2.24	64.5	5.3	30.0
Nicollet	12.8	7.6	6.3	49.8	29 771	32 727	9.9	1.9	2 049	1 111	-317	12 410	2.43	67.3	9.8	25.4
Nobles	12.4	7.7	8.0	48.6	20 832	21 378	2.6	1.8	1 901	953	-501	7 838	2.70	69.8	8.4	27.1
Norman	14.3	10.5	11.3	50.5	7 442	6 852	-7.9	-2.5	362	476	-57	2 776	2.37	64.3	7.4	32.0
Olmsted	12.6	7.5	6.5	51.1	124 277	144 260	16.1	5.0	11 389	4 968	553	57 799	2.50	66.1	9.3	27.5
Otter Tail	16.0	12.0	10.5	49.7	57 159	57 303	0.3	0.7	3 296	3 529	721	24 163	2.32	67.9	6.5	27.8
Pennington	13.5	8.7	7.7	50.2	13 584	13 930	2.5	2.1	961	696	29	5 822	2.36	60.7	9.8	34.3
Pine	15.0	10.5	7.9	46.7	26 530	29 750	12.1	-2.3	1 562	1 363	-806	11 616	2.37	65.3	7.9	28.2
Pipestone	13.7	8.8	11.5	51.5	9 895	9 596	-3.0	-3.4	631	553	-404	3 998	2.30	65.3	9.6	31.0
Polk	13.5	8.7	8.3	49.9	31 369	31 600	0.7	-0.2	2 088	1 769	-377	12 642	2.39	64.5	9.5	29.3
Pope	15.9	11.8	10.9	49.3	11 236	10 995	-2.1	0.4	661	657	59	4 772	2.25	65.8	6.1	29.4
Ramsey	12.3	7.1	5.9	51.3	511 035	508 640	-0.5	5.8	40 535	20 636	10 306	206 156	2.45	58.2	12.3	33.6
Red Lake	15.6	9.5	9.0	49.1	4 299	4 089	-4.9	-0.8	294	203	-140	1 721	2.33	64.7	6.8	31.7
Redwood	13.8	10.0	10.6	50.0	16 815	16 059	-4.5	-3.7	970	966	-619	6 463	2.39	64.1	6.9	32.5
Renville	15.2	9.7	10.6	49.0	17 154	15 730	-8.3	-5.3	930	995	-770	6 378	2.35	65.8	7.1	29.9
Rice	12.3	7.7	6.4	49.9	56 665	64 144	13.2	2.0	3 756	2 396	-185	22 498	2.50	70.2	10.2	25.0
Rock	13.6	9.9	10.6	50.9	9 721	9 687	-0.3	-0.9	580	632	-68	3 933	2.37	67.0	8.6	31.6
Roseau	14.0	8.7	7.0	48.9	16 338	15 629	-4.3	0.9	1 066	707	-228	6 351	2.41	69.3	7.9	26.2
St. Louis	15.3	9.4	7.8	49.7	200 528	200 226	-0.2	0.1	10 768	10 787	623	85 033	2.25	59.1	9.9	32.8
Scott	10.6	5.6	3.7	50.2	89 498	129 928	45.2	9.0	10 047	2 949	4 574	46 214	2.90	76.6	8.3	18.6
Sherburne	11.0	6.2	4.0	48.8	64 417	88 499	37.4	3.6	6 143	2 449	-532	30 283	2.90	76.4	8.8	17.7
Sibley	13.5	8.8	8.7	49.7	15 356	15 226	-0.8	-2.3	918	735	-528	6 025	2.46	66.6	7.0	29.0
Stearns	11.8	7.2	6.3	49.6	133 166	150 642	13.1	2.7	10 204	4 936	-1 048	56 750	2.52	65.2	8.3	24.7
Steele	13.0	8.2	7.9	50.7	33 680	36 576	8.6	0.5	2 508	1 547	-852	14 339	2.50	67.7	8.7	28.2
Stevens	11.9	7.3	9.0	50.3	10 053	9 726	-3.3	0.7	623	442	-81	3 665	2.52	60.4	3.9	31.4
Swift	14.9	10.1	11.3	49.4	11 956	9 783	-18.2	-4.5	571	543	-449	4 230	2.23	63.4	6.8	32.6
Todd	15.4	10.7	8.4	48.8	24 426	24 895	1.9	-2.6	1 690	1 058	-1 264	9 951	2.43	67.5	6.4	28.7
Traverse	14.9	10.6	15.1	50.3	4 134	3 558	-13.9	-4.4	166	266	-48	1 534	2.19	63.5	5.0	32.7
Wabasha	14.9	10.4	8.3	50.2	21 610	21 664	0.2	-2.0	1 240	925	-726	8 929	2.37	69.4	8.3	26.0
Wadena	13.5	10.7	10.8	50.4	13 713	13 843	0.9	0.2	951	981	63	5 737	2.33	63.1	10.2	33.2
Waseca	13.7	8.4	7.8	52.7	19 526	19 136	-2.0	-0.8	1 127	818	-463	7 405	2.41	69.0	9.2	26.3
Washington	13.4	7.7	5.1	50.5	201 130	238 134	18.4	5.7	14 986	7 328	5 523	89 898	2.68	73.2	10.0	21.5
Watonwan	14.2	9.0	10.2	50.3	11 876	11 211	-5.6	-2.3	771	626	-397	4 499	2.44	65.7	8.8	30.5
Wilkin	14.5	9.0	9.1	48.9	7 138	6 576	-7.9	-2.7	365	390	-166	2 763	2.32	65.0	5.9	31.8
Winona	12.8	8.1	7.0	50.6	49 985	51 461	3.0	-1.1	2 488	2 057	-1 013	19 081	2.46	59.1	6.3	31.7
Wright	11.0	6.7	4.5	49.7	89 986	124 700	38.6	5.3	9 603	3 715	610	45 064	2.80	75.5	8.7	20.3
Yellow Medicine	14.8	9.4	10.6	49.0	11 080	10 438	-5.8	-5.4	582	623	-508	4 193	2.37	68.2	8.0	27.1

1. No spouse present.

Table B. States and Counties — **Population, Vital Statistics, Medicare, and Crime**

STATE County	Persons in group quarters, 2015	Daytime population, 2010–2014		Births, 2015		Deaths, 2015		Persons under 65 with no health insurance, 2014		Medicare, 2015			Serious crimes known to police,[2] 2014 Total	
		Number	Employment/residence ratio	Total	Rate[1]	Number	Rate[1]	Number	Percent	Total Beneficiaries	Enrolled in Original Medicare	Enrolled in Medicare Advantage	Number	Rate[3]
	32	33	34	35	36	37	38	39	40	41	42	43	44	45
MINNESOTA—Cont'd														
Fillmore	359	17 733	0.69	260	12.5	223	10.7	1 368	8.3	4 624	2 322	2 302	64	307
Freeborn	637	29 537	0.90	344	11.2	356	11.6	2 019	8.4	6 964	3 156	3 808	541	1 749
Goodhue	880	46 365	1.00	489	10.5	446	9.6	2 568	6.9	8 976	3 773	5 203	903	1 937
Grant	110	5 361	0.79	75	12.6	62	10.4	318	7.0	1 564	756	808	64	1 067
Hennepin	25 572	1 406 771	1.36	16 891	13.9	8 146	6.7	76 678	7.3	170 666	71 872	98 794	42 770	3 529
Houston	257	15 062	0.60	203	10.8	181	9.6	931	6.2	4 035	2 178	1 857	84	447
Hubbard	154	18 323	0.76	217	10.5	188	9.1	1 362	8.8	4 891	2 274	2 617	544	2 621
Isanti	465	31 235	0.63	435	11.3	289	7.5	2 091	6.4	5 599	2 224	3 375	781	2 037
Itasca	1 022	44 060	0.94	448	9.9	500	11.0	2 694	7.6	10 752	5 739	5 013	794	1 735
Jackson	110	10 542	1.05	119	11.7	112	11.0	461	5.6	2 395	1 536	859	103	1 003
Kanabec	246	13 473	0.63	160	10.1	146	9.2	967	7.5	3 052	1 389	1 663	269	1 685
Kandiyohi	1 073	43 540	1.06	595	14.0	359	8.4	2 408	7.0	7 866	3 080	4 786	840	1 976
Kittson	111	4 296	0.90	58	13.1	68	15.3	224	6.6	1 066	574	492	14	311
Koochiching	241	13 078	0.99	112	8.7	132	10.3	853	8.6	3 382	1 625	1 757	295	2 234
Lac qui Parle	154	6 548	0.84	62	9.0	89	12.9	316	6.1	1 637	732	905	39	558
Lake	224	10 676	0.98	101	9.5	129	12.1	521	6.5	2 606	1 554	1 052	74	687
Lake of the Woods	53	3 652	0.84	38	9.7	39	9.9	261	8.6	989	512	477	12	307
Le Sueur	270	22 394	0.63	302	10.9	214	7.7	1 615	7.0	5 756	2 388	3 368	225	807
Lincoln	135	5 156	0.77	71	12.3	78	13.5	306	7.1	1 404	860	544	7	120
Lyon	1 046	27 487	1.13	358	13.9	210	8.2	1 404	6.6	5 169	3 205	1 964	423	1 663
McLeod	476	34 913	0.93	423	11.8	319	8.9	1 866	6.3	7 798	2 934	4 864	642	1 793
Mahnomen	79	6 065	1.27	106	19.3	61	11.1	467	10.3	1 087	637	450	289	5 190
Marshall	76	7 881	0.66	112	11.9	78	8.3	554	7.4	1 958	1 037	921	0	0
Martin	348	20 101	0.96	230	11.4	231	11.5	1 131	7.2	5 342	2 767	2 575	370	1 818
Meeker	353	20 361	0.75	275	11.9	205	8.9	1 277	6.8	4 443	1 525	2 918	348	1 506
Mille Lacs	523	24 851	0.91	313	12.1	258	10.0	1 729	8.3	6 455	2 611	3 844	841	3 258
Morrison	527	30 278	0.83	378	11.5	324	9.9	2 025	7.6	6 787	2 555	4 232	411	1 252
Mower	632	38 507	0.96	501	12.8	341	8.7	2 668	8.3	8 501	5 345	3 156	786	1 994
Murray	163	7 870	0.83	77	9.1	87	10.3	423	6.6	1 999	1 312	687	98	1 152
Nicollet	2 874	31 439	0.92	397	11.9	223	6.7	1 467	5.6	4 444	2 009	2 435	574	1 731
Nobles	385	22 227	1.06	371	17.1	181	8.3	2 206	12.3	3 489	2 393	1 096	267	1 230
Norman	149	6 130	0.81	72	10.8	83	12.5	398	7.7	1 516	841	675	68	1 032
Olmsted	2 657	163 028	1.20	2 190	14.5	962	6.4	7 320	5.7	22 174	13 142	9 032	2 713	1 801
Otter Tail	1 184	54 979	0.91	643	11.1	671	11.6	3 251	7.4	13 883	5 749	8 134	907	1 571
Pennington	327	16 613	1.35	179	12.7	121	8.6	712	6.1	2 509	1 119	1 390	368	2 594
Pine	1 762	26 932	0.81	301	10.3	260	8.9	1 934	8.8	6 111	2 629	3 482	1 476	5 090
Pipestone	205	9 488	1.02	125	13.5	108	11.6	595	8.1	2 136	1 443	693	71	771
Polk	1 279	29 067	0.83	397	12.6	323	10.2	1 896	7.5	5 906	2 984	2 922	489	1 548
Pope	184	10 123	0.85	127	11.5	117	10.6	561	6.7	2 628	1 166	1 462	84	768
Ramsey	17 929	585 283	1.25	7 945	14.8	3 990	7.4	35 912	8.0	103 905	42 967	60 938	19 855	3 732
Red Lake	34	3 379	0.66	53	13.1	22	5.4	253	7.7	822	252	570	14	345
Redwood	373	15 674	0.98	184	11.9	174	11.2	1 008	8.3	3 381	1 722	1 659	232	1 478
Renville	342	14 597	0.90	159	10.6	177	11.8	914	7.7	3 212	1 771	1 441	156	1 035
Rice	7 257	61 123	0.89	697	10.7	456	7.0	3 691	7.5	9 743	4 010	5 733	1 103	1 688
Rock	260	8 974	0.87	110	11.5	104	10.9	518	6.9	2 117	1 245	872	169	1 779
Roseau	191	16 187	1.08	224	14.2	126	8.0	877	6.7	2 673	966	1 707	232	1 493
St. Louis	9 284	208 435	1.08	2 045	10.2	1 998	10.0	10 960	6.8	42 048	21 042	21 006	6 482	3 226
Scott	1 287	109 536	0.64	1 863	13.3	586	4.2	6 489	5.1	11 571	4 446	7 125	2 181	1 567
Sherburne	2 169	68 198	0.53	1 157	12.7	490	5.4	4 430	5.5	7 811	2 973	4 838	1 421	1 568
Sibley	230	12 530	0.66	161	10.8	126	8.5	893	7.3	2 618	1 091	1 527	0	0
Stearns	7 774	161 022	1.12	1 994	13.0	919	6.0	8 172	6.5	29 255	13 338	15 917	4 010	2 626
Steele	594	38 389	1.11	495	13.5	307	8.4	1 631	5.4	6 472	2 668	3 804	773	2 117
Stevens	1 019	10 532	1.16	126	12.8	79	8.0	481	6.6	1 717	983	734	156	1 599
Swift	150	9 437	0.97	108	11.5	92	9.8	507	6.9	2 262	1 213	1 049	99	1 041
Todd	346	21 648	0.74	318	13.1	198	8.2	1 937	10.0	4 838	1 663	3 175	356	1 465
Traverse	100	3 391	0.96	32	9.4	28	8.2	198	7.9	972	560	412	62	1 809
Wabasha	246	17 833	0.67	231	10.9	172	8.1	1 060	6.1	4 900	2 153	2 747	187	873
Wadena	482	14 450	1.12	204	14.8	175	12.7	768	7.2	3 563	1 435	2 128	140	1 013
Waseca	1 318	17 476	0.82	207	10.9	136	7.2	906	6.1	3 446	1 481	1 965	301	1 574
Washington	3 561	204 245	0.68	2 887	11.5	1 473	5.9	9 323	4.3	21 489	7 902	13 587	5 353	2 150
Watonwan	150	10 048	0.80	143	13.0	102	9.3	1 050	11.9	2 325	1 301	1 024	164	1 473
Wilkin	152	5 989	0.83	70	10.9	74	11.5	315	6.0	1 308	661	647	103	1 569
Winona	4 266	51 155	1.00	492	9.6	420	8.2	2 676	6.8	8 534	4 810	3 724	179	349
Wright	1 104	102 770	0.63	1 792	13.7	738	5.6	5 807	5.1	15 842	5 778	10 064	1 919	1 482
Yellow Medicine	290	9 793	0.91	100	10.0	106	10.6	564	7.0	2 434	1 436	998	104	1 031

1. Per 1,000 estimated resident population.　　2. Data for serious crimes have not been adjusted for underreporting; this may affect comparability between geographic areas and over time.
3. Per 100,000 population estimated by the FBI.

Table B. States and Counties — Crime, Education, Money Income, and Poverty

STATE County	Serious crimes known to police, 2014 (cont.)[1] Rate[2] Violent	Property	Education — School enrollment and attainment, 2010-2014 — Enrollment[3] Total	Percent private	Attainment[4] (percent) High school graduate or less	Bachelor's degree or more	Local government expenditures,[5] 2012-2013 Total current spending (mil dol)	Current spending per student (dollars)	Money income, 2010-2014 Per capita income[6] (dollars)	Households Median income (dollars)	Mean income (dollars)	Percent with income of $200,000 or more	Income and poverty, 2014 Median household income (dollars)	Percent below poverty level All persons	Children under 18 years	Children 5 to 17 years in families
	46	47	48	49	50	51	52	53	54	55	56	57	58	59	60	61
MINNESOTA—Cont'd																
Fillmore	53	254	4 780	10.2	45.9	18.7	26.0	10 593	26 051	51 576	63 068	1.7	52 444	11.6	16.9	15.7
Freeborn	113	1 636	6 694	9.2	48.9	15.3	47.4	11 538	26 083	45 569	59 843	2.3	47 203	12.5	18.4	16.8
Goodhue	109	1 828	10 881	12.3	40.6	23.5	73.2	10 645	30 408	57 229	73 238	3.0	60 869	9.6	11.9	11.3
Grant	17	1 051	1 154	9.7	42.4	18.3	11.8	11 039	27 195	49 632	62 371	2.3	48 179	10.5	17.3	16.3
Hennepin	427	3 101	308 985	18.8	25.5	46.4	1 897.8	13 139	38 125	65 033	91 395	8.0	64 490	13.0	17.1	15.9
Houston	69	378	4 344	15.9	42.8	22.0	46.0	9 399	26 719	53 359	63 358	1.7	59 900	8.4	10.7	9.2
Hubbard	120	2 501	3 965	8.5	39.4	24.3	24.3	10 311	25 050	46 412	58 102	1.3	47 944	12.2	19.3	18.1
Isanti	112	1 925	9 744	11.1	47.1	17.1	61.2	10 234	26 406	59 588	70 150	1.8	65 342	7.8	11.7	10.7
Itasca	210	1 525	9 915	8.4	41.2	21.7	71.8	11 064	24 578	47 122	58 443	1.4	48 525	14.7	21.8	19.9
Jackson	29	973	2 294	9.2	43.6	18.6	15.8	10 023	27 942	50 907	64 614	3.3	53 700	9.8	15.0	14.4
Kanabec	144	1 541	3 771	7.3	52.8	13.4	21.2	8 995	22 705	46 872	56 141	1.0	48 908	13.8	21.0	17.8
Kandiyohi	181	1 794	10 214	9.2	41.0	21.9	60.4	10 749	27 550	52 043	67 818	3.0	57 405	11.5	18.7	17.4
Kittson	22	289	915	9.1	44.3	21.2	9.6	13 726	27 867	48 893	62 548	1.9	50 372	9.9	13.6	12.2
Koochiching	182	2 053	2 579	16.1	47.5	18.4	21.8	11 609	24 993	41 725	54 433	1.9	44 113	15.3	22.5	20.0
Lac qui Parle	57	501	1 429	7.1	47.1	18.6	14.9	11 276	28 913	48 426	65 232	4.0	48 245	10.4	14.3	13.5
Lake	139	548	1 946	4.2	41.5	23.2	15.2	10 826	28 058	46 850	61 154	2.0	52 381	10.4	15.3	13.5
Lake of the Woods	77	230	733	2.6	51.9	16.2	6.0	12 490	23 073	45 119	53 141	0.2	44 727	10.7	18.6	17.0
Le Sueur	65	742	6 749	15.2	44.3	21.6	42.2	9 865	28 179	60 296	70 723	2.8	61 665	8.9	10.9	10.1
Lincoln	120	0	1 252	5.9	49.3	19.6	12.6	13 085	25 764	49 122	59 508	1.4	48 449	10.2	13.2	12.1
Lyon	134	1 529	7 198	11.4	42.3	27.2	72.8	17 263	27 787	51 182	68 750	3.0	53 552	11.5	15.7	15.2
McLeod	92	1 701	8 628	14.6	44.9	18.9	50.5	10 072	27 330	56 234	66 770	1.9	60 114	9.9	11.2	10.7
Mahnomen	413	4 777	1 342	8.6	53.4	13.0	16.2	13 032	19 175	39 924	51 366	1.2	39 926	19.6	32.6	32.7
Marshall	0	0	1 987	7.5	50.1	17.9	18.9	14 146	27 877	53 311	64 062	2.2	54 433	9.6	12.8	12.1
Martin	118	1 700	4 446	16.1	49.6	17.9	35.4	11 734	27 629	52 579	63 762	2.9	52 042	12.2	19.5	17.4
Meeker	108	1 398	5 387	10.5	47.9	18.0	26.1	10 355	26 726	54 049	66 278	2.3	54 354	10.0	13.1	12.0
Mille Lacs	155	3 103	6 391	12.7	48.1	15.3	62.2	9 818	23 510	48 763	58 362	1.3	48 434	12.0	17.3	16.2
Morrison	43	1 209	7 481	11.7	49.9	16.4	53.5	10 137	24 091	48 080	58 262	1.9	50 685	11.8	15.8	14.7
Mower	218	1 776	10 142	9.5	45.5	17.9	67.5	11 179	25 209	47 623	61 625	2.2	47 537	12.1	16.3	15.7
Murray	59	1 093	1 795	13.0	48.3	17.2	12.3	11 745	29 107	53 426	65 658	2.9	52 219	9.6	13.3	12.3
Nicollet	142	1 589	10 076	37.2	33.4	32.3	34.8	15 210	27 561	59 963	70 615	2.5	61 279	10.2	11.4	10.5
Nobles	120	1 110	5 122	6.5	54.5	14.4	41.4	11 013	23 668	50 340	62 072	2.9	50 684	13.0	18.1	16.5
Norman	15	1 017	1 483	7.7	50.6	14.7	12.8	11 710	24 886	46 758	58 588	1.6	51 597	13.4	19.0	16.4
Olmsted	157	1 643	38 729	16.8	27.6	40.2	230.7	10 322	34 891	67 089	87 253	6.3	69 430	9.8	12.9	12.1
Otter Tail	118	1 453	11 851	13.3	40.3	23.6	127.2	16 919	27 379	50 914	64 247	2.6	51 510	11.2	16.1	15.2
Pennington	155	2 439	3 370	11.6	43.4	16.6	78.6	36 352	25 584	47 381	59 954	1.5	50 905	9.3	12.7	12.3
Pine	262	4 828	6 198	10.9	54.5	12.6	40.0	10 264	22 129	44 680	54 618	1.1	42 157	17.5	25.1	21.3
Pipestone	33	738	2 030	15.8	49.4	18.0	16.8	11 232	25 102	46 800	57 823	2.1	47 164	12.2	18.1	16.7
Polk	209	1 339	7 826	8.7	41.7	21.3	53.9	10 684	25 823	51 025	62 992	2.3	50 175	12.7	15.8	14.6
Pope	101	667	2 121	8.9	41.4	20.6	14.1	12 755	29 260	51 789	66 608	2.6	51 343	10.4	13.3	12.9
Ramsey	421	3 311	144 790	26.5	32.7	39.8	1 077.3	14 314	30 076	55 460	74 375	4.5	55 070	16.5	24.1	23.4
Red Lake	25	320	858	4.1	50.4	16.1	9.9	13 116	24 278	47 198	56 443	1.0	48 188	9.2	11.5	10.7
Redwood	96	1 382	3 685	15.1	50.4	16.3	26.8	10 667	26 119	47 999	62 065	2.4	49 934	12.4	18.3	16.9
Renville	93	943	3 271	14.6	48.8	15.6	19.0	10 437	28 228	52 000	66 128	2.7	54 386	11.3	17.1	16.4
Rice	153	1 535	20 570	39.1	41.4	27.5	85.3	10 751	26 192	60 365	73 617	3.5	60 317	13.0	16.0	13.3
Rock	1 116	663	2 473	12.1	51.1	18.0	15.2	9 720	25 586	48 403	61 782	2.6	55 352	9.6	12.1	10.8
Roseau	13	1 481	3 663	5.5	46.7	18.0	31.4	10 671	25 787	52 256	63 120	2.2	53 838	9.2	12.3	10.9
St. Louis	241	2 985	51 458	12.8	36.6	26.4	267.2	11 601	26 510	47 138	61 216	2.4	49 714	17.0	19.9	16.9
Scott	93	1 473	39 407	19.0	29.1	38.3	215.3	9 586	35 690	86 510	102 556	8.4	91 688	5.5	6.9	6.3
Sherburne	93	1 475	25 405	13.9	32.6	26.2	183.2	9 667	29 440	73 621	85 179	3.9	76 512	7.2	8.7	7.8
Sibley	0	0	3 614	13.9	52.3	15.8	20.8	10 129	26 709	56 317	65 785	2.1	59 893	9.2	13.5	12.2
Stearns	187	2 440	46 896	20.6	38.7	25.5	253.9	10 612	26 502	55 455	68 623	3.0	55 832	13.4	13.5	12.6
Steele	107	2 010	9 388	16.3	44.2	24.8	63.7	9 776	27 596	55 764	68 734	2.7	57 850	10.9	16.9	15.1
Stevens	133	1 466	3 390	6.1	37.7	26.3	16.4	11 193	27 693	51 181	71 717	2.7	55 292	14.2	11.7	10.1
Swift	84	957	2 012	2.4	49.9	16.6	15.5	10 421	27 546	49 752	62 207	2.4	51 032	10.8	14.5	13.5
Todd	91	1 375	5 473	17.8	50.5	13.8	50.3	15 549	23 062	45 432	56 457	1.8	43 287	17.8	24.9	21.1
Traverse	146	1 663	709	5.8	45.9	16.8	6.1	12 351	29 000	48 750	65 106	3.1	49 536	12.2	19.4	17.7
Wabasha	98	775	4 858	12.7	46.7	20.7	41.8	9 453	29 307	55 994	70 070	2.9	58 752	7.3	10.5	9.8
Wadena	123	890	3 235	6.3	50.2	12.9	30.9	10 689	21 384	38 661	50 346	2.1	41 909	15.8	22.4	20.7
Waseca	78	1 496	4 391	10.9	44.1	19.9	34.0	9 946	25 991	53 830	65 981	2.1	54 183	10.1	13.6	12.7
Washington	85	2 065	67 419	18.9	26.2	41.3	385.6	10 468	37 841	83 182	101 567	9.2	84 113	6.0	6.8	6.0
Watonwan	144	1 329	2 520	8.7	53.1	16.7	20.9	11 363	26 298	50 688	63 084	2.1	48 658	10.4	16.4	15.9
Wilkin	122	1 448	1 536	9.7	40.3	16.4	11.4	10 506	26 557	52 361	61 909	1.6	54 536	10.3	12.7	11.6
Winona	70	279	16 228	16.7	39.7	27.5	64.8	13 203	24 050	48 476	61 143	2.3	49 365	15.8	14.5	13.0
Wright	61	1 421	34 722	11.7	35.4	27.4	256.1	9 967	30 292	73 085	84 127	3.8	76 489	6.0	6.7	5.9
Yellow Medicine	109	922	2 406	6.9	47.7	17.3	16.8	12 620	26 487	52 160	62 813	2.1	51 028	11.2	14.5	13.8

1. Data for serious crimes have not been adjusted for underreporting; this may affect comparability between geographic areas and over time. 2. Per 100,000 population estimated by the FBI.
3. All persons 3 years old and over enrolled in nursery school through college. 4. Persons 25 years old and over. 5. Elementary and secondary education expenditures.
6. Based on population estimated by the American Community Survey, 2010–2014.

Table B. States and Counties — **Personal Income**

STATE County	Personal income, 2014										Earnings, 2014		
	Total (mil dol)	Percent change, 2013–2014	Per capita[1] Dollars	Per capita[1] Rank	Wages and salaries (mil dol)	Supplements to wages and salaries; employer contributions (mil dol) Pension and insurance	Supplements to wages and salaries; employer contributions (mil dol) Government social insurance	Proprietors' income (mil dol)	Dividends, interest, and rent (mil dol)	Personal transfer receipts (mil dol)	Total (mil dol)	Contributions for government social insurance (mil dol) From employee and self-employed	Contributions for government social insurance (mil dol) From employer
	62	63	64	65	66	67	68	69	70	71	72	73	74
MINNESOTA—Cont'd													
Fillmore	844	3.6	40 607	1 107	202	41	16	123	144	181	382	24	16
Freeborn	1 245	0.7	40 374	1 131	475	82	37	159	210	295	752	46	37
Goodhue	2 096	4.0	45 146	665	969	173	76	229	344	375	1 446	86	76
Grant	263	-9.6	44 094	755	74	13	6	46	56	62	139	8	6
Hennepin	77 452	4.9	63 901	93	59 489	7 511	4 362	8 240	16 456	9 286	79 601	4 720	4 362
Houston	839	3.1	44 791	696	162	35	13	75	143	157	286	19	13
Hubbard	747	3.5	36 296	1 724	197	39	16	62	152	216	313	23	16
Isanti	1 485	3.9	38 656	1 369	428	79	34	124	182	304	665	45	34
Itasca	1 656	4.7	36 324	1 719	651	122	53	80	310	496	906	63	53
Jackson	506	-3.8	49 281	422	209	41	17	107	98	91	374	19	17
Kanabec	562	3.9	35 249	1 898	135	28	11	48	80	155	222	16	11
Kandiyohi	1 916	2.4	45 309	649	847	154	68	272	326	383	1 342	82	68
Kittson	232	-16.1	52 265	285	61	12	5	50	45	44	127	6	5
Koochiching	462	-0.7	35 953	1 783	191	38	16	21	74	152	265	19	16
Lac qui Parle	373	-11.9	54 181	228	84	17	6	110	67	78	217	11	6
Lake	447	3.3	41 842	966	193	33	16	31	79	119	274	19	16
Lake of the Woods	172	5.9	43 866	771	49	10	4	14	32	45	77	5	4
Le Sueur	1 209	3.4	43 524	797	369	64	28	133	198	215	594	38	28
Lincoln	275	-2.4	47 570	495	62	12	5	65	48	58	143	7	5
Lyon	1 128	0.2	43 933	767	615	111	46	147	197	209	919	53	46
McLeod	1 445	1.5	40 268	1 142	724	121	60	81	246	297	986	63	60
Mahnomen	176	-6.0	31 893	2 451	66	15	5	7	31	66	94	6	5
Marshall	445	-7.9	47 216	514	105	20	8	68	76	90	201	11	8
Martin	914	-2.4	45 193	661	336	58	25	155	197	211	574	32	25
Meeker	920	2.8	39 813	1 206	257	47	21	107	153	193	433	28	21
Mille Lacs	883	3.5	34 128	2 093	318	63	25	29	121	260	435	30	25
Morrison	1 227	7.7	37 404	1 538	372	76	30	176	195	302	654	38	30
Mower	1 594	0.4	40 537	1 118	739	122	53	168	279	366	1 082	64	53
Murray	435	-8.4	51 379	317	106	22	8	116	76	85	253	12	8
Nicollet	1 408	1.9	42 550	894	579	113	46	90	297	232	827	47	46
Nobles	880	0.6	40 763	1 092	387	71	29	175	156	168	662	34	29
Norman	300	-11.8	45 252	654	65	13	5	72	55	70	155	7	5
Olmsted	7 286	3.9	48 479	457	5 210	703	387	343	1 161	1 032	6 642	395	387
Otter Tail	2 356	2.9	40 871	1 078	839	164	66	235	463	573	1 304	85	66
Pennington	688	1.1	48 923	443	453	75	36	44	155	123	608	36	36
Pine	918	4.3	31 543	2 521	252	58	20	44	147	279	375	27	20
Pipestone	470	1.5	50 618	351	147	29	12	145	79	88	332	15	12
Polk	1 335	-6.0	42 108	942	467	87	38	150	207	304	743	41	38
Pope	509	0.8	46 336	572	179	30	14	67	104	111	290	18	14
Ramsey	25 045	4.8	47 019	521	20 001	2 858	1 463	1 603	4 863	4 586	25 925	1 540	1 463
Red Lake	185	3.2	45 669	622	36	8	3	37	23	36	85	4	3
Redwood	724	-5.4	46 675	547	227	47	17	154	141	147	445	23	17
Renville	755	-5.2	50 247	371	223	40	18	194	141	142	476	20	18
Rice	2 431	4.2	37 320	1 553	1 004	169	80	150	408	444	1 402	88	80
Rock	451	-2.6	47 218	513	135	25	10	120	75	85	290	13	10
Roseau	717	0.6	45 713	619	411	77	33	54	137	118	575	33	33
St. Louis	8 344	4.2	41 523	1 006	4 296	724	341	551	1 411	2 024	5 913	378	341
Scott	6 813	5.3	48 781	447	2 104	309	168	280	878	683	2 861	176	168
Sherburne	3 593	4.8	39 433	1 258	1 102	197	90	128	410	536	1 517	96	90
Sibley	594	-4.5	39 814	1 205	139	28	11	57	107	122	235	14	11
Stearns	6 151	5.1	40 227	1 144	3 642	618	292	491	1 033	1 164	5 044	292	292
Steele	1 548	2.5	42 332	920	915	144	72	113	252	286	1 245	74	72
Stevens	493	0.2	50 350	364	216	41	17	121	107	78	395	18	17
Swift	404	-2.0	42 839	867	137	28	10	82	72	100	258	15	10
Todd	923	5.4	38 037	1 447	219	45	17	187	126	238	467	30	17
Traverse	182	-15.3	53 758	245	44	9	3	42	42	42	97	4	3
Wabasha	898	4.3	42 023	948	253	48	21	89	155	181	411	24	21
Wadena	451	2.8	32 798	2 313	216	41	17	30	78	162	304	20	17
Waseca	744	0.0	39 118	1 308	274	51	23	89	127	154	437	25	23
Washington	13 420	5.0	53 833	241	3 469	547	271	344	2 343	1 531	4 631	297	271
Watonwan	416	-4.3	37 521	1 523	138	29	11	58	77	100	236	13	11
Wilkin	299	-11.3	45 998	595	89	15	7	45	57	61	155	9	7
Winona	2 130	5.6	41 676	986	987	195	78	166	492	386	1 427	81	78
Wright	5 415	5.1	41 677	985	1 595	277	132	330	629	762	2 334	149	132
Yellow Medicine	463	-8.1	45 813	611	148	31	12	72	93	107	263	13	12

1. Based on the resident population estimated as of July 1 of the year shown.

Table B. States and Counties — Earnings, Social Security, and Housing

STATE County	Earnings, 2014 (cont.) Percent by selected industries									Social Security beneficiaries, December 2014		Supplemental Security Income recipients, December 2014	Housing units, 2015	
	Farm	Mining	Construction	Manufacturing	Information: professional, scientific, technical services	Retail trade	Finance, insurance, real estate and leasing	Health care and social assistance	Government	Number	Rate[1]		Total	Percent change, 2010–2014
	75	76	77	78	79	80	81	82	83	84	85	86	87	88
MINNESOTA—Cont'd														
Fillmore	15.8	D	8.9	15.7	3.0	6.5	4.1	7.4	15.9	4 885	235	202	9 859	1.3
Freeborn	12.2	D	5.1	19.2	D	9.0	5.5	15.6	11.6	7 905	257	491	14 211	-0.1
Goodhue	6.0	0.0	4.9	18.9	2.8	5.1	2.6	11.4	15.6	10 145	219	475	20 349	0.1
Grant	22.9	0.0	12.2	3.4	3.7	4.2	4.1	D	14.2	1 485	249	68	3 296	-0.8
Hennepin	0.0	0.1	3.4	8.7	17.9	4.4	16.9	9.3	9.2	179 035	148	26 952	526 537	3.4
Houston	12.6	D	9.5	9.5	D	5.1	2.8	9.7	20.7	4 300	229	217	8 655	0.6
Hubbard	5.5	0.7	5.8	26.0	2.1	8.0	3.6	D	21.1	6 015	292	342	14 600	-0.2
Isanti	-0.7	0.0	7.9	16.4	D	10.1	3.5	20.8	17.0	7 300	190	431	15 553	1.5
Itasca	0.2	6.7	9.2	8.3	2.8	8.3	3.2	15.2	21.1	12 590	277	971	27 254	0.7
Jackson	20.1	0.0	3.8	31.3	D	2.5	2.1	D	9.8	2 445	239	115	4 997	0.1
Kanabec	1.8	0.5	15.4	10.8	2.6	8.5	4.8	D	28.7	3 960	248	230	7 799	-0.6
Kandiyohi	5.8	D	7.0	18.5	4.5	7.8	3.8	D	17.7	9 105	214	708	19 663	1.0
Kittson	34.8	D	3.3	6.1	D	4.1	D	D	16.4	1 155	260	51	2 597	-0.3
Koochiching	1.9	0.0	5.8	24.1	2.7	8.0	5.4	D	23.8	3 680	286	290	7 857	-0.5
Lac qui Parle	31.8	0.0	9.0	10.8	D	5.0	3.4	6.5	16.2	1 810	263	95	3 676	-0.4
Lake	-0.4	D	D	12.9	2.2	5.3	2.7	D	17.5	2 925	274	126	7 849	2.2
Lake of the Woods	7.8	0.0	D	D	D	7.2	D	10.3	21.6	1 205	308	51	3 678	0.2
Le Sueur	5.3	D	8.6	29.7	2.8	4.0	3.8	4.6	11.0	5 535	199	259	12 516	0.8
Lincoln	30.3	D	6.1	1.0	2.8	4.5	2.8	D	9.9	1 510	260	54	3 118	0.3
Lyon	6.7	0.0	6.1	15.3	6.8	6.1	8.9	7.3	18.6	4 725	184	416	11 194	0.9
McLeod	0.5	D	4.5	39.5	3.6	6.3	3.0	13.9	10.7	7 700	215	363	15 715	-0.3
Mahnomen	3.9	0.0	4.5	D		4.2	D	D	59.0	1 260	228	219	2 763	-0.8
Marshall	21.1	D	8.4	9.2	1.9	4.2	D	5.8	16.7	2 195	233	100	4 797	-0.3
Martin	19.4	0.0	3.8	11.5	D	6.6	5.5	D	11.2	5 540	274	381	9 947	-0.6
Meeker	8.4	0.2	10.5	18.0	3.7	6.2	4.4	7.9	15.8	4 995	216	215	10 723	0.5
Mille Lacs	-0.1	D	6.8	10.1	4.5	6.4	3.4	D	38.9	6 235	242	443	12 719	-0.2
Morrison	19.5	0.2	6.8	9.7	5.4	7.2	2.8	D	20.7	7 815	238	580	15 906	1.1
Mower	8.0	0.0	3.5	17.7	D	4.7	2.3	D	14.1	8 915	227	742	16 982	-0.3
Murray	35.7	0.4	8.3	6.9	2.5	4.7	D	D	13.8	2 290	271	97	4 613	1.3
Nicollet	9.3	D	1.7	25.9	D	4.1	2.1	D	22.4	5 500	165	329	13 262	3.0
Nobles	18.1	0.0	3.5	23.8	3.8	6.9	2.9	D	12.0	4 020	186	309	8 588	0.6
Norman	39.0	0.0	D	D	6.4	5.0	D	9.7	13.7	1 730	260	124	3 410	-0.3
Olmsted	0.7	0.0	4.2	9.8	4.4	5.1	2.9	52.4	8.7	24 995	166	2 208	62 299	3.0
Otter Tail	7.9	0.1	7.5	17.9	4.5	7.3	3.3	13.0	15.9	15 680	272	822	35 675	0.2
Pennington	2.9	0.0	3.3	11.1	D	4.6	1.9	D	12.9	2 785	198	200	6 379	1.3
Pine	3.3	D	7.6	3.0	D	7.6	2.9	8.6	44.1	6 945	239	510	17 227	-0.3
Pipestone	30.2	D	6.7	5.7	9.8	5.0	D	5.2	14.3	2 290	246	155	4 478	-0.1
Polk	16.6	0.2	5.5	13.8	3.4	5.7	2.5	D	19.5	6 835	217	607	14 723	0.8
Pope	13.4	0.0	6.3	16.6	1.7	5.2	2.9	D	15.8	2 830	258	129	6 575	2.2
Ramsey	0.0	D	4.3	11.1	9.5	4.1	8.1	12.5	17.4	83 880	157	16 780	218 430	0.6
Red Lake	43.1	D	3.0	D	D	3.8	D	2.5	16.9	905	225	43	1 935	-0.7
Redwood	22.9	D	4.8	18.0	1.6	4.7	4.6	5.3	19.6	3 665	236	218	7 260	-0.2
Renville	40.0	D	3.3	13.4	3.1	2.5	D	D	12.6	3 625	242	211	7 307	-0.7
Rice	3.0	0.2	7.0	19.0	5.5	5.7	3.1	9.2	16.5	10 845	166	763	24 625	0.7
Rock	35.0	D	3.3	7.7	3.3	4.2	11.6	9.0	11.8	2 190	230	104	4 277	0.4
Roseau	6.1	0.0	1.2	57.9	1.1	3.7	2.3	D	10.8	3 080	196	152	7 447	-0.3
St. Louis	0.1	8.2	5.6	5.1	6.8	7.1	4.9	23.7	17.3	46 115	230	5 296	103 411	0.3
Scott	0.6	0.3	11.8	14.5	9.5	5.5	3.1	8.5	19.9	16 065	115	1 171	49 999	6.1
Sherburne	0.1	D	12.0	14.4	3.4	7.0	2.8	13.9	17.6	12 860	141	1 020	33 098	2.2
Sibley	20.9	0.0	9.8	9.8	1.8	3.1	2.2	D	16.1	3 045	204	141	6 548	-0.5
Stearns	4.6	0.2	7.2	13.3	5.8	7.5	6.3	18.1	15.3	26 225	171	2 322	63 218	2.0
Steele	4.7	D	3.3	27.3	D	7.1	16.8	9.8	9.8	7 430	203	501	15 424	0.5
Stevens	27.3	D	4.6	16.3	3.6	4.4	2.6	8.8	17.9	1 820	185	122	4 159	0.0
Swift	14.8	D	4.5	27.4	2.2	3.7	2.8	D	17.6	2 400	254	158	4 812	-0.5
Todd	14.2	D	4.3	36.9	D	4.5	2.5	D	15.3	5 955	245	444	12 984	0.5
Traverse	42.6	0.0	2.9	1.6	D	4.4	D	7.7	15.2	1 080	318	66	2 075	0.1
Wabasha	17.8	D	4.5	23.7	2.0	5.4	3.5	D	14.3	4 990	234	208	10 090	1.0
Wadena	4.9	0.0	5.0	8.3	2.6	6.0	3.1	21.3	21.3	3 770	274	421	7 006	1.6
Waseca	15.0	D	4.4	30.1	2.9	4.8	3.1	8.4	18.4	3 910	206	226	7 915	0.2
Washington	0.6	0.1	5.7	13.0	7.3	8.5	8.6	14.4	15.4	39 185	157	2 056	96 289	4.2
Watonwan	19.9	D	5.4	22.5	1.8	4.4	3.8	8.2	16.5	2 400	219	134	5 029	-0.4
Wilkin	22.2	D	3.0	0.2	D	3.8	D	13.1	13.8	1 370	211	98	3 073	-0.2
Winona	7.2	0.0	3.6	28.2	D	5.5	3.0	8.8	15.4	9 600	188	636	20 974	1.0
Wright	0.8	D	15.6	16.7	3.5	8.4	3.0	9.8	14.7	18 910	145	787	50 345	2.7
Yellow Medicine	25.8	D	7.7	4.5	2.1	4.2	2.0	D	25.4	2 460	245	153	4 745	-0.3

1. Per 1,000 resident population estimated as of July 1 of the year shown.

Table B. States and Counties — Housing, Labor Force, and Employment

STATE County	Housing units, 2010–2014 Occupied units Owner-occupied Total	Percent	Median value[1]	Median owner cost as a percent of income With a mortgage	Without a mortgage[2]	Renter-occupied Median rent[3]	Median rent as a percent of income[2]	Sub-standard units[4] (percent)	Civilian labor force, 2015 Total	Percent change, 2014–2015	Unemployment Total	Rate[5]	Civilian employment,[6] 2010–2014 Percent Total	Management, business, science and arts	Construction, production, and maintenance occupations
	89	90	91	92	93	94	95	96	97	98	99	100	101	102	103
MINNESOTA—Cont'd															
Fillmore	8 424	78.9	138 700	22.7	12.1	585	27.5	2.6	11 416	3.2	467	4.1	10 403	34.8	28.4
Freeborn	13 077	76.0	102 700	21.0	11.3	554	26.9	1.9	16 402	0.6	624	3.8	15 281	25.7	32.2
Goodhue	18 743	76.1	179 900	23.3	12.6	708	30.3	1.5	27 062	0.9	957	3.5	23 625	35.6	27.1
Grant	2 576	80.9	96 000	20.3	12.9	519	26.9	1.2	3 373	2.4	163	4.8	2 961	34.0	27.5
Hennepin	484 868	63.2	227 400	22.6	12.2	934	29.5	2.8	679 549	0.7	22 320	3.3	633 747	47.1	13.6
Houston	7 862	80.3	155 900	22.2	12.6	607	29.8	1.8	10 528	1.3	405	3.8	9 741	34.0	28.6
Hubbard	8 740	81.3	171 300	26.1	12.8	635	27.2	2.5	9 581	1.2	589	6.1	9 482	30.2	26.4
Isanti	13 958	81.4	167 500	24.3	12.5	841	29.5	2.3	20 445	0.7	871	4.3	19 346	28.8	28.5
Itasca	18 821	80.1	152 000	24.4	11.7	648	29.2	2.7	22 600	2.6	1 461	6.5	19 785	30.7	27.3
Jackson	4 442	77.1	100 100	17.9	10.2	538	24.5	1.8	6 364	0.6	257	4.0	5 353	34.8	30.1
Kanabec	6 256	78.8	139 000	25.6	14.0	750	31.1	3.1	8 826	-0.6	596	6.8	7 174	28.0	31.8
Kandiyohi	16 885	74.2	162 000	22.8	12.1	664	31.3	2.0	24 130	1.6	906	3.8	21 693	33.1	29.1
Kittson	1 917	81.2	68 100	18.1	10.0	473	22.3	1.5	2 478	3.4	115	4.6	2 180	32.9	34.7
Koochiching	6 006	76.4	100 200	19.4	11.5	533	32.7	2.6	6 304	-2.3	510	8.1	5 887	28.9	31.2
Lac qui Parle	3 094	81.0	81 300	19.9	10.0	590	26.7	1.0	3 791	3.5	156	4.1	3 461	35.5	29.2
Lake	5 010	82.1	155 100	23.5	10.9	675	30.2	3.3	5 623	-1.4	270	4.8	4 837	29.7	27.3
Lake of the Woods	1 700	87.1	117 600	24.1	13.3	629	30.7	2.1	2 451	2.4	108	4.4	1 986	25.3	38.0
Le Sueur	11 007	81.4	181 500	23.7	12.1	703	27.8	1.6	15 770	1.5	734	4.7	14 467	32.5	31.0
Lincoln	2 469	81.0	90 400	21.0	11.5	522	24.0	0.9	3 405	3.5	121	3.6	2 989	34.7	29.8
Lyon	10 076	67.5	134 700	19.4	10.1	609	24.9	2.2	15 359	0.2	495	3.2	14 119	33.5	30.2
McLeod	14 727	76.1	151 400	22.6	12.8	696	25.0	1.3	20 312	2.1	801	3.9	18 670	32.4	30.0
Mahnomen	2 018	72.6	97 800	20.6	13.5	535	32.7	5.1	2 427	2.5	130	5.4	2 190	27.5	22.6
Marshall	4 072	80.8	90 500	18.5	11.1	513	22.8	1.1	5 767	2.8	396	6.9	4 772	33.3	31.7
Martin	8 780	76.3	103 900	19.8	10.0	638	27.5	1.5	10 488	2.3	429	4.1	10 392	30.4	31.3
Meeker	9 279	78.9	156 000	24.1	12.4	683	28.7	2.0	13 420	4.0	563	4.2	11 423	31.5	33.6
Mille Lacs	10 249	73.6	141 900	24.2	14.3	726	28.3	2.1	12 827	0.8	746	5.8	11 745	30.5	29.7
Morrison	13 494	80.4	152 200	24.6	12.9	643	29.8	1.8	17 847	2.3	966	5.4	16 327	28.8	32.9
Mower	15 511	71.9	108 300	19.8	10.4	711	31.6	2.6	20 477	0.6	660	3.2	19 068	28.0	32.8
Murray	3 768	82.2	97 000	20.4	11.3	547	23.1	0.7	5 150	5.7	225	4.4	4 287	37.9	28.3
Nicollet	12 410	73.2	168 600	22.7	10.0	760	26.9	1.7	20 127	1.5	537	2.7	18 572	36.4	22.4
Nobles	7 838	71.8	107 300	20.3	11.1	602	25.6	7.4	11 546	2.5	372	3.2	10 325	24.3	39.3
Norman	2 776	80.1	84 000	20.3	11.6	565	28.8	2.3	3 435	3.3	162	4.7	3 174	34.7	27.8
Olmsted	57 799	73.9	171 200	20.8	10.0	808	29.1	1.8	83 552	0.3	2 479	3.0	79 169	47.3	15.8
Otter Tail	24 163	79.1	162 000	22.1	11.3	618	29.6	1.8	31 224	0.8	1 311	4.2	27 638	34.0	28.1
Pennington	5 822	74.6	113 400	19.8	11.8	574	27.5	1.6	9 119	2.8	474	5.2	7 514	28.6	26.1
Pine	11 616	78.8	141 600	26.4	13.6	715	29.2	4.4	14 807	1.1	818	5.5	12 937	24.8	29.5
Pipestone	3 998	73.9	89 500	20.5	10.8	569	27.5	2.4	5 007	4.4	164	3.3	4 688	28.6	30.3
Polk	12 642	71.6	130 500	20.2	12.0	629	30.7	1.5	17 443	1.7	731	4.2	15 671	33.0	25.8
Pope	4 772	79.0	146 500	22.4	11.8	654	23.8	1.3	6 571	5.2	218	3.3	5 422	33.6	27.6
Ramsey	206 156	59.3	194 000	22.7	11.7	853	31.1	4.3	280 408	0.8	9 908	3.5	261 376	42.9	16.8
Red Lake	1 721	81.1	89 200	19.3	12.2	506	26.8	1.7	2 332	2.9	136	5.8	2 094	30.1	30.2
Redwood	6 463	78.8	90 400	20.8	11.2	568	26.4	2.2	8 311	3.5	324	3.9	7 627	33.4	28.6
Renville	6 378	78.8	96 500	20.6	10.8	575	24.3	1.6	8 625	4.8	418	4.8	7 550	31.6	34.1
Rice	22 498	75.4	187 100	23.7	12.1	738	29.4	2.3	35 582	1.0	1 272	3.6	33 390	35.4	24.6
Rock	3 933	75.5	123 700	21.5	11.9	619	28.0	1.9	5 919	4.1	127	2.1	4 703	30.6	27.7
Roseau	6 351	77.9	108 900	21.8	11.4	594	26.4	2.4	8 447	-4.5	346	4.1	8 329	27.0	42.6
St. Louis	85 033	70.9	137 200	21.7	11.6	680	32.5	1.8	101 814	-0.8	5 093	5.0	94 870	33.3	21.3
Scott	46 214	83.9	244 700	22.5	10.8	1 000	28.0	1.5	79 078	0.8	2 477	3.1	72 883	41.6	19.5
Sherburne	30 283	81.5	188 600	23.5	10.4	928	30.1	1.9	49 794	0.9	1 985	4.0	46 526	33.2	26.7
Sibley	6 025	79.2	132 000	22.6	12.2	616	25.6	1.4	8 633	4.1	354	4.1	7 795	30.8	35.8
Stearns	56 750	71.4	166 300	22.1	11.5	730	29.3	2.1	88 685	0.8	3 190	3.6	81 665	31.8	25.2
Steele	14 339	76.8	150 600	22.3	11.6	713	32.3	2.1	21 255	-0.6	710	3.3	18 382	31.9	26.0
Stevens	3 665	67.8	134 900	18.7	10.0	536	34.8	1.0	5 737	2.7	159	2.8	5 145	33.4	24.3
Swift	4 230	74.0	93 000	19.0	10.0	569	24.3	1.3	5 206	6.6	314	6.0	4 975	34.3	29.2
Todd	9 951	81.3	129 700	24.9	13.1	561	26.0	4.0	13 050	1.5	571	4.4	11 320	27.0	38.0
Traverse	1 534	80.7	69 300	19.0	10.0	532	23.6	0.3	1 844	7.4	75	4.1	1 661	40.5	24.2
Wabasha	8 929	82.7	156 200	22.7	11.6	707	28.3	0.9	12 086	2.7	438	3.6	11 237	33.5	28.9
Wadena	5 737	74.5	115 500	25.1	13.1	569	30.7	1.5	6 369	3.4	376	5.9	5 793	24.4	33.0
Waseca	7 405	77.9	141 100	20.7	11.9	585	24.4	2.2	9 805	1.1	411	4.2	9 448	32.3	31.5
Washington	89 898	80.7	240 200	22.0	10.1	1 125	28.5	1.5	137 668	0.9	4 338	3.2	128 308	45.2	16.0
Watonwan	4 499	73.3	94 400	18.7	10.0	562	23.9	1.5	6 290	1.8	295	4.7	5 702	29.5	40.4
Wilkin	2 763	76.7	111 400	20.2	10.0	435	25.0	1.4	3 726	3.4	125	3.4	3 393	32.4	31.9
Winona	19 081	70.3	154 700	23.1	10.9	629	29.5	1.8	29 598	0.5	982	3.3	27 914	31.5	25.6
Wright	45 064	84.2	192 800	22.9	11.6	889	30.1	1.7	72 145	1.0	2 647	3.7	67 021	36.1	25.1
Yellow Medicine	4 193	78.5	97 600	20.2	10.0	567	27.5	1.5	5 613	2.0	212	3.8	5 119	32.9	30.1

1. Specified owner-occupied units. 2. A value of 10.0 represents 10 percent or less; a value of 50.0 represents 50 percent or more. 3. Specified renter-occupied units.
4. Overcrowded or lacking complete plumbing facilities. 5. Percent of civilian labor force. 6. Persons 16 years old and over.

Table B. States and Counties — Nonfarm Employment and Agriculture

STATE County	Number of establishments	Total	Health care and social assistance	Manufacturing	Retail trade	Finance and insurance	Professional, scientific, and technical services	Total (mil dol)	Average per employee (dollars)	Number	Fewer than 50 acres	500 acres or more	Farm operators whose principal occupation is farming (percent)
	104	105	106	107	108	109	110	111	112	113	114	115	116
MINNESOTA—Cont'd													
Fillmore	598	4 620	902	840	664	214	125	143	30 961	1 553	24.8	14.8	50.4
Freeborn	809	11 520	D	2 823	1 887	504	211	405	35 113	1 122	33.9	23.4	54.0
Goodhue	1 327	20 676	3 655	4 749	2 620	460	460	860	41 576	1 536	34.2	11.4	47.7
Grant	214	1 525	377	85	241	79	D	55	35 792	542	23.4	25.1	42.3
Hennepin	39 606	875 851	129 880	71 544	76 541	77 921	81 291	52 090	59 473	627	60.3	6.2	65.1
Houston	432	4 025	1 048	456	615	D	D	113	28 036	920	14.9	11.3	48.5
Hubbard	581	4 465	784	910	935	164	76	145	32 446	406	18.7	11.1	51.5
Isanti	820	8 935	2 039	1 527	1 806	326	206	314	35 128	844	43.4	7.8	44.1
Itasca	1 125	13 808	3 444	1 250	2 378	423	606	534	38 691	401	23.2	8.0	45.6
Jackson	320	5 419	1 281	1 498	373	87	59	182	33 620	826	21.3	30.0	59.9
Kanabec	294	2 940	910	417	513	202	96	100	33 896	648	23.1	8.6	50.8
Kandiyohi	1 384	18 799	5 584	2 643	2 850	568	542	644	34 260	1 310	27.0	14.8	44.7
Kittson	145	1 197	309	150	283	59	22	42	34 774	544	10.8	36.2	43.0
Koochiching	382	3 741	615	D	774	D	66	128	34 253	187	9.1	17.6	43.9
Lac qui Parle	210	1 772	D	189	300	D	D	49	27 744	852	18.7	35.2	57.4
Lake	296	3 120	D	D	375	D	D	108	34 705	44	50.0	2.3	29.5
Lake of the Woods	161	1 388	D	D	224	29	D	38	27 534	196	15.3	19.9	36.2
Le Sueur	697	6 980	848	2 434	735	214	149	280	40 083	1 051	35.8	11.4	40.6
Lincoln	207	1 551	551	18	243	55	48	45	28 863	699	17.6	24.5	54.6
Lyon	810	12 921	2 233	2 027	1 976	1 117	D	488	37 767	904	17.7	30.6	64.8
McLeod	965	15 818	2 895	5 341	2 171	416	386	648	40 938	966	32.6	16.6	62.6
Mahnomen	100	1 681	D	D	147	57	D	49	29 435	310	15.8	37.1	52.6
Marshall	260	1 740	288	284	267	116	28	71	41 083	1 148	8.1	33.0	44.9
Martin	623	7 692	1 642	1 335	1 320	351	196	279	36 242	897	20.3	33.2	67.8
Meeker	563	6 271	1 346	1 722	874	177	96	212	33 883	1 147	31.8	13.1	49.4
Mille Lacs	669	8 097	1 790	1 109	997	220	D	242	29 887	731	31.5	7.4	43.2
Morrison	889	8 314	1 646	1 366	1 484	D	202	253	30 399	1 957	18.3	8.7	50.3
Mower	871	13 771	2 794	3 452	1 792	328	262	574	41 689	1 053	30.7	22.5	64.1
Murray	320	2 846	439	D	310	151	470	93	32 527	895	20.7	31.1	59.1
Nicollet	633	12 337	2 339	3 457	974	205	466	473	38 325	764	23.6	20.9	62.6
Nobles	609	9 498	1 571	D	1 492	254	180	343	36 106	995	22.7	26.1	65.7
Norman	181	1 248	408	D	218	D	34	48	38 509	610	7.9	43.9	64.6
Olmsted	3 539	83 892	D	4 412	10 674	1 839	D	4 069	48 508	1 150	35.6	11.6	50.3
Otter Tail	1 672	19 329	4 074	4 351	3 023	572	401	668	34 560	3 033	17.0	13.9	46.6
Pennington	398	8 797	1 263	D	1 007	D	D	361	41 010	515	12.6	25.2	37.5
Pine	613	7 230	1 427	D	1 053	D	116	177	24 469	870	16.6	10.6	47.2
Pipestone	324	3 952	708	573	542	111	D	127	32 086	637	25.1	25.0	57.1
Polk	786	9 524	2 247	2 059	1 408	265	238	324	33 985	1 322	11.6	37.3	56.1
Pope	359	3 577	658	647	343	113	D	137	38 384	931	21.6	16.6	37.1
Ramsey	13 280	298 467	60 124	22 593	26 806	18 630	14 363	16 278	54 539	97	96.9	0.0	83.5
Red Lake	95	744	D	D	142	54	D	22	29 363	322	8.4	29.8	57.1
Redwood	527	5 557	876	866	790	220	59	178	32 059	1 163	19.9	31.2	68.5
Renville	473	4 765	956	1 356	579	179	D	166	34 854	1 061	20.2	32.9	63.4
Rice	1 501	24 152	3 338	3 971	2 716	483	466	850	35 177	1 304	40.9	7.7	45.6
Rock	260	2 659	654	289	409	349	D	79	29 617	689	26.6	23.9	62.1
Roseau	409	7 131	775	4 098	826	168	D	249	34 950	977	9.6	27.2	41.2
St. Louis	5 282	86 432	24 806	4 247	12 265	3 328	3 392	3 458	40 007	685	26.1	6.6	38.4
Scott	3 252	41 373	4 681	6 078	4 981	678	D	2 036	49 208	847	41.0	6.8	51.6
Sherburne	1 970	21 232	4 103	3 054	2 850	410	607	869	40 935	455	41.1	12.5	42.2
Sibley	351	3 333	526	D	369	136	D	113	33 830	949	25.7	20.9	63.8
Stearns	4 363	78 689	16 474	11 407	11 132	3 801	2 419	3 207	40 753	3 501	23.0	8.4	55.4
Steele	1 019	19 638	2 614	D	2 747	D	227	849	43 231	796	38.4	14.2	55.5
Stevens	322	4 445	1 361	D	622	121	103	154	34 674	560	25.2	31.1	56.3
Swift	310	3 215	633	D	389	107	72	110	34 252	801	22.2	26.0	55.2
Todd	543	5 965	1 660	1 649	805	199	D	193	32 397	1 931	18.4	6.8	52.9
Traverse	119	856	298	46	173	37	D	25	29 036	458	22.7	36.7	62.7
Wabasha	563	6 111	908	D	768	173	D	201	32 897	909	24.1	14.2	58.7
Wadena	394	4 053	961	306	736	155	86	129	31 829	643	15.7	6.4	42.8
Waseca	461	5 851	938	D	699	174	146	204	34 931	805	31.3	18.8	55.8
Washington	5 587	73 717	11 377	7 278	12 964	5 212	3 517	2 991	40 578	602	54.0	6.5	57.3
Watonwan	286	3 580	517	D	427	135	45	103	28 837	503	25.0	27.4	60.2
Wilkin	166	1 963	593	D	212	64	D	62	31 607	391	14.8	49.9	68.3
Winona	1 174	21 864	3 397	4 957	2 825	D	491	757	34 619	1 115	22.6	11.9	52.6
Wright	3 209	35 850	5 706	5 437	7 133	714	925	1 390	38 781	1 463	39.2	8.3	48.8
Yellow Medicine	327	3 641	890	215	382	117	44	162	44 630	885	22.7	32.3	60.8

STATE County	Acreage (1,000)	Percent change, 2007–2012	Average size of farm	Total irrigated (1,000)	Total cropland (1,000)	Avg per farm	Avg per acre	Value of machinery and equipment, average per farm (dollars)	Total (mil dol)	Average per farm (dollars)	Crops	Live-stock and poultry products	$10,000 or more	$100,000 or more	Total ($1,000)	Percent of farms
	117	118	119	120	121	122	123	124	125	126	127	128	129	130	131	132
MINNESOTA—Cont'd																
Fillmore	422	-5.3	272	0.2	316.8	1 248 138	4 588	164 626	342.2	220 351	60.6	39.4	62.8	33.5	8 809	70.3
Freeborn	382	-1.7	340	2.4	356.7	1 857 024	5 454	222 874	416.0	370 784	68.8	31.2	64.0	42.7	8 422	76.1
Goodhue	398	0.4	259	4.5	330.0	1 404 395	5 418	191 857	435.7	283 650	60.9	39.1	64.1	36.1	7 646	66.3
Grant	303	-5.8	559	5.0	279.6	2 020 910	3 616	233 819	213.5	393 849	95.2	4.8	46.1	33.0	6 952	92.4
Hennepin	69	3.5	110	0.6	54.3	904 309	8 235	109 024	64.5	102 821	82.7	17.3	44.0	15.8	1 002	33.2
Houston	229	-6.2	249	0.1	129.4	860 452	3 453	133 811	146.3	158 974	51.1	48.9	59.1	28.3	4 864	78.9
Hubbard	117	-7.3	288	19.6	68.9	649 106	2 254	92 340	46.1	113 475	90.7	9.3	40.4	7.1	362	26.8
Isanti	142	12.9	169	3.1	98.9	628 475	3 724	101 475	61.0	72 306	78.5	21.5	40.9	12.0	1 812	45.9
Itasca	84	-9.9	210	D	40.1	395 067	1 884	63 691	11.2	27 870	58.4	41.6	42.1	4.7	286	13.5
Jackson	358	-10.7	433	0.1	330.0	2 646 869	6 110	298 615	376.4	455 643	66.9	33.1	77.2	54.8	6 712	82.9
Kanabec	129	-9.2	199	D	65.9	456 122	2 295	77 170	32.0	49 326	61.5	38.5	39.8	11.1	785	35.5
Kandiyohi	415	-0.5	317	21.0	354.1	1 522 722	4 806	206 989	495.4	378 160	57.4	42.6	48.7	28.6	9 979	82.8
Kittson	470	-13.2	865	D	391.1	1 516 086	1 754	285 081	180.6	331 914	94.5	5.5	44.1	30.9	8 938	86.4
Koochiching	53	-3.1	286	D	24.7	335 963	1 176	73 214	9.1	48 604	56.7	43.3	45.5	7.5	256	19.3
Lac qui Parle	446	8.4	524	4.2	407.9	2 298 670	4 386	298 212	311.8	365 912	81.1	18.9	67.3	50.1	8 663	89.2
Lake	4	9.0	85	0.0	1.5	279 023	3 285	45 000	0.4	8 841	83.5	16.5	20.5	0.0	D	2.3
Lake of the Woods	90	-6.9	461	D	56.2	686 286	1 490	112 276	19.1	97 541	92.4	7.6	45.4	15.3	962	57.7
Le Sueur	242	-3.5	230	0.9	207.5	1 276 799	5 548	158 177	224.3	213 423	63.3	36.7	55.5	26.9	5 726	78.9
Lincoln	291	1.6	416	0.4	256.6	1 614 046	3 878	224 119	198.6	284 117	68.1	31.9	66.1	41.6	7 282	89.0
Lyon	413	-3.7	457	0.0	379.7	2 373 903	5 197	279 675	403.0	445 815	59.9	40.1	73.9	54.8	8 729	83.5
McLeod	264	8.2	273	0.1	237.0	1 471 040	5 385	207 760	234.5	242 789	76.3	23.7	64.9	38.1	7 031	78.3
Mahnomen	216	13.1	696	D	178.5	1 417 135	2 035	281 677	96.0	309 745	93.8	6.2	61.0	40.0	3 698	85.5
Marshall	820	-9.9	714	1.0	740.4	1 506 519	2 109	258 963	322.3	280 777	97.7	2.3	48.3	30.4	15 614	89.4
Martin	429	-4.7	478	0.8	405.6	2 931 235	6 134	300 925	619.6	690 708	53.3	46.7	80.9	61.8	9 526	85.8
Meeker	304	-5.6	265	8.5	259.9	1 101 923	4 160	177 291	291.7	254 347	59.0	41.0	53.0	29.1	6 376	77.8
Mille Lacs	128	2.3	175	0.2	78.9	481 513	2 753	77 425	53.0	72 476	58.8	41.2	47.5	13.7	1 131	44.7
Morrison	437	1.2	223	20.3	256.1	618 675	2 774	154 393	429.9	219 691	26.0	74.0	66.8	27.6	5 626	64.3
Mower	450	7.1	427	3.2	422.9	2 557 820	5 988	260 886	475.8	451 853	68.6	31.4	70.8	46.6	8 929	78.3
Murray	408	-4.9	456	D	374.9	2 572 509	5 644	305 709	365.5	408 348	63.6	36.4	70.9	50.3	9 673	87.5
Nicollet	274	0.1	359	0.0	250.0	2 329 018	6 489	288 609	386.6	506 060	46.1	53.9	78.4	54.3	6 050	84.4
Nobles	381	-9.9	382	D	351.0	2 263 207	5 917	291 514	477.6	480 017	50.8	49.2	79.7	57.8	8 290	83.1
Norman	532	3.8	873	0.9	492.5	2 611 572	2 992	359 020	281.2	461 039	93.6	6.4	69.3	48.5	7 950	85.6
Olmsted	264	-10.7	230	0.2	209.4	1 258 339	5 473	166 763	250.1	217 472	65.8	34.2	58.4	29.4	5 524	70.8
Otter Tail	882	-1.8	291	59.0	623.3	728 802	2 505	127 789	504.3	166 272	64.2	35.8	50.4	20.6	13 475	76.7
Pennington	272	-16.5	528	0.0	225.5	958 184	1 816	167 614	82.4	160 095	90.2	9.8	50.5	24.7	5 827	87.0
Pine	204	-1.9	234	0.5	103.8	472 323	2 018	83 011	65.4	75 223	46.7	53.3	48.2	10.7	1 176	37.1
Pipestone	242	-1.1	380	2.9	206.0	1 994 403	5 250	245 870	307.9	483 356	38.1	61.9	77.7	49.5	4 263	78.6
Polk	1 095	-0.4	828	9.4	991.4	2 403 190	2 902	415 046	594.5	449 722	96.3	3.7	59.2	39.1	17 706	85.2
Pope	334	-7.3	359	28.9	267.5	1 314 806	3 666	183 074	237.7	255 321	72.5	27.5	47.5	29.4	6 786	84.1
Ramsey	1	-23.2	7	0.1	0.4	68 392	9 176	26 876	2.9	30 330	84.3	15.7	29.9	7.2	0	0.0
Red Lake	199	-11.1	617	D	167.7	1 079 854	1 750	181 960	74.8	232 242	87.8	12.2	59.3	32.3	3 215	84.5
Redwood	521	-5.9	448	0.0	489.6	2 835 987	6 325	301 476	518.4	445 711	70.4	29.6	78.3	60.4	10 261	86.1
Renville	622	0.3	586	0.3	589.1	3 547 517	6 055	357 959	710.3	669 506	76.8	23.2	76.5	61.9	10 308	83.4
Rice	237	-6.5	181	0.9	197.3	1 039 649	5 731	131 569	231.6	177 599	63.5	36.5	51.4	21.9	5 113	69.3
Rock	281	0.5	407	1.9	252.7	2 862 247	7 030	286 846	398.4	578 213	44.7	55.3	85.8	62.6	4 542	75.3
Roseau	556	-6.0	569	0.0	445.4	676 111	1 188	161 546	158.4	162 140	86.1	13.9	45.5	22.5	9 192	80.1
St. Louis	127	-14.4	186	D	60.4	349 235	1 880	49 045	17.1	24 904	59.9	40.1	36.9	3.5	245	5.0
Scott	141	20.1	167	0.2	111.6	1 038 302	6 227	115 534	112.2	132 462	61.8	38.2	56.0	22.0	2 679	53.6
Sherburne	112	5.9	247	29.7	88.7	1 062 160	4 301	153 305	88.5	194 532	77.9	22.1	40.7	17.4	1 589	46.6
Sibley	346	0.2	365	0.1	318.6	2 187 458	5 994	250 711	377.0	397 289	63.0	37.0	76.5	49.2	6 433	77.6
Stearns	758	7.0	216	52.0	582.8	844 095	3 901	175 663	808.5	230 933	32.3	67.7	68.1	38.2	16 012	74.0
Steele	238	-10.6	299	0.6	217.9	1 793 508	5 999	217 629	293.1	368 157	66.9	33.1	57.9	36.7	5 456	79.4
Stevens	319	-6.2	570	19.1	297.3	2 547 307	4 467	347 489	441.3	788 107	53.9	46.1	62.5	47.0	5 149	84.1
Swift	361	-7.1	451	27.1	326.6	2 305 811	5 116	259 010	339.2	423 437	71.0	29.0	59.4	40.1	7 598	87.1
Todd	394	4.0	204	14.1	248.1	482 272	2 364	92 717	241.0	124 812	39.3	60.7	60.7	19.4	4 869	62.6
Traverse	348	6.3	761	0.3	335.0	3 384 218	4 448	355 653	264.5	577 596	95.3	4.7	61.6	47.6	7 019	91.7
Wabasha	246	-6.3	270	1.4	177.8	1 269 843	4 698	210 095	231.2	254 341	49.7	50.3	69.3	41.0	5 237	74.4
Wadena	149	-1.5	232	20.0	83.5	412 974	1 784	74 162	57.5	89 401	62.3	37.7	49.6	14.2	1 954	61.7
Waseca	232	-9.0	288	D	213.6	1 692 842	5 881	207 745	303.9	377 523	59.1	40.9	69.6	45.1	5 979	83.5
Washington	81	-0.4	134	3.5	58.5	1 107 086	8 238	108 400	86.4	143 586	90.6	9.4	46.8	17.9	1 090	33.1
Watonwan	237	-11.9	471	3.2	223.3	2 880 443	6 111	300 348	281.0	558 740	64.3	35.7	69.6	52.1	5 266	86.7
Wilkin	444	4.6	1 136	1.9	428.8	4 434 734	3 903	532 286	303.9	777 363	99.0	1.0	71.6	57.5	7 125	86.7
Winona	277	-9.2	249	0.1	180.0	1 165 445	4 686	177 996	282.0	252 939	38.0	62.0	69.4	33.8	5 695	66.8
Wright	288	8.6	197	3.7	231.8	1 055 837	5 361	139 010	227.5	155 519	65.2	34.8	56.0	22.3	4 703	58.9
Yellow Medicine	395	-3.5	446	0.4	364.5	2 043 238	4 578	287 805	322.8	364 741	73.7	26.3	68.6	50.7	9 119	87.5

STATE County	Water use, 2010		Wholesale trade,[1] 2012				Retail trade,[2] 2012				Real estate and rental and leasing,[2] 2012			
	Total water withdrawn (mil gal/day)	Gallons withdrawn per person per day	Number of establish-ments	Number of employees	Sales (mil dol)	Annual payroll (mil dol)	Number of establish-ments	Number of employees	Sales (mil dol)	Annual payroll (mil dol)	Number of establish-ments	Number of employees	Receipts (mil dol)	Annual payroll (mil dol)
	133	134	135	136	137	138	139	140	141	142	143	144	145	146
MINNESOTA—Cont'd														
Fillmore	13.9	668	24	256	362.7	12.1	90	653	189.5	14.2	6	D	D	D
Freeborn	5.7	183	43	516	479.1	24.3	137	1 806	559.8	43.7	22	73	10.2	1.6
Goodhue	617.6	13 372	42	566	582.2	25.8	222	2 356	737.9	55.5	39	109	21.1	3.5
Grant	1.5	253	10	131	957.4	7.9	32	202	60.9	4.4	2	D	D	D
Hennepin	182.2	158	2 046	36 257	32 265.1	2 340.4	4 184	74 958	23 926.9	2 033.8	2 218	17 614	4 192.5	829.4
Houston	2.4	127	16	132	108.0	4.4	70	624	136.2	12.1	4	10	2.4	0.3
Hubbard	11.3	554	3	D	D	D	103	947	216.1	19.3	14	D	D	D
Isanti	4.1	108	24	172	79.9	6.5	97	1 522	482.8	36.8	29	D	D	D
Itasca	196.9	4 370	31	234	133.0	11.1	198	2 347	568.6	50.9	30	82	12.9	2.1
Jackson	2.7	267	14	270	297.2	10.5	43	327	85.2	5.8	7	D	D	D
Kanabec	1.5	95	6	27	9.0	0.8	44	527	130.7	10.1	2	D	D	D
Kandiyohi	11.1	263	70	D	D	D	224	2 988	666.4	61.3	47	130	15.5	2.7
Kittson	1.6	341	15	77	191.2	4.3	31	268	128.4	4.9	2	D	D	D
Koochiching	45.9	3 448	11	50	15.2	1.8	78	749	189.5	16.0	13	33	4.5	0.9
Lac qui Parle	3.5	478	12	122	235.9	5.3	38	309	67.5	5.2	3	7	0.4	0.1
Lake	124.7	11 474	2	D	D	D	43	358	136.0	9.8	9	D	D	D
Lake of the Woods	1.0	237	4	20	18.2	0.7	27	204	53.2	3.7	4	7	0.6	0.1
Le Sueur	23.8	860	28	246	268.8	10.7	86	783	210.7	14.5	23	32	5.6	0.8
Lincoln	2.3	383	6	61	106.9	3.5	38	242	66.9	4.7	4	9	1.3	0.1
Lyon	7.3	282	36	D	D	D	134	2 020	458.9	41.4	29	119	10.3	4.6
McLeod	7.2	197	32	504	260.1	27.3	156	2 113	501.4	42.3	35	92	15.4	2.4
Mahnomen	0.6	115	6	D	D	D	20	161	26.8	2.8	3	D	D	D
Marshall	1.1	114	20	227	431.5	11.2	36	271	123.0	7.2	2	D	D	D
Martin	10.2	487	40	712	1 166.5	44.7	96	1 242	294.5	27.5	17	37	17.3	0.9
Meeker	4.8	204	20	206	224.9	8.8	83	809	250.0	19.3	12	26	5.9	0.9
Mille Lacs	2.6	101	26	238	180.0	7.9	99	1 141	252.6	21.2	26	71	7.8	1.3
Morrison	14.5	437	26	337	238.0	10.6	135	1 487	419.9	32.3	16	49	5.5	0.8
Mower	10.1	259	28	D	D	D	132	1 826	370.0	35.4	21	126	20.1	1.8
Murray	2.1	241	11	131	354.5	6.2	42	266	46.8	4.4	6	26	1.7	0.6
Nicollet	6.6	200	34	415	372.2	19.5	74	869	232.6	23.1	21	135	9.0	3.6
Nobles	6.0	280	35	D	D	D	111	1 471	328.0	30.1	13	46	3.2	0.5
Norman	0.8	115	16	148	171.2	5.6	28	214	47.0	4.3	4	6	0.7	0.1
Olmsted	27.0	187	102	1 210	715.3	58.1	598	10 457	2 447.2	232.4	173	749	143.4	23.0
Otter Tail	104.3	1 820	56	385	738.6	16.8	253	2 903	776.5	64.3	57	95	24.1	2.7
Pennington	2.5	179	20	D	D	D	76	1 028	233.5	20.3	12	D	D	D
Pine	3.1	105	15	60	12.9	1.3	96	1 030	262.9	20.7	15	50	6.0	0.9
Pipestone	3.5	361	20	237	573.1	8.5	52	478	135.5	9.7	3	D	D	D
Polk	13.1	416	44	469	960.5	20.0	109	1 377	331.6	28.5	9	50	3.1	1.2
Pope	16.0	1 458	56	D	D	D	41	311	138.5	7.7	6	7	1.6	0.2
Ramsey	194.9	383	617	10 538	8 499.7	647.1	1 639	26 639	6 557.0	643.7	684	3 885	1 421.2	176.0
Red Lake	2.3	562	5	D	D	D	19	151	61.8	3.5	1	D	D	D
Redwood	3.1	192	30	430	287.2	22.3	72	735	169.6	15.9	15	26	3.1	0.3
Renville	3.5	219	27	261	559.4	13.4	67	514	120.6	9.0	4	8	1.7	0.4
Rice	8.5	133	62	1 013	2 093.8	55.6	202	2 664	683.4	59.6	50	185	48.5	4.0
Rock	3.7	385	17	220	726.3	8.8	40	391	104.0	8.1	10	23	3.0	0.5
Roseau	1.8	115	7	D	D	D	88	876	271.2	16.7	11	32	2.3	0.5
St. Louis	358.3	1 789	206	2 363	1 301.6	114.0	911	11 842	3 008.1	263.3	207	937	154.8	26.9
Scott	18.4	142	152	2 134	2 117.5	132.7	318	4 704	1 337.1	104.4	143	332	72.6	10.9
Sherburne	71.4	807	65	497	353.4	23.2	186	2 778	795.5	65.2	74	162	27.9	4.5
Sibley	3.7	243	17	D	D	D	54	363	75.9	5.7	11	D	D	D
Stearns	36.2	240	183	3 672	2 063.4	161.2	671	10 874	2 917.9	244.9	161	820	132.8	22.7
Steele	6.2	169	44	598	531.4	31.4	178	2 699	568.1	55.5	27	292	18.3	5.4
Stevens	6.2	632	19	99	522.7	4.8	50	545	210.1	12.8	7	18	1.2	0.3
Swift	9.2	936	13	D	D	D	45	373	93.7	7.4	5	73	2.8	1.4
Todd	8.6	346	14	132	178.2	5.1	94	722	156.8	13.0	22	D	D	D
Traverse	0.4	118	11	103	130.5	5.2	23	182	46.7	3.1	2	D	D	D
Wabasha	4.8	221	24	250	191.1	9.7	87	867	223.9	17.7	8	24	2.3	0.3
Wadena	7.0	507	17	391	246.9	17.1	74	750	164.3	17.9	6	D	D	D
Waseca	4.4	231	24	185	180.0	10.0	61	682	180.6	19.1	12	23	2.5	0.4
Washington	391.7	1 645	176	1 817	4 760.1	103.6	699	12 623	2 976.4	267.4	284	1 069	184.9	38.9
Watonwan	3.3	293	14	104	190.1	3.9	40	392	64.3	6.5	5	23	1.1	0.5
Wilkin	0.7	103	13	188	315.2	10.6	26	188	68.4	4.8	6	5	2.7	0.5
Winona	11.7	228	56	D	D	D	164	2 742	681.9	58.1	41	129	21.2	3.0
Wright	365.4	2 930	100	1 135	636.9	61.6	428	6 934	1 713.5	142.5	93	179	48.6	5.5
Yellow Medicine	2.8	265	15	200	647.8	8.3	48	377	100.0	7.0	4	D	D	D

1. Merchant wholesalers, except manufacturers' sales branches and offices.   2. Employer establishments.

Table B. States and Counties — Professional Services, Manufacturing, and Accommodation and Food Services

STATE County	Professional, scientific, and technical services, 2012				Manufacturing, 2012				Accommodation and food services, 2012			
	Number of establishments	Number of employees	Receipts (mil dol)	Annual payroll (mil dol)	Number of establishments	Number of employees	Receipts (mil dol)	Annual payroll (mil dol)	Number of establishments	Number of employees	Sales (mil dol)	Annual payroll (mil dol)
	147	148	149	150	151	152	153	154	155	156	157	158
MINNESOTA—Cont'd												
Fillmore	36	D	D	D	47	800	332.9	31.9	72	437	16.5	4.4
Freeborn	37	235	24.3	9.5	54	2 572	806.5	106.0	73	1 000	36.7	10.4
Goodhue	74	401	53.9	21.9	87	4 839	1 869.4	223.3	111	3 145	246.2	62.6
Grant	12	D	D	D	14	98	16.7	3.0	14	D	D	D
Hennepin	6 831	74 416	14 339.4	5 730.4	1 675	72 307	22 020.7	4 518.2	2 735	66 296	3 791.2	1 108.5
Houston	24	94	7.7	2.5	22	287	54.9	11.3	35	192	8.3	2.2
Hubbard	32	77	6.2	2.1	35	933	325.8	37.7	83	646	30.3	7.3
Isanti	60	D	D	D	70	1 518	394.8	80.0	53	D	D	D
Itasca	78	D	D	D	44	1 231	471.9	63.9	108	1 294	58.9	16.4
Jackson	16	67	7.5	2.0	14	1 359	D	75.3	21	258	8.7	2.2
Kanabec	18	90	6.6	2.1	17	622	116.0	22.5	27	269	11.1	2.6
Kandiyohi	95	538	60.4	21.5	73	2 916	1 140.0	115.0	91	1 427	55.4	15.4
Kittson	7	D	D	D	6	129	D	5.2	8	D	D	D
Koochiching	17	67	4.5	1.7	18	1 021	D	59.8	47	479	24.2	5.8
Lac qui Parle	9	D	D	D	12	283	D	12.1	13	D	D	D
Lake	13	34	3.9	1.5	18	553	167.8	27.4	66	681	36.6	11.0
Lake of the Woods	6	9	0.5	0.2	5	120	D	7.1	38	487	27.7	6.7
Le Sueur	36	D	D	D	52	2 130	883.4	101.4	48	466	18.2	4.9
Lincoln	7	D	D	D	5	15	D	0.5	12	D	D	D
Lyon	49	360	29.8	20.1	36	1 882	1 131.2	76.3	66	1 194	40.1	11.9
McLeod	64	392	32.3	15.5	80	5 465	1 882.5	277.2	64	1 043	39.6	11.2
Mahnomen	3	D	D	D	NA	NA	NA	NA	13	D	D	D
Marshall	11	30	6.9	1.5	17	251	59.7	11.0	23	D	D	D
Martin	39	193	21.3	7.9	39	1 313	1 576.5	59.8	38	749	26.9	7.3
Meeker	33	115	10.8	3.8	55	1 753	828.4	75.9	38	450	14.6	3.9
Mille Lacs	29	D	D	D	40	852	400.9	37.2	67	D	D	D
Morrison	35	195	18.2	8.2	51	1 319	397.7	50.4	89	911	35.5	9.5
Mower	44	D	D	D	36	3 752	D	151.6	71	1 052	44.0	11.3
Murray	15	D	D	D	8	387	D	9.5	24	D	D	D
Nicollet	42	450	46.7	25.0	50	3 678	965.1	131.9	52	759	26.5	7.6
Nobles	34	D	D	D	25	2 856	1 585.0	123.2	42	616	27.9	6.9
Norman	12	D	D	D	NA	NA	NA	NA	14	50	2.1	0.5
Olmsted	278	10 867	1 070.1	668.3	90	9 046	3 209.0	591.8	331	7 596	391.7	111.1
Otter Tail	95	482	48.6	19.3	83	3 875	1 464.5	156.1	149	1 471	69.7	19.7
Pennington	16	D	D	D	17	884	D	38.2	37	1 023	53.8	16.3
Pine	28	D	D	D	26	276	44.3	9.2	65	2 524	232.7	48.8
Pipestone	14	58	13.0	1.5	13	385	92.1	11.3	24	394	10.8	3.1
Polk	48	D	D	D	34	1 526	1 187.8	63.8	61	1 171	48.7	14.9
Pope	23	D	D	D	23	616	113.4	25.8	28	283	11.7	2.7
Ramsey	1 724	13 007	2 300.4	893.6	591	22 817	6 172.0	1 343.7	1 102	21 792	1 080.4	320.4
Red Lake	4	D	D	D	3	D	D	D	14	D	D	D
Redwood	19	58	8.3	2.7	31	1 021	371.8	34.9	39	1 122	98.0	20.8
Renville	24	123	17.8	6.4	23	1 028	559.3	49.6	31	265	8.5	1.9
Rice	137	642	54.3	22.5	77	3 907	1 741.9	189.7	124	2 082	82.6	24.4
Rock	16	85	10.5	4.3	13	267	86.4	9.8	16	205	7.5	1.8
Roseau	24	85	7.8	2.4	24	3 941	2 082.2	147.1	36	533	28.2	7.5
St. Louis	393	D	D	D	213	4 380	D	210.9	530	9 670	525.9	125.7
Scott	426	2 207	229.3	381.8	182	5 671	2 301.5	330.9	193	6 476	581.2	139.3
Sherburne	157	582	60.7	22.1	149	3 078	857.7	157.6	116	2 114	86.3	23.5
Sibley	26	D	D	D	23	1 028	1 018.4	44.3	21	D	D	D
Stearns	311	D	D	D	248	11 231	3 539.4	480.1	360	6 378	266.7	72.2
Steele	59	D	D	D	63	4 535	1 539.8	209.2	84	1 614	61.5	17.4
Stevens	16	99	11.4	4.5	16	776	D	36.1	25	413	16.5	3.9
Swift	16	69	7.7	2.4	16	814	D	46.5	28	252	8.8	2.2
Todd	27	96	6.3	2.6	43	1 509	885.9	63.1	45	384	18.3	4.8
Traverse	3	D	D	D	7	22	5.4	0.9	8	D	D	D
Wabasha	32	D	D	D	34	1 506	523.1	60.1	63	594	20.6	5.6
Wadena	19	54	7.8	2.8	18	342	43.1	10.6	30	322	11.2	2.9
Waseca	31	149	10.1	3.8	28	2 263	1 061.5	99.8	34	351	12.5	3.0
Washington	783	3 673	535.3	207.7	188	6 928	5 767.1	427.3	399	8 618	399.0	115.3
Watonwan	9	36	4.3	1.1	19	1 231	343.2	39.5	23	D	D	D
Wilkin	7	D	D	D	5	11	D	D	13	152	4.3	1.3
Winona	79	360	32.1	11.5	102	4 996	1 567.9	232.0	125	2 124	76.4	20.2
Wright	305	881	98.2	31.7	196	4 776	1 184.9	234.7	190	3 095	123.8	34.0
Yellow Medicine	16	D	D	D	21	261	177.9	11.5	25	605	41.5	10.3

1. Establishment subject to federal tax.

Table B. States and Counties — Health Care and Social Assistance, Other Services, Nonemployer Businesses, and Residential Construction

STATE County	Health care and social assistance, 2012				Other services, 2012				Nonemployer businesses, 2014		Value of residential construction authorized by building permits, 2015	
	Number of establish-ments	Number of employees	Receipts (mil dol)	Annual payroll (mil dol)	Number of establish-ments	Number of employees	Receipts (mil dol)	Annual payroll (mil dol)	Number	Receipts (mil dol)	New Construction ($1,000)	Number of housing units
	159	160	161	162	163	164	165	166	167	168	169	170
MINNESOTA—Cont'd												
Fillmore	49	D	D	D	44	147	12.5	2.5	1 769	71.0	7 975	48
Freeborn	71	2 569	208.3	94.6	66	369	20.1	5.2	1 850	80.7	33 893	138
Goodhue	141	3 780	254.3	123.6	103	483	41.6	10.5	3 029	132.4	16 522	72
Grant	20	511	32.7	16.4	15	39	3.8	0.5	530	24.1	553	3
Hennepin	3 899	128 451	14 036.0	6 012.9	2 651	22 081	2 761.6	721.7	101 629	5 178.9	1 139 582	4 376
Houston	45	1 047	35.7	18.7	41	106	9.8	2.0	1 431	65.0	7 620	43
Hubbard	52	917	85.4	37.0	38	187	14.0	3.0	1 688	62.4	4 019	24
Isanti	78	2 198	217.6	91.0	61	D	D	D	2 635	112.8	27 678	174
Itasca	151	3 495	248.9	112.8	85	387	56.8	9.9	2 983	114.6	28 119	170
Jackson	31	1 421	49.5	23.6	24	95	8.9	1.4	770	34.7	4 103	56
Kanabec	32	938	79.3	32.3	26	85	6.8	1.7	1 041	49.2	2 172	21
Kandiyohi	179	5 189	303.2	164.6	98	599	52.4	10.8	3 117	143.5	17 691	78
Kittson	11	359	19.0	8.7	10	50	4.0	0.7	313	12.1	740	6
Koochiching	41	668	49.7	19.1	27	109	9.4	1.7	834	26.8	1 692	13
Lac qui Parle	15	585	31.6	15.4	15	60	9.0	1.1	614	23.7	2 440	8
Lake	29	473	28.5	11.9	20	177	13.6	4.1	840	31.7	9 299	47
Lake of the Woods	8	D	D	D	10	54	5.3	0.9	355	13.4	4 922	20
Le Sueur	57	844	46.3	19.8	63	D	D	D	1 956	86.1	7 892	52
Lincoln	16	535	32.7	14.1	14	87	10.5	2.0	487	18.1	1 843	9
Lyon	82	2 006	164.5	63.0	51	D	D	D	1 696	74.4	5 340	26
McLeod	113	2 714	223.3	93.4	79	500	38.0	9.3	2 376	104.8	9 742	45
Mahnomen	8	176	12.8	5.0	7	48	4.9	0.9	317	14.0	0	0
Marshall	17	283	13.1	7.1	23	D	D	D	674	23.4	330	2
Martin	64	2 030	139.3	57.1	52	156	14.5	3.0	1 516	63.6	2 200	9
Meeker	57	1 240	81.2	32.4	42	181	14.7	2.6	1 712	68.8	3 263	51
Mille Lacs	71	1 845	104.2	45.5	54	D	D	D	1 829	72.6	9 867	50
Morrison	83	1 749	134.0	54.5	86	341	40.4	7.1	2 351	114.0	14 247	124
Mower	86	2 920	201.5	93.2	91	537	46.7	10.0	1 846	86.0	6 607	38
Murray	17	455	32.6	13.7	22	67	11.2	1.6	737	36.8	3 588	18
Nicollet	78	2 303	152.6	93.6	56	D	D	D	2 113	84.9	26 036	127
Nobles	63	1 298	66.4	31.0	51	294	24.5	5.7	1 268	61.6	2 882	14
Norman	15	401	22.6	11.1	12	38	3.0	0.5	471	23.4	1 886	8
Olmsted	412	20 014	2 408.0	854.4	240	1 846	155.2	46.2	9 609	418.0	264 826	1 622
Otter Tail	172	4 540	285.9	126.7	130	517	46.0	10.3	4 791	204.3	16 848	111
Pennington	40	1 255	108.3	42.5	45	260	15.4	3.9	912	34.8	10 122	72
Pine	76	1 035	73.6	26.3	42	186	22.5	3.8	1 739	72.9	9 696	66
Pipestone	28	738	49.6	19.0	22	71	6.8	1.5	742	36.0	1 969	8
Polk	90	2 512	154.4	71.4	56	301	23.2	5.4	2 148	88.9	13 583	67
Pope	25	666	43.0	20.7	25	75	7.1	1.5	986	42.7	7 862	34
Ramsey	1 850	57 676	5 557.3	2 429.7	1 090	9 996	1 273.8	320.8	36 552	1 525.0	231 602	1 304
Red Lake	6	D	D	D	5	D	D	D	234	13.8	0	0
Redwood	38	865	62.8	23.7	53	237	18.9	4.7	1 033	39.9	6 508	33
Renville	33	1 020	48.1	21.9	33	D	D	D	1 055	51.8	2 747	15
Rice	159	3 193	215.8	101.4	129	606	48.6	12.3	4 146	171.1	29 842	137
Rock	15	634	29.9	11.9	20	75	4.8	1.2	709	34.7	3 581	12
Roseau	30	841	60.8	21.9	36	129	13.1	1.8	1 138	42.4	8 116	63
St. Louis	729	24 700	2 210.0	1 048.0	386	2 505	239.0	58.7	11 539	441.5	114 498	703
Scott	238	4 719	395.9	170.5	221	1 260	108.5	31.7	10 418	521.1	134 938	489
Sherburne	146	4 147	216.9	112.8	147	727	71.0	21.0	6 371	274.1	67 312	323
Sibley	23	568	28.5	13.4	25	D	D	D	1 087	47.5	4 525	22
Stearns	413	14 979	1 619.6	743.1	359	2 344	237.3	58.0	10 316	498.9	116 827	693
Steele	125	2 486	218.1	92.0	89	525	55.0	12.6	2 413	99.2	13 662	69
Stevens	37	1 392	77.0	37.9	22	106	9.8	2.1	643	30.0	3 617	12
Swift	24	674	40.8	16.0	28	114	13.7	2.7	668	26.6	1 571	8
Todd	58	1 546	121.8	63.8	44	129	13.8	2.2	1 691	77.3	7 608	60
Traverse	11	294	14.5	5.8	8	D	D	D	250	11.3	567	4
Wabasha	57	D	D	D	43	149	11.3	2.8	1 549	68.9	8 831	36
Wadena	46	1 073	92.7	34.5	27	117	9.9	1.8	1 016	44.2	3 865	28
Waseca	50	975	56.4	22.0	33	114	10.1	2.2	1 196	56.6	3 575	15
Washington	580	10 469	1 052.7	428.2	397	2 671	194.9	63.4	17 847	810.0	257 377	888
Watonwan	20	484	41.4	15.7	27	115	13.5	2.0	721	28.4	965	6
Wilkin	20	743	61.1	23.4	12	D	D	D	456	43.8	2 488	13
Winona	122	3 195	220.1	90.3	84	429	44.4	10.5	2 890	109.5	12 232	97
Wright	266	6 437	397.7	187.1	225	1 238	90.3	24.3	9 618	416.9	141 067	533
Yellow Medicine	28	1 122	67.3	31.0	22	52	5.8	1.3	807	33.8	1 946	7

Table B. States and Counties — Government Employment and Payroll, and Local Government Finances

STATE County	Full-time equivalent employees	March payroll (dollars)	Administration, judicial, and legal	Police and Corrections	Fire Protection	Highways and transportation	Health and Welfare	Natural resources and utilities	Education and libraries	General revenue Total (mil dol)	Intergovern-mental (mil dol)	Taxes Total (mil dol)	Taxes Per capita Total (dollars)	Property
	171	172	173	174	175	176	177	178	179	180	181	182	183	184
MINNESOTA—Cont'd														
Fillmore	743	2 541 608	12.4	9.9	0.0	8.7	11.1	6.0	50.3	79.4	42.2	20.8	999	988
Freeborn	1 073	4 355 329	8.3	11.4	1.9	7.2	10.0	5.7	54.1	127.7	69.2	36.7	1 183	1 110
Goodhue	1 720	6 840 668	9.9	13.6	2.1	4.3	9.2	6.0	53.4	204.8	92.0	69.5	1 500	1 468
Grant	273	953 527	13.2	7.0	0.0	7.4	8.2	5.8	57.5	34.1	18.5	9.7	1 624	1 620
Hennepin	35 312	195 123 070	8.9	12.4	2.0	3.7	9.4	8.3	54.2	6 392.6	2 496.9	2 262.3	1 910	1 724
Houston	731	2 758 225	7.6	7.3	0.3	4.4	7.9	2.9	66.7	81.1	51.4	19.2	1 022	1 012
Hubbard	660	2 206 385	9.8	10.0	0.0	6.0	8.6	2.6	59.7	84.9	48.1	26.6	1 305	1 278
Isanti	1 257	4 796 343	6.7	9.3	0.1	4.0	7.5	2.3	68.0	131.8	76.3	35.3	924	904
Itasca	1 538	7 554 704	6.6	8.1	0.4	8.7	15.2	3.8	55.3	301.4	126.6	54.1	1 196	1 185
Jackson	515	1 776 829	11.8	7.0	0.2	8.4	20.7	6.0	44.4	50.6	24.7	15.9	1 544	1 531
Kanabec	867	2 925 087	5.0	6.1	0.0	4.3	35.1	1.6	43.5	90.0	33.3	14.7	920	889
Kandiyohi	2 286	9 769 471	6.3	8.2	0.4	2.9	40.7	4.1	36.3	282.7	84.2	49.6	1 170	1 089
Kittson	282	1 417 262	8.1	3.9	0.0	6.1	5.8	4.7	69.0	29.6	16.1	6.4	1 432	1 411
Koochiching	528	2 114 323	5.7	6.7	1.6	5.8	7.4	7.8	61.4	61.1	35.8	8.3	632	626
Lac qui Parle	625	1 888 050	6.9	3.8	0.0	5.1	33.9	3.0	45.7	46.7	21.4	8.4	1 176	1 141
Lake	361	1 980 601	12.9	10.1	0.3	9.4	6.4	8.7	48.8	64.0	33.4	15.7	1 454	1 414
Lake of the Woods	143	726 420	14.0	7.3	0.0	9.2	10.2	5.3	51.7	20.3	13.0	5.1	1 272	1 255
Le Sueur	871	2 940 497	8.0	8.1	0.0	4.7	11.3	5.1	60.6	96.7	50.3	31.2	1 128	1 088
Lincoln	199	603 609	18.2	11.9	0.1	15.9	1.7	6.8	38.3	21.7	9.6	8.1	1 392	1 384
Lyon	1 012	3 496 744	7.5	9.5	0.1	6.3	1.3	11.7	60.6	145.6	71.4	30.6	1 199	1 151
McLeod	1 516	6 615 440	5.8	6.3	0.2	3.2	37.7	10.6	34.8	212.6	66.7	39.1	1 084	1 063
Mahnomen	413	1 411 273	11.1	5.4	0.0	2.8	22.1	3.6	50.5	40.8	24.5	6.0	1 085	1 083
Marshall	459	1 668 424	9.8	5.5	0.5	7.6	16.1	9.7	49.9	55.9	36.6	9.4	991	982
Martin	655	3 114 449	10.3	9.8	0.1	7.4	3.2	9.6	56.8	92.7	49.5	24.0	1 170	1 158
Meeker	1 226	4 903 007	5.1	5.4	0.1	2.7	21.6	3.2	60.7	139.5	63.7	28.6	1 239	1 222
Mille Lacs	1 239	4 213 762	8.0	10.1	0.2	3.3	6.5	3.4	67.4	113.5	71.6	30.4	1 182	1 162
Morrison	1 124	4 203 099	7.6	8.2	0.9	5.8	10.1	2.5	63.7	118.8	71.3	29.8	903	875
Mower	1 542	6 255 175	7.7	8.0	0.8	4.4	8.9	12.3	56.6	166.8	93.6	36.0	915	853
Murray	420	2 070 204	5.7	4.9	0.0	4.6	33.5	2.7	42.5	54.5	22.6	10.9	1 273	1 259
Nicollet	835	3 375 650	8.8	10.9	0.1	6.1	20.8	7.8	43.0	108.0	39.0	29.6	899	839
Nobles	747	5 019 216	4.9	6.5	0.1	3.1	5.4	4.5	73.5	104.9	59.6	21.9	1 019	964
Norman	410	1 309 952	11.1	4.4	0.2	8.7	6.0	6.0	61.5	40.3	26.4	8.4	1 266	1 263
Olmsted	4 101	28 521 111	5.6	8.4	2.3	3.1	9.3	7.4	60.7	672.3	289.4	201.9	1 373	1 242
Otter Tail	2 164	8 240 552	8.0	7.4	0.2	4.7	21.9	3.4	52.3	298.8	109.1	62.1	1 083	1 068
Pennington	640	2 304 729	5.4	8.5	1.6	4.2	7.5	11.0	56.5	114.3	37.7	13.8	984	963
Pine	879	3 660 809	9.4	7.3	0.3	7.0	4.0	1.4	67.8	103.3	61.8	27.4	938	920
Pipestone	661	2 186 364	6.7	4.4	0.1	5.7	33.1	2.8	46.0	72.9	31.8	11.0	1 175	1 146
Polk	1 733	5 824 889	5.7	5.8	1.5	3.5	29.5	8.1	43.7	191.1	112.8	36.5	1 161	1 082
Pope	553	2 333 307	3.9	5.8	0.0	8.4	42.6	1.9	32.2	48.8	23.1	14.2	1 302	1 287
Ramsey	16 492	141 646 187	5.1	8.3	2.7	4.8	6.3	4.1	67.7	2 881.4	1 248.1	805.8	1 549	1 417
Red Lake	258	709 610	7.9	6.0	0.0	6.6	6.3	5.2	67.6	24.0	15.3	4.3	1 044	1 038
Redwood	739	3 232 367	9.3	5.7	0.2	4.8	7.0	5.7	65.2	101.1	39.6	20.4	1 287	1 261
Renville	704	2 316 532	18.7	8.2	0.0	9.5	12.1	4.4	43.1	88.9	34.9	21.9	1 424	1 401
Rice	2 519	10 254 560	4.8	6.6	0.7	2.9	41.2	2.9	39.9	352.9	102.9	62.2	959	916
Rock	396	1 387 361	10.8	6.2	0.1	8.3	1.0	11.6	59.9	45.4	21.6	11.5	1 203	1 152
Roseau	687	2 591 371	8.0	6.4	0.0	5.4	6.6	3.1	69.0	74.6	50.8	14.1	909	899
St. Louis	7 560	37 760 893	7.0	10.6	2.8	7.2	13.4	8.3	44.2	1 073.0	545.0	233.2	1 164	1 026
Scott	3 486	17 619 282	8.6	9.3	0.5	3.5	6.2	5.2	64.4	500.4	232.5	180.8	1 338	1 287
Sherburne	3 233	14 013 536	5.6	10.8	0.4	2.4	4.7	3.2	71.3	366.7	185.3	126.0	1 408	1 391
Sibley	636	2 194 050	9.3	7.3	0.3	6.5	27.2	1.9	46.6	76.3	33.5	18.9	1 250	1 235
Stearns	4 907	24 879 439	7.5	10.1	1.5	2.8	14.9	4.1	56.2	676.6	322.4	196.7	1 297	1 129
Steele	1 297	5 726 547	5.5	10.8	0.9	4.1	6.2	10.3	60.3	147.4	81.6	42.4	1 167	1 112
Stevens	479	1 791 149	11.2	17.4	0.6	6.2	9.0	11.6	40.3	43.2	23.3	12.2	1 258	1 229
Swift	748	2 235 013	8.5	5.5	0.0	5.7	37.9	3.6	34.8	82.8	25.2	13.2	1 379	1 363
Todd	994	3 435 036	8.2	8.5	0.0	4.5	12.5	2.3	58.8	94.8	59.3	21.3	869	840
Traverse	251	735 078	9.6	10.4	0.1	13.3	21.2	2.5	41.3	26.6	9.8	7.7	2 242	2 236
Wabasha	717	2 663 637	12.2	9.5	0.1	4.8	7.6	8.0	55.6	95.1	50.4	27.4	1 278	1 244
Wadena	723	2 230 614	6.7	2.7	0.1	5.3	11.7	4.2	66.3	67.0	41.7	12.2	887	870
Waseca	839	2 685 918	9.1	9.2	1.4	6.3	7.1	5.6	60.1	83.8	42.3	21.8	1 133	1 094
Washington	6 573	28 742 198	7.5	9.9	1.5	2.6	4.9	4.1	68.0	850.9	369.3	318.3	1 304	1 251
Watonwan	544	1 961 440	9.4	7.3	0.3	6.3	9.4	7.3	57.7	52.1	29.2	12.3	1 097	1 083
Wilkin	308	1 120 394	10.9	8.0	0.0	10.2	10.2	7.3	51.6	36.4	21.4	9.3	1 417	1 407
Winona	1 299	5 244 944	8.6	10.3	2.2	4.6	9.2	8.7	54.4	161.3	88.3	44.7	866	816
Wright	4 086	18 042 110	5.5	7.7	0.2	3.1	16.3	2.4	60.5	548.1	243.1	150.9	1 185	1 154
Yellow Medicine	412	1 492 491	12.8	9.7	0.0	10.5	8.7	6.7	48.7	72.8	27.5	13.9	1 364	1 345

1. Based on the resident population estimated as of July 1 of the year shown.

STATE County	Local government finances, 2012 (cont.)							Debt outstanding		Government employment, 2014			Presidential election,[2] 2012		
	Direct general expenditure												Percent of vote cast:		
			Percent of total for:												
	Total (mil dol)	Per capita[1] (dollars)	Education	Health and hospitals	Police protection	Public welfare	Highways	Total (mil dol)	Per capita[1] (dollars)	Federal civilian	Federal military	State and local	Democratic	Republican	All other
	185	186	187	188	189	190	191	192	193	194	195	196	197	198	199

MINNESOTA—Cont'd

STATE County	185	186	187	188	189	190	191	192	193	194	195	196	197	198	199
Fillmore	76.1	3 651	36.6	4.1	4.6	4.1	17.1	66.9	3 213	75	75	1 224	52.7	44.4	2.8
Freeborn	125.1	4 028	42.5	2.8	6.6	6.1	15.4	132.0	4 249	84	111	1 444	57.4	40.2	2.4
Goodhue	204.0	4 403	43.7	3.7	6.0	4.9	10.8	184.3	3 977	124	167	3 927	48.1	49.5	2.3
Grant	31.2	5 248	38.6	0.9	4.1	11.4	16.0	31.1	5 236	31	21	333	51.3	45.7	3.0
Hennepin	7 135.3	6 024	29.8	13.2	5.5	5.6	5.3	9 944.8	8 395	12 814	4 769	83 878	63.4	34.8	1.8
Houston	81.7	4 339	53.8	2.6	5.0	5.5	10.5	57.5	3 052	69	68	1 114	54.3	43.6	2.2
Hubbard	78.2	3 842	35.6	0.3	3.6	14.6	18.2	83.3	4 093	35	75	1 149	41.9	56.3	1.8
Isanti	136.1	3 558	50.4	3.4	6.9	7.7	11.0	169.3	4 426	76	139	1 962	41.1	56.5	2.4
Itasca	350.2	7 744	24.1	20.6	2.5	8.1	14.2	319.0	7 054	162	164	3 293	55.2	42.3	2.6
Jackson	50.2	4 887	33.0	4.1	3.8	7.8	19.0	50.8	4 943	31	37	723	46.6	50.8	2.6
Kanabec	84.8	5 300	27.0	37.5	2.3	6.2	8.2	63.2	3 950	39	58	1 197	44.0	52.7	3.3
Kandiyohi	300.9	7 100	20.9	38.3	5.5	4.8	6.1	333.7	7 875	150	151	3 904	46.2	51.7	2.1
Kittson	33.3	7 415	39.2	0.7	3.3	4.6	22.4	21.5	4 785	59	16	291	58.1	39.6	2.3
Koochiching	70.6	5 344	34.8	3.6	4.7	13.7	11.0	39.7	3 002	183	46	885	53.6	43.5	2.8
Lac qui Parle	48.9	6 880	33.1	26.2	3.0	4.0	16.2	28.8	4 046	37	25	695	51.5	45.6	2.9
Lake	63.2	5 838	24.4	5.5	5.8	10.5	17.5	119.8	11 076	26	38	835	59.9	37.8	2.3
Lake of the Woods	20.1	5 071	32.1	0.5	4.1	7.7	23.1	304.4	76 625	31	14	288	42.0	55.3	2.8
Le Sueur	119.9	4 333	53.4	2.4	3.8	5.4	10.2	161.8	5 845	73	101	1 272	46.6	50.9	2.5
Lincoln	25.1	4 309	25.1	0.5	6.1	11.4	20.4	39.0	6 710	28	21	264	48.5	47.7	3.8
Lyon	146.3	5 727	52.4	0.4	7.1	3.1	11.6	165.7	6 486	118	90	2 746	48.1	49.7	2.2
McLeod	206.8	5 737	26.6	34.0	4.4	4.9	10.2	191.4	5 309	79	130	1 771	39.4	57.8	2.8
Mahnomen	39.5	7 142	44.6	20.1	5.7	5.9	9.3	26.1	4 718	24	20	1 332	61.3	36.0	2.7
Marshall	64.2	6 790	36.8	0.4	2.9	5.0	21.2	37.9	4 006	52	34	576	48.8	48.2	3.0
Martin	94.4	4 613	46.0	0.5	6.6	4.8	14.2	96.9	4 732	63	73	1 248	41.0	56.3	2.7
Meeker	131.9	5 719	44.6	17.9	4.5	5.3	7.4	173.9	7 539	70	84	1 170	42.9	53.7	3.4
Mille Lacs	118.0	4 583	57.3	0.6	3.7	6.4	6.8	133.7	5 195	60	93	3 539	44.8	52.0	3.1
Morrison	121.6	3 680	48.7	1.8	3.7	7.1	14.7	122.4	3 704	428	119	1 875	39.1	58.1	2.8
Mower	168.0	4 268	46.1	1.1	4.6	8.4	11.8	1 198.8	30 447	144	142	2 491	60.5	36.9	2.6
Murray	54.4	6 337	23.7	28.8	4.7	2.0	15.6	37.9	4 418	45	31	603	48.7	48.2	3.1
Nicollet	111.3	3 380	30.7	17.7	4.8	6.8	10.6	144.3	4 383	33	111	2 905	54.2	43.7	2.1
Nobles	104.2	4 852	42.9	3.4	7.6	7.3	10.8	69.0	3 210	86	78	1 396	48.2	49.6	2.3
Norman	40.7	6 134	33.4	1.1	3.5	8.1	19.4	17.3	2 601	34	24	441	62.0	35.1	2.9
Olmsted	687.5	4 675	34.2	1.9	4.8	7.4	9.9	2 857.8	19 432	820	544	7 469	50.6	47.3	2.0
Otter Tail	312.8	5 461	45.3	8.8	3.2	5.1	10.5	310.4	5 419	217	207	3 480	42.4	55.3	2.3
Pennington	122.4	8 695	70.1	0.0	2.8	3.6	4.7	105.6	7 504	69	50	1 596	49.8	47.6	2.6
Pine	95.3	3 262	45.6	1.9	5.8	7.4	12.1	136.2	4 662	311	101	3 241	49.3	47.7	3.0
Pipestone	70.7	7 570	36.9	25.0	2.8	5.3	9.6	31.4	3 359	50	33	936	42.1	55.2	2.6
Polk	182.0	5 792	29.6	1.4	3.7	10.5	14.8	169.8	5 406	100	111	2 550	51.2	46.6	2.2
Pope	48.7	4 470	30.5	12.3	9.7	6.5	14.2	36.7	3 368	39	40	741	50.7	47.0	2.3
Ramsey	2 823.6	5 428	39.6	2.3	6.4	6.6	5.2	4 373.6	8 408	3 250	1 980	55 809	66.0	32.1	2.0
Red Lake	25.7	6 285	56.4	0.3	4.3	4.4	15.8	18.7	4 565	20	15	283	51.1	44.9	4.0
Redwood	94.9	5 987	30.0	25.7	4.1	7.3	11.4	93.1	5 876	64	56	1 933	41.6	55.2	3.2
Renville	96.1	6 251	25.3	21.0	3.3	5.9	14.5	80.0	5 207	62	54	1 053	48.0	48.6	3.4
Rice	342.7	5 285	25.9	37.7	3.6	2.9	5.8	303.1	4 673	129	213	3 569	54.7	43.2	2.2
Rock	42.6	4 461	42.5	0.6	4.4	8.4	12.8	74.6	7 811	28	34	672	41.8	55.8	2.4
Roseau	80.9	5 225	41.7	0.5	3.6	5.4	18.9	44.4	2 870	99	57	970	40.2	57.6	2.1
St. Louis	1 223.1	6 106	33.5	5.6	5.4	6.8	9.4	959.9	4 792	1 404	831	15 015	65.1	32.6	2.3
Scott	487.6	3 608	45.0	0.4	4.6	4.1	15.6	1 025.8	7 590	122	508	9 432	43.5	54.7	1.8
Sherburne	342.7	3 831	57.6	0.7	4.6	4.0	8.4	655.5	7 328	117	327	4 063	39.9	58.1	2.0
Sibley	82.9	5 484	34.0	16.4	4.2	4.8	14.5	70.1	4 636	43	54	736	38.8	58.1	3.1
Stearns	692.0	4 565	39.7	8.6	5.0	4.9	11.1	994.2	6 558	2 170	538	9 649	45.3	52.3	2.4
Steele	144.4	3 975	47.3	1.6	5.1	5.6	14.0	145.9	4 016	73	132	2 045	45.9	51.2	2.9
Stevens	43.9	4 548	36.6	0.3	5.8	5.7	19.8	77.2	7 986	80	32	1 278	49.4	48.1	2.5
Swift	86.6	9 024	19.1	41.7	2.8	4.8	8.8	45.2	4 715	50	34	872	55.4	41.6	2.9
Todd	111.4	4 544	53.4	2.6	3.5	6.4	11.8	81.6	3 330	83	88	1 409	43.1	54.1	2.8
Traverse	29.5	8 562	21.2	13.2	3.7	4.8	17.5	15.5	4 502	25	12	306	51.3	45.8	2.9
Wabasha	100.8	4 696	37.3	2.8	5.5	4.0	15.3	103.1	4 800	60	78	1 006	47.5	49.9	2.6
Wadena	92.1	6 693	61.5	1.4	3.3	12.6	6.8	28.2	2 051	53	49	1 247	40.2	57.6	2.2
Waseca	84.8	4 408	42.7	2.1	5.7	11.6	9.7	75.0	3 897	262	65	1 114	44.5	52.7	2.8
Washington	872.4	3 574	51.1	1.8	5.9	3.6	8.8	1 195.5	4 898	403	903	10 614	51.3	46.9	1.8
Watonwan	57.4	5 127	43.4	1.2	4.2	7.5	11.1	64.3	5 747	52	40	752	48.7	48.0	3.2
Wilkin	36.2	5 494	38.6	2.9	5.1	6.0	20.9	19.1	2 900	24	23	378	45.4	52.3	2.3
Winona	157.7	3 054	44.7	2.6	5.6	6.4	13.8	84.9	1 645	139	171	3 577	58.4	39.3	2.2
Wright	554.0	4 351	45.4	11.5	4.5	3.5	7.8	1 170.5	9 192	185	474	5 639	40.2	57.6	2.2
Yellow Medicine	83.2	8 190	26.8	22.5	2.0	9.0	12.3	76.0	7 477	44	36	1 465	50.6	46.3	3.1

1. Based on the resident population estimated as of July 1 of the year shown.   2. © 2013 Election Data Services, Inc. All rights reserved.

Table B. States and Counties — Land Area and Population

STATE/ County code	CBSA code[1]	County type[2]	STATE County	Land area[3] (sq km) 2010	Total persons 2015	Rank	Per square kilometer	White	Black	American Indian, Alaska Native	Asian and Pacific Islander	Percent Hispanic or Latino[4]	Under 5 years	5 to 17 years	18 to 24 years	25 to 34 years	35 to 44 years	45 to 54 years
				1	2	3	4	5	6	7	8	9	10	11	12	13	14	15
28 000	...	X	MISSISSIPPI	121 531	2 992 333	X	24.6	58.2	37.8	0.8	1.3	3.0	6.5	17.9	10.4	13.1	12.3	13.0
28 001	35020	5	Adams	1 198	31 254	1 403	26.1	38.2	52.9	0.6	0.8	8.0	5.8	15.4	8.4	13.0	12.2	13.3
28 003	18420	7	Alcorn	1 036	37 388	1 243	36.1	83.9	13.0	0.6	0.5	3.1	6.2	17.5	8.2	12.1	12.9	13.3
28 005	32620	8	Amite	1 891	12 574	2 257	6.6	58.1	41.0	0.5	0.4	1.0	5.9	15.2	7.5	10.2	10.1	13.8
28 007	...	6	Attala	1 904	19 043	1 872	10.0	55.4	42.5	0.5	0.5	2.0	7.0	18.1	8.1	10.9	10.9	12.6
28 009	32820	8	Benton	1 053	8 182	2 586	7.8	60.9	36.3	0.8	0.4	2.5	5.2	17.2	8.1	11.3	12.3	15.0
28 011	17380	5	Bolivar	2 270	33 322	1 348	14.7	32.7	64.3	0.3	0.9	2.2	7.5	18.1	11.4	14.1	11.2	12.0
28 013	...	7	Calhoun	1 519	14 717	2 122	9.7	66.4	28.3	0.5	0.3	5.6	6.3	17.9	8.0	11.0	12.0	13.6
28 015	24900	9	Carroll	1 627	10 243	2 413	6.3	64.6	34.1	0.5	0.4	1.3	4.3	15.5	7.7	10.7	11.6	13.6
28 017	...	7	Chickasaw	1 300	17 328	1 960	13.3	51.8	43.8	0.4	0.6	3.9	6.8	18.2	9.7	12.0	11.7	13.3
28 019	...	9	Choctaw	1 083	8 299	2 575	7.7	68.5	30.0	0.5	0.6	1.3	5.6	16.9	8.0	10.6	11.3	14.0
28 021	46980	6	Claiborne	1 262	9 150	2 498	7.3	14.3	83.0	0.4	0.9	1.2	6.1	15.7	18.9	11.2	10.0	10.5
28 023	32940	9	Clarke	1 791	16 006	2 039	8.9	64.1	34.6	0.6	0.4	1.1	5.5	17.6	8.2	11.1	11.7	13.4
28 025	...	7	Clay	1 062	20 048	1 832	18.9	40.1	58.7	0.4	0.4	1.4	6.1	18.0	9.4	11.9	11.5	12.9
28 027	17260	5	Coahoma	1 431	24 620	1 622	17.2	23.0	74.5	0.3	0.8	1.5	8.2	19.4	11.0	12.5	10.8	12.3
28 029	27140	2	Copiah	2 013	28 773	1 464	14.3	45.5	51.2	0.4	0.6	2.8	6.4	17.2	11.2	11.8	11.2	13.1
28 031	...	8	Covington	1 072	19 543	1 850	18.2	62.3	35.9	0.5	0.5	2.1	7.1	17.6	9.0	12.4	11.1	13.1
28 033	32820	1	DeSoto	1 233	173 323	370	140.6	68.6	25.4	0.6	1.8	4.9	6.3	20.4	8.7	12.8	15.0	13.9
28 035	25620	3	Forrest	1 208	75 944	723	62.9	58.7	37.6	0.6	1.5	3.2	6.8	16.3	16.4	14.8	11.3	11.3
28 037	...	9	Franklin	1 460	7 743	2 615	5.3	63.8	36.0	0.6	0.3	0.8	5.6	18.9	7.5	10.7	11.3	13.2
28 039	...	3	George	1 240	23 373	1 663	18.8	88.6	8.9	0.8	0.4	2.2	7.3	19.0	9.3	12.3	12.8	13.3
28 041	...	8	Greene	1 846	13 522	2 200	7.3	71.4	27.6	0.7	0.2	1.0	4.8	15.2	9.5	16.8	15.2	14.1
28 043	24980	7	Grenada	1 093	21 578	1 749	19.7	55.9	42.8	0.5	0.6	1.2	6.2	17.5	9.2	11.5	12.2	13.6
28 045	25060	3	Hancock	1 227	46 420	1 040	37.8	86.2	9.0	1.3	1.5	3.6	5.4	16.7	7.9	11.9	11.9	14.3
28 047	25060	3	Harrison	1 487	201 410	325	135.4	67.4	24.9	1.0	3.9	5.4	7.0	17.3	10.5	14.5	12.3	13.1
28 049	27140	2	Hinds	2 253	242 891	276	107.8	26.7	70.9	0.4	1.1	1.6	6.7	18.5	11.8	14.6	11.8	12.5
28 051	...	6	Holmes	1 960	18 340	1 900	9.4	16.8	81.7	0.3	0.6	0.9	7.7	19.1	12.7	12.3	10.4	12.2
28 053	...	7	Humphreys	1 084	8 669	2 539	8.0	22.7	74.5	0.4	0.5	2.5	7.4	20.0	9.1	12.7	10.3	13.0
28 055	...	9	Issaquena	1 070	1 337	3 092	1.2	34.8	64.2	0.5	0.6	0.9	3.2	11.7	14.3	17.1	10.8	15.3
28 057	46180	7	Itawamba	1 380	23 609	1 654	17.1	91.5	7.1	0.5	0.3	1.4	6.0	16.0	11.2	11.4	12.4	13.5
28 059	25060	3	Jackson	1 872	141 425	452	75.5	69.8	22.4	0.9	2.9	5.5	5.9	18.4	8.8	13.1	12.9	14.1
28 061	29860	9	Jasper	1 751	16 569	2 040	9.5	46.4	52.6	0.4	0.4	1.2	6.8	16.7	8.7	10.9	11.1	13.3
28 063	...	7	Jefferson	1 347	7 507	2 635	5.6	14.4	85.3	0.3	0.1	0.5	6.8	16.4	9.8	13.9	11.5	13.4
28 065	...	8	Jefferson Davis	1 058	11 665	2 313	11.0	38.5	60.0	0.5	0.3	1.1	5.9	15.1	9.3	10.7	11.8	13.3
28 067	29860	4	Jones	1 800	68 215	782	37.9	65.8	29.4	0.7	0.6	4.3	7.2	18.4	9.3	12.6	11.6	12.5
28 069	32940	9	Kemper	1 984	9 969	2 438	5.0	35.2	60.1	3.8	0.3	0.8	4.3	16.5	12.5	11.6	11.8	12.8
28 071	37060	6	Lafayette	1 636	53 154	940	32.5	72.1	24.3	0.6	3.2	2.3	5.4	12.7	26.5	13.8	10.9	9.7
28 073	25620	3	Lamar	1 287	60 618	864	47.1	75.6	21.2	0.6	1.6	2.5	6.9	18.8	9.4	15.6	14.1	12.7
28 075	32940	5	Lauderdale	1 822	78 524	708	43.1	54.2	43.4	0.5	1.1	2.2	6.4	17.6	10.2	13.2	11.9	12.9
28 077	...	8	Lawrence	1 115	12 622	2 254	11.3	66.2	31.6	0.5	0.4	1.9	6.1	17.9	8.3	11.9	11.3	14.3
28 079	...	6	Leake	1 510	22 763	1 696	15.1	48.3	42.0	6.0	0.3	4.2	6.7	21.3	9.1	12.6	11.9	12.0
28 081	46180	5	Lee	1 165	85 300	668	73.2	67.9	29.2	0.5	1.1	2.5	7.0	18.8	8.6	13.0	13.0	13.4
28 083	24900	5	Leflore	1 535	30 999	1 410	20.2	24.4	72.2	0.4	0.7	2.5	7.4	19.6	11.6	13.6	11.8	11.7
28 085	15020	5	Lincoln	1 518	34 649	1 312	22.8	67.5	31.1	0.5	0.5	1.1	6.3	18.4	8.8	12.1	12.6	13.0
28 087	18060	5	Lowndes	1 309	59 710	870	45.6	53.3	44.3	0.5	1.0	1.9	6.7	17.4	10.4	13.7	11.7	13.0
28 089	27140	2	Madison	1 851	103 465	576	55.9	56.5	38.5	0.4	2.6	2.8	6.5	19.1	8.9	13.3	13.4	14.1
28 091	...	6	Marion	1 405	25 563	1 581	18.2	65.8	32.9	0.5	0.6	1.4	6.5	17.7	8.5	12.6	12.0	12.9
28 093	32820	1	Marshall	1 829	35 916	1 276	19.6	48.9	47.8	0.6	0.4	3.3	5.9	16.2	9.8	12.2	12.3	14.2
28 095	...	7	Monroe	1 982	35 827	1 279	18.1	67.7	31.1	0.5	0.4	1.1	5.6	17.4	8.6	11.6	12.0	13.7
28 097	...	7	Montgomery	1 054	10 152	2 424	9.6	53.4	46.0	0.5	0.5	1.2	6.2	16.7	8.4	10.5	10.5	14.3
28 099	...	7	Neshoba	1 477	29 463	1 442	19.9	60.3	22.1	16.6	0.8	2.0	7.4	20.7	8.7	12.0	11.9	12.1
28 101	...	7	Newton	1 497	21 747	1 740	14.5	63.0	30.7	5.1	0.6	1.7	6.8	18.7	10.6	11.2	12.4	12.3
28 103	...	7	Noxubee	1 800	11 043	2 352	6.1	26.8	71.9	0.5	0.4	1.1	6.9	18.4	10.1	12.3	10.8	12.5
28 105	44260	5	Oktibbeha	1 187	49 800	982	42.0	57.8	37.6	0.5	3.7	1.7	5.4	12.6	31.2	13.7	8.8	9.1
28 107	...	6	Panola	1 775	34 167	1 324	19.2	48.3	50.0	0.6	0.5	1.8	7.2	18.7	9.6	12.3	11.8	13.4
28 109	38100	6	Pearl River	2 100	55 191	914	26.3	83.0	13.4	1.3	0.9	3.0	5.9	17.4	9.4	11.3	11.8	13.5
28 111	25620	3	Perry	1 676	12 277	2 278	7.3	78.0	20.9	0.7	0.3	1.3	6.2	17.4	8.7	11.3	11.9	13.8
28 113	32620	7	Pike	1 059	39 956	1 175	37.7	45.6	52.7	0.6	0.8	1.4	7.0	19.6	9.5	11.4	11.7	12.2
28 115	46180	7	Pontotoc	1 289	30 908	1 412	24.0	78.2	15.9	0.7	0.5	6.3	6.8	19.8	8.5	13.0	12.5	13.8
28 117	...	7	Prentiss	1 075	25 459	1 589	23.7	84.1	14.9	0.4	0.4	1.3	6.4	16.5	10.8	12.1	11.6	13.3
28 119	...	6	Quitman	1 049	7 486	2 636	7.1	29.5	69.6	0.7	0.5	1.0	6.8	18.1	9.5	11.4	11.8	13.8
28 121	27140	2	Rankin	2 008	149 039	437	74.2	75.8	20.7	0.5	1.5	2.6	6.3	18.0	7.9	14.6	14.4	13.4
28 123	...	6	Scott	1 578	28 265	1 479	17.9	51.4	37.9	0.6	0.6	10.7	7.6	19.0	9.3	13.0	12.5	12.8
28 125	...	9	Sharkey	1 118	4 585	2 859	4.1	28.9	69.8	0.3	0.5	1.7	7.1	18.2	8.9	10.4	10.6	13.1
28 127	27140	2	Simpson	1 526	27 222	1 523	17.8	62.1	35.7	0.5	0.7	1.6	6.4	18.9	8.7	12.1	11.9	12.9
28 129	...	8	Smith	1 648	16 059	2 036	9.7	75.0	23.8	0.3	0.2	1.5	6.2	18.2	8.4	10.9	11.8	13.4
28 131	...	3	Stone	1 154	18 070	1 914	15.7	77.6	20.2	1.0	0.7	1.7	5.5	16.9	12.7	12.3	12.4	13.2

1. CBSA = Core Based Statistical Area. See Appendix A for explanation. See Appendix B for list of metropolitan areas with component counties. 2. County type code from the Economic Research Service of USDA Rural-Urban Continuum Codes. See Appendix A for definition. 3. Dry land or land partially or temporarily covered by water. 4. May be of any race.

Table B. States and Counties — **Population and Households**

STATE County	55 to 64 years	65 to 74 years	75 years and over	Percent female	Total persons 2000	Total persons 2010	Percent change 2000–2010	Percent change 2010–2015	Births	Deaths	Net migration	Number	Persons per household	Family households	Female family householder[1]	One person
	16	17	18	19	20	21	22	23	24	25	26	27	28	29	30	31
MISSISSIPPI	12.5	8.3	6.0	51.4	2 844 658	2 968 103	4.3	0.8	204 190	155 161	-25 547	1 092 627	2.64	68.7	18.5	27.3
Adams	15.2	9.1	7.6	49.5	34 340	32 297	-5.9	-3.2	1 948	2 135	-840	12 081	2.50	63.4	22.4	34.4
Alcorn	12.7	10.1	6.9	51.1	34 558	37 057	7.2	0.9	2 333	2 288	340	14 651	2.51	67.1	12.4	29.3
Amite	16.3	12.0	9.0	51.4	13 599	13 128	-3.5	-4.2	694	721	-521	5 073	2.53	59.5	13.2	38.9
Attala	12.9	10.8	8.7	52.8	19 661	19 564	-0.5	-2.7	1 331	1 426	-424	7 341	2.58	69.1	20.9	28.7
Benton	13.1	10.7	7.2	50.0	8 026	8 730	8.8	-6.3	490	489	-569	3 040	2.79	66.7	14.4	31.9
Bolivar	12.0	8.4	5.3	53.2	40 633	34 148	-16.0	-2.4	2 823	2 173	-1 489	12 377	2.61	64.8	27.8	30.4
Calhoun	13.6	9.6	8.0	51.9	15 069	14 962	-0.7	-1.6	947	938	-239	5 913	2.47	66.5	15.8	30.9
Carroll	15.6	12.9	8.1	49.0	10 769	10 597	-1.6	-3.3	471	531	-326	3 788	2.69	73.9	14.2	25.3
Chickasaw	12.8	8.6	7.0	51.9	19 440	17 392	-10.5	-0.4	1 316	885	-452	6 560	2.60	69.2	19.3	27.0
Choctaw	14.4	10.8	8.4	51.6	9 758	8 548	-12.4	-2.9	495	457	-309	3 415	2.40	64.4	15.5	34.1
Claiborne	13.4	7.7	6.6	52.5	11 831	9 598	-18.9	-4.7	623	468	-617	3 163	2.80	60.5	27.8	36.7
Clarke	14.1	10.7	7.7	52.7	17 955	16 732	-6.8	-4.3	932	972	-644	6 454	2.55	70.1	19.1	27.2
Clay	13.7	9.1	7.2	53.0	21 979	20 634	-6.1	-2.8	1 186	1 176	-603	7 765	2.59	75.0	25.6	23.2
Coahoma	12.5	7.4	5.9	53.9	30 622	26 145	-14.6	-5.8	2 354	1 587	-2 254	9 350	2.66	66.0	30.7	30.5
Copiah	13.7	8.9	6.5	51.6	28 757	29 449	2.4	-2.3	2 000	1 644	-999	10 004	2.78	69.5	17.6	28.2
Covington	12.6	9.5	7.5	51.1	19 407	19 571	0.8	-0.1	1 385	1 312	-94	6 959	2.76	68.1	18.0	29.4
DeSoto	11.0	7.4	4.4	51.5	107 199	161 264	50.4	7.5	10 787	6 287	7 350	58 957	2.81	75.5	15.0	20.8
Forrest	10.3	7.2	5.5	52.2	72 604	74 932	3.2	1.4	5 683	3 756	-1 031	27 661	2.61	62.5	18.7	28.6
Franklin	14.9	9.4	8.5	51.2	8 448	8 118	-3.9	-4.6	439	488	-303	3 347	2.35	76.8	16.7	22.6
George	11.6	9.4	5.1	49.5	19 144	22 579	17.9	3.5	1 838	1 269	193	7 574	2.96	75.2	11.7	23.6
Greene	11.5	7.9	5.1	40.5	13 299	14 395	8.2	-6.1	714	640	-962	4 257	2.60	69.5	10.9	29.2
Grenada	13.2	9.6	7.0	52.7	23 263	21 906	-5.8	-1.5	1 448	1 473	-329	7 581	2.81	67.8	19.0	30.6
Hancock	14.7	10.6	6.8	50.9	42 967	44 014	2.4	5.5	2 569	2 257	2 105	18 413	2.43	69.4	13.3	26.1
Harrison	12.1	7.8	5.4	50.4	189 601	187 105	-1.3	7.6	14 480	9 359	8 865	74 369	2.53	65.0	17.5	28.9
Hinds	12.1	6.9	5.2	53.2	250 800	245 365	-2.2	-1.0	17 566	10 662	-9 291	88 321	2.70	65.8	24.4	29.6
Holmes	12.0	7.4	6.1	52.2	21 609	19 478	-9.9	-5.8	1 454	1 139	-1 408	6 396	2.86	65.6	31.9	33.1
Humphreys	13.3	8.1	6.2	52.9	11 206	9 375	-16.3	-7.5	701	530	-870	3 051	2.96	64.2	27.7	32.0
Issaquena	13.7	7.2	6.6	40.6	2 274	1 406	-38.2	-4.9	77	63	-88	427	2.32	61.4	16.9	37.0
Itawamba	12.2	10.1	7.4	50.9	22 770	23 401	2.8	0.9	1 354	1 362	177	8 852	2.53	70.9	11.1	27.3
Jackson	12.8	8.6	5.6	50.4	131 420	139 668	6.3	1.3	8 489	6 770	96	50 388	2.76	68.6	15.2	25.9
Jasper	14.5	10.3	7.7	51.3	18 149	17 062	-6.0	-2.9	1 183	954	-733	6 923	2.40	70.3	20.1	28.5
Jefferson	14.2	7.5	6.5	50.2	9 740	7 732	-20.6	-2.9	588	384	-432	2 553	2.80	67.2	31.5	32.1
Jefferson Davis	14.7	11.7	7.6	52.4	13 962	12 480	-10.6	-6.5	790	778	-787	4 947	2.42	66.8	21.1	30.5
Jones	12.9	8.8	6.7	51.4	64 958	67 761	4.3	0.7	5 134	3 806	-710	24 352	2.73	72.1	16.3	24.8
Kemper	13.3	9.4	7.9	49.8	10 453	10 461	0.1	-4.7	470	516	-444	3 661	2.57	61.2	19.7	35.3
Lafayette	9.8	6.6	4.6	51.2	38 744	47 359	22.2	12.2	2 829	1 961	4 699	16 557	2.72	59.7	15.1	31.3
Lamar	11.0	7.0	4.6	51.8	39 070	55 675	42.5	8.9	4 058	2 003	2 843	21 578	2.67	71.7	14.8	23.0
Lauderdale	12.7	8.3	6.8	51.6	78 161	80 261	2.7	-2.2	5 421	4 472	-2 595	29 662	2.58	66.3	20.4	29.8
Lawrence	14.1	9.6	6.6	51.0	13 258	12 929	-2.5	-2.4	834	722	-427	4 829	2.61	74.0	16.7	23.9
Leake	12.0	8.2	6.2	47.9	20 940	23 803	13.7	-4.4	1 633	1 383	-1 302	8 165	2.73	71.4	21.8	26.2
Lee	11.8	8.3	6.1	52.2	75 755	82 910	9.4	2.9	6 137	4 845	915	31 733	2.63	71.1	17.6	25.1
Leflore	11.8	6.8	5.7	51.9	37 947	32 317	-14.8	-4.1	2 516	1 888	-1 943	10 891	2.76	64.1	31.0	33.6
Lincoln	13.3	9.0	6.6	52.2	33 166	34 869	5.1	-0.6	2 426	2 068	-557	13 091	2.61	73.6	19.1	23.7
Lowndes	12.7	8.2	6.3	52.4	61 586	59 779	-2.9	-0.1	4 170	2 991	-1 217	23 431	2.48	65.3	17.7	30.3
Madison	12.4	7.3	5.0	52.1	74 674	95 203	27.5	8.7	6 659	5 365	6 877	36 699	2.64	71.4	14.6	25.1
Marion	13.1	9.2	7.5	51.7	25 595	27 081	5.8	-5.6	1 717	1 831	-1 465	9 903	2.58	73.6	17.6	23.7
Marshall	14.4	9.1	5.9	50.6	34 993	37 139	6.1	-3.3	2 363	2 185	-1 431	13 221	2.62	73.2	19.7	23.2
Monroe	13.5	10.0	7.6	52.0	38 014	36 989	-2.7	-3.1	2 258	2 100	-1 281	13 777	2.61	72.1	16.7	25.7
Montgomery	14.4	11.0	8.0	52.2	12 189	10 925	-10.4	-7.1	638	766	-654	4 169	2.52	69.6	20.3	28.8
Neshoba	12.4	8.1	6.5	52.2	28 684	29 673	3.4	-0.7	2 270	1 786	-678	10 833	2.69	69.4	18.6	28.3
Newton	11.9	9.1	7.1	52.0	21 838	21 720	-0.5	0.1	1 529	1 439	-113	8 113	2.58	74.3	19.1	24.1
Noxubee	13.2	8.6	7.2	51.9	12 548	11 545	-8.0	-4.3	816	662	-729	4 193	2.63	71.2	28.9	24.7
Oktibbeha	9.0	5.7	4.6	50.4	42 902	47 671	11.1	4.5	2 975	1 570	641	17 778	2.47	52.8	14.3	35.3
Panola	12.9	8.5	5.7	51.7	34 274	34 699	1.2	-1.5	2 674	2 073	-1 120	11 868	2.88	64.3	18.4	33.3
Pearl River	13.6	10.6	6.6	50.5	48 621	55 747	14.7	-1.0	3 388	3 159	-818	20 615	2.62	71.1	15.0	25.3
Perry	13.5	10.3	6.8	51.4	12 138	12 250	0.9	0.2	802	674	-164	4 387	2.75	71.1	16.2	27.4
Pike	12.9	8.9	6.7	52.6	38 940	40 407	3.8	-1.1	2 944	2 555	-853	14 809	2.65	64.6	19.3	31.5
Pontotoc	11.6	8.0	6.0	50.4	26 726	29 957	12.1	3.2	2 234	1 428	128	10 223	2.94	72.9	16.1	24.1
Prentiss	12.3	9.4	7.5	50.8	25 556	25 276	-1.1	0.7	1 767	1 372	-132	9 749	2.49	71.8	16.3	25.3
Quitman	13.6	8.7	6.2	52.1	10 117	8 223	-18.7	-9.0	512	554	-747	3 092	2.50	63.7	23.0	32.1
Rankin	12.1	8.0	5.3	51.7	115 327	142 061	23.2	4.9	10 104	5 579	2 492	53 527	2.61	73.5	14.7	22.4
Scott	12.1	8.0	5.7	51.2	28 423	28 264	-0.6	0.0	2 292	1 485	-750	9 767	2.87	70.8	20.5	25.9
Sharkey	15.5	8.5	7.7	53.8	6 580	4 916	-25.3	-6.7	356	296	-391	1 798	2.65	63.1	26.4	32.5
Simpson	13.6	8.9	6.7	51.3	27 639	27 502	-0.5	-1.0	1 799	1 507	-532	9 820	2.71	69.0	16.1	28.2
Smith	13.9	9.8	7.3	51.9	16 182	16 489	1.9	-2.6	1 011	821	-585	6 204	2.62	74.7	18.2	24.1
Stone	12.8	8.9	5.4	50.1	13 622	17 786	30.6	1.6	1 105	901	50	5 763	2.98	75.8	13.8	19.9

1. No spouse present.

Table B. States and Counties — Population, Vital Statistics, Medicare, and Crime

STATE County	Persons in group quarters, 2015	Daytime population, 2010–2014 Number	Daytime population Employment/residence ratio	Births, 2015 Total	Births, 2015 Rate[1]	Deaths, 2015 Number	Deaths, 2015 Rate[1]	Persons under 65 with no health insurance, 2014 Number	Persons under 65... Percent	Medicare, 2015 Total Beneficiaries	Medicare, 2015 Enrolled in Original Medicare	Medicare, 2015 Enrolled in Medicare Advantage	Serious crimes known to police,[2] 2014 Total Number	Serious crimes... Rate[3]
	32	33	34	35	36	37	38	39	40	41	42	43	44	45
MISSISSIPPI	93 979	2 934 283	0.96	38 548	12.9	29 802	10.0	424 433	17.1	544 439	459 550	84 889	95 800	3 200
Adams	2 383	33 144	1.09	363	11.5	410	13.0	4 208	17.6	7 008	5 915	1 093	1 436	4 496
Alcorn	741	37 695	1.03	450	12.0	432	11.6	5 416	17.8	8 808	8 497	311	NA	NA
Amite	116	10 668	0.46	118	9.4	143	11.4	2 068	20.9	2 636	2 345	291	NA	NA
Attala	341	17 671	0.75	246	12.9	262	13.7	2 717	17.7	4 523	3 801	722	NA	NA
Benton	79	6 719	0.40	97	11.8	92	11.2	1 277	18.9	1 966	1 692	274	NA	NA
Bolivar	1 762	33 955	1.00	499	14.9	414	12.3	4 775	17.3	7 073	6 357	716	NA	NA
Calhoun	211	13 336	0.73	188	12.8	171	11.6	2 640	21.9	3 167	2 903	264	NA	NA
Carroll	377	7 785	0.27	94	9.2	106	10.3	1 537	19.8	2 122	2 021	101	NA	NA
Chickasaw	494	16 931	0.93	245	14.1	184	10.6	2 851	20.0	4 225	3 670	555	NA	NA
Choctaw	122	7 464	0.68	101	12.2	107	12.9	1 149	17.3	1 567	1 416	151	78	938
Claiborne	1 110	10 045	1.27	121	13.2	95	10.4	1 194	17.6	1 671	1 271	400	151	1 954
Clarke	52	14 115	0.59	164	10.2	183	11.3	2 293	17.4	3 912	3 422	490	NA	NA
Clay	303	19 113	0.83	211	10.5	224	11.1	2 976	17.9	3 928	3 439	489	378	1 857
Coahoma	707	26 034	1.06	451	18.2	288	11.6	3 520	16.7	4 735	4 367	368	NA	NA
Copiah	999	26 314	0.73	372	12.9	309	10.7	4 345	18.2	6 204	4 648	1 556	NA	NA
Covington	219	17 644	0.73	249	12.8	209	10.7	3 135	19.5	4 088	3 350	738	NA	NA
DeSoto	609	137 557	0.64	2 084	12.1	1 271	7.4	21 080	14.1	22 405	18 486	3 919	NA	NA
Forrest	3 249	86 041	1.31	1 064	14.0	724	9.5	11 140	17.5	17 013	13 825	3 188	NA	NA
Franklin	67	6 889	0.64	74	9.5	73	9.4	1 117	17.4	1 627	1 497	130	NA	NA
George	562	19 785	0.61	336	14.4	227	9.7	3 247	16.7	4 890	3 859	1 031	73	361
Greene	2 398	12 519	0.53	148	10.6	129	9.3	1 730	18.3	1 794	1 581	213	72	523
Grenada	247	23 259	1.20	288	13.3	245	11.3	3 022	16.9	5 327	4 658	669	NA	NA
Hancock	548	45 119	1.00	529	11.4	418	9.0	7 542	20.0	7 778	5 618	2 160	NA	NA
Harrison	5 214	206 657	1.15	2 751	13.7	1 744	8.7	30 640	18.3	34 965	28 825	6 140	8 916	4 490
Hinds	8 989	266 526	1.20	3 249	13.3	2 036	8.4	33 793	16.3	38 399	27 961	10 438	13 113	6 091
Holmes	899	17 500	0.73	256	13.9	244	13.2	2 769	18.4	3 911	3 443	468	NA	NA
Humphreys	83	8 661	0.82	128	14.7	111	12.7	1 503	20.2	1 774	1 555	219	NA	NA
Issaquena	282	1 246	0.90	14	10.3	8	5.9	184	20.5	169	148	21	NA	NA
Itawamba	993	20 274	0.65	243	10.3	247	10.5	3 250	17.4	3 920	3 710	210	352	1 503
Jackson	1 250	136 986	0.94	1 643	11.6	1 305	9.2	20 283	16.9	22 605	17 279	5 326	4 528	3 570
Jasper	87	14 833	0.70	212	12.8	172	10.4	2 473	18.3	3 684	3 099	585	NA	NA
Jefferson	381	7 336	0.84	106	14.1	74	9.8	1 100	17.9	1 413	1 177	236	36	604
Jefferson Davis	111	10 148	0.54	155	13.2	145	12.3	2 003	21.1	2 328	2 101	227	NA	NA
Jones	1 878	70 870	1.10	972	14.2	789	11.6	9 736	17.2	13 783	11 630	2 153	1 686	2 642
Kemper	955	10 319	1.00	90	8.9	96	9.5	1 670	22.1	1 801	1 568	233	86	942
Lafayette	6 118	51 269	1.05	527	10.0	393	7.5	6 803	16.8	5 642	5 151	491	NA	NA
Lamar	309	51 153	0.74	762	12.6	357	5.9	7 780	14.7	5 589	4 421	1 168	1 024	1 792
Lauderdale	3 635	85 003	1.15	1 015	12.9	816	10.3	10 641	16.6	14 856	13 325	1 531	2 741	3 419
Lawrence	0	11 143	0.68	157	12.5	133	10.6	1 810	17.3	3 663	3 243	420	NA	NA
Leake	1 599	21 459	0.76	324	14.1	278	12.1	3 986	22.2	4 405	3 621	784	NA	NA
Lee	1 059	98 274	1.37	1 174	13.8	1 009	11.8	11 593	16.0	17 855	16 575	1 280	NA	NA
Leflore	2 226	34 844	1.32	444	14.2	355	11.4	4 924	19.2	6 144	5 857	287	NA	NA
Lincoln	699	33 592	0.90	471	13.6	382	11.0	4 945	17.0	6 708	5 823	885	NA	NA
Lowndes	1 423	61 651	1.08	792	13.3	561	9.4	7 915	15.8	11 735	10 474	1 261	NA	NA
Madison	1 751	102 523	1.08	1 297	12.6	1 129	11.0	11 345	13.0	13 743	10 996	2 747	1 526	1 729
Marion	718	26 395	0.99	306	11.9	327	12.7	3 987	19.0	5 390	4 447	943	513	1 978
Marshall	1 848	30 233	0.54	448	12.4	434	12.0	5 553	19.1	7 829	6 328	1 501	531	1 461
Monroe	405	33 661	0.80	440	12.3	387	10.8	5 638	19.1	7 467	6 829	638	NA	NA
Montgomery	99	10 089	0.85	109	10.6	122	11.9	1 548	18.4	2 813	2 684	129	NA	NA
Neshoba	394	29 722	1.01	437	14.8	345	11.7	5 266	21.1	4 511	4 058	453	NA	NA
Newton	552	19 187	0.71	299	13.7	296	13.6	3 263	18.3	5 849	5 095	754	NA	NA
Noxubee	159	10 624	0.84	165	14.9	143	12.9	2 040	22.2	2 356	2 244	112	NA	NA
Oktibbeha	4 703	50 115	1.08	571	11.5	365	7.4	7 198	18.3	6 712	6 032	680	1 393	2 823
Panola	315	33 601	0.92	516	15.1	406	11.8	5 275	18.0	6 803	5 765	1 038	1 450	4 480
Pearl River	1 330	47 476	0.61	628	11.4	608	11.0	8 024	18.0	11 393	8 670	2 723	NA	NA
Perry	101	10 717	0.63	153	12.5	116	9.5	1 953	19.3	2 291	2 012	279	NA	NA
Pike	845	41 916	1.12	533	13.3	510	12.8	5 862	17.7	8 895	7 252	1 643	NA	NA
Pontotoc	236	27 914	0.81	416	13.5	248	8.0	4 774	18.0	5 142	4 646	496	NA	NA
Prentiss	877	23 235	0.77	328	12.9	207	8.1	3 721	18.3	6 411	6 107	304	NA	NA
Quitman	137	6 973	0.62	87	11.5	104	13.7	1 307	20.4	1 634	1 503	131	NA	NA
Rankin	5 107	135 761	0.86	1 924	13.0	1 120	7.5	15 140	12.2	21 362	17 011	4 351	1 246	894
Scott	227	29 708	1.13	421	14.9	302	10.7	5 415	22.2	6 169	5 002	1 167	NA	NA
Sharkey	106	4 853	0.97	59	12.8	45	9.8	699	18.1	992	889	103	NA	NA
Simpson	625	24 554	0.72	337	12.3	290	10.6	4 096	18.0	5 200	4 295	905	138	553
Smith	103	13 637	0.57	182	11.3	171	10.6	2 283	17.1	2 553	2 125	428	NA	NA
Stone	1 411	16 472	0.78	215	12.0	164	9.1	2 462	17.5	3 757	2 899	858	292	1 620

1. Per 1,000 estimated resident population. 2. Data for serious crimes have not been adjusted for underreporting; this may affect comparability between geographic areas and over time.
3. Per 100,000 population estimated by the FBI.

Table B. States and Counties — Crime, Education, Money Income, and Poverty

STATE County	Serious crimes known to police, 2014 (cont.)[1] Rate[2] Violent	Property	Education — School enrollment and attainment, 2010–2014 Enrollment[3] Total	Percent private	Attainment[4] (percent) High school graduate or less	Bachelor's degree or more	Local government expenditures,[5] 2012–2013 Total current spending (mil dol)	Current spending per student (dollars)	Money income, 2010–2014 Per capita income[6] (dollars)	Households Median income (dollars)	Mean income (dollars)	Percent with income of $200,000 or more	Income and poverty, 2014 Median household income (dollars)	Percent below poverty level All persons	Children under 18 years	Children 5 to 17 years in families
	46	47	48	49	50	51	52	53	54	55	56	57	58	59	60	61
MISSISSIPPI	278	2 921	814 005	12.8	48.3	20.4	4 023.6	8 130	20 956	39 464	54 881	2.2	39 738	21.9	30.7	29.4
Adams	288	4 208	7 832	9.7	55.2	17.2	35.7	9 469	17 656	28 435	44 380	1.9	32 327	32.9	47.1	46.6
Alcorn	NA	NA	8 738	9.8	55.9	16.2	46.3	7 703	18 758	33 790	46 333	1.0	35 180	21.8	29.1	27.9
Amite	NA	NA	3 060	34.3	60.3	11.5	11.1	10 290	17 140	29 580	41 002	0.8	30 668	23.2	32.2	31.9
Attala	NA	NA	4 767	11.7	55.6	15.1	28.1	7 991	17 894	31 671	45 035	1.3	32 521	23.6	33.3	32.5
Benton	NA	NA	2 124	5.2	65.6	8.6	11.5	9 145	19 734	29 132	48 316	2.0	30 665	25.6	37.8	35.0
Bolivar	NA	NA	10 545	5.9	50.8	21.4	59.2	9 146	16 666	29 255	43 862	1.3	29 297	34.0	43.0	44.3
Calhoun	NA	NA	3 441	8.5	63.0	10.6	18.8	7 352	17 419	29 893	41 845	0.8	33 141	25.0	37.6	32.6
Carroll	NA	NA	2 216	31.6	57.7	13.1	8.5	8 496	19 945	34 060	49 995	0.8	38 219	17.9	25.7	23.6
Chickasaw	NA	NA	4 232	4.7	64.4	10.5	25.2	8 267	16 750	31 301	42 794	1.1	31 616	24.7	35.0	32.5
Choctaw	48	890	2 179	11.2	55.6	13.1	14.8	9 752	17 359	30 768	40 955	0.0	34 548	24.2	34.8	32.3
Claiborne	272	1 683	3 123	7.5	50.6	16.5	16.4	9 607	11 962	23 917	33 674	0.2	26 083	42.6	50.0	48.1
Clarke	NA	NA	4 085	7.3	56.7	12.0	23.3	7 646	18 584	31 478	45 001	0.5	34 910	22.4	32.5	30.0
Clay	319	1 538	5 943	16.7	52.9	19.1	28.0	8 134	18 797	32 844	48 042	1.7	33 939	28.4	42.3	42.9
Coahoma	NA	NA	8 088	12.3	50.4	17.8	46.1	9 335	15 858	27 735	41 886	1.1	28 647	35.0	48.3	49.4
Copiah	NA	NA	7 916	10.5	52.4	13.9	36.1	7 875	18 201	35 199	49 730	1.9	35 314	26.0	37.9	35.1
Covington	NA	NA	4 633	7.9	59.0	14.5	24.4	8 002	16 733	32 162	43 351	0.3	31 835	26.5	36.3	35.2
DeSoto	NA	NA	47 556	12.3	41.3	21.7	212.5	6 488	25 593	58 995	70 158	2.2	58 479	10.1	15.2	14.1
Forrest	NA	NA	24 688	15.4	43.6	26.8	105.9	9 160	20 075	36 538	52 793	1.9	36 808	26.4	33.3	32.5
Franklin	NA	NA	1 983	11.0	56.7	16.7	13.4	8 900	21 294	35 995	53 475	1.5	36 544	20.5	29.2	26.2
George	59	301	5 593	10.2	61.6	11.1	28.3	6 740	20 979	42 472	57 807	1.0	44 811	17.0	23.9	23.1
Greene	109	414	2 946	4.8	64.7	8.7	17.0	7 927	15 427	37 412	48 339	1.4	39 615	23.6	24.7	22.4
Grenada	NA	NA	5 935	11.9	54.3	14.2	31.7	7 318	20 594	33 067	53 538	2.3	33 650	24.8	35.1	34.4
Hancock	NA	NA	10 406	13.1	44.0	22.5	53.9	8 377	22 774	44 069	55 964	1.5	46 288	19.8	28.7	27.7
Harrison	220	4 271	47 996	15.0	43.7	20.8	251.0	8 305	22 224	42 285	55 626	1.7	41 010	18.8	26.6	26.8
Hinds	770	5 321	77 817	17.5	39.0	27.5	340.4	8 350	20 897	38 021	55 190	2.6	38 454	23.6	34.7	33.6
Holmes	NA	NA	5 781	8.8	64.6	12.0	30.1	8 322	11 914	21 399	32 063	0.3	22 640	44.0	58.0	55.5
Humphreys	NA	NA	2 566	9.4	61.3	12.0	14.5	8 234	12 938	24 387	35 994	1.6	25 562	40.3	56.7	56.0
Issaquena	NA	NA	170	26.5	72.8	7.8	NA	NA	14 548	29 583	40 230	0.7	37 096	39.5	47.8	44.3
Itawamba	107	1 396	5 933	5.6	53.6	13.0	26.0	7 246	19 238	36 740	49 990	0.7	38 366	17.2	23.8	23.1
Jackson	243	3 327	36 907	12.0	43.8	20.5	212.7	8 736	24 162	49 145	63 621	2.9	48 018	15.6	22.8	20.9
Jasper	NA	NA	4 061	12.6	57.5	13.3	22.7	9 163	18 398	32 261	44 670	1.9	35 019	22.7	32.0	31.8
Jefferson	235	369	2 121	1.9	54.9	20.4	12.2	8 836	12 518	23 480	34 596	0.3	26 408	38.5	45.2	44.8
Jefferson Davis	NA	NA	2 808	10.0	59.8	14.7	15.6	9 714	15 782	27 063	37 364	0.5	28 271	29.8	43.4	42.2
Jones	199	2 443	16 952	10.8	50.5	17.3	91.2	7 827	19 673	38 044	52 269	2.1	37 367	24.4	35.7	32.5
Kemper	99	843	2 881	8.5	54.2	10.8	11.6	9 880	14 837	30 206	38 237	0.8	33 015	28.2	37.1	33.0
Lafayette	NA	NA	20 424	4.2	34.8	36.9	57.4	8 811	21 838	41 343	60 708	4.0	40 797	25.9	22.4	23.5
Lamar	58	1 734	17 280	10.4	33.6	34.1	79.0	7 850	26 293	51 724	68 648	3.6	51 389	14.2	20.5	19.4
Lauderdale	349	3 070	20 993	10.1	45.4	19.0	107.9	8 305	21 669	37 165	55 519	2.6	38 869	21.7	32.6	30.5
Lawrence	NA	NA	3 080	7.1	54.7	12.8	18.4	8 494	20 186	37 477	51 086	1.5	38 471	22.3	30.7	28.4
Leake	NA	NA	5 979	14.2	60.6	11.6	22.2	7 105	17 178	32 953	48 187	2.9	32 239	27.1	42.6	40.4
Lee	NA	NA	21 148	10.8	44.0	18.4	127.1	8 185	22 496	43 240	58 587	2.5	43 374	19.4	29.6	26.4
Leflore	NA	NA	9 867	8.9	57.6	18.6	51.4	9 057	14 663	24 475	39 070	1.2	26 439	40.1	54.1	52.1
Lincoln	NA	NA	8 588	10.6	52.4	14.7	46.3	7 756	18 597	35 502	48 118	0.8	36 118	21.6	28.7	27.6
Lowndes	NA	NA	16 796	12.0	46.7	21.4	79.3	8 206	21 213	38 672	52 411	1.8	39 937	23.6	34.3	33.0
Madison	155	1 573	29 075	23.2	26.3	46.3	125.5	7 901	34 334	63 156	90 375	8.7	66 671	13.1	18.1	17.5
Marion	208	1 770	6 401	15.8	60.2	12.3	34.7	8 464	18 712	29 010	48 570	1.6	33 428	30.4	40.3	39.3
Marshall	338	1 123	8 232	18.3	62.2	11.3	38.1	7 704	18 526	39 137	50 244	1.1	37 554	21.5	34.1	32.8
Monroe	NA	NA	8 217	6.1	58.1	14.1	55.2	8 027	18 576	36 708	46 981	1.1	36 810	20.1	29.9	28.2
Montgomery	NA	NA	2 446	18.3	59.8	15.7	13.5	9 191	16 761	30 993	41 096	0.3	31 963	24.7	35.9	35.6
Neshoba	NA	NA	8 446	11.2	53.3	13.8	32.9	7 256	18 888	36 830	50 875	2.1	37 686	20.7	29.0	29.9
Newton	NA	NA	5 735	9.1	48.3	15.8	31.1	8 049	21 157	38 265	54 895	1.9	35 185	22.3	31.1	28.7
Noxubee	NA	NA	2 983	16.1	65.5	11.2	17.4	9 676	14 070	26 231	37 401	0.3	28 730	31.3	44.7	42.0
Oktibbeha	158	2 665	22 911	7.4	33.0	42.6	49.3	9 523	20 766	32 348	53 309	2.8	34 429	29.9	31.7	32.8
Panola	513	3 967	8 803	11.8	56.2	14.9	51.8	8 384	19 319	36 651	51 574	1.9	34 526	25.9	39.4	37.7
Pearl River	NA	NA	13 646	13.6	51.4	13.5	71.2	8 213	20 117	40 997	51 578	1.6	38 465	19.3	29.0	26.9
Perry	NA	NA	2 878	9.3	59.4	8.4	16.4	8 479	16 814	33 097	44 237	0.7	32 459	22.6	32.9	30.2
Pike	NA	NA	11 021	14.4	52.8	16.3	56.9	8 102	17 671	31 926	45 331	1.3	30 078	30.5	40.8	40.3
Pontotoc	NA	NA	7 887	5.4	57.8	12.2	42.0	7 184	19 481	40 991	52 759	1.3	40 198	17.7	24.9	23.5
Prentiss	NA	NA	6 313	4.1	60.2	11.8	29.2	7 941	17 595	33 811	44 943	0.8	34 794	22.3	29.9	28.7
Quitman	NA	NA	2 012	12.9	59.7	13.6	11.1	9 015	14 685	24 212	36 758	0.6	26 204	36.2	51.2	47.4
Rankin	60	834	37 021	19.1	38.0	28.7	179.7	7 680	27 508	58 811	73 307	3.8	58 368	11.1	14.9	14.3
Scott	NA	NA	6 973	10.6	62.2	11.2	39.4	7 175	16 965	34 555	46 753	1.3	32 049	26.9	35.7	32.8
Sharkey	NA	NA	1 309	15.0	55.1	21.6	10.4	11 326	15 600	30 688	40 712	0.4	27 877	37.4	54.1	53.0
Simpson	32	521	6 821	19.3	59.5	13.4	33.4	7 897	18 728	36 097	49 282	1.5	34 338	25.9	36.4	33.9
Smith	NA	NA	3 681	13.4	60.6	13.6	22.8	7 949	21 173	37 356	54 511	1.8	38 975	20.8	31.6	29.1
Stone	122	1 498	4 631	16.2	48.2	13.1	21.2	7 748	19 130	45 141	54 323	0.9	41 136	19.5	28.3	26.2

1. Data for serious crimes have not been adjusted for underreporting; this may affect comparability between geographic areas and over time. 2. Per 100,000 population estimated by the FBI.
3. All persons 3 years old and over enrolled in nursery school through college. 4. Persons 25 years old and over. 5. Elementary and secondary education expenditures.
6. Based on population estimated by the American Community Survey, 2010–2014.

STATE County	Total (mil dol)	Percent change, 2013–2014	Per capita[1] Dollars	Rank	Wages and salaries (mil dol)	Pension and insurance	Government social insurance	Proprietors' income (mil dol)	Dividends, interest, and rent (mil dol)	Personal transfer receipts (mil dol)	Total (mil dol)	From employee and self-employed	From employer
	62	63	64	65	66	67	68	69	70	71	72	73	74
MISSISSIPPI................	103 091	2.4	34 431	X	45 443	7 499	3 440	10 084	15 214	26 367	66 466	4 310	3 440
Adams.....................	1 108	0.7	34 908	1 952	430	62	31	170	187	333	693	48	31
Alcorn....................	1 091	2.3	29 182	2 810	504	79	39	68	156	370	690	51	39
Amite.....................	414	3.6	32 765	2 321	75	12	6	75	44	126	168	12	6
Attala....................	566	1.6	29 516	2 779	162	28	13	76	68	185	279	20	13
Benton....................	216	0.0	26 032	3 030	49	10	4	14	21	82	76	7	4
Bolivar...................	1 127	-1.7	33 377	2 215	436	77	32	75	158	379	621	41	32
Calhoun...................	421	0.3	28 526	2 878	119	21	9	39	49	150	189	14	9
Carroll...................	310	-3.8	30 262	2 683	42	8	3	12	43	96	64	7	3
Chickasaw.................	547	4.0	31 621	2 508	192	30	15	67	79	170	304	20	15
Choctaw...................	240	5.5	28 882	2 840	83	16	6	22	29	88	127	9	6
Claiborne.................	264	-2.9	29 086	2 818	186	41	14	13	30	111	254	15	14
Clarke....................	590	1.0	36 172	1 749	114	20	8	42	59	175	184	15	8
Clay......................	706	0.5	34 930	1 950	204	30	15	127	102	195	377	22	15
Coahoma	745	-5.9	30 037	2 708	316	49	24	30	119	309	418	30	24
Copiah....................	897	3.3	31 151	2 563	266	52	21	74	95	287	413	29	21
Covington.................	647	7.3	33 275	2 231	178	33	13	121	73	186	346	20	13
DeSoto....................	6 194	3.8	36 242	1 736	1 966	271	150	516	571	1 011	2 903	196	150
Forrest...................	2 673	2.7	35 024	1 934	1 645	284	123	381	512	689	2 433	151	123
Franklin	235	2.3	29 962	2 719	66	13	5	15	28	83	100	7	5
George....................	708	2.6	30 372	2 669	206	34	15	29	76	186	284	21	15
Greene....................	346	4.1	24 142	3 078	69	15	5	34	31	113	123	9	5
Grenada...................	727	2.5	33 574	2 180	363	61	28	45	90	243	497	34	28
Hancock...................	1 588	4.1	34 555	2 013	739	135	59	143	318	380	1 076	69	59
Harrison..................	6 924	3.3	34 785	1 972	3 861	706	308	470	1 435	1 620	5 345	323	308
Hinds.....................	9 346	2.6	38 344	1 412	5 949	992	437	1 411	1 662	2 114	8 789	540	437
Holmes....................	486	-4.7	26 308	3 018	125	23	10	12	52	244	170	15	10
Humphreys.................	278	-7.3	31 808	2 466	74	14	6	45	38	103	140	9	6
Issaquena	36	-13.6	25 516	3 046	7	1	1	2	8	9	11	1	1
Itawamba..................	723	2.8	30 734	2 623	227	36	17	56	79	224	337	26	17
Jackson...................	4 873	2.4	34 530	2 019	2 638	488	200	215	811	1 092	3 542	227	200
Jasper....................	584	6.3	35 207	1 902	158	28	12	73	61	172	271	17	12
Jefferson.................	229	-3.8	30 198	2 690	46	11	3	16	21	86	76	5	3
Jefferson Davis	357	1.5	30 213	2 687	61	12	5	36	36	129	114	9	5
Jones.....................	2 515	4.8	36 832	1 630	1 261	218	90	311	327	720	1 880	118	90
Kemper....................	292	-1.4	28 753	2 853	241	33	18	25	33	108	317	20	18
Lafayette.................	1 837	4.3	34 703	1 983	867	152	63	208	359	364	1 289	80	63
Lamar.....................	1 875	4.3	31 192	2 556	601	88	45	73	292	362	808	56	45
Lauderdale................	2 756	0.3	34 566	2 012	1 420	234	111	173	453	713	1 939	126	111
Lawrence..................	410	2.1	32 780	2 316	118	19	8	58	40	139	203	13	8
Leake.....................	666	10.0	28 705	2 864	170	31	14	135	63	202	350	19	14
Lee.......................	3 020	2.8	35 429	1 871	2 051	289	157	282	440	683	2 779	180	157
Leflore...................	1 003	-1.1	31 917	2 445	518	94	39	100	190	341	751	47	39
Lincoln...................	1 216	3.5	34 964	1 942	442	66	33	113	130	325	653	45	33
Lowndes...................	2 190	-1.2	36 669	1 654	1 201	199	93	145	357	516	1 638	104	93
Madison	5 959	4.2	58 604	148	2 485	314	180	918	1 157	670	3 897	244	180
Marion....................	837	2.6	32 338	2 398	313	47	23	117	105	270	500	34	23
Marshall..................	1 015	1.0	28 009	2 917	236	36	18	47	97	331	338	28	18
Monroe....................	1 121	2.8	31 132	2 565	402	67	32	79	155	347	580	43	32
Montgomery................	329	1.2	31 665	2 499	88	16	7	18	45	123	128	11	7
Neshoba...................	1 136	4.2	38 565	1 383	467	77	35	276	132	268	855	49	35
Newton....................	704	5.8	32 252	2 409	203	38	15	73	80	233	329	21	15
Noxubee...................	349	-7.8	31 395	2 540	85	17	6	71	37	126	179	10	6
Oktibbeha.................	1 464	2.2	29 636	2 771	756	152	56	92	254	327	1 056	65	56
Panola....................	1 019	-0.5	29 585	2 774	413	65	32	101	120	324	613	43	32
Pearl River...............	1 819	3.3	32 943	2 289	365	65	27	101	228	517	559	47	27
Perry	326	2.9	26 655	3 001	102	15	7	7	33	120	131	11	7
Pike......................	1 192	4.6	29 761	2 749	503	90	38	99	155	404	730	50	38
Pontotoc..................	904	4.0	29 212	2 806	411	58	34	76	94	240	580	40	34
Prentiss..................	692	3.7	27 218	2 966	244	42	19	26	80	240	332	26	19
Quitman...................	214	-7.7	27 921	2 927	41	8	3	14	27	93	66	6	3
Rankin....................	5 922	4.1	39 994	1 176	2 580	369	190	465	763	1 093	3 604	233	190
Scott.....................	841	9.2	29 556	2 777	431	79	35	117	76	261	663	38	35
Sharkey...................	142	-14.7	30 511	2 648	41	7	3	6	24	61	57	4	3
Simpson...................	953	5.6	34 710	1 982	231	40	18	136	91	302	425	26	18
Smith.....................	531	5.2	32 824	2 309	116	21	9	132	45	135	279	13	9
Stone.....................	516	1.8	28 893	2 839	143	25	11	13	65	175	193	15	11

1. Based on the resident population estimated as of July 1 of the year shown.

Table B. States and Counties — Earnings, Social Security, and Housing

STATE County	Earnings, 2014 (cont.) Percent by selected industries									Social Security beneficiaries, December 2014		Supplemental Security Income recipients, December 2014	Housing units, 2015	
	Farm	Mining	Construction	Manufacturing	Information: professional, scientific, technical services	Retail trade	Finance, insurance, real estate and leasing	Health care and social assistance	Government	Number	Rate[1]		Total	Percent change, 2010–2014
	75	76	77	78	79	80	81	82	83	84	85	86	87	88
MISSISSIPPI	3.1	2.1	6.4	12.9	5.5	7.4	5.4	10.7	21.9	640 772	214	125 595	1 300 892	2.1
Adams	0.8	14.3	6.0	4.5	4.4	9.8	4.8	D	12.7	7 940	249	1 873	14 611	-0.3
Alcorn	0.8	0.0	4.5	20.6	2.6	10.7	4.6	10.9	21.0	9 955	267	1 694	17 115	0.2
Amite	17.3	D	5.3	7.5	D	6.7	D	D	11.3	3 210	255	553	6 637	0.0
Attala	5.5	0.5	16.0	10.6	3.3	11.6	3.5	D	20.1	4 345	227	992	9 131	0.1
Benton	6.1	0.0	3.9	9.5	D	D	D	6.2	26.6	2 190	263	558	4 200	0.3
Bolivar	7.6	0.0	3.7	15.4	D	12.3	3.3	14.1	19.6	7 905	234	3 080	14 318	1.7
Calhoun	14.0	0.0	2.0	21.1	2.3	9.2	4.9	D	19.5	3 880	263	711	6 926	0.2
Carroll	0.8	D	16.7	11.2	D	4.7	D	D	24.6	2 315	226	388	5 064	0.2
Chickasaw	13.2	0.0	2.4	38.7	1.6	7.7	2.5	D	13.5	4 635	267	1 013	7 511	0.0
Choctaw	5.0	D	3.0	10.7	D	4.8	D	D	17.7	2 665	321	431	4 156	0.1
Claiborne	3.5	0.0	D	2.9	1.5	2.6	D	D	31.7	2 030	221	695	4 224	0.1
Clarke	8.0	11.8	7.3	10.2	D	6.6	D	D	18.6	4 555	280	817	7 876	0.0
Clay	23.5	D	5.0	10.2	3.8	8.6	3.6	D	11.4	4 830	240	988	9 196	0.2
Coahoma	1.5	0.0	2.5	8.1	4.8	7.9	8.2	D	22.1	5 745	231	2 208	10 738	-0.5
Copiah	6.2	2.3	4.5	29.1	D	7.4	2.4	D	17.7	6 875	238	1 593	12 139	-0.4
Covington	22.4	0.7	7.6	14.9	D	5.8	2.8	D	17.3	4 800	248	1 064	8 517	0.2
DeSoto	0.2	D	9.0	8.6	3.2	10.4	4.9	12.0	12.5	28 185	165	2 763	64 856	5.2
Forrest	0.2	1.0	5.7	7.6	4.4	7.8	5.0	17.2	27.8	14 440	190	2 843	32 722	1.3
Franklin	6.3	D	6.6	3.6	10.4	5.8	D	D	33.4	2 015	259	442	4 160	0.1
George	1.0	D	18.6	7.7	3.7	10.9	3.6	5.9	25.8	5 310	228	786	9 364	0.4
Greene	8.5	2.1	D	D	D	7.0	D	5.2	36.9	2 795	195	439	5 126	0.1
Grenada	0.9	0.0	2.0	28.7	D	9.6	4.7	D	19.3	6 145	284	1 382	10 199	0.4
Hancock	0.0	D	7.5	8.1	11.4	5.1	2.6	D	36.2	10 415	226	1 263	24 083	10.1
Harrison	0.0	D	5.8	5.8	5.0	7.4	4.8	7.8	34.8	38 555	194	6 316	90 749	6.5
Hinds	0.2	4.3	4.1	2.9	8.9	5.4	8.8	14.8	29.9	45 115	185	11 123	104 544	1.1
Holmes	0.7	D	2.7	14.2	3.4	8.1	6.5	D	33.5	4 705	254	2 069	8 420	0.1
Humphreys	19.2	0.0	2.8	24.0	D	5.3	7.4	D	14.2	2 230	254	1 075	3 827	-0.7
Issaquena	21.6	0.0	D	0.0	D	D	D	D	30.1	195	141	69	558	-0.4
Itawamba	2.9	D	11.7	30.6	1.3	6.7	2.6	D	16.9	6 305	269	630	10 172	0.5
Jackson	-0.1	0.3	8.6	38.4	5.4	4.5	3.0	6.2	18.2	29 180	206	3 260	61 365	2.2
Jasper	17.1	5.4	3.8	25.5	4.8	4.9	D	D	16.3	4 705	284	907	8 223	0.1
Jefferson	17.7	D	1.6	D	D	3.3	D	10.9	37.2	1 890	250	744	3 679	0.1
Jefferson Davis	14.9	D	18.0	2.0	2.9	7.3	D	D	25.0	3 200	270	626	5 883	0.2
Jones	4.9	14.8	6.7	19.4	D	5.3	3.9	4.5	17.9	16 060	235	2 696	28 660	0.8
Kemper	3.9	D	58.0	3.6	D	1.6	D	D	9.9	2 270	222	537	4 736	0.3
Lafayette	0.4	D	5.4	7.8	9.0	6.6	6.3	13.8	34.2	7 690	147	963	24 445	7.5
Lamar	1.7	1.3	5.6	1.4	D	15.7	6.9	19.7	13.8	9 765	163	1 504	24 298	0.9
Lauderdale	0.1	D	4.3	7.8	4.6	9.0	5.1	20.3	20.8	16 340	206	3 263	35 013	0.9
Lawrence	18.7	1.1	7.8	29.9	D	4.5	D	3.7	15.8	3 350	267	606	6 043	0.4
Leake	29.8	0.2	D	D	D	7.8	3.0	D	11.3	5 225	225	1 032	9 424	0.1
Lee	0.4	0.0	3.3	19.4	6.3	9.1	6.1	19.4	10.3	18 655	219	3 382	36 303	1.2
Leflore	4.7	D	8.0	11.0	5.3	7.2	3.6	8.8	28.7	7 160	227	2 816	13 163	-0.3
Lincoln	5.3	3.2	7.7	8.8	3.6	9.8	3.9	13.8	14.2	8 095	233	1 399	15 282	0.2
Lowndes	0.1	0.6	8.0	18.8	3.5	8.0	4.1	12.2	22.3	12 830	215	2 470	27 067	1.9
Madison	0.0	6.6	6.2	13.9	14.6	7.3	11.3	8.2	6.4	16 660	164	2 145	41 842	8.5
Marion	8.7	9.3	10.7	4.4	D	8.8	3.7	D	13.4	6 460	251	1 277	11 843	0.1
Marshall	1.8	0.0	11.5	11.7	D	8.4	7.5	D	19.1	8 305	229	1 724	15 139	1.7
Monroe	3.3	1.7	12.9	30.3	D	6.2	2.6	D	13.1	9 815	273	1 418	16 446	-0.1
Montgomery	1.8	0.0	5.4	2.5	3.5	9.1	D	D	24.7	3 205	310	723	5 502	5.9
Neshoba	13.2	D	27.0	3.7	1.3	6.1	1.7	D	31.3	5 730	195	1 050	12 362	0.0
Newton	15.1	0.1	5.8	14.3	1.6	6.5	1.9	D	27.8	6 020	276	1 012	9 375	0.0
Noxubee	27.4	D	3.7	16.4	D	7.9	D	D	21.1	2 790	251	1 017	5 161	-0.2
Oktibbeha	0.5	0.0	3.2	8.2	D	6.0	3.3	6.6	50.0	7 210	146	1 720	21 542	2.8
Panola	2.3	0.1	6.4	16.1	8.0	9.9	4.5	D	17.7	8 190	238	2 172	14 732	0.3
Pearl River	0.4	0.4	9.4	7.5	D	13.2	5.3	D	28.6	13 390	242	1 871	24 699	3.2
Perry	3.4	0.6	2.0	34.2	1.2	5.4	D	10.1	17.4	3 000	246	537	5 525	0.1
Pike	2.8	1.2	2.7	13.8	3.3	13.0	4.9	8.7	26.0	9 735	244	2 391	17 889	0.2
Pontotoc	1.4	0.0	3.1	49.3	2.7	6.0	2.3	D	10.6	7 125	231	901	12 580	1.1
Prentiss	1.8	0.0	6.5	23.1	D	7.2	3.8	D	22.4	6 685	263	723	11 085	0.3
Quitman	11.5	D	D	D	D	D	5.5	D	24.2	1 995	260	767	3 591	0.1
Rankin	1.5	1.8	9.2	7.3	4.8	9.5	8.2	10.8	13.9	27 140	183	2 740	58 726	4.0
Scott	14.8	0.1	4.8	42.5	D	5.7	2.1	5.7	10.5	6 850	241	1 422	11 487	0.1
Sharkey	15.9	D	1.4	0.0	D	8.9	5.9	D	32.5	1 200	259	432	2 122	1.0
Simpson	21.1	0.7	4.7	1.8	D	7.2	4.6	D	16.9	6 675	242	1 384	11 944	0.1
Smith	42.8	D	2.2	20.6	2.8	2.3	D	2.9	9.9	2 840	176	542	7 249	0.2
Stone	1.9	D	3.2	16.9	3.7	9.3	3.7	D	28.7	3 865	216	648	7 281	1.7

1. Per 1,000 resident population estimated as of July 1 of the year shown.

Table B. States and Counties — Housing, Labor Force, and Employment

STATE County	Housing units, 2010–2014 Occupied units		Owner-occupied	Median owner cost as a percent of income		Renter-occupied		Sub-stand-ard units[4] (percent)	Civilian labor force, 2015		Unemployment		Civilian employment,[6] 2010–2014	Percent	
	Total	Percent	Median value[1]	With a mort-gage	Without a mort-gage[2]	Median rent[3]	Median rent as a per-cent of income[2]		Total	Percent change, 2014–2015	Total	Rate[5]	Total	Manage-ment, business, science and arts	Con-struction, produc-tion, and mainte-nance occu-pations
	89	90	91	92	93	94	95	96	97	98	99	100	101	102	103
MISSISSIPPI	1 092 627	68.9	100 800	22.6	11.9	714	32.0	3.4	1 272 661	1.9	83 013	6.5	1 198 828	31.1	27.2
Adams	12 081	66.0	86 800	24.8	13.4	613	34.0	3.4	11 628	0.1	941	8.1	10 748	28.9	24.7
Alcorn	14 651	70.4	82 100	23.1	11.7	608	29.0	3.5	15 795	4.2	908	5.7	14 731	29.2	30.1
Amite	5 073	84.0	67 600	27.2	14.1	636	34.7	2.3	4 566	2.5	352	7.7	4 347	20.5	37.2
Attala	7 341	70.8	71 800	21.1	11.7	538	29.9	3.7	7 055	0.0	545	7.7	6 692	27.1	35.6
Benton	3 040	83.0	74 300	30.1	12.6	583	49.7	3.0	3 041	2.0	244	8.0	3 105	20.2	41.6
Bolivar	12 377	56.2	84 900	23.5	12.6	576	30.8	4.7	13 489	1.3	1 072	7.9	12 459	31.0	23.8
Calhoun	5 913	71.3	62 100	21.8	12.6	503	31.5	2.9	6 159	-1.4	390	6.3	5 813	22.8	42.3
Carroll	3 788	84.5	74 600	18.8	15.5	480	24.7	1.6	3 452	1.2	291	8.4	3 647	30.8	31.2
Chickasaw	6 560	74.4	65 300	26.9	12.0	518	30.5	2.4	7 223	0.1	561	7.8	6 322	17.4	47.2
Choctaw	3 415	71.9	65 100	27.0	13.1	525	28.7	4.2	3 795	6.2	234	6.2	3 003	28.7	36.8
Claiborne	3 163	76.5	54 300	27.8	16.1	551	38.5	6.9	3 097	-0.6	401	12.9	2 503	19.5	27.2
Clarke	6 454	83.9	58 200	24.5	12.7	620	28.4	3.3	6 160	-1.8	490	8.0	6 075	27.8	36.6
Clay	7 765	70.3	78 800	26.4	13.5	640	38.6	2.9	8 093	1.3	779	9.6	7 491	26.7	31.3
Coahoma	9 350	53.8	58 100	23.1	14.1	572	30.5	3.6	9 487	-0.9	975	10.3	8 647	30.6	24.0
Copiah	10 004	76.3	80 700	22.9	12.2	628	30.0	4.0	11 387	1.8	832	7.3	10 387	27.1	31.9
Covington	6 959	82.1	72 300	23.8	12.3	626	32.8	2.2	8 010	2.1	474	5.9	6 898	21.7	35.9
DeSoto	58 957	74.0	151 200	21.3	10.1	955	28.6	2.5	83 862	3.0	4 100	4.9	80 942	33.5	26.1
Forrest	27 661	55.8	115 300	22.3	12.2	719	35.9	2.9	33 321	3.1	2 126	6.4	32 024	33.2	23.0
Franklin	3 347	79.4	71 500	19.9	10.3	522	29.0	2.2	2 972	2.1	232	7.8	3 021	25.1	43.5
George	7 574	86.1	93 800	20.8	10.0	804	40.7	3.1	8 906	-0.3	674	7.6	8 339	27.7	40.4
Greene	4 257	85.4	84 300	21.8	13.5	520	35.6	4.9	4 426	0.6	348	7.9	3 923	26.7	41.8
Grenada	7 581	75.2	88 800	25.2	12.2	535	31.9	2.2	9 549	2.6	583	6.1	8 039	25.6	36.4
Hancock	18 413	73.6	127 800	24.0	12.3	763	30.5	3.7	18 688	1.0	1 227	6.6	18 354	29.9	26.4
Harrison	74 369	59.1	139 600	25.0	11.3	846	32.7	3.4	85 601	0.9	5 181	6.1	83 107	27.7	22.6
Hinds	88 321	59.8	107 000	22.5	10.6	772	35.5	3.7	110 730	2.3	6 737	6.1	105 565	32.5	20.8
Holmes	6 396	66.7	47 900	32.6	16.2	481	30.4	3.9	6 168	0.4	748	12.1	5 566	23.1	36.8
Humphreys	3 051	55.3	63 200	31.7	14.9	551	33.7	6.2	2 485	-3.3	321	12.9	2 610	25.9	37.3
Issaquena	427	64.6	63 500	26.3	14.3	450	30.3	4.2	427	0.0	72	16.9	324	18.2	43.2
Itawamba	8 852	77.9	81 300	22.0	11.3	613	28.5	2.5	10 264	3.6	596	5.8	9 223	28.1	41.3
Jackson	50 388	71.1	120 500	22.7	10.7	836	30.8	2.6	59 519	0.6	4 257	7.2	58 951	30.8	27.0
Jasper	6 923	81.9	70 600	23.9	14.4	712	27.4	3.8	6 472	0.6	509	7.9	6 286	24.3	39.9
Jefferson	2 553	63.1	62 400	27.3	14.8	457	36.2	4.0	2 307	-4.0	344	14.9	1 918	28.7	23.7
Jefferson Davis	4 947	78.9	77 600	27.1	17.4	725	40.2	4.5	4 173	1.4	365	8.7	4 268	21.6	38.4
Jones	24 352	73.3	85 600	21.9	11.9	618	29.3	4.5	26 988	1.1	1 633	6.1	26 538	28.4	34.5
Kemper	3 661	77.8	65 800	24.8	14.2	407	27.1	2.9	3 627	-3.4	378	10.4	3 588	17.5	39.5
Lafayette	16 557	59.3	151 700	21.2	11.3	799	41.8	2.7	24 577	5.5	1 363	5.5	21 711	36.9	19.9
Lamar	21 578	67.0	161 300	21.8	10.6	822	30.9	2.9	28 918	4.0	1 413	4.9	26 733	38.1	20.9
Lauderdale	29 662	65.1	87 800	23.2	11.2	668	29.9	3.6	31 996	-1.9	2 148	6.7	32 410	31.4	22.9
Lawrence	4 829	79.0	84 700	21.4	13.9	652	29.8	2.2	4 810	6.1	357	7.4	4 740	29.7	36.5
Leake	8 165	73.8	74 200	19.7	14.6	605	27.6	6.4	7 996	2.0	505	6.3	8 310	27.7	35.0
Lee	31 733	69.2	111 300	22.1	10.7	661	29.8	2.5	40 185	3.3	2 263	5.6	36 930	30.8	28.4
Leflore	10 891	50.6	70 000	23.0	14.1	556	37.9	5.9	10 586	0.2	1 157	10.9	9 776	30.4	25.3
Lincoln	13 091	74.2	84 200	21.9	12.7	627	33.0	3.6	14 361	4.4	887	6.2	12 990	30.6	31.8
Lowndes	23 431	62.0	113 400	23.4	10.0	706	34.3	2.3	25 375	0.3	1 795	7.1	23 762	30.0	26.9
Madison	36 699	71.4	204 100	20.6	10.0	890	27.7	3.1	51 290	3.0	2 384	4.6	47 611	47.3	15.3
Marion	9 903	75.8	77 500	23.4	13.6	598	41.4	4.4	10 139	2.3	754	7.4	9 134	27.9	31.8
Marshall	13 221	77.4	88 300	24.3	14.1	728	31.7	4.2	14 663	2.0	1 076	7.3	14 081	21.3	35.2
Monroe	13 777	77.0	77 900	22.2	12.4	561	27.7	3.1	15 610	0.9	1 168	7.5	13 912	26.8	32.4
Montgomery	4 169	74.9	73 300	22.3	13.8	597	30.4	3.2	4 251	1.2	335	7.9	3 708	30.7	31.5
Neshoba	10 833	73.8	78 400	22.5	12.0	592	25.2	5.7	10 739	-0.5	667	6.2	12 028	28.9	27.3
Newton	8 113	77.2	71 800	22.1	12.0	623	25.8	3.5	8 820	0.4	550	6.2	8 676	33.6	31.5
Noxubee	4 193	69.8	64 800	30.1	14.6	533	31.2	1.3	4 011	0.1	396	9.9	3 869	20.4	39.8
Oktibbeha	17 778	52.5	134 600	20.7	12.3	713	40.9	2.0	22 553	2.0	1 411	6.3	19 829	42.4	16.6
Panola	11 868	75.1	78 400	21.8	12.6	660	30.3	4.1	13 608	1.3	1 200	8.8	12 288	30.4	30.1
Pearl River	20 615	76.2	112 400	23.7	12.5	790	33.1	3.0	22 779	1.9	1 436	6.3	20 312	31.9	29.1
Perry	4 387	84.0	76 900	22.9	13.0	681	29.6	4.1	4 336	3.0	347	8.0	4 057	22.2	39.5
Pike	14 809	67.2	79 600	23.2	12.4	629	33.9	2.6	14 835	1.9	1 098	7.4	14 414	28.4	31.8
Pontotoc	10 223	75.8	81 300	21.5	11.6	630	25.0	4.0	14 015	3.8	790	5.6	12 869	25.0	39.1
Prentiss	9 749	73.3	76 400	23.9	11.5	518	29.0	1.6	11 070	1.8	677	6.1	9 467	21.6	38.6
Quitman	3 092	66.3	53 800	29.5	13.7	543	34.5	3.1	2 722	-1.1	294	10.8	2 492	30.5	25.9
Rankin	53 527	74.7	151 100	20.2	10.0	889	28.1	2.4	73 278	3.1	3 076	4.2	68 683	41.3	19.3
Scott	9 767	73.8	69 000	22.6	13.0	596	27.2	6.5	13 127	3.5	644	4.9	10 880	24.6	37.8
Sharkey	1 798	59.8	59 100	23.1	10.1	519	30.4	5.6	1 752	-1.2	173	9.9	1 723	35.8	20.0
Simpson	9 820	77.5	76 900	23.1	12.0	604	29.5	6.2	11 107	3.1	660	5.9	10 371	26.0	34.8
Smith	6 204	82.4	76 800	21.1	12.1	594	24.7	5.0	6 831	1.4	375	5.5	6 512	25.0	37.3
Stone	5 763	82.2	107 400	23.9	10.0	706	29.4	3.2	6 447	1.7	483	7.5	6 797	22.5	31.2

1. Specified owner-occupied units.   2. A value of 10.0 represents 10 percent or less; a value of 50.0 represents 50 percent or more.   3. Specified renter-occupied units.   4. Overcrowded or lacking complete plumbing facilities.   5. Percent of civilian labor force.   6. Persons 16 years old and over.

Table B. States and Counties — Nonfarm Employment and Agriculture

	Private nonfarm establishments, employment and payroll, 2014									Agriculture, 2012			
		Employment						Annual payroll		Farms			
											Percent with:		
STATE County	Number of establishments	Total	Health care and social assistance	Manufacturing	Retail trade	Finance and insurance	Professional, scientific, and technical services	Total (mil dol)	Average per employee (dollars)	Number	Fewer than 50 acres	500 acres or more	Farm operators whose principal occupation is farming (percent)
	104	105	106	107	108	109	110	111	112	113	114	115	116
MISSISSIPPI	58 541	912 014	163 145	140 188	140 778	33 377	30 661	32 777	35 939	38 076	28.1	11.8	43.0
Adams	817	10 539	1 825	504	2 189	D	219	351	33 292	189	33.9	10.6	45.0
Alcorn	793	11 555	2 516	2 401	2 208	318	387	379	32 779	505	27.3	5.3	30.9
Amite	165	1 186	157	266	149	D	D	39	32 481	590	27.1	8.6	46.8
Attala	334	4 492	D	728	786	136	59	144	31 975	456	20.4	10.3	34.2
Benton	58	937	134	190	120	D	D	25	26 763	312	16.3	9.0	36.9
Bolivar	729	8 799	1 728	1 517	1 520	268	176	277	31 536	419	23.4	45.8	57.0
Calhoun	262	2 623	502	931	411	D	D	78	29 779	621	20.3	11.9	33.3
Carroll	102	590	D	D	83	20	D	17	29 592	503	18.1	17.7	33.6
Chickasaw	339	5 208	D	3 038	691	D	57	148	28 466	575	20.7	12.2	34.4
Choctaw	112	1 219	218	226	146	23	22	51	41 488	254	15.0	11.4	42.9
Claiborne	103	1 952	467	D	D	D	13	115	59 128	249	16.9	17.7	48.6
Clarke	224	2 874	D	487	324	96	43	100	34 668	329	32.5	4.9	47.4
Clay	351	4 012	624	D	750	123	D	142	35 420	420	20.5	12.1	45.7
Coahoma	559	6 524	1 865	677	1 099	232	230	221	33 837	273	22.0	44.3	63.0
Copiah	436	5 514	693	1 817	787	171	71	156	28 237	506	26.3	8.9	44.5
Covington	329	3 974	489	1 399	568	110	D	119	29 948	493	27.8	6.9	45.8
DeSoto	2 681	47 635	5 973	3 809	8 426	932	909	1 508	31 662	433	44.3	9.7	50.1
Forrest	1 848	31 621	7 888	3 096	4 508	1 046	1 030	1 188	37 565	359	49.0	3.9	36.5
Franklin	116	1 168	340	66	149	D	D	39	33 798	189	19.6	13.2	34.4
George	311	3 514	763	347	995	85	107	112	31 981	573	52.5	1.9	51.5
Greene	114	788	D	D	204	D	D	24	30 602	395	33.2	7.3	37.7
Grenada	553	8 265	1 196	2 567	1 393	221	201	272	32 915	316	17.4	14.9	41.8
Hancock	686	9 378	992	814	1 552	214	1 828	381	40 670	248	46.4	2.0	42.3
Harrison	4 120	70 791	13 783	3 286	11 377	2 554	2 348	2 550	36 018	331	66.2	1.5	36.0
Hinds	5 379	98 269	31 340	3 719	11 235	4 961	5 001	4 253	43 281	1 047	32.5	11.3	39.3
Holmes	242	2 046	422	436	436	89	44	54	26 268	531	18.1	19.0	28.2
Humphreys	152	1 733	183	D	299	63	D	47	27 096	262	21.4	35.9	50.8
Issaquena	9	57	D	NA	NA	D	NA	2	29 263	97	11.3	42.3	53.6
Itawamba	351	5 063	541	2 054	676	174	30	165	32 646	443	15.8	7.0	40.4
Jackson	2 233	43 347	5 295	D	5 107	989	1 570	1 990	45 916	409	62.3	2.4	41.6
Jasper	220	3 203	D	1 480	369	108	63	120	37 513	445	22.0	8.1	47.4
Jefferson	58	653	264	D	87	D	NA	23	35 204	277	22.4	15.5	51.6
Jefferson Davis	153	1 201	D	D	242	D	28	56	46 476	337	23.7	6.5	57.3
Jones	1 316	25 266	2 952	D	3 020	D	449	959	37 941	927	38.2	2.9	49.6
Kemper	133	1 636	D	D	141	52	D	69	42 117	378	15.9	12.7	41.8
Lafayette	1 103	14 642	2 552	1 538	2 639	464	981	484	33 063	449	17.8	8.9	40.3
Lamar	1 298	16 298	3 210	144	4 982	591	732	481	29 527	424	42.0	4.5	34.2
Lauderdale	1 960	31 011	7 368	2 264	5 450	1 652	D	1 083	34 937	373	34.9	6.2	41.8
Lawrence	168	1 697	201	684	D	D	D	82	48 353	397	28.5	6.0	42.3
Leake	293	4 580	625	D	760	D	47	121	26 509	637	25.0	6.4	44.0
Lee	2 411	44 656	7 367	8 614	7 081	2 350	1 248	1 586	35 515	525	34.3	7.8	48.4
Leflore	733	12 461	2 847	2 620	1 773	398	340	391	31 396	300	14.0	43.7	54.7
Lincoln	785	10 126	1 692	785	1 896	348	327	348	34 357	595	30.4	5.9	39.7
Lowndes	1 478	20 422	2 981	3 936	3 546	499	564	820	40 142	413	27.4	15.7	30.3
Madison	2 972	46 526	3 773	6 764	7 022	3 137	3 448	1 908	41 014	685	32.4	14.5	32.7
Marion	586	6 562	878	D	1 231	283	180	217	33 075	552	32.2	5.8	48.7
Marshall	412	6 626	1 397	D	844	309	D	194	29 262	573	25.7	15.4	39.4
Monroe	648	7 853	1 548	2 376	1 091	212	94	289	36 817	726	25.1	13.2	40.8
Montgomery	210	2 399	672	194	475	103	27	69	28 562	345	15.7	14.8	42.3
Neshoba	503	9 034	D	D	1 260	285	354	395	43 699	677	29.1	5.0	52.1
Newton	322	3 438	707	882	626	D	45	118	34 208	562	30.1	7.7	52.3
Noxubee	179	1 694	292	516	323	D	D	52	30 548	565	21.6	20.4	42.3
Oktibbeha	854	11 215	1 629	D	2 016	344	402	314	28 017	402	24.6	12.7	42.8
Panola	600	8 187	1 413	1 751	1 587	316	115	268	32 782	745	14.6	16.4	37.7
Pearl River	810	7 600	1 048	551	1 989	305	375	227	29 924	813	47.6	5.3	42.6
Perry	145	1 556	250	606	265	D	13	74	47 700	310	40.3	3.5	50.3
Pike	962	12 690	2 532	2 440	2 605	397	282	386	30 424	531	35.8	4.0	48.2
Pontotoc	494	11 439	797	7 475	961	215	123	328	28 689	889	29.9	6.6	26.4
Prentiss	482	5 909	767	1 784	893	D	183	165	27 874	504	24.8	6.5	32.1
Quitman	104	729	D	D	136	D	D	18	25 023	347	18.7	27.7	39.2
Rankin	3 484	54 164	8 604	4 212	9 471	2 579	1 371	1 996	36 850	670	43.4	8.7	43.1
Scott	471	9 938	633	5 517	1 192	D	96	304	30 622	716	31.6	6.4	51.5
Sharkey	123	773	207	NA	166	D	16	24	30 401	128	16.4	50.8	61.7
Simpson	423	5 915	2 388	362	997	505	98	161	27 271	606	29.4	5.3	54.1
Smith	172	2 290	D	976	255	64	122	81	35 369	637	27.6	4.9	62.0
Stone	271	2 776	451	D	641	118	98	82	29 497	271	43.9	5.9	42.1

Table B. States and Counties — **Agriculture**

	Agriculture, 2012 (cont.)														
	Land in farms					Value of land and buildings (dollars)			Value of products sold				Percent of farms with sales of:		Government payments	
			Acres								Percent from:					
STATE County	Acreage (1,000)	Percent change, 2007–2012	Average size of farm	Total irrigated (1,000)	Total cropland (1,000)	Average per farm	Average per acre	Value of machinery and equipment, average per farm (dollars)	Total (mil dol)	Average per farm (dollars)	Crops	Livestock and poultry products	$10,000 or more	$100,000 or more	Total ($1,000)	Percent of farms
	117	118	119	120	121	122	123	124	125	126	127	128	129	130	131	132
MISSISSIPPI	10 931	-4.6	287	1 652.0	5 075.6	652 593	2 273	91 910	6 441.0	169 162	46.2	53.8	33.0	12.4	181 205	43.3
Adams	66	-5.6	349	D	20.3	757 720	2 170	73 026	9.9	52 228	85.4	14.6	18.5	4.2	1 107	38.1
Alcorn	94	-0.3	185	D	43.3	345 842	1 866	59 352	20.9	41 461	84.6	15.4	25.1	3.6	795	50.7
Amite	121	10.2	205	0.1	23.0	690 939	3 365	66 768	68.4	115 958	5.6	94.4	32.4	8.8	1 025	43.4
Attala	125	-8.6	275	0.4	29.1	495 542	1 801	48 726	23.1	50 686	54.8	45.2	22.4	4.2	1 359	52.0
Benton	82	-4.3	264	D	29.2	421 772	1 596	49 298	14.5	46 596	72.8	27.2	19.6	6.7	740	56.4
Bolivar	390	-8.8	932	247.8	362.0	2 254 100	2 419	463 976	277.0	661 122	99.9	0.1	70.9	50.1	12 645	85.0
Calhoun	175	-13.3	282	1.2	80.1	520 758	1 844	98 725	78.5	126 446	92.9	7.1	34.5	12.1	3 146	73.4
Carroll	169	-11.1	336	12.3	57.8	631 318	1 879	75 996	36.5	72 620	86.9	13.1	30.0	8.3	2 451	46.1
Chickasaw	166	-7.0	289	3.0	67.2	533 009	1 847	69 757	60.9	105 897	49.6	50.4	34.6	10.3	2 924	65.0
Choctaw	63	-12.0	250	1.0	9.0	492 768	1 973	41 854	11.4	44 945	11.1	88.9	18.9	4.3	444	49.2
Claiborne	83	-11.5	334	D	22.0	671 028	2 011	54 072	11.4	45 864	77.2	22.8	25.3	3.6	1 125	55.0
Clarke	56	-12.9	171	0.4	13.9	404 097	2 358	59 161	33.5	101 763	4.5	95.5	24.9	5.2	160	17.6
Clay	130	-8.6	310	0.8	30.8	507 521	1 639	66 540	92.3	219 655	7.8	92.2	33.3	8.3	1 554	48.6
Coahoma	261	-13.8	956	138.0	226.8	2 411 634	2 523	406 249	179.6	657 799	96.1	3.9	62.3	50.2	10 498	86.4
Copiah	116	-11.8	229	0.2	18.4	523 654	2 286	58 763	61.4	121 336	10.4	89.6	29.1	6.7	527	32.8
Covington	106	-9.0	215	0.6	24.6	631 521	2 941	97 406	203.5	412 838	3.1	96.9	46.5	22.1	617	26.4
DeSoto	119	-16.2	274	17.2	81.2	723 771	2 641	84 483	50.0	115 386	90.2	9.8	24.5	9.0	1 866	25.4
Forrest	43	-6.1	119	0.8	9.8	406 844	3 416	65 822	20.8	58 075	22.8	77.2	27.9	5.8	598	24.2
Franklin	50	6.8	266	0.0	8.8	680 487	2 562	74 143	10.5	55 667	21.7	78.3	27.5	6.3	254	39.7
George	61	-10.6	106	0.5	19.3	357 428	3 361	75 084	22.7	39 620	84.8	15.2	27.2	4.4	421	16.6
Greene	69	34.8	174	0.2	16.2	379 203	2 175	91 420	32.8	83 139	30.5	69.5	26.6	6.8	300	13.2
Grenada	88	-20.8	280	1.1	25.8	511 345	1 828	51 522	11.6	36 775	59.4	40.6	26.9	4.7	1 414	63.6
Hancock	25	-40.2	102	0.1	4.8	403 952	3 964	38 907	2.7	10 988	D	D	27.4	1.6	175	14.1
Harrison	24	12.6	73	0.1	5.6	452 586	6 199	37 532	3.4	10 417	45.8	54.2	19.6	2.1	63	6.9
Hinds	251	-3.5	240	0.5	61.8	549 542	2 292	58 127	73.4	70 106	34.0	66.0	22.0	3.2	3 055	41.2
Holmes	238	4.2	447	51.1	119.8	938 991	2 098	99 501	93.4	175 972	97.7	2.3	25.4	9.8	5 781	66.9
Humphreys	194	-0.5	740	82.7	161.4	1 633 874	2 209	292 195	132.7	506 458	87.2	12.8	55.7	42.4	5 952	84.0
Issaquena	124	2.7	1 282	19.7	75.2	2 458 216	1 917	298 340	53.3	549 691	D	D	52.6	36.1	2 396	88.7
Itawamba	95	1.7	214	0.0	30.2	429 835	2 007	59 011	17.6	39 623	67.5	32.5	29.3	5.9	786	48.8
Jackson	38	-9.3	92	0.2	14.3	347 257	3 778	60 181	14.4	35 164	87.3	12.7	22.0	3.2	277	8.8
Jasper	97	7.1	218	0.0	14.1	436 222	1 998	73 629	97.2	218 366	1.6	98.4	36.2	16.0	545	27.0
Jefferson	86	-14.7	310	0.6	29.9	655 975	2 119	67 863	31.7	114 484	46.7	53.3	32.1	10.8	815	37.5
Jefferson Davis	59	-13.2	175	0.3	10.6	347 445	1 985	54 522	36.0	106 831	4.9	95.1	30.3	7.7	460	36.5
Jones	126	14.7	136	0.4	25.5	433 357	3 189	62 438	217.0	234 063	2.2	97.8	37.6	19.2	1 212	21.6
Kemper	124	-9.1	328	0.1	18.0	569 079	1 738	52 138	20.5	54 119	9.1	90.9	31.2	4.5	619	28.6
Lafayette	109	-4.8	242	0.6	26.9	543 419	2 242	56 581	8.9	19 904	73.3	26.7	22.7	3.1	1 120	50.3
Lamar	64	-12.3	151	0.2	13.2	544 656	3 602	64 014	25.0	59 033	13.8	86.2	36.3	6.4	565	25.0
Lauderdale	69	-17.4	185	0.1	14.6	441 753	2 387	46 413	5.4	14 453	50.1	49.9	21.4	0.8	252	17.2
Lawrence	73	-9.1	183	D	18.2	492 441	2 689	75 239	79.4	199 970	7.3	92.7	40.8	10.3	804	35.5
Leake	106	-16.7	167	0.1	22.6	446 077	2 678	58 912	283.3	444 706	0.9	99.1	38.9	21.4	711	34.5
Lee	133	-9.2	253	0.4	84.7	484 651	1 913	65 162	45.0	85 766	89.3	10.7	31.0	6.9	880	39.2
Leflore	293	-6.9	977	164.1	235.8	1 970 613	2 017	381 793	241.9	806 193	78.3	21.7	55.0	41.0	7 438	81.3
Lincoln	109	-12.8	183	0.2	20.1	547 086	2 997	65 555	69.9	117 405	4.6	95.4	37.3	9.2	615	25.7
Lowndes	119	-8.3	289	4.8	57.3	613 637	2 122	89 651	43.1	104 276	62.2	37.8	33.9	12.1	1 478	47.7
Madison	203	-8.8	296	0.1	68.6	776 399	2 619	67 238	33.3	48 600	82.6	17.4	19.9	6.7	3 611	45.5
Marion	82	-11.3	148	D	18.2	438 998	2 966	75 457	97.3	176 281	2.1	97.9	28.4	13.0	1 259	37.9
Marshall	203	5.3	355	3.5	70.0	699 567	1 972	81 276	32.7	57 079	84.1	15.9	30.7	7.7	1 667	47.3
Monroe	228	14.8	314	0.5	99.6	549 209	1 749	77 127	55.2	76 070	82.2	17.8	28.0	9.6	2 655	54.8
Montgomery	97	-0.1	282	0.7	26.8	501 565	1 779	64 942	20.1	58 339	54.5	45.5	26.4	7.2	1 257	52.2
Neshoba	101	-16.0	150	0.0	20.6	461 393	3 081	79 096	246.5	364 069	0.9	99.1	43.7	21.9	249	16.2
Newton	109	-9.4	194	0.6	22.6	404 137	2 083	65 811	102.4	182 242	4.2	95.8	37.0	15.5	659	22.1
Noxubee	213	-3.8	377	17.3	105.9	815 425	2 161	147 076	140.3	248 235	48.3	51.7	49.7	31.5	2 547	59.6
Oktibbeha	105	3.3	260	0.3	21.7	573 619	2 203	56 042	15.1	37 674	15.0	85.0	24.9	4.7	912	37.8
Panola	273	1.1	366	30.4	134.8	704 463	1 924	87 615	71.9	96 451	91.6	8.4	31.3	9.8	5 745	61.9
Pearl River	118	-12.8	146	1.0	23.0	465 647	3 200	48 637	17.6	21 654	45.7	54.3	28.2	3.4	735	14.8
Perry	44	5.8	140	0.5	12.1	401 719	2 862	68 168	21.8	70 442	23.7	76.3	31.6	7.4	513	23.9
Pike	72	-1.9	136	0.1	14.6	481 913	3 552	55 004	74.4	140 021	2.3	97.7	32.8	7.7	984	38.4
Pontotoc	153	4.7	172	D	64.2	312 294	1 819	55 052	24.7	27 747	76.8	23.2	24.9	5.2	2 249	64.2
Prentiss	93	-8.1	185	0.0	38.4	290 214	1 569	45 899	15.5	30 835	83.6	16.4	23.6	5.6	966	69.4
Quitman	209	-5.3	601	68.7	155.8	1 210 934	2 014	188 674	85.1	245 130	D	D	38.6	24.5	8 654	91.4
Rankin	126	-10.3	188	0.0	28.5	561 387	2 990	65 404	111.2	165 990	8.2	91.8	32.4	12.2	829	20.4
Scott	115	-9.2	161	0.1	27.8	406 497	2 528	85 180	270.8	378 270	1.7	98.3	41.3	16.9	476	20.3
Sharkey	155	-13.5	1 214	61.0	135.2	2 782 797	2 292	455 836	108.2	844 969	96.1	3.9	61.7	45.3	3 767	88.3
Simpson	110	-6.9	181	1.2	28.2	495 135	2 739	80 403	202.4	334 068	3.4	96.6	44.2	21.5	396	16.7
Smith	108	-1.3	170	0.1	26.2	502 821	2 956	74 466	251.1	394 133	3.0	97.0	49.1	25.9	427	11.8
Stone	46	-11.9	169	0.1	7.5	615 882	3 655	58 841	10.7	39 410	D	D	32.5	2.6	298	18.1

STATE County	Water use, 2010		Wholesale trade,[1] 2012				Retail trade,[2] 2012				Real estate and rental and leasing,[2] 2012			
	Total water withdrawn (mil gal/day)	Gallons withdrawn per person per day	Number of establish-ments	Number of employees	Sales (mil dol)	Annual payroll (mil dol)	Number of establish-ments	Number of employees	Sales (mil dol)	Annual payroll (mil dol)	Number of establish-ments	Number of employees	Receipts (mil dol)	Annual payroll (mil dol)
	133	134	135	136	137	138	139	140	141	142	143	144	145	146
MISSISSIPPI	3 933.0	1 325	2 484	30 351	28 303.0	1 373.6	11 594	136 032	37 053.2	2 968.4	2 374	10 235	1 709.3	334.1
Adams	7.5	233	35	265	169.6	10.0	176	2 119	488.7	47.6	36	135	17.6	3.9
Alcorn	6.7	182	35	D	D	D	172	2 119	538.0	49.0	23	225	12.2	3.8
Amite	2.2	165	7	62	14.0	1.5	30	162	39.2	3.5	3	4	0.5	0.1
Attala	4.5	231	13	D	D	D	78	807	192.5	15.5	10	29	3.8	0.8
Benton	2.5	290	NA	NA	NA	NA	16	112	24.4	2.5	NA	NA	NA	NA
Bolivar	440.8	12 910	29	329	763.8	15.0	161	1 535	371.2	31.5	45	126	18.6	3.2
Calhoun	2.8	188	14	175	81.1	5.2	58	401	95.2	8.1	4	10	0.7	0.3
Carroll	8.0	757	4	D	D	D	15	87	22.1	1.5	1	D	D	D
Chickasaw	9.7	558	15	90	69.8	3.1	83	687	153.4	11.7	8	17	2.6	0.5
Choctaw	15.0	1 755	2	D	D	D	27	152	25.1	2.7	1	D	D	D
Claiborne	35.9	3 742	1	D	D	D	24	152	35.3	3.4	NA	NA	NA	NA
Clarke	2.8	166	4	D	D	D	51	322	63.6	5.5	2	D	D	D
Clay	4.2	203	12	119	158.4	5.8	78	792	165.4	15.2	8	20	3.5	0.6
Coahoma	164.0	6 271	28	D	D	D	117	1 043	295.4	24.6	42	255	23.4	5.0
Copiah	10.2	347	15	87	46.3	2.8	83	834	181.5	15.7	8	75	5.0	1.6
Covington	6.3	319	12	68	116.9	2.4	68	522	188.3	12.1	8	27	3.2	0.5
DeSoto	35.7	221	120	2 840	3 232.4	127.2	495	7 957	2 320.9	193.3	97	331	83.8	11.6
Forrest	18.4	245	86	857	574.3	32.9	367	4 470	3 680.2	107.7	92	377	66.1	12.8
Franklin	1.3	158	4	D	D	D	17	113	29.0	2.4	4	30	1.1	0.8
George	3.5	154	11	75	54.2	2.5	77	900	229.5	17.2	6	D	D	D
Greene	8.3	575	3	D	D	D	26	211	48.3	3.9	3	11	0.6	0.1
Grenada	11.9	545	28	D	D	D	120	1 305	415.1	32.2	17	61	13.0	2.4
Hancock	8.2	187	15	64	10.3	3.3	126	1 328	346.2	30.2	28	90	10.0	2.3
Harrison	158.3	846	161	1 537	664.4	65.1	805	10 872	2 859.1	243.0	249	1 100	210.9	35.5
Hinds	60.5	247	270	3 476	2 274.4	166.5	869	11 093	3 072.3	276.4	278	1 544	319.8	66.3
Holmes	36.1	1 880	8	26	32.7	1.0	66	467	98.1	8.9	13	29	2.8	0.4
Humphreys	105.1	11 214	4	D	D	D	34	288	100.4	6.9	2	D	D	D
Issaquena	34.3	24 403	2	D	D	D	NA	NA	NA	NA	NA	NA	NA	NA
Itawamba	11.4	485	8	138	41.9	4.6	70	614	157.1	13.2	4	10	0.7	0.2
Jackson	520.3	3 725	60	564	236.3	22.5	426	4 828	1 220.5	109.0	98	424	49.4	12.7
Jasper	11.1	650	5	D	D	D	39	360	73.0	7.8	5	47	5.2	1.2
Jefferson	1.2	155	NA	NA	NA	NA	14	108	22.0	1.5	1	D	D	D
Jefferson Davis	5.7	460	2	D	D	D	39	207	61.6	4.4	2	D	D	D
Jones	16.4	241	75	D	D	D	241	3 000	796.4	61.7	54	228	64.8	13.0
Kemper	2.3	218	3	D	D	D	25	156	37.8	2.8	4	D	D	D
Lafayette	5.6	118	31	249	161.2	9.1	211	2 576	548.8	53.2	43	97	24.5	3.3
Lamar	12.1	218	36	D	D	D	282	4 802	1 041.4	86.7	61	D	D	D
Lauderdale	11.9	148	78	1 649	1 701.4	74.1	406	5 061	1 488.2	113.4	75	266	58.2	7.9
Lawrence	37.7	2 914	1	D	D	D	36	342	62.5	6.1	1	D	D	D
Leake	5.9	249	6	60	16.9	1.8	78	776	173.0	15.9	4	6	0.2	0.1
Lee	5.2	63	153	1 526	1 049.1	63.6	510	7 242	1 628.1	154.7	96	413	76.0	12.7
Leflore	200.8	6 214	31	D	D	D	154	1 637	465.6	36.2	42	D	D	D
Lincoln	7.4	211	31	D	D	D	159	1 783	540.6	40.8	26	86	13.8	2.9
Lowndes	41.0	685	80	D	D	D	311	3 578	736.5	73.2	63	186	26.3	4.8
Madison	15.1	159	135	2 220	4 549.4	118.2	497	6 698	1 616.9	148.1	139	909	133.7	32.4
Marion	5.1	187	16	163	121.6	5.1	134	1 182	280.1	25.6	25	110	18.3	3.6
Marshall	4.7	126	17	180	96.9	9.5	95	881	185.4	16.8	9	16	1.8	0.3
Monroe	25.0	675	18	182	150.2	8.0	136	1 213	259.2	22.9	14	51	6.0	1.6
Montgomery	1.9	170	3	D	D	D	51	478	144.4	9.0	4	18	1.7	0.4
Neshoba	4.6	156	20	277	448.0	13.2	110	1 180	288.5	25.0	11	256	9.3	6.8
Newton	4.2	194	8	39	8.0	1.1	70	707	137.4	14.2	5	12	1.9	0.2
Noxubee	22.3	1 931	10	80	58.4	1.8	43	320	93.5	7.0	NA	NA	NA	NA
Oktibbeha	6.1	128	15	436	187.3	17.5	163	1 924	472.0	38.3	59	178	30.5	4.8
Panola	36.4	1 049	31	536	576.6	24.2	170	1 555	471.8	33.0	15	66	10.0	2.1
Pearl River	7.2	129	25	D	D	D	172	1 793	477.3	43.4	19	52	7.7	1.1
Perry	22.6	1 842	4	D	D	D	34	250	62.4	4.4	3	D	D	D
Pike	9.4	232	52	383	206.4	13.9	223	2 458	603.8	51.1	39	140	27.1	3.6
Pontotoc	4.1	137	16	148	65.2	3.9	88	950	259.3	19.6	8	18	1.9	0.3
Prentiss	3.7	148	15	72	11.5	1.2	103	948	189.1	17.1	32	61	7.6	1.2
Quitman	135.1	16 431	4	D	D	D	23	128	28.6	2.3	6	D	D	D
Rankin	19.8	140	224	3 551	2 354.5	186.9	509	8 324	2 361.2	190.2	167	818	143.3	28.9
Scott	10.6	374	17	72	56.4	2.3	126	1 188	243.8	23.6	9	35	4.0	1.0
Sharkey	69.6	14 164	9	82	86.7	3.4	24	174	31.5	3.1	13	24	2.7	0.4
Simpson	5.8	210	13	79	27.0	2.6	90	1 020	234.7	20.5	12	41	5.8	1.0
Smith	4.9	298	5	42	15.5	1.2	35	210	47.2	4.0	NA	NA	NA	NA
Stone	4.8	269	10	29	10.9	1.0	54	582	166.6	13.4	8	22	1.5	0.3

1. Merchant wholesalers, except manufacturers' sales branches and offices.   2. Employer establishments.

Table B. States and Counties — Professional Services, Manufacturing, and Accommodation and Food Services

STATE County	Professional, scientific, and technical services, 2012				Manufacturing, 2012				Accommodation and food services, 2012			
	Number of establishments	Number of employees	Receipts (mil dol)	Annual payroll (mil dol)	Number of establishments	Number of employees	Receipts (mil dol)	Annual payroll (mil dol)	Number of establishments	Number of employees	Sales (mil dol)	Annual payroll (mil dol)
	147	148	149	150	151	152	153	154	155	156	157	158
MISSISSIPPI	4 747	30 205	4 023.3	1 449.9	2 252	132 789	66 441.6	5 919.1	5 177	116 238	6 999.2	1 765.0
Adams	52	225	24.8	8.8	18	650	155.0	27.4	89	1 698	89.3	24.0
Alcorn	51	358	27.0	11.2	41	2 118	1 092.7	89.7	69	1 200	55.3	17.0
Amite	9	23	1.6	0.5	6	177	48.3	7.8	3	24	1.4	0.4
Attala	28	62	7.0	2.3	18	656	175.6	20.3	23	D	D	D
Benton	2	D	D	D	6	151	D	5.4	NA	NA	NA	NA
Bolivar	44	173	20.6	7.3	18	1 458	405.8	65.4	53	911	39.4	9.4
Calhoun	18	26	2.3	0.7	18	883	271.1	29.0	10	D	D	D
Carroll	8	16	2.4	0.7	NA	NA	NA	NA	3	16	0.3	0.1
Chickasaw	15	63	4.5	1.7	44	2 817	483.8	87.7	20	D	D	D
Choctaw	8	16	1.5	0.6	6	205	56.8	7.8	8	D	D	D
Claiborne	7	13	1.3	0.3	4	83	D	3.3	11	153	7.7	1.7
Clarke	11	D	D	D	16	494	D	16.1	13	D	D	D
Clay	22	247	20.3	9.7	20	704	656.6	37.9	37	499	22.6	5.9
Coahoma	41	202	31.5	9.9	19	757	288.4	28.5	46	1 244	82.3	20.3
Copiah	28	103	12.1	3.3	20	2 106	626.8	67.6	34	436	16.8	4.1
Covington	18	87	4.3	1.8	11	1 337	432.0	35.0	31	D	D	D
DeSoto	183	989	99.0	27.1	102	3 453	1 269.5	157.5	292	6 498	311.3	80.7
Forrest	187	998	116.5	42.2	64	3 248	942.4	123.6	186	4 332	181.0	50.5
Franklin	9	37	2.6	1.5	3	D	D	D	5	17	0.5	0.1
George	17	100	8.7	2.7	15	300	D	22.1	26	378	15.4	3.6
Greene	4	9	1.0	0.5	4	12	D	0.4	7	D	D	D
Grenada	30	182	21.0	9.4	28	2 239	717.9	90.9	59	940	42.0	10.1
Hancock	96	2 163	316.6	135.0	31	819	D	58.5	86	D	D	D
Harrison	388	2 313	296.4	103.5	109	3 179	1 989.8	163.3	447	18 209	1 537.7	378.0
Hinds	657	5 244	815.6	320.2	131	3 730	1 374.4	183.1	473	9 261	475.6	126.7
Holmes	14	40	7.6	1.8	4	436	D	11.7	16	122	5.5	1.5
Humphreys	5	8	1.2	0.2	4	D	D	D	9	116	4.3	1.0
Issaquena	NA	NA	NA	NA	NA	NA	NA	NA	NA	NA	NA	NA
Itawamba	12	30	3.8	0.9	42	1 542	930.6	50.7	27	404	17.2	4.7
Jackson	208	1 545	179.8	74.1	75	15 152	D	1 119.9	256	D	D	D
Jasper	17	85	9.2	3.4	16	1 599	327.7	52.4	9	D	D	D
Jefferson	NA	NA	NA	NA	NA	NA	NA	NA	5	25	0.9	0.3
Jefferson Davis	13	22	2.5	0.8	4	13	D	D	10	111	4.7	1.1
Jones	95	456	57.2	17.4	61	6 427	1 656.1	245.6	101	D	D	D
Kemper	5	D	D	D	8	415	D	11.2	12	D	D	D
Lafayette	115	924	167.9	52.6	20	1 248	167.6	59.8	128	2 797	135.6	36.9
Lamar	115	740	94.0	35.9	20	177	D	5.8	121	2 475	118.1	31.9
Lauderdale	141	1 063	98.7	40.7	58	2 141	779.4	82.0	175	3 628	174.0	45.7
Lawrence	10	13	1.8	0.4	8	646	D	49.1	11	102	4.0	1.0
Leake	15	40	4.2	1.2	7	D	D	D	22	D	D	D
Lee	187	1 105	109.8	46.2	134	9 087	3 414.0	372.8	205	4 596	199.3	55.5
Leflore	45	317	46.2	13.1	29	D	D	53.2	73	1 285	63.4	16.6
Lincoln	57	265	42.5	13.1	33	1 189	D	53.2	61	984	43.6	10.8
Lowndes	102	514	54.5	26.2	66	4 223	3 543.9	231.2	121	2 163	98.5	26.6
Madison	367	2 907	546.2	180.0	63	5 749	4 568.0	338.7	239	4 681	230.1	60.9
Marion	46	236	22.2	9.1	18	508	75.1	17.3	45	507	22.4	5.5
Marshall	13	D	D	D	27	543	182.5	23.5	31	383	16.3	4.0
Monroe	33	94	11.5	2.5	51	2 356	1 592.6	104.8	47	D	D	D
Montgomery	9	32	3.2	0.7	9	268	D	10.1	21	D	D	D
Neshoba	28	168	22.4	9.1	12	529	175.3	21.6	42	640	27.1	6.6
Newton	21	38	3.9	1.5	15	1 077	D	43.3	26	D	D	D
Noxubee	5	21	1.2	0.2	19	475	139.0	15.6	9	148	6.1	1.7
Oktibbeha	76	441	46.1	15.1	23	1 210	569.1	55.3	108	2 744	125.2	32.8
Panola	31	139	21.1	4.2	31	1 579	631.5	70.7	53	901	42.7	11.2
Pearl River	56	347	28.3	12.9	42	562	224.1	26.2	86	1 158	49.0	13.4
Perry	7	39	4.4	2.1	7	645	D	41.3	6	43	1.9	0.5
Pike	69	291	27.5	11.9	29	2 287	514.9	69.1	76	1 478	68.5	16.2
Pontotoc	24	100	9.8	3.4	71	6 199	1 469.9	185.6	33	492	20.3	5.1
Prentiss	38	165	22.6	5.8	34	1 818	814.2	61.7	28	435	21.8	4.9
Quitman	4	D	D	D	NA	NA	NA	NA	6	D	D	D
Rankin	311	1 356	176.7	54.7	118	3 655	1 553.2	165.9	286	5 399	278.5	71.4
Scott	30	104	6.4	2.4	22	4 883	D	164.6	37	551	26.4	6.2
Sharkey	7	17	1.1	0.3	NA	NA	NA	NA	6	D	D	D
Simpson	27	106	10.0	3.6	11	249	D	8.8	39	599	31.7	6.7
Smith	12	126	11.5	1.7	14	886	321.1	37.3	7	D	D	D
Stone	23	91	6.6	2.4	12	593	251.9	25.3	32	440	21.0	5.2

1. Establishment subject to federal tax.

STATE County	Health care and social assistance, 2012				Other services, 2012				Nonemployer businesses, 2014		Value of residential construction authorized by building permits, 2015	
	Number of establishments	Number of employees	Receipts (mil dol)	Annual payroll (mil dol)	Number of establishments	Number of employees	Receipts (mil dol)	Annual payroll (mil dol)	Number	Receipts (mil dol)	New Construction ($1,000)	Number of housing units
	159	160	161	162	163	164	165	166	167	168	169	170
MISSISSIPPI	6 211	157 620	16 630.6	6 544.7	3 540	19 232	1 951.9	548.9	209 279	8 307.4	1 078 138	6 845
Adams	89	1 903	223.0	80.8	43	196	16.1	4.6	2 375	101.9	2 977	28
Alcorn	103	2 447	271.4	79.4	41	167	13.1	3.5	2 486	111.7	1 373	11
Amite	10	166	12.5	4.5	8	38	4.9	0.8	823	34.0	0	0
Attala	24	D	D	D	22	D	D	D	1 255	50.5	435	5
Benton	8	152	9.5	3.9	5	D	D	D	581	17.6	0	0
Bolivar	90	1 919	149.1	62.5	52	194	15.5	3.8	2 053	69.9	3 636	25
Calhoun	23	468	32.0	13.6	14	D	D	D	944	34.9	300	2
Carroll	5	88	5.5	2.1	7	11	0.9	0.2	667	26.2	NA	NA
Chickasaw	21	391	31.9	15.0	20	D	D	D	1 148	44.5	244	3
Choctaw	8	203	16.5	6.2	8	D	D	D	692	25.2	0	0
Claiborne	13	301	19.2	7.4	6	11	1.1	0.2	357	9.8	0	0
Clarke	18	421	32.9	13.0	17	D	D	D	982	35.7	0	0
Clay	27	696	62.2	25.8	26	113	9.0	2.5	1 359	47.3	1 739	11
Coahoma	82	1 733	184.7	66.0	34	131	8.0	2.2	1 757	57.0	2 703	17
Copiah	34	701	48.0	20.5	25	D	D	D	1 718	49.4	0	0
Covington	30	582	48.1	20.7	24	108	9.3	2.4	1 472	55.6	451	2
DeSoto	266	5 597	637.8	225.0	167	893	88.1	23.2	12 230	528.4	156 770	1 031
Forrest	202	7 779	873.5	421.1	100	648	54.6	15.5	5 281	212.8	8 973	204
Franklin	8	D	D	D	3	D	D	D	475	14.2	0	0
George	36	821	74.9	31.3	17	53	6.3	1.4	1 338	47.5	370	3
Greene	7	D	D	D	7	D	D	D	669	19.8	120	1
Grenada	74	1 323	115.4	45.4	27	103	10.8	2.5	1 404	51.8	1 168	7
Hancock	52	D	D	D	40	291	26.0	9.0	3 312	121.3	79 921	576
Harrison	460	12 318	1 560.5	648.9	271	1 604	155.7	42.7	14 138	579.1	124 965	800
Hinds	742	27 244	3 150.9	1 279.8	405	2 731	299.2	94.4	20 783	766.2	43 486	233
Holmes	35	395	26.9	10.8	12	191	6.2	2.1	1 169	35.3	753	8
Humphreys	20	242	19.7	7.7	11	36	2.0	0.6	581	20.5	0	0
Issaquena	1	D	D	D	NA	NA	NA	NA	85	2.8	NA	NA
Itawamba	29	D	D	D	19	D	D	D	1 301	58.3	635	4
Jackson	277	D	D	D	151	768	65.8	21.6	8 961	336.0	52 303	336
Jasper	12	299	20.5	8.9	11	D	D	D	991	31.2	558	2
Jefferson	14	305	19.6	9.1	5	D	D	D	506	11.5	0	0
Jefferson Davis	12	D	D	D	8	D	D	D	799	22.7	0	0
Jones	108	3 252	283.3	128.7	81	D	D	D	4 319	178.1	4 206	35
Kemper	10	249	14.5	6.9	3	D	D	D	551	12.1	NA	NA
Lafayette	126	2 671	363.2	110.3	63	397	87.9	19.1	3 905	209.2	82 792	672
Lamar	147	3 066	344.9	133.1	61	262	25.9	6.2	4 315	211.5	756	7
Lauderdale	222	7 919	883.6	347.0	131	663	63.0	16.1	4 961	168.6	20 901	115
Lawrence	20	192	14.0	4.8	7	27	3.8	1.0	718	29.4	0	0
Leake	25	598	36.8	16.0	11	40	3.5	1.1	1 184	42.1	0	0
Lee	284	7 976	1 089.4	387.2	128	1 144	105.3	41.5	6 050	257.4	15 277	111
Leflore	81	2 882	245.8	104.8	44	163	12.4	2.8	1 534	68.0	2 762	15
Lincoln	70	1 784	181.2	61.2	48	290	24.6	8.9	2 333	99.6	1 905	9
Lowndes	158	2 949	323.8	111.7	87	462	42.4	11.5	4 003	137.4	10 358	96
Madison	262	4 940	339.3	129.9	156	1 298	151.4	48.5	10 443	599.7	187 846	737
Marion	45	940	63.9	25.3	26	113	10.6	2.8	1 850	68.2	0	0
Marshall	28	1 405	90.8	30.3	29	193	19.3	5.5	2 741	105.4	13 563	107
Monroe	78	1 773	153.8	58.3	42	102	11.3	2.6	2 000	78.6	395	3
Montgomery	20	D	D	D	18	70	5.7	1.4	570	18.8	2 226	84
Neshoba	40	1 070	102.3	43.5	36	146	13.4	3.2	1 683	58.1	0	0
Newton	25	702	57.3	19.6	19	57	4.3	1.0	1 256	44.9	0	0
Noxubee	13	293	22.5	9.9	10	19	1.9	0.4	1 018	27.6	0	0
Oktibbeha	90	1 733	158.0	63.7	64	325	65.7	6.4	3 020	106.7	34 709	252
Panola	67	1 416	136.4	48.9	22	72	7.7	1.7	2 547	86.9	1 443	12
Pearl River	101	1 041	73.9	32.7	49	328	20.7	8.3	3 982	145.5	22 083	181
Perry	19	263	19.3	7.8	7	33	2.6	0.8	738	26.6	60	1
Pike	125	2 758	280.6	119.4	56	299	22.0	6.2	2 833	102.3	17 200	193
Pontotoc	39	D	D	D	32	D	D	D	1 974	79.8	1 317	32
Prentiss	42	858	65.4	25.7	29	101	9.8	2.1	1 507	48.5	2 267	16
Quitman	14	283	15.7	7.5	9	D	D	D	481	12.8	40	1
Rankin	316	8 559	1 023.6	371.7	214	1 114	125.0	35.2	12 037	555.5	123 626	559
Scott	34	D	D	D	39	95	9.7	2.4	1 561	52.2	638	3
Sharkey	12	219	18.9	8.0	11	59	7.0	1.1	386	12.4	400	1
Simpson	51	2 448	150.8	64.9	26	D	D	D	1 908	80.6	5 604	30
Smith	8	221	10.8	4.8	8	22	2.3	0.5	960	34.9	175	2
Stone	22	498	42.5	16.7	9	D	D	D	1 201	46.1	7 595	47

Table B. States and Counties — Government Employment and Payroll, and Local Government Finances

	Government employment and payroll, 2012									Local government finances, 2012				
			March payroll (percent of total)							General revenue				
												Taxes		
													Per capita[1] (dollars)	
STATE County	Full-time equivalent employees	March payroll (dollars)	Adminis-tration, judicial, and legal	Police and Corrections	Fire Protection	Highways and transpor-tation	Health and Welfare	Natural resources and utilities	Education and libraries	Total (mil dol)	Inter-govern-mental (mil dol)	Total (mil dol)	Total	Property
	171	172	173	174	175	176	177	178	179	180	181	182	183	184
MISSISSIPPI	X	X	X	X	X	X	X	X	X	X	X	X	X	X
Adams	1 489	4 260 491	9.2	8.0	2.4	5.1	26.3	5.5	41.4	139.6	46.8	32.7	1 016	894
Alcorn	2 243	7 489 226	3.0	3.6	1.7	1.3	54.6	4.0	31.8	263.0	70.9	24.2	650	610
Amite	299	736 289	14.3	7.8	0.1	5.8	2.2	1.8	66.9	23.6	11.3	6.5	502	498
Attala	932	2 477 820	6.6	4.7	2.3	3.4	21.1	4.4	56.3	69.8	32.7	16.3	850	818
Benton	295	719 394	10.6	6.4	0.0	3.6	0.4	1.7	76.1	18.5	13.0	3.5	406	392
Bolivar	1 582	4 628 258	5.5	13.0	0.3	4.9	0.3	3.0	72.0	119.8	63.2	35.1	1 036	985
Calhoun	797	2 771 233	3.3	2.8	0.0	1.3	49.8	1.3	39.9	46.2	18.3	8.5	575	564
Carroll	314	861 917	13.2	17.2	0.2	6.8	1.7	0.3	60.4	21.1	8.8	6.4	617	604
Chickasaw	881	2 154 461	7.6	9.3	1.7	3.6	8.8	5.2	62.6	53.0	32.3	11.7	673	613
Choctaw	408	952 647	11.6	4.1	0.2	1.9	1.6	2.0	76.1	22.8	12.4	4.5	537	521
Claiborne	496	1 465 091	5.5	6.2	1.5	4.2	22.1	1.6	57.8	34.3	20.9	6.0	640	605
Clarke	690	1 711 804	10.0	5.8	0.8	4.0	1.9	7.4	68.8	41.5	20.7	15.2	917	894
Clay	763	1 943 802	4.0	6.9	4.0	3.4	11.5	2.8	66.9	50.0	29.0	16.2	791	775
Coahoma	1 488	4 098 825	5.5	7.7	3.1	2.8	0.4	13.9	66.3	114.9	75.2	21.5	837	778
Copiah	1 481	4 154 517	5.1	5.7	0.7	2.2	11.5	2.3	72.0	103.1	56.6	17.6	609	584
Covington	1 021	2 828 948	4.9	4.0	0.1	11.3	32.9	1.7	44.1	78.2	25.0	13.0	663	643
DeSoto	5 452	16 140 720	6.4	11.9	7.2	2.5	2.2	3.5	65.3	471.9	208.5	194.3	1 169	1 065
Forrest	6 510	21 206 976	3.1	4.5	2.3	1.8	60.8	2.2	24.8	662.3	117.6	91.2	1 187	1 057
Franklin	363	888 524	9.6	4.0	0.0	5.2	1.8	1.0	78.1	35.6	14.5	5.9	746	704
George	1 085	2 865 559	4.2	7.1	0.4	2.7	30.9	0.7	53.5	89.3	31.9	12.7	553	528
Greene	532	1 305 598	6.9	3.9	0.0	3.1	15.5	1.6	67.6	37.4	20.6	9.4	654	637
Grenada	1 382	4 096 902	5.7	4.4	2.9	2.1	40.8	1.9	40.3	116.3	39.5	20.6	949	909
Hancock	1 924	6 676 661	5.8	6.9	3.4	2.2	23.0	4.5	52.3	287.9	169.1	47.6	1 052	1 011
Harrison	8 736	32 935 719	4.4	8.9	5.2	4.2	30.6	3.3	42.1	1 243.7	542.0	244.1	1 258	1 055
Hinds	10 525	28 655 948	5.9	10.5	4.8	2.2	1.5	4.8	70.4	878.7	450.7	268.0	1 078	1 017
Holmes	1 272	3 625 794	5.9	6.2	0.7	2.4	0.9	1.6	81.9	86.9	59.2	11.7	625	598
Humphreys	384	897 846	4.1	7.0	1.7	2.5	13.2	3.0	68.3	30.0	17.0	9.1	991	961
Issaquena	19	50 080	41.5	24.8	0.0	24.5	6.1	1.7	0.0	5.7	0.8	1.6	1 159	1 141
Itawamba	1 223	4 512 156	2.7	2.6	0.2	1.5	0.6	1.9	90.4	109.5	57.9	13.4	576	538
Jackson	7 975	28 632 767	3.0	5.8	2.5	2.0	45.3	2.4	38.2	857.2	237.3	174.7	1 245	1 188
Jasper	861	2 242 650	7.4	4.2	0.0	4.5	26.0	3.0	54.5	55.7	24.4	18.0	1 092	1 057
Jefferson	478	1 235 476	6.8	10.4	0.0	2.4	29.1	1.1	48.4	43.5	13.0	6.2	816	767
Jefferson Davis	567	1 467 224	8.3	4.6	0.9	4.0	30.4	1.6	49.8	39.7	17.1	8.1	672	658
Jones	4 753	12 100 544	2.7	3.7	2.3	2.1	35.5	1.9	50.3	341.0	127.5	54.3	791	752
Kemper	712	2 430 022	3.8	6.4	0.1	2.1	1.0	0.6	85.7	67.6	39.0	6.3	610	594
Lafayette	1 452	4 109 506	5.9	10.5	4.9	4.1	3.5	5.7	63.4	177.9	50.8	51.3	1 036	964
Lamar	2 053	4 821 922	4.0	6.2	0.6	4.8	0.9	0.5	81.5	123.2	59.9	53.4	924	906
Lauderdale	3 227	9 470 298	9.1	5.9	3.6	6.1	0.0	4.9	68.9	246.0	129.7	76.1	949	901
Lawrence	479	1 248 756	9.0	6.6	0.7	3.8	1.7	1.5	76.3	29.2	16.0	11.0	873	858
Leake	684	1 880 375	16.5	12.0	1.7	3.7	1.5	2.2	61.0	53.2	27.1	11.1	478	447
Lee	4 000	11 007 645	6.2	9.1	3.5	3.3	2.8	6.2	68.2	257.6	136.9	85.3	1 003	974
Leflore	2 494	8 995 576	3.1	4.0	1.8	1.7	57.3	2.3	29.6	240.0	68.2	28.3	913	861
Lincoln	1 177	3 186 542	7.5	6.9	3.7	3.9	0.6	2.4	74.6	84.1	45.5	26.5	760	721
Lowndes	2 233	7 025 354	8.5	12.2	3.9	4.4	1.2	8.3	59.4	183.3	105.0	53.8	901	845
Madison	2 936	9 496 425	7.8	11.0	5.2	3.3	1.3	2.9	67.0	279.8	105.3	131.7	1 337	1 266
Marion	1 327	2 909 454	6.2	11.0	1.8	3.7	1.7	1.0	73.2	79.0	36.5	17.5	662	635
Marshall	1 090	3 348 828	7.9	14.8	1.8	9.2	0.0	8.4	56.4	69.4	40.2	23.0	629	608
Monroe	1 425	3 622 413	13.2	8.0	3.4	7.1	1.1	4.6	60.5	97.7	48.7	27.8	764	733
Montgomery	546	1 639 820	6.9	4.5	1.6	3.8	37.3	2.7	42.6	35.2	16.1	7.1	672	642
Neshoba	938	2 330 410	5.2	9.8	3.5	4.9	0.8	6.3	69.2	84.7	35.9	14.6	489	471
Newton	1 105	3 232 369	4.5	4.7	0.6	1.9	0.9	5.5	81.6	80.7	53.7	13.3	616	581
Noxubee	657	1 978 193	6.6	1.5	0.5	2.2	28.3	0.4	59.1	39.8	18.4	8.4	752	729
Oktibbeha	1 842	5 582 328	2.8	4.7	3.1	1.1	47.2	4.4	36.2	155.8	47.9	35.8	744	726
Panola	1 433	4 200 779	4.8	10.0	2.0	2.8	2.1	3.6	74.4	97.6	58.1	28.7	832	760
Pearl River	2 574	7 161 607	5.5	5.4	1.8	2.1	8.1	3.0	73.4	183.3	100.0	38.8	702	666
Perry	466	1 122 268	9.5	5.9	0.4	5.6	1.3	2.1	74.8	33.9	18.6	9.5	788	759
Pike	2 872	9 325 024	3.8	4.6	1.6	1.6	46.9	2.2	38.5	249.1	83.4	32.7	816	780
Pontotoc	982	3 251 798	6.3	8.7	2.5	3.4	1.2	4.1	73.1	74.0	42.6	18.2	594	546
Prentiss	1 158	3 605 727	3.3	4.8	2.1	1.8	1.3	1.1	85.6	87.2	54.3	15.2	598	572
Quitman	519	1 364 995	6.8	5.4	0.1	5.5	31.8	1.2	49.1	23.7	13.9	7.2	919	878
Rankin	4 244	12 845 764	5.1	11.8	6.8	3.4	0.1	3.9	68.2	344.6	160.2	130.8	901	859
Scott	1 071	2 578 316	6.0	10.4	1.4	2.8	0.9	4.7	73.7	65.2	39.7	17.6	624	583
Sharkey	279	713 380	12.1	7.5	0.1	4.4	1.2	10.7	63.5	17.4	9.5	5.1	1 064	1 028
Simpson	898	2 221 618	6.8	8.7	0.2	5.6	1.2	1.8	73.3	56.8	33.6	17.5	639	614
Smith	568	1 449 509	9.4	8.8	0.0	4.1	1.0	2.8	73.8	37.3	21.8	10.9	667	654
Stone	1 427	5 071 678	2.8	2.3	0.5	0.8	0.4	0.4	92.7	126.2	75.9	12.5	691	645

1. Based on the resident population estimated as of July 1 of the year shown.

Table B. States and Counties — Local Government Finances, Government Employment, and Voting

STATE County	Direct general expenditure Total (mil dol)	Per capita[1] (dollars)	Education	Health and hospitals	Police protection	Public welfare	Highways	Debt outstanding Total (mil dol)	Per capita[1] (dollars)	Government employment, 2014 Federal civilian	Federal military	State and local	Presidential election,[2] 2012 Democratic	Republican	All other
	185	186	187	188	189	190	191	192	193	194	195	196	197	198	199
MISSISSIPPI	X	X	X	X	X	X	X	X	X	25 391	28 329	220 852	43.0	56.2	0.8
Adams	139.6	4 345	30.8	31.5	5.2	0.2	5.9	55.9	1 739	110	176	1 673	57.5	41.8	0.7
Alcorn	255.2	6 866	20.1	53.1	2.1	0.1	2.6	317.3	8 537	90	221	2 938	27.2	71.2	1.6
Amite	19.7	1 524	56.2	1.8	6.7	0.0	13.8	0.3	25	27	75	400	43.8	55.5	0.7
Attala	75.3	3 933	38.1	28.5	2.8	0.2	5.1	32.6	1 702	56	113	1 199	41.9	57.4	0.7
Benton	19.4	2 227	67.1	0.9	4.4	0.2	12.1	3.9	444	48	50	338	48.0	50.2	1.8
Bolivar	121.4	3 582	53.7	4.8	5.9	0.2	8.4	52.7	1 553	76	193	2 743	67.2	31.8	1.0
Calhoun	49.9	3 364	39.2	32.8	3.2	0.1	5.9	14.4	971	36	88	825	35.9	63.5	0.6
Carroll	20.6	1 974	43.6	0.9	2.8	0.0	14.4	13.5	1 292	23	60	341	34.1	65.4	0.4
Chickasaw	52.1	2 994	52.7	1.8	5.1	8.9	7.0	31.3	1 795	42	101	893	50.7	48.5	0.8
Choctaw	30.5	3 651	50.2	10.5	5.3	0.1	10.2	32.0	3 838	34	49	485	35.3	63.6	1.1
Claiborne	35.4	3 783	50.8	3.0	3.9	0.2	5.8	129.3	13 835	28	49	1 661	85.9	13.7	0.4
Clarke	40.6	2 452	65.6	0.9	5.4	0.1	8.0	10.9	661	32	98	778	37.2	62.3	0.6
Clay	52.7	2 577	56.9	0.6	7.8	0.6	8.0	34.3	1 677	56	120	903	59.1	40.3	0.6
Coahoma	119.1	4 634	63.3	0.9	4.4	0.0	4.0	151.1	5 877	64	145	1 911	71.9	27.6	0.5
Copiah	112.0	3 869	65.2	13.0	4.2	0.0	7.0	26.9	930	73	168	1 595	53.2	46.2	0.6
Covington	69.3	3 537	37.9	38.8	3.9	0.1	7.3	13.5	688	66	116	1 265	40.7	58.4	0.9
DeSoto	452.7	2 723	48.5	1.1	8.4	0.0	5.1	539.6	3 246	214	1 026	6 338	30.5	68.8	0.7
Forrest	657.8	8 555	16.6	64.3	2.3	0.0	3.0	378.3	4 920	729	782	10 958	42.8	56.3	1.0
Franklin	33.3	4 206	42.1	31.8	4.6	0.0	7.5	3.6	454	56	47	614	37.0	62.1	0.9
George	87.3	3 806	33.7	44.6	2.8	0.1	6.5	28.7	1 250	43	137	1 406	16.4	82.5	1.1
Greene	39.0	2 727	52.3	0.8	6.9	16.0	9.3	7.5	522	16	68	1 126	23.6	75.3	1.1
Grenada	114.7	5 290	29.2	42.6	4.9	0.0	4.5	98.3	4 534	232	129	1 637	44.4	55.1	0.5
Hancock	284.4	6 285	23.0	16.2	2.7	0.1	4.9	96.7	2 137	1 972	768	2 017	22.1	76.3	1.6
Harrison	1 263.3	6 511	21.1	29.5	4.6	0.2	4.8	919.9	4 741	5 911	8 631	12 880	36.6	62.6	0.9
Hinds	892.8	3 591	57.8	0.8	5.7	0.3	4.2	1 035.1	4 163	4 904	1 484	35 004	69.2	30.3	0.5
Holmes	104.3	5 551	78.5	1.3	3.6	0.2	4.5	35.2	1 870	51	106	1 247	81.4	18.0	0.7
Humphreys	30.1	3 277	50.7	1.4	6.0	0.1	15.6	10.5	1 144	22	52	482	70.9	28.5	0.6
Issaquena	5.9	4 234	0.9	5.4	10.5	0.0	13.4	1.8	1 275	0	0	90	60.9	38.3	0.7
Itawamba	111.8	4 790	82.2	0.5	2.0	0.0	3.7	48.6	2 082	45	136	1 084	20.9	77.0	2.1
Jackson	885.7	6 313	30.2	41.1	3.1	0.1	3.7	521.2	3 715	970	994	8 719	32.7	66.3	1.0
Jasper	52.0	3 145	47.2	13.8	3.9	0.1	13.0	21.9	1 327	52	100	925	54.6	44.9	0.5
Jefferson	38.6	5 053	32.5	24.2	4.3	10.8	4.1	5.0	653	17	47	677	86.7	12.3	1.0
Jefferson Davis	43.5	3 615	47.4	27.4	3.9	0.0	7.0	9.1	759	26	71	644	60.4	39.0	0.6
Jones	365.6	5 326	40.2	37.4	2.4	0.8	3.6	230.8	3 362	218	400	6 924	30.2	68.9	0.9
Kemper	67.4	6 517	80.0	0.6	1.8	0.1	3.5	9.1	878	32	56	623	62.3	37.0	0.6
Lafayette	126.1	2 548	52.3	0.9	7.5	0.0	9.3	146.9	2 968	326	295	7 400	43.3	55.7	1.0
Lamar	128.5	2 224	68.5	0.7	6.9	0.2	7.3	76.2	1 319	45	360	2 371	21.6	77.4	1.1
Lauderdale	232.7	2 900	60.0	3.5	5.9	0.0	5.1	138.1	1 722	810	1 369	5 286	40.3	59.1	0.6
Lawrence	30.1	2 396	64.4	1.7	4.0	0.4	8.9	8.0	634	44	75	704	36.9	62.3	0.8
Leake	54.6	2 344	49.9	15.0	4.7	0.0	8.2	21.7	931	60	128	764	44.4	55.0	0.6
Lee	265.1	3 118	54.1	0.9	7.2	0.2	8.9	210.0	2 470	465	508	5 112	34.4	64.9	0.7
Leflore	246.7	7 972	21.8	53.9	3.5	0.0	2.9	171.6	5 546	105	177	4 035	68.1	31.4	0.5
Lincoln	82.3	2 359	58.3	1.7	7.0	0.0	9.8	29.6	848	89	205	1 667	33.6	65.7	0.7
Lowndes	180.6	3 026	47.7	0.8	6.3	0.1	7.7	210.1	3 521	826	1 664	3 394	48.1	51.0	1.0
Madison	302.7	3 074	49.9	0.4	6.9	0.1	12.3	478.1	4 855	220	602	4 479	42.0	57.5	0.5
Marion	79.2	2 994	45.6	21.5	5.3	0.0	4.2	27.0	1 020	46	151	1 425	34.0	65.4	0.6
Marshall	73.1	1 995	56.1	1.7	6.9	0.1	12.7	20.0	545	75	207	1 200	58.8	40.6	0.7
Monroe	96.6	2 653	58.9	1.2	7.3	0.4	7.6	47.3	1 299	127	214	1 418	41.0	58.2	0.8
Montgomery	37.1	3 497	42.0	24.7	4.2	0.3	9.9	11.3	1 062	28	62	640	45.7	53.8	0.6
Neshoba	87.8	2 947	41.8	32.2	3.5	0.0	5.2	30.9	1 037	83	175	6 059	27.3	72.0	0.7
Newton	81.2	3 757	66.9	1.0	5.1	0.0	5.2	11.7	539	77	128	2 014	32.7	66.8	0.6
Noxubee	40.0	3 569	46.0	25.3	3.7	0.1	6.1	6.0	537	39	66	731	76.3	23.1	0.5
Oktibbeha	178.0	3 694	32.7	38.4	3.7	0.0	4.9	104.4	2 167	241	280	9 654	49.6	49.6	0.8
Panola	102.7	2 980	56.0	1.3	6.9	0.2	7.0	38.1	1 104	111	206	2 209	52.9	46.4	0.6
Pearl River	195.3	3 533	60.8	8.4	3.0	0.1	6.4	65.6	1 186	123	325	3 112	19.2	79.7	1.1
Perry	35.3	2 921	48.4	1.5	4.7	0.1	17.1	88.9	7 358	18	73	547	27.1	71.8	1.1
Pike	242.6	6 051	34.8	43.8	2.9	0.0	2.6	84.1	2 098	111	236	3 514	51.4	47.9	0.7
Pontotoc	80.2	2 621	56.4	1.0	4.0	0.1	6.4	30.1	983	49	185	1 227	23.2	75.6	1.2
Prentiss	89.5	3 525	81.0	0.8	4.2	0.0	3.0	31.5	1 242	46	178	1 524	27.6	70.4	2.0
Quitman	33.0	4 231	64.9	0.9	4.1	0.0	8.6	7.5	959	24	45	347	67.3	32.0	0.7
Rankin	365.9	2 521	50.1	0.9	7.2	0.1	9.8	417.1	2 873	624	860	9 204	22.8	76.3	0.9
Scott	65.3	2 311	62.2	1.9	5.4	0.0	7.7	22.0	779	203	170	1 238	43.1	56.4	0.5
Sharkey	21.1	4 406	71.8	0.6	4.2	0.0	8.3	5.6	1 159	25	27	391	68.2	31.2	0.5
Simpson	63.8	2 330	55.8	1.6	3.8	2.0	6.9	28.1	1 027	42	162	1 621	38.2	60.6	1.2
Smith	36.8	2 253	63.0	1.0	5.3	0.0	13.3	9.9	606	25	97	617	23.7	75.4	0.9
Stone	142.2	7 887	79.3	0.5	3.6	0.0	2.5	30.7	1 701	57	99	1 109	27.5	71.1	1.4

1. Based on the resident population estimated as of July 1 of the year shown. 2. © 2013 Election Data Services, Inc. All rights reserved.

Table B. States and Counties — **Land Area and Population**

STATE/ County code	CBSA code[1]	County type[2]	STATE County	Land area,[3] (sq km) 2010	Total persons 2015	Rank	Per square kilometer	White	Black	American Indian, Alaska Native	Asian and Pacific Islander	Percent Hispanic or Latino[4]	Under 5 years	5 to 17 years	18 to 24 years	25 to 34 years	35 to 44 years	45 to 54 years
				1	2	3	4	5	6	7	8	9	10	11	12	13	14	15
			MISSISSIPPI—Cont'd															
28 133	26940	5	Sunflower	1 807	27 005	1 534	14.9	25.3	72.8	0.4	0.5	1.5	6.3	16.9	11.6	15.9	12.5	13.3
28 135	...	7	Tallahatchie	1 671	14 588	2 131	8.7	36.8	56.4	0.6	1.1	6.2	5.4	15.0	11.2	16.3	13.9	13.0
28 137	32820	1	Tate	1 048	28 296	1 478	27.0	65.7	31.8	0.6	0.6	2.5	5.9	18.3	11.5	11.8	11.6	13.3
28 139	...	7	Tippah	1 186	22 131	1 723	18.7	78.3	17.4	0.5	0.3	4.8	6.2	18.4	9.3	11.7	12.2	14.1
28 141	...	8	Tishomingo	1 099	19 552	1 849	17.8	94.0	3.2	0.6	0.3	2.6	5.3	16.7	8.2	10.6	11.9	14.2
28 143	32820	1	Tunica	1 178	10 343	2 404	8.8	21.3	76.0	0.5	1.2	2.5	8.7	21.6	9.3	14.5	12.4	11.9
28 145	...	7	Union	1 076	28 429	1 475	26.4	79.7	15.7	0.5	0.5	4.6	6.7	18.5	8.6	12.4	13.1	13.2
28 147	...	9	Walthall	1 046	14 638	2 125	14.0	53.8	44.1	0.8	0.6	1.8	5.7	18.9	8.3	11.3	11.8	12.7
28 149	46980	4	Warren	1 524	47 485	1 028	31.2	48.8	48.4	0.5	1.1	2.0	6.5	18.3	8.9	12.3	12.2	13.2
28 151	24740	5	Washington	1 877	48 130	1 017	25.6	26.6	71.1	0.4	0.9	1.3	7.4	19.2	9.8	12.5	11.2	12.6
28 153	...	7	Wayne	2 100	20 566	1 800	9.8	58.8	39.5	0.6	0.4	1.5	6.4	18.3	9.2	12.4	11.9	13.2
28 155	...	9	Webster	1 090	9 899	2 442	9.1	78.4	20.3	0.5	0.5	1.3	5.9	18.3	7.9	12.3	11.5	14.3
28 157	...	8	Wilkinson	1 756	9 122	2 504	5.2	28.9	70.0	0.4	0.3	0.7	6.0	15.7	9.1	15.1	11.3	13.5
28 159	...	7	Winston	1 573	18 317	1 902	11.6	51.2	46.6	1.3	0.4	1.2	5.8	17.9	8.3	11.6	11.9	13.2
28 161	...	7	Yalobusha	1 210	12 447	2 265	10.3	59.5	39.0	0.5	0.4	1.7	6.4	16.4	8.1	11.0	12.2	12.7
28 163	27140	6	Yazoo	2 390	27 387	1 516	11.5	36.8	57.4	0.5	0.8	5.6	6.7	17.6	8.8	16.1	14.5	12.6
29 000	...	X	MISSOURI	178 040	6 083 672	X	34.2	81.9	12.5	1.1	2.5	4.0	6.2	16.8	9.8	13.2	12.1	13.5
29 001	28860	7	Adair	1 469	25 378	1 594	17.3	93.3	2.5	0.8	2.9	2.6	4.6	13.9	26.7	10.6	9.0	10.9
29 003	41140	3	Andrew	1 121	17 296	1 962	15.4	96.6	1.3	0.9	0.6	2.2	5.2	17.7	7.8	10.5	12.5	14.2
29 005	...	9	Atchison	1 418	5 306	2 812	3.7	97.9	0.8	0.7	0.4	1.3	5.5	14.5	7.2	9.8	10.8	13.8
29 007	33020	6	Audrain	1 793	26 096	1 558	14.6	89.4	8.0	0.8	0.9	2.6	6.1	17.3	8.5	13.0	12.4	12.9
29 009	...	6	Barry	2 016	35 829	1 278	17.8	88.3	0.7	2.0	1.5	8.8	6.4	16.6	7.7	10.3	10.6	13.9
29 011	...	6	Barton	1 533	11 880	2 304	7.7	95.4	1.2	2.7	0.9	2.5	5.7	19.3	8.2	10.3	10.8	13.3
29 013	28140	1	Bates	2 167	16 446	2 010	7.6	96.0	1.5	1.4	0.4	2.2	5.9	18.2	7.4	11.2	10.9	13.9
29 015	...	9	Benton	1 824	18 670	1 885	10.2	96.9	0.7	1.4	0.7	1.8	3.9	13.8	5.6	7.7	8.9	13.3
29 017	16020	6	Bollinger	1 600	12 182	2 287	7.6	97.9	0.7	1.2	0.5	0.9	6.0	16.4	7.9	10.3	11.8	15.0
29 019	17860	3	Boone	1 775	174 974	368	98.6	82.3	10.8	1.0	5.3	3.2	6.0	14.5	20.6	15.4	11.4	11.0
29 021	41140	2	Buchanan	1 057	89 100	645	84.3	86.3	7.1	1.0	1.7	6.0	6.7	16.2	10.1	14.3	12.0	13.5
29 023	38740	7	Butler	1 799	42 951	1 115	23.9	91.6	6.4	1.5	1.2	1.7	6.6	17.1	8.0	12.1	11.7	13.2
29 025	28140	1	Caldwell	1 104	9 014	2 511	8.2	96.8	1.1	1.3	0.7	2.0	5.3	18.6	7.4	10.3	11.3	14.2
29 027	27620	3	Callaway	2 162	44 834	1 076	20.7	92.2	5.4	1.3	1.1	2.0	5.7	15.8	11.5	13.1	12.2	14.3
29 029	...	7	Camden	1 699	44 237	1 086	26.0	95.7	0.9	1.1	0.9	2.5	4.5	13.8	6.3	9.6	9.4	13.6
29 031	16020	5	Cape Girardeau	1 498	78 572	707	52.5	88.3	8.7	0.7	1.9	2.2	5.8	15.7	14.7	12.4	11.1	12.3
29 033	...	6	Carroll	1 799	8 992	2 512	5.0	96.0	3.0	0.7	0.8	1.3	6.2	16.5	8.1	9.7	11.8	13.3
29 035	...	9	Carter	1 314	6 263	2 737	4.8	96.4	1.0	1.8	0.6	1.9	6.3	17.6	7.7	11.1	11.3	13.7
29 037	28140	1	Cass	1 805	101 603	590	56.3	90.5	4.6	1.3	1.4	4.3	6.0	19.0	7.9	11.6	12.9	14.1
29 039	...	9	Cedar	1 229	13 934	2 171	11.3	96.5	0.7	1.6	0.8	2.1	5.6	17.3	7.0	9.3	10.3	12.6
29 041	...	9	Chariton	1 946	7 589	2 628	3.9	96.8	2.8	0.5	0.3	1.0	6.3	16.1	6.9	9.9	10.0	13.0
29 043	44180	2	Christian	1 457	83 279	676	57.2	95.2	1.3	1.3	1.1	2.9	6.4	19.7	7.6	13.0	13.4	13.4
29 045	22800	9	Clark	1 307	6 801	2 694	5.2	98.7	0.8	0.6	0.7	0.8	5.9	17.4	7.2	10.3	11.1	14.4
29 047	28140	1	Clay	1 029	235 637	279	229.0	84.7	6.8	1.2	3.2	6.6	6.5	18.5	8.2	14.2	14.0	13.8
29 049	28140	1	Clinton	1 085	20 609	1 797	19.0	95.4	2.3	1.3	0.9	2.1	5.9	17.9	7.7	10.7	12.0	14.5
29 051	27620	3	Cole	1 020	76 720	719	75.2	84.0	12.7	0.8	1.7	2.7	6.2	16.8	9.1	13.7	12.7	14.1
29 053	...	6	Cooper	1 463	17 642	1 938	12.1	90.1	8.3	0.9	0.9	1.6	5.5	16.2	10.0	13.6	11.4	13.4
29 055	...	6	Crawford	1 923	24 526	1 624	12.8	97.0	0.8	1.1	0.6	1.8	6.1	17.4	7.6	11.5	11.4	14.2
29 057	...	8	Dade	1 269	7 595	2 627	6.0	96.6	1.0	2.4	0.7	1.8	4.6	16.5	6.9	9.0	10.9	13.6
29 059	44180	2	Dallas	1 401	16 393	2 017	11.7	96.7	0.7	1.9	0.6	1.8	5.8	17.6	7.2	10.1	10.9	13.9
29 061	...	8	Daviess	1 459	8 253	2 579	5.7	97.4	1.0	0.8	0.5	1.5	6.3	19.8	7.7	9.6	11.3	12.4
29 063	41140	3	DeKalb	1 091	12 687	2 249	11.6	85.5	11.9	0.8	0.7	2.0	4.2	12.6	8.3	16.1	15.2	15.6
29 065	...	7	Dent	1 950	15 593	2 069	8.0	96.6	1.0	1.9	1.3	1.4	5.9	16.9	7.7	10.7	10.6	13.7
29 067	...	6	Douglas	2 107	13 373	2 213	6.3	97.4	0.8	1.8	0.6	1.2	5.6	15.9	6.7	10.0	9.8	13.2
29 069	28380	7	Dunklin	1 401	30 895	1 413	22.1	82.7	11.2	0.8	0.6	6.3	7.3	18.7	8.2	10.9	11.5	13.3
29 071	41180	1	Franklin	2 390	102 426	584	42.9	96.5	1.5	0.8	0.7	1.7	6.2	17.5	8.2	12.0	11.5	15.2
29 073	...	6	Gasconade	1 341	14 858	2 112	11.1	97.2	0.8	0.8	0.8	1.4	5.0	16.2	7.2	9.8	10.6	14.2
29 075	...	8	Gentry	1 273	6 692	2 704	5.3	97.9	1.0	0.6	0.6	1.0	7.5	17.1	8.0	11.1	10.1	13.2
29 077	44180	2	Greene	1 749	288 072	235	164.7	90.8	4.2	1.5	2.6	3.5	6.1	14.9	14.1	14.1	11.6	12.1
29 079	...	7	Grundy	1 127	10 097	2 430	9.0	95.8	1.2	1.1	0.9	2.0	6.8	16.7	9.2	11.4	9.3	12.6
29 081	...	7	Harrison	1 871	8 615	2 544	4.6	96.5	0.8	0.8	0.7	2.2	6.8	17.9	7.2	10.5	10.5	12.3
29 083	...	6	Henry	1 805	21 737	1 741	12.0	95.5	2.0	1.4	0.8	2.1	6.0	16.4	7.0	11.1	11.2	13.5
29 085	...	6	Hickory	1 034	9 201	2 494	8.9	97.0	0.8	2.0	0.5	1.4	3.9	13.1	5.4	7.0	8.6	13.1
29 087	...	8	Holt	1 198	4 484	2 863	3.7	97.3	0.7	1.3	0.5	1.0	5.1	14.7	6.6	9.9	10.8	14.4
29 089	...	3	Howard	1 201	10 139	2 427	8.4	92.5	6.4	1.2	0.6	1.4	5.9	15.8	12.8	11.4	9.8	12.9
29 091	48460	7	Howell	2 402	40 117	1 171	16.7	96.3	0.8	1.7	1.0	2.0	6.6	17.7	8.0	11.6	11.6	13.0
29 093	...	9	Iron	1 425	10 125	2 428	7.1	96.2	2.0	1.7	0.4	1.7	6.0	16.0	7.1	10.6	12.1	14.1
29 095	28140	1	Jackson	1 566	687 623	92	439.1	65.1	24.9	1.2	2.7	8.8	6.8	17.2	8.8	15.1	12.5	13.4

1. CBSA = Core Based Statistical Area. See Appendix A for explanation. See Appendix B for list of metropolitan areas with component counties. 2. County type code from the Economic Research Service of USDA Rural-Urban Continuum Codes. See Appendix A for definition. 3. Dry land or land partially or temporarily covered by water. 4. May be of any race.

Table B. States and Counties — **Population and Households**

STATE County	55 to 64 years	65 to 74 years	75 years and over	Percent female	Total persons 2000	2010	Percent change 2000–2010	2010–2015	Births	Deaths	Net migration	Number	Persons per house-hold	Family house-holds	Female family house-holder[1]	One per-son
	16	17	18	19	20	21	22	23	24	25	26	27	28	29	30	31
MISSISSIPPI—Cont'd																
Sunflower	11.9	6.7	4.8	47.2	34 369	29 450	-14.3	-8.3	1 802	1 535	-2 770	8 451	2.86	69.1	29.6	27.8
Tallahatchie	11.6	7.5	6.0	44.3	14 903	15 383	3.2	-5.2	814	811	-798	4 519	2.48	66.8	23.8	30.2
Tate	12.7	9.3	5.7	51.7	25 370	28 882	13.8	-2.0	1 696	1 443	-817	10 017	2.69	71.8	16.3	24.1
Tippah	12.2	9.4	6.4	50.8	20 826	22 232	6.8	-0.5	1 431	1 329	-213	8 488	2.56	75.0	14.5	21.7
Tishomingo	13.5	11.4	8.2	51.8	19 163	19 596	2.3	-0.2	1 056	1 465	348	7 618	2.52	75.0	15.1	23.6
Tunica	11.4	6.2	4.1	52.9	9 227	10 778	16.8	-4.0	1 022	502	-962	4 031	2.58	64.9	27.5	31.2
Union	11.8	9.0	6.7	51.2	25 362	27 134	7.0	4.8	1 968	1 379	748	10 292	2.65	72.2	14.1	24.2
Walthall	13.6	9.6	8.1	51.9	15 156	15 443	1.9	-5.2	955	930	-844	5 823	2.57	66.1	13.6	30.2
Warren	14.1	8.6	5.9	52.4	49 644	48 773	-1.8	-2.6	3 247	2 613	-1 807	18 367	2.60	66.1	19.5	30.5
Washington	13.6	8.0	5.6	53.2	62 977	51 135	-18.8	-5.9	4 249	3 172	-4 068	18 383	2.69	67.5	29.6	29.1
Wayne	12.7	9.3	6.5	51.9	21 216	20 747	-2.2	-0.9	1 534	1 090	-649	8 031	2.54	68.8	15.4	28.4
Webster	13.2	9.5	7.1	51.0	10 294	10 252	-0.4	-3.4	668	747	-303	4 085	2.44	74.1	18.2	24.1
Wilkinson	13.9	8.7	6.9	46.6	10 312	9 878	-4.2	-7.7	632	588	-820	3 295	2.58	63.5	21.9	33.2
Winston	14.0	9.6	7.8	51.0	20 160	19 198	-4.8	-4.6	1 041	1 138	-795	7 658	2.40	71.2	23.7	26.2
Yalobusha	14.9	10.5	7.8	51.8	13 051	12 678	-2.9	-1.8	808	865	-176	4 808	2.55	67.9	17.0	30.1
Yazoo	11.3	6.7	5.7	44.6	28 149	28 065	-0.3	-2.4	1 938	1 418	-1 140	8 552	2.86	66.8	25.8	29.3
MISSOURI	13.0	8.7	6.7	50.9	5 595 211	5 988 927	7.0	1.6	397 057	295 287	-4 445	2 361 232	2.48	64.9	12.1	29.1
Adair	10.7	7.5	6.1	51.9	24 977	25 607	2.5	-0.9	1 334	1 107	-443	9 608	2.35	54.3	8.2	35.3
Andrew	14.5	9.9	7.5	50.5	16 492	17 291	4.8	0.0	944	865	-43	6 710	2.55	69.9	6.1	24.5
Atchison	14.6	13.4	10.4	50.4	6 430	5 685	-11.6	-6.7	289	392	-277	2 465	2.18	62.4	7.2	31.9
Audrain	13.1	9.1	7.6	54.5	25 853	25 529	-1.3	2.2	1 795	1 517	301	9 381	2.53	66.3	10.0	29.0
Barry	14.3	11.7	8.5	50.2	34 010	35 597	4.7	0.7	2 186	2 088	211	13 398	2.64	69.5	9.3	25.9
Barton	13.9	9.8	8.8	50.7	12 541	12 402	-1.1	-4.2	743	707	-547	5 009	2.43	73.2	8.7	25.4
Bates	13.8	9.8	8.9	50.6	16 653	17 049	2.4	-3.5	1 018	1 088	-538	6 784	2.43	65.4	9.7	29.9
Benton	18.0	17.3	11.5	49.7	17 180	19 056	10.9	-2.0	798	1 460	359	8 273	2.26	68.2	8.0	28.1
Bollinger	14.5	10.8	7.2	50.0	12 029	12 363	2.8	-1.5	715	676	-115	4 790	2.55	68.7	9.5	27.1
Boone	10.6	6.1	4.4	51.6	135 454	162 642	20.1	7.6	11 190	5 291	6 360	66 136	2.40	57.6	9.7	28.9
Buchanan	12.6	8.0	6.6	49.7	85 998	89 201	3.7	-0.1	6 214	4 983	-1 294	33 359	2.57	62.4	13.0	31.5
Butler	13.6	9.8	7.9	51.1	40 867	42 794	4.7	0.4	2 961	2 892	196	16 773	2.50	66.5	13.0	28.7
Caldwell	14.0	10.5	8.4	49.6	8 969	9 424	5.1	-4.4	461	520	-366	3 696	2.43	70.0	9.8	27.5
Callaway	13.2	8.5	5.7	49.2	40 766	44 332	8.7	1.1	2 717	1 917	-209	16 497	2.47	64.6	11.8	29.7
Camden	17.8	16.1	8.7	50.6	37 051	44 002	18.8	0.5	2 136	2 371	578	17 419	2.49	71.1	8.6	24.9
Cape Girardeau	12.5	8.2	7.2	51.6	68 693	75 674	10.2	3.8	4 849	3 787	1 707	29 672	2.48	64.3	10.2	28.4
Carroll	13.7	11.3	9.3	50.8	10 285	9 295	-9.6	-3.3	585	641	-255	3 652	2.48	65.1	9.0	31.4
Carter	14.5	10.7	7.1	51.5	5 941	6 265	5.5	0.0	413	379	-37	2 456	2.54	61.0	11.6	33.7
Cass	12.9	8.8	6.7	51.1	82 092	99 475	21.2	2.1	6 367	4 658	307	37 503	2.65	73.1	10.8	22.0
Cedar	13.7	13.3	10.7	50.4	13 733	13 982	1.8	-0.3	869	1 025	189	5 893	2.33	62.2	9.8	34.8
Chariton	15.2	11.0	11.5	50.3	8 438	7 827	-7.2	-3.0	465	500	-185	2 956	2.54	66.2	7.6	31.6
Christian	12.1	8.7	5.6	51.2	54 285	77 419	42.6	7.6	5 277	2 928	3 351	29 994	2.64	76.0	9.9	20.1
Clark	14.6	10.6	8.5	49.4	7 416	7 129	-3.9	-4.6	405	428	-281	2 859	2.42	63.3	6.5	31.4
Clay	12.0	7.6	5.2	51.0	184 006	221 874	20.6	6.2	16 149	8 434	6 112	87 352	2.58	68.1	11.4	25.6
Clinton	14.0	9.6	7.7	49.6	18 979	20 743	9.3	-0.6	1 158	1 273	-59	8 067	2.49	74.1	11.1	21.2
Cole	13.4	8.0	6.0	49.4	71 397	75 983	6.4	1.0	4 902	3 226	-912	29 307	2.45	65.9	13.0	28.5
Cooper	13.3	8.9	7.6	47.3	16 670	17 601	5.6	0.2	1 038	969	-51	6 520	2.45	67.2	10.1	27.5
Crawford	13.9	10.3	7.4	50.6	22 804	24 696	8.3	-0.7	1 533	1 494	-205	9 427	2.58	67.8	11.9	27.9
Dade	16.4	11.9	10.2	49.2	7 923	7 883	-0.5	-3.7	343	545	-93	3 166	2.38	68.4	11.1	28.5
Dallas	15.0	11.2	8.4	50.1	15 661	16 777	7.1	-2.3	1 026	950	-453	6 348	2.59	75.9	10.9	20.0
Daviess	13.8	11.2	7.7	49.6	8 016	8 433	5.2	-2.1	598	437	-322	3 134	2.60	70.8	6.4	25.3
DeKalb	12.3	8.3	7.4	36.8	11 597	12 892	11.2	-1.6	550	602	-192	3 778	2.47	67.2	7.9	30.0
Dent	14.2	11.2	9.1	50.0	14 927	15 657	4.9	-0.4	912	993	20	5 889	2.62	71.4	12.0	24.5
Douglas	16.6	12.7	9.5	50.6	13 084	13 684	4.6	-2.3	774	805	-283	5 156	2.60	70.2	8.4	26.8
Dunklin	12.8	9.7	7.8	52.1	33 155	31 953	-3.6	-3.3	2 419	2 285	-1 166	12 727	2.44	65.0	16.2	30.6
Franklin	13.8	9.0	6.6	50.3	93 807	101 491	8.2	0.9	6 506	5 066	-606	39 733	2.54	71.0	10.3	24.8
Gasconade	15.4	11.5	10.1	50.6	15 342	15 221	-0.8	-2.4	829	1 040	-131	6 333	2.33	65.1	8.4	30.9
Gentry	13.2	9.3	10.5	51.7	6 861	6 738	-1.8	-0.7	473	454	-57	2 725	2.40	65.5	8.0	31.2
Greene	11.8	8.4	7.0	51.2	240 391	275 178	14.5	4.7	18 671	13 579	7 415	116 632	2.31	59.3	10.2	31.6
Grundy	12.7	10.8	10.4	52.6	10 432	10 261	-1.6	-1.6	792	698	-255	4 150	2.40	65.9	12.0	29.9
Harrison	13.9	10.5	10.6	50.2	8 850	8 957	1.2	-3.8	590	591	-359	3 574	2.39	66.9	7.2	28.3
Henry	14.2	11.6	9.0	50.9	21 997	22 272	1.3	-2.4	1 371	1 622	-243	9 545	2.29	63.7	9.5	29.7
Hickory	17.0	19.0	12.8	51.1	8 940	9 627	7.7	-4.4	378	738	-26	4 134	2.25	67.8	5.8	26.9
Holt	15.6	11.2	11.6	50.7	5 351	4 912	-8.2	-8.7	275	329	-370	2 164	2.12	64.6	7.9	32.0
Howard	14.3	9.4	7.6	50.2	10 212	10 148	-0.6	-0.1	632	494	-109	3 779	2.49	66.0	11.4	30.0
Howell	13.1	10.3	8.3	51.3	37 238	40 400	8.5	-0.7	2 714	2 581	-399	16 060	2.48	68.0	11.2	28.3
Iron	15.4	11.0	7.8	50.7	10 697	10 631	-0.6	-4.8	545	709	-410	4 158	2.42	68.1	11.0	26.5
Jackson	12.6	7.6	6.0	51.6	654 880	674 231	3.0	2.0	50 312	32 038	-4 016	271 965	2.45	59.5	15.0	33.7

1. No spouse present.

Table B. States and Counties — Population, Vital Statistics, Medicare, and Crime

STATE County	Persons in group quarters, 2015	Daytime population, 2010–2014 Number	Employment/residence ratio	Births, 2015 Total	Rate[1]	Deaths, 2015 Number	Rate[1]	Persons under 65 with no health insurance, 2014 Number	Percent	Medicare, 2015 Total Beneficiaries	Enrolled in Original Medicare	Enrolled in Medicare Advantage	Serious crimes known to police,[2] 2014 Total Number	Rate[3]
	32	33	34	35	36	37	38	39	40	41	42	43	44	45
MISSISSIPPI—Cont'd														
Sunflower	3 986	28 367	1.01	325	11.9	280	10.3	3 756	18.5	4 159	3 816	343	NA	NA
Tallahatchie	2 445	14 220	0.77	147	10.0	152	10.4	1 931	18.7	2 505	2 323	182	NA	NA
Tate	1 308	24 321	0.63	297	10.5	295	10.4	4 095	17.9	5 121	4 224	897	NA	NA
Tippah	312	20 803	0.85	287	13.0	223	10.1	3 487	19.0	5 506	5 129	377	3	18
Tishomingo	276	18 189	0.81	207	10.6	284	14.6	2 882	18.6	5 542	5 344	198	87	446
Tunica	104	16 821	2.52	191	18.3	86	8.2	1 377	14.6	1 662	1 331	331	526	5 009
Union	277	27 186	0.97	412	14.6	235	8.3	4 499	19.1	5 376	4 982	394	NA	NA
Walthall	121	12 306	0.49	176	11.9	180	12.2	2 550	20.9	2 708	2 343	365	NA	NA
Warren	525	50 759	1.13	616	12.9	511	10.7	6 426	15.8	8 890	7 489	1 401	2 170	4 518
Washington	726	50 461	1.03	803	16.5	652	13.4	7 864	18.9	10 007	8 415	1 592	3 162	6 772
Wayne	137	18 626	0.73	296	14.4	191	9.3	3 236	18.8	3 320	2 897	423	NA	NA
Webster	57	9 017	0.70	127	12.8	141	14.2	1 504	18.1	2 475	2 343	132	NA	NA
Wilkinson	1 055	9 096	0.88	118	12.9	126	13.7	1 172	17.3	1 814	1 549	265	NA	NA
Winston	442	17 789	0.84	194	10.5	215	11.7	2 713	18.3	3 883	3 401	482	50	268
Yalobusha	155	10 803	0.66	156	12.6	168	13.6	1 740	17.5	3 880	3 489	391	NA	NA
Yazoo	4 118	26 607	0.82	348	12.6	253	9.2	3 572	17.7	4 503	3 962	541	NA	NA
MISSOURI	174 938	6 067 719	1.01	75 559	12.4	56 491	9.3	682 388	13.7	1 087 629	773 135	314 494	203 093	3 349
Adair	2 907	26 580	1.09	249	9.8	210	8.3	2 864	14.8	4 162	3 906	256	772	3 016
Andrew	192	11 736	0.33	186	10.7	169	9.8	1 720	12.1	2 317	2 148	169	268	1 533
Atchison	98	5 149	0.86	53	9.9	67	12.6	554	13.6	1 382	1 303	79	41	759
Audrain	2 549	25 881	1.02	344	13.2	270	10.4	2 831	14.4	4 793	3 948	845	631	2 451
Barry	296	37 653	1.14	411	11.5	380	10.6	5 664	20.1	8 315	5 420	2 895	941	2 646
Barton	90	11 356	0.81	141	11.8	125	10.5	1 726	17.7	2 441	2 000	441	295	2 406
Bates	311	14 453	0.67	202	12.2	194	11.8	2 256	17.0	3 471	2 817	654	520	3 162
Benton	244	16 934	0.68	150	8.0	289	15.4	2 523	19.0	6 303	4 947	1 356	433	2 290
Bollinger	163	9 711	0.44	129	10.5	125	10.2	1 691	16.7	2 493	2 164	329	139	1 108
Boone	9 012	173 589	1.06	2 193	12.6	1 021	5.9	17 744	12.1	21 650	18 293	3 357	5 735	3 316
Buchanan	4 485	98 121	1.21	1 133	12.7	886	9.9	10 150	14.0	16 879	15 343	1 536	4 958	5 516
Butler	873	46 306	1.19	552	12.9	533	12.4	5 950	17.0	10 074	8 911	1 163	2 230	5 162
Caldwell	214	7 223	0.49	85	9.4	96	10.6	1 058	14.8	2 002	1 712	290	116	1 286
Callaway	3 891	38 798	0.71	533	11.9	361	8.1	4 631	13.3	7 330	6 230	1 100	1 206	2 715
Camden	774	44 705	1.05	400	9.1	464	10.5	5 854	17.9	9 633	8 127	1 506	911	2 077
Cape Girardeau	3 832	83 099	1.17	943	12.0	698	8.9	7 708	12.2	14 291	13 044	1 247	2 602	3 345
Carroll	88	8 214	0.76	108	12.0	115	12.8	1 096	15.3	2 243	1 928	315	136	1 494
Carter	40	5 885	0.84	82	13.1	78	12.5	1 015	19.8	1 592	1 368	224	95	1 509
Cass	1 044	79 506	0.56	1 218	12.0	883	8.7	9 350	11.0	14 390	8 906	5 484	2 271	2 249
Cedar	156	12 991	0.81	172	12.3	202	14.5	1 955	18.6	3 684	2 474	1 210	347	2 494
Chariton	213	6 717	0.69	100	13.1	115	15.1	939	16.0	1 658	1 520	138	131	1 728
Christian	582	60 063	0.47	1 024	12.4	593	7.2	9 317	13.3	13 569	7 600	5 969	1 438	1 759
Clark	90	5 701	0.59	74	10.8	67	9.8	963	17.3	1 412	1 289	123	28	408
Clay	2 650	205 307	0.80	3 093	13.2	1 660	7.1	20 287	10.1	35 417	26 991	8 426	10 081	4 332
Clinton	445	16 401	0.56	212	10.4	240	11.7	2 139	12.8	4 192	3 721	471	358	1 742
Cole	4 988	90 723	1.40	943	12.3	641	8.4	7 264	11.9	13 763	12 059	1 704	1 852	2 407
Cooper	1 545	15 984	0.79	199	11.3	178	10.1	1 833	13.8	3 246	2 643	603	428	2 420
Crawford	332	21 926	0.71	307	12.5	278	11.3	3 477	17.3	4 364	3 220	1 144	704	2 867
Dade	133	6 918	0.76	65	8.5	111	14.6	1 006	17.1	1 866	1 177	689	112	1 691
Dallas	199	13 830	0.53	191	11.7	195	11.9	2 689	20.6	3 428	1 969	1 459	309	1 872
Daviess	152	7 022	0.61	119	14.4	77	9.3	1 266	19.3	1 604	1 459	145	79	956
DeKalb	3 542	12 821	1.00	100	7.9	92	7.3	998	13.5	1 560	1 436	124	186	1 448
Dent	201	14 835	0.85	176	11.3	197	12.6	2 580	20.8	3 634	3 290	344	306	1 943
Douglas	123	11 893	0.65	151	11.2	150	11.1	1 979	18.9	2 784	1 528	1 256	206	1 526
Dunklin	662	30 323	0.87	448	14.4	445	14.3	4 228	16.6	7 589	6 642	947	1 507	4 755
Franklin	857	92 949	0.81	1 223	12.0	961	9.4	10 648	12.4	20 894	11 916	8 978	2 545	2 495
Gasconade	250	14 516	0.92	168	11.3	185	12.4	1 741	15.0	3 882	2 897	985	191	1 287
Gentry	177	6 366	0.85	89	13.2	87	12.9	932	17.1	1 578	1 492	86	33	486
Greene	11 252	315 602	1.27	3 573	12.5	2 589	9.0	32 486	14.0	53 456	31 051	22 405	16 612	5 801
Grundy	350	10 269	1.00	166	16.3	128	12.6	1 222	15.6	2 394	2 255	139	164	1 578
Harrison	145	8 493	0.92	110	12.8	122	14.1	1 210	17.9	2 130	2 016	114	118	1 356
Henry	233	21 566	0.94	249	11.4	288	13.2	2 656	15.3	5 949	4 534	1 415	830	3 766
Hickory	75	8 457	0.67	66	7.2	129	14.0	1 370	22.0	2 683	1 744	939	115	1 245
Holt	101	4 256	0.80	53	11.8	60	13.3	534	15.4	1 098	1 006	92	83	1 847
Howard	714	8 647	0.64	120	11.8	78	7.7	1 126	14.4	1 789	1 499	290	140	1 359
Howell	608	42 171	1.11	504	12.6	484	12.1	5 369	16.6	10 341	8 157	2 184	1 327	3 286
Iron	276	10 263	0.96	91	8.9	149	14.6	1 392	17.0	2 774	2 476	298	160	1 554
Jackson	10 907	736 924	1.19	9 555	13.9	6 208	9.1	86 330	14.8	112 175	69 830	42 345	32 865	4 819

1. Per 1,000 estimated resident population. 2. Data for serious crimes have not been adjusted for underreporting; this may affect comparability between geographic areas and over time.
3. Per 100,000 population estimated by the FBI.

Table B. States and Counties — Crime, Education, Money Income, and Poverty

STATE County	Serious crimes known to police, 2014 (cont.)[1] Rate[2]		Education School enrollment and attainment, 2010–2014				Local government expenditures,[5] 2012–2013		Money income, 2010–2014	Households			Income and poverty, 2014	Percent below poverty level		
	Violent	Property	Enrollment[3] Total	Percent private	Attainment[4] (percent) High school graduate or less	Bachelor's degree or more	Total current spending (mil dol)	Current spending per student (dollars)	Per capita income[6] (dollars)	Median income (dollars)	Mean income (dollars)	Percent with income of $200,000 or more	Median household income (dollars)	All persons	Children under 18 years	Children 5 to 17 years in families
	46	47	48	49	50	51	52	53	54	55	56	57	58	59	60	61
MISSISSIPPI—Cont'd																
Sunflower	NA	NA	7 846	12.0	58.4	13.8	38.9	9 209	13 936	27 941	44 024	1.9	29 227	34.8	44.9	43.4
Tallahatchie	NA	NA	3 560	29.1	66.5	9.7	20.2	9 744	13 460	31 860	40 667	0.4	28 456	37.4	47.7	47.1
Tate	NA	NA	8 233	11.3	48.1	16.8	35.6	7 412	21 795	42 902	60 355	3.8	40 975	18.5	26.5	25.1
Tippah	0	18	5 263	8.4	60.5	10.7	31.9	7 702	18 954	35 024	48 003	1.3	37 026	19.1	27.3	25.3
Tishomingo	26	421	4 283	5.4	61.7	11.3	27.0	8 492	18 350	34 499	45 470	1.2	35 550	17.7	26.2	24.6
Tunica	524	4 485	3 032	9.5	54.2	17.6	23.3	10 252	15 298	31 406	40 230	0.5	30 689	27.9	41.9	41.4
Union	NA	NA	7 093	4.5	55.2	14.9	38.2	7 738	19 116	35 389	49 902	1.7	37 667	15.9	23.1	22.4
Walthall	NA	NA	4 111	7.8	61.9	13.0	20.0	8 895	17 684	34 934	45 577	1.0	31 607	26.4	39.8	37.6
Warren	364	4 154	12 934	11.1	44.4	25.2	76.7	8 800	22 368	40 941	56 335	2.6	40 397	21.7	33.0	31.8
Washington	283	6 489	13 964	11.9	52.6	18.7	83.9	8 905	16 738	28 936	43 617	1.9	30 292	35.1	47.5	46.2
Wayne	NA	NA	5 311	4.8	65.0	10.3	30.1	8 381	19 040	29 254	48 984	1.5	35 425	24.7	34.8	31.7
Webster	NA	NA	2 526	13.4	48.7	19.0	14.9	7 990	20 392	33 769	48 608	2.7	34 073	22.1	32.0	29.3
Wilkinson	NA	NA	2 024	19.6	63.5	14.6	12.2	9 435	16 458	32 044	43 078	0.5	27 596	32.5	39.7	38.6
Winston	86	182	4 480	16.3	54.8	17.0	24.0	8 338	19 172	33 969	46 409	0.7	34 403	26.3	40.2	37.1
Yalobusha	NA	NA	2 808	12.9	60.1	11.1	15.2	8 255	18 727	33 900	45 479	1.0	34 494	23.4	33.9	32.3
Yazoo	NA	NA	6 918	19.4	60.6	12.4	34.9	8 172	14 269	27 489	39 995	1.3	30 313	34.6	38.7	39.2
MISSOURI	443	2 906	1 555 899	19.1	43.4	26.7	8 788.6	9 597	26 006	47 764	64 703	3.1	48 288	15.5	21.3	19.5
Adair	293	2 723	10 194	9.3	46.8	28.6	27.5	8 812	19 076	34 976	48 797	1.7	35 425	26.9	23.4	21.0
Andrew	143	1 390	3 856	8.0	50.0	22.4	24.1	8 402	26 086	53 986	66 266	2.7	56 309	10.7	13.3	12.3
Atchison	130	629	1 018	10.0	54.2	21.4	10.0	12 523	25 538	44 216	56 565	2.2	45 997	12.2	17.2	16.1
Audrain	202	2 249	5 705	8.1	61.7	12.3	30.2	8 863	19 797	43 139	52 360	1.5	41 302	17.2	27.5	25.6
Barry	281	2 365	8 148	12.7	59.2	13.3	55.8	8 307	19 680	38 789	49 247	1.1	38 139	20.2	32.7	33.0
Barton	212	2 194	2 870	9.1	55.5	15.3	18.4	8 899	20 275	38 792	49 689	1.0	37 581	19.1	28.1	25.1
Bates	486	2 675	4 019	10.5	61.0	12.1	24.4	8 976	21 369	39 744	51 405	1.1	41 462	18.4	25.9	24.3
Benton	370	1 920	3 431	14.0	59.4	11.8	21.0	7 988	19 412	33 145	43 728	0.5	33 236	19.5	30.8	28.4
Bollinger	136	973	2 913	11.5	63.6	11.5	15.0	7 885	20 186	38 906	49 907	2.2	39 033	20.1	28.5	27.3
Boone	342	2 974	61 590	12.9	26.5	47.7	220.1	9 502	27 098	49 059	67 746	3.8	50 305	19.5	17.7	16.5
Buchanan	412	5 105	22 488	14.3	50.9	19.7	119.9	9 352	22 839	44 971	57 742	1.7	45 431	17.8	26.8	25.5
Butler	498	4 664	10 423	7.9	57.2	14.0	53.1	7 679	19 186	36 160	47 318	1.2	35 774	21.3	32.2	29.8
Caldwell	111	1 175	2 107	6.8	55.8	15.3	16.1	9 834	22 135	41 740	54 171	0.9	43 111	16.2	22.0	19.8
Callaway	335	2 380	11 446	21.0	51.2	21.3	42.4	8 721	22 901	48 264	58 180	1.7	49 384	14.2	20.4	18.6
Camden	244	1 833	8 535	9.8	46.6	22.0	51.9	9 672	23 251	43 498	55 489	2.1	44 410	17.5	27.1	24.6
Cape Girardeau	345	3 001	22 008	12.6	45.1	28.1	84.2	8 411	23 684	45 849	59 646	1.8	47 705	17.0	20.5	18.4
Carroll	198	1 296	2 142	7.5	60.4	17.0	15.1	9 885	23 424	42 582	56 922	2.2	39 017	16.5	24.4	23.3
Carter	270	1 239	1 694	7.9	50.9	14.8	11.1	8 779	19 318	32 656	48 034	3.5	32 170	24.0	35.4	34.9
Cass	167	2 081	26 506	17.3	42.4	24.0	159.9	8 591	28 013	61 046	74 239	2.7	60 970	10.5	14.1	12.3
Cedar	295	2 200	3 171	17.3	58.7	14.3	18.4	7 931	17 744	29 872	41 607	1.1	33 631	21.4	33.0	29.7
Chariton	673	1 055	1 625	18.5	64.1	13.4	11.6	10 680	20 300	40 195	50 492	0.6	43 049	12.0	20.3	20.1
Christian	147	1 612	21 204	14.8	39.7	26.5	115.4	7 878	25 428	52 693	67 252	3.1	51 831	11.3	17.2	14.9
Clark	58	350	1 480	13.2	57.8	10.9	9.2	8 629	23 583	43 497	55 429	0.9	43 298	15.7	23.5	22.1
Clay	758	3 573	60 056	16.1	36.1	30.7	389.1	9 716	29 455	61 184	75 263	3.0	61 598	9.1	12.1	10.6
Clinton	569	1 173	4 745	10.5	47.8	17.5	37.6	8 798	25 307	53 361	64 376	1.4	51 221	12.4	17.0	15.2
Cole	218	2 189	19 464	23.2	40.4	30.9	100.7	8 737	26 254	53 228	67 169	2.1	51 885	13.3	18.0	15.2
Cooper	113	2 307	3 915	12.1	52.4	19.3	22.9	9 087	23 193	44 102	60 283	1.4	42 166	14.0	20.0	18.5
Crawford	171	2 696	5 422	12.6	60.9	13.6	26.7	7 487	19 099	35 829	48 130	0.7	37 379	20.7	30.4	27.8
Dade	181	1 510	1 639	11.2	56.8	15.2	10.4	9 299	20 360	36 209	48 716	1.5	37 173	18.5	27.1	23.7
Dallas	400	1 472	3 368	16.6	61.3	13.9	22.4	8 833	17 663	38 314	46 376	1.4	34 987	21.7	32.8	32.2
Daviess	121	835	1 827	15.7	57.1	15.0	12.3	9 507	19 726	42 188	52 049	1.4	41 610	16.8	27.9	25.9
DeKalb	280	1 168	2 464	8.2	63.4	10.9	10.6	10 176	17 288	44 936	56 071	2.1	42 174	18.6	19.9	19.0
Dent	76	1 866	3 244	9.3	59.4	12.4	17.6	7 975	19 589	37 658	49 108	1.5	34 411	21.6	31.8	29.3
Douglas	170	1 356	2 777	11.8	64.1	9.7	13.8	8 710	16 780	30 879	40 525	0.7	31 805	23.0	35.0	32.7
Dunklin	470	4 285	7 408	4.8	68.3	10.9	48.7	7 961	18 158	31 777	43 497	1.1	31 486	29.8	41.5	40.1
Franklin	179	2 316	24 352	19.5	48.2	18.0	148.3	8 978	24 732	48 661	62 558	2.4	51 978	11.8	16.2	15.1
Gasconade	94	1 193	3 185	10.2	58.4	15.6	24.7	8 516	22 067	42 574	51 595	0.6	44 065	13.5	19.8	18.2
Gentry	15	471	1 407	9.5	55.2	17.3	12.0	10 413	20 223	40 591	49 493	0.8	39 444	15.4	22.0	22.0
Greene	716	5 085	76 093	15.9	37.8	28.7	313.8	8 274	23 765	40 512	55 831	2.3	40 386	20.6	23.9	21.2
Grundy	67	1 511	2 412	7.5	53.5	16.8	14.9	8 594	19 299	37 167	46 634	1.3	37 911	19.2	27.4	25.8
Harrison	69	1 287	1 856	2.8	65.3	12.0	14.1	9 305	19 648	39 342	48 080	0.8	37 486	19.0	26.6	24.5
Henry	250	3 516	4 975	9.5	54.0	15.1	26.7	8 914	22 230	39 880	52 049	1.7	39 232	18.3	26.1	24.2
Hickory	22	1 224	1 642	15.1	59.8	11.2	9.1	10 255	17 804	31 897	39 552	0.2	33 707	22.1	39.5	36.1
Holt	245	1 602	807	5.2	56.2	18.3	7.0	11 475	23 917	41 842	50 944	1.5	41 652	14.4	21.6	20.2
Howard	87	1 272	3 021	35.2	55.6	23.6	12.1	8 266	23 082	44 081	59 684	2.4	44 188	15.6	22.8	20.9
Howell	218	3 068	9 586	7.5	55.3	15.0	46.4	8 578	18 771	33 006	45 617	2.0	32 662	22.1	30.6	28.7
Iron	359	1 195	2 052	4.1	60.2	10.9	18.2	9 622	19 984	37 259	47 774	0.5	33 091	22.1	32.9	31.8
Jackson	702	4 117	170 803	18.1	40.8	28.0	994.3	10 282	26 328	46 917	63 581	2.9	46 185	16.5	23.5	20.8

1. Data for serious crimes have not been adjusted for underreporting; this may affect comparability between geographic areas and over time.   2. Per 100,000 population estimated by the FBI.
3. All persons 3 years old and over enrolled in nursery school through college.   4. Persons 25 years old and over.   5. Elementary and secondary education expenditures.
6. Based on population estimated by the American Community Survey, 2010–2014.

Table B. States and Counties — **Personal Income**

STATE County	Personal income, 2014										Earnings, 2014		
	Total (mil dol)	Percent change, 2013–2014	Per capita[1] Dollars	Per capita[1] Rank	Wages and salaries (mil dol)	Supplements to wages and salaries; employer contributions (mil dol) Pension and insurance	Supplements to wages and salaries; employer contributions (mil dol) Government social insurance	Proprietors' income (mil dol)	Dividends, interest, and rent (mil dol)	Personal transfer receipts (mil dol)	Total (mil dol)	Contributions for government social insurance (mil dol) From employee and self-employed	Contributions for government social insurance (mil dol) From employer
	62	63	64	65	66	67	68	69	70	71	72	73	74

MISSISSIPPI—Cont'd

STATE County	62	63	64	65	66	67	68	69	70	71	72	73	74
Sunflower	739	-3.4	26 863	2 990	298	56	22	54	104	268	431	27	22
Tallahatchie	432	-7.3	29 269	2 799	115	18	9	66	53	134	208	13	9
Tate	890	0.7	31 570	2 516	198	36	15	60	95	251	309	23	15
Tippah	642	3.5	29 137	2 811	207	35	16	43	74	221	301	23	16
Tishomingo	537	3.7	27 655	2 943	189	33	15	24	71	200	261	21	15
Tunica	335	-7.3	31 570	2 516	346	36	28	49	42	99	459	27	28
Union	846	3.2	30 096	2 705	420	60	32	74	111	231	585	41	32
Walthall	426	3.6	28 678	2 867	89	16	7	64	52	151	175	12	7
Warren	1 757	1.9	36 623	1 664	924	170	72	101	286	428	1 268	80	72
Washington	1 590	-0.2	32 475	2 377	657	109	50	127	234	529	942	62	50
Wayne	674	6.6	32 880	2 300	205	33	15	114	88	189	367	22	15
Webster	299	-3.0	29 984	2 718	69	12	5	17	34	112	103	9	5
Wilkinson	242	0.7	26 304	3 019	61	11	5	11	36	96	88	7	5
Winston	585	3.3	31 639	2 503	181	29	13	66	76	191	289	20	13
Yalobusha	367	1.0	29 883	2 733	108	21	8	29	48	146	165	13	8
Yazoo	767	-3.0	27 588	2 949	274	56	21	49	119	248	400	28	21
MISSOURI	252 482	3.6	41 639	X	128 795	21 595	9 324	23 066	45 678	49 233	182 780	10 798	9 324
Adair	792	3.3	30 941	2 594	334	76	24	92	157	204	526	30	24
Andrew	710	2.4	40 882	1 075	83	19	6	75	105	127	183	11	6
Atchison	268	-1.2	49 887	388	57	12	4	79	41	50	152	6	4
Audrain	966	5.2	37 335	1 549	341	77	25	198	138	209	640	33	25
Barry	1 189	5.8	33 329	2 223	539	98	39	183	215	305	859	50	39
Barton	432	-0.5	35 797	1 805	108	25	8	92	65	110	232	12	8
Bates	592	2.2	35 711	1 822	125	30	9	91	94	149	255	15	9
Benton	612	3.4	32 563	2 358	114	27	8	54	106	238	203	18	8
Bollinger	371	1.9	29 957	2 720	56	13	4	40	55	113	113	9	4
Boone	7 154	2.9	41 418	1 017	3 985	915	270	459	1 317	1 077	5 629	295	270
Buchanan	3 234	2.8	36 144	1 757	2 072	373	151	273	513	782	2 869	168	151
Butler	1 477	3.2	34 376	2 049	680	139	52	143	212	506	1 015	64	52
Caldwell	327	8.7	36 193	1 747	54	13	4	66	43	73	137	7	4
Callaway	1 558	2.8	34 810	1 965	592	143	42	102	225	342	880	51	42
Camden	1 549	4.3	35 197	1 904	524	91	41	169	353	443	825	57	41
Cape Girardeau	3 086	3.2	39 547	1 240	1 651	294	120	327	533	603	2 392	140	120
Carroll	434	4.0	47 977	480	84	18	6	101	66	84	209	10	6
Carter	176	-1.7	28 068	2 912	42	11	3	16	28	60	73	6	3
Cass	4 011	3.7	39 757	1 216	891	166	66	209	555	752	1 332	87	66
Cedar	428	3.0	30 681	2 628	89	22	6	46	69	153	163	13	6
Chariton	386	10.9	50 221	374	65	14	5	121	60	74	205	9	5
Christian	2 860	4.6	34 839	1 960	555	110	42	240	371	544	947	66	42
Clark	253	3.8	36 612	1 666	44	11	3	52	35	57	110	6	3
Clay	10 025	4.2	42 898	860	4 837	734	361	917	1 177	1 496	6 850	407	361
Clinton	768	1.9	37 828	1 480	142	32	10	52	122	157	236	15	10
Cole	3 199	2.5	41 790	973	2 222	534	151	215	568	563	3 121	163	151
Cooper	605	2.4	34 416	2 046	188	38	14	56	93	142	297	18	14
Crawford	851	3.4	34 536	2 017	243	47	18	157	113	235	464	31	18
Dade	251	11.7	32 908	2 294	54	13	4	40	40	72	111	7	4
Dallas	501	6.3	30 583	2 643	74	17	6	80	67	159	177	13	6
Daviess	314	9.3	37 867	1 475	46	12	3	83	48	68	144	6	3
DeKalb	318	3.0	25 089	3 061	117	30	8	30	45	78	185	10	8
Dent	478	2.8	30 511	2 648	124	28	9	37	78	158	198	14	9
Douglas	370	6.5	27 316	2 962	74	17	6	85	49	120	182	13	6
Dunklin	1 000	-1.2	31 895	2 450	297	61	23	77	127	383	458	32	23
Franklin	3 913	4.2	38 330	1 418	1 511	276	114	225	617	817	2 126	135	114
Gasconade	542	3.8	36 472	1 691	170	37	13	35	110	142	254	17	13
Gentry	301	10.9	44 134	750	75	15	5	84	43	70	180	7	5
Greene	10 895	4.1	38 112	1 441	6 825	1 148	503	1 070	2 018	2 282	9 546	571	503
Grundy	352	4.2	34 476	2 032	125	29	9	51	57	101	213	12	9
Harrison	321	3.2	37 205	1 567	77	19	5	60	56	87	162	8	5
Henry	860	5.4	39 035	1 317	313	67	22	83	146	245	485	29	22
Hickory	237	3.9	25 654	3 040	36	9	3	22	41	103	69	7	3
Holt	208	-5.2	45 956	597	46	10	3	52	33	45	111	5	3
Howard	371	1.9	36 538	1 681	85	18	7	36	61	93	146	9	7
Howell	1 247	4.5	31 029	2 579	520	106	40	102	199	407	767	51	40
Iron	310	3.5	30 159	2 696	152	27	11	13	40	129	203	14	11
Jackson	28 457	3.5	41 653	991	20 048	3 144	1 450	3 381	4 376	5 479	28 022	1 633	1 450

1. Based on the resident population estimated as of July 1 of the year shown.

Table B. States and Counties — **Earnings, Social Security, and Housing**

STATE County	Farm	Mining	Construction	Manufacturing	Information: professional, scientific, technical services	Retail trade	Finance, insurance, real estate and leasing	Health care and social assistance	Government	Number	Rate[1]	Supplemental Security Income recipients, December 2014	Total	Percent change, 2010–2014
	75	76	77	78	79	80	81	82	83	84	85	86	87	88
MISSISSIPPI—Cont'd														
Sunflower	10.9	0.0	2.5	3.5	1.8	5.5	3.4	6.0	39.6	5 745	209	2 076	9 697	0.1
Tallahatchie	22.3	0.0	2.8	1.2	D	5.5	1.7	D	21.6	3 275	222	1 116	5 541	0.2
Tate	3.6	D	5.6	7.0	D	9.9	4.2	12.6	26.1	6 110	217	976	11 198	2.3
Tippah	3.3	D	5.5	29.7	D	7.7	3.3	D	17.3	6 110	277	1 143	9 725	0.3
Tishomingo	2.2	0.0	5.0	34.3	1.8	7.2	3.1	D	16.7	5 810	299	758	10 320	0.2
Tunica	7.9	0.0	2.1	3.7	D	2.5	1.5	2.1	9.1	1 985	188	739	4 834	0.6
Union	1.9	0.0	3.6	36.0	D	5.8	2.6	D	10.6	6 850	243	818	11 809	2.5
Walthall	18.0	3.5	5.2	12.1	1.9	9.6	4.4	D	17.7	3 760	253	744	7 144	0.2
Warren	0.7	0.2	3.8	14.8	6.9	6.9	3.4	10.9	28.8	10 090	210	2 133	21 880	-0.1
Washington	6.3	D	2.9	8.7	5.4	8.8	3.9	9.5	24.9	11 565	235	4 591	21 609	-0.5
Wayne	22.0	6.7	8.3	7.4	2.2	7.4	2.6	D	16.6	4 720	230	964	9 219	0.1
Webster	7.6	D	4.5	10.7	D	7.6	D	D	19.2	2 625	263	498	4 807	0.1
Wilkinson	3.5	D	2.6	8.9	D	8.5	3.4	D	29.6	2 335	253	772	5 042	0.1
Winston	12.7	D	4.7	18.2	2.6	9.2	2.5	D	13.3	4 955	268	829	8 770	0.3
Yalobusha	3.8	D	6.5	29.7	D	5.9	3.0	2.1	26.1	3 800	310	944	6 384	0.6
Yazoo	2.8	D	3.7	12.3	2.2	5.0	4.7	D	34.3	5 450	196	1 815	10 068	-0.1
MISSOURI	2.1	0.2	5.8	10.6	11.2	6.2	8.0	11.8	15.8	1 246 269	206	142 768	2 746 599	1.2
Adair	4.8	0.0	4.5	7.3	4.2	8.7	3.5	D	24.6	4 865	191	674	11 372	1.0
Andrew	15.3	0.0	11.9	0.7	D	9.8	3.7	D	19.0	3 620	209	198	7 274	-0.4
Atchison	44.6	0.0	2.5	1.3	3.7	4.1	2.6	7.3	12.0	1 480	276	79	2 955	-1.0
Audrain	16.8	0.0	3.9	21.5	2.0	8.4	3.3	D	19.4	5 685	219	599	10 776	-0.7
Barry	11.7	0.1	5.3	26.5	15.5	6.5	4.0	4.7	10.0	8 505	238	958	17 359	-0.9
Barton	26.0	D	6.5	5.3	D	7.7	4.5	5.0	19.7	2 885	240	289	5 561	-0.7
Bates	16.0	0.0	6.3	3.1	6.1	11.8	5.4	7.0	23.5	3 620	219	358	7 800	-0.5
Benton	3.3	0.0	D	6.3	2.6	11.3	9.8	9.3	26.0	6 945	370	532	13 984	-1.2
Bollinger	9.4	D	11.4	5.2	2.9	8.1	D	10.9	20.0	3 035	245	436	5 814	-1.1
Boone	0.5	0.1	5.1	4.4	8.1	7.3	7.1	10.9	37.0	24 680	143	2 772	74 436	7.0
Buchanan	1.1	D	5.9	26.4	5.8	6.5	4.9	15.0	13.8	17 860	199	2 510	38 449	0.1
Butler	1.7	0.0	5.0	13.4	5.5	10.3	4.8	18.3	21.0	12 920	301	2 644	19 640	-0.5
Caldwell	25.4	D	11.8	0.7	4.1	8.0	D	3.9	20.2	2 180	242	160	4 600	-0.1
Callaway	4.8	0.4	5.0	12.9	3.7	4.2	2.6	D	22.6	9 250	207	853	18 535	0.1
Camden	0.5	D	10.5	3.9	5.3	15.1	7.7	15.9	11.9	13 535	307	948	41 292	0.3
Cape Girardeau	1.0	0.1	5.7	11.5	6.7	8.2	4.5	25.9	13.8	16 085	206	1 641	33 153	1.6
Carroll	31.7	0.0	8.7	12.9	2.1	4.9	3.6	D	13.4	2 345	260	191	4 604	-0.6
Carter	1.3	D	14.4	9.3	D	9.3	D	8.0	28.9	1 290	206	202	3 246	0.0
Cass	3.0	0.3	11.1	5.5	4.4	9.2	4.8	9.1	21.0	19 935	197	1 042	40 731	1.8
Cedar	5.3	D	9.7	6.8	3.1	10.5	4.5	10.3	25.4	4 310	309	442	7 165	-0.8
Chariton	37.4	0.0	5.0	3.6	1.1	4.8	4.2	3.9	10.4	1 995	260	150	4 137	-0.7
Christian	0.7	D	13.5	7.3	9.2	9.4	6.1	6.3	17.7	15 845	193	1 071	32 952	4.4
Clark	26.9	D	D	7.0	D	10.3	3.4	3.9	19.1	1 630	237	127	3 450	-0.6
Clay	0.2	0.1	7.3	16.4	16.4	6.6	4.4	7.8	14.7	38 875	167	2 569	95 600	1.8
Clinton	12.8	0.0	6.8	4.2	3.2	5.7	5.5	18.6	24.5	4 565	225	363	8 894	0.2
Cole	0.6	D	5.6	4.2	9.0	6.4	5.6	10.9	39.1	15 675	205	1 297	32 925	2.0
Cooper	10.4	D	7.4	11.2	D	7.7	5.9	7.6	21.3	3 955	225	338	7 434	-0.4
Crawford	0.8	D	5.9	22.4	2.2	26.8	2.9	D	10.1	6 495	264	720	11 918	-0.3
Dade	24.9	D	5.6	9.1	D	5.2	D	1.8	20.4	2 350	309	230	3 927	-1.0
Dallas	8.2	D	D	3.7	2.5	9.7	4.0	D	18.6	4 635	283	531	7 563	-1.3
Daviess	41.4	0.0	8.7	D	D	6.2	2.3	D	16.3	1 935	233	123	4 178	-0.5
DeKalb	11.4	0.0	3.5	1.0	D	7.9	8.0	D	35.7	2 230	176	118	4 292	-0.9
Dent	2.7	0.0	5.2	8.5	2.6	10.2	6.7	D	24.8	4 140	266	593	7 232	-0.7
Douglas	7.0	D	7.3	14.8	D	9.5	3.0	D	13.3	530	39	44	6 438	-1.3
Dunklin	4.9	0.0	3.8	5.7	2.7	11.9	5.8	D	18.6	8 560	273	2 436	14 322	-0.7
Franklin	1.2	0.2	7.8	25.3	4.9	7.2	4.1	12.0	12.1	23 070	226	1 911	44 058	1.5
Gasconade	2.5	D	4.1	29.2	D	7.2	4.0	D	20.5	4 130	277	296	8 116	-1.1
Gentry	45.2	0.0	D	D	D	4.9	2.4	13.2	12.2	1 710	251	166	3 195	-0.4
Greene	0.1	D	4.3	9.6	9.2	7.8	7.0	19.0	13.0	58 385	204	6 822	130 516	4.1
Grundy	15.2	D	4.0	19.9	D	5.9	3.2	10.9	22.0	2 560	251	247	4 999	-0.5
Harrison	27.3	D	2.1	1.1	2.4	13.0	4.6	6.0	24.8	2 370	274	235	4 385	-0.5
Henry	9.7	D	13.0	15.0	2.4	7.6	4.3	8.8	21.6	6 760	307	729	10 864	-0.2
Hickory	16.9	D	D	D	D	12.4	3.5	8.7	24.0	2 975	322	243	6 712	-1.8
Holt	37.3	D	4.2	7.8	D	7.1	3.0	4.3	12.7	1 225	271	74	2 777	-1.0
Howard	14.5	D	4.3	12.0	2.4	6.7	4.3	D	15.0	2 245	221	305	4 532	-1.1
Howell	2.2	0.2	2.8	16.4	5.2	8.2	4.4	18.7	15.4	11 950	298	1 790	18 043	0.1
Iron	1.0	D	D	14.1	0.8	6.7	1.7	10.0	15.6	3 220	314	642	5 268	-1.2
Jackson	0.0	0.0	6.4	6.5	18.5	4.9	11.8	11.4	15.9	125 220	183	17 521	317 140	1.6

1. Per 1,000 resident population estimated as of July 1 of the year shown.

Table B. States and Counties — Housing, Labor Force, and Employment

STATE County	Housing units, 2010–2014 Occupied units — Owner-occupied Total	Percent	Median value[1]	Median owner cost as a percent of income — With a mortgage	Without a mortgage[2]	Renter-occupied Median rent[3]	Median rent as a percent of income[2]	Substandard units[4] (percent)	Civilian labor force, 2015 Total	Percent change, 2014–2015	Unemployment Total	Rate[5]	Civilian employment[6] 2010–2014 Total	Percent — Management, business, science and arts	Construction, production, and maintenance occupations
	89	90	91	92	93	94	95	96	97	98	99	100	101	102	103
MISSISSIPPI—Cont'd															
Sunflower	8 451	58.5	70 600	26.1	12.6	534	31.3	5.7	8 537	-1.6	918	10.8	8 352	28.5	28.7
Tallahatchie	4 519	75.8	66 700	23.5	13.2	488	26.5	4.5	5 887	0.8	448	7.6	3 959	30.0	27.9
Tate	10 017	72.1	114 900	23.5	10.3	703	34.2	4.3	12 024	2.0	860	7.2	11 747	29.2	30.1
Tippah	8 488	75.4	77 700	23.3	10.9	567	28.4	1.9	9 560	9.4	610	6.4	8 387	20.5	43.0
Tishomingo	7 618	76.3	74 500	23.6	10.5	521	26.6	1.8	8 048	5.9	519	6.4	7 400	22.4	40.6
Tunica	4 031	43.8	77 600	21.1	10.3	679	33.7	10.1	4 789	0.5	442	9.2	4 170	24.1	17.6
Union	10 292	71.8	84 200	22.8	10.2	678	31.0	4.7	13 347	3.7	690	5.2	11 133	22.2	38.4
Walthall	5 823	85.6	87 500	27.3	13.5	444	28.2	3.3	5 211	1.0	428	8.2	5 681	28.8	34.8
Warren	18 367	64.9	103 300	21.0	10.5	672	31.9	2.5	21 058	0.4	1 437	6.8	19 798	36.3	21.5
Washington	18 383	54.9	74 000	24.1	13.5	617	37.2	4.0	18 237	-0.8	1 910	10.5	17 103	32.4	22.5
Wayne	8 031	81.7	69 400	23.2	14.3	497	32.0	3.3	7 705	-0.5	614	8.0	7 758	19.9	44.8
Webster	4 085	74.9	71 400	22.0	11.2	499	37.2	3.8	3 984	0.3	292	7.3	3 559	36.0	31.4
Wilkinson	3 295	78.8	55 100	21.4	12.5	431	34.8	4.0	2 923	3.0	311	10.6	3 218	27.4	30.3
Winston	7 658	69.6	75 900	22.1	12.6	577	33.4	3.7	7 173	0.1	599	8.4	6 827	32.9	31.8
Yalobusha	4 808	74.8	70 400	23.9	12.9	396	34.1	3.3	5 028	1.9	358	7.1	4 899	22.7	41.7
Yazoo	8 552	59.9	65 500	23.5	13.9	604	39.0	3.2	9 441	1.7	775	8.2	8 308	27.7	28.2
MISSOURI	2 361 232	67.9	136 700	21.6	11.8	740	29.8	2.0	3 113 769	2.0	155 588	5.0	2 779 991	34.9	21.9
Adair	9 608	60.1	102 700	18.4	11.8	573	36.2	2.0	10 602	-0.1	594	5.6	11 040	35.5	21.5
Andrew	6 710	77.4	125 300	21.0	10.5	703	26.5	1.7	10 011	1.4	417	4.2	8 458	30.7	26.6
Atchison	2 465	69.0	79 900	20.7	12.0	553	21.3	0.8	2 891	0.5	130	4.5	2 665	33.9	28.7
Audrain	9 381	72.9	91 700	20.4	10.9	616	24.5	1.4	11 448	1.7	530	4.6	10 706	26.6	32.0
Barry	13 398	75.3	108 800	22.1	11.2	579	26.7	3.0	15 058	1.5	747	5.0	14 345	26.3	37.4
Barton	5 009	74.8	87 000	21.6	13.1	503	35.5	2.1	5 432	-1.1	296	5.4	5 024	29.2	34.5
Bates	6 784	72.0	100 200	22.4	12.8	600	31.2	1.8	8 362	3.1	504	6.0	7 209	27.0	29.2
Benton	8 273	84.0	105 400	24.8	12.2	589	34.5	3.3	7 274	1.2	472	6.5	6 622	28.1	30.3
Bollinger	4 790	81.7	96 800	21.3	10.5	556	29.9	3.5	5 725	1.3	320	5.6	4 941	26.3	39.8
Boone	66 136	56.7	165 900	20.1	10.0	798	34.0	1.5	100 284	2.5	3 491	3.5	89 118	46.0	12.9
Buchanan	33 359	63.6	108 600	19.9	11.6	681	30.9	1.8	46 861	1.1	2 162	4.6	41 328	26.1	28.3
Butler	16 773	66.1	91 700	19.6	12.0	606	31.2	1.4	19 281	0.8	1 188	6.2	17 814	27.2	26.9
Caldwell	3 696	72.2	88 900	21.9	13.4	643	27.9	2.8	4 480	3.2	201	4.5	3 890	28.8	29.8
Callaway	16 497	74.3	122 400	22.0	10.2	665	26.2	1.9	21 967	0.7	1 030	4.7	19 927	32.9	25.3
Camden	17 419	78.6	167 100	24.2	10.9	656	28.7	2.9	19 029	1.0	1 233	6.5	17 782	30.5	22.0
Cape Girardeau	29 672	64.6	138 000	20.6	10.5	686	29.8	1.9	41 110	0.9	1 770	4.3	37 144	31.9	21.9
Carroll	3 652	76.9	80 900	18.0	11.8	521	30.5	2.2	4 888	3.0	290	5.9	4 023	28.2	30.1
Carter	2 456	71.7	102 900	25.1	12.2	447	28.7	3.1	2 529	-1.2	189	7.5	2 457	33.9	24.1
Cass	37 503	76.6	156 000	22.3	12.5	929	29.1	2.2	54 463	3.0	2 602	4.8	47 738	34.1	25.1
Cedar	5 893	72.4	87 800	23.6	14.4	597	32.2	3.2	5 985	1.9	317	5.3	4 919	28.2	30.0
Chariton	2 956	77.4	71 500	20.0	12.1	478	24.0	2.5	3 920	1.6	183	4.7	3 312	27.2	32.4
Christian	29 994	74.0	141 700	21.3	11.9	745	28.5	2.4	43 444	2.8	1 821	4.2	37 764	35.6	19.9
Clark	2 859	75.6	78 600	19.5	11.7	489	20.6	2.6	3 510	1.9	249	7.1	3 249	25.5	43.3
Clay	87 352	71.0	153 600	21.2	12.3	823	27.0	1.6	133 448	2.9	6 023	4.5	116 388	37.4	20.6
Clinton	8 067	73.2	136 700	21.0	12.3	745	24.8	2.0	11 026	3.0	538	4.9	9 690	26.4	26.9
Cole	29 307	67.8	146 700	19.6	10.0	601	25.1	1.5	39 909	0.5	1 591	4.0	36 323	39.3	18.1
Cooper	6 520	70.7	125 800	19.2	11.2	638	26.9	1.6	7 698	0.5	446	5.8	7 880	28.7	25.3
Crawford	9 427	73.9	106 200	21.1	13.0	610	36.3	2.4	11 051	1.4	665	6.0	9 665	24.6	36.3
Dade	3 166	79.2	78 700	22.6	12.7	564	31.0	3.2	3 619	3.0	185	5.1	3 317	31.7	28.2
Dallas	6 348	79.3	94 600	22.8	10.3	560	24.0	5.1	7 132	2.2	439	6.2	6 161	28.4	30.8
Daviess	3 134	77.2	102 800	23.6	12.7	587	23.9	4.9	4 120	1.9	188	4.6	3 382	30.3	30.7
DeKalb	3 778	65.5	114 300	19.7	12.1	545	26.7	0.8	5 074	1.9	236	4.7	4 300	26.8	28.8
Dent	5 889	71.5	88 900	23.5	11.5	528	28.4	2.8	6 378	1.6	371	5.8	5 961	25.3	30.6
Douglas	5 156	76.8	97 300	24.1	12.4	602	30.8	3.6	5 110	1.5	349	6.8	4 894	20.3	39.6
Dunklin	12 727	62.4	69 900	20.6	12.5	512	30.6	2.2	13 358	1.5	1 063	8.0	11 479	25.8	31.7
Franklin	39 733	75.5	147 500	22.9	11.3	701	27.0	2.4	53 129	1.8	2 683	5.0	47 481	28.4	31.8
Gasconade	6 333	76.1	116 300	21.4	10.7	566	30.4	3.6	7 775	1.9	327	4.2	6 540	25.8	36.0
Gentry	2 725	74.5	83 700	20.4	14.0	499	24.0	4.2	3 686	1.2	155	4.2	2 921	32.3	27.5
Greene	116 632	59.2	128 000	21.3	10.4	694	31.9	1.7	151 650	2.7	6 239	4.1	133 481	34.7	18.9
Grundy	4 150	68.7	75 900	19.7	12.0	584	30.4	3.8	5 011	2.1	206	4.1	4 330	27.6	29.1
Harrison	3 574	73.2	68 400	20.8	13.1	569	24.2	2.5	4 034	1.2	205	5.1	3 847	28.2	28.6
Henry	9 545	72.7	93 200	22.8	13.3	656	29.7	3.1	10 235	1.0	558	5.5	9 235	28.0	32.1
Hickory	4 134	83.1	101 200	26.6	14.6	549	34.3	2.4	3 784	2.2	252	6.7	3 002	26.4	31.9
Holt	2 164	70.1	80 600	20.8	11.3	453	23.7	2.7	2 760	2.1	101	3.7	2 268	33.2	29.1
Howard	3 779	76.2	94 100	21.3	10.0	655	29.6	2.0	5 110	2.3	249	4.9	4 374	31.4	27.0
Howell	16 060	68.2	99 600	22.3	10.7	553	31.6	2.1	16 548	1.5	1 063	6.4	15 993	26.6	32.1
Iron	4 158	70.9	80 700	19.3	10.8	530	26.2	3.3	3 902	-0.8	306	7.8	3 895	21.7	31.3
Jackson	271 965	60.2	125 800	22.2	13.1	800	31.2	1.8	367 142	2.5	21 541	5.9	322 847	35.7	19.4

1. Specified owner-occupied units. 2. A value of 10.0 represents 10 percent or less; a value of 50.0 represents 50 percent or more. 3. Specified renter-occupied units.
4. Overcrowded or lacking complete plumbing facilities. 5. Percent of civilian labor force. 6. Persons 16 years old and over.

Table B. States and Counties — Nonfarm Employment and Agriculture

STATE County	Private nonfarm establishments, employment and payroll, 2014									Agriculture, 2012			
	Number of establish-ments	Employment						Annual payroll		Farms			Farm operators whose principal occupation is farming (percent)
		Total	Health care and social assistance	Manufac-turing	Retail trade	Finance and insurance	Professional, scientific, and technical services	Total (mil dol)	Average per employee (dollars)	Number	Percent with: Fewer than 50 acres	500 acres or more	
	104	105	106	107	108	109	110	111	112	113	114	115	116
MISSISSIPPI—Cont'd													
Sunflower	437	5 134	D	320	984	215	69	160	31 257	350	22.6	44.0	59.7
Tallahatchie	175	1 908	D	D	267	D	48	59	30 969	509	13.6	28.7	38.9
Tate	356	3 840	599	618	798	184	97	113	29 330	569	25.3	14.1	38.8
Tippah	350	4 982	599	1 795	682	D	74	144	28 845	691	25.2	5.4	32.0
Tishomingo	358	4 228	666	1 648	568	D	85	129	30 410	287	22.0	3.8	36.2
Tunica	223	9 139	203	D	483	D	22	251	27 445	108	7.4	62.0	64.8
Union	510	9 271	1 065	3 863	1 162	216	86	334	35 980	688	29.1	6.4	25.3
Walthall	215	1 899	222	367	367	73	D	55	29 074	684	30.7	4.8	49.9
Warren	996	19 114	3 903	2 983	2 455	385	670	653	34 160	238	18.5	19.7	39.9
Washington	1 157	14 653	2 925	1 109	2 943	349	360	446	30 421	284	18.7	47.5	71.1
Wayne	383	4 361	D	833	954	D	120	155	35 557	508	34.4	5.5	48.0
Webster	167	1 465	D	274	224	D	71	49	33 506	362	20.7	11.0	32.9
Wilkinson	132	1 459	330	172	268	D	10	40	27 531	198	17.7	23.7	41.4
Winston	383	4 774	678	1 306	866	95	89	164	34 421	506	27.1	9.5	40.9
Yalobusha	177	2 301	341	905	303	98	D	74	32 287	364	21.2	13.7	50.5
Yazoo	401	4 034	885	D	772	142	157	140	34 598	672	14.3	25.9	49.9
MISSOURI	153 945	2 404 701	404 916	248 347	310 453	130 790	159 837	104 218	43 339	99 171	25.5	13.7	44.2
Adair	635	8 296	2 013	D	1 546	221	618	218	26 239	822	19.6	16.7	44.0
Andrew	292	1 734	338	D	318	57	D	48	27 765	826	29.5	12.8	42.1
Atchison	202	1 283	261	24	318	D	D	35	27 005	395	12.9	36.5	66.6
Audrain	551	6 814	1 172	1 802	1 113	255	120	209	30 693	1 015	18.6	25.1	55.8
Barry	729	13 755	1 951	4 838	1 491	252	D	505	36 721	1 427	31.1	8.4	43.5
Barton	250	2 613	460	372	498	163	D	79	30 178	940	24.0	22.8	45.7
Bates	349	2 783	778	D	611	192	71	78	28 202	1 169	23.4	18.1	46.6
Benton	367	2 266	446	193	689	D	58	52	22 802	800	18.5	13.1	52.8
Bollinger	202	1 371	332	188	313	D	D	35	25 759	788	16.9	12.8	42.4
Boone	4 517	73 688	16 855	3 909	12 273	6 869	3 941	2 688	36 482	1 171	39.5	8.6	38.3
Buchanan	2 294	41 950	8 107	10 015	5 498	1 790	966	1 689	40 252	727	29.4	13.1	44.4
Butler	1 292	15 023	4 306	D	2 624	540	385	482	32 074	509	23.8	24.6	47.9
Caldwell	144	864	D	D	242	54	D	29	33 022	1 035	24.3	10.6	41.0
Callaway	761	11 839	2 286	1 628	1 281	272	D	448	37 832	1 417	28.4	9.7	35.5
Camden	1 409	12 278	2 342	D	3 112	483	652	367	29 915	533	16.3	12.0	42.2
Cape Girardeau	2 399	38 085	9 967	3 887	6 159	1 016	1 170	1 340	35 196	1 139	29.5	10.2	47.8
Carroll	230	1 771	361	185	303	106	D	58	32 834	1 112	18.4	18.2	39.8
Carter	191	981	278	178	157	D	D	20	20 370	196	23.5	17.9	45.4
Cass	1 846	19 588	3 216	2 271	4 175	618	462	596	30 421	1 495	41.1	9.2	46.3
Cedar	282	2 330	635	349	428	99	41	61	26 146	819	19.9	10.4	45.2
Chariton	212	1 285	D	D	240	D	D	37	28 878	1 120	17.1	21.3	47.8
Christian	1 678	14 130	1 856	1 499	2 745	595	1 161	404	28 606	1 177	36.4	5.6	43.8
Clark	143	965	90	D	246	D	D	24	24 576	673	13.5	20.8	40.9
Clay	4 846	93 216	12 684	11 163	11 709	2 326	D	4 508	48 360	578	48.8	10.2	42.6
Clinton	364	2 792	934	131	493	135	89	85	30 370	758	35.1	8.8	38.5
Cole	2 257	32 848	6 260	1 936	5 275	1 862	1 681	1 247	37 970	1 055	24.1	5.4	38.2
Cooper	381	3 862	801	D	737	140	D	106	27 536	928	16.4	17.3	42.8
Crawford	534	5 502	865	1 908	636	D	141	185	33 553	679	20.2	12.8	40.4
Dade	139	1 217	38	D	186	D	D	34	27 753	734	21.5	16.5	47.0
Dallas	273	2 384	D	D	481	D	43	44	18 422	1 188	31.7	7.6	46.8
Daviess	146	862	77	D	196	51	D	22	26 075	1 199	23.4	12.9	36.8
DeKalb	217	1 946	375	D	490	223	D	61	31 565	863	22.7	12.6	40.3
Dent	461	3 706	846	579	514	176	D	124	33 507	673	21.0	13.5	35.7
Douglas	193	2 049	271	672	440	63	D	48	23 441	984	18.6	10.9	43.2
Dunklin	789	8 761	3 040	D	1 443	272	D	194	22 199	345	22.6	42.6	63.5
Franklin	2 572	33 891	3 862	9 030	4 890	1 082	866	1 215	35 855	1 841	33.6	5.1	32.6
Gasconade	414	4 741	947	1 417	690	D	103	123	26 005	859	14.6	10.0	39.1
Gentry	189	1 778	761	D	300	57	D	45	25 496	708	20.2	16.2	40.8
Greene	8 434	146 256	28 493	12 490	18 994	7 381	6 218	5 551	37 953	1 752	48.8	4.5	43.9
Grundy	249	2 731	617	880	441	83	D	83	30 262	689	23.1	12.0	42.7
Harrison	205	1 984	487	D	651	106	D	47	23 939	1 051	18.5	17.4	42.7
Henry	576	6 834	1 755	1 251	1 153	D	129	240	35 130	894	21.8	21.5	54.7
Hickory	144	748	D	D	259	46	16	16	21 218	487	14.4	18.1	56.5
Holt	141	938	D	153	151	D	D	29	31 433	408	20.3	26.7	49.3
Howard	197	2 183	509	D	275	81	45	55	25 355	765	17.0	19.0	36.6
Howell	1 134	13 005	3 544	2 652	2 195	D	305	383	29 450	1 535	24.8	10.1	41.3
Iron	361	2 013	769	74	280	60	D	60	29 838	273	15.4	13.6	46.2
Jackson	17 961	328 883	54 733	25 192	35 539	24 484	27 089	16 078	48 885	701	57.5	5.6	38.7

Table B. States and Counties — **Agriculture**

						Agriculture, 2012 (cont.)									
	Land in farms					Value of land and buildings (dollars)		Value of products sold				Percent of farms with sales of:		Government payments	
			Acres							Percent from:					
STATE County	Acreage (1,000)	Percent change, 2007–2012	Average size of farm	Total irrigated (1,000)	Total cropland (1,000)	Average per farm	Average per acre	Value of machinery and equipment, average per farm (dollars)	Total (mil dol)	Average per farm (dollars)	Crops	Live-stock and poultry products	$10,000 or more	$100,000 or more	Total ($1,000)	Percent of farms
	117	118	119	120	121	122	123	124	125	126	127	128	129	130	131	132
MISSISSIPPI—Cont'd																
Sunflower	373	-1.3	1 065	216.7	323.8	2 077 580	1 951	360 220	273.8	782 283	89.3	10.7	66.9	50.3	10 155	85.1
Tallahatchie	341	7.9	669	112.4	254.8	1 505 411	2 249	200 244	165.0	324 202	99.2	0.8	45.2	22.6	9 164	76.8
Tate	153	-2.5	269	2.2	69.6	540 237	2 008	73 946	44.4	78 025	68.7	31.3	31.1	9.3	2 745	43.8
Tippah	124	-9.9	179	0.3	37.9	291 781	1 628	51 965	22.1	31 961	66.3	33.7	20.0	2.5	932	57.3
Tishomingo	50	-12.7	173	0.7	16.6	319 711	1 852	47 373	6.1	21 167	85.7	14.3	21.6	3.8	420	52.3
Tunica	212	5.3	1 959	101.4	194.5	5 291 852	2 701	598 713	130.1	1 204 222	D	D	73.1	58.3	7 006	89.8
Union	121	-10.4	176	0.1	43.7	364 727	2 073	44 686	17.1	24 785	75.7	24.3	22.7	3.8	1 531	57.8
Walthall	118	-7.8	173	0.1	32.2	516 697	2 992	55 263	79.8	116 722	5.8	94.2	31.9	11.3	1 773	53.7
Warren	125	11.5	524	4.9	43.8	983 702	1 877	103 592	30.6	128 723	98.9	1.1	26.5	10.9	1 648	54.6
Washington	342	2.7	1 206	220.9	313.0	2 563 155	2 126	548 342	271.4	955 764	96.4	3.6	78.9	58.5	9 036	77.1
Wayne	93	8.3	184	0.5	24.0	535 941	2 914	76 234	194.0	381 982	3.5	96.5	45.9	24.6	200	13.8
Webster	81	-3.9	223	0.7	25.8	401 997	1 806	50 633	20.3	56 180	69.6	30.4	25.1	6.9	1 899	68.5
Wilkinson	103	-8.9	521	0.5	15.0	1 170 980	2 248	70 000	7.2	36 182	42.0	58.0	26.3	5.6	829	52.0
Winston	98	2.4	193	0.0	18.8	419 709	2 172	59 943	74.7	147 630	4.5	95.5	27.9	7.1	455	31.4
Yalobusha	95	-4.8	260	1.3	33.4	472 665	1 820	61 310	18.3	50 379	86.4	13.6	25.3	6.6	1 492	56.6
Yazoo	351	-1.3	522	44.8	195.4	1 096 741	2 100	118 775	151.3	225 109	92.5	7.5	34.1	16.4	9 095	74.7
MISSOURI	28 266	-2.6	285	1 180.9	15 259.3	795 444	2 791	88 960	9 164.9	92 415	49.8	50.2	46.8	12.5	323 953	41.7
Adair	273	-2.4	332	0.1	134.0	815 103	2 453	79 223	35.8	43 539	56.3	43.7	44.5	9.9	3 054	50.5
Andrew	199	-16.8	240	D	138.0	855 310	3 558	90 700	57.7	69 831	80.1	19.9	48.9	14.9	3 587	66.8
Atchison	263	-13.5	666	12.2	228.6	3 238 514	4 862	297 134	170.0	430 256	86.5	13.5	73.9	49.9	3 963	84.3
Audrain	436	2.7	430	15.1	354.0	1 643 676	3 822	172 912	151.2	148 960	59.3	40.7	62.2	26.4	5 605	66.0
Barry	268	-7.4	188	0.4	73.6	476 843	2 538	56 169	357.8	250 751	1.8	98.2	51.4	18.3	876	13.0
Barton	332	-4.9	353	11.1	224.0	743 856	2 105	126 076	120.1	127 807	61.0	39.0	56.4	23.0	4 742	59.7
Bates	448	-5.4	383	2.2	278.2	869 524	2 268	113 850	104.1	89 087	61.5	38.6	53.8	14.7	4 369	57.5
Benton	241	8.3	301	0.7	87.2	628 791	2 090	70 250	62.7	78 371	20.8	79.2	52.4	10.3	1 013	29.1
Bollinger	200	-3.7	254	6.8	79.3	511 848	2 014	58 244	31.6	40 128	52.1	47.9	44.8	7.0	1 313	42.0
Boone	241	-7.0	206	5.3	144.4	749 119	3 644	69 631	52.2	44 565	66.0	34.0	34.9	8.1	1 837	31.0
Buchanan	189	-4.5	260	D	136.1	895 721	3 451	91 761	67.5	92 891	89.6	10.4	53.1	15.4	3 153	69.1
Butler	234	-6.6	460	123.6	186.2	1 464 493	3 184	181 733	126.3	248 189	97.4	2.6	52.7	25.0	6 090	52.1
Caldwell	245	-2.2	236	D	153.0	537 488	2 275	54 284	38.9	37 541	62.4	37.6	37.4	6.6	5 312	71.0
Callaway	316	-2.1	223	5.4	160.9	728 630	3 267	79 792	84.9	59 929	40.1	59.9	40.0	8.2	2 756	40.8
Camden	139	-4.0	260	0.1	24.4	566 041	2 177	44 377	17.6	32 951	11.0	89.0	43.7	4.5	100	5.4
Cape Girardeau	253	-16.4	222	11.6	157.3	695 755	3 133	80 699	77.7	68 175	67.2	32.8	45.8	11.8	3 397	54.9
Carroll	432	7.5	388	3.5	320.9	1 216 926	3 134	121 291	130.5	117 322	85.3	14.7	48.6	16.7	7 522	80.2
Carter	74	16.3	376	D	9.6	624 724	1 663	49 066	4.6	23 520	22.7	77.3	31.6	6.1	123	12.8
Cass	319	-2.2	214	2.8	202.4	708 608	3 318	73 090	86.2	57 682	69.8	30.2	36.3	7.5	2 726	34.4
Cedar	190	-0.4	232	D	63.3	422 039	1 822	57 703	23.6	28 797	28.9	71.1	49.7	4.5	639	17.7
Chariton	406	5.7	363	3.9	282.6	1 078 481	2 973	126 969	123.8	110 555	72.1	27.9	53.2	19.3	5 823	73.5
Christian	179	-5.1	152	0.1	53.3	476 400	3 124	48 936	24.3	20 622	14.3	85.7	38.9	3.8	240	7.1
Clark	241	-8.3	358	3.2	150.9	950 793	2 654	103 065	72.1	107 064	71.9	28.1	46.5	17.7	4 399	80.8
Clay	111	-23.1	191	D	57.2	819 787	4 282	92 087	50.4	87 118	38.6	61.4	40.0	11.8	1 079	24.7
Clinton	192	-19.3	253	D	126.9	866 280	3 427	84 827	56.4	74 431	68.5	31.5	39.7	10.3	2 589	48.2
Cole	176	-2.5	167	0.9	67.5	486 792	2 913	62 366	38.4	36 372	27.4	72.6	48.5	5.5	980	30.0
Cooper	307	1.6	331	0.7	190.3	940 300	2 841	108 986	78.3	84 363	57.5	42.5	58.6	16.9	4 120	64.7
Crawford	194	3.9	286	0.0	47.6	595 339	2 080	51 605	15.2	22 392	20.5	79.5	40.4	4.6	344	12.4
Dade	246	-11.1	335	6.5	113.4	733 312	2 192	86 000	69.5	94 661	47.9	52.1	56.1	13.6	1 656	27.9
Dallas	218	-2.2	183	0.2	60.1	426 668	2 326	44 228	47.7	40 160	11.5	88.5	43.7	7.2	612	9.5
Daviess	315	-4.8	263	0.1	210.5	731 193	2 784	71 812	96.6	80 591	40.0	60.0	36.0	9.4	8 392	71.9
DeKalb	243	-6.8	281	0.0	168.3	792 630	2 817	89 886	59.9	69 447	60.8	39.2	48.0	12.4	4 479	66.9
Dent	188	6.5	279	0.4	32.1	447 679	1 602	48 750	17.3	25 779	10.7	89.3	46.2	5.1	307	9.7
Douglas	254	-0.1	258	0.4	45.2	419 160	1 624	41 030	33.3	33 851	8.8	91.2	45.3	6.8	542	8.9
Dunklin	280	-13.9	811	155.8	266.2	3 056 875	3 770	425 835	199.0	576 846	98.9	1.1	69.6	48.7	8 186	75.9
Franklin	292	-2.7	158	1.3	128.9	589 536	3 722	57 212	64.1	34 794	43.1	56.9	34.9	4.9	1 483	26.9
Gasconade	209	-1.7	243	0.4	63.7	596 109	2 451	60 327	25.9	30 207	35.7	64.3	45.4	6.2	853	39.6
Gentry	253	-8.2	358	0.0	160.4	943 222	2 636	84 585	126.6	178 880	28.1	71.9	42.4	13.3	4 831	74.0
Greene	211	-9.2	120	0.3	68.2	442 679	3 683	42 410	41.5	23 669	17.4	82.6	32.9	3.4	609	9.0
Grundy	204	-12.1	296	0.5	139.8	681 840	2 303	67 837	44.7	64 835	36.6	63.4	37.7	9.9	4 432	65.7
Harrison	401	3.2	381	0.1	264.1	951 168	2 494	96 657	76.0	72 288	77.4	22.6	41.9	12.1	8 648	77.3
Henry	358	3.6	400	D	200.2	849 449	2 124	107 462	69.9	78 166	50.1	49.9	56.6	16.2	3 752	48.2
Hickory	182	24.0	374	D	57.3	725 201	1 941	50 281	25.8	52 959	16.3	83.7	47.0	8.0	757	33.7
Holt	200	-15.4	491	19.0	166.5	1 865 299	3 799	204 819	94.9	232 583	95.9	4.1	63.5	33.3	3 139	82.8
Howard	243	-12.0	318	2.8	139.9	807 152	2 537	97 344	47.8	62 455	77.5	22.5	49.2	14.9	3 553	66.1
Howell	354	-8.2	230	0.1	58.5	433 877	1 883	51 521	53.9	35 139	4.5	95.5	41.2	5.9	829	9.6
Iron	71	1.0	258	0.5	17.3	415 751	1 610	44 161	6.0	21 967	14.8	85.2	41.0	4.0	66	5.1
Jackson	111	-20.3	158	0.3	75.1	638 655	4 037	72 385	32.5	46 408	78.2	21.8	35.1	8.8	1 036	29.7

STATE County	Water use, 2010		Wholesale trade,[1] 2012				Retail trade,[2] 2012				Real estate and rental and leasing,[2] 2012			
	Total water withdrawn (mil gal/day)	Gallons withdrawn per person per day	Number of establishments	Number of employees	Sales (mil dol)	Annual payroll (mil dol)	Number of establishments	Number of employees	Sales (mil dol)	Annual payroll (mil dol)	Number of establishments	Number of employees	Receipts (mil dol)	Annual payroll (mil dol)
	133	134	135	136	137	138	139	140	141	142	143	144	145	146
MISSISSIPPI—Cont'd														
Sunflower	366.4	12 441	15	330	443.3	13.5	100	922	244.1	18.8	10	20	3.5	0.5
Tallahatchie	126.0	8 193	7	76	67.2	2.7	40	262	54.1	7.0	5	8	0.8	0.1
Tate	7.4	257	13	44	16.9	1.9	73	799	191.9	17.9	8	17	3.7	0.5
Tippah	4.6	208	15	143	247.8	6.4	77	628	133.8	11.8	6	37	2.7	1.2
Tishomingo	3.2	161	18	166	59.7	4.3	81	597	114.3	12.3	12	20	2.0	0.5
Tunica	155.8	14 454	6	62	84.2	3.2	68	511	107.4	9.0	11	27	10.0	0.9
Union	3.2	118	17	166	200.6	6.7	101	1 039	297.2	22.1	16	37	4.1	0.8
Walthall	3.7	238	4	D	D	D	41	364	111.3	7.4	5	17	2.2	0.6
Warren	217.4	4 458	41	D	D	D	207	2 588	606.9	53.5	43	186	33.5	6.5
Washington	458.9	8 974	70	638	1 152.7	32.8	232	2 937	656.6	56.4	47	159	21.4	4.8
Wayne	6.0	289	21	153	205.9	9.9	83	863	183.9	17.4	9	D	D	D
Webster	1.7	165	4	9	1.8	0.2	43	225	52.6	4.4	NA	NA	NA	NA
Wilkinson	3.5	352	10	48	46.8	1.6	32	283	54.4	6.0	4	D	D	D
Winston	3.1	160	15	247	198.6	9.0	87	870	209.6	18.4	13	116	5.0	2.7
Yalobusha	3.7	288	4	D	D	D	45	354	72.0	6.3	3	26	2.1	0.2
Yazoo	44.9	1 600	19	245	282.1	13.2	94	707	177.4	14.7	18	47	4.7	1.2
MISSOURI	8 568.5	1 431	6 557	96 683	91 916.4	4 978.9	21 456	302 568	90 546.6	7 278.2	6 165	33 447	6 730.0	1 297.9
Adair	3.2	124	21	D	D	D	121	1 538	336.2	30.3	22	78	14.2	2.5
Andrew	19.7	1 140	14	D	D	D	41	332	103.8	6.9	10	D	D	D
Atchison	6.3	1 108	14	133	228.9	5.1	41	316	109.8	7.7	3	5	0.3	0.1
Audrain	13.7	537	20	D	D	D	102	1 108	253.7	21.9	13	37	5.4	0.9
Barry	19.4	545	25	419	321.4	22.5	133	1 439	379.2	29.2	27	80	11.3	1.9
Barton	14.4	1 159	12	191	192.1	6.8	44	501	146.1	9.6	4	8	1.0	0.2
Bates	3.5	207	10	124	90.3	5.2	60	650	171.7	14.2	5	9	0.6	0.2
Benton	4.8	251	10	71	25.8	1.9	67	662	183.0	13.8	9	16	2.9	0.3
Bollinger	14.0	1 129	14	99	66.5	6.5	30	316	73.3	6.6	4	9	0.4	0.1
Boone	18.7	115	135	1 461	631.4	73.2	627	11 563	3 741.0	287.7	227	920	160.6	28.8
Buchanan	78.2	877	102	1 711	1 506.6	76.6	339	5 467	1 369.3	120.6	100	329	59.6	9.9
Butler	339.5	7 933	49	371	193.1	11.7	203	2 610	758.1	56.4	41	181	21.8	6.5
Caldwell	1.2	126	6	62	46.3	2.2	24	208	47.8	3.8	4	D	D	D
Callaway	31.0	700	22	244	100.9	8.7	126	1 259	377.6	25.2	28	83	7.3	1.9
Camden	13.7	310	45	349	169.4	11.6	302	3 072	648.1	67.0	83	232	40.2	6.4
Cape Girardeau	36.5	483	128	1 450	861.4	58.4	415	5 855	1 611.4	131.1	110	340	55.2	9.4
Carroll	5.2	562	12	140	448.8	5.7	40	285	83.3	5.8	7	D	D	D
Carter	0.8	129	7	D	D	D	23	181	31.1	2.5	3	3	0.3	0.1
Cass	5.5	55	59	562	333.5	23.8	252	3 658	984.7	85.0	66	162	35.2	5.2
Cedar	2.0	144	7	58	29.3	1.3	48	483	104.9	9.2	5	22	1.6	0.6
Chariton	1.6	198	14	155	222.3	5.9	43	269	103.7	6.1	12	23	1.1	0.3
Christian	9.4	122	65	550	200.2	23.0	237	2 764	696.8	59.1	67	144	33.4	4.1
Clark	2.4	331	11	154	88.9	5.5	36	258	117.2	4.8	3	5	0.3	0.1
Clay	148.4	669	280	4 156	4 129.6	235.5	582	11 592	3 862.1	299.5	245	1 166	197.5	39.5
Clinton	2.6	124	10	84	132.0	3.0	57	449	158.0	10.8	13	42	4.3	1.0
Cole	9.3	122	77	2 154	974.4	62.8	301	5 114	1 257.9	115.0	62	247	45.8	7.2
Cooper	5.1	291	15	86	102.7	2.8	61	757	301.2	15.8	16	50	6.5	1.0
Crawford	3.2	128	14	110	47.6	5.6	76	636	205.0	14.1	22	71	10.7	2.1
Dade	7.9	1 006	8	506	254.4	15.6	28	181	37.7	2.6	3	4	0.3	0.1
Dallas	2.4	144	9	61	75.0	1.2	47	476	134.8	9.5	7	11	1.9	0.2
Daviess	2.1	251	9	58	31.1	1.8	36	186	70.9	3.8	4	3	0.3	0.1
DeKalb	1.0	75	6	D	D	D	39	529	123.6	10.7	12	D	D	D
Dent	32.5	2 076	6	D	D	D	55	538	127.7	11.2	14	51	2.9	0.7
Douglas	39.6	2 893	8	36	5.3	0.8	40	460	96.9	8.7	4	4	0.4	0.0
Dunklin	111.4	3 485	33	355	218.5	14.0	140	1 495	427.6	32.9	26	529	26.6	9.9
Franklin	1 018.9	10 039	99	981	574.7	36.9	378	4 653	1 396.4	107.9	89	288	28.4	7.8
Gasconade	2.2	146	21	204	86.7	6.7	66	657	171.4	14.4	9	13	1.1	0.3
Gentry	1.9	275	10	56	53.3	2.4	39	283	78.1	6.0	4	131	1.9	0.8
Greene	228.2	829	398	7 106	5 120.2	315.7	1 143	18 649	4 984.2	434.1	406	2 373	329.9	68.8
Grundy	4.2	409	8	88	107.3	3.1	43	413	89.6	8.0	8	24	2.5	0.4
Harrison	1.7	194	14	117	62.9	3.5	47	558	166.0	12.1	7	14	2.3	0.3
Henry	410.1	18 413	22	199	129.1	7.7	117	1 170	275.0	25.7	19	68	9.2	2.0
Hickory	1.4	149	4	15	3.8	0.3	29	236	59.9	4.7	2	D	D	D
Holt	17.0	3 453	9	103	117.3	3.7	22	146	46.4	3.0	2	D	D	D
Howard	9.7	955	9	D	D	D	34	245	53.4	3.5	3	D	D	D
Howell	8.2	203	41	398	229.2	13.2	232	2 085	561.3	45.6	41	131	14.8	3.3
Iron	6.9	648	3	D	D	D	38	262	70.8	4.9	7	19	2.4	0.7
Jackson	644.8	956	832	11 496	10 325.8	676.6	2 228	34 276	9 164.9	846.3	819	5 036	1 232.2	235.8

1. Merchant wholesalers, except manufacturers' sales branches and offices.　　2. Employer establishments.

STATE County	Professional, scientific, and technical services, 2012				Manufacturing, 2012				Accommodation and food services, 2012			
	Number of establish-ments	Number of employees	Receipts (mil dol)	Annual payroll (mil dol)	Number of establish-ments	Number of employees	Receipts (mil dol)	Annual payroll (mil dol)	Number of establish-ments	Number of employees	Sales (mil dol)	Annual payroll (mil dol)
	147	148	149	150	151	152	153	154	155	156	157	158
MISSISSIPPI—Cont'd												
Sunflower	23	71	6.6	2.1	14	293	137.8	9.3	33	358	18.3	4.8
Tallahatchie	10	42	3.7	1.0	4	50	D	1.5	10	90	3.4	0.8
Tate	22	D	D	D	14	784	303.8	30.9	28	403	17.5	4.7
Tippah	15	72	5.6	2.6	27	1 286	400.3	46.5	22	D	D	D
Tishomingo	21	103	5.1	1.5	29	1 345	298.8	49.6	33	D	D	D
Tunica	10	D	D	D	5	319	D	9.8	35	8 231	873.2	204.4
Union	27	84	7.9	3.1	37	3 660	2 379.3	136.5	38	536	26.2	7.1
Walthall	10	22	2.4	0.7	16	469	D	17.0	15	172	8.1	1.6
Warren	96	845	159.4	41.2	37	2 699	D	116.0	111	4 091	345.5	79.0
Washington	80	358	33.5	13.6	34	1 050	711.3	46.6	88	1 868	121.9	29.5
Wayne	40	110	13.7	3.6	11	1 057	279.9	35.6	28	D	D	D
Webster	10	66	4.9	1.5	11	352	D	10.2	10	140	5.7	1.4
Wilkinson	6	D	D	D	5	115	D	4.9	4	D	D	D
Winston	21	95	15.0	2.6	15	1 450	328.9	52.7	30	444	20.8	5.0
Yalobusha	8	45	2.6	0.9	7	857	D	30.9	11	64	4.3	1.0
Yazoo	22	160	11.5	4.3	12	497	D	29.7	25	331	18.2	4.0
MISSOURI	13 279	137 981	24 292.6	8 614.9	6 097	243 208	111 535.4	11 920.8	12 459	239 264	12 430.3	3 409.2
Adair	42	D	D	D	15	638	282.2	24.1	58	D	D	D
Andrew	13	58	3.1	2.0	4	13	2.3	0.5	15	112	4.5	1.1
Atchison	10	D	D	D	5	D	D	0.4	13	132	5.3	1.5
Audrain	22	147	9.1	4.6	36	1 702	1 124.1	68.5	40	441	17.2	4.6
Barry	43	D	D	D	39	4 713	1 391.4	158.8	57	776	33.0	9.0
Barton	13	119	10.6	5.7	17	411	101.9	15.6	17	D	D	D
Bates	21	D	D	D	14	99	D	3.2	28	D	D	D
Benton	23	D	D	D	20	167	D	4.5	47	D	D	D
Bollinger	7	D	D	D	14	154	23.6	5.0	10	110	4.4	1.1
Boone	414	3 570	424.0	156.7	99	3 994	2 042.1	173.3	419	9 006	373.2	104.7
Buchanan	153	D	D	D	89	12 338	D	474.4	183	4 062	180.1	48.6
Butler	48	386	38.3	14.4	46	2 178	545.4	66.9	80	1 678	67.4	18.7
Caldwell	8	D	D	D	6	37	D	0.8	9	D	D	D
Callaway	35	268	33.8	9.5	34	1 605	506.6	69.1	72	910	37.1	10.3
Camden	90	397	51.2	18.1	45	604	131.2	23.2	157	2 633	142.9	40.4
Cape Girardeau	158	1 137	109.6	38.5	95	3 700	2 884.5	181.9	168	4 167	171.0	48.7
Carroll	16	40	3.2	0.8	12	160	D	6.2	13	D	D	D
Carter	5	34	1.4	0.7	18	92	36.1	4.0	12	139	4.3	1.2
Cass	157	D	D	D	59	1 901	557.3	74.0	131	2 133	89.4	25.7
Cedar	14	38	3.1	0.8	20	301	149.1	12.8	32	302	11.0	3.0
Chariton	11	D	D	D	4	78	D	D	16	85	3.0	0.8
Christian	141	D	D	D	100	1 295	274.9	46.1	111	1 774	73.4	23.5
Clark	7	10	0.6	0.2	6	176	D	D	11	102	4.4	1.4
Clay	499	9 242	2 515.1	805.3	195	10 152	8 645.4	579.9	409	9 827	756.4	161.0
Clinton	24	D	D	D	13	105	D	3.1	20	303	13.2	3.7
Cole	231	1 587	238.9	81.4	56	2 293	1 877.5	101.3	166	3 172	132.4	39.4
Cooper	24	80	4.9	2.1	13	374	D	14.0	38	D	D	D
Crawford	26	148	7.4	3.2	47	1 922	345.0	57.9	58	484	23.9	6.7
Dade	3	D	D	D	12	205	64.6	7.2	13	80	2.6	0.8
Dallas	15	D	D	D	15	105	D	2.9	25	254	9.9	2.5
Daviess	5	D	D	D	8	231	D	D	13	82	2.8	0.8
DeKalb	8	20	1.8	0.7	4	23	D	1.3	17	159	7.9	2.0
Dent	16	51	3.5	1.3	21	615	D	30.4	26	D	D	D
Douglas	11	33	3.0	0.8	11	712	D	15.8	16	D	D	D
Dunklin	31	463	11.7	4.4	11	500	D	18.2	44	647	29.6	7.4
Franklin	185	1 174	144.2	42.6	221	9 002	2 617.3	382.3	184	3 157	126.4	38.1
Gasconade	29	117	7.0	2.5	40	1 161	193.2	41.2	46	449	19.4	5.5
Gentry	9	D	D	D	7	228	D	D	13	78	2.2	0.7
Greene	801	5 862	830.7	281.9	295	11 900	4 623.8	521.5	723	14 502	628.1	185.1
Grundy	14	47	2.9	0.9	8	707	D	32.3	13	217	6.9	2.0
Harrison	11	29	1.5	0.6	5	32	D	1.0	21	281	11.4	2.8
Henry	35	141	12.0	3.3	25	1 164	694.8	52.5	56	770	29.7	8.3
Hickory	8	D	D	D	5	D	D	D	17	75	3.1	0.8
Holt	2	D	D	D	7	210	D	6.7	14	112	4.1	1.0
Howard	16	45	4.2	1.4	10	245	57.5	10.2	14	171	5.2	1.7
Howell	64	306	24.9	10.3	69	2 483	672.0	78.5	89	1 241	54.1	14.3
Iron	8	D	D	D	15	88	D	2.2	22	107	4.7	1.3
Jackson	2 044	24 922	5 811.2	1 804.1	634	25 870	10 193.5	1 396.4	1 453	30 594	1 649.0	485.7

1. Establishment subject to federal tax.

Table B. States and Counties — Health Care and Social Assistance, Other Services, Nonemployer Businesses, and Residential Construction

STATE County	Health care and social assistance, 2012				Other services, 2012				Nonemployer businesses, 2014		Value of residential construction authorized by building permits, 2015	
	Number of establishments	Number of employees	Receipts (mil dol)	Annual payroll (mil dol)	Number of establishments	Number of employees	Receipts (mil dol)	Annual payroll (mil dol)	Number	Receipts (mil dol)	New Construction ($1,000)	Number of housing units
	159	160	161	162	163	164	165	166	167	168	169	170
MISSISSIPPI—Cont'd												
Sunflower	63	1 199	104.8	39.0	34	164	13.2	3.7	1 686	48.4	1 338	8
Tallahatchie	15	362	29.6	12.0	14	44	6.4	1.0	871	21.2	48	1
Tate	37	544	51.5	21.3	17	101	7.7	2.7	2 018	71.4	16 434	75
Tippah	31	628	44.5	17.6	10	42	2.5	0.7	1 414	57.8	540	6
Tishomingo	32	D	D	D	22	D	D	D	1 142	39.6	166	2
Tunica	16	190	12.3	4.8	8	D	D	D	699	25.6	1 290	14
Union	51	1 223	111.7	40.7	18	D	D	D	1 965	88.3	1 126	7
Walthall	21	285	14.0	5.4	14	D	D	D	1 085	36.4	0	0
Warren	114	2 997	293.1	108.1	58	307	29.8	7.9	3 078	108.0	340	3
Washington	164	3 083	249.4	99.9	80	556	57.1	16.3	3 516	129.7	2 302	21
Wayne	22	607	45.0	21.8	20	D	D	D	1 343	52.2	0	0
Webster	12	D	D	D	7	D	D	D	833	30.4	110	2
Wilkinson	14	350	29.1	11.5	7	D	D	D	611	21.9	0	0
Winston	28	393	34.8	12.4	17	D	D	D	1 380	60.0	9 163	56
Yalobusha	16	328	23.3	11.0	6	D	D	D	835	27.9	304	10
Yazoo	41	872	73.8	27.5	27	D	D	D	1 542	52.4	950	10
MISSOURI	17 766	399 940	40 089.3	15 746.9	10 357	62 825	6 979.9	1 834.9	397 713	17 198.3	3 146 410	18 344
Adair	101	1 929	159.3	63.3	61	D	D	D	1 515	55.1	6 783	32
Andrew	28	D	D	D	19	D	D	D	1 247	47.2	662	7
Atchison	14	270	16.9	6.7	15	D	D	D	430	17.2	0	0
Audrain	71	1 414	99.4	40.4	45	249	18.8	7.4	1 389	59.4	3 625	28
Barry	71	1 788	99.2	42.8	65	222	15.6	3.9	2 320	78.8	3 980	31
Barton	25	457	30.0	13.2	18	48	4.9	1.3	900	32.5	0	0
Bates	36	D	D	D	21	D	D	D	1 196	43.4	431	3
Benton	34	400	21.4	9.7	32	91	8.3	1.6	1 413	60.2	120	2
Bollinger	20	312	15.2	6.0	16	56	5.3	1.1	745	30.2	0	0
Boone	602	16 725	2 033.5	699.4	327	1 985	187.4	53.2	11 136	539.2	260 589	1 433
Buchanan	315	7 704	852.1	346.6	172	D	D	D	4 046	156.5	26 043	197
Butler	209	4 378	527.8	163.1	65	296	24.0	5.9	2 510	125.7	932	56
Caldwell	14	D	D	D	15	D	D	D	620	20.8	4 438	21
Callaway	64	2 368	128.3	64.9	66	229	19.6	5.5	2 362	83.3	9 002	85
Camden	121	2 143	262.5	84.9	102	358	30.7	8.1	3 854	185.3	38 440	181
Cape Girardeau	317	10 920	1 149.2	455.5	159	798	78.1	19.9	5 293	224.9	34 859	179
Carroll	22	375	24.9	7.9	18	D	D	D	637	23.3	2 743	14
Carter	39	237	8.5	3.9	4	9	1.7	0.3	520	28.9	0	0
Cass	159	3 056	250.2	98.6	140	522	41.2	12.2	6 741	275.4	69 467	315
Cedar	30	646	32.0	15.1	19	34	3.4	0.7	1 087	44.1	758	7
Chariton	14	261	10.8	4.5	14	36	5.9	1.2	618	19.4	190	1
Christian	115	1 434	89.7	37.4	119	429	31.5	9.0	6 584	270.4	115 400	484
Clark	13	60	4.0	1.6	11	37	4.5	0.7	451	18.2	249	5
Clay	553	12 953	1 393.1	591.2	329	1 826	171.1	54.5	14 583	582.4	67 504	337
Clinton	47	D	D	D	33	102	6.7	1.9	1 302	49.2	6 172	27
Cole	252	6 480	711.7	280.5	227	1 441	173.3	52.7	4 713	214.5	15 934	184
Cooper	52	773	45.3	18.7	28	106	8.5	2.2	1 093	41.8	1 180	8
Crawford	60	955	77.2	33.2	28	117	8.4	2.1	1 500	56.9	1 196	10
Dade	10	D	D	D	10	18	2.2	0.6	501	18.5	0	0
Dallas	30	1 021	26.9	13.1	20	D	D	D	1 321	54.6	492	2
Daviess	16	78	6.0	2.2	8	D	D	D	793	41.8	0	0
DeKalb	28	D	D	D	10	D	D	D	650	27.9	200	3
Dent	55	712	42.7	17.8	20	45	3.9	0.9	969	35.5	0	0
Douglas	20	313	16.1	7.0	14	41	4.5	0.8	1 020	36.1	0	0
Dunklin	87	3 270	167.8	57.4	39	136	13.0	2.6	1 843	116.6	3 117	17
Franklin	262	3 747	322.4	153.2	185	869	81.7	23.3	6 614	263.9	65 738	424
Gasconade	34	701	40.7	17.3	33	D	D	D	1 219	44.5	262	3
Gentry	34	777	38.0	17.2	11	26	2.5	0.7	535	18.3	680	4
Greene	820	28 578	3 027.6	1 240.2	599	4 433	401.4	117.0	20 200	927.5	174 299	1 628
Grundy	34	656	48.5	18.8	27	61	5.0	1.2	695	26.7	379	4
Harrison	24	488	29.4	12.1	21	D	D	D	643	27.2	0	0
Henry	55	1 569	122.3	55.1	42	163	10.4	3.2	1 444	51.1	1 222	9
Hickory	9	98	5.4	2.1	11	22	1.9	0.4	711	25.6	NA	NA
Holt	9	D	D	D	9	D	D	D	410	17.9	100	1
Howard	24	493	16.4	8.3	13	D	D	D	699	23.0	1 185	8
Howell	156	3 669	294.1	127.4	66	381	38.9	8.4	3 018	113.7	1 455	14
Iron	93	656	34.8	15.3	27	D	D	D	490	16.2	0	0
Jackson	2 040	54 553	6 169.9	2 405.2	1 236	9 447	1 762.1	312.8	43 159	1 847.5	613 776	4 272

Table B. States and Counties — Government Employment and Payroll, and Local Government Finances

	Government employment and payroll, 2012									Local government finances, 2012				
			March payroll (percent of total)							General revenue				
													Taxes	
														Per capita[1] (dollars)
STATE County	Full-time equivalent employees	March payroll (dollars)	Adminis-tration, judicial, and legal	Police and Corrections	Fire Protection	Highways and transpor-tation	Health and Welfare	Natural resources and utilities	Education and libraries	Total (mil dol)	Inter-govern-mental (mil dol)	Total (mil dol)	Total	Property
	171	172	173	174	175	176	177	178	179	180	181	182	183	184
MISSISSIPPI—Cont'd														
Sunflower	2 017	5 682 629	3.7	5.0	1.7	2.5	30.7	1.5	53.7	155.8	63.4	20.6	724	694
Tallahatchie	772	1 986 175	8.5	7.5	0.2	4.7	29.5	0.9	48.6	34.1	21.3	8.2	542	517
Tate	1 430	4 623 219	2.1	2.6	1.1	1.1	0.9	1.2	90.6	106.6	62.4	20.6	724	690
Tippah	915	2 435 046	6.8	3.3	0.2	2.1	22.7	2.8	61.0	68.1	38.2	11.3	512	467
Tishomingo	694	1 807 779	8.5	7.3	1.2	2.3	1.2	4.4	73.2	46.2	29.7	10.1	515	495
Tunica	738	1 778 465	10.4	23.6	0.0	4.7	6.1	9.7	45.3	86.8	57.0	21.4	2 043	1 507
Union	1 025	2 626 662	4.5	7.6	2.0	3.0	1.3	10.2	71.3	61.0	37.8	16.4	596	576
Walthall	518	1 141 649	3.1	5.7	0.2	3.0	2.1	0.6	83.4	45.4	21.5	8.4	559	539
Warren	1 819	5 138 472	4.6	6.1	7.5	3.0	0.3	7.0	69.2	170.1	68.3	68.7	1 429	1 171
Washington	3 566	9 118 481	5.7	7.2	2.5	3.0	32.4	4.6	43.1	298.0	98.6	52.7	1 060	977
Wayne	1 112	3 158 182	4.3	5.0	0.4	2.8	39.5	1.7	44.9	88.7	32.9	10.5	508	496
Webster	496	1 240 223	6.4	4.4	0.1	3.7	24.5	1.5	58.9	36.7	19.1	6.3	623	599
Wilkinson	427	1 032 081	12.7	10.5	0.3	7.1	2.1	3.0	61.9	56.6	14.2	5.9	630	607
Winston	620	1 506 689	8.7	16.0	2.1	4.3	1.9	2.4	64.2	46.2	24.1	11.5	602	576
Yalobusha	708	1 878 214	6.3	4.5	1.3	4.5	39.0	4.3	40.1	42.2	18.6	8.6	691	675
Yazoo	1 019	2 766 051	5.8	9.4	4.3	6.7	2.3	10.2	60.9	70.1	40.4	21.3	755	728
MISSOURI	X	X	X	X	X	X	X	X	X	X	X	X	X	X
Adair	916	2 496 611	7.3	5.8	2.8	3.2	13.2	5.6	59.0	68.7	23.1	26.9	1 051	570
Andrew	515	1 433 245	5.1	4.2	0.9	3.0	4.0	5.7	76.7	48.4	17.6	23.4	1 345	1 199
Atchison	319	829 091	7.7	5.0	0.1	22.0	10.0	5.1	49.6	22.0	10.2	9.7	1 755	1 294
Audrain	1 347	4 107 516	4.1	5.9	0.2	2.5	49.7	3.5	33.4	133.2	34.7	34.4	1 343	940
Barry	1 307	3 855 776	4.7	5.7	1.8	2.3	1.6	5.6	77.7	94.7	45.3	37.8	1 063	636
Barton	723	2 240 324	3.5	2.9	0.7	1.9	43.2	5.8	41.8	83.5	14.1	10.7	866	674
Bates	840	2 585 067	4.7	5.8	0.3	2.0	37.0	4.7	45.0	43.7	19.9	13.4	805	577
Benton	748	1 949 137	5.2	5.4	0.1	2.8	27.9	2.2	53.8	41.5	16.6	13.2	696	514
Bollinger	361	902 476	5.5	5.4	0.3	4.6	0.0	1.6	82.4	21.6	12.4	7.2	585	414
Boone	6 008	20 052 275	7.9	5.3	3.3	2.8	2.7	11.3	63.5	497.3	161.0	228.2	1 349	805
Buchanan	3 079	9 642 143	5.9	9.4	5.3	3.7	2.5	5.0	66.6	296.5	114.1	129.1	1 439	812
Butler	1 617	4 243 462	2.3	5.6	2.5	3.4	0.0	4.2	79.9	124.9	58.1	43.7	1 015	498
Caldwell	485	1 279 896	6.3	9.6	0.0	2.5	7.8	5.3	68.5	29.5	14.3	7.8	847	648
Callaway	1 265	3 154 685	6.9	9.5	2.6	4.3	5.4	8.0	63.0	88.2	36.4	34.7	782	576
Camden	1 451	4 272 326	7.8	13.4	5.1	5.6	4.2	2.2	60.3	116.5	32.4	68.3	1 557	990
Cape Girardeau	2 602	6 797 882	6.6	9.1	5.9	6.5	1.2	10.3	58.6	207.7	74.1	101.6	1 320	702
Carroll	390	1 096 814	9.3	3.7	1.4	4.2	4.3	6.6	70.1	26.7	11.7	10.0	1 101	852
Carter	278	723 988	1.6	5.8	0.0	2.9	3.2	2.5	72.4	15.4	9.6	3.9	625	446
Cass	4 195	14 748 324	5.3	6.9	4.3	2.7	12.2	4.5	63.7	380.9	126.2	139.6	1 391	927
Cedar	643	1 585 692	4.7	5.5	0.2	3.0	25.1	6.6	54.3	50.4	15.5	11.7	850	590
Chariton	295	762 719	8.8	6.7	0.2	3.7	5.8	6.0	68.4	20.7	8.4	9.5	1 240	969
Christian	2 200	6 653 224	5.3	7.1	2.0	1.8	0.2	4.7	77.8	188.4	89.3	71.0	890	611
Clark	372	840 780	6.1	5.8	0.0	4.4	21.9	7.3	53.6	21.0	7.2	6.3	911	738
Clay	12 186	43 650 964	3.1	4.3	2.0	0.8	42.4	2.3	44.6	1 333.0	239.3	340.1	1 495	1 078
Clinton	670	2 036 971	7.0	9.3	0.4	4.7	2.3	8.2	67.6	52.6	24.6	20.4	993	788
Cole	2 439	7 947 888	7.8	8.8	4.1	4.5	3.5	5.9	65.1	213.9	62.0	116.3	1 523	890
Cooper	744	2 121 619	5.8	7.9	1.4	3.1	23.2	4.8	52.9	62.0	16.7	23.7	1 353	687
Crawford	756	1 998 530	5.7	8.1	0.0	3.7	7.3	5.6	68.1	45.1	21.5	17.0	683	512
Dade	452	949 754	5.1	2.9	0.0	1.2	37.3	2.9	50.6	20.8	9.6	6.2	824	608
Dallas	463	1 037 873	7.3	5.8	0.3	5.2	0.8	2.2	78.1	31.3	18.2	10.5	627	394
Daviess	341	863 936	7.8	3.3	0.0	3.1	2.5	7.8	74.9	20.0	9.8	7.4	895	719
DeKalb	227	666 095	6.8	3.3	0.0	4.5	3.8	6.9	74.5	18.0	7.8	6.8	522	356
Dent	677	1 899 125	6.9	2.7	0.2	3.0	33.8	4.1	48.4	46.0	16.0	9.7	622	406
Douglas	383	1 073 499	10.7	2.4	0.0	4.9	5.0	5.3	70.1	32.6	12.6	16.6	1 225	824
Dunklin	1 473	3 567 888	5.4	6.8	1.4	3.0	1.6	10.3	68.2	82.8	44.0	27.3	859	614
Franklin	3 292	11 002 286	4.9	8.8	2.3	3.4	4.3	2.7	72.9	276.7	102.6	133.5	1 317	868
Gasconade	880	2 347 282	3.9	4.6	0.0	3.4	28.6	4.8	53.1	70.3	15.8	18.8	1 257	905
Gentry	345	893 935	12.0	4.7	0.4	7.4	4.6	5.3	65.1	20.8	9.7	7.8	1 144	911
Greene	10 039	36 380 689	4.7	8.2	3.7	4.6	1.4	13.2	55.1	880.5	308.6	410.2	1 462	763
Grundy	761	1 960 447	2.6	5.1	1.0	3.5	14.2	6.8	64.8	55.4	22.3	10.8	1 048	654
Harrison	594	1 570 497	5.2	2.6	0.2	3.0	37.3	7.0	42.9	43.2	13.0	10.7	1 229	806
Henry	1 267	4 585 264	3.2	3.7	1.3	1.0	61.3	2.7	26.7	117.2	50.1	23.1	1 045	588
Hickory	326	851 720	6.0	4.2	0.0	2.3	0.0	2.3	84.9	21.9	12.6	6.7	714	572
Holt	184	461 150	11.3	6.1	0.0	5.3	1.7	7.2	68.0	16.0	6.1	7.4	1 595	1 143
Howard	396	983 070	7.8	7.5	0.4	5.0	4.3	9.4	64.8	23.9	8.7	11.5	1 135	911
Howell	1 537	3 973 191	5.5	5.3	1.4	3.4	4.8	7.9	71.2	100.7	49.7	31.7	781	439
Iron	459	1 303 360	4.7	4.4	0.6	6.5	6.1	1.8	75.7	26.1	13.0	10.3	991	765
Jackson	27 447	101 433 064	7.4	14.7	9.5	6.2	0.7	5.5	54.6	3 343.9	905.1	1 696.2	2 504	1 116

1. Based on the resident population estimated as of July 1 of the year shown.

Table B. States and Counties — Local Government Finances, Government Employment, and Voting

STATE County	Local government finances, 2012 (cont.) Direct general expenditure Total (mil dol)	Per capita[1] (dollars)	Education	Health and hospitals	Police protection	Public welfare	Highways	Debt outstanding Total (mil dol)	Per capita[1] (dollars)	Government employment, 2014 Federal civilian	Federal military	State and local	Presidential election,[2] 2012 Percent of vote cast: Democratic	Republican	All other
	185	186	187	188	189	190	191	192	193	194	195	196	197	198	199
MISSISSIPPI—Cont'd															
Sunflower	160.1	5 631	46.7	34.5	2.9	0.1	5.4	30.8	1 085	52	141	3 662	70.0	29.0	1.0
Tallahatchie	39.2	2 596	54.2	1.1	5.0	0.0	7.9	12.7	843	36	74	948	59.1	40.1	0.7
Tate	144.1	5 057	68.2	0.5	2.9	0.0	3.0	96.6	3 389	82	162	1 560	39.2	60.1	0.8
Tippah	68.2	3 095	49.3	23.7	3.2	0.2	8.8	13.9	629	57	131	1 152	27.0	71.3	1.7
Tishomingo	53.8	2 746	50.8	1.1	4.8	0.0	7.0	25.8	1 315	59	115	896	23.3	74.2	2.5
Tunica	103.7	9 896	24.0	1.9	8.0	0.7	5.8	114.9	10 965	20	63	898	75.7	23.5	0.8
Union	59.7	2 178	65.6	1.4	6.1	0.0	5.6	32.4	1 180	47	168	1 210	24.5	74.4	1.1
Walthall	45.0	2 981	52.1	26.1	4.3	0.2	4.8	1.9	128	25	89	690	44.4	54.7	0.9
Warren	169.5	3 526	45.5	1.1	6.6	0.2	7.1	264.3	5 496	2 122	329	2 447	48.2	51.2	0.6
Washington	305.6	6 143	28.7	43.2	3.9	0.1	4.1	140.1	2 816	432	310	3 753	67.1	32.4	0.5
Wayne	70.5	3 414	47.5	34.9	3.4	0.1	5.6	14.5	700	37	123	1 240	38.8	60.6	0.6
Webster	31.4	3 130	63.8	1.3	4.6	0.0	7.8	7.1	706	32	60	437	24.7	74.6	0.7
Wilkinson	55.4	5 871	26.6	28.9	2.5	0.1	3.6	35.9	3 804	0	49	527	68.8	30.4	0.9
Winston	45.6	2 397	54.2	1.3	6.9	0.1	7.3	5.2	272	40	109	783	45.5	53.8	0.7
Yalobusha	40.4	3 257	39.3	27.4	4.0	0.0	10.5	17.9	1 447	68	73	798	46.2	53.1	0.7
Yazoo	75.1	2 663	51.5	1.3	5.5	0.3	5.8	42.6	1 510	734	141	1 495	53.3	46.1	0.6
MISSOURI	X	X	X	X	X	X	X	X	X	56 981	35 375	381 156	49.3	49.4	1.3
Adair	66.2	2 589	44.3	3.2	5.6	7.5	7.7	43.5	1 700	73	82	2 415	48.3	49.6	2.1
Andrew	36.8	2 114	65.6	3.0	5.9	1.0	6.2	25.6	1 468	35	59	696	38.1	60.1	1.9
Atchison	22.0	3 990	52.6	2.6	2.8	0.0	17.0	6.5	1 173	29	18	340	33.6	65.1	1.3
Audrain	139.4	5 440	36.1	40.4	2.1	3.8	3.0	68.4	2 669	88	81	2 325	41.1	57.2	1.7
Barry	100.1	2 815	59.9	3.2	4.9	0.0	15.0	67.2	1 892	105	122	1 578	31.6	66.6	1.7
Barton	83.6	6 780	22.2	65.7	1.4	0.0	2.7	35.3	2 861	38	41	897	24.5	74.2	1.3
Bates	44.5	2 660	58.6	0.1	9.7	6.8	7.3	46.0	2 754	56	56	1 111	39.5	58.3	2.2
Benton	41.9	2 209	51.5	5.5	3.4	22.2	5.5	22.9	1 210	95	64	946	37.9	60.2	1.9
Bollinger	21.1	1 700	73.8	1.0	4.3	0.0	7.9	3.1	248	31	42	439	29.2	68.7	2.1
Boone	580.4	3 444	44.8	3.1	4.3	0.2	6.2	2 592.5	15 382	2 466	588	28 559	55.2	43.2	1.6
Buchanan	261.5	2 915	51.6	2.2	9.4	0.7	5.3	599.9	6 688	502	312	6 615	49.1	48.9	2.0
Butler	122.1	2 837	60.0	0.0	6.4	0.0	5.4	48.6	1 129	716	145	2 853	30.7	68.1	1.3
Caldwell	28.6	3 124	59.8	1.8	3.5	5.7	7.6	9.9	1 087	40	30	611	39.7	58.2	2.1
Callaway	85.8	1 936	53.8	4.3	8.4	0.0	6.7	57.3	1 293	119	141	3 800	39.2	58.9	1.8
Camden	113.7	2 593	47.6	3.7	9.0	0.0	11.7	112.7	2 570	81	149	1 847	35.1	63.6	1.3
Cape Girardeau	211.7	2 751	54.0	0.3	5.4	0.0	9.9	197.3	2 564	378	281	5 834	32.7	66.3	1.0
Carroll	27.9	3 076	59.3	3.2	3.9	0.0	11.1	12.4	1 360	45	31	560	33.8	65.1	1.1
Carter	15.8	2 520	74.5	2.8	1.9	0.0	3.9	29.2	4 657	90	21	347	34.0	63.5	2.6
Cass	400.2	3 987	50.4	13.7	3.1	0.3	5.8	468.7	4 669	255	373	4 624	39.5	59.2	1.3
Cedar	37.7	2 733	50.1	29.0	5.1	0.0	2.8	32.6	2 361	66	47	771	32.4	66.0	1.6
Chariton	22.7	2 968	52.9	4.1	2.8	0.0	14.2	3.5	456	42	26	442	42.7	55.5	1.8
Christian	179.8	2 252	67.4	0.5	4.7	1.0	5.5	246.9	3 093	109	280	2 894	31.5	67.3	1.1
Clark	23.6	3 386	46.2	6.2	1.8	17.9	8.0	8.6	1 234	34	23	473	45.5	51.6	3.0
Clay	1 296.4	5 696	31.9	48.7	2.3	0.0	1.9	934.2	4 105	1 084	859	14 340	49.0	49.7	1.2
Clinton	50.6	2 467	62.4	1.9	7.3	0.0	8.9	42.6	2 078	73	68	1 037	43.5	54.6	1.9
Cole	222.3	2 911	50.1	2.6	10.7	0.0	10.0	194.9	2 552	630	271	19 316	36.0	62.9	1.0
Cooper	65.2	3 719	36.8	19.0	3.7	4.9	5.9	51.2	2 925	52	55	1 240	37.3	61.1	1.6
Crawford	44.2	1 780	63.0	8.1	3.6	0.0	5.8	29.0	1 169	33	84	912	38.8	59.6	1.7
Dade	20.9	2 758	51.9	1.1	3.6	23.8	6.9	4.0	526	27	26	508	28.8	69.6	1.6
Dallas	39.6	2 358	42.6	3.7	4.9	0.0	39.8	4.3	254	37	56	597	34.6	63.7	1.7
Daviess	19.9	2 419	62.2	3.1	3.1	0.1	12.4	10.1	1 231	33	28	498	37.0	59.8	3.2
DeKalb	17.0	1 315	62.4	3.4	4.1	0.0	6.0	6.2	478	30	31	1 277	36.1	61.7	2.2
Dent	47.9	3 058	43.1	38.7	4.1	0.0	4.2	2.6	166	58	53	903	29.9	67.8	2.3
Douglas	34.6	2 550	64.0	1.9	3.6	0.0	13.6	7.5	553	48	46	400	31.9	65.6	2.5
Dunklin	76.5	2 405	65.8	1.0	6.7	0.0	5.4	33.5	1 052	98	105	1 579	38.6	59.9	1.5
Franklin	286.0	2 820	58.5	2.0	6.4	0.0	9.3	497.8	4 909	215	349	4 441	43.1	55.5	1.4
Gasconade	55.7	3 719	45.7	31.4	2.9	0.5	4.5	60.7	4 054	52	50	1 002	37.3	61.3	1.4
Gentry	20.3	2 997	59.9	3.6	3.3	0.0	10.5	8.2	1 217	36	23	430	37.5	59.7	2.8
Greene	855.2	3 047	50.1	1.1	8.7	0.2	6.0	1 601.3	5 706	2 052	963	18 702	41.4	57.2	1.3
Grundy	48.8	4 722	61.4	3.0	2.3	10.7	6.0	28.4	2 746	63	34	960	33.3	63.4	3.2
Harrison	40.5	4 640	35.7	40.6	3.2	0.0	7.4	11.6	1 333	42	29	779	32.9	64.2	3.0
Henry	113.3	5 114	25.1	59.5	2.3	0.1	3.3	36.1	1 629	78	75	1 600	43.6	54.6	1.7
Hickory	21.4	2 275	79.2	1.5	2.4	0.0	5.9	11.7	1 244	44	31	302	42.4	55.7	1.8
Holt	15.2	3 273	49.5	0.6	2.4	0.0	13.7	0.8	182	31	15	291	30.5	68.1	1.4
Howard	22.1	2 174	53.2	3.8	5.5	0.3	6.2	33.3	3 276	36	32	481	41.9	55.8	2.3
Howell	94.2	2 317	67.7	2.1	5.1	0.0	5.1	39.4	970	120	136	2 135	33.7	64.5	1.8
Iron	27.4	2 641	71.9	1.5	3.9	0.0	5.6	10.9	1 046	16	34	629	50.1	47.3	2.5
Jackson	3 093.9	4 567	37.7	2.6	9.6	0.3	7.4	6 245.9	9 221	16 105	2 464	43 193	62.1	36.8	1.1

1. Based on the resident population estimated as of July 1 of the year shown. 2. © 2013 Election Data Services, Inc. All rights reserved.

Table B. States and Counties — Land Area and Population

STATE/County code	CBSA code[1]	County type[2]	STATE County	Land area,[3] (sq km) 2010	Total persons 2015	Rank	Per square kilometer	White	Black	American Indian, Alaska Native	Asian and Pacific Islander	Percent Hispanic or Latino[4]	Under 5 years	5 to 17 years	18 to 24 years	25 to 34 years	35 to 44 years	45 to 54 years
				1	2	3	4	5	6	7	8	9	10	11	12	13	14	15
			MISSOURI—Cont'd															
29 097	27900	3	Jasper	1 654	118 596	521	71.7	87.5	3.1	2.9	1.8	7.5	7.1	18.4	9.5	14.1	12.5	12.4
29 099	41180	1	Jefferson	1 701	224 124	291	131.8	96.1	1.6	0.8	1.0	1.8	6.3	17.8	8.0	12.9	13.1	15.1
29 101	47660	4	Johnson	2 148	53 951	929	25.1	88.5	5.8	1.4	3.1	4.0	6.5	15.3	21.1	14.2	10.4	10.8
29 103	...	9	Knox	1 305	3 910	2 910	3.0	97.8	1.2	1.1	0.5	1.2	6.8	17.3	7.7	9.9	9.9	13.4
29 105	30060	6	Laclede	1 981	35 473	1 290	17.9	95.4	1.5	1.6	0.9	2.2	6.6	18.1	7.9	11.8	12.0	14.0
29 107	28140	1	Lafayette	1 628	32 701	1 366	20.1	94.1	3.2	1.2	0.9	2.6	5.8	17.5	8.3	10.8	11.6	14.4
29 109	...	6	Lawrence	1 584	38 180	1 218	24.1	91.2	0.8	1.8	0.6	7.1	6.4	19.1	7.6	10.9	12.1	13.4
29 111	39500	9	Lewis	1 308	10 207	2 417	7.8	94.6	4.1	0.9	0.7	1.6	5.8	17.0	12.1	10.9	10.2	13.3
29 113	41180	1	Lincoln	1 623	54 696	916	33.7	94.9	2.7	0.9	0.9	2.2	6.8	19.7	8.3	12.8	12.6	14.8
29 115	...	7	Linn	1 594	12 308	2 274	7.7	96.6	1.4	0.7	0.4	1.9	5.6	18.3	7.7	10.0	11.0	13.0
29 117	...	6	Livingston	1 379	15 028	2 096	10.9	94.0	3.8	0.9	0.6	1.8	5.8	15.4	8.0	13.0	12.9	12.9
29 119	22220	2	McDonald	1 397	22 643	1 703	16.2	81.8	1.9	4.6	3.1	11.6	6.6	19.7	8.4	11.5	12.4	14.6
29 121	...	7	Macon	2 075	15 335	2 080	7.4	95.5	3.1	0.9	0.9	1.3	5.9	17.7	7.2	10.6	10.9	13.0
29 123	...	7	Madison	1 280	12 408	2 270	9.7	96.2	0.8	0.9	1.1	2.1	5.9	17.4	7.7	11.1	11.8	13.3
29 125	...	8	Maries	1 365	8 963	2 517	6.6	97.5	0.8	1.4	0.6	1.1	4.6	17.3	7.1	10.5	11.1	15.3
29 127	25300	5	Marion	1 132	28 880	1 459	25.5	92.4	6.5	0.7	1.2	1.6	6.3	17.2	9.2	12.2	11.6	13.3
29 129	...	9	Mercer	1 175	3 694	2 925	3.1	97.8	0.8	0.9	1.0	1.0	5.5	18.6	7.3	9.3	10.3	13.3
29 131	...	6	Miller	1 535	25 113	1 605	16.4	96.7	1.0	1.5	0.8	1.9	6.0	17.6	7.7	11.5	11.5	13.7
29 133	...	7	Mississippi	1 066	14 036	2 162	13.2	73.1	25.3	0.6	0.3	2.0	6.6	15.8	8.5	14.0	13.2	13.9
29 135	27620	3	Moniteau	1 075	15 963	2 045	14.8	90.4	4.4	1.1	0.6	4.6	6.5	18.5	8.1	13.2	13.5	14.1
29 137	...	9	Monroe	1 677	8 583	2 548	5.1	95.3	3.7	0.9	0.7	1.2	5.2	17.4	7.5	10.1	10.3	13.6
29 139	...	8	Montgomery	1 389	11 703	2 312	8.4	96.3	2.1	0.9	0.7	1.7	6.0	16.8	7.1	10.7	10.7	14.1
29 141	...	8	Morgan	1 548	20 171	1 822	13.0	96.2	1.3	1.6	0.7	1.9	6.0	16.0	6.9	9.6	9.5	13.2
29 143	...	7	New Madrid	1 748	18 208	1 906	10.4	82.1	16.6	0.8	0.8	1.6	6.1	17.7	7.8	11.2	12.0	13.8
29 145	27900	3	Newton	1 618	58 615	880	36.2	89.5	1.6	4.1	2.7	5.0	6.3	18.1	8.6	11.5	11.5	13.9
29 147	32340	6	Nodaway	2 271	22 810	1 692	10.0	93.8	3.0	0.6	2.0	1.5	4.6	12.3	28.4	11.1	8.8	10.5
29 149	...	9	Oregon	2 046	10 953	2 361	5.4	96.4	1.0	2.8	0.7	1.4	6.1	16.1	7.5	9.0	10.0	14.2
29 151	27620	3	Osage	1 565	13 628	2 197	8.7	98.6	0.6	0.5	0.3	0.7	5.7	17.9	9.0	10.8	12.3	14.9
29 153	...	9	Ozark	1 929	9 409	2 477	4.9	97.3	0.8	1.6	0.4	1.7	4.7	15.1	6.1	8.6	9.4	12.9
29 155	...	7	Pemiscot	1 276	17 482	1 948	13.7	70.8	27.4	0.8	0.5	2.2	7.7	19.2	8.9	11.4	11.7	12.9
29 157	...	7	Perry	1 229	19 183	1 864	15.6	96.3	0.8	0.8	0.8	2.1	6.0	18.0	8.1	11.5	12.2	13.9
29 159	42740	4	Pettis	1 767	42 255	1 125	23.9	87.2	4.1	0.9	1.3	8.3	6.9	18.1	9.0	13.4	11.3	13.2
29 161	40620	5	Phelps	1 740	44 794	1 078	25.7	90.9	3.1	1.6	4.0	2.5	5.8	15.3	17.8	11.9	10.3	12.2
29 163	...	6	Pike	1 736	18 348	1 898	10.6	89.9	8.4	0.6	0.6	2.2	5.9	16.0	8.8	13.5	12.3	14.1
29 165	28140	1	Platte	1 088	96 096	615	88.3	84.6	7.1	1.1	3.9	5.7	6.1	17.8	8.4	13.2	13.7	14.6
29 167	44180	2	Polk	1 646	31 229	1 405	19.0	96.1	1.4	1.5	1.3	2.1	6.1	17.5	12.7	10.6	11.1	12.9
29 169	22780	5	Pulaski	1 417	53 221	937	37.6	72.8	13.7	1.8	5.1	10.7	7.3	15.5	23.0	18.3	11.6	9.5
29 171	...	9	Putnam	1 340	4 858	2 845	3.6	97.5	0.5	0.7	0.7	1.4	4.9	16.3	7.6	9.2	10.1	13.3
29 173	25300	9	Ralls	1 217	10 196	2 418	8.4	96.6	1.7	0.7	0.7	1.2	5.2	16.6	6.8	10.1	11.9	14.7
29 175	33620	6	Randolph	1 250	25 104	1 607	20.1	91.4	7.0	1.0	0.9	1.9	5.8	16.3	9.3	13.8	12.9	14.1
29 177	28140	1	Ray	1 473	22 810	1 692	15.5	95.4	1.9	1.2	0.7	2.3	5.5	17.8	8.0	10.5	12.0	14.8
29 179	...	9	Reynolds	2 094	6 432	2 718	3.1	97.0	1.3	2.2	0.4	1.5	5.0	15.8	6.7	9.9	11.2	13.8
29 181	...	9	Ripley	1 630	13 802	2 182	8.5	96.8	1.1	1.7	0.6	1.2	6.9	15.8	7.6	11.2	11.8	13.5
29 183	41180	1	St. Charles	1 452	385 590	178	265.6	89.4	5.4	0.6	3.1	3.1	6.1	18.2	8.8	13.1	13.3	14.6
29 185	...	8	St. Clair	1 735	9 440	2 472	5.4	96.1	1.1	1.8	0.5	2.3	4.9	14.2	6.4	9.2	9.8	13.6
29 186	...	6	Ste. Genevieve	1 293	17 919	1 921	13.9	95.9	1.3	0.8	1.6	1.0	5.7	16.6	7.9	10.9	11.4	14.9
29 187	22100	4	St. Francois	1 170	66 520	798	56.9	93.4	4.8	0.9	0.6	1.4	5.4	16.0	9.0	14.3	13.4	14.0
29 189	41180	1	St. Louis	1 315	1 003 362	45	763.0	69.2	24.7	0.6	4.7	2.7	5.8	16.5	8.9	12.7	11.7	13.9
29 195	32180	6	Saline	1 957	23 258	1 671	11.9	83.1	6.3	1.0	2.2	9.8	6.3	16.8	11.6	12.2	11.2	12.5
29 197	28860	9	Schuyler	796	4 436	2 869	5.6	97.9	0.6	0.5	0.4	1.1	6.1	19.1	8.0	10.0	11.1	13.0
29 199	...	9	Scotland	1 131	4 854	2 846	4.3	98.5	0.4	0.7	0.4	0.9	8.3	20.0	8.2	10.4	10.0	12.4
29 201	43460	5	Scott	1 088	39 008	1 203	35.9	85.6	12.5	0.9	0.7	2.2	6.9	17.0	8.6	12.2	12.0	13.5
29 203	...	9	Shannon	2 600	8 258	2 578	3.2	96.8	0.8	2.8	0.5	1.8	5.5	16.8	7.8	10.6	10.1	14.3
29 205	...	9	Shelby	1 297	6 128	2 747	4.7	96.9	1.2	0.5	0.3	1.6	5.8	17.3	7.0	10.7	10.8	13.1
29 207	...	7	Stoddard	2 132	29 862	1 433	14.0	96.5	1.5	0.9	0.5	1.7	5.6	16.7	8.1	11.6	12.0	13.6
29 209	14700	8	Stone	1 202	30 943	1 411	25.7	96.5	0.7	1.6	0.6	2.0	4.2	13.5	6.2	8.0	9.4	13.6
29 211	...	9	Sullivan	1 678	6 353	2 728	3.8	79.5	1.6	0.9	0.3	17.5	6.0	17.0	8.1	10.3	12.1	14.3
29 213	14700	6	Taney	1 638	54 592	920	33.3	91.6	1.8	1.8	1.5	5.5	5.8	15.5	10.2	11.6	11.0	12.9
29 215	...	9	Texas	3 049	25 690	1 572	8.4	92.9	4.1	2.1	0.7	2.2	5.6	15.8	8.3	11.8	11.3	13.8
29 217	...	7	Vernon	2 140	20 826	1 786	9.7	96.0	1.3	1.7	0.9	2.0	6.3	18.2	8.7	10.9	11.4	13.7
29 219	41180	1	Warren	1 110	33 513	1 339	30.2	93.5	3.2	0.9	0.9	3.2	6.2	18.2	7.4	11.9	11.4	14.7
29 221	...	1	Washington	1 968	24 788	1 613	12.6	95.6	2.8	1.2	0.5	1.3	5.8	17.2	7.8	12.2	12.9	14.8
29 223	...	9	Wayne	1 966	13 405	2 210	6.8	97.4	1.1	1.5	0.5	1.4	6.0	14.8	6.8	10.0	10.5	14.9
29 225	44180	2	Webster	1 535	37 483	1 240	24.4	96.1	1.5	1.5	0.5	1.9	6.8	20.5	7.8	11.7	12.3	14.0
29 227	...	9	Worth	691	2 057	3 044	3.0	97.9	1.0	0.7	0.6	1.3	5.9	14.5	7.3	9.5	9.1	13.8
29 229	...	6	Wright	1 766	18 268	1 904	10.3	96.6	1.0	1.5	0.6	1.7	6.3	18.8	7.5	10.4	10.6	13.4

1. CBSA = Core Based Statistical Area. See Appendix A for explanation. See Appendix B for list of metropolitan areas with component counties. 2. County type code from the Economic Research Service of USDA Rural-Urban Continuum Codes. See Appendix A for definition. 3. Dry land or land partially or temporarily covered by water. 4. May be of any race.

Table B. States and Counties — **Population and Households**

STATE County	Age (percent) (cont.) 55 to 64 years	65 to 74 years	75 years and over	Percent female	Total persons 2000	2010	Percent change 2000–2010	2010–2015	Components of change, 2010–2015 Births	Deaths	Net migration	Households, 2010–2014 Number	Persons per house-hold	Percent Family house-holds	Female family house-holder[1]	One per-son
	16	17	18	19	20	21	22	23	24	25	26	27	28	29	30	31
MISSOURI—Cont'd																
Jasper	12.0	7.8	6.1	51.1	104 686	117 404	12.1	1.0	8 976	6 024	-1 915	45 236	2.53	64.8	12.3	27.8
Jefferson	13.6	8.4	4.9	50.4	198 099	218 729	10.4	2.5	13 958	9 790	846	81 504	2.68	73.3	11.6	21.2
Johnson	10.0	6.8	5.0	48.8	48 258	52 595	9.0	2.6	3 813	2 002	-481	19 912	2.49	65.6	7.8	22.9
Knox	14.0	11.5	9.5	50.5	4 361	4 131	-5.3	-5.3	271	261	-228	1 742	2.29	67.5	10.6	31.5
Laclede	12.8	9.9	7.0	50.7	32 513	35 571	9.4	-0.3	2 412	1 940	-570	13 745	2.56	72.2	13.3	22.9
Lafayette	13.7	9.7	8.2	50.4	32 960	33 381	1.3	-2.0	1 981	1 858	-798	13 072	2.47	70.0	9.6	26.4
Lawrence	12.8	9.7	8.1	50.5	35 204	38 634	9.7	-1.2	2 569	2 257	-802	14 616	2.58	70.1	9.3	25.3
Lewis	12.7	9.7	8.3	50.0	10 494	10 211	-2.7	0.0	596	534	-56	3 842	2.45	64.9	7.8	29.2
Lincoln	12.7	7.5	4.9	49.8	38 944	52 565	35.0	4.1	3 778	2 169	518	18 521	2.85	73.0	11.0	22.6
Linn	14.3	10.8	9.4	51.4	13 754	12 761	-7.2	-3.5	743	871	-318	4 769	2.58	64.6	8.6	31.9
Livingston	12.7	9.7	9.6	55.9	14 558	15 195	4.4	-1.1	861	1 002	-53	5 674	2.41	64.8	8.7	29.7
McDonald	12.8	8.7	5.3	49.2	21 681	23 083	6.5	-1.9	1 605	1 093	-890	8 208	2.76	68.9	12.2	28.5
Macon	13.7	11.3	9.7	50.9	15 762	15 566	-1.2	-1.5	930	991	-171	6 231	2.44	62.4	8.4	34.7
Madison	13.4	10.9	8.3	50.8	11 800	12 226	3.6	1.5	720	838	258	4 536	2.69	72.2	12.6	22.6
Maries	14.7	11.0	8.4	49.7	8 903	9 178	3.1	-2.3	419	516	-138	3 718	2.42	70.5	9.4	25.2
Marion	13.3	8.9	8.0	51.6	28 289	28 781	1.7	0.3	1 941	1 638	-199	11 287	2.41	66.6	13.5	27.8
Mercer	15.0	10.6	10.2	49.8	3 757	3 785	0.7	-2.4	206	223	-73	1 537	2.39	62.5	9.2	35.4
Miller	14.1	10.3	7.7	50.1	23 564	24 748	5.0	1.5	1 544	1 418	286	9 710	2.53	68.1	10.4	28.8
Mississippi	11.9	9.3	6.9	46.6	13 427	14 358	6.9	-2.2	890	951	-287	5 249	2.44	64.1	18.6	32.4
Moniteau	11.4	8.2	6.6	46.9	14 827	15 607	5.3	2.3	1 088	738	6	5 487	2.61	70.9	9.5	24.7
Monroe	15.2	11.9	8.9	49.4	9 311	8 840	-5.1	-2.9	474	459	-257	3 559	2.41	65.2	8.9	30.5
Montgomery	14.8	10.6	9.2	50.1	12 136	12 236	0.8	-4.4	743	829	-457	4 892	2.39	68.6	10.8	26.7
Morgan	15.1	13.9	9.8	49.7	19 309	20 565	6.5	-1.9	1 320	1 536	-152	8 021	2.49	65.7	8.1	28.7
New Madrid	13.8	10.2	7.4	52.1	19 760	18 960	-4.0	-4.0	1 248	1 247	-733	7 283	2.50	69.1	19.8	26.4
Newton	13.0	10.0	7.4	50.3	52 636	58 112	10.4	0.9	3 865	3 163	-196	22 197	2.60	71.4	8.8	24.0
Nodaway	10.4	7.0	6.9	49.7	21 912	23 370	6.7	-2.4	1 209	985	-809	8 636	2.31	54.4	7.1	32.9
Oregon	15.0	13.2	8.9	50.8	10 344	10 881	5.2	0.7	692	704	80	4 509	2.41	62.3	7.0	33.5
Osage	12.8	9.0	7.7	48.1	13 062	13 885	6.3	-1.9	775	662	-385	5 113	2.65	71.3	6.7	24.3
Ozark	17.1	15.2	11.1	49.5	9 542	9 723	1.9	-3.2	459	649	-108	4 284	2.22	72.0	12.2	24.4
Pemiscot	12.9	8.5	6.9	52.7	20 047	18 296	-8.7	-4.4	1 491	1 201	-1 096	6 914	2.57	62.9	20.2	33.0
Perry	13.6	8.9	7.8	49.9	18 132	18 971	4.6	1.1	1 163	1 043	69	7 443	2.52	71.6	8.3	24.9
Pettis	12.7	8.0	7.3	50.6	39 403	42 201	7.1	0.1	3 069	2 164	-736	16 250	2.55	68.1	10.7	26.7
Phelps	11.8	8.3	6.6	47.6	39 825	45 154	13.4	-0.8	2 814	2 196	-871	16 737	2.51	62.3	9.4	29.2
Pike	12.9	9.3	7.2	44.8	18 351	18 516	0.9	-0.9	1 135	1 013	-250	6 630	2.45	68.6	10.3	26.7
Platte	13.1	7.9	5.0	50.6	73 781	89 317	21.1	7.6	5 999	3 131	3 959	36 842	2.48	66.8	9.7	27.8
Polk	12.1	9.4	7.7	51.2	26 992	31 137	15.4	0.3	2 012	1 793	-58	11 813	2.52	68.2	8.0	26.1
Pulaski	7.3	4.5	3.1	43.2	41 165	52 274	27.0	1.8	4 420	1 479	-1 987	15 528	2.82	65.2	9.7	27.5
Putnam	15.0	13.0	10.6	49.1	5 223	4 979	-4.7	-2.4	285	310	-82	2 245	2.15	63.8	9.3	32.0
Ralls	15.4	12.4	6.8	49.6	9 626	10 167	5.6	0.3	526	471	4	4 034	2.51	74.6	7.6	21.6
Randolph	12.4	8.5	6.9	47.5	24 663	25 414	3.0	-1.2	1 481	1 373	-405	8 640	2.67	66.4	11.4	28.8
Ray	14.1	10.2	6.9	49.9	23 354	23 494	0.6	-2.9	1 290	1 274	-724	8 741	2.61	71.0	10.8	24.7
Reynolds	14.9	12.6	10.1	48.8	6 689	6 694	0.1	-3.9	324	454	-174	2 672	2.42	65.1	8.8	29.5
Ripley	13.6	11.1	8.5	50.7	13 509	14 100	4.4	-2.1	944	985	-256	5 434	2.57	70.0	12.0	26.1
St. Charles	12.6	7.7	5.5	50.9	283 883	360 485	27.0	7.0	23 955	12 670	13 385	137 483	2.65	72.7	9.6	22.8
St. Clair	15.9	14.4	11.7	49.3	9 652	9 805	1.6	-3.7	490	746	-99	4 057	2.31	64.0	9.5	31.6
Ste. Genevieve	15.5	9.5	7.8	49.5	17 842	18 142	1.7	-1.2	943	1 003	-78	7 218	2.46	70.0	8.0	27.5
St. Francois	12.4	8.6	6.7	46.6	55 641	65 365	17.5	1.8	3 911	3 944	1 126	24 868	2.33	65.6	10.8	28.3
St. Louis	13.9	8.8	7.7	52.6	1 016 315	998 883	-1.7	0.4	61 218	49 455	-6 411	402 629	2.44	65.1	14.1	30.0
Saline	12.8	8.9	7.7	50.3	23 756	23 370	-1.6	-0.5	1 609	1 304	-399	8 865	2.47	65.0	13.8	28.7
Schuyler	13.0	10.1	9.6	50.9	4 170	4 431	6.3	0.1	323	265	5	1 745	2.49	69.2	9.3	27.6
Scotland	11.9	9.8	9.1	50.7	4 983	4 853	-2.6	0.0	399	288	-98	1 885	2.53	67.1	9.4	26.3
Scott	13.3	9.5	7.1	51.4	40 422	39 187	-3.1	-0.5	2 712	2 215	-654	15 361	2.51	70.4	15.2	24.4
Shannon	15.4	12.4	7.2	50.1	8 324	8 441	1.4	-2.2	494	461	-170	3 311	2.49	67.7	9.8	26.7
Shelby	14.7	10.7	9.9	50.3	6 799	6 373	-6.3	-3.8	376	417	-188	2 539	2.35	64.8	6.9	32.2
Stoddard	13.3	10.2	8.7	51.3	29 705	29 968	0.9	-0.4	1 923	1 957	-11	12 069	2.42	65.1	9.4	29.8
Stone	17.7	17.2	10.2	51.1	28 658	32 208	12.4	-3.9	1 350	1 914	-513	13 101	2.39	71.2	7.3	24.3
Sullivan	13.9	10.3	8.1	49.2	7 219	6 714	-7.0	-5.4	447	404	-366	2 617	2.47	64.5	10.9	31.4
Taney	13.4	11.7	8.0	51.5	39 703	51 672	30.1	5.7	3 253	2 661	2 273	20 632	2.49	66.3	13.1	27.8
Texas	14.0	10.8	8.7	47.9	23 003	26 008	13.1	-1.2	1 541	1 487	-262	9 217	2.64	68.5	9.0	27.4
Vernon	13.4	10.0	7.7	51.2	20 454	21 159	3.4	-1.6	1 344	1 279	-363	8 101	2.48	68.5	11.7	26.0
Warren	13.6	9.8	6.8	50.1	24 525	32 513	32.6	3.1	2 128	1 427	352	12 337	2.64	72.7	10.8	22.1
Washington	13.8	9.5	5.9	48.4	23 344	25 196	7.9	-1.6	1 546	1 386	-539	9 062	2.65	71.6	11.4	23.5
Wayne	15.1	13.2	8.7	50.2	13 259	13 523	2.0	-0.9	749	1 024	159	5 528	2.40	67.9	12.0	27.8
Webster	12.3	8.7	6.0	49.1	31 045	36 202	16.6	3.5	2 729	1 610	146	12 681	2.81	74.5	9.6	22.2
Worth	15.6	11.5	12.8	50.1	2 382	2 171	-8.9	-5.3	125	149	-88	892	2.29	62.0	5.8	30.2
Wright	13.8	10.6	8.4	51.1	17 955	18 815	4.8	-2.9	1 256	1 167	-619	7 321	2.51	69.4	10.4	27.5

1. No spouse present.

Table B. States and Counties — Population, Vital Statistics, Medicare, and Crime

STATE County	Persons in group quarters, 2015	Daytime population, 2010–2014 Number	Employment/residence ratio	Births, 2015 Total	Rate[1]	Deaths, 2015 Number	Rate[1]	Persons under 65 with no health insurance, 2014 Number	Percent	Medicare, 2015 Total Beneficiaries	Enrolled in Original Medicare	Enrolled in Medicare Advantage	Serious crimes known to police,[2] 2014 Total Number	Rate[3]
	32	33	34	35	36	37	38	39	40	41	42	43	44	45
MISSOURI—Cont'd														
Jasper	2 480	122 778	1.11	1 705	14.4	1 109	9.4	17 305	17.4	24 463	18 754	5 709	6 022	5 183
Jefferson	1 983	166 417	0.48	2 610	11.7	1 970	8.8	23 281	12.1	34 911	20 623	14 288	4 211	1 895
Johnson	3 843	51 126	0.89	735	13.6	380	7.0	5 430	12.2	6 891	5 593	1 298	1 360	2 468
Knox	87	3 716	0.80	56	14.2	42	10.6	682	22.0	920	863	57	39	961
Laclede	345	35 774	1.02	461	13.0	364	10.3	4 920	16.9	8 272	4 719	3 553	948	2 655
Lafayette	724	28 205	0.67	363	11.1	341	10.4	3 293	12.4	6 869	5 118	1 751	419	1 283
Lawrence	559	33 451	0.69	488	12.8	415	10.9	5 697	18.4	7 232	4 468	2 764	1 235	3 239
Lewis	782	8 589	0.67	119	11.7	99	9.7	1 198	15.5	2 193	1 998	195	80	788
Lincoln	632	42 303	0.51	717	13.2	410	7.5	6 608	14.0	8 048	5 562	2 486	730	1 346
Linn	152	12 450	0.99	154	12.5	164	13.3	1 553	15.9	3 149	2 869	280	284	2 311
Livingston	1 616	15 793	1.12	163	10.8	193	12.8	1 592	14.8	3 386	3 038	348	230	1 552
McDonald	157	20 516	0.75	308	13.6	217	9.6	4 703	24.2	3 667	2 570	1 097	573	2 551
Macon	286	14 604	0.86	182	11.8	173	11.2	2 069	17.0	3 565	3 284	281	273	1 756
Madison	165	11 529	0.82	131	10.6	162	13.1	1 708	17.3	2 936	2 576	360	297	2 376
Maries	67	7 048	0.41	66	7.3	92	10.2	1 293	17.9	1 526	1 340	186	109	1 213
Marion	1 368	30 884	1.16	371	12.8	306	10.6	3 197	13.8	6 779	6 117	662	1 180	4 074
Mercer	51	3 931	1.13	36	9.7	40	10.8	514	17.6	765	698	67	24	652
Miller	271	21 731	0.69	299	11.9	253	10.1	3 643	17.8	5 780	4 801	979	647	2 566
Mississippi	1 873	13 746	0.89	155	11.0	165	11.7	1 601	15.8	2 873	2 645	228	392	2 744
Moniteau	1 378	13 765	0.70	206	12.9	145	9.1	2 171	17.7	2 534	2 197	337	129	817
Monroe	128	7 188	0.59	90	10.4	85	9.8	1 136	16.6	2 206	2 008	198	78	888
Montgomery	394	10 281	0.65	130	11.1	153	13.0	1 485	15.9	2 834	2 334	500	176	1 478
Morgan	302	18 954	0.80	256	12.7	281	13.9	3 341	21.9	5 426	4 629	797	456	2 256
New Madrid	332	18 893	1.04	254	13.9	233	12.8	2 320	15.6	3 570	3 208	362	322	1 765
Newton	880	57 725	0.96	720	12.3	584	10.0	8 187	17.1	8 069	6 188	1 881	2 051	3 471
Nodaway	3 620	23 406	1.01	231	10.1	176	7.7	2 049	12.4	3 715	3 505	210	310	1 333
Oregon	121	10 222	0.80	134	12.3	129	11.8	1 632	19.4	2 654	2 178	476	97	880
Osage	405	11 507	0.65	144	10.5	131	9.6	1 425	12.8	2 258	1 984	274	115	842
Ozark	123	8 605	0.68	83	8.8	130	13.8	1 501	21.6	2 689	1 922	767	108	1 134
Pemiscot	202	17 666	0.95	282	16.1	238	13.6	2 170	14.7	3 634	2 919	715	827	4 784
Perry	286	19 395	1.04	215	11.2	209	10.9	2 073	13.0	3 514	3 195	319	265	1 386
Pettis	851	43 927	1.09	571	13.5	378	9.0	6 168	17.5	8 522	7 256	1 266	1 803	4 268
Phelps	3 009	46 356	1.07	515	11.5	415	9.2	5 709	16.0	8 857	7 682	1 175	1 441	3 221
Pike	2 181	18 414	0.98	208	11.3	192	10.4	2 167	16.2	3 493	3 001	492	225	1 201
Platte	869	88 942	0.93	1 154	12.1	595	6.2	7 558	9.3	12 038	9 197	2 841	3 588	3 803
Polk	1 510	28 890	0.82	400	12.8	358	11.5	3 921	16.0	6 776	3 839	2 937	1 020	3 294
Pulaski	10 002	57 952	1.17	822	15.4	265	5.0	5 614	14.2	5 940	5 196	744	1 048	1 940
Putnam	57	4 386	0.75	59	12.2	54	11.1	711	19.4	1 245	1 151	94	34	700
Ralls	54	8 517	0.65	105	10.3	82	8.0	1 063	12.9	1 553	1 371	182	111	1 087
Randolph	2 455	25 485	1.03	276	11.0	243	9.7	2 938	15.5	5 218	4 317	901	538	2 165
Ray	311	18 081	0.47	253	11.1	266	11.6	2 389	12.7	3 797	3 234	563	526	2 291
Reynolds	101	7 111	1.21	61	9.4	93	14.3	878	17.6	1 461	1 300	161	73	1 109
Ripley	63	12 429	0.68	176	12.7	193	13.9	2 124	19.0	3 349	2 968	381	433	3 230
St. Charles	5 440	315 316	0.71	4 642	12.1	2 553	6.7	26 406	8.1	55 494	33 884	21 610	6 064	1 609
St. Clair	207	8 853	0.78	97	10.3	142	15.0	1 311	19.1	2 475	1 849	626	232	2 464
Ste. Genevieve	277	15 884	0.73	192	10.7	185	10.3	2 028	13.8	3 348	2 910	438	273	1 541
St. Francois	6 992	65 072	0.97	732	11.1	748	11.3	7 651	15.4	14 322	12 264	2 058	2 045	3 077
St. Louis	19 416	1 092 295	1.19	11 673	11.6	9 600	9.6	89 221	10.9	180 172	112 746	67 426	26 121	2 604
Saline	1 343	23 088	0.97	298	12.8	234	10.0	2 775	15.1	4 412	3 593	819	511	2 199
Schuyler	47	3 603	0.56	67	15.2	50	11.3	742	21.3	1 184	1 087	97	45	1 036
Scotland	76	4 492	0.83	76	15.7	47	9.7	874	22.4	886	831	55	46	929
Scott	559	39 090	1.00	500	12.8	437	11.2	4 613	14.3	9 554	8 582	972	1 778	4 519
Shannon	80	7 542	0.74	90	10.9	79	9.5	1 229	18.5	1 666	1 356	310	103	1 245
Shelby	198	5 719	0.82	67	10.9	62	10.1	820	17.2	1 528	1 392	136	36	587
Stoddard	690	28 392	0.88	374	12.5	364	12.2	3 858	16.0	7 134	6 056	1 078	508	1 707
Stone	300	27 403	0.65	256	8.3	373	12.0	4 419	19.7	8 275	5 340	2 935	696	2 235
Sullivan	108	6 761	1.08	84	13.1	72	11.2	1 093	21.0	1 417	1 298	119	93	1 455
Taney	1 749	57 994	1.22	632	11.6	496	9.1	9 084	21.6	12 095	8 079	4 016	1 909	3 531
Texas	1 901	24 354	0.84	296	11.5	266	10.4	3 427	18.2	5 541	4 877	664	547	2 139
Vernon	760	20 984	1.00	269	12.9	231	11.1	2 828	16.9	4 787	3 923	864	946	4 521
Warren	317	26 287	0.56	402	12.0	298	8.9	3 960	14.4	5 697	3 463	2 234	840	2 534
Washington	1 091	22 212	0.66	285	11.4	277	11.1	3 509	17.4	4 907	3 920	987	524	2 079
Wayne	133	12 116	0.73	135	10.1	195	14.5	1 887	18.1	4 159	3 515	644	292	2 180
Webster	913	29 973	0.55	546	14.7	318	8.6	5 644	18.4	7 901	3 904	3 997	750	2 052
Worth	52	1 823	0.72	24	11.7	22	10.7	248	15.9	542	521	21	48	2 311
Wright	195	17 539	0.84	243	13.3	223	12.2	3 038	20.7	4 941	3 104	1 837	347	1 886

1. Per 1,000 estimated resident population.   2. Data for serious crimes have not been adjusted for underreporting; this may affect comparability between geographic areas and over time.
3. Per 100,000 population estimated by the FBI.

Table B. States and Counties — Crime, Education, Money Income, and Poverty

STATE County	Serious crimes known to police, 2014 (cont.)[1] Rate[2] Violent	Property	Education — School enrollment and attainment, 2010–2014 — Enrollment[3] Total	Percent private	Attainment[4] (percent) High school graduate or less	Bachelor's degree or more	Local government expenditures,[5] 2012–2013 Total current spending (mil dol)	Current spending per student (dollars)	Money income, 2010–2014 Per capita income[6] (dollars)	Households Median income (dollars)	Mean income (dollars)	Percent with income of $200,000 or more	Income and poverty, 2014 Median household income (dollars)	Percent below poverty level All persons	Children under 18 years	Children 5 to 17 years in families
	46	47	48	49	50	51	52	53	54	55	56	57	58	59	60	61
MISSOURI—Cont'd																
Jasper	411	4 772	30 213	14.0	49.6	21.0	170.8	7 979	21 904	40 914	55 456	1.7	40 047	19.6	25.2	22.3
Jefferson	218	1 677	54 740	16.9	46.3	18.0	322.7	9 134	25 034	55 563	66 365	1.7	58 976	10.6	14.9	13.1
Johnson	169	2 299	17 655	6.6	39.0	26.0	68.0	8 833	22 394	49 978	58 849	1.2	49 949	14.6	16.9	16.4
Knox	0	961	860	26.2	60.2	13.6	5.3	10 488	22 363	35 597	52 319	2.2	37 581	19.4	33.6	33.0
Laclede	255	2 400	8 555	8.6	59.0	14.1	47.0	7 979	19 218	38 693	48 102	0.7	36 895	18.4	26.1	24.3
Lafayette	104	1 179	7 567	15.1	54.3	17.8	47.4	8 980	24 175	51 195	60 749	1.2	48 128	13.4	20.1	19.1
Lawrence	448	2 790	9 426	12.6	56.5	15.6	48.0	7 986	19 463	40 496	50 616	1.2	39 908	18.6	27.2	25.3
Lewis	128	660	2 683	31.0	59.3	13.4	13.3	8 753	19 514	43 000	50 171	0.2	41 891	14.3	23.0	21.1
Lincoln	219	1 127	13 928	15.7	56.3	14.2	73.8	8 242	22 006	53 280	61 490	1.4	53 804	15.7	20.8	19.3
Linn	399	1 912	2 921	6.6	64.4	12.1	22.0	9 465	18 989	37 264	47 266	1.0	37 597	20.0	29.8	26.1
Livingston	169	1 383	3 118	10.2	59.4	17.1	19.8	9 071	21 882	44 754	56 354	1.6	47 937	16.6	23.8	22.6
McDonald	619	1 932	5 965	8.6	56.0	12.3	30.5	8 058	18 093	38 122	47 770	1.7	34 863	22.2	32.3	29.4
Macon	264	1 492	3 583	11.7	57.4	15.7	21.5	9 346	19 970	36 878	48 191	1.6	35 345	17.0	25.6	23.7
Madison	424	1 952	2 724	12.3	60.4	9.9	18.0	8 561	17 459	37 648	44 472	0.8	35 363	20.4	30.2	28.2
Maries	134	1 079	1 865	8.2	58.9	15.3	10.7	7 810	21 316	41 492	50 680	1.2	40 165	16.1	24.0	20.9
Marion	255	3 819	6 884	23.6	54.2	18.4	43.2	8 408	22 731	41 732	56 504	2.0	42 088	18.0	25.8	23.3
Mercer	82	571	809	13.8	60.7	14.2	6.6	10 743	19 906	38 925	47 129	0.0	38 023	15.0	22.1	20.7
Miller	337	2 229	6 257	13.6	57.0	15.4	44.6	8 873	19 969	36 592	48 749	1.9	37 360	17.4	26.6	25.1
Mississippi	497	2 247	2 956	7.5	68.6	10.1	17.3	7 852	15 032	28 436	39 692	0.5	30 661	32.2	40.1	39.5
Moniteau	177	639	3 761	13.9	60.4	17.2	19.6	8 269	19 540	47 386	55 100	0.6	47 158	13.9	20.2	19.4
Monroe	23	866	1 887	12.9	58.7	14.0	13.7	9 050	20 303	40 342	48 561	0.3	41 376	15.8	24.9	22.4
Montgomery	185	1 293	2 718	13.1	61.2	12.1	15.5	8 936	20 529	40 114	49 955	0.7	42 105	16.1	24.5	22.9
Morgan	188	2 068	3 844	21.7	61.6	13.4	16.8	7 992	18 445	34 179	44 935	0.3	36 867	20.7	31.5	29.4
New Madrid	296	1 469	4 061	6.4	65.5	11.9	27.0	9 692	20 896	34 224	51 276	1.2	34 631	23.3	32.9	29.6
Newton	169	3 301	14 681	11.4	47.8	18.8	68.4	7 931	22 350	42 939	58 177	2.2	45 448	14.3	20.4	18.9
Nodaway	120	1 212	9 226	6.2	51.2	23.4	29.4	10 709	18 329	36 237	47 219	1.0	42 956	20.2	17.4	15.9
Oregon	145	734	2 351	1.7	60.2	9.3	15.9	9 012	16 877	29 385	39 910	0.6	29 415	23.9	38.2	35.3
Osage	81	761	3 563	21.9	58.5	17.5	13.7	8 336	23 362	52 479	60 601	0.3	51 958	10.2	13.0	11.7
Ozark	126	1 008	1 645	8.6	60.0	13.6	14.9	9 764	17 324	31 833	39 169	0.0	31 025	22.3	35.0	31.8
Pemiscot	839	3 945	4 523	3.0	64.6	11.4	39.4	10 834	17 387	30 840	42 942	0.6	32 120	28.7	40.2	39.8
Perry	235	1 151	4 698	32.0	58.7	16.1	21.3	8 668	23 539	50 817	59 606	1.6	50 548	11.6	16.3	14.9
Pettis	372	3 896	10 805	12.4	50.1	16.7	52.9	7 855	20 571	39 624	52 529	1.4	40 038	17.6	26.4	24.9
Phelps	422	2 799	15 215	9.9	45.7	28.1	57.3	8 850	20 900	41 942	53 649	1.7	40 710	21.6	26.1	23.7
Pike	133	1 067	3 581	9.9	64.2	12.2	22.4	8 485	18 738	40 120	51 994	1.0	44 408	18.9	26.7	25.8
Platte	668	3 136	25 279	21.8	28.5	39.2	165.1	10 596	35 333	68 638	86 641	5.8	70 874	6.9	9.4	8.4
Polk	368	2 926	8 651	21.7	54.6	17.0	46.9	8 858	19 357	39 336	50 541	0.9	38 344	18.1	27.6	25.8
Pulaski	298	1 642	16 245	14.1	42.9	21.6	81.9	9 000	20 019	49 604	57 512	0.6	47 227	15.9	18.6	18.2
Putnam	0	700	937	14.3	57.0	15.2	6.7	9 237	20 069	36 886	43 859	0.6	34 684	18.6	27.7	25.3
Ralls	69	1 019	2 145	13.8	59.7	13.3	5.7	7 765	23 588	47 837	57 585	1.2	51 738	11.6	16.7	15.0
Randolph	121	2 045	6 260	19.3	54.0	13.9	35.4	9 175	18 263	39 316	49 879	1.4	41 346	18.3	26.3	24.8
Ray	261	2 030	5 695	10.4	57.9	13.9	27.9	8 105	23 957	51 585	62 047	1.2	51 986	15.3	19.9	16.7
Reynolds	228	881	1 282	2.9	70.8	6.2	13.5	12 134	18 791	34 432	44 988	0.3	31 820	21.5	33.6	30.7
Ripley	298	2 932	3 159	8.1	62.6	10.7	18.3	7 915	16 843	31 473	40 625	0.3	30 019	25.1	36.9	34.7
St. Charles	123	1 486	101 934	26.3	32.2	35.5	568.5	9 565	32 473	72 100	86 317	5.1	74 220	6.8	8.9	7.9
St. Clair	414	2 050	1 685	13.4	63.9	11.7	12.2	8 902	18 098	31 875	41 322	0.4	33 986	21.7	33.8	31.6
Ste. Genevieve	361	1 180	4 344	21.4	54.8	12.4	20.9	11 080	23 780	46 244	58 754	1.2	46 874	13.1	18.5	16.9
St. Francois	280	2 797	14 927	12.8	51.7	14.6	88.5	8 253	19 044	37 476	50 007	1.1	40 376	20.3	26.3	23.7
St. Louis	307	2 296	267 410	28.9	29.7	41.4	1 862.2	13 436	35 388	59 520	86 257	7.1	60 093	9.6	13.7	12.6
Saline	176	2 022	6 309	23.9	55.8	18.1	31.5	8 764	19 774	39 027	49 470	0.7	41 112	16.3	23.0	21.1
Schuyler	161	875	953	12.3	61.5	10.4	5.3	8 295	18 631	36 060	47 092	0.9	34 644	18.2	29.5	27.3
Scotland	61	869	986	25.5	60.7	16.9	6.0	9 871	20 556	39 450	52 016	2.0	38 281	16.3	24.9	24.2
Scott	1 047	3 472	9 080	12.8	61.4	14.0	53.4	7 854	20 637	39 076	51 187	1.5	40 532	20.9	31.0	27.2
Shannon	254	991	1 901	9.0	58.2	14.2	17.7	9 034	18 931	33 583	46 199	1.1	27 382	28.2	47.8	43.5
Shelby	16	570	1 400	20.1	54.4	13.6	9.9	9 037	20 256	38 935	48 565	0.6	42 498	16.6	24.1	21.5
Stoddard	134	1 573	6 420	10.1	60.7	13.7	41.2	8 062	23 923	39 229	56 691	1.5	38 329	19.0	26.4	23.6
Stone	466	1 769	6 039	13.9	54.9	15.3	38.4	9 306	21 555	40 136	50 161	1.1	40 642	16.2	27.9	26.4
Sullivan	203	1 252	1 414	4.7	64.3	11.8	10.7	9 919	19 856	37 198	46 161	1.0	36 642	17.7	25.0	22.7
Taney	314	3 217	12 793	23.3	50.2	17.9	69.9	8 679	19 844	37 249	48 707	1.0	35 731	18.7	28.7	27.6
Texas	125	2 014	5 614	10.3	64.1	12.6	32.7	8 327	18 178	35 822	47 438	1.2	33 755	21.5	32.8	32.0
Vernon	545	3 976	5 033	16.6	56.3	14.7	28.5	8 834	20 406	40 508	51 070	1.2	40 267	17.5	26.8	24.3
Warren	410	2 124	7 362	20.3	50.0	16.9	39.7	8 539	25 138	52 512	66 529	2.5	52 959	12.8	19.4	16.5
Washington	302	1 778	5 656	9.3	68.4	7.8	31.5	8 470	17 565	34 282	46 153	1.1	34 581	25.5	39.3	35.4
Wayne	224	1 956	2 470	4.2	63.4	10.2	15.2	8 394	18 707	33 072	44 230	0.5	30 721	26.4	40.8	39.9
Webster	200	1 852	8 932	19.3	55.3	16.0	54.6	7 793	20 183	45 798	55 830	1.3	41 561	17.8	28.1	26.2
Worth	96	2 215	456	8.6	56.7	16.4	3.0	9 075	23 730	42 905	53 784	1.8	38 802	15.5	20.8	20.0
Wright	266	1 619	4 388	12.4	62.7	12.2	28.3	7 968	16 026	30 029	39 978	0.9	31 600	22.7	33.7	31.3

1. Data for serious crimes have not been adjusted for underreporting; this may affect comparability between geographic areas and over time.   2. Per 100,000 population estimated by the FBI.
3. All persons 3 years old and over enrolled in nursery school through college.   4. Persons 25 years old and over.   5. Elementary and secondary education expenditures.
6. Based on population estimated by the American Community Survey, 2010–2014.

| STATE County | Personal income, 2014 | | | | | | | | | | Earnings, 2014 | | |
	Total (mil dol)	Percent change, 2013–2014	Per capita¹ Dollars	Per capita¹ Rank	Wages and salaries (mil dol)	Supplements to wages and salaries; employer contributions (mil dol) Pension and insurance	Supplements to wages and salaries; employer contributions (mil dol) Government social insurance	Proprietors' income (mil dol)	Dividends, interest, and rent (mil dol)	Personal transfer receipts (mil dol)	Total (mil dol)	Contributions for government social insurance (mil dol) From employee and self-employed	Contributions for government social insurance (mil dol) From employer
	62	63	64	65	66	67	68	69	70	71	72	73	74
MISSOURI—Cont'd													
Jasper	4 032	2.6	34 306	2 063	2 289	411	167	319	610	934	3 187	191	167
Jefferson	8 229	4.0	36 947	1 607	1 817	338	139	503	898	1 643	2 797	192	139
Johnson	1 787	3.8	32 871	2 302	782	224	64	162	335	368	1 232	60	64
Knox	184	15.6	46 115	590	33	8	2	65	28	35	108	4	2
Laclede	1 100	4.8	31 039	2 578	439	93	36	101	189	320	669	43	36
Lafayette	1 196	0.4	36 579	1 673	295	65	22	115	180	312	497	31	22
Lawrence	1 152	5.4	30 297	2 678	311	68	23	90	185	320	491	32	23
Lewis	343	2.5	33 812	2 144	83	19	6	57	47	82	164	9	6
Lincoln	1 830	3.8	33 741	2 154	429	87	31	104	200	407	651	43	31
Linn	460	6.2	37 346	1 547	155	30	13	63	81	126	261	16	13
Livingston	531	5.3	35 287	1 892	228	46	17	85	98	135	376	21	17
McDonald	610	8.7	26 733	2 998	235	50	17	71	72	164	372	21	17
Macon	544	3.2	35 121	1 914	165	41	11	85	89	150	303	18	11
Madison	394	4.1	31 820	2 460	115	26	8	25	56	146	174	12	8
Maries	338	3.5	37 469	1 530	42	10	3	70	50	75	125	8	3
Marion	1 076	2.5	37 221	1 566	500	90	39	111	158	291	740	44	39
Mercer	141	20.8	37 949	1 463	34	6	2	49	19	30	92	3	2
Miller	752	6.1	29 925	2 727	220	47	17	107	120	210	390	23	17
Mississippi	441	-5.9	30 952	2 593	129	28	9	73	62	137	240	13	9
Moniteau	519	4.6	32 705	2 333	130	32	9	69	81	106	240	13	9
Monroe	370	4.0	42 530	897	70	17	5	94	49	77	187	8	5
Montgomery	405	2.7	34 188	2 084	99	21	7	51	67	109	178	11	7
Morgan	764	3.9	37 733	1 493	124	27	10	88	237	217	249	17	10
New Madrid	591	-1.5	32 364	2 395	313	55	24	36	70	194	428	27	24
Newton	2 027	4.0	34 589	2 004	792	147	58	158	322	465	1 156	70	58
Nodaway	703	1.7	30 468	2 656	277	68	19	108	121	146	473	24	19
Oregon	288	4.2	26 367	3 015	81	17	8	35	45	115	141	10	8
Osage	527	6.0	38 468	1 399	126	28	9	71	83	94	234	13	9
Ozark	245	0.1	25 864	3 036	11	11	3	22	48	93	81	7	3
Pemiscot	586	-2.8	33 177	2 250	200	46	15	49	74	203	309	19	15
Perry	676	3.0	35 183	1 908	364	69	27	51	92	157	510	30	27
Pettis	1 472	5.1	34 870	1 957	695	135	53	157	230	382	1 039	59	53
Phelps	1 447	2.9	32 258	2 408	689	162	48	72	272	385	971	56	48
Pike	591	1.2	31 883	2 454	203	47	15	67	112	152	332	19	15
Platte	4 667	4.8	49 232	425	2 039	298	150	244	688	569	2 732	162	150
Polk	925	6.2	29 800	2 743	287	68	21	70	148	292	445	28	21
Pulaski	2 073	-4.0	38 794	1 353	1 130	339	105	52	428	346	1 627	70	105
Putnam	184	20.6	38 158	1 432	40	10	3	47	32	50	100	4	3
Ralls	389	0.4	37 967	1 458	159	28	11	52	58	88	251	14	11
Randolph	914	2.1	36 447	1 696	370	78	28	128	117	248	604	36	28
Ray	884	4.3	38 538	1 384	152	37	11	126	101	199	326	20	11
Reynolds	178	1.9	27 068	2 976	71	15	5	7	35	74	98	7	5
Ripley	407	1.9	29 102	2 815	81	20	6	35	51	165	141	11	6
St. Charles	17 329	4.7	45 662	623	6 214	956	457	786	2 184	2 335	8 412	518	457
St. Clair	307	7.1	32 495	2 372	52	13	4	44	51	101	113	8	4
Ste. Genevieve	648	5.1	36 148	1 756	251	41	19	18	103	156	329	22	19
St. Francois	1 967	3.3	29 814	2 741	769	173	57	80	270	649	1 079	71	57
St. Louis	60 653	3.7	60 540	125	35 488	4 775	2 470	4 732	16 324	7 924	47 465	2 818	2 470
Saline	953	2.3	40 813	1 087	320	69	23	219	133	233	630	31	23
Schuyler	120	0.3	27 535	2 953	19	6	1	12	21	36	38	3	1
Scotland	197	6.3	40 494	1 121	39	12	3	66	31	38	119	4	3
Scott	1 496	1.9	38 446	1 402	566	106	44	241	208	404	956	57	44
Shannon	199	1.8	23 890	3 083	38	10	3	25	31	76	76	6	3
Shelby	274	15.4	44 852	689	53	13	4	78	42	56	148	6	4
Stoddard	1 028	-2.6	34 427	2 042	361	69	29	111	141	305	569	37	29
Stone	1 140	5.2	36 651	1 658	196	37	15	175	221	335	423	33	15
Sullivan	288	21.5	44 977	678	21	7	7	102	32	62	232	8	7
Taney	1 653	7.0	30 475	2 654	874	140	72	70	326	507	1 155	76	72
Texas	673	5.0	26 230	3 023	184	50	13	38	128	233	284	19	13
Vernon	736	7.3	35 037	1 929	266	65	19	142	104	205	492	24	19
Warren	1 155	3.9	34 725	1 978	259	51	20	51	160	262	380	27	20
Washington	660	1.8	26 315	3 017	158	42	12	21	68	246	232	17	12
Wayne	360	0.7	26 737	2 997	71	19	5	22	56	152	117	10	5
Webster	1 069	4.0	28 993	2 829	229	51	17	80	144	270	376	27	17
Worth	92	16.4	44 171	746	13	4	1	35	14	17	53	2	1
Wright	471	6.1	25 729	3 038	135	31	10	25	86	192	201	15	10

1. Based on the resident population estimated as of July 1 of the year shown.

Table B. States and Counties — Earnings, Social Security, and Housing

STATE County	Farm	Mining	Construction	Manu-facturing	Information: professional, scientific, technical services	Retail trade	Finance, insur-ance, real estate and leasing	Health care and social assistance	Govern-ment	Number	Rate[1]	Supple-mental Security Income recipients, December 2014	Total	Percent change, 2010–2014
	75	76	77	78	79	80	81	82	83	84	85	86	87	88
MISSOURI—Cont'd														
Jasper	1.3	0.2	5.2	19.2	3.9	8.9	4.4	9.9	12.0	24 240	206	3 616	51 694	2.0
Jefferson	0.1	0.4	11.7	10.4	4.2	8.3	5.4	11.3	18.8	44 255	199	2 911	89 111	1.7
Johnson	3.4	D	5.5	4.8	2.2	5.3	3.6	4.8	56.2	8 320	153	693	21 812	1.3
Knox	47.2	D	3.1	6.4	4.1	3.3	3.0	2.0	11.5	1 050	263	92	2 267	-1.0
Laclede	3.2	0.1	4.0	35.8	2.3	10.4	4.0	9.1	12.3	9 145	258	1 196	15 742	-0.2
Lafayette	11.0	0.0	8.5	8.4	6.5	7.6	4.5	D	22.1	7 625	233	604	14 686	-0.2
Lawrence	11.4	D	6.7	15.7	4.6	7.6	3.0	D	24.4	9 185	242	884	16 523	-0.8
Lewis	27.4	D	3.6	3.4	1.4	6.5	D	D	17.1	2 370	234	201	4 493	-0.9
Lincoln	2.5	1.1	13.0	14.0	D	9.0	4.4	5.0	22.5	10 450	193	923	21 087	0.4
Linn	12.8	0.0	3.3	15.2	7.1	6.1	5.7	9.2	15.1	3 245	263	360	6 374	-0.9
Livingston	12.1	D	6.4	8.4	2.6	8.7	4.5	D	19.0	3 510	233	339	6 737	0.1
McDonald	11.6	D	5.7	35.5	2.0	7.7	1.8	2.8	14.0	4 775	210	633	9 804	-1.2
Macon	10.3	0.0	5.6	15.0	6.0	6.9	3.5	D	28.0	4 110	266	317	7 602	-0.8
Madison	5.7	D	7.5	10.2	D	10.5	D	9.0	24.9	3 510	283	578	5 924	-0.8
Maries	13.1	0.0	D	14.5	D	7.7	D	D	12.0	2 030	225	163	4 556	-1.2
Marion	6.1	D	7.3	10.2	D	8.8	3.8	D	14.0	6 805	236	1 042	12 897	0.6
Mercer	59.7	D	2.4	0.0	D	2.6	2.0	3.4	13.5	855	230	75	2 112	-1.1
Miller	16.1	D	8.9	7.1	2.8	10.9	4.4	D	19.3	5 735	229	587	12 788	0.2
Mississippi	18.2	0.0	D	D	0.9	6.9	3.9	D	21.4	3 410	240	740	5 699	-0.2
Moniteau	17.2	D	12.8	13.3	2.4	6.8	3.4	D	21.7	3 105	196	206	6 121	-0.9
Monroe	41.1	D	2.8	8.1	2.1	2.9	4.4	3.2	16.9	2 070	238	195	4 807	0.2
Montgomery	15.6	0.6	8.4	15.1	1.6	8.1	5.5	6.1	19.2	3 045	258	299	6 162	0.5
Morgan	23.1	D	8.3	9.1	D	12.4	4.2	D	17.7	6 060	300	598	15 370	-0.9
New Madrid	3.2	0.0	3.4	28.0	D	9.8	1.9	D	11.8	4 960	272	987	8 529	0.0
Newton	7.7	D	5.2	12.6	4.2	6.8	2.6	29.2	12.2	13 170	225	971	24 352	0.2
Nodaway	13.3	D	3.5	15.7	3.8	7.2	3.3	10.5	26.6	3 985	173	264	9 668	1.5
Oregon	11.7	D	2.0	7.3	D	9.4	2.5	D	17.4	2 805	258	565	5 418	-1.2
Osage	18.1	0.4	10.0	23.4	1.1	6.5	2.8	4.9	15.8	2 825	206	149	6 534	-0.9
Ozark	13.3	0.0	5.2	4.7	D	8.7	6.8	5.3	26.2	2 300	243	266	5 609	-0.8
Pemiscot	8.9	D	D	D	1.0	8.5	3.8	9.4	25.9	4 510	256	1 433	8 100	-0.7
Perry	3.9	D	9.4	31.2	D	6.5	4.9	D	12.7	4 370	227	363	8 610	0.5
Pettis	6.9	D	4.7	22.8	6.1	7.5	2.8	8.2	17.3	9 035	214	1 223	18 170	-0.4
Phelps	0.3	0.1	4.1	6.5	3.4	8.2	3.7	13.8	39.4	9 310	207	1 204	19 842	1.6
Pike	12.9	D	7.7	5.8	4.1	11.3	3.0	5.9	26.9	4 035	218	425	7 825	-0.6
Platte	0.8	D	5.8	9.2	7.0	7.3	5.7	6.8	11.2	15 135	160	691	40 572	3.4
Polk	6.8	0.2	4.1	2.3	D	8.2	3.7	D	31.7	7 675	247	1 010	13 372	0.5
Pulaski	0.3	D	2.0	D	1.7	3.2	1.6	2.4	79.8	6 535	122	725	18 799	5.0
Putnam	43.8	0.0	D	D	D	5.0	5.1	1.6	23.0	1 385	286	138	2 962	-0.7
Ralls	16.8	0.0	D	49.3	D	3.3	1.0	D	7.7	2 655	258	129	5 126	-1.1
Randolph	2.9	D	3.0	8.3	1.9	16.6	6.1	11.5	17.9	5 375	214	800	10 648	-0.6
Ray	9.3	D	8.8	8.5	3.5	11.1	5.0	D	21.2	5 170	225	341	9 966	-0.2
Reynolds	0.9	D	1.3	12.1	D	3.9	D	12.3	18.9	1 905	291	275	3 994	-0.9
Ripley	6.3	0.0	4.7	12.6	D	10.4	3.3	16.4	24.9	3 960	283	819	6 525	-1.1
St. Charles	0.3	D	7.7	13.5	12.1	8.3	9.2	9.4	12.1	63 730	168	2 712	149 648	6.1
St. Clair	21.8	D	4.3	2.3	D	8.7	3.0	7.9	24.4	2 840	300	281	5 562	-1.4
Ste. Genevieve	2.2	5.9	7.7	7.1	D	5.8	2.9	D	17.6	4 355	242	328	8 626	-0.1
St. Francois	0.2	0.6	6.3	8.1	3.0	8.8	7.0	16.0	28.0	15 900	241	2 648	29 415	3.4
St. Louis	0.0	0.3	5.6	10.3	13.2	5.7	10.6	12.0	8.2	198 715	198	18 166	438 425	0.1
Saline	21.7	0.0	1.7	18.2	2.3	5.2	2.4	D	14.8	4 970	213	617	10 099	-0.2
Schuyler	11.0	0.0	D	D	D	8.6	0.0	3.6	34.1	990	225	114	2 087	-0.7
Scotland	41.7	D	3.1	2.0	D	6.2	2.4	D	26.4	965	199	63	2 342	-1.2
Scott	8.7	D	4.7	12.8	11.4	4.8	3.7	15.1	13.1	9 910	255	1 853	17 053	0.4
Shannon	3.4	D	D	24.3	D	8.6	3.6	D	19.1	1 975	238	337	4 117	-1.1
Shelby	41.0	D	2.3	7.6	2.0	7.8	2.4	D	16.7	1 695	277	124	3 174	-1.0
Stoddard	8.2	0.3	6.2	24.5	2.8	8.4	5.5	D	13.5	8 270	277	1 185	13 598	-0.1
Stone	2.4	D	10.9	1.2	3.3	10.7	12.5	D	13.7	11 070	356	627	20 618	1.2
Sullivan	44.5	D	1.6	D	D	3.4	3.3	2.2	10.2	1 610	249	204	3 326	-1.0
Taney	0.6	0.2	4.0	2.1	4.1	11.1	5.6	D	11.8	17 285	319	1 511	30 142	3.0
Texas	4.1	D	4.9	13.6	2.9	8.2	3.7	D	34.7	7 230	282	832	11 557	-1.1
Vernon	22.1	0.6	3.0	18.1	D	5.5	4.9	D	18.5	5 235	250	712	9 471	-0.3
Warren	3.7	D	9.8	25.5	2.7	6.7	4.1	D	18.2	7 370	222	520	14 957	1.9
Washington	1.1	D	3.9	11.4	D	6.2	3.3	D	38.4	5 945	237	1 223	10 828	-1.7
Wayne	2.7	D	3.6	11.1	D	9.0	3.8	12.6	25.2	3 635	271	702	7 957	-1.6
Webster	9.1	0.3	7.9	12.5	D	10.1	3.8	D	20.1	7 890	214	708	14 498	0.6
Worth	61.6	D	D	D	D	2.8	0.0	1.6	14.8	540	262	42	1 269	-0.9
Wright	10.9	D	3.9	10.2	D	12.5	3.9	D	21.4	5 410	296	878	8 602	-1.1

1. Per 1,000 resident population estimated as of July 1 of the year shown.

Table B. States and Counties — Housing, Labor Force, and Employment

STATE County	Housing units, 2010–2014								Civilian labor force, 2015				Civilian employment,[6] 2010–2014		
	Occupied units										Unemployment			Percent	
		Owner-occupied				Renter-occupied									
				Median owner cost as a percent of income											Con-struction, produc-tion, and mainte-nance occu-pations
	Total	Percent	Median value[1]	With a mort-gage	Without a mort-gage[2]	Median rent[3]	Median rent as a per-cent of income[2]	Sub-stand-ard units[4] (percent)	Total	Percent change, 2014–2015	Total	Rate[5]	Total	Manage-ment, business, science and arts	
	89	90	91	92	93	94	95	96	97	98	99	100	101	102	103

MISSOURI—Cont'd

STATE County	89	90	91	92	93	94	95	96	97	98	99	100	101	102	103
Jasper	45 236	64.9	102 000	20.5	12.4	684	29.8	2.8	58 752	1.6	2 492	4.2	54 376	28.7	27.2
Jefferson	81 504	81.8	150 200	22.3	11.9	770	28.4	2.0	118 670	1.8	5 754	4.8	106 031	29.0	26.6
Johnson	19 912	60.7	142 400	21.7	11.1	732	30.9	2.5	23 357	2.2	1 262	5.4	23 138	31.1	25.9
Knox	1 742	74.7	67 000	21.7	11.9	428	25.3	2.8	2 004	1.5	79	3.9	1 822	32.8	28.6
Laclede	13 745	70.4	99 900	23.0	11.7	601	30.7	3.6	16 151	1.4	1 028	6.4	14 474	25.4	34.8
Lafayette	13 072	76.7	116 900	19.6	11.9	643	28.7	2.0	17 474	2.8	838	4.8	15 204	29.8	31.9
Lawrence	14 616	71.2	92 500	22.9	12.3	626	24.9	3.4	18 129	3.6	886	4.9	15 670	27.1	31.5
Lewis	3 842	72.8	84 300	18.7	11.5	488	23.1	2.5	5 278	2.1	258	4.9	4 851	23.5	33.8
Lincoln	18 521	77.8	145 500	22.5	11.1	759	30.3	1.7	27 135	1.9	1 398	5.2	23 270	25.5	32.5
Linn	4 769	75.1	73 200	20.2	12.5	531	29.0	2.1	5 341	2.1	371	6.9	4 984	26.4	33.1
Livingston	5 674	70.7	98 400	19.3	11.3	601	27.9	1.8	7 365	0.6	316	4.3	6 539	28.3	29.3
McDonald	8 208	70.4	84 200	21.3	11.2	583	26.8	7.2	10 808	4.9	494	4.6	9 288	21.2	38.3
Macon	6 231	74.4	83 800	20.8	12.6	543	28.2	2.3	7 626	2.2	408	5.4	6 499	28.9	29.9
Madison	4 536	75.7	89 600	25.0	11.2	598	31.9	0.4	5 588	1.4	325	5.8	4 783	20.7	37.5
Maries	3 718	74.8	113 200	22.3	10.0	565	26.5	3.2	4 006	0.7	210	5.2	3 535	24.4	36.4
Marion	11 287	67.1	102 500	19.4	11.1	593	27.4	1.3	14 912	1.8	662	4.4	13 020	30.7	29.6
Mercer	1 537	74.1	71 300	18.1	11.6	544	24.0	4.9	1 920	2.5	85	4.4	1 608	32.6	31.6
Miller	9 710	77.9	115 800	23.6	10.6	615	30.3	2.9	11 809	1.2	706	6.0	10 444	23.9	26.8
Mississippi	5 249	62.4	58 800	23.2	12.3	571	30.0	0.9	6 375	1.5	374	5.9	4 936	24.5	28.1
Moniteau	5 487	73.7	110 500	19.5	10.0	537	26.2	2.8	7 463	0.9	365	4.9	6 627	27.8	31.0
Monroe	3 559	75.3	90 200	23.4	11.5	565	24.0	1.5	4 284	2.1	225	5.3	3 747	26.9	35.5
Montgomery	4 892	75.0	102 800	21.9	12.3	623	34.4	1.4	5 783	1.5	288	5.0	5 195	26.6	34.1
Morgan	8 021	77.9	110 300	25.3	13.2	637	28.4	4.4	8 201	2.8	549	6.7	6 900	26.1	29.3
New Madrid	7 283	61.0	74 600	19.1	13.1	534	28.8	1.1	8 695	2.5	538	6.2	7 484	28.0	31.0
Newton	22 197	74.0	107 000	22.0	11.5	631	27.9	1.9	29 017	1.9	1 312	4.5	26 039	28.8	28.3
Nodaway	8 636	55.0	110 100	21.0	11.8	602	33.5	1.6	11 136	0.1	549	4.9	11 422	26.8	27.9
Oregon	4 509	77.0	77 200	23.8	13.9	524	31.7	1.8	4 234	2.0	266	6.3	3 888	22.2	37.3
Osage	5 113	82.2	129 000	19.8	10.0	506	22.5	1.1	7 311	1.0	273	3.7	6 694	27.7	32.7
Ozark	4 284	78.2	87 800	22.7	10.7	502	32.6	6.2	3 718	1.3	294	7.9	3 217	24.7	38.2
Pemiscot	6 914	55.5	65 500	21.2	12.1	539	30.4	2.7	7 156	0.6	649	9.1	6 568	25.8	30.9
Perry	7 443	77.4	123 200	19.7	11.3	686	28.4	2.5	10 401	1.0	433	4.2	9 204	27.0	37.0
Pettis	16 250	68.7	100 100	21.4	11.5	681	32.2	3.6	21 135	2.1	1 113	5.3	18 905	27.4	33.3
Phelps	16 737	61.2	111 800	21.1	10.0	660	31.3	1.7	19 829	1.9	1 052	5.3	18 699	37.5	19.5
Pike	6 630	72.6	90 300	20.8	12.2	606	28.3	2.5	8 228	0.8	378	4.6	7 237	24.6	31.1
Platte	36 842	64.5	186 300	20.6	11.5	873	26.1	1.9	55 677	3.0	2 336	4.2	48 769	41.7	17.7
Polk	11 813	67.3	112 700	21.0	10.1	638	31.4	2.7	14 499	2.6	758	5.2	12 429	29.6	26.9
Pulaski	15 528	52.5	126 000	20.1	10.0	927	26.1	3.3	15 113	-0.9	882	5.8	15 086	34.8	23.8
Putnam	2 245	71.7	85 000	22.8	16.3	512	28.8	1.9	2 536	1.6	101	4.0	2 093	30.9	36.8
Ralls	4 034	81.2	109 100	19.8	11.8	629	24.4	2.5	5 760	1.9	243	4.2	4 987	26.8	32.5
Randolph	8 640	71.9	85 500	20.8	11.9	656	27.9	2.1	10 681	0.9	633	5.9	9 843	27.3	27.0
Ray	8 741	76.2	117 700	22.2	12.2	736	29.9	1.8	11 433	2.5	623	5.4	9 926	25.2	34.7
Reynolds	2 672	78.7	84 500	23.0	10.5	495	32.0	3.5	2 760	2.3	192	7.0	2 319	23.5	40.0
Ripley	5 434	74.4	74 000	22.9	12.6	530	31.8	2.8	5 433	-2.6	430	7.9	5 293	22.3	34.6
St. Charles	137 483	80.0	188 100	20.8	11.7	905	27.7	1.0	217 392	2.3	8 381	3.9	193 425	41.4	16.8
St. Clair	4 057	77.6	81 400	25.0	13.2	443	30.0	5.0	4 025	0.8	277	6.9	3 470	28.9	28.1
Ste. Genevieve	7 218	77.6	126 700	22.6	12.4	608	30.3	1.3	9 173	0.9	486	5.3	8 112	21.4	40.6
St. Francois	24 868	66.3	99 600	21.7	10.9	603	29.5	3.5	26 756	1.5	1 630	6.1	24 859	27.4	26.9
St. Louis	402 629	70.8	173 000	21.5	12.3	873	29.8	1.2	540 801	2.0	24 953	4.6	488 429	43.7	14.0
Saline	8 865	67.5	85 500	21.8	12.6	586	27.3	2.2	11 331	0.6	536	4.7	10 606	28.9	31.1
Schuyler	1 745	73.1	84 500	20.3	15.5	523	23.8	5.7	1 896	0.2	111	5.9	1 856	30.7	35.0
Scotland	1 885	74.9	72 600	24.1	11.6	447	22.1	4.6	2 492	3.9	112	4.5	2 212	32.9	32.0
Scott	15 361	68.1	94 300	18.9	10.8	595	28.6	3.5	20 287	1.9	1 067	5.3	17 751	27.0	31.2
Shannon	3 311	77.6	84 200	22.5	10.4	512	31.8	4.4	3 390	-1.3	273	8.1	3 269	27.2	42.5
Shelby	2 539	73.1	72 000	21.9	11.9	443	24.3	2.8	3 124	2.0	148	4.7	2 859	26.9	36.5
Stoddard	12 069	71.6	87 000	19.5	11.0	541	26.4	2.1	13 377	1.5	881	6.6	12 343	27.7	33.6
Stone	13 101	79.6	150 500	23.0	11.8	725	31.8	1.2	13 698	2.7	1 064	7.8	12 144	27.6	23.7
Sullivan	2 617	69.0	77 100	24.8	13.1	555	21.7	3.3	2 825	2.9	167	5.9	2 783	25.0	40.5
Taney	20 632	61.4	124 400	24.9	11.6	681	30.8	1.6	26 521	2.9	2 128	8.0	22 569	24.1	15.7
Texas	9 217	74.9	100 300	20.8	11.0	531	31.5	2.9	9 541	1.0	632	6.6	9 253	22.8	30.1
Vernon	8 101	69.2	86 600	20.9	10.7	635	28.1	2.5	10 003	1.5	496	5.0	9 514	30.0	27.6
Warren	12 337	79.4	151 800	21.7	11.4	723	28.5	3.1	17 468	1.9	835	4.8	15 039	27.5	32.2
Washington	9 062	77.9	74 500	21.2	10.8	507	27.9	2.6	10 688	1.9	707	6.6	8 784	19.4	37.0
Wayne	5 528	76.4	70 500	21.4	10.0	532	33.7	3.2	5 808	2.6	338	5.8	4 890	23.6	35.6
Webster	12 681	74.1	117 000	20.9	10.0	590	26.9	6.3	16 763	2.7	844	5.0	14 632	25.3	33.1
Worth	892	74.7	60 600	15.3	11.6	328	18.4	0.9	1 239	-4.5	40	3.2	1 009	37.1	29.7
Wright	7 321	73.2	90 100	25.1	10.7	529	27.5	3.1	7 744	1.2	477	6.2	6 645	26.1	34.7

1. Specified owner-occupied units.   2. A value of 10.0 represents 10 percent or less; a value of 50.0 represents 50 percent or more.   3. Specified renter-occupied units.
4. Overcrowded or lacking complete plumbing facilities.   5. Percent of civilian labor force.   6. Persons 16 years old and over.

Table B. States and Counties — Nonfarm Employment and Agriculture

	Private nonfarm establishments, employment and payroll, 2014									Agriculture, 2012			
		Employment						Annual payroll		Farms			
											Percent with:		
STATE County	Number of establishments	Total	Health care and social assistance	Manufacturing	Retail trade	Finance and insurance	Professional, scientific, and technical services	Total (mil dol)	Average per employee (dollars)	Number	Fewer than 50 acres	500 acres or more	Farm operators whose principal occupation is farming (percent)
	104	105	106	107	108	109	110	111	112	113	114	115	116
MISSOURI—Cont'd													
Jasper	2 790	47 215	5 927	8 940	7 878	1 091	1 076	1 761	37 303	1 299	34.9	7.4	39.9
Jefferson	4 076	41 053	7 527	4 021	7 228	1 299	1 014	1 371	33 406	705	41.3	5.4	49.1
Johnson	921	9 892	2 325	1 182	1 770	356	325	281	28 457	1 657	28.5	10.6	40.4
Knox	90	673	37	D	108	52	D	18	26 333	695	15.4	21.7	51.9
Laclede	769	11 065	1 419	4 376	1 805	293	192	325	29 407	1 398	29.2	12.1	41.3
Lafayette	692	6 083	1 137	826	985	249	196	175	28 800	1 174	32.1	14.6	49.2
Lawrence	689	6 616	1 331	1 284	1 287	184	135	208	31 396	1 849	40.1	7.4	41.4
Lewis	191	1 989	295	D	314	91	D	49	24 821	729	19.9	21.3	44.3
Lincoln	884	8 230	1 176	1 181	1 467	331	211	283	34 330	1 162	33.0	13.6	46.3
Linn	291	3 021	494	884	495	149	83	95	31 439	1 039	18.2	17.5	41.0
Livingston	407	4 769	925	523	1 219	D	D	149	31 332	847	20.2	16.1	42.3
McDonald	296	5 459	241	D	942	D	36	161	29 583	926	27.3	6.8	53.6
Macon	346	3 359	518	D	655	163	D	99	29 469	1 291	20.4	14.5	36.9
Madison	290	2 986	D	252	595	D	D	79	26 463	373	19.6	14.2	44.2
Maries	140	1 074	162	172	264	D	D	30	27 605	836	16.6	14.5	46.7
Marion	832	11 763	2 783	1 874	1 879	379	263	397	33 716	704	21.2	14.8	44.0
Mercer	74	412	86	D	73	26	D	11	25 570	567	11.8	21.2	40.9
Miller	661	5 992	473	580	1 820	D	235	174	29 030	1 013	17.1	10.4	42.7
Mississippi	246	2 194	378	85	442	135	70	62	28 351	205	16.6	47.3	70.7
Moniteau	329	2 701	335	D	447	117	72	84	30 932	1 089	20.4	9.5	45.5
Monroe	192	1 586	D	D	266	69	D	41	25 637	1 061	18.2	14.8	39.7
Montgomery	263	2 094	367	D	305	105	19	65	30 857	795	18.9	21.1	49.4
Morgan	478	3 275	D	671	839	120	74	83	25 493	922	24.8	8.6	47.5
New Madrid	434	6 002	880	D	1 357	184	63	224	37 305	317	11.7	56.8	74.8
Newton	1 190	20 810	6 672	2 626	2 069	580	854	712	34 194	1 578	36.8	5.1	39.4
Nodaway	467	6 488	997	1 464	1 114	186	149	186	28 718	1 252	23.2	18.7	46.2
Oregon	214	1 873	619	D	451	51	27	37	19 832	752	19.5	15.4	50.1
Osage	272	3 014	348	1 173	413	D	D	93	30 902	1 115	17.9	10.9	40.8
Ozark	175	869	D	107	158	77	D	20	23 051	639	13.5	20.2	52.7
Pemiscot	448	4 310	1 451	D	709	146	D	131	30 426	227	16.3	53.3	61.2
Perry	488	10 548	1 376	D	1 062	D	139	339	32 131	951	23.1	11.0	34.8
Pettis	1 002	18 488	2 877	4 220	2 375	405	1 483	612	33 083	1 311	28.1	17.5	45.9
Phelps	1 141	13 342	3 466	1 009	2 376	426	348	412	30 879	718	25.5	9.1	39.3
Pike	396	4 495	793	D	672	141	D	138	30 800	1 003	17.7	18.1	39.8
Platte	2 310	38 472	3 314	2 897	6 587	1 969	1 193	1 486	38 616	599	33.1	11.2	44.4
Polk	576	7 338	1 953	483	1 142	205	D	275	37 455	1 505	30.0	9.4	47.0
Pulaski	716	8 320	D	152	1 708	D	387	248	29 795	520	19.2	11.3	39.8
Putnam	84	640	D	D	199	54	22	18	27 386	649	12.2	21.1	45.6
Ralls	199	2 493	D	1 349	184	D	D	111	44 522	723	22.0	20.5	36.9
Randolph	563	7 441	1 413	986	1 183	415	95	257	34 588	818	23.0	10.9	40.3
Ray	351	2 958	552	D	593	122	98	88	29 714	1 162	27.1	9.8	50.9
Reynolds	180	1 340	264	D	123	D	D	58	43 081	363	19.0	11.8	41.6
Ripley	456	2 560	996	D	493	D	D	49	18 955	439	17.3	15.9	42.8
St. Charles	8 170	124 616	16 124	12 461	19 347	10 119	7 038	4 926	39 528	566	34.5	15.7	51.9
St. Clair	180	1 403	515	D	319	D	26	36	25 341	728	20.1	19.0	51.6
Ste. Genevieve	404	4 998	844	1 617	459	153	72	193	38 588	608	22.0	13.2	37.2
St. Francois	1 551	20 176	5 179	D	3 101	1 007	D	549	27 216	627	30.1	5.1	45.3
St. Louis	31 779	570 809	86 103	36 711	68 521	33 902	46 634	30 543	53 509	217	53.5	7.8	49.3
Saline	497	7 904	1 518	2 410	1 007	248	D	229	28 921	959	20.9	26.2	49.9
Schuyler	70	333	D	41	113	21	D	9	27 066	516	22.7	16.3	42.2
Scotland	132	822	D	D	185	44	D	23	27 742	674	19.1	19.1	46.9
Scott	1 074	14 449	3 516	2 791	1 473	446	344	477	33 043	484	32.6	20.2	49.6
Shannon	170	1 203	163	627	D	64	D	23	19 295	452	23.9	13.7	46.7
Shelby	164	963	93	183	218	D	D	27	28 234	709	18.6	26.4	43.2
Stoddard	707	8 566	1 688	2 668	1 307	415	179	273	31 829	907	29.4	23.3	49.1
Stone	650	3 649	457	108	794	D	87	105	28 650	601	26.1	7.8	42.3
Sullivan	109	1 917	231	D	169	50	D	95	49 340	798	12.5	25.2	46.4
Taney	1 758	24 310	2 232	506	5 002	482	402	652	26 833	414	21.5	14.0	47.8
Texas	497	4 091	911	797	718	164	74	111	27 091	1 296	18.7	14.7	51.2
Vernon	534	5 867	1 598	D	930	406	124	174	29 688	1 356	26.6	13.7	43.8
Warren	575	5 951	546	1 335	877	219	140	202	34 015	621	33.8	11.1	40.3
Washington	492	3 374	D	D	545	D	47	92	27 278	531	21.7	9.0	43.9
Wayne	267	1 647	367	370	324	150	37	36	21 833	411	12.4	13.9	44.8
Webster	640	4 944	527	809	1 123	239	196	145	29 240	1 837	35.6	5.7	44.3
Worth	48	241	D	D	63	11	D	6	25 768	384	15.6	16.7	40.9
Wright	401	3 486	456	D	934	D	51	93	26 692	1 246	23.0	11.9	50.2

Table B. States and Counties — **Agriculture**

		Land in farms				Value of land and buildings (dollars)		Value of machinery and equipment, average per farm (dollars)	Value of products sold				Percent of farms with sales of:		Government payments	
			Acres								Percent from:					
STATE County	Acreage (1,000)	Percent change, 2007–2012	Average size of farm	Total irrigated (1,000)	Total cropland (1,000)	Average per farm	Average per acre		Total (mil dol)	Average per farm (dollars)	Crops	Livestock and poultry products	$10,000 or more	$100,000 or more	Total ($1,000)	Percent of farms
	117	118	119	120	121	122	123	124	125	126	127	128	129	130	131	132
MISSOURI—Cont'd																
Jasper	247	-4.7	190	3.5	127.7	443 779	2 337	62 487	100.5	77 336	32.5	67.5	41.6	8.9	2 322	37.0
Jefferson	98	5.7	138	0.3	36.3	471 186	3 407	53 340	13.6	19 325	51.0	49.0	28.9	3.3	255	12.3
Johnson	391	-7.9	236	1.9	219.9	624 016	2 645	95 386	119.9	72 340	38.5	61.5	47.1	9.3	2 968	40.3
Knox	281	10.8	404	D	193.3	1 205 037	2 981	147 283	76.3	109 799	49.5	50.5	53.8	21.2	5 347	73.4
Laclede	320	10.9	229	0.2	89.6	503 814	2 200	50 168	50.4	36 045	15.1	84.9	46.4	7.4	526	10.8
Lafayette	327	-7.4	278	1.8	244.5	1 176 566	4 225	133 569	143.2	122 010	80.6	19.4	57.8	20.8	4 495	57.0
Lawrence	311	-3.6	168	2.3	118.1	431 114	2 562	62 340	204.9	110 819	7.4	92.6	45.3	10.8	1 959	18.6
Lewis	284	8.8	390	2.0	201.3	1 128 680	2 894	139 615	81.2	111 418	64.0	36.0	51.7	19.3	4 159	71.1
Lincoln	281	13.0	242	1.3	191.8	943 589	3 900	91 473	85.6	73 707	55.9	44.1	44.8	12.0	3 161	55.4
Linn	336	1.7	323	0.3	209.0	780 366	2 416	78 069	66.6	64 131	59.0	41.0	48.7	15.5	6 639	67.9
Livingston	284	-8.2	335	0.4	200.5	976 103	2 916	104 609	72.5	85 636	68.9	31.1	49.8	15.6	6 044	70.0
McDonald	187	-6.6	202	0.3	49.5	466 203	2 314	79 172	175.8	189 865	2.1	97.9	44.0	10.9	630	9.9
Macon	386	-2.1	299	0.3	214.7	740 631	2 477	78 400	66.8	51 777	53.6	46.4	41.6	10.1	6 172	58.1
Madison	107	9.0	287	D	24.1	528 405	1 840	54 603	18.4	49 201	9.8	90.2	41.8	6.7	102	13.1
Maries	241	0.4	289	0.2	59.4	563 396	1 951	60 886	35.3	42 176	13.0	87.0	53.8	6.8	435	16.1
Marion	221	-6.6	315	3.0	157.5	1 120 118	3 561	118 102	87.1	123 751	61.6	38.4	48.0	18.2	3 060	71.2
Mercer	227	12.6	400	D	119.4	887 578	2 219	93 078	102.7	181 146	18.6	81.4	40.9	12.5	3 303	67.4
Miller	248	1.2	245	1.4	62.0	544 853	2 221	58 525	103.0	101 659	4.7	95.3	51.2	11.1	549	13.7
Mississippi	245	-5.2	1 195	86.5	232.3	4 962 234	4 153	473 244	157.0	766 000	97.9	2.1	81.5	55.6	3 759	87.8
Moniteau	235	-3.2	216	0.2	99.9	582 663	2 698	67 761	173.5	159 302	9.4	90.6	57.0	13.5	2 018	37.6
Monroe	356	23.4	335	1.1	237.9	1 047 572	3 125	121 686	86.2	81 207	58.0	42.0	40.8	13.2	7 034	75.6
Montgomery	279	12.5	351	3.2	194.0	1 212 507	3 453	132 268	64.0	80 541	73.9	26.1	50.9	20.5	4 635	65.9
Morgan	198	-8.5	215	0.2	77.6	569 115	2 646	63 366	144.8	157 103	8.6	91.4	56.6	21.3	768	17.5
New Madrid	345	-9.5	1 087	196.5	332.5	4 819 981	4 435	524 943	217.1	684 994	99.9	0.1	84.2	65.6	8 243	90.9
Newton	248	0.8	157	0.3	93.4	404 596	2 577	60 035	251.5	159 393	6.0	94.0	44.3	9.5	1 034	17.3
Nodaway	424	-22.0	338	0.3	293.3	1 100 251	3 251	116 792	141.6	113 082	81.0	19.0	58.3	21.6	7 586	72.6
Oregon	254	6.0	338	0.4	35.9	525 161	1 556	53 593	34.5	45 934	3.4	96.6	45.3	6.8	955	26.7
Osage	283	-4.8	254	2.3	82.4	520 062	2 047	73 506	78.7	70 544	17.7	82.3	55.0	9.7	1 003	30.9
Ozark	229	-7.6	358	0.0	29.1	581 482	1 624	60 313	39.2	61 365	5.3	94.7	54.0	10.6	597	8.6
Pemiscot	305	-1.7	1 344	122.7	287.5	4 861 687	3 618	516 802	186.1	819 758	99.9	0.1	79.3	61.7	7 220	80.6
Perry	226	-5.2	238	D	122.0	636 469	2 673	82 989	63.4	66 614	50.1	49.9	52.2	13.4	2 226	64.9
Pettis	420	2.6	320	0.4	263.2	876 005	2 736	116 004	177.0	135 019	30.8	69.2	52.6	19.0	5 117	51.0
Phelps	157	-10.5	219	0.1	27.2	504 223	2 301	51 199	11.7	16 320	15.8	84.2	34.1	2.6	225	12.0
Pike	362	-3.1	361	3.7	226.0	1 247 957	3 461	127 424	87.4	87 094	62.9	37.1	51.7	15.3	4 506	65.7
Platte	153	-14.4	255	1.7	100.7	992 603	3 888	94 775	44.9	74 917	83.7	16.3	41.9	12.0	1 720	48.2
Polk	336	-4.0	223	1.3	102.6	461 553	2 066	49 912	85.2	56 613	10.6	89.4	49.2	10.0	859	15.3
Pulaski	112	-8.6	216	0.1	20.9	421 379	1 948	50 873	12.9	24 752	15.6	84.4	42.1	4.2	110	6.5
Putnam	293	7.3	451	D	124.7	930 538	2 063	91 116	86.1	132 669	19.3	80.7	49.3	18.3	3 373	59.5
Ralls	283	15.5	392	1.1	196.9	1 258 679	3 210	138 203	54.8	75 806	76.5	23.5	39.0	16.7	4 168	76.3
Randolph	209	-5.5	256	1.1	109.1	673 561	2 630	65 106	36.7	44 873	58.5	41.5	35.5	6.2	2 820	53.8
Ray	273	-6.4	235	7.7	174.7	641 818	2 730	86 155	74.5	64 122	71.7	28.3	41.8	10.1	3 721	53.8
Reynolds	97	-9.5	268	0.0	16.5	391 482	1 463	44 970	4.8	13 284	25.3	74.7	35.5	1.1	79	7.4
Ripley	138	0.4	314	12.1	45.1	563 134	1 794	65 385	19.1	43 583	55.8	44.2	40.5	7.3	777	26.7
St. Charles	158	1.3	279	1.1	121.0	1 184 827	4 240	119 919	62.5	110 417	84.8	15.2	53.0	20.7	1 607	55.5
St. Clair	239	-10.0	328	0.5	99.3	542 646	1 656	69 935	33.8	46 482	42.4	57.6	50.7	9.9	1 115	36.4
Ste. Genevieve	163	-13.9	267	0.2	72.3	616 641	2 305	76 181	26.6	43 755	58.6	41.4	46.9	8.7	1 492	46.4
St. Francois	116	3.4	186	0.1	32.0	466 490	2 513	46 496	14.0	22 332	32.9	67.1	36.8	2.6	343	13.1
St. Louis	30	-8.0	137	0.5	15.4	565 189	4 128	69 313	19.1	87 807	97.3	2.7	37.3	11.1	279	20.7
Saline	461	2.6	481	3.5	362.9	1 934 485	4 023	199 556	212.0	221 075	73.3	26.7	66.1	28.7	5 961	79.7
Schuyler	159	4.6	309	D	83.8	687 409	2 226	76 853	30.4	58 917	48.8	51.2	50.2	12.4	2 272	61.8
Scotland	244	5.4	362	D	158.4	1 063 616	2 936	106 022	82.2	121 938	44.7	55.3	53.9	21.5	4 627	70.0
Scott	223	-2.4	461	72.4	192.8	1 878 114	4 077	237 058	188.8	390 035	69.0	31.0	48.6	26.9	4 263	63.8
Shannon	124	11.8	274	0.0	23.0	458 142	1 670	50 407	10.5	23 197	11.5	88.5	37.4	5.8	171	6.6
Shelby	299	3.5	422	1.6	211.0	1 499 389	3 552	149 536	83.0	117 100	71.2	28.8	59.0	24.0	5 033	75.6
Stoddard	448	-2.8	494	226.7	396.3	2 169 982	4 392	245 480	315.0	347 277	81.3	18.7	49.9	26.1	11 137	73.4
Stone	118	-3.1	196	0.1	32.1	465 231	2 369	50 319	34.5	57 393	10.6	89.4	45.3	7.0	368	10.0
Sullivan	323	-3.3	405	D	158.8	751 872	1 858	87 835	149.6	187 526	12.2	87.8	46.5	14.7	5 745	61.3
Taney	116	8.8	280	0.1	18.8	549 092	1 961	49 271	11.7	28 259	10.8	89.2	38.2	4.3	209	10.1
Texas	392	10.4	303	0.1	68.0	496 529	1 641	48 862	42.0	32 416	8.8	91.2	47.4	7.5	565	10.3
Vernon	419	-8.2	309	5.4	244.4	665 520	2 156	99 091	209.0	154 128	29.8	70.2	51.6	13.6	4 561	44.8
Warren	136	-7.3	219	1.1	85.3	850 634	3 880	94 071	31.4	50 589	78.6	21.4	43.3	11.6	1 941	51.2
Washington	124	-9.7	233	0.0	24.3	447 979	1 919	44 347	11.1	20 846	20.8	79.2	37.9	4.7	106	3.6
Wayne	117	10.0	284	D	28.0	433 238	1 527	59 358	7.8	18 949	20.0	80.0	33.8	2.9	356	24.3
Webster	272	0.3	148	0.2	82.9	386 911	2 612	45 690	76.1	41 450	8.4	91.6	45.5	9.0	1 345	8.9
Worth	125	-17.6	326	D	70.0	733 870	2 254	84 737	37.1	96 646	37.1	62.9	43.2	14.1	2 824	84.1
Wright	294	3.4	236	0.2	67.2	424 095	1 797	48 860	47.2	37 913	6.9	93.1	45.8	8.7	1 041	14.4

Table B. States and Counties — Water Use, Wholesale Trade, Retail Trade, and Real Estate

STATE County	Water use, 2010		Wholesale trade,[1] 2012				Retail trade,[2] 2012				Real estate and rental and leasing,[2] 2012			
	Total water withdrawn (mil gal/day)	Gallons withdrawn per person per day	Number of establishments	Number of employees	Sales (mil dol)	Annual payroll (mil dol)	Number of establishments	Number of employees	Sales (mil dol)	Annual payroll (mil dol)	Number of establishments	Number of employees	Receipts (mil dol)	Annual payroll (mil dol)
	133	134	135	136	137	138	139	140	141	142	143	144	145	146
MISSOURI—Cont'd														
Jasper	30.8	262	143	1 695	972.5	70.6	514	7 769	1 987.5	166.1	114	506	75.5	13.2
Jefferson	829.3	3 791	132	1 302	798.0	65.5	484	6 756	1 952.6	162.7	143	465	62.2	14.1
Johnson	9.1	174	20	108	45.6	4.0	148	1 827	508.2	40.2	36	129	25.1	3.4
Knox	1.5	363	8	42	61.2	0.8	16	113	38.1	2.1	NA	NA	NA	NA
Laclede	17.8	500	27	305	196.2	11.3	174	1 813	502.4	42.1	28	72	10.9	1.6
Lafayette	5.7	170	34	319	184.0	11.6	106	1 055	375.5	20.5	16	D	D	D
Lawrence	10.7	276	26	239	92.5	7.1	122	1 320	449.0	31.3	20	48	4.2	0.8
Lewis	2.4	237	8	D	D	D	32	288	85.7	6.1	3	D	D	D
Lincoln	7.2	138	34	245	91.1	9.8	144	1 473	447.8	34.5	28	71	9.0	1.3
Linn	4.8	378	8	50	51.1	1.9	56	535	150.0	11.8	9	D	D	D
Livingston	2.5	163	22	272	126.7	11.4	76	1 167	359.1	26.5	11	37	9.8	0.7
McDonald	6.6	288	10	D	D	D	65	933	221.2	18.6	8	9	2.0	0.3
Macon	3.2	208	14	111	65.7	5.2	67	631	146.5	11.5	12	38	3.5	0.7
Madison	1.4	112	11	185	28.7	6.1	38	505	138.0	11.8	6	23	1.1	0.4
Maries	1.6	177	8	D	D	D	25	222	50.1	3.4	2	D	D	D
Marion	7.7	268	26	321	479.7	14.1	143	1 797	508.5	38.3	27	D	D	D
Mercer	2.2	568	1	D	D	D	13	64	25.0	1.1	1	D	D	D
Miller	4.0	160	13	167	94.6	5.7	119	1 651	377.4	38.8	51	203	30.1	5.3
Mississippi	82.6	5 753	18	191	256.2	6.9	52	474	182.1	9.5	2	D	D	D
Moniteau	3.4	218	10	173	69.8	5.0	55	457	136.2	8.5	5	8	0.5	0.1
Monroe	8.2	931	9	67	78.7	2.2	35	277	80.0	4.8	3	10	1.3	0.2
Montgomery	2.5	202	19	135	110.7	4.8	36	315	98.1	6.1	8	10	1.7	0.2
Morgan	6.5	315	17	56	22.2	1.9	91	762	195.1	16.3	19	39	4.8	0.8
New Madrid	984.5	51 936	32	428	436.0	18.3	77	1 319	495.7	28.0	9	21	3.2	0.5
Newton	9.7	167	41	1 200	1 674.4	48.3	196	2 090	853.8	49.2	29	77	10.5	1.7
Nodaway	3.3	139	17	221	181.4	8.9	72	1 122	260.0	21.2	20	35	5.7	0.6
Oregon	2.0	186	6	D	D	D	44	419	98.8	8.3	7	14	1.5	0.2
Osage	60.8	4 377	6	24	9.3	0.8	49	423	152.5	10.3	5	6	0.5	0.1
Ozark	14.2	1 460	6	32	17.3	0.7	33	214	49.6	3.4	9	16	1.0	0.2
Pemiscot	110.5	6 038	21	233	550.6	10.3	70	688	274.3	13.2	10	D	D	D
Perry	4.7	245	12	348	174.5	15.2	75	978	270.2	23.0	12	19	5.0	0.4
Pettis	9.2	217	35	350	175.4	15.7	174	2 323	615.1	54.4	44	358	37.0	9.4
Phelps	10.4	229	36	365	108.9	13.7	190	2 401	689.2	53.0	40	146	20.0	4.0
Pike	7.4	401	25	314	312.7	11.7	66	686	191.0	15.0	3	8	0.6	0.1
Platte	459.5	5 144	103	1 288	4 053.0	85.4	313	6 054	1 986.7	144.3	126	1 164	178.1	41.4
Polk	5.2	167	23	531	63.0	9.3	110	1 099	299.5	26.3	14	69	6.2	1.3
Pulaski	6.8	129	6	D	D	D	138	1 655	455.2	36.4	46	167	40.6	4.1
Putnam	1.8	364	3	D	D	D	24	176	50.3	3.1	4	14	0.8	0.2
Ralls	1.7	166	16	168	153.4	7.2	34	185	52.4	3.8	2	D	D	D
Randolph	740.2	29 127	17	D	D	D	97	1 118	296.7	25.3	19	63	9.9	1.6
Ray	6.3	266	9	114	186.2	5.7	56	607	138.7	12.6	9	21	1.7	0.4
Reynolds	5.7	851	4	D	D	D	20	122	29.6	2.0	4	9	0.4	0.1
Ripley	31.0	2 201	5	D	D	D	43	435	120.2	8.1	11	136	4.6	1.8
St. Charles	505.1	1 401	336	4 305	9 006.9	246.4	1 085	18 318	4 971.7	437.2	350	1 398	438.4	53.2
St. Clair	1.6	159	4	9	0.6	0.1	33	317	87.9	5.8	3	4	0.2	0.0
Ste. Genevieve	8.1	449	12	133	137.0	6.1	49	462	103.4	10.1	9	27	3.5	0.6
St. Francois	8.2	125	32	657	285.0	24.2	229	3 421	882.8	84.5	61	229	24.4	5.4
St. Louis	535.5	536	1 587	30 594	32 424.2	1 822.0	3 826	67 577	25 262.7	1 882.4	1 309	10 461	2 048.1	504.3
Saline	5.7	243	31	358	382.5	16.0	97	981	253.0	19.1	12	D	D	D
Schuyler	0.4	86	2	D	D	D	24	165	48.4	2.7	NA	NA	NA	NA
Scotland	0.9	176	6	D	D	D	28	162	39.8	3.0	2	D	D	D
Scott	104.6	2 670	53	823	717.9	30.8	181	1 555	415.7	33.2	40	141	17.5	4.0
Shannon	1.3	153	7	D	D	D	19	125	28.4	2.0	7	D	D	D
Shelby	1.8	282	15	97	69.7	3.5	35	223	58.9	4.4	4	5	0.5	0.1
Stoddard	333.0	11 112	37	366	428.5	13.4	118	1 277	424.0	29.6	26	51	6.7	1.2
Stone	4.6	144	17	D	D	D	99	795	216.8	18.9	38	164	19.0	5.8
Sullivan	3.6	539	2	D	D	D	27	184	50.4	3.4	5	4	0.5	0.1
Taney	33.7	651	32	D	D	D	414	4 936	939.9	88.7	116	1 023	152.0	35.8
Texas	3.8	148	22	102	36.7	2.8	83	742	172.5	14.3	10	33	2.7	0.7
Vernon	12.7	599	18	180	80.3	5.7	85	897	238.6	19.1	12	37	6.3	0.8
Warren	3.6	109	25	279	153.3	14.6	88	879	298.0	18.8	25	74	13.8	1.7
Washington	8.3	329	15	46	15.2	1.3	49	510	122.3	9.9	7	16	1.9	0.5
Wayne	1.4	104	11	D	D	D	36	319	72.3	6.3	3	3	0.4	0.0
Webster	4.5	123	32	134	69.6	5.0	109	1 123	376.7	23.8	26	50	4.0	0.9
Worth	0.3	134	4	D	D	D	12	68	18.2	1.2	2	D	D	D
Wright	2.9	156	17	223	89.9	6.9	83	952	245.6	20.0	15	41	3.6	0.6

1. Merchant wholesalers, except manufacturers' sales branches and offices. 2. Employer establishments.

Table B. States and Counties — **Professional Services, Manufacturing, and Accommodation and Food Services**

STATE County	Professional, scientific, and technical services, 2012				Manufacturing, 2012				Accommodation and food services, 2012			
	Number of establishments	Number of employees	Receipts (mil dol)	Annual payroll (mil dol)	Number of establishments	Number of employees	Receipts (mil dol)	Annual payroll (mil dol)	Number of establishments	Number of employees	Sales (mil dol)	Annual payroll (mil dol)
	147	148	149	150	151	152	153	154	155	156	157	158
MISSOURI—Cont'd												
Jasper	180	D	D	D	171	9 161	3 558.8	397.3	261	4 960	214.4	60.2
Jefferson	245	941	88.6	32.7	173	4 369	1 420.5	224.6	279	5 461	228.4	66.2
Johnson	66	D	D	D	30	1 252	D	43.0	100	1 672	66.3	16.4
Knox	4	D	D	D	NA	NA	NA	NA	6	D	D	D
Laclede	41	169	14.0	4.6	59	4 120	1 327.5	139.4	79	1 099	47.9	12.7
Lafayette	47	D	D	D	40	793	D	28.5	61	696	24.2	6.4
Lawrence	44	123	10.7	3.3	47	1 357	629.9	53.6	50	676	24.9	7.2
Lewis	13	D	D	D	6	104	D	3.9	14	113	4.1	1.2
Lincoln	51	184	15.4	5.5	49	981	387.2	51.3	58	D	D	D
Linn	22	98	9.7	3.1	15	1 003	207.5	27.4	20	226	7.8	2.2
Livingston	31	133	10.5	3.4	16	554	152.7	21.4	25	D	D	D
McDonald	13	44	2.6	0.9	23	2 974	611.6	81.9	33	264	13.3	3.3
Macon	23	D	D	D	9	472	D	15.9	32	366	18.4	5.2
Madison	13	74	5.2	1.5	14	281	D	10.2	22	D	D	D
Maries	6	D	D	D	9	165	D	8.4	11	41	1.5	0.4
Marion	45	258	24.9	8.6	39	1 475	1 488.5	72.2	74	1 115	47.0	12.7
Mercer	3	D	D	D	NA	NA	NA	NA	7	D	D	D
Miller	38	274	20.9	10.3	21	488	D	14.5	54	634	31.9	10.0
Mississippi	9	71	7.7	4.3	6	126	D	6.2	20	267	11.5	3.0
Moniteau	15	65	4.8	1.7	28	677	D	28.1	21	D	D	D
Monroe	10	D	D	D	9	218	D	D	18	141	4.7	1.3
Montgomery	8	D	D	D	19	499	154.8	17.1	21	194	6.7	1.9
Morgan	27	86	6.4	2.0	21	609	D	18.1	53	453	19.0	5.3
New Madrid	15	63	5.0	1.9	15	1 561	883.0	89.5	34	474	26.8	5.5
Newton	70	375	38.0	14.8	72	2 499	724.0	89.2	97	1 684	82.8	21.3
Nodaway	27	124	13.3	4.1	22	1 675	D	69.5	45	1 074	36.7	10.5
Oregon	10	D	D	D	11	137	24.0	3.6	14	171	5.8	1.5
Osage	9	17	1.7	0.4	29	988	D	40.1	20	D	D	D
Ozark	9	D	D	D	8	70	D	1.9	22	187	7.5	2.3
Pemiscot	11	44	3.5	0.9	12	825	D	37.0	29	311	15.1	3.3
Perry	27	118	8.8	4.2	37	3 627	1 142.3	115.6	39	618	20.9	5.8
Pettis	67	1 532	101.8	40.6	49	3 955	1 522.4	152.5	80	1 475	59.4	16.6
Phelps	77	327	35.9	11.5	50	912	484.4	43.1	114	1 810	78.1	21.6
Pike	18	522	43.8	11.5	21	555	324.3	22.8	25	D	D	D
Platte	260	D	D	D	49	2 644	1 870.0	127.4	202	5 779	394.3	101.0
Polk	43	D	D	D	22	343	D	12.1	44	780	27.0	7.3
Pulaski	58	639	99.0	45.5	15	123	24.5	D	99	2 280	91.8	39.3
Putnam	3	D	D	D	5	72	D	2.2	4	D	D	D
Ralls	5	19	1.9	0.5	15	1 272	1 405.4	66.2	11	87	3.0	1.0
Randolph	25	106	5.4	1.7	30	1 128	219.0	40.9	51	582	26.5	6.6
Ray	30	D	D	D	14	305	D	16.7	21	229	9.0	2.2
Reynolds	4	D	D	D	26	259	44.2	8.0	15	D	D	D
Ripley	10	D	D	D	30	446	D	11.6	15	195	7.7	1.9
St. Charles	765	6 210	720.9	239.7	256	10 982	6 851.7	614.3	712	16 108	918.4	227.7
St. Clair	9	25	3.3	1.0	8	28	4.9	1.2	16	78	5.4	0.8
Ste. Genevieve	23	81	6.1	2.5	30	1 467	400.4	74.7	29	D	D	D
St. Francois	79	300	33.6	8.7	49	1 474	272.2	55.7	115	1 802	76.3	21.6
St. Louis	3 618	46 440	8 274.0	3 139.6	950	35 884	15 922.9	2 621.7	2 219	47 895	2 628.8	713.8
Saline	29	D	D	D	21	1 948	747.5	68.9	43	522	17.5	5.3
Schuyler	1	D	D	D	3	9	2.9	0.4	3	D	D	D
Scotland	8	D	D	D	9	49	D	1.5	10	60	1.9	0.6
Scott	66	360	47.3	21.5	54	2 412	847.7	94.9	69	1 189	52.8	15.7
Shannon	4	D	D	D	24	372	51.1	8.9	15	64	3.4	0.8
Shelby	11	45	4.7	1.1	8	239	D	8.9	12	85	2.3	0.7
Stoddard	30	157	17.4	5.5	36	2 506	1 242.8	111.5	42	585	24.5	6.9
Stone	34	76	5.6	1.7	22	108	11.6	3.4	92	584	48.9	10.0
Sullivan	4	D	D	D	4	D	D	D	6	D	D	D
Taney	101	413	31.2	12.3	40	360	84.2	14.8	302	7 039	553.0	144.2
Texas	25	80	5.4	1.8	45	698	157.8	24.1	41	D	D	D
Vernon	34	120	11.1	2.9	20	894	D	46.8	36	456	22.3	4.8
Warren	38	145	14.4	4.9	34	1 383	453.2	58.7	49	D	D	D
Washington	13	35	2.0	0.7	19	533	290.1	17.6	22	D	D	D
Wayne	9	D	D	D	25	335	63.1	11.7	20	166	8.9	2.9
Webster	42	D	D	D	45	696	206.2	24.9	35	526	23.5	5.9
Worth	4	D	D	D	3	D	D	D	3	D	D	D
Wright	21	51	5.4	1.2	26	381	D	13.8	23	307	10.8	3.0

1. Establishment subject to federal tax.

STATE County	Health care and social assistance, 2012				Other services, 2012				Nonemployer businesses, 2014		Value of residential construction authorized by building permits, 2015	
	Number of establishments	Number of employees	Receipts (mil dol)	Annual payroll (mil dol)	Number of establishments	Number of employees	Receipts (mil dol)	Annual payroll (mil dol)	Number	Receipts (mil dol)	New Construction ($1,000)	Number of housing units
	159	160	161	162	163	164	165	166	167	168	169	170
MISSOURI—Cont'd												
Jasper	333	6 521	629.5	315.1	225	1 277	99.9	29.8	6 462	262.5	47 236	488
Jefferson	381	6 119	478.7	186.3	334	1 558	143.2	42.4	12 616	488.8	79 522	542
Johnson	100	2 309	200.4	78.6	62	D	D	D	2 952	107.1	26 342	257
Knox	8	38	2.3	0.8	9	D	D	D	359	15.4	0	0
Laclede	78	1 475	135.0	55.4	49	D	D	D	2 587	119.0	2 977	18
Lafayette	62	D	D	D	46	135	11.3	3.0	2 085	85.5	5 775	27
Lawrence	71	1 279	99.0	46.0	38	109	9.2	2.8	2 608	101.9	1 903	10
Lewis	24	311	12.4	5.9	12	D	D	D	630	25.4	250	2
Lincoln	73	D	D	D	61	D	D	D	3 324	121.9	14 606	121
Linn	24	523	37.9	15.2	27	90	9.6	1.9	922	35.0	400	2
Livingston	43	861	74.4	27.8	22	D	D	D	957	36.1	2 983	17
McDonald	26	296	16.7	7.3	17	D	D	D	1 288	51.6	125	1
Macon	31	550	40.5	15.4	26	D	D	D	1 104	46.3	492	2
Madison	29	886	38.9	20.7	16	43	3.4	0.8	703	26.0	528	7
Maries	12	138	8.6	3.0	4	15	2.0	0.2	572	21.2	201	1
Marion	136	2 858	286.2	109.4	57	332	18.2	5.2	1 695	61.6	12 159	63
Mercer	7	D	D	D	8	D	D	D	259	10.5	0	0
Miller	37	495	33.0	13.3	41	D	D	D	1 660	72.5	5 773	26
Mississippi	25	409	19.9	8.0	19	56	4.3	1.1	609	49.3	778	9
Moniteau	32	D	D	D	18	53	3.2	0.8	944	30.9	120	1
Monroe	29	D	D	D	13	D	D	D	600	28.0	12	1
Montgomery	17	382	19.7	8.2	17	D	D	D	829	38.0	3 399	18
Morgan	28	256	13.9	5.2	29	D	D	D	1 657	68.4	750	12
New Madrid	52	886	48.4	17.6	22	58	5.7	1.0	784	22.8	1 112	10
Newton	141	6 401	607.1	273.5	63	219	19.1	5.1	3 771	163.6	4 035	43
Nodaway	51	1 239	94.2	39.5	40	163	10.6	3.1	1 411	48.7	6 448	43
Oregon	38	458	18.1	8.9	15	D	D	D	774	30.4	100	1
Osage	22	D	D	D	14	37	4.2	0.6	942	37.8	0	0
Ozark	10	100	5.8	2.4	13	42	2.7	0.6	766	24.4	68	5
Pemiscot	75	1 276	74.9	32.8	14	45	3.9	1.1	823	30.7	356	9
Perry	51	1 164	86.5	31.9	38	570	17.9	22.3	1 258	49.2	5 558	36
Pettis	136	3 111	229.9	97.5	91	482	34.5	11.2	2 529	112.1	2 063	21
Phelps	148	3 820	343.0	120.7	71	323	24.2	8.3	2 605	96.5	11 882	144
Pike	52	802	49.6	21.5	21	39	5.2	1.2	1 161	45.2	178	12
Platte	201	3 319	354.3	139.8	163	877	94.7	27.0	7 003	323.0	80 467	384
Polk	74	1 924	159.2	63.7	42	218	9.8	2.5	2 264	92.5	2 750	50
Pulaski	62	1 773	158.5	62.7	58	248	19.2	5.9	2 025	70.4	7 590	49
Putnam	10	94	10.1	3.1	6	17	2.0	0.4	423	19.3	0	0
Ralls	13	162	10.0	4.5	12	52	4.9	1.2	709	28.3	50	1
Randolph	72	1 504	128.3	48.0	45	140	10.6	2.5	1 373	53.4	1 766	13
Ray	36	D	D	D	24	D	D	D	1 230	47.0	3 637	19
Reynolds	29	158	7.0	3.0	6	D	D	D	453	17.3	0	0
Ripley	69	796	36.3	16.8	16	46	4.2	0.8	813	33.8	0	0
St. Charles	939	15 694	1 482.9	576.5	592	3 967	336.9	102.9	24 239	1 047.2	499 459	2 292
St. Clair	28	486	22.3	10.4	13	44	4.7	1.0	696	26.4	0	0
Ste. Genevieve	46	815	59.5	23.8	34	138	9.8	2.4	1 077	30.1	1 202	7
St. Francois	244	5 279	379.4	164.4	99	441	32.0	8.9	3 106	111.5	18 275	190
St. Louis	4 190	86 410	9 445.2	3 803.8	1 961	15 935	1 682.2	529.5	72 816	3 745.9	576 373	2 234
Saline	73	1 618	110.8	47.6	35	152	16.8	4.1	1 196	37.7	2 790	41
Schuyler	3	20	1.2	0.7	7	D	D	D	332	14.8	639	3
Scotland	7	D	D	D	15	D	D	D	524	30.9	125	1
Scott	139	2 990	200.0	90.4	61	322	25.5	6.9	2 236	93.3	5 502	64
Shannon	19	215	13.0	4.7	6	15	1.7	0.4	723	30.0	0	0
Shelby	7	102	5.1	2.1	15	38	4.8	0.9	491	20.6	0	0
Stoddard	90	1 499	84.2	36.2	41	137	9.7	3.0	2 004	105.8	2 997	23
Stone	45	458	39.5	12.1	52	273	21.8	6.5	2 721	114.9	26 060	118
Sullivan	10	254	13.9	6.1	10	21	2.8	0.5	392	13.2	65	1
Taney	125	2 363	247.5	91.8	101	556	49.6	12.9	4 374	171.2	26 272	140
Texas	52	968	70.6	28.2	34	69	6.5	1.4	1 759	66.5	528	5
Vernon	71	1 468	91.0	38.0	34	122	7.5	1.8	1 341	58.4	660	9
Warren	56	D	D	D	36	D	D	D	2 042	70.1	22 659	103
Washington	76	776	66.3	22.9	16	56	4.2	1.1	1 015	32.5	0	0
Wayne	40	379	18.1	7.5	10	48	2.1	0.6	693	24.7	0	0
Webster	56	500	26.9	12.2	35	D	D	D	2 937	114.2	7 030	59
Worth	2	D	D	D	5	D	D	D	199	8.1	0	0
Wright	43	492	30.5	11.7	23	77	6.4	1.5	1 273	53.7	335	5

Table B. States and Counties — Government Employment and Payroll, and Local Government Finances

	Government employment and payroll, 2012									Local government finances, 2012				
			March payroll (percent of total)							General revenue				
												Taxes		
													Per capita[1] (dollars)	
STATE County	Full-time equivalent employees	March payroll (dollars)	Administration, judicial, and legal	Police and Corrections	Fire Protection	Highways and transportation	Health and Welfare	Natural resources and utilities	Education and libraries	Total (mil dol)	Inter-governmental (mil dol)	Total (mil dol)	Total	Property
	171	172	173	174	175	176	177	178	179	180	181	182	183	184
MISSOURI—Cont'd														
Jasper	4 406	12 579 406	4.8	9.9	4.0	3.6	1.3	3.8	71.5	389.2	139.5	146.6	1 272	589
Jefferson	6 669	24 871 942	2.8	6.2	4.1	2.5	3.8	3.1	76.7	560.9	238.8	255.4	1 160	796
Johnson	2 208	7 565 488	3.1	4.7	2.1	2.3	37.3	2.7	47.4	195.3	49.7	52.6	967	584
Knox	221	492 621	7.9	5.4	0.0	7.2	22.0	5.2	52.2	12.1	5.9	4.4	1 068	756
Laclede	1 413	3 701 221	5.5	5.9	1.6	12.4	1.2	6.8	65.2	72.4	35.3	26.3	742	477
Lafayette	1 188	3 488 934	7.8	8.3	0.6	3.5	2.3	9.3	67.9	88.1	38.4	34.2	1 034	710
Lawrence	1 155	3 231 901	5.5	6.1	0.7	2.7	6.5	2.7	75.5	76.5	38.1	27.2	706	425
Lewis	450	1 137 169	6.6	5.6	0.1	4.4	19.6	4.3	58.6	29.3	13.4	9.1	892	661
Lincoln	1 917	6 064 837	5.5	7.0	1.3	2.6	24.9	0.7	57.6	159.5	58.6	49.5	928	677
Linn	590	1 568 941	6.7	5.1	0.0	4.8	4.2	7.5	69.7	39.5	19.0	13.4	1 074	641
Livingston	654	1 837 354	4.6	6.8	5.3	2.6	13.9	14.2	51.7	49.5	19.1	16.1	1 073	702
McDonald	606	1 598 982	8.5	7.8	0.1	4.5	1.5	6.0	70.3	51.8	29.8	17.6	770	427
Macon	1 039	2 633 830	3.7	3.4	0.8	3.2	42.4	2.9	43.4	92.8	45.8	29.8	1 914	1 610
Madison	682	1 827 224	2.1	3.5	0.1	2.1	44.4	2.8	42.9	25.4	13.9	8.3	667	425
Maries	323	761 125	7.6	6.0	0.0	6.9	9.4	3.4	66.1	18.2	8.6	7.6	847	638
Marion	1 348	3 816 108	4.3	7.2	3.7	3.7	10.5	8.5	58.2	94.9	33.0	39.1	1 361	752
Mercer	176	501 591	15.9	5.2	0.1	7.0	6.8	4.3	59.8	9.5	4.4	3.9	1 038	887
Miller	1 205	3 202 179	4.4	4.5	1.6	2.3	11.6	1.8	73.2	80.0	30.4	36.5	1 472	1 081
Mississippi	496	1 277 944	12.1	11.0	0.1	3.6	4.4	7.4	61.1	39.2	20.9	12.9	904	600
Moniteau	498	1 342 360	7.0	4.0	0.2	3.3	8.9	4.9	70.4	34.2	15.0	12.7	813	528
Monroe	490	1 220 603	5.4	5.4	0.3	4.2	22.2	8.5	53.6	28.8	12.5	9.7	1 109	878
Montgomery	414	1 189 713	7.9	12.4	0.0	5.3	4.0	3.0	66.0	27.1	9.4	13.0	1 088	730
Morgan	588	1 595 566	8.3	9.3	0.7	4.5	8.1	2.2	61.6	37.0	13.2	17.9	892	558
New Madrid	720	1 973 525	9.1	7.8	0.4	5.1	5.0	6.0	65.2	48.9	21.7	21.3	1 153	837
Newton	1 886	5 757 934	4.6	4.8	2.8	1.7	3.3	2.2	80.6	121.7	59.7	39.0	661	405
Nodaway	726	2 001 480	9.5	5.9	0.8	3.6	4.2	6.4	68.6	62.2	22.3	27.8	1 186	755
Oregon	416	986 254	6.1	4.7	0.0	3.9	0.0	4.8	79.9	22.3	13.8	6.1	554	379
Osage	364	958 029	5.9	4.6	2.7	4.1	8.7	5.2	68.3	23.3	8.9	9.6	696	471
Ozark	375	902 737	3.5	3.0	0.0	3.7	2.8	1.2	83.1	20.2	12.4	5.9	612	453
Pemiscot	869	2 608 472	5.8	7.8	0.7	1.4	2.9	7.8	73.3	61.3	38.4	13.9	770	506
Perry	569	1 561 790	6.3	12.2	0.0	3.8	5.0	9.4	63.2	42.8	15.7	20.2	1 064	628
Pettis	2 440	8 051 066	2.4	3.6	1.7	1.5	41.8	2.5	45.8	222.9	54.6	51.1	1 207	624
Phelps	2 804	9 025 924	2.3	3.7	1.2	1.5	51.9	4.5	33.4	301.2	46.2	39.1	869	478
Pike	681	2 031 713	2.7	3.7	0.2	0.7	28.4	3.3	60.9	45.8	18.4	20.6	1 109	754
Platte	2 626	11 215 330	4.0	6.6	2.9	2.1	4.0	1.9	78.0	290.1	82.7	172.3	1 871	1 274
Polk	1 882	6 311 305	2.0	2.0	0.1	1.6	60.7	1.1	32.3	164.9	36.7	18.1	584	439
Pulaski	1 731	5 423 451	3.5	3.9	1.1	2.3	7.4	5.5	75.3	125.6	76.5	29.6	556	371
Putnam	314	940 189	4.5	2.1	0.0	2.4	55.0	5.9	29.6	17.4	5.2	7.7	1 554	1 199
Ralls	284	692 452	21.1	12.6	0.0	13.9	2.2	4.0	41.7	13.1	5.3	6.2	600	404
Randolph	1 211	3 641 751	3.9	5.9	1.9	2.1	2.9	4.9	77.8	104.1	32.8	33.6	1 328	821
Ray	1 243	21 423 521	0.8	0.5	0.3	0.3	89.8	0.8	7.3	87.1	25.3	21.5	933	704
Reynolds	325	775 935	7.0	5.6	0.0	5.7	4.1	1.6	75.1	20.4	10.7	7.5	1 131	997
Ripley	665	1 587 309	4.3	3.8	0.5	1.9	28.8	2.6	58.2	27.1	17.6	6.3	449	337
St. Charles	12 474	44 955 774	5.7	9.4	5.0	2.8	3.2	4.3	66.6	1 191.7	344.4	666.4	1 808	1 183
St. Clair	558	1 434 103	4.2	10.9	0.0	2.8	35.5	3.2	42.1	48.9	23.1	6.2	654	535
Ste. Genevieve	472	1 571 579	6.8	13.6	0.1	3.5	5.8	7.1	62.2	37.1	12.7	20.0	1 125	724
St. Francois	2 385	7 190 551	2.7	4.3	0.6	1.6	5.1	5.3	80.0	178.1	78.4	65.4	993	571
St. Louis	35 141	147 062 201	4.5	10.0	7.3	2.5	1.6	2.8	69.6	3 629.3	1 051.6	2 133.5	2 133	1 497
Saline	749	2 090 138	7.0	10.8	3.2	5.2	6.6	26.6	39.7	61.0	25.6	21.0	898	647
Schuyler	276	469 325	6.5	3.5	0.0	3.7	25.1	6.2	54.3	12.0	5.3	3.2	735	541
Scotland	479	1 508 783	7.5	3.0	0.0	5.6	60.2	4.1	19.3	31.5	5.9	4.5	918	718
Scott	1 609	5 229 887	4.1	7.7	1.4	1.8	4.2	23.8	53.9	108.4	50.7	38.1	973	559
Shannon	529	555 611	8.1	5.1	0.0	7.2	7.0	5.1	67.1	13.2	8.0	2.9	343	223
Shelby	432	1 223 611	12.6	7.4	0.3	6.2	25.9	5.7	38.5	23.5	9.7	6.6	1 064	756
Stoddard	1 139	2 920 419	5.2	6.2	0.8	8.7	6.5	5.3	66.9	72.2	30.2	21.0	704	560
Stone	846	2 351 044	6.0	5.6	1.1	2.7	0.1	2.1	82.4	74.2	35.5	30.6	969	612
Sullivan	370	985 283	6.2	4.1	0.2	3.8	27.9	5.8	50.1	23.6	9.0	6.6	1 012	748
Taney	1 787	5 327 466	7.7	9.1	3.9	4.1	8.3	6.6	58.2	198.6	59.2	103.3	1 952	978
Texas	1 227	3 278 813	3.7	3.2	0.1	3.2	31.5	5.3	50.4	84.8	28.4	20.4	791	654
Vernon	1 038	3 438 287	4.3	4.0	1.4	1.5	36.6	4.4	47.6	48.3	21.1	19.4	934	559
Warren	943	2 742 942	5.8	9.6	2.2	1.6	5.8	4.1	68.2	70.7	27.9	32.8	1 001	734
Washington	953	2 869 920	3.5	2.5	0.3	2.7	34.5	4.9	50.7	69.6	27.6	13.6	541	368
Wayne	459	1 011 584	9.4	3.6	0.0	7.6	5.0	3.2	71.2	25.2	14.3	7.7	573	378
Webster	946	2 669 213	5.5	5.0	0.3	2.8	11.0	3.5	71.2	63.4	29.0	20.2	556	309
Worth	134	294 433	8.2	2.8	0.0	3.4	21.0	5.8	57.6	6.8	2.2	2.2	1 037	834
Wright	792	2 007 501	4.3	3.8	0.3	2.7	11.1	4.2	73.0	47.2	25.3	12.2	656	392

1. Based on the resident population estimated as of July 1 of the year shown.

Table B. States and Counties — Local Government Finances, Government Employment, and Voting

STATE County	Local government finances, 2012 (cont.)									Government employment, 2014			Presidential election,[2] 2012		
	Direct general expenditure							Debt outstanding					Percent of vote cast:		
	Total (mil dol)	Per capita[1] (dollars)	Education	Health and hospitals	Police protection	Public welfare	Highways	Total (mil dol)	Per capita[1] (dollars)	Federal civilian	Federal military	State and local	Democratic	Republican	All other
			Percent of total for:												
	185	186	187	188	189	190	191	192	193	194	195	196	197	198	199

MISSOURI—Cont'd

STATE County	185	186	187	188	189	190	191	192	193	194	195	196	197	198	199
Jasper	396.9	3 443	54.1	10.7	5.4	0.1	5.6	243.6	2 113	296	423	6 892	32.8	65.9	1.3
Jefferson	583.0	2 648	64.1	2.8	6.2	0.0	7.7	577.7	2 623	285	758	8 194	50.6	48.1	1.4
Johnson	233.9	4 299	31.0	47.8	3.5	0.0	4.6	246.2	4 525	1 182	3 853	5 884	42.9	55.2	1.9
Knox	10.9	2 667	49.1	8.8	4.0	18.8	5.9	0.6	147	31	13	273	37.5	59.9	2.6
Laclede	68.0	1 919	74.1	0.0	4.7	0.0	6.3	34.1	962	85	121	1 518	32.0	66.6	1.4
Lafayette	87.7	2 650	57.3	1.7	5.6	0.1	7.0	105.1	3 177	113	115	2 089	41.6	56.9	1.5
Lawrence	78.1	2 031	67.8	0.8	3.9	5.7	6.5	98.6	2 562	217	129	1 940	30.6	67.7	1.7
Lewis	26.7	2 624	50.7	1.4	3.7	15.5	8.9	11.0	1 085	50	32	595	40.8	57.6	1.6
Lincoln	153.2	2 871	47.7	26.4	4.4	0.0	4.4	139.5	2 615	108	184	2 407	43.5	54.9	1.7
Linn	37.6	3 014	60.3	3.0	4.4	0.0	11.3	26.2	2 102	59	42	783	44.5	52.9	2.6
Livingston	59.6	3 966	50.2	2.8	4.8	8.2	7.4	28.8	1 918	80	46	1 323	37.2	60.9	1.9
McDonald	44.0	1 922	69.8	0.0	4.1	0.0	8.0	31.9	1 393	82	78	883	30.2	67.6	2.2
Macon	48.3	3 102	46.4	1.1	3.5	22.2	8.9	21.2	1 363	74	52	1 597	37.2	61.4	1.4
Madison	30.2	2 426	68.9	0.0	6.2	0.0	6.2	3.9	310	30	42	867	40.6	57.6	1.8
Maries	18.1	2 013	61.7	4.7	4.0	0.0	9.9	10.7	1 187	11	31	340	35.2	62.7	2.1
Marion	99.0	3 444	54.3	3.1	3.7	6.3	4.7	133.0	4 628	101	95	1 895	37.5	61.4	1.2
Mercer	9.9	2 650	69.6	5.6	1.5	0.0	12.0	8.6	2 310	30	13	243	29.7	66.9	3.4
Miller	78.5	3 161	59.5	4.2	3.5	6.0	5.7	46.2	1 860	51	85	1 454	30.8	67.6	1.6
Mississippi	35.3	2 466	49.4	5.6	5.4	0.6	6.5	20.3	1 418	15	42	1 028	42.0	56.6	1.4
Moniteau	32.1	2 054	63.0	5.8	3.2	0.0	6.8	31.2	1 994	48	50	1 045	31.3	67.0	1.7
Monroe	28.8	3 309	49.1	3.2	3.9	16.0	10.7	54.4	6 255	69	29	614	39.5	58.7	1.8
Montgomery	28.9	2 411	56.1	3.6	5.3	0.0	7.9	11.0	913	42	39	651	40.1	58.5	1.4
Morgan	40.7	2 025	46.7	0.1	7.7	7.9	8.7	22.0	1 093	38	68	963	39.0	59.6	1.5
New Madrid	46.5	2 517	59.4	2.4	6.4	0.0	7.6	18.4	995	53	62	957	41.6	56.8	1.6
Newton	127.6	2 161	69.8	3.0	3.0	0.5	3.4	106.0	1 794	144	198	2 631	29.3	69.4	1.3
Nodaway	59.7	2 551	52.7	3.7	4.8	0.0	11.8	64.8	2 766	92	67	2 569	44.0	54.5	1.5
Oregon	21.9	1 990	73.6	1.6	2.2	0.0	5.3	3.9	358	31	37	507	39.4	57.8	2.8
Osage	23.1	1 669	59.8	6.0	2.4	0.0	5.6	11.0	794	35	46	799	26.9	71.5	1.6
Ozark	20.7	2 155	78.4	2.7	3.2	0.1	6.5	0.7	69	20	32	446	35.4	62.3	2.3
Pemiscot	61.8	3 411	67.4	1.6	4.6	0.0	5.4	11.3	624	51	60	1 529	43.0	56.1	0.9
Perry	43.0	2 261	53.4	1.8	6.3	0.0	8.0	19.0	1 001	47	65	1 183	34.8	63.9	1.3
Pettis	213.3	5 041	37.6	44.8	2.5	0.0	4.2	106.8	2 524	145	143	3 201	38.1	60.5	1.4
Phelps	295.8	6 576	23.7	59.1	2.1	0.3	2.9	165.9	3 688	354	232	5 938	38.0	60.2	1.7
Pike	43.7	2 354	53.0	1.6	7.4	0.0	9.9	24.3	1 308	68	56	1 696	44.2	54.2	1.6
Platte	285.1	3 097	65.5	0.9	4.8	0.2	5.0	434.8	4 724	659	344	3 725	46.2	52.6	1.2
Polk	168.1	5 419	28.7	60.0	1.0	0.0	3.1	55.0	1 774	62	101	2 260	33.2	65.4	1.4
Pulaski	139.6	2 621	69.4	2.9	2.8	0.0	4.4	141.0	2 648	3 647	10 496	2 206	35.0	63.7	1.3
Putnam	17.9	3 623	40.9	1.9	1.7	18.6	8.7	7.6	1 551	19	16	481	29.7	68.0	2.3
Ralls	12.4	1 207	50.3	3.6	5.3	0.0	17.2	14.9	1 451	29	35	343	40.1	58.8	1.1
Randolph	103.6	4 090	59.4	15.6	4.7	0.0	3.9	94.5	3 731	68	78	2 123	37.5	60.8	1.7
Ray	82.9	3 594	35.4	24.2	3.6	15.3	8.2	32.9	1 426	48	78	1 356	47.4	50.6	2.0
Reynolds	20.8	3 118	70.7	4.1	2.1	0.5	3.4	4.8	719	19	22	382	43.1	54.2	2.6
Ripley	26.6	1 894	72.9	5.2	4.9	0.0	4.4	1.2	88	59	48	632	33.5	63.5	3.0
St. Charles	1 188.4	3 223	54.5	2.1	6.5	0.1	9.4	1 722.2	4 671	698	1 288	15 440	44.7	54.4	1.0
St. Clair	44.1	4 651	28.5	34.9	1.9	0.0	5.3	16.1	1 703	36	32	523	37.8	59.8	2.4
Ste. Genevieve	38.8	2 184	67.5	3.0	6.6	0.0	7.8	28.1	1 581	29	61	936	56.4	42.3	1.3
St. Francois	177.6	2 694	64.6	4.1	6.8	0.1	6.3	112.4	1 705	134	204	5 687	47.0	51.6	1.4
St. Louis	3 854.3	3 853	55.7	1.6	7.0	0.9	5.2	4 175.7	4 174	5 735	3 438	50 109	59.5	39.6	0.9
Saline	61.1	2 617	55.2	5.4	6.9	0.3	7.5	7.5	323	83	76	1 849	47.8	50.4	1.8
Schuyler	11.1	2 542	46.7	3.1	1.3	22.3	14.5	7.8	1 793	29	15	298	39.1	57.4	3.5
Scotland	35.5	7 289	17.7	58.8	1.2	11.4	5.9	18.8	3 848	21	16	590	37.8	59.5	2.7
Scott	109.3	2 794	52.1	2.0	13.1	0.0	3.9	182.4	4 661	104	132	2 133	34.7	64.1	1.1
Shannon	12.9	1 551	60.4	0.2	2.3	0.0	12.2	2.7	326	17	28	306	42.7	54.1	3.3
Shelby	24.1	3 872	42.9	4.0	2.6	27.1	7.7	6.0	969	35	20	582	33.6	65.3	1.1
Stoddard	67.4	2 263	63.7	5.5	2.6	0.0	6.1	41.2	1 384	145	100	1 323	29.4	69.2	1.4
Stone	68.6	2 173	57.5	0.0	4.0	0.0	7.1	49.4	1 566	37	106	1 121	30.7	68.0	1.3
Sullivan	22.7	3 475	48.2	30.8	2.2	0.1	5.6	9.1	1 389	46	22	434	40.9	56.0	3.1
Taney	188.6	3 561	41.8	3.4	3.9	0.0	6.1	593.9	11 215	175	180	2 224	30.8	68.0	1.1
Texas	72.4	2 804	46.8	37.3	2.0	0.1	3.4	30.6	1 185	67	82	1 881	31.4	66.5	2.1
Vernon	45.8	2 207	64.9	3.0	3.5	0.0	7.3	60.2	2 903	103	70	1 705	38.1	60.1	1.8
Warren	69.9	2 135	57.6	4.6	6.2	0.0	5.1	59.4	1 815	50	114	1 283	43.0	55.7	1.3
Washington	67.9	2 707	49.1	31.2	3.2	0.0	3.5	32.5	1 294	57	82	1 532	49.0	48.9	2.0
Wayne	23.2	1 734	66.5	1.8	4.6	0.0	10.8	24.4	1 824	76	46	541	36.4	61.5	2.1
Webster	62.8	1 727	65.3	0.3	4.1	9.7	6.4	23.5	648	84	124	1 407	34.8	63.8	1.5
Worth	7.6	3 657	53.1	2.9	3.3	20.3	3.2	1.0	466	24	0	159	36.4	60.2	3.4
Wright	48.4	2 598	61.6	0.2	2.3	10.5	5.3	14.9	799	43	62	874	30.0	67.9	2.0

1. Based on the resident population estimated as of July 1 of the year shown.   2. © 2013 Election Data Services, Inc. All rights reserved.

Table B. States and Counties — **Land Area and Population**

STATE/ County code	CBSA code[1]	County type[2]	STATE County	Land area[3] (sq km) 2010	Total persons 2015	Rank	Per square kilometer	White	Black	American Indian, Alaska Native	Asian and Pacific Islander	Percent Hispanic or Latino[4]	Under 5 years	5 to 17 years	18 to 24 years	25 to 34 years	35 to 44 years	45 to 54 years
				1	2	3	4	5	6	7	8	9	10	11	12	13	14	15
			MISSOURI—Cont'd															
29 510	41180	1	St. Louis city	160	315 685	214	1 973.0	45.4	48.5	0.9	3.8	3.8	6.7	13.6	10.6	19.4	12.9	12.7
30 000	...	X	MONTANA	376 962	1 032 949	X	2.7	89.0	1.0	7.7	1.4	3.5	6.0	16.0	9.9	12.6	11.3	12.8
30 001	...	7	Beaverhead	14 353	9 300	2 487	0.6	93.7	0.6	2.6	1.3	3.7	4.5	13.5	14.5	10.1	9.7	11.9
30 003	...	6	Big Horn	12 938	13 242	2 219	1.0	32.0	0.6	63.2	0.9	5.6	10.3	23.2	9.3	12.2	10.0	12.1
30 005	...	9	Blaine	10 949	6 577	2 710	0.6	49.5	0.6	49.0	0.6	2.3	8.7	21.6	9.0	12.1	10.0	12.1
30 007	...	9	Broadwater	3 089	5 689	2 783	1.8	95.9	0.7	2.2	0.7	2.5	5.0	15.7	6.4	8.7	11.1	14.9
30 009	13740	3	Carbon	5 306	10 408	2 399	2.0	95.7	0.6	1.6	0.7	2.3	4.2	14.1	6.3	8.8	10.8	14.4
30 011	...	9	Carter	8 653	1 180	3 100	0.1	97.1	0.5	1.1	0.3	1.2	5.4	11.3	6.7	10.9	6.6	14.0
30 013	24500	3	Cascade	6 988	82 278	681	11.8	89.0	2.4	6.1	1.9	4.1	6.7	15.8	10.5	13.8	10.5	12.4
30 015	...	8	Chouteau	10 289	5 767	2 779	0.6	77.3	0.5	20.6	0.9	2.2	3.8	20.7	8.8	11.0	10.2	12.3
30 017	...	7	Custer	9 799	12 135	2 290	1.2	94.4	0.8	2.6	0.9	3.0	6.3	15.8	8.4	12.7	10.5	13.2
30 019	...	9	Daniels	3 694	1 760	3 071	0.5	95.1	0.8	2.7	0.9	2.0	5.6	15.4	5.6	10.3	9.5	11.8
30 021	...	7	Dawson	6 143	9 625	2 463	1.6	94.2	0.9	3.0	0.7	2.7	6.5	15.8	9.4	13.1	11.0	12.6
30 023	...	7	Deer Lodge	1 908	9 139	2 501	4.8	93.0	0.8	4.5	0.9	3.1	4.0	12.3	9.1	10.6	11.6	14.3
30 025	...	9	Fallon	4 198	3 190	2 958	0.8	96.7	0.5	1.2	0.9	1.7	7.8	18.1	7.3	12.5	11.5	11.7
30 027	...	7	Fergus	11 240	11 427	2 328	1.0	95.6	0.7	2.5	0.6	2.4	5.1	15.2	6.5	10.4	10.8	12.6
30 029	28060	5	Flathead	13 177	96 165	614	7.3	95.2	0.6	2.5	1.4	2.7	5.8	16.6	7.3	11.7	11.7	13.4
30 031	14580	5	Gallatin	6 741	100 739	592	14.9	94.1	0.7	1.7	2.2	3.1	5.8	14.6	16.1	16.2	12.9	11.3
30 033	...	9	Garfield	12 109	1 314	3 095	0.1	98.1	0.4	0.8	0.1	1.2	5.7	17.2	5.7	10.8	10.3	10.9
30 035	...	7	Glacier	7 759	13 647	2 192	1.8	35.5	0.5	63.7	0.7	2.7	9.3	22.0	9.8	13.2	10.6	12.9
30 037	13740	8	Golden Valley	3 044	827	3 116	0.3	93.8	0.8	2.7	1.2	4.1	4.7	15.5	6.1	7.5	8.5	14.7
30 039	...	8	Granite	4 474	3 240	2 955	0.7	96.2	0.7	2.0	0.7	2.1	3.6	12.6	4.8	7.8	9.4	12.8
30 041	...	7	Hill	7 508	16 572	2 003	2.2	73.8	0.9	23.9	1.3	3.3	8.5	18.5	10.2	13.5	10.7	11.4
30 043	25740	3	Jefferson	4 290	11 645	2 316	2.7	95.2	0.8	3.3	0.8	2.3	4.2	16.8	6.4	8.4	10.6	15.4
30 045	...	8	Judith Basin	4 843	1 926	3 055	0.4	97.0	0.2	1.4	0.6	1.7	3.7	15.1	6.9	8.6	9.1	15.8
30 047	...	6	Lake	3 859	29 457	1 444	7.6	72.5	0.7	28.1	1.1	4.1	6.4	17.8	8.0	10.1	10.1	12.3
30 049	25740	5	Lewis and Clark	8 958	66 418	799	7.4	93.7	0.8	3.5	1.3	3.0	5.9	15.9	8.4	12.6	11.4	13.8
30 051	...	9	Liberty	3 704	2 408	3 013	0.7	98.3	0.5	0.9	0.6	0.7	5.7	15.4	8.1	12.1	9.4	14.6
30 053	...	7	Lincoln	9 357	19 052	1 871	2.0	95.3	0.5	2.8	0.8	2.7	4.7	13.7	5.3	8.3	9.7	13.7
30 055	...	9	McCone	6 846	1 683	3 072	0.2	96.6	0.8	1.6	0.2	1.3	3.4	16.5	7.7	9.2	9.5	13.2
30 057	...	9	Madison	9 292	7 915	2 601	0.9	95.9	0.7	1.7	0.6	2.9	3.8	11.9	6.2	9.0	9.7	12.9
30 059	...	9	Meagher	6 195	1 830	3 066	0.3	96.4	0.5	1.5	0.8	1.8	5.8	12.9	7.0	8.7	8.7	12.1
30 061	...	8	Mineral	3 158	4 251	2 882	1.3	94.4	0.9	3.9	1.2	2.9	4.7	13.6	5.3	9.3	8.5	13.3
30 063	33540	3	Missoula	6 717	114 181	538	17.0	92.1	1.0	4.0	2.4	3.1	5.4	14.0	15.6	15.2	11.8	11.6
30 065	...	8	Musselshell	4 838	4 582	2 860	0.9	94.1	0.7	2.5	0.6	3.4	4.8	14.9	6.0	8.2	10.1	14.5
30 067	...	7	Park	7 260	15 972	2 044	2.2	95.4	0.6	2.2	0.9	2.8	4.7	14.4	5.9	10.3	12.8	14.8
30 069	...	9	Petroleum	4 286	475	3 136	0.1	97.3	0.4	1.2	0.0	1.2	2.3	19.6	7.0	6.8	7.8	17.5
30 071	...	9	Phillips	13 313	4 169	2 889	0.3	89.5	0.6	11.2	0.7	2.1	6.1	16.5	7.9	9.2	8.8	15.0
30 073	...	7	Pondera	4 203	6 184	2 743	1.5	83.5	0.7	15.6	0.7	1.9	6.6	17.9	7.5	11.4	10.0	12.9
30 075	...	9	Powder River	8 540	1 773	3 070	0.2	96.5	0.6	2.8	0.5	2.0	2.7	14.6	8.6	7.9	8.8	15.7
30 077	...	7	Powell	6 025	6 840	2 689	1.1	91.6	1.3	5.2	0.9	2.3	4.2	11.4	8.2	12.9	12.5	16.4
30 079	...	9	Prairie	4 498	1 160	3 101	0.3	96.8	1.1	2.5	1.8	2.1	6.5	11.8	5.5	7.1	9.5	11.1
30 081	...	6	Ravalli	6 192	41 373	1 142	6.7	94.6	0.7	2.1	1.1	3.4	4.8	15.5	6.5	8.9	10.4	13.6
30 083	...	7	Richland	5 398	11 960	2 300	2.2	92.6	0.9	3.2	1.0	4.8	7.2	17.5	9.1	13.4	12.6	13.1
30 085	...	7	Roosevelt	6 099	11 476	2 326	1.9	40.3	0.5	59.0	0.8	2.5	9.7	22.3	9.9	13.4	10.7	11.5
30 087	...	8	Rosebud	12 977	9 398	2 478	0.7	60.6	0.7	36.4	1.0	4.1	8.7	20.5	8.3	11.1	10.7	12.4
30 089	...	8	Sanders	7 150	11 336	2 336	1.6	92.9	0.6	6.3	0.8	2.5	4.5	13.7	6.2	7.8	9.2	12.4
30 091	...	9	Sheridan	4 344	3 687	2 927	0.8	95.7	0.9	3.0	0.9	2.2	5.4	15.5	6.8	11.3	10.3	12.4
30 093	15580	5	Silver Bow	1 861	34 622	1 313	18.6	92.6	0.6	3.0	1.1	4.2	5.8	14.7	11.7	11.6	10.8	13.2
30 095	...	8	Stillwater	4 650	9 486	2 471	2.0	95.2	0.5	1.9	0.8	3.3	4.6	16.9	6.3	8.5	11.1	13.9
30 097	...	9	Sweet Grass	4 805	3 634	2 931	0.8	96.8	0.5	1.6	0.9	2.0	4.3	17.9	6.6	8.6	10.4	13.0
30 099	...	8	Teton	5 885	6 104	2 748	1.0	97.0	0.4	3.1	0.6	1.4	6.1	16.9	7.4	9.7	10.1	13.3
30 101	...	7	Toole	4 962	5 087	2 830	1.0	90.6	1.2	6.5	0.9	3.0	5.3	14.6	8.7	13.7	12.1	14.7
30 103	...	8	Treasure	2 531	697	3 129	0.3	94.1	0.4	3.0	0.9	2.7	6.1	11.6	5.5	11.1	7.1	12.6
30 105	...	7	Valley	12 758	7 659	2 621	0.6	87.6	0.8	10.6	1.2	2.2	5.4	17.3	7.2	10.1	10.1	13.3
30 107	...	9	Wheatland	3 686	2 110	3 039	0.6	96.9	1.1	2.3	1.1	1.7	6.8	16.4	6.4	8.9	10.8	10.5
30 109	...	9	Wibaux	2 303	1 130	3 103	0.5	96.2	0.2	1.2	0.7	2.5	4.6	16.7	7.4	9.9	7.7	14.0
30 111	13740	3	Yellowstone	6 820	157 048	408	23.0	89.5	1.3	5.2	1.3	5.2	6.4	17.1	8.6	13.9	12.1	12.9
31 000	...	X	NEBRASKA	198 974	1 896 190	X	9.5	82.0	5.5	1.3	2.7	10.2	6.9	17.9	10.2	13.5	12.0	12.7
31 001	25580	5	Adams	1 459	31 587	1 393	21.6	88.4	1.3	0.8	1.9	8.8	6.3	17.0	11.8	11.5	10.7	12.7
31 003	...	9	Antelope	2 220	6 414	2 722	2.9	96.1	0.5	0.4	0.5	3.0	6.6	16.8	6.6	9.9	9.0	12.9
31 005	...	9	Arthur	1 853	456	3 138	0.2	93.6	0.7	0.9	0.4	5.1	5.7	22.3	5.7	7.9	13.2	11.0
31 007	42420	9	Banner	1 932	788	3 119	0.4	95.1	2.8	0.7	0.1	4.1	6.0	13.0	6.0	9.2	6.4	12.0

1. CBSA = Core Based Statistical Area. See Appendix A for explanation. See Appendix B for list of metropolitan areas with component counties. 2. County type code from the Economic Research Service of USDA Rural-Urban Continuum Codes. See Appendix A for definition. 3. Dry land or land partially or temporarily covered by water. 4. May be of any race.

Table B. States and Counties — Population and Households

STATE County	Age (percent) (cont.)				Population change and components of change, 2000–2015							Households, 2010–2014				
					Total persons		Percent change		Components of change, 2010–2015					Percent		
	55 to 64 years	65 to 74 years	75 years and over	Percent female	2000	2010	2000–2010	2010–2015	Births	Deaths	Net migration	Number	Persons per house-hold	Family house-holds	Female family house-holder[1]	One per-son
	16	17	18	19	20	21	22	23	24	25	26	27	28	29	30	31
MISSOURI—Cont'd																
St. Louis city	12.8	6.3	5.0	51.7	348 189	319 365	-8.3	-1.2	24 976	15 647	-12 153	139 594	2.20	46.7	18.1	44.2
MONTANA	14.7	9.7	7.0	49.8	902 195	989 417	9.7	4.4	64 424	48 198	26 503	407 797	2.40	62.8	8.8	30.2
Beaverhead	16.0	11.5	8.3	48.9	9 202	9 246	0.5	0.6	477	419	-32	4 124	2.12	58.7	6.7	33.3
Big Horn	11.5	6.9	4.4	50.8	12 671	12 865	1.5	2.9	1 450	666	-389	3 503	3.68	78.6	22.3	19.6
Blaine	12.3	7.8	6.4	50.6	7 009	6 491	-7.4	1.3	573	345	-118	2 234	2.87	67.3	17.6	27.8
Broadwater	17.4	13.3	7.7	49.3	4 385	5 612	28.0	1.4	262	257	72	2 469	2.29	69.2	9.5	25.9
Carbon	19.1	13.7	8.6	49.8	9 552	10 078	5.5	3.3	416	472	413	4 305	2.35	63.7	6.0	32.1
Carter	19.9	12.2	13.0	50.0	1 360	1 160	-14.7	1.7	75	71	14	489	2.41	67.5	5.9	28.8
Cascade	13.3	9.1	7.8	49.6	80 357	81 327	1.2	1.2	6 223	4 187	-1 085	33 685	2.36	63.0	10.0	31.6
Chouteau	15.2	9.9	8.2	50.6	5 970	5 813	-2.6	-0.8	237	316	42	2 323	2.46	69.0	10.0	29.0
Custer	14.3	9.6	9.1	50.0	11 696	11 699	0.0	3.7	809	749	380	4 919	2.32	61.5	8.4	33.8
Daniels	16.7	11.8	13.4	49.7	2 017	1 751	-13.2	0.5	107	122	29	882	2.01	58.8	3.5	36.6
Dawson	14.8	8.6	8.2	48.6	9 059	8 963	-1.1	7.4	619	507	569	3 884	2.24	68.9	8.1	26.6
Deer Lodge	17.5	11.8	8.9	46.6	9 417	9 292	-1.3	-1.6	371	645	96	3 909	2.12	57.9	6.7	38.3
Fallon	15.4	7.5	8.2	48.7	2 837	2 890	1.9	10.4	265	149	186	1 197	2.49	67.7	8.0	30.7
Fergus	16.5	12.4	10.6	49.7	11 893	11 586	-2.6	-1.4	624	825	41	4 988	2.20	61.8	4.2	35.4
Flathead	16.2	10.4	6.7	50.2	74 471	90 928	22.1	5.8	5 846	4 221	3 467	37 073	2.46	65.9	7.6	28.2
Gallatin	11.8	6.8	4.4	48.6	67 831	89 513	32.0	12.5	5 938	2 744	7 827	37 495	2.38	60.2	6.0	27.0
Garfield	16.7	13.1	9.5	50.1	1 279	1 209	-5.5	8.7	67	57	86	450	2.42	70.9	4.9	24.7
Glacier	11.4	6.3	4.6	51.1	13 247	13 399	1.1	1.9	1 304	760	-303	4 121	3.16	65.2	18.0	31.3
Golden Valley	18.5	13.3	11.3	48.7	1 042	884	-15.2	-6.4	34	52	-35	319	2.24	65.5	8.2	28.5
Granite	20.1	17.0	11.8	49.5	2 830	3 079	8.8	5.2	104	167	206	1 396	2.20	66.9	5.2	28.7
Hill	13.1	7.9	6.2	49.6	16 673	16 096	-3.5	3.0	1 568	748	-339	6 125	2.61	67.2	10.7	27.5
Jefferson	19.4	12.9	5.8	49.0	10 049	11 403	13.5	2.1	452	528	304	4 497	2.49	71.9	6.5	22.4
Judith Basin	18.3	13.1	9.3	47.9	2 329	2 072	-11.0	-7.0	81	98	-130	899	2.25	65.1	3.6	29.4
Lake	15.5	11.9	7.8	50.8	26 507	28 746	8.4	2.5	1 950	1 427	190	11 916	2.38	66.6	12.3	28.0
Lewis and Clark	15.7	9.7	6.5	50.8	55 716	63 395	13.8	4.8	3 985	2 944	1 960	26 553	2.37	61.9	8.9	31.3
Liberty	15.0	8.9	10.9	52.4	2 158	2 339	8.4	2.9	121	118	63	829	2.44	67.1	4.6	32.1
Lincoln	19.8	15.8	9.0	49.5	18 837	19 687	4.5	-3.2	947	1 212	-373	8 900	2.16	59.5	5.9	34.2
McCone	17.9	11.5	11.0	49.0	1 977	1 734	-12.3	-2.9	78	89	-37	762	2.28	66.8	3.4	30.2
Madison	20.1	16.6	9.8	47.5	6 851	7 691	12.3	2.9	302	357	250	3 389	2.20	59.5	4.0	37.6
Meagher	18.6	14.9	11.2	49.1	1 932	1 891	-2.1	-3.2	99	137	-29	795	2.51	66.5	11.6	29.8
Mineral	18.8	16.1	10.4	47.3	3 884	4 223	8.7	0.7	239	239	14	1 582	2.62	56.3	7.5	36.7
Missoula	12.8	8.3	5.3	49.7	95 802	109 299	14.1	4.5	6 518	4 251	2 558	45 961	2.35	58.2	9.2	29.5
Musselshell	20.0	13.6	7.8	49.8	4 497	4 538	0.9	1.0	216	274	98	1 965	2.39	68.5	3.5	28.9
Park	17.6	11.9	7.6	49.8	15 694	15 636	-0.4	2.1	766	757	331	6 539	2.36	57.6	6.1	37.1
Petroleum	17.9	11.5	9.5	45.4	493	494	0.2	-3.8	17	17	-23	220	2.22	68.6	5.0	27.3
Phillips	16.1	10.5	10.0	50.3	4 601	4 253	-7.6	-2.0	267	280	-65	1 794	2.29	68.5	5.6	28.0
Pondera	14.1	10.4	9.2	51.3	6 424	6 155	-4.2	0.5	385	345	-14	2 306	2.52	64.0	8.5	32.7
Powder River	18.1	12.3	11.3	49.4	1 858	1 743	-6.2	1.7	49	103	77	748	2.23	65.2	8.6	32.4
Powell	15.8	11.0	7.6	38.1	7 180	7 027	-2.1	-2.7	263	387	-65	2 399	2.29	64.1	6.6	29.9
Prairie	18.6	17.9	12.0	49.2	1 199	1 179	-1.7	-1.6	65	90	9	525	2.40	65.5	5.3	31.2
Ravalli	17.2	14.1	9.1	50.3	36 070	40 212	11.5	2.9	2 007	2 201	1 215	16 839	2.39	64.2	8.7	30.1
Richland	14.0	7.6	5.4	47.7	9 667	9 746	0.8	22.7	821	491	1 895	4 294	2.47	63.9	7.1	31.4
Roosevelt	12.0	6.0	4.5	49.7	10 620	10 425	-1.8	10.1	1 231	778	586	3 142	3.39	64.7	16.1	31.7
Rosebud	14.6	8.6	5.0	49.6	9 383	9 235	-1.6	1.8	879	425	-290	3 323	2.78	69.7	10.4	26.7
Sanders	20.2	16.4	9.7	48.9	10 227	11 413	11.6	-0.7	550	663	40	5 153	2.16	66.1	6.7	28.9
Sheridan	17.4	10.1	10.8	49.1	4 105	3 384	-17.6	9.0	191	293	388	1 625	2.10	63.4	7.0	34.4
Silver Bow	14.9	9.6	7.7	49.3	34 606	34 209	-1.1	1.2	2 086	2 117	422	15 275	2.19	56.4	11.7	35.9
Stillwater	18.5	12.5	7.6	49.0	8 195	9 117	11.3	4.0	466	442	326	3 723	2.43	71.7	3.6	25.7
Sweet Grass	15.8	12.9	10.6	50.5	3 609	3 651	1.2	-0.5	161	210	38	1 381	2.59	72.0	3.6	26.4
Teton	14.5	11.5	10.5	50.9	6 445	6 071	-5.8	0.5	404	344	-27	2 339	2.48	67.2	6.2	29.7
Toole	15.3	8.5	7.1	43.6	5 267	5 324	1.1	-4.5	297	228	-314	1 990	2.22	66.7	9.9	29.6
Treasure	19.1	14.9	12.1	48.0	861	718	-16.6	-2.9	39	39	-20	340	2.24	66.5	5.9	33.5
Valley	15.9	10.3	10.5	49.5	7 675	7 369	-4.0	3.9	441	408	253	3 181	2.32	64.2	7.4	32.9
Wheatland	16.4	13.9	10.0	50.2	2 259	2 168	-4.0	-2.7	124	116	-71	901	2.29	63.2	1.2	35.6
Wibaux	15.1	11.6	13.0	48.9	1 068	1 017	-4.8	11.1	67	73	107	437	2.21	64.1	5.7	33.6
Yellowstone	13.6	8.4	6.8	50.9	129 352	147 972	14.4	6.1	10 491	7 238	5 710	61 385	2.42	62.6	10.4	30.3
NEBRASKA	12.5	7.7	6.7	50.2	1 711 263	1 826 341	6.7	3.8	136 434	80 032	14 162	731 347	2.47	65.0	10.0	28.7
Adams	13.4	8.7	7.9	49.9	31 151	31 364	0.7	0.7	2 114	1 599	-319	12 580	2.36	63.8	7.2	29.8
Antelope	15.8	10.9	11.5	50.5	7 452	6 685	-10.3	-4.1	440	355	-321	2 824	2.28	70.1	7.2	26.7
Arthur	12.8	11.3	9.9	51.9	444	460	3.6	-0.9	24	16	-7	189	2.52	64.0	11.6	33.9
Banner	17.8	16.5	13.1	49.5	819	690	-15.8	14.2	28	24	49	310	2.54	75.5	6.5	20.0

1. No spouse present.

Table B. States and Counties — **Population, Vital Statistics, Medicare, and Crime**

STATE County	Persons in group quarters, 2015	Daytime population, 2010–2014 Number	Employment/residence ratio	Births, 2015 Total	Rate[1]	Deaths, 2015 Number	Rate[1]	Persons under 65 with no health insurance, 2014 Number	Percent	Medicare, 2015 Total Beneficiaries	Enrolled in Original Medicare	Enrolled in Medicare Advantage	Serious crimes known to police,[2] 2014 Total Number	Rate[3]
	32	33	34	35	36	37	38	39	40	41	42	43	44	45
MISSOURI—Cont'd														
St. Louis city	11 958	429 406	1.78	4 662	14.7	3 023	9.6	44 385	16.3	44 941	27 820	17 121	25 913	8 134
MONTANA	28 867	1 004 222	1.00	12 593	12.2	9 204	9.0	139 768	16.8	190 426	154 916	35 510	28 625	2 797
Beaverhead	443	9 133	0.96	92	9.9	91	9.8	1 353	19.1	1 978	1 741	237	71	757
Big Horn	137	13 604	1.11	299	22.5	151	11.4	3 009	26.1	1 528	1 419	109	NA	NA
Blaine	220	6 644	1.03	109	16.5	67	10.1	1 488	26.6	958	865	93	11	203
Broadwater	52	4 903	0.69	45	8.0	42	7.4	841	18.9	1 443	1 166	277	46	805
Carbon	53	8 472	0.65	74	7.1	73	7.0	1 380	17.2	2 284	1 778	506	104	997
Carter	11	1 119	0.86	20	17.0	14	11.9	204	23.3	269	244	25	0	0
Cascade	2 526	82 322	1.01	1 177	14.3	748	9.1	10 399	15.6	16 221	12 327	3 894	2 942	3 554
Chouteau	135	5 462	0.84	45	7.7	65	11.1	1 133	23.7	1 084	910	174	NA	NA
Custer	413	11 810	0.99	159	13.1	148	12.2	1 455	15.2	2 423	2 127	296	269	2 234
Daniels	41	1 842	1.03	24	13.5	18	10.1	207	15.5	435	424	11	7	387
Dawson	498	8 962	0.94	124	12.9	83	8.7	1 054	14.0	1 628	1 551	77	277	2 886
Deer Lodge	846	9 069	0.96	68	7.4	118	12.9	1 109	16.6	2 269	2 005	264	241	2 576
Fallon	34	3 203	1.11	53	16.8	25	7.9	308	11.7	481	469	12	21	670
Fergus	465	11 361	0.98	121	10.6	143	12.5	1 554	18.0	2 776	2 189	587	159	1 382
Flathead	992	91 980	0.99	1 166	12.2	849	8.9	12 988	16.7	20 036	15 359	4 677	2 878	3 068
Gallatin	3 265	92 881	1.00	1 199	12.1	531	5.4	11 530	13.8	11 788	9 400	2 388	2 192	2 324
Garfield	0	1 094	0.99	12	9.2	13	9.9	213	21.1	259	241	18	7	530
Glacier	690	13 933	1.06	247	18.1	155	11.3	3 266	27.3	1 533	1 471	62	206	1 488
Golden Valley	89	641	0.71	8	9.5	6	7.1	142	22.4	240	189	51	9	1 051
Granite	40	2 944	0.85	22	6.8	31	9.6	480	21.1	685	603	82	54	1 708
Hill	593	16 841	1.05	309	18.6	142	8.6	2 525	18.1	2 721	2 454	267	572	3 423
Jefferson	230	9 219	0.56	90	7.8	112	9.7	1 269	13.7	2 332	1 913	419	126	1 090
Judith Basin	0	1 886	0.85	15	7.7	13	6.6	375	24.4	464	336	128	10	498
Lake	584	28 037	0.92	375	12.8	295	10.1	5 800	25.2	5 402	4 434	968	804	2 760
Lewis and Clark	1 948	67 679	1.09	779	11.8	594	9.0	7 006	13.0	11 836	9 564	2 272	1 816	2 755
Liberty	403	2 277	1.05	24	10.1	20	8.4	352	18.7	575	546	29	NA	NA
Lincoln	209	19 285	0.98	173	9.1	242	12.7	2 832	19.9	5 762	4 121	1 641	321	1 651
McCone	19	1 628	0.87	20	11.8	16	9.4	309	23.7	D	334	D	13	762
Madison	163	7 482	0.93	54	6.9	57	7.3	1 059	18.5	1 859	1 667	192	48	621
Meagher	174	1 981	0.95	13	7.0	21	11.4	279	20.5	509	498	11	35	1 792
Mineral	22	3 951	0.82	44	10.4	42	9.9	607	19.6	1 355	1 105	250	7	163
Missoula	3 636	114 930	1.07	1 280	11.3	816	7.2	14 557	15.4	18 070	15 015	3 055	3 636	3 228
Musselshell	52	4 579	0.91	37	8.1	52	11.3	720	20.1	1 124	956	168	90	1 932
Park	108	14 839	0.89	149	9.4	154	9.7	2 357	18.5	3 316	2 738	578	116	737
Petroleum	0	548	1.24	2	4.1	0	0.0	69	18.1	89	75	14	3	587
Phillips	127	4 016	0.90	63	15.1	41	9.8	789	23.9	925	866	59	73	1 752
Pondera	645	5 914	0.89	77	12.4	60	9.7	1 148	23.2	1 220	998	222	67	1 075
Powder River	35	1 717	1.01	10	5.6	13	7.3	259	19.1	326	270	56	NA	NA
Powell	1 537	7 147	1.05	43	6.3	75	10.9	738	17.7	1 325	1 159	166	169	2 414
Prairie	21	1 165	0.77	13	11.3	10	8.7	138	17.2	343	303	40	5	424
Ravalli	479	36 843	0.77	372	9.0	431	10.5	5 974	19.1	10 506	8 224	2 282	458	1 142
Richland	34	10 996	1.06	185	15.7	90	7.6	1 435	14.3	1 677	1 647	30	153	1 314
Roosevelt	186	11 410	1.15	252	22.1	193	16.9	2 461	24.8	1 431	1 400	31	198	1 792
Rosebud	65	9 878	1.14	176	18.8	87	9.3	1 500	18.9	1 412	1 237	175	64	684
Sanders	188	11 201	0.96	126	11.1	119	10.5	2 141	26.0	3 325	2 741	584	166	1 459
Sheridan	85	3 685	1.10	41	11.1	47	12.8	417	14.3	874	831	43	92	2 451
Silver Bow	998	34 388	1.00	405	11.7	404	11.7	4 430	15.8	7 158	6 030	1 128	1 643	4 740
Stillwater	112	8 742	0.89	94	10.0	85	9.1	1 003	13.6	2 006	1 546	460	115	1 225
Sweet Grass	45	3 826	1.12	30	8.2	32	8.8	448	16.0	810	707	103	5	136
Teton	461	5 783	0.89	82	13.5	60	9.9	889	18.9	1 329	929	400	71	1 169
Toole	766	5 413	1.09	57	11.2	36	7.0	693	18.7	548	503	45	127	2 491
Treasure	0	730	0.91	8	11.5	6	8.6	99	19.6	205	191	14	NA	NA
Valley	126	7 419	0.97	93	12.2	62	8.1	1 112	18.5	1 779	1 717	62	113	1 465
Wheatland	147	2 130	1.01	25	11.9	20	9.5	395	25.0	494	423	71	2	94
Wibaux	24	923	0.85	21	18.6	13	11.5	174	20.8	D	227	D	2	173
Yellowstone	3 695	154 355	1.03	1 992	12.7	1 373	8.8	19 296	14.9	26 434	20 733	5 701	6 266	4 018
NEBRASKA	52 377	1 872 906	1.02	26 256	13.9	14 697	7.8	173 309	11.0	295 847	256 093	39 754	52 754	2 804
Adams	1 486	31 812	1.03	398	12.6	314	10.0	2 569	10.3	5 431	5 147	284	1 113	3 508
Antelope	70	6 133	0.87	86	13.4	57	8.9	590	12.0	1 316	1 304	12	22	450
Arthur	0	442	0.83	4	8.8	0	0.0	80	22.5	D	101	D	0	0
Banner	0	634	0.63	4	5.2	5	6.5	102	19.2	90	79	11	NA	NA

1. Per 1,000 estimated resident population.   2. Data for serious crimes have not been adjusted for underreporting; this may affect comparability between geographic areas and over time.
3. Per 100,000 population estimated by the FBI.

Table B. States and Counties — Crime, Education, Money Income, and Poverty

STATE County	Serious crimes known to police, 2014 (cont.)[1] Rate[2] Violent	Property	Education — School enrollment and attainment, 2010–2014 Enrollment[3] Total	Percent private	Attainment[4] (percent) High school graduate or less	Bachelor's degree or more	Local government expenditures,[5] 2012–2013 Total current spending (mil dol)	Current spending per student (dollars)	Money income, 2010–2014 Households Per capita income[6] (dollars)	Median income (dollars)	Mean income (dollars)	Percent with income of $200,000 or more	Income and poverty, 2014 Median household income (dollars)	Percent below poverty level All persons	Children under 18 years	Children 5 to 17 years in families
	46	47	48	49	50	51	52	53	54	55	56	57	58	59	60	61
MISSOURI—Cont'd																
St. Louis city	1 706	6 428	82 379	32.1	41.0	30.4	349.9	10 810	23 244	34 800	50 918	2.1	35 681	28.8	42.9	44.1
MONTANA	324	2 473	238 988	12.5	37.4	29.1	1 527.0	10 625	25 977	46 766	62 086	2.7	46 608	15.2	19.2	18.0
Beaverhead	149	607	2 585	3.9	38.1	27.2	12.9	11 077	25 294	42 577	55 941	1.7	41 602	15.1	22.6	21.4
Big Horn	NA	NA	3 674	3.2	48.5	15.8	37.0	15 916	16 279	42 650	55 686	1.3	38 871	30.6	36.3	34.7
Blaine	92	111	1 693	6.2	42.8	17.3	17.8	14 167	17 529	37 065	48 058	1.6	35 740	25.2	31.8	30.6
Broadwater	385	420	1 067	14.4	48.1	21.3	6.3	9 759	27 243	48 211	62 689	3.3	49 758	11.7	16.0	14.7
Carbon	211	786	1 797	6.8	37.2	29.1	16.8	12 184	27 808	48 979	62 503	2.2	47 520	12.7	17.5	15.3
Carter	0	0	233	30.0	46.3	16.4	2.3	18 950	28 271	44 453	63 615	4.3	41 466	14.0	22.3	23.8
Cascade	249	3 305	18 402	11.5	39.1	25.5	109.4	9 502	25 216	45 091	59 133	2.3	42 903	14.3	18.6	18.3
Chouteau	NA	NA	1 515	12.2	41.7	24.4	10.1	15 781	23 085	41 270	57 658	2.7	41 004	19.4	28.6	23.2
Custer	191	2 043	2 589	10.0	39.0	19.5	16.0	9 700	24 876	46 125	58 265	1.9	47 493	11.0	15.7	15.9
Daniels	55	332	285	13.0	37.5	21.2	3.2	12 270	32 686	48 643	66 193	3.3	47 376	10.8	13.0	12.3
Dawson	240	2 647	2 015	8.8	40.3	18.3	14.7	10 970	27 244	49 955	63 740	2.1	50 540	11.7	13.6	13.0
Deer Lodge	374	2 202	1 756	9.1	45.2	18.6	11.4	10 451	23 951	41 015	53 501	1.9	38 178	17.1	22.9	21.5
Fallon	223	447	620	5.5	48.1	16.4	9.4	17 809	32 353	51 595	75 789	4.1	59 102	8.0	9.8	9.6
Fergus	365	1 017	2 200	12.1	41.0	27.6	20.8	12 988	25 867	42 865	56 177	2.1	42 915	14.8	18.3	17.2
Flathead	295	2 773	20 188	14.1	37.3	28.1	126.6	9 340	25 789	46 858	61 904	2.8	47 351	13.6	18.9	17.8
Gallatin	189	2 135	28 435	11.6	23.2	46.7	107.3	9 172	29 468	54 298	71 625	3.9	51 569	13.9	11.9	10.8
Garfield	0	530	203	3.4	53.9	14.6	2.2	11 281	27 218	51 000	63 098	2.4	42 757	15.1	18.1	16.0
Glacier	166	1 322	4 289	10.1	47.0	18.3	37.3	13 673	16 710	33 493	48 931	1.4	33 428	31.8	35.8	34.4
Golden Valley	234	818	133	0.8	51.9	20.8	2.6	18 978	23 356	42 083	48 664	0.3	37 316	20.1	35.5	34.7
Granite	127	1 582	537	7.3	44.0	27.5	4.9	13 013	26 868	49 583	58 411	2.2	47 902	14.4	24.0	21.3
Hill	395	3 028	4 518	8.3	33.7	23.5	38.5	12 335	21 119	44 368	54 828	1.0	43 509	17.6	20.8	20.5
Jefferson	285	804	2 468	17.9	35.0	33.5	15.8	10 156	30 721	61 460	76 258	4.5	61 575	10.4	14.4	11.8
Judith Basin	249	249	375	6.1	40.5	32.1	4.7	18 561	26 274	45 670	59 494	2.1	43 272	14.6	18.1	15.5
Lake	439	2 320	6 396	12.0	40.0	24.9	47.9	11 018	21 927	38 492	53 545	1.8	38 221	22.7	29.7	27.0
Lewis and Clark	375	2 380	15 369	23.3	29.1	37.6	93.5	9 846	28 651	55 594	67 336	2.4	53 572	12.0	15.2	14.2
Liberty	NA	NA	375	17.9	42.7	22.4	3.1	12 725	24 908	46 250	63 565	4.7	37 911	19.1	21.3	19.5
Lincoln	195	1 455	3 896	14.8	45.4	18.9	26.3	10 767	22 464	35 683	47 913	2.1	36 734	19.2	30.1	28.6
McCone	0	762	258	3.1	51.6	17.5	2.9	11 805	29 428	48 194	65 370	4.2	43 132	15.4	21.1	17.5
Madison	78	543	1 415	12.9	37.2	29.4	13.0	15 241	33 124	44 764	71 881	5.0	41 539	12.6	17.3	16.1
Meagher	102	1 690	379	7.4	49.3	18.4	2.9	13 013	19 561	38 144	46 689	0.6	36 903	18.0	30.4	31.6
Mineral	93	70	544	13.4	55.9	12.6	8.8	14 407	20 363	33 060	48 003	2.1	36 449	17.3	28.3	27.0
Missoula	274	2 954	31 319	9.8	27.5	40.2	136.0	10 192	26 559	47 209	63 057	2.9	44 716	15.8	16.4	16.1
Musselshell	429	1 502	1 016	9.2	47.9	15.1	7.3	10 425	23 309	45 096	54 375	0.7	39 827	19.1	29.1	27.2
Park	127	610	2 996	18.5	36.1	33.4	22.0	11 392	25 818	42 506	56 300	2.3	42 942	14.7	18.5	16.6
Petroleum	196	391	75	0.0	48.8	18.0	1.4	15 337	22 567	40 250	49 731	1.8	35 092	17.5	27.4	21.1
Phillips	216	1 536	830	8.4	46.2	19.8	10.9	16 548	22 450	38 426	51 639	0.9	41 595	15.7	20.2	19.2
Pondera	96	978	1 502	15.0	42.8	21.9	13.4	14 114	22 868	40 969	58 361	1.8	39 292	20.3	27.4	25.8
Powder River	NA	NA	347	11.2	37.4	20.5	4.1	15 648	28 849	44 167	61 969	4.0	44 644	12.3	15.9	13.1
Powell	528	1 885	1 115	17.0	45.8	18.9	10.7	14 551	20 650	41 326	54 184	1.8	40 072	20.2	22.6	21.8
Prairie	170	254	212	3.3	58.1	14.0	2.0	14 180	22 028	40 580	49 705	1.0	40 140	12.3	18.6	20.3
Ravalli	182	960	8 588	13.2	43.0	24.2	53.1	9 519	22 516	38 366	52 004	1.5	42 902	17.2	27.2	24.9
Richland	180	1 134	1 977	6.1	44.9	17.3	24.5	12 555	31 840	61 438	77 412	6.2	65 738	8.2	10.6	10.1
Roosevelt	443	1 348	2 756	2.8	56.4	12.6	36.2	14 905	16 720	36 825	51 332	1.7	37 511	23.8	30.6	30.4
Rosebud	192	491	2 328	8.4	41.9	22.9	28.0	16 700	23 118	50 924	62 350	2.3	50 751	20.5	27.0	25.5
Sanders	211	1 248	2 017	22.6	54.0	15.5	19.1	13 735	19 145	31 665	42 387	0.7	32 815	20.7	30.3	28.8
Sheridan	453	1 998	713	10.2	39.1	21.3	8.6	15 610	31 642	47 348	67 292	4.1	52 711	10.2	11.9	10.7
Silver Bow	355	4 385	7 841	18.4	45.8	23.5	42.0	9 501	23 698	37 503	52 278	1.7	39 882	19.5	22.7	21.5
Stillwater	149	1 076	1 919	15.1	43.8	23.5	16.1	11 220	29 298	58 326	69 346	2.8	60 812	8.4	12.2	10.5
Sweet Grass	54	81	820	10.9	42.9	27.8	6.3	11 495	24 437	51 797	63 280	2.2	45 000	12.0	14.4	12.2
Teton	132	1 037	1 289	13.8	43.2	22.4	13.6	11 845	23 871	45 572	58 729	1.2	46 208	13.9	18.7	17.2
Toole	510	1 981	1 032	18.7	48.3	14.4	9.2	12 860	22 837	46 917	57 975	2.3	45 207	17.2	20.7	19.2
Treasure	NA	NA	156	1.9	46.2	19.2	1.5	16 591	22 419	40 682	48 233	0.9	47 089	13.2	19.8	20.5
Valley	78	1 387	1 525	8.1	45.6	17.0	16.2	13 089	26 331	49 198	60 225	2.3	46 328	12.4	18.3	16.8
Wheatland	0	94	278	11.5	59.4	18.9	4.8	14 570	18 935	33 825	45 608	0.0	35 875	19.5	28.2	28.8
Wibaux	0	173	203	13.3	51.1	18.4	2.3	14 400	25 112	39 097	53 862	2.3	43 859	11.7	17.9	16.6
Yellowstone	335	3 682	35 925	14.1	38.4	28.7	212.3	9 311	28 918	51 743	69 931	3.6	51 653	12.3	15.3	13.9
NEBRASKA	280	2 523	511 619	16.9	37.3	29.0	3 513.1	11 579	27 339	52 400	68 081	3.2	52 803	12.3	16.0	14.7
Adams	249	3 259	9 025	21.2	42.6	22.3	65.3	12 916	27 001	51 342	66 368	3.2	48 658	12.5	15.7	14.5
Antelope	41	409	1 427	11.5	44.6	18.3	23.1	20 778	26 312	45 417	60 752	2.4	50 919	14.0	19.0	18.6
Arthur	0	0	131	9.2	26.7	31.6	1.8	18 709	18 709	41 103	48 320	1.6	43 408	10.2	15.7	14.0
Banner	NA	NA	166	16.3	40.7	13.6	2.9	20 743	33 226	46 875	80 051	6.5	48 990	12.4	24.1	25.3

1. Data for serious crimes have not been adjusted for underreporting; this may affect comparability between geographic areas and over time.   2. Per 100,000 population estimated by the FBI.
3. All persons 3 years old and over enrolled in nursery school through college.   4. Persons 25 years old and over.   5. Elementary and secondary education expenditures.
6. Based on population estimated by the American Community Survey, 2010–2014.

Table B. States and Counties — **Personal Income**

STATE County	Personal income, 2014										Earnings, 2014		
	Total (mil dol)	Percent change, 2013–2014	Per capita[1]		Wages and salaries (mil dol)	Supplements to wages and salaries; employer contributions (mil dol)		Proprietors' income (mil dol)	Dividends, interest, and rent (mil dol)	Personal transfer receipts (mil dol)	Total (mil dol)	Contributions for government social insurance (mil dol)	
			Dollars	Rank		Pension and insurance	Government social insurance					From employee and self-employed	From employer
	62	63	64	65	66	67	68	69	70	71	72	73	74
MISSOURI—Cont'd													
St. Louis city	12 485	2.8	39 333	1 276	13 820	2 219	1 001	1 478	2 083	2 939	18 517	1 052	1 001
MONTANA	40 844	3.5	39 903	X	18 365	3 003	1 688	3 990	9 360	7 696	27 045	1 761	1 688
Beaverhead	358	5.1	38 297	1 423	134	26	12	55	88	75	227	13	12
Big Horn	366	3.3	27 586	2 950	191	38	15	23	61	106	267	15	15
Blaine	185	-8.9	27 934	2 924	54	13	5	26	46	50	98	5	5
Broadwater	204	3.6	36 056	1 774	48	9	5	12	46	47	73	5	5
Carbon	423	5.6	40 661	1 101	87	16	8	28	112	83	138	11	8
Carter	64	24.4	54 760	214	12	2	1	29	11	8	44	1	1
Cascade	3 389	4.1	41 163	1 044	1 565	286	148	287	753	670	2 286	145	148
Chouteau	183	-11.2	31 079	2 576	47	9	4	15	55	42	75	5	4
Custer	485	4.9	40 126	1 156	229	36	21	51	92	93	336	22	21
Daniels	56	-24.3	31 356	2 543	27	5	2	-6	20	14	28	3	2
Dawson	392	7.4	41 207	1 035	190	27	19	11	62	67	247	17	19
Deer Lodge	313	1.3	34 257	2 070	113	21	10	14	59	91	158	12	10
Fallon	151	0.0	48 636	452	104	12	8	23	25	19	147	9	8
Fergus	436	-0.8	38 108	1 442	158	29	15	55	113	97	257	17	15
Flathead	3 700	3.8	38 982	1 321	1 582	229	156	406	926	718	2 373	165	156
Gallatin	4 121	5.8	42 350	919	1 983	307	183	443	1 116	476	2 916	182	183
Garfield	51	-8.4	38 826	1 347	10	2	1	16	15	8	29	1	1
Glacier	436	-0.8	31 818	2 461	166	36	14	46	84	114	263	15	14
Golden Valley	36	3.6	42 772	874	7	2	1	4	12	13	13	1	1
Granite	124	6.3	38 624	1 373	28	5	3	17	36	26	53	4	3
Hill	636	-4.4	38 348	1 411	297	52	30	44	153	132	423	27	30
Jefferson	520	3.8	44 950	683	96	18	8	71	96	89	193	14	8
Judith Basin	101	9.2	50 518	359	19	4	2	38	25	14	62	2	2
Lake	915	5.8	31 460	2 532	286	55	25	49	246	279	415	31	25
Lewis and Clark	2 744	3.7	41 665	989	1 554	288	134	174	581	490	2 150	134	134
Liberty	87	-14.7	36 686	1 649	21	4	2	17	34	15	44	2	2
Lincoln	593	3.3	30 996	2 584	183	36	18	39	130	215	276	24	18
McCone	77	-8.4	45 210	660	27	5	2	10	17	13	44	2	2
Madison	347	5.6	44 357	728	139	19	15	39	102	66	212	13	15
Meagher	77	7.8	41 809	969	17	3	1	18	20	20	39	2	1
Mineral	141	3.9	33 213	2 244	35	7	3	11	23	46	56	5	3
Missoula	4 330	4.2	38 422	1 404	2 257	365	211	322	1 111	756	3 154	205	211
Musselshell	172	6.5	37 459	1 532	64	10	5	14	39	48	93	7	5
Park	645	4.5	40 614	1 106	187	28	18	43	200	124	278	20	18
Petroleum	27	4.9	55 984	198	5	1	0	12	4	3	18	0	0
Phillips	151	-4.8	36 040	1 778	46	9	4	22	37	36	82	5	4
Pondera	256	-0.4	41 110	1 048	64	11	6	51	66	51	133	8	6
Powder River	66	3.9	37 166	1 576	4	4	2	17	15	11	41	2	2
Powell	229	4.2	33 075	2 266	94	21	8	18	60	51	141	9	8
Prairie	42	9.0	36 835	1 629	12	3	1	4	12	11	19	1	1
Ravalli	1 488	4.5	36 256	1 730	378	66	36	94	413	373	573	47	36
Richland	718	6.3	62 001	111	433	52	38	91	118	60	613	37	38
Roosevelt	418	0.9	36 891	1 618	149	29	13	37	64	97	227	14	13
Rosebud	334	2.7	35 776	1 812	212	42	19	16	48	74	288	17	19
Sanders	331	2.3	29 094	2 816	85	18	8	28	79	118	139	12	8
Sheridan	189	-17.2	51 020	332	75	11	7	27	46	29	121	7	7
Silver Bow	1 557	2.9	44 883	686	635	110	57	333	273	302	1 136	76	57
Stillwater	400	5.4	43 033	843	202	28	16	40	77	68	287	18	16
Sweet Grass	152	3.8	41 608	1 000	74	11	6	9	50	27	100	7	6
Teton	273	5.5	45 046	676	67	13	6	64	66	47	151	8	6
Toole	225	-5.9	43 781	779	94	18	8	57	58	33	177	10	8
Treasure	41	6.9	59 499	141	7	1	1	11	10	7	20	1	1
Valley	318	-1.0	41 614	998	133	23	13	19	86	67	188	13	13
Wheatland	77	9.2	36 805	1 631	20	4	2	23	19	17	48	2	2
Wibaux	42	2.2	37 401	1 539	13	3	1	9	7	8	25	1	1
Yellowstone	6 651	4.2	42 735	878	3 636	523	331	562	1 247	1 085	5 052	329	331
NEBRASKA	89 479	3.5	47 557	X	43 427	7 368	3 271	14 205	16 457	12 800	68 271	3 838	3 271
Adams	1 325	1.6	42 130	940	608	109	45	140	302	248	903	54	45
Antelope	424	1.1	66 330	79	83	15	6	206	59	55	310	13	6
Arthur	28	72.7	61 653	113	5	1	0	14	4	3	20	0	0
Banner	54	39.6	70 297	57	9	1	1	33	5	4	45	1	1

1. Based on the resident population estimated as of July 1 of the year shown.

STATE County	Farm	Mining	Construction	Manu-facturing	Information: professional, scientific, technical services	Retail trade	Finance, insurance, real estate and leasing	Health care and social assistance	Govern-ment	Number	Rate[1]	Supplemental Security Income recipients, December 2014	Total	Percent change, 2010–2014
	75	76	77	78	79	80	81	82	83	84	85	86	87	88
MISSOURI—Cont'd														
St. Louis city...............	0.0	0.0	D	9.2	15.8	1.6	8.6	15.1	15.1	54 465	172	17 132	175 626	-0.2
MONTANA	3.1	4.6	7.7	4.3	7.8	8.1	5.9	13.4	20.2	212 535	208	18 248	494 198	2.4
Beaverhead..............	20.4	D	5.9	1.3	3.4	6.6	5.5	D	23.8	2 125	228	125	5 243	-0.6
Big Horn.................	7.8	22.8	D	D	1.8	4.2	1.9	D	41.0	2 065	155	331	4 655	-0.9
Blaine...................	21.3	0.7	3.4	0.8	D	6.6	D	5.1	40.3	1 165	176	205	2 808	-1.2
Broadwater..............	10.1	5.1	6.8	20.3	D	6.4	D	7.2	17.5	1 475	262	68	2 689	-0.2
Carbon..................	4.6	3.5	11.1	1.8	6.2	6.9	5.8	8.8	22.1	2 675	257	110	6 452	0.2
Carter...................	71.1	0.0	2.8	0.0	D	2.3	D	D	9.4	290	247	6	806	-0.5
Cascade.................	1.1	0.1	7.1	3.3	6.3	8.3	6.2	16.5	27.5	17 635	214	1 902	37 932	1.8
Chouteau................	21.8	0.0	3.8	1.4	D	6.6	5.6	D	26.4	1 325	225	64	2 854	-0.9
Custer...................	5.8	D	5.3	1.2	3.5	10.4	6.7	12.2	19.5	2 635	218	243	5 609	0.9
Daniels..................	-46.6	D	17.1	D	D	D	D	D	20.4	460	255	11	1 113	0.2
Dawson..................	0.1	10.0	3.4	1.5	4.9	9.0	3.8	D	15.8	1 785	187	105	4 376	3.4
Deer Lodge..............	0.4	0.0	6.9	2.0	6.7	6.2	2.2	27.3	30.9	2 650	290	279	5 112	-0.2
Fallon...................	3.3	34.2	14.5	0.4	D	4.1	2.3	4.8	10.6	570	183	14	1 550	5.4
Fergus...................	9.7	0.1	14.0	5.7	3.7	8.0	5.2	D	19.9	3 015	264	191	5 794	-0.7
Flathead.................	0.2	1.0	8.9	7.4	D	9.2	8.8	17.1	12.9	20 305	214	1 255	47 487	1.1
Gallatin.................	1.2	0.8	12.6	5.2	12.9	10.4	6.5	9.7	17.9	13 165	135	620	45 962	8.7
Garfield.................	56.7	0.0	D	D	D	3.5	D	D	19.3	275	210	10	845	0.1
Glacier..................	10.5	5.5	D	D	2.0	6.6	1.3	4.4	45.9	2 020	147	595	5 314	-0.6
Golden Valley...........	33.5	D	D	D	D	D	D	D	21.8	280	329	23	478	0.4
Granite..................	14.0	2.3	6.8	3.8	D	5.2	D	D	22.4	865	269	34	2 780	-1.5
Hill......................	5.9	0.5	4.7	0.5	7.1	8.5	3.7	D	27.4	2 610	157	436	7 202	-0.7
Jefferson................	4.3	11.4	11.0	5.5	D	12.5	D	D	21.5	2 750	238	155	5 028	-0.5
Judith Basin............	66.0	0.0	D	D	D	1.4	3.1	D	11.8	475	239	28	1 330	-0.4
Lake.....................	0.8	0.5	8.0	5.3	6.5	9.0	3.5	13.7	35.4	8 385	287	838	16 578	-0.1
Lewis and Clark.........	0.7	0.8	4.8	2.3	10.5	6.6	8.3	12.1	36.7	14 075	214	1 107	30 855	2.2
Liberty..................	44.9	D	D	D	D	3.1	D	D	14.3	380	161	46	1 030	-1.2
Lincoln..................	-0.2	2.2	10.1	2.8	4.9	9.0	4.1	15.4	28.2	6 365	333	554	11 451	0.3
McCone..................	24.3	0.0	D	0.0	D	3.1	D	D	12.9	550	323	0	1 004	-0.5
Madison.................	11.8	3.4	7.9	2.0	3.6	4.2	5.2	4.0	12.1	2 220	284	64	6 903	-0.5
Meagher.................	40.7	D	D	D	D	4.4	D	D	14.8	560	300	44	1 422	-0.7
Mineral..................	-0.6	0.0	7.3	D	D	10.2	D	11.3	26.1	1 395	329	158	2 442	-0.2
Missoula.................	-0.1	D	6.2	3.5	D	8.9	6.5	18.0	20.0	20 035	178	2 132	51 869	3.5
Musselshell..............	7.5	46.0	5.4	0.6	2.7	2.7	D	6.5	12.7	1 390	302	101	2 649	-0.2
Park.....................	5.0	0.3	8.1	7.1	6.6	7.9	5.5	11.3	14.0	3 535	223	254	9 372	0.0
Petroleum...............	75.8	D	D	0.0	D	D	0.0	D	11.2	105	215	5	326	0.6
Phillips..................	15.9	D	5.0	1.2	D	7.8	4.5	D	24.2	1 030	246	87	2 314	-0.9
Pondera.................	23.3	2.0	7.5	1.6	2.8	15.4	3.2	D	12.4	1 290	208	176	2 634	-1.0
Powder River............	35.7	D	D	D	D	6.0	D	0.4	20.5	350	197	9	1 010	-1.2
Powell...................	6.1	D	D	D	D	4.0	2.3	D	47.4	1 475	214	127	3 104	0.0
Prairie...................	24.1	0.0	D	D	D	1.5	D	D	46.6	360	316	14	667	-0.9
Ravalli...................	0.0	0.1	9.2	6.4	9.8	9.1	5.4	12.2	20.5	11 895	290	733	19 526	-0.3
Richland.................	4.4	21.0	14.0	4.4	4.8	4.9	4.5	D	7.1	1 655	143	97	5 161	13.4
Roosevelt................	5.6	3.9	4.4	0.6	D	10.7	2.3	D	38.3	1 675	148	416	4 083	0.5
Rosebud.................	4.3	16.7	D	D	D	3.0	1.3	D	30.3	1 635	175	220	4 095	0.9
Sanders.................	1.4	3.0	10.2	5.6	3.6	7.5	3.8	13.3	24.4	3 510	310	240	6 642	-0.5
Sheridan.................	16.1	15.1	D	D	2.7	5.5	3.2	D	16.2	935	254	39	2 134	2.2
Silver Bow...............	0.1	D	3.2	3.9	4.9	9.4	3.7	14.2	15.2	7 970	229	953	16 825	0.6
Stillwater................	7.7	D	D	4.7	3.8	3.5	1.5	D	8.0	2 200	237	86	4 803	0.0
Sweet Grass.............	1.2	D	6.6	2.7	1.7	4.7	3.7	0.6	14.4	900	245	14	2 128	-1.0
Teton....................	31.6	D	6.5	1.7	D	4.6	4.3	5.5	14.0	1 480	245	115	2 876	-0.5
Toole....................	12.8	19.0	D	D	D	3.9	2.8	2.3	24.0	880	171	107	2 341	0.2
Treasure.................	67.5	0.0	1.4	0.0	D	D	D	D	11.5	290	417	0	421	-0.2
Valley...................	5.9	1.2	5.9	0.9	5.1	6.4	D	D	22.8	1 695	222	142	4 834	-0.9
Wheatland...............	37.7	0.0	D	D	D	3.1	2.0	D	14.0	435	208	47	1 189	-0.7
Wibaux..................	32.7	D	D	D	D	0.9	1.3	D	18.5	240	213	9	539	0.2
Yellowstone.............	0.8	3.3	8.3	6.3	9.8	8.3	6.5	16.8	12.1	29 025	187	2 492	67 552	5.6
NEBRASKA................	9.3	0.3	6.3	10.0	7.6	5.5	7.9	10.1	15.4	326 078	173	27 719	820 913	3.0
Adams...................	8.8	0.0	7.0	14.8	3.8	6.3	3.7	D	14.5	6 795	216	543	13 749	3.0
Antelope.................	33.6	D	5.2	16.0	D	3.3	2.8	4.6	7.0	1 540	241	85	3 282	-0.1
Arthur...................	79.5	0.0	D	D	D	D	0.0	D	9.3	90	198	0	252	-0.8
Banner...................	80.0	0.0	D	0.0	0.0	0.0	D	D	6.8	95	127	0	364	-1.4

1. Per 1,000 resident population estimated as of July 1 of the year shown.

Table B. States and Counties — **Housing, Labor Force, and Employment**

STATE County	Housing units, 2010–2014								Civilian labor force, 2015				Civilian employment,[6] 2010–2014		
	Occupied units										Unemployment			Percent	
			Owner-occupied				Renter-occupied								
				Median owner cost as a percent of income											Construction, production, and maintenance occupations
	Total	Percent	Median value[1]	With a mortgage	Without a mortgage[2]	Median rent[3]	Median rent as a percent of income[2]	Sub-standard units[4] (percent)	Total	Percent change, 2014–2015	Total	Rate[5]	Total	Management, business, science and arts	
	89	90	91	92	93	94	95	96	97	98	99	100	101	102	103
MISSOURI—Cont'd															
St. Louis city	139 594	44.2	118 600	23.0	14.1	742	33.1	2.8	163 001	1.6	9 862	6.1	145 366	37.6	15.2
MONTANA	407 797	67.7	187 600	23.3	11.3	696	28.6	2.6	522 728	1.3	21 543	4.1	481 119	35.5	22.2
Beaverhead	4 124	64.6	172 800	21.2	10.6	567	28.7	1.9	5 038	2.8	171	3.4	4 560	37.3	22.4
Big Horn	3 503	63.6	88 400	19.9	10.0	675	23.6	12.1	5 610	-0.4	372	6.6	4 703	33.1	20.1
Blaine	2 234	63.7	78 400	24.7	11.6	469	25.4	3.5	2 425	-1.0	120	4.9	2 537	36.2	28.4
Broadwater	2 469	79.2	178 800	23.0	11.2	618	27.8	3.6	2 504	-0.6	124	5.0	2 712	31.6	33.6
Carbon	4 305	77.2	212 300	22.8	12.5	736	25.4	2.6	5 543	2.2	200	3.6	5 088	34.6	26.0
Carter	489	82.8	81 500	25.6	11.7	475	17.2	4.5	698	0.9	23	3.3	599	52.8	30.6
Cascade	33 685	64.3	159 900	21.8	11.0	629	26.4	2.7	38 888	0.9	1 553	4.0	36 983	33.1	22.0
Chouteau	2 323	63.4	115 100	22.9	10.6	435	19.1	1.7	2 573	-1.4	75	2.9	2 512	42.0	16.9
Custer	4 919	69.1	123 700	18.5	11.7	590	24.8	3.0	6 452	-2.8	211	3.3	6 031	34.1	20.8
Daniels	882	77.7	102 100	18.7	12.1	700	31.7	1.8	966	0.8	25	2.6	1 009	40.3	17.6
Dawson	3 884	69.4	147 900	16.3	10.0	505	24.2	2.8	4 869	-0.6	150	3.1	4 604	34.9	29.8
Deer Lodge	3 909	73.0	124 700	21.8	10.0	510	27.5	2.8	5 291	0.3	207	3.9	3 937	26.3	28.2
Fallon	1 197	71.0	122 800	17.0	10.0	558	19.8	1.6	1 981	-5.1	46	2.3	1 683	31.1	36.5
Fergus	4 988	72.9	120 200	20.3	13.2	664	25.8	2.8	5 771	-0.2	239	4.1	5 774	40.0	24.2
Flathead	37 073	70.1	226 700	27.7	11.8	771	30.6	1.9	45 104	2.4	2 557	5.7	43 071	30.9	24.0
Gallatin	37 495	61.3	263 200	25.1	11.2	850	30.1	2.0	59 742	4.3	1 764	3.0	50 531	39.7	20.2
Garfield	450	77.3	115 000	21.7	11.3	492	15.3	4.4	773	2.7	21	2.7	589	49.7	21.1
Glacier	4 121	58.6	85 800	17.1	10.0	465	23.5	9.0	5 848	-2.5	527	9.0	4 674	34.5	23.7
Golden Valley	319	75.9	86 000	23.6	12.6	766	21.8	6.0	401	1.8	17	4.2	339	31.9	35.7
Granite	1 396	74.3	209 000	22.7	11.7	606	20.7	3.7	1 574	2.4	96	6.1	1 283	36.7	28.6
Hill	6 125	67.7	125 600	19.9	11.1	533	26.8	2.5	7 876	-0.1	334	4.2	7 566	33.1	26.4
Jefferson	4 497	84.1	239 500	22.4	10.0	694	27.3	1.5	5 623	-0.8	226	4.0	5 325	43.7	21.9
Judith Basin	899	74.0	117 000	19.5	12.7	485	18.5	1.2	1 009	3.7	35	3.5	920	48.3	22.7
Lake	11 916	70.3	218 000	27.4	12.1	628	27.4	3.8	12 763	1.5	630	4.9	11 688	35.2	24.9
Lewis and Clark	26 553	71.6	204 600	23.4	10.2	749	27.4	1.8	35 226	-0.6	1 174	3.3	33 121	45.1	14.7
Liberty	829	65.7	88 200	19.8	10.4	501	22.8	3.3	985	0.6	26	2.6	898	41.8	21.4
Lincoln	8 900	78.2	160 500	27.2	12.7	561	28.0	4.1	7 870	-1.3	788	10.0	7 256	30.5	25.9
McCone	762	80.8	109 800	19.5	11.0	481	15.8	2.1	1 080	-1.5	23	2.1	993	53.0	18.4
Madison	3 389	74.7	230 800	28.2	10.7	689	24.6	1.6	4 260	0.0	155	3.6	3 759	37.5	26.1
Meagher	795	74.6	123 400	29.7	12.3	641	25.0	0.3	968	6.0	34	3.5	948	29.5	26.2
Mineral	1 582	75.5	171 300	30.6	13.2	541	31.9	0.9	1 771	0.7	146	8.2	1 536	22.2	28.1
Missoula	45 961	59.2	237 300	24.0	12.3	769	32.5	2.5	61 143	1.3	2 365	3.9	58 050	38.0	16.2
Musselshell	1 965	74.3	135 500	19.8	10.5	547	29.0	4.3	2 436	2.5	103	4.2	2 021	27.4	34.7
Park	6 539	74.9	210 100	27.0	13.7	664	27.4	0.9	8 356	2.9	398	4.8	7 606	36.3	23.9
Petroleum	220	75.0	76 800	27.9	11.7	770	50.0	2.7	293	2.4	15	5.1	253	52.2	22.9
Phillips	1 794	75.0	95 900	20.0	10.7	497	22.8	2.5	2 001	-0.3	101	5.0	1 846	32.5	27.9
Pondera	2 306	68.7	105 800	21.9	12.6	564	25.1	4.0	2 906	1.6	130	4.5	2 755	38.0	25.0
Powder River	748	69.5	99 700	19.4	10.0	580	25.4	2.3	1 080	-0.3	27	2.5	913	44.2	22.9
Powell	2 399	70.5	118 300	20.2	11.6	512	20.1	2.4	3 009	1.8	136	4.5	2 749	34.5	22.9
Prairie	525	86.9	82 900	21.4	10.0	495	50.0	0.8	532	2.7	22	4.1	522	42.5	28.7
Ravalli	16 839	71.4	233 400	28.1	13.1	702	32.6	3.2	19 358	2.3	1 001	5.2	17 274	33.0	24.9
Richland	4 294	67.5	160 700	16.9	10.0	715	23.7	1.0	6 959	-5.7	220	3.2	5 651	26.7	35.8
Roosevelt	3 142	59.7	81 500	17.9	10.2	360	17.6	4.3	4 733	-2.5	246	5.2	3 647	33.3	26.0
Rosebud	3 323	67.4	120 200	18.8	10.3	545	20.1	5.1	4 223	0.5	224	5.3	4 047	36.5	28.1
Sanders	5 153	74.9	172 100	33.0	12.8	636	28.2	3.9	4 753	1.8	390	8.2	4 068	27.2	32.2
Sheridan	1 625	73.5	121 700	19.2	12.0	607	26.8	0.4	2 104	-1.9	52	2.5	1 820	36.1	21.5
Silver Bow	15 275	64.0	122 100	19.6	11.4	595	30.0	1.7	17 315	1.1	738	4.3	16 251	31.9	22.9
Stillwater	3 723	78.8	189 200	20.5	13.4	675	20.6	4.6	4 962	-1.4	183	3.7	4 444	29.0	35.5
Sweet Grass	1 381	72.8	195 800	25.5	10.5	636	26.1	2.5	1 808	0.8	50	2.8	1 674	32.6	35.4
Teton	2 339	76.1	135 600	22.8	12.6	552	26.1	4.2	2 917	0.6	111	3.8	2 705	39.9	23.2
Toole	1 990	60.6	107 400	19.4	10.0	544	25.6	2.2	2 326	-1.6	78	3.4	2 320	31.0	22.7
Treasure	340	65.0	70 600	22.5	14.7	545	19.2	3.5	360	3.2	18	5.0	346	28.6	37.0
Valley	3 181	70.5	110 900	17.2	10.0	509	20.2	1.3	4 434	1.0	137	3.1	3 594	39.4	22.3
Wheatland	901	67.1	81 500	23.5	14.3	525	23.1	7.2	798	1.3	43	5.4	811	40.2	26.1
Wibaux	437	72.5	107 900	17.6	10.6	547	23.6	0.7	552	-0.5	18	3.3	444	36.0	29.1
Yellowstone	61 385	68.5	186 500	21.8	11.0	736	28.5	2.2	81 888	2.4	2 668	3.3	78 079	33.0	22.3
NEBRASKA	731 347	66.5	130 100	20.7	12.2	721	27.2	2.3	1 012 981	-0.1	30 270	3.0	957 508	35.4	23.5
Adams	12 580	70.8	101 900	19.1	10.9	625	24.1	1.4	16 708	-0.2	519	3.1	15 788	32.2	25.8
Antelope	2 824	75.5	77 800	21.0	11.4	487	28.4	1.6	3 629	0.9	92	2.5	3 244	38.3	27.7
Arthur	189	60.3	85 000	18.1	13.5	625	19.4	1.1	226	0.9	10	4.4	202	55.4	22.8
Banner	310	68.4	93 300	19.6	17.5	607	25.6	1.9	441	0.9	15	3.4	415	44.1	21.4

1. Specified owner-occupied units.　2. A value of 10.0 represents 10 percent or less; a value of 50.0 represents 50 percent or more.　3. Specified renter-occupied units.
4. Overcrowded or lacking complete plumbing facilities.　5. Percent of civilian labor force.　6. Persons 16 years old and over.

Table B. States and Counties — Nonfarm Employment and Agriculture

	Private nonfarm establishments, employment and payroll, 2014									Agriculture, 2012			
		Employment						Annual payroll		Farms			
											Percent with:		
STATE County	Number of establishments	Total	Health care and social assistance	Manufacturing	Retail trade	Finance and insurance	Professional, scientific, and technical services	Total (mil dol)	Average per employee (dollars)	Number	Fewer than 50 acres	500 acres or more	Farm operators whose principal occupation is farming (percent)
	104	105	106	107	108	109	110	111	112	113	114	115	116
MISSOURI—Cont'd													
St. Louis city	10 876	223 152	37 342	17 090	9 913	12 970	18 328	11 846	53 084	NA	NA	NA	NA
MONTANA	36 791	363 650	68 523	17 579	58 857	16 071	17 951	13 367	36 758	28 008	28.1	42.2	55.1
Beaverhead	360	2 300	482	45	415	D	D	69	29 978	430	32.3	41.4	56.5
Big Horn	205	2 228	D	D	319	67	D	110	49 452	527	23.3	45.2	50.5
Blaine	146	1 211	274	D	190	45	31	48	40 023	546	9.0	66.7	67.2
Broadwater	129	787	D	D	139	D	D	24	30 592	287	21.6	39.7	54.4
Carbon	407	2 158	284	40	248	D	121	58	26 995	726	24.4	32.6	57.0
Carter	31	145	D	D	30	NA	D	4	26 579	327	6.4	83.2	76.5
Cascade	2 420	29 900	6 609	867	5 275	1 643	1 143	982	32 847	1 105	36.0	29.3	47.8
Chouteau	155	723	D	D	110	D	12	20	28 260	774	5.6	75.6	69.6
Custer	438	4 518	933	84	917	D	107	158	34 929	423	24.8	48.0	60.0
Daniels	71	D	D	D	93	40	14	D	D	338	3.8	71.3	53.8
Dawson	346	2 919	D	40	615	D	72	104	35 719	485	12.8	61.4	57.1
Deer Lodge	244	2 951	D	D	321	65	101	95	32 218	93	31.2	32.3	34.4
Fallon	160	1 287	D	D	159	D	D	69	53 998	295	14.6	62.4	60.3
Fergus	429	3 363	797	336	546	131	79	114	33 882	790	20.1	53.9	62.9
Flathead	3 916	35 041	5 938	2 838	5 721	1 689	1 416	1 233	35 184	1 035	60.4	6.3	49.9
Gallatin	5 127	41 638	5 312	2 981	7 341	1 419	2 741	1 481	35 562	1 163	47.7	18.6	45.0
Garfield	22	135	D	NA	49	D	NA	4	28 585	297	8.8	83.2	76.8
Glacier	253	2 451	441	D	549	48	43	86	35 064	602	12.8	48.5	58.6
Golden Valley	15	D	D	D	D	D	D	D	D	157	8.9	61.1	59.2
Granite	110	521	D	D	92	D	D	16	31 409	163	15.3	52.8	56.4
Hill	535	5 410	1 380	26	1 134	232	150	164	30 347	802	8.7	59.0	53.6
Jefferson	263	1 731	273	D	171	D	D	69	39 696	401	40.4	20.7	40.6
Judith Basin	66	198	D	D	25	D	D	6	30 631	324	12.7	65.4	66.4
Lake	765	5 357	1 164	329	1 157	230	414	162	30 196	1 156	54.8	9.3	45.4
Lewis and Clark	2 186	25 019	5 727	649	3 883	1 687	1 960	944	37 740	703	59.2	17.2	36.6
Liberty	70	314	D	NA	D	23	D	8	26 338	304	3.9	80.6	74.3
Lincoln	613	3 850	901	180	710	127	108	118	30 598	325	49.8	5.8	38.2
McCone	55	367	D	D	89	D	D	13	34 695	489	3.3	73.4	68.3
Madison	362	2 214	D	D	233	67	D	72	32 517	571	28.5	37.5	48.7
Meagher	64	268	D	D	D	D	D	7	24 403	136	22.8	60.3	64.7
Mineral	114	897	D	D	210	D	D	24	27 168	95	50.5	9.5	30.5
Missoula	4 225	49 006	10 261	1 612	8 140	1 941	3 528	1 680	34 273	637	58.4	10.0	38.3
Musselshell	119	937	191	D	135	25	16	46	49 397	356	13.5	43.3	58.1
Park	775	4 724	789	368	721	D	D	149	31 448	564	36.0	36.2	55.1
Petroleum	12	D	D	NA	D	NA	D	1	D	100	6.0	78.0	78.0
Phillips	138	879	D	20	251	46	29	22	25 133	507	13.0	64.1	64.5
Pondera	174	1 352	271	D	219	71	32	44	32 757	505	14.1	59.2	62.2
Powder River	71	333	D	D	85	D	D	10	28 754	328	16.2	74.7	64.9
Powell	163	1 069	D	D	D	D	D	33	31 295	263	31.2	38.8	57.8
Prairie	39	147	D	D	D	D	D	4	24 993	186	11.3	69.4	71.5
Ravalli	1 396	8 553	1 529	820	1 516	375	480	260	30 392	1 438	69.6	5.7	47.0
Richland	578	5 982	D	481	654	149	244	339	56 643	544	12.7	67.3	64.2
Roosevelt	231	2 207	D	D	593	88	28	72	32 550	606	5.9	63.2	55.6
Rosebud	186	2 509	D	D	287	60	D	124	49 226	437	18.1	53.5	57.9
Sanders	351	1 978	493	197	310	64	39	56	28 117	492	31.1	16.3	41.3
Sheridan	174	1 017	315	D	190	70	D	30	29 546	527	2.3	67.6	66.4
Silver Bow	1 140	13 014	3 094	614	2 269	335	530	471	36 196	140	24.3	22.9	43.6
Stillwater	261	2 525	226	D	240	64	61	166	65 836	593	21.8	43.7	56.5
Sweet Grass	160	1 044	D	D	138	D	34	60	57 194	332	18.1	50.6	53.9
Teton	211	1 163	245	D	203	D	34	36	30 617	742	17.0	43.8	58.8
Toole	189	1 649	286	D	239	D	37	58	35 221	423	5.2	75.4	60.0
Treasure	18	51	D	NA	D	D	D	1	26 255	109	11.9	66.1	75.2
Valley	275	2 371	D	D	419	102	71	76	32 100	654	8.7	62.7	66.1
Wheatland	58	372	D	D	D	D	D	10	27 917	154	11.7	65.6	65.6
Wibaux	40	183	D	D	28	D	6	6	32 213	172	6.7	66.9	73.3
Yellowstone	5 543	68 776	13 711	3 375	11 094	3 666	3 424	2 892	42 056	1 330	48.0	21.8	46.9
NEBRASKA	52 991	851 128	124 250	93 135	110 073	60 573	97 943	34 953	41 067	49 969	23.3	37.7	59.7
Adams	970	13 236	2 570	2 712	1 940	373	279	452	34 166	567	25.9	38.8	65.1
Antelope	227	1 413	278	95	283	89	D	44	30 833	767	17.7	39.5	61.0
Arthur	9	D	NA	NA	D	D	D	2	D	85	10.6	81.2	71.8
Banner	10	37	NA	NA	NA	D	NA	1	38 838	193	5.2	63.7	62.7

Table B. States and Counties — **Agriculture**

STATE County	Land in farms — Acreage (1,000) [117]	Percent change, 2007–2012 [118]	Acres — Average size of farm [119]	Acres — Total irrigated (1,000) [120]	Acres — Total cropland (1,000) [121]	Value of land and buildings — Average per farm [122]	Value of land and buildings — Average per acre [123]	Value of machinery and equipment, average per farm (dollars) [124]	Value of products sold — Total (mil dol) [125]	Value of products sold — Average per farm (dollars) [126]	Percent from: Crops [127]	Percent from: Livestock and poultry products [128]	Percent of farms with sales of: $10,000 or more [129]	Percent of farms with sales of: $100,000 or more [130]	Government payments — Total ($1,000) [131]	Government payments — Percent of farms [132]
MISSOURI—Cont'd																
St. Louis city	NA	NA	NA	NA	NA	NA	NA	NA	NA	NA	NA	NA	NA	NA	NA	NA
MONTANA	59 759	-2.7	2 134	1 903.0	17 022.2	1 674 568	785	137 611	4 230.1	151 031	53.3	46.7	50.4	26.2	209 846	44.4
Beaverhead	1 381	11.4	3 211	238.5	178.6	3 580 193	1 115	151 598	142.9	332 270	21.8	78.2	57.9	32.3	368	15.1
Big Horn	3 149	8.6	5 975	46.3	268.1	2 633 651	441	151 454	108.7	206 351	48.8	51.2	53.7	28.8	2 505	32.6
Blaine	2 204	-5.4	4 037	50.5	626.8	2 408 179	597	202 203	113.8	208 509	62.9	37.1	68.9	39.7	8 869	67.2
Broadwater	477	0.4	1 661	39.6	151.3	1 901 303	1 144	166 115	38.1	132 909	56.2	43.8	52.6	27.2	1 700	47.0
Carbon	791	-0.3	1 090	72.8	136.7	1 283 405	1 178	115 977	76.9	105 871	33.8	66.2	52.2	20.4	1 696	35.3
Carter	1 778	4.7	5 437	1.4	234.8	2 923 162	538	205 480	83.2	254 431	14.9	85.1	83.2	51.7	2 009	58.1
Cascade	1 255	-9.1	1 136	33.4	427.7	1 197 706	1 055	96 719	111.1	100 568	48.2	51.8	40.9	16.2	5 952	51.5
Chouteau	2 072	-9.0	2 677	10.4	1 260.3	2 146 671	802	225 031	186.1	240 424	85.5	14.5	66.5	50.4	16 813	81.9
Custer	2 190	3.0	5 177	30.3	139.3	2 082 525	402	132 858	109.2	258 158	19.4	80.6	59.6	35.7	1 847	40.7
Daniels	768	-10.7	2 273	4.1	536.0	1 171 905	516	259 464	95.0	281 074	91.6	8.4	55.6	37.3	5 520	85.8
Dawson	1 258	-8.7	2 594	17.2	399.4	1 163 130	448	171 186	80.4	165 701	69.0	31.0	65.4	36.9	6 390	70.9
Deer Lodge	67	-16.1	716	10.8	11.2	1 154 925	1 613	74 237	5.5	59 613	33.5	66.5	35.5	15.1	60	16.1
Fallon	980	0.1	3 321	0.9	172.1	1 456 376	439	201 753	56.4	191 095	21.4	78.6	65.1	38.0	2 136	74.2
Fergus	1 961	-19.8	2 482	12.4	592.4	2 147 954	865	155 286	145.7	184 456	49.2	50.8	64.3	39.4	6 716	55.1
Flathead	170	-32.5	164	18.2	71.3	819 700	4 994	55 080	34.7	33 504	79.6	20.4	24.2	6.9	707	16.6
Gallatin	703	-9.5	604	79.1	225.1	1 596 942	2 643	97 028	106.0	91 118	55.5	44.5	38.9	15.4	2 741	21.6
Garfield	2 191	-8.4	7 376	1.5	386.1	3 642 283	494	210 761	72.9	245 549	37.1	62.9	78.5	51.2	3 399	60.6
Glacier	1 570	-7.6	2 609	34.1	525.6	1 781 623	683	172 369	105.6	175 380	64.6	35.4	53.5	25.6	6 940	51.3
Golden Valley	708	5.4	4 511	7.0	135.4	2 545 656	564	118 675	21.4	136 242	34.9	65.1	51.0	30.6	2 347	67.5
Granite	285	-5.8	1 751	28.5	27.4	2 233 558	1 276	92 485	19.2	117 497	17.5	82.5	58.3	32.5	152	16.0
Hill	1 598	-5.8	1 992	9.4	1 168.9	1 288 555	647	196 585	164.0	204 451	84.5	15.5	56.0	37.7	17 713	74.4
Jefferson	371	-5.1	926	29.2	50.3	1 049 786	1 134	48 180	22.4	55 920	19.5	80.5	33.2	10.0	519	11.2
Judith Basin	1 034	23.4	3 193	14.0	343.2	2 852 596	893	209 031	92.6	285 664	30.8	69.2	76.2	42.6	2 905	64.5
Lake	556	-12.8	481	80.7	80.7	767 869	1 597	58 202	56.6	48 930	42.9	57.1	42.0	10.6	783	20.2
Lewis and Clark	843	-13.2	1 199	47.5	92.4	1 816 522	1 515	56 963	46.6	66 228	39.5	60.5	27.3	8.4	1 192	14.5
Liberty	898	-0.7	2 954	5.9	604.1	1 795 457	608	271 908	84.7	278 500	81.4	18.6	70.7	51.6	9 709	92.4
Lincoln	47	-8.9	145	3.5	9.8	545 972	3 753	40 302	3.5	10 665	29.1	70.9	18.8	1.8	55	3.4
McCone	1 372	-9.0	2 806	14.2	604.9	1 347 873	480	197 613	102.2	209 053	76.1	23.9	70.3	44.2	7 765	83.6
Madison	1 085	2.3	1 901	111.9	144.9	2 382 159	1 253	124 492	81.3	142 301	33.6	66.4	49.0	23.5	856	15.6
Meagher	812	0.0	5 973	36.1	69.6	5 741 787	961	168 647	39.0	286 809	24.3	75.7	61.8	40.4	533	36.8
Mineral	17	-24.7	179	0.9	4.0	798 084	4 447	32 147	1.1	11 653	23.5	76.6	10.5	2.1	23	13.7
Missoula	247	-12.3	388	16.8	19.9	1 074 215	2 769	40 830	13.6	21 355	29.8	70.2	22.1	4.6	395	9.4
Musselshell	1 018	-10.2	2 859	11.4	124.2	1 412 604	494	87 795	38.1	107 006	27.3	72.7	36.5	18.3	1 854	32.0
Park	774	1.5	1 372	57.1	110.1	3 502 195	2 552	96 943	38.5	68 239	34.1	65.9	47.3	17.4	754	17.7
Petroleum	690	7.7	6 898	11.2	158.3	3 025 110	439	211 460	31.6	316 040	39.0	61.0	77.0	52.0	1 194	69.0
Phillips	2 067	3.0	4 076	33.2	702.0	2 344 404	575	148 256	95.8	188 955	61.0	39.0	63.9	35.9	7 362	68.8
Pondera	957	1.3	1 894	65.8	568.2	1 536 014	811	209 016	113.8	225 259	73.9	26.1	67.3	41.8	8 483	76.4
Powder River	1 589	-1.9	4 843	9.9	171.7	2 666 905	551	151 963	62.4	190 296	13.0	87.0	75.9	48.2	1 530	38.7
Powell	589	-12.1	2 240	53.5	53.5	2 120 281	946	112 894	34.2	130 114	22.3	77.7	48.7	23.6	264	15.6
Prairie	769	0.2	4 135	9.2	119.3	2 331 349	564	147 817	31.2	167 710	47.9	52.1	69.4	41.9	1 749	70.4
Ravalli	235	-10.7	163	61.6	51.3	792 834	4 856	42 915	34.7	24 148	30.2	69.8	25.4	5.4	549	8.6
Richland	1 293	1.1	2 377	62.7	556.5	1 418 388	597	263 978	139.2	255 820	67.3	32.7	65.3	38.1	6 117	73.3
Roosevelt	1 240	-14.6	2 046	16.6	729.0	1 292 137	632	213 368	126.4	208 579	89.4	10.6	58.1	34.5	7 701	79.0
Rosebud	3 142	15.8	7 189	35.9	238.9	2 970 357	413	141 041	91.7	209 929	28.1	71.9	56.5	27.7	2 043	31.6
Sanders	339	-0.9	688	17.5	34.4	817 530	1 187	47 451	14.2	28 917	38.8	61.2	29.9	6.3	501	10.8
Sheridan	1 042	-2.2	1 977	9.2	696.0	1 172 598	593	315 522	129.8	246 207	88.5	11.5	62.2	44.4	7 618	88.0
Silver Bow	70	-31.0	498	4.6	4.4	781 493	1 569	76 293	4.2	30 043	18.4	81.6	30.7	7.1	5	2.9
Stillwater	809	-5.6	1 365	21.6	187.3	1 905 005	1 396	84 403	56.9	95 933	22.8	77.2	48.6	18.7	2 997	42.5
Sweet Grass	856	5.3	2 577	35.8	78.7	2 771 482	1 075	105 373	33.5	100 892	12.8	87.2	49.7	20.8	689	25.0
Teton	975	-15.4	1 314	114.8	548.9	1 381 036	1 051	159 619	140.1	188 811	58.6	41.4	56.5	32.6	8 825	73.3
Toole	1 129	1.2	2 668	6.3	747.3	1 912 251	717	212 683	102.7	242 745	79.8	20.2	65.2	46.1	11 090	85.6
Treasure	618	33.7	5 666	21.9	44.2	2 847 431	503	329 853	46.6	427 202	48.1	51.9	80.7	48.6	548	56.0
Valley	1 635	-20.7	2 499	40.4	788.4	1 240 586	496	243 817	151.5	231 596	78.6	21.4	62.7	38.2	9 013	80.0
Wheatland	874	6.3	5 675	21.7	124.2	2 906 149	512	153 864	46.8	304 071	22.7	77.3	64.9	39.0	1 520	55.2
Wibaux	545	10.7	3 171	1.5	135.7	1 483 262	468	201 831	29.3	170 174	54.3	45.7	75.0	44.8	2 282	85.5
Yellowstone	1 668	3.3	1 254	73.2	351.1	957 953	764	95 176	216.8	163 019	28.0	72.0	38.0	15.5	3 843	30.2
NEBRASKA	45 332	-0.3	907	8 296.6	21 597.4	2 159 268	2 380	230 212	23 068.8	461 661	49.3	50.7	68.5	43.0	392 428	68.7
Adams	341	11.2	601	215.3	284.3	3 170 141	5 278	359 032	418.0	737 136	62.7	37.3	69.5	53.4	5 673	67.4
Antelope	475	-8.0	619	249.7	343.9	2 634 722	4 254	283 301	535.1	697 674	47.9	52.1	74.7	55.9	8 424	73.8
Arthur	453	-0.2	5 327	12.4	29.3	2 247 882	422	174 412	31.5	370 412	29.2	70.8	90.6	57.6	308	24.7
Banner	422	6.9	2 188	15.2	191.6	1 685 534	770	178 580	113.0	585 622	21.3	78.7	68.4	36.3	3 220	77.7

STATE County	Water use, 2010		Wholesale trade,[1] 2012				Retail trade,[2] 2012				Real estate and rental and leasing,[2] 2012			
	Total water withdrawn (mil gal/day)	Gallons withdrawn per person per day	Number of establishments	Number of employees	Sales (mil dol)	Annual payroll (mil dol)	Number of establishments	Number of employees	Sales (mil dol)	Annual payroll (mil dol)	Number of establishments	Number of employees	Receipts (mil dol)	Annual payroll (mil dol)
	133	134	135	136	137	138	139	140	141	142	143	144	145	146
MISSOURI—Cont'd														
St. Louis city	91.5	286	452	7 692	5 916.4	423.3	923	9 422	2 471.9	231.1	411	2 432	1 003.0	102.5
MONTANA	7 645.2	7 727	1 288	13 034	12 645.8	577.1	4 831	55 418	15 623.6	1 346.5	1 726	5 207	835.4	162.3
Beaverhead	483.0	52 234	6	D	D	D	49	423	124.5	9.6	15	72	8.7	2.4
Big Horn	268.1	20 838	6	26	20.8	1.1	47	341	101.4	7.7	8	18	1.8	0.4
Blaine	236.4	36 426	11	53	197.2	1.6	21	165	46.9	3.3	2	D	D	D
Broadwater	192.4	34 284	7	28	17.7	1.3	15	131	77.7	3.1	1	D	D	D
Carbon	400.2	39 709	15	D	D	D	50	D	D	D	24	30	2.5	0.5
Carter	1.6	1 379	NA	NA	NA	NA	6	34	14.7	0.8	3	D	D	D
Cascade	166.9	2 052	112	D	D	D	352	4 859	1 359.7	117.4	121	349	62.1	9.8
Chouteau	42.1	7 242	15	79	195.8	3.0	22	114	46.8	2.5	4	3	0.5	0.0
Custer	151.5	12 950	19	161	64.3	5.3	54	806	256.7	21.1	16	23	3.3	0.5
Daniels	3.9	2 204	5	16	38.4	0.7	16	96	51.4	2.5	NA	NA	NA	NA
Dawson	79.0	8 810	17	181	323.9	6.9	47	493	151.8	11.9	12	41	11.3	3.2
Deer Lodge	39.6	4 259	1	D	D	D	28	290	75.2	6.2	8	14	1.0	0.3
Fallon	7.0	2 419	6	D	D	D	15	137	34.7	3.0	5	2	0.3	0.1
Fergus	50.0	4 316	15	D	D	D	65	464	150.3	11.0	21	53	6.0	1.1
Flathead	61.7	679	103	958	1 283.5	38.6	473	5 317	1 515.9	138.3	223	791	86.9	21.0
Gallatin	333.2	3 722	127	1 025	600.7	40.2	582	6 760	1 710.3	166.7	332	824	152.6	25.9
Garfield	4.5	3 706	NA	NA	NA	NA	6	78	13.1	1.0	NA	NA	NA	NA
Glacier	128.1	9 561	8	52	108.7	2.2	44	448	128.7	11.2	7	5	1.0	0.1
Golden Valley	39.6	44 830	1	D	D	D	1	D	D	D	NA	NA	NA	NA
Granite	72.0	23 368	3	16	5.8	0.7	19	101	24.3	1.9	3	D	D	D
Hill	10.8	673	26	221	367.1	9.3	88	1 029	286.4	23.9	24	64	7.1	1.4
Jefferson	91.0	7 979	8	30	13.6	1.3	28	185	51.7	3.5	7	13	0.7	0.2
Judith Basin	16.8	8 127	5	25	13.0	0.9	6	20	5.6	0.3	2	D	D	D
Lake	390.6	13 587	20	59	21.8	1.5	122	1 069	268.3	26.4	37	39	6.0	0.9
Lewis and Clark	154.1	2 430	63	516	332.7	21.3	276	3 735	998.6	91.5	98	315	68.3	11.9
Liberty	29.0	12 407	7	49	59.3	1.9	10	44	12.8	1.3	2	D	D	D
Lincoln	18.2	924	11	47	35.4	1.1	83	693	172.6	15.2	24	51	5.7	0.8
McCone	25.6	14 758	3	D	D	D	10	73	24.8	1.6	1	D	D	D
Madison	434.4	56 479	3	D	D	D	44	225	59.5	4.1	25	D	D	D
Meagher	217.2	114 839	1	D	D	D	13	64	14.3	1.0	2	D	D	D
Mineral	5.2	1 238	2	D	D	D	16	215	49.3	4.1	2	D	D	D
Missoula	85.6	783	151	1 838	1 220.7	81.5	570	7 931	2 044.0	180.0	206	918	130.6	29.7
Musselshell	73.5	16 197	4	14	6.7	0.5	19	186	42.0	3.2	3	D	D	D
Park	193.5	12 373	8	18	6.0	0.6	100	669	205.4	17.6	33	41	5.8	1.1
Petroleum	49.5	100 142	NA	NA	NA	NA	2	D	D	D	1	D	D	D
Phillips	244.2	57 409	4	44	98.9	1.8	26	212	39.2	4.0	3	2	1.0	0.1
Pondera	243.5	39 574	13	133	244.5	7.3	25	227	55.9	4.7	2	D	D	D
Powder River	31.4	18 038	1	D	D	D	12	107	24.6	1.9	2	D	D	D
Powell	138.4	19 695	2	D	D	D	18	181	46.0	5.1	4	7	1.1	0.2
Prairie	72.2	61 213	NA	NA	NA	NA	5	24	6.5	0.3	1	D	D	D
Ravalli	168.9	4 200	42	151	182.9	5.6	166	1 482	330.6	31.3	44	90	8.6	1.7
Richland	259.7	26 649	24	238	470.5	9.8	57	652	215.8	17.1	23	184	54.7	11.7
Roosevelt	86.4	8 289	10	D	D	D	41	530	159.2	11.0	10	23	1.0	0.2
Rosebud	195.7	21 190	1	D	D	D	28	240	56.4	4.4	7	26	8.1	0.7
Sanders	62.2	5 446	9	52	9.6	0.9	53	325	78.0	6.4	10	20	1.2	0.2
Sheridan	20.2	5 954	5	D	D	D	27	193	61.1	4.0	1	D	D	D
Silver Bow	40.7	1 191	37	348	189.3	14.3	172	2 203	610.1	51.7	47	137	15.1	3.2
Stillwater	87.0	9 540	5	14	74.9	0.9	33	243	103.2	4.7	4	8	1.0	0.1
Sweet Grass	154.1	42 205	4	22	2.9	0.5	21	139	39.5	2.8	6	9	1.4	0.2
Teton	427.0	70 308	11	48	114.0	1.8	27	190	69.7	4.9	5	D	D	D
Toole	8.6	1 619	9	50	222.3	3.0	24	221	83.5	5.2	8	15	1.6	0.2
Treasure	90.1	125 501	1	D	D	D	3	D	D	D	NA	NA	NA	NA
Valley	191.6	25 999	14	203	248.0	9.6	47	366	158.7	8.7	6	17	1.6	0.5
Wheatland	126.9	58 552	1	D	D	D	9	71	16.7	1.2	NA	NA	NA	NA
Wibaux	3.5	3 412	NA	NA	NA	NA	4	22	6.3	0.4	NA	NA	NA	NA
Yellowstone	437.5	2 956	306	4 690	3 193.3	231.3	734	10 298	3 272.2	277.7	271	914	164.3	30.2
NEBRASKA	8 036.3	4 400	2 720	34 409	42 619.0	1 675.4	7 279	105 953	30 470.7	2 440.4	2 001	10 068	1 732.0	388.5
Adams	128.1	4 083	63	703	949.4	32.0	144	1 876	453.3	42.7	60	131	24.2	2.9
Antelope	83.1	12 432	22	225	535.0	9.7	37	275	70.2	4.7	4	2	0.5	0.1
Arthur	5.5	11 935	NA	NA	NA	NA	2	D	D	D	NA	NA	NA	NA
Banner	17.5	25 333	NA	NA	NA	NA	NA	NA	NA	NA	NA	NA	NA	NA

1. Merchant wholesalers, except manufacturers' sales branches and offices.   2. Employer establishments.

STATE County	Professional, scientific, and technical services, 2012				Manufacturing, 2012				Accommodation and food services, 2012			
	Number of establish-ments	Number of employees	Receipts (mil dol)	Annual payroll (mil dol)	Number of establish-ments	Number of employees	Receipts (mil dol)	Annual payroll (mil dol)	Number of establish-ments	Number of employees	Sales (mil dol)	Annual payroll (mil dol)
	147	148	149	150	151	152	153	154	155	156	157	158
MISSOURI—Cont'd												
St. Louis city	1 009	17 461	3 015.1	1 200.0	484	17 422	10 737.0	975.2	1 036	22 069	1 255.7	371.4
MONTANA	3 545	16 660	2 191.9	798.8	1 237	15 729	11 535.2	714.5	3 458	46 251	2 420.5	649.5
Beaverhead	25	72	5.3	1.5	13	37	6.8	1.2	48	425	18.3	5.0
Big Horn	15	39	3.0	1.2	3	15	D	D	27	234	17.2	3.5
Blaine	13	26	4.8	1.6	5	13	3.4	0.5	12	56	2.6	0.6
Broadwater	9	28	2.5	0.7	6	159	D	6.8	21	118	5.4	1.4
Carbon	28	D	D	D	10	D	D	D	51	490	24.8	7.4
Carter	5	9	0.6	0.1	NA	NA	NA	NA	2	D	D	D
Cascade	202	1 159	131.8	50.3	62	964	955.3	45.0	240	3 887	194.7	51.5
Chouteau	9	27	2.2	0.6	7	17	5.9	0.7	18	D	D	D
Custer	28	99	7.9	3.1	13	79	D	2.2	39	543	28.5	6.8
Daniels	3	D	D	D	NA	NA	NA	NA	9	D	D	D
Dawson	24	71	6.5	2.3	4	37	D	1.6	34	502	25.7	6.4
Deer Lodge	26	112	15.6	4.9	4	87	D	D	30	275	10.9	2.6
Fallon	9	16	2.3	0.5	3	9	D	D	18	104	6.9	1.4
Fergus	34	82	7.8	2.0	26	273	60.6	11.9	47	413	18.5	4.9
Flathead	375	1 347	184.6	56.1	182	2 367	620.8	105.3	363	4 362	247.9	67.7
Gallatin	655	2 415	298.0	113.5	188	2 363	491.0	99.5	410	7 193	348.1	96.5
Garfield	NA	NA	NA	NA	NA	NA	NA	NA	5	28	1.1	0.2
Glacier	11	64	6.8	1.8	4	20	2.3	0.5	51	335	38.3	8.7
Golden Valley	1	D	D	D	NA	NA	NA	NA	4	13	0.5	0.1
Granite	5	3	0.7	0.2	5	15	2.2	0.5	16	101	8.3	2.9
Hill	30	206	20.6	10.4	7	18	2.9	0.7	56	758	35.0	9.2
Jefferson	25	36	5.2	1.7	12	234	D	14.6	21	191	7.1	2.1
Judith Basin	4	11	2.1	0.3	NA	NA	NA	NA	10	27	1.4	0.3
Lake	52	352	71.8	20.2	35	497	72.4	15.4	76	630	33.5	8.6
Lewis and Clark	250	1 661	209.8	84.0	58	525	D	22.1	198	3 083	142.0	39.6
Liberty	4	10	0.6	0.2	NA	NA	NA	NA	5	32	0.7	0.2
Lincoln	35	84	8.2	2.5	24	137	16.8	4.0	64	488	26.4	7.3
McCone	1	D	D	D	NA	NA	NA	NA	5	18	0.6	0.1
Madison	28	60	5.5	1.9	11	69	D	1.8	55	220	15.8	4.0
Meagher	3	3	0.2	0.1	NA	NA	NA	NA	15	52	2.2	0.5
Mineral	6	37	2.7	1.1	7	200	D	7.6	19	120	4.8	1.4
Missoula	501	2 865	325.4	137.2	102	1 351	310.6	49.1	342	6 106	317.4	84.0
Musselshell	8	15	1.5	0.5	3	6	1.7	0.3	13	D	D	D
Park	74	181	23.7	7.6	29	338	58.9	14.1	118	1 130	75.2	22.3
Petroleum	1	D	D	D	NA	NA	NA	NA	2	D	D	D
Phillips	9	28	2.4	0.7	5	13	1.9	0.5	16	109	4.7	1.2
Pondera	10	36	3.0	1.2	8	89	D	3.1	16	141	4.8	1.2
Powder River	4	D	D	D	NA	NA	NA	NA	12	57	2.9	0.6
Powell	9	32	3.3	0.9	8	185	D	D	22	D	D	D
Prairie	4	5	0.8	0.3	NA	NA	NA	NA	6	19	0.6	0.1
Ravalli	122	514	27.3	25.5	84	703	132.4	25.7	96	841	38.4	11.6
Richland	40	228	46.6	13.6	12	371	D	14.6	44	569	38.4	8.9
Roosevelt	11	21	2.0	0.8	NA	NA	NA	NA	24	256	13.7	3.1
Rosebud	5	15	1.4	0.3	3	7	D	D	33	247	10.8	2.6
Sanders	24	35	3.5	0.9	20	185	37.6	6.4	39	320	12.5	3.6
Sheridan	11	28	3.3	1.1	NA	NA	NA	NA	15	137	6.9	1.7
Silver Bow	107	654	73.9	30.8	35	492	D	31.5	147	2 244	102.4	28.7
Stillwater	24	55	6.0	1.7	11	441	D	25.6	25	174	11.0	2.6
Sweet Grass	12	28	4.4	1.0	10	53	D	2.0	16	140	6.4	2.0
Teton	10	36	3.7	1.0	7	15	3.0	0.5	19	107	5.2	1.2
Toole	12	36	5.0	1.5	4	30	7.0	1.3	27	202	12.0	2.7
Treasure	2	D	D	D	NA	NA	NA	NA	4	13	0.4	0.1
Valley	19	75	6.5	2.5	6	39	D	1.0	34	367	16.4	4.4
Wheatland	3	7	1.4	0.2	NA	NA	NA	NA	11	54	3.5	0.6
Wibaux	4	8	0.8	0.4	NA	NA	NA	NA	4	37	1.5	0.5
Yellowstone	604	3 578	618.7	198.5	183	3 185	6 880.3	185.8	404	7 935	452.2	121.3
NEBRASKA	4 448	74 514	5 726.7	3 639.3	1 844	92 409	57 499.2	4 002.8	4 326	70 128	3 094.5	855.4
Adams	62	306	31.4	12.2	57	2 448	1 858.9	101.8	81	1 354	53.0	13.7
Antelope	12	29	4.6	1.1	9	85	D	4.1	15	D	D	D
Arthur	1	D	D	D	NA	NA	NA	NA	1	D	D	D
Banner	NA	NA	NA	NA	NA	NA	NA	NA	NA	NA	NA	NA

1. Establishment subject to federal tax.

STATE County	Health care and social assistance, 2012				Other services, 2012				Nonemployer businesses, 2014		Value of residential construction authorized by building permits, 2015	
	Number of establishments	Number of employees	Receipts (mil dol)	Annual payroll (mil dol)	Number of establishments	Number of employees	Receipts (mil dol)	Annual payroll (mil dol)	Number	Receipts (mil dol)	New Construction ($1,000)	Number of housing units
	159	160	161	162	163	164	165	166	167	168	169	170
MISSOURI—Cont'd												
St. Louis city	1 219	35 572	4 162.1	1 389.0	629	4 529	647.7	151.1	21 249	808.5	87 445	548
MONTANA	3 512	65 657	6 469.5	2 555.4	2 278	10 917	1 222.0	302.8	86 186	3 852.5	827 389	4 826
Beaverhead	40	487	41.1	19.0	21	58	4.0	1.0	863	35.2	391	3
Big Horn	21	D	D	D	9	22	2.3	0.6	491	17.3	0	0
Blaine	15	366	31.1	12.7	10	D	D	D	303	8.1	0	0
Broadwater	7	106	7.0	3.0	9	D	D	D	480	23.3	0	0
Carbon	32	D	D	D	20	D	D	D	1 131	47.6	812	4
Carter	2	D	D	D	2	D	D	D	105	5.4	90	1
Cascade	262	6 363	711.9	269.1	155	871	76.6	21.7	4 743	203.2	50 884	226
Chouteau	11	130	9.5	4.9	6	9	0.3	0.1	354	15.5	2 334	9
Custer	49	978	67.2	31.3	27	123	14.2	3.2	881	39.0	1 390	4
Daniels	4	D	D	D	5	D	D	D	136	7.4	0	0
Dawson	29	631	45.0	20.7	30	97	9.4	2.3	652	28.3	1 527	7
Deer Lodge	52	1 278	110.6	51.7	12	45	5.0	1.3	465	17.9	1 520	15
Fallon	5	D	D	D	9	21	3.6	0.7	333	15.0	2 976	28
Fergus	47	855	52.9	25.3	32	122	11.1	2.1	1 031	43.3	0	0
Flathead	339	5 537	572.5	232.6	227	937	87.1	22.7	10 102	479.0	57 499	281
Gallatin	385	4 387	437.5	173.1	269	1 314	155.9	40.3	11 579	544.1	300 899	1 496
Garfield	1	D	D	D	2	D	D	D	132	5.3	150	1
Glacier	18	962	55.3	22.5	17	85	28.6	2.7	732	27.4	0	0
Golden Valley	2	D	D	D	1	D	D	D	84	4.6	NA	NA
Granite	4	D	D	D	3	6	0.3	0.1	294	12.9	NA	NA
Hill	58	1 374	102.1	44.4	37	173	18.3	3.9	936	30.1	4 123	32
Jefferson	22	225	13.9	5.3	10	34	4.1	1.3	990	41.1	583	2
Judith Basin	3	6	0.1	0.0	1	D	D	D	184	7.5	NA	NA
Lake	77	1 182	98.1	43.7	50	141	11.0	2.9	2 346	89.7	2 261	27
Lewis and Clark	271	5 376	610.0	219.5	200	1 156	126.8	41.6	5 337	238.5	30 343	171
Liberty	3	D	D	D	3	D	D	D	150	5.7	NA	NA
Lincoln	56	866	60.1	27.3	36	114	10.5	2.5	1 578	60.7	79	1
McCone	3	D	D	D	2	D	D	D	184	6.6	0	0
Madison	19	141	12.3	5.2	15	D	D	D	1 035	44.5	1 250	5
Meagher	7	D	D	D	2	D	D	D	175	7.0	NA	NA
Mineral	13	145	8.7	4.9	7	4	1.4	0.3	329	11.2	0	0
Missoula	489	9 292	965.9	351.1	287	1 889	258.2	56.0	9 678	444.9	47 913	574
Musselshell	9	178	11.1	3.8	8	17	1.7	0.3	367	14.5	138	1
Park	55	850	60.0	27.7	49	181	16.3	4.8	2 124	84.5	5 826	36
Petroleum	1	D	D	D	1	D	D	D	40	1.7	NA	NA
Phillips	9	184	9.5	4.8	13	37	3.9	0.9	381	15.4	364	2
Pondera	18	317	20.9	9.1	12	28	3.1	0.5	433	15.2	0	0
Powder River	1	D	D	D	7	D	D	D	178	6.3	NA	NA
Powell	16	184	14.7	5.6	5	18	1.9	0.5	477	20.7	6 681	25
Prairie	3	D	D	D	2	D	D	D	76	3.0	NA	NA
Ravalli	133	1 459	103.3	46.0	81	246	22.3	5.2	4 297	179.2	2 318	17
Richland	32	676	59.1	21.2	30	117	12.6	3.4	966	51.4	1 778	9
Roosevelt	12	D	D	D	11	58	3.1	0.6	541	20.6	300	1
Rosebud	17	300	13.0	6.1	14	77	5.3	1.9	495	12.5	230	1
Sanders	39	407	28.1	12.0	14	60	5.4	1.2	1 028	40.4	41	1
Sheridan	12	366	18.0	7.9	9	20	3.2	0.6	351	19.6	292	1
Silver Bow	159	3 303	287.5	127.1	72	289	34.1	7.2	2 189	90.9	5 009	72
Stillwater	24	259	14.5	5.4	10	18	3.0	0.5	827	35.7	0	0
Sweet Grass	6	24	1.1	0.3	10	28	2.1	0.5	426	18.7	150	1
Teton	18	238	11.8	5.6	11	14	2.8	0.6	565	25.0	181	1
Toole	12	D	D	D	11	25	2.2	0.4	336	14.0	320	2
Treasure	1	D	D	D	1	D	D	D	60	2.0	0	0
Valley	24	603	43.1	19.5	20	63	6.9	1.5	527	17.6	590	3
Wheatland	4	D	D	D	3	5	0.3	0.1	149	6.7	NA	NA
Wibaux	3	D	D	D	NA	NA	NA	NA	89	2.9	824	6
Yellowstone	558	12 676	1 527.6	583.0	368	2 134	234.8	58.7	11 451	586.7	295 323	1 760
NEBRASKA	5 410	125 469	12 869.4	4 907.3	3 989	21 832	2 841.3	612.5	129 519	5 597.1	1 317 315	8 096
Adams	116	2 495	247.7	103.7	55	307	33.0	6.8	2 135	89.4	13 575	68
Antelope	15	305	22.9	8.8	20	40	4.5	0.8	632	27.0	1 741	8
Arthur	NA	NA	NA	NA	2	D	D	D	47	2.9	NA	NA
Banner	NA	NA	NA	NA	1	D	D	D	47	1.7	NA	NA

Table B. States and Counties — Government Employment and Payroll, and Local Government Finances

STATE County	Government employment and payroll, 2012									Local government finances, 2012				
			March payroll (percent of total)							General revenue				
												Taxes		
													Per capita[1] (dollars)	
	Full-time equivalent employees	March payroll (dollars)	Administration, judicial, and legal	Police and Corrections	Fire Protection	Highways and transportation	Health and Welfare	Natural resources and utilities	Education and libraries	Total (mil dol)	Inter-governmental (mil dol)	Total (mil dol)	Total	Property
	171	172	173	174	175	176	177	178	179	180	181	182	183	184
MISSOURI—Cont'd														
St. Louis city	15 033	62 103 817	5.6	17.2	5.7	20.6	1.5	12.9	34.1	2 385.3	762.8	924.8	2 907	1 228
MONTANA	X	X	X	X	X	X	X	X	X	X	X	X	X	X
Beaverhead	518	1 862 160	5.1	4.6	0.4	2.9	54.8	1.7	29.5	66.4	12.9	10.3	1 104	1 099
Big Horn	748	2 839 698	3.5	4.0	0.0	3.4	4.1	1.1	82.8	62.2	38.7	13.7	1 049	1 040
Blaine	358	1 163 514	11.3	3.8	0.0	6.0	0.6	3.7	73.6	31.5	20.8	7.2	1 083	1 053
Broadwater	160	477 725	12.8	12.5	0.0	5.0	4.9	1.1	62.3	14.4	6.3	5.4	935	924
Carbon	377	1 229 196	11.7	8.3	1.5	6.6	1.7	4.4	62.9	33.2	13.2	15.7	1 547	1 457
Carter	67	178 052	5.5	6.2	0.0	11.1	1.6	2.3	58.2	7.1	3.5	2.6	2 229	2 201
Cascade	2 704	9 771 107	6.8	13.0	3.8	5.6	3.7	6.9	59.0	238.3	103.2	77.2	944	913
Chouteau	318	956 267	6.0	6.6	0.0	4.7	29.2	2.6	49.0	26.4	10.3	9.2	1 565	1 560
Custer	539	1 661 688	7.8	7.4	3.4	4.8	3.2	3.6	68.6	42.2	19.5	9.9	832	817
Daniels	99	271 126	13.7	7.5	0.1	5.3	5.9	3.5	61.2	10.7	3.8	5.1	2 865	1 845
Dawson	486	1 501 541	7.2	15.3	1.5	5.5	7.5	3.6	57.4	42.3	16.8	12.8	1 387	1 374
Deer Lodge	264	898 579	8.3	14.8	4.3	3.9	1.1	6.9	59.7	28.1	15.5	7.9	855	847
Fallon	190	709 670	11.6	5.6	3.4	9.5	5.9	6.1	55.5	33.9	25.4	5.0	1 645	1 614
Fergus	520	1 621 405	6.8	8.4	2.1	15.7	1.2	2.9	61.6	43.5	22.6	14.7	1 286	1 268
Flathead	2 820	10 913 778	6.6	7.4	3.2	3.5	3.5	3.7	70.8	292.8	116.8	111.5	1 216	1 179
Gallatin	2 434	9 405 208	8.1	11.0	3.8	2.9	5.0	5.6	60.7	253.4	77.2	121.2	1 309	1 215
Garfield	115	230 472	8.7	3.3	2.9	6.0	24.2	7.0	41.9	7.0	2.6	2.3	1 862	1 861
Glacier	700	2 311 773	4.2	4.6	0.0	3.2	3.2	2.5	81.1	52.7	34.1	13.8	1 008	1 004
Golden Valley	58	147 171	10.6	3.5	0.0	4.0	0.0	0.3	80.9	4.9	2.7	1.9	2 302	2 299
Granite	179	573 451	9.2	4.8	0.0	3.8	33.5	2.9	44.5	15.4	5.5	4.2	1 364	1 358
Hill	793	2 599 436	4.3	6.6	2.9	3.9	3.3	3.7	74.5	62.6	35.3	17.8	1 085	1 070
Jefferson	303	957 909	14.8	9.2	0.0	4.0	5.0	1.6	64.0	29.3	15.5	10.6	927	924
Judith Basin	121	355 407	6.9	3.6	0.0	13.7	0.1	1.1	72.7	9.7	4.7	3.9	1 915	1 915
Lake	962	3 993 744	4.2	5.9	0.2	1.6	3.5	2.9	80.7	85.3	44.4	27.2	940	933
Lewis and Clark	1 872	7 755 463	7.5	9.0	2.6	3.9	8.6	5.4	59.9	213.1	82.3	69.8	1 076	1 054
Liberty	111	316 696	12.4	8.7	0.0	7.1	6.6	4.8	58.9	8.2	3.8	3.3	1 372	1 372
Lincoln	599	1 992 630	12.4	7.4	0.5	3.8	2.7	4.3	65.2	57.6	31.7	14.9	766	754
McCone	168	326 681	15.1	4.8	0.1	1.2	1.9	4.1	42.3	8.6	3.2	4.3	2 540	2 486
Madison	459	1 488 288	7.5	4.1	0.2	3.8	40.5	2.0	39.5	41.8	10.9	17.1	2 205	2 194
Meagher	122	326 266	10.3	7.3	0.0	3.7	0.0	4.5	46.8	8.8	3.1	3.4	1 746	1 742
Mineral	297	957 709	7.9	6.9	0.3	1.9	33.5	1.3	47.5	23.2	8.6	6.0	1 442	1 403
Missoula	3 035	11 623 602	8.8	11.6	6.2	6.3	5.7	3.6	55.2	333.0	140.7	131.9	1 189	1 156
Musselshell	259	845 308	4.5	3.3	0.0	3.2	25.2	1.6	61.7	22.2	9.1	7.4	1 596	1 532
Park	528	1 727 963	10.9	8.8	4.3	3.9	4.6	4.7	62.0	50.7	22.2	18.0	1 154	1 123
Petroleum	36	121 984	11.4	0.0	0.0	5.5	0.0	6.6	74.9	4.7	3.4	0.9	1 705	1 703
Phillips	229	653 111	10.8	5.9	0.1	6.4	3.3	8.6	61.5	21.3	11.3	6.4	1 542	1 503
Pondera	212	607 909	10.4	10.1	0.2	5.9	1.8	7.3	62.5	34.1	12.3	7.0	1 132	1 127
Powder River	137	334 388	14.5	7.2	0.0	8.8	27.7	1.7	37.3	12.1	5.0	3.7	2 074	1 968
Powell	199	625 409	10.4	7.0	0.5	5.1	2.6	2.8	69.0	21.5	10.6	6.4	906	902
Prairie	95	225 508	8.2	3.7	0.0	5.1	32.5	1.7	42.7	7.5	2.4	1.9	1 617	1 608
Ravalli	1 130	3 297 468	9.0	9.9	0.2	2.5	1.0	3.9	72.3	96.2	49.5	36.0	885	874
Richland	560	1 708 186	7.9	8.6	0.2	7.8	4.4	8.1	58.4	72.7	47.2	9.4	866	853
Roosevelt	704	2 186 188	5.4	5.6	0.2	3.3	10.8	2.9	70.0	63.5	42.5	12.7	1 161	1 154
Rosebud	641	1 932 124	5.8	8.0	0.0	6.1	4.9	5.7	68.6	65.9	31.0	16.0	1 705	1 689
Sanders	390	1 112 745	8.1	9.8	0.3	5.2	3.6	1.9	69.3	33.6	16.5	12.8	1 123	1 122
Sheridan	333	1 098 598	7.7	3.6	1.6	5.2	44.9	1.5	34.4	19.8	10.2	5.6	1 551	1 542
Silver Bow	995	3 780 881	7.3	11.3	8.8	7.4	1.2	11.1	51.5	120.3	54.8	39.2	1 139	1 112
Stillwater	340	1 123 218	10.5	6.8	1.0	7.0	2.4	1.8	70.1	29.0	12.6	12.5	1 360	1 350
Sweet Grass	197	563 456	9.7	3.8	0.0	3.5	28.6	2.5	49.1	22.0	6.9	6.1	1 698	1 696
Teton	434	1 416 652	5.6	3.0	0.1	2.9	31.7	6.4	49.4	34.6	11.1	9.4	1 552	1 512
Toole	386	1 266 882	7.5	5.0	0.0	3.8	44.2	2.8	34.4	36.1	9.0	7.8	1 492	1 473
Treasure	44	114 460	17.8	4.4	0.0	4.5	6.2	7.2	53.1	3.7	1.5	1.7	2 261	2 258
Valley	402	1 205 227	6.6	9.6	0.0	6.9	3.9	4.9	66.3	36.1	17.0	11.6	1 551	1 486
Wheatland	160	440 257	19.4	6.3	0.0	12.1	3.4	4.6	49.3	9.4	4.2	4.2	1 974	1 965
Wibaux	61	199 748	22.1	5.7	0.0	16.7	2.2	0.8	52.4	6.8	4.9	1.2	1 174	1 124
Yellowstone	4 840	19 590 185	5.0	8.6	4.7	4.9	8.9	6.0	55.1	469.5	175.3	161.7	1 065	989
NEBRASKA	X	X	X	X	X	X	X	X	X	X	X	X	X	X
Adams	2 340	8 844 524	2.4	3.7	1.5	2.0	0.5	13.9	70.2	174.2	49.6	89.6	2 849	2 506
Antelope	558	1 836 977	2.9	2.2	0.0	3.6	29.5	1.6	60.0	30.0	8.2	17.8	2 718	2 366
Arthur	35	130 066	6.4	2.0	0.0	4.7	0.0	27.0	59.3	5.8	0.9	4.6	9 488	9 335
Banner	61	179 960	9.3	1.7	0.0	7.8	0.0	0.0	79.6	4.4	1.3	2.8	3 726	3 499

1. Based on the resident population estimated as of July 1 of the year shown.

Items 171—184

Table B. States and Counties — Local Government Finances, Government Employment, and Voting

STATE County	Total (mil dol)	Per capita[1] (dollars)	Education	Health and hospitals	Police protection	Public welfare	Highways	Total (mil dol)	Per capita[1] (dollars)	Federal civilian	Federal military	State and local	Demo-cratic	Republican	All other
	185	186	187	188	189	190	191	192	193	194	195	196	197	198	199
MISSOURI—Cont'd															
St. Louis city	2 326.2	7 311	33.4	1.7	10.8	0.0	1.1	3 993.6	12 552	13 820	1 585	21 248	83.7	15.5	0.8
MONTANA	X	X	X	X	X	X	X	X	X	12 998	8 104	74 061	47.3	49.5	3.2
Beaverhead	83.3	8 915	24.9	55.9	2.2	0.0	3.8	91.0	9 739	185	43	822	33.9	63.2	2.9
Big Horn	70.6	5 404	65.3	1.6	3.9	0.0	4.8	34.0	2 603	381	64	1 906	67.4	31.2	1.4
Blaine	33.0	4 932	63.3	2.3	5.1	0.0	8.2	3.4	513	184	31	495	58.2	39.0	2.8
Broadwater	14.1	2 447	49.7	2.6	9.1	0.2	5.3	4.7	809	43	27	194	31.8	65.8	2.4
Carbon	34.2	3 380	55.4	0.7	7.0	0.2	11.0	23.7	2 339	87	50	486	42.5	54.1	3.4
Carter	7.6	6 469	34.7	9.5	5.5	0.1	25.5	0.4	371	12	0	99	15.5	80.1	4.3
Cascade	242.5	2 968	53.0	1.0	9.7	1.4	5.2	90.0	1 101	1 627	3 544	4 052	49.9	47.6	2.4
Chouteau	26.7	4 530	44.1	21.5	3.3	0.0	8.4	4.1	697	33	28	431	39.2	57.1	3.7
Custer	40.6	3 415	62.2	2.4	7.6	0.1	8.1	9.5	801	184	57	893	41.6	55.9	2.5
Daniels	9.9	5 552	39.1	7.1	5.2	0.0	8.9	3.2	1 792	17	0	109	32.0	64.7	3.4
Dawson	38.5	4 159	54.9	3.1	5.4	1.0	7.1	8.2	884	31	44	730	35.9	59.5	4.5
Deer Lodge	30.1	3 259	41.6	2.0	6.6	2.8	4.8	4.9	531	82	40	872	67.0	29.6	3.4
Fallon	38.0	12 574	45.8	4.0	2.8	0.0	17.5	0.2	57	12	15	268	22.2	74.3	3.5
Fergus	44.0	3 847	53.6	2.3	4.8	0.0	11.5	9.5	831	142	54	878	31.0	65.9	3.1
Flathead	299.8	3 272	56.2	3.9	5.8	1.2	5.0	178.9	1 952	735	459	4 146	36.9	58.5	4.6
Gallatin	262.4	2 834	48.1	1.3	10.1	4.2	4.1	247.8	2 676	602	471	8 870	50.3	46.9	2.8
Garfield	7.3	5 772	36.8	2.4	2.5	23.3	14.2	0.6	450	23	0	116	15.1	82.3	2.6
Glacier	51.7	3 768	77.0	2.8	4.0	0.1	4.7	22.4	1 630	430	63	1 868	68.9	29.2	1.9
Golden Valley	4.5	5 323	65.4	0.9	4.3	0.5	4.7	0.0	5	0	0	70	25.3	69.9	4.9
Granite	15.6	5 012	35.1	0.6	6.3	26.8	7.6	2.0	654	35	15	198	35.0	59.1	5.9
Hill	62.8	3 840	76.1	0.8	4.8	0.0	3.2	16.7	1 020	158	78	1 969	54.3	42.1	3.6
Jefferson	31.9	2 799	57.0	3.8	8.3	0.0	5.0	4.6	400	40	55	704	40.7	55.8	3.5
Judith Basin	9.6	4 741	53.8	0.9	3.4	0.0	18.1	3.4	1 658	31	10	140	32.1	64.8	3.1
Lake	86.4	2 980	61.8	0.9	5.2	0.3	4.0	23.2	799	97	139	2 812	48.6	46.7	4.7
Lewis and Clark	212.2	3 270	47.9	4.1	8.6	3.1	5.3	156.7	2 415	1 993	322	9 049	52.1	45.5	2.4
Liberty	7.9	3 293	47.0	5.3	10.3	0.0	12.1	1.8	772	19	10	122	36.7	59.3	4.0
Lincoln	58.1	2 979	51.4	6.8	7.7	0.1	7.8	18.2	932	424	92	698	32.8	61.8	5.4
McCone	8.6	5 082	52.1	3.7	4.1	0.8	13.0	2.4	1 422	18	0	142	29.4	66.5	4.0
Madison	42.1	5 447	35.2	13.7	4.0	18.5	7.6	7.0	907	64	37	463	35.2	61.8	3.0
Meagher	10.9	5 666	29.5	3.3	0.7	0.0	6.7	0.3	179	24	0	103	30.8	64.6	4.6
Mineral	24.9	5 975	42.3	33.5	3.9	0.0	3.9	5.6	1 346	56	21	239	42.4	52.8	4.9
Missoula	338.7	3 052	44.0	5.5	7.0	0.8	5.2	188.8	1 701	1 315	537	9 376	61.8	35.1	3.0
Musselshell	23.0	4 926	37.1	29.7	2.1	0.0	4.3	1.8	390	14	22	247	27.6	68.6	3.9
Park	60.3	3 873	58.7	2.2	5.8	0.5	3.5	26.2	1 681	70	77	623	46.9	49.2	3.9
Petroleum	4.6	8 926	53.5	1.5	1.5	0.0	8.0	0.4	812	0	0	51	22.7	75.7	1.7
Phillips	22.5	5 449	53.5	1.7	4.2	0.0	11.5	7.9	1 903	77	20	303	30.1	67.0	2.9
Pondera	34.1	5 531	42.2	35.4	3.5	1.5	3.2	14.5	2 348	30	27	326	42.4	55.0	2.6
Powder River	12.1	6 877	33.4	1.6	5.0	22.2	16.5	0.1	69	10	0	182	20.0	77.3	2.7
Powell	23.3	3 289	58.1	0.9	6.4	0.4	8.2	1.7	234	79	26	1 023	36.3	59.8	3.9
Prairie	7.4	6 390	28.9	2.4	3.9	29.4	8.6	2.0	1 732	36	0	126	28.7	68.4	2.9
Ravalli	99.9	2 460	64.0	1.1	7.3	0.5	5.0	31.4	773	509	198	1 362	38.0	58.9	3.1
Richland	76.0	7 032	41.5	1.4	4.3	0.9	22.5	6.1	568	76	56	692	26.6	70.5	2.9
Roosevelt	58.9	5 389	63.9	10.7	5.5	0.5	4.5	9.1	836	164	54	1 521	61.8	35.5	2.7
Rosebud	68.3	7 269	51.2	7.9	4.8	0.3	4.7	257.2	27 372	241	45	1 424	50.4	46.4	3.2
Sanders	36.1	3 162	60.5	4.1	6.1	0.0	8.2	4.9	428	133	54	492	33.7	60.9	5.4
Sheridan	21.8	6 087	50.6	2.2	6.1	1.6	16.8	1.9	517	72	18	262	47.5	49.2	3.3
Silver Bow	113.4	3 297	39.5	4.4	5.9	0.1	4.1	60.4	1 757	235	200	2 378	68.8	28.4	2.8
Stillwater	30.5	3 315	64.5	0.6	4.5	0.1	6.8	2.6	287	37	45	421	32.4	64.1	3.5
Sweet Grass	22.6	6 259	30.6	0.8	5.2	32.8	6.0	1.4	398	28	18	308	26.0	71.7	2.3
Teton	35.3	5 826	43.7	23.0	0.8	4.8	5.1	8.3	1 372	55	27	426	39.5	57.3	3.2
Toole	36.4	6 970	29.7	40.6	6.4	0.0	6.6	14.4	2 766	162	21	485	34.7	62.1	3.2
Treasure	3.8	5 182	44.6	5.5	3.4	0.1	10.4	0.5	679	0	0	54	32.1	64.6	3.3
Valley	35.4	4 717	51.9	2.2	5.0	0.1	10.3	8.7	1 160	161	37	613	42.1	54.2	3.7
Wheatland	8.9	4 252	54.8	5.6	6.4	0.1	6.6	3.2	1 505	20	10	128	29.5	67.0	3.6
Wibaux	6.5	6 114	36.4	10.7	5.5	0.0	16.1	1.2	1 157	0	0	108	26.0	67.6	6.4
Yellowstone	506.3	3 333	47.8	7.1	5.8	0.2	6.1	224.5	1 478	1 683	778	7 186	45.5	51.8	2.7
NEBRASKA	X	X	X	X	X	X	X	X	X	16 693	12 624	144 987	41.6	56.5	1.9
Adams	180.4	5 735	72.7	0.4	3.1	0.2	6.2	136.0	4 322	110	111	2 248	35.5	62.5	2.1
Antelope	34.5	5 275	71.6	0.0	2.2	0.0	12.9	7.4	1 136	31	23	465	23.8	74.8	1.4
Arthur	4.1	8 356	45.4	0.2	0.8	0.0	11.7	0.0	0	0	0	50	14.8	82.5	2.7
Banner	4.4	5 725	68.1	0.3	1.3	0.0	14.7	0.0	0	0	0	68	14.9	83.7	1.4

1. Based on the resident population estimated as of July 1 of the year shown.   2. © 2013 Election Data Services, Inc. All rights reserved.

STATE/ County code	CBSA code[1]	County type[2]	STATE County	Land area[3] (sq km) 2010	Total persons 2015	Rank	Per square kilometer	White	Black	American Indian, Alaska Native	Asian and Pacific Islander	Percent Hispanic or Latino[4]	Under 5 years	5 to 17 years	18 to 24 years	25 to 34 years	35 to 44 years	45 to 54 years
				1	2	3	4	5	6	7	8	9	10	11	12	13	14	15
			NEBRASKA—Cont'd															
31 009	...	9	Blaine	1 841	487	3 135	0.3	99.8	0.6	0.4	0.4	0.2	8.3	15.1	7.5	7.9	9.3	15.7
31 011	...	9	Boone	1 778	5 315	2 811	3.0	97.4	0.5	0.5	0.4	1.7	5.6	17.4	7.7	9.6	9.2	13.4
31 013	...	7	Box Butte	2 785	11 337	2 335	4.1	84.3	1.1	3.5	0.9	11.9	7.1	18.2	7.5	11.6	11.5	11.6
31 015	...	9	Boyd	1 398	2 006	3 048	1.4	96.5	0.2	1.2	1.0	2.0	4.6	16.4	6.1	7.2	8.8	12.0
31 017	...	9	Brown	3 163	2 946	2 981	0.9	97.9	0.6	1.0	0.4	1.2	4.7	15.4	7.0	8.6	9.8	13.4
31 019	28260	5	Buffalo	2 507	48 863	1 001	19.5	88.3	1.5	0.6	1.9	8.5	7.0	16.4	16.0	13.9	11.3	11.0
31 021	...	8	Burt	1 273	6 585	2 708	5.2	94.5	0.9	2.1	0.6	2.7	5.4	17.0	6.5	9.0	9.6	13.0
31 023	...	6	Butler	1 515	8 115	2 593	5.4	96.2	0.6	0.7	0.6	2.8	5.8	17.8	7.1	9.6	10.5	14.1
31 025	36540	2	Cass	1 444	25 512	1 585	17.7	95.6	0.9	0.9	0.9	3.1	6.0	18.6	7.2	10.1	12.2	15.0
31 027	...	9	Cedar	1 917	8 564	2 550	4.5	97.8	0.3	0.6	0.4	1.5	5.3	19.2	7.7	8.9	9.3	13.3
31 029	...	9	Chase	2 317	3 956	2 904	1.7	87.0	0.4	0.4	0.3	12.6	5.7	18.3	6.7	10.3	10.9	12.4
31 031	...	7	Cherry	15 437	5 848	2 769	0.4	91.8	0.8	6.4	1.0	2.8	5.4	16.4	7.1	10.1	11.1	12.7
31 033	...	7	Cheyenne	3 098	10 167	2 421	3.3	91.0	0.7	1.0	1.9	6.6	6.2	17.9	7.3	13.2	12.1	13.6
31 035	...	9	Clay	1 482	6 309	2 734	4.3	89.7	0.8	0.7	0.6	8.9	6.3	18.0	7.4	10.2	10.6	13.3
31 037	...	7	Colfax	1 066	10 520	2 394	9.9	54.2	1.9	0.6	0.7	42.9	8.2	21.4	8.5	12.7	11.6	12.8
31 039	...	7	Cuming	1 478	9 125	2 503	6.2	89.7	0.7	0.5	0.5	9.6	5.5	18.9	7.3	10.1	9.5	13.7
31 041	...	7	Custer	6 671	10 806	2 372	1.6	96.1	0.9	0.8	0.5	2.6	6.1	17.2	7.2	10.1	10.6	13.1
31 043	43580	3	Dakota	684	20 781	1 791	30.4	53.2	4.4	2.8	3.8	37.6	8.0	21.0	9.8	12.9	11.7	12.6
31 045	...	7	Dawes	3 617	9 055	2 508	2.5	87.7	2.5	4.7	2.8	4.3	5.1	13.3	21.8	10.3	8.7	10.9
31 047	30420	7	Dawson	2 624	23 886	1 647	9.1	62.0	4.1	0.7	1.0	33.3	7.5	20.3	8.9	11.9	11.8	12.1
31 049	...	9	Deuel	1 139	1 921	3 056	1.7	93.2	0.7	1.0	0.6	5.5	5.2	15.8	6.2	8.9	10.2	14.1
31 051	43580	3	Dixon	1 233	5 797	2 774	4.7	86.8	0.8	0.7	0.3	12.0	5.8	19.0	7.4	9.5	10.7	12.5
31 053	23340	4	Dodge	1 369	36 706	1 260	26.8	86.7	1.3	0.8	1.0	11.3	6.4	17.2	9.2	11.4	11.3	12.8
31 055	36540	2	Douglas	851	550 064	120	646.4	72.7	12.5	1.1	3.9	11.9	7.6	18.2	9.4	16.1	12.9	12.7
31 057	...	9	Dundy	2 382	1 799	3 069	0.8	92.1	1.1	0.9	0.6	6.5	3.9	17.2	7.3	8.4	11.1	12.2
31 059	...	9	Fillmore	1 490	5 619	2 793	3.8	95.0	0.8	0.7	0.7	3.9	4.9	15.7	7.3	9.9	9.4	14.4
31 061	...	9	Franklin	1 491	2 985	2 973	2.0	98.2	0.4	0.8	0.5	1.9	4.5	14.7	6.8	8.5	9.5	13.5
31 063	...	9	Frontier	2 524	2 624	2 998	1.0	96.7	0.4	0.7	0.4	2.3	3.9	16.6	11.8	9.8	9.5	11.4
31 065	...	9	Furnas	1 863	4 862	2 844	2.6	95.9	0.7	0.7	0.6	3.2	5.1	17.5	6.8	9.1	10.0	12.6
31 067	13100	6	Gage	2 205	21 900	1 736	9.9	96.2	1.0	1.2	0.7	2.1	5.7	16.4	7.3	10.0	10.9	14.4
31 069	...	9	Garden	4 414	1 918	3 058	0.4	94.3	0.9	1.3	0.4	4.5	3.9	13.8	5.8	9.3	9.0	14.3
31 071	...	9	Garfield	1 476	2 028	3 046	1.4	98.6	0.5	0.3	0.2	1.4	3.0	15.9	6.7	8.7	8.6	12.7
31 073	30420	9	Gosper	1 187	1 973	3 051	1.7	95.0	1.2	1.1	0.6	4.1	5.9	17.7	7.0	9.7	9.7	14.0
31 075	...	9	Grant	2 010	641	3 132	0.3	97.9	0.3	0.8	0.3	1.5	7.9	12.6	5.5	12.6	8.1	15.5
31 077	...	9	Greeley	1 476	2 429	3 010	1.6	96.9	0.8	0.6	0.3	2.2	5.2	19.0	5.9	9.3	9.5	12.7
31 079	24260	5	Hall	1 415	61 680	851	43.6	70.3	2.6	0.7	1.6	25.9	7.6	19.1	9.0	13.1	12.5	12.8
31 081	24260	7	Hamilton	1 406	9 190	2 495	6.5	96.5	0.8	0.6	0.3	3.0	5.8	18.8	7.9	10.4	10.9	14.0
31 083	...	9	Harlan	1 433	3 452	2 941	2.4	97.6	0.3	0.7	0.4	2.1	6.8	15.1	6.7	7.9	9.3	13.7
31 085	...	9	Hayes	1 847	932	3 109	0.5	95.3	0.8	0.3	0.3	3.8	4.7	15.1	7.5	10.0	7.4	12.0
31 087	...	9	Hitchcock	1 839	2 883	2 985	1.6	96.1	0.6	1.0	0.4	3.3	5.7	16.0	6.0	10.5	9.7	12.5
31 089	...	7	Holt	6 248	10 313	2 407	1.7	95.3	0.5	0.6	0.4	3.9	7.1	16.9	6.7	9.6	9.5	13.6
31 091	...	9	Hooker	1 868	732	3 125	0.4	96.7	0.0	2.8	0.1	1.4	6.2	14.1	5.2	7.6	10.7	10.2
31 093	24260	9	Howard	1 475	6 409	2 723	4.3	96.6	0.8	0.7	0.4	2.4	5.9	17.9	7.0	10.2	11.5	13.8
31 095	...	7	Jefferson	1 477	7 263	2 648	4.9	96.0	1.0	0.9	0.5	3.3	5.6	16.4	6.2	10.2	10.2	12.6
31 097	...	8	Johnson	974	5 173	2 824	5.3	80.8	6.4	1.3	1.7	10.5	4.8	15.0	7.7	13.7	13.2	14.9
31 099	28260	7	Kearney	1 337	6 585	2 708	4.9	94.4	0.5	0.7	0.6	5.4	6.2	18.2	7.1	10.7	11.5	13.2
31 101	...	7	Keith	2 750	8 063	2 595	2.9	92.1	0.9	1.1	0.7	6.6	4.5	16.1	6.6	9.7	10.3	13.6
31 103	...	9	Keya Paha	2 002	804	3 118	0.4	99.1	0.1	0.6	0.6	0.6	5.8	14.2	5.4	7.5	9.1	13.2
31 105	...	6	Kimball	2 465	3 689	2 926	1.5	89.7	0.7	2.2	1.2	8.4	5.8	16.2	7.2	10.8	9.2	12.7
31 107	...	9	Knox	2 871	8 543	2 554	3.0	87.8	0.6	9.8	0.6	2.6	6.1	18.0	6.6	8.3	9.3	12.7
31 109	30700	2	Lancaster	2 169	306 468	222	141.3	84.7	4.9	1.1	4.8	6.5	6.7	16.4	15.3	14.3	12.1	11.5
31 111	35820	5	Lincoln	6 641	35 656	1 284	5.4	89.7	1.3	0.9	1.2	8.3	6.3	18.1	7.8	11.7	12.2	12.5
31 113	35820	9	Logan	1 478	777	3 120	0.5	95.9	0.5	1.7	0.3	2.1	6.0	18.1	7.1	11.2	10.9	12.1
31 115	...	9	Loup	1 472	585	3 134	0.4	97.3	0.5	0.2	0.0	2.2	4.1	16.2	4.9	8.3	7.7	12.9
31 117	35820	9	McPherson	2 225	475	3 136	0.2	97.4	1.2	0.6	0.0	1.6	3.8	21.5	5.0	8.4	9.4	15.5
31 119	35740	5	Madison	1 483	35 039	1 304	23.6	82.6	2.0	1.4	1.1	14.2	7.3	17.4	10.1	12.8	10.7	12.7
31 121	24260	7	Merrick	1 256	7 787	2 610	6.2	94.0	0.7	1.0	1.4	4.0	5.6	17.7	7.6	10.7	11.0	14.4
31 123	...	9	Morrill	3 688	4 854	2 846	1.3	83.6	0.6	1.4	0.7	15.0	5.4	19.1	7.2	10.4	12.0	12.5
31 125	...	9	Nance	1 144	3 595	2 935	3.1	97.4	0.6	0.7	0.2	2.3	6.2	16.2	6.8	9.9	10.3	13.4
31 127	...	7	Nemaha	1 055	7 046	2 670	6.7	96.0	1.5	0.9	0.8	2.5	6.1	15.1	13.0	12.3	9.0	12.3
31 129	...	9	Nuckolls	1 490	4 329	2 878	2.9	96.9	0.5	0.8	0.4	2.5	4.3	16.4	6.2	9.1	9.5	12.2
31 131	...	6	Otoe	1 594	15 984	2 042	10.0	91.0	1.0	0.8	1.0	6.7	6.1	17.3	7.3	10.5	11.4	13.7
31 133	...	9	Pawnee	1 116	2 659	2 995	2.4	97.7	0.9	0.8	0.8	1.8	5.4	16.7	6.7	8.3	9.1	12.7
31 135	...	9	Perkins	2 288	2 944	2 982	1.3	95.4	0.5	0.3	0.4	3.7	6.6	17.5	6.0	9.9	10.5	12.3
31 137	...	7	Phelps	1 398	9 296	2 488	6.6	93.3	0.8	0.6	0.6	5.3	7.0	16.8	8.1	11.1	10.4	13.4
31 139	35740	9	Pierce	1 485	7 208	2 656	4.9	97.7	0.5	0.5	0.4	1.6	6.1	18.8	7.6	10.6	10.8	14.5

1. CBSA = Core Based Statistical Area. See Appendix A for explanation. See Appendix B for list of metropolitan areas with component counties. 2. County type code from the Economic Research Service of USDA Rural-Urban Continuum Codes. See Appendix A for definition. 3. Dry land or land partially or temporarily covered by water. 4. May be of any race.

Table B. States and Counties — **Population and Households**

STATE County	55 to 64 years (16)	65 to 74 years (17)	75 years and over (18)	Percent female (19)	Total persons 2000 (20)	2010 (21)	Percent change 2000–2010 (22)	2010–2015 (23)	Births (24)	Deaths (25)	Net migration (26)	Number (27)	Persons per household (28)	Family households (29)	Female family householder[1] (30)	One person (31)
NEBRASKA—Cont'd																
Blaine	14.3	11.7	10.1	48.0	583	478	-18.0	1.9	22	22	1	250	2.38	70.0	5.6	21.6
Boone	15.5	9.7	11.9	49.8	6 259	5 505	-12.0	-3.5	321	325	-171	2 236	2.37	68.1	6.8	29.4
Box Butte	16.4	8.5	7.5	49.9	12 158	11 308	-7.0	0.3	803	584	-173	4 807	2.31	65.7	9.2	31.1
Boyd	16.2	15.1	13.7	51.1	2 438	2 099	-13.9	-4.4	89	144	-30	948	2.15	61.0	3.6	36.3
Brown	16.8	11.4	12.9	50.8	3 525	3 143	-10.8	-6.3	146	201	-113	1 509	2.01	68.1	13.1	29.6
Buffalo	11.5	6.9	6.0	50.3	42 259	46 102	9.1	6.0	3 664	1 767	844	18 018	2.50	64.0	8.0	26.4
Burt	15.7	11.0	12.8	50.5	7 791	6 858	-12.0	-4.0	370	511	-134	2 882	2.28	67.3	7.6	29.5
Butler	14.5	10.0	10.6	49.2	8 767	8 395	-4.2	-3.3	492	509	-242	3 556	2.29	67.9	7.8	26.6
Cass	14.8	9.3	6.8	49.6	24 334	25 241	3.7	1.1	1 481	1 224	35	9 754	2.57	71.8	6.8	24.4
Cedar	15.0	9.6	11.7	49.4	9 615	8 852	-7.9	-3.3	545	516	-311	3 528	2.43	67.7	4.3	29.6
Chase	15.0	9.6	11.2	51.2	4 068	3 966	-2.5	-0.3	232	271	33	1 698	2.31	68.8	6.7	27.3
Cherry	15.7	10.5	10.9	50.0	6 148	5 713	-7.1	2.4	367	315	77	2 603	2.16	69.9	4.5	26.3
Cheyenne	13.6	8.1	8.1	50.2	9 830	9 998	1.7	1.7	675	469	-38	4 382	2.27	63.2	8.6	33.6
Clay	15.1	10.4	8.7	49.4	7 039	6 542	-7.1	-3.6	392	370	-251	2 624	2.41	71.3	7.3	25.2
Colfax	11.7	6.4	6.7	48.5	10 441	10 515	0.7	0.0	922	405	-495	3 670	2.83	71.3	8.0	24.3
Cuming	13.5	9.9	11.6	49.9	10 203	9 139	-10.4	-0.2	575	512	-76	3 834	2.33	68.7	5.7	29.3
Custer	14.7	10.6	10.3	50.2	11 793	10 943	-7.2	-1.3	642	702	-104	4 746	2.25	68.5	8.3	27.4
Dakota	11.3	7.2	5.5	50.0	20 253	21 006	3.7	-1.1	1 930	790	-1 401	7 248	2.84	75.2	13.1	20.2
Dawes	12.3	8.9	8.7	50.6	9 060	9 182	1.3	-1.4	527	421	-254	3 745	2.13	59.5	8.5	33.1
Dawson	12.4	8.2	6.8	49.2	24 365	24 326	-0.2	-1.8	2 004	1 099	-1 323	8 731	2.73	71.8	11.6	24.7
Deuel	16.1	11.4	12.1	50.2	2 098	1 941	-7.5	-1.0	84	111	20	840	2.30	61.8	5.0	33.6
Dixon	15.4	10.6	9.2	49.7	6 339	6 000	-5.3	-3.4	389	316	-276	2 348	2.47	70.6	7.8	27.4
Dodge	12.8	9.3	9.6	50.7	36 160	36 685	1.5	0.1	2 503	2 222	-279	15 162	2.36	66.3	9.0	28.5
Douglas	11.6	6.5	4.9	50.7	463 585	517 116	11.5	6.4	43 969	19 902	9 768	206 522	2.51	61.9	12.7	31.0
Dundy	16.5	11.2	12.0	49.6	2 292	2 008	-12.4	-10.4	78	156	-125	888	2.16	68.9	4.5	26.9
Fillmore	15.5	10.7	12.2	50.2	6 634	5 890	-11.2	-4.6	272	450	-91	2 430	2.27	66.3	7.0	30.2
Franklin	16.9	12.5	13.3	50.0	3 574	3 225	-9.8	-7.4	141	189	-166	1 405	2.19	67.5	7.3	27.9
Frontier	15.8	10.9	10.3	48.5	3 099	2 756	-11.1	-4.8	129	93	-146	1 079	2.22	65.0	5.3	29.7
Furnas	16.3	11.3	11.5	50.3	5 324	4 959	-6.9	-2.0	244	357	23	2 215	2.18	62.6	7.0	35.5
Gage	14.9	9.9	10.5	50.5	22 993	22 311	-3.0	-1.8	1 261	1 450	-241	9 119	2.34	64.8	8.0	29.9
Garden	16.2	12.3	15.4	48.9	2 292	2 057	-10.3	-6.8	98	143	-93	878	2.15	66.3	5.7	30.6
Garfield	17.4	12.5	14.4	50.1	1 902	2 049	7.7	-1.0	80	158	53	870	2.21	60.3	5.1	37.1
Gosper	15.1	10.7	10.2	48.0	2 143	2 044	-4.6	-3.5	112	115	-80	749	2.62	71.3	7.9	24.2
Grant	18.1	10.8	8.9	47.0	747	614	-17.8	4.4	48	29	6	273	2.25	67.8	6.2	31.5
Greeley	14.7	10.4	13.3	49.3	2 714	2 538	-6.5	-4.3	148	139	-119	1 028	2.40	66.1	5.6	32.8
Hall	11.8	7.5	6.7	49.7	53 534	58 607	9.5	5.2	4 945	2 690	785	22 418	2.65	66.2	12.5	26.9
Hamilton	14.6	9.2	8.5	49.7	9 403	9 114	-3.1	0.8	522	415	-21	3 564	2.51	73.5	8.4	22.3
Harlan	16.4	13.5	10.8	48.5	3 786	3 423	-9.6	0.8	209	207	33	1 518	2.24	63.2	6.4	34.9
Hayes	18.5	11.8	13.0	48.2	1 068	967	-9.5	-3.6	60	26	-75	462	2.48	76.6	3.0	20.8
Hitchcock	15.8	11.9	11.9	49.6	3 111	2 908	-6.5	-0.9	170	187	-16	1 351	2.10	59.6	6.1	36.9
Holt	15.8	10.1	10.7	50.6	11 551	10 435	-9.7	-1.2	738	618	-248	4 424	2.31	65.9	4.1	28.5
Hooker	17.0	13.0	15.9	51.6	783	736	-6.0	-0.5	39	52	15	309	2.04	66.3	0.0	32.0
Howard	13.6	10.8	9.4	49.2	6 567	6 274	-4.5	2.2	395	312	72	2 605	2.41	66.1	6.9	29.7
Jefferson	16.4	11.1	11.4	50.3	8 333	7 547	-9.4	-3.8	403	559	-138	3 319	2.22	65.0	7.6	30.0
Johnson	13.7	8.2	8.7	40.5	4 488	5 217	16.2	-0.8	229	294	16	1 927	2.14	61.8	8.8	34.0
Kearney	14.2	9.4	9.4	50.9	6 882	6 489	-5.7	1.5	418	366	60	2 646	2.44	68.9	7.7	26.1
Keith	16.1	13.5	9.7	50.0	8 875	8 368	-5.7	-3.6	396	476	-194	3 769	2.15	62.9	7.3	31.3
Keya Paha	16.4	12.6	15.7	51.1	983	824	-16.2	-2.4	39	37	-14	375	1.98	65.6	5.6	29.6
Kimball	15.4	11.7	11.0	49.3	4 089	3 821	-6.6	-3.5	210	236	-100	1 628	2.28	61.1	7.8	37.3
Knox	15.1	11.2	12.6	51.1	9 374	8 701	-7.2	-1.8	543	606	-109	3 721	2.24	65.3	5.7	30.8
Lancaster	11.5	6.9	5.3	50.0	250 291	285 407	14.0	7.4	21 289	10 160	9 635	116 533	2.41	60.8	9.8	29.5
Lincoln	14.2	9.2	7.9	50.5	34 632	36 288	4.8	-1.7	2 235	1 818	-1 091	15 032	2.35	63.6	8.5	31.1
Logan	16.1	10.0	8.4	50.3	774	763	-1.4	1.8	58	27	-17	322	2.29	63.7	3.7	31.1
Loup	21.1	15.3	9.5	48.3	712	628	-11.8	-6.8	27	24	-42	244	2.29	74.6	6.1	18.4
McPherson	16.5	9.4	10.4	50.0	533	539	1.1	-11.9	14	14	-62	188	2.24	80.9	1.6	17.6
Madison	13.4	7.8	7.8	50.4	35 226	34 876	-1.0	0.5	2 696	1 811	-757	14 049	2.42	65.8	11.3	28.9
Merrick	14.1	9.6	9.3	50.1	8 204	7 855	-4.3	-0.9	483	436	-100	3 331	2.28	65.2	7.2	26.3
Morrill	15.3	9.2	9.0	49.3	5 440	5 042	-7.3	-3.7	279	288	-203	2 028	2.35	66.9	12.0	29.9
Nance	16.7	9.5	11.1	49.9	4 038	3 735	-7.5	-3.7	210	235	-113	1 548	2.27	66.1	8.5	31.5
Nemaha	14.0	9.3	8.7	50.7	7 576	7 248	-4.3	-2.8	404	419	-157	2 898	2.31	62.9	7.3	30.6
Nuckolls	16.2	12.6	13.6	50.3	5 057	4 500	-11.0	-3.8	214	305	-68	2 054	2.13	67.2	5.9	30.5
Otoe	14.0	9.8	10.0	50.8	15 396	15 740	2.2	1.6	1 004	990	212	6 448	2.40	68.2	8.9	28.0
Pawnee	15.5	11.9	13.7	50.1	3 087	2 773	-10.2	-4.1	155	184	-72	1 292	2.10	61.8	5.1	35.6
Perkins	15.2	10.3	11.6	49.3	3 200	2 970	-7.2	-0.9	198	158	-47	1 244	2.33	66.6	3.3	27.5
Phelps	13.1	9.4	10.7	50.3	9 747	9 188	-5.7	1.2	611	573	40	3 769	2.37	67.3	4.1	29.4
Pierce	13.5	9.1	9.0	49.5	7 857	7 266	-7.5	-0.8	434	348	-130	2 908	2.43	70.1	6.4	28.1

1. No spouse present.

Table B. States and Counties — Population, Vital Statistics, Medicare, and Crime

STATE County	Persons in group quarters, 2015	Daytime population, 2010–2014 Number	Employment/residence ratio	Births, 2015 Total	Rate[1]	Deaths, 2015 Number	Rate[1]	Persons under 65 with no health insurance, 2014 Number	Percent	Medicare, 2015 Total Beneficiaries	Enrolled in Original Medicare	Enrolled in Medicare Advantage	Serious crimes known to police,[2] 2014 Total Number	Rate[3]
	32	33	34	35	36	37	38	39	40	41	42	43	44	45
NEBRASKA—Cont'd														
Blaine	0	519	0.76	2	4.0	3	6.1	93	23.6	D	101	D	NA	NA
Boone	97	5 502	1.04	63	11.8	66	12.4	429	10.3	1 210	1 154	56	NA	NA
Box Butte	186	11 654	1.06	169	14.9	103	9.1	1 014	10.7	2 045	1 913	132	206	1 819
Boyd	29	1 982	0.91	12	6.0	20	9.9	196	13.6	D	610	D	NA	NA
Brown	38	3 098	1.01	29	9.9	35	11.9	317	14.3	D	799	D	33	1 146
Buffalo	2 082	48 438	1.04	728	15.0	348	7.2	3 882	9.7	6 683	6 023	660	960	1 983
Burt	130	5 973	0.77	70	10.6	96	14.6	484	9.7	1 676	1 513	163	NA	NA
Butler	166	7 228	0.74	97	11.9	92	11.3	595	9.2	1 725	1 614	111	51	614
Cass	298	18 814	0.50	270	10.6	233	9.1	1 691	7.9	4 348	3 693	655	315	1 239
Cedar	148	7 951	0.82	111	12.9	94	10.9	836	12.4	1 689	1 326	363	25	287
Chase	66	4 195	1.10	43	10.8	54	13.6	440	14.0	D	854	D	36	897
Cherry	55	5 880	1.04	79	13.6	59	10.2	662	14.7	D	1 246	D	44	757
Cheyenne	103	10 913	1.16	133	13.1	75	7.4	721	8.5	1 741	1 638	103	243	2 396
Clay	90	5 696	0.77	74	11.7	74	11.7	649	12.8	1 437	1 423	14	NA	NA
Colfax	94	10 593	1.02	186	17.7	67	6.4	1 588	17.6	2 108	2 006	102	NA	NA
Cuming	135	8 636	0.90	110	12.1	81	8.9	906	12.8	1 786	1 661	125	28	312
Custer	126	10 652	0.97	133	12.3	125	11.6	1 145	13.6	2 388	2 364	24	99	918
Dakota	259	21 902	1.10	357	17.2	130	6.3	3 128	17.5	1 909	1 335	574	586	2 841
Dawes	1 157	9 183	1.01	97	10.7	76	8.4	1 007	15.3	1 637	1 381	256	141	1 553
Dawson	299	24 023	0.98	399	16.7	190	7.9	3 383	16.8	3 673	3 159	514	495	2 045
Deuel	19	1 697	0.75	19	9.9	17	8.8	182	12.4	D	466	D	10	515
Dixon	82	4 902	0.66	75	13.0	50	8.6	548	11.9	1 994	1 496	498	90	1 653
Dodge	1 203	36 499	0.99	492	13.4	400	10.9	3 416	11.8	7 572	6 682	890	834	2 283
Douglas	12 556	583 559	1.19	8 497	15.5	3 713	6.8	55 013	11.7	73 402	54 871	18 531	23 058	4 254
Dundy	28	1 961	0.99	16	8.7	28	15.2	216	15.0	D	425	D	NA	NA
Fillmore	192	5 760	1.00	51	9.1	83	14.8	429	10.1	D	1 325	D	NA	NA
Franklin	23	2 774	0.74	27	8.9	29	9.6	253	11.1	D	840	D	13	426
Frontier	113	2 457	0.93	26	9.7	16	6.0	247	12.3	531	488	43	NA	NA
Furnas	80	4 916	1.00	51	10.5	63	12.9	463	12.4	1 323	1 303	20	4	82
Gage	516	20 610	0.88	239	11.0	256	11.8	1 574	9.2	4 777	4 387	390	621	3 049
Garden	34	1 861	0.92	16	8.4	15	7.8	183	13.3	643	581	62	NA	NA
Garfield	52	1 985	1.03	19	9.4	17	8.5	200	13.8	568	552	16	NA	NA
Gosper	44	1 691	0.70	19	9.7	14	7.1	154	9.9	513	440	73	14	715
Grant	3	639	0.97	9	14.3	3	4.8	75	15.1	D	178	D	NA	NA
Greeley	56	2 272	0.80	26	10.6	26	10.6	354	18.8	D	585	D	NA	NA
Hall	1 130	64 907	1.15	988	16.0	504	8.2	7 770	14.9	10 434	9 442	992	2 619	4 272
Hamilton	117	8 470	0.86	103	11.3	77	8.4	652	8.7	1 696	1 604	92	86	943
Harlan	47	3 147	0.80	44	12.7	29	8.4	292	11.1	D	763	D	NA	NA
Hayes	0	942	0.66	10	10.7	4	4.3	178	25.4	D	93	D	NA	NA
Hitchcock	30	2 430	0.66	31	10.7	36	12.5	277	12.6	D	777	D	29	1 010
Holt	141	10 541	1.02	149	14.4	115	11.1	1 117	13.6	2 311	2 297	14	32	306
Hooker	26	772	1.25	8	11.0	8	11.0	57	11.1	D	213	D	0	0
Howard	70	4 906	0.56	82	12.8	51	8.0	531	10.5	1 316	1 294	22	NA	NA
Jefferson	91	7 535	1.01	79	10.8	89	12.2	615	10.9	1 846	1 690	156	NA	NA
Johnson	1 022	5 013	0.92	39	7.5	50	9.7	381	11.6	965	920	45	19	370
Kearney	81	6 172	0.89	77	11.7	64	9.7	471	8.8	1 196	1 138	58	115	1 750
Keith	43	8 046	0.96	73	9.0	75	9.3	703	11.3	1 929	1 766	163	137	1 694
Keya Paha	0	643	0.79	10	12.4	3	3.7	124	21.6	176	176	0	2	255
Kimball	42	3 835	1.04	39	10.6	33	8.9	352	12.4	875	848	27	39	1 060
Knox	218	7 976	0.86	114	13.4	95	11.1	1 038	16.2	2 136	1 892	244	28	327
Lancaster	15 112	301 276	1.05	4 056	13.3	1 927	6.3	25 166	10.0	40 270	36 075	4 195	10 455	3 481
Lincoln	600	36 861	1.05	405	11.3	336	9.4	2 873	9.8	7 460	6 021	1 439	1 205	3 342
Logan	0	692	0.87	11	14.4	7	9.2	105	17.1	193	169	24	NA	NA
Loup	0	495	0.78	5	8.5	5	8.5	80	18.3	D	83	D	NA	NA
McPherson	0	352	0.63	2	4.1	2	4.1	71	17.9	97	85	12	NA	NA
Madison	1 096	38 258	1.17	504	14.4	353	10.1	3 622	12.5	6 912	5 976	936	755	2 132
Merrick	196	6 867	0.77	100	12.9	79	10.2	718	11.6	1 494	1 393	101	58	743
Morrill	81	4 552	0.84	53	10.9	44	9.1	570	14.5	1 028	939	89	23	618
Nance	142	3 200	0.74	35	9.8	33	9.2	338	12.1	755	725	30	NA	NA
Nemaha	518	7 582	1.11	78	11.0	58	8.2	526	9.7	1 351	1 295	56	53	742
Nuckolls	53	4 134	0.87	43	9.9	56	12.9	348	10.8	1 173	1 126	47	NA	NA
Otoe	337	14 503	0.84	195	12.2	174	10.9	1 220	9.7	2 894	2 627	267	NA	NA
Pawnee	35	2 590	0.87	41	15.3	28	10.5	270	13.6	D	707	D	45	1 668
Perkins	34	3 085	1.10	39	13.4	24	8.2	272	12.1	601	584	17	11	378
Phelps	258	9 635	1.10	122	13.2	94	10.2	675	9.3	1 871	1 852	19	166	1 798
Pierce	109	6 044	0.68	90	12.5	69	9.6	559	9.5	1 230	1 218	12	NA	NA

1. Per 1,000 estimated resident population.   2. Data for serious crimes have not been adjusted for underreporting; this may affect comparability between geographic areas and over time.
3. Per 100,000 population estimated by the FBI.

Table B. States and Counties — Crime, Education, Money Income, and Poverty

STATE County	Serious crimes known to police, 2014 (cont.)[1] Rate[2] Violent	Property	Education — School enrollment and attainment, 2010–2014 — Enrollment[3] Total	Percent private	Attainment[4] (percent) High school graduate or less	Bachelor's degree or more	Local government expenditures,[5] 2012–2013 Total current spending (mil dol)	Current spending per student (dollars)	Money income, 2010–2014 Per capita income[6] (dollars)	Households Median income (dollars)	Mean income (dollars)	Percent with income of $200,000 or more	Income and poverty, 2014 Median household income (dollars)	Percent below poverty level All persons	Children under 18 years	Children 5 to 17 years in families
	46	47	48	49	50	51	52	53	54	55	56	57	58	59	60	61
NEBRASKA—Cont'd																
Blaine	NA	NA	158	2.5	43.3	15.7	2.3	21 575	23 684	48 214	59 510	1.6	38 228	15.7	22.0	23.7
Boone	NA	NA	1 239	18.1	51.3	15.4	12.8	15 336	25 985	47 450	62 360	4.2	52 914	10.3	13.2	11.8
Box Butte	238	1 580	2 910	8.7	44.7	15.5	23.3	11 740	24 865	49 367	58 414	1.6	55 465	11.4	16.9	15.3
Boyd	NA	NA	384	4.2	50.6	18.6	5.7	17 021	22 783	40 083	49 081	0.6	39 964	13.9	20.2	18.0
Brown	0	1 146	614	12.5	47.3	19.6	9.9	19 948	24 287	34 645	47 924	1.5	42 348	12.8	18.2	16.0
Buffalo	205	1 779	15 056	8.2	33.0	32.8	87.9	11 574	25 154	52 562	64 926	2.2	51 550	12.5	14.5	13.2
Burt	NA	NA	1 428	3.5	45.6	16.5	16.0	12 387	24 841	46 988	57 758	1.6	49 345	10.6	15.8	14.3
Butler	60	554	1 963	25.0	49.7	14.0	13.7	13 371	28 525	49 241	67 979	2.7	54 240	9.2	11.7	10.2
Cass	130	1 109	6 450	14.1	37.4	24.5	42.6	11 325	30 413	65 560	77 900	3.5	66 522	6.9	10.3	8.8
Cedar	46	241	2 097	21.1	49.0	16.5	17.1	15 161	26 702	49 507	65 016	3.2	54 421	10.4	14.1	12.6
Chase	199	697	855	2.7	45.8	19.0	10.2	12 833	30 881	48 450	71 718	3.2	52 749	9.3	10.8	9.3
Cherry	172	585	1 098	15.1	40.1	20.4	12.2	15 576	24 942	46 817	57 165	1.7	43 564	13.3	21.6	19.7
Cheyenne	375	2 022	2 440	5.7	35.4	23.8	19.5	11 674	29 728	54 094	67 310	2.7	55 964	9.0	11.8	10.5
Clay	NA	NA	1 502	6.0	44.4	17.5	19.5	13 025	25 664	50 682	62 703	2.2	55 758	11.3	16.4	14.5
Colfax	NA	NA	2 692	8.9	61.0	14.1	27.4	11 366	23 688	52 086	65 210	2.8	50 758	10.3	15.1	14.3
Cuming	22	290	2 162	28.1	48.8	18.1	19.2	12 145	25 363	49 872	59 893	2.0	56 047	9.1	11.7	9.9
Custer	121	798	2 361	12.0	43.4	20.3	25.4	14 350	26 105	44 336	59 647	2.2	45 644	13.4	19.0	17.5
Dakota	165	2 676	5 488	13.1	61.4	11.9	48.7	11 506	20 735	48 508	57 622	1.3	50 289	14.8	22.1	18.1
Dawes	143	1 409	2 959	6.4	30.3	39.1	13.7	11 899	22 654	41 267	52 939	1.4	40 667	18.8	21.8	18.6
Dawson	145	1 900	6 394	3.4	57.3	15.1	59.6	11 188	21 046	48 104	56 361	1.1	47 366	13.7	20.1	17.1
Deuel	0	515	484	2.1	42.0	18.5	7.2	16 465	28 163	50 764	63 205	2.7	44 109	11.8	19.1	17.4
Dixon	0	1 653	1 453	3.4	51.4	16.6	14.2	13 386	24 173	49 634	60 218	1.8	52 601	10.7	15.8	12.7
Dodge	186	2 097	8 766	22.2	50.1	18.6	69.3	11 902	24 754	47 991	59 916	2.1	50 043	12.9	17.3	14.8
Douglas	483	3 771	153 534	21.2	32.6	36.6	999.0	10 868	29 123	53 444	73 091	4.3	52 842	14.0	18.3	17.3
Dundy	NA	NA	352	12.2	39.7	21.8	5.8	14 708	29 111	47 636	64 920	5.9	45 624	13.8	20.9	18.1
Fillmore	NA	NA	1 219	9.6	46.2	19.7	13.5	15 045	26 873	52 063	62 553	2.4	54 556	10.1	13.8	12.6
Franklin	0	426	642	3.4	45.9	17.8	4.5	14 226	26 349	45 707	59 717	3.3	44 794	13.6	18.9	16.6
Frontier	NA	NA	684	9.4	42.1	16.9	9.1	15 588	25 361	48 713	60 550	2.1	48 543	13.7	17.9	15.3
Furnas	21	62	1 128	15.9	45.6	18.1	15.1	14 016	22 554	40 765	50 139	1.4	44 461	12.7	19.4	17.1
Gage	496	2 553	4 814	11.3	45.3	20.5	41.1	12 627	25 166	49 021	59 378	1.8	50 861	11.0	15.8	14.0
Garden	NA	NA	323	9.3	41.4	22.0	4.0	16 110	28 149	41 410	58 983	2.8	38 645	15.6	24.3	21.2
Garfield	NA	NA	421	2.6	49.5	12.8	4.4	12 052	21 939	41 776	48 389	1.1	40 436	11.8	14.6	12.1
Gosper	51	664	522	7.9	43.5	18.0	3.3	13 966	24 856	50 063	60 936	0.5	55 319	9.1	14.7	14.0
Grant	NA	NA	172	8.1	44.3	18.6	2.4	16 524	21 471	45 268	49 042	0.4	47 537	11.0	17.3	19.5
Greeley	NA	NA	547	15.9	49.5	15.1	7.3	16 310	23 902	43 226	54 784	1.9	43 858	12.7	18.7	16.2
Hall	243	4 029	15 141	10.8	48.6	17.7	138.3	11 398	24 075	49 178	61 677	2.0	48 499	14.7	19.3	17.2
Hamilton	143	800	2 260	13.0	37.2	24.8	19.3	12 168	28 982	58 382	73 630	4.2	62 191	6.9	9.6	9.1
Harlan	NA	NA	668	7.9	47.8	14.5	4.0	14 208	24 417	46 859	54 151	1.1	46 744	11.4	16.8	16.3
Hayes	NA	NA	272	4.8	40.6	19.0	2.4	20 033	24 590	48 750	59 784	3.9	48 856	14.5	18.0	16.2
Hitchcock	70	940	581	8.6	42.2	15.3	6.1	21 935	22 958	35 938	49 053	0.7	40 496	13.8	21.0	19.6
Holt	96	210	2 258	13.4	43.0	20.1	22.8	14 224	24 624	45 782	58 386	2.0	46 667	12.5	17.0	16.6
Hooker	0	0	109	8.3	39.3	23.6	2.9	16 842	22 940	38 011	50 935	2.3	40 732	9.6	13.6	13.6
Howard	NA	NA	1 518	11.8	49.7	18.7	8.9	11 760	27 363	48 750	64 784	2.1	51 040	11.5	14.5	13.3
Jefferson	NA	NA	1 672	6.6	53.5	13.2	19.8	12 583	25 291	44 449	57 392	2.4	44 947	11.5	16.7	15.0
Johnson	117	253	978	11.8	54.9	13.2	9.7	12 664	20 624	44 057	56 151	2.4	48 511	13.9	16.8	15.3
Kearney	137	1 613	1 493	9.4	40.0	24.9	16.3	13 001	26 991	55 670	63 515	2.4	56 791	9.6	13.4	12.0
Keith	49	1 645	1 576	19.0	39.2	22.0	20.7	18 569	26 605	42 326	58 350	1.2	45 192	12.0	20.4	17.4
Keya Paha	0	255	126	2.4	52.3	15.8	2.1	22 011	28 104	39 028	54 907	2.4	41 138	20.5	31.1	29.2
Kimball	326	734	738	4.9	49.0	15.9	6.8	12 447	25 133	42 219	55 976	1.7	45 771	11.7	18.0	16.2
Knox	82	245	1 888	12.1	48.5	18.9	22.5	14 831	26 287	43 709	58 611	2.1	42 745	14.9	21.8	19.7
Lancaster	315	3 166	89 346	16.6	29.6	36.2	435.9	10 395	27 512	51 916	68 201	3.3	52 011	14.0	16.0	14.7
Lincoln	258	3 084	9 139	16.0	41.3	19.9	57.9	10 029	26 896	49 250	63 292	2.0	49 770	14.5	18.6	16.3
Logan	NA	NA	158	8.2	38.3	20.4	2.7	12 748	24 599	45 179	58 050	1.9	50 761	9.4	13.1	11.7
Loup	NA	NA	125	4.0	47.9	14.4	1.8	20 466	25 806	55 125	62 918	3.7	49 132	15.5	23.9	20.4
McPherson	NA	NA	64	9.4	36.4	25.6	1.8	18 657	25 760	57 763	62 027	1.1	62 280	13.9	26.8	23.1
Madison	141	1 991	9 081	21.4	40.1	21.3	60.3	10 818	25 279	47 622	61 567	3.1	51 836	13.7	17.9	16.6
Merrick	26	718	1 837	8.5	45.2	16.0	11.6	11 821	25 403	49 637	62 610	2.0	50 893	10.4	15.2	13.3
Morrill	27	591	1 134	8.7	45.8	17.0	12.7	14 269	23 268	45 000	55 149	2.2	46 961	14.0	20.1	17.0
Nance	NA	NA	746	6.3	48.1	14.4	10.2	13 090	25 499	46 220	59 434	2.3	48 535	11.7	15.5	14.1
Nemaha	56	686	2 078	8.5	41.6	27.1	18.9	16 960	26 837	47 875	66 410	3.2	49 162	13.6	16.5	15.2
Nuckolls	NA	NA	859	7.3	50.4	16.1	6.1	13 324	23 935	42 404	52 066	1.1	43 249	13.4	19.4	16.9
Otoe	NA	NA	3 604	16.0	46.5	22.0	28.7	11 290	25 700	51 316	61 957	1.5	51 527	10.0	13.4	12.0
Pawnee	0	1 668	511	16.4	56.9	14.5	7.1	14 573	25 138	38 462	54 027	1.5	42 977	12.2	21.6	20.2
Perkins	69	309	598	21.2	38.9	20.7	6.3	15 649	29 634	56 333	67 420	3.5	56 080	10.4	14.5	13.5
Phelps	87	1 711	2 078	10.9	37.3	23.8	22.9	14 467	27 126	51 396	64 883	2.0	54 137	9.5	12.6	12.2
Pierce	NA	NA	1 799	18.0	44.2	20.4	15.5	12 370	25 938	52 178	63 808	2.3	53 489	10.0	13.2	11.9

1. Data for serious crimes have not been adjusted for underreporting; this may affect comparability between geographic areas and over time. 2. Per 100,000 population estimated by the FBI.
3. All persons 3 years old and over enrolled in nursery school through college. 4. Persons 25 years old and over. 5. Elementary and secondary education expenditures.
6. Based on population estimated by the American Community Survey, 2010–2014.

Table B. States and Counties — **Personal Income**

STATE County	Personal income, 2014 Total (mil dol)	Percent change, 2013–2014	Per capita[1] Dollars	Per capita[1] Rank	Wages and salaries (mil dol)	Supplements to wages and salaries; employer contributions (mil dol) Pension and insurance	Supplements — Government social insurance	Proprietors' income (mil dol)	Dividends, interest, and rent (mil dol)	Personal transfer receipts (mil dol)	Earnings, 2014 Total (mil dol)	Contributions for government social insurance (mil dol) From employee and self-employed	Contributions — From employer
	62	63	64	65	66	67	68	69	70	71	72	73	74
NEBRASKA—Cont'd													
Blaine	35	48.3	69 036	63	5	1	0	18	7	4	25	0	0
Boone	347	-1.6	64 836	88	85	16	6	158	54	42	265	8	6
Box Butte	513	7.1	45 255	653	256	38	31	98	75	98	423	25	31
Boyd	102	16.4	50 072	383	17	4	1	41	15	22	63	3	1
Brown	178	19.5	60 491	126	43	9	3	84	25	28	139	4	3
Buffalo	2 250	4.1	46 657	548	1 055	187	77	360	498	287	1 679	96	77
Burt	316	-13.8	48 088	475	71	14	5	80	46	62	171	8	5
Butler	377	-4.3	45 707	620	113	21	8	79	65	63	220	11	8
Cass	1 173	0.0	45 950	599	211	39	15	130	198	183	395	23	15
Cedar	456	-9.6	52 988	267	102	20	7	181	72	58	310	12	7
Chase	238	5.1	59 787	137	70	13	5	100	39	31	188	7	5
Cherry	350	28.9	60 729	121	79	15	6	159	56	44	259	8	6
Cheyenne	592	7.1	58 358	152	334	47	23	100	103	71	503	28	23
Clay	313	12.3	49 580	409	109	22	8	82	51	48	221	10	8
Colfax	466	-0.1	44 341	729	193	38	15	135	62	57	381	17	15
Cuming	782	8.3	86 661	19	149	26	11	462	82	68	648	20	11
Custer	579	7.6	53 952	237	162	32	12	211	86	88	418	16	12
Dakota	731	-2.2	35 071	1 920	510	93	39	97	84	130	739	43	39
Dawes	333	15.4	36 858	1 624	119	26	10	73	60	69	228	12	10
Dawson	946	5.0	39 255	1 289	426	85	32	209	139	160	752	37	32
Deuel	85	6.3	43 665	789	20	4	1	16	19	16	41	2	1
Dixon	269	-8.3	46 609	551	69	14	5	76	39	37	165	7	5
Dodge	1 489	-0.1	40 537	1 118	642	119	49	176	276	297	985	60	49
Douglas	28 668	4.6	52 772	276	17 386	2 594	1 295	3 986	5 961	3 418	25 261	1 528	1 295
Dundy	136	11.5	72 014	49	28	5	2	52	30	19	87	3	2
Fillmore	322	-9.5	56 868	176	92	18	6	82	60	52	198	9	6
Franklin	143	2.7	46 378	567	27	6	2	31	36	28	65	3	2
Frontier	146	-0.5	54 039	232	32	6	2	64	19	17	104	4	2
Furnas	254	13.6	51 951	297	73	15	5	70	46	50	163	7	5
Gage	1 039	-3.2	47 942	482	330	66	24	202	162	228	622	35	24
Garden	109	27.1	56 994	173	21	4	2	40	21	20	67	2	2
Garfield	101	9.8	50 518	359	27	6	2	35	21	18	70	3	2
Gosper	105	4.9	53 506	255	21	4	1	27	22	16	53	2	1
Grant	35	40.3	55 924	199	6	1	0	15	8	5	23	1	0
Greeley	116	-1.4	46 706	546	23	5	2	43	22	20	73	3	2
Hall	2 370	3.2	38 538	1 384	1 401	251	104	223	448	410	1 979	119	104
Hamilton	450	-4.7	49 210	428	140	25	10	87	77	66	262	14	10
Harlan	163	8.5	46 753	541	30	6	2	53	27	31	91	3	2
Hayes	73	38.9	78 580	30	9	2	1	44	8	4	55	1	1
Hitchcock	126	5.0	43 435	801	33	8	2	28	21	30	71	4	2
Holt	520	0.0	49 971	386	174	31	12	160	83	92	377	19	12
Hooker	37	35.0	50 581	354	10	2	1	14	5	7	28	1	1
Howard	285	1.4	44 769	698	56	12	4	65	40	49	137	6	4
Jefferson	354	-1.5	48 262	465	126	23	10	79	69	66	239	12	10
Johnson	208	-2.8	40 070	1 167	62	16	4	56	29	35	137	6	4
Kearney	400	-0.4	60 273	129	86	16	6	144	62	59	253	11	6
Keith	372	4.2	45 866	610	115	21	8	87	66	72	232	12	8
Keya Paha	58	15.7	71 933	52	6	1	0	34	9	7	42	1	0
Kimball	184	8.9	49 633	402	75	13	6	33	32	34	127	8	6
Knox	392	1.8	46 236	578	97	20	7	123	61	77	247	10	7
Lancaster	13 064	4.1	43 287	815	7 404	1 332	548	879	2 574	1 827	10 164	610	548
Lincoln	1 654	8.0	46 195	581	743	116	75	345	231	320	1 279	75	75
Logan	31	-10.7	41 076	1 051	7	1	0	8	4	6	17	1	0
Loup	44	44.1	75 240	39	4	1	0	23	5	5	28	0	0
McPherson	40	83.7	79 900	28	3	1	0	26	5	3	30	0	0
Madison	1 551	1.6	44 089	756	851	156	62	246	260	258	1 315	75	62
Merrick	343	-4.1	44 181	741	95	17	7	82	54	64	200	10	7
Morrill	294	15.3	60 468	127	62	11	4	136	35	40	214	7	4
Nance	174	-4.3	48 799	446	44	8	3	46	23	30	101	4	3
Nemaha	317	-9.2	44 172	745	158	31	10	52	56	60	251	13	10
Nuckolls	202	-3.4	46 169	582	52	10	4	59	34	43	124	6	4
Otoe	681	-2.3	43 138	832	238	46	18	93	122	124	395	22	18
Pawnee	134	-3.3	49 630	403	32	7	2	45	21	24	87	3	2
Perkins	193	5.5	66 586	76	54	10	4	94	29	21	162	5	4
Phelps	532	6.8	57 873	161	200	39	14	190	76	78	443	17	14
Pierce	338	-5.7	46 891	529	79	15	6	78	51	50	178	9	6

1. Based on the resident population estimated as of July 1 of the year shown.

STATE County	Earnings, 2014 (cont.)									Social Security beneficiaries, December 2014			Housing units, 2015	
	Percent by selected industries											Supplemental Security Income recipients, December 2014		
	Farm	Mining	Construction	Manufacturing	Information: professional, scientific, technical services	Retail trade	Finance, insurance, real estate and leasing	Health care and social assistance	Government	Number	Rate[1]		Total	Percent change, 2010–2014
	75	76	77	78	79	80	81	82	83	84	85	86	87	88
NEBRASKA—Cont'd														
Blaine	76.3	0.0	D	0.0	0.0	D	D	D	14.6	110	220	0	323	-0.9
Boone	54.5	0.0	2.1	4.5	0.8	2.9	1.9	3.3	12.2	1 255	235	50	2 636	-0.5
Box Butte	18.2	0.0	2.2	4.8	2.5	3.5	2.3	3.5	13.9	1 850	163	183	5 420	-1.1
Boyd	38.4	D	1.3	1.0	D	2.7	3.1	3.6	15.1	635	313	32	1 371	-1.4
Brown	51.7	0.0	3.1	1.0	D	4.4	D	2.2	16.1	860	292	48	1 840	-1.2
Buffalo	5.4	0.1	5.4	18.9	D	7.7	3.7	15.1	13.8	7 460	154	450	20 008	5.0
Burt	35.8	0.0	4.3	5.5	D	3.7	3.7	4.7	15.2	1 830	278	124	3 461	-0.2
Butler	28.0	D	4.7	18.6	D	2.9	D	D	15.5	1 900	231	90	4 057	0.1
Cass	17.1	3.8	5.6	8.1	3.1	7.0	4.6	5.0	17.8	4 930	193	210	11 283	1.5
Cedar	41.7	D	5.9	4.4	2.2	3.6	3.4	2.9	11.1	1 865	217	56	4 130	-0.4
Chase	44.9	D	3.3	0.8	D	7.0	3.4	1.2	12.9	905	228	41	1 932	-0.7
Cherry	55.5	D	4.8	0.9	2.5	4.8	1.1	3.9	11.7	1 350	234	74	3 178	0.7
Cheyenne	11.2	D	2.7	3.8	1.9	6.5	1.8	6.6	8.2	1 970	195	121	4 976	1.8
Clay	32.9	D	7.4	9.5	D	2.8	D	3.6	19.0	1 430	226	53	2 991	-0.3
Colfax	25.8	D	D	D	1.5	2.6	1.5	D	9.2	1 540	146	83	4 146	1.2
Cuming	51.0	D	2.6	16.0	1.4	1.7	2.4	3.5	5.6	2 100	233	66	4 210	0.1
Custer	43.5	0.0	5.5	9.4	2.3	4.1	3.0	D	10.6	2 520	235	127	5 587	0.1
Dakota	3.4	D	5.4	41.8	D	4.0	8.3	3.1	9.3	3 305	160	286	7 755	1.6
Dawes	22.0	D	3.8	0.3	2.4	10.3	2.7	9.9	27.5	1 935	213	112	4 212	-0.9
Dawson	21.1	D	3.2	23.0	2.8	5.3	3.0	D	16.4	4 325	180	320	10 153	0.3
Deuel	23.6	0.0	D	0.0	D	7.6	D	6.2	21.1	515	266	24	1 030	-1.3
Dixon	38.7	0.0	D	D	D	1.4	1.1	2.0	11.8	1 230	213	50	2 700	0.4
Dodge	6.9	0.1	4.2	20.0	3.1	8.9	4.1	D	18.1	8 200	223	514	16 633	0.3
Douglas	0.0	D	8.2	6.8	12.2	5.3	11.8	12.1	11.0	79 985	147	10 076	229 086	4.3
Dundy	54.5	0.0	3.9	1.0	D	1.8	1.1	2.4	13.5	465	246	19	1 115	-0.9
Fillmore	32.4	0.0	8.7	5.6	D	3.5	5.2	3.8	17.2	1 450	257	52	2 920	0.2
Franklin	36.0	0.0	2.5	0.0	D	5.7	D	3.5	22.7	745	244	64	1 724	-0.6
Frontier	40.2	0.0	D	D	D	2.0	6.4	D	14.7	390	144	18	1 566	-0.5
Furnas	39.8	0.0	3.0	4.8	5.7	3.1	D	7.7	14.8	1 480	303	95	2 709	-0.4
Gage	17.3	D	3.7	21.4	1.9	6.6	3.0	D	17.5	5 430	251	382	10 412	-0.3
Garden	55.6	0.0	D	D	D	6.3	D	4.2	14.8	590	309	26	1 297	-1.3
Garfield	29.9	D	4.5	4.8	2.1	4.7	D	D	11.1	555	278	23	1 181	0.3
Gosper	50.9	0.0	D	D	D	1.2	D	0.4	13.9	520	265	11	1 280	1.2
Grant	69.7	0.0	1.7	0.0	D	4.5	0.0	D	12.6	160	258	0	388	1.0
Greeley	50.6	0.0	2.6	1.3	D	D	3.1	0.3	14.9	625	252	30	1 294	-0.5
Hall	2.4	D	6.3	20.9	3.8	8.5	5.3	12.0	15.7	10 500	171	923	24 333	3.3
Hamilton	22.4	0.0	4.6	11.6	5.5	5.5	3.3	D	10.7	1 950	214	67	4 066	2.5
Harlan	52.9	D	2.0	0.7	D	4.4	D	D	15.1	870	250	39	2 363	-0.5
Hayes	80.2	D	D	D	D	D	D	0.2	6.2	100	107	9	510	-0.2
Hitchcock	16.8	6.5	5.2	15.5	D	2.1	1.0	0.5	19.1	845	292	47	1 729	-1.9
Holt	25.3	0.3	3.1	6.6	1.8	5.7	4.0	D	10.6	2 500	241	163	5 223	0.2
Hooker	52.2	0.0	D	D	D	1.5	D	D	13.1	225	310	0	436	1.2
Howard	39.4	0.5	2.9	1.9	1.9	4.6	2.9	3.9	23.7	1 495	235	64	3 026	2.5
Jefferson	27.7	0.2	6.3	11.7	2.8	6.3	2.5	8.0	11.5	1 980	271	169	3 905	-0.3
Johnson	29.3	0.0	4.6	4.7	D	3.7	5.6	4.0	34.8	1 040	201	55	2 169	-1.0
Kearney	29.7	0.0	3.1	32.6	D	1.4	D	D	9.4	1 535	233	90	2 933	1.6
Keith	26.1	D	5.4	5.1	3.1	8.4	4.5	7.9	11.8	2 300	284	120	5 367	-1.1
Keya Paha	81.6	0.0	D	D	D	D	D	D	6.5	180	224	0	543	-1.1
Kimball	7.9	16.0	2.7	13.8	D	5.3	D	D	15.6	995	270	47	1 937	-1.3
Knox	46.8	0.0	2.5	2.7	D	4.4	2.6	D	19.2	2 310	272	128	4 884	2.0
Lancaster	0.7	D	5.7	8.6	9.1	6.1	10.1	13.1	21.8	44 455	147	4 798	126 503	4.7
Lincoln	16.1	D	4.2	3.8	2.9	6.3	3.2	13.8	14.2	6 530	183	725	16 618	0.2
Logan	53.2	0.0	D	D	D	1.3	D	0.7	19.4	170	226	10	395	0.0
Loup	82.8	0.0	0.0	0.0	0.0	D	D	D	8.9	160	273	10	440	3.5
McPherson	89.0	0.0	0.0	D	D	D	D	0.0	6.7	90	180	0	281	-0.7
Madison	8.1	D	4.4	15.8	3.9	7.8	4.9	14.7	15.7	6 805	193	584	15 147	0.9
Merrick	26.0	D	13.9	8.0	1.7	3.2	3.7	D	13.4	1 890	243	153	3 771	1.9
Morrill	45.6	D	2.3	1.2	D	3.3	D	D	13.0	1 130	233	91	2 424	-0.7
Nance	36.5	D	D	D	1.8	3.1	3.1	6.3	18.1	815	229	58	1 853	2.9
Nemaha	13.9	0.0	1.8	6.2	D	3.3	D	5.0	53.9	1 525	213	130	3 496	-0.1
Nuckolls	33.8	0.0	2.7	D	D	6.0	4.0	15.9	13.3	1 250	286	66	2 447	-0.7
Otoe	16.0	0.0	5.2	18.4	D	6.2	3.2	D	21.2	3 345	211	203	7 078	0.8
Pawnee	48.1	D	D	13.1	0.5	3.4	2.3	3.1	17.2	770	286	45	1 607	1.2
Perkins	49.3	0.0	7.7	2.8	D	1.7	1.5	11.6	615	213	18	1 440	-0.7
Phelps	39.4	D	D	D	1.9	3.6	3.4	D	9.5	2 160	235	120	4 213	0.9
Pierce	28.8	0.3	6.7	5.4	D	3.9	3.7	7.9	10.7	1 495	208	50	3 241	0.6

1. Per 1,000 resident population estimated as of July 1 of the year shown.

Table B. States and Counties — Housing, Labor Force, and Employment

STATE County	Housing units, 2010–2014							Civilian labor force, 2015		Unemployment		Civilian employment,[6] 2010–2014		
	Occupied units												Percent	
		Owner-occupied				Renter-occupied								
				Median owner cost as a percent of income										Con-struction, produc-tion, and mainte-nance occu-pations
	Total	Percent	Median value[1]	With a mort-gage	Without a mort-gage[2]	Median rent[3]	Median rent as a per-cent of income[2]	Sub-stand-ard units[4] (percent)	Total	Percent change, 2014–2015	Total	Rate[5]	Total	Manage-ment, business, science and arts
	89	90	91	92	93	94	95	96	97	98	99	100	101	102	103

NEBRASKA—Cont'd

STATE County	89	90	91	92	93	94	95	96	97	98	99	100	101	102	103
Blaine	250	52.0	92 000	21.6	10.0	711	18.8	2.4	275	0.0	12	4.4	316	42.7	34.5
Boone	2 236	79.0	86 500	21.0	11.3	578	18.7	1.9	3 045	0.6	75	2.5	2 751	36.2	28.2
Box Butte	4 807	64.0	93 000	18.3	10.0	551	28.0	2.8	5 634	-2.1	172	3.1	5 521	30.8	37.1
Boyd	948	79.4	54 100	24.3	12.1	395	28.8	1.8	1 098	-0.3	29	2.6	980	42.2	26.6
Brown	1 509	67.1	73 100	19.8	15.9	497	20.1	0.7	1 403	-1.3	52	3.7	1 564	38.6	21.2
Buffalo	18 018	64.2	142 800	20.3	11.6	706	27.6	1.4	27 295	-0.8	661	2.4	26 474	32.1	24.1
Burt	2 882	77.2	85 300	20.6	13.9	590	24.6	1.8	3 632	1.2	131	3.6	3 144	31.5	27.2
Butler	3 556	76.5	101 200	20.4	11.2	614	23.3	4.5	4 793	-0.9	134	2.8	4 273	29.6	38.3
Cass	9 754	80.5	148 300	22.1	13.8	748	26.6	1.8	13 283	0.2	435	3.3	13 094	33.0	26.1
Cedar	3 528	80.8	96 300	19.2	11.8	568	26.5	1.6	4 705	0.6	112	2.4	4 443	34.0	28.0
Chase	1 698	77.6	87 900	19.9	11.5	567	21.7	0.4	2 355	0.2	45	1.9	2 102	37.5	26.0
Cherry	2 603	64.3	106 900	22.5	10.1	513	19.7	3.3	3 447	0.8	79	2.3	3 244	38.8	21.6
Cheyenne	4 382	66.9	108 400	17.5	12.3	590	24.3	2.1	5 801	0.8	125	2.2	5 546	34.6	21.1
Clay	2 624	77.1	80 100	18.9	11.4	541	21.2	1.9	3 416	-1.5	99	2.9	3 207	34.1	33.7
Colfax	3 670	74.3	87 200	19.1	10.9	615	20.1	6.1	5 597	-0.6	147	2.6	5 165	21.8	48.7
Cuming	3 834	69.1	90 700	18.9	11.2	570	21.1	1.3	4 883	-1.5	129	2.6	4 730	31.7	32.0
Custer	4 746	73.3	83 700	20.6	13.0	578	21.6	1.3	6 330	3.0	140	2.2	5 660	32.9	31.0
Dakota	7 248	64.8	107 700	20.2	12.9	672	25.9	5.5	11 070	0.1	389	3.5	10 400	22.2	37.7
Dawes	3 745	63.3	108 700	18.7	14.5	522	31.8	2.3	5 270	-0.4	136	2.6	4 733	39.9	17.5
Dawson	8 731	68.4	89 700	20.6	12.6	648	23.7	5.5	13 180	-1.3	417	3.2	12 187	23.4	43.9
Deuel	840	76.3	67 100	18.9	10.2	629	18.8	1.7	1 083	-0.9	27	2.5	1 027	27.7	28.9
Dixon	2 348	76.6	78 800	19.5	11.8	574	24.3	2.4	3 089	0.9	102	3.3	2 952	30.2	36.2
Dodge	15 162	66.6	110 100	19.4	12.9	692	25.3	2.1	19 209	-0.2	626	3.3	18 163	25.4	29.6
Douglas	206 522	61.9	143 300	21.5	12.9	808	29.3	2.7	287 805	0.3	9 449	3.3	273 523	38.9	17.8
Dundy	888	64.9	70 000	17.3	10.6	453	17.3	0.0	1 228	-4.0	26	2.1	945	40.8	33.9
Fillmore	2 430	76.3	76 700	17.5	10.6	578	20.4	0.9	3 244	-0.2	95	2.9	3 056	33.5	29.6
Franklin	1 405	83.3	56 100	18.1	11.5	479	26.5	1.4	1 535	-2.8	37	2.4	1 560	33.2	28.5
Frontier	1 079	75.4	84 000	20.4	11.4	601	19.0	0.6	1 542	-0.8	39	2.5	1 298	33.2	26.5
Furnas	2 215	73.6	61 400	22.1	12.8	524	20.6	1.7	2 752	1.4	73	2.7	2 300	34.8	28.9
Gage	9 119	72.2	107 900	19.9	12.3	631	25.0	0.9	11 091	-0.1	398	3.6	10 953	34.2	27.2
Garden	878	79.3	73 300	22.6	12.2	558	22.8	2.3	1 199	0.3	29	2.4	983	31.5	25.1
Garfield	870	75.9	84 800	24.4	11.0	334	24.8	0.8	1 206	0.2	29	2.4	929	27.9	28.6
Gosper	749	75.0	104 000	20.6	11.4	614	19.9	0.5	1 081	-5.0	27	2.5	1 051	24.2	27.0
Grant	273	68.5	47 200	27.3	10.7	616	17.5	0.0	432	0.7	10	2.3	345	36.8	35.4
Greeley	1 028	80.1	59 300	22.0	12.8	526	16.9	1.8	1 272	-0.2	39	3.1	1 138	33.4	31.0
Hall	22 418	63.9	118 300	21.0	12.4	656	25.6	3.6	31 826	-1.9	1 246	3.9	30 971	25.7	32.8
Hamilton	3 564	79.8	111 600	19.2	10.9	646	28.5	0.8	4 692	-1.7	134	2.9	4 696	34.5	27.3
Harlan	1 518	78.6	73 800	18.8	13.1	552	21.9	1.1	1 805	0.0	39	2.2	1 619	31.3	30.7
Hayes	462	69.3	70 900	26.1	11.4	495	19.0	1.1	627	-0.3	15	2.4	624	40.5	34.8
Hitchcock	1 351	72.9	56 900	18.3	13.8	640	35.3	3.3	1 331	-0.9	43	3.2	1 374	32.2	31.1
Holt	4 424	74.1	94 500	20.0	13.1	606	23.8	1.0	5 943	0.2	142	2.4	5 443	33.3	28.0
Hooker	309	80.9	72 300	21.3	15.4	579	37.5	0.6	414	-2.4	17	4.1	344	33.4	25.9
Howard	2 605	76.0	100 600	21.1	13.5	559	25.8	0.5	3 319	-1.5	121	3.6	3 259	32.5	30.6
Jefferson	3 319	78.4	68 000	18.8	13.1	471	22.5	0.4	4 311	0.1	117	2.7	3 760	29.3	30.0
Johnson	1 927	72.9	76 800	20.1	12.9	583	19.4	1.7	2 140	-1.5	70	3.3	2 128	31.0	29.9
Kearney	2 646	71.1	100 700	19.0	11.8	711	23.7	1.1	3 842	-0.3	85	2.2	3 479	26.5	34.3
Keith	3 769	69.2	95 000	19.1	13.5	606	25.4	0.2	4 739	1.4	125	2.6	4 177	30.7	28.7
Keya Paha	375	76.0	74 300	26.0	12.6	475	12.8	2.1	629	1.5	14	2.2	482	50.6	25.1
Kimball	1 628	66.6	75 100	22.8	13.4	624	21.7	1.7	2 083	-6.6	74	3.6	1 750	31.7	32.7
Knox	3 721	73.9	79 500	19.2	12.1	440	22.3	1.7	4 768	0.6	151	3.2	4 204	33.6	28.9
Lancaster	116 533	59.5	150 000	20.6	11.2	727	29.5	2.3	168 402	0.0	4 393	2.6	157 745	38.6	19.4
Lincoln	15 032	67.1	113 100	20.8	13.5	628	24.3	2.0	18 601	-0.8	538	2.9	17 497	26.2	31.9
Logan	322	69.3	102 400	23.2	11.3	517	20.5	3.1	492	-0.8	14	2.8	352	31.5	28.7
Loup	244	78.3	75 400	28.5	10.0	492	17.5	0.0	381	0.0	13	3.4	310	43.5	30.3
McPherson	188	68.6	132 700	18.1	12.1	657	13.8	4.3	472	7.5	9	1.9	203	36.9	31.5
Madison	14 049	64.1	115 300	19.7	12.2	609	26.0	2.5	19 359	-0.8	530	2.7	18 512	28.8	29.9
Merrick	3 331	72.8	83 900	19.4	12.1	550	26.3	0.2	4 057	-1.5	150	3.7	4 135	31.0	28.3
Morrill	2 028	68.8	80 600	21.1	12.2	626	27.5	2.3	2 668	-0.6	77	2.9	2 399	25.8	34.0
Nance	1 548	76.7	71 000	18.0	11.0	532	28.6	1.4	2 078	0.2	51	2.5	1 832	33.6	31.8
Nemaha	2 898	69.6	90 200	17.2	12.2	552	24.2	2.9	3 723	-0.2	137	3.7	3 389	32.9	27.1
Nuckolls	2 054	74.2	54 700	18.8	11.2	515	22.8	1.9	2 419	0.5	61	2.5	2 242	32.7	28.5
Otoe	6 448	74.8	117 200	20.1	12.2	656	26.4	0.9	8 238	-0.3	269	3.3	8 054	29.8	29.0
Pawnee	1 292	75.9	56 700	20.5	13.4	468	23.3	3.3	1 693	2.2	44	2.6	1 264	40.5	28.2
Perkins	1 244	77.8	88 300	17.5	11.0	603	24.9	0.2	1 842	-0.7	34	1.8	1 495	43.0	27.8
Phelps	3 769	72.9	106 400	19.0	11.2	613	22.6	0.4	5 025	-0.7	119	2.4	4 768	28.9	32.6
Pierce	2 908	79.3	98 500	20.6	11.9	563	19.5	1.2	4 199	-1.1	107	2.5	3 649	34.5	29.6

1. Specified owner-occupied units.   2. A value of 10.0 represents 10 percent or less; a value of 50.0 represents 50 percent or more.   3. Specified renter-occupied units.
4. Overcrowded or lacking complete plumbing facilities.   5. Percent of civilian labor force.   6. Persons 16 years old and over.

Table B. States and Counties — Nonfarm Employment and Agriculture

	Private nonfarm establishments, employment and payroll, 2014									Agriculture, 2012			
STATE County		Employment						Annual payroll		Farms			
											Percent with:		
	Number of establishments	Total	Health care and social assistance	Manufacturing	Retail trade	Finance and insurance	Professional, scientific, and technical services	Total (mil dol)	Average per employee (dollars)	Number	Fewer than 50 acres	500 acres or more	Farm operators whose principal occupation is farming (percent)
	104	105	106	107	108	109	110	111	112	113	114	115	116
NEBRASKA—Cont'd													
Blaine	7	D	NA	NA	D	D	NA	D	D	117	14.5	66.7	76.1
Boone	200	1 455	313	113	248	76	34	47	32 579	646	12.7	42.4	68.3
Box Butte	309	2 927	599	D	439	D	90	97	33 166	466	17.8	48.7	59.9
Boyd	64	388	D	D	69	33	D	10	24 683	266	14.7	56.0	59.4
Brown	132	915	D	D	279	43	D	25	27 401	328	24.1	51.2	68.3
Buffalo	1 583	22 081	3 937	3 125	3 757	642	676	754	34 146	1 046	29.4	31.4	53.2
Burt	200	1 621	184	D	164	D	D	58	35 664	560	22.9	35.0	63.0
Butler	200	2 195	389	787	301	D	46	79	36 178	840	23.8	32.5	58.2
Cass	536	3 530	D	455	572	230	144	124	34 995	731	34.1	31.1	54.2
Cedar	295	1 941	D	D	351	120	100	61	31 572	939	20.8	29.9	58.7
Chase	156	1 083	D	D	278	D	D	37	34 371	342	11.7	54.1	64.9
Cherry	227	1 807	D	D	391	47	75	46	25 672	566	14.8	70.8	80.4
Cheyenne	300	4 528	D	342	906	167	71	248	54 703	555	10.6	54.1	58.9
Clay	194	1 166	D	82	D	D	26	39	33 678	457	25.2	42.5	67.0
Colfax	250	3 541	293	D	339	103	D	129	36 333	554	22.6	30.3	66.1
Cuming	351	2 554	357	311	380	193	112	86	33 798	918	26.1	25.1	61.2
Custer	380	2 934	612	D	587	166	89	94	31 952	1 352	21.1	43.3	62.9
Dakota	430	10 773	597	D	921	D	99	409	37 982	243	35.0	28.3	42.4
Dawes	283	2 224	574	D	618	D	57	64	28 699	493	11.8	52.7	53.5
Dawson	688	9 715	1 176	3 430	1 635	277	221	311	32 014	806	24.9	39.0	64.6
Deuel	62	340	30	NA	103	D	D	8	24 776	237	14.3	51.1	58.2
Dixon	104	1 079	D	D	73	45	D	34	31 767	570	24.9	31.1	60.5
Dodge	1 004	15 239	2 562	3 104	2 636	479	196	503	33 006	767	29.6	28.3	68.3
Douglas	15 136	305 146	46 322	21 049	36 224	35 622	20 297	14 682	48 113	396	58.3	13.6	44.4
Dundy	62	337	96	27	D	14	D	12	36 822	251	8.0	55.0	55.0
Fillmore	230	1 749	299	292	213	158	D	60	34 429	472	13.1	48.5	72.5
Franklin	74	418	D	NA	114	44	D	12	27 529	338	11.2	47.9	67.8
Frontier	64	394	39	D	76	45	14	13	33 421	317	15.8	51.1	60.6
Furnas	158	1 264	391	122	188	63	14	44	34 706	389	16.7	48.3	67.1
Gage	683	7 390	1 822	1 529	1 066	229	142	238	32 259	1 263	26.6	27.4	49.6
Garden	54	396	D	D	65	D	D	7	18 404	261	20.3	51.7	69.7
Garfield	98	584	120	D	129	D	24	14	24 777	226	16.8	41.2	58.0
Gosper	67	303	D	28	29	28	D	10	34 013	260	13.1	55.0	63.1
Grant	31	107	D	D	D	D	D	2	20 355	80	13.8	65.0	75.0
Greeley	67	377	D	14	98	37	NA	10	25 467	389	9.0	47.8	68.9
Hall	1 822	30 308	4 207	7 476	5 134	1 221	624	1 068	35 253	593	29.3	34.2	59.9
Hamilton	304	2 676	332	473	313	111	93	103	38 468	572	22.7	40.2	72.0
Harlan	102	623	D	D	95	49	D	17	27 639	360	19.7	40.6	60.6
Hayes	21	53	D	D	D	D	D	2	30 302	235	8.1	60.0	67.7
Hitchcock	65	397	D	D	75	D	NA	16	40 872	299	10.4	50.8	59.5
Holt	412	3 477	858	D	620	181	83	109	31 443	1 279	14.3	49.4	64.4
Hooker	30	114	D	D	38	D	D	4	32 623	82	11.0	76.8	54.9
Howard	152	985	D	D	212	D	32	28	28 048	682	26.1	29.0	59.1
Jefferson	232	2 520	D	D	393	D	47	79	31 444	627	21.9	33.2	55.5
Johnson	115	902	D	D	147	D	D	25	27 346	587	22.7	25.0	49.1
Kearney	174	1 876	611	277	D	77	D	57	30 290	344	15.1	56.1	78.5
Keith	354	2 447	294	D	546	180	D	73	29 869	388	14.7	46.4	72.2
Keya Paha	23	D	NA	NA	D	D	4	1	D	244	11.9	66.0	73.0
Kimball	129	1 179	D	D	202	D	D	45	37 981	402	9.0	52.5	52.5
Knox	261	1 646	336	46	377	169	64	42	25 574	1 080	17.5	38.1	68.3
Lancaster	8 111	129 360	23 621	11 639	18 072	10 063	8 434	5 062	39 132	1 836	51.1	14.9	34.2
Lincoln	1 061	11 732	2 805	340	2 223	499	447	383	32 683	1 168	29.8	39.2	59.2
Logan	24	86	D	D	D	D	D	2	24 419	149	22.8	46.3	63.8
Loup	12	D	NA	NA	D	D	NA	D	D	138	12.3	49.3	62.3
McPherson	6	D	NA	NA	D	D	NA	0	D	118	11.9	71.2	59.3
Madison	1 337	18 422	2 715	3 306	3 052	698	628	640	34 727	753	25.9	29.9	59.2
Merrick	240	1 630	D	285	180	84	36	63	38 799	492	27.8	33.7	57.1
Morrill	114	721	D	D	213	46	11	23	31 275	512	19.3	42.6	61.1
Nance	104	485	D	NA	97	45	D	12	24 184	355	22.8	34.9	64.2
Nemaha	188	1 477	360	D	242	111	D	43	29 150	451	16.0	33.3	57.6
Nuckolls	181	1 092	D	D	240	D	38	30	27 191	435	16.3	43.7	55.2
Otoe	458	5 030	D	1 385	805	206	86	159	31 556	897	29.8	29.7	49.3
Pawnee	64	510	113	D	65	50	D	16	31 925	540	12.4	34.1	52.0
Perkins	125	822	D	D	137	40	D	30	36 024	394	8.6	57.1	65.7
Phelps	333	3 887	863	D	440	147	94	137	35 295	405	16.3	54.1	72.3
Pierce	226	1 545	349	121	D	D	44	48	30 853	677	21.1	30.9	60.4

Table B. States and Counties — **Agriculture**

STATE County	Acreage (1,000) [117]	Percent change, 2007–2012 [118]	Average size of farm [119]	Total irrigated (1,000) [120]	Total cropland (1,000) [121]	Average per farm [122]	Average per acre [123]	Value of machinery and equipment, average per farm (dollars) [124]	Total (mil dol) [125]	Average per farm (dollars) [126]	Crops [127]	Live-stock and poultry products [128]	$10,000 or more [129]	$100,000 or more [130]	Total ($1,000) [131]	Percent of farms [132]
NEBRASKA—Cont'd																
Blaine	403	-9.2	3 440	7.0	32.6	1 760 274	512	95 709	34.7	296 214	16.3	83.7	76.9	39.3	293	32.5
Boone	434	7.2	672	184.7	326.9	2 964 181	4 408	289 596	453.4	701 850	42.9	57.1	83.4	59.0	5 870	78.8
Box Butte	675	0.7	1 449	141.6	337.5	1 547 721	1 068	292 384	299.3	642 170	56.3	43.7	65.2	43.3	4 279	68.2
Boyd	291	15.6	1 094	5.2	98.0	1 504 169	1 375	147 015	62.9	236 477	30.2	69.8	72.9	32.3	913	75.9
Brown	725	9.6	2 212	40.2	109.4	1 584 393	716	138 912	195.4	595 826	20.1	79.9	66.5	43.3	1 694	38.4
Buffalo	581	-5.2	555	240.8	342.3	2 074 083	3 737	226 212	395.1	377 751	68.9	31.1	67.5	40.6	8 102	64.9
Burt	310	12.7	553	37.6	278.5	2 886 561	5 216	245 725	226.9	405 252	66.2	33.8	72.3	50.4	4 598	77.0
Butler	370	3.9	441	110.8	306.6	2 179 969	4 948	258 019	276.4	329 043	66.9	33.1	67.0	42.9	6 657	78.6
Cass	345	22.8	472	3.5	304.3	2 732 765	5 792	210 464	149.3	204 291	93.9	6.1	60.7	41.6	4 746	66.5
Cedar	466	-1.7	497	139.0	371.7	2 189 874	4 408	211 296	388.7	413 987	42.0	58.0	75.6	45.4	6 256	73.7
Chase	541	-2.6	1 583	159.7	290.6	3 112 181	1 966	393 310	414.9	1 213 085	44.2	55.8	65.2	52.6	6 032	76.9
Cherry	3 757	-0.1	6 637	50.9	358.5	3 521 118	531	181 652	246.8	435 974	32.4	67.6	78.3	55.7	3 354	27.2
Cheyenne	703	-6.8	1 267	48.7	499.3	1 131 528	893	203 490	205.7	370 593	43.6	56.4	65.0	38.6	7 026	85.4
Clay	331	-9.5	723	191.7	259.1	3 712 295	5 133	386 182	355.1	776 978	59.6	40.4	77.9	58.4	5 141	73.7
Colfax	258	20.8	465	66.8	224.9	2 460 460	5 291	266 197	337.9	609 935	34.2	65.8	77.8	45.5	5 060	75.8
Cuming	363	0.8	395	52.4	312.6	2 120 511	5 364	285 514	1 081.3	1 177 889	12.9	87.1	79.3	49.3	6 797	76.8
Custer	1 504	-6.9	1 112	261.5	484.9	2 110 533	1 898	187 440	845.3	625 226	34.7	65.3	70.6	40.8	7 479	55.4
Dakota	158	-5.2	650	29.3	136.0	3 120 123	4 799	228 041	73.0	300 317	89.4	10.6	56.4	28.8	2 079	68.3
Dawes	824	-2.9	1 671	21.4	172.7	1 243 284	744	109 030	75.6	153 410	27.8	72.2	62.1	37.9	2 428	67.5
Dawson	630	-1.6	782	248.5	321.8	2 429 274	3 106	263 305	826.3	1 025 163	34.3	65.7	71.3	48.9	6 166	55.2
Deuel	277	-0.8	1 168	17.4	216.1	1 167 042	999	226 080	70.6	297 971	57.3	42.7	69.2	43.9	2 383	69.6
Dixon	299	20.3	525	24.0	226.3	2 176 037	4 148	211 812	169.1	296 716	42.0	58.0	63.0	35.4	4 695	73.7
Dodge	330	-2.5	430	118.0	305.0	2 414 327	5 611	281 532	326.0	425 043	60.7	39.3	72.2	48.9	5 602	74.3
Douglas	86	2.1	217	19.8	76.3	1 352 033	6 217	152 404	58.0	146 513	93.4	6.6	47.0	23.7	1 378	40.9
Dundy	521	-12.4	2 075	94.8	208.6	2 820 614	1 359	377 386	195.6	779 363	54.1	45.9	69.3	51.8	3 944	73.3
Fillmore	328	-9.3	696	211.0	296.4	3 835 816	5 513	473 146	334.8	709 335	78.0	22.0	84.1	68.9	5 465	81.4
Franklin	288	-1.3	851	85.8	166.2	2 527 118	2 969	260 417	119.1	352 447	87.0	13.0	78.4	48.2	3 802	81.1
Frontier	452	-4.9	1 426	53.3	174.7	2 093 385	1 468	232 278	124.6	393 145	53.1	46.9	70.7	41.0	3 205	74.4
Furnas	436	-2.3	1 120	66.4	282.7	2 622 414	2 341	282 820	181.6	466 720	54.2	45.8	69.9	44.2	5 719	82.3
Gage	534	-1.1	423	63.8	422.0	1 477 063	3 491	156 753	244.5	193 561	71.5	28.5	60.9	35.7	9 908	75.5
Garden	1 026	-2.1	3 932	35.7	149.4	2 403 636	611	180 276	113.6	435 341	33.3	66.7	65.5	44.1	1 714	70.1
Garfield	346	-5.4	1 531	22.5	70.7	1 517 035	991	146 903	64.8	286 597	34.9	65.1	74.3	42.9	1 373	48.7
Gosper	290	28.5	1 115	98.8	171.8	3 529 077	3 165	330 900	139.1	534 885	79.2	20.8	76.5	55.8	3 628	73.5
Grant	493	-0.4	6 167	1.7	41.0	3 407 063	552	136 288	29.0	362 063	D	D	71.3	53.8	226	8.8
Greeley	338	19.8	870	88.2	154.4	2 807 974	3 229	210 997	187.6	482 134	45.5	54.5	75.1	47.0	3 064	74.0
Hall	330	0.4	556	207.6	245.4	2 484 954	4 470	292 526	353.1	595 405	65.9	34.1	69.5	52.1	4 755	64.6
Hamilton	304	-4.6	532	235.5	273.2	3 430 491	6 446	346 014	353.2	617 547	77.1	22.9	77.4	62.4	5 705	77.6
Harlan	313	-10.9	869	93.3	211.8	2 677 533	3 082	261 208	223.5	620 828	56.6	43.4	67.8	44.2	2 989	68.1
Hayes	385	-15.1	1 639	57.1	186.1	2 121 255	1 294	253 677	163.4	695 383	44.9	55.1	70.2	50.2	4 320	92.8
Hitchcock	399	14.8	1 335	21.5	207.4	1 723 151	1 290	204 060	63.6	212 803	67.4	32.6	71.2	42.1	3 553	79.9
Holt	1 414	-7.7	1 106	280.2	600.5	2 314 973	2 093	217 735	636.4	497 540	51.7	48.3	77.2	43.2	7 584	53.2
Hooker	437	-4.4	5 327	3.1	15.7	2 361 890	443	104 793	17.3	210 500	10.9	89.1	81.7	35.4	897	34.1
Howard	312	12.0	458	115.4	182.5	1 350 003	2 949	186 560	246.3	361 128	45.5	54.5	71.7	39.9	3 603	70.1
Jefferson	352	8.2	562	92.8	270.7	2 206 616	3 928	230 150	219.6	350 234	62.2	37.8	66.3	39.4	5 179	74.8
Johnson	198	12.6	337	14.3	132.9	856 930	2 545	107 278	74.6	127 112	58.7	41.3	54.7	26.7	3 405	79.9
Kearney	294	-9.4	854	194.5	242.8	4 508 817	5 283	440 390	407.4	1 184 375	56.9	43.1	84.0	72.4	5 065	80.2
Keith	541	-6.9	1 395	115.3	253.9	2 593 289	1 859	276 216	228.3	588 492	60.7	39.3	65.7	44.3	3 371	67.0
Keya Paha	466	-3.7	1 909	20.1	98.0	1 480 037	775	148 684	107.1	438 848	27.2	72.8	77.9	43.0	733	40.6
Kimball	598	13.3	1 487	34.4	384.8	1 289 806	868	160 933	60.8	151 256	83.5	16.5	51.0	30.6	5 236	87.3
Knox	628	17.0	581	63.9	326.6	1 612 287	2 774	174 033	312.8	289 671	29.9	70.1	69.4	35.1	7 276	74.4
Lancaster	489	16.0	266	21.4	402.6	1 219 781	4 580	123 412	177.8	96 822	82.5	17.5	42.8	18.1	8 810	59.5
Lincoln	1 423	-11.1	1 219	239.8	432.3	1 749 910	1 436	196 783	782.7	670 087	33.8	66.2	62.2	33.0	5 832	45.5
Logan	330	-9.2	2 216	23.0	61.4	2 518 114	1 136	213 148	42.0	281 846	62.5	37.5	63.1	39.6	1 180	53.0
Loup	283	-20.2	2 051	8.2	29.3	1 519 891	741	106 181	32.1	232 406	24.2	75.8	68.8	37.7	772	58.7
McPherson	471	-13.2	3 990	7.1	20.2	1 789 517	449	88 102	30.1	255 144	19.5	80.5	70.3	39.8	167	18.6
Madison	352	11.6	467	122.0	291.0	2 250 416	4 817	236 368	303.7	403 263	49.2	50.8	71.8	40.2	7 057	69.5
Merrick	235	-5.2	478	167.4	200.2	1 833 841	3 838	280 335	275.2	559 394	58.6	41.4	66.1	47.8	4 182	72.6
Morrill	799	-11.4	1 561	128.6	240.5	1 440 148	923	169 750	345.2	674 223	33.1	66.9	68.9	45.1	3 595	69.7
Nance	208	-8.0	586	63.3	133.7	2 003 290	3 417	204 239	145.9	410 927	49.3	50.7	70.4	46.8	3 285	73.5
Nemaha	253	19.1	562	11.4	211.4	2 284 878	4 068	234 035	108.1	239 772	89.3	10.7	67.4	42.4	4 984	80.9
Nuckolls	350	13.9	804	65.2	230.4	3 033 191	3 773	259 074	168.4	387 140	81.8	18.2	82.8	54.7	4 756	79.3
Otoe	388	20.4	432	8.4	321.9	1 856 521	4 295	174 511	158.5	176 670	84.1	15.9	61.3	36.8	5 428	69.3
Pawnee	269	23.5	498	7.3	180.1	1 288 361	2 588	153 443	75.7	140 241	75.7	24.3	58.7	29.6	4 461	78.3
Perkins	557	-0.3	1 413	127.9	432.1	3 208 183	2 271	350 124	233.1	591 713	78.2	21.8	76.9	56.3	7 804	85.8
Phelps	331	-2.6	818	231.9	265.0	3 684 978	4 504	546 160	738.8	1 824 185	35.7	64.3	85.7	76.3	6 054	77.3
Pierce	329	3.9	486	130.0	260.6	2 102 468	4 324	270 908	261.2	385 832	56.4	43.6	72.8	41.1	5 154	70.3

Table B. States and Counties — Water Use, Wholesale Trade, Retail Trade, and Real Estate

STATE County	Water use, 2010 Total water withdrawn (mil gal/day)	Gallons withdrawn per person per day	Wholesale trade,[1] 2012 Number of establishments	Number of employees	Sales (mil dol)	Annual payroll (mil dol)	Retail trade,[2] 2012 Number of establishments	Number of employees	Sales (mil dol)	Annual payroll (mil dol)	Real estate and rental and leasing,[2] 2012 Number of establishments	Number of employees	Receipts (mil dol)	Annual payroll (mil dol)
	133	134	135	136	137	138	139	140	141	142	143	144	145	146
NEBRASKA—Cont'd														
Blaine	3.1	6 444	NA	NA	NA	NA	2	D	D	D	NA	NA	NA	NA
Boone	60.9	11 055	16	213	518.4	10.3	38	257	85.8	4.6	5	D	D	D
Box Butte	101.8	9 002	20	196	173.0	8.2	47	412	96.5	7.8	10	16	2.8	0.3
Boyd	9.1	4 350	3	16	8.4	0.5	11	74	14.4	1.0	1	D	D	D
Brown	51.1	16 232	4	D	D	D	31	259	68.1	5.3	2	D	D	D
Buffalo	230.8	5 007	77	902	1 254.5	43.0	236	3 677	967.0	78.9	55	156	39.0	4.4
Burt	10.6	1 550	16	180	128.0	6.2	29	179	33.8	2.5	4	5	0.3	0.0
Butler	51.2	6 100	14	129	216.5	6.9	27	298	64.2	4.8	4	3	0.3	0.1
Cass	18.4	728	17	D	D	D	70	627	177.8	13.2	20	21	3.3	0.5
Cedar	28.4	3 209	24	161	120.3	7.2	46	377	111.0	8.0	8	14	1.4	0.3
Chase	144.2	36 364	16	222	536.5	10.0	30	260	92.3	7.4	4	7	0.2	0.1
Cherry	44.7	7 826	7	102	222.5	2.3	38	422	87.3	7.6	9	7	1.4	0.2
Cheyenne	43.3	4 327	13	113	194.6	5.6	52	1 508	1 081.6	46.1	7	9	1.5	0.2
Clay	121.3	18 546	24	174	289.5	8.6	25	200	135.9	4.1	2	D	D	D
Colfax	24.1	2 294	17	131	214.2	7.6	43	342	106.0	7.6	6	14	1.4	0.2
Cuming	12.8	1 395	24	163	220.5	7.4	50	378	206.0	7.5	4	5	0.9	0.1
Custer	169.1	15 460	15	120	77.8	5.4	63	483	143.4	10.6	7	10	0.7	0.1
Dakota	7.4	350	15	249	219.1	12.3	68	897	198.7	18.5	13	D	D	D
Dawes	7.9	861	4	23	10.4	0.7	58	581	169.9	13.8	10	10	1.1	0.2
Dawson	182.7	7 511	34	433	680.1	19.5	107	1 398	423.4	34.4	19	D	D	D
Deuel	28.0	14 405	3	D	D	D	11	118	94.8	2.1	1	D	D	D
Dixon	9.6	1 597	8	35	93.3	1.7	9	61	11.7	0.8	1	D	D	D
Dodge	36.0	980	63	640	1 127.7	31.8	162	2 427	1 097.3	59.0	36	172	24.1	4.2
Douglas	386.0	746	750	10 775	12 685.1	594.8	1 749	34 754	8 586.0	839.3	713	5 700	977.6	258.1
Dundy	108.0	53 800	5	D	D	D	10	46	12.3	1.1	1	D	D	D
Fillmore	120.6	20 467	24	199	281.1	8.1	30	234	65.0	3.9	5	4	0.4	0.0
Franklin	37.5	11 622	9	68	90.2	2.2	12	102	20.4	2.0	1	D	D	D
Frontier	36.0	13 059	6	D	D	D	12	65	19.2	1.2	1	D	D	D
Furnas	32.8	6 622	10	D	D	D	33	204	52.9	3.8	1	D	D	D
Gage	24.9	1 115	36	349	369.5	15.5	112	1 036	262.4	23.0	14	23	3.7	0.6
Garden	27.9	13 578	3	D	D	D	12	65	11.9	0.9	NA	NA	NA	NA
Garfield	12.7	6 193	3	D	D	D	22	138	29.6	2.1	1	D	D	D
Gosper	57.3	28 048	6	41	101.4	1.6	5	24	3.7	0.3	4	D	D	D
Grant	2.1	3 453	3	D	D	D	4	20	3.3	0.2	NA	NA	NA	NA
Greeley	51.5	20 280	4	49	50.4	2.4	15	92	41.6	1.9	2	D	D	D
Hall	132.6	2 263	98	1 296	910.4	66.9	297	4 864	1 256.3	110.1	77	296	54.3	9.0
Hamilton	142.7	15 642	14	284	545.3	14.7	40	309	116.5	6.1	7	9	3.1	0.7
Harlan	37.2	10 876	10	46	63.2	2.0	18	97	34.4	2.0	1	D	D	D
Hayes	41.6	43 020	NA	NA	NA	NA	2	D	D	D	NA	NA	NA	NA
Hitchcock	24.6	8 473	5	D	D	D	13	71	15.8	1.4	NA	NA	NA	NA
Holt	358.2	34 327	30	374	424.0	16.2	80	615	159.9	11.2	13	17	4.2	0.4
Hooker	2.6	3 519	NA	NA	NA	NA	5	34	7.2	0.6	NA	NA	NA	NA
Howard	168.0	26 771	8	55	43.7	1.9	27	212	52.9	3.8	NA	NA	NA	NA
Jefferson	40.6	5 376	13	D	D	D	33	570	176.9	10.1	4	15	0.7	0.3
Johnson	6.9	1 326	4	D	D	D	26	144	44.8	2.9	4	23	3.6	0.3
Kearney	103.6	15 958	14	182	246.1	8.5	20	160	33.4	3.0	3	3	0.6	0.1
Keith	119.8	14 315	19	154	135.2	6.7	63	560	241.5	12.3	17	44	3.9	0.7
Keya Paha	22.1	26 796	2	D	D	D	3	9	5.0	0.2	NA	NA	NA	NA
Kimball	29.1	7 618	4	D	D	D	22	173	50.3	4.2	3	D	D	D
Knox	33.1	3 800	13	118	151.0	4.4	54	384	82.2	6.5	7	29	1.7	0.6
Lancaster	22.0	77	278	4 169	3 139.7	169.3	1 016	17 165	4 322.6	388.1	344	1 715	255.1	56.5
Lincoln	263.4	7 257	46	D	D	D	194	2 180	728.8	49.2	43	104	17.8	2.6
Logan	12.3	16 107	2	D	D	D	2	D	D	D	NA	NA	NA	NA
Loup	9.1	14 320	1	D	D	D	1	D	D	D	NA	NA	NA	NA
McPherson	6.9	12 801	NA	NA	NA	NA	2	D	D	D	NA	NA	NA	NA
Madison	40.5	1 162	64	1 730	2 252.8	78.7	212	3 061	815.2	67.6	59	172	24.8	4.2
Merrick	111.9	14 264	24	198	369.2	9.5	33	204	72.1	3.7	5	10	1.1	0.5
Morrill	213.9	42 422	12	120	71.0	5.9	20	163	37.2	2.9	3	3	0.4	0.0
Nance	36.4	9 751	5	23	52.0	0.9	16	100	25.4	2.0	1	D	D	D
Nemaha	727.0	100 304	9	57	69.5	2.5	37	235	57.7	4.6	5	10	0.8	0.1
Nuckolls	62.4	13 860	16	114	172.0	5.4	26	231	73.8	4.8	1	D	D	D
Otoe	314.8	19 998	21	171	239.4	8.0	80	833	202.5	16.9	15	63	11.9	1.9
Pawnee	4.9	1 771	1	D	D	D	10	76	15.7	1.4	NA	NA	NA	NA
Perkins	96.5	32 495	14	121	218.7	6.0	19	120	56.8	3.5	3	15	1.0	0.1
Phelps	153.9	16 748	28	378	851.6	17.3	48	404	116.5	9.3	9	13	2.7	0.2
Pierce	54.4	7 480	14	D	D	D	36	200	69.6	3.5	3	3	0.5	0.1

1. Merchant wholesalers, except manufacturers' sales branches and offices.   2. Employer establishments.

Table B. States and Counties — Professional Services, Manufacturing, and Accommodation and Food Services

STATE County	Professional, scientific, and technical services, 2012				Manufacturing, 2012				Accommodation and food services, 2012			
	Number of establish-ments	Number of employees	Receipts (mil dol)	Annual payroll (mil dol)	Number of establish-ments	Number of employees	Receipts (mil dol)	Annual payroll (mil dol)	Number of establish-ments	Number of employees	Sales (mil dol)	Annual payroll (mil dol)
	147	148	149	150	151	152	153	154	155	156	157	158
NEBRASKA—Cont'd												
Blaine	NA	NA	NA	NA	NA	NA	NA	NA	1	D	D	D
Boone	8	25	5.5	0.9	11	112	D	5.4	11	94	3.2	0.8
Box Butte	22	93	8.8	2.6	8	328	D	16.2	32	339	14.7	3.9
Boyd	1	D	D	D	5	16	D	0.3	6	20	0.6	0.1
Brown	6	19	1.5	0.4	3	24	D	D	10	87	2.9	0.7
Buffalo	104	630	77.1	27.0	58	3 306	1 785.0	147.3	143	3 084	121.7	33.9
Burt	8	72	20.8	3.8	8	76	22.2	2.8	15	67	2.8	0.6
Butler	9	D	D	D	10	571	D	23.9	15	D	D	D
Cass	37	127	10.3	5.2	19	381	170.5	19.2	41	D	D	D
Cedar	13	D	D	D	12	198	D	9.3	12	87	2.2	0.5
Chase	8	D	D	D	4	22	D	D	9	D	D	D
Cherry	18	62	7.4	1.7	8	23	5.1	0.9	23	300	14.0	3.8
Cheyenne	15	D	D	D	8	273	120.8	15.0	35	520	28.1	6.9
Clay	7	D	D	D	7	67	D	2.5	8	31	1.0	0.3
Colfax	11	58	8.0	1.6	3	D	D	D	19	D	D	D
Cuming	22	104	15.7	3.3	14	323	245.8	14.3	25	290	15.4	2.6
Custer	27	96	9.9	2.6	9	D	D	D	31	313	10.7	3.1
Dakota	25	D	D	D	36	D	D	D	40	526	25.1	7.2
Dawes	18	D	D	D	4	10	1.5	0.3	37	457	17.4	4.9
Dawson	57	D	D	D	26	D	D	D	61	D	D	D
Deuel	3	4	0.3	0.1	NA	NA	NA	NA	5	D	D	D
Dixon	1	D	D	D	NA	NA	NA	NA	6	17	1.1	0.1
Dodge	49	183	20.6	7.0	60	3 402	1 955.3	140.1	97	1 476	56.3	15.8
Douglas	1 742	55 558	3 260.3	2 757.2	431	20 560	10 990.1	904.0	1 258	24 758	1 170.2	342.9
Dundy	5	D	D	D	5	15	2.7	0.4	4	27	1.2	0.3
Fillmore	10	24	2.5	0.7	13	221	415.1	8.7	13	81	2.7	0.6
Franklin	4	15	1.5	0.4	NA	NA	NA	NA	6	33	1.3	0.3
Frontier	3	15	0.9	0.3	NA	NA	NA	NA	3	D	D	D
Furnas	5	18	1.2	0.4	7	98	D	4.4	12	D	D	D
Gage	33	125	10.6	3.8	40	1 252	727.0	56.1	49	628	27.4	6.7
Garden	3	D	D	D	NA	NA	NA	NA	3	32	1.0	0.2
Garfield	7	D	D	D	8	117	D	3.7	9	63	1.8	0.3
Gosper	3	D	D	D	NA	NA	NA	NA	3	D	D	D
Grant	2	D	D	D	NA	NA	NA	NA	5	12	0.1	0.0
Greeley	NA	NA	NA	NA	3	9	D	D	4	9	0.6	0.1
Hall	109	638	69.7	25.2	74	7 241	6 021.9	280.1	156	2 515	114.9	33.0
Hamilton	16	69	13.0	2.7	19	443	D	21.7	19	169	6.8	2.0
Harlan	8	D	D	D	5	37	D	D	14	91	3.6	0.8
Hayes	2	D	D	D	NA	NA	NA	NA	2	D	D	D
Hitchcock	NA	NA	NA	NA	3	85	188.0	3.6	5	17	0.6	0.1
Holt	21	63	7.7	2.8	20	190	D	6.8	41	386	12.8	3.2
Hooker	1	D	D	D	NA	NA	NA	NA	4	7	0.3	0.0
Howard	10	26	3.5	0.9	5	10	2.1	0.3	10	69	2.5	0.5
Jefferson	11	D	D	D	16	572	178.4	20.6	19	160	6.7	1.5
Johnson	4	11	0.7	0.2	4	D	D	D	10	57	2.0	0.5
Kearney	10	27	2.0	0.6	9	260	209.2	12.2	12	118	3.1	1.0
Keith	28	119	9.9	3.6	15	254	D	8.0	46	514	22.9	6.1
Keya Paha	4	5	0.2	0.0	NA	NA	NA	NA	NA	NA	NA	NA
Kimball	9	20	1.5	0.3	8	263	38.7	8.9	16	110	4.0	0.9
Knox	17	D	D	D	6	23	6.4	0.9	22	98	3.5	0.7
Lancaster	842	9 135	1 292.4	460.9	235	12 011	5 963.3	596.5	672	13 483	598.3	156.9
Lincoln	78	D	D	D	17	D	200.8	D	94	D	D	D
Logan	1	D	D	D	NA	NA	NA	NA	1	D	D	D
Loup	NA	NA	NA	NA	NA	NA	NA	NA	1	D	D	D
McPherson	NA	NA	NA	NA	NA	NA	NA	NA	1	D	D	D
Madison	88	702	51.5	20.6	55	3 092	D	132.6	101	1 644	64.6	17.8
Merrick	8	34	4.2	1.4	16	254	D	11.8	13	99	4.4	1.0
Morrill	1	D	D	D	3	36	D	1.4	18	147	4.2	1.1
Nance	5	D	D	D	NA	NA	NA	NA	14	D	D	D
Nemaha	8	36	2.1	0.7	3	D	D	D	20	253	7.0	2.5
Nuckolls	14	31	2.6	0.7	3	6	D	D	9	D	D	D
Otoe	26	85	7.3	2.1	17	1 512	D	66.9	40	398	13.9	4.4
Pawnee	4	D	D	D	5	D	D	D	5	33	0.8	0.2
Perkins	7	25	1.6	0.5	3	10	D	D	3	7	0.6	0.1
Phelps	25	89	11.2	3.6	7	D	D	D	22	316	11.3	3.1
Pierce	11	D	D	D	11	D	D	D	10	99	2.2	0.6

1. Establishment subject to federal tax.

STATE County	Health care and social assistance, 2012				Other services, 2012				Nonemployer businesses, 2014		Value of residential construction authorized by building permits, 2015	
	Number of establish-ments	Number of employees	Receipts (mil dol)	Annual payroll (mil dol)	Number of establish-ments	Number of employees	Receipts (mil dol)	Annual payroll (mil dol)	Number	Receipts (mil dol)	New Construction ($1,000)	Number of housing units
	159	160	161	162	163	164	165	166	167	168	169	170
NEBRASKA—Cont'd												
Blaine	NA	NA	NA	NA	NA	NA	NA	NA	45	1.4	NA	NA
Boone	19	244	14.0	4.7	10	26	3.1	0.8	523	22.2	0	0
Box Butte	29	607	50.5	20.0	31	105	11.7	2.3	705	25.0	1 096	6
Boyd	9	108	5.2	2.1	4	11	1.6	0.2	206	8.0	0	0
Brown	11	181	11.5	4.8	11	28	3.1	0.8	310	9.7	0	0
Buffalo	177	4 012	453.6	165.4	112	D	D	D	3 709	174.1	39 218	210
Burt	17	227	12.5	5.6	13	72	8.5	2.4	537	24.9	1 262	5
Butler	15	373	28.3	13.0	15	D	D	D	655	25.9	400	3
Cass	29	423	26.6	9.8	35	120	9.0	2.4	1 858	75.9	20 602	121
Cedar	13	191	10.2	4.2	25	D	D	D	728	40.7	3 363	14
Chase	10	142	11.6	5.2	12	D	D	D	386	21.8	1 265	3
Cherry	19	345	23.9	9.5	18	36	4.8	0.8	565	21.6	5 226	36
Cheyenne	19	510	45.6	16.9	23	67	6.6	1.8	668	32.4	4 909	25
Clay	16	154	5.4	2.6	8	D	D	D	547	27.7	1 999	10
Colfax	15	344	36.0	8.6	27	76	8.1	1.9	574	27.1	2 363	11
Cuming	26	385	40.9	14.6	33	132	21.1	3.8	736	38.2	5 144	20
Custer	41	713	44.0	19.8	28	59	7.2	1.2	1 095	43.3	4 837	25
Dakota	32	520	33.7	12.2	36	240	54.8	14.1	1 031	52.0	4 609	24
Dawes	33	630	44.1	21.3	19	51	3.1	0.8	676	20.7	803	4
Dawson	73	1 143	92.1	34.5	62	D	D	D	1 385	63.8	9 791	57
Deuel	3	19	1.0	0.4	3	D	D	D	176	9.2	0	0
Dixon	11	99	4.6	1.8	11	D	D	D	482	23.2	1 376	6
Dodge	114	2 662	231.7	85.4	92	377	36.4	8.9	2 257	105.2	14 347	50
Douglas	1 742	47 573	5 673.5	2 121.5	1 067	8 179	1 287.2	251.7	35 681	1 718.2	350 120	2 788
Dundy	8	D	D	D	3	D	D	D	161	7.5	200	1
Fillmore	14	288	20.5	8.7	22	63	9.4	1.4	476	21.9	300	1
Franklin	7	166	9.1	3.6	7	19	1.4	0.2	256	9.2	532	3
Frontier	8	40	1.0	0.5	4	D	D	D	224	9.9	50	1
Furnas	20	359	24.6	10.9	14	D	D	D	419	20.2	799	4
Gage	58	1 780	114.4	48.2	66	242	21.6	5.6	1 561	55.8	3 271	15
Garden	4	D	D	D	4	9	0.5	0.1	202	8.1	300	2
Garfield	7	D	D	D	8	17	1.7	0.4	232	8.7	678	6
Gosper	7	9	0.4	0.2	1	D	D	D	186	8.7	3 277	13
Grant	NA	NA	NA	NA	2	D	D	D	103	4.1	0	0
Greeley	3	10	0.1	0.1	2	D	D	D	246	13.5	220	1
Hall	185	D	D	D	145	987	92.7	21.6	3 790	169.9	35 318	232
Hamilton	19	D	D	D	23	D	D	D	825	34.1	3 401	14
Harlan	8	172	11.2	5.0	6	D	D	D	332	12.0	810	6
Hayes	1	D	D	D	NA	NA	NA	NA	75	3.4	295	2
Hitchcock	2	D	D	D	2	D	D	D	224	9.9	0	0
Holt	33	870	75.4	29.2	37	D	D	D	1 261	75.0	3 023	15
Hooker	1	D	D	D	4	4	0.5	0.1	101	3.3	351	2
Howard	10	D	D	D	12	D	D	D	503	20.1	4 709	30
Jefferson	16	411	28.1	11.9	17	D	D	D	461	22.2	2 030	7
Johnson	14	274	22.3	9.4	8	21	1.8	0.3	306	10.5	160	1
Kearney	14	604	27.7	13.2	13	D	D	D	463	20.2	3 991	14
Keith	23	339	32.1	10.6	24	94	8.7	2.2	761	33.6	2 779	15
Keya Paha	NA	NA	NA	NA	3	D	D	D	117	4.6	0	0
Kimball	7	97	9.1	4.0	10	D	D	D	294	12.0	290	4
Knox	19	375	24.2	9.1	12	29	3.3	0.6	669	25.7	4 126	29
Lancaster	971	23 204	2 364.8	939.4	667	4 152	578.3	130.7	20 171	782.1	372 300	2 500
Lincoln	140	D	D	D	79	398	38.3	10.1	2 235	87.7	13 128	76
Logan	1	D	D	D	3	15	0.3	0.2	70	3.3	NA	NA
Loup	NA	NA	NA	NA	1	D	D	D	73	2.3	1 648	9
McPherson	NA	NA	NA	NA	NA	NA	NA	NA	37	1.7	0	0
Madison	164	D	D	D	106	542	44.3	14.0	2 575	109.6	12 558	62
Merrick	17	343	24.3	9.1	22	48	7.3	1.2	630	25.1	3 951	24
Morrill	8	135	12.6	4.3	6	D	D	D	379	14.3	0	0
Nance	10	165	7.4	3.5	13	D	D	D	275	10.8	2 899	7
Nemaha	21	369	30.8	13.6	17	73	4.5	1.1	507	20.8	430	2
Nuckolls	15	385	28.3	11.4	23	48	4.4	0.8	355	15.3	450	3
Otoe	42	853	66.9	26.5	36	129	11.4	2.9	1 162	44.2	7 179	29
Pawnee	7	116	8.8	3.9	5	14	0.9	0.2	250	9.1	1 160	7
Perkins	7	230	16.5	6.2	10	D	D	D	301	15.9	1 010	3
Phelps	21	813	59.7	24.7	30	104	21.1	2.9	846	35.7	6 488	28
Pierce	17	D	D	D	13	22	2.6	0.6	646	29.7	2 865	11

Table B. States and Counties — Government Employment and Payroll, and Local Government Finances

	Government employment and payroll, 2012									Local government finances, 2012				
			March payroll (percent of total)							General revenue				
													Taxes	
														Per capita[1] (dollars)
STATE County	Full-time equivalent employees	March payroll (dollars)	Administration, judicial, and legal	Police and Corrections	Fire Protection	Highways and transportation	Health and Welfare	Natural resources and utilities	Education and libraries	Total (mil dol)	Inter-governmental (mil dol)	Total (mil dol)	Total	Property
	171	172	173	174	175	176	177	178	179	180	181	182	183	184
NEBRASKA—Cont'd														
Blaine	38	116 097	9.8	2.6	0.0	4.4	0.0	0.8	82.3	3.5	0.8	2.4	4 720	4 449
Boone	460	1 692 880	3.4	2.8	0.0	3.1	53.1	1.6	35.2	48.2	4.1	17.4	3 205	2 668
Box Butte	797	2 934 530	5.1	4.9	0.6	2.6	34.3	4.7	46.8	73.9	15.5	21.5	1 898	1 550
Boyd	117	356 840	12.6	1.7	0.0	16.0	0.2	10.9	57.9	9.3	3.1	5.0	2 429	2 227
Brown	260	870 487	5.2	3.3	0.0	3.3	24.0	16.3	47.5	23.9	5.2	7.5	2 470	2 176
Buffalo	1 737	6 480 217	6.2	9.5	0.9	3.9	2.1	3.9	71.0	175.2	52.8	86.9	1 830	1 377
Burt	405	1 151 444	8.6	6.4	0.0	7.3	1.0	16.5	58.3	32.4	6.0	19.8	2 978	2 657
Butler	460	1 583 569	5.4	4.9	0.0	7.3	25.9	17.6	38.5	51.3	15.3	24.0	2 892	2 645
Cass	930	3 065 349	8.2	11.0	0.0	5.1	1.0	3.6	70.6	95.9	27.6	43.8	1 744	1 516
Cedar	483	1 415 097	8.1	3.5	0.0	8.8	0.8	13.3	64.8	39.6	9.7	20.9	2 385	2 173
Chase	332	1 110 424	4.3	4.0	0.0	4.7	35.2	7.8	44.0	41.9	4.1	13.9	3 412	3 043
Cherry	255	767 776	8.8	7.8	0.0	8.5	0.8	7.7	65.2	38.3	6.2	15.0	2 611	2 227
Cheyenne	473	1 711 606	5.9	6.9	0.1	6.1	2.1	17.6	59.6	50.6	16.3	25.0	2 484	1 966
Clay	462	1 297 168	6.4	2.9	0.0	4.4	10.6	4.8	67.8	36.0	7.3	21.7	3 380	3 083
Colfax	471	1 687 680	7.1	4.2	0.1	3.4	0.0	8.5	76.2	45.8	15.6	25.2	2 364	2 089
Cuming	453	1 421 997	8.3	5.2	0.0	7.6	0.8	11.8	65.0	41.8	8.7	22.9	2 521	2 184
Custer	710	2 846 682	7.1	7.6	0.6	7.7	7.1	24.5	41.2	53.1	11.4	26.7	2 483	2 199
Dakota	972	3 563 243	6.5	7.2	0.4	2.2	0.4	6.2	75.7	80.5	44.9	26.9	1 286	955
Dawes	367	1 249 160	8.1	6.9	0.0	5.6	4.6	6.3	67.5	30.8	10.5	13.6	1 487	1 140
Dawson	1 718	5 640 576	3.0	5.6	0.0	2.6	22.8	12.1	52.5	153.2	47.5	40.1	1 657	1 368
Deuel	141	507 062	13.6	7.1	0.0	10.8	0.8	3.1	63.8	13.1	2.9	7.5	3 787	3 435
Dixon	423	1 293 730	7.0	5.2	0.0	4.4	0.1	2.3	78.0	31.8	9.3	14.9	2 525	2 324
Dodge	2 164	10 158 631	3.6	5.2	1.1	2.6	42.4	7.4	36.3	221.5	79.5	60.9	1 672	1 359
Douglas	24 079	100 381 103	3.6	9.6	4.0	3.5	4.4	25.2	48.9	2 457.4	796.5	1 177.7	2 217	1 587
Dundy	208	669 425	6.4	3.2	0.0	3.8	42.5	2.5	41.3	17.3	2.2	6.8	3 356	3 043
Fillmore	362	1 220 014	6.9	3.1	0.1	6.7	29.9	2.4	49.5	43.0	5.2	18.2	3 154	2 687
Franklin	266	1 622 165	12.8	12.9	0.0	7.6	20.4	27.8	17.9	14.4	3.0	5.2	1 628	1 517
Frontier	255	1 135 230	18.7	2.7	0.0	9.6	0.0	22.2	46.4	17.7	4.4	9.4	3 436	3 195
Furnas	443	1 409 219	6.3	2.7	0.2	3.0	18.5	17.2	51.3	28.8	8.9	13.3	2 701	2 216
Gage	894	3 582 464	6.7	7.0	2.9	7.2	0.7	19.7	53.9	82.2	27.8	39.6	1 814	1 546
Garden	214	658 334	5.9	3.2	0.9	5.3	49.9	2.8	31.7	16.1	1.9	6.4	3 289	2 928
Garfield	99	296 601	11.6	3.8	0.0	6.2	0.0	8.4	68.2	7.8	2.6	4.1	2 026	1 771
Gosper	141	396 475	7.9	4.8	0.0	10.0	27.7	9.6	37.4	12.4	1.6	6.8	3 334	3 090
Grant	58	138 009	9.1	2.9	0.0	8.9	0.0	0.0	78.7	4.2	0.6	3.2	5 083	4 808
Greeley	162	445 160	7.7	2.9	0.0	5.1	0.0	6.8	77.0	13.4	3.4	7.4	3 018	2 769
Hall	2 737	10 820 863	5.4	7.6	3.9	3.5	0.6	18.3	59.8	240.9	94.1	101.1	1 675	1 264
Hamilton	408	1 264 730	9.1	7.2	0.0	7.2	3.0	5.2	67.5	39.3	8.1	21.3	2 363	2 061
Harlan	208	554 731	9.8	4.8	0.0	6.6	36.0	7.8	31.8	21.6	4.7	5.2	1 526	1 274
Hayes	59	140 504	6.9	0.0	0.0	17.5	0.0	1.1	74.5	4.9	1.1	3.3	3 501	3 306
Hitchcock	135	502 076	5.5	9.7	0.0	8.5	0.6	32.9	42.8	12.2	2.7	6.3	2 166	1 952
Holt	457	1 501 263	9.1	4.7	0.0	9.6	2.1	8.2	65.9	52.2	11.5	29.0	2 791	2 328
Hooker	94	243 859	6.4	2.5	0.0	3.0	31.7	0.0	53.1	6.6	1.1	3.3	4 499	4 234
Howard	489	1 673 314	3.0	2.5	0.0	3.5	30.8	15.6	43.1	39.6	8.7	12.1	1 910	1 679
Jefferson	388	1 330 833	4.5	5.1	0.5	4.1	1.7	10.5	71.7	34.4	8.5	21.1	2 812	2 496
Johnson	311	1 042 290	4.4	2.9	0.0	4.2	35.4	11.8	40.5	31.4	6.4	12.0	2 329	2 119
Kearney	491	1 419 422	5.9	3.6	0.2	4.7	23.6	1.7	59.6	37.0	4.9	21.7	3 345	3 061
Keith	405	1 305 826	7.9	6.0	2.7	4.6	0.5	4.9	72.0	34.2	10.9	18.9	2 304	1 808
Keya Paha	48	112 765	9.7	2.6	0.0	8.1	0.1	0.9	76.3	3.9	0.8	2.8	3 476	3 285
Kimball	327	1 077 444	7.5	4.5	0.0	4.9	31.5	6.3	43.8	23.2	8.1	9.0	2 386	2 123
Knox	455	1 410 392	6.9	5.2	0.0	6.0	0.5	11.5	69.5	39.5	15.7	18.5	2 154	1 898
Lancaster	10 733	45 755 791	5.1	7.8	4.0	4.4	4.3	11.6	61.0	979.6	313.6	469.5	1 600	1 150
Lincoln	1 720	6 235 856	4.7	7.5	3.4	4.1	1.7	7.3	69.6	279.7	58.1	71.6	1 983	1 637
Logan	59	160 033	10.8	4.2	0.0	4.3	0.0	2.4	77.5	4.8	1.4	3.0	3 927	3 676
Loup	40	120 306	13.9	4.4	0.0	11.3	0.0	1.2	68.0	3.9	1.3	2.1	3 615	3 416
McPherson	37	88 185	16.1	0.0	0.0	8.0	0.0	0.1	75.8	3.0	0.5	2.2	4 361	4 232
Madison	1 848	7 112 436	4.2	6.2	2.5	3.0	2.2	7.2	74.5	181.2	50.7	86.6	2 472	2 061
Merrick	402	1 076 825	8.5	3.7	0.0	5.6	31.5	5.5	44.2	35.9	7.1	13.5	1 732	1 569
Morrill	306	1 053 262	7.6	5.7	0.1	4.9	0.1	9.8	68.4	37.2	13.6	10.5	2 152	1 947
Nance	276	922 483	9.8	3.4	0.0	6.6	22.8	3.9	52.2	23.2	3.7	11.8	3 167	2 896
Nemaha	407	1 469 356	4.6	3.0	0.0	3.2	23.9	9.1	55.9	43.7	12.6	14.0	1 959	1 690
Nuckolls	283	687 707	10.1	4.5	0.0	6.4	0.3	41.3	36.3	18.3	8.3	7.3	1 653	1 451
Otoe	850	2 831 957	5.7	5.8	1.1	4.0	15.2	13.1	52.1	63.3	14.6	30.7	1 948	1 590
Pawnee	199	600 056	5.0	2.2	0.0	4.6	35.8	3.6	47.4	19.2	4.6	6.3	2 267	2 041
Perkins	326	1 063 703	7.6	5.6	0.0	8.0	47.1	0.7	29.4	27.8	2.7	9.8	3 327	2 981
Phelps	471	1 581 446	8.2	8.0	0.0	6.4	0.6	7.7	68.6	46.7	11.6	24.5	2 663	2 090
Pierce	446	1 313 225	5.7	3.6	0.0	4.0	19.8	2.4	64.0	35.8	6.4	16.9	2 364	2 111

1. Based on the resident population estimated as of July 1 of the year shown.

Table B. States and Counties — Local Government Finances, Government Employment, and Voting

STATE County	Local government finances, 2012 (cont.)									Government employment, 2014			Presidential election,[2] 2012		
	Direct general expenditure							Debt outstanding					Percent of vote cast:		
				Percent of total for:											
	Total (mil dol)	Per capita[1] (dollars)	Education	Health and hospitals	Police protection	Public welfare	Highways	Total (mil dol)	Per capita[1] (dollars)	Federal civilian	Federal military	State and local	Democratic	Republican	All other
	185	186	187	188	189	190	191	192	193	194	195	196	197	198	199
NEBRASKA—Cont'd															
Blaine	3.5	6 794	68.8	0.0	1.3	0.1	13.6	0.2	409	26	0	56	13.6	84.2	2.2
Boone	44.3	8 176	31.0	48.5	1.6	0.2	8.2	3.3	617	30	19	634	26.2	72.0	1.8
Box Butte	77.0	6 806	35.7	37.0	2.5	2.0	3.9	22.0	1 940	37	41	1 017	37.9	58.9	3.2
Boyd	9.7	4 699	58.5	0.6	1.5	0.2	13.1	3.5	1 709	16	0	228	22.5	75.6	1.9
Brown	24.8	8 204	40.4	26.1	2.3	0.3	10.6	32.9	10 893	20	11	410	19.8	77.1	3.1
Buffalo	185.9	3 916	56.3	0.0	5.0	0.1	9.3	209.9	4 423	136	171	3 895	30.4	67.9	1.7
Burt	33.4	5 018	48.1	0.0	2.4	7.6	14.7	21.0	3 159	36	24	526	41.7	56.3	2.0
Butler	46.9	5 656	32.0	32.2	1.7	0.4	12.1	67.8	8 175	46	30	617	31.0	66.6	2.4
Cass	93.1	3 704	51.2	0.3	3.0	4.3	10.9	110.7	4 404	66	93	1 359	39.2	58.7	2.1
Cedar	36.7	4 202	50.3	0.2	2.2	11.6	13.5	12.1	1 386	100	31	599	28.5	69.8	1.7
Chase	45.4	11 179	31.0	33.0	1.0	7.2	9.0	27.2	6 701	25	14	492	18.5	80.1	1.4
Cherry	38.0	6 630	32.1	37.2	1.7	0.3	10.5	8.0	1 401	51	21	529	19.6	77.1	3.3
Cheyenne	49.4	4 909	41.1	0.6	3.5	0.7	11.0	57.6	5 724	35	37	784	24.2	73.8	1.9
Clay	34.4	5 370	60.7	0.6	1.7	7.2	11.3	9.1	1 421	158	23	592	25.7	71.8	2.5
Colfax	46.8	4 390	67.4	0.0	2.2	0.1	9.4	40.1	3 760	71	38	627	35.1	63.0	1.9
Cuming	41.2	4 546	53.9	0.1	3.2	10.9	11.1	33.8	3 720	33	33	742	31.2	66.8	2.0
Custer	58.1	5 407	49.7	9.3	2.4	0.2	14.8	69.4	6 462	47	39	875	21.4	77.1	1.5
Dakota	78.7	3 764	62.6	0.2	7.4	0.1	7.6	134.6	6 433	79	76	1 090	46.8	51.5	1.7
Dawes	29.9	3 268	45.6	1.0	4.2	5.9	7.9	6.6	723	132	29	1 076	34.0	62.9	3.0
Dawson	147.3	6 083	43.0	30.0	3.4	0.3	4.0	105.3	4 347	105	88	2 104	30.0	68.4	1.6
Deuel	13.9	7 026	54.5	0.2	3.3	12.7	8.4	6.2	3 140	0	0	213	24.5	73.7	1.8
Dixon	37.0	6 247	66.9	0.5	2.1	6.9	10.0	11.9	2 016	39	21	411	33.9	63.9	2.3
Dodge	228.6	6 277	38.1	39.7	2.7	0.1	4.4	108.2	2 971	110	132	2 961	43.0	55.0	2.0
Douglas	2 356.0	4 435	50.4	2.4	4.8	0.7	3.5	5 801.4	10 920	5 645	2 220	34 749	51.5	46.9	1.6
Dundy	16.6	8 200	35.5	42.3	1.9	0.1	6.9	4.4	2 201	12	0	231	21.4	76.8	1.8
Fillmore	52.3	9 062	29.1	41.2	1.9	5.3	7.7	42.5	7 369	31	20	708	32.6	64.9	2.4
Franklin	15.0	4 719	33.2	32.0	1.8	0.8	12.7	4.5	1 407	23	11	328	28.5	69.5	2.0
Frontier	20.5	7 466	46.9	0.1	2.3	0.1	8.9	3.3	1 221	19	10	331	24.9	73.6	1.5
Furnas	28.2	5 750	56.4	1.0	2.4	0.6	7.4	29.1	5 927	33	18	535	23.9	74.1	2.0
Gage	86.9	3 984	52.5	1.0	5.5	0.3	9.7	60.4	2 770	90	78	1 918	44.0	53.5	2.5
Garden	15.6	7 995	28.9	43.5	2.2	0.1	10.1	6.3	3 250	20	0	192	24.9	74.2	1.0
Garfield	7.9	3 915	57.3	0.0	2.5	0.1	10.1	2.3	1 144	0	0	154	20.6	77.7	1.7
Gosper	10.9	5 386	31.3	0.1	3.2	25.6	12.4	14.3	7 034	12	0	163	24.8	74.0	1.1
Grant	3.8	6 037	69.2	0.0	2.1	0.4	9.7	0.6	886	0	0	75	11.2	86.6	2.2
Greeley	13.1	5 331	58.5	0.6	2.1	10.6	11.9	0.6	256	10	0	274	38.2	59.6	2.2
Hall	244.4	4 050	57.3	0.2	5.0	0.4	4.7	235.9	3 910	664	224	4 362	36.9	61.0	2.1
Hamilton	38.8	4 301	50.9	10.9	3.5	0.3	6.8	21.3	2 363	32	33	566	27.8	70.6	1.6
Harlan	18.5	5 430	23.7	38.1	1.7	0.1	10.0	8.8	2 568	30	13	260	22.8	75.3	2.0
Hayes	4.6	4 815	56.7	0.0	1.7	0.1	23.0	3.0	3 102	10	0	76	15.4	83.4	1.3
Hitchcock	14.2	4 921	60.3	0.0	1.9	12.2	13.1	25.6	8 853	12	11	295	25.1	72.6	2.3
Holt	51.3	4 932	45.5	0.4	1.7	4.7	17.2	22.9	2 199	47	38	798	21.9	75.3	2.8
Hooker	6.6	9 034	46.4	0.1	1.6	24.9	5.3	2.7	3 706	0	0	107	17.1	81.1	1.8
Howard	38.9	6 142	41.7	32.5	1.3	0.1	6.8	35.9	5 667	33	23	605	36.1	61.6	2.2
Jefferson	40.6	5 402	53.7	1.6	3.4	0.3	20.6	11.0	1 468	34	27	562	41.1	56.9	2.0
Johnson	34.2	6 653	29.7	38.9	1.2	0.3	9.9	24.3	4 729	37	15	828	43.3	54.1	2.6
Kearney	35.5	5 473	48.5	23.6	1.5	0.3	10.0	27.7	4 274	27	24	475	27.8	70.6	1.6
Keith	39.6	4 813	60.0	0.5	6.0	0.4	7.6	23.7	2 887	37	30	524	24.5	74.1	1.3
Keya Paha	3.8	4 669	59.2	0.1	1.4	0.2	21.0	0.1	63	0	0	73	21.6	76.7	1.7
Kimball	23.1	6 099	29.0	29.9	2.7	0.3	7.3	8.6	2 260	17	14	422	24.2	74.3	1.4
Knox	36.1	4 212	62.9	0.2	2.2	0.2	15.1	13.8	1 609	50	30	1 060	30.7	66.8	2.5
Lancaster	1 063.8	3 626	52.7	2.0	4.3	0.9	6.6	2 798.4	9 538	3 088	1 106	29 990	51.6	46.6	1.8
Lincoln	277.0	7 674	31.2	44.8	2.8	0.1	3.5	165.3	4 578	249	130	2 629	31.0	66.5	2.5
Logan	4.4	5 741	67.1	0.1	2.1	0.1	12.6	0.0	0	0	0	75	19.5	78.6	1.9
Loup	3.6	6 161	52.9	0.1	1.5	0.1	13.6	0.2	387	0	0	65	21.9	76.8	1.3
McPherson	2.7	5 281	63.8	0.0	1.7	0.0	16.4	0.2	424	0	0	42	15.4	81.9	2.7
Madison	170.2	4 860	59.2	2.5	5.3	4.1	7.9	156.1	4 457	193	127	3 545	29.5	68.7	1.8
Merrick	35.5	4 565	36.4	31.5	2.4	0.0	9.6	24.0	3 084	26	28	548	28.7	69.2	2.0
Morrill	33.2	6 781	39.2	26.6	3.3	9.2	5.8	13.5	2 752	22	18	534	23.7	73.4	2.9
Nance	23.3	6 270	46.3	24.6	3.0	0.1	9.3	5.5	1 467	18	13	380	32.2	65.4	2.5
Nemaha	44.9	6 283	42.5	30.4	2.7	0.2	5.5	29.2	4 079	30	24	1 588	35.7	61.4	2.9
Nuckolls	18.8	4 230	39.6	0.3	2.4	0.5	14.2	17.6	3 963	27	16	352	29.6	67.4	3.0
Otoe	67.1	4 260	45.5	16.1	3.2	0.4	12.3	89.9	5 710	61	57	1 265	41.1	56.9	2.0
Pawnee	19.3	6 965	36.0	32.5	1.5	0.2	10.3	5.3	1 916	23	10	286	34.9	62.1	3.0
Perkins	25.8	8 812	27.1	49.1	2.1	0.3	6.5	3.1	1 070	18	11	370	21.8	76.9	1.3
Phelps	43.9	4 769	54.3	0.1	2.5	4.2	9.8	37.5	4 071	58	33	731	23.5	75.1	1.4
Pierce	33.9	4 731	50.9	15.7	2.6	6.0	10.0	8.7	1 213	26	26	390	24.3	73.9	1.8

1. Based on the resident population estimated as of July 1 of the year shown. 2. © 2013 Election Data Services, Inc. All rights reserved.

Table B. States and Counties — **Land Area and Population**

STATE/ County code	CBSA code[1]	County type[2]	STATE County	Land area,[3] (sq km) 2010	Total persons 2015	Rank	Per square kilometer	White	Black	American Indian, Alaska Native	Asian and Pacific Islander	Percent Hispanic or Latino[4]	Under 5 years	5 to 17 years	18 to 24 years	25 to 34 years	35 to 44 years	45 to 54 years
				1	2	3	4	5	6	7	8	9	10	11	12	13	14	15
			NEBRASKA—Cont'd															
31 141	18100	5	Platte	1 746	32 847	1 363	18.8	81.7	0.7	0.7	0.8	16.6	7.4	18.6	8.7	11.8	11.4	13.1
31 143	...	9	Polk	1 135	5 202	2 820	4.6	95.5	0.4	0.6	0.4	3.8	5.7	17.9	6.8	8.9	10.9	13.4
31 145	...	7	Red Willow	1 857	10 829	2 370	5.8	93.0	1.4	0.9	0.7	5.1	6.1	16.3	9.7	11.3	10.4	12.8
31 147	...	7	Richardson	1 429	8 094	2 594	5.7	94.2	0.8	4.2	0.9	1.9	5.2	15.6	6.9	9.5	9.8	13.9
31 149	...	9	Rock	2 612	1 381	3 088	0.5	98.7	0.2	0.9	0.6	2.2	4.8	16.2	5.4	10.4	9.4	11.6
31 151	...	6	Saline	1 487	14 282	2 149	9.6	73.3	1.2	0.7	2.2	22.9	6.9	17.3	13.3	11.0	11.7	12.7
31 153	36540	2	Sarpy	619	175 692	366	283.8	84.5	5.4	0.9	3.5	8.3	7.8	20.4	8.7	15.0	14.1	13.4
31 155	36540	2	Saunders	1 943	21 016	1 773	10.8	96.5	0.8	0.7	0.7	2.2	6.2	18.7	7.4	10.4	10.9	15.2
31 157	42420	5	Scotts Bluff	1 915	36 261	1 269	18.9	74.5	0.9	1.9	1.1	22.7	6.8	17.7	8.5	12.0	11.3	12.1
31 159	30700	2	Seward	1 480	17 110	1 974	11.6	96.5	1.0	0.8	0.8	2.3	5.9	17.3	13.6	10.3	10.7	12.8
31 161	...	9	Sheridan	6 322	5 220	2 817	0.8	85.5	0.9	11.1	0.9	4.6	4.9	17.7	6.0	10.0	10.2	11.2
31 163	...	9	Sherman	1 465	3 091	2 966	2.1	97.4	0.6	0.5	0.5	1.9	5.1	15.8	6.3	7.7	9.5	12.9
31 165	42420	9	Sioux	5 353	1 260	3 098	0.2	93.4	0.7	1.7	0.5	4.8	5.4	16.1	6.3	8.7	10.7	13.5
31 167	35740	9	Stanton	1 108	5 937	2 759	5.4	93.8	1.1	1.0	0.3	4.8	6.0	19.9	7.9	11.6	11.2	14.2
31 169	...	9	Thayer	1 486	5 163	2 826	3.5	96.8	0.8	0.7	0.6	2.2	5.2	16.7	7.1	8.7	9.2	12.9
31 171	...	9	Thomas	1 847	684	3 130	0.4	97.4	0.4	0.6	0.4	1.7	8.3	15.0	5.8	10.3	11.8	11.5
31 173	...	8	Thurston	1 019	7 064	2 668	6.9	40.4	1.1	55.5	0.8	4.5	10.1	25.5	10.1	11.5	9.2	10.7
31 175	...	9	Valley	1 471	4 154	2 891	2.8	97.2	0.5	0.4	0.5	2.2	5.4	17.6	6.8	9.2	10.5	12.6
31 177	36540	2	Washington	1 010	20 248	1 819	20.0	96.1	1.1	0.6	0.7	2.5	5.4	18.4	9.1	9.8	11.5	15.4
31 179	...	6	Wayne	1 147	9 367	2 481	8.2	91.8	2.2	0.9	1.2	5.6	5.7	13.8	25.8	10.1	8.7	10.5
31 181	...	9	Webster	1 489	3 625	2 932	2.4	93.5	1.4	1.1	1.0	4.6	5.8	15.9	8.1	8.3	9.8	14.1
31 183	...	9	Wheeler	1 490	750	3 124	0.5	98.6	0.3	0.4	0.5	0.9	6.4	13.7	7.3	8.4	11.1	13.3
31 185	...	7	York	1 483	13 806	2 181	9.3	92.4	1.9	0.9	1.0	4.9	6.6	16.0	9.9	12.2	10.2	12.7
32 000	...	X	NEVADA	284 332	2 890 845	X	10.2	54.1	9.4	1.5	10.6	27.8	6.2	17.1	9.0	14.3	13.5	13.5
32 001	21980	6	Churchill	12 770	24 200	1 637	1.9	77.0	2.9	5.2	4.8	13.2	6.5	16.7	8.6	12.9	10.7	13.2
32 003	29820	1	Clark	20 439	2 114 801	14	103.5	48.1	11.9	1.0	12.5	30.3	6.4	17.4	9.0	14.7	14.1	13.5
32 005	23820	4	Douglas	1 838	47 710	1 024	26.0	83.4	1.2	2.7	3.0	12.2	4.1	14.2	6.5	9.7	9.6	13.8
32 007	21220	5	Elko	44 470	51 935	963	1.2	68.9	1.6	5.5	2.0	24.2	7.2	20.9	9.5	14.6	12.7	13.9
32 009	...	9	Esmeralda	9 277	829	3 115	0.1	73.5	2.9	5.7	1.3	19.2	3.2	13.9	5.5	10.8	11.1	12.9
32 011	21220	9	Eureka	10 815	2 016	3 047	0.2	83.1	1.8	3.0	1.6	14.0	6.9	16.1	7.5	10.6	11.7	16.2
32 013	49080	7	Humboldt	24 969	17 019	1 980	0.7	68.3	1.4	4.7	1.6	26.1	7.8	19.5	8.7	13.7	12.5	13.6
32 015	...	7	Lander	14 219	5 903	2 761	0.4	70.9	1.1	4.4	1.3	24.0	8.1	18.7	8.8	13.2	10.8	14.3
32 017	...	8	Lincoln	27 540	5 036	2 834	0.2	87.8	3.9	2.1	1.7	7.8	4.0	18.7	8.9	10.8	11.6	12.2
32 019	22280	6	Lyon	5 183	52 585	950	10.1	78.8	1.8	3.5	2.9	15.9	5.3	17.0	7.1	11.0	11.3	13.6
32 021	...	7	Mineral	9 720	4 478	2 864	0.5	68.2	5.1	15.6	3.5	10.8	6.1	13.0	7.2	10.6	8.4	13.1
32 023	37220	6	Nye	47 091	42 477	1 121	0.9	79.9	3.0	2.5	2.9	14.4	4.3	13.7	6.3	8.4	8.8	13.2
32 027	...	8	Pershing	15 635	6 634	2 706	0.4	68.2	4.5	3.9	2.0	23.3	4.6	13.9	8.8	14.1	14.7	17.1
32 029	39900	2	Storey	681	3 987	2 903	5.9	86.5	2.0	2.6	3.0	7.8	2.2	10.3	5.6	7.4	9.6	15.0
32 031	39900	2	Washoe	16 323	446 903	155	27.4	66.5	3.0	2.0	7.7	23.5	6.0	16.4	9.6	14.4	12.2	13.5
32 033	...	7	White Pine	22 988	9 811	2 450	0.4	75.7	5.2	4.9	1.7	15.0	6.3	15.1	8.6	15.0	12.5	14.0
32 510	16180	3	Carson City	375	54 521	922	145.4	70.7	2.4	2.9	3.3	22.9	5.2	15.3	8.4	12.1	11.4	14.0
33 000	...	X	NEW HAMPSHIRE	23 187	1 330 608	X	57.4	92.6	1.7	0.7	3.1	3.3	4.9	15.3	9.7	11.6	11.9	15.8
33 001	29060	4	Belknap	1 037	60 641	862	58.5	96.1	1.1	0.8	1.6	1.6	4.7	14.8	7.1	10.5	11.2	15.3
33 003	...	8	Carroll	2 411	47 285	1 030	19.6	97.2	0.8	0.9	0.9	1.4	3.8	13.0	6.5	8.6	9.8	15.2
33 005	28300	4	Cheshire	1 830	75 909	724	41.5	95.8	1.1	0.9	2.0	1.7	4.7	13.9	12.1	11.7	10.6	14.4
33 007	13620	7	Coos	4 648	31 212	1 406	6.7	96.6	1.0	1.1	0.8	1.7	4.2	13.5	6.9	9.9	11.3	15.1
33 009	17200	5	Grafton	4 426	89 320	643	20.2	92.9	1.5	1.1	4.2	2.2	4.3	12.9	13.5	12.0	10.4	13.6
33 011	31700	2	Hillsborough	2 269	406 678	170	179.2	87.8	2.8	0.6	4.4	6.0	5.4	16.3	8.9	12.7	12.8	16.2
33 013	18180	4	Merrimack	2 419	147 994	440	61.2	94.5	1.6	0.8	2.3	1.9	4.8	15.2	9.7	11.3	12.0	15.7
33 015	14460	1	Rockingham	1 799	301 777	224	167.7	94.5	1.1	0.6	2.5	2.6	4.6	16.1	7.8	11.0	12.3	17.4
33 017	14460	1	Strafford	956	126 825	492	132.7	92.9	1.7	0.8	3.9	2.2	5.0	14.4	16.3	11.9	11.6	14.2
33 019	17200	7	Sullivan	1 392	42 967	1 114	30.9	96.8	1.0	1.1	1.0	1.5	4.7	15.0	7.1	10.6	11.6	15.6
34 000	...	X	NEW JERSEY	19 047	8 958 013	X	470.3	58.0	13.6	0.5	10.0	19.3	6.0	16.6	8.9	12.8	13.1	15.0
34 001	12100	2	Atlantic	1 439	274 219	246	190.6	58.2	15.7	0.6	8.9	18.5	6.1	16.1	9.6	11.9	11.9	14.9
34 003	35620	1	Bergen	603	938 506	53	1 556.4	59.7	5.9	0.3	17.1	18.5	5.2	16.4	8.1	11.7	13.5	15.6
34 005	37980	1	Burlington	2 068	450 226	153	217.7	70.5	17.6	0.7	5.9	7.5	5.2	16.5	8.8	12.1	12.5	15.8
34 007	37980	1	Camden	573	510 923	133	891.7	59.7	19.6	0.6	6.4	15.6	6.3	17.0	8.8	13.6	12.7	14.4
34 009	36140	3	Cape May	651	94 727	618	145.5	87.1	5.2	0.5	1.5	7.3	4.9	13.0	8.3	10.2	9.4	14.0
34 011	47220	3	Cumberland	1 253	155 854	414	124.4	49.5	20.3	1.4	1.8	29.3	6.8	17.0	8.8	14.8	13.6	13.7
34 013	35620	1	Essex	327	797 434	75	2 438.6	33.3	39.8	0.6	5.8	22.2	6.7	17.4	9.5	13.6	14.2	14.5
34 015	37980	1	Gloucester	834	291 479	233	349.5	80.9	11.1	0.5	3.6	5.7	5.5	17.5	9.1	12.1	12.9	15.4
34 017	35620	1	Hudson	120	674 836	97	5 623.6	30.4	11.9	0.5	15.5	43.1	7.0	13.4	9.1	20.9	15.6	12.9
34 019	35620	1	Hunterdon	1 108	125 488	498	113.3	87.6	2.7	0.3	4.4	6.2	3.9	17.2	8.4	8.3	11.3	18.7

1. CBSA = Core Based Statistical Area. See Appendix A for explanation. See Appendix B for list of metropolitan areas with component counties. 2. County type code from the Economic Research Service of USDA Rural-Urban Continuum Codes. See Appendix A for definition. 3. Dry land or land partially or temporarily covered by water. 4. May be of any race.

Table B. States and Counties — **Population and Households**

| | Population, 2014 (cont.) | | | | Population change and components of change, 2000–2015 | | | | | | | Households, 2010–2014 | | | | |
| | Age (percent) (cont.) | | | | Total persons | | Percent change | | Components of change, 2010–2015 | | | | | Percent | | |
STATE County	55 to 64 years	65 to 74 years	75 years and over	Percent female	2000	2010	2000– 2010	2010– 2015	Births	Deaths	Net migration	Number	Persons per household	Family households	Female family householder[1]	One person
	16	17	18	19	20	21	22	23	24	25	26	27	28	29	30	31
NEBRASKA—Cont'd																
Platte	13.2	8.0	7.8	49.4	31 662	32 237	1.8	1.9	2 515	1 382	-583	12 666	2.53	66.8	8.1	29.1
Polk	16.3	10.1	10.1	50.2	5 639	5 406	-4.1	-3.8	273	332	-109	2 238	2.31	68.5	6.8	27.6
Red Willow	14.5	8.8	10.1	50.0	11 448	11 055	-3.4	-2.0	655	609	-249	4 661	2.28	63.2	5.8	31.2
Richardson	15.4	11.3	12.4	50.4	9 531	8 363	-12.3	-3.2	501	591	-159	3 715	2.17	60.9	5.8	37.3
Rock	20.3	10.6	11.2	49.8	1 756	1 528	-13.0	-9.6	69	103	-129	692	2.00	63.4	4.5	34.5
Saline	12.1	7.5	7.5	49.2	13 843	14 200	2.6	0.6	992	715	-179	5 156	2.57	68.7	10.3	24.5
Sarpy	10.4	6.1	4.1	49.9	122 595	158 840	29.6	10.6	13 484	4 399	7 750	60 844	2.71	73.8	10.6	21.5
Saunders	13.8	9.5	7.9	49.4	19 830	20 780	4.8	1.1	1 255	971	-63	8 070	2.55	69.2	6.7	26.6
Scotts Bluff	13.9	9.1	8.6	51.6	36 951	36 970	0.1	-1.9	2 603	2 120	-1 139	14 659	2.45	66.1	11.9	28.2
Seward	12.8	8.6	8.0	48.9	16 496	16 750	1.5	2.1	1 031	830	135	6 224	2.50	71.3	5.8	25.2
Sheridan	16.6	11.4	12.0	51.0	6 198	5 469	-11.8	-4.6	299	370	-137	2 292	2.28	62.8	9.2	33.0
Sherman	16.5	12.3	13.9	50.7	3 318	3 152	-5.0	-1.9	159	187	-51	1 343	2.28	66.6	8.2	29.7
Sioux	18.1	9.9	11.2	49.4	1 475	1 311	-11.1	-3.9	48	34	-56	557	2.30	68.8	4.7	29.3
Stanton	14.2	8.0	7.0	49.6	6 455	6 129	-5.1	-3.1	405	216	-393	2 312	2.63	75.6	10.1	22.4
Thayer	15.4	11.3	13.4	51.1	6 055	5 228	-13.7	-1.2	310	401	40	2 331	2.16	67.1	4.9	30.1
Thomas	17.5	11.2	8.6	47.0	729	647	-11.2	5.7	46	26	8	324	2.30	71.0	5.6	28.1
Thurston	10.8	6.2	5.9	50.6	7 171	6 940	-3.2	1.8	741	391	-234	2 076	3.30	70.9	20.7	25.2
Valley	14.1	12.2	11.6	50.2	4 647	4 260	-8.3	-2.5	269	284	-81	1 901	2.21	69.3	6.5	27.7
Washington	14.3	9.1	6.9	50.0	18 780	20 234	7.7	0.1	1 116	854	-230	7 794	2.54	72.6	6.1	24.2
Wayne	11.3	6.7	7.4	49.2	9 851	9 595	-2.6	-2.4	530	303	-412	3 548	2.31	64.8	6.3	28.7
Webster	15.0	11.0	12.0	51.3	4 061	3 812	-6.1	-4.9	188	292	-92	1 555	2.32	62.8	5.0	33.4
Wheeler	17.9	12.3	9.7	49.3	886	818	-7.7	-8.3	37	25	-60	388	2.19	59.3	4.9	36.1
York	13.8	8.9	9.7	51.3	14 598	13 665	-6.4	1.0	920	745	-39	5 599	2.32	65.8	6.6	30.9
NEVADA	12.2	8.8	5.3	49.7	1 998 257	2 700 691	35.2	7.0	185 956	111 222	111 180	1 005 958	2.71	64.5	12.9	27.7
Churchill	13.4	10.9	7.1	49.4	23 982	24 877	3.7	-2.7	1 655	1 350	-1 013	9 431	2.54	66.4	10.9	28.2
Clark	11.5	8.3	5.0	50.0	1 375 765	1 951 269	41.8	8.4	139 109	75 710	96 780	715 415	2.77	64.6	14.0	27.5
Douglas	17.6	14.9	9.6	49.8	41 259	46 997	13.9	1.5	1 890	2 312	1 092	19 765	2.37	68.7	8.3	25.0
Elko	11.9	6.0	3.3	47.9	45 291	48 942	8.1	6.1	3 731	1 382	628	17 587	2.85	72.5	7.7	20.9
Esmeralda	16.7	13.6	12.4	43.4	971	784	-19.3	5.7	38	54	56	467	2.19	51.8	6.4	40.5
Eureka	16.0	9.3	5.6	46.5	1 651	1 987	20.4	1.5	80	66	11	769	2.27	59.7	2.1	36.2
Humboldt	13.5	7.0	3.7	47.8	16 106	16 525	2.6	3.0	1 378	599	-238	6 092	2.76	66.6	7.9	29.0
Lander	12.9	8.4	4.8	49.0	5 794	5 775	-0.3	2.2	453	173	-145	2 075	2.83	70.5	8.4	21.2
Lincoln	14.0	12.2	7.6	46.0	4 165	5 345	28.3	-5.8	153	243	-206	1 916	2.57	67.2	7.5	31.2
Lyon	14.9	12.8	6.9	49.4	34 501	51 980	50.7	1.2	2 991	2 739	386	19 728	2.59	68.3	10.7	24.4
Mineral	16.5	14.8	10.3	51.3	5 071	4 771	-5.9	-6.1	278	433	-133	1 917	2.35	55.7	12.8	35.9
Nye	17.5	17.4	10.5	49.5	32 485	43 945	35.3	-3.3	1 950	3 359	-157	17 803	2.39	66.9	9.2	25.8
Pershing	13.1	9.0	4.8	36.7	6 693	6 753	0.9	-1.8	307	243	-188	2 111	2.30	73.3	9.0	21.4
Storey	22.1	18.9	8.9	48.0	3 399	4 010	18.0	-0.6	102	142	-15	1 823	2.13	63.0	5.7	32.0
Washoe	13.2	9.2	5.4	49.7	339 486	421 427	24.1	6.0	28 291	18 499	15 025	164 461	2.57	61.9	11.2	29.6
White Pine	13.4	8.7	6.4	42.7	9 181	10 030	9.2	-2.2	558	468	-273	3 373	2.66	61.5	4.6	33.8
Carson City	14.4	10.9	8.3	48.9	52 457	55 274	5.4	-1.4	2 992	3 450	-430	21 225	2.48	61.4	12.5	31.3
NEW HAMPSHIRE	14.9	9.3	6.6	50.6	1 235 786	1 316 466	6.5	1.1	66 109	56 574	4 853	519 580	2.46	66.8	9.6	25.4
Belknap	16.5	11.9	7.9	50.8	56 325	60 092	6.7	0.9	2 873	3 357	952	25 010	2.37	67.8	10.5	25.9
Carroll	18.6	14.5	10.0	50.4	43 666	47 820	9.5	-1.1	1 911	2 636	204	21 279	2.21	66.3	7.0	27.1
Cheshire	15.3	10.1	7.2	51.1	73 825	77 117	4.5	-1.6	3 617	3 551	-1 161	30 659	2.34	63.3	9.9	27.4
Coos	17.3	12.1	9.7	49.0	33 111	33 052	-0.2	-5.6	1 345	2 168	-980	14 395	2.13	63.1	10.5	31.4
Grafton	15.3	10.5	7.6	50.7	81 743	89 114	9.0	0.2	3 998	4 104	359	35 127	2.35	62.3	9.0	29.6
Hillsborough	13.8	8.1	5.8	50.4	380 841	400 721	5.2	1.5	22 839	15 656	-1 179	154 236	2.56	67.6	10.6	24.6
Merrimack	15.2	9.3	6.8	50.7	136 225	146 442	7.5	1.1	7 103	6 711	858	57 040	2.46	66.5	9.3	26.4
Rockingham	15.5	9.2	6.0	50.5	277 359	295 220	6.4	2.2	13 688	11 208	4 333	117 284	2.52	69.8	8.6	23.1
Strafford	12.8	7.9	5.8	51.3	112 233	123 146	9.7	3.0	6 612	4 980	1 995	46 891	2.48	64.0	10.2	25.2
Sullivan	16.5	11.3	7.6	50.6	40 458	43 742	8.1	-1.8	2 123	2 203	-528	17 659	2.42	67.0	9.9	25.8
NEW JERSEY	12.9	8.1	6.6	51.2	8 414 350	8 791 936	4.5	1.9	546 887	373 269	1 112	3 188 498	2.72	69.3	13.5	25.8
Atlantic	13.8	9.1	6.7	51.6	252 552	274 549	8.7	-0.1	17 369	13 523	-4 110	101 166	2.65	66.6	16.3	27.9
Bergen	13.4	8.5	7.5	51.6	884 118	905 117	2.4	3.7	48 170	36 649	24 017	335 671	2.71	71.6	11.2	24.5
Burlington	13.5	8.5	7.0	50.9	423 394	448 728	6.0	0.3	23 956	19 893	-2 134	164 736	2.66	70.2	11.7	25.1
Camden	13.0	8.0	6.3	51.7	508 932	513 678	0.9	-0.5	33 558	23 834	-12 084	187 121	2.70	67.3	16.2	27.4
Cape May	16.3	13.5	10.5	51.2	102 326	97 265	-4.9	-2.6	4 690	6 758	-279	41 069	2.28	65.0	9.6	30.5
Cumberland	11.7	7.7	5.9	48.4	146 438	156 898	7.1	-0.7	10 987	7 512	-4 179	50 399	2.87	69.8	19.3	24.8
Essex	11.8	6.9	5.4	51.9	793 633	783 987	-1.2	1.7	54 833	31 089	-9 276	277 745	2.77	64.9	20.1	30.1
Gloucester	13.4	8.2	5.9	51.4	254 673	288 288	13.2	1.1	15 961	12 832	-163	104 435	2.73	72.6	12.5	22.6
Hudson	10.4	6.1	4.7	50.2	608 975	634 277	4.2	6.4	51 596	20 446	10 270	246 135	2.63	61.7	17.2	28.9
Hunterdon	16.4	9.3	6.4	50.6	121 989	127 351	4.4	-1.5	4 758	4 548	-2 031	46 951	2.59	73.1	7.8	22.7

1. No spouse present.

Table B. States and Counties — Population, Vital Statistics, Medicare, and Crime

STATE County	Persons in group quarters, 2015	Daytime population, 2010–2014 Number	Daytime population, 2010–2014 Employment/residence ratio	Births, 2015 Total	Births, 2015 Rate[1]	Deaths, 2015 Number	Deaths, 2015 Rate[1]	Persons under 65 with no health insurance, 2014 Number	Persons under 65 with no health insurance, 2014 Percent	Medicare, 2015 Total Beneficiaries	Medicare, 2015 Enrolled in Original Medicare	Medicare, 2015 Enrolled in Medicare Advantage	Serious crimes known to police,[2] 2014 Total Number	Serious crimes known to police,[2] 2014 Total Rate[3]
	32	33	34	35	36	37	38	39	40	41	42	43	44	45
NEBRASKA—Cont'd														
Platte	483	34 367	1.11	476	14.5	263	8.0	3 228	11.9	4 965	4 685	280	496	1 521
Polk	109	4 411	0.67	57	10.9	55	10.5	424	10.1	992	979	13	79	1 503
Red Willow	366	11 492	1.09	121	11.2	125	11.5	874	10.3	2 256	2 233	23	288	2 615
Richardson	151	7 366	0.78	103	12.7	118	14.5	740	12.0	2 072	2 042	30	70	866
Rock	29	1 448	1.02	14	10.0	16	11.5	219	19.5	D	364	D	1	72
Saline	1 023	14 615	1.04	183	12.8	124	8.7	1 527	13.6	2 391	2 346	45	290	2 002
Sarpy	1 083	141 336	0.72	2 556	14.7	910	5.2	10 998	7.1	17 665	14 761	2 904	2 268	1 318
Saunders	341	16 331	0.56	227	10.8	180	8.6	1 400	8.2	3 647	3 227	420	237	1 130
Scotts Bluff	853	37 458	1.03	473	13.0	365	10.0	4 406	15.0	7 681	6 773	908	921	2 555
Seward	1 286	15 061	0.77	186	10.9	143	8.4	980	7.5	2 747	2 629	118	137	915
Sheridan	102	4 775	0.77	57	10.9	62	11.8	703	17.6	1 259	1 106	153	NA	NA
Sherman	55	2 571	0.63	32	10.4	37	12.0	301	13.3	710	641	69	23	742
Sioux	0	1 046	0.65	9	7.0	5	3.9	168	16.5	D	113	D	NA	NA
Stanton	0	4 949	0.63	79	13.1	32	5.3	510	9.9	547	460	87	45	732
Thayer	120	5 373	1.08	69	13.3	81	15.6	410	10.5	1 334	1 317	17	65	1 252
Thomas	2	760	1.03	7	10.2	3	4.4	66	12.1	140	129	11	NA	NA
Thurston	58	7 482	1.23	146	20.8	79	11.3	1 052	17.5	921	882	39	7	103
Valley	36	4 434	1.07	51	12.2	49	11.7	414	13.0	1 025	1 009	16	NA	NA
Washington	529	18 339	0.82	228	11.3	163	8.0	1 061	6.4	3 183	2 640	543	213	1 052
Wayne	1 085	9 212	0.95	102	10.9	39	4.2	732	10.4	1 233	1 092	141	NA	NA
Webster	154	3 377	0.78	33	9.0	59	16.2	318	11.5	960	918	42	26	710
Wheeler	0	901	1.10	6	7.9	3	4.0	98	16.5	D	140	D	1	134
York	768	14 905	1.15	180	13.0	137	9.9	895	8.4	2 789	2 756	33	257	1 840
NEVADA	36 736	2 766 719	1.00	36 036	12.6	22 345	7.8	416 208	17.3	409 739	261 194	148 545	92 583	3 261
Churchill	346	24 446	1.01	321	13.3	248	10.3	3 351	17.2	4 736	4 269	467	826	3 426
Clark	23 123	2 009 615	1.01	26 841	12.8	15 447	7.4	315 827	17.8	269 825	157 271	112 554	72 994	3 532
Douglas	229	45 685	0.93	377	7.9	480	10.1	5 198	14.6	9 354	8 407	947	837	1 759
Elko	787	49 069	0.92	836	16.0	319	6.1	6 985	14.8	4 983	4 831	152	1 482	2 755
Esmeralda	1	1 009	0.91	16	19.3	3	3.6	121	20.0	D	167	D	10	1 170
Eureka	1	5 614	5.39	12	6.0	6	3.0	190	11.1	D	258	D	42	1 984
Humboldt	191	17 435	1.06	257	15.0	103	6.0	2 716	17.8	2 229	2 115	114	251	1 416
Lander	16	5 920	1.00	86	14.5	31	5.2	748	14.4	727	706	21	167	2 714
Lincoln	239	5 366	1.05	38	7.5	51	10.0	796	20.3	2 726	2 134	592	50	950
Lyon	360	44 444	0.63	580	11.1	546	10.5	7 023	17.0	11 698	9 119	2 579	965	1 859
Mineral	52	4 702	1.05	50	11.1	101	22.5	519	15.5	1 153	989	164	NA	NA
Nye	424	42 291	0.95	354	8.4	618	14.6	5 555	18.4	14 171	7 408	6 763	883	2 087
Pershing	1 655	6 875	1.07	59	8.9	39	5.9	701	16.8	708	687	21	123	1 763
Storey	5	3 153	0.56	20	5.1	16	4.1	352	12.5	281	255	26	120	3 026
Washoe	5 293	428 959	0.99	5 495	12.4	3 622	8.2	58 428	15.7	71 618	49 026	22 592	12 055	2 735
White Pine	1 267	10 370	1.09	111	11.2	84	8.5	932	12.9	1 575	1 538	37	128	1 260
Carson City	2 747	61 766	1.32	583	10.7	631	11.6	6 766	16.3	13 494	12 014	1 480	1 035	1 906
NEW HAMPSHIRE	41 762	1 283 239	0.94	12 562	9.5	10 980	8.3	118 870	11.0	242 729	223 618	19 111	28 643	2 159
Belknap	928	55 920	0.86	535	8.8	707	11.7	6 174	12.8	14 975	13 671	1 304	1 800	2 987
Carroll	509	46 509	0.95	353	7.5	537	11.3	5 498	15.4	12 680	11 899	781	924	2 223
Cheshire	4 485	74 150	0.94	647	8.5	648	8.5	6 994	11.8	15 321	14 048	1 273	1 537	2 565
Coos	1 420	31 307	0.94	260	8.3	404	12.8	3 599	15.0	8 584	8 241	343	507	1 594
Grafton	6 978	101 600	1.28	762	8.5	776	8.7	8 826	13.1	18 247	16 963	1 284	1 782	2 096
Hillsborough	7 964	388 664	0.93	4 302	10.6	3 097	7.6	35 777	10.4	64 761	58 805	5 956	9 289	2 360
Merrimack	7 108	149 994	1.04	1 331	9.0	1 258	8.5	12 582	10.6	27 315	25 075	2 240	2 394	1 828
Rockingham	2 497	283 149	0.91	2 707	9.0	2 152	7.1	23 218	9.2	51 792	47 640	4 152	4 881	1 694
Strafford	9 158	115 191	0.86	1 268	10.0	988	7.8	12 153	12.1	20 193	18 742	1 451	3 321	2 655
Sullivan	715	36 755	0.69	397	9.2	413	9.6	4 049	11.7	8 861	8 534	327	716	1 873
NEW JERSEY	186 013	8 596 195	0.93	103 006	11.5	72 065	8.1	940 315	12.6	1 371 126	1 124 559	246 567	178 339	1 995
Atlantic	6 215	280 898	1.04	3 167	11.5	2 678	9.7	34 377	15.1	48 514	43 093	5 421	9 170	3 315
Bergen	10 414	901 820	0.96	9 351	10.0	6 901	7.4	93 391	12.0	143 521	120 717	22 804	10 541	1 132
Burlington	13 362	432 908	0.92	4 526	10.0	3 896	8.6	28 938	7.8	74 523	60 294	14 229	7 506	1 661
Camden	7 478	474 367	0.84	6 294	12.3	4 566	8.9	53 848	12.4	84 036	66 028	18 008	15 449	3 009
Cape May	2 611	94 886	0.97	842	8.9	1 281	13.5	8 575	12.0	24 928	22 024	2 904	3 765	3 934
Cumberland	12 013	157 860	1.01	1 929	12.3	1 397	8.9	18 876	15.1	26 583	22 108	4 475	6 931	4 397
Essex	23 466	810 271	1.06	10 303	12.9	6 073	7.6	113 132	16.5	101 011	75 832	25 179	23 449	2 960
Gloucester	4 223	254 687	0.75	3 022	10.4	2 538	8.7	20 538	8.3	43 413	35 192	8 221	6 640	2 281
Hudson	9 428	601 537	0.84	10 265	15.3	4 057	6.0	110 211	18.6	69 726	50 161	19 565	13 028	1 951
Hunterdon	3 721	118 780	0.87	873	6.9	916	7.3	6 373	6.2	19 557	17 637	1 920	870	690

1. Per 1,000 estimated resident population. 2. Data for serious crimes have not been adjusted for underreporting; this may affect comparability between geographic areas and over time.
3. Per 100,000 population estimated by the FBI.

Table B. States and Counties — Crime, Education, Money Income, and Poverty

STATE County	Serious crimes known to police, 2014 (cont.)[1] Rate[2] Violent	Property	School enrollment and attainment, 2010–2014 Enrollment[3] Total	Percent private	Attainment[4] (percent) High school graduate or less	Bachelor's degree or more	Local government expenditures,[5] 2012–2013 Total current spending (mil dol)	Current spending per student (dollars)	Money income, 2010–2014 Per capita income[6] (dollars)	Households Median income (dollars)	Mean income (dollars)	Percent with income of $200,000 or more	Income and poverty, 2014 Median household income (dollars)	Percent below poverty level All persons	Children under 18 years	Children 5 to 17 years in families
	46	47	48	49	50	51	52	53	54	55	56	57	58	59	60	61
NEBRASKA—Cont'd																
Platte	83	1 438	8 486	22.6	42.6	20.6	57.5	12 520	25 815	55 391	64 975	2.6	61 768	8.4	11.4	10.8
Polk	0	1 503	1 220	11.6	40.9	19.5	17.4	13 966	29 567	54 375	69 263	4.0	58 162	8.0	12.2	10.8
Red Willow	73	2 543	2 488	8.8	42.2	19.6	19.6	11 321	23 912	43 627	56 268	1.5	43 842	11.7	16.5	15.2
Richardson	0	866	1 869	7.2	48.8	21.7	16.9	13 798	24 703	40 765	53 133	1.4	44 282	14.4	20.9	18.5
Rock	0	72	257	5.1	48.4	20.1	3.3	17 244	28 158	48 854	59 285	2.9	46 051	15.0	22.0	19.4
Saline	110	1 892	4 206	23.3	51.5	14.3	33.1	11 654	21 230	46 814	56 808	1.5	51 805	10.1	12.7	12.8
Sarpy	70	1 248	50 641	16.5	27.6	36.6	266.1	10 519	30 539	70 121	82 407	3.9	74 008	5.3	7.0	6.6
Saunders	52	1 077	5 403	23.4	40.1	24.5	30.8	11 188	29 175	60 487	73 615	3.6	61 961	8.2	11.2	9.5
Scotts Bluff	164	2 391	9 453	12.9	43.2	21.2	74.6	11 381	24 417	46 443	59 807	2.0	47 194	15.6	21.9	20.2
Seward	53	861	5 056	32.7	37.4	26.8	36.9	14 328	27 579	59 503	73 397	4.1	61 802	8.2	8.9	7.8
Sheridan	NA	NA	1 213	5.9	42.8	24.1	11.6	13 280	22 665	40 489	51 632	1.4	40 351	16.0	25.6	22.3
Sherman	64	677	737	0.5	53.2	14.5	6.5	13 677	24 505	46 301	55 328	0.7	43 883	12.1	18.4	16.6
Sioux	NA	NA	273	13.2	39.9	25.1	2.6	22 894	27 669	40 625	59 727	2.9	47 313	16.0	22.9	21.0
Stanton	16	716	1 634	10.5	40.8	19.4	5.4	11 787	28 682	53 532	71 359	2.1	55 955	9.2	13.4	11.9
Thayer	212	1 040	1 018	9.1	46.5	17.8	13.5	16 720	27 626	45 213	62 302	2.3	49 517	10.7	15.2	13.3
Thomas	NA	NA	171	5.8	35.0	24.2	2.0	19 206	28 421	52 105	66 235	3.7	39 537	15.4	26.1	29.0
Thurston	29	74	2 314	5.1	46.0	15.6	29.1	16 792	18 251	40 494	58 262	2.4	41 344	34.0	44.2	42.6
Valley	NA	NA	804	8.8	49.8	17.4	9.0	13 679	24 165	42 708	54 741	1.7	44 726	12.3	15.3	14.0
Washington	74	978	5 599	18.8	36.5	29.8	35.4	10 144	30 438	68 207	79 189	3.6	69 191	7.4	9.0	7.7
Wayne	NA	NA	3 852	4.1	29.0	36.4	26.1	17 024	25 523	53 808	67 245	3.5	53 290	13.6	12.0	11.1
Webster	164	546	855	7.7	44.9	18.5	8.0	12 750	22 328	41 107	51 872	1.2	40 979	12.7	15.6	14.5
Wheeler	0	134	156	1.3	47.3	18.6	2.2	19 138	27 996	44 107	61 438	3.4	45 400	12.6	19.9	20.6
York	21	1 819	3 419	26.3	40.8	24.1	22.4	11 903	28 271	50 922	67 733	3.2	51 335	10.6	14.5	14.0
NEVADA	636	2 625	684 277	11.1	43.8	22.5	3 622.3	8 339	26 515	52 205	69 351	3.4	51 487	15.4	22.2	20.2
Churchill	236	3 190	5 990	5.0	45.9	14.4	40.3	10 771	23 823	46 195	58 398	0.8	46 840	13.2	17.7	17.2
Clark	743	2 790	495 640	11.6	44.9	22.2	2 555.2	8 066	26 040	52 070	69 106	3.4	51 241	15.6	23.1	21.0
Douglas	164	1 595	10 100	13.3	33.0	25.6	56.5	9 207	34 090	58 940	79 596	4.8	60 322	10.3	16.5	14.0
Elko	454	2 302	13 589	7.4	44.8	17.5	93.5	9 494	29 762	72 280	83 733	4.9	72 648	10.8	14.8	12.9
Esmeralda	117	1 053	203	1.5	56.1	13.3	2.0	30 299	20 513	31 528	43 148	0.0	47 180	14.0	18.4	17.5
Eureka	378	1 606	447	9.4	42.8	22.9	7.5	27 856	31 057	68 403	71 378	0.5	70 535	9.8	13.0	12.9
Humboldt	322	1 095	4 550	7.0	53.6	12.4	34.4	9 814	26 547	62 632	71 421	2.3	67 423	10.7	14.7	14.0
Lander	569	2 145	1 414	12.4	55.9	9.8	13.7	12 508	29 302	76 558	78 379	1.4	74 347	11.0	14.8	14.3
Lincoln	19	931	1 428	8.5	48.9	15.1	12.8	13 090	23 523	40 550	61 528	1.7	45 629	15.1	19.5	16.9
Lyon	277	1 581	11 898	9.3	45.6	15.9	80.3	9 949	22 709	47 143	57 303	0.9	48 576	13.7	20.6	19.0
Mineral	NA	NA	870	2.9	48.4	10.8	6.9	13 814	23 222	38 664	50 744	1.6	40 714	19.0	32.4	32.0
Nye	144	1 943	7 852	11.2	50.8	13.4	55.7	10 347	23 035	41 757	54 697	1.1	42 881	16.8	28.4	26.2
Pershing	616	1 147	1 540	4.9	56.5	11.8	11.4	16 100	18 623	48 165	60 745	0.4	52 001	18.5	21.1	19.3
Storey	706	2 320	589	7.8	37.4	20.7	6.4	15 440	37 215	64 835	78 112	5.1	55 291	8.4	13.7	12.3
Washoe	371	2 364	112 515	10.3	37.9	27.9	546.5	8 408	28 621	52 910	72 122	4.1	52 862	15.4	19.2	17.6
White Pine	305	955	2 308	8.8	48.9	15.5	16.7	11 629	25 857	55 337	70 589	1.7	57 243	13.7	16.6	16.2
Carson City	295	1 611	13 344	8.0	42.8	20.4	82.4	10 502	25 893	50 108	64 360	2.2	45 639	19.3	26.8	24.1
NEW HAMPSHIRE	196	1 963	323 195	21.4	37.1	34.4	2 598.9	13 721	33 821	65 986	84 480	5.7	66 469	9.2	12.6	11.1
Belknap	229	2 758	12 484	19.0	39.2	29.2	129.1	14 829	31 044	60 782	74 952	3.2	59 831	10.0	15.2	13.8
Carroll	202	2 021	8 956	17.7	37.3	32.2	98.5	17 558	32 860	52 393	73 585	3.9	57 556	10.7	17.5	15.7
Cheshire	194	2 371	19 773	16.2	42.4	30.8	141.8	16 574	29 591	56 139	72 719	3.1	56 008	11.8	15.3	13.9
Coos	145	1 450	6 166	9.8	52.5	17.8	64.1	15 290	24 737	42 407	54 461	2.1	42 491	14.9	22.6	20.8
Grafton	158	1 938	23 501	32.5	37.1	37.5	204.8	17 955	31 221	55 045	76 182	5.1	56 353	11.6	15.5	14.6
Hillsborough	272	2 088	100 771	24.3	36.6	35.5	721.9	12 670	34 767	70 906	89 012	6.7	71 233	8.7	12.1	10.7
Merrimack	147	1 680	35 772	24.8	36.8	33.7	317.3	13 316	31 579	65 226	79 697	4.3	62 429	9.5	13.2	11.4
Rockingham	119	1 575	71 171	19.2	32.9	38.0	621.6	13 270	39 605	79 368	99 678	8.2	79 653	6.1	8.4	7.4
Strafford	249	2 406	35 924	14.7	37.0	33.2	211.6	13 328	29 757	59 580	76 381	4.2	58 577	11.8	14.1	12.2
Sullivan	162	1 711	8 677	18.9	46.9	27.4	97.3	15 730	29 073	56 851	68 946	3.1	57 142	10.4	16.1	14.7
NEW JERSEY	261	1 734	2 288 364	18.9	40.4	36.4	24 972.4	17 572	36 359	72 062	98 286	9.8	71 968	11.1	15.8	14.8
Atlantic	384	2 931	68 354	13.8	48.6	24.4	833.0	18 329	27 411	54 392	71 779	4.3	54 208	15.1	23.6	22.0
Bergen	81	1 050	232 524	21.6	33.5	46.1	2 447.9	18 298	43 194	83 686	116 079	13.6	84 309	7.6	8.9	8.9
Burlington	167	1 493	114 836	17.7	37.5	35.3	1 250.2	17 604	37 511	79 612	100 022	8.7	80 479	7.2	9.3	8.5
Camden	465	2 544	134 445	17.2	44.1	29.7	1 488.0	18 970	30 667	61 842	80 892	5.3	61 685	13.0	19.1	18.3
Cape May	239	3 694	18 792	12.9	45.9	29.2	257.1	19 903	33 499	57 394	77 949	5.0	55 409	13.0	19.5	18.6
Cumberland	511	3 886	37 541	9.9	62.7	13.8	504.4	18 695	22 425	50 603	65 299	2.6	45 438	19.5	28.1	28.4
Essex	648	2 312	219 369	18.0	45.0	32.3	2 714.2	23 340	32 327	54 499	87 496	9.2	54 603	16.7	23.4	21.5
Gloucester	113	2 168	77 764	15.3	43.0	28.7	783.8	16 092	33 609	76 213	91 614	6.5	78 983	8.2	10.5	9.5
Hudson	360	1 592	153 514	18.4	43.8	36.8	1 597.6	20 153	32 678	58 973	83 368	7.7	57 720	17.7	27.0	29.2
Hunterdon	44	645	32 252	17.8	28.4	48.3	406.8	19 151	50 846	106 519	136 413	19.0	103 876	4.7	4.6	3.9

1. Data for serious crimes have not been adjusted for underreporting; this may affect comparability between geographic areas and over time.   2. Per 100,000 population estimated by the FBI.
3. All persons 3 years old and over enrolled in nursery school through college.   4. Persons 25 years old and over.   5. Elementary and secondary education expenditures.
6. Based on population estimated by the American Community Survey, 2010–2014.

Table B. States and Counties — **Personal Income**

STATE County	Personal income, 2014										Earnings, 2014		
	Total (mil dol)	Percent change, 2013–2014	Per capita[1] Dollars	Rank	Wages and salaries (mil dol)	Supplements to wages and salaries; employer contributions (mil dol) Pension and insurance	Government social insurance	Proprietors' income (mil dol)	Dividends, interest, and rent (mil dol)	Personal transfer receipts (mil dol)	Total (mil dol)	Contributions for government social insurance (mil dol) From employee and self-employed	From employer
	62	63	64	65	66	67	68	69	70	71	72	73	74
NEBRASKA—Cont'd													
Platte	1 491	1.5	45 651	625	773	151	57	305	245	206	1 286	67	57
Polk	269	-3.8	51 010	333	53	10	4	93	41	38	160	6	4
Red Willow	522	10.5	48 069	477	210	38	16	118	93	94	384	20	16
Richardson	359	-3.0	44 109	753	90	18	7	70	65	77	186	10	7
Rock	115	42.5	79 579	29	19	4	1	66	15	10	89	2	1
Saline	561	-4.8	39 332	1 277	285	56	23	83	86	98	447	24	23
Sarpy	7 434	5.0	43 170	827	3 362	633	266	197	1 187	946	4 460	258	266
Saunders	924	0.4	44 188	739	195	38	14	126	145	150	373	20	14
Scotts Bluff	1 596	5.4	43 777	780	723	123	60	315	228	302	1 221	73	60
Seward	778	2.1	45 377	645	260	46	20	124	129	114	449	24	20
Sheridan	280	18.8	53 172	264	58	12	4	97	45	42	172	6	4
Sherman	120	-4.8	39 172	1 300	26	6	2	25	20	27	59	3	2
Sioux	90	28.7	68 725	67	9	2	1	52	11	7	63	1	1
Stanton	259	-9.1	42 692	882	80	13	5	66	35	32	164	7	5
Thayer	294	-1.8	56 225	193	102	19	7	78	62	51	206	10	7
Thomas	44	39.0	63 815	94	10	2	1	17	8	6	30	1	1
Thurston	330	-9.8	47 409	505	126	25	9	107	43	56	267	10	9
Valley	191	8.0	45 317	647	64	14	5	52	36	38	134	6	5
Washington	968	-0.4	47 783	489	429	75	30	72	175	137	607	36	30
Wayne	397	-7.6	42 142	938	144	30	10	97	70	58	282	12	10
Webster	170	5.7	46 530	556	35	7	2	56	27	34	100	4	2
Wheeler	104	47.0	135 907	3	10	2	1	81	8	5	93	1	1
York	673	-3.6	48 343	463	310	54	23	103	137	114	491	27	23
NEVADA	115 672	5.6	40 742	X	57 653	10 009	4 266	8 114	25 604	18 890	80 042	4 571	4 266
Churchill	1 066	5.0	44 440	722	384	92	30	261	163	214	766	40	30
Clark	81 821	5.9	39 533	1 243	42 091	6 930	3 167	5 795	17 219	13 268	57 983	3 333	3 167
Douglas	2 715	5.0	57 113	169	788	138	59	133	1 048	405	1 118	71	59
Elko	2 200	0.9	41 702	981	1 127	194	79	93	244	241	1 492	81	79
Esmeralda	41	13.8	49 841	390	22	4	1	0	6	8	28	2	1
Eureka	70	1.4	34 531	2 018	401	57	26	4	10	8	487	28	26
Humboldt	743	1.4	43 025	845	443	86	30	56	94	95	615	32	30
Lander	307	2.6	51 055	329	249	42	16	13	28	34	320	17	16
Lincoln	137	7.5	26 440	3 010	61	19	4	5	23	43	89	4	4
Lyon	1 643	5.8	31 720	2 488	489	107	35	70	236	421	701	46	35
Mineral	157	3.4	34 822	1 964	58	16	4	5	30	54	83	5	4
Nye	1 452	5.7	34 332	2 055	549	100	39	112	242	484	800	55	39
Pershing	205	10.0	30 655	2 633	101	27	6	21	24	40	154	6	6
Storey	140	3.0	35 867	1 798	204	30	19	7	29	27	259	15	19
Washoe	20 336	5.7	46 211	580	9 169	1 733	662	1 297	5 676	2 981	12 861	729	662
White Pine	400	5.2	39 908	1 191	222	58	13	16	54	77	310	15	13
Carson City	2 238	5.8	41 046	1 055	1 294	376	77	228	476	491	1 975	92	77
NEW HAMPSHIRE	70 020	4.8	52 773	X	33 048	5 024	2 315	5 935	13 175	10 162	46 322	2 848	2 315
Belknap	3 071	4.5	50 929	335	1 066	184	78	235	664	565	1 562	103	78
Carroll	2 316	3.1	48 861	444	721	126	54	235	693	485	1 136	79	54
Cheshire	3 567	3.5	46 861	533	1 435	249	103	387	749	628	2 174	137	103
Coos	1 255	2.9	39 651	1 231	452	97	34	93	227	383	676	47	34
Grafton	4 563	4.5	50 895	336	2 888	438	211	470	1 057	737	4 007	241	211
Hillsborough	22 438	5.0	55 378	206	11 937	1 662	819	1 803	4 228	2 870	16 221	983	819
Merrimack	7 220	4.7	49 061	433	3 729	656	263	534	1 323	1 182	5 182	310	263
Rockingham	18 291	5.1	60 844	118	7 805	1 069	542	1 750	3 033	2 045	11 167	687	542
Strafford	5 350	5.2	42 592	890	2 407	434	166	286	835	889	3 292	201	166
Sullivan	1 949	4.6	45 214	658	609	109	45	143	365	379	906	60	45
NEW JERSEY	515 020	4.7	57 620	X	240 628	39 437	18 426	43 312	90 987	73 415	341 803	20 274	18 426
Atlantic	11 927	3.7	43 336	810	6 059	1 128	505	1 123	1 936	2 630	8 815	530	505
Bergen	68 651	5.0	73 536	47	29 380	4 367	2 271	7 006	15 200	6 940	43 024	2 522	2 271
Burlington	24 171	3.7	53 747	246	11 685	2 036	961	1 827	3 737	3 672	16 510	977	961
Camden	23 960	3.8	46 886	530	10 289	1 882	851	1 537	3 595	4 861	14 559	897	851
Cape May	4 940	3.7	51 812	302	1 591	345	145	462	1 259	1 140	2 542	168	145
Cumberland	5 582	3.6	35 468	1 863	2 736	604	233	434	778	1 538	4 008	243	233
Essex	46 406	5.2	58 319	153	22 487	4 002	1 700	3 990	9 723	7 393	32 179	1 861	1 700
Gloucester	13 559	3.9	46 603	553	4 785	958	404	638	1 669	2 308	6 786	421	404
Hudson	33 515	5.4	50 088	381	18 476	2 899	1 328	3 295	4 358	5 099	25 998	1 513	1 328
Hunterdon	9 826	4.5	77 944	33	3 169	490	236	884	1 680	875	4 779	286	236

1. Based on the resident population estimated as of July 1 of the year shown.

STATE County	Earnings, 2014 (cont.) Percent by selected industries									Social Security beneficiaries, December 2014		Supplemental Security Income recipients, December 2014	Housing units, 2015	
	Farm	Mining	Construction	Manufacturing	Information: professional, scientific, technical services	Retail trade	Finance, insurance, real estate and leasing	Health care and social assistance	Government	Number	Rate[1]		Total	Percent change, 2010–2014
	75	76	77	78	79	80	81	82	83	84	85	86	87	88
NEBRASKA—Cont'd														
Platte	15.4	0.0	5.1	31.3	2.7	5.2	3.6	7.0	11.9	6 325	193	312	13 641	2.0
Polk	46.6	D	3.3	0.5	D	4.1	D	4.6	15.6	1 065	202	50	2 710	-0.7
Red Willow	20.3	1.6	4.1	7.8	3.1	7.7	4.1	10.2	14.5	2 430	224	151	5 272	0.1
Richardson	27.4	0.2	3.8	7.8	D	5.7	3.0	D	14.8	2 260	277	147	4 369	-0.5
Rock	68.0	0.0	D	D	D	1.3	2.8	0.7	10.4	370	262	18	909	-0.5
Saline	12.9	0.0	1.2	37.6	1.1	3.7	2.1	D	16.1	2 515	175	148	5 786	0.4
Sarpy	0.5	0.0	7.5	4.1	9.3	5.7	8.6	4.7	28.2	22 260	129	1 231	67 144	8.4
Saunders	26.5	D	9.1	5.8	4.3	5.6	4.3	D	20.4	4 120	197	183	9 447	2.5
Scotts Bluff	8.2	D	4.2	7.0	3.7	6.2	5.5	15.4	14.5	8 205	225	854	16 320	-0.5
Seward	18.5	0.0	6.5	17.0	2.1	3.8	3.9	D	14.3	3 075	180	137	7 051	2.6
Sheridan	53.9	D	1.1	2.5	D	4.3	D	1.3	17.2	1 105	210	52	2 898	-1.3
Sherman	35.9	0.0	1.9	1.2	D	4.6	D	5.1	20.5	775	252	26	1 936	-0.3
Sioux	88.9	0.0	0.0	0.0	D	0.7	D	D	6.2	255	195	5	822	0.9
Stanton	33.5	D	D	D	D	0.7	1.4	0.4	8.4	995	164	20	2 652	0.7
Thayer	31.1	D	4.3	19.1	0.8	2.9	3.8	3.0	16.0	1 405	269	75	2 744	0.5
Thomas	60.2	D	D	D	D	4.5	D	D	13.7	195	284	0	400	-0.5
Thurston	38.4	0.0	2.2	5.2	D	1.9	D	5.3	32.8	1 105	159	214	2 415	0.3
Valley	29.7	D	3.8	3.0	D	5.4	D	3.0	23.3	1 105	262	62	2 281	0.4
Washington	6.9	D	10.6	18.5	5.3	10.0	3.3	D	21.5	3 850	190	155	8 460	1.9
Wayne	30.6	0.0	2.0	13.2	1.7	3.4	5.7	7.3	22.3	1 500	160	75	3 868	2.4
Webster	52.5	D	D	D	D	3.7	D	4.6	14.8	945	258	82	1 900	-0.6
Wheeler	89.0	0.0	0.2	0.0	0.0	D	D	0.0	2.9	160	209	0	574	-0.3
York	14.4	D	4.4	11.1	4.3	5.8	4.8	D	13.8	3 095	223	172	6 285	0.9
NEVADA	0.3	2.1	6.5	3.8	8.4	7.2	5.9	9.0	16.8	475 811	168	50 919	1 209 756	3.1
Churchill	2.8	1.3	8.3	4.2	D	7.6	5.0	8.6	25.3	5 465	227	493	10 687	-1.3
Clark	0.0	0.1	6.5	2.7	8.7	7.4	6.1	8.8	15.7	320 495	155	38 973	871 807	3.7
Douglas	0.1	D	7.2	11.7	7.4	6.9	5.7	8.0	15.0	13 565	285	396	23 890	0.9
Elko	1.7	15.7	12.2	1.1	2.8	6.1	1.9	5.7	17.2	5 995	114	492	20 778	6.2
Esmeralda	0.7	D	D	D	D	D	0.0	0.0	16.5	255	309	16	824	-3.3
Eureka	1.1	D	D	0.0	D	D	0.2	D	D	270	136	18	1 036	-3.7
Humboldt	4.0	37.4	5.4	2.6	D	6.2	1.0	D	17.9	2 495	145	223	7 258	1.9
Lander	3.1	68.4	D	D	D	2.5	D	0.4	13.1	890	149	86	2 619	1.7
Lincoln	5.1	0.8	D	D	D	5.2	2.3	D	46.3	1 065	208	63	2 731	0.0
Lyon	4.6	5.6	5.2	18.1	3.7	14.3	2.7	D	19.5	13 260	256	876	22 448	-0.4
Mineral	-1.2	14.2	D	D	D	D	D	D	43.7	1 320	293	144	2 783	-1.6
Nye	7.0	14.4	4.1	1.0	18.2	6.7	1.5	7.4	15.7	15 060	357	1 014	21 662	-3.1
Pershing	13.9	38.3	D	D	D	3.3	D	D	31.9	940	140	63	2 405	-2.4
Storey	0.0	D	6.6	18.6	D	D	D	D	6.8	965	247	12	1 984	-0.3
Washoe	0.1	1.2	6.8	6.7	9.2	6.8	6.9	11.4	17.7	79 385	180	6 915	188 977	2.2
White Pine	0.3	36.9	3.5	0.3	1.2	4.0	1.3	D	36.0	1 775	178	145	4 422	-1.7
Carson City	0.2	D	3.6	9.0	5.5	6.9	4.8	14.4	37.9	12 610	231	990	23 445	-0.4
NEW HAMPSHIRE	0.1	0.1	6.5	12.0	11.9	8.6	9.3	12.5	12.9	283 983	214	19 671	622 561	1.3
Belknap	0.2	0.2	7.6	9.9	7.4	12.1	4.9	14.4	15.8	16 990	281	1 047	37 790	1.1
Carroll	-0.1	D	12.8	4.3	6.9	11.9	6.7	12.4	15.1	14 365	303	729	40 370	1.4
Cheshire	0.4	D	8.8	13.9	5.4	10.1	6.6	13.8	14.3	18 135	238	1 246	35 015	0.7
Coos	0.0	0.1	7.0	5.3	2.8	9.9	3.7	17.8	26.0	10 450	330	909	21 264	-0.3
Grafton	0.4	0.1	4.1	10.4	8.7	7.0	3.9	23.5	10.9	20 115	225	1 065	51 832	1.4
Hillsborough	0.0	0.0	5.7	14.6	15.9	8.0	11.4	11.1	10.1	76 450	189	7 134	168 074	1.2
Merrimack	0.3	0.2	6.5	8.6	7.9	8.0	8.9	14.4	21.8	32 490	220	2 213	63 818	0.4
Rockingham	0.1	0.1	7.5	10.6	14.1	9.1	8.8	9.0	8.9	59 555	198	2 344	129 359	2.1
Strafford	0.2	0.1	5.0	11.2	7.1	7.6	14.9	13.4	22.0	24 625	195	2 136	52 669	1.9
Sullivan	0.5	D	8.3	26.0	5.7	10.4	5.2	8.0	15.0	10 805	251	848	22 344	0.0
NEW JERSEY	0.1	0.2	5.4	7.6	15.5	6.2	9.6	11.3	15.6	1 568 016	175	181 606	3 593 604	1.1
Atlantic	0.7	D	6.5	D	6.2	7.1	3.8	15.1	23.8	56 410	205	6 891	127 865	1.0
Bergen	0.0	D	6.0	7.1	15.7	6.5	7.0	14.9	9.8	160 020	172	12 084	355 116	0.8
Burlington	0.2	D	5.2	8.5	11.7	7.1	11.2	11.8	18.1	87 735	195	5 911	177 994	1.4
Camden	0.1	D	5.7	7.3	10.4	7.2	5.0	18.5	19.0	96 345	189	16 647	206 210	0.6
Cape May	0.2	0.1	10.2	D	4.8	10.2	6.5	11.8	27.7	27 985	293	1 812	99 010	0.7
Cumberland	1.8	0.3	5.8	14.2	2.9	6.9	2.7	14.6	28.1	30 520	194	5 737	56 360	0.9
Essex	0.0	D	3.7	4.8	14.8	3.8	11.7	11.0	22.1	117 215	147	29 253	314 763	0.6
Gloucester	0.9	0.1	9.1	9.0	6.3	10.7	3.5	10.3	23.2	55 125	189	4 560	112 381	2.4
Hudson	0.0	D	2.8	2.9	16.6	4.9	27.0	6.6	15.7	80 955	121	21 784	277 811	2.8
Hunterdon	0.3	D	8.7	4.4	17.1	9.3	10.9	10.5	14.8	23 230	185	907	49 964	1.0

1. Per 1,000 resident population estimated as of July 1 of the year shown.

Table B. States and Counties — **Housing, Labor Force, and Employment**

STATE County	Housing units, 2010–2014 Occupied units Owner-occupied Total	Percent	Median value[1]	Median owner cost as a percent of income With a mortgage	Without a mortgage[2]	Renter-occupied Median rent[3]	Median rent as a percent of income[2]	Substandard units[4] (percent)	Civilian labor force, 2015 Total	Percent change, 2014–2015	Unemployment Total	Rate[5]	Civilian employment,[6] 2010–2014 Total	Percent Management, business, science and arts	Construction, production, and maintenance occupations
	89	90	91	92	93	94	95	96	97	98	99	100	101	102	103
NEBRASKA—Cont'd															
Platte	12 666	71.9	122 700	19.6	11.4	643	22.5	2.9	17 236	-0.6	509	3.0	17 417	28.2	35.5
Polk	2 238	74.8	97 600	20.4	10.4	607	21.1	1.1	2 952	-0.5	74	2.5	2 799	35.7	31.4
Red Willow	4 661	72.4	84 000	17.8	14.5	569	24.0	1.7	6 160	-2.2	162	2.6	5 600	26.8	28.2
Richardson	3 715	74.9	67 900	18.7	12.3	497	22.3	1.2	4 337	1.3	139	3.2	4 039	33.1	29.4
Rock	692	79.6	63 500	18.6	11.5	574	13.6	1.9	876	-1.0	23	2.6	759	42.6	29.5
Saline	5 156	65.8	94 800	20.6	11.6	668	26.2	2.9	7 326	1.1	214	2.9	6 963	29.5	37.2
Sarpy	60 844	69.9	162 100	21.0	11.2	863	26.1	2.1	90 294	0.4	2 523	2.8	86 041	41.1	17.5
Saunders	8 070	78.5	147 300	21.9	13.6	721	22.4	0.6	11 045	0.1	336	3.0	10 564	35.8	24.1
Scotts Bluff	14 659	69.1	104 100	22.0	14.3	678	28.2	2.9	18 716	-0.3	636	3.4	18 218	28.5	26.4
Seward	6 224	73.3	142 700	19.7	12.4	655	24.4	0.8	8 886	0.2	254	2.9	8 377	36.0	27.6
Sheridan	2 292	68.7	67 600	22.6	13.1	553	22.9	1.4	2 755	-1.0	74	2.7	2 546	40.7	21.8
Sherman	1 343	78.8	83 900	21.4	13.3	594	18.3	0.7	1 721	-0.5	50	2.9	1 507	37.2	30.5
Sioux	557	73.4	86 600	31.3	14.1	475	17.6	0.0	805	-0.4	20	2.5	677	44.9	18.9
Stanton	2 312	82.9	101 200	20.7	11.2	651	22.8	1.1	3 553	-0.8	91	2.6	3 206	31.6	32.8
Thayer	2 331	78.2	60 100	18.9	12.1	456	21.3	1.5	3 001	-1.2	71	2.4	2 450	36.9	27.1
Thomas	324	72.8	84 300	20.4	10.0	525	18.5	0.6	439	2.3	13	3.0	442	40.3	26.9
Thurston	2 076	64.3	68 800	17.5	11.5	498	24.5	11.0	2 989	-1.2	158	5.3	2 431	37.1	23.2
Valley	1 901	72.7	77 600	18.3	11.9	444	26.0	0.6	2 093	-1.4	59	2.8	2 247	34.7	27.8
Washington	7 794	79.8	173 500	21.9	12.3	695	25.1	1.0	11 114	0.5	329	3.0	10 876	38.2	23.8
Wayne	3 548	63.8	107 800	17.9	10.0	569	23.3	3.6	5 575	0.0	143	2.6	5 298	35.6	23.5
Webster	1 555	76.8	67 700	20.6	12.9	474	22.3	1.8	1 743	0.7	62	3.6	1 678	35.0	30.5
Wheeler	388	76.5	87 400	23.6	12.0	606	20.0	1.3	566	1.1	14	2.5	533	43.9	31.9
York	5 599	68.0	112 600	19.6	11.3	617	23.3	0.5	7 397	-0.1	216	2.9	7 278	33.2	25.8
NEVADA	1 005 958	55.7	167 100	25.5	10.8	980	30.5	4.7	1 425 714	1.7	96 162	6.7	1 240 614	27.8	18.4
Churchill	9 431	60.3	144 900	22.9	10.3	838	28.0	3.2	10 570	-3.4	742	7.0	9 527	28.0	29.5
Clark	715 415	53.1	163 100	25.9	10.8	1 009	30.8	5.0	1 047 528	2.2	71 265	6.8	903 785	26.6	17.0
Douglas	19 765	71.1	267 200	27.2	11.5	1 035	30.8	1.8	22 602	0.5	1 529	6.8	20 387	31.2	20.0
Elko	17 587	71.2	183 900	19.3	10.0	923	22.4	4.2	27 176	-4.2	1 413	5.2	25 436	25.7	32.7
Esmeralda	467	59.7	70 900	20.4	12.8	443	20.7	10.5	524	-2.1	24	4.6	368	23.9	46.5
Eureka	769	68.3	89 300	15.7	10.0	654	13.1	5.3	1 004	-3.6	60	6.0	878	34.3	33.6
Humboldt	6 092	72.9	152 900	18.4	10.0	781	22.5	4.4	8 593	-4.6	504	5.9	7 758	21.0	40.8
Lander	2 075	79.5	104 700	14.5	10.0	708	19.7	3.0	3 419	0.9	223	6.5	2 550	23.5	53.5
Lincoln	1 916	64.6	139 500	23.2	10.0	588	28.6	1.0	1 961	0.6	122	6.2	1 704	33.6	21.8
Lyon	19 728	71.9	129 300	26.5	11.0	922	28.9	3.2	21 678	-5.8	2 047	9.4	19 752	26.3	29.5
Mineral	1 917	67.1	84 400	18.5	12.4	508	19.9	7.1	1 611	-3.4	169	10.5	1 691	26.7	28.8
Nye	17 803	70.3	102 300	26.6	12.0	803	31.3	2.5	16 370	-0.2	1 422	8.7	13 937	24.7	24.5
Pershing	2 111	66.1	119 900	19.5	11.1	625	24.1	8.3	2 536	-3.1	173	6.8	2 054	28.7	35.1
Storey	1 823	92.9	181 300	26.2	11.3	699	21.5	0.0	1 884	1.4	138	7.3	1 818	36.2	21.5
Washoe	164 461	57.1	201 100	25.7	11.4	908	31.1	4.6	228 227	1.9	14 244	6.2	202 147	33.2	18.8
White Pine	3 373	73.1	120 700	17.5	10.0	768	23.4	2.6	4 928	0.2	266	5.4	3 916	33.5	27.7
Carson City	21 225	58.2	188 000	24.3	12.1	837	29.0	4.0	25 103	-0.1	1 821	7.3	22 906	31.4	20.8
NEW HAMPSHIRE	519 580	71.0	237 400	25.2	16.6	1 001	29.8	1.9	741 189	0.1	25 463	3.4	693 329	39.6	20.2
Belknap	25 010	74.9	220 600	25.7	16.6	899	28.6	1.7	31 478	-0.2	1 050	3.3	30 307	36.8	22.6
Carroll	21 279	79.6	225 400	26.1	15.1	907	31.8	2.4	23 731	-1.7	850	3.6	23 031	33.1	20.0
Cheshire	30 659	70.4	191 200	25.3	18.4	938	32.7	1.8	41 689	-0.6	1 354	3.2	39 483	35.6	24.0
Coos	14 395	70.3	127 600	24.4	16.6	677	28.9	1.9	14 807	-2.3	703	4.7	15 012	30.0	25.1
Grafton	35 127	68.0	212 800	24.0	15.9	892	28.6	2.4	48 196	-0.4	1 396	2.9	44 957	42.1	18.9
Hillsborough	154 236	66.9	245 900	24.8	16.2	1 067	29.8	2.0	228 523	0.1	8 232	3.6	213 597	41.0	19.5
Merrimack	57 040	72.0	227 300	25.8	17.0	942	30.7	2.0	80 704	0.0	2 518	3.1	76 062	40.0	19.5
Rockingham	117 284	76.6	279 800	25.5	16.2	1 114	28.6	1.3	177 897	0.9	6 471	3.6	163 155	41.9	18.8
Strafford	46 891	65.2	217 900	26.2	17.4	973	31.9	2.3	70 703	0.3	2 209	3.1	65 865	36.7	21.0
Sullivan	17 659	74.8	170 700	24.7	17.3	856	28.9	1.4	23 461	-1.0	680	2.9	21 860	34.7	26.0
NEW JERSEY	3 188 498	65.0	319 900	27.5	18.4	1 188	32.2	3.7	4 543 780	0.7	254 953	5.6	4 235 089	40.7	17.6
Atlantic	101 166	67.7	230 200	30.1	19.1	1 043	35.4	3.8	127 666	-3.8	11 962	9.4	127 647	29.5	16.2
Bergen	335 671	64.8	443 500	28.6	19.3	1 340	31.0	2.4	485 316	1.1	22 093	4.6	451 145	46.5	14.0
Burlington	164 736	77.4	247 800	25.2	16.7	1 208	31.9	1.5	232 359	1.2	12 078	5.2	221 024	42.4	16.0
Camden	187 121	67.7	202 900	26.4	19.2	983	34.1	2.3	255 354	1.0	16 046	6.3	239 788	38.4	18.0
Cape May	41 069	75.3	307 000	28.2	18.5	1 042	34.4	1.4	48 896	0.2	5 307	10.9	42 999	34.4	17.9
Cumberland	50 399	66.6	165 700	26.3	17.5	978	36.5	4.3	67 387	-0.1	5 846	8.7	62 500	25.7	27.7
Essex	277 745	45.2	358 100	29.9	19.8	1 069	33.3	5.4	375 624	-0.1	25 220	6.7	353 763	37.1	18.6
Gloucester	104 435	79.9	219 000	25.5	17.5	1 052	33.4	1.4	149 669	1.0	8 866	5.9	140 827	40.8	18.6
Hudson	246 135	32.0	337 900	30.6	21.3	1 194	29.1	7.5	362 265	0.8	19 057	5.3	331 881	38.6	19.4
Hunterdon	46 951	83.8	393 500	25.2	16.1	1 332	30.8	1.4	66 112	0.5	2 707	4.1	64 801	50.6	12.9

1. Specified owner-occupied units. 2. A value of 10.0 represents 10 percent or less; a value of 50.0 represents 50 percent or more. 3. Specified renter-occupied units.
4. Overcrowded or lacking complete plumbing facilities. 5. Percent of civilian labor force. 6. Persons 16 years old and over.

Table B. States and Counties — Nonfarm Employment and Agriculture

	Private nonfarm establishments, employment and payroll, 2014								Agriculture, 2012			
	Employment						Annual payroll		Farms			
											Percent with:	
STATE County	Number of establishments	Total	Health care and social assistance	Manufacturing	Retail trade	Finance and insurance	Professional, scientific, and technical services	Total (mil dol)	Average per employee (dollars)	Number	Fewer than 50 acres	500 acres or more	Farm operators whose principal occupation is farming (percent)
	104	105	106	107	108	109	110	111	112	113	114	115	116
NEBRASKA—Cont'd													
Platte	1 014	15 770	1 425	5 326	2 099	520	400	587	37 234	942	24.3	31.0	64.9
Polk	149	940	253	D	130	45	D	26	27 929	466	23.2	39.7	66.1
Red Willow	422	3 939	638	D	905	225	126	121	30 669	405	26.7	39.0	47.4
Richardson	256	1 755	414	D	316	88	D	51	28 972	736	21.6	28.7	55.7
Rock	45	D	D	D	D	D	D	10	D	247	14.2	68.0	61.1
Saline	301	4 895	546	2 007	467	146	49	214	43 636	756	22.9	32.3	56.6
Sarpy	3 442	46 905	4 958	3 020	8 707	1 577	3 947	1 902	40 552	396	57.6	15.4	39.4
Saunders	535	3 732	654	445	617	208	117	117	31 444	1 204	30.4	25.1	55.8
Scotts Bluff	1 094	12 701	2 880	1 042	2 439	468	354	430	33 848	966	30.6	22.7	49.7
Seward	445	5 625	813	1 161	538	D	D	176	31 230	992	36.4	23.3	47.0
Sheridan	166	1 000	D	D	228	102	30	25	24 673	536	16.2	50.9	68.5
Sherman	86	541	D	D	117	D	D	14	26 250	414	12.1	38.9	60.9
Sioux	13	38	D	NA	17	D	D	1	28 184	354	8.2	63.6	71.2
Stanton	110	D	D	D	91	D	D	D	D	619	20.8	29.9	64.6
Thayer	215	2 077	D	D	190	111	41	73	34 960	432	15.7	44.9	63.9
Thomas	22	143	NA	D	6	D	D	6	38 469	87	14.9	70.1	66.7
Thurston	124	1 517	161	D	208	D	D	61	39 969	367	25.3	45.2	65.7
Valley	182	1 349	354	D	297	70	D	39	28 788	402	13.9	49.3	73.1
Washington	564	6 402	885	1 160	1 130	240	175	298	46 538	821	40.0	21.4	58.0
Wayne	248	3 193	498	D	353	279	152	88	27 533	518	24.7	33.0	67.0
Webster	91	662	162	NA	156	41	D	19	28 804	423	21.5	42.6	53.9
Wheeler	20	97	NA	D	D	D	NA	2	18 887	198	17.2	56.6	67.7
York	511	6 011	952	808	950	D	141	208	34 550	541	21.1	43.4	70.6
NEVADA	61 625	1 090 071	108 667	41 572	140 879	34 322	56 214	43 673	40 065	4 137	53.2	18.9	53.0
Churchill	485	5 100	705	373	856	151	366	187	36 685	672	63.1	7.6	54.3
Clark	42 031	797 871	76 305	18 913	104 745	25 280	41 981	31 099	38 977	252	78.6	2.0	46.8
Douglas	1 618	16 083	1 348	1 791	2 026	356	817	586	36 412	255	65.1	7.5	62.4
Elko	1 081	20 665	1 548	248	2 470	279	488	1 037	50 161	552	37.0	31.5	53.4
Esmeralda	13	D	NA	D	D	D	NA	D	D	38	23.7	31.6	63.2
Eureka	41	1 813	D	D	D	D	D	149	82 432	101	8.9	49.5	68.3
Humboldt	395	6 721	631	224	1 029	82	74	366	54 390	359	36.2	38.2	54.6
Lander	101	1 520	D	D	246	D	D	81	53 236	124	37.1	47.6	62.1
Lincoln	91	595	109	D	186	D	18	17	28 424	185	35.7	20.5	43.8
Lyon	779	9 631	522	2 081	1 283	170	340	354	36 716	462	60.0	15.4	56.1
Mineral	60	1 119	D	D	D	D	21	41	36 882	119	67.2	1.7	27.7
Nye	658	7 389	763	D	1 483	145	173	258	34 883	198	63.6	15.2	51.0
Pershing	76	1 154	D	D	D	D	D	60	52 192	154	29.2	37.7	81.8
Storey	87	588	D	D	74	NA	D	17	28 452	6	100.0	0.0	0.0
Washoe	11 655	173 135	22 360	14 561	22 513	5 717	10 097	7 403	42 756	479	69.3	7.1	44.1
White Pine	196	2 854	273	D	416	45	D	152	53 254	160	40.6	26.3	43.8
Carson City	1 930	20 718	3 645	2 917	3 289	1 004	1 141	887	42 823	21	81.0	4.8	47.6
NEW HAMPSHIRE	37 396	563 323	88 007	66 151	97 453	29 079	29 915	26 937	47 817	4 391	55.5	3.5	48.0
Belknap	1 786	21 009	3 881	2 535	5 117	D	666	821	39 070	302	55.6	1.7	42.4
Carroll	1 833	16 986	2 786	910	3 718	398	534	548	32 285	291	53.6	3.4	52.6
Cheshire	1 904	27 644	3 627	4 664	5 716	1 321	617	1 103	39 899	407	53.6	5.7	47.4
Coos	849	8 984	2 102	654	1 760	311	141	295	32 802	293	38.2	6.5	50.2
Grafton	2 871	48 171	11 200	5 527	7 537	883	1 613	2 325	48 270	500	38.0	7.2	45.2
Hillsborough	10 889	180 527	28 859	26 505	28 018	10 330	10 772	9 693	53 691	688	64.0	1.5	50.0
Merrimack	3 979	60 791	12 350	5 595	10 258	3 423	2 758	2 627	43 217	600	55.7	3.8	49.2
Rockingham	9 490	129 125	15 166	12 286	26 494	6 630	8 697	6 106	47 290	658	69.6	0.8	48.8
Strafford	2 581	36 242	6 614	4 383	6 518	D	1 353	1 646	45 422	354	58.2	1.1	48.6
Sullivan	913	11 664	1 319	3 092	2 316	460	182	455	39 050	298	51.3	5.7	43.0
NEW JERSEY	230 600	3 526 716	561 829	221 901	456 680	192 521	317 085	202 658	57 464	9 071	71.2	3.1	49.5
Atlantic	6 365	110 726	17 978	1 492	16 780	2 751	4 383	3 981	35 949	402	69.4	2.2	61.4
Bergen	31 573	439 344	73 101	32 634	63 504	15 903	34 466	26 559	60 451	60	88.3	0.0	48.3
Burlington	10 531	180 008	26 321	15 710	24 432	16 297	18 283	9 305	51 690	838	69.5	5.0	56.4
Camden	11 402	170 942	39 532	11 332	23 846	4 638	11 779	7 764	45 420	175	81.1	1.1	50.3
Cape May	3 788	25 547	4 538	471	6 499	1 048	1 033	986	38 581	152	75.7	1.3	48.0
Cumberland	2 883	44 491	10 481	7 377	7 281	1 190	1 017	1 664	37 406	583	61.7	5.3	55.2
Essex	18 751	289 817	54 776	17 891	26 872	21 399	24 685	16 972	58 560	13	100.0	0.0	53.8
Gloucester	5 884	88 224	13 780	7 054	16 902	1 663	3 497	3 552	40 257	584	74.3	2.6	45.0
Hudson	13 149	209 244	27 212	7 954	22 950	35 075	10 982	14 470	69 155	0	0.0	0.0	0.0
Hunterdon	3 865	44 220	7 525	3 596	7 148	D	4 047	3 091	69 906	1 447	71.9	1.9	43.7

Table B. States and Counties — **Agriculture**

STATE County	Land in farms — Acreage (1,000)	Land in farms — Percent change, 2007–2012	Acres — Average size of farm	Acres — Total irrigated (1,000)	Acres — Total cropland (1,000)	Value of land and buildings (dollars) — Average per farm	Value of land and buildings (dollars) — Average per acre	Value of machinery and equipment, average per farm (dollars)	Value of products sold — Total (mil dol)	Value of products sold — Average per farm (dollars)	Percent from: Crops	Percent from: Livestock and poultry products	Percent of farms with sales of: $10,000 or more	Percent of farms with sales of: $100,000 or more	Government payments — Total ($1,000)	Government payments — Percent of farms
	117	118	119	120	121	122	123	124	125	126	127	128	129	130	131	132
NEBRASKA—Cont'd																
Platte	426	0.1	453	194.0	351.5	2 302 510	5 088	284 312	652.1	692 256	36.3	63.7	75.7	53.7	6 298	74.1
Polk	245	-8.9	526	151.0	212.2	3 128 150	5 943	329 976	326.2	700 084	51.2	48.8	80.3	64.4	3 710	79.2
Red Willow	420	-6.0	1 036	53.1	241.6	1 651 696	1 594	224 978	180.5	445 701	45.7	54.3	64.4	37.5	3 807	61.5
Richardson	319	14.3	434	4.7	245.8	1 653 332	3 812	171 026	162.0	220 139	71.0	29.0	65.4	38.2	6 434	82.2
Rock	645	2.0	2 610	36.3	146.9	2 813 632	1 078	195 603	97.8	395 903	40.2	59.8	82.6	53.8	1 332	36.0
Saline	362	21.3	479	108.1	296.7	2 306 246	4 818	261 522	208.8	276 152	82.3	17.7	65.9	41.4	5 966	80.8
Sarpy	92	-9.0	232	10.4	82.2	1 380 134	5 959	127 424	63.6	160 553	75.4	24.6	45.5	24.5	1 340	58.1
Saunders	469	9.8	390	105.6	412.0	2 054 154	5 268	198 767	380.5	316 033	59.0	41.0	65.2	37.4	7 393	72.3
Scotts Bluff	445	23.6	461	199.2	239.7	860 445	1 867	172 940	390.1	403 791	41.2	58.8	62.1	31.2	3 579	62.3
Seward	355	6.7	358	129.9	294.3	1 799 861	5 031	216 676	308.5	311 017	59.7	40.3	59.3	34.5	6 718	71.2
Sheridan	1 534	-0.4	2 863	60.7	275.5	1 983 683	693	201 590	167.5	312 541	50.0	50.0	62.5	35.1	3 179	57.3
Sherman	281	4.1	679	71.1	127.7	1 609 171	2 369	172 713	114.2	275 754	68.3	31.7	78.7	42.8	2 093	70.5
Sioux	1 224	-5.2	3 459	39.5	94.0	1 981 486	573	151 356	146.0	412 446	20.3	79.7	74.6	44.1	1 338	46.0
Stanton	254	7.9	411	28.4	195.1	1 798 275	4 375	202 628	182.1	294 158	35.1	64.9	67.7	35.4	3 656	77.9
Thayer	326	-7.1	755	135.5	254.0	3 114 514	4 123	323 176	249.4	577 278	74.7	25.3	78.7	56.9	4 259	81.5
Thomas	368	-13.5	4 225	2.9	8.0	2 125 345	503	114 736	22.4	257 770	D	D	73.6	37.9	438	18.4
Thurston	248	24.0	675	11.9	215.9	3 406 256	5 049	284 038	197.7	538 651	47.3	52.7	72.2	57.8	3 744	80.1
Valley	349	-1.9	869	93.1	150.7	1 919 602	2 209	248 953	205.1	510 179	46.5	53.5	76.9	52.2	2 783	75.1
Washington	248	14.2	302	17.3	209.8	1 820 340	6 024	180 247	163.5	199 117	62.8	37.2	54.9	32.6	4 069	59.3
Wayne	280	1.2	540	49.8	238.4	2 363 431	4 373	235 147	203.3	392 380	45.7	54.3	75.5	43.8	3 410	77.4
Webster	302	-1.1	715	55.0	177.8	2 021 950	2 830	228 965	226.9	536 404	40.4	59.6	76.8	45.2	3 545	71.6
Wheeler	357	-0.9	1 804	39.4	90.9	2 208 793	1 225	254 586	259.8	1 312 323	13.6	86.4	74.7	51.5	1 407	52.5
York	340	-1.9	628	252.4	313.1	3 534 628	5 631	429 436	415.4	767 861	72.9	27.1	81.0	65.1	6 039	74.5
NEVADA	5 914	0.8	1 429	687.8	756.9	1 324 673	927	134 626	764.1	184 710	47.9	52.1	42.0	21.2	3 253	8.2
Churchill	197	50.0	294	53.6	56.3	713 604	2 431	110 594	89.9	133 833	34.5	65.5	44.6	18.3	414	7.3
Clark	16	-82.3	62	3.7	4.4	347 790	5 611	66 325	6.8	27 083	48.2	51.8	33.7	4.4	34	3.6
Douglas	101	10.9	396	25.6	18.6	1 141 780	2 884	76 525	D	D	D	D	36.9	12.2	D	0.8
Elko	2 127	2.0	3 853	132.2	170.4	1 908 208	495	122 257	95.6	173 221	15.3	84.7	42.4	23.6	398	6.5
Esmeralda	35	38.7	911	17.5	19.2	1 631 211	1 791	350 737	13.1	345 974	98.2	1.8	60.5	60.5	0	0.0
Eureka	639	-18.5	6 325	46.7	49.1	4 087 158	646	288 782	36.0	356 634	81.2	18.8	72.3	59.4	D	3.0
Humboldt	809	6.9	2 253	137.5	165.3	2 233 571	991	271 593	135.3	376 983	75.7	24.3	48.7	37.9	703	26.7
Lander	314	-7.4	2 532	37.2	44.6	1 880 298	743	211 121	39.3	316 581	68.9	31.1	55.6	46.8	132	15.3
Lincoln	D	D	D	22.0	22.4	1 074 735	D	145 276	23.2	125 487	60.2	39.8	41.6	21.6	34	5.9
Lyon	366	40.4	792	87.7	78.3	1 738 119	2 194	137 630	133.0	287 959	43.8	56.2	44.2	21.4	485	5.8
Mineral	D	D	D	D	D	863 597	D	38 882	0.9	7 429	56.4	43.6	25.2	0.8	0	0.0
Nye	65	-28.3	329	20.0	26.4	703 429	2 139	127 217	70.5	356 035	D	D	36.9	12.6	62	6.1
Pershing	299	22.5	1 943	52.8	57.4	1 813 416	933	262 714	62.8	407 474	52.5	47.5	63.6	42.9	779	29.2
Storey	0	D	14	D	D	550 167	38 384	29 833	D	D	D	D	0.0	0.0	0	0.0
Washoe	443	-8.9	924	15.4	13.7	752 190	814	53 073	16.5	34 543	49.6	50.4	27.8	6.7	75	4.0
White Pine	193	D	1 208	32.7	24.3	987 431	817	150 775	20.7	129 069	43.9	56.1	40.6	22.5	120	7.5
Carson City	D	D	D	D	D	665 048	D	108 429	5.8	275 476	D	D	23.8	19.0	0	0.0
NEW HAMPSHIRE	474	0.5	108	2.6	98.3	449 848	4 167	56 426	190.9	43 477	52.8	47.2	26.6	6.0	3 472	10.6
Belknap	24	2.2	79	0.3	5.7	431 990	5 462	54 798	7.8	25 712	61.2	38.8	22.2	5.0	194	7.3
Carroll	29	-8.4	101	0.2	3.9	479 337	4 751	50 859	5.5	18 801	63.2	36.8	24.1	2.7	203	9.6
Cheshire	63	31.2	156	0.1	9.2	455 386	2 928	52 337	17.3	42 582	39.6	60.4	31.4	6.9	231	7.9
Coos	57	11.6	194	0.0	12.5	462 461	2 386	65 020	14.2	48 461	34.6	65.4	28.7	6.5	200	14.7
Grafton	82	-17.6	165	0.1	17.2	489 910	2 974	61 806	29.8	59 662	19.5	80.5	28.8	8.0	753	19.8
Hillsborough	48	-5.0	69	0.7	11.1	450 385	6 495	52 282	22.5	32 759	69.8	30.2	22.8	7.0	261	6.8
Merrimack	65	0.5	108	0.6	13.7	430 238	3 974	58 167	45.3	75 443	77.7	22.3	30.5	6.8	686	13.0
Rockingham	36	7.2	55	0.3	9.0	406 448	7 428	49 995	18.4	27 964	68.9	31.1	23.7	4.6	352	7.9
Strafford	31	19.2	87	0.3	7.7	425 040	4 904	61 031	12.8	36 144	47.0	53.0	30.5	3.1	295	10.7
Sullivan	39	-9.7	131	0.1	8.3	515 507	3 937	66 409	17.3	58 091	30.8	69.2	23.5	8.1	296	9.4
NEW JERSEY	715	-2.5	79	88.4	456.8	1 008 402	12 792	81 470	1 006.9	111 006	88.5	11.5	36.1	12.3	7 596	11.4
Atlantic	29	-2.9	73	11.3	18.9	903 438	12 320	135 682	125.4	312 040	98.2	1.8	51.7	25.4	247	8.2
Bergen	1	21.7	24	0.1	0.5	1 005 933	42 148	74 700	5.2	86 600	96.3	3.7	60.0	20.0	D	1.7
Burlington	96	11.8	114	13.1	52.3	1 108 438	9 686	98 032	100.9	120 390	95.4	4.6	45.3	14.4	1 939	13.4
Camden	7	-18.5	41	2.5	4.7	513 600	12 583	67 920	16.0	91 526	99.2	0.8	32.6	12.0	20	5.7
Cape May	7	-7.8	48	2.2	4.3	557 868	11 534	51 809	8.0	52 809	93.4	6.6	40.1	10.5	D	2.0
Cumberland	65	-7.1	111	19.3	49.7	889 362	8 035	130 184	170.4	292 216	97.2	2.8	50.9	22.1	520	14.9
Essex	0	-30.4	10	0.0	0.0	624 923	63 469	61 769	1.9	148 462	D	D	69.2	38.5	0	0.0
Gloucester	43	-7.3	74	9.0	32.0	882 231	11 909	93 639	87.7	150 154	93.9	6.1	33.6	15.6	700	13.0
Hudson	0	0.0	0	0.0	0.0	0	0	0	0.0	0	0.0	0.0	0.0	0.0	0	0.0
Hunterdon	96	-4.0	66	1.2	58.3	1 088 382	16 401	59 249	67.2	46 445	85.3	14.7	26.3	5.1	724	10.8

STATE County	Water use, 2010		Wholesale trade,[1] 2012				Retail trade,[2] 2012				Real estate and rental and leasing,[2] 2012			
	Total water withdrawn (mil gal/day)	Gallons withdrawn per person per day	Number of establish-ments	Number of employees	Sales (mil dol)	Annual payroll (mil dol)	Number of establish-ments	Number of employees	Sales (mil dol)	Annual payroll (mil dol)	Number of establish-ments	Number of employees	Receipts (mil dol)	Annual payroll (mil dol)
	133	134	135	136	137	138	139	140	141	142	143	144	145	146
NEBRASKA—Cont'd														
Platte	124.5	3 861	51	543	851.1	26.9	161	2 112	541.2	45.6	38	120	21.7	2.8
Polk	65.5	12 107	8	115	211.9	6.2	24	128	50.2	2.8	1	D	D	D
Red Willow	39.9	3 608	22	246	193.8	12.5	80	929	329.2	21.6	15	37	2.7	0.4
Richardson	2.9	343	26	137	473.1	5.0	44	331	94.1	7.2	6	16	1.7	0.5
Rock	21.6	14 174	4	D	D	D	7	44	6.8	0.7	NA	NA	NA	NA
Saline	46.1	3 245	21	175	316.6	9.1	43	536	129.2	11.1	8	18	2.6	0.3
Sarpy	35.1	221	183	2 932	4 040.2	161.1	367	7 301	2 926.4	174.8	146	580	163.2	22.0
Saunders	104.3	5 020	31	193	235.6	9.0	67	566	161.7	12.3	17	22	1.8	0.4
Scotts Bluff	518.7	14 031	56	D	D	D	178	D	D	D	46	116	19.8	3.0
Seward	51.2	3 057	27	258	528.2	14.1	47	521	105.6	10.7	9	11	2.6	0.3
Sheridan	54.4	9 947	12	206	104.3	4.8	42	236	55.7	3.8	2	D	D	D
Sherman	45.1	14 293	3	32	15.2	1.2	17	134	59.1	3.0	1	D	D	D
Sioux	99.0	75 484	1	D	D	D	3	D	D	D	NA	NA	NA	NA
Stanton	19.0	3 105	3	D	D	D	13	83	17.9	1.4	NA	NA	NA	NA
Thayer	79.1	15 132	25	215	524.6	12.3	31	173	56.1	3.4	3	D	D	D
Thomas	1.4	2 148	1	D	D	D	4	25	8.0	0.4	NA	NA	NA	NA
Thurston	5.9	853	8	99	103.3	3.5	24	219	73.0	4.7	4	D	D	D
Valley	120.0	28 174	8	76	225.5	3.3	33	267	116.5	6.0	2	D	D	D
Washington	445.8	22 032	18	D	D	D	56	1 106	747.4	42.4	15	20	2.6	0.5
Wayne	15.8	1 641	12	122	63.4	3.2	40	352	69.6	5.9	7	16	1.2	0.5
Webster	42.0	11 020	13	D	D	D	19	163	29.3	2.4	NA	NA	NA	NA
Wheeler	40.5	49 450	3	D	D	D	2	D	D	D	NA	NA	NA	NA
York	138.2	10 112	37	390	427.0	17.6	70	979	290.2	20.9	19	47	5.6	0.9
NEVADA	2 623.1	971	2 501	27 649	19 841.7	1 516.2	8 135	129 977	38 234.2	3 454.1	3 866	22 412	4 981.2	814.7
Churchill	191.8	7 708	15	78	39.1	2.9	69	966	235.1	23.4	32	113	12.5	2.6
Clark	486.6	249	1 630	16 747	11 597.1	958.8	5 712	95 369	27 971.7	2 531.6	2 794	17 855	3 700.3	647.4
Douglas	111.6	2 374	41	341	211.6	18.3	172	1 793	516.6	46.8	126	D	D	D
Elko	357.1	7 314	57	D	D	D	161	2 359	946.5	63.8	41	249	35.0	7.3
Esmeralda	25.8	32 950	1	D	D	D	1	D	D	D	NA	NA	NA	NA
Eureka	306.2	154 076	2	D	D	D	7	29	10.2	0.6	NA	NA	NA	NA
Humboldt	282.4	17 086	18	122	71.4	8.1	78	989	325.3	25.6	9	D	D	D
Lander	164.0	28 391	4	34	38.4	2.2	20	235	52.0	6.0	3	4	0.8	0.1
Lincoln	54.1	10 123	2	D	D	D	16	D	D	D	3	D	D	D
Lyon	222.1	4 274	38	749	206.4	24.6	97	1 188	465.5	29.1	33	D	D	D
Mineral	3.1	658	2	D	D	D	15	95	31.3	3.0	NA	NA	NA	NA
Nye	63.9	1 455	9	96	55.4	4.5	117	1 404	397.1	34.1	34	79	7.7	1.8
Pershing	82.8	12 261	2	D	D	D	16	131	48.4	3.3	1	D	D	D
Storey	2.0	491	NA	NA	NA	NA	20	41	6.0	0.9	1	D	D	D
Washoe	132.9	315	584	8 064	6 401.9	414.6	1 391	21 603	6 167.0	580.0	671	D	D	D
White Pine	119.8	11 943	7	64	33.7	2.2	31	408	111.0	9.6	7	D	D	D
Carson City	17.0	307	89	519	276.4	25.2	212	3 139	918.2	92.6	111	304	51.7	9.5
NEW HAMPSHIRE	1 214.6	923	1 543	21 140	18 029.2	1 307.9	6 127	95 660	26 018.2	2 403.6	1 338	7 044	1 593.1	309.7
Belknap	9.3	155	50	447	214.2	23.9	342	4 907	1 357.5	127.0	78	420	62.0	12.3
Carroll	5.0	104	39	310	99.2	14.5	363	3 558	877.7	88.9	69	237	36.1	8.6
Cheshire	7.9	103	59	1 151	637.4	47.0	368	5 839	1 692.5	150.1	60	229	45.1	8.0
Coos	13.6	411	21	295	89.3	7.5	182	1 800	566.6	45.2	25	68	11.9	2.5
Grafton	12.2	137	78	713	487.9	42.6	519	7 712	2 034.2	199.5	144	454	70.5	15.3
Hillsborough	55.1	137	537	6 822	4 749.3	470.5	1 584	26 984	7 724.7	700.9	387	2 697	565.9	123.8
Merrimack	216.2	1 476	148	3 176	2 823.3	162.5	624	10 124	2 819.7	243.0	143	848	319.9	41.4
Rockingham	871.2	2 951	487	6 804	8 203.7	455.3	1 587	26 066	6 764.5	625.5	303	1 286	316.8	55.9
Strafford	19.0	154	85	1 037	385.9	58.1	385	6 378	1 619.4	166.9	93	560	78.1	22.7
Sullivan	5.1	117	39	385	339.1	26.0	173	2 292	561.2	56.5	36	245	86.7	19.2
NEW JERSEY	5 670.7	645	12 760	208 830	288 467.8	14 976.8	31 722	436 299	133 665.7	12 676.0	8 749	53 751	17 327.6	2 813.1
Atlantic	60.1	219	188	D	D	D	1 227	16 099	4 292.7	394.9	227	1 383	351.1	52.0
Bergen	116.3	128	2 720	36 346	77 906.6	2 730.3	3 807	56 423	20 349.2	2 662.1	1 357	7 550	2 481.5	417.9
Burlington	109.5	244	492	10 202	14 927.4	618.5	1 428	23 654	6 868.6	645.4	364	3 340	886.7	201.7
Camden	57.5	112	572	8 133	4 906.7	442.3	1 730	23 577	6 445.8	593.9	398	2 660	601.1	116.3
Cape May	79.6	818	60	D	D	D	669	5 803	1 639.4	166.2	218	681	148.7	26.0
Cumberland	58.9	375	152	3 223	2 422.4	133.6	512	7 201	2 049.0	175.0	120	471	96.2	15.8
Essex	33.2	42	987	14 029	13 657.7	913.7	2 710	26 114	9 204.6	720.2	879	5 267	1 258.8	214.8
Gloucester	72.2	251	296	7 307	16 524.4	437.2	954	16 728	4 452.9	398.7	171	1 228	256.1	63.9
Hudson	209.4	330	757	15 906	26 043.1	1 009.8	2 118	23 126	6 647.6	611.5	636	3 698	1 238.8	199.0
Hunterdon	89.7	699	143	1 868	1 030.6	150.0	493	6 561	2 350.0	190.2	104	415	123.8	25.3

1. Merchant wholesalers, except manufacturers' sales branches and offices.   2. Employer establishments.

STATE County	Professional, scientific, and technical services, 2012				Manufacturing, 2012				Accommodation and food services, 2012			
	Number of establishments	Number of employees	Receipts (mil dol)	Annual payroll (mil dol)	Number of establishments	Number of employees	Receipts (mil dol)	Annual payroll (mil dol)	Number of establishments	Number of employees	Sales (mil dol)	Annual payroll (mil dol)
	147	148	149	150	151	152	153	154	155	156	157	158
NEBRASKA—Cont'd												
Platte	65	465	55.7	23.1	74	5 492	4 438.5	261.6	75	968	40.9	10.5
Polk	12	18	1.9	0.4	6	53	D	1.6	6	37	1.4	0.2
Red Willow	28	123	13.9	4.4	14	293	D	14.3	30	524	21.5	6.0
Richardson	13	63	4.2	1.5	14	193	40.4	7.1	21	193	6.1	1.7
Rock	2	D	D	D	NA	NA	NA	NA	4	15	0.4	0.1
Saline	16	43	4.6	1.2	19	2 654	2 175.0	125.9	27	309	10.6	2.6
Sarpy	297	2 588	354.6	156.8	76	2 699	791.9	139.3	255	4 718	224.7	62.7
Saunders	45	119	15.0	4.9	22	288	104.6	9.5	42	D	D	D
Scotts Bluff	68	D	D	D	39	847	270.7	33.7	100	D	D	D
Seward	29	106	21.4	3.3	20	1 197	576.8	57.3	30	453	18.6	4.4
Sheridan	8	29	3.8	0.7	NA	NA	NA	NA	21	133	4.8	1.3
Sherman	6	13	0.9	0.3	3	10	D	D	8	61	2.5	0.6
Sioux	1	D	D	D	NA	NA	NA	NA	2	D	D	D
Stanton	2	D	D	D	NA	NA	NA	NA	5	60	1.7	0.4
Thayer	9	18	2.3	0.6	11	524	D	15.3	12	115	7.6	1.1
Thomas	1	D	D	D	NA	NA	NA	NA	NA	NA	NA	NA
Thurston	9	D	D	D	6	246	D	10.1	8	65	2.5	0.5
Valley	14	D	D	D	9	74	D	3.2	9	D	D	D
Washington	47	163	20.1	6.5	26	1 134	1 549.7	69.9	52	441	16.1	4.4
Wayne	16	56	10.7	2.7	12	893	217.6	28.6	23	393	11.5	2.5
Webster	2	D	D	D	NA	NA	NA	NA	4	24	0.6	0.2
Wheeler	NA	NA	NA	NA	NA	NA	NA	NA	5	8	0.2	0.1
York	29	122	14.5	4.8	28	777	359.3	34.9	39	710	32.2	8.7
NEVADA	8 102	47 934	7 758.5	2 832.1	1 706	38 123	14 719.1	1 979.3	5 815	296 762	27 481.5	8 555.6
Churchill	43	354	23.4	10.4	18	248	D	12.8	50	586	35.9	9.4
Clark	5 645	35 253	5 825.0	2 128.2	894	17 390	5 673.8	782.0	4 050	250 601	24 283.8	7 612.3
Douglas	238	786	115.6	37.2	74	1 129	713.0	55.1	126	5 326	445.8	125.1
Elko	98	666	123.7	32.7	24	D	D	D	138	5 036	442.7	121.4
Esmeralda	1	D	D	D	NA	NA	NA	NA	1	D	D	D
Eureka	4	D	D	D	NA	NA	NA	NA	5	34	1.5	0.4
Humboldt	19	96	10.3	3.6	13	241	120.0	12.0	62	1 161	84.1	15.7
Lander	1	D	D	D	NA	NA	NA	NA	14	145	6.2	1.6
Lincoln	6	20	2.4	0.6	NA	NA	NA	NA	19	D	D	D
Lyon	62	324	34.8	13.1	81	1 708	729.9	85.9	67	613	31.2	7.9
Mineral	5	22	1.5	0.6	NA	NA	NA	NA	10	D	D	D
Nye	50	155	12.5	4.3	14	60	D	1.7	81	1 401	96.5	22.5
Pershing	2	D	D	D	6	128	D	D	13	113	5.8	1.8
Storey	6	7	0.5	0.2	6	91	17.3	3.1	14	71	9.4	2.4
Washoe	1 619	9 029	1 435.4	539.9	442	13 974	6 427.4	840.4	973	28 138	1 860.8	580.8
White Pine	8	25	2.1	0.9	6	23	D	0.8	33	553	31.2	9.4
Carson City	295	1 180	170.1	60.0	122	2 798	634.0	162.7	159	2 740	133.4	41.2
NEW HAMPSHIRE	3 825	30 159	3 947.8	1 697.5	1 851	66 636	18 895.6	3 923.8	3 606	54 047	2 942.3	890.9
Belknap	147	D	D	D	86	2 483	673.3	117.2	223	2 603	157.9	50.7
Carroll	133	D	D	D	74	1 069	225.8	41.2	313	4 034	247.0	70.6
Cheshire	147	628	69.2	30.0	127	4 719	1 101.6	230.1	172	2 543	128.7	40.0
Coos	37	114	11.3	4.3	37	731	189.3	31.0	111	1 747	81.0	31.2
Grafton	254	1 537	210.1	98.4	115	5 758	1 593.9	300.2	378	5 112	296.7	92.2
Hillsborough	1 335	10 986	1 721.0	737.1	554	25 287	7 450.8	1 732.0	897	14 781	762.2	229.8
Merrimack	433	2 850	402.7	171.8	206	5 548	1 577.3	291.1	307	4 965	238.7	75.2
Rockingham	1 049	8 202	1 109.2	462.4	425	14 055	4 580.4	824.8	853	13 804	810.2	237.3
Strafford	235	1 720	217.6	95.3	137	4 428	924.4	228.1	282	3 676	182.8	52.2
Sullivan	55	180	21.1	9.0	90	2 559	578.8	128.0	70	782	37.1	11.8
NEW JERSEY	29 390	307 549	58 738.2	24 013.0	7 758	230 697	108 855.0	14 094.8	20 127	291 933	19 673.6	5 386.8
Atlantic	579	D	D	D	96	1 730	285.4	72.3	860	46 661	4 008.5	1 282.5
Bergen	4 067	37 178	6 945.7	2 557.1	1 107	33 434	12 577.6	2 133.9	2 331	28 682	2 016.7	518.2
Burlington	1 323	D	D	D	343	15 380	5 496.6	1 046.9	914	14 391	771.4	206.5
Camden	1 444	D	D	D	389	11 340	D	613.9	998	14 598	789.4	210.9
Cape May	214	D	D	D	66	615	98.2	21.5	903	5 888	593.0	160.0
Cumberland	207	D	D	D	162	8 055	2 812.0	351.2	265	3 555	173.7	43.6
Essex	2 213	28 745	6 117.7	2 678.1	720	17 556	5 942.0	921.7	1 550	20 633	1 378.7	368.3
Gloucester	514	D	D	D	235	8 056	12 683.6	440.2	483	7 832	406.6	108.0
Hudson	1 335	11 261	1 961.4	898.8	378	7 865	2 682.9	363.9	1 381	15 540	1 214.5	287.1
Hunterdon	561	4 111	888.9	350.4	141	3 485	1 400.2	198.5	312	3 518	206.3	54.9

1. Establishment subject to federal tax.

Table B. States and Counties — Health Care and Social Assistance, Other Services, Nonemployer Businesses, and Residential Construction

STATE County	Health care and social assistance, 2012				Other services, 2012				Nonemployer businesses, 2014		Value of residential construction authorized by building permits, 2015	
	Number of establishments	Number of employees	Receipts (mil dol)	Annual payroll (mil dol)	Number of establishments	Number of employees	Receipts (mil dol)	Annual payroll (mil dol)	Number	Receipts (mil dol)	New Construction ($1,000)	Number of housing units
	159	160	161	162	163	164	165	166	167	168	169	170
NEBRASKA—Cont'd												
Platte	82	1 551	179.9	55.9	78	360	26.7	8.4	2 203	91.8	15 072	71
Polk	9	273	17.4	7.2	9	17	2.8	0.5	446	14.4	993	5
Red Willow	50	604	60.9	22.5	33	90	10.1	2.4	863	32.2	3 846	24
Richardson	26	D	D	D	22	66	4.8	0.8	639	20.4	2 787	45
Rock	4	D	D	D	5	7	0.9	0.2	215	10.6	453	3
Saline	26	525	37.9	16.4	26	96	6.2	1.8	792	32.9	3 692	20
Sarpy	302	4 733	387.5	146.4	225	1 219	110.5	30.3	9 659	366.6	229 345	897
Saunders	31	672	38.8	17.6	27	D	D	D	1 735	64.4	17 905	95
Scotts Bluff	128	D	D	D	76	D	D	D	2 541	106.3	3 174	14
Seward	36	761	53.7	24.0	38	134	15.4	3.5	1 306	41.0	9 486	48
Sheridan	17	208	12.2	6.4	18	42	3.1	0.6	461	18.5	212	3
Sherman	6	D	D	D	6	11	0.9	0.1	266	11.1	418	2
Sioux	1	D	D	D	1	D	D	D	121	3.7	568	2
Stanton	7	D	D	D	4	23	2.7	0.4	451	19.7	5 720	26
Thayer	11	416	25.8	11.1	21	60	16.3	1.4	412	20.2	1 483	8
Thomas	NA	NA	NA	NA	1	D	D	D	81	4.5	1 007	5
Thurston	9	277	32.6	14.7	8	24	3.2	0.8	271	11.9	1 532	8
Valley	18	111	5.9	2.5	14	67	6.0	1.3	394	16.2	1 190	5
Washington	40	926	67.4	31.7	41	D	D	D	1 502	64.2	23 191	86
Wayne	24	458	31.7	14.2	20	D	D	D	601	23.7	3 003	26
Webster	9	189	10.7	4.7	5	17	2.1	0.3	277	9.2	1 700	9
Wheeler	NA	NA	NA	NA	1	D	D	D	85	4.4	0	0
York	41	1 063	79.9	35.5	57	253	20.6	5.0	1 042	44.7	5 514	21
NEVADA	6 308	108 585	13 928.5	5 094.7	3 538	25 386	2 608.9	706.5	199 538	10 288.0	2 141 757	14 083
Churchill	41	714	81.1	30.6	42	171	12.2	3.5	1 141	45.1	5 459	24
Clark	4 426	75 019	9 714.9	3 493.8	2 344	17 926	1 602.8	476.8	148 576	7 394.1	1 407 544	10 605
Douglas	121	1 310	165.9	59.1	69	514	41.2	15.1	5 123	342.1	51 079	140
Elko	125	D	D	D	70	D	D	D	2 311	105.4	31 684	236
Esmeralda	NA	NA	NA	NA	1	D	D	D	68	2.0	NA	NA
Eureka	1	D	D	D	1	D	D	D	116	4.8	NA	NA
Humboldt	37	628	55.0	22.2	36	D	D	D	863	34.3	6 324	51
Lander	9	D	D	D	4	D	D	D	274	8.5	295	2
Lincoln	6	128	7.4	3.3	2	D	D	D	272	8.5	2 107	8
Lyon	38	D	D	D	42	202	20.7	5.3	2 571	127.2	39 004	179
Mineral	6	D	D	D	4	D	D	D	166	6.8	0	0
Nye	61	821	82.6	24.3	49	203	16.8	4.4	2 238	86.1	NA	NA
Pershing	6	107	9.0	3.6	4	D	D	D	197	5.0	0	0
Storey	1	D	D	D	3	D	D	D	279	11.6	1 228	7
Washoe	1 190	D	D	D	728	D	D	D	29 985	1 682.3	585 308	2 780
White Pine	16	301	44.6	16.7	13	D	D	D	456	15.8	2 414	8
Carson City	224	3 744	510.8	182.9	126	660	62.8	19.0	4 902	408.2	9 311	43
NEW HAMPSHIRE	3 578	87 099	9 616.5	4 086.4	2 879	16 603	1 554.9	473.3	103 345	5 762.2	736 931	3 763
Belknap	137	3 536	358.6	148.0	147	626	49.1	13.8	5 583	299.1	71 148	364
Carroll	142	2 693	267.9	100.4	111	432	39.6	11.1	5 469	286.0	60 012	209
Cheshire	157	3 954	334.7	156.5	144	938	77.2	22.6	5 953	302.4	26 119	212
Coos	102	2 469	214.2	91.1	68	377	40.5	12.6	2 213	89.1	6 154	33
Grafton	273	10 236	1 482.4	659.8	207	D	D	D	7 949	429.2	69 297	244
Hillsborough	1 094	28 561	3 089.1	1 339.9	824	5 516	490.3	160.3	28 189	1 609.6	171 801	921
Merrimack	410	12 310	1 239.7	550.0	411	1 995	257.0	68.2	10 985	579.0	64 852	378
Rockingham	866	15 640	1 697.7	671.8	676	3 639	335.9	104.1	25 986	1 634.5	207 558	1 041
Strafford	302	6 486	834.3	327.4	204	1 192	111.9	32.9	7 772	381.8	50 361	313
Sullivan	95	1 214	97.8	41.4	87	D	D	D	3 246	151.5	9 627	48
NEW JERSEY	26 935	540 875	60 375.2	24 325.0	18 327	108 216	11 607.8	3 150.1	653 271	37 997.5	4 051 996	30 560
Atlantic	846	17 487	1 969.3	780.4	563	3 588	293.9	85.2	16 335	801.3	112 218	710
Bergen	3 664	70 990	9 303.0	3 642.8	2 423	12 297	1 376.8	366.9	89 950	6 110.6	486 319	2 671
Burlington	1 215	25 242	2 710.6	1 006.5	778	4 560	363.7	118.9	26 968	1 568.6	116 797	892
Camden	1 535	38 296	4 238.4	1 821.5	920	5 873	478.1	149.4	28 904	1 503.4	88 894	1 040
Cape May	278	4 767	443.7	186.8	296	1 237	96.3	32.4	8 029	461.3	181 526	614
Cumberland	417	8 593	872.1	338.7	240	1 253	97.1	27.3	5 985	274.6	26 226	237
Essex	2 534	53 168	6 274.3	2 462.1	1 639	12 502	1 220.6	360.6	63 431	3 317.2	281 585	3 214
Gloucester	689	13 076	1 298.2	541.2	502	2 838	223.8	66.5	15 464	749.4	74 916	738
Hudson	1 412	26 740	2 397.6	1 000.5	1 092	5 024	439.1	125.3	51 315	2 364.9	656 156	5 060
Hunterdon	363	7 216	794.4	323.9	272	1 466	120.6	38.5	11 803	780.4	51 511	425

Table B. States and Counties — Government Employment and Payroll, and Local Government Finances

STATE County	Full-time equivalent employees	March payroll (dollars)	Administration, judicial, and legal	Police and Corrections	Fire Protection	Highways and transportation	Health and Welfare	Natural resources and utilities	Education and libraries	Total (mil dol)	Intergovernmental (mil dol)	Total (mil dol)	Per capita¹ Total	Per capita¹ Property
	171	172	173	174	175	176	177	178	179	180	181	182	183	184
NEBRASKA—Cont'd														
Platte	3 477	20 266 212	1.3	2.8	0.3	1.8	0.3	79.5	13.4	163.8	34.4	61.8	1 892	1 373
Polk	420	1 380 326	5.6	2.1	0.0	3.0	15.0	11.8	58.7	37.3	5.7	21.1	3 974	3 451
Red Willow	459	1 542 403	5.5	7.0	2.8	3.6	3.4	14.8	59.2	39.4	13.2	18.3	1 666	1 234
Richardson	419	1 193 885	9.7	4.8	0.6	7.6	0.0	12.0	63.6	30.7	8.7	18.1	2 182	1 949
Rock	140	411 891	13.3	2.7	0.0	6.6	35.8	2.2	35.4	13.0	2.1	4.8	3 482	3 134
Saline	632	2 291 344	7.0	11.3	0.3	4.0	0.9	7.0	67.4	70.4	19.1	28.7	1 969	1 723
Sarpy	5 078	18 211 968	6.6	10.7	1.5	2.7	1.0	2.9	72.0	450.7	142.5	250.1	1 508	1 248
Saunders	810	2 374 236	6.4	9.1	0.3	4.5	15.3	6.0	56.4	83.3	19.9	36.4	1 747	1 563
Scotts Bluff	2 061	7 164 008	4.8	7.4	1.1	2.8	2.5	7.6	73.3	182.1	72.1	64.7	1 751	1 338
Seward	680	2 373 107	7.0	6.7	0.0	6.0	0.7	9.6	68.9	55.3	12.4	35.6	2 103	1 821
Sheridan	512	1 548 088	13.3	3.5	0.0	6.0	29.3	9.8	37.6	40.3	9.6	11.2	2 111	1 872
Sherman	144	428 471	12.6	3.9	0.0	9.3	0.2	2.5	70.1	13.6	4.9	7.3	2 338	2 074
Sioux	56	132 554	19.8	4.1	0.0	17.1	0.0	2.1	56.8	4.9	1.0	3.0	2 305	2 122
Stanton	142	497 786	10.8	7.3	0.0	12.3	0.9	19.3	48.7	13.2	4.4	6.8	1 111	1 047
Thayer	412	1 461 621	5.5	2.0	0.0	5.1	41.8	4.4	38.2	41.8	5.4	16.6	3 236	3 029
Thomas	60	133 894	17.6	0.2	0.0	4.3	2.3	11.2	63.8	4.0	0.7	2.8	4 143	3 988
Thurston	545	1 799 779	5.2	2.2	0.0	2.7	22.5	1.8	65.3	52.7	28.4	8.7	1 244	1 115
Valley	518	1 666 812	3.3	2.5	0.0	3.6	47.1	17.8	25.3	53.3	10.2	13.7	3 233	2 920
Washington	750	2 779 921	6.4	9.0	0.0	4.2	8.1	3.5	68.0	69.7	16.2	43.5	2 146	1 843
Wayne	341	1 199 613	9.9	5.1	0.0	9.4	0.0	6.2	69.3	36.1	12.9	18.5	1 940	1 746
Webster	258	1 370 728	10.8	2.2	0.0	8.5	14.9	37.0	25.2	25.0	5.9	8.3	2 228	1 836
Wheeler	43	129 479	13.7	4.4	0.0	13.0	0.0	0.4	68.2	4.3	0.9	3.2	3 984	3 805
York	557	2 016 974	7.4	11.4	2.9	4.0	1.6	20.2	51.6	58.5	16.3	32.4	2 356	1 736
NEVADA	X	X	X	X	X	X	X	X	X	X	X	X	X	X
Churchill	944	3 773 220	10.4	12.8	0.4	2.3	1.9	7.4	51.3	114.7	52.6	27.8	1 142	921
Clark	51 796	300 406 553	8.1	16.4	5.9	3.4	8.6	10.1	45.3	8 606.7	3 678.4	2 735.1	1 367	869
Douglas	1 543	6 734 261	11.5	13.8	10.6	2.6	1.1	9.0	47.4	190.9	73.5	79.1	1 682	1 414
Elko	1 843	7 360 751	11.7	10.6	2.2	3.0	2.9	4.9	62.8	202.1	112.9	62.5	1 220	871
Esmeralda	82	243 932	21.0	20.4	0.0	9.4	1.5	2.3	37.8	7.7	4.9	1.6	2 030	2 012
Eureka	151	777 513	15.5	14.0	0.0	9.5	5.9	8.6	42.4	52.6	15.1	33.5	16 737	16 592
Humboldt	805	3 278 576	10.2	13.2	0.3	2.8	19.5	2.9	48.7	119.3	53.7	33.6	1 972	1 745
Lander	301	1 258 391	12.7	11.1	0.0	4.5	25.4	3.4	42.8	97.8	10.8	72.9	12 271	11 925
Lincoln	324	1 339 919	8.9	8.4	0.1	6.3	17.9	11.0	44.6	43.9	32.2	5.0	930	812
Lyon	1 568	6 140 208	8.1	8.1	3.5	1.3	1.3	10.4	64.0	160.6	98.5	45.8	892	708
Mineral	326	1 115 225	7.2	7.3	1.2	2.2	44.5	6.8	29.7	44.0	21.3	4.5	977	861
Nye	1 197	5 104 254	15.1	13.0	3.6	2.6	5.5	2.8	53.7	149.5	78.9	54.1	1 259	1 117
Pershing	319	1 109 998	11.6	9.0	0.3	4.2	22.5	5.0	44.3	34.1	14.3	8.8	1 300	1 263
Storey	188	901 189	19.1	15.5	16.1	3.8	0.0	4.0	34.8	29.3	7.0	16.6	4 219	4 028
Washoe	13 423	56 391 305	10.3	14.1	5.5	4.2	4.2	8.5	50.6	1 707.2	748.2	591.5	1 376	997
White Pine	513	2 356 531	8.8	7.1	1.5	3.7	40.7	2.2	32.8	71.2	22.1	18.0	1 791	1 611
Carson City	1 396	6 652 347	9.5	13.4	7.3	4.2	3.5	6.4	53.3	189.1	96.1	54.9	1 001	717
NEW HAMPSHIRE	X	X	X	X	X	X	X	X	X	X	X	X	X	X
Belknap	2 709	10 085 919	5.6	9.4	4.9	3.9	5.2	2.9	67.2	286.0	77.2	174.6	2 894	2 867
Carroll	2 191	7 449 385	6.3	9.2	2.5	4.0	7.7	3.0	65.3	220.7	71.1	131.4	2 763	2 740
Cheshire	3 313	11 134 351	6.0	8.9	2.9	3.9	7.7	4.1	65.0	326.6	110.7	178.9	2 328	2 314
Coos	1 565	5 117 863	3.6	6.6	2.3	4.9	20.1	3.2	58.8	159.6	71.8	67.1	2 091	2 079
Grafton	4 014	15 506 186	5.7	9.6	3.8	4.9	5.6	2.9	66.7	413.3	113.5	253.8	2 845	2 823
Hillsborough	13 991	56 054 764	4.1	10.8	6.0	4.5	3.9	3.8	65.8	1 458.9	470.6	808.2	2 006	1 981
Merrimack	5 875	21 465 982	6.0	10.6	5.3	4.2	7.6	3.1	61.7	555.7	176.5	328.2	2 236	2 219
Rockingham	10 620	43 247 180	4.5	10.2	6.0	2.4	3.9	2.7	68.4	1 174.1	314.0	771.3	2 590	2 568
Strafford	4 327	16 109 116	5.0	11.0	4.3	2.9	5.3	4.6	64.6	465.8	153.2	257.6	2 076	2 027
Sullivan	1 670	6 151 956	5.3	6.7	2.1	4.8	8.2	3.5	67.8	169.0	64.2	91.6	2 126	2 114
NEW JERSEY	X	X	X	X	X	X	X	X	X	X	X	X	X	X
Atlantic	14 001	71 971 044	5.3	13.7	4.7	1.7	5.3	3.8	63.4	1 749.6	507.4	1 016.6	3 691	3 639
Bergen	32 531	187 619 946	3.6	14.1	2.2	2.4	3.4	3.1	69.8	4 811.6	664.9	3 480.7	3 788	3 728
Burlington	17 657	91 624 216	4.0	9.2	2.6	2.9	2.3	3.0	75.0	2 079.2	596.9	1 183.3	2 622	2 584
Camden	20 756	110 518 829	3.6	10.7	3.0	3.5	5.8	2.8	67.4	3 281.1	1 305.1	1 230.4	2 396	2 359
Cape May	5 885	27 086 618	8.8	13.8	3.3	3.6	9.4	7.3	49.4	701.1	152.6	449.5	4 667	4 561
Cumberland	7 697	36 180 326	5.2	9.1	0.8	1.2	4.3	5.3	72.5	886.9	544.0	234.1	1 483	1 435
Essex	27 848	164 987 769	6.6	19.3	7.5	1.4	6.3	6.8	50.7	4 140.4	1 433.6	2 242.3	2 846	2 712
Gloucester	12 453	61 264 381	3.9	10.6	0.6	1.8	6.9	3.4	70.7	1 465.5	472.5	747.5	2 581	2 536
Hudson	18 627	101 485 405	7.4	23.1	8.9	1.9	5.7	4.8	45.5	2 886.1	1 144.0	1 243.6	1 906	1 849
Hunterdon	5 140	25 927 699	5.8	5.6	0.8	4.7	2.2	2.5	77.1	623.8	82.1	477.9	3 762	3 722

1. Based on the resident population estimated as of July 1 of the year shown.

STATE County	Local government finances, 2012 (cont.)									Government employment, 2014			Presidential election,[2] 2012		
	Direct general expenditure							Debt outstanding					Percent of vote cast:		
			Percent of total for:												
	Total (mil dol)	Per capita[1] (dollars)	Educa-tion	Health and hospitals	Police protec-tion	Public welfare	High-ways	Total (mil dol)	Per capita[1] (dollars)	Federal civilian	Federal military	State and local	Demo-cratic	Republi-can	All other
	185	186	187	188	189	190	191	192	193	194	195	196	197	198	199
NEBRASKA—Cont'd															
Platte	113.1	3 461	56.1	0.4	3.7	0.6	15.1	2 372.1	72 585	86	119	2 470	28.3	69.8	1.9
Polk	34.4	6 457	55.6	18.0	1.4	0.1	7.2	36.4	6 843	25	19	514	26.3	71.6	2.1
Red Willow	41.1	3 746	48.6	0.9	4.2	0.6	6.1	41.9	3 815	68	39	1 056	24.1	74.0	1.8
Richardson	30.5	3 684	56.0	0.2	3.6	0.5	13.4	14.8	1 787	37	29	564	38.1	59.0	2.8
Rock	12.2	8 902	28.5	45.3	2.3	0.2	9.0	0.5	363	0	0	210	17.4	79.9	2.7
Saline	69.9	4 800	47.6	15.1	3.0	5.7	7.4	56.7	3 893	57	49	1 459	50.9	46.4	2.7
Sarpy	475.3	2 866	55.1	0.8	7.4	0.2	4.2	984.0	5 933	3 245	6 193	6 706	41.2	57.1	1.8
Saunders	75.5	3 628	42.1	21.4	3.2	0.2	8.3	105.7	5 074	105	76	1 459	36.9	60.6	2.5
Scotts Bluff	188.1	5 089	58.5	0.3	4.2	1.6	3.8	124.2	3 361	159	131	3 070	32.2	65.9	1.9
Seward	66.4	3 923	62.3	0.1	3.8	0.8	11.4	73.7	4 351	48	58	1 096	35.9	61.7	2.4
Sheridan	37.7	7 085	31.7	24.7	2.1	9.8	6.1	9.5	1 782	26	19	629	18.4	78.8	2.7
Sherman	13.4	4 324	49.2	0.3	3.1	0.3	17.7	6.5	2 098	11	11	298	37.2	60.4	2.4
Sioux	4.8	3 666	52.8	0.0	2.8	0.0	23.8	0.0	0	11	0	80	16.0	82.4	1.6
Stanton	13.6	2 232	42.0	0.7	4.3	0.5	31.8	14.5	2 388	19	22	274	26.6	71.4	2.0
Thayer	43.3	8 429	33.8	38.7	2.7	0.2	7.2	11.5	2 243	34	19	635	32.3	65.8	1.9
Thomas	4.0	5 904	53.0	0.5	3.1	0.0	7.9	0.8	1 214	0	0	92	13.1	84.9	2.1
Thurston	60.1	8 565	48.8	36.6	1.1	0.1	3.6	70.6	10 050	220	25	1 432	52.7	45.7	1.6
Valley	51.9	12 276	20.8	38.7	0.9	0.1	4.8	58.0	13 716	32	15	641	29.1	68.4	2.5
Washington	65.2	3 221	57.9	0.1	4.7	0.2	11.9	202.8	10 013	46	73	1 578	36.0	62.3	1.8
Wayne	43.1	4 516	51.6	0.3	2.5	0.4	9.5	23.9	2 503	37	31	1 067	32.8	65.7	1.5
Webster	23.9	6 404	33.4	19.3	2.3	5.0	13.2	9.5	2 548	24	13	307	30.4	67.9	1.8
Wheeler	4.1	5 045	61.1	0.0	2.5	0.0	23.7	0.6	806	0	0	61	21.8	75.9	2.3
York	55.4	4 034	45.6	2.4	5.0	0.3	13.4	105.0	7 641	55	48	1 160	24.5	73.8	1.7
NEVADA	X	X	X	X	X	X	X	X	X	18 121	18 550	131 509	55.1	42.7	2.2
Churchill	117.7	4 831	40.0	0.3	7.9	1.8	3.2	48.9	2 005	587	717	1 295	32.9	64.4	2.6
Clark	9 171.7	4 584	29.1	8.3	9.6	2.7	7.2	21 727.8	10 860	12 366	15 709	83 157	58.5	39.5	2.0
Douglas	187.5	3 990	36.5	0.3	5.7	2.5	2.5	82.9	1 764	88	134	2 149	41.2	56.5	2.3
Elko	209.5	4 091	47.0	0.9	7.2	0.7	5.0	51.6	1 008	352	147	3 303	28.3	68.5	3.2
Esmeralda	8.2	10 566	34.9	3.8	14.2	0.4	10.2	1.0	1 279	0	0	90	23.7	69.0	7.3
Eureka	40.5	20 245	25.6	2.0	4.9	0.3	18.1	0.0	0	0	0	206	19.3	75.7	5.0
Humboldt	102.4	6 005	35.6	26.8	6.8	1.0	6.9	5.9	344	146	48	1 372	33.7	63.3	3.0
Lander	42.2	7 095	31.4	24.0	6.2	2.0	4.2	0.0	0	68	17	494	27.5	69.7	2.8
Lincoln	42.9	7 928	28.0	0.6	5.4	1.6	11.1	9.9	1 834	40	14	570	24.6	71.1	4.3
Lyon	173.5	3 380	52.1	0.6	14.8	3.1	4.1	198.7	3 872	64	145	2 010	39.8	57.6	2.6
Mineral	39.6	8 513	17.4	39.2	5.2	0.6	3.6	14.3	3 064	68	14	492	46.9	49.0	4.1
Nye	174.9	4 071	43.6	4.0	14.2	1.5	4.9	134.2	3 123	118	121	1 633	41.3	54.5	4.2
Pershing	35.1	5 199	33.9	28.5	4.8	1.5	1.5	18.6	2 751	16	14	706	36.7	58.6	4.8
Storey	27.2	6 900	26.2	0.0	10.5	0.8	8.2	58.6	14 880	0	11	228	45.6	51.6	2.9
Washoe	1 673.2	3 892	35.9	1.1	6.6	4.3	3.3	4 470.2	10 398	3 485	1 279	23 818	55.2	42.6	2.1
White Pine	67.7	6 746	27.2	38.8	5.4	1.6	6.0	14.1	1 407	192	25	1 208	32.0	63.5	4.5
Carson City	205.0	3 738	48.3	2.1	8.1	1.2	5.3	391.1	7 131	517	147	8 778	49.1	48.2	2.7
NEW HAMPSHIRE	X	X	X	X	X	X	X	X	X	7 413	4 613	82 921	54.1	44.5	1.4
Belknap	273.9	4 541	53.3	0.3	6.3	6.1	4.4	96.2	1 595	138	199	4 159	50.0	48.8	1.2
Carroll	240.5	5 057	57.3	1.0	4.6	7.3	6.0	161.9	3 404	131	157	2 967	52.4	46.1	1.5
Cheshire	326.5	4 248	59.3	0.8	4.3	5.5	5.6	178.9	2 328	156	241	5 376	63.0	35.5	1.5
Coos	150.6	4 691	46.4	1.2	3.9	16.3	6.1	37.2	1 158	389	101	2 705	58.3	40.1	1.6
Grafton	440.6	4 940	56.2	0.8	4.4	4.8	5.7	258.1	2 895	511	279	6 776	63.0	35.5	1.5
Hillsborough	1 496.1	3 713	52.0	0.6	6.1	3.8	4.7	1 157.0	2 872	3 870	1 362	17 741	51.2	47.5	1.3
Merrimack	608.7	4 147	55.4	0.5	5.3	7.4	4.5	341.5	2 327	815	472	15 903	56.3	42.5	1.3
Rockingham	1 129.6	3 793	60.9	0.4	6.4	4.0	3.7	523.7	1 758	1 010	1 255	13 509	49.9	48.8	1.3
Strafford	444.5	3 582	51.7	0.1	5.7	7.3	4.8	294.8	2 375	305	405	11 338	59.5	39.2	1.3
Sullivan	166.1	3 857	51.2	0.5	4.3	11.4	5.9	81.8	1 900	88	142	2 447	58.2	40.3	1.5
NEW JERSEY	X	X	X	X	X	X	X	X	X	48 999	25 070	545 412	57.3	41.7	1.0
Atlantic	1 718.6	6 240	52.7	0.6	6.1	2.1	1.7	1 314.6	4 773	2 608	919	20 990	57.0	41.9	1.1
Bergen	4 857.2	5 286	54.3	5.8	7.0	1.3	2.6	3 581.0	3 897	2 565	1 878	45 546	54.3	44.9	0.8
Burlington	2 064.4	4 574	62.3	1.5	4.2	2.2	3.1	2 370.1	5 251	5 213	6 075	24 576	58.8	40.2	1.0
Camden	3 129.5	6 094	51.5	4.2	4.5	3.4	4.0	3 660.4	7 128	2 378	1 062	29 673	67.6	31.3	1.1
Cape May	808.9	8 400	33.8	1.5	5.3	4.4	4.9	673.4	6 992	446	1 029	8 317	45.0	53.7	1.3
Cumberland	880.4	5 580	60.1	2.7	3.8	3.4	2.5	354.4	2 246	646	295	12 989	60.1	38.5	1.4
Essex	4 300.2	5 459	38.9	3.3	8.3	2.9	1.3	3 851.1	4 889	8 966	1 634	65 935	76.0	23.4	0.6
Gloucester	1 410.5	4 871	58.9	0.8	4.6	2.2	1.9	1 385.8	4 785	473	583	19 644	55.4	43.3	1.3
Hudson	2 833.2	4 343	33.2	3.1	8.5	2.8	1.8	3 638.2	5 577	5 597	1 473	38 664	72.9	26.2	0.9
Hunterdon	605.4	4 765	66.0	1.2	3.5	0.8	6.1	565.1	4 448	251	249	8 274	42.6	56.0	1.4

1. Based on the resident population estimated as of July 1 of the year shown.   2. © 2013 Election Data Services, Inc. All rights reserved.

Table B. States and Counties — **Land Area and Population**

STATE/ County code	CBSA code[1]	County type[2]	STATE County	Land area[3] (sq km) 2010	Total persons 2015	Rank	Per square kilometer	White	Black	American Indian, Alaska Native	Asian and Pacific Islander	Percent Hispanic or Latino[4]	Under 5 years	5 to 17 years	18 to 24 years	25 to 34 years	35 to 44 years	45 to 54 years
				1	2	3	4	5	6	7	8	9	10	11	12	13	14	15
			NEW JERSEY—Cont'd															
34 021	45940	2	Mercer	582	371 398	184	638.1	53.1	20.4	0.5	11.2	16.6	5.9	16.0	11.2	12.5	13.3	14.7
34 023	35620	1	Middlesex	800	840 900	69	1 051.1	46.4	10.0	0.5	24.6	19.9	6.0	16.0	9.7	14.1	14.0	14.4
34 025	35620	1	Monmouth	1 214	628 715	106	517.9	76.8	7.6	0.4	6.1	10.5	5.2	17.1	8.4	10.6	12.1	16.5
34 027	35620	1	Morris	1 192	499 509	138	419.1	73.9	3.6	0.3	11.0	12.8	5.1	17.1	8.3	10.8	12.8	16.9
34 029	35620	1	Ocean	1 629	588 721	109	361.4	86.0	3.5	0.3	2.4	8.9	6.8	16.7	7.6	10.8	10.5	12.9
34 031	35620	1	Passaic	478	510 916	134	1 068.9	43.8	11.3	0.4	5.9	39.5	6.9	17.4	10.1	13.3	13.0	14.0
34 033	37980	1	Salem	860	64 180	818	74.6	77.0	14.7	0.7	1.5	8.0	5.7	16.5	8.4	11.6	11.8	14.6
34 035	35620	1	Somerset	782	333 654	202	426.7	60.0	9.6	0.3	17.4	14.2	5.5	17.7	7.8	10.8	13.6	16.9
34 037	35620	1	Sussex	1 344	143 673	447	106.9	88.6	2.3	0.4	2.6	7.3	4.6	17.0	8.5	9.7	12.0	17.7
34 039	35620	1	Union	266	555 786	119	2 089.4	43.3	21.8	0.4	5.9	30.0	6.5	17.4	8.8	12.9	14.0	15.1
34 041	10900	2	Warren	924	106 869	559	115.7	84.7	4.6	0.4	3.3	8.4	4.6	16.6	8.7	10.6	12.1	17.0
35 000	...	X	**NEW MEXICO**	314 161	2 085 109	X	6.6	40.2	2.3	9.3	2.1	47.7	6.6	17.5	10.0	13.4	11.7	12.7
35 001	10740	2	Bernalillo	3 007	676 685	96	225.0	41.7	3.2	4.7	3.3	49.0	6.3	16.6	9.6	15.1	12.5	13.0
35 003	...	9	Catron	17 932	3 456	2 940	0.2	77.2	1.1	3.8	0.7	19.9	3.2	10.8	5.3	6.4	6.3	10.7
35 005	40740	5	Chaves	15 709	65 764	805	4.2	41.7	1.9	1.3	1.2	54.9	7.3	19.9	10.3	12.7	10.9	12.2
35 006	24380	6	Cibola	11 757	27 329	1 518	2.3	22.1	1.4	39.4	0.9	37.9	7.4	17.1	9.5	13.9	12.2	12.7
35 007	...	7	Colfax	9 733	12 414	2 269	1.3	48.7	0.8	2.0	0.7	49.0	4.8	14.2	7.7	10.3	9.4	13.1
35 009	17580	5	Curry	3 638	50 398	980	13.9	52.0	6.6	1.4	2.4	39.7	8.6	18.4	12.8	17.2	11.1	10.6
35 011	...	9	De Baca	6 016	1 828	3 068	0.3	57.3	0.6	2.6	0.7	40.8	5.8	16.1	6.3	10.0	8.6	13.8
35 013	29740	3	Dona Ana	9 861	214 295	302	21.7	29.6	1.8	1.2	1.5	66.7	7.2	18.2	14.9	12.6	10.7	11.3
35 015	16100	5	Eddy	10 815	57 578	892	5.3	50.4	1.7	1.6	0.9	46.2	7.0	19.2	9.3	13.7	11.5	12.5
35 017	43500	7	Grant	10 261	28 609	1 469	2.8	48.2	1.1	1.5	1.0	49.7	5.5	15.3	8.4	10.0	9.8	11.3
35 019	...	7	Guadalupe	7 849	4 371	2 873	0.6	16.7	1.6	1.8	1.3	79.9	4.9	15.7	8.2	15.0	11.7	13.5
35 021	...	9	Harding	5 505	698	3 128	0.1	55.8	0.9	0.4	0.7	43.4	4.0	10.8	5.7	8.3	6.3	13.3
35 023	...	7	Hidalgo	8 901	4 423	2 871	0.5	41.1	1.1	0.8	0.8	57.4	6.5	16.8	9.1	11.5	9.0	14.5
35 025	26020	5	Lea	11 372	71 180	758	6.3	39.4	4.0	1.2	0.7	55.7	8.6	21.8	10.1	14.9	12.1	11.7
35 027	...	7	Lincoln	12 512	19 420	1 853	1.6	64.8	0.8	3.4	0.7	31.6	4.9	13.6	6.5	8.9	8.7	13.2
35 028	31060	6	Los Alamos	283	17 785	1 931	62.8	75.2	1.1	1.5	7.3	16.6	5.5	17.7	6.7	9.8	12.2	15.8
35 029	19700	6	Luna	7 680	24 518	1 625	3.2	32.9	1.1	1.2	0.8	65.1	7.6	18.4	9.3	11.0	9.9	11.4
35 031	23700	4	McKinley	14 115	76 708	720	5.4	11.3	1.3	74.5	1.2	14.0	9.0	21.7	11.0	13.8	11.5	12.0
35 033	...	8	Mora	5 002	4 596	2 858	0.9	18.2	0.5	0.8	0.4	80.8	4.4	14.8	7.5	9.8	9.2	14.2
35 035	10460	4	Otero	17 128	64 362	816	3.8	52.7	4.2	6.6	2.3	36.5	7.6	16.6	11.0	14.1	10.7	11.7
35 037	...	7	Quay	7 445	8 455	2 560	1.1	52.0	1.8	1.6	1.4	44.9	6.3	14.9	7.0	9.7	9.7	13.1
35 039	21580	6	Rio Arriba	15 179	39 465	1 189	2.6	13.8	0.5	14.2	0.6	71.7	7.1	17.2	8.6	11.5	11.5	13.1
35 041	38780	7	Roosevelt	6 339	19 120	1 867	3.0	55.3	2.3	1.8	2.1	39.8	7.6	17.2	19.1	13.0	10.2	10.3
35 043	10740	2	Sandoval	9 611	139 394	456	14.5	46.8	2.6	12.8	2.2	37.4	5.8	18.8	8.2	12.1	12.7	13.6
35 045	22140	3	San Juan	14 279	118 737	520	8.3	42.2	1.1	38.0	0.9	19.5	7.3	20.0	9.2	14.0	11.9	12.2
35 047	29780	6	San Miguel	12 214	27 967	1 487	2.3	19.7	1.5	1.5	0.9	77.0	5.4	14.5	10.9	11.3	10.6	13.8
35 049	42140	3	Santa Fe	4 945	148 686	438	30.1	44.2	1.0	3.1	1.7	51.3	4.8	14.6	7.7	11.3	11.8	13.8
35 051	...	6	Sierra	10 823	11 282	2 341	1.0	68.2	1.0	2.5	0.7	29.3	4.0	11.2	5.8	8.2	7.2	12.0
35 053	...	6	Socorro	17 215	17 256	1 966	1.0	36.9	1.2	12.2	1.7	49.2	6.2	17.2	11.4	11.8	10.3	12.6
35 055	45340	7	Taos	5 706	32 907	1 359	5.8	37.3	0.6	6.3	1.0	56.2	5.1	14.0	6.9	10.3	10.8	13.7
35 057	10740	2	Torrance	8 663	15 485	2 074	1.8	54.6	2.0	3.0	1.0	41.3	5.3	16.9	8.4	11.1	11.0	13.2
35 059	...	9	Union	9 903	4 201	2 886	0.4	55.6	2.1	2.2	1.0	41.3	4.9	13.6	8.7	14.5	12.3	13.2
35 061	10740	2	Valencia	2 761	75 737	727	27.4	35.3	1.3	4.1	0.9	59.5	6.2	18.4	9.0	11.9	11.7	13.8
36 000	...	X	**NEW YORK**	122 057	19 795 791	X	162.2	57.8	15.5	0.7	9.1	18.6	6.0	15.4	10.0	14.4	12.7	14.1
36 001	10580	2	Albany	1 354	309 381	219	228.5	75.5	13.6	0.6	6.8	5.7	5.0	13.9	14.8	13.0	11.2	13.5
36 003	...	7	Allegany	2 666	47 462	1 029	17.8	95.6	1.7	0.6	1.7	1.5	5.1	15.6	15.1	10.4	10.2	12.7
36 005	35620	1	Bronx	109	1 455 444	26	13 352.7	10.9	30.4	0.6	4.2	54.7	7.6	17.9	11.4	15.3	12.8	13.3
36 007	13780	2	Broome	1 828	196 567	333	107.5	86.5	6.3	0.7	5.0	3.9	5.1	14.5	14.2	11.3	10.2	13.5
36 009	36460	4	Cattaraugus	3 389	77 922	711	23.0	92.6	2.3	3.7	1.2	2.0	5.8	16.9	9.5	11.0	11.0	13.9
36 011	12180	4	Cayuga	1 791	78 288	710	43.7	92.3	4.9	0.7	1.0	2.8	5.2	15.2	8.9	12.2	11.6	15.1
36 013	27460	4	Chautauqua	2 746	130 779	479	47.6	89.8	3.3	0.9	1.0	7.0	5.3	15.6	10.4	11.5	10.7	13.7
36 015	21300	3	Chemung	1 055	87 071	662	82.5	89.2	8.1	0.7	2.0	2.9	6.0	15.8	9.2	12.2	11.5	14.2
36 017	...	6	Chenango	2 314	48 844	1 002	21.1	96.2	1.4	0.8	1.0	2.2	5.4	15.9	8.2	10.5	11.3	14.7
36 019	38460	5	Clinton	2 688	81 251	687	30.2	91.2	4.6	0.8	1.8	2.8	4.8	13.5	13.8	12.4	11.9	15.0
36 021	26460	6	Columbia	1 644	61 509	852	37.4	88.9	5.8	0.6	2.3	4.5	4.3	14.2	7.8	10.0	10.9	15.7
36 023	18860	4	Cortland	1 292	48 494	1 009	37.5	94.4	2.5	0.8	1.6	2.7	4.8	14.8	18.4	10.9	10.5	13.2
36 025	...	6	Delaware	3 736	46 053	1 045	12.3	93.3	2.2	0.6	1.3	3.7	4.8	13.5	10.3	9.6	9.8	14.0
36 027	35620	2	Dutchess	2 061	295 754	232	143.5	74.4	10.9	0.6	4.6	11.6	4.8	15.4	11.4	11.2	11.8	16.1
36 029	15380	1	Erie	2 701	922 578	56	341.6	77.8	14.1	0.9	3.7	5.1	5.4	15.3	10.1	13.5	11.1	14.1
36 031	...	6	Essex	4 647	38 478	1 209	8.3	93.1	3.2	0.8	1.0	3.1	4.2	13.1	7.7	11.6	11.6	15.0
36 033	31660	5	Franklin	4 219	50 660	978	12.0	83.0	6.1	8.2	0.9	3.3	5.2	14.6	10.4	14.0	12.4	14.9
36 035	24100	4	Fulton	1 283	53 992	928	42.1	94.3	2.4	0.6	1.0	2.8	5.0	15.8	8.2	11.6	11.9	15.2

1. CBSA = Core Based Statistical Area. See Appendix A for explanation. See Appendix B for list of metropolitan areas with component counties.   2. County type code from the Economic Research Service of USDA Rural-Urban Continuum Codes. See Appendix A for definition.   3. Dry land or land partially or temporarily covered by water.   4. May be of any race.

Table B. States and Counties — Population and Households

STATE County	Age (percent) (cont.) 55 to 64 years	65 to 74 years	75 years and over	Percent female	Population change Total persons 2000	2010	Percent change 2000–2010	2010–2015	Components of change, 2010–2015 Births	Deaths	Net migration	Households, 2010–2014 Number	Persons per house-hold	Percent Family house-holds	Female family house-holder[1]	One per-son
	16	17	18	19	20	21	22	23	24	25	26	27	28	29	30	31
NEW JERSEY—Cont'd																
Mercer	12.7	7.6	6.2	51.0	350 761	367 508	4.8	1.1	22 442	14 970	-3 182	131 475	2.66	67.5	13.1	26.8
Middlesex	12.4	7.4	6.0	50.8	750 162	809 860	8.0	3.8	51 269	30 358	10 811	282 182	2.83	72.5	12.3	22.8
Monmouth	14.5	8.8	6.8	51.4	615 301	630 378	2.5	-0.3	32 511	28 383	-5 534	233 730	2.66	69.5	10.6	25.8
Morris	13.7	8.5	6.9	51.0	470 212	492 279	4.7	1.5	24 706	19 278	2 589	179 776	2.71	71.7	8.5	23.9
Ocean	12.8	11.4	10.5	51.9	510 916	576 565	12.8	2.1	42 643	36 833	6 120	221 720	2.59	67.2	9.8	28.7
Passaic	12.0	7.4	5.7	51.3	489 049	501 624	2.6	1.9	37 342	18 978	-8 548	162 097	3.06	72.9	18.5	23.5
Salem	14.2	9.6	7.6	51.3	64 285	66 083	2.8	-2.9	3 752	3 726	-2 018	24 665	2.60	68.6	14.9	26.4
Somerset	13.6	7.8	6.3	51.3	297 490	323 441	8.7	3.2	18 187	11 959	3 851	115 941	2.80	72.8	9.7	23.2
Sussex	15.8	9.1	5.6	50.4	144 166	148 869	3.3	-3.5	6 855	6 086	-5 787	54 248	2.67	73.8	9.5	21.5
Union	12.3	7.1	5.9	51.2	522 541	536 499	2.7	3.6	36 435	20 831	4 695	185 688	2.90	71.3	16.1	24.6
Warren	14.5	8.9	7.1	51.2	102 437	108 692	6.1	-1.7	4 867	4 783	-1 916	41 548	2.54	69.8	10.4	25.0
NEW MEXICO	12.9	9.0	6.3	50.5	1 819 046	2 059 192	13.2	1.3	140 807	87 604	-27 115	764 684	2.66	65.1	14.1	28.9
Bernalillo	12.7	8.2	5.9	51.0	556 678	662 555	19.0	2.1	43 424	27 144	-1 871	263 719	2.51	61.7	14.0	31.2
Catron	22.4	21.9	13.0	48.0	3 543	3 725	5.1	-7.2	111	179	-136	1 440	2.41	59.1	3.1	39.4
Chaves	12.0	8.1	6.7	50.2	61 382	65 645	6.9	0.2	4 922	3 404	-1 193	23 506	2.71	69.9	16.8	26.1
Cibola	13.0	8.2	6.1	48.9	25 595	27 213	6.3	0.4	2 079	1 345	-639	8 354	3.04	68.4	18.3	28.2
Colfax	16.8	13.8	9.9	49.1	14 189	13 750	-3.1	-9.7	688	754	-1 266	5 369	2.38	61.5	12.4	34.0
Curry	9.7	6.3	5.2	48.1	45 044	48 376	7.4	4.2	4 893	1 920	-959	18 223	2.69	67.4	13.3	28.1
De Baca	15.8	13.0	10.8	49.8	2 240	2 022	-9.7	-9.6	85	135	-137	601	3.23	60.2	4.7	34.8
Dona Ana	11.0	8.0	6.1	50.8	174 682	209 241	19.8	2.4	16 207	7 771	-3 594	74 623	2.79	69.4	16.1	23.9
Eddy	12.7	7.6	6.3	49.5	51 658	53 829	4.2	7.0	4 375	2 854	2 297	20 190	2.68	69.6	12.2	26.1
Grant	15.6	13.8	10.3	50.5	31 002	29 514	-4.8	-3.1	1 655	1 793	-771	12 229	2.34	60.8	12.9	33.8
Guadalupe	13.2	9.0	8.9	43.4	4 680	4 687	0.1	-6.7	212	212	-345	1 269	3.12	62.2	16.1	33.5
Harding	20.8	14.5	16.3	47.0	810	695	-14.2	0.4	29	38	14	212	3.09	60.8	3.8	35.4
Hidalgo	13.5	10.6	8.5	49.4	5 932	4 894	-17.5	-9.6	288	218	-550	1 858	2.49	69.6	17.1	29.1
Lea	10.3	5.8	4.6	48.5	55 511	64 727	16.6	10.0	6 005	2 775	3 300	21 331	3.04	75.3	12.0	20.1
Lincoln	17.8	16.1	10.2	50.3	19 411	20 497	5.6	-5.3	981	994	-993	8 640	2.31	61.4	10.6	31.9
Los Alamos	15.7	9.4	7.2	49.2	18 343	17 950	-2.1	-0.9	883	605	-467	7 495	2.38	67.8	6.0	27.1
Luna	11.7	11.3	9.5	50.0	25 016	25 095	0.3	-2.3	2 051	1 516	-1 057	9 120	2.69	62.0	14.6	32.6
McKinley	10.5	6.2	4.4	52.0	74 798	71 491	-4.4	7.3	6 424	2 894	1 720	17 862	4.05	69.9	23.0	27.6
Mora	17.4	13.1	9.6	48.3	5 180	4 881	-5.8	-5.8	225	207	-292	1 525	3.08	54.0	6.9	40.6
Otero	11.9	9.2	7.2	49.0	62 298	63 799	2.4	0.9	4 653	2 911	-1 064	23 907	2.62	67.8	13.5	27.9
Quay	15.6	13.9	9.8	51.3	10 155	9 041	-11.0	-6.5	531	598	-531	3 319	2.64	58.0	11.8	39.4
Rio Arriba	14.5	9.9	6.6	50.8	41 190	40 247	-2.3	-1.9	3 004	2 028	-1 603	14 245	2.77	64.9	15.5	29.6
Roosevelt	10.0	6.9	5.7	50.0	18 018	19 846	10.1	-3.7	1 566	788	-1 537	7 198	2.63	65.6	13.5	26.4
Sandoval	13.5	9.5	5.6	50.9	89 908	131 563	46.3	6.0	7 801	5 030	4 681	47 965	2.80	71.0	12.7	23.0
San Juan	12.4	7.4	5.6	50.6	113 801	130 045	14.3	-8.7	9 862	4 866	-16 381	40 693	3.09	73.5	16.8	22.7
San Miguel	15.1	11.2	7.2	50.6	30 126	29 393	-2.4	-4.9	1 686	1 388	-1 684	11 306	2.40	55.4	15.7	38.2
Santa Fe	16.4	12.6	7.1	51.3	129 292	144 171	11.5	3.1	7 188	5 586	2 689	61 313	2.34	58.4	11.1	33.6
Sierra	17.7	18.8	15.2	50.2	13 270	11 988	-9.7	-5.9	525	1 194	-41	4 686	2.46	52.6	8.0	43.7
Socorro	13.7	9.9	6.8	49.1	18 078	17 864	-1.2	-3.4	1 182	901	-886	5 161	3.31	61.2	16.8	33.3
Taos	17.0	13.8	8.5	51.0	29 979	32 940	9.9	-0.1	1 644	1 421	-293	13 239	2.45	58.1	12.4	36.1
Torrance	16.1	11.5	6.5	47.6	16 911	16 383	-3.1	-5.5	803	757	-946	5 656	2.68	68.6	12.5	28.8
Union	13.1	10.4	9.3	43.1	4 174	4 551	9.0	-7.7	221	243	-314	1 602	2.42	60.9	9.4	33.9
Valencia	13.5	9.5	6.0	49.8	66 152	76 574	15.8	-1.1	4 604	3 135	-2 266	26 828	2.79	71.3	14.3	24.1
NEW YORK	12.7	8.1	6.6	51.5	18 976 457	19 378 087	2.1	2.2	1 260 125	792 242	-22 308	7 255 528	2.62	63.9	14.8	29.6
Albany	13.2	8.4	7.0	51.7	294 565	304 208	3.3	1.7	16 404	14 040	3 353	122 945	2.35	55.8	11.7	34.9
Allegany	13.9	9.5	7.5	49.4	49 927	48 923	-2.0	-3.0	2 548	2 400	-1 525	18 407	2.36	65.3	9.7	28.6
Bronx	10.4	6.3	4.9	52.8	1 332 650	1 385 107	3.9	5.1	113 689	49 415	7 212	480 323	2.85	66.0	31.5	30.0
Broome	13.7	9.0	8.5	50.9	200 536	200 600	0.0	-2.0	10 844	10 956	-3 856	79 438	2.37	60.2	11.3	32.0
Cattaraugus	14.8	9.6	7.5	50.5	83 955	80 354	-4.3	-3.0	4 831	4 307	-2 789	31 798	2.41	63.5	10.4	29.7
Cayuga	14.6	9.5	7.6	48.9	81 963	80 020	-2.4	-2.2	4 092	3 852	-1 794	30 907	2.44	64.4	11.3	29.3
Chautauqua	14.7	9.7	8.4	50.5	139 750	134 894	-3.5	-3.1	7 186	7 401	-3 725	54 226	2.34	62.2	12.3	31.0
Chemung	14.1	9.2	7.8	50.4	91 070	88 842	-2.4	-2.0	5 176	4 809	-2 066	35 390	2.35	62.7	12.4	29.9
Chenango	15.1	10.9	8.0	50.0	51 401	50 478	-1.8	-3.2	2 687	2 867	-1 462	19 560	2.51	64.6	10.8	27.7
Clinton	13.5	8.7	6.6	48.6	79 894	82 131	2.8	-1.1	4 024	3 634	-1 306	31 976	2.32	64.6	10.8	26.7
Columbia	16.3	12.0	8.8	49.8	63 094	63 096	0.0	-2.5	2 870	3 438	-998	25 095	2.39	65.1	12.0	28.3
Cortland	12.5	8.5	6.4	51.2	48 599	49 306	1.5	-1.6	2 475	2 254	-1 018	18 045	2.53	59.8	10.2	32.3
Delaware	16.1	12.7	9.2	49.7	48 055	47 989	-0.1	-4.0	2 130	2 821	-1 114	19 370	2.31	61.6	9.6	33.2
Dutchess	13.9	8.7	6.8	50.2	280 150	297 448	6.2	-0.6	14 112	12 584	-3 294	106 898	2.61	67.4	10.9	26.7
Erie	13.9	8.8	7.8	51.6	950 265	919 064	-3.3	0.4	52 266	50 387	3 571	381 783	2.34	60.5	13.8	33.0
Essex	15.8	11.7	9.3	47.9	38 851	39 361	1.3	-2.2	1 680	2 083	-482	15 571	2.32	63.6	9.4	30.3
Franklin	13.4	8.7	6.2	45.1	51 134	51 606	0.9	-1.8	2 712	2 335	-1 301	19 131	2.37	64.7	11.8	28.5
Fulton	14.3	10.1	7.9	50.5	55 073	55 524	0.8	-2.8	2 810	3 160	-1 118	22 440	2.38	64.6	12.3	27.6

1. No spouse present.

Table B. States and Counties — **Population, Vital Statistics, Medicare, and Crime**

STATE County	Persons in group quarters, 2015	Daytime population, 2010–2014		Births, 2015		Deaths, 2015		Persons under 65 with no health insurance, 2014		Medicare, 2015			Serious crimes known to police,[2] 2014 Total	
		Number	Employ- ment/ resi- dence ratio	Total	Rate[1]	Number	Rate[1]	Number	Percent	Total Beneficiaries	Enrolled in Original Medicare	Enrolled in Medicare Advantage	Number	Rate[3]
	32	33	34	35	36	37	38	39	40	41	42	43	44	45
NEW JERSEY—Cont'd														
Mercer	19 420	420 992	1.30	4 157	11.2	2 870	7.7	35 429	11.7	59 008	48 867	10 141	7 866	2 117
Middlesex	23 478	806 389	0.95	9 381	11.2	5 976	7.1	83 799	11.9	110 258	90 516	19 742	13 341	1 598
Monmouth	7 345	592 083	0.87	6 051	9.6	5 519	8.8	53 105	10.1	106 784	90 707	16 077	11 438	1 814
Morris	8 772	532 908	1.14	4 557	9.1	3 648	7.3	33 605	8.1	74 617	66 187	8 430	4 943	985
Ocean	7 142	513 639	0.71	8 100	13.8	6 890	11.7	54 893	12.1	139 266	112 356	26 910	9 739	1 663
Passaic	11 037	466 235	0.82	6 966	13.6	3 608	7.1	69 273	15.9	71 233	55 275	15 958	11 207	2 209
Salem	1 257	60 899	0.84	701	10.9	743	11.5	5 861	11.0	12 551	10 904	1 647	1 605	2 467
Somerset	4 098	345 236	1.10	3 354	10.1	2 434	7.3	22 490	7.9	42 408	38 031	4 377	3 989	1 199
Sussex	1 742	117 735	0.60	1 250	8.7	1 204	8.3	10 776	8.8	23 494	20 988	2 506	1 421	976
Union	6 821	519 460	0.90	6 881	12.4	3 981	7.2	73 763	15.5	76 109	60 017	16 092	12 303	2 230
Warren	1 970	92 605	0.71	1 036	9.7	889	8.3	9 062	10.2	19 586	17 625	1 961	1 527	1 424
NEW MEXICO	43 082	2 075 756	1.00	26 286	12.6	17 050	8.2	295 204	17.1	343 091	224 953	118 138	86 336	4 140
Bernalillo	11 943	699 672	1.09	8 059	11.9	5 477	8.1	87 375	15.4	106 556	49 275	57 281	38 737	5 737
Catron	106	3 632	0.98	24	6.9	19	5.4	514	22.2	1 208	1 000	208	6	168
Chaves	1 782	63 449	0.91	927	14.1	624	9.5	10 364	19.0	11 335	9 700	1 635	3 863	5 882
Cibola	2 556	27 313	0.99	372	13.6	266	9.7	3 988	18.9	3 458	2 820	638	641	2 350
Colfax	408	13 373	1.02	131	10.4	142	11.3	1 398	14.9	3 120	2 574	546	329	2 549
Curry	1 484	51 266	1.05	938	18.5	356	7.0	7 225	16.5	7 059	6 288	771	2 652	5 211
De Baca	9	1 947	0.97	12	6.6	23	12.6	324	23.5	499	454	45	8	426
Dona Ana	4 576	206 636	0.93	2 925	13.7	1 498	7.0	33 147	18.5	33 714	22 546	11 168	7 132	3 337
Eddy	995	58 035	1.13	920	16.1	528	9.3	6 423	13.4	9 102	8 318	784	2 401	4 308
Grant	590	29 225	0.99	303	10.5	331	11.5	2 944	13.6	7 352	5 599	1 753	NA	NA
Guadalupe	570	4 626	1.03	37	8.4	39	8.8	483	15.6	862	700	162	112	2 486
Harding	0	690	1.18	6	8.7	5	7.3	84	17.8	199	173	26	NA	NA
Hidalgo	64	4 810	1.04	52	11.6	44	9.8	599	16.4	972	723	249	98	2 133
Lea	2 065	68 373	1.05	1 218	17.3	499	7.1	10 860	17.9	8 073	7 798	275	2 482	3 609
Lincoln	116	19 623	0.93	177	9.1	179	9.2	2 915	20.2	5 178	4 053	1 125	581	3 134
Los Alamos	94	25 644	1.87	167	9.4	98	5.5	586	4.0	2 754	2 531	223	NA	NA
Luna	551	25 071	1.01	400	16.3	270	11.0	3 848	20.2	5 976	3 985	1 991	1 090	4 451
McKinley	775	73 439	1.02	1 222	16.2	579	7.7	17 252	26.2	8 061	7 350	711	3 156	4 292
Mora	8	4 280	0.68	43	9.4	30	6.5	574	16.2	1 163	948	215	23	495
Otero	2 295	65 019	0.98	887	13.7	575	8.9	9 482	18.1	10 546	8 627	1 919	1 553	2 386
Quay	22	8 865	1.01	80	9.5	93	11.0	1 054	16.3	2 285	1 916	369	237	2 772
Rio Arriba	425	36 685	0.77	538	13.6	418	10.6	6 355	19.3	7 410	5 246	2 164	834	2 090
Roosevelt	1 078	18 859	0.86	315	16.3	142	7.3	3 167	19.7	2 623	2 350	273	489	2 458
Sandoval	761	113 687	0.62	1 449	10.5	1 024	7.4	15 041	13.0	18 761	9 231	9 530	2 804	2 053
San Juan	1 746	127 664	1.01	1 826	15.0	986	8.1	20 607	19.4	17 228	16 350	878	3 155	2 518
San Miguel	1 300	27 468	0.86	296	10.5	261	9.3	3 221	14.5	6 168	4 854	1 314	NA	NA
Santa Fe	2 627	148 718	1.03	1 323	8.9	1 064	7.2	23 172	19.9	30 450	20 708	9 742	4 483	3 033
Sierra	265	12 008	1.06	112	9.9	217	19.2	1 329	17.9	3 939	2 763	1 176	NA	NA
Socorro	580	17 654	1.01	216	12.5	158	9.1	2 582	18.6	2 885	2 101	784	693	3 965
Taos	470	32 719	0.98	303	9.2	278	8.4	4 884	19.1	7 418	5 724	1 694	945	2 865
Torrance	615	14 608	0.73	139	8.9	153	9.8	2 062	16.9	2 669	1 379	1 290	286	1 843
Union	662	4 444	1.02	38	9.0	38	9.0	552	19.6	870	815	55	62	1 436
Valencia	1 544	66 254	0.62	831	11.0	636	8.4	10 793	17.2	13 198	6 054	7 144	3 161	4 160
NEW YORK	574 606	19 934 173	1.04	238 831	12.1	154 974	7.8	1 654 986	10.1	3 096 477	1 847 784	1 248 693	414 680	2 100
Albany	17 659	376 958	1.47	3 100	10.0	2 679	8.7	18 101	7.3	48 751	27 010	21 741	9 212	2 989
Allegany	4 358	45 358	0.85	465	9.8	447	9.4	3 028	8.5	8 913	5 416	3 497	644	1 342
Bronx	44 084	1 252 959	0.70	21 663	15.0	10 175	7.0	173 351	13.9	171 867	69 953	101 914	(6)	(6)
Broome	10 784	205 627	1.08	2 057	10.4	2 086	10.6	11 189	7.2	42 583	26 750	15 833	6 402	3 248
Cattaraugus	2 599	76 674	0.92	896	11.4	812	10.4	6 023	9.5	17 345	9 332	8 013	1 513	1 923
Cayuga	4 121	71 798	0.79	736	9.4	689	8.8	4 679	7.5	14 394	10 364	4 030	1 611	2 026
Chautauqua	6 117	132 687	0.98	1 342	10.2	1 360	10.4	8 193	7.9	29 250	15 552	13 698	3 589	2 702
Chemung	4 569	90 209	1.04	920	10.5	921	10.6	4 457	6.5	18 519	12 408	6 111	2 151	2 430
Chenango	793	47 776	0.90	500	10.2	542	11.0	3 388	8.5	10 913	7 018	3 895	938	1 900
Clinton	6 797	81 513	0.99	733	9.0	689	8.5	5 074	8.1	16 651	13 707	2 944	1 359	1 665
Columbia	2 021	57 755	0.84	532	8.6	641	10.4	4 268	8.9	13 779	9 623	4 156	955	1 570
Cortland	3 800	47 468	0.92	473	9.7	406	8.3	2 854	7.5	8 164	6 035	2 129	678	1 384
Delaware	2 413	46 595	0.97	366	7.9	537	11.6	3 345	9.6	10 042	7 387	2 655	795	1 746
Dutchess	19 546	275 617	0.84	2 614	8.8	2 509	8.5	19 181	8.2	51 865	41 441	10 424	4 812	1 627
Erie	28 316	949 219	1.07	10 098	10.9	9 538	10.3	51 633	6.9	176 720	69 191	107 529	28 429	3 085
Essex	2 394	38 363	0.96	308	8.0	411	10.7	2 514	8.8	8 656	6 983	1 673	397	1 026
Franklin	6 075	52 066	1.03	502	9.9	477	10.8	4 086	10.8	8 720	6 618	2 102	847	1 635
Fulton	1 402	50 368	0.81	509	9.4	564	10.4	3 945	9.0	10 964	6 076	4 888	1 472	2 703

1. Per 1,000 estimated resident population.　　2. Data for serious crimes have not been adjusted for underreporting; this may affect comparability between geographic areas and over time.
3. Per 100,000 population estimated by the FBI.　　6. Bronx, Kings, Queens, and Richmond counties are included with New York county.

Table B. States and Counties — Crime, Education, Money Income, and Poverty

STATE County	Serious crimes known to police, 2014 (cont.)[1] Rate[2]		Education — School enrollment and attainment, 2010–2014				Education — Local government expenditures,[5] 2012–2013		Money income, 2010–2014		Households		Income and poverty, 2014		Percent below poverty level	
			Enrollment[3]		Attainment[4] (percent)											
	Violent	Property	Total	Percent private	High school graduate or less	Bachelor's degree or more	Total current spending (mil dol)	Current spending per student (dollars)	Per capita income[6] (dollars)	Median income (dollars)	Mean income (dollars)	Percent with income of $200,000 or more	Median household income (dollars)	All persons	Children under 18 years	Children 5 to 17 years in families
	46	47	48	49	50	51	52	53	54	55	56	57	58	59	60	61
NEW JERSEY—Cont'd																
Mercer	343	1 774	102 670	24.3	38.3	39.8	1 078.0	18 652	38 076	74 118	104 437	11.5	73 750	11.8	16.1	14.0
Middlesex	155	1 443	219 255	14.8	37.6	40.7	2 050.3	16 984	34 616	80 118	98 447	9.2	77 330	8.3	10.8	11.0
Monmouth	142	1 673	163 664	21.4	33.2	42.0	1 821.9	18 026	43 548	85 605	115 245	13.7	87 220	8.2	10.5	9.9
Morris	61	924	128 957	22.5	29.1	50.6	1 385.2	17 840	48 928	99 142	132 542	17.5	100 511	5.0	5.6	5.1
Ocean	100	1 563	141 059	32.2	46.5	26.3	1 210.0	16 561	30 951	61 839	79 508	4.7	62 937	11.9	20.8	18.3
Passaic	394	1 815	136 440	13.7	52.1	26.2	1 558.9	19 440	27 795	59 513	81 138	6.5	58 030	18.2	27.4	26.2
Salem	261	2 205	15 580	13.1	52.3	20.4	199.1	17 454	28 987	60 768	74 346	3.4	56 645	13.1	19.7	17.8
Somerset	59	1 140	85 142	20.0	28.2	52.0	939.4	17 470	48 646	100 903	134 595	17.9	100 194	5.0	6.5	6.1
Sussex	51	926	36 980	19.1	37.4	33.1	444.0	19 944	38 454	87 397	103 174	9.0	82 048	6.2	7.0	6.0
Union	376	1 854	142 612	15.7	44.3	32.3	1 711.2	19 167	35 411	69 396	99 818	10.5	68 172	11.1	15.9	15.4
Warren	72	1 352	26 614	17.4	44.9	29.5	291.6	16 791	34 016	70 934	87 399	6.5	71 294	8.3	10.6	9.7
NEW MEXICO	597	3 542	567 018	10.3	42.4	26.1	2 951.6	9 012	23 948	44 968	62 136	2.9	44 905	20.6	28.0	26.2
Bernalillo	827	4 911	186 321	14.1	35.9	32.3	797.4	8 475	26 916	48 390	66 203	3.6	47 192	18.7	24.5	22.6
Catron	84	84	556	21.4	42.1	20.7	5.7	18 099	19 254	39 342	44 330	2.2	33 256	22.2	42.8	40.1
Chaves	647	5 235	18 482	8.9	48.3	18.4	100.8	8 520	20 356	40 541	55 339	1.4	38 403	23.4	32.4	28.7
Cibola	554	1 796	7 329	10.5	55.8	11.7	37.3	9 947	16 362	36 279	46 954	0.8	35 081	28.8	37.6	35.9
Colfax	232	2 317	2 875	7.7	46.4	20.6	22.1	11 657	20 975	35 189	47 328	0.9	37 156	20.5	30.6	27.2
Curry	318	4 893	14 148	8.4	43.4	20.4	77.4	8 070	21 886	40 318	56 191	1.4	42 620	19.2	27.3	26.7
De Baca	320	107	513	0.0	53.6	11.6	4.6	15 801	25 942	37 961	52 687	1.5	33 789	20.6	32.1	31.6
Dona Ana	286	3 051	68 552	4.2	43.9	27.4	353.6	8 696	20 058	38 426	55 193	2.3	38 974	27.9	39.4	36.0
Eddy	617	3 690	13 863	7.1	51.9	16.8	96.2	9 107	27 630	51 303	71 493	3.1	57 007	14.1	18.5	17.3
Grant	NA	NA	6 901	8.2	42.2	25.6	43.4	9 913	23 411	38 923	54 221	1.3	38 221	19.1	27.8	25.3
Guadalupe	666	1 820	1 036	11.4	64.7	12.8	9.9	13 429	15 192	27 957	42 909	0.7	29 147	25.8	33.1	30.7
Harding	NA	NA	113	2.7	54.9	23.9	3.0	36 134	18 565	31 500	46 688	0.5	40 380	14.8	19.0	18.1
Hidalgo	501	1 632	1 022	3.3	53.7	15.6	10.1	14 213	19 400	35 048	46 867	0.2	34 304	24.5	33.6	31.9
Lea	475	3 133	18 178	8.9	58.2	12.6	111.1	7 925	22 962	55 248	69 446	3.2	58 994	16.6	20.9	18.9
Lincoln	297	2 837	4 170	8.6	40.1	26.1	31.0	10 562	24 732	41 710	55 565	2.3	39 995	20.1	33.2	31.9
Los Alamos	NA	NA	4 651	11.2	13.8	64.0	37.3	10 562	50 723	105 989	120 502	14.8	108 477	4.2	4.6	3.8
Luna	837	3 614	6 227	8.4	63.0	13.9	51.6	9 424	15 549	28 489	38 929	0.6	27 268	30.6	38.3	38.4
McKinley	766	3 527	22 457	9.0	60.0	11.4	138.0	10 368	12 800	29 812	43 338	1.4	29 497	35.8	42.9	45.7
Mora	108	387	1 519	3.0	60.3	8.0	2.1	28 413	18 950	24 425	37 593	0.0	27 627	24.2	35.3	31.8
Otero	300	2 087	16 669	6.3	45.6	17.2	66.0	8 881	19 803	40 614	51 754	1.4	41 736	20.2	29.7	28.7
Quay	480	2 293	1 860	1.0	54.5	13.8	17.4	11 562	16 719	29 042	39 232	0.2	29 069	23.9	36.0	35.8
Rio Arriba	559	1 531	9 601	10.9	51.9	15.5	66.8	11 380	19 483	38 635	50 136	1.1	34 902	24.1	30.9	29.5
Roosevelt	141	2 317	7 046	4.9	44.8	22.8	35.6	10 037	17 668	36 567	46 599	0.4	36 108	24.0	28.5	28.1
Sandoval	215	1 838	38 167	10.8	35.5	28.6	181.9	8 646	26 916	57 092	73 442	4.0	56 142	12.6	16.3	14.8
San Juan	535	1 983	34 310	5.9	49.9	15.2	211.3	8 814	21 992	48 824	64 655	2.5	47 520	21.0	29.4	28.5
San Miguel	NA	NA	7 338	11.5	47.6	19.9	53.6	11 736	18 355	28 292	42 659	0.7	32 964	25.5	33.6	33.2
Santa Fe	267	2 766	33 891	17.5	33.6	39.9	146.9	9 052	32 454	52 958	75 123	5.5	52 628	14.2	21.0	18.4
Sierra	NA	NA	1 578	7.2	50.8	18.9	13.6	10 030	18 589	28 855	37 854	0.3	29 036	23.8	40.0	38.4
Socorro	498	3 467	5 496	5.3	55.7	19.2	25.5	11 198	17 969	33 570	51 859	2.4	32 285	31.0	42.6	40.3
Taos	430	2 434	7 307	7.7	37.6	28.9	42.0	11 052	22 107	35 823	49 812	1.3	36 125	19.2	29.9	28.4
Torrance	322	1 521	3 792	6.0	50.4	16.2	40.5	10 091	18 278	34 720	48 826	0.8	37 311	27.6	37.1	32.7
Union	93	1 343	903	12.1	55.6	19.0	8.5	14 168	20 511	36 176	51 183	1.9	36 684	19.4	23.7	22.4
Valencia	904	3 256	20 147	8.7	50.1	16.5	109.4	8 575	19 646	42 012	53 660	1.0	40 591	24.5	30.1	29.5
NEW YORK	382	1 718	4 997 148	23.6	41.6	33.7	55 065.8	19 818	32 829	58 687	85 736	7.3	58 771	16.0	22.9	21.7
Albany	339	2 650	84 131	23.7	34.0	38.7	687.6	18 866	32 624	59 940	78 285	4.5	60 371	13.5	18.5	16.9
Allegany	204	1 138	14 393	27.9	52.0	19.1	127.4	18 465	20 881	42 726	53 827	1.1	42 655	18.3	26.5	22.8
Bronx	(7)	(7)	401 135	18.4	57.5	18.3	(7)	(7)	18 269	34 284	49 661	1.7	33 871	31.5	43.0	43.5
Broome	299	2 948	53 936	7.7	43.5	26.2	472.7	17 298	24 820	46 368	60 688	2.6	46 283	17.2	23.6	21.2
Cattaraugus	208	1 714	18 825	19.7	53.0	18.0	234.2	17 351	22 486	43 503	55 277	1.4	43 892	16.2	23.4	21.2
Cayuga	245	1 781	17 976	15.5	47.7	20.2	155.8	16 019	25 070	51 792	62 824	1.8	52 792	12.7	19.8	18.9
Chautauqua	267	2 434	32 237	8.9	47.4	21.1	332.6	16 430	22 483	42 720	53 971	1.1	41 757	19.3	28.8	27.5
Chemung	186	2 243	20 391	14.5	46.0	22.9	180.4	14 937	25 967	49 685	64 707	2.8	48 880	18.2	26.6	23.5
Chenango	162	1 738	11 358	9.3	53.0	17.2	149.3	19 084	22 339	44 427	55 265	1.2	46 387	16.7	24.6	22.6
Clinton	148	1 517	20 190	9.6	50.2	22.4	208.3	18 791	25 279	50 985	64 485	2.2	51 576	16.6	19.3	17.7
Columbia	132	1 439	12 528	15.1	42.7	28.5	147.7	19 656	32 665	58 625	78 941	4.2	55 047	11.6	18.0	16.1
Cortland	102	1 282	15 456	6.9	46.4	22.7	108.9	16 441	23 581	48 404	61 284	1.5	48 357	13.8	18.5	16.6
Delaware	167	1 579	10 000	4.9	51.1	20.5	134.7	21 116	23 911	44 183	56 099	1.3	45 860	14.4	22.6	20.8
Dutchess	214	1 413	81 757	28.2	37.1	33.4	826.9	19 281	33 962	72 471	90 923	6.9	70 925	10.2	12.9	11.4
Erie	441	2 644	233 913	17.4	38.2	31.2	2 117.0	17 775	28 512	51 050	67 277	3.2	50 134	15.2	22.9	20.7
Essex	176	850	7 706	15.1	45.6	23.8	87.7	22 130	26 755	50 322	64 341	1.9	50 182	12.0	18.2	17.6
Franklin	158	1 477	10 733	14.7	51.8	17.7	146.6	19 142	22 322	47 110	58 932	1.9	45 704	18.5	24.6	23.1
Fulton	130	2 573	11 923	8.2	52.7	15.7	134.0	15 761	24 265	45 722	58 147	1.7	45 409	17.8	25.8	24.3

1. Data for serious crimes have not been adjusted for underreporting; this may affect comparability between geographic areas and over time.   2. Per 100,000 population estimated by the FBI.
3. All persons 3 years old and over enrolled in nursery school through college.   4. Persons 25 years old and over.   5. Elementary and secondary education expenditures.
6. Based on population estimated by the American Community Survey, 2010–2014.   7. Bronx, Kings, Queens, and Richmond counties are included with New York county.

Table B. States and Counties — **Personal Income**

	Personal income, 2014										Earnings, 2014		
			Per capita[1]			Supplements to wages and salaries; employer contributions (mil dol)						Contributions for government social insurance (mil dol)	
STATE County	Total (mil dol)	Percent change, 2013–2014	Dollars	Rank	Wages and salaries (mil dol)	Pension and insurance	Government social insurance	Proprietors' income (mil dol)	Dividends, interest, and rent (mil dol)	Personal transfer receipts (mil dol)	Total (mil dol)	From employee and self-employed	From employer
	62	63	64	65	66	67	68	69	70	71	72	73	74

STATE County	62	63	64	65	66	67	68	69	70	71	72	73	74
NEW JERSEY—Cont'd													
Mercer	22 246	4.6	59 875	135	15 137	2 495	1 123	1 582	4 297	3 115	20 337	1 166	1 123
Middlesex	43 894	5.1	52 486	280	25 976	4 087	2 005	3 684	6 501	5 866	35 751	2 077	2 005
Monmouth	41 544	4.6	66 019	80	13 744	2 341	1 106	2 937	7 895	5 058	20 128	1 226	1 106
Morris	41 382	4.7	82 810	25	23 082	3 186	1 651	4 415	7 549	3 392	32 334	1 851	1 651
Ocean	26 020	4.8	44 381	727	6 997	1 423	603	1 810	4 568	6 141	10 833	778	603
Passaic	22 230	4.8	43 687	787	8 886	1 670	728	1 568	3 404	4 466	12 852	791	728
Salem	2 773	3.2	42 850	866	1 249	275	98	132	390	662	1 754	109	98
Somerset	27 846	4.8	83 731	22	16 081	2 080	1 093	2 942	5 099	2 116	22 196	1 270	1 093
Sussex	7 659	4.0	52 851	273	1 784	362	148	502	1 115	1 050	2 795	183	148
Union	31 687	5.0	57 306	167	15 329	2 479	1 098	2 277	5 471	4 218	21 183	1 249	1 098
Warren	5 201	4.7	48 645	451	1 705	327	140	267	764	875	2 439	156	140
NEW MEXICO	77 356	5.1	37 091	X	36 645	6 427	2 917	5 694	14 089	17 685	51 684	3 242	2 917
Bernalillo	26 137	4.0	38 690	1 365	15 306	2 551	1 235	1 571	4 910	5 304	20 663	1 291	1 235
Catron	114	7.5	32 092	2 430	24	7	2	11	28	39	43	3	2
Chaves	2 331	9.3	35 377	1 884	777	141	61	388	366	619	1 367	80	61
Cibola	692	4.4	25 302	3 055	298	64	24	24	96	235	410	27	24
Colfax	472	6.3	37 205	1 567	167	37	14	50	92	143	269	18	14
Curry	2 192	7.6	43 006	847	984	212	91	341	365	424	1 628	76	91
De Baca	73	18.0	40 160	1 151	18	4	1	13	16	24	37	2	1
Dona Ana	6 537	5.0	30 593	2 641	2 779	579	225	490	1 100	1 809	4 074	255	225
Eddy	2 951	9.3	52 323	283	1 585	234	116	458	526	486	2 393	148	116
Grant	1 045	5.0	35 908	1 789	396	87	30	51	191	357	564	39	30
Guadalupe	128	10.4	28 730	2 859	41	9	3	13	18	51	66	4	3
Harding	36	28.6	53 296	260	9	2	1	11	8	7	23	1	1
Hidalgo	172	5.9	37 642	1 504	65	17	5	23	31	50	111	6	5
Lea	3 163	10.5	45 185	662	1 925	243	141	546	298	497	2 856	170	141
Lincoln	751	5.8	38 115	1 439	216	39	18	66	219	212	339	25	18
Los Alamos	1 107	2.3	62 619	105	1 246	112	95	33	216	94	1 486	92	95
Luna	717	4.0	29 055	2 821	275	63	23	48	112	276	410	29	23
McKinley	1 763	5.0	23 789	3 085	732	181	61	25	260	640	998	63	61
Mora	148	6.6	32 262	2 406	24	7	2	11	26	61	44	4	2
Otero	2 190	2.4	33 653	2 166	909	218	80	84	469	529	1 291	75	80
Quay	299	6.2	35 176	1 910	100	21	8	20	54	116	149	10	8
Rio Arriba	1 232	4.3	30 976	2 589	341	76	27	55	171	414	499	36	27
Roosevelt	739	7.0	37 852	1 476	218	51	17	137	100	177	423	19	17
Sandoval	4 966	4.6	36 088	1 767	1 347	211	104	144	706	998	1 806	131	104
San Juan	4 481	5.0	36 197	1 745	2 453	404	185	271	585	939	3 313	206	185
San Miguel	897	6.5	31 760	2 479	275	75	22	45	153	372	417	29	22
Santa Fe	7 155	4.4	48 291	464	2 816	503	213	449	2 149	1 215	3 980	259	213
Sierra	392	6.3	34 621	1 995	102	23	8	28	83	176	161	13	8
Socorro	566	5.8	32 712	2 331	206	53	16	63	88	179	337	18	16
Taos	1 092	5.4	32 998	2 279	351	66	30	83	264	343	529	39	30
Torrance	448	8.0	28 714	2 863	122	26	10	43	60	159	200	13	10
Union	139	8.2	32 393	2 389	43	9	3	17	25	39	73	4	3
Valencia	2 231	4.8	29 422	2 788	495	102	45	83	304	700	725	57	45
NEW YORK	1 098 103	4.0	55 611	X	600 733	106 816	44 132	103 802	208 669	190 197	855 482	45 108	44 132
Albany	16 309	3.3	52 921	271	12 671	3 561	1 075	1 502	2 689	2 871	18 810	923	1 075
Allegany	1 581	4.7	33 128	2 257	522	186	48	113	193	423	869	48	48
Bronx	46 364	4.0	32 238	2 411	12 596	2 217	1 091	4 328	4 946	14 913	20 232	1 202	1 091
Broome	7 491	1.4	37 958	1 461	3 631	1 043	316	484	1 131	1 859	5 474	301	316
Cattaraugus	2 782	2.4	35 395	1 878	1 179	380	105	211	365	754	1 874	103	105
Cayuga	2 977	3.0	37 774	1 487	1 106	316	100	260	391	682	1 782	93	100
Chautauqua	4 529	2.8	34 296	2 064	1 860	531	171	309	615	1 348	2 871	163	171
Chemung	3 407	2.6	38 820	1 348	1 696	425	147	187	433	862	2 454	136	147
Chenango	1 813	3.4	36 684	1 651	768	227	67	131	241	468	1 194	66	67
Clinton	3 078	2.8	37 709	1 496	1 381	427	125	242	405	741	2 175	113	125
Columbia	2 851	3.0	45 889	607	851	242	76	193	532	623	1 363	77	76
Cortland	1 762	2.5	35 950	1 784	699	210	63	172	227	406	1 143	60	63
Delaware	1 692	4.0	36 332	1 718	637	211	57	160	282	456	1 066	59	57
Dutchess	13 984	4.1	47 151	517	5 720	1 331	487	659	2 220	2 508	8 198	444	487
Erie	41 288	3.1	44 740	700	21 544	4 964	1 856	3 104	6 091	8 693	31 469	1 691	1 856
Essex	1 546	3.5	39 963	1 182	583	194	53	104	279	382	933	51	53
Franklin	1 782	0.8	34 754	1 975	742	306	65	110	233	457	1 223	63	65
Fulton	2 049	2.7	37 879	1 472	643	185	59	147	253	581	1 034	62	59

1. Based on the resident population estimated as of July 1 of the year shown.

Table B. States and Counties — Earnings, Social Security, and Housing

STATE County	Farm	Mining	Construction	Manu-facturing	Information: professional, scientific, technical services	Retail trade	Finance, insurance, real estate and leasing	Health care and social assistance	Govern-ment	Social Security beneficiaries, December 2014 Number	Rate[1]	Supplemental Security Income recipients, December 2014	Housing units, 2015 Total	Percent change, 2010–2014
	75	76	77	78	79	80	81	82	83	84	85	86	87	88
NEW JERSEY—Cont'd														
Mercer	0.0	D	3.0	5.9	20.7	4.1	10.9	9.5	19.5	65 715	177	9 623	144 487	0.9
Middlesex	0.0	0.8	4.9	8.5	18.5	5.6	7.6	8.2	13.7	128 715	154	12 976	299 592	1.6
Monmouth	0.1	0.0	8.9	3.6	17.5	8.2	8.8	14.9	15.0	118 365	188	8 178	260 686	0.9
Morris	0.0	D	4.5	11.0	19.8	5.7	11.5	8.7	9.2	84 745	170	4 442	191 287	0.8
Ocean	0.0	0.8	10.1	3.1	7.4	10.2	5.0	18.9	21.9	154 510	264	7 311	280 494	0.9
Passaic	0.0	0.2	6.7	11.6	8.0	8.6	5.3	12.9	20.2	80 320	158	14 820	176 850	0.4
Salem	1.7	0.0	D	14.9	4.0	4.3	2.3	10.3	19.3	14 830	229	1 635	27 632	0.8
Somerset	0.0	0.2	3.4	11.5	25.1	5.3	9.3	6.2	7.1	50 560	152	2 867	125 877	2.2
Sussex	0.1	0.2	9.0	5.6	8.3	9.6	4.1	14.2	22.8	27 555	190	1 667	62 327	0.7
Union	0.0	D	6.1	14.1	15.4	5.3	5.8	10.3	14.3	85 710	155	11 085	201 486	1.0
Warren	0.9	0.2	D	12.5	5.2	9.1	2.4	13.5	19.0	21 450	201	1 416	45 412	1.1
NEW MEXICO	2.5	6.2	5.8	4.1	11.5	6.7	5.0	11.2	26.9	399 987	192	64 059	914 952	1.5
Bernalillo	0.0	0.2	6.1	4.2	16.4	6.7	6.5	12.9	26.1	119 950	178	17 770	288 992	1.7
Catron	16.3	D	6.0	1.4	D	D	D	D	45.0	1 390	393	77	3 275	-0.4
Chaves	15.0	9.2	4.1	4.6	5.3	8.8	3.4	12.8	19.1	12 920	196	2 260	26 688	0.0
Cibola	0.8	D	2.0	0.8	D	7.6	1.8	D	41.4	4 615	169	801	11 072	-0.3
Colfax	7.4	2.2	5.9	1.9	2.5	7.8	5.0	6.0	33.6	3 675	290	409	10 063	0.4
Curry	17.2	D	3.7	3.1	2.8	4.8	2.3	8.8	38.6	7 440	146	1 630	20 891	4.1
De Baca	34.1	0.0	3.5	D	D	6.9	D	6.7	26.1	525	287	80	1 338	-0.4
Dona Ana	3.4	0.0	5.4	3.8	8.3	6.2	3.7	14.7	33.8	37 595	176	8 076	84 646	3.9
Eddy	1.9	37.9	7.1	4.1	2.9	4.8	3.4	6.0	11.8	10 495	185	1 353	23 691	4.9
Grant	2.9	25.9	4.1	D	2.5	6.4	2.3	7.9	35.2	8 605	297	878	14 626	-0.5
Guadalupe	16.4	D	2.9	D	D	10.8	D	13.3	33.8	1 015	228	252	2 382	-0.5
Harding	36.0	D	D	D	D	D	D	0.0	23.2	220	325	13	526	0.0
Hidalgo	17.4	0.0	D	D	D	5.0	D	D	51.4	1 140	251	171	2 380	-0.5
Lea	5.0	36.2	9.8	4.4	2.5	4.8	3.9	D	8.3	9 290	133	1 581	25 581	2.7
Lincoln	3.7	D	8.0	0.8	6.9	11.4	5.8	11.9	21.5	5 820	296	367	17 705	1.1
Los Alamos	0.0	0.0	1.1	0.2	73.8	1.1	2.1	3.5	8.6	2 975	168	75	8 301	-0.6
Luna	2.7	0.2	5.0	8.3	D	10.7	2.1	D	39.0	6 910	281	1 433	10 936	-0.6
McKinley	-0.5	D	3.1	4.2	2.3	10.1	2.6	11.3	48.3	10 580	143	4 623	25 740	-0.3
Mora	13.6	D	D	D	D	5.8	2.9	D	37.9	1 430	312	310	3 218	-0.4
Otero	1.0	0.4	5.3	0.6	5.0	5.7	2.6	9.5	55.6	12 750	196	1 445	30 926	-0.2
Quay	8.6	0.0	5.1	0.9	1.9	8.0	4.0	D	33.6	2 640	312	428	5 547	-0.4
Rio Arriba	2.1	0.5	5.0	1.2	D	7.7	2.3	14.7	45.7	8 415	212	1 594	19 506	-0.7
Roosevelt	30.3	D	3.5	5.3	2.2	5.0	2.2	D	29.3	3 080	157	641	8 322	1.9
Sandoval	0.5	0.6	6.1	23.9	6.9	6.6	3.6	6.8	22.8	26 690	194	2 783	54 690	4.6
San Juan	1.1	23.5	7.6	2.4	2.5	7.2	3.2	11.1	20.5	20 860	168	4 019	49 661	0.6
San Miguel	2.3	0.1	4.3	0.9	2.3	6.8	3.4	D	50.6	7 245	256	1 926	15 506	-0.6
Santa Fe	0.0	1.4	4.5	1.1	8.9	8.9	9.9	13.7	30.7	34 465	233	2 872	71 873	0.8
Sierra	9.2	D	8.4	1.9	2.5	8.0	3.0	D	32.5	4 415	390	562	8 261	-1.1
Socorro	16.8	D	1.4	2.2	7.7	4.5	1.3	D	44.1	3 940	227	1 099	7 979	-1.0
Taos	0.2	5.1	8.1	1.1	6.3	9.6	5.0	16.1	23.4	8 940	271	1 165	20 388	0.6
Torrance	15.4	D	5.5	5.5	D	8.5	1.4	5.4	27.5	3 515	226	600	7 735	-0.8
Union	20.6	D	D	D	D	6.2	D	11.9	25.4	955	224	115	2 298	-0.3
Valencia	2.8	D	7.9	4.2	2.9	10.1	3.5	8.4	32.5	15 485	204	2 651	30 209	0.4
NEW YORK	0.3	0.1	4.3	4.4	16.7	4.9	18.9	10.6	16.7	3 482 978	176	653 601	8 206 739	1.2
Albany	0.1	D	5.9	3.3	12.2	5.2	8.1	10.6	35.5	59 710	193	7 280	138 713	0.7
Allegany	3.3	0.8	4.9	18.1	2.8	4.9	1.6	7.0	35.3	11 070	232	1 424	25 974	-0.6
Bronx	0.0	D	6.5	2.9	6.0	5.9	7.0	29.1	12.0	190 730	132	106 921	523 690	2.3
Broome	0.1	0.2	5.6	11.5	7.1	6.9	4.5	16.3	27.3	46 390	235	6 742	89 640	-1.0
Cattaraugus	1.8	0.7	3.3	15.9	2.8	7.5	2.9	D	36.5	19 315	246	2 548	40 941	-0.4
Cayuga	6.7	D	5.3	13.9	5.5	7.6	2.2	11.6	28.8	17 845	226	1 746	36 451	-0.1
Chautauqua	2.8	0.6	4.4	21.6	3.4	7.6	2.6	11.7	26.5	33 005	250	4 625	66 672	-0.4
Chemung	0.1	3.1	5.0	15.1	3.6	6.8	5.3	15.0	25.3	21 310	244	3 196	38 340	-0.1
Chenango	2.8	0.2	3.8	27.5	4.4	5.9	8.3	6.4	26.4	12 920	262	1 608	24 905	0.8
Clinton	3.4	D	4.2	10.6	3.5	8.5	2.1	15.8	34.1	18 640	228	2 755	35 970	0.2
Columbia	1.7	D	6.7	6.4	5.9	7.5	4.0	17.7	27.7	15 655	253	1 472	32 853	0.2
Cortland	2.3	0.1	4.6	16.7	5.0	7.4	4.2	D	26.7	9 685	198	1 202	20 503	-0.3
Delaware	1.8	1.5	5.5	24.3	5.7	5.5	3.3	8.4	29.8	12 795	275	1 144	31 178	-0.2
Dutchess	0.1	D	6.0	13.4	6.5	6.7	4.4	15.1	25.4	58 565	198	5 445	119 233	0.5
Erie	0.2	0.4	4.4	11.5	9.1	5.9	8.2	12.7	21.4	203 710	221	27 788	421 840	0.4
Essex	0.4	1.0	7.9	7.6	4.1	6.7	2.8	10.6	38.3	10 035	260	1 075	25 790	0.7
Franklin	3.3	D	2.8	2.0	3.4	5.5	1.7	14.5	53.9	11 725	229	1 828	25 274	-0.1
Fulton	0.3	D	4.8	8.7	5.1	9.6	3.3	17.4	26.8	14 715	272	2 090	28 656	0.3

1. Per 1,000 resident population estimated as of July 1 of the year shown.

Table B. States and Counties — Housing, Labor Force, and Employment

STATE County	Housing units, 2010–2014 Occupied units Owner-occupied Total	Percent	Median value[1]	Median owner cost as a percent of income With a mortgage	Without a mortgage[2]	Renter-occupied Median rent[3]	Median rent as a percent of income[2]	Substandard units[4] (percent)	Civilian labor force, 2015 Total	Percent change, 2014–2015	Unemployment Total	Rate[5]	Civilian employment,[6] 2010–2014 Total	Percent Management, business, science and arts	Construction, production, and maintenance occupations
	89	90	91	92	93	94	95	96	97	98	99	100	101	102	103
NEW JERSEY—Cont'd															
Mercer	131 475	65.1	280 400	25.5	16.1	1 135	31.6	2.9	199 062	2.1	9 611	4.8	177 007	43.9	14.9
Middlesex	282 182	65.2	325 000	27.1	17.6	1 292	29.3	4.1	440 343	1.2	21 935	5.0	400 296	43.9	17.4
Monmouth	233 730	74.8	386 900	27.2	17.2	1 241	34.5	1.9	331 623	1.2	16 458	5.0	305 912	43.4	15.2
Morris	179 776	75.5	426 700	26.2	16.6	1 353	28.1	1.7	263 272	0.5	11 127	4.2	255 325	49.5	12.7
Ocean	221 720	81.1	264 100	28.8	19.6	1 337	38.0	2.2	268 585	0.9	16 120	6.0	242 930	34.4	19.7
Passaic	162 097	54.2	343 100	30.7	21.2	1 174	37.1	9.5	249 659	0.5	17 135	6.9	228 233	32.3	24.9
Salem	24 665	70.9	189 000	24.4	18.3	999	35.7	1.6	31 445	0.8	2 222	7.1	28 973	32.2	28.3
Somerset	115 941	77.5	396 500	26.1	16.3	1 420	28.4	1.9	174 497	0.5	7 709	4.4	167 982	51.0	13.3
Sussex	54 248	84.1	277 600	27.4	17.9	1 219	37.2	1.2	77 573	0.1	4 068	5.2	74 954	39.6	18.9
Union	185 688	59.8	353 300	28.8	19.4	1 181	33.2	7.2	279 864	0.2	16 394	5.9	264 233	36.0	22.0
Warren	41 548	73.5	261 000	27.4	19.0	999	30.9	1.9	57 209	0.2	2 992	5.2	52 869	35.3	21.1
NEW MEXICO	764 684	68.2	159 300	23.2	10.0	774	30.5	4.6	919 893	-0.2	60 651	6.6	875 947	35.6	20.6
Bernalillo	263 719	62.4	185 500	23.5	10.0	800	31.4	3.3	318 387	-0.1	18 874	5.9	309 188	40.4	16.5
Catron	1 440	87.2	159 000	26.7	10.4	744	35.6	2.0	1 261	6.9	101	8.0	1 128	28.5	28.6
Chaves	23 506	65.4	99 100	20.2	10.0	684	29.0	4.5	27 248	1.4	1 734	6.4	27 153	29.7	27.6
Cibola	8 354	74.8	86 700	21.6	10.0	587	32.2	11.7	9 151	1.8	724	7.9	9 684	25.9	25.6
Colfax	5 369	67.6	117 300	25.6	11.7	594	28.1	1.8	5 965	-3.1	366	6.1	5 162	32.5	20.3
Curry	18 223	59.4	129 000	20.9	10.0	715	30.6	2.1	21 751	0.3	1 071	4.9	20 686	26.2	32.3
De Baca	601	82.7	84 800	24.9	10.0	460	23.3	1.2	854	2.0	43	5.0	738	28.7	36.0
Dona Ana	74 623	64.7	137 300	23.5	10.3	705	33.4	4.6	93 179	-0.3	6 868	7.4	88 340	32.4	20.9
Eddy	20 190	73.5	116 200	17.4	10.0	738	23.7	4.3	29 366	1.8	1 439	4.9	24 718	27.9	33.6
Grant	12 229	75.6	128 800	22.0	10.0	642	31.3	3.0	12 303	-1.0	810	6.6	11 125	36.4	21.9
Guadalupe	1 269	78.4	81 500	23.4	12.6	493	28.9	1.9	1 642	1.5	117	7.1	1 300	29.8	17.3
Harding	212	83.0	63 800	35.0	12.4	675	35.0	1.9	280	-10.8	24	8.6	199	32.2	28.1
Hidalgo	1 858	67.5	75 700	20.2	10.6	446	26.7	4.7	2 127	-0.4	134	6.3	1 878	26.4	25.7
Lea	21 331	70.6	101 400	17.7	10.0	760	22.9	5.6	29 428	-3.7	1 827	6.2	28 199	24.5	37.7
Lincoln	8 640	77.6	155 400	25.8	12.9	765	25.7	7.2	8 613	-1.4	502	5.8	8 162	31.1	20.6
Los Alamos	7 495	75.0	280 700	17.7	10.0	974	21.1	1.1	8 396	-0.4	342	4.1	8 960	69.2	7.0
Luna	9 120	67.4	84 700	27.9	10.7	548	27.4	4.8	10 817	-4.0	1 900	17.6	8 644	23.6	27.7
McKinley	17 862	73.0	70 600	20.5	10.0	546	24.3	20.9	24 107	0.9	2 331	9.7	22 410	29.2	23.9
Mora	1 525	78.1	81 500	17.8	13.4	635	44.7	4.7	2 248	0.0	219	9.7	1 513	28.2	25.1
Otero	23 907	64.7	101 400	22.5	10.0	775	27.2	4.2	24 709	0.0	1 536	6.2	22 243	27.2	23.4
Quay	3 319	75.5	73 000	24.1	11.8	422	24.9	3.4	3 188	-2.0	230	7.2	3 027	26.5	22.9
Rio Arriba	14 245	78.0	140 900	22.7	10.0	644	32.5	5.2	16 329	0.1	1 310	8.0	15 669	33.8	18.4
Roosevelt	7 198	59.2	115 800	22.2	10.0	697	36.3	4.7	8 023	-1.3	442	5.5	8 392	28.0	22.5
Sandoval	47 965	81.0	175 800	24.7	10.0	997	30.7	4.7	60 693	-0.3	4 081	6.7	57 758	40.0	17.5
San Juan	40 693	73.2	144 100	20.6	10.0	756	27.4	9.7	55 257	0.4	3 893	7.0	51 532	27.4	28.0
San Miguel	11 306	72.8	117 700	26.8	13.6	636	39.4	2.7	10 988	0.6	849	7.7	9 974	30.9	17.5
Santa Fe	61 313	69.4	272 700	26.5	10.0	930	36.0	3.6	71 658	0.1	3 891	5.4	69 661	43.3	14.3
Sierra	4 686	75.9	91 100	23.2	12.5	576	31.0	2.6	4 003	2.5	366	9.1	4 107	25.0	20.4
Socorro	5 161	72.5	112 500	22.9	11.8	580	27.5	3.6	6 460	0.1	489	7.6	5 662	38.0	21.0
Taos	13 239	72.5	211 900	26.1	11.5	762	37.0	4.8	14 743	-1.5	1 365	9.3	13 963	36.0	17.8
Torrance	5 656	80.4	107 400	24.5	15.0	688	33.4	5.3	5 449	-1.7	492	9.0	5 339	34.9	21.6
Union	1 602	63.4	90 200	19.9	13.9	639	26.1	3.2	1 892	-0.2	84	4.4	1 602	40.1	24.1
Valencia	26 828	79.0	133 500	24.9	10.4	737	36.1	3.9	29 378	-0.2	2 197	7.5	27 831	28.4	25.0
NEW YORK	7 255 528	53.8	283 700	25.3	14.9	1 117	32.1	5.4	9 679 327	0.9	513 077	5.3	9 137 540	38.9	16.8
Albany	122 945	58.8	208 600	22.1	12.7	918	29.3	1.2	158 773	0.8	7 007	4.4	154 002	43.6	12.8
Allegany	18 407	73.3	69 100	20.4	13.7	604	31.8	3.2	23 311	-0.3	1 345	5.8	20 416	32.0	27.7
Bronx	480 323	19.1	366 400	32.2	13.4	1 060	35.3	12.3	615 993	0.7	47 691	7.7	548 477	24.0	18.4
Broome	79 438	66.1	108 300	20.9	12.9	701	33.2	1.8	86 925	-1.4	5 257	6.0	88 182	35.4	19.8
Cattaraugus	31 798	71.7	83 000	21.2	13.7	617	28.8	3.1	36 302	-1.1	2 252	6.2	34 402	28.0	26.7
Cayuga	30 907	72.0	109 000	20.7	13.2	666	28.2	1.7	37 566	-0.3	2 026	5.4	36 664	31.6	25.3
Chautauqua	54 226	69.9	84 100	20.0	13.6	611	30.5	2.1	57 869	0.0	3 544	6.1	58 065	30.0	27.5
Chemung	35 390	68.3	97 800	18.5	12.5	707	32.7	1.1	37 960	-0.8	2 247	5.9	38 756	33.5	22.3
Chenango	19 560	75.8	91 800	21.6	14.2	612	29.3	2.5	23 148	-0.4	1 291	5.6	21 390	30.8	28.4
Clinton	31 976	68.3	125 200	21.1	12.0	736	31.9	2.0	36 013	-0.1	2 134	5.9	35 880	32.4	22.1
Columbia	25 095	72.0	222 800	24.9	14.9	870	29.0	1.5	31 524	0.4	1 284	4.1	29 809	37.1	21.1
Cortland	18 045	66.1	105 200	21.5	13.5	675	27.6	2.0	23 816	0.4	1 399	5.9	23 587	32.9	22.9
Delaware	19 370	74.2	133 600	23.8	14.0	672	29.7	3.5	19 686	-1.9	1 191	6.0	20 131	30.5	27.3
Dutchess	106 898	69.5	282 100	27.5	16.8	1 124	32.7	2.4	143 390	0.6	6 567	4.6	143 344	40.1	17.4
Erie	381 783	65.1	126 700	20.6	13.3	738	29.9	1.2	449 176	0.0	24 346	5.4	437 327	37.9	17.5
Essex	15 571	73.5	145 800	21.8	14.3	789	29.5	2.3	17 385	-1.1	1 062	6.1	17 586	33.9	22.4
Franklin	19 131	71.7	98 500	20.4	13.2	655	30.5	1.9	20 446	-0.5	1 334	6.5	20 090	31.1	20.8
Fulton	22 440	69.3	107 500	22.7	13.8	701	31.2	1.6	23 465	-0.1	1 541	6.6	24 133	27.7	27.0

1. Specified owner-occupied units.　　2. A value of 10.0 represents 10 percent or less; a value of 50.0 represents 50 percent or more.　　3. Specified renter-occupied units.
4. Overcrowded or lacking complete plumbing facilities.　　5. Percent of civilian labor force.　　6. Persons 16 years old and over.

Table B. States and Counties — **Nonfarm Employment and Agriculture**

| | Private nonfarm establishments, employment and payroll, 2014 | | | | | | | | | Agriculture, 2012 | | | |
| | | | | | | | | | | | | | |

| STATE County | Number of establish-ments | \multicolumn{6}{c}{Employment} | | | | Annual payroll | | \multicolumn{4}{c}{Farms} |
		Total	Health care and social assistance	Manufac-turing	Retail trade	Finance and insurance	Professional, scientific, and technical services	Total (mil dol)	Average per employee (dollars)	Number	Percent with: Fewer than 50 acres	500 acres or more	Farm operators whose principal occu-pation is farming (percent)
	104	105	106	107	108	109	110	111	112	113	114	115	116
NEW JERSEY—Cont'd													
Mercer	9 627	182 255	30 928	6 902	19 591	15 405	22 196	12 049	66 109	272	71.0	2.9	46.0
Middlesex	21 560	383 660	47 421	27 883	39 081	14 198	54 246	23 378	60 935	198	73.2	5.1	43.9
Monmouth	18 997	228 837	41 808	9 011	40 156	10 560	20 561	11 048	48 278	823	82.4	2.4	57.2
Morris	16 771	286 394	35 524	12 937	30 113	18 101	41 662	21 194	74 003	366	79.0	0.8	43.4
Ocean	12 552	134 831	33 265	5 044	28 741	3 591	6 533	4 879	36 189	178	82.0	1.7	51.1
Passaic	11 941	150 645	28 489	16 843	23 686	4 738	7 560	6 737	44 723	78	92.3	0.0	48.7
Salem	1 147	18 309	2 905	3 972	1 902	473	437	1 041	56 870	825	60.4	6.5	53.3
Somerset	9 914	184 296	22 210	12 015	19 490	11 330	25 578	14 758	80 078	400	71.0	3.5	33.3
Sussex	3 254	30 254	6 041	2 296	5 986	988	1 294	1 197	39 557	885	69.5	1.9	47.5
Union	13 668	202 369	32 351	15 845	25 646	5 973	13 024	12 068	59 632	8	100.0	0.0	37.5
Warren	2 455	27 906	5 382	3 642	5 975	585	995	1 248	44 715	784	65.3	3.2	49.4
NEW MEXICO	43 748	602 632	115 814	26 449	95 707	22 586	46 523	23 629	39 210	24 721	51.3	25.3	50.1
Bernalillo	15 771	244 760	48 449	12 230	35 898	10 555	19 770	9 555	39 040	1 006	80.9	7.4	44.2
Catron	56	362	114	D	60	D	D	10	28 249	351	14.5	40.2	63.0
Chaves	1 426	17 005	3 526	851	3 439	701	936	592	34 829	595	39.7	36.1	55.3
Cibola	316	4 943	1 435	D	820	103	D	173	35 011	522	54.4	26.1	44.4
Colfax	415	3 406	508	127	596	183	82	97	28 510	290	13.4	41.4	47.9
Curry	1 067	12 770	2 840	D	2 468	485	D	379	29 697	600	16.8	49.7	45.0
De Baca	46	245	D	D	53	D	D	6	25 196	203	39.9	39.4	60.1
Dona Ana	3 546	50 861	13 190	2 371	8 034	1 649	5 064	1 594	31 337	2 184	85.6	4.5	37.7
Eddy	1 398	22 732	2 795	1 312	3 017	569	859	1 184	52 084	551	41.0	31.4	56.4
Grant	624	6 885	1 512	122	1 244	240	135	275	39 873	407	30.7	33.9	45.7
Guadalupe	94	967	78	D	D	24	D	25	25 831	372	19.9	55.9	62.4
Harding	8	D	D	NA	D	D	NA	D	D	202	5.4	61.4	66.8
Hidalgo	94	826	162	D	244	D	D	20	24 201	171	24.6	55.0	66.1
Lea	1 724	26 136	2 352	873	3 319	488	524	1 395	53 361	460	29.6	44.1	55.4
Lincoln	689	5 068	546	83	1 208	296	144	137	26 964	362	30.7	43.9	55.5
Los Alamos	362	D	1 002	44	406	D	D	D	D	9	100.0	0.0	88.9
Luna	392	4 301	D	329	1 008	D	81	112	26 050	190	26.3	36.8	61.6
McKinley	973	15 783	4 584	D	3 454	420	229	478	30 255	2 297	38.9	35.6	60.3
Mora	45	308	124	D	D	D	NA	8	24 432	597	31.5	19.6	64.8
Otero	958	11 651	2 136	197	2 296	335	600	332	28 517	486	49.4	22.6	48.1
Quay	230	1 996	348	43	472	103	52	48	23 854	553	13.0	53.7	52.4
Rio Arriba	549	6 215	1 794	D	1 150	224	74	215	34 647	1 892	63.4	14.3	44.2
Roosevelt	345	3 570	611	D	690	138	70	106	29 655	680	17.4	47.5	50.7
Sandoval	1 671	23 029	3 587	2 788	3 279	766	809	841	36 526	1 029	63.8	14.2	45.3
San Juan	2 793	39 206	6 667	1 685	6 257	1 015	1 314	1 843	47 002	2 628	61.7	20.8	54.2
San Miguel	436	5 845	3 011	64	913	174	95	156	26 729	877	19.4	39.9	53.5
Santa Fe	4 711	45 219	8 071	754	9 657	1 718	2 345	1 784	39 456	715	67.0	13.4	43.6
Sierra	219	2 193	698	D	432	71	37	56	25 736	256	35.9	36.3	67.6
Socorro	228	2 913	D	75	460	75	238	85	29 057	704	60.2	20.0	55.0
Taos	1 071	8 418	1 440	132	1 548	212	296	237	28 179	983	75.3	7.4	35.6
Torrance	225	1 912	D	D	520	42	D	51	26 696	589	16.1	40.7	53.0
Union	100	920	D	D	129	D	D	27	28 946	353	5.7	73.1	58.6
Valencia	904	10 196	1 905	D	2 361	341	285	268	26 303	1 607	87.4	2.7	43.1
NEW YORK	536 890	7 858 425	1 459 585	423 971	935 555	536 065	626 610	492 706	62 698	35 537	32.6	8.4	57.4
Albany	9 398	175 816	34 385	7 322	22 801	12 113	16 341	8 072	45 911	494	42.5	3.6	46.6
Allegany	801	11 744	1 729	2 305	1 325	195	245	372	31 712	784	23.3	6.9	51.8
Bronx	17 466	246 446	99 902	5 664	29 907	3 987	3 894	10 733	43 552	1	100.0	0.0	100.0
Broome	4 261	71 889	15 066	7 428	11 735	2 772	3 689	2 744	38 175	563	34.1	3.0	48.8
Cattaraugus	1 626	22 718	3 451	3 907	3 980	637	530	785	34 573	1 038	26.6	7.5	51.8
Cayuga	1 653	19 535	3 703	3 381	3 548	343	473	698	35 712	891	33.2	12.7	59.4
Chautauqua	2 908	41 289	7 998	9 523	6 360	866	961	1 317	31 898	1 515	35.2	4.8	54.3
Chemung	1 810	31 795	6 662	5 197	5 340	994	721	1 249	39 287	372	27.2	4.3	53.8
Chenango	933	13 635	1 863	4 262	1 805	D	373	560	41 097	828	22.9	8.1	56.3
Clinton	1 863	25 422	4 882	3 569	5 248	432	709	871	34 253	603	26.9	11.6	57.5
Columbia	1 723	15 450	4 158	1 451	2 930	405	549	579	37 474	494	42.1	9.7	61.5
Cortland	1 026	16 196	3 490	2 985	2 341	D	985	509	31 447	518	23.0	9.1	52.1
Delaware	1 041	10 222	1 886	3 078	1 598	330	195	418	40 934	704	27.7	9.5	62.2
Dutchess	7 478	93 981	18 669	7 178	14 634	2 931	7 783	4 296	45 714	678	44.5	7.2	54.3
Erie	22 565	414 626	73 145	44 691	54 763	28 438	28 777	17 651	42 570	1 044	45.3	5.1	57.4
Essex	1 152	9 886	1 921	D	1 815	D	253	349	35 328	261	29.5	11.1	55.6
Franklin	965	10 443	3 268	528	1 859	240	360	334	31 999	688	23.0	8.4	59.4
Fulton	1 176	14 025	3 328	1 850	2 486	297	398	477	33 976	211	37.0	6.6	57.3

Table B. States and Counties — **Agriculture**

STATE County	Land in farms — Acreage (1,000) [117]	Percent change, 2007–2012 [118]	Average size of farm [119]	Total irrigated (1,000) [120]	Total cropland (1,000) [121]	Value of land and buildings — Average per farm [122]	Average per acre [123]	Value of machinery and equipment, average per farm (dollars) [124]	Value of products sold — Total (mil dol) [125]	Average per farm (dollars) [126]	Percent from: Crops [127]	Live-stock and poultry products [128]	Percent of farms with sales of: $10,000 or more [129]	$100,000 or more [130]	Government payments — Total ($1,000) [131]	Percent of farms [132]
NEW JERSEY—Cont'd																
Mercer	20	-9.1	73	1.1	12.4	1 474 301	20 310	59 195	19.7	72 533	83.1	16.9	43.0	11.0	310	14.3
Middlesex	17	-7.8	87	2.7	12.3	1 716 202	19 686	104 551	29.3	147 732	98.6	1.4	46.0	20.2	130	15.2
Monmouth	39	-11.7	47	3.7	25.1	1 021 639	21 581	73 476	84.4	102 565	79.6	20.4	38.6	12.8	169	6.2
Morris	14	-15.1	40	0.7	7.2	914 418	23 148	75 101	28.4	77 560	95.8	4.2	33.6	8.5	61	2.2
Ocean	8	-19.0	45	0.7	2.9	691 534	15 446	55 247	11.6	64 888	84.3	15.7	41.0	11.2	112	5.6
Passaic	1	-26.6	19	0.1	0.2	581 667	31 204	58 385	3.4	44 051	92.5	7.5	26.9	6.4	D	1.3
Salem	102	5.5	123	18.1	81.2	974 698	7 895	107 623	112.0	135 749	84.0	16.0	37.5	17.6	1 386	22.2
Somerset	35	6.2	87	0.5	20.2	1 779 905	20 497	72 478	23.2	58 015	89.2	10.8	34.0	8.5	128	7.0
Sussex	61	-6.5	69	0.3	27.9	735 954	10 672	48 488	18.7	21 078	62.1	37.9	23.4	5.2	370	8.1
Union	0	-23.8	12	0.0	0.1	1 513 000	126 083	85 375	2.4	294 875	D	D	62.5	37.5	0	0.0
Warren	72	-3.6	92	1.7	46.4	942 751	10 230	77 084	91.2	116 333	59.9	40.1	31.9	11.4	773	17.3
NEW MEXICO	43 201	-0.1	1 748	680.3	1 976.7	755 185	432	60 316	2 550.1	103 157	24.2	75.8	24.4	7.0	70 588	22.3
Bernalillo	351	47.5	349	5.3	12.5	395 200	1 134	33 582	18.1	18 023	41.5	58.5	13.0	1.9	172	8.6
Catron	1 078	-27.3	3 070	5.4	3.1	1 311 014	427	62 142	12.7	36 302	1.3	98.7	27.4	8.8	613	13.7
Chaves	2 483	1.2	4 173	49.8	63.0	1 503 955	360	147 017	388.1	652 267	11.6	88.4	53.6	30.9	4 688	32.9
Cibola	1 559	5.4	2 987	D	3.9	930 634	312	37 464	D	D	D	D	14.8	1.3	500	26.1
Colfax	1 963	-6.8	6 769	10.3	23.9	2 682 179	396	76 979	35.7	123 255	6.0	94.0	47.2	17.9	918	23.1
Curry	881	-0.8	1 468	62.2	479.0	849 413	579	157 685	447.3	745 525	7.0	93.0	42.0	19.5	8 250	72.2
De Baca	1 068	-0.2	5 261	8.1	11.2	1 301 429	247	90 015	24.0	118 064	36.9	63.1	55.7	27.1	1 868	58.6
Dona Ana	660	12.0	302	76.3	93.8	540 877	1 790	75 238	351.0	160 729	47.5	52.5	23.9	8.1	1 453	9.5
Eddy	1 142	3.1	2 073	43.3	53.0	926 314	447	123 615	119.6	216 995	42.2	57.8	45.6	15.6	2 481	35.2
Grant	1 064	-12.3	2 615	4.0	8.4	980 442	375	52 437	14.5	35 732	14.3	85.7	33.2	5.9	1 329	15.0
Guadalupe	1 643	17.0	4 417	3.8	17.7	1 176 723	266	43 145	17.7	47 605	2.1	97.9	32.0	9.1	2 853	36.0
Harding	1 034	9.5	5 119	D	21.3	1 447 842	283	58 356	13.5	66 807	2.1	97.9	39.6	14.4	1 289	40.1
Hidalgo	930	-9.6	5 440	9.6	12.9	1 347 661	248	97 895	29.2	170 491	57.9	42.1	73.1	24.6	1 228	46.2
Lea	1 982	-16.2	4 309	51.6	117.0	1 461 422	339	136 552	188.9	410 709	21.6	78.4	48.0	23.0	5 045	37.8
Lincoln	1 553	-11.3	4 291	2.0	5.1	1 519 177	354	62 006	16.9	46 588	3.2	96.8	42.8	11.6	2 709	26.0
Los Alamos	0	88.9	2	D	D	28 889	15 294	6 556	D	D	D	D	0.0	0.0	0	0.0
Luna	550	-15.8	2 896	20.6	37.2	1 228 332	424	174 526	62.5	328 853	63.9	36.1	58.4	30.5	1 472	52.6
McKinley	3 023	-4.7	1 316	1.9	44.1	414 200	315	22 288	8.4	3 652	7.4	92.6	5.1	0.4	845	29.7
Mora	778	-14.9	1 303	7.6	13.3	723 692	555	45 174	11.6	19 469	9.9	90.1	21.1	3.2	1 839	18.8
Otero	1 224	8.6	2 518	6.0	D	1 057 944	420	53 058	14.6	30 113	55.0	45.0	30.2	5.3	1 183	12.1
Quay	1 518	1.9	2 745	7.0	216.2	919 353	335	76 897	36.8	66 526	6.4	93.6	33.5	10.8	6 471	71.1
Rio Arriba	1 433	-1.9	757	29.2	66.8	548 193	724	43 273	19.0	10 031	37.5	62.5	19.8	1.4	1 277	14.5
Roosevelt	1 349	-9.7	1 984	46.1	290.3	966 632	487	120 344	264.3	388 712	6.9	93.1	39.9	13.2	8 038	62.4
Sandoval	950	60.6	923	9.4	17.8	482 790	523	31 229	10.6	10 288	52.9	47.1	16.2	1.0	815	10.0
San Juan	2 580	58.2	982	85.9	115.6	341 496	348	41 084	71.3	27 135	88.9	11.1	13.3	1.2	1 023	14.0
San Miguel	2 350	4.9	2 680	4.6	22.4	1 010 876	377	43 104	18.6	21 244	5.1	94.9	21.4	2.7	1 639	16.5
Santa Fe	718	26.0	1 004	8.9	13.1	848 969	846	39 010	12.8	17 869	75.1	24.9	15.0	2.7	394	5.7
Sierra	1 250	-7.0	4 883	12.4	19.4	1 396 238	286	91 934	39.3	153 699	44.6	55.4	55.9	20.7	1 418	37.1
Socorro	1 271	-11.1	1 806	18.9	21.4	890 670	493	67 983	77.2	109 726	15.3	84.7	37.2	11.9	1 539	9.5
Taos	313	-31.4	319	14.5	24.6	373 969	1 173	30 988	8.4	8 561	41.0	59.0	10.8	1.6	440	9.0
Torrance	1 865	3.8	3 166	25.0	47.9	1 151 192	364	79 518	58.5	99 355	39.9	60.1	32.6	9.3	3 259	27.7
Union	1 967	-10.3	5 573	26.0	66.1	2 047 037	367	96 062	98.1	278 011	17.2	82.8	66.3	31.4	2 900	49.3
Valencia	670	32.4	417	23.1	23.4	392 418	942	48 432	55.8	34 701	23.8	76.2	13.8	2.6	641	6.3
NEW YORK	7 184	0.1	202	59.8	4 217.0	525 587	2 600	117 163	5 415.1	152 380	41.5	58.5	49.2	20.0	74 511	26.4
Albany	63	3.9	128	0.4	36.5	397 650	3 099	73 182	46.0	93 030	67.6	32.4	38.3	8.3	384	16.8
Allegany	150	-0.3	192	0.1	71.3	335 583	1 750	70 612	73.4	93 569	28.5	71.5	36.4	12.8	1 099	27.0
Bronx	D	D	D	0.0	0.0	D	D	D	D	D	D	D	100.0	0.0	0	0.0
Broome	80	-8.0	142	0.1	38.1	371 162	2 623	66 933	30.7	54 552	22.9	77.1	34.3	5.9	770	18.7
Cattaraugus	197	7.5	190	0.9	97.3	359 361	1 891	91 609	99.1	95 503	25.3	74.7	41.8	14.7	1 895	31.4
Cayuga	238	-4.4	268	0.4	181.7	860 439	3 215	216 304	293.5	329 376	33.8	66.2	59.1	29.6	2 791	35.8
Chautauqua	237	0.3	156	0.9	129.5	322 390	2 065	95 881	161.8	106 831	45.6	54.4	54.3	18.9	2 502	19.8
Chemung	58	-10.8	156	0.2	28.1	376 065	2 407	75 599	16.0	43 143	41.2	58.8	28.5	8.6	482	22.8
Chenango	167	-5.7	202	0.2	79.3	370 505	1 835	87 490	65.9	79 630	22.3	77.7	45.4	19.3	2 117	30.9
Clinton	147	-1.3	244	0.1	74.0	494 534	2 025	144 806	149.0	247 096	28.4	71.6	46.9	19.7	1 660	24.7
Columbia	95	-10.5	193	1.4	56.9	1 008 441	5 223	115 555	66.5	134 664	54.0	46.0	55.1	20.6	674	19.8
Cortland	115	-7.9	222	0.2	60.4	423 170	1 906	104 708	62.9	121 423	21.4	78.6	47.5	15.6	984	35.7
Delaware	146	-12.1	207	0.2	59.3	515 442	2 492	83 908	47.7	67 736	19.5	80.5	46.9	17.5	1 248	33.7
Dutchess	112	9.9	166	0.8	45.6	860 500	5 187	97 681	49.0	72 304	53.1	46.9	49.1	16.7	427	10.3
Erie	143	-4.5	137	1.9	93.8	404 428	2 959	112 551	133.1	127 535	46.3	53.7	42.2	16.4	1 863	23.9
Essex	55	9.2	210	0.1	20.0	443 410	2 110	75 100	11.7	44 862	47.6	52.4	34.1	8.0	209	13.0
Franklin	145	10.8	211	0.6	74.8	354 044	1 680	100 096	84.2	122 334	23.2	76.8	48.4	18.3	1 583	26.0
Fulton	32	-5.9	151	0.1	14.7	324 464	2 148	74 938	9.3	44 081	36.2	63.8	41.2	10.0	269	18.5

Table B. States and Counties — Water Use, Wholesale Trade, Retail Trade, and Real Estate

STATE County	Water use, 2010		Wholesale trade,[1] 2012				Retail trade,[2] 2012				Real estate and rental and leasing,[2] 2012			
	Total water withdrawn (mil gal/day)	Gallons withdrawn per person per day	Number of establishments	Number of employees	Sales (mil dol)	Annual payroll (mil dol)	Number of establishments	Number of employees	Sales (mil dol)	Annual payroll (mil dol)	Number of establishments	Number of employees	Receipts (mil dol)	Annual payroll (mil dol)
	133	134	135	136	137	138	139	140	141	142	143	144	145	146
NEW JERSEY—Cont'd														
Mercer	477.6	1 303	354	D	D	D	1 305	18 794	5 127.4	477.9	347	1 934	729.3	91.8
Middlesex	67.9	84	1 580	33 984	40 540.7	2 614.2	2 611	38 315	11 869.8	982.7	680	5 893	2 421.8	349.8
Monmouth	79.9	127	803	6 856	4 888.8	409.3	2 627	38 150	11 026.1	1 008.7	672	3 948	824.6	164.5
Morris	105.0	213	912	14 194	21 280.6	1 103.1	1 823	29 044	9 346.9	854.7	606	5 457	2 863.2	427.4
Ocean	574.6	997	388	2 761	1 295.7	127.9	1 869	26 568	7 695.4	724.1	546	2 525	468.2	92.8
Passaic	221.2	441	755	11 293	9 132.5	774.4	1 834	22 841	7 294.0	580.7	412	2 274	942.0	120.4
Salem	3 054.1	46 216	36	713	1 825.4	36.6	176	1 932	627.0	43.4	42	174	28.5	6.1
Somerset	13.6	42	495	12 184	25 544.7	1 040.4	1 086	18 878	5 609.3	510.5	294	1 286	442.8	62.4
Sussex	16.8	112	122	1 083	459.6	58.0	413	5 658	1 819.8	146.0	86	316	62.9	11.1
Union	147.8	276	853	15 361	14 069.6	1 380.5	1 941	24 757	7 376.3	646.2	532	3 070	1 058.3	147.7
Warren	26.1	240	95	D	D	D	389	6 076	1 573.8	143.0	58	181	43.1	6.6
NEW MEXICO	3 161.0	1 535	1 646	17 448	10 720.4	814.6	6 590	90 792	25 179.3	2 214.5	2 369	9 754	1 960.4	368.7
Bernalillo	149.0	225	791	10 150	5 620.8	495.7	2 076	33 334	9 548.2	857.5	942	4 274	818.2	150.5
Catron	20.0	5 366	1	D	D	D	13	68	10.7	0.9	NA	NA	NA	NA
Chaves	241.3	3 676	46	446	190.4	17.8	233	3 138	895.1	72.7	78	267	45.8	10.1
Cibola	11.1	408	7	D	D	D	70	864	256.7	19.1	12	36	5.8	1.1
Colfax	47.8	3 477	9	D	D	D	77	640	151.6	13.5	26	104	6.7	1.4
Curry	164.0	3 390	46	425	199.8	15.4	190	2 492	624.4	56.0	61	207	30.8	5.6
De Baca	51.8	25 628	1	D	D	D	8	54	13.0	1.1	1	D	D	D
Dona Ana	397.2	1 899	102	D	D	D	496	7 916	1 965.4	167.7	209	690	116.6	18.9
Eddy	193.5	3 594	54	558	1 075.3	23.3	191	2 674	798.7	67.0	55	283	89.5	14.7
Grant	46.5	1 576	14	109	43.3	4.1	114	1 222	257.1	25.1	40	126	15.2	2.8
Guadalupe	24.6	5 249	1	D	D	D	16	258	126.6	4.2	2	D	D	D
Harding	3.2	4 604	NA	NA	NA	NA	3	D	D	D	NA	NA	NA	NA
Hidalgo	61.6	12 585	2	D	D	D	26	237	157.7	4.8	1	D	D	D
Lea	175.5	2 711	92	D	D	D	214	2 830	919.8	71.1	91	774	247.8	53.2
Lincoln	23.3	1 135	10	D	D	D	135	1 184	279.7	26.9	60	152	22.8	3.3
Los Alamos	3.6	202	3	D	D	D	28	472	103.2	10.9	22	66	17.1	2.6
Luna	109.7	4 371	14	D	D	D	74	972	210.0	19.2	23	47	7.7	1.3
McKinley	13.8	193	44	D	D	D	227	3 271	996.7	72.6	42	158	28.4	5.4
Mora	12.7	2 600	NA	NA	NA	NA	7	D	D	D	1	D	D	D
Otero	30.1	472	24	D	D	D	186	2 185	567.7	50.6	52	151	18.7	3.5
Quay	41.6	4 597	2	D	D	D	41	461	263.9	8.7	8	13	0.9	0.4
Rio Arriba	107.1	2 660	10	55	43.7	1.0	83	1 068	254.6	27.4	24	64	7.2	1.4
Roosevelt	173.6	8 748	11	87	70.7	2.8	52	650	156.8	14.8	11	26	3.9	0.6
Sandoval	65.5	498	40	235	88.8	8.7	189	3 397	942.3	79.4	75	198	39.7	7.8
San Juan	343.7	2 643	156	1 412	663.0	73.8	450	6 210	1 801.6	157.4	107	750	205.0	36.8
San Miguel	38.5	1 309	8	D	D	D	81	921	220.9	20.5	18	49	6.3	1.2
Santa Fe	49.8	345	111	867	773.2	37.4	813	8 981	2 324.5	250.1	280	933	181.8	36.9
Sierra	42.8	3 567	2	D	D	D	43	474	102.1	9.0	9	17	2.5	0.4
Socorro	129.4	7 241	1	D	D	D	39	483	119.8	10.6	11	32	3.1	0.6
Taos	106.5	3 232	17	D	D	D	211	1 438	304.1	32.0	62	213	19.3	4.4
Torrance	55.6	3 396	9	D	D	D	43	494	154.0	9.8	2	D	D	D
Union	63.2	13 900	NA	NA	NA	NA	21	131	33.2	2.5	1	D	D	D
Valencia	163.6	2 136	18	D	D	D	140	2 212	601.3	50.0	43	D	D	D
NEW YORK	10 574.5	546	28 853	325 663	341 735.0	19 833.3	77 463	905 325	251 167.7	23 641.2	32 033	166 315	56 409.8	8 654.4
Albany	50.0	164	394	4 810	4 329.6	252.9	1 305	21 436	5 762.8	538.6	412	2 637	565.5	101.6
Allegany	5.7	116	18	131	94.9	4.5	145	1 396	271.1	26.8	19	34	6.1	1.3
Bronx	0.2	0	676	10 510	10 994.5	587.4	3 932	27 777	6 872.8	616.4	2 235	8 856	1 899.7	302.1
Broome	47.3	236	196	3 870	2 968.8	163.5	719	11 290	2 741.2	246.2	160	834	180.3	27.5
Cattaraugus	13.7	171	49	709	637.7	26.4	339	4 084	1 091.5	90.4	45	257	29.1	7.7
Cayuga	9.6	120	63	912	623.4	43.6	260	3 535	874.7	78.5	59	178	29.1	4.4
Chautauqua	436.2	3 234	109	1 405	693.2	58.8	508	6 313	1 437.9	132.3	88	560	447.5	19.9
Chemung	9.8	111	85	1 193	765.0	51.5	350	5 044	1 174.8	115.8	84	382	106.6	17.0
Chenango	7.7	153	24	D	D	D	170	1 953	512.8	41.7	24	D	D	D
Clinton	15.4	188	90	1 293	709.1	56.4	368	5 354	1 385.3	115.3	76	280	45.0	8.4
Columbia	8.5	134	53	729	306.1	30.1	267	2 770	748.8	67.9	58	181	21.7	4.2
Cortland	6.1	123	33	D	D	D	177	2 415	694.4	54.0	40	146	24.4	4.2
Delaware	455.5	9 493	30	573	256.8	29.6	183	1 784	472.7	39.1	30	75	10.7	1.8
Dutchess	77.9	262	214	1 909	4 342.1	130.8	1 046	14 155	3 792.7	349.9	325	1 324	246.3	45.7
Erie	482.8	525	998	18 454	19 343.2	1 011.2	3 343	52 423	12 106.1	1 139.3	785	5 883	862.2	190.9
Essex	22.2	564	15	169	82.5	4.9	214	2 192	514.0	49.2	31	D	D	D
Franklin	13.3	257	23	203	149.2	6.8	185	1 855	501.8	45.2	33	94	12.6	2.3
Fulton	6.4	116	50	465	244.9	21.2	205	2 382	675.3	57.4	30	118	18.2	3.6

1. Merchant wholesalers, except manufacturers' sales branches and offices.   2. Employer establishments.

Table B. States and Counties — Professional Services, Manufacturing, and Accommodation and Food Services

STATE County	Professional, scientific, and technical services, 2012				Manufacturing, 2012				Accommodation and food services, 2012			
	Number of establishments	Number of employees	Receipts (mil dol)	Annual payroll (mil dol)	Number of establishments	Number of employees	Receipts (mil dol)	Annual payroll (mil dol)	Number of establishments	Number of employees	Sales (mil dol)	Annual payroll (mil dol)
	147	148	149	150	151	152	153	154	155	156	157	158
NEW JERSEY—Cont'd												
Mercer	1 591	21 394	5 318.1	2 127.7	246	7 070	2 220.3	378.2	812	11 894	731.4	201.0
Middlesex	4 053	50 970	10 318.6	3 919.9	742	28 277	15 784.9	1 765.7	1 685	21 988	1 387.2	361.2
Monmouth	2 621	20 213	3 516.5	1 446.3	426	8 551	3 053.1	440.2	1 652	23 082	1 318.9	356.7
Morris	2 665	36 232	8 207.1	3 128.9	529	14 358	5 178.0	835.8	1 284	18 783	1 235.0	337.9
Ocean	1 091	5 988	839.5	301.7	278	5 069	1 400.0	231.1	1 145	12 911	801.5	203.7
Passaic	1 051	7 060	1 023.8	413.3	716	18 337	5 214.5	1 030.3	975	10 172	648.0	156.1
Salem	80	D	D	D	38	2 617	D	187.3	106	1 691	89.2	22.8
Somerset	1 827	25 815	5 063.6	2 307.5	300	12 329	4 974.7	1 007.3	798	11 509	739.9	210.9
Sussex	335	1 357	181.3	67.8	119	1 932	465.8	100.1	294	3 455	222.3	52.7
Union	1 389	16 181	1 875.4	1 171.6	619	20 790	20 139.4	1 727.9	1 134	12 856	819.1	211.9
Warren	230	D	D	D	108	3 854	2 050.3	227.0	245	2 294	122.2	32.1
NEW MEXICO	4 687	44 175	7 618.8	2 771.8	1 389	26 731	29 102.4	1 349.2	4 177	82 601	4 349.7	1 250.4
Bernalillo	2 261	18 714	3 488.9	1 101.8	575	11 976	D	569.9	1 394	31 736	1 702.6	495.5
Catron	4	D	D	D	4	13	D	0.6	12	38	1.7	0.4
Chaves	108	994	172.6	64.1	37	877	770.2	37.5	128	2 300	107.8	28.5
Cibola	17	D	D	D	6	38	D	1.1	36	584	27.5	7.7
Colfax	23	D	D	D	13	98	D	3.7	64	1 091	67.0	21.9
Curry	88	535	49.7	19.0	25	534	D	28.5	83	1 949	78.2	22.3
De Baca	1	D	D	D	NA	NA	NA	NA	5	D	D	D
Dona Ana	339	D	D	D	128	2 520	D	87.1	319	6 813	285.2	80.7
Eddy	77	593	54.1	33.5	35	1 459	D	112.1	111	2 083	118.0	31.0
Grant	47	D	D	D	14	121	D	3.6	78	862	33.1	9.6
Guadalupe	2	D	D	D	NA	NA	NA	NA	23	302	15.4	4.3
Harding	NA	NA	NA	NA	NA	NA	NA	NA	1	D	D	D
Hidalgo	4	D	D	D	NA	NA	NA	NA	16	207	9.6	2.7
Lea	82	569	82.1	30.8	37	854	D	68.0	138	2 261	132.1	30.2
Lincoln	53	D	D	D	17	67	D	2.6	99	1 185	60.5	18.0
Los Alamos	65	D	D	D	8	47	D	2.0	37	450	23.8	6.3
Luna	20	D	D	D	12	287	D	9.0	56	770	32.4	8.7
McKinley	43	D	D	D	24	383	D	26.7	143	2 508	119.4	31.5
Mora	NA	NA	NA	NA	NA	NA	NA	NA	3	D	D	D
Otero	71	D	D	D	28	190	D	5.1	108	2 422	164.7	45.1
Quay	12	D	D	D	4	24	D	1.3	33	536	22.9	6.0
Rio Arriba	35	D	D	D	22	95	D	2.9	66	1 089	70.7	20.3
Roosevelt	16	D	D	D	14	329	449.8	14.6	30	587	20.5	6.2
Sandoval	172	760	94.1	39.6	60	3 747	D	243.4	156	3 482	161.0	50.9
San Juan	256	D	D	D	85	1 318	268.6	62.8	197	4 253	201.8	56.3
San Miguel	35	D	D	D	9	48	9.1	1.5	58	719	34.4	8.9
Santa Fe	625	2 604	356.9	151.5	138	719	131.0	27.5	421	9 049	592.4	179.9
Sierra	15	D	D	D	5	121	D	3.0	39	390	15.8	4.7
Socorro	24	D	D	D	5	64	D	2.2	41	621	24.8	6.8
Taos	97	D	D	D	39	104	D	2.6	151	1 974	92.2	31.5
Torrance	13	D	D	D	11	132	D	4.5	26	D	D	D
Union	7	D	D	D	NA	NA	NA	NA	14	171	6.3	1.8
Valencia	75	D	D	D	27	523	D	23.6	91	D	D	D
NEW YORK	59 302	588 820	133 638.8	49 200.3	16 475	426 621	148 879.9	22 073.3	49 731	679 146	49 285.5	13 734.3
Albany	1 116	14 737	3 110.3	1 023.3	231	7 327	3 547.4	423.5	1 011	15 417	866.6	240.8
Allegany	49	199	20.4	7.2	46	2 433	841.8	108.8	92	1 175	50.0	12.4
Bronx	671	3 704	376.9	147.0	323	6 197	1 477.9	251.5	1 735	15 924	1 005.1	250.4
Broome	312	D	D	D	173	7 718	2 200.8	403.1	522	7 985	387.4	104.5
Cattaraugus	96	518	67.8	23.8	74	4 669	1 558.6	286.1	213	2 835	128.6	36.4
Cayuga	92	477	44.4	19.9	88	3 143	1 065.7	155.1	182	1 977	89.5	25.5
Chautauqua	194	1 108	87.5	33.3	197	9 474	5 107.5	428.6	347	4 735	208.7	57.7
Chemung	111	774	83.5	36.1	85	5 495	1 247.0	278.8	202	3 534	154.5	43.3
Chenango	64	316	26.3	8.8	74	3 443	1 661.4	165.3	94	769	34.7	10.0
Clinton	128	734	67.1	26.7	78	3 161	1 279.4	138.5	187	2 648	139.2	38.3
Columbia	175	562	73.5	27.5	73	1 290	462.6	53.7	161	1 419	72.7	20.8
Cortland	82	1 036	99.7	51.1	66	3 163	711.4	146.5	134	2 574	101.0	28.7
Delaware	75	219	21.2	5.8	36	3 593	1 557.2	195.7	124	1 060	44.6	12.4
Dutchess	775	4 010	624.7	224.1	198	8 544	2 481.9	668.2	784	9 107	499.5	136.0
Erie	2 138	28 912	3 598.2	1 656.1	1 008	42 606	15 835.4	2 250.2	2 279	41 143	1 871.9	551.5
Essex	71	D	D	D	28	782	213.1	56.6	201	2 360	150.3	47.2
Franklin	65	410	33.4	17.3	28	460	250.2	19.9	115	846	51.2	13.0
Fulton	77	300	26.2	8.9	71	1 724	712.2	66.3	131	1 209	56.1	15.8

1. Establishment subject to federal tax.

Table B. States and Counties — Health Care and Social Assistance, Other Services, Nonemployer Businesses, and Residential Construction

STATE County	Health care and social assistance, 2012				Other services, 2012				Nonemployer businesses, 2014		Value of residential construction authorized by building permits, 2015	
	Number of establish-ments	Number of employees	Receipts (mil dol)	Annual payroll (mil dol)	Number of establish-ments	Number of employees	Receipts (mil dol)	Annual payroll (mil dol)	Number	Receipts (mil dol)	New Construction ($1,000)	Number of housing units
	159	160	161	162	163	164	165	166	167	168	169	170
NEW JERSEY—Cont'd												
Mercer	1 165	28 970	2 981.0	1 326.6	815	6 403	1 245.5	239.1	23 914	1 386.6	107 634	896
Middlesex	2 195	46 302	5 084.5	2 039.8	1 569	10 342	1 635.7	398.2	53 731	3 041.2	387 679	2 990
Monmouth	2 382	40 905	4 809.5	1 842.3	1 477	8 532	738.0	223.9	52 370	3 472.3	281 564	1 399
Morris	1 727	34 457	4 235.4	1 784.5	1 200	7 548	802.0	232.2	41 655	2 922.4	243 864	2 262
Ocean	1 537	30 984	3 185.9	1 246.7	1 061	5 433	489.4	129.6	38 545	2 144.7	483 404	2 621
Passaic	1 431	25 884	2 516.8	1 059.9	956	4 962	443.6	118.5	37 023	1 903.5	60 776	507
Salem	165	3 312	319.9	122.3	100	386	29.1	7.5	2 807	127.6	4 429	43
Somerset	1 173	21 653	2 475.7	980.8	714	4 882	643.1	156.7	26 211	1 787.9	155 205	1 551
Sussex	361	6 319	551.2	232.3	300	1 285	112.4	33.1	10 861	594.0	34 759	216
Union	1 551	31 943	3 370.8	1 367.2	1 188	6 710	646.0	211.4	41 051	2 333.0	187 006	2 185
Warren	295	4 571	543.1	218.3	222	1 095	112.9	29.0	6 919	352.7	29 527	289
NEW MEXICO	4 967	116 557	11 236.6	4 588.0	2 962	17 464	1 798.6	501.4	121 343	4 827.8	872 141	4 599
Bernalillo	1 893	48 404	5 278.0	2 143.7	1 096	7 326	750.0	217.2	39 958	1 647.8	264 522	1 291
Catron	7	120	2.7	1.7	5	D	D	D	363	12.3	NA	NA
Chaves	176	3 778	331.1	133.6	79	396	33.7	9.6	3 120	137.5	12 446	70
Cibola	49	1 532	150.8	53.9	23	85	7.3	2.0	1 085	30.6	NA	NA
Colfax	39	593	52.5	25.4	28	87	8.6	2.1	804	30.3	4 956	14
Curry	118	2 829	225.6	87.1	76	468	40.0	9.4	1 890	82.0	14 397	58
De Baca	5	D	D	D	3	D	D	D	120	4.0	NA	NA
Dona Ana	496	12 122	1 010.7	418.4	234	1 124	86.4	26.3	12 134	457.5	150 247	760
Eddy	114	2 875	275.8	112.9	85	501	48.4	12.5	2 499	128.2	36 148	252
Grant	81	1 645	139.1	58.5	45	172	10.9	2.9	1 541	43.4	2 639	15
Guadalupe	9	D	D	D	9	D	D	D	154	5.2	NA	NA
Harding	1	D	D	D	NA	NA	NA	NA	58	2.8	NA	NA
Hidalgo	10	133	7.6	3.3	3	D	D	D	208	10.0	NA	NA
Lea	112	2 329	207.9	78.7	105	800	122.2	31.3	3 076	203.4	42 090	420
Lincoln	47	598	63.8	25.4	40	204	14.8	3.9	1 899	71.6	15 345	61
Los Alamos	67	1 095	102.6	41.2	24	203	11.2	2.8	1 078	37.5	3 034	9
Luna	50	855	76.3	30.1	28	83	6.6	1.6	1 002	29.9	1 194	7
McKinley	107	4 407	374.3	155.3	78	469	55.3	10.8	3 912	79.1	1 150	4
Mora	5	119	4.3	2.5	4	D	D	D	306	6.7	NA	NA
Otero	101	2 241	210.4	81.4	67	357	21.3	6.3	3 203	105.6	0	0
Quay	26	406	37.9	11.9	23	112	13.1	2.8	375	14.0	NA	NA
Rio Arriba	84	1 878	141.5	63.0	23	115	12.2	3.3	1 941	59.4	0	0
Roosevelt	32	752	57.3	23.2	17	69	8.1	1.7	768	33.0	3 898	30
Sandoval	201	3 058	284.8	107.2	109	583	45.2	16.1	7 825	275.3	165 626	918
San Juan	275	6 819	682.5	291.7	226	1 571	164.1	54.5	5 266	245.0	28 033	118
San Miguel	73	2 950	178.1	80.2	28	150	7.5	2.1	1 390	39.6	0	0
Santa Fe	513	8 697	961.0	384.4	335	1 892	268.6	66.4	16 248	750.3	26 627	110
Sierra	20	784	40.2	19.4	19	106	10.1	2.1	711	22.0	0	0
Socorro	29	736	48.7	24.6	12	D	D	D	753	19.5	345	4
Taos	103	1 476	120.9	53.7	57	229	18.3	5.3	3 342	103.7	8 614	74
Torrance	21	273	10.0	5.1	8	D	D	D	806	26.7	NA	NA
Union	13	D	D	D	10	34	2.9	0.6	296	8.6	NA	NA
Valencia	90	2 685	117.5	57.7	63	D	D	D	3 212	105.3	9 323	86
NEW YORK	56 734	1 468 987	155 666.1	65 180.0	45 646	271 689	39 709.2	9 395.1	1 674 297	84 227.0	10 826 337	74 611
Albany	1 017	33 297	3 522.5	1 396.7	810	5 994	691.9	220.5	17 822	904.0	226 758	1 097
Allegany	100	1 793	119.8	50.7	75	263	20.0	4.4	2 530	88.5	6 149	49
Bronx	2 145	98 945	10 001.3	4 584.1	1 757	8 242	782.4	224.0	116 145	3 288.4	570 944	4 682
Broome	435	14 852	1 527.8	612.6	341	1 937	151.1	43.6	10 066	422.8	24 849	152
Cattaraugus	175	3 585	324.5	123.1	123	666	53.8	13.7	3 838	140.9	10 890	77
Cayuga	198	4 036	302.4	136.8	131	518	41.1	9.8	4 210	160.8	17 052	108
Chautauqua	279	8 791	623.9	263.5	253	1 448	105.7	24.1	6 987	260.7	14 661	79
Chemung	211	6 421	621.6	294.0	128	670	57.3	15.6	3 893	141.6	20 143	78
Chenango	107	2 025	158.6	65.3	77	256	22.5	6.4	2 796	108.4	13 027	263
Clinton	239	5 147	499.7	231.6	116	560	50.1	13.0	3 985	159.8	23 116	145
Columbia	153	3 929	330.5	150.5	99	335	35.2	9.5	5 990	267.9	40 067	209
Cortland	127	3 591	231.6	106.1	93	401	35.2	9.0	2 368	88.8	8 865	73
Delaware	114	2 167	152.1	63.3	83	417	75.1	10.5	3 579	136.9	8 304	47
Dutchess	901	18 607	2 004.6	847.0	591	2 592	279.2	73.3	21 043	981.7	69 689	293
Erie	2 675	74 944	7 532.5	3 154.4	1 752	11 023	1 059.9	283.5	46 740	2 111.8	285 488	1 482
Essex	151	1 978	140.3	61.6	67	282	29.4	7.4	3 053	151.0	27 779	90
Franklin	170	3 276	285.0	126.0	72	225	19.5	5.0	2 773	101.5	10 478	58
Fulton	182	4 128	260.4	113.7	85	486	38.5	11.5	2 818	103.8	9 282	55

Table B. States and Counties — Government Employment and Payroll, and Local Government Finances

STATE County	Full-time equivalent employees	March payroll (dollars)	Adminis-tration, judicial, and legal	Police and Corrections	Fire Protection	Highways and transpor-tation	Health and Welfare	Natural resources and utilities	Education and libraries	Total (mil dol)	Inter-govern-mental (mil dol)	Total (mil dol)	Per capita[1] Total	Per capita[1] Property
	171	172	173	174	175	176	177	178	179	180	181	182	183	184
NEW JERSEY—Cont'd														
Mercer	15 352	84 285 619	4.4	12.4	3.3	2.0	4.4	4.9	64.8	2 164.5	711.0	1 168.1	3 172	3 117
Middlesex	26 592	147 425 663	4.2	13.0	2.6	1.8	4.3	3.9	68.2	3 819.6	965.9	2 247.0	2 730	2 672
Monmouth	27 427	142 190 760	5.3	14.3	0.7	3.0	5.2	3.7	66.3	3 459.7	822.0	2 117.8	3 365	3 308
Morris	19 889	108 738 326	4.6	10.9	0.8	2.8	3.7	5.8	68.0	2 618.5	372.1	1 893.1	3 801	3 744
Ocean	20 430	99 202 051	5.5	14.5	0.4	3.0	4.9	5.2	63.9	2 394.3	580.3	1 531.1	2 638	2 603
Passaic	15 817	88 473 333	5.1	16.3	5.0	2.0	8.1	4.7	57.7	2 251.4	742.8	1 305.1	2 595	2 566
Salem	3 305	15 720 003	5.8	12.2	0.0	2.4	4.8	2.4	69.6	394.8	172.3	152.1	2 313	2 287
Somerset	13 026	68 430 732	3.9	11.5	0.6	3.4	3.0	2.1	73.5	1 611.4	277.0	1 174.0	3 583	3 530
Sussex	5 561	30 640 722	5.9	8.8	0.2	3.9	3.0	1.3	75.3	772.0	189.2	484.5	3 286	3 255
Union	23 222	130 750 946	5.8	13.4	5.4	2.2	5.9	2.3	63.3	3 230.4	1 130.6	1 723.2	3 168	3 100
Warren	4 346	20 547 388	6.3	9.9	0.9	3.6	6.8	2.0	68.4	536.8	183.8	292.4	2 716	2 688
NEW MEXICO	X	X	X	X	X	X	X	X	X	X	X	X	X	X
Bernalillo	22 833	89 838 327	6.2	16.3	6.5	6.3	5.2	6.3	51.7	2 451.4	1 173.3	882.0	1 310	743
Catron	146	386 239	12.7	8.6	0.0	7.4	4.7	1.5	64.1	15.7	10.9	2.6	698	511
Chaves	2 443	7 710 245	4.6	11.3	4.7	3.4	1.7	6.7	65.0	249.1	177.0	44.9	682	436
Cibola	909	2 491 571	7.4	11.5	1.3	2.3	1.9	3.3	70.0	97.5	46.9	12.3	451	248
Colfax	652	2 023 377	9.7	9.4	4.3	3.0	9.7	10.8	51.3	63.7	33.7	19.3	1 463	839
Curry	2 120	6 374 697	3.9	9.1	4.6	2.6	2.3	2.7	74.0	176.6	105.3	49.5	991	345
De Baca	134	371 334	8.8	11.3	0.0	8.7	3.7	10.9	56.5	13.8	7.8	2.5	1 319	841
Dona Ana	7 916	26 726 295	5.8	10.4	2.7	2.6	2.1	5.9	66.7	732.8	425.3	209.7	978	447
Eddy	2 143	8 178 370	5.4	14.2	5.2	4.3	2.1	6.4	59.3	275.0	129.3	115.7	2 126	1 225
Grant	1 747	5 905 715	4.3	7.8	1.4	2.5	44.2	2.7	35.9	187.1	80.4	29.7	1 009	473
Guadalupe	390	1 120 471	7.2	4.4	2.0	4.0	2.5	2.3	74.8	29.2	18.8	6.1	1 319	617
Harding	70	190 631	18.3	3.6	0.0	12.0	4.9	3.4	55.3	10.0	6.0	3.0	4 246	2 506
Hidalgo	293	795 504	9.1	17.5	0.0	4.5	3.0	5.4	58.2	28.3	19.6	4.7	976	778
Lea	3 191	11 349 323	4.4	10.8	3.6	2.9	15.4	4.7	55.7	413.1	170.9	153.5	2 314	1 380
Lincoln	853	2 783 245	8.5	11.0	3.3	4.9	5.2	9.6	53.8	99.8	41.5	37.7	1 857	1 135
Los Alamos	1 400	5 075 436	10.8	6.3	17.0	4.7	1.3	11.9	40.5	138.8	77.2	49.3	2 712	875
Luna	1 233	3 637 272	6.8	12.9	1.8	1.9	2.6	2.4	66.6	103.9	67.8	23.4	936	513
McKinley	3 373	9 383 425	3.6	7.5	2.2	1.6	1.9	3.4	78.5	249.0	155.9	62.8	861	271
Mora	208	516 517	10.0	3.6	0.0	4.3	0.8	0.5	79.2	16.8	10.9	2.4	506	430
Otero	1 662	5 122 202	6.3	14.5	0.3	2.5	2.3	4.7	67.9	147.4	86.7	40.4	612	307
Quay	563	1 605 317	7.9	9.3	0.4	3.2	4.0	8.7	65.3	54.3	38.6	8.0	912	461
Rio Arriba	1 378	4 062 743	9.2	7.6	1.7	2.7	5.6	3.5	67.3	133.9	69.5	50.2	1 244	819
Roosevelt	849	2 598 517	4.7	9.9	3.2	3.4	1.0	3.2	73.2	65.0	40.9	14.6	714	505
Sandoval	3 959	13 152 644	7.2	11.4	4.7	3.3	1.2	5.4	66.3	399.2	201.9	135.8	1 002	605
San Juan	5 857	21 149 302	4.2	11.0	2.6	2.0	1.9	8.4	68.4	491.8	290.9	126.9	987	702
San Miguel	1 294	3 946 008	6.9	7.5	1.7	1.8	1.8	6.1	72.8	102.3	63.7	27.0	933	408
Santa Fe	4 848	18 022 225	9.3	12.0	6.4	3.8	4.1	9.6	48.1	527.4	253.9	199.3	1 361	807
Sierra	644	2 455 286	6.7	6.0	0.0	1.9	22.5	6.1	54.0	49.9	22.0	12.6	1 060	582
Socorro	721	1 882 356	6.5	9.1	3.0	3.6	4.4	6.7	63.5	61.4	43.7	9.7	551	305
Taos	1 245	3 508 311	12.0	9.6	1.7	3.3	3.5	5.5	61.6	118.8	59.8	45.9	1 400	624
Torrance	904	2 576 995	5.9	5.6	0.5	2.0	1.4	1.7	82.4	69.5	50.0	14.8	923	704
Union	203	666 897	11.2	10.4	3.2	8.9	2.6	4.7	56.6	23.5	13.2	5.9	1 327	768
Valencia	2 378	6 663 270	5.6	7.4	1.3	1.2	2.2	2.4	79.8	195.8	120.3	56.4	736	383
NEW YORK	X	X	X	X	X	X	X	X	X	X	X	X	X	X
Albany	12 459	58 755 137	5.6	15.4	3.5	2.8	8.7	5.3	57.2	1 776.2	540.6	885.9	2 900	2 024
Allegany	2 326	8 539 230	7.1	8.0	0.7	8.2	7.3	2.7	64.1	300.9	162.2	113.9	2 356	1 929
Bronx	(3)	(3)	(3)	(3)	(3)	(3)	(3)	(3)	(3)	(3)	(3)	(3)	(3)	(3)
Broome	9 618	36 733 525	4.9	8.4	2.7	4.4	10.5	3.0	64.3	1 182.8	494.6	520.5	2 628	1 756
Cattaraugus	4 623	18 563 190	6.2	8.6	1.7	8.0	12.2	3.6	59.1	526.9	273.4	184.2	2 318	1 675
Cayuga	3 237	14 564 325	6.1	8.2	3.3	5.0	9.9	3.2	63.1	427.9	185.0	169.5	2 131	1 441
Chautauqua	6 787	27 243 053	4.8	7.7	2.9	6.8	9.0	2.9	65.0	772.7	364.8	268.8	2 013	1 539
Chemung	3 853	14 858 297	5.0	9.7	2.9	4.0	13.2	3.8	59.7	476.3	219.3	175.3	1 971	1 236
Chenango	2 731	10 005 930	6.4	7.7	1.8	9.2	7.9	1.6	64.4	295.2	157.3	105.1	2 106	1 541
Clinton	3 949	16 260 748	5.3	6.0	0.9	6.0	11.3	2.6	65.0	458.8	198.9	190.2	2 329	1 643
Columbia	3 025	13 243 189	8.0	8.1	0.4	9.6	12.9	2.0	57.7	374.6	114.6	212.1	3 394	2 596
Cortland	2 146	9 594 343	7.0	14.5	2.0	8.9	10.2	5.2	50.7	258.6	118.1	110.0	2 223	1 645
Delaware	2 262	8 403 397	8.5	6.5	0.1	11.8	10.9	1.5	59.1	286.6	118.1	136.3	2 410	1 645
Dutchess	12 054	60 953 575	5.6	9.6	3.0	3.7	5.7	1.9	69.4	1 683.1	521.2	964.5	3 244	2 611
Erie	35 259	161 616 876	3.7	12.8	3.3	2.9	5.3	5.1	65.4	5 298.2	2 255.2	2 176.7	2 368	1 547
Essex	1 990	7 313 826	9.9	6.1	1.3	9.8	14.0	4.4	53.3	255.8	76.1	132.5	3 401	2 621
Franklin	2 713	9 538 618	5.8	5.4	0.9	6.2	10.0	2.2	68.0	305.3	153.8	104.0	2 008	1 575
Fulton	2 664	9 331 227	4.7	7.9	2.7	4.8	13.2	1.3	64.4	301.1	138.4	121.2	2 207	1 595

1. Based on the resident population estimated as of July 1 of the year shown. 3. Bronx, Kings, Queens, and Richmond counties are included with New York county.

STATE County	Local government finances, 2012 (cont.)									Government employment, 2014			Presidential election,[2] 2012		
	Direct general expenditure							Debt outstanding					Percent of vote cast:		
			Percent of total for:												
	Total (mil dol)	Per capita[1] (dollars)	Education	Health and hospitals	Police protection	Public welfare	Highways	Total (mil dol)	Per capita[1] (dollars)	Federal civilian	Federal military	State and local	Democratic	Republican	All other
	185	186	187	188	189	190	191	192	193	194	195	196	197	198	199
NEW JERSEY—Cont'd															
Mercer	2 145.5	5 825	52.3	0.9	5.3	4.3	1.4	1 928.9	5 237	2 362	741	39 569	67.4	31.4	1.2
Middlesex	3 874.0	4 707	54.1	1.1	5.8	2.4	1.7	4 163.4	5 059	2 113	1 766	52 815	60.4	38.5	1.1
Monmouth	3 411.5	5 420	54.8	1.1	6.0	2.1	2.9	2 733.3	4 343	2 087	1 485	33 368	47.6	51.3	1.1
Morris	2 580.5	5 182	55.7	1.5	5.7	1.5	3.1	2 056.9	4 130	5 402	1 102	26 034	45.5	53.6	0.9
Ocean	2 437.7	4 200	51.2	0.6	6.8	3.2	3.4	2 209.0	3 805	2 969	1 344	25 107	40.2	58.6	1.3
Passaic	2 262.2	4 499	45.8	2.5	6.7	5.0	2.2	1 387.8	2 760	1 048	1 014	28 080	60.4	38.7	0.8
Salem	408.1	6 204	53.4	1.9	3.9	2.2	4.2	399.9	6 081	151	129	4 193	51.2	47.2	1.6
Somerset	1 638.3	4 999	58.6	2.0	5.3	1.0	4.6	1 441.4	4 399	1 719	668	16 205	52.5	46.4	1.1
Sussex	733.7	4 976	63.4	1.4	3.9	2.2	4.2	551.0	3 737	320	295	7 582	38.9	59.6	1.5
Union	3 281.6	6 033	53.5	2.9	6.2	1.6	1.8	2 546.6	4 681	1 469	1 115	32 147	63.7	35.5	0.9
Warren	573.8	5 330	58.0	1.8	4.0	3.5	3.9	237.2	2 203	216	214	5 704	42.2	56.2	1.7
NEW MEXICO	X	X	X	X	X	X	X	X	X	29 538	17 563	161 766	56.9	41.8	1.3
Bernalillo	2 337.5	3 471	48.0	2.0	9.0	1.6	5.0	3 333.0	4 949	13 800	5 185	53 770	60.0	38.7	1.3
Catron	17.1	4 674	36.7	2.0	4.1	0.6	7.9	9.9	2 693	100	0	215	31.4	66.2	2.4
Chaves	248.0	3 771	52.6	0.0	6.6	2.3	4.4	107.2	1 630	255	173	3 989	37.1	61.7	1.2
Cibola	102.5	3 749	38.6	30.4	2.4	3.0	2.9	41.6	1 521	320	65	2 917	64.1	34.4	1.5
Colfax	65.2	4 931	40.3	5.9	6.4	0.7	7.3	52.6	3 979	56	32	1 431	54.7	43.9	1.4
Curry	185.3	3 711	57.6	0.2	5.2	0.7	4.3	71.0	1 422	837	4 837	2 512	32.3	66.5	1.2
De Baca	13.6	7 072	35.8	17.8	4.5	0.1	4.9	5.2	2 717	15	0	492	33.4	64.8	0.9
Dona Ana	719.6	3 356	57.5	1.3	6.7	1.9	4.1	440.1	2 052	3 640	557	16 817	58.1	40.5	1.3
Eddy	252.5	4 640	47.2	2.8	8.5	1.6	5.2	120.4	2 213	611	144	3 226	36.6	62.2	1.2
Grant	196.6	6 690	26.5	40.7	4.6	2.8	2.6	102.5	3 489	207	74	3 292	59.2	39.3	1.5
Guadalupe	26.2	5 682	37.7	0.7	4.4	6.5	5.2	22.0	4 789	24	10	400	70.9	28.2	0.9
Harding	10.9	15 478	46.4	1.6	4.0	0.1	7.1	5.9	8 396	17	0	91	41.5	57.2	1.3
Hidalgo	27.3	5 693	43.1	2.0	15.9	0.6	2.6	9.5	1 987	292	12	385	50.9	48.0	1.1
Lea	416.5	6 278	45.5	12.6	5.6	1.1	7.8	219.2	3 304	88	177	3 573	27.4	71.6	1.0
Lincoln	102.5	5 048	37.3	4.2	6.6	0.5	5.9	89.0	4 382	103	51	1 087	36.5	61.9	1.7
Los Alamos	168.1	9 258	31.9	0.0	4.1	1.6	6.7	190.8	10 505	253	49	1 640	52.6	45.7	1.6
Luna	99.5	3 974	55.3	2.0	7.7	1.0	3.5	25.7	1 027	531	63	1 567	51.7	46.4	1.9
McKinley	255.3	3 497	63.0	1.1	4.0	1.8	3.8	145.8	1 997	2 446	191	5 004	71.4	27.5	1.1
Mora	17.2	3 658	55.5	0.3	2.6	0.0	3.0	10.3	2 189	44	12	254	78.6	20.6	0.8
Otero	149.2	2 258	50.7	0.5	8.4	3.1	9.6	138.3	2 094	1 706	4 209	4 542	39.6	58.8	1.6
Quay	53.7	6 124	48.7	5.9	4.7	3.6	4.1	28.0	3 197	47	22	888	38.7	59.2	2.1
Rio Arriba	130.8	3 245	54.4	0.5	4.5	1.1	2.9	101.6	2 519	324	103	4 469	75.0	24.1	0.9
Roosevelt	64.4	3 152	61.8	0.1	6.6	2.2	4.8	18.8	922	53	48	2 177	34.3	64.2	1.6
Sandoval	384.6	2 836	51.6	0.1	6.8	1.0	6.1	599.5	4 422	359	357	7 255	55.7	43.0	1.3
San Juan	551.0	4 287	55.6	3.3	6.3	1.2	4.3	2 140.3	16 652	1 496	321	9 843	38.8	59.9	1.3
San Miguel	108.9	3 769	60.5	0.3	4.2	0.7	4.8	73.4	2 539	143	70	3 663	79.7	19.1	1.1
Santa Fe	578.2	3 950	45.8	1.3	6.0	2.2	3.5	916.2	6 259	956	385	16 196	76.9	21.9	1.2
Sierra	50.5	4 245	27.8	29.9	10.1	1.0	8.1	29.4	2 475	109	29	767	42.9	55.0	2.1
Socorro	72.0	4 091	47.8	0.2	3.8	0.0	4.6	25.8	1 466	192	44	2 420	59.5	38.4	2.1
Taos	129.6	3 953	49.9	1.4	3.2	2.6	3.3	125.3	3 823	283	85	1 934	81.8	17.0	1.2
Torrance	69.7	4 348	66.8	0.8	2.8	0.8	2.9	231.1	14 425	75	39	946	44.5	53.8	1.7
Union	21.1	4 754	42.4	8.0	5.7	1.5	6.6	13.0	2 941	50	0	288	28.2	70.4	1.3
Valencia	184.9	2 413	64.8	0.5	5.8	0.6	3.4	196.9	2 570	106	194	4 015	53.2	45.5	1.4
NEW YORK	X	X	X	X	X	X	X	X	X	114 773	58 273	1 282 136	62.9	36.0	1.0
Albany	1 817.9	5 952	40.0	3.9	5.2	11.2	3.9	2 211.1	7 239	5 006	671	58 924	63.8	34.4	1.8
Allegany	309.4	6 398	47.0	2.5	1.8	9.8	11.7	294.0	6 080	116	71	3 925	38.2	60.0	1.8
Bronx	(3)		(3)	(3)	(3)	(3)	(3)	(3)		4 282	2 371	16 658	88.7	10.9	0.4
Broome	1 232.1	6 221	48.7	3.4	2.9	12.0	3.8	1 229.8	6 209	527	306	18 498	53.2	45.2	1.6
Cattaraugus	550.0	6 922	49.6	5.9	2.3	13.2	7.5	513.3	6 460	241	149	9 431	43.9	54.5	1.6
Cayuga	442.3	5 560	52.0	4.7	3.2	9.3	6.8	308.3	3 875	135	122	5 612	53.3	44.8	1.8
Chautauqua	806.8	6 042	50.1	3.0	2.9	12.8	6.0	665.7	4 985	301	205	8 906	49.6	48.6	1.8
Chemung	467.0	5 252	42.9	3.0	3.0	18.1	8.9	490.6	5 518	210	136	6 050	48.8	50.0	1.1
Chenango	297.2	5 953	57.1	3.1	1.6	8.2	7.3	216.1	4 329	89	79	4 122	48.4	49.6	2.0
Clinton	495.0	6 062	54.0	4.9	1.9	11.3	5.6	401.8	4 921	695	122	7 134	60.7	37.8	1.6
Columbia	381.3	6 100	48.0	4.5	2.2	13.2	9.0	225.4	3 607	160	98	4 594	55.9	42.5	1.6
Cortland	277.6	5 611	47.3	4.6	3.0	10.4	8.5	199.2	4 027	108	75	3 886	54.2	44.2	1.6
Delaware	281.8	5 961	44.9	3.5	1.5	9.4	12.5	208.3	4 406	124	73	4 536	46.4	51.6	2.0
Dutchess	1 642.8	5 525	55.5	3.6	3.3	7.6	4.0	1 417.6	4 768	1 186	451	18 689	53.7	45.1	1.2
Erie	5 644.5	6 141	44.0	10.5	3.7	9.5	3.2	5 158.7	5 613	8 204	1 728	65 229	58.0	40.5	1.5
Essex	273.6	7 022	36.7	6.8	1.3	10.7	9.0	306.9	7 877	334	59	4 055	55.9	42.6	1.5
Franklin	335.9	6 486	56.1	3.6	1.2	11.1	5.6	277.2	5 352	159	74	7 574	60.4	38.2	1.4
Fulton	288.3	5 250	49.7	2.7	2.5	16.8	5.0	192.0	3 496	77	87	3 431	44.5	53.7	1.8

1. Based on the resident population estimated as of July 1 of the year shown.　2. © 2013 Election Data Services, Inc. All rights reserved.　3. Bronx, Kings, Queens, and Richmond counties are included with New York county.

Table B. States and Counties — **Land Area and Population**

				Population, 2015				Population and population characteristics, 2014										
								Race alone or in combination, not Hispanic or Latino (percent)					Age (percent)					
STATE/ County code	CBSA code[1]	County type[2]	STATE County	Land area,[3] (sq km) 2010	Total persons 2015	Rank	Per square kilometer	White	Black	American Indian, Alaska Native	Asian and Pacific Islander	Percent Hispanic or Latino[4]	Under 5 years	5 to 17 years	18 to 24 years	25 to 34 years	35 to 44 years	45 to 54 years
				1	2	3	4	5	6	7	8	9	10	11	12	13	14	15

			NEW YORK—Cont'd															
36 037	12860	4	Genesee	1 277	58 937	877	46.2	92.4	3.8	1.5	1.0	3.0	5.2	15.5	9.2	11.7	11.2	15.4
36 039	...	6	Greene	1 676	47 625	1 026	28.4	87.5	6.6	0.8	1.3	5.5	4.4	12.8	9.7	10.7	11.4	15.5
36 041	...	8	Hamilton	4 448	4 712	2 854	1.1	96.9	1.4	0.8	0.8	1.4	3.4	11.7	6.1	7.2	9.0	14.7
36 043	46540	2	Herkimer	3 656	63 100	838	17.3	96.0	1.7	0.5	0.9	2.1	5.4	15.7	9.1	11.0	10.9	14.4
36 045	48060	4	Jefferson	3 286	117 635	525	35.8	84.4	7.0	1.0	2.8	7.3	8.7	16.1	13.0	17.0	11.5	11.4
36 047	35620	1	Kings	183	2 636 735	8	14 408.4	37.0	31.9	0.6	12.8	19.5	7.6	15.7	9.4	18.0	13.9	12.3
36 049	...	6	Lewis	3 301	26 957	1 536	8.2	96.9	1.3	0.6	0.7	1.7	6.3	17.3	8.2	11.3	11.4	14.4
36 051	40380	1	Livingston	1 636	64 717	813	39.6	91.9	3.1	0.6	1.9	3.4	4.3	14.4	15.8	10.2	10.7	14.7
36 053	45060	2	Madison	1 696	71 849	752	42.4	94.8	2.4	1.0	1.3	2.0	4.7	15.6	13.2	10.4	10.7	15.0
36 055	40380	1	Monroe	1 702	749 600	84	440.4	73.2	15.8	0.6	4.3	8.1	5.6	15.8	10.8	13.7	11.3	14.0
36 057	11220	4	Montgomery	1 044	49 642	984	47.5	84.6	2.6	0.6	1.1	12.6	5.9	16.7	8.3	12.1	11.7	13.5
36 059	35620	1	Nassau	737	1 361 350	28	1 847.2	63.3	11.8	0.4	9.7	16.1	5.4	16.7	9.0	11.3	12.2	15.3
36 061	35620	1	New York	59	1 644 518	20	27 873.2	48.7	13.6	0.5	13.3	25.9	5.2	9.5	9.6	22.7	14.7	12.7
36 063	15380	1	Niagara	1 353	212 652	305	157.2	88.2	8.2	1.6	1.6	2.6	5.2	15.2	9.1	11.9	11.3	15.0
36 065	46540	2	Oneida	3 140	232 500	281	74.0	84.5	7.1	0.6	4.2	5.3	5.8	15.5	9.9	12.2	11.2	14.3
36 067	45060	2	Onondaga	2 016	468 463	146	232.4	79.9	12.4	1.3	4.3	4.6	5.8	16.1	10.7	13.1	11.3	14.3
36 069	40380	1	Ontario	1 668	109 561	550	65.7	92.0	3.0	0.6	1.7	4.3	5.0	15.9	9.6	10.6	11.1	15.3
36 071	35620	2	Orange	2 102	377 647	179	179.7	67.8	10.8	0.7	3.3	19.4	6.5	19.4	10.8	11.1	12.4	15.0
36 073	40380	1	Orleans	1 013	41 582	1 133	41.0	88.1	7.2	1.1	0.8	4.7	4.9	15.3	9.8	12.0	11.5	16.0
36 075	35620	2	Oswego	2 465	120 146	515	48.7	95.6	1.4	0.9	1.1	2.3	5.5	16.1	11.7	11.8	11.2	15.5
36 077	36580	6	Otsego	2 594	60 636	863	23.4	93.1	2.5	0.6	1.9	3.5	4.1	12.6	17.7	9.5	9.5	13.5
36 079	35620	1	Putnam	597	99 042	597	165.9	82.1	3.0	0.4	3.0	13.1	4.5	16.9	8.5	10.1	12.4	18.0
36 081	35620	1	Queens	281	2 339 150	11	8 324.4	27.3	19.1	0.8	26.9	28.0	6.3	14.1	9.0	16.3	14.3	14.1
36 083	10580	2	Rensselaer	1 690	160 266	401	94.8	86.1	7.7	0.6	3.1	4.5	5.3	14.8	10.8	13.5	11.8	14.6
36 085	35620	1	Richmond	151	474 558	144	3 142.8	63.7	10.4	0.5	8.8	18.1	5.8	16.4	9.2	13.0	13.1	14.7
36 087	35620	1	Rockland	449	326 037	205	726.1	64.6	12.2	0.4	7.2	17.2	7.5	20.2	9.4	11.4	11.2	13.5
36 089	36300	5	St. Lawrence	6 942	111 007	545	16.0	93.1	2.7	1.5	1.6	2.2	5.5	15.2	14.5	11.8	11.1	13.5
36 091	10580	2	Saratoga	2 098	226 249	287	107.8	92.2	2.2	0.5	3.1	3.0	5.1	16.0	8.4	11.6	13.0	15.9
36 093	10580	2	Schenectady	530	154 604	420	291.7	78.5	11.8	1.1	5.7	6.7	6.0	16.1	9.5	12.7	12.2	14.4
36 095	10580	2	Schoharie	1 611	31 330	1 402	19.4	94.3	1.8	0.7	1.1	3.1	4.6	14.2	11.3	10.0	10.9	14.8
36 097	...	6	Schuyler	850	18 186	1 908	21.4	97.4	1.6	0.7	0.8	1.7	5.1	14.5	8.1	10.6	11.2	15.2
36 099	42900	6	Seneca	838	34 833	1 308	41.6	90.7	5.6	0.8	1.0	3.1	5.1	15.0	9.4	13.0	11.3	14.1
36 101	18500	4	Steuben	3 602	97 631	604	27.1	95.2	2.2	0.7	1.8	1.6	5.7	16.6	8.3	11.3	11.5	14.5
36 103	35620	1	Suffolk	2 362	1 501 587	24	635.7	70.4	7.8	0.5	4.5	18.2	5.4	16.9	9.4	11.3	12.6	16.2
36 105	...	4	Sullivan	2 507	74 877	737	29.9	74.9	9.4	0.8	2.1	15.0	5.9	15.7	8.6	11.4	11.5	15.5
36 107	13780	2	Tioga	1 343	49 453	990	36.8	96.3	1.3	0.6	1.1	1.7	5.2	16.7	7.8	10.6	11.1	15.5
36 109	27060	3	Tompkins	1 229	104 926	565	85.4	80.5	5.0	0.8	11.9	4.7	4.2	11.2	27.8	12.7	9.8	10.7
36 111	28740	3	Ulster	2 912	180 143	358	61.9	81.9	6.9	0.8	2.7	9.7	4.5	14.0	9.9	11.9	12.0	15.4
36 113	24020	3	Warren	2 245	64 688	814	28.8	95.6	1.7	0.7	1.3	2.2	4.7	14.2	8.0	11.1	11.1	15.5
36 115	24020	3	Washington	2 153	62 230	845	28.9	93.6	3.4	0.6	0.8	2.5	4.9	14.9	8.6	11.9	12.3	15.6
36 117	40380	1	Wayne	1 564	91 446	637	58.5	92.1	4.1	0.7	1.1	4.0	5.4	16.6	8.3	10.9	11.6	15.2
36 119	35620	1	Westchester	1 115	976 396	47	875.7	56.3	14.4	0.5	6.8	23.7	5.7	17.2	8.9	11.4	13.1	15.2
36 121	...	6	Wyoming	1 535	41 013	1 151	26.7	90.4	5.9	0.6	0.7	3.2	4.8	14.4	8.3	13.8	12.9	16.0
36 123	40380	6	Yates	876	25 048	1 608	28.6	96.5	1.4	0.5	0.7	2.2	6.4	16.9	11.2	9.9	9.5	12.8
37 000	...	X	NORTH CAROLINA	125 920	10 042 802	X	79.8	65.6	22.4	1.7	3.2	9.0	6.1	16.9	9.9	13.0	13.1	13.8
37 001	15500	3	Alamance	1 098	158 276	406	144.1	66.8	19.7	0.8	1.9	12.1	5.8	17.1	9.9	11.9	12.5	14.2
37 003	25860	2	Alexander	673	37 325	1 244	55.5	88.6	6.5	0.6	1.3	4.4	5.0	16.0	7.9	10.9	13.0	14.8
37 005	...	9	Alleghany	609	10 837	2 368	17.8	84.0	2.1	0.7	0.9	9.5	4.3	13.8	7.2	8.7	11.2	14.3
37 007	...	1	Anson	1 376	25 759	1 569	18.7	45.8	48.3	1.0	1.2	3.5	4.9	15.6	9.2	13.4	12.8	14.1
37 009	...	9	Ashe	1 104	27 020	1 533	24.5	93.3	1.1	0.6	0.6	5.3	4.7	13.8	6.8	9.9	11.7	14.0
37 011	...	8	Avery	640	17 689	1 934	27.6	90.2	4.6	0.8	0.8	4.7	3.9	12.2	9.8	12.5	13.5	14.2
37 013	47820	6	Beaufort	2 142	47 651	1 025	22.2	67.1	25.5	0.6	0.7	7.5	5.4	15.7	7.5	9.8	11.5	13.0
37 015	...	9	Bertie	1 811	20 199	1 821	11.2	35.4	60.8	0.9	0.8	1.6	4.4	14.3	8.7	12.1	10.8	14.1
37 017	...	6	Bladen	2 264	34 318	1 322	15.2	55.9	34.8	2.7	0.6	7.7	5.1	16.4	8.3	10.7	12.0	13.3
37 019	34820	2	Brunswick	2 194	122 765	507	56.0	82.8	11.7	1.3	1.0	4.8	4.5	12.7	6.1	9.5	10.5	12.2
37 021	11700	2	Buncombe	1 701	253 178	263	148.8	85.5	7.3	1.0	1.7	6.5	5.3	14.1	8.4	13.6	13.1	13.3
37 023	25860	2	Burke	1 313	88 842	647	67.7	84.0	7.5	0.7	4.1	5.9	4.8	15.0	9.5	10.9	12.0	15.2
37 025	16740	1	Cabarrus	937	196 762	332	210.0	70.6	17.4	0.7	3.1	10.0	6.3	19.9	8.3	12.0	14.9	14.7
37 027	25860	2	Caldwell	1 221	81 287	686	66.6	89.3	5.7	0.7	0.8	5.0	5.1	16.0	8.1	10.4	12.9	15.4
37 029	21020	8	Camden	623	10 309	2 410	16.5	82.3	13.6	1.0	3.0	2.6	4.5	19.5	7.4	10.2	13.9	16.3
37 031	33980	4	Carteret	1 311	68 879	773	52.5	87.9	6.9	1.1	1.8	4.3	4.5	13.9	7.3	10.9	11.3	14.2
37 033	...	8	Caswell	1 101	22 941	1 685	20.8	62.7	34.3	0.8	0.6	3.6	4.7	14.3	7.8	10.8	12.0	15.1
37 035	25860	2	Catawba	1 033	155 056	416	150.1	78.2	9.5	0.6	4.3	8.9	5.7	17.2	8.7	11.1	13.0	14.7
37 037	20500	2	Chatham	1 767	70 928	761	40.1	72.6	13.2	0.7	2.1	12.8	4.8	15.5	6.4	9.1	11.9	13.8
37 039	...	9	Cherokee	1 180	27 178	1 524	23.0	93.8	2.1	2.7	0.9	2.8	4.4	13.5	6.5	8.7	10.5	12.9

1. CBSA = Core Based Statistical Area. See Appendix A for explanation. See Appendix B for list of metropolitan areas with component counties. Service of USDA Rural-Urban Continuum Codes. See Appendix A for definition. 3. Dry land or land partially or temporarily covered by water. 2. County type code from the Economic Research 4. May be of any race.

Table B. States and Counties — **Population and Households**

STATE County	55 to 64 years	65 to 74 years	75 years and over	Percent female	2000	2010	2000–2010	2010–2015	Births	Deaths	Net migration	Number	Persons per house-hold	Family house-holds	Female family house-holder[1]	One per-son
	16	17	18	19	20	21	22	23	24	25	26	27	28	29	30	31
NEW YORK—Cont'd																
Genesee	14.5	9.2	8.0	50.1	60 370	60 033	-0.6	-1.8	3 137	3 247	-1 029	23 967	2.45	67.0	9.4	27.0
Greene	15.5	11.7	8.2	47.9	48 195	49 218	2.1	-3.2	2 240	2 652	-1 122	18 102	2.49	64.4	10.2	30.5
Hamilton	21.0	16.6	10.2	49.3	5 379	4 843	-10.0	-2.7	176	309	9	1 639	2.85	65.2	6.3	29.0
Herkimer	14.7	10.3	8.5	50.7	64 427	64 486	0.1	-2.1	3 493	3 489	-1 359	26 583	2.37	64.5	11.7	28.9
Jefferson	10.1	7.0	5.2	47.7	111 738	116 232	4.0	1.2	11 491	4 703	-5 617	44 822	2.52	67.6	11.4	26.3
Kings	11.0	6.8	5.4	52.6	2 465 326	2 504 710	1.6	5.3	219 990	84 610	1 339	925 371	2.74	63.2	20.0	28.9
Lewis	14.5	9.0	7.7	49.4	26 944	27 074	0.5	-0.4	1 703	1 309	-567	10 726	2.50	70.7	8.8	23.5
Livingston	14.0	8.9	6.9	49.9	64 328	65 219	1.4	-0.8	2 839	2 774	-598	24 242	2.42	65.3	11.1	26.5
Madison	14.5	9.2	6.7	50.8	69 441	73 453	5.8	-2.2	3 560	3 166	-1 953	26 407	2.55	66.6	10.5	27.5
Monroe	13.2	8.5	7.0	51.7	735 343	744 402	1.2	0.7	44 410	33 898	-5 197	298 915	2.41	61.0	14.4	31.7
Montgomery	14.2	9.3	8.3	50.7	49 708	50 257	1.1	-1.2	3 071	2 987	-656	19 655	2.49	63.1	11.9	31.1
Nassau	13.7	8.6	7.8	51.5	1 334 544	1 339 762	0.4	1.6	74 159	57 419	7 416	441 912	3.01	76.6	12.0	19.8
New York	11.3	7.9	6.4	52.8	1 537 195	1 585 874	3.2	3.7	100 400	53 400	15 520	745 089	2.09	41.4	11.5	47.3
Niagara	15.0	9.5	7.9	51.3	219 846	216 487	-1.5	-1.8	11 430	12 326	-2 609	88 252	2.39	62.7	12.4	32.2
Oneida	13.6	9.3	8.2	50.2	235 469	234 890	-0.2	-1.0	13 904	13 024	-2 956	90 821	2.43	61.8	12.6	31.8
Onondaga	13.4	8.2	7.1	51.7	458 336	467 027	1.9	0.3	27 986	21 538	-4 623	185 089	2.43	61.3	13.6	31.6
Ontario	14.9	10.2	7.5	50.9	100 224	108 097	7.9	1.4	5 452	5 453	1 412	44 198	2.38	64.9	10.5	28.3
Orange	12.2	7.3	5.2	50.0	341 367	372 782	9.2	1.3	25 660	13 461	-7 076	124 901	2.90	71.7	12.1	23.8
Orleans	14.3	9.3	6.9	50.3	44 171	42 876	-2.9	-3.0	2 175	2 192	-1 276	15 894	2.47	67.4	14.2	27.0
Oswego	13.7	8.6	5.9	50.0	122 377	122 109	-0.2	-1.6	7 020	5 485	-3 315	45 300	2.57	66.5	12.5	25.4
Otsego	14.5	10.5	8.1	51.4	61 676	62 249	0.9	-2.6	2 767	3 141	-1 094	23 798	2.36	62.9	9.6	28.1
Putnam	14.8	9.0	5.8	50.2	95 745	99 750	4.2	-0.7	4 455	3 561	-1 544	34 164	2.85	76.9	9.5	19.7
Queens	12.3	7.5	6.1	51.5	2 229 379	2 230 541	0.1	4.9	159 979	75 367	29 029	780 069	2.89	67.4	16.2	26.3
Rensselaer	14.0	8.8	6.5	50.6	152 538	159 427	4.5	0.5	9 043	7 909	-191	63 995	2.40	61.6	12.1	29.8
Richmond	13.3	8.5	6.1	51.6	443 728	468 730	5.6	1.2	28 530	18 457	-3 539	165 079	2.81	74.2	14.4	22.6
Rockland	11.9	8.2	6.7	51.0	286 753	311 687	8.7	4.6	25 128	11 022	788	98 394	3.16	75.7	10.6	20.7
St. Lawrence	13.1	8.7	6.6	49.1	111 931	111 941	0.0	-0.8	6 463	5 370	-1 972	41 579	2.41	63.6	11.6	28.5
Saratoga	14.0	9.4	6.4	50.6	200 635	219 613	9.5	3.0	11 769	9 057	3 963	89 876	2.43	64.6	8.8	28.0
Schenectady	13.4	8.2	7.4	51.3	146 555	154 721	5.6	-0.1	9 394	7 895	-1 408	57 846	2.60	61.4	12.3	33.0
Schoharie	15.6	11.0	7.6	50.2	31 582	32 744	3.7	-4.3	1 405	1 444	-1 255	12 739	2.41	64.1	9.3	28.8
Schuyler	16.1	11.1	8.1	49.6	19 224	18 339	-4.6	-0.8	889	1 022	-70	7 759	2.32	63.3	8.2	28.3
Seneca	14.7	10.0	7.5	47.8	33 342	35 244	5.7	-1.2	2 003	1 670	-644	13 485	2.38	61.2	9.8	29.8
Steuben	14.6	9.7	7.7	50.4	98 726	98 994	0.3	-1.4	5 792	5 052	-2 042	41 285	2.35	62.7	10.3	30.9
Suffolk	13.1	8.6	6.7	50.7	1 419 369	1 493 291	5.2	0.6	83 659	62 034	-12 179	496 780	2.96	74.9	12.3	20.8
Sullivan	14.7	10.3	6.5	48.7	73 966	77 541	4.8	-3.4	4 499	3 796	-3 119	28 954	2.51	62.8	12.9	30.6
Tioga	15.1	10.1	7.8	50.3	51 784	51 123	-1.3	-3.3	2 677	2 220	-2 020	20 178	2.48	69.5	10.6	26.4
Tompkins	11.2	7.2	5.1	50.7	96 501	101 594	5.3	3.3	4 636	3 382	2 081	38 340	2.34	52.6	8.2	32.3
Ulster	15.0	10.0	7.4	50.2	177 749	182 531	2.7	-1.3	8 562	8 495	-2 337	69 388	2.45	63.9	11.0	30.1
Warren	15.5	11.4	8.4	51.1	63 303	65 705	3.8	-1.5	3 205	3 428	-732	27 699	2.32	63.9	12.0	29.1
Washington	14.6	10.0	7.2	48.2	61 042	63 216	3.6	-1.6	3 228	3 180	-910	24 165	2.46	69.0	12.0	24.9
Wayne	14.8	9.7	6.8	50.5	93 765	93 750	0.0	-2.5	5 211	4 368	-2 965	36 479	2.49	68.8	11.1	25.3
Westchester	12.9	8.2	7.5	51.7	923 459	949 092	2.8	2.9	56 334	37 027	9 658	342 956	2.73	69.6	13.0	26.6
Wyoming	14.4	9.3	6.2	45.7	43 424	42 131	-3.0	-2.7	2 035	1 854	-1 254	15 691	2.41	66.8	9.2	27.4
Yates	14.9	10.6	7.8	51.3	24 621	25 351	3.0	-1.2	1 630	1 306	-583	9 642	2.49	69.7	10.8	23.7
NORTH CAROLINA	12.5	8.7	6.0	51.3	8 049 313	9 535 692	18.5	5.3	630 511	432 400	297 064	3 742 514	2.54	66.4	13.8	27.9
Alamance	12.5	9.0	7.1	52.3	130 800	151 241	15.6	4.7	9 271	8 046	5 558	61 046	2.45	67.1	14.5	28.6
Alexander	13.6	11.5	7.4	49.2	33 603	37 193	10.7	0.4	1 874	1 823	-99	13 721	2.64	68.0	10.0	28.1
Alleghany	16.0	14.0	10.5	50.3	10 677	11 155	4.5	-2.9	481	661	-117	4 752	2.27	69.5	8.1	26.2
Anson	13.7	9.5	6.9	48.2	25 275	26 948	6.6	-4.4	1 357	1 534	-1 031	9 549	2.55	65.6	19.5	30.2
Ashe	15.3	13.6	10.0	50.4	24 384	27 281	11.9	-1.0	1 271	1 760	174	11 746	2.28	70.8	11.1	25.0
Avery	13.5	11.8	8.6	45.5	17 167	17 795	3.7	-0.6	756	978	109	7 174	2.13	67.7	7.7	26.3
Beaufort	15.6	13.1	8.4	51.9	44 958	47 773	6.3	-0.3	2 592	2 926	192	18 894	2.49	65.4	13.1	31.3
Bertie	15.7	10.6	9.2	49.9	19 773	21 293	7.7	-5.1	957	1 294	-820	7 662	2.53	64.5	18.1	32.0
Bladen	15.5	11.3	7.4	51.8	32 278	35 190	9.0	-2.5	1 880	2 083	-656	14 407	2.38	65.5	18.7	30.9
Brunswick	17.5	18.5	8.5	51.4	73 143	107 431	46.9	14.3	5 478	6 338	15 774	48 331	2.32	69.8	11.1	25.8
Buncombe	14.1	10.4	7.7	52.0	206 330	238 308	15.5	6.2	13 645	12 645	13 002	101 645	2.34	59.2	10.3	32.7
Burke	14.1	10.6	7.7	50.1	89 148	90 914	2.0	-2.3	4 486	5 297	-1 243	34 597	2.52	67.2	13.7	27.9
Cabarrus	11.3	7.5	5.0	51.2	131 063	178 182	36.0	10.4	12 172	7 548	13 635	65 693	2.79	72.5	12.1	23.6
Caldwell	14.3	10.9	7.0	50.6	77 415	83 029	7.3	-2.1	4 176	4 745	-1 112	31 354	2.59	65.8	11.9	31.2
Camden	13.4	9.2	5.6	49.9	6 885	9 980	45.0	3.3	471	341	214	3 609	2.79	77.8	14.1	18.6
Carteret	16.2	13.2	8.6	50.7	59 383	66 469	11.9	3.6	3 258	3 927	3 026	29 352	2.27	64.7	11.8	30.3
Caswell	15.8	11.7	7.8	49.2	23 501	23 719	0.9	-3.3	1 099	1 386	-597	8 608	2.57	71.0	15.3	25.9
Catawba	13.4	9.7	6.5	50.9	141 685	154 356	8.9	0.5	9 265	8 174	-470	58 424	2.60	69.4	12.3	25.1
Chatham	14.9	13.5	10.1	52.1	49 329	63 491	28.7	11.7	3 282	3 267	7 164	26 474	2.46	69.1	9.9	26.7
Cherokee	16.8	16.6	10.1	51.3	24 298	27 444	12.9	-1.0	1 141	1 876	449	10 503	2.54	67.9	10.1	28.0

1. No spouse present.

Table B. States and Counties — Population, Vital Statistics, Medicare, and Crime

STATE County	Persons in group quarters, 2015	Daytime population, 2010–2014 Number	Employ-ment/resi-dence ratio	Births, 2015 Total	Rate[1]	Deaths, 2015 Number	Rate[1]	Persons under 65 with no health insurance, 2014 Number	Percent	Medicare, 2015 Total Beneficiaries	Enrolled in Original Medicare	Enrolled in Medicare Advantage	Serious crimes known to police,[2] 2014 Total Number	Rate[3]
	32	33	34	35	36	37	38	39	40	41	42	43	44	45
NEW YORK—Cont'd														
Genesee	1 951	56 256	0.88	578	9.8	615	10.4	3 821	8.0	12 584	5 355	7 229	1 536	2 586
Greene	3 211	44 795	0.80	426	8.9	507	10.6	3 156	8.9	10 280	6 832	3 448	709	1 466
Hamilton	82	4 461	0.83	31	6.6	66	14.0	334	9.7	1 422	1 030	392	63	1 322
Herkimer	1 420	54 794	0.66	664	10.5	664	10.5	4 234	8.3	12 461	7 665	4 796	1 143	1 915
Jefferson	6 165	122 470	1.07	2 195	18.6	919	7.8	8 096	8.2	18 337	13 671	4 666	2 563	2 180
Kings	35 148	2 283 569	0.74	41 719	15.9	16 883	6.4	282 455	12.4	311 582	170 555	141 027	(6)	(6)
Lewis	316	23 518	0.69	315	11.6	262	9.7	2 117	9.4	5 006	3 657	1 349	271	996
Livingston	6 085	57 440	0.75	531	8.2	510	7.9	3 393	6.9	11 753	4 390	7 363	906	1 402
Madison	4 575	64 534	0.75	666	9.2	575	8.0	4 055	7.2	12 858	8 420	4 438	1 165	1 613
Monroe	26 362	780 733	1.09	8 461	11.3	6 462	8.6	42 806	7.0	135 859	43 395	92 464	21 491	2 858
Montgomery	925	48 330	0.92	607	12.2	541	10.9	3 389	8.3	11 409	6 693	4 716	1 261	2 528
Nassau	20 828	1 271 046	0.88	14 113	10.4	10 991	8.1	80 572	7.2	227 803	166 469	61 334	17 569	1 295
New York	66 848	3 146 768	2.79	18 669	11.4	10 924	6.7	120 131	8.9	236 436	143 195	93 241	(6)187 769	(6)2 216
Niagara	4 117	191 632	0.76	2 191	10.3	2 310	10.8	12 454	7.2	44 861	19 916	24 945	6 225	2 909
Oneida	12 988	241 473	1.07	2 634	11.3	2 429	10.4	14 281	7.8	48 772	31 731	17 041	5 853	2 505
Onondaga	17 176	497 780	1.14	5 270	11.2	4 081	8.7	27 481	7.2	84 026	53 818	30 208	13 012	2 772
Ontario	3 386	110 009	1.02	1 041	9.5	1 021	9.3	6 352	7.2	21 974	8 592	13 382	2 210	2 018
Orange	11 331	349 657	0.85	4 984	13.2	2 652	7.0	26 102	8.2	54 265	44 538	9 727	7 919	2 102
Orleans	2 734	38 852	0.79	409	9.8	398	9.5	3 076	9.3	7 710	3 399	4 311	692	1 642
Oswego	4 932	108 384	0.74	1 326	11.0	1 037	8.6	8 134	8.2	22 808	14 731	8 077	2 630	2 172
Otsego	5 360	62 789	1.04	524	8.6	614	10.1	4 084	9.0	13 010	10 238	2 772	873	1 416
Putnam	2 420	78 200	0.56	826	8.3	690	7.0	6 069	7.3	15 060	12 064	2 996	770	787
Queens	26 901	1 925 679	0.66	30 432	13.1	15 125	6.5	315 982	15.9	294 696	152 401	142 295	(6)	(6)
Rensselaer	5 915	139 000	0.74	1 780	11.1	1 514	9.5	8 705	6.7	28 019	15 886	12 133	4 289	2 676
Richmond	7 094	396 749	0.63	5 387	11.4	3 820	8.1	31 670	7.9	75 354	42 328	33 026	(6)	(6)
Rockland	7 002	291 161	0.81	5 204	16.0	2 287	7.0	24 101	8.9	49 225	39 482	9 743	3 728	1 152
St. Lawrence	11 354	109 915	0.95	1 194	10.7	1 019	9.1	7 469	8.9	22 026	17 345	4 681	1 741	1 632
Saratoga	3 466	195 142	0.76	2 264	10.0	1 850	8.2	10 089	5.4	38 389	21 420	16 969	2 991	1 328
Schenectady	4 513	149 114	0.92	1 733	11.2	1 461	9.4	9 939	7.7	32 605	17 877	14 728	5 123	3 291
Schoharie	1 421	28 863	0.77	251	8.0	280	8.9	2 038	8.3	6 333	4 570	1 763	388	1 224
Schuyler	203	16 254	0.73	158	8.7	180	9.9	1 095	7.4	3 661	2 416	1 245	164	885
Seneca	2 808	32 928	0.85	378	10.8	313	9.0	2 369	9.0	6 088	3 305	2 783	734	2 067
Steuben	1 743	97 667	0.97	1 078	11.0	978	10.0	6 578	8.2	20 596	13 862	6 734	1 523	1 543
Suffolk	28 781	1 411 790	0.88	15 568	10.4	12 262	8.2	109 506	8.7	248 520	190 226	58 294	26 062	1 735
Sullivan	3 809	72 501	0.86	824	10.9	739	9.8	6 580	10.7	14 989	13 219	1 770	1 675	2 187
Tioga	517	42 428	0.66	546	11.0	434	8.7	2 753	6.8	9 716	6 151	3 565	490	978
Tompkins	13 249	114 245	1.23	842	8.0	604	5.8	6 391	8.1	13 671	10 563	3 108	2 611	2 504
Ulster	11 651	166 311	0.82	1 602	8.9	1 641	9.1	13 094	9.2	34 540	26 004	8 536	3 267	1 806
Warren	698	71 253	1.19	623	9.6	640	9.9	3 777	7.3	16 074	9 725	6 349	1 235	1 890
Washington	3 149	53 005	0.64	591	9.5	628	10.1	4 281	8.7	12 593	7 599	4 994	704	1 115
Wayne	1 120	80 878	0.72	994	10.8	808	8.8	5 989	7.8	19 442	7 865	11 577	1 658	1 796
Westchester	27 921	940 885	0.95	10 699	11.0	7 179	7.4	81 967	10.3	148 769	108 629	40 140	12 046	1 238
Wyoming	3 832	38 739	0.84	384	9.3	326	7.9	2 263	7.3	7 335	3 167	4 168	382	922
Yates	1 251	23 166	0.81	305	12.2	252	10.0	2 449	12.5	5 464	2 526	2 938	322	1 281
NORTH CAROLINA	252 683	9 752 385	1.00	120 676	12.1	85 357	8.5	1 254 138	15.2	1 704 453	1 179 402	525 051	318 464	3 203
Alamance	4 599	145 208	0.88	1 784	11.3	1 535	9.8	21 046	16.5	29 566	13 707	15 859	4 880	3 140
Alexander	1 326	31 801	0.66	358	9.6	363	9.7	4 743	16.2	7 103	5 003	2 100	859	2 327
Alleghany	110	10 759	0.95	95	8.7	130	12.0	1 713	21.0	3 185	2 118	1 067	150	1 375
Anson	2 748	25 158	0.88	253	9.8	276	10.6	3 240	16.7	4 994	3 970	1 024	923	4 244
Ashe	379	24 964	0.81	233	8.6	348	12.9	4 104	19.8	6 803	4 897	1 906	273	1 004
Avery	2 521	18 932	1.18	135	7.6	189	10.7	2 459	20.7	4 506	3 356	1 150	243	1 404
Beaufort	515	47 876	1.02	474	10.0	585	12.3	5 791	15.6	12 409	10 564	1 845	1 406	2 994
Bertie	1 636	19 678	0.86	171	8.4	259	12.8	2 157	14.4	4 858	4 359	499	488	2 420
Bladen	355	35 464	1.04	357	10.4	438	12.7	5 190	18.6	6 606	5 004	1 602	939	2 696
Brunswick	962	103 985	0.79	1 073	8.9	1 342	11.1	15 005	17.4	33 540	27 064	6 476	2 618	2 286
Buncombe	7 818	259 838	1.13	2 658	10.6	2 492	9.9	30 085	15.0	52 421	38 644	13 777	7 103	2 840
Burke	2 550	86 262	0.89	849	9.6	976	11.0	12 227	17.2	17 734	12 055	5 679	2 278	2 580
Cabarrus	1 391	170 275	0.82	2 395	12.3	1 466	7.5	22 327	13.4	29 892	19 544	10 348	4 091	2 157
Caldwell	976	75 561	0.80	796	9.8	916	11.3	11 269	17.0	17 207	11 122	6 085	2 658	3 245
Camden	17	7 104	0.32	94	9.1	59	5.7	1 170	13.3	1 591	1 415	176	93	907
Carteret	986	63 924	0.87	636	9.2	783	11.4	8 664	16.3	14 812	12 359	2 453	1 232	1 785
Caswell	1 270	17 718	0.36	214	9.3	242	10.5	2 754	15.8	4 497	2 620	1 877	519	2 245
Catawba	2 361	167 277	1.19	1 733	11.2	1 588	10.3	19 696	15.4	32 974	22 583	10 391	4 841	3 126
Chatham	788	55 550	0.63	632	9.1	671	9.6	8 158	15.7	9 954	5 611	4 343	1 369	2 021
Cherokee	434	27 125	1.00	216	8.0	350	12.9	3 809	19.2	8 213	6 215	1 998	811	2 979

1. Per 1,000 estimated resident population. 2. Data for serious crimes have not been adjusted for underreporting; this may affect comparability between geographic areas and over time.
3. Per 100,000 population estimated by the FBI. 6. Bronx, Kings, Queens, and Richmond counties are included with New York county.

Table B. States and Counties — Crime, Education, Money Income, and Poverty

STATE County	Serious crimes known to police, 2014 (cont.)[1] Rate[2] Violent	Property	School enrollment and attainment, 2010–2014 Enrollment[3] Total	Percent private	Attainment[4] (percent) High school graduate or less	Bachelor's degree or more	Local government expenditures,[5] 2012–2013 Total current spending (mil dol)	Current spending per student (dollars)	Money income, 2010–2014 Per capita income[6] (dollars)	Households Median income (dollars)	Mean income (dollars)	Percent with income of $200,000 or more	Income and poverty, 2014 Median household income (dollars)	Percent below poverty level All persons	Children under 18 years	Children 5 to 17 years in families
	46	47	48	49	50	51	52	53	54	55	56	57	58	59	60	61
NEW YORK—Cont'd																
Genesee	222	2 364	13 824	11.9	46.9	20.2	144.5	16 528	25 721	50 573	63 416	1.6	52 410	12.0	17.1	15.8
Greene	209	1 257	8 445	12.7	50.3	20.1	126.3	19 718	25 770	49 864	65 390	2.4	52 597	11.1	20.0	20.0
Hamilton	42	1 280	859	5.9	42.5	23.8	17.9	35 563	29 974	52 939	63 710	2.7	49 137	11.4	20.6	18.0
Herkimer	221	1 694	15 307	9.9	45.6	21.3	158.8	16 410	23 607	45 649	56 640	1.4	44 148	16.5	23.0	20.7
Jefferson	185	1 994	29 388	13.0	45.4	20.5	276.6	14 686	23 681	48 613	60 174	2.0	49 781	15.1	22.6	24.9
Kings	(7)	(7)	671 262	28.9	48.0	31.6	(7)	(7)	25 932	46 958	69 599	4.9	47 547	23.4	33.1	32.7
Lewis	151	845	6 119	10.1	57.5	14.2	72.2	17 019	23 723	46 990	59 166	1.6	47 542	14.3	23.2	22.3
Livingston	104	1 298	18 125	11.9	45.9	23.9	135.5	16 561	23 981	52 200	62 604	1.6	49 920	14.7	18.9	16.6
Madison	132	1 481	19 461	23.2	43.0	27.2	166.4	16 154	25 786	53 584	67 771	3.1	51 600	11.8	17.5	15.9
Monroe	320	2 538	202 424	24.8	35.0	35.9	1 969.5	18 433	29 170	52 501	70 767	3.8	51 371	14.2	22.2	20.1
Montgomery	116	2 412	11 701	14.5	53.0	16.3	117.7	15 775	23 809	44 167	58 106	1.8	40 923	18.9	27.3	25.9
Nassau	153	1 141	353 230	26.4	33.9	42.3	5 005.6	24 744	42 949	98 401	128 206	16.5	98 312	6.7	9.3	8.4
New York	(7)598	(7)1 618	337 582	45.1	26.5	59.3	(7)22 278.7	(7)22 518	63 610	71 656	132 838	17.7	75 459	17.7	23.5	26.9
Niagara	390	2 518	49 993	16.7	45.3	22.9	480.0	16 130	26 710	49 091	63 175	2.2	49 274	13.4	18.0	16.6
Oneida	281	2 224	55 965	14.0	45.4	23.1	544.8	16 112	25 633	48 931	63 439	2.4	48 350	17.7	28.6	26.1
Onondaga	331	2 441	128 035	26.2	36.6	33.5	1 178.4	16 765	29 156	54 498	71 456	4.0	52 892	16.1	23.7	22.1
Ontario	146	1 872	27 142	21.5	37.2	31.6	270.6	16 254	30 346	57 318	73 918	3.8	58 473	11.5	15.2	14.7
Orange	242	1 860	108 825	22.2	41.3	28.6	1 229.3	20 090	30 561	70 794	88 441	6.5	69 228	13.4	20.8	18.9
Orleans	154	1 488	9 212	11.2	54.7	16.2	98.3	15 265	22 350	48 015	57 666	1.0	46 577	15.5	21.5	19.2
Oswego	200	1 972	32 865	9.0	54.0	17.7	365.5	17 541	23 472	47 646	60 820	1.8	46 926	19.6	27.9	24.8
Otsego	146	1 270	17 746	14.6	44.7	27.2	139.5	18 399	24 263	47 884	61 290	2.3	43 104	18.9	22.3	20.4
Putnam	58	729	25 561	17.6	34.3	38.2	363.1	23 644	40 967	96 262	116 931	13.7	94 334	6.3	7.0	6.0
Queens	(7)	(7)	551 047	21.7	46.9	30.2	(7)	(7)	26 580	57 210	74 140	4.3	56 866	15.4	21.0	20.3
Rensselaer	314	2 361	41 330	30.1	38.9	28.5	358.4	17 715	30 285	60 140	74 105	3.2	59 925	13.0	20.0	18.3
Richmond	(7)	(7)	122 240	23.9	43.6	30.6	(7)	(7)	32 091	74 043	90 681	7.1	70 299	14.5	20.9	19.9
Rockland	126	1 026	93 884	41.7	35.6	40.7	950.9	23 595	34 833	85 808	109 174	12.9	83 162	14.7	25.5	21.6
St. Lawrence	127	1 505	31 399	23.1	48.8	21.6	275.2	17 586	22 908	44 454	58 928	2.1	43 518	18.9	26.4	23.9
Saratoga	94	1 234	53 696	20.3	31.9	38.0	472.9	15 181	35 860	70 581	87 334	5.7	71 885	7.2	9.6	8.9
Schenectady	405	2 885	38 622	16.7	40.6	29.8	418.3	16 536	28 609	57 025	71 184	3.4	56 508	13.2	20.9	19.7
Schoharie	63	1 161	7 556	8.0	50.6	19.1	88.4	19 843	26 097	51 873	64 152	2.6	48 718	15.9	21.5	18.3
Schuyler	70	815	3 802	13.3	50.0	18.0	40.4	18 409	24 529	49 225	58 511	0.6	48 135	15.4	23.9	21.5
Seneca	208	1 859	7 135	20.7	48.3	19.6	76.8	18 626	23 823	48 932	60 595	1.4	49 809	14.2	21.1	19.5
Steuben	162	1 381	22 302	11.2	48.1	20.8	266.0	17 309	25 596	46 773	61 179	2.0	46 849	16.6	24.1	21.3
Suffolk	122	1 613	389 080	14.9	39.9	33.5	5 465.5	21 944	37 427	88 323	109 783	11.3	85 886	7.7	10.4	9.7
Sullivan	253	1 934	17 665	13.3	48.7	21.1	238.8	24 259	25 336	49 388	63 971	3.0	48 908	16.3	25.8	24.6
Tioga	102	876	11 759	11.9	45.5	23.8	127.6	16 083	28 803	56 167	71 107	3.3	52 195	11.4	18.0	16.6
Tompkins	123	2 381	42 314	51.4	25.8	50.3	209.0	19 154	27 829	52 836	72 701	4.9	51 880	18.7	17.2	15.4
Ulster	183	1 622	42 965	13.7	40.4	30.1	527.3	21 935	30 868	58 592	77 548	5.0	56 718	13.7	17.3	15.5
Warren	104	1 786	13 737	11.6	42.6	28.3	168.1	17 987	30 662	56 601	71 229	3.3	54 585	13.3	20.5	18.2
Washington	127	988	13 492	11.5	54.3	18.5	152.4	16 887	23 877	51 494	61 153	1.6	47 547	14.6	20.4	17.8
Wayne	182	1 614	21 500	13.0	47.5	21.3	260.6	17 820	25 643	51 597	63 553	1.7	49 191	12.9	18.4	16.2
Westchester	226	1 012	255 359	25.3	33.3	46.0	3 463.9	23 561	48 487	83 422	133 325	17.3	83 152	10.4	13.3	12.3
Wyoming	109	813	8 608	14.0	53.2	14.7	72.8	16 749	23 708	53 012	61 921	1.1	53 783	12.3	16.9	15.5
Yates	84	1 197	5 997	35.2	49.3	24.3	41.7	17 728	25 436	50 061	66 161	3.4	48 368	14.5	23.7	23.3
NORTH CAROLINA	330	2 873	2 549 268	14.3	41.4	27.8	12 383.1	8 390	25 608	46 693	64 555	3.4	46 596	17.2	24.1	22.6
Alamance	372	2 768	39 532	20.0	46.2	21.0	181.0	7 914	23 324	42 592	57 401	2.2	41 296	17.9	24.4	21.8
Alexander	157	2 169	8 250	15.2	58.8	13.0	45.1	8 382	20 112	41 676	51 367	1.0	43 043	16.4	22.9	21.0
Alleghany	110	1 265	1 972	8.1	54.1	17.4	16.1	10 700	19 452	35 319	44 851	0.9	35 266	20.5	34.2	29.4
Anson	405	3 840	5 739	6.1	63.0	10.7	38.8	10 618	17 091	33 388	44 676	1.5	32 508	25.0	35.9	33.1
Ashe	55	949	5 338	6.6	50.4	18.6	30.8	9 299	21 149	36 244	48 831	1.1	36 488	20.9	31.2	27.9
Avery	133	1 271	3 700	22.0	48.6	20.1	22.9	10 200	21 541	38 138	54 824	3.2	37 131	19.8	31.7	29.2
Beaufort	300	2 693	10 964	8.0	50.0	17.8	62.0	8 545	21 789	40 671	51 834	1.3	40 357	18.8	28.8	27.6
Bertie	134	2 286	4 365	12.1	63.2	11.1	27.8	9 742	16 557	29 388	41 901	0.3	31 217	27.7	38.9	33.4
Bladen	207	2 489	8 656	8.4	55.3	11.5	49.6	9 486	19 059	29 532	44 665	1.1	33 521	25.6	35.8	34.4
Brunswick	141	2 144	20 525	13.2	41.5	25.4	111.2	8 939	27 260	46 955	62 156	2.3	47 387	15.7	30.0	28.7
Buncombe	245	2 595	55 575	17.3	35.2	35.1	266.7	8 885	26 930	45 642	62 346	2.9	47 296	13.9	20.5	19.8
Burke	156	2 424	20 433	7.9	52.2	17.4	112.8	8 454	20 346	37 735	50 451	1.3	39 275	20.5	30.1	27.0
Cabarrus	105	2 052	51 204	12.0	40.2	26.2	281.4	7 832	25 544	53 935	69 595	3.1	55 250	12.2	16.7	15.0
Caldwell	137	3 108	18 476	7.6	56.3	13.4	103.1	8 323	19 397	34 853	47 498	1.4	38 653	18.8	27.7	25.2
Camden	29	878	2 968	8.1	37.3	19.3	16.8	8 686	26 388	62 194	71 831	1.7	61 730	9.7	14.2	12.2
Carteret	130	1 655	14 408	10.1	39.4	24.2	76.0	8 729	27 975	47 179	63 111	2.7	48 824	14.7	24.3	21.7
Caswell	190	2 055	4 988	12.0	60.1	10.7	26.4	9 186	19 057	38 318	47 938	0.8	42 730	19.9	29.2	27.5
Catawba	254	2 872	37 443	13.5	47.6	21.5	201.7	8 157	23 355	45 397	60 064	2.5	45 080	16.2	23.2	21.5
Chatham	179	1 842	14 088	14.6	38.3	36.2	78.2	9 253	32 369	57 140	78 606	6.0	56 797	13.9	21.0	19.3
Cherokee	224	2 755	5 729	10.8	48.9	18.4	32.8	9 237	18 556	34 507	44 116	0.4	34 620	21.0	33.0	30.5

1. Data for serious crimes have not been adjusted for underreporting; this may affect comparability between geographic areas and over time.   2. Per 100,000 population estimated by the FBI.
3. All persons 3 years old and over enrolled in nursery school through college.   4. Persons 25 years old and over.   5. Elementary and secondary education expenditures.
6. Based on population estimated by the American Community Survey, 2010–2014.   7. Bronx, Kings, Queens, and Richmond counties are included with New York county.

Table B. States and Counties — **Personal Income**

STATE County	Personal income, 2014 Total (mil dol)	Percent change, 2013–2014	Per capita[1] Dollars	Per capita[1] Rank	Wages and salaries (mil dol)	Supplements to wages and salaries; employer contributions (mil dol) Pension and insurance	Government social insurance	Proprietors' income (mil dol)	Dividends, interest, and rent (mil dol)	Personal transfer receipts (mil dol)	Earnings, 2014 Total (mil dol)	Contributions for government social insurance (mil dol) From employee and self-employed	From employer
	62	63	64	65	66	67	68	69	70	71	72	73	74
NEW YORK—Cont'd													
Genesee	2 311	2.7	39 064	1 313	909	273	83	199	299	510	1 465	76	83
Greene	1 862	3.3	38 812	1 350	602	209	54	111	301	471	976	56	54
Hamilton	236	10.0	50 157	379	66	33	6	10	55	55	115	7	6
Herkimer	2 313	1.4	36 283	1 726	631	200	57	152	300	630	1 039	62	57
Jefferson	5 167	1.5	43 384	807	2 666	834	256	300	980	929	4 056	180	256
Kings	104 604	4.4	39 898	1 193	24 900	4 417	2 185	5 957	13 865	26 582	37 459	2 210	2 185
Lewis	1 132	3.3	41 579	1 001	253	101	23	122	138	221	499	24	23
Livingston	2 363	2.1	36 579	1 673	742	271	68	201	295	517	1 282	68	68
Madison	2 726	3.3	37 663	1 501	846	239	76	198	383	567	1 359	74	76
Monroe	34 439	2.8	45 927	602	18 776	3 812	1 603	3 327	4 833	6 951	27 518	1 473	1 603
Montgomery	1 805	1.8	36 252	1 733	733	181	68	65	237	521	1 048	62	68
Nassau	100 019	4.5	73 618	46	36 043	6 862	3 000	9 302	21 150	12 135	55 207	2 906	3 000
New York	242 170	4.4	148 002	2	281 820	38 231	17 016	45 047	72 548	18 214	382 115	19 320	17 016
Niagara	8 344	2.5	39 077	1 310	2 970	773	269	316	1 048	2 086	4 328	254	269
Oneida	8 938	1.2	38 383	1 409	4 309	1 249	376	528	1 296	2 303	6 462	349	376
Onondaga	20 712	2.9	44 237	738	11 858	2 686	1 014	1 526	2 940	4 221	17 083	894	1 014
Ontario	5 037	2.8	45 915	605	2 387	534	200	402	699	943	3 523	189	200
Orange	16 876	4.7	44 870	688	6 317	1 651	558	860	2 144	3 141	9 387	490	558
Orleans	1 332	-0.1	31 720	2 488	517	192	48	42	164	365	798	44	48
Oswego	4 180	2.3	34 570	2 010	1 429	457	123	133	472	1 091	2 143	123	123
Otsego	2 167	2.5	35 448	1 868	969	277	84	92	345	532	1 422	78	84
Putnam	5 617	4.5	56 458	185	1 308	312	114	242	854	755	1 977	112	114
Queens	91 718	4.4	39 507	1 247	28 229	4 649	2 461	5 093	12 167	23 552	40 432	2 351	2 461
Rensselaer	6 858	2.8	42 926	855	2 576	684	223	308	916	1 374	3 791	208	223
Richmond	22 414	4.1	47 360	508	4 565	795	402	946	2 743	5 418	6 707	418	402
Rockland	17 252	4.8	53 270	261	6 459	1 403	544	1 251	2 679	2 969	9 658	516	544
St. Lawrence	3 696	3.0	33 179	2 249	1 482	498	133	250	471	999	2 363	125	133
Saratoga	12 744	3.5	56 662	180	4 000	864	346	780	2 294	1 675	5 990	327	346
Schenectady	6 889	3.0	44 238	737	3 451	692	288	241	1 024	1 431	4 673	259	288
Schoharie	1 101	3.3	34 877	1 955	322	110	29	55	148	272	515	29	29
Schuyler	688	2.9	37 253	1 561	183	56	17	73	86	179	330	19	17
Seneca	1 224	1.2	35 082	1 919	531	159	45	123	171	297	859	46	45
Steuben	3 854	2.8	39 167	1 302	2 005	435	165	223	540	904	2 828	155	165
Suffolk	85 255	4.3	56 725	179	36 645	7 627	3 017	5 121	13 466	13 509	52 410	2 786	3 017
Sullivan	2 990	3.2	39 368	1 270	982	307	88	163	459	831	1 541	87	88
Tioga	1 916	1.5	38 416	1 405	629	151	53	118	241	430	950	57	53
Tompkins	3 945	3.1	37 686	1 498	2 471	503	219	253	728	635	3 445	176	219
Ulster	7 515	4.2	41 648	993	2 486	751	221	383	1 256	1 740	3 841	215	221
Warren	2 957	3.0	45 509	637	1 551	342	138	187	486	636	2 219	122	138
Washington	2 224	3.6	35 657	1 830	689	235	63	132	287	547	1 119	61	63
Wayne	3 493	2.6	37 944	1 464	1 146	371	103	148	402	850	1 768	100	103
Westchester	85 375	4.6	87 777	16	29 626	5 158	2 258	6 184	20 903	8 640	43 226	2 275	2 258
Wyoming	1 528	4.1	37 091	1 587	583	202	54	155	184	322	994	47	54
Yates	831	3.2	32 970	2 282	242	74	22	63	145	220	401	22	22
NORTH CAROLINA	389 513	4.7	39 171	X	201 553	33 711	15 444	28 486	66 458	77 962	279 194	16 849	15 444
Alamance	5 422	4.3	34 801	1 968	2 323	383	184	325	825	1 245	3 215	213	184
Alexander	1 232	7.0	32 956	2 287	304	59	25	166	151	307	553	36	25
Alleghany	354	5.1	32 540	2 365	101	22	8	45	79	116	176	12	8
Anson	805	6.0	31 230	2 552	269	62	20	79	94	252	431	26	20
Ashe	847	3.7	31 215	2 554	252	48	20	95	153	266	415	29	20
Avery	546	5.8	30 715	2 625	217	43	18	62	118	156	340	22	18
Beaufort	1 731	2.3	36 372	1 710	604	117	46	114	301	523	881	60	46
Bertie	650	3.8	32 312	2 403	210	50	16	57	76	235	333	21	16
Bladen	1 135	3.3	32 743	2 325	444	96	34	171	130	360	744	42	34
Brunswick	4 192	6.0	35 279	1 894	1 175	218	93	262	847	1 298	1 748	135	93
Buncombe	9 553	4.6	38 128	1 438	5 042	861	395	600	2 132	2 102	6 899	436	395
Burke	2 848	4.6	31 827	2 457	1 098	226	86	302	411	803	1 712	113	86
Cabarrus	7 400	6.5	38 521	1 387	2 727	462	206	565	896	1 259	3 960	247	206
Caldwell	2 452	4.4	30 091	2 707	836	159	67	116	356	740	1 177	86	67
Camden	406	1.9	39 320	1 281	65	11	5	21	60	74	102	7	5
Carteret	3 021	3.7	43 903	770	778	151	60	246	708	665	1 235	84	60
Caswell	680	3.4	29 443	2 785	105	26	8	43	89	225	181	15	8
Catawba	5 678	4.0	36 742	1 641	3 395	574	276	250	958	1 286	4 494	283	276
Chatham	3 544	6.1	51 593	308	539	97	42	341	798	586	1 020	71	42
Cherokee	762	3.6	28 064	2 913	258	51	21	59	126	314	389	30	21

1. Based on the resident population estimated as of July 1 of the year shown.

STATE County	Earnings, 2014 (cont.)									Social Security beneficiaries, December 2014		Housing units, 2015		
	Percent by selected industries													
	Farm	Mining	Construction	Manu-facturing	Infor-mation: professional, scientific, technical services	Retail trade	Finance, insur-ance, real estate and leasing	Health care and social assistance	Govern-ment	Number	Rate[1]	Supple-mental Security Income recipients, December 2014	Total	Percent change, 2010–2014
	75	76	77	78	79	80	81	82	83	84	85	86	87	88
NEW YORK—Cont'd														
Genesee	6.2	0.3	5.5	14.3	2.6	6.5	2.8	8.9	30.8	13 640	231	1 144	25 647	0.3
Greene	0.7	D	4.8	6.5	4.7	7.6	3.2	6.2	41.5	12 265	256	1 386	29 307	0.3
Hamilton	0.0	D	6.3	D	D	6.2	D	D	62.6	1 730	368	61	8 777	0.9
Herkimer	3.3	0.2	6.5	15.7	2.5	7.8	2.1	9.3	30.9	15 875	249	1 636	33 323	-0.1
Jefferson	2.4	0.1	4.5	4.0	2.5	5.9	2.0	8.8	59.0	21 280	179	2 724	59 123	2.0
Kings	0.0	D	6.3	3.0	9.6	7.8	9.0	24.9	10.9	325 230	124	136 594	1 025 752	2.5
Lewis	14.1	D	5.6	14.0	2.7	5.4	1.4	D	36.8	6 215	229	595	15 314	1.4
Livingston	5.3	D	7.5	9.8	2.8	7.6	2.2	8.1	37.4	13 665	211	1 202	27 353	1.2
Madison	4.0	D	6.4	12.4	5.0	7.1	3.4	11.8	24.6	15 175	210	1 421	31 761	0.0
Monroe	0.1	0.0	5.6	12.5	14.2	5.1	6.4	13.1	15.2	156 170	208	25 290	324 824	1.3
Montgomery	2.9	0.6	3.6	17.1	2.4	8.7	2.3	20.8	22.9	11 990	241	1 815	23 188	0.5
Nassau	0.0	D	6.0	3.2	14.3	7.5	9.9	17.2	17.7	253 660	187	16 932	466 818	-0.3
New York	0.0	0.1	1.4	0.7	25.2	2.8	32.6	4.8	12.0	251 745	154	71 223	869 866	2.7
Niagara	1.3	D	5.0	16.2	4.9	7.9	2.8	12.3	27.8	52 495	246	5 758	99 141	0.0
Oneida	0.8	0.1	3.3	8.8	6.1	7.2	7.8	15.5	33.0	54 995	236	8 289	103 861	-0.3
Onondaga	0.4	0.1	5.0	9.2	10.8	6.2	7.5	12.7	21.0	95 920	205	14 170	204 970	1.3
Ontario	1.8	0.1	8.0	13.8	5.8	9.3	3.8	11.1	20.3	25 345	231	1 847	49 903	3.4
Orange	0.4	0.1	4.5	5.9	7.5	9.2	3.7	13.9	32.7	63 975	170	6 707	140 297	2.4
Orleans	4.1	0.3	3.1	17.4	1.3	4.2	4.7	D	45.6	9 455	225	945	18 503	0.4
Oswego	0.8	0.2	5.1	11.4	3.0	7.1	2.3	10.6	32.3	26 590	220	3 295	53 661	0.1
Otsego	2.1	D	2.8	4.9	3.7	7.9	6.4	26.0	26.4	14 385	236	1 347	30 692	-0.3
Putnam	0.1	0.0	9.4	D	D	5.5	4.3	17.8	27.3	18 240	184	796	38 336	0.3
Queens	0.0	D	12.9	3.5	5.2	6.3	8.5	17.1	10.7	322 655	139	73 130	849 505	1.7
Rensselaer	0.4	0.3	7.1	9.0	9.4	5.4	4.2	12.1	27.7	31 835	199	4 060	71 872	0.6
Richmond	0.0	0.0	11.3	D	8.0	8.3	4.7	26.5	10.9	87 850	186	14 661	179 001	1.3
Rockland	0.0	D	6.8	9.7	10.3	6.5	5.4	14.0	21.7	55 420	171	5 050	104 825	0.7
St. Lawrence	4.3	0.2	4.2	9.1	2.6	7.1	2.0	D	37.8	25 175	225	3 722	52 251	0.2
Saratoga	0.6	0.6	8.3	12.7	9.8	7.2	9.7	9.3	18.9	46 295	206	2 780	102 564	4.0
Schenectady	0.0	D	3.8	13.6	21.0	5.5	4.1	13.9	19.2	32 620	211	5 184	68 180	0.3
Schoharie	3.1	D	8.6	2.4	3.3	7.6	5.4	9.5	37.6	7 745	245	672	17 217	-0.1
Schuyler	6.3	D	11.3	11.6	3.0	7.5	D	D	25.8	4 780	261	403	9 577	1.3
Seneca	4.5	D	4.3	27.9	D	7.6	1.9	D	31.6	7 995	229	752	16 210	1.0
Steuben	2.3	0.4	2.2	14.7	15.6	5.2	4.4	8.7	22.4	23 510	239	2 974	48 768	-0.2
Suffolk	0.2	0.2	7.4	8.3	10.4	6.6	9.4	11.4	22.1	287 450	191	20 566	570 670	0.1
Sullivan	0.6	0.5	4.4	4.0	3.5	6.5	5.4	18.9	36.3	16 910	223	2 601	49 745	1.1
Tioga	1.4	0.2	4.2	39.6	D	5.1	1.8	4.8	20.7	11 835	237	1 186	22 162	-0.2
Tompkins	0.8	1.3	2.2	8.0	7.5	5.2	3.5	D	15.0	15 470	148	1 500	42 272	1.4
Ulster	0.6	0.2	5.1	5.7	5.6	9.0	4.5	12.6	34.3	40 605	225	4 255	83 801	0.2
Warren	0.1	0.3	6.6	11.0	7.7	8.7	5.2	15.9	17.1	17 905	276	1 575	39 180	1.2
Washington	6.2	0.7	7.2	18.3	D	6.2	1.5	7.3	38.1	14 950	240	1 634	29 028	0.6
Wayne	4.3	0.4	6.1	20.6	2.5	5.9	2.3	7.1	31.9	22 645	246	2 266	41 447	1.0
Westchester	0.0	D	6.6	4.2	15.0	5.6	12.6	12.7	17.8	166 390	171	17 378	369 623	-0.3
Wyoming	15.0	D	2.6	10.5	D	5.6	1.9	D	39.8	9 035	219	649	18 058	0.5
Yates	15.2	0.0	4.2	14.0	2.3	6.4	2.6	D	23.4	6 065	242	537	13 743	1.9
NORTH CAROLINA	1.5	0.1	5.4	11.9	10.1	6.4	8.2	10.3	19.4	1 948 531	196	235 300	4 490 948	3.8
Alamance	0.3	0.1	5.7	16.4	4.3	7.9	5.2	21.3	11.3	32 665	209	3 369	68 493	2.8
Alexander	9.1	D	4.1	30.1	4.8	4.7	3.1	6.2	18.0	8 875	238	626	16 163	-0.2
Alleghany	12.4	D	8.7	13.5	D	6.5	4.1	D	17.4	3 425	315	346	8 136	0.5
Anson	11.8	D	2.3	18.1	D	4.8	1.7	D	28.5	5 880	225	1 078	11 507	-0.6
Ashe	9.0	D	11.7	11.2	D	8.8	5.5	11.1	14.1	7 805	288	792	17 493	0.9
Avery	5.0	D	8.7	1.6	D	8.1	4.3	D	22.5	4 615	260	412	14 041	1.1
Beaufort	4.4	0.0	5.2	22.7	4.2	7.9	4.3	9.7	16.5	13 580	286	1 884	25 472	3.2
Bertie	14.6	D	1.6	26.1	D	2.7	D	D	21.8	5 745	282	1 304	9 727	-1.0
Bladen	18.1	0.0	2.7	35.3	D	3.4	1.7	D	17.5	8 360	242	1 634	17 636	-0.5
Brunswick	1.5	D	9.6	4.6	D	8.5	6.2	11.4	17.0	38 530	324	2 324	83 080	7.2
Buncombe	0.4	0.1	5.1	11.0	7.4	8.2	5.5	21.6	15.4	57 400	229	5 796	116 638	2.9
Burke	0.8	D	3.9	26.2	3.1	6.4	3.1	17.6	21.9	22 430	253	2 008	40 615	-0.6
Cabarrus	0.5	D	6.9	8.5	4.6	10.2	3.7	6.7	20.3	32 650	170	3 133	76 892	6.9
Caldwell	0.8	D	4.6	22.5	2.9	7.5	2.9	12.1	17.8	20 760	255	1 830	37 643	0.0
Camden	9.7	0.0	6.4	1.5	D	4.7	3.1	2.0	22.8	1 920	187	128	4 155	1.2
Carteret	0.6	0.0	7.3	4.0	5.2	11.2	6.2	10.3	23.4	18 065	263	1 250	48 982	1.7
Caswell	13.3	D	7.0	9.3	D	4.8	D	8.6	35.0	6 090	265	714	10 591	-0.3
Catawba	0.5	D	3.3	27.8	4.6	7.8	2.9	10.9	12.4	34 190	221	3 018	67 872	0.0
Chatham	4.0	D	8.8	12.6	10.0	5.7	5.6	11.7	13.6	16 855	246	930	30 498	6.1
Cherokee	2.9	D	D	9.9	8.5	10.6	5.2	D	20.4	9 360	346	840	17 733	1.2

1. Per 1,000 resident population estimated as of July 1 of the year shown.

STATE County	Housing units, 2010–2014								Civilian labor force, 2015				Civilian employment,[6] 2010–2014		
	Occupied units										Unemployment			Percent	
			Owner-occupied			Renter-occupied									
				Median owner cost as a percent of income											
	Total	Percent	Median value[1]	With a mort-gage	Without a mort-gage[2]	Median rent[3]	Median rent as a per-cent of income[2]	Sub-stand-ard units[4] (percent)	Total	Percent change, 2014–2015	Total	Rate[5]	Total	Manage-ment, business, science and arts	Con-struction, produc-tion, and mainte-nance occu-pations
	89	90	91	92	93	94	95	96	97	98	99	100	101	102	103
NEW YORK—Cont'd															
Genesee	23 967	73.1	105 200	21.3	14.2	722	29.5	1.7	30 152	0.2	1 521	5.0	29 812	30.0	28.1
Greene	18 102	75.2	174 200	25.5	15.7	836	34.3	1.5	20 836	0.4	1 197	5.7	19 638	34.5	23.8
Hamilton	1 639	81.8	163 100	22.0	13.3	629	19.9	0.8	2 453	0.8	166	6.8	1 993	35.7	19.9
Herkimer	26 583	70.3	95 100	20.2	13.6	621	29.5	2.1	28 914	0.0	1 814	6.3	28 987	32.5	23.3
Jefferson	44 822	55.8	135 200	21.8	13.4	941	28.5	2.4	46 610	-0.2	3 144	6.7	44 448	32.0	21.3
Kings	925 371	29.5	557 500	32.8	16.7	1 189	33.1	11.2	1 242 051	1.1	72 945	5.9	1 138 762	37.5	15.4
Lewis	10 726	75.8	111 900	20.9	12.8	684	33.0	1.8	11 771	-1.0	832	7.1	11 838	29.0	34.5
Livingston	24 242	73.9	119 200	22.3	13.8	711	34.2	2.4	31 149	0.4	1 669	5.4	30 527	35.1	24.9
Madison	26 407	75.6	122 400	22.5	13.8	730	27.2	1.3	33 434	-0.2	1 904	5.7	32 835	38.2	23.1
Monroe	298 915	64.5	136 600	21.8	13.5	820	33.5	1.5	365 058	-0.1	18 863	5.2	356 881	42.1	16.0
Montgomery	19 655	67.3	101 100	22.2	16.9	702	30.7	3.1	22 318	0.0	1 492	6.7	21 629	30.1	28.7
Nassau	441 912	80.2	447 700	29.1	19.1	1 559	34.0	2.7	695 815	1.3	30 009	4.3	656 248	43.5	13.8
New York	745 089	22.6	838 400	19.5	10.0	1 480	28.5	6.0	931 558	1.6	44 910	4.8	868 961	58.9	6.2
Niagara	88 252	70.9	106 700	20.7	14.2	655	30.4	1.3	101 622	-0.1	6 335	6.2	99 821	31.6	22.8
Oneida	90 821	66.4	111 900	20.7	13.1	707	30.0	1.6	103 051	-0.3	5 557	5.4	103 962	35.5	20.5
Onondaga	185 089	65.2	134 200	21.0	13.1	771	30.2	1.6	224 505	-0.3	11 150	5.0	219 556	40.3	16.3
Ontario	44 198	73.1	140 100	21.1	14.2	789	30.1	1.8	55 067	0.3	2 652	4.8	53 329	38.5	20.5
Orange	124 901	69.6	268 500	27.8	18.0	1 156	36.1	4.1	178 292	1.4	8 426	4.7	170 479	34.6	20.1
Orleans	15 894	76.6	91 300	23.1	17.0	638	32.8	3.2	18 026	-0.3	1 166	6.5	17 642	26.1	33.2
Oswego	45 300	72.2	92 900	21.2	13.6	725	32.7	2.3	54 888	-0.5	3 956	7.2	52 651	28.9	28.9
Otsego	23 798	74.0	139 000	22.8	13.9	775	35.2	3.1	29 796	-0.9	1 588	5.3	28 274	36.2	21.1
Putnam	34 164	82.7	362 400	27.6	17.7	1 234	34.1	2.0	50 742	0.7	2 202	4.3	50 404	43.3	16.3
Queens	780 069	43.8	446 800	32.0	14.9	1 350	33.8	9.7	1 181 681	1.5	58 871	5.0	1 083 846	31.7	19.1
Rensselaer	63 995	65.2	177 700	23.0	14.1	871	29.4	1.7	81 816	0.6	3 871	4.7	79 637	39.1	19.1
Richmond	165 079	68.8	439 600	28.6	15.5	1 177	32.6	4.4	225 115	1.2	12 962	5.8	207 199	38.8	17.3
Rockland	98 394	69.0	424 400	28.7	18.0	1 329	36.6	7.0	152 086	1.6	6 982	4.6	144 787	43.4	14.3
St. Lawrence	41 579	70.6	86 200	21.0	13.4	698	31.2	3.1	47 023	-0.3	3 263	6.9	45 019	33.5	20.9
Saratoga	89 876	71.3	230 900	22.3	13.0	978	26.8	0.9	116 864	0.8	4 922	4.2	113 075	43.9	16.2
Schenectady	57 846	66.7	166 900	23.1	14.4	849	32.9	1.4	76 734	0.6	3 655	4.8	73 761	38.2	17.1
Schoharie	12 739	76.3	146 200	23.4	15.3	729	30.8	2.0	14 864	0.6	868	5.8	14 469	32.1	26.2
Schuyler	7 759	78.1	99 700	21.2	12.8	620	25.7	2.7	8 613	-0.1	565	6.6	8 301	30.2	26.8
Seneca	13 485	73.1	95 400	21.0	13.8	692	30.5	1.9	15 908	2.3	829	5.2	15 337	31.1	27.1
Steuben	41 285	70.1	89 800	20.8	12.6	664	25.8	2.2	43 914	-0.6	2 810	6.4	43 596	34.0	27.1
Suffolk	496 780	79.3	376 800	29.3	19.5	1 519	35.1	2.8	776 358	1.2	37 212	4.8	731 119	37.6	19.0
Sullivan	28 954	65.1	168 800	28.1	16.5	851	32.3	2.7	33 811	1.4	1 869	5.5	32 340	30.7	23.9
Tioga	20 178	78.5	110 500	20.0	12.7	641	28.8	1.4	23 529	-1.3	1 325	5.6	24 148	35.8	25.5
Tompkins	38 340	56.1	171 000	21.5	12.9	965	34.3	1.9	55 371	0.9	2 255	4.1	49 324	51.9	12.4
Ulster	69 388	69.5	226 600	27.0	17.6	1 014	34.6	1.9	88 438	0.3	4 339	4.9	85 667	38.8	19.1
Warren	27 699	70.0	191 800	23.1	13.9	856	30.9	1.6	32 442	0.3	1 822	5.6	31 794	35.3	20.3
Washington	24 165	73.5	144 100	24.4	14.2	805	31.8	2.2	28 761	0.5	1 469	5.1	28 439	27.6	30.9
Wayne	36 479	78.0	110 400	21.1	14.5	689	31.4	1.7	44 518	0.0	2 409	5.4	43 389	33.5	28.8
Westchester	342 956	61.9	509 200	27.0	18.5	1 354	33.0	4.5	479 520	1.7	22 113	4.6	461 126	45.8	13.1
Wyoming	15 691	74.9	101 800	20.4	11.9	594	28.4	0.8	18 421	0.2	1 056	5.7	18 561	27.4	32.7
Yates	9 642	77.3	121 600	22.7	12.3	665	29.7	2.8	11 804	0.8	594	5.0	11 688	31.3	26.8
NORTH CAROLINA	3 742 514	65.8	153 600	22.6	11.9	790	30.6	2.8	4 769 251	1.7	273 773	5.7	4 287 690	35.9	22.6
Alamance	61 046	66.0	135 800	22.6	12.2	743	30.9	3.2	77 083	0.5	4 123	5.3	69 707	31.6	26.3
Alexander	13 721	77.8	120 700	20.5	10.0	576	29.8	3.5	17 546	0.6	873	5.0	16 127	25.2	38.6
Alleghany	4 752	75.9	145 500	23.3	14.0	577	32.2	1.6	4 484	2.3	277	6.2	4 167	29.1	34.8
Anson	9 549	69.4	78 700	23.0	15.3	676	31.4	2.6	10 853	-0.5	711	6.6	9 707	21.0	39.3
Ashe	11 746	76.7	151 300	27.0	10.6	648	34.6	1.4	12 326	-0.6	743	6.0	11 904	28.2	31.9
Avery	7 174	76.5	144 700	28.1	10.2	706	33.0	4.2	7 610	-0.4	454	6.0	7 023	24.1	26.8
Beaufort	18 894	70.2	116 600	24.7	15.3	653	31.5	1.9	20 144	0.4	1 335	6.6	18 420	29.9	30.7
Bertie	7 662	73.2	79 300	24.6	16.8	620	39.1	2.5	8 630	1.4	627	7.3	7 118	24.8	40.0
Bladen	14 407	68.2	86 100	23.8	15.7	614	35.7	2.8	14 857	4.1	1 185	8.0	12 896	24.8	38.9
Brunswick	48 331	75.3	179 800	26.4	12.4	860	33.7	1.6	48 509	1.9	3 496	7.2	44 038	29.8	23.9
Buncombe	101 645	63.9	189 500	23.6	11.5	828	29.9	2.7	130 911	2.4	5 688	4.3	115 720	38.5	17.9
Burke	34 597	71.7	111 700	22.3	10.5	626	31.2	2.7	39 574	0.7	2 264	5.7	36 825	28.0	31.2
Cabarrus	65 693	72.5	167 700	22.5	11.9	808	28.9	3.1	96 803	2.9	5 011	5.2	84 448	36.8	22.2
Caldwell	31 354	71.3	107 000	21.9	12.2	619	34.3	1.7	35 501	0.2	2 240	6.3	33 197	24.6	34.5
Camden	3 609	85.2	216 000	26.5	12.7	1 143	35.8	2.7	4 612	1.4	267	5.8	4 365	39.2	21.6
Carteret	29 352	70.2	193 500	24.5	13.2	780	28.3	2.0	31 399	1.2	1 864	5.9	29 727	34.0	22.4
Caswell	8 608	74.8	97 700	23.3	12.0	605	33.5	1.8	9 622	-0.1	614	6.4	9 186	24.8	31.6
Catawba	58 424	70.3	133 100	21.1	10.3	685	28.4	3.1	74 774	0.3	4 161	5.6	70 161	30.8	29.2
Chatham	26 474	78.5	219 000	23.5	11.4	786	29.7	2.0	32 900	2.2	1 564	4.8	29 075	39.5	24.2
Cherokee	10 503	82.5	137 800	25.7	11.6	637	32.2	2.4	11 170	0.7	725	6.5	9 428	25.4	29.5

1. Specified owner-occupied units. 2. A value of 10.0 represents 10 percent or less; a value of 50.0 represents 50 percent or more. 3. Specified renter-occupied units.
4. Overcrowded or lacking complete plumbing facilities. 5. Percent of civilian labor force. 6. Persons 16 years old and over.

Table B. States and Counties — **Nonfarm Employment and Agriculture**

STATE County	Private nonfarm establishments, employment and payroll, 2014									Agriculture, 2012			
	Number of establishments	Employment						Annual payroll		Farms			Farm operators whose principal occupation is farming (percent)
		Total	Health care and social assistance	Manufacturing	Retail trade	Finance and insurance	Professional, scientific, and technical services	Total (mil dol)	Average per employee (dollars)	Number	Percent with: Fewer than 50 acres	500 acres or more	
	104	105	106	107	108	109	110	111	112	113	114	115	116
NEW YORK—Cont'd													
Genesee	1 348	16 566	2 891	3 084	2 709	388	314	575	34 734	549	35.3	12.0	56.5
Greene	1 138	10 869	1 169	834	2 192	359	222	319	29 369	273	31.9	5.9	51.3
Hamilton	196	839	34	D	174	D	D	24	28 959	26	34.6	0.0	42.3
Herkimer	1 127	12 379	2 229	3 052	1 997	279	197	402	32 500	687	21.0	7.9	59.7
Jefferson	2 435	29 831	6 176	2 305	6 975	739	898	1 027	34 441	876	20.5	17.2	57.4
Kings	54 723	562 928	185 927	21 405	72 108	15 888	19 688	21 820	38 761	10	100.0	0.0	60.0
Lewis	528	4 637	1 135	1 074	801	D	125	166	35 696	634	18.3	12.5	60.4
Livingston	1 239	13 183	1 973	1 983	2 594	248	380	429	32 520	661	34.2	14.7	55.8
Madison	1 430	17 019	3 079	2 769	2 610	515	680	571	33 569	838	27.3	10.6	58.2
Monroe	17 499	343 350	64 018	36 338	42 097	12 275	22 942	14 896	43 383	475	54.5	10.1	66.7
Montgomery	1 071	15 169	3 943	3 255	2 607	318	248	502	33 092	659	23.2	9.3	67.2
Nassau	47 823	545 065	106 541	16 407	78 441	35 136	43 306	27 618	50 668	55	90.9	1.8	47.3
New York	105 998	2 188 523	243 205	18 786	153 104	287 334	304 064	232 409	106 194	6	100.0	0.0	0.0
Niagara	4 512	59 594	10 343	8 280	10 834	1 364	1 752	2 055	34 481	760	47.2	7.0	52.9
Oneida	4 908	89 372	19 816	9 417	12 278	6 524	3 482	3 238	36 229	1 066	25.7	8.3	56.7
Onondaga	11 809	217 506	40 370	17 922	29 468	11 557	15 747	9 237	42 467	681	44.1	8.8	54.9
Ontario	2 878	44 462	8 267	5 927	9 281	831	1 381	1 853	41 676	853	40.9	10.6	58.0
Orange	9 189	112 409	20 175	7 553	23 576	3 028	6 036	4 167	37 071	658	42.1	4.6	60.6
Orleans	655	7 918	1 239	2 382	1 072	D	99	259	32 691	487	41.9	9.2	55.2
Oswego	2 153	23 571	4 647	3 010	4 504	630	596	949	40 247	657	32.6	5.3	54.5
Otsego	1 415	19 141	5 921	951	3 286	1 161	608	714	37 291	995	26.2	6.8	57.3
Putnam	2 874	20 755	5 119	1 257	3 172	667	1 251	878	42 288	72	72.2	4.2	50.0
Queens	47 510	537 442	126 834	21 332	62 102	D	14 556	24 338	45 285	6	66.7	0.0	16.7
Rensselaer	2 962	42 702	9 156	2 914	5 937	1 356	3 314	1 888	44 213	495	34.1	8.7	52.3
Richmond	9 044	96 645	30 678	1 125	16 204	2 364	3 483	3 670	37 971	8	100.0	0.0	50.0
Rockland	9 546	103 615	22 991	8 009	14 219	3 243	5 438	4 656	44 934	23	82.6	0.0	65.2
St. Lawrence	1 959	26 606	6 175	2 430	5 206	668	628	970	36 449	1 303	13.7	10.8	60.2
Saratoga	5 198	67 946	9 196	6 459	11 065	4 157	4 138	2 982	43 889	583	46.5	4.5	61.9
Schenectady	3 073	48 689	11 801	4 352	7 560	2 202	D	2 118	43 492	169	41.4	3.6	46.2
Schoharie	570	5 315	1 009	276	1 059	259	181	176	33 129	532	22.0	6.8	62.0
Schuyler	382	3 684	D	598	694	57	67	121	32 774	393	30.8	5.3	50.4
Seneca	716	8 957	1 239	1 435	2 408	148	118	309	34 489	584	30.5	9.1	69.3
Steuben	1 800	25 801	6 071	4 298	4 611	1 002	D	1 323	51 266	1 667	19.3	11.4	51.4
Suffolk	48 831	562 520	93 060	53 033	81 755	22 013	47 243	28 915	51 403	604	70.4	1.5	69.2
Sullivan	1 922	18 636	5 425	1 194	2 815	649	555	605	32 454	321	38.6	7.2	59.5
Tioga	814	10 694	1 122	1 203	1 325	220	D	532	49 711	536	22.9	8.8	54.1
Tompkins	2 361	47 972	5 631	2 569	5 111	1 078	2 332	1 767	36 842	558	43.9	6.8	50.5
Ulster	4 727	45 384	9 193	3 514	8 986	2 024	1 595	1 529	33 688	486	48.4	5.1	67.3
Warren	2 306	31 200	6 468	3 728	6 012	1 146	888	1 211	38 815	117	60.7	0.0	54.7
Washington	1 049	10 449	1 864	3 010	1 789	224	210	386	36 968	851	31.1	11.6	55.6
Wayne	1 720	19 905	3 097	5 934	3 203	538	592	746	37 492	873	38.3	8.6	62.2
Westchester	31 692	377 803	77 135	10 761	50 944	21 743	25 728	24 584	65 072	131	74.8	1.5	58.8
Wyoming	785	9 135	1 170	1 819	1 439	405	342	315	34 497	713	33.0	14.9	62.8
Yates	540	5 091	925	887	755	100	118	152	29 816	919	27.1	3.6	66.6
NORTH CAROLINA	219 897	3 560 448	560 309	408 132	469 243	172 319	203 500	155 372	43 638	50 218	48.1	6.8	48.9
Alamance	3 138	51 102	8 405	8 439	8 950	1 512	1 284	1 809	35 395	732	42.5	4.6	41.7
Alexander	557	7 141	531	3 217	827	163	133	204	28 579	603	55.4	5.0	53.2
Alleghany	251	2 094	508	D	318	D	D	61	29 227	567	43.0	4.6	49.7
Anson	385	5 143	864	1 412	709	92	118	154	29 968	429	26.8	9.3	55.7
Ashe	513	5 163	1 083	851	1 041	192	D	163	31 505	1 140	47.6	2.1	46.4
Avery	500	4 538	837	148	760	D	68	125	27 546	483	63.1	0.8	46.2
Beaufort	1 075	13 248	2 207	2 921	2 301	414	270	452	34 125	364	39.8	21.7	50.5
Bertie	315	3 423	1 010	624	390	70	48	135	39 407	325	30.8	23.1	64.0
Bladen	512	8 633	1 291	4 166	883	D	143	319	36 907	492	42.3	12.4	53.3
Brunswick	2 298	23 815	3 943	1 407	4 830	D	687	803	33 717	254	52.8	7.1	42.9
Buncombe	7 607	107 803	23 559	11 197	17 425	2 613	4 427	4 047	37 541	1 060	64.8	0.9	51.0
Burke	1 439	22 385	4 313	7 796	2 951	368	424	725	32 395	486	58.8	1.6	50.6
Cabarrus	4 057	58 214	9 404	5 630	12 070	986	1 670	2 105	36 157	589	52.0	4.2	50.1
Caldwell	1 306	17 114	3 276	4 447	2 795	351	293	536	31 324	411	56.9	1.7	44.8
Camden	108	525	D	D	94	22	33	15	28 926	60	41.7	36.7	65.0
Carteret	1 911	18 039	3 347	923	4 175	509	443	546	30 292	125	64.8	7.2	48.8
Caswell	230	1 550	376	166	335	45	35	40	25 718	543	32.2	6.6	49.9
Catawba	4 023	78 234	11 521	21 616	9 655	1 319	1 857	3 032	38 755	698	55.6	1.7	41.8
Chatham	1 338	13 040	2 615	1 865	2 089	238	508	405	31 065	1 138	47.0	1.9	45.2
Cherokee	573	6 151	1 117	1 324	1 382	170	222	188	30 565	255	54.1	3.9	54.5

Table B. States and Counties — Agriculture

	Agriculture, 2012 (cont.)															
	Land in farms					Value of land and buildings (dollars)		Value of machinery and equipment, average per farm (dollars)	Value of products sold				Percent of farms with sales of:		Government payments	
			Acres								Percent from:					
STATE County	Acreage (1,000)	Percent change, 2007–2012	Average size of farm	Total irrigated (1,000)	Total cropland (1,000)	Average per farm	Average per acre		Total (mil dol)	Average per farm (dollars)	Crops	Live-stock and poultry products	$10,000 or more	$100,000 or more	Total ($1,000)	Percent of farms
	117	118	119	120	121	122	123	124	125	126	127	128	129	130	131	132
NEW YORK—Cont'd																
Genesee	187	2.1	341	6.3	143.3	898 004	2 632	213 681	237.0	431 607	36.0	64.0	48.1	25.9	2 111	45.5
Greene	43	-3.0	157	0.7	18.7	588 198	3 736	65 901	22.4	82 022	43.5	56.5	40.3	6.2	911	23.8
Hamilton	2	361.8	80	D	0.3	145 692	1 823	28 538	0.3	13 385	D	D	19.2	7.7	0	0.0
Herkimer	140	0.2	204	0.1	76.4	393 428	1 927	92 482	70.4	102 536	25.1	74.9	57.9	21.0	1 414	32.0
Jefferson	291	10.9	332	0.3	173.5	544 535	1 640	133 429	183.6	209 551	24.7	75.3	51.6	24.1	2 974	31.5
Kings	D	D	D	0.0	D	951 000	D	15 000	2.0	199 300	D	D	60.0	40.0	0	0.0
Lewis	182	8.7	287	0.1	97.2	478 692	1 670	145 063	137.0	216 151	17.2	82.8	64.0	35.3	2 400	37.7
Livingston	195	-12.4	295	0.2	149.6	854 528	2 897	176 086	186.8	282 614	43.2	56.8	44.3	22.5	2 425	41.9
Madison	187	-0.4	224	0.8	111.0	456 792	2 042	116 047	117.7	140 489	26.4	73.6	52.0	24.7	2 231	29.2
Monroe	99	-25.8	208	0.9	79.5	737 682	3 551	142 223	90.6	190 695	89.8	10.2	46.1	19.2	1 331	21.7
Montgomery	131	5.5	199	0.2	85.9	458 426	2 299	108 599	86.8	131 701	24.8	75.2	60.8	22.8	1 523	32.0
Nassau	3	108.2	49	0.1	0.3	894 000	18 333	51 509	6.2	113 546	47.9	52.1	47.3	21.8	0	0.0
New York	D	D	D	0.0	D	D	D	47 000	D	D	D	D	16.7	0.0	0	0.0
Niagara	143	0.1	188	3.0	118.5	430 664	2 292	136 736	122.7	161 415	62.2	37.8	45.1	14.9	1 684	27.1
Oneida	205	6.7	192	0.2	118.7	383 145	1 991	109 238	113.2	106 181	37.3	62.7	48.2	21.7	2 155	31.5
Onondaga	150	-0.2	221	1.3	101.8	696 072	3 155	166 094	152.1	223 275	31.8	68.2	50.2	19.2	1 688	32.5
Ontario	193	-3.2	226	0.9	148.2	727 475	3 222	149 744	180.3	211 402	42.8	57.2	53.0	25.2	2 675	32.8
Orange	88	8.7	134	2.7	45.8	740 827	5 537	116 939	100.7	153 035	71.5	28.5	59.3	22.9	2 006	27.8
Orleans	135	-3.3	277	4.6	109.5	720 725	2 598	232 292	150.3	308 672	92.1	7.9	46.0	25.5	1 883	39.4
Oswego	94	-6.0	143	0.6	45.4	289 994	2 022	85 426	47.6	72 454	47.3	52.7	39.7	11.6	555	17.8
Otsego	181	2.4	182	0.2	85.5	407 769	2 245	80 409	66.8	67 096	35.6	64.4	42.7	15.8	1 391	21.8
Putnam	6	4.8	82	D	1.6	448 681	5 468	42 181	3.3	45 222	92.2	7.8	29.2	13.9	24	6.9
Queens	0	D	74	0.0	0.4	377 833	5 129	82 333	0.2	26 833	95.7	5.0	100.0	0.0	0	0.0
Rensselaer	89	4.4	179	0.6	50.6	616 113	3 436	104 002	53.1	107 204	52.9	47.1	48.3	16.0	733	30.5
Richmond	D	D	D	0.0	D	440 750	D	D	1.0	120 125	100.0	0.0	50.0	50.0	0	0.0
Rockland	1	D	23	0.1	0.2	1 980 870	86 616	71 913	1.7	75 391	96.5	3.5	56.5	21.7	0	0.0
St. Lawrence	357	2.8	274	0.6	172.1	388 063	1 417	95 682	187.4	143 794	20.7	79.3	48.3	16.7	2 569	20.7
Saratoga	79	4.2	135	0.3	43.8	647 986	4 791	109 096	80.0	137 166	24.3	75.7	43.2	12.9	613	14.2
Schenectady	20	3.9	118	0.1	9.1	406 036	3 454	77 172	4.2	24 621	70.7	29.3	36.7	5.3	101	7.1
Schoharie	98	3.0	185	0.7	55.0	421 389	2 279	86 735	39.5	74 248	39.0	61.0	49.1	13.9	1 105	31.0
Schuyler	69	4.3	176	0.2	38.0	503 155	2 857	92 982	44.5	113 160	29.1	70.9	47.6	17.6	375	16.0
Seneca	130	1.7	223	0.4	98.0	656 699	2 945	168 820	118.9	203 640	44.2	55.8	67.1	39.4	1 017	28.9
Steuben	406	9.1	243	1.2	221.7	446 421	1 834	105 887	187.2	112 301	43.4	56.6	44.6	16.4	3 112	29.8
Suffolk	36	4.6	60	11.8	23.2	696 702	11 697	138 692	239.8	397 050	85.3	14.7	63.7	32.0	790	7.1
Sullivan	54	6.8	168	0.1	22.8	617 897	3 683	74 601	27.1	84 424	15.0	85.0	44.5	13.1	274	18.1
Tioga	108	1.0	201	0.7	50.7	396 076	1 968	83 879	36.7	68 560	30.8	69.2	42.2	14.6	1 112	36.9
Tompkins	91	-16.5	163	0.3	54.4	448 507	2 757	113 717	67.4	120 772	33.7	66.3	43.7	16.1	900	25.8
Ulster	71	-3.3	147	4.2	26.1	738 835	5 042	103 237	55.9	115 019	83.0	17.0	43.0	12.6	328	10.1
Warren	10	11.4	81	0.1	1.5	325 487	3 997	58 376	D	D	D	D	28.2	11.1	D	0.9
Washington	189	-6.6	223	0.6	101.9	539 925	2 426	111 270	139.1	163 510	19.4	80.6	53.3	21.0	2 914	28.6
Wayne	179	6.3	205	1.9	126.3	508 517	2 479	166 179	205.6	235 517	72.7	27.3	60.5	31.2	2 084	27.5
Westchester	8	-9.0	59	0.1	1.5	952 855	16 102	104 863	8.8	67 176	47.6	52.4	46.6	17.6	D	2.3
Wyoming	226	3.6	317	3.4	159.5	828 938	2 617	216 229	318.5	446 711	24.5	75.5	52.7	29.3	3 057	35.1
Yates	127	0.7	138	0.6	88.1	546 444	3 956	115 875	117.0	127 336	37.6	62.4	75.1	45.8	1 081	17.1
NORTH CAROLINA	8 415	-0.7	168	174.5	4 745.0	726 944	4 338	92 882	12 588.1	250 670	34.2	65.8	37.3	16.6	120 129	28.7
Alamance	84	-4.9	114	0.9	31.8	538 171	4 715	60 452	32.9	44 986	46.8	53.2	30.3	9.2	470	17.5
Alexander	59	6.7	97	0.6	20.9	578 788	5 949	70 687	187.7	311 227	5.8	94.2	45.6	28.9	177	6.8
Alleghany	91	18.6	160	D	32.9	770 166	4 803	70 547	36.3	64 092	56.6	43.4	44.1	11.5	590	23.1
Anson	84	-7.9	195	1.1	28.3	725 956	3 725	97 247	193.9	451 900	8.7	91.3	49.4	30.3	551	36.6
Ashe	112	3.7	99	0.2	33.1	561 065	5 687	54 833	54.5	47 790	74.4	25.6	38.1	7.9	216	10.4
Avery	28	1.5	58	0.4	11.6	407 195	6 968	55 195	17.2	35 607	96.1	3.9	44.5	8.1	71	4.8
Beaufort	148	-7.5	407	2.6	129.3	1 244 750	3 056	218 201	121.6	334 074	84.7	15.3	49.2	34.6	3 011	71.7
Bertie	147	-0.4	452	4.2	95.4	1 220 674	2 703	219 246	225.2	692 822	37.4	62.6	68.9	49.2	3 200	74.8
Bladen	117	-7.7	238	4.6	52.9	784 878	3 291	106 965	308.5	627 110	19.3	80.7	46.7	26.2	1 102	38.8
Brunswick	45	3.1	179	1.2	27.4	769 642	4 302	92 492	58.2	229 197	48.0	52.0	34.3	12.6	427	24.8
Buncombe	71	-0.8	67	0.9	17.2	580 025	8 601	48 772	54.4	51 333	72.1	27.9	22.0	4.1	1 481	17.4
Burke	34	18.3	71	1.8	12.9	376 290	5 318	50 689	45.4	93 364	25.0	75.0	30.5	9.9	70	4.5
Cabarrus	66	-0.8	112	0.3	29.9	823 779	7 325	65 380	55.9	94 829	24.8	75.2	25.3	6.3	427	14.3
Caldwell	32	-1.6	78	0.4	11.8	430 625	5 521	45 667	17.8	43 294	53.7	46.3	26.0	7.3	145	6.6
Camden	49	-10.6	822	0.0	46.8	2 334 567	2 841	450 750	48.9	815 217	D	D	56.7	40.0	603	40.0
Carteret	63	13.4	503	0.2	45.5	1 653 072	3 288	92 024	29.2	233 656	98.9	1.2	33.6	15.2	363	18.4
Caswell	97	-5.1	179	1.7	24.8	514 319	2 877	64 361	34.2	63 063	51.7	48.3	29.3	8.5	946	35.4
Catawba	67	-6.7	96	0.7	29.3	519 109	5 400	59 158	67.3	96 430	29.4	70.6	32.2	9.6	447	16.0
Chatham	112	7.3	98	1.2	26.7	487 262	4 961	47 006	163.9	144 033	5.5	94.5	40.3	11.0	546	11.6
Cherokee	21	5.0	84	D	7.6	483 376	5 746	59 451	D	D	D	D	23.1	5.5	232	14.1

Table B. States and Counties — Water Use, Wholesale Trade, Retail Trade, and Real Estate

STATE County	Water use, 2010		Wholesale trade,[1] 2012				Retail trade,[2] 2012				Real estate and rental and leasing,[2] 2012			
	Total water withdrawn (mil gal/day)	Gallons withdrawn per person per day	Number of establishments	Number of employees	Sales (mil dol)	Annual payroll (mil dol)	Number of establishments	Number of employees	Sales (mil dol)	Annual payroll (mil dol)	Number of establishments	Number of employees	Receipts (mil dol)	Annual payroll (mil dol)
	133	134	135	136	137	138	139	140	141	142	143	144	145	146
NEW YORK—Cont'd														
Genesee	22.9	381	76	1 165	1 187.1	51.6	219	2 561	785.8	59.1	29	150	25.2	5.1
Greene	7.1	143	27	1 007	724.6	63.0	198	2 329	610.4	53.8	43	181	27.1	7.7
Hamilton	1.1	219	NA	NA	NA	NA	33	169	41.6	4.3	7	8	0.9	0.2
Herkimer	11.9	185	30	545	162.1	25.3	187	2 016	543.9	44.9	34	113	15.0	2.4
Jefferson	24.2	208	67	870	345.2	34.7	476	6 849	1 937.9	161.4	119	588	103.9	17.8
Kings	27.6	11	3 457	28 586	16 522.9	1 176.8	9 931	65 979	20 533.1	1 623.7	4 327	15 248	3 765.5	530.6
Lewis	9.2	340	7	D	D	D	74	792	258.7	19.8	12	D	D	D
Livingston	15.6	238	51	560	458.9	24.0	219	2 501	633.6	55.0	40	206	22.9	5.8
Madison	4.0	55	36	434	151.0	16.9	222	2 688	745.5	61.9	43	148	12.1	3.5
Monroe	121.9	164	788	10 459	6 131.6	562.0	2 349	40 491	9 494.1	902.0	835	6 237	1 091.2	233.4
Montgomery	10.6	211	44	D	D	D	179	2 461	673.3	55.4	22	80	10.2	1.9
Nassau	532.2	397	2 856	28 767	27 959.1	1 860.3	6 145	77 488	24 105.6	2 206.3	2 331	9 580	3 054.1	532.1
New York	29.4	19	7 678	84 273	128 760.9	6 385.0	11 691	148 493	44 040.0	5 027.8	9 627	70 399	33 323.0	4 826.9
Niagara	367.5	1 698	179	2 187	1 506.4	95.0	735	10 233	2 521.6	212.7	144	563	81.8	16.1
Oneida	36.3	155	175	2 081	1 087.5	90.9	830	11 889	3 012.2	263.6	170	686	111.9	20.0
Onondaga	109.2	234	591	10 750	17 113.3	559.0	1 682	28 932	6 916.0	639.1	588	3 756	662.3	150.5
Ontario	17.5	162	113	1 285	660.2	65.9	527	9 194	2 021.4	193.8	94	423	53.8	10.1
Orange	374.4	1 004	455	6 661	8 298.4	304.8	1 512	23 117	6 221.1	530.6	374	1 407	407.3	51.5
Orleans	7.4	171	17	281	130.4	14.3	95	1 097	252.4	22.6	20	61	9.4	1.3
Oswego	985.4	8 070	58	504	368.3	21.8	353	4 392	1 258.4	101.6	69	205	29.6	5.0
Otsego	7.4	119	46	460	308.8	19.6	290	3 373	917.0	78.7	53	215	32.7	6.9
Putnam	6.7	67	101	905	516.3	50.3	329	3 037	952.2	79.7	89	209	33.9	7.9
Queens	1 244.3	558	2 971	24 171	16 059.4	1 250.3	7 388	59 829	17 003.2	1 542.4	2 840	11 679	3 100.3	509.9
Rensselaer	22.1	139	101	1 200	2 270.2	67.3	424	5 814	1 572.2	138.4	101	464	103.0	15.5
Richmond	350.6	748	342	1 416	1 460.0	75.0	1 273	15 926	3 816.0	353.5	312	1 151	377.5	43.8
Rockland	133.3	428	504	4 697	3 892.0	282.0	1 154	14 253	4 153.7	382.2	443	1 498	281.1	55.0
St. Lawrence	23.9	214	46	446	175.0	19.9	414	5 139	1 446.6	116.3	57	167	32.7	5.0
Saratoga	39.4	179	176	3 133	2 332.0	181.5	724	10 871	2 980.0	250.5	213	975	233.2	33.5
Schenectady	40.7	263	78	774	519.3	37.3	480	7 256	1 821.1	167.3	111	510	112.4	19.5
Schoharie	169.7	5 183	19	118	54.9	4.4	95	1 049	319.0	23.9	15	46	7.2	1.5
Schuyler	20.7	1 131	3	D	D	D	59	633	141.4	12.9	5	D	D	D
Seneca	8.2	233	27	410	202.5	13.1	183	2 360	489.9	43.9	19	77	26.0	1.9
Steuben	17.7	178	40	277	122.4	9.3	326	4 238	1 074.0	95.9	51	232	32.5	8.7
Suffolk	604.0	404	2 838	37 819	32 383.0	2 260.5	6 524	79 498	23 693.4	2 182.4	1 677	6 519	1 868.5	303.8
Sullivan	102.6	1 322	43	584	363.6	21.5	291	2 673	771.5	66.5	111	398	55.5	9.6
Tioga	6.3	123	25	331	396.9	14.3	132	1 367	372.9	32.4	12	23	3.3	0.6
Tompkins	232.7	2 291	36	454	259.0	21.6	349	5 071	1 112.0	105.5	112	609	121.6	20.5
Ulster	458.2	2 511	159	1 504	810.4	71.3	733	8 606	2 324.9	211.8	195	732	116.6	22.0
Warren	54.2	824	59	575	190.4	21.0	447	6 436	1 549.1	149.5	74	240	45.0	8.9
Washington	32.6	516	30	D	D	D	186	1 759	498.8	42.4	17	46	4.8	1.0
Wayne	475.6	5 072	62	607	245.7	22.7	267	3 276	822.6	75.5	58	223	24.7	4.2
Westchester	2 044.6	2 154	1 286	16 494	20 313.9	1 493.5	3 802	48 739	14 514.2	1 395.5	1 966	8 041	2 436.5	399.2
Wyoming	18.8	447	26	219	121.9	9.8	128	1 479	376.0	33.0	18	99	11.3	2.8
Yates	76.6	3 024	10	127	41.0	3.4	92	814	208.9	17.8	22	79	10.2	2.5
NORTH CAROLINA	12 420.1	1 303	9 713	136 174	105 275.6	7 853.7	34 288	446 373	120 691.0	10 421.2	10 140	47 155	9 301.7	1 942.6
Alamance	23.9	158	143	1 642	627.2	70.0	624	8 756	2 108.4	178.0	119	607	142.0	24.4
Alexander	4.2	114	17	111	47.8	4.5	86	834	194.8	17.6	10	18	1.6	0.3
Alleghany	5.5	497	3	4	1.1	0.7	41	296	67.9	5.9	10	19	1.7	0.3
Anson	9.5	354	11	203	109.4	10.3	73	726	181.3	14.7	9	D	D	D
Ashe	17.5	641	22	214	101.9	7.0	106	1 020	273.0	22.4	24	48	7.9	1.8
Avery	19.9	1 120	18	D	D	D	82	742	195.5	15.6	32	D	D	D
Beaufort	89.9	1 882	51	477	360.7	20.7	189	2 300	548.4	51.4	36	133	16.6	2.8
Bertie	20.8	978	14	126	145.6	4.7	50	357	95.9	6.7	4	5	0.2	0.1
Bladen	93.2	2 647	22	174	226.7	6.9	91	823	199.5	15.9	14	27	5.2	0.7
Brunswick	1 384.0	12 882	69	544	237.1	21.6	371	4 423	1 125.8	100.7	128	556	85.0	20.2
Buncombe	300.6	1 261	265	2 532	1 286.7	110.6	1 135	16 104	3 884.2	381.4	393	1 287	238.0	43.0
Burke	38.9	428	48	431	226.2	17.4	260	2 541	680.5	54.9	50	128	15.0	3.0
Cabarrus	22.7	127	191	2 454	1 600.3	115.7	708	11 637	2 920.3	247.7	171	645	115.6	18.8
Caldwell	19.7	237	64	411	202.3	16.4	256	2 740	701.0	58.2	58	137	16.7	3.4
Camden	6.1	614	3	17	4.1	0.4	17	94	24.9	1.7	4	4	1.2	0.1
Carteret	10.7	160	47	272	85.7	9.8	363	3 885	972.8	89.3	118	529	63.7	13.5
Caswell	4.2	178	5	D	D	D	49	309	63.9	6.5	1	D	D	D
Catawba	1 076.7	6 975	238	5 320	4 053.8	244.5	715	9 502	2 607.3	222.3	187	534	130.5	17.0
Chatham	246.4	3 880	52	311	115.0	12.6	175	2 089	583.0	43.6	36	80	15.0	2.5
Cherokee	21.8	794	15	149	84.4	4.4	130	1 302	363.6	28.6	26	67	15.4	1.8

1. Merchant wholesalers, except manufacturers' sales branches and offices.   2. Employer establishments.

Table B. States and Counties — Professional Services, Manufacturing, and Accommodation and Food Services

STATE County	Professional, scientific, and technical services, 2012				Manufacturing, 2012				Accommodation and food services, 2012			
	Number of establish-ments	Number of employees	Receipts (mil dol)	Annual payroll (mil dol)	Number of establish-ments	Number of employees	Receipts (mil dol)	Annual payroll (mil dol)	Number of establish-ments	Number of employees	Sales (mil dol)	Annual payroll (mil dol)
	147	148	149	150	151	152	153	154	155	156	157	158
NEW YORK—Cont'd												
Genesee	76	322	28.3	11.5	95	2 632	983.0	125.8	144	1 910	89.9	25.2
Greene	76	258	27.5	9.9	29	735	339.8	D	191	2 675	99.2	29.4
Hamilton	2	D	D	D	3	8	D	D	57	234	22.8	4.8
Herkimer	61	184	18.3	5.9	60	2 561	666.2	119.4	168	1 469	71.3	19.9
Jefferson	142	1 092	115.9	45.4	66	2 247	770.5	102.6	335	4 117	198.8	57.0
Kings	4 346	23 391	3 467.9	1 312.8	1 756	18 296	3 644.1	731.0	4 809	34 099	2 453.4	615.5
Lewis	23	82	9.5	2.5	25	1 371	532.7	58.1	64	480	19.1	5.5
Livingston	98	374	31.7	10.9	55	2 106	635.9	91.1	142	2 123	80.4	23.4
Madison	121	681	66.5	27.7	58	2 407	885.5	109.2	164	2 024	86.4	23.8
Monroe	1 973	21 387	3 187.1	1 263.9	887	38 958	14 610.3	2 315.5	1 662	26 555	1 300.3	370.6
Montgomery	61	252	25.1	7.5	74	3 578	839.0	134.3	117	948	49.2	12.0
Nassau	6 835	43 568	6 915.5	2 542.9	1 043	16 580	5 196.7	893.7	3 483	43 996	2 938.8	818.0
New York	17 504	289 103	88 609.6	31 491.6	2 063	21 220	4 970.9	899.1	9 634	206 517	20 382.6	6 032.2
Niagara	325	1 810	234.9	86.1	273	7 987	3 134.9	463.1	521	9 841	1 055.9	183.3
Oneida	408	3 645	555.6	210.0	236	9 807	3 481.3	462.0	559	10 870	791.3	199.6
Onondaga	1 179	13 456	2 065.5	767.9	436	18 565	7 576.0	1 034.6	1 146	18 791	918.7	265.5
Ontario	239	1 469	195.5	79.9	167	6 718	2 671.0	332.4	302	4 879	237.3	72.3
Orange	872	5 909	648.5	248.4	318	7 105	2 592.4	336.9	847	9 601	575.2	150.4
Orleans	35	168	15.0	5.2	36	2 026	764.6	96.5	57	692	28.4	7.9
Oswego	135	546	55.0	19.7	85	2 669	2 131.1	139.6	290	3 599	153.2	41.2
Otsego	116	623	54.1	19.6	58	877	203.8	37.7	210	2 560	148.5	37.6
Putnam	311	1 246	208.6	74.9	87	1 478	308.6	74.3	195	1 604	100.4	26.3
Queens	3 248	13 293	1 585.1	669.1	1 294	22 240	4 438.1	972.5	4 558	40 510	3 139.1	749.9
Rensselaer	280	3 464	460.4	193.0	95	3 383	D	176.2	348	4 009	209.2	58.6
Richmond	873	3 535	663.0	169.2	136	999	285.3	44.8	770	7 805	472.6	109.8
Rockland	1 272	5 270	1 616.3	341.6	251	8 416	9 613.2	601.3	769	7 762	501.2	140.1
St. Lawrence	107	611	55.8	21.1	77	2 639	1 302.9	149.6	256	2 904	131.6	34.0
Saratoga	605	3 852	608.6	210.2	138	5 259	1 977.4	331.6	524	8 089	446.4	128.6
Schenectady	276	3 772	207.5	284.3	110	4 490	1 709.3	283.0	339	3 846	191.7	54.9
Schoharie	36	208	18.4	6.5	21	239	D	9.5	62	459	23.1	6.5
Schuyler	15	38	2.5	0.7	35	574	D	30.4	62	572	34.9	9.2
Seneca	35	139	14.4	3.8	40	1 318	674.2	68.8	72	744	35.3	11.0
Steuben	133	1 707	89.4	157.7	77	4 314	1 237.0	212.9	223	2 562	132.2	34.0
Suffolk	5 622	43 771	6 531.9	2 657.2	2 067	51 967	15 887.4	2 800.5	3 624	45 646	2 990.4	810.8
Sullivan	167	D	D	D	51	1 224	354.0	41.0	243	1 572	139.6	34.7
Tioga	55	D	D	D	44	1 228	438.2	48.6	89	829	36.2	10.6
Tompkins	274	2 312	356.6	124.1	93	2 766	861.1	150.4	334	4 408	231.7	65.4
Ulster	443	1 601	189.3	69.1	170	3 518	D	170.2	546	6 655	367.3	117.4
Warren	168	876	106.7	40.0	76	3 767	928.9	206.4	413	3 992	306.1	85.9
Washington	61	235	35.1	9.2	87	2 942	1 206.2	152.3	127	758	38.0	9.7
Wayne	105	589	116.2	26.9	137	5 702	1 656.8	241.8	165	1 732	71.7	19.1
Westchester	4 205	28 162	4 976.7	2 187.8	601	11 776	4 492.9	584.9	2 460	26 862	2 020.0	562.8
Wyoming	62	351	41.9	10.8	44	1 878	473.7	76.3	81	747	31.7	9.0
Yates	31	118	10.6	3.9	44	836	188.5	33.3	55	382	22.7	6.4
NORTH CAROLINA	22 855	196 287	31 947.9	12 940.3	8 953	403 593	202 344.6	18 191.2	19 496	358 602	18 622.3	5 040.6
Alamance	218	1 375	133.0	55.8	200	9 268	3 138.4	399.3	293	5 761	254.4	71.8
Alexander	37	123	11.5	4.2	69	3 284	591.5	107.7	38	D	D	D
Alleghany	12	40	3.1	0.9	17	444	D	15.6	22	211	10.8	3.3
Anson	27	116	10.0	3.2	20	1 428	393.3	54.5	29	401	16.8	4.7
Ashe	24	58	3.5	1.3	20	1 122	232.7	36.1	46	573	23.7	6.7
Avery	29	66	7.2	2.1	13	174	20.5	5.2	59	593	45.6	12.9
Beaufort	88	341	26.2	9.5	64	2 661	1 462.1	152.1	73	1 141	50.1	12.5
Bertie	11	51	4.9	1.5	11	D	D	42.4	15	166	6.5	1.6
Bladen	33	143	17.7	5.0	28	5 565	1 904.3	178.5	46	448	25.6	6.3
Brunswick	196	637	57.7	22.2	71	1 520	1 983.0	101.4	271	3 436	180.8	48.7
Buncombe	873	4 336	473.4	206.2	287	13 805	2 839.5	590.9	735	14 976	880.1	254.3
Burke	110	464	44.3	16.3	126	7 475	2 804.6	288.8	127	2 102	97.2	25.2
Cabarrus	338	1 505	193.8	73.3	162	5 427	1 757.9	237.4	346	8 214	428.0	113.7
Caldwell	79	324	31.9	10.5	121	6 098	1 158.1	197.1	117	D	D	D
Camden	7	28	3.0	1.5	NA	NA	NA	NA	3	28	1.5	0.4
Carteret	122	447	49.2	18.9	61	981	343.7	32.9	229	3 318	164.4	48.3
Caswell	13	37	3.5	1.4	9	172	33.3	5.6	13	D	D	D
Catawba	322	1 627	654.5	71.2	411	20 830	5 850.9	809.8	342	6 737	290.7	83.7
Chatham	145	468	59.6	22.2	72	1 538	487.4	66.7	103	1 674	91.3	25.5
Cherokee	37	250	15.7	8.3	26	1 168	317.1	41.8	61	817	41.0	11.3

1. Establishment subject to federal tax.

Table B. States and Counties — Health Care and Social Assistance, Other Services, Nonemployer Businesses, and Residential Construction

STATE County	Health care and social assistance, 2012				Other services, 2012				Nonemployer businesses, 2014		Value of residential construction authorized by building permits, 2015	
	Number of establishments	Number of employees	Receipts (mil dol)	Annual payroll (mil dol)	Number of establishments	Number of employees	Receipts (mil dol)	Annual payroll (mil dol)	Number	Receipts (mil dol)	New Construction ($1,000)	Number of housing units
	159	160	161	162	163	164	165	166	167	168	169	170
NEW YORK—Cont'd												
Genesee	141	3 053	221.6	98.7	100	626	51.8	15.0	2 925	224.6	13 533	95
Greene	94	1 254	88.1	38.8	83	373	32.7	8.2	3 410	136.4	19 430	97
Hamilton	6	25	1.7	0.8	7	D	D	D	478	19.5	6 338	29
Herkimer	109	2 334	184.1	70.5	94	552	32.1	8.3	3 308	137.7	16 283	74
Jefferson	277	6 183	536.8	247.5	187	912	83.3	21.0	5 031	194.0	17 368	147
Kings	6 394	184 851	16 419.6	7 123.6	4 675	18 153	1 622.5	431.4	260 250	10 855.1	3 219 703	26 026
Lewis	49	1 071	83.2	41.4	43	164	21.1	4.7	1 685	72.0	10 789	110
Livingston	143	2 019	140.2	61.2	88	337	39.3	8.6	3 516	144.1	10 466	69
Madison	166	3 027	272.9	110.7	98	349	30.6	7.1	4 242	173.4	24 468	124
Monroe	1 949	63 159	5 819.8	2 425.3	1 151	7 580	772.3	209.4	44 660	2 060.6	258 878	1 880
Montgomery	177	3 970	356.9	149.6	87	558	57.5	15.4	2 456	92.0	4 126	25
Nassau	5 771	111 832	13 166.2	5 522.1	4 068	21 377	2 140.6	587.0	135 574	9 089.3	393 115	1 086
New York	8 106	251 513	34 680.5	13 322.5	9 778	92 777	21 846.1	4 572.6	225 724	17 804.0	1 503 732	12 267
Niagara	512	10 096	789.4	345.9	341	1 593	109.0	31.0	9 415	364.4	45 076	195
Oneida	615	19 043	1 636.6	730.7	407	3 677	219.0	74.3	12 108	471.2	28 729	172
Onondaga	1 294	38 389	4 379.2	1 717.8	876	5 965	613.6	178.1	27 646	1 265.3	117 573	925
Ontario	274	8 001	685.0	340.7	211	1 252	98.6	30.5	6 858	294.1	105 163	494
Orange	961	20 593	2 176.8	957.3	749	3 963	460.3	108.4	24 048	1 105.7	162 517	1 091
Orleans	78	1 544	96.0	46.2	63	209	20.6	4.7	1 758	70.4	2 958	19
Oswego	206	4 897	347.9	156.5	183	699	57.4	13.7	5 409	186.8	22 091	145
Otsego	170	6 049	675.4	281.4	103	617	51.3	11.6	4 403	166.6	26 732	168
Putnam	261	5 055	559.1	239.5	233	1 035	118.0	32.3	8 970	436.8	17 156	58
Queens	5 047	122 646	12 103.5	5 098.2	4 645	19 428	1 863.4	500.0	240 308	8 843.8	1 586 010	12 667
Rensselaer	354	9 708	732.3	349.1	244	1 361	122.5	48.0	8 694	338.3	28 936	254
Richmond	1 308	30 614	2 960.7	1 274.1	869	3 779	342.3	85.5	34 602	1 550.9	100 509	541
Rockland	1 164	22 289	2 083.5	900.8	731	4 364	350.9	106.5	26 808	1 576.3	81 972	502
St. Lawrence	260	6 640	581.7	259.6	170	706	64.8	14.5	4 969	174.7	29 662	288
Saratoga	544	8 412	761.2	317.9	321	1 668	145.3	45.5	15 376	729.4	280 429	1 786
Schenectady	435	11 854	1 005.7	439.2	205	D	D	D	8 562	326.8	51 387	464
Schoharie	62	1 039	69.9	30.7	31	D	D	D	1 832	68.9	3 929	22
Schuyler	39	836	57.5	27.4	34	D	D	D	1 125	35.4	7 710	71
Seneca	63	1 335	82.0	40.4	49	233	19.1	4.6	1 800	76.7	4 087	27
Steuben	238	5 701	488.2	227.8	148	663	59.6	14.5	5 236	203.3	10 428	65
Suffolk	4 736	95 248	10 416.2	4 491.2	3 945	19 049	2 048.8	520.1	126 453	6 925.5	690 849	1 218
Sullivan	250	5 491	412.0	186.4	160	456	66.6	12.0	5 537	224.2	42 881	271
Tioga	68	1 045	54.3	26.7	65	205	20.3	4.8	2 762	103.1	13 557	97
Tompkins	271	5 283	483.0	199.8	152	966	122.9	23.9	7 371	274.4	40 961	279
Ulster	514	8 991	741.4	312.4	322	1 229	114.9	28.6	16 206	675.8	72 158	307
Warren	283	6 574	569.0	261.1	140	817	84.1	26.0	4 717	228.9	53 438	301
Washington	105	1 535	96.2	44.5	78	271	28.6	7.7	3 765	144.5	7 762	80
Wayne	151	3 061	215.0	102.9	133	434	36.2	9.0	4 803	193.4	22 529	140
Westchester	3 592	79 057	9 638.2	4 111.1	2 819	15 205	2 013.8	539.3	94 864	6 368.3	269 569	816
Wyoming	68	1 183	94.2	40.9	62	246	21.7	5.7	2 056	88.6	3 915	32
Yates	50	975	64.1	28.0	45	147	12.3	2.7	1 941	92.7	9 892	50
NORTH CAROLINA	22 977	529 570	55 227.5	21 757.0	13 716	80 710	9 141.5	2 321.3	706 538	28 822.5	9 707 931	54 757
Alamance	379	8 367	801.9	369.4	190	1 097	100.7	29.2	9 624	350.5	122 046	1 032
Alexander	43	559	33.5	14.6	36	139	9.8	2.1	2 253	81.3	17 070	65
Alleghany	27	517	31.1	13.8	10	D	D	D	908	33.1	8 805	17
Anson	45	826	50.7	24.7	21	D	D	D	1 285	43.4	5 120	36
Ashe	51	1 136	73.3	35.1	32	118	10.4	2.8	2 360	88.3	16 294	77
Avery	41	746	72.2	25.4	25	180	20.4	5.1	1 664	57.2	22 111	47
Beaufort	120	2 392	186.5	77.6	80	384	32.1	8.6	3 293	127.1	17 822	148
Bertie	57	1 344	63.4	28.5	18	62	5.3	1.4	868	24.4	3 752	18
Bladen	56	998	52.7	19.8	29	D	D	D	1 795	63.8	6 502	42
Brunswick	221	3 576	326.6	127.5	119	463	45.3	12.0	9 993	400.1	536 126	2 325
Buncombe	844	20 510	2 518.2	1 012.7	456	2 461	261.7	69.8	25 330	1 037.4	320 589	1 353
Burke	187	4 495	461.5	183.6	99	434	41.1	11.1	5 165	196.8	31 900	224
Cabarrus	343	6 008	568.1	244.2	266	1 435	119.0	31.6	13 715	509.8	229 583	1 763
Caldwell	132	2 924	234.4	88.5	79	397	39.0	10.9	4 958	185.4	28 491	168
Camden	5	24	1.4	0.6	7	D	D	D	676	20.5	5 006	20
Carteret	191	3 165	283.7	120.4	143	598	51.3	15.5	6 298	255.5	78 330	345
Caswell	29	467	23.7	11.6	14	D	D	D	1 077	33.6	12 502	56
Catawba	382	11 445	1 153.6	446.6	223	1 410	109.8	31.8	10 538	485.0	62 624	348
Chatham	127	2 581	179.1	67.4	83	306	36.8	8.7	5 745	245.0	165 659	596
Cherokee	76	1 217	96.7	41.9	35	103	7.6	2.2	2 170	75.3	21 220	132

Table B. States and Counties — Government Employment and Payroll, and Local Government Finances

	Government employment and payroll, 2012									Local government finances, 2012				
			March payroll (percent of total)							General revenue				
													Taxes	
														Per capita[1] (dollars)
STATE County	Full-time equivalent employees	March payroll (dollars)	Administration, judicial, and legal	Police and Corrections	Fire Protection	Highways and transportation	Health and Welfare	Natural resources and utilities	Education and libraries	Total (mil dol)	Inter-governmental (mil dol)	Total (mil dol)	Total	Property
	171	172	173	174	175	176	177	178	179	180	181	182	183	184
NEW YORK—Cont'd														
Genesee	3 495	13 011 030	5.1	5.8	1.6	4.1	10.0	1.1	70.6	378.8	154.3	137.4	2 290	1 468
Greene	2 313	9 425 632	7.2	6.0	0.0	7.6	11.6	1.6	64.8	291.0	101.2	151.7	3 117	2 471
Hamilton	511	1 883 521	13.9	3.7	0.5	18.0	10.6	5.4	45.2	54.6	10.1	40.8	8 548	7 863
Herkimer	3 357	17 320 913	6.2	16.3	10.9	9.4	4.5	5.4	45.2	354.3	171.8	137.0	2 124	1 648
Jefferson	5 239	20 682 670	6.0	6.1	2.2	6.7	6.7	3.0	66.9	631.5	312.9	217.3	1 807	1 154
Kings	(3)	(3)	(3)	(3)	(3)	(3)	(3)	(3)	(3)	(3)	(3)	(3)	(3)	(3)
Lewis	1 643	6 393 465	5.3	4.0	0.1	9.3	34.1	0.3	46.2	221.0	80.0	54.5	2 001	1 591
Livingston	2 962	11 287 932	7.2	8.2	0.0	6.5	18.2	2.0	56.7	340.1	136.2	132.2	2 039	1 556
Madison	2 860	10 880 867	5.6	7.3	1.1	8.0	7.4	2.2	66.8	324.2	144.9	143.1	1 977	1 638
Monroe	32 909	147 986 255	4.0	10.2	3.5	2.4	4.8	4.9	68.8	4 246.2	1 878.0	1 825.1	2 441	1 824
Montgomery	2 237	9 439 506	8.2	8.8	2.4	6.9	5.7	2.1	64.3	270.8	126.1	103.0	2 062	1 500
Nassau	60 368	360 394 360	4.0	11.4	0.7	2.4	9.9	3.6	66.2	10 545.3	2 263.0	7 088.6	5 254	4 380
New York	(3)411 393	(3)36 392 993	(3)3.2	(3)18.6	(3)5.3	(3)14.2	(3)17.3	(3)4.7	(3)33.2	(3)89 561.8	(3)30 794.6	(3)42 487.9	(3)5 096	(3)2 183
Niagara	8 942	40 897 207	4.2	9.3	3.5	3.3	5.7	3.9	65.8	1 197.2	504.4	461.1	2 144	1 505
Oneida	10 265	43 288 880	5.1	9.3	3.3	5.7	6.1	4.4	65.3	1 243.2	607.6	466.1	1 996	1 316
Onondaga	21 333	98 896 686	3.5	9.2	2.8	3.6	6.0	5.0	68.2	2 768.2	1 213.5	1 131.6	2 424	1 706
Ontario	5 314	22 633 286	7.3	8.2	1.0	4.3	6.4	3.2	68.2	617.9	231.6	291.0	2 682	1 907
Orange	15 475	79 024 558	5.0	9.7	1.3	3.8	7.6	2.1	69.2	2 388.1	851.1	1 242.0	3 316	2 623
Orleans	1 883	7 322 413	5.8	7.3	1.3	4.6	12.9	1.4	65.5	215.9	108.4	76.5	1 785	1 393
Oswego	5 833	24 108 601	4.0	4.7	1.8	4.8	6.7	1.2	74.7	720.3	332.9	266.4	2 189	1 640
Otsego	2 867	10 320 001	6.5	5.1	1.5	9.1	12.9	1.2	62.0	319.5	134.0	135.1	2 189	1 567
Putnam	3 780	21 486 132	6.3	9.6	0.0	4.8	5.6	1.1	71.4	620.4	156.8	423.9	4 256	3 653
Queens	(3)	(3)	(3)	(3)	(3)	(3)	(3)	(3)	(3)	(3)	(3)	(3)	(3)	(3)
Rensselaer	7 740	35 240 411	5.4	10.0	1.8	3.0	10.0	3.2	65.6	935.0	383.9	372.9	2 333	1 782
Richmond	(3)	(3)	(3)	(3)	(3)	(3)	(3)	(3)	(3)	(3)	(3)	(3)	(3)	(3)
Rockland	12 621	72 071 900	6.2	11.8	0.2	3.4	10.5	3.3	63.3	2 081.2	511.7	1 307.8	4 116	3 491
St. Lawrence	5 029	19 319 273	5.7	6.1	1.0	8.5	20.0	3.1	54.2	629.7	288.6	207.1	1 845	1 390
Saratoga	8 393	36 185 319	5.4	6.8	1.4	6.5	7.0	2.5	68.7	1 010.7	328.4	547.9	2 467	1 874
Schenectady	6 336	30 200 971	4.8	10.8	2.9	3.7	8.4	3.1	64.2	840.2	334.0	398.5	2 569	1 914
Schoharie	1 588	6 242 263	7.0	4.8	0.1	8.7	8.1	2.1	67.7	198.0	92.7	86.5	2 696	2 164
Schuyler	713	2 598 532	9.7	8.4	0.0	8.0	12.3	2.8	55.9	92.6	40.4	41.0	2 213	1 616
Seneca	1 397	5 203 170	7.6	6.3	0.0	6.3	10.3	4.6	63.8	187.5	82.2	75.2	2 129	1 460
Steuben	5 430	22 838 751	6.3	4.7	1.6	6.5	9.0	2.5	68.7	603.0	285.7	219.9	2 220	1 686
Suffolk	63 444	372 480 221	4.1	12.0	1.0	2.5	5.0	2.8	71.0	10 433.2	3 062.8	6 438.8	4 295	3 385
Sullivan	3 903	18 183 844	6.0	6.2	4.1	7.1	11.7	2.9	59.7	571.4	182.8	285.0	3 711	3 207
Tioga	2 377	8 831 267	4.9	6.4	0.5	4.3	7.4	1.1	72.8	263.8	126.3	98.9	1 959	1 607
Tompkins	4 530	19 870 493	5.0	6.2	2.8	4.4	7.3	3.5	68.0	531.9	184.0	252.8	2 465	1 857
Ulster	8 282	38 442 668	5.7	7.7	1.3	4.8	8.8	1.7	68.0	1 095.2	330.4	630.3	3 467	2 848
Warren	3 395	12 916 351	7.7	10.3	0.3	8.0	7.0	4.0	60.4	411.0	122.0	230.3	3 513	2 589
Washington	3 303	11 817 292	4.2	5.9	0.6	5.8	10.6	1.3	70.1	334.5	150.3	129.8	2 063	1 703
Wayne	4 573	16 899 070	5.7	6.6	0.1	4.5	9.5	2.2	70.0	506.8	227.4	194.1	2 088	1 627
Westchester	42 725	278 687 815	4.6	13.0	4.0	2.1	14.4	4.1	55.6	8 694.6	1 905.2	4 937.7	5 135	4 223
Wyoming	1 997	7 253 253	6.6	6.7	0.7	6.2	29.3	3.6	45.9	224.2	78.4	71.1	1 698	1 279
Yates	984	3 705 476	8.7	13.4	0.2	8.3	6.2	2.9	58.0	114.7	43.0	58.3	2 300	1 770
NORTH CAROLINA	X	X	X	X	X	X	X	X	X	X	X	X	X	X
Alamance	5 835	17 822 770	4.1	10.8	2.8	1.7	7.8	5.8	64.0	420.3	210.4	147.7	960	694
Alexander	1 147	3 312 277	3.5	5.4	1.2	0.1	15.0	1.1	71.6	79.1	47.9	22.9	622	467
Alleghany	425	1 164 658	3.2	4.3	0.0	1.2	5.7	2.7	76.9	29.9	16.8	10.5	964	802
Anson	1 315	3 876 045	2.9	6.4	2.5	0.6	7.2	4.8	74.4	91.7	58.9	20.0	760	612
Ashe	790	2 611 411	5.6	7.1	0.0	1.1	16.3	2.1	65.4	64.2	34.4	23.7	876	672
Avery	815	1 974 739	6.6	9.8	1.1	1.1	14.1	2.6	59.8	51.3	22.8	24.5	1 387	1 109
Beaufort	2 278	5 974 850	4.5	7.2	2.1	0.6	8.3	10.0	62.5	173.8	99.8	49.9	1 050	812
Bertie	997	3 093 286	5.9	4.6	0.1	0.6	4.8	2.9	80.8	51.4	32.6	12.0	580	454
Bladen	1 399	4 935 403	2.7	6.3	0.5	0.4	11.2	2.6	74.0	133.3	64.5	29.1	834	667
Brunswick	3 900	12 967 182	6.8	10.3	1.5	1.3	19.2	7.5	47.9	393.3	118.2	177.6	1 582	1 215
Buncombe	8 896	30 002 974	4.8	8.2	3.6	1.6	11.7	7.3	59.6	751.0	306.2	322.9	1 321	936
Burke	3 144	9 746 027	4.9	6.5	1.0	0.9	9.1	5.9	70.6	228.4	129.8	66.9	739	594
Cabarrus	7 505	25 676 197	3.6	8.3	4.5	1.2	14.4	6.7	58.7	601.3	252.6	258.8	1 403	1 100
Caldwell	3 445	10 357 515	2.9	6.0	2.1	0.6	13.9	3.0	69.5	257.1	164.6	64.8	791	595
Camden	352	1 014 214	1.0	5.8	0.0	0.0	0.0	4.2	71.8	30.3	17.1	11.7	1 163	952
Carteret	2 554	7 543 452	5.4	9.0	4.8	1.2	10.1	4.3	60.9	338.2	84.6	98.9	1 462	1 061
Caswell	710	2 061 989	3.0	5.5	0.0	0.0	17.8	1.7	67.9	51.5	32.9	13.2	569	464
Catawba	7 515	27 058 433	3.4	5.6	2.5	1.6	35.0	3.0	45.2	716.3	255.5	171.8	1 113	804
Chatham	1 616	6 230 991	4.0	6.8	0.3	0.8	10.6	4.0	68.1	164.8	66.0	78.0	1 182	977
Cherokee	1 091	3 381 536	5.0	8.1	0.0	1.1	13.2	8.0	61.9	84.3	45.8	26.1	966	704

1. Based on the resident population estimated as of July 1 of the year shown. 3. Bronx, Kings, Queens, and Richmond counties are included with New York county.

STATE County	Local government finances, 2012 (cont.)									Government employment, 2014			Presidential election,[2] 2012		
	Direct general expenditure							Debt outstanding					Percent of vote cast:		
			Percent of total for:												
	Total (mil dol)	Per capita[1] (dollars)	Education	Health and hospitals	Police protection	Public welfare	Highways	Total (mil dol)	Per capita[1] (dollars)	Federal civilian	Federal military	State and local	Democratic	Republican	All other
	185	186	187	188	189	190	191	192	193	194	195	196	197	198	199
NEW YORK—Cont'd															
Genesee	380.9	6 350	48.2	3.3	2.6	11.4	6.0	207.2	3 454	589	94	5 211	40.1	58.5	1.5
Greene	302.4	6 212	48.5	5.4	2.1	9.8	9.4	211.7	4 350	90	73	4 258	44.1	54.0	1.8
Hamilton	53.0	11 093	36.6	5.7	1.7	2.5	16.4	24.5	5 123	19	0	889	35.9	62.8	1.3
Herkimer	352.7	5 467	56.7	3.1	1.8	9.3	8.9	252.1	3 907	102	101	4 343	44.5	53.8	1.7
Jefferson	631.0	5 247	49.6	3.4	2.6	9.2	6.9	554.7	4 612	3 184	16 970	8 352	46.8	52.0	1.2
Kings	(3)		(3)	(3)	(3)	(3)	(3)	(3)	(3)	7 481	4 415	30 062	79.4	20.0	0.6
Lewis	250.8	9 211	33.2	34.9	1.3	6.5	7.0	120.5	4 427	59	44	2 324	44.8	53.6	1.6
Livingston	328.9	5 074	44.9	5.5	2.8	18.2	7.8	282.5	4 359	134	95	6 158	45.3	53.2	1.5
Madison	345.6	4 774	52.0	4.3	2.3	7.4	8.1	456.5	6 307	125	110	4 224	49.3	48.5	2.2
Monroe	4 348.7	5 815	50.1	4.2	4.3	10.9	3.2	3 397.3	4 543	2 714	1 272	44 763	58.3	40.5	1.2
Montgomery	305.0	6 106	50.5	2.2	2.0	7.7	5.3	285.4	5 714	95	80	2 579	45.0	53.1	1.9
Nassau	11 105.9	8 231	48.3	7.2	8.7	5.9	3.1	9 302.1	6 894	5 202	2 602	74 285	53.8	45.4	0.7
New York	(3)84 366.2	(3)10 120	(3)26.6	(3)10.0	(3)6.0	(3)15.1	(3)1.9	(3)168 630.0	(3)20 227	22 425	2 749	419 036	85.7	13.5	0.8
Niagara	1 203.8	5 596	48.1	2.7	3.7	8.2	5.8	966.3	4 492	986	373	13 172	49.7	48.7	1.6
Oneida	1 300.4	5 568	52.4	2.6	3.1	11.0	5.5	1 381.4	5 915	2 244	406	23 723	46.1	52.2	1.6
Onondaga	3 043.0	6 518	47.4	3.2	3.3	10.4	4.6	3 160.9	6 771	4 375	852	36 471	59.3	38.9	1.8
Ontario	612.2	5 642	54.1	2.3	2.9	8.5	6.6	594.8	5 481	1 452	174	7 344	49.2	49.3	1.5
Orange	2 555.9	6 825	54.6	4.6	3.7	10.5	3.3	1 906.2	5 090	4 696	6 506	21 955	51.6	47.4	1.0
Orleans	216.3	5 050	53.5	3.8	2.2	13.7	6.1	184.0	4 295	81	64	3 904	39.9	58.6	1.5
Oswego	722.5	5 936	55.7	2.6	2.1	8.4	6.2	668.5	5 493	251	215	8 987	50.3	47.9	1.8
Otsego	326.6	5 293	47.1	2.7	1.6	14.9	9.2	292.6	4 742	127	92	4 799	52.0	46.1	1.9
Putnam	630.2	6 327	61.1	2.1	4.6	3.9	5.1	400.1	4 017	138	158	4 463	45.8	53.3	1.0
Queens	(3)		(3)	(3)	(3)	(3)	(3)	(3)		14 016	3 786	23 575	75.1	24.3	0.6
Rensselaer	989.2	6 189	51.6	3.4	3.1	13.0	3.7	809.6	5 065	357	267	11 244	53.7	44.4	1.9
Richmond	(3)		(3)	(3)	(3)	(3)	(3)	(3)		1 012	1 230	5 404	47.6	51.7	0.7
Rockland	2 333.3	7 343	45.2	11.3	4.7	6.4	4.3	1 968.4	6 195	473	516	18 075	52.6	46.7	0.6
St. Lawrence	626.2	5 579	45.3	11.0	2.3	10.4	8.4	441.9	3 937	584	266	9 798	57.5	41.1	1.4
Saratoga	1 019.1	4 588	54.8	5.8	3.1	8.2	5.3	814.5	3 667	394	2 021	11 796	50.9	47.5	1.6
Schenectady	849.4	5 476	48.9	2.4	3.7	14.9	3.5	691.5	4 458	599	255	8 896	55.3	42.6	2.0
Schoharie	201.5	6 278	47.0	3.9	1.2	7.5	15.0	132.3	4 121	74	49	2 545	41.8	56.1	2.1
Schuyler	91.9	4 963	40.6	6.3	1.9	11.2	10.5	63.1	3 409	47	29	1 119	45.7	52.8	1.5
Seneca	180.7	5 118	46.5	4.6	2.7	8.7	6.0	331.8	9 398	89	52	2 879	50.4	47.8	1.8
Steuben	616.7	6 226	58.5	3.7	1.6	11.1	8.0	529.5	5 345	1 022	158	6 936	40.9	57.8	1.3
Suffolk	11 000.9	7 338	53.4	3.5	5.3	5.4	3.3	9 786.8	6 528	11 412	2 656	92 244	52.6	46.6	0.9
Sullivan	549.1	7 150	46.8	4.4	2.6	12.2	8.2	363.9	4 739	185	117	5 641	54.1	44.6	1.3
Tioga	265.1	5 251	53.3	3.7	1.7	7.4	7.4	230.5	4 566	152	86	2 469	44.1	54.3	1.7
Tompkins	541.1	5 276	48.3	4.4	2.7	8.0	5.5	696.7	6 794	267	169	5 981	70.2	28.1	1.7
Ulster	1 119.8	6 160	51.1	2.0	2.8	12.1	5.4	695.1	3 823	451	292	13 178	61.0	37.4	1.7
Warren	406.2	6 198	44.0	4.8	3.3	10.1	9.1	365.7	5 580	194	107	4 602	50.6	47.9	1.5
Washington	349.4	5 552	55.7	4.3	1.6	11.5	6.6	209.9	3 336	120	96	4 890	49.5	48.7	1.7
Wayne	528.4	5 684	56.8	4.2	2.3	10.7	5.9	364.9	3 926	179	151	7 145	44.3	54.2	1.4
Westchester	8 708.4	9 055	42.2	12.9	4.6	6.4	1.7	6 138.8	6 383	4 466	1 540	55 737	63.4	35.8	0.8
Wyoming	218.6	5 217	34.6	26.6	2.8	7.6	9.3	135.9	3 244	95	61	4 192	36.1	62.3	1.6
Yates	112.7	4 445	44.0	5.8	4.2	8.7	10.8	161.3	6 365	62	39	1 234	47.6	51.3	1.0
NORTH CAROLINA	X	X	X	X	X	X	X	X	X	69 014	132 343	652 309	49.7	49.4	0.9
Alamance	427.7	2 779	50.9	3.4	8.3	5.8	1.6	182.0	1 183	216	377	6 833	44.9	54.2	0.9
Alexander	79.9	2 168	57.3	6.5	5.6	7.5	0.5	21.9	594	54	90	1 912	29.9	68.3	1.7
Alleghany	28.9	2 648	55.4	5.1	5.7	7.6	0.2	8.2	749	50	27	607	38.4	59.4	2.2
Anson	92.1	3 494	62.0	2.8	6.7	6.7	1.0	5.0	191	48	58	2 487	60.2	39.2	0.7
Ashe	66.1	2 439	50.5	2.7	5.8	13.7	1.2	26.9	992	56	66	1 143	37.3	60.6	2.2
Avery	52.4	2 970	45.9	4.8	9.0	7.8	1.8	12.6	717	44	38	1 546	27.4	71.5	1.1
Beaufort	192.0	4 042	45.1	2.4	4.2	6.6	1.0	78.5	1 653	114	117	2 731	41.1	58.5	0.4
Bertie	49.9	2 417	57.0	0.9	7.9	10.3	1.0	16.3	788	90	47	1 349	65.2	34.6	0.2
Bladen	137.6	3 942	46.1	22.2	4.7	6.1	1.2	40.6	1 164	100	85	2 356	50.7	48.7	0.6
Brunswick	396.3	3 530	32.7	9.9	9.3	4.9	1.6	543.6	4 843	413	351	4 761	40.5	58.5	1.0
Buncombe	800.5	3 274	41.8	1.9	10.0	8.4	2.1	617.7	2 527	2 992	668	13 249	56.3	42.4	1.3
Burke	231.0	2 553	56.9	2.9	7.1	6.7	0.9	69.8	771	139	214	7 157	39.8	59.0	1.2
Cabarrus	593.1	3 214	47.0	1.8	6.9	5.0	1.7	669.7	3 630	267	474	13 330	40.4	58.9	0.7
Caldwell	274.4	3 349	49.9	21.1	4.8	6.2	1.3	60.2	735	126	200	4 191	34.4	64.1	1.6
Camden	29.0	2 871	58.0	0.3	6.4	4.2	0.0	8.6	849	13	26	462	33.1	65.1	1.7
Carteret	311.1	4 600	29.2	39.1	5.8	4.1	1.4	132.7	1 963	268	396	4 570	32.2	66.9	1.0
Caswell	54.4	2 344	50.3	5.5	16.1	11.3	0.1	23.2	1 000	40	54	1 304	51.0	47.9	1.0
Catawba	685.5	4 441	36.4	32.8	4.4	5.5	1.4	324.5	2 102	355	380	9 440	36.9	61.9	1.2
Chatham	177.4	2 689	45.4	4.2	15.7	6.3	0.6	171.9	2 605	115	169	2 390	54.3	44.6	1.1
Cherokee	85.8	3 180	51.5	5.7	5.1	7.8	0.4	29.5	1 092	88	66	1 543	30.1	68.7	1.3

1. Based on the resident population estimated as of July 1 of the year shown.   2. © 2013 Election Data Services, Inc. All rights reserved.   3. Bronx, Kings, Queens, and Richmond counties are included with New York county.

Table B. States and Counties — Land Area and Population

STATE/ County code	CBSA code[1]	County type[2]	STATE County	Land area,[3] (sq km) 2010	Total persons 2015	Rank	Per square kilometer	White	Black	American Indian, Alaska Native	Asian and Pacific Islander	Percent Hispanic or Latino[4]	Under 5 years	5 to 17 years	18 to 24 years	25 to 34 years	35 to 44 years	45 to 54 years
				1	2	3	4	5	6	7	8	9	10	11	12	13	14	15
			NORTH CAROLINA—Cont'd															
37 041	...	7	Chowan	447	14 394	2 141	32.2	61.6	34.4	0.7	0.9	3.2	5.4	15.6	7.4	10.4	10.0	13.3
37 043	...	9	Clay	556	10 703	2 378	19.3	95.0	1.6	1.0	0.5	3.0	4.3	13.5	6.5	8.1	10.3	12.1
37 045	43140	4	Cleveland	1 202	96 879	609	80.6	74.9	21.7	0.6	1.3	3.1	5.7	16.6	9.8	10.8	11.8	14.5
37 047	...	6	Columbus	2 428	56 694	900	23.4	61.4	30.7	3.9	0.6	4.9	5.5	16.8	8.7	11.8	11.9	13.7
37 049	35100	5	Craven	1 836	103 451	577	56.3	68.4	22.5	1.1	3.5	7.1	7.0	15.5	13.2	13.5	10.4	11.1
37 051	22180	2	Cumberland	1 689	323 838	209	191.7	48.2	38.3	2.5	4.2	11.0	8.2	17.6	12.7	16.9	11.8	11.8
37 053	47260	1	Currituck	678	25 263	1 599	37.3	89.2	6.9	1.1	1.3	3.7	5.1	17.0	7.6	11.1	12.7	16.6
37 055	28620	5	Dare	993	35 663	1 283	35.9	89.4	3.5	1.0	1.0	6.8	5.3	14.3	6.4	11.2	12.1	15.1
37 057	49180	4	Davidson	1 431	164 622	389	115.0	82.2	9.8	0.9	1.7	6.8	5.3	17.4	8.0	10.8	12.9	15.3
37 059	49180	2	Davie	684	41 753	1 131	61.0	86.5	7.3	0.7	1.0	6.4	5.1	16.8	7.7	9.1	12.2	15.1
37 061	...	6	Duplin	2 114	59 159	876	28.0	52.8	25.5	0.7	0.6	21.7	6.6	18.2	8.7	11.7	12.6	13.2
37 063	20500	2	Durham	741	300 952	225	406.1	43.6	38.4	1.0	5.5	13.3	7.0	15.0	10.5	18.1	14.5	12.4
37 065	40580	3	Edgecombe	1 309	54 150	927	41.4	37.8	57.7	0.7	0.6	4.2	6.4	16.8	9.1	11.6	11.1	13.3
37 067	49180	2	Forsyth	1 057	369 019	185	349.1	59.1	26.6	0.8	2.7	12.6	6.3	17.4	10.0	12.8	12.6	13.8
37 069	39580	2	Franklin	1 273	63 710	825	50.0	64.8	26.9	1.0	0.9	8.0	5.6	17.4	8.8	11.1	13.0	15.1
37 071	16740	1	Gaston	922	213 442	303	231.5	76.1	16.6	0.9	1.8	6.4	6.1	17.0	8.7	12.0	13.6	14.6
37 073	47260	8	Gates	882	11 431	2 327	13.0	64.1	34.2	1.3	0.7	2.0	5.0	16.6	8.1	9.9	10.9	16.6
37 075	...	9	Graham	756	8 616	2 543	11.4	89.2	1.0	7.8	0.6	3.2	5.4	15.8	7.4	10.2	11.0	13.6
37 077	37080	6	Granville	1 377	58 674	879	42.6	59.8	32.4	0.9	1.1	7.6	4.9	16.4	9.4	10.9	13.3	16.0
37 079	...	3	Greene	689	21 134	1 767	30.7	48.1	36.1	0.9	0.5	14.6	5.8	15.8	8.5	13.5	13.7	14.2
37 081	24660	2	Guilford	1 672	517 600	130	309.6	53.8	34.4	1.1	5.1	7.6	6.1	16.7	11.0	13.6	13.0	13.7
37 083	40260	4	Halifax	1 875	52 456	953	28.0	40.0	53.4	4.2	1.0	2.7	5.5	16.4	8.8	11.1	10.9	14.2
37 085	20380	4	Harnett	1 541	128 140	487	83.2	64.8	22.2	1.7	2.1	11.9	7.5	19.7	9.6	15.4	13.7	12.6
37 087	11700	2	Haywood	1 434	59 868	868	41.7	94.3	1.5	1.1	0.6	3.7	4.4	14.0	7.2	10.1	11.5	14.2
37 089	11700	2	Henderson	966	112 655	541	116.6	85.4	3.9	1.0	1.5	9.9	4.9	14.8	6.6	10.0	11.6	13.2
37 091	...	7	Hertford	914	24 184	1 639	26.5	34.8	59.8	1.7	1.0	3.8	5.3	14.5	11.2	11.8	11.3	13.5
37 093	22180	2	Hoke	1 012	52 671	948	52.0	43.9	34.9	9.8	2.5	12.5	9.3	19.4	8.7	18.5	13.7	12.0
37 095	...	9	Hyde	1 587	5 526	2 802	3.5	62.0	29.9	0.9	0.5	8.0	4.4	13.5	7.4	13.6	13.7	13.4
37 097	16740	4	Iredell	1 486	169 866	377	114.3	78.1	12.7	0.7	2.7	7.3	5.6	18.3	8.6	11.1	13.5	15.7
37 099	19000	6	Jackson	1 271	41 265	1 145	32.5	82.9	2.7	9.8	1.3	5.1	4.2	12.4	18.9	11.4	10.3	11.5
37 101	39580	2	Johnston	2 049	185 660	349	90.6	70.4	16.1	0.9	1.1	13.4	6.5	19.9	8.1	11.7	15.0	14.9
37 103	35100	8	Jones	1 219	10 013	2 433	8.2	59.3	31.8	1.2	0.7	4.4	4.5	14.5	8.1	10.9	10.0	14.0
37 105	41820	4	Lee	660	59 660	872	90.4	59.6	20.1	1.0	1.4	19.5	7.0	18.3	8.8	12.4	12.8	13.3
37 107	28820	4	Lenoir	1 038	58 106	884	56.0	51.1	41.1	0.7	0.9	7.5	5.9	17.0	8.8	11.0	11.1	13.7
37 109	16740	4	Lincoln	772	81 035	689	105.0	86.3	6.2	0.7	0.8	7.2	5.0	16.9	8.0	10.4	13.7	16.0
37 111	32000	6	McDowell	1 141	44 989	1 073	39.4	89.5	4.4	0.9	0.9	5.5	5.2	15.5	7.9	11.1	12.8	14.5
37 113	...	7	Macon	1 335	34 201	1 323	25.6	90.6	2.0	1.0	0.9	6.6	4.9	14.0	7.0	9.6	9.8	12.6
37 115	11700	2	Madison	1 164	21 139	1 766	18.2	94.6	2.1	1.0	0.7	2.7	4.9	14.2	11.0	9.9	11.8	13.6
37 117	...	6	Martin	1 195	23 357	1 665	19.5	53.1	43.1	0.6	0.6	3.6	5.2	15.5	8.0	9.7	10.7	13.9
37 119	16740	1	Mecklenburg	1 357	1 034 070	41	762.0	50.3	32.2	0.9	6.0	12.7	7.0	17.6	9.4	16.5	15.2	13.6
37 121	...	9	Mitchell	573	15 246	2 084	26.6	93.8	1.0	0.9	0.6	4.6	4.6	14.1	7.2	10.2	11.0	14.1
37 123	...	6	Montgomery	1 274	27 548	1 509	21.6	64.6	18.9	0.8	1.6	15.1	6.1	17.1	8.3	10.6	12.0	13.1
37 125	38240	4	Moore	1 807	94 352	621	52.2	78.7	13.7	1.4	1.6	6.3	5.4	15.8	6.9	10.8	11.4	12.7
37 127	40580	3	Nash	1 400	93 919	623	67.1	52.8	39.9	1.2	1.2	6.6	5.8	17.1	9.0	11.0	12.3	14.4
37 129	48900	2	New Hanover	496	220 358	295	444.3	78.3	15.0	1.0	2.1	5.4	5.3	14.1	13.1	13.6	12.8	12.7
37 131	40260	9	Northampton	1 390	20 426	1 811	14.7	39.1	58.2	0.8	0.5	2.0	5.1	13.9	7.9	9.7	9.6	14.0
37 133	27340	3	Onslow	1 975	186 311	346	94.3	70.8	16.8	1.4	3.8	12.2	9.8	15.5	21.5	18.9	10.0	8.4
37 135	20500	2	Orange	1 031	141 354	453	137.1	71.7	12.7	1.0	8.7	8.4	4.7	15.7	18.6	12.4	11.9	13.3
37 137	35100	9	Pamlico	872	12 781	2 244	14.7	75.7	20.7	1.0	0.9	3.5	3.8	12.7	6.8	10.1	9.9	13.3
37 139	21020	7	Pasquotank	588	39 829	1 178	67.7	56.7	38.0	0.9	2.0	4.7	6.1	15.6	11.4	14.0	11.5	13.2
37 141	48900	2	Pender	2 253	57 611	890	25.6	76.1	17.3	1.2	1.0	6.4	5.5	16.9	7.9	10.9	12.9	14.5
37 143	21020	9	Perquimans	640	13 440	2 206	21.0	72.7	24.9	0.8	0.6	2.3	4.7	15.5	6.3	10.3	10.1	13.2
37 145	20500	2	Person	1 016	39 259	1 191	38.6	67.6	28.0	1.0	0.6	4.2	5.4	16.4	8.2	10.4	12.5	14.6
37 147	24780	3	Pitt	1 689	175 842	365	104.1	57.7	35.2	0.7	2.4	5.9	6.1	15.8	18.4	13.8	12.0	11.6
37 149	...	8	Polk	616	20 366	1 814	33.1	89.3	5.0	0.7	0.7	5.6	3.6	13.7	6.8	7.8	9.7	13.9
37 151	24660	2	Randolph	2 027	142 799	448	70.4	81.3	6.6	0.9	1.4	11.2	5.8	17.8	8.3	11.0	12.9	14.9
37 153	40460	4	Richmond	1 227	45 437	1 064	37.0	59.3	31.7	3.3	1.4	6.4	6.2	17.4	9.7	11.3	12.6	13.5
37 155	31300	4	Robeson	2 458	134 197	471	54.6	28.2	25.3	39.6	1.1	8.1	7.2	18.7	11.0	12.3	12.6	12.8
37 157	24660	2	Rockingham	1 465	91 758	633	62.6	74.3	19.6	0.9	0.9	5.9	5.1	15.8	7.9	10.4	12.1	15.2
37 159	16740	4	Rowan	1 324	139 142	457	105.1	74.2	16.9	0.8	1.4	8.2	5.6	17.2	9.2	11.8	12.3	14.3
37 161	22580	2	Rutherford	1 461	66 390	800	45.4	85.4	10.8	0.8	0.8	4.1	5.3	16.1	8.0	10.0	12.1	14.5
37 163	...	6	Sampson	2 447	63 724	823	26.0	53.4	26.6	2.3	0.7	18.4	6.5	18.2	8.7	11.2	12.8	13.6
37 165	29900	6	Scotland	826	35 509	1 288	43.0	46.2	39.6	12.0	1.1	2.9	6.5	17.1	10.2	11.4	12.2	13.3
37 167	10620	6	Stanly	1 023	60 714	861	59.3	82.6	11.9	0.6	2.2	3.9	5.5	16.2	9.2	11.5	12.0	14.4
37 169	49180	2	Stokes	1 163	46 351	1 043	39.9	92.3	4.5	0.8	0.5	2.9	4.5	15.5	8.0	9.7	12.3	16.0
37 171	34340	4	Surry	1 378	72 743	746	52.8	85.2	4.2	0.6	0.9	10.1	5.3	16.9	8.1	10.1	12.5	14.6

1. CBSA = Core Based Statistical Area. See Appendix A for explanation. See Appendix B for list of metropolitan areas with component counties.   2. County type code from the Economic Research Service of USDA Rural-Urban Continuum Codes. See Appendix A for definition.   3. Dry land or land partially or temporarily covered by water.   4. May be of any race.

Table B. States and Counties — **Population and Households**

STATE County	55 to 64 years	65 to 74 years	75 years and over	Percent female	Total persons 2000	Total persons 2010	2000–2010	2010–2015	Births	Deaths	Net migration	Number	Persons per house-hold	Family house-holds	Female family house-holder[1]	One per-son
	16	17	18	19	20	21	22	23	24	25	26	27	28	29	30	31
NORTH CAROLINA—Cont'd																
Chowan	15.5	12.8	9.6	52.4	14 526	14 793	1.8	-2.7	790	939	-236	6 036	2.39	67.8	17.0	28.0
Clay	17.0	17.2	11.0	50.8	8 775	10 587	20.6	1.1	429	703	399	4 351	2.42	66.8	6.2	29.1
Cleveland	13.7	10.3	6.8	51.8	96 287	98 083	1.9	-1.2	5 635	5 985	-847	37 407	2.56	66.8	13.7	29.2
Columbus	13.8	10.5	7.2	50.7	54 749	58 098	6.1	-2.4	3 329	3 572	-1 223	22 131	2.47	65.0	16.3	31.4
Craven	12.1	9.7	7.4	49.2	91 436	103 505	13.2	-0.1	8 308	5 177	-3 375	39 930	2.52	69.3	13.5	26.4
Cumberland	10.2	6.4	4.4	51.0	302 963	319 431	5.4	1.4	29 972	12 316	-13 696	122 288	2.56	65.8	17.9	28.8
Currituck	15.0	9.5	5.4	50.3	18 190	23 547	29.5	7.3	1 273	1 111	1 528	9 124	2.64	74.0	9.9	19.6
Dare	16.9	11.9	6.8	50.6	29 967	33 920	13.2	5.1	1 890	1 582	1 363	14 852	2.31	66.4	9.5	25.6
Davidson	13.5	10.0	6.8	51.0	147 246	162 878	10.6	1.1	9 023	8 659	1 050	64 254	2.51	69.4	12.7	26.0
Davie	14.8	10.9	8.3	51.1	34 835	41 222	18.3	1.3	1 963	2 130	695	16 117	2.54	70.5	11.1	25.9
Duplin	13.1	9.3	6.5	50.8	49 063	58 505	19.2	1.1	4 004	2 647	-665	22 027	2.66	68.6	13.8	25.4
Durham	11.4	6.6	4.5	52.1	223 314	269 974	20.9	11.5	22 600	9 499	17 059	113 564	2.37	59.1	15.1	31.8
Edgecombe	14.8	9.8	7.2	53.6	55 606	56 551	1.7	-4.2	3 407	3 098	-2 738	20 987	2.60	67.6	23.1	27.8
Forsyth	12.6	8.2	6.2	52.5	306 067	350 670	14.6	5.2	24 091	16 100	10 347	141 901	2.45	62.9	13.9	31.6
Franklin	13.8	9.3	5.9	50.4	47 260	60 592	28.2	5.1	3 530	2 761	2 279	23 395	2.57	70.8	13.5	25.1
Gaston	13.0	9.0	6.1	51.6	190 365	206 083	8.3	3.6	13 231	11 400	5 355	79 209	2.59	67.7	14.8	27.8
Gates	15.2	10.6	7.2	51.2	10 516	12 186	15.9	-6.2	543	595	-660	4 508	2.62	74.2	15.0	23.0
Graham	14.3	12.9	9.4	50.6	7 993	8 861	10.9	-2.8	482	566	-156	3 392	2.54	72.3	9.0	25.6
Granville	13.8	9.3	6.0	49.0	48 498	57 532	18.6	2.0	2 924	2 540	635	19 983	2.70	69.8	15.1	26.9
Greene	13.9	8.6	6.2	45.8	18 974	21 362	12.6	-1.1	1 151	965	-434	7 143	2.69	68.4	17.1	29.0
Guilford	12.2	7.9	5.9	52.5	421 048	488 406	16.0	6.0	32 061	20 856	17 818	198 560	2.44	63.0	15.6	30.5
Halifax	14.7	10.3	8.0	52.2	57 370	54 691	-4.7	-4.1	3 067	3 520	-1 802	21 554	2.43	66.2	22.5	30.7
Harnett	10.3	6.8	4.4	50.5	91 025	114 678	26.0	11.7	9 603	4 706	8 382	41 601	2.84	72.2	14.2	23.5
Haywood	14.9	13.6	10.2	51.9	54 033	59 036	9.3	1.4	2 898	3 726	1 569	26 261	2.22	66.7	11.3	28.8
Henderson	14.4	13.5	11.0	51.7	89 173	106 742	19.7	5.5	5 640	6 816	6 776	45 534	2.35	66.1	8.8	29.3
Hertford	15.0	9.8	7.6	50.6	22 601	24 658	9.1	-1.9	1 244	1 388	-340	8 700	2.49	67.1	22.6	29.4
Hoke	9.9	5.4	3.0	50.6	33 646	46 952	39.5	12.2	4 923	1 595	2 279	16 534	2.95	74.6	18.0	21.7
Hyde	16.4	10.0	7.7	44.5	5 826	5 810	-0.3	-4.9	266	270	-285	2 112	2.39	71.4	20.6	24.3
Iredell	12.6	8.8	5.8	50.9	122 660	159 440	30.0	6.5	9 251	7 597	8 469	60 277	2.68	73.0	12.9	23.3
Jackson	13.1	11.2	6.5	50.9	33 121	40 271	21.6	2.5	2 030	1 718	770	15 872	2.33	61.1	10.5	31.7
Johnston	11.6	7.8	4.5	50.9	121 965	168 878	38.5	9.9	11 757	6 575	11 203	61 333	2.83	75.6	13.2	20.1
Jones	16.2	12.5	9.2	51.3	10 381	10 153	-2.2	-1.4	520	687	-112	4 113	2.44	67.8	14.2	28.7
Lee	12.4	8.8	6.2	50.8	49 040	57 866	18.0	3.1	4 233	2 741	346	21 239	2.73	69.7	14.3	25.7
Lenoir	14.6	10.1	7.7	52.2	59 648	59 495	-0.3	-2.3	3 494	3 657	-1 170	23 571	2.45	66.0	19.1	29.7
Lincoln	14.0	10.2	5.7	50.2	63 780	78 265	22.7	3.5	4 054	3 730	2 420	30 114	2.60	73.9	11.5	21.8
McDowell	14.5	10.9	7.7	49.8	42 151	44 996	6.7	0.0	2 397	2 556	201	17 142	2.56	67.9	12.9	27.0
Macon	15.7	15.1	11.3	51.4	29 811	33 922	13.8	0.8	1 729	2 205	754	15 504	2.15	64.9	9.8	29.8
Madison	14.8	11.9	7.9	50.3	19 635	20 774	5.8	1.8	983	1 182	552	8 353	2.38	68.4	10.1	26.3
Martin	16.4	12.0	8.6	53.0	25 593	24 505	-4.3	-4.7	1 260	1 663	-823	9 465	2.51	66.9	14.4	30.2
Mecklenburg	10.6	6.1	4.0	51.9	695 454	919 666	32.2	12.4	73 198	28 720	68 393	371 921	2.56	62.3	14.6	30.1
Mitchell	15.5	13.3	10.1	50.5	15 687	15 581	-0.7	-2.2	747	1 100	-1	6 396	2.35	70.6	9.7	26.0
Montgomery	14.3	11.1	7.4	51.4	26 822	27 798	3.6	-0.9	1 692	1 450	-505	10 625	2.50	65.1	13.3	30.2
Moore	13.2	12.7	11.2	52.0	74 769	88 247	18.0	6.9	5 186	5 488	6 091	36 947	2.42	66.7	10.3	29.4
Nash	14.0	9.7	6.7	51.9	87 420	95 839	9.6	-2.0	5 748	5 187	-2 503	37 159	2.50	65.2	15.6	30.3
New Hanover	12.6	9.4	6.4	52.0	160 307	202 683	26.4	8.7	11 785	9 050	14 420	87 176	2.33	58.2	11.3	31.8
Northampton	16.7	13.0	10.0	51.8	22 086	22 098	0.1	-7.6	952	1 409	-1 178	8 564	2.40	65.3	22.6	31.6
Onslow	7.4	5.0	3.5	45.4	150 355	177 772	18.2	4.8	22 825	4 861	-9 895	61 147	2.76	72.1	13.1	22.7
Orange	12.2	7.0	4.2	52.2	118 227	133 702	13.1	5.7	6 481	3 927	5 214	51 419	2.47	60.7	10.0	29.3
Pamlico	17.3	15.7	10.4	48.7	12 934	13 144	1.6	-2.8	474	775	-93	5 145	2.41	71.8	10.3	25.9
Pasquotank	12.8	8.9	6.5	50.8	34 897	40 661	16.5	-2.0	2 608	2 135	-1 384	14 608	2.60	69.9	16.9	24.8
Pender	14.3	10.6	6.5	50.0	41 082	52 201	27.1	10.4	3 123	2 505	4 597	20 154	2.62	68.9	11.2	26.8
Perquimans	15.5	14.7	9.7	51.9	11 368	13 453	18.3	-0.1	695	760	38	5 473	2.45	72.4	11.2	23.1
Person	15.1	10.2	7.3	51.4	35 623	39 464	10.8	-0.5	2 174	2 213	-182	15 326	2.53	69.7	16.4	24.8
Pitt	11.0	6.7	4.6	52.8	133 798	168 148	25.7	4.6	11 192	6 187	2 731	66 427	2.50	60.2	16.5	29.2
Polk	17.1	14.8	12.7	52.2	18 324	20 510	11.9	-0.7	733	1 416	544	8 764	2.28	65.7	9.5	29.7
Randolph	13.2	9.7	6.4	50.6	130 454	141 752	8.7	0.7	8 417	7 192	-140	54 254	2.60	70.9	12.9	25.2
Richmond	13.2	9.5	6.5	51.1	46 564	46 639	0.2	-2.6	2 876	2 795	-1 282	18 260	2.46	64.4	17.7	30.4
Robeson	12.3	8.0	5.0	51.6	123 339	134 168	8.8	0.0	9 940	6 632	-3 189	45 446	2.89	71.2	23.6	24.8
Rockingham	15.0	10.6	7.8	51.7	91 928	93 640	1.9	-2.0	4 959	5 692	-1 081	37 691	2.42	68.4	14.7	27.8
Rowan	13.3	9.5	6.8	50.7	130 340	138 442	6.2	0.5	8 078	8 042	454	52 002	2.57	68.6	14.0	26.8
Rutherford	14.6	11.6	7.9	51.6	62 899	67 809	7.8	-2.1	3 543	4 350	-523	26 778	2.46	70.5	14.2	26.3
Sampson	13.0	9.2	6.8	50.8	60 161	63 431	5.4	0.5	4 456	3 275	-882	23 413	2.69	67.5	16.3	27.7
Scotland	13.4	9.6	6.5	50.8	35 998	36 157	0.4	-1.8	2 378	2 064	-1 007	12 931	2.62	66.5	22.6	29.9
Stanly	13.5	10.4	7.2	50.2	58 100	60 585	4.3	0.2	3 434	3 431	151	23 484	2.49	68.9	11.8	27.5
Stokes	14.8	11.3	7.8	50.9	44 711	47 401	6.0	-2.2	2 091	2 621	-630	18 855	2.46	72.3	12.1	25.5
Surry	13.6	10.8	8.2	51.1	71 219	73 673	3.4	-1.3	4 007	4 414	-650	29 380	2.46	68.9	12.7	27.8

1. No spouse present.

Table B. States and Counties — Population, Vital Statistics, Medicare, and Crime

STATE County	Persons in group quarters, 2015	Daytime population, 2010–2014 Number	Employ-ment/resi-dence ratio	Births, 2015 Total	Rate[1]	Deaths, 2015 Number	Rate[1]	Persons under 65 with no health insurance, 2014 Number	Percent	Medicare, 2015 Total Beneficiaries	Enrolled in Original Medicare	Enrolled in Medicare Advantage	Serious crimes known to police,[2] 2014 Total Number	Rate[3]
	32	33	34	35	36	37	38	39	40	41	42	43	44	45
NORTH CAROLINA—Cont'd														
Chowan	273	13 944	0.87	146	10.1	176	12.1	1 831	16.3	3 614	3 223	391	337	2 285
Clay	100	9 378	0.68	83	7.8	135	12.7	1 437	19.0	3 251	2 586	665	303	2 856
Cleveland	2 105	93 101	0.89	1 062	11.0	1 181	12.2	11 140	14.1	22 964	17 531	5 433	2 059	2 228
Columbus	2 894	54 727	0.86	630	11.1	694	12.2	8 067	18.2	13 117	11 028	2 089	2 846	5 058
Craven	4 997	108 245	1.08	1 493	14.4	991	9.5	11 884	14.5	22 120	19 906	2 214	2 903	2 781
Cumberland	7 784	352 757	1.20	5 619	17.3	2 438	7.5	37 935	13.4	47 147	35 660	11 487	17 223	5 251
Currituck	192	18 727	0.53	268	10.7	209	8.3	3 154	15.0	4 051	3 570	481	401	1 628
Dare	152	36 294	1.10	337	9.5	303	8.6	4 882	17.2	7 038	6 297	741	1 249	3 533
Davidson	1 785	137 495	0.63	1 731	10.5	1 685	10.3	21 051	15.5	27 349	12 080	15 269	4 063	2 504
Davie	380	34 190	0.59	363	8.7	379	9.1	4 793	14.4	8 698	4 065	4 633	885	2 173
Duplin	358	56 159	0.86	761	12.8	514	8.7	11 610	23.2	9 076	7 490	1 586	1 357	2 277
Durham	12 895	335 740	1.39	4 375	14.7	1 915	6.4	37 687	15.1	37 159	26 134	11 025	14 474	4 935
Edgecombe	1 211	52 546	0.85	609	11.2	620	11.4	6 523	14.5	8 546	7 067	1 479	2 069	3 889
Forsyth	10 566	382 117	1.15	4 573	12.5	3 067	8.3	46 575	15.3	66 548	29 501	37 047	18 434	5 057
Franklin	1 647	50 016	0.54	680	10.7	549	8.7	9 093	17.5	9 373	6 523	2 850	1 182	1 883
Gaston	3 260	191 097	0.80	2 499	11.8	2 212	10.4	28 052	15.8	40 854	27 297	13 557	6 609	3 320
Gates	61	8 830	0.38	93	8.1	117	10.2	1 351	14.3	2 277	1 871	406	NA	NA
Graham	93	8 002	0.76	86	10.0	100	11.6	1 274	19.0	2 060	1 566	494	NA	NA
Granville	4 244	55 349	0.89	547	9.3	520	8.9	6 753	14.6	9 082	6 249	2 833	1 673	2 857
Greene	2 477	18 772	0.68	202	9.5	214	10.1	3 183	20.1	2 807	2 380	427	50	235
Guilford	16 502	550 911	1.22	6 181	12.0	4 240	8.2	63 324	14.8	84 173	40 869	43 304	17 666	3 450
Halifax	1 397	51 285	0.87	571	10.8	695	13.2	6 537	15.5	13 874	11 153	2 721	2 304	4 376
Harnett	3 298	99 505	0.54	1 918	15.0	961	7.5	17 013	15.5	13 825	10 716	3 109	3 755	2 941
Haywood	707	55 075	0.84	559	9.4	738	12.4	6 914	15.3	15 751	11 103	4 648	1 683	2 895
Henderson	1 292	104 220	0.90	1 088	9.7	1 328	11.9	14 256	17.1	30 391	22 590	7 801	1 966	1 780
Hertford	2 572	25 276	1.10	237	9.8	275	11.3	2 786	15.6	5 150	4 456	694	783	3 307
Hoke	773	40 196	0.50	916	17.6	313	6.0	7 917	17.0	4 139	2 978	1 161	1 275	2 431
Hyde	762	5 875	1.06	48	8.6	41	7.3	694	17.4	981	827	154	NA	NA
Iredell	1 302	160 477	0.96	1 792	10.6	1 508	9.0	20 771	14.7	28 913	19 461	9 452	4 153	2 501
Jackson	3 591	42 026	1.08	375	9.1	315	7.7	6 108	20.2	7 227	5 424	1 803	889	2 160
Johnston	1 534	147 079	0.63	2 267	12.4	1 317	7.2	25 247	16.0	23 484	17 984	5 500	3 806	2 185
Jones	90	8 153	0.51	96	9.6	126	12.5	1 339	17.0	2 337	1 987	350	NA	NA
Lee	1 026	60 532	1.06	770	12.9	526	8.8	8 754	17.5	13 177	10 270	2 907	1 735	2 905
Lenoir	1 201	62 802	1.16	664	11.4	732	12.6	7 518	15.8	14 047	12 087	1 960	2 731	4 695
Lincoln	708	67 879	0.69	776	9.6	746	9.3	10 201	15.3	14 742	10 901	3 841	1 722	2 146
McDowell	1 668	43 096	0.89	453	10.1	494	11.0	5 547	15.5	10 415	7 419	2 996	1 525	3 457
Macon	415	33 520	0.97	334	9.8	407	12.0	5 181	20.8	10 721	9 209	1 512	889	2 622
Madison	1 306	17 661	0.62	192	9.1	232	11.0	2 431	15.2	4 963	3 693	1 270	238	1 209
Martin	155	22 144	0.80	242	10.3	295	12.6	2 805	15.1	5 789	5 050	739	893	3 790
Mecklenburg	16 328	1 099 268	1.28	14 320	14.0	5 978	5.8	133 436	14.9	118 246	80 148	38 098	39 794	3 937
Mitchell	231	15 445	1.01	146	9.5	205	13.4	1 881	16.1	4 014	2 979	1 035	NA	NA
Montgomery	1 008	27 310	0.97	303	11.0	267	9.7	4 313	20.1	5 231	3 917	1 314	765	2 992
Moore	858	88 925	0.95	1 039	11.1	1 096	11.7	10 546	15.0	23 806	18 177	5 629	2 014	2 226
Nash	1 904	97 511	1.06	1 081	11.5	988	10.5	11 949	15.4	22 568	18 214	4 354	2 984	3 180
New Hanover	6 850	225 529	1.16	2 279	10.4	1 819	8.3	25 641	14.5	39 444	32 724	6 720	9 127	4 261
Northampton	749	19 959	0.81	161	7.9	273	13.3	2 244	14.7	5 087	4 210	877	536	3 063
Onslow	13 405	186 721	1.04	4 348	23.4	995	5.4	17 953	11.5	19 140	16 505	2 635	NA	NA
Orange	9 303	144 611	1.11	1 190	8.5	744	5.3	13 974	12.1	18 717	12 006	6 711	3 255	2 288
Pamlico	696	11 555	0.71	89	6.9	151	11.8	1 450	16.2	3 201	2 815	386	317	2 449
Pasquotank	2 345	40 621	1.02	502	12.6	366	9.2	4 864	15.6	7 996	6 900	1 096	1 368	3 430
Pender	1 090	43 934	0.54	610	10.7	497	8.7	7 440	16.3	10 836	8 881	1 955	1 160	2 079
Perquimans	84	11 441	0.57	129	9.6	132	9.8	1 567	15.4	3 483	3 044	439	178	1 303
Person	443	34 473	0.70	430	11.0	428	10.9	4 688	14.6	7 287	4 628	2 659	876	2 228
Pitt	6 467	173 430	1.01	2 128	12.1	1 256	7.2	21 566	14.4	25 402	21 368	4 034	6 114	3 532
Polk	349	17 916	0.70	154	7.6	266	13.1	2 610	17.7	5 675	4 510	1 165	283	1 433
Randolph	1 292	127 574	0.76	1 597	11.2	1 427	10.0	20 213	17.0	28 020	12 960	15 060	4 708	3 296
Richmond	1 099	44 596	0.90	522	11.5	526	11.5	6 651	17.7	10 328	8 819	1 509	2 600	5 598
Robeson	4 145	130 500	0.90	1 853	13.8	1 319	9.8	24 581	21.7	24 764	18 998	5 766	5 271	3 911
Rockingham	1 059	85 827	0.82	958	10.4	1 121	12.2	11 186	15.0	21 316	10 229	11 087	2 825	3 118
Rowan	4 536	132 437	0.89	1 533	11.0	1 523	11.0	19 050	16.9	26 142	15 676	10 466	3 891	2 901
Rutherford	1 222	63 766	0.86	653	9.8	832	12.5	8 243	15.5	14 683	11 554	3 129	1 696	2 709
Sampson	1 076	59 465	0.83	840	13.2	660	10.3	10 762	20.3	10 635	8 305	2 330	1 707	2 692
Scotland	2 567	37 603	1.15	437	12.3	398	11.2	4 514	16.3	7 124	5 618	1 506	1 658	4 703
Stanly	2 034	55 774	0.81	677	11.2	675	11.1	7 137	14.7	13 470	9 928	3 542	1 242	2 502
Stokes	457	37 117	0.49	389	8.4	513	11.1	5 428	14.5	9 268	3 541	5 727	1 208	2 598
Surry	968	72 726	0.98	741	10.2	853	11.7	10 947	18.6	18 192	8 846	9 346	2 423	3 318

1. Per 1,000 estimated resident population.   2. Data for serious crimes have not been adjusted for underreporting; this may affect comparability between geographic areas and over time.
3. Per 100,000 population estimated by the FBI.

STATE County	Serious crimes known to police, 2014 (cont.)[1] Rate[2]		Education School enrollment and attainment, 2010–2014				Local government expenditures,[5] 2012–2013		Money income, 2010–2014				Income and poverty, 2014			
			Enrollment[3]		Attainment[4] (percent)					Households				Percent below poverty level		
	Violent	Property	Total	Percent private	High school graduate or less	Bachelor's degree or more	Total current spending (mil dol)	Current spending per student (dollars)	Per capita income[6] (dollars)	Median income (dollars)	Mean income (dollars)	Percent with income of $200,000 or more	Median household income (dollars)	All persons	Children under 18 years	Children 5 to 17 years in families
	46	47	48	49	50	51	52	53	54	55	56	57	58	59	60	61
NORTH CAROLINA—Cont'd																
Chowan	312	1 973	3 312	8.1	49.8	20.9	25.3	10 939	21 179	37 154	52 093	1.4	38 887	23.2	36.0	33.8
Clay	245	2 611	2 324	11.0	42.0	20.1	13.4	9 685	21 935	36 089	51 289	1.4	37 072	18.5	30.3	27.8
Cleveland	223	2 005	24 230	11.6	51.8	16.5	142.1	8 910	20 512	39 197	51 305	1.5	39 444	21.1	30.8	28.5
Columbus	473	4 585	13 533	6.6	50.9	12.7	77.4	8 720	19 289	34 597	47 926	1.0	34 321	24.3	35.4	32.3
Craven	236	2 545	25 163	12.4	41.2	21.6	120.4	8 013	24 582	47 295	60 587	2.3	43 972	16.4	26.2	25.7
Cumberland	512	4 739	95 894	15.1	36.9	22.9	433.0	8 181	23 204	44 778	58 139	1.8	42 582	17.6	25.6	24.5
Currituck	199	1 429	5 686	9.9	46.3	19.2	35.3	9 020	26 703	58 676	70 427	1.4	58 024	11.2	17.2	15.4
Dare	238	3 295	7 262	10.6	33.0	29.4	54.3	10 664	30 958	55 520	71 875	3.8	54 642	11.0	18.5	18.1
Davidson	187	2 318	39 375	11.1	52.6	17.9	199.4	7 673	22 465	42 866	55 796	1.6	43 346	16.9	23.3	21.8
Davie	155	2 018	9 900	14.5	46.4	25.6	54.5	8 167	26 739	49 591	66 937	4.3	47 592	13.8	21.3	19.2
Duplin	240	2 037	14 278	8.2	58.3	10.4	82.2	8 638	17 677	34 787	46 666	1.0	34 109	27.7	37.6	38.6
Durham	650	4 285	79 074	27.3	30.2	45.6	343.7	10 390	29 801	52 038	72 793	4.7	50 745	16.6	22.2	23.0
Edgecombe	472	3 417	13 967	7.3	58.7	10.7	59.1	8 605	17 652	33 892	44 998	0.9	31 615	25.9	38.1	36.0
Forsyth	556	4 501	94 235	20.0	39.3	32.1	457.9	8 499	26 670	46 003	65 866	3.7	45 944	19.7	27.6	26.0
Franklin	145	1 738	15 044	16.5	50.8	18.2	70.2	8 085	21 836	42 763	55 729	1.5	48 166	15.4	22.6	21.3
Gaston	374	2 947	50 140	13.7	47.6	18.5	239.6	7 535	22 654	42 158	57 034	2.0	42 056	16.7	23.3	21.9
Gates	NA	NA	2 758	12.5	54.6	12.5	19.0	10 650	22 207	49 894	56 790	0.4	48 413	15.6	24.4	22.1
Graham	NA	NA	1 774	11.3	52.7	16.6	13.2	10 572	20 525	37 161	49 271	1.5	33 824	20.6	32.8	31.7
Granville	294	2 563	14 308	13.6	50.3	17.7	71.5	8 257	22 756	49 655	60 774	1.4	49 342	15.9	19.3	18.6
Greene	28	207	4 973	7.4	56.2	9.7	34.5	10 433	18 477	39 498	49 952	1.6	37 263	28.3	38.2	34.5
Guilford	388	3 062	139 569	13.8	37.3	33.7	670.1	9 035	26 322	45 050	64 739	3.4	44 828	17.3	25.4	23.4
Halifax	458	3 919	12 765	10.2	59.4	11.9	78.8	9 995	18 728	32 834	45 572	1.2	31 674	23.5	34.6	32.1
Harnett	255	2 686	36 683	17.5	46.0	18.3	149.9	7 290	20 274	44 417	56 723	1.5	45 380	20.5	27.3	25.4
Haywood	246	2 649	12 014	8.6	42.3	23.8	65.7	8 613	24 870	41 795	55 256	1.9	42 812	15.2	26.7	24.7
Henderson	125	1 655	22 022	13.8	38.5	28.3	111.2	8 199	25 617	46 257	59 491	1.9	47 286	12.9	22.0	22.0
Hertford	325	2 982	6 327	26.0	54.9	14.3	32.5	10 251	17 289	32 201	45 365	1.1	30 056	25.8	35.3	31.0
Hoke	124	2 307	14 677	16.4	43.1	18.4	67.3	8 007	19 036	43 754	54 760	1.0	44 175	19.5	28.3	29.2
Hyde	NA	NA	1 088	17.8	58.3	11.2	10.2	17 500	19 796	44 425	51 654	2.2	36 891	21.9	28.7	27.0
Iredell	249	2 252	40 770	9.5	41.5	25.1	212.4	7 786	27 125	51 889	71 309	4.2	54 026	12.7	18.5	16.7
Jackson	204	1 956	12 349	5.1	40.8	29.3	32.6	8 895	21 033	36 705	50 035	1.3	38 130	23.5	27.8	25.9
Johnston	194	1 992	47 650	10.8	45.9	20.0	273.5	8 114	22 589	49 799	62 209	1.3	50 055	15.3	21.6	20.1
Jones	NA	NA	2 028	13.4	49.4	13.7	14.4	11 722	20 634	37 288	48 813	1.5	38 928	22.2	36.6	34.7
Lee	181	2 724	14 650	9.5	46.3	20.2	82.6	8 260	21 556	46 309	56 952	1.1	46 073	18.5	27.5	25.8
Lenoir	841	3 854	15 169	8.7	51.2	13.9	76.8	8 218	19 330	35 687	46 886	1.0	35 991	22.1	35.5	33.2
Lincoln	160	1 986	18 093	9.0	46.7	19.9	89.1	7 513	25 693	48 664	65 563	3.6	49 676	16.0	21.2	19.1
McDowell	152	3 305	10 276	9.8	55.8	13.9	58.8	8 883	18 730	36 271	46 142	0.9	37 881	17.6	27.1	25.7
Macon	127	2 495	6 384	9.4	44.1	22.4	41.0	9 073	24 120	38 491	53 124	2.3	37 884	18.1	33.2	30.5
Madison	30	1 179	4 820	24.4	52.2	20.3	23.8	9 150	20 791	38 251	50 256	1.0	38 445	19.9	29.4	27.0
Martin	552	3 238	5 744	5.2	54.4	12.9	35.5	9 803	19 313	36 132	46 670	0.8	35 930	19.7	32.4	30.6
Mecklenburg	522	3 414	266 681	19.6	30.2	41.5	1 188.2	8 224	32 817	56 472	82 890	6.9	59 049	15.2	21.1	19.8
Mitchell	NA	NA	3 366	10.3	53.4	16.4	20.1	9 846	21 388	37 487	50 758	1.8	36 795	19.2	28.5	27.3
Montgomery	227	2 765	6 235	7.8	54.3	14.9	38.6	9 024	19 193	32 715	48 685	1.7	38 530	21.1	31.1	28.8
Moore	171	2 054	19 409	14.1	35.7	32.0	111.3	8 620	29 570	50 393	70 008	4.8	51 650	15.5	23.9	23.2
Nash	449	2 731	24 732	13.6	50.6	18.4	156.2	9 312	23 056	43 341	57 359	2.2	43 348	18.2	26.2	25.9
New Hanover	465	3 797	56 999	12.2	30.9	37.2	222.0	8 591	29 742	49 582	69 727	4.1	49 905	18.0	23.2	21.5
Northampton	274	2 789	4 567	10.4	60.5	11.1	24.9	10 987	18 546	31 468	43 512	0.3	32 063	25.8	38.1	37.2
Onslow	NA	NA	46 286	13.8	38.5	18.4	198.2	7 762	21 583	46 141	56 091	1.2	47 201	14.3	19.5	20.7
Orange	148	2 140	50 640	10.9	23.8	56.2	209.1	10 511	35 406	57 261	92 658	11.1	60 304	14.1	13.1	11.8
Pamlico	270	2 179	2 544	13.3	45.2	19.9	15.2	11 405	24 854	44 762	60 714	2.0	43 097	17.9	32.1	29.8
Pasquotank	346	3 084	10 992	10.8	45.3	18.9	52.8	8 803	22 446	45 664	59 539	2.3	44 596	18.8	27.6	26.7
Pender	190	1 889	12 568	10.7	45.7	21.6	70.6	8 058	23 383	44 526	60 499	2.6	45 453	15.4	20.9	20.7
Perquimans	161	1 142	2 837	8.4	52.9	16.7	18.0	9 746	23 260	45 391	57 106	2.1	41 328	17.1	29.2	26.7
Person	186	2 042	9 459	11.5	53.3	14.0	43.5	8 797	21 191	43 381	52 916	1.2	45 841	18.7	26.2	23.7
Pitt	416	3 116	61 926	7.9	38.3	28.8	197.0	8 282	23 439	42 011	58 633	2.6	41 765	23.4	27.0	27.7
Polk	40	1 392	3 840	6.9	40.0	30.0	26.3	10 765	26 686	47 534	60 197	1.7	45 464	14.7	25.2	22.5
Randolph	155	3 142	33 175	9.0	56.2	14.1	187.0	7 956	20 892	41 782	53 195	1.0	41 770	16.7	26.1	23.8
Richmond	422	5 176	11 916	10.9	56.0	13.1	66.7	8 473	17 982	34 060	44 445	1.2	34 665	24.7	37.2	36.0
Robeson	443	3 468	36 795	4.1	59.6	12.4	204.9	8 312	15 460	30 581	42 918	1.1	30 414	33.1	46.6	44.7
Rockingham	200	2 918	20 654	9.9	56.5	13.1	115.3	8 477	21 138	38 946	50 595	1.1	39 606	19.4	28.7	25.4
Rowan	371	2 530	34 121	16.1	50.8	17.2	171.5	8 506	21 149	41 925	54 197	1.4	44 973	18.0	28.7	26.3
Rutherford	134	2 574	15 599	9.8	50.2	16.4	80.6	8 996	19 686	36 863	47 831	1.2	35 629	21.5	31.9	28.5
Sampson	213	2 479	15 845	6.5	59.6	12.1	99.1	8 275	19 463	35 731	50 438	1.4	33 876	29.0	36.8	35.1
Scotland	644	4 059	9 600	10.0	57.1	15.0	64.7	10 310	15 787	30 834	41 185	0.5	32 782	28.9	41.6	37.8
Stanly	248	2 254	14 154	16.2	51.7	15.6	70.5	7 984	20 880	42 010	52 497	0.9	41 921	16.5	22.0	20.8
Stokes	260	2 338	9 479	9.7	57.9	13.6	60.1	8 705	21 406	41 944	52 118	1.0	45 065	13.8	20.9	18.7
Surry	175	3 142	15 564	8.4	54.2	15.2	97.5	8 432	20 164	35 894	49 460	1.3	37 915	18.9	25.6	23.8

1. Data for serious crimes have not been adjusted for underreporting; this may affect comparability between geographic areas and over time.   2. Per 100,000 population estimated by the FBI.
3. All persons 3 years old and over enrolled in nursery school through college.   4. Persons 25 years old and over.   5. Elementary and secondary education expenditures.
6. Based on population estimated by the American Community Survey, 2010–2014.

Table B. States and Counties — Personal Income

STATE County	Personal income, 2014										Earnings, 2014		
	Total (mil dol)	Percent change, 2013–2014	Per capita[1] Dollars	Per capita[1] Rank	Wages and salaries (mil dol)	Supplements to wages and salaries; employer contributions (mil dol) Pension and insurance	Supplements to wages and salaries; employer contributions (mil dol) Government social insurance	Proprietors' income (mil dol)	Dividends, interest, and rent (mil dol)	Personal transfer receipts (mil dol)	Total (mil dol)	Contributions for government social insurance (mil dol) From employee and self-employed	Contributions for government social insurance (mil dol) From employer
	62	63	64	65	66	67	68	69	70	71	72	73	74

NORTH CAROLINA— Cont'd

STATE County	62	63	64	65	66	67	68	69	70	71	72	73	74
Chowan	511	3.0	35 054	1 923	175	33	13	39	110	160	260	18	13
Clay	298	3.5	28 176	2 904	63	13	5	11	65	117	93	9	5
Cleveland	3 077	4.0	31 699	2 492	1 305	242	105	135	430	1 001	1 788	123	105
Columbus	1 757	1.0	30 852	2 608	575	116	44	159	248	619	895	60	44
Craven	4 121	3.4	39 436	1 256	2 186	525	184	189	901	943	3 085	169	184
Cumberland	12 267	3.2	37 592	1 513	8 322	2 115	743	556	2 998	2 852	11 735	567	743
Currituck	968	4.0	38 760	1 357	243	41	20	55	153	178	359	24	20
Dare	1 556	3.4	44 328	730	638	109	55	137	379	273	939	58	55
Davidson	5 685	4.3	34 650	1 991	1 649	291	132	517	719	1 380	2 589	181	132
Davie	1 680	4.1	40 542	1 116	395	67	32	79	287	360	572	42	32
Duplin	2 129	6.6	35 546	1 848	670	142	52	612	234	468	1 477	66	52
Durham	12 612	5.0	42 830	868	13 543	1 848	978	1 095	2 078	1 923	17 464	1 014	978
Edgecombe	1 768	3.1	32 176	2 420	658	139	51	91	304	594	940	62	51
Forsyth	15 137	4.8	41 437	1 016	9 389	1 390	721	1 070	2 793	2 823	12 570	770	721
Franklin	2 001	5.0	31 826	2 458	490	92	37	173	230	480	792	53	37
Gaston	7 686	4.9	36 404	1 704	2 800	476	224	509	1 182	1 876	4 009	267	224
Gates	374	1.6	32 368	2 394	50	11	4	19	50	95	84	7	4
Graham	244	4.2	28 264	2 899	74	14	7	20	33	89	116	9	7
Granville	1 938	3.5	33 123	2 258	884	222	65	88	272	434	1 259	76	65
Greene	656	6.7	31 087	2 573	139	35	10	144	70	170	328	16	10
Guilford	20 661	4.7	40 344	1 133	13 344	2 034	1 026	1 494	3 674	3 773	17 898	1 083	1 026
Halifax	1 715	1.7	32 376	2 390	568	120	43	75	238	620	807	59	43
Harnett	3 968	4.7	31 324	2 544	842	169	66	366	538	913	1 443	93	66
Haywood	2 018	4.0	33 930	2 126	618	117	47	134	371	639	916	69	47
Henderson	3 948	5.0	35 518	1 853	1 398	241	109	186	918	1 084	1 934	140	109
Hertford	699	3.8	28 752	2 854	347	64	27	49	93	236	487	31	27
Hoke	1 486	4.3	28 790	2 847	267	62	21	99	177	368	449	28	21
Hyde	187	2.9	32 987	2 280	74	16	6	40	37	43	136	6	6
Iredell	6 792	6.0	40 747	1 094	3 290	494	249	339	1 009	1 226	4 372	274	249
Jackson	1 268	4.6	30 935	2 596	563	118	40	75	252	317	797	51	40
Johnston	6 337	5.1	34 930	1 950	1 742	329	133	516	708	1 283	2 719	172	133
Jones	392	3.7	38 925	1 329	59	12	4	62	60	106	138	7	4
Lee	2 067	2.8	34 648	1 992	989	185	79	111	364	517	1 363	85	79
Lenoir	2 181	3.5	37 297	1 556	1 033	213	79	212	334	632	1 537	91	79
Lincoln	2 864	6.1	35 879	1 796	813	145	65	66	377	628	1 089	76	65
McDowell	1 303	4.7	28 985	2 830	561	122	47	48	167	427	778	53	47
Macon	1 150	4.5	33 937	2 123	385	69	31	67	289	360	553	42	31
Madison	613	4.1	28 964	2 833	132	29	10	44	103	200	215	17	10
Martin	811	3.2	34 567	2 011	288	55	22	54	109	273	418	27	22
Mecklenburg	49 715	6.1	49 099	432	40 559	5 236	2 968	5 576	7 953	5 879	54 339	3 151	2 968
Mitchell	452	4.0	29 501	2 781	181	37	15	11	70	154	243	18	15
Montgomery	886	5.4	32 334	2 400	330	65	27	74	140	241	496	31	27
Moore	3 873	4.3	41 613	999	1 327	212	102	274	1 023	911	1 915	130	102
Nash	3 539	4.1	37 505	1 524	1 609	304	126	207	529	889	2 247	141	126
New Hanover	8 668	4.4	40 076	1 165	4 587	768	347	838	1 959	1 708	6 540	397	347
Northampton	635	0.3	31 042	2 577	188	36	15	36	92	238	275	21	15
Onslow	8 355	2.0	44 538	713	4 305	1 218	406	277	1 816	1 237	6 206	264	406
Orange	7 441	3.3	52 989	266	3 647	818	231	434	1 823	780	5 130	285	231
Pamlico	491	2.2	37 926	1 466	102	23	8	27	104	144	159	12	8
Pasquotank	1 366	2.1	34 331	2 056	651	142	50	76	221	353	919	55	50
Pender	1 764	4.8	31 366	2 542	396	74	30	122	272	472	623	43	30
Perquimans	481	1.5	35 742	1 814	72	15	5	35	86	144	127	10	5
Person	1 296	3.4	33 113	2 259	391	77	31	58	164	366	558	39	31
Pitt	6 209	4.1	35 410	1 877	3 288	669	236	342	1 035	1 356	4 535	264	236
Polk	770	4.0	37 842	1 477	158	30	13	46	217	210	248	20	13
Randolph	4 554	4.8	31 896	2 449	1 624	305	131	286	584	1 193	2 346	158	131
Richmond	1 372	3.6	29 991	2 717	497	103	42	93	175	510	735	51	42
Robeson	3 590	2.8	26 639	3 005	1 331	281	103	216	419	1 354	1 932	126	103
Rockingham	2 993	3.8	32 638	2 348	1 003	190	80	132	426	901	1 405	103	80
Rowan	4 379	4.5	31 587	2 514	1 964	365	158	115	679	1 256	2 603	174	158
Rutherford	1 890	3.7	28 379	2 884	641	130	52	119	290	648	943	69	52
Sampson	2 294	6.4	35 821	1 802	654	128	49	440	313	590	1 271	59	49
Scotland	1 033	2.0	29 039	2 824	449	85	36	49	145	391	618	43	36
Stanly	1 974	4.3	32 571	2 356	660	127	52	142	296	541	981	67	52
Stokes	1 473	4.3	31 742	2 481	237	49	18	84	169	401	389	33	18
Surry	2 447	4.8	33 538	2 190	991	186	79	168	407	709	1 424	96	79

1. Based on the resident population estimated as of July 1 of the year shown.

Table B. States and Counties — Earnings, Social Security, and Housing

STATE County	Farm	Mining	Construction	Manu-facturing	Information: professional, scientific, technical services	Retail trade	Finance, insurance, real estate and leasing	Health care and social assistance	Govern-ment	Number	Rate[1]	Supplemental Security Income recipients, December 2014	Total	Percent change, 2010–2014
	75	76	77	78	79	80	81	82	83	84	85	86	87	88
NORTH CAROLINA—Cont'd														
Chowan	6.1	0.0	5.6	8.8	5.7	7.2	3.5	D	17.0	4 160	285	599	7 255	-0.5
Clay	-3.1	0.0	D	D	D	15.1	4.3	D	27.6	3 625	341	292	7 244	1.5
Cleveland	1.5	D	5.3	24.4	2.8	8.0	2.9	D	16.2	24 680	254	3 222	43 254	-0.3
Columbus	8.1	0.0	3.7	17.1	2.5	8.3	4.2	13.6	20.5	14 710	258	3 113	25 847	-0.7
Craven	0.7	D	3.2	7.3	5.6	5.4	2.8	8.8	52.2	22 930	220	2 559	46 055	2.3
Cumberland	0.4	D	3.1	4.2	4.4	4.7	2.3	5.4	62.9	53 190	163	10 065	144 426	6.6
Currituck	0.5	D	9.7	0.9	D	10.5	10.7	D	18.1	4 795	192	315	15 218	5.3
Dare	0.0	D	9.5	3.2	D	12.9	13.8	5.6	19.4	8 015	228	310	34 187	2.1
Davidson	0.9	0.0	7.2	20.3	3.3	7.1	3.5	9.5	13.4	37 765	230	3 203	73 136	0.7
Davie	1.5	0.3	7.4	18.2	D	8.5	4.8	D	15.0	10 150	246	588	18 222	-0.1
Duplin	29.8	0.0	3.3	18.3	D	3.6	1.3	3.4	12.0	11 080	186	1 773	25 466	-1.0
Durham	0.1	D	2.2	21.1	17.4	2.9	7.4	16.4	9.2	41 605	141	6 170	130 230	8.3
Edgecombe	4.8	D	5.2	15.7	D	9.4	2.5	D	23.5	13 105	239	2 838	24 627	-0.8
Forsyth	0.2	0.1	3.6	10.7	8.3	6.9	10.3	17.3	9.4	70 060	192	8 409	161 895	3.2
Franklin	5.6	D	11.2	21.2	D	5.7	2.6	8.3	16.6	12 690	202	1 478	27 057	1.8
Gaston	0.1	D	5.0	25.2	4.3	8.2	3.9	16.4	13.3	46 515	220	5 535	90 398	1.9
Gates	12.0	0.0	D	D	1.9	5.4	4.3	4.1	30.6	2 600	225	317	5 222	0.3
Graham	2.3	0.0	24.1	D	D	5.7	4.2	4.7	21.5	2 545	294	288	5 931	0.0
Granville	1.9	D	3.9	25.8	1.7	3.7	2.0	D	44.5	12 065	207	1 397	23 372	2.4
Greene	27.5	0.0	7.0	3.8	D	3.8	4.7	6.5	28.6	4 310	203	779	8 161	-0.6
Guilford	0.2	0.1	4.8	14.5	9.1	6.4	9.7	11.8	11.5	92 395	180	11 384	225 123	3.3
Halifax	2.8	0.0	4.3	15.5	2.3	9.6	3.4	10.4	27.7	14 450	273	3 973	25 671	-0.4
Harnett	3.9	D	11.1	6.1	5.7	10.5	4.6	D	21.5	21 250	168	2 946	49 751	6.5
Haywood	0.8	D	6.4	19.0	4.9	11.5	4.4	13.3	19.5	18 315	308	1 696	35 111	0.4
Henderson	2.1	D	6.6	18.2	4.7	8.8	4.4	15.1	16.3	32 490	293	1 936	55 664	1.7
Hertford	5.9	0.0	5.3	17.4	D	6.9	2.6	D	16.1	5 555	228	1 270	10 502	-1.2
Hoke	7.9	D	8.9	20.6	D	5.4	2.1	D	25.1	6 975	135	1 168	20 165	10.7
Hyde	29.7	0.0	6.9	2.8	2.4	4.0	3.0	3.3	25.2	1 165	206	178	3 350	0.1
Iredell	1.3	0.0	5.9	17.1	D	7.7	3.2	9.2	11.0	33 610	201	2 615	70 906	2.7
Jackson	0.6	D	6.5	3.2	D	6.6	2.9	11.0	45.3	8 720	213	692	26 709	2.9
Johnston	4.0	0.1	10.4	18.7	4.1	8.6	3.7	6.7	18.4	32 275	178	3 864	71 144	5.1
Jones	35.4	0.0	7.6	0.9	D	3.4	D	D	20.7	2 590	257	390	4 851	0.3
Lee	1.0	0.3	5.0	35.0	D	7.7	3.0	10.9	12.8	11 895	200	1 511	24 247	0.5
Lenoir	8.5	D	6.9	23.1	3.8	6.0	4.1	8.2	20.4	15 170	260	2 850	27 206	-0.8
Lincoln	1.3	D	9.8	23.9	5.2	8.4	3.2	5.2	18.7	17 580	220	1 542	34 241	1.8
McDowell	1.1	0.8	4.0	41.2	D	8.0	1.9	8.3	16.2	12 105	269	1 391	20 936	0.6
Macon	1.2	0.1	9.9	6.5	11.5	11.3	5.7	13.7	16.4	11 550	341	787	25 379	0.5
Madison	2.4	D	6.4	8.6	D	6.1	3.7	D	21.8	5 685	269	776	10 704	0.9
Martin	8.4	0.0	5.4	24.7	D	7.8	7.1	D	17.3	6 795	290	1 111	11 521	-1.6
Mecklenburg	0.1	0.0	5.6	5.4	14.7	5.3	18.2	6.3	10.4	130 895	129	17 869	427 826	7.4
Mitchell	0.7	D	D	5.2	1.7	9.0	3.2	15.5	21.5	4 615	301	467	8 742	0.3
Montgomery	5.5	D	5.8	31.2	D	8.0	D	D	17.3	6 415	234	749	16 041	0.8
Moore	4.0	D	6.8	5.0	D	7.4	5.2	27.5	12.6	25 015	269	1 471	45 719	4.0
Nash	3.0	D	5.2	23.6	6.0	7.5	4.2	9.1	15.5	22 295	237	3 770	42 456	0.4
New Hanover	0.0	D	6.9	9.5	12.8	9.1	7.4	12.1	19.3	42 640	197	4 316	107 090	5.6
Northampton	6.4	D	5.4	9.5	D	15.2	D	D	21.2	5 890	286	1 264	11 512	-1.4
Onslow	1.5	D	3.0	0.8	2.1	4.3	1.8	3.0	74.3	23 285	126	2 927	76 926	12.8
Orange	0.4	0.0	2.2	2.1	7.8	5.2	8.8	5.6	56.6	19 285	138	1 472	56 697	2.1
Pamlico	5.8	D	7.5	4.3	4.2	11.2	3.0	D	27.9	3 985	309	276	7 564	0.4
Pasquotank	1.8	0.0	3.1	4.3	6.6	9.1	4.7	13.6	37.2	8 455	213	1 278	16 915	0.5
Pender	10.3	D	10.5	6.3	D	7.0	4.5	D	23.4	12 440	222	1 202	27 559	3.2
Perquimans	15.0	0.0	6.5	1.7	D	5.5	D	D	24.5	4 005	298	380	7 036	0.7
Person	3.8	0.0	6.7	16.5	3.3	8.1	2.8	10.4	17.6	9 980	255	1 158	18 220	0.1
Pitt	2.0	D	4.0	10.6	4.5	7.0	4.5	12.2	35.9	28 745	164	5 997	77 332	3.1
Polk	2.5	0.0	7.7	5.8	D	5.7	6.1	25.1	17.2	6 365	313	312	11 495	0.6
Randolph	3.1	0.1	6.0	35.0	2.7	5.9	3.2	9.5	13.9	32 710	229	3 389	61 232	0.3
Richmond	6.4	1.2	6.3	18.2	4.0	8.6	2.3	12.2	19.9	11 100	243	2 175	21 102	1.8
Robeson	5.1	0.0	4.6	15.8	2.3	8.0	3.4	18.8	23.1	27 730	206	7 814	52 219	-1.0
Rockingham	1.8	D	5.6	26.2	D	8.5	3.1	11.9	15.4	24 865	271	3 174	43 566	-0.3
Rowan	0.9	0.4	5.0	18.0	3.5	7.1	3.0	10.1	22.1	32 305	233	2 888	60 241	0.0
Rutherford	1.1	D	5.7	17.4	6.8	9.4	3.6	14.5	18.0	17 880	269	2 169	33 915	0.1
Sampson	35.7	0.0	3.0	12.6	2.1	5.2	1.7	D	17.1	14 415	225	2 274	27 056	-0.7
Scotland	2.2	D	3.9	20.8	2.4	8.1	3.1	17.4	19.6	8 985	252	1 939	15 132	-0.4
Stanly	2.8	D	7.7	20.6	2.9	8.4	4.1	12.9	18.7	14 445	238	1 361	27 260	0.6
Stokes	3.7	0.0	7.7	16.8	D	8.1	D	12.5	23.5	11 235	242	894	21 842	-0.4
Surry	3.6	0.3	14.7	12.7	D	9.2	3.8	D	16.4	19 910	273	2 264	33 516	-0.4

1. Per 1,000 resident population estimated as of July 1 of the year shown.

Table B. States and Counties — Housing, Labor Force, and Employment

STATE County	Housing units, 2010–2014								Civilian labor force, 2015				Civilian employment,[6] 2010–2014		
	Occupied units										Unemployment			Percent	
		Owner-occupied				Renter-occupied									
				Median owner cost as a percent of income											Con-struction, produc-tion, and mainte-nance occu-pations
				With a mort-gage	Without a mort-gage[2]		Median rent as a per-cent of income[2]	Sub-stand-ard units[4]		Percent change, 2014–2015				Manage-ment, business, science and arts	
	Total	Percent	Median value[1]			Median rent[3]		(percent)	Total		Total	Rate[5]	Total		
	89	90	91	92	93	94	95	96	97	98	99	100	101	102	103
NORTH CAROLINA—Cont'd															
Chowan	6 036	66.8	138 000	25.6	16.3	725	37.7	6.1	5 662	-0.2	410	7.2	5 735	35.2	24.0
Clay	4 351	78.3	146 400	23.9	12.9	668	36.9	1.9	4 100	0.0	251	6.1	3 940	28.6	22.1
Cleveland	37 407	68.3	104 100	22.0	11.8	655	34.0	2.4	45 926	0.0	2 970	6.5	39 842	27.7	28.3
Columbus	22 131	69.0	83 600	25.1	13.2	591	34.0	2.3	22 615	-1.7	1 720	7.6	20 843	26.0	28.7
Craven	39 930	63.3	153 500	23.9	12.9	886	29.9	2.0	41 439	1.0	2 535	6.1	39 686	31.5	25.4
Cumberland	122 288	53.7	128 600	23.0	11.9	866	29.9	2.2	126 488	-0.7	9 319	7.4	117 557	33.2	21.2
Currituck	9 124	81.5	223 600	25.9	10.1	973	33.7	1.3	12 758	0.6	748	5.9	11 559	25.2	29.5
Dare	14 852	69.1	284 400	28.6	12.8	1 041	28.2	1.3	20 242	0.8	1 509	7.5	18 512	30.8	21.9
Davidson	64 254	72.6	131 500	22.2	11.2	642	27.8	2.7	79 038	1.0	4 386	5.5	71 552	27.8	30.7
Davie	16 117	80.4	164 100	20.9	12.0	685	27.0	2.1	19 841	1.0	1 000	5.0	18 107	33.6	25.5
Duplin	22 027	67.0	86 000	23.7	13.8	626	31.3	5.5	26 657	0.4	1 543	5.8	24 382	25.1	41.4
Durham	113 564	54.4	180 200	21.3	10.8	877	30.6	3.1	155 994	2.2	7 815	5.0	139 643	49.5	14.2
Edgecombe	20 987	62.6	81 700	23.7	15.5	649	32.4	3.8	23 078	-0.5	2 219	9.6	21 732	22.8	33.1
Forsyth	141 901	63.1	150 300	21.8	10.9	731	31.2	3.0	179 226	1.3	9 874	5.5	161 027	39.6	19.4
Franklin	23 395	74.3	127 200	24.4	14.0	716	30.8	2.8	29 044	2.8	1 700	5.9	26 155	32.0	27.5
Gaston	79 209	67.1	124 000	22.8	12.2	723	32.4	3.7	103 234	2.6	6 160	6.0	90 343	29.1	28.2
Gates	4 508	80.3	144 500	23.0	14.1	751	31.3	2.7	5 225	0.7	288	5.5	4 947	26.8	32.5
Graham	3 392	82.0	122 300	20.7	10.0	576	23.9	2.0	3 178	-4.0	386	12.1	3 103	26.5	34.3
Granville	19 983	74.7	137 800	22.7	12.6	752	27.4	2.9	28 556	1.6	1 424	5.0	23 840	33.4	28.4
Greene	7 143	69.7	86 100	22.9	13.8	597	27.3	5.4	9 492	1.0	525	5.5	8 259	23.4	35.1
Guilford	198 560	60.1	155 500	22.9	11.3	761	30.7	2.7	256 090	1.3	15 058	5.9	232 121	36.5	19.8
Halifax	21 554	62.5	86 400	22.9	16.2	663	36.5	2.0	20 875	-1.8	1 853	8.9	19 380	26.0	29.6
Harnett	41 601	66.1	133 400	23.2	13.0	782	29.4	3.3	50 167	1.8	3 379	6.7	45 298	31.2	26.0
Haywood	26 261	72.9	157 200	24.0	11.5	726	30.3	2.1	27 858	2.2	1 454	5.2	24 613	31.7	25.9
Henderson	45 534	73.7	181 600	22.8	10.0	749	32.4	2.6	50 697	2.5	2 398	4.7	45 162	33.2	24.8
Hertford	8 700	63.7	81 300	24.3	15.1	625	30.4	3.6	9 238	-1.4	654	7.1	8 284	29.4	27.4
Hoke	16 534	66.6	143 500	24.3	12.8	778	32.2	4.1	19 339	-0.1	1 560	8.1	16 862	29.5	26.5
Hyde	2 112	76.5	80 500	18.8	11.7	769	23.6	0.7	2 178	-0.7	199	9.1	2 322	29.4	31.6
Iredell	60 277	72.8	168 000	22.6	10.7	808	29.2	2.6	81 897	2.6	4 486	5.5	73 376	33.4	27.5
Jackson	15 872	66.4	173 200	25.6	10.0	620	34.7	2.1	18 518	1.0	1 129	6.1	17 512	30.0	16.2
Johnston	61 333	71.3	143 500	22.0	12.1	781	33.0	2.9	88 283	3.0	4 551	5.2	78 546	34.2	24.9
Jones	4 113	70.6	97 300	24.0	13.1	652	32.1	2.5	4 547	1.5	265	5.8	4 224	30.3	31.2
Lee	21 239	67.2	132 900	21.2	12.9	688	27.4	3.9	26 005	4.1	1 890	7.3	25 408	28.9	29.7
Lenoir	23 571	60.2	92 600	22.6	15.3	662	31.6	2.4	27 876	0.2	1 790	6.4	24 449	27.7	31.3
Lincoln	30 114	77.7	152 700	21.5	11.1	664	29.0	2.3	40 637	2.7	2 207	5.4	36 154	29.6	30.8
McDowell	17 142	70.2	101 300	21.7	10.8	575	27.5	2.6	21 325	2.5	1 180	5.5	17 130	26.3	30.6
Macon	15 504	73.3	166 800	25.2	10.0	747	34.4	3.1	15 168	1.0	933	6.2	12 823	28.7	21.3
Madison	8 353	72.7	158 100	26.6	10.1	631	27.3	2.3	9 613	2.3	545	5.7	8 870	27.1	28.4
Martin	9 465	70.5	86 200	23.9	16.5	620	26.7	2.9	9 731	-1.4	750	7.7	9 062	32.0	31.7
Mecklenburg	371 921	58.7	181 800	21.9	11.6	913	29.4	2.6	562 314	2.8	30 143	5.4	484 396	41.6	16.3
Mitchell	6 396	77.9	122 500	24.7	11.3	563	36.2	2.7	6 335	-3.0	439	6.9	5 854	29.9	31.7
Montgomery	10 625	69.6	88 600	23.0	12.1	544	31.0	4.6	11 683	1.9	665	5.7	10 362	27.6	37.2
Moore	36 947	74.7	199 000	22.4	11.8	740	29.1	2.0	38 190	0.1	2 220	5.8	35 356	38.8	18.7
Nash	37 159	64.1	119 200	22.8	13.3	744	32.3	3.5	43 937	-0.5	3 221	7.3	40 636	29.5	28.1
New Hanover	87 176	57.6	212 300	24.2	12.8	902	32.5	3.1	113 185	2.6	6 054	5.3	101 353	39.2	15.9
Northampton	8 564	71.2	82 800	24.1	15.9	640	36.3	1.7	7 849	-1.1	599	7.6	7 322	26.9	31.6
Onslow	61 147	53.7	154 100	24.2	12.0	962	31.4	2.4	63 959	0.1	3 856	6.0	59 460	29.2	22.3
Orange	51 419	60.3	272 700	21.8	10.7	918	31.7	2.3	74 172	2.2	3 415	4.6	67 849	55.7	10.9
Pamlico	5 145	79.5	159 700	25.3	12.4	739	31.8	3.6	5 366	1.4	325	6.1	5 315	29.7	29.1
Pasquotank	14 608	63.3	162 800	26.3	14.6	837	32.2	4.8	17 402	0.8	1 284	7.4	16 867	30.9	24.6
Pender	20 154	77.5	154 500	24.8	14.1	799	31.3	3.4	25 825	2.2	1 575	6.1	22 719	29.4	29.4
Perquimans	5 473	77.0	163 000	26.6	14.5	722	33.0	1.3	5 153	1.2	367	7.1	4 777	34.3	28.3
Person	15 326	71.7	113 600	23.4	10.3	637	33.7	3.9	18 132	1.2	1 221	6.7	16 382	27.1	29.4
Pitt	66 427	53.9	133 400	22.0	13.4	738	33.0	2.5	87 628	0.4	5 339	6.1	80 199	38.1	18.9
Polk	8 764	75.7	173 600	25.1	10.0	720	25.6	1.9	8 699	3.6	445	5.1	8 223	33.6	28.7
Randolph	54 254	74.0	119 400	23.1	11.9	644	29.9	3.4	67 250	1.1	3 805	5.7	62 085	26.0	35.1
Richmond	18 260	64.0	79 500	22.5	12.6	606	33.2	2.4	17 220	0.5	1 359	7.9	16 808	28.0	31.6
Robeson	45 446	64.0	67 600	23.4	13.5	601	31.8	5.2	51 630	1.0	4 365	8.5	47 000	25.2	34.0
Rockingham	37 691	70.0	105 600	22.3	11.2	612	31.4	2.1	41 484	1.1	2 733	6.6	38 286	25.5	32.6
Rowan	52 002	67.8	128 700	22.6	11.7	725	30.3	2.5	63 805	2.4	3 842	6.0	56 028	28.8	30.2
Rutherford	26 778	72.1	106 500	22.5	12.2	604	29.3	2.9	25 046	-1.5	1 963	7.8	24 903	27.3	34.3
Sampson	23 413	69.8	87 700	22.6	13.7	598	29.8	4.5	29 549	-0.1	1 760	6.0	26 511	25.9	37.3
Scotland	12 931	64.3	78 700	24.0	14.2	607	37.2	3.5	11 889	-0.8	1 271	10.7	10 973	31.7	26.7
Stanly	23 484	72.5	128 000	23.0	12.6	645	32.0	2.9	28 779	1.0	1 538	5.3	25 290	29.6	28.5
Stokes	18 855	79.5	116 700	22.0	10.6	614	30.7	2.9	21 991	1.2	1 188	5.4	19 793	26.8	34.9
Surry	29 380	72.0	114 100	23.0	12.5	615	28.7	3.3	33 341	1.1	1 822	5.5	30 420	28.3	31.2

1. Specified owner-occupied units. 2. A value of 10.0 represents 10 percent or less; a value of 50.0 represents 50 percent or more. 3. Specified renter-occupied units.
4. Overcrowded or lacking complete plumbing facilities. 5. Percent of civilian labor force. 6. Persons 16 years old and over.

Table B. States and Counties — **Nonfarm Employment and Agriculture**

STATE County	Private nonfarm establishments, employment and payroll, 2014									Agriculture, 2012			
	Number of establishments	Employment						Annual payroll		Farms			Farm operators whose principal occupation is farming (percent)
		Total	Health care and social assistance	Manufacturing	Retail trade	Finance and insurance	Professional, scientific, and technical services	Total (mil dol)	Average per employee (dollars)	Number	Percent with:		
											Fewer than 50 acres	500 acres or more	
	104	105	106	107	108	109	110	111	112	113	114	115	116
NORTH CAROLINA—Cont'd													
Chowan	351	3 660	1 008	D	466	94	112	123	33 583	141	32.6	27.7	73.0
Clay	207	1 479	301	D	374	36	48	38	25 435	154	56.5	0.6	53.2
Cleveland	1 907	27 679	5 089	5 212	3 843	513	941	987	35 650	1 036	43.3	3.7	35.3
Columbus	997	11 459	2 918	2 052	2 268	D	271	401	34 967	731	41.6	11.4	48.2
Craven	2 133	27 477	6 270	3 128	4 738	824	1 787	1 008	36 700	256	45.3	14.1	59.8
Cumberland	5 689	92 537	19 268	6 834	16 603	1 928	5 073	3 080	33 281	389	41.4	10.8	45.8
Currituck	608	4 648	228	39	943	D	127	166	35 794	82	46.3	28.0	56.1
Dare	1 849	13 331	936	263	3 468	409	388	435	32 659	9	55.6	22.2	88.9
Davidson	2 723	44 818	D	8 978	5 111	829	1 028	1 665	37 161	1 062	54.7	1.6	45.3
Davie	796	8 359	1 208	1 392	1 389	209	206	265	31 724	640	53.4	1.9	47.2
Duplin	817	12 847	1 639	5 673	1 768	222	146	384	29 912	940	37.4	11.3	62.7
Durham	6 948	171 271	24 814	12 454	15 077	7 928	26 816	10 789	62 996	232	62.5	2.6	44.8
Edgecombe	737	12 307	2 502	2 862	1 514	172	139	395	32 081	272	34.9	19.5	52.2
Forsyth	8 247	156 618	23 342	14 584	20 595	10 093	6 995	7 409	47 309	662	65.7	1.2	50.6
Franklin	940	9 495	1 131	D	1 405	155	208	390	41 091	542	40.8	9.0	39.7
Gaston	3 917	62 250	11 535	13 003	9 380	1 170	1 335	2 280	36 632	520	54.8	1.0	39.8
Gates	117	789	114	140	189	D	D	19	23 773	182	33.5	14.3	44.0
Graham	169	1 653	270	D	D	41	20	55	33 306	107	54.2	0.0	39.3
Granville	843	11 836	2 103	3 835	1 311	305	210	430	36 343	589	37.0	5.4	50.6
Greene	232	1 883	D	129	297	42	D	52	27 716	260	31.9	18.8	62.7
Guilford	13 205	254 674	36 404	32 067	27 808	12 889	11 503	10 938	42 951	962	56.9	4.2	43.9
Halifax	965	12 564	2 916	2 191	2 319	316	223	388	30 897	341	28.2	27.3	49.3
Harnett	1 609	19 249	3 757	1 330	3 242	568	433	583	30 263	797	55.6	9.2	47.9
Haywood	1 340	14 235	3 321	1 698	2 914	408	443	445	31 293	597	58.8	2.5	42.2
Henderson	2 502	31 089	6 621	5 988	5 198	803	904	1 104	35 527	468	68.6	2.8	52.1
Hertford	499	7 498	2 144	953	1 240	D	107	254	33 834	162	37.7	24.7	64.8
Hoke	417	5 015	1 092	1 436	819	75	D	127	25 269	202	47.0	13.4	54.0
Hyde	164	858	D	64	115	D	D	26	29 963	158	39.9	27.8	55.1
Iredell	4 432	61 861	8 889	10 422	8 462	1 340	3 096	2 640	42 682	1 203	47.3	5.2	55.9
Jackson	925	11 714	2 140	277	1 709	188	328	368	31 403	245	59.6	0.8	44.5
Johnston	3 064	38 094	5 199	6 968	7 935	826	868	1 310	34 397	1 175	50.6	7.1	46.6
Jones	126	778	170	30	102	D	D	26	32 886	170	35.9	15.3	60.0
Lee	1 253	22 711	2 758	8 612	3 056	360	270	804	35 407	246	47.6	6.9	43.9
Lenoir	1 233	21 257	3 979	4 191	2 997	587	539	670	31 537	401	37.4	17.0	64.3
Lincoln	1 539	17 312	2 462	3 437	2 972	419	467	586	33 827	651	53.6	1.8	35.5
McDowell	704	13 140	1 672	5 849	1 595	183	158	415	31 560	334	53.6	1.5	46.1
Macon	1 052	9 153	D	661	1 872	442	206	285	31 109	326	62.0	0.6	42.3
Madison	296	3 090	560	D	416	45	37	75	24 194	719	49.0	1.1	38.4
Martin	434	5 292	1 272	1 000	966	158	116	144	27 232	357	22.1	23.5	61.6
Mecklenburg	29 301	569 552	66 098	26 147	56 112	65 570	46 852	32 921	57 801	237	64.1	2.5	47.7
Mitchell	369	4 034	900	563	724	88	D	121	29 916	286	62.9	0.3	37.1
Montgomery	483	6 597	1 023	2 342	782	D	66	213	32 268	250	44.0	6.0	63.6
Moore	2 213	29 404	8 817	1 718	4 475	990	1 126	1 063	36 163	718	51.9	3.3	47.9
Nash	2 050	35 586	5 939	D	5 196	1 430	877	1 342	37 700	430	39.8	14.9	56.5
New Hanover	6 922	87 723	15 875	4 304	14 818	2 866	5 934	3 501	39 911	50	74.0	2.0	52.0
Northampton	264	3 969	624	505	D	D	26	131	33 088	319	25.1	24.1	65.8
Onslow	2 757	34 547	5 210	1 078	8 097	1 013	1 840	946	27 394	347	48.4	7.2	54.2
Orange	3 170	41 624	15 838	926	5 857	1 845	2 195	1 703	40 925	645	54.0	2.6	47.8
Pamlico	262	2 539	593	D	413	46	D	69	27 208	80	40.0	31.3	68.8
Pasquotank	907	10 864	2 406	624	2 433	476	276	350	32 173	136	39.7	30.9	66.2
Pender	980	8 143	1 526	690	1 541	94	D	256	31 457	335	51.3	7.8	49.9
Perquimans	200	1 355	167	D	241	50	D	40	29 339	185	27.0	30.8	68.6
Person	660	7 757	1 284	1 550	1 446	185	129	266	34 292	395	36.5	12.9	50.6
Pitt	3 533	57 990	15 688	5 319	8 604	2 044	2 003	2 062	35 563	391	34.8	21.5	59.3
Polk	468	3 666	1 501	316	405	106	125	104	28 466	290	55.2	1.4	50.0
Randolph	2 507	39 739	5 039	14 806	4 242	1 055	600	1 288	32 403	1 486	46.7	2.8	48.6
Richmond	797	11 315	2 092	3 379	1 880	243	138	342	30 249	277	40.1	5.4	49.8
Robeson	1 791	29 831	7 064	6 715	4 891	1 181	583	900	30 183	941	45.2	13.2	56.3
Rockingham	1 688	22 136	3 159	6 090	3 723	D	490	755	34 128	902	44.5	3.8	46.1
Rowan	2 527	42 623	D	7 844	4 531	682	819	1 743	40 903	1 011	55.2	4.2	36.2
Rutherford	1 245	15 119	2 601	3 411	2 481	324	246	464	30 720	638	51.4	2.2	48.4
Sampson	982	13 654	2 450	3 508	2 196	D	280	420	30 786	1 067	36.3	13.0	55.2
Scotland	609	9 651	2 358	1 672	1 561	187	101	294	30 487	150	32.0	16.7	51.3
Stanly	1 277	16 289	3 175	3 297	2 615	361	281	500	30 670	664	54.7	4.8	44.3
Stokes	619	5 377	1 149	909	902	104	193	167	31 077	926	40.4	2.4	50.9
Surry	1 647	26 212	4 032	3 704	4 146	624	364	932	35 543	1 256	49.2	2.2	48.5

STATE County	Acreage (1,000) [117]	Percent change, 2007–2012 [118]	Average size of farm [119]	Total irrigated (1,000) [120]	Total cropland (1,000) [121]	Average per farm [122]	Average per acre [123]	Value of machinery and equipment, average per farm (dollars) [124]	Total (mil dol) [125]	Average per farm (dollars) [126]	Crops [127]	Livestock and poultry products [128]	$10,000 or more [129]	$100,000 or more [130]	Total ($1,000) [131]	Percent of farms [132]
NORTH CAROLINA—Cont'd																
Chowan	58	-22.1	412	5.0	47.5	1 307 021	3 169	343 525	70.7	501 582	81.4	18.6	70.2	46.1	1 586	72.3
Clay	12	21.7	76	0.2	4.3	380 760	4 990	38 864	3.2	20 636	80.3	19.7	20.1	2.6	209	26.6
Cleveland	117	0.9	113	0.2	47.2	463 430	4 116	58 367	127.7	123 296	17.2	82.8	30.7	11.3	834	23.6
Columbus	159	4.5	218	2.4	116.3	660 404	3 032	132 025	196.5	268 835	42.1	57.9	46.5	19.7	3 374	56.0
Craven	71	-0.4	276	0.9	51.5	853 684	3 094	150 055	55.5	216 820	68.0	32.0	43.8	25.0	1 471	55.9
Cumberland	82	-6.8	212	3.4	47.7	660 437	3 121	119 159	104.8	269 383	40.3	59.7	40.1	18.0	1 021	38.8
Currituck	35	28.2	431	0.2	32.1	1 762 451	4 088	244 244	25.9	315 537	99.9	0.1	51.2	28.0	507	48.8
Dare	D	D	D	0.0	D	1 553 333	D	159 111	1.1	125 333	D	D	44.4	22.2	D	22.2
Davidson	87	-4.6	82	0.8	40.8	504 619	6 138	56 573	54.6	51 412	39.8	60.2	25.1	7.1	616	15.6
Davie	60	-14.7	93	0.1	30.0	575 472	6 178	50 453	25.4	39 625	49.7	50.3	28.0	6.3	227	11.3
Duplin	231	-6.9	246	11.7	155.0	1 001 313	4 076	159 549	1 276.4	1 357 895	10.5	89.5	69.7	53.0	3 324	41.0
Durham	21	-20.3	90	0.4	6.5	771 086	8 578	50 358	9.4	40 517	83.1	16.9	26.7	4.7	237	23.7
Edgecombe	127	-9.4	466	5.9	90.4	1 226 103	2 634	266 243	156.0	573 618	62.9	37.1	47.1	31.6	2 479	71.3
Forsyth	40	-7.2	61	0.2	19.7	507 905	8 309	46 530	16.1	24 311	89.3	10.7	20.4	3.0	254	15.4
Franklin	117	3.6	216	3.8	59.5	921 013	4 271	108 980	81.5	150 308	69.2	30.8	31.9	12.7	1 070	36.5
Gaston	42	11.6	81	0.1	15.1	488 746	6 062	41 181	17.1	32 792	30.0	70.0	23.3	5.0	186	14.2
Gates	63	-16.5	348	3.8	45.2	1 210 253	3 480	152 918	66.8	367 126	45.9	54.1	46.7	30.8	980	70.3
Graham	7	-4.8	64	0.0	1.4	385 037	6 026	55 776	1.7	15 972	32.2	67.8	32.7	1.9	94	15.0
Granville	101	-21.5	171	2.0	27.9	703 173	4 108	50 185	22.8	38 769	84.2	15.8	28.0	7.0	1 224	47.0
Greene	101	9.8	389	2.1	69.4	1 517 792	3 900	167 331	274.0	1 053 758	27.7	72.3	66.2	44.2	2 286	73.8
Guilford	91	-6.0	94	1.5	41.7	583 445	6 185	63 998	58.2	60 500	56.2	43.8	28.3	8.8	962	14.8
Halifax	196	-0.9	574	3.5	120.4	1 362 000	2 371	216 636	128.3	376 211	67.7	32.3	42.5	30.2	6 355	73.0
Harnett	120	7.2	150	2.3	77.0	803 863	5 349	95 246	190.3	238 732	38.7	61.3	35.5	19.8	3 369	38.8
Haywood	49	-12.9	82	0.4	10.1	519 586	6 334	39 461	14.1	23 660	45.5	54.5	23.8	4.5	773	23.1
Henderson	36	-5.8	76	3.4	17.4	596 389	7 807	67 859	61.8	132 139	87.6	12.4	36.8	14.1	1 427	8.8
Hertford	83	5.6	513	5.6	53.7	1 226 611	2 393	231 747	146.4	903 531	36.8	63.2	54.3	38.9	1 813	72.2
Hoke	59	-2.7	290	0.7	37.4	929 153	3 204	113 114	96.8	479 327	26.1	73.9	44.1	22.8	855	43.6
Hyde	108	30.1	681	0.5	83.1	1 674 475	2 460	333 924	133.4	844 373	D	D	47.5	29.7	1 787	79.1
Iredell	152	10.1	127	0.9	75.4	761 847	6 014	74 110	165.9	137 929	22.4	77.6	39.7	16.2	1 528	12.6
Jackson	16	21.5	66	0.1	6.2	638 514	9 656	51 196	8.2	33 502	93.6	6.4	29.4	6.1	90	11.0
Johnston	195	0.4	166	3.6	133.7	809 586	4 883	105 065	265.2	225 684	57.9	42.1	39.1	18.5	4 347	39.2
Jones	59	-14.1	349	1.1	45.3	931 588	2 668	189 171	185.6	1 091 594	16.6	83.4	55.9	38.8	2 130	57.6
Lee	39	7.9	159	1.3	15.0	663 992	4 180	71 622	34.7	141 252	49.5	50.5	32.9	12.2	569	19.5
Lenoir	122	-11.2	304	3.7	94.2	1 027 628	3 375	183 147	312.4	778 973	31.1	68.9	62.1	44.1	3 454	64.3
Lincoln	56	-6.4	85	0.2	25.6	475 570	5 571	55 046	56.5	86 731	17.2	82.8	27.6	7.5	350	18.1
McDowell	25	8.4	75	0.2	6.1	430 174	5 770	59 126	25.2	75 392	68.3	31.7	23.1	7.5	110	5.1
Macon	23	7.3	70	0.1	5.2	530 994	7 631	48 359	5.6	17 295	36.0	64.0	20.6	1.5	91	9.8
Madison	56	-15.7	78	0.2	10.2	423 822	5 414	31 459	5.7	7 861	67.5	32.5	18.1	0.8	859	34.6
Martin	127	20.6	356	0.8	88.7	1 004 266	2 819	192 616	100.3	281 070	84.3	15.7	61.3	37.8	4 684	85.4
Mecklenburg	15	-19.3	65	0.5	5.9	1 341 371	20 591	136 338	D	D	D	D	30.4	5.9	D	5.9
Mitchell	19	-15.2	68	0.0	4.3	356 112	5 271	34 846	2.5	8 703	80.4	19.6	24.1	0.3	119	13.6
Montgomery	35	-17.6	140	1.2	9.7	574 648	4 099	95 416	122.3	489 116	7.6	92.4	48.4	30.8	162	9.6
Moore	82	3.0	115	1.6	19.2	611 519	5 325	58 081	162.4	226 213	9.3	90.7	34.8	14.3	635	10.7
Nash	141	-8.4	327	6.0	91.5	1 246 505	3 812	153 670	184.4	428 723	60.8	39.2	50.5	32.6	1 705	50.5
New Hanover	3	-34.8	58	0.1	1.2	819 980	14 231	42 980	5.4	107 060	99.0	1.0	46.0	20.0	80	14.0
Northampton	163	4.6	510	3.2	109.5	1 335 680	2 618	218 533	133.0	416 821	56.9	43.1	59.2	35.4	5 226	85.6
Onslow	58	4.4	166	1.5	38.4	634 349	3 819	115 625	187.7	540 928	15.6	84.4	46.4	30.5	1 001	38.3
Orange	57	-5.6	88	0.8	21.8	587 984	6 693	53 744	30.6	47 462	50.5	49.5	31.9	6.4	611	22.6
Pamlico	47	1.4	585	2.4	39.4	1 682 463	2 877	334 763	35.8	448 100	D	D	53.8	38.8	881	63.8
Pasquotank	72	-15.6	531	D	67.7	1 678 897	3 159	307 206	69.0	507 537	99.4	0.6	58.1	40.4	969	52.2
Pender	56	-9.4	166	1.7	30.5	704 096	4 229	93 278	173.6	518 069	19.5	80.5	40.6	25.1	1 532	33.7
Perquimans	80	17.0	433	0.9	72.4	1 405 173	3 245	296 043	98.8	534 081	59.9	40.1	78.4	60.0	1 749	75.1
Person	95	-3.3	241	2.8	49.5	916 124	3 797	106 694	41.0	103 868	88.5	11.5	33.9	15.7	851	43.5
Pitt	172	0.2	439	3.6	131.7	1 397 719	3 181	233 246	215.9	552 194	51.5	48.5	60.1	38.9	3 877	57.3
Polk	24	14.8	83	0.1	7.1	609 310	7 332	49 707	D	D	D	D	20.7	5.2	56	13.1
Randolph	157	6.4	106	1.2	57.1	505 668	4 792	63 355	236.4	159 079	10.1	89.9	35.1	14.9	961	13.1
Richmond	48	16.3	172	1.5	19.4	707 336	4 119	72 953	165.2	596 390	7.1	92.9	48.7	32.5	610	27.4
Robeson	266	-0.9	282	6.5	198.6	828 756	2 937	136 951	409.6	435 310	35.2	64.8	45.7	24.4	4 522	51.1
Rockingham	112	-4.2	124	3.4	37.2	503 050	4 045	50 227	32.8	36 368	74.3	25.7	25.5	5.7	726	27.6
Rowan	121	4.5	120	1.1	65.9	677 980	5 658	79 407	84.0	83 067	60.5	39.5	29.5	8.0	458	12.6
Rutherford	60	-9.6	93	0.2	16.1	376 525	4 035	35 348	22.8	35 751	14.3	85.7	22.7	3.9	313	14.4
Sampson	292	-9.3	273	16.3	179.3	1 086 479	3 975	186 084	1 258.8	1 179 750	17.7	82.3	66.3	46.2	3 373	53.7
Scotland	69	4.8	460	2.2	33.4	1 654 193	3 600	113 933	82.2	547 833	24.5	75.5	50.7	34.7	427	44.7
Stanly	93	-11.0	140	0.5	54.5	720 660	5 141	85 458	96.5	145 354	33.8	66.2	27.1	11.0	928	26.5
Stokes	92	0.6	99	0.5	30.8	380 308	3 847	46 631	31.4	33 949	36.4	63.6	22.2	4.2	1 065	26.6
Surry	127	10.8	101	1.1	56.3	463 494	4 588	84 900	198.9	158 387	22.9	77.1	34.1	10.7	1 293	26.1

Table B. States and Counties — Water Use, Wholesale Trade, Retail Trade, and Real Estate

STATE County	Water use, 2010		Wholesale trade,[1] 2012				Retail trade,[2] 2012				Real estate and rental and leasing,[2] 2012			
	Total water withdrawn (mil gal/day)	Gallons withdrawn per person per day	Number of establishments	Number of employees	Sales (mil dol)	Annual payroll (mil dol)	Number of establishments	Number of employees	Sales (mil dol)	Annual payroll (mil dol)	Number of establishments	Number of employees	Receipts (mil dol)	Annual payroll (mil dol)
	133	134	135	136	137	138	139	140	141	142	143	144	145	146
NORTH CAROLINA—Cont'd														
Chowan	7.0	475	20	231	196.7	9.0	56	479	119.2	9.5	12	29	3.8	0.6
Clay	1.3	119	1	D	D	D	45	422	134.4	10.7	5	9	0.8	0.1
Cleveland	43.4	442	77	1 223	1 309.4	43.4	373	3 656	962.1	83.5	78	253	39.2	7.0
Columbus	43.1	741	37	357	295.2	17.4	217	2 125	553.1	47.2	35	85	14.3	2.1
Craven	37.3	361	75	D	D	D	394	4 358	1 213.6	103.3	99	336	43.4	9.9
Cumberland	45.7	143	164	2 628	1 028.8	103.2	1 049	15 587	4 374.2	365.3	326	D	D	D
Currituck	5.6	240	17	103	58.7	3.9	127	879	275.2	23.9	47	D	D	D
Dare	8.7	257	33	D	D	D	420	3 372	863.9	89.5	131	D	D	D
Davidson	27.2	167	148	1 904	1 032.2	77.9	466	4 824	1 301.8	108.6	91	D	D	D
Davie	6.4	155	33	349	160.1	15.9	112	1 258	360.2	28.9	29	D	D	D
Duplin	38.5	658	34	441	473.1	15.2	180	1 762	466.4	37.5	25	84	5.5	2.1
Durham	33.8	126	198	8 508	6 468.7	981.8	939	14 512	3 402.1	329.8	295	1 661	367.1	70.6
Edgecombe	15.3	270	17	359	206.0	11.2	141	1 416	372.1	29.9	39	90	24.4	3.3
Forsyth	49.5	141	380	6 070	4 220.3	285.3	1 361	19 642	5 569.4	479.4	373	1 791	313.9	65.9
Franklin	9.5	156	35	414	150.2	17.7	129	1 385	353.7	29.9	30	88	16.8	4.2
Gaston	851.7	4 133	198	2 756	2 037.7	120.2	637	9 035	2 329.5	203.3	148	742	151.2	26.1
Gates	2.9	234	7	30	23.0	1.1	26	191	43.6	3.8	1	D	D	D
Graham	39.1	4 408	2	D	D	D	33	226	44.5	4.6	3	3	0.3	0.0
Granville	8.2	137	24	D	D	D	132	1 306	350.0	29.0	34	87	11.3	1.9
Greene	7.6	357	4	D	D	D	45	303	83.5	5.3	2	D	D	D
Guilford	66.0	135	957	14 160	14 111.4	788.0	1 851	26 619	6 979.7	664.7	656	4 338	711.8	171.7
Halifax	31.7	580	25	D	D	D	236	2 448	607.0	50.9	39	138	13.6	2.7
Harnett	27.7	241	53	D	D	D	268	3 037	869.4	66.8	69	226	19.6	5.3
Haywood	101.2	1 714	36	195	109.1	10.7	254	2 768	811.0	66.3	68	170	24.1	4.2
Henderson	19.4	182	111	1 236	740.5	46.8	407	4 653	1 330.8	114.2	109	282	52.3	9.0
Hertford	10.7	432	17	96	38.7	3.2	101	1 122	254.9	22.8	12	32	5.4	0.8
Hoke	26.2	559	9	83	49.6	3.3	79	806	257.7	16.7	19	D	D	D
Hyde	1.8	312	12	89	84.8	2.4	36	166	30.4	2.8	6	53	4.5	1.5
Iredell	26.0	163	231	1 803	1 233.0	92.9	619	7 783	2 249.9	181.9	167	469	85.5	16.7
Jackson	5.1	127	16	D	D	D	157	1 519	403.7	34.0	54	184	21.5	5.4
Johnston	29.7	176	95	1 051	897.6	56.0	548	7 446	2 134.2	159.1	89	377	64.5	11.3
Jones	3.7	362	7	D	D	D	26	112	33.7	2.5	NA	NA	NA	NA
Lee	11.8	204	41	D	D	D	238	3 021	832.2	67.6	51	165	28.6	5.7
Lenoir	29.6	498	64	847	478.3	34.6	239	2 746	728.9	67.1	42	161	27.8	4.9
Lincoln	26.9	343	72	848	332.9	38.0	237	2 945	789.8	68.7	52	94	16.1	3.0
McDowell	11.1	246	30	209	393.2	9.6	125	1 597	457.8	35.9	24	54	5.5	1.2
Macon	278.1	8 198	20	94	33.8	2.8	222	1 757	432.5	43.8	56	93	14.4	2.6
Madison	2.7	132	5	21	6.8	0.3	41	408	111.5	7.6	15	17	2.2	0.6
Martin	63.6	2 594	21	163	77.3	5.6	75	914	249.1	19.9	10	28	4.8	0.7
Mecklenburg	2 804.9	3 050	1 811	28 413	21 895.9	1 802.7	3 378	52 469	14 756.9	1 291.7	1 678	9 686	2 279.5	533.3
Mitchell	4.1	265	9	28	25.0	1.1	61	679	182.1	14.4	16	42	5.3	1.4
Montgomery	6.1	220	23	185	62.7	7.9	83	719	189.8	15.7	12	18	2.3	0.3
Moore	21.1	240	61	360	224.4	16.0	352	4 380	1 094.9	97.0	97	230	32.6	7.1
Nash	20.6	215	111	2 045	2 693.9	98.1	410	5 059	1 234.5	110.3	87	374	49.0	11.3
New Hanover	42.4	209	282	2 531	1 189.4	122.7	1 027	13 512	3 871.7	336.5	378	2 111	355.7	76.9
Northampton	21.4	970	16	D	D	D	49	415	131.2	9.3	4	12	0.4	0.1
Onslow	32.3	182	50	304	139.1	11.9	545	7 716	2 213.0	177.9	187	664	127.0	20.7
Orange	24.2	181	83	678	510.4	33.2	386	5 621	1 385.3	151.1	153	558	95.7	20.0
Pamlico	3.8	286	9	D	D	D	41	412	100.1	9.3	12	40	2.7	0.8
Pasquotank	5.3	131	34	496	176.3	17.1	193	2 504	698.3	58.1	36	166	26.2	4.8
Pender	12.6	241	33	306	179.4	13.3	147	1 484	386.7	30.6	47	203	39.8	9.4
Perquimans	2.9	212	8	63	36.8	2.1	32	232	66.4	4.6	7	55	4.7	3.5
Person	1 014.8	25 714	22	320	176.0	14.5	126	1 409	378.4	29.3	19	52	7.9	1.1
Pitt	28.8	171	144	1 597	1 028.7	69.5	633	8 597	2 354.8	193.0	176	681	115.5	22.7
Polk	2.6	126	10	D	D	D	67	467	100.8	8.9	21	85	4.5	1.4
Randolph	23.4	165	148	1 753	836.6	80.9	395	4 137	1 107.9	89.7	79	235	46.2	6.7
Richmond	18.6	399	22	D	D	D	192	1 899	449.8	41.6	36	115	10.1	2.0
Robeson	37.2	277	71	1 050	604.4	34.3	390	4 921	1 395.6	117.3	60	211	27.1	4.3
Rockingham	133.4	1 424	52	769	397.6	24.6	324	3 530	866.3	77.0	56	153	15.9	3.4
Rowan	197.6	1 427	124	1 679	888.2	59.3	402	4 221	1 194.6	95.6	85	312	36.6	8.0
Rutherford	11.6	170	41	511	166.0	23.5	233	2 511	600.1	54.2	41	86	10.8	2.5
Sampson	37.9	597	43	788	450.6	35.7	191	2 219	593.0	50.2	33	94	17.0	3.0
Scotland	7.3	203	18	311	564.5	9.0	139	1 461	351.7	30.0	23	39	9.5	1.3
Stanly	9.5	157	49	328	177.7	16.4	232	2 609	618.1	55.4	36	145	22.4	4.3
Stokes	1 283.4	27 076	18	69	12.8	2.3	104	881	222.1	18.2	23	D	D	D
Surry	26.5	360	63	732	396.1	23.7	336	3 903	1 067.1	88.3	68	220	27.2	5.6

1. Merchant wholesalers, except manufacturers' sales branches and offices.　2. Employer establishments.

Table B. States and Counties — Professional Services, Manufacturing, and Accommodation and Food Services

STATE County	Professional, scientific, and technical services, 2012				Manufacturing, 2012				Accommodation and food services, 2012			
	Number of establish-ments	Number of employees	Receipts (mil dol)	Annual payroll (mil dol)	Number of establish-ments	Number of employees	Receipts (mil dol)	Annual payroll (mil dol)	Number of establish-ments	Number of employees	Sales (mil dol)	Annual payroll (mil dol)
	147	148	149	150	151	152	153	154	155	156	157	158
NORTH CAROLINA—Cont'd												
Chowan	26	138	13.5	4.5	18	493	451.2	20.5	28	430	19.1	5.1
Clay	13	40	3.4	1.4	8	156	D	5.6	18	166	8.6	2.4
Cleveland	131	747	104.7	29.5	118	5 325	1 821.2	232.2	159	2 262	109.1	28.6
Columbus	60	205	20.4	7.0	35	1 943	900.9	94.6	95	1 005	52.2	12.6
Craven	221	1 813	213.8	95.0	66	3 377	1 261.4	158.0	197	D	D	D
Cumberland	547	6 670	904.9	371.3	102	6 182	3 827.0	312.8	633	13 451	629.4	172.7
Currituck	40	115	14.2	4.9	15	43	D	1.4	70	D	D	D
Dare	130	D	D	D	36	398	47.8	13.9	325	D	D	D
Davidson	202	805	81.5	29.4	247	8 405	2 470.2	317.9	230	3 780	163.2	46.6
Davie	78	273	20.5	7.4	43	1 237	448.7	50.2	65	1 005	43.1	11.5
Duplin	53	168	15.4	5.7	32	5 482	2 056.7	169.6	63	921	44.1	10.7
Durham	1 123	32 330	5 726.0	2 810.4	171	11 001	8 955.5	782.2	709	14 103	832.5	226.9
Edgecombe	47	174	11.9	5.2	34	3 000	1 028.9	120.2	53	766	38.1	9.5
Forsyth	928	6 669	942.7	397.4	315	14 325	14 759.1	732.1	728	14 604	713.6	201.7
Franklin	69	247	30.4	12.8	53	2 327	1 047.3	126.8	51	633	27.8	7.6
Gaston	296	1 292	125.0	48.8	276	12 709	5 021.4	544.8	329	6 015	297.4	74.4
Gates	8	32	2.5	0.7	7	133	D	5.7	4	D	D	D
Graham	8	25	2.2	0.8	8	D	D	D	22	214	14.6	4.2
Granville	59	257	24.2	9.4	47	4 229	3 020.6	197.2	73	979	52.4	12.1
Greene	10	44	3.4	1.6	13	103	D	5.3	15	D	D	D
Guilford	1 439	D	D	D	641	32 428	26 932.2	1 690.3	1 143	22 863	1 158.5	319.5
Halifax	53	246	14.8	6.0	33	1 583	486.3	81.2	100	1 968	86.6	20.8
Harnett	116	437	47.8	18.4	63	1 566	358.4	58.5	135	2 305	99.1	26.0
Haywood	117	461	48.3	15.5	34	1 811	D	100.7	160	2 114	102.7	30.0
Henderson	222	821	87.6	30.9	123	5 858	2 625.0	281.7	207	2 925	170.0	48.1
Hertford	19	103	8.5	3.5	16	883	D	55.2	50	748	29.0	7.3
Hoke	30	143	7.0	2.9	13	2 011	1 654.1	66.7	24	477	16.5	4.3
Hyde	5	D	D	D	6	34	D	D	29	D	D	D
Iredell	381	2 671	438.4	124.9	280	9 940	3 628.9	459.9	345	6 011	289.6	76.9
Jackson	84	378	34.8	11.9	17	166	64.5	9.0	104	3 553	548.5	88.6
Johnston	255	845	91.4	31.6	109	6 399	3 712.6	323.3	262	4 949	243.0	61.2
Jones	6	20	1.9	0.5	5	28	D	1.2	6	D	D	D
Lee	80	304	26.5	90.5	73	8 039	2 751.5	340.9	106	1 816	84.2	23.0
Lenoir	64	498	112.4	23.8	46	3 374	D	135.8	99	1 776	78.4	20.9
Lincoln	117	471	53.2	18.2	109	3 974	1 884.9	165.4	101	1 649	75.4	20.2
McDowell	36	162	13.8	6.1	53	5 206	1 324.2	192.5	72	1 006	46.5	12.3
Macon	69	206	16.1	6.1	25	676	181.2	25.5	105	1 194	63.3	20.6
Madison	21	34	3.3	0.9	17	357	D	14.1	25	273	12.2	4.0
Martin	19	133	8.8	2.9	15	786	557.4	30.1	44	673	25.7	7.0
Mecklenburg	3 935	47 897	8 741.1	3 404.2	796	24 964	11 150.0	1 364.6	2 333	49 178	2 845.1	776.0
Mitchell	16	66	4.9	2.0	25	347	56.5	14.1	35	391	19.4	5.0
Montgomery	18	65	5.9	1.7	57	2 275	803.2	77.4	39	D	D	D
Moore	215	1 331	176.2	65.3	84	1 777	781.5	74.4	204	4 650	236.7	69.4
Nash	154	892	97.2	37.3	85	6 582	3 184.4	335.6	191	3 948	166.7	46.5
New Hanover	860	5 650	1 071.2	288.7	170	4 515	2 449.5	321.5	657	12 919	623.3	171.5
Northampton	11	29	2.2	0.8	9	444	246.4	19.2	14	123	4.6	1.3
Onslow	246	1 748	198.1	69.5	40	1 049	271.0	34.2	347	6 640	353.1	86.9
Orange	538	2 132	316.3	130.1	73	862	161.4	41.8	311	5 585	283.0	81.1
Pamlico	23	51	4.9	1.4	14	130	D	5.1	31	D	D	D
Pasquotank	63	334	35.3	13.4	27	726	D	37.4	92	1 774	76.9	19.4
Pender	77	202	19.3	6.7	37	753	191.4	28.0	89	1 032	50.5	14.0
Perquimans	13	33	1.8	0.8	5	D	D	D	13	218	8.6	2.2
Person	32	126	10.3	3.4	34	1 717	841.2	67.2	56	905	41.3	10.5
Pitt	311	1 893	247.9	84.4	87	4 905	2 160.8	248.8	362	8 055	357.6	96.7
Polk	37	135	12.4	4.2	20	304	78.2	9.3	34	352	14.4	4.4
Randolph	165	624	55.8	18.6	293	14 850	4 557.3	510.6	202	3 190	158.6	41.6
Richmond	45	171	12.8	4.0	42	2 775	794.4	87.6	66	949	42.3	10.5
Robeson	110	D	D	D	61	6 421	3 081.4	227.0	173	3 039	139.1	34.2
Rockingham	113	D	D	D	85	6 311	4 268.3	267.6	149	2 132	91.1	24.2
Rowan	177	851	87.9	29.4	186	7 529	3 856.6	327.2	219	3 619	163.2	44.5
Rutherford	78	250	21.3	7.4	71	2 639	672.5	115.4	123	1 590	71.8	19.7
Sampson	55	289	22.9	8.3	47	3 413	821.8	106.9	79	D	D	D
Scotland	27	117	9.4	3.8	30	1 662	984.2	74.8	58	923	43.8	11.3
Stanly	69	315	41.5	11.6	92	3 066	832.9	119.2	119	1 687	70.6	19.7
Stokes	39	141	11.8	4.4	25	896	489.7	33.1	52	721	35.1	9.1
Surry	96	355	33.4	11.2	93	3 511	967.8	122.4	160	2 403	105.4	28.7

1. Establishment subject to federal tax.

Table B. States and Counties — **Health Care and Social Assistance, Other Services, Nonemployer Businesses, and Residential Construction**

STATE County	Health care and social assistance, 2012				Other services, 2012				Nonemployer businesses, 2014		Value of residential construction authorized by building permits, 2015	
	Number of establishments	Number of employees	Receipts (mil dol)	Annual payroll (mil dol)	Number of establishments	Number of employees	Receipts (mil dol)	Annual payroll (mil dol)	Number	Receipts (mil dol)	New Construction ($1,000)	Number of housing units
	159	160	161	162	163	164	165	166	167	168	169	170
NORTH CAROLINA—Cont'd												
Chowan	62	1 194	94.1	39.2	16	80	5.9	1.9	976	33.1	2 656	10
Clay	23	270	14.9	6.5	11	D	D	D	1 062	34.5	9 596	39
Cleveland	227	5 245	496.8	195.7	121	607	58.8	16.3	5 422	177.6	12 014	60
Columbus	169	3 353	246.5	97.1	51	D	D	D	3 370	112.3	4 112	31
Craven	241	7 319	715.4	300.9	143	711	58.2	15.6	5 648	217.2	41 428	354
Cumberland	778	20 384	2 106.5	958.1	417	2 403	221.4	59.4	17 167	638.6	195 884	1 112
Currituck	27	248	18.0	7.6	43	201	22.2	5.6	2 023	95.1	85 727	288
Dare	92	D	D	D	95	404	33.6	9.7	5 251	269.5	85 086	268
Davidson	196	13 615	1 634.9	566.3	185	709	73.9	18.1	10 956	414.4	100 709	389
Davie	63	1 122	79.5	34.5	53	189	15.7	3.9	2 965	116.2	30 219	193
Duplin	105	1 969	133.2	60.1	52	203	17.4	5.0	3 157	128.1	8 640	36
Durham	772	25 680	3 785.0	1 271.4	433	4 298	708.8	175.8	21 776	787.2	356 928	3 060
Edgecombe	105	2 502	203.1	73.3	46	D	D	D	2 493	75.5	6 690	32
Forsyth	793	22 194	2 115.1	861.5	528	3 078	369.2	86.2	25 429	989.9	174 257	1 383
Franklin	81	1 162	86.9	34.7	60	219	19.9	5.2	3 975	151.0	62 299	353
Gaston	471	11 455	1 177.4	486.2	285	1 432	113.7	34.0	12 980	503.0	268 300	1 361
Gates	13	137	7.0	3.7	10	44	3.9	0.8	532	17.9	4 577	24
Graham	10	D	D	D	7	D	D	D	685	24.3	3 339	20
Granville	93	2 089	149.3	62.5	44	118	13.6	3.7	3 054	94.1	49 731	259
Greene	43	671	35.2	15.8	13	D	D	D	1 017	32.9	4 725	53
Guilford	1 289	33 134	3 512.8	1 373.9	804	5 091	830.0	155.1	39 226	1 701.5	386 055	1 814
Halifax	130	3 022	223.0	97.1	71	D	D	D	2 551	70.5	13 711	47
Harnett	175	3 533	302.4	114.4	97	383	35.6	8.8	6 418	247.5	110 978	747
Haywood	141	3 047	314.1	128.9	96	417	36.4	10.8	4 737	168.6	32 071	119
Henderson	292	6 339	581.9	236.3	174	860	84.3	24.7	8 854	341.7	110 928	616
Hertford	82	2 189	155.8	64.7	36	D	D	D	950	30.6	6 777	75
Hoke	65	946	49.5	20.8	24	101	7.5	1.9	2 283	62.0	54 894	274
Hyde	10	D	D	D	3	D	D	D	581	21.0	1 123	6
Iredell	455	6 805	758.7	298.5	272	1 696	149.9	39.2	13 052	608.4	351 615	1 356
Jackson	91	1 900	201.6	84.4	54	205	26.5	6.2	3 074	119.5	78 695	191
Johnston	300	5 165	457.1	177.1	200	868	74.2	21.3	11 853	512.5	265 635	1 545
Jones	15	188	47.7	9.3	5	12	1.1	0.3	581	19.4	1 558	15
Lee	160	2 732	249.7	93.8	84	393	27.9	9.2	3 519	141.6	17 660	81
Lenoir	176	4 333	305.5	133.8	81	522	45.7	13.1	3 180	111.7	6 341	38
Lincoln	137	2 343	223.5	86.8	130	491	41.6	12.3	5 531	228.2	74 268	444
McDowell	91	1 630	119.4	44.9	40	293	21.8	6.7	2 474	84.6	29 674	142
Macon	91	1 546	134.1	53.4	93	354	31.1	8.7	3 227	112.0	12 989	85
Madison	30	652	37.9	16.2	11	38	4.2	0.9	1 846	69.9	20 865	73
Martin	74	1 462	95.3	37.7	19	D	D	D	1 246	43.4	0	0
Mecklenburg	2 576	61 634	8 163.9	3 031.5	1 698	12 608	1 767.5	413.7	87 844	3 996.0	1 345 474	9 056
Mitchell	38	886	97.6	29.3	27	84	6.1	1.7	1 125	34.2	3 456	23
Montgomery	55	1 031	61.4	29.7	34	200	11.5	4.7	1 550	57.6	2 343	28
Moore	275	8 294	913.4	374.0	137	709	56.7	16.8	7 370	335.5	128 094	562
Nash	243	4 050	349.4	143.4	138	D	D	D	5 585	210.8	35 061	231
New Hanover	756	12 485	1 277.4	511.7	440	2 566	226.8	65.5	19 376	932.9	315 604	1 812
Northampton	32	693	26.4	12.8	17	D	D	D	923	29.7	4 826	25
Onslow	257	5 765	491.7	197.5	210	1 172	89.9	26.6	8 866	325.8	113 726	894
Orange	391	12 581	1 389.9	600.6	196	1 699	271.2	59.1	12 601	530.3	171 907	691
Pamlico	37	557	43.0	20.8	19	109	11.4	2.6	1 026	39.4	12 001	66
Pasquotank	138	2 540	225.1	97.3	62	D	D	D	2 566	80.2	13 519	86
Pender	89	1 305	97.3	38.5	55	193	17.4	5.1	4 089	148.9	84 581	546
Perquimans	16	183	8.9	4.5	11	D	D	D	961	30.2	5 344	26
Person	83	1 278	98.9	35.2	43	158	17.0	4.4	2 048	69.1	12 198	64
Pitt	510	16 075	1 880.0	681.9	183	1 104	93.9	25.1	10 300	387.1	73 208	538
Polk	58	1 457	104.4	43.8	26	D	D	D	1 881	75.1	18 010	61
Randolph	238	5 136	363.9	164.1	170	709	77.9	19.7	9 595	359.8	43 874	211
Richmond	98	2 042	177.2	73.2	56	272	16.2	4.8	1 917	64.0	7 059	188
Robeson	286	8 151	581.0	256.4	80	358	26.9	7.7	7 468	236.2	20 481	105
Rockingham	170	3 440	287.5	110.4	121	525	39.6	11.1	4 941	168.6	36 605	187
Rowan	263	8 202	837.0	406.4	142	682	58.0	18.0	9 019	327.4	74 173	294
Rutherford	132	2 951	245.8	90.6	68	377	27.7	9.1	4 107	165.6	22 163	110
Sampson	130	2 719	179.4	76.3	64	292	25.4	7.5	3 386	135.8	10 182	76
Scotland	114	2 358	236.0	97.2	32	117	10.2	2.3	1 746	54.2	2 907	29
Stanly	174	3 190	251.4	98.7	81	390	32.2	10.2	3 936	146.2	13 343	92
Stokes	51	1 156	107.1	36.4	47	D	D	D	2 886	112.0	15 476	75
Surry	171	5 086	411.6	173.2	96	487	39.4	11.2	4 815	204.5	21 617	154

Table B. States and Counties — Government Employment and Payroll, and Local Government Finances

STATE County	Government employment and payroll, 2012									Local government finances, 2012				
			March payroll (percent of total)							General revenue				
													Taxes	
														Per capita[1] (dollars)
	Full-time equivalent employees	March payroll (dollars)	Adminis-tration, judicial, and legal	Police and Corrections	Fire Protection	Highways and transpor-tation	Health and Welfare	Natural resources and utilities	Education and libraries	Total (mil dol)	Inter-govern-mental (mil dol)	Total (mil dol)	Total	Property
	171	172	173	174	175	176	177	178	179	180	181	182	183	184
NORTH CAROLINA— Cont'd														
Chowan	470	1 457 821	1.5	4.5	1.5	0.7	1.5	4.7	79.9	47.9	24.9	15.3	1 036	830
Clay	374	1 096 838	4.9	8.6	0.1	2.1	18.6	3.2	58.6	30.3	17.7	10.0	938	759
Cleveland	5 555	17 029 077	1.4	2.7	1.1	0.6	40.8	3.7	48.8	997.0	173.6	81.7	838	665
Columbus	2 576	8 631 036	7.0	13.2	4.0	1.6	9.8	5.6	57.3	181.2	110.5	43.2	750	595
Craven	5 760	21 786 606	3.1	4.6	1.8	1.3	49.5	4.0	34.0	683.8	247.7	93.3	890	647
Cumberland	18 665	65 054 561	1.3	6.1	1.9	0.8	41.4	3.9	38.6	1 026.5	546.0	340.9	1 052	756
Currituck	1 085	3 605 883	4.2	9.0	1.4	0.2	12.9	4.4	63.7	101.1	28.3	49.2	2 044	1 156
Dare	1 891	6 914 953	10.6	12.1	4.0	0.9	18.7	6.6	40.2	195.1	51.6	121.3	3 507	2 197
Davidson	5 783	17 327 794	4.1	6.9	2.6	0.9	8.4	4.1	68.7	408.7	228.5	125.0	765	602
Davie	1 378	4 164 460	3.3	9.1	0.2	0.6	15.6	2.8	66.1	100.6	51.4	36.9	892	723
Duplin	2 596	7 169 108	4.4	6.0	0.9	1.1	11.3	3.0	71.0	166.7	96.1	42.2	702	533
Durham	9 926	33 408 797	6.2	5.0	0.4	2.0	10.8	7.2	66.1	1 014.8	394.0	460.1	1 645	1 286
Edgecombe	2 085	7 168 867	2.6	6.9	1.2	0.7	10.7	5.5	70.6	170.1	100.0	37.8	676	569
Forsyth	13 925	45 845 272	4.9	9.9	5.3	1.5	7.4	5.9	62.7	1 198.2	555.3	456.5	1 275	995
Franklin	1 848	5 584 621	4.4	7.9	0.4	0.3	14.6	2.9	65.1	141.2	69.1	51.6	840	681
Gaston	7 249	25 015 194	7.4	6.7	2.8	2.9	12.2	6.4	59.7	643.2	307.9	230.9	1 110	864
Gates	371	1 271 812	3.9	2.8	0.0	1.1	5.8	2.3	82.4	29.7	19.3	7.6	641	522
Graham	358	999 021	5.0	6.3	0.1	2.3	19.0	2.4	60.3	29.4	18.8	7.3	834	661
Granville	1 871	5 604 572	7.1	8.1	0.7	1.1	4.5	5.4	70.7	198.6	73.9	47.4	785	648
Greene	792	2 460 297	7.1	5.1	0.0	2.0	11.7	8.9	63.9	57.2	35.0	8.8	409	388
Guilford	18 710	71 857 919	4.6	10.1	4.0	2.3	6.6	6.4	63.8	1 781.8	770.6	726.5	1 450	1 146
Halifax	2 529	8 099 327	3.1	5.7	1.4	1.3	12.8	5.1	68.3	190.1	109.1	47.9	886	669
Harnett	3 872	13 569 140	4.6	12.1	0.4	1.1	9.2	4.4	66.9	288.8	164.5	83.5	684	544
Haywood	3 238	11 027 848	3.6	5.3	0.5	0.6	44.4	2.8	39.6	310.3	118.9	68.8	1 168	882
Henderson	4 495	15 113 386	3.5	6.2	0.7	0.5	37.6	2.5	46.9	628.0	121.4	105.7	976	755
Hertford	1 107	3 318 864	2.9	8.6	0.6	0.6	10.8	4.2	66.9	79.7	46.0	21.1	863	629
Hoke	1 946	6 883 544	2.2	5.4	0.2	1.0	6.2	1.3	80.3	121.2	74.9	31.7	626	463
Hyde	303	895 248	4.8	5.1	0.0	0.0	17.4	6.5	63.4	29.6	15.5	8.8	1 500	1 122
Iredell	5 871	18 788 013	4.4	8.0	3.5	0.6	9.3	4.8	66.7	482.4	216.0	188.6	1 159	907
Jackson	1 418	4 256 176	4.4	6.6	0.0	1.0	11.8	4.0	65.6	109.9	53.3	43.4	1 072	832
Johnston	7 756	24 977 350	2.3	4.6	1.2	0.6	24.0	3.4	62.5	698.3	273.2	164.7	942	743
Jones	494	1 149 556	4.9	6.6	0.0	0.2	13.5	4.3	66.8	28.8	17.3	6.8	664	556
Lee	3 038	10 911 112	3.3	6.5	2.0	1.2	5.3	3.7	57.7	206.8	113.6	67.5	1 130	854
Lenoir	2 634	8 323 127	3.5	7.1	2.0	2.2	10.0	8.6	63.7	209.1	121.6	56.5	955	735
Lincoln	2 462	7 572 141	4.1	8.7	1.3	1.3	14.4	4.8	63.7	182.3	86.5	68.9	868	682
McDowell	1 584	3 817 801	1.8	2.8	0.5	0.8	1.5	2.4	89.3	105.4	60.6	31.8	708	497
Macon	1 378	3 815 292	6.5	9.2	0.5	1.5	16.3	5.7	56.3	100.9	48.1	36.6	1 081	971
Madison	876	2 682 447	3.6	4.9	0.2	0.3	14.0	3.1	71.6	52.3	29.4	15.8	761	620
Martin	1 141	3 472 186	4.5	5.3	2.4	1.3	15.0	4.7	65.2	85.6	46.7	22.7	948	699
Mecklenburg	60 489	285 037 206	2.7	6.4	2.0	1.6	56.6	3.0	26.7	8 195.0	1 390.6	1 863.3	1 923	1 419
Mitchell	1 336	2 250 773	2.5	3.7	0.0	0.0	5.6	2.2	79.0	52.4	33.1	13.0	844	617
Montgomery	1 174	3 454 946	3.3	6.9	0.0	0.7	9.4	3.4	74.1	81.0	47.9	21.9	792	630
Moore	3 494	11 423 864	5.9	7.9	2.5	1.7	12.6	3.7	62.8	269.6	121.4	108.4	1 201	948
Nash	6 656	23 448 806	3.3	5.8	2.6	2.0	39.4	6.2	39.5	555.5	191.0	99.1	1 035	775
New Hanover	11 962	45 527 134	2.5	6.8	2.5	1.2	49.3	4.7	29.7	1 468.2	274.1	326.8	1 562	1 109
Northampton	777	2 301 803	10.7	8.8	0.0	0.6	20.3	6.4	49.8	67.1	36.8	21.0	982	870
Onslow	5 873	18 455 158	3.9	7.0	1.9	1.2	10.7	4.8	66.2	585.4	209.5	152.5	832	536
Orange	5 385	18 675 410	6.4	8.5	3.1	3.3	8.9	7.6	55.3	495.0	178.9	247.0	1 791	1 537
Pamlico	537	1 656 218	4.6	6.6	0.2	0.4	9.9	5.9	70.1	42.4	25.2	12.6	965	785
Pasquotank	3 546	11 505 340	5.8	3.9	1.2	1.0	34.4	2.5	33.1	251.3	70.2	38.8	955	676
Pender	1 621	5 227 407	6.3	8.7	1.1	0.4	9.8	2.7	65.8	149.8	76.0	58.2	1 074	864
Perquimans	396	1 289 198	8.5	2.8	0.0	0.0	8.3	6.7	68.4	34.0	18.9	10.8	795	634
Person	1 548	5 009 176	3.6	7.9	2.5	1.2	11.6	4.6	65.6	119.0	63.0	39.6	1 007	800
Pitt	6 107	20 619 861	3.8	8.9	3.2	2.0	4.2	10.9	60.2	555.7	265.7	167.7	972	677
Polk	658	2 004 992	5.0	7.0	0.0	2.3	8.7	5.2	70.0	53.2	24.8	21.2	1 045	877
Randolph	4 527	16 669 167	4.3	8.3	2.7	1.2	7.8	3.4	68.3	345.4	185.5	117.9	828	644
Richmond	2 132	5 122 800	4.4	8.9	2.0	1.6	14.1	4.9	62.7	142.5	82.7	39.5	848	648
Robeson	6 145	18 365 522	4.4	13.6	1.4	1.1	12.5	5.8	59.7	414.1	250.9	103.1	761	522
Rockingham	3 543	11 125 272	5.5	9.4	2.7	1.5	10.3	3.0	62.8	267.2	141.9	84.2	908	715
Rowan	5 594	16 509 444	3.8	6.2	1.8	1.2	7.6	4.3	71.8	395.5	204.5	128.5	930	719
Rutherford	3 135	8 814 742	3.6	6.0	1.3	1.0	9.8	3.6	57.5	200.1	101.7	53.6	796	593
Sampson	2 770	7 777 872	2.8	6.0	0.4	0.4	11.9	2.4	71.5	212.9	127.6	48.5	759	539
Scotland	1 728	5 628 337	3.5	5.7	0.4	0.9	9.5	5.0	72.9	112.7	68.9	30.4	843	662
Stanly	2 443	7 501 977	4.3	7.7	2.6	2.1	13.1	6.3	62.1	184.7	101.2	51.9	857	641
Stokes	1 636	4 531 305	4.4	6.7	2.3	0.1	12.8	2.1	70.0	122.3	78.2	33.7	720	593
Surry	3 820	12 472 258	2.4	4.5	0.8	0.5	33.1	2.1	53.9	321.4	128.8	65.4	889	603

1. Based on the resident population estimated as of July 1 of the year shown.

STATE County	Local government finances, 2012 (cont.)										Government employment, 2014			Presidential election,[2] 2012		
	Direct general expenditure							Debt outstanding						Percent of vote cast:		
			Percent of total for:													
	Total (mil dol)	Per capita[1] (dollars)	Education	Health and hospitals	Police protection	Public welfare	Highways	Total (mil dol)	Per capita[1] (dollars)	Federal civilian	Federal military	State and local	Demo-cratic	Republi-can	All other
	185	186	187	188	189	190	191	192	193	194	195	196	197	198	199
NORTH CAROLINA—Cont'd															
Chowan	47.4	3 208	53.9	0.4	10.6	6.8	2.3	21.8	1 475	33	35	848	49.1	50.2	0.7
Clay	30.1	2 831	45.1	6.7	10.1	14.8	0.1	11.8	1 114	18	26	518	31.3	66.9	1.8
Cleveland	561.2	5 758	30.2	48.9	3.5	3.9	0.5	167.5	1 719	166	236	5 595	39.6	59.5	0.9
Columbus	177.1	3 072	58.4	4.6	6.2	8.6	0.7	63.1	1 095	122	134	3 649	45.6	53.5	0.9
Craven	658.8	6 288	21.8	54.9	3.8	3.5	0.8	179.3	1 712	5 355	8 985	6 990	43.4	55.8	0.8
Cumberland	1 088.1	3 358	50.4	3.7	7.9	6.3	1.3	508.0	1 568	14 328	48 218	23 166	58.5	40.9	0.6
Currituck	92.8	3 854	37.2	6.0	8.8	4.4	0.1	60.9	2 529	37	62	1 163	33.7	65.2	1.2
Dare	214.0	6 189	25.3	7.8	9.4	3.9	1.4	229.3	6 632	234	183	2 812	44.7	54.0	1.3
Davidson	418.5	2 563	60.4	2.9	6.7	5.2	1.1	214.7	1 315	164	403	6 510	32.7	66.2	1.1
Davie	101.9	2 459	54.9	7.3	7.9	6.1	0.9	31.0	749	67	102	1 599	30.3	68.6	1.0
Duplin	161.0	2 681	57.6	5.6	6.5	7.2	1.1	40.0	667	135	150	3 284	45.0	54.4	0.6
Durham	1 130.0	4 041	36.7	5.4	7.7	4.9	2.8	1 199.0	4 288	5 974	863	15 023	75.6	23.6	0.8
Edgecombe	174.9	3 125	52.2	4.1	6.7	12.0	1.1	31.7	567	180	134	4 188	67.1	32.6	0.3
Forsyth	1 295.8	3 618	44.3	6.0	8.5	3.9	2.2	1 426.9	3 984	1 620	919	18 881	54.8	44.3	0.8
Franklin	146.8	2 389	50.6	6.0	5.3	7.7	1.0	126.9	2 064	82	152	2 403	49.1	49.8	1.1
Gaston	705.2	3 389	45.5	9.1	9.5	5.7	2.2	453.5	2 180	335	517	9 325	37.2	62.2	0.6
Gates	29.2	2 457	67.6	0.6	4.9	6.5	0.1	8.9	752	24	29	530	52.2	47.0	0.8
Graham	26.4	3 040	48.5	6.1	10.0	8.9	1.3	9.5	1 093	32	21	484	30.3	67.7	2.0
Granville	202.2	3 345	38.7	26.8	6.4	4.7	0.7	131.9	2 182	1 475	135	6 743	52.9	46.3	0.8
Greene	57.7	2 693	65.9	4.7	3.8	7.2	0.7	25.4	1 185	35	47	1 853	46.8	52.7	0.4
Guilford	1 919.4	3 832	43.8	4.5	7.5	4.2	2.9	2 139.4	4 271	3 879	1 288	29 951	58.8	40.4	0.8
Halifax	185.9	3 442	51.7	6.0	5.5	8.7	1.6	112.0	2 073	124	128	4 233	64.0	35.7	0.3
Harnett	319.1	2 613	48.6	4.3	6.4	3.5	1.3	272.9	2 234	118	316	5 517	41.2	57.9	0.8
Haywood	325.8	5 531	28.2	47.8	4.0	5.8	1.3	100.5	1 706	116	146	3 442	45.4	53.1	1.5
Henderson	411.4	3 800	31.5	38.2	5.0	4.9	1.3	200.9	1 856	188	273	5 253	38.9	59.9	1.2
Hertford	78.3	3 203	52.5	7.5	6.9	8.5	1.0	105.4	4 314	61	54	1 604	70.5	29.0	0.5
Hoke	115.8	2 291	61.0	2.2	4.8	7.7	0.8	96.8	1 915	51	126	2 125	59.0	40.3	0.7
Hyde	31.1	5 313	35.0	17.4	4.4	5.8	0.0	21.2	3 614	41	12	651	50.3	49.1	0.6
Iredell	484.3	2 977	49.9	1.9	7.8	5.0	2.0	564.7	3 470	248	412	8 447	37.3	61.7	1.0
Jackson	117.6	2 908	51.0	4.9	4.2	6.3	0.6	47.1	1 164	54	94	7 232	52.0	46.6	1.5
Johnston	707.4	4 044	42.4	30.3	4.0	3.6	1.0	672.2	3 843	218	446	9 098	37.7	61.4	0.8
Jones	28.7	2 798	50.8	6.3	6.8	10.5	0.5	4.3	418	23	25	549	45.5	53.9	0.6
Lee	211.6	3 544	60.3	1.6	7.1	4.8	1.1	152.3	2 550	155	146	3 220	45.3	53.7	1.0
Lenoir	226.0	3 816	45.8	3.1	5.0	6.3	0.8	200.6	3 387	186	142	5 847	49.7	49.8	0.4
Lincoln	184.5	2 326	52.4	5.8	7.2	7.4	0.6	203.5	2 566	98	196	3 628	32.7	66.0	1.3
McDowell	115.5	2 567	60.9	1.8	4.8	9.3	1.1	20.1	447	77	107	2 510	35.7	62.7	1.5
Macon	106.3	3 138	46.9	3.4	10.5	5.7	2.0	49.0	1 446	166	83	1 639	38.4	59.9	1.7
Madison	53.5	2 579	46.9	5.8	7.8	10.1	0.9	10.7	515	60	49	943	48.4	50.0	1.6
Martin	89.4	3 730	50.1	10.1	7.7	7.3	1.2	36.3	1 513	50	58	1 516	52.1	47.5	0.4
Mecklenburg	7 529.3	7 770	17.3	51.9	4.4	2.3	1.8	7 935.0	8 189	5 572	2 583	69 097	61.8	37.4	0.7
Mitchell	54.4	3 537	64.7	2.0	5.5	8.9	0.2	3.0	192	50	37	1 116	28.5	70.1	1.4
Montgomery	78.0	2 820	58.5	5.5	7.0	5.5	1.1	28.8	1 042	51	66	1 691	43.9	54.9	1.2
Moore	304.5	3 372	46.2	2.7	12.1	4.3	1.8	140.3	1 553	150	241	4 455	38.9	60.3	0.9
Nash	589.1	6 155	29.3	42.9	4.8	3.1	1.6	113.0	1 181	203	230	5 887	49.0	50.4	0.6
New Hanover	1 459.0	6 973	21.3	49.4	4.8	2.5	1.1	1 476.2	7 055	882	710	18 783	48.8	50.2	1.0
Northampton	68.1	3 176	37.6	9.0	6.4	10.1	1.8	37.7	1 759	44	49	1 161	65.0	34.6	0.4
Onslow	563.2	3 073	38.6	24.7	6.7	6.5	1.0	439.4	2 398	7 015	45 767	8 053	38.8	60.3	0.8
Orange	485.2	3 518	44.0	6.5	6.9	6.2	1.4	328.7	2 383	225	363	39 071	71.8	27.1	1.1
Pamlico	43.2	3 303	51.1	3.1	4.3	7.4	0.9	13.7	1 044	26	52	901	42.3	57.0	0.8
Pasquotank	254.1	6 261	28.0	49.1	4.4	3.4	1.2	135.3	3 334	726	877	4 124	56.5	42.8	0.7
Pender	152.0	2 804	46.6	4.9	6.0	6.5	0.6	184.1	3 396	94	166	2 482	41.7	57.3	0.9
Perquimans	34.1	2 515	51.3	2.5	8.3	7.0	1.1	30.1	2 218	33	33	632	42.6	56.6	0.8
Person	126.4	3 218	53.5	5.5	6.7	8.5	0.7	200.1	5 097	52	96	1 872	45.3	53.8	0.8
Pitt	557.6	3 232	46.8	1.8	9.9	5.2	2.1	400.7	2 322	595	458	24 323	54.1	45.3	0.6
Polk	49.0	2 420	52.7	2.7	8.4	8.4	1.3	16.1	796	42	50	879	41.6	56.7	1.7
Randolph	349.0	2 450	59.5	2.6	7.6	5.8	1.4	147.2	1 033	198	351	6 101	28.2	70.5	1.3
Richmond	150.1	3 220	56.1	3.4	6.8	7.0	1.1	48.8	1 047	82	111	2 993	50.3	48.8	1.0
Robeson	429.7	3 171	54.2	4.0	5.7	7.6	1.3	103.7	765	279	325	8 521	56.5	42.7	0.8
Rockingham	263.7	2 844	53.2	2.0	6.8	7.4	2.1	167.2	1 803	146	225	4 129	41.5	57.4	1.1
Rowan	420.9	3 046	54.8	2.5	6.5	5.4	1.5	263.4	1 906	2 408	333	6 682	38.0	60.8	1.2
Rutherford	191.7	2 848	53.0	6.6	6.5	6.8	1.1	113.5	1 685	105	162	3 473	33.6	65.4	1.1
Sampson	232.7	3 639	52.4	12.4	4.0	6.9	0.7	122.1	1 909	106	156	4 135	45.5	53.9	0.6
Scotland	112.8	3 125	56.5	1.8	7.2	8.7	1.5	27.4	758	44	82	2 275	57.3	42.2	0.4
Stanly	179.1	2 956	54.3	4.3	6.6	5.6	1.2	61.7	1 019	140	145	3 484	31.1	67.8	1.0
Stokes	117.6	2 514	64.2	4.7	5.2	6.5	0.4	62.1	1 328	66	114	1 834	31.6	66.6	1.7
Surry	324.4	4 410	40.1	37.5	3.8	3.5	0.8	112.5	1 530	165	179	4 492	35.5	63.4	1.1

1. Based on the resident population estimated as of July 1 of the year shown.   2. © 2013 Election Data Services, Inc. All rights reserved.

Table B. States and Counties — **Land Area and Population**

STATE/ County code	CBSA code[1]	County type[2]	STATE County	Land area,[3] (sq km) 2010	Population, 2015 Total persons 2015	Rank	Per square kilometer	White	Black	American Indian, Alaska Native	Asian and Pacific Islander	Percent Hispanic or Latino[4]	Under 5 years	5 to 17 years	18 to 24 years	25 to 34 years	35 to 44 years	45 to 54 years
				1	2	3	4	5	6	7	8	9	10	11	12	13	14	15
			NORTH CAROLINA—Cont'd															
37 173	...	8	Swain	1 368	14 434	2 136	10.6	67.5	2.1	29.0	1.0	4.7	6.3	16.4	9.3	11.4	11.8	13.0
37 175	14820	6	Transylvania	980	33 211	1 351	33.9	92.0	4.9	1.0	0.8	3.2	3.9	12.5	8.3	9.0	10.0	12.5
37 177	28620	9	Tyrrell	1 008	4 070	2 896	4.0	54.8	36.8	0.7	2.6	6.7	5.4	12.6	8.2	14.2	12.2	14.2
37 179	16740	1	Union	1 636	222 742	293	136.2	74.9	12.4	0.7	2.7	11.0	6.0	22.5	8.7	9.8	14.9	16.0
37 181	25780	4	Vance	657	44 568	1 082	67.8	41.9	50.8	0.6	0.8	7.2	6.7	17.5	9.5	11.0	11.7	13.4
37 183	39580	2	Wake	2 163	1 024 198	42	473.5	62.7	21.5	0.8	7.2	10.0	6.5	18.5	9.4	14.7	15.6	14.5
37 185	...	8	Warren	1 110	20 155	1 823	18.2	39.5	51.7	5.7	0.7	4.0	4.7	14.2	8.3	10.7	10.4	13.6
37 187	...	7	Washington	902	12 385	2 272	13.7	46.5	48.9	0.6	0.6	4.8	5.6	15.8	8.4	9.0	10.2	13.4
37 189	14380	6	Watauga	810	52 906	943	65.3	93.6	2.3	0.9	1.5	3.5	3.4	9.9	29.9	11.0	9.2	10.7
37 191	24140	3	Wayne	1 432	124 132	502	86.7	56.0	32.1	0.9	2.0	11.1	6.8	17.3	10.4	13.2	11.9	13.1
37 193	35900	6	Wilkes	1 954	68 502	780	35.1	89.2	4.9	0.6	0.6	5.8	4.9	16.3	7.7	10.1	12.2	14.5
37 195	48980	4	Wilson	954	81 714	684	85.7	49.5	39.7	0.6	1.4	10.1	6.2	17.5	8.9	11.6	12.1	13.6
37 197	49180	2	Yadkin	867	37 585	1 236	43.4	85.6	3.8	0.5	0.4	10.6	5.4	16.5	8.2	10.1	12.3	15.5
37 199	...	8	Yancey	810	17 587	1 941	21.7	93.7	1.3	0.8	0.4	4.9	4.9	14.4	7.4	9.3	11.8	13.8
38 000	...	X	**NORTH DAKOTA**	178 711	756 927	X	4.2	88.2	2.5	6.1	1.8	3.2	6.9	15.9	12.7	14.6	11.1	12.1
38 001	...	9	Adams	2 558	2 359	3 018	0.9	97.5	1.1	1.6	1.1	1.2	5.5	13.8	6.5	9.5	9.1	13.4
38 003	...	6	Barnes	3 863	11 099	2 348	2.9	94.0	2.0	1.7	1.6	1.6	5.4	15.0	10.4	11.3	9.8	13.0
38 005	...	9	Benson	3 597	6 753	2 699	1.9	43.9	0.5	54.4	0.7	2.1	10.2	24.0	9.3	11.6	9.0	11.8
38 007	...	9	Billings	2 976	936	3 108	0.3	93.1	0.3	0.5	3.6	1.8	5.8	13.2	7.8	14.2	11.5	13.4
38 009	...	9	Bottineau	4 321	6 716	2 702	1.6	94.5	1.2	3.5	0.8	2.0	6.3	14.7	9.0	10.1	9.8	13.0
38 011	...	9	Bowman	3 009	3 294	2 954	1.1	93.8	0.9	1.5	0.3	4.7	6.5	17.8	7.6	11.5	10.0	11.2
38 013	...	9	Burke	2 858	2 308	3 024	0.8	96.2	1.0	1.5	0.9	2.1	8.0	15.4	7.1	13.4	9.2	13.8
38 015	13900	3	Burleigh	4 229	92 991	628	22.0	92.2	1.6	4.8	1.1	1.9	6.6	16.1	10.1	14.8	12.2	12.7
38 017	22020	3	Cass	4 571	171 512	375	37.5	90.1	4.2	1.9	3.2	2.4	6.9	15.2	15.9	16.9	12.2	11.3
38 019	...	9	Cavalier	3 856	3 828	2 916	1.0	97.0	0.5	1.8	0.5	1.1	5.2	14.5	7.0	8.4	8.5	13.4
38 021	...	9	Dickey	2 930	5 104	2 828	1.7	95.1	1.2	1.3	0.8	3.4	5.8	16.8	10.0	10.2	10.1	11.9
38 023	...	9	Divide	3 265	2 450	3 009	0.8	94.2	1.3	1.2	0.8	3.9	5.8	15.1	7.7	11.2	8.8	13.0
38 025	...	9	Dunn	5 202	4 646	2 856	0.9	84.4	1.2	10.2	1.9	3.8	6.7	16.0	8.6	15.0	10.5	14.0
38 027	...	9	Eddy	1 632	2 365	3 017	1.4	92.5	1.0	4.9	0.6	3.1	5.5	16.7	6.4	9.6	8.8	13.0
38 029	...	8	Emmons	3 912	3 402	2 943	0.9	97.8	0.4	1.2	0.4	1.1	4.4	15.5	7.4	6.0	9.0	14.1
38 031	...	9	Foster	1 646	3 356	2 948	2.0	97.0	0.6	1.4	0.7	1.2	5.3	16.0	7.3	10.3	10.2	13.8
38 033	...	9	Golden Valley	2 592	1 845	3 064	0.7	94.9	1.1	1.5	0.5	2.7	5.9	17.7	7.3	10.5	11.2	12.5
38 035	24220	3	Grand Forks	3 720	70 916	762	19.1	87.6	4.0	3.6	3.2	3.8	6.7	13.7	22.8	15.0	9.7	10.2
38 037	...	8	Grant	4 297	2 388	3 015	0.6	96.9	0.7	2.7	0.6	1.0	5.8	12.7	6.3	7.6	8.8	13.4
38 039	...	9	Griggs	1 836	2 314	3 022	1.3	98.2	0.4	0.8	0.1	0.8	4.6	13.9	6.0	8.0	8.2	12.5
38 041	...	9	Hettinger	2 932	2 704	2 991	0.9	94.2	1.2	3.7	0.5	2.3	6.4	16.3	7.0	11.5	9.5	13.1
38 043	...	8	Kidder	3 500	2 417	3 011	0.7	94.8	0.6	0.5	0.7	3.8	5.3	16.0	6.7	10.3	9.6	13.2
38 045	...	9	LaMoure	2 968	4 125	2 893	1.4	98.9	0.6	0.9	0.2	1.1	5.3	15.8	6.4	8.5	9.5	12.7
38 047	...	9	Logan	2 571	1 935	3 054	0.8	97.7	0.7	1.1	0.4	0.9	5.4	15.9	6.7	8.2	9.6	13.1
38 049	33500	9	McHenry	4 854	5 968	2 757	1.2	96.4	0.6	1.3	0.6	2.7	6.3	17.0	7.5	11.3	11.4	13.6
38 051	...	9	McIntosh	2 525	2 759	2 989	1.1	97.8	0.5	1.1	0.7	2.1	5.5	13.5	6.1	8.7	7.5	13.0
38 053	...	9	McKenzie	7 149	12 826	2 241	1.8	78.4	1.6	14.4	0.8	6.8	8.0	21.4	9.7	16.0	12.2	12.8
38 055	...	8	McLean	5 467	9 744	2 455	1.8	91.0	0.6	7.5	0.3	2.1	5.9	16.1	6.1	10.2	10.6	12.5
38 057	...	6	Mercer	2 701	8 853	2 527	3.3	94.6	0.7	2.6	0.7	2.5	6.4	15.9	6.9	11.3	10.0	15.2
38 059	13900	3	Morton	4 989	30 310	1 424	6.1	92.4	1.3	4.6	0.9	2.7	6.8	16.5	8.3	15.1	11.9	13.2
38 061	...	9	Mountrail	4 728	10 331	2 405	2.2	67.6	1.2	27.6	0.6	6.2	8.3	16.8	10.6	15.5	12.2	11.4
38 063	...	8	Nelson	2 543	2 968	2 976	1.2	95.9	1.0	2.7	0.2	2.0	4.9	13.8	5.9	9.2	8.3	13.1
38 065	13900	8	Oliver	1 871	1 846	3 063	1.0	94.1	0.6	3.2	0.6	2.5	6.5	16.1	7.2	9.4	8.9	14.6
38 067	...	9	Pembina	2 897	7 091	2 666	2.4	93.5	0.7	2.9	0.6	3.7	5.2	15.5	7.0	10.2	9.9	12.8
38 069	...	7	Pierce	2 638	4 312	2 879	1.6	94.1	0.8	4.8	0.2	1.4	6.3	15.8	7.4	10.0	9.9	13.4
38 071	...	7	Ramsey	3 074	11 630	2 317	3.8	87.9	0.8	10.7	1.0	2.5	6.5	15.9	9.4	12.0	10.1	13.4
38 073	...	8	Ransom	2 233	5 448	2 806	2.4	96.7	0.9	1.4	0.6	1.9	5.6	17.3	7.2	9.4	11.1	14.0
38 075	33500	9	Renville	2 272	2 571	3 001	1.1	96.5	1.0	1.2	0.7	2.3	6.6	15.7	7.7	11.3	10.5	14.6
38 077	47420	6	Richland	3 719	16 402	2 013	4.4	93.6	1.2	3.1	1.1	2.7	5.4	16.0	15.1	10.6	9.8	12.8
38 079	...	9	Rolette	2 339	14 649	2 124	6.3	22.4	0.7	77.0	0.3	1.6	10.3	23.5	9.7	12.1	10.8	12.4
38 081	...	9	Sargent	2 224	3 876	2 911	1.7	95.0	0.8	1.5	0.9	2.9	5.4	15.7	8.0	9.8	10.7	14.1
38 083	...	9	Sheridan	2 518	1 310	3 096	0.5	96.7	0.5	2.7	0.7	1.3	4.0	13.1	5.5	9.0	7.7	13.6
38 085	13900	8	Sioux	2 834	4 370	2 874	1.5	17.0	0.8	79.9	0.5	3.8	12.2	25.4	10.6	13.1	11.1	12.3
38 087	...	9	Slope	3 147	767	3 122	0.2	94.8	0.8	1.8	0.1	3.0	7.2	15.2	6.0	10.7	8.4	13.7
38 089	19860	7	Stark	3 457	32 154	1 379	9.3	90.5	2.0	1.9	1.7	4.9	7.6	16.7	11.0	17.3	10.9	12.3
38 091	...	8	Steele	1 845	1 956	3 052	1.1	97.4	0.3	1.5	0.3	1.3	5.7	14.8	6.6	9.5	9.5	13.8
38 093	27420	7	Stutsman	5 754	21 103	1 769	3.7	94.5	1.3	2.3	1.0	2.1	5.6	14.8	10.7	12.2	10.9	13.2
38 095	...	9	Towner	2 654	2 272	3 026	0.9	95.9	0.7	4.4	0.3	0.8	6.7	15.0	6.2	9.1	6.8	15.2
38 097	...	8	Traill	2 232	8 014	2 597	3.6	94.8	1.1	1.8	0.8	3.2	6.4	15.9	9.9	10.8	10.3	13.4
38 099	...	6	Walsh	3 320	10 897	2 365	3.3	86.7	0.5	2.2	0.7	11.1	6.4	16.2	7.5	10.6	9.7	13.5

1. CBSA = Core Based Statistical Area. See Appendix A for explanation. See Appendix B for list of metropolitan areas with component counties. Service of USDA Rural-Urban Continuum Codes. See Appendix A for definition.   3. Dry land or land partially or temporarily covered by water.   2. County type code from the Economic Research Service of USDA.   4. May be of any race.

Table B. States and Counties — **Population and Households**

STATE County	55 to 64 years	65 to 74 years	75 years and over	Percent female	2000	2010	2000–2010	2010–2015	Births	Deaths	Net migration	Number	Persons per household	Family households	Female family householder[1]	One person
	16	17	18	19	20	21	22	23	24	25	26	27	28	29	30	31
NORTH CAROLINA—Cont'd																
Swain	13.3	11.3	7.2	51.7	12 968	13 981	7.8	3.2	1 044	961	384	5 357	2.58	67.1	12.8	28.6
Transylvania	15.3	15.7	12.8	51.6	29 334	33 090	12.8	0.4	1 425	2 046	754	13 735	2.31	67.7	8.7	28.5
Tyrrell	13.9	10.9	8.5	46.3	4 149	4 407	6.2	-7.6	222	208	-334	1 455	2.49	70.9	15.4	26.9
Union	10.8	7.2	4.1	50.6	123 677	201 307	62.8	10.6	12 432	6 532	15 093	69 464	2.98	80.5	10.5	16.1
Vance	13.9	9.7	6.7	53.2	42 954	45 419	5.7	-1.9	3 020	2 554	-1 358	16 651	2.65	64.5	20.9	31.1
Wake	10.7	6.1	3.9	51.3	627 846	901 021	43.5	13.7	65 702	25 029	80 608	355 647	2.62	66.3	11.6	26.9
Warren	16.6	12.5	9.1	49.5	19 972	20 975	5.0	-3.9	977	1 194	-582	7 866	2.50	65.4	17.1	30.7
Washington	16.5	11.9	9.2	53.0	13 723	13 218	-3.7	-6.3	676	790	-723	5 126	2.47	65.7	21.0	30.4
Watauga	11.9	8.6	5.6	50.0	42 695	51 079	19.6	3.6	1 842	1 743	1 839	20 224	2.30	52.1	7.4	29.8
Wayne	12.7	8.3	6.2	50.8	113 329	122 623	8.2	1.2	8 988	5 944	-1 505	47 480	2.55	67.4	18.2	27.5
Wilkes	14.5	11.5	8.4	50.7	65 632	69 340	5.6	-1.2	3 526	3 950	-421	27 355	2.49	69.4	10.6	27.0
Wilson	13.7	9.4	6.9	52.6	73 814	81 234	10.1	0.6	5 020	4 338	-352	32 026	2.49	66.3	17.9	29.4
Yadkin	13.7	10.6	7.7	50.4	36 348	38 406	5.7	-2.1	2 069	2 101	-761	15 174	2.49	69.3	10.8	28.4
Yancey	15.0	13.6	9.9	50.8	17 774	17 818	0.2	-1.3	879	1 137	75	7 230	2.42	71.5	9.6	25.3
NORTH DAKOTA	12.5	7.3	6.9	48.7	642 200	672 591	4.7	12.5	53 765	31 480	61 105	292 616	2.32	60.8	7.8	31.2
Adams	17.0	11.6	13.6	51.3	2 593	2 343	-9.6	0.7	120	140	32	1 098	2.07	69.4	4.6	24.7
Barnes	14.9	10.0	10.2	50.0	11 775	11 066	-6.0	0.3	626	681	100	4 918	2.13	61.6	5.4	30.0
Benson	12.0	6.9	5.3	48.5	6 964	6 660	-4.4	1.4	770	397	-250	2 331	2.89	70.1	19.4	27.1
Billings	16.3	9.4	8.3	44.6	888	783	-11.8	19.5	61	13	114	361	2.24	63.2	3.0	36.3
Bottineau	15.7	12.0	9.3	47.8	7 149	6 429	-10.1	4.5	374	393	308	3 000	2.09	61.6	4.9	34.1
Bowman	16.0	10.0	9.5	48.3	3 242	3 151	-2.8	4.5	232	237	168	1 330	2.34	62.9	3.3	33.9
Burke	15.1	9.9	8.1	46.7	2 242	1 968	-12.2	17.3	160	112	285	988	2.17	57.6	4.7	39.0
Burleigh	13.0	7.7	6.8	50.2	69 416	81 308	17.1	14.4	6 385	3 488	8 505	35 767	2.32	62.8	9.0	29.2
Cass	10.7	5.8	5.0	49.3	123 138	149 778	21.6	14.5	12 527	4 960	13 781	67 013	2.28	54.8	7.7	33.6
Cavalier	16.4	12.7	13.9	49.3	4 831	3 993	-17.3	-4.1	221	261	-87	1 759	2.17	64.9	3.4	32.2
Dickey	13.5	10.5	11.3	50.3	5 757	5 289	-8.1	-3.5	289	371	-114	2 211	2.22	64.2	4.9	31.4
Divide	15.3	11.1	12.0	48.3	2 283	2 071	-9.3	18.3	148	133	374	1 065	2.04	63.8	2.9	33.6
Dunn	15.0	7.2	7.1	46.5	3 600	3 536	-1.8	31.4	288	172	996	1 473	2.60	72.3	6.4	21.7
Eddy	16.3	11.6	12.2	49.6	2 757	2 385	-13.5	-0.8	135	240	83	1 074	2.13	58.3	8.9	33.8
Emmons	15.9	12.7	14.9	48.7	4 331	3 550	-18.0	-4.2	141	266	-6	1 618	2.12	62.1	4.6	36.2
Foster	15.1	9.1	13.0	50.1	3 759	3 343	-11.1	0.4	180	207	68	1 576	2.09	67.5	7.5	29.1
Golden Valley	16.3	9.2	9.4	49.5	1 924	1 680	-12.7	9.8	107	94	161	766	2.29	57.8	4.3	39.4
Grand Forks	10.7	6.2	5.0	48.5	66 109	66 861	1.1	6.1	5 134	2 475	1 302	28 045	2.26	54.7	7.7	33.3
Grant	17.7	14.3	13.4	49.1	2 841	2 394	-15.7	-0.3	135	146	27	1 137	2.05	60.4	3.5	34.8
Griggs	18.0	14.4	14.3	49.0	2 754	2 420	-12.1	-4.4	104	197	-9	1 068	2.12	65.5	4.6	32.8
Hettinger	13.2	10.3	12.6	51.5	2 715	2 477	-8.8	9.2	164	181	233	1 088	2.23	70.5	6.2	26.5
Kidder	17.9	10.0	10.9	48.7	2 753	2 435	-11.6	-0.7	143	78	-55	1 097	2.21	74.4	2.7	24.2
LaMoure	16.5	11.1	14.3	48.7	4 701	4 139	-12.0	-0.3	213	225	34	1 898	2.14	64.5	4.3	32.7
Logan	14.1	11.8	15.2	49.2	2 308	1 990	-13.8	-2.8	106	133	-27	866	2.17	66.1	2.9	31.6
McHenry	13.9	9.7	9.3	47.5	5 987	5 395	-9.9	10.6	353	301	507	2 576	2.19	64.7	6.8	32.4
McIntosh	14.4	11.2	20.0	51.2	3 390	2 809	-17.1	-1.8	134	280	97	1 336	2.00	62.4	6.2	34.4
McKenzie	11.6	4.9	3.4	46.6	5 737	6 360	10.9	101.7	808	286	5 819	2 755	2.96	68.7	8.2	25.9
McLean	17.1	12.7	8.9	48.9	9 311	8 962	-3.7	8.7	595	549	729	4 078	2.23	67.9	5.4	29.2
Mercer	17.3	9.4	7.6	48.1	8 644	8 424	-2.5	5.1	544	433	329	3 666	2.29	67.1	6.8	29.4
Morton	13.3	8.2	6.8	49.4	25 303	27 471	8.6	10.3	2 219	1 367	1 916	11 820	2.35	65.3	7.7	28.4
Mountrail	12.9	6.4	4.5	44.8	6 631	7 673	15.7	34.6	782	391	2 202	3 108	2.75	70.1	12.0	26.4
Nelson	16.8	13.9	14.1	49.2	3 715	3 126	-15.9	-5.1	159	309	-10	1 499	1.99	60.6	7.1	36.3
Oliver	18.6	11.5	7.2	48.9	2 065	1 846	-10.6	0.0	109	59	-37	783	2.34	69.9	2.3	26.4
Pembina	17.8	10.5	11.1	48.6	8 585	7 413	-13.7	-4.3	407	448	-309	3 299	2.14	64.0	5.9	31.2
Pierce	14.4	10.2	12.6	49.3	4 675	4 357	-6.8	-1.0	256	342	47	1 943	2.16	62.0	2.6	35.2
Ramsey	14.3	9.4	9.0	49.4	12 066	11 451	-5.1	1.6	834	689	71	5 003	2.21	56.8	9.6	37.6
Ransom	14.9	9.3	11.3	48.9	5 890	5 457	-7.4	-0.2	317	395	79	2 307	2.29	63.0	5.1	34.2
Renville	14.6	8.9	10.0	47.4	2 610	2 470	-5.4	4.1	166	137	71	1 079	2.31	65.5	4.5	29.9
Richland	14.5	7.7	8.1	48.4	17 998	16 321	-9.3	0.5	901	698	-123	6 616	2.28	64.8	6.8	28.0
Rolette	11.0	6.1	4.1	50.9	13 674	13 937	1.9	5.1	1 590	792	-83	4 728	3.00	73.9	25.2	23.5
Sargent	16.5	11.2	8.5	47.4	4 366	3 829	-12.3	1.2	200	164	18	1 712	2.24	63.4	5.0	29.6
Sheridan	18.1	13.4	15.5	50.2	1 710	1 321	-22.7	-0.8	74	54	-30	620	2.13	70.6	2.6	28.2
Sioux	8.0	4.5	2.8	50.0	4 044	4 153	2.7	5.2	507	254	-43	1 098	3.87	73.9	29.3	22.5
Slope	18.4	10.3	10.1	46.0	767	727	-5.2	5.5	49	12	8	318	2.25	69.8	7.9	28.9
Stark	11.5	5.9	6.9	47.4	22 636	24 199	6.9	32.9	2 277	1 176	6 763	10 887	2.40	63.1	7.3	27.7
Steele	16.4	12.0	11.7	49.1	2 258	1 975	-12.5	-1.0	104	85	-50	936	2.12	60.6	2.9	34.5
Stutsman	15.0	8.8	8.8	48.9	21 908	21 100	-3.7	0.0	1 238	1 251	55	9 050	2.14	59.7	9.6	35.4
Towner	17.5	11.2	12.3	49.1	2 876	2 246	-21.9	1.2	139	140	29	1 018	2.21	62.2	8.4	36.5
Traill	14.3	9.2	9.8	49.1	8 477	8 121	-4.2	-1.3	496	472	-126	3 334	2.32	60.5	5.8	34.7
Walsh	15.0	10.3	10.7	49.3	12 389	11 119	-10.3	-2.0	721	709	-188	4 922	2.16	63.1	6.9	33.0

1. No spouse present.

Table B. States and Counties — Population, Vital Statistics, Medicare, and Crime

STATE County	Persons in group quarters, 2015	Daytime population, 2010–2014 Number	Daytime population Employment/residence ratio	Births, 2015 Total	Births Rate[1]	Deaths, 2015 Number	Deaths Rate[1]	Persons under 65 with no health insurance, 2014 Number	Percent	Medicare, 2015 Total Beneficiaries	Enrolled in Original Medicare	Enrolled in Medicare Advantage	Serious crimes known to police,[2] 2014 Total Number	Rate[3]
	32	33	34	35	36	37	38	39	40	41	42	43	44	45
NORTH CAROLINA—Cont'd														
Swain	243	15 042	1.19	209	14.6	195	13.6	2 399	20.7	3 397	2 922	475	250	1 773
Transylvania	1 048	31 384	0.88	291	8.8	371	11.2	3 765	16.4	9 431	7 030	2 401	555	1 685
Tyrrell	523	4 280	1.05	40	9.8	34	8.3	633	22.6	778	673	105	60	1 483
Union	2 158	177 685	0.67	2 404	10.9	1 286	5.8	25 265	13.2	22 603	16 591	6 012	4 680	2 167
Vance	805	44 458	0.97	574	12.9	496	11.1	5 891	15.9	10 327	7 134	3 193	2 748	6 138
Wake	21 028	975 514	1.05	12 755	12.6	5 177	5.1	105 435	12.0	117 785	78 841	38 944	14 893	1 498
Warren	1 019	18 146	0.64	189	9.4	239	11.8	2 674	17.8	4 162	2 968	1 194	512	2 754
Washington	146	12 757	0.98	128	10.3	139	11.1	1 474	14.9	3 119	2 716	403	303	2 397
Watauga	5 719	54 937	1.13	352	6.7	339	6.4	5 852	14.8	7 217	5 123	2 094	865	1 637
Wayne	2 976	121 945	0.96	1 698	13.7	1 235	9.9	17 397	16.7	22 485	18 082	4 403	4 608	3 764
Wilkes	958	66 512	0.90	662	9.6	772	11.2	9 885	18.1	15 904	9 188	6 716	1 718	2 486
Wilson	1 511	85 259	1.11	936	11.5	854	10.5	12 060	18.0	15 913	13 313	2 600	2 966	3 723
Yadkin	304	33 042	0.68	371	9.8	394	10.5	5 133	16.7	8 232	3 406	4 826	952	2 630
Yancey	165	15 733	0.71	166	9.4	202	11.5	2 216	16.5	4 930	3 504	1 426	154	878
NORTH DAKOTA	26 601	739 885	1.09	11 170	14.9	5 879	7.9	57 168	9.3	113 112	94 245	18 867	17 565	2 375
Adams	57	2 251	0.93	20	8.5	23	9.7	203	11.4	628	551	77	12	506
Barnes	520	10 722	0.93	126	11.3	122	11.0	787	9.2	2 260	1 861	399	199	1 767
Benson	16	6 743	0.99	147	21.6	81	11.9	910	15.4	918	851	67	36	518
Billings	9	899	1.09	15	16.3	4	4.3	106	14.2	D	74	D	8	883
Bottineau	262	6 405	0.95	78	11.7	76	11.4	615	12.1	1 499	1 428	71	71	1 038
Bowman	63	3 208	1.01	51	15.6	33	10.1	296	11.3	722	644	78	17	524
Burke	2	1 968	0.83	34	15.0	21	9.2	175	9.5	D	450	D	14	581
Burleigh	3 417	88 836	1.06	1 278	13.9	681	7.4	5 475	7.3	14 388	11 255	3 133	2 134	2 356
Cass	5 490	172 889	1.16	2 523	14.9	1 013	6.0	12 023	8.3	19 717	15 591	4 126	4 341	2 603
Cavalier	71	3 791	0.93	43	11.2	43	11.2	269	9.5	967	863	104	28	720
Dickey	206	5 073	0.94	63	12.3	68	13.3	400	10.3	1 117	980	137	27	513
Divide	70	2 419	1.15	35	14.3	19	7.8	150	8.0	D	432	D	3	126
Dunn	130	4 689	1.38	72	15.9	17	3.7	485	12.8	494	425	69	71	1 632
Eddy	89	2 167	0.83	26	11.0	42	17.7	189	10.5	564	501	63	26	1 075
Emmons	54	3 399	0.94	29	8.5	50	14.6	345	14.0	975	713	262	36	1 033
Foster	49	3 499	1.08	39	11.6	37	11.0	228	8.7	770	625	145	NA	NA
Golden Valley	52	1 792	0.98	19	10.3	9	4.9	151	10.6	D	366	D	10	535
Grand Forks	4 181	71 835	1.10	1 007	14.3	455	6.4	5 385	9.2	9 370	7 798	1 572	1 960	2 800
Grant	18	2 260	0.92	27	11.4	25	10.5	334	19.6	609	466	143	8	336
Griggs	47	2 293	0.95	20	8.6	36	15.6	173	10.5	623	525	98	8	351
Hettinger	183	2 541	0.97	36	13.4	21	7.8	209	10.8	673	551	122	41	1 508
Kidder	0	2 190	0.81	28	11.6	8	3.3	262	13.7	517	332	185	23	945
LaMoure	66	4 054	0.96	45	10.9	36	8.7	359	11.7	977	774	203	10	239
Logan	69	1 894	0.94	23	11.8	23	11.8	266	19.0	491	365	126	10	515
McHenry	49	4 664	0.62	68	11.4	52	8.7	548	11.3	1 287	1 067	220	40	657
McIntosh	98	2 854	1.05	31	11.2	50	18.1	231	12.1	903	671	232	7	255
McKenzie	156	11 004	1.66	246	20.7	47	3.9	1 104	10.9	834	817	17	244	2 372
McLean	150	9 036	0.94	114	11.8	96	9.9	764	10.2	2 244	1 869	375	156	1 610
Mercer	126	9 296	1.18	108	12.3	90	10.2	587	8.1	1 582	1 306	276	48	554
Morton	699	23 713	0.70	459	15.3	236	7.8	2 242	8.9	5 001	3 767	1 234	753	2 555
Mountrail	557	11 072	1.53	162	16.1	67	6.7	1 140	13.1	1 153	1 128	25	168	1 700
Nelson	79	2 899	0.88	28	9.3	54	18.0	219	10.1	993	948	45	49	1 581
Oliver	2	2 109	1.33	21	11.4	6	3.2	145	9.7	260	203	57	7	370
Pembina	147	7 638	1.10	80	11.3	85	12.0	552	10.0	1 616	1 381	235	62	867
Pierce	242	4 519	1.06	53	12.2	59	13.6	382	11.7	950	641	309	65	1 448
Ramsey	470	11 939	1.07	159	13.7	123	10.6	1 001	11.0	2 493	2 434	59	404	3 476
Ransom	182	5 283	0.94	56	10.3	80	14.7	387	9.0	1 172	1 024	148	47	846
Renville	52	2 388	0.88	34	13.2	23	8.9	156	7.4	D	457	D	51	1 923
Richland	1 101	16 037	0.97	186	11.3	135	8.2	1 200	9.3	2 562	2 001	561	296	1 804
Rolette	122	14 157	0.96	301	20.5	186	12.7	2 340	18.2	1 630	1 588	42	35	237
Sargent	39	4 853	1.49	47	12.1	24	6.2	234	7.5	938	835	103	25	637
Sheridan	1	1 175	0.79	23	17.5	7	5.3	135	14.4	359	295	64	21	1 606
Sioux	44	5 003	1.54	96	21.7	69	15.6	635	15.9	314	287	27	1	22
Slope	0	692	0.94	10	13.0	0	0.0	63	10.3	82	71	11	2	259
Stark	718	29 180	1.14	555	17.7	229	7.3	2 071	7.9	4 100	3 523	577	796	2 709
Steele	1	1 844	0.86	20	10.2	11	5.6	134	9.0	382	338	44	2	102
Stutsman	1 657	21 789	1.07	245	11.6	227	10.7	1 457	9.1	4 338	3 151	1 187	546	2 576
Towner	34	2 231	0.94	35	15.3	20	8.8	168	9.6	542	525	17	3	128
Traill	353	7 705	0.90	98	12.2	93	11.6	490	7.7	1 573	1 342	231	48	578
Walsh	331	11 149	1.02	150	13.7	134	12.3	937	10.9	2 347	2 038	309	213	1 911

1. Per 1,000 estimated resident population. 2. Data for serious crimes have not been adjusted for underreporting; this may affect comparability between geographic areas and over time.
3. Per 100,000 population estimated by the FBI.

Table B. States and Counties — Crime, Education, Money Income, and Poverty

STATE County	Serious crimes known to police, 2014 (cont.)[1] Rate[2] Violent	Property	Education — Enrollment[3] Total	Percent private	Attainment[4] (percent) High school graduate or less	Bachelor's degree or more	Local government expenditures,[5] 2012–2013 Total current spending (mil dol)	Current spending per student (dollars)	Money income, 2010–2014 Per capita income[6] (dollars)	Households Median income (dollars)	Mean income (dollars)	Percent with income of $200,000 or more	Income and poverty, 2014 Median household income (dollars)	Percent below poverty level All persons	Children under 18 years	Children 5 to 17 years in families
	46	47	48	49	50	51	52	53	54	55	56	57	58	59	60	61
NORTH CAROLINA—Cont'd																
Swain	206	1 567	3 140	7.4	50.3	15.3	19.5	9 375	19 312	34 632	46 954	1.0	34 788	19.3	28.8	27.9
Transylvania	143	1 543	6 933	22.2	39.6	29.0	35.8	9 961	24 551	43 959	57 095	1.9	44 490	16.2	28.8	26.5
Tyrrell	222	1 261	956	5.1	69.1	8.0	8.6	14 391	16 217	34 056	44 044	0.6	32 773	28.3	37.1	37.8
Union	168	1 999	63 632	16.6	37.7	32.3	319.6	7 861	28 765	65 893	85 553	6.3	64 381	10.8	14.5	12.0
Vance	646	5 493	11 493	8.6	59.0	12.7	63.5	8 892	18 815	34 075	47 841	1.4	33 609	27.0	38.6	36.4
Wake	126	1 373	280 792	17.8	24.9	48.3	1 175.7	7 788	33 727	66 579	88 385	7.2	66 950	11.5	14.3	13.1
Warren	226	2 528	4 007	13.1	57.3	15.2	26.4	10 683	19 022	34 953	47 064	1.0	33 869	22.8	34.5	33.1
Washington	261	2 136	2 967	9.2	60.3	9.5	19.1	10 537	18 794	33 115	44 462	0.9	32 867	26.8	43.3	39.4
Watauga	114	1 524	21 462	5.1	32.0	38.0	42.6	9 369	21 801	35 491	53 651	2.7	41 942	26.2	19.2	18.2
Wayne	372	3 392	32 345	12.5	47.4	17.2	153.4	7 765	21 818	41 172	53 833	1.6	36 890	23.3	35.8	33.4
Wilkes	207	2 279	15 060	8.9	58.3	12.9	84.0	8 091	18 441	32 157	45 315	1.5	33 398	23.4	29.5	28.1
Wilson	409	3 314	19 942	15.2	53.7	18.4	101.1	8 057	21 426	39 332	52 943	1.5	39 268	23.9	39.2	39.3
Yadkin	282	2 348	8 167	6.3	57.2	13.0	48.7	8 297	22 338	38 652	54 011	2.0	40 801	17.2	27.0	24.7
Yancey	28	849	3 728	17.0	50.1	18.7	21.8	9 361	21 330	39 008	50 700	1.4	35 974	20.6	30.3	27.9
NORTH DAKOTA	265	2 110	177 759	10.9	36.1	27.3	1 214.6	11 980	30 894	55 579	73 272	4.1	60 227	11.1	13.7	12.3
Adams	84	421	335	5.7	41.6	23.9	3.6	12 633	33 132	48 553	69 036	5.8	45 710	10.2	14.1	13.2
Barnes	231	1 536	2 632	5.7	42.7	24.3	15.8	14 133	32 698	54 009	74 187	3.7	52 376	10.3	13.8	11.8
Benson	14	503	1 861	1.6	52.0	12.5	17.2	15 908	19 443	38 729	56 016	3.0	39 342	29.9	41.3	38.1
Billings	0	883	112	0.0	48.6	19.5	2.3	32 222	42 832	64 306	97 146	9.7	75 096	7.7	9.0	8.6
Bottineau	102	936	1 330	7.9	42.1	17.9	12.6	15 306	31 638	52 593	72 214	3.6	56 965	9.7	11.7	10.5
Bowman	62	462	597	4.7	45.0	20.0	7.6	12 666	34 290	63 750	81 396	4.2	60 946	7.4	10.4	9.5
Burke	124	456	470	6.8	45.7	18.5	4.9	15 408	33 174	55 455	72 847	5.0	62 875	8.3	9.6	9.4
Burleigh	246	2 110	21 114	22.2	30.9	33.4	127.0	10 533	33 644	64 370	80 119	4.5	66 734	8.2	9.0	7.9
Cass	296	2 308	46 775	11.1	25.5	37.4	239.9	11 149	31 415	52 993	72 977	4.4	53 755	11.3	12.4	11.2
Cavalier	77	643	697	14.3	37.7	19.0	6.3	14 349	36 141	61 989	80 793	4.0	54 057	9.0	13.6	12.0
Dickey	95	418	1 253	19.2	43.7	25.0	8.2	9 803	27 056	50 634	62 723	3.5	51 817	11.7	15.7	13.9
Divide	0	126	250	0.0	43.2	23.3	4.4	12 968	41 003	58 036	90 603	6.2	67 344	8.3	12.0	10.8
Dunn	276	1 356	834	7.7	44.4	19.3	8.1	16 669	38 216	69 063	98 811	9.6	72 018	9.5	12.9	11.5
Eddy	41	1 034	475	2.3	43.7	19.9	5.3	14 732	29 059	47 917	63 980	1.8	47 596	10.7	13.9	11.5
Emmons	29	1 005	725	5.5	51.4	14.8	7.5	13 181	28 042	40 375	59 917	3.3	44 282	13.2	19.4	16.3
Foster	NA	NA	663	3.0	43.1	20.0	5.4	9 828	30 060	55 089	66 989	2.5	54 593	8.0	9.8	8.4
Golden Valley	107	428	439	0.2	33.8	22.1	4.9	15 451	28 359	38 542	66 235	2.9	53 420	10.7	15.4	13.9
Grand Forks	216	2 584	23 050	7.0	31.7	32.6	102.5	11 796	27 772	47 050	65 785	3.9	50 435	16.7	16.8	14.9
Grant	84	252	410	5.1	50.7	17.2	3.5	14 139	31 092	43 317	66 678	5.5	39 679	16.1	23.8	22.0
Griggs	88	264	410	6.3	46.5	18.4	5.7	15 304	29 528	51 528	64 580	3.5	51 192	9.5	11.2	9.8
Hettinger	0	1 508	511	8.8	48.7	16.0	6.2	13 872	28 719	51 176	68 426	4.2	50 038	11.1	14.5	12.6
Kidder	123	822	505	0.6	44.0	19.1	4.9	12 207	32 233	56 058	72 448	5.7	46 923	14.1	17.9	15.3
LaMoure	48	191	750	12.8	43.6	22.1	10.7	13 636	33 368	54 393	73 349	4.2	53 721	9.7	12.2	10.4
Logan	0	515	376	3.5	57.0	14.0	4.9	13 300	30 798	49 821	69 269	3.0	44 696	11.9	17.9	16.2
McHenry	49	608	1 073	14.4	48.6	15.7	12.3	13 328	29 987	51 161	66 919	3.8	48 887	12.3	15.8	13.8
McIntosh	146	109	422	0.7	53.0	18.1	5.4	13 574	27 384	37 750	56 875	2.4	40 258	13.0	18.3	17.5
McKenzie	447	1 925	2 017	9.8	40.6	21.1	15.5	12 925	34 688	67 578	96 913	9.4	81 209	8.6	11.9	9.7
McLean	83	1 528	1 815	5.0	43.8	17.6	19.4	11 919	31 187	53 778	69 635	2.8	56 616	10.1	14.9	13.2
Mercer	81	473	1 650	3.9	40.5	19.8	14.5	11 269	31 584	66 712	72 766	3.4	74 047	7.3	8.8	7.8
Morton	248	2 308	6 508	17.4	38.6	25.3	47.4	11 084	30 293	58 949	72 761	3.3	54 637	9.2	12.1	10.8
Mountrail	263	1 437	2 114	7.7	39.6	18.6	20.4	12 524	33 839	66 250	84 444	6.5	66 807	9.3	14.2	14.2
Nelson	129	1 452	507	8.3	38.0	19.4	6.6	14 513	30 411	50 640	62 517	3.1	45 040	10.8	16.2	14.6
Oliver	106	264	339	11.2	45.4	19.6	3.0	14 765	31 194	62 708	74 245	1.8	62 010	10.6	20.8	19.6
Pembina	126	741	1 441	6.8	48.5	18.8	14.4	13 683	29 093	51 613	64 025	2.6	56 298	8.9	11.3	10.0
Pierce	89	1 359	767	10.0	47.9	15.3	7.6	12 915	24 729	43 125	54 622	1.9	39 572	11.6	14.6	13.0
Ramsey	189	3 286	2 619	7.3	39.0	22.8	25.6	14 260	28 670	47 361	64 055	3.1	51 097	12.3	18.2	16.6
Ransom	108	738	1 234	3.4	47.4	18.6	10.2	10 846	28 896	53 472	66 712	3.0	56 270	8.4	11.7	9.9
Renville	75	1 848	517	5.4	36.5	16.9	9.0	14 763	31 781	63 480	74 143	3.1	60 957	7.7	10.0	9.1
Richland	140	1 664	4 376	7.6	35.6	22.4	30.4	13 266	28 499	56 396	68 377	2.6	57 177	9.7	12.3	10.2
Rolette	27	210	2 988	1.4	40.1	20.0	39.4	13 125	15 825	32 781	46 321	1.5	35 630	31.6	41.1	38.1
Sargent	51	586	800	2.5	43.1	20.1	8.6	13 314	32 086	56 845	71 569	3.0	58 467	7.3	9.8	8.5
Sheridan	153	1 453	213	12.2	50.3	16.9	2.1	19 046	33 010	50 395	71 106	4.0	44 990	16.1	26.8	22.9
Sioux	22	0	1 382	8.9	44.0	17.4	9.7	22 901	16 287	40 152	59 876	2.0	33 950	33.6	42.0	39.7
Slope	0	259	90	8.9	45.0	23.6	0.6	37 563	33 389	65 577	74 048	3.8	55 664	9.4	7.1	6.1
Stark	191	2 518	6 374	13.5	40.9	24.3	39.8	10 998	33 396	70 243	81 136	4.3	76 672	7.6	8.7	7.9
Steele	51	51	377	3.4	39.5	17.4	3.7	16 652	33 619	53 438	73 458	3.2	59 408	7.1	11.4	10.2
Stutsman	231	2 345	4 865	21.7	49.8	22.3	38.6	13 323	29 361	50 926	66 541	3.2	53 333	11.6	14.4	12.6
Towner	0	128	457	3.3	41.1	18.8	3.1	11 732	34 103	56 574	72 310	4.3	51 961	10.9	17.4	14.6
Traill	72	506	2 067	4.4	34.3	27.9	17.0	12 678	29 736	53 641	70 476	2.9	58 995	8.9	11.3	10.2
Walsh	144	1 767	2 207	4.4	48.9	18.1	25.4	13 748	29 322	49 780	65 124	2.3	51 754	10.9	13.6	12.0

1. Data for serious crimes have not been adjusted for underreporting; this may affect comparability between geographic areas and over time.　2. Per 100,000 population estimated by the FBI.
3. All persons 3 years old and over enrolled in nursery school through college.　4. Persons 25 years old and over.　5. Elementary and secondary education expenditures.
6. Based on population estimated by the American Community Survey, 2010–2014.

Table B. States and Counties — **Personal Income**

STATE County	Personal income, 2014										Earnings, 2014		
			Per capita[1]			Supplements to wages and salaries; employer contributions (mil dol)						Contributions for government social insurance (mil dol)	
	Total (mil dol)	Percent change, 2013–2014	Dollars	Rank	Wages and salaries (mil dol)	Pension and insurance	Government social insurance	Proprietors' income (mil dol)	Dividends, interest, and rent (mil dol)	Personal transfer receipts (mil dol)	Total (mil dol)	From employee and self-employed	From employer
	62	63	64	65	66	67	68	69	70	71	72	73	74
NORTH CAROLINA— Cont'd													
Swain	424	5.0	29 712	2 758	226	41	18	16	75	141	301	20	18
Transylvania	1 094	3.9	33 112	2 260	298	55	23	76	305	335	453	36	23
Tyrrell	124	3.5	30 098	2 704	36	9	3	19	18	37	66	4	3
Union	8 998	7.3	41 166	1 043	2 544	427	199	489	1 127	1 210	3 659	224	199
Vance	1 340	2.6	30 024	2 711	528	102	42	57	198	476	728	51	42
Wake	49 629	5.2	49 695	400	27 925	3 997	2 076	2 941	8 372	5 135	36 939	2 166	2 076
Warren	574	6.7	28 356	2 889	134	28	9	34	87	206	204	15	9
Washington	405	-0.4	32 221	2 414	102	23	8	21	62	154	153	12	8
Watauga	1 629	4.4	30 998	2 583	809	159	59	109	377	325	1 136	70	59
Wayne	4 378	3.2	35 181	1 909	1 849	405	149	324	722	1 088	2 726	152	149
Wilkes	2 133	4.7	30 988	2 586	768	160	58	160	363	688	1 147	79	58
Wilson	2 934	2.5	36 044	1 777	1 728	311	133	194	426	771	2 366	144	133
Yadkin	1 205	4.3	31 890	2 452	339	62	28	79	158	341	509	36	28
Yancey	525	4.2	29 783	2 745	121	25	10	34	99	186	190	16	10
NORTH DAKOTA	41 265	4.8	55 802	X	24 022	3 012	1 904	4 275	8 070	5 055	33 214	1 946	1 904
Adams	103	6.3	43 369	808	40	6	3	16	20	23	65	4	3
Barnes	552	-4.7	49 559	410	199	31	17	97	132	101	343	21	17
Benson	218	-3.7	31 909	2 446	89	18	7	21	40	63	135	8	7
Billings	79	17.9	87 254	17	29	4	2	8	24	4	43	2	2
Bottineau	379	-8.6	57 030	172	126	19	11	67	96	61	223	13	11
Bowman	212	3.8	65 368	84	85	11	6	41	48	25	143	8	6
Burke	217	6.2	96 495	10	56	8	5	46	41	16	115	5	5
Burleigh	4 832	6.6	53 387	258	2 846	371	225	415	955	603	3 857	237	225
Cass	8 803	5.1	52 711	277	5 469	701	429	1 037	1 914	902	7 636	461	429
Cavalier	265	-5.0	68 781	65	69	10	6	99	53	36	184	7	6
Dickey	304	-2.2	59 072	145	79	12	7	50	120	48	147	8	7
Divide	156	4.4	64 209	90	64	8	5	33	43	20	110	6	5
Dunn	356	7.7	80 900	26	246	22	18	55	70	27	341	18	18
Eddy	109	-3.7	45 726	617	29	5	3	23	19	26	59	3	3
Emmons	141	-5.9	41 294	1 028	35	6	3	31	31	33	76	4	3
Foster	166	-1.8	49 314	420	76	10	6	36	34	28	129	7	6
Golden Valley	78	4.5	42 800	871	32	5	3	5	26	12	45	3	3
Grand Forks	3 098	4.1	44 177	743	1 869	308	155	215	674	435	2 547	146	155
Grant	103	9.5	43 810	777	24	4	2	24	20	24	54	3	2
Griggs	124	-7.3	53 389	257	38	6	3	26	32	25	73	4	3
Hettinger	147	7.7	55 144	210	35	6	3	12	26	22	55	4	3
Kidder	122	0.6	50 133	380	27	4	2	38	25	22	71	3	2
LaMoure	247	9.8	59 497	142	59	10	5	83	53	35	157	7	5
Logan	129	19.4	66 350	78	22	4	2	57	24	20	85	3	2
McHenry	312	1.2	52 089	292	61	11	5	60	44	48	138	7	5
McIntosh	139	8.5	49 745	395	37	6	3	39	30	34	86	4	3
McKenzie	887	19.7	80 640	27	933	81	76	91	182	48	1 181	66	76
McLean	535	-1.3	55 838	204	190	32	16	58	105	86	295	17	16
Mercer	446	3.6	51 034	331	329	58	28	17	80	64	432	25	28
Morton	1 326	4.1	44 464	718	551	77	50	14	222	217	692	44	50
Mountrail	688	16.8	70 326	56	598	58	44	56	131	67	755	43	44
Nelson	157	-3.3	51 480	313	38	6	3	33	35	40	80	4	3
Oliver	85	-4.1	45 911	606	65	10	5	10	17	13	91	5	5
Pembina	351	-1.2	49 188	430	174	26	17	31	99	62	247	14	17
Pierce	174	-2.1	39 408	1 263	70	11	6	32	35	39	118	7	6
Ramsey	493	-2.7	42 640	885	231	37	19	38	109	105	326	21	19
Ransom	240	-3.3	43 999	762	85	13	8	26	49	52	132	8	8
Renville	145	-13.1	56 073	195	49	6	4	21	31	22	80	5	4
Richland	680	-7.1	41 400	1 019	324	49	27	34	160	115	434	27	27
Rolette	448	2.3	30 621	2 637	168	42	14	37	65	150	260	15	14
Sargent	199	-14.6	50 530	356	120	19	10	26	60	29	175	9	10
Sheridan	32	-10.3	24 393	3 074	8	2	1	-6	12	14	5	1	1
Sioux	109	-1.4	24 680	3 070	70	15	5	7	14	41	98	5	5
Slope	44	-25.4	57 069	170	20	2	1	9	12	6	33	1	1
Stark	2 719	14.6	89 515	15	1 681	151	121	250	337	177	2 203	135	121
Steele	105	-24.8	53 524	254	32	5	3	20	33	13	60	3	3
Stutsman	1 023	0.7	48 420	458	457	69	38	186	204	177	750	46	38
Towner	110	-2.5	47 706	490	27	5	2	29	26	23	63	3	2
Traill	362	-9.0	44 845	690	145	23	14	21	88	69	202	12	14
Walsh	510	-7.8	46 480	559	203	30	18	68	121	101	320	20	18

1. Based on the resident population estimated as of July 1 of the year shown.

Table B. States and Counties — Earnings, Social Security, and Housing

STATE County	Earnings, 2014 (cont.) Percent by selected industries									Social Security beneficiaries, December 2014		Supplemental Security Income recipients, December 2014	Housing units, 2015	
	Farm	Mining	Construction	Manu-facturing	Infor-mation: professional, scientific, technical services	Retail trade	Finance, insur-ance, real estate and leasing	Health care and social assistance	Govern-ment	Number	Rate[1]		Total	Percent change, 2010–2014
	75	76	77	78	79	80	81	82	83	84	85	86	87	88
NORTH CAROLINA—Cont'd														
Swain	0.3	0.0	D	8.1	1.6	5.7	2.0	D	44.3	3 960	277	358	8 817	1.1
Transylvania	2.2	D	8.9	6.5	D	9.1	6.7	15.5	17.5	10 050	305	594	19 372	1.1
Tyrrell	22.5	0.0	5.5	5.5	D	6.1	D	D	33.5	915	222	137	2 050	-0.9
Union	3.4	D	13.0	19.6	5.3	7.6	3.6	4.6	15.8	31 580	145	2 376	77 794	6.7
Vance	1.9	D	3.3	11.9	5.3	10.7	3.3	16.9	18.5	10 905	245	2 313	19 916	-0.8
Wake	0.1	0.2	6.4	7.2	20.5	5.9	8.1	9.3	14.8	125 605	126	12 391	411 435	10.6
Warren	10.1	0.0	3.6	9.5	2.3	3.9	2.6	6.5	32.6	5 645	279	959	11 715	-0.8
Washington	7.7	0.0	2.1	13.9	2.4	7.4	3.3	8.4	30.4	3 590	286	674	6 412	-1.2
Watauga	0.8	0.2	5.8	2.4	5.3	9.4	5.0	17.4	30.4	8 910	170	633	33 130	3.1
Wayne	8.0	D	3.7	12.2	3.5	6.8	3.3	11.6	32.1	25 645	206	4 554	53 290	0.6
Wilkes	5.6	D	3.9	18.3	D	7.5	3.7	6.7	19.4	18 510	269	2 025	33 018	-0.1
Wilson	3.6	0.1	7.2	28.7	5.6	6.1	4.9	8.8	12.2	17 875	220	2 864	35 762	0.7
Yadkin	7.8	0.0	8.2	23.5	4.9	5.7	2.7	6.4	14.9	9 445	250	796	17 208	-0.8
Yancey	5.8	D	13.3	9.5	3.7	9.1	3.5	D	21.5	5 640	321	631	11 067	0.3
NORTH DAKOTA	4.1	11.3	10.2	5.0	6.3	5.9	7.0	9.8	14.8	124 372	168	8 224	362 960	14.3
Adams	19.2	D	4.8	2.3	1.9	10.0	3.5	27.5	9.9	695	295	17	1 413	2.6
Barnes	11.8	D	8.2	11.0	4.1	5.4	4.5	10.7	16.5	2 685	242	142	5 808	1.8
Benson	11.2	0.0	11.3	D	D	1.8	D	1.1	53.1	1 175	171	181	3 001	1.7
Billings	8.2	D	2.4	0.0	D	1.6	D	0.0	24.3	135	148	0	547	13.0
Bottineau	13.2	19.5	8.1	3.6	D	6.6	4.0	D	15.8	1 660	250	52	4 439	2.3
Bowman	20.3	11.9	12.2	1.2	2.7	4.8	D	9.2	9.0	720	222	23	1 743	3.6
Burke	29.2	9.3	6.8	0.0	D	D	2.2	0.5	17.3	490	219	16	1 429	6.6
Burleigh	0.1	1.8	9.1	2.4	9.0	7.3	7.2	18.9	19.5	15 575	172	866	41 248	15.4
Cass	0.5	0.1	9.0	7.8	11.0	7.1	12.9	13.0	12.0	22 065	132	1 813	78 241	15.2
Cavalier	45.9	D	7.9	0.3	D	3.5	D	4.4	7.3	1 070	277	27	2 340	1.3
Dickey	27.0	0.0	5.2	8.0	D	5.9	D	12.1	9.9	1 220	238	69	2 651	0.6
Divide	21.5	16.9	D	D	D	2.8	2.7	D	11.0	550	226	15	1 496	13.0
Dunn	10.6	36.0	D	D	D	1.6	D	1.1	4.8	660	149	29	2 412	13.1
Eddy	34.5	2.6	D	D	D	3.6	D	14.1	13.8	630	266	39	1 346	1.7
Emmons	33.3	0.0	8.7	0.3	D	6.0	D	9.3	15.5	1 000	292	34	2 122	1.8
Foster	24.4	D	5.9	D	D	6.7	3.6	9.5	10.4	810	241	27	1 818	0.9
Golden Valley	-3.5	D	D	D	D	5.2	5.5	12.1	18.4	360	197	9	1 027	6.2
Grand Forks	1.7	0.6	7.7	4.4	5.6	9.3	5.1	16.8	29.2	9 870	140	736	32 238	9.9
Grant	38.6	0.0	3.9	5.0	D	2.4	0.0	12.2	13.0	705	299	26	1 711	1.2
Griggs	26.7	0.0	6.5	10.9	D	4.2	D	6.9	11.8	690	298	24	1 464	0.2
Hettinger	15.9	0.0	7.2	2.8	D	4.3	0.0	6.6	17.8	615	232	17	1 431	1.2
Kidder	50.9	D	3.9	0.2	D	2.6	D	2.5	11.2	565	233	25	1 691	1.0
LaMoure	44.4	0.0	3.4	2.3	1.3	4.5	D	2.7	11.5	1 040	253	55	2 255	0.8
Logan	57.2	0.0	D	D	D	2.1	D	D	8.7	590	303	17	1 159	1.3
McHenry	38.0	D	D	D	3.1	1.8	2.3	2.8	14.1	1 295	217	54	3 106	5.4
McIntosh	44.2	0.0	2.2	3.9	D	3.8	2.9	14.9	10.3	905	328	43	1 858	0.0
McKenzie	2.9	20.9	25.5	0.1	D	2.4	3.0	D	8.5	1 015	92	46	5 862	89.7
McLean	13.7	D	8.8	2.1	D	3.0	3.2	D	14.8	2 315	241	88	6 088	8.9
Mercer	-0.6	D	15.4	0.3	2.4	3.3	2.1	D	6.2	1 805	206	50	4 691	5.4
Morton	2.1	3.0	10.4	10.2	10.9	8.2	4.8	9.1	13.2	5 490	184	308	14 393	19.2
Mountrail	2.3	27.2	16.1	1.3	D	3.8	1.8	1.6	5.6	1 425	146	62	4 933	19.8
Nelson	38.4	0.0	D	D	D	1.6	D	10.4	14.4	1 015	334	29	1 945	0.9
Oliver	9.0	D	10.9	1.1	D	D	D	D	5.4	405	219	0	930	2.8
Pembina	13.9	0.2	11.2	16.8	D	4.4	D	4.3	22.0	1 780	250	79	3 879	0.5
Pierce	17.6	0.0	D	5.4	2.4	6.3	D	D	11.5	1 055	241	46	2 224	1.1
Ramsey	-0.1	D	7.5	3.7	4.7	11.1	9.5	D	24.6	2 610	225	198	5 809	3.5
Ransom	16.0	D	6.1	11.2	D	5.8	5.0	11.5	18.1	1 245	229	45	2 678	0.8
Renville	14.5	32.6	4.7	5.0	D	1.5	D	4.7	13.8	560	217	13	1 415	2.1
Richland	2.9	D	8.2	27.1	4.3	5.6	3.2	6.5	21.8	3 125	191	137	7 674	2.3
Rolette	6.4	D	6.5	3.8	0.5	5.9	D	D	61.8	2 190	149	839	5 516	2.7
Sargent	15.8	D	D	D	D	2.5	D	1.3	7.9	940	240	38	2 082	3.9
Sheridan	-157.1	0.0	D	D	D	D	D	D	89.9	435	329	25	899	0.6
Sioux	7.5	0.0	1.7	D	D	D	0.0	D	84.1	450	101	208	1 333	1.7
Slope	35.1	D	0.8	0.0	D	0.0	0.0	0.0	3.8	190	248	0	437	0.2
Stark	-0.4	33.1	11.0	5.3	4.3	4.9	5.1	4.3	6.0	4 425	145	225	14 354	33.7
Steele	38.5	0.0	11.0	8.8	D	4.6	D	D	10.5	395	202	0	1 196	2.1
Stutsman	8.4	0.1	5.8	11.4	3.8	6.2	5.4	D	15.6	4 665	220	391	10 109	2.5
Towner	40.1	0.0	D	D	D	2.4	D	D	11.2	635	276	17	1 449	0.0
Traill	6.2	D	5.5	15.1	1.9	3.7	5.1	D	19.3	1 745	216	57	3 817	1.0
Walsh	11.2	0.3	5.3	9.1	3.9	4.1	11.7	D	17.9	2 700	246	142	5 589	1.7

1. Per 1,000 resident population estimated as of July 1 of the year shown.

Table B. States and Counties — Housing, Labor Force, and Employment

	Housing units, 2010–2014								Civilian labor force, 2015				Civilian employment,[6] 2010–2014		
	Occupied units										Unemployment			Percent	
	Owner-occupied			Median owner cost as a percent of income		Renter-occupied									
STATE County	Total	Percent	Median value[1]	With a mortgage	Without a mortgage[2]	Median rent[3]	Median rent as a percent of income[2]	Sub-standard units[4] (percent)	Total	Percent change, 2014–2015	Total	Rate[5]	Total	Management, business, science and arts	Construction, production, and mainte-nance occupations
	89	90	91	92	93	94	95	96	97	98	99	100	101	102	103
NORTH CAROLINA—Cont'd															
Swain	5 357	74.2	123 100	22.7	10.0	582	28.1	3.4	6 675	3.0	524	7.9	5 329	27.5	19.2
Transylvania	13 735	77.5	181 300	21.7	10.0	647	30.9	1.2	13 503	1.3	744	5.5	13 335	31.0	24.5
Tyrrell	1 455	74.7	101 800	28.1	15.9	619	28.2	0.8	1 580	1.9	148	9.4	1 348	15.0	39.9
Union	69 464	81.0	193 500	22.3	11.2	869	31.5	2.7	111 919	3.1	5 398	4.8	96 452	38.1	20.9
Vance	16 651	64.0	99 800	24.0	13.3	656	34.0	3.0	18 105	0.4	1 557	8.6	17 269	25.2	27.4
Wake	355 647	64.9	229 200	20.7	10.0	935	28.5	2.7	539 432	3.2	25 088	4.7	483 498	49.3	12.5
Warren	7 866	70.7	97 400	26.1	15.2	700	33.5	3.0	7 245	0.5	606	8.4	7 143	25.7	28.8
Washington	5 126	68.1	82 600	24.2	15.1	638	38.7	1.6	4 986	-1.0	440	8.8	4 290	22.1	37.1
Watauga	20 224	57.4	225 600	24.5	11.2	822	50.0	1.1	27 500	1.9	1 351	4.9	24 288	33.5	15.0
Wayne	47 480	60.6	108 000	22.5	12.2	705	30.6	3.3	53 947	0.3	3 291	6.1	50 820	29.1	31.4
Wilkes	27 355	73.7	110 500	24.5	13.1	586	34.5	3.1	29 614	0.4	1 697	5.7	26 024	25.1	30.9
Wilson	32 026	60.0	114 700	24.5	14.4	727	32.2	3.2	36 646	-2.5	3 504	9.6	33 908	29.4	28.3
Yadkin	15 174	77.0	120 300	23.6	12.0	591	27.4	3.2	17 709	1.2	884	5.0	16 227	27.5	33.9
Yancey	7 230	75.8	142 800	22.8	10.9	611	30.4	3.4	7 434	-0.9	442	5.9	6 993	28.4	30.2
NORTH DAKOTA	292 616	65.1	142 000	18.9	10.0	676	25.3	1.8	414 347	-0.2	11 287	2.7	379 972	34.8	25.1
Adams	1 098	72.2	111 900	16.7	10.5	456	18.9	1.5	1 116	0.0	32	2.9	1 297	44.5	25.6
Barnes	4 918	69.7	92 000	18.2	10.0	560	22.3	0.5	5 648	0.6	179	3.2	5 815	34.2	28.7
Benson	2 331	65.0	54 500	16.9	11.0	410	20.1	10.0	2 499	-0.9	113	4.5	2 488	36.0	27.3
Billings	361	73.4	122 500	17.8	10.0	823	13.2	3.0	472	-4.1	14	3.0	516	36.0	34.3
Bottineau	3 000	75.7	94 000	17.4	10.0	599	24.4	1.3	3 251	-0.5	139	4.3	3 221	31.4	27.8
Bowman	1 330	74.1	128 700	17.5	10.0	569	15.7	0.6	1 851	-2.5	34	1.8	1 666	32.7	32.3
Burke	988	66.3	98 400	14.4	10.0	598	23.0	2.4	1 176	-9.7	38	3.2	1 099	27.7	35.1
Burleigh	35 767	70.5	182 300	19.6	10.0	720	23.9	2.3	48 739	2.4	1 141	2.3	48 257	38.1	21.4
Cass	67 013	52.6	164 600	20.1	10.1	694	26.2	1.3	95 023	2.3	2 091	2.2	92 761	38.4	20.7
Cavalier	1 759	86.9	68 000	14.1	10.0	496	18.6	0.1	2 077	0.9	57	2.7	1 952	41.4	25.6
Dickey	2 211	71.8	83 800	18.4	10.0	511	22.5	0.8	2 572	-0.9	47	1.8	2 711	33.4	27.1
Divide	1 065	82.4	88 200	16.9	10.0	546	25.1	0.7	1 839	-2.1	33	1.8	1 230	44.1	22.0
Dunn	1 473	80.6	118 700	13.4	10.0	750	20.1	2.8	4 046	-6.1	76	1.9	1 989	31.0	34.7
Eddy	1 074	73.4	64 300	15.7	10.0	425	18.8	0.1	1 293	-0.2	60	4.6	1 232	40.8	26.6
Emmons	1 618	81.2	72 700	20.1	11.8	413	23.0	1.1	1 558	-0.5	77	4.9	1 628	38.1	26.2
Foster	1 576	74.7	91 500	16.1	10.0	488	27.7	1.3	1 631	-0.4	47	2.9	1 771	35.0	30.7
Golden Valley	766	72.2	95 000	17.3	10.0	508	27.8	5.0	978	0.0	22	2.2	936	36.6	22.5
Grand Forks	28 045	51.6	154 000	19.4	10.0	715	31.0	1.4	37 400	0.8	899	2.4	37 254	35.8	20.2
Grant	1 137	77.4	71 900	20.1	11.1	442	25.1	1.8	1 325	1.8	41	3.1	1 255	43.6	25.3
Griggs	1 068	75.4	73 500	15.9	10.0	443	22.9	0.0	1 162	-2.2	27	2.3	1 213	34.4	26.5
Hettinger	1 088	81.0	86 600	16.2	10.0	502	18.3	2.4	1 554	0.8	38	2.4	1 182	38.6	27.3
Kidder	1 097	80.7	76 700	18.3	10.0	535	26.6	0.4	1 358	5.8	49	3.6	1 322	42.4	24.5
LaMoure	1 898	78.3	81 800	17.2	10.0	550	25.9	0.6	2 289	1.0	56	2.4	2 106	37.9	28.7
Logan	866	83.6	66 100	15.7	10.7	627	28.1	1.5	958	3.0	26	2.7	947	38.2	28.3
McHenry	2 576	80.4	89 200	19.1	10.2	506	20.7	2.5	3 290	-0.7	137	4.2	2 765	29.6	34.4
McIntosh	1 336	82.6	57 200	18.9	10.7	482	23.1	0.7	1 265	1.2	39	3.1	1 337	33.6	25.0
McKenzie	2 755	68.6	170 800	13.3	10.0	633	17.3	3.6	9 172	-0.5	212	2.3	4 115	35.1	31.8
McLean	4 078	77.1	117 800	17.2	10.0	542	21.6	1.5	4 918	0.3	179	3.6	4 470	32.5	28.8
Mercer	3 666	82.4	118 800	16.6	10.0	584	23.8	0.9	4 257	2.3	177	4.2	4 347	27.7	33.3
Morton	11 820	77.3	156 400	21.0	10.6	710	26.4	1.3	16 361	2.2	491	3.0	15 891	34.2	23.4
Mountrail	3 108	68.3	110 500	14.7	10.0	663	17.4	3.9	8 113	-10.7	154	1.9	4 561	31.3	28.5
Nelson	1 499	80.7	65 300	17.5	10.0	438	19.9	0.3	1 532	-0.4	57	3.7	1 572	32.5	28.6
Oliver	783	83.4	111 100	16.0	10.0	529	19.9	1.7	902	2.0	51	5.7	836	33.7	31.8
Pembina	3 299	77.2	73 800	16.2	10.7	519	22.1	1.2	3 619	0.2	191	5.3	3 684	29.6	30.3
Pierce	1 943	73.3	85 000	18.3	11.7	558	27.5	1.4	1 842	1.7	78	4.2	2 142	34.1	29.5
Ramsey	5 003	63.6	93 500	17.9	10.0	512	23.5	2.1	5 671	-0.4	191	3.4	6 038	33.6	21.5
Ransom	2 307	70.1	98 500	19.0	10.0	564	22.8	0.7	2 783	1.6	68	2.4	2 779	31.8	37.2
Renville	1 079	77.1	110 700	16.6	10.0	612	20.6	0.9	1 343	-4.8	44	3.3	1 337	36.8	30.6
Richland	6 616	73.4	103 700	18.7	10.0	501	23.4	1.3	8 652	1.3	232	2.7	8 821	32.5	30.2
Rolette	4 728	69.7	64 300	16.8	11.9	369	26.7	6.1	4 858	1.1	493	10.1	4 889	37.2	20.5
Sargent	1 712	77.9	72 100	17.8	10.0	569	18.9	0.4	2 268	4.4	41	1.8	2 062	30.7	40.6
Sheridan	620	86.0	59 100	18.3	10.0	397	31.4	1.1	733	0.8	36	4.9	717	39.7	29.0
Sioux	1 098	42.7	60 900	14.6	10.7	463	15.1	13.5	1 335	2.3	56	4.2	1 300	38.8	14.2
Slope	318	84.3	60 800	12.6	10.0	675	15.0	3.1	455	-11.5	12	2.6	389	50.6	29.8
Stark	10 887	71.4	182 200	17.5	10.0	748	24.7	2.3	20 373	-4.8	528	2.6	15 434	28.8	31.1
Steele	936	73.0	77 100	15.4	10.0	445	17.3	1.6	1 063	3.1	23	2.2	1 018	30.2	36.0
Stutsman	9 050	67.0	102 000	17.7	10.0	613	24.7	0.3	10 715	2.4	273	2.5	11 121	30.9	26.9
Towner	1 018	77.7	66 800	15.8	10.0	442	23.8	0.5	1 271	2.6	34	2.7	1 140	45.6	19.1
Traill	3 334	73.1	97 800	19.1	10.1	561	23.9	1.7	4 464	-0.2	125	2.8	4 131	34.4	28.8
Walsh	4 922	75.2	73 300	17.3	10.0	504	24.8	1.2	5 609	0.3	231	4.1	5 633	31.1	33.3

1. Specified owner-occupied units.　　2. A value of 10.0 represents 10 percent or less; a value of 50.0 represents 50 percent or more.　　3. Specified renter-occupied units.
4. Overcrowded or lacking complete plumbing facilities.　　5. Percent of civilian labor force.　　6. Persons 16 years old and over.

Table B. States and Counties — Nonfarm Employment and Agriculture

	Private nonfarm establishments, employment and payroll, 2014								Agriculture, 2012			
		Employment					Annual payroll		Farms			
										Percent with:		
STATE County	Number of establishments	Total	Health care and social assistance	Manufacturing	Retail trade	Finance and insurance	Professional, scientific, and technical services	Total (mil dol)	Average per employee (dollars)	Number	Fewer than 50 acres	500 acres or more	Farm operators whose principal occupation is farming (percent)
	104	105	106	107	108	109	110	111	112	113	114	115	116

NORTH CAROLINA—Cont'd

Swain	351	3 461	D	D	536	77	D	106	30 621	94	62.8	1.1	26.6
Transylvania	790	7 108	1 432	534	1 432	221	D	211	29 740	221	63.8	2.3	46.6
Tyrrell	82	488	28	D	144	D	6	12	24 770	78	21.8	28.2	57.7
Union	4 215	50 005	5 419	10 369	6 984	999	1 389	1 896	37 913	1 059	55.6	6.8	53.0
Vance	839	12 469	2 221	1 398	2 258	245	292	394	31 623	242	36.4	10.7	36.8
Wake	26 755	425 283	56 166	13 170	54 803	22 410	48 902	21 797	51 254	783	57.0	4.5	49.0
Warren	255	2 210	601	D	368	D	41	57	25 864	256	34.0	11.7	42.6
Washington	233	2 904	646	D	465	D	D	109	37 591	156	25.6	30.1	59.0
Watauga	1 550	16 972	3 107	614	3 520	340	649	515	30 344	609	49.4	2.0	44.7
Wayne	2 145	33 742	7 284	6 061	5 888	1 135	730	1 115	33 048	563	40.1	18.1	60.9
Wilkes	1 167	17 815	2 826	4 176	2 410	355	478	587	32 936	972	44.9	3.9	50.6
Wilson	1 723	31 592	4 954	7 526	3 651	D	673	1 252	39 636	297	42.4	17.8	61.3
Yadkin	581	9 019	994	2 346	792	138	173	275	30 449	952	55.6	2.7	44.9
Yancey	320	3 168	421	D	564	78	D	103	32 454	450	57.3	0.7	31.1
NORTH DAKOTA	24 698	360 970	59 713	24 862	51 115	17 594	15 641	17 363	48 100	30 961	11.0	48.8	56.6
Adams	102	776	D	D	177	D	D	26	33 888	392	12.8	48.7	60.2
Barnes	380	3 989	1 051	592	491	157	91	127	31 867	855	11.6	40.6	52.4
Benson	99	1 146	31	D	D	D	D	36	31 021	563	6.9	54.2	64.5
Billings	61	390	NA	NA	D	D	D	26	66 985	197	4.6	68.5	68.0
Bottineau	279	2 053	252	117	393	130	D	87	42 377	863	8.5	41.7	48.8
Bowman	166	1 399	D	D	226	86	D	55	39 225	348	8.6	55.5	54.3
Burke	96	576	22	NA	88	37	D	26	45 696	488	6.4	47.3	54.3
Burleigh	3 016	47 295	11 045	1 139	7 572	2 092	2 334	2 185	46 193	1 014	23.1	34.7	42.3
Cass	5 321	100 247	17 486	8 677	13 204	7 953	5 852	4 405	43 937	968	21.0	49.8	66.3
Cavalier	165	1 217	224	D	212	86	D	47	38 758	667	7.5	57.1	63.4
Dickey	222	1 804	390	195	310	62	D	54	29 810	543	11.0	45.7	53.8
Divide	123	962	D	D	95	32	D	44	45 625	452	5.5	54.4	54.6
Dunn	199	2 749	D	D	187	D	D	188	68 245	628	13.1	56.5	66.1
Eddy	79	498	204	D	65	21	D	16	31 769	331	8.8	50.2	46.2
Emmons	127	738	183	D	D	52	D	22	29 892	609	6.6	58.1	55.2
Foster	147	1 250	252	D	226	61	9	52	41 697	310	10.3	49.7	61.0
Golden Valley	76	488	D	NA	D	D	D	19	38 045	251	7.2	58.6	62.2
Grand Forks	1 911	33 024	7 069	2 224	6 034	997	1 611	1 201	36 367	970	12.3	35.8	62.7
Grant	74	439	191	D	29	D	D	13	30 339	508	8.3	59.4	65.2
Griggs	97	723	D	D	52	32	D	23	32 054	456	6.6	45.8	52.9
Hettinger	100	451	D	D	71	50	D	17	37 089	494	5.9	54.0	54.9
Kidder	66	530	D	D	77	38	D	18	33 525	559	6.4	54.2	49.7
LaMoure	158	985	139	50	144	D	NA	36	36 934	642	8.6	49.2	59.0
Logan	71	441	D	D	56	D	D	13	28 717	379	7.4	56.2	58.3
McHenry	129	783	D	D	207	48	D	29	36 894	911	9.2	48.8	64.8
McIntosh	114	952	358	D	134	D	D	27	28 700	471	7.4	51.4	59.7
McKenzie	512	6 793	267	D	524	127	247	531	78 221	574	10.5	59.4	61.1
McLean	258	2 533	457	D	337	123	D	136	53 517	868	7.3	51.6	51.6
Mercer	245	4 222	499	D	454	127	58	249	58 884	422	12.3	46.2	54.3
Morton	829	9 661	1 652	882	1 129	374	D	457	47 310	887	20.3	47.9	55.2
Mountrail	409	5 189	239	D	729	D	D	368	70 979	670	4.6	57.9	66.4
Nelson	117	795	279	D	101	60	D	24	29 882	603	6.8	35.8	36.5
Oliver	41	653	14	D	D	D	D	53	80 493	290	13.4	48.3	53.4
Pembina	284	2 832	D	697	408	108	D	109	38 353	584	12.3	45.0	62.3
Pierce	159	1 465	D	D	289	D	53	53	36 331	521	7.5	53.7	58.3
Ramsey	416	4 620	810	D	940	271	57	150	32 361	573	11.0	48.5	51.5
Ransom	188	1 675	383	405	253	D	48	53	31 924	548	11.7	36.3	48.7
Renville	107	705	D	D	D	D	16	29	40 628	304	8.2	68.1	73.4
Richland	534	6 574	670	2 085	947	167	147	230	35 014	854	15.6	47.9	64.3
Rolette	198	2 373	560	D	485	103	D	71	29 830	649	9.1	38.8	48.8
Sargent	128	2 215	70	D	150	45	D	106	47 692	537	6.5	45.4	55.9
Sheridan	43	146	25	D	D	D	D	4	28 664	370	7.8	53.5	54.6
Sioux	26	1 014	D	D	D	D	D	27	27 069	176	10.8	67.0	66.5
Slope	20	109	NA	NA	D	NA	NA	11	97 239	221	9.5	62.4	62.0
Stark	1 235	17 451	2 084	1 072	2 459	501	598	1 028	58 936	837	20.2	39.1	48.6
Steele	59	497	D	143	92	48	D	21	42 109	355	8.7	52.4	63.1
Stutsman	681	9 437	2 722	850	1 342	528	216	335	35 532	1 028	10.1	49.8	55.2
Towner	85	512	D	D	46	53	D	15	28 982	529	7.2	62.4	61.1
Traill	304	2 874	D	473	321	153	36	113	39 370	468	17.3	48.3	63.7
Walsh	409	3 548	686	575	528	154	97	121	34 154	962	13.7	38.9	47.3

Table B. States and Counties — **Agriculture**

STATE County	Acreage (1,000)	Percent change, 2007–2012	Average size of farm	Total irrigated (1,000)	Total cropland (1,000)	Average per farm	Average per acre	Value of machinery and equipment, average per farm (dollars)	Total (mil dol)	Average per farm (dollars)	Crops	Live-stock and poultry products	$10,000 or more	$100,000 or more	Total ($1,000)	Percent of farms
	117	118	119	120	121	122	123	124	125	126	127	128	129	130	131	132
NORTH CAROLINA—Cont'd																
Swain	D	D	D	0.0	D	349 085	D	37 309	0.7	7 202	48.3	51.7	16.0	1.1	17	10.6
Transylvania	18	11.7	81	0.4	6.6	716 964	8 838	43 715	20.4	92 131	81.5	18.5	34.8	11.3	200	12.7
Tyrrell	65	19.9	828	0.0	57.8	2 107 192	2 545	343 936	59.6	763 474	D	D	62.8	42.3	772	83.3
Union	202	13.2	190	0.4	148.3	1 075 361	5 647	112 638	535.8	505 977	24.0	76.0	43.6	25.9	1 807	17.4
Vance	55	-0.4	227	1.6	19.5	784 640	3 460	79 628	17.3	71 463	97.7	2.3	26.4	11.2	446	45.9
Wake	84	-0.9	108	3.2	44.4	1 029 967	9 575	68 049	65.2	83 324	94.1	5.9	33.0	9.6	848	24.8
Warren	66	-9.6	257	0.8	26.0	657 488	2 562	60 867	25.6	100 156	53.7	46.3	37.9	14.5	678	57.4
Washington	91	-5.7	586	4.4	75.9	1 767 526	3 017	301 814	68.4	438 237	95.5	4.5	52.6	35.9	1 639	76.3
Watauga	56	21.8	92	0.0	14.5	684 361	7 474	51 750	15.3	25 108	38.4	61.6	34.5	5.1	222	22.5
Wayne	191	9.1	340	4.8	146.8	1 400 607	4 124	199 504	577.2	1 025 265	27.4	72.6	61.5	44.8	2 943	56.5
Wilkes	111	1.0	114	0.1	36.2	553 577	4 842	80 330	284.9	293 140	6.6	93.4	42.1	19.1	329	6.6
Wilson	111	6.4	375	1.4	86.4	1 431 529	3 817	266 391	179.6	604 822	84.3	15.7	46.5	30.6	1 876	62.3
Yadkin	100	-4.5	106	0.5	53.5	555 887	5 267	68 082	124.7	130 956	26.8	73.2	33.8	12.3	921	25.7
Yancey	31	-7.3	69	0.1	6.2	446 533	6 482	28 402	5.7	12 758	71.8	28.2	23.8	2.7	532	23.3
NORTH DAKOTA	39 263	-1.0	1 268	218.4	27 147.2	1 808 801	1 426	300 285	10 950.7	353 693	88.3	11.7	59.0	40.6	381 710	80.1
Adams	601	-4.1	1 534	D	380.0	1 236 143	806	192 020	107.5	274 329	77.3	22.7	54.1	36.7	4 734	81.9
Barnes	937	3.3	1 096	1.7	836.5	2 449 174	2 235	342 849	376.4	440 175	97.5	2.5	54.9	39.5	11 719	83.6
Benson	802	5.6	1 425	1.2	644.4	1 841 764	1 293	354 654	240.6	427 405	92.7	7.3	62.0	46.0	7 551	83.5
Billings	722	-0.3	3 666	0.0	131.3	2 888 964	788	226 416	36.7	186 127	48.1	51.9	78.7	41.1	1 365	68.5
Bottineau	899	-12.6	1 042	D	773.0	1 408 030	1 351	275 319	254.0	294 359	95.1	4.9	53.3	34.9	9 818	83.4
Bowman	730	1.3	2 099	1.5	372.6	1 577 514	752	251 733	111.4	320 164	54.1	45.9	61.5	41.4	4 005	80.2
Burke	595	4.3	1 219	D	434.6	1 023 576	839	247 330	105.1	215 455	91.7	8.3	50.4	32.4	5 413	86.9
Burleigh	951	8.1	938	4.6	494.7	1 320 447	1 408	162 938	179.6	177 132	72.9	27.1	50.2	23.6	5 300	53.9
Cass	1 107	6.6	1 144	9.3	1 044.5	3 277 384	2 865	455 639	567.1	585 855	96.8	3.2	68.0	54.3	14 691	78.3
Cavalier	940	7.7	1 410	0.0	871.5	2 681 525	1 902	456 447	334.5	501 547	98.2	1.8	65.1	54.4	15 805	92.2
Dickey	633	-9.2	1 166	16.3	481.1	2 629 105	2 254	359 029	266.8	491 398	88.2	11.8	57.8	43.1	10 047	79.4
Divide	565	-20.2	1 250	2.4	419.2	807 018	646	241 810	93.8	207 496	90.9	9.1	55.1	38.3	4 848	90.5
Dunn	1 031	-1.2	1 642	0.4	374.3	1 498 726	913	250 261	124.8	198 707	60.6	39.4	72.3	39.3	3 189	70.9
Eddy	396	5.1	1 196	0.2	288.7	1 600 341	1 338	283 166	105.1	317 538	90.2	9.8	52.0	37.2	4 696	87.9
Emmons	744	-14.7	1 222	3.9	443.9	1 439 232	1 178	269 821	171.3	281 255	80.9	19.1	62.7	47.0	5 117	87.8
Foster	374	-6.5	1 206	2.6	314.3	2 254 016	1 868	422 081	169.4	546 484	80.4	19.6	65.5	51.3	4 700	78.4
Golden Valley	562	-1.4	2 241	D	242.6	1 887 992	843	258 785	59.6	237 327	73.3	26.7	63.3	38.2	4 251	79.7
Grand Forks	816	-1.1	842	18.9	749.2	1 768 300	2 101	322 178	428.8	442 023	94.8	5.2	51.3	39.3	11 254	90.9
Grant	1 050	-0.8	2 067	2.4	504.0	1 904 955	922	235 537	157.1	309 232	70.3	29.7	68.1	45.9	5 753	84.8
Griggs	445	9.7	977	2.8	342.4	1 781 884	1 824	254 471	127.8	280 325	91.5	8.5	53.7	35.5	8 891	88.4
Hettinger	716	1.1	1 449	0.0	558.5	1 624 585	1 121	263 455	159.0	321 927	91.4	8.6	49.4	34.4	8 615	88.7
Kidder	780	3.6	1 396	15.0	429.8	1 290 878	925	198 445	148.3	265 326	72.2	27.8	59.9	40.4	4 079	84.6
LaMoure	726	5.5	1 131	7.4	611.3	2 445 422	2 163	342 617	292.4	455 500	88.9	11.1	63.6	50.9	7 967	85.7
Logan	572	-1.0	1 508	1.5	333.3	1 541 950	1 022	285 359	172.1	454 087	50.0	50.0	63.1	48.3	3 296	90.0
McHenry	1 061	-2.0	1 165	1.2	624.8	1 047 299	899	161 514	198.2	217 581	72.3	27.7	56.4	34.7	8 289	77.9
McIntosh	590	7.3	1 252	D	397.2	1 472 964	1 176	214 769	139.8	296 754	75.3	24.7	66.7	42.7	3 350	79.6
McKenzie	1 064	-1.0	1 854	19.9	425.6	1 366 373	737	246 225	114.4	199 387	69.0	31.0	62.9	38.5	4 116	70.0
McLean	1 113	-4.3	1 282	7.4	838.7	1 681 880	1 312	307 744	293.4	338 025	92.3	7.7	62.2	41.6	11 766	82.8
Mercer	503	-1.3	1 192	1.4	231.0	1 135 981	953	188 306	76.7	181 765	73.3	26.7	65.6	32.5	2 572	70.9
Morton	1 220	4.7	1 375	7.6	549.1	1 405 868	1 022	208 989	225.2	253 934	67.6	32.4	62.8	34.6	5 558	62.0
Mountrail	964	-7.0	1 438	0.2	578.8	1 308 849	910	278 960	154.9	231 166	86.8	13.2	60.3	37.0	7 195	77.0
Nelson	560	1.9	929	2.1	474.9	1 092 551	1 175	230 488	145.8	241 725	93.3	6.7	37.3	24.5	9 207	95.5
Oliver	395	4.4	1 360	5.9	165.1	1 388 955	1 021	192 590	85.5	294 810	60.2	39.8	74.8	39.3	2 057	75.2
Pembina	692	6.6	1 185	5.7	632.8	3 054 467	2 577	574 476	406.0	695 164	98.7	1.3	60.3	44.9	8 554	77.7
Pierce	598	2.9	1 148	1.0	479.8	1 180 380	1 028	257 340	142.1	272 649	90.5	9.5	55.9	41.8	6 473	90.6
Ramsey	698	-2.3	1 219	D	622.7	1 696 558	1 392	394 349	236.1	412 005	96.7	3.3	51.0	41.2	10 448	85.3
Ransom	502	-4.9	915	14.8	339.3	1 673 436	1 828	213 192	179.3	327 126	85.4	14.6	50.2	32.5	9 311	81.6
Renville	500	-9.8	1 645	0.0	445.8	2 659 974	1 617	536 164	156.4	514 605	97.8	2.2	80.6	66.1	6 902	84.2
Richland	869	-4.1	1 017	3.7	788.5	3 021 842	2 970	437 697	535.7	627 234	95.1	4.9	67.7	54.3	15 676	82.2
Rolette	534	-5.9	823	D	365.5	925 470	1 124	187 112	107.9	166 301	90.8	9.2	50.7	24.8	5 631	68.1
Sargent	513	1.5	955	13.7	432.5	2 265 119	2 372	338 054	243.4	453 311	90.3	9.7	55.5	45.8	9 185	87.2
Sheridan	514	2.7	1 388	D	347.3	1 297 773	935	230 697	107.8	291 295	91.1	8.9	53.8	38.9	4 293	82.7
Sioux	573	-21.5	3 256	D	155.9	2 912 585	894	265 188	62.7	356 421	47.1	52.9	71.6	52.3	1 476	58.5
Slope	674	-12.3	3 051	D	245.0	2 603 290	853	329 502	67.6	305 688	72.0	28.0	64.3	41.6	3 166	72.4
Stark	830	-0.9	991	0.8	498.8	1 345 419	1 358	207 119	152.6	182 298	77.8	22.2	52.9	27.4	4 741	66.3
Steele	426	5.9	1 200	6.0	397.0	2 218 885	1 850	483 662	210.6	593 158	98.3	1.7	63.7	57.2	6 646	94.6
Stutsman	1 303	9.2	1 267	8.2	1 030.6	2 212 500	1 746	385 059	464.6	451 914	90.0	10.0	60.1	41.3	13 278	78.3
Towner	645	6.3	1 220	0.4	573.3	1 565 902	1 283	320 216	196.8	372 049	91.2	8.8	60.5	53.1	7 528	87.1
Traill	548	0.8	1 170	2.0	526.2	3 395 635	2 901	477 162	308.8	659 887	99.3	0.7	68.2	54.9	8 804	80.6
Walsh	802	0.9	834	3.4	714.5	1 982 913	2 377	308 740	424.0	440 783	98.3	1.7	49.7	37.8	14 445	87.1

Table B. States and Counties — Water Use, Wholesale Trade, Retail Trade, and Real Estate

STATE County	Water use, 2010 Total water withdrawn (mil gal/day)	Gallons withdrawn per person per day	Wholesale trade,[1] 2012 Number of establishments	Number of employees	Sales (mil dol)	Annual payroll (mil dol)	Retail trade,[2] 2012 Number of establishments	Number of employees	Sales (mil dol)	Annual payroll (mil dol)	Real estate and rental and leasing,[2] 2012 Number of establishments	Number of employees	Receipts (mil dol)	Annual payroll (mil dol)
	133	134	135	136	137	138	139	140	141	142	143	144	145	146
NORTH CAROLINA—Cont'd														
Swain	15.0	1 073	4	D	D	D	96	472	107.1	9.1	7	23	2.0	0.4
Transylvania	811.1	24 513	15	D	D	D	125	1 352	311.3	30.2	48	91	13.4	2.7
Tyrrell	0.6	134	1	D	D	D	20	135	36.0	2.3	2	D	D	D
Union	42.2	210	266	2 658	1 449.1	126.9	492	6 803	1 943.6	156.4	144	304	60.2	11.2
Vance	9.8	216	31	D	D	D	179	2 186	527.9	49.0	51	211	27.5	5.1
Wake	114.5	127	1 082	18 108	18 602.6	1 401.0	3 161	51 026	14 359.3	1 264.2	1 320	7 360	1 683.3	391.9
Warren	2.6	123	9	21	10.2	0.6	44	314	72.4	6.0	9	D	D	D
Washington	5.8	438	12	185	174.1	4.1	48	465	127.7	8.7	4	D	D	D
Watauga	11.0	215	37	299	140.2	14.7	318	3 471	762.9	70.2	100	382	55.2	10.0
Wayne	34.3	280	95	1 822	1 244.8	74.4	464	5 709	1 557.5	125.8	63	257	29.3	7.1
Wilkes	14.3	206	47	D	D	D	223	2 500	1 365.2	53.5	44	185	46.8	7.0
Wilson	26.0	320	99	D	D	D	319	3 606	992.7	83.6	76	247	43.1	6.3
Yadkin	15.3	399	29	222	87.7	7.8	108	760	242.9	16.0	14	D	D	D
Yancey	12.8	716	7	24	3.7	0.4	61	522	144.9	12.3	17	D	D	D
NORTH DAKOTA	1 147.1	1 705	1 430	18 880	28 150.8	1 078.2	3 185	47 186	15 519.8	1 204.4	912	5 157	1 445.1	247.5
Adams	0.5	222	10	49	120.6	1.7	16	169	43.1	4.1	2	D	D	D
Barnes	2.2	194	22	192	329.6	9.2	48	479	121.7	10.3	11	86	4.5	1.8
Benson	2.1	321	14	86	228.9	4.1	9	55	12.3	1.4	2	D	D	D
Billings	2.1	2 669	1	D	D	D	10	D	D	D	1	D	D	D
Bottineau	3.2	496	16	120	99.0	5.6	34	337	95.5	6.8	8	16	1.1	0.1
Bowman	2.1	673	13	123	96.6	7.6	19	251	93.2	5.5	3	2	0.2	0.0
Burke	1.1	549	6	60	454.5	3.6	10	96	38.5	2.5	3	2	0.7	0.1
Burleigh	16.2	199	132	2 094	1 483.2	113.2	373	6 905	1 995.1	177.7	132	404	107.3	13.9
Cass	17.2	115	333	6 020	5 497.7	335.9	645	12 500	3 790.4	302.8	277	1 716	302.9	64.8
Cavalier	0.9	215	15	D	D	D	29	213	125.7	5.2	1	D	D	D
Dickey	7.6	1 431	16	152	450.1	7.0	41	324	96.3	7.2	1	D	D	D
Divide	2.2	1 067	2	D	D	D	9	86	21.1	1.8	1	D	D	D
Dunn	3.0	834	8	50	86.8	2.7	13	161	69.1	3.5	1	D	D	D
Eddy	2.0	818	4	D	D	D	10	72	16.7	1.7	2	D	D	D
Emmons	5.7	1 606	14	95	236.9	3.5	20	106	30.7	2.3	NA	NA	NA	NA
Foster	1.8	523	19	119	210.8	6.6	28	247	133.0	7.2	2	D	D	D
Golden Valley	0.6	339	5	68	87.3	3.2	15	134	72.7	2.8	NA	NA	NA	NA
Grand Forks	17.5	262	92	1 235	1 214.9	65.6	314	5 860	1 562.2	130.9	79	504	86.1	14.7
Grant	9.6	3 989	8	50	98.4	2.4	10	31	7.2	0.7	1	D	D	D
Griggs	3.1	1 269	6	104	66.5	5.2	12	60	18.1	1.4	1	D	D	D
Hettinger	0.3	113	4	D	D	D	14	87	128.6	2.7	2	D	D	D
Kidder	13.9	5 696	6	17	27.9	0.7	8	66	48.4	1.7	2	D	D	D
LaMoure	5.3	1 285	23	213	391.6	9.9	16	142	133.1	3.8	2	D	D	D
Logan	2.8	1 392	6	D	D	D	11	46	30.5	1.7	1	D	D	D
McHenry	22.0	4 085	5	D	D	D	17	122	26.5	2.5	5	D	D	D
McIntosh	0.9	313	11	103	277.1	3.5	19	140	52.1	3.6	3	9	0.8	0.1
McKenzie	37.7	5 925	14	172	263.6	25.7	24	301	166.1	10.6	15	69	27.6	5.0
McLean	21.6	2 407	20	216	528.9	9.4	38	293	132.5	7.2	2	D	D	D
Mercer	372.6	44 230	6	28	21.5	1.5	39	420	125.2	9.6	5	5	0.3	0.1
Morton	51.2	1 865	34	D	D	D	99	1 230	586.1	40.3	43	118	16.8	3.3
Mountrail	3.4	446	12	140	406.4	9.1	41	475	274.0	15.4	6	16	1.1	0.3
Nelson	1.0	326	13	107	449.2	6.2	19	103	31.5	1.6	4	4	0.1	0.0
Oliver	433.1	234 588	1	D	D	D	2	D	D	D	NA	NA	NA	NA
Pembina	2.1	286	35	352	847.9	13.4	45	403	82.9	7.8	3	1	0.3	0.0
Pierce	1.3	287	11	112	201.5	5.3	22	263	92.6	6.2	2	D	D	D
Ramsey	0.3	26	29	207	622.1	11.0	80	962	311.7	27.1	6	192	7.4	4.6
Ransom	10.6	1 933	13	187	292.1	10.4	30	252	66.2	4.8	4	4	0.7	0.1
Renville	1.4	579	12	89	250.5	4.3	13	142	81.1	3.7	2	D	D	D
Richland	6.2	379	34	D	D	D	75	899	277.3	19.6	18	50	5.6	1.1
Rolette	2.1	149	7	48	103.6	2.9	45	496	132.9	9.7	2	D	D	D
Sargent	4.5	1 183	12	74	145.1	2.9	17	124	20.9	1.8	4	D	D	D
Sheridan	0.4	310	3	D	D	D	6	20	5.5	0.2	2	D	D	D
Sioux	0.7	166	NA	NA	NA	NA	8	D	D	D	NA	NA	NA	NA
Slope	6.1	8 391	NA	NA	NA	NA	1	D	D	D	NA	NA	NA	NA
Stark	3.2	132	53	745	1 186.8	44.7	160	2 050	883.4	62.8	43	211	72.4	12.0
Steele	0.8	400	6	D	D	D	10	61	34.4	1.7	1	D	D	D
Stutsman	9.1	430	39	470	875.5	24.3	101	1 328	379.1	32.3	28	79	20.9	2.0
Towner	0.5	205	8	64	193.8	3.4	13	51	30.4	1.3	2	D	D	D
Traill	1.1	132	30	334	1 733.4	16.3	42	313	97.2	7.1	7	9	0.7	0.2
Walsh	1.0	92	35	374	599.7	18.9	58	535	123.1	10.4	11	13	1.0	0.3

1. Merchant wholesalers, except manufacturers' sales branches and offices.   2. Employer establishments.

— **Professional Services, Manufacturing, and Accommodation and Food Services**

STATE County	Professional, scientific, and technical services, 2012				Manufacturing, 2012				Accommodation and food services, 2012			
	Number of establish-ments	Number of employees	Receipts (mil dol)	Annual payroll (mil dol)	Number of establish-ments	Number of employees	Receipts (mil dol)	Annual payroll (mil dol)	Number of establish-ments	Number of employees	Sales (mil dol)	Annual payroll (mil dol)
	147	148	149	150	151	152	153	154	155	156	157	158
NORTH CAROLINA—Cont'd												
Swain	11	D	D	D	11	414	D	17.1	82	765	50.0	12.4
Transylvania	67	D	D	D	24	440	61.1	18.3	83	1 106	68.5	21.3
Tyrrell	3	D	D	D	3	105	9.6	2.3	6	D	D	D
Union	395	1 221	156.5	54.2	231	9 760	3 645.4	444.3	264	4 159	192.9	50.8
Vance	46	196	16.4	6.9	41	1 581	756.2	66.1	67	1 239	57.0	15.0
Wake	4 332	40 850	7 315.9	3 072.9	576	12 902	13 105.2	696.6	2 102	42 326	2 165.2	606.3
Warren	14	52	3.8	0.9	9	494	128.9	14.7	23	207	8.9	2.3
Washington	12	66	7.5	1.8	12	780	394.6	47.0	27	D	D	D
Watauga	149	723	47.9	20.0	47	667	108.0	23.6	174	3 416	142.1	43.2
Wayne	147	816	76.0	27.4	83	5 833	1 691.3	243.8	186	3 284	161.7	42.0
Wilkes	83	418	36.5	15.0	73	4 288	1 156.1	138.7	105	1 568	65.7	17.9
Wilson	112	769	95.4	36.3	91	7 809	13 159.9	393.6	138	2 749	139.3	34.2
Yadkin	41	230	20.6	8.1	41	2 064	748.3	79.1	58	875	34.4	9.6
Yancey	17	75	5.0	1.5	12	686	145.0	28.9	21	282	11.6	3.4
NORTH DAKOTA	1 722	13 715	1 846.9	735.7	745	23 541	14 427.4	1 042.8	1 935	35 698	2 045.1	521.3
Adams	4	D	D	D	NA	NA	NA	NA	11	D	D	D
Barnes	15	79	9.6	3.6	10	500	D	23.1	31	356	14.1	3.4
Benson	6	14	1.9	0.9	4	102	D	D	16	D	D	D
Billings	3	5	1.0	0.3	3	13	D	D	14	131	19.0	5.4
Bottineau	20	67	6.4	2.9	10	92	D	4.6	28	237	11.0	2.7
Bowman	4	D	D	D	7	35	D	1.0	17	118	5.1	1.2
Burke	4	D	D	D	NA	NA	NA	NA	12	48	4.4	0.5
Burleigh	308	1 969	314.8	118.4	68	900	D	39.3	173	4 980	242.1	70.7
Cass	481	D	D	D	186	8 566	3 451.1	395.7	388	9 671	446.8	130.9
Cavalier	6	16	1.3	0.6	5	14	3.1	0.6	18	D	D	D
Dickey	9	37	2.6	0.9	13	225	60.0	9.4	19	145	4.6	1.1
Divide	6	15	1.6	0.4	3	6	D	D	7	D	D	D
Dunn	4	16	2.2	0.9	5	D	D	D	9	165	24.6	3.5
Eddy	4	10	1.1	0.2	NA	NA	NA	NA	11	30	1.4	0.3
Emmons	9	12	0.9	0.3	3	6	D	D	10	88	2.8	0.8
Foster	7	10	3.4	0.5	3	D	D	D	10	125	5.2	1.5
Golden Valley	5	18	1.8	0.5	NA	NA	NA	NA	4	D	D	D
Grand Forks	130	1 473	167.2	79.1	55	2 166	590.7	78.4	196	4 191	177.6	52.5
Grant	3	7	0.6	0.1	3	27	D	D	6	D	D	D
Griggs	9	43	4.7	1.6	5	155	21.4	5.1	11	D	D	D
Hettinger	5	15	0.9	0.4	3	5	D	D	5	35	1.3	0.2
Kidder	4	D	D	D	3	6	D	D	8	43	2.0	0.6
LaMoure	2	D	D	D	7	52	D	1.9	16	D	D	D
Logan	2	D	D	D	NA	NA	NA	NA	9	57	1.3	0.3
McHenry	6	14	2.1	0.6	4	D	D	D	7	24	1.3	0.3
McIntosh	6	24	1.6	0.6	4	109	D	3.3	10	D	D	D
McKenzie	32	134	46.7	13.9	5	17	1.6	0.4	28	460	31.8	6.5
McLean	7	20	1.6	0.5	5	67	D	3.2	28	181	9.8	2.1
Mercer	11	69	7.2	2.2	7	35	5.7	0.9	30	348	12.4	3.5
Morton	61	D	D	D	36	913	D	56.0	52	D	D	D
Mountrail	18	44	8.9	2.3	3	D	D	D	30	167	18.8	3.1
Nelson	5	12	0.8	0.3	3	57	D	1.4	15	106	3.4	0.8
Oliver	3	D	D	D	5	D	D	0.7	3	9	0.3	0.1
Pembina	14	27	2.8	0.6	15	520	477.1	22.5	20	D	D	D
Pierce	13	58	4.4	1.1	NA	NA	NA	NA	12	171	5.6	1.5
Ramsey	19	61	7.9	2.4	9	219	D	9.8	47	681	29.6	7.9
Ransom	15	52	4.7	1.3	8	405	D	12.3	19	129	4.8	1.2
Renville	7	14	1.1	0.3	NA	NA	NA	NA	10	30	1.4	0.2
Richland	32	D	D	D	35	1 871	1 276.7	87.2	47	821	89.6	16.1
Rolette	6	8	0.9	0.3	8	231	D	7.4	25	582	43.1	12.5
Sargent	9	34	3.5	1.5	6	D	D	D	14	D	D	D
Sheridan	4	D	D	D	3	43	D	D	2	D	D	D
Sioux	2	D	D	D	NA	NA	NA	NA	6	D	D	D
Slope	NA	NA	NA	NA	NA	NA	NA	NA	1	D	D	D
Stark	71	430	75.9	23.3	28	898	431.8	44.6	80	1 431	111.6	25.8
Steele	3	3	0.3	0.1	8	158	D	4.9	5	20	1.0	0.1
Stutsman	34	174	16.4	6.4	24	902	500.6	37.7	60	926	40.2	11.9
Towner	8	21	1.9	0.5	4	49	D	1.0	9	32	1.3	0.3
Traill	10	31	3.1	1.4	15	311	D	12.3	26	203	7.7	2.0
Walsh	24	88	8.5	3.0	10	522	111.2	17.8	36	259	12.0	2.7

1. Establishment subject to federal tax.

Table B. States and Counties — Health Care and Social Assistance, Other Services, Nonemployer Businesses, and Residential Construction

STATE County	Health care and social assistance, 2012				Other services, 2012				Nonemployer businesses, 2014		Value of residential construction authorized by building permits, 2015	
	Number of establishments	Number of employees	Receipts (mil dol)	Annual payroll (mil dol)	Number of establishments	Number of employees	Receipts (mil dol)	Annual payroll (mil dol)	Number	Receipts (mil dol)	New Construction ($1,000)	Number of housing units
	159	160	161	162	163	164	165	166	167	168	169	170
NORTH CAROLINA—Cont'd												
Swain	31	736	89.3	26.7	18	D	D	D	1 330	42.8	10 160	52
Transylvania	70	1 589	148.7	57.5	46	248	21.0	6.0	3 075	120.4	31 918	82
Tyrrell	8	D	D	D	7	44	4.2	1.4	285	9.8	65	1
Union	292	5 038	533.9	201.5	281	1 255	109.2	32.8	16 510	728.5	285 198	1 396
Vance	101	2 512	205.0	83.0	48	225	22.7	6.1	2 511	89.6	6 968	74
Wake	2 688	47 097	5 110.4	2 066.2	1 699	12 705	1 463.3	420.1	80 548	3 675.8	1 764 682	10 089
Warren	23	446	20.0	9.7	12	D	D	D	994	31.3	15 129	48
Washington	34	665	34.7	15.0	11	D	D	D	654	20.1	999	8
Watauga	140	3 419	624.9	144.3	82	349	28.4	7.6	4 639	203.2	85 634	397
Wayne	254	6 896	606.6	265.8	142	939	69.3	20.3	6 089	232.5	39 671	248
Wilkes	147	2 783	233.7	91.5	72	338	23.2	8.4	4 467	176.5	26 704	159
Wilson	200	5 103	408.7	169.3	114	619	54.4	15.0	4 658	172.9	31 024	114
Yadkin	52	982	60.4	24.8	35	D	D	D	2 416	88.2	2 177	4
Yancey	32	D	D	D	24	86	7.5	2.2	1 599	53.2	6 071	50
NORTH DAKOTA	1 856	56 639	5 418.4	2 414.4	1 716	9 232	1 064.0	253.7	53 588	2 847.4	953 024	6 256
Adams	13	D	D	D	9	D	D	D	225	9.2	1 034	6
Barnes	37	1 156	53.4	26.8	28	147	10.5	2.9	891	48.6	6 465	30
Benson	6	50	1.5	0.8	3	10	1.8	0.2	297	12.0	50	1
Billings	NA	NA	NA	NA	4	14	1.7	0.4	89	4.7	1 161	5
Bottineau	6	256	14.3	6.8	9	D	D	D	692	31.1	4 865	20
Bowman	11	226	16.7	8.3	14	D	D	D	276	13.6	531	3
Burke	5	D	D	D	2	D	D	D	216	12.2	905	4
Burleigh	271	10 591	1 080.5	488.2	254	1 691	208.8	53.8	7 120	415.0	120 231	776
Cass	439	15 347	1 909.7	815.0	380	2 549	278.0	71.4	11 711	685.8	332 270	2 138
Cavalier	10	242	15.7	5.7	11	D	D	D	384	16.6	1 695	5
Dickey	23	409	31.5	13.0	20	67	5.9	1.6	415	13.0	793	3
Divide	6	D	D	D	5	D	D	D	217	10.4	500	1
Dunn	4	D	D	D	11	D	D	D	345	25.9	8 685	40
Eddy	9	223	11.3	6.5	7	D	D	D	194	7.8	1 100	11
Emmons	11	213	10.1	5.7	7	12	0.7	0.1	272	10.5	0	0
Foster	11	302	22.9	10.1	7	17	1.2	0.3	291	10.4	800	4
Golden Valley	5	114	7.0	3.3	7	28	1.2	0.4	179	7.6	3 052	12
Grand Forks	160	6 865	668.9	301.2	148	827	103.2	21.7	3 968	192.0	67 391	462
Grant	7	224	12.1	5.3	5	D	D	D	208	8.9	551	5
Griggs	5	D	D	D	7	D	D	D	205	9.0	110	1
Hettinger	10	110	5.1	2.6	8	D	D	D	203	8.3	0	0
Kidder	6	47	1.7	0.8	3	D	D	D	238	11.1	440	2
LaMoure	13	D	D	D	13	49	4.4	0.9	360	14.7	500	1
Logan	7	148	4.6	2.5	7	D	D	D	186	7.0	0	0
McHenry	6	D	D	D	7	D	D	D	418	17.5	2 118	10
McIntosh	10	308	17.0	8.9	7	19	1.0	0.2	269	11.1	500	3
McKenzie	9	184	15.1	6.1	27	112	10.6	2.6	788	58.8	71 642	745
McLean	19	443	23.8	12.0	19	D	D	D	729	29.2	10 412	49
Mercer	18	445	26.7	12.7	16	44	4.0	0.9	617	18.6	8 316	43
Morton	64	1 627	99.3	48.3	58	D	D	D	2 300	134.7	58 064	288
Mountrail	13	196	12.5	6.2	19	83	10.1	2.5	754	53.0	9 247	48
Nelson	10	256	11.5	5.6	12	D	D	D	297	10.5	650	3
Oliver	4	D	D	D	2	D	D	D	124	4.7	4 538	18
Pembina	16	336	19.1	7.2	18	D	D	D	583	22.0	0	0
Pierce	9	D	D	D	14	D	D	D	382	16.5	1 248	5
Ramsey	41	888	56.7	26.1	28	131	10.9	2.2	878	37.1	5 075	36
Ransom	25	420	26.5	11.9	22	75	6.5	1.3	367	14.6	500	2
Renville	7	D	D	D	3	D	D	D	178	6.5	1 330	8
Richland	45	578	35.6	18.7	38	143	11.2	3.0	1 133	57.3	5 909	31
Rolette	25	549	54.7	24.7	9	D	D	D	705	22.4	0	0
Sargent	7	65	3.0	1.8	8	31	5.1	0.8	300	13.4	4 830	30
Sheridan	2	D	D	D	5	D	D	D	114	5.4	572	4
Sioux	1	D	D	D	2	D	D	D	100	3.9	0	0
Slope	NA	NA	NA	NA	1	D	D	D	60	4.1	800	4
Stark	91	1 927	131.4	60.4	79	585	78.6	16.0	2 648	167.6	48 310	206
Steele	1	D	D	D	4	7	1.2	0.2	135	8.5	405	3
Stutsman	62	2 423	154.8	88.7	54	299	23.6	6.9	1 379	57.3	13 556	65
Towner	3	D	D	D	6	30	2.5	0.4	225	8.9	0	0
Traill	20	595	34.4	17.5	23	80	15.9	2.2	589	24.7	2 927	12
Walsh	39	726	45.8	21.7	38	101	7.0	1.9	779	36.1	460	4

Table B. States and Counties — Government Employment and Payroll, and Local Government Finances

	Government employment and payroll, 2012									Local government finances, 2012				
			March payroll (percent of total)							General revenue				
												Taxes		
													Per capita[1] (dollars)	
STATE County	Full-time equivalent employees	March payroll (dollars)	Administration, judicial, and legal	Police and Corrections	Fire Protection	Highways and transportation	Health and Welfare	Natural resources and utilities	Education and libraries	Total (mil dol)	Inter-govern-mental (mil dol)	Total (mil dol)	Total	Property
	171	172	173	174	175	176	177	178	179	180	181	182	183	184
NORTH CAROLINA—Cont'd														
Swain	570	1 634 935	2.8	6.9	0.0	0.2	15.2	3.5	58.7	39.0	24.0	8.3	586	366
Transylvania	1 211	3 349 488	5.1	9.9	0.5	1.7	16.3	4.8	52.7	82.0	34.9	38.2	1 162	930
Tyrrell	212	788 126	5.4	5.1	0.0	0.3	6.1	4.4	76.8	19.0	12.0	4.7	1 091	930
Union	6 960	22 437 486	4.7	8.5	1.4	0.7	5.2	5.8	72.3	593.9	274.3	239.3	1 148	942
Vance	2 151	6 716 262	3.1	6.3	2.9	1.8	9.0	3.0	71.8	166.4	101.2	37.4	828	618
Wake	31 235	120 436 016	3.6	9.3	3.7	3.7	7.3	6.6	61.6	3 180.9	1 227.2	1 366.9	1 436	1 077
Warren	682	2 143 055	2.8	7.9	0.0	0.0	10.7	3.8	61.2	57.4	29.8	20.1	976	845
Washington	551	1 546 357	6.0	8.2	0.0	0.4	15.3	5.7	59.9	40.0	25.2	10.3	805	588
Watauga	1 481	4 632 704	6.0	11.0	2.1	4.5	13.2	7.1	47.6	137.3	56.5	63.0	1 214	855
Wayne	5 237	14 176 474	3.0	6.2	2.1	1.3	9.2	6.0	66.2	346.7	199.6	101.5	817	585
Wilkes	3 431	10 259 077	2.0	4.8	0.3	0.9	32.4	1.6	56.6	184.5	95.3	58.2	840	635
Wilson	3 417	11 244 041	5.5	9.5	3.3	2.4	11.6	11.2	53.8	288.2	140.0	90.5	1 105	863
Yadkin	1 268	3 737 818	3.9	5.9	0.1	0.5	11.5	3.0	70.9	88.3	50.5	29.0	763	624
Yancey	773	2 283 963	4.6	6.2	0.2	1.0	23.0	3.1	60.9	45.5	25.0	17.2	973	798
NORTH DAKOTA	X	X	X	X	X	X	X	X	X	X	X	X	X	X
Adams	92	255 672	10.2	8.6	0.0	6.4	7.5	3.3	62.1	8.2	3.6	3.0	1 313	1 054
Barnes	418	1 392 699	15.6	9.1	0.5	3.9	5.1	9.8	55.6	66.9	40.2	17.6	1 597	1 448
Benson	305	941 315	6.1	1.3	0.6	5.7	5.8	1.7	78.6	27.9	19.5	4.6	683	672
Billings	71	278 902	16.6	9.9	1.1	28.8	4.2	4.9	31.5	14.4	10.4	1.7	1 884	1 457
Bottineau	258	801 858	8.7	5.1	0.1	7.5	5.5	8.6	64.2	29.2	15.4	8.8	1 337	1 194
Bowman	154	498 076	10.9	6.0	0.1	7.5	7.8	4.7	63.1	25.9	15.6	5.2	1 630	1 395
Burke	132	476 712	12.0	4.9	0.0	8.5	2.8	2.4	67.3	11.4	4.8	4.8	2 215	1 096
Burleigh	2 640	9 881 026	4.2	8.2	4.2	3.6	6.6	9.1	61.0	347.2	171.6	100.7	1 174	925
Cass	4 659	18 693 995	4.8	9.4	2.9	4.9	9.6	7.5	60.1	694.2	293.1	246.4	1 578	1 145
Cavalier	150	482 792	10.3	7.1	0.0	7.2	5.9	7.5	58.4	17.1	7.4	6.7	1 688	1 662
Dickey	177	602 013	11.3	6.4	0.0	5.8	12.2	3.2	59.7	28.7	12.8	9.2	1 751	1 617
Divide	112	399 142	14.1	7.5	0.0	19.6	4.6	5.6	47.0	17.6	9.2	3.7	1 673	1 505
Dunn	163	514 670	8.7	4.7	0.8	11.8	6.5	2.4	65.0	27.2	19.0	3.9	992	865
Eddy	101	291 076	9.8	5.2	0.0	6.4	5.8	4.1	67.8	12.9	6.6	3.2	1 370	1 257
Emmons	160	461 725	8.9	3.7	0.1	7.4	1.9	9.4	68.6	16.2	7.3	6.2	1 777	1 711
Foster	109	345 480	14.5	2.4	0.1	5.2	6.9	1.6	67.7	14.4	6.3	5.0	1 462	1 302
Golden Valley	168	598 525	4.4	2.4	0.0	4.3	3.1	1.4	83.6	12.6	6.8	3.5	1 923	1 846
Grand Forks	2 414	9 092 121	5.6	9.8	3.4	6.3	6.5	11.9	54.2	280.6	106.1	94.4	1 399	1 054
Grant	103	251 784	10.0	5.5	0.0	9.2	10.7	3.2	60.2	8.5	3.8	3.4	1 448	1 414
Griggs	112	363 293	9.3	4.3	0.0	8.1	9.0	2.0	65.6	13.5	5.4	5.3	2 241	2 176
Hettinger	147	439 881	7.5	2.1	0.1	8.1	4.0	22.4	54.8	15.0	6.5	5.4	2 133	1 985
Kidder	100	305 849	4.8	4.8	0.0	1.6	8.6	4.8	75.3	16.0	7.8	3.7	1 533	1 484
LaMoure	228	740 715	7.4	3.3	0.0	6.3	2.2	19.6	60.3	63.8	47.3	9.5	2 316	2 252
Logan	83	243 512	4.2	4.7	0.0	5.7	6.1	5.0	73.3	10.5	5.6	3.9	2 040	2 023
McHenry	239	766 397	8.6	2.6	0.1	4.2	4.4	4.0	74.9	20.6	10.3	7.3	1 263	1 225
McIntosh	139	432 649	7.6	5.1	0.1	10.8	4.4	16.0	55.9	10.7	5.5	3.7	1 328	1 289
McKenzie	313	1 128 904	9.9	9.8	0.0	9.8	6.5	4.0	57.4	54.1	24.6	7.4	930	751
McLean	438	1 374 148	6.7	7.0	0.0	5.7	12.1	3.3	64.5	43.6	23.1	11.4	1 229	1 093
Mercer	347	1 135 199	9.4	9.5	0.0	9.4	2.8	4.7	62.2	34.8	17.4	9.3	1 093	917
Morton	946	3 200 962	5.4	9.1	1.2	7.7	8.1	5.9	61.5	106.1	48.2	35.2	1 253	1 139
Mountrail	385	1 261 569	8.3	7.4	0.0	8.6	6.2	3.5	65.1	85.8	57.9	12.5	1 434	1 307
Nelson	146	457 045	9.7	3.0	0.0	8.5	4.7	8.9	63.6	17.3	8.0	6.7	2 183	2 144
Oliver	76	233 042	14.9	6.8	0.0	9.6	2.9	7.5	56.4	9.0	3.8	3.7	2 018	1 749
Pembina	393	1 633 628	6.4	4.3	0.0	3.1	4.1	45.4	36.2	40.0	15.7	16.1	2 221	2 125
Pierce	154	464 990	7.2	8.4	0.0	4.1	5.0	3.6	69.5	21.3	8.8	5.5	1 245	1 151
Ramsey	543	1 755 199	7.3	12.7	1.3	4.3	10.4	5.8	57.4	84.1	57.8	15.4	1 331	1 034
Ransom	223	692 010	8.7	4.1	0.8	4.5	6.6	5.2	68.5	23.4	12.3	7.8	1 436	1 220
Renville	140	452 741	8.2	6.0	0.0	8.7	3.5	2.3	70.0	19.2	9.5	5.9	2 288	2 255
Richland	582	2 019 868	4.8	9.7	0.0	6.5	9.5	7.4	61.0	75.6	33.2	29.0	1 787	1 613
Rolette	726	2 856 302	1.9	2.3	0.2	1.2	3.8	2.8	87.6	53.9	43.3	5.9	409	382
Sargent	167	536 100	9.7	3.9	0.0	3.3	5.4	6.8	70.4	21.4	9.5	8.1	2 073	2 002
Sheridan	59	160 666	12.8	0.0	0.0	8.5	0.2	3.7	73.9	5.6	2.2	2.9	2 255	2 229
Sioux	129	394 909	4.4	0.8	1.7	4.0	0.3	1.7	86.3	11.5	9.3	1.5	349	348
Slope	36	114 876	15.1	4.2	0.0	6.9	0.2	2.1	68.6	5.2	3.3	1.0	1 297	1 208
Stark	970	3 430 314	4.3	17.8	1.0	4.4	10.3	9.5	51.8	103.5	43.2	33.0	1 232	836
Steele	76	279 013	12.8	4.5	0.1	2.6	1.4	2.1	76.4	12.4	4.6	4.9	2 441	2 369
Stutsman	738	2 551 998	5.2	10.8	0.9	5.8	9.7	7.6	58.2	88.6	38.8	29.6	1 413	1 195
Towner	120	341 158	12.4	5.1	0.0	10.5	3.7	3.7	63.4	10.1	3.9	3.9	1 695	1 626
Traill	299	1 042 936	6.6	4.5	0.0	5.7	5.6	2.7	74.1	35.7	16.3	11.8	1 468	1 367
Walsh	425	1 396 845	7.5	5.6	0.0	5.1	6.2	9.3	63.8	46.8	22.8	16.0	1 451	1 295

1. Based on the resident population estimated as of July 1 of the year shown.

STATE County	Total (mil dol)	Per capita[1] (dollars)	Education	Health and hospitals	Police protection	Public welfare	Highways	Total (mil dol)	Per capita[1] (dollars)	Federal civilian	Federal military	State and local	Demo-cratic	Republi-can	All other
	185	186	187	188	189	190	191	192	193	194	195	196	197	198	199
NORTH CAROLINA—Cont'd															
Swain	40.3	2 852	47.4	5.4	7.2	14.3	0.2	10.7	758	194	35	2 343	48.4	50.0	1.6
Transylvania	80.6	2 453	45.7	4.8	9.9	7.4	1.1	13.0	395	125	79	1 371	43.0	55.6	1.4
Tyrrell	18.9	4 355	54.4	1.2	9.5	7.3	0.7	10.3	2 385	18	0	460	48.8	50.3	0.9
Union	614.4	2 946	53.1	2.0	6.1	4.7	1.0	748.0	3 587	249	537	10 223	36.2	62.9	0.9
Vance	164.7	3 650	56.0	9.8	6.5	7.1	0.6	48.5	1 074	86	109	2 712	63.1	36.4	0.5
Wake	3 282.9	3 448	42.3	4.0	6.5	3.3	2.2	9 085.4	9 542	5 149	2 976	77 835	56.7	42.3	1.0
Warren	54.2	2 635	50.1	5.1	10.5	10.6	0.3	7.2	348	33	48	1 325	69.5	30.0	0.5
Washington	43.9	3 443	43.6	0.4	7.2	13.8	1.5	7.6	594	29	31	941	58.1	41.4	0.6
Watauga	128.3	2 473	32.3	4.5	9.1	5.1	3.7	134.7	2 596	105	121	6 204	51.3	47.0	1.7
Wayne	344.7	2 774	55.1	4.8	6.3	6.3	1.4	151.3	1 217	1 213	4 580	8 125	45.4	54.0	0.5
Wilkes	183.3	2 645	60.4	4.2	5.5	7.8	0.6	49.6	715	181	168	4 287	30.1	68.3	1.7
Wilson	278.4	3 401	41.7	5.4	8.2	8.1	1.5	192.4	2 351	118	198	5 239	52.8	46.7	0.4
Yadkin	87.9	2 308	57.4	4.6	6.9	10.0	0.9	50.3	1 322	66	93	1 422	26.4	72.4	1.2
Yancey	44.5	2 522	51.4	2.5	6.4	10.3	0.6	14.3	810	32	43	846	46.2	51.9	1.9
NORTH DAKOTA	X	X	X	X	X	X	X	X	X	9 104	11 615	66 852	44.6	53.3	2.1
Adams	8.2	3 529	45.9	0.0	4.8	3.9	18.8	0.1	33	16	16	131	34.2	62.0	3.8
Barnes	64.0	5 811	34.3	4.3	8.8	3.5	21.8	18.2	1 650	76	71	1 086	48.1	49.6	2.2
Benson	27.4	4 053	65.7	0.2	1.4	3.3	17.2	0.6	85	153	46	1 379	66.1	32.6	1.3
Billings	17.0	18 828	14.4	6.5	9.0	0.0	56.2	0.1	133	54	0	125	22.8	75.2	2.0
Bottineau	32.3	4 914	41.2	2.2	4.2	0.0	32.5	11.5	1 748	75	43	639	39.4	58.6	2.0
Bowman	21.3	6 655	38.7	2.4	2.9	1.6	30.5	1.3	409	23	22	239	29.1	67.5	3.4
Burke	10.7	4 949	47.9	0.4	2.6	2.0	26.1	0.1	67	98	15	174	30.3	67.9	1.8
Burleigh	313.0	3 649	41.6	1.2	5.7	1.7	12.7	181.5	2 116	1 057	586	10 512	37.3	60.9	1.7
Cass	703.9	4 508	39.9	0.1	5.6	3.0	13.2	1 204.5	7 713	2 263	1 104	12 304	52.7	45.6	1.7
Cavalier	16.8	4 263	40.9	2.0	4.3	4.3	23.7	11.4	2 878	36	25	203	43.7	53.0	3.4
Dickey	36.5	6 935	38.3	1.4	3.0	1.6	13.3	34.3	6 520	25	33	303	39.8	58.2	1.9
Divide	23.6	10 577	21.6	1.5	4.6	0.7	33.8	0.9	389	32	16	157	41.0	55.7	3.3
Dunn	24.7	6 221	37.5	0.0	3.7	1.5	33.1	0.3	74	15	29	284	32.1	65.7	2.3
Eddy	13.4	5 660	43.4	0.1	4.4	2.5	14.8	1.6	686	23	15	168	50.0	47.0	2.9
Emmons	14.9	4 274	52.4	1.3	1.9	2.0	14.2	3.8	1 081	25	23	223	29.7	67.0	3.3
Foster	13.8	4 065	45.3	1.9	3.7	2.8	14.1	10.6	3 116	26	22	219	41.6	55.4	3.0
Golden Valley	12.7	7 062	41.7	1.5	3.3	2.2	17.1	4.6	2 568	12	12	176	24.0	73.4	2.6
Grand Forks	251.5	3 728	47.0	1.0	5.1	1.4	4.7	705.5	10 456	1 037	1 993	9 872	51.7	46.6	1.7
Grant	8.1	3 453	49.5	18.0	2.5	2.6	12.7	1.2	524	25	16	138	21.1	44.2	34.8
Griggs	13.1	5 527	43.9	3.5	2.8	2.9	21.9	3.7	1 562	21	15	176	45.5	51.9	2.6
Hettinger	16.2	6 357	49.8	0.0	2.6	2.3	14.4	1.9	738	18	17	185	30.1	66.2	3.6
Kidder	15.9	6 560	32.7	24.9	1.7	1.4	20.1	2.4	973	22	16	158	34.4	61.2	4.4
LaMoure	23.0	5 581	54.0	0.0	2.5	2.6	15.6	7.0	1 691	45	27	300	38.7	58.5	2.8
Logan	8.8	4 566	63.4	1.0	2.8	0.2	13.9	1.7	867	19	13	140	28.3	68.7	3.0
McHenry	20.8	3 592	61.0	0.0	2.3	2.7	13.3	1.0	180	48	40	332	40.6	56.9	2.5
McIntosh	10.1	3 663	56.1	1.5	2.9	2.7	15.9	1.7	619	18	18	182	37.8	59.8	2.4
McKenzie	61.8	7 738	29.9	3.0	3.5	1.3	31.4	15.2	1 897	49	73	1 634	34.4	64.1	1.5
McLean	38.0	4 086	53.6	1.4	4.7	3.8	12.0	18.4	1 973	125	63	716	39.4	58.4	2.2
Mercer	37.5	4 418	49.3	0.5	5.7	1.3	17.4	59.3	6 990	39	58	545	33.6	63.4	3.0
Morton	106.7	3 797	49.8	2.5	5.2	2.3	6.9	103.5	3 685	94	196	1 581	38.3	59.3	2.4
Mountrail	86.5	9 907	36.3	0.5	1.9	1.2	37.1	26.9	3 081	41	62	654	50.3	47.9	1.9
Nelson	16.3	5 277	44.9	2.6	2.2	1.3	18.7	14.3	4 644	26	20	228	51.8	45.7	2.6
Oliver	7.8	4 256	42.5	0.0	3.8	0.0	8.3	20.2	10 993	0	12	103	31.9	65.6	2.5
Pembina	37.7	5 190	45.2	0.5	3.9	2.4	8.5	14.9	2 043	235	81	548	45.2	52.1	2.8
Pierce	24.3	5 462	53.5	2.7	4.5	1.9	9.5	4.3	974	19	28	252	37.0	60.8	2.2
Ramsey	75.8	6 569	35.0	0.9	2.9	2.1	20.4	33.0	2 865	160	74	1 369	48.6	49.6	1.8
Ransom	25.2	4 634	45.6	1.6	2.9	1.7	12.3	21.6	3 965	37	35	482	56.4	41.0	2.6
Renville	20.6	8 041	40.3	0.1	2.1	0.0	28.2	3.6	1 387	23	17	203	37.5	59.4	3.1
Richland	75.3	4 645	43.3	4.4	4.5	1.9	13.1	88.9	5 482	65	108	1 880	46.4	51.6	2.0
Rolette	53.3	3 703	79.0	1.4	2.2	2.2	5.1	6.0	419	916	97	1 995	75.1	23.0	1.9
Sargent	19.0	4 886	48.6	1.5	1.7	2.4	13.8	11.5	2 940	38	26	249	57.9	40.4	1.8
Sheridan	5.5	4 306	39.7	1.2	1.7	1.0	20.2	0.2	179	11	0	100	28.5	69.1	2.4
Sioux	11.0	2 521	85.3	0.0	0.5	4.1	5.3	3.0	686	225	29	1 316	83.1	15.6	1.3
Slope	3.6	4 734	14.2	2.9	4.4	0.0	33.2	0.4	538	0	0	35	25.8	72.3	1.9
Stark	96.5	3 605	41.6	0.9	4.4	3.4	11.2	19.1	712	179	199	2 195	34.3	63.5	2.2
Steele	11.3	5 664	42.7	0.0	2.8	4.2	26.4	5.7	2 876	14	13	111	59.5	39.1	1.4
Stutsman	83.3	3 978	42.4	3.2	5.0	2.2	13.9	57.9	2 766	178	130	1 881	41.5	56.2	2.3
Towner	8.9	3 844	45.7	5.0	3.3	2.3	18.6	2.2	931	19	15	121	51.9	44.8	3.3
Traill	35.4	4 390	54.9	0.9	3.8	2.9	12.5	42.5	5 269	41	52	867	52.9	45.7	1.5
Walsh	51.9	4 703	54.4	1.3	4.4	2.5	9.7	23.8	2 156	61	71	1 094	47.6	49.5	2.9

1. Based on the resident population estimated as of July 1 of the year shown. 2.

Table B. States and Counties — **Land Area and Population**

				Population, 2015				Population and population characteristics, 2014										
								Race alone or in combination, not Hispanic or Latino (percent)					Age (percent)					
STATE/ County code	CBSA code[1]	County type[2]	STATE County	Land area,[3] (sq km) 2010	Total persons 2015	Rank	Per square kilometer	White	Black	American Indian, Alaska Native	Asian and Pacific Islander	Percent Hispanic or Latino[4]	Under 5 years	5 to 17 years	18 to 24 years	25 to 34 years	35 to 44 years	45 to 54 years
				1	2	3	4	5	6	7	8	9	10	11	12	13	14	15
			NORTH DAKOTA—Cont'd															
38 101	33500	5	Ward	5 214	71 275	757	13.7	87.2	4.7	3.1	2.2	5.1	7.9	15.3	15.5	17.6	11.3	10.8
38 103	...	9	Wells	3 292	4 168	2 890	1.3	98.0	0.7	1.2	0.3	1.1	5.4	13.8	6.6	8.2	8.5	14.4
38 105	48780	7	Williams	5 380	35 294	1 294	6.6	88.1	2.5	5.7	1.2	5.2	8.3	17.2	10.9	18.1	11.8	12.7
39 000	...	X	**OHIO**	105 829	11 613 423	X	109.7	81.9	13.5	0.7	2.5	3.5	6.0	16.8	9.5	12.7	12.1	13.8
39 001	...	6	Adams	1 512	28 024	1 483	18.5	98.0	1.0	1.2	0.4	0.8	6.1	18.5	7.6	10.8	12.5	14.0
39 003	30620	3	Allen	1 042	104 425	567	100.2	84.0	14.1	0.7	1.2	2.8	6.1	17.2	10.6	11.9	11.6	13.0
39 005	11740	4	Ashland	1 095	53 213	938	48.6	96.9	1.4	0.5	0.9	1.2	6.0	17.2	10.3	11.1	11.2	13.2
39 007	11780	4	Ashtabula	1 818	98 632	600	54.3	91.9	4.8	0.8	0.7	3.8	5.7	16.9	7.9	11.2	11.8	14.6
39 009	11900	4	Athens	1 304	65 886	803	50.5	91.7	3.6	1.1	4.1	1.8	4.3	11.3	29.8	12.4	9.7	10.4
39 011	47540	4	Auglaize	1 040	45 876	1 051	44.1	97.2	1.0	0.5	0.8	1.5	6.1	18.2	8.0	10.9	11.6	14.1
39 013	48540	3	Belmont	1 378	69 154	772	50.2	94.4	5.0	0.5	0.7	0.9	4.9	14.2	8.2	12.4	11.9	13.9
39 015	17140	1	Brown	1 269	43 839	1 094	34.5	97.7	1.4	0.7	0.5	0.8	5.8	17.6	7.8	11.1	12.6	14.4
39 017	17140	1	Butler	1 210	376 353	180	311.0	84.7	9.0	0.6	3.4	4.5	6.2	18.1	12.2	11.8	12.3	13.7
39 019	15940	2	Carroll	1 022	27 811	1 499	27.2	97.5	1.1	0.8	0.5	1.2	4.8	16.7	7.6	9.9	11.7	14.5
39 021	46500	6	Champaign	1 110	38 987	1 204	35.1	95.4	3.4	0.9	0.9	1.5	5.9	17.5	8.7	10.8	12.1	14.7
39 023	44220	3	Clark	1 029	135 959	466	132.1	87.0	10.6	0.9	1.2	3.1	5.9	17.0	8.8	11.4	11.4	13.6
39 025	17140	1	Clermont	1 171	201 973	323	172.5	95.5	2.0	0.6	1.6	1.7	6.0	18.2	8.0	12.2	12.8	14.8
39 027	48940	6	Clinton	1 058	41 917	1 127	39.6	95.2	3.4	0.7	0.9	1.6	6.4	17.6	9.4	11.6	12.0	13.8
39 029	41400	4	Columbiana	1 378	104 806	566	76.1	95.7	3.0	0.6	0.6	1.5	5.3	15.6	7.6	11.2	12.3	14.3
39 031	18740	6	Coshocton	1 461	36 569	1 263	25.0	97.1	1.9	0.6	0.5	0.9	6.0	17.5	7.7	11.4	11.5	13.7
39 033	15340	4	Crawford	1 041	42 306	1 124	40.6	97.0	1.6	0.5	0.6	1.5	5.5	16.5	8.0	10.5	12.0	13.7
39 035	17460	1	Cuyahoga	1 184	1 255 921	31	1 060.7	61.7	30.7	0.7	3.5	5.4	5.8	15.8	9.2	13.1	11.6	13.9
39 037	24820	6	Darke	1 549	52 076	959	33.6	97.3	1.2	0.5	0.6	1.5	5.9	18.3	7.9	10.2	11.6	14.1
39 039	19580	4	Defiance	1 066	38 352	1 212	36.0	87.7	2.5	0.6	0.6	9.6	5.8	17.7	9.0	11.6	11.8	12.9
39 041	18140	1	Delaware	1 148	193 013	341	168.1	88.4	4.2	0.5	6.2	2.4	6.1	21.5	7.5	10.3	15.9	15.4
39 043	41780	3	Erie	652	75 550	731	115.9	86.4	10.4	0.8	0.9	4.0	5.2	15.7	8.2	10.8	10.9	14.1
39 045	18140	1	Fairfield	1 306	151 408	429	115.9	89.3	7.9	0.8	1.8	2.1	5.6	18.8	8.5	11.7	13.3	14.8
39 047	47920	6	Fayette	1 052	28 679	1 467	27.3	95.1	3.4	0.7	1.0	1.9	6.4	17.7	8.0	11.6	12.4	13.8
39 049	18140	1	Franklin	1 378	1 251 722	32	908.4	68.0	23.5	0.9	5.3	5.1	7.2	16.5	10.3	17.7	13.3	12.8
39 051	45780	2	Fulton	1 050	42 537	1 120	40.5	90.6	1.0	0.5	0.6	8.2	5.9	18.3	8.3	10.9	11.8	14.1
39 053	38580	6	Gallia	1 208	30 142	1 428	25.0	95.6	3.4	1.0	0.8	1.2	6.1	16.9	8.5	11.7	11.7	13.6
39 055	17460	1	Geauga	1 036	94 102	622	90.8	96.7	1.7	0.4	1.0	1.4	5.1	19.0	8.1	8.1	10.6	15.4
39 057	19380	2	Greene	1 072	164 427	390	153.4	86.2	8.4	0.9	4.0	2.7	5.5	15.2	12.8	13.2	11.0	13.3
39 059	15740	6	Guernsey	1 353	39 258	1 192	29.0	96.7	2.7	0.9	0.7	1.0	5.9	16.9	8.0	11.4	11.6	14.1
39 061	17140	1	Hamilton	1 051	807 598	74	768.4	68.6	27.2	0.6	2.9	2.9	6.6	16.6	9.7	14.6	11.7	13.4
39 063	22300	4	Hancock	1 376	75 573	730	54.9	91.4	2.5	0.5	2.2	5.0	6.1	16.5	9.5	12.9	11.8	13.7
39 065	...	6	Hardin	1 218	31 682	1 391	26.0	96.6	1.6	0.7	1.1	1.5	5.9	17.4	16.2	10.2	11.3	12.2
39 067	...	6	Harrison	1 042	15 450	2 076	14.8	96.5	3.1	0.6	0.4	0.8	5.2	15.8	7.2	9.8	11.2	14.2
39 069	...	6	Henry	1 077	27 816	1 498	25.8	91.6	1.0	0.6	0.6	7.3	6.2	17.7	7.9	11.1	11.8	13.7
39 071	...	6	Highland	1 432	43 026	1 111	30.0	96.9	2.3	0.8	0.5	0.9	6.0	18.2	7.9	11.3	12.4	13.7
39 073	18140	6	Hocking	1 091	28 491	1 472	26.1	97.9	1.2	0.9	0.4	0.9	5.6	17.5	7.7	10.8	12.4	14.3
39 075	...	7	Holmes	1 094	43 909	1 092	40.1	98.6	0.6	0.3	0.3	1.0	9.1	24.1	9.8	12.1	11.0	11.1
39 077	35940	4	Huron	1 273	58 469	882	45.9	92.2	1.9	0.7	0.6	6.1	6.1	18.6	8.3	11.4	12.3	14.0
39 079	27160	7	Jackson	1 089	32 596	1 369	29.9	97.4	1.2	1.2	0.5	1.0	6.2	17.9	7.9	12.1	12.7	13.5
39 081	48260	3	Jefferson	1 058	67 347	789	63.7	92.5	6.7	0.6	0.8	1.4	4.8	14.7	9.7	10.5	11.2	13.7
39 083	34540	4	Knox	1 361	61 061	858	44.9	96.9	1.6	0.6	1.0	1.4	6.2	17.1	11.7	10.8	11.1	13.2
39 085	17460	1	Lake	589	229 245	283	389.2	90.8	4.5	0.4	1.7	4.0	5.0	15.9	7.9	11.4	11.8	14.9
39 087	26580	2	Lawrence	1 174	61 109	857	52.1	96.3	3.0	0.7	0.6	0.9	5.6	16.9	8.0	11.8	12.8	14.1
39 089	18140	1	Licking	1 768	170 570	376	96.5	93.3	4.8	0.8	1.3	1.7	6.0	17.6	9.0	11.4	12.5	14.6
39 091	13340	4	Logan	1 187	45 386	1 067	38.2	95.7	3.1	0.7	1.1	1.4	6.0	18.0	7.9	11.0	12.1	14.2
39 093	17460	1	Lorain	1 272	305 147	223	239.9	81.4	9.4	0.8	1.5	9.2	5.6	17.1	8.8	11.0	12.5	14.5
39 095	45780	2	Lucas	883	433 689	163	491.2	72.3	20.8	0.8	2.2	6.7	6.4	16.9	10.0	13.5	11.9	13.2
39 097	18140	1	Madison	1 207	44 094	1 088	36.5	90.4	7.4	0.7	1.3	1.7	5.2	16.0	8.4	13.3	14.8	15.5
39 099	49660	2	Mahoning	1 066	231 900	282	217.5	78.4	16.3	0.7	1.2	5.4	5.1	15.3	8.8	11.2	11.4	13.6
39 101	32020	4	Marion	1 046	65 355	808	62.5	90.6	7.3	0.7	0.8	2.4	5.8	15.3	8.7	12.8	12.8	14.7
39 103	17460	1	Medina	1 091	176 395	363	161.7	95.4	1.9	0.5	1.5	1.9	5.3	18.3	7.7	10.5	13.0	15.7
39 105	...	6	Meigs	1 114	23 257	1 672	20.9	98.1	1.4	0.8	0.4	0.5	5.4	16.3	7.2	11.3	12.4	14.4
39 107	16380	7	Mercer	1 198	40 968	1 153	34.2	96.6	0.8	0.5	0.9	1.8	6.5	18.9	8.4	11.1	10.8	13.1
39 109	19380	2	Miami	1 053	104 224	571	99.0	94.6	3.3	0.6	1.7	1.5	5.7	17.5	7.7	11.5	12.3	14.0
39 111	...	8	Monroe	1 180	14 409	2 138	12.2	98.8	0.9	0.9	0.3	0.5	5.4	15.6	7.0	9.9	11.3	13.9
39 113	19380	2	Montgomery	1 195	532 258	126	445.4	74.2	22.4	0.8	2.7	2.6	6.2	16.3	9.5	13.1	11.5	13.5
39 115	...	6	Morgan	1 079	14 777	2 119	13.7	95.9	4.9	1.6	0.7	0.8	5.1	16.6	7.7	10.4	11.3	14.4
39 117	18140	1	Morrow	1 052	35 074	1 301	33.3	97.6	1.1	0.8	0.7	1.4	5.8	18.4	7.6	10.6	12.9	14.5
39 119	49780	4	Muskingum	1 721	86 290	666	50.1	94.2	5.8	0.9	0.8	1.0	6.0	17.3	9.2	11.6	11.8	13.7
39 121	...	6	Noble	1 031	14 326	2 147	13.9	95.9	3.1	0.8	0.3	0.6	4.7	13.5	6.4	9.3	8.8	13.3

1. CBSA = Core Based Statistical Area. See Appendix A for explanation. See Appendix B for list of metropolitan areas with component counties.
See Appendix A for definition.
2. County type code from the Economic Research Service of USDA Rural-Urban Continuum Codes. See Appendix A for definition.
3. Dry land or land partially or temporarily covered by water.
4. May be of any race.

Table B. States and Counties — **Population and Households**

STATE County	55 to 64 years	65 to 74 years	75 years and over	Percent female	2000	2010	2000–2010	2010–2015	Births	Deaths	Net migration	Number	Persons per house-hold	Family house-holds	Female family house-holder[1]	One per-son
	16	17	18	19	20	21	22	23	24	25	26	27	28	29	30	31
NORTH DAKOTA—Cont'd																
Ward	10.1	5.8	5.7	47.3	58 795	61 675	4.9	15.6	6 079	2 552	6 028	25 495	2.48	62.7	8.1	28.7
Wells	16.1	12.3	14.8	49.8	5 102	4 207	-17.5	-0.9	200	354	111	1 970	2.08	65.2	4.9	33.5
Williams	11.6	4.7	4.7	45.7	19 761	22 398	13.3	57.6	2 744	1 181	11 202	11 113	2.38	61.8	6.0	28.3
OHIO	13.6	8.7	6.8	51.1	11 353 140	11 536 725	1.6	0.7	728 569	586 523	-57 852	4 570 015	2.46	64.4	12.9	29.8
Adams	13.9	9.9	6.8	50.7	27 330	28 550	4.5	-1.8	1 782	1 692	-591	10 734	2.61	69.7	13.0	26.5
Allen	13.6	8.6	7.3	49.6	108 473	106 331	-2.0	-1.8	6 738	5 623	-2 976	40 191	2.52	67.2	14.7	27.9
Ashland	13.8	9.6	7.8	51.0	52 523	53 139	1.2	0.1	3 249	2 836	-399	20 339	2.51	70.0	9.4	25.1
Ashtabula	14.6	9.9	7.5	49.7	102 728	101 497	-1.2	-2.8	5 797	6 006	-2 593	38 933	2.49	65.2	12.1	28.9
Athens	10.7	6.8	4.6	50.1	62 223	64 773	4.1	1.7	2 894	2 491	711	22 208	2.49	54.7	9.0	32.4
Auglaize	14.2	8.8	8.1	50.4	46 611	45 949	-1.4	-0.2	2 813	2 492	-523	18 115	2.50	69.4	8.0	25.8
Belmont	15.6	10.2	8.7	49.0	70 226	70 400	0.2	-1.8	3 686	4 638	-190	28 007	2.35	65.2	9.4	30.8
Brown	13.9	9.7	7.0	50.4	42 285	44 846	6.1	-2.2	2 644	2 463	-1 204	16 587	2.65	73.3	12.7	22.5
Butler	12.6	7.6	5.6	51.0	332 807	368 130	10.6	2.2	23 815	16 030	304	134 934	2.67	69.6	12.0	24.2
Carroll	15.5	11.4	7.9	49.8	28 836	28 836	0.0	-3.6	1 453	1 583	-862	10 922	2.57	72.6	7.5	22.6
Champaign	13.7	9.9	6.8	50.2	38 890	40 097	3.1	-2.8	2 095	1 973	-1 211	15 163	2.56	72.9	11.7	23.0
Clark	14.0	10.0	7.9	51.5	144 742	138 333	-4.4	-1.7	8 393	8 695	-2 034	54 969	2.44	65.2	14.3	29.3
Clermont	14.1	8.5	5.5	50.7	177 977	197 363	10.9	2.3	12 340	8 353	573	74 187	2.67	71.7	10.3	23.7
Clinton	14.0	8.9	6.4	50.6	40 543	42 037	3.7	-0.3	2 659	2 239	-495	16 052	2.54	70.4	11.7	25.2
Columbiana	15.4	10.2	8.0	49.6	112 075	107 841	-3.8	-2.8	5 767	6 206	-2 441	42 184	2.44	67.8	11.6	26.8
Coshocton	14.5	10.0	7.8	50.5	36 655	36 901	0.7	-0.9	2 361	2 096	-531	14 561	2.49	68.8	11.0	27.0
Crawford	14.3	10.5	9.0	51.3	46 966	43 784	-6.8	-3.4	2 487	2 707	-1 164	17 625	2.41	66.8	10.1	28.6
Cuyahoga	14.1	8.6	7.8	52.4	1 393 978	1 280 109	-8.2	-1.9	78 646	71 237	-29 885	534 721	2.32	57.6	16.1	36.8
Darke	13.6	10.2	8.4	50.8	53 309	52 959	-0.7	-1.7	3 262	2 968	-1 176	20 929	2.48	67.5	9.9	28.8
Defiance	14.3	9.4	7.5	50.6	39 500	39 035	-1.2	-1.7	2 326	1 991	-1 020	15 332	2.48	70.5	11.7	23.7
Delaware	11.9	7.1	4.4	50.4	109 989	174 189	58.4	10.8	11 366	5 106	12 142	65 029	2.75	76.3	7.5	19.9
Erie	15.4	11.1	8.6	51.2	79 551	77 079	-3.1	-2.0	4 188	4 761	-1 020	31 998	2.34	64.2	11.7	30.4
Fairfield	12.8	8.6	5.9	50.2	122 759	146 152	19.1	3.6	8 757	6 081	2 349	54 581	2.66	72.3	10.9	23.1
Fayette	13.6	9.5	7.0	50.6	28 433	29 030	2.1	-1.2	1 864	1 805	-444	11 532	2.46	66.3	12.8	28.6
Franklin	11.3	6.4	4.5	51.3	1 068 978	1 163 545	8.8	7.6	97 094	46 358	38 692	474 683	2.47	58.4	14.3	32.4
Fulton	14.6	9.0	7.1	50.6	42 084	42 698	1.5	-0.4	2 622	2 111	-800	16 333	2.58	73.7	8.7	23.6
Gallia	14.2	9.9	7.5	50.7	31 069	30 934	-0.4	-2.6	1 989	1 881	-835	11 502	2.60	70.3	12.2	25.8
Geauga	15.6	10.4	7.7	50.6	90 895	93 410	2.8	0.7	4 838	4 049	-112	34 753	2.67	74.4	8.8	21.3
Greene	13.4	8.8	6.8	50.8	147 886	161 569	9.3	1.8	9 320	7 011	534	63 549	2.43	66.1	10.7	28.3
Guernsey	14.6	10.0	7.5	50.7	40 792	40 087	-1.7	-2.1	2 405	2 322	-802	15 564	2.52	68.2	11.9	26.7
Hamilton	13.2	7.6	6.5	51.9	845 303	802 374	-5.1	0.7	57 463	40 207	-10 260	329 062	2.39	59.1	15.1	34.3
Hancock	13.4	8.9	7.1	51.0	71 295	74 782	4.9	1.1	4 797	3 601	-461	30 795	2.38	65.2	10.9	29.4
Hardin	12.1	8.3	6.4	50.5	31 945	32 058	0.4	-1.2	2 017	1 645	-763	11 438	2.58	67.0	11.3	27.8
Harrison	16.9	11.1	8.5	50.7	15 856	15 864	0.1	-2.6	833	1 048	-171	6 333	2.44	69.3	10.1	26.1
Henry	14.1	9.1	8.5	50.8	29 210	28 215	-3.4	-1.4	1 722	1 406	-847	11 075	2.49	70.2	8.8	24.8
Highland	13.5	9.8	7.2	51.1	40 875	43 589	6.6	-1.3	2 827	2 440	-928	16 837	2.54	68.9	11.6	26.1
Hocking	14.5	10.4	6.8	50.3	28 241	29 375	4.0	-3.0	1 661	1 572	-823	11 426	2.49	69.8	10.8	26.4
Holmes	10.3	6.9	5.6	50.1	38 943	42 366	8.8	3.6	4 153	1 540	-1 040	12 516	3.38	81.0	6.4	17.1
Huron	13.7	9.0	6.5	50.8	59 487	59 626	0.2	-1.9	3 829	3 014	-1 973	22 507	2.59	70.4	12.0	23.9
Jackson	14.0	9.3	6.4	50.7	32 641	33 225	1.8	-1.9	2 249	2 093	-771	13 204	2.47	68.0	13.2	27.5
Jefferson	15.9	10.6	8.9	51.5	73 894	69 709	-5.7	-3.4	3 449	4 991	-621	28 176	2.35	65.3	11.9	29.9
Knox	13.6	9.4	7.0	51.0	54 500	60 930	11.8	0.2	3 770	3 119	-495	22 642	2.54	68.2	9.8	25.9
Lake	15.1	10.0	7.9	51.2	227 511	230 038	1.1	-0.3	11 963	12 285	-451	94 089	2.41	65.4	10.7	29.5
Lawrence	13.8	10.0	7.1	51.1	62 319	62 450	0.2	-2.1	3 672	3 477	-1 413	23 622	2.60	67.4	13.7	28.2
Licking	13.5	9.1	6.1	51.0	145 491	166 480	14.4	2.5	10 313	7 831	1 653	64 146	2.56	69.9	10.9	25.1
Logan	14.4	9.6	6.9	50.7	46 005	45 858	-0.3	-1.0	2 877	2 474	-856	18 471	2.44	69.9	12.4	24.3
Lorain	14.1	9.3	7.0	50.7	284 664	301 356	5.9	1.3	17 751	15 121	925	117 134	2.50	68.4	13.8	26.9
Lucas	13.5	8.2	6.4	51.5	455 054	441 815	-2.9	-1.8	29 792	22 739	-14 888	178 121	2.40	60.4	15.9	32.9
Madison	12.9	8.1	5.8	45.5	40 213	43 430	8.0	1.5	2 225	2 025	478	14 676	2.59	70.4	11.2	25.5
Mahoning	15.4	9.9	9.2	51.3	257 555	238 823	-7.3	-2.9	12 530	15 915	-3 022	97 624	2.34	62.1	15.0	33.3
Marion	13.9	9.1	6.9	46.9	66 217	66 501	0.4	-1.7	4 040	3 616	-1 471	24 586	2.42	68.5	13.0	26.6
Medina	14.0	9.3	6.2	50.6	151 095	172 333	14.1	2.4	9 315	7 275	1 812	65 950	2.62	73.0	9.0	22.6
Meigs	15.0	10.3	7.7	50.9	23 072	23 771	3.0	-2.2	1 285	1 366	-402	9 486	2.46	69.0	10.9	26.0
Mercer	14.3	8.8	8.1	49.8	40 924	40 814	-0.3	0.4	2 879	2 123	-658	15 923	2.53	70.0	7.6	25.6
Miami	14.0	10.0	7.3	50.6	98 868	102 506	3.7	1.7	6 132	5 230	834	41 169	2.48	67.6	10.3	27.1
Monroe	15.3	12.5	9.2	49.7	15 180	14 642	-3.5	-1.6	801	917	-161	6 056	2.38	68.5	9.2	27.2
Montgomery	13.4	9.0	7.6	51.9	559 062	535 141	-4.3	-0.5	35 091	30 084	-7 266	222 673	2.32	60.2	15.2	34.5
Morgan	14.7	10.9	8.8	50.2	14 897	15 048	1.0	-1.8	740	829	-157	6 056	2.44	72.1	11.2	24.3
Morrow	14.4	9.3	6.5	49.7	31 628	34 827	10.1	0.7	2 017	1 622	-152	12 640	2.74	73.7	9.7	21.4
Muskingum	13.7	9.3	7.4	51.6	84 585	86 074	1.8	0.3	5 442	4 922	-242	34 160	2.46	67.0	13.8	27.5
Noble	20.2	14.8	8.9	41.7	14 058	14 645	4.2	-2.2	757	647	-409	4 916	2.44	68.7	7.9	28.9

1. No spouse present.

Table B. States and Counties — **Population, Vital Statistics, Medicare, and Crime**

STATE County	Persons in group quarters, 2015	Daytime population, 2010–2014 Number	Daytime population, 2010–2014 Employ-ment/resi-dence ratio	Births, 2015 Total	Births, 2015 Rate[1]	Deaths, 2015 Number	Deaths, 2015 Rate[1]	Persons under 65 with no health insurance, 2014 Number	Persons under 65 with no health insurance, 2014 Percent	Medicare, 2015 Total Beneficiaries	Medicare, 2015 Enrolled in Original Medicare	Medicare, 2015 Enrolled in Medicare Advantage	Serious crimes known to police,[2] 2014 Total Number	Serious crimes known to police,[2] 2014 Total Rate[3]
	32	33	34	35	36	37	38	39	40	41	42	43	44	45
NORTH DAKOTA—Cont'd														
Ward	3 410	68 189	1.06	1 267	18.0	477	6.8	5 438	9.2	8 824	7 666	1 158	1 678	2 404
Wells	114	4 313	1.05	35	8.4	42	10.1	286	9.4	1 197	1 141	56	47	1 113
Williams	546	35 337	1.56	699	20.7	214	6.3	2 327	8.0	3 348	3 310	38	1 787	5 618
OHIO	312 145	11 572 238	1.00	139 884	12.1	111 722	9.6	947 102	9.9	2 047 074	1 201 461	845 613	357 558	3 084
Adams	338	25 697	0.73	325	11.6	311	11.1	2 949	12.7	6 379	4 342	2 037	455	1 623
Allen	5 929	112 323	1.15	1 282	12.2	1 057	10.1	8 343	10.0	19 926	14 592	5 334	3 862	3 672
Ashland	2 230	49 516	0.84	626	11.8	543	10.2	5 187	12.3	9 677	5 791	3 886	841	1 589
Ashtabula	3 425	92 998	0.82	1 084	11.0	1 098	11.1	8 975	11.3	21 013	15 335	5 678	NA	NA
Athens	9 958	65 726	1.03	541	8.3	463	7.1	5 388	11.1	9 792	6 337	3 455	1 247	1 958
Auglaize	525	43 729	0.90	540	11.8	475	10.4	3 026	8.0	10 221	7 467	2 754	384	1 111
Belmont	3 836	63 843	0.79	720	10.4	812	11.7	5 371	10.1	14 055	6 948	7 107	681	1 145
Brown	575	36 215	0.54	479	10.9	474	10.8	3 900	10.7	7 856	4 627	3 229	559	1 275
Butler	11 441	349 467	0.87	4 493	12.0	3 190	8.5	31 205	9.9	57 391	32 842	24 549	10 943	3 059
Carroll	405	23 653	0.60	270	9.6	324	11.6	2 533	11.2	4 318	2 281	2 037	246	984
Champaign	781	33 932	0.67	372	9.5	383	9.8	3 242	10.1	7 000	3 805	3 195	751	1 908
Clark	2 861	128 177	0.84	1 571	11.5	1 633	12.0	11 922	10.8	28 539	14 360	14 179	6 145	4 539
Clermont	1 717	162 371	0.61	2 303	11.4	1 620	8.0	15 718	9.1	26 193	14 342	11 851	5 703	2 835
Clinton	1 158	42 059	1.01	510	12.2	418	10.0	3 333	9.7	8 294	5 123	3 171	832	2 203
Columbiana	3 952	93 336	0.71	1 105	10.5	1 174	11.2	8 991	10.8	23 280	14 276	9 004	617	750
Coshocton	428	34 437	0.84	458	12.5	376	10.3	3 658	12.3	7 054	5 015	2 039	561	1 525
Crawford	579	39 685	0.81	471	11.1	507	12.0	3 618	10.7	10 058	7 069	2 989	1 645	4 309
Cuyahoga	29 887	1 401 095	1.24	15 082	12.0	13 150	10.5	103 272	10.0	229 248	131 711	97 537	38 478	3 569
Darke	606	48 121	0.81	638	12.2	576	11.0	4 274	10.1	9 917	7 011	2 906	678	1 349
Defiance	749	37 322	0.92	428	11.1	390	10.1	3 107	9.9	8 328	6 385	1 943	643	1 673
Delaware	2 291	164 588	0.81	2 245	11.7	1 045	5.5	8 822	5.3	17 769	9 644	8 125	2 547	1 620
Erie	1 678	76 527	1.00	816	10.8	891	11.8	5 551	9.2	18 178	13 698	4 480	1 945	2 838
Fairfield	3 324	123 100	0.64	1 713	11.4	1 224	8.1	10 053	8.0	23 834	12 136	11 698	3 701	2 845
Fayette	593	29 318	1.04	343	12.0	318	11.1	2 603	11.0	5 172	2 843	2 329	1 181	4 103
Franklin	27 778	1 311 504	1.19	19 099	15.4	9 158	7.4	119 761	11.2	158 467	83 314	75 153	49 469	4 146
Fulton	391	40 363	0.89	532	12.5	406	9.5	3 000	8.5	8 550	5 744	2 806	469	1 229
Gallia	819	31 904	1.10	380	12.6	350	11.6	2 945	12.1	6 930	5 068	1 862	1 064	3 497
Geauga	864	83 644	0.77	931	9.9	770	8.2	7 781	10.1	15 184	9 315	5 869	703	747
Greene	8 494	168 499	1.07	1 799	10.9	1 394	8.5	12 090	9.3	19 949	11 534	8 415	3 898	2 439
Guernsey	510	39 329	0.97	461	11.7	441	11.2	3 623	11.2	8 760	5 959	2 801	693	1 771
Hamilton	20 793	925 280	1.33	10 948	13.6	7 774	9.6	68 434	10.1	140 120	81 009	59 111	34 335	4 462
Hancock	1 582	84 037	1.24	937	12.4	671	8.9	5 260	8.5	12 982	9 347	3 635	1 786	2 439
Hardin	2 145	28 983	0.78	387	12.2	316	10.0	2 478	9.9	5 598	4 112	1 486	690	2 185
Harrison	232	13 688	0.70	160	10.3	206	13.3	1 315	10.6	3 677	2 252	1 425	107	723
Henry	346	25 501	0.80	311	11.2	250	9.0	1 962	8.6	5 430	4 006	1 424	448	1 670
Highland	484	38 835	0.72	554	12.9	461	10.7	4 138	11.7	7 618	5 071	2 547	835	1 941
Hocking	312	24 925	0.65	313	10.9	294	10.3	2 492	10.5	5 473	3 806	1 667	444	1 557
Holmes	765	45 661	1.14	778	17.7	316	7.2	8 701	22.9	3 617	1 961	1 656	326	747
Huron	578	55 644	0.86	748	12.8	549	9.4	5 287	10.7	12 887	9 958	2 929	NA	NA
Jackson	325	31 476	0.88	434	13.3	380	11.6	3 197	11.7	6 263	4 576	1 687	852	2 604
Jefferson	2 337	64 237	0.85	693	10.3	943	14.0	5 017	9.5	16 707	10 567	6 140	NA	NA
Knox	3 485	56 784	0.84	715	11.7	578	9.5	4 849	10.1	10 971	7 084	3 887	1 265	2 080
Lake	2 815	210 509	0.83	2 276	9.9	2 346	10.2	17 424	9.4	45 583	27 131	18 452	NA	NA
Lawrence	669	51 570	0.56	690	11.2	697	11.4	5 241	10.3	13 683	10 586	3 097	1 525	2 503
Licking	3 403	148 713	0.76	1 982	11.7	1 525	9.0	12 081	8.6	28 216	16 058	12 158	4 408	3 136
Logan	450	44 889	0.97	556	12.2	484	10.6	4 023	10.7	9 094	6 279	2 815	1 113	2 572
Lorain	8 966	273 387	0.78	3 385	11.1	2 843	9.3	21 774	8.8	54 315	35 078	19 237	NA	NA
Lucas	10 123	456 528	1.10	5 645	13.0	4 344	10.0	35 243	9.7	75 011	44 425	30 586	11 822	2 860
Madison	5 227	41 099	0.88	433	9.8	364	8.3	3 117	9.5	7 667	3 646	4 021	796	1 853
Mahoning	7 837	236 764	1.01	2 417	10.4	2 948	12.7	18 540	10.1	51 427	25 777	25 650	8 153	3 583
Marion	6 047	66 569	1.02	746	11.4	690	10.5	5 124	10.3	13 730	8 984	4 746	2 868	4 355
Medina	1 198	147 818	0.70	1 807	10.3	1 398	7.9	10 677	7.2	29 214	16 690	12 524	1 736	988
Meigs	212	19 190	0.48	231	9.9	256	11.0	2 220	11.7	4 447	3 327	1 120	334	1 490
Mercer	439	38 493	0.89	579	14.1	392	9.6	2 966	8.8	7 326	5 199	2 127	609	1 491
Miami	1 055	97 953	0.89	1 211	11.6	968	9.3	7 738	9.1	20 888	12 795	8 093	2 908	2 933
Monroe	165	14 010	0.89	150	10.4	193	13.4	1 153	10.2	3 268	1 665	1 603	66	540
Montgomery	14 951	555 002	1.09	6 662	12.5	5 715	10.7	46 961	10.8	107 411	55 713	51 698	20 599	3 909
Morgan	188	12 574	0.58	125	8.5	137	9.3	1 385	11.7	2 755	1 792	963	250	1 679
Morrow	366	26 833	0.48	373	10.6	313	8.9	3 015	10.3	4 825	2 980	1 845	355	1 144
Muskingum	1 741	85 488	0.99	1 023	11.9	938	10.9	7 503	10.7	19 521	13 521	6 000	2 776	3 326
Noble	2 684	13 954	0.86	142	9.9	122	8.5	1 030	11.0	1 825	1 181	644	NA	NA

1. Per 1,000 estimated resident population.   2. Data for serious crimes have not been adjusted for underreporting; this may affect comparability between geographic areas and over time.
3. Per 100,000 population estimated by the FBI.

Table B. States and Counties — Crime, Education, Money Income, and Poverty

STATE County	Serious crimes known to police, 2014 (cont.)[1] Rate[2] Violent	Property	Education — School enrollment and attainment, 2010–2014 — Enrollment[3] Total	Percent private	Attainment[4] (percent) High school graduate or less	Bachelor's degree or more	Local government expenditures,[5] 2012–2013 Total current spending (mil dol)	Current spending per student (dollars)	Money income, 2010–2014 Per capita income[6] (dollars)	Households Median income (dollars)	Mean income (dollars)	Percent with income of $200,000 or more	Income and poverty, 2014 Median household income (dollars)	Percent below poverty level All persons	Children under 18 years	Children 5 to 17 years in families
	46	47	48	49	50	51	52	53	54	55	56	57	58	59	60	61
NORTH DAKOTA—Cont'd																
Ward	271	2 133	15 739	8.8	36.2	25.3	106.3	11 118	29 564	59 301	73 857	3.4	62 526	8.5	10.6	9.4
Wells	47	1 066	671	8.9	49.9	19.7	7.4	13 286	29 980	44 770	62 537	2.9	51 470	10.9	13.6	11.9
Williams	516	5 103	5 556	8.0	39.8	19.1	51.1	12 417	41 984	82 823	104 811	8.7	86 354	6.9	9.0	8.6
OHIO	285	2 799	3 007 872	18.0	45.6	25.6	19 171.9	11 197	26 520	48 849	65 491	3.2	49 349	15.8	22.7	20.8
Adams	96	1 527	6 341	7.0	67.1	9.8	45.4	9 301	17 695	34 733	45 040	0.5	34 116	24.8	33.3	31.5
Allen	386	3 286	28 660	17.8	51.4	17.2	161.7	11 172	22 585	43 648	57 005	2.0	43 602	18.0	24.9	24.2
Ashland	68	1 521	13 975	31.0	56.9	19.7	91.7	10 664	22 441	47 034	58 215	1.5	47 369	14.6	21.0	19.4
Ashtabula	NA	NA	23 438	12.3	59.4	13.4	153.9	10 704	20 284	40 304	50 374	0.8	39 757	21.5	32.1	28.1
Athens	99	1 859	28 458	4.4	42.2	28.8	99.1	13 355	17 069	33 773	46 547	1.2	34 216	29.9	31.4	27.5
Auglaize	52	1 059	11 213	10.2	50.5	18.2	79.9	10 137	25 033	52 773	62 998	1.4	52 650	8.3	12.1	11.3
Belmont	118	1 027	14 023	12.3	55.1	14.9	82.0	9 585	23 285	43 045	55 596	1.8	41 983	16.1	24.5	21.1
Brown	57	1 218	10 208	6.3	64.9	11.4	74.1	10 296	22 088	44 899	57 066	2.0	46 484	15.0	23.0	22.2
Butler	223	2 835	106 127	13.8	44.7	28.1	617.7	10 950	27 394	56 998	73 643	3.9	58 558	14.4	20.3	19.2
Carroll	80	904	6 482	9.8	62.7	10.6	31.5	9 317	22 359	45 660	56 996	2.0	46 177	13.5	21.4	19.0
Champaign	109	1 799	9 744	18.9	56.7	16.0	75.7	10 456	23 573	49 840	60 340	1.6	50 302	11.3	17.7	16.1
Clark	369	4 171	33 975	18.3	50.2	18.2	217.1	10 699	22 941	43 011	56 194	1.5	42 029	18.2	27.6	24.9
Clermont	106	2 729	49 656	18.5	46.1	26.2	266.2	9 836	28 708	60 552	75 606	4.1	62 158	11.2	15.4	14.5
Clinton	90	2 113	10 815	15.9	55.1	15.2	70.6	8 699	22 828	45 909	58 250	1.8	49 453	13.7	20.4	20.2
Columbiana	51	699	23 013	11.0	59.7	13.6	156.2	10 881	22 573	43 707	55 886	1.6	42 645	15.9	23.5	21.5
Coshocton	92	1 433	7 917	15.5	64.8	12.1	52.5	10 680	20 799	41 569	51 654	0.9	41 547	18.1	27.4	25.5
Crawford	144	4 165	9 738	13.4	57.5	12.6	67.3	10 051	21 938	41 377	52 431	0.8	39 881	15.4	24.7	23.0
Cuyahoga	561	3 008	324 356	25.8	40.6	30.3	2 288.5	14 915	27 892	44 203	64 370	3.8	44 138	19.6	30.0	28.1
Darke	117	1 231	12 384	10.6	62.6	11.6	82.2	9 613	22 582	43 323	55 355	1.3	46 610	12.2	17.0	15.2
Defiance	104	1 569	9 850	21.6	55.2	16.3	59.0	9 263	23 539	48 853	58 751	1.7	53 026	11.7	18.1	15.7
Delaware	82	1 538	53 598	21.9	24.0	51.1	282.3	10 095	41 357	91 936	114 403	11.8	97 802	4.8	5.1	4.6
Erie	133	2 705	17 631	14.2	49.4	21.1	173.3	14 711	26 909	48 204	63 409	2.6	49 234	13.9	22.3	20.2
Fairfield	153	2 692	39 985	16.3	42.8	26.2	235.3	9 689	28 099	60 704	74 690	3.6	59 921	9.6	13.9	12.7
Fayette	205	3 898	6 799	8.7	61.7	13.8	42.2	9 039	21 033	40 576	51 778	1.5	44 947	15.8	25.3	23.6
Franklin	422	3 724	333 461	16.8	35.8	36.7	2 255.2	13 463	28 807	51 890	70 522	4.2	53 164	17.3	24.6	23.6
Fulton	84	1 145	11 090	12.4	51.6	16.7	113.9	14 887	26 070	52 872	67 389	2.0	54 666	10.5	14.8	13.2
Gallia	151	3 346	7 493	12.3	61.2	14.7	60.6	13 851	21 049	37 494	53 946	1.5	36 675	26.1	37.9	33.0
Geauga	30	717	23 397	26.6	37.1	36.0	140.3	12 172	35 407	70 487	94 494	8.0	72 264	7.8	11.5	10.2
Greene	114	2 325	50 201	20.8	33.5	36.9	236.3	11 076	30 629	58 775	76 826	4.9	59 382	13.2	18.1	17.1
Guernsey	135	1 636	8 842	14.5	58.2	13.2	58.3	12 056	21 559	40 420	53 073	1.0	41 940	17.2	26.4	24.7
Hamilton	457	4 005	214 884	24.5	38.0	34.3	1 333.6	13 313	30 062	48 927	71 440	5.0	48 973	17.6	24.4	22.9
Hancock	117	2 321	19 488	23.7	45.1	24.9	141.8	10 351	26 612	50 166	64 032	3.2	51 498	12.7	18.2	16.7
Hardin	95	2 090	9 607	29.8	62.0	14.5	44.2	10 239	20 011	42 670	53 386	0.9	45 195	19.0	24.8	21.9
Harrison	203	521	3 114	7.6	62.1	9.5	15.7	10 087	22 180	41 819	54 033	1.3	42 582	16.9	25.6	23.0
Henry	63	1 607	7 154	13.1	53.7	14.8	64.0	14 373	24 604	52 526	61 823	1.7	53 645	10.2	15.0	14.3
Highland	67	1 873	10 358	8.3	61.2	11.2	69.1	9 119	19 587	39 855	49 149	0.8	41 611	19.3	27.6	25.3
Hocking	102	1 456	7 148	9.6	57.6	13.7	39.6	9 928	21 253	42 792	53 398	1.0	42 374	17.5	26.1	23.7
Holmes	18	728	9 371	39.5	77.8	7.8	41.5	9 763	17 716	47 625	58 906	1.9	50 069	12.4	18.5	17.9
Huron	NA	NA	14 824	14.7	59.8	13.1	107.2	9 655	22 666	49 315	58 912	1.3	47 824	13.4	19.9	18.4
Jackson	113	2 491	7 629	12.8	59.9	17.3	49.4	9 497	20 250	37 393	49 363	1.1	41 161	20.0	30.2	27.4
Jefferson	NA	NA	15 922	24.7	53.7	15.2	99.3	10 740	22 591	40 816	53 388	1.5	40 148	20.0	31.1	27.3
Knox	112	1 968	15 502	32.3	53.3	21.4	88.4	11 374	23 926	48 953	62 534	2.4	46 908	15.1	21.4	20.3
Lake	NA	NA	54 474	18.1	42.5	26.0	380.8	11 682	29 556	56 809	71 065	3.1	58 697	8.9	13.4	12.1
Lawrence	141	2 362	14 505	9.5	58.9	14.8	125.1	12 805	21 760	42 981	54 252	1.3	41 608	17.5	27.4	25.6
Licking	125	3 010	44 647	18.3	48.3	22.6	287.8	11 008	27 082	55 777	69 859	2.9	57 308	13.5	20.6	18.7
Logan	102	2 470	10 439	12.8	62.0	14.8	82.1	12 396	23 897	48 416	59 002	1.6	50 753	17.0	27.2	22.5
Lorain	NA	NA	79 615	19.1	45.2	22.3	452.7	10 683	26 487	52 610	67 033	2.8	52 331	14.7	21.7	19.3
Lucas	782	2 078	119 530	18.4	43.5	24.2	687.5	13 243	24 683	41 751	58 921	2.8	42 344	20.7	29.4	25.1
Madison	70	1 784	10 271	15.1	54.7	15.7	74.8	11 340	23 994	54 331	69 322	3.2	52 996	12.6	17.1	15.6
Mahoning	281	3 302	57 624	14.9	49.9	21.5	380.1	12 511	23 628	41 350	55 344	2.0	41 316	18.9	28.7	25.2
Marion	200	4 154	14 555	9.6	56.7	12.5	127.2	13 902	20 986	42 904	55 496	1.2	42 240	21.3	27.3	25.4
Medina	47	941	45 038	15.6	39.2	29.9	267.2	9 751	31 291	66 296	81 455	4.6	68 405	7.0	9.6	8.3
Meigs	129	1 361	4 952	11.1	61.3	11.9	35.7	10 592	19 097	35 970	47 023	0.4	38 081	22.6	32.7	29.3
Mercer	95	1 395	9 731	6.7	57.0	15.9	88.2	10 825	24 362	52 033	62 314	1.8	52 606	8.9	11.7	10.6
Miami	102	2 831	25 316	12.1	49.8	19.7	173.4	11 320	25 654	51 847	62 943	1.8	51 868	10.6	15.7	14.8
Monroe	57	483	2 820	12.8	64.5	10.3	26.8	10 815	22 337	41 394	52 960	1.3	40 646	15.7	23.0	21.6
Montgomery	362	3 546	146 434	21.5	40.7	24.8	841.7	12 128	25 171	43 281	58 890	2.4	42 994	19.7	30.3	27.3
Morgan	262	1 417	3 256	7.6	60.4	10.7	21.0	10 273	21 010	38 696	51 918	1.4	37 923	18.1	27.6	25.3
Morrow	58	1 086	8 601	13.3	58.6	13.8	50.0	9 512	22 825	51 444	62 033	0.9	49 846	12.1	21.1	19.8
Muskingum	182	3 144	21 507	13.6	57.8	14.6	172.2	11 901	20 887	40 937	51 491	1.1	41 814	19.1	27.2	24.4
Noble	NA	NA	2 232	7.9	70.9	9.5	18.3	10 876	20 719	37 126	49 011	0.9	43 953	16.3	20.0	18.6

1. Data for serious crimes have not been adjusted for underreporting; this may affect comparability between geographic areas and over time.　2. Per 100,000 population estimated by the FBI.
3. All persons 3 years old and over enrolled in nursery school through college.　4. Persons 25 years old and over.　5. Elementary and secondary education expenditures.
6. Based on population estimated by the American Community Survey, 2010–2014.

Table B. States and Counties — **Personal Income**

	Personal income, 2014					Supplements to wages and salaries; employer contributions (mil dol)					Earnings, 2014	Contributions for government social insurance (mil dol)	
STATE County	Total (mil dol)	Percent change, 2013–2014	Per capita[1] Dollars	Per capita[1] Rank	Wages and salaries (mil dol)	Pension and insurance	Government social insurance	Proprietors' income (mil dol)	Dividends, interest, and rent (mil dol)	Personal transfer receipts (mil dol)	Total (mil dol)	From employee and self-employed	From employer
	62	63	64	65	66	67	68	69	70	71	72	73	74
NORTH DAKOTA—Cont'd													
Ward	3 887	4.9	56 024	197	2 145	313	185	296	727	414	2 939	168	185
Wells	215	-6.8	51 325	318	67	10	7	38	65	44	122	7	7
Williams	3 905	13.9	121 538	4	3 499	259	246	200	458	172	4 203	240	246
OHIO	489 695	3.8	42 236	X	255 254	45 257	18 664	39 285	74 485	98 057	358 460	20 335	18 664
Adams	798	3.7	28 374	2 885	218	55	15	81	93	291	369	24	15
Allen	3 799	2.9	36 169	1 752	2 197	428	167	294	514	931	3 086	177	167
Ashland	1 803	3.7	33 995	2 114	708	140	54	142	242	413	1 045	63	54
Ashtabula	3 314	3.6	33 412	2 213	1 171	249	92	182	404	1 042	1 694	107	92
Athens	2 005	4.4	30 977	2 588	887	277	47	106	315	516	1 317	55	47
Auglaize	1 900	4.0	41 443	1 014	860	161	65	132	314	347	1 217	69	65
Belmont	2 638	4.8	37 973	1 457	1 037	188	73	225	341	655	1 522	95	73
Brown	1 433	3.9	32 478	2 376	315	78	23	121	161	408	537	35	23
Butler	15 295	4.5	40 878	1 076	7 068	1 223	521	1 329	1 955	2 792	10 142	579	521
Carroll	1 002	3.8	35 541	1 849	285	53	22	111	121	251	471	30	22
Champaign	1 443	1.1	36 883	1 619	452	90	33	124	166	327	699	42	33
Clark	4 995	3.7	36 580	1 672	1 948	379	147	281	721	1 374	2 755	171	147
Clermont	8 667	4.8	43 002	849	2 559	432	191	705	1 046	1 487	3 887	236	191
Clinton	1 494	2.4	35 713	1 820	687	139	53	164	209	351	1 043	59	53
Columbiana	3 581	3.6	33 885	2 131	1 183	248	91	248	432	1 002	1 770	112	91
Coshocton	1 257	3.6	34 421	2 045	449	94	35	165	151	343	743	45	35
Crawford	1 453	1.5	34 198	2 080	511	109	39	97	200	420	757	48	39
Cuyahoga	61 128	3.6	48 521	455	40 682	6 551	2 960	6 577	11 111	11 970	56 769	3 194	2 960
Darke	2 014	4.1	38 586	1 379	701	138	56	286	273	433	1 180	66	56
Defiance	1 417	4.1	36 798	1 633	728	127	56	152	166	326	1 063	61	56
Delaware	12 064	4.8	63 790	95	4 632	676	326	1 027	1 623	968	6 661	379	326
Erie	3 261	3.2	43 003	848	1 412	280	109	394	511	717	2 196	126	109
Fairfield	6 064	3.9	40 324	1 136	1 595	314	118	395	748	1 099	2 421	146	118
Fayette	1 013	1.6	35 189	1 905	407	78	31	106	131	279	622	36	31
Franklin	55 608	4.5	45 158	664	39 860	7 065	2 749	4 898	8 221	8 866	54 572	2 825	2 749
Fulton	1 656	2.7	38 885	1 333	715	137	55	168	205	319	1 075	62	55
Gallia	1 038	1.7	34 163	2 088	432	106	32	71	151	350	642	38	32
Geauga	5 285	3.9	56 043	196	1 470	259	114	362	1 083	649	2 205	131	114
Greene	7 178	4.0	43 817	776	3 994	932	305	458	1 276	1 226	5 689	298	305
Guernsey	1 364	3.9	34 453	2 036	646	129	48	95	165	406	918	56	48
Hamilton	41 323	4.2	51 229	322	30 774	4 574	2 190	3 711	8 810	6 737	41 250	2 341	2 190
Hancock	3 286	4.0	43 624	791	2 137	352	157	318	450	547	2 964	171	157
Hardin	1 033	3.1	32 491	2 373	330	73	26	118	123	246	546	29	26
Harrison	535	5.4	34 434	2 041	182	38	14	22	62	150	255	17	14
Henry	1 060	0.4	37 953	1 462	451	94	35	100	142	237	681	37	35
Highland	1 289	2.6	29 955	2 721	369	91	27	91	160	401	578	35	27
Hocking	934	3.6	32 502	2 370	228	58	16	53	110	277	355	22	16
Holmes	1 439	6.8	32 778	2 318	679	124	55	425	186	203	1 284	66	55
Huron	2 096	2.1	35 698	1 828	910	170	81	155	276	502	1 316	80	81
Jackson	1 071	3.9	32 701	2 334	391	83	30	68	142	334	572	36	30
Jefferson	2 334	2.6	34 481	2 031	877	181	70	124	293	739	1 252	81	70
Knox	2 311	3.6	37 782	1 486	897	167	69	179	381	538	1 311	79	69
Lake	10 088	3.4	44 010	761	4 357	804	327	487	1 356	1 911	5 975	353	327
Lawrence	2 027	2.5	32 892	2 298	466	108	35	69	218	678	678	47	35
Licking	6 748	4.0	39 835	1 202	2 200	413	165	382	906	1 308	3 159	188	165
Logan	1 768	2.7	38 860	1 340	875	149	66	192	206	375	1 282	76	66
Lorain	12 139	3.9	39 901	1 192	4 360	843	328	509	1 560	2 577	6 039	363	328
Lucas	17 717	4.2	40 702	1 099	9 981	1 813	745	1 600	2 431	4 127	14 140	793	745
Madison	1 604	1.2	36 527	1 684	651	136	46	149	212	298	982	52	46
Mahoning	9 323	3.4	39 978	1 178	3 931	758	300	982	1 427	2 437	5 971	357	300
Marion	2 200	2.8	33 474	2 200	987	217	74	204	265	606	1 482	84	74
Medina	8 267	4.1	46 966	524	2 579	459	195	462	1 046	1 201	3 696	222	195
Meigs	676	3.1	28 963	2 834	123	32	9	31	73	232	195	15	9
Mercer	1 762	5.2	43 158	829	747	149	55	258	261	289	1 209	62	55
Miami	4 187	3.4	40 301	1 139	1 677	310	127	201	608	836	2 316	139	127
Monroe	441	4.0	30 453	2 657	125	28	9	32	62	137	195	14	9
Montgomery	21 778	3.7	40 851	1 083	12 047	2 135	910	1 446	3 864	4 903	16 538	951	910
Morgan	444	5.8	29 880	2 734	97	23	7	32	55	142	159	11	7
Morrow	1 155	2.3	32 869	2 303	195	49	13	73	126	275	330	21	13
Muskingum	3 031	3.5	35 319	1 891	1 317	262	97	157	392	834	1 833	111	97
Noble	387	2.4	26 913	2 988	134	34	9	24	49	98	202	11	9

1. Based on the resident population estimated as of July 1 of the year shown.

Table B. States and Counties — Earnings, Social Security, and Housing

STATE County	Farm	Mining	Construction	Manu-facturing	Information: professional, scientific, technical services	Retail trade	Finance, insurance, real estate and leasing	Health care and social assistance	Govern-ment	Social Security beneficiaries, December 2014 Number	Rate[1]	Supplemental Security Income recipients, December 2014	Housing units, 2015 Total	Percent change, 2010–2014
	75	76	77	78	79	80	81	82	83	84	85	86	87	88
NORTH DAKOTA—Cont'd														
Ward	1.0	9.2	10.9	1.4	4.8	7.5	6.0	10.7	25.4	9 225	133	567	32 561	21.8
Wells	24.4	D	5.4	1.7	1.3	D	5.5	D	10.5	1 210	289	46	2 505	1.0
Williams	1.1	42.3	12.5	1.0	4.0	3.2	5.7	2.2	3.1	3 545	110	197	18 598	77.7
OHIO	0.6	0.6	5.3	14.6	9.1	6.0	8.0	12.9	15.3	2 267 508	196	313 259	5 156 307	0.6
Adams	2.3	0.9	8.3	15.4	3.1	9.5	3.6	9.7	22.5	6 660	237	1 784	12 797	-1.4
Allen	0.8	0.1	4.8	24.4	3.8	6.9	3.5	18.2	13.1	21 960	209	3 200	44 799	-0.4
Ashland	1.6	0.3	7.0	20.0	7.2	7.0	3.1	D	14.4	11 250	212	765	22 087	-0.2
Ashtabula	0.6	1.3	5.5	27.1	3.6	6.9	3.2	14.6	16.1	23 045	232	3 181	45 828	-0.6
Athens	0.2	D	3.7	D	4.4	6.8	3.4	12.7	51.3	9 385	145	2 664	26 204	-0.7
Auglaize	4.6	D	5.1	44.3	3.0	5.2	2.7	8.3	11.1	9 515	207	541	19 665	0.4
Belmont	0.3	19.2	D	3.8	D	9.6	9.2	10.9	14.6	16 780	242	2 116	32 072	-1.2
Brown	1.3	D	D	8.5	3.0	7.0	3.7	D	21.3	10 465	237	1 367	19 409	0.6
Butler	0.2	0.2	7.1	17.7	3.9	7.7	9.9	10.5	13.0	64 575	173	7 258	149 891	1.1
Carroll	3.2	4.7	17.9	17.9	2.9	6.6	2.7	5.8	11.5	6 725	238	494	13 572	-0.9
Champaign	5.1	D	5.2	36.7	D	5.3	3.4	D	15.7	8 450	216	615	16 664	-0.5
Clark	0.6	0.3	3.9	15.7	3.9	6.7	9.1	14.2	15.9	30 660	225	4 055	61 102	-0.5
Clermont	0.2	D	7.6	11.3	10.2	8.7	10.8	9.0	12.6	37 470	186	2 757	82 250	2.0
Clinton	2.2	D	3.0	22.6	3.4	6.2	5.0	D	14.1	8 565	205	1 049	18 034	-0.5
Columbiana	2.0	1.2	6.0	19.3	2.6	9.9	3.6	14.1	18.0	24 940	236	3 218	46 584	-1.1
Coshocton	3.1	4.7	5.6	24.5	D	6.9	3.2	10.5	12.1	8 485	232	916	16 322	-1.3
Crawford	3.0	D	4.9	23.9	4.4	6.5	6.6	D	15.0	10 960	258	1 164	19 965	-1.0
Cuyahoga	0.0	D	3.8	10.4	12.6	4.3	11.2	15.1	13.4	251 120	199	51 346	618 165	-0.6
Darke	9.7	D	8.4	23.0	D	5.9	5.2	10.4	10.7	11 980	229	903	22 716	-0.1
Defiance	4.5	0.0	3.5	34.9	3.1	9.0	4.9	D	11.6	8 810	229	789	16 693	-0.2
Delaware	0.2	D	4.0	7.8	11.9	6.3	15.4	6.7	8.2	24 930	132	1 227	70 560	6.3
Erie	0.9	D	4.0	19.8	3.0	6.9	4.1	12.9	15.9	18 670	246	1 682	37 678	-0.4
Fairfield	0.6	0.3	8.0	12.1	4.1	9.3	5.6	15.6	18.1	27 855	185	2 459	59 977	2.2
Fayette	4.4	0.0	6.2	16.7	2.2	11.9	6.1	D	16.6	6 490	226	931	12 670	-0.2
Franklin	0.0	0.4	4.6	5.2	12.6	5.5	11.6	11.2	19.6	168 160	136	33 029	545 058	3.4
Fulton	2.2	D	9.1	35.4	D	6.0	2.7	8.7	13.2	8 545	201	423	17 363	-0.3
Gallia	0.3	D	2.8	5.8	D	7.9	5.3	D	16.1	7 160	236	1 702	13 755	-1.2
Geauga	0.7	D	11.9	22.7	5.0	7.8	4.3	9.3	11.8	18 305	195	753	36 838	0.7
Greene	0.2	D	3.1	4.6	15.7	5.7	4.4	6.3	47.1	28 700	174	2 638	69 320	1.6
Guernsey	0.4	5.6	11.2	20.9	4.8	7.3	3.4	12.9	15.2	9 635	243	1 537	19 092	-0.5
Hamilton	0.0	D	4.5	10.8	13.2	4.1	9.6	14.1	9.9	142 995	177	24 993	377 685	0.1
Hancock	0.9	D	3.7	28.5	4.3	6.1	2.9	9.5	7.1	15 095	201	1 096	33 312	0.4
Hardin	14.7	0.0	2.9	23.0	2.2	5.4	3.3	D	14.7	6 355	200	677	13 087	-0.1
Harrison	1.9	22.3	13.9	8.0	D	3.4	2.5	7.4	15.3	3 765	242	579	8 069	-1.2
Henry	5.2	D	8.7	32.8	D	5.1	3.7	8.9	17.5	6 100	219	364	11 911	-0.4
Highland	4.1	0.4	6.4	20.3	D	9.7	5.9	10.0	24.1	10 095	234	1 485	19 191	-1.0
Hocking	0.3	D	9.0	14.4	2.5	7.7	6.8	8.2	30.4	6 580	229	1 016	13 301	-0.8
Holmes	5.8	0.9	17.9	31.6	2.4	7.9	3.0	D	7.4	4 780	109	406	13 582	-0.6
Huron	2.9	D	10.2	29.2	2.7	5.3	3.5	10.3	11.7	12 245	209	1 134	25 117	-0.3
Jackson	0.3	1.2	6.7	30.8	2.1	8.6	3.6	11.5	16.2	7 515	229	1 585	14 567	-0.1
Jefferson	0.1	D	D	7.3	3.6	7.9	3.1	D	14.6	17 810	263	2 697	32 483	-1.0
Knox	1.5	0.6	9.1	29.8	3.2	6.6	2.7	11.0	12.4	12 555	206	1 172	25 505	1.5
Lake	0.5	D	5.6	29.0	5.0	7.5	4.1	9.7	13.0	49 690	217	2 812	102 068	0.9
Lawrence	0.2	0.0	11.7	5.8	2.9	9.0	3.6	16.7	25.2	14 965	243	3 653	27 349	-0.9
Licking	1.7	0.4	7.5	14.0	6.5	9.6	8.1	11.7	16.2	33 500	198	3 225	70 092	1.2
Logan	2.1	0.2	3.9	41.3	3.6	4.6	2.8	7.7	10.4	9 740	214	858	23 155	-0.1
Lorain	0.6	0.1	5.5	24.2	4.0	7.7	4.2	11.2	18.0	62 130	204	7 129	129 295	1.8
Lucas	0.1	0.1	6.2	16.0	7.7	6.7	6.0	17.6	15.4	84 485	194	18 016	202 471	-0.1
Madison	3.7	0.0	5.9	24.3	D	6.1	2.6	D	22.0	7 390	168	625	15 943	0.0
Mahoning	0.2	0.7	6.7	11.0	5.9	7.6	8.6	15.9	15.9	56 890	244	8 918	111 305	-0.5
Marion	2.6	D	3.6	27.9	5.8	6.8	3.4	15.6	16.6	14 415	219	2 310	27 796	-0.1
Medina	0.4	0.1	9.1	16.4	6.1	8.6	5.2	9.1	12.4	32 735	186	1 434	71 133	2.8
Meigs	2.1	6.2	8.9	4.0	D	10.7	4.1	D	30.2	5 475	235	1 190	10 992	-1.8
Mercer	11.9	D	7.2	30.6	D	6.8	4.2	5.2	13.0	8 345	204	440	17 702	0.4
Miami	0.7	D	5.8	29.0	D	7.5	3.6	8.9	13.4	22 340	215	1 714	44 290	0.1
Monroe	2.5	D	17.3	D	2.0	7.0	4.9	D	19.9	3 700	256	482	7 452	-1.5
Montgomery	0.1	0.0	4.5	12.2	11.6	5.1	7.2	18.9	16.0	110 315	207	16 168	254 323	-0.2
Morgan	0.8	D	5.6	22.4	D	7.1	3.5	9.5	22.8	3 950	267	585	7 806	-1.1
Morrow	5.8	0.5	7.5	18.4	D	6.7	3.9	D	27.3	7 005	200	568	14 093	-0.4
Muskingum	0.7	4.3	4.1	10.0	4.6	9.4	4.1	D	16.7	20 640	240	3 500	37 699	-1.0
Noble	1.1	15.7	10.2	4.2	5.3	4.7	4.4	5.4	30.5	2 660	185	281	6 048	-0.1

1. Per 1,000 resident population estimated as of July 1 of the year shown.

Table B. States and Counties — Housing, Labor Force, and Employment

STATE County	Housing units, 2010–2014 Occupied units — Owner-occupied Total	Percent	Median value[1]	Median owner cost as a percent of income — With a mortgage	Without a mortgage[2]	Renter-occupied — Median rent[3]	Median rent as a percent of income[2]	Sub-standard units[4] (percent)	Civilian labor force, 2015 — Total	Percent change, 2014–2015	Unemployment — Total	Rate[5]	Civilian employment,[6] 2010–2014 — Total	Percent — Management, business, science and arts	Construction, production, and maintenance occupations
	89	90	91	92	93	94	95	96	97	98	99	100	101	102	103
NORTH DAKOTA—Cont'd															
Ward	25 495	62.1	171 300	20.0	10.0	825	26.7	1.8	34 440	-0.6	1 065	3.1	34 530	29.3	28.1
Wells	1 970	77.8	66 800	15.8	10.0	448	21.9	2.2	2 196	-0.2	86	3.9	2 065	32.4	28.6
Williams	11 113	67.9	174 200	14.4	10.0	756	18.7	3.2	29 032	-9.1	647	2.2	15 000	27.5	36.5
OHIO	4 570 015	66.9	129 600	21.9	12.6	729	29.9	1.7	5 700 351	0.0	277 330	4.9	5 303 013	34.7	23.3
Adams	10 734	71.0	88 300	23.9	12.8	544	34.8	3.6	10 586	0.7	839	7.9	10 050	25.9	34.8
Allen	40 191	67.6	106 200	20.6	12.4	652	32.2	2.1	48 106	-0.5	2 326	4.8	46 238	26.3	29.3
Ashland	20 339	72.0	119 900	22.7	12.5	681	24.1	3.0	25 564	0.1	1 301	5.1	23 272	29.3	31.3
Ashtabula	38 933	72.3	107 300	22.7	13.4	631	33.9	2.0	44 400	-1.2	2 656	6.0	41 267	25.1	33.3
Athens	22 208	56.5	113 900	22.5	12.2	703	43.1	1.8	27 502	-0.4	1 697	6.2	26 580	36.0	16.8
Auglaize	18 115	74.3	131 500	20.5	11.5	652	24.2	1.4	24 490	1.4	899	3.7	22 409	29.6	34.2
Belmont	28 007	75.0	89 700	19.6	11.2	554	26.8	0.9	31 298	-1.7	1 982	6.3	29 706	25.9	29.7
Brown	16 587	77.8	114 700	23.5	13.5	666	27.1	1.9	19 681	0.0	1 216	6.2	18 260	26.7	31.7
Butler	134 934	69.9	156 300	21.7	12.1	815	30.4	1.8	187 121	0.3	8 550	4.6	175 534	36.2	21.2
Carroll	10 922	78.5	110 900	22.6	11.5	607	28.0	3.2	13 521	-0.4	800	5.9	12 375	24.3	36.6
Champaign	15 163	74.2	121 100	22.2	12.5	708	28.4	1.2	19 995	0.3	873	4.4	17 779	28.0	33.9
Clark	54 969	66.0	104 200	21.1	12.0	669	31.2	2.1	64 200	-1.2	3 207	5.0	58 478	28.8	27.5
Clermont	74 187	74.7	152 400	21.4	12.4	765	28.5	1.2	102 877	0.3	4 613	4.5	96 188	35.2	22.9
Clinton	16 052	65.2	118 300	22.6	12.7	685	27.7	1.6	16 845	-0.6	1 033	6.1	18 321	27.6	30.4
Columbiana	42 184	71.6	97 600	20.3	11.3	607	26.9	1.6	49 556	-1.1	2 909	5.9	46 461	25.0	33.0
Coshocton	14 561	73.9	95 600	22.0	11.0	571	28.0	2.1	16 052	1.8	1 007	6.3	15 288	22.6	40.5
Crawford	17 625	70.0	87 100	21.4	12.0	642	27.6	1.0	19 164	-2.2	1 110	5.8	17 864	26.6	35.3
Cuyahoga	534 721	60.2	123 300	23.1	14.1	736	31.5	1.5	610 001	-1.0	30 488	5.0	575 119	38.8	17.7
Darke	20 929	72.0	110 000	21.7	12.2	589	27.1	1.4	26 310	0.6	1 117	4.2	23 441	24.3	39.7
Defiance	15 332	74.7	107 400	21.0	11.7	647	27.3	1.8	18 605	-1.8	915	4.9	17 916	25.8	35.5
Delaware	65 029	81.6	248 600	21.9	11.7	927	27.3	1.1	101 620	1.2	3 542	3.5	91 842	52.1	12.1
Erie	31 998	68.4	131 900	21.9	13.0	710	26.6	1.0	36 957	-1.2	2 081	5.6	35 679	29.6	25.6
Fairfield	54 581	71.7	163 300	21.5	11.0	794	30.0	2.0	75 367	0.9	3 247	4.3	69 568	35.7	21.1
Fayette	11 532	61.3	107 800	23.5	12.8	701	30.8	2.0	14 066	-0.5	693	4.9	12 311	25.5	29.3
Franklin	474 683	54.4	150 000	22.2	12.8	834	29.3	2.4	654 086	1.0	26 604	4.1	601 107	40.9	16.1
Fulton	16 333	78.9	128 600	21.5	12.8	664	27.8	2.0	22 444	0.3	1 102	4.9	20 239	28.4	34.0
Gallia	11 502	75.2	93 000	22.7	12.9	585	25.6	2.7	12 195	-1.7	792	6.5	11 479	28.9	30.6
Geauga	34 753	85.6	219 500	22.9	12.3	818	26.2	2.1	48 751	-0.7	1 964	4.0	45 634	39.5	21.7
Greene	63 549	67.2	158 300	21.4	12.2	851	28.8	0.9	80 098	0.5	3 514	4.4	74 509	44.0	16.6
Guernsey	15 564	74.1	94 400	21.1	11.4	591	31.0	1.9	19 143	0.3	1 197	6.3	16 365	26.5	33.8
Hamilton	329 062	59.0	143 000	22.1	12.9	708	31.3	1.9	402 663	0.3	18 067	4.5	379 018	39.9	16.7
Hancock	30 795	70.7	124 500	20.6	11.1	664	27.3	0.6	40 757	0.8	1 489	3.7	36 826	32.5	29.8
Hardin	11 438	69.6	94 700	20.8	12.7	650	29.1	2.6	14 922	-1.2	698	4.7	13 496	24.5	33.6
Harrison	6 333	77.8	86 300	21.4	11.8	630	28.5	2.5	7 229	-1.7	452	6.3	6 822	23.5	38.1
Henry	11 075	79.6	110 600	20.5	12.8	682	26.8	1.4	13 538	-1.5	760	5.6	13 316	28.5	37.0
Highland	16 837	71.3	98 900	24.1	12.1	622	31.1	2.5	16 991	-1.9	1 077	6.3	16 364	24.7	40.0
Hocking	11 426	74.6	109 500	21.9	12.2	574	29.0	2.8	13 284	0.8	727	5.5	12 336	29.3	30.7
Holmes	12 516	77.2	155 300	21.9	10.1	557	22.4	5.7	20 578	3.4	702	3.4	18 335	19.4	46.3
Huron	22 507	72.8	115 600	21.3	12.1	622	27.4	2.3	27 490	-1.4	1 824	6.6	26 822	23.3	38.9
Jackson	13 204	68.8	90 700	22.2	13.8	634	32.0	2.2	12 995	-1.7	979	7.5	13 090	30.6	33.4
Jefferson	28 176	71.2	86 300	19.6	12.3	594	29.1	1.6	29 552	-0.8	2 192	7.4	28 009	27.6	27.0
Knox	22 642	70.7	133 300	22.7	12.9	691	28.5	2.3	31 038	-0.3	1 445	4.7	27 763	30.4	30.8
Lake	94 089	74.9	148 200	22.2	12.7	808	29.3	1.1	123 388	-0.9	5 379	4.4	115 917	35.4	22.4
Lawrence	23 622	74.1	97 300	20.9	12.2	644	29.6	2.5	25 336	-1.9	1 468	5.8	24 356	30.6	27.1
Licking	64 146	72.5	150 800	21.8	12.7	746	29.8	1.7	87 474	0.9	3 837	4.4	81 206	34.1	22.6
Logan	18 471	73.9	117 100	20.9	13.1	707	28.0	3.0	23 459	1.6	969	4.1	20 374	27.0	38.9
Lorain	117 134	71.7	138 000	21.9	12.7	747	31.3	1.6	149 186	-0.8	8 035	5.4	137 710	32.9	24.6
Lucas	178 121	61.6	106 300	22.2	13.2	664	32.0	1.3	209 263	0.2	11 115	5.3	192 857	32.4	23.3
Madison	14 676	70.7	146 200	21.6	13.4	741	27.0	2.3	20 682	1.1	825	4.0	18 411	29.6	29.4
Mahoning	97 624	68.8	96 900	21.7	12.5	629	31.3	1.1	107 101	-0.8	6 544	6.1	101 829	30.6	24.1
Marion	24 586	68.4	97 400	20.6	11.9	702	31.2	1.6	27 920	0.2	1 427	5.1	26 065	27.9	34.2
Medina	65 950	79.1	180 100	22.0	11.8	832	28.5	1.5	94 213	-0.8	3 752	4.0	88 073	37.5	21.7
Meigs	9 486	79.7	83 100	22.4	12.4	567	31.3	2.1	9 088	-1.1	750	8.3	8 560	27.0	33.7
Mercer	15 923	77.4	127 200	20.6	11.6	650	25.6	1.4	23 104	2.0	753	3.3	20 382	24.8	39.9
Miami	41 169	70.5	134 200	21.4	11.4	741	27.3	1.3	52 238	0.3	2 306	4.4	48 284	30.3	31.1
Monroe	6 056	77.4	88 300	19.6	10.0	521	27.0	1.7	5 545	-5.6	552	10.0	5 618	23.2	39.6
Montgomery	222 673	61.6	110 500	22.8	13.8	731	31.5	1.5	249 429	0.1	12 474	5.0	234 178	35.2	20.4
Morgan	6 056	77.0	88 600	20.6	10.2	537	34.6	3.1	6 740	1.1	489	7.3	5 799	27.6	36.1
Morrow	12 640	81.8	132 600	22.8	13.1	662	30.0	2.3	16 936	0.8	840	5.0	15 884	26.0	37.4
Muskingum	34 160	67.6	106 300	21.4	12.9	637	30.6	1.8	39 073	-0.7	2 402	6.1	36 896	26.4	29.3
Noble	4 916	82.0	83 100	22.8	11.4	596	33.0	3.3	4 936	-2.9	364	7.4	4 299	24.9	35.7

1. Specified owner-occupied units. 2. A value of 10.0 represents 10 percent or less; a value of 50.0 represents 50 percent or more. 3. Specified renter-occupied units.
4. Overcrowded or lacking complete plumbing facilities. 5. Percent of civilian labor force. 6. Persons 16 years old and over.

Table B. States and Counties — Nonfarm Employment and Agriculture

STATE County	Private nonfarm establishments, employment and payroll, 2014									Agriculture, 2012			
	Number of establishments	Employment						Annual payroll		Farms			
		Total	Health care and social assistance	Manufac-turing	Retail trade	Finance and insurance	Professional, scientific, and technical services	Total (mil dol)	Average per employee (dollars)	Number	Percent with:		Farm operators whose principal occu-pation is farming (percent)
											Fewer than 50 acres	500 acres or more	
	104	105	106	107	108	109	110	111	112	113	114	115	116
NORTH DAKOTA—Cont'd													
Ward	2 148	28 965	4 601	528	6 318	996	945	1 339	46 242	961	15.3	47.9	60.1
Wells	195	1 347	445	D	240	86	D	43	31 886	543	8.1	50.8	56.9
Williams	1 539	25 952	1 280	361	2 482	402	742	2 002	77 130	758	8.8	52.1	52.4
OHIO	250 535	4 636 844	821 510	642 967	560 265	248 251	239 703	203 868	43 967	75 462	41.1	8.3	43.9
Adams	361	4 069	1 076	D	876	164	100	141	34 659	1 351	38.0	4.2	37.2
Allen	2 436	44 435	10 922	7 274	5 956	1 180	905	1 747	39 321	904	38.8	11.8	42.9
Ashland	1 021	16 279	2 458	3 805	2 046	326	D	556	34 175	1 034	36.4	5.4	46.8
Ashtabula	1 941	24 606	5 250	5 873	3 636	561	876	842	34 213	1 099	41.6	6.7	46.8
Athens	1 024	12 328	3 101	291	2 729	388	577	376	30 539	722	31.2	3.3	37.8
Auglaize	973	19 233	2 512	8 373	2 127	346	438	761	39 584	1 040	34.6	9.8	42.5
Belmont	1 471	19 256	4 220	860	4 183	795	567	641	33 301	700	27.1	4.9	42.1
Brown	528	6 139	1 474	769	973	174	127	179	29 092	1 379	40.4	5.7	39.7
Butler	7 002	126 095	15 789	17 773	17 885	7 934	3 242	5 344	42 381	865	51.0	6.6	43.9
Carroll	472	5 137	670	1 524	721	86	107	162	31 629	733	33.2	5.5	40.9
Champaign	596	9 310	956	3 879	966	211	282	358	38 497	873	46.0	11.6	46.2
Clark	2 321	40 253	7 429	5 879	5 628	3 026	1 273	1 399	34 746	785	53.2	11.3	49.6
Clermont	3 524	48 803	5 780	5 142	9 692	2 387	2 640	2 068	42 384	822	60.1	5.0	38.6
Clinton	723	13 865	1 893	3 134	1 568	353	D	532	38 368	759	42.2	15.5	53.1
Columbiana	2 037	26 548	5 526	5 863	4 080	614	420	847	31 916	1 045	44.7	4.5	42.0
Coshocton	635	9 206	2 012	2 351	1 339	187	107	342	37 155	1 122	32.6	5.4	40.6
Crawford	828	13 070	2 927	4 068	1 289	676	504	435	33 294	634	33.1	18.6	50.9
Cuyahoga	33 016	664 773	141 315	69 685	62 232	45 335	40 735	33 123	49 827	114	87.7	0.0	40.4
Darke	1 138	15 871	2 275	5 483	1 980	582	282	572	36 054	1 693	41.8	10.8	41.2
Defiance	810	13 549	1 947	3 231	2 309	603	242	515	37 983	1 030	37.5	12.1	38.5
Delaware	4 230	76 684	6 889	5 479	12 006	14 413	3 677	3 831	49 958	755	56.4	9.9	43.8
Erie	1 822	29 977	4 972	6 802	4 548	619	611	1 092	36 418	345	42.9	12.2	48.1
Fairfield	2 613	34 460	6 852	4 347	6 827	854	983	1 122	32 568	1 184	51.2	8.2	43.2
Fayette	577	9 490	1 110	1 704	2 546	160	65	303	31 880	504	35.5	24.2	56.5
Franklin	27 388	608 429	111 782	31 202	65 492	54 347	40 306	29 707	48 826	388	62.9	8.2	40.5
Fulton	935	14 491	1 942	6 500	1 695	376	221	584	40 323	825	42.4	13.3	42.8
Gallia	553	9 069	D	388	1 514	350	67	358	39 436	957	34.6	2.7	39.0
Geauga	2 744	28 158	4 433	7 329	3 650	679	1 095	1 166	41 401	959	55.2	2.2	49.8
Greene	3 042	49 576	6 653	3 535	9 293	1 189	9 308	1 926	38 843	800	61.6	9.0	39.4
Guernsey	864	13 754	2 897	2 687	1 830	D	D	505	36 719	1 228	36.6	1.6	34.6
Hamilton	20 954	468 724	86 316	39 568	44 836	32 940	39 902	25 025	53 390	295	67.1	3.1	42.4
Hancock	1 712	41 537	5 004	11 552	4 092	663	1 289	1 821	43 840	831	32.7	15.4	45.5
Hardin	460	6 862	662	1 854	906	209	83	219	31 971	793	31.3	14.1	52.2
Harrison	262	2 895	D	373	279	D	30	131	45 391	444	26.6	6.8	46.2
Henry	560	8 058	1 264	2 791	952	233	197	319	39 540	848	33.1	15.7	47.9
Highland	671	8 046	1 605	1 457	1 635	565	113	268	33 267	1 412	38.3	7.9	45.1
Hocking	467	4 925	1 019	779	787	D	93	142	28 733	367	38.4	3.0	40.9
Holmes	1 173	18 199	1 562	7 047	2 017	378	269	573	31 506	1 969	36.7	2.4	50.0
Huron	1 120	16 443	2 522	5 170	2 075	418	403	639	38 884	865	38.7	12.7	47.1
Jackson	598	8 539	1 377	3 063	1 375	D	150	266	31 157	526	32.3	4.9	41.8
Jefferson	1 272	19 023	4 546	1 237	3 055	365	296	652	34 257	493	26.0	4.1	39.4
Knox	1 054	18 270	3 127	4 729	2 170	424	337	813	44 495	1 374	45.8	5.5	44.6
Lake	5 996	86 124	10 986	19 399	13 228	2 021	3 119	3 723	43 223	214	70.6	1.4	55.6
Lawrence	811	10 277	2 731	821	1 859	281	290	341	33 220	592	26.2	1.9	41.9
Licking	2 897	47 805	7 520	7 763	6 835	3 640	1 843	1 823	38 130	1 484	51.1	5.7	39.8
Logan	833	15 213	2 047	4 670	1 654	295	777	634	41 671	868	40.4	12.3	39.2
Lorain	5 518	84 068	14 216	16 071	13 532	2 160	3 377	3 345	39 785	768	52.7	6.0	46.4
Lucas	9 627	197 169	38 266	19 480	23 833	5 936	9 915	7 934	40 240	330	52.7	12.4	58.2
Madison	681	11 831	1 362	3 277	1 749	149	D	465	39 270	699	40.1	21.9	53.2
Mahoning	5 559	88 782	20 919	8 623	12 399	2 413	3 639	3 175	35 764	578	44.5	4.2	48.3
Marion	1 111	21 225	4 494	6 559	2 825	399	283	754	35 502	578	34.1	16.6	41.9
Medina	3 986	50 979	6 834	8 504	9 027	2 482	2 030	2 029	39 792	920	63.0	4.0	50.2
Meigs	298	2 425	D	63	544	D	57	66	27 263	588	27.0	3.2	53.2
Mercer	970	15 473	2 189	4 241	1 982	568	312	560	36 209	1 208	35.3	12.0	45.0
Miami	2 099	35 171	4 670	10 844	4 717	726	837	1 334	37 928	1 068	54.6	10.0	41.8
Monroe	252	2 637	D	140	368	174	D	118	44 677	823	26.5	2.8	41.9
Montgomery	11 457	225 682	49 878	26 993	26 188	11 115	12 124	9 909	43 907	770	63.8	6.6	42.7
Morgan	158	1 828	309	606	299	90	39	59	32 209	510	22.2	5.5	39.4
Morrow	381	3 646	1 001	D	454	68	150	119	32 725	824	43.9	8.7	43.0
Muskingum	1 737	27 255	6 420	2 689	4 602	604	431	970	35 601	1 259	35.3	4.8	38.4
Noble	213	1 983	379	301	318	88	D	58	29 325	595	27.2	4.2	33.3

Table B. States and Counties — **Agriculture**

STATE County	Land in farms — Acreage (1,000) [117]	Percent change, 2007–2012 [118]	Acres — Average size of farm [119]	Total irrigated (1,000) [120]	Total cropland (1,000) [121]	Value of land and buildings (dollars) — Average per farm [122]	Average per acre [123]	Value of machinery and equipment, average per farm (dollars) [124]	Value of products sold — Total (mil dol) [125]	Average per farm (dollars) [126]	Percent from: Crops [127]	Live-stock and poultry products [128]	Percent of farms with sales of: $10,000 or more [129]	$100,000 or more [130]	Government payments — Total ($1,000) [131]	Percent of farms [132]
NORTH DAKOTA—Cont'd																
Ward	1 073	0.7	1 117	0.2	829.4	1 716 400	1 537	298 381	274.5	285 596	93.3	6.7	62.7	39.2	9 875	71.4
Wells	738	-2.5	1 359	0.8	622.3	2 198 269	1 617	364 245	272.0	500 842	95.1	4.9	58.2	44.6	7 746	85.6
Williams	1 063	-7.1	1 403	15.6	739.1	1 044 598	745	289 881	178.7	235 756	93.8	6.2	59.4	36.7	6 315	72.2
OHIO	13 961	0.0	185	46.6	10 748.6	894 933	4 837	116 896	10 064.1	133 366	65.6	34.4	47.4	20.3	228 858	45.9
Adams	172	-6.3	128	0.2	84.4	365 260	2 862	59 237	38.9	28 798	68.6	31.4	33.6	6.6	2 316	55.4
Allen	183	-2.2	203	D	163.0	1 070 715	5 284	144 872	144.1	159 393	76.2	23.8	61.7	30.3	3 593	74.4
Ashland	153	1.6	148	0.2	110.9	677 328	4 578	93 800	103.6	100 214	53.0	47.0	52.5	17.5	2 061	45.4
Ashtabula	166	2.6	151	0.2	109.0	494 527	3 275	114 303	82.3	74 846	74.4	25.6	38.8	13.2	1 609	28.7
Athens	90	10.1	125	0.1	28.0	348 506	2 781	47 575	9.5	13 224	57.2	42.8	21.3	2.1	320	16.8
Auglaize	210	-1.5	202	0.0	191.5	1 220 936	6 044	176 234	190.6	183 235	60.6	39.4	66.1	34.0	5 338	77.1
Belmont	113	-12.3	162	0.0	35.0	540 911	3 344	59 970	20.1	28 764	21.9	78.1	37.4	4.1	613	9.7
Brown	206	-14.1	150	0.1	139.3	539 260	3 602	89 819	82.6	59 891	88.5	11.5	41.8	12.2	3 795	57.9
Butler	146	14.8	169	0.3	116.4	986 918	5 845	107 817	65.0	75 191	80.4	19.6	36.6	12.4	2 379	32.4
Carroll	106	-9.1	145	0.4	58.4	539 031	3 718	86 621	39.2	53 478	51.6	48.4	40.5	10.2	989	28.0
Champaign	190	-7.2	218	3.7	164.9	1 166 636	5 359	147 490	130.4	149 386	86.6	13.4	49.7	24.6	3 854	56.2
Clark	174	-1.7	222	1.6	149.8	1 141 031	5 138	147 288	145.1	184 896	80.4	19.6	45.1	23.8	2 754	47.6
Clermont	121	15.7	147	0.2	88.5	752 370	5 106	83 123	58.0	70 583	93.3	6.7	25.5	8.4	1 264	29.7
Clinton	208	-4.7	274	0.1	187.7	1 360 628	4 962	172 278	163.8	215 867	90.5	9.5	60.1	34.8	3 825	63.8
Columbiana	128	-2.4	122	0.3	81.7	594 740	4 861	98 871	99.3	95 020	38.4	61.6	45.0	15.4	1 509	24.8
Coshocton	170	-0.8	151	0.6	88.7	518 983	3 430	87 948	81.7	72 781	39.9	60.1	39.2	13.4	1 530	30.7
Crawford	240	9.3	379	0.1	221.9	1 772 235	4 681	250 994	193.1	304 645	74.0	26.0	67.2	43.7	4 734	75.6
Cuyahoga	3	-10.4	23	0.1	0.6	391 509	17 113	56 079	10.2	89 605	98.5	1.5	25.4	8.8	12	3.5
Darke	340	-3.0	201	1.1	311.6	1 425 144	7 097	175 760	559.5	330 475	32.2	67.8	65.2	32.9	6 902	69.5
Defiance	225	-3.4	219	0.0	198.1	980 354	4 483	116 630	113.5	110 232	75.9	24.1	48.4	21.8	6 297	85.8
Delaware	141	2.0	187	0.8	123.4	1 108 061	5 937	144 164	121.9	161 464	88.5	11.5	45.0	20.5	2 396	45.2
Erie	83	-0.9	242	0.4	71.9	1 137 035	4 708	184 907	88.2	255 583	92.2	7.8	56.8	31.6	1 343	55.1
Fairfield	207	16.3	175	0.3	162.9	833 232	4 773	114 217	105.8	89 394	79.4	20.6	36.5	15.8	3 782	48.0
Fayette	197	-10.0	390	0.0	180.6	2 134 145	5 473	226 067	143.5	284 808	87.9	12.1	59.9	39.3	4 144	73.0
Franklin	62	4.1	160	0.3	53.5	983 101	6 151	118 101	48.2	124 299	96.2	3.8	44.8	17.5	853	37.9
Fulton	195	6.2	237	0.5	179.6	1 315 518	5 556	166 076	175.7	213 023	69.4	30.6	60.7	35.4	4 204	67.3
Gallia	116	-0.9	121	0.2	34.6	393 862	3 254	51 183	15.1	15 827	51.6	48.4	22.6	2.9	734	23.6
Geauga	67	18.1	70	0.3	32.7	494 216	7 094	47 118	43.6	45 477	41.0	59.0	40.0	9.1	345	5.6
Greene	146	-10.3	182	0.6	124.7	1 095 626	6 012	120 653	95.9	119 883	90.7	9.3	39.6	17.1	2 173	46.6
Guernsey	144	4.5	117	0.0	51.7	336 147	2 871	49 570	21.5	17 502	36.6	63.4	24.9	2.9	291	10.2
Hamilton	22	1.5	73	0.2	10.0	533 654	7 282	73 278	23.6	80 153	61.3	38.7	32.5	10.5	257	13.2
Hancock	230	-7.1	277	0.0	212.8	1 310 924	4 731	164 752	160.2	192 834	91.7	8.3	71.2	41.2	4 142	77.1
Hardin	248	-3.5	313	0.4	222.6	1 527 226	4 887	171 834	272.5	343 571	53.8	46.2	61.9	34.6	4 779	72.1
Harrison	95	2.2	215	0.0	38.1	645 957	3 007	68 225	18.2	41 081	42.6	57.4	32.9	7.9	245	14.4
Henry	236	1.6	278	0.6	221.4	1 570 350	5 645	170 375	155.5	183 383	91.6	8.4	72.3	36.0	4 449	85.6
Highland	265	-2.0	187	0.2	197.7	677 928	3 619	97 353	128.6	91 069	82.6	17.4	43.9	16.3	6 128	62.6
Hocking	38	-9.3	104	0.0	14.0	372 025	3 585	44 937	5.3	14 450	80.2	19.8	22.9	2.7	212	19.3
Holmes	221	17.7	112	0.3	124.1	653 282	5 822	64 655	204.9	104 045	20.9	79.1	59.6	24.3	1 796	12.9
Huron	238	8.6	275	3.2	208.7	1 235 467	4 485	165 143	190.7	220 421	81.0	19.0	55.8	32.1	3 680	57.9
Jackson	72	-0.3	136	0.1	27.2	321 939	2 362	58 485	10.7	20 293	44.2	55.8	29.3	5.9	525	32.3
Jefferson	68	-1.6	139	0.0	25.9	381 974	2 755	68 801	7.8	15 880	48.4	51.6	30.2	3.4	218	19.9
Knox	186	-6.2	135	0.1	128.7	647 124	4 779	91 124	121.4	88 386	66.0	34.0	42.4	15.0	2 491	35.7
Lake	17	6.6	80	1.9	8.6	604 140	7 550	111 075	81.8	382 351	99.4	0.6	48.1	17.8	23	8.9
Lawrence	65	-1.8	109	0.1	17.0	266 258	2 441	50 843	4.8	8 189	57.3	42.7	15.7	1.5	366	18.2
Licking	224	-0.8	151	0.2	161.4	738 829	4 894	103 000	194.8	131 270	52.2	47.8	36.8	12.1	2 331	25.5
Logan	213	5.8	245	0.3	177.7	1 221 374	4 979	135 014	147.9	170 409	82.6	17.4	49.5	23.4	4 046	58.8
Lorain	123	-1.1	160	1.4	102.7	750 453	4 698	125 251	179.1	233 203	89.7	10.3	51.8	20.6	1 519	41.5
Lucas	63	0.2	191	1.5	59.7	1 103 406	5 778	138 709	66.2	200 521	95.2	4.8	58.2	31.8	964	55.2
Madison	263	6.2	377	0.1	244.2	1 917 923	5 092	202 773	193.8	277 230	79.4	20.6	58.4	39.9	5 148	66.0
Mahoning	75	17.0	130	0.9	54.5	644 289	4 968	119 341	65.4	113 234	45.9	54.1	48.1	19.9	847	32.9
Marion	189	-8.5	327	D	174.8	1 562 507	4 773	199 900	151.4	261 990	74.2	25.8	55.0	32.0	4 497	73.5
Medina	95	-0.5	103	0.6	72.4	656 848	6 363	94 628	60.5	65 797	70.1	29.9	37.1	11.6	1 274	20.8
Meigs	76	-2.5	129	0.3	24.6	312 980	2 428	53 207	14.5	24 622	66.8	33.2	29.1	4.3	748	17.9
Mercer	273	-6.8	226	0.1	248.7	1 775 939	7 854	213 011	596.4	493 681	25.7	74.3	76.3	49.7	7 650	79.1
Miami	184	-6.5	173	2.3	164.8	983 794	5 703	103 808	110.0	102 998	91.9	8.1	51.2	21.7	3 147	59.2
Monroe	111	11.9	135	0.0	29.7	311 759	2 308	58 011	13.7	16 612	32.4	67.6	23.2	2.6	264	6.3
Montgomery	124	11.8	161	1.2	104.7	944 141	5 858	111 271	76.8	99 695	84.6	15.4	38.8	13.0	1 656	44.4
Morgan	95	-6.9	187	0.0	30.0	448 463	2 403	64 149	12.2	23 975	41.5	58.5	34.1	5.1	370	22.7
Morrow	168	1.6	204	0.2	139.2	952 987	4 682	131 218	131.7	159 848	70.9	29.1	50.7	20.0	2 689	43.8
Muskingum	173	4.1	138	0.1	79.2	449 031	3 263	70 551	58.1	46 149	51.8	48.2	34.4	7.8	1 298	24.1
Noble	86	-3.6	145	0.1	28.8	368 677	2 547	55 652	9.8	16 403	37.1	62.9	31.9	2.2	78	4.9

Table B. States and Counties — Water Use, Wholesale Trade, Retail Trade, and Real Estate

STATE County	Water use, 2010		Wholesale trade,[1] 2012				Retail trade,[2] 2012				Real estate and rental and leasing,[2] 2012			
	Total water withdrawn (mil gal/day)	Gallons withdrawn per person per day	Number of establishments	Number of employees	Sales (mil dol)	Annual payroll (mil dol)	Number of establishments	Number of employees	Sales (mil dol)	Annual payroll (mil dol)	Number of establishments	Number of employees	Receipts (mil dol)	Annual payroll (mil dol)
	133	134	135	136	137	138	139	140	141	142	143	144	145	146
NORTH DAKOTA—Cont'd														
Ward...............	7.7	125	102	1 621	2 898.0	100.1	297	5 634	1 902.3	162.9	79	735	195.1	37.9
Wells...............	1.0	226	19	D	D	D	36	209	80.4	4.5	3	D	D	D
Williams...........	21.1	942	91	1 527	1 868.5	119.2	114	1 833	797.5	62.2	77	819	573.6	82.4
OHIO	9 442.8	819	11 744	182 791	155 426.0	9 627.2	36 531	549 152	153 554.0	13 099.3	9 932	60 966	16 132.7	2 441.8
Adams..............	588.8	20 622	9	114	77.9	3.9	77	853	224.9	18.0	8	27	3.0	0.8
Allen...............	34.6	325	124	2 287	1 388.8	91.6	417	6 072	1 641.5	134.3	85	376	55.2	11.0
Ashland............	5.6	105	39	D	D	D	156	2 036	486.1	46.1	31	156	12.8	3.4
Ashtabula..........	189.6	1 868	48	385	220.1	14.2	327	3 635	1 081.1	80.6	70	199	26.7	5.3
Athens.............	9.5	147	28	D	D	D	192	2 783	695.1	58.7	61	213	24.8	4.5
Auglaize...........	10.8	234	35	D	D	D	165	2 096	491.8	43.1	31	193	14.4	5.9
Belmont............	179.5	2 550	38	D	D	D	299	3 837	1 042.5	82.2	54	320	44.1	8.0
Brown..............	4.8	107	23	138	72.3	4.5	102	979	256.4	21.6	14	51	6.0	1.0
Butler.............	131.6	357	435	9 727	8 239.8	545.4	1 011	17 718	7 072.0	482.8	264	1 283	289.6	45.7
Carroll............	3.1	107	17	D	D	D	65	671	204.9	16.8	12	57	6.7	1.5
Champaign..........	9.4	233	25	D	D	D	95	980	271.3	21.4	22	56	10.3	1.5
Clark..............	25.8	187	88	2 274	2 697.8	111.4	403	5 708	1 541.5	128.0	95	468	56.8	12.5
Clermont...........	384.0	1 946	148	1 560	1 051.1	83.5	520	9 185	2 659.3	227.7	140	608	105.3	19.7
Clinton............	4.1	98	29	383	425.2	17.4	127	1 531	443.1	37.0	27	186	37.4	5.4
Columbiana.........	10.3	96	88	1 108	584.6	49.7	338	3 922	1 126.4	88.9	55	215	25.7	5.9
Coshocton..........	147.3	3 993	16	D	D	D	107	1 219	307.3	25.5	18	D	D	D
Crawford...........	5.5	125	35	D	D	D	135	1 330	348.9	30.4	27	64	7.3	1.3
Cuyahoga...........	466.0	364	1 930	31 718	21 584.9	1 742.5	4 302	59 458	15 072.5	1 412.8	1 534	13 977	4 931.1	691.5
Darke..............	8.5	161	56	628	528.3	25.4	170	1 956	480.6	43.3	36	131	14.3	3.9
Defiance...........	11.2	286	33	445	422.8	19.7	150	2 344	593.9	54.0	25	95	13.5	2.2
Delaware...........	28.3	162	151	D	D	D	587	11 363	3 178.6	273.5	162	697	146.6	28.0
Erie...............	34.2	443	65	743	1 145.5	35.5	309	4 531	1 072.4	96.7	74	282	41.0	9.2
Fairfield..........	14.6	100	75	D	D	D	412	6 930	1 678.8	151.1	130	491	63.7	10.5
Fayette............	4.2	146	25	D	D	D	183	2 411	675.2	44.9	15	58	20.8	1.5
Franklin...........	177.8	153	1 274	25 263	20 890.3	1 441.5	3 613	65 130	21 384.9	1 810.6	1 394	9 626	2 688.7	420.3
Fulton.............	4.5	104	42	429	382.8	15.7	157	1 651	433.7	37.4	19	70	6.1	1.6
Gallia.............	1 109.4	35 863	17	209	68.3	6.3	120	1 320	336.3	28.7	22	65	9.0	1.6
Geauga.............	9.8	105	135	1 382	592.0	74.1	283	3 696	1 007.8	87.6	65	299	30.3	10.1
Greene.............	15.6	97	79	979	1 101.9	46.9	505	9 080	2 121.3	192.5	128	472	96.7	13.6
Guernsey...........	6.5	163	23	D	D	D	144	1 667	547.0	37.8	34	99	25.3	2.6
Hamilton...........	382.5	477	1 112	18 946	15 311.6	1 065.9	2 821	44 091	11 558.5	1 077.1	979	6 913	1 634.4	313.1
Hancock............	19.2	257	72	964	953.4	47.8	263	4 090	1 103.7	90.6	60	432	55.4	14.2
Hardin.............	4.6	143	16	115	216.4	4.8	90	930	200.0	18.0	13	49	8.0	0.8
Harrison...........	1.3	83	8	D	D	D	33	281	70.9	5.1	5	D	D	D
Henry..............	11.7	413	26	221	305.7	9.6	79	943	290.7	19.0	19	75	24.6	2.2
Highland...........	3.4	78	14	131	95.8	4.4	139	1 532	393.0	34.1	26	65	10.1	1.7
Hocking............	3.0	101	5	D	D	D	67	799	213.2	17.5	28	110	10.2	2.5
Holmes.............	6.4	151	60	631	332.2	22.7	157	1 976	456.7	45.1	15	40	10.3	1.2
Huron..............	7.1	120	46	607	601.6	27.7	174	1 993	538.4	43.5	47	151	23.3	4.0
Jackson............	2.3	70	20	123	60.4	4.3	117	1 410	339.5	29.9	24	79	10.4	2.1
Jefferson..........	1 734.0	24 875	45	D	D	D	216	3 082	723.2	65.7	43	196	23.1	6.0
Knox...............	9.0	147	43	D	D	D	177	2 051	585.2	47.6	38	137	16.7	3.2
Lake...............	818.4	3 558	296	2 993	1 406.6	149.5	789	12 537	3 505.0	293.4	189	711	150.6	23.6
Lawrence...........	9.4	150	20	180	100.3	6.3	154	1 870	553.8	42.4	22	59	8.1	1.5
Licking............	19.9	119	96	1 574	1 634.8	76.6	444	6 954	2 454.9	167.9	110	357	69.0	10.3
Logan..............	6.1	134	28	1 381	748.8	63.3	148	1 685	442.3	38.2	32	153	28.4	4.0
Lorain.............	464.5	1 541	246	2 943	1 826.6	130.4	814	12 995	3 707.3	310.4	192	1 116	116.2	26.5
Lucas..............	685.3	1 551	440	6 310	5 058.6	327.0	1 459	23 721	5 977.9	561.0	411	2 688	2 530.9	161.2
Madison............	7.0	162	23	D	D	D	103	1 719	1 116.1	44.8	30	87	13.6	1.9
Mahoning...........	7.4	31	279	3 666	1 814.7	178.6	893	12 319	3 104.3	262.6	177	2 348	184.5	59.3
Marion.............	12.4	186	36	541	620.1	25.7	181	2 822	745.3	69.5	44	191	28.9	6.0
Medina.............	9.7	56	233	3 012	1 536.8	162.5	486	8 741	2 651.4	199.7	131	487	85.4	13.7
Meigs..............	9.0	379	7	68	13.2	1.7	63	510	155.5	10.1	8	16	1.8	0.2
Mercer.............	8.9	218	49	1 039	790.3	39.4	168	1 930	496.5	46.4	28	69	10.2	1.7
Miami..............	16.5	161	84	820	740.7	35.7	307	4 558	1 239.3	108.0	73	300	44.1	8.8
Monroe.............	2.9	197	6	D	D	D	47	360	74.4	6.5	1	D	D	D
Montgomery.........	141.2	264	521	7 997	15 523.2	450.6	1 675	26 113	6 490.7	605.1	534	3 167	524.5	110.7
Morgan.............	1.7	114	6	D	D	D	26	268	54.5	4.8	3	D	D	D
Morrow.............	3.4	99	14	D	D	D	51	475	164.1	9.7	6	11	2.2	0.2
Muskingum..........	16.5	192	54	868	707.1	33.6	338	4 448	1 117.8	94.1	56	265	41.2	8.3
Noble..............	1.3	89	5	28	16.7	1.1	34	327	105.0	6.7	3	2	0.7	0.1

1. Merchant wholesalers, except manufacturers' sales branches and offices.　　2. Employer establishments.

Table B. States and Counties — Professional Services, Manufacturing, and Accommodation and Food Services

STATE County	Professional, scientific, and technical services, 2012				Manufacturing, 2012				Accommodation and food services, 2012			
	Number of establishments	Number of employees	Receipts (mil dol)	Annual payroll (mil dol)	Number of establishments	Number of employees	Receipts (mil dol)	Annual payroll (mil dol)	Number of establishments	Number of employees	Sales (mil dol)	Annual payroll (mil dol)
	147	148	149	150	151	152	153	154	155	156	157	158
NORTH DAKOTA—Cont'd												
Ward	144	763	116.9	49.4	54	561	D	21.8	173	3 932	211.6	59.1
Wells	9	25	2.0	0.8	7	51	30.0	1.9	17	114	4.8	1.0
Williams	99	558	123.8	37.5	33	250	125.1	12.4	94	2 152	259.1	44.0
OHIO	23 961	233 876	35 970.8	14 219.9	14 482	627 124	313 630.0	33 135.4	23 432	437 293	20 652.8	5 742.7
Adams	26	D	D	D	24	542	103.7	29.8	35	508	21.4	5.8
Allen	164	952	75.8	33.0	124	7 318	15 270.4	448.1	234	4 521	211.3	54.3
Ashland	69	962	127.1	42.8	83	3 655	1 069.9	156.6	91	1 500	61.9	17.2
Ashtabula	118	D	D	D	147	6 167	2 449.5	313.9	229	2 706	121.5	30.8
Athens	71	580	86.0	23.6	38	176	D	6.4	143	2 860	107.2	29.1
Auglaize	70	434	56.8	17.2	83	7 339	2 961.6	363.5	90	1 341	50.5	14.2
Belmont	81	551	55.9	20.1	45	893	D	37.5	127	2 374	112.2	31.4
Brown	28	131	9.2	3.5	32	526	95.1	21.4	67	825	33.0	9.3
Butler	590	3 574	441.6	174.1	402	17 369	10 342.8	997.0	640	12 799	611.8	166.0
Carroll	25	118	9.6	3.5	40	1 366	368.6	55.1	41	485	17.9	5.3
Champaign	47	271	14.6	14.2	41	3 393	1 387.0	170.0	48	701	29.9	7.6
Clark	166	1 172	141.2	58.3	158	6 116	2 832.4	275.0	235	4 288	197.0	53.2
Clermont	385	2 826	469.6	154.5	169	5 182	1 248.5	262.3	280	6 030	285.3	81.9
Clinton	49	D	D	D	41	2 604	1 029.1	128.4	74	1 371	75.2	17.6
Columbiana	106	435	36.3	13.8	171	5 294	1 443.2	213.0	174	2 587	102.9	28.0
Coshocton	29	132	10.8	3.1	52	2 358	1 195.1	113.0	51	717	32.8	9.2
Crawford	45	357	74.1	13.2	80	3 374	1 045.9	149.9	84	987	41.6	10.9
Cuyahoga	4 016	41 345	6 848.8	2 750.9	1 890	69 606	24 399.4	4 048.8	2 959	53 954	2 738.6	758.7
Darke	69	280	30.3	8.8	72	4 475	1 855.5	216.8	88	1 015	43.0	11.0
Defiance	45	221	20.5	7.4	43	3 278	1 018.0	203.5	81	1 228	50.1	13.2
Delaware	534	3 692	667.1	222.2	135	5 463	3 012.0	303.4	421	9 496	460.2	134.1
Erie	117	D	D	D	103	5 465	2 021.6	291.7	263	5 848	305.9	77.6
Fairfield	196	910	76.3	28.9	107	4 219	1 277.9	207.0	244	4 767	203.0	59.6
Fayette	21	72	8.3	2.1	25	1 670	1 343.7	75.9	59	1 053	46.9	12.5
Franklin	3 472	40 628	7 092.6	2 737.0	814	28 991	12 574.1	1 461.7	2 797	57 229	2 980.8	843.3
Fulton	47	D	D	D	93	6 102	3 394.5	290.9	73	936	35.3	10.3
Gallia	29	87	8.7	2.4	22	452	D	22.4	53	886	43.4	11.5
Geauga	349	1 109	207.7	58.4	195	7 259	2 787.3	353.1	171	2 404	98.7	28.5
Greene	437	8 729	1 756.2	651.4	102	3 221	877.9	170.4	311	6 674	319.9	86.5
Guernsey	43	235	30.7	11.1	55	2 634	1 562.7	120.8	89	1 465	71.0	18.0
Hamilton	2 536	40 955	6 599.1	2 839.3	990	45 901	23 167.3	2 800.1	1 853	39 506	2 004.4	569.6
Hancock	136	758	97.8	38.6	94	9 903	4 821.3	491.4	181	4 063	169.8	48.3
Hardin	25	85	7.0	2.4	30	1 722	475.5	73.3	51	868	37.2	12.1
Harrison	13	27	2.4	0.7	12	368	92.3	13.6	27	198	7.9	2.3
Henry	24	91	9.8	3.3	45	3 100	2 313.6	158.0	49	D	D	D
Highland	40	132	11.0	2.9	27	1 698	585.9	68.6	63	878	36.4	9.6
Hocking	26	D	D	D	24	847	287.1	39.3	57	885	45.8	12.6
Holmes	30	267	35.1	11.2	253	6 028	1 483.4	200.9	67	1 374	61.0	17.9
Huron	80	410	33.1	14.4	87	5 436	2 336.8	232.4	107	1 474	60.9	15.5
Jackson	36	153	11.6	3.3	32	3 492	D	117.6	53	884	35.8	9.8
Jefferson	87	D	D	D	35	1 333	D	76.0	142	1 808	76.2	20.0
Knox	54	335	33.4	12.1	69	4 976	2 166.3	300.4	91	1 438	60.7	16.5
Lake	555	3 056	413.5	170.9	617	19 183	6 045.2	970.0	529	9 279	406.8	111.6
Lawrence	42	271	18.0	7.8	34	915	D	30.6	66	1 124	58.9	14.3
Licking	229	1 795	144.3	114.4	151	7 809	2 958.9	358.2	280	4 975	212.7	61.7
Logan	54	766	62.7	27.2	48	4 584	6 790.1	305.7	98	1 214	56.5	15.0
Lorain	448	3 297	276.1	111.4	379	16 010	7 328.0	892.4	514	8 536	397.0	104.6
Lucas	864	8 875	1 182.6	474.5	460	18 286	27 736.6	1 154.6	1 025	19 099	823.0	237.3
Madison	42	D	D	D	44	2 895	1 157.9	135.8	46	844	36.0	10.6
Mahoning	447	3 570	307.8	142.2	326	8 756	1 978.7	398.9	490	9 022	397.2	105.6
Marion	71	303	29.8	9.6	71	5 966	3 681.7	276.5	106	1 893	86.9	22.1
Medina	407	2 028	230.8	83.7	277	8 543	2 970.4	405.6	288	4 897	223.0	61.9
Meigs	11	D	D	D	7	D	D	1.6	28	372	16.4	4.6
Mercer	44	295	31.7	10.6	82	3 807	1 136.9	172.5	85	1 192	44.8	11.9
Miami	159	1 000	112.6	41.6	216	10 888	3 923.9	542.3	188	3 816	159.8	45.7
Monroe	11	D	D	D	9	D	D	D	18	163	5.9	1.6
Montgomery	1 121	12 095	1 713.7	727.6	730	26 188	8 239.2	1 466.6	1 112	22 321	1 028.7	296.6
Morgan	8	D	D	D	9	582	D	27.8	16	159	5.1	1.5
Morrow	33	D	D	D	26	844	D	45.6	29	350	17.6	4.6
Muskingum	106	452	55.6	17.1	72	2 699	867.7	126.2	167	3 102	139.5	39.7
Noble	12	D	D	D	13	299	101.9	D	17	D	D	D

1. Establishment subject to federal tax.

Table B. States and Counties — Health Care and Social Assistance, Other Services, Nonemployer Businesses, and Residential Construction

STATE County	Health care and social assistance, 2012				Other services, 2012				Nonemployer businesses, 2014		Value of residential construction authorized by building permits, 2015	
	Number of establishments	Number of employees	Receipts (mil dol)	Annual payroll (mil dol)	Number of establishments	Number of employees	Receipts (mil dol)	Annual payroll (mil dol)	Number	Receipts (mil dol)	New Construction ($1,000)	Number of housing units
	159	160	161	162	163	164	165	166	167	168	169	170
NORTH DAKOTA—Cont'd												
Ward	152	D	D	D	134	751	69.7	19.7	4 457	225.0	46 728	304
Wells	17	461	21.8	10.8	16	D	D	D	364	15.6	400	2
Williams	65	1 485	131.6	57.6	78	467	82.0	17.0	2 734	177.0	101 357	803
OHIO	28 237	798 770	80 915.7	33 141.0	18 851	127 366	13 221.5	3 491.3	757 764	32 874.5	3 982 890	20 047
Adams	48	1 057	67.1	28.3	25	64	26.1	2.2	1 962	74.3	625	4
Allen	307	11 307	1 256.5	501.7	197	1 264	92.0	25.5	5 457	208.5	16 101	77
Ashland	112	2 220	188.6	71.4	91	563	44.3	14.7	3 421	152.9	11 133	67
Ashtabula	217	5 453	420.3	171.9	158	646	47.5	10.9	6 101	243.5	14 051	88
Athens	144	3 058	287.7	101.6	80	417	27.6	7.5	3 254	106.9	23 733	91
Auglaize	97	2 259	169.4	60.0	89	529	38.2	11.9	2 734	108.9	23 903	108
Belmont	208	4 715	311.7	127.6	124	654	41.0	12.0	3 298	139.9	4 974	52
Brown	58	1 461	112.6	42.2	42	180	13.1	3.8	2 800	106.9	10 038	63
Butler	730	15 022	1 491.8	566.6	520	4 178	373.1	108.0	21 795	926.9	160 521	1 027
Carroll	39	753	41.6	17.4	46	224	16.8	4.0	1 923	84.9	0	0
Champaign	49	1 362	89.1	35.5	48	165	14.0	3.1	2 165	89.8	6 394	37
Clark	313	10 029	912.0	334.8	212	1 363	134.3	40.5	6 748	257.9	16 571	63
Clermont	291	5 950	527.0	211.9	289	1 688	147.8	43.8	13 113	564.3	71 142	420
Clinton	90	1 751	176.2	64.2	60	260	21.5	6.2	2 752	107.5	7 215	37
Columbiana	291	5 444	415.4	161.9	184	857	69.0	18.4	5 993	250.6	6 721	50
Coshocton	84	1 783	143.5	56.0	60	267	22.0	5.0	2 312	91.5	780	13
Crawford	98	2 313	176.8	70.1	73	310	27.1	6.3	2 187	81.0	906	6
Cuyahoga	3 593	137 744	14 792.8	6 409.1	2 495	18 586	2 072.3	568.0	90 292	4 052.0	203 527	744
Darke	77	2 284	186.6	74.3	106	405	24.9	7.0	3 522	143.2	10 072	44
Defiance	85	2 403	194.0	80.8	70	386	31.2	7.1	2 176	88.3	3 389	22
Delaware	395	6 795	541.6	243.4	270	2 266	458.8	94.2	16 124	888.9	215 643	950
Erie	208	5 406	489.8	224.1	138	710	47.5	14.3	4 721	193.0	22 094	85
Fairfield	303	6 114	564.4	241.0	171	1 031	101.5	30.4	10 362	435.7	91 574	342
Fayette	53	1 432	114.4	45.8	40	193	10.7	3.2	1 519	56.4	7 834	46
Franklin	3 325	104 976	11 693.1	4 509.2	1 912	17 718	2 309.3	597.1	91 486	4 154.0	843 224	5 373
Fulton	93	2 330	197.1	76.4	71	254	25.9	6.0	2 977	127.9	10 193	68
Gallia	70	2 473	227.0	97.3	37	241	17.9	5.4	1 909	71.2	428	5
Geauga	237	3 833	360.2	157.2	176	1 179	108.6	36.7	10 643	606.1	46 070	132
Greene	341	5 861	608.5	219.4	212	1 244	99.7	27.9	9 657	385.9	124 224	393
Guernsey	123	2 653	221.2	74.6	60	276	31.0	6.1	2 388	106.3	5 322	38
Hamilton	2 371	80 058	10 054.4	4 272.5	1 488	11 624	1 292.3	344.2	56 359	2 607.7	186 896	893
Hancock	183	5 107	523.6	192.3	137	892	99.6	22.9	4 373	190.0	23 902	99
Hardin	48	645	48.9	18.9	32	117	8.9	2.3	1 545	59.5	3 487	29
Harrison	27	513	39.9	15.0	19	61	5.7	1.2	862	43.9	255	1
Henry	52	1 371	81.3	36.0	42	304	19.7	5.2	1 652	72.5	5 672	27
Highland	97	1 650	128.4	50.9	42	154	13.1	2.9	2 984	128.0	435	8
Hocking	47	1 075	74.7	29.9	35	199	22.2	4.2	1 908	75.0	8 103	49
Holmes	60	1 397	153.1	41.2	53	184	21.5	5.0	5 092	301.1	645	5
Huron	102	2 711	269.6	111.4	105	544	41.3	11.6	3 067	132.2	8 951	56
Jackson	74	1 372	120.4	42.5	40	157	16.7	3.6	1 674	58.4	15 771	65
Jefferson	155	4 577	438.1	164.5	101	590	41.0	11.9	2 986	104.3	1 569	8
Knox	130	2 971	231.6	93.2	77	499	42.7	11.7	4 748	214.8	21 588	121
Lake	608	11 077	944.7	408.2	470	2 718	214.6	66.8	15 242	672.8	91 159	539
Lawrence	123	D	D	D	55	281	28.2	6.3	2 763	98.5	1 164	11
Licking	262	7 491	625.0	254.5	203	1 190	103.1	27.8	11 687	490.9	69 198	280
Logan	94	2 122	180.1	69.5	67	505	79.3	13.1	2 848	116.2	12 414	82
Lorain	616	13 559	1 290.7	534.4	454	2 641	260.3	62.6	17 007	673.0	164 594	847
Lucas	1 275	38 102	4 107.7	1 677.1	731	5 136	444.5	130.0	24 657	1 063.1	93 209	390
Madison	73	D	D	D	46	159	11.9	3.3	2 694	110.6	9 398	41
Mahoning	767	19 562	1 823.7	717.0	382	2 612	216.7	58.4	15 426	609.6	28 181	127
Marion	157	4 315	369.2	151.5	95	648	40.1	11.0	3 098	109.2	5 476	31
Medina	369	7 484	580.7	238.2	300	1 639	128.9	41.0	13 084	612.5	152 987	676
Meigs	41	473	30.4	11.9	17	53	6.7	1.4	1 113	35.1	427	4
Mercer	76	2 104	132.6	57.7	86	436	43.3	10.9	2 691	124.9	14 873	66
Miami	197	4 449	374.8	135.0	178	900	81.3	20.7	6 615	250.1	38 826	151
Monroe	18	D	D	D	23	D	D	D	1 086	38.7	0	0
Montgomery	1 466	48 822	5 573.6	2 243.7	852	6 243	682.6	157.5	31 772	1 270.1	90 680	436
Morgan	16	340	20.2	7.7	13	D	D	D	859	29.6	8 350	39
Morrow	47	D	D	D	24	80	7.3	2.0	2 578	117.6	5 344	27
Muskingum	194	6 011	603.1	266.2	159	1 093	86.6	23.9	5 282	203.4	7 557	79
Noble	20	D	D	D	20	D	D	D	755	31.1	3 790	26

Table B. States and Counties — Government Employment and Payroll, and Local Government Finances

	Government employment and payroll, 2012									Local government finances, 2012				
			March payroll (percent of total)							General revenue				
												Taxes		
													Per capita[1] (dollars)	
STATE County	Full-time equivalent employees	March payroll (dollars)	Administration, judicial, and legal	Police and Corrections	Fire Protection	Highways and transportation	Health and Welfare	Natural resources and utilities	Education and libraries	Total (mil dol)	Inter-governmental (mil dol)	Total (mil dol)	Total	Property
	171	172	173	174	175	176	177	178	179	180	181	182	183	184
NORTH DAKOTA— Cont'd														
Ward	2 136	7 851 589	4.3	7.5	2.8	4.2	5.4	5.7	68.4	241.7	117.3	80.2	1 238	819
Wells	201	657 258	11.8	3.8	0.0	9.3	11.4	5.1	54.7	18.7	8.8	6.5	1 519	1 436
Williams	864	3 064 820	7.6	11.5	0.1	4.9	6.8	4.6	59.1	140.3	49.9	59.7	2 236	1 126
OHIO	X	X	X	X	X	X	X	X	X	X	X	X	X	X
Adams	1 309	4 554 288	8.6	6.3	1.2	4.8	20.7	12.5	44.5	95.0	57.8	28.2	996	856
Allen	4 029	14 917 726	8.3	9.1	4.8	3.4	9.8	5.8	55.9	394.8	197.5	125.6	1 195	774
Ashland	1 952	6 407 247	7.9	9.8	3.4	8.4	11.1	4.1	54.7	148.8	65.0	62.1	1 172	812
Ashtabula	3 445	13 283 345	8.6	8.3	6.3	6.3	10.0	5.8	52.9	379.5	210.8	114.5	1 141	880
Athens	2 322	8 135 468	7.7	8.6	2.5	4.0	14.9	8.3	53.4	218.6	106.3	74.7	1 161	793
Auglaize	1 848	6 837 964	8.1	11.1	3.6	6.2	9.8	11.2	48.9	165.8	68.7	63.4	1 383	791
Belmont	2 607	9 128 313	8.1	10.6	2.1	10.5	11.9	10.3	46.0	191.0	101.3	63.6	913	616
Brown	1 467	5 037 757	10.7	6.4	1.0	3.0	3.9	4.5	68.2	139.2	79.2	35.6	803	573
Butler	12 086	48 616 602	7.6	9.8	5.5	2.6	6.4	6.6	59.8	1 333.8	510.2	553.1	1 493	1 108
Carroll	814	2 533 284	12.9	4.6	0.1	10.7	12.6	3.6	53.6	67.3	39.5	18.9	663	541
Champaign	1 507	5 457 874	8.0	11.9	3.0	4.5	7.3	4.2	60.0	133.3	67.8	46.2	1 167	749
Clark	5 386	19 627 638	7.6	10.0	4.2	2.3	8.2	4.4	57.6	501.3	270.1	168.3	1 227	774
Clermont	5 289	20 437 759	7.0	10.5	7.4	2.9	8.3	2.8	59.9	577.6	246.3	251.2	1 262	1 074
Clinton	1 809	5 888 599	9.0	8.5	2.2	3.7	8.2	6.6	60.3	157.7	71.7	54.0	1 288	849
Columbiana	3 495	11 243 471	8.0	8.4	2.1	5.7	10.5	5.6	58.7	309.6	171.8	94.5	887	570
Coshocton	1 280	4 337 624	6.8	5.0	9.6	5.4	10.8	3.0	57.6	122.4	67.8	38.8	1 056	791
Crawford	1 254	4 325 266	5.9	4.7	3.6	1.8	1.1	5.5	77.2	151.9	72.7	51.8	1 209	747
Cuyahoga	62 490	287 120 691	6.2	10.3	5.0	6.7	17.9	8.2	44.0	8 188.0	2 777.4	3 498.3	2 765	1 595
Darke	1 735	6 310 491	7.2	9.5	3.5	3.8	9.0	4.8	60.8	161.4	77.3	60.1	1 145	652
Defiance	1 658	5 904 403	6.0	5.9	1.8	3.6	22.5	5.1	51.1	159.4	60.4	46.4	1 200	722
Delaware	5 621	21 810 855	6.5	8.3	8.6	3.5	6.9	3.8	60.6	594.5	125.1	379.4	2 096	1 582
Erie	3 210	12 237 910	9.9	7.7	6.1	3.6	6.5	6.6	58.0	347.1	131.6	140.7	1 841	1 302
Fairfield	4 930	17 614 468	7.6	7.4	6.0	3.4	7.0	5.5	62.0	533.2	218.0	227.0	1 539	972
Fayette	1 569	5 994 441	8.4	7.6	3.1	4.0	30.8	6.0	35.4	151.4	51.3	42.0	1 454	900
Franklin	43 936	204 420 126	7.5	12.0	8.0	4.8	6.8	5.9	53.0	6 852.6	2 645.8	3 248.5	2 717	1 632
Fulton	1 714	6 275 872	9.2	6.4	2.8	7.9	4.5	5.4	60.4	175.3	77.4	66.6	1 566	1 017
Gallia	1 230	4 310 190	10.5	5.0	0.3	10.5	8.6	3.8	60.0	121.8	67.0	35.1	1 144	879
Geauga	2 853	10 934 381	6.8	10.3	1.9	6.2	6.6	5.0	60.8	321.0	103.8	177.1	1 890	1 605
Greene	5 165	20 150 214	7.8	10.0	5.1	2.9	8.5	4.8	58.8	586.4	206.6	277.8	1 698	1 294
Guernsey	1 477	4 435 295	10.2	6.1	1.9	6.0	6.7	6.6	52.4	132.8	73.2	38.5	968	624
Hamilton	30 330	130 350 382	7.8	13.0	8.0	5.1	7.5	8.7	47.8	4 236.2	1 499.4	1 927.5	2 403	1 479
Hancock	2 432	8 819 684	8.0	8.9	4.5	4.6	9.6	8.0	55.4	271.6	110.7	109.9	1 453	890
Hardin	1 423	4 258 899	9.1	8.7	1.2	4.7	11.9	3.6	57.1	110.9	55.5	32.7	1 034	564
Harrison	710	1 856 484	14.6	4.5	0.0	15.6	8.0	4.7	51.0	49.7	28.0	13.6	864	670
Henry	1 481	5 408 211	10.0	3.9	0.9	3.5	8.5	11.1	57.7	117.5	56.0	44.6	1 592	1 074
Highland	2 293	6 286 414	5.2	4.7	1.8	3.3	31.1	2.7	50.4	172.7	76.0	41.2	959	563
Hocking	914	2 885 727	10.2	5.6	1.4	5.5	5.2	3.2	67.0	114.8	42.6	28.6	978	747
Holmes	1 321	4 844 879	5.9	5.2	1.1	8.0	34.0	1.8	43.4	120.7	39.0	36.0	838	671
Huron	2 467	10 437 634	6.6	7.8	2.4	4.1	4.3	21.4	48.4	200.0	86.9	77.4	1 306	715
Jackson	1 363	4 190 837	9.9	7.6	2.0	7.6	8.5	6.5	56.1	108.3	64.9	23.7	718	505
Jefferson	2 754	8 388 400	8.2	12.7	2.8	7.2	11.7	7.8	48.7	279.5	143.1	76.7	1 121	730
Knox	2 080	6 852 809	7.4	6.9	4.1	5.9	8.2	4.9	60.0	183.1	81.3	75.5	1 244	918
Lake	9 604	40 201 055	7.4	10.0	6.0	4.6	9.6	6.7	54.4	980.1	328.7	481.4	2 097	1 489
Lawrence	2 540	8 380 560	7.9	7.5	1.5	3.4	6.7	4.8	67.2	216.7	128.7	37.7	607	431
Licking	5 717	20 737 584	8.7	10.0	5.7	3.6	5.5	4.6	60.9	579.7	236.0	255.6	1 525	1 041
Logan	1 959	6 311 962	5.8	5.7	2.0	5.4	16.7	4.0	58.9	181.6	83.8	65.2	1 434	1 028
Lorain	11 564	45 174 817	6.2	9.7	3.8	2.9	8.7	7.0	60.5	1 201.2	540.9	467.7	1 551	1 088
Lucas	14 739	62 111 336	9.0	11.4	8.7	4.8	10.1	5.0	50.5	2 086.3	910.4	780.9	1 783	1 087
Madison	1 659	6 453 004	10.2	8.0	6.0	3.9	8.2	4.3	57.6	145.7	58.9	62.4	1 448	1 020
Mahoning	8 773	31 345 985	6.1	10.6	3.5	4.0	7.9	7.9	58.9	868.3	433.7	320.4	1 363	887
Marion	2 295	8 158 244	7.0	10.0	5.7	2.9	9.1	2.6	60.7	238.0	129.7	65.6	990	651
Medina	5 924	23 018 921	7.1	9.8	2.3	4.3	7.5	6.6	61.1	592.1	209.5	282.6	1 627	1 274
Meigs	1 067	3 103 267	7.9	7.6	0.0	6.4	10.2	11.3	53.7	74.8	52.2	14.0	593	473
Mercer	1 924	6 814 130	6.9	4.9	1.1	2.5	23.6	3.3	56.9	205.3	75.3	58.0	1 418	907
Miami	3 473	13 601 040	7.3	8.3	2.8	3.5	7.7	7.6	59.9	385.2	159.1	157.7	1 531	850
Monroe	802	1 932 268	10.9	3.9	0.2	9.0	13.4	7.6	53.8	74.7	47.7	17.9	1 229	1 062
Montgomery	22 502	93 151 363	7.9	9.7	4.7	6.0	8.0	8.2	54.1	2 605.5	1 042.9	1 055.0	1 974	1 302
Morgan	442	1 318 311	13.5	4.8	0.0	6.2	1.1	3.1	69.8	48.1	33.5	10.1	676	539
Morrow	1 452	4 922 890	11.2	5.3	0.3	5.8	24.4	1.2	49.4	129.7	48.6	32.8	939	663
Muskingum	3 889	12 275 435	6.0	8.2	2.0	4.2	10.5	5.2	60.2	370.0	202.8	113.8	1 324	918
Noble	445	1 384 468	17.5	1.9	0.0	7.5	11.4	15.2	45.8	48.2	22.3	17.2	1 183	1 099

1. Based on the resident population estimated as of July 1 of the year shown.

Table B. States and Counties — Local Government Finances, Government Employment, and Voting

STATE County	Direct general expenditure — Total (mil dol)	Per capita[1] (dollars)	Education	Health and hospitals	Police protection	Public welfare	Highways	Debt outstanding — Total (mil dol)	Per capita[1] (dollars)	Federal civilian	Federal military	State and local	Democratic	Republican	All other
	185	186	187	188	189	190	191	192	193	194	195	196	197	198	199
NORTH DAKOTA—Cont'd															
Ward	230.0	3 550	57.5	0.3	5.1	2.2	10.8	95.7	1 477	1 137	5 664	4 422	39.6	58.8	1.6
Wells	18.0	4 209	46.4	1.9	3.5	4.3	18.7	9.3	2 176	28	27	270	35.4	61.8	2.9
Williams	130.1	4 872	37.2	3.2	4.7	0.9	16.5	127.0	4 757	73	212	2 196	31.2	67.1	1.7
OHIO	X	X	X	X	X	X	X	X	X	76 023	36 046	683 874	51.5	46.9	1.6
Adams	85.9	3 030	56.6	4.4	3.7	6.7	8.9	48.9	1 726	69	72	1 450	36.6	60.7	2.7
Allen	385.4	3 665	49.5	5.4	6.9	4.3	6.7	180.7	1 719	326	258	5 819	38.8	59.6	1.6
Ashland	147.7	2 789	50.7	9.1	6.1	3.4	7.9	51.1	966	101	132	2 303	37.0	60.2	2.8
Ashtabula	389.2	3 877	53.0	7.0	3.8	6.1	7.1	243.8	2 429	191	265	4 367	55.8	42.2	2.0
Athens	231.8	3 605	47.4	7.2	2.6	14.9	4.9	68.3	1 062	229	156	10 603	66.6	31.3	2.0
Auglaize	176.4	3 848	52.8	1.4	5.8	4.8	6.3	154.1	3 362	86	117	2 249	28.6	69.8	1.5
Belmont	186.0	2 669	48.0	6.2	2.5	6.5	6.8	55.5	797	161	170	3 829	50.3	47.6	2.1
Brown	134.7	3 035	63.4	3.5	6.0	3.2	5.5	58.8	1 325	83	113	1 886	37.3	60.6	2.1
Butler	1 326.8	3 580	50.2	3.7	7.9	4.7	5.8	1 987.8	5 364	557	958	20 088	38.0	60.6	1.4
Carroll	59.8	2 092	47.0	8.7	3.5	6.9	10.6	17.3	605	46	72	956	46.0	50.9	3.1
Champaign	144.3	3 648	59.7	3.7	3.5	3.9	6.6	60.2	1 522	65	99	1 809	39.1	59.0	1.9
Clark	474.6	3 459	49.3	5.8	5.9	6.2	3.3	206.0	1 502	552	348	6 482	47.9	50.4	1.8
Clermont	582.2	2 924	49.6	6.2	6.8	6.0	5.4	332.6	1 671	294	518	7 184	33.1	65.5	1.4
Clinton	150.9	3 602	49.6	3.5	5.9	5.2	7.7	60.1	1 434	124	106	2 290	34.0	64.3	1.8
Columbiana	314.7	2 954	56.2	3.2	5.1	8.9	6.3	123.5	1 160	593	264	4 484	45.1	52.8	2.1
Coshocton	116.3	3 163	50.7	9.0	6.0	6.2	9.6	60.1	1 634	71	94	1 494	45.6	51.4	3.0
Crawford	163.0	3 804	50.5	4.3	4.1	5.0	8.0	99.7	2 328	84	109	1 791	39.1	58.2	2.7
Cuyahoga	8 005.7	6 328	36.6	14.5	5.9	3.6	2.9	11 286.9	8 922	15 807	3 609	77 817	68.9	30.0	1.1
Darke	165.9	3 160	56.8	4.8	5.9	4.6	7.2	76.5	1 457	104	134	2 107	30.9	67.0	2.1
Defiance	164.9	4 263	38.1	17.8	4.2	3.1	5.7	96.2	2 486	86	98	1 954	43.8	54.2	2.0
Delaware	580.7	3 207	51.8	3.6	4.6	2.2	6.9	734.5	4 057	211	484	7 260	39.7	59.3	1.1
Erie	360.9	4 724	52.1	2.5	5.2	3.9	4.2	232.7	3 046	304	193	4 943	56.1	42.3	1.6
Fairfield	537.8	3 647	55.2	5.3	4.9	3.9	3.7	791.1	5 364	234	404	6 563	40.7	57.8	1.6
Fayette	143.4	4 966	32.8	26.1	3.8	3.7	4.5	83.9	2 906	51	73	1 708	37.6	60.7	1.6
Franklin	6 511.1	5 446	38.1	3.0	6.3	6.0	4.2	8 029.0	6 716	12 672	3 587	117 553	59.7	39.0	1.3
Fulton	197.2	4 637	67.2	2.5	4.2	2.4	4.5	104.1	2 450	90	109	2 520	45.1	53.2	1.7
Gallia	123.5	4 023	57.7	2.3	5.6	5.4	6.2	74.2	2 416	78	76	1 679	35.9	61.9	2.2
Geauga	314.3	3 355	48.5	9.3	6.8	2.6	8.8	302.2	3 225	99	242	4 083	41.6	56.9	1.5
Greene	655.1	4 004	53.0	4.0	6.4	4.0	4.8	524.5	3 206	13 745	3 041	11 184	40.1	58.5	1.3
Guernsey	125.8	3 159	48.1	3.5	4.9	8.6	7.9	38.7	973	114	101	2 215	44.0	53.1	2.9
Hamilton	4 409.2	5 497	37.9	6.8	6.8	4.4	3.4	5 717.7	7 129	8 660	2 140	47 659	53.0	46.0	1.0
Hancock	295.5	3 905	53.3	7.9	3.8	2.7	4.3	240.6	3 180	153	191	3 207	37.5	60.6	1.9
Hardin	110.3	3 489	43.3	1.9	7.5	10.6	8.3	59.1	1 869	76	77	1 422	38.2	59.1	2.7
Harrison	46.0	2 927	48.6	1.1	3.7	9.2	14.1	4.8	305	52	40	710	47.3	49.7	3.0
Henry	116.8	4 166	57.4	9.8	4.3	0.3	7.0	51.0	1 819	67	71	2 017	42.6	55.5	1.9
Highland	157.5	3 663	45.3	24.8	5.4	4.0	5.4	55.6	1 293	95	110	2 345	35.7	62.1	2.2
Hocking	118.1	4 036	34.2	34.9	4.9	5.2	5.5	21.9	748	46	74	1 739	48.3	49.1	2.6
Holmes	122.6	2 851	35.9	29.5	3.5	5.1	8.0	35.7	830	62	112	1 554	28.3	69.5	2.3
Huron	227.6	3 839	59.2	1.8	3.8	5.5	5.6	177.4	2 992	139	151	2 403	47.2	50.4	2.4
Jackson	103.5	3 142	55.6	4.5	4.9	6.5	7.1	74.9	2 274	67	84	1 462	38.6	58.7	2.7
Jefferson	274.2	4 010	48.3	6.7	5.3	3.8	7.4	154.1	2 253	163	169	3 127	49.1	48.9	2.1
Knox	190.4	3 137	48.2	3.8	2.8	3.7	12.6	94.4	1 554	101	149	2 618	39.0	58.9	2.0
Lake	960.6	4 184	51.1	7.4	6.8	2.5	5.5	411.1	1 790	457	611	11 139	49.6	48.7	1.7
Lawrence	214.4	3 452	60.9	5.7	3.5	4.9	4.0	51.1	822	122	158	3 025	41.4	56.7	1.9
Licking	578.6	3 453	56.4	0.8	6.3	6.5	4.5	386.9	2 309	358	441	7 380	41.2	57.0	1.8
Logan	185.1	4 071	51.9	5.6	4.3	4.6	6.6	117.8	2 592	118	119	2 115	35.7	62.3	1.9
Lorain	1 206.9	4 003	55.2	4.3	5.8	3.9	4.7	1 730.7	5 741	1 105	788	14 280	58.1	40.2	1.7
Lucas	1 896.4	4 330	37.6	9.4	7.1	4.9	3.8	2 289.2	5 226	1 899	1 197	27 927	65.0	33.5	1.5
Madison	152.8	3 549	60.2	4.9	4.6	3.8	5.7	137.1	3 184	71	101	3 034	37.4	60.8	1.8
Mahoning	851.8	3 622	47.9	5.8	7.8	3.8	4.3	531.9	2 262	1 175	598	13 637	62.2	35.6	2.1
Marion	232.6	3 512	58.7	1.2	4.1	2.2	4.0	316.2	4 773	111	179	3 786	44.4	53.3	2.4
Medina	715.8	4 121	54.5	3.6	4.6	2.1	11.9	431.2	2 483	279	481	6 750	45.2	53.3	1.5
Meigs	70.8	3 002	53.3	2.8	2.8	10.1	10.2	25.4	1 075	65	60	1 058	39.5	58.1	2.4
Mercer	196.0	4 794	46.2	26.1	3.3	3.1	7.9	89.2	2 183	97	105	2 703	27.5	71.0	1.5
Miami	405.1	3 930	56.7	3.4	6.0	3.1	5.3	280.3	2 720	182	266	4 624	34.8	63.3	1.9
Monroe	83.7	5 754	66.8	2.8	2.6	8.8	8.9	2.9	200	48	37	718	53.1	43.9	3.0
Montgomery	2 652.7	4 965	44.5	3.0	6.4	8.6	5.3	2 338.6	4 377	4 222	4 046	27 281	52.4	46.2	1.4
Morgan	43.8	2 938	48.1	4.6	5.2	8.6	11.1	11.3	760	41	38	643	44.9	52.1	3.1
Morrow	139.5	3 994	47.5	22.8	1.4	3.0	5.3	60.5	1 733	48	90	1 567	37.1	60.5	2.4
Muskingum	340.0	3 956	54.4	3.3	4.9	6.1	6.4	122.4	1 424	219	218	5 243	45.4	52.6	2.0
Noble	36.8	2 523	50.8	2.9	4.1	7.6	14.3	3.0	208	23	30	932	40.1	55.9	4.0

1. Based on the resident population estimated as of July 1 of the year shown.   2. © 2013 Election Data Services, Inc. All rights reserved.

Table B. States and Counties — **Land Area and Population**

STATE/ County code	CBSA code[1]	County type[2]	STATE County	Land area,[3] (sq km) 2010	Total persons 2015	Rank	Per square kilometer	White	Black	American Indian, Alaska Native	Asian and Pacific Islander	Percent Hispanic or Latino[4]	Under 5 years	5 to 17 years	18 to 24 years	25 to 34 years	35 to 44 years	45 to 54 years
								Race alone or in combination, not Hispanic or Latino (percent)					Age (percent)					
				1	2	3	4	5	6	7	8	9	10	11	12	13	14	15
			OHIO—Cont'd															
39 123	38840	2	Ottawa	660	40 877	1 158	61.9	93.7	1.6	0.5	0.6	4.9	4.4	15.1	6.9	9.2	10.7	14.4
39 125	...	6	Paulding	1 079	18 976	1 875	17.6	93.9	1.5	0.8	0.4	4.5	5.7	18.3	7.5	11.0	11.7	14.2
39 127	18140	6	Perry	1 057	35 985	1 273	34.0	98.0	0.9	1.1	0.3	0.8	5.9	18.3	8.2	11.6	12.3	14.6
39 129	18140	1	Pickaway	1 298	56 998	896	43.9	94.5	4.3	0.7	0.7	1.3	5.5	16.6	9.3	12.9	13.9	14.7
39 131	...	7	Pike	1 140	28 217	1 480	24.8	97.0	1.7	1.4	0.6	0.9	5.9	18.0	8.1	11.0	12.8	14.2
39 133	10420	2	Portage	1 262	162 275	395	128.6	91.6	5.3	0.7	2.3	1.6	4.4	14.9	16.6	11.1	11.0	13.9
39 135	...	2	Preble	1 098	41 329	1 143	37.6	97.9	1.0	0.8	0.9	0.7	5.5	17.9	7.5	11.1	11.9	14.3
39 137	...	6	Putnam	1 250	34 042	1 326	27.2	93.2	0.6	0.3	0.4	5.9	6.7	18.9	8.5	10.9	11.3	14.1
39 139	31900	3	Richland	1 283	121 707	510	94.9	88.0	10.5	0.7	1.0	1.7	5.7	16.1	8.7	11.9	12.0	13.6
39 141	17060	4	Ross	1 785	77 170	716	43.2	92.0	7.2	1.1	0.9	1.1	5.4	16.2	8.0	12.5	13.6	15.2
39 143	23380	4	Sandusky	1 058	59 679	871	56.4	87.2	4.2	0.6	0.6	9.6	5.9	17.4	8.0	11.3	12.0	13.9
39 145	39020	4	Scioto	1 580	76 825	717	48.6	95.1	3.4	1.3	0.6	1.2	5.7	16.3	9.2	12.5	12.5	13.2
39 147	45660	4	Seneca	1 427	55 610	911	39.0	91.8	3.4	0.5	0.9	4.8	5.1	17.2	10.9	11.4	11.5	13.3
39 149	43380	4	Shelby	1 056	48 901	1 000	46.3	94.9	3.4	0.5	1.4	1.6	6.4	19.6	8.3	10.9	12.2	14.3
39 151	15940	2	Stark	1 490	375 165	183	251.8	89.2	9.2	0.8	1.2	1.9	5.5	16.5	9.0	11.6	11.6	13.8
39 153	10420	2	Summit	1 069	541 968	121	507.0	80.3	15.9	0.7	3.3	1.9	5.7	16.0	9.0	12.7	11.9	14.2
39 155	49660	2	Trumbull	1 601	203 751	319	127.3	89.1	9.5	0.7	0.8	1.6	5.2	15.8	8.1	10.9	11.4	14.0
39 157	35420	4	Tuscarawas	1 470	92 916	629	63.2	96.2	1.4	0.6	0.6	2.4	5.9	17.0	7.8	11.7	11.9	13.5
39 159	18140	1	Union	1 118	54 277	925	48.5	92.5	3.2	0.6	3.6	1.5	5.8	19.6	8.2	12.5	15.6	15.4
39 161	46780	6	Van Wert	1 060	28 562	1 470	26.9	95.8	1.7	0.4	0.6	2.8	5.9	17.6	8.2	10.9	11.7	13.5
39 163	...	9	Vinton	1 068	13 048	2 230	12.2	98.3	1.1	1.0	0.4	0.7	5.6	17.7	8.1	11.0	12.8	14.6
39 165	17140	1	Warren	1 039	224 469	290	216.0	89.1	3.9	0.5	5.3	2.6	5.9	20.0	7.7	11.2	14.2	15.7
39 167	31930	3	Washington	1 637	61 112	856	37.3	96.7	1.9	0.9	1.1	1.1	5.0	15.1	9.1	10.9	11.4	13.9
39 169	49300	4	Wayne	1 437	116 063	529	80.8	95.3	2.4	0.6	1.2	1.8	6.5	18.1	10.1	11.3	11.3	13.1
39 171	...	7	Williams	1 090	37 120	1 249	34.1	94.2	1.5	0.6	0.8	4.1	5.8	17.3	7.9	11.4	11.9	13.9
39 173	45780	2	Wood	1 599	129 730	482	81.1	90.1	3.2	0.6	2.2	5.3	5.4	15.3	17.4	12.2	11.2	12.1
39 175	...	7	Wyandot	1 054	22 243	1 721	21.1	96.2	0.8	0.5	0.8	2.7	6.0	17.4	7.7	11.2	12.2	13.5
40 000	...	X	**OKLAHOMA**	177 660	3 911 338	X	22.0	71.9	8.8	12.3	2.8	9.8	6.8	17.7	10.1	13.7	12.2	12.6
40 001	...	6	Adair	1 485	22 004	1 731	14.8	51.6	0.9	50.6	0.9	6.2	6.8	20.0	9.0	11.4	12.4	13.5
40 003	...	9	Alfalfa	2 244	5 868	2 766	2.6	86.6	4.9	5.1	0.7	5.0	5.4	14.1	6.3	10.9	15.0	16.6
40 005	...	7	Atoka	2 527	13 793	2 184	5.5	77.9	4.8	19.1	1.0	3.5	5.6	16.7	8.3	12.6	12.0	13.1
40 007	...	9	Beaver	4 700	5 427	2 810	1.2	75.1	1.2	2.3	0.4	22.9	5.5	19.8	8.1	10.4	11.6	13.5
40 009	21120	7	Beckham	2 336	23 768	1 650	10.2	77.8	4.9	4.1	1.2	14.1	8.0	17.4	9.6	16.3	12.4	12.3
40 011	...	6	Blaine	2 405	9 833	2 448	4.1	77.9	4.7	11.9	0.8	9.2	8.2	18.2	8.3	10.5	10.2	12.7
40 013	20460	6	Bryan	2 343	44 884	1 075	19.2	79.0	2.6	19.0	1.1	5.6	6.8	16.9	10.2	13.6	11.6	12.0
40 015	...	6	Caddo	3 311	29 343	1 446	8.9	62.7	4.2	26.3	0.7	11.3	6.7	18.3	8.6	13.2	11.9	13.4
40 017	36420	1	Canadian	2 322	133 378	475	57.4	81.4	3.7	7.1	3.9	8.0	6.8	19.6	7.8	14.7	14.4	13.1
40 019	11620	5	Carter	2 129	48 689	1 004	22.9	76.1	8.6	13.4	1.6	6.7	6.9	18.6	8.1	12.4	12.6	12.8
40 021	45140	6	Cherokee	1 941	48 447	1 010	25.0	57.8	2.3	41.6	1.0	6.6	6.1	17.0	15.3	11.9	11.0	11.7
40 023	...	7	Choctaw	1 995	14 997	2 098	7.5	67.8	12.8	21.5	0.9	3.8	6.2	18.2	7.7	10.7	11.1	12.9
40 025	...	9	Cimarron	4 752	2 216	3 030	0.5	76.7	1.0	2.3	0.7	21.4	5.9	18.2	6.7	10.4	10.2	11.8
40 027	36420	1	Cleveland	1 395	274 458	245	196.7	78.1	6.0	7.8	5.4	7.9	5.9	16.4	15.0	15.0	12.5	12.1
40 029	...	9	Coal	1 338	5 651	2 789	4.2	78.8	1.8	23.7	0.7	3.9	5.7	18.2	8.7	9.8	11.1	12.1
40 031	30020	3	Comanche	2 769	124 648	501	45.0	61.8	19.2	7.6	4.7	12.6	7.4	16.8	13.3	16.9	12.2	11.8
40 033	30020	6	Cotton	1 639	5 996	2 752	3.7	81.8	3.4	12.0	0.7	7.2	5.9	18.0	8.0	10.8	11.3	14.2
40 035	...	6	Craig	1 972	14 818	2 114	7.5	73.0	4.5	27.4	1.1	3.2	5.4	16.5	8.3	11.5	11.9	14.6
40 037	46140	2	Creek	2 461	70 892	763	28.8	83.1	3.4	15.4	0.9	3.7	6.2	17.9	8.1	11.6	12.0	13.7
40 039	48220	7	Custer	2 561	29 744	1 436	11.6	72.5	3.8	8.1	1.9	16.4	7.6	16.9	17.3	14.0	10.1	10.6
40 041	...	6	Delaware	1 912	41 459	1 139	21.7	72.1	0.8	29.8	1.5	3.5	4.8	16.5	7.4	9.6	10.6	13.1
40 043	...	9	Dewey	2 589	4 995	2 837	1.9	86.4	1.6	7.2	1.2	6.0	6.8	19.4	7.7	10.8	10.4	12.5
40 045	...	9	Ellis	3 190	4 231	2 884	1.3	89.4	1.2	3.4	0.6	7.5	5.4	18.0	7.2	9.6	11.6	12.1
40 047	21420	5	Garfield	2 741	63 569	828	23.2	79.7	4.5	4.4	3.9	11.4	7.4	18.3	9.2	14.2	11.3	12.1
40 049	...	6	Garvin	2 077	27 755	1 502	13.4	81.0	3.5	11.9	1.0	7.6	6.7	18.2	8.1	12.3	11.8	12.6
40 051	36420	1	Grady	2 850	54 648	919	19.2	85.9	3.2	8.8	0.9	5.3	6.0	18.4	8.5	12.4	12.6	13.8
40 053	...	9	Grant	2 592	4 523	2 862	1.7	92.0	2.0	3.8	0.5	4.3	6.1	17.6	7.0	10.4	10.4	13.6
40 055	...	7	Greer	1 656	6 070	2 749	3.7	78.2	8.4	4.4	0.6	11.3	5.2	14.7	8.1	16.4	12.7	13.3
40 057	...	9	Harmon	1 391	2 788	2 988	2.0	62.7	8.7	3.2	0.7	27.2	7.5	17.3	7.9	11.9	10.2	12.6
40 059	...	9	Harper	2 691	3 754	2 922	1.4	77.9	0.7	1.7	0.4	20.1	7.2	18.3	7.8	11.0	10.8	13.5
40 061	...	6	Haskell	1 493	12 845	2 238	8.6	78.8	1.2	22.0	1.0	4.0	6.0	18.2	8.0	11.3	11.1	12.8
40 063	...	7	Hughes	2 084	13 735	2 187	6.6	70.6	6.5	23.9	0.7	4.7	4.9	16.7	8.5	13.1	12.3	12.8
40 065	11060	5	Jackson	2 079	25 574	1 580	12.3	67.1	8.2	3.2	2.3	22.8	8.3	17.4	10.8	14.8	11.4	12.0
40 067	...	8	Jefferson	1 965	6 276	2 736	3.2	82.6	2.0	9.7	0.6	9.7	6.5	17.7	7.3	10.5	11.0	12.9
40 069	...	7	Johnston	1 665	10 980	2 357	6.6	77.6	2.9	21.4	1.1	4.6	6.2	17.3	9.6	11.7	11.1	13.2
40 071	38620	6	Kay	2 382	45 366	1 068	19.0	80.3	3.1	13.4	1.0	7.2	7.1	18.1	9.1	11.5	11.1	12.1
40 073	...	6	Kingfisher	2 326	15 584	2 070	6.7	80.1	1.8	5.4	0.5	15.0	7.4	19.7	8.1	11.8	11.7	13.6

1. CBSA = Core Based Statistical Area. See Appendix A for explanation. See Appendix B for list of metropolitan areas with component counties.   2. County type code from the Economic Research Service of USDA Rural-Urban Continuum Codes. See Appendix A for definition.   3. Dry land or land partially or temporarily covered by water.   4. May be of any race.

	Population, 2014 (cont.)				Population change and components of change, 2000–2015							Households, 2010–2014				
	Age (percent) (cont.)				Total persons		Percent change		Components of change, 2010–2015					Percent		
STATE County	55 to 64 years	65 to 74 years	75 years and over	Percent female	2000	2010	2000–2010	2010–2015	Births	Deaths	Net migration	Number	Persons per house-hold	Family house-holds	Female family house-holder[1]	One per-son
	16	17	18	19	20	21	22	23	24	25	26	27	28	29	30	31
OHIO—Cont'd																
Ottawa	17.2	13.0	9.1	50.5	40 985	41 434	1.1	-1.3	1 798	2 454	41	17 366	2.33	69.6	8.8	26.1
Paulding	14.6	9.9	7.1	50.2	20 293	19 614	-3.3	-3.3	1 151	974	-793	7 798	2.46	70.0	7.7	25.5
Perry	14.0	9.3	5.7	50.0	34 078	36 052	5.8	-0.2	2 268	1 825	-463	13 637	2.62	72.6	11.6	23.7
Pickaway	12.7	8.5	6.1	47.2	52 727	55 698	5.6	2.3	3 171	2 619	763	19 435	2.67	72.6	11.0	23.1
Pike	13.7	9.2	7.1	50.2	27 695	28 709	3.7	-1.7	1 833	1 692	-594	10 944	2.56	67.2	14.2	27.8
Portage	13.5	8.7	6.0	51.0	152 061	161 421	6.2	0.5	7 726	7 063	357	61 042	2.54	65.4	11.6	26.2
Preble	14.6	10.0	7.2	50.4	42 337	42 270	-0.2	-2.2	2 311	2 360	-853	16 151	2.57	71.5	11.6	24.2
Putnam	14.1	8.1	7.4	49.8	34 726	34 499	-0.7	-1.3	2 416	1 567	-1 317	13 006	2.61	73.9	6.6	22.5
Richland	14.0	9.8	8.3	49.2	128 852	124 475	-3.4	-2.2	7 345	7 123	-2 961	48 211	2.40	64.2	12.2	31.2
Ross	13.9	9.0	6.2	47.5	73 345	78 064	6.4	-1.1	4 374	4 184	-989	28 209	2.53	68.9	13.5	26.1
Sandusky	14.6	9.3	7.6	50.8	61 792	60 944	-1.4	-2.1	3 512	3 233	-1 514	23 831	2.48	67.9	12.0	27.3
Scioto	13.7	9.2	7.6	50.8	79 195	79 499	0.4	-3.4	4 694	4 907	-2 306	29 558	2.54	63.8	10.9	30.1
Seneca	14.3	8.8	7.5	50.0	58 683	56 745	-3.3	-2.0	3 066	3 043	-1 178	21 539	2.47	68.5	12.1	26.1
Shelby	13.6	8.3	6.4	49.8	47 910	49 423	3.2	-1.1	3 240	2 202	-1 546	18 616	2.61	72.5	9.6	22.4
Stark	14.4	9.7	8.0	51.5	378 098	375 584	-0.7	-0.1	21 895	21 095	-792	149 756	2.44	66.1	12.4	28.7
Summit	14.3	8.9	7.3	51.5	542 899	541 786	-0.2	-0.4	32 305	29 111	-2 339	220 710	2.41	62.7	13.1	31.5
Trumbull	15.2	10.6	8.7	51.2	225 116	210 307	-6.6	-3.1	11 040	13 007	-4 243	86 565	2.35	64.4	13.5	31.2
Tuscarawas	14.3	9.7	8.2	50.6	90 914	92 582	1.8	0.4	5 840	5 163	-351	36 366	2.51	69.7	10.8	26.1
Union	11.6	6.8	4.4	52.5	40 909	52 267	27.8	3.8	3 206	1 731	472	18 291	2.73	75.0	9.2	21.1
Van Wert	14.2	9.6	8.4	51.3	29 659	28 744	-3.1	-0.6	1 720	1 595	-365	11 388	2.48	69.1	9.4	27.1
Vinton	15.0	9.4	6.1	50.4	12 806	13 435	4.9	-2.9	755	745	-365	5 137	2.57	70.7	11.8	24.8
Warren	12.2	7.7	5.4	49.8	158 383	212 868	34.4	5.4	12 765	8 077	6 694	77 328	2.74	75.9	8.3	19.7
Washington	15.3	10.8	8.4	50.9	63 251	61 778	-2.3	-1.1	3 230	3 704	-87	24 923	2.40	65.4	9.5	29.8
Wayne	13.4	9.0	7.2	50.5	111 564	114 514	2.6	1.4	8 094	5 540	-977	42 593	2.61	71.2	9.5	25.0
Williams	14.3	9.6	7.9	50.3	39 188	37 642	-3.9	-1.4	2 262	1 981	-793	15 001	2.42	65.8	10.4	28.8
Wood	12.5	7.8	6.1	50.7	121 065	125 488	3.7	3.4	7 145	5 321	2 146	49 561	2.45	62.5	9.1	28.5
Wyandot	14.1	9.3	8.6	50.7	22 908	22 615	-1.3	-1.6	1 365	1 229	-497	9 327	2.38	66.5	8.7	27.0
OKLAHOMA	12.3	8.3	6.2	50.5	3 450 654	3 751 616	8.7	4.3	278 907	197 438	76 903	1 450 117	2.56	66.5	12.5	28.1
Adair	12.3	9.0	5.5	49.7	21 038	22 683	7.8	-3.0	1 542	1 241	-949	7 942	2.80	74.4	15.6	22.1
Alfalfa	13.8	9.4	8.4	39.9	6 105	5 642	-7.6	4.0	316	355	293	2 067	2.26	65.3	7.3	28.4
Atoka	13.7	10.7	7.3	47.7	13 879	14 183	2.2	-2.7	878	717	-450	5 208	2.42	71.8	14.2	24.7
Beaver	13.9	9.4	7.7	50.0	5 857	5 636	-3.8	-3.7	313	219	-295	2 089	2.64	72.7	6.8	24.5
Beckham	11.7	6.6	5.7	46.5	19 799	22 119	11.7	7.5	2 006	1 240	867	7 770	2.72	66.3	13.5	27.6
Blaine	14.2	9.6	8.2	50.2	11 976	11 943	-0.3	-17.7	830	617	-2 474	3 703	2.17	66.6	13.2	28.5
Bryan	12.0	9.9	7.0	51.3	36 534	42 416	16.1	5.8	2 993	2 448	1 884	16 713	2.54	63.8	12.2	29.8
Caddo	12.4	8.9	6.8	48.2	30 150	29 600	-1.8	-0.9	2 224	1 836	-589	10 245	2.74	68.9	13.2	26.1
Canadian	11.5	7.4	4.7	50.5	87 697	115 541	31.8	15.4	8 819	4 571	13 197	42 622	2.83	74.2	10.0	21.6
Carter	13.0	8.7	7.0	51.3	45 621	47 726	4.6	2.0	3 443	3 248	758	17 475	2.72	67.0	11.9	28.9
Cherokee	11.8	9.1	6.1	50.8	42 521	46 985	10.5	3.1	3 250	2 524	736	16 873	2.70	66.3	13.0	29.0
Choctaw	13.8	11.4	8.0	51.4	15 342	15 205	-0.9	-1.4	1 005	1 049	-146	6 067	2.47	62.2	15.3	34.5
Cimarron	14.3	11.6	10.9	50.0	3 148	2 475	-21.4	-10.5	141	140	-265	993	2.37	68.1	10.7	28.2
Cleveland	11.1	7.1	4.8	50.1	208 016	255 761	23.0	7.3	15 968	9 746	11 935	98 174	2.58	66.5	11.1	25.2
Coal	14.0	11.1	9.2	51.1	6 031	5 925	-1.8	-4.6	330	418	-208	2 346	2.47	68.6	11.9	28.7
Comanche	10.4	6.2	4.8	48.0	114 996	124 098	7.9	0.4	10 548	5 123	-4 960	44 104	2.63	66.0	15.5	28.4
Cotton	13.5	10.4	7.8	49.9	6 614	6 193	-6.4	-3.2	375	433	-145	2 420	2.50	70.8	10.7	26.1
Craig	13.1	10.8	8.0	48.7	14 950	15 025	0.5	-1.4	864	1 095	101	5 521	2.48	66.7	10.6	29.7
Creek	13.5	10.0	6.9	50.5	67 367	69 967	3.9	1.3	4 550	4 369	637	26 232	2.66	71.5	11.1	25.1
Custer	10.4	6.7	6.4	50.0	26 142	27 469	5.1	8.3	2 530	1 499	1 244	10 302	2.61	67.2	9.1	23.7
Delaware	15.0	14.2	8.7	50.9	37 077	41 489	11.9	-0.1	2 067	2 675	633	16 520	2.48	68.6	10.7	27.3
Dewey	13.1	10.8	8.6	51.0	4 743	4 810	1.4	3.8	348	366	196	1 840	2.56	67.3	5.6	28.7
Ellis	15.9	10.4	9.8	50.6	4 075	4 151	1.9	1.9	213	269	128	1 744	2.31	68.4	6.8	29.8
Garfield	12.4	7.9	7.3	50.2	57 813	60 580	4.8	4.9	5 067	3 572	1 539	23 816	2.52	69.4	12.8	26.9
Garvin	13.3	9.5	7.6	50.7	27 210	27 576	1.3	0.6	2 020	1 977	187	10 380	2.60	66.3	10.7	29.7
Grady	13.4	8.9	6.0	50.3	45 516	52 431	15.2	4.2	3 249	2 752	1 766	19 717	2.66	74.0	10.4	23.0
Grant	14.3	9.9	10.8	50.9	5 144	4 527	-12.0	-0.1	275	313	40	1 966	2.26	64.9	8.0	32.2
Greer	11.3	9.0	9.2	42.6	6 061	6 239	2.9	-2.7	366	396	-119	2 211	2.27	62.6	9.4	34.5
Harmon	13.2	9.6	9.8	51.8	3 283	2 922	-11.0	-4.6	190	176	-150	1 175	2.36	69.5	14.5	27.5
Harper	13.6	8.2	9.6	50.5	3 562	3 685	3.5	1.9	314	251	3	1 493	2.47	69.1	7.1	28.9
Haskell	12.8	11.7	8.1	49.8	11 792	12 769	8.3	0.6	811	772	84	4 806	2.65	69.3	10.6	26.6
Hughes	12.9	10.3	8.5	46.5	14 154	14 003	-1.1	-1.9	761	978	-68	4 696	2.58	67.0	12.3	30.0
Jackson	11.6	7.6	6.1	50.3	28 439	26 446	-7.0	-3.3	2 315	1 268	-1 924	10 407	2.45	65.4	10.4	28.8
Jefferson	14.6	11.1	8.4	49.5	6 818	6 472	-5.1	-3.0	401	485	-113	2 473	2.51	68.7	9.9	28.8
Johnston	13.1	10.4	7.4	51.1	10 513	10 957	4.2	0.2	698	742	87	4 265	2.52	66.8	13.8	31.0
Kay	13.1	9.7	8.4	50.6	48 080	46 562	-3.2	-2.6	3 372	2 960	-1 500	18 272	2.45	64.3	12.0	31.0
Kingfisher	12.6	7.9	7.2	50.2	13 926	15 029	7.9	3.7	1 069	753	242	5 737	2.62	72.7	11.1	25.3

1. No spouse present.

Table B. States and Counties — Population, Vital Statistics, Medicare, and Crime

STATE County	Persons in group quarters, 2015	Daytime population, 2010–2014 Number	Employment/residence ratio	Births, 2015 Total	Rate[1]	Deaths, 2015 Number	Rate[1]	Persons under 65 with no health insurance, 2014 Number	Percent	Medicare, 2015 Total Beneficiaries	Enrolled in Original Medicare	Enrolled in Medicare Advantage	Serious crimes known to police,[2] 2014 Total Number	Rate[3]
	32	33	34	35	36	37	38	39	40	41	42	43	44	45
OHIO—Cont'd														
Ottawa	495	37 540	0.80	334	8.2	462	11.3	2 632	8.3	10 133	6 910	3 223	564	1 637
Paulding	85	15 914	0.60	211	11.1	173	9.1	1 645	10.5	3 573	2 568	1 005	184	978
Perry	307	29 019	0.51	443	12.3	362	10.1	3 406	11.2	7 312	4 903	2 409	594	1 707
Pickaway	4 558	48 622	0.68	611	10.7	519	9.1	4 183	9.5	9 172	4 744	4 428	1 493	2 642
Pike	496	29 612	1.12	352	12.5	330	11.7	2 789	11.9	4 957	3 715	1 242	360	1 271
Portage	7 876	144 182	0.78	1 492	9.2	1 343	8.3	13 034	10.0	25 359	13 503	11 856	2 794	1 831
Preble	386	35 212	0.65	446	10.8	435	10.5	3 183	9.3	7 831	4 468	3 363	420	1 299
Putnam	303	28 742	0.68	467	13.7	298	8.7	2 261	7.9	6 006	4 554	1 452	250	767
Richland	7 404	124 665	1.04	1 398	11.5	1 359	11.2	10 250	10.9	26 802	19 621	7 181	5 689	4 880
Ross	5 740	77 673	1.00	838	10.9	780	10.1	6 009	10.0	16 058	10 228	5 830	3 239	4 154
Sandusky	901	59 484	0.96	640	10.7	593	9.9	4 794	9.7	10 513	7 384	3 129	1 339	2 453
Scioto	3 403	76 016	0.91	883	11.5	923	12.0	6 710	10.9	16 333	12 639	3 694	2 815	3 613
Seneca	2 605	50 834	0.79	593	10.7	542	9.7	4 084	9.2	12 024	9 273	2 751	637	1 491
Shelby	589	52 976	1.17	618	12.6	406	8.3	3 316	8.0	7 784	5 276	2 508	1 164	2 414
Stark	9 082	369 003	0.96	4 280	11.4	3 938	10.5	26 023	8.6	80 911	38 910	42 001	11 219	3 272
Summit	10 356	558 502	1.07	5 624	11.4	5 624	10.4	41 494	9.3	96 296	46 660	49 636	16 807	3 362
Trumbull	3 905	198 557	0.89	2 141	10.5	2 442	11.9	18 374	11.3	45 712	23 428	22 284	5 045	2 681
Tuscarawas	1 251	87 830	0.88	1 137	12.2	966	10.4	8 905	11.8	18 861	10 478	8 383	714	775
Union	2 784	58 640	1.23	627	11.6	328	6.1	2 971	6.6	5 479	3 066	2 413	508	948
Van Wert	396	26 988	0.87	349	12.2	301	10.6	2 199	9.5	4 978	3 535	1 443	507	1 782
Vinton	68	11 018	0.53	138	10.5	150	11.4	1 282	11.5	2 267	1 610	657	229	1 727
Warren	5 744	201 397	0.84	2 396	10.7	1 662	7.4	12 862	6.9	27 937	15 395	12 542	2 652	1 290
Washington	1 717	60 738	0.97	615	10.1	690	11.3	4 775	9.9	14 137	11 098	3 039	687	1 131
Wayne	3 661	111 344	0.93	1 605	13.8	1 054	9.1	12 091	12.9	21 462	12 026	9 436	1 930	1 775
Williams	990	37 900	1.03	435	11.7	373	10.0	3 015	10.0	7 596	5 103	2 493	NA	NA
Wood	6 750	130 505	1.04	1 395	10.8	1 048	8.1	8 515	8.1	20 060	11 637	8 423	1 944	1 635
Wyandot	251	20 453	0.80	253	11.4	239	10.7	1 714	9.4	4 640	3 239	1 401	159	736
OKLAHOMA	109 973	3 810 216	0.99	53 966	13.9	38 052	9.8	576 768	17.9	647 630	529 696	117 934	131 726	3 397
Adair	92	20 607	0.78	312	14.1	270	12.2	4 771	25.5	3 940	3 744	196	458	2 074
Alfalfa	1 054	5 689	0.99	66	11.3	52	8.9	632	16.8	1 095	1 050	45	51	863
Atoka	750	12 841	0.76	178	12.9	116	8.4	2 360	22.4	2 567	2 398	169	250	1 805
Beaver	43	5 040	0.79	72	13.2	45	8.2	897	19.8	889	862	27	82	1 477
Beckham	1 921	25 359	1.25	408	17.2	257	10.8	3 130	16.5	3 098	2 938	160	593	2 463
Blaine	107	10 017	1.05	171	17.3	105	10.6	1 502	18.6	2 034	1 924	110	153	1 580
Bryan	1 134	42 612	0.95	555	12.4	514	11.5	6 881	19.1	8 581	7 944	637	1 448	3 240
Caddo	1 932	27 324	0.79	415	14.1	365	12.4	5 585	24.6	5 767	5 467	300	596	2 013
Canadian	2 488	96 580	0.56	1 792	13.6	913	6.9	14 291	12.7	15 542	11 257	4 285	4 259	3 306
Carter	913	51 436	1.15	684	14.0	637	13.1	7 437	18.3	10 334	9 467	867	2 661	5 457
Cherokee	2 008	45 659	0.88	614	12.7	480	9.9	10 142	25.8	7 444	6 705	739	1 382	2 862
Choctaw	172	14 987	0.96	185	12.3	202	13.4	2 694	22.4	3 598	3 339	259	385	2 564
Cimarron	7	2 252	0.88	31	13.8	20	8.9	468	26.6	549	534	15	30	1 300
Cleveland	10 543	222 131	0.67	2 977	10.9	1 894	7.0	31 838	13.9	28 133	22 799	5 334	9 452	3 465
Coal	61	5 411	0.79	59	10.3	78	13.7	1 068	23.3	1 209	1 131	78	73	1 245
Comanche	10 320	129 078	1.06	1 958	15.7	1 027	8.2	16 182	16.0	17 036	16 108	928	5 745	4 598
Cotton	48	5 412	0.71	78	12.9	92	15.2	944	18.8	1 223	1 164	59	33	536
Craig	1 050	15 258	1.08	164	11.2	212	14.4	2 343	21.0	4 684	4 184	500	201	1 378
Creek	1 062	61 837	0.70	853	12.1	879	12.4	9 870	17.0	13 072	8 813	4 259	1 474	2 087
Custer	1 517	28 798	1.02	510	17.2	277	9.3	4 983	20.5	4 414	4 139	275	612	2 047
Delaware	356	37 422	0.74	434	10.5	526	12.7	7 185	22.8	8 706	7 484	1 222	466	1 126
Dewey	93	4 717	0.95	85	17.1	76	15.3	758	19.3	1 079	1 046	33	69	1 421
Ellis	46	3 892	0.88	39	9.3	55	13.2	462	14.0	844	760	84	96	2 298
Garfield	1 808	62 773	1.04	984	15.6	638	10.1	8 944	17.0	11 244	10 540	704	2 459	3 921
Garvin	317	28 351	1.09	403	14.6	321	11.6	4 552	20.2	6 228	5 702	526	683	2 501
Grady	1 081	45 303	0.66	624	11.5	496	9.1	7 544	16.8	8 330	7 181	1 149	968	1 791
Grant	73	4 310	0.90	57	12.6	50	11.1	504	14.2	974	931	43	46	1 015
Greer	1 145	5 477	0.71	77	12.6	62	10.1	662	16.8	1 230	1 192	38	44	713
Harmon	100	2 762	0.89	37	13.2	36	12.9	512	23.5	581	550	31	111	3 881
Harper	41	3 606	0.92	73	19.2	68	17.9	635	20.5	770	748	22	25	650
Haskell	78	12 139	0.85	173	13.4	138	10.7	2 441	23.8	2 963	2 686	277	85	647
Hughes	1 565	13 113	0.84	150	10.9	173	12.6	2 263	23.2	2 770	2 524	246	219	1 588
Jackson	697	26 785	1.04	426	16.6	202	7.9	3 571	16.4	3 940	3 795	145	752	2 890
Jefferson	144	5 683	0.72	79	12.6	85	13.5	1 098	22.2	1 551	1 438	113	73	1 135
Johnston	292	10 456	0.85	146	13.2	162	14.7	1 865	21.1	2 256	2 120	136	110	1 000
Kay	1 273	46 896	1.06	648	14.3	552	12.1	6 717	18.5	10 087	9 057	1 030	1 830	4 024
Kingfisher	155	14 672	0.93	215	13.8	132	8.5	2 432	18.6	2 651	2 428	223	215	1 401

1. Per 1,000 estimated resident population.   2. Data for serious crimes have not been adjusted for underreporting; this may affect comparability between geographic areas and over time.
3. Per 100,000 population estimated by the FBI.

Table B. States and Counties — Crime, Education, Money Income, and Poverty

STATE County	Serious crimes known to police, 2014 (cont.)[1] Rate[2] Violent	Property	Education School enrollment and attainment, 2010–2014 Enrollment[3] Total	Percent private	Attainment[4] (percent) High school graduate or less	Bachelor's degree or more	Local government expenditures,[5] 2012–2013 Total current spending (mil dol)	Current spending per student (dollars)	Money income, 2010–2014 Per capita income[6] (dollars)	Households Median income (dollars)	Mean income (dollars)	Percent with income of $200,000 or more	Income and poverty, 2014 Median household income (dollars)	Percent below poverty level All persons	Children under 18 years	Children 5 to 17 years in families
	46	47	48	49	50	51	52	53	54	55	56	57	58	59	60	61
OHIO—Cont'd																
Ottawa	107	1 529	8 737	11.3	47.4	21.4	73.0	11 313	28 703	53 599	67 380	2.5	50 345	10.1	15.6	14.1
Paulding	27	952	4 627	12.1	59.6	12.7	35.2	11 617	23 565	45 404	58 814	2.3	47 358	12.3	18.1	16.1
Perry	124	1 583	8 777	8.8	61.6	11.0	62.8	10 894	19 580	41 892	50 743	1.0	43 341	17.8	25.1	22.9
Pickaway	124	2 518	13 730	10.1	58.0	16.4	95.5	10 157	24 341	55 678	68 025	2.1	54 868	13.2	19.0	17.6
Pike	67	1 204	6 518	6.3	67.0	11.4	64.1	13 373	20 292	39 989	51 758	1.1	40 512	21.9	32.7	29.6
Portage	111	1 720	48 325	10.1	47.4	25.5	248.3	11 065	25 926	53 027	66 233	2.4	52 047	14.2	18.2	15.4
Preble	68	1 231	10 120	9.0	57.8	12.2	65.4	10 076	23 603	48 147	59 789	1.4	49 516	13.0	19.9	18.6
Putnam	64	702	8 884	11.8	50.3	20.2	61.7	10 415	26 600	61 036	68 961	2.1	56 519	7.8	9.6	8.9
Richland	218	4 662	28 503	19.3	54.6	15.9	200.6	13 157	21 959	42 042	54 461	1.4	41 948	15.9	23.4	21.7
Ross	210	3 944	18 310	8.9	58.6	15.0	125.9	11 242	21 536	43 450	57 808	2.0	42 466	19.2	27.2	24.1
Sandusky	86	2 367	15 055	15.7	52.3	14.1	92.5	10 919	23 236	46 099	57 401	1.3	46 447	14.5	21.2	19.1
Scioto	184	3 429	19 506	8.1	57.4	14.4	129.9	11 067	20 045	36 945	51 031	1.4	37 625	27.2	36.1	32.8
Seneca	147	1 344	14 889	26.4	56.0	14.7	68.0	12 081	22 552	44 947	56 982	1.7	45 003	17.5	25.6	21.4
Shelby	114	2 300	12 741	12.3	56.0	15.6	82.9	9 650	25 603	51 266	66 900	2.3	50 774	10.7	16.0	14.5
Stark	318	2 954	96 427	17.2	48.9	21.5	574.5	10 143	24 821	46 290	60 719	2.3	47 745	14.9	21.6	20.0
Summit	335	3 027	139 190	16.0	41.7	29.9	862.9	11 886	28 389	50 082	67 927	3.8	50 453	13.4	20.3	18.5
Trumbull	219	2 461	45 671	12.1	56.6	17.4	330.4	11 438	23 139	43 226	54 573	1.4	43 160	17.2	28.3	26.8
Tuscarawas	38	737	21 565	11.5	61.3	14.7	151.8	9 877	22 617	44 656	55 942	1.4	46 128	13.4	18.3	17.6
Union	50	897	13 858	12.3	45.6	26.0	75.0	9 714	28 648	64 758	81 842	4.7	69 900	7.7	9.2	8.0
Van Wert	112	1 670	6 965	16.3	57.5	15.4	54.6	11 197	23 686	46 436	58 499	1.4	49 565	11.0	14.8	14.0
Vinton	60	1 667	3 259	5.8	66.6	8.7	24.3	10 693	18 198	37 984	46 106	0.3	37 633	23.7	36.3	32.2
Warren	58	1 232	59 867	18.2	34.9	38.7	363.8	10 140	33 421	73 177	93 473	8.1	72 973	5.8	7.5	6.7
Washington	79	1 052	13 692	20.4	53.5	16.6	86.4	10 659	23 933	43 512	57 326	2.3	45 048	15.7	21.2	20.3
Wayne	107	1 668	28 881	23.1	56.9	20.2	181.4	11 631	23 151	49 244	61 579	1.9	50 106	13.9	20.4	18.8
Williams	NA	NA	9 084	13.7	57.1	13.7	57.4	10 088	21 413	42 455	52 395	1.0	42 214	14.2	21.6	20.4
Wood	66	1 569	41 938	10.3	37.3	30.8	214.2	12 749	27 210	52 758	68 414	2.9	54 996	13.5	12.3	11.2
Wyandot	79	657	5 335	9.3	59.7	13.0	32.4	9 325	23 266	46 904	56 695	1.5	47 905	10.0	13.8	12.5
OKLAHOMA	406	2 991	992 868	10.9	45.0	23.8	5 176.3	7 672	24 695	46 235	62 871	2.9	47 524	16.6	22.4	21.1
Adair	389	1 684	5 798	2.9	63.5	12.9	42.1	8 985	15 692	33 325	42 838	0.6	31 386	27.2	36.7	35.4
Alfalfa	118	745	995	6.8	52.8	20.3	10.3	11 589	26 103	47 684	67 730	3.5	51 885	16.6	18.3	17.4
Atoka	116	1 689	3 210	6.5	60.2	13.1	21.1	9 263	18 587	37 519	50 937	2.0	35 910	21.8	30.7	28.9
Beaver	90	1 387	1 334	3.9	54.3	17.9	12.0	10 802	25 610	52 386	67 146	3.0	56 664	10.5	15.7	14.1
Beckham	158	2 305	4 774	7.2	56.2	16.9	28.6	7 069	25 654	49 027	72 820	5.0	46 625	15.0	19.0	18.6
Blaine	165	1 415	1 946	2.9	55.2	16.7	18.4	9 850	21 130	44 183	57 761	3.1	44 309	18.4	25.2	24.9
Bryan	206	3 034	10 701	6.3	50.5	20.7	59.9	8 022	20 964	38 743	52 551	1.9	38 187	19.1	26.2	25.1
Caddo	250	1 763	7 003	2.4	56.8	15.0	45.5	8 479	18 870	40 170	50 788	1.2	39 933	23.5	28.9	25.6
Canadian	418	2 888	32 810	10.6	37.2	25.4	167.2	6 840	28 160	64 200	77 579	3.6	68 421	7.7	10.1	9.3
Carter	929	4 528	11 776	12.8	55.5	18.2	74.0	7 955	22 118	43 280	57 746	2.2	44 402	16.5	22.1	21.2
Cherokee	249	2 614	13 570	7.0	44.9	23.4	62.9	8 392	18 893	37 230	49 684	1.2	38 027	20.6	28.6	27.7
Choctaw	306	2 258	3 359	2.3	60.4	14.2	21.5	8 095	18 739	30 282	43 979	1.3	29 652	26.8	37.6	35.3
Cimarron	130	1 170	557	10.2	53.0	17.5	5.3	12 073	24 946	45 647	59 248	3.0	41 800	18.0	25.9	24.1
Cleveland	318	3 146	82 091	9.8	35.7	31.0	313.0	7 152	27 386	55 626	71 787	3.3	58 205	12.6	14.2	13.0
Coal	85	1 160	1 379	3.6	61.2	13.0	12.8	10 531	20 968	38 141	51 914	1.5	36 566	20.9	26.1	24.6
Comanche	739	3 860	33 421	5.3	44.3	20.4	172.3	7 587	23 035	46 302	60 463	2.3	46 071	18.6	24.0	21.7
Cotton	16	520	1 442	7.4	57.0	16.0	9.6	8 807	21 410	45 877	54 398	0.7	41 469	17.8	24.8	22.4
Craig	137	1 241	3 189	7.7	56.5	13.9	24.0	8 251	19 936	38 273	50 047	1.0	36 953	19.2	26.1	23.9
Creek	212	1 875	16 549	7.9	54.3	15.0	97.5	7 473	22 736	44 003	58 647	2.3	46 614	15.8	23.0	20.9
Custer	164	1 883	8 635	4.6	49.2	27.3	40.1	7 685	22 993	45 056	60 817	2.2	45 574	15.9	18.5	18.6
Delaware	143	984	8 413	5.9	54.1	16.4	53.8	7 981	21 476	36 198	52 171	2.1	36 424	18.8	30.8	28.9
Dewey	21	1 400	1 122	4.8	51.6	22.6	11.6	10 951	25 721	49 087	65 394	4.1	50 348	12.4	16.8	15.2
Ellis	215	2 082	874	2.4	46.2	24.9	10.7	12 445	28 458	50 060	67 956	3.8	52 032	12.0	16.6	15.0
Garfield	319	3 602	14 809	11.3	49.6	21.5	83.5	7 632	24 647	46 726	61 754	2.6	49 136	14.5	19.3	18.3
Garvin	205	2 296	5 637	7.1	60.0	15.0	43.3	8 024	21 315	38 716	53 667	2.2	40 774	19.2	23.9	23.2
Grady	200	1 591	13 067	5.7	51.5	17.2	66.8	7 144	24 286	51 394	63 209	2.7	51 199	12.1	17.2	15.9
Grant	66	949	975	4.2	46.0	22.1	8.9	10 924	28 135	48 345	65 030	2.9	49 774	12.3	15.8	14.2
Greer	97	616	1 236	1.5	55.2	13.2	8.0	8 432	19 837	41 020	52 872	3.2	34 872	25.2	28.5	25.9
Harmon	280	3 601	626	3.4	49.9	20.5	4.8	8 673	21 012	31 285	50 986	2.0	33 750	24.8	33.9	33.8
Harper	52	598	892	7.5	56.0	17.9	7.0	9 102	23 484	47 703	57 095	1.1	49 204	10.6	14.8	14.1
Haskell	30	616	2 944	3.5	59.8	11.4	19.9	8 484	18 910	35 764	46 521	1.0	35 313	24.5	36.5	34.1
Hughes	131	1 457	2 955	3.5	60.3	11.1	21.5	8 982	18 007	34 439	50 428	2.8	34 837	23.4	29.1	26.3
Jackson	288	2 602	6 562	8.2	44.4	19.8	39.2	7 653	22 569	42 029	56 268	1.5	41 370	17.2	23.0	23.5
Jefferson	109	1 026	1 390	3.4	61.7	11.4	11.3	9 574	18 828	34 080	47 012	0.8	32 645	23.0	31.1	29.5
Johnston	100	900	2 829	8.7	51.7	17.9	16.4	8 376	19 742	37 845	49 670	1.2	35 977	20.1	26.6	25.0
Kay	517	3 507	11 267	8.3	46.0	19.7	67.9	8 044	22 741	41 806	55 392	1.9	41 514	18.2	25.6	26.6
Kingfisher	91	1 310	4 017	8.3	49.7	19.4	28.6	8 344	26 791	58 890	68 159	2.2	59 525	10.0	13.8	13.0

1. Data for serious crimes have not been adjusted for underreporting; this may affect comparability between geographic areas and over time.   2. Per 100,000 population estimated by the FBI.
3. All persons 3 years old and over enrolled in nursery school through college.   4. Persons 25 years old and over.   5. Elementary and secondary education expenditures.
6. Based on population estimated by the American Community Survey, 2010–2014.

Table B. States and Counties — **Personal Income**

STATE County	Personal income, 2014										Earnings, 2014		
	Total (mil dol)	Percent change, 2013–2014	Per capita[1] Dollars	Per capita[1] Rank	Wages and salaries (mil dol)	Supplements to wages and salaries; employer contributions (mil dol) Pension and insurance	Supplements to wages and salaries; employer contributions (mil dol) Government social insurance	Proprietors' income (mil dol)	Dividends, interest, and rent (mil dol)	Personal transfer receipts (mil dol)	Total (mil dol)	Contributions for government social insurance (mil dol) From employee and self-employed	Contributions for government social insurance (mil dol) From employer
	62	63	64	65	66	67	68	69	70	71	72	73	74
OHIO—Cont'd													
Ottawa	1 818	4.0	44 178	742	594	124	45	120	286	418	884	55	45
Paulding	692	4.9	36 429	1 699	174	41	13	86	90	156	315	15	13
Perry	1 113	2.8	31 086	2 574	230	53	16	32	110	327	332	23	16
Pickaway	1 978	1.4	34 785	1 972	598	151	39	144	235	441	932	49	39
Pike	907	3.9	32 093	2 429	469	74	35	96	100	314	675	42	35
Portage	6 306	3.6	38 956	1 323	2 453	556	167	382	873	1 218	3 559	190	167
Preble	1 445	1.6	34 757	1 974	409	83	30	90	188	364	612	37	30
Putnam	1 458	1.9	42 671	883	444	88	34	155	201	238	721	40	34
Richland	4 168	3.7	34 180	2 086	1 999	411	153	210	607	1 118	2 773	163	153
Ross	2 487	2.6	32 228	2 413	1 225	268	91	112	302	694	1 695	96	91
Sandusky	2 193	2.6	36 440	1 698	1 063	226	83	120	268	524	1 492	87	83
Scioto	2 443	2.5	31 627	2 505	909	216	68	108	293	897	1 300	78	68
Seneca	1 921	2.3	34 516	2 025	711	153	56	99	249	501	1 019	62	56
Shelby	1 900	3.6	38 809	1 352	1 303	221	99	151	253	347	1 774	99	99
Stark	15 183	3.9	40 409	1 129	6 853	1 240	524	1 196	2 166	3 462	9 814	587	524
Summit	24 258	3.7	44 761	699	13 119	2 234	961	1 737	3 706	4 614	18 051	1 043	961
Trumbull	7 101	3.2	34 611	1 997	2 943	553	229	360	1 036	2 076	4 085	261	229
Tuscarawas	3 351	4.1	36 115	1 761	1 422	288	109	211	456	794	2 030	120	109
Union	2 291	3.0	42 610	888	1 793	273	129	93	246	303	2 288	127	129
Van Wert	1 045	2.4	36 705	1 644	418	86	32	104	135	238	639	36	32
Vinton	388	5.6	29 299	2 796	83	23	6	15	46	134	126	8	6
Warren	10 991	4.9	49 584	408	4 085	667	298	507	1 355	1 361	5 557	321	298
Washington	2 274	4.5	37 151	1 578	1 154	219	89	145	332	568	1 607	97	89
Wayne	4 071	4.8	35 232	1 900	2 004	383	148	356	609	839	2 890	163	148
Williams	1 351	3.1	36 241	1 737	666	138	53	114	174	315	971	56	53
Wood	5 311	4.0	40 986	1 063	2 889	549	218	307	758	884	3 963	215	218
Wyandot	830	2.2	37 122	1 581	362	73	28	84	109	176	546	29	28
OKLAHOMA	169 228	4.7	43 637	X	75 618	12 597	5 739	27 855	28 651	30 196	121 809	6 481	5 739
Adair	567	2.2	25 534	3 044	162	38	13	63	66	201	277	16	13
Alfalfa	284	6.5	49 026	436	87	18	6	70	55	38	181	8	6
Atoka	421	5.4	30 524	2 645	115	23	9	77	51	129	224	13	9
Beaver	297	5.8	54 222	226	80	15	6	108	44	34	209	7	6
Beckham	1 047	5.3	44 188	739	616	78	46	249	151	156	989	51	46
Blaine	407	5.4	41 027	1 058	132	23	10	77	63	83	243	12	10
Bryan	1 357	5.2	30 514	2 646	575	103	43	206	206	395	835	50	43
Caddo	897	4.0	30 605	2 639	281	62	21	107	152	238	471	27	21
Canadian	5 410	6.0	41 747	975	1 438	227	109	370	724	764	2 144	126	109
Carter	2 132	4.8	43 671	788	1 041	173	80	339	351	438	1 633	90	80
Cherokee	1 424	3.6	29 452	2 783	540	102	38	141	224	401	821	47	38
Choctaw	469	5.4	30 959	2 590	147	31	12	55	55	177	246	15	12
Cimarron	127	13.2	55 292	209	27	5	2	55	17	20	89	2	2
Cleveland	11 062	3.9	40 985	1 064	3 342	611	251	954	1 898	1 716	5 159	289	251
Coal	208	9.0	35 904	1 790	45	9	3	33	31	56	90	5	3
Comanche	4 651	1.7	37 195	1 572	2 374	559	206	236	890	954	3 376	168	206
Cotton	250	2.8	40 718	1 097	51	12	3	38	35	53	105	5	3
Craig	533	10.0	36 559	1 680	203	42	16	94	74	155	355	19	16
Creek	2 774	4.1	39 281	1 286	816	135	64	323	435	627	1 338	81	64
Custer	1 215	3.7	41 192	1 037	606	99	45	197	208	186	947	50	45
Delaware	1 281	3.3	30 905	2 602	289	54	23	162	229	397	528	34	23
Dewey	266	6.1	54 034	234	72	13	5	86	40	39	176	8	5
Ellis	282	13.3	68 053	70	61	11	5	124	46	26	201	7	5
Garfield	2 842	4.5	45 050	675	1 429	235	107	296	523	506	2 067	115	107
Garvin	1 133	6.1	41 099	1 049	484	81	37	144	162	272	745	43	37
Grady	2 073	4.7	38 500	1 393	532	88	41	270	284	391	931	53	41
Grant	234	-1.5	52 018	293	80	13	6	58	47	36	157	7	6
Greer	161	6.6	26 195	3 024	44	10	3	21	27	57	78	5	3
Harmon	103	-1.5	36 852	1 625	27	6	2	25	16	27	61	3	2
Harper	175	8.0	45 958	596	45	9	3	41	29	27	98	4	3
Haskell	458	2.7	35 551	1 845	112	21	10	115	54	133	258	13	10
Hughes	473	5.1	34 284	2 067	121	23	9	101	63	133	254	13	9
Jackson	992	4.0	38 154	1 433	442	109	38	91	191	207	680	34	38
Jefferson	221	11.6	35 148	1 912	47	9	4	39	28	62	98	5	4
Johnston	357	6.3	32 187	2 419	101	22	8	46	44	119	177	11	8
Kay	1 783	0.3	39 207	1 295	808	128	62	245	298	421	1 242	73	62
Kingfisher	699	4.4	45 005	677	299	46	21	139	113	101	505	26	21

1. Based on the resident population estimated as of July 1 of the year shown.

Table B. States and Counties — Earnings, Social Security, and Housing

STATE County	Earnings, 2014 (cont.) — Percent by selected industries									Social Security beneficiaries, December 2014		Supplemental Security Income recipients, December 2014	Housing units, 2015	
	Farm	Mining	Construction	Manufacturing	Information: professional, scientific, technical services	Retail trade	Finance, insurance, real estate and leasing	Health care and social assistance	Government	Number	Rate[1]		Total	Percent change, 2010–2014
	75	76	77	78	79	80	81	82	83	84	85	86	87	88
OHIO—Cont'd														
Ottawa	1.2	D	6.1	18.0	D	6.9	5.1	8.8	16.1	11 010	268	550	28 035	0.5
Paulding	23.8	0.3	3.8	23.5	1.9	5.2	3.0	D	19.4	4 445	234	370	8 691	-0.7
Perry	0.7	4.5	14.6	12.8	2.5	6.9	2.8	D	25.7	7 810	217	1 325	15 124	-0.6
Pickaway	6.3	D	5.9	22.1	D	6.4	3.5	D	28.5	10 780	190	1 179	21 137	-0.6
Pike	1.2	D	8.5	5.3	D	5.0	2.3	11.1	13.0	6 380	226	1 561	12 538	0.5
Portage	0.2	1.0	5.1	20.9	4.6	6.6	4.0	7.3	26.4	29 465	182	2 463	68 194	1.1
Preble	8.2	D	4.3	35.9	D	7.3	2.8	D	16.4	9 500	229	748	17 837	-0.3
Putnam	8.5	D	9.2	35.9	2.4	5.5	3.2	5.4	12.6	6 560	192	326	13 794	0.5
Richland	1.5	0.0	5.9	22.0	4.5	8.0	4.2	14.0	18.1	28 610	235	3 438	54 199	-0.7
Ross	1.0	0.1	3.1	20.6	2.7	7.1	2.7	18.7	27.4	15 765	204	2 849	31 756	-1.2
Sandusky	1.2	D	6.3	39.3	2.1	6.4	4.3	D	13.1	13 530	225	1 262	26 174	-0.8
Scioto	0.2	D	4.5	8.8	3.8	8.1	4.1	26.5	24.6	17 165	222	5 608	34 141	0.0
Seneca	2.0	0.9	7.2	24.1	3.2	7.8	D	9.4	15.7	12 155	218	1 124	23 895	-0.9
Shelby	3.1	0.0	6.6	50.5	D	3.9	1.9	D	8.7	9 530	195	856	20 190	0.1
Stark	0.5	2.3	6.4	20.0	5.7	6.9	6.1	16.4	12.3	84 520	225	9 685	165 746	0.3
Summit	0.0	0.1	5.2	12.7	9.0	6.6	6.3	15.3	12.1	106 825	197	14 491	245 294	0.1
Trumbull	0.2	0.3	4.9	25.2	2.8	8.5	4.1	13.1	15.3	52 700	257	6 070	95 345	-0.8
Tuscarawas	1.6	3.6	6.5	24.4	4.0	7.6	3.8	11.9	14.6	20 690	223	1 966	39 943	-0.7
Union	0.9	D	3.0	39.8	14.9	3.5	1.9	3.1	10.4	7 640	142	520	20 277	4.4
Van Wert	9.8	D	4.1	27.9	D	5.5	8.7	12.1	12.7	6 555	230	462	12 680	0.5
Vinton	1.0	D	7.2	22.7	D	3.5	D	D	29.1	3 040	230	711	6 186	-1.7
Warren	0.2	0.0	5.6	15.6	9.3	8.0	9.2	9.4	11.7	34 460	155	1 866	84 766	5.0
Washington	0.5	4.1	9.6	18.6	3.9	6.6	5.1	17.7	11.1	15 080	247	1 933	28 020	-1.2
Wayne	4.1	3.4	5.7	31.7	3.0	6.0	4.3	D	13.8	22 180	192	1 896	46 071	0.5
Williams	3.1	D	3.9	42.6	D	6.2	2.3	10.3	12.4	8 395	226	613	16 533	-0.8
Wood	1.1	0.1	6.5	28.1	4.3	4.9	3.9	7.1	17.9	21 290	164	1 376	53 927	1.0
Wyandot	10.2	1.8	9.9	34.3	D	5.1	3.2	D	15.0	4 920	220	336	9 862	-0.1
OKLAHOMA	1.9	14.0	6.1	8.9	6.6	6.2	5.7	9.4	17.8	749 794	193	96 975	1 711 453	2.8
Adair	13.1	D	3.8	22.1	1.5	6.3	2.2	8.9	26.5	4 755	215	906	9 242	1.1
Alfalfa	18.9	D	5.4	1.4	D	4.3	3.6	2.4	15.3	1 145	198	93	2 743	-0.7
Atoka	3.3	5.4	5.5	4.3	D	11.8	5.3	D	25.6	3 280	237	534	6 334	0.5
Beaver	33.9	15.2	D	D	D	1.6	D	0.6	11.5	1 015	185	49	2 659	-0.4
Beckham	2.4	31.6	10.0	2.9	D	10.0	6.1	D	5.9	3 900	164	557	10 037	4.0
Blaine	14.7	6.3	10.4	14.5	2.9	5.4	D	4.2	15.9	2 115	214	191	5 178	-0.3
Bryan	2.8	D	4.4	7.0	4.1	6.3	3.7	11.9	33.8	9 615	217	1 686	19 989	2.1
Caddo	11.8	6.2	8.9	1.0	4.4	7.1	D	D	29.4	5 945	202	976	13 183	0.3
Canadian	1.3	13.5	8.7	14.5	4.5	7.0	4.9	5.6	16.6	20 460	158	1 265	47 635	4.0
Carter	0.5	17.2	6.5	16.1	4.5	7.2	4.7	10.9	11.0	11 225	230	1 602	21 532	1.8
Cherokee	4.8	0.4	5.1	1.5	2.0	8.5	4.1	7.8	49.2	9 865	204	1 557	21 748	1.4
Choctaw	7.7	D	4.1	2.6	3.7	7.0	D	10.7	26.5	4 085	270	899	7 518	0.0
Cimarron	57.8	D	D	D	D	2.6	2.5	D	12.6	610	267	31	1 573	-0.9
Cleveland	0.1	3.4	9.0	5.5	8.9	8.9	6.0	9.4	28.6	41 695	154	3 381	112 393	7.2
Coal	10.3	13.0	4.7	4.0	D	6.0	D	8.2	20.7	1 385	240	252	2 801	-0.3
Comanche	0.5	0.7	3.9	8.3	4.2	6.0	3.9	5.3	54.0	19 520	156	3 224	51 696	1.9
Cotton	22.0	D	3.2	0.6	D	2.2	3.3	2.9	40.0	1 380	225	139	3 007	-0.3
Craig	14.1	D	3.1	5.1	D	7.9	3.7	7.6	25.4	4 375	300	733	6 727	-0.3
Creek	0.8	7.5	13.0	20.9	D	5.8	4.0	9.8	13.6	16 695	236	1 636	30 092	1.1
Custer	4.0	15.5	5.0	12.1	4.4	6.7	4.5	D	15.5	4 635	157	557	12 492	2.4
Delaware	11.5	D	8.5	7.8	D	8.5	4.9	D	22.7	11 565	279	1 409	24 915	0.4
Dewey	10.4	29.5	14.8	2.7	3.3	4.7	2.8	2.2	11.2	1 290	261	68	2 439	-0.2
Ellis	30.3	27.3	1.6	0.1	D	3.3	D	2.1	10.1	920	223	43	2 273	-0.5
Garfield	0.9	18.6	5.5	7.1	7.0	6.3	4.2	9.3	16.6	12 305	195	1 304	26 856	0.1
Garvin	1.9	20.0	12.1	13.0	3.1	7.8	3.3	6.0	11.8	7 015	255	911	12 827	0.0
Grady	6.2	14.6	10.7	8.8	4.3	7.4	5.0	D	15.3	10 690	198	1 156	22 584	1.6
Grant	16.3	26.3	11.1	0.3	D	2.7	D	2.7	10.3	1 055	235	74	2 483	-0.1
Greer	18.9	D	1.5	D	D	5.3	D	12.5	37.0	1 415	230	201	2 731	-0.3
Harmon	36.8	0.3	D	D	D	3.5	D	2.9	23.6	690	245	158	1 544	0.0
Harper	41.9	5.3	D	D	D	3.1	3.5	2.5	21.0	850	221	45	1 889	-1.0
Haskell	16.0	8.1	5.5	14.6	D	6.7	D	18.5	12.2	3 300	256	536	6 065	0.6
Hughes	20.5	19.7	3.8	4.9	2.4	6.0	D	D	18.1	3 430	248	471	6 242	1.0
Jackson	5.3	D	2.8	7.0	3.3	6.6	3.5	4.2	50.5	4 595	178	703	12 148	0.6
Jefferson	30.7	5.7	D	D	D	5.5	5.5	D	20.1	1 680	267	248	3 390	0.4
Johnston	6.0	8.1	2.9	14.0	D	5.1	D	15.3	27.3	2 720	245	430	5 145	0.4
Kay	1.5	7.4	8.8	12.0	D	8.3	3.7	8.3	15.8	11 160	245	1 125	21 626	-0.4
Kingfisher	5.0	36.7	5.4	5.5	8.7	5.4	3.0	3.4	8.0	2 355	152	145	6 483	1.2

1. Per 1,000 resident population estimated as of July 1 of the year shown.

Table B. States and Counties — Housing, Labor Force, and Employment

STATE County	Housing units, 2010–2014								Civilian labor force, 2015				Civilian employment,[6] 2010–2014		
	Occupied units							Sub-stand-ard units[4] (percent)		Percent change, 2014–2015	Unemployment			Percent	
	Owner-occupied					Renter-occupied								Manage-ment, business, science and arts	Con-struction, produc-tion, and mainte-nance occu-pations
				Median owner cost as a percent of income											
	Total	Percent	Median value[1]	With a mort-gage	Without a mort-gage[2]	Median rent[3]	Median rent as a per-cent of income[2]		Total		Total	Rate[5]	Total		
	89	90	91	92	93	94	95	96	97	98	99	100	101	102	103
OHIO—Cont'd															
Ottawa	17 366	79.9	135 800	21.8	12.4	703	28.6	1.1	21 089	-1.9	1 392	6.6	19 309	29.6	30.1
Paulding	7 798	76.8	94 800	19.6	11.8	588	27.8	2.1	8 945	-0.8	428	4.8	8 498	24.7	41.6
Perry	13 637	73.5	89 900	21.9	12.2	581	30.7	2.1	15 953	0.9	1 030	6.5	14 648	25.9	34.6
Pickaway	19 435	73.4	147 500	22.0	12.7	762	28.1	1.8	26 024	0.9	1 225	4.7	24 364	31.6	27.6
Pike	10 944	70.2	93 100	22.8	12.0	670	35.3	3.2	10 388	-1.1	769	7.4	9 803	31.9	31.5
Portage	61 042	69.1	149 300	21.9	12.4	799	31.0	1.3	87 007	0.2	4 224	4.9	81 540	30.8	25.5
Preble	16 151	76.5	115 900	22.6	13.6	708	28.7	1.5	21 021	-0.5	1 012	4.8	19 344	25.3	34.0
Putnam	13 006	82.9	134 300	19.3	10.0	692	24.5	1.0	18 644	0.0	727	3.9	17 655	32.2	34.7
Richland	48 211	68.9	102 400	22.1	11.6	625	27.9	1.2	53 647	-1.6	2 986	5.6	50 171	27.5	29.6
Ross	28 209	71.1	109 400	20.8	12.3	662	30.0	2.8	33 774	0.3	1 805	5.3	29 387	27.4	30.8
Sandusky	23 831	74.3	109 400	21.7	12.0	623	28.5	0.8	31 283	0.0	1 514	4.8	28 143	24.0	38.7
Scioto	29 558	68.9	90 800	20.8	12.8	550	31.9	2.1	29 632	-0.8	2 269	7.7	27 721	32.4	23.9
Seneca	21 539	71.8	97 200	19.7	12.1	635	26.8	0.9	27 478	1.1	1 316	4.8	25 327	24.8	37.9
Shelby	18 616	73.4	126 000	21.1	12.1	688	26.9	1.8	24 133	2.0	1 034	4.3	23 146	27.1	38.4
Stark	149 756	69.4	121 700	21.2	11.8	679	29.1	1.3	186 772	-0.8	9 835	5.3	171 407	31.1	24.9
Summit	220 710	67.0	133 700	21.6	12.7	742	30.4	1.2	272 921	0.3	13 498	4.9	255 341	37.0	19.9
Trumbull	86 565	71.3	97 700	21.3	12.1	630	30.1	1.3	91 662	-1.0	5 917	6.5	87 320	27.1	29.7
Tuscarawas	36 366	72.1	109 800	20.9	12.0	653	29.1	1.5	45 614	0.7	2 444	5.4	42 541	25.7	33.3
Union	18 291	76.9	173 400	22.6	13.8	797	27.6	1.2	27 121	1.2	1 030	3.8	24 814	36.3	25.6
Van Wert	11 388	76.1	90 000	20.3	10.8	635	26.5	1.4	14 451	0.3	597	4.1	12 960	25.5	39.1
Vinton	5 137	74.9	79 400	22.7	12.8	642	32.2	4.2	5 480	-0.6	361	6.6	5 105	26.1	34.4
Warren	77 328	77.3	187 800	21.5	11.9	936	27.1	0.9	111 471	0.4	4 619	4.1	103 989	44.1	16.9
Washington	24 923	75.4	108 200	20.4	10.8	592	29.1	1.5	28 362	0.5	1 695	6.0	25 914	29.8	28.3
Wayne	42 593	73.2	135 300	22.0	10.9	666	27.6	3.0	59 826	0.5	2 354	3.9	53 500	29.2	32.2
Williams	15 001	74.7	96 200	21.3	12.8	630	30.0	1.4	19 074	1.5	840	4.4	16 614	22.9	41.9
Wood	49 561	67.2	145 700	21.2	12.8	726	29.0	1.3	69 446	0.4	2 989	4.3	63 426	36.1	22.8
Wyandot	9 327	71.4	105 600	20.0	10.6	610	25.7	1.0	12 384	0.2	453	3.7	10 852	25.8	41.4
OKLAHOMA	1 450 117	66.5	115 000	20.9	10.8	717	28.5	3.1	1 842 054	2.5	78 207	4.2	1 699 610	33.1	24.9
Adair	7 942	70.4	74 700	21.5	11.0	529	26.2	4.9	8 195	1.3	483	5.9	8 372	24.2	38.7
Alfalfa	2 067	75.3	64 000	16.5	10.0	621	23.1	0.8	3 152	2.0	91	2.9	2 224	34.1	32.4
Atoka	5 208	76.1	84 700	21.6	11.9	592	29.4	2.6	4 843	0.9	308	6.4	4 843	29.4	32.3
Beaver	2 089	75.8	87 200	18.6	10.0	633	15.2	0.6	3 077	-0.6	82	2.7	2 636	31.8	35.6
Beckham	7 770	62.9	110 600	20.2	10.0	700	19.9	1.8	12 523	-1.8	603	4.8	9 654	24.8	35.3
Blaine	3 703	73.0	74 400	18.0	10.2	562	24.8	2.3	4 567	1.9	169	3.7	3 633	33.1	22.8
Bryan	16 713	63.6	87 900	19.8	11.3	665	29.4	3.9	18 353	2.8	809	4.4	18 562	30.1	27.2
Caddo	10 245	71.2	76 200	18.9	10.6	538	23.8	3.4	11 937	7.2	595	5.0	11 058	27.8	33.3
Canadian	42 622	77.4	141 600	21.2	10.0	859	25.7	1.9	67 910	3.1	2 363	3.5	60 707	36.0	21.4
Carter	17 475	69.9	94 600	19.8	10.8	668	26.3	3.1	22 810	3.6	999	4.4	20 563	28.2	28.1
Cherokee	16 873	65.7	106 300	21.6	10.6	588	28.9	4.2	19 373	4.6	969	5.0	19 125	33.7	23.4
Choctaw	6 067	69.6	76 100	21.1	11.4	549	31.7	3.7	5 972	2.8	443	7.4	5 422	26.9	30.0
Cimarron	993	72.2	63 300	17.7	10.0	395	17.6	3.3	1 401	10.0	31	2.2	1 147	35.0	31.9
Cleveland	98 174	66.4	142 800	20.8	10.8	828	30.0	2.7	139 063	2.5	4 710	3.4	130 389	38.5	18.4
Coal	2 346	72.0	71 900	19.4	10.0	562	27.8	5.4	2 347	2.1	173	7.4	2 238	29.8	35.1
Comanche	44 104	56.1	114 400	21.1	10.0	770	27.5	2.3	50 169	1.8	2 110	4.2	48 706	31.5	24.0
Cotton	2 420	75.9	74 300	18.6	12.1	590	24.6	3.6	2 958	3.9	118	4.0	2 564	32.7	27.0
Craig	5 521	78.3	88 400	20.9	10.5	605	28.4	2.7	6 285	3.8	292	4.6	5 829	26.4	30.0
Creek	26 232	75.7	104 800	21.5	11.1	664	26.8	3.9	31 702	2.4	1 512	4.8	29 602	28.2	31.9
Custer	10 302	60.0	115 100	19.3	11.0	614	24.4	3.3	15 827	-0.4	616	3.9	13 711	30.8	28.3
Delaware	16 520	77.1	109 400	26.0	12.0	607	29.0	4.0	17 481	2.2	842	4.8	15 682	27.7	29.9
Dewey	1 840	72.6	77 900	16.1	11.0	609	15.7	2.5	2 468	2.8	88	3.6	2 058	32.6	36.0
Ellis	1 744	76.5	77 500	14.9	10.0	644	17.8	1.0	2 428	3.9	94	3.9	1 874	37.9	30.6
Garfield	23 816	65.9	93 500	20.5	10.1	674	22.7	3.2	29 973	1.1	1 154	3.9	27 993	26.3	31.5
Garvin	10 380	70.1	85 900	20.3	11.6	598	25.0	3.1	13 017	3.1	586	4.5	10 803	27.1	33.7
Grady	19 717	76.1	108 800	20.6	10.0	662	25.8	3.0	26 420	4.0	1 139	4.3	23 433	29.7	30.1
Grant	1 966	75.2	65 100	18.2	10.0	588	20.1	1.2	3 354	19.4	93	2.8	2 107	33.0	33.8
Greer	2 211	66.6	66 500	19.6	10.7	588	24.6	3.8	2 205	8.5	120	5.4	2 314	31.1	28.3
Harmon	1 175	67.7	46 400	16.8	10.7	457	27.8	2.0	1 306	2.2	44	3.4	1 107	34.6	28.1
Harper	1 493	78.4	69 700	16.7	10.0	545	23.4	1.1	2 046	3.9	60	2.9	1 855	29.4	33.6
Haskell	4 806	73.0	79 600	22.0	10.3	574	28.6	2.8	4 503	3.8	344	7.6	4 656	25.9	36.3
Hughes	4 696	77.4	64 100	19.7	11.9	575	28.1	2.5	5 792	2.7	419	7.2	4 545	26.7	32.9
Jackson	10 407	59.2	88 100	19.5	11.3	685	26.2	3.7	10 968	2.9	436	4.0	10 960	28.4	28.9
Jefferson	2 473	75.0	57 900	20.6	12.8	456	27.7	2.6	2 685	4.0	149	5.5	2 512	23.4	35.0
Johnston	4 265	71.9	77 800	18.7	11.9	569	27.9	4.2	3 976	9.5	253	6.4	3 992	32.9	35.8
Kay	18 272	70.1	76 200	19.6	11.5	621	25.7	3.2	19 377	0.5	1 063	5.5	19 767	29.3	28.8
Kingfisher	5 737	76.9	117 900	19.2	10.0	700	23.1	2.8	8 379	5.3	252	3.0	7 433	31.8	32.6

1. Specified owner-occupied units.   2. A value of 10.0 represents 10 percent or less; a value of 50.0 represents 50 percent or more.   3. Specified renter-occupied units.
4. Overcrowded or lacking complete plumbing facilities.   5. Percent of civilian labor force.   6. Persons 16 years old and over.

| | Private nonfarm establishments, employment and payroll, 2014 | | | | | | | | Agriculture, 2012 | | | |
| | Employment | | | | | | Annual payroll | | Farms | | Percent with: | |
STATE County	Number of establish-ments	Total	Health care and social assistance	Manufac-turing	Retail trade	Finance and insurance	Professional, scientific, and technical services	Total (mil dol)	Average per employee (dollars)	Number	Fewer than 50 acres	500 acres or more	Farm operators whose principal occupation is farming (percent)
	104	105	106	107	108	109	110	111	112	113	114	115	116
OHIO—Cont'd													
Ottawa	1 016	10 047	1 695	2 073	1 359	D	170	427	42 470	620	45.2	8.4	40.5
Paulding	298	3 520	586	1 236	380	99	74	113	31 988	676	34.8	18.2	39.8
Perry	419	3 758	787	670	652	194	D	113	30 073	699	39.1	4.9	29.3
Pickaway	777	11 129	2 238	2 282	1 433	305	200	434	39 032	803	39.6	18.3	52.3
Pike	404	6 985	1 609	1 287	906	217	D	366	52 351	490	27.6	5.3	38.0
Portage	3 001	44 531	5 910	9 620	7 896	758	1 248	1 686	37 860	847	56.6	3.0	42.9
Preble	638	8 507	1 111	2 995	1 239	250	218	306	36 022	1 088	45.9	11.9	41.8
Putnam	732	9 174	777	3 525	1 062	287	201	331	36 041	1 272	27.6	12.2	40.8
Richland	2 613	43 022	7 686	8 362	6 302	1 022	928	1 449	33 678	1 010	37.2	5.0	52.0
Ross	1 215	22 505	6 156	4 235	3 701	465	406	1 013	45 024	980	35.1	9.0	48.1
Sandusky	1 302	22 885	3 177	9 192	2 512	D	415	868	37 930	737	36.9	14.8	47.2
Scioto	1 273	17 900	6 466	1 491	3 133	488	544	568	31 754	689	39.2	4.9	40.3
Seneca	1 141	16 658	2 558	3 914	2 218	402	374	535	32 141	1 113	28.4	14.7	41.3
Shelby	976	23 170	1 999	11 551	1 913	338	D	1 088	46 965	986	32.4	11.1	41.3
Stark	8 212	138 303	27 929	24 527	20 092	6 065	4 198	5 150	37 240	1 168	56.1	3.3	46.5
Summit	13 418	246 552	45 814	29 976	30 146	10 188	15 861	11 070	44 898	304	72.4	1.6	41.4
Trumbull	4 094	68 435	11 521	14 463	9 783	1 683	1 540	2 697	39 405	888	41.6	4.2	46.7
Tuscarawas	2 169	30 613	5 297	7 544	4 544	675	879	1 078	35 225	1 014	39.2	4.7	41.3
Union	997	24 257	1 672	5 538	1 946	338	3 208	1 407	57 999	995	48.2	11.1	44.5
Van Wert	550	9 628	1 410	3 536	1 083	736	290	362	37 581	655	29.2	23.1	55.7
Vinton	137	1 848	347	D	155	D	20	56	30 497	226	25.7	3.5	36.3
Warren	4 060	75 153	10 495	9 872	9 703	4 845	3 716	3 624	48 225	942	67.3	4.7	42.3
Washington	1 407	21 847	4 558	3 530	2 806	728	635	900	41 210	1 122	31.0	2.7	48.7
Wayne	2 462	39 201	5 576	12 060	4 798	1 173	1 579	1 535	39 153	1 928	41.7	5.2	52.0
Williams	827	15 000	1 979	6 864	1 300	260	213	536	35 758	984	35.6	9.8	37.5
Wood	2 751	51 081	5 219	11 628	6 199	842	2 037	2 138	41 860	1 091	42.4	13.7	44.6
Wyandot	510	7 807	764	3 386	790	248	74	281	36 009	593	32.2	21.2	42.2
OKLAHOMA	92 430	1 359 851	216 386	136 360	180 524	58 121	70 078	58 150	42 762	80 245	25.0	19.0	42.1
Adair	219	2 891	572	D	542	D	79	89	30 758	1 129	26.5	10.5	43.8
Alfalfa	132	1 299	D	D	200	73	D	61	46 783	645	6.8	41.4	55.5
Atoka	276	2 260	382	185	449	D	46	66	29 058	1 103	17.9	16.1	37.0
Beaver	158	1 377	D	D	109	D	30	63	45 893	965	6.1	40.3	32.7
Beckham	876	10 968	1 157	D	1 782	331	355	513	46 741	1 016	15.0	28.0	33.0
Blaine	289	2 404	375	D	332	143	47	82	34 189	798	8.5	35.5	54.1
Bryan	757	10 579	2 142	1 117	1 545	632	364	308	29 079	1 484	23.9	13.9	40.9
Caddo	454	4 385	683	75	801	208	D	152	34 776	1 461	12.3	26.7	46.5
Canadian	2 531	27 420	2 857	3 196	3 823	857	1 611	1 098	40 052	1 307	32.8	19.3	47.1
Carter	1 572	20 649	3 392	3 191	3 077	673	644	805	38 993	1 321	22.6	15.7	34.1
Cherokee	733	8 909	2 663	D	1 743	307	132	256	28 707	1 233	29.4	8.5	38.8
Choctaw	283	3 482	1 217	89	D	115	82	91	26 232	965	18.4	18.7	50.3
Cimarron	74	364	D	D	84	37	D	9	25 769	554	3.4	52.0	49.6
Cleveland	5 621	70 651	12 864	3 664	12 097	2 478	3 774	2 399	33 949	1 081	53.6	4.8	45.1
Coal	92	840	195	73	176	D	D	26	30 463	571	16.5	23.1	43.1
Comanche	2 162	31 938	6 177	3 534	5 680	1 680	954	1 066	33 382	1 107	22.6	23.7	43.8
Cotton	75	1 088	51	D	97	44	D	35	31 878	500	11.4	37.0	51.4
Craig	335	3 962	1 250	330	653	217	83	129	32 445	1 263	21.9	13.9	43.9
Creek	1 389	16 906	2 211	4 603	2 051	462	D	677	40 068	1 777	39.0	6.9	31.6
Custer	924	10 770	1 638	1 231	1 944	363	355	437	40 607	877	15.7	36.7	41.7
Delaware	729	7 269	1 264	629	1 480	286	D	203	27 942	1 345	27.7	8.0	46.4
Dewey	150	941	D	60	221	59	23	36	38 208	743	7.1	41.6	40.5
Ellis	117	1 063	162	D	221	56	D	40	38 009	760	5.3	39.7	42.2
Garfield	1 700	22 785	4 174	2 081	3 554	782	574	872	38 262	1 098	16.8	31.5	46.8
Garvin	705	8 031	1 155	1 200	1 266	282	164	332	41 345	1 498	25.3	15.3	36.5
Grady	1 119	11 998	1 809	1 408	1 556	439	D	399	33 216	1 666	26.8	17.6	45.3
Grant	126	1 169	157	D	D	D	D	55	46 733	801	8.1	36.6	50.1
Greer	90	683	219	D	159	D	D	19	27 682	498	5.4	38.6	40.2
Harmon	53	458	125	D	66	D	D	13	29 024	366	4.6	43.7	44.3
Harper	106	661	134	D	120	D	D	22	33 590	532	4.7	49.1	46.1
Haskell	226	2 471	D	D	484	64	46	71	28 820	864	19.8	14.5	46.9
Hughes	222	2 314	768	D	414	71	32	60	26 070	921	15.4	20.7	47.8
Jackson	532	7 960	D	D	1 359	295	D	270	33 968	694	16.7	34.6	44.2
Jefferson	100	844	D	D	118	78	D	26	31 032	417	8.4	42.0	48.2
Johnston	186	1 743	439	D	254	D	35	66	37 846	645	18.0	16.3	42.6
Kay	1 133	15 313	2 241	2 610	2 129	451	476	573	37 420	993	22.7	25.0	43.5
Kingfisher	470	5 367	513	D	613	190	D	251	46 708	1 021	13.0	33.7	49.8

Table B. States and Counties — Agriculture

STATE County	Land in farms Acreage (1,000) [117]	Percent change, 2007–2012 [118]	Acres Average size of farm [119]	Total irrigated (1,000) [120]	Total cropland (1,000) [121]	Value of land and buildings (dollars) Average per farm [122]	Average per acre [123]	Value of machinery and equipment, average per farm (dollars) [124]	Value of products sold Total (mil dol) [125]	Average per farm (dollars) [126]	Percent from: Crops [127]	Live-stock and poultry products [128]	Percent of farms with sales of: $10,000 or more [129]	$100,000 or more [130]	Government payments Total ($1,000) [131]	Percent of farms [132]
OHIO—Cont'd																
Ottawa	113	-2.1	182	1.5	103.6	863 753	4 753	119 450	79.1	127 503	98.5	1.5	59.5	26.8	2 390	74.0
Paulding	221	-13.6	327	0.0	205.3	1 583 920	4 848	188 343	187.2	276 864	55.0	45.0	57.8	27.5	5 581	86.1
Perry	107	9.5	153	0.0	67.8	556 103	3 625	82 957	37.1	53 074	82.3	17.7	31.3	7.2	866	21.3
Pickaway	294	1.7	366	0.8	265.8	1 752 654	4 792	200 377	172.3	214 609	78.8	21.2	51.4	28.0	6 106	64.8
Pike	97	20.8	199	0.7	53.2	631 647	3 176	71 429	26.9	54 855	85.3	14.7	35.5	8.4	992	35.7
Portage	83	0.7	98	0.4	58.7	511 001	5 195	78 929	43.7	51 571	73.7	26.3	32.9	7.8	618	18.5
Preble	224	-2.8	206	0.2	195.1	1 083 226	5 256	148 121	154.8	142 302	65.9	34.1	50.6	24.9	4 689	55.9
Putnam	306	0.6	240	0.6	287.2	1 208 173	5 029	175 040	243.2	191 203	74.8	25.2	78.0	41.4	5 606	84.4
Richland	161	9.6	159	0.1	120.3	789 172	4 962	110 557	128.7	127 408	51.7	48.3	55.0	29.5	1 806	32.5
Ross	222	-0.9	226	D	153.7	816 043	3 607	92 039	79.8	81 432	87.5	12.5	35.5	14.3	6 567	57.1
Sandusky	181	0.1	246	0.8	166.3	1 159 189	4 709	160 579	135.3	183 525	93.5	6.5	65.9	37.9	3 636	76.5
Scioto	94	-7.5	137	0.1	42.0	385 210	2 813	67 393	22.2	32 229	63.5	36.5	25.5	6.1	995	25.5
Seneca	291	7.8	261	0.2	258.1	1 272 024	4 873	163 428	174.6	156 848	85.0	15.0	69.7	33.2	4 919	80.8
Shelby	206	-5.4	209	0.0	183.2	1 245 277	5 952	149 865	207.9	210 807	59.5	40.5	68.6	37.9	3 948	77.1
Stark	136	-1.7	116	0.5	105.4	640 866	5 514	101 840	130.7	111 895	50.6	49.4	46.0	16.5	1 693	26.5
Summit	17	9.1	54	0.3	9.6	459 954	8 451	59 490	11.3	37 118	86.7	13.3	32.2	7.6	112	8.2
Trumbull	114	-9.0	128	0.1	77.5	514 001	4 007	112 287	66.5	74 841	72.0	28.0	44.7	14.8	1 117	30.4
Tuscarawas	138	-3.2	136	0.0	78.4	521 749	3 831	95 939	92.3	91 066	25.6	74.4	38.4	12.5	1 562	25.1
Union	242	10.6	243	0.2	216.6	1 248 834	5 136	151 144	169.0	169 875	84.5	15.5	48.0	22.9	4 372	58.6
Van Wert	227	-7.8	347	0.8	214.8	2 177 867	6 276	212 111	209.7	320 087	73.0	27.0	78.0	48.7	5 103	85.0
Vinton	33	-9.3	148	0.0	11.8	358 668	2 427	42 867	4.7	20 805	82.4	17.6	27.9	2.7	195	35.8
Warren	107	13.0	113	0.7	80.2	809 270	7 150	85 670	66.7	70 815	91.1	8.9	30.7	10.1	1 061	24.3
Washington	139	12.0	124	1.8	49.5	331 367	2 676	58 988	30.5	27 165	59.2	40.8	30.7	5.4	1 152	22.1
Wayne	272	9.4	141	0.8	209.6	878 912	6 238	113 697	381.0	197 614	27.2	72.8	64.0	28.8	4 320	29.2
Williams	208	-2.1	211	1.3	181.6	809 134	3 828	101 897	126.0	128 026	66.2	33.8	44.0	20.6	5 771	79.3
Wood	268	-2.8	246	1.0	252.2	1 429 592	5 821	162 243	227.7	208 712	85.0	15.0	63.2	34.8	5 520	80.8
Wyandot	221	0.6	372	0.0	202.0	1 872 809	5 029	211 556	196.7	331 749	66.8	33.2	63.1	38.1	4 364	86.0
OKLAHOMA	34 356	-2.1	428	479.8	11 279.0	573 858	1 340	74 209	7 129.6	88 848	26.3	73.7	40.8	10.0	256 845	37.1
Adair	252	1.1	223	0.2	44.5	441 987	1 979	56 876	164.2	145 455	1.5	98.5	41.5	10.7	1 278	20.4
Alfalfa	545	0.4	845	1.3	326.6	1 201 132	1 421	186 451	168.5	261 298	36.7	63.3	72.1	34.3	5 814	82.8
Atoka	353	-13.5	320	0.1	59.9	447 024	1 396	52 142	24.5	22 249	17.1	82.9	35.4	2.8	1 311	23.5
Beaver	1 116	-1.2	1 156	24.6	351.9	772 084	668	100 918	187.0	193 772	17.6	82.4	37.8	15.8	7 765	74.1
Beckham	568	9.3	559	6.2	159.8	617 433	1 105	74 880	44.3	43 574	43.5	56.5	35.2	9.1	5 558	66.4
Blaine	522	-10.9	654	3.1	247.1	778 357	1 190	124 377	138.2	173 231	30.2	69.8	65.3	21.2	4 901	77.8
Bryan	441	-10.1	297	8.1	111.8	526 677	1 771	56 929	60.9	41 060	31.9	68.1	40.2	6.3	1 971	26.3
Caddo	708	-5.6	484	30.3	276.1	647 626	1 337	93 927	128.9	88 215	46.9	53.1	54.2	15.2	9 454	61.7
Canadian	501	-1.6	383	10.0	253.8	737 861	1 926	107 595	145.8	111 524	35.7	64.3	44.0	16.1	4 250	42.1
Carter	457	13.3	346	1.1	79.5	545 662	1 579	53 157	33.0	24 953	17.0	83.0	30.2	4.6	1 055	14.8
Cherokee	236	-4.2	191	1.1	46.0	453 732	2 370	56 633	138.7	112 483	75.8	24.2	33.4	3.6	1 083	15.0
Choctaw	330	1.3	342	1.1	63.2	503 597	1 471	63 712	47.5	49 178	13.2	86.8	44.7	8.1	1 810	29.3
Cimarron	1 157	10.8	2 089	39.4	426.9	1 055 505	505	132 971	376.7	679 890	17.4	82.6	46.8	29.8	9 997	86.6
Cleveland	134	-16.3	124	1.4	36.1	386 582	3 125	42 396	14.9	13 764	44.7	55.3	19.7	2.2	585	12.1
Coal	274	1.6	479	0.4	45.1	603 704	1 260	65 790	22.4	39 282	18.5	81.5	43.8	8.4	856	20.0
Comanche	463	-6.9	418	0.7	137.1	577 613	1 381	62 284	47.4	42 794	35.9	64.1	40.3	9.5	2 995	43.9
Cotton	400	9.0	800	0.1	185.5	900 322	1 126	122 376	64.4	128 862	46.0	54.0	61.0	24.2	5 699	79.0
Craig	462	1.1	366	D	110.9	582 744	1 592	61 639	97.3	77 075	11.9	88.1	51.1	8.4	1 725	33.9
Creek	347	-8.1	195	0.4	71.1	349 067	1 788	43 752	23.5	13 238	19.0	81.0	23.5	2.1	384	8.3
Custer	623	9.5	710	8.2	254.9	951 593	1 340	134 592	103.2	117 636	48.3	51.7	58.6	20.4	6 729	69.3
Delaware	283	-8.3	211	0.1	62.4	488 390	2 319	62 352	254.4	189 144	1.8	98.2	48.9	13.8	1 183	27.9
Dewey	625	6.1	841	2.4	165.1	852 131	1 013	90 935	42.0	56 580	49.7	50.3	51.4	13.3	5 420	76.6
Ellis	758	5.6	998	8.7	168.7	796 726	798	83 476	119.8	157 616	11.0	89.0	45.5	15.3	4 705	74.5
Garfield	666	0.4	607	8.4	433.0	870 574	1 434	146 813	151.8	138 239	61.8	38.2	64.4	24.7	9 317	69.1
Garvin	463	-7.5	309	1.1	111.0	488 585	1 580	72 700	44.9	29 975	38.2	61.8	39.6	6.3	2 210	32.0
Grady	583	-4.1	350	14.3	182.7	563 619	1 610	77 691	138.9	83 344	21.0	79.0	40.3	9.8	3 014	33.0
Grant	582	-8.0	727	1.3	409.2	992 482	1 365	152 116	96.9	120 953	73.4	26.6	58.9	24.2	8 734	87.3
Greer	402	7.0	806	3.7	142.9	690 175	856	99 878	32.7	65 681	61.5	38.5	54.0	17.1	4 991	84.5
Harmon	341	5.7	931	25.2	167.1	886 842	953	143 131	53.6	146 579	51.7	48.3	48.1	20.8	4 837	86.6
Harper	618	0.1	1 161	5.9	201.9	884 026	761	78 647	148.7	279 560	9.4	90.6	47.4	20.1	5 563	82.0
Haskell	256	-11.8	296	0.5	46.7	448 627	1 514	60 922	98.8	114 407	2.5	97.5	45.7	10.6	810	23.4
Hughes	436	-1.1	474	1.8	64.0	590 418	1 247	68 746	90.2	97 958	6.1	93.9	41.4	7.5	2 392	36.4
Jackson	479	0.9	690	14.1	295.6	690 865	1 001	154 581	53.2	76 591	78.7	21.3	45.5	20.3	7 021	77.2
Jefferson	475	3.3	1 140	0.1	79.3	1 153 223	1 011	87 902	82.4	197 511	7.5	92.5	63.3	24.0	1 921	59.7
Johnston	284	-15.1	440	0.5	40.9	591 054	1 344	55 721	21.6	33 541	17.6	82.4	42.5	4.8	766	33.6
Kay	484	-1.6	488	1.8	307.1	659 226	1 352	109 617	86.7	87 312	66.5	33.5	54.7	17.3	8 096	67.4
Kingfisher	568	0.2	556	9.1	327.5	757 269	1 362	135 742	161.8	158 497	39.2	60.8	65.2	27.9	4 945	69.9

STATE County	Water use, 2010		Wholesale trade,[1] 2012				Retail trade,[2] 2012				Real estate and rental and leasing,[2] 2012			
	Total water withdrawn (mil gal/day)	Gallons withdrawn per person per day	Number of establishments	Number of employees	Sales (mil dol)	Annual payroll (mil dol)	Number of establishments	Number of employees	Sales (mil dol)	Annual payroll (mil dol)	Number of establishments	Number of employees	Receipts (mil dol)	Annual payroll (mil dol)
	133	134	135	136	137	138	139	140	141	142	143	144	145	146
OHIO—Cont'd														
Ottawa	37.1	896	27	156	127.5	6.4	144	1 433	427.7	38.2	44	120	15.1	3.4
Paulding	2.6	132	15	201	120.1	7.7	48	385	113.0	7.6	6	D	D	D
Perry	2.7	75	15	D	D	D	70	626	173.4	13.1	10	16	2.7	0.4
Pickaway	23.4	420	38	D	D	D	124	1 402	437.9	32.6	25	85	12.7	2.1
Pike	7.6	263	14	133	46.9	4.5	79	890	219.1	18.4	10	71	11.1	2.1
Portage	50.5	313	138	2 930	2 204.2	174.6	438	7 363	1 944.3	159.4	105	621	108.5	25.6
Preble	5.0	118	26	221	159.9	8.8	106	1 319	415.5	29.3	13	70	13.3	2.3
Putnam	6.1	178	35	354	297.1	13.6	110	1 054	274.8	21.6	10	28	2.5	0.8
Richland	17.0	137	104	1 993	939.2	78.9	438	6 528	1 501.2	139.9	102	417	49.2	9.1
Ross	40.9	524	44	D	D	D	236	3 582	938.9	77.8	51	198	34.7	6.2
Sandusky	14.7	241	47	662	764.0	28.1	199	2 366	629.2	54.7	34	172	17.8	3.5
Scioto	11.8	149	25	D	D	D	253	3 085	784.0	70.0	45	246	30.4	5.6
Seneca	6.5	115	49	646	504.3	27.0	159	2 064	586.5	49.8	29	71	10.6	1.6
Shelby	8.0	161	43	979	543.0	35.6	142	1 754	490.0	39.2	37	132	15.4	3.6
Stark	45.2	120	329	4 584	2 551.8	212.6	1 261	19 983	5 330.3	453.5	284	1 295	215.7	41.5
Summit	24.3	45	821	13 158	7 841.2	752.5	1 755	29 142	8 439.7	745.7	476	2 570	473.6	92.7
Trumbull	176.8	840	170	2 528	2 288.6	124.1	685	9 608	2 495.3	201.1	135	1 323	200.4	47.1
Tuscarawas	38.8	419	81	758	321.3	28.6	361	4 334	1 180.3	95.1	61	267	38.0	7.4
Union	14.3	272	55	689	2 150.6	38.2	121	1 911	631.1	50.4	42	158	24.2	4.2
Van Wert	6.5	226	28	D	D	D	87	1 202	282.7	24.6	13	56	16.5	3.1
Vinton	0.8	61	1	D	D	D	30	209	43.7	3.4	1	D	D	D
Warren	23.4	110	167	3 371	3 109.6	221.0	532	9 726	2 924.2	246.2	151	664	124.7	20.3
Washington	777.3	12 582	68	D	D	D	227	2 724	756.3	62.9	39	D	D	D
Wayne	16.6	145	124	D	D	D	366	4 524	1 060.0	100.6	62	217	46.9	7.0
Williams	4.9	130	46	680	413.0	25.1	125	1 266	326.6	25.4	23	80	13.3	2.5
Wood	11.7	94	167	2 958	2 057.6	137.0	385	6 264	1 813.4	134.2	117	527	127.2	20.7
Wyandot	7.4	328	27	342	270.2	13.8	66	786	228.8	16.2	8	D	D	D
OKLAHOMA	3 168.2	845	3 909	50 660	71 892.9	2 718.6	13 051	168 839	50 256.2	4 055.1	4 000	21 261	4 269.6	898.0
Adair	10.3	452	8	63	27.9	1.7	58	549	123.4	9.4	7	12	1.4	0.4
Alfalfa	8.2	1 456	9	D	D	D	24	163	57.1	3.4	1	D	D	D
Atoka	24.4	1 721	9	35	34.0	1.2	45	438	129.8	9.8	7	D	D	D
Beaver	42.0	7 452	6	D	D	D	19	106	37.5	1.8	5	5	1.6	0.1
Beckham	11.2	508	36	547	305.4	29.2	141	1 657	715.4	41.0	40	421	138.4	27.2
Blaine	10.3	863	13	D	D	D	47	272	89.7	4.5	4	D	D	D
Bryan	13.9	327	28	D	D	D	124	1 441	432.8	31.5	26	70	12.2	2.4
Caddo	65.9	2 227	17	237	191.5	9.4	89	767	283.9	19.1	9	39	12.1	1.4
Canadian	15.3	132	102	877	512.8	42.6	255	3 567	1 306.8	88.1	123	721	212.0	41.9
Carter	438.1	9 212	64	866	872.1	32.3	247	2 700	889.7	65.6	70	345	83.0	16.6
Cherokee	9.6	203	16	738	111.3	16.4	143	1 710	390.6	33.7	35	146	25.8	3.5
Choctaw	9.4	617	6	31	27.6	1.1	43	481	118.8	9.5	3	8	0.5	0.1
Cimarron	55.4	22 347	6	17	30.3	1.0	11	81	38.5	1.7	NA	NA	NA	NA
Cleveland	39.1	153	140	1 360	737.9	70.9	710	10 983	3 168.9	262.2	335	1 479	231.0	52.6
Coal	3.3	552	2	D	D	D	20	153	41.9	3.1	1	D	D	D
Comanche	25.4	204	62	D	D	D	409	5 286	1 407.8	117.9	125	D	D	D
Cotton	6.8	1 095	2	D	D	D	15	124	36.9	1.6	1	D	D	D
Craig	2.0	134	16	135	73.4	5.8	62	720	204.9	15.7	5	9	1.3	0.2
Creek	216.7	3 096	64	1 061	579.7	49.4	181	1 877	570.5	43.7	34	103	14.2	2.9
Custer	9.0	327	36	338	442.9	21.7	149	1 655	530.9	37.2	45	383	96.6	34.7
Delaware	7.2	174	19	100	26.0	3.4	141	1 428	369.2	30.7	36	279	45.2	11.6
Dewey	30.0	6 239	8	25	17.5	1.0	33	246	74.9	3.8	2	D	D	D
Ellis	23.3	5 602	5	69	39.6	3.9	25	269	53.0	3.0	1	D	D	D
Garfield	9.8	162	73	D	D	D	267	3 387	926.8	84.3	80	328	57.5	12.4
Garvin	44.6	1 617	25	177	105.5	7.2	110	1 117	433.7	30.3	12	36	15.6	2.2
Grady	37.1	707	42	525	324.9	25.9	152	1 602	491.7	34.7	33	164	38.8	8.1
Grant	15.3	3 369	10	40	69.6	1.5	19	D	D	D	1	D	D	D
Greer	4.5	723	4	26	7.8	0.7	13	145	30.2	2.7	2	D	D	D
Harmon	31.0	10 620	1	D	D	D	13	D	D	D	1	D	D	D
Harper	9.0	2 432	3	D	D	D	17	127	26.5	2.4	3	D	D	D
Haskell	5.0	388	4	60	18.9	1.5	33	473	142.9	10.2	4	6	0.7	0.1
Hughes	9.3	664	5	D	D	D	47	427	111.5	7.8	8	34	3.2	1.2
Jackson	74.2	2 805	24	D	D	D	99	1 241	358.3	27.0	20	146	20.1	3.1
Jefferson	12.3	1 904	3	D	D	D	25	149	46.0	2.4	1	D	D	D
Johnston	4.6	418	9	68	36.1	2.3	34	229	61.1	4.7	3	5	0.4	0.1
Kay	46.5	998	43	D	D	D	183	2 126	631.8	48.2	40	132	22.6	4.0
Kingfisher	10.3	683	22	331	450.2	16.1	53	556	198.9	14.1	4	4	2.3	0.5

1. Merchant wholesalers, except manufacturers' sales branches and offices.   2. Employer establishments.

Table B. States and Counties — Professional Services, Manufacturing, and Accommodation and Food Services

STATE County	Professional, scientific, and technical services, 2012				Manufacturing, 2012				Accommodation and food services, 2012			
	Number of establishments	Number of employees	Receipts (mil dol)	Annual payroll (mil dol)	Number of establishments	Number of employees	Receipts (mil dol)	Annual payroll (mil dol)	Number of establishments	Number of employees	Sales (mil dol)	Annual payroll (mil dol)
	147	148	149	150	151	152	153	154	155	156	157	158
OHIO—Cont'd												
Ottawa	54	D	D	D	53	2 150	811.8	117.7	165	1 703	115.1	30.4
Paulding	12	52	3.2	1.2	38	1 132	282.8	44.9	25	296	11.0	2.7
Perry	21	D	D	D	22	738	D	28.4	47	355	16.6	4.1
Pickaway	56	429	28.7	9.9	35	2 221	900.0	125.1	70	1 254	51.4	14.0
Pike	21	D	D	D	22	1 388	D	88.8	36	597	28.7	7.2
Portage	224	D	D	D	244	9 585	3 010.8	468.2	304	4 925	250.5	61.7
Preble	38	188	11.4	4.9	55	2 761	1 141.7	148.9	56	882	37.4	10.6
Putnam	35	171	18.0	6.0	53	3 209	2 677.9	145.8	60	D	D	D
Richland	187	925	113.1	36.0	168	8 064	3 122.7	385.9	239	4 556	190.1	54.1
Ross	74	645	37.1	15.7	33	4 270	3 928.5	276.6	123	2 486	115.2	30.7
Sandusky	85	431	39.1	12.2	108	8 458	3 878.0	388.4	117	1 844	76.4	19.8
Scioto	80	792	74.0	37.4	43	1 439	1 190.6	64.3	142	2 485	112.8	29.9
Seneca	69	377	29.3	11.9	79	3 498	1 262.6	152.8	106	1 481	53.4	14.5
Shelby	52	364	48.0	18.6	122	10 052	7 166.1	536.9	80	1 300	58.2	14.4
Stark	675	D	D	D	506	22 667	12 182.9	1 061.2	769	13 844	630.1	174.7
Summit	1 500	14 776	2 443.4	856.7	837	27 965	9 557.1	1 402.7	1 195	21 494	974.7	268.9
Trumbull	306	1 436	175.5	49.5	218	15 764	9 668.4	1 095.3	396	11 386	516.3	156.0
Tuscarawas	140	D	D	D	211	7 401	2 276.1	346.3	194	2 700	112.1	30.6
Union	93	2 362	706.6	211.2	53	6 143	10 102.7	424.9	80	1 335	63.9	17.5
Van Wert	36	141	14.7	6.3	39	3 323	1 505.7	130.2	45	798	31.2	7.8
Vinton	7	D	D	D	15	453	98.2	27.5	13	D	D	D
Warren	473	3 934	567.7	234.9	198	9 523	3 803.4	493.3	350	7 767	386.6	107.1
Washington	96	D	D	D	88	3 628	D	222.3	112	D	D	D
Wayne	153	1 668	117.3	88.3	254	10 257	3 203.8	471.4	171	2 937	125.6	36.6
Williams	40	301	23.3	11.2	113	6 337	2 466.3	274.4	71	927	35.0	9.7
Wood	216	1 658	195.1	93.1	179	11 030	4 256.0	623.3	322	6 468	263.9	73.2
Wyandot	23	76	7.9	2.0	41	3 055	958.8	130.8	49	568	22.6	5.5
OKLAHOMA	9 470	71 997	10 991.3	4 115.2	3 610	133 064	74 295.4	6 416.0	7 403	143 561	7 121.2	1 908.3
Adair	17	D	D	D	16	1 075	485.0	38.3	20	198	7.2	2.2
Alfalfa	9	D	D	D	NA	NA	NA	NA	8	44	3.1	0.7
Atoka	10	D	D	D	17	178	47.0	6.6	25	D	D	D
Beaver	18	D	D	D	3	29	D	D	9	D	D	D
Beckham	80	273	47.2	14.3	17	D	D	D	72	999	51.9	10.7
Blaine	21	183	17.1	7.0	7	391	D	16.8	16	129	6.0	1.5
Bryan	63	382	39.7	15.0	35	1 076	243.2	35.3	76	1 573	73.5	21.1
Caddo	34	D	D	D	10	46	D	1.6	36	339	14.1	3.6
Canadian	232	846	172.5	59.6	79	2 979	1 035.6	114.1	171	3 310	160.6	41.7
Carter	134	722	61.5	33.7	43	2 984	4 853.5	178.2	116	2 397	106.7	29.4
Cherokee	45	129	10.4	2.8	21	107	15.1	3.5	88	1 226	53.1	13.5
Choctaw	18	D	D	D	11	133	D	2.7	24	542	18.1	8.1
Cimarron	4	D	D	D	NA	NA	NA	NA	10	82	4.1	1.0
Cleveland	676	3 166	396.5	131.5	132	3 659	1 495.7	158.7	506	11 290	512.4	140.7
Coal	2	D	D	D	5	73	D	2.9	6	D	D	D
Comanche	162	1 129	114.8	49.8	45	3 487	D	183.7	227	4 863	220.5	66.2
Cotton	6	14	1.0	0.4	4	8	D	D	7	64	2.7	0.6
Craig	24	D	D	D	14	440	89.9	16.8	25	345	14.4	3.7
Creek	104	299	35.1	10.4	124	4 057	1 649.9	212.4	90	D	D	D
Custer	74	D	D	D	32	1 184	429.8	57.3	68	1 284	61.3	14.4
Delaware	54	D	D	D	27	693	87.1	22.0	63	1 816	165.8	40.2
Dewey	4	D	D	D	4	28	D	1.4	6	64	1.9	0.6
Ellis	9	29	6.1	0.8	NA	NA	NA	NA	8	D	D	D
Garfield	118	D	D	D	61	2 451	1 668.7	96.5	125	2 198	112.7	26.8
Garvin	61	D	D	D	31	1 067	2 819.8	53.9	49	660	33.1	7.9
Grady	105	300	35.7	11.5	64	1 505	564.1	57.0	62	1 240	53.2	13.6
Grant	6	D	D	D	3	12	2.1	0.3	5	D	D	D
Greer	9	D	D	D	NA	NA	NA	NA	6	55	1.8	0.5
Harmon	4	D	D	D	NA	NA	NA	NA	2	D	D	D
Harper	7	D	D	D	NA	NA	NA	NA	6	D	D	D
Haskell	23	D	D	D	7	70	D	D	13	D	D	D
Hughes	9	D	D	D	6	29	D	1.0	19	202	7.2	2.1
Jackson	41	D	D	D	13	821	225.6	D	56	1 103	42.0	11.4
Jefferson	5	D	D	D	7	28	D	0.9	8	78	3.0	0.8
Johnston	12	D	D	D	9	285	D	9.4	9	D	D	D
Kay	90	509	52.8	21.7	65	2 983	D	171.0	90	1 350	65.2	15.9
Kingfisher	27	277	41.3	18.4	18	470	130.2	22.5	34	370	16.7	4.4

1. Establishment subject to federal tax.

Table B. States and Counties — **Health Care and Social Assistance, Other Services, Nonemployer Businesses, and Residential Construction**

STATE County	Health care and social assistance, 2012				Other services, 2012				Nonemployer businesses, 2014		Value of residential construction authorized by building permits, 2015	
	Number of establishments	Number of employees	Receipts (mil dol)	Annual payroll (mil dol)	Number of establishments	Number of employees	Receipts (mil dol)	Annual payroll (mil dol)	Number	Receipts (mil dol)	New Construction ($1,000)	Number of housing units
	159	160	161	162	163	164	165	166	167	168	169	170
OHIO—Cont'd												
Ottawa	76	1 771	123.0	49.8	79	311	28.6	8.4	2 906	122.8	31 162	138
Paulding	32	604	36.0	15.8	17	61	6.0	1.2	1 040	40.1	2 477	16
Perry	61	709	40.0	18.5	28	158	11.4	2.4	2 144	72.7	7 230	42
Pickaway	86	2 266	189.6	73.5	51	179	18.2	4.3	3 269	128.2	7 180	55
Pike	60	1 610	118.0	44.4	21	69	6.6	1.4	1 485	56.2	16 242	66
Portage	267	5 974	418.5	181.0	227	1 518	120.6	40.8	10 040	444.3	66 448	406
Preble	61	975	60.4	21.6	59	235	20.8	5.4	2 462	95.9	6 367	32
Putnam	54	990	49.0	20.9	55	274	30.3	6.4	2 020	80.0	9 350	38
Richland	316	7 570	674.5	274.6	209	1 186	108.4	25.3	6 809	277.5	15 906	62
Ross	158	6 268	754.2	373.1	85	490	35.3	9.7	3 904	140.2	1 426	20
Sandusky	160	3 660	283.4	113.3	99	635	42.3	14.1	3 148	107.3	9 840	98
Scioto	214	6 155	591.9	206.7	89	336	30.4	6.8	3 981	126.6	3 401	146
Seneca	145	2 536	180.6	69.9	104	505	32.0	8.2	2 839	104.5	4 862	33
Shelby	98	1 929	169.1	64.1	69	342	36.3	9.7	2 673	114.1	17 591	61
Stark	996	28 010	2 455.5	1 090.0	694	4 770	460.7	131.2	23 649	973.8	105 900	558
Summit	1 519	45 181	4 649.6	1 869.0	1 084	7 398	853.5	202.2	37 471	1 615.1	143 247	561
Trumbull	578	10 720	991.1	378.8	313	1 771	128.1	36.8	12 576	524.3	13 364	77
Tuscarawas	200	5 156	397.5	157.3	190	1 096	125.2	27.8	6 001	260.8	11 997	68
Union	78	1 732	166.1	63.3	68	354	29.6	8.9	3 465	159.4	109 768	396
Van Wert	60	1 505	113.3	41.8	45	234	20.2	3.6	1 607	66.6	3 210	17
Vinton	22	D	D	D	8	D	D	D	678	21.9	0	0
Warren	433	9 527	853.7	325.5	244	1 944	175.3	56.3	15 639	755.5	249 373	962
Washington	139	5 586	453.2	195.2	110	D	D	D	3 719	162.3	2 367	21
Wayne	235	5 274	415.5	178.6	169	891	97.0	20.4	8 783	414.5	44 698	211
Williams	65	2 006	169.7	71.6	66	372	30.3	7.1	2 193	85.4	5 296	30
Wood	243	4 906	384.2	164.5	210	1 433	126.7	38.6	7 578	321.3	56 563	257
Wyandot	37	772	55.6	21.1	56	240	21.5	5.6	1 387	53.6	4 301	18
OKLAHOMA	10 654	213 226	22 795.4	8 289.9	5 411	32 388	4 037.3	939.7	275 014	13 180.5	2 216 234	11 545
Adair	17	562	33.0	16.5	11	28	1.9	0.4	1 383	47.3	2 504	13
Alfalfa	11	111	6.6	2.9	6	D	D	D	407	16.8	160	2
Atoka	22	466	26.2	9.8	15	D	D	D	984	48.0	0	0
Beaver	6	75	7.1	2.3	11	D	D	D	472	21.6	0	0
Beckham	87	1 235	111.5	39.4	39	247	33.4	7.6	1 947	127.7	2 397	10
Blaine	27	365	21.3	10.0	14	28	3.5	0.4	742	31.0	195	1
Bryan	124	2 092	204.5	66.4	34	159	12.8	3.6	2 898	145.8	6 680	53
Caddo	34	618	29.7	13.1	19	88	12.4	3.3	1 567	68.4	1 163	7
Canadian	233	2 849	228.1	88.7	159	1 006	184.0	32.9	9 764	435.3	56 886	225
Carter	217	3 790	323.6	121.1	93	974	148.1	46.4	3 487	164.7	12 158	61
Cherokee	114	2 633	244.7	106.7	41	279	20.4	5.8	2 922	121.4	6 785	60
Choctaw	40	975	59.7	27.0	13	D	D	D	962	45.2	2 700	36
Cimarron	4	D	D	D	4	D	D	D	207	9.4	0	0
Cleveland	755	12 359	1 158.1	435.8	308	1 761	301.9	44.6	20 452	951.4	189 351	944
Coal	11	242	10.4	5.5	4	D	D	D	442	19.1	108	1
Comanche	275	6 918	704.6	271.8	136	830	69.0	20.9	4 796	199.7	17 910	100
Cotton	7	42	5.1	1.4	5	16	1.6	0.3	335	12.4	0	0
Craig	74	1 329	83.1	43.5	16	43	4.4	1.2	933	38.1	55	2
Creek	113	2 166	147.1	56.4	82	306	35.9	8.1	4 672	207.0	24 337	202
Custer	92	1 668	158.5	59.7	51	302	30.3	8.3	2 214	109.1	6 556	31
Delaware	84	1 440	133.1	47.2	54	241	21.8	5.3	2 768	121.2	8 842	72
Dewey	9	D	D	D	9	42	8.4	1.1	514	27.8	NA	NA
Ellis	10	192	15.5	6.9	5	D	D	D	347	17.5	95	1
Garfield	208	4 158	427.0	151.8	118	586	58.8	14.5	4 264	191.8	16 716	74
Garvin	64	1 277	78.3	30.7	26	129	23.9	4.8	2 165	115.9	2 589	29
Grady	87	D	D	D	65	328	37.1	8.2	3 720	188.4	20 484	105
Grant	7	119	5.1	2.5	4	D	D	D	337	15.8	0	0
Greer	17	D	D	D	7	15	1.5	0.2	294	13.1	0	0
Harmon	6	122	8.5	3.8	2	D	D	D	160	7.7	NA	NA
Harper	9	127	7.5	3.5	6	D	D	D	317	11.2	250	1
Haskell	29	819	53.7	22.3	11	31	2.4	0.4	1 044	45.6	932	6
Hughes	40	D	D	D	10	D	D	D	775	35.4	0	0
Jackson	48	1 389	111.1	47.6	34	151	10.6	2.7	1 384	54.9	5 368	35
Jefferson	7	D	D	D	3	D	D	D	417	16.2	NA	NA
Johnston	30	586	31.8	15.3	10	32	3.3	0.8	615	23.5	486	6
Kay	143	2 252	176.8	65.7	75	335	31.6	8.3	2 592	102.3	2 903	16
Kingfisher	39	479	33.3	13.6	29	D	D	D	1 563	83.4	7 344	22

Table B. States and Counties — Government Employment and Payroll, and Local Government Finances

STATE County	Government employment and payroll, 2012		March payroll (percent of total)							Local government finances, 2012				
										General revenue		Taxes		
													Per capita[1] (dollars)	
	Full-time equivalent employees	March payroll (dollars)	Administration, judicial, and legal	Police and Corrections	Fire Protection	Highways and transportation	Health and Welfare	Natural resources and utilities	Education and libraries	Total (mil dol)	Inter-governmental (mil dol)	Total (mil dol)	Total	Property
	171	172	173	174	175	176	177	178	179	180	181	182	183	184
OHIO—Cont'd														
Ottawa	1 807	6 970 433	8.9	9.2	2.9	11.6	10.2	7.2	48.1	169.9	58.3	72.2	1 746	1 408
Paulding	840	2 899 437	7.0	5.4	0.3	5.0	30.9	2.1	47.9	78.4	30.7	20.4	1 057	705
Perry	1 584	4 562 693	8.5	5.7	0.8	9.1	10.2	4.3	60.2	119.5	77.0	27.9	775	640
Pickaway	2 330	14 643 979	43.7	3.1	0.9	1.5	14.8	1.6	34.2	261.8	90.0	68.3	1 211	848
Pike	1 231	4 378 557	9.2	6.9	1.1	6.4	9.9	6.4	59.2	142.7	70.7	26.2	920	694
Portage	6 776	25 510 983	5.9	7.0	4.0	6.3	23.8	3.4	48.7	675.5	218.5	230.1	1 425	1 010
Preble	1 714	6 190 256	11.3	8.4	1.2	8.8	6.9	4.8	52.3	137.6	66.2	50.4	1 204	713
Putnam	1 034	3 725 218	9.3	7.5	0.0	5.3	1.5	3.8	72.3	126.1	61.7	46.9	1 371	814
Richland	5 091	18 513 991	8.5	9.4	5.0	4.1	11.2	8.3	52.0	473.0	237.7	163.9	1 336	864
Ross	2 848	9 604 595	8.8	6.4	2.9	4.7	10.0	4.2	62.4	240.8	134.0	79.9	1 032	625
Sandusky	2 171	7 625 048	7.2	8.4	1.7	3.5	12.3	6.5	58.8	231.5	116.4	82.4	1 362	773
Scioto	2 809	9 457 558	7.1	6.9	2.7	3.9	7.6	6.7	64.1	259.9	167.7	61.3	781	581
Seneca	1 825	6 110 506	9.4	11.2	4.5	4.6	9.9	4.4	55.0	195.7	93.8	60.1	1 073	657
Shelby	1 460	5 397 171	6.3	6.1	4.3	3.0	5.5	5.6	68.3	184.8	82.0	67.4	1 370	761
Stark	11 531	42 201 589	4.3	6.8	4.8	4.1	1.9	6.1	71.3	1 313.7	628.2	474.7	1 266	949
Summit	20 065	81 863 137	7.5	10.7	5.8	4.7	7.7	7.2	54.5	2 401.2	877.7	1 094.2	2 023	1 303
Trumbull	7 911	27 957 859	8.3	9.9	5.3	3.3	10.3	6.6	55.2	724.1	366.6	245.2	1 182	844
Tuscarawas	3 307	11 310 698	8.3	7.0	2.8	5.4	6.0	9.0	58.9	309.5	126.6	106.5	1 152	825
Union	2 131	8 121 953	6.0	5.6	3.5	2.1	30.6	3.2	47.7	262.5	68.5	90.7	1 720	1 149
Van Wert	1 050	4 217 502	8.6	7.4	2.1	8.6	3.4	13.7	52.1	118.7	67.2	36.2	1 260	753
Vinton	591	1 697 854	7.1	2.3	0.0	6.1	13.7	1.9	66.2	47.0	34.8	7.8	590	511
Warren	5 863	22 314 741	4.2	7.3	6.2	2.1	0.6	3.3	75.2	748.9	233.0	383.6	1 766	1 359
Washington	2 326	7 490 510	7.9	9.4	3.2	6.0	8.9	3.7	59.9	189.5	93.8	66.4	1 080	769
Wayne	4 495	16 994 820	7.3	7.8	2.6	5.0	22.5	5.7	48.6	484.9	177.5	144.9	1 261	926
Williams	1 758	5 321 575	7.9	5.7	0.7	4.6	15.8	10.1	54.0	135.0	50.2	50.2	1 339	733
Wood	4 470	17 275 956	8.6	10.8	3.6	3.3	9.2	6.1	56.1	532.6	184.0	232.7	1 815	1 163
Wyandot	1 084	3 936 981	8.9	7.2	0.8	3.5	33.2	5.1	40.6	97.2	30.4	25.4	1 124	531
OKLAHOMA	X	X	X	X	X	X	X	X	X	X	X	X	X	X
Adair	986	2 539 434	3.7	4.1	0.2	2.8	2.6	7.8	77.6	58.2	42.9	7.8	352	205
Alfalfa	248	605 307	12.0	6.9	0.5	12.8	1.7	4.7	59.3	13.7	4.5	6.9	1 225	981
Atoka	901	3 031 357	2.1	2.9	0.0	0.7	13.5	14.8	65.5	69.1	37.2	9.2	658	295
Beaver	349	1 030 481	7.5	3.5	0.0	11.8	12.7	7.2	56.4	23.3	11.7	9.1	1 626	1 124
Beckham	996	2 808 433	5.1	8.4	3.6	5.8	2.7	8.0	63.2	78.3	28.3	36.4	1 577	607
Blaine	619	1 556 580	6.7	6.5	0.9	6.6	23.9	4.9	49.9	45.9	14.5	14.0	1 429	639
Bryan	1 434	4 012 582	7.3	9.9	3.7	4.8	3.9	6.2	62.9	108.1	53.8	36.2	833	407
Caddo	1 563	4 548 760	3.7	5.7	1.7	6.2	8.5	8.8	64.8	96.6	61.1	21.0	708	392
Canadian	3 819	11 398 884	4.8	10.1	3.4	2.2	6.5	2.2	69.3	291.7	123.9	127.1	1 037	614
Carter	1 811	5 386 589	5.3	10.5	3.1	4.9	1.1	6.3	67.9	152.0	61.4	59.3	1 233	591
Cherokee	2 005	6 302 718	3.9	5.1	1.3	3.4	35.5	5.3	44.2	165.4	56.2	22.0	457	230
Choctaw	795	2 289 614	6.3	3.7	1.7	3.9	19.7	5.9	57.8	37.7	23.4	8.9	588	233
Cimarron	196	450 099	9.5	5.4	0.0	14.3	1.7	5.6	54.3	9.9	3.7	3.1	1 291	950
Cleveland	9 950	35 955 536	3.3	6.4	4.0	1.7	32.0	2.8	48.9	893.3	214.7	278.1	1 047	619
Coal	319	840 600	8.4	5.3	4.4	7.5	6.5	3.4	64.6	24.3	13.0	8.5	1 425	897
Comanche	6 240	22 060 234	3.6	5.7	3.0	2.1	37.2	3.2	44.6	505.2	159.3	103.2	817	354
Cotton	263	656 798	7.9	5.3	1.5	6.9	1.4	7.9	66.9	18.1	12.3	3.0	492	352
Craig	859	2 734 367	4.9	5.6	1.6	5.0	35.0	3.8	42.2	46.2	23.2	13.9	943	509
Creek	2 475	7 871 373	5.1	6.6	4.0	2.5	1.9	5.1	74.1	169.5	81.2	61.8	874	489
Custer	1 316	3 555 785	5.3	7.5	2.4	3.8	17.0	5.5	56.6	88.8	32.3	37.3	1 306	656
Delaware	1 264	3 298 724	6.6	7.0	0.4	4.1	1.2	4.6	74.6	80.2	42.1	28.6	690	467
Dewey	334	940 532	8.5	5.7	0.5	11.7	14.3	4.1	54.3	35.1	7.3	21.9	4 581	2 207
Ellis	243	705 922	9.0	9.1	0.0	18.9	2.9	2.2	56.6	31.4	7.5	8.4	2 051	1 616
Garfield	2 242	6 971 075	5.4	9.4	5.9	4.5	1.4	5.0	66.7	176.9	68.5	75.4	1 232	577
Garvin	1 260	3 212 232	6.5	6.6	2.1	5.0	14.9	6.4	57.8	92.3	43.7	25.1	920	451
Grady	1 921	5 776 643	3.4	5.2	3.6	3.2	26.9	2.4	54.3	157.9	56.1	41.4	779	442
Grant	233	634 768	12.0	7.0	0.1	21.2	0.0	6.1	53.1	15.2	6.4	5.9	1 313	1 043
Greer	288	950 821	5.8	5.3	2.0	1.0	29.5	6.4	48.4	16.6	9.5	2.9	481	285
Harmon	242	611 023	7.5	4.4	0.0	5.4	40.8	2.6	38.3	7.4	4.3	1.9	648	388
Harper	266	708 452	8.7	5.5	0.0	9.6	26.4	4.5	45.3	14.8	7.0	5.9	1 592	1 096
Haskell	614	1 704 293	4.5	5.0	0.0	5.1	27.6	1.6	53.4	31.8	20.1	7.0	543	274
Hughes	768	2 037 752	4.4	2.9	0.8	3.3	28.1	3.9	55.8	38.4	20.3	12.6	908	604
Jackson	1 759	6 015 452	3.3	4.6	2.2	1.8	47.3	5.6	33.9	146.2	38.1	20.7	788	304
Jefferson	350	958 729	7.0	3.6	0.7	3.6	15.4	11.0	58.0	49.9	41.2	3.0	470	281
Johnston	410	1 050 719	7.1	6.5	0.6	3.4	2.9	5.1	73.6	22.7	13.6	6.2	561	357
Kay	2 026	5 686 908	6.0	8.0	6.7	4.3	2.5	9.9	60.6	149.2	58.1	50.8	1 108	557
Kingfisher	634	1 825 978	7.8	7.8	3.3	9.1	1.5	4.9	65.1	48.4	22.2	18.8	1 254	825

1. Based on the resident population estimated as of July 1 of the year shown.

STATE County	Total (mil dol) [185]	Per capita[1] (dollars) [186]	Education [187]	Health and hospitals [188]	Police protection [189]	Public welfare [190]	Highways [191]	Total (mil dol) [192]	Per capita[1] (dollars) [193]	Federal civilian [194]	Federal military [195]	State and local [196]	Democratic [197]	Republican [198]	All other [199]
OHIO—Cont'd															
Ottawa	183.7	4 444	50.5	4.7	6.9	9.8	7.3	162.5	3 930	179	146	2 090	52.2	46.0	1.7
Paulding	83.9	4 350	53.2	21.6	2.3	1.9	7.4	20.8	1 079	49	49	1 047	42.6	54.4	2.9
Perry	127.1	3 530	59.9	5.5	4.7	7.4	7.0	19.6	543	59	92	1 514	47.1	50.1	2.7
Pickaway	245.9	4 360	42.1	29.7	3.7	2.8	4.2	155.1	2 750	86	135	3 765	38.3	60.0	1.8
Pike	136.0	4 775	54.3	20.5	2.3	3.4	5.2	25.3	889	78	72	1 375	48.2	49.3	2.5
Portage	676.4	4 190	37.6	28.6	4.0	3.4	4.1	295.0	1 827	306	411	15 251	53.5	44.5	2.0
Preble	135.2	3 229	56.4	4.3	5.3	6.0	7.0	22.8	546	73	107	1 788	33.3	64.6	2.1
Putnam	148.9	4 353	62.5	3.1	4.2	4.4	6.0	72.4	2 117	73	88	1 551	28.3	70.0	1.8
Richland	480.9	3 920	52.3	8.7	5.0	4.8	5.5	209.0	1 703	587	298	7 257	42.1	55.7	2.2
Ross	234.3	3 026	58.4	0.5	5.1	7.8	4.6	264.6	3 418	1 627	186	4 977	45.4	52.6	2.0
Sandusky	231.1	3 819	59.9	4.6	7.5	4.6	4.8	105.5	1 744	110	154	3 243	51.4	46.7	1.9
Scioto	262.2	3 341	61.1	5.0	1.9	4.1	4.6	211.5	2 694	167	193	5 256	45.8	52.2	2.0
Seneca	196.2	3 502	52.9	6.1	6.7	3.7	7.6	729.9	13 029	123	137	2 615	47.7	50.4	2.0
Shelby	185.3	3 769	51.8	0.7	3.4	11.7	9.7	191.1	3 887	72	125	2 377	30.9	67.3	1.8
Stark	1 278.7	3 411	55.1	4.6	5.7	5.0	5.4	444.1	1 185	926	982	18 083	51.7	46.3	2.0
Summit	2 276.4	4 209	43.9	4.8	5.6	4.3	3.4	4 224.1	7 811	1 999	1 397	29 542	57.6	41.1	1.3
Trumbull	736.8	3 552	53.3	5.9	6.4	5.6	3.7	248.1	1 196	508	549	9 356	60.0	37.6	2.4
Tuscarawas	292.0	3 160	50.0	4.4	5.1	6.3	5.1	119.9	1 297	254	237	4 858	50.1	47.6	2.3
Union	256.7	4 870	31.4	31.2	3.9	1.4	6.7	364.0	6 906	62	134	3 286	35.1	63.2	1.7
Van Wert	130.4	4 536	67.9	0.9	3.8	2.9	7.3	64.6	2 247	48	73	1 365	35.3	62.6	2.1
Vinton	47.0	3 548	53.9	4.2	3.0	10.0	10.2	7.8	588	19	34	657	43.6	53.5	2.9
Warren	743.8	3 424	50.7	0.4	7.2	6.1	4.8	599.3	2 759	268	585	9 549	31.4	67.5	1.1
Washington	192.0	3 124	48.4	9.0	6.4	6.0	9.1	94.7	1 541	209	154	2 806	41.3	56.9	1.8
Wayne	466.4	4 061	44.9	24.0	3.9	6.3	4.1	103.7	903	253	291	6 518	41.6	56.3	2.1
Williams	124.0	3 304	51.6	1.0	5.4	10.9	7.1	67.6	1 801	79	94	2 074	44.4	53.7	1.9
Wood	538.0	4 197	50.7	2.8	4.6	11.9	5.6	402.7	3 142	206	333	11 489	52.7	45.6	1.7
Wyandot	101.5	4 489	33.1	34.8	4.5	8.4	7.7	18.8	830	55	57	1 410	40.6	57.1	2.2
OKLAHOMA	X	X	X	X	X	X	X	X	X	46 348	33 988	289 059	34.4	65.6	0.0
Adair	58.1	2 606	75.3	1.7	3.3	0.0	6.3	8.0	359	41	85	1 557	30.7	69.3	0.0
Alfalfa	13.7	2 424	57.6	1.3	4.0	0.0	1.2	6.6	1 158	35	18	543	16.9	83.1	0.0
Atoka	56.5	4 036	38.0	13.0	4.0	0.0	9.5	27.1	1 931	39	50	1 126	28.1	71.9	0.0
Beaver	21.3	3 811	59.5	6.4	2.9	0.1	14.8	3.5	632	30	21	491	10.8	89.2	0.0
Beckham	65.5	2 839	44.5	3.2	6.9	0.0	8.4	42.2	1 830	47	83	1 086	22.0	78.0	0.0
Blaine	43.3	4 420	45.4	22.1	2.7	0.0	10.7	12.1	1 232	56	38	855	24.6	75.4	0.0
Bryan	107.3	2 473	57.5	3.2	6.5	0.0	4.5	150.1	3 458	101	166	5 576	32.2	67.8	0.0
Caddo	102.4	3 449	54.1	1.6	3.8	0.0	12.2	21.8	736	518	105	2 290	34.7	65.3	0.0
Canadian	275.3	2 246	65.8	0.4	5.8	0.0	4.1	217.3	1 773	575	556	5 758	23.9	76.1	0.0
Carter	138.7	2 885	55.4	3.2	6.9	0.0	8.9	72.9	1 517	94	185	3 334	29.7	70.3	0.0
Cherokee	168.8	3 505	38.7	45.6	2.0	0.0	2.6	38.5	800	267	178	7 558	43.9	56.1	0.0
Choctaw	38.5	2 537	57.0	7.0	5.1	0.5	14.4	11.0	728	42	57	1 414	33.3	66.7	0.0
Cimarron	9.8	4 126	56.2	20.2	2.6	0.0	5.2	1.3	527	16	0	260	12.0	88.0	0.0
Cleveland	909.8	3 425	38.7	32.5	4.4	0.0	4.9	703.2	2 647	701	1 054	23 110	38.0	62.0	0.0
Coal	24.2	4 050	54.5	2.2	3.3	0.0	16.0	1.2	199	17	22	388	26.4	73.6	0.0
Comanche	515.7	4 080	36.9	40.3	4.3	0.0	3.0	244.6	1 935	4 165	11 449	9 990	41.2	58.8	0.0
Cotton	18.1	2 940	59.1	0.3	2.7	0.0	14.7	9.2	1 490	25	23	937	27.8	72.2	0.0
Craig	47.8	3 238	66.7	1.2	4.4	0.0	10.2	13.5	915	56	52	1 670	35.0	65.0	0.0
Creek	169.8	2 404	59.1	3.0	5.7	0.0	7.1	161.0	2 279	255	267	3 173	29.2	70.8	0.0
Custer	81.3	2 850	57.0	0.1	7.9	0.0	10.2	57.0	1 999	175	107	2 735	25.3	74.7	0.0
Delaware	80.1	1 934	71.5	1.7	5.9	0.0	2.4	56.3	1 357	79	158	2 552	33.1	66.9	0.0
Dewey	31.7	6 636	49.7	0.2	2.9	9.2	14.3	8.2	1 718	29	18	392	15.7	84.3	0.0
Ellis	30.2	7 367	36.1	47.3	0.6	0.0	4.4	13.0	3 179	20	16	369	14.8	85.2	0.0
Garfield	196.4	3 209	47.9	2.4	5.3	0.1	7.4	189.6	3 098	453	1 432	3 487	24.5	75.5	0.0
Garvin	89.3	3 271	48.3	13.4	4.7	0.0	8.8	23.0	841	78	104	1 711	28.2	71.8	0.0
Grady	154.9	2 916	45.5	28.8	4.1	0.0	7.2	30.5	575	85	202	2 536	26.6	73.4	0.0
Grant	14.3	3 176	61.0	1.3	3.6	0.0	8.2	4.8	1 069	31	17	326	21.9	78.1	0.0
Greer	17.2	2 824	46.1	10.9	6.9	0.0	14.6	3.8	617	28	19	573	26.8	73.2	0.0
Harmon	8.0	2 738	65.6	4.3	8.1	0.0	0.4	0.3	109	22	10	297	30.6	69.4	0.0
Harper	17.7	4 809	42.7	7.9	3.9	0.0	26.2	2.4	653	24	14	414	14.1	85.9	0.0
Haskell	31.5	2 434	63.9	0.9	4.0	0.2	11.6	2.2	171	57	49	580	31.5	68.5	0.0
Hughes	38.5	2 780	61.1	4.7	3.7	0.0	13.2	24.3	1 755	39	47	951	35.3	64.7	0.0
Jackson	175.1	6 672	28.3	40.8	3.6	0.0	5.4	32.6	1 243	1 315	1 393	2 405	25.2	74.8	0.0
Jefferson	21.5	3 367	52.8	2.1	2.8	0.0	12.1	30.4	4 768	28	24	381	32.8	67.2	0.0
Johnston	21.5	1 952	72.5	4.2	4.8	0.0	3.1	3.8	343	48	41	985	31.6	68.4	0.0
Kay	166.0	3 621	41.7	1.9	7.4	0.0	9.5	127.9	2 790	97	170	4 238	29.2	70.8	0.0
Kingfisher	52.9	3 526	63.6	1.6	4.5	0.0	9.8	16.6	1 106	45	59	844	15.8	84.2	0.0

1. Based on the resident population estimated as of July 1 of the year shown.   2. © 2013 Election Data Services, Inc. All rights reserved.

Table B. States and Counties — **Land Area and Population**

STATE/ County code	CBSA code[1]	County type[2]	STATE County	Land area[3] (sq km) 2010	Total persons 2015	Rank	Per square kilometer	White	Black	American Indian, Alaska Native	Asian and Pacific Islander	Percent Hispanic or Latino[4]	Under 5 years	5 to 17 years	18 to 24 years	25 to 34 years	35 to 44 years	45 to 54 years
				1	2	3	4	5	6	7	8	9	10	11	12	13	14	15
			OKLAHOMA—Cont'd															
40 075	...	6	Kiowa	2 629	9 144	2 500	3.5	78.6	5.5	8.5	0.8	10.8	6.5	17.3	7.6	11.2	10.8	13.3
40 077	...	7	Latimer	1 870	10 483	2 396	5.6	75.1	2.0	27.2	0.7	3.4	6.2	16.5	10.6	11.1	10.3	13.1
40 079	22900	2	Le Flore	4 116	49 605	985	12.1	77.5	2.9	17.6	1.0	6.6	6.1	17.9	8.6	12.0	12.1	13.1
40 081	36420	1	Lincoln	2 466	35 042	1 303	14.2	87.9	2.5	10.8	0.7	3.1	5.9	18.7	7.9	10.7	11.6	14.2
40 083	36420	1	Logan	1 927	45 996	1 049	23.9	81.4	9.9	6.1	1.1	5.6	5.8	17.9	10.9	11.4	12.4	13.3
40 085	...	9	Love	1 331	9 870	2 445	7.4	76.5	2.9	9.5	0.9	14.6	6.7	18.5	8.1	11.9	10.8	12.6
40 087	36420	1	McClain	1 478	38 066	1 219	25.8	84.7	1.4	10.6	0.9	7.5	6.3	19.5	7.9	12.0	13.0	13.9
40 089	...	7	McCurtain	4 791	33 048	1 355	6.9	69.4	9.9	20.0	1.7	5.5	7.3	18.4	8.5	11.3	11.6	13.1
40 091	...	6	McIntosh	1 602	19 990	1 836	12.5	75.4	4.5	24.2	0.9	2.5	5.0	15.1	7.0	9.5	10.0	13.5
40 093	...	9	Major	2 473	7 771	2 611	3.1	87.4	1.4	3.4	0.8	9.1	7.4	17.6	7.0	11.4	10.7	12.8
40 095	...	6	Marshall	961	16 232	2 029	16.9	72.5	2.2	14.5	0.7	16.3	6.4	17.4	7.5	10.1	10.9	13.2
40 097	...	6	Mayes	1 697	40 887	1 156	24.1	74.6	1.0	29.6	0.7	3.2	6.4	17.9	8.4	11.6	11.7	13.2
40 099	...	7	Murray	1 079	13 936	2 170	12.9	80.1	2.4	17.6	0.8	5.6	5.8	17.7	7.4	11.7	11.5	12.8
40 101	34780	4	Muskogee	2 099	69 699	770	33.2	64.2	12.7	24.5	1.1	5.8	7.0	17.5	9.1	13.0	12.0	12.6
40 103	...	6	Noble	1 896	11 554	2 319	6.1	85.8	2.6	11.4	0.9	3.3	5.6	18.6	7.6	11.3	11.6	14.1
40 105	...	6	Nowata	1 465	10 539	2 392	7.2	76.3	3.3	26.5	0.6	2.7	5.9	17.5	8.1	11.0	10.9	13.9
40 107	...	6	Okfuskee	1 602	12 181	2 288	7.6	67.9	8.9	25.0	0.9	4.0	6.8	16.7	8.4	12.2	12.4	13.9
40 109	36420	1	Oklahoma	1 836	776 864	79	423.1	61.5	17.0	5.8	4.2	16.2	7.8	17.7	9.6	15.8	12.5	12.2
40 111	46140	2	Okmulgee	1 806	39 187	1 196	21.7	70.3	10.4	23.0	0.9	3.7	6.1	17.7	10.1	11.6	10.9	13.0
40 113	46140	2	Osage	5 818	47 887	1 019	8.2	70.4	12.1	20.4	0.6	3.3	5.2	17.6	7.9	11.0	11.3	13.9
40 115	33060	6	Ottawa	1 219	31 981	1 382	26.2	76.2	1.7	25.3	2.1	5.3	6.9	17.9	10.2	11.1	11.4	12.4
40 117	46140	2	Pawnee	1 471	16 436	2 011	11.2	83.2	1.6	17.9	0.8	2.8	6.2	18.1	7.6	10.4	11.6	13.8
40 119	44660	4	Payne	1 773	80 850	692	45.6	82.1	4.9	8.3	5.3	4.5	5.7	13.6	27.9	13.7	9.5	9.3
40 121	32540	5	Pittsburg	3 381	44 610	1 080	13.2	77.2	4.6	20.4	0.9	4.6	6.3	15.9	8.1	13.1	11.6	13.4
40 123	10220	7	Pontotoc	1 866	38 194	1 217	20.5	73.7	3.8	23.5	1.3	4.8	7.0	16.7	11.7	14.0	11.0	12.1
40 125	43060	4	Pottawatomie	2 040	71 875	751	35.2	78.7	4.3	17.0	1.4	4.9	6.7	17.6	10.0	12.8	12.2	12.9
40 127	...	9	Pushmataha	3 615	11 183	2 344	3.1	78.3	1.6	21.8	0.6	3.2	5.6	16.0	7.4	10.5	10.3	13.7
40 129	...	9	Roger Mills	2 956	3 788	2 921	1.3	86.0	1.4	6.8	0.8	6.9	6.6	19.1	6.4	12.2	11.1	12.4
40 131	46140	2	Rogers	1 750	90 802	640	51.9	80.4	1.8	20.0	1.7	4.2	5.7	18.9	9.0	11.7	12.3	14.4
40 133	...	7	Seminole	1 639	25 548	1 582	15.6	71.9	6.3	23.8	0.8	4.5	6.5	18.9	9.0	11.1	11.3	13.3
40 135	22900	2	Sequoyah	1 744	41 153	1 146	23.6	73.0	2.6	28.9	1.0	3.8	5.8	18.3	8.4	11.3	12.3	14.1
40 137	20340	4	Stephens	2 254	44 581	1 081	19.8	85.0	2.8	8.6	0.9	7.0	6.4	17.4	8.0	12.0	11.5	12.8
40 139	25100	7	Texas	5 287	21 489	1 756	4.1	48.1	3.3	1.7	2.7	46.1	8.1	19.5	11.5	14.7	13.1	12.1
40 141	...	6	Tillman	2 256	7 515	2 634	3.3	63.6	8.5	4.8	0.8	25.4	6.2	18.2	8.0	11.9	10.7	13.5
40 143	46140	2	Tulsa	1 477	639 242	102	432.8	68.4	12.0	9.8	3.5	11.8	7.4	18.2	9.3	14.6	12.8	12.7
40 145	46140	2	Wagoner	1 454	76 559	721	52.7	79.0	4.8	15.8	2.1	5.7	6.2	18.9	7.7	12.6	13.2	13.5
40 147	12780	4	Washington	1 076	52 021	960	48.3	79.6	3.7	15.0	2.2	5.7	6.4	17.3	8.5	12.0	11.3	12.5
40 149	...	7	Washita	2 598	11 661	2 314	4.5	86.3	1.7	4.6	0.4	9.6	6.7	17.4	7.4	12.9	11.1	12.9
40 151	...	7	Woods	3 332	9 304	2 485	2.8	86.6	4.2	4.0	1.5	6.5	5.9	14.4	17.7	14.2	9.8	10.9
40 153	49260	7	Woodward	3 218	21 559	1 751	6.7	82.6	2.4	4.0	1.1	12.1	7.5	18.3	8.7	15.1	12.6	12.6
41 000	...	X	OREGON	248 608	4 028 977	X	16.2	79.9	2.5	2.4	6.0	12.5	5.8	15.8	9.2	13.7	13.0	12.9
41 001	...	7	Baker	7 947	16 005	2 040	2.0	93.5	1.1	2.4	1.2	3.9	5.2	14.2	6.7	10.4	9.8	12.6
41 003	18700	3	Benton	1 751	87 572	659	50.0	85.0	1.6	1.6	8.0	7.0	4.1	12.7	22.6	12.9	9.9	10.6
41 005	38900	1	Clackamas	4 844	401 515	173	82.9	85.8	1.5	1.6	5.9	8.4	5.3	16.9	8.1	11.7	12.7	14.4
41 007	11820	4	Clatsop	2 147	37 831	1 230	17.6	88.5	1.2	2.2	2.8	8.1	5.3	14.3	8.3	12.4	10.9	12.8
41 009	38900	1	Columbia	1 703	49 600	986	29.1	92.1	1.1	2.9	2.4	4.6	5.1	17.2	7.5	10.7	12.3	14.4
41 011	18300	5	Coos	4 134	63 121	837	15.3	89.3	0.9	5.1	2.3	6.0	4.9	13.5	7.2	10.7	10.0	12.6
41 013	39260	6	Crook	7 716	21 630	1 747	2.8	90.1	0.5	2.4	1.1	7.4	4.3	15.1	6.4	9.1	11.0	12.9
41 015	15060	7	Curry	4 215	22 483	1 708	5.3	90.2	0.8	4.2	1.6	6.6	4.3	11.2	5.6	8.0	8.5	12.5
41 017	13460	3	Deschutes	7 817	175 268	367	22.4	89.8	0.8	1.7	2.1	7.8	5.3	16.1	7.1	12.3	13.1	13.1
41 019	40700	4	Douglas	13 043	107 490	355	8.3	91.4	0.8	3.6	2.0	5.2	5.1	14.4	7.3	10.4	10.2	12.7
41 021	...	9	Gilliam	3 120	1 859	3 062	0.6	91.1	0.6	2.1	1.9	6.5	6.1	13.7	5.7	8.4	10.6	13.0
41 023	...	9	Grant	11 729	7 185	2 659	0.6	94.2	0.7	2.6	1.4	3.4	4.7	13.8	5.5	8.8	9.5	12.1
41 025	...	7	Harney	26 245	7 200	2 657	0.3	90.1	1.1	5.2	1.1	4.8	5.1	15.2	7.4	9.8	10.6	12.7
41 027	26220	6	Hood River	1 352	23 137	1 678	17.1	66.4	0.7	1.6	2.5	31.0	6.6	18.4	8.3	12.3	12.7	13.9
41 029	32780	3	Jackson	7 209	212 567	306	29.5	84.7	1.2	2.4	2.5	12.0	5.7	15.3	8.2	12.0	11.3	12.5
41 031	...	6	Jefferson	4 612	22 666	1 702	4.9	62.2	1.0	17.7	1.6	19.6	6.7	17.4	8.4	11.6	11.3	12.8
41 033	24420	4	Josephine	4 247	84 745	669	20.0	90.1	0.9	2.9	1.9	7.0	4.9	14.6	7.0	9.8	10.1	12.6
41 035	28900	5	Klamath	15 387	66 016	802	4.3	82.5	1.3	5.8	1.9	11.9	6.0	15.5	9.1	11.6	10.8	12.7
41 037	...	7	Lake	21 080	7 829	2 607	0.4	88.5	1.3	4.0	1.4	7.8	4.2	14.2	6.5	9.9	11.5	14.1
41 039	21660	2	Lane	11 793	362 895	188	30.8	86.6	1.7	2.7	4.6	8.3	4.9	14.2	13.2	12.5	11.5	12.2
41 041	35440	4	Lincoln	2 538	47 038	1 032	18.5	86.2	0.9	5.3	2.2	8.5	5.0	12.0	6.5	10.0	10.0	12.3
41 043	10540	4	Linn	5 931	120 547	514	20.3	88.8	0.9	2.6	2.1	8.4	6.2	17.0	8.2	12.7	11.9	12.7
41 045	36620	6	Malheur	25 609	30 380	1 422	1.2	63.2	1.5	1.7	2.2	33.1	7.0	18.1	9.8	13.1	12.2	12.0
41 047	41420	2	Marion	3 062	330 700	204	108.0	69.3	1.7	2.1	4.0	25.7	6.8	18.6	9.7	13.5	12.5	12.3

1. CBSA = Core Based Statistical Area. See Appendix A for explanation. See Appendix B for list of metropolitan areas with component counties.   2. County type code from the Economic Research Service of USDA Rural-Urban Continuum Codes. See Appendix A for definition.   3. Dry land or land partially or temporarily covered by water.   4. May be of any race.

Table B. States and Counties — **Population and Households**

STATE County	55 to 64 years	65 to 74 years	75 years and over	Percent female	2000	2010	2000–2010	2010–2015	Births	Deaths	Net migration	Number	Persons per house-hold	Family house-holds	Female family house-holder[1]	One per-son
	16	17	18	19	20	21	22	23	24	25	26	27	28	29	30	31
OKLAHOMA—Cont'd																
Kiowa	14.3	10.9	8.0	50.8	10 227	9 446	-7.6	-3.2	580	681	-179	3 974	2.31	63.5	13.6	30.3
Latimer	13.0	10.6	8.6	49.4	10 692	11 154	4.3	-6.0	578	584	-655	4 101	2.55	70.1	11.9	26.0
Le Flore	13.2	10.1	6.8	50.0	48 109	50 384	4.7	-1.5	3 169	3 145	-823	18 255	2.66	69.7	12.3	25.9
Lincoln	13.9	10.2	6.8	50.1	32 080	34 273	6.8	2.2	2 124	1 838	444	13 342	2.55	71.3	11.1	25.0
Logan	13.2	8.9	6.1	50.5	33 924	41 853	23.4	9.9	2 507	1 826	3 195	15 146	2.76	73.7	10.2	23.3
Love	13.1	10.9	7.4	50.5	8 831	9 421	6.7	4.8	670	594	366	3 243	2.92	74.9	10.1	21.8
McClain	12.7	9.0	5.7	50.4	27 740	34 506	24.4	10.3	2 205	1 662	2 967	13 014	2.74	75.5	8.9	21.7
McCurtain	12.9	9.9	7.1	51.0	34 402	33 154	-3.6	-0.3	2 486	2 032	-499	12 891	2.53	70.8	14.5	26.4
McIntosh	15.2	14.1	10.5	50.5	19 456	20 252	4.1	-1.3	1 147	1 692	218	8 158	2.45	68.5	10.2	27.8
Major	14.4	9.4	9.3	50.9	7 545	7 527	-0.2	3.2	574	413	97	3 066	2.45	71.0	7.2	26.0
Marshall	13.7	12.2	8.6	50.3	13 184	15 836	20.1	2.5	956	936	351	6 003	2.62	66.1	8.8	29.6
Mayes	13.7	10.3	6.8	50.3	38 369	41 264	7.5	-0.9	2 692	2 551	-436	15 802	2.56	69.8	10.5	26.9
Murray	14.0	10.9	8.2	50.0	12 623	13 488	6.9	3.3	836	972	535	5 229	2.54	69.0	10.1	26.1
Muskogee	12.7	9.1	6.9	51.2	69 451	70 988	2.2	-1.8	4 981	4 705	-1 645	26 574	2.52	67.1	14.5	28.2
Noble	13.6	9.6	8.0	50.6	11 411	11 561	1.3	-0.1	729	673	-67	4 562	2.46	73.0	9.8	24.2
Nowata	13.8	10.7	8.2	50.8	10 569	10 536	-0.3	0.0	606	699	111	4 104	2.52	71.0	10.5	26.0
Okfuskee	12.6	10.2	6.9	46.6	11 814	12 191	3.2	-0.1	907	833	-89	4 196	2.62	69.7	13.8	26.3
Oklahoma	11.8	7.1	5.4	51.1	660 448	718 627	8.8	8.1	65 092	35 662	28 874	287 998	2.53	62.4	13.9	31.2
Okmulgee	13.3	9.9	7.4	50.7	39 685	40 069	1.0	-2.2	2 694	2 699	-876	15 008	2.55	64.9	14.2	30.9
Osage	14.6	10.9	7.6	49.7	44 437	47 480	6.8	0.9	2 369	2 463	264	18 433	2.52	69.7	10.8	26.6
Ottawa	12.0	10.3	7.7	51.0	33 194	31 848	-4.1	0.4	2 349	2 286	8	11 988	2.59	68.8	13.2	27.3
Pawnee	14.3	10.8	7.3	50.1	16 612	16 579	-0.2	-0.9	997	1 052	-79	6 323	2.59	70.3	11.1	25.1
Payne	9.2	6.2	4.9	48.9	68 190	77 350	13.4	4.5	4 797	2 879	1 557	30 182	2.34	54.4	8.4	30.8
Pittsburg	13.4	10.4	7.7	49.2	43 953	45 837	4.3	-2.7	2 851	3 079	-886	18 477	2.32	66.0	12.5	28.8
Pontotoc	11.7	8.7	7.0	51.2	35 143	37 492	6.7	1.9	2 906	2 274	67	14 650	2.50	64.0	13.9	29.4
Pottawatomie	12.2	9.1	6.5	52.3	65 521	69 442	6.0	3.5	4 937	4 082	1 524	26 033	2.59	70.1	13.2	26.2
Pushmataha	14.2	12.7	9.5	51.0	11 667	11 572	-0.8	-3.4	688	833	-227	4 784	2.34	62.8	12.0	33.1
Roger Mills	14.1	9.8	8.5	49.5	3 436	3 647	6.1	3.9	272	169	18	1 307	2.84	68.6	8.9	26.9
Rogers	12.7	9.1	6.3	50.2	70 641	86 906	23.0	4.5	5 288	4 117	2 550	33 129	2.64	75.9	9.9	20.8
Seminole	12.8	9.7	7.4	50.9	24 894	25 482	2.4	0.3	1 799	1 734	42	9 266	2.68	69.6	14.1	26.7
Sequoyah	12.8	10.2	6.8	50.6	38 972	42 439	8.9	-3.0	2 241	2 556	-994	15 522	2.66	72.5	13.7	24.0
Stephens	13.9	9.6	8.4	51.3	43 182	45 048	4.3	-1.0	2 880	2 850	-491	17 850	2.48	66.7	10.7	30.1
Texas	10.5	5.7	4.7	46.8	20 107	20 640	2.7	4.1	1 806	684	-235	7 166	2.92	73.4	10.1	22.3
Tillman	13.2	10.0	8.2	50.1	9 287	7 992	-13.9	-6.0	524	453	-502	3 029	2.46	69.4	14.2	27.6
Tulsa	12.0	7.3	5.6	51.3	563 299	603 440	7.1	5.9	49 327	29 482	15 962	243 509	2.49	63.6	13.9	30.5
Wagoner	13.1	9.6	5.3	50.5	57 491	73 087	27.1	4.8	4 559	3 229	2 082	27 086	2.75	75.8	11.0	20.3
Washington	13.5	9.5	9.1	51.4	48 996	50 977	4.0	2.0	3 316	3 106	913	21 109	2.41	66.2	11.1	29.4
Washita	13.3	8.5	8.0	49.8	11 508	11 629	1.1	0.3	760	752	40	4 585	2.49	71.8	8.5	26.0
Woods	11.1	7.8	8.3	46.2	9 089	8 878	-2.3	4.8	553	524	375	3 393	2.35	58.0	7.7	34.5
Woodward	11.4	7.9	6.0	47.0	18 486	20 081	8.6	7.4	1 694	1 044	824	7 246	2.71	68.2	10.2	27.5
OREGON	13.6	9.4	6.5	50.5	3 421 399	3 831 073	12.0	5.2	238 882	174 286	129 687	1 522 988	2.50	63.4	10.6	27.9
Baker	16.3	14.1	10.6	49.5	16 741	16 138	-3.6	-0.8	912	1 054	71	7 197	2.15	63.3	8.5	31.8
Benton	12.8	8.3	6.0	49.9	78 153	85 581	9.5	2.3	3 807	2 872	980	33 376	2.42	55.5	7.1	28.6
Clackamas	14.8	9.8	6.4	50.8	338 391	375 998	11.1	6.8	20 953	16 365	20 028	147 736	2.58	69.1	9.9	24.3
Clatsop	16.7	12.0	7.3	50.6	35 630	37 037	3.9	2.1	2 198	1 991	588	15 746	2.31	61.3	10.5	31.8
Columbia	15.6	10.8	6.4	50.3	43 560	49 353	13.3	0.5	2 558	2 143	-150	18 772	2.61	71.5	10.4	23.5
Coos	16.9	13.9	10.1	50.7	62 779	63 043	0.4	0.1	3 245	4 524	1 237	25 847	2.38	60.0	9.3	32.5
Crook	17.0	15.1	9.1	50.6	19 182	20 978	9.4	3.1	985	1 184	838	8 977	2.30	64.8	8.6	28.5
Curry	18.8	18.0	13.3	50.7	21 137	22 364	5.8	0.5	945	1 849	965	10 296	2.14	58.2	7.3	33.3
Deschutes	14.8	11.5	6.8	50.7	115 367	157 733	36.7	11.1	9 073	6 954	15 127	64 917	2.49	66.8	9.1	25.5
Douglas	16.2	13.3	10.3	50.7	100 399	107 667	7.2	0.0	5 673	7 216	1 516	43 730	2.41	66.5	10.7	26.2
Gilliam	18.3	12.5	11.6	49.9	1 915	1 871	-2.3	-0.6	97	95	-20	879	2.17	61.7	7.5	35.7
Grant	18.4	15.2	12.1	50.5	7 935	7 445	-6.2	-3.5	324	396	-181	3 164	2.27	64.2	7.5	30.8
Harney	16.7	13.0	9.5	49.4	7 609	7 422	-2.5	-3.0	436	417	-226	3 083	2.30	70.3	9.1	26.7
Hood River	13.6	7.8	6.3	49.9	20 411	22 346	9.5	3.5	1 516	899	150	8 251	2.62	65.1	7.6	25.0
Jackson	14.9	11.6	8.6	51.4	181 269	203 206	12.1	4.6	12 227	11 636	8 380	82 977	2.44	64.1	11.4	29.0
Jefferson	13.8	11.3	6.6	48.1	19 009	21 720	14.3	4.4	1 553	1 019	385	7 800	2.69	71.7	14.7	22.6
Josephine	16.1	14.3	10.6	51.2	75 726	82 713	9.2	2.5	4 335	6 047	3 687	34 187	2.39	64.0	10.3	29.7
Klamath	15.1	11.4	7.8	50.1	63 775	66 380	4.1	-0.5	4 185	3 845	-667	27 148	2.39	66.0	12.1	26.5
Lake	16.5	13.7	9.3	46.9	7 422	7 895	6.4	-0.8	388	416	-46	3 616	2.04	57.5	5.4	35.3
Lane	14.2	10.2	7.2	50.9	322 959	351 715	8.9	3.2	18 637	17 367	9 570	145 627	2.38	59.1	10.7	29.0
Lincoln	19.2	15.6	9.2	51.4	44 479	46 032	3.5	2.2	2 272	2 969	1 768	20 672	2.20	61.5	8.3	31.5
Linn	13.9	10.1	7.2	50.5	103 069	116 672	13.2	3.3	7 582	6 130	2 237	44 942	2.60	68.0	11.6	25.1
Malheur	11.9	8.5	7.2	45.5	31 615	31 312	-1.0	-3.0	2 287	1 508	-1 720	10 235	2.64	67.7	11.5	28.1
Marion	12.2	8.3	6.1	50.1	284 834	315 335	10.7	4.9	23 109	13 765	5 782	113 883	2.72	69.0	13.7	25.6

1. No spouse present.

Table B. States and Counties — Population, Vital Statistics, Medicare, and Crime

STATE County	Persons in group quarters, 2015	Daytime population, 2010–2014		Births, 2015		Deaths, 2015		Persons under 65 with no health insurance, 2014		Medicare, 2015			Serious crimes known to police,[2] 2014 Total	
		Number	Employ-ment/resi-dence ratio	Total	Rate[1]	Number	Rate[1]	Number	Percent	Total Beneficiaries	Enrolled in Original Medicare	Enrolled in Medicare Advantage	Number	Rate[3]
	32	33	34	35	36	37	38	39	40	41	42	43	44	45
OKLAHOMA—Cont'd														
Kiowa	171	8 637	0.81	110	11.9	121	13.1	1 426	19.3	2 193	2 032	161	190	2 037
Latimer	575	10 837	0.98	93	8.8	100	9.5	1 691	20.5	1 681	1 543	138	169	1 580
Le Flore	1 616	46 390	0.80	672	13.5	664	13.4	9 352	23.5	11 020	9 484	1 536	1 209	2 435
Lincoln	386	29 125	0.63	433	12.4	323	9.3	4 859	17.1	6 179	5 091	1 088	635	1 846
Logan	2 182	33 287	0.46	489	10.7	362	7.9	5 859	15.8	5 117	4 099	1 018	773	1 715
Love	88	10 922	1.33	129	13.1	113	11.5	1 520	19.1	1 926	1 804	122	128	1 302
McClain	194	29 718	0.62	430	11.4	312	8.3	5 095	16.1	6 737	5 816	921	683	1 845
McCurtain	454	32 892	0.98	506	15.3	425	12.9	5 683	21.1	7 060	6 384	676	982	2 970
McIntosh	345	18 672	0.77	240	12.0	312	15.6	3 219	21.5	5 488	5 036	452	446	2 169
Major	77	7 234	0.89	118	15.2	67	8.6	1 121	17.9	1 488	1 431	57	98	1 267
Marshall	329	15 104	0.86	174	10.8	145	9.0	3 044	24.0	3 565	3 303	262	253	1 577
Mayes	566	38 870	0.86	524	12.8	522	12.8	6 718	20.1	8 082	6 821	1 261	762	1 871
Murray	313	12 937	0.88	174	12.5	190	13.7	2 014	18.4	2 771	2 594	177	274	1 989
Muskogee	3 526	73 391	1.11	911	13.1	881	12.6	11 910	21.5	15 630	13 967	1 663	2 412	3 437
Noble	273	11 156	0.93	141	12.2	117	10.1	1 526	16.2	2 097	1 982	115	171	1 496
Nowata	157	8 776	0.57	119	11.3	132	12.5	1 726	20.6	2 295	2 105	190	137	1 295
Okfuskee	1 228	11 202	0.73	162	13.3	160	13.1	1 979	21.6	2 436	2 181	255	296	2 382
Oklahoma	14 818	848 454	1.30	12 689	16.4	6 748	8.7	120 120	18.3	119 935	90 756	29 179	34 472	4 507
Okmulgee	1 374	36 749	0.80	504	12.9	513	13.1	5 808	18.7	7 936	6 892	1 044	964	2 452
Osage	1 504	39 089	0.54	450	9.4	526	11.0	6 257	16.6	3 839	3 225	614	1 074	2 229
Ottawa	968	31 926	0.99	476	14.9	490	15.3	5 233	20.6	7 379	6 683	696	741	2 289
Pawnee	194	14 184	0.65	181	11.0	173	10.6	2 484	18.7	3 439	3 020	419	190	1 151
Payne	7 767	80 640	1.05	913	11.3	554	6.9	11 579	18.2	11 054	10 527	527	2 361	2 967
Pittsburg	2 429	46 197	1.05	555	12.4	553	12.4	7 163	20.8	9 530	8 791	739	1 437	3 231
Pontotoc	1 696	39 554	1.10	550	14.4	488	12.8	6 120	20.0	7 374	6 782	592	1 463	3 837
Pottawatomie	3 055	67 312	0.88	933	13.0	786	10.9	10 191	17.6	13 717	11 124	2 593	2 941	4 107
Pushmataha	110	10 640	0.83	141	12.6	155	13.9	1 817	21.2	2 785	2 509	276	160	1 434
Roger Mills	11	3 878	1.08	56	14.8	20	5.3	536	17.5	698	677	21	75	1 987
Rogers	1 216	75 645	0.69	1 062	11.8	799	8.8	10 869	14.4	12 948	8 933	4 015	1 297	1 447
Seminole	581	24 701	0.92	341	13.4	333	13.1	4 449	21.7	5 159	4 536	623	633	2 488
Sequoyah	464	37 028	0.70	500	12.1	526	12.8	7 174	21.1	8 799	7 279	1 520	1 138	2 778
Stephens	540	44 449	0.98	540	12.1	523	11.7	6 265	17.3	8 708	7 709	999	1 728	3 847
Texas	572	20 999	0.95	357	16.5	135	6.2	4 365	23.0	2 235	2 082	153	362	1 614
Tillman	267	7 227	0.81	92	12.2	70	9.3	1 267	21.2	1 643	1 541	102	194	2 535
Tulsa	9 874	677 981	1.21	9 427	14.8	5 753	9.1	92 793	17.2	108 250	73 223	35 027	28 040	4 469
Wagoner	319	53 474	0.37	822	10.8	638	8.4	10 828	16.9	6 340	4 327	2 013	1 689	2 212
Washington	798	52 759	1.05	630	12.1	629	12.1	6 844	16.4	11 624	10 601	1 023	1 109	2 143
Washita	206	10 036	0.68	142	12.2	149	12.8	1 769	18.6	2 312	2 170	142	189	1 614
Woods	1 004	9 816	1.21	109	11.7	95	10.2	977	14.2	1 581	1 480	101	108	1 188
Woodward	1 240	21 643	1.10	339	15.8	243	11.3	2 955	17.0	3 167	3 007	160	583	2 704
OREGON	86 962	3 945 098	1.03	46 091	11.5	33 700	8.4	378 857	11.6	706 615	376 408	330 207	123 529	3 111
Baker	409	15 887	0.97	177	11.0	201	12.5	1 410	12.0	4 396	4 150	246	423	2 633
Benton	4 467	87 448	1.04	693	8.0	566	6.5	7 031	10.1	11 544	6 036	5 508	2 620	3 004
Clackamas	2 912	353 971	0.83	4 172	10.5	3 238	8.1	31 753	9.6	67 232	24 386	42 846	NA	NA
Clatsop	896	38 268	1.06	409	10.9	380	10.1	3 471	11.7	8 842	6 579	2 263	924	2 981
Columbia	372	40 221	0.54	511	10.3	448	9.0	3 885	9.5	9 389	4 298	5 091	661	1 388
Coos	1 228	62 705	1.00	618	9.8	855	13.6	5 803	12.4	17 632	15 591	2 041	2 164	3 613
Crook	215	20 040	0.90	209	9.8	225	10.5	2 137	13.5	5 651	4 279	1 372	536	2 567
Curry	318	22 084	0.97	172	7.7	355	15.9	1 967	12.9	7 603	6 706	897	291	1 367
Deschutes	1 217	162 915	1.00	1 822	10.5	1 343	7.8	16 562	12.0	35 277	24 038	11 239	4 379	2 595
Douglas	1 734	106 639	0.99	1 074	10.0	1 338	12.5	9 518	11.7	29 087	19 181	9 906	3 123	3 009
Gilliam	21	2 103	1.21	18	9.5	21	11.1	135	9.2	511	484	27	30	1 519
Grant	95	7 270	0.98	58	8.1	69	9.6	634	12.2	1 995	1 607	388	87	1 196
Harney	157	7 276	1.01	90	12.5	68	9.5	823	15.3	1 743	1 612	131	156	2 193
Hood River	791	23 176	1.05	293	12.7	170	7.4	2 780	14.2	3 544	2 608	936	410	1 796
Jackson	3 572	206 942	1.00	2 361	11.2	2 181	10.3	21 410	12.9	48 594	32 093	16 501	9 061	4 300
Jefferson	898	21 132	0.91	309	13.7	229	10.2	2 958	17.1	4 631	3 358	1 273	620	2 938
Josephine	1 542	81 578	0.95	867	10.3	1 103	13.1	7 481	12.0	23 456	14 051	9 405	2 896	3 457
Klamath	1 054	65 524	0.98	784	11.9	757	11.5	6 967	13.4	14 235	11 005	3 230	1 936	2 967
Lake	468	7 984	1.04	82	10.5	80	10.2	883	15.7	1 927	1 763	164	NA	NA
Lane	7 815	355 871	1.01	3 636	10.1	3 344	9.3	34 733	12.0	71 163	33 865	37 298	NA	NA
Lincoln	806	46 399	1.01	426	9.1	536	11.5	4 858	14.1	12 628	9 872	2 756	1 737	3 725
Linn	1 191	113 685	0.90	1 440	12.0	1 247	10.4	10 106	10.3	26 375	12 646	13 729	4 028	3 364
Malheur	3 373	34 087	1.32	431	14.2	253	8.3	3 438	15.4	5 730	5 084	646	821	3 017
Marion	10 725	327 251	1.05	4 438	13.5	2 677	8.2	36 430	13.5	52 352	20 615	31 737	11 416	3 492

1. Per 1,000 estimated resident population. 2. Data for serious crimes have not been adjusted for underreporting; this may affect comparability between geographic areas and over time.
3. Per 100,000 population estimated by the FBI.

Table B. States and Counties — Crime, Education, Money Income, and Poverty

STATE County	Serious crimes known to police, 2014 (cont.)[1] Rate[2] Violent	Property	Education — School enrollment and attainment, 2010–2014 Enrollment[3] Total	Percent private	Attainment[4] (percent) High school graduate or less	Bachelor's degree or more	Local government expenditures,[5] 2012–2013 Total current spending (mil dol)	Current spending per student (dollars)	Money income, 2010–2014 Per capita income[6] (dollars)	Households Median income (dollars)	Mean income (dollars)	Percent with income of $200,000 or more	Income and poverty, 2014 Median household income (dollars)	Percent below poverty level All persons	Children under 18 years	Children 5 to 17 years in families
	46	47	48	49	50	51	52	53	54	55	56	57	58	59	60	61
OKLAHOMA—Cont'd																
Kiowa	289	1 747	2 180	5.4	50.5	18.5	14.6	8 821	23 062	37 431	54 466	2.0	36 699	19.1	25.6	24.4
Latimer	290	1 290	2 776	5.9	49.1	14.1	12.0	8 721	22 065	39 563	54 615	2.2	35 522	20.7	27.4	25.6
Le Flore	213	2 222	11 881	4.5	57.8	12.9	80.4	7 915	18 390	35 970	48 083	1.0	36 627	24.0	31.1	28.8
Lincoln	189	1 657	8 222	9.0	55.1	13.1	41.0	7 302	22 752	43 746	57 196	1.6	46 083	14.9	19.8	18.3
Logan	144	1 570	11 501	12.2	42.3	26.5	35.1	7 552	26 284	54 303	72 589	4.3	55 602	13.8	17.4	15.9
Love	81	1 221	2 149	9.2	59.6	16.1	13.1	7 609	20 151	44 461	54 600	1.9	52 662	12.5	22.0	20.8
McClain	92	1 754	9 161	6.2	47.5	21.5	50.6	6 888	26 582	55 741	70 139	2.8	58 392	10.2	13.9	13.0
McCurtain	200	2 770	7 941	6.5	59.9	14.2	59.2	8 645	17 691	33 012	44 384	1.0	34 964	20.9	29.0	28.5
McIntosh	170	1 998	3 992	6.1	55.8	13.5	27.7	8 264	19 891	36 718	46 837	0.9	33 450	22.4	32.5	31.0
Major	26	1 241	1 687	6.3	54.2	16.2	9.1	8 201	27 225	50 319	66 509	3.3	54 107	11.8	16.3	15.8
Marshall	137	1 440	3 707	6.4	54.8	14.2	23.0	7 658	20 831	39 028	53 247	1.8	38 517	18.0	25.9	24.4
Mayes	346	1 525	9 827	6.4	52.8	15.9	59.0	8 057	20 848	42 076	52 156	1.1	41 806	17.6	23.7	22.8
Murray	167	1 822	2 904	2.5	57.8	20.2	17.8	7 042	22 809	46 536	56 692	1.8	43 783	15.1	19.7	17.9
Muskogee	735	2 702	17 991	8.5	49.8	18.7	104.0	7 588	20 312	40 133	52 112	1.2	41 015	22.2	30.9	28.7
Noble	175	1 321	2 862	2.6	47.7	21.3	18.3	8 545	22 996	44 775	58 235	1.9	46 874	13.4	18.4	16.7
Nowata	265	1 031	2 582	7.8	56.7	13.1	15.2	8 099	20 142	40 203	49 147	0.7	39 706	16.1	23.2	21.6
Okfuskee	249	2 132	2 733	7.6	58.6	10.5	28.6	6 472	16 664	35 586	46 266	0.8	34 172	25.0	28.7	27.3
Oklahoma	595	3 912	197 912	14.4	39.1	30.2	941.3	7 441	27 114	46 584	67 734	4.1	48 226	17.9	25.4	24.2
Okmulgee	252	2 200	9 785	4.9	51.4	14.5	54.3	7 880	20 198	38 683	50 277	1.0	38 183	21.5	29.4	27.6
Osage	235	1 995	11 708	9.0	54.3	16.2	34.8	9 060	22 530	44 748	56 833	1.4	48 014	16.6	24.0	21.9
Ottawa	182	2 107	7 992	6.2	52.4	13.8	47.0	7 711	18 231	36 616	46 576	0.8	35 580	22.1	32.9	31.5
Pawnee	273	878	3 783	10.5	55.6	16.5	20.0	7 531	21 660	43 947	54 694	1.4	43 476	15.4	22.6	20.7
Payne	264	2 704	32 260	4.5	36.0	36.4	87.6	8 145	21 452	37 637	54 842	2.8	41 037	23.7	21.6	19.4
Pittsburg	148	3 083	9 424	8.9	52.1	15.6	67.3	8 530	22 719	41 339	55 380	1.9	39 900	21.7	29.3	27.7
Pontotoc	422	3 414	9 840	5.5	46.5	27.1	59.3	8 372	21 556	42 566	53 160	1.1	41 423	17.3	21.3	19.6
Pottawatomie	459	3 647	17 729	13.4	49.2	18.0	99.2	7 470	21 682	44 250	56 974	2.1	45 710	17.5	25.0	23.7
Pushmataha	242	1 192	2 233	3.9	58.5	12.2	20.6	8 916	20 108	32 462	45 332	1.4	32 215	23.1	33.2	31.2
Roger Mills	132	1 854	862	4.9	46.8	21.2	12.4	14 792	26 104	53 194	68 157	4.2	56 139	12.3	16.7	15.7
Rogers	221	1 226	23 329	13.0	42.2	23.1	107.5	7 562	27 488	57 843	72 399	3.0	56 465	10.0	13.8	12.4
Seminole	279	2 209	6 366	4.5	54.8	13.4	43.3	8 417	18 797	35 607	49 198	1.7	35 964	24.7	33.5	30.1
Sequoyah	315	2 463	10 029	4.8	58.1	13.1	68.1	7 906	18 639	37 483	47 871	0.9	35 592	27.9	37.7	35.8
Stephens	158	3 689	10 533	6.5	54.0	17.5	60.9	7 374	23 577	43 519	57 846	2.2	42 967	15.5	21.5	21.2
Texas	214	1 400	5 655	5.5	57.7	19.5	36.7	8 208	22 569	50 172	63 989	1.4	49 780	13.6	19.3	19.6
Tillman	248	2 287	1 771	2.8	62.1	16.1	14.6	9 253	18 449	36 592	47 025	1.0	35 274	23.8	33.1	30.9
Tulsa	591	3 878	161 827	18.1	37.5	30.0	883.1	7 643	27 995	48 926	69 143	4.1	50 507	14.8	20.4	19.0
Wagoner	270	1 942	19 748	11.9	45.8	21.5	45.7	6 768	25 239	56 189	68 132	2.0	58 921	9.8	14.4	13.6
Washington	186	1 957	11 992	13.4	43.8	26.1	60.9	7 385	27 514	48 870	66 061	3.8	49 056	13.9	18.6	18.6
Washita	307	1 306	2 733	5.4	53.8	17.6	18.6	8 357	24 213	47 300	60 763	2.4	47 391	13.9	19.0	17.5
Woods	99	1 089	2 479	9.1	44.0	25.7	14.1	10 708	25 494	52 188	64 073	2.1	48 831	14.3	17.0	16.6
Woodward	278	2 425	4 628	5.0	53.2	18.8	29.0	7 610	25 767	54 387	68 624	2.9	56 067	12.3	16.3	16.3
OREGON	232	2 879	967 378	14.7	35.1	30.1	5 557.8	9 543	27 173	50 521	67 671	3.5	51 088	16.4	21.3	19.3
Baker	454	2 178	3 284	13.2	42.4	20.4	23.7	9 675	23 890	40 576	52 412	2.0	38 966	20.6	29.2	28.3
Benton	127	2 877	32 497	7.3	20.4	51.4	81.2	9 368	27 233	49 338	68 121	3.9	54 089	18.9	13.0	12.6
Clackamas	NA	NA	93 395	16.3	31.0	32.0	537.6	9 246	33 126	64 700	84 551	5.8	65 555	9.5	12.6	11.5
Clatsop	187	2 794	8 116	10.5	34.8	23.6	51.8	10 368	26 281	47 337	61 112	2.0	45 132	15.4	22.7	20.6
Columbia	90	1 297	11 209	11.7	44.4	17.1	69.5	8 861	26 316	54 605	67 308	2.1	57 517	12.0	16.8	14.8
Coos	144	3 470	11 134	8.8	44.2	18.8	98.0	10 367	22 993	39 193	53 112	1.7	39 956	19.8	30.1	28.9
Crook	196	2 370	4 214	11.3	52.3	14.7	29.7	9 386	20 533	36 158	47 297	0.7	38 155	18.3	27.2	23.6
Curry	99	1 268	3 111	13.1	39.0	22.2	22.8	9 708	24 056	41 939	50 998	1.0	40 524	17.1	25.3	24.7
Deschutes	181	2 414	38 497	12.0	30.5	31.3	235.4	9 490	28 054	49 584	68 088	3.5	52 387	13.2	17.8	16.8
Douglas	206	2 803	22 325	11.2	44.2	15.9	148.4	10 353	22 074	40 820	52 220	1.3	41 504	19.9	28.5	25.7
Gilliam	0	1 519	341	6.2	44.0	18.8	6.9	23 646	27 401	46 490	59 515	1.6	51 978	11.7	20.1	20.8
Grant	41	1 155	1 349	10.2	44.3	19.5	13.8	15 354	22 878	37 258	49 846	1.1	41 304	16.8	27.1	24.8
Harney	70	2 123	1 595	16.3	47.4	16.9	16.2	15 383	20 455	35 828	47 761	0.8	36 340	21.3	31.6	26.9
Hood River	158	1 638	5 365	7.3	42.6	32.0	44.8	10 818	26 497	56 417	71 159	3.6	54 063	14.6	20.1	18.1
Jackson	319	3 981	45 877	11.2	38.4	25.1	279.8	9 729	24 460	44 086	58 914	2.2	44 835	18.1	25.9	22.3
Jefferson	190	2 749	5 309	6.0	46.8	16.0	42.2	11 583	21 997	46 588	58 408	1.4	42 753	21.2	32.2	30.2
Josephine	222	3 235	16 462	10.2	43.1	17.3	99.3	9 292	22 412	37 447	53 650	2.1	37 230	20.6	33.3	30.2
Klamath	218	2 749	15 636	10.1	43.5	19.6	94.6	9 942	21 740	39 534	52 279	1.4	39 234	21.9	29.1	26.6
Lake	NA	NA	1 469	4.3	47.8	18.3	14.0	11 623	22 020	34 535	48 346	0.7	40 328	19.3	28.1	24.9
Lane	NA	NA	96 173	10.2	33.9	28.2	443.9	9 761	24 720	43 685	59 120	2.2	44 976	18.4	20.1	17.0
Lincoln	347	3 377	7 647	12.6	39.7	24.3	52.7	10 019	25 130	42 429	55 305	1.8	40 226	18.8	30.3	30.0
Linn	109	3 255	29 084	10.2	41.9	17.5	197.8	8 945	21 363	44 965	54 361	0.9	44 358	19.1	26.8	24.9
Malheur	294	2 723	7 992	12.1	50.0	13.7	58.0	11 145	16 683	34 380	48 292	1.9	35 094	28.7	38.3	37.4
Marion	237	3 255	84 165	15.4	43.4	21.7	586.5	9 867	22 202	47 360	60 378	1.8	48 554	17.7	25.1	22.6

1. Data for serious crimes have not been adjusted for underreporting; this may affect comparability between geographic areas and over time.   2. Per 100,000 population estimated by the FBI.
3. All persons 3 years old and over enrolled in nursery school through college.   4. Persons 25 years old and over.   5. Elementary and secondary education expenditures.
6. Based on population estimated by the American Community Survey, 2010–2014.

Table B. States and Counties — **Personal Income**

STATE County	Total (mil dol) [62]	Percent change, 2013–2014 [63]	Per capita¹ Dollars [64]	Per capita¹ Rank [65]	Wages and salaries (mil dol) [66]	Pension and insurance [67]	Government social insurance [68]	Proprietors' income (mil dol) [69]	Dividends, interest, and rent (mil dol) [70]	Personal transfer receipts (mil dol) [71]	Total (mil dol) [72]	From employee and self-employed [73]	From employer [74]
OKLAHOMA—Cont'd													
Kiowa	314	2.3	33 594	2 176	86	19	6	47	50	94	158	9	6
Latimer	364	1.4	34 087	2 101	148	31	11	36	52	112	226	13	11
Le Flore	1 562	2.7	31 395	2 540	540	97	43	189	184	493	870	51	43
Lincoln	1 176	4.3	33 968	2 117	266	48	20	129	165	270	463	29	20
Logan	2 040	5.9	45 064	672	273	46	21	462	234	308	802	39	21
Love	346	6.5	35 380	1 883	173	41	13	25	56	88	251	14	13
McClain	1 527	6.2	40 912	1 070	342	55	26	106	204	278	529	32	26
McCurtain	1 001	1.7	30 286	2 680	391	76	34	123	116	336	623	37	34
McIntosh	663	3.8	32 987	2 280	131	25	11	65	93	251	232	18	11
Major	375	10.1	48 348	462	133	23	9	91	53	55	257	12	9
Marshall	559	4.8	34 520	2 023	166	30	13	68	76	156	277	17	13
Mayes	1 398	5.4	34 244	2 072	533	93	42	104	187	371	772	48	42
Murray	549	5.3	39 775	1 210	218	49	16	50	84	125	333	19	16
Muskogee	2 335	2.9	33 376	2 216	1 247	254	100	194	366	694	1 796	105	100
Noble	436	3.6	37 976	1 456	204	37	15	37	84	93	293	17	15
Nowata	359	2.0	34 154	2 089	59	12	5	42	48	90	119	8	5
Okfuskee	350	5.9	28 685	2 866	83	19	6	44	51	118	152	9	6
Oklahoma	39 106	4.9	51 038	330	24 182	3 890	1 807	8 045	6 821	5 604	37 923	1 947	1 807
Okmulgee	1 232	3.8	31 509	2 524	371	73	28	76	167	399	549	37	28
Osage	1 765	5.8	36 775	1 636	281	54	21	366	211	362	722	37	21
Ottawa	1 057	-0.1	32 924	2 291	385	75	29	103	160	319	593	36	29
Pawnee	552	2.6	33 626	2 171	149	29	12	53	75	147	244	16	12
Payne	3 052	7.4	38 028	1 449	1 501	306	108	436	510	485	2 351	122	108
Pittsburg	1 564	2.3	35 057	1 922	706	141	55	131	281	419	1 033	61	55
Pontotoc	1 498	5.9	39 422	1 261	713	141	53	157	244	348	1 065	59	53
Pottawatomie	2 519	4.7	35 084	1 916	829	145	63	265	410	619	1 302	78	63
Pushmataha	336	2.9	30 225	2 686	92	20	7	43	49	123	163	11	7
Roger Mills	186	12.7	49 555	412	38	8	3	39	56	24	88	4	3
Rogers	3 813	4.8	42 451	903	1 377	219	107	442	490	658	2 145	122	107
Seminole	831	3.4	32 693	2 335	283	55	22	117	132	246	477	28	22
Sequoyah	1 266	3.6	30 617	2 638	274	59	22	101	186	415	456	32	22
Stephens	2 205	5.2	49 556	411	765	111	57	616	334	389	1 548	79	57
Texas	992	9.1	45 417	639	399	73	30	313	114	108	816	29	30
Tillman	288	10.8	37 793	1 484	76	16	5	70	40	70	168	7	5
Tulsa	35 510	5.0	56 401	186	18 161	2 600	1 379	8 130	7 193	4 510	30 270	1 547	1 379
Wagoner	2 629	3.7	34 735	1 977	374	65	29	87	309	533	556	42	29
Washington	2 430	4.4	46 788	537	1 162	183	83	328	469	440	1 755	100	83
Washita	400	2.8	34 678	1 987	93	18	7	47	69	85	164	9	7
Woods	394	7.6	42 421	910	176	34	12	63	116	61	286	15	12
Woodward	1 179	6.4	54 746	216	565	80	41	309	192	130	996	48	41
OREGON	163 653	5.7	41 220	X	85 068	12 306	7 481	12 431	31 399	33 524	117 285	7 458	7 481
Baker	542	6.4	33 723	2 157	186	37	17	37	133	173	278	19	17
Benton	3 427	4.4	39 698	1 227	1 760	339	148	259	827	513	2 507	152	148
Clackamas	19 240	5.3	48 713	449	7 312	917	657	1 596	3 636	2 685	10 483	683	657
Clatsop	1 414	4.6	37 726	1 494	649	107	61	104	285	376	922	61	61
Columbia	1 814	5.3	36 680	1 652	395	70	37	59	254	463	560	43	37
Coos	2 278	5.8	36 469	1 693	837	161	79	165	428	771	1 243	87	79
Crook	716	7.8	34 088	2 100	264	43	24	70	147	233	401	29	24
Curry	798	4.4	35 720	1 817	223	40	21	53	188	284	337	27	21
Deschutes	7 101	7.0	41 675	987	2 855	418	270	758	1 810	1 519	4 301	289	270
Douglas	3 693	5.7	34 521	2 021	1 403	247	133	263	671	1 249	2 047	148	133
Gilliam	79	4.0	40 766	1 091	34	7	3	9	17	18	53	3	3
Grant	261	8.7	36 392	1 705	91	24	8	23	58	74	145	9	8
Harney	255	10.8	35 720	1 817	86	22	8	26	51	75	143	8	8
Hood River	942	4.9	41 177	1 041	451	68	43	65	230	166	627	36	43
Jackson	7 915	5.8	37 637	1 505	3 273	511	308	679	1 724	2 106	4 771	326	308
Jefferson	683	7.9	30 757	2 620	240	52	22	18	111	240	331	23	22
Josephine	2 807	5.7	33 577	2 179	860	138	83	194	556	1 025	1 275	101	83
Klamath	2 183	5.2	33 356	2 218	850	154	81	142	382	720	1 227	83	81
Lake	285	11.6	36 364	1 711	96	24	8	37	63	78	165	9	8
Lane	13 393	5.3	37 374	1 542	6 077	996	557	989	2 697	3 293	8 619	573	557
Lincoln	1 681	4.9	36 227	1 740	641	112	60	119	379	505	932	67	60
Linn	4 087	6.2	34 239	2 075	1 734	272	164	177	633	1 263	2 347	161	164
Malheur	840	7.4	27 661	2 942	444	93	40	64	157	298	641	39	40
Marion	11 614	6.8	35 614	1 839	5 977	1 119	534	968	1 937	3 059	8 598	529	534

1. Based on the resident population estimated as of July 1 of the year shown.

Table B. States and Counties — Earnings, Social Security, and Housing

STATE County	Earnings, 2014 (cont.) Percent by selected industries									Social Security beneficiaries, December 2014		Housing units, 2015		
	Farm	Mining	Construction	Manu-facturing	Information: professional, scientific, technical services	Retail trade	Finance, insur-ance, real estate and leasing	Health care and social assistance	Govern-ment	Number	Rate[1]	Supple-mental Security Income recipients, December 2014	Total	Percent change, 2010–2014
	75	76	77	78	79	80	81	82	83	84	85	86	87	88
OKLAHOMA—Cont'd														
Kiowa	18.8	10.3	D	D	D	6.5	4.4	7.7	22.3	2 455	265	358	5 172	-0.8
Latimer	3.4	12.9	15.0	D	D	3.9	1.8	4.9	23.8	2 555	240	343	4 978	0.0
Le Flore	11.1	13.9	6.2	6.6	D	6.5	2.8	5.1	28.2	12 575	252	2 118	21 754	1.4
Lincoln	1.5	D	12.8	9.6	3.1	8.0	8.7	D	17.9	7 485	216	746	15 225	0.1
Logan	1.3	21.1	12.2	4.4	D	6.2	11.4	7.9	8.8	8 090	179	661	17 265	0.4
Love	3.2	1.1	3.2	1.9	D	3.8	2.6	D	57.0	2 485	254	228	4 532	-0.1
McClain	4.6	11.2	16.0	2.8	5.0	11.5	4.3	6.7	17.4	7 485	201	641	15 011	7.3
McCurtain	6.6	D	5.8	22.4	D	8.1	2.7	D	18.9	8 365	253	1 624	15 580	0.3
McIntosh	2.8	3.8	6.9	1.3	D	15.9	4.7	D	24.5	6 775	337	934	13 456	0.8
Major	16.4	29.0	6.7	7.6	D	4.5	D	2.3	8.2	1 695	218	84	3 663	-0.2
Marshall	3.0	3.4	2.7	31.9	2.2	6.6	6.0	9.0	14.7	4 135	257	433	10 034	0.3
Mayes	2.6	2.8	13.2	23.9	D	9.6	2.5	D	19.6	9 800	240	1 219	19 255	0.1
Murray	3.1	5.4	6.1	6.2	D	6.4	1.8	D	43.7	3 355	243	354	6 781	0.5
Muskogee	1.1	0.5	5.6	14.2	3.1	7.1	3.6	D	33.1	15 575	223	2 826	30 894	0.0
Noble	6.3	2.0	2.6	D	D	3.7	3.1	D	20.1	2 675	232	243	5 317	-0.4
Nowata	13.7	7.6	6.3	12.0	0.0	4.0	4.9	9.7	19.5	2 420	231	234	4 825	-0.1
Okfuskee	10.9	7.5	5.7	4.0	D	5.7	D	10.1	37.0	2 840	233	614	5 296	0.3
Oklahoma	0.0	17.3	4.3	5.7	7.8	5.6	6.7	11.1	17.7	124 960	163	19 404	334 327	4.5
Okmulgee	2.5	3.5	4.0	19.3	3.0	8.1	3.7	D	31.7	10 415	266	1 710	17 799	-0.5
Osage	9.5	20.1	10.6	7.0	3.7	5.6	2.7	D	19.7	10 890	227	881	21 528	1.8
Ottawa	7.8	1.8	3.0	11.4	1.9	6.9	3.0	11.0	38.9	8 040	251	1 271	14 051	-0.1
Pawnee	4.3	D	5.4	2.7	11.7	8.3	D	6.7	24.9	3 715	227	368	7 722	-0.3
Payne	0.5	11.1	6.4	5.0	4.4	8.3	4.2	4.4	37.2	12 265	153	1 362	35 468	4.3
Pittsburg	0.7	12.3	6.0	7.6	D	7.9	3.4	D	34.6	11 535	259	1 517	22 929	1.3
Pontotoc	1.6	7.7	4.0	7.3	6.0	5.8	4.5	10.6	37.7	8 410	220	1 262	16 776	1.1
Pottawatomie	1.4	7.8	5.7	12.8	D	7.2	4.0	10.1	22.4	16 040	223	2 056	29 692	1.9
Pushmataha	4.1	D	7.2	2.7	D	7.9	5.3	17.0	27.5	3 020	271	533	6 113	0.0
Roger Mills	25.5	10.4	D	D	D	4.1	D	0.5	25.1	745	197	77	1 901	-0.2
Rogers	1.1	1.2	16.0	27.6	D	4.7	3.0	5.9	17.4	17 955	200	1 273	36 835	4.8
Seminole	6.1	D	5.4	13.1	2.3	6.1	3.0	D	20.4	5 780	227	1 049	11 654	0.1
Sequoyah	2.1	1.3	5.4	1.6	5.4	12.9	4.3	D	32.7	10 715	259	1 985	18 904	1.3
Stephens	0.8	D	4.2	12.1	D	6.0	4.7	7.1	7.2	10 495	236	1 070	20 702	0.2
Texas	33.2	3.8	3.4	16.4	6.6	3.9	2.3	2.0	10.3	2 770	127	166	8 173	-0.4
Tillman	33.7	0.7	D	D	D	2.9	D	2.2	21.1	1 860	244	307	4 046	-0.8
Tulsa	0.0	14.8	6.2	10.5	8.9	5.5	6.9	10.6	6.8	109 280	173	14 787	279 871	4.3
Wagoner	3.1	0.7	13.1	24.9	2.8	8.4	3.4	D	18.2	14 750	195	1 201	31 169	5.0
Washington	0.6	37.7	3.1	6.4	4.6	5.4	4.1	9.1	7.2	12 825	247	1 130	23 691	1.0
Washita	14.8	17.0	6.0	3.1	3.7	5.4	6.2	3.8	22.8	2 385	206	235	5 456	-0.4
Woods	10.4	32.0	4.2	2.6	D	6.3	4.9	D	18.7	1 730	187	96	4 441	-0.8
Woodward	6.6	36.6	8.8	4.4	2.0	4.4	3.9	4.6	8.6	3 715	173	280	8 938	1.1
OREGON	1.5	0.1	5.9	12.7	10.1	6.6	6.2	12.3	17.1	798 156	201	85 136	1 718 409	2.6
Baker	7.8	D	3.8	9.2	4.7	8.5	3.3	D	25.3	5 000	311	455	8 830	0.0
Benton	1.5	0.1	3.0	11.8	11.3	5.3	2.9	14.7	31.3	14 610	169	1 000	37 695	4.0
Clackamas	1.7	0.0	8.4	13.7	11.4	7.4	7.4	13.2	10.3	76 265	193	5 201	162 217	3.4
Clatsop	0.5	D	5.6	15.1	3.2	10.0	3.3	14.1	20.6	9 620	257	807	21 928	1.8
Columbia	1.5	0.8	7.0	16.8	D	8.0	4.7	8.4	22.1	11 640	235	1 010	20 764	0.3
Coos	2.4	0.1	4.4	8.7	3.9	8.6	3.2	11.7	29.8	19 770	316	2 340	30 484	-0.4
Crook	4.4	0.1	7.3	9.7	7.3	4.8	1.9	8.2	20.7	6 545	311	453	10 396	1.9
Curry	3.0	D	6.4	10.2	5.6	10.6	3.8	D	22.4	8 650	389	633	12 647	0.3
Deschutes	0.0	0.1	10.2	6.2	11.8	8.9	7.1	18.0	14.2	39 350	231	2 254	83 873	4.7
Douglas	1.3	0.5	4.5	15.3	4.4	7.3	3.5	13.2	23.5	33 380	312	3 255	49 160	0.5
Gilliam	25.0	0.0	6.4	D	D	2.4	D	2.8	22.4	520	270	36	1 154	-0.2
Grant	8.9	D	D	D	3.8	5.7	D	D	44.8	2 240	312	166	4 297	-1.1
Harney	16.4	0.0	D	D	2.2	7.2	1.9	5.6	45.1	2 025	283	229	3 802	-0.9
Hood River	8.8	0.0	3.8	13.3	12.0	7.6	2.5	13.6	13.0	4 060	178	259	9 586	3.4
Jackson	0.8	0.1	7.1	9.4	6.4	10.4	4.9	18.5	15.6	53 595	255	4 670	92 844	2.1
Jefferson	1.9	D	1.9	16.9	D	5.6	1.9	9.0	42.6	5 620	252	657	9 778	-0.4
Josephine	0.6	D	5.7	11.3	4.3	11.5	5.6	19.6	15.6	26 400	316	2 775	38 136	0.4
Klamath	4.2	0.1	4.4	8.2	D	8.8	3.3	14.9	25.2	16 950	259	1 998	32 815	0.1
Lake	17.0	D	4.1	6.6	3.2	5.4	2.0	D	41.1	2 220	283	241	4 396	-1.0
Lane	0.7	0.2	5.5	11.1	8.4	8.6	5.6	15.9	19.9	79 785	223	9 089	159 288	2.0
Lincoln	1.2	D	5.8	8.7	4.2	10.1	3.3	11.8	26.2	14 930	322	1 296	30 857	0.8
Linn	2.2	D	6.7	23.0	3.2	7.0	2.9	11.2	16.7	27 605	231	3 300	49 164	0.7
Malheur	7.0	D	2.2	5.2	D	9.8	2.5	12.4	32.6	6 310	208	955	11 638	-0.5
Marion	2.8	0.2	6.5	5.9	5.0	6.9	5.1	16.1	30.8	62 145	191	7 214	123 467	2.1

1. Per 1,000 resident population estimated as of July 1 of the year shown.

Table B. States and Counties — Housing, Labor Force, and Employment

STATE County	Housing units, 2010–2014 Occupied units Total	Percent	Owner-occupied Median value[1]	Median owner cost as a percent of income With a mortgage	Without a mortgage[2]	Renter-occupied Median rent[3]	Median rent as a percent of income[2]	Sub-standard units[4] (percent)	Civilian labor force, 2015 Total	Percent change, 2014–2015	Unemployment Total	Rate[5]	Civilian employment,[6] 2010–2014 Percent Total	Management, business, science and arts	Construction, production, and maintenance occupations
	89	90	91	92	93	94	95	96	97	98	99	100	101	102	103
OKLAHOMA—Cont'd															
Kiowa	3 974	65.9	59 900	18.1	10.2	509	25.9	3.3	4 220	4.1	190	4.5	3 987	29.9	29.3
Latimer	4 101	67.7	77 800	18.9	10.0	500	25.2	3.5	3 911	-1.2	308	7.9	3 998	31.8	31.5
Le Flore	18 255	73.6	79 700	21.7	12.0	568	28.2	3.7	19 892	2.7	1 327	6.7	18 151	25.7	32.9
Lincoln	13 342	76.9	94 200	20.3	10.0	601	29.2	3.7	16 037	3.6	718	4.5	14 618	27.3	32.2
Logan	15 146	78.3	138 800	20.4	10.0	681	24.3	3.4	21 624	3.1	790	3.7	19 619	35.2	23.7
Love	3 243	74.5	84 900	19.3	10.9	621	22.4	3.0	5 986	10.2	206	3.4	4 110	26.0	33.6
McClain	13 014	80.3	151 200	21.3	10.8	685	24.0	2.3	18 803	3.8	671	3.6	16 628	32.8	25.2
McCurtain	12 891	69.2	73 900	22.0	11.1	564	27.7	4.4	14 844	4.9	1 143	7.7	12 361	24.2	38.0
McIntosh	8 158	78.5	83 900	22.2	10.8	576	29.9	4.1	7 097	0.9	597	8.4	7 209	28.7	30.5
Major	3 066	74.7	87 100	18.8	10.0	549	19.9	2.4	4 374	0.4	137	3.1	3 601	26.9	36.6
Marshall	6 003	78.8	85 300	20.1	10.5	606	25.8	4.2	6 816	-1.6	360	5.3	6 076	22.4	35.5
Mayes	15 802	74.1	100 500	21.4	11.0	628	26.9	4.5	19 495	3.9	817	4.2	16 648	28.9	32.5
Murray	5 229	69.7	87 100	19.8	10.0	615	21.3	4.2	6 785	3.7	277	4.1	6 152	28.2	26.0
Muskogee	26 574	67.5	90 200	20.8	10.8	632	31.0	2.4	29 831	1.9	1 483	5.0	27 580	29.0	28.6
Noble	4 562	74.7	84 200	19.6	11.0	590	31.4	2.6	5 683	2.7	195	3.4	5 220	33.5	29.1
Nowata	4 104	79.1	74 600	19.0	12.0	627	27.0	3.9	4 861	2.3	266	5.5	4 238	27.3	34.0
Okfuskee	4 196	73.4	71 400	20.7	10.0	497	29.3	3.9	4 567	2.6	260	5.7	4 049	28.4	32.3
Oklahoma	287 998	59.3	129 800	21.6	11.4	768	30.0	3.2	378 342	2.4	14 316	3.8	347 274	35.8	20.9
Okmulgee	15 008	69.4	77 600	20.1	11.3	613	27.1	2.3	16 414	2.7	1 052	6.4	15 017	28.7	27.6
Osage	18 433	77.6	97 300	20.5	11.5	633	27.3	3.3	21 581	3.0	1 091	5.1	19 591	28.9	30.7
Ottawa	11 988	71.4	81 600	21.8	11.1	619	29.8	4.7	14 431	4.6	718	5.0	13 066	26.2	28.4
Pawnee	6 323	75.5	85 300	21.2	11.1	624	26.2	3.7	7 566	3.6	423	5.6	6 898	27.4	34.5
Payne	30 182	50.7	132 700	22.2	10.3	711	37.4	2.5	38 563	0.5	1 316	3.4	37 280	37.8	19.8
Pittsburg	18 477	71.8	89 400	19.7	10.3	661	28.8	3.5	17 471	1.8	969	5.5	18 504	27.9	28.5
Pontotoc	14 650	66.0	102 000	22.2	10.0	635	29.6	4.0	18 308	3.1	708	3.9	17 310	32.6	24.5
Pottawatomie	26 033	69.6	100 200	19.9	10.2	657	28.1	3.3	32 947	2.6	1 433	4.3	29 633	31.3	27.2
Pushmataha	4 784	74.4	75 600	19.5	11.7	501	31.1	4.3	4 915	4.7	373	7.6	4 163	31.8	29.2
Roger Mills	1 307	75.7	86 500	16.2	10.0	496	23.1	2.8	1 857	3.5	75	4.0	1 616	30.5	32.2
Rogers	33 129	78.5	142 900	21.3	10.0	792	26.6	3.2	44 818	2.6	1 893	4.2	41 476	34.0	26.5
Seminole	9 266	73.8	70 500	21.3	10.1	537	26.4	4.1	9 654	1.0	635	6.6	9 508	26.0	32.1
Sequoyah	15 522	70.9	88 000	20.7	11.1	618	30.9	4.5	17 033	2.1	1 044	6.1	15 789	27.2	29.7
Stephens	17 850	70.3	95 100	19.8	10.7	634	26.5	2.8	20 555	1.3	1 174	5.7	18 520	29.2	30.0
Texas	7 166	62.6	90 700	18.8	10.0	668	20.9	7.7	9 838	5.3	308	3.1	10 918	25.4	40.0
Tillman	3 029	73.5	51 700	20.4	11.9	574	25.4	3.3	3 375	2.5	141	4.2	3 089	29.0	33.0
Tulsa	243 509	60.6	136 100	21.2	11.4	764	28.9	3.0	318 047	2.1	12 722	4.0	295 886	36.1	21.2
Wagoner	27 086	80.8	139 000	20.9	10.8	771	27.7	2.5	36 404	2.4	1 473	4.0	34 175	31.0	26.9
Washington	21 109	73.3	109 900	19.4	10.4	669	27.7	2.2	24 661	0.9	1 026	4.2	22 696	35.1	21.9
Washita	4 585	70.6	76 200	16.7	10.0	666	19.9	2.6	5 637	0.7	300	5.3	5 145	30.2	32.3
Woods	3 393	68.4	88 000	15.9	10.0	594	21.3	1.4	5 454	3.2	144	2.6	4 235	31.0	25.1
Woodward	7 246	71.7	108 700	16.6	10.0	654	22.7	2.4	10 515	-2.3	516	4.9	9 500	28.3	37.0
OREGON	1 522 988	61.5	234 100	25.5	12.7	894	32.5	3.4	1 969 467	1.6	112 354	5.7	1 752 414	36.7	20.9
Baker	7 197	65.9	152 400	22.4	12.3	626	29.8	3.6	6 691	-0.3	462	6.9	6 411	36.1	23.8
Benton	33 376	57.4	268 400	22.9	10.2	845	39.0	2.4	45 171	1.8	1 945	4.3	39 691	48.8	13.8
Clackamas	147 736	68.5	295 600	25.8	12.9	1 001	30.3	2.9	204 481	1.8	10 651	5.2	180 798	37.8	20.0
Clatsop	15 746	62.7	248 300	26.6	12.5	825	32.0	3.6	18 301	1.5	1 017	5.6	17 001	27.5	24.3
Columbia	18 772	73.2	208 700	23.9	12.2	801	31.7	1.8	22 896	2.3	1 651	7.2	20 369	29.7	31.2
Coos	25 847	66.2	172 100	25.7	13.3	728	33.7	2.2	25 914	-0.6	1 957	7.6	23 444	27.1	25.3
Crook	8 977	68.5	159 800	29.5	11.4	724	33.4	3.2	8 934	-1.0	761	8.5	7 640	23.3	25.3
Curry	10 296	65.4	211 300	29.0	11.9	825	32.7	2.7	8 630	0.0	732	8.5	7 889	29.7	23.3
Deschutes	64 917	65.0	243 400	27.3	12.7	931	33.4	2.1	84 185	3.8	5 024	6.0	71 744	37.0	19.2
Douglas	43 730	68.6	170 700	25.8	12.5	776	32.1	3.2	44 255	0.4	3 388	7.7	39 200	27.3	28.0
Gilliam	879	61.8	125 600	20.4	10.5	704	24.0	1.4	810	-1.9	53	6.5	884	25.2	41.5
Grant	3 164	73.6	141 100	24.0	12.0	615	29.0	2.1	3 077	-2.0	273	8.9	2 835	33.0	26.4
Harney	3 083	67.7	104 400	22.1	11.6	558	25.9	5.6	3 301	0.6	241	7.3	2 913	38.1	24.8
Hood River	8 251	64.2	309 500	26.2	11.8	867	28.8	4.4	13 576	-1.2	644	4.7	11 181	34.9	28.9
Jackson	82 977	62.4	217 200	27.6	14.0	885	35.9	3.2	97 648	1.0	6 751	6.9	86 204	32.1	20.8
Jefferson	7 800	65.9	158 100	24.6	11.3	753	25.3	3.3	9 613	2.3	712	7.4	8 039	23.7	31.6
Josephine	34 187	66.0	212 600	27.9	12.6	823	36.7	3.1	33 162	1.1	2 605	7.9	28 331	30.6	23.7
Klamath	27 148	65.8	154 600	24.4	11.2	738	34.1	3.2	28 444	-0.6	2 273	8.0	26 125	30.3	26.3
Lake	3 616	63.4	141 400	25.5	11.4	562	29.0	3.1	3 458	-1.1	271	7.8	3 310	29.4	28.8
Lane	145 627	59.3	214 300	26.0	12.6	857	35.3	2.4	171 388	1.2	10 194	5.9	156 185	34.6	20.3
Lincoln	20 672	65.0	221 800	27.4	13.6	825	30.9	3.5	20 484	-0.4	1 386	6.8	19 701	27.1	20.4
Linn	44 942	65.7	171 700	25.0	12.5	808	33.2	3.1	54 608	0.9	3 760	6.9	47 990	28.2	29.1
Malheur	10 235	60.4	127 300	22.5	11.8	594	36.3	5.8	11 964	-0.7	772	6.5	10 607	28.9	30.4
Marion	113 883	59.6	186 300	26.1	12.5	798	32.6	5.5	152 400	2.0	9 293	6.1	133 824	30.4	25.5

1. Specified owner-occupied units.   2. A value of 10.0 represents 10 percent or less; a value of 50.0 represents 50 percent or more.   3. Specified renter-occupied units.
4. Overcrowded or lacking complete plumbing facilities.   5. Percent of civilian labor force.   6. Persons 16 years old and over.

Table B. States and Counties — Nonfarm Employment and Agriculture

| | Private nonfarm establishments, employment and payroll, 2014 | | | | | | | | | Agriculture, 2012 | | | |
STATE County	Number of establish-ments	Employment Total	Health care and social assistance	Manufac-turing	Retail trade	Finance and insurance	Professional, scientific, and technical services	Annual payroll Total (mil dol)	Average per employee (dollars)	Farms Number	Percent with: Fewer than 50 acres	500 acres or more	Farm operators whose principal occu-pation is farming (percent)
	104	105	106	107	108	109	110	111	112	113	114	115	116
OKLAHOMA—Cont'd													
Kiowa	190	1 730	494	D	289	D	33	52	29 899	667	9.0	44.8	53.2
Latimer	166	1 838	414	D	287	63	58	64	34 884	691	27.2	13.9	36.3
Le Flore	814	8 409	2 701	398	1 578	420	281	268	31 925	1 843	32.2	8.4	48.0
Lincoln	564	5 807	644	755	785	435	126	205	35 313	2 121	26.0	10.6	43.9
Logan	799	6 310	1 112	374	1 071	D	203	184	29 090	1 203	27.2	14.8	37.1
Love	150	4 608	136	D	144	D	D	134	28 985	621	22.9	15.5	45.7
McClain	845	7 514	888	417	1 489	247	276	261	34 786	1 239	39.9	12.2	38.7
McCurtain	596	8 757	1 698	2 551	1 225	249	82	266	30 423	1 577	28.0	8.1	39.9
McIntosh	357	3 065	807	75	904	146	120	90	29 417	1 018	25.8	9.4	36.7
Major	265	2 460	D	D	294	77	53	127	51 678	901	13.7	32.6	45.3
Marshall	282	3 714	468	1 207	589	D	91	125	33 626	525	26.5	15.6	40.8
Mayes	804	10 000	1 068	2 885	1 690	303	348	386	38 575	1 551	36.6	7.7	42.5
Murray	282	3 277	482	380	636	154	65	112	34 220	470	22.1	17.0	37.4
Muskogee	1 411	22 569	5 617	3 489	3 302	604	517	831	36 816	1 735	34.2	8.4	46.0
Noble	227	4 414	370	D	D	155	45	182	41 246	828	15.5	27.5	39.4
Nowata	158	1 430	334	276	137	67	D	40	27 708	889	22.5	14.3	44.2
Okfuskee	168	2 495	D	D	196	D	D	79	31 479	881	18.5	15.7	39.5
Oklahoma	23 290	372 366	59 129	21 192	46 039	18 408	25 566	17 597	47 257	1 180	56.6	5.7	44.4
Okmulgee	694	7 525	2 224	1 417	1 263	308	177	216	28 673	1 329	32.3	10.8	44.6
Osage	598	5 911	743	352	817	165	102	192	32 480	1 325	28.5	25.6	47.8
Ottawa	592	9 002	1 545	1 502	981	289	309	257	28 601	1 020	36.4	7.9	38.6
Pawnee	259	2 978	478	227	442	D	D	114	38 340	813	21.4	18.2	31.5
Payne	1 823	23 067	3 373	1 722	4 269	918	1 142	749	32 481	1 466	34.9	10.5	34.1
Pittsburg	943	11 235	2 517	1 156	2 054	426	365	400	35 619	1 567	27.1	15.8	39.8
Pontotoc	967	12 509	3 507	1 080	1 757	1 049	324	427	34 172	1 313	26.9	10.1	38.2
Pottawatomie	1 295	18 086	2 708	2 889	2 979	686	712	563	31 125	1 643	32.0	9.6	39.6
Pushmataha	189	2 018	837	131	314	127	D	49	24 098	732	15.4	15.8	47.0
Roger Mills	90	559	D	D	93	D	D	21	37 034	678	9.9	42.6	49.6
Rogers	1 715	27 270	2 962	7 466	2 460	723	788	1 291	47 349	1 733	47.8	8.1	33.8
Seminole	472	5 706	1 069	692	843	244	106	195	34 251	1 054	20.7	10.5	36.2
Sequoyah	582	6 867	2 246	159	1 197	D	113	167	24 270	1 204	37.7	6.9	42.6
Stephens	1 101	12 949	2 167	2 133	1 993	650	603	494	38 188	1 286	23.6	17.1	33.0
Texas	487	8 078	392	D	981	257	126	360	44 519	1 024	8.4	42.6	38.7
Tillman	142	1 214	241	D	164	70	18	38	31 595	556	8.1	44.4	52.2
Tulsa	18 606	329 662	50 355	38 824	39 118	15 020	20 551	15 824	48 002	1 036	57.6	3.8	40.0
Wagoner	912	8 486	741	D	1 451	D	225	306	36 024	1 090	44.7	7.5	35.0
Washington	1 187	20 143	2 937	1 007	2 375	725	1 519	1 005	49 912	811	37.5	9.5	41.2
Washita	244	1 641	263	D	294	94	41	56	34 224	973	12.3	36.2	50.5
Woods	294	3 191	D	D	544	157	57	135	42 331	751	13.6	41.9	52.2
Woodward	794	8 846	1 041	469	1 269	320	188	416	47 065	882	15.3	33.9	39.1
OREGON	109 875	1 444 041	227 540	161 572	196 582	60 484	85 552	65 715	45 508	35 439	61.5	10.6	49.9
Baker	516	4 035	679	509	797	135	187	133	32 890	645	31.0	28.7	60.5
Benton	2 103	24 947	5 706	1 892	3 515	603	2 283	1 025	41 071	886	71.4	5.6	46.3
Clackamas	11 244	134 580	20 286	16 384	18 769	5 594	8 391	6 068	45 088	3 745	81.4	1.1	41.1
Clatsop	1 438	13 881	1 901	D	2 838	250	320	477	34 329	199	55.3	2.5	45.7
Columbia	897	7 886	1 512	1 271	1 368	281	264	239	30 264	751	69.9	2.4	45.7
Coos	1 528	17 381	3 758	1 508	2 953	431	412	597	34 321	654	41.4	9.5	56.9
Crook	477	3 853	475	860	597	D	99	129	33 488	551	49.9	16.7	51.0
Curry	664	4 868	1 051	667	945	190	99	152	31 281	197	37.6	21.3	60.4
Deschutes	6 260	56 454	9 972	4 230	9 835	1 870	2 788	2 144	37 978	1 283	78.9	3.0	44.0
Douglas	2 423	27 865	5 060	3 782	4 385	879	852	1 012	36 331	1 927	50.9	8.1	48.3
Gilliam	72	793	D	NA	101	D	D	29	37 137	170	4.1	77.6	63.5
Grant	239	1 370	379	D	216	91	60	47	34 428	398	28.1	36.9	54.3
Harney	186	1 239	353	8	274	D	62	40	32 316	497	21.5	42.3	57.1
Hood River	999	9 991	1 855	1 345	1 395	D	409	303	30 307	554	74.9	0.5	56.7
Jackson	5 951	67 428	12 986	6 196	11 771	2 248	2 222	2 447	36 285	1 722	72.1	2.4	56.2
Jefferson	363	3 829	562	1 135	504	70	48	128	33 438	474	42.2	18.4	53.2
Josephine	1 906	20 344	4 525	2 609	4 234	659	533	653	32 096	617	76.3	0.6	55.8
Klamath	1 504	16 696	3 116	2 024	2 981	1 085	612	592	35 435	955	38.7	19.4	63.7
Lake	195	1 230	309	229	157	49	42	43	34 854	373	21.4	40.2	70.2
Lane	9 558	120 985	22 831	13 417	19 364	5 359	5 244	4 496	37 163	2 660	73.9	2.9	44.5
Lincoln	1 558	14 080	D	874	2 910	256	315	431	30 586	362	63.3	3.9	48.3
Linn	2 441	33 472	5 027	7 038	4 770	1 071	859	1 239	37 011	2 083	64.8	6.7	48.7
Malheur	704	8 099	1 555	D	1 911	D	209	240	29 675	1 113	33.9	20.8	64.1
Marion	7 734	98 245	18 877	9 566	16 159	3 239	3 849	3 484	35 466	2 567	72.5	5.6	47.1

STATE County	Land in farms Acreage (1,000)	Percent change, 2007–2012	Average size of farm	Total irrigated (1,000)	Total cropland (1,000)	Value of land and buildings (dollars) Average per farm	Average per acre	Value of machinery and equipment, average per farm (dollars)	Value of products sold Total (mil dol)	Average per farm (dollars)	Percent from: Crops	Live-stock and poultry products	Percent of farms with sales of: $10,000 or more	$100,000 or more	Government payments Total ($1,000)	Percent of farms
	117	118	119	120	121	122	123	124	125	126	127	128	129	130	131	132
OKLAHOMA—Cont'd																
Kiowa	593	5.1	890	2.7	302.3	854 510	961	144 499	107.8	161 627	59.1	40.9	61.3	28.0	8 081	79.2
Latimer	221	3.3	319	0.1	38.2	425 538	1 333	56 986	24.6	35 570	8.5	91.5	34.6	4.6	1 268	15.8
Le Flore	395	-15.3	214	6.1	103.7	425 397	1 985	57 896	287.3	155 883	6.6	93.4	38.0	12.0	2 522	25.6
Lincoln	454	-6.9	214	0.8	106.5	369 323	1 724	54 060	38.7	18 260	26.8	73.2	31.7	3.2	1 147	16.3
Logan	367	-9.0	305	1.1	133.7	575 341	1 884	63 051	44.0	36 563	47.2	52.8	37.2	5.5	2 181	38.3
Love	219	-16.2	353	1.1	48.8	611 282	1 730	56 594	23.9	38 472	19.5	80.5	40.7	7.4	1 234	29.0
McClain	283	-16.1	228	1.7	78.9	466 267	2 043	61 161	48.5	39 117	26.2	73.8	32.6	7.7	1 349	24.8
McCurtain	317	-6.8	201	1.5	70.3	349 785	1 742	57 386	163.1	103 452	7.2	92.8	36.6	7.8	1 573	24.0
McIntosh	236	-4.4	232	0.2	58.1	357 114	1 541	52 882	22.3	21 872	13.1	86.9	37.7	3.6	672	23.3
Major	537	3.8	596	10.1	217.0	668 974	1 122	95 212	105.4	116 986	39.2	60.8	59.4	20.3	3 795	65.7
Marshall	192	21.6	365	0.7	41.8	610 888	1 672	64 185	18.4	34 983	20.8	79.2	37.0	5.3	830	24.0
Mayes	285	-9.0	184	0.4	85.2	388 246	2 112	56 484	76.0	48 985	8.0	92.0	37.0	6.8	1 628	24.2
Murray	208	5.6	443	0.0	24.3	613 813	1 386	65 602	28.0	59 557	8.2	91.8	36.6	4.9	709	33.0
Muskogee	350	-6.5	202	7.3	120.2	356 096	1 765	55 445	50.6	29 140	42.3	57.7	33.9	4.0	2 161	29.6
Noble	443	-5.2	535	1.9	193.3	762 217	1 425	79 824	61.3	73 995	48.4	51.6	51.1	16.2	4 809	64.4
Nowata	292	-17.6	329	0.1	64.8	544 327	1 657	53 998	40.0	45 009	12.3	87.7	46.1	5.5	1 267	31.7
Okfuskee	320	7.0	363	0.7	60.1	463 053	1 276	57 190	34.7	39 373	13.3	86.7	39.7	5.3	922	26.4
Oklahoma	144	-9.8	122	2.3	47.9	378 664	3 099	43 969	20.4	17 300	71.0	29.0	19.7	3.6	502	14.4
Okmulgee	300	2.0	226	0.7	78.0	406 784	1 801	51 241	27.1	20 421	27.7	72.3	30.5	3.8	908	21.6
Osage	1 217	-5.7	918	1.3	131.4	968 906	1 055	58 483	121.5	91 682	6.2	93.8	42.9	11.2	4 433	23.2
Ottawa	193	-18.8	189	0.2	87.9	436 945	2 306	76 215	117.6	115 291	43.1	56.9	39.0	7.8	1 622	25.5
Pawnee	286	-3.9	352	0.0	52.2	468 352	1 331	55 888	26.7	32 864	14.6	85.4	37.8	7.4	1 400	30.3
Payne	350	-2.0	239	0.4	105.1	451 118	1 891	52 108	34.1	23 231	26.5	73.5	33.4	4.1	1 737	23.5
Pittsburg	524	-4.3	334	1.8	95.6	454 824	1 361	54 429	41.6	26 535	15.7	84.3	35.4	4.8	1 898	16.1
Pontotoc	325	-14.4	247	0.9	69.0	434 772	1 759	49 674	36.0	27 438	17.6	82.3	34.4	2.4	1 242	16.4
Pottawatomie	335	-15.1	204	0.9	86.9	358 388	1 756	52 875	35.4	21 523	24.0	76.0	26.0	2.7	1 346	14.2
Pushmataha	297	2.4	406	D	37.9	462 504	1 138	44 060	14.6	19 939	9.7	90.3	36.9	4.4	2 454	23.9
Roger Mills	719	0.0	1 061	5.3	117.5	1 093 820	1 031	96 844	46.0	67 827	28.1	71.9	47.8	14.0	4 532	58.1
Rogers	302	-18.7	174	1.0	71.8	429 069	2 464	44 947	66.4	38 290	11.7	88.3	31.2	4.5	1 186	15.5
Seminole	243	-3.0	231	0.2	48.0	325 588	1 411	46 705	38.1	36 162	10.4	89.6	29.9	2.2	875	20.8
Sequoyah	215	-7.3	179	3.3	63.8	357 679	2 002	52 061	55.5	46 084	23.0	77.0	31.2	3.9	1 620	9.1
Stephens	481	2.3	374	0.1	75.9	474 056	1 268	58 719	44.2	32 782	12.5	87.5	35.1	5.8	2 539	29.9
Texas	1 287	6.7	1 257	153.0	678.8	1 005 370	800	180 940	1 013.9	990 157	15.0	85.0	42.1	19.9	12 943	78.5
Tillman	541	16.7	974	10.6	290.0	977 950	1 004	163 739	102.4	184 257	53.7	46.3	62.4	25.7	6 753	79.0
Tulsa	106	-19.0	103	4.7	42.7	372 738	3 635	35 707	21.0	20 313	70.3	29.7	23.9	2.9	692	10.0
Wagoner	199	-24.3	182	4.0	78.6	443 074	2 428	53 862	33.8	31 050	57.8	42.2	31.1	4.7	1 257	26.2
Washington	231	1.9	285	D	55.6	476 007	1 672	50 665	37.4	46 086	19.2	80.8	35.4	7.5	590	22.3
Washita	633	7.2	651	7.0	343.6	780 371	1 199	136 291	114.7	117 867	54.3	45.7	64.5	23.2	10 153	80.5
Woods	808	-3.0	1 077	2.8	231.1	1 167 659	1 085	114 887	82.5	109 875	43.0	57.0	55.7	23.7	4 609	71.0
Woodward	715	-8.7	810	4.6	149.9	898 007	1 108	85 655	116.5	132 078	13.4	86.6	46.1	13.4	4 264	56.5
OREGON	16 302	-0.6	460	1 629.7	4 690.4	865 613	1 882	90 222	4 883.7	137 805	66.5	33.5	35.6	13.1	85 840	15.1
Baker	711	-0.1	1 102	100.9	107.5	1 117 372	1 014	118 667	93.3	144 583	49.4	50.6	52.2	21.6	1 883	25.7
Benton	124	8.2	140	11.3	68.2	830 059	5 932	68 867	103.3	116 597	78.2	21.8	28.6	10.4	486	6.4
Clackamas	163	-11.0	43	22.2	84.0	585 754	13 486	53 573	325.2	86 833	76.7	23.3	27.5	7.1	607	3.8
Clatsop	16	-22.7	82	0.7	5.3	456 739	5 548	53 940	11.5	58 010	12.3	87.7	22.1	6.0	50	6.0
Columbia	57	-1.9	75	1.9	18.0	414 475	5 493	41 466	39.4	52 413	D	D	17.6	1.6	232	4.1
Coos	157	8.1	241	11.2	20.9	776 687	3 225	60 953	50.4	77 018	21.5	78.6	43.6	12.2	678	10.7
Crook	823	8.0	1 493	61.9	57.0	1 357 530	909	76 437	42.3	76 766	32.1	67.9	38.3	9.4	554	9.3
Curry	63	-14.8	322	3.2	5.2	1 095 939	3 408	71 112	21.4	108 411	44.9	55.1	53.8	19.3	524	17.3
Deschutes	131	1.3	102	34.0	28.9	716 430	7 015	52 158	20.6	16 033	54.1	45.9	22.1	2.4	241	3.4
Douglas	382	-3.7	198	14.6	49.2	611 961	3 084	44 231	64.8	33 629	36.3	63.7	27.3	4.7	730	5.3
Gilliam	723	-1.4	4 255	6.5	331.7	2 117 900	498	293 047	44.1	259 141	84.6	15.4	50.6	40.0	7 931	90.0
Grant	656	-13.8	1 649	31.6	96.4	1 326 967	805	79 166	25.4	63 719	22.3	77.7	50.8	14.8	900	14.8
Harney	1 505	3.0	3 029	165.7	223.0	1 660 966	548	163 302	88.9	178 966	41.7	58.3	55.7	30.0	1 414	24.9
Hood River	26	-4.2	47	14.1	16.3	885 421	19 000	90 121	77.1	139 200	D	D	49.8	26.9	777	13.4
Jackson	214	-12.3	124	36.5	32.8	582 023	4 682	40 415	64.1	37 240	57.6	42.4	25.7	3.4	252	3.8
Jefferson	817	15.2	1 724	41.1	62.9	1 104 840	641	154 973	65.0	137 198	72.7	27.3	40.7	19.4	1 182	32.7
Josephine	28	-25.1	46	9.0	8.4	460 319	10 052	35 806	18.8	30 481	D	D	25.0	4.7	129	2.9
Klamath	650	-3.7	681	159.9	205.2	1 004 853	1 475	136 301	181.5	190 037	56.5	43.5	48.7	21.8	1 951	21.4
Lake	657	-5.2	1 762	148.9	131.1	1 791 244	1 017	171 150	85.6	229 614	52.6	47.4	61.7	33.8	716	20.6
Lane	220	-10.6	83	19.3	100.0	563 427	6 824	49 734	142.5	53 574	74.6	25.4	23.5	5.6	575	5.1
Lincoln	30	-3.1	83	0.4	5.1	400 392	4 795	35 680	5.5	15 293	30.6	69.4	22.7	1.7	93	3.6
Linn	331	-12.0	159	28.7	227.5	769 891	4 840	89 696	241.2	115 812	77.1	22.9	31.3	11.7	882	6.8
Malheur	1 077	-8.0	967	183.0	204.8	1 136 094	1 174	174 964	359.3	322 829	50.7	49.3	68.3	32.6	2 574	40.2
Marion	286	-7.0	111	84.9	213.8	885 406	7 942	130 593	592.9	230 953	81.5	18.5	41.0	17.7	1 583	9.8

Table B. States and Counties — Water Use, Wholesale Trade, Retail Trade, and Real Estate

STATE County	Water use, 2010		Wholesale trade,[1] 2012				Retail trade,[2] 2012				Real estate and rental and leasing,[2] 2012			
	Total water withdrawn (mil gal/day)	Gallons withdrawn per person per day	Number of establishments	Number of employees	Sales (mil dol)	Annual payroll (mil dol)	Number of establishments	Number of employees	Sales (mil dol)	Annual payroll (mil dol)	Number of establishments	Number of employees	Receipts (mil dol)	Annual payroll (mil dol)
	133	134	135	136	137	138	139	140	141	142	143	144	145	146
OKLAHOMA—Cont'd														
Kiowa	13.8	1 456	8	D	D	D	40	286	58.3	5.5	4	11	1.1	0.2
Latimer	2.9	261	5	54	73.5	3.9	24	259	52.5	5.1	4	D	D	D
Le Flore	23.7	470	21	D	D	D	145	1 490	406.8	30.3	22	44	5.9	0.9
Lincoln	21.3	620	27	183	117.3	8.1	87	814	239.1	17.3	19	69	9.9	2.1
Logan	11.2	267	15	63	26.3	2.4	87	1 001	343.9	22.2	40	155	30.2	4.5
Love	5.5	585	5	12	9.4	0.5	26	176	77.4	3.8	6	D	D	D
McClain	8.1	234	18	103	38.7	3.8	118	1 389	463.6	37.5	27	66	39.7	4.5
McCurtain	9.9	298	27	97	86.7	3.7	100	1 156	275.2	24.4	19	78	8.0	1.8
McIntosh	5.0	246	6	28	14.6	1.6	68	847	289.7	18.7	12	D	D	D
Major	17.3	2 300	16	100	55.5	3.9	32	264	93.7	5.3	6	D	D	D
Marshall	7.2	452	5	64	19.0	4.0	52	542	159.8	12.2	9	31	2.5	0.6
Mayes	111.1	2 692	34	344	382.6	18.1	137	1 663	466.8	35.2	20	41	5.4	0.7
Murray	21.3	1 577	7	D	D	D	48	578	196.9	14.2	11	D	D	D
Muskogee	48.0	677	57	1 022	509.1	45.7	258	3 194	927.9	75.8	56	211	29.6	5.7
Noble	35.6	3 079	8	81	30.9	2.3	32	326	127.6	7.5	7	17	2.1	0.2
Nowata	51.1	4 845	9	79	33.6	2.1	18	129	36.8	2.7	7	22	1.3	0.5
Okfuskee	5.8	479	4	15	2.3	0.2	28	210	88.7	4.8	2	D	D	D
Oklahoma	131.1	182	1 128	18 305	43 903.7	1 065.3	2 909	42 001	13 117.1	1 116.5	1 136	6 497	1 502.8	293.8
Okmulgee	18.9	471	21	D	D	D	123	1 315	341.0	26.3	16	36	4.7	0.9
Osage	19.1	402	15	D	D	D	88	869	216.3	16.8	17	95	21.2	4.7
Ottawa	4.9	152	21	180	44.6	6.4	100	993	232.9	20.8	19	46	6.8	1.2
Pawnee	13.3	800	5	D	D	D	39	423	115.7	8.8	6	37	8.9	1.9
Payne	11.9	153	50	D	D	D	297	4 027	1 021.0	84.7	85	298	53.0	8.3
Pittsburg	17.3	377	39	D	D	D	176	2 047	603.8	46.3	44	181	34.5	6.8
Pontotoc	152.5	4 066	41	407	438.3	18.7	167	1 809	437.4	37.8	42	293	65.5	12.6
Pottawatomie	22.9	330	38	305	180.3	12.6	238	2 904	755.0	63.6	47	162	23.5	4.5
Pushmataha	1.3	110	2	D	D	D	36	328	70.6	5.0	7	22	6.2	0.7
Roger Mills	7.8	2 137	2	D	D	D	16	92	31.6	1.7	1	D	D	D
Rogers	90.3	1 039	73	957	1 885.4	53.1	205	2 530	777.3	62.6	77	222	48.4	7.5
Seminole	342.0	13 423	23	386	161.7	14.2	75	862	233.5	17.6	14	31	6.7	1.4
Sequoyah	10.4	244	14	D	D	D	118	1 179	387.7	24.9	14	37	3.8	0.6
Stephens	137.0	3 040	48	D	D	D	194	1 961	550.4	43.9	26	106	23.9	3.8
Texas	301.9	14 629	33	D	D	D	76	890	226.5	18.4	15	42	4.3	0.8
Tillman	11.4	1 431	11	100	83.8	3.7	21	177	27.8	2.7	NA	NA	NA	NA
Tulsa	15.4	26	996	14 271	13 182.2	854.3	2 315	36 091	10 454.5	894.5	919	6 119	981.5	242.8
Wagoner	14.1	192	36	244	117.8	11.4	115	1 360	389.7	29.0	28	41	4.3	1.0
Washington	11.6	228	29	173	194.6	7.4	181	2 270	652.2	53.8	42	195	29.5	5.9
Washita	9.1	780	7	131	49.9	5.6	46	283	86.0	5.5	8	69	9.5	2.3
Woods	11.3	1 277	21	186	218.8	9.0	46	465	168.6	10.2	6	10	2.0	0.2
Woodward	24.4	1 217	42	D	D	D	114	1 224	435.2	30.3	33	148	31.4	7.2
OREGON	6 734.5	1 758	4 393	59 523	48 325.3	3 233.0	13 879	187 402	49 481.1	4 831.5	5 644	26 016	4 649.6	902.8
Baker	496.0	30 744	15	84	30.5	3.0	86	797	198.9	17.6	10	39	4.1	1.7
Benton	38.8	454	44	346	452.5	22.6	262	3 455	731.0	82.5	105	453	53.3	10.2
Clackamas	299.2	796	563	8 015	5 388.6	456.3	1 188	18 541	5 125.3	486.9	564	2 440	451.9	96.8
Clatsop	65.5	1 769	22	210	110.4	9.1	284	2 756	704.1	67.4	75	239	30.4	6.0
Columbia	39.5	801	16	D	D	D	120	1 349	318.1	31.5	37	108	12.8	2.6
Coos	27.5	435	42	399	287.8	15.3	262	2 930	745.8	73.8	58	215	26.4	5.1
Crook	225.6	10 755	13	D	D	D	70	583	184.2	14.6	24	33	6.5	0.8
Curry	21.2	948	12	35	14.6	0.7	97	988	244.6	23.8	45	81	10.1	1.5
Deschutes	157.5	998	215	1 262	794.9	57.1	755	9 365	2 476.6	244.0	388	1 252	186.1	40.0
Douglas	72.3	671	54	D	D	D	378	4 419	1 103.4	102.1	120	329	43.4	7.6
Gilliam	18.9	10 086	5	D	D	D	11	52	10.5	1.1	NA	NA	NA	NA
Grant	130.8	17 574	7	D	D	D	38	241	67.4	5.6	10	20	1.2	0.4
Harney	422.9	56 975	3	D	D	D	27	279	107.3	7.2	8	22	2.1	0.4
Hood River	83.1	3 718	24	360	110.5	14.7	157	1 287	315.4	33.5	31	71	10.0	2.0
Jackson	392.4	1 931	206	1 771	828.4	76.8	865	11 223	3 202.7	297.5	306	1 043	164.1	26.3
Jefferson	172.1	7 925	20	194	156.4	9.5	47	506	133.1	11.3	24	65	6.0	1.6
Josephine	30.2	365	49	D	D	D	312	4 150	987.9	105.1	106	354	44.8	8.5
Klamath	661.6	9 967	49	533	210.9	21.0	237	2 902	757.5	69.9	72	199	23.5	5.2
Lake	465.5	58 958	8	D	D	D	30	200	74.9	4.8	5	D	D	D
Lane	224.2	637	384	4 860	2 852.0	229.0	1 270	18 265	4 291.5	449.9	505	2 115	314.3	58.4
Lincoln	28.9	627	27	D	D	D	307	2 758	580.8	62.2	74	320	40.2	7.0
Linn	122.6	1 051	110	1 396	1 066.7	61.3	343	4 753	1 181.6	112.6	112	360	48.5	10.2
Malheur	616.4	19 684	36	584	340.7	17.6	120	1 834	534.5	45.8	29	55	9.0	1.4
Marion	281.5	893	264	3 694	3 190.0	177.6	1 103	15 497	3 862.2	377.0	417	1 991	269.7	58.6

1. Merchant wholesalers, except manufacturers' sales branches and offices. 2. Employer establishments.

Professional Services, Manufacturing, and Accommodation and Food Services

STATE County	Professional, scientific, and technical services, 2012				Manufacturing, 2012				Accommodation and food services, 2012			
	Number of establish-ments	Number of employees	Receipts (mil dol)	Annual payroll (mil dol)	Number of establish-ments	Number of employees	Receipts (mil dol)	Annual payroll (mil dol)	Number of establish-ments	Number of employees	Sales (mil dol)	Annual payroll (mil dol)
	147	148	149	150	151	152	153	154	155	156	157	158
OKLAHOMA—Cont'd												
Kiowa	16	D	D	D	5	D	D	D	15	D	D	D
Latimer	17	D	D	D	NA	NA	NA	NA	8	D	D	D
Le Flore	86	307	22.1	6.9	30	492	D	17.9	47	D	D	D
Lincoln	40	129	16.7	4.0	29	790	231.5	31.3	44	564	22.6	6.2
Logan	60	160	18.5	5.2	23	363	97.6	14.7	60	837	37.3	9.8
Love	14	D	D	D	5	111	D	4.6	29	579	53.8	10.4
McClain	72	269	40.4	10.4	22	385	103.5	13.9	62	1 110	46.3	12.8
McCurtain	34	D	D	D	29	2 477	1 342.0	91.7	53	691	37.0	7.5
McIntosh	37	D	D	D	14	62	9.5	2.2	34	465	20.8	5.4
Major	17	D	D	D	8	44	D	1.5	11	D	D	D
Marshall	23	D	D	D	20	1 097	245.2	43.8	28	289	17.4	4.1
Mayes	60	D	D	D	58	2 608	1 224.7	130.6	72	940	40.2	10.4
Murray	27	D	D	D	16	451	D	21.5	30	339	17.6	4.8
Muskogee	93	D	D	D	55	3 660	1 489.7	181.3	133	2 384	104.4	27.7
Noble	14	D	D	D	9	1 451	D	80.4	22	D	D	D
Nowata	8	D	D	D	11	254	D	11.3	9	D	D	D
Okfuskee	6	D	D	D	7	132	D	4.5	7	D	D	D
Oklahoma	2 947	22 906	3 372.4	1 360.6	701	21 353	7 681.0	948.9	1 780	39 515	1 909.4	525.0
Okmulgee	44	192	15.1	4.9	34	1 438	533.8	66.3	49	737	32.1	8.0
Osage	45	D	D	D	28	270	D	11.7	43	554	24.7	7.6
Ottawa	50	333	32.3	11.5	43	1 495	D	57.2	58	2 101	228.3	40.2
Pawnee	26	124	36.3	5.4	17	250	D	10.5	22	D	D	D
Payne	150	1 195	131.6	50.4	64	1 538	473.0	62.3	181	3 661	155.0	41.9
Pittsburg	98	422	46.8	18.0	31	999	332.7	50.2	96	1 560	74.2	18.2
Pontotoc	80	342	35.6	12.4	32	1 114	270.3	41.1	69	1 374	62.1	16.7
Pottawatomie	106	681	95.3	29.4	57	2 911	1 112.5	134.5	120	2 528	107.9	29.7
Pushmataha	14	D	D	D	7	85	D	2.7	15	124	4.4	1.2
Roger Mills	6	D	D	D	NA	NA	NA	NA	4	D	D	D
Rogers	135	782	110.8	44.2	150	6 775	3 040.1	365.1	109	3 258	308.2	77.7
Seminole	27	D	D	D	24	738	129.7	29.1	35	553	23.6	6.0
Sequoyah	41	126	10.5	3.2	22	104	D	4.4	59	D	D	D
Stephens	82	427	49.8	15.7	62	2 512	1 935.5	132.0	77	1 098	50.1	12.8
Texas	31	D	D	D	11	D	D	D	50	670	29.2	7.2
Tillman	8	D	D	D	5	D	D	D	10	86	3.5	0.9
Tulsa	2 382	19 526	3 446.4	1 198.9	903	37 197	18 770.2	1 997.1	1 519	30 477	1 425.3	414.5
Wagoner	72	199	18.0	6.1	61	2 163	746.5	111.5	69	D	D	D
Washington	89	D	D	D	36	965	253.2	53.4	111	1 831	91.0	23.2
Washita	20	D	D	D	10	39	D	1.4	14	D	D	D
Woods	23	D	D	D	5	40	D	1.9	33	332	19.2	3.8
Woodward	53	D	D	D	24	498	448.4	32.2	55	862	50.9	11.6
OREGON	11 663	84 493	11 386.1	5 841.1	5 289	D	D	D	10 610	150 482	8 466.8	2 438.5
Baker	40	172	18.4	5.4	29	494	105.1	18.0	56	557	27.5	8.2
Benton	284	1 996	332.6	125.1	93	1 613	412.7	71.4	209	3 087	142.8	41.6
Clackamas	1 231	7 805	1 215.9	525.9	553	15 789	5 371.5	901.1	777	11 638	637.5	188.3
Clatsop	87	326	22.1	7.2	47	1 671	905.8	103.1	248	3 138	210.1	59.7
Columbia	78	275	23.3	8.6	52	1 350	458.3	64.6	85	964	42.9	12.3
Coos	115	439	44.3	16.2	70	1 352	315.7	48.4	165	2 129	126.2	34.9
Crook	34	109	12.2	3.7	30	728	150.8	25.4	44	479	23.7	8.0
Curry	36	105	16.6	2.8	20	578	176.0	27.4	107	880	46.5	12.2
Deschutes	708	2 631	332.0	120.7	279	3 672	801.8	165.8	498	7 635	435.6	133.5
Douglas	157	777	64.4	26.5	126	3 640	1 017.3	158.4	262	3 391	217.2	57.2
Gilliam	3	D	D	D	NA	NA	NA	NA	9	68	1.5	0.6
Grant	18	D	D	D	4	D	D	D	24	135	6.0	1.8
Harney	11	45	2.8	1.2	4	D	D	D	32	186	11.5	2.9
Hood River	125	423	84.4	18.2	63	1 055	304.3	44.5	96	1 306	62.1	19.3
Jackson	506	D	D	D	308	5 370	1 624.6	217.4	586	7 381	382.2	112.5
Jefferson	21	55	3.8	1.3	19	838	168.3	32.4	45	404	21.3	5.9
Josephine	140	563	40.6	13.5	106	2 190	434.8	89.6	199	2 483	124.5	35.8
Klamath	125	625	107.1	24.7	56	1 662	449.9	63.8	171	1 978	110.7	30.1
Lake	12	D	D	D	11	190	34.5	7.2	31	144	6.6	1.6
Lane	948	5 301	583.9	226.2	529	12 345	4 039.3	581.3	937	13 627	711.8	203.7
Lincoln	95	289	27.6	9.8	50	965	579.4	61.0	274	3 593	216.4	63.4
Linn	164	802	84.8	27.8	181	6 318	2 253.6	355.2	216	2 796	130.4	35.5
Malheur	46	185	17.2	7.1	35	1 078	D	34.2	84	1 008	50.8	13.6
Marion	664	3 815	448.4	170.5	352	9 155	2 540.3	347.6	667	D	D	D

1. Establishment subject to federal tax.

Table B. States and Counties — Health Care and Social Assistance, Other Services, Nonemployer Businesses, and Residential Construction

STATE County	Health care and social assistance, 2012				Other services, 2012				Nonemployer businesses, 2014		Value of residential construction authorized by building permits, 2015	
	Number of establish-ments	Number of employees	Receipts (mil dol)	Annual payroll (mil dol)	Number of establish-ments	Number of employees	Receipts (mil dol)	Annual payroll (mil dol)	Number	Receipts (mil dol)	New Construction ($1,000)	Number of housing units
	159	160	161	162	163	164	165	166	167	168	169	170
OKLAHOMA—Cont'd												
Kiowa	24	577	30.6	13.8	8	28	3.5	0.8	634	32.0	0	0
Latimer	25	357	23.0	9.2	8	D	D	D	757	32.3	0	0
Le Flore	95	2 706	202.8	86.1	44	D	D	D	2 993	125.9	8 776	77
Lincoln	57	D	D	D	21	D	D	D	2 500	123.5	2 245	12
Logan	61	D	D	D	52	176	19.8	3.9	3 639	176.1	13 014	66
Love	10	133	5.5	2.6	6	62	3.1	1.3	638	29.3	0	0
McClain	68	D	D	D	48	D	D	D	3 317	165.8	55 551	269
McCurtain	60	1 634	79.5	37.0	37	146	11.1	3.8	2 174	97.0	525	3
McIntosh	49	916	71.0	25.3	23	102	13.1	3.1	1 463	66.9	4 772	35
Major	14	231	13.3	6.4	11	D	D	D	700	31.0	1 111	5
Marshall	26	590	70.0	23.2	14	50	4.2	1.1	1 051	48.0	525	4
Mayes	86	955	101.6	35.3	46	132	10.6	2.6	2 617	108.2	2 650	43
Murray	31	595	42.3	16.4	11	32	2.8	0.6	860	38.3	1 219	12
Muskogee	230	5 700	616.6	250.4	84	587	57.9	14.6	3 879	171.2	9 150	64
Noble	18	395	24.3	9.8	13	66	5.4	1.2	793	27.3	215	2
Nowata	16	D	D	D	10	30	2.2	0.6	670	27.3	872	13
Okfuskee	43	1 619	104.4	30.0	10	9	3.0	0.7	730	29.8	0	0
Oklahoma	2 873	56 884	7 921.4	2 618.1	1 414	9 503	1 063.4	285.5	61 275	3 172.6	948 012	4 383
Okmulgee	124	2 032	117.5	50.5	39	174	12.7	2.9	2 231	87.9	1 108	8
Osage	42	732	37.4	15.8	24	76	9.5	1.9	3 081	129.4	16 302	88
Ottawa	72	1 402	110.0	47.6	33	138	12.5	2.8	1 817	74.5	508	8
Pawnee	29	459	27.8	11.4	9	29	2.8	0.8	1 031	45.9	155	2
Payne	160	3 570	305.4	118.4	109	763	167.3	20.9	5 072	220.8	57 226	500
Pittsburg	116	2 560	218.9	87.2	54	340	24.5	7.3	2 697	121.0	6 511	73
Pontotoc	130	3 418	350.1	128.5	46	194	18.0	4.5	2 889	124.4	3 264	27
Pottawatomie	167	2 451	257.4	100.5	72	350	27.9	8.2	4 316	203.3	11 514	63
Pushmataha	24	732	43.3	16.6	7	28	2.5	0.7	780	30.0	0	0
Roger Mills	5	D	D	D	3	D	D	D	362	22.0	0	0
Rogers	193	2 953	268.3	108.2	83	392	43.2	11.7	6 435	296.2	87 643	498
Seminole	43	1 079	81.4	28.1	21	D	D	D	1 421	61.7	1 469	8
Sequoyah	79	2 345	105.4	46.6	29	D	D	D	2 699	110.0	6 155	59
Stephens	101	2 121	177.1	63.3	69	361	68.5	11.3	3 168	162.4	5 812	37
Texas	39	500	44.8	18.0	28	110	12.3	2.2	1 193	55.2	976	5
Tillman	18	298	18.3	7.2	7	D	D	D	453	13.6	0	0
Tulsa	2 063	48 166	5 808.5	2 135.3	1 184	8 068	1 123.9	251.1	48 362	2 461.2	499 029	2 636
Wagoner	76	816	52.8	21.9	58	172	25.9	4.9	5 159	236.7	58 193	340
Washington	172	3 091	284.1	113.0	78	473	38.5	11.9	3 162	169.3	8 589	47
Washita	14	297	13.9	7.4	10	27	3.3	0.6	850	42.6	0	0
Woods	20	D	D	D	18	D	D	D	804	34.0	150	1
Woodward	81	1 029	96.4	34.9	41	262	34.3	8.7	1 480	84.8	7 037	42
OREGON	12 475	217 584	24 956.8	9 689.3	6 894	37 941	4 435.0	1 149.1	269 901	12 597.9	3 591 958	17 510
Baker	53	664	54.6	22.9	37	D	D	D	1 088	36.0	4 640	21
Benton	271	5 258	588.1	258.8	147	891	153.8	30.3	5 696	229.3	39 562	142
Clackamas	1 136	17 962	2 424.2	896.7	677	D	D	D	29 208	1 578.4	494 630	1 831
Clatsop	137	2 163	213.9	89.8	91	D	D	D	2 802	137.0	73 731	208
Columbia	114	1 239	62.2	25.8	64	D	D	D	2 609	105.8	22 668	98
Coos	193	3 539	350.3	143.7	86	D	D	D	3 616	149.6	5 234	29
Crook	35	D	D	D	41	D	D	D	1 402	58.6	26 475	90
Curry	89	885	79.9	31.4	28	D	D	D	1 806	74.4	9 442	40
Deschutes	608	9 398	1 114.0	442.5	329	1 526	156.8	41.9	16 143	828.6	473 441	2 227
Douglas	312	4 830	544.3	244.2	135	657	134.1	17.3	5 650	235.0	44 053	172
Gilliam	9	D	D	D	5	D	D	D	104	2.7	NA	NA
Grant	22	D	D	D	14	D	D	D	467	17.2	NA	NA
Harney	22	309	29.8	10.8	14	D	D	D	512	15.3	1 415	7
Hood River	96	1 759	130.8	59.4	55	244	20.7	6.1	1 864	88.9	25 788	98
Jackson	674	12 116	1 443.8	510.7	315	1 836	157.3	51.0	16 447	734.1	159 429	717
Jefferson	40	622	51.2	24.1	22	D	D	D	995	44.3	11 229	45
Josephine	269	4 376	418.5	151.1	103	D	D	D	5 702	233.1	45 516	237
Klamath	203	3 067	323.5	122.2	102	D	D	D	3 354	147.8	21 943	90
Lake	21	292	28.6	12.1	10	D	D	D	466	18.8	170	4
Lane	1 135	20 576	2 247.4	828.6	611	3 480	443.9	97.7	22 905	982.8	157 338	721
Lincoln	119	1 657	169.4	73.8	111	D	D	D	3 416	179.2	27 776	150
Linn	216	4 660	422.3	174.0	142	D	D	D	5 783	241.1	80 934	365
Malheur	112	1 563	133.1	53.6	57	D	D	D	1 326	55.7	7 468	31
Marion	971	17 456	1 787.0	758.3	484	2 394	215.7	66.8	16 112	744.6	213 671	1 004

Table B. States and Counties — Government Employment and Payroll, and Local Government Finances

	Government employment and payroll, 2012									Local government finances, 2012				
			March payroll (percent of total)							General revenue				
													Taxes	
													Per capita[1] (dollars)	
STATE County	Full-time equivalent employees	March payroll (dollars)	Administration, judicial, and legal	Police and Corrections	Fire Protection	Highways and transportation	Health and Welfare	Natural resources and utilities	Education and libraries	Total (mil dol)	Intergovernmental (mil dol)	Total (mil dol)	Total	Property
	171	172	173	174	175	176	177	178	179	180	181	182	183	184
OKLAHOMA—Cont'd														
Kiowa	554	1 581 546	4.8	5.3	0.8	4.5	36.0	6.1	41.7	28.0	15.7	7.6	812	529
Latimer	754	2 593 866	3.2	2.1	0.0	3.7	15.7	2.1	72.9	31.9	13.6	7.0	636	318
Le Flore	1 864	5 014 735	3.3	6.0	0.4	3.5	3.6	5.5	75.8	125.0	71.3	28.8	578	300
Lincoln	1 059	2 802 834	6.5	7.7	1.4	5.3	0.3	7.8	70.0	71.7	38.3	21.4	627	358
Logan	875	2 347 456	7.2	7.5	3.8	5.0	0.6	6.6	67.9	60.0	30.1	18.4	421	259
Love	481	1 481 165	6.9	3.8	0.0	3.5	40.8	1.2	43.6	19.3	11.3	5.6	581	387
McClain	1 466	3 975 638	5.5	7.7	3.1	4.0	13.2	3.3	60.7	113.4	39.8	57.3	1 609	1 149
McCurtain	1 454	3 983 530	2.5	5.7	1.1	5.2	4.9	5.0	74.7	93.6	55.4	21.0	632	354
McIntosh	617	1 761 398	8.2	6.9	0.0	2.0	1.7	6.5	74.4	51.2	28.1	16.0	778	358
Major	407	1 118 428	9.8	3.5	0.5	9.3	27.6	2.4	45.6	26.8	10.8	7.7	1 002	610
Marshall	530	1 477 680	5.8	6.2	1.0	4.3	3.0	4.0	74.8	36.0	20.4	10.5	660	446
Mayes	1 472	4 043 970	8.9	5.6	0.7	3.0	3.2	7.1	70.0	95.9	51.9	32.6	792	421
Murray	655	1 707 493	6.8	7.5	3.1	2.3	19.7	11.8	48.5	44.1	24.1	10.4	762	306
Muskogee	3 141	8 727 804	4.0	8.5	4.5	4.3	6.8	5.1	65.6	275.3	85.7	75.6	1 071	547
Noble	622	1 661 200	5.9	6.7	2.5	6.0	18.5	6.1	53.2	44.6	16.7	14.0	1 213	863
Nowata	422	1 000 994	6.4	5.5	1.0	6.4	3.0	5.6	71.4	24.0	14.4	5.9	556	321
Okfuskee	460	1 098 562	3.9	6.1	0.0	6.2	0.9	3.6	76.5	34.2	24.4	6.6	531	326
Oklahoma	24 286	88 713 472	5.8	14.1	10.2	3.4	2.9	6.5	56.5	2 544.3	761.2	1 182.3	1 594	722
Okmulgee	1 552	4 277 777	5.1	5.1	2.9	3.2	3.2	5.9	73.4	89.1	52.5	23.2	586	272
Osage	1 130	2 941 818	9.3	7.0	1.1	14.2	11.3	6.8	48.8	74.5	39.5	19.7	410	229
Ottawa	1 421	4 097 793	5.8	5.3	2.3	2.7	1.7	8.0	73.0	80.7	44.3	21.1	654	269
Pawnee	597	1 604 091	5.8	5.4	1.0	3.9	18.9	7.0	56.7	35.2	20.6	8.5	514	277
Payne	3 634	11 234 115	4.8	7.5	4.2	1.9	31.7	8.2	40.1	192.3	66.9	89.1	1 137	592
Pittsburg	2 380	5 927 369	5.7	11.0	5.4	4.2	4.8	9.9	55.6	254.4	76.4	76.1	1 689	1 039
Pontotoc	1 436	4 130 846	4.3	6.5	3.1	5.4	2.1	5.4	70.4	103.9	50.5	34.4	905	337
Pottawatomie	2 336	6 720 266	6.0	7.2	4.0	2.8	0.1	7.4	71.9	167.8	93.6	52.1	737	301
Pushmataha	607	1 521 960	2.8	3.2	1.8	5.1	17.4	5.2	63.2	38.1	21.2	5.6	504	248
Roger Mills	256	746 029	12.5	6.7	0.0	25.4	12.9	5.1	34.8	20.6	10.5	6.4	1 687	1 138
Rogers	2 835	7 580 674	6.2	6.2	5.0	5.0	1.0	15.1	60.3	197.1	79.1	87.2	986	621
Seminole	1 164	2 881 448	5.7	5.9	2.6	4.0	1.0	5.8	73.2	80.4	47.5	19.7	772	340
Sequoyah	1 722	4 751 418	4.1	6.5	0.8	2.8	13.0	2.9	69.8	115.2	65.1	22.1	534	266
Stephens	1 530	4 875 145	5.7	8.9	3.8	3.6	0.3	5.9	70.1	109.2	51.3	39.9	891	426
Texas	1 138	3 387 767	5.5	7.8	2.0	6.4	23.7	3.4	50.3	93.1	28.0	34.4	1 601	1 035
Tillman	545	1 405 251	6.0	9.3	2.4	4.7	24.1	6.9	45.0	21.8	14.4	3.8	490	335
Tulsa	23 532	78 482 436	5.7	10.6	6.5	3.9	2.1	5.2	62.5	2 206.7	679.3	1 020.7	1 663	890
Wagoner	1 330	3 590 004	7.0	7.2	2.6	4.0	2.4	9.2	64.5	85.8	39.9	34.9	465	232
Washington	1 747	5 123 970	4.5	9.2	5.9	3.5	2.6	6.6	65.7	123.9	52.2	47.3	915	518
Washita	621	1 807 048	6.4	5.9	0.7	7.4	8.9	3.3	66.3	43.9	25.8	12.0	1 030	518
Woods	575	1 537 398	8.0	4.6	2.6	8.1	31.6	4.9	39.0	38.5	13.1	16.6	1 883	804
Woodward	891	2 568 486	5.9	8.6	3.5	5.0	7.2	4.7	61.8	69.5	25.7	32.5	1 583	708
OREGON	X	X	X	X	X	X	X	X	X	X	X	X	X	X
Baker	487	1 718 138	10.0	12.3	6.0	4.4	2.9	7.2	54.6	56.2	31.8	15.5	977	900
Benton	1 834	7 923 562	9.3	13.4	6.2	3.8	7.4	9.4	45.7	259.6	93.0	115.4	1 335	1 185
Clackamas	10 411	44 609 746	8.2	11.7	6.1	3.3	4.7	6.1	57.9	1 431.7	520.8	623.0	1 623	1 458
Clatsop	1 540	5 672 121	8.9	12.5	2.7	5.7	8.3	8.9	49.7	172.7	53.4	71.3	1 912	1 596
Columbia	1 444	6 022 192	7.2	9.3	8.1	2.1	0.4	16.3	52.3	192.4	87.9	59.7	1 211	1 123
Coos	3 079	13 113 856	2.7	5.5	1.8	2.4	45.7	3.7	37.5	386.2	116.4	74.2	1 187	1 048
Crook	584	2 274 092	9.3	15.0	2.6	3.8	3.7	7.2	51.7	72.1	28.3	22.8	1 099	940
Curry	803	3 143 734	7.1	10.1	0.4	5.5	38.6	5.6	31.1	90.5	25.4	26.9	1 211	1 076
Deschutes	4 773	21 188 503	8.1	12.1	5.4	2.6	5.0	7.0	55.3	649.0	217.1	283.8	1 749	1 579
Douglas	3 555	13 196 754	6.3	8.9	6.6	3.1	10.3	6.1	57.1	374.6	196.1	94.6	883	829
Gilliam	145	510 580	18.3	7.1	1.3	10.8	8.3	8.3	45.2	24.4	3.8	15.2	7 770	6 077
Grant	485	1 961 339	5.0	4.3	0.1	3.5	41.5	3.5	38.1	55.0	23.8	7.9	1 083	1 049
Harney	427	1 530 704	6.7	5.9	0.4	3.5	37.4	2.0	42.0	51.3	21.5	7.2	998	925
Hood River	639	2 757 629	6.9	8.8	4.6	6.5	3.0	12.1	54.2	95.2	38.6	26.4	1 171	1 023
Jackson	4 931	20 369 335	9.1	14.6	6.5	6.1	5.2	6.8	50.0	668.0	291.3	260.8	1 263	1 068
Jefferson	1 028	3 923 905	4.1	6.5	1.3	1.7	29.3	8.4	46.4	112.4	50.4	24.0	1 101	997
Josephine	2 192	8 995 230	6.6	12.9	2.5	3.4	1.3	3.1	68.4	243.6	119.9	70.8	854	781
Klamath	1 819	7 192 100	5.9	8.2	6.2	6.2	7.0	7.1	56.2	234.1	125.3	59.4	901	796
Lake	460	1 602 079	5.2	5.5	1.6	6.9	38.3	7.3	33.1	51.6	18.7	10.7	1 372	1 263
Lane	11 647	50 155 119	7.2	10.9	5.2	6.9	4.1	11.4	48.1	1 390.4	585.1	463.2	1 306	1 120
Lincoln	1 465	6 826 571	10.2	14.7	2.9	4.9	8.2	27.9	29.0	200.9	55.6	104.1	2 255	1 881
Linn	3 984	16 207 525	6.1	11.2	5.6	4.0	5.1	4.9	61.9	447.9	223.4	146.4	1 237	1 133
Malheur	1 459	4 992 780	4.9	8.6	1.3	2.7	8.2	7.2	66.0	146.8	85.7	25.2	821	712
Marion	12 046	53 396 211	5.2	8.9	3.6	3.2	3.6	3.7	69.6	1 311.4	678.7	400.1	1 250	1 131

1. Based on the resident population estimated as of July 1 of the year shown.

Table B. States and Counties — Local Government Finances, Government Employment, and Voting

STATE County	Direct general expenditure Total (mil dol)	Per capita[1] (dollars)	Percent of total for: Education	Health and hospitals	Police protection	Public welfare	Highways	Debt outstanding Total (mil dol)	Per capita[1] (dollars)	Government employment, 2014 Federal civilian	Federal military	State and local	Presidential election,[2] 2012 Percent of vote cast: Democratic	Republican	All other
	185	186	187	188	189	190	191	192	193	194	195	196	197	198	199
OKLAHOMA—Cont'd															
Kiowa	28.9	3 103	50.8	1.7	5.1	0.0	11.2	18.6	1 994	44	35	676	32.6	67.4	0.0
Latimer	33.5	3 038	45.3	21.6	2.5	0.0	11.1	4.0	365	27	39	1 165	31.5	68.5	0.0
Le Flore	128.2	2 571	63.3	5.2	3.9	0.1	7.2	41.9	840	168	185	4 602	30.7	69.3	0.0
Lincoln	69.8	2 043	62.1	1.0	6.3	0.0	9.1	22.4	656	84	131	1 707	25.1	74.9	0.0
Logan	60.7	1 390	56.3	2.5	8.0	0.0	8.8	34.1	782	60	165	1 299	31.3	68.7	0.0
Love	22.3	2 329	73.8	2.7	1.9	0.0	7.2	4.8	506	23	37	2 804	32.7	67.3	0.0
McClain	115.0	3 229	69.2	1.7	5.3	0.0	6.8	54.5	1 531	65	142	1 630	24.1	75.9	0.0
McCurtain	89.7	2 703	65.8	3.0	3.2	0.0	7.5	40.6	1 222	132	125	2 364	26.5	73.5	0.0
McIntosh	48.8	2 370	65.3	1.5	5.7	0.0	9.6	27.7	1 344	37	76	1 151	40.4	59.6	0.0
Major	27.0	3 519	43.6	21.9	3.4	0.2	15.4	8.4	1 096	27	29	433	14.8	85.2	0.0
Marshall	35.6	2 234	67.7	3.5	3.9	0.0	4.1	8.2	513	21	61	781	30.6	69.4	0.0
Mayes	94.4	2 293	68.5	1.3	6.4	0.0	6.3	46.9	1 140	64	154	2 387	36.0	64.0	0.0
Murray	43.2	3 162	41.5	28.0	3.6	0.0	4.3	20.9	1 532	68	52	2 855	29.8	70.2	0.0
Muskogee	284.3	4 027	38.4	31.9	3.5	0.0	3.0	95.6	1 354	2 870	256	6 411	42.5	57.5	0.0
Noble	44.7	3 877	46.3	20.3	3.8	0.0	12.0	32.4	2 812	34	43	1 269	23.2	76.8	0.0
Nowata	24.4	2 295	64.3	0.0	4.0	0.0	11.1	7.8	734	28	40	504	31.8	68.2	0.0
Okfuskee	34.0	2 753	77.0	0.0	2.3	0.0	10.3	17.9	1 449	26	42	1 163	35.9	64.1	0.0
Oklahoma	2 264.8	3 053	44.4	0.4	10.3	0.2	5.6	2 878.7	3 881	25 461	8 684	58 714	41.6	58.4	0.0
Okmulgee	89.9	2 270	65.7	0.5	4.7	0.0	7.2	96.2	2 428	119	145	3 377	41.5	58.5	0.0
Osage	73.9	1 543	50.5	8.5	2.4	0.8	12.7	17.6	367	183	189	2 620	38.1	61.9	0.0
Ottawa	87.3	2 709	53.9	2.6	5.3	0.0	11.8	33.9	1 051	101	119	5 462	38.2	61.8	0.0
Pawnee	33.0	2 003	61.8	3.2	3.7	0.0	10.4	20.5	1 247	227	62	940	31.3	68.7	0.0
Payne	185.3	2 363	48.5	0.4	11.8	0.1	8.4	115.8	1 477	240	290	14 655	36.5	63.5	0.0
Pittsburg	209.1	4 642	32.4	36.3	4.6	0.0	4.1	129.8	2 882	1 628	164	3 938	31.7	68.3	0.0
Pontotoc	100.3	2 643	61.6	0.6	5.6	0.0	7.3	22.3	586	158	139	6 675	31.6	68.4	0.0
Pottawatomie	171.7	2 427	59.2	0.4	6.1	0.0	8.2	62.2	879	138	265	6 285	30.8	69.2	0.0
Pushmataha	38.0	3 395	55.0	22.5	3.5	0.2	8.3	9.5	847	29	42	896	28.3	71.7	0.0
Roger Mills	21.1	5 590	33.6	1.3	3.6	0.0	42.2	0.7	196	38	14	356	16.0	84.0	0.0
Rogers	198.7	2 249	54.8	0.9	4.1	0.0	9.8	136.5	1 544	440	340	6 333	28.0	72.0	0.0
Seminole	79.1	3 109	54.5	1.3	3.6	0.0	6.2	27.2	1 070	140	95	1 954	34.7	65.3	0.0
Sequoyah	115.1	2 781	61.2	12.8	4.0	0.7	4.6	67.9	1 639	132	174	3 065	32.0	68.0	0.0
Stephens	108.9	2 432	55.9	0.5	5.5	0.0	9.4	48.1	1 074	79	169	2 079	24.0	76.0	0.0
Texas	98.3	4 570	36.3	26.0	2.2	0.1	7.6	39.3	1 829	73	82	1 691	14.7	85.3	0.0
Tillman	23.0	2 944	65.1	1.9	5.6	0.0	12.8	6.9	884	37	28	727	32.2	67.8	0.0
Tulsa	2 175.2	3 544	44.8	4.4	6.3	0.8	7.9	3 349.0	5 456	3 304	2 423	31 480	37.8	62.2	0.0
Wagoner	88.4	1 178	62.5	2.4	6.7	0.0	8.5	84.6	1 128	68	305	1 841	29.1	70.9	0.0
Washington	127.7	2 473	49.2	0.7	6.0	0.0	8.3	98.7	1 911	92	196	2 425	27.7	72.3	0.0
Washita	39.5	3 402	50.0	0.3	4.5	0.0	20.5	17.5	1 502	37	43	724	22.0	78.0	0.0
Woods	34.4	3 894	39.3	5.7	3.4	0.0	14.9	7.3	829	29	32	1 127	22.3	77.7	0.0
Woodward	71.3	3 469	43.9	1.0	6.2	0.0	7.9	53.7	2 613	84	78	1 602	17.4	82.6	0.0
OREGON	X	X	X	X	X	X	X	X	X	27 503	11 927	238 169	56.7	40.4	2.9
Baker	54.2	3 408	42.8	7.5	5.5	1.6	8.5	12.0	754	215	42	865	32.0	64.4	3.7
Benton	259.2	2 999	46.3	7.4	9.6	0.0	4.2	233.8	2 705	508	254	10 581	64.3	32.8	2.8
Clackamas	1 519.2	3 958	45.7	4.4	7.2	1.0	4.3	2 524.7	6 577	1 031	1 137	13 618	53.9	43.6	2.5
Clatsop	169.8	4 551	35.4	2.0	7.8	5.6	4.9	220.8	5 921	196	494	2 391	57.7	38.8	3.5
Columbia	192.3	3 902	51.6	1.9	4.3	0.2	3.0	214.6	4 353	65	133	1 747	54.1	42.0	3.9
Coos	396.6	6 341	32.9	41.8	2.9	0.1	2.5	240.2	3 841	326	387	4 786	46.5	49.6	3.9
Crook	64.9	3 132	41.4	3.3	7.3	0.2	6.7	59.1	2 852	297	56	868	35.1	61.5	3.4
Curry	101.4	4 557	23.1	33.1	4.3	2.7	5.0	92.8	4 173	82	101	1 011	42.4	53.9	3.7
Deschutes	663.5	4 089	49.1	3.5	7.4	0.4	5.0	1 093.2	6 736	871	459	7 610	48.7	49.0	2.4
Douglas	388.7	3 627	47.5	11.2	5.7	0.2	5.6	258.0	2 407	1 370	322	5 903	38.3	58.4	3.2
Gilliam	26.0	13 296	30.4	4.8	3.1	0.9	11.5	62.9	32 197	10	0	216	38.7	58.4	2.9
Grant	58.7	8 019	29.3	28.9	3.0	0.6	14.1	17.9	2 444	282	19	684	25.7	71.2	3.0
Harney	51.9	7 203	32.1	38.3	1.6	0.5	8.2	34.0	4 719	241	19	725	25.8	70.5	3.7
Hood River	99.3	4 399	46.3	2.2	2.8	0.6	8.1	98.9	4 381	111	60	1 074	64.1	33.2	2.7
Jackson	678.0	3 285	42.6	5.3	8.6	0.0	6.1	887.0	4 297	1 720	562	8 732	48.6	48.5	2.9
Jefferson	108.0	4 966	39.6	27.4	3.8	0.4	3.9	71.9	3 306	129	58	2 268	44.3	52.9	2.8
Josephine	253.3	3 055	59.6	2.9	7.1	0.1	5.0	145.0	1 748	264	222	2 748	41.4	54.6	4.0
Klamath	233.2	3 538	47.7	4.6	6.8	0.2	7.6	72.7	1 103	870	186	3 763	31.9	65.0	3.1
Lake	52.0	6 689	27.7	39.5	2.5	0.3	10.2	44.6	5 745	249	20	754	25.9	71.5	2.5
Lane	1 390.2	3 921	44.2	5.1	6.9	2.2	4.3	1 580.1	4 457	1 586	1 038	23 241	62.3	34.9	2.8
Lincoln	229.9	4 981	36.4	6.6	7.4	0.1	6.6	316.8	6 864	332	194	3 283	59.7	36.8	3.5
Linn	449.1	3 794	51.6	3.6	6.2	0.4	4.4	449.9	3 801	318	321	5 950	42.6	54.0	3.4
Malheur	157.2	5 132	62.3	4.3	3.4	0.2	3.8	62.8	2 050	227	73	2 886	28.3	68.6	3.1
Marion	1 325.2	4 141	57.0	3.6	5.0	0.2	4.6	1 931.4	6 036	1 250	862	32 400	49.6	47.4	3.0

1. Based on the resident population estimated as of July 1 of the year shown. 2. © 2013 Election Data Services, Inc. All rights reserved.

Table B. States and Counties — Land Area and Population

STATE/ County code	CBSA code[1]	County type[2]	STATE County	Land area,[3] (sq km) 2010	Total persons 2015	Rank	Per square kilometer	White	Black	American Indian, Alaska Native	Asian and Pacific Islander	Percent Hispanic or Latino[4]	Under 5 years	5 to 17 years	18 to 24 years	25 to 34 years	35 to 44 years	45 to 54 years
				1	2	3	4	5	6	7	8	9	10	11	12	13	14	15
			OREGON—Cont'd															
41 049	25840	6	Morrow	5 262	11 190	2 342	2.1	62.6	0.9	2.1	1.4	35.2	7.0	21.0	8.8	10.5	12.0	12.2
41 051	38900	1	Multnomah	1 117	790 294	76	707.5	74.6	6.6	1.9	9.7	11.2	5.9	13.8	8.5	18.5	16.0	13.0
41 053	41420	2	Polk	1 919	79 391	700	41.4	82.2	1.2	3.1	3.5	13.0	5.8	17.5	13.0	11.1	11.3	11.8
41 055	...	9	Sherman	2 133	1 680	3 073	0.8	91.5	0.9	2.1	0.9	6.8	3.6	14.4	6.5	9.3	10.4	13.9
41 057	...	6	Tillamook	2 856	25 653	1 576	9.0	86.7	0.8	2.3	2.1	10.3	5.4	13.7	6.8	10.3	10.2	12.5
41 059	25840	5	Umatilla	8 328	76 531	722	9.2	69.1	1.2	4.3	1.7	25.8	7.2	18.7	9.4	13.3	12.6	12.5
41 061	29260	7	Union	5 275	25 790	1 564	4.9	91.5	1.0	2.1	3.1	4.5	6.0	16.0	12.3	11.4	10.1	11.1
41 063	...	9	Wallowa	8 149	6 856	2 687	0.8	95.3	1.1	1.7	1.2	2.8	5.0	13.3	4.7	9.8	8.8	12.4
41 065	45520	6	Wasco	6 168	25 775	1 567	4.2	77.5	0.8	4.4	2.3	17.0	6.1	16.4	8.1	12.0	10.8	12.0
41 067	38900	1	Washington	1 876	574 326	112	306.1	71.0	2.7	1.3	12.5	16.3	6.6	17.8	8.3	15.2	15.0	13.6
41 069	...	9	Wheeler	4 441	1 358	3 089	0.3	92.5	1.3	2.9	2.1	5.2	4.1	11.5	5.3	7.6	8.9	11.4
41 071	38900	1	Yamhill	1 854	102 659	583	55.4	80.3	1.3	2.4	3.0	15.7	5.7	17.6	10.9	12.0	12.4	12.8
42 000	...	X	**PENNSYLVANIA**	115 883	12 802 503	X	110.5	79.2	11.6	0.5	3.7	6.6	5.6	15.5	9.6	12.8	11.8	14.1
42 001	23900	4	Adams	1 343	102 295	587	76.2	90.6	2.2	0.5	1.2	6.6	5.1	15.6	9.8	10.5	11.4	15.0
42 003	38300	1	Allegheny	1 891	1 230 459	34	650.7	81.1	14.4	0.5	4.0	1.9	5.3	13.8	9.3	14.9	11.4	13.5
42 005	38300	1	Armstrong	1 692	67 052	791	39.6	98.2	1.3	0.3	0.4	0.7	5.0	14.7	7.3	10.4	11.7	15.0
42 007	38300	1	Beaver	1 126	168 871	379	150.0	91.6	7.5	0.5	0.8	1.4	5.1	14.5	8.0	11.3	11.1	14.6
42 009	...	6	Bedford	2 622	48 586	1 008	18.5	97.8	1.0	0.4	0.5	1.1	5.0	15.7	7.3	9.9	11.8	14.9
42 011	39740	2	Berks	2 218	415 271	166	187.2	75.3	5.1	0.4	1.8	18.6	5.9	17.0	9.9	11.9	11.9	14.5
42 013	11020	3	Blair	1 362	125 593	497	92.2	96.1	1.6	0.4	1.0	1.2	5.5	15.0	8.9	11.4	11.6	13.6
42 015	42380	6	Bradford	2 972	61 281	854	20.6	97.3	0.9	0.7	0.9	1.5	6.0	16.2	7.4	10.6	10.8	14.7
42 017	37980	1	Bucks	1 565	627 367	107	400.9	86.6	4.4	0.4	5.2	4.9	4.9	16.4	8.0	10.9	11.9	16.2
42 019	38300	1	Butler	2 042	186 818	345	91.5	95.9	1.7	0.4	1.5	1.3	5.0	15.9	8.8	11.1	12.1	15.5
42 021	27780	3	Cambria	1 783	136 411	464	76.5	94.5	4.3	0.3	0.9	1.5	4.9	14.4	9.2	10.4	11.3	13.6
42 023	...	7	Cameron	1 026	4 732	2 852	4.6	98.6	1.0	0.6	0.6	0.7	4.6	12.9	7.0	9.1	10.0	15.0
42 025	10900	2	Carbon	988	63 960	820	64.7	93.5	2.0	0.5	0.8	4.1	4.6	15.1	6.9	10.9	11.8	15.3
42 027	44300	3	Centre	2 875	160 580	400	55.9	87.3	4.1	0.4	6.3	2.8	4.1	11.3	26.0	13.6	10.4	11.4
42 029	37980	1	Chester	1 944	515 939	131	265.4	81.9	6.8	0.4	5.3	7.1	5.7	17.8	9.0	11.4	12.6	15.4
42 031	...	6	Clarion	1 556	39 498	1 186	25.4	95.7	1.5	0.4	1.0	0.7	5.0	13.8	14.4	10.8	10.6	13.2
42 033	20180	4	Clearfield	2 965	80 994	690	27.3	93.8	2.8	0.3	0.9	2.9	4.7	14.0	8.2	11.8	12.8	15.3
42 035	30820	6	Clinton	2 300	39 441	1 190	17.1	96.6	2.2	0.4	0.9	1.4	5.5	14.8	16.0	10.7	10.8	12.2
42 037	14100	4	Columbia	1 251	66 672	796	53.3	94.4	2.2	0.5	1.5	2.6	4.6	13.4	16.7	10.5	10.6	13.2
42 039	32740	4	Crawford	2 622	86 484	664	33.0	96.2	2.5	0.5	0.8	1.2	5.5	15.9	9.5	10.8	11.1	13.9
42 041	25420	2	Cumberland	1 413	246 338	272	174.3	89.2	4.4	0.5	4.4	3.4	5.3	15.0	10.1	13.0	12.2	14.0
42 043	25420	2	Dauphin	1 360	272 983	249	200.7	70.3	19.0	0.6	4.2	8.3	6.2	16.3	8.4	13.6	12.1	14.1
42 045	37980	1	Delaware	476	563 894	116	1 184.7	70.1	21.6	0.6	6.1	3.5	6.0	16.4	10.3	12.8	11.8	14.1
42 047	...	7	Elk	2 143	30 872	1 414	14.4	98.5	0.7	0.4	0.6	0.8	4.9	14.9	7.2	9.5	11.1	16.2
42 049	21500	2	Erie	2 070	278 045	244	134.3	87.2	8.4	0.5	1.8	3.8	5.8	16.1	10.7	12.9	11.3	13.4
42 051	38300	1	Fayette	2 047	133 628	473	65.3	93.5	5.6	0.5	0.6	1.1	5.0	14.5	7.7	11.4	12.0	14.4
42 053	...	9	Forest	1 106	7 410	2 640	6.7	75.2	18.7	0.5	0.4	5.9	1.5	5.9	10.9	17.5	12.7	14.8
42 055	16540	4	Franklin	2 000	153 638	422	76.8	90.4	4.3	0.5	1.4	5.0	6.1	16.9	7.8	11.7	12.2	13.9
42 057	...	8	Fulton	1 133	14 629	2 127	12.9	97.4	1.6	0.6	0.3	1.2	5.2	16.3	7.3	10.4	12.3	14.7
42 059	...	6	Greene	1 492	37 519	1 238	25.1	94.6	3.8	0.7	0.6	1.4	4.9	14.2	10.1	12.1	12.9	14.1
42 061	26500	6	Huntingdon	2 265	45 668	1 057	20.2	92.0	6.0	0.4	0.7	1.8	4.5	14.2	9.6	12.3	12.5	14.3
42 063	26860	4	Indiana	2 142	86 966	663	40.6	94.8	3.2	0.4	1.4	1.4	5.0	13.3	17.3	10.6	10.0	12.6
42 065	...	7	Jefferson	1 690	44 430	1 085	26.3	98.3	0.8	0.6	0.4	0.8	5.7	15.5	8.0	11.1	11.2	14.1
42 067	...	6	Juniata	1 014	24 737	1 617	24.4	95.5	1.0	0.4	0.7	3.1	5.5	17.0	7.3	10.9	11.7	14.1
42 069	42540	2	Lackawanna	1 189	211 917	309	178.2	88.8	3.3	0.4	2.6	6.2	5.2	14.8	9.6	12.3	11.4	13.9
42 071	29540	2	Lancaster	2 444	536 624	125	219.6	84.4	4.3	0.4	2.5	9.8	6.6	17.6	9.4	12.6	11.5	13.3
42 073	35260	4	Lawrence	928	88 082	654	94.9	94.4	5.2	0.4	0.8	1.2	5.4	15.1	8.5	10.4	11.2	13.8
42 075	30140	3	Lebanon	937	137 067	462	146.3	85.4	2.5	0.4	1.6	11.4	6.2	16.7	8.5	11.4	11.8	13.6
42 077	10900	2	Lehigh	894	360 685	189	403.5	69.4	6.3	0.4	3.8	21.4	5.9	16.8	9.1	12.7	12.4	14.1
42 079	42540	2	Luzerne	2 306	318 449	213	138.1	86.0	4.2	0.3	1.4	9.1	5.0	14.6	9.2	12.0	11.8	14.5
42 081	48700	3	Lycoming	3 182	116 048	530	36.5	92.5	5.7	0.5	0.9	2.0	5.6	15.1	9.9	12.7	11.1	13.7
42 083	14620	7	McKean	2 536	42 412	1 123	16.7	94.2	2.9	0.6	0.8	2.1	4.9	15.2	9.3	11.6	12.3	14.1
42 085	49660	2	Mercer	1 742	114 234	537	65.6	92.0	6.7	0.5	1.0	1.3	4.9	15.4	10.0	10.3	11.0	13.9
42 087	30380	4	Mifflin	1 065	46 500	1 037	43.7	97.3	1.2	0.4	0.8	1.3	6.0	16.6	7.4	10.8	11.2	14.1
42 089	20700	4	Monroe	1 575	166 397	384	105.6	69.4	13.9	0.8	2.9	14.5	4.5	16.8	10.9	10.2	11.4	16.5
42 091	37980	1	Montgomery	1 251	819 264	72	654.9	78.7	10.0	0.4	8.1	4.8	5.6	16.4	8.0	12.5	12.6	14.9
42 093	14100	6	Montour	337	18 557	1 887	55.1	93.3	1.9	0.4	3.0	2.4	5.9	14.8	7.1	12.8	10.8	14.2
42 095	10900	2	Northampton	957	300 813	226	314.3	80.1	5.9	0.4	3.4	12.0	5.0	15.6	10.0	11.5	11.9	14.6
42 097	44980	4	Northumberland	1 187	93 246	627	78.6	94.2	2.8	0.4	0.6	3.1	5.3	14.6	7.5	12.1	11.8	14.2
42 099	25420	2	Perry	1 428	45 685	1 055	32.0	97.1	1.3	0.6	0.8	1.7	5.9	16.2	7.9	11.1	12.4	15.2
42 101	37980	1	Philadelphia	347	1 567 442	23	4 517.1	37.2	42.6	0.8	7.7	13.6	7.1	15.1	11.4	18.1	12.2	12.2
42 103	35620	1	Pike	1 411	55 949	907	39.7	82.8	6.0	0.8	1.6	10.2	3.8	16.0	8.1	8.6	10.9	16.7

1. CBSA = Core Based Statistical Area. See Appendix A for explanation. See Appendix B for list of metropolitan areas with component counties.   2. County type code from the Economic Research Service of USDA Rural-Urban Continuum Codes. See Appendix A for definition.   3. Dry land or land partially or temporarily covered by water.   4. May be of any race.

Table B. States and Counties — **Population and Households**

STATE County	Population, 2014 (cont.) Age (percent) (cont.) 55 to 64 years	65 to 74 years	75 years and over	Percent female	Population change and components of change, 2000–2015 Total persons 2000	2010	Percent change 2000–2010	2010–2015	Components of change, 2010–2015 Births	Deaths	Net migration	Households, 2010–2014 Number	Persons per house-hold	Percent Family house-holds	Female family house-holder[1]	One per-son
	16	17	18	19	20	21	22	23	24	25	26	27	28	29	30	31
OREGON—Cont'd																
Morrow	14.0	8.7	5.8	48.8	10 995	11 173	1.6	0.2	814	409	-381	3 714	3.01	73.8	11.0	23.0
Multnomah	12.3	7.2	4.8	50.6	660 486	735 189	11.3	7.5	49 956	29 191	33 971	308 595	2.40	54.4	10.8	32.8
Polk	12.6	9.7	7.4	51.7	62 380	75 403	20.9	5.3	4 547	3 379	2 641	28 253	2.64	69.1	9.6	23.2
Sherman	17.2	13.1	11.7	50.4	1 934	1 765	-8.7	-4.8	84	75	-94	791	2.25	57.5	6.3	33.8
Tillamook	17.6	14.2	9.2	49.6	24 262	25 250	4.1	1.6	1 302	1 473	673	10 213	2.40	63.1	9.0	29.8
Umatilla	12.3	8.1	6.0	47.7	70 548	75 889	7.6	0.8	5 774	3 254	-1 747	26 901	2.69	67.5	13.5	26.7
Union	14.5	10.4	8.2	50.9	24 530	25 744	4.9	0.2	1 596	1 356	-137	10 134	2.46	64.1	7.2	27.1
Wallowa	19.3	15.2	11.5	51.1	7 226	7 008	-3.0	-2.2	307	421	-5	3 018	2.24	61.5	10.9	35.3
Wasco	14.7	11.2	8.7	50.4	23 791	25 213	6.0	2.2	1 564	1 559	497	9 595	2.47	67.5	11.8	28.0
Washington	11.7	7.0	4.8	50.7	445 342	529 849	19.0	8.4	37 759	16 027	22 167	203 901	2.65	67.5	10.2	25.2
Wheeler	18.0	18.5	14.7	49.2	1 547	1 441	-6.9	-5.8	53	91	-44	666	1.99	63.5	5.1	33.2
Yamhill	13.0	8.8	6.8	50.1	84 992	99 193	16.7	3.5	5 829	4 390	1 847	34 149	2.79	71.9	11.2	22.5
PENNSYLVANIA	13.8	9.0	7.7	51.1	12 281 054	12 702 887	3.4	0.8	746 467	671 050	32 402	4 957 736	2.49	64.6	12.0	29.6
Adams	14.5	10.3	8.0	50.7	91 292	101 417	11.1	0.9	5 385	4 983	202	37 956	2.57	71.5	9.5	23.5
Allegheny	14.5	8.9	8.4	51.8	1 281 666	1 223 348	-4.6	0.6	69 531	71 409	11 571	527 445	2.26	57.8	11.8	35.3
Armstrong	15.7	10.9	9.3	50.4	72 392	68 938	-4.8	-2.7	3 575	4 444	-955	28 616	2.36	67.7	9.9	28.3
Beaver	15.6	10.2	9.5	51.6	181 412	170 539	-6.0	-1.0	9 008	10 865	452	70 336	2.37	65.7	11.6	30.0
Bedford	15.0	11.0	9.4	50.1	49 984	49 768	-0.4	-2.4	2 556	2 816	-921	20 145	2.42	69.9	9.5	26.7
Berks	13.1	8.6	7.3	50.8	373 638	411 572	10.2	0.9	25 594	19 438	-1 904	153 857	2.60	69.1	12.3	24.7
Blair	14.7	10.2	9.1	51.2	129 144	127 078	-1.6	-1.2	7 207	8 477	-485	50 948	2.42	65.4	11.4	30.4
Bradford	14.8	11.1	8.5	50.5	62 761	62 622	-0.2	-2.1	3 703	3 557	-1 344	24 338	2.54	68.4	9.5	26.5
Bucks	15.0	9.2	7.5	51.0	597 635	625 255	4.6	0.3	30 924	29 329	-75	231 959	2.66	71.5	9.4	24.0
Butler	14.7	9.2	7.8	50.6	174 083	183 862	5.6	1.6	9 481	9 763	2 980	74 138	2.42	67.9	8.5	26.5
Cambria	15.8	10.5	9.9	50.8	152 598	143 674	-5.8	-5.1	6 965	9 484	-4 651	57 959	2.29	63.9	11.3	31.7
Cameron	17.6	13.8	10.0	50.5	5 974	5 085	-14.9	-6.9	239	340	-245	2 214	2.19	62.6	9.1	33.0
Carbon	15.6	11.1	8.5	50.5	58 802	65 250	11.0	-2.0	3 092	4 135	-172	25 764	2.48	68.1	11.1	25.7
Centre	10.7	6.9	5.6	47.6	135 758	153 981	13.4	4.3	6 759	4 959	4 868	57 283	2.44	56.6	6.5	28.7
Chester	13.6	8.2	6.3	50.8	433 501	499 146	15.1	3.4	28 953	19 568	7 313	185 306	2.65	70.1	8.4	23.9
Clarion	14.1	9.8	8.2	51.2	41 765	39 989	-4.3	-1.2	2 054	2 202	-366	15 846	2.38	62.5	8.1	28.2
Clearfield	14.3	10.2	8.7	47.7	83 382	81 644	-2.1	-0.8	3 888	4 883	317	31 863	2.40	66.4	9.0	29.6
Clinton	12.8	9.3	7.9	51.0	37 914	39 241	3.5	0.5	2 243	2 082	74	14 947	2.48	65.9	10.3	26.5
Columbia	13.8	9.4	7.7	51.7	64 151	67 296	4.9	-0.9	3 245	3 518	-353	26 413	2.39	63.0	9.8	26.6
Crawford	14.9	10.7	7.7	51.1	90 366	88 765	-1.8	-2.6	4 904	5 156	-1 856	34 713	2.43	66.7	10.4	27.6
Cumberland	13.4	9.3	7.8	50.6	213 674	235 408	10.2	4.6	13 456	11 564	8 830	95 835	2.36	64.4	8.6	29.6
Dauphin	14.1	8.6	6.7	51.6	251 798	268 100	6.5	1.8	18 052	12 725	106	109 027	2.41	63.0	13.7	30.7
Delaware	13.5	7.8	7.2	52.0	550 864	558 726	1.4	0.9	35 189	28 536	-786	204 571	2.63	66.8	14.3	28.5
Elk	15.8	10.6	9.9	49.9	35 112	31 946	-9.0	-3.4	1 522	2 032	-526	13 375	2.33	66.0	10.0	31.1
Erie	14.0	8.6	7.2	50.7	280 843	280 566	-0.1	-0.9	16 756	14 534	-4 356	109 700	2.44	63.2	12.8	30.4
Fayette	15.6	10.6	8.9	50.7	148 644	136 607	-8.1	-2.2	7 304	9 451	-769	53 987	2.42	63.7	11.9	31.6
Forest	15.3	13.2	8.2	32.9	4 946	7 716	56.0	-4.0	186	441	-58	2 075	2.04	60.1	7.9	34.9
Franklin	13.2	10.0	8.2	51.0	129 313	149 618	15.7	2.7	9 793	7 518	1 533	58 298	2.56	68.8	9.2	26.6
Fulton	14.0	11.7	8.0	49.6	14 261	14 844	4.1	-1.4	802	721	-248	5 981	2.46	70.5	8.2	24.3
Greene	14.7	9.8	7.2	48.1	40 672	38 686	-4.9	-3.0	2 005	2 323	-821	14 383	2.35	66.3	11.4	27.7
Huntingdon	13.8	10.7	8.1	46.9	45 586	46 027	1.0	-0.8	2 267	2 395	-236	17 231	2.37	67.7	8.3	28.4
Indiana	13.9	9.3	7.8	49.9	89 605	88 893	-0.8	-2.2	4 457	4 645	-1 666	34 398	2.41	63.0	8.1	28.3
Jefferson	15.0	10.1	9.3	50.2	45 932	45 199	-1.6	-1.7	2 625	2 935	-414	18 583	2.38	66.0	9.7	29.8
Juniata	13.6	10.7	9.1	50.1	22 821	24 636	8.0	0.4	1 398	1 308	-119	9 329	2.62	71.0	7.9	24.2
Lackawanna	14.1	9.9	8.9	51.7	213 295	214 436	0.5	-1.2	11 564	13 881	-61	85 335	2.41	64.2	11.9	31.9
Lancaster	12.8	8.6	7.8	51.1	470 658	519 448	10.4	3.3	37 164	24 537	4 010	194 503	2.64	70.3	9.2	24.1
Lawrence	15.6	10.1	9.8	51.7	94 643	91 140	-3.7	-3.4	4 768	5 820	-1 918	36 616	2.39	66.8	12.0	29.3
Lebanon	13.4	9.8	8.6	50.9	120 327	133 577	11.0	2.6	8 500	7 504	2 347	51 793	2.55	70.1	10.9	25.6
Lehigh	12.9	8.5	7.5	51.3	312 090	349 626	12.0	3.2	21 837	17 269	6 672	133 684	2.58	66.9	13.2	27.3
Luzerne	14.0	10.0	9.0	50.7	319 250	320 918	0.5	-0.8	16 605	20 909	2 361	129 335	2.38	63.6	13.5	31.5
Lycoming	14.2	9.4	8.1	50.8	120 044	116 108	-3.3	-0.1	6 722	6 541	-162	46 008	2.42	64.9	11.0	28.6
McKean	14.5	9.7	8.5	48.8	45 936	43 450	-5.4	-2.4	2 286	2 779	-506	17 340	2.31	64.5	12.7	30.0
Mercer	14.8	10.2	9.7	50.8	120 293	116 674	-3.0	-2.1	5 996	7 349	-1 157	46 128	2.35	66.2	12.6	29.9
Mifflin	13.6	10.9	9.4	50.9	46 486	46 683	0.4	-0.4	2 956	2 702	-404	18 822	2.45	66.6	11.0	27.3
Monroe	14.8	9.2	5.9	50.6	138 687	169 842	22.5	-2.0	7 487	7 159	-3 585	57 661	2.87	73.3	12.9	20.7
Montgomery	13.6	8.6	7.8	51.4	750 097	799 884	6.6	2.4	46 843	38 269	10 846	307 953	2.56	68.3	9.4	26.5
Montour	14.8	9.7	9.9	52.2	18 236	18 267	0.2	1.6	1 062	1 110	309	7 380	2.41	63.8	9.3	31.2
Northampton	13.9	9.3	8.1	50.9	267 066	297 735	11.5	1.0	15 321	14 788	2 333	112 790	2.56	69.2	11.1	25.1
Northumberland	14.7	10.5	9.2	49.8	94 556	94 514	0.0	-1.3	5 023	6 034	-147	39 170	2.29	64.4	10.8	30.3
Perry	15.4	9.8	6.1	49.7	43 602	45 965	5.4	-0.6	2 820	2 200	-866	18 077	2.50	70.5	9.8	23.4
Philadelphia	11.4	6.9	5.6	52.7	1 517 550	1 526 006	0.6	2.7	119 525	75 775	456	580 297	2.58	53.1	20.6	39.5
Pike	15.5	12.4	7.9	49.8	46 302	57 366	23.9	-2.5	2 057	2 359	-1 296	21 183	2.66	72.0	9.3	23.9

1. No spouse present.

Table B. States and Counties — Population, Vital Statistics, Medicare, and Crime

STATE County	Persons in group quarters, 2015	Daytime population, 2010–2014 Number	Daytime population Employment/residence ratio	Births, 2015 Total	Births, 2015 Rate[1]	Deaths, 2015 Number	Deaths, 2015 Rate[1]	Persons under 65 with no health insurance, 2014 Number	Persons under 65 ... Percent	Medicare, 2015 Total Beneficiaries	Medicare, 2015 Enrolled in Original Medicare	Medicare, 2015 Enrolled in Medicare Advantage	Serious crimes known to police,[2] 2014 Total Number	Serious crimes ... Total Rate[3]
	32	33	34	35	36	37	38	39	40	41	42	43	44	45
OREGON—Cont'd														
Morrow	23	11 374	1.03	143	12.8	74	6.6	1 373	14.5	1 752	1 476	276	244	2 137
Multnomah	19 556	855 907	1.26	9 627	12.3	5 682	7.2	74 363	11.1	107 878	41 557	66 321	43 289	5 573
Polk	1 915	65 649	0.65	863	11.0	658	8.4	7 036	11.2	16 780	6 772	10 008	2 280	2 945
Sherman	0	1 888	1.13	14	8.3	12	7.1	145	11.3	464	373	91	18	1 042
Tillamook	464	25 224	0.99	246	9.6	280	11.0	2 629	13.9	6 676	4 949	1 727	530	2 083
Umatilla	4 044	76 383	0.99	1 100	14.4	618	8.1	8 271	13.3	12 109	10 284	1 825	2 050	2 678
Union	734	25 546	0.98	312	12.1	268	10.4	2 316	11.4	5 583	4 948	635	559	2 172
Wallowa	108	6 890	1.00	60	8.8	68	9.9	600	12.1	2 063	1 933	130	60	884
Wasco	741	25 775	1.04	306	11.9	284	11.1	3 032	15.0	5 775	4 344	1 431	724	2 824
Washington	7 052	546 260	1.00	7 215	12.7	3 219	5.7	52 338	10.7	64 697	25 451	39 246	10 645	1 889
Wheeler	27	1 321	0.94	10	7.3	13	9.5	134	14.7	382	296	86	10	729
Yamhill	6 022	92 425	0.81	1 105	10.8	840	8.2	9 447	11.7	16 919	8 118	8 801	2 075	2 044
PENNSYLVANIA	430 357	12 700 590	0.99	141 956	11.1	128 630	10.1	1 047 882	10.2	2 404 652	1 365 715	1 038 937	287 180	2 246
Adams	3 963	87 700	0.72	1 044	10.2	945	9.3	8 141	10.2	18 706	12 721	5 985	1 224	1 205
Allegheny	36 751	1 319 509	1.15	13 512	11.0	13 639	11.1	79 587	8.0	233 723	76 194	157 529	29 394	2 384
Armstrong	650	58 000	0.65	658	9.8	875	13.0	5 160	9.6	17 279	5 675	11 604	688	1 013
Beaver	3 255	150 434	0.75	1 713	10.1	2 067	12.2	11 680	8.7	37 895	11 997	25 898	4 073	2 460
Bedford	551	45 339	0.82	492	10.1	519	10.6	4 491	11.6	11 485	5 657	5 828	633	1 331
Berks	11 846	392 495	0.89	4 908	11.8	3 682	8.9	39 628	11.7	74 096	46 747	27 349	8 699	2 102
Blair	3 751	132 152	1.10	1 377	10.9	1 627	12.9	9 419	9.4	29 903	14 423	15 480	2 368	1 878
Bradford	577	64 417	1.07	663	10.8	689	11.2	5 374	10.9	13 893	10 108	3 785	1 129	1 814
Bucks	8 128	570 067	0.82	5 854	9.3	5 761	9.2	35 816	6.9	109 314	70 512	38 802	10 254	1 635
Butler	5 817	185 253	1.00	1 842	9.9	1 883	10.1	10 824	7.2	36 171	14 469	21 702	2 616	1 408
Cambria	6 431	138 186	0.95	1 270	9.3	1 748	12.8	9 275	8.9	34 368	12 439	21 929	2 707	1 937
Cameron	92	4 927	0.99	43	9.0	60	12.6	374	10.2	1 366	1 019	347	58	1 198
Carbon	699	53 741	0.61	583	9.1	771	12.0	5 416	10.5	14 506	11 578	2 928	1 273	1 969
Centre	19 633	163 826	1.11	1 286	8.0	991	6.2	11 322	9.4	20 708	10 430	10 278	1 970	1 265
Chester	13 545	500 054	0.97	5 517	10.7	3 891	7.6	36 810	8.6	72 966	54 219	18 747	6 857	1 344
Clarion	2 076	37 620	0.89	385	9.8	415	10.5	3 480	11.3	8 087	5 321	2 766	590	1 515
Clearfield	5 718	80 675	0.98	732	9.0	919	11.3	6 390	10.5	18 242	11 073	7 169	1 593	1 965
Clinton	2 433	37 377	0.87	429	10.9	387	9.8	3 401	11.2	7 413	4 201	3 212	730	1 819
Columbia	4 306	65 368	0.94	600	9.0	690	10.3	5 008	9.7	14 173	8 169	6 004	1 188	1 782
Crawford	3 855	84 761	0.92	921	10.6	930	10.7	8 575	12.6	19 525	13 208	6 317	1 256	1 443
Cumberland	12 554	249 628	1.09	2 636	10.8	2 176	8.9	16 817	8.8	47 629	28 095	19 534	3 813	1 572
Dauphin	6 783	319 189	1.38	3 455	12.7	2 427	8.9	23 059	10.2	47 464	23 348	24 116	7 509	2 765
Delaware	22 506	514 189	0.82	6 700	11.9	5 365	9.5	42 794	9.3	92 518	63 755	28 763	13 741	2 442
Elk	355	31 151	0.97	274	8.8	361	11.6	2 120	8.6	7 346	5 949	1 397	553	1 762
Erie	12 863	285 312	1.04	3 155	11.3	2 718	9.8	24 067	10.7	53 380	28 053	25 327	6 587	2 351
Fayette	4 244	123 258	0.77	1 425	10.6	1 813	13.5	11 216	10.6	31 591	12 706	18 885	2 951	2 192
Forest	2 522	8 436	1.51	37	5.0	77	10.3	426	12.2	1 635	1 070	565	109	1 432
Franklin	2 560	142 006	0.86	1 850	12.1	1 529	10.0	15 281	12.3	30 378	22 930	7 448	3 321	2 176
Fulton	122	13 625	0.83	147	10.1	137	9.4	1 211	10.4	3 336	2 581	755	200	1 368
Greene	3 013	40 294	1.15	390	10.4	429	11.4	2 544	8.9	7 740	3 764	3 976	772	2 051
Huntingdon	4 865	42 743	0.82	438	9.6	499	10.9	3 423	10.5	9 774	6 035	3 739	586	1 366
Indiana	5 594	88 196	1.00	815	9.3	867	9.9	8 028	11.9	17 683	6 457	11 226	1 441	1 648
Jefferson	774	42 773	0.89	491	11.0	522	11.7	3 588	10.1	10 483	6 638	3 845	412	918
Juniata	292	21 371	0.69	262	10.6	254	10.3	2 631	13.3	4 754	2 551	2 203	265	1 096
Lackawanna	8 080	217 302	1.03	2 219	10.5	2 539	12.0	16 581	9.9	46 026	32 725	13 301	4 326	2 044
Lancaster	12 782	512 851	0.94	7 247	13.5	4 816	9.0	58 557	13.4	96 072	59 597	36 475	9 261	1 741
Lawrence	2 087	83 668	0.84	897	10.2	1 077	12.2	6 574	9.4	22 279	8 735	13 544	1 903	2 157
Lebanon	3 614	125 728	0.85	1 595	11.7	1 435	10.5	12 097	11.1	27 565	16 486	11 079	2 350	1 729
Lehigh	8 947	367 194	1.08	4 242	11.8	3 259	9.1	33 629	11.4	66 298	43 901	22 397	9 145	2 567
Luzerne	11 991	321 085	1.00	3 188	10.0	3 960	12.4	27 351	10.9	68 625	50 925	17 700	8 077	2 532
Lycoming	5 480	119 392	1.05	1 283	11.0	1 297	11.2	10 027	10.9	24 558	16 219	8 339	2 479	2 121
McKean	3 256	41 947	0.94	448	10.5	510	12.0	3 376	10.5	9 349	7 274	2 075	762	1 777
Mercer	6 796	117 885	1.04	1 139	9.9	1 444	12.6	8 828	10.2	26 954	14 171	12 783	2 360	2 055
Mifflin	559	44 372	0.88	557	12.0	505	10.9	4 803	13.0	10 476	5 791	4 685	764	1 640
Monroe	4 371	156 808	0.84	1 424	8.5	1 458	8.7	16 177	11.7	28 423	22 860	5 563	4 401	2 644
Montgomery	21 732	872 180	1.15	8 850	10.8	7 497	9.2	43 479	6.5	142 230	98 446	43 784	15 053	1 847
Montour	844	25 171	1.79	188	10.1	213	11.5	1 133	7.8	3 961	1 943	2 018	219	1 178
Northampton	10 746	274 131	0.82	2 857	9.5	2 841	9.5	22 527	9.4	58 823	42 193	16 630	5 713	1 903
Northumberland	3 733	84 536	0.76	939	10.0	1 082	11.6	8 814	12.1	21 594	13 822	7 772	1 667	1 774
Perry	658	33 551	0.45	516	11.3	416	9.1	4 386	11.5	8 759	4 552	4 207	677	1 490
Philadelphia	57 227	1 656 538	1.18	22 319	14.3	14 797	9.5	190 767	14.4	229 723	120 450	109 273	68 761	4 410
Pike	478	46 722	0.56	400	7.1	470	8.4	4 937	11.2	9 071	7 921	1 150	907	1 608

1. Per 1,000 estimated resident population. 2. Data for serious crimes have not been adjusted for underreporting; this may affect comparability between geographic areas and over time.
3. Per 100,000 population estimated by the FBI.

Table B. States and Counties — Crime, Education, Money Income, and Poverty

STATE County	Serious crimes known to police, 2014 (cont.)[1] Rate[2] Violent	Property	Education — School enrollment and attainment, 2010–2014 — Enrollment[3] Total	Percent private	Attainment[4] (percent) High school graduate or less	Bachelor's degree or more	Local government expenditures,[5] 2012–2013 Total current spending (mil dol)	Current spending per student (dollars)	Money income, 2010–2014 Per capita income[6] (dollars)	Households Median income (dollars)	Mean income (dollars)	Percent with income of $200,000 or more	Income and poverty, 2014 Median household income (dollars)	Percent below poverty level All persons	Children under 18 years	Children 5 to 17 years in families
	46	47	48	49	50	51	52	53	54	55	56	57	58	59	60	61
OREGON—Cont'd																
Morrow	184	1 953	2 963	4.8	58.4	10.2	23.5	9 611	20 750	50 443	59 837	1.3	51 839	16.3	22.3	20.2
Multnomah	467	5 106	186 702	20.1	28.8	40.3	998.2	10 779	31 047	52 845	73 748	4.9	53 519	18.6	23.2	21.0
Polk	220	2 725	21 600	10.3	36.6	28.9	59.0	9 056	23 891	51 880	63 754	1.9	52 626	14.1	17.2	15.5
Sherman	58	984	340	16.2	42.9	18.5	3.6	14 618	27 427	39 960	60 594	3.7	53 277	14.2	23.4	20.3
Tillamook	114	1 969	4 728	13.3	47.9	19.5	38.5	12 078	22 417	43 037	53 181	1.9	41 662	17.5	25.9	23.0
Umatilla	209	2 469	19 679	7.0	45.9	15.8	146.7	10 655	20 887	47 185	57 929	1.7	44 780	18.0	25.2	23.2
Union	128	2 044	6 718	15.0	41.7	22.7	35.5	9 425	22 857	43 265	56 400	2.5	44 841	17.7	22.0	21.1
Wallowa	0	884	1 302	11.3	40.6	25.1	14.1	16 756	23 996	41 522	52 345	1.2	39 743	15.8	26.1	24.6
Wasco	129	2 695	5 706	11.3	43.2	18.7	39.9	11 205	21 865	43 226	56 879	1.7	44 010	16.8	23.4	22.8
Washington	154	1 736	144 217	17.5	28.6	39.7	792.5	9 192	31 587	65 272	82 645	5.4	66 315	12.5	16.0	14.5
Wheeler	219	511	226	14.2	46.6	16.1	4.4	13 813	24 154	34 808	48 883	1.4	33 387	23.3	39.5	37.7
Yamhill	123	1 921	26 951	24.3	44.0	22.4	153.3	9 212	24 018	53 864	67 182	2.7	52 903	15.4	20.5	18.4
PENNSYLVANIA	314	1 932	3 115 016	23.9	47.8	28.1	24 371.8	13 864	28 912	53 115	72 210	4.4	53 224	13.6	19.2	17.8
Adams	103	1 102	24 311	28.0	55.5	21.2	276.2	20 032	27 701	60 068	72 454	2.9	60 179	10.8	14.8	13.1
Allegheny	401	1 983	294 258	25.7	37.1	36.9	2 286.7	15 859	32 378	52 390	73 790	4.8	52 385	13.1	18.5	17.8
Armstrong	105	909	13 357	12.3	60.9	14.6	115.1	15 328	24 266	45 375	57 137	1.7	44 326	13.8	21.0	19.2
Beaver	285	2 175	36 634	17.3	48.1	22.6	313.3	13 956	26 925	50 242	63 450	2.3	51 041	11.7	17.0	16.3
Bedford	90	1 241	9 754	14.1	64.2	13.7	87.7	12 522	23 075	44 692	55 748	1.3	46 890	13.6	20.0	18.3
Berks	328	1 774	106 133	17.2	54.2	22.7	944.1	13 729	26 998	55 798	70 581	3.4	55 936	14.3	21.4	21.4
Blair	235	1 643	26 951	14.3	58.6	18.6	229.4	13 023	23 785	43 871	57 078	2.2	43 343	15.0	20.6	19.0
Bradford	182	1 633	12 925	11.9	60.4	17.0	130.7	13 539	24 431	48 418	60 943	2.5	47 242	12.9	18.7	17.6
Bucks	92	1 543	152 149	24.1	37.8	36.5	1 385.5	16 018	37 910	76 824	100 029	9.2	77 823	6.6	8.3	7.1
Butler	93	1 315	46 165	16.0	42.4	31.7	312.2	11 345	31 818	59 365	78 255	5.0	60 851	8.9	10.4	8.8
Cambria	173	1 764	31 743	21.4	57.3	18.9	228.6	12 404	23 191	42 304	55 093	1.6	42 703	15.3	23.6	21.6
Cameron	103	1 095	838	7.9	62.5	14.6	9.7	14 007	25 087	41 157	54 054	1.4	40 257	14.2	22.0	21.3
Carbon	213	1 755	13 440	13.9	57.7	15.0	119.4	13 449	25 294	49 913	61 788	1.4	49 252	13.0	21.3	18.8
Centre	82	1 184	60 473	8.1	39.1	40.4	193.1	14 954	25 803	50 295	67 748	3.9	51 573	17.9	12.2	11.5
Chester	134	1 210	135 576	25.2	30.9	48.8	1 158.3	16 651	42 323	86 093	113 912	13.4	85 613	7.3	9.2	8.2
Clarion	139	1 376	10 294	7.8	59.1	19.3	97.9	16 625	22 341	42 880	54 538	1.9	43 202	15.1	19.2	17.6
Clearfield	260	1 705	15 742	11.9	63.9	13.2	169.1	14 639	21 102	41 510	51 471	0.8	40 230	16.5	22.0	19.8
Clinton	164	1 655	10 848	11.6	59.4	17.2	58.1	13 462	21 595	44 329	55 066	0.8	44 224	17.4	23.3	21.5
Columbia	180	1 602	18 735	8.3	56.9	21.2	82.6	13 085	23 913	46 367	60 293	1.9	46 938	14.3	17.5	15.3
Crawford	99	1 344	19 902	24.5	57.9	19.6	149.7	13 018	22 421	43 622	55 796	1.7	43 969	14.9	22.5	21.2
Cumberland	98	1 475	58 914	22.9	43.7	32.8	350.5	13 693	32 179	61 417	78 710	4.6	62 692	9.1	12.8	10.9
Dauphin	370	2 395	63 931	18.2	46.4	28.2	486.6	13 724	29 536	54 337	71 612	3.9	52 907	13.4	20.6	19.2
Delaware	416	2 027	154 488	33.7	40.1	35.5	1 132.2	16 337	33 539	64 174	89 186	7.5	62 867	11.0	15.1	13.9
Elk	70	1 692	6 268	24.9	60.4	15.4	43.2	11 556	24 071	46 576	55 774	1.2	46 965	10.5	14.4	13.1
Erie	228	2 124	71 984	23.9	50.2	25.6	502.3	13 085	24 505	45 703	60 677	2.4	45 476	16.4	23.4	21.4
Fayette	184	2 009	26 545	12.5	63.6	13.9	217.4	12 606	21 319	38 879	50 835	1.2	36 902	20.2	30.7	28.7
Forest	460	972	918	30.4	68.5	9.2	10.4	19 796	13 680	36 037	44 643	0.7	37 794	21.9	41.2	36.5
Franklin	149	2 027	32 972	17.2	57.4	19.1	250.5	10 985	25 540	53 394	64 629	1.7	50 434	11.9	17.1	14.7
Fulton	260	1 108	3 117	10.9	66.6	12.7	28.8	13 047	23 192	48 452	56 803	1.0	48 084	13.3	20.8	17.6
Greene	244	1 807	7 963	22.2	61.3	17.0	76.6	14 597	22 847	46 485	60 401	1.4	49 897	16.5	21.8	20.1
Huntingdon	201	1 166	9 370	23.0	63.8	14.3	64.4	11 460	20 918	44 163	53 336	0.9	44 531	15.1	21.2	17.2
Indiana	300	1 348	24 413	8.9	54.7	23.3	167.2	16 972	23 577	45 168	58 810	2.2	42 611	17.0	21.9	20.5
Jefferson	107	811	9 212	13.4	62.7	14.3	72.7	14 997	21 952	42 295	52 337	1.0	43 810	13.3	21.1	19.8
Juniata	87	1 009	5 019	22.3	69.9	12.2	28.7	9 677	22 134	47 269	56 657	1.2	48 944	12.3	18.4	16.6
Lackawanna	196	1 848	51 485	32.4	48.4	25.7	350.4	12 588	25 624	46 056	62 117	2.7	45 098	15.4	20.4	19.6
Lancaster	165	1 577	127 322	25.6	54.3	24.7	949.3	13 988	26 892	57 120	71 532	3.3	57 369	10.5	15.3	13.9
Lawrence	211	1 946	19 326	16.6	55.8	19.4	158.1	12 702	23 519	43 991	56 257	1.7	44 903	13.2	20.5	18.6
Lebanon	149	1 580	30 660	23.2	58.5	19.8	221.1	11 553	27 060	56 173	68 738	2.5	53 861	10.9	17.1	16.3
Lehigh	228	2 339	86 632	22.1	46.5	28.1	712.0	14 619	28 139	55 681	72 478	4.1	58 283	12.8	19.5	17.6
Luzerne	264	2 268	71 795	22.4	50.9	21.4	551.7	12 548	25 091	45 118	60 052	2.3	44 222	15.8	24.4	21.6
Lycoming	218	1 903	26 777	15.2	54.0	19.4	222.2	13 719	23 531	45 877	57 790	1.8	45 211	16.2	22.6	20.9
McKean	303	1 474	9 934	13.7	59.4	15.6	98.7	15 646	23 034	42 913	53 141	1.2	44 723	16.6	24.8	22.3
Mercer	218	1 837	26 608	24.1	55.1	20.5	256.6	15 933	23 195	43 715	56 696	1.6	43 559	14.6	25.0	22.6
Mifflin	137	1 502	9 128	20.4	68.2	11.9	94.0	17 759	20 772	40 947	50 364	1.3	40 957	16.3	25.0	22.3
Monroe	218	2 426	45 184	14.9	47.3	23.2	435.0	15 532	25 266	57 748	70 343	2.8	59 492	13.3	19.6	17.4
Montgomery	148	1 699	205 170	30.3	31.4	46.2	1 775.8	16 934	41 699	79 926	107 410	11.0	79 576	7.1	8.9	8.2
Montour	301	877	3 812	16.1	50.9	28.3	29.3	12 455	30 455	53 604	73 559	4.8	54 547	11.2	17.0	15.9
Northampton	168	1 735	75 521	28.2	45.7	27.2	633.3	14 826	30 116	61 041	77 946	4.4	61 510	10.0	13.8	12.5
Northumberland	237	1 536	17 995	17.4	65.6	14.3	190.8	15 952	22 633	41 560	53 843	1.2	40 429	15.9	23.2	21.8
Perry	207	1 283	9 637	16.8	58.0	16.1	76.5	12 245	26 242	57 417	65 619	1.7	54 920	8.7	14.5	13.6
Philadelphia	1 022	3 388	416 404	33.7	52.9	24.5	2 905.9	20 194	22 542	37 460	55 353	2.6	39 037	25.8	36.9	36.6
Pike	144	1 465	13 507	12.8	45.7	22.9	118.3	14 046	27 935	58 906	72 426	2.9	58 375	10.6	16.4	14.5

1. Data for serious crimes have not been adjusted for underreporting; this may affect comparability between geographic areas and over time. 2. Per 100,000 population estimated by the FBI.
3. All persons 3 years old and over enrolled in nursery school through college. 4. Persons 25 years old and over. 5. Elementary and secondary education expenditures.
6. Based on population estimated by the American Community Survey, 2010–2014.

Table B. States and Counties — **Personal Income**

STATE County	Total (mil dol)	Percent change, 2013–2014	Per capita[1] Dollars	Per capita[1] Rank	Wages and salaries (mil dol)	Pension and insurance	Government social insurance	Proprietors' income (mil dol)	Dividends, interest, and rent (mil dol)	Personal transfer receipts (mil dol)	Total (mil dol)	From employee and self-employed	From employer
	62	63	64	65	66	67	68	69	70	71	72	73	74
OREGON—Cont'd													
Morrow	470	8.4	42 033	947	266	45	25	107	54	91	442	19	25
Multnomah	36 588	5.5	47 106	519	25 923	3 611	2 273	3 657	6 875	5 690	35 465	2 152	2 273
Polk	2 672	6.0	34 296	2 064	660	130	61	98	476	641	948	69	61
Sherman	99	2.0	58 011	156	38	8	3	27	17	20	77	3	3
Tillamook	927	8.0	36 564	1 678	322	60	30	98	205	274	510	33	30
Umatilla	2 632	4.6	34 318	2 059	1 187	210	115	170	393	670	1 682	104	115
Union	883	4.9	34 384	2 047	380	72	37	46	162	259	535	36	37
Wallowa	284	8.5	41 663	990	81	18	8	41	68	80	148	9	8
Wasco	994	7.4	38 974	1 322	430	73	39	104	169	256	647	37	39
Washington	26 299	5.4	46 713	544	17 665	1 873	1 393	975	4 902	3 501	21 906	1 364	1 393
Wheeler	44	12.7	32 131	2 427	10	2	1	3	12	15	16	1	1
Yamhill	3 713	6.0	36 488	1 688	1 366	233	128	229	692	842	1 956	123	128
PENNSYLVANIA	609 679	3.6	47 679	X	296 487	53 170	23 391	55 611	103 602	116 997	428 659	25 309	23 391
Adams	4 351	3.5	42 776	873	1 352	279	115	330	709	807	2 075	127	115
Allegheny	66 458	3.2	53 976	235	40 887	6 393	3 155	7 430	11 227	11 369	57 865	3 369	3 155
Armstrong	2 758	3.0	40 683	1 100	744	167	61	338	369	698	1 310	87	61
Beaver	6 959	2.6	41 084	1 050	2 333	506	195	309	859	1 764	3 344	224	195
Bedford	1 729	2.2	35 330	1 889	564	122	50	205	228	464	941	61	50
Berks	17 729	3.8	42 856	864	8 081	1 596	657	1 284	2 744	3 620	11 619	685	657
Blair	4 829	3.4	38 336	1 415	2 382	510	209	295	744	1 321	3 396	212	209
Bradford	2 375	4.2	38 448	1 401	1 156	224	92	189	386	554	1 660	103	92
Bucks	39 177	3.7	62 514	106	13 305	2 195	1 072	3 182	6 591	5 121	19 755	1 174	1 072
Butler	9 112	3.3	49 004	438	4 267	792	340	499	1 363	1 544	5 897	352	340
Cambria	5 170	2.1	37 536	1 521	2 100	466	185	290	782	1 570	3 041	202	185
Cameron	198	1.4	41 153	1 046	80	19	7	11	37	59	117	8	7
Carbon	2 505	4.2	38 866	1 338	602	148	52	254	348	618	1 056	70	52
Centre	6 345	4.3	39 973	1 180	3 455	1 349	270	506	1 151	993	5 580	278	270
Chester	36 905	4.7	71 971	50	17 762	2 515	1 266	4 121	6 769	3 572	25 663	1 445	1 266
Clarion	1 407	2.0	36 239	1 738	497	140	42	139	231	390	819	50	42
Clearfield	3 105	2.6	38 245	1 425	1 151	259	98	190	409	799	1 698	110	98
Clinton	1 428	4.5	35 917	1 787	554	143	47	140	185	346	883	53	47
Columbia	2 430	2.2	36 209	1 744	993	252	84	176	360	579	1 505	92	84
Crawford	3 055	2.8	35 046	1 925	1 191	265	101	282	421	851	1 838	116	101
Cumberland	11 734	3.9	48 137	472	6 610	1 204	537	743	2 118	1 907	9 094	528	537
Dauphin	12 338	3.0	45 453	638	9 581	2 071	749	912	1 852	2 373	13 313	741	749
Delaware	31 139	3.7	55 313	207	12 918	2 106	989	1 883	5 746	4 996	17 896	1 064	989
Elk	1 319	4.4	42 290	928	633	134	54	61	198	315	882	55	54
Erie	10 637	2.0	38 200	1 429	5 280	1 123	431	536	1 712	2 658	7 371	446	431
Fayette	4 969	2.0	37 055	1 592	1 536	353	132	365	684	1 504	2 386	166	132
Forest	174	3.1	23 209	3 096	96	34	8	10	41	65	148	9	8
Franklin	6 111	4.0	39 972	1 181	2 378	488	203	438	986	1 267	3 507	211	203
Fulton	524	4.6	35 779	1 811	215	47	18	50	78	137	330	20	18
Greene	1 629	3.8	43 047	841	939	169	71	151	207	361	1 330	80	71
Huntingdon	1 585	4.3	34 653	1 990	469	128	40	115	219	417	751	48	40
Indiana	3 236	2.9	36 900	1 616	1 545	381	122	444	483	791	2 493	146	122
Jefferson	1 611	2.1	36 094	1 765	606	128	51	130	249	453	915	60	51
Juniata	908	4.0	36 607	1 667	213	48	19	133	127	206	413	26	19
Lackawanna	8 761	3.4	41 187	1 038	4 023	806	338	608	1 456	2 175	5 775	358	338
Lancaster	22 246	4.6	41 712	979	10 133	1 822	832	2 582	3 824	4 139	15 369	892	832
Lawrence	3 402	2.4	38 322	1 419	1 223	252	104	224	463	963	1 802	121	104
Lebanon	5 595	3.6	41 034	1 056	1 974	453	167	436	865	1 171	3 030	180	167
Lehigh	16 178	4.9	45 211	659	9 701	1 601	752	1 144	2 518	3 061	13 198	780	752
Luzerne	12 677	3.3	39 760	1 215	5 926	1 221	506	748	2 020	3 149	8 401	520	506
Lycoming	4 633	4.0	39 766	1 214	2 377	502	194	257	739	1 043	3 329	202	194
McKean	1 674	2.5	39 329	1 279	683	161	56	143	300	430	1 043	65	56
Mercer	4 138	2.4	36 023	1 779	1 955	398	164	182	641	1 204	2 699	175	164
Mifflin	1 565	3.5	33 621	2 173	589	128	49	171	203	459	937	60	49
Monroe	6 037	4.2	36 297	1 723	2 269	537	192	282	835	1 306	3 280	200	192
Montgomery	61 947	4.1	75 835	38	33 250	4 590	2 466	6 621	15 796	6 514	46 926	2 675	2 466
Montour	1 016	3.3	54 521	220	987	161	65	155	129	179	1 369	77	65
Northampton	13 619	4.7	45 299	652	5 068	974	424	556	2 203	2 639	7 023	440	424
Northumberland	3 398	2.0	36 172	1 749	1 082	252	93	183	542	921	1 610	108	93
Perry	1 740	3.6	38 135	1 435	261	72	22	127	234	371	482	33	22
Philadelphia	66 495	4.0	42 617	887	41 579	7 136	3 241	10 888	9 444	17 501	62 844	3 565	3 241
Pike	2 196	4.3	39 078	1 309	377	98	33	123	359	506	631	46	33

1. Based on the resident population estimated as of July 1 of the year shown.

STATE County	Farm	Mining	Construction	Manu-facturing	Information: professional, scientific, technical services	Retail trade	Finance, insurance, real estate and leasing	Health care and social assistance	Government	Number	Rate[1]	Supplemental Security Income recipients, December 2014	Total	Percent change, 2010–2014
	75	76	77	78	79	80	81	82	83	84	85	86	87	88
OREGON—Cont'd														
Morrow	30.9	D	5.6	22.0	D	1.3	1.0	1.6	11.7	2 080	186	223	4 478	0.8
Multnomah	0.1	D	5.7	7.0	15.0	5.1	8.6	11.0	17.5	114 960	148	20 854	336 248	3.5
Polk	4.8	D	6.0	11.4	D	4.9	2.5	12.2	31.4	16 700	214	1 362	31 166	2.9
Sherman	36.8	0.0	D	D	D	D	D	0.6	31.6	510	300	38	913	-0.5
Tillamook	11.5	0.0	5.8	13.3	2.8	6.7	3.0	10.5	23.2	7 760	306	532	18 573	1.2
Umatilla	5.0	0.1	4.7	9.3	3.4	6.8	2.7	D	26.4	13 815	180	1 732	29 836	0.5
Union	2.2	0.0	4.7	14.4	3.6	8.7	3.1	16.1	25.4	6 035	235	620	11 590	0.9
Wallowa	18.9	0.0	6.1	3.9	3.6	7.2	4.8	D	26.4	2 325	341	152	4 090	-0.4
Wasco	14.8	D	4.2	5.1	7.3	9.6	2.4	19.4	21.1	6 120	240	666	11 428	-0.5
Washington	0.6	0.1	5.1	26.1	D	5.6	5.8	8.0	7.2	78 460	139	7 076	222 015	4.5
Wheeler	25.2	0.0	D	D	D	D	D	D	34.0	495	361	31	890	-0.6
Yamhill	6.9	0.2	6.0	22.3	4.2	6.6	3.5	12.3	15.0	19 660	193	1 557	37 966	2.3
PENNSYLVANIA	0.6	1.4	5.7	10.2	13.1	5.5	8.5	13.8	13.7	2 722 892	213	374 111	5 602 813	0.6
Adams	4.5	D	7.4	19.5	5.3	6.6	3.9	D	15.4	23 235	228	1 113	41 462	1.6
Allegheny	0.0	2.7	5.5	5.8	15.4	4.7	10.9	14.2	9.8	265 800	216	35 830	590 680	0.3
Armstrong	0.6	17.6	6.3	11.4	4.5	6.9	3.3	13.7	15.2	17 805	263	1 997	32 338	-0.6
Beaver	0.1	0.9	5.1	16.3	6.8	7.4	3.2	15.9	16.4	43 465	257	4 829	78 327	0.1
Bedford	4.9	D	11.9	12.3	D	9.2	3.0	8.0	15.4	12 985	265	1 222	24 012	0.2
Berks	1.7	0.1	6.2	19.1	7.3	7.0	5.2	13.3	14.0	85 070	205	10 643	164 904	0.1
Blair	1.4	0.4	4.9	13.8	6.1	8.2	3.1	19.6	16.6	30 445	242	4 841	56 011	-0.5
Bradford	1.9	11.5	6.2	16.2	3.2	6.0	4.7	19.2	12.7	15 920	258	1 944	30 124	0.5
Bucks	0.2	0.2	10.0	11.4	12.9	7.4	6.7	13.3	10.5	127 025	203	7 148	247 207	0.5
Butler	0.2	1.7	6.4	16.3	8.1	7.1	4.0	10.2	14.6	41 020	220	3 395	80 787	3.4
Cambria	0.2	1.1	4.4	8.2	7.9	7.8	6.0	22.2	17.8	38 270	278	5 113	65 126	-0.8
Cameron	0.3	D	D	50.2	D	2.6	D	4.5	21.9	1 560	326	139	4 387	-1.5
Carbon	0.2	0.2	5.0	11.5	20.0	7.4	3.2	15.8	16.8	16 855	262	1 393	34 387	0.3
Centre	0.6	1.2	4.3	5.1	8.0	5.1	3.7	9.8	49.8	23 405	147	1 588	65 478	3.5
Chester	1.0	0.6	4.9	8.0	20.3	5.4	15.5	8.8	8.0	86 330	168	4 314	196 755	2.2
Clarion	1.1	9.0	6.4	10.5	3.2	7.6	3.4	14.0	27.1	9 710	246	1 321	20 233	1.4
Clearfield	0.1	3.8	4.5	8.3	3.5	8.4	3.6	20.2	19.3	20 775	256	2 538	38 579	-0.2
Clinton	4.8	D	7.2	22.5	4.9	6.2	2.3	D	23.3	9 060	229	1 020	18 985	-0.5
Columbia	1.0	D	5.9	20.0	5.2	7.9	3.1	11.5	21.8	15 545	232	1 528	29 594	0.3
Crawford	3.2	1.6	4.6	25.2	3.6	6.7	3.1	15.9	15.9	22 265	256	3 108	44 309	-0.8
Cumberland	0.8	0.0	4.0	6.3	10.7	6.0	10.5	12.8	17.1	49 550	203	2 637	103 561	3.6
Dauphin	0.4	0.0	4.1	8.2	7.4	3.8	8.8	15.0	24.8	54 860	202	7 597	122 194	1.5
Delaware	0.0	D	6.3	9.5	10.5	5.5	12.1	13.1	11.7	103 995	185	12 263	221 874	-0.5
Elk	0.0	1.0	4.1	49.9	2.5	5.0	2.2	11.2	10.0	8 625	277	685	17 529	-0.3
Erie	0.3	0.2	4.1	21.6	4.9	6.8	8.0	17.0	16.6	61 595	221	11 420	120 094	0.8
Fayette	0.3	5.0	6.6	9.6	4.6	9.0	2.6	15.2	19.9	35 790	267	8 344	62 971	0.3
Forest	0.2	9.3	D	D	D	1.9	D	10.7	56.5	1 785	238	162	8 652	-1.2
Franklin	4.6	0.1	4.6	19.2	4.6	6.9	3.2	14.9	17.3	34 990	229	2 553	64 325	1.7
Fulton	5.3	D	9.5	39.2	D	3.7	1.8	9.8	13.9	3 920	268	391	7 109	-0.2
Greene	-0.2	D	7.9	1.7	4.5	4.6	2.9	D	14.7	8 845	234	1 716	16 441	-0.1
Huntingdon	5.9	1.1	6.4	9.7	2.5	6.0	4.0		29.4	11 090	242	1 218	22 397	0.1
Indiana	0.6	18.3	5.7	5.1	3.3	5.6	3.4	9.3	21.4	20 245	231	2 808	38 602	0.9
Jefferson	0.7	11.5	4.8	23.5	3.7	6.2	2.7	14.9	14.1	11 765	264	1 520	22 424	0.0
Juniata	9.3	D	10.4	27.3	D	6.2	3.7	6.3	11.9	5 605	226	496	11 009	0.3
Lackawanna	0.1	0.3	6.2	10.0	8.0	8.1	7.6	17.6	14.1	53 855	253	6 840	98 370	1.6
Lancaster	3.7	0.2	10.1	16.3	7.1	7.0	6.5	13.5	9.8	107 425	201	9 957	207 090	2.0
Lawrence	0.9	0.6	11.8	14.9	4.8	6.8	6.0	14.9	14.6	24 030	271	3 661	40 675	-0.7
Lebanon	5.1	D	4.9	17.6	5.1	7.2	2.9	13.2	20.7	31 400	231	2 472	56 464	1.6
Lehigh	0.2	D	4.6	10.1	7.7	5.4	5.6	20.0	9.8	73 910	206	10 826	143 847	0.9
Luzerne	0.0	0.5	4.7	11.5	6.8	7.3	6.4	15.4	16.3	78 730	247	10 128	148 211	-0.4
Lycoming	0.5	7.3	5.9	16.1	5.0	6.4	4.6	13.9	18.4	27 080	232	3 381	52 671	0.3
McKean	0.2	16.7	4.6	22.0	2.4	5.3	1.9	12.2	16.4	11 140	261	1 710	21 004	-1.0
Mercer	0.5	1.3	3.8	22.5	3.1	8.0	5.8	18.1	13.7	30 655	267	4 095	51 562	-0.3
Mifflin	4.4	0.0	6.2	25.4	2.3	9.5	3.3	16.2	12.9	12 020	258	1 442	21 513	-0.1
Monroe	0.1	0.1	4.3	14.5	4.0	8.5	3.3	12.2	28.1	34 140	204	3 027	80 720	0.4
Montgomery	0.0	0.1	7.6	9.4	20.4	4.9	13.3	12.0	6.7	152 475	187	8 607	328 589	0.9
Montour	0.7	D	4.9	2.2	D	2.3	7.6	D	7.5	4 520	243	488	8 048	1.1
Northampton	0.1	0.1	5.6	15.3	8.0	6.6	7.0	10.2	15.8	66 825	223	5 785	121 581	1.0
Northumberland	3.1	0.7	5.4	17.9	3.6	6.1	2.9	13.0	18.4	24 340	260	2 880	44 874	-0.5
Perry	10.6	D	12.3	6.1	3.4	8.3	4.3	7.2	25.8	10 050	221	769	20 540	0.6
Philadelphia	0.0	0.0	1.9	2.9	24.1	3.0	9.1	15.5	16.0	256 780	164	110 676	672 588	0.4
Pike	0.2	0.7	D	D	D	9.6	4.5	8.2	31.1	14 115	251	674	38 547	0.5

1. Per 1,000 resident population estimated as of July 1 of the year shown.

Table B. States and Counties — **Housing, Labor Force, and Employment**

STATE County	Housing units, 2010–2014								Civilian labor force, 2015				Civilian employment,[6] 2010–2014		
	Occupied units							Sub-stand-ard units[4] (percent)			Unemployment		Percent		
			Owner-occupied			Renter-occupied									
				Median owner cost as a percent of income											
	Total	Percent	Median value[1]	With a mortgage	Without a mortgage[2]	Median rent[3]	Median rent as a percent of income[2]		Total	Percent change, 2014–2015	Total	Rate[5]	Total	Manage-ment, business, science and arts	Con-struction, produc-tion, and mainte-nance occu-pations
	89	90	91	92	93	94	95	96	97	98	99	100	101	102	103

OREGON—Cont'd

STATE County	89	90	91	92	93	94	95	96	97	98	99	100	101	102	103
Morrow	3 714	69.8	122 200	20.7	11.3	647	28.9	7.6	5 528	0.9	320	5.8	4 711	26.2	40.7
Multnomah	308 595	53.7	270 200	25.7	13.9	941	32.9	4.0	427 659	1.9	21 350	5.0	383 634	42.6	16.8
Polk	28 253	64.8	212 100	24.2	12.2	796	32.7	3.5	36 384	2.4	2 084	5.7	31 383	35.3	21.7
Sherman	791	64.7	139 900	22.0	12.2	734	29.3	1.6	890	1.0	56	6.3	779	36.8	28.4
Tillamook	10 213	70.7	226 400	27.9	12.5	821	35.0	1.9	11 314	1.3	653	5.8	9 919	25.1	34.5
Umatilla	26 901	61.6	141 900	21.9	11.2	680	25.8	5.8	35 196	-0.3	2 288	6.5	31 906	28.3	31.1
Union	10 134	64.1	159 800	21.5	11.5	680	33.4	3.2	11 635	0.3	737	6.3	10 773	29.4	24.5
Wallowa	3 018	70.3	209 200	23.6	13.4	689	33.4	1.5	3 255	1.4	257	7.9	2 990	37.3	22.1
Wasco	9 595	64.5	177 000	24.9	12.5	734	33.9	2.4	12 979	-4.4	741	5.7	10 517	26.4	27.4
Washington	203 901	60.6	279 100	24.4	12.0	1 015	29.9	3.4	299 458	2.1	14 287	4.8	269 223	43.4	16.8
Wheeler	666	70.9	126 800	29.0	14.5	561	22.3	2.3	705	-3.4	37	5.2	587	35.8	28.3
Yamhill	34 149	67.0	218 800	25.5	12.6	904	31.8	3.3	51 073	2.0	2 728	5.3	43 676	29.7	28.0
PENNSYLVANIA	4 957 736	69.5	164 900	22.7	13.5	832	30.4	1.7	6 423 906	0.5	330 048	5.1	5 946 480	36.5	21.7
Adams	37 956	76.9	194 100	23.7	13.5	844	30.5	2.1	55 038	-0.1	2 241	4.1	50 550	29.5	31.6
Allegheny	527 445	65.3	124 800	20.1	12.9	771	28.8	1.0	647 803	0.2	31 201	4.8	605 650	43.1	14.8
Armstrong	28 616	76.2	93 400	20.0	12.2	607	25.9	1.2	33 342	0.6	2 130	6.4	30 602	27.0	33.0
Beaver	70 336	72.8	117 300	20.6	12.9	642	28.1	1.1	85 989	0.1	5 041	5.9	79 843	32.1	23.8
Bedford	20 145	79.8	120 100	21.9	12.3	620	28.2	2.1	24 129	-0.5	1 420	5.9	22 328	25.7	34.4
Berks	153 857	71.7	169 200	23.7	14.8	849	32.1	2.0	213 249	1.1	10 151	4.8	196 201	31.4	27.7
Blair	50 948	72.0	108 500	20.1	12.5	630	28.9	1.2	61 018	0.2	3 053	5.0	57 590	30.1	25.2
Bradford	24 338	75.0	123 700	21.0	12.1	666	27.6	2.7	31 515	-0.3	1 800	5.7	26 878	27.7	34.8
Bucks	231 959	77.2	307 600	24.7	14.9	1 128	31.4	1.3	338 412	1.0	15 289	4.5	320 281	41.9	17.7
Butler	74 138	76.4	173 100	20.8	12.1	756	28.9	1.1	97 620	0.3	4 468	4.6	91 043	36.4	22.1
Cambria	57 959	73.8	86 800	19.7	13.3	561	27.9	1.1	62 363	-0.9	3 981	6.4	58 867	32.2	24.0
Cameron	2 214	70.5	69 600	20.0	11.6	557	26.3	0.5	2 268	-1.3	158	7.0	2 250	23.3	43.9
Carbon	25 764	79.0	145 200	25.6	14.4	750	31.9	1.5	31 667	0.3	1 848	5.8	29 065	26.3	31.2
Centre	57 283	60.4	193 500	21.9	11.4	894	36.4	2.9	77 888	0.4	2 969	3.8	73 751	43.8	16.4
Chester	185 306	75.3	323 600	23.4	13.8	1 192	29.3	1.6	276 442	1.0	10 198	3.7	258 128	47.9	15.2
Clarion	15 846	70.2	108 200	19.5	10.8	596	30.3	2.2	18 241	-1.0	1 040	5.7	17 239	29.9	29.1
Clearfield	31 863	77.2	87 100	22.0	13.9	586	28.8	1.3	36 410	-0.7	2 343	6.4	34 329	26.5	31.4
Clinton	14 947	71.6	113 800	21.8	14.2	675	28.6	1.4	18 819	-0.7	1 259	6.7	17 459	24.4	31.0
Columbia	26 413	70.4	137 000	20.9	14.0	710	31.2	1.2	33 867	-1.1	1 856	5.5	30 699	30.0	27.9
Crawford	34 713	74.0	103 300	21.6	13.0	611	28.0	2.9	41 256	0.1	2 075	5.0	37 725	30.6	30.5
Cumberland	95 835	70.9	185 900	21.8	12.1	871	28.0	1.5	127 912	1.5	4 949	3.9	120 082	38.7	19.4
Dauphin	109 027	64.3	159 200	21.9	12.4	846	28.9	1.5	141 108	1.3	6 353	4.5	131 130	37.9	19.2
Delaware	204 571	69.9	233 400	24.3	15.0	978	32.5	1.3	291 908	0.7	13 828	4.7	266 310	41.7	16.0
Elk	13 375	79.4	90 400	18.9	11.7	563	27.6	0.3	16 331	-0.1	784	4.8	14 939	22.6	43.6
Erie	109 700	66.5	117 200	20.7	12.4	685	30.9	1.6	134 873	0.2	7 185	5.3	127 697	33.1	23.7
Fayette	53 987	71.7	87 000	20.8	12.9	588	28.0	2.1	58 480	0.1	4 238	7.2	53 669	26.0	29.7
Forest	2 075	81.5	84 800	23.2	12.1	505	25.3	2.0	1 883	-2.4	145	7.7	1 585	28.5	22.5
Franklin	58 298	72.6	174 300	23.4	11.7	801	28.3	1.8	77 739	1.7	3 723	4.8	70 570	31.4	28.7
Fulton	5 981	78.5	156 300	23.5	11.3	641	25.7	2.1	7 445	2.1	447	6.0	6 531	23.4	37.5
Greene	14 383	73.1	93 300	19.0	10.8	624	28.0	0.8	18 281	-1.2	1 058	5.8	15 002	29.4	31.0
Huntingdon	17 231	76.2	115 900	21.6	12.5	558	27.6	1.9	19 665	-0.9	1 338	6.8	18 616	28.6	31.5
Indiana	34 398	71.4	107 000	20.6	12.1	678	31.8	3.1	41 917	-2.9	2 561	6.1	39 174	28.9	28.5
Jefferson	18 583	74.4	88 700	20.8	11.5	580	26.6	2.6	21 004	0.8	1 241	5.9	19 739	25.3	35.7
Juniata	9 329	77.5	142 400	22.9	11.6	587	26.5	2.8	11 969	1.0	574	4.8	11 075	25.7	38.5
Lackawanna	85 335	66.5	145 900	23.0	14.9	702	28.5	1.2	106 388	-0.2	6 035	5.7	97 535	33.8	22.6
Lancaster	194 503	69.4	187 300	23.5	12.8	896	31.4	2.1	275 869	1.3	10 997	4.0	256 207	32.7	27.5
Lawrence	36 616	74.2	97 200	21.4	13.2	625	30.7	1.9	42 219	-0.8	2 589	6.1	39 557	30.4	26.7
Lebanon	51 793	71.4	164 500	22.6	12.6	761	27.6	1.8	70 133	0.1	3 071	4.4	64 169	30.0	27.8
Lehigh	133 684	67.0	193 900	23.9	14.5	923	33.0	2.1	184 342	0.7	9 583	5.2	166 747	35.0	22.7
Luzerne	129 335	67.9	121 700	21.8	14.5	688	29.3	1.5	158 303	-0.4	9 952	6.3	145 606	30.9	24.4
Lycoming	46 008	70.0	134 600	22.4	14.0	699	29.3	1.8	60 975	-0.8	3 574	5.9	53 701	29.1	27.5
McKean	17 340	73.4	74 700	19.5	11.5	613	30.9	1.2	18 987	-1.6	1 119	5.9	17 793	29.6	32.2
Mercer	46 128	74.0	105 100	20.8	12.7	612	29.5	2.0	53 046	0.0	2 815	5.3	49 751	29.7	26.1
Mifflin	18 822	72.3	96 700	23.3	13.8	621	27.1	4.0	20 979	-0.5	1 170	5.6	19 487	24.0	37.1
Monroe	57 661	79.5	183 100	28.4	17.0	1 038	33.9	1.9	80 651	1.1	5 046	6.3	75 207	33.0	21.9
Montgomery	307 953	72.6	290 800	23.5	14.1	1 146	29.4	1.1	441 254	1.1	17 770	4.0	415 553	48.6	14.3
Montour	7 380	72.9	157 900	20.7	12.2	722	26.9	0.6	9 167	-0.8	384	4.2	8 555	39.4	22.5
Northampton	112 790	72.3	208 900	24.3	15.3	952	32.0	1.9	156 515	0.8	8 010	5.1	142 588	34.7	23.0
Northumberland	39 170	71.5	100 500	21.1	13.8	609	27.9	1.6	43 489	-0.9	2 572	5.9	40 974	27.3	30.1
Perry	18 077	79.5	158 700	23.0	12.3	723	26.2	2.0	24 232	1.0	1 046	4.3	22 522	28.0	31.6
Philadelphia	580 297	52.9	143 200	25.0	15.3	915	34.7	3.0	696 194	0.8	47 914	6.9	625 086	35.9	16.1
Pike	21 183	84.6	189 200	26.4	14.8	1 101	36.6	1.4	25 160	0.1	1 586	6.3	24 013	30.2	24.0

1. Specified owner-occupied units.   2. A value of 10.0 represents 10 percent or less; a value of 50.0 represents 50 percent or more.   3. Specified renter-occupied units.
4. Overcrowded or lacking complete plumbing facilities.   5. Percent of civilian labor force.   6. Persons 16 years old and over.

Table B. States and Counties — **Nonfarm Employment and Agriculture**

	Private nonfarm establishments, employment and payroll, 2014									Agriculture, 2012			
		Employment						Annual payroll		Farms			
											Percent with:		
STATE County	Number of establishments	Total	Health care and social assistance	Manufacturing	Retail trade	Finance and insurance	Professional, scientific, and technical services	Total (mil dol)	Average per employee (dollars)	Number	Fewer than 50 acres	500 acres or more	Farm operators whose principal occupation is farming (percent)
	104	105	106	107	108	109	110	111	112	113	114	115	116
OREGON—Cont'd													
Morrow	189	3 628	D	1 369	109	D	D	152	41 990	401	27.7	51.9	63.1
Multnomah	25 872	401 261	60 200	33 064	40 700	19 666	31 051	20 379	50 787	598	84.8	1.7	44.5
Polk	1 362	13 169	2 553	1 845	1 440	265	389	420	31 926	1 143	66.0	5.2	52.2
Sherman	53	448	D	NA	D	D	D	16	34 996	186	5.4	76.3	73.7
Tillamook	702	6 600	D	1 321	1 128	163	109	219	33 253	280	45.4	3.2	68.2
Umatilla	1 541	21 438	3 121	2 505	2 959	489	670	720	33 587	1 603	49.0	25.0	49.0
Union	734	7 125	1 455	1 303	1 388	D	224	236	33 100	829	46.4	18.2	46.9
Wallowa	366	1 658	404	108	308	D	75	53	32 131	522	37.0	27.4	47.9
Wasco	680	7 632	1 702	350	1 561	227	308	486	63 615	670	39.4	24.2	52.1
Washington	14 688	249 517	27 590	35 117	30 647	12 770	20 482	15 215	60 979	1 643	74.4	3.0	44.7
Wheeler	27	170	D	NA	D	D	NA	3	15 959	153	10.5	51.0	58.8
Yamhill	2 347	26 478	4 640	6 072	3 447	705	616	1 024	38 675	2 028	73.7	3.8	47.0
PENNSYLVANIA	298 297	5 255 409	973 465	548 672	660 341	266 219	321 707	248 561	47 296	59 309	39.3	4.1	51.7
Adams	1 930	28 076	4 479	5 462	3 426	552	1 156	1 001	35 648	1 188	48.2	6.3	50.9
Allegheny	33 614	703 336	132 413	35 504	73 771	49 280	55 754	35 282	50 164	428	50.7	0.9	41.6
Armstrong	1 320	14 409	3 416	1 589	2 078	676	403	502	34 813	783	25.0	6.1	42.0
Beaver	3 445	50 618	10 155	8 058	7 158	889	2 460	1 919	37 921	646	45.2	1.9	47.5
Bedford	1 032	12 873	1 730	2 070	2 167	324	198	413	32 086	1 210	25.0	6.5	50.6
Berks	8 274	149 151	24 997	30 352	20 609	5 627	6 357	6 527	43 764	2 039	47.8	3.5	61.4
Blair	3 174	50 319	9 880	7 011	8 885	1 651	1 825	1 719	34 164	525	35.8	5.9	58.5
Bradford	1 383	19 952	4 702	3 427	3 081	799	551	841	42 154	1 629	25.8	7.6	45.8
Bucks	18 952	244 396	39 531	25 588	38 056	8 354	15 529	10 758	44 020	827	71.1	2.7	51.3
Butler	4 815	80 370	13 153	12 344	11 278	2 265	6 636	3 592	44 693	1 061	39.9	4.1	45.6
Cambria	3 286	47 647	12 045	4 518	6 896	2 073	2 695	1 646	34 546	551	33.4	5.6	37.4
Cameron	112	1 613	197	975	132	D	15	54	33 247	36	25.0	11.1	50.0
Carbon	1 140	13 372	2 991	1 738	2 114	302	209	389	29 067	195	46.2	2.6	37.4
Centre	3 290	45 984	8 657	3 989	8 015	1 281	3 096	1 715	37 296	1 192	40.1	4.8	57.4
Chester	14 024	244 291	33 700	15 880	28 935	24 842	23 578	16 298	66 713	1 730	57.1	2.5	60.7
Clarion	933	10 982	2 912	1 497	1 791	296	239	331	30 142	652	22.1	6.3	39.3
Clearfield	2 014	26 170	5 711	2 754	4 873	D	621	909	34 720	533	34.3	4.3	45.0
Clinton	760	10 657	1 348	2 843	1 829	D	215	379	35 575	469	37.1	3.8	51.0
Columbia	1 392	22 893	3 971	5 238	3 419	581	811	794	34 693	944	37.3	4.6	39.8
Crawford	2 020	27 502	5 262	7 233	3 737	540	774	915	33 258	1 351	31.1	6.0	51.5
Cumberland	5 805	115 978	16 720	8 699	16 050	9 482	8 278	5 019	43 271	1 415	47.0	3.5	53.1
Dauphin	6 718	141 108	32 987	7 881	15 338	10 140	7 144	6 806	48 229	811	49.0	2.7	44.9
Delaware	12 675	214 886	39 322	15 094	25 778	12 951	12 319	11 868	55 232	76	64.5	0.0	48.7
Elk	882	14 499	1 811	7 001	1 496	233	299	549	37 892	271	45.4	1.5	33.6
Erie	6 176	112 761	23 617	20 045	15 859	D	3 702	4 258	37 759	1 422	41.2	4.1	48.7
Fayette	2 676	36 687	7 739	3 156	6 199	591	1 108	1 226	33 424	941	34.0	3.4	47.8
Forest	107	1 225	466	D	100	D	D	39	31 751	56	25.0	3.6	41.1
Franklin	3 017	48 464	7 774	8 579	7 428	1 139	1 748	1 767	36 461	1 596	35.9	6.3	60.8
Fulton	262	D	D	D	336	D	D	D	D	656	22.6	5.2	38.6
Greene	762	14 203	1 314	357	2 365	317	257	754	53 060	876	27.2	3.3	40.4
Huntingdon	829	9 529	1 918	1 202	1 478	425	273	289	30 291	833	25.1	7.1	45.9
Indiana	1 894	26 933	4 559	2 325	5 250	D	996	1 010	37 517	1 166	38.0	3.9	50.2
Jefferson	1 147	14 023	2 942	3 388	1 754	276	428	501	35 754	577	25.0	5.7	51.5
Juniata	461	5 923	741	2 515	599	250	D	180	30 456	737	42.3	3.0	47.6
Lackawanna	5 372	96 324	24 583	8 710	12 955	5 491	3 110	3 360	34 879	303	25.1	1.3	43.6
Lancaster	12 414	220 898	35 953	33 882	30 338	7 163	10 311	8 931	40 430	5 657	44.1	1.3	72.2
Lawrence	1 994	27 359	6 917	3 793	3 532	1 222	768	947	34 603	659	33.4	3.6	50.4
Lebanon	2 641	44 254	8 264	9 055	6 853	950	1 133	1 589	35 898	1 219	48.2	2.3	58.9
Lehigh	8 448	169 299	38 179	17 315	21 701	5 969	6 801	8 530	50 384	486	58.8	5.8	56.2
Luzerne	7 169	131 081	24 572	16 629	18 295	5 024	6 192	4 894	37 339	556	38.8	3.6	42.3
Lycoming	2 826	46 628	8 577	7 926	7 682	1 521	1 606	1 773	38 027	1 207	32.4	3.7	44.0
McKean	1 044	13 223	2 627	3 353	1 779	D	203	473	35 792	290	37.2	3.1	36.9
Mercer	2 794	45 667	10 475	8 375	7 330	1 489	772	1 564	34 244	1 185	32.3	4.1	45.1
Mifflin	959	13 750	3 162	D	2 207	339	156	492	35 789	808	35.4	2.1	49.0
Monroe	3 350	45 985	6 674	D	9 468	966	2 836	1 728	37 576	283	53.0	2.5	55.1
Montgomery	25 984	495 469	78 354	39 959	59 048	36 123	45 955	29 282	59 099	596	75.2	1.0	55.0
Montour	450	14 550	7 421	D	717	D	480	950	65 324	459	43.1	1.5	45.3
Northampton	6 237	97 821	13 186	11 202	13 563	4 312	4 262	4 084	41 751	498	62.9	6.0	50.6
Northumberland	1 639	24 382	5 901	4 250	3 353	607	500	844	34 623	847	43.0	6.5	54.7
Perry	777	6 310	1 074	656	1 140	265	203	162	25 611	889	32.6	4.8	50.6
Philadelphia	27 395	594 334	143 942	21 182	51 258	29 363	47 386	32 447	54 594	22	81.8	0.0	45.5
Pike	886	8 200	979	D	1 917	172	226	214	26 043	50	46.0	14.0	34.0

Table B. States and Counties — **Agriculture**

STATE County	Land in farms — Acreage (1,000)	Percent change, 2007–2012	Acres — Average size of farm	Total irrigated (1,000)	Total cropland (1,000)	Value of land and buildings (dollars) — Average per farm	Average per acre	Value of machinery and equipment, average per farm (dollars)	Value of products sold — Total (mil dol)	Average per farm (dollars)	Percent from: Crops	Live-stock and poultry products	Percent of farms with sales of: $10,000 or more	$100,000 or more	Government payments — Total ($1,000)	Percent of farms
	117	118	119	120	121	122	123	124	125	126	127	128	129	130	131	132
OREGON—Cont'd																
Morrow	1 165	5.5	2 906	65.6	486.4	2 762 863	951	302 516	568.1	1 416 736	34.3	65.7	50.4	34.9	11 900	61.1
Multnomah	30	5.2	50	4.6	17.4	598 075	11 928	72 756	68.9	115 278	D	D	30.1	9.5	242	6.0
Polk	145	-13.1	127	20.4	101.0	777 650	6 141	85 558	149.8	131 099	77.6	22.4	33.3	12.8	912	16.1
Sherman	514	-0.1	2 762	2.2	365.1	1 645 672	596	308 538	54.5	292 914	D	D	61.8	44.6	8 820	93.5
Tillamook	37	-3.3	131	7.1	14.5	817 064	6 259	115 754	117.1	418 361	2.6	97.4	53.6	38.6	1 553	34.3
Umatilla	1 308	-9.6	816	147.8	769.7	1 332 795	1 633	163 995	423.3	264 089	87.9	12.1	42.1	22.2	18 381	40.8
Union	412	-15.6	497	49.0	119.2	768 875	1 548	101 823	68.4	82 473	75.0	25.0	39.0	12.2	2 713	30.0
Wallowa	453	-14.3	867	38.0	88.5	1 094 554	1 263	101 395	46.6	89 310	47.5	52.5	45.8	20.5	2 746	38.5
Wasco	1 427	50.3	2 130	50.6	210.0	1 605 100	753	118 193	89.8	134 005	88.7	11.3	41.3	18.4	6 871	39.3
Washington	136	6.1	83	20.3	82.0	774 189	9 371	81 491	238.0	144 840	94.7	5.3	38.5	12.8	1 544	15.0
Wheeler	649	-14.3	4 242	10.4	24.8	2 749 542	648	97 634	14.2	92 536	22.9	77.1	45.1	19.6	748	26.1
Yamhill	177	-1.9	87	22.1	108.5	801 316	9 162	76 411	280.9	138 487	78.9	21.1	32.8	10.8	2 466	16.2
PENNSYLVANIA	7 704	-1.3	130	39.0	4 546.1	704 712	5 425	89 730	7 400.8	124 783	37.6	62.4	48.1	19.9	86 359	27.0
Adams	171	-1.9	144	2.2	125.6	898 623	6 232	113 572	201.7	169 817	56.5	43.5	48.6	19.2	1 818	28.5
Allegheny	35	-8.4	81	0.2	14.1	428 841	5 269	53 269	10.4	24 292	84.2	15.8	31.3	5.1	41	7.9
Armstrong	129	5.6	165	0.2	66.6	474 018	2 875	83 686	35.9	45 800	56.3	43.7	42.1	9.2	924	24.8
Beaver	56	-16.8	86	0.2	28.5	415 333	4 809	67 373	20.9	32 373	52.0	48.0	32.8	6.0	500	16.1
Bedford	210	-0.6	173	0.1	104.3	640 069	3 692	95 976	122.8	101 504	29.7	70.3	48.1	21.7	1 863	29.4
Berks	234	5.2	115	1.6	182.3	1 015 554	8 859	120 253	528.7	259 299	42.6	57.4	58.5	30.2	3 646	28.3
Blair	90	3.1	172	0.3	63.3	783 611	4 565	106 916	107.7	205 145	16.2	83.8	54.1	29.0	1 416	32.6
Bradford	308	15.5	189	0.2	163.3	700 259	3 704	89 510	128.8	79 063	22.6	77.4	43.1	15.3	6 994	43.0
Bucks	64	-15.6	77	0.8	48.0	950 716	12 280	89 245	62.4	75 475	75.1	24.9	41.0	13.7	579	13.7
Butler	136	4.9	128	0.6	77.1	609 486	4 747	89 819	52.9	49 863	69.6	30.4	41.3	10.0	1 502	26.6
Cambria	77	-12.6	140	0.1	45.4	457 327	3 277	82 508	32.6	59 240	55.5	44.5	42.3	8.5	775	31.9
Cameron	6	22.1	173	0.0	1.6	337 472	1 955	55 528	0.7	19 222	45.4	54.6	44.4	0.0	55	38.9
Carbon	21	5.6	109	0.2	13.4	710 523	6 547	99 005	9.3	47 892	91.4	8.6	46.7	8.2	191	42.1
Centre	162	9.1	136	1.1	84.9	736 207	5 416	86 739	91.6	76 830	34.3	65.7	47.2	20.0	1 985	30.3
Chester	164	-1.4	95	1.2	107.1	1 242 743	13 070	110 712	660.7	381 933	81.0	19.0	52.6	27.7	1 631	15.8
Clarion	116	-12.2	178	0.1	60.5	524 998	2 951	75 406	36.1	55 423	55.7	44.3	41.7	10.3	960	33.3
Clearfield	69	10.4	130	0.1	34.8	344 137	2 649	68 355	13.7	25 687	53.2	46.8	36.4	6.9	392	21.6
Clinton	53	-6.9	112	0.8	29.1	608 542	5 414	85 166	60.6	129 122	20.2	79.8	57.1	31.8	951	29.2
Columbia	123	0.1	130	0.6	85.1	610 161	4 693	89 506	74.4	78 762	65.5	34.5	40.7	13.8	2 088	48.9
Crawford	228	-1.9	169	0.3	130.3	475 734	2 822	91 693	116.1	85 918	44.3	55.7	46.3	15.4	2 095	26.6
Cumberland	155	-1.6	109	1.6	119.7	853 018	7 793	95 594	195.4	138 061	30.4	69.6	55.3	26.6	1 997	28.5
Dauphin	129	44.5	160	0.7	60.0	724 409	4 541	94 716	122.6	151 158	23.4	76.6	49.3	20.1	724	27.1
Delaware	5	8.3	62	0.1	1.2	857 868	13 799	57 684	9.8	128 697	99.0	1.0	32.9	6.6	D	2.6
Elk	23	-29.4	87	0.0	9.7	296 376	3 420	49 461	4.2	15 605	47.6	52.4	30.6	2.2	66	8.5
Erie	169	-2.6	119	0.9	96.2	407 705	3 438	75 158	91.7	64 469	76.5	23.5	41.5	12.8	1 693	20.5
Fayette	113	-19.8	120	0.0	55.2	398 345	3 321	66 763	27.0	28 717	52.6	47.4	31.6	5.3	588	17.7
Forest	8	-22.8	148	0.0	2.5	356 125	2 408	69 071	1.8	32 500	38.8	61.2	35.7	5.4	25	17.9
Franklin	265	9.0	166	2.8	201.8	1 101 504	6 646	133 634	413.8	259 277	21.6	78.4	66.3	40.4	4 302	34.1
Fulton	112	8.4	171	0.1	61.1	622 541	3 639	84 477	53.0	80 755	24.7	75.3	41.9	12.0	1 033	53.5
Greene	112	-25.2	128	D	36.3	385 629	3 007	66 540	14.6	16 637	39.3	60.7	28.3	2.2	189	7.2
Huntingdon	158	6.8	190	0.8	77.2	728 200	3 832	89 801	93.5	112 249	19.5	80.5	42.3	14.4	2 274	35.4
Indiana	154	-18.1	132	D	85.4	369 054	2 799	70 768	67.3	57 725	58.4	41.6	38.3	9.9	1 078	22.7
Jefferson	91	4.9	158	0.1	53.2	410 645	2 596	71 778	27.7	48 057	44.9	55.1	44.5	10.2	436	16.1
Juniata	91	-6.8	124	0.3	53.8	622 389	5 039	92 383	101.4	137 639	14.1	85.9	51.4	24.6	1 913	44.6
Lackawanna	33	-17.6	108	0.1	16.1	529 017	4 894	68 812	13.2	43 687	71.2	28.8	32.0	7.3	127	17.5
Lancaster	439	3.3	78	6.1	332.0	973 388	12 509	101 987	1 475.0	260 731	17.7	82.3	74.2	48.4	5 843	18.4
Lawrence	80	-12.9	122	0.1	46.8	501 196	4 105	84 781	38.5	58 451	53.5	46.5	48.7	10.3	652	25.9
Lebanon	121	7.0	100	1.5	97.4	1 052 028	10 562	122 164	348.9	286 245	13.1	86.9	64.1	37.6	2 250	26.6
Lehigh	76	-9.8	157	0.8	63.2	1 308 144	8 329	109 327	90.8	186 899	69.6	30.4	51.4	14.4	701	25.3
Luzerne	61	-8.5	110	0.3	34.4	491 933	4 489	67 198	21.0	37 757	82.2	17.8	31.7	9.2	970	41.4
Lycoming	158	-1.2	131	0.6	79.7	559 934	4 265	73 065	72.2	59 819	53.8	46.2	41.6	13.2	2 246	39.1
McKean	36	-12.5	125	0.0	13.2	258 072	2 062	49 907	5.0	17 076	49.3	50.7	31.4	4.5	192	24.5
Mercer	163	-5.1	138	0.1	97.7	470 815	3 420	88 056	82.7	69 747	56.5	43.5	47.8	14.8	1 376	29.9
Mifflin	91	-3.8	112	0.1	53.2	550 040	4 908	76 090	94.0	116 365	17.7	82.3	55.6	24.8	1 361	26.6
Monroe	26	-9.2	94	0.1	13.0	735 583	7 861	71 198	11.0	38 777	66.8	33.2	35.7	8.5	174	15.5
Montgomery	31	-26.6	52	0.8	18.7	725 669	14 051	52 896	25.6	42 943	71.9	28.1	39.8	8.1	293	10.6
Montour	43	-13.5	95	0.1	29.6	519 508	5 483	62 275	47.4	103 322	60.1	39.9	44.2	17.6	678	36.4
Northampton	66	-3.7	132	0.3	55.6	1 084 882	8 218	115 108	43.5	87 341	82.9	17.1	44.6	16.9	845	23.3
Northumberland	130	-12.3	153	1.4	92.8	748 819	4 898	101 762	154.3	182 218	37.0	63.0	54.0	24.7	2 014	43.1
Perry	135	-6.4	152	0.3	81.3	767 425	5 051	104 962	140.4	157 931	19.7	80.3	52.2	25.5	1 816	36.2
Philadelphia	0	8.8	13	0.0	0.1	587 318	45 337	29 864	0.8	34 909	94.7	5.2	50.0	9.1	0	0.0
Pike	28	2.5	565	0.0	3.4	1 037 120	1 835	55 680	3.0	59 300	91.3	8.7	40.0	10.0	D	6.0

Table B. States and Counties — Water Use, Wholesale Trade, Retail Trade, and Real Estate

STATE County	Water use, 2010 Total water withdrawn (mil gal/day)	Gallons withdrawn per person per day	Wholesale trade,[1] 2012 Number of establish-ments	Number of employees	Sales (mil dol)	Annual payroll (mil dol)	Retail trade,[2] 2012 Number of establish-ments	Number of employees	Sales (mil dol)	Annual payroll (mil dol)	Real estate and rental and leasing,[2] 2012 Number of establish-ments	Number of employees	Receipts (mil dol)	Annual payroll (mil dol)
	133	134	135	136	137	138	139	140	141	142	143	144	145	146
OREGON—Cont'd														
Morrow	412.1	36 879	11	60	51.2	3.8	13	79	19.6	2.1	10	11	1.4	0.2
Multnomah	58.3	79	1 233	21 805	21 267.8	1 275.5	2 888	37 805	9 982.9	1 016.1	1 373	8 734	1 569.3	369.5
Polk	42.6	565	29	264	100.9	10.4	125	1 546	360.7	36.9	59	167	19.4	3.0
Sherman	11.3	6 380	4	D	D	D	7	D	D	D	NA	NA	NA	NA
Tillamook	47.5	1 882	9	105	42.3	3.2	114	1 032	248.9	24.4	27	91	8.0	1.7
Umatilla	383.3	5 051	65	953	738.7	45.4	224	2 922	802.8	70.8	60	148	21.1	4.0
Union	206.1	8 006	22	209	140.3	8.4	103	1 313	318.5	31.6	17	70	9.6	1.8
Wallowa	138.6	19 773	2	D	D	D	51	284	63.6	7.0	18	D	D	D
Wasco	125.6	4 982	25	628	213.6	14.6	123	1 506	389.4	37.1	42	102	10.9	2.6
Washington	103.5	195	734	9 915	8 667.6	618.5	1 573	28 336	8 389.7	790.3	809	4 492	1 207.1	158.0
Wheeler	35.9	24 892	1	D	D	D	6	D	D	D	2	D	D	D
Yamhill	75.7	763	70	D	D	D	283	3 325	886.6	84.9	102	263	36.4	6.1
PENNSYLVANIA	8 134.9	640	12 568	195 004	191 170.1	11 203.8	43 952	643 903	178 794.9	15 330.6	9 438	58 585	13 364.0	2 617.5
Adams	20.2	199	61	D	D	D	333	3 231	801.2	74.4	47	210	35.8	7.0
Allegheny	641.5	524	1 497	21 265	27 237.9	1 195.1	4 423	72 737	20 553.7	1 730.3	1 291	9 005	2 208.0	414.5
Armstrong	180.4	2 617	35	525	217.2	24.2	215	2 105	551.2	42.1	27	270	33.8	10.0
Beaver	432.3	2 535	112	1 508	1 179.5	74.3	517	7 307	1 590.2	149.3	92	398	83.2	14.2
Bedford	17.8	358	39	382	350.6	21.8	183	2 088	576.2	43.0	11	86	21.2	4.9
Berks	57.1	139	354	6 912	4 277.4	362.2	1 256	20 219	5 719.4	494.3	246	1 249	213.0	41.4
Blair	22.8	179	119	1 832	2 258.4	80.7	561	8 383	2 286.7	189.4	87	349	72.9	11.3
Bradford	11.9	191	49	D	D	D	252	3 127	903.7	72.7	30	223	52.6	9.9
Bucks	182.4	292	1 152	14 950	12 999.7	854.9	2 408	38 063	10 185.1	975.9	589	3 494	855.9	147.2
Butler	15.7	85	253	4 444	3 353.8	249.0	680	11 085	2 902.2	245.0	148	714	160.4	23.9
Cambria	27.1	189	115	1 365	664.9	51.0	561	6 927	1 733.8	148.6	86	408	48.3	12.2
Cameron	0.8	157	2	D	D	D	17	174	30.9	3.3	1	D	D	D
Carbon	25.1	385	19	D	D	D	194	2 142	562.6	49.3	36	121	21.1	3.4
Centre	45.4	295	90	873	538.9	42.5	481	7 570	1 748.7	155.7	133	1 036	255.5	34.7
Chester	191.4	384	711	12 642	19 155.1	1 204.8	1 517	27 549	12 474.9	984.2	457	2 360	781.2	143.1
Clarion	5.1	126	30	385	167.3	14.2	185	1 879	460.4	40.7	21	104	11.0	3.4
Clearfield	304.3	3 727	68	771	703.6	30.4	350	4 731	1 331.3	105.4	43	344	35.9	8.7
Clinton	16.9	430	18	D	D	D	121	1 773	582.6	39.5	37	165	26.6	4.3
Columbia	10.4	155	46	419	118.4	15.8	236	3 413	904.8	70.4	43	205	33.9	6.4
Crawford	14.0	157	57	372	136.3	12.8	317	3 577	973.5	85.5	51	176	24.5	4.3
Cumberland	33.0	140	189	2 607	2 666.3	124.9	858	16 016	4 812.9	376.3	222	1 366	316.8	66.3
Dauphin	100.4	374	295	6 839	6 655.5	390.2	981	15 280	3 943.9	348.2	218	1 608	505.1	90.5
Delaware	782.2	1 399	522	6 961	5 482.3	536.3	1 700	24 271	6 468.8	602.2	409	2 945	776.4	169.8
Elk	21.6	676	26	D	D	D	124	1 496	314.5	28.8	11	46	6.3	1.2
Erie	49.4	176	264	3 127	1 242.5	145.7	958	15 221	3 752.8	326.4	182	1 042	158.5	32.3
Fayette	45.1	330	107	1 002	496.6	37.7	487	6 040	1 638.8	129.7	69	299	50.9	9.9
Forest	2.0	264	1	D	D	D	18	101	24.8	2.0	1	D	D	D
Franklin	19.1	127	108	D	D	D	486	7 106	1 809.5	157.6	87	328	54.9	10.4
Fulton	2.9	193	12	142	139.8	4.6	42	374	102.9	7.3	3	12	1.2	0.5
Greene	35.7	922	26	350	302.8	17.5	138	2 444	883.7	63.3	12	47	6.7	1.1
Huntingdon	14.0	306	29	344	94.9	11.6	141	1 424	354.3	28.8	10	28	9.8	1.0
Indiana	59.8	673	67	D	D	D	309	5 016	1 318.8	112.7	45	163	26.2	3.8
Jefferson	4.7	105	39	441	245.5	17.9	176	1 857	556.2	37.7	24	128	32.2	4.6
Juniata	3.8	154	18	133	54.5	5.0	69	601	204.4	13.1	6	12	1.3	0.2
Lackawanna	52.1	243	251	3 800	4 374.5	168.9	916	13 197	3 186.3	278.2	138	690	128.5	21.1
Lancaster	78.2	151	582	10 776	8 764.0	496.7	1 917	29 783	6 899.6	669.6	342	2 009	396.6	79.1
Lawrence	100.3	1 101	86	D	D	D	292	3 391	838.7	75.6	44	279	29.7	7.0
Lebanon	14.6	109	99	2 679	3 913.7	112.7	431	6 597	1 695.7	158.6	70	309	40.5	7.8
Lehigh	50.9	146	408	9 182	8 062.4	577.2	1 239	20 261	5 550.4	467.5	315	1 587	324.0	58.2
Luzerne	85.3	266	300	5 656	3 435.9	242.3	1 247	18 177	8 097.0	413.8	210	923	214.7	34.0
Lycoming	16.0	138	108	2 110	1 271.2	82.6	503	7 404	1 878.1	154.7	89	618	120.0	24.4
McKean	12.9	298	31	D	D	D	158	1 551	401.8	34.7	16	62	6.4	1.4
Mercer	30.6	263	89	1 099	644.7	42.4	516	7 109	1 527.3	147.2	72	275	101.6	7.8
Mifflin	9.3	199	35	D	D	D	162	2 063	539.4	46.9	23	71	11.0	1.7
Monroe	33.1	195	97	D	D	D	634	8 710	2 140.4	187.8	123	507	86.8	15.2
Montgomery	114.8	143	1 237	19 422	17 692.1	1 444.8	3 261	56 471	16 036.3	1 489.8	931	7 713	1 767.3	412.8
Montour	18.8	1 030	13	149	190.2	6.1	54	662	167.2	13.6	6	18	2.9	0.6
Northampton	267.2	897	250	3 917	9 979.8	192.8	873	13 238	3 627.4	316.9	178	726	260.6	27.4
Northumberland	22.9	242	56	945	1 152.0	46.6	280	3 188	909.7	76.7	38	182	37.4	7.7
Perry	3.9	85	16	144	81.4	6.1	134	1 166	317.8	25.6	10	23	3.4	0.7
Philadelphia	374.8	246	1 047	16 940	13 181.9	973.0	4 506	50 185	12 241.3	1 165.5	1 079	8 856	1 951.0	443.5
Pike	4.6	79	15	98	31.8	5.4	134	1 862	471.4	40.0	40	442	41.9	10.9

1. Merchant wholesalers, except manufacturers' sales branches and offices.   2. Employer establishments.

Table B. States and Counties — Professional Services, Manufacturing, and Accommodation and Food Services

STATE County	Professional, scientific, and technical services, 2012				Manufacturing, 2012				Accommodation and food services, 2012			
	Number of establish- ments	Number of employees	Receipts (mil dol)	Annual payroll (mil dol)	Number of establish- ments	Number of employees	Receipts (mil dol)	Annual payroll (mil dol)	Number of establish- ments	Number of employees	Sales (mil dol)	Annual payroll (mil dol)
	147	148	149	150	151	152	153	154	155	156	157	158
OREGON—Cont'd												
Morrow	3	6	1.2	0.2	11	1 120	753.5	46.9	19	125	6.8	2.0
Multnomah	3 682	31 457	5 611.6	2 186.1	1 095	32 206	10 278.1	1 633.4	2 799	42 709	2 506.2	736.3
Polk	117	407	36.2	12.6	60	1 801	424.7	68.1	142	D	D	D
Sherman	1	D	D	D	NA	NA	NA	NA	7	60	4.6	1.2
Tillamook	41	D	D	D	30	1 224	708.3	55.8	120	950	51.2	14.5
Umatilla	102	844	74.3	36.3	70	2 522	858.1	90.3	163	2 903	194.5	47.1
Union	47	225	19.2	7.9	28	1 097	275.9	43.1	65	806	33.8	9.4
Wallowa	24	82	7.5	2.6	15	85	D	2.9	47	139	9.7	2.3
Wasco	48	267	25.0	10.0	30	273	93.6	10.8	85	1 288	66.7	20.8
Washington	1 750	21 129	1 788.4	2 119.1	708	D	D	D	1 141	17 404	970.6	277.9
Wheeler	NA	NA	NA	NA	NA	NA	NA	NA	5	18	0.9	0.2
Yamhill	200	638	67.4	24.7	225	5 407	1 893.6	280.4	195	2 486	129.3	40.0
PENNSYLVANIA	29 297	316 658	54 833.8	22 621.5	13 988	543 641	231 396.2	28 057.8	27 646	439 159	23 504.2	6 377.4
Adams	126	D	D	D	113	5 745	2 148.7	240.8	222	3 521	185.7	53.0
Allegheny	3 864	59 880	11 007.2	4 362.7	1 086	36 428	16 279.5	2 073.3	3 170	57 039	2 940.6	827.4
Armstrong	77	361	37.8	11.5	65	1 468	324.1	62.6	95	1 153	42.7	11.0
Beaver	254	3 560	262.0	143.0	175	7 556	4 615.0	397.5	309	4 456	191.8	51.1
Bedford	45	194	18.5	4.7	64	2 065	863.0	83.5	107	1 607	78.6	24.7
Berks	703	D	D	D	498	29 439	10 905.1	1 547.9	754	12 294	548.8	155.6
Blair	221	1 789	208.3	74.8	135	6 943	2 115.6	298.8	280	4 634	199.4	56.5
Bradford	88	549	64.0	21.4	61	3 921	1 975.5	185.0	125	1 576	76.2	20.4
Bucks	2 331	18 164	3 140.0	1 196.9	1 045	27 061	9 681.4	1 428.8	1 385	21 398	1 136.1	302.9
Butler	426	7 354	2 293.3	622.6	266	12 782	4 630.0	687.1	363	6 841	326.6	89.7
Cambria	228	3 359	380.3	168.2	127	5 232	1 798.8	241.6	300	4 070	179.0	47.8
Cameron	6	D	D	D	23	858	D	38.2	13	D	D	D
Carbon	60	241	19.8	9.7	55	1 678	415.0	68.8	116	1 939	112.0	29.9
Centre	365	3 204	432.1	191.2	145	3 960	1 053.5	181.9	311	6 352	289.0	79.7
Chester	2 239	20 472	4 199.5	1 774.2	533	16 067	6 633.5	961.4	932	15 867	846.1	251.0
Clarion	38	238	22.1	9.9	33	1 293	471.2	52.1	95	1 400	57.4	14.2
Clearfield	106	610	56.1	19.7	108	2 613	962.4	99.9	179	2 407	99.5	27.1
Clinton	48	235	24.0	7.9	47	2 836	1 676.8	130.3	83	1 266	58.0	15.3
Columbia	92	677	54.0	22.0	73	5 484	1 613.4	224.9	159	2 484	109.3	29.6
Crawford	115	800	84.1	32.2	277	7 093	1 759.2	318.1	185	2 349	102.8	27.4
Cumberland	649	7 932	1 161.1	522.0	186	7 550	3 776.4	353.2	506	9 403	465.0	129.1
Dauphin	712	7 608	1 178.0	481.8	186	7 679	3 228.9	404.2	679	12 533	718.3	199.6
Delaware	1 525	12 084	2 383.7	903.0	367	12 929	7 364.9	974.8	1 105	16 283	878.1	236.0
Elk	40	1 020	26.4	17.0	135	6 587	1 732.6	295.0	72	763	28.3	7.1
Erie	412	3 028	375.8	135.3	476	21 490	9 437.7	1 179.0	630	10 877	485.4	128.2
Fayette	137	961	143.0	40.5	111	3 088	1 324.2	157.8	285	4 101	211.8	62.0
Forest	2	D	D	D	5	D	D	D	21	125	7.5	1.8
Franklin	223	2 067	234.8	100.3	196	8 182	3 180.0	403.9	270	D	D	D
Fulton	12	31	1.8	0.5	15	D	D	D	18	255	10.5	3.1
Greene	39	230	23.1	7.4	24	370	101.5	15.8	59	1 087	53.3	14.4
Huntingdon	54	256	17.5	7.6	43	1 884	667.4	75.8	84	964	50.3	13.6
Indiana	125	D	D	D	89	2 570	509.6	101.4	178	2 955	117.6	30.0
Jefferson	69	380	42.1	13.9	101	3 475	887.6	151.7	94	942	41.6	10.2
Juniata	22	60	4.3	1.1	59	1 977	337.1	64.7	31	371	15.4	4.4
Lackawanna	488	2 922	363.3	132.4	237	8 611	D	370.4	590	8 685	411.7	107.9
Lancaster	957	12 486	1 249.1	1 037.2	856	33 212	13 655.7	1 638.7	998	17 833	878.4	246.9
Lawrence	138	D	D	D	140	3 465	1 819.4	192.3	163	2 163	89.0	23.9
Lebanon	197	1 083	151.2	48.6	205	8 099	2 743.8	336.5	232	3 320	146.1	40.5
Lehigh	754	D	D	D	378	15 977	9 889.5	867.6	735	12 283	633.0	175.9
Luzerne	575	5 266	528.3	207.3	314	16 701	6 628.0	728.6	740	10 730	515.6	134.1
Lycoming	200	2 151	184.5	74.5	160	8 162	3 186.7	371.5	296	4 696	237.9	62.6
McKean	60	202	16.3	6.2	51	3 290	1 615.8	170.4	102	954	44.6	11.3
Mercer	164	801	77.1	26.6	186	7 405	3 309.4	351.2	254	4 138	188.3	47.6
Mifflin	38	164	11.7	3.6	86	3 696	1 163.0	184.0	84	1 107	45.2	12.3
Monroe	306	D	D	D	111	4 449	D	358.1	387	8 392	724.8	155.1
Montgomery	3 696	45 260	7 823.6	3 663.3	987	39 566	14 574.7	2 433.5	1 901	29 320	1 723.2	489.4
Montour	37	449	134.9	25.4	18	424	140.7	13.9	39	708	38.7	9.9
Northampton	590	4 342	588.8	252.6	328	11 374	4 081.2	571.4	678	11 011	941.1	198.3
Northumberland	104	534	45.0	17.4	78	3 710	1 194.3	150.7	172	1 549	66.2	17.8
Perry	50	218	18.1	6.6	36	665	102.6	22.0	71	449	21.1	5.2
Philadelphia	2 845	47 158	10 464.6	4 249.2	765	22 558	19 718.6	1 198.5	3 669	53 533	3 551.7	982.4
Pike	77	243	30.6	8.6	20	150	27.1	6.2	103	1 826	127.2	36.3

1. Establishment subject to federal tax.

STATE County	Health care and social assistance, 2012				Other services, 2012				Nonemployer businesses, 2014		Value of residential construction authorized by building permits, 2015	
	Number of establishments	Number of employees	Receipts (mil dol)	Annual payroll (mil dol)	Number of establishments	Number of employees	Receipts (mil dol)	Annual payroll (mil dol)	Number	Receipts (mil dol)	New Construction ($1,000)	Number of housing units
	159	160	161	162	163	164	165	166	167	168	169	170
OREGON—Cont'd												
Morrow	15	139	9.8	3.6	12	31	2.8	0.8	516	24.8	3 624	15
Multnomah	2 950	62 033	7 703.7	2 988.1	1 867	12 391	1 810.6	423.2	65 899	3 148.0	768 440	4 832
Polk	191	2 531	168.6	75.0	87	332	25.7	7.5	4 009	159.4	60 198	293
Sherman	4	23	0.3	0.1	2	D	D	D	105	4.4	NA	NA
Tillamook	52	810	87.3	36.0	44	D	D	D	1 826	83.3	23 055	98
Umatilla	207	2 923	312.6	115.8	104	500	58.4	17.3	3 401	146.6	16 112	84
Union	103	1 388	127.5	55.3	54	D	D	D	1 577	60.5	4 659	19
Wallowa	35	412	33.9	13.4	19	D	D	D	747	32.5	3 722	16
Wasco	74	1 769	148.2	78.4	48	173	13.4	4.1	1 373	50.6	NA	NA
Washington	1 722	25 903	3 238.1	1 205.9	843	5 106	530.2	179.2	35 141	1 690.0	652 401	3 338
Wheeler	5	D	D	D	1	D	D	D	144	5.9	NA	NA
Yamhill	260	4 241	433.6	151.6	133	D	D	D	5 690	253.5	92 837	349
PENNSYLVANIA	36 552	955 479	96 329.2	39 326.6	25 231	154 319	17 736.7	4 366.6	799 663	38 648.9	4 406 389	22 854
Adams	182	4 634	448.2	167.1	150	909	75.1	19.8	6 475	266.9	50 501	240
Allegheny	4 423	123 336	12 756.2	5 392.7	2 872	19 874	2 346.4	604.4	77 932	3 680.4	533 473	2 957
Armstrong	188	3 504	246.4	106.5	113	499	38.4	10.5	3 574	153.2	4 854	25
Beaver	470	9 380	779.6	351.2	316	1 324	113.6	30.6	8 601	343.1	23 399	104
Bedford	120	1 769	148.9	54.8	95	373	27.1	6.8	3 268	152.2	7 610	49
Berks	827	25 605	2 588.9	1 067.0	767	4 046	363.5	101.5	24 160	1 132.4	74 107	416
Blair	438	11 356	1 149.5	472.4	283	1 573	118.4	36.7	6 089	289.5	24 723	117
Bradford	148	4 744	561.0	228.0	120	558	43.9	11.3	3 495	155.4	22 837	121
Bucks	2 014	40 065	3 735.6	1 582.5	1 424	8 400	746.1	234.1	51 033	2 893.1	221 571	1 066
Butler	608	12 564	1 198.6	493.0	388	2 309	203.4	54.3	11 596	547.1	220 826	964
Cambria	540	11 708	1 047.3	444.7	312	1 690	133.9	34.2	6 180	249.2	12 406	47
Cameron	11	D	D	D	11	62	3.5	0.6	224	7.7	0	0
Carbon	160	3 302	219.0	97.4	91	310	28.7	6.8	3 334	144.8	10 153	59
Centre	363	7 882	767.4	316.6	249	1 471	131.7	37.0	9 489	454.0	91 172	389
Chester	1 440	34 065	3 442.7	1 431.8	1 042	8 068	1 969.8	300.6	41 146	2 480.8	218 678	1 299
Clarion	137	3 052	197.3	84.0	72	494	53.1	11.3	2 401	112.3	13 169	73
Clearfield	260	6 187	576.4	238.7	165	1 169	90.7	26.1	4 235	176.9	19 561	192
Clinton	71	1 241	98.3	39.3	66	315	30.9	5.5	1 837	73.3	7 196	41
Columbia	164	D	D	D	114	493	48.6	9.8	3 198	135.2	29 275	153
Crawford	238	5 129	424.6	183.6	174	816	70.2	16.4	5 472	238.0	11 866	57
Cumberland	662	15 684	1 650.9	675.6	535	4 185	521.6	130.0	15 332	758.5	141 630	831
Dauphin	820	26 291	2 182.0	899.1	685	4 728	580.5	175.7	15 753	716.2	117 872	715
Delaware	1 608	39 002	3 952.6	1 724.6	1 116	6 740	863.0	212.3	40 100	2 078.5	80 975	349
Elk	108	2 117	146.6	66.5	78	340	21.9	5.4	1 601	64.8	5 395	40
Erie	850	24 899	2 216.5	923.1	563	3 591	322.7	80.2	13 951	595.0	43 855	267
Fayette	408	7 929	619.8	259.5	240	1 181	118.1	28.1	6 245	266.3	38 506	164
Forest	10	456	35.9	14.2	6	13	1.2	0.2	273	11.0	454	2
Franklin	305	8 178	820.5	349.3	287	1 558	131.5	32.7	8 944	380.5	44 392	231
Fulton	25	D	D	D	27	97	9.7	2.1	950	42.6	4 974	26
Greene	105	1 588	141.3	52.5	72	369	46.9	10.3	1 543	63.3	6 773	36
Huntingdon	95	1 859	147.4	61.7	79	301	27.3	5.5	2 492	106.9	9 652	48
Indiana	252	4 406	360.6	149.4	151	954	109.1	25.6	4 941	231.6	10 245	53
Jefferson	150	2 991	236.6	100.0	103	426	32.6	7.9	2 950	132.9	746	6
Juniata	34	561	37.3	14.2	32	108	9.9	2.5	1 817	90.5	6 661	35
Lackawanna	730	19 120	1 805.5	768.9	401	2 181	180.8	53.0	11 916	577.3	133 851	593
Lancaster	1 110	34 977	3 387.5	1 411.1	1 031	6 339	588.6	161.3	40 764	2 115.6	214 161	1 154
Lawrence	291	6 467	501.7	214.0	174	853	71.5	19.5	4 960	209.9	9 390	53
Lebanon	279	8 165	772.4	341.9	233	1 086	110.1	27.5	8 107	366.2	60 062	384
Lehigh	1 170	40 184	4 351.2	1 715.9	719	4 730	428.3	127.0	21 794	961.0	132 327	680
Luzerne	967	23 680	2 273.1	934.5	559	2 803	292.8	71.8	16 573	811.6	44 264	204
Lycoming	287	8 233	825.8	345.7	240	1 546	152.8	35.4	6 190	282.6	37 055	159
McKean	151	2 764	209.7	88.5	95	472	37.9	9.1	2 112	86.1	4 808	30
Mercer	410	10 413	866.4	358.8	251	1 144	97.7	22.7	6 479	308.5	21 603	107
Mifflin	127	3 113	251.0	104.4	67	249	21.1	5.2	2 646	111.7	10 504	66
Monroe	393	7 031	643.1	276.0	309	1 571	115.7	37.0	10 218	466.0	35 527	152
Montgomery	3 023	71 373	7 980.2	3 199.4	1 908	11 847	1 609.1	359.9	68 190	4 194.8	257 643	1 402
Montour	100	D	D	D	35	234	62.0	8.7	1 045	47.5	6 891	37
Northampton	776	13 343	1 137.2	468.0	547	2 875	233.2	71.8	17 553	848.2	64 627	328
Northumberland	206	5 305	340.8	149.5	146	772	46.7	13.8	4 434	203.8	9 646	51
Perry	80	1 007	49.6	23.6	65	245	22.9	4.8	2 863	121.6	16 078	69
Philadelphia	3 920	152 972	17 972.6	6 847.5	2 493	17 972	2 408.7	632.4	84 805	3 153.2	690 914	3 666
Pike	86	961	64.2	26.0	97	950	70.1	19.4	3 803	179.5	20 722	76

STATE County	Government employment and payroll, 2012									Local government finances, 2012				
	Full-time equivalent employees	March payroll (dollars)	March payroll (percent of total)							General revenue				
													Taxes	
			Administration, judicial, and legal	Police and Corrections	Fire Protection	Highways and transportation	Health and Welfare	Natural resources and utilities	Education and libraries	Total (mil dol)	Intergovernmental (mil dol)	Total (mil dol)	Per capita[1] (dollars)	
													Total	Property
	171	172	173	174	175	176	177	178	179	180	181	182	183	184
OREGON—Cont'd														
Morrow	611	2 174 057	7.8	9.3	1.6	5.2	17.4	6.6	45.7	79.1	31.3	21.7	1 928	1 801
Multnomah	29 478	148 927 675	7.5	11.9	4.2	13.6	6.4	9.0	42.8	4 680.8	1 700.4	1 856.1	2 445	1 660
Polk	1 230	4 842 625	12.3	13.6	2.4	1.9	8.6	6.6	52.1	138.5	77.6	42.1	552	500
Sherman	121	446 146	20.7	9.6	8.8	9.9	11.4	7.5	29.5	23.4	4.3	6.6	3 808	3 775
Tillamook	1 081	4 310 792	8.6	7.5	1.5	5.0	4.7	26.1	44.4	116.8	36.6	46.1	1 822	1 701
Umatilla	2 519	9 346 604	6.6	11.0	3.9	3.0	1.9	7.4	65.3	307.6	163.2	86.2	1 122	1 020
Union	750	2 655 712	8.7	12.0	2.8	4.4	0.9	8.8	60.1	87.0	50.9	20.7	802	722
Wallowa	382	1 406 470	6.1	5.5	0.3	3.8	43.8	3.1	36.5	46.2	14.1	8.6	1 262	1 113
Wasco	982	3 676 060	6.9	6.4	4.7	3.8	3.2	15.2	58.1	115.4	52.3	37.4	1 468	1 319
Washington	14 620	63 993 061	6.8	11.2	6.7	2.5	2.0	7.5	60.1	1 882.7	665.8	834.1	1 523	1 366
Wheeler	106	329 289	21.3	2.9	0.0	9.3	0.0	7.4	57.6	8.1	5.1	1.6	1 126	1 092
Yamhill	2 820	11 200 226	7.7	9.1	4.6	1.7	6.0	8.9	59.7	320.3	146.1	104.5	1 043	942
PENNSYLVANIA	X	X	X	X	X	X	X	X	X	X	X	X	X	X
Adams	2 548	9 790 732	7.8	9.5	0.9	2.6	2.1	3.4	73.2	374.0	165.8	167.3	1 648	1 256
Allegheny	43 945	195 375 705	6.5	12.8	2.4	11.5	5.4	5.9	53.8	6 769.1	2 823.5	2 739.2	2 228	1 525
Armstrong	2 222	7 529 691	6.9	7.0	0.0	4.1	6.8	5.5	68.9	227.1	114.7	81.0	1 185	1 004
Beaver	5 422	21 094 763	6.4	10.1	0.3	4.8	6.7	6.8	64.1	785.3	350.5	233.6	1 372	1 124
Bedford	1 369	4 444 835	5.3	5.6	0.8	4.2	1.7	5.0	77.4	128.7	70.2	45.3	918	675
Berks	14 566	69 528 665	6.1	16.3	5.1	2.6	4.7	5.3	58.7	2 039.3	792.5	835.6	2 021	1 642
Blair	4 030	13 533 958	4.8	8.4	2.3	5.0	8.5	7.0	62.6	402.4	214.5	126.2	993	707
Bradford	2 246	8 350 493	7.8	4.9	0.5	5.3	11.4	1.9	67.4	247.1	119.2	78.6	1 252	972
Bucks	18 333	88 124 851	6.0	11.7	0.6	4.0	4.0	3.9	68.9	2 731.2	688.4	1 517.1	2 419	2 074
Butler	4 890	20 031 417	6.5	6.1	0.5	3.3	5.6	4.7	72.2	629.8	252.7	262.6	1 420	1 090
Cambria	4 484	15 273 184	8.2	8.3	1.4	5.9	5.7	6.0	63.9	555.1	293.7	143.3	1 012	781
Cameron	214	664 238	8.3	4.9	0.0	5.0	7.5	2.5	70.2	17.3	9.0	6.0	1 223	1 052
Carbon	2 113	7 282 054	7.7	9.6	0.0	3.5	11.6	5.7	60.5	211.1	71.9	108.6	1 671	1 438
Centre	3 965	14 048 206	7.5	8.6	0.0	7.9	9.9	5.8	58.3	455.2	154.4	216.4	1 394	1 018
Chester	13 231	61 935 244	7.1	9.3	0.2	2.2	4.5	2.8	71.3	2 107.9	567.4	1 254.5	2 476	2 063
Clarion	1 226	4 224 897	6.3	6.9	0.0	3.1	1.8	3.0	78.3	155.3	103.3	39.4	993	773
Clearfield	2 608	9 251 789	4.9	5.4	0.0	3.3	1.6	4.7	78.9	261.5	141.7	88.1	1 086	853
Clinton	1 129	4 364 621	9.8	5.9	2.2	2.6	11.0	7.0	59.8	138.0	54.0	44.3	1 121	835
Columbia	1 917	7 059 353	6.5	11.0	0.0	3.3	2.0	3.1	73.5	197.2	86.4	83.5	1 248	914
Crawford	2 501	8 880 019	8.6	8.3	1.6	5.0	10.3	5.8	59.4	270.2	125.4	98.7	1 127	906
Cumberland	7 023	27 433 306	6.6	8.7	0.0	2.7	6.7	4.9	68.9	914.8	308.3	434.2	1 820	1 330
Dauphin	10 041	42 265 280	7.7	13.4	1.0	4.7	1.7	5.4	64.3	1 441.8	522.5	527.9	1 958	1 407
Delaware	18 047	76 207 314	10.5	9.6	1.0	2.0	6.2	4.1	65.6	2 712.5	932.9	1 199.8	2 138	1 938
Elk	1 009	3 366 414	8.9	6.3	0.0	12.9	2.6	6.2	61.7	108.1	52.0	37.3	1 181	901
Erie	8 523	32 472 819	5.3	9.7	2.6	5.6	3.9	6.0	65.7	1 197.6	616.5	364.0	1 297	1 046
Fayette	3 546	14 568 652	6.8	9.1	0.4	5.2	7.7	9.3	61.2	411.7	262.1	104.7	772	570
Forest	197	632 875	20.3	3.4	0.0	3.6	5.7	3.9	62.0	19.5	9.4	7.5	980	863
Franklin	3 820	13 644 359	7.7	8.8	1.7	2.3	9.1	6.1	63.5	415.1	130.8	191.4	1 265	978
Fulton	454	1 468 178	11.3	2.6	0.0	2.5	0.0	2.1	81.0	47.4	25.7	16.4	1 112	912
Greene	1 301	4 613 569	10.4	5.2	0.0	6.2	4.1	7.8	65.3	144.0	67.6	57.8	1 518	1 258
Huntingdon	1 125	3 453 282	9.3	7.1	0.0	3.2	3.8	5.2	70.1	118.4	66.3	38.4	837	613
Indiana	2 289	9 093 274	6.9	6.4	0.1	4.5	4.9	5.1	70.9	313.8	170.3	97.7	1 107	879
Jefferson	1 211	4 334 856	6.6	7.0	0.0	4.9	1.4	6.4	72.3	125.7	68.4	38.4	858	661
Juniata	563	1 993 044	11.0	5.3	1.3	2.6	0.1	1.9	75.5	49.2	23.8	21.6	867	690
Lackawanna	6 361	25 493 690	6.8	11.8	3.2	4.1	6.5	6.5	59.1	757.3	291.3	324.8	1 515	1 101
Lancaster	12 622	54 624 168	5.9	11.7	0.8	2.8	3.4	3.5	70.9	1 833.2	668.6	843.7	1 601	1 327
Lawrence	2 433	9 509 559	8.0	8.4	1.5	4.9	1.0	3.8	71.8	318.9	174.0	106.5	1 185	905
Lebanon	4 116	14 939 586	6.1	9.0	1.7	2.8	9.0	5.5	65.4	485.8	160.6	191.5	1 416	1 136
Lehigh	11 303	49 829 858	7.3	10.7	1.9	4.5	9.3	4.5	60.4	1 670.5	674.3	669.0	1 883	1 523
Luzerne	9 404	36 055 331	7.5	12.5	3.5	3.7	4.7	5.2	62.1	1 080.5	466.5	439.6	1 369	1 039
Lycoming	3 615	14 906 594	7.7	7.9	1.8	4.3	2.7	6.0	68.7	451.3	198.0	155.7	1 329	953
McKean	1 616	5 647 554	6.9	7.4	1.5	4.5	8.7	8.2	62.2	167.7	97.2	44.6	1 033	829
Mercer	3 570	12 446 506	8.5	9.8	1.2	3.2	1.2	4.2	70.1	402.4	216.5	133.0	1 150	861
Mifflin	1 135	4 324 228	8.8	6.8	1.1	5.0	2.7	9.1	64.8	153.4	81.3	46.8	1 002	733
Monroe	5 957	25 067 544	5.7	4.3	0.0	5.4	1.6	1.5	80.9	719.0	225.3	441.5	2 616	2 404
Montgomery	23 690	112 151 487	6.4	12.2	0.4	2.4	5.0	4.0	68.6	3 430.1	888.0	2 054.1	2 541	2 087
Montour	515	1 746 307	6.4	6.4	0.0	4.4	0.9	6.3	73.4	92.9	26.6	26.3	1 431	915
Northampton	10 782	47 706 434	7.1	11.9	1.8	2.5	7.7	4.9	61.8	1 411.9	496.8	671.7	2 244	1 804
Northumberland	3 162	10 304 053	9.0	7.6	0.0	3.1	16.2	4.4	59.0	273.2	137.2	88.2	934	631
Perry	1 241	4 130 390	6.3	5.0	0.0	3.3	5.0	1.5	77.8	139.6	62.3	60.0	1 312	977
Philadelphia	60 937	311 591 353	8.6	18.6	4.6	16.9	6.0	8.1	36.4	11 133.9	5 530.3	4 080.0	2 636	743
Pike	1 166	4 430 795	9.4	13.5	0.0	2.5	4.3	1.7	67.0	128.4	48.7	71.2	1 252	1 185

1. Based on the resident population estimated as of July 1 of the year shown.

Table B. States and Counties — Local Government Finances, Government Employment, and Voting

STATE County	Local government finances, 2012 (cont.) Direct general expenditure							Debt outstanding		Government employment, 2014			Presidential election,[2] 2012 Percent of vote cast:		
	Total (mil dol)	Per capita[1] (dollars)	Education	Health and hospitals	Police protection	Public welfare	Highways	Total (mil dol)	Per capita[1] (dollars)	Federal civilian	Federal military	State and local	Democratic	Republican	All other
	185	186	187	188	189	190	191	192	193	194	195	196	197	198	199
OREGON—Cont'd															
Morrow	78.1	6 947	32.8	11.0	4.6	0.3	5.8	136.8	12 168	58	36	737	34.7	61.8	3.4
Multnomah	4 425.0	5 828	31.5	4.6	5.2	4.0	6.5	7 864.7	10 358	12 270	2 430	58 086	76.7	20.6	2.7
Polk	140.8	1 844	43.0	8.4	8.3	1.0	5.6	271.5	3 556	73	206	4 988	48.4	48.9	2.6
Sherman	18.9	10 932	20.7	4.0	4.0	1.4	11.8	3.5	2 023	133	0	185	36.8	60.6	2.7
Tillamook	118.4	4 684	38.3	7.8	3.6	0.3	5.5	166.8	6 595	109	105	1 649	53.2	43.3	3.5
Umatilla	311.2	4 051	58.5	1.4	4.4	0.0	4.1	422.0	5 493	513	198	6 211	37.2	59.8	3.1
Union	90.0	3 495	44.0	3.4	5.7	0.4	5.1	30.5	1 185	231	68	2 013	36.6	60.2	3.2
Wallowa	44.0	6 453	31.6	33.8	3.6	0.8	8.6	38.3	5 620	95	18	506	33.4	63.5	3.1
Wasco	106.5	4 180	48.5	2.2	4.8	0.4	4.4	159.3	6 251	284	67	1 686	51.9	44.8	3.3
Washington	1 940.6	3 543	44.5	2.9	7.1	0.0	5.6	2 532.1	4 623	714	1 507	20 127	59.8	37.7	2.5
Wheeler	9.5	6 659	47.9	0.8	2.6	1.5	12.0	2.0	1 419	0	0	108	34.6	61.3	4.1
Yamhill	320.3	3 195	49.5	5.9	5.8	0.1	3.1	445.1	4 439	468	259	3 769	47.8	49.1	3.1
PENNSYLVANIA	X	X	X	X	X	X	X	X	X	95 728	36 262	648 716	54.7	44.3	1.0
Adams	458.0	4 513	68.9	3.6	1.4	3.2	2.7	405.6	3 997	708	262	3 441	39.6	59.2	1.1
Allegheny	6 640.6	5 402	42.9	7.9	4.6	4.6	3.0	13 494.2	10 977	12 735	3 632	52 478	57.3	41.8	0.9
Armstrong	246.9	3 609	57.6	1.5	1.2	7.5	5.0	239.3	3 498	191	180	2 673	37.0	61.6	1.3
Beaver	789.6	4 638	46.6	3.5	3.0	14.1	3.9	1 928.6	11 328	296	447	7 451	47.9	50.8	1.3
Bedford	155.3	3 148	66.4	0.0	0.4	2.0	4.8	224.7	4 556	102	130	2 152	27.0	71.8	1.2
Berks	2 024.3	4 896	54.5	3.4	4.1	7.2	2.8	3 478.7	8 413	911	1 080	21 684	53.9	44.7	1.4
Blair	409.0	3 217	49.0	3.1	3.0	8.6	3.9	474.2	3 730	983	328	7 613	37.3	61.6	1.1
Bradford	244.7	3 898	54.4	2.0	1.6	7.3	6.2	751.2	11 963	211	164	2 950	40.0	58.4	1.6
Bucks	2 875.9	4 586	57.6	0.8	5.5	7.0	4.5	3 960.3	6 316	1 094	1 677	21 653	53.8	45.1	1.1
Butler	656.7	3 550	51.5	4.2	2.4	9.5	4.4	1 305.0	7 055	2 777	489	8 512	35.7	63.1	1.2
Cambria	571.5	4 037	49.2	3.2	5.7	14.0	3.6	641.5	4 531	1 036	378	7 021	49.4	48.7	1.9
Cameron	19.1	3 864	59.4	3.8	1.2	2.5	5.9	30.2	6 117	14	13	387	39.2	58.9	1.9
Carbon	219.0	3 370	60.5	0.1	2.6	4.4	3.4	265.0	4 076	105	171	2 558	50.0	48.1	1.9
Centre	453.5	2 923	51.0	2.2	3.5	7.9	6.1	486.7	3 136	450	453	47 555	55.4	43.5	1.1
Chester	2 204.4	4 352	57.7	5.2	3.8	3.4	3.3	2 995.8	5 914	2 371	1 345	23 283	54.2	45.0	0.8
Clarion	168.8	4 258	67.2	3.0	1.9	2.5	3.4	87.7	2 213	105	100	3 439	38.0	60.4	1.5
Clearfield	261.5	3 221	66.6	0.0	3.5	3.1	4.8	310.5	3 824	252	203	4 598	43.0	55.2	1.8
Clinton	137.3	3 474	41.4	0.3	1.3	4.6	4.0	99.3	2 514	138	101	3 038	48.0	50.7	1.3
Columbia	207.5	3 102	63.6	0.0	3.1	3.7	4.7	212.5	3 176	144	168	5 167	47.1	51.6	1.3
Crawford	281.4	3 212	48.8	2.8	1.9	9.1	5.8	238.2	2 719	263	224	3 930	44.0	54.4	1.6
Cumberland	1 033.3	4 330	58.9	3.0	2.8	6.7	2.5	1 275.7	5 346	4 438	1 389	12 962	42.6	56.3	1.1
Dauphin	1 554.4	5 764	46.5	4.7	3.9	9.1	2.6	2 450.3	9 087	2 582	760	38 756	54.0	45.0	1.0
Delaware	2 744.1	4 891	50.1	2.1	4.9	11.1	2.0	4 601.2	8 200	2 117	1 485	23 713	60.2	38.8	1.0
Elk	92.2	2 921	46.8	0.2	2.8	1.8	8.2	287.8	9 123	104	83	1 290	51.1	46.8	2.1
Erie	1 203.4	4 288	44.0	5.6	2.7	14.2	3.5	1 705.3	6 076	1 522	758	15 847	59.3	39.4	1.2
Fayette	427.6	3 152	56.8	10.4	1.2	3.1	3.6	909.8	6 706	359	349	6 158	49.2	49.6	1.2
Forest	20.2	2 638	52.6	4.6	0.8	4.0	10.1	11.6	1 515	67	13	941	42.5	55.9	1.6
Franklin	452.7	2 992	54.1	4.1	1.9	5.5	4.8	619.1	4 092	2 271	409	5 968	33.3	65.8	0.9
Fulton	47.5	3 214	61.6	0.0	3.7	4.3	4.1	65.3	4 419	30	39	716	25.0	73.6	1.4
Greene	138.0	3 624	59.6	4.6	1.0	1.6	6.1	149.4	3 923	128	93	2 485	49.0	49.4	1.6
Huntingdon	134.9	2 937	57.1	1.3	1.8	2.3	5.0	147.7	3 216	127	110	2 951	35.5	63.0	1.4
Indiana	303.7	3 442	61.2	0.1	1.0	6.1	4.2	387.8	4 396	204	227	7 488	45.7	52.9	1.4
Jefferson	139.0	3 104	60.2	0.0	1.5	3.9	5.0	213.5	4 770	102	118	1 871	34.3	64.1	1.6
Juniata	46.0	1 848	65.2	0.1	0.9	2.6	5.4	13.7	550	69	66	696	31.6	66.8	1.6
Lackawanna	820.1	3 824	47.2	0.3	3.9	6.6	3.0	968.6	4 516	927	556	10 022	62.6	36.6	0.8
Lancaster	2 018.4	3 831	55.1	5.4	4.3	5.1	3.3	3 447.0	6 543	1 222	1 397	19 367	43.7	55.5	0.9
Lawrence	334.2	3 719	50.8	2.1	3.0	11.6	4.1	469.7	5 226	208	233	3 450	46.8	51.9	1.3
Lebanon	507.4	3 752	47.7	2.2	2.9	15.0	5.1	705.4	5 215	2 962	358	5 216	40.0	58.9	1.2
Lehigh	1 756.6	4 945	46.2	3.6	3.3	11.2	2.9	3 948.1	11 114	816	951	16 165	57.1	41.6	1.3
Luzerne	1 193.5	3 718	54.0	0.4	3.0	3.8	4.8	1 386.1	4 318	3 130	845	14 770	53.6	45.2	1.2
Lycoming	560.5	4 783	43.8	0.0	2.2	3.1	4.4	997.6	8 514	359	300	8 996	37.3	61.5	1.2
McKean	182.4	4 229	57.8	3.7	2.0	4.1	3.6	130.5	3 026	419	105	2 004	40.5	57.8	1.6
Mercer	435.3	3 764	63.5	2.3	3.0	2.6	3.9	444.6	3 844	246	310	5 061	49.1	49.4	1.6
Mifflin	166.3	3 555	61.5	4.0	1.7	0.4	3.1	218.1	4 664	89	123	1 713	32.6	66.2	1.2
Monroe	739.9	4 384	67.9	0.1	3.0	3.9	2.5	1 201.0	7 115	3 396	464	8 412	57.6	41.3	1.0
Montgomery	3 494.4	4 322	56.9	1.9	5.0	6.2	3.6	4 364.3	5 398	2 564	2 291	32 787	60.0	39.2	0.8
Montour	79.5	4 333	44.5	0.0	1.9	1.3	3.9	895.8	48 800	34	49	1 448	41.9	57.0	1.1
Northampton	1 501.3	5 017	49.8	3.1	4.0	11.6	2.7	2 550.6	8 523	1 104	781	13 720	55.5	43.2	1.3
Northumberland	266.3	2 820	54.3	3.8	5.1	7.1	3.9	255.4	2 704	170	243	4 220	42.2	56.0	1.7
Perry	128.6	2 813	61.7	2.5	0.8	7.4	4.3	107.1	2 343	82	121	1 838	32.4	66.1	1.5
Philadelphia	9 802.9	6 334	34.2	13.8	6.2	5.8	1.1	18 737.5	12 107	29 902	5 182	73 241	83.1	16.3	0.6
Pike	135.9	2 388	49.0	0.4	1.9	5.8	3.9	42.8	752	219	149	2 330	47.3	51.5	1.1

1. Based on the resident population estimated as of July 1 of the year shown.   2. © 2013 Election Data Services, Inc. All rights reserved.

Table B. States and Counties — **Land Area and Population**

STATE/County code	CBSA code[1]	County type[2]	STATE County	Land area[3] (sq km) 2010	Total persons 2015	Rank	Per square kilometer	White	Black	American Indian, Alaska Native	Asian and Pacific Islander	Percent Hispanic or Latino[4]	Under 5 years	5 to 17 years	18 to 24 years	25 to 34 years	35 to 44 years	45 to 54 years
				1	2	3	4	5	6	7	8	9	10	11	12	13	14	15
			PENNSYLVANIA—Cont'd															
42 105	...	9	Potter	2 801	17 093	1 977	6.1	97.8	0.7	0.7	0.6	1.1	5.6	15.6	7.3	9.7	10.2	14.1
42 107	39060	4	Schuylkill	2 017	144 590	444	71.7	92.9	3.4	0.4	0.8	3.6	4.7	14.8	7.4	11.7	12.5	14.9
42 109	42780	7	Snyder	851	40 444	1 165	47.5	96.1	1.4	0.4	0.9	2.2	5.6	16.3	12.0	11.3	11.3	13.6
42 111	43740	4	Somerset	2 783	75 522	732	27.1	95.4	3.0	0.4	0.5	1.4	4.4	13.9	7.4	11.3	12.3	14.7
42 113	...	8	Sullivan	1 165	6 328	2 732	5.4	94.3	3.6	0.7	0.6	1.8	3.4	8.9	9.7	8.8	9.4	14.5
42 115	...	6	Susquehanna	2 133	41 666	1 132	19.5	97.1	0.8	0.5	0.6	1.8	4.8	14.9	7.5	9.9	10.7	15.5
42 117	...	6	Tioga	2 936	41 877	1 128	14.3	97.5	1.3	0.6	0.8	1.3	5.8	14.2	10.6	11.2	10.5	13.6
42 119	30260	4	Union	818	44 954	1 074	55.0	85.5	7.2	0.6	2.1	5.7	4.4	13.7	13.1	13.8	13.5	13.5
42 121	36340	4	Venango	1 746	53 119	941	30.4	97.1	1.8	0.5	0.7	1.1	5.3	15.0	7.3	10.2	11.0	14.4
42 123	47620	6	Warren	2 290	40 396	1 167	17.6	97.8	0.8	0.6	0.7	0.9	4.9	14.9	7.3	10.2	10.8	14.9
42 125	38300	1	Washington	2 220	208 261	313	93.8	94.3	4.2	0.5	1.2	1.5	5.0	14.8	8.8	10.7	11.7	14.7
42 127	...	6	Wayne	1 879	51 198	972	27.2	91.7	3.7	0.5	0.8	4.2	4.1	13.5	7.4	10.8	11.6	15.6
42 129	38300	1	Westmoreland	2 661	357 956	192	134.5	95.5	3.3	0.4	1.2	1.1	4.6	14.2	7.9	10.2	11.2	15.1
42 131	42540	2	Wyoming	1 029	27 800	1 500	27.0	96.5	1.3	0.6	0.8	1.8	5.0	15.4	8.9	11.0	11.6	14.3
42 133	49620	2	York	2 342	442 867	158	189.1	86.3	6.5	0.5	1.8	6.5	5.7	16.7	8.4	12.0	12.5	15.0
44 000	...	X	**RHODE ISLAND**	2 678	1 056 298	X	394.4	76.2	6.8	1.0	4.1	14.0	5.2	15.0	11.1	13.2	11.9	14.5
44 001	39300	1	Bristol	63	49 084	995	779.1	94.5	1.5	0.6	2.5	4.2	4.0	15.6	10.9	9.7	10.8	15.5
44 003	39300	1	Kent	436	164 801	387	378.0	91.5	2.3	0.8	3.1	4.2	4.9	14.5	7.5	12.5	12.4	15.8
44 005	39300	1	Newport	265	82 423	679	311.0	88.7	4.7	1.0	2.7	5.2	4.4	14.0	9.3	11.9	11.4	14.6
44 007	39300	1	Providence	1 061	633 473	104	597.1	65.8	9.6	1.1	4.9	20.9	5.8	15.3	11.5	14.7	12.3	13.9
44 009	39300	1	Washington	853	126 517	493	148.3	92.9	2.0	1.4	2.7	3.0	3.8	14.2	15.0	8.7	9.9	15.0
45 000	...	X	**SOUTH CAROLINA**	77 857	4 896 146	X	62.9	65.2	28.2	0.8	2.0	5.4	6.0	16.4	10.0	13.0	12.3	13.4
45 001	24940	6	Abbeville	1 270	24 932	1 609	19.6	70.0	29.0	0.6	0.6	1.2	5.4	16.1	9.8	10.0	11.2	13.3
45 003	12260	2	Aiken	2 774	165 829	385	59.8	68.6	25.6	1.0	1.3	5.4	5.7	16.4	8.6	12.6	11.5	13.7
45 005	...	6	Allendale	1 057	9 433	2 474	8.9	23.9	72.9	0.5	0.6	2.9	5.1	14.4	9.4	14.3	12.4	13.9
45 007	24860	3	Anderson	1 853	194 692	337	105.1	79.0	17.2	0.6	1.2	3.5	6.0	17.3	8.5	11.6	12.4	13.9
45 009	...	7	Bamberg	1 019	14 880	2 109	14.6	36.6	61.2	0.6	0.6	1.9	5.1	15.0	14.7	9.5	9.9	13.1
45 011	...	6	Barnwell	1 420	21 725	1 743	15.3	52.6	44.5	0.9	1.0	2.5	7.0	18.3	8.8	11.0	11.4	13.6
45 013	25940	2	Beaufort	1 493	179 589	359	120.3	68.7	19.5	0.6	1.9	11.4	5.8	14.1	9.6	11.8	10.5	10.8
45 015	16700	2	Berkeley	2 846	202 786	322	71.3	66.1	25.7	1.2	3.5	6.1	6.8	17.6	10.2	14.6	13.2	13.4
45 017	17900	2	Calhoun	987	14 781	2 118	15.0	54.6	42.0	0.7	0.7	3.2	5.2	15.1	7.8	10.1	11.2	14.6
45 019	16700	2	Charleston	2 373	389 262	177	164.0	64.7	29.0	0.7	2.2	5.1	6.1	14.1	10.0	17.3	12.3	12.8
45 021	23500	4	Cherokee	1 017	56 194	906	55.3	74.5	21.3	0.8	0.8	4.1	6.3	17.6	9.5	12.0	12.7	13.8
45 023	16740	6	Chester	1 504	32 267	1 378	21.5	60.2	37.8	1.0	0.7	1.8	6.3	16.8	8.3	11.2	11.6	14.6
45 025	...	6	Chesterfield	2 070	46 017	1 048	22.2	62.6	33.3	1.0	0.8	3.9	5.8	17.2	8.8	11.2	12.4	14.9
45 027	...	6	Clarendon	1 572	33 775	1 332	21.5	48.1	48.6	0.5	0.8	3.0	5.1	15.3	10.1	11.0	10.4	13.0
45 029	...	6	Colleton	2 736	37 731	1 234	13.8	57.7	38.8	1.2	0.7	3.1	6.0	17.0	8.1	10.9	10.9	13.9
45 031	22500	3	Darlington	1 453	67 548	786	46.5	56.2	41.5	0.7	0.7	2.0	5.8	17.2	9.3	10.8	12.2	13.7
45 033	...	6	Dillon	1 049	31 234	1 404	29.8	48.2	47.0	3.1	0.6	2.5	7.1	18.6	9.1	11.8	11.8	13.2
45 035	16700	2	Dorchester	1 485	152 478	425	102.7	67.0	26.7	1.2	2.7	4.9	6.5	19.1	8.7	13.9	13.6	14.7
45 037	12260	2	Edgefield	1 296	26 514	1 546	20.5	57.3	37.1	0.6	0.7	5.7	4.4	14.9	9.1	12.7	13.2	15.1
45 039	17900	2	Fairfield	1 777	22 747	1 697	12.8	39.1	59.4	0.7	0.6	1.9	4.9	15.6	8.4	10.0	11.2	14.8
45 041	22500	3	Florence	2 072	138 900	459	67.0	53.9	42.6	0.7	1.7	2.4	6.5	17.7	9.4	12.5	12.5	13.2
45 043	23860	4	Georgetown	2 107	61 298	853	29.1	63.8	32.8	0.6	0.7	3.2	4.9	15.1	7.3	9.2	10.6	12.8
45 045	24860	2	Greenville	2 033	491 863	140	241.9	70.7	18.9	0.6	2.7	8.8	6.4	17.0	9.4	13.6	13.2	13.8
45 047	24940	4	Greenwood	1 178	69 838	768	59.3	61.3	32.2	0.5	1.2	5.8	6.3	16.7	10.0	12.3	11.8	13.3
45 049	...	6	Hampton	1 450	20 049	1 831	13.8	42.0	53.7	0.7	0.7	3.9	5.7	16.8	8.8	12.7	13.0	13.8
45 051	34820	3	Horry	2 937	309 199	220	105.3	78.9	14.3	1.0	1.7	6.1	5.2	14.1	8.2	12.3	11.7	13.1
45 053	25940	6	Jasper	1 697	27 824	1 497	16.4	42.1	44.0	0.5	1.0	14.0	6.0	15.5	9.9	13.8	12.2	13.6
45 055	17900	2	Kershaw	1 882	63 603	827	33.8	70.0	25.6	0.7	1.0	4.2	5.9	17.7	7.9	11.5	12.0	14.1
45 057	16740	4	Lancaster	1 422	85 842	667	60.4	71.4	23.1	0.6	1.1	5.0	5.7	16.2	7.4	12.1	13.4	13.3
45 059	24860	2	Laurens	1 849	66 623	797	36.0	69.4	26.3	0.6	0.6	4.4	5.9	16.5	9.9	11.3	11.7	14.0
45 061	...	6	Lee	1 062	17 896	1 923	16.9	34.0	63.4	0.6	0.7	2.1	4.9	15.8	10.0	13.6	11.4	13.7
45 063	17900	2	Lexington	1 810	281 833	241	155.7	77.3	15.6	0.9	2.2	5.8	6.1	17.5	8.3	13.2	13.3	14.3
45 065	...	8	McCormick	930	9 706	2 457	10.4	49.5	49.0	0.5	0.7	1.2	3.2	9.7	6.0	11.1	10.4	13.6
45 067	...	6	Marion	1 267	31 747	1 387	25.1	40.0	56.5	0.9	0.9	2.7	6.1	17.2	9.0	11.1	11.6	12.8
45 069	13500	6	Marlboro	1 242	27 494	1 512	22.1	41.5	51.5	5.1	0.7	3.2	5.4	15.3	8.6	14.4	13.7	14.1
45 071	35140	6	Newberry	1 632	38 012	1 221	23.3	61.0	31.2	0.5	0.8	7.5	5.8	16.2	9.9	11.2	11.5	13.2
45 073	42860	6	Oconee	1 622	75 713	728	46.7	86.4	8.4	0.7	1.0	4.8	5.4	15.0	8.0	10.8	11.0	13.1
45 075	36700	4	Orangeburg	2 865	89 208	644	31.1	34.6	62.4	1.0	1.3	2.1	6.3	16.3	11.3	11.8	10.4	13.1
45 077	24860	2	Pickens	1 286	121 691	511	94.6	87.5	7.5	0.6	2.2	3.4	4.9	14.7	18.1	11.4	11.0	12.7
45 079	17900	2	Richland	1 961	407 051	169	207.6	45.6	47.2	0.8	3.4	5.1	5.9	16.0	15.9	14.8	12.4	12.4
45 081	17900	2	Saluda	1 173	20 053	1 829	17.1	58.9	26.1	0.6	0.5	14.9	6.3	15.8	8.1	12.4	11.8	13.6
45 083	43900	2	Spartanburg	2 093	297 302	231	142.0	70.4	21.6	0.6	2.7	6.4	6.3	17.4	9.8	12.4	12.5	13.9

1. CBSA = Core Based Statistical Area. See Appendix A for explanation. See Appendix B for list of metropolitan areas with component counties. 2. County type code from the Economic Research Service of USDA Rural-Urban Continuum Codes. See Appendix A for definition. 3. Dry land or land partially or temporarily covered by water. 4. May be of any race.

Table B. States and Counties — **Population and Households**

STATE County	55 to 64 years	65 to 74 years	75 years and over	Percent female	2000	2010	2000–2010	2010–2015	Births	Deaths	Net migration	Number	Persons per household	Family households	Female family householder[1]	One person
	16	17	18	19	20	21	22	23	24	25	26	27	28	29	30	31
PENNSYLVANIA—Cont'd																
Potter	15.6	12.2	9.6	50.0	18 080	17 458	-3.4	-2.1	1 043	1 071	-271	6 848	2.51	66.8	8.7	28.7
Schuylkill	14.5	10.3	9.0	48.9	150 336	148 289	-1.4	-2.5	7 178	9 971	-690	59 122	2.37	65.3	11.5	29.6
Snyder	13.2	9.2	7.5	50.6	37 546	39 709	5.8	1.9	2 321	1 842	266	14 414	2.61	72.2	8.2	22.9
Somerset	15.6	10.7	9.6	48.1	80 023	77 748	-2.8	-2.9	3 551	4 958	-789	29 748	2.43	69.3	8.4	27.0
Sullivan	18.4	14.9	12.0	47.7	6 556	6 428	-2.0	-1.6	273	578	196	2 476	2.41	63.4	5.9	32.4
Susquehanna	16.6	11.7	8.3	49.6	42 238	43 356	2.6	-3.9	2 119	2 329	-1 519	17 265	2.45	67.7	8.9	27.0
Tioga	14.5	11.1	8.5	50.5	41 373	41 983	1.5	-0.3	2 322	2 338	-60	16 802	2.43	68.0	8.9	26.1
Union	11.9	8.4	7.7	45.0	41 624	44 949	8.0	0.0	2 134	1 976	-128	15 058	2.36	68.5	9.3	24.5
Venango	16.7	11.0	8.9	50.8	57 565	54 983	-4.5	-3.4	2 924	3 434	-1 291	22 412	2.36	67.6	11.1	28.4
Warren	16.3	11.4	9.3	49.8	43 863	41 815	-4.7	-3.4	2 152	2 657	-830	17 029	2.38	65.2	8.6	30.3
Washington	15.4	10.3	8.7	51.1	202 897	207 820	2.4	0.2	10 495	13 049	3 164	83 644	2.43	65.8	10.2	29.0
Wayne	16.3	12.6	8.1	46.9	47 722	52 825	10.7	-3.1	2 166	3 072	-874	19 362	2.49	68.2	9.0	27.4
Westmoreland	16.1	11.1	9.6	51.2	369 993	365 169	-1.3	-2.0	16 593	22 852	-589	151 489	2.34	66.6	10.5	29.1
Wyoming	15.3	11.3	7.1	49.6	28 080	28 276	0.7	-1.7	1 511	1 563	-397	10 895	2.52	67.7	9.6	25.9
York	13.7	9.1	6.8	50.5	381 751	434 998	13.9	1.8	26 031	19 839	2 062	168 278	2.55	70.2	10.9	24.6
RHODE ISLAND	13.5	8.5	7.2	51.5	1 048 319	1 052 931	0.4	0.3	57 570	50 264	-3 445	409 569	2.47	62.5	13.8	30.2
Bristol	14.8	9.6	9.1	51.8	50 648	49 875	-1.5	-1.6	1 849	2 592	-106	19 167	2.41	66.9	9.7	27.6
Kent	15.0	9.5	7.9	51.7	167 090	166 158	-0.6	-0.8	8 352	9 011	-613	68 428	2.39	62.7	10.9	30.5
Newport	15.0	10.9	8.4	50.9	85 433	83 141	-2.7	-0.9	3 768	3 644	-700	34 833	2.27	60.0	10.0	32.2
Providence	12.4	7.5	6.7	51.5	621 602	626 663	0.8	1.1	38 749	29 319	-2 151	237 650	2.53	61.8	16.5	30.9
Washington	15.4	10.3	7.6	51.7	123 546	127 094	2.9	-0.5	4 852	5 698	125	49 491	2.43	65.8	9.6	26.5
SOUTH CAROLINA	13.1	9.6	6.1	51.4	4 012 012	4 625 401	15.3	5.9	301 101	228 566	190 997	1 795 715	2.56	67.1	15.2	27.8
Abbeville	14.8	11.6	7.8	51.5	26 167	25 416	-2.9	-1.9	1 341	1 425	-384	9 752	2.49	68.4	15.5	27.8
Aiken	14.0	10.4	7.1	51.5	142 552	160 106	12.3	3.6	9 781	8 589	4 212	63 609	2.52	67.7	15.1	28.5
Allendale	14.2	10.3	5.9	46.1	11 211	10 419	-7.1	-9.5	539	590	-932	3 456	2.55	63.8	25.0	33.8
Anderson	13.2	10.0	7.0	51.7	165 740	187 123	12.9	4.0	11 797	10 380	5 830	73 669	2.54	69.7	13.2	26.5
Bamberg	14.4	10.6	7.7	51.8	16 658	15 987	-4.0	-6.9	833	909	-978	5 777	2.50	61.3	18.3	36.6
Barnwell	14.0	9.8	6.2	52.3	23 478	22 621	-3.7	-4.0	1 567	1 354	-1 128	8 434	2.61	66.2	21.0	29.5
Beaufort	13.2	14.9	9.2	50.9	120 937	162 233	34.1	10.7	10 828	7 311	13 296	65 054	2.50	68.6	10.0	26.3
Berkeley	11.9	8.0	4.2	50.2	142 651	177 850	24.7	14.0	13 608	6 482	16 929	67 423	2.75	71.2	14.3	23.9
Calhoun	16.2	12.4	7.3	51.3	15 185	15 176	-0.1	-2.6	743	889	-284	6 135	2.42	69.6	16.8	27.2
Charleston	12.9	8.8	5.7	51.6	309 969	350 204	13.0	11.2	25 188	15 486	27 965	145 991	2.42	58.8	14.0	31.9
Cherokee	12.9	9.3	5.9	51.5	52 537	55 467	5.6	1.3	3 569	3 088	342	20 647	2.66	67.7	16.1	28.5
Chester	14.5	10.1	6.6	51.5	34 068	33 140	-2.7	-2.6	2 081	2 023	-877	12 237	2.65	68.1	19.9	28.9
Chesterfield	13.8	9.9	6.1	51.3	42 768	46 738	9.3	-1.5	2 717	2 603	-799	17 837	2.56	68.7	16.7	28.0
Clarendon	15.2	12.4	7.4	50.7	32 502	34 966	7.6	-3.4	1 845	1 944	-1 009	12 768	2.57	66.6	18.9	29.9
Colleton	14.6	11.3	7.3	52.1	38 264	38 892	1.6	-3.0	2 363	2 577	-1 010	14 678	2.57	67.6	19.6	28.4
Darlington	14.5	10.1	6.4	52.8	67 394	68 683	1.9	-1.7	4 134	4 252	-912	26 267	2.55	69.5	19.4	26.5
Dillon	13.3	9.0	6.0	52.7	30 722	32 062	4.4	-2.6	2 291	1 912	-1 221	11 703	2.65	69.9	23.8	27.1
Dorchester	12.0	7.5	4.1	51.2	96 413	136 589	41.7	11.6	9 614	4 852	10 556	51 450	2.74	72.5	15.4	23.7
Edgefield	14.7	10.1	5.8	45.9	24 595	26 978	9.7	-1.7	1 046	1 069	-508	9 043	2.63	71.7	16.0	25.5
Fairfield	17.0	11.1	6.9	52.2	23 454	23 956	2.1	-5.0	1 190	1 510	-863	9 402	2.44	66.5	20.0	30.7
Florence	13.1	9.1	5.9	53.2	125 761	136 888	8.8	1.5	9 343	7 646	381	51 794	2.60	69.7	20.3	26.4
Georgetown	16.1	15.1	9.0	52.4	55 797	60 158	7.8	1.9	3 099	3 642	1 496	23 309	2.57	68.7	14.2	27.3
Greenville	12.3	8.5	5.7	51.4	379 616	451 219	18.9	9.0	32 346	20 241	27 561	176 955	2.57	67.1	13.3	28.3
Greenwood	12.5	9.5	7.6	53.2	66 271	69 661	5.1	0.3	4 693	3 659	-837	26 760	2.51	65.5	16.8	29.9
Hampton	13.4	9.8	6.0	48.4	21 386	21 090	-1.4	-4.9	1 192	1 096	-1 144	7 463	2.58	66.9	19.3	30.0
Horry	14.8	13.3	7.2	51.5	196 629	269 291	37.0	14.8	16 180	15 101	38 306	115 764	2.43	64.0	12.3	29.0
Jasper	13.5	9.9	5.5	48.4	20 678	24 777	19.8	12.3	1 724	1 177	2 523	8 749	2.89	67.5	18.3	27.3
Kershaw	14.4	9.9	6.5	51.5	52 647	61 570	16.9	3.3	3 748	3 294	1 565	24 061	2.57	71.3	15.5	24.7
Lancaster	13.1	12.0	6.8	50.9	61 351	76 652	24.9	12.0	4 868	4 093	8 238	29 104	2.67	70.1	17.1	26.9
Laurens	13.9	9.9	6.5	51.5	69 567	66 539	-4.4	0.1	4 017	4 156	186	25 312	2.53	71.2	17.8	24.8
Lee	14.4	9.6	6.5	47.8	20 119	19 222	-4.5	-6.9	961	1 173	-1 156	6 471	2.62	68.1	24.2	28.8
Lexington	13.1	8.8	5.5	51.1	216 014	262 397	21.5	7.4	17 168	11 663	13 368	105 081	2.54	68.3	13.6	26.1
McCormick	16.2	19.6	10.3	44.9	9 958	10 233	2.8	-5.2	299	641	-195	4 058	2.14	70.2	15.6	26.6
Marion	15.1	10.5	6.5	53.8	35 466	33 062	-6.8	-4.0	2 120	2 238	-1 168	11 782	2.73	68.9	23.3	27.7
Marlboro	13.3	9.6	5.6	46.8	28 818	28 933	0.4	-5.0	1 586	1 697	-1 302	9 645	2.60	67.4	20.4	29.6
Newberry	14.1	10.8	7.2	51.4	36 108	37 508	3.9	1.3	2 344	2 165	327	14 230	2.56	71.0	17.7	25.7
Oconee	15.1	13.3	8.3	50.5	66 215	74 275	12.2	1.9	4 086	4 415	1 814	30 319	2.44	69.2	12.7	26.3
Orangeburg	13.7	10.2	6.9	53.1	91 582	92 495	1.0	-3.6	5 818	5 485	-3 551	33 836	2.61	65.7	20.6	31.0
Pickens	11.9	9.0	6.2	50.2	110 757	119 226	7.6	2.1	6 347	5 812	1 749	44 091	2.54	65.4	9.8	26.3
Richland	11.2	6.9	4.4	51.5	320 677	384 506	19.9	5.9	25 334	14 794	11 836	144 647	2.51	60.9	17.3	31.6
Saluda	13.7	10.7	7.6	49.6	19 181	19 872	3.6	0.9	1 278	1 057	-44	7 113	2.76	69.3	14.0	26.1
Spartanburg	12.6	9.0	6.0	51.5	253 791	284 305	12.0	4.6	18 785	14 825	8 900	108 383	2.60	70.3	15.8	25.5

1. No spouse present.

Table B. States and Counties — Population, Vital Statistics, Medicare, and Crime

STATE County	Persons in group quarters, 2015	Daytime population, 2010–2014 Number	Employment/residence ratio	Births, 2015 Total	Rate[1]	Deaths, 2015 Number	Rate[1]	Persons under 65 with no health insurance, 2014 Number	Percent	Medicare, 2015 Total Beneficiaries	Enrolled in Original Medicare	Enrolled in Medicare Advantage	Serious crimes known to police,[2] 2014 Total Number	Rate[3]
	32	33	34	35	36	37	38	39	40	41	42	43	44	45
PENNSYLVANIA—Cont'd														
Potter	217	17 393	0.99	199	11.6	208	12.1	1 427	10.7	4 222	2 986	1 236	207	1 222
Schuylkill	6 843	136 954	0.84	1 331	9.2	1 811	12.5	11 878	10.6	33 221	23 162	10 059	2 541	1 756
Snyder	2 468	38 635	0.93	456	11.3	342	8.5	4 335	13.8	7 498	4 043	3 455	579	1 513
Somerset	4 955	72 228	0.85	650	8.6	931	12.3	6 194	10.9	17 830	6 994	10 836	870	1 142
Sullivan	440	5 957	0.82	53	8.4	102	16.1	615	13.4	1 718	1 213	505	76	1 199
Susquehanna	282	36 337	0.66	408	9.8	419	10.0	3 938	11.8	8 895	6 956	1 939	506	1 276
Tioga	1 787	41 639	0.96	417	9.9	451	10.7	3 692	11.4	9 621	7 199	2 422	528	1 240
Union	8 862	47 494	1.15	412	9.2	391	8.7	3 173	10.8	7 550	4 695	2 855	409	912
Venango	1 301	52 975	0.95	532	10.0	662	12.4	4 434	10.5	12 990	8 404	4 586	872	1 626
Warren	760	39 817	0.92	418	10.3	507	12.5	3 085	9.7	9 193	7 336	1 857	616	1 515
Washington	5 618	200 091	0.92	2 042	9.8	2 473	11.9	13 383	8.1	46 401	15 712	30 689	3 898	1 896
Wayne	3 909	48 263	0.82	410	8.0	540	10.5	3 988	10.7	16 251	13 574	2 677	724	1 414
Westmoreland	7 038	337 107	0.85	3 144	8.8	4 374	12.2	23 181	8.3	82 817	25 980	56 837	5 864	1 640
Wyoming	631	27 941	0.98	279	10.0	308	11.0	2 203	9.8	6 485	4 431	2 054	411	1 471
York	8 741	402 626	0.83	4 993	11.3	3 832	8.7	30 937	8.5	79 644	50 927	28 717	8 253	1 877
RHODE ISLAND	41 638	1 032 746	0.96	10 984	10.4	9 533	9.0	74 089	8.6	185 920	111 170	74 750	25 248	2 393
Bristol	2 778	40 884	0.64	346	7.1	524	10.7	2 251	5.9	9 252	5 076	4 176	684	1 389
Kent	1 477	155 207	0.88	1 601	9.7	1 655	10.0	7 818	5.7	33 280	18 851	14 429	3 257	1 969
Newport	3 277	85 660	1.07	724	8.8	727	8.8	4 134	6.4	16 770	12 312	4 458	1 987	2 406
Providence	27 162	632 288	1.01	7 389	11.7	5 477	8.7	53 734	10.4	103 152	59 640	43 512	17 326	2 744
Washington	6 944	118 707	0.88	924	7.3	1 150	9.1	6 152	6.2	23 466	15 291	8 175	1 912	1 511
SOUTH CAROLINA	136 532	4 691 496	0.98	57 905	11.9	45 097	9.3	635 365	16.1	896 240	677 054	219 186	191 269	3 958
Abbeville	903	21 355	0.59	257	10.3	257	10.3	3 283	16.8	4 572	3 191	1 381	605	2 622
Aiken	2 443	159 776	0.95	1 836	11.1	1 698	10.3	21 548	16.1	32 942	25 679	7 263	6 600	3 980
Allendale	1 367	10 335	1.11	96	10.0	112	11.7	1 150	16.9	1 819	1 099	720	178	2 257
Anderson	2 888	177 460	0.84	2 308	11.9	2 006	10.4	24 961	15.8	38 799	26 531	12 268	10 786	5 608
Bamberg	1 249	14 792	0.84	151	10.0	165	11.0	1 823	15.8	2 931	2 038	893	521	3 390
Barnwell	285	21 488	0.90	288	13.2	271	12.4	2 948	16.1	4 367	3 158	1 209	996	4 508
Beaufort	5 035	172 443	1.05	2 089	11.8	1 477	8.3	22 121	17.3	41 489	34 366	7 123	5 313	3 040
Berkeley	3 607	161 754	0.68	2 667	13.3	1 351	6.7	25 701	15.1	21 763	16 883	4 880	5 600	2 822
Calhoun	157	11 645	0.46	126	8.5	179	12.1	2 008	16.9	2 245	1 631	614	402	2 738
Charleston	10 396	422 484	1.32	4 968	12.9	3 121	8.1	48 986	15.5	67 649	54 548	13 101	12 662	3 342
Cherokee	819	54 546	0.94	667	11.9	571	10.2	7 868	16.7	10 242	6 971	3 271	2 026	3 603
Chester	218	28 908	0.69	368	11.4	409	12.7	4 393	16.4	7 063	5 314	1 749	1 245	3 820
Chesterfield	872	44 822	0.91	531	11.5	529	11.5	7 035	18.3	8 391	6 951	1 440	1 649	3 562
Clarendon	1 446	31 804	0.76	350	10.3	379	11.2	4 649	18.0	7 375	5 490	1 885	1 401	4 077
Colleton	389	35 707	0.82	437	11.6	549	14.5	5 791	18.9	8 144	5 889	2 255	1 859	4 934
Darlington	1 363	64 041	0.84	779	11.5	816	12.1	9 365	16.8	13 021	10 570	2 451	2 867	4 212
Dillon	483	30 482	0.90	428	13.7	357	11.4	4 984	19.0	5 783	4 425	1 358	1 967	6 313
Dorchester	1 872	115 923	0.59	1 907	12.7	1 003	6.7	17 803	13.8	20 401	15 855	4 546	5 426	3 715
Edgefield	2 918	23 614	0.70	205	7.7	235	8.9	3 199	16.4	3 306	2 358	948	458	1 733
Fairfield	277	21 266	0.76	215	9.4	299	13.1	3 012	16.2	4 597	3 265	1 332	906	3 934
Florence	3 287	147 203	1.16	1 750	12.6	1 461	10.5	17 106	14.7	28 268	24 139	4 129	6 414	4 647
Georgetown	560	59 925	0.98	591	9.7	724	11.9	8 657	18.9	17 726	14 311	3 415	2 385	3 931
Greenville	11 839	498 201	1.15	6 309	12.9	3 977	8.2	62 306	15.5	81 536	55 214	26 322	19 328	4 010
Greenwood	2 457	70 987	1.05	873	12.5	735	10.5	9 622	17.3	15 668	11 885	3 783	3 311	4 728
Hampton	1 484	19 682	0.87	220	10.9	221	10.9	2 630	16.7	4 581	3 362	1 219	567	3 364
Horry	2 955	284 819	1.01	3 185	10.5	3 066	10.1	49 555	21.1	69 732	57 600	12 132	16 896	5 709
Jasper	1 336	22 584	0.70	340	12.4	228	8.3	4 926	22.9	3 559	2 482	1 077	1 076	3 957
Kershaw	403	56 240	0.76	714	11.3	663	10.5	7 923	15.0	13 090	10 485	2 605	1 614	2 562
Lancaster	2 066	70 833	0.72	992	11.7	824	9.8	10 826	16.5	12 145	9 941	2 204	2 991	3 660
Laurens	2 424	61 509	0.81	744	11.2	804	12.1	9 244	17.3	13 136	9 078	4 058	2 811	4 230
Lee	1 706	16 168	0.57	182	10.0	254	14.0	2 375	17.6	3 230	2 454	776	764	4 193
Lexington	2 309	255 072	0.88	3 280	11.7	2 252	8.1	37 590	15.9	43 928	34 485	9 443	8 259	3 000
McCormick	1 160	9 428	0.79	59	6.0	136	13.9	873	15.5	3 331	2 288	1 043	157	1 583
Marion	203	28 901	0.69	402	12.6	424	13.3	4 390	16.7	7 470	5 983	1 487	2 096	6 551
Marlboro	3 182	27 208	0.88	301	10.9	318	11.5	3 612	17.6	6 083	4 753	1 330	1 323	4 741
Newberry	1 209	37 049	0.97	469	12.4	410	10.8	5 324	17.7	8 352	6 210	2 142	1 088	2 888
Oconee	792	73 577	0.96	739	9.8	863	11.4	10 146	17.3	18 943	14 420	4 523	2 396	3 171
Orangeburg	3 127	90 800	0.99	1 042	11.6	1 085	12.1	12 294	17.1	18 990	13 009	5 981	4 299	4 801
Pickens	6 772	110 175	0.81	1 243	10.3	1 126	9.3	15 524	16.2	24 443	16 265	8 178	4 655	3 862
Richland	31 113	432 084	1.20	4 844	12.0	2 938	7.3	42 957	13.1	54 339	43 161	11 178	19 952	4 932
Saluda	259	17 852	0.73	235	11.7	205	10.2	3 393	20.8	2 932	2 117	815	361	1 785
Spartanburg	8 206	293 598	1.04	3 587	12.1	2 882	9.8	39 653	16.3	60 583	38 121	22 462	9 989	3 399

1. Per 1,000 estimated resident population. 2. Data for serious crimes have not been adjusted for underreporting; this may affect comparability between geographic areas and over time.
3. Per 100,000 population estimated by the FBI.

Table B. States and Counties — Crime, Education, Money Income, and Poverty

STATE County	Serious crimes known to police, 2014 (cont.)[1] Rate[2] Violent	Property	Education — School enrollment and attainment, 2010–2014 Enrollment[3] Total	Percent private	Attainment[4] (percent) High school graduate or less	Bachelor's degree or more	Local government expenditures,[5] 2012–2013 Total current spending (mil dol)	Current spending per student (dollars)	Money income, 2010–2014 Per capita income[6] (dollars)	Households Median income (dollars)	Mean income (dollars)	Percent with income of $200,000 or more	Income and poverty, 2014 Median household income (dollars)	Percent below poverty level All persons	Children under 18 years	Children 5 to 17 years in families
	46	47	48	49	50	51	52	53	54	55	56	57	58	59	60	61
PENNSYLVANIA—Cont'd																
Potter	183	1 039	3 602	10.7	61.6	15.4	34.1	13 602	22 997	41 862	55 561	1.8	40 323	14.3	22.8	21.6
Schuylkill	158	1 598	29 472	14.5	61.2	14.9	236.7	13 596	23 249	45 020	56 276	1.3	43 169	13.5	18.5	16.7
Snyder	167	1 346	9 736	34.6	63.5	16.6	57.4	11 633	23 886	48 718	63 982	2.8	49 117	13.1	20.3	18.4
Somerset	105	1 037	14 415	14.7	63.4	14.9	127.4	13 119	22 618	44 255	56 017	1.6	45 706	13.5	21.0	19.6
Sullivan	79	1 121	976	11.5	61.1	15.6	11.8	18 792	23 418	41 786	54 872	1.6	44 191	14.4	22.4	21.8
Susquehanna	96	1 180	8 557	16.4	58.7	16.7	98.9	14 800	25 454	49 948	61 638	2.0	49 552	12.8	19.7	17.8
Tioga	101	1 139	9 720	12.4	55.2	19.4	70.9	12 796	23 596	45 863	58 213	2.0	47 360	16.3	23.2	20.6
Union	74	839	11 723	46.8	56.7	21.3	52.7	13 257	22 858	48 827	66 158	3.9	47 996	13.4	14.9	13.5
Venango	125	1 501	11 173	12.8	60.5	15.9	86.2	13 852	22 923	43 291	54 160	1.0	43 810	16.2	25.2	23.0
Warren	152	1 362	8 127	15.7	56.5	18.4	59.2	12 711	25 054	44 391	58 649	1.3	44 651	14.1	24.1	22.3
Washington	167	1 729	47 510	17.9	48.9	26.6	387.1	13 733	29 816	55 323	72 318	4.2	55 796	10.7	14.1	12.1
Wayne	102	1 313	9 977	16.7	54.4	19.6	77.4	15 432	24 132	49 285	61 440	2.1	48 663	13.9	19.8	17.1
Westmoreland	165	1 475	77 682	18.0	46.8	26.2	609.7	12 534	28 654	51 593	67 177	3.1	53 536	10.1	13.6	13.0
Wyoming	79	1 393	6 076	21.3	57.5	17.9	55.1	14 571	25 306	51 021	63 384	2.1	55 882	10.9	17.5	15.9
York	206	1 671	104 031	19.5	52.9	22.5	849.3	13 141	28 454	58 906	72 536	3.0	58 471	10.2	15.1	14.4
RHODE ISLAND	219	2 174	273 474	25.9	42.0	31.4	2 127.8	14 415	30 765	56 423	76 618	5.1	54 797	14.8	21.2	19.2
Bristol	65	1 324	13 346	38.0	33.1	43.5	103.7	15 239	38 312	69 240	97 565	9.4	68 246	8.0	9.0	7.8
Kent	115	1 854	37 238	20.4	39.0	30.1	361.2	16 196	34 110	62 976	80 766	4.8	61 923	9.3	12.5	11.2
Newport	180	2 226	19 894	34.2	30.7	44.9	162.4	16 492	41 326	72 702	95 539	8.7	69 203	9.5	13.3	11.5
Providence	290	2 455	166 752	27.9	47.4	26.4	1 230.7	15 033	26 690	49 139	67 581	3.8	47 278	18.3	26.6	24.7
Washington	73	1 438	36 244	13.2	30.5	43.8	269.9	17 316	36 805	72 784	92 845	7.5	70 705	10.4	12.0	9.8
SOUTH CAROLINA	498	3 460	1 201 061	14.6	45.0	25.3	6 981.8	9 514	24 222	45 033	61 196	2.7	45 337	17.9	26.4	25.1
Abbeville	316	2 306	6 008	19.4	58.0	12.3	27.5	8 676	18 303	35 409	45 773	1.0	35 525	21.4	29.8	26.7
Aiken	370	3 610	39 217	12.5	45.8	24.8	208.6	8 451	25 093	45 597	61 681	2.4	48 537	16.6	28.4	26.0
Allendale	469	1 788	2 204	7.3	63.1	12.7	19.4	14 597	12 277	25 495	33 438	0.1	25 530	39.9	48.7	46.4
Anderson	546	5 062	46 337	14.0	49.5	19.2	262.8	8 394	22 216	41 822	56 000	1.8	43 124	16.7	23.8	21.9
Bamberg	416	2 974	4 481	12.6	48.4	18.3	26.0	11 590	19 136	32 738	48 582	1.5	30 349	29.7	41.0	37.2
Barnwell	738	3 770	6 020	10.8	58.2	11.7	42.3	10 071	18 695	33 639	46 511	0.3	32 205	27.0	42.3	39.2
Beaufort	469	2 570	34 946	16.2	32.7	37.4	229.0	11 201	32 290	57 295	79 308	6.4	55 427	12.9	24.6	23.9
Berkeley	307	2 515	49 285	16.4	44.1	21.6	268.8	8 686	24 474	51 844	65 032	2.5	52 436	13.7	20.7	20.3
Calhoun	368	2 370	3 555	20.6	54.8	16.8	18.1	10 549	23 042	41 727	55 812	1.8	41 209	19.3	29.2	28.0
Charleston	418	2 923	93 185	17.9	32.1	40.0	510.3	11 441	31 198	52 083	75 060	5.6	52 752	16.8	25.7	24.3
Cherokee	363	3 240	13 560	12.8	60.3	14.7	81.2	8 993	19 185	34 766	49 219	1.2	38 947	22.3	31.6	29.8
Chester	706	3 114	7 618	12.7	60.5	13.0	54.1	9 800	18 433	33 151	46 555	1.0	37 537	22.5	33.5	32.4
Chesterfield	402	3 160	10 695	8.1	64.4	12.4	67.9	9 086	17 317	31 692	42 916	0.8	34 949	26.4	35.0	30.6
Clarendon	512	3 565	7 796	14.9	59.2	13.6	47.0	9 220	17 517	32 243	44 814	1.4	32 268	27.0	39.1	36.3
Colleton	865	4 068	8 953	8.2	57.5	14.1	56.3	9 188	18 517	32 224	46 110	1.3	35 558	23.0	35.1	34.6
Darlington	436	3 776	16 544	13.1	56.8	16.1	92.6	9 021	19 800	35 494	50 157	1.4	35 640	25.3	36.1	33.0
Dillon	867	5 447	7 529	8.7	67.3	8.3	48.4	8 155	15 010	28 847	39 119	0.5	30 516	29.8	41.8	41.4
Dorchester	412	3 302	39 162	16.2	39.8	24.9	228.5	8 808	24 633	54 452	66 043	2.2	56 388	12.8	19.1	19.0
Edgefield	117	1 616	6 061	11.3	55.5	18.6	35.9	10 224	20 809	44 704	57 191	0.9	44 129	17.5	26.5	24.4
Fairfield	677	3 256	4 747	15.0	58.8	15.2	41.8	13 816	20 993	36 213	49 428	1.6	35 490	23.1	34.5	31.7
Florence	490	4 158	36 984	13.6	50.2	21.5	215.8	9 287	22 522	42 321	58 239	2.4	42 232	19.5	28.2	27.5
Georgetown	458	3 473	12 764	10.1	46.5	23.8	100.4	10 321	24 483	41 578	59 677	3.3	44 283	19.6	31.6	30.8
Greenville	584	3 427	117 626	23.3	39.9	31.6	620.2	8 421	27 097	49 968	68 855	3.8	49 659	14.7	21.5	20.4
Greenwood	578	4 149	17 968	7.6	49.9	23.0	102.8	8 733	21 050	36 045	52 213	1.9	38 878	22.1	33.1	31.5
Hampton	611	2 753	4 682	7.6	63.5	11.1	39.2	11 419	19 849	34 494	48 856	1.5	33 644	23.8	34.8	32.5
Horry	536	5 173	59 783	9.1	44.5	22.9	413.3	10 333	23 693	42 322	56 003	2.0	42 830	17.6	29.9	29.8
Jasper	276	3 681	5 913	17.8	61.9	13.0	37.1	12 748	17 606	37 801	46 297	0.9	37 715	24.5	41.2	41.4
Kershaw	317	2 244	15 012	11.7	50.1	20.0	90.2	8 675	21 851	43 203	55 266	1.9	45 411	17.4	25.3	23.7
Lancaster	497	3 163	17 570	8.2	50.4	20.3	103.3	8 753	21 943	42 906	55 811	1.8	44 854	19.7	30.3	28.3
Laurens	582	3 648	15 687	12.1	58.0	14.3	81.7	9 128	19 953	38 300	50 209	1.2	38 268	21.1	30.5	29.5
Lee	653	3 540	4 408	14.5	65.3	9.7	21.9	9 754	15 095	30 939	42 187	0.2	31 510	27.8	36.3	34.7
Lexington	340	2 660	68 769	12.9	39.5	28.7	372.1	9 819	27 026	54 170	68 230	3.0	54 098	13.8	20.1	18.6
McCormick	121	1 462	1 547	10.9	53.4	17.7	11.6	14 146	21 730	38 919	53 365	2.7	38 694	24.6	41.0	39.6
Marion	700	5 851	7 905	11.9	59.0	15.0	51.4	9 869	16 743	29 884	42 642	0.9	32 283	30.1	48.0	45.0
Marlboro	914	3 827	6 140	4.8	69.2	9.0	41.0	9 514	14 925	28 765	40 536	1.0	31 170	31.4	46.5	40.7
Newberry	289	2 598	8 989	15.3	56.0	17.8	59.5	10 060	22 073	41 971	55 795	1.9	42 000	19.4	30.3	27.9
Oconee	449	2 723	16 569	10.7	50.2	22.1	109.1	10 330	24 321	41 197	58 663	2.6	39 548	17.5	23.7	22.3
Orangeburg	530	4 270	24 649	14.6	54.7	18.8	154.1	11 087	17 645	33 615	44 954	1.0	31 382	30.8	43.1	41.1
Pickens	316	3 546	38 653	9.3	48.6	22.4	131.1	7 832	21 090	41 501	54 701	1.5	41 375	19.5	21.9	20.0
Richland	805	4 128	124 348	16.3	32.7	36.2	780.5	11 626	25 920	48 674	65 975	3.2	49 782	16.1	22.2	20.9
Saluda	242	1 543	4 009	9.5	63.8	12.2	20.7	9 467	19 601	38 216	50 218	1.3	42 286	20.6	32.7	33.6
Spartanburg	380	3 019	74 362	15.4	47.4	21.9	456.7	9 742	22 330	43 555	57 559	1.9	44 050	17.7	26.7	26.1

1. Data for serious crimes have not been adjusted for underreporting; this may affect comparability between geographic areas and over time.   2. Per 100,000 population estimated by the FBI.
3. All persons 3 years old and over enrolled in nursery school through college.   4. Persons 25 years old and over.   5. Elementary and secondary education expenditures.
6. Based on population estimated by the American Community Survey, 2010–2014.

Table B. States and Counties — **Personal Income**

STATE County	Personal income, 2014										Earnings, 2014		
	Total (mil dol)	Percent change, 2013–2014	Per capita[1] Dollars	Per capita[1] Rank	Wages and salaries (mil dol)	Supplements to wages and salaries; employer contributions (mil dol) Pension and insurance	Supplements to wages and salaries; employer contributions (mil dol) Government social insurance	Proprietors' income (mil dol)	Dividends, interest, and rent (mil dol)	Personal transfer receipts (mil dol)	Total (mil dol)	Contributions for government social insurance (mil dol) From employee and self-employed	Contributions for government social insurance (mil dol) From employer
	62	63	64	65	66	67	68	69	70	71	72	73	74
PENNSYLVANIA—Cont'd													
Potter	617	3.1	35 867	1 798	218	55	18	95	90	174	385	24	18
Schuylkill	5 517	3.5	37 839	1 478	1 979	444	170	312	834	1 459	2 905	189	170
Snyder	1 455	3.4	36 084	1 768	532	122	47	127	214	395	828	50	47
Somerset	2 715	2.2	35 615	1 838	949	225	80	241	447	727	1 495	98	80
Sullivan	239	4.7	37 752	1 489	65	17	6	15	60	72	103	7	6
Susquehanna	1 570	1.9	37 459	1 532	377	90	30	148	293	359	645	44	30
Tioga	1 453	2.7	34 360	2 053	541	135	44	101	244	384	822	52	44
Union	1 556	3.2	34 666	1 989	721	159	61	168	263	295	1 109	63	61
Venango	1 935	2.1	36 151	1 755	743	186	62	68	289	632	1 059	71	62
Warren	1 542	3.2	37 883	1 471	601	138	49	136	251	405	925	59	49
Washington	10 047	3.0	48 258	466	4 974	815	379	756	1 556	1 987	6 923	427	379
Wayne	1 797	3.4	34 962	1 943	574	138	48	110	365	494	871	59	48
Westmoreland	15 963	2.9	44 425	723	5 790	1 107	480	868	2 458	3 598	8 244	539	480
Wyoming	1 048	3.8	37 270	1 559	486	92	40	57	172	238	674	42	40
York	18 969	3.3	43 037	842	8 007	1 527	660	839	2 884	3 560	11 033	672	660
RHODE ISLAND	51 027	5.0	48 359	X	24 528	3 968	1 997	4 055	8 966	10 285	34 549	2 295	1 997
Bristol	3 274	3.9	66 737	75	623	111	52	202	923	406	987	74	52
Kent	8 494	4.6	51 438	316	3 583	555	302	477	1 243	1 590	4 917	339	302
Newport	4 735	4.5	57 488	164	2 221	426	194	239	1 295	762	3 080	194	194
Providence	27 669	5.4	43 782	778	15 618	2 389	1 247	2 657	4 084	6 444	21 911	1 445	1 247
Washington	6 855	4.4	54 128	231	2 484	487	202	480	1 421	1 084	3 654	243	202
SOUTH CAROLINA	177 242	4.7	36 677	X	85 576	14 253	6 560	11 748	29 557	40 138	118 138	7 551	6 560
Abbeville	738	4.4	29 570	2 775	221	45	18	55	91	243	339	26	18
Aiken	6 139	3.3	37 265	1 560	2 883	412	220	443	935	1 414	3 958	263	220
Allendale	275	-1.4	28 315	2 894	130	24	9	18	38	96	181	12	9
Anderson	6 599	4.9	34 228	2 077	2 470	426	190	379	899	1 708	3 465	242	190
Bamberg	451	4.1	29 701	2 761	152	31	12	30	56	160	224	16	12
Barnwell	597	2.2	27 202	2 969	190	38	15	27	90	213	270	20	15
Beaufort	8 113	4.6	46 137	588	2 938	536	241	511	2 726	1 578	4 225	267	241
Berkeley	6 900	5.9	34 810	1 965	2 250	346	168	627	925	1 317	3 390	218	168
Calhoun	530	0.3	35 642	1 834	190	37	15	69	72	143	311	21	15
Charleston	18 229	5.2	47 843	486	11 918	2 011	910	1 908	4 162	2 788	16 747	969	910
Cherokee	1 582	4.0	28 230	2 901	707	123	58	69	193	495	957	67	58
Chester	947	3.5	29 298	2 797	350	62	27	49	117	318	488	35	27
Chesterfield	1 328	2.7	28 790	2 847	548	95	43	71	147	403	758	53	43
Clarendon	925	1.1	27 112	2 973	239	48	18	56	139	362	360	30	18
Colleton	1 207	5.0	31 966	2 440	374	69	29	62	183	393	534	40	29
Darlington	2 227	1.7	32 840	2 307	948	160	71	76	279	656	1 256	87	71
Dillon	768	1.0	24 674	3 071	283	51	23	13	89	299	372	29	23
Dorchester	4 929	6.0	33 199	2 245	1 210	204	92	51	656	1 086	1 558	112	92
Edgefield	782	3.6	29 435	2 786	225	45	18	29	108	206	317	22	18
Fairfield	723	2.6	31 449	2 533	563	95	43	26	93	227	728	46	43
Florence	5 065	3.5	36 380	1 709	2 749	456	204	354	735	1 299	3 763	240	204
Georgetown	2 418	3.7	39 788	1 209	928	150	71	218	587	662	1 369	96	71
Greenville	19 692	5.6	40 791	1 089	12 372	1 767	945	1 396	2 930	3 544	16 481	1 025	945
Greenwood	2 288	3.8	32 913	2 293	1 169	226	87	114	357	662	1 596	105	87
Hampton	555	1.8	27 216	2 967	201	39	15	30	80	183	286	20	15
Horry	9 555	6.4	31 973	2 438	4 095	637	334	713	1 755	2 830	5 778	403	334
Jasper	660	4.1	24 301	3 075	309	52	24	60	79	206	445	30	24
Kershaw	2 256	3.0	35 720	1 817	727	126	56	158	295	561	1 067	72	56
Lancaster	2 905	6.5	34 936	1 948	1 021	163	76	200	373	742	1 460	103	76
Laurens	2 005	4.8	30 131	2 701	841	143	66	62	255	692	1 112	80	66
Lee	482	-2.6	26 275	3 020	126	25	10	40	60	185	200	15	10
Lexington	11 098	5.0	39 935	1 189	4 715	777	356	807	1 560	1 989	6 654	421	356
McCormick	306	3.4	31 092	2 571	61	14	4	8	66	120	87	9	4
Marion	943	3.0	29 520	2 778	228	44	18	106	102	330	395	30	18
Marlboro	690	0.3	24 717	3 068	309	58	24	18	92	264	409	30	24
Newberry	1 273	3.1	33 686	2 163	490	95	37	46	188	351	668	46	37
Oconee	2 691	3.7	35 794	1 807	1 143	214	86	91	501	728	1 535	108	86
Orangeburg	2 675	2.1	29 691	2 763	1 170	211	92	131	353	892	1 604	111	92
Pickens	3 902	4.7	32 419	2 385	1 441	266	104	150	604	961	1 962	137	104
Richland	15 585	4.8	38 811	1 351	10 478	1 882	790	885	2 655	2 959	14 034	816	790
Saluda	603	0.3	30 107	2 703	145	32	11	30	76	167	219	16	11
Spartanburg	10 739	4.8	36 583	1 671	5 904	910	446	862	1 871	2 410	8 122	524	446

1. Based on the resident population estimated as of July 1 of the year shown.

Table B. States and Counties — Earnings, Social Security, and Housing

STATE County	Earnings, 2014 (cont.)									Social Security beneficiaries, December 2014			Housing units, 2015	
	Percent by selected industries													
	Farm	Mining	Construction	Manu-facturing	Infor-mation: professional, scientific, technical services	Retail trade	Finance, insur-ance, real estate and leasing	Health care and social assistance	Govern-ment	Number	Rate[1]	Supple-mental Security Income recipients, December 2014	Total	Percent change, 2010–2014
	75	76	77	78	79	80	81	82	83	84	85	86	87	88
PENNSYLVANIA—Cont'd														
Potter	4.1	0.6	6.8	10.0	18.5	4.8	3.9	D	17.1	4 930	286	472	12 814	-0.9
Schuylkill	1.9	2.4	4.1	22.5	4.0	6.5	3.0	13.7	18.5	37 980	261	3 935	69 113	-0.3
Snyder	5.7	D	5.0	23.4	3.0	10.9	2.7	D	19.0	8 835	219	652	16 140	0.7
Somerset	2.3	6.7	5.1	10.5	5.2	6.9	4.8	12.1	21.1	20 360	267	2 402	37 889	-0.6
Sullivan	1.9	D	11.7	D	D	6.4	D	D	25.1	1 950	308	139	6 298	-0.1
Susquehanna	1.7	16.9	10.8	4.4	4.7	7.2	4.1	8.0	19.6	10 635	254	873	23 020	0.2
Tioga	3.2	6.1	4.5	13.8	5.1	7.6	4.6	D	23.1	10 940	260	1 120	21 506	0.7
Union	5.9	D	4.8	7.1	2.6	5.4	3.5	D	23.2	8 380	187	552	17 078	0.5
Venango	-0.1	1.8	3.3	26.1	2.5	7.7	3.1	14.2	22.4	15 335	287	2 145	27 228	-0.9
Warren	0.7	7.2	3.4	18.0	3.8	7.2	5.6	13.1	15.7	11 085	272	994	23 332	-1.0
Washington	0.1	9.4	11.4	10.2	8.3	5.0	5.9	10.8	10.3	51 235	246	5 339	94 124	1.2
Wayne	1.5	0.6	10.6	3.5	7.0	9.4	5.1	14.4	28.0	14 070	274	1 042	31 903	0.8
Westmoreland	0.1	2.9	7.8	15.6	6.9	7.8	4.2	12.3	13.9	95 480	266	8 918	168 225	0.0
Wyoming	3.6	11.0	5.4	28.2	D	6.0	1.9	D	11.6	6 900	245	588	13 314	0.5
York	0.4	0.3	8.2	19.7	6.9	6.5	4.3	13.5	14.6	92 080	209	8 688	181 068	1.3
RHODE ISLAND	0.1	D	5.1	8.8	11.6	5.7	10.2	14.6	16.8	216 029	205	33 280	462 578	-0.2
Bristol	0.0	0.0	6.0	D	7.2	4.9	5.4	13.4	17.8	10 950	223	661	20 787	-0.3
Kent	0.0	D	5.2	11.1	10.7	9.0	9.0	15.3	13.5	38 430	233	3 458	73 593	-0.1
Newport	0.1	D	4.3	D	11.8	5.6	4.9	7.7	37.0	18 470	224	1 371	41 951	0.4
Providence	0.0	0.0	5.1	6.9	12.8	4.6	12.4	15.8	13.7	120 505	191	26 212	263 219	-0.6
Washington	0.3	0.2	4.8	17.6	6.9	8.5	4.4	12.6	22.3	27 675	219	1 578	63 028	1.3
SOUTH CAROLINA	0.3	0.1	5.7	14.4	8.9	7.3	7.1	9.5	20.5	1 040 971	216	118 354	2 210 082	3.4
Abbeville	2.3	0.0	6.0	32.7	3.7	4.5	1.9	3.1	21.0	6 535	262	644	12 004	-0.6
Aiken	-0.2	0.2	8.9	13.3	12.0	6.0	5.7	7.6	11.5	37 520	228	3 925	74 504	3.1
Allendale	5.4	0.0	0.8	32.7	D	3.0	D	D	27.8	2 245	232	632	4 451	-0.8
Anderson	0.3	0.1	5.8	25.0	4.1	9.6	3.2	8.3	20.2	47 175	245	4 763	86 084	1.5
Bamberg	4.6	0.0	2.4	20.9	3.7	6.0	D	7.5	22.5	3 680	242	717	7 604	-1.5
Barnwell	1.3	0.0	4.0	27.9	D	8.9	1.8	D	26.0	5 230	238	1 146	10 378	-1.0
Beaufort	0.2	0.1	6.9	1.1	8.4	8.3	8.2	8.8	32.8	44 625	255	2 002	95 287	2.4
Berkeley	0.2	D	9.9	14.7	20.7	7.2	3.3	3.7	16.4	33 310	168	2 670	79 154	7.9
Calhoun	1.7	0.0	13.4	33.1	D	3.1	D	D	11.4	3 810	256	418	7 298	-0.5
Charleston	0.1	0.0	5.5	8.8	11.0	7.0	8.2	11.1	25.1	68 470	180	7 402	180 681	6.3
Cherokee	0.6	D	D	36.8	1.8	7.4	3.2	D	12.9	13 675	244	1 624	24 052	0.2
Chester	2.1	0.0	6.5	34.5	4.7	5.4	2.0	D	17.2	8 485	262	1 178	14 582	-0.8
Chesterfield	1.2	D	4.1	36.7	2.6	6.2	1.7	9.0	13.4	10 595	230	1 576	21 260	-1.0
Clarendon	1.3	0.0	4.9	5.8	7.1	11.8	3.2	7.4	34.8	9 430	277	1 787	17 419	-0.3
Colleton	0.2	D	5.5	8.2	D	9.3	5.2	15.1	19.0	10 225	271	1 817	19 676	-1.1
Darlington	0.2	0.0	3.6	29.2	2.3	6.2	2.4	9.9	12.6	16 475	243	2 945	30 215	-0.3
Dillon	-4.6	0.0	2.3	22.2	D	11.2	3.6	D	19.4	7 235	231	1 653	13 545	-1.4
Dorchester	0.2	D	5.8	20.9	4.7	9.2	3.5	8.4	20.9	26 095	176	3 372	58 621	6.2
Edgefield	3.8	D	4.0	17.4	1.9	6.4	2.4	D	32.3	5 635	213	820	10 655	0.9
Fairfield	1.0	D	2.4	36.0	11.2	2.3	0.6	2.8	10.1	5 640	246	874	11 677	0.0
Florence	0.4	D	3.7	11.8	7.8	8.2	13.3	13.3	19.7	30 215	217	5 991	59 210	0.9
Georgetown	0.5	0.1	7.4	13.7	6.5	8.1	6.4	11.6	21.7	18 940	312	1 632	34 262	1.8
Greenville	0.0	0.1	6.6	13.7	12.6	6.1	7.4	9.7	11.6	93 305	193	9 067	203 433	4.1
Greenwood	0.1	D	3.8	26.0	3.2	7.0	3.1	11.9	24.3	16 465	237	1 765	31 210	0.5
Hampton	0.5	0.0	4.3	14.0	D	8.1	D	D	30.1	4 530	222	813	9 007	-1.5
Horry	0.5	D	7.1	3.4	6.7	11.9	12.6	11.1	16.3	82 650	277	5 996	196 116	5.4
Jasper	0.5	0.0	12.4	2.8	D	20.3	5.2	13.4	16.1	5 075	188	683	11 077	7.6
Kershaw	2.9	1.4	7.2	19.7	4.1	9.3	6.7	6.2	16.9	14 365	227	1 252	28 191	2.6
Lancaster	1.1	0.0	3.8	14.1	22.0	9.7	3.7	11.5	12.8	20 490	247	1 722	35 063	7.3
Laurens	0.6	D	3.2	39.1	4.8	5.2	1.4	D	17.4	17 970	270	2 506	30 613	-0.3
Lee	8.5	0.0	4.3	15.2	D	6.2	D	D	26.6	4 270	232	750	7 659	-1.5
Lexington	-0.1	0.1	7.3	10.7	7.5	8.8	5.8	7.1	19.0	51 550	186	4 495	119 716	5.0
McCormick	1.3	0.0	D	11.6	D	4.4	D	D	49.8	3 475	352	312	5 476	0.4
Marion	1.6	D	6.7	9.5	D	14.4	5.9	D	18.3	8 365	262	1 694	14 762	-1.3
Marlboro	1.0	D	1.7	37.0	7.5	6.9	2.3	D	25.7	6 975	250	1 478	11 928	-1.2
Newberry	1.2	0.0	5.9	39.6	D	6.7	1.8	D	18.2	9 475	251	1 041	17 982	0.3
Oconee	0.4	D	4.9	27.8	D	6.4	2.9	6.7	14.6	21 730	289	1 536	39 255	1.3
Orangeburg	0.4	0.0	4.6	22.5	2.7	10.1	3.7	7.4	26.5	21 545	240	4 050	42 086	-1.0
Pickens	0.0	D	4.7	19.8	4.3	9.2	3.7	8.7	33.2	26 445	219	2 290	52 416	2.3
Richland	0.0	D	3.6	5.6	11.2	5.2	11.4	11.6	30.4	63 975	159	8 694	168 973	4.5
Saluda	11.3	D	3.1	37.2	D	4.9	1.3	D	21.0	4 390	219	465	9 262	-0.3
Spartanburg	0.1	0.1	5.3	26.1	5.4	6.4	4.7	8.1	15.3	65 300	222	7 143	125 343	2.2

1. Per 1,000 resident population estimated as of July 1 of the year shown.

Table B. States and Counties — Housing, Labor Force, and Employment

STATE County	Housing units, 2010–2014 Occupied units — Owner-occupied Total	Percent	Median value[1]	Median owner cost as a percent of income — With a mortgage	Without a mortgage[2]	Renter-occupied — Median rent[3]	Median rent as a percent of income[2]	Sub-standard units[4] (percent)	Civilian labor force, 2015 Total	Percent change, 2014–2015	Unemployment Total	Rate[5]	Civilian employment[6] 2010–2014 Total	Percent — Management, business, science and arts	Construction, production, and maintenance occupations
	89	90	91	92	93	94	95	96	97	98	99	100	101	102	103
PENNSYLVANIA—Cont'd															
Potter	6 848	77.7	100 300	22.3	13.3	595	29.3	1.7	7 449	-1.5	503	6.8	7 090	29.0	36.4
Schuylkill	59 122	75.1	93 800	22.1	14.6	627	27.0	1.1	68 256	-1.0	4 166	6.1	63 551	27.7	32.2
Snyder	14 414	75.6	139 400	21.7	12.4	689	26.1	2.7	20 054	1.0	911	4.5	19 037	26.7	31.8
Somerset	29 748	78.0	97 400	21.6	13.1	572	26.1	1.3	34 396	-1.7	2 286	6.6	33 249	27.8	31.9
Sullivan	2 476	83.3	139 400	22.7	14.1	569	30.1	1.4	3 042	-0.5	182	6.0	2 503	25.3	37.5
Susquehanna	17 265	77.4	145 800	22.3	13.7	715	29.0	1.4	21 505	0.4	1 161	5.4	19 250	27.1	34.1
Tioga	16 802	75.1	121 300	22.0	13.6	684	28.8	1.5	20 398	-0.2	1 290	6.3	18 240	29.3	32.3
Union	15 058	72.2	154 000	23.4	13.2	715	28.6	1.8	19 313	1.0	835	4.3	17 776	33.1	25.7
Venango	22 412	76.3	80 800	20.0	11.3	586	28.5	1.1	24 397	-1.1	1 408	5.8	24 090	28.6	30.2
Warren	17 029	77.2	89 300	19.8	11.8	585	26.3	1.5	19 980	-0.9	969	4.8	18 378	31.2	31.1
Washington	83 644	76.3	147 000	19.5	11.3	652	27.2	1.1	106 529	0.4	5 754	5.4	98 955	34.4	23.6
Wayne	19 362	79.1	178 600	27.3	13.5	783	34.3	1.2	22 240	-0.4	1 261	5.7	21 273	27.6	28.2
Westmoreland	151 489	76.0	137 200	20.2	12.3	651	27.3	0.8	183 521	0.2	9 587	5.2	172 631	34.5	24.3
Wyoming	10 895	78.1	157 800	22.5	13.7	701	29.1	2.0	14 224	-0.3	839	5.9	12 935	25.7	33.1
York	168 278	75.0	170 900	23.7	14.4	838	30.0	1.4	232 848	1.0	10 718	4.6	215 874	32.4	27.2
RHODE ISLAND	409 569	60.3	241 200	25.8	15.6	923	30.9	2.1	554 557	-0.3	33 124	6.0	511 362	36.4	18.8
Bristol	19 167	71.7	330 600	25.5	17.0	968	32.9	1.4	26 254	0.2	1 338	5.1	24 343	47.1	13.7
Kent	68 428	70.2	211 700	25.4	15.8	981	30.7	1.2	91 172	-0.2	5 030	5.5	84 914	36.1	19.1
Newport	34 833	62.6	346 500	25.2	14.1	1 130	29.0	1.0	44 108	0.0	2 282	5.2	40 882	42.8	13.8
Providence	237 650	53.4	215 800	26.3	16.2	884	31.3	2.8	323 300	-0.3	20 660	6.4	296 361	33.0	20.6
Washington	49 491	73.6	314 900	25.0	14.4	1 044	29.8	0.9	69 723	-0.2	3 814	5.5	64 862	44.3	15.2
SOUTH CAROLINA	1 795 715	68.6	137 600	22.5	11.3	784	31.6	2.3	2 257 083	1.8	134 507	6.0	2 031 997	32.6	23.9
Abbeville	9 752	78.2	89 000	23.0	12.9	583	39.7	2.0	10 423	-1.2	717	6.9	9 361	26.7	34.6
Aiken	63 609	73.5	126 900	21.0	10.8	705	30.3	2.1	73 562	1.1	4 354	5.9	68 521	34.5	26.6
Allendale	3 456	64.8	55 800	24.6	17.4	580	31.4	2.0	2 763	-3.4	316	11.4	2 846	21.6	37.9
Anderson	73 669	72.4	124 500	21.8	10.1	669	32.0	2.2	88 383	2.2	4 755	5.4	79 245	28.9	28.6
Bamberg	5 777	79.1	67 300	21.1	13.5	553	36.9	3.2	5 482	-1.2	576	10.5	5 564	27.6	29.0
Barnwell	8 434	74.2	72 200	23.7	13.7	632	33.4	3.7	8 453	-2.0	755	8.9	8 107	25.0	34.1
Beaufort	65 054	69.7	272 900	27.6	11.9	1 042	30.3	2.9	71 344	3.0	3 877	5.4	68 431	32.4	18.1
Berkeley	67 423	69.5	151 100	23.5	11.3	982	32.0	1.9	92 754	2.3	5 082	5.5	81 461	31.4	25.7
Calhoun	6 135	78.4	98 400	21.4	13.2	707	30.3	2.3	6 966	1.5	490	7.0	6 393	26.4	35.2
Charleston	145 991	60.4	236 900	25.2	13.3	973	34.0	1.9	196 913	2.7	9 534	4.8	177 364	39.2	17.1
Cherokee	20 647	68.2	84 100	21.3	11.7	647	28.9	3.1	23 392	-0.9	1 674	7.2	21 085	25.4	34.2
Chester	12 237	73.8	84 200	21.4	11.5	598	32.6	2.2	13 621	1.7	1 130	8.3	12 381	20.6	36.5
Chesterfield	17 837	69.9	78 000	22.8	10.9	589	37.7	2.8	21 330	0.8	1 307	6.1	17 882	24.2	34.8
Clarendon	12 768	71.8	87 700	24.4	12.0	572	30.7	3.8	13 077	1.0	1 015	7.8	11 329	26.3	30.4
Colleton	14 678	73.5	85 200	26.1	14.4	702	32.3	2.4	16 745	0.9	1 167	7.0	14 378	23.7	29.9
Darlington	26 267	69.1	86 200	20.1	11.3	617	32.4	2.6	30 054	1.3	2 225	7.4	25 743	27.0	30.1
Dillon	11 703	64.6	64 100	22.7	13.9	544	29.2	4.6	12 629	0.5	1 093	8.7	11 006	17.5	36.6
Dorchester	51 450	70.0	164 400	23.8	11.8	966	31.8	1.5	71 848	2.5	3 910	5.4	64 848	33.9	22.7
Edgefield	9 043	77.0	110 400	20.5	11.7	580	27.8	3.6	10 700	1.7	680	6.4	10 080	26.6	35.0
Fairfield	9 402	69.8	95 700	24.9	13.6	665	31.7	1.0	10 167	1.6	811	8.0	8 886	26.0	35.9
Florence	51 794	65.8	118 100	20.6	10.5	668	29.9	2.4	65 412	1.1	4 299	6.6	57 320	34.3	20.5
Georgetown	23 309	76.9	155 300	27.9	13.4	832	32.3	1.6	25 247	2.0	2 112	8.4	22 847	29.6	23.6
Greenville	176 955	66.4	154 500	20.9	10.0	763	29.2	2.0	240 641	2.4	11 917	5.0	215 311	36.8	21.6
Greenwood	26 760	65.5	101 100	20.7	11.1	645	33.1	2.9	31 304	-0.9	1 978	6.3	28 214	30.9	30.5
Hampton	7 463	76.7	78 800	22.5	16.0	643	28.4	3.5	8 323	0.4	708	8.5	7 788	22.4	29.7
Horry	115 764	69.3	157 700	26.5	11.9	833	33.9	3.4	136 476	2.0	9 596	7.0	125 690	27.8	17.8
Jasper	8 749	71.0	94 400	29.7	12.4	761	31.1	3.3	11 733	2.9	601	5.1	11 744	18.0	31.8
Kershaw	24 061	77.6	113 500	23.3	11.3	683	25.6	1.6	28 889	1.9	1 725	6.0	25 799	29.6	29.1
Lancaster	29 104	75.8	147 300	23.1	11.0	652	33.1	2.2	35 971	2.3	2 278	6.3	31 680	27.9	26.6
Laurens	25 312	71.2	81 000	20.5	10.3	664	31.6	2.2	30 497	2.3	1 981	6.5	26 998	24.0	35.2
Lee	6 471	74.6	64 500	24.2	12.4	604	33.8	3.5	6 467	0.5	551	8.5	6 117	23.0	30.3
Lexington	105 081	73.8	139 200	20.5	10.0	832	29.6	1.9	144 101	2.1	6 988	4.8	129 729	35.9	22.0
McCormick	4 058	78.6	105 300	26.5	11.8	518	31.7	0.7	3 454	-0.7	248	7.2	2 995	22.2	32.7
Marion	11 782	67.2	75 900	23.1	13.2	521	36.8	2.0	12 858	0.3	1 290	10.0	11 642	26.3	32.0
Marlboro	9 645	67.0	58 400	20.7	12.6	552	33.4	4.2	9 673	-2.7	977	10.1	9 276	22.0	39.2
Newberry	14 230	73.0	104 500	21.2	11.1	654	29.9	2.4	18 831	1.8	1 002	5.3	16 084	26.6	34.9
Oconee	30 319	74.8	138 700	22.9	10.1	690	33.2	2.2	34 437	1.0	1 999	5.8	28 894	31.6	28.6
Orangeburg	33 836	68.3	86 900	23.3	13.2	667	34.2	2.9	37 194	-1.5	3 997	10.7	33 771	28.2	29.2
Pickens	44 091	69.3	120 600	20.9	10.5	706	34.2	1.8	55 946	2.3	3 217	5.8	50 154	33.3	25.6
Richland	144 647	59.8	148 000	22.2	11.1	868	32.4	1.8	197 036	1.9	11 164	5.7	179 668	39.0	15.4
Saluda	7 113	71.6	88 900	22.5	12.1	638	24.7	3.1	8 862	2.6	462	5.2	7 907	22.1	40.7
Spartanburg	108 383	68.6	123 200	21.1	10.0	700	30.8	2.5	139 121	1.9	7 949	5.7	125 017	30.6	28.6

1. Specified owner-occupied units. 2. A value of 10.0 represents 10 percent or less; a value of 50.0 represents 50 percent or more. 3. Specified renter-occupied units.
4. Overcrowded or lacking complete plumbing facilities. 5. Percent of civilian labor force. 6. Persons 16 years old and over.

Table B. States and Counties — Nonfarm Employment and Agriculture

| STATE County | Private nonfarm establishments, employment and payroll, 2014 | | | | | | | | | Agriculture, 2012 | | | |
	Number of establish-ments	Employment Total	Health care and social assistance	Manufac-turing	Retail trade	Finance and insurance	Professional, scientific, and technical services	Annual payroll Total (mil dol)	Average per employee (dollars)	Farms Number	Percent with: Fewer than 50 acres	500 acres or more	Farm operators whose principal occu-pation is farming (percent)
	104	105	106	107	108	109	110	111	112	113	114	115	116
PENNSYLVANIA—Cont'd													
Potter	349	4 230	918	511	549	D	140	154	36 442	442	23.8	9.3	55.9
Schuylkill	2 812	40 196	7 236	9 379	5 653	953	1 066	1 443	35 897	791	41.5	5.4	49.7
Snyder	875	14 882	1 639	3 846	3 027	295	188	418	28 090	933	46.7	2.9	47.9
Somerset	1 688	18 761	3 445	2 889	2 650	729	611	658	35 060	1 140	22.5	7.2	48.3
Sullivan	161	1 231	456	D	258	D	D	31	25 054	179	24.6	8.9	50.3
Susquehanna	886	7 146	1 123	584	1 284	211	258	225	31 550	1 005	29.7	5.5	51.0
Tioga	887	11 125	2 119	2 186	1 922	392	276	410	36 822	1 125	21.0	7.0	49.5
Union	902	15 882	4 144	1 398	1 652	390	345	549	34 556	613	37.8	2.3	61.5
Venango	1 196	16 234	3 353	4 050	2 533	382	361	559	34 464	464	33.0	5.4	48.1
Warren	923	14 084	3 080	2 974	2 233	D	291	516	36 604	602	34.7	4.5	39.0
Washington	5 091	83 500	13 248	9 560	8 581	1 515	3 245	4 393	52 617	1 915	36.1	1.8	44.6
Wayne	1 295	12 282	2 544	621	2 549	467	300	393	31 977	711	24.9	4.1	50.4
Westmoreland	8 683	123 755	20 900	18 985	18 379	2 848	6 261	4 979	40 236	1 274	37.3	3.1	46.2
Wyoming	667	11 354	648	D	1 345	209	362	704	61 978	508	30.9	3.1	46.1
York	8 611	159 950	23 402	31 617	22 290	3 651	5 392	6 407	40 057	2 171	56.6	4.4	48.9
RHODE ISLAND	28 132	421 578	86 190	39 275	48 991	26 751	22 380	19 511	46 281	1 243	71.1	0.9	49.8
Bristol	1 227	14 219	3 305	1 578	1 374	219	453	448	31 531	42	73.8	0.0	57.1
Kent	4 668	68 240	12 080	6 129	11 258	5 113	4 238	2 874	42 115	126	65.9	1.6	41.3
Newport	2 715	30 089	4 864	2 030	4 098	1 310	2 923	1 385	46 039	214	72.4	0.9	55.6
Providence	15 563	263 991	58 257	22 576	25 622	18 824	12 278	12 720	48 184	425	73.2	0.2	45.6
Washington	3 739	41 953	7 613	6 961	6 639	956	1 637	1 881	44 846	436	69.7	1.4	52.8
SOUTH CAROLINA	102 297	1 617 249	221 357	219 826	229 453	67 780	83 937	62 406	38 588	25 266	44.1	8.1	41.0
Abbeville	329	4 475	468	2 085	445	125	46	146	32 604	574	32.2	5.9	34.1
Aiken	2 690	48 978	6 217	6 614	6 752	1 161	D	2 231	45 561	1 102	46.5	4.6	33.9
Allendale	125	1 646	D	830	D	D	D	68	41 576	141	22.0	27.0	54.6
Anderson	3 623	55 098	8 257	11 025	8 635	1 082	1 970	2 000	36 301	1 498	50.9	2.9	35.6
Bamberg	264	3 077	546	1 004	422	96	58	94	30 462	315	19.4	15.6	40.3
Barnwell	359	4 739	785	1 709	761	121	D	153	32 216	397	36.5	11.8	44.6
Beaufort	4 940	52 003	7 362	527	9 600	2 753	3 029	1 736	33 384	137	56.9	16.1	39.4
Berkeley	2 760	40 857	2 422	5 473	6 644	947	2 951	1 819	44 511	373	57.4	9.7	45.8
Calhoun	239	3 422	353	1 455	197	39	24	144	42 221	412	31.1	14.3	45.4
Charleston	12 358	190 684	29 573	15 162	27 647	6 309	16 596	7 998	41 944	359	64.1	3.6	42.9
Cherokee	955	17 452	1 159	5 654	2 748	296	190	543	31 101	490	43.1	3.9	31.4
Chester	531	6 610	D	2 213	913	147	123	256	38 683	477	33.5	8.6	39.8
Chesterfield	681	12 636	1 747	5 461	1 288	207	75	445	35 253	717	36.8	7.9	34.0
Clarendon	459	5 484	D	698	1 291	241	63	148	26 942	422	29.6	17.1	55.2
Colleton	713	7 220	1 325	729	1 531	274	225	227	31 377	530	40.4	13.0	42.1
Darlington	1 098	17 552	2 310	3 127	2 213	416	255	764	43 543	385	36.9	20.0	46.2
Dillon	470	7 428	1 176	2 128	1 101	171	D	186	25 097	228	21.1	24.6	46.5
Dorchester	2 152	24 651	2 817	4 194	4 120	692	832	840	34 079	411	48.7	7.5	46.7
Edgefield	310	4 611	507	1 177	412	57	51	162	35 219	389	40.1	9.0	36.2
Fairfield	286	5 181	660	979	592	D	D	299	57 626	194	32.5	10.3	40.2
Florence	3 044	55 643	13 095	6 292	8 759	4 237	2 433	2 013	36 173	632	33.4	11.1	44.3
Georgetown	1 774	18 471	3 636	2 084	2 862	521	774	665	36 028	209	39.7	13.9	44.0
Greenville	12 315	218 473	26 020	27 191	25 475	7 963	15 449	8 975	41 080	1 101	62.7	1.4	33.9
Greenwood	1 330	22 693	4 445	5 589	3 491	496	1 206	819	36 081	476	44.1	4.6	49.6
Hampton	325	3 253	D	631	592	126	92	117	36 087	323	28.5	18.6	46.1
Horry	8 294	99 390	10 664	2 618	21 885	3 491	3 132	2 865	28 830	938	44.1	9.8	50.5
Jasper	576	6 642	1 192	255	1 741	D	152	231	34 740	115	40.9	23.5	65.2
Kershaw	1 103	15 335	2 265	3 226	2 252	520	392	538	35 114	483	44.7	6.8	39.3
Lancaster	1 256	16 637	2 501	D	2 915	1 010	463	683	41 039	577	47.1	4.0	47.1
Laurens	929	16 112	1 878	6 030	1 631	380	D	599	37 155	826	40.0	5.3	35.4
Lee	187	1 744	214	D	375	69	44	49	28 251	386	26.2	16.8	45.3
Lexington	6 212	94 192	13 199	8 838	15 884	3 006	3 345	3 397	36 060	1 011	56.2	3.8	42.0
McCormick	87	951	211	275	115	22	D	26	27 849	93	24.7	21.5	35.5
Marion	497	5 197	613	800	1 051	213	80	142	27 281	275	40.7	17.1	41.8
Marlboro	327	5 065	1 011	1 973	919	121	53	159	31 441	224	26.8	20.1	44.6
Newberry	719	11 041	1 260	4 630	1 355	171	141	373	33 817	594	36.2	7.7	38.9
Oconee	1 473	19 852	2 602	5 288	2 906	418	470	773	38 931	884	60.7	1.7	39.3
Orangeburg	1 621	25 892	4 137	7 309	3 945	684	383	860	33 202	1 056	34.2	12.7	42.2
Pickens	1 984	28 992	3 698	4 991	4 659	616	811	844	29 121	727	69.6	1.1	44.0
Richland	8 761	157 927	27 196	9 813	18 610	18 967	11 122	6 630	41 979	398	52.0	4.5	38.9
Saluda	247	3 602	443	D	348	D	D	104	28 935	587	30.7	9.2	44.6
Spartanburg	6 146	121 579	14 433	27 278	14 042	2 021	4 823	5 117	42 085	1 338	57.6	1.4	43.7

Table B. States and Counties — **Agriculture**

	Land in farms					Value of land and buildings (dollars)		Value of machinery and equipment, average per farm (dollars)	Value of products sold				Percent of farms with sales of:		Government payments	
			Acres								Percent from:					
STATE County	Acreage (1,000)	Percent change, 2007– 2012	Average size of farm	Total irrigated (1,000)	Total cropland (1,000)	Average per farm	Average per acre		Total (mil dol)	Average per farm (dollars)	Crops	Live-stock and poultry products	$10,000 or more	$100,000 or more	Total ($1,000)	Percent of farms
	117	118	119	120	121	122	123	124	125	126	127	128	129	130	131	132
PENNSYLVANIA—Cont'd																
Potter	97	9.3	219	0.0	42.0	601 247	2 749	87 593	35.5	80 204	31.7	68.3	36.2	12.9	1 364	52.0
Schuylkill	106	-10.8	134	1.7	72.1	860 377	6 436	105 598	165.9	209 675	46.3	53.7	47.0	21.0	1 486	42.7
Snyder	91	-9.0	98	0.8	59.7	568 781	5 820	67 891	165.5	177 377	16.4	83.6	56.2	24.9	1 273	25.3
Somerset	215	3.8	188	0.1	119.4	495 161	2 631	91 144	104.2	91 411	26.0	74.0	52.8	21.1	1 602	30.9
Sullivan	37	34.7	209	0.0	15.4	645 698	3 084	97 117	9.5	53 168	26.7	73.3	33.5	8.9	461	43.6
Susquehanna	166	5.2	166	0.1	73.7	675 315	4 079	80 360	43.3	43 106	20.7	79.3	35.2	11.3	1 585	35.2
Tioga	205	11.4	182	0.2	109.0	626 933	3 438	78 940	80.3	71 340	26.5	73.5	43.6	13.3	2 590	42.0
Union	93	46.2	152	0.1	52.7	820 065	5 391	101 024	136.0	221 811	19.1	80.9	73.2	45.0	713	27.2
Venango	62	-5.0	133	0.0	29.0	410 136	3 093	81 901	15.8	33 998	64.5	35.5	39.2	6.7	489	22.8
Warren	82	-17.2	137	0.1	27.6	321 166	2 346	63 495	20.7	34 464	32.9	67.1	28.9	6.6	464	15.9
Washington	206	-2.5	107	0.8	86.4	489 897	4 558	68 244	35.4	18 492	53.1	46.9	28.1	2.7	841	10.9
Wayne	113	21.6	159	0.1	43.2	592 875	3 730	76 821	32.4	45 502	21.0	79.0	43.5	11.4	696	20.0
Westmoreland	143	-14.6	112	0.4	81.9	534 291	4 758	92 900	48.6	38 155	55.6	44.4	37.1	7.1	1 118	25.3
Wyoming	69	-11.8	135	0.1	32.4	542 844	4 011	79 911	14.6	28 772	57.3	42.7	32.7	7.7	633	31.7
York	262	-10.4	121	0.8	195.0	910 957	7 547	87 005	234.1	107 814	62.9	37.1	45.3	16.5	2 746	22.2
RHODE ISLAND	70	2.6	56	4.0	22.6	786 093	14 041	56 065	59.7	47 990	82.1	17.9	35.7	8.7	2 345	15.3
Bristol	D	D	D	0.1	1.1	977 024	D	52 190	2.7	63 548	80.4	19.5	47.6	16.7	D	2.4
Kent	D	D	D	0.2	1.9	790 095	D	39 087	4.4	34 548	80.4	19.6	38.1	7.9	D	7.9
Newport	12	13.9	54	0.5	6.5	1 201 720	22 248	63 850	14.6	68 365	83.1	16.9	47.2	12.6	390	22.4
Providence	D	D	D	0.6	4.9	600 586	D	41 569	14.1	33 127	77.8	22.2	31.3	5.2	949	17.9
Washington	27	10.8	63	2.6	8.2	743 369	11 870	71 654	23.9	54 865	84.6	15.4	32.6	9.6	936	12.6
SOUTH CAROLINA	4 971	1.7	197	159.2	1 967.3	586 518	2 981	72 400	3 040.1	120 323	42.6	57.4	27.0	8.6	46 616	26.9
Abbeville	92	0.9	160	D	23.7	444 972	2 775	52 261	9.6	16 786	31.0	69.0	26.1	1.2	631	19.9
Aiken	154	-3.1	140	1.3	55.8	532 257	3 800	54 850	96.3	87 426	16.3	83.7	26.9	7.1	892	16.1
Allendale	124	-0.7	882	6.5	39.1	1 949 496	2 211	94 773	25.6	181 532	89.3	10.7	27.0	12.8	946	68.8
Anderson	159	-8.1	106	0.6	46.5	463 880	4 367	51 636	62.8	41 918	D	D	23.5	4.3	779	12.3
Bamberg	93	-25.9	294	7.4	36.6	650 460	2 215	93 587	37.2	118 187	69.9	30.1	36.5	15.6	1 408	67.9
Barnwell	88	-5.2	221	4.4	37.5	539 234	2 437	79 058	48.4	121 867	D	D	29.5	13.9	1 091	48.9
Beaufort	42	-14.6	308	3.2	6.4	1 041 226	3 382	99 153	D	D	D	D	32.1	6.6	51	10.9
Berkeley	75	42.4	201	0.4	19.5	718 094	3 568	54 810	6.9	18 413	87.5	12.5	27.1	4.3	388	18.8
Calhoun	118	7.1	287	14.9	64.5	802 779	2 794	154 303	79.7	193 354	69.6	30.4	40.0	19.4	1 632	45.9
Charleston	35	-15.0	99	1.6	8.8	615 329	6 234	49 072	D	D	D	D	28.1	5.8	76	4.7
Cherokee	65	3.0	132	D	16.6	399 810	3 033	43 643	24.0	49 078	40.7	59.3	20.8	2.0	625	15.9
Chester	96	-14.6	200	0.5	19.0	564 608	2 820	65 338	42.6	89 329	D	D	29.8	6.1	376	10.3
Chesterfield	131	-6.8	183	1.2	42.4	500 552	2 739	59 743	121.2	169 050	D	D	23.2	7.8	1 047	37.1
Clarendon	174	12.3	412	8.5	98.1	758 033	1 840	152 725	139.6	330 829	53.2	46.8	42.2	20.1	1 972	68.7
Colleton	188	7.4	354	2.8	45.9	955 200	2 697	90 266	33.6	63 330	95.4	4.6	28.7	6.6	707	36.2
Darlington	177	2.4	459	7.3	113.7	1 132 418	2 465	182 395	129.2	335 509	58.4	41.6	45.7	26.5	2 806	47.3
Dillon	107	1.7	468	1.3	75.2	1 218 289	2 602	169 167	132.2	579 724	38.6	61.4	43.4	28.1	2 245	69.3
Dorchester	75	14.6	181	2.1	34.5	623 706	3 440	74 095	50.0	121 572	47.1	52.9	28.5	10.7	853	29.2
Edgefield	81	6.4	210	6.0	20.9	619 203	2 955	80 298	44.7	114 854	73.3	26.7	23.7	5.1	540	24.2
Fairfield	45	-14.2	229	D	7.3	640 268	2 791	51 732	30.9	159 237	5.0	95.0	26.8	6.7	137	9.8
Florence	156	-1.7	247	1.8	94.3	546 794	2 215	91 321	54.0	85 517	98.4	1.6	35.1	11.6	2 303	49.8
Georgetown	66	15.1	318	0.5	12.4	747 407	2 354	71 541	12.8	61 287	98.3	1.7	23.0	8.6	313	56.5
Greenville	73	0.3	66	1.6	20.6	430 060	6 498	38 996	16.6	15 044	81.7	18.4	15.8	1.7	180	5.3
Greenwood	86	21.0	180	0.2	12.7	432 540	2 407	46 794	6.7	14 023	33.3	66.7	23.3	1.7	311	11.1
Hampton	139	9.7	431	6.3	51.7	1 032 814	2 398	85 718	34.6	107 266	98.8	1.2	31.6	13.3	1 584	64.4
Horry	178	8.5	189	5.6	108.0	571 035	3 016	93 665	101.3	107 988	78.6	21.4	31.4	14.0	2 149	45.7
Jasper	69	31.6	597	D	8.7	1 620 974	2 717	69 043	6.4	55 626	93.5	6.5	26.1	5.2	60	17.4
Kershaw	83	-3.1	172	1.1	16.7	524 702	3 058	60 770	147.2	304 687	3.3	96.7	23.6	10.8	499	16.6
Lancaster	65	-0.2	113	0.3	14.0	443 986	3 936	45 899	78.0	135 208	4.5	95.5	24.4	7.5	86	8.8
Laurens	123	-5.7	148	0.7	35.0	503 297	3 389	47 098	40.9	49 530	D	D	28.8	4.8	1 085	15.0
Lee	142	1.0	369	9.2	93.2	835 806	2 265	151 886	118.6	307 225	51.3	48.7	31.6	18.9	2 289	66.8
Lexington	108	19.2	107	10.7	49.0	424 407	3 984	64 111	164.6	162 818	25.9	74.1	27.2	10.1	660	13.2
McCormick	30	20.5	323	D	3.6	570 806	1 767	42 785	5.2	55 946	22.6	77.4	21.5	5.4	155	32.3
Marion	80	15.4	292	1.1	44.5	679 087	2 328	107 269	40.6	147 815	69.8	30.2	29.5	14.2	931	66.5
Marlboro	113	-7.5	506	2.7	71.1	1 096 866	2 169	123 723	61.8	276 063	73.5	26.5	33.0	23.2	2 154	62.5
Newberry	104	3.7	176	0.8	31.7	476 949	2 711	66 958	139.5	234 891	D	D	31.1	7.2	1 004	22.2
Oconee	68	-4.0	77	0.3	15.4	407 562	5 308	49 633	121.4	137 313	5.0	95.0	21.4	7.9	382	6.3
Orangeburg	283	-1.5	268	25.4	152.9	677 763	2 528	124 560	231.5	219 264	53.8	46.2	33.3	16.3	3 506	43.9
Pickens	45	-12.3	62	0.8	13.0	344 880	5 575	41 396	8.4	11 611	66.3	33.7	12.5	1.0	167	4.0
Richland	61	3.5	153	2.0	31.1	536 626	3 511	68 653	30.0	75 472	76.9	23.1	24.6	5.8	507	10.1
Saluda	108	-1.7	184	4.4	29.6	524 673	2 853	81 700	126.3	215 130	21.8	78.2	37.0	11.6	750	25.6
Spartanburg	102	-7.3	76	1.9	37.7	377 862	4 964	38 547	34.6	25 829	56.6	43.4	18.1	2.2	833	8.1

Table B. States and Counties — Water Use, Wholesale Trade, Retail Trade, and Real Estate

STATE County	Water use, 2010 — Total water withdrawn (mil gal/day)	Gallons withdrawn per person per day	Wholesale trade,[1] 2012 — Number of establishments	Number of employees	Sales (mil dol)	Annual payroll (mil dol)	Retail trade,[2] 2012 — Number of establishments	Number of employees	Sales (mil dol)	Annual payroll (mil dol)	Real estate and rental and leasing,[2] 2012 — Number of establishments	Number of employees	Receipts (mil dol)	Annual payroll (mil dol)
	133	134	135	136	137	138	139	140	141	142	143	144	145	146
PENNSYLVANIA—Cont'd														
Potter	6.3	358	6	D	D	D	68	546	152.7	13.6	5	16	1.0	0.2
Schuylkill	36.7	247	99	1 562	916.6	55.0	504	5 677	1 381.9	119.1	60	240	40.7	6.6
Snyder	276.6	6 967	26	D	D	D	198	2 867	630.2	54.9	13	47	11.1	1.7
Somerset	29.7	382	65	894	443.1	34.6	253	2 643	781.1	60.2	46	151	43.6	5.8
Sullivan	0.6	95	2	D	D	D	30	279	64.7	4.5	4	D	D	D
Susquehanna	4.4	102	34	267	569.9	8.6	146	1 269	533.6	28.0	15	88	24.5	4.7
Tioga	8.0	190	28	394	237.7	17.5	155	2 002	563.9	44.5	23	56	8.9	1.6
Union	6.4	142	30	D	D	D	130	1 561	479.2	37.0	28	158	19.0	3.4
Venango	8.2	149	43	D	D	D	204	2 565	636.9	53.9	26	79	12.6	1.9
Warren	14.0	334	27	211	142.0	8.8	130	2 394	674.6	55.4	18	71	7.3	1.4
Washington	357.6	1 721	227	3 257	2 869.3	186.9	691	8 657	2 342.1	194.5	145	772	221.8	38.3
Wayne	5.8	110	24	D	D	D	223	2 560	711.1	60.4	27	62	11.5	2.0
Westmoreland	40.0	110	330	5 958	7 333.3	308.5	1 258	18 183	4 671.7	416.7	262	1 106	240.4	38.0
Wyoming	13.1	464	18	389	106.5	14.5	114	1 334	393.5	28.0	9	27	10.4	2.0
York	2 641.2	6 072	359	6 685	4 340.8	301.4	1 297	21 024	5 192.4	463.9	258	1 470	263.7	51.8
RHODE ISLAND	375.5	357	1 158	15 697	22 310.4	1 000.2	3 795	47 688	12 063.9	1 206.6	1 058	5 615	1 119.8	218.5
Bristol	1.6	32	48	385	204.9	21.5	145	1 355	288.1	32.2	43	127	24.2	3.8
Kent	4.0	24	213	2 683	1 670.6	156.9	676	11 126	2 984.2	285.3	177	1 298	261.8	49.5
Newport	11.7	142	69	390	331.1	22.0	430	4 211	1 116.5	116.3	112	769	100.9	23.1
Providence	330.8	528	701	11 014	19 000.6	720.6	1 996	24 365	5 999.4	594.4	598	3 063	659.5	130.0
Washington	27.4	216	127	1 225	1 103.3	79.3	548	6 631	1 675.7	178.4	128	358	73.5	12.2
SOUTH CAROLINA	6 782.2	1 466	4 337	54 949	45 520.9	2 806.2	17 586	220 438	58 093.8	4 954.6	4 692	23 189	4 334.4	825.9
Abbeville	4.4	172	6	52	22.1	2.1	62	439	91.4	7.6	2	D	D	D
Aiken	207.9	1 298	69	505	399.4	20.0	508	6 601	1 749.5	139.6	106	331	53.6	9.8
Allendale	12.8	1 229	8	46	55.2	1.8	26	136	33.9	2.7	4	D	D	D
Anderson	266.7	1 425	167	2 514	2 641.3	105.6	697	8 472	2 189.6	188.1	125	422	91.7	13.1
Bamberg	5.4	337	6	D	D	D	56	462	95.3	9.6	2	D	D	D
Barnwell	5.6	247	4	D	D	D	74	782	167.1	14.9	10	18	2.2	0.4
Beaufort	24.4	150	113	470	295.6	21.4	734	9 080	2 090.5	203.1	379	1 718	267.1	62.8
Berkeley	571.4	3 213	151	2 343	3 248.3	125.6	396	6 173	1 730.6	141.6	130	699	132.4	26.1
Calhoun	91.5	6 031	9	D	D	D	35	224	65.9	3.6	3	D	D	D
Charleston	53.5	153	468	5 049	2 875.4	264.4	1 935	26 034	6 707.7	628.9	695	3 295	599.2	118.4
Cherokee	11.5	208	22	432	131.6	14.6	235	2 648	800.6	49.4	39	153	24.2	2.6
Chester	5.3	160	12	175	302.1	10.0	100	828	234.1	17.1	14	D	D	D
Chesterfield	9.7	207	27	305	96.4	10.0	135	1 271	317.7	22.8	16	37	4.1	0.8
Clarendon	6.4	183	16	113	74.2	3.8	124	1 247	336.3	24.9	16	34	3.9	1.0
Colleton	12.3	316	28	195	107.2	7.3	157	1 635	408.3	32.5	44	144	22.5	3.7
Darlington	216.8	3 156	73	592	859.7	25.3	235	2 246	536.6	45.2	37	102	46.5	2.7
Dillon	5.6	174	20	443	391.7	15.4	121	1 159	394.2	22.2	21	62	4.9	1.1
Dorchester	33.6	246	73	562	215.3	27.5	297	3 697	973.2	78.7	104	332	65.0	11.3
Edgefield	11.4	422	8	125	62.7	6.1	54	405	152.1	9.5	8	22	1.7	0.5
Fairfield	772.0	32 227	10	D	D	D	54	539	224.9	12.1	11	D	D	D
Florence	42.8	313	158	2 493	1 585.7	105.5	701	8 277	2 149.6	178.9	130	555	104.3	19.7
Georgetown	833.2	13 850	40	280	135.3	10.2	303	2 776	703.3	62.9	86	417	54.8	13.0
Greenville	41.7	93	711	9 278	10 153.0	521.9	1 757	24 790	6 380.5	593.2	534	2 681	838.1	113.6
Greenwood	13.0	186	49	421	837.9	19.1	275	3 224	758.9	67.6	44	D	D	D
Hampton	8.3	394	10	182	118.2	10.0	92	678	164.8	13.2	7	23	2.1	0.8
Horry	141.7	526	238	1 605	734.3	65.4	1 666	20 687	5 240.2	455.3	590	4 496	506.6	131.1
Jasper	29.2	1 178	27	258	146.8	12.6	104	1 425	574.8	40.5	18	69	13.6	3.2
Kershaw	11.2	182	16	70	43.5	4.8	178	2 122	586.3	44.0	32	83	14.0	3.2
Lancaster	20.5	268	47	1 106	719.7	38.8	238	2 673	732.9	60.3	43	D	D	D
Laurens	7.3	109	32	227	115.2	10.6	180	1 680	412.1	32.8	20	50	6.3	1.0
Lee	3.9	203	11	80	138.2	3.8	42	381	86.0	7.3	2	D	D	D
Lexington	257.7	982	302	5 744	3 889.3	292.0	1 046	15 123	3 974.5	338.3	243	1 277	227.9	43.8
McCormick	1.5	149	1	D	D	D	22	122	31.9	2.1	2	D	D	D
Marion	4.5	135	21	338	208.4	16.5	128	1 042	239.0	21.0	10	30	3.5	0.9
Marlboro	32.7	1 130	13	114	43.5	4.2	98	704	185.5	14.9	13	29	4.3	0.6
Newberry	9.3	247	26	238	160.5	10.0	133	1 389	428.1	29.2	17	65	14.9	2.2
Oconee	2 537.7	34 167	39	388	201.2	13.4	254	2 920	741.0	63.9	64	153	26.0	5.5
Orangeburg	32.4	351	66	529	387.8	21.6	370	4 070	1 016.6	80.2	53	241	25.7	7.9
Pickens	48.8	409	66	403	301.3	21.5	324	4 215	1 163.1	97.9	68	345	44.5	9.4
Richland	78.0	203	417	5 489	4 191.3	303.2	1 254	18 443	4 780.7	433.4	408	2 792	736.4	133.1
Saluda	6.1	308	8	45	14.4	1.4	49	414	115.1	8.5	4	D	D	D
Spartanburg	42.1	148	414	5 813	5 340.5	297.1	1 069	13 459	3 966.7	316.7	227	999	180.6	37.3

1. Merchant wholesalers, except manufacturers' sales branches and offices.   2. Employer establishments.

Table B. States and Counties — Professional Services, Manufacturing, and Accommodation and Food Services

STATE County	Professional, scientific, and technical services, 2012				Manufacturing, 2012				Accommodation and food services, 2012			
	Number of establishments	Number of employees	Receipts (mil dol)	Annual payroll (mil dol)	Number of establishments	Number of employees	Receipts (mil dol)	Annual payroll (mil dol)	Number of establishments	Number of employees	Sales (mil dol)	Annual payroll (mil dol)
	147	148	149	150	151	152	153	154	155	156	157	158
PENNSYLVANIA—Cont'd												
Potter	23	113	12.9	4.9	23	513	69.5	19.0	40	254	12.3	2.9
Schuylkill	157	1 040	113.9	49.6	177	8 882	3 400.0	397.6	271	2 671	124.4	31.5
Snyder	44	204	17.3	7.0	62	3 627	678.7	139.7	85	1 743	79.9	20.6
Somerset	96	D	D	D	107	2 854	836.1	130.8	165	3 112	137.2	39.2
Sullivan	10	16	1.7	0.7	5	D	D	D	26	D	D	D
Susquehanna	46	213	26.1	8.5	61	659	124.0	23.8	83	752	44.1	10.8
Tioga	53	306	29.4	11.8	42	2 316	591.7	90.9	104	1 451	65.5	16.9
Union	68	345	25.1	10.0	38	1 343	353.3	55.9	92	2 165	89.3	24.1
Venango	69	365	46.7	14.4	80	4 048	1 388.1	219.2	112	1 325	55.0	15.2
Warren	52	277	25.3	12.6	61	2 652	3 515.5	136.9	78	904	42.3	10.8
Washington	408	3 276	608.1	189.3	247	9 931	3 561.9	514.0	396	6 603	318.0	81.4
Wayne	84	305	30.9	11.0	53	523	104.1	20.1	158	1 490	144.6	39.6
Westmoreland	705	5 812	1 053.4	328.6	556	18 854	7 681.5	920.2	756	12 356	516.6	143.6
Wyoming	48	292	33.6	12.7	30	2 541	D	156.9	60	763	33.7	7.9
York	705	5 671	635.2	279.4	568	31 890	11 489.4	1 602.6	791	13 391	593.3	165.9
RHODE ISLAND	2 997	21 165	3 338.2	1 310.1	1 509	39 608	11 262.2	2 076.5	2 973	44 063	2 481.3	705.9
Bristol	109	381	52.9	19.8	92	1 633	325.1	70.6	124	1 496	72.8	19.9
Kent	503	2 948	418.3	160.4	218	7 609	2 643.0	439.1	467	8 013	412.0	118.5
Newport	326	3 168	545.6	229.0	74	1 860	284.1	148.0	358	5 945	411.2	121.4
Providence	1 719	13 021	2 040.1	803.1	962	21 885	6 126.4	1 026.7	1 563	23 354	1 242.9	351.4
Washington	340	1 647	281.3	97.9	163	6 621	1 883.6	392.1	461	5 255	342.4	94.7
SOUTH CAROLINA	9 721	79 824	12 721.7	4 817.3	3 854	207 396	99 160.8	10 082.1	9 828	185 282	9 763.8	2 650.5
Abbeville	17	43	3.4	0.9	34	1 686	598.8	71.9	26	332	12.5	3.8
Aiken	243	4 751	1 548.2	471.3	82	6 845	4 639.3	390.4	253	D	D	D
Allendale	6	D	D	D	6	719	447.0	35.3	6	D	D	D
Anderson	278	1 822	209.0	74.8	196	10 223	5 435.0	439.9	383	6 019	272.2	75.5
Bamberg	17	66	7.5	1.9	21	823	177.0	32.6	21	235	9.7	2.5
Barnwell	24	D	D	D	20	1 918	564.1	83.1	32	419	16.9	4.3
Beaufort	554	2 876	339.1	144.8	71	524	82.2	20.2	501	10 502	656.6	193.0
Berkeley	246	2 735	477.7	164.5	88	5 106	6 261.6	332.3	241	4 605	195.9	52.6
Calhoun	13	D	D	D	22	1 278	D	80.6	10	D	D	D
Charleston	1 561	15 343	2 760.7	1 096.9	288	13 984	5 668.1	818.4	1 192	26 575	1 640.0	455.0
Cherokee	48	179	16.2	6.0	58	5 455	3 050.6	220.7	86	1 758	73.4	20.5
Chester	32	157	19.9	6.8	40	2 245	1 140.7	105.3	41	536	25.5	6.6
Chesterfield	27	81	7.0	2.0	49	4 375	1 345.2	188.7	63	848	37.8	9.7
Clarendon	18	77	9.5	4.7	18	403	235.2	13.6	58	624	28.3	7.1
Colleton	45	229	34.3	9.3	26	620	137.8	20.1	70	1 205	65.6	18.5
Darlington	60	255	26.5	8.0	50	3 092	1 693.0	171.0	88	1 188	53.2	13.7
Dillon	24	302	8.4	4.0	16	2 214	470.1	54.2	56	872	34.8	9.4
Dorchester	194	796	102.4	34.6	89	4 439	2 026.4	228.4	183	2 879	132.4	36.2
Edgefield	17	42	4.4	1.1	20	1 213	389.5	41.5	22	D	D	D
Fairfield	15	D	D	D	18	754	232.3	30.9	24	234	9.1	2.5
Florence	208	2 429	267.8	104.8	98	5 860	2 633.5	308.5	296	5 423	272.5	71.9
Georgetown	168	837	129.0	34.9	45	2 010	1 032.6	115.9	171	2 819	152.0	44.5
Greenville	1 529	14 537	2 095.5	888.9	555	26 782	9 628.1	1 280.1	1 073	19 791	999.9	271.7
Greenwood	119	1 166	140.8	58.2	62	5 498	2 478.9	251.8	135	2 387	102.5	26.1
Hampton	16	D	D	D	15	621	156.6	26.5	31	347	16.6	3.6
Horry	670	3 059	342.9	121.5	145	2 693	759.8	121.4	1 218	25 903	1 716.7	451.1
Jasper	25	123	13.6	5.4	19	190	46.2	7.3	54	687	32.3	8.9
Kershaw	77	D	D	D	58	3 122	1 419.7	149.0	91	1 308	55.5	14.8
Lancaster	88	559	73.8	28.6	47	1 916	1 292.5	87.0	95	1 491	65.9	16.5
Laurens	46	186	13.3	6.6	78	5 398	1 728.2	230.9	84	1 275	56.6	14.7
Lee	11	D	D	D	11	214	D	11.1	18	234	10.1	2.7
Lexington	579	3 175	367.3	140.1	206	8 527	3 620.3	402.0	513	10 122	455.2	127.3
McCormick	6	D	D	D	5	298	D	12.5	7	D	D	D
Marion	22	69	4.9	1.8	19	714	214.1	26.9	44	708	32.0	8.2
Marlboro	14	55	4.6	1.4	20	1 912	881.9	76.8	27	317	14.7	4.0
Newberry	42	153	12.3	4.4	44	4 831	1 651.5	185.2	61	826	36.6	9.0
Oconee	117	469	42.1	16.8	76	5 151	2 135.2	242.5	119	1 672	81.5	19.2
Orangeburg	80	334	42.9	16.1	70	6 332	2 470.4	275.8	175	3 222	152.1	37.5
Pickens	157	846	92.1	34.2	113	4 713	1 500.8	200.3	235	4 212	186.9	48.9
Richland	1 213	13 037	2 328.9	859.4	204	9 355	5 375.0	536.0	844	17 706	862.2	238.3
Saluda	14	D	D	D	8	1 953	D	52.0	18	D	D	D
Spartanburg	452	4 804	692.5	263.5	397	23 972	15 038.1	1 288.2	550	10 059	477.9	128.0

1. Establishment subject to federal tax.

Table B. States and Counties — Health Care and Social Assistance, Other Services, Nonemployer Businesses, and Residential Construction

STATE County	Health care and social assistance, 2012				Other services, 2012				Nonemployer businesses, 2014		Value of residential construction authorized by building permits, 2015	
	Number of establishments	Number of employees	Receipts (mil dol)	Annual payroll (mil dol)	Number of establishments	Number of employees	Receipts (mil dol)	Annual payroll (mil dol)	Number	Receipts (mil dol)	New Construction ($1,000)	Number of housing units
	159	160	161	162	163	164	165	166	167	168	169	170
PENNSYLVANIA—Cont'd												
Potter	33	907	88.3	36.1	27	115	8.9	1.9	1 297	59.0	2 016	12
Schuylkill	336	7 975	597.1	259.1	250	1 103	83.9	24.3	6 736	316.5	22 708	99
Snyder	83	1 134	104.6	39.4	69	286	27.4	6.1	2 884	145.1	11 638	79
Somerset	193	3 627	292.2	119.0	143	654	52.9	12.9	4 609	182.1	25 569	104
Sullivan	16	D	D	D	13	61	2.3	0.6	481	22.4	1 682	8
Susquehanna	65	1 136	77.9	34.3	70	291	24.5	5.5	3 202	167.2	16 633	70
Tioga	104	1 901	153.8	62.4	69	255	27.8	6.0	2 561	108.4	4 629	28
Union	144	3 740	315.4	142.1	66	306	23.5	5.9	2 714	136.6	10 957	46
Venango	170	3 475	226.6	114.7	107	419	35.6	8.4	2 905	110.1	9 815	47
Warren	107	3 221	254.0	114.2	85	529	31.4	7.4	2 160	87.8	3 432	22
Washington	690	13 512	1 301.5	518.0	421	2 455	227.6	63.9	12 479	647.1	154 688	657
Wayne	125	2 510	188.0	80.0	103	706	55.4	15.5	3 887	181.7	22 942	94
Westmoreland	1 155	20 603	1 809.4	737.8	805	4 447	477.2	105.5	21 305	948.9	97 384	393
Wyoming	67	687	42.1	18.8	52	237	24.5	6.5	1 774	79.4	5 148	34
York	924	24 161	2 604.4	1 031.9	783	5 242	651.3	139.7	25 586	1 187.3	137 570	778
RHODE ISLAND	3 236	84 067	8 223.0	3 556.0	2 276	13 046	1 444.6	390.9	75 223	3 381.9	211 614	998
Bristol	126	2 848	133.7	70.6	121	449	34.9	10.8	4 227	203.2	8 748	43
Kent	570	11 802	1 113.1	455.6	369	2 083	219.7	60.9	11 197	516.9	23 831	149
Newport	250	4 845	375.1	154.4	208	1 133	120.4	35.0	7 606	356.2	35 344	134
Providence	1 898	57 002	5 943.2	2 600.1	1 310	8 075	940.3	249.7	40 843	1 757.5	76 144	423
Washington	392	7 570	658.1	275.4	268	1 306	129.3	34.6	11 350	548.1	67 547	249
SOUTH CAROLINA	9 848	212 444	22 941.3	8 687.3	6 666	44 374	4 464.9	1 302.3	319 046	13 344.5	6 242 696	31 030
Abbeville	27	486	37.9	15.6	23	67	6.7	1.4	1 370	48.5	4 695	26
Aiken	310	6 330	519.8	199.6	169	950	79.6	20.4	10 267	355.3	148 129	683
Allendale	12	283	22.5	8.5	8	D	D	D	515	12.6	2 665	2
Anderson	365	8 273	928.6	343.8	235	3 448	371.8	169.8	11 815	470.8	156 936	864
Bamberg	41	693	36.4	20.5	23	D	D	D	803	18.9	947	5
Barnwell	34	723	48.5	20.6	26	131	16.9	4.0	1 345	35.5	3 094	27
Beaufort	426	5 819	661.3	222.0	309	2 700	244.6	82.6	14 965	795.2	582 878	1 783
Berkeley	210	2 318	154.7	65.5	187	1 068	86.9	26.2	11 725	455.6	395 506	1 960
Calhoun	22	D	D	D	16	D	D	D	862	33.7	2 516	15
Charleston	1 250	30 476	4 338.2	1 412.0	768	5 340	579.2	155.9	34 304	1 765.3	780 605	3 936
Cherokee	75	1 180	84.5	36.1	70	319	32.0	7.8	2 465	80.3	9 834	87
Chester	49	707	75.3	27.2	36	141	12.3	3.4	1 644	53.3	5 332	15
Chesterfield	90	1 624	125.4	47.2	40	119	8.7	2.3	2 304	75.2	8 122	56
Clarendon	41	1 456	95.5	41.2	33	194	13.2	4.1	2 071	68.5	7 377	37
Colleton	71	1 443	158.5	60.6	35	145	9.6	2.4	2 835	104.7	11 048	48
Darlington	96	2 444	218.8	83.4	79	345	29.9	7.6	3 696	125.1	17 011	154
Dillon	47	1 170	87.2	37.1	37	83	7.3	1.6	1 595	46.7	1 987	19
Dorchester	209	3 170	271.0	100.7	165	832	67.7	23.0	9 053	342.7	171 534	694
Edgefield	20	526	34.3	14.1	24	65	5.9	1.5	1 413	49.5	15 929	76
Fairfield	27	D	D	D	12	D	D	D	1 376	41.9	7 015	33
Florence	354	13 444	1 565.1	585.4	196	1 348	135.8	32.3	8 665	327.8	41 627	270
Georgetown	215	3 742	467.2	164.1	115	619	44.0	12.7	5 153	211.4	68 831	299
Greenville	1 120	21 857	2 261.7	996.1	706	5 185	651.9	157.1	35 914	1 634.1	796 617	4 338
Greenwood	144	4 752	585.2	207.9	78	548	33.4	10.1	3 798	137.1	12 306	120
Hampton	28	520	39.8	17.1	23	105	7.8	1.8	1 174	39.1	973	5
Horry	657	10 903	1 274.1	443.5	504	2 720	279.6	65.9	22 736	1 051.4	630 917	3 829
Jasper	44	975	89.8	27.6	42	162	14.1	3.5	1 575	70.5	69 078	319
Kershaw	96	D	D	D	82	373	29.3	8.4	3 977	139.7	42 535	299
Lancaster	136	2 266	229.0	88.2	97	495	50.3	27.5	5 126	195.4	341 008	1 109
Laurens	90	2 033	179.0	68.5	60	278	24.4	7.3	3 130	107.5	17 077	114
Lee	25	323	18.9	8.3	14	D	D	D	849	24.3	549	5
Lexington	527	12 620	1 058.8	436.7	491	2 905	277.8	88.1	18 494	771.1	436 515	1 897
McCormick	9	214	12.1	5.0	7	D	D	D	518	17.1	8 460	37
Marion	60	711	51.2	24.2	36	112	9.6	2.2	1 663	47.2	1 873	13
Marlboro	43	971	73.1	27.9	22	45	4.0	1.1	986	27.6	1 702	11
Newberry	58	1 175	107.3	42.0	55	232	20.0	5.9	1 838	61.9	15 458	78
Oconee	139	2 882	274.5	107.9	94	542	40.5	12.6	4 511	169.2	70 345	256
Orangeburg	220	3 904	381.9	158.5	98	474	37.5	10.6	4 926	165.2	9 887	89
Pickens	195	3 459	296.7	121.6	137	692	117.3	17.6	7 347	304.0	124 714	580
Richland	944	26 658	3 202.5	1 277.0	609	4 986	475.4	141.8	25 916	1 083.2	261 814	2 368
Saluda	21	D	D	D	14	D	D	D	951	36.1	6 215	30
Spartanburg	583	D	D	D	413	2 940	326.3	80.2	18 525	834.0	236 332	1 399

	Government employment and payroll, 2012								Local government finances, 2012				
		March payroll (percent of total)							General revenue				
											Taxes		
												Per capita[1] (dollars)	
STATE County	Full-time equivalent employees	March payroll (dollars)	Administration, judicial, and legal	Police and Corrections	Fire Protection	Highways and transportation	Health and Welfare	Natural resources and utilities	Education and libraries	Total (mil dol)	Intergovernmental (mil dol)	Total (mil dol)	Total	Property
	171	172	173	174	175	176	177	178	179	180	181	182	183	184
PENNSYLVANIA— Cont'd														
Potter	590	2 437 639	12.0	6.7	1.0	7.4	0.9	10.0	61.5	73.9	41.6	21.8	1 241	1 052
Schuylkill	4 186	15 090 961	8.1	8.5	0.1	3.8	7.3	7.1	64.1	485.2	233.0	166.2	1 130	842
Snyder	1 018	3 558 017	6.3	8.1	0.0	2.9	3.5	3.8	74.2	107.4	42.7	49.5	1 247	859
Somerset	2 210	7 165 165	8.8	4.3	0.0	5.7	1.8	4.2	70.6	225.8	112.7	81.2	1 055	857
Sullivan	201	742 784	15.2	1.7	1.1	5.2	3.8	5.3	67.2	22.1	7.8	11.8	1 822	1 657
Susquehanna	1 464	5 097 993	5.6	5.6	0.6	4.5	1.7	2.4	79.2	139.9	73.6	54.2	1 268	1 138
Tioga	1 450	4 927 182	7.0	6.0	0.6	3.5	10.4	7.0	64.2	150.3	76.5	54.9	1 290	1 005
Union	883	3 323 742	9.7	6.0	0.0	3.9	4.3	8.9	66.1	157.6	75.7	51.5	1 145	812
Venango	2 052	6 987 537	7.7	7.9	3.0	3.8	5.2	5.7	65.4	196.8	112.6	57.2	1 053	811
Warren	1 409	4 668 630	8.7	7.2	1.1	5.4	17.0	2.6	57.5	113.1	58.7	41.3	1 004	762
Washington	5 853	22 585 416	6.8	9.1	1.4	4.1	7.0	4.9	65.0	790.8	371.8	291.3	1 396	1 069
Wayne	2 592	9 809 084	4.6	4.1	0.0	2.0	28.2	1.9	57.7	212.3	71.7	119.1	2 293	2 175
Westmoreland	10 354	41 162 785	6.1	8.6	0.9	4.3	6.4	9.3	63.6	1 302.8	557.8	500.8	1 378	1 099
Wyoming	947	3 123 745	15.3	5.7	0.0	2.7	0.3	2.0	71.4	97.3	46.7	41.6	1 479	1 225
York	12 293	50 416 660	6.7	12.2	1.5	2.7	6.3	3.6	64.5	1 771.5	572.5	787.5	1 799	1 467
RHODE ISLAND	X	X	X	X	X	X	X	X	X	X	X	X	X	X
Bristol	1 397	7 178 253	3.0	7.9	2.0	3.0	1.9	4.4	77.5	205.0	41.5	148.0	3 011	2 942
Kent	4 694	24 743 968	2.8	9.9	10.7	2.0	1.3	3.7	68.1	624.4	144.3	407.2	2 470	2 403
Newport	2 527	11 716 139	5.0	10.6	9.2	2.6	0.2	5.5	65.4	364.6	76.1	229.2	2 793	2 650
Providence	17 322	86 400 418	3.8	11.7	9.5	2.0	0.4	5.9	66.0	2 313.9	791.5	1 215.6	1 935	1 896
Washington	4 199	20 282 486	4.3	9.4	3.8	3.0	1.3	3.8	73.7	552.3	102.2	401.4	3 187	3 138
SOUTH CAROLINA	X	X	X	X	X	X	X	X	X	X	X	X	X	X
Abbeville	815	2 384 457	7.4	9.5	1.1	1.8	7.5	8.4	63.9	60.8	30.4	21.1	840	689
Aiken	4 376	15 335 939	9.0	9.9	1.0	4.3	3.0	6.2	65.7	401.1	181.9	160.3	984	738
Allendale	625	1 746 281	7.6	6.7	0.0	2.9	29.6	2.5	49.5	29.1	16.4	9.0	902	790
Anderson	5 484	17 493 225	6.4	10.0	1.2	2.0	1.3	5.3	72.7	476.2	210.0	176.3	931	827
Bamberg	819	2 552 389	7.1	5.8	0.6	1.4	37.3	0.9	45.9	39.6	22.1	13.7	867	775
Barnwell	1 118	3 299 448	5.3	8.6	0.4	1.1	16.7	7.6	59.3	70.5	38.2	23.1	1 038	893
Beaufort	5 616	22 420 841	6.5	9.3	6.0	1.7	27.9	4.2	42.3	768.1	132.7	391.8	2 332	1 843
Berkeley	4 857	15 229 373	6.7	8.6	2.0	1.9	2.3	2.1	74.3	476.5	201.9	143.2	755	670
Calhoun	495	1 790 689	3.0	5.0	0.5	1.8	4.1	1.1	81.6	33.4	14.6	15.0	1 004	980
Charleston	13 396	47 281 757	9.0	15.4	8.8	3.6	4.8	11.4	43.8	1 612.3	402.2	924.2	2 531	1 581
Cherokee	1 933	5 953 218	3.7	7.2	1.7	1.1	6.9	7.7	68.8	146.3	65.3	61.5	1 104	806
Chester	1 174	3 574 024	8.6	9.3	2.2	0.6	4.9	8.2	64.8	79.0	35.9	29.6	909	770
Chesterfield	1 558	4 244 462	5.6	8.8	0.8	1.2	1.7	2.9	77.8	100.3	53.6	36.7	796	594
Clarendon	1 529	4 986 545	5.1	7.6	1.8	1.2	37.8	2.0	42.4	136.5	40.9	33.6	977	747
Colleton	1 758	4 967 648	10.1	9.9	7.4	1.9	2.9	2.2	63.4	116.4	49.6	49.9	1 307	1 182
Darlington	2 194	6 310 138	4.5	9.9	1.9	2.4	4.0	4.0	70.6	151.5	78.7	44.0	646	554
Dillon	1 167	2 987 274	6.2	10.5	1.5	1.1	5.2	3.0	70.1	74.9	42.2	21.2	675	561
Dorchester	4 560	14 338 815	6.9	8.6	2.2	1.2	2.7	4.6	73.0	360.3	155.5	139.0	976	789
Edgefield	1 053	2 997 459	5.4	8.0	0.1	1.3	20.4	4.5	59.7	56.1	29.4	18.1	688	606
Fairfield	1 055	3 207 938	8.3	8.3	1.2	2.5	4.8	5.3	67.8	73.7	26.6	41.9	1 793	1 684
Florence	4 772	15 317 333	6.1	8.9	1.8	2.8	7.2	5.8	66.2	387.1	172.1	134.7	976	696
Georgetown	2 430	7 765 625	7.3	7.7	6.1	2.1	3.9	7.3	63.7	209.0	63.2	106.1	1 762	1 609
Greenville	21 594	81 147 575	3.3	5.4	3.5	1.1	44.4	4.7	36.9	2 639.7	456.3	485.5	1 038	884
Greenwood	2 547	7 901 666	5.9	7.9	1.9	1.7	4.3	10.3	62.2	563.0	100.6	69.9	1 002	786
Hampton	938	2 724 640	7.1	11.8	1.3	1.6	5.2	2.5	69.3	58.5	31.0	21.3	1 028	897
Horry	9 820	34 724 743	8.4	11.7	5.0	3.5	2.7	7.6	58.9	1 161.7	254.9	609.6	2 160	1 278
Jasper	809	2 603 546	11.5	13.8	11.9	2.4	1.3	2.1	56.6	69.7	25.2	37.2	1 441	1 298
Kershaw	2 730	9 680 043	3.3	4.0	1.9	0.5	41.5	2.8	45.5	255.3	130.9	56.4	904	774
Lancaster	2 327	7 452 417	5.3	8.0	1.9	1.0	4.2	8.2	68.9	189.5	79.8	80.0	1 012	782
Laurens	2 310	7 353 314	3.4	6.7	2.3	0.9	31.0	8.0	45.9	214.0	83.0	50.0	755	651
Lee	612	1 602 678	12.0	8.7	1.3	2.9	9.6	3.4	62.1	41.4	23.3	12.5	672	517
Lexington	14 886	59 502 218	2.4	4.2	1.3	0.5	41.6	2.7	46.6	1 461.3	374.4	370.5	1 370	1 163
McCormick	304	811 090	7.2	12.7	0.0	1.9	8.7	11.9	53.4	21.6	7.9	10.9	1 095	1 058
Marion	1 230	3 302 618	5.6	10.1	1.2	1.8	3.5	3.5	72.9	78.2	42.6	22.7	700	520
Marlboro	985	2 122 399	9.2	11.9	1.6	1.6	3.1	6.4	62.6	68.7	37.5	16.6	591	514
Newberry	1 757	5 725 610	5.0	8.2	1.1	1.3	25.7	9.1	48.9	109.3	44.6	46.1	1 227	1 069
Oconee	2 527	8 134 083	7.1	8.0	2.1	2.9	2.0	10.1	66.8	184.8	66.5	95.0	1 272	1 175
Orangeburg	4 563	16 266 007	3.4	5.4	0.2	1.1	46.5	2.7	38.9	425.4	101.6	103.8	1 135	920
Pickens	3 247	10 077 389	5.7	8.6	2.0	3.3	4.7	5.9	66.7	262.7	109.4	112.3	939	722
Richland	13 444	45 241 826	6.4	9.8	3.8	1.6	2.7	7.7	65.0	1 390.8	394.8	589.3	1 496	1 309
Saluda	474	1 331 037	7.6	11.4	2.9	2.3	1.5	2.7	69.2	35.8	16.8	14.0	705	629
Spartanburg	14 164	55 750 441	3.2	4.9	1.6	0.6	47.1	3.9	37.9	1 488.8	350.6	322.9	1 118	988

1. Based on the resident population estimated as of July 1 of the year shown.

Table B. States and Counties — Local Government Finances, Government Employment, and Voting

STATE County	Local government finances, 2012 (cont.)									Government employment, 2014			Presidential election,[2] 2012		
	Direct general expenditure							Debt outstanding					Percent of vote cast:		
			Percent of total for:												
	Total (mil dol)	Per capita[1] (dollars)	Education	Health and hospitals	Police protection	Public welfare	Highways	Total (mil dol)	Per capita[1] (dollars)	Federal civilian	Federal military	State and local	Democratic	Republican	All other
	185	186	187	188	189	190	191	192	193	194	195	196	197	198	199
PENNSYLVANIA—Cont'd															
Potter	70.3	3 999	50.7	1.3	1.0	9.1	10.6	81.5	4 636	43	46	1 038	30.6	68.1	1.3
Schuylkill	520.8	3 541	55.0	1.5	2.5	6.8	4.7	555.0	3 774	627	373	7 212	44.9	53.5	1.6
Snyder	122.1	3 077	62.0	2.4	4.4	0.0	4.2	222.5	5 610	89	102	2 148	34.8	64.0	1.3
Somerset	213.0	2 768	61.0	0.1	2.5	5.7	5.5	286.3	3 720	193	191	4 231	36.6	61.7	1.7
Sullivan	25.1	3 889	63.1	2.1	0.7	2.7	8.5	9.0	1 396	19	16	365	39.5	59.0	1.5
Susquehanna	148.2	3 471	72.6	0.9	1.4	2.1	5.8	59.8	1 401	103	112	1 817	43.5	55.1	1.4
Tioga	137.5	3 229	52.4	0.0	1.2	10.9	7.3	119.5	2 807	144	109	2 879	35.5	63.0	1.5
Union	203.9	4 535	63.4	1.3	1.3	2.6	2.9	249.6	5 553	1 557	99	1 419	42.1	56.7	1.2
Venango	206.3	3 800	58.4	2.1	1.5	7.2	5.3	271.4	5 001	105	140	3 395	39.6	58.9	1.5
Warren	109.9	2 672	58.9	0.5	2.9	0.7	5.6	93.3	2 267	164	107	1 879	46.1	52.3	1.6
Washington	804.7	3 855	54.3	1.5	2.6	11.8	4.2	903.0	4 326	450	570	9 900	47.0	51.8	1.2
Wayne	210.9	4 059	64.5	2.4	0.7	4.4	3.0	262.7	5 056	518	127	2 503	43.3	55.6	1.1
Westmoreland	1 328.7	3 656	53.4	2.5	2.9	10.3	4.0	1 848.5	5 087	810	969	14 361	41.1	57.8	1.1
Wyoming	92.1	3 276	63.0	0.1	3.2	5.3	6.8	54.9	1 953	62	74	1 136	45.6	53.2	1.3
York	1 790.5	4 089	47.4	3.5	3.3	9.2	2.6	2 454.1	5 605	3 989	1 325	16 248	42.7	56.3	1.1
RHODE ISLAND	X	X	X	X	X	X	X	X	X	10 246	7 303	54 254	63.3	35.0	1.7
Bristol	201.6	4 102	66.6	0.2	4.1	0.1	4.2	147.6	3 004	89	230	2 043	62.6	35.9	1.5
Kent	593.7	3 601	58.4	0.1	6.4	0.5	2.8	449.3	2 725	718	797	7 396	57.7	40.5	1.8
Newport	357.9	4 363	48.4	2.1	8.0	0.4	3.0	203.9	2 486	4 472	2 668	3 351	60.9	37.6	1.6
Providence	2 229.9	3 549	53.2	0.2	8.2	0.1	2.8	1 836.7	2 923	4 399	3 001	29 578	66.9	31.5	1.6
Washington	532.3	4 226	67.5	0.5	5.4	0.4	3.5	302.1	2 398	568	607	11 886	59.0	39.2	1.8
SOUTH CAROLINA	X	X	X	X	X	X	X	X	X	32 167	53 136	315 623	44.9	53.9	1.2
Abbeville	59.7	2 377	50.1	3.0	7.7	0.0	1.3	24.7	985	38	99	1 341	41.8	56.9	1.3
Aiken	373.4	2 294	57.5	1.3	7.7	0.1	2.4	155.5	955	687	669	7 057	37.4	61.4	1.2
Allendale	27.5	2 758	69.3	1.7	5.0	0.0	1.5	14.8	1 477	17	34	1 083	75.3	23.5	1.2
Anderson	483.1	2 551	63.5	0.3	6.2	0.2	2.1	1 327.5	7 010	306	785	11 697	32.7	66.0	1.3
Bamberg	61.7	3 917	76.9	0.2	5.2	0.0	0.8	38.4	2 439	33	57	981	65.0	33.9	1.2
Barnwell	71.5	3 218	57.8	0.4	6.7	0.2	2.1	37.0	1 667	49	89	1 510	50.3	48.7	1.0
Beaufort	752.2	4 476	32.2	19.6	6.0	1.1	2.3	1 451.5	8 637	2 312	9 866	7 574	44.1	54.9	0.9
Berkeley	500.4	2 637	57.1	1.2	5.3	0.4	2.8	2 158.7	11 375	875	819	7 941	42.8	55.9	1.3
Calhoun	36.1	2 418	56.3	3.7	6.6	1.8	1.0	42.7	2 864	23	61	764	51.3	47.8	0.9
Charleston	1 363.0	3 733	36.6	1.0	11.9	0.2	4.7	2 857.4	7 825	9 055	11 686	36 962	53.5	45.2	1.2
Cherokee	132.3	2 378	65.3	1.5	6.6	5.1	2.3	1 423.8	25 579	104	227	2 212	34.7	64.1	1.2
Chester	89.7	2 756	62.9	3.1	5.0	0.0	0.4	59.0	1 811	57	132	1 570	53.5	45.2	1.3
Chesterfield	104.7	2 271	63.2	0.0	8.7	0.0	2.6	194.8	4 224	88	186	2 029	47.9	50.9	1.2
Clarendon	138.9	4 044	34.7	40.8	4.1	0.0	1.0	88.7	2 583	58	134	2 257	55.8	43.5	0.8
Colleton	127.8	3 350	47.8	0.7	8.0	0.8	3.0	141.2	3 701	92	161	1 984	49.7	49.2	1.0
Darlington	148.0	2 173	64.2	0.4	7.0	0.0	2.0	103.9	1 525	142	274	3 037	49.4	49.6	1.0
Dillon	76.7	2 441	64.6	0.3	6.0	3.0	2.1	10.2	324	79	126	1 438	55.2	43.8	1.0
Dorchester	349.2	2 451	64.0	1.4	6.0	0.0	7.4	507.4	3 561	187	605	6 058	41.6	57.1	1.3
Edgefield	58.3	2 211	67.5	2.4	6.3	0.5	2.0	25.9	981	408	97	1 243	44.1	55.0	1.0
Fairfield	86.5	3 704	53.6	6.2	5.9	0.0	1.7	21.4	917	37	93	1 422	65.3	33.7	1.0
Florence	382.5	2 773	59.5	5.9	6.5	0.2	1.7	270.2	1 958	581	588	12 421	48.0	51.2	0.9
Georgetown	194.2	3 227	56.8	1.4	5.1	0.6	2.7	502.9	8 355	118	283	4 793	46.9	52.1	1.0
Greenville	2 628.6	5 621	23.1	51.4	2.7	0.2	1.1	3 479.0	7 440	1 870	1 998	29 191	37.2	61.0	1.8
Greenwood	506.5	7 261	23.9	58.7	2.1	0.0	0.7	466.2	6 684	135	276	6 917	41.6	57.3	1.1
Hampton	68.8	3 318	69.0	2.5	7.3	0.9	1.8	31.5	1 522	339	78	1 138	62.2	36.8	1.0
Horry	1 100.1	3 897	39.1	12.4	5.6	0.1	5.5	1 603.2	5 679	592	1 221	15 304	37.1	61.7	1.3
Jasper	67.2	2 600	51.4	0.2	8.9	0.4	1.9	79.1	3 062	51	106	1 291	60.9	38.0	1.1
Kershaw	253.6	4 068	36.7	41.9	2.8	0.2	1.0	291.1	4 669	92	258	3 242	40.1	58.8	1.0
Lancaster	185.7	2 347	54.7	4.0	5.6	0.0	2.8	219.5	2 775	93	334	3 540	42.0	56.8	1.2
Laurens	231.7	3 499	34.1	32.5	3.9	0.1	2.1	194.1	2 931	100	266	3 735	40.2	58.3	1.4
Lee	37.3	1 999	57.1	4.7	6.6	0.1	2.1	54.1	2 902	27	67	1 069	65.1	33.6	1.3
Lexington	1 529.8	5 658	44.1	37.4	3.3	0.0	0.9	1 531.8	5 665	612	1 137	19 126	30.4	68.4	1.1
McCormick	18.6	1 873	57.9	5.8	5.0	0.0	2.0	32.0	3 218	78	35	799	52.7	46.6	0.8
Marion	79.9	2 460	61.3	1.8	8.6	0.0	2.4	5.2	159	68	133	1 490	63.3	35.7	1.0
Marlboro	80.0	2 841	65.4	1.7	6.2	2.2	0.0	67.2	2 386	368	101	1 466	62.5	36.7	0.8
Newberry	116.7	3 107	49.9	1.3	5.2	0.5	1.6	134.2	3 573	90	151	2 283	40.6	58.2	1.2
Oconee	188.2	2 522	59.7	0.5	7.2	0.2	3.1	171.5	2 298	135	306	3 912	30.5	68.0	1.6
Orangeburg	436.4	4 771	34.3	43.8	4.1	0.1	3.6	296.9	3 246	203	363	6 941	68.6	30.5	0.9
Pickens	329.4	2 752	64.3	1.5	5.1	0.1	3.3	469.0	3 919	179	480	9 383	25.9	72.1	2.0
Richland	1 388.2	3 525	44.0	0.2	4.6	0.1	1.1	5 237.8	13 300	9 144	10 467	46 078	64.0	35.1	0.9
Saluda	34.3	1 725	55.3	2.1	7.5	0.1	2.3	31.1	1 565	32	81	917	38.6	60.3	1.0
Spartanburg	1 501.9	5 202	32.3	48.4	2.8	0.4	1.0	1 018.7	3 528	490	1 179	19 232	38.4	60.0	1.5

1. Based on the resident population estimated as of July 1 of the year shown.   2. © 2013 Election Data Services, Inc. All rights reserved.

STATE/ County code	CBSA code[1]	County type[2]	STATE County	Land area,[3] (sq km) 2010	Total persons 2015	Rank	Per square kilometer	White	Black	American Indian, Alaska Native	Asian and Pacific Islander	Percent Hispanic or Latino[4]	Under 5 years	5 to 17 years	18 to 24 years	25 to 34 years	35 to 44 years	45 to 54 years
				1	2	3	4	5	6	7	8	9	10	11	12	13	14	15
			SOUTH CAROLINA—Cont'd															
45 085	44940	3	Sumter	1 723	107 480	556	62.4	47.7	47.4	0.8	2.0	3.8	7.1	17.5	11.1	13.4	11.3	12.9
45 087	43900	6	Union	1 332	27 777	1 501	20.9	66.5	32.4	0.6	0.5	1.2	5.4	16.4	8.0	10.4	12.1	14.3
45 089	...	6	Williamsburg	2 419	32 535	1 372	13.4	32.1	65.0	0.6	0.6	2.3	5.3	16.4	8.7	11.7	11.8	13.1
45 091	16740	1	York	1 763	251 195	266	142.5	73.2	20.2	1.3	2.2	5.0	6.3	18.5	8.9	12.3	14.0	14.6
46 000	...	X	**SOUTH DAKOTA**	196 350	858 469	X	4.4	84.9	2.4	9.5	1.7	3.6	7.1	17.6	10.0	13.1	11.2	12.6
46 003	...	9	Aurora	1 835	2 733	2 990	1.5	92.8	0.8	2.2	0.8	4.4	6.5	19.8	6.8	10.7	10.1	12.6
46 005	26700	7	Beadle	3 260	18 372	1 897	5.6	81.2	2.0	1.4	6.5	9.6	8.4	17.4	8.1	12.4	9.9	13.2
46 007	...	9	Bennett	3 068	3 423	2 942	1.1	38.5	1.1	61.0	1.1	3.4	9.6	24.0	10.6	11.1	10.3	11.5
46 009	...	9	Bon Homme	1 460	6 985	2 678	4.8	89.3	1.6	8.0	0.4	2.2	4.5	14.9	8.5	13.3	11.6	14.1
46 011	15100	7	Brookings	2 052	33 897	1 330	16.5	91.8	1.7	1.7	3.3	2.5	6.1	13.6	28.2	12.9	9.5	9.4
46 013	10100	5	Brown	4 437	38 785	1 207	8.7	90.3	2.0	4.1	2.4	2.4	6.8	16.9	10.0	13.5	10.9	12.7
46 015	...	9	Brule	2 117	5 281	2 814	2.5	87.9	0.9	10.8	0.7	2.4	7.0	18.4	7.8	10.4	10.9	13.4
46 017	...	9	Buffalo	1 221	2 095	3 041	1.7	19.3	1.2	77.0	0.4	3.5	13.3	27.3	10.0	13.9	10.6	9.1
46 019	...	6	Butte	5 827	10 283	2 412	1.8	93.5	1.0	3.4	0.7	3.7	6.3	17.9	7.6	11.4	9.9	13.1
46 021	...	9	Campbell	1 900	1 397	3 086	0.7	98.0	0.9	1.2	0.5	1.4	3.8	12.8	7.1	7.5	7.6	17.9
46 023	...	9	Charles Mix	2 842	9 383	2 479	3.3	65.9	0.9	33.2	0.7	2.5	8.6	20.9	8.4	10.2	9.6	11.9
46 025	...	9	Clark	2 480	3 659	2 929	1.5	95.2	1.6	0.5	0.2	2.8	8.3	15.6	7.3	11.1	9.5	12.2
46 027	46820	6	Clay	1 068	13 964	2 168	13.1	90.2	2.3	3.8	2.6	2.8	5.7	12.4	31.5	12.5	8.4	8.9
46 029	47980	7	Codington	1 783	27 939	1 489	15.7	94.4	1.0	2.7	1.1	1.9	7.0	17.3	9.3	12.7	11.6	13.3
46 031	...	9	Corson	6 396	4 197	2 888	0.7	34.2	0.9	63.0	0.9	3.9	9.4	25.2	9.8	12.1	10.2	12.1
46 033	39660	8	Custer	4 033	8 446	2 561	2.1	92.6	1.1	4.5	0.8	3.0	3.9	13.0	4.8	8.0	8.9	14.6
46 035	33580	7	Davison	1 128	19 858	1 839	17.6	93.5	1.3	3.4	1.0	2.4	6.3	16.7	10.5	12.7	10.9	12.5
46 037	...	9	Day	2 662	5 539	2 800	2.1	88.8	0.9	9.7	1.0	2.1	5.7	16.3	6.4	9.6	9.1	12.5
46 039	...	9	Deuel	1 613	4 333	2 876	2.7	95.2	1.1	0.9	0.3	3.1	5.5	17.5	6.8	9.6	11.0	13.9
46 041	...	9	Dewey	5 963	5 685	2 784	1.0	25.5	0.7	73.1	0.7	3.5	11.7	23.4	10.1	12.5	10.3	12.7
46 043	...	9	Douglas	1 118	2 977	2 974	2.7	96.3	0.8	2.7	0.3	1.3	6.3	16.6	7.1	8.8	8.5	12.3
46 045	10100	9	Edmunds	2 916	3 999	2 902	1.4	97.5	0.5	1.1	0.4	1.6	5.5	17.2	7.3	9.0	10.0	14.4
46 047	...	7	Fall River	4 506	6 867	2 685	1.5	87.6	1.5	8.7	1.3	3.7	3.3	14.6	6.4	8.4	9.5	13.2
46 049	...	9	Faulk	2 543	2 337	3 020	0.9	98.6	0.6	0.8	0.4	1.1	6.1	16.3	7.8	8.9	8.6	13.5
46 051	...	7	Grant	1 765	7 142	2 662	4.0	95.2	1.1	1.5	0.6	2.8	5.7	16.7	7.6	9.0	11.2	14.2
46 053	...	9	Gregory	2 629	4 201	2 886	1.6	90.1	0.9	9.0	0.9	1.4	5.7	17.1	6.6	8.6	10.2	12.2
46 055	...	8	Haakon	4 689	1 861	3 061	0.4	94.5	2.1	4.0	1.4	1.5	6.3	16.0	5.5	9.0	10.7	10.8
46 057	...	9	Hamlin	1 314	6 047	2 750	4.6	95.4	0.6	1.0	0.4	3.3	9.5	21.8	7.6	10.3	10.4	11.5
46 059	...	9	Hand	3 721	3 348	2 950	0.9	97.6	0.4	0.8	0.6	1.2	5.2	15.8	7.1	10.0	8.1	14.1
46 061	33580	8	Hanson	1 125	3 385	2 946	3.0	98.9	0.4	0.8	0.4	0.8	9.7	23.3	6.7	9.6	11.9	12.0
46 063	...	9	Harding	6 919	1 267	3 097	0.2	95.0	0.7	3.1	0.5	2.1	7.8	14.6	7.3	13.0	10.3	14.2
46 065	38180	7	Hughes	1 921	17 555	1 942	9.1	85.2	1.4	11.9	0.9	2.8	7.0	16.8	7.8	13.8	11.7	13.7
46 067	...	8	Hutchinson	2 105	7 301	2 645	3.5	95.4	1.0	1.6	0.3	2.0	6.8	16.8	6.8	8.7	10.7	12.0
46 069	...	9	Hyde	2 229	1 397	3 086	0.6	89.0	0.8	9.8	0.6	1.6	5.0	16.4	7.2	10.6	8.9	11.7
46 071	...	8	Jackson	4 828	3 321	2 952	0.7	45.9	1.3	53.4	0.6	3.3	10.9	23.2	9.8	11.1	9.2	12.1
46 073	...	9	Jerauld	1 363	1 997	3 049	1.5	94.1	0.4	0.8	0.5	4.9	6.7	16.4	4.2	10.1	9.8	11.1
46 075	...	9	Jones	2 511	924	3 110	0.4	93.9	1.1	4.8	1.7	2.3	5.1	16.0	5.8	9.5	10.8	13.6
46 077	...	9	Kingsbury	2 155	4 990	2 838	2.3	96.1	0.9	1.4	0.5	2.3	6.3	15.8	7.0	9.8	9.8	13.8
46 079	...	6	Lake	1 459	12 622	2 254	8.7	95.3	1.2	1.4	1.2	2.4	5.5	14.2	11.2	10.3	9.2	12.7
46 081	43940	6	Lawrence	2 072	24 827	1 611	12.0	92.8	1.2	3.3	1.1	3.2	4.7	13.7	13.0	11.7	10.2	12.2
46 083	43620	3	Lincoln	1 495	52 849	944	35.4	95.1	1.8	1.0	1.7	1.8	8.3	20.9	6.9	15.6	14.9	12.1
46 085	...	9	Lyman	4 253	3 876	2 911	0.9	60.2	0.9	39.0	0.6	2.3	8.3	20.4	8.6	12.0	10.2	12.1
46 087	43620	3	McCook	1 487	5 599	2 795	3.8	95.9	0.6	0.9	0.3	3.0	7.0	19.2	7.0	9.9	10.7	13.1
46 089	...	9	McPherson	2 944	2 415	3 012	0.8	97.7	0.5	0.7	0.3	1.6	5.7	16.5	6.0	7.8	9.1	12.1
46 091	...	9	Marshall	2 171	4 769	2 849	2.2	84.1	1.1	7.9	0.3	7.3	6.2	15.2	8.3	12.2	9.8	13.2
46 093	39660	3	Meade	8 990	26 986	1 535	3.0	90.6	2.4	4.1	1.5	4.1	6.3	17.7	11.6	14.1	11.2	12.2
46 095	...	9	Mellette	3 386	2 050	3 045	0.6	45.4	1.2	55.0	0.6	3.0	9.4	21.4	9.6	10.0	9.4	12.9
46 097	...	8	Miner	1 477	2 236	3 027	1.5	96.8	1.2	0.8	0.5	2.1	5.6	18.1	7.0	8.6	9.3	14.1
46 099	43620	3	Minnehaha	2 091	185 197	350	88.6	86.3	5.5	3.3	2.4	4.9	7.7	17.4	9.6	15.7	12.4	13.0
46 101	...	8	Moody	1 345	6 430	2 719	4.8	80.9	1.5	14.6	1.6	3.7	7.5	18.0	7.4	11.0	10.2	14.2
46 102	...	7	Oglala Lakota	5 423	14 373	2 144	2.7	6.6	0.4	90.3	0.4	3.7	11.7	26.4	11.6	14.5	10.5	10.6
46 103	39660	3	Pennington	7 191	108 702	552	15.1	83.3	2.2	11.1	1.9	4.9	7.0	17.0	8.9	14.0	11.4	12.4
46 105	...	9	Perkins	7 435	3 019	2 970	0.4	96.0	0.5	2.1	0.4	1.4	5.2	16.3	7.0	9.5	9.6	13.1
46 107	...	9	Potter	2 230	2 320	3 021	1.0	96.0	0.6	2.1	0.7	1.9	5.4	15.2	5.9	8.1	8.7	12.9
46 109	...	9	Roberts	2 852	10 311	2 409	3.6	61.3	0.9	38.0	0.8	2.4	8.7	19.7	8.5	9.5	9.9	12.1
46 111	...	9	Sanborn	1 475	2 355	3 019	1.6	97.0	0.5	1.3	0.4	2.4	6.4	15.8	7.2	11.9	9.6	13.3
46 115	...	7	Spink	3 895	6 524	2 715	1.7	95.8	0.9	2.2	0.2	2.2	5.9	18.1	7.9	10.8	9.3	13.1
46 117	38180	9	Stanley	3 741	2 954	2 979	0.8	90.3	1.4	9.5	0.5	1.4	5.9	18.0	7.1	11.8	11.6	14.0
46 119	38180	9	Sully	2 608	1 426	3 082	0.5	95.5	1.3	3.2	0.2	2.5	4.9	16.7	6.6	10.9	9.5	14.8
46 121	...	9	Todd	3 596	9 959	2 439	2.8	12.3	0.5	84.6	0.4	3.7	13.0	27.4	10.4	14.2	10.1	9.4

1. CBSA = Core Based Statistical Area. See Appendix A for explanation. See Appendix B for list of metropolitan areas with component counties.   2. County type code from the Economic Research Service of USDA Rural-Urban Continuum Codes. See Appendix A for definition.   3. Dry land or land partially or temporarily covered by water.   4. May be of any race.

Table B. States and Counties — **Population and Households**

STATE County	55 to 64 years (16)	65 to 74 years (17)	75 years and over (18)	Percent female (19)	2000 (20)	2010 (21)	2000–2010 (22)	2010–2015 (23)	Births (24)	Deaths (25)	Net migration (26)	Number (27)	Persons per household (28)	Family households (29)	Female family householder[1] (30)	One person (31)
SOUTH CAROLINA—Cont'd																
Sumter	12.2	8.3	6.2	51.8	104 646	107 463	2.7	0.0	7 939	5 353	-2 608	40 024	2.63	68.7	19.5	27.6
Union	14.8	10.7	7.8	52.5	29 881	28 963	-3.1	-4.1	1 621	1 934	-856	11 739	2.37	67.6	17.0	29.6
Williamsburg	15.0	10.9	7.0	51.5	37 217	34 419	-7.5	-5.5	1 791	2 143	-1 552	11 788	2.69	65.3	22.8	31.2
York	12.4	8.2	4.9	51.7	164 614	226 071	37.3	11.1	15 339	9 821	18 935	87 905	2.63	71.0	13.1	24.1
SOUTH DAKOTA	13.1	8.1	7.1	49.7	754 844	814 191	7.9	5.4	63 534	37 773	18 191	327 101	2.45	64.4	9.6	29.5
Aurora	13.8	9.3	10.4	48.5	3 058	2 710	-11.4	0.8	192	143	-9	1 098	2.37	68.1	5.6	28.4
Beadle	13.9	8.1	8.6	49.3	17 023	17 398	2.2	5.6	1 707	1 016	292	7 460	2.31	61.4	9.8	33.8
Bennett	10.7	6.0	6.3	52.2	3 574	3 431	-4.0	-0.2	371	165	-204	1 088	3.11	71.3	19.5	25.6
Bon Homme	13.1	9.1	10.9	42.0	7 260	7 067	-2.7	-1.2	330	384	-32	2 499	2.26	66.1	4.4	30.2
Brookings	9.8	5.6	4.8	49.0	28 220	31 965	13.3	6.0	2 123	1 029	842	12 318	2.34	58.4	7.0	29.7
Brown	13.0	7.8	8.3	50.7	35 460	36 531	3.0	6.2	2 587	1 954	1 661	15 794	2.28	61.3	8.8	33.7
Brule	14.8	7.8	9.5	51.1	5 364	5 255	-2.0	0.5	400	290	-78	2 065	2.42	72.3	12.2	24.3
Buffalo	8.6	4.7	2.5	50.2	2 032	1 912	-5.9	9.6	275	93	7	543	3.70	75.7	25.4	20.3
Butte	15.3	10.5	8.0	49.7	9 094	10 110	11.2	1.7	683	534	20	4 080	2.48	60.9	6.2	31.8
Campbell	18.5	11.1	13.6	48.5	1 782	1 466	-17.7	-4.7	62	65	-51	676	2.12	59.2	3.1	39.5
Charles Mix	12.4	8.9	9.1	50.0	9 350	9 129	-2.4	2.8	834	473	-121	3 196	2.75	66.3	12.8	29.6
Clark	15.6	9.8	10.6	49.3	4 143	3 691	-10.9	-0.9	272	248	-66	1 453	2.27	59.3	2.8	36.6
Clay	9.5	6.0	5.2	50.7	13 537	13 864	2.4	0.7	796	502	-213	5 185	2.25	47.3	5.0	30.8
Codington	13.3	7.9	7.6	49.9	25 897	27 227	5.1	2.6	2 019	1 249	-23	11 666	2.32	59.9	9.2	33.0
Corson	10.8	6.1	4.4	48.7	4 181	4 050	-3.1	3.6	455	239	-84	1 212	3.40	74.9	20.5	20.8
Custer	21.3	16.3	9.3	50.3	7 275	8 216	12.9	2.8	376	416	282	3 680	2.16	65.8	5.4	28.9
Davison	13.1	7.9	9.4	50.1	18 741	19 504	4.1	1.8	1 373	1 071	65	8 524	2.21	61.3	7.9	33.7
Day	16.1	12.4	12.0	49.2	6 267	5 710	-8.9	-3.0	322	395	-100	2 564	2.14	62.2	9.6	35.6
Deuel	14.7	10.6	10.3	48.4	4 498	4 364	-3.0	-0.7	241	197	-58	1 837	2.33	67.8	5.9	29.3
Dewey	9.4	5.5	4.5	51.6	5 972	5 301	-11.2	7.2	753	373	9	1 676	3.25	69.5	22.0	24.4
Douglas	15.1	10.9	13.9	50.4	3 458	3 002	-13.2	-0.8	177	218	4	1 285	2.25	67.9	4.3	27.9
Edmunds	15.3	10.4	10.9	49.0	4 367	4 071	-6.8	-1.8	235	236	-46	1 589	2.31	65.4	4.0	30.7
Fall River	18.5	14.7	11.4	49.3	7 453	7 094	-4.8	-3.2	298	571	23	3 161	2.10	55.5	8.4	39.0
Faulk	15.4	10.1	13.2	49.5	2 640	2 364	-10.5	-1.1	145	125	-41	949	2.21	60.2	2.2	33.5
Grant	15.7	10.4	9.6	48.8	7 847	7 356	-6.3	-2.9	424	416	-226	3 125	2.27	71.5	6.3	25.3
Gregory	15.6	11.6	12.6	49.4	4 792	4 271	-10.9	-1.6	254	323	3	1 989	2.11	60.9	8.0	36.5
Haakon	18.4	11.0	12.2	49.9	2 196	1 937	-11.8	-3.9	107	118	-54	877	2.33	69.9	5.4	26.9
Hamlin	11.5	9.2	8.3	49.8	5 540	5 903	6.6	2.4	619	357	-123	2 087	2.74	73.8	3.6	21.1
Hand	15.3	9.8	14.7	49.5	3 741	3 431	-8.3	-2.4	203	211	-91	1 464	2.24	63.6	5.3	33.7
Hanson	13.2	10.1	3.6	48.6	3 139	3 331	6.1	1.6	259	103	-74	1 026	3.05	71.4	3.7	26.0
Harding	17.1	8.8	6.9	48.2	1 353	1 255	-7.2	1.0	78	45	-27	504	2.37	65.1	4.4	31.2
Hughes	14.2	8.3	8.6	51.0	16 481	17 022	3.3	3.1	1 260	720	0	7 140	2.29	60.0	5.6	36.7
Hutchinson	14.5	9.4	14.3	50.9	8 075	7 343	-9.1	-0.6	486	572	29	2 932	2.25	66.6	7.7	31.7
Hyde	16.3	10.2	13.8	49.5	1 671	1 420	-15.0	-1.6	77	78	-15	541	2.63	67.5	6.8	29.8
Jackson	10.2	6.7	6.6	49.8	2 930	3 031	3.4	9.6	381	161	70	1 058	2.93	72.0	9.8	21.4
Jerauld	16.8	11.7	13.2	49.7	2 295	2 071	-9.8	-3.6	132	134	-75	887	2.27	68.1	8.6	27.8
Jones	17.4	10.4	11.3	53.9	1 193	1 006	-15.7	-8.2	54	47	-100	437	1.84	52.2	4.3	46.5
Kingsbury	16.0	10.1	11.4	49.4	5 815	5 148	-11.5	-3.1	324	357	-142	2 311	2.16	66.0	3.3	28.9
Lake	17.2	11.9	7.9	48.3	11 276	11 200	-0.7	12.7	690	556	1 255	4 722	2.35	64.5	7.1	30.9
Lawrence	16.1	10.2	8.3	50.0	21 802	24 097	10.5	3.0	1 240	1 128	596	10 483	2.21	62.1	7.7	31.2
Lincoln	11.0	6.1	4.2	50.4	24 131	44 823	85.7	17.9	4 146	1 042	4 802	17 650	2.71	75.5	8.8	19.8
Lyman	13.3	8.5	6.7	47.4	3 895	3 755	-3.6	3.2	359	161	-68	1 446	2.64	67.2	12.4	28.8
McCook	13.5	9.6	9.9	49.7	5 832	5 618	-3.7	-0.3	395	403	-40	2 191	2.45	63.6	7.0	24.1
McPherson	14.6	11.5	16.7	51.4	2 904	2 459	-15.3	-1.8	132	177	-1	1 028	2.00	63.8	10.6	35.1
Marshall	15.4	10.6	9.2	45.4	4 576	4 656	1.7	2.4	318	285	85	1 738	2.54	61.3	6.3	33.5
Meade	13.2	8.1	5.7	47.7	24 253	25 456	5.0	6.0	1 687	931	770	10 244	2.47	72.3	8.1	22.7
Mellette	11.7	8.0	7.6	47.2	2 083	2 048	-1.7	0.1	173	109	-65	697	2.94	71.7	24.4	25.8
Miner	15.4	9.8	12.0	49.7	2 884	2 389	-17.2	-6.4	117	158	-104	1 004	2.27	60.4	5.6	35.6
Minnehaha	12.0	6.8	5.4	49.8	148 281	169 476	14.3	9.3	14 988	6 741	7 239	68 906	2.48	63.4	11.2	29.3
Moody	14.7	9.2	7.9	49.7	6 595	6 486	-1.7	-0.9	472	261	-251	2 707	2.30	69.0	10.2	27.8
Oglala Lakota	7.8	4.2	2.6	51.6	12 466	13 586	9.0	5.8	1 809	720	-277	2 929	4.68	81.9	42.6	16.2
Pennington	13.8	8.6	6.8	49.8	88 565	100 937	14.0	7.7	8 154	4 235	3 732	41 155	2.46	63.7	11.0	29.2
Perkins	16.3	11.2	11.8	49.0	3 363	2 982	-11.3	1.2	183	220	72	1 343	2.19	61.8	6.5	36.1
Potter	15.5	13.6	14.7	51.6	2 693	2 329	-13.5	-0.4	118	179	58	1 048	2.13	62.7	6.4	35.5
Roberts	13.4	9.6	8.6	50.0	10 016	10 149	1.3	1.6	972	591	-213	3 602	2.78	68.4	11.4	26.8
Sanborn	17.0	9.0	9.9	48.1	2 675	2 355	-12.0	0.0	170	143	-8	1 072	2.10	60.1	4.9	33.2
Spink	15.3	9.1	10.5	49.5	7 454	6 415	-13.9	1.7	412	380	72	2 623	2.39	64.5	5.9	30.9
Stanley	14.5	10.6	6.5	48.2	2 772	2 966	7.0	-0.4	189	90	-99	1 223	2.44	65.7	10.7	25.3
Sully	17.8	9.2	9.5	46.0	1 556	1 373	-11.8	3.9	86	43	16	611	2.37	65.6	1.8	30.1
Todd	8.3	4.6	2.7	51.4	9 050	9 612	6.2	3.6	1 430	548	-533	2 745	3.57	74.5	36.0	22.0

1. No spouse present.

Table B. States and Counties — Population, Vital Statistics, Medicare, and Crime

STATE County	Persons in group quarters, 2015	Daytime population, 2010–2014 Number	Employ-ment/resi-dence ratio	Births, 2015 Total	Births, 2015 Rate[1]	Deaths, 2015 Number	Deaths, 2015 Rate[1]	Persons under 65 with no health insurance, 2014 Number	Percent	Medicare, 2015 Total Beneficiaries	Enrolled in Original Medicare	Enrolled in Medicare Advantage	Serious crimes known to police,[2] 2014 Total Number	Rate[3]
	32	33	34	35	36	37	38	39	40	41	42	43	44	45
SOUTH CAROLINA—Cont'd														
Sumter	2 799	108 055	1.01	1 495	13.9	1 046	9.7	15 054	16.8	20 030	16 325	3 705	4 780	4 395
Union	504	26 399	0.82	317	11.4	356	12.8	3 363	15.0	6 787	4 524	2 263	1 019	3 647
Williamsburg	1 437	31 599	0.82	329	10.1	384	11.8	4 134	16.2	6 797	4 820	1 977	1 164	3 537
York	3 956	216 903	0.83	2 990	12.0	1 931	7.8	29 260	14.0	43 662	33 410	10 252	6 425	2 637
SOUTH DAKOTA	34 019	837 413	1.01	12 344	14.4	6 972	8.1	81 569	11.6	147 875	120 539	27 336	18 688	2 190
Aurora	96	2 784	1.04	45	16.4	23	8.4	279	13.1	521	424	97	10	367
Beadle	620	17 942	1.00	346	18.9	193	10.5	2 166	14.6	4 077	3 305	772	403	2 206
Bennett	37	3 291	0.87	69	20.1	35	10.2	589	20.3	445	431	14	56	1 619
Bon Homme	1 544	6 489	0.81	57	8.1	67	9.6	531	12.3	1 481	1 274	207	2	28
Brookings	3 594	33 636	1.05	426	12.7	194	5.8	2 755	10.4	3 763	3 088	675	468	1 408
Brown	1 365	38 573	1.05	506	13.1	354	9.1	2 993	9.5	6 948	6 208	740	675	1 835
Brule	132	5 444	1.05	69	13.0	49	9.2	644	15.1	1 014	858	156	NA	NA
Buffalo	3	1 985	0.96	54	25.8	28	13.4	336	18.1	141	141	0	NA	NA
Butte	111	8 697	0.69	137	13.3	97	9.4	1 226	14.8	1 991	1 500	491	169	1 626
Campbell	0	1 362	0.89	16	11.5	6	4.3	119	11.3	548	475	73	5	384
Charles Mix	589	9 480	1.07	168	18.0	102	10.9	1 399	19.2	1 721	1 559	162	65	810
Clark	489	3 479	0.91	60	16.4	41	11.2	443	15.4	802	576	226	9	251
Clay	2 244	13 771	0.97	154	11.0	82	5.9	1 329	12.9	1 664	1 374	290	319	2 283
Codington	381	28 664	1.07	399	14.3	229	8.2	2 305	9.8	4 937	3 257	1 680	600	2 140
Corson	1	3 942	0.85	88	21.0	47	11.2	747	20.7	689	649	40	13	305
Custer	254	7 699	0.82	67	7.9	75	8.9	751	12.3	2 155	1 777	378	102	1 196
Davison	769	21 143	1.14	265	13.3	190	9.6	1 695	10.7	3 762	3 236	526	667	3 349
Day	139	5 417	0.91	53	9.6	78	14.1	666	16.0	1 393	1 100	293	NA	NA
Deuel	50	4 116	0.90	43	9.9	31	7.2	402	11.9	897	625	272	24	556
Dewey	19	5 859	1.19	149	26.2	90	15.8	1 064	21.6	699	673	26	11	194
Douglas	178	3 011	1.01	31	10.5	36	12.2	342	15.4	762	630	132	5	165
Edmunds	420	3 497	0.75	48	12.0	36	9.0	323	10.4	846	751	95	2	50
Fall River	232	7 109	1.05	63	9.2	98	14.3	650	13.3	2 217	1 898	319	NA	NA
Faulk	497	2 379	1.01	29	12.4	14	6.0	166	9.2	578	553	25	10	418
Grant	104	7 499	1.06	84	11.7	76	10.6	680	11.8	1 719	1 127	592	NA	NA
Gregory	44	4 152	0.96	53	12.6	52	12.3	553	17.6	1 148	951	197	NA	NA
Haakon	36	2 152	1.06	21	11.3	10	5.4	215	15.3	460	398	62	NA	NA
Hamlin	245	5 222	0.74	120	19.9	63	10.5	573	11.7	1 016	708	308	65	1 087
Hand	61	3 263	0.95	43	12.8	25	7.5	261	10.4	672	612	60	12	355
Hanson	520	2 464	0.44	50	14.7	14	4.1	354	12.0	1 260	1 076	184	15	438
Harding	29	1 377	1.17	17	13.5	6	4.8	171	16.7	181	159	22	1	79
Hughes	772	18 089	1.07	249	14.2	152	8.6	1 537	10.6	2 750	2 460	290	535	3 033
Hutchinson	832	6 612	0.83	107	14.7	103	14.2	693	12.8	1 828	1 397	431	25	352
Hyde	38	1 550	1.11	19	13.6	9	6.4	133	12.5	313	292	21	NA	NA
Jackson	42	3 089	0.93	77	23.3	25	7.6	651	23.8	398	361	37	NA	NA
Jerauld	176	2 301	1.25	26	13.0	21	10.5	187	12.5	510	450	60	2	97
Jones	0	768	0.92	10	10.6	6	6.4	157	20.8	213	187	26	NA	NA
Kingsbury	203	4 689	0.83	63	12.5	60	11.9	387	9.8	1 362	1 144	218	NA	NA
Lake	874	11 514	0.95	131	10.5	108	8.7	889	9.4	3 050	2 561	489	NA	NA
Lawrence	1 072	24 180	0.98	227	9.2	204	8.2	2 534	13.1	4 835	3 821	1 014	664	2 643
Lincoln	284	37 040	0.58	765	14.7	197	3.8	2 794	6.0	2 372	1 756	616	1 134	2 217
Lyman	35	3 725	0.94	70	18.1	21	5.4	604	19.0	594	529	65	NA	NA
McCook	312	4 674	0.68	79	14.1	73	13.0	450	10.0	988	812	176	47	829
McPherson	347	2 329	0.93	28	11.6	27	11.2	253	14.6	486	441	45	1	41
Marshall	373	4 512	0.93	65	13.7	47	9.9	624	16.7	928	833	95	52	1 084
Meade	797	21 522	0.67	325	12.1	191	7.1	2 771	12.3	4 003	3 216	787	297	1 073
Mellette	49	1 884	0.75	36	17.3	13	6.3	342	20.1	310	294	16	21	1 003
Miner	80	2 228	0.90	24	10.6	21	9.2	188	10.5	513	468	45	14	603
Minnehaha	6 275	192 795	1.17	2 948	16.0	1 286	7.0	15 074	9.7	31 260	24 236	7 024	5 216	2 861
Moody	164	5 713	0.78	92	14.3	49	7.6	730	13.9	956	798	158	55	861
Oglala Lakota	91	14 913	1.30	334	23.4	142	9.9	2 367	18.7	1 017	1 003	14	NA	NA
Pennington	2 566	109 528	1.09	1 582	14.6	839	7.7	11 319	12.6	20 416	16 622	3 794	3 702	3 460
Perkins	65	3 027	1.00	41	13.5	30	9.9	406	17.6	773	664	109	13	425
Potter	63	2 282	0.97	18	7.7	30	12.9	220	13.1	691	663	28	10	415
Roberts	281	10 123	0.96	198	19.2	108	10.5	1 417	17.1	1 816	1 499	317	55	535
Sanborn	174	1 944	0.68	37	15.8	20	8.5	283	15.1	503	437	66	NA	NA
Spink	403	6 481	0.98	78	11.9	64	9.8	578	11.2	1 482	1 329	153	35	525
Stanley	0	2 557	0.74	35	11.8	13	4.4	326	13.2	527	465	62	7	235
Sully	0	1 412	0.94	15	10.5	2	1.4	139	11.9	224	203	21	2	137
Todd	28	10 196	1.12	257	25.8	115	11.6	1 458	16.6	D	663	D	NA	NA

1. Per 1,000 estimated resident population.   2. Data for serious crimes have not been adjusted for underreporting; this may affect comparability between geographic areas and over time.
3. Per 100,000 population estimated by the FBI.

Table B. States and Counties — Crime, Education, Money Income, and Poverty

STATE County	Serious crimes known to police, 2014 (cont.)[1] Rate[2]		Education						Money income, 2010–2014				Income and poverty, 2014			
			School enrollment and attainment, 2010–2014				Local government expenditures,[5] 2012–2013			Households				Percent below poverty level		
			Enrollment[3]		Attainment[4] (percent)											
	Violent	Property	Total	Percent private	High school graduate or less	Bachelor's degree or more	Total current spending (mil dol)	Current spending per student (dollars)	Per capita income[6] (dollars)	Median income (dollars)	Mean income (dollars)	Percent with income of $200,000 or more	Median household income (dollars)	All persons	Children under 18 years	Children 5 to 17 years in families
	46	47	48	49	50	51	52	53	54	55	56	57	58	59	60	61
SOUTH CAROLINA—Cont'd																
Sumter	647	3 748	30 245	17.2	48.6	18.9	143.8	8 563	20 395	40 662	52 688	1.3	37 906	23.2	32.7	32.5
Union	523	3 124	6 419	9.0	57.9	13.6	35.8	8 648	19 253	35 221	45 623	0.6	37 501	19.6	29.2	27.0
Williamsburg	523	3 015	8 743	12.3	62.1	12.0	49.2	10 642	15 933	27 485	41 634	1.0	29 609	28.3	44.2	40.2
York	398	2 238	63 414	10.4	40.5	28.6	372.9	9 214	26 875	53 568	70 628	3.8	54 196	14.6	19.0	18.0
SOUTH DAKOTA	327	1 864	218 108	12.9	40.8	26.7	1 118.9	8 470	26 311	50 338	65 425	3.0	51 059	14.1	18.4	16.1
Aurora	37	330	650	12.3	50.6	18.5	6.4	10 991	24 074	47 024	57 955	2.1	50 896	10.8	14.5	12.9
Beadle	301	1 905	4 030	11.9	49.2	20.3	22.6	8 509	24 265	44 258	57 791	1.9	49 583	15.1	22.0	21.3
Bennett	318	1 301	1 129	7.0	47.9	16.5	5.6	11 486	16 032	34 697	50 949	2.6	34 326	34.8	45.5	41.1
Bon Homme	14	14	1 336	5.2	51.7	17.6	10.8	9 564	21 983	42 795	58 608	2.7	47 987	15.2	18.3	16.0
Brookings	99	1 309	13 589	4.8	32.0	41.4	35.9	8 427	24 694	48 406	62 713	2.6	52 930	14.1	11.5	10.5
Brown	242	1 593	9 841	18.8	41.3	26.9	40.4	7 647	27 958	52 469	65 170	3.1	53 150	11.8	13.2	11.4
Brule	NA	NA	1 081	13.7	47.7	21.4	11.3	9 673	22 083	46 698	55 819	1.8	47 224	14.8	19.0	16.5
Buffalo	NA	NA	655	23.2	60.7	8.6	NA	NA	11 719	31 758	40 981	0.0	21 658	40.7	47.5	44.6
Butte	173	1 453	2 486	16.5	48.1	18.2	13.6	7 856	22 459	41 731	53 460	1.7	41 446	15.8	22.6	20.0
Campbell	0	384	303	1.3	54.0	19.3	1.4	11 913	31 665	39 167	71 777	4.0	49 895	9.4	9.5	8.9
Charles Mix	125	685	2 521	19.2	49.0	18.0	18.7	10 971	19 901	41 220	54 410	2.8	41 395	24.0	31.4	27.9
Clark	84	167	723	5.1	47.6	20.2	5.6	9 045	28 434	49 016	70 863	4.1	48 024	13.8	25.6	23.7
Clay	279	2 004	6 769	4.0	33.1	43.1	10.4	8 604	21 044	36 627	53 973	1.4	43 453	24.9	18.3	16.4
Codington	225	1 915	6 795	11.0	48.8	20.3	34.1	7 596	25 624	47 891	60 754	2.4	52 892	10.3	13.6	12.1
Corson	0	305	1 248	1.2	52.2	14.1	12.6	14 742	15 854	32 892	52 897	1.9	31 420	38.6	45.2	39.1
Custer	47	1 149	1 437	14.5	35.5	27.4	8.0	9 207	28 855	50 903	65 781	3.8	51 244	10.7	18.7	17.3
Davison	346	3 002	4 844	19.9	38.4	26.4	25.4	8 172	25 544	50 061	59 413	1.5	48 675	12.3	14.7	13.0
Day	NA	NA	1 158	3.6	51.3	17.8	6.4	8 767	23 651	37 901	50 815	1.5	43 305	16.3	19.7	17.6
Deuel	46	510	930	2.4	48.7	22.1	4.2	7 789	28 810	52 717	67 654	3.3	51 246	10.1	12.8	11.2
Dewey	0	194	1 612	1.9	53.3	14.9	5.0	14 451	15 404	33 704	49 403	1.6	34 936	27.2	32.7	32.5
Douglas	99	66	628	24.7	54.3	18.1	3.3	10 209	27 978	49 360	64 896	5.3	49 251	11.6	14.4	12.9
Edmunds	0	50	851	11.0	45.4	23.6	6.2	9 532	27 271	54 229	66 975	2.5	57 148	10.5	13.9	12.0
Fall River	NA	NA	1 123	7.3	42.1	21.6	11.7	10 405	25 191	43 239	52 875	0.9	42 007	17.0	24.4	19.5
Faulk	0	418	528	23.3	45.5	20.6	3.0	9 199	25 494	42 781	62 825	2.8	46 633	13.2	21.3	20.2
Grant	NA	NA	1 416	10.4	56.0	17.2	10.5	9 022	26 219	51 277	62 027	2.0	52 816	10.0	13.5	11.7
Gregory	NA	NA	820	6.6	52.1	17.5	7.7	10 586	23 879	37 321	51 431	2.0	36 836	18.3	27.0	23.5
Haakon	NA	NA	432	4.4	47.0	18.6	2.7	8 947	24 265	42 950	58 451	2.6	43 699	12.0	15.3	14.0
Hamlin	0	1 087	1 455	10.3	50.9	19.3	11.8	9 073	25 861	56 134	70 987	4.2	53 944	10.4	12.8	12.2
Hand	0	355	656	10.7	49.2	20.2	4.2	9 664	27 345	46 951	61 022	3.0	51 201	10.0	12.0	10.0
Hanson	58	380	1 003	17.0	44.3	24.8	3.0	7 002	23 460	57 857	71 999	2.5	61 945	8.1	15.2	14.2
Harding	0	79	309	2.3	37.4	30.5	2.7	15 056	23 472	47 917	57 888	3.4	49 220	11.2	14.8	15.9
Hughes	431	2 602	3 763	10.4	35.7	32.1	19.3	7 389	29 501	57 614	70 476	1.9	58 340	11.0	14.9	12.9
Hutchinson	14	338	1 599	8.5	46.7	26.1	13.3	9 377	26 093	43 688	60 382	2.7	48 879	13.2	20.4	18.4
Hyde	NA	NA	269	1.1	56.3	17.6	2.8	10 249	27 010	53 036	67 866	1.7	49 184	10.1	8.4	7.0
Jackson	NA	NA	944	4.4	41.2	20.2	4.1	10 960	19 333	45 610	55 467	3.4	31 922	33.9	43.3	40.5
Jerauld	0	97	475	13.5	51.9	16.7	3.2	10 016	28 985	49 236	66 758	2.3	48 773	14.9	18.5	16.8
Jones	NA	NA	121	6.6	46.8	17.3	2.0	11 131	26 504	38 750	49 344	0.2	44 876	13.1	23.2	20.0
Kingsbury	NA	NA	990	5.7	44.7	23.2	10.0	9 443	28 092	52 522	63 817	2.7	51 837	10.1	13.1	12.2
Lake	NA	NA	3 477	5.4	40.3	28.4	16.9	8 404	28 245	50 378	66 980	2.9	53 175	9.5	11.4	10.3
Lawrence	179	2 464	6 116	7.8	38.6	29.5	24.3	8 243	28 120	44 267	63 673	3.3	45 945	13.6	18.2	15.3
Lincoln	268	1 949	13 559	18.8	27.0	41.0	47.4	7 354	34 624	75 877	92 263	5.8	79 857	4.3	4.9	4.2
Lyman	NA	NA	975	7.9	46.9	19.1	5.3	13 610	20 923	44 922	56 138	1.2	40 639	24.9	35.1	30.7
McCook	0	829	1 310	15.6	43.8	22.6	11.4	9 540	27 830	56 603	71 992	2.6	57 741	10.0	13.2	11.8
McPherson	41	0	447	7.4	48.9	16.9	4.2	11 510	22 515	37 602	51 362	1.9	38 469	17.0	25.4	22.4
Marshall	229	854	1 061	10.5	41.5	21.1	5.9	8 282	26 460	51 579	68 070	3.3	50 155	12.0	18.9	17.4
Meade	90	982	6 518	8.6	40.6	21.5	21.4	7 620	27 114	52 967	67 274	3.0	54 771	10.4	14.9	12.9
Mellette	191	812	639	4.4	48.7	17.5	4.9	11 007	14 882	35 478	42 875	0.6	34 237	33.2	43.3	39.7
Miner	43	560	518	8.5	48.0	24.5	5.6	9 921	31 017	48 241	74 027	4.2	49 159	12.4	15.1	12.9
Minnehaha	372	2 489	45 311	18.7	38.6	29.3	237.1	7 705	27 143	53 391	67 490	2.9	55 107	11.5	14.1	12.6
Moody	204	657	1 535	5.7	42.3	25.6	8.2	8 992	26 995	50 651	65 988	2.9	53 654	12.3	14.8	13.6
Oglala Lakota	NA	NA	4 932	7.5	48.7	12.5	22.5	15 645	9 226	26 383	38 572	1.8	27 244	52.2	53.5	47.1
Pennington	497	2 962	26 890	13.7	36.3	27.9	146.0	8 290	26 906	50 564	66 213	3.4	48 379	14.1	20.2	17.3
Perkins	33	393	577	17.2	49.3	18.8	4.8	12 466	25 458	38 635	56 604	4.2	39 936	15.2	18.7	15.6
Potter	0	415	435	8.7	50.9	20.0	3.9	10 624	26 923	44 931	58 822	2.9	52 758	11.0	16.3	14.4
Roberts	126	409	2 592	2.0	51.9	15.8	16.8	10 725	22 674	48 441	61 217	2.6	45 911	20.4	28.5	26.4
Sanborn	NA	NA	394	12.4	50.0	16.1	1.8	8 944	27 076	49 375	59 141	2.9	46 281	14.7	20.9	19.5
Spink	15	510	1 449	9.5	46.3	22.0	12.0	9 280	27 971	49 627	69 662	5.6	48 125	11.7	16.7	13.9
Stanley	134	101	639	5.0	43.6	26.8	4.7	10 497	30 188	57 930	72 877	5.6	67 172	8.8	12.3	10.4
Sully	0	137	342	9.6	44.5	26.3	3.3	12 373	36 707	61 806	85 320	6.9	59 879	6.3	6.7	5.8
Todd	NA	NA	3 562	6.7	47.4	13.9	23.8	11 547	11 101	30 539	38 117	0.6	27 481	47.4	52.8	46.9

1. Data for serious crimes have not been adjusted for underreporting; this may affect comparability between geographic areas and over time. 2. Per 100,000 population estimated by the FBI.
3. All persons 3 years old and over enrolled in nursery school through college. 4. Persons 25 years old and over. 5. Elementary and secondary education expenditures.
6. Based on population estimated by the American Community Survey, 2010–2014.

Table B. States and Counties — **Personal Income**

STATE County	Total (mil dol) [62]	Percent change, 2013–2014 [63]	Per capita¹ Dollars [64]	Per capita¹ Rank [65]	Wages and salaries (mil dol) [66]	Pension and insurance [67]	Government social insurance [68]	Proprietors' income (mil dol) [69]	Dividends, interest, and rent (mil dol) [70]	Personal transfer receipts (mil dol) [71]	Earnings Total (mil dol) [72]	From employee and self-employed [73]	From employer [74]
SOUTH CAROLINA— Cont'd													
Sumter	3 893	2.9	36 077	1 770	1 825	395	153	179	670	994	2 552	149	153
Union	799	3.7	28 673	2 868	269	49	21	32	97	299	371	29	21
Williamsburg	876	2.1	26 792	2 994	369	83	28	35	113	342	515	37	28
York	9 299	6.9	37 903	1 468	3 701	578	282	455	1 104	1 662	5 017	323	282
SOUTH DAKOTA	38 631	2.0	45 279	X	17 030	2 927	1 267	6 092	8 381	5 827	27 317	1 553	1 267
Aurora	136	-8.4	49 476	416	28	5	2	48	25	17	83	3	2
Beadle	869	0.9	47 818	487	328	58	24	177	198	126	588	33	24
Bennett	114	12.6	33 094	2 263	27	8	2	30	18	29	67	3	2
Bon Homme	260	-6.6	37 050	1 593	60	14	4	67	57	47	146	7	4
Brookings	1 380	4.3	41 416	1 018	723	164	54	174	322	153	1 115	60	54
Brown	1 794	1.0	46 712	545	844	144	64	275	408	249	1 326	81	64
Brule	255	-4.7	48 032	478	65	12	5	91	50	38	173	7	5
Buffalo	56	10.5	27 017	2 980	20	6	2	14	7	17	40	2	2
Butte	353	9.9	34 310	2 061	99	18	8	66	67	71	190	11	8
Campbell	66	-6.3	47 868	485	18	3	1	17	15	11	40	2	1
Charles Mix	397	-6.4	42 772	874	108	24	8	139	75	75	279	12	8
Clark	190	-10.3	52 011	294	37	7	3	65	48	24	112	4	3
Clay	590	-3.9	42 367	917	210	55	15	185	104	81	466	24	15
Codington	1 202	2.1	43 030	844	608	102	46	124	289	180	880	54	46
Corson	135	16.0	32 360	2 396	32	8	2	48	19	31	90	3	2
Custer	353	7.4	41 853	965	84	19	6	43	85	70	152	10	6
Davison	946	1.5	47 551	496	467	76	35	161	228	140	739	44	35
Day	248	-2.5	44 401	726	63	12	5	55	65	48	134	7	5
Deuel	228	-3.5	52 774	275	60	12	5	76	40	30	153	7	5
Dewey	225	16.8	39 664	1 230	79	20	6	58	33	50	163	7	6
Douglas	156	-9.8	52 459	281	42	8	3	52	30	24	105	4	3
Edmunds	204	7.0	51 130	327	50	9	4	64	46	27	127	5	4
Fall River	291	10.8	42 492	900	101	23	10	42	68	78	176	10	10
Faulk	127	11.4	53 943	239	24	4	2	52	24	19	83	2	2
Grant	318	6.2	43 957	763	163	27	12	52	68	58	254	15	12
Gregory	168	-5.3	39 947	1 184	45	9	3	38	38	37	96	5	3
Haakon	115	30.3	62 068	109	30	6	2	50	20	14	87	3	2
Hamlin	210	-6.3	35 045	1 926	68	12	5	16	45	34	101	6	5
Hand	194	-3.8	58 027	155	49	8	4	71	38	24	132	5	4
Hanson	213	-9.2	62 354	108	23	4	2	49	64	36	78	4	2
Harding	72	21.4	57 828	162	24	4	2	30	12	6	60	2	2
Hughes	845	6.2	47 899	484	443	94	32	104	175	108	674	37	32
Hutchinson	366	-11.1	50 840	338	89	16	7	120	78	56	232	10	7
Hyde	65	-26.4	46 351	569	22	4	2	15	18	10	42	2	2
Jackson	95	20.3	28 927	2 837	23	6	2	26	14	22	58	2	2
Jerauld	103	-11.3	51 291	319	55	10	4	29	24	17	98	5	4
Jones	56	-19.9	57 624	163	14	3	1	20	12	6	38	1	1
Kingsbury	264	-2.5	51 977	296	66	13	5	65	51	39	150	7	5
Lake	615	-0.1	49 707	398	183	37	14	108	156	106	341	21	14
Lawrence	1 035	3.7	41 976	954	387	66	29	86	277	178	568	38	29
Lincoln	2 851	5.3	55 305	208	855	118	62	208	601	211	1 243	76	62
Lyman	143	-29.9	36 902	1 615	45	10	3	30	30	28	88	4	3
McCook	283	-12.1	50 071	384	50	9	4	99	43	39	162	8	4
McPherson	106	12.8	43 470	798	20	4	1	31	29	20	56	2	1
Marshall	218	-0.9	46 534	555	64	11	5	62	44	31	142	6	5
Meade	1 238	7.6	45 943	601	286	68	23	356	201	158	732	40	23
Mellette	65	24.5	30 829	2 610	10	3	1	18	9	17	33	1	1
Miner	102	-11.7	44 102	754	24	5	2	23	24	18	53	2	2
Minnehaha	8 485	4.6	46 398	565	5 545	804	405	1 031	1 683	1 154	7 785	476	405
Moody	283	-12.0	44 445	721	82	17	6	48	59	39	153	8	6
Oglala Lakota	335	7.7	23 546	3 092	149	39	11	29	31	137	228	11	11
Pennington	4 486	4.7	41 440	1 015	2 377	413	183	168	1 181	848	3 142	194	183
Perkins	152	21.4	49 997	385	36	8	3	59	28	23	107	4	3
Potter	197	4.5	84 194	21	30	5	2	105	42	19	143	6	2
Roberts	333	-2.8	32 145	2 426	117	26	9	40	71	78	191	11	9
Sanborn	96	-10.6	41 137	1 047	21	5	2	19	20	15	47	2	2
Spink	353	-7.1	53 477	256	90	20	7	98	83	73	214	9	7
Stanley	170	-10.4	56 839	177	49	8	4	32	39	16	93	4	4
Sully	125	1.8	87 019	18	23	3	2	65	24	8	94	2	2
Todd	236	4.5	23 923	3 081	100	26	7	25	27	86	158	8	7

1. Based on the resident population estimated as of July 1 of the year shown.

Table B. States and Counties — Earnings, Social Security, and Housing

STATE County	Earnings, 2014 (cont.) Percent by selected industries									Social Security beneficiaries, December 2014		Supplemental Security Income recipients, December 2014	Housing units, 2015	
	Farm	Mining	Construction	Manufacturing	Information: professional, scientific, technical services	Retail trade	Finance, insurance, real estate and leasing	Health care and social assistance	Government	Number	Rate[1]		Total	Percent change, 2010–2014
	75	76	77	78	79	80	81	82	83	84	85	86	87	88
SOUTH CAROLINA—Cont'd														
Sumter	0.7	0.0	6.0	15.4	4.3	5.6	2.6	11.2	36.9	22 720	210	4 268	47 183	2.5
Union	2.6	D	2.6	24.0	1.6	7.1	5.5	D	26.8	8 335	298	1 046	13 987	-1.2
Williamsburg	1.1	0.0	4.4	31.9	D	4.9	D	D	23.9	8 705	266	1 972	15 137	-1.4
York	0.6	0.0	4.8	15.8	8.5	8.3	9.3	10.2	13.6	43 620	178	3 728	101 588	7.8
SOUTH DAKOTA	9.8	0.3	6.2	10.6	5.5	7.2	8.5	13.6	16.4	165 499	194	14 905	380 331	4.6
Aurora	47.5	0.0	D	D	D	3.5	D	11.1	10.4	600	219	26	1 330	0.5
Beadle	13.9	D	5.2	22.5	2.2	6.0	5.4	D	13.1	3 580	196	406	8 388	1.0
Bennett	41.6	0.0	7.0	D	D	5.2	D	D	26.9	530	154	163	1 257	-0.5
Bon Homme	31.5	D	5.1	5.0	2.4	5.3	3.3	D	19.8	1 550	221	81	2 960	1.0
Brookings	7.1	D	5.2	27.1	3.5	5.5	3.4	3.7	25.8	4 325	130	278	13 999	6.6
Brown	1.6	D	7.0	16.6	4.4	8.4	8.4	15.0	13.1	7 270	188	544	17 672	5.8
Brule	39.9	D	5.6	0.5	2.9	6.0	3.5	7.0	11.2	1 150	216	118	2 509	3.1
Buffalo	35.7	0.0	D	0.0	D	D	D	D	56.8	200	96	110	607	-0.3
Butte	13.2	D	12.2	4.5	4.3	9.7	3.9	6.7	14.8	2 320	225	201	4 695	1.6
Campbell	47.6	0.0	D	D	D	3.7	D	1.9	7.8	445	324	16	978	-0.2
Charles Mix	37.4	0.0	5.1	1.7	2.2	4.4	3.6	D	21.1	1 865	202	267	3 857	0.2
Clark	50.7	0.0	7.5	6.4	D	3.8	D	3.6	8.9	780	213	81	1 814	6.1
Clay	10.5	D	5.2	11.7	3.7	5.1	4.0	7.8	34.8	1 865	133	165	5 831	3.4
Codington	3.5	0.1	6.9	21.6	5.1	9.4	6.4	13.0	13.5	5 500	197	362	12 848	3.6
Corson	54.2	0.0	0.8	0.0	1.2	1.0	D	0.9	31.3	570	136	242	1 534	-0.4
Custer	5.9	1.7	11.8	0.7	D	6.2	4.7	D	27.2	2 475	293	102	4 949	6.9
Davison	5.2	D	6.9	21.9	6.7	9.7	4.4	13.0	9.9	4 255	214	376	9 261	4.6
Day	32.9	0.0	7.5	6.3	D	5.7	D	6.6	13.8	1 570	282	103	3 706	2.1
Deuel	37.3	0.0	12.1	10.3	D	3.7	2.5	4.2	6.9	1 025	237	34	2 214	0.5
Dewey	27.5	D	2.3	0.2	D	6.3	1.7	D	48.2	885	156	356	2 000	-0.1
Douglas	41.5	D	5.9	4.0	D	2.6	D	D	7.7	745	253	40	1 439	0.0
Edmunds	38.1	0.0	4.7	5.1	D	6.3	3.0	D	11.6	880	221	30	2 018	2.6
Fall River	23.1	0.6	2.0	0.4	2.5	3.9	1.9	D	35.5	2 285	333	187	4 167	-0.5
Faulk	63.6	0.0	2.1	D	D	D	2.5	D	7.0	530	226	46	1 156	1.8
Grant	11.9	0.6	15.6	17.9	1.7	6.2	5.8	D	6.7	1 910	265	94	3 580	1.5
Gregory	26.3	D	7.7	0.7	2.0	8.9	5.9	D	12.7	1 180	280	96	2 509	0.2
Haakon	48.7	0.0	D	D	5.6	4.6	3.2	D	6.9	480	260	0	1 009	-0.4
Hamlin	16.1	0.0	12.0	15.7	D	6.8	4.6	4.0	19.9	1 055	176	59	2 853	3.4
Hand	52.0	0.0	3.0	1.0	D	3.2	D	D	7.6	890	265	55	1 812	-0.2
Hanson	52.0	D	9.9	7.4	D	1.8	2.7	D	9.8	1 395	410	33	1 180	0.3
Harding	44.2	D	17.8	0.0	D	2.0	D	D	9.3	190	152	0	737	0.8
Hughes	6.5	D	3.7	0.6	6.8	7.3	7.5	10.8	39.5	3 330	189	246	7 895	3.6
Hutchinson	40.5	0.0	4.0	5.1	1.3	4.8	3.1	D	8.1	1 895	262	92	3 371	0.6
Hyde	39.6	0.0	D	D	D	4.6	D	D	19.3	345	247	17	702	-0.8
Jackson	42.9	0.0	D	D	D	4.0	D	D	30.3	485	148	135	1 188	-0.4
Jerauld	20.4	0.0	D	D	D	2.0	D	D	5.2	545	272	30	1 069	-0.1
Jones	48.4	0.0	D	D	D	7.5	2.7	1.3	15.2	230	238	8	604	2.5
Kingsbury	38.3	0.0	5.3	13.0	D	3.7	D	5.4	9.0	1 295	255	72	2 745	0.9
Lake	8.4	D	6.1	22.9	5.0	7.2	4.9	7.9	17.0	3 510	285	153	5 677	2.1
Lawrence	0.3	D	8.3	4.5	4.1	10.7	5.2	13.6	17.9	5 665	229	358	13 544	6.2
Lincoln	1.9	0.1	9.9	12.8	D	7.4	16.3	12.3	6.1	6 850	133	210	19 539	9.3
Lyman	33.9	0.0	D	D	D	5.3	2.1	0.3	35.8	730	189	81	1 729	1.5
McCook	26.1	0.0	3.5	D	3.2	3.6	2.7	6.2	7.8	1 240	220	75	2 525	1.4
McPherson	57.2	0.1	1.2	3.3	D	3.1	0.0	6.2	11.7	730	301	47	1 419	0.1
Marshall	42.8	D	6.7	14.9	2.4	4.0	D	D	10.9	1 040	221	65	2 581	1.9
Meade	8.3	D	13.0	2.1	7.2	5.5	6.3	7.8	26.0	4 775	177	280	11 616	5.5
Mellette	52.2	0.0	D	0.0	D	3.2	D	1.0	29.1	355	169	118	834	-0.5
Miner	41.9	0.0	D	3.4	D	3.5	D	7.8	13.7	560	243	31	1 330	1.7
Minnehaha	0.5	D	5.6	8.5	8.3	7.9	14.9	20.7	10.0	31 805	174	2 952	77 750	8.7
Moody	25.2	0.0	11.1	9.3	1.2	2.4	1.9	D	21.8	1 240	194	49	2 840	0.6
Oglala Lakota	11.5	0.0	1.3	D	D	D	D	1.6	73.1	1 505	106	1 112	3 580	-0.4
Pennington	0.5	0.1	6.7	4.6	6.5	8.6	7.0	19.2	23.4	22 905	212	2 012	47 180	5.0
Perkins	49.0	0.0	5.5	D	D	4.5	D	4.1	10.5	830	273	52	1 729	-0.6
Potter	26.3	0.0	3.5	1.8	D	45.8	D	2.9	5.0	540	231	14	1 499	-0.1
Roberts	13.9	D	5.2	7.6	2.0	5.5	D	8.9	38.2	2 070	200	223	4 947	0.9
Sanborn	43.6	0.0	D	D	D	2.0	D	D	14.0	525	225	20	1 186	1.2
Spink	37.5	0.0	5.1	6.2	D	3.0	6.1	D	21.7	1 525	232	168	3 176	1.2
Stanley	29.9	D	28.4	0.0	3.2	7.4	D	1.1	11.0	585	197	17	1 464	5.6
Sully	71.6	0.0	D	D	D	3.1	2.3	D	5.5	295	207	5	875	3.6
Todd	15.4	0.0	1.0	D	D	3.5	D	D	68.3	995	100	600	3 131	-0.4

1. Per 1,000 resident population estimated as of July 1 of the year shown.

Table B. States and Counties — Housing, Labor Force, and Employment

STATE County	Housing units, 2010–2014 Occupied units Owner-occupied Total	Percent	Median value[1]	Median owner cost as a percent of income With a mortgage	Without a mortgage[2]	Renter-occupied Median rent[3]	Median rent as a percent of income[2]	Sub-standard units[4] (percent)	Civilian labor force, 2015 Total	Percent change, 2014–2015	Unemployment Total	Rate[5]	Civilian employment,[6] 2010–2014 Total	Percent Management, business, science and arts	Construction, production, and maintenance occupations
	89	90	91	92	93	94	95	96	97	98	99	100	101	102	103
SOUTH CAROLINA—Cont'd															
Sumter..........................	40 024	64.5	108 300	21.5	11.8	735	29.5	3.1	44 413	0.3	3 047	6.9	41 109	29.0	27.7
Union..........................	11 739	72.2	74 300	20.1	12.3	617	30.9	1.8	11 674	1.8	914	7.8	10 793	23.0	37.6
Williamsburg..................	11 788	73.6	65 600	25.3	15.1	583	32.8	2.7	12 818	1.6	1 183	9.2	11 269	23.3	31.6
York..........................	87 905	70.5	158 700	21.3	10.0	812	30.5	1.9	125 099	2.3	6 856	5.5	109 270	36.0	21.4
SOUTH DAKOTA..............	327 101	68.0	135 700	21.0	10.9	648	26.2	2.9	452 303	0.8	14 222	3.1	425 816	35.0	23.4
Aurora..........................	1 098	80.1	71 200	17.6	11.8	583	20.9	2.6	1 601	-0.7	36	2.2	1 377	34.6	29.9
Beadle..........................	7 460	65.3	91 600	18.4	10.6	548	24.6	4.8	9 550	1.0	255	2.7	9 153	27.3	32.1
Bennett..........................	1 088	57.9	52 100	23.7	12.1	461	26.0	16.1	1 140	0.1	59	5.2	1 169	39.8	20.3
Bon Homme....................	2 499	79.6	69 200	19.9	10.6	509	28.8	3.6	3 075	2.0	82	2.7	2 913	39.5	23.3
Brookings	12 318	59.1	152 000	22.6	10.2	666	29.9	1.0	18 587	1.9	548	2.9	18 590	34.3	26.9
Brown..........................	15 794	70.2	138 100	19.8	12.0	590	25.5	1.3	21 155	0.3	570	2.7	20 569	33.7	27.0
Brule..........................	2 065	70.8	94 300	21.1	12.0	518	18.2	2.9	2 570	-0.2	70	2.7	2 526	37.8	21.5
Buffalo..........................	543	40.7	42 900	19.2	13.7	610	17.2	17.5	717	-2.6	53	7.4	677	35.9	22.5
Butte..........................	4 080	73.6	110 500	23.7	12.5	582	30.1	0.8	5 137	0.6	177	3.4	4 995	28.3	33.0
Campbell..........................	676	82.5	54 600	18.2	11.5	564	28.9	0.9	858	0.5	26	3.0	701	44.9	20.5
Charles Mix....................	3 196	71.0	75 800	19.6	11.3	501	24.1	5.4	4 015	-0.4	139	3.5	3 891	35.5	22.4
Clark..........................	1 453	77.8	74 800	18.8	10.8	532	19.8	2.5	1 995	-0.1	73	3.7	1 803	35.1	27.8
Clay..........................	5 185	52.0	136 000	20.7	10.0	676	41.8	1.5	7 038	-1.1	219	3.1	7 141	38.7	17.7
Codington....................	11 666	68.8	138 500	21.0	11.4	600	25.0	2.7	15 463	0.3	483	3.1	15 130	25.4	29.7
Corson..........................	1 212	51.1	55 800	11.8	12.4	427	21.7	12.7	1 498	0.1	78	5.2	1 246	41.2	23.9
Custer..........................	3 680	81.3	205 100	24.4	12.9	775	24.6	2.8	3 974	-0.1	171	4.3	3 723	40.5	21.8
Davison..........................	8 524	63.8	124 600	19.4	10.0	597	24.5	0.8	11 415	0.8	295	2.6	10 425	35.7	23.6
Day	2 564	72.9	77 700	22.1	12.0	487	31.3	2.1	2 920	1.1	144	4.9	2 667	34.6	26.2
Deuel..........................	1 837	83.8	99 500	18.7	10.3	438	17.3	1.4	2 327	-0.7	117	5.0	2 255	35.3	32.4
Dewey..........................	1 676	60.1	56 400	17.0	12.2	450	20.0	12.3	2 326	-2.3	268	11.5	1 877	46.8	18.5
Douglas	1 285	78.5	71 800	17.4	10.3	550	19.0	0.9	1 704	-1.5	42	2.5	1 550	37.8	23.3
Edmunds..........................	1 589	80.5	102 400	17.6	10.0	497	21.6	0.2	2 245	0.2	56	2.5	2 152	35.0	28.1
Fall River	3 161	67.0	88 800	23.9	11.6	589	26.8	2.0	3 025	0.2	135	4.5	3 143	33.8	24.9
Faulk..........................	949	77.1	78 600	23.5	10.0	483	21.2	3.1	1 145	-0.1	31	2.7	1 145	45.7	21.5
Grant..........................	3 125	78.9	103 800	20.9	10.0	470	23.4	1.5	4 866	3.3	144	3.0	3 935	29.8	31.9
Gregory..........................	1 989	70.2	59 000	21.9	10.5	484	31.8	2.7	2 081	0.0	66	3.2	2 008	39.5	21.9
Haakon..........................	877	81.0	72 900	23.1	10.0	633	18.4	1.7	1 104	1.0	25	2.3	984	46.6	18.8
Hamlin..........................	2 087	77.0	114 800	21.4	10.0	581	24.3	5.4	3 157	0.5	107	3.4	2 839	30.8	36.0
Hand..........................	1 464	72.6	89 100	21.8	10.6	464	22.3	1.0	1 851	0.9	44	2.4	1 645	35.7	26.7
Hanson..........................	1 026	86.5	106 400	22.3	11.9	604	22.8	1.7	1 826	0.6	61	3.3	1 665	38.3	28.2
Harding..........................	504	71.6	76 600	20.6	10.6	569	18.7	0.8	778	0.1	19	2.4	660	40.6	35.9
Hughes..........................	7 140	64.3	166 700	20.4	10.0	579	23.1	2.4	9 983	-0.2	245	2.5	9 703	45.2	16.0
Hutchinson	2 932	77.3	71 900	18.7	11.1	563	28.7	1.1	3 688	0.4	93	2.5	3 669	38.8	26.1
Hyde..........................	541	82.3	72 300	16.1	11.2	496	14.0	3.0	709	-0.7	21	3.0	819	38.7	25.0
Jackson	1 058	59.6	53 400	19.8	11.3	442	15.2	12.8	1 320	-1.6	57	4.3	1 269	49.8	19.3
Jerauld..........................	887	75.0	70 500	20.2	12.3	504	16.5	2.8	1 133	-5.8	26	2.3	1 021	34.0	35.2
Jones..........................	437	71.4	64 600	21.3	12.7	386	19.0	1.1	593	-2.8	18	3.0	482	38.6	21.2
Kingsbury	2 311	75.0	86 200	16.9	10.2	457	19.2	1.3	2 793	-3.5	85	3.0	2 637	36.7	28.9
Lake..........................	4 722	71.9	121 800	18.8	11.7	503	23.1	0.4	6 569	3.5	237	3.6	6 412	32.1	26.4
Lawrence..........................	10 483	66.5	172 600	23.6	11.6	595	27.1	2.1	12 884	1.6	421	3.3	12 663	29.8	23.0
Lincoln..........................	17 650	77.3	191 000	20.9	10.0	840	23.3	1.2	30 133	1.9	685	2.3	27 081	45.5	17.1
Lyman..........................	1 446	67.7	72 400	17.3	11.2	501	16.3	7.6	1 810	-0.1	86	4.8	1 749	42.0	19.2
McCook	2 191	80.4	101 600	19.3	10.0	583	22.5	2.0	3 199	1.2	76	2.4	2 988	34.7	27.3
McPherson	1 028	77.1	57 500	21.4	10.7	246	12.6	0.0	1 128	-0.4	38	3.4	1 035	40.9	22.2
Marshall..........................	1 738	72.5	96 300	19.2	11.5	494	19.9	2.0	2 507	-1.1	98	3.9	2 256	33.9	30.8
Meade	10 244	71.0	158 100	22.9	12.4	770	29.6	3.5	13 345	0.3	429	3.2	12 912	30.9	26.4
Mellette	697	64.0	55 200	21.8	10.0	430	20.8	9.6	817	-1.4	43	5.3	789	47.8	26.5
Miner	1 004	78.9	64 600	17.5	12.8	447	18.0	1.5	1 233	-0.9	31	2.5	1 186	40.5	27.4
Minnehaha..........................	68 906	63.7	152 900	21.1	10.0	698	26.8	2.6	106 517	1.8	2 916	2.7	97 176	33.3	21.5
Moody..........................	2 707	70.7	113 000	22.3	12.2	540	20.7	2.3	3 943	-1.1	137	3.5	3 380	42.0	27.8
Oglala Lakota	2 929	54.5	20 000	14.1	12.1	431	19.1	38.3	3 600	-1.0	417	11.6	3 114	41.7	16.4
Pennington	41 155	66.6	154 900	22.8	12.1	781	28.5	2.8	54 234	0.3	1 753	3.2	52 607	33.2	19.9
Perkins	1 343	70.7	58 000	20.2	10.1	442	26.8	1.8	1 591	2.2	51	3.2	1 483	39.5	27.5
Potter..........................	1 048	82.6	64 800	17.0	13.1	539	27.2	0.1	1 199	-0.4	39	3.3	1 142	32.7	27.4
Roberts..........................	3 602	68.6	87 300	20.1	10.6	495	23.9	2.9	4 901	0.5	218	4.4	4 381	36.7	25.7
Sanborn..........................	1 072	73.8	75 400	18.7	10.0	510	20.8	0.8	1 229	-1.6	32	2.6	1 266	31.3	34.8
Spink	2 623	73.1	68 100	18.0	10.0	510	22.3	0.5	3 382	-0.6	106	3.1	3 196	35.8	25.5
Stanley	1 223	78.3	131 300	22.0	12.1	641	27.1	2.9	1 859	-0.4	45	2.4	1 700	37.6	26.7
Sully	611	72.8	99 400	18.3	10.0	618	13.1	2.1	881	-0.8	22	2.5	808	40.2	31.2
Todd..........................	2 745	45.8	45 100	25.4	10.4	469	20.5	18.1	3 051	-2.3	227	7.4	2 853	33.1	18.7

1. Specified owner-occupied units. 2. A value of 10.0 represents 10 percent or less; a value of 50.0 represents 50 percent or more. 3. Specified renter-occupied units.
4. Overcrowded or lacking complete plumbing facilities. 5. Percent of civilian labor force. 6. Persons 16 years old and over.

Table B. States and Counties — Nonfarm Employment and Agriculture

	Private nonfarm establishments, employment and payroll, 2014									Agriculture, 2012			
	Employment						Annual payroll		Farms			
											Percent with:	
STATE County	Number of establish-ments	Total	Health care and social assistance	Manufac-turing	Retail trade	Finance and insurance	Professional, scientific, and technical services	Total (mil dol)	Average per employee (dollars)	Number	Fewer than 50 acres	500 acres or more	Farm operators whose principal occu-pation is farming (percent)
	104	105	106	107	108	109	110	111	112	113	114	115	116
SOUTH CAROLINA—Cont'd													
Sumter	1 777	31 005	5 325	5 492	4 455	794	1 120	1 025	33 070	515	44.3	14.2	45.8
Union	429	6 435	D	1 446	819	182	D	192	29 764	264	33.0	7.2	33.7
Williamsburg	497	7 134	811	D	871	160	D	253	35 482	679	28.9	15.8	38.3
York	4 633	69 198	8 794	9 355	10 072	4 688	2 591	2 765	39 955	1 004	48.3	4.7	35.8
SOUTH DAKOTA	26 198	347 819	65 356	44 065	52 061	26 365	11 805	13 161	37 839	31 989	19.6	43.6	58.9
Aurora	86	601	D	57	D	46	D	18	29 388	442	12.2	47.5	60.6
Beadle	564	7 134	1 467	1 655	1 115	377	124	228	31 977	754	19.4	43.4	55.6
Bennett	62	643	170	D	138	D	D	17	26 905	219	7.3	68.5	68.0
Bon Homme	176	1 091	337	129	D	84	D	32	28 905	671	20.3	38.3	54.7
Brookings	879	13 138	1 477	4 262	1 806	588	621	480	36 545	1 023	31.7	23.9	46.2
Brown	1 282	18 672	2 969	2 887	3 031	977	510	666	35 650	1 056	23.6	38.9	57.4
Brule	222	1 881	469	25	255	71	45	51	27 125	407	21.4	47.2	61.9
Buffalo	10	162	25	D	D	NA	D	4	24 123	78	7.7	66.7	75.6
Butte	313	2 309	D	193	433	87	D	75	32 332	659	21.1	35.2	57.7
Campbell	60	266	24	D	23	D	D	8	31 711	242	7.9	56.6	63.2
Charles Mix	282	2 447	521	99	427	126	D	63	25 823	759	14.1	45.1	67.2
Clark	118	643	D	D	78	D	D	21	32 944	597	11.6	48.1	58.1
Clay	297	3 411	754	D	766	77	142	81	23 834	461	27.1	37.3	64.4
Codington	1 110	14 098	1 739	3 551	2 769	794	266	501	35 543	713	30.9	29.6	44.6
Corson	36	199	D	NA	D	D	NA	7	33 337	323	6.5	73.7	79.3
Custer	271	1 303	D	30	248	D	40	47	36 195	446	33.0	32.5	54.3
Davison	720	11 403	2 172	1 800	2 085	332	649	372	32 638	427	26.5	31.1	48.2
Day	179	1 518	293	262	246	D	D	44	29 308	693	14.0	35.9	46.0
Deuel	141	1 771	180	D	D	D	D	87	48 885	664	26.5	28.6	53.6
Dewey	83	562	143	D	87	56	D	21	36 552	342	14.6	65.2	55.6
Douglas	108	958	D	D	137	D	D	27	28 547	434	15.0	42.9	72.4
Edmunds	122	903	170	69	123	53	31	31	34 620	422	9.7	60.7	62.6
Fall River	201	2 425	1 537	27	242	40	41	132	54 502	327	18.7	51.1	64.5
Faulk	71	458	D	D	68	D	D	13	29 203	280	6.4	70.7	75.4
Grant	283	3 217	421	596	508	141	D	111	34 426	618	22.0	39.6	64.6
Gregory	190	1 110	317	33	257	D	29	29	25 781	505	10.1	52.3	65.3
Haakon	80	629	D	D	91	D	D	20	31 324	287	2.8	72.8	73.2
Hamlin	183	1 154	170	D	132	56	41	46	39 585	489	28.6	30.3	52.8
Hand	120	1 063	275	46	D	58	44	31	29 004	415	6.5	64.6	68.7
Hanson	71	294	D	D	D	29	D	11	36 990	370	16.8	44.1	60.0
Harding	41	418	D	NA	29	D	D	23	55 727	250	5.6	80.4	79.2
Hughes	660	6 538	1 107	D	1 403	485	306	220	33 581	338	33.1	34.3	50.0
Hutchinson	235	2 177	661	308	324	106	D	67	30 769	802	16.5	40.5	60.3
Hyde	43	458	D	NA	70	D	D	17	36 367	207	11.6	63.8	81.2
Jackson	50	280	D	NA	108	D	D	6	22 279	299	7.7	70.6	70.6
Jerauld	81	1 284	D	D	58	D	14	44	34 203	233	18.5	46.4	49.8
Jones	52	272	D	NA	90	D	D	8	28 235	163	4.3	72.4	73.0
Kingsbury	171	1 420	239	413	167	113	17	47	33 146	518	14.9	45.8	64.1
Lake	365	3 713	608	904	514	144	145	133	35 877	502	29.1	30.3	51.6
Lawrence	997	9 806	D	566	1 421	280	285	282	28 725	312	28.8	17.9	42.0
Lincoln	1 329	14 621	2 668	2 357	1 723	1 228	452	586	40 086	899	34.8	27.5	50.3
Lyman	73	619	D	NA	260	37	D	14	22 572	430	6.3	62.3	53.7
McCook	184	1 039	265	D	182	D	D	27	26 158	568	25.0	37.5	53.5
McPherson	81	361	D	D	D	53	D	10	26 443	398	12.6	54.0	60.6
Marshall	146	1 210	D	393	193	51	D	43	35 683	518	14.5	41.5	53.7
Meade	697	5 271	D	334	701	167	166	231	43 893	891	21.2	50.4	56.9
Mellette	22	D	D	NA	D	D	D	3	D	229	3.1	76.4	83.8
Miner	80	510	D	38	64	D	D	16	31 106	486	17.5	36.8	55.6
Minnehaha	5 523	116 138	D	11 644	15 176	12 712	4 335	4 954	42 659	1 157	39.7	23.2	52.0
Moody	165	1 657	239	337	176	24	D	53	31 914	513	29.2	25.7	63.0
Oglala Lakota	67	1 755	D	D	207	16	D	54	31 041	174	4.6	69.5	77.0
Pennington	3 737	48 048	9 156	2 793	8 772	3 436	1 827	1 728	35 963	599	24.5	38.4	52.1
Perkins	126	770	127	D	D	45	13	23	29 288	437	8.9	72.3	69.6
Potter	101	803	138	D	87	D	D	28	35 027	247	11.3	56.3	68.0
Roberts	232	2 234	555	D	385	104	25	60	26 991	876	19.2	35.0	54.3
Sanborn	55	D	D	D	D	D	D	13	D	402	10.2	41.5	47.0
Spink	189	1 376	324	D	183	83	D	47	33 864	675	11.4	56.7	67.0
Stanley	112	1 103	17	D	137	41	D	35	31 636	183	7.1	71.0	66.1
Sully	70	335	D	D	86	D	D	13	37 919	191	6.3	66.0	72.8
Todd	60	1 394	D	D	258	D	D	42	30 347	231	10.4	63.2	70.6

Table B. States and Counties — **Agriculture**

Agriculture, 2012 (cont.)

STATE County	Acreage (1,000) [117]	Percent change, 2007–2012 [118]	Average size of farm [119]	Total irrigated (1,000) [120]	Total cropland (1,000) [121]	Average per farm [122]	Average per acre [123]	Value of machinery and equipment, average per farm (dollars) [124]	Total (mil dol) [125]	Average per farm (dollars) [126]	Crops [127]	Live-stock and poultry products [128]	$10,000 or more [129]	$100,000 or more [130]	Total ($1,000) [131]	Percent of farms [132]
SOUTH CAROLINA—Cont'd																
Sumter	176	14.7	342	8.9	69.5	792 967	2 320	105 033	130.5	253 379	36.9	63.1	27.2	10.9	1 870	57.3
Union	47	4.0	179	0.1	9.0	394 534	2 201	43 322	15.3	58 121	12.3	87.7	29.5	1.9	303	14.4
Williamsburg	224	7.2	331	0.8	91.8	689 383	2 086	83 346	61.8	91 032	83.2	16.8	29.9	12.8	2 763	60.1
York	124	-0.2	123	0.7	38.1	621 009	5 031	48 627	96.8	96 452	D	D	23.4	4.1	572	14.6
SOUTH DAKOTA	43 257	-0.9	1 352	378.7	19 147.3	2 281 027	1 687	241 373	10 170.2	317 929	59.7	40.3	65.0	40.7	283 797	71.3
Aurora	442	21.2	1 000	D	267.7	2 361 032	2 361	226 367	127.3	287 910	53.6	46.4	71.7	45.5	3 875	81.4
Beadle	794	3.1	1 053	11.2	576.9	3 014 625	2 864	295 423	300.2	398 088	63.3	36.7	66.3	46.9	7 071	74.9
Bennett	606	-19.5	2 769	6.6	178.6	1 564 995	565	198 361	62.2	283 799	35.8	64.2	76.7	51.1	2 139	73.5
Bon Homme	352	13.9	524	6.6	277.2	1 529 963	2 920	189 478	107.9	160 744	38.3	61.7	66.0	30.3	4 954	86.3
Brookings	449	-2.9	439	16.9	327.4	1 870 065	4 261	195 803	312.5	305 506	51.9	48.1	52.9	29.9	7 038	68.3
Brown	1 079	-0.6	1 022	6.4	854.5	2 980 409	2 917	318 692	520.6	493 029	88.9	11.1	56.9	40.7	17 500	66.3
Brule	514	-0.9	1 263	3.7	263.9	2 876 440	2 278	244 592	150.9	370 715	51.0	49.0	70.0	42.8	2 702	68.8
Buffalo	296	-5.1	3 797	6.3	87.0	4 488 474	1 182	380 705	45.7	585 256	50.3	49.7	70.5	50.0	912	78.2
Butte	1 135	-0.5	1 722	45.4	116.8	1 066 480	619	99 675	75.4	114 340	23.0	77.0	67.2	26.1	3 255	46.7
Campbell	360	-10.1	1 489	2.3	211.0	1 898 711	1 275	321 665	98.9	408 607	62.8	37.2	71.1	51.7	2 928	85.5
Charles Mix	692	4.8	912	15.3	448.9	2 146 680	2 353	264 441	227.9	300 271	45.2	54.8	70.2	44.9	5 433	87.7
Clark	609	19.7	1 020	7.3	401.3	2 584 074	2 534	297 191	249.4	417 714	64.0	36.0	66.2	51.1	5 326	83.9
Clay	259	-3.0	561	20.8	237.6	2 481 560	4 422	279 267	96.8	210 037	82.3	17.7	64.2	46.6	4 323	79.4
Codington	369	0.6	518	4.3	255.9	1 389 913	2 684	168 854	172.4	241 811	62.8	37.2	56.2	33.4	3 757	62.6
Corson	1 242	-3.2	3 846	D	346.4	2 514 418	654	240 712	117.1	362 492	50.9	49.1	86.4	60.4	3 165	66.3
Custer	623	3.7	1 397	3.1	46.9	1 600 944	1 146	76 119	26.0	58 325	11.0	89.0	47.8	15.7	1 285	19.7
Davison	275	-1.5	645	1.7	210.2	2 187 288	3 393	215 440	78.8	184 515	63.7	36.3	55.7	31.4	2 594	65.6
Day	570	0.5	823	0.3	395.0	1 571 924	1 911	211 440	189.7	273 775	83.5	16.5	51.7	32.5	6 718	78.6
Deuel	342	7.8	515	1.1	207.6	1 519 508	2 951	183 530	177.8	267 700	52.5	47.5	54.2	32.2	4 206	78.2
Dewey	1 182	-18.5	3 455	0.0	214.4	1 979 599	573	171 526	69.3	202 535	42.2	57.8	76.9	44.7	4 224	64.9
Douglas	270	19.8	622	2.1	192.3	1 774 048	2 854	210 823	117.5	270 668	35.4	64.6	81.1	50.5	2 807	79.3
Edmunds	697	6.1	1 652	1.0	492.8	3 620 645	2 192	451 389	271.4	643 123	68.7	31.3	74.2	58.3	5 097	81.5
Fall River	1 089	14.6	3 330	7.5	63.8	1 714 394	515	112 138	116.9	357 364	5.5	94.5	59.3	30.3	1 885	40.4
Faulk	616	0.2	2 199	0.5	382.8	4 275 536	1 945	559 368	216.3	772 596	72.3	27.7	83.9	66.4	5 575	87.9
Grant	429	17.9	694	3.4	290.7	2 075 218	2 992	261 960	240.8	389 675	56.4	43.6	66.0	48.1	4 517	70.6
Gregory	635	-3.0	1 257	0.5	239.1	1 534 659	1 221	156 531	94.1	186 410	42.4	57.6	73.5	37.4	2 245	79.4
Haakon	1 133	-1.5	3 949	0.1	324.6	2 375 324	601	186 188	77.1	268 700	43.0	57.0	75.6	50.2	4 539	73.5
Hamlin	311	0.4	636	7.9	241.7	2 272 331	3 572	285 902	188.2	384 920	66.3	33.7	59.1	39.9	4 136	74.8
Hand	905	0.7	2 181	4.5	565.6	4 161 320	1 908	431 607	284.4	685 390	69.6	30.4	77.1	58.1	5 362	85.3
Hanson	274	25.1	741	1.1	212.2	2 773 749	3 745	316 603	110.7	299 054	60.7	39.3	67.6	46.8	2 701	75.1
Harding	1 467	-8.1	5 869	0.7	179.7	2 465 216	420	212 876	70.4	281 628	24.3	75.7	80.0	55.6	2 729	61.6
Hughes	431	4.8	1 275	9.8	269.5	2 502 944	1 963	213 530	107.3	317 577	81.2	18.8	54.7	32.8	3 532	62.1
Hutchinson	513	0.7	640	4.0	409.7	2 103 788	3 287	263 249	186.2	232 226	38.3	61.7	69.1	38.4	7 192	85.2
Hyde	515	7.0	2 486	0.3	216.3	3 454 498	1 390	317 135	94.3	455 705	66.9	33.1	80.7	57.5	2 441	75.4
Jackson	1 158	-2.2	3 873	0.6	176.6	3 077 278	795	179 492	51.9	173 619	34.6	65.4	71.2	41.8	2 083	58.2
Jerauld	333	1.3	1 428	1.4	181.6	2 811 747	1 968	300 974	99.3	426 206	62.4	37.6	67.8	40.8	2 191	73.4
Jones	612	17.9	3 757	0.7	210.1	2 730 785	727	235 785	65.3	400 319	61.5	38.5	74.8	58.3	2 535	81.0
Kingsbury	521	9.1	1 006	2.1	382.3	3 338 884	3 319	324 201	278.3	537 182	63.0	37.0	75.3	55.8	5 135	74.9
Lake	262	-16.9	521	1.8	207.3	2 128 008	4 081	237 606	168.8	336 323	66.6	33.4	56.6	41.8	3 352	75.5
Lawrence	159	18.9	509	2.7	29.7	722 071	1 419	76 962	19.1	61 064	12.7	87.3	41.0	11.9	315	22.1
Lincoln	366	9.8	407	2.9	329.9	2 211 686	5 440	198 632	172.3	191 619	60.0	40.0	61.4	33.1	6 946	71.4
Lyman	1 029	5.3	2 392	8.7	456.4	2 398 733	1 003	253 705	136.8	318 044	69.5	30.5	65.6	47.0	6 670	81.6
McCook	363	-0.1	639	D	299.5	2 713 745	4 248	278 900	157.0	276 347	61.6	38.4	65.0	40.1	3 979	72.9
McPherson	573	10.5	1 439	1.3	286.8	2 201 472	1 530	274 035	159.4	400 425	53.1	46.9	71.4	42.0	3 081	76.9
Marshall	532	-0.4	1 027	D	316.0	2 296 672	2 235	328 147	306.8	592 357	47.6	52.4	58.7	39.6	8 084	82.2
Meade	2 033	-8.0	2 281	4.0	349.8	1 537 875	674	117 736	116.4	130 688	21.8	78.2	60.3	28.5	4 935	42.4
Mellette	699	-4.2	3 051	D	117.4	2 181 253	715	174 258	46.2	201 799	30.1	69.9	82.5	52.8	1 048	65.1
Miner	357	19.1	735	D	231.5	2 361 718	3 212	260 222	123.7	254 517	60.6	39.4	57.4	40.1	4 341	82.5
Minnehaha	408	-3.2	353	1.7	322.4	1 814 344	5 146	191 197	270.2	233 576	60.8	39.2	56.3	34.4	5 753	67.2
Moody	254	-13.3	496	3.2	208.8	2 525 815	5 094	216 696	215.0	419 047	61.1	38.9	59.8	40.7	4 100	76.2
Oglala Lakota	1 101	-17.4	6 329	0.5	97.8	2 910 178	460	155 874	32.3	185 563	27.0	73.0	77.0	36.8	1 772	45.4
Pennington	1 074	-9.4	1 793	5.8	222.8	1 253 793	699	110 694	65.7	109 760	45.0	55.0	55.9	23.7	2 942	30.7
Perkins	1 631	-10.8	3 732	0.2	393.2	2 007 828	538	177 826	125.0	286 087	34.6	65.4	77.6	51.5	4 913	77.1
Potter	538	4.1	2 178	D	357.3	4 354 235	1 999	489 332	157.0	635 684	89.5	10.5	70.9	54.7	3 783	78.1
Roberts	623	5.1	711	2.3	429.3	1 800 643	2 531	225 765	251.2	286 725	79.7	20.3	57.1	36.6	9 142	79.2
Sanborn	360	13.2	896	D	221.8	2 130 490	2 377	270 057	118.8	295 401	58.4	41.6	60.9	39.8	3 561	78.1
Spink	945	4.1	1 400	19.2	714.7	4 166 481	2 976	425 689	447.6	663 096	74.7	25.3	72.3	56.4	12 003	87.4
Stanley	791	-14.1	4 323	0.2	219.4	3 968 497	918	248 842	64.0	349 896	63.7	36.3	77.6	50.3	2 309	62.3
Sully	628	3.2	3 289	24.6	501.0	5 131 304	1 560	595 026	225.6	1 181 042	82.7	17.3	77.5	61.3	3 981	77.0
Todd	860	-1.1	3 723	7.2	125.2	1 902 965	511	163 303	59.7	258 268	26.7	73.3	72.3	42.4	398	37.2

Table B. States and Counties — Water Use, Wholesale Trade, Retail Trade, and Real Estate

STATE County	Water use, 2010		Wholesale trade,[1] 2012				Retail trade,[2] 2012				Real estate and rental and leasing,[2] 2012			
	Total water withdrawn (mil gal/day)	Gallons withdrawn per person per day	Number of establishments	Number of employees	Sales (mil dol)	Annual payroll (mil dol)	Number of establishments	Number of employees	Sales (mil dol)	Annual payroll (mil dol)	Number of establishments	Number of employees	Receipts (mil dol)	Annual payroll (mil dol)
	133	134	135	136	137	138	139	140	141	142	143	144	145	146
SOUTH CAROLINA—Cont'd														
Sumter	23.5	219	69	635	342.0	28.8	398	4 416	1 096.8	85.4	78	258	28.9	6.4
Union	4.7	161	14	102	43.4	4.4	99	905	195.7	16.9	14	134	8.2	3.1
Williamsburg	5.4	155	19	249	145.1	8.6	115	927	225.2	18.0	17	45	4.5	1.0
York	217.1	960	233	4 335	3 237.0	292.2	656	9 498	2 845.2	218.4	202	717	125.3	25.3
SOUTH DAKOTA	625.8	769	1 317	15 827	20 411.1	756.9	3 843	49 867	13 791.8	1 127.3	962	3 526	582.8	105.7
Aurora	0.8	284	6	48	65.4	1.5	8	59	10.8	1.1	2	D	D	D
Beadle	5.7	329	28	351	615.6	17.8	79	1 084	257.8	23.7	31	155	14.0	2.5
Bennett	26.2	7 648	NA	NA	NA	NA	15	126	32.3	2.4	NA	NA	NA	NA
Bon Homme	6.9	976	11	101	76.2	2.9	32	206	47.1	3.7	4	7	0.4	0.1
Brookings	17.0	532	29	252	451.6	12.5	121	1 679	375.9	34.7	45	169	21.1	4.4
Brown	8.8	241	80	1 048	1 914.6	48.7	201	2 956	809.5	75.0	57	251	31.3	7.0
Brule	3.9	742	12	104	102.0	4.3	41	299	99.1	6.4	4	4	0.2	0.1
Buffalo	15.4	8 044	NA	NA	NA	NA	2	D	D	D	NA	NA	NA	NA
Butte	17.2	1 698	6	D	D	D	49	429	157.4	11.4	8	16	1.2	0.4
Campbell	15.8	10 764	5	D	D	D	6	25	10.9	0.4	1	D	D	D
Charles Mix	19.9	2 178	14	182	180.8	5.8	52	445	99.8	7.5	3	D	D	D
Clark	8.2	2 208	8	D	D	D	14	91	34.8	2.0	1	D	D	D
Clay	5.5	397	8	44	30.2	1.8	45	665	122.8	11.3	11	20	3.2	0.4
Codington	12.8	469	58	773	580.6	36.0	184	2 667	649.1	56.0	50	126	20.3	3.1
Corson	1.8	447	4	D	D	D	6	43	15.1	1.1	NA	NA	NA	NA
Custer	12.5	1 525	1	D	D	D	31	261	68.1	4.8	9	16	6.3	0.3
Davison	1.6	80	35	D	D	D	130	2 030	530.4	47.3	26	D	D	D
Day	8.5	1 490	9	139	212.7	4.8	29	264	62.2	4.6	2	D	D	D
Deuel	2.9	671	6	30	37.6	1.1	23	116	46.1	3.0	1	D	D	D
Dewey	1.1	208	5	73	50.1	2.0	14	97	22.0	1.2	4	22	0.9	0.2
Douglas	4.3	1 419	6	D	D	D	18	119	36.4	1.9	2	D	D	D
Edmunds	3.0	747	13	202	472.5	8.8	16	126	44.4	2.7	4	6	0.2	0.0
Fall River	7.1	1 001	3	D	D	D	31	239	68.5	4.1	7	11	1.1	0.2
Faulk	0.9	389	10	48	113.5	2.4	13	95	29.6	2.2	1	D	D	D
Grant	20.4	2 766	13	129	193.2	6.2	46	501	127.5	10.9	9	18	2.2	0.3
Gregory	3.1	716	6	27	39.7	1.0	29	221	67.0	4.5	2	D	D	D
Haakon	6.3	3 242	8	102	232.1	2.7	16	99	29.0	2.0	1	D	D	D
Hamlin	1.6	276	11	142	149.8	7.7	18	117	38.5	2.6	2	D	D	D
Hand	1.1	329	11	158	89.1	5.0	21	186	36.2	2.8	1	D	D	D
Hanson	1.6	477	7	D	D	D	4	32	6.2	0.5	1	D	D	D
Harding	0.8	622	NA	NA	NA	NA	7	33	11.4	0.6	NA	NA	NA	NA
Hughes	46.8	2 752	23	D	D	D	105	1 393	347.2	30.6	30	D	D	D
Hutchinson	1.9	261	28	336	480.0	12.5	41	321	81.1	6.2	2	D	D	D
Hyde	0.8	528	5	58	173.1	2.9	8	97	21.3	1.3	1	D	D	D
Jackson	2.1	683	2	D	D	D	14	118	33.6	1.8	NA	NA	NA	NA
Jerauld	1.2	594	5	D	D	D	9	65	21.3	1.5	2	D	D	D
Jones	2.7	2 674	2	D	D	D	12	87	32.8	2.0	NA	NA	NA	NA
Kingsbury	6.1	1 189	8	112	240.5	5.2	23	141	34.1	2.5	2	D	D	D
Lake	8.0	716	17	198	371.4	11.5	46	491	162.3	12.2	12	28	2.3	0.4
Lawrence	23.1	959	19	52	38.8	2.1	142	1 380	434.0	35.2	63	184	22.2	4.6
Lincoln	5.4	120	55	390	667.6	19.5	126	1 571	490.6	45.9	54	268	39.2	8.8
Lyman	5.5	1 475	4	D	D	D	16	301	54.5	5.0	1	D	D	D
McCook	1.6	287	10	73	100.0	3.4	24	161	52.1	2.9	6	D	D	D
McPherson	1.4	582	2	D	D	D	10	61	14.2	1.1	1	D	D	D
Marshall	8.8	1 881	10	60	69.1	2.5	24	194	74.3	4.6	1	D	D	D
Meade	10.3	403	21	D	D	D	78	615	211.0	16.2	23	75	11.6	1.9
Mellette	4.5	2 202	NA	NA	NA	NA	7	56	11.6	0.8	1	D	D	D
Miner	0.5	213	4	D	D	D	13	65	17.8	1.3	2	D	D	D
Minnehaha	34.2	202	359	5 704	3 841.7	291.7	798	14 467	4 264.7	332.8	229	1 189	254.0	44.9
Moody	4.4	680	4	31	18.8	1.6	20	188	50.5	3.0	5	5	0.5	0.1
Oglala Lakota	0.9	67	1	D	D	D	10	189	51.4	3.2	NA	NA	NA	NA
Pennington	51.8	513	158	1 858	1 248.7	83.0	574	8 278	2 250.8	198.6	160	554	97.2	15.8
Perkins	1.6	550	5	D	D	D	19	108	24.8	2.2	3	D	D	D
Potter	5.0	2 130	7	94	577.3	5.3	17	123	21.8	1.6	2	D	D	D
Roberts	8.8	862	14	101	421.8	4.8	41	359	112.5	6.6	2	D	D	D
Sanborn	0.7	301	4	19	25.5	0.8	5	D	D	D	NA	NA	NA	NA
Spink	18.3	2 846	18	202	491.8	11.6	23	184	46.1	3.6	3	4	0.6	0.1
Stanley	4.5	1 514	3	D	D	D	15	133	53.2	3.8	4	D	D	D
Sully	27.2	19 825	5	D	D	D	11	88	42.6	2.4	3	D	D	D
Todd	39.4	4 097	1	D	D	D	15	196	43.0	3.0	3	D	D	D

1. Merchant wholesalers, except manufacturers' sales branches and offices.   2. Employer establishments.

Table B. States and Counties — Professional Services, Manufacturing, and Accommodation and Food Services

STATE County	Professional, scientific, and technical services, 2012				Manufacturing, 2012				Accommodation and food services, 2012			
	Number of establishments	Number of employees	Receipts (mil dol)	Annual payroll (mil dol)	Number of establishments	Number of employees	Receipts (mil dol)	Annual payroll (mil dol)	Number of establishments	Number of employees	Sales (mil dol)	Annual payroll (mil dol)
	147	148	149	150	151	152	153	154	155	156	157	158
SOUTH CAROLINA—Cont'd												
Sumter	126	714	75.8	23.2	71	5 524	1 817.5	214.6	158	2 951	127.0	34.9
Union	22	100	5.7	1.8	28	1 483	524.5	63.7	36	485	21.0	6.0
Williamsburg	26	95	10.5	2.8	35	2 110	1 778.0	97.2	27	D	D	D
York	455	2 240	297.2	102.9	213	8 310	3 111.1	439.6	392	7 094	336.9	89.6
SOUTH DAKOTA	1 822	11 144	1 315.4	482.3	1 025	41 931	16 882.6	1 764.7	2 363	37 974	1 873.7	514.2
Aurora	8	D	D	D	5	44	D	1.5	14	35	1.6	0.4
Beadle	28	114	11.0	4.0	31	1 646	495.1	55.7	48	525	21.7	5.4
Bennett	4	5	0.3	0.1	NA	NA	NA	NA	5	46	1.6	0.4
Bon Homme	6	20	1.8	0.5	13	320	D	11.6	14	65	2.4	0.5
Brookings	71	348	43.3	16.2	40	4 565	2 282.1	206.1	84	1 540	55.9	16.0
Brown	80	430	54.7	18.4	40	2 827	D	114.8	108	1 951	81.1	23.8
Brule	22	41	3.3	1.2	3	12	4.6	0.5	24	209	11.4	2.7
Buffalo	1	D	D	D	NA	NA	NA	NA	1	D	D	D
Butte	21	84	6.5	2.5	16	123	60.9	5.2	30	257	11.4	3.3
Campbell	4	7	0.3	0.1	3	48	D	D	7	D	D	D
Charles Mix	10	52	4.5	1.4	8	86	D	3.1	21	438	19.8	7.2
Clark	6	18	2.4	0.4	8	121	D	3.6	9	20	1.3	0.4
Clay	14	50	2.8	1.1	10	275	D	11.5	43	837	28.4	7.5
Codington	72	294	46.2	10.6	78	3 388	1 029.9	140.7	92	1 884	82.6	22.6
Corson	NA	NA	NA	NA	NA	NA	NA	NA	3	D	D	D
Custer	19	D	D	D	12	43	D	1.2	54	366	31.1	7.9
Davison	48	D	D	D	39	1 676	D	75.4	67	1 365	55.9	15.2
Day	5	24	2.2	0.7	13	219	61.5	9.4	17	168	5.2	1.4
Deuel	5	D	D	D	4	D	D	D	13	88	4.3	1.0
Dewey	4	11	0.4	0.1	NA	NA	NA	NA	6	18	1.7	0.2
Douglas	5	10	0.8	0.2	9	105	14.4	3.1	5	D	D	D
Edmunds	6	21	2.6	0.7	5	63	D	2.5	9	72	2.3	0.7
Fall River	13	49	3.1	1.1	8	24	5.5	0.8	37	336	13.5	3.5
Faulk	3	D	D	D	3	13	D	D	13	49	2.5	0.3
Grant	14	46	4.7	1.6	14	580	844.6	25.9	25	286	10.5	2.3
Gregory	8	26	2.3	0.6	6	59	D	D	19	95	3.8	0.8
Haakon	5	14	1.7	0.5	4	62	D	D	7	36	1.6	0.3
Hamlin	3	D	D	D	8	233	D	8.9	11	33	1.4	0.2
Hand	9	30	3.5	1.1	6	40	D	1.6	13	95	3.0	0.6
Hanson	2	D	D	D	3	54	D	D	4	15	0.7	0.1
Harding	NA	NA	NA	NA	NA	NA	NA	NA	3	23	1.0	0.2
Hughes	53	279	35.9	12.3	6	44	D	2.1	51	984	40.9	11.7
Hutchinson	11	30	2.8	1.0	11	214	76.8	8.2	18	D	D	D
Hyde	2	D	D	D	NA	NA	NA	NA	1	D	D	D
Jackson	1	D	D	D	NA	NA	NA	NA	10	39	4.5	1.0
Jerauld	6	8	1.9	0.2	NA	NA	NA	NA	6	42	2.6	0.7
Jones	2	D	D	D	NA	NA	NA	NA	14	78	4.3	1.2
Kingsbury	7	20	2.2	0.5	12	401	75.1	14.3	13	101	3.5	0.9
Lake	29	126	18.1	4.6	21	872	374.0	32.1	36	463	14.3	4.0
Lawrence	69	263	24.8	8.5	41	445	130.9	17.1	137	2 704	197.1	46.4
Lincoln	82	D	D	D	69	2 313	D	97.6	53	D	D	D
Lyman	1	D	D	D	NA	NA	NA	NA	14	173	9.7	2.5
McCook	10	D	D	D	4	8	D	0.2	18	D	D	D
McPherson	4	D	D	D	7	47	4.7	1.6	5	20	0.7	0.2
Marshall	11	21	2.1	0.6	8	355	174.7	16.3	13	115	3.7	1.0
Meade	50	D	D	D	35	225	D	8.3	74	671	43.6	10.9
Mellette	1	D	D	D	NA	NA	NA	NA	4	10	0.4	0.1
Miner	3	16	1.1	0.4	4	32	D	1.3	8	D	D	D
Minnehaha	480	4 148	476.7	201.5	176	10 763	3 612.6	479.0	444	10 517	493.8	147.2
Moody	9	16	1.1	0.4	11	326	88.5	14.1	15	D	D	D
Oglala Lakota	2	D	D	D	NA	NA	NA	NA	10	305	20.3	5.9
Pennington	303	1 928	223.8	76.8	117	2 115	524.3	85.9	352	6 418	351.8	98.3
Perkins	5	11	0.8	0.2	4	D	D	D	8	D	D	D
Potter	3	D	D	D	4	44	D	1.6	12	65	4.8	1.0
Roberts	15	31	3.7	1.0	11	272	D	7.3	18	171	4.6	1.0
Sanborn	7	20	1.9	0.4	NA	NA	NA	NA	6	25	1.2	0.2
Spink	8	36	4.8	1.4	7	72	D	3.3	13	126	4.8	1.2
Stanley	4	D	D	D	3	D	D	D	13	D	D	D
Sully	2	D	D	D	NA	NA	NA	NA	8	D	D	D
Todd	2	D	D	D	3	37	7.0	1.4	3	19	0.6	0.2

1. Establishment subject to federal tax.

Table B. States and Counties — **Health Care and Social Assistance, Other Services, Nonemployer Businesses, and Residential Construction**

STATE County	Health care and social assistance, 2012				Other services, 2012				Nonemployer businesses, 2014		Value of residential construction authorized by building permits, 2015	
	Number of establish-ments	Number of employees	Receipts (mil dol)	Annual payroll (mil dol)	Number of establish-ments	Number of employees	Receipts (mil dol)	Annual payroll (mil dol)	Number	Receipts (mil dol)	New Construction ($1,000)	Number of housing units
	159	160	161	162	163	164	165	166	167	168	169	170
SOUTH CAROLINA—Cont'd												
Sumter	188	5 504	471.1	184.1	130	996	77.4	27.8	6 153	209.8	27 545	217
Union	30	D	D	D	30	132	8.0	2.3	1 066	30.2	3 750	19
Williamsburg	55	797	55.3	22.5	35	D	D	D	1 744	45.4	7 780	60
York	445	8 980	897.0	307.6	283	2 070	188.3	61.7	15 888	625.0	675 625	2 749
SOUTH DAKOTA	2 298	63 494	6 211.7	2 558.4	1 805	8 371	939.5	214.1	63 384	2 992.0	740 741	4 482
Aurora	10	D	D	D	6	D	D	D	234	8.9	2 520	9
Beadle	50	1 409	87.8	40.4	51	175	16.5	4.2	1 052	47.3	8 420	26
Bennett	5	156	9.1	5.1	2	D	D	D	155	5.5	0	0
Bon Homme	21	367	22.0	9.1	14	D	D	D	477	19.6	2 801	14
Brookings	75	1 396	99.0	43.4	66	354	64.9	9.1	2 034	93.9	28 680	264
Brown	112	2 867	240.5	116.1	79	D	D	D	2 842	139.2	14 934	174
Brule	24	457	24.7	10.8	17	69	8.8	1.9	467	21.4	4 423	24
Buffalo	3	D	D	D	1	D	D	D	40	0.5	0	0
Butte	31	282	18.8	8.1	22	D	D	D	906	35.9	4 380	38
Campbell	4	25	0.8	0.5	2	D	D	D	130	5.6	170	1
Charles Mix	22	524	31.9	14.5	26	D	D	D	698	23.1	3 139	15
Clark	10	140	6.1	2.4	11	D	D	D	257	10.9	3 386	10
Clay	30	721	50.5	17.8	24	113	12.1	2.5	846	35.0	7 530	74
Codington	89	1 691	191.5	65.1	79	327	31.2	7.8	2 106	93.6	20 803	120
Corson	6	19	1.0	0.6	NA	NA	NA	NA	161	5.1	0	0
Custer	20	D	D	D	16	78	6.6	2.1	893	38.0	14 994	98
Davison	79	D	D	D	52	D	D	D	1 415	63.9	11 007	66
Day	19	291	18.1	6.3	14	D	D	D	480	21.1	5 293	33
Deuel	5	161	10.6	4.2	5	D	D	D	369	17.9	0	0
Dewey	9	149	18.7	7.2	6	D	D	D	237	9.7	488	5
Douglas	7	265	13.6	6.7	11	28	4.3	0.7	256	12.8	1 105	7
Edmunds	11	197	8.8	3.8	6	D	D	D	386	21.4	2 855	15
Fall River	22	D	D	D	16	67	4.5	1.1	576	21.4	1 076	7
Faulk	4	D	D	D	5	D	D	D	214	10.3	810	4
Grant	24	415	30.1	11.4	18	72	7.3	1.5	648	26.4	4 038	17
Gregory	15	317	18.1	7.4	12	D	D	D	513	19.5	1 660	7
Haakon	7	D	D	D	4	17	1.6	0.5	219	10.5	200	2
Hamlin	12	198	6.5	2.9	7	16	2.3	0.4	413	18.5	3 985	22
Hand	8	229	13.5	6.8	11	19	1.5	0.2	329	14.8	2 390	9
Hanson	2	D	D	D	1	D	D	D	312	11.3	1 778	11
Harding	4	D	D	D	1	D	D	D	175	7.5	721	5
Hughes	58	1 269	110.1	45.7	76	347	50.8	11.6	1 505	61.4	9 897	51
Hutchinson	17	651	40.2	18.8	14	D	D	D	574	20.1	2 037	7
Hyde	3	D	D	D	2	D	D	D	114	5.3	0	0
Jackson	1	D	D	D	5	10	0.8	0.1	191	6.0	0	0
Jerauld	4	131	9.6	3.8	7	16	1.4	0.3	155	6.8	830	3
Jones	2	D	D	D	2	D	D	D	112	5.1	370	9
Kingsbury	14	240	13.2	5.3	13	33	3.0	0.6	479	23.0	3 485	18
Lake	33	694	40.7	18.5	20	D	D	D	1 037	45.8	7 981	41
Lawrence	87	1 401	126.3	54.9	58	233	21.0	5.3	2 376	107.4	58 158	198
Lincoln	132	3 237	232.2	96.7	80	D	D	D	4 385	253.8	38 397	172
Lyman	2	D	D	D	3	D	D	D	248	10.3	275	2
McCook	17	251	13.5	5.2	13	D	D	D	456	22.5	3 300	14
McPherson	7	53	3.2	1.1	6	D	D	D	194	7.9	2 065	11
Marshall	13	175	10.7	4.0	7	27	3.7	0.8	360	20.5	5 255	20
Meade	45	D	D	D	50	151	20.8	4.1	2 181	95.8	25 272	146
Mellette	2	D	D	D	1	D	D	D	100	3.5	254	2
Miner	9	156	7.2	3.3	4	12	1.3	0.4	202	9.5	1 695	12
Minnehaha	462	20 372	2 348.8	970.6	375	2 326	256.5	67.7	13 004	684.0	255 858	1 726
Moody	15	203	13.9	6.0	6	D	D	D	430	20.5	5 439	17
Oglala Lakota	13	285	30.3	10.4	3	11	0.8	0.2	350	7.5	NA	NA
Pennington	343	D	D	D	268	1 572	193.3	39.2	7 940	368.8	88 493	554
Perkins	16	142	7.8	3.4	16	38	3.3	0.9	255	9.6	0	0
Potter	13	70	6.4	2.8	8	D	D	D	261	14.5	200	1
Roberts	23	532	32.7	14.8	16	42	3.2	0.8	596	21.6	6 159	28
Sanborn	4	D	D	D	4	D	D	D	191	6.4	905	5
Spink	17	359	18.3	8.3	12	D	D	D	499	25.5	4 422	23
Stanley	3	D	D	D	11	D	D	D	297	15.3	4 275	19
Sully	3	D	D	D	2	D	D	D	164	8.6	1 782	8
Todd	7	283	37.6	16.2	3	7	0.4	0.1	216	4.2	0	0

Table B. States and Counties — Government Employment and Payroll, and Local Government Finances

	Government employment and payroll, 2012									Local government finances, 2012				
			March payroll (percent of total)							General revenue				
													Taxes	
														Per capita[1] (dollars)
STATE County	Full-time equivalent employees	March payroll (dollars)	Adminis- tration, judicial, and legal	Police and Corrections	Fire Protection	Highways and transpor- tation	Health and Welfare	Natural resources and utilities	Education and libraries	Total (mil dol)	Inter- govern- mental (mil dol)	Total (mil dol)	Total	Property
	171	172	173	174	175	176	177	178	179	180	181	182	183	184
SOUTH CAROLINA— Cont'd														
Sumter	6 341	17 021 292	4.2	6.1	1.7	1.8	1.6	3.3	80.4	271.8	124.5	114.5	1 060	719
Union	1 425	4 994 326	5.2	7.0	0.2	1.0	39.3	5.0	41.2	156.7	60.9	39.0	1 380	1 287
Williamsburg	1 213	3 312 602	4.2	7.9	1.6	5.2	5.0	3.6	71.8	89.9	50.4	26.4	785	649
York	6 735	24 865 548	7.3	9.2	2.7	1.3	1.7	7.5	67.9	705.5	262.8	328.3	1 399	1 188
SOUTH DAKOTA	X	X	X	X	X	X	X	X	X	X	X	X	X	X
Aurora	140	322 496	9.8	3.3	0.0	8.6	1.1	1.5	66.8	11.3	4.4	5.5	2 022	1 782
Beadle	584	1 871 207	6.9	12.0	1.9	6.5	2.6	6.6	60.1	58.6	17.5	28.6	1 609	1 176
Bennett	147	346 133	7.8	7.3	0.0	5.0	1.7	2.9	72.7	11.6	7.6	3.2	943	754
Bon Homme	246	662 539	7.1	6.3	0.0	9.5	0.7	8.4	67.8	20.1	7.9	9.7	1 383	1 174
Brookings	1 332	4 813 095	7.8	6.0	0.3	3.2	25.9	9.5	35.5	157.9	19.7	49.9	1 530	1 086
Brown	1 246	3 689 884	7.8	11.6	5.1	6.3	2.4	10.7	55.2	123.6	32.4	67.9	1 819	1 288
Brule	271	673 549	6.8	6.7	0.0	5.9	4.3	5.0	71.0	23.2	8.9	9.4	1 779	1 325
Buffalo	8	22 528	50.6	21.1	0.0	22.9	5.5	0.0	0.0	0.8	0.4	0.4	192	185
Butte	371	1 001 042	7.3	7.8	0.0	4.9	3.0	11.2	62.8	30.3	11.5	12.6	1 233	945
Campbell	48	126 932	22.4	4.9	0.0	20.2	1.5	5.8	43.7	4.7	1.5	2.4	1 718	1 442
Charles Mix	442	1 244 510	5.7	6.5	0.0	4.7	3.0	7.5	71.5	43.1	25.6	13.6	1 477	1 206
Clark	179	456 728	7.7	2.5	0.0	10.5	1.0	1.7	74.5	13.4	3.7	8.2	2 276	2 032
Clay	330	1 043 813	10.4	13.3	0.4	5.7	5.0	14.2	48.1	31.3	7.5	16.6	1 174	904
Codington	1 090	3 894 294	3.6	7.6	3.8	3.8	1.7	14.6	62.8	104.2	32.6	43.8	1 587	1 028
Corson	271	904 657	3.0	2.6	0.0	2.6	0.1	2.2	88.7	21.6	17.7	2.5	623	555
Custer	232	684 633	12.9	6.8	0.0	6.7	2.7	5.5	65.3	24.6	3.9	16.5	1 973	1 606
Davison	843	2 644 986	5.7	9.5	3.2	6.0	2.9	7.3	64.6	80.5	25.5	35.2	1 779	1 145
Day	198	482 927	10.0	8.0	0.0	11.7	0.7	5.9	61.4	17.2	6.4	8.5	1 510	1 240
Deuel	127	393 062	16.5	8.2	0.0	17.0	0.4	1.9	51.5	10.7	2.3	7.0	1 607	1 351
Dewey	249	617 513	9.8	3.1	0.0	5.4	0.5	3.0	76.8	18.8	15.2	2.6	474	405
Douglas	103	390 547	16.4	4.6	0.0	12.5	2.5	2.3	56.5	11.6	4.6	5.2	1 737	1 444
Edmunds	292	715 008	7.1	3.1	0.0	7.8	38.4	2.4	38.6	22.4	5.8	9.6	2 374	2 086
Fall River	314	938 839	8.8	7.6	0.0	7.0	1.0	10.3	60.3	26.8	9.4	11.3	1 614	1 321
Faulk	160	527 286	5.6	4.5	0.5	2.3	56.7	2.0	27.9	16.8	4.1	5.1	2 160	1 927
Grant	245	716 131	9.0	6.4	0.0	8.2	1.2	3.8	68.1	23.2	5.9	13.7	1 887	1 505
Gregory	203	581 904	10.2	4.7	0.0	9.2	1.1	2.4	71.6	14.3	5.6	7.1	1 664	1 354
Haakon	81	213 827	13.1	5.5	0.0	16.5	0.4	2.6	58.3	6.5	2.3	3.6	1 879	1 523
Hamlin	251	731 928	6.3	2.3	0.0	5.0	20.2	5.1	60.7	25.7	8.6	10.9	1 835	1 641
Hand	128	359 355	11.0	4.7	0.0	11.4	0.2	8.6	63.0	11.0	2.9	6.5	1 921	1 624
Hanson	122	328 179	9.5	3.1	0.0	9.0	0.2	1.6	71.2	10.7	3.6	5.8	1 710	1 577
Harding	80	208 002	15.2	4.0	0.0	10.1	0.3	2.9	63.3	10.2	6.4	3.1	2 343	2 124
Hughes	626	1 983 352	7.7	12.8	0.3	6.2	2.7	9.5	57.1	62.6	25.1	25.5	1 463	989
Hutchinson	312	1 009 609	5.2	3.1	0.0	6.2	0.4	1.3	82.1	25.8	8.2	14.2	1 970	1 677
Hyde	72	227 594	10.2	2.5	0.0	8.4	0.0	1.6	77.3	7.5	1.8	4.3	2 988	2 608
Jackson	115	288 915	10.3	3.2	0.0	5.1	1.0	2.8	74.9	7.4	4.2	2.7	835	680
Jerauld	90	237 116	13.3	5.9	0.0	10.4	1.6	8.1	58.2	8.7	2.5	4.4	2 169	1 851
Jones	52	131 432	19.8	7.6	0.0	10.4	0.0	7.8	54.5	4.5	1.4	2.5	2 475	1 992
Kingsbury	244	603 141	5.3	3.1	0.0	8.6	0.5	3.3	72.9	19.8	5.2	12.1	2 312	2 048
Lake	462	1 563 214	5.5	6.2	2.0	5.6	2.5	13.5	62.4	39.3	10.2	19.2	1 628	1 310
Lawrence	692	2 469 903	12.9	15.3	0.3	6.8	1.3	10.2	51.2	81.2	20.9	45.9	1 883	1 338
Lincoln	1 033	2 768 370	9.1	4.4	0.0	3.8	0.9	2.0	77.7	90.9	26.1	51.6	1 069	947
Lyman	133	337 375	11.7	3.3	0.0	7.7	3.0	3.7	67.3	10.3	4.3	4.8	1 278	913
McCook	186	538 315	9.8	4.8	0.0	8.7	1.8	2.2	71.0	17.3	5.5	9.8	1 740	1 508
McPherson	123	336 878	14.7	3.6	0.0	5.4	0.4	2.0	72.6	9.5	2.9	5.6	2 295	1 958
Marshall	176	472 048	9.8	7.5	0.0	9.0	0.7	2.0	69.8	18.3	6.1	9.2	1 978	1 696
Meade	671	2 100 253	11.4	12.6	0.3	4.8	2.3	5.9	59.2	71.1	19.6	32.1	1 233	1 036
Mellette	114	303 196	8.5	5.7	0.0	4.1	0.4	0.8	78.5	7.4	5.3	1.6	750	650
Miner	106	326 794	11.4	7.0	0.0	13.4	1.2	6.7	59.0	10.3	3.2	6.3	2 717	2 393
Minnehaha	5 678	21 221 355	6.2	10.8	4.4	3.8	2.4	6.0	65.2	616.7	171.2	329.3	1 882	1 201
Moody	202	536 978	10.4	8.8	0.0	7.4	2.5	6.9	57.6	17.4	5.8	9.2	1 422	1 220
Oglala Lakota	423	1 199 764	0.8	0.3	0.0	0.8	0.1	0.1	98.0	32.0	30.4	0.8	60	34
Pennington	4 148	12 984 488	4.9	10.8	1.8	2.6	2.5	4.4	67.5	388.6	116.3	197.4	1 891	1 300
Perkins	118	328 373	10.9	5.6	0.1	9.6	2.5	6.3	62.1	12.4	5.3	5.7	1 878	1 506
Potter	120	307 306	11.7	3.9	0.0	9.7	0.1	2.7	67.9	9.5	3.0	5.6	2 367	2 004
Roberts	404	1 039 666	5.9	3.7	0.0	5.7	2.4	2.0	77.9	33.8	13.8	12.6	1 220	986
Sanborn	116	293 325	10.3	3.6	0.0	17.9	1.1	1.1	64.9	9.9	3.4	5.4	2 323	2 120
Spink	406	1 160 424	5.6	3.5	0.0	5.0	32.9	2.4	50.2	35.9	9.8	13.7	2 078	1 808
Stanley	129	372 565	10.6	5.4	0.0	9.7	1.2	9.7	61.3	12.9	5.5	6.2	2 082	1 623
Sully	83	220 042	14.4	4.9	0.0	19.2	0.0	3.4	56.8	8.2	1.3	6.2	4 370	3 985
Todd	452	1 136 660	0.9	0.9	0.0	1.9	0.0	0.5	95.5	33.5	29.5	2.7	275	165

1. Based on the resident population estimated as of July 1 of the year shown.

Table B. States and Counties — Local Government Finances, Government Employment, and Voting

STATE County	Local government finances, 2012 (cont.)									Government employment, 2014			Presidential election,[2] 2012		
	Direct general expenditure							Debt outstanding					Percent of vote cast:		
			Percent of total for:												
	Total (mil dol)	Per capita[1] (dollars)	Education	Health and hospitals	Police protection	Public welfare	Highways	Total (mil dol)	Per capita[1] (dollars)	Federal civilian	Federal military	State and local	Democratic	Republican	All other
	185	186	187	188	189	190	191	192	193	194	195	196	197	198	199
SOUTH CAROLINA—Cont'd															
Sumter	256.2	2 371	55.2	1.2	7.1	0.3	2.5	245.3	2 270	1 286	5 791	5 446	57.3	41.9	0.8
Union	153.8	5 444	47.1	30.4	4.0	0.0	1.3	64.7	2 291	69	113	1 929	43.8	55.0	1.2
Williamsburg	98.8	2 939	50.1	2.9	6.6	0.2	2.4	85.8	2 551	365	129	1 969	68.6	30.4	1.0
York	690.0	2 941	56.4	0.2	5.6	0.3	5.3	1 179.4	5 026	403	995	11 851	40.5	58.2	1.4
SOUTH DAKOTA	X	X	X	X	X	X	X	X	X	11 107	8 210	65 160	44.7	53.2	2.1
Aurora	10.8	3 945	58.5	0.4	3.0	0.2	16.5	1.6	575	19	16	197	43.8	53.1	3.1
Beadle	52.6	2 962	43.9	0.4	4.7	0.5	16.7	29.0	1 634	291	106	1 001	45.3	52.6	2.2
Bennett	9.4	2 748	64.2	0.1	4.4	0.1	6.8	1.2	356	26	21	349	46.1	50.8	3.1
Bon Homme	17.7	2 516	62.3	1.6	3.0	0.2	15.6	31.0	4 403	29	33	591	43.1	53.9	3.0
Brookings	154.9	4 746	25.5	21.6	2.6	0.2	6.1	90.0	2 758	151	185	5 916	51.7	46.1	2.2
Brown	117.1	3 136	36.3	1.3	5.8	0.9	19.9	125.1	3 352	474	225	2 687	51.9	46.3	1.8
Brule	20.0	3 782	59.2	3.2	3.6	0.4	11.2	7.8	1 479	35	31	355	39.6	57.7	2.7
Buffalo	0.8	373	0.0	0.1	9.4	0.1	48.9	0.0	0	142	13	319	73.3	25.2	1.5
Butte	26.8	2 623	51.6	0.6	5.1	0.1	7.2	14.4	1 409	52	62	599	30.7	66.3	3.0
Campbell	4.2	2 981	36.0	0.6	4.6	0.0	22.5	0.4	298	0	0	74	28.5	69.2	2.3
Charles Mix	36.8	3 989	58.4	1.9	2.5	0.1	9.6	8.3	898	180	53	1 099	45.4	53.0	1.6
Clark	12.5	3 493	42.0	1.9	2.9	0.4	29.1	4.5	1 242	28	19	231	42.8	54.9	2.3
Clay	28.7	2 034	37.0	1.5	8.1	0.3	17.6	30.7	2 172	33	73	3 423	61.0	36.8	2.2
Codington	112.1	4 060	54.8	0.3	6.8	0.1	7.1	80.3	2 910	189	167	1 971	45.9	52.3	1.8
Corson	23.4	5 738	86.2	0.1	2.0	0.0	5.0	0.0	0	66	25	566	59.5	38.1	2.4
Custer	27.8	3 331	34.7	5.4	4.4	0.4	11.1	31.7	3 801	183	50	520	32.7	64.5	2.7
Davison	79.9	4 042	50.0	4.3	4.8	0.5	9.4	39.7	2 006	117	116	1 279	42.0	56.0	2.0
Day	17.9	3 188	37.1	0.7	3.2	0.3	29.6	10.3	1 840	60	33	372	55.7	42.8	1.5
Deuel	11.0	2 511	38.7	3.1	3.5	0.4	20.6	3.8	861	24	26	239	47.5	49.1	3.4
Dewey	20.6	3 719	81.8	0.2	1.5	0.0	11.1	1.0	189	362	34	1 203	65.8	32.6	1.6
Douglas	13.1	4 408	29.4	0.6	2.1	0.1	14.6	4.2	1 429	24	17	162	24.1	73.6	2.2
Edmunds	19.8	4 926	31.7	14.2	1.7	12.6	18.5	5.7	1 415	20	22	323	39.5	58.4	2.1
Fall River	27.6	3 962	45.4	2.5	5.3	0.5	9.0	13.8	1 973	473	40	575	35.1	61.6	3.2
Faulk	15.6	6 550	19.0	49.2	1.5	0.1	14.5	9.5	4 005	18	11	124	35.7	62.0	2.3
Grant	24.5	3 375	44.5	0.6	3.4	0.2	18.1	33.2	4 576	31	43	348	46.6	50.9	2.4
Gregory	13.6	3 189	55.3	0.9	3.5	0.2	17.9	4.1	966	32	25	257	34.3	63.3	2.4
Haakon	5.9	3 054	42.6	5.8	5.5	0.1	21.5	1.1	586	19	11	100	16.2	81.4	2.3
Hamlin	22.8	3 851	49.4	1.4	2.0	13.5	15.0	12.1	2 042	24	35	466	37.4	59.6	3.0
Hand	10.6	3 130	41.2	0.5	4.5	0.1	26.1	19.0	5 596	17	20	202	35.7	62.0	2.3
Hanson	11.6	3 434	65.3	0.5	1.6	0.3	16.2	6.0	1 773	0	18	188	39.5	58.7	1.8
Harding	10.1	7 661	50.7	0.5	2.4	0.4	25.4	8.7	6 600	24	0	100	18.4	78.3	3.3
Hughes	62.3	3 568	31.3	0.8	5.8	0.2	8.1	67.4	3 862	281	102	3 696	35.9	62.6	1.6
Hutchinson	27.0	3 751	58.0	0.4	2.3	0.4	18.5	16.9	2 349	43	39	418	34.4	63.3	2.2
Hyde	6.9	4 834	48.1	0.3	2.2	0.2	22.1	3.4	2 354	0	0	180	28.8	69.7	1.5
Jackson	6.7	2 101	64.9	0.5	3.6	0.1	11.3	0.1	43	109	20	213	38.4	59.0	2.6
Jerauld	8.5	4 170	41.2	4.0	3.2	0.4	21.3	7.5	3 682	10	11	121	49.0	49.4	1.5
Jones	4.6	4 509	46.3	0.5	2.9	0.0	21.7	0.2	192	0	0	131	23.4	73.8	2.7
Kingsbury	18.6	3 559	52.1	0.8	2.8	0.4	20.1	7.7	1 482	38	30	270	45.9	51.5	2.6
Lake	36.5	3 105	51.8	0.5	4.3	0.3	14.7	90.9	7 721	60	70	1 144	49.3	48.6	2.1
Lawrence	77.3	3 170	35.3	0.4	7.0	0.2	6.3	116.0	4 753	158	143	1 893	40.9	56.3	2.8
Lincoln	90.3	1 871	58.4	0.4	3.1	0.3	11.9	267.9	5 547	50	311	1 447	41.6	56.8	1.6
Lyman	9.2	2 439	55.2	0.9	3.3	0.2	15.6	1.7	440	79	23	640	43.3	54.5	2.3
McCook	15.8	2 821	51.5	2.0	4.3	1.1	18.5	9.6	1 716	27	32	263	41.4	55.9	2.7
McPherson	9.4	3 852	48.9	0.7	3.2	0.2	24.6	1.4	581	10	13	146	32.1	66.5	1.4
Marshall	17.1	3 652	35.5	1.2	4.5	1.6	22.5	18.4	3 939	23	26	337	57.6	41.1	1.4
Meade	75.4	2 895	52.2	1.6	5.1	0.0	8.9	43.4	1 666	1 418	161	1 399	32.3	64.8	2.9
Mellette	6.7	3 182	72.5	0.9	4.5	0.0	7.6	0.1	43	14	12	234	44.2	52.8	3.0
Miner	10.4	4 490	36.7	2.2	3.5	0.3	27.2	3.8	1 655	18	14	154	49.7	47.4	3.0
Minnehaha	640.2	3 657	45.9	1.7	5.7	0.6	9.2	652.2	3 726	2 489	1 128	8 396	49.5	48.7	1.8
Moody	17.2	2 661	47.1	1.8	6.6	1.5	18.2	8.8	1 373	110	38	657	51.1	46.3	2.6
Oglala Lakota	33.5	2 386	97.4	0.1	0.3	0.0	1.0	0.0	1	632	86	2 423	88.7	9.9	1.4
Pennington	412.8	3 956	45.6	1.3	6.0	0.5	8.9	401.2	3 844	1 446	3 815	6 239	38.5	59.6	1.9
Perkins	12.2	4 029	44.2	1.4	4.2	1.5	18.1	0.6	203	27	18	230	29.6	65.4	5.0
Potter	9.5	4 047	43.5	2.0	3.4	0.0	20.1	1.6	667	16	14	161	33.5	65.1	1.5
Roberts	30.3	2 938	57.6	0.5	2.8	0.1	10.2	9.6	930	189	61	1 338	58.9	39.3	1.8
Sanborn	8.5	3 645	45.3	1.1	3.6	0.1	31.4	2.8	1 215	16	13	153	41.4	55.4	3.1
Spink	34.6	5 228	34.4	27.8	3.5	0.4	14.0	21.8	3 298	42	38	971	47.4	50.8	1.8
Stanley	13.1	4 413	38.6	0.8	6.2	0.1	30.5	9.4	3 157	10	18	191	32.8	65.5	1.7
Sully	7.0	4 938	44.2	0.2	5.0	0.4	25.5	3.3	2 332	11	0	115	28.0	69.7	2.3
Todd	28.4	2 854	92.0	0.1	0.7	0.0	2.9	1.4	137	265	60	2 007	78.1	20.2	1.7

1. Based on the resident population estimated as of July 1 of the year shown.   2. © 2013 Election Data Services, Inc. All rights reserved.

Table B. States and Counties — **Land Area and Population**

STATE/ County code	CBSA code[1]	County type[2]	STATE County	Land area[3] (sq km) 2010	Total persons 2015	Rank	Per square kilometer	White	Black	American Indian, Alaska Native	Asian and Pacific Islander	Percent Hispanic or Latino[4]	Under 5 years	5 to 17 years	18 to 24 years	25 to 34 years	35 to 44 years	45 to 54 years
				1	2	3	4	5	6	7	8	9	10	11	12	13	14	15
			SOUTH DAKOTA—Cont'd															
46 123	...	7	Tripp	4 176	5 434	2 808	1.3	84.2	0.6	15.2	0.9	1.7	6.2	16.3	8.4	9.4	9.8	13.9
46 125	43620	3	Turner	1 598	8 209	2 584	5.1	96.5	0.8	1.3	0.5	2.2	6.0	17.3	6.4	10.2	11.0	13.9
46 127	43580	3	Union	1 193	14 909	2 106	12.5	94.0	1.3	1.4	1.5	3.2	6.1	19.3	7.6	11.0	12.1	14.0
46 129	...	7	Walworth	1 835	5 443	2 807	3.0	84.2	1.0	15.8	0.5	1.8	6.0	16.6	6.5	10.6	9.1	12.5
46 135	49460	7	Yankton	1 350	22 702	1 700	16.8	91.4	2.2	3.6	1.0	3.3	5.8	15.3	8.9	12.7	11.6	14.1
46 137	...	9	Ziebach	5 080	2 803	2 987	0.6	27.5	0.8	70.9	1.0	3.7	6.3	29.5	11.9	12.1	11.7	13.0
47 000	...	X	**TENNESSEE**	106 798	6 600 299	X	61.8	76.1	17.6	0.8	2.1	5.0	6.1	16.7	9.6	13.1	12.8	13.7
47 001	28940	2	Anderson	873	75 749	726	86.8	91.8	5.1	1.0	1.7	2.5	5.3	15.8	7.9	11.2	12.1	14.2
47 003	43180	6	Bedford	1 227	47 183	1 031	38.5	79.5	8.8	0.7	1.4	11.8	6.7	19.5	9.0	12.1	13.1	13.3
47 005	...	7	Benton	1 021	16 129	2 033	15.8	94.4	3.1	1.2	0.8	2.2	5.1	14.6	7.2	9.7	11.4	14.5
47 007	...	8	Bledsoe	1 053	14 502	2 133	13.8	87.5	6.2	0.9	0.4	2.1	3.9	13.4	7.8	12.1	14.4	16.1
47 009	28940	2	Blount	1 447	127 253	491	87.9	93.0	3.5	0.9	1.2	3.0	5.1	16.0	8.3	11.0	12.4	14.7
47 011	17420	3	Bradley	851	104 091	574	122.3	88.5	5.3	0.8	1.4	5.4	5.6	16.8	10.2	12.4	12.9	13.9
47 013	28940	6	Campbell	1 244	39 752	1 179	32.0	97.7	0.7	1.0	0.5	1.2	5.2	15.8	8.0	10.6	12.9	14.3
47 015	34980	1	Cannon	688	13 840	2 179	20.1	96.2	2.3	0.9	0.6	1.8	5.4	15.8	8.0	11.4	12.3	15.1
47 017	...	6	Carroll	1 552	27 910	1 491	18.0	87.2	11.3	0.9	0.5	2.4	6.0	15.6	10.0	10.2	11.4	13.8
47 019	27740	3	Carter	884	56 486	902	63.9	97.1	2.0	0.7	0.6	1.7	4.9	14.1	8.6	11.7	12.1	14.4
47 021	34980	1	Cheatham	783	39 741	1 180	50.8	94.6	2.3	0.9	0.9	2.8	5.6	18.0	8.1	11.6	13.5	16.2
47 023	27180	3	Chester	740	17 471	1 949	23.6	87.2	10.4	0.9	0.7	2.5	4.9	17.0	14.4	10.9	11.8	12.4
47 025	...	6	Claiborne	1 126	31 709	1 389	28.2	96.7	1.5	0.9	0.8	1.1	4.7	14.9	9.5	11.6	12.4	13.8
47 027	...	8	Clay	613	7 771	2 611	12.7	96.4	2.2	0.7	0.4	2.0	5.4	15.1	7.0	9.0	11.3	14.7
47 029	35460	6	Cocke	1 126	35 162	1 296	31.2	95.3	2.7	1.0	0.6	2.2	5.2	15.6	7.7	10.1	12.3	14.7
47 031	46100	4	Coffee	1 111	54 277	925	48.9	90.9	4.7	0.8	1.3	4.0	6.0	17.9	8.4	11.8	12.1	14.0
47 033	27180	8	Crockett	688	14 601	2 130	21.2	76.7	14.1	0.5	0.6	9.7	5.8	18.6	8.0	11.9	11.7	13.8
47 035	18900	7	Cumberland	1 764	58 229	883	33.0	95.9	0.9	0.9	0.7	2.7	5.0	13.3	6.8	9.2	9.9	12.4
47 037	34980	1	Davidson	1 305	678 889	95	520.2	58.7	28.6	0.8	4.1	9.9	7.0	14.6	10.4	19.1	13.8	12.6
47 039	...	9	Decatur	865	11 660	2 315	13.5	92.7	3.4	0.7	0.9	2.9	4.9	15.1	7.3	10.2	11.3	13.5
47 041	...	6	DeKalb	788	19 182	1 865	24.3	90.7	2.0	0.8	0.5	7.5	5.8	16.7	7.8	11.8	12.1	14.2
47 043	34980	1	Dickson	1 269	51 487	969	40.6	91.6	5.2	0.9	0.8	3.1	5.9	17.5	8.1	12.2	13.0	14.8
47 045	20540	5	Dyer	1 327	37 893	1 227	28.6	81.8	15.3	0.7	0.8	3.1	6.5	17.5	8.7	11.5	12.4	14.0
47 047	32820	1	Fayette	1 825	39 165	1 198	21.5	69.2	27.7	0.6	0.8	2.5	5.4	15.5	7.0	10.7	12.0	14.6
47 049	...	9	Fentress	1 291	17 917	1 922	13.9	97.7	0.6	0.8	0.4	1.3	5.0	16.9	7.5	9.8	11.8	14.2
47 051	46100	6	Franklin	1 436	41 449	1 140	28.9	90.8	5.8	1.2	1.2	2.8	4.9	16.1	11.1	9.9	11.7	13.2
47 053	...	4	Gibson	1 561	49 399	993	31.6	78.4	19.2	0.6	0.5	2.5	6.4	17.9	8.1	11.6	12.5	13.4
47 055	...	6	Giles	1 582	28 846	1 455	18.3	86.8	11.4	1.0	0.8	2.1	5.3	15.7	8.6	10.8	11.6	14.6
47 057	28940	3	Grainger	727	22 846	1 689	31.4	96.5	1.1	0.7	0.3	2.7	4.9	16.2	7.7	10.1	12.9	15.3
47 059	24620	6	Greene	1 611	68 580	778	42.6	94.1	2.7	0.7	0.7	2.8	4.7	15.4	8.4	10.3	12.4	14.4
47 061	...	8	Grundy	934	13 441	2 205	14.4	97.4	0.9	1.3	0.4	1.1	5.2	16.4	7.9	10.7	12.3	13.3
47 063	34100	3	Hamblen	417	63 402	832	152.0	83.9	4.9	0.7	1.3	10.9	6.2	17.2	8.1	11.4	13.0	14.1
47 065	16860	2	Hamilton	1 405	354 098	194	252.0	73.0	20.3	0.8	2.6	5.1	5.9	15.3	9.7	13.6	12.6	13.4
47 067	...	8	Hancock	576	6 572	2 711	11.4	99.0	0.9	1.0	0.5	0.4	5.6	15.6	7.6	11.1	12.1	13.6
47 069	...	6	Hardeman	1 730	25 707	1 571	14.9	56.0	42.0	0.6	0.9	1.6	4.9	15.1	9.1	14.2	12.9	14.4
47 071	...	6	Hardin	1 495	25 756	1 570	17.2	93.5	4.4	0.9	0.7	2.0	5.2	15.6	7.9	9.9	11.7	14.8
47 073	28700	3	Hawkins	1 261	56 471	904	44.8	96.7	1.9	0.8	0.6	1.4	5.1	16.0	7.6	10.4	12.5	14.8
47 075	...	6	Haywood	1 381	18 023	1 917	13.1	46.1	49.9	0.4	0.3	4.2	5.8	17.9	8.7	11.3	11.4	13.8
47 077	...	6	Henderson	1 347	28 015	1 485	20.8	89.1	9.2	0.6	0.5	2.3	5.9	17.5	8.0	11.9	12.6	14.3
47 079	37540	7	Henry	1 456	32 147	1 380	22.1	88.8	8.9	0.8	0.6	2.3	5.0	16.0	7.2	10.4	11.4	13.7
47 081	34980	1	Hickman	1 586	24 363	1 630	15.4	92.1	5.6	1.1	0.4	2.1	5.5	16.4	8.3	12.6	13.0	15.1
47 083	...	8	Houston	519	8 149	2 590	15.7	93.8	4.1	1.0	0.8	2.3	5.0	16.8	8.2	10.7	12.0	13.5
47 085	...	6	Humphreys	1 375	18 135	1 910	13.2	94.5	3.4	0.9	0.6	2.0	5.9	16.2	8.0	10.4	12.3	13.9
47 087	18260	8	Jackson	799	11 509	2 325	14.4	97.7	0.9	1.1	0.3	2.0	4.9	14.2	7.7	9.7	11.8	14.4
47 089	34100	3	Jefferson	710	53 240	936	75.0	93.4	2.8	0.8	0.7	3.5	5.2	15.6	9.5	10.7	11.8	14.6
47 091	...	6	Johnson	773	17 830	1 928	23.1	95.1	2.7	0.7	0.5	1.8	4.3	13.2	7.7	12.0	13.3	15.0
47 093	28940	2	Knox	1 316	451 324	152	343.0	84.8	9.8	0.8	2.7	3.9	5.8	15.6	12.3	13.3	12.6	13.4
47 095	...	9	Lake	429	7 576	2 630	17.7	69.1	28.9	0.9	0.4	2.0	4.5	11.1	10.8	17.5	15.2	13.8
47 097	...	6	Lauderdale	1 222	26 936	1 537	22.0	61.9	35.6	0.9	0.8	2.3	5.6	17.6	9.4	14.4	13.2	14.0
47 099	29980	6	Lawrence	1 598	42 564	1 118	26.6	95.4	2.4	1.0	0.7	1.9	6.8	18.2	8.1	11.3	11.8	13.6
47 101	...	6	Lewis	731	11 854	2 305	16.2	94.8	2.8	1.0	0.8	2.2	5.8	16.3	7.6	10.4	12.4	13.3
47 103	...	6	Lincoln	1 477	33 743	1 334	22.8	88.9	7.8	1.3	0.7	3.1	5.6	16.8	7.8	10.9	11.6	14.5
47 105	28940	2	Loudon	594	51 130	973	86.1	89.6	1.9	0.7	1.0	7.9	5.3	14.6	6.9	9.8	11.0	12.9
47 107	11940	4	McMinn	1 114	52 639	949	47.3	91.5	4.7	1.2	1.0	3.3	5.6	16.1	8.6	10.7	12.1	14.2
47 109	...	6	McNairy	1 458	26 066	1 559	17.9	91.9	6.7	0.8	0.4	2.0	5.9	16.8	7.9	10.5	12.2	13.6
47 111	34980	1	Macon	795	23 177	1 674	29.2	93.3	0.9	0.8	0.8	4.9	7.0	17.6	8.7	11.9	12.5	14.3
47 113	27180	3	Madison	1 443	97 610	605	67.6	58.1	37.9	0.5	1.4	3.6	6.6	16.4	11.2	12.4	11.9	13.4
47 115	16860	2	Marion	1 290	28 487	1 473	22.1	93.4	4.6	1.0	0.7	1.7	5.1	16.1	8.0	11.1	12.2	14.3

1. CBSA = Core Based Statistical Area. See Appendix A for explanation. See Appendix B for list of metropolitan areas with component counties.   2. County type code from the Economic Research Service of USDA Rural-Urban Continuum Codes. See Appendix A for definition.   3. Dry land or land partially or temporarily covered by water.   4. May be of any race.

Table B. States and Counties — Population and Households

STATE County	Age (percent) (cont.) 55 to 64 years	65 to 74 years	75 years and over	Percent female	Total persons 2000	2010	Percent change 2000–2010	2010–2015	Components of change 2010–2015 Births	Deaths	Net migration	Households, 2010–2014 Number	Persons per household	Family households	Female family householder[1]	One person
	16	17	18	19	20	21	22	23	24	25	26	27	28	29	30	31
SOUTH DAKOTA—Cont'd																
Tripp	14.5	10.1	11.5	50.5	6 430	5 644	-12.2	-3.7	347	345	-211	2 595	2.09	60.7	8.3	34.8
Turner	14.8	10.2	10.3	49.6	8 849	8 347	-5.7	-1.7	461	527	-89	3 494	2.34	68.4	6.1	27.4
Union	14.4	8.8	6.7	49.4	12 584	14 399	14.4	3.5	855	593	259	5 861	2.50	66.9	4.9	29.5
Walworth	14.4	11.4	12.9	51.1	5 974	5 438	-9.0	0.1	369	410	42	2 376	2.24	59.7	8.0	36.5
Yankton	14.1	9.0	8.5	48.1	21 652	22 438	3.6	1.2	1 375	1 104	33	8 840	2.33	63.1	8.0	30.8
Ziebach	8.8	3.8	2.9	49.0	2 519	2 801	11.2	0.1	203	65	-135	792	3.58	77.0	29.4	19.8
TENNESSEE	12.9	9.0	6.1	51.3	5 689 283	6 346 275	11.5	4.0	420 465	324 079	154 490	2 487 349	2.53	66.7	13.5	28.1
Anderson	14.7	10.4	8.5	51.5	71 330	75 126	5.3	0.8	4 190	4 763	1 248	30 393	2.44	65.3	12.6	30.4
Bedford	11.9	8.9	5.5	50.9	37 586	45 058	19.9	4.7	3 250	2 326	1 138	16 608	2.72	73.7	12.1	21.4
Benton	15.1	13.7	8.7	50.5	16 537	16 489	-0.3	-2.2	831	1 252	80	6 837	2.36	66.2	10.4	29.4
Bledsoe	14.0	11.3	6.9	42.7	12 367	12 869	4.1	12.7	623	659	1 534	4 480	2.68	71.4	10.5	23.7
Blount	14.0	11.0	7.5	51.5	105 823	123 016	16.2	3.4	6 742	6 722	3 919	48 674	2.52	69.5	10.5	26.4
Bradley	12.3	9.4	6.4	51.3	87 965	98 963	12.5	5.2	6 240	5 008	3 741	37 823	2.59	68.9	12.5	26.2
Campbell	13.9	11.6	7.7	51.3	39 854	40 716	2.2	-2.4	2 188	2 771	-336	15 902	2.51	67.5	13.1	29.0
Cannon	13.9	10.3	7.8	50.2	12 826	13 801	7.6	0.3	734	855	163	5 405	2.52	69.2	12.3	26.6
Carroll	13.2	11.3	8.4	51.4	29 475	28 505	-3.3	-2.1	1 641	2 088	-157	11 096	2.48	66.3	11.3	30.9
Carter	14.4	11.6	8.1	51.0	56 742	57 424	1.2	-1.6	2 774	3 453	-310	24 090	2.31	67.8	11.9	28.6
Cheatham	13.8	8.5	4.7	50.2	35 912	39 108	8.9	1.6	2 291	1 858	181	14 520	2.68	73.6	11.3	21.0
Chester	11.9	9.4	7.3	52.1	15 540	17 131	10.2	2.0	1 018	898	167	5 943	2.70	71.2	13.8	26.5
Claiborne	14.6	11.4	7.1	51.1	29 862	32 213	7.9	-1.6	1 651	2 209	41	12 696	2.41	67.5	12.5	29.1
Clay	13.9	14.0	9.7	51.1	7 976	7 860	-1.5	-1.1	414	569	25	3 174	2.43	69.9	9.1	28.4
Cocke	15.2	11.9	7.3	51.6	33 565	35 662	6.2	-1.4	2 025	2 477	-19	14 788	2.37	67.8	14.9	28.2
Coffee	12.9	9.7	7.2	51.2	48 014	52 795	10.0	2.8	3 410	3 354	1 415	21 131	2.48	69.1	13.5	27.4
Crockett	12.6	9.8	7.6	52.1	14 532	14 584	0.4	0.1	926	881	-10	5 572	2.58	68.0	11.8	28.1
Cumberland	14.5	17.0	11.9	51.3	46 802	56 050	19.8	3.9	2 916	3 992	3 073	23 923	2.36	68.0	8.4	28.0
Davidson	11.5	6.4	4.7	51.8	569 891	626 662	10.0	8.3	51 742	26 614	27 578	259 557	2.41	55.7	14.6	35.4
Decatur	15.0	13.0	9.7	50.9	11 731	11 750	0.2	-0.8	628	899	182	5 045	2.27	68.3	12.2	28.4
DeKalb	14.0	10.7	6.8	50.4	17 423	18 721	7.4	2.5	1 186	1 253	521	6 998	2.66	69.7	11.8	26.3
Dickson	13.4	8.9	6.1	50.8	43 156	49 654	15.1	3.7	3 184	2 587	1 151	18 469	2.68	72.6	13.4	24.3
Dyer	12.8	9.9	6.7	51.7	37 279	38 337	2.8	-1.2	2 498	2 231	-753	15 088	2.49	70.8	14.7	24.9
Fayette	16.1	11.6	7.1	50.5	28 806	38 413	33.4	2.0	2 221	1 889	286	14 681	2.60	74.5	11.4	22.1
Fentress	14.8	12.7	7.3	51.0	16 625	17 959	8.0	-0.2	992	1 218	164	7 326	2.42	67.7	11.8	27.7
Franklin	14.1	11.1	7.9	51.2	39 270	41 052	4.5	1.0	2 066	2 500	847	16 126	2.42	70.3	11.5	23.9
Gibson	12.6	9.5	8.0	52.3	48 152	49 683	3.2	-0.6	3 224	3 437	-76	19 255	2.52	67.6	14.8	29.1
Giles	14.5	11.2	7.7	51.4	29 447	29 485	0.1	-1.8	1 570	1 797	-308	11 327	2.50	69.5	13.9	25.8
Grainger	14.4	11.9	6.6	49.8	20 659	22 652	9.6	0.9	1 180	1 375	381	8 888	2.54	71.2	8.7	24.9
Greene	14.4	12.0	8.0	50.9	62 909	68 831	9.4	-0.4	3 280	4 383	799	28 489	2.34	67.9	12.0	28.0
Grundy	13.5	12.7	8.0	50.5	14 332	13 708	-4.4	-1.9	824	1 027	-109	5 331	2.51	68.1	14.1	28.1
Hamblen	12.4	10.4	7.3	51.3	58 128	62 541	7.6	1.4	4 066	3 785	595	24 401	2.54	68.8	13.0	26.8
Hamilton	13.5	9.1	6.9	51.8	307 896	336 465	9.3	5.2	21 746	17 519	13 441	135 974	2.46	65.1	13.6	29.4
Hancock	15.9	11.0	7.5	50.5	6 786	6 819	0.5	-3.6	349	518	-61	2 819	2.32	64.1	13.3	32.9
Hardeman	13.1	9.8	6.5	45.6	28 105	27 253	-3.0	-5.7	1 430	1 447	-1 499	8 712	2.64	68.1	18.7	28.8
Hardin	14.9	12.2	8.8	51.6	25 578	26 025	1.7	-1.0	1 444	1 846	150	9 889	2.58	67.0	11.5	28.9
Hawkins	14.4	11.9	7.4	50.9	53 563	56 836	6.1	-0.6	2 828	3 502	237	23 414	2.40	70.0	11.6	26.5
Haywood	14.9	9.3	6.8	53.5	19 797	18 787	-5.1	-4.1	1 188	972	-1 019	6 995	2.60	61.8	18.4	34.1
Henderson	13.0	10.3	6.5	51.5	25 522	27 793	8.9	0.8	1 704	1 574	114	10 916	2.54	69.5	11.0	27.5
Henry	14.8	12.8	8.8	51.5	31 115	32 330	3.9	-0.6	1 764	2 326	363	13 317	2.38	67.4	10.5	29.2
Hickman	13.6	9.4	6.2	47.5	22 295	24 699	10.8	-1.4	1 434	1 376	-402	8 812	2.59	71.0	10.4	25.9
Houston	14.2	11.5	8.0	51.2	8 088	8 426	4.2	-3.3	430	514	-176	3 311	2.46	67.0	7.4	28.1
Humphreys	14.4	11.2	7.8	50.4	17 929	18 538	3.4	-2.2	1 066	1 221	-234	7 360	2.46	67.4	10.4	28.5
Jackson	16.4	13.2	7.6	49.9	10 984	11 614	5.7	-0.9	503	750	151	4 552	2.50	71.7	14.5	25.5
Jefferson	13.6	11.7	7.3	50.9	44 294	51 570	16.4	3.2	2 749	2 939	1 742	19 979	2.53	71.1	11.0	24.6
Johnson	14.1	12.7	7.8	46.5	17 499	18 244	4.3	-2.3	806	1 075	-177	7 110	2.28	67.4	9.0	29.5
Knox	12.4	8.4	6.1	51.4	382 032	432 234	13.1	4.4	27 194	21 517	13 088	180 558	2.37	60.3	10.2	33.2
Lake	12.4	8.3	6.4	36.1	7 954	7 832	-1.5	-3.3	345	483	-108	2 150	2.38	66.5	22.3	29.9
Lauderdale	12.2	8.4	5.4	47.7	27 101	27 815	2.6	-3.2	1 558	1 446	-976	9 833	2.52	68.3	19.6	28.0
Lawrence	12.7	10.1	7.4	51.0	39 926	41 869	4.9	1.7	2 960	2 631	416	15 932	2.61	71.2	11.4	26.0
Lewis	15.4	11.2	7.5	51.1	11 367	12 161	7.0	-2.5	669	705	-281	4 768	2.47	69.0	9.3	26.2
Lincoln	14.4	10.5	7.9	51.1	31 340	33 361	6.4	1.1	1 844	2 075	638	13 702	2.41	67.6	11.8	28.5
Loudon	15.0	15.0	9.5	51.1	39 086	48 559	24.2	5.3	2 801	3 101	2 724	19 912	2.48	74.7	9.2	22.1
McMinn	13.9	11.0	7.7	51.3	49 015	52 266	6.6	0.7	2 968	3 379	790	20 187	2.54	68.7	10.0	28.2
McNairy	13.7	11.6	7.8	50.9	24 653	26 076	5.8	0.0	1 483	1 778	259	9 796	2.63	67.5	10.7	30.0
Macon	12.5	9.5	6.0	51.3	20 386	22 242	9.1	4.2	1 667	1 402	657	8 640	2.58	71.1	13.4	22.7
Madison	13.2	8.6	6.3	52.8	91 837	98 294	7.0	-0.7	6 581	4 818	-2 409	36 253	2.60	66.7	16.7	28.9
Marion	14.9	11.2	6.9	50.9	27 776	28 232	1.6	0.9	1 603	1 821	478	11 282	2.48	71.4	13.9	25.0

1. No spouse present.

Table B. States and Counties — **Population, Vital Statistics, Medicare, and Crime**

STATE County	Persons in group quarters, 2015	Daytime population, 2010–2014 Number	Employment/ residence ratio	Births, 2015 Total	Rate[1]	Deaths, 2015 Number	Rate[1]	Persons under 65 with no health insurance, 2014 Number	Percent	Medicare, 2015 Total Beneficiaries	Enrolled in Original Medicare	Enrolled in Medicare Advantage	Serious crimes known to police,[2] 2014 Total Number	Rate[3]
	32	33	34	35	36	37	38	39	40	41	42	43	44	45
SOUTH DAKOTA—Cont'd														
Tripp	131	5 400	0.95	70	12.8	64	11.7	746	17.7	1 235	1 121	114	37	677
Turner	152	6 679	0.61	84	10.2	101	12.3	733	11.2	1 865	1 403	462	79	944
Union	89	15 901	1.16	148	9.9	110	7.4	942	7.4	2 741	2 141	600	123	948
Walworth	152	5 328	0.93	75	13.7	71	13.0	512	12.5	1 160	1 110	50	94	1 694
Yankton	2 296	23 942	1.12	270	11.9	191	8.4	1 853	10.9	4 463	3 653	810	570	2 502
Ziebach	0	2 588	0.73	31	11.0	18	6.4	545	21.4	D	114	D	5	176
TENNESSEE	153 726	6 493 932	1.02	81 261	12.4	62 474	9.5	765 026	14.1	1 187 963	768 467	419 496	240 295	3 669
Anderson	1 183	90 953	1.50	777	10.3	896	11.9	7 758	12.8	16 521	10 568	5 953	NA	NA
Bedford	545	42 730	0.84	634	13.5	432	9.2	7 354	18.6	8 179	5 746	2 433	1 030	2 229
Benton	162	15 192	0.80	157	9.7	244	15.1	1 968	15.8	4 592	3 719	873	319	1 959
Bledsoe	2 521	11 777	0.66	117	8.1	130	9.0	1 617	17.2	2 217	1 655	562	124	964
Blount	2 005	116 401	0.85	1 322	10.4	1 266	10.0	13 293	13.1	26 129	15 337	10 792	2 420	1 922
Bradley	2 809	99 491	0.96	1 240	12.0	995	9.6	13 220	15.7	20 192	12 585	7 607	4 316	4 198
Campbell	519	36 731	0.74	415	10.4	542	13.6	4 929	15.5	10 367	5 445	4 922	1 443	3 587
Cannon	164	10 588	0.42	129	9.4	149	10.8	1 712	15.3	2 907	2 003	904	133	963
Carroll	975	26 084	0.78	306	10.9	388	13.8	3 006	13.7	7 569	6 099	1 470	629	2 199
Carter	910	46 800	0.55	506	9.0	687	12.2	7 007	15.7	11 326	5 737	5 589	1 650	2 871
Cheatham	283	30 374	0.50	447	11.3	351	8.8	4 647	13.6	6 004	3 311	2 693	971	2 446
Chester	1 291	14 679	0.62	207	11.9	171	9.8	1 828	13.8	2 733	2 209	524	305	1 752
Claiborne	1 257	29 397	0.79	320	10.1	420	13.3	3 648	14.8	7 980	4 327	3 653	776	2 465
Clay	96	7 144	0.76	75	9.7	101	13.0	947	16.1	1 482	1 243	239	100	1 286
Cocke	294	31 990	0.74	388	11.0	475	13.5	4 267	15.0	9 413	5 005	4 408	1 495	4 207
Coffee	557	56 887	1.18	668	12.4	615	11.4	6 502	14.7	12 516	9 447	3 069	1 880	3 505
Crockett	194	13 195	0.76	173	11.8	159	10.9	2 167	18.0	3 114	2 694	420	320	2 187
Cumberland	636	56 633	0.98	541	9.3	785	13.5	6 623	16.2	17 945	14 192	3 753	2 264	3 908
Davidson	26 717	749 624	1.32	10 223	15.2	5 268	7.8	93 801	16.4	89 170	49 132	40 038	32 658	4 887
Decatur	213	10 576	0.75	140	12.0	184	15.7	1 445	16.2	2 751	2 188	563	278	2 381
DeKalb	298	18 016	0.87	223	11.6	214	11.1	2 822	18.0	4 162	2 277	1 885	447	2 313
Dickson	617	44 945	0.76	628	12.3	464	9.1	6 053	14.2	9 185	5 826	3 359	1 558	3 083
Dyer	516	38 602	1.03	463	12.2	419	11.1	3 928	12.5	8 388	7 035	1 353	2 006	5 239
Fayette	424	30 100	0.49	419	10.7	398	10.2	3 880	12.4	5 639	4 068	1 571	681	1 752
Fentress	132	16 677	0.79	188	10.5	223	12.5	2 331	16.4	4 872	3 978	894	460	2 562
Franklin	2 051	38 678	0.85	408	9.9	442	10.7	4 261	13.4	8 554	6 368	2 186	806	1 953
Gibson	991	44 624	0.74	618	12.5	634	12.8	5 185	12.9	11 333	9 418	1 915	1 567	3 164
Giles	609	27 694	0.88	312	10.8	332	11.5	3 285	14.3	6 467	5 214	1 253	713	2 488
Grainger	151	18 414	0.49	226	9.9	256	11.2	2 997	16.2	5 640	2 701	2 939	439	1 929
Greene	1 752	67 695	0.97	651	9.5	836	12.2	8 054	15.1	17 425	9 993	7 432	1 723	2 522
Grundy	180	12 058	0.65	162	12.1	178	13.2	1 776	16.8	3 595	2 454	1 141	301	2 233
Hamblen	918	67 697	1.20	764	12.1	709	11.2	8 690	16.9	13 818	8 021	5 797	2 240	3 535
Hamilton	9 958	385 658	1.26	4 171	11.8	3 395	9.6	37 436	13.1	67 041	43 337	23 704	17 270	4 899
Hancock	149	5 856	0.60	64	9.7	95	14.4	774	14.6	1 369	755	614	146	2 192
Hardeman	3 804	25 518	0.87	269	10.4	276	10.7	2 552	14.1	5 527	4 372	1 155	759	2 901
Hardin	371	25 006	0.89	269	10.4	350	13.6	3 118	15.3	6 108	5 102	1 006	905	3 468
Hawkins	456	48 463	0.61	525	9.3	712	12.6	5 824	12.8	13 880	5 902	7 978	1 413	2 482
Haywood	174	16 739	0.77	226	12.5	204	11.3	2 161	14.3	3 311	2 478	833	839	4 625
Henderson	218	26 042	0.82	317	11.3	295	10.5	3 190	13.8	6 147	4 814	1 333	757	2 686
Henry	491	32 372	1.01	337	10.5	447	13.9	3 813	15.3	8 648	7 171	1 477	1 095	3 394
Hickman	1 511	19 759	0.49	293	12.0	250	10.3	3 001	15.7	4 972	3 056	1 916	508	2 096
Houston	177	7 192	0.61	82	10.0	85	10.4	949	14.4	1 917	1 497	420	103	1 245
Humphreys	205	18 335	1.00	193	10.6	224	12.4	2 039	14.0	4 227	3 298	929	330	1 812
Jackson	177	9 676	0.50	88	7.7	147	12.8	1 392	15.4	2 179	1 696	483	202	1 754
Jefferson	1 804	45 549	0.69	518	9.8	599	11.3	5 789	14.0	14 026	7 921	6 105	1 340	2 556
Johnson	1 809	16 810	0.79	162	9.1	199	11.1	1 892	15.2	4 957	2 845	2 112	621	3 460
Knox	12 096	467 812	1.13	5 205	11.6	4 226	9.4	46 068	12.3	77 748	44 254	33 494	19 896	4 434
Lake	2 523	7 782	1.03	57	7.5	95	12.5	576	13.8	1 386	1 246	140	130	1 682
Lauderdale	2 490	26 640	0.89	281	10.4	273	10.1	2 910	13.9	5 153	3 954	1 199	1 004	3 602
Lawrence	407	38 328	0.77	572	13.5	490	11.5	5 327	15.4	10 877	8 744	2 133	1 264	3 002
Lewis	217	10 614	0.68	131	11.0	125	10.5	1 624	16.9	2 303	1 682	621	334	2 796
Lincoln	283	29 762	0.73	338	10.0	383	11.4	3 926	14.4	7 386	5 392	1 994	923	2 733
Loudon	480	45 829	0.80	531	10.4	565	11.1	6 062	15.9	14 652	8 618	6 034	1 145	2 244
McMinn	951	51 465	0.95	583	11.1	635	12.1	5 750	13.6	12 025	8 315	3 710	2 099	3 997
McNairy	313	24 514	0.82	268	10.3	333	12.8	3 154	15.0	7 845	6 458	1 387	585	2 230
Macon	269	19 477	0.65	333	14.4	270	11.7	3 311	17.2	4 104	2 813	1 291	340	1 487
Madison	4 428	113 638	1.37	1 237	12.6	929	9.5	10 165	12.7	18 360	14 679	3 681	4 492	4 533
Marion	250	25 214	0.73	324	11.4	343	12.1	3 461	15.0	5 861	3 889	1 972	578	2 029

1. Per 1,000 estimated resident population.   2. Data for serious crimes have not been adjusted for underreporting; this may affect comparability between geographic areas and over time.
3. Per 100,000 population estimated by the FBI.

Table B. States and Counties — Crime, Education, Money Income, and Poverty

STATE County	Serious crimes known to police, 2014 (cont.)[1] Rate[2]		Education School enrollment and attainment, 2010–2014 Enrollment[3]		Attainment[4] (percent)		Local government expenditures,[5] 2012–2013		Money income, 2010–2014	Households			Income and poverty, 2014	Percent below poverty level		
	Violent	Property	Total	Percent private	High school graduate or less	Bachelor's degree or more	Total current spending (mil dol)	Current spending per student (dollars)	Per capita income[6] (dollars)	Median income (dollars)	Mean income (dollars)	Percent with income of $200,000 or more	Median household income (dollars)	All persons	Children under 18 years	Children 5 to 17 years in families
	46	47	48	49	50	51	52	53	54	55	56	57	58	59	60	61
SOUTH DAKOTA—Cont'd																
Tripp	128	549	1 127	6.5	45.4	21.8	8.1	8 483	24 308	36 978	52 558	2.7	40 545	19.9	27.9	24.4
Turner	48	896	1 823	9.2	46.6	19.9	13.6	8 782	26 263	51 343	61 784	1.9	55 708	10.2	12.3	10.8
Union	154	794	3 863	15.5	36.9	32.7	24.7	8 605	37 326	64 513	91 958	9.0	72 041	6.3	8.5	7.1
Walworth	144	1 550	1 267	12.9	48.5	22.5	7.6	8 798	27 095	42 643	60 509	1.9	41 831	15.9	21.3	18.2
Yankton	299	2 204	5 253	20.6	42.4	26.7	22.9	7 395	26 831	50 044	64 755	3.3	47 363	13.8	16.5	13.6
Ziebach	0	176	978	2.0	53.2	13.1	9.9	14 640	12 764	32 500	42 639	0.0	32 025	44.6	48.9	34.3
TENNESSEE	608	3 061	1 595 882	17.1	48.1	24.4	8 221.1	8 208	24 811	44 621	62 344	3.1	44 357	18.2	25.9	24.3
Anderson	NA	NA	16 281	13.7	48.4	23.6	121.7	9 935	25 353	44 199	61 081	2.3	46 689	15.6	23.8	21.7
Bedford	346	1 882	11 033	9.8	62.3	13.3	58.2	7 066	19 855	40 989	53 016	1.3	42 252	19.1	28.4	27.7
Benton	190	1 769	3 134	6.3	66.7	10.0	19.5	8 483	19 168	34 087	43 985	0.7	34 382	21.4	33.0	31.5
Bledsoe	140	824	2 757	14.1	65.6	10.2	16.4	8 065	16 631	34 450	45 955	1.2	34 948	28.5	35.4	33.3
Blount	272	1 649	27 627	14.7	48.7	21.7	154.8	8 464	24 507	46 518	60 940	2.3	47 175	14.7	21.8	20.1
Bradley	544	3 654	25 541	23.2	50.5	19.3	120.3	7 581	22 294	41 575	57 306	1.8	43 065	17.5	24.0	22.8
Campbell	370	3 217	8 200	12.9	69.9	9.5	42.9	7 282	17 242	32 616	41 744	0.5	33 333	22.7	34.3	31.8
Cannon	181	782	2 718	7.1	65.8	12.8	15.8	7 446	20 974	39 438	52 332	0.7	41 068	16.4	23.2	21.2
Carroll	252	1 948	6 638	17.4	60.8	15.6	37.2	7 835	19 461	36 168	48 176	1.4	36 627	20.8	28.2	27.9
Carter	231	2 639	12 210	13.2	58.1	16.1	66.7	8 122	19 385	32 754	44 972	1.1	34 354	24.6	33.2	30.8
Cheatham	315	2 131	9 665	14.6	54.4	19.3	47.4	7 101	23 730	52 138	62 739	1.7	51 475	12.7	19.2	17.0
Chester	276	1 477	4 707	27.3	57.1	15.6	19.3	6 864	19 059	41 028	52 982	2.3	40 980	20.1	25.3	23.4
Claiborne	394	2 071	7 310	28.3	67.3	12.3	38.6	8 185	18 322	32 884	44 033	1.0	33 640	24.0	34.1	30.8
Clay	244	1 042	1 413	6.7	71.3	13.3	9.0	8 242	16 802	29 812	39 115	0.2	30 744	24.0	35.0	34.0
Cocke	523	3 683	6 304	6.0	69.4	9.4	44.7	8 026	18 113	30 888	42 188	0.9	30 860	27.8	40.4	36.7
Coffee	464	3 041	12 295	7.9	55.6	18.2	82.9	8 804	21 123	39 656	52 976	1.8	45 235	16.8	25.6	23.5
Crockett	492	1 695	3 338	9.3	64.6	12.0	22.0	7 189	19 270	37 298	48 742	1.2	37 853	19.0	26.2	25.9
Cumberland	343	3 564	10 257	11.5	56.3	17.8	54.0	7 210	21 674	38 350	49 929	1.3	40 839	16.6	29.2	27.2
Davidson	1 120	3 767	162 247	30.7	37.7	36.5	810.7	9 800	28 971	47 434	68 794	4.3	48 195	19.9	31.5	30.6
Decatur	231	2 150	2 316	6.1	63.3	13.3	12.2	7 210	23 760	37 219	54 251	2.9	37 417	19.9	27.7	26.1
DeKalb	269	2 044	3 956	6.6	65.9	13.8	21.9	7 219	22 451	37 409	58 461	2.7	38 595	20.1	29.4	28.9
Dickson	455	2 628	11 606	12.9	60.2	13.5	64.3	7 606	22 191	45 056	57 614	2.3	45 914	14.3	21.1	19.4
Dyer	737	4 503	9 270	6.8	55.8	19.9	54.5	7 997	22 925	41 426	57 117	2.2	43 425	19.6	28.4	26.9
Fayette	275	1 477	8 574	32.2	48.8	22.7	30.4	7 966	28 946	55 623	74 448	4.9	56 573	14.7	21.2	20.0
Fentress	201	2 361	3 710	3.9	71.3	10.2	18.4	7 706	16 283	29 784	39 402	0.8	30 299	28.1	37.7	34.2
Franklin	346	1 606	10 149	21.6	56.1	18.7	46.9	8 002	23 099	42 663	57 973	2.8	43 851	16.5	23.8	21.5
Gibson	545	2 619	11 942	8.5	55.4	15.4	69.9	7 559	20 189	37 460	50 264	1.1	37 498	19.5	27.0	25.6
Giles	283	2 205	6 493	15.6	62.0	14.6	32.7	8 067	20 182	38 739	49 731	1.3	41 326	16.9	25.4	23.5
Grainger	180	1 749	4 664	10.1	67.2	11.1	26.5	7 253	18 475	34 566	46 255	1.4	35 704	21.9	31.4	28.6
Greene	328	2 194	13 867	10.8	60.8	15.5	78.6	7 721	19 998	35 860	47 295	1.1	36 740	17.7	24.9	22.5
Grundy	341	1 892	2 697	9.9	72.6	9.7	18.4	7 970	15 581	26 856	39 107	1.3	28 086	26.1	37.2	34.6
Hamblen	472	3 064	13 706	8.5	60.4	16.1	76.0	7 400	20 675	38 600	51 539	1.5	37 410	23.4	33.7	29.9
Hamilton	640	4 259	84 924	21.8	40.3	28.1	375.3	8 587	27 464	47 880	67 422	3.8	48 380	15.9	22.0	20.9
Hancock	195	1 996	1 421	10.2	67.2	10.1	9.3	9 558	15 464	26 528	35 875	0.5	27 323	29.5	42.8	40.6
Hardeman	688	2 213	5 265	11.7	68.2	9.2	33.7	8 302	14 954	30 260	41 951	0.6	35 321	25.3	32.6	31.0
Hardin	410	3 058	5 175	14.8	64.7	12.4	30.3	8 153	20 949	34 084	51 737	2.4	36 285	21.7	30.3	28.7
Hawkins	297	2 185	11 847	6.9	62.0	13.0	65.1	8 014	21 259	37 432	50 938	1.1	39 506	19.6	27.6	26.2
Haywood	1 064	3 561	4 805	7.9	64.9	12.4	27.6	8 156	18 998	33 922	46 634	1.6	35 470	24.7	34.5	31.9
Henderson	443	2 242	6 816	9.9	59.9	13.2	37.3	7 569	19 847	38 696	49 600	1.5	39 303	19.1	27.4	25.5
Henry	319	3 075	7 086	8.7	61.7	16.3	39.7	8 004	21 941	38 694	52 223	1.8	37 151	20.5	30.7	30.0
Hickman	371	1 725	5 341	12.5	67.2	11.2	28.9	7 832	18 147	38 032	49 735	0.8	37 443	20.2	29.3	27.9
Houston	242	1 003	1 916	6.4	64.8	11.0	10.9	7 667	19 230	38 637	47 898	1.5	39 753	19.1	27.4	25.1
Humphreys	209	1 603	4 122	7.3	58.5	13.6	23.5	7 547	21 883	41 152	52 937	1.3	42 837	17.6	26.3	25.0
Jackson	208	1 546	2 128	4.0	70.9	9.5	12.7	8 032	18 452	33 500	44 991	0.9	35 379	23.4	35.1	34.0
Jefferson	277	2 279	11 467	16.8	57.3	15.1	55.7	7 376	21 603	41 426	54 816	1.3	41 235	17.8	25.6	24.4
Johnson	579	2 880	3 105	13.1	67.3	9.3	20.6	8 862	17 273	31 711	41 297	1.0	31 330	26.4	35.3	33.1
Knox	481	3 952	112 176	16.9	36.3	34.5	462.4	7 848	28 255	47 543	67 521	4.0	47 199	17.7	23.0	20.8
Lake	181	1 501	1 432	10.5	72.5	8.2	7.6	7 941	11 875	29 214	41 849	0.8	28 524	41.9	44.0	42.3
Lauderdale	814	2 787	6 685	5.9	68.5	10.1	37.1	7 845	15 715	31 185	42 955	1.0	33 595	24.8	31.7	29.5
Lawrence	511	2 492	9 644	13.9	63.2	11.9	52.6	7 682	19 298	37 371	50 183	1.1	34 614	21.8	29.2	27.6
Lewis	385	2 411	2 220	14.1	60.5	12.7	13.6	6 958	17 962	36 114	44 360	0.2	36 255	20.3	31.8	30.5
Lincoln	391	2 342	7 353	16.5	57.7	16.3	40.1	7 279	21 686	41 328	51 747	1.0	41 802	16.5	22.4	20.7
Loudon	231	2 013	8 931	14.6	47.7	25.6	56.4	7 622	28 191	50 619	69 191	3.8	53 945	13.6	22.0	19.9
McMinn	489	3 508	11 679	17.8	59.3	14.8	60.9	7 447	20 615	39 644	50 893	1.0	39 528	17.4	25.2	23.5
McNairy	385	1 845	5 772	11.2	65.4	11.4	33.5	7 568	17 516	32 214	44 244	0.7	34 882	23.5	28.9	26.9
Macon	223	1 264	5 010	7.8	70.2	9.0	25.1	6 520	17 386	34 156	44 931	0.5	36 886	19.3	29.4	28.4
Madison	883	3 650	26 712	28.2	46.3	25.1	114.4	8 557	23 398	42 069	59 880	2.8	43 113	20.9	29.2	26.6
Marion	253	1 776	6 324	12.2	59.5	15.3	34.7	7 481	21 127	40 998	51 895	0.9	40 766	20.6	30.8	27.9

1. Data for serious crimes have not been adjusted for underreporting; this may affect comparability between geographic areas and over time.   2. Per 100,000 population estimated by the FBI.
3. All persons 3 years old and over enrolled in nursery school through college.   4. Persons 25 years old and over.   5. Elementary and secondary education expenditures.
6. Based on population estimated by the American Community Survey, 2010–2014.

Table B. States and Counties — **Personal Income**

STATE County	Personal income, 2014										Earnings, 2014		
	Total (mil dol)	Percent change, 2013–2014	Per capita[1] Dollars	Per capita[1] Rank	Wages and salaries (mil dol)	Supplements to wages and salaries; employer contributions (mil dol) Pension and insurance	Supplements to wages and salaries; employer contributions (mil dol) Government social insurance	Proprietors' income (mil dol)	Dividends, interest, and rent (mil dol)	Personal transfer receipts (mil dol)	Total (mil dol)	Contributions for government social insurance (mil dol) From employee and self-employed	Contributions for government social insurance (mil dol) From employer
	62	63	64	65	66	67	68	69	70	71	72	73	74
SOUTH DAKOTA—Cont'd													
Tripp	250	-3.5	45 411	640	73	13	5	74	46	49	166	7	5
Turner	449	-11.2	54 248	225	74	15	6	177	62	60	272	14	6
Union	1 173	-0.8	78 030	32	478	62	32	151	341	91	723	43	32
Walworth	237	-0.1	43 066	839	76	14	6	32	60	51	129	8	6
Yankton	882	-0.7	38 870	1 337	482	85	36	71	186	160	674	40	36
Ziebach	76	39.4	26 823	2 992	12	3	1	37	9	15	53	1	1
TENNESSEE	264 965	3.7	40 457	X	129 859	20 482	9 137	35 161	37 563	54 826	194 640	11 658	9 137
Anderson	3 048	3.4	40 361	1 132	2 169	297	153	516	401	707	3 135	188	153
Bedford	1 537	4.2	32 969	2 284	700	134	50	202	214	363	1 086	64	50
Benton	527	1.8	32 659	2 344	133	31	10	33	72	189	208	17	10
Bledsoe	299	6.3	21 432	3 106	59	20	4	38	39	116	122	8	4
Blount	4 685	4.0	37 085	1 588	2 051	333	148	450	674	1 066	2 982	190	148
Bradley	4 090	4.4	39 715	1 220	1 674	294	124	775	544	857	2 868	170	124
Campbell	1 216	2.1	30 473	2 655	331	69	25	88	151	471	513	40	25
Cannon	471	2.9	34 218	2 078	76	17	6	68	60	128	166	12	6
Carroll	941	-0.4	33 184	2 248	271	55	21	63	107	341	410	30	21
Carter	1 740	2.2	30 588	2 642	368	78	27	173	239	586	647	50	27
Cheatham	1 476	4.3	37 122	1 581	329	70	24	167	161	292	590	38	24
Chester	511	2.0	29 417	2 790	123	28	9	58	56	152	218	15	9
Claiborne	944	2.3	29 879	2 735	309	65	23	53	116	347	450	34	23
Clay	268	5.1	34 471	2 033	52	13	4	60	28	84	129	8	4
Cocke	999	2.8	28 236	2 900	271	57	20	60	113	382	408	33	20
Coffee	2 000	4.6	37 295	1 557	1 038	176	75	294	260	513	1 582	95	75
Crockett	535	-0.4	36 472	1 691	153	32	11	104	52	154	301	19	11
Cumberland	1 916	4.3	33 039	2 273	607	108	44	216	343	687	975	75	44
Davidson	36 296	5.5	54 307	223	24 686	3 238	1 700	10 190	5 249	4 658	39 814	2 197	1 700
Decatur	395	-0.2	33 878	2 134	134	26	10	38	47	151	207	15	10
DeKalb	630	4.0	32 681	2 337	206	40	16	87	83	177	349	22	16
Dickson	1 714	4.1	33 883	2 132	591	105	44	164	197	425	904	59	44
Dyer	1 400	1.3	36 918	1 610	595	119	44	199	175	396	958	58	44
Fayette	1 985	1.4	50 890	337	335	61	24	411	209	328	831	51	24
Fentress	552	1.6	30 894	2 603	150	31	11	84	64	214	276	20	11
Franklin	1 432	4.0	34 579	2 008	435	87	33	126	204	389	680	45	33
Gibson	1 711	-0.8	34 595	2 000	497	102	37	185	195	551	822	54	37
Giles	1 011	4.2	35 047	1 924	370	68	27	82	145	294	547	37	27
Grainger	663	4.1	29 011	2 826	127	28	10	51	75	219	215	18	10
Greene	2 467	3.1	36 098	1 764	942	172	71	142	281	984	1 326	91	71
Grundy	375	0.4	27 927	2 925	66	18	5	42	44	149	131	11	5
Hamblen	2 038	3.0	32 328	2 401	1 142	202	81	162	260	587	1 587	101	81
Hamilton	15 493	4.0	44 112	752	9 137	1 472	651	1 831	2 546	2 936	13 091	771	651
Hancock	154	5.5	23 104	3 098	26	9	2	4	20	73	41	4	2
Hardeman	701	0.0	27 011	2 982	254	58	19	54	85	256	384	26	19
Hardin	915	2.2	35 383	1 882	305	59	22	105	138	312	491	34	22
Hawkins	1 692	2.0	29 830	2 740	479	97	36	66	199	574	677	55	36
Haywood	540	-7.6	29 707	2 759	196	44	14	43	75	182	297	19	14
Henderson	866	2.7	30 916	2 598	291	53	22	62	109	259	428	29	22
Henry	1 170	1.2	36 345	1 715	408	88	31	175	185	356	702	43	31
Hickman	658	4.3	26 982	2 984	134	33	10	34	71	223	211	17	10
Houston	262	5.4	31 728	2 484	50	13	4	24	34	93	91	7	4
Humphreys	622	4.5	34 278	2 068	276	56	20	49	86	190	401	20	20
Jackson	398	3.3	34 379	2 048	55	14	4	109	37	126	182	13	4
Jefferson	1 618	3.8	30 715	2 625	520	95	38	113	217	494	766	55	38
Johnson	515	3.4	28 837	2 843	157	36	11	29	67	189	232	18	11
Knox	19 297	4.0	43 012	846	10 695	1 651	759	2 317	3 112	3 321	15 421	910	759
Lake	180	-5.8	23 582	3 090	58	17	4	9	25	84	89	6	4
Lauderdale	697	-0.7	25 468	3 049	216	50	16	40	85	249	322	22	16
Lawrence	1 266	2.4	29 950	2 722	353	73	27	130	147	407	583	41	27
Lewis	334	4.8	28 071	2 910	78	19	6	34	38	121	138	10	6
Lincoln	1 204	2.6	35 789	1 808	345	73	25	117	165	316	559	36	25
Loudon	2 035	3.8	40 084	1 163	584	96	42	105	405	514	827	60	42
McMinn	1 716	3.6	32 606	2 353	712	120	54	153	200	505	1 040	70	54
McNairy	730	1.8	27 774	2 934	198	50	15	52	86	284	314	24	15
Macon	682	4.4	29 651	2 769	163	37	12	86	78	209	298	20	12
Madison	3 689	1.7	37 571	1 514	2 302	429	166	423	530	873	3 320	193	166
Marion	945	3.6	33 252	2 237	262	50	19	55	111	280	386	29	19

1. Based on the resident population estimated as of July 1 of the year shown.

Table B. States and Counties — Earnings, Social Security, and Housing

STATE County	Earnings, 2014 (cont.) Percent by selected industries									Social Security beneficiaries, December 2014		Supplemental Security Income recipients, December 2014	Housing units, 2015	
	Farm	Mining	Construction	Manufacturing	Information: professional, scientific, technical services	Retail trade	Finance, insurance, real estate and leasing	Health care and social assistance	Government	Number	Rate[1]		Total	Percent change, 2010–2014
	75	76	77	78	79	80	81	82	83	84	85	86	87	88
SOUTH DAKOTA—Cont'd														
Tripp	37.8	D	4.8	1.6	3.6	8.0	D	D	11.2	1 400	255	167	3 071	0.0
Turner	22.9	D	5.1	36.2	2.0	1.9	D	D	6.1	1 850	224	85	3 993	1.4
Union	4.4	0.0	2.7	18.1	5.1	4.0	8.8	14.4	5.3	2 835	189	92	6 834	8.8
Walworth	12.1	D	4.5	0.8	D	10.3	5.1	D	14.3	1 655	300	131	3 004	0.0
Yankton	9.4	D	3.1	25.3	D	6.5	5.0	15.1	16.3	4 905	216	420	9 851	2.1
Ziebach	72.2	0.0	D	D	D	D	D	D	16.1	155	55	87	984	-0.3
TENNESSEE	0.4	0.2	6.1	12.1	8.8	6.8	7.7	15.5	14.2	1 371 562	209	183 890	2 892 305	2.9
Anderson	-0.1	D	6.3	27.8	22.7	4.1	3.8	8.7	11.9	19 465	258	2 241	34 835	0.3
Bedford	3.5	D	7.6	35.2	D	5.9	4.5	D	11.0	9 600	207	1 081	18 676	1.7
Benton	-1.8	D	6.0	15.3	D	10.2	6.2	D	26.7	5 250	326	588	8 967	-0.1
Bledsoe	13.0	D	9.4	D	D	4.6	3.0	4.5	43.9	3 280	226	446	5 684	-0.6
Blount	-0.1	D	12.7	18.7	3.6	8.4	6.3	7.4	15.1	30 950	245	2 698	56 378	2.0
Bradley	1.7	D	5.8	21.2	3.2	6.5	3.3	D	9.6	23 230	225	2 546	42 878	3.6
Campbell	-0.3	0.6	11.0	14.7	2.5	9.9	5.8	D	20.1	11 555	290	2 505	20 438	2.4
Cannon	1.6	D	18.1	7.7	D	5.4	D	D	19.3	3 440	251	388	6 058	0.3
Carroll	1.2	D	4.3	10.5	D	6.3	6.3	D	20.4	7 765	275	1 085	13 170	0.0
Carter	0.0	D	11.9	9.0	3.5	11.6	5.5	D	21.0	16 320	290	2 189	27 822	0.3
Cheatham	-0.1	D	15.1	24.3	D	6.5	3.6	D	14.7	7 895	199	788	15 869	1.3
Chester	-0.4	0.0	D	11.0	D	8.6	4.7	D	22.2	4 060	234	424	7 023	0.6
Claiborne	0.5	5.2	3.7	18.9	1.9	6.2	5.4	D	22.1	9 345	296	2 007	15 089	1.5
Clay	10.7	D	4.6	8.0	D	6.9	3.1	D	17.7	2 415	312	296	4 257	-0.6
Cocke	1.9	D	D	23.4	1.6	10.5	3.2	D	24.7	10 680	303	2 070	17 345	-0.7
Coffee	1.1	0.0	5.2	17.6	D	6.4	3.3	10.4	13.9	13 285	248	1 557	23 641	0.9
Crockett	1.7	0.0	6.5	26.0	2.6	15.0	7.2	D	14.9	3 580	245	459	6 386	-0.6
Cumberland	0.7	D	7.2	15.0	4.7	10.1	4.6	13.9	13.6	21 230	367	1 540	28 828	2.4
Davidson	0.0	0.2	5.1	3.6	13.7	5.1	9.5	25.3	8.8	98 180	147	15 850	298 788	5.2
Decatur	-1.4	D	6.5	13.2	D	6.6	D	29.3	16.9	3 655	312	484	6 829	-0.6
DeKalb	4.0	0.0	D	23.3	13.2	5.4	2.6	D	16.0	4 885	254	726	9 451	0.5
Dickson	-0.4	D	10.2	22.0	3.0	9.3	4.5	13.7	15.8	10 740	212	1 213	21 229	2.0
Dyer	2.6	0.0	11.2	25.9	D	7.8	5.1	10.9	15.4	9 340	247	1 526	16 809	0.6
Fayette	0.5	D	6.5	25.1	D	10.9	8.7	5.0	9.4	9 535	244	1 292	16 433	4.9
Fentress	4.7	D	9.1	5.6	2.3	10.8	4.6	D	15.0	5 750	322	1 100	8 927	-0.4
Franklin	3.9	0.9	5.0	21.2	D	7.7	3.3	D	16.7	10 600	256	1 006	19 030	1.8
Gibson	4.9	0.0	7.9	16.4	3.7	10.3	6.5	D	19.3	12 820	259	1 744	22 435	2.0
Giles	-0.3	D	8.5	32.3	D	7.6	3.3	D	13.7	7 710	268	770	13 880	0.3
Grainger	0.7	D	10.4	24.5	D	7.3	D	3.7	24.1	6 545	287	1 103	10 868	-0.2
Greene	2.0	D	4.3	24.9	2.3	9.0	3.9	D	16.4	20 425	299	2 541	32 169	0.4
Grundy	2.1	D	7.8	7.7	D	10.4	4.1	11.0	29.7	3 835	285	704	6 367	-0.5
Hamblen	0.3	D	4.3	32.1	2.6	8.3	3.3	12.5	13.2	16 045	255	2 102	27 024	0.2
Hamilton	0.0	D	6.4	13.2	7.6	6.7	9.1	12.6	17.0	72 420	206	8 807	156 385	3.5
Hancock	0.1	0.0	2.6	4.2	D	9.3	D	15.0	52.2	1 880	284	504	3 595	-0.8
Hardeman	0.9	0.0	5.4	29.2	D	5.0	D	D	25.7	6 555	253	1 398	10 848	0.0
Hardin	0.4	D	7.1	30.0	3.1	10.1	5.5	D	17.8	8 075	312	1 139	13 980	0.3
Hawkins	-0.1	D	3.1	35.9	D	6.2	2.2	D	19.6	16 995	300	2 097	26 843	-0.1
Haywood	2.1	0.0	3.7	25.9	2.5	6.6	4.8	6.5	23.1	4 440	244	979	8 409	1.1
Henderson	1.7	0.0	4.7	18.9	1.9	8.7	9.8	D	18.5	7 200	257	943	12 803	0.1
Henry	6.9	D	5.5	19.0	2.9	8.6	6.6	D	21.2	9 635	299	964	16 998	-0.3
Hickman	-1.8	0.0	D	13.3	2.8	5.3	2.2	D	30.9	5 720	235	723	10 294	-0.2
Houston	2.2	0.0	11.2	12.9	D	6.3	3.2	16.4	28.6	2 205	267	309	4 167	-0.5
Humphreys	0.3	D	7.2	33.4	5.5	5.6	2.5	D	21.0	4 930	272	531	8 873	0.1
Jackson	-0.3	0.3	13.4	7.9	D	5.6	D	D	14.8	3 420	298	432	5 809	-0.4
Jefferson	0.9	D	D	17.0	D	7.7	3.8	D	16.2	14 080	267	1 456	23 672	0.7
Johnson	0.9	D	5.4	22.1	3.0	5.3	3.4	9.0	24.2	5 360	299	768	8 905	-0.6
Knox	0.0	0.1	6.3	5.3	11.1	8.0	7.9	16.5	15.0	85 055	190	10 170	200 478	2.8
Lake	10.5	0.0	D	D	D	4.2	1.4	9.7	51.1	1 490	194	361	2 608	0.4
Lauderdale	4.8	0.0	2.5	20.4	D	6.4	5.2	8.1	29.8	5 995	219	1 299	11 276	0.2
Lawrence	2.9	D	6.1	18.1	3.5	10.2	4.1	D	19.4	10 920	258	1 334	18 141	-0.2
Lewis	-0.4	0.0	6.6	9.4	2.6	13.0	2.2	D	23.1	3 290	277	325	5 450	-0.4
Lincoln	4.1	D	6.4	27.1	D	8.6	3.4	4.4	21.1	8 370	249	787	15 338	0.6
Loudon	3.5	D	7.1	20.3	4.0	8.2	5.0	7.7	15.4	15 295	302	1 035	22 403	3.1
McMinn	1.1	D	5.4	37.3	D	7.8	4.6	D	12.4	13 575	258	1 699	23 247	-0.4
McNairy	1.5	0.0	5.4	23.3	D	6.7	2.6	D	22.7	7 810	299	1 251	11 981	0.4
Macon	5.7	0.0	7.5	12.5	6.1	13.1	6.2	D	19.6	5 505	239	714	9 992	1.3
Madison	0.3	D	8.6	17.1	3.9	7.4	4.4	13.2	22.2	20 935	213	3 341	42 805	2.2
Marion	-0.3	D	5.5	25.5	D	10.4	2.9	8.5	18.5	7 920	279	1 136	13 078	1.0

1. Per 1,000 resident population estimated as of July 1 of the year shown.

Table B. States and Counties — Housing, Labor Force, and Employment

STATE County	Housing units, 2010–2014								Civilian labor force, 2015				Civilian employment,[6] 2010–2014		
	Occupied units										Unemployment			Percent	
			Owner-occupied			Renter-occupied									
				Median owner cost as a percent of income											
	Total	Percent	Median value[1]	With a mortgage	Without a mortgage[2]	Median rent[3]	Median rent as a percent of income[2]	Sub-standard units[4] (percent)	Total	Percent change, 2014–2015	Total	Rate[5]	Total	Management, business, science and arts	Construction, production, and maintenance occupations
	89	90	91	92	93	94	95	96	97	98	99	100	101	102	103
SOUTH DAKOTA—Cont'd															
Tripp	2 595	65.2	75 000	19.7	13.2	558	33.1	1.7	3 104	-1.2	85	2.7	2 854	45.0	26.9
Turner	3 494	78.5	97 300	23.1	11.4	600	23.3	0.9	4 731	1.2	128	2.7	4 345	34.8	29.6
Union	5 861	74.7	153 600	18.4	10.0	764	22.9	0.8	8 102	0.7	279	3.4	7 476	41.5	20.1
Walworth	2 376	64.6	72 800	20.7	11.3	518	20.5	1.9	2 311	-2.7	126	5.5	2 576	33.3	24.8
Yankton	8 840	70.8	125 300	19.4	10.0	571	27.0	0.8	11 672	2.2	309	2.6	11 295	32.0	26.2
Ziebach	792	49.7	65 700	19.3	10.3	449	30.2	12.4	1 009	0.1	50	5.0	939	49.9	21.4
TENNESSEE	2 487 349	67.1	139 900	22.7	11.0	757	30.9	2.4	3 062 776	0.5	176 752	5.8	2 835 895	33.6	24.2
Anderson	30 393	69.2	131 700	21.3	10.4	701	28.2	1.4	33 411	0.7	1 990	6.0	31 618	34.4	23.0
Bedford	16 608	69.4	113 200	22.1	11.5	667	30.0	5.2	19 418	-0.6	1 277	6.6	19 032	25.7	37.4
Benton	6 837	77.3	82 200	23.2	11.6	562	35.2	3.5	6 775	0.5	531	7.8	6 068	22.8	36.4
Bledsoe	4 480	77.7	105 000	25.0	11.2	523	33.2	4.7	4 255	-1.0	338	7.9	4 454	23.0	39.5
Blount	48 674	73.4	163 600	23.2	10.0	744	29.9	1.6	59 500	0.8	3 155	5.3	54 795	32.2	24.6
Bradley	37 823	67.0	141 400	22.3	10.6	711	31.4	2.6	49 042	-0.6	2 639	5.4	43 193	28.6	28.5
Campbell	15 902	70.8	89 200	22.6	12.7	551	31.3	1.7	14 792	0.1	1 193	8.1	13 913	23.9	32.6
Cannon	5 405	75.5	116 600	25.4	11.3	606	25.7	1.9	5 910	1.8	343	5.8	5 629	22.3	36.8
Carroll	11 096	75.2	83 100	21.9	11.1	551	31.2	1.8	12 232	-2.5	1 050	8.6	10 984	30.0	30.6
Carter	24 090	70.6	103 400	22.1	12.1	563	32.0	2.1	23 656	-1.0	1 573	6.6	23 444	28.5	27.3
Cheatham	14 520	80.7	156 500	24.0	10.5	920	41.5	2.3	20 182	1.5	987	4.9	18 308	30.0	27.9
Chester	5 943	72.5	102 000	22.1	10.7	656	28.8	2.4	8 159	-0.2	496	6.1	6 899	29.3	29.7
Claiborne	12 696	72.7	97 800	23.7	10.6	518	31.2	1.5	12 684	-0.3	932	7.3	11 643	26.4	34.3
Clay	3 174	75.2	94 800	23.9	12.6	514	28.5	1.7	3 002	-0.1	271	9.0	2 821	23.3	35.0
Cocke	14 788	69.9	98 600	24.4	11.2	551	32.5	3.2	14 451	-0.9	1 148	7.9	13 842	21.6	34.1
Coffee	21 131	66.1	118 000	22.6	11.9	662	29.4	4.0	24 289	-0.9	1 364	5.6	21 217	31.8	28.2
Crockett	5 572	68.2	86 200	21.8	12.5	656	30.7	2.8	6 833	-1.1	450	6.6	5 980	27.3	34.4
Cumberland	23 923	79.4	139 700	23.3	10.0	635	30.6	1.6	22 955	-0.9	1 660	7.2	20 068	27.3	29.4
Davidson	259 557	54.0	167 400	23.6	11.5	859	30.7	2.9	364 254	1.9	16 259	4.5	329 631	39.3	17.2
Decatur	5 045	77.7	86 800	21.6	10.3	540	33.6	1.9	4 702	-2.2	383	8.1	4 569	29.7	31.3
DeKalb	6 998	72.5	117 100	23.1	10.0	535	25.5	2.0	7 382	-1.2	518	7.0	7 601	27.0	38.1
Dickson	18 469	72.0	141 400	22.5	10.8	735	32.1	2.0	24 053	1.7	1 336	5.6	21 723	27.5	30.6
Dyer	15 088	64.0	99 800	20.3	11.6	616	27.5	2.5	16 713	0.4	1 227	7.3	16 003	29.5	33.5
Fayette	14 681	79.5	177 400	22.7	10.0	631	26.6	2.5	17 768	-0.6	1 137	6.4	17 053	32.6	27.8
Fentress	7 326	77.7	92 100	24.5	12.9	530	30.6	2.4	7 034	-0.4	519	7.4	6 090	27.4	34.2
Franklin	16 126	75.8	106 800	22.7	11.2	619	26.3	1.8	19 526	-0.9	1 037	5.3	16 609	29.6	33.3
Gibson	19 255	72.1	88 900	23.9	11.8	607	29.5	2.5	21 045	-1.1	1 594	7.6	19 805	28.0	29.1
Giles	11 327	72.0	103 700	22.4	11.7	581	31.8	1.8	14 533	1.8	746	5.1	11 788	27.9	36.1
Grainger	8 888	81.1	93 700	23.0	11.8	525	28.1	2.8	9 216	-0.3	626	6.8	8 598	24.4	40.0
Greene	28 489	71.4	109 800	22.4	10.3	561	27.8	2.6	30 665	1.3	2 031	6.6	27 753	28.5	33.2
Grundy	5 331	76.2	80 200	24.5	13.4	515	29.2	4.9	4 896	-4.2	387	7.9	4 449	22.4	36.5
Hamblen	24 401	68.3	124 400	22.5	11.4	644	33.1	1.7	26 510	0.4	1 681	6.3	25 084	26.1	36.0
Hamilton	135 974	64.6	157 200	21.4	10.5	759	30.3	2.0	167 197	1.2	9 132	5.5	161 007	37.3	20.3
Hancock	2 819	75.5	77 400	23.9	11.8	367	20.8	3.9	2 079	0.2	208	10.0	2 267	23.1	40.0
Hardeman	8 712	70.2	84 300	26.4	12.4	594	36.8	2.0	9 312	-3.0	722	7.8	8 206	23.7	36.1
Hardin	9 889	78.5	97 100	25.1	11.3	598	28.4	2.7	10 244	-2.4	760	7.4	9 216	24.3	34.3
Hawkins	23 414	75.9	109 500	22.0	11.4	603	28.0	1.6	23 592	-1.4	1 541	6.5	22 082	27.2	35.6
Haywood	6 995	62.2	93 800	24.8	12.6	629	32.7	3.6	7 667	-1.5	658	8.6	7 297	24.6	37.5
Henderson	10 916	75.3	97 000	21.1	11.5	600	28.6	2.2	12 237	-0.1	1 006	8.2	11 119	27.0	35.8
Henry	13 317	73.6	91 400	21.9	10.2	609	28.0	2.2	13 923	-0.3	931	6.7	12 368	25.8	32.0
Hickman	8 812	77.9	96 500	23.1	10.0	640	39.9	4.2	10 487	1.2	603	5.7	9 394	23.5	35.7
Houston	3 311	73.6	92 000	21.9	12.0	559	26.9	3.7	3 214	-2.8	285	8.9	3 063	20.7	44.3
Humphreys	7 360	78.0	106 000	22.5	11.8	595	26.7	1.9	8 474	0.8	587	6.9	7 227	27.4	36.9
Jackson	4 552	78.2	102 800	24.9	12.8	515	31.4	1.3	4 462	-0.4	359	8.0	3 946	25.6	40.8
Jefferson	19 979	73.3	122 700	22.5	11.2	656	26.8	2.3	23 223	0.5	1 518	6.5	22 402	26.4	31.0
Johnson	7 110	77.7	100 800	26.4	10.8	492	29.5	5.0	7 307	2.1	425	5.8	6 299	24.9	32.7
Knox	180 558	64.5	158 400	21.7	10.5	785	30.4	1.6	228 557	0.9	10 938	4.8	211 194	40.0	17.0
Lake	2 150	57.0	73 700	20.7	13.2	435	26.7	3.3	1 977	-6.2	174	8.8	1 817	25.3	24.2
Lauderdale	9 833	61.8	78 600	24.5	13.3	610	29.6	3.3	9 655	-2.0	879	9.1	9 155	25.3	33.1
Lawrence	15 932	74.2	98 300	22.3	10.8	563	30.4	3.7	17 640	-0.3	1 195	6.8	16 660	23.9	36.0
Lewis	4 768	78.0	94 800	24.1	12.2	561	26.4	2.3	4 792	-1.6	361	7.5	4 509	27.4	32.8
Lincoln	13 702	73.6	108 100	23.3	11.4	606	26.7	2.0	15 124	-1.7	748	4.9	14 284	26.3	35.9
Loudon	19 912	76.5	177 600	21.4	10.0	714	27.9	1.9	21 930	0.3	1 257	5.7	19 811	31.1	28.7
McMinn	20 187	74.6	116 200	21.8	11.2	590	30.8	1.7	22 608	0.7	1 474	6.5	20 860	26.6	37.4
McNairy	9 796	73.3	85 800	23.5	13.5	546	31.3	2.0	8 785	-2.1	768	8.7	8 913	26.5	38.1
Macon	8 640	71.1	99 000	24.0	12.3	539	25.8	3.6	10 034	0.4	536	5.3	9 311	21.3	42.8
Madison	36 253	64.8	114 600	22.7	11.3	758	36.3	1.6	46 644	0.0	2 823	6.1	42 390	32.9	22.5
Marion	11 282	73.3	115 700	23.0	10.6	617	31.1	3.2	11 768	0.8	813	6.9	11 505	26.6	35.5

1. Specified owner-occupied units.　　2. A value of 10.0 represents 10 percent or less; a value of 50.0 represents 50 percent or more.　　3. Specified renter-occupied units.
4. Overcrowded or lacking complete plumbing facilities.　　5. Percent of civilian labor force.　　6. Persons 16 years old and over.

Table B. States and Counties — Nonfarm Employment and Agriculture

STATE County	Private nonfarm establishments, employment and payroll, 2014									Agriculture, 2012			
	Number of establish-ments	Employment						Annual payroll		Farms			
		Total	Health care and social assistance	Manufac-turing	Retail trade	Finance and insurance	Professional, scientific, and technical services	Total (mil dol)	Average per employee (dollars)	Number	Fewer than 50 acres	500 acres or more	Farm operators whose principal occu-pation is farming (percent)
	104	105	106	107	108	109	110	111	112	113	114	115	116

SOUTH DAKOTA—Cont'd													
Tripp	210	1 671	D	D	383	D	52	47	28 351	629	12.6	58.8	65.5
Turner	266	1 595	372	188	237	D	D	51	31 684	794	26.4	30.6	57.4
Union	495	8 738	1 040	1 647	506	971	189	416	47 610	527	24.5	37.6	63.6
Walworth	218	2 032	384	D	359	82	82	59	29 058	256	18.0	48.8	60.5
Yankton	736	10 580	1 897	2 842	1 725	D	229	385	36 374	692	23.0	34.0	57.2
Ziebach	43	276	59	D	D	D	D	8	27 739	240	8.8	75.0	72.5
TENNESSEE	131 504	2 453 470	391 560	308 546	316 203	110 664	116 294	103 559	42 209	68 050	39.4	5.5	41.8
Anderson	1 503	37 860	3 741	9 981	3 384	919	8 936	2 176	57 466	441	52.4	1.4	34.0
Bedford	761	13 930	1 034	4 529	1 505	418	214	506	36 309	1 411	36.2	7.6	47.1
Benton	304	3 341	695	757	654	145	48	93	27 976	463	24.8	6.7	43.4
Bledsoe	94	526	93	55	D	45	D	14	27 511	579	28.5	5.4	40.6
Blount	2 248	41 175	6 250	D	5 642	2 303	D	1 776	43 135	980	52.0	2.7	45.6
Bradley	1 897	38 779	5 036	7 692	5 282	1 812	728	1 426	36 783	807	50.7	4.2	40.8
Campbell	588	7 311	1 874	1 691	1 528	270	D	206	28 198	370	41.9	1.4	41.9
Cannon	174	1 474	375	D	213	47	D	48	32 554	717	36.7	3.6	43.1
Carroll	431	6 145	1 603	914	735	281	97	191	31 097	732	31.3	7.9	40.2
Carter	702	9 085	2 060	1 048	1 770	329	173	245	26 955	493	51.7	1.6	37.7
Cheatham	551	5 842	596	D	834	152	135	218	37 395	415	38.8	2.9	46.5
Chester	234	2 995	396	427	439	105	D	77	25 793	391	32.5	4.3	26.6
Claiborne	410	7 068	1 160	1 869	796	256	146	227	32 073	945	36.3	3.6	40.2
Clay	107	1 118	D	D	148	34	D	30	27 099	424	23.6	7.8	47.2
Cocke	471	5 919	903	1 579	1 389	199	88	186	31 450	625	39.8	1.0	44.6
Coffee	1 208	20 007	3 069	4 541	3 004	781	2 471	810	40 480	895	47.4	7.9	36.0
Crockett	223	2 452	470	D	267	80	37	85	34 632	369	35.8	17.6	45.3
Cumberland	1 058	14 325	2 776	2 484	2 573	453	272	459	32 044	764	39.4	7.5	36.8
Davidson	18 619	418 413	77 616	18 717	39 578	21 213	33 274	20 636	49 319	360	49.2	2.2	40.8
Decatur	209	2 995	1 145	411	343	106	43	102	34 132	405	22.2	7.2	40.7
DeKalb	282	4 059	581	1 810	503	93	D	139	34 300	637	37.2	4.9	38.8
Dickson	904	13 153	2 111	3 496	2 247	456	199	446	33 878	1 143	36.7	3.8	33.8
Dyer	776	12 174	1 872	3 659	2 118	487	173	426	35 015	449	34.5	22.5	50.6
Fayette	581	6 555	578	1 689	891	D	D	261	39 878	745	33.0	12.8	41.3
Fentress	233	4 452	630	289	575	172	47	122	27 431	536	38.4	6.5	45.5
Franklin	678	10 837	1 705	2 920	1 401	260	177	409	37 750	861	48.0	5.3	40.0
Gibson	927	10 764	2 027	2 160	2 085	420	214	339	31 511	830	40.0	13.3	40.8
Giles	527	8 112	951	3 045	1 264	281	131	301	37 054	1 692	28.9	4.4	40.7
Grainger	223	2 318	202	955	372	D	D	68	29 541	885	40.7	0.8	43.3
Greene	1 092	21 694	4 343	5 929	2 806	D	370	690	31 805	2 529	49.8	1.4	46.9
Grundy	164	1 313	360	295	276	D	D	33	24 958	278	42.1	2.5	34.5
Hamblen	1 265	26 816	4 024	9 035	3 875	515	292	931	34 720	569	49.4	1.9	48.7
Hamilton	8 740	180 791	26 139	25 734	20 382	11 546	7 639	7 106	39 303	561	53.8	3.2	39.2
Hancock	45	371	165	NA	106	D	D	12	31 563	457	28.9	4.4	40.0
Hardeman	356	5 364	1 124	D	624	168	D	180	33 639	579	24.2	11.2	31.6
Hardin	486	6 366	1 155	1 789	1 215	196	74	234	36 806	589	29.2	11.9	37.4
Hawkins	583	9 544	1 367	3 786	1 349	242	D	333	34 926	1 437	42.7	1.3	45.4
Haywood	312	4 516	D	D	620	D	D	172	38 134	413	31.2	19.9	44.8
Henderson	484	6 466	980	1 677	1 088	D	104	189	29 306	844	24.6	6.5	32.0
Henry	703	8 406	1 422	1 433	1 607	337	278	268	31 837	826	30.4	10.8	41.3
Hickman	249	2 268	555	537	287	D	D	73	32 316	639	27.4	8.1	39.7
Houston	106	1 070	D	221	140	39	D	29	27 136	338	29.9	6.8	47.9
Humphreys	328	3 864	635	1 253	602	D	D	171	44 342	598	30.3	12.0	36.8
Jackson	96	936	128	D	116	28	D	38	40 865	499	32.5	5.6	38.7
Jefferson	658	10 402	1 188	1 669	1 794	265	150	353	33 921	981	45.9	1.4	43.7
Johnson	241	2 951	639	568	390	111	44	110	37 296	476	45.0	1.9	37.0
Knox	10 949	207 005	33 441	10 502	30 053	10 396	9 333	8 259	39 897	912	55.8	1.0	45.5
Lake	75	601	D	NA	144	D	NA	16	26 221	60	16.7	41.7	58.3
Lauderdale	293	4 752	696	1 023	706	183	35	153	32 156	457	34.4	15.5	37.4
Lawrence	699	8 370	1 291	1 715	1 581	254	206	246	29 447	1 559	36.4	5.6	42.3
Lewis	208	1 936	568	304	420	77	41	51	26 278	222	40.5	5.9	44.6
Lincoln	584	7 555	864	2 795	1 345	212	139	261	34 518	1 595	33.1	6.1	37.6
Loudon	896	12 205	1 462	2 714	1 900	321	382	454	37 189	685	49.5	2.3	41.3
McMinn	879	15 034	2 130	5 558	2 148	522	239	567	37 728	1 043	44.8	3.9	44.1
McNairy	395	4 364	838	949	612	138	D	130	29 883	658	26.0	5.9	38.4
Macon	324	3 311	636	814	694	D	D	98	29 619	879	33.8	3.2	43.2
Madison	2 549	50 611	11 832	8 451	7 167	1 264	1 292	1 842	36 396	592	31.3	10.0	46.8
Marion	423	5 637	780	1 517	1 197	156	73	181	32 040	280	33.2	8.6	41.4

Table B. States and Counties — **Agriculture**

	Agriculture, 2012 (cont.)															
	Land in farms					Value of land and buildings (dollars)		Value of machinery and equipment, average per farm (dollars)	Value of products sold				Percent of farms with sales of:		Government payments	
			Acres								Percent from:					
STATE County	Acreage (1,000)	Percent change, 2007–2012	Average size of farm	Total irrigated (1,000)	Total cropland (1,000)	Average per farm	Average per acre		Total (mil dol)	Average per farm (dollars)	Crops	Live-stock and poultry products	$10,000 or more	$100,000 or more	Total ($1,000)	Percent of farms
	117	118	119	120	121	122	123	124	125	126	127	128	129	130	131	132
SOUTH DAKOTA—Cont'd																
Tripp	1 019	0.5	1 620	2.7	477.8	1 810 404	1 118	224 453	229.0	364 110	37.8	62.2	74.6	49.9	5 336	83.1
Turner	384	3.5	484	18.3	329.3	2 089 242	4 316	248 820	182.2	229 447	55.4	44.6	67.3	36.3	5 690	72.5
Union	288	3.4	547	41.4	259.3	2 743 670	5 012	281 402	158.4	300 653	67.2	32.8	70.2	45.2	4 998	80.8
Walworth	445	0.1	1 737	1.9	245.7	2 572 492	1 481	343 938	117.8	460 305	75.6	24.4	62.1	47.3	3 077	78.1
Yankton	328	1.7	474	15.5	265.0	1 962 231	4 142	221 565	117.4	169 691	48.4	51.6	62.4	33.1	4 604	81.5
Ziebach	1 108	4.7	4 618	0.0	175.6	2 194 488	475	163 100	49.8	207 504	38.7	61.3	75.0	42.9	2 580	56.7
TENNESSEE	10 868	-0.9	160	146.4	5 329.7	569 416	3 565	69 244	3 611.0	53 065	57.8	42.2	30.2	6.1	67 665	23.8
Anderson	36	-10.7	81	0.1	10.2	475 961	5 856	61 673	3.6	8 102	21.2	78.8	13.2	1.6	36	7.3
Bedford	232	0.5	165	0.5	88.6	629 255	3 821	62 006	107.3	76 062	9.8	90.2	37.7	8.9	811	18.9
Benton	88	21.2	190	0.0	38.5	425 503	2 241	67 212	10.8	23 348	67.9	32.1	29.4	3.9	606	39.1
Bledsoe	102	11.1	177	0.8	42.6	619 174	3 506	74 772	42.7	73 789	24.9	75.1	42.3	11.2	96	10.5
Blount	101	2.4	103	0.6	42.8	700 027	6 811	59 394	17.0	17 341	36.6	63.4	28.7	3.4	234	11.1
Bradley	87	-9.4	107	0.1	28.6	583 543	5 439	57 476	115.7	143 376	5.5	94.5	30.1	11.3	217	8.7
Campbell	33	-2.0	91	0.1	11.5	338 165	3 736	58 478	3.3	9 041	22.3	77.7	18.9	1.1	50	9.2
Cannon	96	-17.5	134	0.1	38.5	415 745	3 097	55 290	21.1	29 431	49.3	50.7	27.3	5.7	381	14.1
Carroll	178	-1.0	243	2.0	121.4	595 486	2 450	92 384	62.2	84 956	95.1	4.9	25.4	6.7	2 510	50.3
Carter	40	2.3	82	0.0	12.4	427 787	5 238	49 771	8.6	17 377	18.9	81.1	24.1	2.8	95	13.4
Cheatham	52	-17.0	126	0.2	20.8	539 161	4 270	71 566	11.4	27 436	73.7	26.3	30.1	6.3	155	18.3
Chester	61	-15.1	156	0.5	28.1	300 294	1 928	52 100	10.0	25 683	80.8	19.2	25.1	4.6	404	48.8
Claiborne	121	-2.6	129	0.0	34.4	394 144	3 066	52 611	18.7	19 773	12.1	87.9	25.0	1.7	380	31.2
Clay	80	2.5	188	0.0	27.3	522 627	2 779	67 042	36.3	85 526	12.0	88.0	44.3	9.0	373	24.3
Cocke	61	-4.8	98	0.8	20.4	358 320	3 668	49 451	27.9	44 584	36.7	63.3	22.4	2.7	189	16.6
Coffee	145	3.5	162	2.6	79.0	572 818	3 540	80 251	60.8	67 884	64.7	35.3	32.5	10.1	1 075	22.3
Crockett	131	-12.5	354	4.2	112.1	1 003 241	2 836	150 220	62.1	168 247	95.5	4.5	48.2	22.0	2 946	69.1
Cumberland	129	5.3	169	0.1	49.5	643 314	3 807	70 047	34.1	44 685	37.9	62.1	29.7	5.0	264	10.2
Davidson	35	-15.8	97	0.4	11.3	601 725	6 221	58 703	D	D	D	D	16.1	1.1	55	4.2
Decatur	77	1.2	191	0.0	25.0	410 128	2 150	60 484	8.1	20 037	55.6	44.4	30.1	2.5	301	34.3
DeKalb	90	-6.0	141	1.0	33.5	451 124	3 209	64 680	62.7	98 447	91.4	8.6	31.4	5.2	154	17.9
Dickson	149	6.7	130	0.2	46.1	432 552	3 329	52 872	14.0	12 209	40.0	60.0	23.6	1.7	153	11.6
Dyer	212	-11.3	471	16.5	188.3	1 182 490	2 508	188 944	108.4	241 408	94.9	5.1	51.4	26.9	2 426	63.3
Fayette	229	0.7	307	5.3	147.4	965 636	3 141	113 322	75.3	101 050	90.2	9.8	26.8	9.1	2 515	44.0
Fentress	91	7.7	169	0.0	26.3	543 444	3 207	70 149	41.0	76 515	8.9	91.1	41.4	9.5	400	17.4
Franklin	125	-13.1	146	1.9	74.8	567 243	3 897	82 614	81.4	94 565	43.9	56.1	37.0	10.9	683	23.9
Gibson	286	-0.2	345	5.0	250.2	1 065 437	3 090	153 169	145.2	174 923	94.6	5.4	39.2	16.6	4 101	62.3
Giles	270	3.3	160	2.4	88.4	468 997	2 938	62 255	45.8	27 075	36.8	63.2	32.8	3.3	955	19.3
Grainger	85	-7.2	96	0.4	25.8	366 236	3 803	49 200	18.9	21 367	57.7	42.3	27.2	2.4	233	22.4
Greene	226	-1.4	89	0.4	90.8	362 074	4 052	56 139	85.6	33 859	15.3	84.7	26.9	3.6	1 135	23.6
Grundy	33	-22.5	119	0.5	14.2	340 791	2 864	50 061	17.7	63 507	48.4	51.6	33.5	6.8	61	9.7
Hamblen	59	-15.2	103	D	27.3	484 123	4 682	60 812	29.0	51 051	38.3	61.7	28.8	3.7	313	13.5
Hamilton	52	-4.2	93	0.1	19.7	527 171	5 654	57 647	12.4	22 182	16.9	83.1	19.6	2.9	114	5.7
Hancock	64	6.2	141	D	15.6	323 665	2 297	44 394	5.5	11 993	10.3	89.7	28.7	1.5	162	28.2
Hardeman	154	4.0	266	1.1	78.2	678 563	2 554	73 984	30.3	52 252	87.2	12.8	22.3	6.0	1 411	50.4
Hardin	126	15.0	214	1.9	59.9	542 166	2 531	66 596	22.1	37 554	81.7	18.3	31.2	6.3	849	39.0
Hawkins	133	-11.7	93	0.2	42.3	326 872	3 522	45 740	18.1	12 602	36.4	63.6	20.9	1.1	451	26.8
Haywood	219	2.4	531	14.2	197.0	1 916 540	3 608	210 751	125.6	304 107	98.6	1.4	40.7	23.0	3 018	70.0
Henderson	162	-1.9	192	0.1	79.8	424 276	2 207	64 594	35.3	41 831	73.9	26.1	31.4	5.9	1 264	50.4
Henry	205	5.8	248	4.4	131.6	688 305	2 779	98 464	91.6	110 849	62.1	37.9	36.3	14.8	2 181	48.8
Hickman	121	7.7	189	0.4	39.3	452 828	2 394	56 521	12.9	20 233	50.4	49.6	32.1	2.7	291	20.3
Houston	50	6.6	149	D	11.8	337 740	2 269	57 231	9.0	26 521	4.9	95.1	26.3	7.4	94	12.4
Humphreys	123	4.3	207	0.3	40.8	587 381	2 844	66 271	15.3	25 517	56.4	43.6	28.9	4.2	343	12.2
Jackson	74	-2.5	148	0.0	19.5	427 545	2 894	46 649	5.0	9 928	47.5	52.5	17.2	1.0	452	23.8
Jefferson	96	-5.9	97	0.5	37.7	526 143	5 400	55 272	30.7	31 318	15.3	84.7	26.7	3.3	441	16.3
Johnson	47	8.8	100	0.0	16.1	474 284	4 764	55 954	9.1	19 046	24.0	76.0	29.6	3.6	226	21.2
Knox	65	-21.2	72	0.2	24.5	549 549	7 670	49 402	14.6	16 035	59.3	40.7	17.5	1.0	241	10.0
Lake	80	-5.2	1 329	15.4	78.1	4 373 900	3 291	611 450	51.8	863 000	99.8	0.2	83.3	51.7	868	90.0
Lauderdale	201	4.5	439	13.2	172.5	1 373 934	3 127	155 593	97.3	212 827	97.2	2.8	32.6	17.5	2 290	65.4
Lawrence	236	-1.1	151	0.8	105.5	400 664	2 649	55 580	65.3	41 875	51.0	49.0	34.3	5.6	1 223	23.8
Lewis	31	-13.6	138	0.1	9.6	360 077	2 602	44 788	3.1	13 860	15.8	84.2	27.0	4.5	46	14.4
Lincoln	266	1.9	167	4.0	108.2	562 043	3 371	70 241	110.5	69 283	33.5	66.5	37.2	6.7	1 066	17.5
Loudon	69	-9.9	101	0.1	33.1	549 140	5 422	77 477	77.5	113 093	77.3	22.7	24.7	4.2	177	17.7
McMinn	122	-0.1	117	0.2	48.2	480 752	4 098	61 846	37.9	36 379	12.1	87.9	24.7	4.0	473	13.0
McNairy	130	5.9	198	D	61.5	426 061	2 157	58 903	23.0	35 026	87.3	12.7	23.9	4.0	929	47.7
Macon	122	-4.6	139	0.2	47.6	474 719	3 424	56 597	44.7	50 857	59.8	40.2	33.0	7.4	869	34.6
Madison	166	-6.3	280	7.9	117.9	706 385	2 520	101 103	66.0	111 552	94.4	5.6	30.9	11.0	2 288	61.8
Marion	51	0.3	181	0.1	22.0	533 475	2 942	88 682	13.1	46 918	46.3	53.7	33.6	8.2	183	11.8

STATE County	Water use, 2010		Wholesale trade,[1] 2012				Retail trade,[2] 2012				Real estate and rental and leasing,[2] 2012			
	Total water withdrawn (mil gal/day)	Gallons withdrawn per person per day	Number of establishments	Number of employees	Sales (mil dol)	Annual payroll (mil dol)	Number of establishments	Number of employees	Sales (mil dol)	Annual payroll (mil dol)	Number of establishments	Number of employees	Receipts (mil dol)	Annual payroll (mil dol)
	133	134	135	136	137	138	139	140	141	142	143	144	145	146
SOUTH DAKOTA—Cont'd														
Tripp	11.5	2 032	14	132	130.1	5.2	47	384	104.3	8.4	4	2	0.4	0.0
Turner	4.4	524	16	107	250.4	4.9	33	269	46.6	4.1	4	D	D	D
Union	6.8	472	35	641	1 135.3	39.1	46	422	153.2	7.8	21	40	9.1	1.9
Walworth	13.5	2 473	9	73	351.0	3.3	41	366	88.8	6.6	6	D	D	D
Yankton	19.3	859	32	240	213.8	10.3	121	1 554	368.6	34.5	21	51	7.6	1.4
Ziebach	0.5	168	4	D	D	D	8	62	15.8	0.9	2	D	D	D
TENNESSEE	7 696.6	1 213	5 828	92 537	111 718.4	4 863.3	22 615	306 078	91 641.6	7 420.3	5 470	30 593	6 178.4	1 220.0
Anderson	307.7	4 096	41	449	591.5	19.5	242	3 510	916.1	76.6	57	184	38.5	6.9
Bedford	16.0	354	24	D	D	D	150	1 502	407.6	34.3	31	154	27.4	5.1
Benton	2.5	149	11	D	D	D	59	631	150.9	13.5	4	9	1.5	0.2
Bledsoe	3.1	238	3	D	D	D	19	127	53.2	3.8	4	6	0.9	0.2
Blount	16.0	130	86	D	D	D	360	5 651	1 441.2	144.2	84	334	70.7	10.9
Bradley	19.0	192	60	D	D	D	363	4 676	1 335.0	111.7	62	D	D	D
Campbell	4.7	115	13	58	46.9	2.5	132	1 492	401.5	33.0	24	62	8.1	1.5
Cannon	2.0	143	5	D	D	D	34	213	61.2	4.7	2	D	D	D
Carroll	5.6	198	14	D	D	D	98	846	204.4	16.6	13	57	7.1	0.9
Carter	20.2	351	12	D	D	D	131	1 692	431.2	35.0	23	61	9.5	1.6
Cheatham	4.4	112	10	D	D	D	76	797	225.8	18.0	17	37	7.4	0.9
Chester	1.9	110	8	38	35.3	1.1	57	440	132.9	10.0	8	15	2.8	0.3
Claiborne	4.3	132	10	D	D	D	86	768	170.1	16.5	19	48	5.3	1.2
Clay	13.7	1 744	2	D	D	D	26	159	37.7	2.8	6	25	1.5	0.2
Cocke	6.9	193	5	D	D	D	112	1 271	341.0	28.7	17	113	5.9	1.5
Coffee	9.3	176	38	456	269.6	20.1	255	2 834	827.6	67.1	39	144	20.9	4.2
Crockett	4.3	298	15	272	352.2	16.4	39	266	78.5	5.1	5	12	3.8	0.2
Cumberland	8.3	147	38	D	D	D	229	2 632	750.3	61.1	39	139	19.1	3.6
Davidson	163.4	261	923	17 595	17 607.0	1 115.0	2 575	37 506	10 138.3	989.0	897	6 348	1 410.7	284.0
Decatur	2.2	189	4	D	D	D	45	335	76.5	7.1	4	7	0.5	0.1
DeKalb	3.1	164	9	D	D	D	51	493	107.3	10.0	10	15	1.7	0.5
Dickson	6.2	125	28	525	513.7	22.7	179	2 198	714.7	49.8	32	74	10.8	1.8
Dyer	13.5	352	40	D	D	D	169	2 053	580.8	50.8	25	72	12.8	3.2
Fayette	6.9	179	24	D	D	D	86	924	216.1	19.8	14	24	4.4	0.6
Fentress	2.3	130	5	10	5.4	0.3	50	599	145.6	12.4	6	92	10.0	2.8
Franklin	41.1	1 000	12	D	D	D	144	1 379	410.4	32.4	16	D	D	D
Gibson	8.6	173	32	367	310.4	15.7	192	1 992	505.8	42.5	26	71	18.0	2.2
Giles	5.4	181	25	273	189.1	12.4	124	1 342	317.1	27.8	9	37	2.6	0.9
Grainger	4.4	195	1	D	D	D	51	351	89.9	7.3	10	7	1.4	0.2
Greene	12.6	184	31	365	181.8	12.3	205	2 642	686.2	56.2	34	129	18.4	2.6
Grundy	2.6	187	3	4	0.6	0.1	47	306	72.1	5.9	1	D	D	D
Hamblen	10.0	161	50	D	D	D	265	3 888	978.7	93.5	53	165	33.2	4.6
Hamilton	1 968.0	5 849	437	5 317	2 904.0	266.3	1 410	19 752	5 236.5	485.2	375	2 092	418.4	97.5
Hancock	0.7	103	2	D	D	D	16	107	24.7	1.8	3	D	D	D
Hardeman	4.2	155	11	76	69.5	3.0	77	629	147.9	12.6	6	22	1.5	0.5
Hardin	29.4	1 128	15	98	228.0	4.2	113	1 269	396.7	30.6	20	55	8.3	2.0
Hawkins	355.5	6 255	19	167	89.1	6.2	113	1 233	303.1	25.1	24	91	11.3	2.6
Haywood	7.6	407	10	107	68.1	3.5	59	630	207.6	12.7	9	30	3.2	0.9
Henderson	4.0	145	15	224	56.5	5.8	103	1 094	296.9	23.5	8	D	D	D
Henry	5.7	177	25	581	159.4	18.4	139	1 604	489.5	40.5	26	84	15.2	2.2
Hickman	3.3	134	13	58	45.3	2.1	48	293	71.4	5.9	5	16	0.8	0.2
Houston	1.4	171	1	D	D	D	21	154	35.3	3.2	2	D	D	D
Humphreys	737.3	39 775	13	86	111.3	5.4	65	585	185.7	12.0	8	19	1.3	0.3
Jackson	1.1	97	4	D	D	D	22	102	30.9	1.8	1	D	D	D
Jefferson	8.2	160	18	D	D	D	126	1 786	640.4	38.4	26	132	28.8	4.3
Johnson	2.8	152	4	D	D	D	55	453	108.8	8.3	14	34	3.5	0.4
Knox	71.8	166	655	9 371	5 382.5	494.3	1 764	29 577	7 926.7	733.1	559	3 312	618.3	123.8
Lake	5.3	679	6	D	D	D	21	154	29.8	2.6	3	8	1.0	0.2
Lauderdale	6.7	239	19	818	1 545.9	35.0	78	688	161.7	14.5	17	56	18.0	2.1
Lawrence	6.6	157	33	258	157.6	9.2	172	1 512	384.2	34.2	18	61	8.2	1.4
Lewis	2.1	169	5	D	D	D	41	394	179.5	10.1	3	6	0.7	0.1
Lincoln	9.5	286	22	248	385.1	11.7	128	1 240	316.8	30.7	19	122	8.5	2.8
Loudon	18.2	374	41	D	D	D	150	1 857	484.0	41.7	32	131	14.8	3.5
McMinn	68.9	1 318	29	D	D	D	172	1 940	542.4	42.9	33	132	18.2	3.3
McNairy	4.2	160	15	130	44.2	6.3	83	615	154.8	14.0	8	30	3.9	0.7
Macon	3.5	155	10	78	18.7	2.0	70	666	177.4	14.7	16	50	3.4	0.5
Madison	16.6	168	141	1 485	808.6	65.7	469	7 050	1 902.6	162.4	104	546	86.8	16.9
Marion	4.0	142	19	159	69.1	6.2	99	1 112	336.2	25.4	5	21	2.6	0.5

1. Merchant wholesalers, except manufacturers' sales branches and offices. 2. Employer establishments.

Table B. States and Counties — **Professional Services, Manufacturing, and Accommodation and Food Services**

STATE County	Professional, scientific, and technical services, 2012				Manufacturing, 2012				Accommodation and food services, 2012			
	Number of establishments	Number of employees	Receipts (mil dol)	Annual payroll (mil dol)	Number of establishments	Number of employees	Receipts (mil dol)	Annual payroll (mil dol)	Number of establishments	Number of employees	Sales (mil dol)	Annual payroll (mil dol)
	147	148	149	150	151	152	153	154	155	156	157	158
SOUTH DAKOTA—Cont'd												
Tripp	15	51	6.4	1.7	6	68	D	D	23	166	8.0	2.0
Turner	15	43	9.0	1.6	11	172	D	7.6	20	86	3.5	0.7
Union	49	188	30.9	9.8	23	1 502	D	63.3	40	416	18.5	4.6
Walworth	18	90	9.6	2.8	4	103	D	D	28	428	27.1	6.7
Yankton	45	228	28.4	9.1	29	2 808	849.2	114.8	65	1 013	44.8	12.3
Ziebach	2	D	D	D	NA	NA	NA	NA	4	D	D	D
TENNESSEE	10 863	104 552	14 199.5	6 129.5	5 823	293 646	139 960.5	14 180.5	12 004	241 348	12 499.0	3 546.5
Anderson	201	9 551	871.7	742.0	94	9 177	2 224.0	598.3	132	2 690	127.1	35.0
Bedford	48	218	18.8	6.0	52	3 882	1 121.4	138.4	54	833	40.2	10.9
Benton	14	56	4.2	1.3	19	596	96.3	19.1	30	D	D	D
Bledsoe	6	8	0.6	0.2	7	D	9.9	D	4	D	D	D
Blount	175	D	D	D	107	5 417	3 761.4	306.1	210	4 526	229.8	68.3
Bradley	142	853	76.2	32.0	113	7 961	D	339.8	178	3 538	168.3	44.5
Campbell	26	D	D	D	34	980	235.9	38.6	55	D	D	D
Cannon	12	27	1.9	0.6	14	290	26.1	8.8	10	D	D	D
Carroll	29	114	9.2	3.6	26	727	612.5	35.5	32	398	19.5	4.3
Carter	44	141	12.2	3.7	35	1 007	188.4	40.2	65	1 203	48.5	15.4
Cheatham	37	140	21.8	4.9	39	1 905	820.2	83.4	40	545	26.0	6.7
Chester	13	D	D	D	20	388	76.1	16.7	25	D	D	D
Claiborne	29	D	D	D	32	1 860	327.9	56.7	29	463	23.6	5.7
Clay	4	9	0.7	0.1	9	274	D	7.0	10	D	D	D
Cocke	27	102	7.5	2.4	30	1 486	659.6	69.1	65	915	48.2	13.1
Coffee	83	3 159	361.0	174.2	79	4 443	D	211.8	108	1 893	89.8	23.6
Crockett	10	D	D	D	14	238	127.9	13.7	10	D	D	D
Cumberland	68	248	30.5	7.7	58	2 099	678.0	79.4	97	1 570	101.2	24.9
Davidson	1 930	24 182	4 021.7	1 641.1	552	18 154	7 319.4	851.8	1 714	40 106	2 573.8	759.3
Decatur	16	D	D	D	22	443	117.0	19.0	20	159	7.9	1.7
DeKalb	24	105	7.8	2.9	20	2 359	672.0	80.2	22	284	13.1	3.8
Dickson	53	199	20.5	7.7	47	3 214	775.7	132.0	92	1 396	67.1	19.0
Dyer	45	191	18.5	5.9	40	3 705	1 455.6	146.6	58	949	42.4	10.8
Fayette	32	338	15.5	8.1	46	1 831	814.3	85.5	42	557	22.5	5.4
Fentress	14	43	3.7	0.8	20	298	39.1	10.6	19	D	D	D
Franklin	37	D	D	D	45	D	3 643.1	D	55	D	D	D
Gibson	47	219	14.3	4.8	58	2 620	737.8	116.9	65	985	45.0	11.0
Giles	36	151	12.8	5.2	43	2 376	1 040.2	107.9	46	639	24.8	6.4
Grainger	10	D	D	D	25	867	138.8	25.7	14	D	D	D
Greene	81	279	31.2	9.3	96	5 209	1 771.1	226.8	117	1 658	77.8	21.5
Grundy	7	D	D	D	16	359	D	8.6	13	157	7.2	1.9
Hamblen	70	281	24.8	10.1	101	8 609	3 235.8	357.6	110	1 995	99.2	26.1
Hamilton	787	7 803	1 053.0	390.3	411	25 092	12 127.5	1 323.1	830	17 426	903.3	256.9
Hancock	1	D	D	D	NA	NA	NA	NA	3	38	1.8	0.5
Hardeman	13	44	3.0	0.6	22	1 566	D	57.3	25	229	13.1	3.1
Hardin	31	94	7.5	2.1	34	1 674	743.9	91.7	54	653	31.7	8.2
Hawkins	34	90	11.5	3.1	41	3 475	1 328.3	151.3	67	911	38.1	10.8
Haywood	15	80	4.6	2.0	17	1 798	597.8	73.5	32	288	14.5	3.5
Henderson	32	D	D	D	35	1 202	362.4	48.2	37	656	26.2	6.2
Henry	40	264	18.3	8.4	39	1 358	277.8	51.4	65	798	33.1	9.2
Hickman	9	34	2.4	0.9	24	544	124.4	18.5	22	D	D	D
Houston	5	21	2.3	0.5	7	207	23.2	6.8	16	D	D	D
Humphreys	14	66	4.7	2.0	23	1 353	2 099.1	95.2	40	385	18.1	5.0
Jackson	5	D	D	D	NA	NA	NA	NA	5	D	D	D
Jefferson	40	157	23.9	4.1	43	1 596	988.3	60.5	68	1 070	53.1	14.5
Johnson	14	44	7.4	1.3	18	758	165.4	32.6	22	254	9.3	2.7
Knox	1 153	D	D	D	360	11 934	4 816.9	645.3	934	21 794	1 039.3	315.2
Lake	2	D	D	D	NA	NA	NA	NA	11	135	5.2	1.4
Lauderdale	13	33	3.4	0.8	12	953	209.1	36.4	19	D	D	D
Lawrence	42	177	19.9	5.5	50	1 683	397.6	64.6	49	851	44.6	10.8
Lewis	15	36	2.6	0.8	20	259	46.0	8.1	17	D	D	D
Lincoln	38	154	14.3	4.9	31	2 363	D	79.7	48	545	26.7	6.6
Loudon	53	D	D	D	50	2 804	1 424.2	136.8	77	1 366	64.6	19.3
McMinn	52	350	17.4	5.5	62	4 642	2 196.6	248.2	92	1 539	69.6	18.3
McNairy	19	68	6.2	1.6	49	1 328	352.1	47.6	31	435	15.4	4.4
Macon	25	53	6.3	1.7	35	771	214.2	27.3	24	221	12.0	2.6
Madison	171	1 810	129.4	70.3	101	8 726	4 374.7	406.6	221	4 750	222.5	62.9
Marion	20	77	6.1	2.7	27	1 374	D	59.6	51	D	D	D

1. Establishment subject to federal tax.

Table B. States and Counties — Health Care and Social Assistance, Other Services, Nonemployer Businesses, and Residential Construction

STATE County	Health care and social assistance, 2012				Other services, 2012				Nonemployer businesses, 2014		Value of residential construction authorized by building permits, 2015	
	Number of establishments	Number of employees	Receipts (mil dol)	Annual payroll (mil dol)	Number of establishments	Number of employees	Receipts (mil dol)	Annual payroll (mil dol)	Number	Receipts (mil dol)	New Construction ($1,000)	Number of housing units
	159	160	161	162	163	164	165	166	167	168	169	170
SOUTH DAKOTA—Cont'd												
Tripp	19	434	31.6	13.2	16	75	6.4	1.3	542	28.8	1 590	11
Turner	25	412	21.1	10.4	10	D	D	D	753	33.3	3 639	14
Union	57	1 070	143.3	54.5	30	D	D	D	1 319	82.0	34 437	137
Walworth	12	397	26.0	12.1	20	106	6.6	1.9	450	18.7	3 076	22
Yankton	72	2 028	193.2	83.9	58	243	21.8	5.0	1 545	65.4	17 608	134
Ziebach	8	D	D	D	1	D	D	D	63	2.2	NA	NA
TENNESSEE	14 897	380 453	42 383.7	16 227.9	8 117	55 990	6 525.8	1 711.4	487 341	22 033.7	5 596 464	32 219
Anderson	189	4 140	424.7	164.7	111	491	44.8	13.1	4 587	190.3	24 699	120
Bedford	96	986	86.8	32.6	38	257	19.5	6.2	2 917	122.5	28 187	161
Benton	38	672	51.6	18.0	19	D	D	D	1 034	34.4	515	3
Bledsoe	9	D	D	D	2	D	D	D	828	29.0	0	0
Blount	247	6 554	561.5	249.4	161	896	85.3	28.8	8 631	361.9	105 343	631
Bradley	230	4 659	622.9	188.2	94	851	70.9	21.4	6 870	340.3	64 606	578
Campbell	69	2 191	172.8	68.3	32	D	D	D	2 437	96.3	20 415	191
Cannon	17	377	24.8	11.3	10	D	D	D	1 040	43.1	1 388	11
Carroll	67	1 721	111.5	49.8	23	D	D	D	1 543	56.1	987	6
Carter	81	1 782	147.9	59.7	40	D	D	D	3 269	112.3	13 144	110
Cheatham	46	567	44.5	17.2	26	D	D	D	3 374	150.2	22 339	121
Chester	28	455	26.9	12.4	10	D	D	D	1 009	44.8	1 256	13
Claiborne	52	1 227	84.4	37.9	32	D	D	D	1 866	76.4	12 185	87
Clay	9	373	13.0	6.0	3	D	D	D	715	22.1	1 994	13
Cocke	40	1 017	102.7	37.5	26	D	D	D	2 210	68.3	85	2
Coffee	197	3 056	305.8	107.0	70	278	21.4	5.9	3 459	134.9	17 126	132
Crockett	29	515	31.6	13.3	10	D	D	D	914	35.7	0	0
Cumberland	138	3 018	386.0	91.9	66	580	33.4	12.8	4 385	189.2	54 323	262
Davidson	1 819	62 989	8 547.7	3 158.0	1 225	11 665	1 369.2	407.5	65 079	3 400.6	1 386 523	8 197
Decatur	27	1 019	67.4	39.5	10	D	D	D	791	28.1	0	0
DeKalb	29	533	40.9	15.7	16	D	D	D	1 327	48.7	6 763	51
Dickson	122	2 129	260.3	85.4	45	D	D	D	3 741	158.2	41 118	211
Dyer	108	2 005	200.6	71.7	45	207	20.8	5.2	2 386	89.7	7 013	64
Fayette	54	611	44.1	20.0	29	113	9.7	2.7	3 275	155.9	60 898	236
Fentress	29	D	D	D	15	D	D	D	1 495	70.9	167	2
Franklin	84	1 577	149.7	53.3	50	273	30.7	6.5	2 687	92.4	21 991	127
Gibson	111	2 106	139.7	56.2	53	D	D	D	2 888	117.2	18 117	98
Giles	57	889	77.5	28.3	28	D	D	D	1 753	75.6	8 719	70
Grainger	15	232	11.9	5.6	14	D	D	D	1 475	59.3	6 558	37
Greene	136	4 034	298.1	127.4	60	356	27.9	8.0	4 088	150.1	17 653	105
Grundy	18	379	24.4	11.7	8	D	D	D	1 209	42.4	909	3
Hamblen	164	4 246	358.7	147.7	73	349	28.6	8.9	3 609	158.1	14 799	79
Hamilton	1 038	26 382	3 179.1	1 255.6	580	D	D	D	24 986	1 251.0	249 936	1 639
Hancock	12	182	16.6	5.7	2	D	D	D	416	10.6	0	0
Hardeman	40	1 149	76.9	36.5	16	D	D	D	1 452	49.0	8 796	88
Hardin	59	1 155	100.4	40.4	23	D	D	D	1 811	73.1	834	9
Hawkins	54	1 433	102.5	41.7	44	D	D	D	3 008	94.9	10 719	91
Haywood	27	470	37.7	15.4	21	D	D	D	1 093	39.9	2 403	16
Henderson	56	886	60.1	22.9	34	D	D	D	1 786	67.6	1 438	9
Henry	83	1 466	142.0	53.3	52	D	D	D	2 281	101.0	1 341	15
Hickman	23	D	D	D	15	D	D	D	1 707	62.7	9 383	53
Houston	15	408	28.5	12.6	5	D	D	D	517	22.8	275	1
Humphreys	30	595	47.3	15.1	22	D	D	D	1 148	44.2	1 083	10
Jackson	9	D	D	D	4	D	D	D	794	24.9	0	0
Jefferson	66	1 434	132.5	42.1	41	177	13.8	4.1	3 058	122.4	29 688	109
Johnson	23	575	42.8	17.1	9	D	D	D	1 039	36.3	200	1
Knox	1 244	36 221	4 262.2	1 514.8	730	5 946	547.5	191.1	34 486	1 797.6	307 784	1 737
Lake	11	D	D	D	4	D	D	D	337	8.0	321	6
Lauderdale	30	611	62.9	17.6	13	D	D	D	1 336	53.4	1 528	11
Lawrence	76	1 311	107.0	38.8	40	119	10.7	3.2	2 842	117.1	1 509	8
Lewis	26	492	23.9	10.7	10	D	D	D	884	39.2	452	5
Lincoln	54	843	59.4	25.7	37	D	D	D	2 299	97.3	1 404	8
Loudon	97	1 796	142.9	55.0	46	216	27.6	6.0	3 410	149.2	61 123	272
McMinn	108	1 805	177.0	62.4	48	219	18.9	5.0	2 996	121.9	1 716	15
McNairy	47	799	63.9	24.5	20	D	D	D	1 684	65.6	347	3
Macon	37	657	50.7	19.2	22	D	D	D	1 666	70.7	13 357	144
Madison	313	11 842	1 172.9	484.4	131	D	D	D	6 578	291.4	35 016	201
Marion	44	D	D	D	31	D	D	D	1 776	75.8	19 596	92

Table B. States and Counties — Government Employment and Payroll, and Local Government Finances

	Government employment and payroll, 2012									Local government finances, 2012				
			March payroll (percent of total)							General revenue				
													Taxes	
														Per capita[1] (dollars)
STATE County	Full-time equivalent employees	March payroll (dollars)	Administration, judicial, and legal	Police and Corrections	Fire Protection	Highways and transportation	Health and Welfare	Natural resources and utilities	Education and libraries	Total (mil dol)	Inter-governmental (mil dol)	Total (mil dol)	Total	Property
	171	172	173	174	175	176	177	178	179	180	181	182	183	184
SOUTH DAKOTA— Cont'd														
Tripp	313	855 393	8.1	15.4	0.0	7.0	3.8	9.9	55.0	19.6	5.9	10.3	1 882	1 410
Turner	279	817 829	8.0	3.7	0.0	8.8	0.3	5.1	73.1	26.4	8.0	14.2	1 711	1 477
Union	512	1 673 489	7.8	8.7	0.3	5.6	0.6	5.0	68.1	61.5	22.0	30.6	2 059	1 752
Walworth	221	589 011	7.5	16.1	0.1	6.5	1.9	2.6	64.6	20.6	9.1	7.9	1 440	1 024
Yankton	681	2 403 085	7.3	8.7	0.5	6.7	3.4	8.0	64.3	65.0	16.6	35.8	1 586	1 147
Ziebach	95	280 194	7.1	2.1	0.0	3.4	0.6	0.4	86.0	6.0	4.4	1.4	474	432
TENNESSEE	X	X	X	X	X	X	X	X	X	X	X	X	X	X
Anderson	3 051	10 709 572	8.9	7.5	4.2	3.4	1.7	10.8	62.8	221.7	89.4	94.0	1 246	741
Bedford	2 341	6 860 633	3.8	5.9	2.6	2.3	32.4	8.2	44.3	114.2	59.7	38.4	842	542
Benton	474	1 606 363	5.8	8.8	0.2	3.6	4.0	12.7	63.7	37.9	21.5	12.7	775	443
Bledsoe	594	1 386 704	5.7	6.0	0.0	3.7	3.2	3.2	63.4	34.4	25.2	6.2	483	381
Blount	6 070	20 455 931	4.4	6.6	1.8	2.2	37.0	5.4	41.5	528.9	111.3	129.7	1 044	749
Bradley	3 454	10 166 787	4.0	11.4	6.6	3.1	10.6	1.9	61.3	246.4	112.5	81.3	804	494
Campbell	1 510	4 358 532	4.9	7.7	2.4	5.5	4.9	19.0	54.0	98.1	55.2	27.6	684	390
Cannon	555	1 372 374	3.7	6.2	1.4	2.5	4.5	3.9	73.3	29.2	18.5	7.5	546	395
Carroll	1 139	3 140 304	5.3	9.1	1.3	4.5	0.7	12.9	62.8	71.5	41.1	18.0	635	428
Carter	1 973	5 071 600	5.5	8.9	2.0	4.0	1.2	9.8	68.0	111.1	63.2	34.7	606	404
Cheatham	1 170	3 416 461	8.9	8.5	1.2	3.8	4.2	5.4	66.2	87.0	44.5	32.3	824	545
Chester	583	1 479 520	6.9	10.4	1.3	4.6	3.5	4.5	63.6	35.4	21.8	9.2	537	327
Claiborne	1 693	4 650 708	4.4	4.7	0.0	1.8	36.9	4.7	46.4	101.7	41.7	19.7	620	402
Clay	346	836 185	8.5	6.7	0.0	5.7	8.6	7.4	60.8	19.6	11.9	5.0	642	405
Cocke	1 225	3 330 780	5.4	6.8	3.2	4.8	1.6	3.4	73.7	82.1	45.4	25.0	704	410
Coffee	2 224	6 075 717	5.2	8.5	3.3	2.4	3.8	13.4	59.9	153.4	61.5	58.5	1 099	624
Crockett	563	1 474 498	6.0	8.0	0.1	3.9	5.1	5.6	69.5	39.4	25.3	9.5	647	455
Cumberland	1 971	4 871 298	10.5	9.2	1.5	7.6	3.6	6.6	59.6	116.9	58.5	44.1	773	397
Davidson	22 627	87 554 648	6.2	13.1	7.2	2.6	9.0	12.5	47.7	2 674.3	751.4	1 227.6	1 894	1 220
Decatur	576	1 686 615	5.4	7.1	0.0	3.3	24.4	5.4	52.2	40.6	17.7	8.4	718	421
DeKalb	735	1 938 173	2.6	5.5	0.0	2.8	3.4	27.2	58.1	43.2	24.6	12.8	677	446
Dickson	1 972	5 546 728	7.3	6.8	2.6	2.4	3.9	17.9	57.6	141.4	60.1	55.8	1 108	644
Dyer	1 460	4 541 888	6.2	11.6	5.0	4.0	2.4	8.4	60.7	128.0	69.8	34.0	890	593
Fayette	1 075	2 824 788	9.0	14.5	2.4	0.3	4.2	5.6	62.7	63.0	30.1	24.0	622	428
Fentress	636	1 503 203	9.4	7.6	0.0	4.8	9.5	5.6	62.4	35.7	20.4	10.5	583	350
Franklin	1 139	3 326 510	2.9	9.5	1.7	3.7	1.6	11.4	69.2	91.2	43.8	33.8	829	597
Gibson	1 945	5 303 575	3.3	10.5	3.0	4.3	1.1	8.6	68.2	134.8	75.7	35.9	723	550
Giles	1 369	3 634 496	12.1	7.4	0.5	8.8	4.0	4.5	61.5	61.4	31.0	24.0	827	523
Grainger	662	1 667 581	3.5	8.8	0.0	0.6	5.1	2.8	78.1	45.9	30.1	11.3	496	384
Greene	2 317	6 964 692	4.1	9.6	2.3	3.1	6.4	13.2	60.6	142.8	69.9	48.8	709	420
Grundy	608	1 426 124	5.2	4.3	0.0	3.5	2.0	5.6	77.2	32.3	23.7	6.9	507	359
Hamblen	1 973	6 233 306	5.6	9.2	4.7	2.5	1.7	12.8	60.0	162.1	67.7	63.4	1 011	537
Hamilton	14 734	56 385 621	6.4	7.3	3.0	3.5	37.2	11.3	30.7	1 780.1	395.6	494.7	1 432	1 127
Hancock	347	800 025	10.1	7.0	0.2	6.6	20.3	2.7	53.2	20.3	13.2	2.7	407	312
Hardeman	1 079	2 839 972	5.5	9.2	1.0	3.5	5.9	11.2	62.9	64.6	37.7	18.1	684	425
Hardin	1 366	3 651 007	4.5	6.1	0.3	2.3	39.7	2.3	43.0	104.2	34.3	23.2	893	480
Hawkins	2 067	6 744 656	3.8	5.3	0.4	2.2	8.6	5.8	73.1	111.4	61.3	40.6	717	506
Haywood	942	2 633 709	7.9	9.5	3.1	3.5	5.1	9.8	55.4	60.5	32.7	17.9	982	679
Henderson	1 113	2 867 377	7.3	13.1	1.5	3.4	1.2	16.3	56.3	63.0	35.8	20.0	714	394
Henry	1 119	3 290 953	5.3	9.3	2.1	1.8	1.8	14.7	63.3	150.2	42.7	24.7	765	442
Hickman	1 002	2 269 272	16.1	6.3	0.5	2.3	4.1	5.8	61.1	54.5	34.7	13.4	554	369
Houston	381	990 105	9.2	11.3	0.4	5.4	8.2	5.2	59.0	21.6	14.5	4.9	585	382
Humphreys	1 002	3 913 409	14.1	4.3	0.1	2.3	9.0	4.1	63.2	46.8	26.1	15.5	851	526
Jackson	425	1 046 407	9.7	7.7	0.0	7.2	3.9	4.7	66.8	24.4	16.5	5.7	497	349
Jefferson	1 433	4 289 878	5.4	8.6	1.0	4.2	5.2	9.0	66.5	126.4	54.0	43.3	829	545
Johnson	620	1 243 277	8.2	8.9	0.0	5.0	2.1	6.1	68.5	37.2	23.2	8.9	494	360
Knox	13 135	45 220 953	5.5	12.5	2.9	3.2	3.7	15.3	55.2	1 270.2	389.9	630.9	1 430	810
Lake	321	873 740	15.6	15.9	0.2	6.0	4.5	10.1	47.6	18.1	11.6	3.5	457	287
Lauderdale	1 033	2 753 225	7.4	11.7	2.0	4.8	4.6	4.1	64.7	70.8	41.8	18.4	664	441
Lawrence	1 270	4 176 846	6.6	9.0	1.9	3.7	3.6	13.3	60.8	96.9	50.8	33.0	783	468
Lewis	515	1 074 509	10.9	12.0	0.6	6.6	1.4	6.6	61.8	31.6	21.1	6.6	554	298
Lincoln	1 457	3 836 126	5.1	6.7	1.8	3.0	1.0	26.5	54.5	110.1	39.6	20.1	599	348
Loudon	1 628	5 601 296	4.4	6.8	2.4	2.3	1.4	30.5	50.4	114.9	46.7	47.0	944	641
McMinn	2 013	6 789 227	4.8	5.9	1.4	2.2	24.9	7.7	47.8	109.5	59.5	34.1	651	417
McNairy	1 044	2 736 738	6.7	5.8	0.7	3.7	0.6	11.6	68.0	61.0	40.2	14.3	547	361
Macon	840	2 132 533	7.7	8.1	1.0	0.1	5.9	5.3	70.4	49.3	29.8	13.4	597	355
Madison	7 853	28 936 219	2.2	6.4	2.6	1.2	64.3	4.4	18.6	921.0	113.3	137.5	1 393	781
Marion	942	2 790 775	7.6	7.6	0.6	2.9	2.4	9.1	69.0	67.8	35.6	24.6	870	523

1. Based on the resident population estimated as of July 1 of the year shown.

Table B. States and Counties — Local Government Finances, Government Employment, and Voting

STATE County	Total (mil dol) 185	Per capita[1] (dollars) 186	Education 187	Health and hospitals 188	Police protection 189	Public welfare 190	Highways 191	Total (mil dol) 192	Per capita[1] (dollars) 193	Federal civilian 194	Federal military 195	State and local 196	Democratic 197	Republican 198	All other 199
SOUTH DAKOTA—Cont'd															
Tripp	20.4	3 717	42.1	1.5	4.2	0.3	17.5	16.4	2 990	29	33	368	32.2	65.5	2.3
Turner	25.7	3 093	49.0	0.7	4.4	0.2	18.6	21.3	2 563	26	49	399	38.6	58.3	3.1
Union	61.7	4 151	39.7	0.2	4.0	0.0	10.5	55.2	3 718	54	91	734	42.1	56.0	1.9
Walworth	18.8	3 440	49.6	0.6	5.7	0.1	11.1	8.2	1 510	30	32	387	34.8	62.9	2.2
Yankton	61.7	2 730	45.1	1.7	5.7	0.5	12.7	62.1	2 746	200	124	1 703	47.7	49.7	2.5
Ziebach	6.0	2 081	73.9	0.5	2.6	0.0	10.9	0.0	0	0	17	166	62.2	35.0	2.8
TENNESSEE	X	X	X	X	X	X	X	X	X	48 894	22 021	374 601	41.8	56.9	1.3
Anderson	264.4	3 506	58.7	2.4	7.0	0.0	3.3	316.3	4 194	893	239	4 183	36.1	62.3	1.6
Bedford	117.2	2 572	51.0	2.6	5.8	0.2	4.7	126.0	2 764	63	146	2 261	32.4	65.9	1.7
Benton	36.9	2 254	60.4	2.4	7.0	0.3	8.6	25.4	1 550	55	51	1 008	40.8	57.0	2.1
Bledsoe	29.7	2 318	58.9	3.4	3.8	0.3	6.6	28.6	2 232	19	38	1 013	31.7	66.2	2.1
Blount	501.3	4 037	31.7	37.6	3.9	0.0	2.2	1 376.5	11 085	237	416	7 430	29.5	68.9	1.6
Bradley	234.0	2 314	53.1	8.4	7.2	0.1	4.8	222.5	2 200	204	319	4 778	24.5	74.2	1.3
Campbell	109.0	2 696	46.6	2.9	5.5	0.1	5.8	125.9	3 115	77	125	1 958	30.6	67.6	1.8
Cannon	28.5	2 064	58.3	3.3	7.4	0.4	8.5	13.9	1 008	28	43	606	36.9	60.9	2.3
Carroll	72.3	2 547	58.4	0.4	6.1	0.2	7.2	63.9	2 250	77	87	1 533	34.2	64.0	1.8
Carter	118.2	2 060	67.1	0.7	5.7	0.0	4.3	105.8	1 845	75	176	2 585	25.7	72.8	1.5
Cheatham	93.0	2 367	69.6	2.1	5.4	0.3	4.2	61.6	1 568	73	125	1 502	33.5	65.1	1.4
Chester	35.0	2 039	59.3	1.0	5.7	0.4	11.6	19.6	1 140	31	51	1 016	27.8	71.0	1.2
Claiborne	96.3	3 036	42.5	32.9	3.7	0.0	3.6	69.4	2 188	55	96	2 010	29.5	68.9	1.6
Clay	20.9	2 663	48.6	6.1	6.2	0.2	10.9	14.3	1 818	43	24	441	41.7	56.0	2.3
Cocke	89.1	2 504	59.3	1.2	4.9	0.0	6.9	71.6	2 014	61	111	1 928	26.8	71.7	1.6
Coffee	162.9	3 060	57.5	2.0	5.5	0.1	4.0	222.3	4 176	463	223	3 226	34.3	63.7	2.0
Crockett	40.8	2 791	61.9	3.1	4.8	0.9	7.7	29.0	1 982	34	46	848	32.6	66.2	1.3
Cumberland	113.1	1 983	49.3	6.2	5.6	0.0	4.0	134.0	2 349	100	182	2 397	30.7	67.8	1.5
Davidson	2 727.2	4 207	31.0	8.4	7.3	1.2	1.6	6 313.0	9 738	7 874	2 478	38 216	59.9	38.9	1.2
Decatur	37.9	3 249	38.3	26.2	3.3	0.3	5.7	26.0	2 228	26	36	757	32.9	65.1	2.0
DeKalb	40.9	2 165	55.5	3.0	7.5	0.1	5.8	23.6	1 246	36	60	980	40.1	57.8	2.1
Dickson	126.9	2 520	53.8	2.4	7.4	0.0	4.2	145.3	2 885	82	160	2 472	38.5	59.8	1.7
Dyer	131.4	3 436	50.7	0.2	7.3	0.6	6.4	99.2	2 594	98	119	2 696	30.5	68.2	1.2
Fayette	62.3	1 611	54.0	3.2	7.9	0.0	9.2	51.2	1 325	51	122	1 475	35.8	63.2	1.0
Fentress	35.1	1 954	57.6	4.3	4.7	0.6	7.7	14.5	810	35	56	795	27.2	71.1	1.8
Franklin	85.2	2 091	56.5	0.5	7.5	0.1	5.2	83.2	2 040	128	125	2 068	37.9	60.5	1.6
Gibson	141.6	2 854	58.9	2.2	5.8	0.4	6.0	112.6	2 270	147	155	2 804	34.8	63.6	1.6
Giles	61.6	2 118	59.8	4.3	3.0	0.1	8.6	25.0	859	67	90	1 401	39.5	59.0	1.5
Grainger	44.5	1 960	64.7	3.7	4.6	0.0	7.6	29.5	1 301	52	72	969	27.5	70.6	1.9
Greene	138.3	2 009	61.2	3.2	5.4	0.0	7.0	106.4	1 546	218	211	3 443	28.8	69.5	1.7
Grundy	31.5	2 310	69.9	0.6	3.4	0.2	7.5	12.0	880	20	42	822	42.6	55.3	2.1
Hamblen	158.5	2 526	53.0	0.6	6.2	0.2	4.7	224.6	3 579	172	198	3 569	30.0	68.4	1.6
Hamilton	1 693.1	4 900	23.2	34.8	4.9	0.9	2.5	1 512.3	4 377	5 705	1 146	21 496	43.6	55.4	1.1
Hancock	20.0	2 979	49.9	15.8	3.9	0.2	7.0	17.1	2 543	0	21	465	27.0	70.9	2.2
Hardeman	62.6	2 361	60.6	2.7	6.6	0.1	7.3	28.4	1 071	54	70	1 863	52.7	46.5	0.8
Hardin	104.9	4 042	36.7	35.8	2.7	2.7	4.6	72.4	2 789	108	81	1 637	27.8	70.5	1.6
Hawkins	108.4	1 915	66.6	0.9	4.8	0.3	4.8	126.4	2 234	144	179	2 306	28.2	70.1	1.7
Haywood	64.2	3 520	54.9	2.6	5.5	0.0	5.8	26.7	1 465	96	57	1 129	60.3	39.0	0.8
Henderson	60.8	2 170	65.5	0.2	6.4	0.1	5.4	92.9	3 314	55	88	1 365	27.9	70.8	1.3
Henry	154.5	4 776	27.8	50.9	2.8	0.0	4.3	81.7	2 525	110	132	2 491	38.0	60.4	1.6
Hickman	52.0	2 151	60.6	3.4	4.7	0.0	9.9	46.4	1 921	52	73	1 213	41.9	56.3	1.8
Houston	20.6	2 448	57.1	4.4	4.1	0.4	9.8	13.7	1 623	21	26	578	50.0	47.9	2.0
Humphreys	43.2	2 363	55.4	1.0	7.3	0.0	8.5	7.4	405	236	57	1 032	47.5	50.4	2.1
Jackson	23.3	2 034	61.8	2.9	4.3	0.2	9.2	4.9	428	25	36	538	49.4	48.5	2.0
Jefferson	135.7	2 600	53.6	3.3	4.7	9.4	4.4	112.4	2 153	112	165	2 317	27.9	70.6	1.4
Johnson	35.0	1 933	61.4	0.7	5.0	0.2	7.3	18.8	1 038	38	51	1 034	27.9	70.1	2.0
Knox	1 174.3	2 661	40.8	2.1	7.9	0.2	2.6	2 290.6	5 191	3 538	1 463	31 171	37.7	60.7	1.5
Lake	17.1	2 221	49.1	3.9	6.9	0.5	10.4	23.7	3 088	16	16	919	45.8	52.5	1.7
Lauderdale	69.4	2 504	56.8	2.7	7.3	0.6	7.8	45.4	1 639	51	78	1 911	46.3	52.8	0.9
Lawrence	93.3	2 217	57.9	3.0	6.7	0.0	7.8	110.6	2 628	114	133	2 014	32.2	66.0	1.8
Lewis	31.4	2 639	46.3	0.6	5.1	0.1	5.8	17.0	1 431	27	37	658	37.3	61.0	1.6
Lincoln	111.8	3 338	38.2	35.1	4.0	0.0	4.7	92.5	2 760	50	106	2 195	28.1	70.3	1.6
Loudon	111.4	2 238	57.9	0.6	7.1	0.2	4.5	662.5	13 305	136	160	2 040	27.3	71.3	1.4
McMinn	110.6	2 110	58.7	0.9	5.3	0.0	5.6	28.0	534	93	164	2 136	29.5	69.1	1.4
McNairy	55.7	2 129	62.1	0.2	4.9	0.0	6.8	28.4	1 086	78	82	1 381	30.0	68.5	1.5
Macon	53.2	2 366	60.7	4.0	6.0	0.1	7.6	27.7	1 232	37	72	1 188	28.0	69.9	2.1
Madison	890.5	9 027	13.8	63.1	3.2	0.0	1.8	1 017.8	10 317	415	301	11 623	46.1	53.1	0.8
Marion	61.4	2 169	58.5	0.8	8.3	0.0	5.6	57.5	2 034	63	89	1 305	39.4	59.0	1.6

1. Based on the resident population estimated as of July 1 of the year shown. 2. © 2013 Election Data Services, Inc. All rights reserved.

Table B. States and Counties — **Land Area and Population**

STATE/ County code	CBSA code[1]	County type[2]	STATE County	Land area,[3] (sq km) 2010	Total persons 2015	Rank	Per square kilometer	White	Black	American Indian, Alaska Native	Asian and Pacific Islander	Percent Hispanic or Latino[4]	Under 5 years	5 to 17 years	18 to 24 years	25 to 34 years	35 to 44 years	45 to 54 years
				1	2	3	4	5	6	7	8	9	10	11	12	13	14	15
			TENNESSEE—Cont'd															
47 117	30280	6	Marshall	972	31 552	1 394	32.5	87.4	7.5	0.8	0.8	5.0	5.7	18.0	8.1	11.7	13.3	14.3
47 119	34980	4	Maury	1 588	87 757	657	55.3	81.6	12.9	0.7	1.1	5.3	6.5	17.0	8.0	13.4	12.7	13.4
47 121	...	8	Meigs	505	11 830	2 306	23.4	95.6	2.0	1.1	0.6	1.7	4.8	15.7	7.2	9.8	12.8	15.0
47 123	...	6	Monroe	1 646	45 771	1 053	27.8	92.6	2.7	1.3	0.7	3.9	5.2	16.4	7.9	10.7	12.0	13.9
47 125	17300	3	Montgomery	1 396	193 479	339	138.6	68.2	20.9	1.3	4.1	9.6	8.7	18.5	12.0	19.0	13.2	11.2
47 127	46100	9	Moore	335	6 322	2 733	18.9	94.7	2.7	0.9	0.8	1.9	3.8	16.3	7.4	9.9	12.6	14.0
47 129	28940	6	Morgan	1 352	21 498	1 754	15.9	94.1	4.0	1.1	0.4	1.2	4.2	15.5	8.4	13.1	14.1	14.9
47 131	46460	7	Obion	1 411	30 639	1 417	21.7	85.1	11.5	0.6	0.5	3.8	5.8	16.4	7.9	11.1	12.4	13.4
47 133	18260	7	Overton	1 123	22 129	1 724	19.7	97.5	1.2	0.9	0.5	1.3	5.5	16.8	7.9	10.2	12.3	13.8
47 135	...	8	Perry	1 074	7 929	2 600	7.4	94.3	3.1	1.5	0.5	2.2	5.5	16.1	7.6	10.7	11.3	12.8
47 137	...	9	Pickett	422	5 146	2 827	12.2	98.7	0.3	0.7	0.3	1.5	3.9	14.7	6.7	8.7	10.7	14.6
47 139	17420	3	Polk	1 126	16 773	1 992	14.9	97.0	1.0	1.3	0.4	1.7	4.7	15.9	7.6	9.9	12.9	15.1
47 141	18260	4	Putnam	1 039	74 553	738	71.8	89.9	2.8	0.7	1.6	5.8	5.8	15.4	14.7	12.2	11.4	12.3
47 143	19420	6	Rhea	817	32 526	1 373	39.8	92.3	2.7	1.1	0.7	4.5	5.5	17.6	9.3	11.0	12.1	13.5
47 145	28940	4	Roane	934	52 753	947	56.5	94.6	3.3	1.1	0.9	1.7	4.6	15.2	7.1	9.5	11.6	14.7
47 147	34980	1	Robertson	1 234	68 570	779	55.6	85.5	8.3	0.7	0.8	6.2	6.7	18.4	8.0	12.6	13.1	14.7
47 149	34980	1	Rutherford	1 604	298 612	229	186.2	75.4	14.9	0.7	3.9	7.2	6.5	18.6	13.2	14.4	14.4	13.2
47 151	...	6	Scott	1 379	21 950	1 734	15.9	98.4	0.5	0.8	0.4	0.7	6.3	18.2	8.4	11.4	13.4	14.0
47 153	16860	2	Sequatchie	689	14 811	2 116	21.5	94.8	0.9	1.0	0.5	3.3	5.2	16.6	7.7	10.4	12.7	13.9
47 155	42940	4	Sevier	1 535	95 946	617	62.5	92.0	1.4	0.9	1.5	5.6	5.5	15.6	8.3	11.5	12.7	14.4
47 157	32820	1	Shelby	1 977	938 069	54	474.5	38.3	53.6	0.6	3.0	6.0	7.2	18.3	10.3	14.3	12.9	13.2
47 159	34980	1	Smith	814	19 295	1 860	23.7	94.5	2.7	1.0	0.4	2.6	5.7	17.7	8.1	11.6	12.0	15.7
47 161	...	3	Stewart	1 190	13 259	2 218	11.1	93.8	2.5	1.6	1.4	2.5	5.1	16.4	7.6	10.6	11.9	15.1
47 163	28700	3	Sullivan	1 071	156 791	410	146.4	95.1	3.0	0.7	1.0	1.7	5.0	14.9	7.9	10.6	12.3	14.4
47 165	34980	1	Sumner	1 371	175 989	364	128.4	87.0	7.6	0.7	1.8	4.3	6.0	18.4	8.0	12.0	13.7	14.7
47 167	32820	1	Tipton	1 187	61 870	848	52.1	77.5	19.2	1.0	1.3	2.5	6.1	19.5	9.0	12.3	12.9	14.7
47 169	34980	1	Trousdale	296	8 042	2 596	27.2	87.2	10.1	1.1	0.5	3.0	5.5	17.3	8.8	11.5	12.6	14.5
47 171	27740	3	Unicoi	482	17 860	1 927	37.1	94.8	0.7	0.8	0.3	4.4	4.4	15.0	7.0	10.3	11.8	14.4
47 173	28940	2	Union	579	19 119	1 868	33.0	98.4	0.7	1.1	0.4	1.5	6.5	16.9	7.7	11.3	12.3	14.7
47 175	...	9	Van Buren	708	5 677	2 786	8.0	98.0	1.0	0.9	0.4	1.3	4.2	14.8	7.3	9.4	12.4	13.9
47 177	32660	6	Warren	1 121	40 435	1 166	36.1	87.5	3.8	0.8	0.8	8.3	5.9	17.7	7.9	11.7	13.1	13.8
47 179	27740	3	Washington	846	126 302	495	149.3	91.2	5.0	0.7	1.8	3.3	5.2	14.5	12.3	12.2	12.4	13.4
47 181	...	8	Wayne	1 901	16 748	1 995	8.8	91.8	6.5	0.9	0.4	1.8	4.4	14.0	8.4	13.5	13.5	14.6
47 183	32280	7	Weakley	1 503	33 960	1 328	22.6	88.7	8.8	0.7	1.5	2.3	5.2	14.1	17.2	11.0	10.5	12.5
47 185	...	7	White	976	26 521	1 544	27.2	95.0	2.6	0.9	0.6	2.1	5.9	16.0	7.7	11.5	11.6	14.0
47 187	34980	1	Williamson	1 509	211 672	310	140.3	86.9	4.9	0.5	4.4	4.7	5.8	22.3	7.4	9.3	14.9	16.0
47 189	34980	1	Wilson	1 478	128 991	485	87.2	87.6	7.6	0.8	1.9	3.7	5.8	18.4	7.8	11.2	13.9	15.2
48 000	...	X	**TEXAS**	676 587	27 469 114	X	40.6	44.7	12.3	0.7	5.0	38.6	7.3	19.1	10.2	14.6	13.5	12.9
48 001	37300	5	Anderson	2 752	57 580	891	20.9	60.8	21.6	0.7	0.8	17.0	5.1	14.1	8.1	15.9	16.1	15.1
48 003	11380	6	Andrews	3 887	18 105	1 912	4.7	42.4	2.1	1.0	0.8	54.6	9.3	21.3	10.0	15.3	11.9	12.1
48 005	31260	5	Angelina	2 066	88 255	652	42.7	62.3	15.6	0.7	1.2	21.2	7.0	19.1	9.2	12.5	12.2	12.9
48 007	18580	2	Aransas	653	25 350	1 595	38.8	69.2	1.9	1.4	2.3	26.7	4.6	14.1	7.4	10.0	9.6	12.3
48 009	48660	3	Archer	2 339	8 715	2 535	3.7	89.8	1.4	1.3	0.7	8.2	3.5	18.1	8.3	10.4	10.9	15.8
48 011	11100	3	Armstrong	2 355	1 947	3 053	0.8	89.2	2.0	1.5	0.5	8.5	6.1	17.3	6.3	9.7	11.8	12.1
48 013	41700	1	Atascosa	3 159	48 435	1 011	15.3	35.7	1.1	0.7	0.5	62.5	7.3	20.6	9.2	12.7	12.2	12.5
48 015	26420	1	Austin	1 674	29 563	1 438	17.7	64.6	9.5	0.7	0.7	26.0	6.2	18.0	8.1	10.5	11.5	13.4
48 017	...	7	Bailey	2 141	7 210	2 655	3.4	36.9	1.3	0.5	0.6	60.6	9.4	20.9	9.1	12.0	10.9	11.2
48 019	41700	1	Bandera	2 049	21 269	1 763	10.4	80.0	1.1	1.4	0.7	17.9	4.1	13.4	6.3	8.2	9.3	15.3
48 021	12420	1	Bastrop	2 300	80 527	694	35.0	56.2	7.9	1.0	1.2	35.0	6.1	19.3	8.2	11.5	12.7	14.4
48 023	...	6	Baylor	2 247	3 618	2 933	1.6	84.4	3.4	0.9	0.6	12.4	5.8	15.5	6.9	9.6	9.9	13.1
48 025	13300	4	Bee	2 280	32 874	1 361	14.4	33.3	8.4	0.5	0.8	57.7	5.9	15.4	11.9	17.3	14.4	13.4
48 027	28660	2	Bell	2 722	334 941	201	123.0	51.0	22.8	1.1	5.2	23.5	8.7	19.0	12.2	17.3	12.5	11.2
48 029	41700	1	Bexar	3 211	1 897 753	17	591.0	30.3	7.8	0.6	3.4	59.1	7.2	19.0	10.8	15.6	13.3	12.5
48 031	...	8	Blanco	1 837	11 004	2 356	6.0	79.3	1.3	1.0	0.7	18.9	4.0	15.2	6.4	8.9	10.6	14.3
48 033	...	9	Borden	2 324	648	3 131	0.3	81.2	0.9	1.4	0.2	16.8	5.4	16.3	7.2	9.8	10.9	16.6
48 035	...	6	Bosque	2 546	17 891	1 925	7.0	80.4	2.3	1.0	0.7	17.2	5.4	16.4	6.8	8.9	10.4	13.4
48 037	45500	3	Bowie	2 292	93 389	625	40.7	66.5	25.3	1.3	1.5	7.3	6.5	17.4	9.1	13.4	13.0	13.1
48 039	26420	1	Brazoria	3 516	346 312	196	98.5	51.3	13.5	0.7	6.8	29.2	7.1	19.7	8.5	13.9	14.5	13.8
48 041	17780	3	Brazos	1 516	215 037	300	141.8	58.5	11.3	0.6	6.2	24.8	6.2	14.3	28.1	15.7	10.3	9.2
48 043	...	7	Brewster	16 016	9 145	2 499	0.6	54.3	1.5	1.2	1.4	43.2	6.3	13.3	8.1	14.1	11.0	12.5
48 045	...	9	Briscoe	2 331	1 505	3 081	0.6	69.1	3.4	1.0	0.4	27.7	5.5	16.3	6.0	10.2	12.1	13.6
48 047	...	6	Brooks	2 443	7 230	2 652	3.0	8.4	0.7	0.2	1.2	89.0	9.2	18.8	9.9	12.2	9.3	11.3
48 049	15220	5	Brown	2 446	37 896	1 226	15.5	74.6	4.1	1.1	0.7	21.0	5.6	17.3	8.9	11.7	11.5	12.7
48 051	17780	3	Burleson	1 707	17 460	1 951	10.2	66.5	13.2	0.8	0.6	20.1	5.9	16.8	7.9	10.4	10.4	14.1
48 053	...	6	Burnet	2 575	45 463	1 062	17.7	75.7	2.6	1.0	0.9	22.1	5.3	16.3	8.0	10.8	11.0	13.0

1. CBSA = Core Based Statistical Area. See Appendix A for explanation. See Appendix B for list of metropolitan areas with component counties. 2. County type code from the Economic Research Service of USDA Rural-Urban Continuum Codes. See Appendix A for definition. 3. Dry land or land partially or temporarily covered by water. 4. May be of any race.

Table B. States and Counties — **Population and Households**

	Population, 2014 (cont.) Age (percent) (cont.)				Population change and components of change, 2000–2015 Total persons		Percent change		Components of change, 2010–2015			Households, 2010–2014			Percent	
STATE County	55 to 64 years	65 to 74 years	75 years and over	Percent female	2000	2010	2000–2010	2010–2015	Births	Deaths	Net migration	Number	Persons per house-hold	Family house-holds	Female family house-holder[1]	One per-son
	16	17	18	19	20	21	22	23	24	25	26	27	28	29	30	31
TENNESSEE—Cont'd																
Marshall	13.7	9.5	5.6	50.9	26 767	30 617	14.4	3.1	1 909	1 567	589	11 724	2.61	70.7	14.0	25.1
Maury	14.1	8.9	6.0	51.6	69 498	80 959	16.5	8.4	5 782	4 190	5 079	32 112	2.54	68.1	13.8	27.2
Meigs	14.9	13.5	6.3	49.9	11 086	11 753	6.0	0.7	598	758	233	4 677	2.47	69.8	13.4	23.9
Monroe	14.4	12.5	7.1	50.5	38 961	44 517	14.3	2.8	2 653	2 583	1 169	17 497	2.54	73.5	8.5	24.0
Montgomery	8.8	5.2	3.3	50.1	134 768	172 337	27.9	12.3	17 411	5 829	9 221	64 818	2.76	73.1	14.6	21.2
Moore	15.2	12.3	8.5	50.8	5 740	6 362	10.8	-0.6	279	333	30	2 444	2.55	72.7	10.5	22.5
Morgan	13.6	9.9	6.2	45.2	19 757	21 987	11.3	-2.2	1 032	1 143	-335	7 342	2.56	71.6	11.5	24.3
Obion	14.1	11.1	7.8	51.6	32 450	31 807	-2.0	-3.7	1 798	2 039	-901	12 496	2.47	71.3	16.3	23.8
Overton	14.1	11.8	7.6	50.7	20 118	22 078	9.7	0.2	1 238	1 488	302	8 719	2.50	70.1	8.7	27.3
Perry	15.0	12.9	8.1	49.5	7 631	7 915	3.7	0.2	522	538	11	3 247	2.38	67.5	11.7	28.1
Pickett	15.5	14.8	10.4	49.8	4 945	5 077	2.7	1.4	202	338	176	2 252	2.22	78.4	9.3	18.6
Polk	14.5	12.0	7.4	50.2	16 050	16 825	4.8	-0.3	810	1 112	252	6 619	2.49	72.0	10.4	24.9
Putnam	11.8	9.5	6.7	50.6	62 315	72 367	16.1	3.0	4 655	3 857	1 429	29 423	2.38	63.5	11.9	27.5
Rhea	13.5	10.9	6.7	50.8	28 400	31 809	12.0	2.3	2 028	1 870	606	12 307	2.55	67.0	13.7	27.2
Roane	16.1	12.5	8.7	50.9	51 910	54 180	4.4	-2.6	2 509	3 575	-309	22 070	2.39	64.8	10.1	30.0
Robertson	12.9	8.2	5.3	50.9	54 433	66 288	21.8	3.4	4 675	3 234	792	24 435	2.71	74.0	13.0	21.8
Rutherford	10.2	6.0	3.6	50.7	182 023	262 604	44.3	13.7	19 755	8 534	24 031	98 454	2.74	69.2	12.4	23.2
Scott	12.7	9.6	5.9	50.8	21 127	22 228	5.2	-1.3	1 428	1 416	-285	8 294	2.63	66.7	10.9	28.2
Sequatchie	14.3	12.2	6.9	50.8	11 370	14 119	24.2	4.9	803	802	658	5 635	2.52	73.6	12.6	23.7
Sevier	14.2	11.2	6.5	50.9	71 170	89 876	26.3	6.8	5 425	4 893	5 264	36 253	2.53	70.6	11.2	24.0
Shelby	12.3	6.9	4.7	52.4	897 472	927 640	3.4	1.1	72 402	40 540	-20 671	345 475	2.66	64.3	20.8	30.4
Smith	13.8	9.9	5.5	50.5	17 712	19 162	8.2	0.7	1 190	1 134	67	7 387	2.56	70.4	8.2	26.3
Stewart	14.5	11.8	7.1	49.7	12 370	13 324	7.7	-0.5	685	832	94	5 245	2.52	70.6	9.9	25.9
Sullivan	14.5	11.6	8.7	51.6	153 048	156 823	2.5	0.0	8 260	10 307	2 145	66 279	2.32	66.1	11.8	29.5
Sumner	12.6	9.0	5.6	51.2	130 449	160 657	23.2	9.5	10 408	7 171	11 654	61 408	2.69	74.8	12.4	21.5
Tipton	12.4	8.1	5.0	50.7	51 271	61 081	19.1	1.3	3 908	2 791	-419	21 486	2.82	76.6	17.0	20.5
Trousdale	14.2	9.7	5.8	50.4	7 259	7 869	8.4	2.2	478	435	131	2 928	2.64	69.8	16.2	25.5
Unicoi	15.4	12.3	9.5	50.8	17 667	18 313	3.7	-2.5	828	1 346	71	7 579	2.33	66.1	7.1	31.7
Union	14.3	10.6	5.8	50.4	17 808	19 109	7.3	0.1	1 061	1 062	-1	7 241	2.62	71.5	13.3	23.9
Van Buren	17.1	13.7	7.2	50.1	5 508	5 548	0.7	2.3	294	299	147	2 089	2.62	72.3	14.1	24.0
Warren	13.1	9.9	6.9	50.6	38 276	39 840	4.1	1.5	2 529	2 407	441	15 440	2.54	67.3	12.6	29.0
Washington	13.0	10.0	7.0	51.1	107 198	122 979	14.7	2.7	7 024	6 867	3 013	52 330	2.29	63.9	11.2	28.8
Wayne	13.2	10.6	7.7	44.9	16 842	17 021	1.1	-1.6	768	1 019	-15	6 018	2.46	71.3	10.6	26.6
Weakley	12.4	9.5	7.5	51.1	34 895	35 021	0.4	-3.0	1 862	1 892	-1 006	13 654	2.35	64.3	11.9	28.4
White	14.0	11.2	8.0	51.2	23 102	25 834	11.8	2.7	1 584	1 839	894	9 827	2.61	70.3	10.6	27.6
Williamson	12.8	7.1	4.5	51.2	126 638	183 180	44.6	15.6	10 784	5 213	22 613	68 119	2.84	78.8	7.1	18.8
Wilson	13.2	9.2	5.3	50.9	88 809	114 011	28.4	13.1	7 249	4 961	12 263	43 817	2.70	73.7	12.1	22.7
TEXAS	11.0	6.8	4.7	50.4	20 851 820	25 146 105	20.6	9.2	2 028 029	920 595	1 199 941	9 013 582	2.83	69.6	14.4	24.9
Anderson	11.9	8.2	5.6	39.0	55 109	58 458	6.1	-1.5	3 072	3 246	-618	16 610	2.75	74.4	11.8	27.0
Andrews	10.1	5.4	4.5	48.9	13 004	14 786	13.7	22.4	1 626	589	2 265	5 412	2.96	75.3	9.8	21.7
Angelina	11.9	8.4	6.6	51.1	80 130	86 771	8.3	1.7	6 438	4 507	-459	30 840	2.73	73.8	15.7	23.0
Aransas	15.2	16.0	10.6	50.5	22 497	23 158	2.9	9.5	1 363	1 789	2 418	9 550	2.46	68.7	8.6	25.9
Archer	14.9	10.3	7.8	49.9	8 854	9 055	2.3	-3.8	371	355	-329	3 336	2.63	76.4	4.7	20.3
Armstrong	15.4	12.0	9.4	50.7	2 148	1 901	-11.5	2.4	125	134	50	665	2.82	76.8	7.8	18.2
Atascosa	11.6	8.3	5.6	50.3	38 628	44 911	16.3	7.8	3 415	2 036	2 153	15 161	3.03	77.1	14.3	19.7
Austin	14.7	10.6	7.0	50.4	23 590	28 411	20.4	4.1	1 769	1 407	829	10 786	2.64	71.8	9.5	26.0
Bailey	11.5	7.8	7.3	49.3	6 594	7 165	8.7	0.6	605	300	-276	2 400	2.90	74.5	10.2	23.7
Bandera	18.9	15.7	8.9	50.5	17 645	20 485	16.1	3.8	867	999	860	8 569	2.36	69.3	8.0	26.7
Bastrop	13.9	8.7	5.0	49.1	57 733	74 169	28.5	8.6	4 826	3 175	4 489	25 314	2.90	73.5	10.9	22.3
Baylor	14.1	13.2	11.9	51.9	4 093	3 726	-9.0	-2.9	181	304	27	1 806	1.98	54.9	7.6	43.7
Bee	10.3	6.6	4.8	40.0	32 359	31 861	-1.5	3.2	1 985	1 240	367	8 933	2.75	70.9	17.9	25.1
Bell	9.2	5.8	4.0	50.0	237 974	310 238	30.4	8.0	33 172	10 147	1 279	106 743	2.93	72.2	15.2	23.5
Bexar	10.5	6.5	4.7	50.8	1 392 931	1 714 774	23.1	10.7	139 762	63 181	103 719	613 290	2.86	67.9	16.5	26.4
Blanco	18.1	14.1	8.3	49.6	8 418	10 491	24.6	4.9	425	597	690	4 086	2.57	70.2	9.3	26.5
Borden	13.3	10.4	10.1	46.5	729	641	-12.1	1.1	41	27	-2	256	2.64	78.5	5.9	19.9
Bosque	14.8	13.7	10.2	50.5	17 204	18 212	5.9	-1.8	1 002	1 245	-95	6 961	2.53	68.8	8.4	27.3
Bowie	12.2	8.8	6.6	49.5	89 306	92 565	3.6	0.9	6 357	5 154	-335	33 766	2.60	68.8	17.5	27.3
Brazoria	11.4	6.7	4.2	49.3	241 767	313 127	29.5	10.6	24 643	11 091	19 030	109 817	2.87	74.2	12.5	21.8
Brazos	7.9	4.7	3.5	49.3	152 415	194 851	27.8	10.4	13 941	4 840	10 758	72 191	2.59	55.1	11.6	27.5
Brewster	15.2	11.9	7.6	50.1	8 866	9 232	4.1	-0.9	601	376	-328	4 071	2.24	54.3	6.5	38.0
Briscoe	12.4	12.7	11.2	50.5	1 790	1 637	-8.5	-8.1	69	81	-124	635	2.52	75.4	12.6	23.1
Brooks	11.1	10.0	8.2	50.4	7 976	7 223	-9.4	0.1	681	417	-241	2 346	2.95	67.5	23.7	31.0
Brown	13.1	11.2	8.1	50.4	37 674	38 106	1.1	-0.6	2 192	2 434	40	13 329	2.70	70.0	10.4	26.0
Burleson	15.3	10.4	8.8	50.3	16 470	17 187	4.4	1.6	976	1 001	286	6 243	2.73	70.9	11.2	26.9
Burnet	14.5	12.1	9.0	51.1	34 147	42 727	25.1	6.4	2 475	2 286	2 354	16 774	2.59	70.5	10.2	25.2

1. No spouse present.

Table B. States and Counties — Population, Vital Statistics, Medicare, and Crime

STATE County	Persons in group quarters, 2015	Daytime population, 2010–2014 Number	Employ-ment/resi-dence ratio	Births, 2015 Total	Births Rate[1]	Deaths, 2015 Number	Deaths Rate[1]	Persons under 65 with no health insurance, 2014 Number	Percent	Medicare, 2015 Total Beneficiaries	Enrolled in Original Medicare	Enrolled in Medicare Advantage	Serious crimes known to police,[2] 2014 Total Number	Rate[3]
	32	33	34	35	36	37	38	39	40	41	42	43	44	45
TENNESSEE—Cont'd														
Marshall	359	28 569	0.81	367	11.7	303	9.6	3 914	14.9	5 716	3 900	1 816	652	2 081
Maury	1 009	77 164	0.85	1 111	12.8	870	10.0	9 682	13.4	17 473	12 337	5 136	2 319	2 740
Meigs	128	9 965	0.52	119	10.1	140	11.9	1 368	14.8	2 964	1 934	1 030	358	3 073
Monroe	500	42 932	0.87	525	11.5	498	10.9	6 089	16.9	10 896	6 382	4 514	1 324	2 907
Montgomery	3 422	162 490	0.76	3 434	17.9	1 166	6.1	20 288	11.9	20 204	15 528	4 676	6 243	3 330
Moore	104	5 297	0.64	59	9.3	48	7.6	670	13.5	771	634	137	89	1 411
Morgan	2 232	18 594	0.51	208	9.6	220	10.2	2 218	14.0	3 548	1 902	1 646	369	1 681
Obion	461	31 657	1.02	325	10.6	394	12.8	3 595	14.5	8 055	6 994	1 061	1 173	3 779
Overton	286	19 324	0.66	223	10.1	286	13.0	2 700	15.4	4 857	3 968	889	379	1 713
Perry	123	7 469	0.85	102	12.9	94	11.9	998	16.3	1 958	1 370	588	93	1 181
Pickett	74	4 402	0.67	37	7.2	52	10.2	590	15.5	1 137	933	204	48	939
Polk	244	13 952	0.56	170	10.2	198	11.8	2 040	15.3	4 496	3 214	1 282	375	2 246
Putnam	2 548	79 985	1.23	885	11.9	733	9.8	9 206	15.4	18 062	14 291	3 771	2 576	3 483
Rhea	924	34 820	1.21	395	12.1	375	11.5	3 806	14.6	7 563	5 558	2 005	815	2 488
Roane	646	48 693	0.77	452	8.6	672	12.7	5 430	13.2	13 482	8 046	5 436	1 420	2 845
Robertson	703	56 211	0.64	887	13.0	604	8.8	8 101	13.9	11 226	6 411	4 815	1 775	2 618
Rutherford	4 893	260 117	0.88	3 941	13.4	1 710	5.8	30 944	12.1	32 655	19 812	12 843	8 094	2 827
Scott	264	20 788	0.82	288	13.1	265	12.1	2 695	14.7	4 584	2 950	1 634	430	1 953
Sequatchie	188	12 013	0.57	162	11.0	167	11.3	1 721	14.6	2 680	1 877	803	437	2 941
Sevier	982	92 314	0.99	1 051	11.0	955	10.0	15 115	19.5	20 464	11 231	9 233	3 075	3 247
Shelby	18 113	1 011 562	1.18	13 730	14.6	7 943	8.5	122 149	15.0	129 460	92 793	36 667	57 798	6 118
Smith	159	17 031	0.73	242	12.6	195	10.2	2 275	14.2	3 493	2 404	1 089	328	1 716
Stewart	92	11 527	0.63	125	9.4	167	12.6	1 592	14.9	2 923	2 320	603	244	1 821
Sullivan	2 632	165 607	1.14	1 594	10.2	1 867	11.9	17 493	14.2	40 352	17 049	23 303	5 448	3 471
Sumner	1 252	144 004	0.71	2 106	12.1	1 466	8.4	17 130	11.7	27 387	15 037	12 350	2 842	1 659
Tipton	963	47 473	0.47	738	11.9	568	9.2	6 178	11.7	9 456	7 229	2 227	2 001	3 234
Trousdale	130	6 443	0.57	96	12.0	80	10.0	1 022	15.2	1 440	874	566	224	2 858
Unicoi	405	17 549	0.91	157	8.8	256	14.3	2 161	15.5	4 922	2 743	2 179	297	1 643
Union	152	15 517	0.44	176	9.2	204	10.7	2 589	16.3	3 416	1 520	1 896	551	2 877
Van Buren	94	4 700	0.60	59	10.5	44	7.8	688	15.7	1 013	781	232	128	2 283
Warren	580	39 187	0.96	494	12.3	429	10.7	5 953	18.1	9 610	7 129	2 481	1 124	2 803
Washington	4 250	132 800	1.14	1 319	10.5	1 253	9.9	13 435	13.3	28 155	15 360	12 795	3 622	2 864
Wayne	2 164	15 893	0.81	143	8.5	201	12.0	1 784	15.1	3 270	2 554	716	163	960
Weakley	1 887	31 838	0.80	356	10.5	341	10.0	3 433	12.9	6 371	5 516	855	612	1 779
White	382	23 864	0.77	310	11.7	331	12.5	3 098	14.8	6 612	4 941	1 671	803	3 039
Williamson	1 153	210 825	1.18	2 197	10.5	1 054	5.1	13 645	7.6	24 178	14 992	9 186	2 471	1 215
Wilson	1 247	104 860	0.74	1 457	11.5	1 017	8.0	11 966	11.3	18 920	11 670	7 250	2 693	2 169
TEXAS	600 329	26 085 940	1.00	398 088	14.6	182 479	6.7	4 976 322	21.4	3 389 498	2 270 594	1 118 904	923 348	3 425
Anderson	14 376	57 673	0.98	587	10.2	629	10.9	7 721	21.1	10 036	7 425	2 611	1 376	2 363
Andrews	80	15 539	0.92	353	19.9	99	5.6	3 243	20.7	1 878	1 498	380	515	2 950
Angelina	2 961	88 505	1.03	1 251	14.2	897	10.2	16 219	22.4	17 255	12 676	4 579	3 293	3 733
Aransas	458	22 163	0.81	285	11.3	353	14.0	4 204	23.3	6 170	3 897	2 273	1 128	4 540
Archer	56	6 784	0.50	78	8.9	59	6.7	1 405	19.5	1 229	1 050	179	NA	NA
Armstrong	54	1 513	0.53	27	13.9	22	11.3	311	20.5	405	334	71	16	810
Atascosa	388	41 874	0.76	681	14.2	408	8.5	8 396	20.5	6 658	3 910	2 748	856	1 784
Austin	215	26 617	0.84	340	11.6	271	9.3	4 630	19.4	5 655	4 407	1 248	541	1 855
Bailey	106	6 543	0.83	110	15.5	40	5.6	1 773	30.7	1 072	928	144	122	1 705
Bandera	320	16 472	0.52	169	8.0	195	9.2	3 285	21.1	4 935	3 748	1 187	311	1 498
Bastrop	2 420	62 335	0.58	1 045	13.2	632	8.0	15 034	23.0	12 014	8 891	3 123	1 830	2 384
Baylor	66	3 625	0.98	30	8.3	43	11.9	589	21.9	1 011	855	156	90	2 490
Bee	7 673	32 117	0.97	402	12.2	205	6.2	4 298	19.9	4 136	2 645	1 491	610	1 834
Bell	8 303	335 379	1.10	6 301	19.0	2 007	6.0	43 885	15.1	38 675	26 184	12 491	11 381	3 431
Bexar	43 081	1 835 014	1.06	27 684	14.7	12 646	6.7	300 596	18.7	243 374	137 714	105 660	97 028	5 229
Blanco	101	9 938	0.85	70	6.4	117	10.7	2 038	24.4	2 660	2 123	537	121	1 115
Borden	0	624	0.82	14	21.5	7	10.8	72	13.9	50	37	13	11	1 719
Bosque	267	15 543	0.64	198	11.1	223	12.5	3 380	25.1	4 463	2 985	1 478	210	1 278
Bowie	6 250	99 803	1.19	1 199	12.8	969	10.4	13 450	18.3	17 834	14 119	3 715	4 232	4 484
Brazoria	10 697	279 667	0.69	4 890	14.3	2 255	6.6	45 605	15.7	40 894	26 864	14 030	6 482	1 925
Brazos	14 105	204 448	1.03	2 766	13.0	1 018	4.8	34 752	19.5	18 896	15 166	3 730	6 144	2 974
Brewster	45	9 315	1.01	111	12.1	57	6.2	1 582	21.5	1 829	1 346	483	172	1 838
Briscoe	0	1 461	0.80	10	6.6	8	5.3	413	35.4	395	321	74	9	589
Brooks	56	7 753	1.24	133	18.4	75	10.4	1 342	23.1	1 515	972	543	138	1 891
Brown	1 709	38 604	1.05	404	10.7	418	11.1	6 140	21.0	8 563	6 959	1 604	1 200	3 163
Burleson	197	15 005	0.67	182	10.5	192	11.1	3 268	23.6	3 617	2 672	945	202	1 169
Burnet	1 243	40 907	0.84	493	11.0	450	10.0	8 085	23.9	11 639	8 788	2 851	900	2 080

1. Per 1,000 estimated resident population.   2. Data for serious crimes have not been adjusted for underreporting; this may affect comparability between geographic areas and over time.
3. Per 100,000 population estimated by the FBI.

Table B. States and Counties — Crime, Education, Money Income, and Poverty

STATE County	Serious crimes known to police, 2014 (cont.)[1] Rate[2]		Education						Money income, 2010–2014				Income and poverty, 2014			
			School enrollment and attainment, 2010–2014				Local government expenditures,[5] 2012–2013			Households				Percent below poverty level		
			Enrollment[3]		Attainment[4] (percent)											
	Violent	Property	Total	Percent private	High school graduate or less	Bachelor's degree or more	Total current spending (mil dol)	Current spending per student (dollars)	Per capita income[6] (dollars)	Median income (dollars)	Mean income (dollars)	Percent with income of $200,000 or more	Median household income (dollars)	All persons	Children under 18 years	Children 5 to 17 years in families
	46	47	48	49	50	51	52	53	54	55	56	57	58	59	60	61
TENNESSEE—Cont'd																
Marshall	575	1 507	6 813	13.3	60.1	13.2	40.6	7 580	21 241	41 822	54 439	1.2	42 839	15.5	22.0	19.7
Maury	419	2 320	18 344	17.7	50.0	18.6	93.2	7 783	23 259	46 565	58 254	2.2	51 303	15.5	22.4	21.3
Meigs	386	2 687	2 439	5.7	65.3	7.8	14.3	7 942	18 465	33 061	45 595	0.3	34 801	20.8	28.7	25.5
Monroe	369	2 538	8 782	10.0	64.0	11.2	54.1	7 535	19 880	37 202	50 561	1.4	37 392	20.6	30.0	28.0
Montgomery	596	2 734	53 481	12.5	39.9	24.0	242.8	7 928	22 867	50 693	61 882	2.0	50 935	13.9	17.3	17.6
Moore	111	1 300	1 474	12.3	57.0	13.9	8.4	8 264	25 687	43 393	64 952	2.3	50 358	12.5	20.6	18.1
Morgan	159	1 521	4 156	9.0	71.6	7.3	25.3	7 619	16 927	38 003	49 584	0.8	36 390	23.4	29.0	26.2
Obion	383	3 395	7 389	8.9	59.4	15.4	42.0	8 006	21 929	40 327	53 496	1.7	40 683	20.8	31.6	28.9
Overton	253	1 459	4 907	7.4	65.0	13.2	25.6	7 462	18 679	34 913	46 345	0.6	35 884	18.9	26.5	24.2
Perry	216	965	1 568	13.7	64.8	12.7	9.9	8 524	16 597	31 750	40 341	0.2	33 776	23.6	33.4	29.2
Pickett	78	861	851	0.7	65.3	12.3	5.8	7 687	20 590	35 510	49 081	0.1	31 996	19.2	29.7	25.2
Polk	198	2 048	3 511	9.5	65.9	10.2	20.8	7 832	20 825	39 434	51 344	1.9	36 643	20.3	27.8	25.6
Putnam	370	3 112	19 943	6.4	53.4	22.8	87.6	7 906	21 470	34 780	52 821	1.9	37 693	20.8	25.9	25.8
Rhea	284	2 204	7 684	11.5	63.7	11.7	38.3	7 239	19 764	37 512	49 994	1.9	37 952	22.0	31.0	28.4
Roane	339	2 506	10 349	9.5	54.3	17.7	60.1	8 411	23 478	41 726	54 950	1.5	43 269	18.0	25.5	24.4
Robertson	478	2 140	16 516	18.5	54.4	16.9	83.2	7 227	24 049	53 748	64 400	1.9	52 640	13.4	18.6	17.5
Rutherford	390	2 437	82 869	11.5	39.8	28.9	363.5	7 635	25 057	55 096	68 013	2.4	53 799	14.7	16.2	15.2
Scott	218	1 735	5 291	4.3	70.1	10.5	32.2	7 295	17 680	30 206	45 606	0.8	31 397	24.5	31.8	30.2
Sequatchie	370	2 570	3 164	11.5	58.7	13.1	16.3	7 003	22 300	42 182	54 629	1.0	44 111	18.7	29.5	28.4
Sevier	302	2 945	18 647	11.4	56.1	15.4	123.4	8 419	22 125	42 499	55 246	1.9	39 905	17.7	26.5	25.7
Shelby	1 306	4 812	263 191	19.8	40.4	29.8	1 461.3	9 480	25 913	46 213	67 555	4.1	44 015	23.0	34.5	33.2
Smith	272	1 444	4 458	10.1	66.1	11.0	24.0	7 431	21 354	43 988	54 745	1.3	43 659	15.0	21.8	20.4
Stewart	403	1 418	3 230	7.2	56.9	12.4	18.3	8 258	21 598	41 089	52 709	1.0	41 590	17.5	26.5	24.5
Sullivan	430	3 041	33 427	13.5	50.5	21.2	191.6	8 669	24 085	39 577	56 070	2.3	38 840	18.5	28.2	25.0
Sumner	246	1 413	42 014	14.0	44.4	24.0	211.4	7 430	28 393	56 193	75 068	4.1	58 291	11.3	16.9	15.4
Tipton	711	2 523	16 419	8.5	53.1	14.8	87.5	7 402	23 205	53 133	64 592	1.6	52 339	15.4	20.7	19.8
Trousdale	485	2 373	1 933	8.6	67.6	11.9	9.0	7 049	20 298	37 211	51 484	2.5	40 251	17.5	25.9	23.5
Unicoi	277	1 366	3 734	5.5	62.4	13.4	19.7	7 483	21 162	34 346	49 206	1.0	37 632	20.1	29.3	26.9
Union	313	2 564	4 040	13.4	70.8	8.6	37.4	6 315	18 053	36 009	45 989	1.2	37 453	22.6	33.3	30.8
Van Buren	232	2 051	1 154	18.1	71.6	12.4	6.8	8 633	19 945	34 250	49 473	1.0	34 884	20.6	31.5	28.7
Warren	434	2 369	9 064	11.3	65.1	13.1	50.3	7 591	20 048	34 592	49 380	1.8	36 942	19.0	28.2	25.4
Washington	316	2 549	33 593	11.5	42.8	30.8	135.6	8 072	26 083	42 935	61 094	3.2	43 212	16.7	22.0	20.9
Wayne	277	683	3 132	4.8	69.4	8.2	19.9	7 945	15 812	31 225	42 574	0.6	33 573	23.3	30.9	28.8
Weakley	204	1 576	10 671	5.3	56.4	19.5	33.5	7 396	19 516	35 845	48 089	1.3	36 205	21.5	26.7	25.0
White	242	2 797	5 510	9.7	65.8	11.9	28.8	7 020	17 529	33 933	44 165	0.5	35 400	21.9	29.7	29.5
Williamson	118	1 097	56 751	23.5	22.2	54.1	310.0	8 339	42 675	91 743	119 922	14.9	97 936	5.6	6.0	5.3
Wilson	323	1 846	29 402	18.7	44.4	26.7	147.0	7 347	28 435	60 095	74 869	3.5	60 955	10.1	14.0	12.5
TEXAS	406	3 019	7 366 632	10.9	43.7	27.1	40 962.5	8 299	26 513	52 576	73 913	5.0	53 067	17.2	24.5	23.3
Anderson	299	2 064	12 659	6.2	57.1	11.3	74.1	8 890	18 623	42 511	58 518	2.4	42 471	20.4	25.4	24.4
Andrews	538	2 412	3 963	4.3	58.0	13.6	29.0	8 021	29 363	61 250	85 059	6.5	66 878	10.7	14.1	13.9
Angelina	340	3 393	22 796	4.9	53.3	15.3	140.1	8 256	21 521	42 374	59 568	2.1	42 128	17.9	25.9	24.2
Aransas	427	4 114	4 033	7.6	45.8	19.5	31.1	9 814	25 906	42 247	61 419	2.9	44 551	17.5	32.0	31.6
Archer	NA	NA	2 141	6.2	47.6	20.3	16.2	8 731	28 250	58 274	73 061	3.8	58 867	9.4	13.7	11.4
Armstrong	152	658	448	4.5	35.7	24.4	4.0	10 801	27 199	61 250	73 589	0.9	55 177	11.0	15.9	15.1
Atascosa	119	1 665	12 271	6.6	61.0	13.6	79.9	8 895	21 957	50 756	66 425	2.2	52 785	16.9	24.4	23.3
Austin	274	1 581	7 100	12.6	47.7	19.5	47.7	8 534	27 490	54 603	70 416	3.5	58 792	11.2	18.3	17.2
Bailey	168	1 537	1 951	6.2	65.5	10.2	13.3	8 893	18 082	41 982	50 060	0.9	36 821	19.9	29.8	29.5
Bandera	96	1 402	3 886	12.2	42.3	21.5	25.3	9 320	26 900	48 587	64 006	3.1	50 107	13.5	23.8	21.4
Bastrop	317	2 068	18 602	9.9	51.5	17.3	129.2	8 372	23 605	53 382	67 274	2.3	52 886	14.7	22.2	21.0
Baylor	249	2 241	804	1.5	46.6	22.4	5.5	9 368	30 573	33 019	60 118	4.9	36 027	18.3	29.3	27.6
Bee	183	1 650	6 914	11.9	60.6	8.9	42.4	8 670	16 509	41 738	55 836	3.2	40 680	24.9	29.7	28.9
Bell	391	3 040	95 028	11.0	39.0	22.2	527.5	7 955	23 335	51 027	64 517	2.4	51 048	14.2	21.0	21.6
Bexar	454	4 775	521 988	13.6	42.0	26.5	2 685.3	8 334	24 525	50 867	68 216	3.8	50 699	18.3	26.4	25.5
Blanco	92	1 023	2 242	13.6	41.4	27.9	18.0	10 732	28 113	51 740	70 515	3.7	57 177	12.0	20.4	18.6
Borden	313	1 406	136	0.0	37.5	33.1	4.6	19 310	47 823	73 333	134 916	8.2	61 750	10.3	14.2	14.2
Bosque	116	1 162	3 978	7.5	52.6	15.4	24.1	10 496	24 290	44 339	60 521	2.9	44 397	15.0	23.5	21.9
Bowie	553	3 931	22 712	6.8	48.2	18.8	153.5	8 527	22 977	42 917	60 259	2.7	41 883	20.1	30.9	28.4
Brazoria	178	1 746	88 797	10.0	39.9	27.9	481.6	7 588	30 134	69 092	86 683	5.8	73 788	9.9	13.3	12.4
Brazos	285	2 689	87 474	5.7	36.2	38.3	220.7	8 235	22 243	39 060	59 765	3.8	41 641	26.4	24.7	23.5
Brewster	171	1 667	2 380	8.6	34.7	36.3	14.8	11 723	27 095	38 589	60 131	2.3	40 179	13.8	22.5	23.0
Briscoe	0	589	344	7.0	49.9	20.7	4.4	10 870	22 197	36 696	55 051	2.5	42 139	16.7	29.1	27.9
Brooks	260	1 631	1 469	1.2	70.6	11.0	17.0	11 019	14 353	22 176	39 322	0.7	27 875	32.4	45.5	47.1
Brown	301	2 863	9 184	12.9	54.7	16.4	58.2	8 765	20 533	40 982	53 377	2.3	41 316	17.5	27.4	24.9
Burleson	145	1 024	3 803	12.1	57.5	13.7	25.4	8 965	23 223	49 533	60 331	1.9	48 140	16.2	25.4	22.8
Burnet	250	1 830	9 530	10.2	47.4	23.3	64.1	8 831	25 757	50 712	64 166	3.1	53 203	14.0	23.9	22.0

1. Data for serious crimes have not been adjusted for underreporting; this may affect comparability between geographic areas and over time. 2. Per 100,000 population estimated by the FBI.
3. All persons 3 years old and over enrolled in nursery school through college. 4. Persons 25 years old and over. 5. Elementary and secondary education expenditures.
6. Based on population estimated by the American Community Survey, 2010–2014.

Table B. States and Counties — **Personal Income**

STATE County	Personal income, 2014										Earnings, 2014		
			Per capita[1]			Supplements to wages and salaries; employer contributions (mil dol)						Contributions for government social insurance (mil dol)	
	Total (mil dol)	Percent change, 2013–2014	Dollars	Rank	Wages and salaries (mil dol)	Pension and insurance	Government social insurance	Proprietors' income (mil dol)	Dividends, interest, and rent (mil dol)	Personal transfer receipts (mil dol)	Total (mil dol)	From employee and self-employed	From employer
	62	63	64	65	66	67	68	69	70	71	72	73	74
TENNESSEE—Cont'd													
Marshall	1 012	5.0	32 369	2 392	317	65	23	90	125	256	495	32	23
Maury	3 134	4.7	36 646	1 659	1 327	235	98	286	368	718	1 947	121	98
Meigs	389	6.6	33 223	2 243	75	19	6	63	47	121	162	12	6
Monroe	1 332	3.9	29 449	2 784	500	97	38	102	164	439	737	52	38
Montgomery	7 543	3.0	39 708	1 225	1 811	349	132	596	1 274	1 329	2 888	169	132
Moore	230	6.2	36 474	1 690	77	24	6	14	32	60	121	7	6
Morgan	589	1.6	27 205	2 968	114	30	8	71	57	189	223	17	8
Obion	1 105	0.0	35 704	1 826	367	68	27	127	176	321	589	38	27
Overton	623	3.5	28 279	2 897	159	38	12	56	75	211	264	20	12
Perry	225	3.3	28 822	2 844	59	14	5	23	37	93	101	8	5
Pickett	156	4.4	30 395	2 666	31	7	2	16	22	61	57	5	2
Polk	512	5.1	30 603	2 640	77	20	6	30	57	164	133	11	6
Putnam	2 527	3.7	34 077	2 107	1 278	265	92	259	465	653	1 895	115	92
Rhea	1 006	3.1	30 823	2 612	500	109	38	49	122	316	696	45	38
Roane	1 867	2.6	35 390	1 880	1 029	143	68	61	265	582	1 301	88	68
Robertson	2 394	2.6	35 160	1 911	838	171	62	192	252	515	1 262	78	62
Rutherford	10 457	5.5	36 194	1 746	5 338	890	379	1 241	1 117	1 608	7 849	449	379
Scott	580	2.7	26 374	3 014	185	44	14	39	60	233	282	21	14
Sequatchie	475	4.1	32 305	2 404	88	22	7	28	60	157	144	12	7
Sevier	3 077	4.1	32 350	2 397	1 295	208	101	339	447	793	1 943	127	101
Shelby	41 969	2.5	44 705	703	26 404	3 782	1 801	5 121	6 378	7 356	37 108	2 132	1 801
Smith	651	2.9	34 231	2 076	201	41	14	74	95	163	330	21	14
Stewart	496	0.5	37 381	1 541	140	35	11	29	75	134	215	14	11
Sullivan	5 798	2.5	36 918	1 610	3 241	560	224	376	886	1 579	4 401	285	224
Sumner	6 703	5.1	38 813	1 349	2 053	337	148	403	833	1 278	2 942	191	148
Tipton	2 072	1.5	33 626	2 171	399	84	29	125	222	481	637	44	29
Trousdale	429	6.1	53 567	250	49	12	4	203	28	77	268	14	4
Unicoi	596	1.6	33 185	2 247	238	46	19	28	75	222	331	24	19
Union	499	2.4	26 104	3 027	79	20	6	21	60	173	125	12	6
Van Buren	150	3.3	26 648	3 002	28	8	2	16	20	63	55	5	2
Warren	1 228	3.0	30 731	2 624	505	92	37	86	168	384	720	48	37
Washington	4 653	2.9	36 859	1 623	2 375	463	170	319	691	1 097	3 327	204	170
Wayne	448	2.6	26 492	3 008	136	36	10	22	54	166	204	15	10
Weakley	1 120	-0.2	32 584	2 354	423	104	31	143	158	336	702	41	31
White	774	3.3	29 430	2 787	234	46	17	72	96	264	370	27	17
Williamson	14 727	6.4	71 761	53	6 972	788	452	2 413	2 180	967	10 625	598	452
Wilson	5 167	5.6	41 214	1 034	1 672	246	118	429	612	885	2 464	157	118
TEXAS	1 231 085	6.0	45 669	X	633 344	86 984	42 544	186 179	196 117	178 115	949 051	48 106	42 544
Anderson	1 833	4.0	31 815	2 464	818	137	55	205	238	448	1 216	66	55
Andrews	960	10.7	54 928	213	505	63	32	161	73	95	761	38	32
Angelina	3 258	4.1	37 132	1 579	1 481	244	101	330	490	832	2 156	119	101
Aransas	1 081	5.9	43 292	813	257	39	18	77	279	272	391	27	18
Archer	459	7.1	52 139	289	82	15	5	114	64	66	217	10	5
Armstrong	85	1.4	43 290	814	15	3	1	10	16	19	29	1	1
Atascosa	1 776	5.7	37 172	1 575	643	91	42	223	276	374	999	55	42
Austin	1 361	5.4	46 741	542	496	68	34	141	243	232	738	41	34
Bailey	311	21.2	44 960	681	95	19	6	104	35	57	224	7	6
Bandera	854	5.9	40 868	1 080	113	20	7	73	194	195	213	15	7
Bastrop	2 372	6.6	30 383	2 667	604	110	42	177	359	535	932	56	42
Baylor	149	10.8	41 473	1 012	45	8	3	28	21	45	84	4	3
Bee	960	2.7	29 203	2 808	404	73	25	111	157	229	613	32	25
Bell	13 168	2.6	40 007	1 174	7 394	1 691	616	792	2 294	2 462	10 492	480	616
Bexar	75 825	5.6	40 857	1 082	40 787	6 492	2 913	9 560	13 250	13 036	59 752	3 027	2 913
Blanco	627	6.9	57 949	158	124	20	8	173	160	89	326	15	8
Borden	32	-7.7	48 928	442	8	2	0	2	13	4	11	1	0
Bosque	680	3.3	38 229	1 428	147	29	9	81	125	175	267	15	9
Bowie	3 339	3.2	35 795	1 806	1 627	310	118	250	595	847	2 306	127	118
Brazoria	14 377	6.5	42 519	898	5 442	836	360	884	1 414	1 982	7 522	405	360
Brazos	6 848	6.5	32 740	2 327	3 852	760	240	480	1 298	967	5 332	247	240
Brewster	372	4.9	40 576	1 112	161	32	11	33	87	72	237	13	11
Briscoe	64	-9.8	41 914	958	12	3	1	18	12	14	33	1	1
Brooks	263	7.0	36 606	1 668	116	24	8	28	28	100	176	10	8
Brown	1 233	5.9	32 743	2 325	553	99	39	107	182	408	799	47	39
Burleson	692	5.3	40 097	1 160	192	29	13	73	106	155	306	18	13
Burnet	1 963	6.1	43 688	786	567	87	38	282	529	387	974	56	38

1. Based on the resident population estimated as of July 1 of the year shown.

Table B. States and Counties — **Earnings, Social Security, and Housing**

STATE County	Farm	Mining	Construction	Manu-facturing	Information: professional, scientific, technical services	Retail trade	Finance, insurance, real estate and leasing	Health care and social assistance	Govern-ment	Number	Rate[1]	Supple-mental Security Income recipients, December 2014	Total	Percent change, 2010–2014
	75	76	77	78	79	80	81	82	83	84	85	86	87	88
TENNESSEE—Cont'd														
Marshall	2.0	D	6.9	29.9	2.8	8.3	3.5	4.5	21.8	7 125	228	785	13 347	1.7
Maury	0.2	D	6.6	17.5	4.6	7.0	9.4	11.1	20.2	18 365	215	1 915	36 251	2.8
Meigs	0.5	D	12.6	26.8	D	4.5	D	3.6	18.0	3 550	303	558	5 691	1.1
Monroe	0.5	D	3.2	39.7	2.8	8.0	2.6	8.1	14.1	12 760	281	1 762	20 866	0.4
Montgomery	0.5	D	9.8	9.8	6.1	9.7	6.2	11.8	22.1	25 255	133	3 396	78 305	11.7
Moore	6.1	D	4.3	D	D	1.4	0.8	D	30.6	1 620	256	73	2 986	2.4
Morgan	2.0	D	7.0	5.8	D	5.4	6.3	D	32.1	5 305	244	626	8 882	-0.4
Obion	8.1	D	5.8	15.2	D	12.0	5.7	8.7	15.7	8 565	277	1 034	14 561	-0.7
Overton	0.0	1.4	8.9	17.7	2.6	8.5	6.0	13.5	21.9	6 260	285	697	10 246	-0.5
Perry	-1.5	D	4.6	21.3	D	7.0	D	D	23.8	2 375	303	259	4 570	-0.6
Pickett	4.9	D	D	4.4	D	10.5	5.2	12.5	23.8	1 705	335	226	3 454	-0.2
Polk	11.7	D	4.9	7.9	D	8.8	D	D	33.0	5 145	308	636	8 486	6.2
Putnam	-0.3	0.2	6.2	14.6	5.5	9.1	6.5	10.5	27.0	17 205	231	2 179	33 203	4.1
Rhea	0.2	D	3.3	26.1	1.9	4.6	2.1	D	43.3	7 830	240	1 162	14 456	0.6
Roane	-0.2	D	2.4	4.9	46.2	6.0	1.5	D	17.1	15 485	294	1 907	25 523	-0.7
Robertson	1.7	D	9.0	31.6	2.5	7.2	3.8	5.2	15.9	13 260	195	1 271	26 612	2.0
Rutherford	0.0	D	6.1	25.3	5.5	6.4	6.4	12.0	15.1	39 965	138	3 891	112 105	8.9
Scott	-0.3	4.7	7.6	21.5	D	8.7	3.3	D	25.7	5 770	262	1 525	9 856	-0.5
Sequatchie	1.4	4.8	5.0	7.8	D	9.3	9.0	D	30.9	4 350	294	458	6 386	0.3
Sevier	0.0	D	D	3.8	3.3	12.5	9.7	5.5	15.6	23 600	249	1 984	56 409	0.9
Shelby	0.0	0.0	5.0	9.5	6.2	6.1	8.8	12.4	14.3	151 505	161	34 287	404 286	1.5
Smith	2.0	D	D	22.9	2.0	5.8	4.0	D	17.0	4 415	232	490	8 617	1.0
Stewart	1.5	0.0	13.4	11.3	D	4.0	5.8	4.6	49.1	3 450	260	429	6 770	-0.1
Sullivan	0.0	D	7.9	27.2	5.4	7.0	4.1	17.7	10.4	44 890	286	4 841	74 191	0.6
Sumner	0.4	D	10.1	16.2	8.0	7.3	5.6	12.1	14.9	33 420	193	2 610	68 854	4.4
Tipton	0.9	D	11.2	18.3	D	8.6	3.2	D	25.0	11 585	187	1 488	23 530	1.4
Trousdale	1.0	0.1	D	4.5	17.2	11.0	12.4	18.4	9.9	1 935	242	275	3 442	2.2
Unicoi	0.5	D	5.6	36.9	D	4.8	1.6	8.3	15.1	5 295	295	633	8 839	0.1
Union	-1.9	D	D	17.2	D	8.8	D	3.3	33.5	4 815	254	757	9 108	1.7
Van Buren	1.4	D	8.7	18.7	D	3.7	D	D	36.3	1 785	318	182	2 647	-0.6
Warren	1.7	0.0	5.2	31.2	D	7.5	3.3	11.6	15.0	10 040	251	1 628	17 838	0.1
Washington	0.4	D	4.1	9.1	6.4	8.0	6.5	21.7	23.3	29 450	234	3 334	59 404	3.8
Wayne	2.7	D	2.0	9.8	D	5.7	4.5	15.0	38.3	4 385	260	509	7 238	-0.7
Weakley	8.3	1.6	2.2	9.5	D	5.5	13.6	D	27.2	7 915	232	895	15 527	0.2
White	0.4	D	4.9	23.8	D	9.2	3.2	12.1	15.9	7 425	282	985	11 649	1.2
Williamson	0.0	D	5.6	1.6	18.0	6.4	14.9	20.3	6.1	27 310	133	990	75 994	10.9
Wilson	-0.2	0.1	9.3	12.2	5.2	13.1	6.2	9.2	11.9	23 960	191	1 642	50 215	10.2
TEXAS	0.6	9.5	7.5	8.9	11.2	5.6	8.0	8.7	13.7	3 842 249	142	666 301	10 587 752	6.1
Anderson	0.8	7.2	4.7	2.5	5.2	6.3	5.2	12.8	24.5	9 505	165	1 290	20 155	0.2
Andrews	1.1	37.3	11.8	3.0	D	3.1	5.4	D	10.9	2 185	125	264	6 194	6.5
Angelina	0.6	3.6	5.4	13.2	5.2	7.8	3.9	19.3	16.6	18 035	205	3 162	36 310	2.0
Aransas	-0.4	D	11.3	0.9	7.1	13.4	6.2	D	14.1	7 550	303	651	15 844	3.2
Archer	11.2	35.6	3.5	2.2	D	3.6	1.1	D	13.6	1 765	200	110	4 139	0.8
Armstrong	21.7	0.0	6.8	0.0	D	1.7	D	10.5	22.1	460	236	18	900	-0.4
Atascosa	1.1	23.3	9.9	2.7	3.5	7.7	8.7	D	13.1	9 020	189	1 628	17 929	1.7
Austin	1.2	3.4	13.9	15.0	11.1	11.9	5.2	4.3	10.3	5 900	203	552	13 036	0.9
Bailey	44.3	0.0	2.2	3.3	D	2.9	2.0	1.5	12.5	1 340	193	170	2 780	-0.1
Bandera	2.0	D	14.4	1.3	9.0	6.8	6.7	D	18.2	6 130	293	376	11 626	0.6
Bastrop	0.2	3.8	11.1	7.4	4.5	11.2	4.3	7.0	24.6	13 870	177	1 887	29 796	1.6
Baylor	20.1	D	6.6	0.9	D	4.7	D	D	13.6	1 080	301	128	2 651	-0.5
Bee	1.0	23.8	3.6	2.1	6.5	10.3	2.9	D	27.7	4 720	143	1 054	10 668	0.2
Bell	0.1	0.2	6.1	3.9	4.1	5.0	3.0	12.0	51.7	46 450	141	7 668	135 698	8.2
Bexar	0.0	3.7	6.8	4.3	10.0	6.4	11.8	10.7	22.0	279 260	150	55 984	684 164	3.2
Blanco	2.0	D	22.5	3.6	D	4.5	7.1	D	9.3	2 765	256	135	5 721	3.5
Borden	19.9	D	D	D	D	D	0.0	D	40.9	105	161	6	385	0.0
Bosque	16.2	D	10.7	11.1	3.2	5.4	4.0	D	22.7	4 425	250	351	9 642	0.2
Bowie	0.9	0.7	4.0	3.9	4.0	8.6	7.7	19.5	27.7	19 570	210	4 127	39 238	1.9
Brazoria	0.3	3.2	17.8	24.0	5.4	6.3	3.6	6.1	13.5	44 760	132	5 469	129 521	9.5
Brazos	0.4	4.3	6.4	5.7	8.3	7.2	4.5	10.0	36.7	20 815	99	3 498	85 223	9.7
Brewster	2.8	1.1	5.4	1.0	13.0	5.4	4.6	D	35.5	1 995	218	213	5 442	1.1
Briscoe	48.4	0.3	D	D	D	4.6	5.0	D	15.0	395	257	40	953	0.0
Brooks	6.8	17.5	3.0	0.0	D	5.4	D	5.1	38.9	1 735	240	563	3 232	-0.2
Brown	0.2	2.6	6.0	22.5	D	9.5	4.3	D	18.7	9 355	249	1 286	18 528	1.3
Burleson	3.2	17.2	8.2	6.9	D	11.5	3.7	D	12.9	4 000	232	504	8 925	1.1
Burnet	-0.1	2.2	15.0	7.9	6.9	9.1	7.5	10.2	13.7	10 460	235	651	21 740	4.3

1. Per 1,000 resident population estimated as of July 1 of the year shown.

Table B. States and Counties — Housing, Labor Force, and Employment

STATE County	Housing units, 2010–2014								Civilian labor force, 2015				Civilian employment,[6] 2010–2014		
	Occupied units							Substandard units[4] (percent)		Percent change, 2014–2015	Unemployment			Percent	
	Owner-occupied					Renter-occupied									
				Median owner cost as a percent of income											
	Total	Percent	Median value[1]	With a mortgage	Without a mortgage[2]	Median rent[3]	Median rent as a percent of income[2]		Total		Total	Rate[5]	Total	Management, business, science and arts	Construction, production, and maintenance occupations
	89	90	91	92	93	94	95	96	97	98	99	100	101	102	103
TENNESSEE—Cont'd															
Marshall	11 724	73.7	111 000	21.2	11.5	643	29.5	2.8	14 702	1.4	844	5.7	13 385	25.5	33.8
Maury	32 112	69.7	138 000	22.7	11.0	692	29.9	2.0	41 959	1.7	2 209	5.3	37 631	31.1	24.3
Meigs	4 677	77.5	94 000	25.0	10.5	572	27.1	5.0	4 857	-0.6	378	7.8	3 766	17.8	47.7
Monroe	17 497	73.6	113 700	23.0	10.9	577	30.3	3.4	19 037	-0.3	1 223	6.4	16 355	22.9	37.6
Montgomery	64 818	60.9	143 400	22.1	10.1	856	28.7	2.7	78 128	0.9	4 656	6.0	71 463	31.2	23.9
Moore	2 444	83.3	141 700	20.7	11.2	660	21.8	2.0	3 311	0.4	154	4.7	2 955	23.0	33.6
Morgan	7 342	79.9	91 100	22.0	12.2	644	27.9	3.0	7 829	0.3	597	7.6	6 860	24.9	30.0
Obion	12 496	68.5	89 100	20.1	12.2	580	29.3	1.1	12 475	-3.0	1 108	8.9	12 183	26.5	33.0
Overton	8 719	78.0	90 400	22.3	11.0	539	24.2	3.8	9 068	-0.9	663	7.3	8 319	27.1	34.5
Perry	3 247	75.3	83 900	26.2	10.0	537	31.5	4.2	3 104	1.6	217	7.0	2 764	25.4	34.2
Pickett	2 252	80.0	95 400	21.9	10.0	460	27.9	1.4	2 408	5.3	187	7.8	2 183	32.9	32.8
Polk	6 619	80.0	110 900	23.6	10.9	625	31.6	2.6	7 330	-1.2	495	6.8	6 343	23.8	33.5
Putnam	29 423	61.7	139 200	23.2	11.0	607	35.1	2.8	32 419	0.8	1 943	6.0	30 372	32.9	22.4
Rhea	12 307	69.3	102 100	21.8	10.3	577	32.2	2.4	13 101	-1.6	992	7.6	12 371	24.7	39.6
Roane	22 070	72.8	120 000	21.8	11.2	686	31.4	2.3	22 729	0.5	1 494	6.6	20 986	30.7	27.6
Robertson	24 435	76.5	151 900	23.4	11.5	820	26.0	1.8	34 102	1.5	1 688	4.9	31 155	31.2	30.2
Rutherford	98 454	66.8	157 400	22.2	10.0	881	30.0	2.7	152 997	1.9	7 021	4.6	135 350	34.1	23.5
Scott	8 294	75.2	80 000	23.7	13.0	521	32.7	1.2	8 081	-2.3	774	9.6	7 701	24.6	37.6
Sequatchie	5 635	75.9	134 100	21.2	10.0	630	32.1	5.9	5 797	0.8	387	6.7	5 758	28.1	31.7
Sevier	36 253	66.2	158 000	23.0	10.0	724	29.5	3.3	49 991	1.9	3 071	6.1	43 813	24.6	20.0
Shelby	345 475	58.0	131 700	23.9	12.5	861	34.5	3.2	429 430	-0.4	28 535	6.6	419 148	35.0	21.7
Smith	7 387	74.8	113 800	22.5	10.0	563	30.0	3.2	8 494	1.5	485	5.7	7 844	24.1	35.9
Stewart	5 245	80.7	120 500	22.2	12.2	615	30.1	0.9	5 139	-2.0	404	7.9	4 863	31.5	31.3
Sullivan	66 279	74.0	122 700	21.0	10.3	598	29.6	1.6	69 138	-1.3	4 113	5.9	66 121	31.1	23.2
Sumner	61 408	72.3	174 700	23.2	10.4	860	28.7	1.9	88 328	1.8	4 148	4.7	79 506	34.2	22.4
Tipton	21 486	73.2	138 500	21.6	11.0	754	29.3	1.3	27 328	-0.4	1 999	7.3	26 648	29.8	30.0
Trousdale	2 928	75.1	117 800	24.5	12.9	549	34.3	0.5	3 722	1.1	221	5.9	3 344	22.7	28.8
Unicoi	7 579	73.9	109 100	19.7	11.0	583	33.6	2.7	7 059	-1.2	575	8.1	6 770	26.9	35.0
Union	7 241	78.8	99 300	24.0	10.0	550	32.7	3.7	7 263	0.3	500	6.9	6 734	22.9	37.7
Van Buren	2 089	85.3	79 300	22.4	11.2	454	30.0	1.7	2 061	-2.6	170	8.2	2 252	26.6	30.6
Warren	15 440	70.0	94 000	21.6	10.9	558	28.4	2.5	17 812	1.9	1 025	5.8	15 870	26.0	36.2
Washington	52 330	66.6	146 300	22.0	10.0	680	30.2	1.4	57 677	-0.4	3 304	5.7	56 855	38.2	18.0
Wayne	6 018	82.1	77 000	23.6	11.8	470	25.4	0.4	6 311	-2.5	469	7.4	5 662	23.6	34.1
Weakley	13 654	65.9	92 400	19.6	11.4	567	30.8	1.5	15 648	-1.7	1 101	7.0	14 306	31.3	27.7
White	9 827	75.8	95 800	23.8	10.8	578	34.9	2.5	11 350	-1.0	709	6.2	9 907	23.3	37.2
Williamson	68 119	81.0	336 400	21.6	10.0	1 132	29.6	1.1	105 943	1.8	4 319	4.1	94 345	54.6	10.1
Wilson	43 817	78.2	192 900	22.6	10.4	858	32.1	1.6	63 873	1.8	2 995	4.7	57 041	34.2	20.6
TEXAS	9 013 582	62.7	131 400	22.2	11.9	870	29.5	5.5	13 078 323	0.4	583 963	4.5	11 809 010	34.9	22.8
Anderson	16 610	72.6	80 300	20.9	12.7	715	30.1	4.9	22 824	4.7	910	4.0	20 147	23.3	27.1
Andrews	5 412	76.9	95 500	16.7	10.0	869	23.5	4.5	9 303	-2.4	323	3.5	7 597	22.2	40.6
Angelina	30 840	66.1	86 000	20.7	11.4	750	30.8	5.2	37 370	-1.0	2 106	5.6	35 533	27.0	29.5
Aransas	9 550	72.3	133 300	26.0	14.5	819	36.0	3.7	10 092	-1.1	514	5.1	9 295	29.9	26.3
Archer	3 336	81.8	98 500	19.0	10.8	652	28.7	1.9	4 180	-1.5	185	4.4	4 201	34.4	30.2
Armstrong	665	77.9	107 400	16.7	10.0	712	18.4	3.3	988	-1.6	27	2.7	934	40.3	26.1
Atascosa	15 161	74.0	85 400	20.4	11.0	731	21.6	8.8	20 621	1.2	984	4.8	19 223	24.5	34.0
Austin	10 786	75.6	157 800	22.9	11.9	846	26.9	3.1	14 154	0.1	646	4.6	13 251	31.5	32.7
Bailey	2 400	64.8	66 200	21.8	10.0	587	23.9	14.5	2 761	-6.7	119	4.3	3 261	27.9	30.4
Bandera	8 569	80.9	146 600	21.3	11.6	800	29.4	2.6	9 180	0.6	366	4.0	8 867	36.6	22.3
Bastrop	25 314	79.0	121 500	23.0	12.4	856	28.6	5.6	37 336	1.7	1 449	3.9	31 911	30.2	28.6
Baylor	1 806	73.2	76 600	23.4	14.5	469	26.4	2.7	1 624	-1.7	58	3.6	1 410	34.5	31.3
Bee	8 933	64.4	72 300	20.6	13.4	781	27.2	6.7	10 367	-3.4	651	6.3	10 191	20.8	29.5
Bell	106 743	56.0	124 500	21.5	11.0	865	28.3	2.9	135 742	0.6	6 355	4.7	125 180	32.1	21.3
Bexar	613 290	58.9	126 100	22.0	11.5	862	29.6	5.0	874 901	1.0	33 500	3.8	803 439	34.6	19.3
Blanco	4 086	78.1	171 900	22.5	12.7	739	28.3	3.4	5 739	1.0	180	3.1	4 753	38.0	23.1
Borden	256	66.8	83 900	13.0	10.0	1 083	25.0	0.8	414	-2.1	12	2.9	288	55.2	23.6
Bosque	6 961	76.2	86 600	19.6	12.4	618	23.5	3.8	8 057	-1.0	365	4.5	7 046	28.6	30.6
Bowie	33 766	66.2	99 800	20.8	11.3	713	31.3	2.7	39 300	-0.9	1 904	4.8	36 893	28.6	26.2
Brazoria	109 817	73.4	148 800	20.7	10.2	888	26.7	4.4	167 023	0.2	7 628	4.6	150 463	40.5	23.2
Brazos	72 191	45.3	154 400	22.1	11.6	862	39.9	4.2	105 943	1.5	3 592	3.4	95 940	39.8	18.4
Brewster	4 071	59.2	112 500	20.8	10.0	629	23.7	5.3	3 913	-3.8	157	4.0	4 522	40.3	17.4
Briscoe	635	77.5	57 100	19.5	10.0	540	28.8	2.4	601	-5.7	23	3.8	711	36.7	32.3
Brooks	2 346	64.8	49 400	21.9	14.4	498	29.3	7.3	2 603	-3.8	260	10.0	2 335	23.3	20.3
Brown	13 329	69.7	86 500	22.1	12.4	661	29.1	1.8	15 878	0.2	693	4.4	15 102	29.1	27.0
Burleson	6 243	81.3	91 400	19.7	10.0	684	26.7	5.6	7 695	1.4	340	4.4	6 982	29.4	29.5
Burnet	16 774	72.9	153 000	23.4	13.3	859	28.8	3.0	21 141	-1.7	779	3.7	18 556	29.1	25.0

1. Specified owner-occupied units.   2. A value of 10.0 represents 10 percent or less; a value of 50.0 represents 50 percent or more.   3. Specified renter-occupied units.
4. Overcrowded or lacking complete plumbing facilities.   5. Percent of civilian labor force.   6. Persons 16 years old and over.

STATE County	Number of establish-ments	Total	Health care and social assistance	Manufac-turing	Retail trade	Finance and insurance	Professional, scientific, and technical services	Total (mil dol)	Average per employee (dollars)	Number	Fewer than 50 acres	500 acres or more	Farm operators whose principal occupation is farming (percent)
	104	105	106	107	108	109	110	111	112	113	114	115	116
TENNESSEE—Cont'd													
Marshall	473	7 981	731	3 469	1 106	203	94	286	35 836	1 025	34.4	5.4	50.4
Maury	1 677	24 546	5 264	3 570	4 159	1 742	607	967	39 393	1 513	39.4	6.3	40.0
Meigs	104	1 472	103	817	215	33	D	48	32 889	317	28.7	5.4	39.1
Monroe	698	10 891	1 300	4 506	1 595	310	177	358	32 886	872	42.0	4.0	48.2
Montgomery	2 728	41 482	7 455	5 552	8 639	1 304	1 710	1 293	31 161	783	38.6	7.8	34.4
Moore	61	D	148	D	79	D	D	D	D	358	32.1	7.8	45.3
Morgan	160	1 600	409	357	237	47	D	51	31 583	413	32.9	1.4	48.9
Obion	640	9 598	1 119	2 639	1 656	428	109	290	30 176	568	32.6	16.5	57.0
Overton	291	3 504	752	789	505	D	83	110	31 300	922	39.6	4.1	32.9
Perry	116	1 409	447	489	195	49	D	41	29 009	246	19.5	6.1	40.2
Pickett	82	607	140	D	86	D	7	20	33 288	316	34.2	3.5	30.4
Polk	207	1 459	D	D	382	D	D	40	27 467	255	45.5	6.7	58.0
Putnam	1 729	27 500	5 457	4 207	4 938	948	526	912	33 154	898	46.1	3.1	33.9
Rhea	498	8 243	1 047	3 407	1 170	D	78	259	31 418	411	40.1	5.6	44.8
Roane	732	8 517	2 226	1 003	1 670	D	577	243	28 487	519	45.9	1.2	34.9
Robertson	1 095	17 776	1 960	6 404	2 278	412	250	643	36 165	1 180	46.6	6.6	45.3
Rutherford	4 758	101 022	11 912	15 799	13 408	3 685	2 524	4 111	40 695	1 327	46.5	4.6	41.8
Scott	315	3 488	687	990	668	137	D	103	29 637	302	30.8	3.0	43.4
Sequatchie	181	1 952	470	161	450	D	D	52	26 456	188	39.4	8.5	38.8
Sevier	2 599	35 441	2 244	1 480	7 813	928	749	921	25 978	603	40.1	1.3	41.3
Shelby	19 372	426 313	67 908	26 734	48 420	15 947	16 640	20 576	48 264	411	53.3	7.8	42.1
Smith	262	3 787	473	1 204	600	111	D	135	35 743	850	24.4	4.4	45.1
Stewart	149	1 474	221	D	252	61	D	51	34 277	350	28.0	7.1	38.6
Sullivan	3 310	64 500	12 753	8 324	8 324	1 905	1 854	2 770	42 941	1 074	58.0	1.8	34.8
Sumner	2 987	42 382	5 984	7 724	5 965	1 529	2 345	1 650	38 933	1 355	48.6	4.1	40.7
Tipton	697	8 928	1 484	1 814	1 649	295	136	271	30 301	520	44.6	10.6	42.9
Trousdale	115	1 033	207	D	211	64	D	27	25 905	290	32.8	4.5	37.6
Unicoi	247	3 656	366	1 655	496	87	D	144	39 326	93	60.2	0.0	31.2
Union	190	1 585	D	474	352	42	D	42	26 408	408	38.0	1.5	42.4
Van Buren	35	444	D	D	31	D	D	14	31 658	245	42.0	5.7	55.1
Warren	714	10 136	1 468	3 579	1 575	321	D	344	33 908	1 122	41.5	6.3	50.4
Washington	2 809	50 984	13 892	4 386	8 674	2 732	2 963	1 863	36 539	1 312	55.6	2.1	49.0
Wayne	208	2 606	621	566	332	178	D	79	30 505	664	19.4	7.7	35.2
Weakley	565	7 581	1 635	1 375	1 147	244	122	209	27 605	861	33.7	12.8	45.5
White	366	5 150	796	1 907	789	138	D	172	33 393	927	38.9	5.0	38.9
Williamson	6 333	104 390	13 431	2 354	13 438	10 817	8 588	6 175	59 158	1 160	46.5	3.5	43.6
Wilson	2 436	35 339	4 110	3 291	5 745	1 048	1 029	1 348	38 152	1 473	37.4	3.7	41.8
TEXAS	557 721	9 920 214	1 411 362	807 515	1 242 045	495 507	664 995	501 457	50 549	248 809	37.7	15.8	42.1
Anderson	940	11 738	2 267	368	1 916	327	228	440	37 468	2 001	38.3	6.5	39.4
Andrews	403	5 683	D	387	476	D	217	334	58 852	169	37.3	39.1	30.8
Angelina	1 857	30 525	7 821	4 866	4 818	832	992	1 058	34 645	975	47.5	3.3	39.8
Aransas	503	4 131	498	35	1 024	160	121	113	27 429	100	49.0	8.0	34.0
Archer	201	1 539	281	D	106	D	D	62	40 561	531	17.1	36.2	47.1
Armstrong	38	323	D	NA	D	D	D	8	24 700	281	5.7	55.5	45.9
Atascosa	757	11 462	1 235	296	1 920	297	269	582	50 787	1 987	29.8	15.0	37.4
Austin	609	7 722	709	1 470	983	D	234	307	39 748	2 098	38.5	7.2	36.1
Bailey	142	1 458	D	D	216	D	37	41	28 263	494	9.5	39.3	46.6
Bandera	355	2 956	327	D	323	85	106	84	28 513	1 002	36.3	17.9	45.7
Bastrop	1 175	12 475	1 769	1 048	2 739	376	432	416	33 362	2 083	40.2	6.7	49.0
Baylor	117	935	D	D	108	D	26	21	22 527	277	7.6	38.3	58.1
Bee	481	5 567	1 079	D	1 144	D	204	214	38 363	974	31.6	16.9	45.2
Bell	4 925	87 549	24 453	6 061	13 791	3 368	3 129	3 298	37 665	2 533	50.8	6.3	34.2
Bexar	34 489	688 074	110 745	31 891	86 877	58 685	42 966	29 659	43 105	2 457	56.8	4.8	41.4
Blanco	263	1 907	167	D	232	82	95	79	41 248	792	29.8	24.6	41.7
Borden	8	D	NA	NA	D	NA	D	1	D	114	7.0	58.8	50.9
Bosque	291	2 500	589	469	383	135	D	82	32 945	1 265	26.1	17.9	41.6
Bowie	2 187	32 450	6 940	2 021	6 263	1 387	881	1 070	32 981	1 619	44.4	6.9	40.4
Brazoria	5 153	83 160	8 646	13 996	14 051	2 247	3 461	4 005	48 165	3 091	61.8	8.6	36.4
Brazos	4 094	61 500	9 194	5 116	10 326	1 549	3 055	2 090	33 988	1 412	46.0	7.5	34.7
Brewster	280	2 469	522	40	395	D	44	64	25 980	202	17.3	52.5	51.0
Briscoe	37	151	D	D	D	D	D	4	27 642	282	5.0	44.7	46.5
Brooks	126	1 582	D	NA	314	111	D	45	28 722	374	19.5	21.7	43.3
Brown	905	13 146	3 714	2 279	2 005	418	222	396	30 112	1 918	33.7	13.5	36.5
Burleson	333	3 063	302	375	665	115	116	123	40 179	1 429	30.9	10.6	49.1
Burnet	1 145	10 604	1 585	828	2 151	325	425	372	35 084	1 481	36.5	12.5	35.6

Table B. States and Counties — **Agriculture**

STATE County	Acreage (1,000) 117	Percent change, 2007–2012 118	Average size of farm 119	Total irrigated (1,000) 120	Total cropland (1,000) 121	Average per farm 122	Average per acre 123	Value of machinery and equipment, average per farm (dollars) 124	Total (mil dol) 125	Average per farm (dollars) 126	Crops 127	Livestock and poultry products 128	$10,000 or more 129	$100,000 or more 130	Total ($1,000) 131	Percent of farms 132
TENNESSEE—Cont'd																
Marshall	162	6.9	158	0.0	62.5	477 125	3 017	54 191	38.7	37 764	12.0	88.0	32.5	6.8	534	20.7
Maury	242	7.1	160	0.5	90.1	584 794	3 649	59 194	43.3	28 632	36.7	63.3	29.1	4.0	886	16.1
Meigs	53	7.7	167	0.1	20.0	587 246	3 520	57 767	6.9	21 647	19.3	80.7	30.9	3.8	153	19.6
Monroe	111	19.5	127	0.1	48.1	571 742	4 507	62 169	33.1	37 969	22.4	77.6	26.3	6.4	282	13.9
Montgomery	147	-2.7	188	0.7	77.1	811 156	4 310	79 954	47.3	60 350	77.0	23.0	35.0	8.9	1 031	31.5
Moore	59	13.3	164	0.0	14.8	578 542	3 528	69 791	22.6	63 045	D	D	38.0	9.8	128	13.4
Morgan	55	4.0	134	0.0	19.5	460 262	3 427	57 613	15.1	36 567	7.8	92.2	24.9	3.9	70	6.3
Obion	253	0.4	445	6.1	211.8	1 418 014	3 186	191 794	141.0	248 166	72.5	27.5	48.9	23.1	3 270	65.7
Overton	123	7.2	133	0.1	36.1	433 815	3 250	49 648	16.4	17 787	19.3	80.7	31.0	2.9	345	17.8
Perry	48	-6.3	194	0.0	13.8	384 012	1 981	41 463	2.4	9 951	33.9	66.1	26.0	1.6	155	31.3
Pickett	42	10.2	132	0.0	14.5	384 127	2 905	53 035	12.0	37 842	9.2	90.8	36.7	3.8	144	23.4
Polk	36	9.8	139	0.1	16.3	623 392	4 470	73 286	38.0	149 188	9.0	91.0	35.7	16.1	180	11.8
Putnam	96	-7.7	107	D	31.4	461 269	4 329	51 198	11.5	12 845	23.2	76.8	24.9	2.3	236	13.6
Rhea	58	2.7	140	0.8	24.4	490 925	3 499	56 000	16.8	40 886	55.2	44.8	28.5	4.4	194	16.3
Roane	47	-10.7	90	0.0	14.0	460 058	5 085	48 503	4.9	9 357	21.0	79.0	21.0	0.8	70	9.2
Robertson	209	-8.0	177	2.3	140.7	862 760	4 869	106 988	134.9	114 306	83.8	16.2	37.9	13.5	1 789	31.5
Rutherford	176	7.2	133	0.7	70.4	647 736	4 878	58 704	28.4	21 424	54.3	45.7	26.5	3.1	691	11.8
Scott	39	25.9	130	D	14.9	366 026	2 824	54 722	4.3	14 189	10.1	89.9	11.3	0.7	56	9.3
Sequatchie	31	7.0	163	D	10.0	528 037	3 236	72 968	7.0	37 404	15.1	84.9	31.9	8.0	66	17.0
Sevier	56	-1.6	92	0.0	17.1	545 836	5 926	48 391	5.3	8 713	22.1	77.9	24.0	0.7	61	13.8
Shelby	82	-11.3	199	4.3	60.4	913 324	4 586	77 803	31.8	77 387	94.2	5.8	26.3	8.0	733	22.9
Smith	130	2.0	153	0.2	36.8	405 628	2 658	52 353	18.9	22 205	40.3	59.7	32.2	3.3	507	19.5
Stewart	61	9.5	173	0.2	20.7	455 657	2 629	73 034	8.2	23 537	68.6	31.4	27.4	3.4	176	22.6
Sullivan	85	3.4	79	0.1	31.7	436 682	5 526	46 955	17.8	16 535	9.8	90.2	20.5	2.2	254	16.3
Sumner	167	-8.9	123	0.2	68.7	600 046	4 864	57 937	47.2	34 830	51.7	48.3	27.4	5.4	1 321	22.0
Tipton	155	-8.7	299	5.7	127.3	887 075	2 967	121 448	67.6	130 064	96.8	3.2	33.1	13.3	2 213	44.0
Trousdale	41	-6.2	142	0.1	13.9	548 321	3 854	65 507	8.2	28 259	36.4	63.6	41.4	4.5	90	24.1
Unicoi	5	14.4	58	D	1.9	321 409	5 511	32 602	D	D	D	D	9.7	2.2	7	7.5
Union	45	-1.5	111	0.0	12.8	320 044	2 887	57 931	3.3	8 039	14.1	85.9	20.8	0.7	183	17.6
Van Buren	37	6.1	151	D	11.0	561 576	3 721	60 033	5.6	22 727	17.5	82.5	29.4	3.3	221	20.0
Warren	163	1.7	146	5.4	83.7	519 646	3 569	73 327	88.2	78 595	79.6	20.4	48.1	13.3	531	13.9
Washington	112	-5.8	85	0.9	49.4	546 271	6 417	67 845	38.6	29 405	33.5	66.5	28.3	5.3	381	22.4
Wayne	133	15.7	201	0.2	36.7	404 798	2 014	52 301	22.3	33 581	15.1	84.9	39.8	4.7	533	20.3
Weakley	254	-0.6	295	3.2	203.8	878 358	2 976	140 220	129.6	150 479	66.0	34.0	42.5	19.0	2 897	51.8
White	122	-7.6	131	0.1	39.6	494 409	3 766	60 759	25.4	27 435	14.9	85.1	41.3	2.7	344	16.5
Williamson	139	-14.3	120	0.5	52.4	882 452	7 376	54 664	23.6	20 338	46.1	53.9	24.7	3.8	254	12.2
Wilson	188	-2.4	128	0.2	57.2	566 389	4 432	47 804	18.4	12 470	16.5	83.5	27.6	1.5	423	11.3
TEXAS	130 153	-0.2	523	4 489.2	29 147.5	876 614	1 676	72 180	25 375.6	101 988	29.0	71.0	29.7	7.0	643 993	21.1
Anderson	375	8.4	187	0.9	70.3	458 514	2 446	50 885	44.6	22 278	30.6	69.4	24.5	2.6	835	5.3
Andrews	752	-7.0	4 450	5.0	71.5	1 459 077	328	91 710	12.6	74 426	46.3	53.7	24.3	12.4	1 436	34.9
Angelina	117	1.5	120	0.2	21.7	378 739	3 157	45 106	46.4	47 639	9.2	90.8	24.3	3.3	168	2.6
Aransas	40	-21.8	398	0.0	2.6	679 110	1 704	43 180	1.1	10 750	18.4	81.6	14.0	2.0	93	24.0
Archer	541	6.7	1 020	0.2	115.6	1 002 917	984	87 567	76.8	144 674	16.6	83.4	53.5	21.8	2 480	40.7
Armstrong	434	-15.9	1 545	4.6	143.0	1 623 819	1 051	116 189	19.2	68 349	42.1	57.9	38.8	16.7	2 637	76.2
Atascosa	665	3.4	335	26.7	108.1	655 914	1 959	57 840	85.0	42 778	32.7	67.3	25.2	4.1	1 512	16.8
Austin	370	10.8	176	4.3	71.2	720 469	4 086	48 374	43.5	20 754	40.1	59.9	32.1	3.1	1 256	12.1
Bailey	472	-1.0	955	48.5	307.7	768 374	805	162 789	292.4	592 000	10.9	89.1	38.3	21.9	8 049	80.4
Bandera	402	22.2	402	0.6	34.1	1 082 003	2 694	42 303	11.2	11 166	11.3	88.7	16.3	0.8	455	7.1
Bastrop	388	-3.6	186	2.9	60.3	695 536	3 738	49 157	35.3	16 955	33.7	66.3	26.0	2.7	1 678	12.0
Baylor	544	-0.6	1 963	1.9	146.8	2 039 458	1 039	143 347	44.7	161 509	33.2	66.8	57.0	24.2	2 780	77.6
Bee	539	-1.7	553	5.1	70.4	1 032 344	1 866	56 745	26.0	26 739	38.2	61.8	25.6	4.4	1 051	17.9
Bell	421		166	3.1	170.5	509 341	3 062	64 187	84.9	33 510	69.0	31.0	22.5	3.8	2 125	16.3
Bexar	343	-19.5	140	8.3	89.1	597 423	4 281	44 547	72.4	29 462	75.6	24.4	17.1	2.7	706	10.0
Blanco	364	-8.0	460	0.5	22.1	2 172 696	4 728	46 035	19.1	24 172	47.3	52.7	27.4	1.8	481	9.3
Borden	464	6.7	4 073	5.0	63.1	2 381 579	585	242 132	9.4	82 781	56.6	43.4	36.8	16.7	1 527	74.6
Bosque	570	3.4	450	0.7	70.3	1 089 916	2 420	55 434	78.3	61 894	64.1	35.9	31.9	5.2	466	11.2
Bowie	273	-6.4	169	5.9	77.8	382 695	2 269	51 216	66.0	40 780	21.2	78.8	29.4	5.4	1 209	13.1
Brazoria	631	19.3	204	20.4	175.9	619 773	3 036	59 444	118.2	38 252	60.5	39.5	21.8	3.5	4 831	9.4
Brazos	299	8.5	212	7.3	41.9	798 834	3 771	53 654	95.0	67 278	13.1	86.9	26.3	4.2	1 409	8.6
Brewster	1 913	9.5	9 469	0.5	47.1	4 436 252	469	85 431	9.9	49 025	10.5	89.5	31.2	12.4	1 041	15.8
Briscoe	524	-4.1	1 859	22.8	139.6	1 550 957	834	128 057	20.4	72 465	62.6	37.4	36.5	20.2	3 481	84.4
Brooks	573	4.4	1 532	1.1	26.0	1 628 016	1 063	53 329	50.8	135 743	1.1	98.9	26.7	2.9	320	25.4
Brown	595	6.3	310	3.5	84.6	635 187	2 046	45 413	40.7	21 209	18.5	81.5	22.1	2.1	1 191	18.0
Burleson	335	-7.1	235	19.6	81.2	674 186	2 873	67 470	90.1	63 022	38.1	61.9	32.7	5.6	1 432	10.9
Burnet	485	0.6	328	1.7	44.7	1 089 307	3 324	42 226	14.7	9 935	25.3	74.7	19.4	1.6	588	6.6

Table B. States and Counties — Water Use, Wholesale Trade, Retail Trade, and Real Estate

STATE County	Water use, 2010 Total water withdrawn (mil gal/day)	Gallons withdrawn per person per day	Wholesale trade,[1] 2012 Number of establishments	Number of employees	Sales (mil dol)	Annual payroll (mil dol)	Retail trade,[2] 2012 Number of establishments	Number of employees	Sales (mil dol)	Annual payroll (mil dol)	Real estate and rental and leasing,[2] 2012 Number of establishments	Number of employees	Receipts (mil dol)	Annual payroll (mil dol)
	133	134	135	136	137	138	139	140	141	142	143	144	145	146
TENNESSEE—Cont'd														
Marshall	4.8	155	14	D	D	D	102	1 033	289.1	23.3	16	35	4.7	0.8
Maury	13.4	165	61	977	474.0	46.8	327	4 023	1 132.0	94.1	68	238	46.4	7.6
Meigs	1.5	130	1	D	D	D	29	198	51.9	3.9	4	6	0.3	0.1
Monroe	10.2	228	23	133	36.7	4.6	141	1 630	412.1	36.4	27	44	6.6	1.0
Montgomery	25.4	148	77	1 020	587.5	46.0	533	8 205	2 146.2	199.1	145	623	103.9	19.2
Moore	1.7	270	2	D	D	D	15	80	16.3	1.3	1	D	D	D
Morgan	2.4	108	3	D	D	D	33	253	54.2	4.2	1	D	D	D
Obion	8.9	281	33	423	301.5	14.5	142	1 826	457.7	40.1	22	60	7.3	1.3
Overton	3.0	134	8	D	D	D	63	498	164.1	10.9	8	D	D	D
Perry	1.9	239	1	D	D	D	29	188	40.2	3.6	3	3	0.4	0.1
Pickett	0.9	177	1	D	D	D	26	121	30.0	2.7	1	D	D	D
Polk	4.7	276	5	D	D	D	46	370	84.3	7.1	4	D	D	D
Putnam	15.5	215	65	1 150	427.2	52.2	349	4 782	1 282.9	104.4	63	172	34.2	4.5
Rhea	24.9	781	7	D	D	D	107	1 150	281.1	22.7	21	97	8.4	1.7
Roane	272.2	5 023	20	D	D	D	151	1 746	472.3	39.4	20	65	11.1	1.9
Robertson	9.7	146	39	739	724.1	23.5	172	2 313	675.2	58.2	35	95	12.2	2.1
Rutherford	38.8	148	219	6 361	14 847.0	287.0	829	12 376	3 515.3	281.7	188	990	314.0	44.2
Scott	2.7	122	4	15	9.8	0.6	67	633	153.3	13.8	10	13	2.5	0.4
Sequatchie	1.4	96	9	55	83.4	1.4	37	391	104.0	9.1	7	21	4.1	0.5
Sevier	13.4	149	38	D	D	D	645	7 349	1 561.1	150.9	146	1 185	143.2	32.0
Shelby	646.3	697	1 180	24 270	35 454.3	1 374.8	3 056	46 778	22 058.5	1 261.1	923	6 988	1 437.0	306.3
Smith	2.8	144	7	D	D	D	60	579	158.9	14.4	9	21	2.6	0.5
Stewart	1 291.4	96 924	3	8	1.4	0.2	37	289	86.6	6.3	4	18	1.3	0.2
Sullivan	512.0	3 265	174	1 733	1 006.2	67.9	547	8 149	2 095.9	187.4	110	443	77.7	13.2
Sumner	622.2	3 873	117	1 572	2 117.7	72.8	449	5 756	1 503.6	136.8	131	785	152.0	41.4
Tipton	9.1	148	18	D	D	D	145	1 667	393.6	33.3	25	80	10.5	2.2
Trousdale	1.2	155	3	D	D	D	30	234	56.2	4.4	1	D	D	D
Unicoi	6.2	336	8	D	D	D	37	505	129.5	11.1	6	19	2.4	0.7
Union	1.8	94	7	D	D	D	40	346	87.6	6.8	4	D	D	D
Van Buren	1.4	243	1	D	D	D	10	60	9.4	0.8	2	D	D	D
Warren	10.6	266	26	D	D	D	157	1 618	376.4	34.6	22	51	11.8	1.5
Washington	23.3	190	118	1 259	791.3	52.2	520	8 260	2 011.5	174.7	114	588	91.7	18.0
Wayne	2.3	135	5	D	D	D	45	335	65.0	5.8	5	D	D	D
Weakley	5.4	153	27	295	243.0	13.6	123	1 178	297.4	24.5	20	57	9.3	1.1
White	4.4	168	15	D	D	D	82	811	209.4	18.6	14	32	2.4	0.6
Williamson	4.1	23	237	2 762	10 285.7	186.4	766	12 866	3 968.6	354.4	249	1 397	500.8	77.0
Wilson	17.0	149	88	1 646	1 362.9	88.5	403	5 471	1 432.6	123.7	106	542	94.8	18.5
TEXAS	24 796.7	986	27 752	408 692	691 242.6	24 826.1	78 281	1 150 148	356 116.4	28 835.5	26 639	169 941	38 757.4	7 751.8
Anderson	28.7	491	33	D	D	D	164	1 913	572.1	47.1	34	124	34.7	5.8
Andrews	64.0	4 329	15	D	D	D	30	344	169.8	12.5	15	114	26.7	8.5
Angelina	15.2	175	62	808	360.6	35.2	324	4 580	1 274.7	109.4	79	329	54.4	10.8
Aransas	0.7	29	8	63	10.5	1.1	73	920	288.9	25.0	36	79	13.3	1.9
Archer	7.0	768	13	D	D	D	14	102	25.5	1.8	3	D	D	D
Armstrong	4.7	2 462	3	D	D	D	4	D	D	D	1	D	D	D
Atascosa	41.2	917	38	D	D	D	115	1 709	564.7	38.8	35	226	66.5	11.6
Austin	7.0	246	23	679	728.8	34.1	83	939	272.4	22.4	20	47	9.5	1.5
Bailey	65.2	9 096	19	D	D	D	21	229	49.0	4.3	NA	NA	NA	NA
Bandera	3.4	165	5	28	8.1	1.1	49	299	81.2	5.7	8	18	2.8	0.6
Bastrop	223.3	3 011	34	D	D	D	175	2 462	867.8	59.6	44	132	24.8	3.7
Baylor	6.0	1 602	6	35	30.9	1.4	16	99	24.0	1.7	1	D	D	D
Bee	8.5	266	12	D	D	D	78	1 050	330.6	26.1	27	98	17.8	3.7
Bell	73.6	237	126	2 616	3 630.5	135.2	922	13 098	3 626.1	293.2	299	1 486	217.9	50.4
Bexar	1 342.1	783	1 464	D	D	D	4 845	80 840	26 480.6	1 994.5	1 718	13 472	3 054.2	601.3
Blanco	2.2	212	8	D	D	D	32	209	68.7	4.7	4	9	1.1	0.2
Borden	6.7	10 374	NA	NA	NA	NA	1	D	D	D	NA	NA	NA	NA
Bosque	9.7	533	10	77	22.0	2.9	53	417	90.7	8.1	10	23	2.1	0.5
Bowie	16.0	173	90	D	D	D	413	6 170	1 611.3	146.2	102	455	93.3	17.3
Brazoria	856.3	2 734	228	1 865	1 636.4	102.3	797	13 282	3 686.3	314.0	248	1 566	392.8	77.3
Brazos	67.9	349	140	1 704	1 191.8	86.6	629	9 807	2 672.0	207.8	231	1 299	260.8	43.5
Brewster	3.7	403	11	D	D	D	49	405	87.7	8.0	21	148	5.4	1.2
Briscoe	26.8	16 359	4	D	D	D	6	23	6.3	0.4	1	D	D	D
Brooks	3.3	457	2	D	D	D	18	297	85.8	6.7	4	10	2.1	0.3
Brown	16.0	420	35	D	D	D	181	1 872	509.0	41.5	36	132	20.0	3.9
Burleson	29.3	1 705	18	D	D	D	58	653	293.2	17.9	6	14	3.1	0.6
Burnet	16.9	396	41	336	163.1	14.8	182	2 015	617.7	52.1	46	148	25.8	5.2

1. Merchant wholesalers, except manufacturers' sales branches and offices.   2. Employer establishments.

Table B. States and Counties — Professional Services, Manufacturing, and Accommodation and Food Services

STATE County	Professional, scientific, and technical services, 2012				Manufacturing, 2012				Accommodation and food services, 2012			
	Number of establishments	Number of employees	Receipts (mil dol)	Annual payroll (mil dol)	Number of establishments	Number of employees	Receipts (mil dol)	Annual payroll (mil dol)	Number of establishments	Number of employees	Sales (mil dol)	Annual payroll (mil dol)
	147	148	149	150	151	152	153	154	155	156	157	158
TENNESSEE—Cont'd												
Marshall	30	88	7.7	2.2	45	2 656	1 085.2	128.0	45	512	25.5	6.4
Maury	104	620	57.8	23.4	76	3 582	1 902.1	201.5	158	2 859	123.1	35.4
Meigs	3	D	D	D	11	753	233.0	28.2	15	D	D	D
Monroe	42	197	16.2	6.1	60	4 333	1 509.3	171.6	82	918	41.7	10.6
Montgomery	177	1 677	235.5	78.7	68	5 519	2 256.0	258.2	338	6 157	296.8	81.1
Moore	4	D	D	D	5	D	D	D	8	D	D	D
Morgan	6	D	D	D	20	330	63.3	12.8	8	D	D	D
Obion	32	119	14.1	4.3	39	2 439	1 195.0	82.2	57	822	33.4	8.4
Overton	22	D	D	D	28	D	D	D	25	D	D	D
Perry	4	D	D	D	11	515	D	17.2	8	D	D	D
Pickett	3	5	0.4	0.1	8	86	14.8	2.2	12	D	D	D
Polk	8	14	2.2	0.5	9	108	D	5.4	18	296	9.3	2.5
Putnam	141	584	70.8	25.4	99	4 301	1 214.4	162.2	159	3 666	158.8	45.1
Rhea	29	79	6.0	2.0	29	3 544	848.6	121.0	48	792	30.7	8.0
Roane	56	D	D	D	23	1 096	270.1	40.5	68	1 359	52.0	15.1
Robertson	64	208	21.2	7.3	78	5 788	1 793.0	218.1	91	1 536	65.6	18.4
Rutherford	340	2 304	265.6	117.2	200	14 761	11 539.0	818.0	469	11 020	502.7	146.5
Scott	13	41	3.8	2.1	31	738	113.7	22.2	24	387	14.4	3.9
Sequatchie	13	42	4.0	1.7	8	111	D	5.1	15	D	D	D
Sevier	151	779	69.9	25.3	69	939	263.2	41.2	508	11 751	832.7	221.2
Shelby	1 762	17 349	2 496.2	1 055.5	580	24 360	22 412.7	1 417.0	1 659	36 739	1 889.7	529.1
Smith	16	D	D	D	17	959	D	41.9	21	D	D	D
Stewart	4	D	D	D	9	194	37.1	6.2	19	D	D	D
Sullivan	266	1 875	232.4	89.4	143	15 287	6 361.4	1 030.5	317	6 340	286.4	82.4
Sumner	210	1 837	213.7	92.7	173	6 127	2 158.4	271.7	231	4 416	195.6	58.1
Tipton	33	131	11.1	3.3	26	1 591	446.3	56.2	63	882	39.5	10.1
Trousdale	8	35	2.5	0.8	6	195	D	6.8	9	108	4.3	1.1
Unicoi	7	16	2.0	0.6	19	1 698	440.7	90.4	32	344	15.9	4.1
Union	11	D	D	D	14	544	125.9	19.2	9	161	7.4	2.0
Van Buren	1	D	D	D	6	D	D	D	1	D	D	D
Warren	40	117	10.4	3.4	57	3 276	1 311.7	141.4	51	770	32.3	8.2
Washington	222	2 751	218.3	102.0	116	4 536	1 503.7	179.2	283	6 344	278.5	80.8
Wayne	10	19	1.4	0.4	21	530	79.9	16.4	17	170	7.1	2.0
Weakley	23	91	8.3	2.4	25	1 033	D	34.7	58	816	35.5	8.8
White	18	32	3.4	0.7	40	1 910	561.1	82.2	28	D	D	D
Williamson	792	7 610	1 465.0	580.1	119	2 237	558.3	92.9	437	9 418	485.2	138.0
Wilson	185	D	D	D	108	2 851	1 281.6	143.6	212	4 345	190.0	56.8
TEXAS	62 322	639 561	122 086.2	47 256.4	19 782	767 024	702 603.1	42 529.8	48 721	976 390	54 480.8	14 743.8
Anderson	81	238	32.0	10.6	24	245	D	10.8	68	D	D	D
Andrews	24	D	D	D	7	387	135.9	15.3	26	372	21.4	5.1
Angelina	147	768	91.7	33.6	65	4 602	1 451.6	177.8	144	3 162	141.5	40.1
Aransas	37	153	20.8	4.9	7	26	D	0.8	74	1 032	50.5	13.4
Archer	9	D	D	D	11	D	D	D	8	D	D	D
Armstrong	1	D	D	D	NA	NA	NA	NA	1	D	D	D
Atascosa	44	240	34.2	10.8	21	216	D	8.3	62	951	52.3	13.6
Austin	49	235	23.8	10.9	33	2 085	D	117.2	49	521	28.7	7.5
Bailey	12	38	4.2	1.5	7	148	D	5.2	14	212	7.9	2.3
Bandera	35	104	10.5	3.4	11	35	D	1.0	49	559	26.6	8.6
Bastrop	101	416	46.1	14.6	59	990	284.4	42.0	109	2 273	138.0	39.8
Baylor	7	24	1.4	0.8	4	44	D	1.1	9	71	5.5	0.7
Bee	38	D	D	D	9	92	D	4.3	56	725	40.5	10.5
Bell	365	3 505	407.6	164.2	136	5 724	1 962.5	237.3	584	11 467	552.0	149.9
Bexar	3 963	40 811	6 684.3	2 557.1	873	30 474	14 766.1	1 478.3	3 612	88 432	5 006.7	1 365.3
Blanco	26	D	D	D	13	109	26.4	4.6	27	277	11.5	3.6
Borden	1	D	D	D	NA	NA	NA	NA	NA	NA	NA	NA
Bosque	22	48	5.7	2.3	16	431	115.2	19.2	22	172	10.1	2.3
Bowie	156	846	86.5	29.2	56	1 840	462.7	78.9	184	4 141	193.8	55.7
Brazoria	456	2 433	316.1	126.5	212	12 119	32 864.6	1 016.8	474	9 303	462.5	127.2
Brazos	401	2 690	523.0	134.3	100	4 480	1 063.6	178.3	436	9 491	446.5	121.5
Brewster	17	49	5.6	1.6	11	27	5.9	0.9	40	617	31.5	8.5
Briscoe	1	D	D	D	NA	NA	NA	NA	3	10	0.3	0.1
Brooks	9	25	2.3	0.5	NA	NA	NA	NA	21	289	15.6	4.3
Brown	54	D	D	D	31	2 292	1 222.0	107.5	81	1 270	59.9	16.4
Burleson	23	149	12.4	4.2	15	353	D	16.9	40	266	14.1	3.3
Burnet	84	473	33.5	14.6	52	687	259.9	33.2	110	1 545	89.0	25.6

1. Establishment subject to federal tax.

STATE County	Health care and social assistance, 2012				Other services, 2012				Nonemployer businesses, 2014		Value of residential construction authorized by building permits, 2015	
	Number of establishments	Number of employees	Receipts (mil dol)	Annual payroll (mil dol)	Number of establishments	Number of employees	Receipts (mil dol)	Annual payroll (mil dol)	Number	Receipts (mil dol)	New Construction ($1,000)	Number of housing units
	159	160	161	162	163	164	165	166	167	168	169	170
TENNESSEE—Cont'd												
Marshall	56	724	57.3	19.8	25	111	11.9	2.8	1 932	81.4	18 200	107
Maury	213	5 384	539.7	208.3	107	661	60.5	18.1	5 971	248.9	167 981	875
Meigs	10	D	D	D	7	D	D	D	682	29.0	9 463	45
Monroe	72	1 480	118.5	42.1	40	D	D	D	2 712	117.1	3 940	66
Montgomery	331	7 170	662.2	251.9	184	975	76.1	21.2	9 305	440.8	160 739	1 263
Moore	6	187	12.5	7.5	5	9	0.6	0.1	439	19.8	4 956	27
Morgan	15	370	33.2	13.1	7	D	D	D	1 134	38.0	0	0
Obion	86	D	D	D	39	D	D	D	1 846	65.8	5 385	74
Overton	35	D	D	D	18	D	D	D	1 805	68.6	114	3
Perry	14	396	26.1	10.8	8	D	D	D	584	26.2	781	4
Pickett	5	D	D	D	4	D	D	D	450	22.1	NA	NA
Polk	18	395	30.9	12.7	8	22	2.0	0.4	1 065	39.7	27 739	154
Putnam	228	5 719	511.9	214.5	115	D	D	D	5 869	261.5	74 335	563
Rhea	68	968	68.2	28.4	26	89	7.6	2.1	1 634	55.2	1 890	12
Roane	91	1 892	128.8	53.5	46	192	20.3	5.0	3 019	118.9	613	8
Robertson	122	1 908	176.3	70.4	69	209	21.7	5.5	4 946	225.1	46 652	277
Rutherford	524	13 614	1 376.6	586.1	301	2 632	282.7	78.4	19 604	907.9	535 890	3 557
Scott	41	1 002	65.2	23.7	16	D	D	D	1 326	58.5	242	4
Sequatchie	22	D	D	D	8	21	1.8	0.4	1 059	34.7	140	3
Sevier	150	2 281	198.9	67.3	144	846	78.6	22.3	7 843	365.1	55 545	319
Shelby	2 338	68 016	8 166.7	3 140.9	1 202	10 502	1 938.8	366.1	79 157	2 924.6	322 598	2 325
Smith	26	D	D	D	12	D	D	D	1 323	54.1	6 639	41
Stewart	15	195	18.2	8.1	11	D	D	D	808	27.0	0	0
Sullivan	444	12 341	1 521.5	567.3	220	D	D	D	9 667	406.0	59 964	514
Sumner	334	5 369	599.5	219.1	197	944	98.6	24.6	14 164	694.8	213 021	1 074
Tipton	84	1 314	141.3	45.5	41	160	20.1	4.9	3 908	131.2	17 304	105
Trousdale	23	233	19.3	6.1	6	D	D	D	567	27.2	7 876	69
Unicoi	26	747	44.7	18.3	19	D	D	D	801	29.1	475	4
Union	20	177	11.6	4.8	15	47	4.9	1.3	1 203	46.3	9 375	64
Van Buren	2	D	D	D	2	D	D	D	380	12.6	0	0
Warren	98	1 428	114.7	43.6	48	D	D	D	2 905	121.0	7 518	52
Washington	351	14 010	1 641.3	737.0	175	910	69.9	22.6	7 954	362.6	83 295	575
Wayne	31	402	34.3	12.7	12	39	4.7	1.0	860	31.7	0	0
Weakley	81	1 582	134.6	50.9	37	168	15.2	4.2	1 690	71.8	4 713	23
White	38	856	68.3	24.3	27	D	D	D	1 921	77.4	8 745	87
Williamson	634	11 192	1 456.1	591.2	323	2 109	200.2	60.5	24 164	1 644.4	736 172	2 304
Wilson	268	3 941	392.5	151.2	149	1 091	95.2	31.3	10 363	504.8	284 100	1 357
TEXAS	61 342	1 345 664	145 035.1	54 570.6	34 116	259 128	30 172.2	8 454.5	2 150 702	107 536.9	29 086 961	175 443
Anderson	141	2 214	216.2	78.4	60	308	22.3	7.8	3 106	131.8	1 148	7
Andrews	26	475	64.0	22.8	23	D	D	D	1 290	96.0	5 064	22
Angelina	285	7 839	588.4	240.8	119	818	152.6	32.8	5 271	261.6	7 752	54
Aransas	44	518	46.2	14.8	47	150	14.1	3.4	2 624	119.3	35 038	179
Archer	12	D	D	D	10	D	D	D	874	49.4	1 178	6
Armstrong	4	93	3.1	1.6	2	D	D	D	168	7.9	600	1
Atascosa	80	1 309	115.4	43.0	48	217	23.8	5.2	3 335	154.7	7 111	43
Austin	44	D	D	D	31	114	11.6	2.8	2 695	138.2	3 156	19
Bailey	15	251	16.9	6.6	12	37	3.9	0.8	374	23.6	0	0
Bandera	24	339	21.4	8.4	32	105	11.4	2.8	2 238	108.4	0	0
Bastrop	108	1 983	155.1	62.7	78	330	31.1	8.6	5 947	268.6	14 445	127
Baylor	13	511	19.3	8.6	15	D	D	D	273	11.4	150	1
Bee	50	D	D	D	38	187	18.3	4.7	1 499	59.3	512	7
Bell	524	22 484	2 849.6	1 245.3	409	2 898	202.5	72.7	16 167	674.1	314 516	2 042
Bexar	4 314	110 407	12 143.6	4 363.8	2 461	17 571	1 645.4	478.9	127 915	5 897.4	808 959	4 404
Blanco	18	159	7.8	3.6	15	44	7.4	1.4	1 335	67.3	1 952	10
Borden	NA	NA	NA	NA	NA	NA	NA	NA	55	3.1	NA	NA
Bosque	20	606	42.2	16.4	21	69	5.4	1.4	1 456	66.9	470	5
Bowie	289	7 151	798.4	295.4	154	979	87.0	26.4	5 255	225.9	17 313	285
Brazoria	627	8 038	646.5	273.7	369	2 558	237.6	75.3	23 328	1 043.6	666 126	3 365
Brazos	399	8 166	1 040.0	376.0	266	1 939	374.6	53.6	12 732	598.9	248 814	1 616
Brewster	24	548	30.0	12.1	20	D	D	D	960	32.8	1 356	11
Briscoe	3	4	0.2	0.1	1	D	D	D	131	5.3	NA	NA
Brooks	20	339	10.7	5.3	11	31	3.3	0.7	586	14.7	0	0
Brown	136	3 126	206.2	77.2	69	381	24.3	6.9	2 470	105.9	16 848	126
Burleson	16	D	D	D	26	115	11.4	3.7	1 399	62.6	873	9
Burnet	106	1 302	145.3	51.5	71	303	24.0	6.9	4 975	276.3	76 117	307

Table B. States and Counties — Government Employment and Payroll, and Local Government Finances

STATE County	Full-time equivalent employees	March payroll (dollars)	Administration, judicial, and legal	Police and Corrections	Fire Protection	Highways and transportation	Health and Welfare	Natural resources and utilities	Education and libraries	Total (mil dol)	Intergovernmental (mil dol)	Taxes Total (mil dol)	Per capita Total	Per capita Property
	171	172	173	174	175	176	177	178	179	180	181	182	183	184
TENNESSEE—Cont'd														
Marshall	1 203	3 538 766	7.5	9.0	3.9	2.6	5.0	17.4	52.4	86.1	36.7	29.2	947	612
Maury	4 616	17 056 047	3.2	6.1	2.9	2.0	47.4	6.3	30.7	499.9	86.1	89.0	1 086	702
Meigs	438	942 766	9.9	10.0	0.1	7.3	3.2	2.3	67.2	24.7	17.0	5.2	441	333
Monroe	1 373	3 993 045	7.7	8.8	1.3	3.3	4.4	9.7	64.2	96.5	51.5	31.4	696	447
Montgomery	6 061	19 419 026	4.6	11.0	3.6	3.7	5.7	6.1	63.4	519.4	202.5	207.0	1 122	681
Moore	237	724 102	2.2	14.7	0.1	9.4	3.2	8.5	61.9	15.5	8.0	5.6	884	707
Morgan	796	1 965 391	7.2	7.4	0.0	4.6	5.8	5.4	68.9	42.3	28.2	10.4	475	387
Obion	1 057	3 471 219	8.5	14.0	3.5	4.1	0.4	7.6	60.8	80.5	42.6	24.7	789	436
Overton	829	2 041 789	5.5	9.1	0.7	4.4	6.6	7.0	65.6	46.5	30.0	11.5	520	304
Perry	339	836 675	10.6	3.6	0.0	5.3	3.5	5.7	67.5	22.6	13.7	5.6	716	537
Pickett	180	540 892	11.1	15.0	0.6	9.3	3.5	4.7	55.8	13.0	8.2	3.4	670	349
Polk	595	1 517 421	15.7	1.5	0.0	7.2	2.1	5.6	67.4	36.3	22.3	11.2	674	514
Putnam	4 261	15 613 316	2.1	4.8	1.2	1.6	55.8	4.6	27.7	418.9	71.7	81.6	1 114	597
Rhea	1 269	3 661 964	5.1	6.0	0.8	2.6	18.6	8.5	54.3	86.8	39.8	20.0	621	367
Roane	1 700	6 055 393	5.5	6.7	3.8	2.6	1.3	17.4	61.6	147.3	59.5	50.7	948	593
Robertson	2 143	5 842 234	11.7	12.9	2.0	4.7	1.8	7.6	58.5	164.1	73.4	70.3	1 050	658
Rutherford	8 751	29 120 491	7.0	11.2	3.9	1.2	3.2	8.8	62.0	738.4	270.4	325.5	1 186	718
Scott	1 044	2 569 027	6.5	7.4	0.9	5.4	5.6	10.3	56.6	56.6	33.7	12.4	560	370
Sequatchie	429	1 170 657	6.1	8.5	0.0	0.5	5.6	7.1	71.3	32.3	19.5	9.3	645	457
Sevier	3 747	12 103 289	4.1	9.3	3.0	4.0	3.5	8.2	62.6	359.9	83.9	186.0	2 010	703
Shelby	39 378	138 123 866	7.0	15.4	7.3	4.6	11.4	14.4	38.1	4 311.3	1 448.6	1 719.3	1 828	1 235
Smith	725	1 800 266	8.4	11.3	0.6	6.1	2.0	7.1	61.0	45.3	25.5	13.2	693	395
Stewart	498	1 358 521	8.2	10.6	0.2	5.1	5.7	3.5	65.2	36.1	23.5	9.2	693	470
Sullivan	5 719	18 566 959	5.4	9.7	3.3	4.6	4.4	5.7	64.8	404.7	154.7	177.3	1 131	800
Sumner	5 626	16 827 689	5.9	10.4	4.6	1.7	3.7	8.6	63.7	406.0	171.8	163.0	981	658
Tipton	2 180	6 476 685	4.4	8.2	2.1	2.7	0.9	8.0	72.1	146.0	87.1	41.2	668	453
Trousdale	275	758 540	10.0	16.9	0.0	0.0	4.0	1.1	68.0	18.5	11.4	4.6	596	490
Unicoi	819	2 543 400	3.6	3.8	1.5	4.4	24.1	4.2	48.7	63.6	21.5	9.0	495	392
Union	593	1 652 593	8.9	6.9	0.0	4.2	0.9	6.7	72.2	47.6	34.6	8.9	466	312
Van Buren	275	698 479	8.3	7.1	1.3	19.0	5.9	2.5	55.9	13.1	8.7	3.1	554	397
Warren	1 148	3 625 874	6.8	9.9	2.3	1.1	6.3	13.7	58.4	97.8	53.6	31.0	779	452
Washington	4 114	12 590 200	5.8	10.1	3.4	7.7	2.2	15.3	53.6	294.8	106.3	133.5	1 068	712
Wayne	611	1 515 515	5.5	10.2	0.2	4.9	1.5	4.4	71.7	45.0	23.8	10.1	595	364
Weakley	1 333	3 550 802	5.6	11.2	2.3	5.4	9.1	13.8	50.6	73.0	37.4	20.2	579	318
White	908	2 433 483	6.9	8.8	0.8	3.2	3.5	9.7	65.1	53.2	31.7	14.3	548	338
Williamson	8 184	27 964 745	5.4	6.5	3.3	2.0	20.1	5.4	55.8	754.7	175.6	348.2	1 805	1 175
Wilson	3 881	11 949 351	7.0	10.1	4.4	3.3	1.0	8.4	64.6	281.9	110.9	131.1	1 102	707
TEXAS	X	X	X	X	X	X	X	X	X	X	X	X	X	X
Anderson	1 888	5 360 452	8.0	11.5	3.0	3.1	0.6	3.8	69.2	124.5	47.1	61.2	1 052	867
Andrews	1 090	4 021 801	5.8	6.7	0.0	2.3	33.8	5.1	46.1	121.7	9.4	81.6	5 063	4 756
Angelina	4 483	13 382 100	4.8	8.0	2.7	2.0	11.2	3.8	66.5	300.9	135.8	97.6	1 114	832
Aransas	888	2 584 176	9.4	13.5	0.0	5.1	2.4	5.8	61.2	78.8	13.5	50.4	2 117	1 856
Archer	436	1 231 876	8.0	6.2	0.0	2.7	1.6	4.3	76.7	26.8	10.9	12.0	1 378	1 224
Armstrong	112	284 475	10.7	2.6	0.0	2.6	2.2	3.2	77.2	9.5	3.3	3.2	1 666	1 480
Atascosa	2 208	6 519 286	5.0	7.2	0.0	2.0	13.3	3.4	67.8	191.3	123.7	49.0	1 056	822
Austin	1 209	3 635 525	7.8	10.5	0.0	3.4	2.6	5.7	69.1	87.7	23.7	51.5	1 801	1 613
Bailey	547	1 435 208	5.2	6.9	0.0	2.6	29.6	1.9	53.0	36.8	12.6	9.8	1 375	1 158
Bandera	640	2 084 125	8.5	10.8	0.2	3.9	4.1	2.5	68.5	46.4	8.5	32.2	1 567	1 462
Bastrop	2 838	9 520 485	5.2	12.2	0.0	2.3	0.8	3.0	76.0	243.4	86.4	112.0	1 498	1 314
Baylor	318	889 487	6.6	4.2	0.0	2.8	45.1	5.7	34.2	22.6	4.9	3.9	1 085	880
Bee	1 435	4 453 164	5.0	5.5	1.3	2.9	4.8	5.0	74.6	114.4	63.6	30.2	930	752
Bell	16 055	50 764 685	4.5	8.6	3.4	1.9	2.7	4.5	73.5	1 144.1	497.9	378.1	1 171	912
Bexar	76 821	296 304 428	4.1	8.7	3.4	4.0	10.0	11.6	57.2	7 217.6	2 547.6	2 991.4	1 675	1 345
Blanco	357	1 339 398	8.8	7.8	0.0	1.9	0.2	3.3	77.7	39.5	6.7	29.4	2 761	2 644
Borden	74	200 651	18.7	3.1	0.0	8.2	0.0	0.5	68.4	14.0	2.2	11.3	18 268	18 188
Bosque	689	2 029 654	8.4	7.1	0.0	2.6	0.4	2.1	77.7	47.1	20.0	22.7	1 253	1 100
Bowie	4 233	13 543 434	5.4	7.5	2.7	2.3	0.7	7.1	73.2	292.7	128.5	118.6	1 273	993
Brazoria	12 753	42 706 512	5.9	10.5	0.7	2.7	5.3	4.6	69.2	1 184.7	316.7	617.5	1 901	1 646
Brazos	7 250	22 942 099	8.3	13.0	5.1	4.6	3.7	12.3	47.5	549.9	134.9	310.5	1 547	1 241
Brewster	439	1 264 854	9.4	14.2	0.0	3.7	0.7	6.1	63.5	31.3	14.9	12.8	1 373	1 071
Briscoe	68	181 356	19.1	3.9	0.0	5.1	1.2	13.9	56.0	4.9	1.8	2.3	1 491	1 329
Brooks	470	1 100 857	8.0	8.1	0.4	3.7	1.2	7.4	70.9	40.5	15.5	18.6	2 598	2 321
Brown	1 839	5 391 982	6.8	9.8	2.3	3.3	10.4	7.5	59.2	125.8	54.0	52.8	1 397	1 099
Burleson	707	1 886 727	9.3	7.8	0.0	4.3	0.7	3.5	74.3	46.7	14.9	26.1	1 507	1 240
Burnet	1 778	6 073 530	9.9	14.7	4.3	2.7	0.2	7.3	59.5	155.5	24.4	99.6	2 293	2 003

1. Based on the resident population estimated as of July 1 of the year shown.

Table B. States and Counties — Local Government Finances, Government Employment, and Voting

STATE County	Total (mil dol)	Per capita[1] (dollars)	Education	Health and hospitals	Police protection	Public welfare	Highways	Total (mil dol)	Per capita[1] (dollars)	Federal civilian	Federal military	State and local	Democratic	Republican	All other
	185	186	187	188	189	190	191	192	193	194	195	196	197	198	199
TENNESSEE—Cont'd															
Marshall	82.9	2 684	52.1	3.0	8.4	0.2	5.3	93.9	3 039	60	98	1 633	38.3	59.8	1.9
Maury	491.1	5 990	19.6	56.1	3.7	0.0	3.1	294.5	3 592	172	268	6 268	38.7	60.1	1.2
Meigs	23.1	1 979	63.8	2.5	5.7	0.5	8.0	7.5	637	28	37	487	32.4	66.0	1.6
Monroe	104.4	2 314	64.5	4.7	5.5	0.1	5.1	101.6	2 250	89	142	1 983	30.1	68.5	1.4
Montgomery	461.9	2 504	57.1	3.0	7.0	0.0	4.1	4 359.0	23 630	1 161	629	9 033	45.5	53.4	1.1
Moore	15.3	2 419	59.1	2.9	4.2	0.1	11.9	10.0	1 582	0	20	864	29.8	68.1	2.1
Morgan	41.9	1 911	64.0	5.8	4.0	0.4	6.2	30.5	1 389	35	61	1 309	28.9	69.1	2.0
Obion	81.3	2 595	55.8	0.3	6.3	3.1	8.4	30.1	960	110	97	1 581	32.2	66.3	1.6
Overton	44.3	1 997	60.0	3.6	4.9	0.1	6.9	44.2	1 992	40	69	1 242	42.3	55.6	2.2
Perry	21.2	2 699	47.8	5.5	4.8	0.0	8.5	8.1	1 031	17	24	434	44.3	53.2	2.5
Pickett	13.0	2 545	48.4	5.3	3.9	0.0	10.4	3.4	663	0	16	284	32.0	66.9	1.2
Polk	34.7	2 079	61.1	2.7	6.5	0.1	8.0	19.5	1 171	70	52	758	32.7	65.6	1.7
Putnam	420.4	5 740	22.0	57.2	3.4	0.0	2.3	286.9	3 919	229	231	8 243	35.7	62.6	1.7
Rhea	100.3	3 111	50.3	17.1	4.9	0.0	5.3	141.2	4 378	1 172	101	1 686	26.2	72.4	1.4
Roane	135.7	2 538	58.0	2.9	4.6	0.2	4.6	117.8	2 203	455	165	3 342	31.0	67.3	1.7
Robertson	151.2	2 259	56.5	3.0	9.4	0.0	4.9	198.9	2 971	80	214	3 543	33.7	64.8	1.4
Rutherford	715.7	2 608	53.2	2.1	8.2	1.5	4.4	983.5	3 583	2 740	922	15 234	39.8	58.9	1.4
Scott	55.5	2 502	62.9	3.9	4.5	2.5	6.6	69.2	3 121	85	69	1 416	25.4	72.7	1.9
Sequatchie	28.3	1 960	60.8	3.3	6.5	0.0	5.5	20.7	1 434	13	46	912	31.6	66.4	2.0
Sevier	377.1	4 076	36.1	2.9	5.4	0.1	6.1	1 420.7	15 357	337	299	4 630	25.3	73.4	1.2
Shelby	4 592.5	4 882	44.5	8.2	8.9	1.1	2.0	5 549.0	5 898	13 714	3 841	54 005	63.4	36.0	0.6
Smith	46.3	2 421	56.5	3.9	7.0	0.1	6.8	37.3	1 955	126	60	943	38.7	58.9	2.4
Stewart	34.1	2 565	59.2	4.6	6.3	0.0	7.3	35.9	2 697	497	42	672	44.9	53.7	1.5
Sullivan	439.1	2 801	49.3	2.5	6.5	0.0	4.1	464.0	2 959	482	491	7 462	28.7	70.0	1.3
Sumner	387.5	2 333	56.0	2.5	7.6	0.1	4.7	365.1	2 198	466	544	7 306	32.0	66.9	1.2
Tipton	139.6	2 263	63.6	0.7	6.7	0.1	6.6	67.3	1 091	94	192	2 616	31.3	67.8	0.9
Trousdale	20.8	2 672	57.7	2.4	6.2	0.2	9.5	0.0	0	31	25	461	45.5	52.1	2.3
Unicoi	70.8	3 884	31.1	44.7	3.2	0.3	5.1	50.1	2 748	67	56	861	29.2	69.4	1.5
Union	45.7	2 387	70.7	3.8	4.1	0.2	4.9	34.2	1 787	22	60	833	28.6	69.8	1.6
Van Buren	17.4	3 085	70.1	3.3	3.6	0.0	8.9	9.0	1 604	0	18	381	38.5	58.7	2.9
Warren	107.0	2 687	60.0	3.5	4.8	0.0	5.4	47.1	1 181	88	125	1 863	38.3	59.5	2.2
Washington	308.7	2 467	44.9	1.3	7.5	0.5	5.7	609.5	4 872	2 604	424	9 462	32.5	66.0	1.4
Wayne	44.4	2 612	47.4	0.4	4.4	17.6	6.9	31.8	1 874	30	47	1 603	24.5	73.7	1.7
Weakley	68.4	1 967	54.8	0.5	6.6	11.4	8.3	23.7	682	115	106	3 729	33.6	64.7	1.7
White	50.7	1 943	60.1	2.7	5.8	0.3	5.6	21.8	835	52	82	1 299	35.0	63.3	1.8
Williamson	720.3	3 734	44.7	20.8	4.0	0.0	4.3	886.6	4 596	431	649	10 109	29.8	69.3	1.0
Wilson	304.2	2 557	61.0	0.4	7.4	0.0	4.9	398.5	3 350	183	394	4 919	31.1	67.6	1.3
TEXAS	X	X	X	X	X	X	X	X	X	193 961	172 297	1 617 690	43.7	55.5	0.9
Anderson	133.7	2 297	64.2	0.2	4.5	0.4	4.2	165.8	2 850	124	90	5 475	27.8	71.4	0.8
Andrews	109.9	6 817	50.8	29.4	3.5	0.0	1.1	185.6	11 518	14	36	1 225	17.1	82.4	0.5
Angelina	307.3	3 509	57.1	10.2	4.5	0.3	4.2	395.7	4 517	322	177	6 747	32.2	67.1	0.7
Aransas	80.8	3 391	53.6	1.1	9.5	1.2	4.4	116.6	4 897	18	51	1 036	30.7	68.4	0.8
Archer	26.8	3 072	60.0	1.1	6.2	0.4	7.7	257.0	29 423	22	83	491	17.0	82.4	0.7
Armstrong	8.5	4 369	44.7	28.9	3.6	0.2	4.8	4.2	2 172	0	0	133	12.9	86.5	0.6
Atascosa	210.7	4 536	43.4	9.8	2.8	0.8	23.3	433.1	9 325	54	98	2 472	44.4	55.0	0.6
Austin	84.2	2 944	55.5	4.8	7.5	0.0	7.6	104.0	3 635	74	60	1 403	24.1	75.0	1.0
Bailey	34.7	4 873	39.4	36.7	4.8	0.0	3.9	50.9	7 137	23	14	578	29.4	69.9	0.7
Bandera	43.7	2 128	59.1	2.9	6.1	0.5	5.8	35.4	1 721	14	43	717	24.2	74.6	1.2
Bastrop	242.4	3 242	50.0	11.5	5.2	0.6	5.9	413.3	5 529	374	157	3 524	45.1	53.3	1.6
Baylor	20.8	5 731	29.9	49.2	3.4	0.6	3.5	3.0	829	19	0	231	22.3	76.8	0.9
Bee	111.6	3 432	71.0	1.4	3.1	1.8	2.5	62.7	1 928	36	52	3 260	44.7	54.8	0.5
Bell	1 144.2	3 542	60.4	2.5	4.9	0.5	2.7	1 912.0	5 919	10 222	39 737	19 540	44.7	54.5	0.8
Bexar	7 362.8	4 123	44.0	14.4	5.4	2.0	2.3	18 461.5	10 338	34 009	32 977	106 140	52.4	46.8	0.7
Blanco	38.6	3 621	55.5	0.1	3.6	0.0	9.2	37.3	3 505	57	22	491	29.7	69.2	1.1
Borden	23.8	38 584	84.8	0.0	0.6	0.1	3.3	22.5	36 494	0	0	84	11.1	87.5	1.4
Bosque	45.2	2 493	68.1	0.1	4.3	0.7	4.0	30.9	1 705	66	36	1 176	23.5	75.4	1.1
Bowie	279.8	3 004	63.0	0.3	4.7	0.4	5.3	243.0	2 609	3 827	198	6 305	30.7	68.7	0.6
Brazoria	1 133.2	3 489	48.6	5.5	5.0	0.2	6.1	3 469.8	10 684	454	744	17 665	34.8	64.3	0.9
Brazos	577.4	2 877	45.4	2.3	6.2	0.4	5.6	1 281.3	6 385	728	471	35 122	34.9	63.9	1.2
Brewster	31.8	3 412	50.6	3.2	7.7	0.4	6.8	9.3	995	281	19	1 058	50.5	47.6	1.9
Briscoe	3.7	2 339	51.9	0.1	4.3	0.0	11.3	7.8	4 998	10	0	110	24.7	74.3	1.0
Brooks	42.3	5 904	45.4	2.3	10.2	0.3	5.0	40.3	5 626	344	15	512	75.7	24.1	0.3
Brown	120.7	3 191	51.3	7.8	5.5	0.5	4.3	150.8	3 986	124	74	2 722	18.8	80.3	0.9
Burleson	42.2	2 441	59.8	0.6	4.9	0.0	11.0	23.6	1 367	46	35	780	30.8	68.2	1.0
Burnet	148.6	3 420	46.0	1.6	5.8	0.4	3.8	219.9	5 061	74	90	2 397	27.3	71.4	1.3

1. Based on the resident population estimated as of July 1 of the year shown.   2. © 2013 Election Data Services, Inc. All rights reserved.

STATE/ County code	CBSA code[1]	County type[2]	STATE County	Land area,[3] (sq km) 2010	Population, 2015			Population and population characteristics, 2014										
								Race alone or in combination, not Hispanic or Latino (percent)					Age (percent)					
					Total persons 2015	Rank	Per square kilometer	White	Black	American Indian, Alaska Native	Asian and Pacific Islander	Percent Hispanic or Latino[4]	Under 5 years	5 to 17 years	18 to 24 years	25 to 34 years	35 to 44 years	45 to 54 years
				1	2	3	4	5	6	7	8	9	10	11	12	13	14	15
			TEXAS—Cont'd															
48 055	12420	1	Caldwell	1 412	40 522	1 164	28.7	42.8	6.6	0.6	1.1	49.8	5.7	18.5	11.9	13.0	12.5	12.9
48 057	38920	3	Calhoun	1 313	21 895	1 737	16.7	44.5	2.9	0.6	5.0	47.9	6.6	18.5	9.1	12.2	11.5	13.2
48 059	10180	3	Callahan	2 329	13 557	2 198	5.8	87.9	2.0	1.1	1.0	9.4	5.4	16.8	7.0	10.8	11.2	13.9
48 061	15180	2	Cameron	2 307	422 156	164	183.0	10.1	0.5	0.2	0.8	88.7	8.7	22.9	10.7	12.1	12.6	11.0
48 063	...	6	Camp	507	12 682	2 250	25.0	59.0	17.5	0.7	1.1	23.4	6.7	19.4	8.8	11.3	11.4	12.3
48 065	11100	3	Carson	2 383	5 969	2 756	2.5	87.5	1.5	1.7	0.9	10.1	5.6	19.6	7.5	10.8	11.4	13.5
48 067	...	6	Cass	2 427	30 313	1 423	12.5	77.6	17.6	1.0	0.8	4.3	5.9	16.5	7.6	10.2	11.2	13.2
48 069	...	6	Castro	2 317	7 656	2 622	3.3	34.4	2.2	0.5	0.5	62.5	9.0	21.5	9.0	11.1	11.4	11.5
48 071	26420	1	Chambers	1 547	38 863	1 205	25.1	68.7	8.8	0.7	1.5	21.3	6.7	21.0	8.9	13.1	13.9	13.9
48 073	27380	6	Cherokee	2 727	51 542	967	18.9	62.5	15.1	0.8	0.8	22.0	6.9	18.7	9.5	11.5	12.2	12.6
48 075	...	7	Childress	1 804	7 088	2 667	3.9	59.8	10.2	0.8	1.0	29.6	5.5	15.4	12.2	18.7	11.9	10.4
48 077	48660	3	Clay	2 820	10 360	2 402	3.7	92.2	1.3	1.9	0.7	5.4	4.9	16.7	7.0	9.3	10.7	14.6
48 079	...	9	Cochran	2 008	2 953	2 980	1.5	38.1	4.5	0.8	0.5	57.2	7.8	20.5	9.4	13.3	9.7	13.2
48 081	...	8	Coke	2 361	3 238	2 956	1.4	77.2	1.2	1.4	0.6	21.2	5.1	14.6	6.1	9.5	8.5	14.4
48 083	...	6	Coleman	3 268	8 338	2 568	2.6	78.8	3.1	1.1	0.7	17.7	5.7	16.3	6.5	9.0	10.7	13.1
48 085	19100	1	Collin	2 179	914 127	57	419.5	62.3	9.9	0.9	14.0	15.1	6.5	20.7	8.0	12.8	16.5	15.3
48 087	...	9	Collingsworth	2 379	3 044	2 969	1.3	61.0	5.5	1.9	0.6	32.4	7.5	20.8	7.5	12.2	9.8	12.3
48 089	...	6	Colorado	2 487	20 870	1 780	8.4	58.4	12.9	0.4	0.9	28.3	5.7	17.2	8.1	10.1	10.0	13.2
48 091	41700	1	Comal	1 449	129 048	484	89.1	70.2	2.3	0.8	1.4	26.6	5.7	17.4	7.7	10.9	11.9	14.2
48 093	...	7	Comanche	2 429	13 430	2 207	5.5	71.6	0.8	0.8	0.5	27.4	6.1	17.1	7.4	9.6	10.0	13.2
48 095	...	8	Concho	2 548	4 081	2 895	1.6	41.2	2.0	0.4	0.7	56.4	3.4	9.5	7.3	17.4	19.5	14.8
48 097	23620	6	Cooke	2 266	39 229	1 193	17.3	78.0	3.6	1.5	1.2	17.0	6.5	17.7	9.0	11.6	10.7	13.1
48 099	28660	2	Coryell	2 725	75 503	733	27.7	62.2	18.0	1.3	4.1	17.9	7.3	17.5	12.4	19.6	14.7	11.3
48 101	...	9	Cottle	2 332	1 426	3 082	0.6	64.5	10.2	0.6	0.4	24.1	4.0	17.8	7.1	9.5	9.2	13.5
48 103	...	6	Crane	2 033	5 048	2 832	2.5	34.8	2.6	1.1	0.4	62.1	8.4	21.6	10.0	13.8	11.6	13.1
48 105	...	7	Crockett	7 271	3 710	2 923	0.5	34.6	0.7	0.7	0.8	64.5	7.5	18.1	8.2	12.5	11.8	12.6
48 107	31180	3	Crosby	2 332	5 977	2 754	2.6	41.8	4.2	0.5	0.2	54.1	7.1	19.7	8.3	10.6	11.1	11.9
48 109	...	9	Culberson	9 875	2 236	3 027	0.2	22.7	1.7	1.7	2.0	73.5	7.5	17.6	8.8	11.8	10.7	13.0
48 111	...	7	Dallam	3 893	7 121	2 665	1.8	54.1	2.3	1.2	1.2	43.0	9.3	22.7	9.3	14.2	12.5	12.8
48 113	19100	1	Dallas	2 257	2 553 385	9	1 131.3	32.1	22.9	0.7	6.3	39.3	7.7	19.2	9.8	16.1	14.1	13.0
48 115	29500	7	Dawson	2 332	13 520	2 201	5.8	37.5	6.1	0.5	0.7	54.9	7.1	18.0	10.9	16.2	11.8	11.0
48 117	25820	6	Deaf Smith	3 877	18 952	1 877	4.9	27.4	1.4	0.5	0.6	70.6	9.1	22.9	10.0	12.7	11.6	11.2
48 119	...	1	Delta	665	5 217	2 818	7.8	83.1	9.0	2.4	1.2	7.2	5.3	16.7	7.7	10.1	10.5	13.2
48 121	19100	1	Denton	2 275	780 612	77	343.1	63.5	9.9	1.0	8.6	19.0	6.6	19.5	9.6	15.0	15.8	14.5
48 123	...	6	DeWitt	2 354	20 797	1 790	8.8	56.8	9.1	0.4	0.7	33.9	6.4	15.8	7.3	11.6	12.3	13.8
48 125	...	8	Dickens	2 335	2 206	3 032	0.9	63.9	5.4	1.3	1.1	29.7	6.2	12.8	8.6	13.2	13.6	11.2
48 127	...	6	Dimmit	3 442	10 980	2 357	3.2	12.5	1.2	0.2	0.5	86.6	8.3	22.1	9.8	12.3	11.1	11.1
48 129	...	8	Donley	2 401	3 499	2 939	1.5	83.5	5.7	0.9	0.8	10.9	5.6	14.1	13.8	9.5	9.0	11.1
48 131	...	7	Duval	4 645	11 388	2 331	2.5	10.0	1.0	0.3	0.3	88.6	7.2	18.5	10.7	12.3	11.4	12.3
48 133	...	6	Eastland	2 400	18 171	1 909	7.6	80.4	2.7	1.0	0.8	15.9	5.5	15.9	10.7	10.5	10.0	12.3
48 135	36220	3	Ector	2 325	159 436	405	68.6	36.7	4.6	0.8	1.2	57.3	9.0	20.8	11.0	16.2	12.0	11.4
48 137	...	9	Edwards	5 485	1 894	3 059	0.3	44.3	0.6	0.8	0.3	54.4	5.6	14.5	7.4	8.7	9.4	11.7
48 139	19100	1	Ellis	2 423	163 632	392	67.5	64.5	9.7	0.9	1.0	25.1	6.4	20.6	9.4	12.3	13.3	14.0
48 141	21340	2	El Paso	2 623	835 593	70	318.6	14.0	3.5	0.5	1.6	81.0	8.1	20.1	11.8	14.2	12.6	11.8
48 143	44500	7	Erath	2 805	41 122	1 148	14.7	76.1	2.0	1.1	1.0	19.8	6.0	14.8	21.8	12.1	10.0	11.1
48 145	47380	6	Falls	1 983	17 142	1 970	8.6	52.2	24.2	0.8	0.8	22.2	6.3	15.0	9.0	13.6	11.8	14.0
48 147	...	6	Fannin	2 307	33 693	1 336	14.6	81.1	7.5	1.9	0.8	10.5	5.3	15.7	8.7	12.0	12.2	14.0
48 149	...	6	Fayette	2 461	25 110	1 606	10.2	72.9	7.0	0.5	0.5	19.8	5.0	15.9	7.2	9.2	10.0	13.4
48 151	...	8	Fisher	2 328	3 827	2 917	1.6	68.0	3.7	0.9	0.4	27.9	4.4	16.3	8.4	9.5	10.5	12.9
48 153	...	6	Floyd	2 570	5 901	2 763	2.3	39.7	3.6	0.5	0.4	56.0	7.7	19.4	8.4	10.7	11.0	11.8
48 155	...	9	Foard	1 824	1 220	3 099	0.7	75.5	5.8	0.6	0.8	18.8	4.8	16.6	7.7	8.7	9.8	15.2
48 157	26420	1	Fort Bend	2 231	716 087	88	321.0	36.4	20.9	0.6	19.7	24.0	6.7	21.2	8.5	12.5	15.3	14.3
48 159	...	8	Franklin	737	10 651	2 383	14.5	80.6	5.0	1.2	1.0	13.7	5.9	18.3	7.1	10.9	10.1	13.3
48 161	...	7	Freestone	2 273	19 691	1 847	8.7	68.7	16.4	1.0	0.8	14.8	5.9	17.2	7.0	11.5	13.3	13.4
48 163	...	6	Frio	2 936	18 793	1 880	6.4	16.6	3.4	0.4	2.2	77.6	7.0	17.4	13.4	18.0	12.3	10.9
48 165	...	7	Gaines	3 891	20 051	1 830	5.2	58.4	1.9	0.7	0.6	39.8	9.9	25.2	9.6	13.8	11.6	11.5
48 167	26420	1	Galveston	980	322 225	211	328.8	59.5	13.6	0.8	4.0	23.7	6.4	18.2	9.0	13.2	13.0	14.2
48 169	...	6	Garza	2 314	6 415	2 720	2.8	42.8	6.7	0.6	0.4	50.0	4.6	13.8	13.9	19.6	12.2	13.8
48 171	23240	7	Gillespie	2 741	25 963	1 560	9.5	77.2	0.6	0.7	0.7	21.6	5.0	14.4	6.8	8.5	9.2	12.1
48 173	13700	8	Glasscock	2 332	1 315	3 094	0.6	63.4	1.5	1.0	0.3	34.1	6.0	19.9	9.4	9.9	14.7	12.4
48 175	47020	3	Goliad	2 207	7 531	2 633	3.4	59.6	4.7	0.8	0.5	35.9	4.7	17.0	7.9	9.7	10.4	13.8
48 177	...	6	Gonzales	2 763	20 573	1 799	7.4	43.7	6.7	0.5	0.6	49.5	7.1	19.4	8.9	11.8	11.2	12.7
48 179	37420	6	Gray	2 398	23 210	1 673	9.7	65.8	5.2	1.5	0.8	26.7	7.3	18.4	8.2	13.3	12.8	12.9
48 181	43300	3	Grayson	2 416	125 467	499	51.9	78.9	6.8	2.4	1.6	12.6	6.1	17.6	9.0	11.8	11.5	13.5
48 183	30980	3	Gregg	708	124 108	503	175.3	60.2	20.8	0.9	1.7	18.0	7.6	18.1	10.3	13.7	11.9	12.6
48 185	...	6	Grimes	2 040	27 512	1 510	13.5	60.3	16.5	0.9	0.8	22.9	5.6	16.4	8.6	12.5	12.4	14.0

1. CBSA = Core Based Statistical Area. See Appendix A for explanation. See Appendix B for list of metropolitan areas with component counties. 2. County type code from the Economic Research Service of USDA Rural-Urban Continuum Codes. See Appendix A for definition. 3. Dry land or land partially or temporarily covered by water. 4. May be of any race.

Table B. States and Counties — Population and Households

STATE County	55 to 64 years	65 to 74 years	75 years and over	Percent female	2000	2010	2000–2010	2010–2015	Births	Deaths	Net migration	Number	Persons per house-hold	Family house-holds	Female family house-holder[1]	One per-son
	16	17	18	19	20	21	22	23	24	25	26	27	28	29	30	31

TEXAS—Cont'd

STATE County	55 to 64 years	65 to 74 years	75 years and over	Percent female	2000	2010	2000–2010	2010–2015	Births	Deaths	Net migration	Number	Persons per house-hold	Family house-holds	Female family house-holder[1]	One per-son
Caldwell	12.2	7.7	5.5	49.6	32 194	38 057	18.2	6.5	2 488	1 506	1 447	12 059	2.92	69.9	15.2	23.5
Calhoun	12.9	9.3	6.8	49.0	20 647	21 381	3.6	2.4	1 520	1 073	51	7 873	2.71	73.3	13.1	22.1
Callahan	14.8	11.3	8.8	50.7	12 905	13 544	5.0	0.1	660	880	253	5 220	2.57	63.8	9.5	32.7
Cameron	9.6	6.9	5.5	51.7	335 227	406 219	21.2	3.9	39 172	12 855	-10 664	119 695	3.44	79.7	21.3	18.0
Camp	12.8	9.7	7.6	51.6	11 549	12 401	7.4	2.3	1 029	735	35	4 410	2.80	72.0	15.2	26.0
Carson	14.5	9.5	7.6	50.3	6 516	6 182	-5.1	-3.4	304	344	-148	2 324	2.59	75.9	9.7	21.3
Cass	14.1	12.3	9.0	51.6	30 438	30 464	0.1	-0.5	1 868	2 136	-30	11 757	2.54	67.4	13.7	29.5
Castro	12.5	7.1	7.0	49.0	8 285	8 062	-2.7	-5.0	663	277	-781	2 501	3.17	74.6	10.9	21.7
Chambers	11.7	7.1	3.7	49.7	26 031	35 096	34.8	10.7	2 463	1 335	2 618	12 551	2.89	79.1	6.2	17.4
Cherokee	12.5	9.4	6.7	48.9	46 659	50 836	9.0	1.4	3 947	2 583	-584	17 527	2.75	73.7	15.3	22.8
Childress	10.5	8.1	7.2	41.0	7 688	7 041	-8.4	0.7	386	346	25	2 367	2.42	68.9	11.6	24.9
Clay	16.4	11.6	8.7	49.8	11 006	10 752	-2.3	-3.6	485	600	-245	4 163	2.52	70.4	7.3	26.5
Cochran	11.2	7.6	7.3	50.5	3 730	3 127	-16.2	-5.6	242	123	-283	1 000	2.92	74.7	12.1	23.5
Coke	15.0	14.5	12.4	51.3	3 864	3 319	-14.1	-2.4	144	268	57	1 541	2.02	67.2	9.1	28.2
Coleman	15.4	13.3	10.2	49.8	9 235	8 895	-3.7	-6.3	471	626	-403	3 505	2.44	74.3	12.3	23.5
Collin	10.5	6.2	3.5	50.9	491 675	782 351	59.1	16.8	55 573	18 760	92 719	296 878	2.81	74.0	10.1	21.3
Collingsworth	12.4	9.3	8.3	51.1	3 206	3 057	-4.6	-0.4	238	198	-52	1 127	2.64	69.1	9.7	28.3
Colorado	15.1	11.2	9.5	49.9	20 390	20 874	2.4	0.0	1 295	1 402	77	7 702	2.65	72.9	9.1	25.6
Comal	14.8	10.7	6.7	50.7	78 021	108 477	39.0	19.0	7 120	5 218	18 155	43 063	2.66	73.7	10.2	21.9
Comanche	13.7	13.1	9.8	50.9	14 026	13 974	-0.4	-3.9	831	881	-503	5 096	2.66	65.6	10.1	31.8
Concho	12.5	8.9	6.8	30.1	3 966	4 087	3.1	-0.1	123	160	30	821	3.21	78.4	9.6	19.6
Cooke	14.0	10.0	7.5	50.4	36 363	38 437	5.7	2.1	2 765	2 096	127	14 615	2.59	72.3	12.0	23.7
Coryell	8.2	5.5	3.5	50.4	74 978	75 388	0.5	0.2	5 354	2 085	-3 338	20 910	3.04	76.6	13.1	20.2
Cottle	14.4	13.5	11.0	52.3	1 904	1 505	-21.0	-5.2	76	110	-33	706	2.25	71.1	10.5	26.1
Crane	10.4	6.5	4.8	50.2	3 996	4 375	9.5	15.4	396	180	455	1 611	2.79	72.4	7.4	23.2
Crockett	14.2	8.4	6.6	50.3	4 099	3 719	-9.3	-0.2	280	177	-93	1 418	2.67	75.4	7.2	18.1
Crosby	12.5	10.5	8.4	50.7	7 072	6 059	-14.3	-1.4	375	359	-94	2 208	2.68	74.8	13.4	22.3
Culberson	13.9	9.4	7.4	51.2	2 975	2 398	-19.4	-6.8	153	74	-240	868	2.63	65.1	13.2	32.6
Dallam	10.6	5.6	3.1	48.5	6 222	6 703	7.7	6.2	737	212	-105	2 299	3.00	69.2	13.4	27.9
Dallas	10.4	5.7	3.9	50.7	2 218 899	2 367 643	6.7	7.8	204 953	78 415	63 233	868 717	2.78	65.4	16.3	28.6
Dawson	10.2	7.5	7.2	44.8	14 985	13 833	-7.7	-2.3	986	707	-598	4 363	2.65	69.6	13.7	28.1
Deaf Smith	10.6	6.2	5.6	50.4	18 561	19 372	4.4	-2.2	1 801	791	-1 444	6 210	3.06	73.9	12.4	23.9
Delta	14.6	13.2	8.7	50.5	5 327	5 231	-1.8	-0.3	314	368	16	1 926	2.68	69.6	12.7	27.5
Denton	10.2	5.7	3.0	50.8	432 976	662 615	53.0	17.8	49 809	16 228	82 701	250 472	2.78	71.2	11.2	21.9
DeWitt	13.5	9.9	9.4	47.9	20 013	20 097	0.4	3.5	1 333	1 263	600	6 921	2.69	68.0	13.6	30.2
Dickens	13.6	10.9	10.0	42.4	2 762	2 444	-11.5	-9.7	108	122	-214	928	2.26	65.2	8.9	33.0
Dimmit	11.0	8.1	6.2	50.9	10 248	9 996	-2.5	9.8	977	419	456	3 635	2.87	68.3	16.8	30.0
Donley	13.6	12.6	10.8	51.5	3 828	3 728	-2.6	-6.1	179	264	-145	1 277	2.63	68.8	12.8	28.3
Duval	10.4	9.4	7.8	48.4	13 120	11 782	-10.2	-3.3	877	681	-602	3 920	2.82	69.0	16.5	28.4
Eastland	14.0	11.6	9.5	50.8	18 297	18 583	1.6	-2.2	1 056	1 279	-184	6 970	2.51	61.8	10.6	33.3
Ector	10.0	5.4	4.1	49.6	121 123	137 133	13.2	16.3	14 509	6 096	13 854	50 214	2.85	71.1	16.2	23.6
Edwards	16.7	15.7	10.3	49.7	2 162	2 002	-7.4	-5.4	121	79	-139	799	2.52	65.3	9.1	32.3
Ellis	12.0	7.4	4.4	50.6	111 360	149 610	34.3	9.4	10 542	5 709	9 097	51 814	2.95	78.4	12.4	17.9
El Paso	10.0	6.2	5.1	51.0	679 622	800 647	17.8	4.4	71 950	25 659	-11 514	257 600	3.14	75.4	20.1	21.3
Erath	10.5	7.8	5.9	50.9	33 001	37 890	14.8	8.5	2 544	1 627	2 166	14 696	2.55	61.3	9.9	27.3
Falls	13.0	9.3	8.0	52.3	18 576	17 866	-3.8	-4.1	1 045	933	-776	5 496	2.87	64.2	15.2	33.4
Fannin	13.3	11.0	7.9	47.0	31 242	33 915	8.6	-0.7	1 749	2 132	99	11 795	2.61	70.3	12.3	25.5
Fayette	15.5	12.7	11.0	50.8	21 804	24 554	12.6	2.3	1 269	1 562	795	9 748	2.48	68.3	6.4	28.9
Fisher	14.9	11.7	11.3	50.4	4 344	3 974	-8.5	-3.7	171	261	-51	1 619	2.37	65.4	8.8	30.9
Floyd	12.3	9.5	9.3	50.3	7 771	6 446	-17.1	-8.5	432	344	-649	2 400	2.58	74.6	15.3	22.9
Foard	12.3	12.8	12.1	51.4	1 622	1 336	-17.6	-8.7	64	94	-80	519	2.16	51.1	6.7	46.2
Fort Bend	12.0	6.2	3.3	50.9	354 452	584 832	65.0	22.4	43 942	14 020	99 425	198 316	3.16	82.6	12.8	15.0
Franklin	14.1	11.9	8.5	51.0	9 458	10 605	12.1	0.4	580	594	92	4 228	2.48	70.4	9.6	25.8
Freestone	13.5	10.5	7.7	48.2	17 867	19 817	10.9	-0.6	1 176	1 119	-168	7 351	2.47	71.6	15.9	25.6
Frio	9.3	6.7	4.9	41.3	16 252	17 217	5.9	9.2	1 361	649	885	4 854	3.08	75.9	17.1	20.1
Gaines	9.0	5.0	4.3	49.4	14 467	17 526	21.1	14.4	1 971	618	1 097	5 483	3.35	78.6	9.2	17.9
Galveston	13.2	7.7	5.0	50.6	250 158	291 304	16.4	10.6	20 864	12 605	22 097	111 953	2.65	68.5	12.8	26.1
Garza	10.6	6.0	5.4	35.4	4 872	6 461	32.6	-0.7	334	267	-120	1 607	2.52	70.5	18.5	26.8
Gillespie	15.6	14.9	13.6	51.5	20 814	24 837	19.3	4.5	1 286	1 798	1 610	10 606	2.33	68.0	8.1	29.2
Glasscock	13.2	9.1	5.3	45.8	1 406	1 226	-12.8	7.3	69	38	71	470	2.52	75.1	1.1	22.8
Goliad	16.1	11.6	8.7	50.1	6 928	7 210	4.1	4.5	336	367	334	2 978	2.42	73.0	12.0	24.0
Gonzales	12.6	9.0	7.2	49.5	18 628	19 807	6.3	3.9	1 462	1 031	321	6 397	3.09	71.0	16.0	26.0
Gray	11.7	8.0	7.3	47.5	22 744	22 535	-0.9	3.0	1 768	1 300	227	8 403	2.51	65.6	9.7	30.9
Grayson	13.4	9.8	7.2	51.2	110 595	120 873	9.3	3.8	7 888	6 955	3 638	46 747	2.56	69.2	12.9	25.4
Gregg	11.9	7.6	6.6	51.0	111 379	121 764	9.3	1.9	9 989	6 510	-1 175	45 511	2.60	67.7	16.2	28.3
Grimes	14.4	9.9	6.1	45.5	23 552	26 568	12.8	3.6	1 646	1 338	608	9 001	2.61	69.4	15.0	27.1

1. No spouse present.

Table B. States and Counties — **Population, Vital Statistics, Medicare, and Crime**

STATE County	Persons in group quarters, 2015	Daytime population, 2010–2014 Number	Employ-ment/ resi-dence ratio	Births, 2015 Total	Births, 2015 Rate[1]	Deaths, 2015 Number	Deaths, 2015 Rate[1]	Persons under 65 with no health insurance, 2014 Number	Percent	Medicare, 2015 Total Beneficiaries	Enrolled in Original Medicare	Enrolled in Medicare Advantage	Serious crimes known to police,[2] 2014 Total Number	Rate[3]
	32	33	34	35	36	37	38	39	40	41	42	43	44	45
TEXAS—Cont'd														
Caldwell	3 370	31 935	0.56	489	12.2	298	7.4	7 939	24.0	6 007	4 463	1 544	787	1 977
Calhoun	250	24 946	1.38	307	14.1	212	9.7	3 709	20.4	3 647	3 144	503	565	2 842
Callahan	74	10 904	0.50	127	9.4	172	12.7	2 208	20.5	2 752	2 144	608	202	1 482
Cameron	3 845	412 786	0.98	7 403	17.6	2 556	6.1	119 223	32.8	53 597	32 424	21 173	15 087	3 569
Camp	67	11 670	0.83	225	17.8	121	9.6	2 653	25.5	2 799	2 086	713	397	3 175
Carson	26	5 505	0.79	55	9.2	60	10.0	881	17.7	1 015	808	207	67	1 114
Cass	366	27 454	0.76	376	12.4	415	13.7	4 487	18.9	7 393	5 525	1 868	912	3 027
Castro	63	7 552	0.85	113	14.6	48	6.2	2 184	32.9	1 052	940	112	188	2 330
Chambers	228	34 804	0.88	492	12.8	230	6.0	5 868	17.4	2 888	2 017	871	1 087	2 900
Cherokee	2 953	48 195	0.86	757	14.8	487	9.5	9 994	24.9	7 939	5 655	2 284	1 487	2 913
Childress	1 454	7 188	1.04	65	9.2	64	9.0	765	16.7	1 244	965	279	NA	NA
Clay	68	7 735	0.41	99	9.5	117	11.3	1 638	19.9	1 687	1 434	253	152	1 450
Cochran	78	2 881	0.87	41	14.0	9	3.1	711	29.0	544	441	103	131	4 355
Coke	39	2 847	0.70	27	8.3	49	15.1	521	22.0	807	646	161	30	936
Coleman	39	7 844	0.77	79	9.4	109	13.0	1 584	24.5	2 299	1 924	375	NA	NA
Collin	4 500	789 346	0.89	10 948	12.2	4 071	4.5	100 851	12.7	79 722	57 800	21 922	16 724	1 903
Collingsworth	49	2 760	0.79	39	12.9	25	8.2	796	32.3	599	518	81	16	510
Colorado	335	20 233	0.94	247	11.9	251	12.1	3 388	20.8	4 184	3 614	570	291	1 394
Comal	1 084	112 951	0.94	1 507	11.9	986	7.8	16 575	16.4	24 940	17 876	7 064	3 122	2 564
Comanche	140	12 645	0.77	158	11.7	178	13.2	3 101	29.8	3 101	2 494	607	315	2 310
Concho	1 627	4 271	1.17	17	4.2	29	7.1	351	19.3	573	459	114	3	74
Cooke	680	37 399	0.93	539	13.8	406	10.4	6 954	22.1	6 568	5 217	1 351	NA	NA
Coryell	11 424	66 172	0.66	1 038	13.7	410	5.4	8 558	14.9	7 860	5 724	2 136	1 461	1 900
Cottle	0	1 535	0.91	12	8.4	12	8.4	300	28.2	421	337	84	14	966
Crane	89	4 427	0.91	83	16.6	17	3.4	940	21.6	535	430	105	48	977
Crockett	49	4 100	1.13	47	12.5	22	5.9	734	22.8	608	523	85	51	1 321
Crosby	62	5 478	0.78	65	11.0	68	11.5	1 235	26.0	1 129	803	326	35	720
Culberson	12	2 283	0.96	30	13.3	11	4.9	542	28.9	445	357	88	15	663
Dallam	40	7 395	1.13	146	20.5	31	4.4	1 960	30.3	1 399	1 193	206	187	2 603
Dallas	32 145	2 770 233	1.28	39 555	15.6	15 695	6.2	559 465	25.0	286 077	193 085	92 992	93 245	3 691
Dawson	1 812	13 530	0.99	193	14.3	127	9.4	2 456	25.1	2 205	1 812	393	486	3 496
Deaf Smith	380	19 719	1.05	338	17.7	172	9.0	4 636	27.7	2 495	2 037	458	559	2 904
Delta	61	4 249	0.47	64	12.3	55	10.5	878	21.6	1 250	1 064	186	66	1 251
Denton	10 861	577 965	0.64	10 063	13.1	3 499	4.6	98 012	14.5	55 407	38 471	16 936	14 355	1 912
DeWitt	1 832	20 482	1.01	275	13.3	225	10.9	2 668	17.6	3 599	3 110	489	590	2 841
Dickens	315	2 318	0.97	22	10.0	12	5.4	366	25.4	534	438	96	17	750
Dimmit	93	14 622	1.99	212	19.3	78	7.1	1 901	20.2	1 692	1 148	544	438	3 908
Donley	280	3 358	0.81	32	9.1	49	14.0	628	25.5	824	683	141	58	1 652
Duval	543	11 305	0.92	162	14.1	143	12.5	1 977	22.0	2 200	1 453	747	NA	NA
Eastland	892	18 343	0.99	210	11.5	244	13.4	3 137	22.9	4 336	3 374	962	445	2 543
Ector	2 439	145 038	1.00	3 070	19.6	1 196	7.6	30 970	22.6	17 973	14 398	3 575	7 375	4 797
Edwards	5	1 921	0.87	21	11.1	8	4.2	442	32.1	750	595	155	32	1 709
Ellis	1 739	132 338	0.69	2 137	13.2	1 172	7.3	27 755	20.0	23 165	17 350	5 815	3 200	2 028
El Paso	16 022	822 148	0.99	13 615	16.3	5 118	6.1	180 615	25.0	108 268	52 740	55 528	20 101	2 393
Erath	3 741	38 542	0.96	491	12.0	327	8.0	8 424	26.6	5 669	4 395	1 274	780	1 930
Falls	2 016	15 469	0.66	196	11.4	166	9.7	3 024	24.5	2 749	1 826	923	187	1 215
Fannin	3 125	29 995	0.71	335	9.9	430	12.7	5 323	21.3	6 783	5 568	1 215	441	1 411
Fayette	450	23 832	0.92	257	10.3	288	11.5	4 125	21.9	6 059	5 027	1 032	421	1 679
Fisher	22	3 367	0.71	29	7.6	52	13.6	620	21.2	843	670	173	152	3 937
Floyd	35	5 936	0.88	75	12.6	62	10.4	1 212	25.2	1 201	895	306	125	2 793
Foard	30	1 098	0.87	9	7.2	10	8.0	239	24.9	385	333	52	0	0
Fort Bend	5 080	498 478	0.55	9 223	13.2	3 116	4.4	87 638	14.3	47 773	29 860	17 913	12 516	1 858
Franklin	91	10 718	1.03	118	11.1	128	12.1	1 795	21.4	1 791	1 384	407	163	1 516
Freestone	1 596	18 861	0.90	220	11.2	194	9.9	3 311	22.5	3 474	2 768	706	268	1 357
Frio	3 371	19 897	1.32	287	15.4	132	7.1	2 893	22.1	2 328	1 613	715	475	2 580
Gaines	84	18 117	0.95	407	20.7	127	6.5	5 483	31.3	1 758	1 478	280	227	1 169
Galveston	4 915	272 821	0.79	4 146	13.0	2 629	8.3	48 824	18.1	45 872	32 907	12 965	9 911	3 170
Garza	2 139	6 626	1.16	61	9.5	35	5.4	824	22.9	793	554	239	64	1 011
Gillespie	319	25 234	1.00	247	9.6	342	13.3	4 495	24.7	7 026	5 787	1 239	363	1 414
Glasscock	0	1 496	1.56	12	9.2	7	5.4	209	19.1	143	129	14	11	869
Goliad	93	5 963	0.53	64	8.5	62	8.2	961	16.2	1 334	1 077	257	115	1 517
Gonzales	327	20 701	1.08	288	14.1	195	9.5	4 605	27.2	3 698	2 983	715	652	3 168
Gray	2 018	22 543	0.98	343	14.7	244	10.5	3 984	22.1	4 234	3 522	712	1 024	4 384
Grayson	2 180	117 745	0.92	1 533	12.3	1 284	10.3	21 994	21.8	25 470	20 248	5 222	2 961	2 417
Gregg	4 241	143 640	1.39	1 879	15.2	1 252	10.1	22 093	21.5	25 351	19 271	6 080	5 349	4 307
Grimes	2 989	25 035	0.82	329	12.1	207	7.6	4 979	24.7	4 701	3 441	1 260	600	2 212

1. Per 1,000 estimated resident population. 2. Data for serious crimes have not been adjusted for underreporting; this may affect comparability between geographic areas and over time.
3. Per 100,000 population estimated by the FBI.

Table B. States and Counties — Crime, Education, Money Income, and Poverty

STATE County	Serious crimes known to police, 2014 (cont.)[1] Rate[2] Violent	Property	Education — School enrollment and attainment, 2010–2014 Enrollment[3] Total	Per-cent private	Attainment[4] (percent) High school grad-uate or less	Bach-elor's degree or more	Local government expenditures,[5] 2012–2013 Total current spending (mil dol)	Current spend-ing per student (dollars)	Money income, 2010–2014 Per capita income[6] (dollars)	Households Median income (dollars)	Mean income (dollars)	Percent with income of $200,000 or more	Income and poverty, 2014 Median house-hold income (dollars)	Percent below poverty level All per-sons	Children under 18 years	Children 5 to 17 years in families
	46	47	48	49	50	51	52	53	54	55	56	57	58	59	60	61
TEXAS—Cont'd																
Caldwell	201	1 776	9 952	6.6	56.9	15.6	53.6	8 126	20 368	47 435	60 371	2.4	47 227	16.0	23.7	22.7
Calhoun	372	2 469	5 343	4.8	53.1	15.8	34.9	8 209	24 142	47 546	63 795	3.0	46 705	17.3	25.5	24.4
Callahan	110	1 372	2 875	13.7	51.5	13.4	22.3	9 142	22 008	42 102	54 241	2.3	40 796	16.3	22.6	21.0
Cameron	259	3 310	129 486	4.0	59.9	16.1	912.1	9 142	14 898	33 390	48 892	1.7	32 215	34.5	47.0	45.7
Camp	432	2 743	3 179	2.8	56.0	14.3	30.1	11 929	18 873	38 154	51 307	1.5	37 801	23.9	35.5	34.9
Carson	266	848	1 550	4.8	39.9	22.6	13.3	10 205	27 062	63 424	70 670	2.1	58 425	8.6	11.5	10.2
Cass	378	2 649	6 495	3.5	59.2	12.7	51.1	9 042	20 534	36 342	48 840	1.0	39 256	19.1	30.2	29.6
Castro	124	2 206	2 083	3.3	67.0	13.9	16.7	9 616	22 198	40 470	65 710	2.0	42 966	19.4	28.8	27.9
Chambers	277	2 623	9 867	5.7	47.3	18.8	69.0	9 679	30 102	72 239	86 528	4.4	77 281	10.7	11.9	11.1
Cherokee	380	2 533	12 992	8.9	55.1	15.9	86.0	7 993	19 683	38 949	55 326	1.9	38 465	20.1	29.2	29.5
Childress	NA	NA	1 686	9.4	50.8	20.0	10.0	8 812	20 982	48 682	60 805	2.1	39 025	22.0	28.1	26.4
Clay	124	1 326	2 290	10.4	49.1	16.9	17.2	10 467	25 729	50 025	64 332	2.6	50 993	13.5	17.9	16.1
Cochran	166	4 189	767	3.1	63.2	13.7	12.1	15 506	18 318	41 071	53 608	1.2	39 870	20.7	29.8	27.8
Coke	31	905	662	1.8	46.6	17.1	5.9	11 631	28 741	40 822	59 247	3.4	41 593	14.9	21.8	20.5
Coleman	NA	NA	1 529	1.7	58.1	14.0	13.1	10 003	21 332	34 692	50 389	1.1	37 497	22.6	35.6	32.4
Collin	159	1 744	244 429	13.3	22.2	49.4	1 418.7	7 958	38 575	84 233	106 923	10.7	86 634	7.0	9.0	8.8
Collingsworth	32	478	685	6.1	52.6	18.7	5.6	9 423	21 594	42 798	54 721	1.8	38 655	19.3	29.9	27.9
Colorado	187	1 207	4 267	12.1	58.0	17.5	32.3	9 215	24 112	45 262	62 094	3.4	46 484	16.0	25.1	23.5
Comal	301	2 264	27 353	14.0	34.7	33.2	198.9	7 424	33 020	64 987	87 170	6.3	64 533	9.2	13.8	12.6
Comanche	264	2 046	2 883	6.1	56.5	18.3	21.0	9 441	19 125	35 692	47 431	0.9	38 280	19.7	31.5	29.9
Concho	0	74	685	7.9	67.9	11.8	4.8	9 901	20 503	52 844	65 314	2.9	40 837	26.5	26.6	26.1
Cooke	NA	NA	9 241	11.0	46.2	20.5	54.3	8 738	25 823	51 222	66 755	2.6	57 378	15.3	22.8	21.3
Coryell	181	1 719	22 529	8.7	43.4	15.5	93.6	8 023	19 410	49 783	61 361	1.5	47 018	14.8	21.6	20.7
Cottle	483	483	318	11.9	56.6	15.2	2.9	13 114	19 813	34 833	43 256	0.6	32 722	20.9	31.7	26.9
Crane	142	834	1 248	2.8	59.5	11.8	13.5	12 637	24 344	52 451	68 664	2.4	61 098	9.5	11.6	11.1
Crockett	181	1 140	685	1.8	60.7	11.1	9.9	12 346	24 862	51 594	64 425	0.6	49 614	13.7	19.4	18.7
Crosby	103	617	1 505	5.0	61.9	11.6	15.7	12 378	19 740	38 668	54 364	2.2	36 627	24.1	36.8	33.0
Culberson	0	663	447	1.3	72.1	11.7	5.5	12 734	16 120	35 302	41 340	2.0	33 637	24.7	37.2	36.8
Dallam	612	1 990	1 871	11.9	57.5	11.1	16.6	8 737	20 528	41 105	57 605	2.0	43 523	12.4	18.9	18.7
Dallas	443	3 248	667 714	13.0	45.5	28.7	3 577.5	8 157	27 195	49 925	73 982	5.3	50 118	19.3	29.0	27.9
Dawson	403	3 093	3 108	4.3	65.5	10.1	28.5	10 980	19 725	39 746	58 857	3.2	41 876	20.2	26.2	26.1
Deaf Smith	301	2 602	5 564	6.5	62.1	14.8	36.0	8 139	17 855	42 995	54 896	1.5	41 499	19.2	27.9	26.8
Delta	38	1 213	1 167	7.6	50.9	17.0	7.0	9 063	20 251	40 988	52 060	1.3	38 304	20.0	29.3	26.3
Denton	167	1 745	219 368	12.1	27.0	41.0	966.1	8 204	34 528	74 662	95 025	8.1	74 569	8.7	9.8	8.3
DeWitt	611	2 229	4 235	6.5	60.8	13.3	33.6	11 403	26 104	48 082	70 884	4.7	45 717	18.0	26.1	25.7
Dickens	88	661	405	1.0	53.1	14.4	5.2	12 935	20 353	38 397	49 416	0.9	35 924	22.1	29.9	30.1
Dimmit	143	3 766	2 963	6.9	60.1	10.4	22.8	9 338	20 822	38 140	58 272	2.8	36 856	25.0	35.1	33.0
Donley	541	1 111	978	10.9	48.8	16.7	6.6	11 241	21 264	40 719	51 932	1.5	37 263	19.4	30.7	30.2
Duval	NA	NA	2 481	3.7	67.5	7.0	25.9	10 199	21 334	32 479	58 363	4.3	35 069	26.0	33.9	33.0
Eastland	200	2 343	4 277	8.0	54.1	14.0	27.4	9 101	22 171	35 221	55 588	2.5	36 591	19.9	28.2	27.2
Ector	911	3 886	40 237	10.4	55.1	14.3	219.9	7 418	25 726	54 903	72 400	4.0	55 555	12.8	18.6	17.9
Edwards	107	1 603	284	0.0	56.1	24.3	7.5	14 247	28 407	41 726	53 301	1.9	35 554	22.5	37.4	36.8
Ellis	114	1 914	44 489	10.6	45.8	21.2	253.4	7 857	25 924	61 898	75 484	4.0	61 157	11.0	16.7	16.1
El Paso	364	2 029	264 240	7.2	49.5	20.8	1 520.3	8 554	18 705	40 783	56 319	2.2	40 081	23.4	31.7	32.0
Erath	151	1 779	13 365	5.2	43.9	25.6	46.3	8 305	21 306	40 711	54 662	2.1	41 914	21.8	23.5	23.1
Falls	195	1 020	4 171	6.0	62.5	11.4	26.7	11 344	16 749	33 587	46 497	0.5	35 491	23.7	31.4	31.1
Fannin	147	1 264	7 494	7.4	52.8	15.6	50.2	9 080	20 784	44 432	56 221	1.6	43 211	17.1	22.7	20.3
Fayette	263	1 416	5 312	11.7	57.0	16.1	35.0	9 467	28 403	48 711	68 136	4.0	49 830	10.9	17.5	16.3
Fisher	285	3 652	742	4.3	53.5	14.1	6.5	11 775	25 235	42 063	57 578	1.2	44 519	15.4	22.6	19.7
Floyd	469	2 324	1 558	6.9	52.7	17.2	14.5	11 005	22 375	40 993	58 320	1.8	36 898	23.7	37.1	36.3
Foard	0	0	209	2.9	48.5	20.9	2.7	12 393	21 105	34 375	44 337	0.0	33 442	17.3	25.1	22.9
Fort Bend	267	1 591	197 123	14.0	29.6	42.3	1 254.9	7 541	35 024	86 407	109 414	12.6	88 516	8.8	12.4	10.9
Franklin	233	1 284	2 326	15.2	47.8	22.0	13.7	8 461	28 058	44 000	70 297	5.7	42 099	16.4	26.4	24.0
Freestone	167	1 190	4 489	3.2	55.0	12.1	38.8	10 661	23 008	44 072	59 198	1.9	46 526	16.7	22.8	22.0
Frio	299	2 281	4 344	5.3	67.5	7.9	32.0	9 908	15 732	35 681	52 791	2.3	34 206	26.0	32.2	31.0
Gaines	46	1 123	4 709	23.6	69.9	11.2	42.9	12 770	21 690	54 434	69 778	3.1	50 709	14.0	19.1	18.5
Galveston	274	2 895	83 148	10.2	38.3	28.3	605.6	7 850	31 030	61 744	82 091	6.3	58 333	14.3	19.9	19.3
Garza	79	932	1 263	7.6	66.4	8.9	10.1	12 389	17 389	49 479	66 320	5.8	49 947	28.0	29.2	26.7
Gillespie	51	1 364	4 904	20.2	39.4	33.3	33.6	9 328	30 757	52 414	71 627	5.0	52 814	12.5	20.3	18.4
Glasscock	0	869	293	0.0	43.5	24.8	5.7	19 599	39 169	81 563	104 283	15.7	73 335	8.6	12.0	11.1
Goliad	211	1 306	1 484	3.2	49.6	15.3	13.8	10 063	30 556	49 702	73 832	5.4	49 369	15.3	24.1	21.6
Gonzales	661	2 507	5 034	11.9	60.1	14.7	37.8	9 168	20 794	41 263	58 980	2.6	42 291	18.3	28.5	27.5
Gray	492	3 891	5 476	8.6	50.6	14.5	34.1	8 337	22 285	45 179	59 481	1.3	49 012	14.2	18.3	17.6
Grayson	272	2 145	30 272	11.7	44.6	20.2	184.2	8 670	24 614	47 631	62 838	2.7	49 261	15.3	22.4	21.9
Gregg	443	3 864	31 702	10.8	44.6	19.9	213.1	8 859	24 137	46 391	62 642	2.9	50 020	18.2	26.5	24.8
Grimes	498	1 714	6 034	7.7	57.3	11.6	41.9	9 619	20 858	46 652	60 589	2.6	44 795	18.6	24.6	23.2

1. Data for serious crimes have not been adjusted for underreporting; this may affect comparability between geographic areas and over time.   2. Per 100,000 population estimated by the FBI.
3. All persons 3 years old and over enrolled in nursery school through college.   4. Persons 25 years old and over.   5. Elementary and secondary education expenditures.
6. Based on population estimated by the American Community Survey, 2010–2014.

Table B. States and Counties — **Personal Income**

STATE County	Personal income, 2014										Earnings, 2014		
			Per capita[1]			Supplements to wages and salaries; employer contributions (mil dol)						Contributions for government social insurance (mil dol)	
	Total (mil dol)	Percent change, 2013–2014	Dollars	Rank	Wages and salaries (mil dol)	Pension and insurance	Government social insurance	Proprietors' income (mil dol)	Dividends, interest, and rent (mil dol)	Personal transfer receipts (mil dol)	Total (mil dol)	From employee and self-employed	From employer
	62	63	64	65	66	67	68	69	70	71	72	73	74
TEXAS—Cont'd													
Caldwell	1 166	6.0	29 283	2 798	320	54	22	121	175	303	518	30	22
Calhoun	850	5.1	39 013	1 319	688	114	46	113	107	184	961	50	46
Callahan	488	5.0	36 138	1 758	88	16	6	35	77	126	145	10	6
Cameron	10 599	4.2	25 211	3 057	4 476	905	320	836	1 310	3 415	6 537	357	320
Camp	454	7.3	35 936	1 786	148	26	10	61	75	119	245	13	10
Carson	270	-1.7	44 901	684	352	33	23	49	34	41	456	24	23
Cass	1 025	4.4	33 870	2 136	280	53	19	120	139	343	472	29	19
Castro	412	20.0	52 974	268	107	16	7	186	35	59	316	6	7
Chambers	1 792	6.3	46 986	523	688	108	45	55	181	229	896	49	45
Cherokee	1 650	3.8	32 422	2 384	540	107	35	221	225	473	902	48	35
Childress	182	-1.7	25 621	3 041	82	20	5	17	31	56	124	6	5
Clay	517	7.5	49 808	393	71	13	4	140	67	95	228	10	4
Cochran	134	-0.4	45 610	628	34	7	2	42	15	28	85	2	2
Coke	109	6.6	33 588	2 178	24	6	2	13	20	36	44	3	2
Coleman	301	4.7	35 709	1 823	69	15	4	42	60	103	130	8	4
Collin	52 359	6.8	59 146	144	22 074	2 512	1 471	6 819	6 678	3 715	32 876	1 659	1 471
Collingsworth	113	-3.8	37 409	1 536	37	7	3	14	22	33	61	3	3
Colorado	940	4.4	45 389	644	307	48	21	103	169	213	479	27	21
Comal	6 139	7.1	49 626	404	1 891	261	132	455	1 075	1 008	2 739	158	132
Comanche	535	14.0	39 449	1 253	126	25	8	125	82	142	284	13	8
Concho	97	0.6	23 920	3 082	34	6	2	12	19	30	55	3	2
Cooke	2 195	5.7	56 631	182	834	117	57	724	329	334	1 732	82	57
Coryell	2 469	1.7	32 678	2 338	539	121	35	113	598	492	807	41	35
Cottle	80	0.7	56 269	190	21	4	1	7	26	19	33	2	1
Crane	224	7.2	45 308	650	118	18	7	40	15	29	183	9	7
Crockett	158	13.2	41 534	1 004	77	13	5	26	30	26	120	6	5
Crosby	196	-21.1	33 250	2 238	58	10	4	21	29	67	94	5	4
Culberson	82	3.2	36 353	1 713	41	8	3	6	11	25	58	3	3
Dallam	428	11.6	60 007	130	161	22	12	191	37	48	386	14	12
Dallas	131 991	5.4	52 406	282	101 873	11 775	6 872	28 267	25 277	15 083	148 787	7 454	6 872
Dawson	448	-5.1	33 539	2 189	178	32	11	58	76	117	280	14	11
Deaf Smith	780	18.0	40 652	1 102	287	48	19	256	79	146	610	21	19
Delta	188	7.7	35 889	1 793	32	9	2	19	22	56	62	4	2
Denton	35 398	7.3	46 987	522	10 205	1 392	700	1 968	4 089	3 365	14 266	755	700
DeWitt	982	8.9	47 470	499	365	60	22	115	267	207	561	30	22
Dickens	65	4.4	29 421	2 789	21	5	1	3	12	24	30	2	1
Dimmit	533	8.4	48 078	476	360	52	26	44	62	101	482	25	26
Donley	139	-6.8	39 130	1 306	30	7	2	33	23	34	72	3	2
Duval	459	5.2	39 800	1 208	191	31	13	29	47	142	264	15	13
Eastland	1 245	5.9	68 513	69	368	56	25	367	300	210	817	39	25
Ector	7 244	11.4	47 069	520	4 684	525	307	778	693	913	6 294	330	307
Edwards	74	6.3	39 359	1 272	16	4	1	14	18	20	34	2	1
Ellis	5 946	5.9	37 322	1 551	1 936	298	139	396	608	1 026	2 769	156	139
El Paso	26 518	3.6	31 816	2 463	12 596	2 629	951	2 639	4 009	5 973	18 816	946	951
Erath	1 291	8.8	32 150	2 423	527	100	35	197	213	282	859	40	35
Falls	569	5.6	33 517	2 194	125	31	8	93	72	173	257	13	8
Fannin	1 146	5.2	33 958	2 118	271	61	19	104	149	324	454	28	19
Fayette	1 172	6.6	47 200	515	396	64	26	86	303	249	572	34	26
Fisher	164	-6.9	42 920	856	36	7	2	10	24	41	55	3	2
Floyd	241	-3.5	40 591	1 110	67	12	4	68	31	62	153	6	4
Foard	52	6.7	40 967	1 066	10	2	1	8	9	17	20	1	1
Fort Bend	37 525	8.6	54 753	215	9 045	1 127	589	3 113	4 213	2 902	13 874	720	589
Franklin	410	6.6	38 688	1 366	115	17	9	93	57	100	234	12	9
Freestone	716	7.0	36 255	1 732	298	50	20	119	123	163	486	26	20
Frio	650	11.3	35 084	1 916	415	56	27	42	71	137	540	29	27
Gaines	706	-4.0	36 333	1 717	315	49	20	144	78	97	528	24	20
Galveston	14 741	6.3	46 917	526	4 924	928	320	861	2 175	2 274	7 032	364	320
Garza	449	4.3	69 782	60	78	13	5	290	43	42	386	15	5
Gillespie	1 307	5.8	51 224	323	360	58	25	111	498	263	555	35	25
Glasscock	85	-9.1	65 970	81	19	3	1	8	37	6	32	1	1
Goliad	304	7.4	40 243	1 143	65	12	4	13	64	67	93	6	4
Gonzales	852	14.2	41 629	996	289	50	18	164	172	177	522	22	18
Gray	1 094	8.0	47 461	500	473	72	31	228	210	178	804	39	31
Grayson	4 575	4.7	37 034	1 595	1 875	284	133	288	678	1 171	2 580	152	133
Gregg	6 149	4.3	49 913	387	3 891	493	277	1 163	880	1 116	5 825	303	277
Grimes	951	5.9	34 996	1 937	424	67	28	71	151	205	590	33	28

1. Based on the resident population estimated as of July 1 of the year shown.

STATE County	Farm	Mining	Construction	Manu-facturing	Infor-mation: professional, scientific, technical services	Retail trade	Finance, insur-ance, real estate and leasing	Health care and social assistance	Govern-ment	Number	Rate[1]	Supple-mental Security Income recipients, December 2014	Total	Percent change, 2010–2014
	75	76	77	78	79	80	81	82	83	84	85	86	87	88
TEXAS—Cont'd														
Caldwell	0.5	8.5	12.9	5.5	3.0	8.3	5.0	11.7	17.4	7 080	178	1 072	14 087	2.4
Calhoun	0.5	1.8	18.1	47.0	D	4.6	3.8	2.4	8.0	4 250	195	567	11 810	3.5
Callahan	0.4	8.7	17.7	6.9	3.1	10.9	3.4	5.6	22.0	3 330	246	327	6 595	0.7
Cameron	0.7	0.2	3.8	5.2	3.9	9.4	4.2	20.6	28.3	61 070	145	23 087	147 492	3.9
Camp	11.1	0.8	9.8	3.1	D	8.2	5.9	D	12.1	2 765	219	483	5 686	0.5
Carson	6.2	1.3	D	0.6	2.0	D	0.1	4.5	1 165	194	56	2 773	-0.4
Cass	4.3	3.4	7.0	22.2	2.4	7.4	3.3	D	17.3	8 240	272	1 235	14 432	0.4
Castro	63.2	1.0	0.8	0.9	D	2.9	1.6	D	9.0	1 240	159	156	3 183	0.5
Chambers	0.1	7.3	6.9	32.6	D	4.3	7.1	D	13.2	5 795	152	509	14 799	11.3
Cherokee	9.2	3.8	7.4	12.0	D	5.7	4.3	D	22.9	10 355	203	1 472	20 997	0.7
Childress	6.2	0.2	D	D	4.8	8.5	4.8	5.7	44.7	1 305	185	178	2 861	-0.8
Clay	11.6	D	6.0	4.6	D	5.4	3.4	D	11.2	2 605	251	175	5 156	0.1
Cochran	48.5	9.6	D	D	D	2.9	1.3	2.0	20.2	600	205	115	1 357	-0.2
Coke	5.6	15.2	9.1	D	D	6.9	D	2.1	29.4	935	288	79	2 666	0.0
Coleman	2.9	9.9	9.5	2.8	4.7	8.2	7.7	D	21.0	2 420	288	279	5 525	-0.3
Collin	0.0	2.6	6.0	8.6	20.3	6.3	12.0	9.8	8.6	93 990	106	7 949	337 778	12.2
Collingsworth	17.6	0.0	D	D	D	3.0	D	D	17.2	640	212	75	1 607	-0.6
Colorado	2.0	6.6	10.8	20.5	D	6.9	4.9	D	11.3	4 915	238	511	10 566	0.4
Comal	-0.3	1.8	13.8	7.0	7.0	11.0	4.8	10.2	12.3	25 990	211	1 486	53 248	13.0
Comanche	25.2	1.6	5.7	2.3	6.4	8.8	3.4	4.0	16.0	3 680	273	364	7 272	0.7
Concho	14.4	D	D	D	1.0	2.9	D	9.7	24.0	660	163	61	1 646	0.5
Cooke	0.4	41.5	4.1	15.9	D	4.3	2.7	D	9.0	7 775	200	628	16 720	0.7
Coryell	1.0	D	8.6	2.5	D	8.0	5.0	D	43.3	9 950	132	1 156	26 168	3.9
Cottle	19.8	0.3	D	D	D	6.0	D	4.0	18.4	440	308	52	958	-1.0
Crane	1.1	D	D	D	D	2.2	D	2.9	11.6	660	134	100	1 662	1.8
Crockett	7.6	42.6	D	D	D	4.9	3.1	0.6	15.7	700	185	49	1 871	0.3
Crosby	21.5	D	D	D	D	11.9	D	6.3	22.2	1 295	220	184	2 913	0.4
Culberson	8.5	D	D	D	D	14.1	D	D	33.6	570	252	120	1 153	1.4
Dallam	28.1	D	8.1	9.8	4.9	3.4	5.1	1.0	4.1	945	133	104	2 906	2.8
Dallas	0.0	5.7	6.1	7.1	16.7	4.6	13.8	8.9	8.7	303 195	120	65 546	985 403	4.5
Dawson	8.5	12.0	5.7	1.6	2.0	16.2	3.1	D	27.1	2 455	182	435	5 203	-0.3
Deaf Smith	33.9	D	3.8	13.8	2.7	5.4	2.7	1.8	10.8	2 825	147	426	7 065	-0.2
Delta	22.6	0.0	D	D	D	1.8	D	D	22.2	1 410	270	184	2 468	0.4
Denton	0.2	1.5	7.7	8.6	11.3	7.6	8.0	11.1	15.6	78 455	104	6 153	288 294	12.6
DeWitt	-0.1	20.0	8.9	12.1	3.6	6.3	8.8	D	19.9	4 570	221	524	9 176	0.0
Dickens	8.5	D	D	D	D	5.3	D	1.7	25.1	580	263	51	1 282	0.0
Dimmit	2.2	26.8	18.7	1.5	D	3.2	2.4	D	17.8	2 005	182	622	4 364	0.3
Donley	38.0	D	D	D	D	6.3	2.6	4.6	24.5	880	250	88	2 135	-0.3
Duval	-0.9	26.2	9.0	D	D	2.9	D	3.6	23.4	2 465	214	666	5 543	0.4
Eastland	0.8	43.8	3.7	1.9	D	3.7	8.9	D	12.1	4 565	250	594	10 253	0.0
Ector	0.0	22.6	11.7	8.1	4.1	5.8	5.6	5.1	9.7	19 355	125	3 521	57 025	7.5
Edwards	21.8	D	D	D	D	9.4	D	D	27.1	410	218	83	1 611	0.3
Ellis	0.5	0.5	10.1	26.5	3.6	7.7	3.4	6.6	14.1	24 700	155	2 871	58 088	6.8
El Paso	0.0	0.1	6.8	6.1	5.1	7.5	4.6	10.2	36.0	121 445	145	29 876	289 443	7.1
Erath	12.9	1.6	8.4	10.5	D	7.0	3.8	9.0	20.6	6 290	155	557	17 550	3.3
Falls	12.9	D	5.2	3.0	D	7.7	D	7.4	31.0	3 555	207	739	7 727	0.0
Fannin	1.8	2.0	7.7	8.1	2.4	8.6	4.5	8.3	34.4	7 670	227	849	14 268	0.5
Fayette	1.4	9.1	7.1	8.5	4.7	10.0	7.8	8.3	17.3	6 220	250	431	13 879	0.1
Fisher	11.8	D	D	D	D	3.6	0.0	4.1	27.1	980	256	100	2 206	-0.3
Floyd	40.8	D	2.3	2.4	D	3.8	D	2.9	17.0	1 280	214	173	2 996	-0.3
Foard	33.9	0.0	D	D	D	4.9	D	D	20.9	405	319	35	789	0.0
Fort Bend	0.1	6.7	14.6	12.0	9.2	7.2	6.0	8.3	10.3	69 680	101	10 047	233 243	18.5
Franklin	15.7	D	8.1	D	D	3.9	D	14.3	9.6	2 235	211	193	5 791	0.4
Freestone	2.2	26.0	16.8	2.1	3.1	6.8	2.4	D	14.8	3 770	192	402	9 305	0.4
Frio	3.8	33.1	3.9	0.7	D	4.0	3.3	D	13.9	2 765	149	727	5 904	1.0
Gaines	4.7	26.5	15.2	1.7	1.5	7.4	2.6	D	13.9	2 005	104	316	6 375	1.2
Galveston	0.0	1.6	8.4	13.5	6.8	7.3	7.2	6.8	26.3	50 635	161	6 815	142 337	7.4
Garza	0.1	62.3	6.9	2.7	D	1.4	2.8	D	5.6	895	139	110	2 220	-0.8
Gillespie	-0.4	1.6	15.4	7.8	5.9	11.0	5.8	17.7	11.7	7 820	307	293	12 954	1.4
Glasscock	18.4	D	D	D	0.7	3.8	D	D	21.0	155	120	0	582	0.3
Goliad	-6.1	14.1	7.3	2.3	D	5.6	2.7	D	24.3	1 730	230	200	3 720	0.3
Gonzales	24.3	11.3	2.7	10.8	2.2	5.4	3.1	D	15.3	3 865	189	544	8 837	0.5
Gray	7.5	26.1	5.4	18.4	D	5.2	2.4	5.6	10.0	4 360	186	362	10 090	-0.7
Grayson	0.4	1.1	9.2	15.4	4.5	8.2	7.1	18.0	13.5	27 225	221	3 052	54 653	1.7
Gregg	-0.1	17.8	10.8	10.8	7.2	7.2	4.5	11.3	7.1	23 935	194	4 622	51 648	4.3
Grimes	-0.4	2.1	7.2	30.7	D	5.2	4.5	D	17.8	5 125	189	712	11 009	0.9

1. Per 1,000 resident population estimated as of July 1 of the year shown.

Table B. States and Counties — Housing, Labor Force, and Employment

STATE County	Housing units, 2010–2014								Civilian labor force, 2015				Civilian employment,[6] 2010–2014		
	Occupied units							Sub-stand-ard units[4] (percent)			Unemployment			Percent	
	Owner-occupied					Renter-occupied									
				Median owner cost as a percent of income											
	Total	Percent	Median value[1]	With a mortgage	Without a mortgage[2]	Median rent[3]	Median rent as a percent of income[2]		Total	Percent change, 2014–2015	Total	Rate[5]	Total	Management, business, science and arts	Construction, production, and maintenance occupations
	89	90	91	92	93	94	95	96	97	98	99	100	101	102	103
TEXAS—Cont'd															
Caldwell	12 059	66.4	106 100	22.8	12.0	776	28.8	6.0	17 557	1.8	756	4.3	15 958	25.3	29.7
Calhoun	7 873	70.7	99 600	19.7	10.2	742	29.7	6.6	11 831	6.7	456	3.9	9 099	29.5	35.3
Callahan	5 220	81.9	74 200	19.1	12.3	641	25.1	4.6	5 781	-0.8	247	4.3	5 293	24.9	31.4
Cameron	119 695	67.1	77 400	24.4	12.8	648	32.7	12.5	164 295	-1.2	11 692	7.1	145 012	28.0	21.9
Camp	4 410	68.9	87 100	22.6	13.3	660	25.0	8.2	5 061	-3.0	316	6.2	4 737	25.1	36.9
Carson	2 324	88.6	89 000	18.1	10.0	609	19.4	2.3	3 114	-1.2	100	3.2	2 922	32.9	31.4
Cass	11 757	74.4	76 300	21.0	12.2	569	29.1	3.8	12 107	-1.4	835	6.9	12 018	20.8	35.3
Castro	2 501	70.2	69 600	21.7	12.8	651	29.7	8.4	3 646	-4.0	126	3.5	3 391	26.2	41.0
Chambers	12 551	82.4	145 200	19.0	11.5	889	23.1	3.0	17 895	0.3	950	5.3	15 336	34.8	36.9
Cherokee	17 527	71.2	81 800	22.4	12.5	670	30.7	5.1	20 794	-1.8	1 083	5.2	19 853	26.7	30.9
Childress	2 367	66.6	66 000	14.4	13.6	671	29.4	0.5	2 872	0.3	91	3.2	2 793	33.4	19.8
Clay	4 163	83.8	81 700	19.5	11.7	619	23.0	2.4	4 935	-1.7	219	4.4	4 828	30.2	28.6
Cochran	1 000	79.5	31 500	19.2	10.0	451	17.8	10.6	1 324	-5.3	68	5.1	1 177	22.7	46.2
Coke	1 541	72.2	79 800	21.3	11.1	556	29.3	1.2	1 402	-2.5	58	4.1	1 436	44.3	25.0
Coleman	3 505	68.0	58 400	26.6	11.6	543	27.0	1.2	3 062	-1.9	172	5.6	3 536	28.1	28.6
Collin	296 878	67.2	211 900	21.6	11.2	1 086	26.7	2.3	484 121	2.1	17 632	3.6	429 486	51.7	11.0
Collingsworth	1 127	82.3	66 200	20.1	12.3	465	21.3	0.8	1 265	0.5	46	3.6	1 398	29.9	34.9
Colorado	7 702	78.9	109 100	20.4	11.8	681	23.6	2.8	9 903	-3.6	394	4.0	8 978	30.2	32.3
Comal	43 063	75.8	209 100	21.7	10.6	975	29.0	4.1	60 421	1.0	2 248	3.7	52 534	37.9	20.4
Comanche	5 096	74.8	69 300	23.6	12.6	569	26.7	6.4	5 367	-3.0	231	4.3	4 962	31.4	33.4
Concho	821	78.0	83 300	19.2	10.7	532	24.5	1.0	1 372	-3.0	45	3.3	1 094	35.3	31.0
Cooke	14 615	69.7	114 800	20.6	12.4	731	28.2	5.5	20 010	-2.6	736	3.7	18 017	26.5	32.1
Coryell	20 910	57.4	97 900	20.4	10.2	942	27.0	2.9	24 857	0.5	1 190	4.8	22 204	30.5	20.9
Cottle	706	74.6	39 300	24.3	11.8	246	22.7	0.4	546	-9.8	39	7.1	679	30.8	21.4
Crane	1 611	73.3	73 800	16.6	10.0	635	22.4	5.2	1 829	-8.8	106	5.8	1 927	20.7	43.1
Crockett	1 418	71.1	49 600	19.0	10.0	592	14.2	4.8	1 989	3.0	117	5.9	1 794	20.1	42.8
Crosby	2 208	64.4	53 100	19.5	10.9	596	24.5	7.3	2 643	-2.0	115	4.4	2 481	26.6	33.5
Culberson	868	70.7	46 200	21.9	14.4	480	31.6	4.7	1 034	2.2	45	4.4	996	18.5	27.5
Dallam	2 299	65.1	70 700	22.1	10.0	718	23.7	4.0	3 980	2.0	89	2.2	3 365	24.9	40.3
Dallas	868 717	52.0	129 200	24.0	12.9	895	29.3	7.0	1 274 040	1.9	54 348	4.3	1 161 634	33.2	24.0
Dawson	4 363	71.3	58 800	17.2	11.5	524	24.4	2.7	4 790	-2.2	218	4.6	4 679	24.9	31.2
Deaf Smith	6 210	66.6	81 600	22.7	11.0	651	23.9	7.5	8 813	-3.2	283	3.2	8 210	26.9	38.9
Delta	1 926	79.5	73 200	23.2	12.5	632	40.9	2.3	2 596	-2.1	120	4.6	1 883	30.3	29.8
Denton	250 472	64.7	189 000	21.5	11.8	968	28.5	2.5	423 135	2.2	15 119	3.6	373 978	43.6	14.9
DeWitt	6 921	78.2	86 300	18.7	10.0	641	27.0	5.6	10 146	1.3	406	4.0	8 315	25.6	33.5
Dickens	928	75.8	47 400	16.5	13.2	478	18.3	2.2	709	-4.8	33	4.7	819	36.5	26.0
Dimmit	3 635	71.4	58 400	17.7	12.1	570	22.9	9.4	7 150	-6.6	335	4.7	4 239	18.5	27.9
Donley	1 277	76.9	61 400	19.1	12.6	556	23.1	4.0	1 600	-1.2	68	4.3	1 413	38.6	20.5
Duval	3 920	71.1	53 800	22.8	13.0	719	21.1	12.0	5 255	-5.0	431	8.2	4 252	17.7	34.2
Eastland	6 970	73.2	58 700	24.0	12.2	559	20.9	6.2	8 060	-3.6	385	4.8	7 074	27.9	29.1
Ector	50 214	65.5	96 800	19.0	10.0	849	25.1	7.2	79 869	-3.0	3 682	4.6	67 350	23.3	35.2
Edwards	799	89.0	71 100	14.5	14.0	479	17.4	3.4	868	0.1	41	4.7	885	23.4	32.8
Ellis	51 814	72.7	140 200	21.5	12.2	898	30.5	4.1	80 632	2.0	3 186	4.0	72 667	31.7	26.9
El Paso	257 600	61.8	112 800	23.6	11.4	741	30.2	7.2	343 495	-0.3	17 954	5.2	320 384	29.5	22.5
Erath	14 696	59.5	112 200	22.3	11.3	702	34.8	3.4	20 030	-0.3	785	3.9	19 051	30.0	28.9
Falls	5 496	73.0	64 400	22.2	13.2	594	25.5	4.8	6 454	-1.4	277	4.3	6 245	27.3	30.7
Fannin	11 795	74.3	92 300	21.0	13.3	672	33.3	3.8	15 389	0.7	641	4.2	13 197	31.4	29.8
Fayette	9 748	76.6	130 800	19.1	12.3	696	24.3	1.6	12 711	-2.8	428	3.4	11 570	24.6	33.9
Fisher	1 619	73.2	61 700	19.2	11.6	553	20.1	4.7	1 802	-3.3	71	3.9	1 796	28.8	30.7
Floyd	2 400	67.9	62 200	17.0	11.7	620	27.5	5.0	2 749	-7.3	154	5.6	2 754	30.5	33.2
Foard	519	71.7	45 400	27.5	14.3	451	26.2	1.0	555	-4.0	24	4.3	463	28.9	21.2
Fort Bend	198 316	78.7	189 500	22.3	11.3	1 187	27.4	3.5	348 961	0.6	15 013	4.3	300 816	48.4	14.6
Franklin	4 228	76.2	101 800	22.2	11.3	645	25.1	2.8	4 521	-2.9	224	5.0	4 379	27.2	28.8
Freestone	7 351	77.0	78 200	19.9	12.3	649	24.1	3.4	7 482	-4.6	407	5.4	8 049	27.4	31.3
Frio	4 854	69.2	63 400	24.3	12.5	696	23.5	14.2	9 864	-4.6	377	3.8	6 440	16.9	32.5
Gaines	5 483	78.4	89 500	16.6	10.0	697	19.2	8.3	9 336	-0.3	303	3.2	7 524	24.6	45.1
Galveston	111 953	67.3	150 300	21.6	11.8	910	30.4	3.5	157 727	0.1	7 869	5.0	140 542	39.0	21.1
Garza	1 607	74.2	71 300	16.5	10.6	718	24.5	1.1	2 125	-5.3	79	3.7	1 903	29.4	28.7
Gillespie	10 606	74.6	218 600	25.2	12.4	874	32.2	4.0	12 585	0.5	366	2.9	11 345	33.9	21.1
Glasscock	470	66.2	182 500	14.4	10.0	1 106	20.8	2.3	823	-0.8	24	2.9	555	43.1	31.2
Goliad	2 978	84.5	113 700	14.7	11.9	664	21.7	3.9	3 550	-0.6	155	4.4	3 018	30.1	32.6
Gonzales	6 397	71.0	81 400	22.0	12.1	576	24.5	10.0	9 689	-2.5	360	3.7	8 407	23.2	36.9
Gray	8 403	73.9	73 200	19.2	10.7	644	27.0	3.0	9 307	-4.9	526	5.7	9 521	25.7	33.9
Grayson	46 747	67.6	105 800	21.7	13.0	784	28.2	3.3	60 503	0.3	2 422	4.0	53 283	31.3	25.7
Gregg	45 511	61.8	122 900	20.6	11.1	764	30.3	4.0	59 424	-2.8	2 956	5.0	54 953	27.8	28.9
Grimes	9 001	75.4	95 800	19.7	12.0	655	30.4	6.7	11 462	-3.1	618	5.4	9 820	25.4	35.7

1. Specified owner-occupied units.   2. A value of 10.0 represents 10 percent or less; a value of 50.0 represents 50 percent or more.   3. Specified renter-occupied units.
4. Overcrowded or lacking complete plumbing facilities.   5. Percent of civilian labor force.   6. Persons 16 years old and over.

Table B. States and Counties — Nonfarm Employment and Agriculture

STATE County	Number of establishments	Total	Health care and social assistance	Manufacturing	Retail trade	Finance and insurance	Professional, scientific, and technical services	Total (mil dol)	Average per employee (dollars)	Number	Fewer than 50 acres	500 acres or more	Farm operators whose principal occupation is farming (percent)
	104	105	106	107	108	109	110	111	112	113	114	115	116
TEXAS—Cont'd													
Caldwell	580	6 116	1 206	774	1 184	185	112	197	32 288	1 623	42.7	8.3	40.1
Calhoun	429	8 449	590	D	991	190	590	543	64 290	264	29.2	31.4	46.6
Callahan	209	1 439	191	141	306	58	72	50	35 006	992	27.6	21.3	43.3
Cameron	6 312	100 798	31 505	4 656	18 218	3 266	3 413	2 660	26 393	1 305	66.3	11.5	45.4
Camp	222	2 551	D	224	403	106	27	103	40 284	487	40.0	6.2	41.3
Carson	118	661	D	33	119	D	14	31	46 581	386	15.5	46.6	51.0
Cass	498	5 772	906	1 694	961	205	126	206	35 736	1 024	29.6	5.2	43.1
Castro	167	1 056	D	43	206	51	90	32	30 350	532	9.0	51.5	54.3
Chambers	558	10 174	528	D	647	D	218	623	61 225	734	56.0	17.7	39.6
Cherokee	766	10 456	2 291	2 317	1 394	329	217	341	32 598	1 574	34.2	6.5	46.9
Childress	155	1 199	68	NA	401	67	40	32	26 623	383	5.2	34.5	41.3
Clay	129	812	163	D	222	D	D	22	27 441	861	16.4	27.1	43.4
Cochran	51	293	119	D	D	D	D	8	28 901	288	4.9	47.6	51.7
Coke	61	250	NA	D	87	D	D	7	27 440	443	9.3	40.6	44.9
Coleman	213	1 455	260	89	280	90	46	36	24 602	906	10.9	36.5	46.7
Collin	20 610	354 722	42 986	18 662	48 025	41 389	37 974	20 773	58 561	2 264	64.9	4.4	33.0
Collingsworth	62	485	D	D	74	D	D	16	33 363	383	6.3	41.3	45.2
Colorado	567	6 465	851	1 926	955	184	127	226	34 891	1 575	28.3	13.0	48.6
Comal	3 150	41 385	6 031	2 990	6 350	921	1 312	1 588	38 373	1 104	44.8	9.3	36.9
Comanche	268	2 444	622	D	483	156	85	74	30 140	1 435	26.8	18.6	50.6
Concho	49	717	172	D	78	D	D	24	33 753	401	5.7	51.4	56.9
Cooke	890	13 797	1 114	3 138	1 839	383	237	617	44 686	1 946	40.0	10.9	42.2
Coryell	706	9 974	1 214	474	1 980	420	829	249	24 930	1 308	31.3	16.8	42.3
Cottle	27	153	D	D	D	D	D	3	19 065	264	6.4	44.7	32.2
Crane	87	1 243	D	D	130	D	D	68	55 070	27	29.6	66.7	51.9
Crockett	126	1 389	29	D	225	D	D	71	51 309	216	4.2	68.1	63.4
Crosby	98	622	136	D	130	D	12	24	37 921	431	8.6	43.4	51.0
Culberson	57	612	D	D	227	D	D	15	23 871	77	9.1	75.3	68.8
Dallam	206	1 665	D	68	243	69	68	60	36 094	371	5.9	62.3	59.0
Dallas	63 485	1 361 547	167 794	98 299	121 661	97 439	132 261	79 353	58 281	839	68.2	5.0	39.7
Dawson	293	2 816	D	126	689	134	D	111	39 559	596	7.2	42.8	55.0
Deaf Smith	397	5 270	535	1 610	768	190	201	198	37 556	621	11.3	55.2	64.6
Delta	60	D	D	NA	37	D	D	D	D	529	33.1	10.2	41.2
Denton	13 062	191 536	24 290	12 304	28 404	12 305	9 790	8 101	42 296	3 203	73.2	3.8	34.9
DeWitt	458	5 403	1 002	521	697	246	116	230	42 576	1 711	24.1	14.0	45.7
Dickens	45	238	24	D	55	D	D	8	35 496	437	4.8	34.3	35.5
Dimmit	245	5 762	428	57	501	D	D	339	58 871	367	23.2	35.7	36.8
Donley	83	472	100	D	110	16	D	10	22 015	380	8.9	29.7	44.5
Duval	171	2 776	395	D	246	55	42	126	45 456	1 436	11.0	25.0	45.5
Eastland	456	5 824	1 059	580	845	146	D	237	40 756	1 174	17.3	18.6	33.6
Ector	3 686	63 283	7 049	4 672	8 387	1 403	1 690	3 539	55 926	264	70.5	14.4	28.8
Edwards	38	176	D	D	76	D	D	4	24 222	419	6.4	50.6	51.1
Ellis	2 643	37 683	3 490	9 679	5 438	869	759	1 395	37 022	2 264	48.4	8.2	40.8
El Paso	13 875	223 489	41 337	13 793	38 117	6 546	9 631	6 965	31 164	657	81.6	7.6	39.7
Erath	936	12 412	1 624	2 767	2 001	324	353	419	33 757	2 161	30.2	13.7	44.6
Falls	212	1 729	423	D	433	78	D	49	28 260	1 263	26.5	13.2	53.4
Fannin	447	4 800	1 223	692	903	150	113	168	34 939	2 515	41.4	8.5	43.2
Fayette	731	7 458	D	1 110	1 283	278	196	252	33 813	2 822	30.8	6.7	41.5
Fisher	67	547	108	D	76	46	15	23	41 302	588	8.5	38.4	38.6
Floyd	161	1 021	238	D	127	D	D	32	31 154	589	7.3	39.4	39.9
Foard	29	172	76	D	31	D	D	4	22 262	194	8.8	42.3	46.4
Fort Bend	11 358	145 249	21 988	14 485	25 430	4 107	9 711	6 621	45 583	1 286	46.6	9.7	47.1
Franklin	167	5 815	D	D	302	93	31	105	18 108	520	28.1	12.1	47.5
Freestone	343	3 829	D	D	498	D	81	173	45 112	1 517	30.3	11.8	45.6
Frio	333	5 590	691	109	690	122	D	290	51 803	651	20.0	35.3	50.8
Gaines	402	3 932	D	226	498	91	D	180	45 680	644	10.6	50.2	55.9
Galveston	5 479	79 740	14 519	5 988	12 541	3 631	4 227	3 208	40 235	612	63.2	8.7	45.4
Garza	135	1 438	D	24	217	D	10	53	36 802	277	8.7	46.9	43.7
Gillespie	929	8 552	1 603	669	1 585	277	315	265	31 018	1 847	30.5	19.9	41.5
Glasscock	28	276	NA	D	D	D	D	15	54 815	186	4.3	70.4	59.7
Goliad	124	760	D	D	115	D	D	30	40 114	1 175	27.9	17.2	44.4
Gonzales	430	4 955	727	1 343	828	185	114	182	36 637	1 674	23.1	18.9	46.1
Gray	609	6 878	837	949	1 118	177	219	300	43 605	417	15.3	47.7	35.7
Grayson	2 517	39 698	8 412	7 088	6 320	1 909	926	1 335	33 629	2 562	50.8	5.6	44.1
Gregg	4 096	68 188	10 482	9 819	9 559	2 224	2 437	2 921	42 836	527	59.0	4.2	42.9
Grimes	397	5 937	375	2 408	678	D	144	283	47 733	1 683	37.3	10.5	39.7

Table B. States and Counties — **Agriculture**

STATE County	Acreage (1,000)	Percent change, 2007–2012	Average size of farm	Total irrigated (1,000)	Total cropland (1,000)	Average per farm	Average per acre	Value of machinery and equipment, average per farm (dollars)	Total (mil dol)	Average per farm (dollars)	Crops	Live-stock and poultry products	$10,000 or more	$100,000 or more	Total ($1,000)	Percent of farms
	117	118	119	120	121	122	123	124	125	126	127	128	129	130	131	132
TEXAS—Cont'd																
Caldwell	310	1.9	191	0.6	55.9	632 375	3 306	45 283	62.9	38 779	17.8	82.2	22.2	2.7	1 076	10.2
Calhoun	184	-20.1	697	5.8	60.5	1 223 477	1 755	114 295	42.1	159 489	67.2	32.8	49.2	20.5	1 664	46.2
Callahan	563	5.7	568	0.7	87.2	857 079	1 510	49 690	29.9	30 142	19.5	80.5	28.7	4.9	1 943	26.1
Cameron	310	-11.4	237	112.3	209.2	697 056	2 937	84 762	160.4	122 916	91.9	8.1	32.1	13.3	4 851	45.4
Camp	78	14.1	161	0.7	20.4	418 072	2 602	73 626	137.7	282 686	2.2	97.8	37.8	9.0	118	5.5
Carson	485	-9.8	1 256	49.4	269.8	1 156 262	920	200 505	83.0	214 990	61.0	39.0	44.8	23.8	5 875	75.1
Cass	168	-5.1	164	0.2	38.9	337 149	2 060	50 023	67.6	66 010	7.8	92.2	27.3	5.1	128	4.1
Castro	548	-3.4	1 030	154.9	411.0	1 131 530	1 098	323 836	1 312.1	2 466 429	11.9	88.1	62.0	45.5	10 759	80.5
Chambers	254	-5.1	346	15.2	92.8	690 097	1 996	80 785	25.6	34 868	58.8	41.2	27.1	7.9	3 018	17.2
Cherokee	301	2.4	191	1.4	67.8	472 935	2 470	58 168	134.0	85 123	66.9	33.1	34.1	5.7	736	3.9
Childress	444	11.1	1 159	9.2	142.1	891 243	769	90 394	19.9	51 883	65.5	34.5	38.6	11.2	3 104	80.4
Clay	633	-4.4	735	1.7	99.2	1 158 323	1 577	71 052	79.8	92 695	15.6	84.4	48.0	13.0	2 098	34.5
Cochran	449	-8.2	1 558	67.8	268.5	1 048 688	673	204 642	100.8	349 955	D	D	35.8	25.3	7 287	87.2
Coke	484	-1.4	1 093	1.0	49.0	1 141 964	1 045	62 172	7.0	15 826	29.4	70.6	26.0	3.4	967	34.5
Coleman	726	3.8	801	1.0	135.5	1 210 947	1 512	68 786	28.4	31 320	40.1	59.9	41.3	7.5	2 499	49.2
Collin	313	7.6	138	6.2	136.6	732 661	5 303	45 315	77.8	34 369	65.3	34.7	19.2	3.4	1 307	7.2
Collingsworth	495	-3.5	1 292	27.3	164.1	1 075 068	832	152 681	43.1	112 556	69.4	30.6	47.3	18.8	4 307	79.6
Colorado	485	-8.0	308	20.1	136.2	1 019 175	3 309	68 878	68.0	43 162	65.4	34.6	35.9	7.6	4 361	17.0
Comal	205	6.5	186	0.4	14.1	974 562	5 248	42 853	D	D	D	D	14.5	0.5	131	5.2
Comanche	517	-10.7	360	18.1	133.8	865 152	2 401	69 521	158.1	110 199	16.9	83.1	42.4	8.4	1 563	21.0
Concho	502	-9.0	1 251	2.1	106.6	1 979 873	1 583	117 608	22.8	56 933	62.3	37.7	54.6	13.2	3 244	67.8
Cooke	504	10.6	259	0.4	132.4	845 941	3 267	60 599	63.3	32 538	29.2	70.8	36.9	7.1	1 361	19.2
Coryell	463	-5.2	354	0.4	85.8	861 112	2 432	52 811	68.6	52 408	23.6	76.4	30.2	5.0	959	16.1
Cottle	565	5.6	2 139	2.9	98.4	1 323 023	619	96 019	15.9	60 246	33.5	66.5	33.3	9.1	2 297	14.8
Crane	239	-36.3	8 858	D	D	5 228 185	590	51 926	1.4	52 222	1.6	98.4	55.6	14.8	56	14.8
Crockett	1 546	-3.5	7 158	0.1	8.0	4 508 931	630	78 523	13.9	64 324	0.3	99.7	46.3	16.7	2 214	33.3
Crosby	558	1.0	1 296	111.7	299.6	1 107 218	855	231 005	71.6	166 100	93.9	6.1	53.1	36.2	7 549	88.6
Culberson	1 618	17.8	21 013	6.0	64.5	7 180 273	342	134 844	13.7	178 364	48.1	51.9	57.1	28.6	680	27.3
Dallam	852	-9.1	2 296	175.6	388.4	2 164 833	943	330 364	651.7	1 756 642	25.5	74.5	55.3	40.7	7 262	76.8
Dallas	84	-4.8	100	1.4	35.9	460 257	4 611	52 857	44.5	53 026	85.9	14.1	17.8	4.4	280	6.9
Dawson	558	-1.8	936	61.2	481.2	738 569	789	188 577	73.1	122 700	97.0	3.0	38.9	23.0	11 185	91.9
Deaf Smith	924	-2.4	1 487	119.9	606.7	1 470 176	989	259 588	1 379.1	2 220 734	5.8	94.2	50.4	37.5	13 023	78.9
Delta	131	-1.2	248	D	65.0	452 815	1 826	60 987	29.3	55 475	53.6	46.4	40.8	5.3	801	33.8
Denton	384	9.5	120	3.3	131.9	731 687	6 111	52 478	137.0	42 771	25.8	74.2	18.1	3.2	1 210	7.6
DeWitt	536	-2.3	314	0.6	49.7	819 210	2 613	61 814	61.4	35 856	12.4	87.6	40.9	4.7	1 068	10.0
Dickens	573	-0.3	1 310	13.4	128.3	958 899	732	87 062	18.5	42 394	43.7	56.3	31.1	8.5	3 468	78.9
Dimmit	677	-4.4	1 845	4.8	44.3	2 875 932	1 559	62 379	35.2	95 956	24.3	75.7	25.9	6.5	730	14.4
Donley	585	-0.7	1 540	14.9	68.0	1 659 213	1 078	89 887	95.1	250 337	14.1	85.9	36.3	12.9	2 000	63.4
Duval	960	-6.0	668	D	60.0	872 009	1 305	38 103	14.8	10 309	6.5	93.5	20.5	1.3	2 814	37.0
Eastland	504	-3.2	429	8.9	91.5	852 450	1 987	56 647	27.9	23 744	30.5	69.5	36.4	4.5	1 428	24.0
Ector	429	1.2	1 624	0.8	3.6	786 019	484	48 008	2.2	8 296	28.9	71.1	16.3	1.5	211	5.3
Edwards	970	-2.7	2 315	1.1	13.0	2 907 783	1 256	48 630	8.2	19 485	7.4	92.6	28.9	5.5	2 070	25.8
Ellis	474	7.0	209	0.4	224.4	665 859	3 181	73 345	91.4	40 367	73.7	26.3	24.1	4.5	2 825	24.3
El Paso	209	24.2	319	24.9	53.3	617 767	1 938	93 251	45.5	69 308	87.0	13.0	25.7	9.4	768	9.3
Erath	608	-2.5	281	12.3	124.4	903 801	3 215	72 397	256.4	118 670	7.2	92.8	32.2	7.2	1 814	8.5
Falls	383	-14.1	303	5.1	174.3	589 978	1 947	82 715	135.3	107 123	40.7	59.3	41.3	12.2	4 706	29.1
Fannin	514	8.4	204	1.2	200.0	523 141	2 561	54 400	71.1	28 287	56.0	44.0	28.2	4.9	2 381	20.3
Fayette	492	-13.0	174	1.1	95.4	738 387	4 235	49 415	66.4	23 515	20.8	79.2	32.0	2.3	1 428	15.1
Fisher	495	-9.2	842	2.6	210.1	911 269	1 083	109 594	31.1	52 872	64.8	35.2	36.6	11.9	4 632	78.7
Floyd	582	-7.3	988	96.7	392.9	1 131 611	1 145	188 253	282.7	480 039	D	D	37.0	21.2	9 002	89.8
Foard	368	-2.0	1 898	1.9	98.2	1 401 794	739	100 098	13.8	71 273	44.8	55.2	47.4	22.7	1 505	69.6
Fort Bend	339	-11.4	264	10.3	135.9	1 080 498	4 095	75 835	103.8	80 705	88.5	11.5	36.2	10.7	4 101	29.2
Franklin	113	-15.4	217	0.8	27.9	623 454	2 869	67 423	86.0	165 339	4.4	95.6	48.1	14.6	171	7.3
Freestone	421	5.4	278	0.4	47.1	583 104	2 100	56 028	44.1	29 059	13.1	86.9	30.5	4.1	433	6.7
Frio	713	10.5	1 096	60.5	152.9	2 238 931	2 043	113 647	183.7	282 138	59.4	40.6	35.9	16.0	2 765	26.3
Gaines	775	-18.2	1 203	227.0	570.6	1 167 174	970	255 823	180.5	280 233	97.2	2.8	53.4	38.4	17 390	83.5
Galveston	90	-13.4	146	0.4	17.6	527 309	3 604	49 598	D	D	D	D	24.3	1.0	756	8.3
Garza	456	-11.1	1 645	8.1	82.1	1 141 856	694	92 982	12.4	44 711	70.4	29.6	35.7	13.4	2 696	74.4
Gillespie	652	-0.1	353	1.9	66.4	1 504 356	4 260	41 480	46.1	24 981	24.5	75.5	28.0	3.1	1 901	20.8
Glasscock	434	-9.6	2 332	25.3	134.7	2 086 946	895	302 559	25.9	139 129	89.3	10.7	51.1	30.6	5 362	69.4
Goliad	495	5.4	421	0.7	33.0	871 038	2 068	55 077	19.4	16 549	19.6	80.4	29.7	3.8	751	9.4
Gonzales	610	-6.8	364	7.8	69.0	1 176 904	3 231	69 381	517.8	309 295	4.5	95.5	44.0	11.6	1 202	12.7
Gray	515	1.1	1 235	21.6	161.2	1 096 012	888	129 902	207.7	498 026	11.7	88.3	42.9	16.1	3 299	61.4
Grayson	431	7.7	168	3.5	176.4	632 363	3 757	58 110	91.9	35 889	72.7	27.3	24.6	4.3	1 948	14.2
Gregg	48	6.3	91	0.4	8.2	353 905	3 881	45 812	3.6	6 844	37.3	62.7	15.7	0.8	41	0.8
Grimes	417	-4.6	248	1.6	56.7	957 864	3 865	59 447	48.1	28 551	23.0	77.0	31.0	3.7	755	5.8

Table B. States and Counties — Water Use, Wholesale Trade, Retail Trade, and Real Estate

STATE County	Water use, 2010		Wholesale trade,[1] 2012				Retail trade,[2] 2012				Real estate and rental and leasing,[2] 2012			
	Total water withdrawn (mil gal/day)	Gallons withdrawn per person per day	Number of establishments	Number of employees	Sales (mil dol)	Annual payroll (mil dol)	Number of establishments	Number of employees	Sales (mil dol)	Annual payroll (mil dol)	Number of establishments	Number of employees	Receipts (mil dol)	Annual payroll (mil dol)
	133	134	135	136	137	138	139	140	141	142	143	144	145	146
TEXAS—Cont'd														
Caldwell	21.6	567	18	D	D	D	81	1 035	345.2	26.7	21	55	7.4	1.3
Calhoun	49.6	2 319	16	D	D	D	63	927	435.3	31.4	20	146	35.2	5.9
Callahan	2.7	200	7	32	11.7	1.0	38	330	157.0	10.5	8	D	D	D
Cameron	281.5	693	317	D	D	D	1 119	16 624	4 124.8	353.2	312	1 338	185.5	32.2
Camp	4.3	344	9	82	34.0	2.9	50	371	111.2	8.4	7	D	D	D
Carson	80.6	13 044	7	D	D	D	20	150	57.4	2.7	1	D	D	D
Cass	33.2	1 091	8	D	D	D	88	883	218.4	18.4	18	33	5.0	0.7
Castro	324.4	40 237	12	142	117.2	6.2	33	185	55.0	3.6	8	16	2.9	0.3
Chambers	265.5	7 565	32	407	138.9	18.5	85	588	283.2	13.7	22	68	37.5	3.4
Cherokee	68.1	1 339	31	D	D	D	132	1 438	383.2	31.8	29	60	8.8	1.6
Childress	9.3	1 318	3	D	D	D	29	370	90.4	7.3	4	D	D	D
Clay	5.4	500	3	D	D	D	28	226	88.8	6.4	5	D	D	D
Cochran	65.9	21 059	3	D	D	D	12	68	50.2	1.7	NA	NA	NA	NA
Coke	34.8	10 491	2	D	D	D	14	66	32.4	1.6	NA	NA	NA	NA
Coleman	52.6	5 915	7	48	23.3	2.1	32	259	68.2	5.0	10	15	1.6	0.4
Collin	327.8	419	817	13 530	18 366.8	1 074.2	2 433	44 931	14 623.9	1 209.9	928	6 910	1 363.0	316.6
Collingsworth	44.5	14 540	5	D	D	D	14	74	15.8	1.6	NA	NA	NA	NA
Colorado	143.7	6 886	32	262	151.7	9.7	101	905	256.5	21.3	18	194	49.0	7.9
Comal	44.4	410	123	D	D	D	380	5 498	1 894.5	147.7	165	800	131.4	29.0
Comanche	28.4	2 033	22	D	D	D	49	430	138.1	10.2	9	27	1.9	0.7
Concho	7.8	1 899	1	D	D	D	12	73	17.1	1.1	1	D	D	D
Cooke	12.4	323	46	D	D	D	145	1 787	543.4	43.4	30	102	21.5	3.1
Coryell	3.7	49	11	D	D	D	120	1 704	493.6	36.2	37	112	14.3	3.0
Cottle	2.0	1 336	NA	NA	NA	NA	5	44	11.6	1.0	NA	NA	NA	NA
Crane	23.5	5 365	4	23	16.9	1.3	12	109	30.2	2.0	2	D	D	D
Crockett	11.7	3 154	4	36	36.3	2.3	19	181	72.9	4.7	3	D	D	D
Crosby	74.7	12 327	8	D	D	D	19	133	35.8	2.8	2	D	D	D
Culberson	39.2	16 351	1	D	D	D	17	247	136.7	4.1	2	D	D	D
Dallam	329.6	49 172	20	354	394.1	14.3	23	203	89.8	5.8	5	D	D	D
Dallas	307.4	130	3 657	67 700	80 605.0	4 255.0	7 518	112 656	35 957.9	3 151.9	3 490	32 478	7 691.3	1 679.2
Dawson	79.0	5 712	21	104	78.5	4.8	43	659	316.8	19.0	7	D	D	D
Deaf Smith	173.9	8 978	34	D	D	D	66	747	275.8	17.7	14	53	4.5	1.0
Delta	2.6	501	3	17	16.3	0.6	14	33	11.7	0.6	2	D	D	D
Denton	166.3	251	513	8 395	16 900.0	539.7	1 625	26 041	8 274.0	645.1	582	3 180	655.5	129.7
DeWitt	6.6	326	14	213	124.9	11.4	61	667	220.2	16.2	13	195	52.1	10.3
Dickens	8.8	3 588	NA	NA	NA	NA	9	57	11.9	1.0	2	D	D	D
Dimmit	11.2	1 116	6	191	174.6	13.1	28	446	142.6	11.2	9	35	3.5	0.9
Donley	26.8	7 289	1	D	D	D	20	113	27.9	1.9	6	9	1.7	0.4
Duval	9.3	789	9	74	24.8	2.5	29	240	78.6	4.7	3	29	6.0	1.0
Eastland	9.8	527	12	D	D	D	81	807	314.0	19.2	19	34	4.6	0.9
Ector	60.2	439	298	4 659	3 608.8	330.5	451	7 286	2 711.7	218.7	176	1 482	604.9	101.9
Edwards	0.9	455	NA	NA	NA	NA	7	83	21.7	2.2	2	D	D	D
Ellis	23.4	156	113	D	D	D	360	5 007	1 459.4	115.4	122	381	66.0	10.7
El Paso	277.5	347	952	D	D	D	2 322	34 934	9 180.6	753.5	699	3 143	617.3	108.0
Erath	16.1	425	35	D	D	D	172	1 831	535.2	41.5	40	111	15.8	2.8
Falls	10.9	611	9	D	D	D	52	419	97.5	8.4	5	19	3.9	0.9
Fannin	55.1	1 624	11	D	D	D	80	924	281.9	24.3	12	121	8.9	3.1
Fayette	24.7	1 005	34	D	D	D	125	1 134	368.6	28.5	32	109	20.4	3.3
Fisher	7.8	1 968	2	D	D	D	13	70	15.6	1.4	1	D	D	D
Floyd	93.3	14 469	12	D	D	D	22	131	31.5	2.5	1	D	D	D
Foard	2.9	2 141	1	D	D	D	7	31	7.4	0.5	NA	NA	NA	NA
Fort Bend	995.3	1 700	579	5 593	6 110.2	302.2	1 423	23 132	7 147.2	561.9	457	1 521	428.0	61.4
Franklin	5.4	505	4	16	5.1	0.7	27	269	105.9	6.1	9	16	2.1	0.3
Freestone	816.1	41 182	13	168	127.5	9.6	63	498	221.3	11.3	12	102	22.6	5.2
Frio	56.4	3 276	13	D	D	D	54	619	250.4	12.7	11	30	6.4	1.2
Gaines	333.6	19 037	27	374	362.2	25.9	45	498	108.9	10.3	12	22	3.8	0.7
Galveston	57.3	197	197	1 701	1 933.8	83.5	876	11 165	3 523.0	294.5	283	1 422	252.3	50.3
Garza	14.3	2 219	4	D	D	D	21	203	58.5	3.4	5	13	4.1	0.6
Gillespie	7.4	297	33	D	D	D	167	1 490	327.8	33.7	39	182	24.1	6.5
Glasscock	56.7	46 215	2	D	D	D	1	D	D	D	NA	NA	NA	NA
Goliad	391.7	54 325	3	13	3.3	0.3	15	128	41.0	2.0	2	D	D	D
Gonzales	19.5	985	20	277	228.2	13.1	72	770	238.6	15.7	9	15	3.4	0.5
Gray	24.6	1 093	31	447	1 065.5	31.3	100	1 082	314.8	25.0	30	118	23.7	4.8
Grayson	22.3	185	100	905	906.6	36.6	417	5 685	1 620.2	137.9	109	327	48.9	8.6
Gregg	90.4	743	252	3 592	2 395.6	194.3	664	9 190	2 639.8	233.0	199	1 220	411.8	62.5
Grimes	308.2	11 585	19	195	189.0	9.5	67	713	213.1	16.7	14	44	5.1	1.2

1. Merchant wholesalers, except manufacturers' sales branches and offices.   2. Employer establishments.

Table B. States and Counties — Professional Services, Manufacturing, and Accommodation and Food Services

STATE County	Professional, scientific, and technical services, 2012				Manufacturing, 2012				Accommodation and food services, 2012			
	Number of establishments	Number of employees	Receipts (mil dol)	Annual payroll (mil dol)	Number of establishments	Number of employees	Receipts (mil dol)	Annual payroll (mil dol)	Number of establishments	Number of employees	Sales (mil dol)	Annual payroll (mil dol)
	147	148	149	150	151	152	153	154	155	156	157	158
TEXAS—Cont'd												
Caldwell	32	108	6.7	2.2	19	699	153.4	24.3	59	740	41.1	10.5
Calhoun	27	D	D	D	19	3 274	11 074.5	304.2	61	619	32.9	8.2
Callahan	11	49	6.8	2.1	10	126	D	4.9	19	D	D	D
Cameron	488	2 359	258.4	81.1	204	4 414	1 709.6	D	660	12 582	635.1	171.7
Camp	9	25	4.5	1.4	8	202	D	8.3	8	D	D	D
Carson	6	D	D	D	3	D	D	D	10	D	D	D
Cass	28	135	10.1	3.9	23	1 257	D	66.0	43	495	18.8	4.9
Castro	12	107	10.4	4.1	7	42	D	1.9	12	77	3.1	0.8
Chambers	32	190	29.1	10.1	30	2 135	D	184.1	54	876	48.7	12.2
Cherokee	56	277	48.0	12.9	66	2 711	458.5	93.6	58	828	39.4	10.4
Childress	11	43	5.0	1.2	NA	NA	NA	NA	26	344	16.6	4.0
Clay	6	D	D	D	NA	NA	NA	NA	7	D	D	D
Cochran	4	5	0.5	0.1	NA	NA	NA	NA	2	D	D	D
Coke	3	D	D	D	NA	NA	NA	NA	6	D	D	D
Coleman	20	35	4.3	1.0	10	168	D	7.2	20	D	D	D
Collin	3 138	D	D	D	419	18 588	8 652.9	1 309.7	1 620	34 192	1 892.3	540.8
Collingsworth	5	D	D	D	NA	NA	NA	NA	4	35	1.2	0.3
Colorado	37	88	11.5	3.5	37	1 597	556.6	78.7	44	578	33.4	7.4
Comal	304	1 340	188.4	58.3	110	3 244	960.3	134.7	318	5 723	304.9	80.1
Comanche	24	85	10.6	3.7	7	131	D	5.3	19	D	D	D
Concho	2	D	D	D	4	27	D	D	5	D	D	D
Cooke	65	223	25.4	8.9	57	2 953	999.7	133.0	71	1 325	61.6	16.6
Coryell	69	780	88.1	36.5	21	293	D	12.4	80	1 316	60.7	15.5
Cottle	NA	NA	NA	NA	NA	NA	NA	NA	4	D	D	D
Crane	5	24	2.3	1.0	NA	NA	NA	NA	6	D	D	D
Crockett	5	14	0.8	0.3	NA	NA	NA	NA	19	269	14.2	2.8
Crosby	3	D	D	D	3	28	D	1.0	5	D	D	D
Culberson	1	D	D	D	NA	NA	NA	NA	15	174	9.5	2.4
Dallam	14	D	D	D	7	57	D	2.4	20	249	13.8	3.2
Dallas	8 837	125 146	23 867.3	10 053.0	2 347	94 078	37 035.6	4 801.6	5 059	107 611	6 753.1	1 887.8
Dawson	18	D	D	D	15	121	22.0	5.7	27	335	17.8	4.1
Deaf Smith	28	224	25.1	9.5	25	1 469	1 084.2	59.8	27	D	D	D
Delta	4	D	D	D	NA	NA	NA	NA	4	D	D	D
Denton	1 626	8 428	1 246.8	446.6	366	12 933	6 886.9	651.8	1 117	22 142	1 138.8	307.1
DeWitt	37	121	14.8	4.8	18	594	D	16.1	51	440	27.3	6.2
Dickens	4	D	D	D	NA	NA	NA	NA	5	36	1.7	0.4
Dimmit	8	D	D	D	4	84	11.2	2.7	30	399	32.8	5.5
Donley	10	D	D	D	NA	NA	NA	NA	9	103	4.1	1.2
Duval	7	56	6.4	1.4	NA	NA	NA	NA	17	75	5.7	1.0
Eastland	28	365	51.8	21.6	20	511	D	20.9	46	530	24.9	6.6
Ector	227	1 832	205.4	80.1	251	4 756	1 706.3	265.7	261	6 150	389.0	94.0
Edwards	2	D	D	D	NA	NA	NA	NA	5	D	D	D
Ellis	179	D	D	D	160	8 301	4 129.7	407.5	207	3 753	177.7	49.5
El Paso	1 201	D	D	D	504	D	13 643.2	D	1 476	28 733	1 384.4	375.2
Erath	68	324	32.8	11.9	40	2 463	D	114.6	98	1 682	71.4	18.8
Falls	8	24	6.4	0.9	8	90	D	5.1	15	D	D	D
Fannin	30	130	10.3	3.3	27	606	135.7	20.3	38	D	D	D
Fayette	64	201	21.8	7.0	39	951	314.0	38.6	74	925	44.5	11.8
Fisher	4	D	D	D	NA	NA	NA	NA	6	D	D	D
Floyd	7	17	1.1	0.4	7	38	11.4	1.8	10	46	2.0	0.4
Foard	1	D	D	D	NA	NA	NA	NA	3	11	0.6	0.1
Fort Bend	1 505	10 000	1 749.9	911.6	342	13 045	4 791.5	722.0	889	16 733	885.3	244.6
Franklin	13	29	2.5	0.8	NA	NA	NA	NA	14	D	D	D
Freestone	28	68	8.2	2.7	12	222	D	7.9	30	549	25.0	6.5
Frio	13	68	4.0	1.7	3	50	D	2.2	40	449	34.2	6.5
Gaines	15	72	7.0	2.8	17	158	31.9	7.8	27	D	D	D
Galveston	541	6 889	778.8	347.9	154	6 236	41 294.9	613.6	646	14 121	763.3	212.4
Garza	6	9	0.8	0.2	NA	NA	NA	NA	9	D	D	D
Gillespie	71	D	D	D	56	544	114.7	20.7	104	1 472	72.7	22.9
Glasscock	2	D	D	D	NA	NA	NA	NA	1	D	D	D
Goliad	14	25	3.3	1.5	4	69	D	D	16	109	5.7	1.6
Gonzales	39	106	10.9	3.6	23	1 456	554.5	52.5	38	473	24.6	5.5
Gray	46	413	65.2	27.6	21	927	453.0	52.5	40	816	35.0	8.9
Grayson	227	844	99.0	32.7	112	6 886	2 574.9	288.3	224	4 305	200.2	57.1
Gregg	382	2 759	357.5	143.4	176	9 075	3 582.7	486.9	322	6 608	307.4	86.3
Grimes	26	142	16.1	5.5	37	2 617	1 501.4	138.9	34	323	20.3	4.7

1. Establishment subject to federal tax.

Table B. States and Counties — Health Care and Social Assistance, Other Services, Nonemployer Businesses, and Residential Construction

STATE County	Health care and social assistance, 2012				Other services, 2012				Nonemployer businesses, 2014		Value of residential construction authorized by building permits, 2015	
	Number of establish-ments	Number of employees	Receipts (mil dol)	Annual payroll (mil dol)	Number of establish-ments	Number of employees	Receipts (mil dol)	Annual payroll (mil dol)	Number	Receipts (mil dol)	New Construction ($1,000)	Number of housing units
	159	160	161	162	163	164	165	166	167	168	169	170
TEXAS—Cont'd												
Caldwell	65	1 279	93.7	46.7	33	106	11.9	3.0	2 648	123.5	44 997	268
Calhoun	34	582	44.8	17.9	34	244	28.4	8.8	1 425	64.8	16 298	81
Callahan	11	118	6.0	2.5	8	40	2.8	0.9	1 240	54.8	781	4
Cameron	1 003	31 018	1 911.3	844.7	402	2 159	163.6	44.6	30 897	1 207.3	143 131	1 285
Camp	22	459	41.0	13.1	9	D	D	D	786	33.1	450	8
Carson	4	D	D	D	8	D	D	D	411	13.1	1 755	7
Cass	46	1 096	63.5	29.2	37	186	16.9	4.8	1 776	83.7	1 619	16
Castro	5	165	14.0	5.2	14	49	7.4	1.4	460	25.0	0	0
Chambers	31	D	D	D	28	104	9.1	2.5	2 595	128.9	64 203	317
Cherokee	83	2 521	179.2	87.3	42	171	15.1	3.9	3 041	132.4	873	5
Childress	20	360	33.3	12.4	11	27	2.9	0.6	372	14.3	0	0
Clay	11	D	D	D	7	D	D	D	793	40.3	263	2
Cochran	9	96	6.9	2.8	3	D	D	D	170	6.5	0	0
Coke	1	D	D	D	4	D	D	D	307	14.0	0	0
Coleman	14	344	22.6	8.2	14	D	D	D	756	43.9	0	0
Collin	2 690	35 757	4 766.3	1 665.7	1 036	7 810	1 154.4	276.8	81 518	4 481.2	2 875 678	14 137
Collingsworth	5	D	D	D	5	16	0.8	0.1	194	6.3	0	0
Colorado	43	1 165	92.4	37.7	35	128	10.9	2.8	1 872	92.2	385	5
Comal	305	5 472	497.2	202.0	218	1 821	94.9	50.8	12 588	683.1	382 254	1 742
Comanche	19	466	32.6	13.3	19	46	3.3	0.9	975	42.3	0	0
Concho	6	141	10.5	4.7	2	D	D	D	214	7.7	285	2
Cooke	84	1 135	100.8	41.5	55	411	37.5	13.7	3 372	193.1	4 908	40
Coryell	57	1 136	70.1	30.9	75	360	29.2	7.8	2 717	115.8	31 691	250
Cottle	4	46	1.3	0.7	1	D	D	D	135	3.6	0	0
Crane	9	167	13.4	6.2	3	D	D	D	319	13.3	90	2
Crockett	6	35	2.6	1.3	5	25	2.1	0.5	334	13.5	NA	NA
Crosby	10	157	9.6	4.0	6	D	D	D	387	13.5	335	5
Culberson	4	D	D	D	2	D	D	D	190	6.2	35	1
Dallam	10	D	D	D	21	D	D	D	465	27.1	3 121	20
Dallas	6 754	155 579	19 683.2	7 652.7	3 427	32 368	4 510.7	1 244.5	221 267	12 351.0	2 830 893	21 698
Dawson	14	378	42.6	10.5	23	79	6.2	1.7	687	32.5	0	0
Deaf Smith	21	505	39.5	16.0	37	174	17.5	3.8	1 193	65.1	837	10
Delta	6	299	6.7	3.1	5	16	1.3	0.2	361	13.3	677	3
Denton	1 462	21 835	2 473.8	893.3	743	4 951	497.3	145.7	63 520	3 223.1	2 014 435	7 887
DeWitt	39	D	D	D	34	191	31.9	6.0	1 529	92.0	1 865	13
Dickens	5	D	D	D	3	D	D	D	143	3.6	NA	NA
Dimmit	24	419	45.1	13.0	19	D	D	D	754	32.2	1 561	6
Donley	9	99	4.8	2.3	8	20	2.5	0.6	267	10.1	0	0
Duval	19	351	14.5	9.0	6	D	D	D	816	36.3	NA	NA
Eastland	53	885	45.2	21.2	37	132	11.4	3.1	1 383	63.8	0	0
Ector	293	7 384	823.7	297.6	250	2 276	340.1	83.5	11 204	728.6	111 046	612
Edwards	3	13	0.6	0.1	3	D	D	D	208	8.5	NA	NA
Ellis	259	3 610	326.6	125.6	170	786	71.1	18.6	13 117	643.6	238 490	1 337
El Paso	1 523	D	D	D	907	5 672	464.4	129.3	55 159	2 378.4	603 056	4 491
Erath	75	1 839	152.9	56.8	73	381	40.5	9.2	3 043	147.9	13 834	218
Falls	27	470	42.9	13.7	18	44	2.8	0.9	931	42.1	661	5
Fannin	49	1 211	128.3	49.1	34	122	12.5	2.5	2 290	104.5	2 274	21
Fayette	64	D	D	D	51	278	22.1	6.8	2 517	124.3	829	8
Fisher	8	129	9.4	4.2	7	18	2.1	0.4	257	10.6	NA	NA
Floyd	15	265	18.3	7.7	14	37	3.9	0.9	346	10.1	280	4
Foard	5	D	D	D	3	D	D	D	127	5.6	NA	NA
Fort Bend	1 490	18 644	1 809.7	648.0	566	3 481	366.9	101.0	61 222	3 090.6	1 113 815	9 278
Franklin	21	3 787	85.5	42.1	18	109	7.1	1.7	779	42.8	125	1
Freestone	29	631	45.3	15.7	26	88	10.2	1.9	1 230	54.4	586	3
Frio	31	786	42.6	16.4	16	D	D	D	1 026	46.6	905	8
Gaines	15	300	29.9	10.0	31	D	D	D	1 703	133.2	360	1
Galveston	556	12 280	1 211.2	495.9	419	2 455	368.2	73.9	22 937	1 123.8	523 965	2 447
Garza	11	177	9.3	4.4	4	11	2.0	0.2	366	19.7	0	0
Gillespie	84	1 611	138.5	66.4	53	269	26.4	6.4	3 602	175.3	8 135	41
Glasscock	NA	NA	NA	NA	1	D	D	D	129	8.3	NA	NA
Goliad	10	107	4.5	1.8	7	10	0.4	0.1	593	28.5	150	3
Gonzales	31	734	49.2	22.2	30	89	8.6	2.2	1 347	58.1	2 951	18
Gray	58	879	87.3	31.7	45	170	19.9	5.0	1 320	76.9	430	2
Grayson	381	9 105	809.1	337.4	139	834	81.0	27.5	9 538	445.1	44 351	340
Gregg	435	10 345	1 323.8	420.7	246	1 979	256.7	80.9	9 200	498.5	37 897	229
Grimes	23	D	D	D	18	D	D	D	2 069	103.7	1 616	17

Table B. States and Counties — Government Employment and Payroll, and Local Government Finances

| | Government employment and payroll, 2012 | | | | | | | | | Local government finances, 2012 | | | | |
| | Full-time equivalent employees | March payroll (dollars) | March payroll (percent of total) | | | | | | | General revenue | | | Taxes | |
STATE County			Administration, judicial, and legal	Police and Corrections	Fire Protection	Highways and transportation	Health and Welfare	Natural resources and utilities	Education and libraries	Total (mil dol)	Intergovernmental (mil dol)	Total (mil dol)	Per capita[1] (dollars) Total	Property
	171	172	173	174	175	176	177	178	179	180	181	182	183	184
TEXAS—Cont'd														
Caldwell	1 295	4 627 444	7.7	8.7	1.9	2.0	2.0	4.0	73.2	94.8	42.5	38.1	983	834
Calhoun	989	2 883 600	7.4	10.3	2.1	7.4	2.5	3.0	65.2	113.6	11.0	59.8	2 767	2 477
Callahan	610	1 550 184	5.1	6.1	0.1	2.1	0.9	3.3	80.5	36.2	16.2	14.8	1 095	992
Cameron	21 552	67 816 703	3.9	8.4	2.8	2.4	1.6	5.2	74.0	1 662.8	982.8	420.5	1 012	795
Camp	508	1 428 009	4.7	3.7	0.0	2.7	0.0	6.7	81.7	31.5	14.9	13.1	1 056	885
Carson	384	1 061 435	13.7	2.8	0.0	2.8	2.7	4.8	64.8	23.9	6.1	15.1	2 453	2 374
Cass	1 554	4 198 540	6.2	6.2	1.2	1.7	13.0	3.1	67.7	95.7	40.0	32.1	1 064	938
Castro	547	1 382 117	5.7	6.3	0.0	3.1	22.6	2.8	59.3	40.7	18.5	9.6	1 182	1 099
Chambers	1 626	5 773 846	8.8	6.1	0.0	3.1	10.0	6.3	64.8	164.5	34.4	100.6	2 780	2 551
Cherokee	1 869	5 488 563	6.6	9.7	2.3	2.5	5.7	2.1	69.7	129.7	67.3	48.0	938	770
Childress	583	1 738 210	4.7	11.1	1.6	1.8	46.8	4.4	29.0	62.7	9.4	6.1	867	753
Clay	559	1 694 976	3.7	2.8	0.0	4.0	14.3	8.9	63.3	47.0	12.1	16.9	1 605	1 445
Cochran	322	904 022	9.5	5.0	0.0	3.0	15.4	3.4	63.0	25.0	7.6	15.4	5 071	4 948
Coke	281	838 152	5.9	2.3	0.0	2.1	28.4	5.7	54.6	19.7	5.9	9.5	2 954	2 830
Coleman	629	1 691 631	4.4	5.0	0.9	13.7	19.1	6.3	48.7	34.6	18.7	11.3	1 301	1 096
Collin	28 433	113 769 771	4.6	8.7	4.4	3.5	1.7	4.9	69.6	3 611.2	681.0	1 995.2	2 390	2 038
Collingsworth	212	542 831	8.4	5.4	0.0	4.5	10.4	2.8	67.4	13.8	5.2	4.4	1 449	1 266
Colorado	861	2 596 959	7.5	9.0	0.0	6.1	1.1	3.8	71.4	68.4	17.2	35.5	1 716	1 501
Comal	4 722	16 455 274	5.9	10.7	5.6	2.4	1.7	4.9	65.1	413.5	81.4	279.4	2 443	2 055
Comanche	808	2 419 843	5.0	9.4	3.7	2.4	31.9	1.8	45.5	44.9	19.7	15.0	1 088	940
Concho	164	494 362	12.1	5.4	0.0	4.2	27.0	5.6	44.3	14.7	3.5	6.1	1 522	1 335
Cooke	2 150	7 756 968	4.6	7.0	2.3	2.2	22.1	3.1	58.0	192.9	53.2	71.4	1 846	1 489
Coryell	2 637	8 819 482	4.6	7.6	1.9	0.9	12.3	2.8	67.6	181.4	80.4	52.0	674	538
Cottle	98	244 407	17.9	5.3	0.0	6.5	0.0	11.3	51.6	5.8	2.0	2.8	1 867	1 769
Crane	326	1 145 731	9.6	10.7	0.0	1.4	1.7	18.9	57.2	40.3	6.9	31.6	6 922	6 690
Crockett	357	1 200 438	6.5	5.5	0.5	4.8	18.8	4.6	54.0	42.3	5.4	32.0	8 555	8 552
Crosby	396	1 113 076	6.6	6.1	0.0	1.6	0.7	8.5	76.2	24.3	14.0	7.8	1 271	1 153
Culberson	191	571 285	13.3	8.3	0.0	6.0	1.7	9.4	60.5	20.8	4.5	8.8	3 852	3 344
Dallam	459	1 265 633	7.6	10.7	0.5	2.5	1.7	3.2	73.1	27.7	8.8	15.1	2 154	1 701
Dallas	105 099	440 691 940	4.7	11.6	5.3	7.3	14.2	4.5	50.8	12 510.2	3 260.1	5 736.3	2 338	1 792
Dawson	1 027	2 968 415	3.1	5.5	0.8	1.9	24.1	9.3	55.0	56.2	16.2	34.3	2 514	2 311
Deaf Smith	1 045	3 343 534	6.0	8.2	0.3	2.5	18.1	3.3	61.2	124.1	26.6	28.5	1 470	1 181
Delta	249	617 205	10.2	5.7	0.1	0.9	0.0	6.2	76.6	18.1	9.8	6.9	1 304	1 174
Denton	21 018	80 654 351	6.5	9.2	4.5	1.3	2.5	6.0	68.8	2 022.8	459.3	1 266.0	1 790	1 527
DeWitt	1 484	4 135 234	4.5	4.4	0.5	2.2	24.6	3.4	59.6	97.2	42.1	29.7	1 450	1 280
Dickens	132	357 360	9.4	5.8	0.0	5.1	0.0	3.9	70.5	10.8	3.0	6.0	2 586	2 419
Dimmit	818	1 945 225	7.2	5.4	0.0	1.0	23.0	4.5	58.2	46.5	21.1	19.9	1 904	1 452
Donley	386	1 127 365	14.0	2.9	0.0	2.0	12.1	7.2	61.3	18.4	8.5	4.9	1 371	1 208
Duval	1 069	2 869 544	5.5	8.4	0.0	5.8	26.4	3.4	49.4	84.6	22.4	23.2	1 983	1 875
Eastland	1 310	3 783 362	4.4	5.2	0.7	1.4	13.7	3.5	70.8	84.5	34.9	24.4	1 322	1 079
Ector	6 915	26 339 816	4.0	7.3	3.2	1.3	27.3	2.1	53.3	690.5	140.4	269.5	1 467	1 389
Edwards	196	461 967	5.6	6.6	0.5	3.6	2.2	2.7	77.7	11.0	3.0	7.2	3 657	3 565
Ellis	6 187	19 866 741	5.2	9.5	4.1	1.8	0.8	3.8	73.5	481.2	162.1	262.5	1 705	1 483
El Paso	38 262	139 590 880	4.5	10.3	3.7	3.1	8.1	3.0	65.5	3 339.7	1 610.5	1 090.4	1 318	1 018
Erath	1 440	4 169 914	6.4	10.7	3.0	2.6	13.7	4.5	57.7	97.3	38.9	48.4	1 230	1 006
Falls	755	2 249 164	5.5	10.4	1.3	2.6	0.2	6.9	72.4	45.7	26.5	12.5	711	588
Fannin	1 308	3 305 390	7.2	6.5	4.5	3.2	0.4	4.6	72.9	79.2	36.7	29.9	885	758
Fayette	1 047	3 070 054	8.5	11.9	0.0	5.3	5.8	7.8	59.5	68.3	15.9	38.4	1 557	1 347
Fisher	274	819 484	9.8	4.3	0.0	4.0	33.9	2.2	42.7	20.3	6.0	7.5	1 949	1 549
Floyd	494	1 401 943	6.0	6.3	0.0	3.0	29.3	3.2	52.2	29.3	12.8	7.3	1 148	1 016
Foard	109	252 340	7.9	2.2	0.0	27.8	2.3	4.6	52.5	6.5	3.6	2.6	1 980	1 699
Fort Bend	16 162	56 081 173	6.1	10.9	2.4	2.1	1.2	2.8	73.5	1 700.0	419.7	1 031.0	1 644	1 484
Franklin	376	1 062 026	10.1	8.0	0.0	4.2	0.1	6.2	71.2	29.0	7.2	17.8	1 676	1 502
Freestone	870	2 743 049	6.9	7.9	0.0	2.8	1.7	3.3	77.1	162.3	33.5	110.1	5 642	5 300
Frio	734	2 179 421	2.5	6.3	0.0	4.5	0.2	6.1	79.7	65.4	34.3	19.5	1 102	928
Gaines	1 152	3 808 818	1.9	4.1	0.0	3.9	20.6	2.9	66.0	125.0	15.5	87.9	4 775	4 628
Galveston	16 441	61 971 543	4.8	11.2	1.9	2.4	3.8	5.1	69.9	1 645.8	615.8	806.4	2 684	2 330
Garza	293	892 400	9.4	14.2	0.0	2.3	1.8	3.0	68.2	25.0	4.6	15.2	2 373	2 062
Gillespie	1 151	3 952 390	6.0	8.2	0.8	2.5	3.0	27.3	49.9	76.0	11.8	50.4	2 005	1 655
Glasscock	71	223 571	6.0	3.1	0.0	7.3	0.0	3.2	74.8	20.5	1.8	16.3	12 932	12 861
Goliad	327	1 001 812	9.8	6.6	0.0	4.9	0.3	2.6	69.7	27.2	7.6	18.0	2 453	2 250
Gonzales	1 193	3 267 421	6.8	6.0	0.5	2.5	24.1	5.5	54.2	101.3	40.1	26.2	1 309	1 024
Gray	994	2 974 220	9.1	9.3	4.4	4.3	1.5	4.0	66.4	72.0	21.7	36.7	1 599	1 291
Grayson	5 248	18 290 717	5.6	9.2	3.5	2.7	4.2	4.8	69.0	414.8	144.6	188.3	1 544	1 271
Gregg	5 913	19 287 172	4.5	10.7	5.5	1.7	6.6	4.4	64.2	499.5	162.8	256.1	2 088	1 490
Grimes	917	2 789 960	7.3	9.4	0.7	2.4	1.2	2.1	74.4	77.3	25.0	42.7	1 594	1 464

1. Based on the resident population estimated as of July 1 of the year shown.

Table B. States and Counties — **Local Government Finances, Government Employment, and Voting**

STATE County	Total (mil dol) 185	Per capita[1] (dollars) 186	Education 187	Health and hospitals 188	Police protection 189	Public welfare 190	Highways 191	Total (mil dol) 192	Per capita[1] (dollars) 193	Federal civilian 194	Federal military 195	State and local 196	Democratic 197	Republican 198	All other 199
TEXAS—Cont'd															
Caldwell	103.3	2 667	49.6	3.3	5.2	0.3	3.5	64.6	1 669	57	76	1 611	46.4	52.4	1.2
Calhoun	106.7	4 938	37.9	23.7	4.3	0.2	4.4	73.3	3 392	34	98	1 329	39.7	59.7	0.6
Callahan	33.7	2 494	68.1	0.5	5.7	0.0	2.9	34.4	2 546	45	28	594	18.6	80.3	1.1
Cameron	1 613.4	3 883	61.9	0.8	4.4	0.5	3.7	1 801.3	4 335	3 224	969	27 511	64.1	35.3	0.7
Camp	30.6	2 461	71.8	0.2	3.9	0.1	5.5	43.1	3 459	30	26	584	38.0	61.3	0.8
Carson	23.0	3 741	59.9	1.1	2.8	0.0	5.0	34.1	5 539	14	12	426	13.6	85.5	0.9
Cass	91.1	3 021	59.3	15.9	3.7	0.3	2.8	50.0	1 659	64	62	1 610	29.5	69.9	0.7
Castro	33.2	4 069	51.2	27.7	4.5	0.0	3.7	20.0	2 445	19	16	620	31.4	68.2	0.4
Chambers	168.5	4 656	51.2	9.0	4.2	0.4	4.6	360.8	9 968	53	79	1 920	24.0	75.1	0.9
Cherokee	167.4	3 268	66.5	4.9	3.9	0.1	4.5	85.5	1 669	67	99	4 026	28.1	71.2	0.7
Childress	54.2	7 712	18.8	64.6	2.7	0.0	2.7	6.3	898	21	12	1 071	21.6	77.6	0.7
Clay	46.1	4 377	39.2	17.7	2.7	0.1	5.6	119.9	11 385	24	21	507	20.3	78.9	0.8
Cochran	27.0	8 873	69.4	12.8	3.0	0.0	3.8	0.1	27	12	0	329	26.9	71.7	1.4
Coke	16.5	5 122	42.6	0.1	3.0	32.6	4.0	24.2	7 483	11	0	341	19.1	79.8	1.1
Coleman	34.1	3 930	44.6	22.9	4.1	0.1	3.7	15.9	1 837	40	17	555	17.4	81.3	1.3
Collin	4 140.4	4 961	43.1	0.7	3.6	0.1	8.6	16 872.8	20 216	1 528	1 914	42 803	36.8	62.3	0.9
Collingsworth	16.5	5 436	37.3	43.5	4.4	0.0	1.5	12.6	4 138	16	0	215	19.6	78.9	1.5
Colorado	71.5	3 453	50.2	14.9	5.5	0.1	5.4	63.0	3 042	46	42	1 010	30.0	69.4	0.6
Comal	446.0	3 899	56.1	0.9	6.3	0.6	5.0	943.7	8 251	164	254	5 524	25.7	73.2	1.1
Comanche	42.2	3 069	50.8	15.3	4.6	0.2	5.8	30.9	2 246	43	28	981	25.6	73.1	1.3
Concho	12.3	3 067	36.9	29.2	4.3	0.0	4.1	3.9	977	26	0	224	23.9	74.9	1.2
Cooke	191.9	4 961	48.0	22.9	5.0	0.1	3.7	159.4	4 119	58	79	2 787	20.3	79.0	0.7
Coryell	215.6	2 792	43.6	12.0	4.0	0.3	22.6	217.4	2 815	192	504	5 937	36.1	63.0	0.9
Cottle	5.4	3 651	50.1	1.6	2.9	0.1	3.3	1.4	940	10	0	141	26.5	72.2	1.3
Crane	40.9	8 956	77.6	0.0	3.1	0.0	1.6	6.3	1 384	0	10	371	21.9	77.0	1.1
Crockett	42.8	11 437	63.2	0.7	1.7	0.8	5.5	6.0	1 614	0	0	399	33.1	66.4	0.5
Crosby	24.1	3 941	70.8	0.1	3.8	1.1	3.7	0.5	83	15	12	449	35.7	63.8	0.5
Culberson	18.7	8 167	29.9	32.6	5.7	0.0	3.2	2.8	1 224	87	0	200	64.8	33.9	1.3
Dallam	28.3	4 044	60.6	0.3	5.2	0.0	6.8	30.2	4 320	15	15	271	19.0	79.9	1.1
Dallas	11 949.9	4 870	37.6	17.2	5.8	0.7	2.6	27 138.7	11 060	25 315	5 902	143 996	57.3	42.0	0.7
Dawson	56.4	4 132	73.5	0.6	3.9	0.1	3.1	165.8	12 154	51	24	1 270	28.1	70.9	0.9
Deaf Smith	135.2	6 983	26.5	25.1	2.4	0.1	2.8	2 436.8	125 866	47	39	1 272	26.3	73.1	0.7
Delta	15.4	2 898	62.3	0.0	6.5	0.3	5.4	19.5	3 660	16	11	301	26.9	72.2	0.8
Denton	2 006.9	2 837	52.0	1.7	5.6	0.1	6.2	6 231.1	8 810	1 628	1 582	32 614	37.5	61.6	0.9
DeWitt	94.1	4 596	46.6	28.3	3.1	0.2	3.8	56.7	2 773	32	39	2 172	25.9	73.8	0.3
Dickens	13.9	5 980	66.7	0.3	4.5	0.0	7.7	7.5	3 235	11	0	160	24.1	75.1	0.8
Dimmit	42.2	4 036	66.0	0.3	4.0	0.0	3.8	95.0	9 081	273	23	1 029	75.0	24.4	0.6
Donley	19.7	5 489	76.6	0.0	1.8	2.7	1.6	21.5	5 966	11	0	405	17.2	81.3	1.5
Duval	69.0	5 890	36.6	35.9	4.0	0.7	3.7	59.2	5 053	139	23	997	74.8	24.4	0.8
Eastland	81.8	4 441	62.6	14.7	2.7	0.2	2.9	42.9	2 328	50	417	1 456	19.5	79.4	1.1
Ector	691.3	4 790	36.3	40.0	3.5	0.0	2.4	385.4	2 670	164	314	9 348	25.6	73.6	0.8
Edwards	10.4	5 270	76.7	0.0	6.7	0.0	2.3	2.5	1 271	21	0	137	33.4	65.0	1.5
Ellis	446.9	2 903	57.1	0.3	6.0	0.3	3.9	1 320.0	8 573	214	327	6 887	28.5	70.7	0.8
El Paso	3 257.4	3 937	52.3	15.6	4.9	0.4	0.9	4 034.1	4 876	12 497	28 234	53 979	65.9	33.4	0.8
Erath	86.0	2 188	55.2	1.6	7.4	0.4	5.3	109.6	2 786	77	83	3 734	22.3	76.8	0.9
Falls	44.4	2 519	65.6	1.1	5.3	0.8	6.2	13.4	762	406	31	1 155	39.7	59.4	0.8
Fannin	76.7	2 268	61.1	2.7	7.1	0.7	5.8	54.2	1 601	711	63	1 890	29.6	69.2	1.2
Fayette	68.1	2 756	56.7	3.7	5.9	0.8	7.7	47.6	1 928	68	51	1 569	28.1	70.8	1.1
Fisher	21.3	5 529	41.6	30.6	4.6	0.1	5.1	3.0	779	17	0	302	38.5	60.7	0.8
Floyd	29.6	4 646	49.4	29.9	3.4	0.0	1.0	5.9	923	28	12	506	29.0	70.8	0.3
Foard	4.6	3 531	56.3	4.7	6.8	0.2	7.6	0.1	79	0	0	98	36.8	60.8	2.4
Fort Bend	1 722.6	2 746	46.9	0.7	4.7	0.3	7.2	5 183.8	8 264	697	1 447	22 104	48.5	50.9	0.6
Franklin	25.1	2 364	51.5	0.1	5.6	0.4	9.6	29.4	2 760	19	22	430	23.1	75.5	1.4
Freestone	159.6	8 177	39.9	10.8	11.9	0.0	12.6	91.4	4 681	33	38	1 390	27.9	71.4	0.7
Frio	58.9	3 327	54.3	3.8	5.2	0.0	3.8	93.0	5 256	98	31	1 280	59.2	40.5	0.3
Gaines	132.6	7 199	63.4	14.7	1.8	0.0	4.5	120.9	6 566	25	40	1 376	16.0	83.2	0.8
Galveston	1 667.3	5 549	43.5	4.3	5.0	0.5	5.1	3 060.4	10 185	890	1 021	24 523	39.8	59.3	0.9
Garza	22.3	3 480	59.5	0.1	9.6	0.7	5.7	14.9	2 330	12	0	375	21.4	77.5	1.1
Gillespie	76.0	3 023	58.0	2.8	9.2	0.3	5.1	26.7	1 061	47	52	1 114	20.9	77.5	1.6
Glasscock	21.4	16 992	83.0	6.7	0.3	0.0	0.7	8.1	6 411	0	0	135	9.3	90.1	0.5
Goliad	22.9	3 113	65.5	4.1	7.2	0.8	7.3	16.0	2 182	18	15	446	36.4	62.9	0.8
Gonzales	101.6	5 069	39.0	28.7	5.0	0.0	3.6	43.0	2 146	64	42	1 446	34.5	64.8	0.7
Gray	70.1	3 049	52.0	0.4	5.0	0.2	5.4	80.6	3 506	39	44	1 529	14.2	85.1	0.7
Grayson	423.3	3 471	54.8	3.3	5.1	0.0	6.0	717.6	5 885	319	252	6 106	30.6	68.5	1.0
Gregg	514.7	4 196	54.4	5.9	5.3	0.0	4.4	916.0	7 468	340	248	7 124	30.9	68.5	0.6
Grimes	84.3	3 146	51.8	0.3	3.8	0.0	6.3	95.1	3 549	48	50	1 796	32.5	66.8	0.7

1. Based on the resident population estimated as of July 1 of the year shown. 2. © 2013 Election Data Services, Inc. All rights reserved.

Table B. States and Counties — Land Area and Population

STATE/ County code	CBSA code[1]	County type[2]	STATE County	Population, 2015				Population and population characteristics, 2014										
								Race alone or in combination, not Hispanic or Latino (percent)					Age (percent)					
				Land area[3] (sq km) 2010	Total persons 2015	Rank	Per square kilometer	White	Black	American Indian, Alaska Native	Asian and Pacific Islander	Percent Hispanic or Latino[4]	Under 5 years	5 to 17 years	18 to 24 years	25 to 34 years	35 to 44 years	45 to 54 years
				1	2	3	4	5	6	7	8	9	10	11	12	13	14	15
			TEXAS—Cont'd															
48 187	41700	1	Guadalupe	1 842	151 249	430	82.1	53.8	7.9	0.8	2.5	37.0	6.3	19.8	9.1	12.5	13.9	14.2
48 189	38380	4	Hale	2 602	34 360	1 320	13.2	36.0	5.3	0.6	0.7	58.4	8.0	19.7	11.7	13.7	11.6	12.0
48 191	...	9	Hall	2 288	3 138	2 962	1.4	58.9	7.3	0.8	0.2	34.8	5.4	18.2	8.5	9.4	9.2	12.5
48 193	...	6	Hamilton	2 165	8 159	2 589	3.8	86.9	1.2	0.7	0.8	11.3	5.2	15.6	7.1	9.3	10.1	12.6
48 195	...	7	Hansford	2 382	5 610	2 794	2.4	53.0	0.9	0.6	0.4	45.2	6.9	22.1	8.7	10.8	12.3	12.9
48 197	...	7	Hardeman	1 800	3 840	2 915	2.1	70.5	6.4	1.1	0.9	22.8	6.3	17.3	7.0	10.8	11.9	12.2
48 199	13140	2	Hardin	2 307	55 865	908	24.2	87.9	6.0	0.8	0.9	5.6	6.4	18.4	8.2	12.4	12.5	13.6
48 201	26420	1	Harris	4 412	4 538 028	3	1 028.6	32.5	19.1	0.5	7.4	41.7	7.7	19.4	9.9	16.2	14.3	12.7
48 203	32220	4	Harrison	2 331	66 746	794	28.6	65.2	23.0	0.9	1.0	12.5	6.6	18.3	10.5	12.0	11.9	12.8
48 205	...	9	Hartley	3 787	6 193	2 742	1.6	64.8	7.6	0.7	0.8	26.2	5.3	15.8	5.8	14.6	17.8	16.2
48 207	...	6	Haskell	2 339	5 737	2 780	2.5	69.5	4.4	1.0	1.0	25.5	5.1	14.9	8.9	11.8	11.2	12.7
48 209	12420	1	Hays	1 756	194 739	336	110.9	57.5	4.1	0.8	2.0	37.0	6.0	17.6	17.5	14.0	12.8	11.6
48 211	...	9	Hemphill	2 347	4 264	2 881	1.8	66.0	0.7	1.1	1.0	32.5	8.7	22.9	7.9	12.6	12.4	12.3
48 213	11980	4	Henderson	2 263	79 545	699	35.2	80.4	7.0	1.3	0.8	12.0	5.5	16.5	8.1	10.6	10.9	13.2
48 215	32580	2	Hidalgo	4 069	842 304	68	207.0	7.3	0.5	0.1	1.1	91.1	9.7	23.9	11.1	13.2	13.0	10.6
48 217	...	6	Hill	2 483	34 855	1 307	14.0	72.8	7.1	0.9	0.6	20.1	6.0	17.9	8.3	10.9	10.6	12.3
48 219	30220	6	Hockley	2 353	23 433	1 661	10.0	48.8	4.1	0.7	0.6	46.7	7.4	19.5	12.4	13.3	10.8	11.9
48 221	19100	4	Hood	1 089	55 423	912	50.9	86.5	1.1	1.2	0.8	11.5	5.2	15.4	6.9	10.5	9.9	12.8
48 223	44860	6	Hopkins	1 987	36 223	1 270	18.2	75.6	7.8	1.0	0.9	16.3	6.7	18.5	8.4	11.6	11.6	13.0
48 225	...	7	Houston	3 188	22 785	1 694	7.1	63.0	25.7	0.7	0.7	10.9	5.1	14.5	7.6	11.4	12.3	14.6
48 227	13700	5	Howard	2 333	37 206	1 246	15.9	52.0	6.5	1.1	1.3	40.4	6.0	15.8	10.9	15.2	12.2	16.0
48 229	21340	8	Hudspeth	11 839	3 379	2 947	0.3	19.8	1.3	0.7	0.7	78.2	6.4	18.1	10.1	10.2	10.8	13.1
48 231	19100	1	Hunt	2 176	89 844	642	41.3	74.6	8.6	1.4	1.8	14.9	6.2	17.7	9.9	12.1	11.8	14.0
48 233	14420	6	Hutchinson	2 298	21 734	1 742	9.5	73.0	3.3	2.3	0.8	22.3	7.3	19.1	8.5	12.2	12.3	12.2
48 235	41660	3	Irion	2 724	1 554	3 078	0.6	70.3	2.2	1.3	0.9	27.6	6.4	15.9	7.9	11.4	10.3	15.3
48 237	...	6	Jack	2 359	8 878	2 522	3.8	78.4	4.3	0.9	0.6	16.2	6.0	15.7	9.9	13.3	12.0	14.8
48 239	...	6	Jackson	2 148	14 816	2 115	6.9	60.9	7.0	0.8	0.8	31.5	6.9	19.1	8.2	12.0	11.3	12.5
48 241	...	6	Jasper	2 432	35 506	1 289	14.6	75.7	17.2	0.8	1.0	6.6	6.7	17.7	8.0	11.3	10.9	13.5
48 243	...	9	Jeff Davis	5 865	2 156	3 036	0.4	65.1	1.7	1.1	0.8	34.0	1.9	10.1	5.5	7.9	9.2	14.2
48 245	13140	2	Jefferson	2 270	254 308	262	112.0	43.4	34.1	0.7	4.1	18.9	6.8	16.9	10.2	14.6	12.4	13.2
48 247	...	6	Jim Hogg	2 943	5 200	2 821	1.8	7.0	0.6	0.4	0.7	91.8	9.0	21.1	8.2	12.6	11.2	11.4
48 249	10860	4	Jim Wells	2 240	41 382	1 141	18.5	19.1	0.7	0.4	0.5	79.6	8.1	20.1	9.9	12.9	11.5	11.9
48 251	19100	1	Johnson	1 877	159 990	402	85.2	75.4	3.4	1.1	1.6	20.0	6.5	19.9	8.8	12.7	12.9	14.0
48 253	10180	3	Jones	2 405	19 970	1 837	8.3	60.1	12.7	0.7	0.7	27.2	4.8	13.1	9.8	16.8	15.0	14.5
48 255	...	6	Karnes	1 936	14 975	2 101	7.7	39.1	8.2	0.5	0.4	52.6	5.8	15.4	10.6	16.9	13.1	12.3
48 257	19100	1	Kaufman	2 022	114 690	534	56.7	68.7	10.9	1.0	1.3	19.4	6.9	20.7	8.2	12.9	14.0	13.7
48 259	41700	1	Kendall	1 716	40 384	1 168	23.5	75.7	1.1	1.0	1.3	22.4	4.9	18.5	7.8	9.3	11.6	14.4
48 261	28780	9	Kenedy	3 777	407	3 139	0.1	20.9	2.4	1.7	0.5	71.8	7.3	18.3	8.3	15.0	8.8	13.8
48 263	...	9	Kent	2 337	764	3 123	0.3	79.9	1.5	2.0	0.3	18.1	3.4	18.1	5.5	11.1	8.9	12.9
48 265	28500	4	Kerr	2 858	50 955	975	17.8	71.3	2.0	1.1	1.2	25.7	5.1	14.3	8.4	9.7	9.1	12.1
48 267	...	7	Kimble	3 240	4 388	2 872	1.4	72.9	0.5	0.9	0.9	25.5	4.9	14.1	6.4	8.9	10.5	12.2
48 269	...	9	King	2 359	282	3 140	0.1	82.1	1.1	1.9	0.8	17.2	7.6	13.0	6.5	11.1	11.8	14.9
48 271	...	9	Kinney	3 523	3 549	2 938	1.0	41.7	1.5	1.0	0.5	56.9	4.5	14.6	9.2	10.9	11.8	10.7
48 273	28780	4	Kleberg	2 283	31 857	1 386	14.0	22.4	3.9	0.5	2.7	72.1	7.3	17.2	21.0	13.8	9.8	9.5
48 275	...	9	Knox	2 203	3 860	2 913	1.8	60.4	5.8	1.0	0.4	33.7	7.5	18.6	7.6	10.6	10.7	11.6
48 277	37580	4	Lamar	2 350	49 440	991	21.0	77.2	14.3	2.5	1.1	7.5	6.5	17.1	9.0	11.4	11.4	13.4
48 279	...	6	Lamb	2 632	13 385	2 211	5.1	41.0	4.6	0.8	0.4	53.9	8.3	19.9	8.8	11.5	10.8	12.7
48 281	28660	2	Lampasas	1 846	20 588	1 798	11.2	74.9	4.3	1.8	2.1	18.9	5.9	17.5	7.8	10.6	11.8	14.4
48 283	...	6	La Salle	3 851	7 631	2 625	2.0	14.1	0.7	0.6	0.5	84.4	6.7	14.0	18.2	17.2	11.1	10.7
48 285	...	6	Lavaca	2 512	19 836	1 841	7.9	75.4	6.9	0.5	0.5	17.7	6.0	17.6	7.3	10.0	10.4	12.7
48 287	...	6	Lee	1 629	16 898	1 987	10.4	65.5	11.6	0.7	0.8	23.0	5.7	16.9	8.6	11.0	11.3	14.3
48 289	...	8	Leon	2 779	17 086	1 978	6.1	74.7	7.7	1.0	1.0	14.3	5.7	15.7	6.9	10.2	9.9	12.5
48 291	26420	1	Liberty	3 000	79 654	698	26.6	67.6	11.0	1.0	0.9	20.7	6.8	18.3	9.5	13.6	12.9	13.9
48 293	...	6	Limestone	2 345	23 320	1 668	9.9	61.1	18.2	0.8	0.7	20.9	6.3	16.8	8.9	12.9	11.7	12.4
48 295	...	9	Lipscomb	2 414	3 569	2 821	1.5	65.7	1.4	1.7	0.9	31.5	6.2	20.5	8.7	13.8	10.8	12.7
48 297	...	6	Live Oak	2 693	12 229	2 283	4.5	56.9	4.6	1.0	0.8	37.5	4.9	15.1	8.1	13.6	11.8	13.3
48 299	...	7	Llano	2 419	19 796	1 844	8.2	88.3	1.4	1.2	0.7	9.8	4.3	11.3	5.5	7.3	8.0	12.0
48 301	...	9	Loving	1 733	112	3 141	0.1	74.7	0.0	3.4	0.0	20.7	9.3	20.9	1.2	14.0	3.5	14.0
48 303	31180	3	Lubbock	2 320	299 453	227	129.1	55.9	7.5	0.7	2.7	33.9	6.8	17.4	17.2	14.6	11.0	10.9
48 305	31180	6	Lynn	2 310	5 724	2 781	2.5	49.7	2.5	0.8	0.3	47.9	7.1	20.2	8.2	11.3	10.7	13.8
48 307	...	7	McCulloch	2 760	8 341	2 567	3.0	65.8	2.5	0.6	0.6	31.1	6.2	17.2	7.5	10.4	10.4	12.3
48 309	47380	3	McLennan	2 686	245 671	273	91.5	58.7	15.0	0.7	2.0	25.2	7.1	17.7	15.0	12.8	11.0	11.7
48 311	...	8	McMullen	2 951	820	3 117	0.3	60.2	1.5	0.9	0.5	37.8	4.1	16.4	7.1	10.7	9.7	14.7
48 313	...	6	Madison	1 207	14 065	2 159	11.7	57.4	20.3	0.7	1.0	22.2	5.7	15.8	11.8	17.5	13.1	11.0
48 315	...	8	Marion	986	10 160	2 423	10.3	72.7	22.7	1.7	1.0	4.1	4.5	13.9	6.7	9.4	9.8	14.8
48 317	33260	6	Martin	2 370	5 641	2 792	2.4	52.0	2.1	0.8	0.5	45.7	8.9	21.3	9.7	13.9	10.8	13.3

1. CBSA = Core Based Statistical Area. See Appendix A for explanation. See Appendix B for list of metropolitan areas with component counties. 2. County type code from the Economic Research Service of USDA Rural-Urban Continuum Codes. See Appendix A for definition. 3. Dry land or land partially or temporarily covered by water. 4. May be of any race.

Table B. States and Counties — **Population and Households**

STATE County	55 to 64 years	65 to 74 years	75 years and over	Percent female	2000	2010	2000–2010	2010–2015	Births	Deaths	Net migration	Number	Persons per household	Family households	Female family householder[1]	One person
	16	17	18	19	20	21	22	23	24	25	26	27	28	29	30	31
TEXAS—Cont'd																
Guadalupe	11.2	7.8	5.2	50.6	89 023	131 537	47.8	15.0	9 064	4 822	14 987	47 768	2.89	75.8	12.7	20.8
Hale	10.3	7.0	6.0	48.1	36 602	36 273	-0.9	-5.3	2 789	1 613	-3 178	11 644	2.84	72.2	15.5	24.6
Hall	13.2	12.5	11.1	51.2	3 782	3 353	-11.3	-6.4	169	236	-137	1 176	2.72	67.8	11.4	29.5
Hamilton	14.3	13.6	12.2	50.9	8 229	8 517	3.5	-4.2	462	669	-154	3 084	2.61	71.0	8.5	27.6
Hansford	11.8	7.8	6.7	49.3	5 369	5 613	4.5	-0.1	414	242	-169	1 988	2.75	73.5	7.6	24.0
Hardeman	14.8	11.0	8.8	49.1	4 724	4 139	-12.4	-7.2	204	201	-299	1 706	2.35	60.7	12.9	34.4
Hardin	13.2	9.1	6.1	50.6	48 073	54 635	13.7	2.3	3 646	2 780	377	20 746	2.64	73.5	11.5	22.9
Harris	10.6	5.7	3.5	50.2	3 400 578	4 093 076	20.4	10.9	357 198	124 765	216 236	1 462 002	2.89	68.2	15.5	26.2
Harrison	13.0	8.8	6.1	51.1	62 110	65 629	5.7	1.7	4 450	3 190	-60	23 544	2.78	72.4	14.2	24.0
Hartley	10.0	7.7	6.8	38.3	5 537	6 062	9.5	2.2	332	171	-52	1 817	2.52	74.0	4.2	22.3
Haskell	13.7	11.0	10.6	47.1	6 093	5 899	-3.2	-2.7	241	425	31	2 297	2.21	67.1	8.3	29.6
Hays	10.4	6.4	3.6	50.2	97 589	157 127	61.0	23.9	11 280	4 569	30 260	58 749	2.78	64.4	9.8	23.2
Hemphill	10.7	7.2	5.3	49.2	3 351	3 807	13.6	12.0	347	165	273	1 410	2.82	76.7	8.2	21.3
Henderson	14.3	12.2	8.7	51.2	73 277	78 536	7.2	1.3	4 741	5 182	1 405	29 820	2.60	69.0	11.0	26.4
Hidalgo	8.1	5.8	4.6	51.2	569 463	774 774	36.1	8.7	84 955	20 499	2 143	221 150	3.61	82.1	20.3	15.3
Hill	13.4	11.6	8.5	50.9	32 321	35 089	8.6	-0.7	2 146	2 041	-322	13 108	2.60	69.9	11.6	25.7
Hockley	11.2	7.6	5.9	50.6	22 716	22 935	1.0	2.2	1 739	1 069	-173	8 122	2.77	75.1	13.2	20.9
Hood	15.2	13.8	10.3	50.9	41 100	51 173	24.5	8.3	3 073	3 148	4 222	21 104	2.45	67.5	8.5	27.8
Hopkins	12.8	9.9	7.3	50.7	31 960	35 161	10.0	3.0	2 407	1 962	533	13 243	2.64	75.2	12.2	21.2
Houston	13.9	11.2	9.4	47.1	23 185	23 732	2.4	-4.0	1 247	1 560	-651	7 911	2.56	64.8	13.8	32.8
Howard	11.6	6.5	5.8	43.1	33 627	35 012	4.1	6.3	2 311	1 946	1 824	11 192	2.68	65.6	13.6	29.5
Hudspeth	14.1	11.0	6.2	49.3	3 344	3 476	3.9	-2.8	228	87	-234	1 022	2.95	72.6	14.7	26.3
Hunt	12.9	9.1	6.2	50.6	76 596	86 129	12.4	4.3	5 672	4 487	2 499	30 697	2.76	68.3	11.5	26.8
Hutchinson	13.8	7.9	6.8	50.0	23 857	22 249	-6.7	-2.3	1 586	1 195	-834	8 390	2.59	65.9	13.1	31.5
Irion	14.6	10.8	7.5	48.2	1 771	1 599	-9.7	-2.8	88	64	-68	625	2.60	76.0	10.2	22.4
Jack	11.8	9.4	6.9	44.1	8 763	9 044	3.2	-1.8	499	431	-203	2 959	2.62	68.7	7.3	25.6
Jackson	13.3	8.9	7.8	50.1	14 391	14 075	-2.2	5.3	997	710	464	5 216	2.71	69.2	10.5	27.1
Jasper	13.7	10.6	7.6	50.8	35 604	35 710	0.3	-0.6	2 380	2 116	-429	12 511	2.79	67.9	12.1	29.6
Jeff Davis	21.4	19.2	10.7	49.7	2 207	2 342	6.1	-7.9	67	100	-151	1 051	2.11	66.9	5.8	31.5
Jefferson	12.4	7.2	6.2	48.8	252 051	252 273	0.1	0.8	18 251	12 575	-3 502	92 771	2.55	64.0	17.8	31.5
Jim Hogg	10.7	9.5	6.4	49.8	5 281	5 300	0.4	-1.9	472	277	-283	1 773	2.95	72.0	17.7	26.3
Jim Wells	11.5	8.0	6.1	50.6	39 326	40 838	3.8	1.3	3 387	2 086	-747	13 488	3.03	75.8	19.2	21.4
Johnson	12.0	8.1	5.1	50.0	126 811	150 943	19.0	6.0	10 408	6 440	5 035	53 255	2.84	76.8	10.8	19.3
Jones	11.7	8.1	6.2	37.1	20 785	20 198	-2.8	-1.1	903	948	-154	5 641	2.28	66.2	10.2	30.3
Karnes	11.3	7.3	7.2	41.7	15 446	14 824	-4.0	1.0	859	802	86	4 460	2.65	69.2	14.1	29.5
Kaufman	11.8	7.4	4.4	50.8	71 313	103 346	44.9	11.0	7 747	4 454	7 789	35 177	3.01	78.2	13.6	17.6
Kendall	14.3	11.3	7.9	51.2	23 743	33 415	40.7	20.9	1 742	1 769	6 886	13 119	2.71	76.2	8.2	20.6
Kenedy	13.5	8.0	7.3	48.3	414	416	0.5	-2.2	19	6	-26	131	4.01	78.6	19.1	21.4
Kent	13.2	13.0	13.9	50.7	859	808	-5.9	-5.4	46	64	-25	374	2.16	59.9	8.8	38.5
Kerr	14.6	14.1	12.7	51.8	43 653	49 625	13.7	2.7	2 621	3 659	2 178	20 353	2.36	64.6	11.3	31.2
Kimble	16.6	15.0	11.5	50.7	4 468	4 607	3.1	-4.8	206	275	-149	2 064	2.16	66.1	11.1	28.2
King	17.6	9.5	8.0	50.4	356	286	-19.7	-1.4	10	4	-9	127	2.28	64.6	3.9	27.6
Kinney	13.1	12.7	12.6	43.9	3 379	3 598	6.5	-1.4	164	195	-8	1 157	2.87	69.0	7.3	27.8
Kleberg	9.0	7.0	5.4	48.8	31 549	32 061	1.6	-0.6	2 554	1 275	-1 513	11 059	2.74	66.7	16.5	23.3
Knox	12.6	9.6	11.1	50.3	4 253	3 719	-12.6	3.8	261	275	168	1 528	2.38	63.8	14.5	33.6
Lamar	12.7	10.7	7.7	51.7	48 499	49 789	2.7	-0.7	3 427	3 226	-638	18 965	2.57	69.6	14.2	26.8
Lamb	11.6	8.2	8.1	50.0	14 709	13 977	-5.0	-4.2	1 045	799	-845	4 784	2.85	71.0	12.8	25.3
Lampasas	13.8	10.6	7.5	50.8	17 762	19 677	10.8	4.6	1 259	975	580	7 409	2.66	75.4	9.7	20.0
La Salle	8.9	7.7	5.5	41.3	5 866	6 886	17.4	10.8	504	250	469	1 860	3.34	68.6	14.2	29.8
Lavaca	14.1	11.4	10.4	51.3	19 210	19 263	0.3	3.0	1 108	1 259	735	7 751	2.45	71.9	9.0	25.9
Lee	14.5	9.9	7.8	49.7	15 657	16 610	6.1	1.7	999	798	107	5 967	2.69	71.1	7.9	24.4
Leon	14.8	13.8	9.6	50.4	15 335	16 801	9.6	1.7	1 084	1 147	319	6 170	2.70	72.6	12.1	23.0
Liberty	12.4	8.0	4.7	50.8	70 154	75 646	7.8	5.3	5 577	3 792	2 152	25 088	2.82	73.7	13.2	22.2
Limestone	13.5	10.2	7.3	48.1	22 051	23 386	6.1	-0.3	1 537	1 344	-208	8 183	2.73	70.1	12.8	27.6
Lipscomb	12.8	7.4	7.0	48.8	3 057	3 302	8.0	8.1	251	157	167	1 173	2.88	67.8	7.0	29.0
Live Oak	13.3	11.2	8.6	46.2	12 309	11 528	-6.3	6.1	628	587	673	3 738	2.70	71.0	10.6	25.1
Llano	17.9	18.9	15.0	51.7	17 044	19 301	13.2	2.6	823	1 538	1 117	8 651	2.20	62.9	7.6	34.3
Loving	22.1	12.8	2.3	41.9	67	82	22.4	36.6	7	5	30	33	2.70	45.5	6.1	39.4
Lubbock	10.3	6.5	5.3	50.6	242 628	278 831	14.9	7.4	21 391	12 015	10 843	106 885	2.57	62.6	14.1	28.2
Lynn	12.8	8.3	7.5	49.6	6 550	5 915	-9.7	-3.2	416	251	-353	2 158	2.66	73.2	18.1	23.5
McCulloch	14.4	12.2	9.5	50.2	8 205	8 283	1.0	0.7	491	591	167	3 055	2.65	66.1	8.9	31.1
McLennan	11.2	7.3	6.1	51.2	213 517	234 906	10.0	4.6	18 253	10 547	3 156	85 893	2.68	66.8	15.1	26.3
McMullen	14.5	10.2	12.7	48.8	851	707	-16.9	16.0	44	47	123	251	2.57	67.7	8.8	29.9
Madison	10.5	8.4	6.3	42.0	12 940	13 667	5.6	2.9	808	647	213	3 839	2.56	70.7	13.7	25.6
Marion	17.1	14.1	9.5	51.1	10 941	10 536	-3.7	-3.6	514	812	-94	4 439	2.30	63.1	10.6	32.2
Martin	9.9	7.4	4.8	50.2	4 746	4 799	1.1	17.5	484	208	561	1 563	3.21	77.5	12.5	19.6

1. No spouse present.

Table B. States and Counties — **Population, Vital Statistics, Medicare, and Crime**

STATE County	Daytime population, 2010–2014 — Persons in group quarters, 2015	Daytime population — Number	Daytime population — Employment/residence ratio	Births, 2015 — Total	Births, 2015 — Rate[1]	Deaths, 2015 — Number	Deaths, 2015 — Rate[1]	Persons under 65 with no health insurance, 2014 — Number	Persons under 65 with no health insurance, 2014 — Percent	Medicare, 2015 — Total Beneficiaries	Medicare, 2015 — Enrolled in Original Medicare	Medicare, 2015 — Enrolled in Medicare Advantage	Serious crimes known to police,[2] 2014 Total — Number	Serious crimes — Rate[3]
	32	33	34	35	36	37	38	39	40	41	42	43	44	45
TEXAS—Cont'd														
Guadalupe	1 925	114 730	0.62	1 812	12.1	986	6.6	21 379	16.9	19 609	14 255	5 354	3 246	2 207
Hale	2 818	36 065	1.01	480	13.9	307	8.9	6 418	23.4	5 378	4 163	1 215	1 065	2 968
Hall	43	3 384	1.10	31	9.9	34	10.9	736	30.9	747	621	126	39	1 206
Hamilton	227	8 105	0.93	82	10.0	109	13.3	1 516	25.0	1 881	1 267	614	96	1 374
Hansford	62	5 272	0.89	78	14.0	32	5.7	1 242	26.5	874	776	98	34	772
Hardeman	21	3 877	0.89	34	8.7	35	9.0	810	25.8	918	764	154	75	2 251
Hardin	378	43 982	0.53	709	12.7	514	9.2	8 159	17.3	9 697	6 120	3 577	854	1 526
Harris	47 997	4 565 367	1.15	70 499	15.7	25 441	5.7	950 262	23.9	439 023	254 043	184 980	200 021	4 519
Harrison	1 415	62 680	0.85	860	12.9	636	9.5	11 133	20.2	9 928	7 602	2 326	1 585	2 342
Hartley	1 461	6 296	1.09	74	12.0	30	4.9	877	23.0	139	115	24	101	1 641
Haskell	530	5 593	0.87	45	7.8	61	10.6	925	23.1	1 341	1 085	256	63	1 064
Hays	8 040	150 653	0.76	2 334	12.3	924	4.9	31 069	19.6	19 198	13 754	5 444	3 889	2 136
Hemphill	46	4 686	1.35	67	15.9	24	5.7	807	22.2	496	441	55	81	1 890
Henderson	1 288	70 500	0.72	909	11.4	1 017	12.8	15 903	25.7	13 498	9 915	3 583	2 215	2 802
Hidalgo	7 305	795 157	0.96	16 293	19.5	4 221	5.0	247 930	33.8	87 337	55 678	31 659	30 676	3 689
Hill	790	30 980	0.71	391	11.2	377	10.8	6 566	24.0	7 661	5 779	1 882	727	2 077
Hockley	832	22 962	0.98	316	13.4	203	8.6	4 131	21.0	3 386	2 528	858	711	2 977
Hood	759	47 507	0.77	632	11.6	601	11.0	8 441	20.8	13 943	10 353	3 590	1 078	2 035
Hopkins	451	33 882	0.89	443	12.3	366	10.2	7 448	25.2	6 612	5 706	906	375	1 044
Houston	2 789	23 082	0.99	242	10.6	281	12.3	3 606	23.1	5 080	3 970	1 110	455	1 988
Howard	6 072	36 215	1.04	459	12.4	334	9.1	5 260	20.0	5 258	4 346	912	1 880	5 122
Hudspeth	86	3 643	1.29	35	10.6	9	2.7	829	32.4	527	318	209	23	696
Hunt	2 490	84 094	0.91	1 096	12.3	896	10.0	16 109	22.1	15 020	12 555	2 465	2 785	3 273
Hutchinson	206	22 369	1.05	308	14.1	204	9.4	3 968	21.5	3 709	3 128	581	707	3 527
Irion	0	1 971	1.48	19	12.2	8	5.1	194	15.1	269	230	39	46	2 831
Jack	1 102	8 934	0.99	90	10.1	64	7.2	1 503	23.6	1 420	1 175	245	222	2 465
Jackson	217	13 845	0.92	192	13.0	114	7.7	2 399	19.7	2 411	1 926	485	216	1 456
Jasper	939	35 140	0.94	460	12.9	396	11.1	5 050	17.8	6 885	5 000	1 885	1 078	3 006
Jeff Davis	88	2 413	1.12	10	4.6	19	8.8	428	29.3	569	459	110	12	535
Jefferson	16 084	278 837	1.26	3 502	13.8	2 478	9.8	46 960	23.1	41 562	26 788	14 774	10 924	4 298
Jim Hogg	16	5 247	0.99	92	17.6	48	9.2	1 067	24.4	879	636	243	22	417
Jim Wells	357	43 472	1.13	650	15.7	371	9.0	7 195	20.4	7 620	4 463	3 157	1 713	4 151
Johnson	2 694	129 427	0.64	2 069	13.0	1 244	7.8	27 778	20.6	26 878	15 418	11 460	3 126	1 995
Jones	5 249	19 351	0.85	176	8.8	154	7.7	2 539	21.2	2 678	2 164	514	593	2 979
Karnes	2 642	17 088	1.45	178	11.9	153	10.3	1 769	17.4	2 725	2 170	555	376	2 466
Kaufman	1 348	87 871	0.59	1 574	13.9	902	8.0	19 976	20.6	19 484	13 978	5 506	2 111	1 909
Kendall	527	34 017	0.87	344	8.7	363	9.2	5 279	17.0	9 476	7 110	2 366	524	1 338
Kenedy	0	798	2.38	2	4.9	0	0.0	88	25.7	57	43	14	12	2 899
Kent	36	907	1.12	13	16.8	8	10.3	119	21.1	178	139	39	11	1 355
Kerr	1 952	50 179	1.01	518	10.2	698	13.8	8 213	23.0	14 885	12 515	2 370	1 119	2 220
Kimble	45	4 254	0.87	35	7.9	47	10.7	908	28.0	1 051	860	191	52	1 159
King	0	300	1.06	0	0.0	0	0.0	48	22.3	D	22	D	1	348
Kinney	332	3 612	1.01	29	8.2	41	11.6	574	25.0	852	634	218	NA	NA
Kleberg	1 933	31 708	0.97	507	15.9	237	7.4	6 218	23.7	4 416	2 569	1 847	1 385	4 283
Knox	107	3 969	1.13	52	13.5	44	11.4	842	28.0	743	627	116	28	736
Lamar	611	50 199	1.02	664	13.4	650	13.1	9 066	22.6	11 039	9 836	1 203	1 673	3 368
Lamb	187	13 516	0.94	197	14.6	129	9.6	2 929	26.0	2 480	1 904	576	352	2 735
Lampasas	221	16 911	0.63	258	12.6	167	8.2	3 884	23.7	4 429	3 249	1 180	463	2 504
La Salle	1 632	9 147	1.90	96	12.7	38	5.0	1 226	25.2	1 008	663	345	49	649
Lavaca	414	17 550	0.78	206	10.4	235	11.9	3 279	21.4	5 408	4 570	838	272	1 373
Lee	481	15 515	0.85	192	11.4	147	8.8	2 785	20.8	2 863	2 194	669	310	1 850
Leon	104	16 991	1.03	202	11.9	215	12.7	3 208	25.0	4 879	3 715	1 164	194	1 236
Liberty	4 983	67 930	0.68	1 106	14.0	738	9.4	14 889	23.5	13 338	8 127	5 211	2 631	3 384
Limestone	1 590	23 964	1.05	276	11.8	259	11.1	4 239	23.5	4 318	3 129	1 189	827	3 525
Lipscomb	36	3 175	0.85	55	15.4	35	9.8	800	26.5	545	476	69	41	1 150
Live Oak	1 156	13 173	1.37	122	10.0	101	8.3	1 676	19.3	1 580	1 139	441	276	2 293
Llano	162	18 109	0.84	170	8.7	296	15.1	2 866	22.3	5 470	4 156	1 314	346	1 764
Loving	0	394	6.35	0	0.0	0	0.0	13	16.0	D	12	D	11	11 000
Lubbock	12 352	288 104	1.01	4 268	14.4	2 442	8.2	46 772	18.7	39 784	26 835	12 949	14 146	4 828
Lynn	43	4 967	0.66	81	14.1	35	6.1	1 122	23.4	1 010	782	228	58	1 014
McCulloch	107	8 565	1.09	86	10.4	108	13.1	1 452	22.7	1 955	1 699	256	114	1 354
McLennan	9 275	245 972	1.06	3 565	14.6	2 038	8.3	42 547	21.0	37 823	26 087	11 736	8 722	3 615
McMullen	0	1 682	4.12	10	12.3	9	11.1	96	15.5	157	111	46	45	5 740
Madison	2 597	14 770	1.26	153	11.0	120	8.6	2 253	24.0	2 115	1 598	517	343	2 469
Marion	161	8 677	0.56	101	10.0	130	12.8	1 626	21.2	2 128	1 616	512	337	3 291
Martin	48	5 089	1.00	108	19.5	37	6.7	1 003	21.1	714	607	107	118	2 151

1. Per 1,000 estimated resident population.   2. Data for serious crimes have not been adjusted for underreporting; this may affect comparability between geographic areas and over time.
3. Per 100,000 population estimated by the FBI.

Table B. States and Counties — Crime, Education, Money Income, and Poverty

STATE County	Serious crimes known to police, 2014 (cont.)[1] Rate[2]		Education — School enrollment and attainment, 2010–2014 Enrollment[3]		Attainment[4] (percent)		Local government expenditures,[5] 2012–2013		Money income, 2010–2014 — Households				Income and poverty, 2014 — Percent below poverty level		
	Violent	Property	Total	Percent private	High school graduate or less	Bachelor's degree or more	Total current spending (mil dol)	Current spending per student (dollars)	Per capita income[6] (dollars)	Median income (dollars)	Mean income (dollars)	Percent with income of $200,000 or more	Median household income (dollars)	All persons	Children under 18 years	Children 5 to 17 years in families
	46	47	48	49	50	51	52	53	54	55	56	57	58	59	60	61
TEXAS—Cont'd																
Guadalupe	186	2 021	39 978	12.4	42.8	25.2	176.5	7 337	26 696	62 412	75 798	3.1	61 825	10.4	14.7	14.3
Hale	198	2 771	10 011	12.1	61.2	14.3	63.8	8 321	18 061	42 303	52 565	1.8	40 213	24.0	32.5	30.4
Hall	186	1 020	787	3.0	58.3	12.4	6.0	11 129	18 314	33 205	47 762	1.5	33 324	24.5	38.6	34.5
Hamilton	129	1 245	1 558	4.5	51.9	19.0	13.8	9 229	23 734	42 211	58 638	2.7	41 207	16.2	26.2	24.7
Hansford	318	454	1 495	5.2	53.9	21.9	16.3	11 381	23 631	46 181	63 796	3.3	50 698	12.7	18.0	16.1
Hardeman	30	2 221	940	6.6	56.2	18.9	9.6	13 105	20 373	37 656	47 298	1.1	36 992	18.7	29.4	28.8
Hardin	164	1 361	13 263	10.7	52.1	15.4	85.8	8 073	25 326	52 438	66 565	2.6	53 872	12.9	17.3	16.6
Harris	718	3 801	1 218 501	11.0	44.2	29.0	6 029.3	8 132	28 454	53 822	79 900	6.5	54 230	17.3	25.1	24.4
Harrison	371	1 971	16 764	14.0	50.6	18.6	107.8	8 329	23 452	46 969	62 808	3.0	48 461	17.1	22.7	22.1
Hartley	341	1 300	1 174	28.0	56.6	21.4	4.1	11 140	23 563	65 132	78 950	4.1	64 182	10.5	10.5	9.9
Haskell	101	963	1 090	5.1	57.7	16.6	10.4	11 019	23 421	42 645	57 826	3.5	35 607	25.1	34.9	33.7
Hays	253	1 883	60 263	6.5	32.2	36.8	246.1	7 955	27 080	58 878	75 993	5.2	59 569	17.5	17.4	16.8
Hemphill	373	1 517	1 198	4.0	47.0	22.2	9.6	9 825	29 473	58 281	81 187	4.1	66 505	8.9	12.7	12.1
Henderson	314	2 489	17 208	7.4	52.9	15.5	85.2	8 236	21 857	40 299	55 124	1.9	40 921	20.2	31.1	30.0
Hidalgo	329	3 360	265 253	5.7	61.5	16.4	1 868.5	9 112	14 525	34 952	50 323	1.7	34 368	33.5	45.5	44.3
Hill	157	1 920	8 467	6.1	51.9	14.6	62.1	9 551	21 041	40 994	55 296	1.7	41 521	21.8	32.2	29.2
Hockley	423	2 554	7 069	5.1	50.1	16.1	51.3	10 414	22 630	50 485	63 702	2.6	50 124	14.4	21.0	21.0
Hood	170	1 866	10 092	13.7	42.5	24.1	66.7	8 898	29 659	54 397	72 094	4.4	55 472	12.4	20.4	19.1
Hopkins	150	894	8 349	8.0	55.7	15.2	56.1	8 536	21 674	45 158	57 395	2.3	44 076	20.3	32.8	32.0
Houston	188	1 800	4 505	4.8	56.9	13.9	29.5	9 852	17 830	32 855	48 127	1.3	33 698	25.9	37.4	33.7
Howard	687	4 436	8 376	7.0	53.4	13.0	47.3	8 257	21 080	47 994	62 668	2.2	47 299	17.5	22.7	22.1
Hudspeth	91	605	837	3.1	73.3	8.4	9.3	13 055	13 660	23 350	37 479	1.1	32 086	26.7	38.8	37.6
Hunt	402	2 871	23 689	8.2	51.5	17.4	121.1	8 745	22 446	44 898	59 716	2.1	43 385	20.5	30.2	27.5
Hutchinson	659	2 869	5 537	7.8	49.7	13.2	38.0	8 885	24 231	47 191	59 979	2.1	51 508	13.9	18.3	16.8
Irion	62	2 769	387	4.7	52.9	13.1	3.9	12 807	30 444	54 886	77 767	5.4	63 054	8.6	13.5	13.4
Jack	178	2 287	1 737	9.8	60.4	10.8	14.2	11 651	23 126	45 130	69 140	2.9	52 030	14.9	19.1	17.8
Jackson	175	1 281	3 485	9.0	53.3	16.5	29.0	8 434	23 368	50 856	61 508	1.7	52 185	14.7	19.9	18.5
Jasper	323	2 682	8 172	9.9	60.0	10.3	57.3	8 799	19 969	39 176	52 820	1.0	41 017	17.7	27.6	26.0
Jeff Davis	312	223	385	1.3	37.1	38.4	5.2	15 198	28 902	51 357	63 939	1.4	46 364	13.1	29.2	27.1
Jefferson	652	3 646	61 766	8.4	50.5	18.0	383.9	9 380	23 563	42 368	60 909	3.1	41 147	21.2	32.3	30.1
Jim Hogg	114	304	1 218	0.5	59.3	13.0	10.9	9 766	19 746	38 013	53 891	4.4	36 929	22.5	32.9	32.2
Jim Wells	582	3 570	10 988	6.3	61.6	10.7	74.4	8 614	20 977	42 463	61 627	2.7	46 200	20.2	28.5	28.0
Johnson	155	1 840	40 519	12.2	49.5	16.6	257.8	8 056	24 787	58 221	70 472	2.5	55 926	13.3	19.0	18.2
Jones	317	2 663	3 565	6.0	65.0	9.3	27.9	10 459	15 309	42 287	55 073	2.2	41 079	23.4	27.4	26.9
Karnes	223	2 243	2 938	5.6	62.9	12.4	23.1	9 668	22 966	44 650	74 816	5.5	43 986	22.3	30.0	28.4
Kaufman	223	1 686	29 429	9.7	48.1	18.5	192.5	7 565	24 959	61 459	72 764	2.6	57 585	13.8	19.2	17.8
Kendall	130	1 208	9 600	16.3	30.9	40.7	64.7	7 883	36 169	74 320	98 525	9.1	77 764	8.3	12.4	10.9
Kenedy	483	2 415	145	6.9	63.1	14.3	2.2	26 639	13 959	36 563	45 163	0.0	38 451	17.9	30.3	29.2
Kent	246	1 108	120	0.8	48.1	23.3	3.3	23 069	25 222	46 842	60 133	1.9	43 026	12.4	20.1	17.1
Kerr	232	1 988	10 489	17.8	40.4	28.3	56.9	8 452	26 108	42 930	61 407	3.1	44 113	17.6	28.7	27.1
Kimble	111	1 047	631	2.1	53.9	16.8	5.7	8 370	27 544	40 000	60 305	2.9	38 750	18.5	34.0	32.9
King	0	348	39	0.0	55.2	22.4	3.6	37 375	30 871	54 583	67 820	5.5	64 203	10.7	16.7	17.6
Kinney	NA	NA	738	6.1	55.9	13.2	6.2	9 921	15 689	32 473	43 431	0.0	39 335	21.0	24.9	22.7
Kleberg	696	3 587	11 704	5.2	47.2	24.4	49.6	9 496	19 230	37 725	54 665	2.3	40 884	22.8	28.5	27.4
Knox	79	657	839	0.8	57.9	13.2	8.5	11 193	19 470	37 018	47 037	0.3	36 929	21.3	33.4	31.1
Lamar	364	3 003	12 261	7.9	49.9	16.2	75.5	8 740	21 523	41 130	54 328	2.1	41 009	18.6	28.8	27.0
Lamb	241	2 494	3 688	3.8	59.8	14.1	30.6	9 747	19 555	37 161	53 136	2.7	37 111	22.6	31.8	29.8
Lampasas	141	2 363	4 570	7.0	40.3	21.1	32.4	8 697	24 134	48 862	64 193	2.4	50 699	14.4	24.1	22.6
La Salle	80	570	1 661	2.5	71.5	13.5	14.7	11 395	17 184	35 554	56 153	2.8	38 012	28.1	35.7	37.6
Lavaca	162	1 212	4 123	18.2	60.8	15.3	33.6	8 718	25 196	45 780	62 273	2.6	47 041	13.8	19.9	18.2
Lee	269	1 582	4 081	12.9	55.9	17.0	26.9	8 942	24 604	52 452	66 277	3.3	52 895	13.0	18.7	17.6
Leon	45	1 192	3 266	2.5	51.3	17.0	31.5	10 302	25 946	48 763	66 216	3.9	45 159	13.5	21.1	21.1
Liberty	439	2 946	18 478	7.9	61.6	8.8	119.2	8 105	20 370	47 722	60 511	2.1	47 123	17.4	23.4	22.6
Limestone	367	3 158	5 019	4.8	58.0	13.6	38.8	9 452	20 550	39 484	53 895	1.3	37 256	19.6	28.5	27.6
Lipscomb	140	1 010	815	5.5	53.8	21.1	10.3	11 981	29 596	61 151	79 970	4.1	60 810	10.6	13.2	12.2
Live Oak	357	1 936	2 388	4.1	55.5	15.9	18.2	10 397	21 357	44 579	57 600	1.3	51 481	15.5	20.7	19.0
Llano	158	1 606	3 220	9.4	39.9	26.8	18.8	10 280	34 348	45 205	74 313	5.1	45 096	14.9	29.1	28.8
Loving	1 000	10 000	8	0.0	76.3	2.6	NA	NA	25 629	65 625	57 394	0.0	55 819	9.3	19.2	16.7
Lubbock	764	4 065	97 505	9.4	40.5	28.0	409.4	8 605	24 454	45 529	63 652	3.6	45 719	17.7	21.3	21.0
Lynn	87	926	1 447	8.4	55.8	17.7	15.4	11 846	22 767	41 541	58 562	3.3	41 589	18.3	28.2	26.4
McCulloch	48	1 307	1 566	3.6	54.3	15.7	15.7	10 134	21 654	40 908	54 426	1.6	39 649	18.9	30.2	27.6
McLennan	400	3 216	74 049	22.7	45.2	22.1	378.1	8 891	21 852	42 544	58 596	2.5	43 488	19.7	27.8	26.7
McMullen	128	5 612	113	0.0	59.3	4.4	4.1	16 631	36 277	45 208	84 579	3.6	61 571	9.2	13.5	11.2
Madison	274	2 196	3 018	2.8	62.1	10.0	21.5	8 307	15 222	40 879	53 501	1.3	39 030	21.5	28.3	26.5
Marion	645	2 646	2 069	12.3	58.4	14.5	11.5	9 221	22 610	34 363	49 850	2.7	34 452	23.1	35.6	34.1
Martin	219	1 933	1 331	5.2	57.4	17.3	12.6	11 776	26 286	52 232	77 777	7.2	61 896	12.5	16.5	15.9

1. Data for serious crimes have not been adjusted for underreporting; this may affect comparability between geographic areas and over time.   2. Per 100,000 population estimated by the FBI.
3. All persons 3 years old and over enrolled in nursery school through college.   4. Persons 25 years old and over.   5. Elementary and secondary education expenditures.
6. Based on population estimated by the American Community Survey, 2010–2014.

Table B. States and Counties — **Personal Income**

STATE County	Personal income, 2014										Earnings, 2014		
	Total (mil dol)	Percent change, 2013–2014	Per capita[1] Dollars	Per capita[1] Rank	Wages and salaries (mil dol)	Supplements to wages and salaries; employer contributions (mil dol) Pension and insurance	Supplements to wages and salaries; employer contributions (mil dol) Government social insurance	Proprietors' income (mil dol)	Dividends, interest, and rent (mil dol)	Personal transfer receipts (mil dol)	Total (mil dol)	Contributions for government social insurance (mil dol) From employee and self-employed	Contributions for government social insurance (mil dol) From employer
	62	63	64	65	66	67	68	69	70	71	72	73	74
TEXAS—Cont'd													
Guadalupe	5 660	6.5	38 439	1 403	1 403	228	96	239	859	1 039	1 967	115	96
Hale	1 081	0.4	31 143	2 564	430	74	30	183	140	283	718	34	30
Hall	113	-10.0	36 054	1 775	32	6	2	19	16	35	59	3	2
Hamilton	412	4.9	50 220	375	87	17	6	29	179	92	139	8	6
Hansford	413	17.9	75 035	40	133	21	8	156	44	37	318	9	8
Hardeman	146	2.3	37 222	1 565	41	9	3	15	29	47	67	4	3
Hardin	2 406	7.3	43 262	818	556	86	41	246	244	488	928	55	41
Harris	252 695	6.4	56 896	175	162 733	18 643	10 348	58 353	40 727	25 668	250 078	12 308	10 348
Harrison	2 915	4.6	43 297	812	1 344	208	91	471	387	565	2 114	111	91
Hartley	326	21.8	53 573	249	99	18	6	156	46	23	279	5	6
Haskell	209	-4.5	36 268	1 729	61	11	4	29	31	62	105	6	4
Hays	6 468	8.5	34 959	1 944	2 243	378	152	615	990	974	3 387	174	152
Hemphill	310	13.1	74 072	44	145	21	9	86	92	19	262	11	9
Henderson	2 782	5.2	35 086	1 915	591	110	40	266	406	849	1 008	67	40
Hidalgo	19 741	4.9	23 753	3 086	8 229	1 593	567	2 602	2 075	5 854	12 991	672	567
Hill	1 259	5.5	36 121	1 760	346	62	24	112	184	349	543	33	24
Hockley	994	-2.5	42 167	935	581	79	38	204	109	200	901	45	38
Hood	2 376	5.9	44 056	758	787	99	53	149	482	526	1 088	70	53
Hopkins	1 314	8.0	36 572	1 675	512	82	35	192	187	317	822	43	35
Houston	790	8.7	34 720	1 979	329	51	19	40	124	244	439	27	19
Howard	1 331	4.1	36 313	1 721	608	119	42	216	201	265	985	49	42
Hudspeth	88	3.2	27 317	2 961	60	16	5	9	17	22	91	4	5
Hunt	2 948	5.2	33 312	2 225	1 289	244	87	204	342	770	1 824	101	87
Hutchinson	881	3.4	40 463	1 124	595	99	41	77	101	175	812	43	41
Irion	96	4.5	60 959	116	55	7	3	14	24	11	79	4	3
Jack	421	10.5	47 543	497	211	26	13	90	78	63	341	18	13
Jackson	596	3.5	40 467	1 123	251	41	17	62	77	132	370	20	17
Jasper	1 342	6.5	37 747	1 490	437	74	29	137	160	379	677	40	29
Jeff Davis	76	3.1	34 495	2 028	25	5	2	6	22	19	38	2	2
Jefferson	9 971	6.5	39 532	1 244	6 817	1 153	474	820	1 502	2 297	9 264	494	474
Jim Hogg	175	8.7	33 296	2 226	92	20	6	9	26	53	128	7	6
Jim Wells	1 769	3.6	42 782	872	1 084	125	69	234	211	444	1 513	83	69
Johnson	5 986	5.7	38 016	1 452	1 997	299	137	563	691	1 186	2 996	170	137
Jones	573	-1.2	28 720	2 862	213	46	12	64	76	162	335	17	12
Karnes	604	13.0	40 545	1 115	282	45	18	56	141	134	400	22	18
Kaufman	4 154	6.4	37 348	1 546	1 133	187	77	346	405	749	1 743	97	77
Kendall	2 565	6.3	65 960	82	601	83	41	124	683	295	848	49	41
Kenedy	23	12.6	56 300	188	52	5	3	9	5	2	69	3	3
Kent	35	14.8	44 827	692	10	3	1	5	7	9	19	1	1
Kerr	2 228	4.7	44 059	757	706	116	50	259	723	513	1 131	67	50
Kimble	182	2.2	41 000	1 060	56	10	3	16	44	45	86	5	3
King	17	29.6	63 985	92	8	1	0	5	3	1	15	0	0
Kinney	107	2.9	30 314	2 675	37	11	3	4	24	32	54	3	3
Kleberg	1 099	3.4	34 148	2 090	534	120	38	80	169	277	772	39	38
Knox	151	2.4	39 229	1 291	60	10	4	23	19	43	96	5	4
Lamar	1 859	4.7	37 540	1 518	803	129	57	242	247	523	1 232	69	57
Lamb	492	1.6	36 248	1 734	158	28	11	114	49	122	311	12	11
Lampasas	940	2.7	46 618	549	154	29	11	72	194	218	266	16	11
La Salle	341	12.0	45 591	631	242	27	15	23	88	52	308	17	15
Lavaca	858	6.9	43 525	796	237	40	16	74	207	215	366	22	16
Lee	724	5.1	43 241	822	348	51	23	59	116	138	481	27	23
Leon	676	10.4	40 093	1 162	301	41	21	71	127	185	434	25	21
Liberty	2 722	5.4	34 839	1 960	764	122	51	242	261	639	1 179	68	51
Limestone	789	6.3	33 551	2 185	332	72	21	67	105	257	492	27	21
Lipscomb	165	6.7	46 304	574	64	11	4	19	40	21	97	5	4
Live Oak	538	7.1	44 484	715	231	44	16	84	112	93	376	19	16
Llano	771	8.6	39 508	1 246	165	27	11	31	245	238	233	19	11
Loving	3	27.2	33 453	2 204	2	0	0	0	1	0	2	0	0
Lubbock	11 066	5.0	37 644	1 503	5 529	925	367	1 202	1 679	2 090	8 022	409	367
Lynn	179	-26.5	31 026	2 580	55	12	4	-1	27	51	69	4	4
McCulloch	349	1.9	42 574	892	135	22	9	60	52	91	227	12	9
McLennan	8 634	4.7	35 467	1 864	4 595	738	322	669	1 382	1 874	6 323	346	322
McMullen	57	5.5	71 176	54	45	6	3	3	28	5	58	3	3
Madison	432	8.3	31 177	2 559	163	29	11	39	87	117	242	13	11
Marion	351	5.4	34 591	2 003	64	13	5	29	49	130	111	8	5
Martin	269	1.9	49 193	429	89	16	6	24	49	39	135	7	6

1. Based on the resident population estimated as of July 1 of the year shown.

Table B. States and Counties — Earnings, Social Security, and Housing

STATE County	Earnings, 2014 (cont.) Percent by selected industries									Social Security beneficiaries, December 2014		Supplemental Security Income recipients, December 2014	Housing units, 2015	
	Farm	Mining	Construction	Manu-facturing	Infor-mation: professional, scientific, technical services	Retail trade	Finance, insurance, real estate and leasing	Health care and social assistance	Govern-ment	Number	Rate[1]		Total	Percent change, 2010–2014
	75	76	77	78	79	80	81	82	83	84	85	86	87	88
TEXAS—Cont'd														
Guadalupe	0.4	2.0	8.0	23.9	3.9	7.5	4.1	6.3	18.3	24 065	163	1 930	55 007	10.0
Hale	15.7	0.7	4.2	4.8	D	9.3	3.0	D	17.5	5 795	167	927	13 494	-0.3
Hall	23.9	0.0	D	D	14.3	4.0	5.5	5.0	19.6	840	271	91	1 934	-0.5
Hamilton	8.2	D	10.7	8.6	3.5	11.5	2.9	9.1	23.7	2 225	272	155	4 562	-0.1
Hansford	47.2	22.4	2.5	1.0	D	1.8	D	D	9.6	945	171	51	2 346	0.3
Hardeman	12.6	4.2	D	D	D	6.5	3.5	4.0	30.8	970	247	120	2 401	-0.7
Hardin	-0.2	9.6	16.3	7.0	6.4	9.7	3.7	10.6	12.0	11 275	203	1 244	23 782	5.2
Harris	0.0	15.3	7.7	9.0	13.0	4.0	6.7	6.4	8.0	493 220	111	106 039	1 720 441	7.6
Harrison	0.3	25.3	5.8	23.9	D	4.3	6.1	D	8.3	13 305	200	1 944	28 121	1.5
Hartley	63.0	0.1	D	D	D	1.8	D	D	15.6	640	105	10	1 994	2.5
Haskell	7.8	15.8	2.9	0.8	D	11.2	D	9.6	20.0	1 415	245	163	3 440	-0.1
Hays	0.0	1.0	11.2	9.1	7.5	11.3	4.7	9.0	21.6	23 360	126	2 159	72 978	22.8
Hemphill	9.9	29.5	8.2	1.0	2.6	D	8.5	1.1	9.0	530	127	23	1 688	3.6
Henderson	1.1	6.4	9.8	10.4	6.0	10.5	4.1	D	17.5	21 430	270	2 323	40 104	1.3
Hidalgo	0.7	2.7	5.3	3.1	4.2	10.3	4.5	18.9	25.1	101 130	122	42 814	264 604	6.6
Hill	1.3	3.0	18.6	9.4	5.8	10.0	3.0	D	20.0	8 575	247	965	16 148	0.2
Hockley	2.0	41.1	8.2	2.4	D	3.1	2.3	D	10.9	4 055	172	546	9 304	0.1
Hood	0.0	30.5	8.2	5.9	4.2	8.0	7.4	6.8	10.0	14 660	272	772	25 673	2.9
Hopkins	10.0	D	9.9	11.5	D	8.6	4.3	5.1	14.4	7 620	213	965	15 234	1.4
Houston	1.8	5.7	8.8	9.6	10.0	5.1	9.5	6.0	19.8	5 565	245	876	11 563	0.3
Howard	0.7	21.4	6.6	11.3	3.3	5.5	3.5	D	23.6	5 690	156	869	13 139	0.1
Hudspeth	11.5	D	D	D	D	1.8	D	1.2	68.9	590	184	177	1 532	0.3
Hunt	0.8	D	5.4	33.8	3.7	7.5	3.0	6.9	21.1	18 150	204	2 527	37 012	0.8
Hutchinson	0.6	27.2	24.2	14.8	D	4.0	2.0	D	9.7	4 215	193	388	10 579	-0.5
Irion	4.1	60.9	D	D	D	1.5	D	D	7.7	330	210	19	857	0.1
Jack	0.0	57.0	7.5	1.3	D	1.3	2.1	2.1	8.8	1 475	166	109	4 115	0.5
Jackson	2.9	10.5	17.1	D	4.6	4.2	2.3	2.7	14.7	3 040	206	317	6 605	0.2
Jasper	0.4	3.2	15.8	17.7	D	7.7	4.6	D	15.4	8 730	245	1 329	16 901	0.6
Jeff Davis	5.8	D	D	D	D	3.8	D	10.4	37.2	640	293	39	1 618	0.3
Jefferson	0.0	0.9	13.4	23.3	8.3	6.5	3.6	10.5	12.6	46 065	182	9 257	108 123	3.5
Jim Hogg	0.9	7.2	1.7	2.3	D	6.7	D	D	42.0	980	187	283	2 448	0.3
Jim Wells	0.9	42.7	3.0	3.7	2.5	4.8	6.2	D	7.7	8 140	197	1 904	16 249	0.6
Johnson	0.3	8.1	11.2	15.8	4.5	7.8	3.7	7.2	13.3	27 620	176	2 956	59 690	5.2
Jones	2.7	22.7	5.7	3.8	1.6	4.3	4.3	2.5	35.8	3 440	174	402	7 403	-0.2
Karnes	-1.5	18.4	4.3	4.7	D	10.0	3.6	D	22.4	2 835	191	450	5 885	4.1
Kaufman	0.3	1.3	10.8	13.8	D	8.4	3.9	7.1	19.8	18 785	169	2 438	39 457	3.0
Kendall	0.2	2.0	13.1	6.0	12.2	13.8	8.4	8.6	12.9	7 995	206	349	15 291	8.8
Kenedy	18.5	D	0.0	0.0	D	D	D	D	6.5	65	158	13	233	0.0
Kent	29.6	0.0	D	0.0	D	3.3	D	10.1	38.8	185	236	13	552	0.0
Kerr	0.4	2.7	10.3	5.7	6.6	12.0	6.4	15.4	17.6	15 330	303	1 018	24 105	1.1
Kimble	2.1	D	10.2	4.5	D	9.1	17.6	2.8	20.5	1 150	259	126	3 373	0.1
King	43.0	0.0	0.0	0.0	D	0.0	0.0	0.0	25.0	45	172	0	186	0.0
Kinney	6.2	D	D	D	D	2.6	D	1.4	59.8	935	267	125	1 941	0.1
Kleberg	1.7	7.3	4.9	2.2	D	6.8	3.8	D	40.9	5 035	157	1 156	13 274	3.8
Knox	18.3	28.0	D	D	D	5.2	D	1.6	21.3	840	218	120	2 044	0.0
Lamar	1.2	0.5	12.6	26.2	D	7.9	4.0	13.1	12.9	12 020	243	2 017	22 620	0.6
Lamb	36.3	0.2	3.5	6.8	1.7	5.3	3.3	3.4	15.4	2 580	190	425	6 102	-0.4
Lampasas	-1.3	0.8	11.7	9.5	3.2	21.6	4.4	D	19.2	4 710	233	459	9 240	6.0
La Salle	1.0	59.0	7.0	0.0	D	1.3	0.7	D	15.2	1 210	162	327	2 903	5.7
Lavaca	2.0	10.6	7.1	18.5	3.9	7.2	4.1	D	13.3	5 170	263	441	10 372	0.3
Lee	0.4	12.7	30.6	6.8	4.6	4.0	5.9	D	13.7	3 455	207	316	7 610	1.5
Leon	7.2	16.0	24.7	16.7	1.8	3.9	3.8	1.0	10.2	5 155	307	440	9 557	0.5
Liberty	0.1	6.6	10.1	14.2	D	9.1	3.5	D	19.2	13 080	167	2 086	29 811	3.7
Limestone	1.4	10.4	3.7	8.1	1.4	6.4	4.4	10.2	31.9	5 290	226	838	10 563	0.2
Lipscomb	7.6	23.5	D	D	D	2.0	D	0.2	18.6	570	160	31	1 515	0.2
Live Oak	-0.4	37.3	5.3	11.0	3.3	4.0	4.5	1.8	15.5	2 310	191	231	6 126	1.0
Llano	-0.4	1.1	9.8	3.9	4.0	6.3	8.6	D	19.8	7 295	375	417	14 922	4.5
Loving	2.0	4.0	D	D	0.0	0.0	0.0	0.0	41.2	10	115	0	50	0.0
Lubbock	0.2	2.2	6.7	3.7	7.5	9.0	7.7	15.4	23.6	44 125	150	6 700	123 099	7.0
Lynn	3.7	D	3.7	2.7	D	4.0	D	2.0	37.2	1 125	196	166	2 676	0.0
McCulloch	0.7	23.8	4.1	15.8	1.7	7.7	2.8	4.6	14.0	2 100	256	321	4 279	-0.5
McLennan	0.2	0.5	7.3	17.6	5.5	6.3	8.5	10.5	16.2	42 760	176	7 364	98 656	3.7
McMullen	4.0	45.6	D	D	0.7	D	D	D	13.4	165	205	13	487	0.4
Madison	5.8	D	18.0	2.5	3.7	12.4	4.4	6.4	25.6	2 525	182	299	5 192	1.9
Marion	0.2	D	4.1	17.6	D	11.1	D	D	17.3	3 255	322	520	6 258	0.7
Martin	4.7	8.0	D	D	D	7.1	D	3.0	20.2	165	30	10	1 866	0.8

1. Per 1,000 resident population estimated as of July 1 of the year shown.

Table B. States and Counties — Housing, Labor Force, and Employment

STATE County	Housing units, 2010–2014								Civilian labor force, 2015				Civilian employment,[6] 2010–2014		
	Occupied units										Unemployment		Percent		
			Owner-occupied			Renter-occupied									
				Median owner cost as a percent of income			Median rent as a percent of income[2]	Sub-stand-ard units[4] (percent)		Percent change, 2014–2015				Manage-ment, business, science and arts	Con-struction, produc-tion, and mainte-nance occu-pations
	Total	Percent	Median value[1]	With a mort-gage	Without a mort-gage[2]	Median rent[3]			Total		Total	Rate[5]	Total		
	89	90	91	92	93	94	95	96	97	98	99	100	101	102	103
TEXAS—Cont'd															
Guadalupe	47 768	77.7	158 700	21.6	11.6	882	25.7	3.6	72 288	1.0	2 568	3.6	65 304	34.3	23.8
Hale	11 644	62.9	71 100	20.1	10.0	596	26.4	6.2	12 919	-4.5	833	6.4	14 602	23.4	34.3
Hall	1 176	68.9	42 000	21.6	12.3	487	31.7	2.0	1 206	-4.6	66	5.5	1 203	22.4	31.4
Hamilton	3 084	73.0	95 200	19.4	14.4	613	26.3	3.9	3 499	-1.9	164	4.7	3 276	26.6	28.8
Hansford	1 988	76.7	76 800	17.7	10.0	609	29.6	5.7	3 103	-4.3	92	3.0	2 597	29.1	39.4
Hardeman	1 706	71.2	42 600	19.2	11.0	495	31.2	2.8	1 623	-1.5	81	5.0	1 611	37.7	28.3
Hardin	20 746	78.4	99 000	18.5	10.4	805	26.0	3.3	25 221	-0.6	1 420	5.6	23 895	30.9	30.7
Harris	1 462 002	55.7	133 400	22.5	11.7	895	29.8	6.5	2 239 426	0.4	103 800	4.6	2 021 179	34.5	24.4
Harrison	23 544	74.2	110 900	20.9	11.4	690	24.2	3.8	31 349	-2.6	1 662	5.3	28 931	29.5	30.5
Hartley	1 817	64.7	143 100	17.9	10.0	726	27.0	6.3	2 981	2.8	63	2.1	2 332	40.0	24.1
Haskell	2 297	76.1	47 900	19.9	10.0	407	28.3	5.1	2 596	-3.6	91	3.5	2 244	36.1	28.8
Hays	58 749	65.1	175 700	23.5	12.1	954	39.7	4.2	96 012	2.1	3 310	3.4	82 122	38.3	16.8
Hemphill	1 410	73.3	110 800	19.6	10.0	701	19.3	2.9	2 301	-9.6	73	3.2	1 902	28.5	29.8
Henderson	29 820	75.5	88 100	23.7	13.8	739	32.1	3.7	34 240	-1.4	1 685	4.9	30 048	26.3	29.3
Hidalgo	221 150	67.9	78 900	24.1	13.1	658	33.1	15.0	331 632	-0.1	26 299	7.9	291 917	26.1	24.0
Hill	13 108	72.4	84 600	21.4	13.5	655	28.2	5.3	15 584	-1.9	719	4.6	14 274	25.3	31.5
Hockley	8 122	69.5	79 300	17.9	10.0	671	25.3	4.2	11 745	-2.8	491	4.2	10 665	26.6	32.2
Hood	21 104	77.0	150 600	23.0	11.7	875	31.5	3.3	24 367	0.5	1 105	4.5	21 874	33.9	25.9
Hopkins	13 243	71.6	93 300	22.3	11.7	683	28.3	5.1	16 954	-3.1	720	4.2	15 069	28.2	32.3
Houston	7 911	70.3	74 900	21.4	13.8	630	37.2	3.4	9 924	1.2	450	4.5	7 791	23.3	28.1
Howard	11 192	68.3	70 400	17.7	10.4	723	24.7	3.3	13 286	-2.2	618	4.7	13 419	26.7	29.0
Hudspeth	1 022	82.5	41 900	27.5	16.6	660	36.3	12.0	1 230	-1.7	71	5.8	1 088	25.0	32.8
Hunt	30 697	69.2	92 000	21.8	12.7	753	33.3	4.9	39 186	1.6	1 839	4.7	35 749	30.9	27.8
Hutchinson	8 390	76.8	68 200	17.9	10.0	703	26.9	2.9	9 821	-6.6	438	4.5	9 433	24.4	33.9
Irion	625	76.3	104 400	19.8	10.5	763	27.6	2.2	821	-1.4	30	3.7	749	35.9	29.9
Jack	2 959	74.7	79 000	16.7	10.4	770	24.2	2.8	4 086	-5.1	174	4.3	3 254	22.9	41.1
Jackson	5 216	75.0	84 700	18.0	11.3	745	19.7	4.2	7 392	-3.1	279	3.8	6 066	26.8	39.5
Jasper	12 511	77.7	87 400	20.1	11.4	661	32.8	3.6	13 934	-3.5	1 050	7.5	12 216	25.0	32.0
Jeff Davis	1 051	73.4	106 900	16.7	10.0	929	16.3	6.5	1 089	-5.1	36	3.3	1 104	35.0	27.0
Jefferson	92 771	63.7	96 400	21.8	12.0	747	31.3	3.5	108 580	-1.4	7 577	7.0	102 202	28.5	27.4
Jim Hogg	1 773	75.2	71 300	18.2	12.5	591	27.5	4.0	2 045	-7.0	148	7.2	1 928	27.3	37.6
Jim Wells	13 488	71.2	67 400	19.9	12.1	727	26.4	8.1	19 336	-3.8	1 533	7.9	16 895	27.3	29.8
Johnson	53 255	74.6	114 100	20.8	12.3	881	26.9	4.5	74 614	0.3	3 278	4.4	68 595	31.2	30.2
Jones	5 641	78.4	65 200	18.1	13.2	619	23.0	2.6	5 725	-1.4	315	5.5	5 200	26.8	29.2
Karnes	4 460	75.7	77 900	18.7	10.0	589	29.6	9.0	6 494	3.5	276	4.3	4 954	29.8	31.7
Kaufman	35 177	77.4	131 500	23.6	13.1	889	31.4	4.3	54 638	1.9	2 232	4.1	48 472	33.6	25.1
Kendall	13 119	72.8	286 400	23.1	12.3	1 004	28.2	4.0	18 785	0.6	622	3.3	16 405	48.1	15.6
Kenedy	131	30.5	166 700	0.0	10.0	711	35.6	9.2	284	-16.2	8	2.8	195	25.1	28.2
Kent	374	74.6	66 100	14.2	10.5	525	46.8	4.0	505	-1.4	13	2.6	427	38.2	27.9
Kerr	20 353	71.0	153 100	23.0	12.7	782	28.5	5.0	21 257	-0.8	794	3.7	20 662	32.6	19.0
Kimble	2 064	76.1	84 500	22.3	13.8	545	33.1	1.0	2 001	-5.3	75	3.7	2 064	31.0	26.6
King	127	37.0	71 700	0.0	19.2	775	15.0	8.7	219	-2.2	7	3.2	180	38.9	38.9
Kinney	1 157	82.8	68 400	22.3	13.9	600	28.7	4.1	1 170	-4.6	77	6.6	1 129	28.3	26.7
Kleberg	11 059	52.6	77 100	20.7	11.2	736	29.9	6.8	14 363	-5.9	867	6.0	13 342	31.7	25.2
Knox	1 528	70.4	42 200	16.8	11.1	457	28.1	4.1	1 690	-2.8	64	3.8	1 522	26.9	32.8
Lamar	18 965	65.6	84 100	19.5	12.0	645	30.3	3.8	22 364	1.0	1 074	4.8	21 273	26.2	29.6
Lamb	4 784	70.0	58 700	19.6	12.2	603	26.1	5.9	5 541	-8.1	500	9.0	5 656	26.7	34.6
Lampasas	7 409	74.8	128 400	20.6	13.4	771	27.6	2.3	8 990	0.3	398	4.4	8 336	31.3	28.6
La Salle	1 860	67.6	69 200	22.7	12.3	417	29.5	9.8	4 287	-6.3	177	4.1	2 323	21.6	41.9
Lavaca	7 751	79.1	99 100	19.1	10.4	617	23.4	6.3	8 786	-2.1	338	3.8	8 679	32.1	34.0
Lee	5 967	75.4	115 900	21.7	11.5	733	27.4	3.6	9 320	-0.2	334	3.6	7 540	27.8	26.5
Leon	6 170	84.7	89 600	19.7	11.9	601	26.7	4.3	6 949	-3.7	371	5.3	6 992	28.8	33.4
Liberty	25 088	77.8	84 900	21.7	12.5	739	26.5	6.9	31 068	0.3	2 134	6.9	27 614	23.7	37.1
Limestone	8 183	75.1	83 800	22.4	12.6	690	28.4	4.3	8 596	-6.6	436	5.1	9 531	29.2	31.7
Lipscomb	1 173	71.6	87 800	14.5	10.0	649	14.8	2.9	1 728	-1.2	68	3.9	1 614	30.2	44.1
Live Oak	3 738	81.4	87 700	19.4	12.6	700	24.4	3.3	5 789	-5.3	238	4.1	3 906	27.4	31.7
Llano	8 651	77.6	160 000	21.8	13.0	712	29.4	2.2	8 139	0.6	350	4.3	7 570	30.2	19.8
Loving	33	36.4	85 000	0.0	32.5	842	41.7	0.0	78	0.0	4	5.1	57	15.8	21.1
Lubbock	106 885	57.2	109 900	21.3	11.7	807	33.3	3.8	148 287	0.3	5 089	3.4	139 582	33.8	19.6
Lynn	2 158	71.9	72 200	22.0	10.0	625	31.5	2.5	2 815	-1.6	113	4.0	2 559	30.6	28.9
McCulloch	3 055	78.5	71 800	21.8	13.5	650	32.8	5.7	3 931	-4.4	189	4.8	3 644	25.3	35.9
McLennan	85 893	58.7	112 100	22.6	12.8	767	32.5	3.3	112 492	-0.4	4 620	4.1	106 831	32.0	23.5
McMullen	251	81.3	64 100	19.3	12.2	513	10.9	0.0	961	-9.3	20	2.1	361	13.9	34.6
Madison	3 839	70.7	87 700	26.1	10.4	678	24.1	8.2	5 106	1.6	219	4.3	3 968	25.9	29.9
Marion	4 439	75.7	78 300	22.6	12.0	566	29.2	1.4	4 412	-1.5	288	6.5	3 962	27.9	31.9
Martin	1 563	74.6	90 500	19.5	10.0	707	23.1	7.5	2 582	-3.9	91	3.5	2 286	24.4	38.1

1. Specified owner-occupied units.   2.   A value of 10.0 represents 10 percent or less; a value of 50.0 represents 50 percent or more.   3.   Specified renter-occupied units.
4.   Overcrowded or lacking complete plumbing facilities.   5.   Percent of civilian labor force.   6.   Persons 16 years old and over.

Table B. States and Counties — Nonfarm Employment and Agriculture

STATE County	Private nonfarm establishments, employment and payroll, 2014									Agriculture, 2012			
	Number of establish-ments	Employment						Annual payroll		Farms			Farm operators whose principal occu-pation is farming (percent)
		Total	Health care and social assistance	Manufac-turing	Retail trade	Finance and insurance	Professional, scientific, and technical services	Total (mil dol)	Average per employee (dollars)	Number	Percent with:		
											Fewer than 50 acres	500 acres or more	
	104	105	106	107	108	109	110	111	112	113	114	115	116
TEXAS—Cont'd													
Guadalupe	1 927	30 511	3 038	7 209	4 347	547	682	1 225	40 143	2 241	48.3	6.1	35.7
Hale	695	9 062	1 186	660	1 488	D	172	306	33 782	899	11.7	39.6	48.8
Hall	72	511	87	D	87	D	D	18	35 280	390	3.8	44.1	39.5
Hamilton	210	1 457	D	221	344	33	37	48	33 091	1 001	17.1	21.8	42.2
Hansford	155	1 207	D	D	D	92	44	50	41 080	263	5.7	62.7	70.0
Hardeman	83	684	150	D	113	57	D	26	37 534	357	8.4	42.0	37.5
Hardin	820	8 894	952	674	2 198	233	335	346	38 853	660	64.8	4.1	33.2
Harris	97 513	2 012 118	250 426	170 003	202 587	77 820	183 683	131 332	65 271	2 207	70.1	4.5	35.0
Harrison	1 323	20 818	1 751	5 054	2 066	983	1 025	853	40 997	1 298	43.4	7.1	41.1
Hartley	119	1 191	276	D	D	32	D	42	35 107	255	6.7	65.5	64.7
Haskell	146	1 099	114	D	312	57	39	31	28 348	503	8.7	40.4	50.1
Hays	3 660	46 675	6 051	3 715	11 580	966	1 854	1 514	32 438	1 439	52.1	6.5	34.3
Hemphill	167	1 651	179	D	185	D	30	79	47 646	232	12.1	58.6	55.6
Henderson	1 285	12 802	2 136	1 723	2 723	432	755	397	30 977	1 961	45.2	6.2	42.4
Hidalgo	11 780	181 601	55 588	6 008	37 203	6 329	5 750	4 974	27 389	2 161	57.9	14.7	51.4
Hill	626	7 157	1 213	1 065	1 454	201	149	232	32 369	1 884	34.6	11.0	43.6
Hockley	523	7 917	1 573	249	895	241	88	406	51 225	781	14.7	34.1	45.6
Hood	1 241	13 536	2 199	467	2 737	464	413	546	40 363	1 286	57.1	6.8	42.8
Hopkins	737	10 534	1 193	1 951	1 678	451	164	367	34 803	2 113	31.5	8.8	42.0
Houston	353	3 643	771	632	644	148	97	129	35 281	1 505	23.3	13.2	49.9
Howard	709	9 895	1 570	864	1 460	299	206	385	38 928	475	21.3	34.3	48.8
Hudspeth	32	315	D	D	59	D	NA	11	34 730	167	13.2	53.9	60.5
Hunt	1 379	21 599	3 141	6 892	3 542	411	517	1 015	47 013	4 206	58.7	3.6	31.9
Hutchinson	480	6 556	413	1 714	943	158	221	363	55 345	247	27.1	38.9	44.1
Irion	65	609	D	NA	D	D	D	43	71 015	155	22.6	52.3	43.9
Jack	233	2 216	47	D	182	D	57	107	48 420	864	17.1	23.8	42.0
Jackson	312	4 870	272	D	551	123	D	222	45 527	811	23.7	25.2	45.3
Jasper	612	8 847	2 360	D	1 436	276	222	310	35 041	894	59.5	2.0	36.9
Jeff Davis	55	401	84	NA	47	D	D	10	24 848	84	16.7	69.0	57.1
Jefferson	5 606	100 209	16 505	14 957	14 315	2 403	4 805	5 076	50 649	764	48.0	18.3	45.5
Jim Hogg	92	964	204	76	207	48	D	38	39 836	263	15.2	45.2	39.2
Jim Wells	939	16 343	4 388	646	1 632	324	294	723	44 243	1 047	32.7	16.0	33.5
Johnson	2 686	36 399	3 648	5 380	5 242	806	1 013	1 469	40 358	3 023	61.4	4.3	35.6
Jones	275	2 583	592	D	236	115	39	98	37 877	1 014	25.0	20.9	37.6
Karnes	338	4 823	D	396	530	109	D	263	54 483	1 288	17.5	13.1	45.6
Kaufman	1 773	22 813	3 360	3 670	3 899	629	593	781	34 218	3 041	59.3	4.2	38.5
Kendall	1 150	11 127	1 588	967	2 415	D	776	435	39 134	1 387	42.4	13.6	39.3
Kenedy	16	150	NA	NA	NA	NA	NA	8	55 313	28	0.0	89.3	67.9
Kent	14	101	D	NA	D	D	NA	6	59 455	194	8.8	44.3	31.4
Kerr	1 390	15 188	3 819	566	2 812	538	674	556	36 610	1 034	28.9	20.6	38.9
Kimble	134	930	D	D	282	D	D	25	27 161	602	15.4	48.2	46.7
King	NA	NA	NA	NA	NA	NA	NA	NA	NA	59	0.0	59.3	23.7
Kinney	33	370	D	NA	D	NA	D	10	26 451	196	12.8	57.1	43.4
Kleberg	569	7 473	1 627	125	1 627	320	D	231	30 931	401	50.9	10.2	37.7
Knox	88	658	122	NA	D	D	D	28	42 705	228	8.8	47.4	56.1
Lamar	1 156	16 283	3 259	4 221	2 502	519	376	583	35 827	1 843	32.0	11.7	34.6
Lamb	247	2 556	376	D	393	D	74	90	35 035	933	10.1	37.3	52.3
Lampasas	391	3 630	681	D	656	121	94	108	29 885	1 017	37.0	17.2	46.3
La Salle	135	2 155	126	NA	283	D	D	155	71 996	446	11.9	44.6	42.2
Lavaca	481	5 340	1 008	D	812	319	115	194	36 304	2 617	29.8	7.7	40.7
Lee	414	5 029	316	344	646	232	125	259	51 550	1 807	33.8	7.2	35.0
Leon	359	4 355	105	791	546	121	62	260	59 703	1 962	30.3	11.6	52.2
Liberty	1 060	13 274	1 820	1 683	2 556	339	380	543	40 889	1 470	50.7	7.6	46.0
Limestone	402	5 204	1 069	969	1 029	254	70	177	34 085	1 526	24.1	14.2	50.4
Lipscomb	91	880	D	D	D	71	8	39	44 398	277	6.5	56.0	46.2
Live Oak	303	3 923	D	D	453	88	113	210	53 502	892	13.5	28.5	42.3
Llano	444	3 839	655	78	544	173	D	110	28 695	740	25.8	31.6	42.7
Loving	2	D	NA	NA	NA	D	NA	D	D	10	0.0	100.0	80.0
Lubbock	7 015	110 878	22 911	5 236	18 227	5 701	4 139	3 797	34 247	1 116	36.0	26.8	45.6
Lynn	83	658	147	61	80	60	D	25	38 040	455	8.6	49.5	60.4
McCulloch	216	2 482	242	D	452	99	D	103	41 322	619	13.1	36.0	46.2
McLennan	5 036	100 004	17 120	13 936	11 929	4 662	2 504	3 534	35 338	3 278	55.3	5.8	38.8
McMullen	48	597	D	D	61	D	D	39	64 598	238	7.1	64.3	50.4
Madison	230	2 940	D	36	730	85	D	98	33 347	970	28.8	10.4	45.8
Marion	152	1 541	382	299	204	37	D	46	29 942	247	34.8	6.1	34.8
Martin	103	1 168	D	D	159	33	D	61	52 638	414	13.5	42.3	57.0

Table B. States and Counties — **Agriculture**

STATE County	Acreage (1,000) 117	Percent change, 2007–2012 118	Average size of farm 119	Total irrigated (1,000) 120	Total cropland (1,000) 121	Average per farm 122	Average per acre 123	Value of machinery and equipment, average per farm (dollars) 124	Total (mil dol) 125	Average per farm (dollars) 126	Crops 127	Live-stock and poultry products 128	$10,000 or more 129	$100,000 or more 130	Total ($1,000) 131	Percent of farms 132
TEXAS—Cont'd																
Guadalupe	383	-0.5	171	1.9	112.1	614 506	3 595	50 088	61.6	27 484	49.2	50.8	25.0	4.0	2 230	12.2
Hale	641	8.8	713	202.2	479.7	844 726	1 185	232 068	409.9	455 984	31.5	68.5	47.2	30.4	15 250	85.4
Hall	509	-4.6	1 305	27.8	186.3	1 006 900	771	121 005	24.8	63 464	74.3	25.7	36.2	13.3	4 834	83.8
Hamilton	446	-5.3	445	0.6	75.6	1 105 527	2 482	58 377	55.8	55 772	19.2	80.8	40.4	6.8	1 233	23.7
Hansford	567	-3.2	2 155	98.1	294.4	1 994 289	925	403 190	783.2	2 977 973	14.1	85.9	74.1	50.2	4 906	81.7
Hardeman	355	-4.2	993	4.5	130.9	869 655	875	82 580	25.4	71 042	36.1	63.9	45.7	8.7	2 043	80.1
Hardin	69	-24.9	104	1.7	22.7	320 964	3 092	62 642	D	D	D	D	18.0	2.0	414	2.1
Harris	236	-8.7	107	5.9	59.9	572 259	5 342	45 283	65.2	29 538	72.8	27.2	20.8	3.4	1 072	6.2
Harrison	200	-0.6	154	0.5	40.9	437 530	2 845	50 800	19.0	14 631	26.2	73.8	23.5	1.9	274	3.3
Hartley	903	-0.9	3 541	155.5	270.3	3 557 855	1 005	348 706	1 180.9	4 630 969	16.4	83.6	68.2	60.0	4 317	72.5
Haskell	567	14.6	1 128	27.5	298.5	834 078	740	144 797	38.7	76 881	74.0	26.0	42.1	16.5	5 201	84.9
Hays	245	4.0	170	1.0	30.3	1 055 578	6 200	33 647	15.0	10 403	48.9	51.1	12.7	1.5	469	4.5
Hemphill	576	4.9	2 482	3.2	39.8	1 837 310	740	115 043	110.6	476 517	2.7	97.3	46.1	19.8	1 293	50.4
Henderson	346	8.5	176	1.4	81.9	525 054	2 979	50 080	49.5	25 253	35.0	65.0	26.8	3.0	193	1.8
Hidalgo	795	10.0	368	183.6	465.6	1 117 900	3 038	115 296	452.8	209 517	91.7	8.3	33.2	14.2	9 106	20.0
Hill	504	-4.0	268	0.9	231.9	602 704	2 252	72 047	119.9	63 662	67.1	32.9	33.4	8.1	3 921	28.7
Hockley	484	-0.1	619	106.9	400.1	643 108	1 038	182 472	78.7	100 790	89.1	10.9	37.5	20.0	10 093	81.6
Hood	224	9.0	174	2.8	43.3	712 228	4 085	52 253	18.7	14 574	45.7	54.3	20.5	2.2	162	5.8
Hopkins	423	8.2	200	1.3	127.7	442 861	2 214	64 010	205.9	97 466	6.3	93.7	40.3	9.8	1 817	9.2
Houston	468	6.2	311	6.0	83.6	697 706	2 244	55 639	49.6	32 944	28.1	71.9	34.7	4.9	1 461	14.6
Howard	498	-4.7	1 049	4.2	161.9	796 236	759	88 682	13.9	29 187	33.5	66.5	18.7	4.8	4 460	62.1
Hudspeth	2 251	-0.3	13 480	18.1	48.3	7 586 677	563	134 042	34.5	206 455	71.7	28.3	65.3	22.2	1 323	35.9
Hunt	455	17.0	108	5.4	180.3	330 262	3 056	41 054	69.3	16 485	64.6	35.4	18.7	1.9	1 324	8.4
Hutchinson	521	-6.5	2 109	35.1	97.8	1 606 478	762	154 777	55.9	226 219	57.5	42.5	39.3	21.9	1 984	30.4
Irion	496	-20.6	3 201	0.7	10.7	3 005 394	939	70 394	7.5	48 148	10.3	89.7	47.1	9.7	904	25.8
Jack	528	-8.4	611	0.4	35.8	1 195 220	1 956	55 066	22.5	26 042	10.1	89.9	35.3	5.9	751	11.9
Jackson	442	-10.3	545	13.1	151.8	1 151 591	2 114	118 181	101.8	125 568	72.7	27.3	48.3	16.5	6 538	36.6
Jasper	88	-8.1	99	0.4	16.3	310 437	3 149	49 808	10.1	11 263	55.8	44.2	18.2	0.7	26	1.3
Jeff Davis	1 255	-9.8	14 941	0.1	3.6	7 177 381	480	76 583	D	D	D	D	38.1	23.8	792	26.2
Jefferson	354	6.2	463	22.4	112.7	767 829	1 657	88 914	38.0	49 778	56.8	43.2	31.8	10.1	3 631	22.3
Jim Hogg	645	0.7	2 452	D	9.6	3 272 540	1 335	58 118	11.1	42 323	D	D	36.1	6.1	1 349	33.1
Jim Wells	504	8.9	481	4.8	192.0	878 878	1 827	85 848	82.9	79 137	42.5	57.5	25.5	4.8	2 904	22.5
Johnson	429	29.5	142	2.4	119.9	578 482	4 077	50 827	78.9	26 083	25.3	74.7	20.4	2.8	834	6.3
Jones	563	-1.8	555	3.6	301.9	617 260	1 112	88 348	43.3	42 685	68.6	31.4	29.2	8.4	5 627	53.7
Karnes	465	11.3	361	0.9	82.7	937 215	2 598	66 483	27.6	21 428	38.8	61.2	32.2	3.4	1 683	18.9
Kaufman	449	6.5	148	1.4	130.5	502 007	3 399	42 963	59.0	19 395	34.4	65.6	19.8	2.3	637	2.8
Kendall	370	8.0	267	0.9	27.5	1 277 133	4 788	32 921	12.5	9 034	16.9	83.1	19.3	1.2	835	6.3
Kenedy	916	0.8	32 728	0.7	3.1	21 522 643	658	288 179	23.7	845 964	D	D	75.0	28.6	44	10.7
Kent	563	-0.8	2 903	1.1	39.3	2 479 716	854	68 263	D	D	D	D	31.4	10.8	1 687	74.2
Kerr	582	-5.1	563	1.9	44.2	1 483 207	2 634	38 048	10.8	10 448	12.2	87.8	18.3	1.6	597	7.6
Kimble	694	12.0	1 153	8.5	15.5	2 044 718	1 773	53 435	D	D	D	D	23.8	2.8	2 269	26.4
King	418	-23.0	7 078	D	23.4	4 304 051	608	122 169	6.6	111 661	D	D	37.3	15.3	748	78.0
Kinney	577	-4.1	2 943	1.2	16.6	3 539 699	1 203	48 612	4.7	24 031	24.7	75.3	32.1	5.1	903	20.9
Kleberg	484	-2.9	1 207	0.1	71.2	2 274 983	1 884	79 327	61.8	154 157	D	D	25.4	4.7	1 570	27.9
Knox	451	-8.7	1 976	21.6	189.7	1 528 439	773	192 219	59.0	258 829	32.4	67.6	64.5	27.2	3 240	82.0
Lamar	497	-4.7	269	7.0	175.8	582 745	2 163	67 187	84.9	46 058	47.7	52.3	36.2	6.5	5 129	25.7
Lamb	616	-2.9	661	179.5	469.1	764 255	1 157	226 869	575.3	616 598	20.3	79.7	46.5	30.3	14 489	85.7
Lampasas	445	6.9	437	0.2	50.3	1 097 964	2 511	49 163	16.1	15 867	18.1	81.9	25.6	3.0	530	11.1
La Salle	635	-2.2	1 423	7.0	44.0	2 777 861	1 952	69 648	18.7	41 890	63.9	36.1	28.0	6.5	1 007	15.9
Lavaca	547	-3.5	209	4.3	80.8	612 201	2 931	46 957	61.9	23 655	20.3	79.7	36.4	3.3	1 440	10.4
Lee	318	-2.3	176	0.9	44.1	563 382	3 199	42 538	38.6	21 340	33.4	66.6	31.0	1.8	935	11.9
Leon	594	4.4	303	0.8	74.0	759 197	2 506	63 997	148.7	75 810	6.7	93.3	32.8	4.6	1 172	6.9
Liberty	287	-3.7	195	5.2	101.1	488 804	2 505	70 376	34.9	23 768	42.1	57.9	22.9	3.3	1 494	6.1
Limestone	487	-3.8	319	0.3	80.9	603 233	1 891	55 660	48.3	31 641	25.6	74.4	38.2	5.0	2 192	15.3
Lipscomb	591	3.5	2 135	23.3	118.4	1 725 505	808	137 588	52.7	190 188	16.9	83.1	44.8	23.5	2 756	75.1
Live Oak	541	7.9	606	0.7	55.7	1 161 267	1 916	63 307	17.9	20 082	15.8	84.2	34.9	4.5	1 774	26.2
Llano	528	-2.0	714	0.8	21.3	1 930 442	2 705	51 043	13.8	18 600	10.4	89.6	32.2	3.2	890	12.3
Loving	380	-11.1	37 952	0.0	0.6	7 543 900	199	74 000	0.9	91 200	0.0	100.0	90.0	30.0	136	60.0
Lubbock	503	-2.6	450	155.5	423.8	834 394	1 853	174 972	174.8	156 631	54.8	45.2	39.0	22.0	10 896	61.6
Lynn	472	-4.4	1 038	71.6	406.7	933 648	900	261 402	67.6	148 560	97.3	2.7	55.6	32.3	9 808	90.1
McCulloch	614	0.3	992	0.9	90.1	1 838 354	1 852	79 971	22.6	36 454	38.2	61.8	36.7	9.5	3 014	39.9
McLennan	554	4.5	169	3.5	244.0	437 533	2 591	54 417	183.1	55 852	40.9	59.1	21.2	4.5	3 662	17.3
McMullen	517	2.2	2 174	D	19.3	3 055 197	1 405	85 521	8.3	35 025	5.2	94.8	31.5	7.6	239	8.0
Madison	291	6.7	300	2.3	35.3	840 584	2 799	79 825	82.9	85 423	D	D	33.5	4.4	1 087	10.6
Marion	40	-5.1	162	0.2	8.3	361 308	2 224	40 939	3.4	13 563	16.5	83.5	16.6	0.8	62	4.9
Martin	454	-0.9	1 096	17.1	279.6	1 130 809	1 032	160 903	20.3	48 949	88.8	11.2	26.1	13.8	5 158	80.9

Table B. States and Counties — Water Use, Wholesale Trade, Retail Trade, and Real Estate

STATE County	Water use, 2010 Total water withdrawn (mil gal/day)	Gallons withdrawn per person per day	Wholesale trade,[1] 2012 Number of establish-ments	Number of employees	Sales (mil dol)	Annual payroll (mil dol)	Retail trade,[2] 2012 Number of establish-ments	Number of employees	Sales (mil dol)	Annual payroll (mil dol)	Real estate and rental and leasing,[2] 2012 Number of establish-ments	Number of employees	Receipts (mil dol)	Annual payroll (mil dol)
	133	134	135	136	137	138	139	140	141	142	143	144	145	146
TEXAS—Cont'd														
Guadalupe	61.1	465	92	D	D	D	270	3 756	1 166.8	90.5	89	373	70.1	14.2
Hale	208.4	5 744	45	D	D	D	114	1 464	346.9	29.0	31	103	15.9	2.4
Hall	30.9	9 219	2	D	D	D	15	94	48.3	1.7	1	D	D	D
Hamilton	2.5	298	6	85	32.9	3.7	52	366	87.1	7.8	1	D	D	D
Hansford	119.6	21 302	18	98	148.0	3.7	24	213	74.2	5.3	4	4	0.9	0.1
Hardeman	6.1	1 476	7	D	D	D	15	135	33.4	2.3	NA	NA	NA	NA
Hardin	6.5	119	19	D	D	D	155	2 033	712.6	51.4	26	54	7.3	1.4
Harris	443.8	108	6 363	100 988	340 775.7	6 909.3	12 644	189 299	61 669.4	4 940.5	4 930	37 842	9 174.7	1 850.8
Harrison	32.5	495	58	D	D	D	192	2 069	647.6	49.5	62	288	45.3	10.9
Hartley	311.1	51 321	10	78	85.2	4.2	13	D	D	D	5	13	4.2	1.0
Haskell	33.3	5 640	1	D	D	D	27	298	89.8	7.0	NA	NA	NA	NA
Hays	19.7	125	117	D	D	D	619	10 400	2 471.3	208.4	177	680	161.8	21.6
Hemphill	8.6	2 267	13	D	D	D	23	148	64.8	3.9	9	96	24.4	5.6
Henderson	37.6	478	34	D	D	D	230	2 599	671.8	58.0	56	201	26.4	5.8
Hidalgo	470.2	607	841	D	D	D	2 219	33 566	9 296.8	733.9	497	2 209	445.0	61.9
Hill	7.5	212	21	D	D	D	151	1 427	409.7	28.1	28	86	12.0	2.1
Hockley	126.9	5 533	23	D	D	D	61	850	221.0	18.8	12	63	13.4	4.7
Hood	25.6	501	55	396	222.5	19.5	195	2 394	747.6	60.6	70	376	50.0	11.9
Hopkins	37.7	1 073	31	904	1 176.6	42.2	147	1 659	496.7	37.5	28	116	15.8	2.7
Houston	10.1	426	11	D	D	D	60	640	160.7	13.6	9	45	4.8	1.2
Howard	29.6	846	27	D	D	D	108	D	D	D	41	156	30.1	4.5
Hudspeth	120.0	34 508	NA	NA	NA	NA	10	41	11.3	0.6	NA	NA	NA	NA
Hunt	17.2	200	51	D	D	D	247	3 428	966.3	90.9	66	182	28.5	4.8
Hutchinson	94.4	4 260	19	D	D	D	79	867	205.2	17.7	11	93	17.0	2.2
Irion	3.7	2 289	2	D	D	D	4	17	1.6	0.2	NA	NA	NA	NA
Jack	6.1	679	7	D	D	D	26	187	38.7	3.9	7	12	2.4	0.3
Jackson	90.4	6 419	15	124	230.1	7.4	38	511	165.6	10.8	10	D	D	D
Jasper	44.7	1 251	29	D	D	D	127	1 457	425.7	32.5	23	78	14.0	2.3
Jeff Davis	2.7	1 170	1	D	D	D	6	51	7.9	0.8	4	9	2.4	0.4
Jefferson	242.7	962	273	2 964	2 451.0	156.3	992	13 877	3 968.3	348.1	264	1 759	372.3	73.9
Jim Hogg	0.8	158	4	D	D	D	20	209	72.8	4.6	3	D	D	D
Jim Wells	7.0	171	39	D	D	D	142	1 708	641.6	43.8	46	527	128.1	30.9
Johnson	25.3	168	124	1 160	604.6	52.8	381	4 843	1 513.4	119.0	108	610	125.6	28.9
Jones	15.6	770	23	108	538.5	4.4	34	216	158.4	5.9	6	D	D	D
Karnes	5.1	344	13	69	45.3	2.7	39	479	192.0	11.9	11	8	2.1	0.5
Kaufman	59.6	577	62	D	D	D	291	3 480	1 021.0	84.9	50	150	27.6	4.8
Kendall	4.9	148	51	D	D	D	152	2 107	941.0	66.1	47	116	24.3	4.2
Kenedy	1.3	3 005	NA	NA	NA	NA	NA	NA	NA	NA	1	D	D	D
Kent	16.8	20 792	NA	NA	NA	NA	3	D	D	D	NA	NA	NA	NA
Kerr	10.1	203	44	D	D	D	215	3 006	791.7	72.0	84	229	31.7	8.2
Kimble	17.0	3 679	NA	NA	NA	NA	34	239	97.5	6.0	3	7	1.6	0.4
King	4.1	14 231	NA	NA	NA	NA	NA	NA	NA	NA	NA	NA	NA	NA
Kinney	2.2	620	2	D	D	D	8	58	9.8	0.8	2	D	D	D
Kleberg	3.2	100	5	D	D	D	110	1 490	524.3	33.8	27	D	D	D
Knox	26.9	7 220	11	D	D	D	15	139	31.6	2.1	3	4	0.2	0.1
Lamar	29.2	587	43	D	D	D	212	2 426	678.6	57.3	48	161	22.4	4.9
Lamb	184.9	13 231	19	172	123.6	8.4	40	374	93.0	7.8	1	D	D	D
Lampasas	3.5	176	6	D	D	D	51	604	208.9	15.1	14	42	9.5	2.0
La Salle	6.8	985	6	72	33.9	3.3	22	238	134.4	4.9	5	D	D	D
Lavaca	10.3	535	15	D	D	D	90	772	178.8	15.3	12	39	8.5	1.2
Lee	8.6	515	19	D	D	D	62	618	151.6	12.8	14	111	39.9	5.5
Leon	6.0	354	13	D	D	D	66	558	156.8	10.9	13	51	9.3	2.4
Liberty	56.6	748	45	500	239.1	25.8	197	2 468	796.6	60.9	32	192	33.0	8.3
Limestone	30.6	1 307	10	D	D	D	93	966	263.8	20.6	14	47	6.1	1.1
Lipscomb	30.2	9 140	4	D	D	D	20	120	98.1	3.6	1	D	D	D
Live Oak	5.3	455	15	D	D	D	39	347	263.0	9.5	10	40	20.1	1.8
Llano	74.5	3 859	15	236	79.0	10.1	68	480	135.3	11.0	22	39	9.1	1.4
Loving	2.1	26 098	NA	NA	NA	NA	NA	NA	NA	NA	NA	NA	NA	NA
Lubbock	131.7	472	377	5 273	4 815.9	259.1	1 046	16 460	4 796.6	405.0	394	1 559	270.4	49.7
Lynn	54.5	9 214	4	D	D	D	8	76	18.5	1.7	3	D	D	D
McCulloch	12.3	1 485	9	180	57.7	10.5	39	481	139.0	10.6	5	8	0.9	0.2
McLennan	73.7	314	239	2 976	1 634.7	123.0	846	11 099	3 223.8	250.4	223	1 512	286.8	63.8
McMullen	1.8	2 546	NA	NA	NA	NA	4	D	D	D	2	D	D	D
Madison	4.3	312	6	D	D	D	37	655	244.8	17.9	13	47	14.6	1.2
Marion	9.9	937	2	D	D	D	28	192	61.3	4.6	7	8	1.4	0.2
Martin	38.5	8 029	7	D	D	D	12	144	88.7	4.6	1	D	D	D

1. Merchant wholesalers, except manufacturers' sales branches and offices.   2. Employer establishments.

Table B. States and Counties — **Professional Services, Manufacturing, and Accommodation and Food Services**

STATE County	Professional, scientific, and technical services, 2012				Manufacturing, 2012				Accommodation and food services, 2012			
	Number of establishments	Number of employees	Receipts (mil dol)	Annual payroll (mil dol)	Number of establishments	Number of employees	Receipts (mil dol)	Annual payroll (mil dol)	Number of establishments	Number of employees	Sales (mil dol)	Annual payroll (mil dol)
	147	148	149	150	151	152	153	154	155	156	157	158
TEXAS—Cont'd												
Guadalupe	132	568	54.5	19.5	111	5 290	2 542.7	231.0	176	3 082	153.7	39.8
Hale	47	D	D	D	23	2 631	2 414.6	90.2	53	985	44.5	12.2
Hall	3	D	D	D	3	35	D	D	12	D	D	D
Hamilton	13	37	4.2	1.0	15	234	38.2	6.6	17	179	8.7	2.4
Hansford	9	39	4.8	1.8	3	16	2.1	0.6	12	D	D	D
Hardeman	3	D	D	D	NA	NA	NA	NA	8	D	D	D
Hardin	49	258	29.6	15.8	24	658	D	33.6	75	1 188	50.7	13.9
Harris	12 925	192 436	44 873.8	17 280.7	4 082	164 479	200 035.4	10 303.2	7 946	166 626	10 106.1	2 710.0
Harrison	115	825	141.8	53.9	77	4 454	2 856.9	183.1	106	1 784	78.2	23.1
Hartley	7	D	D	D	NA	NA	NA	NA	4	14	0.9	0.1
Haskell	7	D	D	D	NA	NA	NA	NA	17	120	5.6	1.2
Hays	381	1 870	198.0	77.7	136	3 908	1 179.0	203.9	361	7 110	348.3	99.3
Hemphill	10	35	15.3	1.4	4	21	D	1.0	12	91	8.0	1.8
Henderson	93	3 061	264.5	68.9	62	1 665	265.1	63.7	135	1 755	77.9	20.5
Hidalgo	886	5 381	566.0	169.6	268	5 713	1 675.4	216.0	1 014	19 468	985.9	247.1
Hill	38	139	15.7	5.2	40	850	265.3	34.0	69	954	43.9	12.5
Hockley	28	D	D	D	15	199	D	8.5	39	547	25.8	7.1
Hood	124	369	47.5	15.2	32	400	D	15.4	101	1 452	66.1	19.0
Hopkins	49	250	66.4	11.5	44	1 840	910.7	69.6	52	791	39.2	12.0
Houston	27	95	8.6	2.1	20	511	160.0	24.5	32	380	16.9	4.2
Howard	45	D	D	D	23	640	D	41.8	76	D	D	D
Hudspeth	1	D	D	D	NA	NA	NA	NA	5	24	1.1	0.3
Hunt	84	424	61.9	14.4	70	7 508	3 089.7	556.3	116	2 052	98.6	26.0
Hutchinson	33	208	25.2	10.5	22	1 712	D	156.7	46	709	31.3	8.8
Irion	4	4	0.7	0.1	NA	NA	NA	NA	1	D	D	D
Jack	10	D	D	D	5	50	D	2.1	17	D	D	D
Jackson	22	134	10.0	3.9	11	D	D	D	20	258	11.9	3.3
Jasper	43	151	18.2	4.1	19	1 335	771.2	90.0	56	777	31.7	8.5
Jeff Davis	5	D	D	D	NA	NA	NA	NA	13	159	8.9	2.4
Jefferson	510	5 909	985.5	383.2	202	13 123	80 760.5	1 106.7	478	10 150	485.5	132.2
Jim Hogg	1	D	D	D	6	69	D	4.1	10	82	3.5	0.8
Jim Wells	62	273	66.6	12.9	20	620	454.7	35.9	84	1 345	74.2	17.4
Johnson	199	1 032	131.0	45.3	161	4 977	1 498.0	245.1	230	3 690	170.9	47.6
Jones	14	44	4.4	1.7	11	182	D	5.5	16	D	D	D
Karnes	17	113	15.3	3.9	8	284	D	14.6	32	427	29.0	5.4
Kaufman	116	556	66.8	21.0	95	3 210	1 100.1	165.3	161	2 618	127.0	34.3
Kendall	136	793	131.1	46.6	36	1 003	D	41.1	96	1 486	64.7	20.7
Kenedy	NA	NA	NA	NA	NA	NA	NA	NA	1	D	D	D
Kent	NA	NA	NA	NA	NA	NA	NA	NA	1	D	D	D
Kerr	134	684	70.6	27.3	44	586	D	23.4	131	1 991	122.8	35.7
Kimble	10	D	D	D	6	68	D	2.8	15	D	D	D
King	NA	NA	NA	NA	NA	NA	NA	NA	NA	NA	NA	NA
Kinney	NA	NA	NA	NA	NA	NA	NA	NA	4	20	0.8	0.2
Kleberg	32	D	D	D	16	98	D	5.1	76	D	D	D
Knox	2	D	D	D	NA	NA	NA	NA	5	D	D	D
Lamar	53	D	D	D	56	3 525	2 152.6	177.8	105	1 568	73.1	20.4
Lamb	17	48	4.6	1.1	6	D	D	17.8	16	D	D	D
Lampasas	40	98	8.5	3.1	23	539	D	18.4	33	458	19.8	5.3
La Salle	1	D	D	D	NA	NA	NA	NA	18	D	D	D
Lavaca	40	136	17.1	5.8	35	1 554	377.5	54.6	31	371	19.5	4.9
Lee	26	117	15.9	4.6	19	418	108.6	20.8	38	316	15.9	4.0
Leon	20	D	D	D	20	751	D	48.8	42	346	18.0	3.9
Liberty	88	333	38.0	11.4	35	1 262	D	78.8	95	1 403	67.5	17.4
Limestone	25	71	7.3	2.4	11	818	193.2	33.5	40	430	22.1	5.2
Lipscomb	4	D	D	D	NA	NA	NA	NA	5	D	D	D
Live Oak	21	D	D	D	6	D	D	D	33	312	27.6	5.4
Llano	38	104	10.6	3.9	17	62	D	2.3	51	1 047	64.2	21.1
Loving	NA	NA	NA	NA	NA	NA	NA	NA	NA	NA	NA	NA
Lubbock	631	3 860	482.3	175.9	240	4 984	1 572.9	216.1	627	D	D	D
Lynn	6	D	D	D	3	63	D	1.9	6	D	D	D
McCulloch	20	D	D	D	12	435	D	16.8	23	265	11.5	2.9
McLennan	369	2 583	331.4	139.6	232	14 194	D	677.1	487	D	D	D
McMullen	3	D	D	D	NA	NA	NA	NA	3	6	0.5	0.1
Madison	19	73	8.4	2.3	8	33	6.8	1.5	36	386	23.0	4.9
Marion	10	D	D	D	9	182	D	7.4	21	211	11.2	2.8
Martin	4	12	1.3	0.7	NA	NA	NA	NA	6	D	D	D

1. Establishment subject to federal tax.

STATE County	Health care and social assistance, 2012				Other services, 2012				Nonemployer businesses, 2014		Value of residential construction authorized by building permits, 2015	
	Number of establishments	Number of employees	Receipts (mil dol)	Annual payroll (mil dol)	Number of establishments	Number of employees	Receipts (mil dol)	Annual payroll (mil dol)	Number	Receipts (mil dol)	New Construction ($1,000)	Number of housing units
	159	160	161	162	163	164	165	166	167	168	169	170
TEXAS—Cont'd												
Guadalupe	189	3 077	275.1	107.5	141	923	76.9	22.3	9 502	415.0	278 685	1 313
Hale	84	1 058	104.5	36.0	49	345	24.7	7.5	2 095	88.7	2 730	16
Hall	7	87	4.3	2.1	6	46	4.0	1.3	212	6.8	0	0
Hamilton	24	531	35.7	16.5	22	38	5.4	1.5	729	31.9	598	6
Hansford	7	D	D	D	12	42	4.9	1.3	512	26.3	401	3
Hardeman	13	210	18.3	7.7	10	51	3.1	0.9	282	11.9	0	0
Hardin	65	D	D	D	52	D	D	D	3 729	142.0	42 782	232
Harris	10 433	232 131	29 549.4	10 842.4	5 820	58 629	7 505.2	2 234.1	387 455	20 157.5	4 793 594	33 975
Harrison	123	1 881	203.6	66.2	77	923	89.0	32.8	4 521	208.7	13 178	54
Hartley	7	D	D	D	12	D	D	D	347	25.8	NA	NA
Haskell	11	D	D	D	15	55	5.7	1.0	443	17.4	75	2
Hays	309	5 778	603.3	220.8	203	1 170	114.0	35.3	15 174	715.4	402 067	2 626
Hemphill	10	169	12.7	5.7	8	D	D	D	423	26.1	158	1
Henderson	126	2 180	215.6	84.3	69	295	24.9	7.0	5 964	301.5	9 838	47
Hidalgo	2 048	54 356	3 479.0	1 471.2	571	3 701	350.3	84.2	68 931	2 671.8	620 741	4 306
Hill	50	1 168	79.0	33.0	38	178	11.6	3.2	2 374	105.7	614	7
Hockley	46	1 089	74.8	28.8	27	D	D	D	1 330	61.3	580	4
Hood	131	2 352	242.5	89.9	82	534	38.1	11.7	5 263	262.8	25 678	144
Hopkins	76	1 416	120.2	47.4	48	221	17.4	4.8	2 776	138.9	4 426	16
Houston	37	768	53.9	21.6	27	144	13.4	3.9	1 377	50.6	0	0
Howard	67	1 699	163.7	51.4	40	D	D	D	1 656	87.4	10 519	100
Hudspeth	2	D	D	D	3	4	0.1	0.0	224	8.1	NA	NA
Hunt	175	3 165	308.8	118.2	93	409	32.2	10.3	6 415	290.9	23 786	102
Hutchinson	44	486	49.7	16.7	34	223	25.8	6.9	1 100	50.9	5 150	48
Irion	1	D	D	D	3	D	D	D	207	14.7	0	0
Jack	13	D	D	D	12	87	16.2	2.7	816	50.4	0	0
Jackson	16	303	24.9	9.9	26	63	6.5	1.4	1 015	51.4	2 071	13
Jasper	80	2 341	107.3	47.8	35	137	11.5	2.9	2 446	100.9	1 077	11
Jeff Davis	4	D	D	D	5	D	D	D	261	8.6	NA	NA
Jefferson	810	17 453	1 760.8	625.3	362	2 712	286.6	81.2	15 283	682.4	95 208	599
Jim Hogg	11	645	13.9	8.0	4	9	0.7	0.2	421	10.5	NA	NA
Jim Wells	114	4 355	211.2	96.0	69	381	63.0	15.8	3 050	148.7	1 533	12
Johnson	240	D	D	D	183	1 110	118.5	42.2	11 958	564.8	123 808	747
Jones	20	632	32.3	15.2	16	54	3.8	1.1	1 208	52.8	0	0
Karnes	27	437	30.7	12.6	15	57	3.4	0.8	990	49.1	7 491	45
Kaufman	160	3 412	235.5	100.1	112	557	63.1	22.3	9 566	442.2	65 333	578
Kendall	129	1 548	125.3	44.9	69	365	30.6	8.4	5 002	324.7	58 426	190
Kenedy	NA	NA	NA	NA	4	D	D	D	20	0.3	NA	NA
Kent	2	D	D	D	NA	NA	NA	NA	61	2.6	NA	NA
Kerr	176	3 826	370.5	164.1	101	537	61.7	15.2	5 320	285.3	15 735	63
Kimble	8	141	8.6	4.1	6	19	1.4	0.4	616	20.0	0	0
King	NA	NA	NA	NA	NA	NA	NA	NA	0	0.0	NA	NA
Kinney	2	D	D	D	3	D	D	D	162	4.6	390	2
Kleberg	67	1 599	115.8	45.5	46	D	D	D	1 522	53.5	8 105	55
Knox	8	166	10.7	4.5	10	D	D	D	272	12.9	0	0
Lamar	177	3 747	326.1	121.7	86	425	39.7	10.4	3 815	166.5	3 033	40
Lamb	27	429	23.8	10.9	17	D	D	D	735	28.8	179	1
Lampasas	25	747	45.7	19.3	22	153	16.7	4.2	1 475	62.3	1 774	18
La Salle	9	D	D	D	4	14	1.5	0.4	550	19.9	1 502	22
Lavaca	38	981	65.3	24.5	47	140	13.3	2.6	1 748	85.4	1 917	19
Lee	29	325	20.8	8.3	25	85	9.3	2.2	1 397	60.4	1 169	8
Leon	19	291	11.6	5.5	25	114	6.9	2.0	1 522	72.2	800	5
Liberty	102	D	D	D	71	491	55.1	16.8	4 961	214.5	31 487	306
Limestone	49	1 120	84.0	31.2	21	D	D	D	1 371	57.7	305	2
Lipscomb	3	10	0.5	0.2	7	12	1.8	0.2	332	16.3	0	0
Live Oak	12	250	8.7	3.6	14	D	D	D	1 032	54.3	1 385	10
Llano	31	605	46.5	19.3	22	63	6.9	1.7	2 055	108.7	31 235	76
Loving	NA	NA	NA	NA	NA	NA	NA	NA	14	0.3	NA	NA
Lubbock	848	22 202	2 519.2	866.0	460	D	D	D	20 487	1 055.2	306 713	1 850
Lynn	6	131	9.2	3.1	6	D	D	D	338	12.9	85	1
McCulloch	16	267	19.9	8.2	19	78	6.3	1.8	698	25.1	0	0
McLennan	547	16 602	1 484.1	627.5	361	2 364	233.2	64.5	14 643	671.3	209 381	1 502
McMullen	1	D	D	D	NA	NA	NA	NA	140	6.1	NA	NA
Madison	19	306	24.8	11.3	15	D	D	D	1 010	48.4	295	3
Marion	13	354	15.7	9.7	13	D	D	D	703	30.4	156	1
Martin	7	135	11.6	4.7	8	21	3.2	0.6	438	22.9	580	5

Table B. States and Counties — Government Employment and Payroll, and Local Government Finances

		Government employment and payroll, 2012								Local government finances, 2012				
			March payroll (percent of total)							General revenue			Taxes	
														Per capita[1] (dollars)
STATE County	Full-time equivalent employees	March payroll (dollars)	Adminis-tration, judicial, and legal	Police and Corrections	Fire Protection	Highways and transpor-tation	Health and Welfare	Natural resources and utilities	Education and libraries	Total (mil dol)	Inter-govern-mental (mil dol)	Total (mil dol)	Total	Property
	171	172	173	174	175	176	177	178	179	180	181	182	183	184
TEXAS—Cont'd														
Guadalupe	4 848	17 546 517	6.1	10.0	2.4	1.9	15.8	3.7	58.3	422.8	109.1	182.6	1 306	1 097
Hale	1 782	7 262 318	4.1	6.3	2.1	1.0	6.9	2.2	76.9	114.8	52.3	44.9	1 233	1 018
Hall	222	559 195	7.2	8.3	0.0	3.6	2.3	5.4	72.7	14.8	8.2	4.0	1 202	1 007
Hamilton	539	1 700 689	4.8	3.1	0.0	3.4	41.0	2.4	45.4	45.9	10.7	12.7	1 528	1 340
Hansford	494	1 557 868	4.9	2.9	0.1	2.2	32.4	1.8	53.8	31.7	6.9	19.4	3 509	3 267
Hardeman	417	1 303 943	5.8	4.2	0.7	1.9	46.4	3.2	37.5	42.6	8.4	16.1	3 932	3 714
Hardin	2 150	6 172 176	6.7	7.8	0.0	2.1	0.7	3.2	78.4	141.1	61.5	64.0	1 160	1 008
Harris	166 045	659 443 824	4.4	11.0	3.4	5.0	8.8	2.9	62.2	19 260.3	5 471.7	9 235.2	2 171	1 765
Harrison	2 833	8 500 249	3.8	8.6	2.9	1.9	0.3	3.6	77.3	193.7	50.6	119.6	1 773	1 592
Hartley	92	266 990	18.2	0.7	0.0	0.0	0.4	1.3	72.8	11.2	1.1	8.7	1 410	1 297
Haskell	331	767 433	9.1	5.5	0.1	3.6	22.4	5.8	53.3	22.1	9.1	7.4	1 260	1 097
Hays	7 053	24 108 223	5.6	10.9	2.6	1.5	6.6	5.7	64.1	545.5	162.4	287.7	1 703	1 398
Hemphill	358	1 141 524	8.4	5.9	0.0	4.6	27.8	4.3	48.3	47.6	3.4	36.2	8 863	8 415
Henderson	2 818	8 513 766	7.2	8.3	1.6	1.5	0.2	3.2	76.9	203.3	68.1	103.6	1 309	1 130
Hidalgo	39 042	129 583 687	3.7	6.7	1.7	1.6	2.9	3.9	78.6	3 159.2	1 926.2	864.1	1 071	868
Hill	1 782	5 391 972	5.2	8.8	1.2	2.0	0.1	2.7	79.5	122.0	52.4	48.3	1 376	1 175
Hockley	1 746	5 964 084	3.8	4.6	0.6	1.5	0.5	1.6	86.7	146.0	48.8	70.9	3 073	2 862
Hood	1 577	5 364 527	10.6	11.6	0.3	2.2	0.8	4.5	68.5	134.0	27.6	93.9	1 804	1 536
Hopkins	1 924	6 315 574	4.5	5.5	2.0	2.2	35.9	2.7	46.4	157.4	43.9	43.8	1 235	1 002
Houston	827	2 210 644	8.8	8.8	0.6	3.0	1.9	5.5	70.3	60.8	24.7	26.3	1 135	940
Howard	2 006	6 202 628	4.2	6.9	2.7	2.0	15.7	7.1	59.9	146.9	52.2	61.9	1 747	1 467
Hudspeth	286	780 976	7.7	13.3	0.0	2.9	1.1	7.6	67.2	19.0	10.0	7.0	2 108	2 025
Hunt	4 073	13 501 049	5.0	7.3	2.3	1.6	26.3	8.0	48.4	331.7	94.9	108.8	1 250	1 039
Hutchinson	1 204	3 868 672	7.3	8.9	2.7	2.5	1.7	5.0	70.3	90.0	30.2	42.4	1 935	1 693
Irion	111	320 492	16.7	8.2	0.0	4.3	0.8	7.7	60.9	14.0	1.4	12.0	7 598	7 380
Jack	453	1 551 359	5.7	9.9	0.3	1.9	21.3	3.8	56.6	35.4	3.7	28.0	3 118	2 834
Jackson	834	2 725 347	5.8	6.2	1.3	2.4	17.9	11.4	54.8	75.0	21.3	27.7	1 942	1 729
Jasper	1 516	4 363 997	5.7	7.7	0.0	3.0	2.1	6.7	72.0	103.2	47.1	43.9	1 222	1 064
Jeff Davis	113	390 447	7.2	8.1	0.0	0.0	1.2	1.2	81.3	9.9	6.7	3.0	1 289	1 181
Jefferson	10 830	41 244 326	6.6	14.9	6.1	3.8	6.0	8.0	53.1	1 149.2	304.3	568.5	2 258	1 850
Jim Hogg	316	819 818	7.4	11.3	0.9	0.2	7.1	5.0	62.8	22.9	9.1	11.0	2 095	1 786
Jim Wells	1 854	5 562 478	7.3	10.0	2.6	4.3	1.8	3.2	68.8	136.7	63.1	61.1	1 463	914
Johnson	6 428	20 663 672	6.4	10.8	3.7	2.3	0.9	4.4	69.6	540.8	136.3	306.3	1 996	1 658
Jones	1 148	3 124 966	5.6	5.9	0.0	1.6	32.6	5.2	48.8	55.2	25.7	15.1	754	677
Karnes	676	1 956 116	5.9	7.8	0.1	2.4	17.7	3.7	62.1	49.9	22.4	22.9	1 501	1 339
Kaufman	4 535	15 218 689	4.8	9.9	1.3	2.3	10.1	6.4	64.2	385.5	158.1	186.8	1 750	1 528
Kendall	1 662	5 537 436	9.0	8.0	1.1	3.0	1.6	5.5	70.6	133.9	20.6	100.2	2 786	2 470
Kenedy	35	84 678	6.2	3.9	0.0	0.0	0.5	0.4	86.0	11.6	0.2	10.5	24 369	24 346
Kent	75	243 441	11.6	3.7	0.1	21.1	0.0	2.6	60.8	8.5	1.3	6.8	8 151	8 082
Kerr	1 700	5 612 578	8.7	13.7	6.0	3.2	1.3	4.7	60.4	120.6	27.6	78.6	1 580	1 286
Kimble	171	555 031	11.3	14.1	0.0	6.0	2.2	4.9	60.8	13.0	3.2	6.7	1 472	1 379
King	59	195 445	17.5	2.0	0.0	2.6	0.0	0.5	77.5	9.5	1.7	7.1	25 620	25 616
Kinney	195	518 153	13.2	15.7	0.0	1.2	4.8	4.1	59.5	14.4	8.6	3.8	1 046	948
Kleberg	1 554	3 973 033	8.5	14.3	3.3	6.7	4.0	5.3	56.2	170.5	58.0	63.5	1 984	1 710
Knox	325	851 631	7.1	3.5	0.0	2.7	26.8	6.9	52.1	19.7	7.7	5.6	1 486	1 218
Lamar	2 237	7 154 454	5.0	8.6	0.2	1.3	0.9	4.5	77.8	165.7	68.1	68.9	1 384	1 087
Lamb	779	2 277 980	7.5	10.4	1.2	3.2	3.0	4.3	70.1	61.1	24.1	21.0	1 499	1 349
Lampasas	821	2 377 321	5.2	9.7	1.6	2.7	0.6	3.2	72.8	53.7	20.4	26.9	1 339	1 135
La Salle	315	950 554	9.0	9.5	0.0	3.2	0.2	4.1	71.9	22.1	6.6	13.4	1 887	1 739
Lavaca	808	2 421 042	9.6	8.5	3.3	4.6	17.2	10.0	41.0	73.1	14.0	28.2	1 446	1 296
Lee	700	2 033 290	5.6	8.6	0.0	3.2	0.0	4.3	74.9	49.3	14.2	29.5	1 776	1 564
Leon	757	2 170 423	7.7	7.0	0.0	3.1	1.2	2.4	78.4	47.5	14.0	28.8	1 714	1 601
Liberty	2 976	8 829 594	6.7	8.2	1.1	2.8	0.4	3.1	76.8	210.0	86.8	98.0	1 280	1 101
Limestone	1 302	3 748 599	6.3	12.5	1.9	3.5	15.2	4.0	56.2	116.3	27.5	51.1	2 165	1 970
Lipscomb	247	785 351	10.0	5.2	0.0	6.1	4.3	3.8	69.9	21.9	4.9	15.8	4 530	4 351
Live Oak	529	1 441 098	7.4	10.9	0.0	3.7	1.5	5.4	67.2	34.0	9.9	21.0	1 801	1 538
Llano	637	1 790 590	16.6	12.9	0.0	4.0	0.3	8.5	56.3	64.8	6.8	51.0	2 670	2 571
Loving	12	46 971	59.5	22.6	0.0	14.3	0.0	3.6	0.0	4.4	0.6	3.4	48 366	47 718
Lubbock	12 902	47 474 349	4.7	10.5	4.4	1.1	28.6	5.7	43.9	1 264.7	335.5	406.2	1 421	1 107
Lynn	453	1 252 881	5.2	5.1	0.0	1.3	20.1	4.2	62.8	30.1	12.7	8.8	1 516	1 374
McCulloch	585	1 662 784	6.4	5.5	1.5	2.1	23.0	8.4	50.7	33.3	13.2	11.4	1 371	1 168
McLennan	10 401	35 092 132	5.7	11.4	3.1	2.0	4.5	8.6	63.6	1 172.8	436.4	367.8	1 541	1 222
McMullen	82	296 876	20.7	8.4	0.0	8.2	1.7	1.9	58.1	10.8	0.8	9.1	12 590	12 296
Madison	473	1 465 387	9.1	5.4	0.0	2.2	0.6	3.0	77.1	37.7	16.3	14.6	1 066	920
Marion	304	892 993	8.9	7.6	0.0	4.1	0.5	2.4	76.0	19.4	6.6	11.1	1 074	952
Martin	332	1 249 120	9.9	4.5	0.0	9.6	23.0	3.5	48.5	39.6	3.4	28.7	5 722	5 575

1. Based on the resident population estimated as of July 1 of the year shown.

Table B. States and Counties — Local Government Finances, Government Employment, and Voting

	Local government finances, 2012 (cont.)									Government employment, 2014			Presidential election,[2] 2012		
	Direct general expenditure							Debt outstanding					Percent of vote cast:		
STATE County	Total (mil dol)	Per capita[1] (dollars)	Percent of total for:					Total (mil dol)	Per capita[1] (dollars)	Federal civilian	Federal military	State and local	Demo-cratic	Republi-can	All other
			Educa-tion	Health and hospitals	Police protec-tion	Public welfare	High-ways								
	185	186	187	188	189	190	191	192	193	194	195	196	197	198	199

TEXAS—Cont'd

STATE County	185	186	187	188	189	190	191	192	193	194	195	196	197	198	199
Guadalupe	411.4	2 942	44.3	19.5	5.0	0.8	3.8	852.5	6 096	199	301	5 828	34.0	65.0	0.9
Hale	116.3	3 196	62.2	9.1	7.7	0.6	2.8	79.2	2 177	75	66	2 333	27.2	72.1	0.6
Hall	13.5	4 104	66.2	1.9	3.1	0.1	5.0	0.2	72	18	0	257	25.6	73.6	0.8
Hamilton	41.2	4 960	31.5	48.5	2.0	0.3	2.3	24.5	2 949	28	17	660	22.8	76.1	1.0
Hansford	29.9	5 415	58.4	21.3	2.2	0.0	2.5	26.3	4 772	17	11	617	11.4	87.9	0.7
Hardeman	52.1	12 765	19.2	41.9	2.9	17.5	2.7	3.2	781	18	0	410	23.4	75.2	1.4
Hardin	129.3	2 342	65.3	0.6	6.8	0.5	3.7	120.4	2 181	70	114	2 267	19.0	80.2	0.8
Harris	18 773.0	4 413	44.4	10.5	5.7	0.1	4.8	54 673.5	12 853	24 683	10 052	240 670	50.4	48.8	0.7
Harrison	211.9	3 142	59.8	0.1	4.4	0.4	3.4	272.1	4 034	124	135	3 195	34.0	65.4	0.6
Hartley	10.5	1 709	39.9	0.0	7.7	0.2	15.4	0.2	32	0	10	848	12.6	86.2	1.2
Haskell	22.2	3 760	53.2	17.8	3.7	0.0	7.7	2.3	395	24	11	422	33.0	65.6	1.4
Hays	604.2	3 575	42.7	5.8	5.4	0.3	6.3	1 700.9	10 065	198	408	12 246	48.1	50.2	1.7
Hemphill	40.3	9 878	51.7	16.2	2.1	0.1	5.1	11.9	2 915	0	0	435	13.8	85.7	0.6
Henderson	213.8	2 703	68.0	1.9	5.3	0.0	3.7	147.7	1 868	86	163	3 414	27.3	71.9	0.8
Hidalgo	3 161.8	3 920	67.1	2.0	3.8	0.5	2.9	3 738.4	4 635	3 891	1 752	51 385	69.0	30.3	0.7
Hill	125.8	3 583	69.5	0.2	4.8	0.9	4.9	161.8	4 607	91	71	2 179	28.9	70.2	0.9
Hockley	161.5	7 000	72.9	0.5	2.3	0.2	2.4	78.0	3 383	39	47	1 925	23.5	75.8	0.7
Hood	131.2	2 521	60.0	0.3	6.6	0.1	3.8	144.0	2 767	93	110	1 901	22.5	76.6	0.9
Hopkins	166.2	4 685	40.6	33.8	3.5	0.0	3.4	140.0	3 947	73	74	2 261	27.3	72.0	0.7
Houston	60.7	2 619	51.0	8.0	6.2	0.1	5.3	62.1	2 682	77	41	1 631	30.8	68.1	1.1
Howard	188.2	5 315	65.7	10.8	3.1	0.2	2.0	576.8	16 289	889	63	2 666	26.3	72.5	1.2
Hudspeth	19.7	5 893	49.6	0.3	7.1	0.2	7.3	2.3	676	356	0	288	47.9	51.0	1.1
Hunt	326.3	3 747	36.3	30.6	4.6	0.2	2.6	436.0	5 007	251	252	6 980	29.1	69.7	1.2
Hutchinson	107.0	4 880	47.7	23.7	4.7	0.1	2.3	102.9	4 693	68	45	1 491	15.1	84.0	0.9
Irion	11.6	7 395	70.4	0.2	3.8	0.0	4.9	6.1	3 865	0	0	121	20.1	78.8	1.1
Jack	45.5	5 070	74.2	0.0	3.7	0.0	2.4	80.2	8 928	18	16	576	15.5	83.6	0.8
Jackson	78.6	5 513	49.1	25.8	3.2	0.1	3.9	106.4	7 462	30	30	1 049	25.7	73.6	0.7
Jasper	96.3	2 680	59.7	2.7	8.6	0.0	5.7	89.0	2 478	77	72	2 032	28.6	70.6	0.8
Jeff Davis	9.6	4 176	59.9	0.4	3.0	0.1	0.2	0.3	132	26	0	220	37.9	60.6	1.5
Jefferson	1 153.5	4 581	41.4	4.2	7.0	0.6	5.6	5 050.2	20 055	1 868	715	15 816	50.8	48.6	0.6
Jim Hogg	22.0	4 186	44.7	0.9	5.9	2.1	11.8	5.1	979	267	11	366	73.6	26.0	0.4
Jim Wells	136.5	3 268	62.9	0.3	5.4	0.2	3.5	108.5	2 599	76	108	2 203	57.8	41.7	0.6
Johnson	466.6	3 041	55.2	0.5	6.0	0.3	3.6	1 105.1	7 202	223	322	6 990	25.8	73.3	0.9
Jones	52.9	2 651	52.3	25.3	1.5	0.0	3.3	40.8	2 041	63	33	2 277	26.3	72.4	1.3
Karnes	43.7	2 867	55.3	6.6	2.9	0.5	5.2	10.2	671	57	25	1 629	38.9	60.4	0.7
Kaufman	387.6	3 631	51.9	6.6	4.1	0.3	7.0	686.1	6 427	179	229	6 251	31.8	67.5	0.7
Kendall	128.4	3 571	58.1	1.2	6.7	0.2	4.5	314.6	8 750	53	79	1 684	21.5	77.5	1.1
Kenedy	11.2	25 935	97.1	0.0	0.4	0.0	0.5	2.3	5 397	0	0	86	53.5	46.5	0.0
Kent	8.2	9 762	93.8	0.1	0.5	0.0	0.6	0.0	11	0	0	184	22.1	76.3	1.6
Kerr	109.6	2 202	53.6	0.5	9.0	0.7	3.7	92.9	1 865	494	102	2 701	24.7	74.3	1.0
Kimble	12.1	2 660	49.4	6.6	3.6	0.0	5.0	15.9	3 487	14	0	358	18.6	80.7	0.8
King	6.3	22 880	69.2	0.0	1.3	0.0	7.6	6.0	21 884	0	0	66	4.9	92.6	2.5
Kinney	13.4	3 722	44.0	4.4	9.1	0.6	3.6	2.9	792	151	0	296	40.8	58.5	0.7
Kleberg	174.6	5 453	30.3	33.2	3.9	0.0	12.4	115.3	3 599	933	410	3 949	53.2	46.0	0.8
Knox	18.2	4 797	47.6	28.6	3.0	0.3	3.7	1.1	293	28	0	413	26.8	72.1	1.1
Lamar	164.5	3 303	65.4	1.9	5.1	1.8	4.5	148.6	2 982	149	102	2 957	28.6	70.5	0.9
Lamb	58.4	4 171	54.5	18.7	5.0	0.0	4.5	16.0	1 139	37	28	971	25.5	73.9	0.6
Lampasas	51.3	2 552	61.5	0.3	7.0	0.3	5.8	67.4	3 353	42	41	993	24.9	74.0	1.0
La Salle	18.2	2 554	68.9	0.1	1.4	0.3	5.5	31.9	4 493	116	12	641	59.2	40.2	0.6
Lavaca	68.8	3 532	36.2	22.8	5.2	0.2	7.3	31.6	1 625	57	40	934	22.7	76.5	0.7
Lee	48.0	2 889	56.5	0.5	6.1	0.7	6.6	75.0	4 518	22	34	1 224	31.4	67.6	1.0
Leon	49.2	2 929	78.9	0.0	2.9	0.1	4.5	50.5	3 005	46	35	829	20.1	79.1	0.8
Liberty	200.4	2 617	61.0	0.6	5.8	0.5	5.2	218.2	2 850	109	152	4 297	27.7	71.4	0.9
Limestone	124.3	5 268	41.5	12.6	11.7	0.3	4.7	91.4	3 877	50	45	3 060	32.9	66.4	0.7
Lipscomb	21.7	6 247	73.2	0.5	3.5	0.1	5.7	7.8	2 241	19	0	377	12.3	87.0	0.6
Live Oak	41.2	3 535	63.8	0.2	3.3	0.0	5.5	61.8	5 297	256	23	592	23.4	74.1	0.8
Llano	64.4	3 376	59.1	0.1	6.5	0.0	4.8	33.0	1 727	28	40	801	23.4	75.6	1.0
Loving	1.8	25 817	0.0	0.0	11.2	0.0	10.5	0.0	0	0	0	20	15.2	84.8	0.0
Lubbock	1 336.0	4 675	34.3	32.4	4.8	0.0	2.2	2 306.4	8 071	1 273	639	27 091	31.3	68.0	0.8
Lynn	28.7	4 967	57.9	19.6	4.2	0.0	3.2	5.0	865	20	12	536	29.6	69.6	0.8
McCulloch	37.3	4 484	41.7	24.2	3.9	0.0	4.2	38.1	4 581	26	17	621	24.2	75.2	0.6
McLennan	1 142.6	4 787	41.4	2.5	5.0	0.6	1.6	11 590.0	48 553	2 631	575	14 264	37.7	61.6	0.8
McMullen	9.6	13 263	74.2	0.8	4.8	0.2	7.4	23.3	32 058	0	0	144	24.6	74.5	0.9
Madison	33.7	2 466	63.1	0.8	7.5	2.9	5.7	33.0	2 410	16	23	1 185	28.1	71.0	0.9
Marion	19.4	1 875	65.3	1.5	8.2	0.0	7.5	15.3	1 483	36	21	375	38.7	60.4	1.0
Martin	116.9	23 298	19.8	76.2	0.5	0.0	0.4	67.3	13 408	13	11	437	18.3	81.0	0.7

1. Based on the resident population estimated as of July 1 of the year shown. 2. © 2013 Election Data Services, Inc. All rights reserved.

Table B. States and Counties — Land Area and Population

STATE/ County code	CBSA code[1]	County type[2]	STATE County	Land area[3] (sq km) 2010	Total persons 2015	Rank	Per square kilometer	White	Black	American Indian, Alaska Native	Asian and Pacific Islander	Percent Hispanic or Latino[4]	Under 5 years	5 to 17 years	18 to 24 years	25 to 34 years	35 to 44 years	45 to 54 years
				1	2	3	4	5	6	7	8	9	10	11	12	13	14	15
			TEXAS—Cont'd															
48 319	...	9	Mason	2 406	4 032	2 901	1.7	75.0	0.9	0.7	0.4	23.7	4.1	16.1	6.4	8.4	9.9	12.4
48 321	13060	4	Matagorda	2 850	36 770	1 258	12.9	46.6	11.0	0.7	2.3	40.4	7.1	18.4	9.1	12.0	10.6	13.2
48 323	20580	5	Maverick	3 313	57 706	888	17.4	3.3	0.4	1.0	0.5	94.8	9.0	22.9	11.6	12.5	12.0	11.0
48 325	41700	1	Medina	3 433	48 417	1 012	14.1	45.6	2.5	0.7	1.0	50.9	5.5	18.4	10.3	11.9	11.6	14.0
48 327	...	8	Menard	2 336	2 164	3 034	0.9	62.4	1.6	0.5	0.5	35.3	4.8	12.9	6.3	8.6	7.6	13.3
48 329	33260	3	Midland	2 332	161 077	399	69.1	49.5	6.5	0.8	1.8	42.4	8.4	19.2	10.2	16.9	12.0	11.8
48 331	...	6	Milam	2 634	24 513	1 626	9.3	64.2	9.6	0.8	0.9	25.5	6.3	18.5	8.3	10.0	10.8	12.9
48 333	...	9	Mills	1 938	4 900	2 840	2.5	81.0	1.4	0.7	0.5	17.2	4.9	17.5	7.0	8.3	9.9	12.3
48 335	...	7	Mitchell	2 360	9 067	2 506	3.8	49.1	10.7	0.9	0.7	39.2	5.3	14.7	12.6	17.3	13.5	12.1
48 337	...	6	Montague	2 411	19 262	1 861	8.0	87.5	1.0	1.5	0.6	10.5	6.0	17.0	7.1	10.8	10.6	13.4
48 339	26420	1	Montgomery	2 698	537 559	124	199.2	69.9	5.0	0.8	3.2	22.5	6.8	20.0	8.5	12.6	13.8	14.1
48 341	20300	6	Moore	2 330	22 255	1 717	9.6	35.4	2.7	0.9	8.7	52.5	9.5	21.8	10.4	13.8	12.1	11.8
48 343	...	6	Morris	653	12 516	2 260	19.2	67.2	23.7	1.3	0.9	9.2	6.3	16.6	8.1	11.3	10.7	11.8
48 345	...	8	Motley	2 563	1 148	3 102	0.4	80.0	2.1	1.0	0.7	16.5	3.7	16.2	5.6	10.2	10.4	10.9
48 347	34860	5	Nacogdoches	2 452	65 664	806	26.8	61.6	18.5	0.9	1.9	18.6	7.2	16.3	20.1	11.8	9.8	10.8
48 349	18620	4	Navarro	2 615	48 323	1 015	18.5	59.4	14.1	0.8	1.8	25.6	7.3	18.9	9.1	11.4	11.6	13.1
48 351	13140	8	Newton	2 418	13 986	2 165	5.8	75.1	20.5	1.3	0.9	3.6	5.6	16.1	9.3	11.4	11.7	14.2
48 353	45020	6	Nolan	2 362	15 107	2 091	6.4	58.6	5.1	0.7	0.7	35.9	6.6	19.2	9.3	11.9	11.2	12.0
48 355	18580	2	Nueces	2 172	359 715	190	165.6	31.7	3.9	0.6	2.3	62.3	6.8	18.5	10.3	14.6	12.3	12.5
48 357	...	7	Ochiltree	2 377	10 747	2 374	4.5	46.8	0.9	0.9	0.9	51.7	8.9	22.6	9.6	13.5	12.8	12.1
48 359	11100	8	Oldham	3 886	2 069	3 043	0.5	79.9	3.9	1.4	1.6	14.6	4.0	24.1	6.8	11.5	12.9	13.3
48 361	13140	2	Orange	864	84 260	671	97.5	82.8	9.1	1.1	1.4	6.9	6.7	18.0	8.8	12.6	12.2	13.6
48 363	33420	6	Palo Pinto	2 465	27 895	1 493	11.3	76.9	2.9	1.0	0.9	19.9	6.6	17.7	8.5	11.0	11.1	13.1
48 365	...	6	Panola	2 077	23 766	1 651	11.4	73.9	16.2	0.9	0.7	9.1	6.4	17.8	8.8	11.9	11.7	12.4
48 367	19100	1	Parker	2 340	126 042	496	53.9	86.1	1.9	1.4	1.0	11.4	5.7	18.8	8.5	11.2	12.4	15.1
48 369	...	7	Parmer	2 281	9 749	2 454	4.3	36.3	1.4	0.4	0.4	62.2	8.2	20.9	10.2	13.1	11.1	12.7
48 371	...	7	Pecos	12 338	16 203	2 030	1.3	27.0	3.9	0.7	1.3	67.6	7.6	16.9	9.0	15.5	13.6	13.8
48 373	...	6	Polk	2 738	46 972	1 033	17.2	71.9	11.5	2.3	0.9	14.4	5.6	14.9	8.1	11.6	11.6	13.3
48 375	11100	3	Potter	2 353	121 802	509	51.8	47.5	10.4	1.0	5.0	37.2	8.3	19.2	9.5	15.4	12.6	12.4
48 377	...	7	Presidio	9 985	6 876	2 684	0.7	14.3	1.2	0.6	1.6	82.0	7.1	18.9	8.9	10.3	11.1	11.5
48 379	...	8	Rains	594	11 161	2 346	18.8	87.4	3.2	1.5	1.1	8.2	5.0	15.2	6.7	9.5	10.4	13.7
48 381	11100	3	Randall	2 361	130 269	481	55.2	75.2	3.3	1.0	2.0	19.5	6.6	17.7	10.4	14.8	12.4	12.1
48 383	...	6	Reagan	3 044	3 792	2 919	1.2	31.2	2.9	0.5	0.6	66.0	8.4	21.9	9.2	13.6	11.8	13.4
48 385	...	9	Real	1 811	3 307	2 953	1.8	71.2	1.2	1.7	0.8	26.8	5.2	12.0	7.3	7.8	9.1	12.5
48 387	...	6	Red River	2 685	12 455	2 264	4.6	74.3	17.6	1.7	0.5	7.2	5.2	15.0	7.5	10.3	10.7	13.5
48 389	37780	7	Reeves	6 826	14 732	2 121	2.2	19.3	5.1	0.3	1.1	74.2	6.0	16.5	12.4	16.1	15.0	12.4
48 391	...	6	Refugio	1 995	7 289	2 647	3.7	43.4	6.2	0.8	0.8	49.8	6.0	17.1	8.8	10.3	10.7	13.0
48 393	...	9	Roberts	2 393	916	3 111	0.4	88.9	0.8	1.3	0.9	11.0	4.2	20.5	6.0	13.1	10.1	14.2
48 395	17780	3	Robertson	2 216	16 659	2 001	7.5	59.7	20.3	0.8	1.0	19.8	6.7	17.7	8.5	11.0	10.8	12.8
48 397	19100	1	Rockwall	329	90 861	639	276.2	74.1	6.4	0.9	3.4	17.0	6.1	21.6	7.9	11.2	15.1	14.9
48 399	...	6	Runnels	2 722	10 551	2 391	3.9	63.0	2.5	0.8	0.7	33.9	5.5	18.6	7.6	11.1	10.2	12.8
48 401	30980	3	Rusk	2 393	53 070	942	22.2	66.2	18.2	0.9	0.8	16.3	6.5	16.6	9.1	13.6	12.8	13.5
48 403	...	9	Sabine	1 273	10 368	2 401	8.1	87.5	8.0	1.1	0.6	4.3	4.3	14.3	6.5	8.3	8.7	13.0
48 405	...	9	San Augustine	1 374	8 473	2 559	6.2	69.7	23.1	0.7	0.6	7.4	6.0	14.4	7.1	9.2	9.4	13.3
48 407	...	1	San Jacinto	1 474	27 413	1 515	18.6	76.3	10.5	1.2	0.8	12.7	5.5	16.9	7.8	9.8	10.8	13.4
48 409	18580	2	San Patricio	1 796	67 357	788	37.5	41.0	2.0	0.7	1.3	56.0	7.1	20.2	9.4	13.0	12.1	12.6
48 411	...	7	San Saba	2 940	5 901	2 763	2.0	65.5	2.4	1.0	0.4	28.0	5.8	15.1	9.2	12.7	8.7	11.5
48 413	...	8	Schleicher	3 395	3 211	2 957	0.9	45.9	1.7	0.4	0.4	52.2	5.8	23.4	7.1	13.4	10.6	11.9
48 415	43660	7	Scurry	2 345	17 615	1 940	7.5	55.1	5.0	0.6	0.7	39.3	7.5	18.0	10.1	13.9	12.2	12.7
48 417	...	8	Shackelford	2 368	3 350	2 949	1.4	85.7	1.6	0.7	0.8	11.6	5.7	17.8	8.0	9.8	11.2	14.3
48 419	...	6	Shelby	2 061	25 402	1 593	12.3	63.5	17.5	0.6	1.1	18.0	7.2	19.2	8.5	11.8	11.9	12.9
48 421	...	9	Sherman	2 391	3 072	2 967	1.3	56.2	1.4	0.9	0.4	42.2	7.0	20.8	9.4	11.1	12.2	14.3
48 423	46340	3	Smith	2 387	222 936	292	93.4	61.6	18.0	0.7	1.9	18.6	7.0	17.9	10.2	13.4	11.8	12.2
48 425	19100	8	Somervell	483	8 739	2 534	18.1	78.5	1.4	1.4	1.1	19.5	5.1	18.4	8.5	10.3	11.7	13.9
48 427	40100	4	Starr	3 168	63 795	821	20.1	3.8	0.2	0.1	0.3	95.5	10.4	22.7	11.6	12.7	12.2	10.8
48 429	...	7	Stephens	2 322	9 440	2 472	4.1	73.9	2.6	0.9	0.6	23.0	5.4	16.9	9.5	12.7	10.8	12.7
48 431	...	8	Sterling	2 392	1 352	3 091	0.6	59.5	2.6	1.4	0.2	37.6	5.5	21.2	7.2	13.8	10.7	12.2
48 433	...	8	Stonewall	2 373	1 410	3 085	0.6	80.0	3.7	1.1	1.3	15.7	5.5	16.9	5.6	9.3	9.6	13.1
48 435	...	7	Sutton	3 766	3 913	2 909	1.0	38.5	0.5	0.2	0.4	60.8	7.8	17.7	9.0	11.8	11.6	13.5
48 437	...	6	Swisher	2 306	7 533	2 632	3.3	49.6	7.9	0.9	0.3	42.1	6.8	18.6	9.3	13.2	10.4	12.1
48 439	19100	1	Tarrant	2 237	1 982 498	15	886.2	50.9	16.2	0.9	6.0	27.8	7.3	19.8	9.5	14.8	13.9	12.3
48 441	10180	3	Taylor	2 371	136 051	465	57.4	67.1	8.0	0.9	2.6	23.6	7.3	17.3	14.8	14.4	10.5	11.2
48 443	...	9	Terrell	6 107	837	3 114	0.1	48.5	1.7	1.0	2.7	50.7	5.8	14.2	7.7	12.2	13.3	10.5
48 445	...	6	Terry	2 302	12 739	2 247	5.5	41.7	4.6	0.5	0.5	53.0	7.9	19.0	9.7	14.4	10.9	12.3
48 447	...	9	Throckmorton	2 363	1 579	3 076	0.7	85.7	1.2	1.2	0.6	11.8	4.7	16.8	6.9	10.4	9.0	13.4
48 449	34420	7	Titus	1 052	32 623	1 367	31.0	47.6	9.9	0.7	1.1	41.6	8.0	21.1	10.2	12.1	12.4	12.3

1. CBSA = Core Based Statistical Area. See Appendix A for explanation. See Appendix B for list of metropolitan areas with component counties.   2. County type code from the Economic Research Service of USDA Rural-Urban Continuum Codes. See Appendix A for definition.   3. Dry land or land partially or temporarily covered by water.   4. May be of any race.

Table B. States and Counties — Population and Households

	Population, 2014 (cont.)				Population change and components of change, 2000–2015							Households, 2010–2014				
	Age (percent) (cont.)				Total persons		Percent change		Components of change, 2010–2015					Percent		
STATE County	55 to 64 years	65 to 74 years	75 years and over	Percent female	2000	2010	2000–2010	2010–2015	Births	Deaths	Net migration	Number	Persons per house-hold	Family house-holds	Female family house-holder[1]	One per-son
	16	17	18	19	20	21	22	23	24	25	26	27	28	29	30	31
TEXAS—Cont'd																
Mason	15.5	15.8	11.6	50.3	3 738	4 012	7.3	0.5	194	233	65	1 678	2.42	68.8	6.9	28.2
Matagorda	13.8	9.1	6.8	50.2	37 957	36 702	-3.3	0.2	2 740	1 855	-757	13 143	2.75	69.1	15.6	28.3
Maverick	9.5	6.5	4.9	50.6	47 297	54 258	14.7	6.4	5 624	1 868	-341	16 091	3.43	80.9	20.0	17.9
Medina	12.8	9.2	6.3	48.4	39 304	46 006	17.1	5.2	2 747	1 992	1 630	15 221	2.90	78.0	13.8	18.4
Menard	16.4	16.3	13.8	50.0	2 360	2 242	-5.0	-3.5	102	165	7	886	2.42	66.7	11.5	31.5
Midland	11.3	5.3	4.8	49.8	116 009	136 875	18.0	17.7	13 442	5 350	16 022	51 609	2.80	70.6	13.0	24.0
Milam	13.8	10.6	8.8	50.3	24 238	24 753	2.1	-1.0	1 606	1 446	-429	9 279	2.58	66.2	12.5	31.0
Mills	14.9	13.7	11.5	51.0	5 151	4 936	-4.2	-0.7	239	325	46	1 798	2.61	71.4	5.7	28.3
Mitchell	10.7	7.5	6.3	39.9	9 698	9 403	-3.0	-3.6	528	462	-384	2 690	2.53	70.6	10.4	26.3
Montague	13.8	12.1	9.4	50.8	19 117	19 720	3.2	-2.3	1 206	1 402	-203	8 090	2.38	67.7	10.2	28.6
Montgomery	12.2	7.6	4.4	50.5	293 768	455 764	55.1	17.9	34 609	16 798	62 072	168 279	2.88	73.9	10.5	21.5
Moore	10.4	5.8	4.4	47.9	20 121	21 904	8.9	1.6	2 196	682	-1 151	6 836	3.22	77.2	13.7	19.0
Morris	14.3	11.3	9.7	52.0	13 048	12 934	-0.9	-3.2	835	860	-398	4 967	2.54	74.1	15.7	24.7
Motley	14.5	15.8	12.7	48.4	1 426	1 210	-15.1	-5.1	48	88	-23	462	2.54	62.6	3.7	34.6
Nacogdoches	11.0	7.5	5.5	52.3	59 203	64 524	9.0	1.8	4 726	2 909	-769	23 708	2.52	63.8	13.6	29.9
Navarro	12.5	9.5	6.7	50.5	45 124	47 831	6.0	1.0	3 574	2 613	-523	17 660	2.67	72.5	15.9	22.7
Newton	14.0	10.8	6.8	48.4	15 072	14 445	-4.2	-3.2	734	854	-359	4 823	2.90	66.0	10.3	30.4
Nolan	12.8	9.5	7.4	49.7	15 802	15 217	-3.7	-0.5	1 077	923	-299	5 449	2.69	65.4	14.9	29.4
Nueces	12.0	7.5	5.5	50.7	313 645	340 223	8.5	5.7	25 457	14 356	8 777	125 458	2.72	68.7	17.5	24.6
Ochiltree	10.2	6.0	4.3	49.1	9 006	10 223	13.5	5.1	925	409	0	3 770	2.78	74.5	11.2	21.2
Oldham	13.4	8.1	5.8	48.9	2 185	2 052	-6.1	0.8	124	72	-28	643	2.49	72.9	9.3	25.5
Orange	13.1	8.6	6.5	50.5	84 966	81 837	-3.7	3.0	5 809	4 705	1 352	31 373	2.61	71.3	12.6	24.9
Palo Pinto	13.8	11.0	7.3	50.9	27 026	28 111	4.0	-0.8	1 935	1 649	-446	10 413	2.66	67.7	12.0	28.3
Panola	14.1	9.6	7.3	50.5	22 756	23 796	4.6	-0.1	1 562	1 415	-180	8 979	2.61	70.0	14.0	26.1
Parker	13.6	9.3	5.5	50.0	88 495	116 927	32.1	7.8	6 922	5 131	7 052	42 887	2.72	74.6	8.6	21.4
Parmer	11.1	6.9	5.8	48.3	10 016	10 269	2.5	-5.1	796	349	-945	3 278	3.05	76.4	12.3	17.8
Pecos	11.2	7.1	5.3	43.3	16 809	15 507	-7.7	4.5	1 216	577	97	4 546	2.96	68.5	10.3	29.2
Polk	15.0	12.9	7.0	46.4	41 133	45 413	10.4	3.4	2 668	3 203	2 137	17 195	2.42	72.5	16.0	24.6
Potter	11.0	6.4	5.2	48.7	113 546	121 073	6.6	0.6	10 834	6 026	-4 117	43 002	2.70	64.1	16.3	30.7
Presidio	11.2	11.2	9.8	50.1	7 304	7 817	7.0	-12.0	629	238	-1 352	2 646	2.82	69.3	13.1	28.4
Rains	15.9	14.5	9.1	50.0	9 139	10 914	19.4	2.3	527	639	393	4 188	2.60	72.1	12.5	25.0
Randall	12.4	7.8	5.8	50.8	104 312	120 725	15.7	7.9	8 717	5 116	5 875	48 942	2.51	68.3	10.4	25.4
Reagan	11.4	5.5	4.7	47.7	3 326	3 367	1.2	12.6	348	113	190	1 200	2.89	79.3	9.5	17.3
Real	17.5	16.7	11.8	50.6	3 047	3 309	8.6	-0.1	172	265	98	1 208	2.70	64.7	14.4	23.2
Red River	15.0	12.9	10.0	51.7	14 314	12 864	-10.1	-3.2	755	954	-215	5 144	2.41	64.8	13.1	32.4
Reeves	9.4	6.7	5.3	39.9	13 137	13 783	4.9	6.9	942	515	516	3 705	3.09	66.3	14.3	28.4
Refugio	13.4	11.3	9.3	50.5	7 828	7 383	-5.7	-1.3	442	401	-99	2 771	2.56	71.2	16.1	25.2
Roberts	13.1	12.5	6.1	50.8	887	929	4.7	-1.4	53	48	-15	348	2.66	79.9	4.9	20.1
Robertson	14.0	10.5	8.0	50.5	16 000	16 622	3.9	0.2	1 074	948	-48	6 002	2.72	70.3	17.5	27.2
Rockwall	11.4	7.2	4.6	51.0	43 080	78 337	81.8	16.0	5 124	2 575	9 850	27 733	2.98	81.8	11.0	14.8
Runnels	13.6	10.9	9.7	50.0	11 495	10 501	-8.6	0.5	572	710	170	3 739	2.73	74.9	14.7	23.4
Rusk	12.8	8.7	6.4	47.1	47 372	53 304	12.5	-0.4	3 415	2 813	-824	17 794	2.77	70.5	12.7	26.4
Sabine	16.3	17.3	11.3	50.7	10 469	10 835	3.5	-4.3	488	819	-118	3 965	2.63	63.4	9.6	33.2
San Augustine	15.4	13.9	11.4	51.3	8 946	8 864	-0.9	-4.4	535	718	-193	3 117	2.73	61.0	12.4	35.1
San Jacinto	15.9	12.3	7.7	49.6	22 246	26 378	18.6	3.9	1 466	1 425	1 049	9 285	2.87	78.2	12.6	18.8
San Patricio	11.3	8.4	5.8	49.8	67 138	64 807	-3.5	3.9	4 967	3 149	685	22 621	2.86	75.0	14.9	21.1
San Saba	14.2	13.1	9.7	47.7	6 186	6 131	-0.9	-3.8	333	347	-217	2 098	2.53	61.9	9.1	32.6
Schleicher	12.7	9.2	5.9	48.9	2 935	3 461	17.9	-7.2	199	118	-343	1 028	3.18	75.6	16.1	22.4
Scurry	11.9	7.0	6.7	46.0	16 361	16 921	3.4	4.1	1 354	907	246	5 894	2.60	71.4	11.7	25.8
Shackelford	14.7	9.9	8.6	51.2	3 302	3 378	2.3	-0.8	177	159	-38	1 360	2.44	70.1	8.7	27.5
Shelby	12.5	9.2	7.0	50.5	25 224	25 448	0.9	-0.2	1 898	1 476	-428	9 564	2.66	66.9	14.8	29.7
Sherman	11.3	7.7	6.3	47.7	3 186	3 034	-4.8	1.3	212	122	-42	1 007	2.99	75.4	7.8	22.9
Smith	12.0	8.6	6.9	51.7	174 706	209 721	20.0	6.3	15 984	10 232	7 184	79 089	2.65	68.2	13.6	26.8
Somervell	13.9	10.7	7.4	50.7	6 809	8 490	24.7	2.9	468	445	202	3 265	2.53	74.0	10.2	23.5
Starr	8.3	6.4	4.9	51.4	53 597	60 968	13.8	4.6	7 194	1 986	-2 436	16 073	3.82	83.1	23.2	15.4
Stephens	12.9	10.5	8.5	49.7	9 674	9 630	-0.5	-2.0	567	575	-179	3 469	2.54	70.3	10.5	28.2
Sterling	12.8	8.6	8.1	47.8	1 393	1 143	-17.9	18.3	81	79	203	475	2.78	77.5	10.3	20.8
Stonewall	14.3	11.0	14.8	51.9	1 693	1 490	-12.0	-5.4	66	107	-51	588	2.31	66.2	5.1	32.3
Sutton	12.6	9.3	6.8	49.7	4 077	4 128	1.3	-5.2	277	161	-341	1 458	2.72	76.4	10.8	19.5
Swisher	11.6	9.2	8.9	47.7	8 378	7 854	-6.3	-4.1	577	381	-485	2 664	2.69	71.5	8.0	25.1
Tarrant	10.9	6.2	4.1	51.1	1 446 219	1 809 531	25.1	9.6	146 261	60 862	85 886	667 362	2.79	69.1	14.3	25.7
Taylor	10.6	7.4	6.5	51.1	126 555	131 510	3.9	3.5	10 664	6 655	432	49 482	2.57	66.2	13.2	27.1
Terrell	13.4	12.8	10.1	46.8	1 081	984	-9.0	-14.9	46	55	-140	407	1.99	55.8	7.6	36.6
Terry	11.2	7.8	6.7	47.2	12 761	12 651	-0.9	0.7	1 033	635	-295	3 985	2.90	68.9	17.4	27.6
Throckmorton	13.6	12.6	12.7	51.0	1 850	1 641	-11.3	-3.8	88	93	-50	722	2.16	62.6	8.2	36.6
Titus	10.7	7.6	5.6	50.5	28 118	32 334	15.0	0.9	2 589	1 353	-958	10 532	3.05	74.7	13.0	22.0

1. No spouse present.

Table B. States and Counties — **Population, Vital Statistics, Medicare, and Crime**

STATE County	Persons in group quarters, 2015	Daytime population, 2010–2014 Number	Employment/residence ratio	Births, 2015 Total	Rate[1]	Deaths, 2015 Number	Rate[1]	Persons under 65 with no health insurance, 2014 Number	Percent	Medicare, 2015 Total Beneficiaries	Enrolled in Original Medicare	Enrolled in Medicare Advantage	Serious crimes known to police,[2] 2014 Total Number	Rate[3]
	32	33	34	35	36	37	38	39	40	41	42	43	44	45
TEXAS—Cont'd														
Mason	3	3 867	0.90	37	9.1	42	10.4	1 002	34.0	1 086	904	182	77	1 839
Matagorda	341	35 560	0.93	525	14.3	353	9.6	6 683	22.0	6 422	4 821	1 601	1 220	3 313
Maverick	996	53 225	0.87	1 103	19.2	364	6.3	15 151	30.7	8 684	5 821	2 863	1 355	2 389
Medina	2 383	39 802	0.62	548	11.4	403	8.4	7 702	20.1	7 141	4 524	2 617	652	1 390
Menard	38	2 188	0.99	24	11.1	22	10.2	466	31.5	610	518	92	15	700
Midland	1 647	157 358	1.15	2 834	17.9	1 035	6.5	26 465	19.1	16 076	12 974	3 102	4 583	2 929
Milam	406	22 359	0.78	316	13.0	258	10.6	4 214	21.8	5 236	3 244	1 992	546	2 255
Mills	146	4 720	0.91	49	10.0	60	12.3	1 048	29.3	1 185	787	398	31	629
Mitchell	2 079	8 978	0.90	104	11.5	67	7.4	1 317	22.5	1 391	1 133	258	198	2 091
Montague	271	17 950	0.80	226	11.7	267	13.8	3 504	23.1	4 833	4 132	701	481	2 590
Montgomery	3 439	435 866	0.77	7 065	13.4	3 575	6.8	77 042	17.0	64 354	40 184	24 170	9 493	1 849
Moore	135	22 916	1.07	430	19.3	127	5.7	5 098	25.8	2 197	1 893	304	470	2 301
Morris	146	12 694	0.98	160	12.7	149	11.8	2 079	20.8	3 248	2 233	1 015	358	2 774
Motley	0	1 150	0.95	7	6.1	15	13.0	235	28.6	331	262	69	13	1 082
Nacogdoches	4 971	64 749	0.98	883	13.5	563	8.6	13 013	25.0	10 047	7 932	2 115	1 884	2 855
Navarro	708	46 964	0.94	682	14.2	527	10.9	9 484	23.8	9 562	7 648	1 914	1 759	3 751
Newton	728	12 164	0.56	141	10.0	178	12.7	2 048	18.7	2 495	1 825	670	81	572
Nolan	409	15 600	1.08	223	14.8	173	11.5	2 536	20.7	2 971	2 413	558	382	2 530
Nueces	6 087	357 890	1.06	5 046	14.1	2 769	7.7	63 245	20.7	51 892	25 832	26 060	17 671	4 940
Ochiltree	51	11 521	1.21	182	17.0	72	6.7	2 540	26.5	1 135	1 030	105	86	778
Oldham	278	2 291	1.30	30	14.5	8	3.9	241	15.8	396	325	71	20	939
Orange	641	75 414	0.79	1 178	14.0	887	10.6	11 269	16.0	15 639	10 145	5 494	2 289	2 731
Palo Pinto	265	26 511	0.87	380	13.6	341	12.2	6 079	26.7	5 201	4 411	790	759	2 707
Panola	401	24 014	1.01	306	12.9	243	10.2	3 833	19.7	4 240	3 375	865	864	3 590
Parker	1 148	99 807	0.63	1 357	10.9	1 010	8.1	17 059	16.5	17 442	13 254	4 188	2 103	1 731
Parmer	77	11 265	1.25	159	16.2	35	3.6	2 632	30.7	1 281	1 170	111	92	924
Pecos	2 090	16 388	1.11	254	15.8	93	5.8	2 658	22.4	2 084	1 660	424	391	2 467
Polk	4 409	44 639	0.93	531	11.4	632	13.6	7 852	23.8	16 728	12 268	4 460	1 236	2 675
Potter	7 138	145 669	1.45	2 044	16.7	1 108	9.1	25 444	25.0	30 262	23 871	6 391	6 026	4 914
Presidio	0	7 341	0.95	121	17.4	53	7.6	1 785	32.5	1 626	1 348	278	27	381
Rains	69	9 163	0.59	102	9.2	110	9.9	2 060	24.5	2 567	2 062	505	128	1 145
Randall	2 572	99 877	0.60	1 725	13.3	990	7.6	17 071	15.7	4 872	3 926	946	5 429	4 216
Reagan	30	4 187	1.41	91	24.1	15	4.0	808	24.1	395	342	53	0	0
Real	72	3 255	0.89	38	11.4	49	14.7	703	29.6	1 070	904	166	23	680
Red River	183	10 753	0.58	160	12.8	180	14.4	2 306	24.1	3 160	2 705	455	304	2 438
Reeves	3 134	15 320	1.28	202	13.9	92	6.3	2 305	24.2	1 928	1 654	274	285	2 020
Refugio	115	6 921	0.88	85	11.7	35	4.8	1 112	19.4	1 674	1 305	369	117	1 593
Roberts	0	779	0.64	10	10.9	6	6.5	86	11.4	134	101	33	14	1 716
Robertson	183	15 789	0.88	207	12.5	162	9.8	3 285	24.6	3 035	2 337	698	383	2 310
Rockwall	758	73 589	0.75	1 016	11.4	507	5.7	10 706	13.9	10 483	7 848	2 635	1 155	1 320
Runnels	185	9 868	0.86	103	9.8	116	11.1	1 966	24.0	2 507	2 222	285	189	1 829
Rusk	4 844	49 118	0.76	618	11.6	541	10.2	8 904	21.9	7 517	5 704	1 813	1 369	2 647
Sabine	101	10 090	0.83	101	9.8	127	12.3	1 686	22.8	3 787	2 982	805	162	1 705
San Augustine	225	8 374	0.83	100	11.7	134	15.7	1 378	21.6	2 093	1 556	537	198	2 246
San Jacinto	129	20 672	0.37	297	10.9	256	9.4	4 822	22.3	4 021	2 536	1 485	613	2 258
San Patricio	662	58 257	0.74	1 004	15.0	535	8.0	11 127	19.6	12 280	6 252	6 028	2 186	3 261
San Saba	627	5 800	0.96	59	10.1	59	10.1	1 206	30.2	1 263	965	298	55	913
Schleicher	2	3 146	0.91	39	12.2	16	5.0	637	23.8	476	394	82	16	506
Scurry	1 712	17 619	1.07	261	14.9	167	9.6	2 813	21.0	2 638	2 150	488	644	3 676
Shackelford	33	3 367	1.01	35	10.5	30	9.0	562	20.7	622	525	97	31	911
Shelby	158	24 932	0.93	373	14.6	301	11.8	5 862	27.5	4 884	3 793	1 091	584	2 345
Sherman	24	2 875	0.87	45	14.6	10	3.3	740	28.1	445	399	46	35	1 117
Smith	5 059	220 534	1.06	3 147	14.2	1 965	8.9	39 070	21.5	40 238	30 782	9 456	7 096	3 269
Somervell	294	9 441	1.24	95	10.9	91	10.5	1 263	17.8	1 405	1 012	393	72	822
Starr	818	59 313	0.86	1 378	21.7	363	5.7	17 767	32.4	8 663	6 766	1 897	1 140	1 821
Stephens	638	9 265	0.94	115	12.2	88	9.4	1 827	26.2	1 751	1 424	327	139	1 506
Sterling	35	1 413	1.09	22	16.3	19	14.1	213	19.4	224	182	42	6	480
Stonewall	27	1 424	1.03	14	10.0	13	9.3	241	23.1	365	321	44	5	350
Sutton	13	4 177	1.10	53	13.4	21	5.3	769	23.2	641	607	34	23	572
Swisher	647	7 216	0.79	111	14.7	65	8.6	1 347	24.1	1 522	1 330	192	150	1 926
Tarrant	22 485	1 867 376	0.98	28 572	14.5	12 277	6.2	341 744	19.8	212 526	121 614	90 912	71 745	3 679
Taylor	4 808	137 237	1.06	2 041	15.1	1 343	9.9	21 335	18.9	22 992	18 266	4 726	6 089	4 488
Terrell	0	827	1.05	2	2.3	8	9.2	191	26.7	219	171	48	14	1 582
Terry	1 170	12 142	0.89	202	15.8	129	10.1	2 502	25.4	1 989	1 388	601	324	2 520
Throckmorton	13	1 521	0.91	20	12.5	17	10.6	318	26.6	371	321	50	5	312
Titus	492	35 771	1.24	484	14.9	242	7.4	7 322	26.3	4 847	3 794	1 053	952	2 897

1. Per 1,000 estimated resident population.   2. Data for serious crimes have not been adjusted for underreporting; this may affect comparability between geographic areas and over time.
3. Per 100,000 population estimated by the FBI.

Table B. States and Counties — Crime, Education, Money Income, and Poverty

STATE County	Serious crimes known to police, 2014 (cont.)[1] Rate[2] Violent	Property	Education — School enrollment and attainment, 2010–2014 — Enrollment[3] Total	Percent private	Attainment[4] (percent) High school graduate or less	Bachelor's degree or more	Local government expenditures[5] 2012–2013 Total current spending (mil dol)	Current spending per student (dollars)	Money income, 2010–2014 Per capita income[6] (dollars)	Households Median income (dollars)	Mean income (dollars)	Percent with income of $200,000 or more	Income and poverty, 2014 Median household income (dollars)	Percent below poverty level All persons	Children under 18 years	Children 5 to 17 years in families
	46	47	48	49	50	51	52	53	54	55	56	57	58	59	60	61
TEXAS—Cont'd																
Mason	96	1 743	597	16.6	47.6	24.1	7.2	9 999	27 512	45 536	63 184	3.9	42 820	14.8	25.1	22.4
Matagorda	326	2 987	8 608	8.9	59.0	14.9	69.8	9 964	22 072	40 410	57 392	2.2	41 587	22.1	30.1	29.7
Maverick	178	2 211	17 753	4.1	64.8	12.1	125.5	8 318	14 516	32 536	47 100	1.4	32 248	26.5	35.5	35.7
Medina	143	1 247	12 299	10.1	50.0	18.8	76.6	8 226	22 848	56 338	68 409	2.9	53 440	14.3	21.9	19.8
Menard	514	187	632	0.0	54.6	19.2	4.5	13 212	20 055	34 091	50 644	2.5	32 580	22.7	39.8	39.4
Midland	326	2 603	38 793	14.9	40.9	25.0	211.9	8 407	34 885	66 966	95 762	8.4	74 811	9.9	14.1	14.0
Milam	235	2 020	5 846	7.3	56.7	16.0	41.0	8 940	21 465	37 183	54 510	2.6	41 849	18.3	28.6	26.6
Mills	20	608	1 239	7.3	44.0	23.9	10.8	12 738	22 615	44 241	57 405	3.1	38 564	17.1	25.6	23.0
Mitchell	243	1 848	2 215	6.2	56.4	9.9	16.1	11 020	17 330	45 769	59 074	1.3	41 363	20.7	25.2	24.0
Montague	162	2 429	4 272	9.9	51.1	16.3	30.6	9 010	26 109	45 897	61 556	2.6	48 996	14.8	21.8	20.2
Montgomery	179	1 670	132 163	13.1	38.0	31.7	685.7	7 241	33 455	68 840	93 694	9.3	70 929	10.9	15.5	14.6
Moore	245	2 057	6 316	4.2	61.9	13.0	44.5	8 544	19 434	48 149	58 989	1.4	42 839	14.6	20.4	20.4
Morris	333	2 441	2 785	5.6	52.3	12.8	20.2	9 081	20 124	39 387	51 806	1.5	37 954	18.6	29.9	29.2
Motley	0	1 082	317	1.6	47.8	19.5	2.7	14 564	20 712	34 853	49 345	0.6	37 936	17.5	31.0	27.6
Nacogdoches	288	2 567	21 862	3.8	47.0	25.0	90.4	8 312	20 299	39 126	53 760	1.9	38 895	22.7	28.7	29.8
Navarro	354	3 397	12 298	4.9	53.6	16.7	79.5	8 141	20 491	40 976	55 472	1.8	43 091	20.3	31.8	29.2
Newton	64	508	2 939	6.9	63.2	6.9	20.3	9 970	20 509	36 890	53 635	2.4	39 135	20.2	29.9	27.4
Nolan	391	2 140	3 849	3.3	54.6	12.9	31.7	10 231	20 097	37 342	51 806	1.7	38 742	17.9	29.5	27.4
Nueces	646	4 294	92 810	8.2	47.0	20.4	518.7	8 418	24 875	49 368	66 423	3.1	51 222	16.8	23.1	21.2
Ochiltree	127	652	2 936	8.2	59.6	14.0	19.6	8 157	23 989	51 115	65 923	2.1	61 773	10.7	14.6	13.8
Oldham	141	798	662	4.8	36.5	30.3	13.5	15 021	23 377	51 250	74 091	5.0	54 458	15.6	32.9	26.5
Orange	307	2 425	19 880	7.7	52.6	13.8	126.2	8 283	24 938	48 766	64 961	2.4	48 834	16.0	22.1	20.3
Palo Pinto	175	2 532	5 926	6.8	55.5	15.9	44.5	8 494	23 503	41 370	60 656	3.1	40 862	18.6	26.0	25.4
Panola	349	3 241	5 438	6.8	52.6	11.4	39.7	10 050	25 326	51 794	63 545	2.4	48 822	15.5	21.5	19.8
Parker	125	1 606	29 748	13.4	38.0	25.6	157.2	8 126	30 934	64 979	84 267	5.8	67 655	9.9	14.8	13.6
Parmer	80	844	2 824	8.2	62.1	15.8	23.5	9 589	20 169	46 308	60 130	2.0	41 813	14.6	20.4	19.9
Pecos	366	2 101	3 301	4.1	66.0	11.5	31.6	10 309	19 974	49 421	60 921	1.0	44 817	17.8	21.6	21.8
Polk	331	2 343	9 234	8.5	58.0	12.1	62.5	8 951	20 225	39 412	53 400	1.9	41 401	18.5	30.5	29.6
Potter	622	4 292	32 869	7.3	51.5	15.1	306.3	8 160	19 967	37 758	54 086	1.8	38 224	21.5	30.2	29.8
Presidio	113	268	1 849	1.0	64.7	22.0	22.6	12 757	16 176	30 983	42 152	0.3	34 258	21.8	33.9	34.1
Rains	98	1 047	2 251	6.4	57.2	11.4	13.6	8 192	22 933	46 531	56 229	1.2	47 834	14.9	26.2	24.8
Randall	534	3 682	34 483	7.1	30.8	30.7	88.9	9 635	30 376	60 895	76 264	3.8	64 636	9.7	12.7	12.2
Reagan	0	0	942	5.2	70.0	11.0	9.9	11 166	23 814	52 692	66 353	4.3	62 376	11.2	13.0	12.8
Real	0	680	573	3.3	48.5	20.0	2.5	9 511	19 806	37 019	47 218	0.2	37 294	18.7	33.6	36.8
Red River	297	2 142	2 641	8.1	60.6	14.2	23.3	10 420	19 128	31 344	44 845	1.7	34 340	20.1	30.6	29.2
Reeves	390	1 631	2 864	3.0	65.9	10.6	25.7	10 538	18 099	44 950	57 068	2.2	39 006	24.8	27.3	25.3
Refugio	245	1 348	1 547	2.7	55.3	10.3	17.0	12 190	24 090	44 688	61 662	2.9	43 654	16.9	26.0	24.0
Roberts	245	1 471	222	3.6	34.9	34.3	2.9	13 391	35 797	73 182	93 927	6.3	69 424	7.3	10.3	9.2
Robertson	537	1 773	4 029	9.4	59.2	17.0	40.7	12 615	21 216	43 371	55 250	1.6	43 194	19.0	29.3	28.9
Rockwall	90	1 229	24 573	13.9	30.2	36.7	152.8	7 878	34 850	86 597	101 939	8.2	84 692	6.8	8.9	8.1
Runnels	135	1 693	2 484	3.0	61.2	13.7	20.5	9 892	20 081	38 684	52 480	1.6	38 607	18.1	26.8	24.2
Rusk	298	2 349	11 811	7.8	54.3	13.3	68.8	8 547	22 084	46 924	62 306	3.1	46 427	16.6	23.1	21.6
Sabine	358	1 347	1 955	3.0	60.2	12.2	14.4	9 111	18 626	33 951	46 614	1.9	35 701	19.0	30.3	27.6
San Augustine	250	1 997	1 684	6.8	64.9	10.0	9.0	10 917	18 177	29 293	43 377	1.7	32 826	23.9	37.7	37.5
San Jacinto	243	2 015	5 806	4.3	61.8	12.3	30.7	8 740	24 037	46 969	65 558	3.8	43 087	18.6	29.5	27.2
San Patricio	340	2 921	16 922	6.0	52.7	14.8	126.8	8 677	23 741	51 760	66 097	2.6	51 958	15.8	23.6	22.0
San Saba	149	763	1 271	6.1	51.8	13.5	10.0	10 209	19 595	38 065	47 031	1.7	38 000	20.3	32.9	32.1
Schleicher	0	506	945	4.6	54.8	20.4	6.3	10 699	23 074	44 643	62 172	3.8	50 361	13.6	19.2	16.4
Scurry	485	3 191	4 547	5.3	50.3	15.4	32.5	9 875	23 967	50 829	70 281	3.4	56 444	14.1	18.3	18.2
Shackelford	147	764	827	7.7	47.2	24.3	7.0	11 117	25 602	50 857	62 315	3.3	55 130	13.1	19.3	18.1
Shelby	333	2 012	5 969	5.4	59.5	13.8	53.1	9 379	21 084	36 250	53 984	2.8	35 772	22.0	31.8	31.5
Sherman	96	1 022	774	8.0	52.2	21.2	8.2	8 479	23 728	49 219	68 681	4.1	49 309	13.4	17.1	15.3
Smith	342	2 927	58 714	11.1	40.5	25.2	272.8	8 242	24 924	46 669	65 384	3.5	45 363	18.1	25.9	22.7
Somervell	69	754	2 295	3.5	41.1	27.0	19.3	11 415	26 708	51 190	68 508	5.7	51 733	12.1	19.9	17.3
Starr	271	1 549	19 241	2.3	75.0	9.6	167.6	9 519	11 935	25 906	40 552	0.7	26 699	35.4	44.4	43.9
Stephens	173	1 333	2 123	7.5	54.5	16.5	12.2	8 371	21 145	43 082	54 390	1.6	44 110	20.8	32.3	29.0
Sterling	240	240	278	2.2	52.7	26.6	3.3	12 333	19 762	50 509	54 285	2.1	59 854	11.8	18.3	16.3
Stonewall	0	350	328	1.5	57.3	17.7	3.1	12 071	23 895	42 321	58 059	5.1	42 780	15.5	21.7	19.7
Sutton	224	348	1 061	1.7	52.6	17.8	11.8	12 664	24 723	48 986	63 507	3.8	60 435	13.2	19.9	20.2
Swisher	295	1 631	1 789	6.6	58.8	15.6	16.2	10 205	18 046	37 833	49 103	1.0	37 527	20.9	28.9	27.0
Tarrant	400	3 279	537 691	13.7	39.1	29.7	2 726.9	7 941	28 541	57 727	78 103	5.2	58 127	15.2	21.7	20.4
Taylor	442	4 046	38 531	25.4	42.7	24.6	196.8	8 489	23 472	44 695	60 491	2.3	45 559	15.9	21.7	21.1
Terrell	113	1 469	115	3.5	56.4	16.9	2.9	25 284	31 894	40 781	60 287	2.2	39 503	18.1	24.9	24.0
Terry	257	2 264	3 480	4.1	61.2	12.8	24.2	10 090	22 211	39 494	63 443	3.1	38 752	21.2	29.0	28.1
Throckmorton	0	312	277	4.3	46.4	20.7	3.7	11 879	24 926	40 833	54 146	2.1	43 618	14.2	21.3	18.8
Titus	344	2 553	9 309	5.4	56.0	14.2	57.3	8 005	19 178	42 856	57 283	1.6	40 680	20.6	29.7	27.8

1. Data for serious crimes have not been adjusted for underreporting; this may affect comparability between geographic areas and over time.   2. Per 100,000 population estimated by the FBI.
3. All persons 3 years old and over enrolled in nursery school through college.   4. Persons 25 years old and over.   5. Elementary and secondary education expenditures.
6. Based on population estimated by the American Community Survey, 2010–2014.

Table B. States and Counties — **Personal Income**

STATE County	Personal income, 2014 Total (mil dol)	Percent change, 2013–2014	Per capita[1] Dollars	Per capita[1] Rank	Wages and salaries (mil dol)	Supplements to wages and salaries; employer contributions (mil dol) Pension and insurance	Government social insurance	Proprietors' income (mil dol)	Dividends, interest, and rent (mil dol)	Personal transfer receipts (mil dol)	Earnings, 2014 Total (mil dol)	Contributions for government social insurance (mil dol) From employee and self-employed	From employer
	62	63	64	65	66	67	68	69	70	71	72	73	74
TEXAS—Cont'd													
Mason	162	6.2	39 689	1 228	39	8	2	32	44	39	82	5	2
Matagorda	1 363	3.2	37 324	1 550	565	104	37	111	183	326	816	44	37
Maverick	1 454	5.7	25 490	3 047	570	131	40	119	127	481	861	48	40
Medina	1 699	4.9	35 478	1 860	355	67	22	131	283	381	575	34	22
Menard	72	8.0	33 538	2 190	14	3	1	11	16	24	29	2	1
Midland	15 032	9.7	96 463	11	6 574	732	414	5 501	2 175	854	13 220	595	414
Milam	904	4.6	37 276	1 558	279	43	18	128	120	255	468	27	18
Mills	173	8.2	35 472	1 862	47	9	3	21	40	53	80	5	3
Mitchell	290	0.0	31 964	2 441	105	24	6	26	40	72	162	8	6
Montague	961	7.3	49 513	413	247	38	16	178	155	207	479	26	16
Montgomery	28 983	7.7	55 849	203	8 744	1 090	578	2 541	4 224	2 997	12 953	692	578
Moore	833	10.5	37 604	1 511	457	89	30	176	77	122	752	32	30
Morris	482	2.0	37 831	1 479	234	37	17	70	58	150	358	20	17
Motley	42	2.0	36 247	1 735	11	2	1	9	8	11	23	1	1
Nacogdoches	2 112	6.1	32 337	2 399	811	154	54	280	351	538	1 299	65	54
Navarro	1 700	4.4	35 276	1 895	618	111	43	169	246	477	941	54	43
Newton	407	6.4	28 802	2 846	50	13	3	13	42	125	80	7	3
Nolan	551	4.3	36 501	1 687	258	45	17	49	87	153	369	21	17
Nueces	15 118	5.0	42 439	905	8 059	1 303	571	2 633	2 343	2 897	12 565	633	571
Ochiltree	652	14.2	60 573	123	320	39	20	237	84	54	615	25	20
Oldham	105	23.4	50 645	350	50	8	4	35	14	14	96	3	4
Orange	3 332	7.2	39 933	1 190	1 138	187	77	148	346	810	1 550	94	77
Palo Pinto	1 027	5.1	36 560	1 679	391	60	25	101	176	258	578	33	25
Panola	1 050	5.5	44 173	744	515	71	34	177	152	216	798	42	34
Parker	5 926	6.2	48 118	473	1 535	213	104	608	912	839	2 459	135	104
Parmer	464	18.4	46 800	535	205	35	15	176	43	63	431	12	15
Pecos	520	8.8	32 710	2 332	297	49	18	39	62	112	404	21	18
Polk	1 664	3.3	36 102	1 763	413	75	27	113	370	670	629	49	27
Potter	4 951	4.8	40 706	1 098	3 439	574	246	1 210	642	994	5 469	267	246
Presidio	228	-5.3	32 614	2 351	91	21	7	26	45	62	145	7	7
Rains	351	5.2	31 775	2 476	60	12	4	33	50	108	108	8	4
Randall	5 377	6.5	41 938	956	1 277	175	82	329	884	743	1 862	109	82
Reagan	222	8.3	59 221	143	135	18	9	30	22	23	192	9	9
Real	94	4.0	27 896	2 929	20	4	1	8	27	43	33	3	1
Red River	438	7.6	35 219	1 901	83	18	6	33	65	159	139	10	6
Reeves	391	11.1	27 247	2 965	172	34	11	40	54	103	257	13	11
Refugio	331	4.7	45 306	651	123	19	8	26	59	80	175	10	8
Roberts	42	7.2	45 578	632	7	2	0	4	12	5	13	1	0
Robertson	730	5.5	44 251	736	178	33	12	148	118	166	370	18	12
Rockwall	4 431	6.7	50 460	361	1 015	144	70	346	582	456	1 576	85	70
Runnels	377	1.5	36 152	1 754	116	22	8	37	56	109	183	11	8
Rusk	1 921	4.3	35 633	1 836	725	110	48	174	263	431	1 057	60	48
Sabine	355	4.5	34 318	2 059	79	16	6	28	65	145	129	10	6
San Augustine	280	5.4	32 516	2 368	56	13	4	38	43	118	111	7	4
San Jacinto	857	6.6	31 607	2 511	81	18	5	37	124	259	140	13	5
San Patricio	2 604	4.2	38 920	1 330	1 003	174	72	124	364	586	1 372	77	72
San Saba	195	7.5	34 718	1 980	51	11	3	29	40	58	95	5	3
Schleicher	141	12.1	44 732	701	52	8	3	16	19	24	80	4	3
Scurry	901	4.5	51 998	295	525	64	31	176	119	128	796	40	31
Shackelford	325	7.8	97 227	8	107	14	7	153	50	30	280	12	7
Shelby	1 023	9.1	40 083	1 164	330	56	23	225	123	259	634	30	23
Sherman	201	26.0	65 049	87	38	6	2	113	16	15	160	2	2
Smith	9 465	4.9	43 249	821	4 376	637	303	1 689	1 589	1 829	7 005	366	303
Somervell	356	4.6	40 991	1 062	249	47	16	34	57	71	346	18	16
Starr	1 461	5.2	23 215	3 095	459	126	31	116	120	550	732	40	31
Stephens	500	6.4	53 179	263	141	26	9	205	63	90	381	17	9
Sterling	72	10.8	53 564	252	30	6	2	4	25	10	42	2	2
Stonewall	73	11.2	52 132	290	27	5	2	8	17	18	42	2	2
Sutton	264	11.8	66 362	77	222	23	13	57	39	33	315	16	13
Swisher	313	15.7	41 310	1 026	69	15	4	121	36	64	210	6	4
Tarrant	89 814	5.7	46 169	582	44 883	6 204	3 161	13 057	13 606	11 363	67 305	3 428	3 161
Taylor	5 719	5.5	42 318	924	2 690	461	197	776	1 043	1 122	4 125	210	197
Terrell	51	8.0	55 079	212	22	5	2	2	15	10	30	2	2
Terry	431	-8.5	33 826	2 143	170	28	11	53	50	116	261	13	11
Throckmorton	84	11.3	51 935	298	21	4	1	20	13	19	47	2	1
Titus	1 013	6.0	31 171	2 560	562	109	40	112	126	253	822	42	40

1. Based on the resident population estimated as of July 1 of the year shown.

STATE County	Farm	Mining	Construction	Manu-facturing	Information: professional, scientific, technical services	Retail trade	Finance, insurance, real estate and leasing	Health care and social assistance	Govern-ment	Number	Rate[1]	Supplemental Security Income recipients, December 2014	Total	Percent change, 2010–2014
	75	76	77	78	79	80	81	82	83	84	85	86	87	88
TEXAS—Cont'd														
Mason	7.6	D	5.6	2.2	D	3.8	7.5	4.3	16.0	1 180	290	84	2 750	0.6
Matagorda	4.8	6.7	8.4	2.8	4.4	5.3	3.4	D	15.6	7 120	195	1 131	19 217	2.2
Maverick	1.1	1.0	3.6	3.8	2.6	9.6	2.7	D	40.7	10 040	176	3 728	18 142	3.9
Medina	1.8	9.4	9.2	1.0	4.5	9.2	5.2	D	26.4	8 820	184	1 151	18 157	0.9
Menard	20.6	8.8	D	D	D	8.4	6.3	D	28.8	645	300	61	1 704	0.1
Midland	0.0	56.7	3.8	3.9	4.6	3.2	3.8	2.7	4.6	19 215	123	2 362	59 511	9.5
Milam	4.5	3.3	17.6	12.9	2.3	5.0	4.2	11.2	13.1	5 855	241	817	11 384	0.7
Mills	7.5	D	6.7	4.6	D	13.3	4.5	12.8	20.6	1 305	267	119	2 852	0.2
Mitchell	0.0	25.4	2.4	1.7	D	6.5	D	2.5	38.2	1 550	171	225	4 053	-0.3
Montague	0.8	41.2	5.0	4.4	6.1	6.3	4.3	D	13.1	5 095	262	419	10 173	0.4
Montgomery	0.0	14.3	9.7	9.1	10.3	6.8	6.4	8.1	11.3	74 770	144	7 343	202 474	14.0
Moore	15.0	6.3	D	D	D	4.9	1.8	D	12.3	2 545	114	280	7 996	1.5
Morris	5.4	D	2.0	48.2	12.8	2.6	D	2.2	8.7	3 105	245	411	6 024	0.0
Motley	34.0	0.0	D	D	D	7.0	D	D	21.9	345	299	30	779	0.0
Nacogdoches	7.3	1.2	9.1	12.1	3.3	7.6	4.8	12.1	24.0	11 370	174	2 027	28 042	2.3
Navarro	-0.1	3.5	12.8	16.8	3.1	7.2	4.8	10.6	18.1	10 480	218	1 709	20 468	1.2
Newton	-2.7	D	3.4	6.7	D	7.7	D	11.8	35.0	2 810	199	586	7 171	0.4
Nolan	-0.5	12.1	6.9	13.9	3.3	8.6	3.7	D	23.3	3 240	214	571	7 103	-0.7
Nueces	0.8	14.5	11.6	7.4	5.9	5.7	4.7	11.4	16.2	58 785	165	12 978	147 925	4.9
Ochiltree	15.8	46.5	7.3	0.6	1.7	3.4	1.7	1.0	6.6	1 300	121	111	4 061	0.0
Oldham	39.8	D	21.0	D	D	1.0	D	D	16.0	470	227	30	846	0.6
Orange	-0.3	2.5	11.5	33.9	3.5	7.1	4.2	4.6	14.8	18 120	217	2 561	36 482	3.3
Palo Pinto	0.7	16.4	5.4	22.3	D	7.4	3.7	D	16.6	6 405	229	772	15 323	0.7
Panola	2.8	21.5	24.5	5.8	3.8	4.7	2.7	3.9	9.4	5 090	214	649	11 000	0.7
Parker	0.6	15.2	11.7	8.4	5.6	8.4	4.2	7.1	11.7	22 110	180	1 342	48 246	3.5
Parmer	45.7	D	D	D	1.0	1.6	D	D	9.3	1 450	147	148	3 795	-0.1
Pecos	1.8	22.7	6.1	0.4	D	6.5	3.5	2.4	27.4	2 310	145	389	5 604	0.3
Polk	-0.8	2.0	8.2	12.1	4.3	10.9	4.5	8.9	24.0	18 575	402	1 709	24 397	7.6
Potter	0.1	5.4	5.7	9.3	7.7	7.2	6.7	14.8	17.4	18 535	152	3 157	49 435	4.6
Presidio	19.9	D	D	D	D	5.5	2.0	D	49.1	1 725	245	659	3 832	0.2
Rains	0.0	D	14.2	5.3	D	12.2	D	D	20.5	2 920	265	257	5 298	0.6
Randall	6.3	1.5	9.6	5.1	6.1	10.3	4.5	7.8	12.1	20 120	156	1 243	53 919	4.5
Reagan	0.8	40.5	3.4	0.0	0.6	1.7	D	0.3	10.7	450	120	49	1 398	1.9
Real	0.4	D	10.2	3.7	D	10.2	D	12.8	25.1	1 245	371	141	2 601	0.1
Red River	11.2	3.9	9.9	9.8	2.2	4.6	5.5	12.7	22.7	3 570	286	513	6 865	0.6
Reeves	5.3	13.4	3.2	0.2	1.6	7.4	2.7	2.7	35.3	2 230	155	464	4 624	-0.3
Refugio	-0.5	37.9	12.3	0.1	D	5.2	4.0	D	21.0	1 815	249	234	3 738	0.3
Roberts	21.6	D	D	0.0	D	D	D	D	0.0	150	163	0	439	0.0
Robertson	8.5	22.4	13.9	1.4	2.1	4.5	2.7	3.3	14.3	3 680	224	658	8 587	1.2
Rockwall	-0.2	0.6	10.3	6.4	9.7	10.4	6.8	17.2	13.1	11 935	136	730	31 610	13.1
Runnels	3.0	5.1	12.3	19.3	D	5.8	3.6	7.0	21.6	2 650	255	329	5 272	-0.5
Rusk	3.0	20.1	13.8	7.7	D	5.0	3.8	5.9	11.9	9 925	186	1 236	21 378	0.9
Sabine	4.1	9.5	D	D	D	7.4	3.8	11.1	19.1	3 640	352	332	8 028	0.5
San Augustine	21.0	D	5.7	2.5	2.0	6.5	2.8	11.4	18.6	2 420	282	450	5 356	0.3
San Jacinto	-3.8	1.9	10.9	5.5	7.5	6.4	4.7	5.0	31.6	6 795	251	1 225	13 142	-0.3
San Patricio	1.3	7.6	20.1	12.2	5.0	5.9	2.2	4.4	25.1	12 885	193	2 477	27 230	2.7
San Saba	3.7	5.0	3.6	5.5	D	8.3	D	4.4	25.7	1 430	245	165	3 168	-0.3
Schleicher	11.6	29.0	15.9	1.1	D	1.8	D	3.8	15.4	545	173	59	1 493	0.3
Scurry	0.3	49.0	5.0	2.6	1.3	4.1	2.1	D	12.1	2 920	168	338	7 202	3.4
Shackelford	2.0	79.9	1.1	2.4	D	1.2	1.4	D	4.1	725	218	61	1 756	0.1
Shelby	17.5	13.2	8.0	15.6	D	6.0	3.4	4.1	11.3	5 540	217	1 025	11 956	0.7
Sherman	73.2	D	D	D	D	2.0	1.6	D	8.4	345	112	20	1 292	3.2
Smith	0.4	16.2	4.7	6.8	7.6	8.0	5.6	20.2	11.2	42 925	195	5 549	88 852	1.8
Somervell	1.0	D	5.6	1.1	9.8	2.1	1.3	D	13.7	1 625	188	117	3 738	1.7
Starr	2.5	3.4	3.7	0.3	1.4	9.0	1.8	D	46.1	9 660	153	5 019	19 656	0.7
Stephens	0.2	57.8	6.6	6.5	D	3.0	4.2	3.1	9.5	2 075	221	254	4 925	-0.3
Sterling	2.9	39.5	D	D	D	3.0	D	D	17.7	240	178	30	616	0.2
Stonewall	19.8	16.2	D	D	D	3.5	D	D	27.2	370	265	28	928	0.0
Sutton	2.2	42.1	5.2	3.0	D	1.8	D	D	7.7	745	188	68	2 023	-0.4
Swisher	55.3	D	1.3	2.2	D	3.6	D	D	17.9	1 630	215	157	3 204	-0.5
Tarrant	0.0	7.4	6.8	12.4	8.0	6.0	8.4	9.7	11.5	245 855	126	35 990	747 684	4.6
Taylor	0.4	9.3	7.1	3.2	6.3	6.8	6.4	13.7	21.8	24 360	180	3 888	56 933	2.1
Terrell	7.4	0.0	D	D	1.9	3.2	D	1.9	46.3	225	252	27	700	0.0
Terry	9.3	20.1	2.6	3.2	D	14.9	2.6	D	22.0	2 230	175	388	4 860	0.7
Throckmorton	16.8	36.2	D	D	D	1.2	D	2.4	16.8	405	251	26	1 079	0.0
Titus	2.8	3.5	4.6	30.0	1.9	8.6	3.8	6.9	18.2	5 590	172	771	12 099	0.4

1. Per 1,000 resident population estimated as of July 1 of the year shown.

Table B. States and Counties — Housing, Labor Force, and Employment

STATE County	Housing units, 2010–2014 Occupied units — Owner-occupied Total	Percent	Median value[1]	Median owner cost as a percent of income — With a mortgage	Without a mortgage[2]	Renter-occupied Median rent[3]	Median rent as a percent of income[2]	Sub-standard units[4] (percent)	Civilian labor force, 2015 Total	Percent change, 2014–2015	Unemployment Total	Rate[5]	Civilian employment,[6] 2010–2014 Total	Percent — Management, business, science and arts	Construction, production, and maintenance occupations
	89	90	91	92	93	94	95	96	97	98	99	100	101	102	103

TEXAS—Cont'd

STATE County	89	90	91	92	93	94	95	96	97	98	99	100	101	102	103
Mason	1 678	82.1	165 500	27.2	11.6	707	27.3	2.7	1 823	-3.9	70	3.8	1 907	28.9	32.1
Matagorda	13 143	68.3	91 300	20.1	12.8	662	27.6	4.6	17 190	3.1	1 166	6.8	15 572	23.5	34.7
Maverick	16 091	70.3	85 900	26.0	14.3	593	27.7	13.9	23 564	0.7	2 525	10.7	20 043	22.1	27.8
Medina	15 221	79.1	115 500	20.1	11.5	701	25.2	4.8	20 564	0.8	901	4.4	19 293	30.9	25.6
Menard	886	73.4	58 400	25.5	11.3	605	26.2	5.2	862	-2.7	45	5.2	822	26.8	30.5
Midland	51 609	67.6	157 300	19.9	10.0	1 035	26.7	4.5	88 456	-2.7	3 052	3.5	73 777	32.5	27.9
Milam	9 279	67.3	79 600	20.6	12.3	661	29.5	4.1	10 090	-1.3	534	5.3	9 474	30.0	28.9
Mills	1 798	82.9	100 000	23.9	11.4	535	31.1	2.3	2 036	-0.6	74	3.6	1 879	32.6	26.4
Mitchell	2 690	72.6	45 800	19.6	10.0	564	21.5	0.7	2 745	-5.5	157	5.7	2 748	29.5	33.1
Montague	8 090	73.7	91 800	21.2	13.0	721	32.5	2.8	9 761	-3.7	418	4.3	8 260	30.3	33.8
Montgomery	168 279	72.5	169 800	21.7	11.6	994	27.3	5.2	255 338	0.6	10 892	4.3	224 133	37.6	21.7
Moore	6 836	68.9	87 600	19.3	10.0	639	25.2	8.9	11 129	-1.5	353	3.2	10 797	21.9	43.0
Morris	4 967	72.3	66 000	19.9	11.8	627	26.1	4.8	5 328	-5.3	473	8.9	4 701	27.7	31.7
Motley	462	72.7	55 400	21.0	13.4	543	28.0	3.9	485	-2.4	18	3.7	473	39.3	27.9
Nacogdoches	23 708	56.7	108 900	21.2	10.9	719	30.6	4.3	28 197	-1.5	1 339	4.7	27 466	33.5	27.1
Navarro	17 660	68.1	79 600	23.0	12.5	697	29.1	5.5	22 868	-1.2	977	4.3	20 067	24.9	32.8
Newton	4 823	76.9	73 800	24.6	10.5	578	24.4	1.5	5 497	-1.1	410	7.5	5 003	25.3	31.6
Nolan	5 449	69.4	54 700	18.0	12.0	560	25.1	3.1	6 906	-2.0	284	4.1	6 352	26.1	30.7
Nueces	125 458	58.1	111 100	22.3	12.1	866	29.9	5.3	167 125	-0.6	8 237	4.9	159 189	29.4	24.8
Ochiltree	3 770	70.3	77 600	17.9	10.3	684	19.7	6.9	5 299	-4.9	227	4.3	4 843	20.8	41.4
Oldham	643	75.7	87 300	22.4	11.0	822	42.3	2.5	922	-2.0	28	3.0	770	41.6	22.9
Orange	31 373	76.1	94 000	21.0	10.0	753	28.0	3.0	37 334	-1.5	2 445	6.5	35 368	28.2	31.4
Palo Pinto	10 413	71.1	80 200	20.9	12.5	699	29.9	4.6	13 098	-2.1	697	5.3	11 677	26.8	34.5
Panola	8 979	79.7	89 300	19.3	10.0	640	24.8	3.3	11 653	-7.2	609	5.2	10 334	23.1	37.9
Parker	42 887	78.1	157 900	20.6	11.8	904	28.6	3.4	59 407	0.5	2 475	4.2	54 205	36.7	24.8
Parmer	3 278	69.8	83 800	21.9	10.0	635	19.8	5.3	4 975	-3.0	122	2.5	4 676	23.4	42.9
Pecos	4 546	68.0	68 600	17.0	10.9	649	22.5	4.5	6 890	0.4	356	5.2	6 372	19.1	37.7
Polk	17 195	79.1	78 300	22.7	12.1	642	29.4	5.3	16 936	-1.7	1 038	6.1	15 554	25.7	29.6
Potter	43 002	58.0	86 100	22.6	11.3	707	30.2	5.7	56 556	-0.5	1 903	3.4	53 353	25.2	29.6
Presidio	2 646	67.5	44 900	18.9	10.4	400	22.0	6.7	3 107	-8.9	337	10.8	2 857	28.9	24.4
Rains	4 188	81.7	98 500	23.0	14.1	683	26.8	4.5	5 396	-0.1	247	4.6	4 533	28.2	33.3
Randall	48 942	68.8	144 400	19.5	11.1	814	27.4	2.3	68 441	-0.6	2 009	2.9	64 378	36.9	17.9
Reagan	1 200	72.7	70 300	16.3	11.9	731	14.0	4.3	1 955	-5.9	89	4.6	1 670	20.2	46.8
Real	1 208	75.6	113 500	19.4	13.2	726	31.6	2.3	1 070	1.0	56	5.2	1 039	35.7	22.9
Red River	5 144	73.1	69 100	20.0	13.7	508	30.1	2.1	4 923	-0.3	313	6.4	4 604	23.8	37.2
Reeves	3 705	71.6	40 600	16.4	11.1	616	22.8	5.2	5 641	-2.0	272	4.8	4 920	23.9	27.9
Refugio	2 771	77.7	66 500	17.5	11.0	635	29.2	4.7	3 343	-7.1	178	5.3	3 046	23.2	31.3
Roberts	348	87.6	104 700	14.2	10.5	813	14.6	2.0	455	1.1	19	4.2	422	45.7	23.5
Robertson	6 002	71.1	79 800	20.6	11.6	597	33.3	3.2	7 206	0.8	347	4.8	6 558	28.4	30.7
Rockwall	27 733	81.4	187 600	22.1	13.5	1 225	26.9	3.0	44 391	2.3	1 669	3.8	40 068	45.7	16.0
Runnels	3 739	75.4	65 400	18.9	13.5	569	23.8	1.2	4 685	-5.8	175	3.7	4 217	24.1	32.3
Rusk	17 794	76.4	96 700	18.8	10.6	687	26.4	3.2	23 436	-3.2	1 111	4.7	21 927	25.1	36.8
Sabine	3 965	87.9	80 700	21.6	13.5	542	27.7	3.6	3 491	-1.4	329	9.4	2 925	22.2	35.9
San Augustine	3 117	80.2	69 300	22.7	14.1	487	30.3	2.8	2 792	-1.2	257	9.2	2 424	24.1	40.3
San Jacinto	9 285	82.0	87 800	24.4	11.6	683	28.9	4.4	11 260	-1.3	639	5.7	9 931	24.9	36.4
San Patricio	22 621	68.1	90 600	20.8	12.2	799	26.0	7.7	30 558	-0.4	1 982	6.5	28 602	27.8	30.0
San Saba	2 098	76.3	69 400	21.8	11.8	575	34.9	2.4	2 231	0.0	81	3.6	2 340	24.8	40.5
Schleicher	1 028	71.4	83 500	20.9	10.0	506	20.0	8.6	1 681	-5.6	79	4.7	1 525	29.7	36.1
Scurry	5 894	73.5	88 800	19.2	10.0	696	24.8	5.0	8 210	-4.7	339	4.1	7 300	24.4	36.0
Shackelford	1 360	77.1	72 300	20.4	12.3	575	28.3	2.0	2 100	-11.5	59	2.8	1 506	34.2	27.6
Shelby	9 564	72.1	68 300	20.6	10.5	575	31.5	2.7	11 420	-1.7	607	5.3	10 453	25.3	40.3
Sherman	1 007	75.9	77 400	19.8	10.0	624	20.9	4.5	1 430	-5.0	41	2.9	1 412	30.7	39.2
Smith	79 089	65.9	126 400	22.4	12.3	841	30.6	4.8	102 736	0.5	4 648	4.5	95 623	33.7	23.2
Somervell	3 265	70.8	141 300	19.8	12.1	835	24.4	5.3	4 173	0.9	209	5.0	3 839	38.4	28.1
Starr	16 073	76.6	65 400	19.2	13.2	500	33.8	13.1	25 757	-0.9	3 502	13.6	20 734	21.6	26.2
Stephens	3 469	75.0	76 700	22.4	11.5	526	28.0	2.3	4 106	-4.3	174	4.2	3 622	26.1	35.4
Sterling	475	73.5	74 400	18.3	10.0	661	38.9	5.7	753	-7.3	26	3.5	586	33.1	29.2
Stonewall	588	77.6	54 200	18.7	11.8	310	29.4	4.1	666	-4.4	29	4.4	560	35.7	27.7
Sutton	1 458	67.9	79 300	26.6	12.8	612	21.3	4.5	1 742	-13.8	105	6.0	1 836	23.7	46.5
Swisher	2 664	73.1	68 200	18.3	12.3	576	35.2	4.5	2 735	-5.1	131	4.8	2 783	27.1	32.7
Tarrant	667 362	61.2	137 700	22.4	12.3	899	29.6	4.7	992 840	0.2	41 251	4.2	901 695	36.1	22.0
Taylor	49 482	59.6	99 100	20.2	11.8	777	30.5	3.0	63 654	-1.2	2 356	3.7	59 808	30.5	21.0
Terrell	407	64.4	54 300	13.9	11.6	743	15.5	0.0	446	-6.9	22	4.9	377	18.0	30.8
Terry	3 985	70.4	65 000	20.3	10.4	648	27.9	4.1	5 409	-3.6	256	4.7	4 881	31.7	29.2
Throckmorton	722	69.4	64 400	14.1	12.1	428	24.3	2.5	787	-5.5	26	3.3	714	28.2	30.3
Titus	10 532	70.0	88 900	22.0	11.4	627	26.4	9.5	12 672	-1.8	741	5.8	13 740	22.3	43.0

1. Specified owner-occupied units.   2. A value of 10.0 represents 10 percent or less; a value of 50.0 represents 50 percent or more.   3. Specified renter-occupied units.
4. Overcrowded or lacking complete plumbing facilities.   5. Percent of civilian labor force.   6. Persons 16 years old and over.

Table B. States and Counties — **Nonfarm Employment and Agriculture**

STATE County		Private nonfarm establishments, employment and payroll, 2014								Agriculture, 2012			
		Employment						Annual payroll		Farms			
											Percent with:		
	Number of establish-ments	Total	Health care and social assistance	Manufac-turing	Retail trade	Finance and insurance	Professional, scientific, and technical services	Total (mil dol)	Average per employee (dollars)	Number	Fewer than 50 acres	500 acres or more	Farm operators whose principal occu-pation is farming (percent)
	104	105	106	107	108	109	110	111	112	113	114	115	116
TEXAS—Cont'd													
Mason	139	939	139	31	154	59	D	25	26 639	640	11.1	43.4	48.9
Matagorda	709	8 048	1 295	643	1 313	217	158	421	52 361	856	28.5	27.9	47.7
Maverick	798	12 208	4 053	587	2 646	381	191	286	23 441	294	53.4	20.4	34.4
Medina	702	6 946	938	D	1 188	D	435	222	31 913	1 976	31.9	15.9	50.2
Menard	47	D	D	D	47	D	D	4	D	325	14.5	45.2	48.6
Midland	5 147	87 738	6 797	3 106	9 281	2 029	4 640	5 992	68 293	540	47.6	19.8	24.3
Milam	411	4 341	1 077	208	628	D	134	180	41 523	1 909	32.6	12.2	44.9
Mills	111	882	178	D	204	D	D	24	27 596	870	20.3	26.0	43.1
Mitchell	140	1 526	D	D	291	49	D	64	41 641	482	12.2	25.9	32.2
Montague	435	4 242	528	207	675	179	D	189	44 637	1 454	26.2	15.3	39.8
Montgomery	10 282	144 894	16 984	11 988	23 002	5 241	9 435	8 249	56 929	1 601	63.1	3.7	30.7
Moore	445	7 907	D	3 493	885	159	102	332	41 983	261	10.0	58.2	64.8
Morris	229	4 261	148	D	301	121	116	192	45 025	412	34.7	8.7	50.0
Motley	27	173	D	D	D	D	D	3	17 168	224	3.6	53.1	39.3
Nacogdoches	1 302	17 398	3 231	3 518	2 799	553	480	546	31 385	1 196	28.6	7.6	43.0
Navarro	931	14 004	2 519	2 990	2 212	391	301	469	33 475	2 573	41.0	9.2	47.6
Newton	126	1 036	340	D	162	32	64	27	26 403	450	57.8	2.2	31.3
Nolan	352	4 326	513	886	784	154	79	158	36 607	478	15.1	32.4	39.7
Nueces	7 903	139 655	27 715	7 310	18 663	3 793	6 394	5 821	41 679	754	43.4	21.1	36.3
Ochiltree	369	4 254	D	47	410	124	D	245	57 661	348	8.3	54.3	51.1
Oldham	41	568	D	D	36	D	NA	17	30 246	159	7.5	64.8	46.5
Orange	1 356	19 051	1 388	5 272	3 264	573	505	960	50 380	671	79.7	3.9	43.7
Palo Pinto	628	6 331	809	1 217	1 126	142	248	236	37 280	1 329	42.2	15.6	32.7
Panola	488	7 657	679	954	869	191	230	351	45 853	1 079	34.6	10.1	43.4
Parker	2 447	28 284	3 038	2 596	5 440	678	959	1 161	41 032	4 370	66.1	3.5	35.3
Parmer	210	3 199	D	D	167	87	D	120	37 664	570	8.6	47.9	59.3
Pecos	347	4 156	545	D	772	166	68	184	44 328	291	13.1	67.7	45.0
Polk	708	8 435	1 375	D	1 732	345	254	280	33 185	738	40.2	8.5	48.6
Potter	3 618	61 359	13 644	D	9 188	3 228	2 201	2 360	38 461	258	35.3	31.4	38.0
Presidio	119	950	D	D	233	57	D	20	21 200	162	8.6	63.6	45.1
Rains	159	1 343	133	D	419	D	218	35	26 103	682	47.5	7.9	44.7
Randall	2 464	32 030	4 433	4 714	5 842	1 132	815	1 113	34 737	892	30.5	27.4	36.4
Reagan	131	1 575	D	D	74	D	D	90	56 998	135	5.2	71.9	51.1
Real	80	535	99	D	72	D	D	11	21 015	241	19.9	40.7	44.4
Red River	168	1 469	388	316	265	87	25	45	30 358	1 139	22.3	17.1	45.7
Reeves	235	2 798	D	D	480	27	46	140	49 857	240	11.7	51.7	43.3
Refugio	156	1 968	249	9	288	D	22	91	46 490	259	31.3	35.9	43.2
Roberts	18	134	NA	NA	D	D	D	6	44 821	107	2.8	73.8	58.9
Robertson	271	2 688	319	D	385	98	32	127	47 112	1 520	28.7	12.0	49.5
Rockwall	1 962	22 034	3 993	1 149	4 543	649	1 093	772	35 043	440	71.8	6.4	35.7
Runnels	234	2 198	D	435	451	D	D	74	33 710	925	12.4	29.6	45.8
Rusk	836	12 059	1 494	D	1 403	D	847	532	44 121	1 390	30.9	7.8	35.1
Sabine	159	1 556	333	D	305	61	D	51	32 729	201	36.3	4.5	46.8
San Augustine	119	1 131	397	D	221	48	D	36	31 689	305	23.3	9.8	52.5
San Jacinto	209	1 033	119	147	228	D	29	33	32 285	791	48.5	2.8	44.6
San Patricio	1 057	16 027	1 770	D	2 596	D	581	704	43 941	701	47.9	21.8	41.8
San Saba	153	851	169	41	203	25	42	22	25 811	744	19.9	33.7	48.8
Schleicher	57	500	D	D	54	23	D	26	52 608	310	10.6	60.6	44.8
Scurry	450	5 934	490	103	854	133	140	318	53 605	677	16.4	32.9	39.0
Shackelford	126	1 339	D	120	78	D	D	83	62 229	233	7.7	47.6	43.3
Shelby	505	6 950	674	2 591	949	510	144	238	34 244	1 048	26.4	8.3	53.3
Sherman	59	332	D	D	D	29	D	13	38 861	313	5.8	59.1	48.6
Smith	5 734	90 521	22 096	7 023	12 389	5 104	4 664	3 719	41 087	2 961	54.8	3.0	45.3
Somervell	195	3 640	469	49	219	51	96	199	54 589	350	38.6	14.0	37.7
Starr	564	9 567	5 304	34	1 850	D	133	184	19 209	1 165	16.8	26.3	39.5
Stephens	265	2 283	230	385	339	110	56	95	41 482	452	7.3	40.9	30.3
Sterling	59	453	D	D	D	D	D	25	54 232	73	4.1	80.8	56.2
Stonewall	51	443	D	NA	40	D	D	18	39 745	356	5.3	45.5	34.0
Sutton	140	1 285	D	D	141	D	D	61	47 163	218	6.9	71.1	54.1
Swisher	146	1 030	D	128	148	D	D	29	28 266	565	9.6	46.5	54.2
Tarrant	39 633	756 293	95 267	77 741	99 334	45 008	36 297	35 785	47 317	1 278	74.0	3.6	28.7
Taylor	3 374	53 589	11 411	2 119	8 293	2 773	1 764	1 847	34 470	1 149	29.8	19.1	38.7
Terrell	13	45	D	NA	D	D	D	2	36 178	86	0.0	86.0	57.0
Terry	240	2 509	510	D	444	97	45	90	35 838	630	11.4	37.5	55.7
Throckmorton	50	289	114	D	22	D	D	8	26 630	275	5.5	49.1	49.1
Titus	629	14 424	2 251	6 074	1 867	446	153	461	31 993	801	35.8	5.7	37.5

Table B. States and Counties — **Agriculture**

STATE County	Acreage (1,000) [117]	Percent change, 2007–2012 [118]	Average size of farm [119]	Total irrigated (1,000) [120]	Total cropland (1,000) [121]	Value of land and buildings — Average per farm [122]	Average per acre [123]	Value of machinery and equipment, average per farm (dollars) [124]	Total (mil dol) [125]	Average per farm (dollars) [126]	Percent from: Crops [127]	Live-stock and poultry products [128]	$10,000 or more [129]	$100,000 or more [130]	Government payments Total ($1,000) [131]	Percent of farms [132]
TEXAS—Cont'd																
Mason	551	2.8	861	3.0	28.9	2 039 833	2 368	59 491	51.4	80 389	9.7	90.3	43.8	8.4	1 749	32.5
Matagorda	568	-1.7	664	32.7	177.0	1 315 683	1 983	126 209	129.7	151 522	59.4	40.6	48.7	16.2	5 271	34.6
Maverick	541	14.2	1 840	13.0	13.8	2 169 796	1 179	59 840	32.6	110 912	8.0	92.0	24.1	8.5	410	7.5
Medina	834	11.4	422	51.4	141.4	1 095 775	2 598	66 329	115.5	58 461	56.2	43.8	28.5	7.2	3 298	19.4
Menard	537	9.2	1 651	1.5	20.7	2 408 895	1 459	54 991	9.6	29 646	13.0	87.0	42.8	7.1	1 249	30.8
Midland	404	-11.4	749	10.7	62.4	1 072 641	1 432	83 080	17.2	31 876	65.7	34.3	17.6	5.0	1 866	23.5
Milam	528	-2.0	277	2.5	143.0	990 114	3 581	65 371	144.7	75 814	26.6	73.4	33.1	7.2	3 451	22.0
Mills	471	-0.6	542	3.3	57.5	1 204 675	2 223	58 645	43.0	49 462	12.6	87.4	40.9	4.8	1 277	22.2
Mitchell	573	-0.3	1 189	4.2	146.7	938 568	789	84 627	21.2	43 956	61.0	39.0	24.1	8.7	7 078	77.8
Montague	489	-3.7	336	0.6	74.0	840 349	2 500	59 290	44.9	30 902	18.7	81.3	32.9	5.7	1 034	14.4
Montgomery	155	-8.6	97	1.2	31.6	573 034	5 905	48 231	23.8	14 888	48.2	51.8	18.4	2.4	227	3.4
Moore	524	-5.4	2 006	122.4	263.6	1 884 521	939	303 854	605.0	2 318 107	19.4	80.6	57.1	39.8	6 010	68.6
Morris	92	7.2	223	0.0	18.1	468 248	2 100	55 663	46.9	113 922	4.9	95.1	41.3	10.4	99	9.2
Motley	595	3.6	2 658	4.2	65.8	1 960 781	738	69 571	12.8	57 143	24.5	75.5	42.0	15.2	1 767	74.6
Nacogdoches	265	-0.1	221	0.3	43.7	558 234	2 521	73 452	322.4	269 544	1.8	98.2	37.0	11.8	595	7.3
Navarro	558	-4.9	217	0.9	146.1	445 243	2 053	57 970	66.4	25 798	47.3	52.7	27.4	3.5	2 633	13.6
Newton	59	-0.8	131	0.0	8.9	261 813	2 004	54 300	2.9	6 551	35.4	64.7	17.1	0.7	D	0.7
Nolan	465	-13.9	973	3.3	118.2	1 093 607	1 124	81 916	23.8	49 847	52.0	48.0	26.2	7.5	3 074	57.3
Nueces	524	2.9	695	0.4	362.6	1 076 476	1 549	160 967	84.9	112 557	92.2	7.8	33.2	12.9	5 340	34.7
Ochiltree	545	-6.0	1 565	48.2	304.6	1 566 761	1 001	223 842	424.6	1 220 129	14.6	85.4	59.2	33.0	6 098	77.3
Oldham	830	-5.7	5 223	3.4	94.8	3 082 126	590	134 522	113.0	710 415	2.4	97.6	45.9	27.0	2 473	81.8
Orange	53	-17.2	79	0.4	6.7	261 493	3 323	47 335	4.3	6 461	44.2	55.8	11.3	0.9	112	1.5
Palo Pinto	593	7.6	446	0.7	55.4	1 074 703	2 407	51 951	53.8	40 472	18.4	81.6	24.8	4.0	489	6.5
Panola	227	4.4	211	0.7	38.6	442 762	2 101	66 066	93.3	86 466	6.0	94.0	34.5	5.8	156	4.7
Parker	494	12.0	113	2.2	93.9	567 100	5 012	49 848	74.3	17 000	20.8	79.2	17.3	2.5	294	2.4
Parmer	554	-1.3	971	163.0	444.7	1 010 667	1 040	277 575	1 329.5	2 332 523	9.9	90.1	59.3	42.1	11 381	83.3
Pecos	2 948	1.4	10 130	13.9	63.7	5 133 601	507	136 553	47.5	163 127	58.1	41.9	47.1	17.5	2 077	33.3
Polk	139	5.7	189	0.4	23.2	515 232	2 732	57 919	7.8	10 618	30.7	69.3	25.2	1.5	106	2.4
Potter	569	-0.8	2 204	3.1	54.2	1 208 547	548	66 465	21.0	81 287	7.7	92.3	29.5	12.0	1 092	22.1
Presidio	1 656	6.1	10 219	0.6	24.5	4 712 426	461	101 093	D	D	D	D	34.6	13.6	555	21.6
Rains	117	19.7	171	0.2	34.3	432 129	2 522	43 035	15.3	22 361	31.2	68.8	26.5	4.7	329	6.5
Randall	571	-0.7	640	15.9	250.8	642 873	1 004	77 600	540.3	605 734	2.9	97.1	29.8	10.0	5 003	42.9
Reagan	699	2.2	5 174	12.1	46.7	2 516 941	486	233 267	11.1	82 259	64.3	35.7	50.4	22.2	1 681	63.0
Real	321	-13.9	1 330	0.5	5.5	1 966 274	1 478	38 465	1.6	6 842	12.2	87.8	14.5	0.4	270	15.8
Red River	449	-0.2	394	2.8	94.7	654 453	1 662	73 917	53.5	46 997	26.5	73.5	42.0	7.5	1 949	18.9
Reeves	1 236	18.8	5 149	10.6	98.2	1 384 817	269	85 475	54.2	225 858	20.0	80.0	33.8	15.4	2 698	58.3
Refugio	475	-3.2	1 833	1.2	86.5	1 673 463	913	151 490	43.0	166 201	76.1	23.9	46.3	18.1	1 669	33.6
Roberts	562	15.9	5 257		49.3	3 455 290	657	143 140	16.4	153 271	31.5	68.5	57.0	31.8	1 122	57.9
Robertson	468	2.7	308	19.7	107.9	736 551	2 394	70 166	136.4	89 766	24.3	75.7	37.0	6.3	2 945	13.7
Rockwall	45	21.3	103	0.1	14.1	602 114	5 836	38 743	4.1	9 348	48.8	51.2	14.3	1.1	63	2.7
Runnels	666	1.5	720	4.5	247.9	931 382	1 294	89 466	47.4	51 272	62.3	37.7	42.8	10.9	6 002	68.8
Rusk	274	-8.8	197	0.4	47.5	431 437	2 186	58 886	75.3	54 175	25.6	74.4	24.7	3.3	295	2.4
Sabine	29	-8.5	144	0.2	4.6	392 557	2 718	84 005	14.7	73 274	3.8	96.2	31.3	3.0	22	9.0
San Augustine	73	0.3	239	0.0	8.9	552 167	2 310	122 351	63.2	207 262	2.0	98.0	42.6	11.1	25	6.2
San Jacinto	112	17.2	141	0.5	24.3	400 991	2 835	54 541	8.5	10 783	27.9	72.1	19.3	1.4	110	1.6
San Patricio	374	1.2	534	5.6	247.7	852 438	1 597	189 071	86.2	122 989	79.2	20.8	32.5	14.6	3 794	36.9
San Saba	671	-6.5	902	3.6	53.2	2 198 733	2 438	66 862	30.0	40 351	31.1	68.9	43.1	8.9	1 166	18.8
Schleicher	834	4.1	2 689	1.4	32.5	2 490 152	926	79 410	13.6	43 903	20.6	79.4	46.1	10.6	2 325	46.8
Scurry	494	-4.8	730	3.7	206.4	620 700	850	98 991	29.0	42 876	44.9	55.1	23.3	7.4	4 295	69.3
Shackelford	505	-8.5	2 168	D	55.0	2 371 000	1 093	83 609	22.3	95 854	11.6	88.4	54.5	15.9	1 604	53.2
Shelby	197	-0.3	188	1.8	36.4	550 712	2 927	92 111	473.3	451 610	2.1	97.9	46.6	21.6	334	3.9
Sherman	583	-0.2	1 863	126.6	339.1	2 006 652	1 077	378 847	590.4	1 886 121	21.9	78.1	46.3	37.7	6 153	83.1
Smith	302	0.0	102	2.5	77.1	386 589	3 786	43 300	76.8	25 934	77.5	22.5	18.6	2.6	189	1.8
Somervell	91	10.6	261	0.1	12.3	1 016 549	3 894	47 343	4.3	12 294	27.5	72.5	22.0	2.3	42	5.4
Starr	669	2.4	574	8.6	131.3	1 015 723	1 770	66 303	108.5	93 173	25.0	75.0	23.5	4.4	4 099	40.3
Stephens	517	20.4	1 143	D	54.4	1 599 708	1 399	58 681	9.2	20 392	11.6	88.4	37.6	3.1	777	30.3
Sterling	585	1.2	8 015	0.6	12.7	4 225 370	527	140 699	D	D	D	D	71.2	27.4	712	39.7
Stonewall	473	-2.6	1 328	0.7	79.5	955 171	719	52 202	47.4	133 275	5.3	94.7	35.4	6.2	2 288	80.9
Sutton	911	1.8	4 179	1.3	11.0	3 946 307	944	77 894	10.9	49 872	4.6	95.5	45.9	15.1	1 066	26.6
Swisher	546	-3.1	966	65.3	351.1	888 986	921	164 150	586.8	1 038 602	7.6	92.4	45.7	21.2	10 082	86.9
Tarrant	146	-5.6	114	0.9	38.0	722 473	6 339	54 282	34.6	27 076	72.8	27.2	18.0	4.1	109	2.8
Taylor	579	-0.1	504	1.1	158.9	570 210	1 132	55 372	37.6	32 746	27.7	72.3	23.8	4.1	3 600	37.7
Terrell	1 101	-15.5	12 800	0.3	2.0	4 976 860	389	57 116	3.1	35 686	D	D	39.5	9.3	507	22.1
Terry	442	-11.0	702	98.2	377.0	799 537	1 139	189 140	125.8	199 687	70.2	29.8	46.2	27.9	13 162	88.6
Throckmorton	508	-11.5	1 847	D	107.6	2 215 240	1 199	84 844	24.8	90 316	35.1	64.9	54.2	11.6	1 749	60.0
Titus	147	-11.9	183	D	31.1	471 061	2 575	53 954	81.2	101 401	4.5	95.5	35.3	6.1	112	7.6

Table B. States and Counties — Water Use, Wholesale Trade, Retail Trade, and Real Estate

STATE County	Water use, 2010 — Total water withdrawn (mil gal/day)	Gallons withdrawn per person per day	Wholesale trade,[1] 2012 — Number of establishments	Number of employees	Sales (mil dol)	Annual payroll (mil dol)	Retail trade,[2] 2012 — Number of establishments	Number of employees	Sales (mil dol)	Annual payroll (mil dol)	Real estate and rental and leasing,[2] 2012 — Number of establishments	Number of employees	Receipts (mil dol)	Annual payroll (mil dol)
	133	134	135	136	137	138	139	140	141	142	143	144	145	146
TEXAS—Cont'd														
Mason	5.2	1 306	8	D	D	D	25	140	36.4	2.6	4	5	2.0	0.2
Matagorda	210.5	5 736	31	123	104.9	4.5	128	1 241	324.6	25.7	33	170	32.1	7.5
Maverick	56.2	1 035	44	D	D	D	166	2 511	585.6	49.4	26	71	12.5	1.9
Medina	52.7	1 145	24	D	D	D	100	1 112	436.7	30.3	25	42	5.3	0.9
Menard	2.8	1 240	4	D	D	D	9	49	11.9	0.8	NA	NA	NA	NA
Midland	35.3	258	265	4 659	3 749.7	289.5	503	7 463	2 930.6	216.9	266	D	D	D
Milam	45.7	1 844	16	138	110.5	5.3	64	681	186.9	14.6	16	38	5.0	0.9
Mills	5.2	1 062	1	D	D	D	23	203	65.2	5.3	2	D	D	D
Mitchell	18.0	1 911	4	10	4.3	0.6	30	284	71.3	6.2	2	D	D	D
Montague	10.9	554	22	68	35.2	3.0	69	686	192.6	15.3	9	12	3.1	0.4
Montgomery	89.2	196	501	4 711	9 996.3	290.2	1 313	21 292	6 297.8	535.2	482	2 134	489.6	108.6
Moore	156.4	7 139	29	D	D	D	75	898	276.4	19.4	13	31	5.0	0.8
Morris	29.4	2 270	12	631	212.7	35.0	39	316	63.6	6.1	7	33	4.8	0.8
Motley	6.4	5 322	3	D	D	D	4	24	3.3	0.4	NA	NA	NA	NA
Nacogdoches	16.1	250	45	D	D	D	241	2 944	880.8	70.7	54	168	29.3	4.5
Navarro	51.2	1 073	29	D	D	D	163	2 039	539.2	46.1	48	136	19.4	3.3
Newton	6.2	429	4	D	D	D	32	177	73.3	3.5	NA	NA	NA	NA
Nolan	11.3	743	19	D	D	D	53	691	210.1	14.5	10	47	5.3	0.7
Nueces	235.0	691	361	4 987	5 153.6	264.8	1 128	17 030	5 138.3	418.1	414	2 868	667.2	132.2
Ochiltree	58.5	5 721	30	D	D	D	37	448	127.2	11.0	16	90	44.2	5.5
Oldham	5.8	2 836	2	D	D	D	7	D	D	D	NA	NA	NA	NA
Orange	411.3	5 026	36	D	D	D	269	3 130	909.6	71.8	59	272	58.3	8.7
Palo Pinto	50.4	1 794	23	267	121.4	11.8	118	1 089	281.8	23.1	28	91	16.9	3.2
Panola	17.4	733	23	D	D	D	81	939	228.7	20.7	26	155	24.8	6.1
Parker	22.6	193	97	1 053	779.1	41.6	316	4 515	1 772.7	128.0	88	302	55.0	9.5
Parmer	239.6	23 332	26	201	426.9	6.7	25	167	43.9	3.3	4	4	0.6	0.1
Pecos	145.1	9 356	16	166	135.6	8.0	58	645	185.9	14.4	9	64	11.8	2.2
Polk	558.9	12 308	19	99	45.9	4.3	128	1 738	474.6	40.9	30	87	17.6	3.0
Potter	5.6	46	169	D	D	D	555	D	D	D	167	827	162.2	29.0
Presidio	5.3	682	2	D	D	D	27	212	51.3	3.6	2	D	D	D
Rains	2.2	202	5	D	D	D	27	408	149.0	11.2	5	10	1.5	0.2
Randall	26.8	222	79	D	D	D	352	5 343	1 805.1	142.0	142	D	D	D
Reagan	25.6	7 594	5	D	D	D	9	60	29.2	1.6	1	D	D	D
Real	1.0	311	3	4	1.0	0.1	12	45	14.6	1.0	4	6	0.9	0.1
Red River	7.1	550	5	D	D	D	40	249	54.8	4.2	5	5	0.7	0.1
Reeves	56.9	4 129	7	D	D	D	29	425	162.0	9.0	8	29	8.1	1.1
Refugio	12.0	1 624	5	D	D	D	22	252	101.1	5.0	7	29	3.9	0.7
Roberts	21.1	22 680	NA	NA	NA	NA	2	D	D	D	NA	NA	NA	NA
Robertson	433.8	26 099	2	D	D	D	49	370	148.6	8.1	7	39	7.7	2.1
Rockwall	0.6	7	66	D	D	D	251	4 179	1 444.8	108.4	76	289	56.0	9.1
Runnels	7.8	743	5	D	D	D	47	473	139.8	10.3	2	D	D	D
Rusk	1 594.9	29 906	27	255	152.4	11.8	126	1 410	442.1	34.2	22	68	12.7	2.7
Sabine	2.2	202	1	D	D	D	31	310	65.6	5.4	4	2	0.1	0.0
San Augustine	3.1	350	4	12	2.9	0.4	24	215	58.2	4.8	6	10	0.6	0.2
San Jacinto	2.9	109	7	D	D	D	29	229	59.6	4.5	13	D	D	D
San Patricio	11.4	176	38	D	D	D	150	2 298	712.2	52.4	54	162	26.4	4.2
San Saba	7.0	1 137	9	61	14.1	1.1	35	198	45.3	3.7	3	3	0.2	0.1
Schleicher	2.7	766	3	D	D	D	10	56	12.3	1.2	NA	NA	NA	NA
Scurry	38.9	2 297	25	D	D	D	63	739	242.3	18.1	14	88	16.6	4.4
Shackelford	1.8	524	8	53	24.1	2.8	14	100	16.1	2.0	5	8	0.7	0.2
Shelby	13.5	530	10	D	D	D	93	1 087	302.1	24.3	22	91	9.8	2.5
Sherman	213.9	70 501	6	D	D	D	10	92	28.5	2.7	1	D	D	D
Smith	30.8	147	215	D	D	D	829	11 883	3 388.9	293.6	281	1 477	301.0	61.6
Somervell	2 043.9	240 736	6	46	25.8	1.9	30	218	47.8	4.3	10	17	2.4	0.3
Starr	26.2	429	24	D	D	D	135	1 735	435.4	33.6	14	45	5.6	0.9
Stephens	36.8	3 826	6	D	D	D	36	380	84.0	8.4	6	D	D	D
Sterling	2.0	1 724	2	D	D	D	3	D	D	D	1	D	D	D
Stonewall	2.5	1 698	2	D	D	D	6	35	8.9	0.6	1	D	D	D
Sutton	3.2	766	8	D	D	D	20	139	49.5	3.0	3	D	D	D
Swisher	104.4	13 296	13	55	23.4	1.8	20	152	51.5	2.9	3	6	0.4	0.1
Tarrant	286.1	158	1 944	34 600	30 173.3	1 974.7	5 705	91 200	28 908.8	2 381.7	1 826	12 190	2 647.1	528.7
Taylor	3.6	27	146	1 803	2 007.0	90.0	563	7 825	2 223.5	185.7	166	885	150.3	27.1
Terrell	1.5	1 514	NA	NA	NA	NA	4	19	5.0	0.4	NA	NA	NA	NA
Terry	132.5	10 473	18	D	D	D	43	453	131.5	10.1	8	D	D	D
Throckmorton	1.4	853	6	17	5.9	0.5	5	19	7.1	0.4	NA	NA	NA	NA
Titus	1 950.7	60 330	31	D	D	D	133	1 732	477.8	41.7	25	65	10.4	1.6

1. Merchant wholesalers, except manufacturers' sales branches and offices.   2. Employer establishments.

STATE County	Professional, scientific, and technical services, 2012				Manufacturing, 2012				Accommodation and food services, 2012			
	Number of establish-ments	Number of employees	Receipts (mil dol)	Annual payroll (mil dol)	Number of establish-ments	Number of employees	Receipts (mil dol)	Annual payroll (mil dol)	Number of establish-ments	Number of employees	Sales (mil dol)	Annual payroll (mil dol)
	147	148	149	150	151	152	153	154	155	156	157	158
TEXAS—Cont'd												
Mason	14	D	D	D	6	29	5.3	1.2	14	D	D	D
Matagorda	43	162	11.8	4.2	28	513	1 657.5	41.4	84	1 045	51.5	14.0
Maverick	40	D	D	D	14	339	49.0	9.0	72	2 103	211.4	34.6
Medina	62	380	32.8	11.7	21	247	D	9.2	73	872	41.7	11.1
Menard	2	D	D	D	NA	NA	NA	NA	3	24	1.1	0.3
Midland	495	4 727	1 004.8	266.6	142	D	D	D	298	D	D	D
Milam	41	117	9.1	3.3	14	278	D	14.9	44	381	16.7	4.1
Mills	7	D	D	D	8	59	D	1.6	10	100	4.0	1.1
Mitchell	10	35	4.6	1.2	NA	NA	NA	NA	15	D	D	D
Montague	39	112	18.6	4.6	15	270	D	8.2	30	418	16.2	4.5
Montgomery	1 341	8 823	1 351.7	629.7	407	10 599	D	571.8	782	16 697	944.9	253.2
Moore	21	D	D	D	14	D	D	165.0	47	685	32.6	8.7
Morris	15	D	D	D	15	1 945	1 327.1	136.4	20	275	12.1	3.1
Motley	1	D	D	D	NA	NA	NA	NA	3	10	0.3	0.1
Nacogdoches	94	D	D	D	59	3 883	1 258.7	113.2	115	2 516	99.7	27.7
Navarro	59	298	24.0	8.0	55	2 834	1 046.9	115.2	63	1 017	50.7	13.0
Newton	9	58	4.1	1.5	6	81	D	1.3	3	27	0.4	0.2
Nolan	28	D	D	D	11	665	203.7	38.3	39	506	26.2	6.2
Nueces	812	5 789	849.1	309.6	193	7 063	41 840.9	514.2	849	17 049	892.8	242.4
Ochiltree	23	167	30.6	11.5	9	40	7.3	1.3	19	270	16.3	3.6
Oldham	NA	NA	NA	NA	NA	NA	NA	NA	9	54	2.0	0.5
Orange	92	501	57.9	23.0	74	5 287	6 340.3	426.6	140	2 002	101.2	25.5
Palo Pinto	39	211	33.7	8.6	33	1 325	460.4	55.2	73	1 023	47.1	13.2
Panola	39	206	25.3	8.0	16	905	281.9	29.6	30	419	17.8	4.8
Parker	208	892	115.3	37.7	127	2 360	582.9	109.6	190	3 237	152.0	42.0
Parmer	9	23	1.8	0.4	6	D	D	D	6	D	D	D
Pecos	16	60	2.4	1.8	4	14	D	D	43	627	36.6	7.8
Polk	73	340	30.5	10.1	25	1 227	362.5	58.1	57	940	44.5	11.9
Potter	322	1 967	414.6	115.3	125	11 535	D	716.9	366	D	D	D
Presidio	5	14	0.5	0.2	3	13	D	D	23	185	9.5	2.5
Rains	13	D	D	D	7	85	D	3.0	20	154	7.1	1.8
Randall	199	2 294	123.3	66.7	72	1 297	D	65.8	184	3 387	164.3	43.0
Reagan	7	26	1.8	0.6	NA	NA	NA	NA	7	D	D	D
Real	5	D	D	D	5	23	D	0.9	13	74	4.9	1.1
Red River	8	25	3.2	1.1	14	242	D	8.6	15	D	D	D
Reeves	16	D	D	D	3	6	2.0	D	32	434	33.9	6.4
Refugio	4	20	2.1	0.8	4	5	0.3	0.1	21	D	D	D
Roberts	1	D	D	D	NA	NA	NA	NA	1	D	D	D
Robertson	17	38	4.4	1.0	8	70	D	3.0	26	327	15.8	4.9
Rockwall	226	D	D	D	55	1 081	285.0	56.3	169	3 686	194.1	56.5
Runnels	13	D	D	D	14	505	297.9	18.8	17	D	D	D
Rusk	75	793	150.0	53.9	34	1 297	333.1	51.7	67	D	D	D
Sabine	16	D	D	D	4	309	D	D	15	77	3.9	0.7
San Augustine	7	D	D	D	5	85	D	2.3	7	D	D	D
San Jacinto	22	D	D	D	14	137	D	7.4	11	111	4.4	1.4
San Patricio	78	436	58.0	23.8	38	3 861	D	260.3	125	2 052	103.0	24.1
San Saba	16	39	4.2	1.2	7	30	D	1.4	18	D	D	D
Schleicher	4	D	D	D	NA	NA	NA	NA	1	D	D	D
Scurry	23	D	D	D	16	119	43.0	5.1	49	591	29.4	7.1
Shackelford	5	D	D	D	6	148	D	6.6	9	D	D	D
Shelby	32	133	19.7	4.5	23	2 465	577.3	72.1	34	D	D	D
Sherman	1	D	D	D	NA	NA	NA	NA	2	D	D	D
Smith	596	4 265	689.9	244.8	189	6 739	5 066.1	318.0	405	9 236	427.1	124.3
Somervell	14	59	9.7	3.8	6	33	D	1.1	28	455	23.0	7.4
Starr	30	D	D	D	6	29	2.3	0.6	51	648	35.5	8.2
Stephens	20	92	8.2	2.6	15	348	D	13.7	18	D	D	D
Sterling	2	D	D	D	NA	NA	NA	NA	3	D	D	D
Stonewall	3	D	D	D	NA	NA	NA	NA	5	22	0.8	0.2
Sutton	10	21	1.6	0.4	4	D	D	D	15	203	12.0	2.7
Swisher	7	25	1.5	0.7	8	75	D	3.1	13	D	D	D
Tarrant	4 314	39 363	6 258.9	2 258.2	1 568	70 421	45 771.0	3 894.9	3 474	77 362	4 483.6	1 188.2
Taylor	274	1 775	183.3	72.7	95	2 098	913.9	87.8	301	6 435	303.2	85.3
Terrell	2	D	D	D	NA	NA	NA	NA	5	11	0.4	0.0
Terry	15	61	4.7	1.2	5	22	D	0.8	23	280	15.4	3.4
Throckmorton	2	D	D	D	NA	NA	NA	NA	4	D	D	D
Titus	29	D	D	D	40	5 865	1 341.0	162.5	62	1 229	54.8	15.2

1. Establishment subject to federal tax.

Table B. States and Counties — **Health Care and Social Assistance, Other Services, Nonemployer Businesses, and Residential Construction**

STATE County	Health care and social assistance, 2012				Other services, 2012				Nonemployer businesses, 2014		Value of residential construction authorized by building permits, 2015	
	Number of establishments	Number of employees	Receipts (mil dol)	Annual payroll (mil dol)	Number of establishments	Number of employees	Receipts (mil dol)	Annual payroll (mil dol)	Number	Receipts (mil dol)	New Construction ($1,000)	Number of housing units
	159	160	161	162	163	164	165	166	167	168	169	170
TEXAS—Cont'd												
Mason	11	98	5.1	2.7	8	19	2.5	0.4	584	22.6	586	3
Matagorda	79	1 418	151.0	48.1	60	282	31.9	9.3	2 678	121.0	21 634	85
Maverick	96	4 039	213.0	84.4	37	145	9.5	2.5	4 449	164.0	10 007	95
Medina	69	935	55.0	25.4	40	200	18.0	4.4	3 236	148.3	5 869	36
Menard	2	D	D	D	2	D	D	D	281	10.3	NA	NA
Midland	398	7 196	817.7	299.7	264	2 138	337.4	73.6	15 951	1 269.9	204 438	1 025
Milam	38	791	51.8	22.9	32	117	10.7	2.6	1 630	71.5	878	14
Mills	13	156	7.9	3.7	7	D	D	D	452	16.0	NA	NA
Mitchell	8	D	D	D	5	17	1.2	0.3	506	20.3	150	1
Montague	40	643	46.1	19.4	37	122	11.1	2.7	1 864	105.7	395	2
Montgomery	1 015	15 877	2 147.8	724.1	579	4 253	353.2	111.7	44 231	2 628.3	1 358 461	7 024
Moore	43	680	49.6	21.7	27	109	11.9	2.6	1 065	66.7	2 697	14
Morris	23	257	11.9	5.8	17	78	9.9	2.0	796	28.2	0	0
Motley	1	D	D	D	2	D	D	D	112	3.9	NA	NA
Nacogdoches	202	3 339	353.7	119.6	85	427	37.1	9.6	3 941	174.1	2 227	21
Navarro	130	2 338	163.0	65.3	63	214	21.0	5.1	3 185	152.2	18 981	98
Newton	9	D	D	D	5	D	D	D	617	21.9	NA	NA
Nolan	32	D	D	D	15	D	D	D	1 040	39.8	0	0
Nueces	1 045	28 174	2 640.5	984.5	522	4 501	525.5	143.9	23 594	1 087.1	216 546	1 217
Ochiltree	20	D	D	D	24	101	11.6	2.8	810	48.2	775	5
Oldham	2	D	D	D	2	D	D	D	184	8.2	1 188	4
Orange	141	1 419	119.6	43.3	85	D	D	D	4 744	181.7	45 860	301
Palo Pinto	49	670	89.0	31.5	37	145	16.9	3.9	2 152	112.1	1 366	7
Panola	43	653	56.1	19.7	27	126	12.7	3.2	1 612	76.2	1 565	7
Parker	207	D	D	D	150	914	79.0	23.9	12 134	691.9	87 592	395
Parmer	9	140	14.3	4.9	19	D	D	D	508	25.6	235	3
Pecos	17	470	51.9	17.6	23	114	10.6	3.1	928	35.6	753	7
Polk	72	1 413	121.7	45.6	43	268	19.6	5.5	3 590	171.0	93 098	471
Potter	460	D	D	D	237	1 916	253.5	60.9	8 152	450.2	159 119	804
Presidio	4	41	2.6	1.3	4	14	0.5	0.2	776	27.6	1 366	7
Rains	12	144	7.8	3.1	12	D	D	D	837	40.3	280	2
Randall	235	D	D	D	162	D	D	D	10 204	483.3	12 501	64
Reagan	5	D	D	D	8	D	D	D	385	18.9	0	0
Real	10	199	8.5	4.3	2	D	D	D	463	20.2	0	0
Red River	16	395	29.8	12.2	7	D	D	D	915	39.7	707	9
Reeves	10	D	D	D	11	D	D	D	661	33.2	540	3
Refugio	8	257	23.0	7.3	7	23	1.9	0.6	483	25.6	518	4
Roberts	NA	NA	NA	NA	NA	NA	NA	NA	90	3.2	NA	NA
Robertson	18	D	D	D	24	139	19.2	5.5	1 223	56.6	17 468	87
Rockwall	234	3 578	472.7	146.0	96	741	53.4	16.9	8 770	502.9	297 742	1 046
Runnels	19	387	24.8	12.0	14	D	D	D	888	37.4	450	2
Rusk	73	1 596	104.0	41.2	41	275	23.2	7.6	3 131	143.1	1 516	13
Sabine	14	320	12.7	6.3	14	45	3.7	0.9	722	29.4	405	3
San Augustine	17	393	20.8	8.4	5	D	D	D	537	20.3	0	0
San Jacinto	11	138	7.4	3.1	12	40	4.6	1.0	1 775	79.6	34 435	177
San Patricio	97	1 722	113.9	50.0	64	342	42.4	11.4	4 458	186.0	89 656	757
San Saba	17	194	15.3	4.6	6	D	D	D	590	20.6	255	2
Schleicher	3	D	D	D	1	D	D	D	303	13.7	390	2
Scurry	22	538	60.3	19.5	29	251	38.3	9.4	1 112	57.0	981	6
Shackelford	4	D	D	D	7	8	1.0	0.2	488	27.5	NA	NA
Shelby	40	820	49.2	19.4	30	D	D	D	1 723	88.1	0	0
Sherman	2	D	D	D	4	7	0.5	0.1	232	10.7	957	11
Smith	640	21 211	2 527.9	969.6	347	2 613	252.8	87.5	17 750	926.3	132 119	470
Somervell	15	D	D	D	12	D	D	D	745	41.7	1 894	9
Starr	100	5 009	170.5	85.9	21	D	D	D	6 718	193.8	404	9
Stephens	19	314	19.5	9.6	17	56	4.5	1.1	895	57.9	96	2
Sterling	2	D	D	D	2	D	D	D	168	9.5	NA	NA
Stonewall	6	D	D	D	3	6	0.5	0.1	145	6.6	NA	NA
Sutton	4	61	7.4	2.9	9	13	2.1	0.5	420	15.8	1 952	10
Swisher	10	206	15.7	5.9	15	D	D	D	489	16.7	0	0
Tarrant	4 575	91 404	11 276.2	4 009.1	2 390	19 504	2 118.4	563.0	158 872	7 546.1	1 963 388	8 984
Taylor	389	11 883	1 026.5	403.9	224	1 763	145.6	40.3	9 862	486.3	80 316	531
Terrell	1	D	D	D	2	D	D	D	85	2.4	NA	NA
Terry	21	446	31.9	12.1	22	63	5.1	1.6	622	27.4	170	3
Throckmorton	3	D	D	D	4	8	0.6	0.1	228	11.1	NA	NA
Titus	88	D	D	D	41	204	19.9	4.8	1 720	76.0	10 824	142

Table B. States and Counties — Government Employment and Payroll, and Local Government Finances

STATE County	Government employment and payroll, 2012		March payroll (percent of total)							Local government finances, 2012				
										General revenue			Taxes	
														Per capita[1] (dollars)	
	Full-time equivalent employees	March payroll (dollars)	Administration, judicial, and legal	Police and Corrections	Fire Protection	Highways and transportation	Health and Welfare	Natural resources and utilities	Education and libraries	Total (mil dol)	Intergovernmental (mil dol)	Total (mil dol)	Total	Property
	171	172	173	174	175	176	177	178	179	180	181	182	183	184
TEXAS—Cont'd														
Mason	187	574 614	8.5	5.1	0.0	5.6	6.2	8.5	64.4	12.7	4.9	6.2	1 550	1 351
Matagorda	1 950	6 092 071	4.5	8.9	0.0	2.4	17.9	4.6	60.5	272.8	55.1	91.7	2 509	2 321
Maverick	3 274	9 420 323	4.8	5.7	1.7	2.4	2.2	3.5	79.0	215.5	121.7	45.7	826	606
Medina	2 042	6 076 041	4.7	6.4	0.0	2.1	11.3	4.7	68.9	144.1	64.8	47.3	1 012	893
Menard	160	407 534	7.5	8.8	0.0	1.5	18.9	3.1	58.6	9.7	3.2	4.0	1 788	1 631
Midland	6 743	26 604 150	5.0	7.8	4.1	1.5	30.2	1.5	47.9	761.2	127.7	334.2	2 279	1 657
Milam	1 010	3 486 020	6.1	8.9	0.2	4.0	1.5	3.6	74.9	75.2	30.4	35.9	1 485	1 337
Mills	267	764 983	7.7	3.6	0.0	3.0	2.7	4.7	78.1	16.6	9.4	5.5	1 135	994
Mitchell	583	1 683 044	7.8	5.5	0.2	3.5	33.1	3.1	46.1	46.4	10.5	19.0	2 033	1 894
Montague	1 080	3 133 643	3.8	5.6	1.7	2.8	25.9	4.1	52.2	89.9	35.1	30.6	1 565	1 349
Montgomery	15 517	53 618 969	5.3	8.9	4.3	1.6	4.2	3.6	70.3	1 469.3	416.6	880.8	1 816	1 602
Moore	1 387	4 297 575	5.7	7.6	1.6	2.0	18.7	4.0	59.3	101.2	21.6	47.4	2 125	1 879
Morris	525	1 489 068	7.2	8.0	0.0	2.6	0.2	4.5	77.3	33.3	11.9	17.9	1 399	1 218
Motley	53	139 031	14.8	3.4	0.0	11.8	4.1	2.8	61.5	4.2	1.7	2.0	1 659	1 542
Nacogdoches	3 209	11 081 415	3.8	5.6	2.6	0.8	27.6	2.8	56.3	249.0	82.9	70.1	1 062	894
Navarro	2 582	8 615 927	4.3	7.4	1.8	2.3	3.2	3.1	74.7	198.0	85.4	69.3	1 444	1 208
Newton	492	1 402 695	9.9	5.3	0.0	3.1	1.3	4.5	74.9	46.4	14.2	18.8	1 321	1 309
Nolan	1 074	3 200 019	5.7	6.5	2.3	1.6	30.0	3.7	48.4	92.2	25.3	33.8	2 265	1 854
Nueces	15 002	50 012 628	4.7	10.3	4.3	5.0	3.5	5.4	62.9	1 333.3	434.9	623.4	1 793	1 377
Ochiltree	750	1 938 537	5.3	7.0	1.8	3.2	23.4	3.9	53.5	38.3	10.0	24.3	2 264	1 986
Oldham	268	808 206	6.5	4.6	0.0	1.8	0.0	1.4	85.2	17.9	9.3	4.2	2 028	1 796
Orange	3 533	11 142 459	7.8	12.4	2.2	3.6	1.2	10.2	61.9	284.3	105.6	118.8	1 432	1 208
Palo Pinto	1 439	4 512 709	5.6	7.4	0.8	3.8	30.1	2.6	48.2	125.0	32.7	53.6	1 926	1 663
Panola	1 035	3 674 945	5.9	7.4	0.6	4.5	0.6	2.7	77.7	119.5	26.6	78.0	3 248	3 005
Parker	3 910	13 841 811	8.1	6.9	2.5	2.7	2.3	3.6	72.3	342.4	84.3	203.7	1 701	1 506
Parmer	674	1 770 342	9.3	9.6	0.0	4.1	7.1	4.4	65.0	56.5	17.4	22.7	2 231	2 142
Pecos	928	3 033 599	8.3	7.8	0.0	4.3	11.7	7.2	58.4	127.5	16.7	76.1	4 873	4 588
Polk	1 509	6 360 260	11.3	19.6	0.1	3.8	2.1	6.1	56.0	118.9	38.8	47.9	1 049	878
Potter	8 893	30 669 359	4.8	10.2	6.1	3.0	6.5	3.7	64.1	740.4	307.7	290.5	2 375	1 650
Presidio	514	1 310 951	9.3	7.0	0.0	3.7	6.0	5.4	67.8	35.4	22.2	7.8	1 041	903
Rains	490	1 074 762	8.2	7.5	0.0	2.1	0.3	4.6	75.7	30.7	11.0	16.4	1 498	1 297
Randall	1 728	5 466 299	10.7	21.4	1.0	1.7	0.6	1.5	61.9	119.8	28.9	76.8	614	566
Reagan	366	1 075 023	9.6	7.2	0.4	4.0	23.8	3.8	50.1	44.4	3.9	33.4	9 618	8 897
Real	97	286 334	19.1	8.8	0.0	5.7	12.5	1.5	51.9	7.4	1.1	5.5	1 637	1 475
Red River	579	1 522 449	5.6	7.7	1.5	3.4	0.0	3.7	77.9	37.1	22.5	10.9	857	736
Reeves	1 448	3 858 596	5.2	36.7	1.3	1.5	16.8	4.5	33.4	149.1	13.2	27.3	1 981	1 689
Refugio	551	1 642 349	7.4	7.5	0.7	4.5	25.8	3.6	49.3	40.3	10.7	21.9	3 017	2 809
Roberts	81	227 300	16.9	8.7	0.0	5.2	2.4	7.8	59.0	9.8	1.4	7.9	9 265	8 938
Robertson	905	2 580 494	9.2	10.0	0.0	3.8	0.5	5.5	69.4	85.5	23.3	56.6	3 421	3 199
Rockwall	3 263	11 181 638	8.8	10.5	1.2	0.8	0.1	2.9	74.8	283.0	72.7	179.3	2 159	1 870
Runnels	671	2 087 986	8.8	8.8	0.6	3.6	22.7	8.6	45.9	42.1	20.2	12.8	1 230	1 099
Rusk	1 692	6 115 196	8.9	12.8	1.3	2.9	0.5	7.7	64.0	130.2	38.5	76.0	1 407	1 267
Sabine	470	1 232 799	8.2	5.9	0.0	2.1	12.7	6.2	63.1	31.3	14.1	9.8	938	790
San Augustine	376	978 889	9.7	7.9	0.0	4.2	0.9	5.0	71.7	33.0	20.0	10.7	1 214	1 066
San Jacinto	778	2 008 317	6.5	5.3	0.1	3.0	0.8	1.6	81.9	49.7	19.2	26.2	965	899
San Patricio	3 506	9 765 866	4.9	8.3	1.0	2.9	7.6	7.3	67.8	239.0	100.4	101.3	1 544	1 330
San Saba	434	1 149 764	5.8	3.1	0.0	36.7	1.6	5.8	45.2	25.2	16.5	6.7	1 112	1 001
Schleicher	239	526 633	7.5	4.0	0.0	5.0	19.5	5.6	57.3	13.1	4.2	6.5	2 000	1 918
Scurry	995	3 410 030	6.1	6.6	1.3	2.1	20.3	2.2	60.2	121.2	28.5	57.3	3 345	2 945
Shackelford	207	556 026	10.6	6.6	0.0	5.6	3.6	4.5	68.0	12.7	3.6	7.4	2 193	1 913
Shelby	1 249	3 791 323	5.4	6.0	0.5	2.4	0.0	3.4	81.5	78.9	40.8	30.6	1 176	971
Sherman	266	825 372	8.9	3.5	0.0	4.4	16.5	9.6	54.1	17.5	2.5	11.5	3 752	3 455
Smith	8 764	29 028 100	7.6	10.8	2.8	1.5	6.8	3.6	65.8	648.3	207.0	325.4	1 515	1 170
Somervell	476	1 533 907	6.3	9.3	0.2	6.9	1.2	3.4	65.6	85.7	11.9	48.2	5 603	5 421
Starr	4 112	12 165 296	5.7	7.0	1.5	2.0	8.1	2.5	71.6	268.0	173.1	50.8	825	734
Stephens	543	1 467 714	8.2	6.9	1.9	2.5	26.7	3.6	48.8	27.8	5.2	19.3	2 044	1 781
Sterling	86	271 999	21.3	6.6	0.0	4.1	0.0	5.7	60.3	15.5	4.1	9.5	8 008	7 790
Stonewall	209	553 406	6.8	2.8	0.0	10.2	50.6	1.9	26.7	13.8	2.1	5.9	3 967	3 683
Sutton	312	1 080 664	8.3	4.9	0.0	4.6	23.3	3.3	51.3	24.7	7.3	14.2	3 596	3 274
Swisher	403	1 118 598	6.5	7.0	0.0	2.6	0.9	4.3	77.3	36.9	14.7	7.6	964	823
Tarrant	76 274	291 509 259	6.4	12.5	4.8	1.5	9.8	4.8	58.6	7 673.3	2 064.9	3 815.1	2 029	1 629
Taylor	5 091	16 346 681	6.1	13.5	5.9	1.9	5.4	4.7	60.8	427.2	176.5	186.9	1 401	997
Terrell	108	366 799	22.2	0.0	0.0	7.7	5.5	4.7	44.6	12.5	1.9	9.9	10 751	10 482
Terry	926	2 466 610	5.9	8.0	1.0	2.6	26.1	3.6	51.2	56.3	12.9	26.6	2 108	1 903
Throckmorton	113	346 336	4.5	0.0	0.0	1.3	25.5	5.9	62.6	9.8	3.2	3.9	2 462	2 280
Titus	2 456	7 751 640	2.6	4.2	1.3	1.2	29.0	2.5	58.4	124.8	50.8	52.8	1 617	1 410

1. Based on the resident population estimated as of July 1 of the year shown.

Table B. States and Counties — Local Government Finances, Government Employment, and Voting

	Local government finances, 2012 (cont.)									Government employment, 2014			Presidential election,[2] 2012		
	Direct general expenditure							Debt outstanding					Percent of vote cast:		
			Percent of total for:												
STATE County	Total (mil dol)	Per capita[1] (dollars)	Education	Health and hospitals	Police protection	Public welfare	Highways	Total (mil dol)	Per capita[1] (dollars)	Federal civilian	Federal military	State and local	Democratic	Republican	All other
	185	186	187	188	189	190	191	192	193	194	195	196	197	198	199
TEXAS—Cont'd															
Mason	11.2	2 787	63.4	2.7	6.9	0.1	5.9	3.4	853	16	0	274	25.7	72.8	1.5
Matagorda	250.1	6 844	32.2	45.6	2.8	0.0	2.5	242.4	6 631	80	75	2 312	35.9	63.3	0.8
Maverick	219.2	3 958	56.6	2.8	3.8	0.0	8.5	215.3	3 888	896	116	5 059	78.2	21.2	0.6
Medina	151.4	3 238	58.2	13.0	3.7	0.4	3.0	135.1	2 888	59	94	2 892	32.7	66.6	0.7
Menard	9.9	4 437	46.2	0.0	6.1	23.8	3.2	1.6	696	0	0	190	29.0	69.9	1.1
Midland	747.6	5 098	34.2	40.2	3.6	0.0	1.3	587.4	4 005	513	319	8 302	21.0	78.2	0.8
Milam	70.4	2 914	62.9	2.6	4.1	0.6	7.3	71.3	2 950	49	49	1 197	36.4	62.4	1.1
Mills	17.5	3 633	61.9	2.4	3.5	0.4	4.0	5.4	1 116	15	10	329	18.3	80.5	1.2
Mitchell	47.8	5 118	43.4	36.9	2.7	0.1	3.9	37.5	4 017	23	15	1 154	24.1	74.7	1.2
Montague	91.2	4 662	32.2	41.0	3.2	0.2	3.8	35.2	1 798	43	40	1 289	20.1	78.6	1.4
Montgomery	1 474.0	3 039	50.5	6.5	5.6	0.1	4.0	4 045.0	8 339	802	1 069	24 456	23.3	75.9	0.8
Moore	95.6	4 283	47.6	26.8	5.1	0.1	0.9	47.9	2 146	62	46	1 619	20.7	78.8	0.6
Morris	30.0	2 343	68.2	0.1	4.2	0.6	3.3	10.3	804	25	26	636	39.2	60.2	0.7
Motley	4.0	3 301	70.6	4.0	1.7	0.1	5.8	0.1	49	12	0	96	11.3	87.9	0.8
Nacogdoches	257.8	3 903	37.6	34.4	3.9	0.9	1.9	196.8	2 981	146	131	5 428	35.9	63.4	0.7
Navarro	194.1	4 045	64.8	2.1	5.7	0.3	4.2	235.6	4 910	97	98	3 318	33.1	66.2	0.7
Newton	45.7	3 222	44.4	0.0	8.1	1.7	3.7	33.4	2 356	25	28	619	33.3	65.5	1.2
Nolan	90.3	6 050	47.2	28.5	3.6	0.0	3.1	76.3	5 116	41	30	1 612	30.0	68.8	1.1
Nueces	1 384.5	3 982	48.2	4.5	6.3	0.1	3.8	2 805.4	8 069	6 198	2 911	21 561	47.3	51.8	0.9
Ochiltree	30.1	2 806	68.7	0.5	3.5	0.0	4.9	31.4	2 924	19	22	784	7.8	91.7	0.5
Oldham	17.7	8 594	83.4	0.0	4.2	0.0	2.0	4.6	2 220	0	0	278	11.1	88.4	0.5
Orange	269.5	3 248	46.6	0.7	7.3	0.2	3.2	736.8	8 880	98	172	4 118	26.0	73.1	0.9
Palo Pinto	119.5	4 289	40.7	32.3	3.8	0.0	3.5	91.1	3 271	55	58	1 721	25.3	73.4	1.3
Panola	120.9	5 033	70.2	0.4	3.5	0.2	6.0	54.6	2 272	72	48	1 389	25.3	74.2	0.5
Parker	370.5	3 095	53.1	7.2	4.5	0.0	11.8	720.3	6 017	162	253	5 059	21.9	77.1	1.0
Parmer	51.6	5 067	48.1	20.9	4.1	4.3	4.2	28.1	2 758	65	20	822	19.4	80.0	0.7
Pecos	125.4	8 031	44.7	24.0	3.2	0.0	4.0	74.8	4 792	52	29	1 879	36.8	61.8	1.3
Polk	109.6	2 400	62.3	0.6	6.0	0.2	7.5	278.0	6 089	84	86	2 926	30.9	68.1	0.9
Potter	749.2	6 124	53.7	5.1	5.8	0.0	2.4	762.3	6 231	1 906	389	13 012	29.8	69.2	1.0
Presidio	41.0	5 442	67.0	0.7	1.8	0.0	1.4	21.5	2 854	329	14	649	71.3	27.8	0.9
Rains	31.1	2 840	44.9	2.6	3.6	0.5	6.4	25.3	2 316	20	23	461	24.7	74.3	1.0
Randall	116.9	935	49.6	1.1	7.6	0.1	3.1	128.5	1 027	181	261	4 204	18.3	80.9	0.8
Reagan	38.8	11 153	53.5	17.4	3.8	0.3	7.7	32.0	9 222	11	0	378	19.8	80.0	0.2
Real	6.9	2 039	48.7	0.5	9.4	2.4	11.7	0.3	75	0	0	202	23.0	76.0	0.9
Red River	37.7	2 968	74.1	0.1	2.9	1.4	1.5	18.4	1 453	38	25	681	30.5	68.5	1.0
Reeves	138.8	10 063	21.0	12.8	3.3	0.0	1.6	136.0	9 859	74	23	1 544	52.2	47.0	0.8
Refugio	40.6	5 594	55.7	13.7	4.6	0.0	5.7	20.5	2 822	36	15	679	42.4	56.9	0.7
Roberts	9.1	10 678	90.1	0.4	2.2	0.0	2.1	0.7	768	0	0	97	7.9	92.1	0.0
Robertson	89.0	5 381	81.1	0.1	3.4	0.3	3.2	84.0	5 080	42	34	1 023	39.9	59.3	0.8
Rockwall	297.5	3 584	49.5	0.4	5.7	0.2	5.2	881.6	10 619	89	180	3 421	26.5	72.7	0.9
Runnels	43.0	4 112	51.2	23.8	1.8	0.0	4.7	11.5	1 101	37	21	788	18.6	80.6	0.7
Rusk	130.1	2 408	66.3	0.4	4.6	0.1	6.1	181.9	3 368	70	100	2 422	26.6	72.9	0.5
Sabine	29.1	2 787	50.7	22.5	5.3	0.0	6.3	11.3	1 081	48	21	476	22.1	76.9	1.0
San Augustine	28.0	3 179	73.4	1.6	6.1	0.0	0.7	34.8	3 949	20	17	413	35.7	63.0	1.2
San Jacinto	46.2	1 704	66.1	0.2	5.1	0.5	6.7	34.4	1 269	23	56	894	30.4	68.7	1.0
San Patricio	237.2	3 616	57.1	6.5	5.8	0.3	3.2	231.1	3 524	90	1 686	3 864	41.4	58.0	0.6
San Saba	18.5	3 087	57.6	1.7	4.5	1.1	6.8	15.9	2 642	23	11	486	19.8	79.0	1.2
Schleicher	13.7	4 190	45.0	27.0	0.7	0.0	3.4	34.9	10 699	11	0	269	24.8	74.4	0.8
Scurry	113.5	6 628	57.4	17.4	3.7	0.1	3.7	74.5	4 348	34	32	1 671	19.5	79.3	1.2
Shackelford	11.4	3 400	61.4	4.1	6.5	0.0	5.6	0.9	262	12	0	227	13.8	85.3	0.9
Shelby	75.6	2 905	71.6	0.6	5.1	0.0	6.1	42.1	1 619	76	53	1 304	27.6	71.9	0.5
Sherman	18.7	6 099	54.0	15.6	4.5	0.0	6.0	3.1	1 017	0	0	270	12.5	86.7	0.9
Smith	645.1	3 003	55.0	5.1	5.6	0.2	3.4	1 145.0	5 330	642	478	12 851	29.8	69.4	0.8
Somervell	86.1	10 008	49.0	29.8	3.5	0.5	3.8	65.4	7 610	13	17	860	22.6	75.8	1.6
Starr	254.5	4 130	66.2	11.4	3.9	0.0	3.6	277.9	4 510	749	129	5 175	84.5	15.2	0.3
Stephens	27.4	2 898	46.7	2.5	5.2	0.1	3.9	19.2	2 029	17	18	679	17.8	81.4	0.9
Sterling	17.5	14 668	64.5	1.9	2.1	15.3	2.0	10.2	8 554	0	0	160	15.7	84.0	0.3
Stonewall	23.1	15 635	13.2	76.1	1.3	0.0	2.7	0.1	57	11	0	231	28.0	71.3	0.7
Sutton	22.3	5 656	62.2	17.0	3.3	0.1	3.4	1.6	405	0	0	428	24.1	75.3	0.5
Swisher	30.7	3 895	48.7	32.1	4.0	0.0	0.8	3.2	409	26	14	757	32.1	66.4	1.5
Tarrant	7 651.9	4 070	42.5	12.1	6.9	0.1	3.7	19 647.2	10 450	14 407	5 316	94 273	43.7	55.4	0.8
Taylor	402.0	3 012	53.5	4.7	7.8	0.6	3.1	263.9	1 977	1 027	4 516	8 435	26.8	72.3	0.9
Terrell	12.1	13 215	63.5	3.9	7.6	0.0	8.3	21.1	22 972	65	0	122	35.8	62.2	1.9
Terry	59.1	4 683	48.8	27.3	3.7	0.4	3.1	17.6	1 397	22	24	1 096	32.2	67.3	0.5
Throckmorton	9.9	6 177	38.7	32.3	0.8	0.0	11.7	0.2	137	0	0	179	19.8	80.1	0.1
Titus	127.0	3 889	67.0	0.4	4.2	0.1	6.4	228.1	6 985	90	66	2 822	34.0	65.2	0.8

1. Based on the resident population estimated as of July 1 of the year shown.   2. © 2013 Election Data Services, Inc. All rights reserved.

Table B. States and Counties — **Land Area and Population**

STATE/ County code	CBSA code[1]	County type[2]	STATE County	Land area[3] (sq km) 2010	Total persons 2015	Rank	Per square kilometer	White	Black	American Indian, Alaska Native	Asian and Pacific Islander	Percent Hispanic or Latino[4]	Under 5 years	5 to 17 years	18 to 24 years	25 to 34 years	35 to 44 years	45 to 54 years
					Population, 2015			Population and population characteristics, 2014										
								Race alone or in combination, not Hispanic or Latino (percent)					Age (percent)					
				1	2	3	4	5	6	7	8	9	10	11	12	13	14	15
			TEXAS—Cont'd															
48 451	41660	3	Tom Green	3 942	118 105	523	30.0	56.2	4.4	0.8	1.8	38.0	6.8	16.8	12.7	15.5	10.7	11.4
48 453	12420	1	Travis	2 565	1 176 558	36	458.7	51.3	8.7	0.7	7.2	33.9	6.9	16.2	10.0	19.9	15.8	12.7
48 455	26660	8	Trinity	1 796	14 402	2 140	8.0	80.0	10.3	1.2	0.6	9.2	4.7	14.9	6.7	9.3	10.1	12.9
48 457	...	6	Tyler	2 394	21 347	1 762	8.9	80.5	11.6	1.1	0.5	7.7	5.3	14.1	8.9	13.2	11.3	12.8
48 459	30980	3	Upshur	1 510	40 603	1 162	26.9	82.5	9.2	1.5	0.8	7.9	6.3	17.8	8.3	11.3	11.1	13.8
48 461	...	8	Upton	3 215	3 651	2 930	1.1	44.1	2.1	1.4	0.5	52.6	8.2	20.3	8.2	13.4	11.6	11.2
48 463	46620	7	Uvalde	4 020	27 245	1 521	6.8	28.2	0.8	0.4	0.8	69.9	7.6	20.2	10.9	12.3	11.4	11.0
48 465	19620	5	Val Verde	8 145	48 988	996	6.0	17.3	1.6	0.4	0.9	80.5	8.3	20.6	11.3	13.9	11.8	11.1
48 467	...	6	Van Zandt	2 182	53 547	935	24.5	85.8	3.4	1.4	0.7	10.2	5.6	17.9	7.5	10.1	11.4	13.6
48 469	47020	3	Victoria	2 285	92 382	631	40.4	47.0	6.6	0.5	1.5	45.2	7.2	18.6	9.5	14.0	11.6	12.1
48 471	26660	4	Walker	2 031	70 699	764	34.8	58.1	23.1	0.7	1.5	17.8	4.2	11.3	19.7	14.7	13.3	14.2
48 473	26420	1	Waller	1 330	48 656	1 005	36.6	44.3	25.3	0.7	1.0	29.8	6.3	17.7	20.7	10.0	10.2	12.1
48 475	...	6	Ward	2 164	11 721	2 310	5.4	43.3	4.5	1.0	0.9	51.6	8.0	20.0	9.4	14.2	11.3	11.8
48 477	14780	6	Washington	1 564	34 765	1 310	22.2	65.7	17.9	0.5	1.9	15.1	5.9	16.6	11.1	10.4	10.5	12.7
48 479	29700	3	Webb	8 706	269 721	251	31.0	3.8	0.3	0.1	0.6	95.1	10.0	24.0	11.6	13.4	13.2	11.1
48 481	20900	4	Wharton	2 813	41 486	1 137	14.7	46.3	13.5	0.4	0.6	39.6	6.7	19.3	9.3	12.2	11.0	12.8
48 483	...	9	Wheeler	2 369	5 657	2 788	2.4	69.7	3.0	1.0	0.9	27.5	6.9	19.4	8.1	12.1	11.3	11.8
48 485	48660	3	Wichita	1 626	131 705	477	81.0	68.1	11.0	1.4	3.0	18.2	6.6	16.1	13.6	15.1	11.2	11.9
48 487	46900	6	Wilbarger	2 514	13 027	2 231	5.2	61.4	8.9	1.4	1.3	28.7	6.7	16.9	9.8	12.8	11.0	12.5
48 489	39700	6	Willacy	1 530	21 903	1 735	14.3	9.7	2.0	0.3	0.7	87.6	6.5	18.8	13.3	15.4	12.9	10.9
48 491	12420	1	Williamson	2 896	508 514	136	175.6	63.6	6.9	0.8	6.9	23.9	6.8	20.3	7.9	14.0	16.4	13.6
48 493	41700	1	Wilson	2 082	47 520	1 027	22.8	59.0	1.8	0.8	0.6	38.6	5.7	19.1	8.2	11.1	12.4	15.1
48 495	...	6	Winkler	2 178	8 005	2 598	3.7	39.0	2.3	0.7	0.6	58.3	8.1	22.3	9.9	13.5	12.0	12.7
48 497	19100	1	Wise	2 342	62 953	839	26.9	78.9	1.7	1.3	0.8	18.4	6.5	18.6	8.4	12.0	12.1	14.9
48 499	...	6	Wood	1 671	43 356	1 105	25.9	84.2	5.3	1.1	0.7	9.6	4.9	14.8	7.9	9.2	9.5	12.3
48 501	...	7	Yoakum	2 071	8 546	2 553	4.1	34.8	1.4	0.7	0.5	62.8	9.5	22.8	9.1	13.0	10.7	12.1
48 503	...	6	Young	2 368	18 270	1 903	7.7	79.7	1.8	1.0	0.7	17.9	6.7	17.3	7.7	11.1	11.0	12.7
48 505	49820	6	Zapata	2 586	14 374	2 143	5.6	5.6	0.3	0.2	0.2	93.8	10.1	23.3	10.8	13.3	11.9	10.4
48 507	...	7	Zavala	3 360	12 235	2 281	3.6	6.4	0.5	0.2	0.1	93.8	8.9	21.7	12.6	12.4	11.0	10.7
49 000	...	X	UTAH	212 818	2 995 919	X	14.1	81.1	1.5	1.4	4.4	13.5	8.6	22.2	11.3	15.0	13.1	10.4
49 001	...	9	Beaver	6 708	6 354	2 727	0.9	86.5	0.6	1.3	2.1	10.9	8.2	24.1	8.7	11.0	12.1	10.4
49 003	36260	4	Box Elder	14 881	52 097	958	3.5	88.8	0.6	1.3	1.9	9.1	8.6	24.2	8.7	12.6	12.4	10.8
49 005	30860	3	Cache	3 017	120 783	513	40.0	85.5	0.9	1.0	3.7	10.5	9.3	21.8	18.9	14.3	11.1	8.4
49 007	39220	7	Carbon	3 829	20 479	1 806	5.3	84.5	1.0	1.6	1.3	13.2	7.7	19.2	9.5	12.9	11.5	10.6
49 009	...	8	Daggett	1 805	1 109	3 105	0.6	93.7	1.2	1.0	0.8	4.2	5.2	17.8	5.9	12.6	11.2	11.6
49 011	36260	2	Davis	774	336 043	199	434.2	86.7	1.8	0.8	4.0	9.1	8.9	24.4	9.4	14.6	13.8	10.7
49 013	...	6	Duchesne	8 394	20 862	1 782	2.5	87.4	0.8	4.8	1.3	8.1	10.4	23.8	8.6	14.7	12.0	9.8
49 015	...	9	Emery	11 557	10 370	2 400	0.9	92.1	0.6	0.9	1.0	6.3	7.6	23.4	7.5	11.4	11.7	10.8
49 017	...	9	Garfield	13 404	5 009	2 835	0.4	90.9	0.7	2.2	1.9	5.6	6.1	19.2	7.0	11.1	10.5	11.7
49 019	...	7	Grand	9 509	9 516	2 469	1.0	84.5	1.1	4.3	1.6	10.0	6.9	15.8	6.8	13.1	13.0	12.9
49 021	16260	4	Iron	8 538	48 368	1 013	5.7	87.9	0.7	2.5	2.1	8.3	8.4	20.8	16.0	13.1	11.1	9.2
49 023	39340	2	Juab	8 786	10 594	2 387	1.2	94.1	0.6	1.3	0.9	4.7	8.9	26.2	9.0	11.7	12.8	10.2
49 025	...	6	Kane	10 335	7 131	2 663	0.7	93.0	0.8	2.4	1.0	4.5	5.8	17.1	7.4	11.1	10.1	11.2
49 027	...	7	Millard	17 023	12 645	2 253	0.7	85.4	0.6	1.4	1.3	12.8	8.2	23.2	8.3	10.7	10.7	10.5
49 029	36260	2	Morgan	1 578	11 065	2 350	7.0	95.9	0.5	0.6	0.9	2.7	8.4	26.9	8.4	9.6	13.1	11.6
49 031	...	9	Piute	1 963	1 517	3 080	0.8	90.9	0.6	0.9	0.6	7.7	3.6	22.1	6.8	6.9	9.8	10.3
49 033	...	8	Rich	2 665	2 311	3 023	0.9	94.2	0.6	1.3	0.3	4.6	7.0	22.7	6.8	10.9	11.3	10.5
49 035	41620	2	Salt Lake	1 923	1 107 314	39	575.8	74.4	2.1	1.1	6.6	17.8	8.1	20.2	9.7	16.7	14.2	11.4
49 037	...	7	San Juan	20 254	15 772	2 055	0.8	48.4	0.7	46.7	1.2	5.1	8.1	24.1	10.8	11.3	11.2	11.6
49 039	...	6	Sanpete	4 118	28 778	1 463	7.0	87.4	1.1	1.4	2.2	9.8	6.5	21.1	15.9	12.0	11.8	10.1
49 041	...	7	Sevier	4 948	20 984	1 775	4.2	92.9	0.5	1.4	0.9	4.9	7.0	23.2	8.1	11.7	12.4	10.6
49 043	44920	2	Summit	4 848	39 633	1 183	8.2	85.8	0.7	0.7	2.5	11.6	6.0	20.2	7.9	11.9	13.9	15.9
49 045	41620	2	Tooele	17 978	62 952	840	3.5	85.2	1.2	1.5	2.0	11.8	8.5	26.0	8.4	13.3	15.0	11.2
49 047	46860	7	Uintah	11 602	37 928	1 224	3.3	85.3	0.7	7.9	1.5	8.0	9.8	24.0	9.2	16.3	12.6	9.8
49 049	39340	2	Utah	5 189	575 205	111	110.9	85.2	0.9	0.9	4.0	11.2	10.2	24.7	16.6	14.4	12.2	8.2
49 051	25720	6	Wasatch	3 045	29 161	1 450	9.6	85.0	0.6	0.8	1.7	12.8	7.9	25.0	8.3	12.5	14.7	11.7
49 053	41100	3	Washington	6 284	155 602	415	24.8	86.7	0.9	1.6	2.6	10.0	7.3	21.1	8.8	12.4	10.9	9.4
49 055	...	9	Wayne	6 373	2 692	2 992	0.4	93.9	0.6	0.7	1.7	4.9	6.1	21.0	7.4	9.7	10.9	11.5
49 057	36260	2	Weber	1 492	243 645	275	163.3	78.8	1.7	1.1	2.7	17.7	8.0	21.1	9.7	15.3	13.1	11.3
50 000	...	X	VERMONT	23 871	626 042	X	26.2	95.1	1.7	1.1	2.1	1.8	4.9	14.6	10.8	11.5	11.4	14.6
50 001	...	6	Addison	1 985	37 035	1 254	18.7	94.8	1.5	0.8	2.6	2.2	4.3	14.0	14.0	9.5	10.9	14.7
50 003	13540	6	Bennington	1 748	36 317	1 267	20.8	96.2	1.4	0.7	1.3	1.8	4.7	14.8	9.3	9.3	10.0	14.8
50 005	...	7	Caledonia	1 681	30 780	1 415	18.3	96.7	1.1	1.3	1.1	1.5	4.8	15.6	9.7	10.6	11.5	13.9

1. CBSA = Core Based Statistical Area. See Appendix A for explanation. See Appendix B for list of metropolitan areas with component counties. See Appendix A for definition.   3. Dry land or land partially or temporarily covered by water.   2. County type code from the Economic Research Service of USDA Rural-Urban Continuum Codes. See Appendix A for definition.   4. May be of any race.

Table B. States and Counties — Population and Households

STATE County	Age (percent) (cont.) 55 to 64 years	65 to 74 years	75 years and over	Percent female	Population change and components of change, 2000-2015 Total persons 2000	2010	Percent change 2000-2010	2010-2015	Components of change, 2010-2015 Births	Deaths	Net migration	Households, 2010-2014 Number	Persons per household	Percent Family households	Female family householder[1]	One person
	16	17	18	19	20	21	22	23	24	25	26	27	28	29	30	31
TEXAS—Cont'd																
Tom Green	11.7	7.8	6.7	50.3	104 010	110 224	6.0	7.1	8 117	5 190	5 029	42 361	2.53	65.0	13.0	29.6
Travis	10.3	5.2	3.2	49.6	812 280	1 024 347	26.1	14.9	83 235	26 208	93 195	419 496	2.55	57.2	11.5	30.8
Trinity	16.1	14.6	10.7	51.8	13 779	14 675	6.5	-1.9	692	1 117	164	5 078	2.83	63.9	8.3	34.0
Tyler	13.7	11.9	8.7	45.9	20 871	21 766	4.3	-1.9	1 163	1 314	-206	8 154	2.36	71.5	11.3	25.5
Upshur	14.4	10.0	7.1	50.5	35 291	39 316	11.4	3.3	2 570	2 200	1 000	14 219	2.76	72.6	9.7	23.7
Upton	13.3	6.9	6.9	49.0	3 404	3 349	-1.6	9.0	281	161	202	1 183	2.77	73.8	7.5	24.3
Uvalde	10.5	8.9	7.1	50.7	25 926	26 405	1.8	3.2	2 152	1 321	7	8 622	3.04	71.9	15.3	23.2
Val Verde	9.3	7.7	6.1	49.2	44 856	48 879	9.0	0.2	4 618	1 850	-2 760	15 055	3.16	75.9	12.9	21.5
Van Zandt	14.1	11.5	8.3	50.9	48 140	52 582	9.2	1.8	3 040	3 308	1 233	18 903	2.74	70.2	10.4	25.7
Victoria	12.3	8.2	6.3	50.9	84 088	86 793	3.2	6.4	6 903	3 992	2 693	32 207	2.72	71.3	15.6	24.6
Walker	11.1	6.8	4.6	41.2	61 758	67 861	9.9	4.2	3 231	2 649	2 208	20 681	2.32	58.9	13.8	30.0
Waller	11.3	7.3	4.2	50.2	32 663	43 237	32.4	12.5	3 099	1 478	3 701	13 655	2.99	73.2	14.0	20.2
Ward	11.1	7.7	6.4	50.3	10 909	10 658	-2.3	10.0	937	536	689	3 916	2.76	68.6	14.6	28.8
Washington	14.0	10.3	9.4	50.7	30 373	33 708	11.0	3.1	2 148	1 957	810	11 917	2.69	70.7	13.9	25.9
Webb	8.1	5.0	3.6	51.2	193 117	250 304	29.6	7.8	28 941	6 465	-2 935	68 502	3.74	82.2	22.7	15.0
Wharton	13.1	8.4	7.3	50.7	41 188	41 280	0.2	0.5	2 834	2 138	-489	14 492	2.81	67.8	13.6	29.0
Wheeler	13.3	9.6	7.6	48.9	5 284	5 410	2.4	4.6	367	335	214	2 281	2.42	70.8	10.3	24.9
Wichita	11.6	7.3	6.5	48.4	131 664	131 669	0.0	0.0	9 345	6 826	-2 583	47 818	2.47	64.4	13.2	30.5
Wilbarger	13.5	9.4	7.5	51.0	14 676	13 535	-7.8	-3.8	870	778	-570	5 253	2.39	64.2	15.1	31.9
Willacy	9.7	7.1	5.4	45.4	20 082	22 134	10.2	-1.0	1 688	847	-1 088	5 461	3.59	81.0	24.0	17.6
Williamson	10.1	6.8	4.1	50.9	249 967	422 613	69.1	20.3	32 278	11 260	63 513	158 283	2.86	72.7	10.5	22.2
Wilson	13.7	9.0	5.8	49.9	32 408	42 913	32.4	10.7	2 622	1 849	3 717	15 598	2.82	80.0	10.9	16.7
Winkler	10.6	6.4	4.5	48.7	7 173	7 110	-0.9	12.6	655	296	531	2 659	2.74	71.4	12.9	24.4
Wise	13.2	9.0	5.4	49.6	48 793	59 119	21.2	6.5	4 054	2 637	2 316	20 694	2.87	77.4	10.8	18.7
Wood	14.9	15.7	10.9	50.6	36 752	41 961	14.2	3.3	2 148	3 147	2 258	16 076	2.55	70.0	9.4	25.5
Yoakum	10.8	6.8	5.1	50.6	7 322	7 879	7.6	8.5	844	294	111	2 594	3.09	79.0	11.2	19.4
Young	14.0	10.2	9.2	50.6	17 943	18 550	3.4	-1.5	1 211	1 310	-196	7 268	2.49	71.6	11.0	25.1
Zapata	8.6	7.0	4.6	49.6	12 182	14 018	15.1	2.5	1 510	450	-708	4 424	3.21	81.7	23.6	17.0
Zavala	10.1	7.0	5.5	49.9	11 600	11 677	0.7	4.8	1 076	428	-95	3 556	3.29	72.2	23.0	25.3
UTAH	9.4	5.9	4.2	49.7	2 233 169	2 763 888	23.8	8.4	270 428	81 869	43 920	896 194	3.14	75.1	9.6	19.5
Beaver	11.9	8.0	5.6	48.7	6 005	6 629	10.4	-4.1	598	270	-611	2 163	2.94	75.0	10.8	23.4
Box Elder	10.6	6.5	5.7	49.4	42 745	49 975	16.9	4.2	4 573	1 800	-695	16 223	3.09	81.1	7.3	16.9
Cache	7.7	4.8	3.8	50.1	91 391	112 656	23.3	7.2	12 582	2 568	-2 012	35 505	3.16	75.6	7.6	16.7
Carbon	13.4	8.7	6.6	50.3	20 422	21 403	4.8	-4.3	1 619	1 138	-1 395	7 834	2.61	67.6	8.8	27.6
Daggett	14.4	13.3	7.9	44.1	921	1 061	15.2	4.5	63	29	20	276	2.14	66.7	4.3	31.5
Davis	9.1	5.3	3.8	49.6	238 994	306 486	28.2	9.6	30 536	7 973	6 896	96 711	3.27	81.2	9.2	15.3
Duchesne	9.7	6.4	4.6	48.9	14 371	18 609	29.5	12.1	2 251	685	656	6 738	2.82	79.7	8.8	17.5
Emery	12.9	8.9	5.7	49.2	10 860	10 976	1.1	-5.5	835	441	-1 001	3 628	2.96	80.1	8.7	17.4
Garfield	15.3	11.0	8.0	47.8	4 735	5 172	9.2	-3.2	321	229	-275	1 815	2.69	68.8	8.8	25.6
Grand	15.5	9.4	6.4	50.1	8 485	9 225	8.7	3.2	668	384	7	3 822	2.41	57.1	7.3	37.5
Iron	9.8	7.0	4.4	50.0	33 779	46 163	36.7	4.8	4 413	1 467	-772	15 135	3.02	71.5	9.3	21.4
Juab	9.4	6.8	4.8	48.9	8 238	10 246	24.4	3.4	950	387	-225	3 066	3.33	82.7	9.6	15.7
Kane	15.8	13.7	7.8	50.0	6 046	7 125	17.8	0.1	418	370	-49	2 925	2.43	63.6	5.3	28.0
Millard	12.2	9.1	7.0	49.0	12 405	12 503	0.8	1.1	986	493	-379	4 210	2.94	76.3	9.6	20.5
Morgan	10.7	7.0	4.4	49.1	7 129	9 469	32.8	16.9	845	266	1 019	2 941	3.38	86.9	2.8	11.7
Piute	15.7	13.7	11.0	48.5	1 435	1 557	8.5	-2.6	75	69	-67	557	3.37	73.2	7.0	25.3
Rich	13.1	10.9	6.8	48.7	1 961	2 264	15.5	2.1	176	64	-53	627	3.63	80.4	6.7	17.1
Salt Lake	10.1	5.7	3.9	49.8	898 387	1 029 581	14.6	7.5	94 669	31 493	15 649	348 110	3.02	70.5	10.8	23.0
San Juan	11.0	7.1	4.8	50.2	14 413	14 749	2.3	6.9	1 290	493	256	4 038	3.60	73.3	14.7	24.1
Sanpete	9.9	7.6	5.2	47.7	22 763	27 822	22.2	3.4	2 080	919	-230	7 945	3.15	76.4	6.8	18.1
Sevier	11.2	8.7	7.0	49.1	18 842	20 801	10.4	0.9	1 616	999	-421	7 112	2.85	75.3	7.9	23.3
Summit	14.3	7.0	2.8	48.9	29 736	36 327	22.2	9.1	2 282	715	1 804	13 425	2.81	72.8	7.1	20.3
Tooele	9.0	5.3	3.3	49.5	40 735	58 218	42.9	8.1	5 227	1 681	1 152	18 400	3.23	80.3	10.4	16.3
Uintah	9.3	5.1	3.9	49.1	25 224	32 584	29.2	16.4	3 678	1 082	2 735	11 048	3.10	75.8	8.6	20.1
Utah	6.6	4.2	3.0	49.6	368 536	516 640	40.2	11.3	62 938	10 967	6 441	145 469	3.62	82.2	8.1	12.3
Wasatch	10.5	6.2	3.2	48.6	15 215	23 525	54.6	24.0	2 147	616	4 067	7 752	3.28	79.4	7.9	17.7
Washington	10.7	10.8	8.8	50.5	90 354	138 115	52.9	12.7	11 792	5 878	11 397	47 905	2.98	75.9	8.8	19.8
Wayne	14.6	11.9	6.9	49.2	2 509	2 778	10.7	-3.1	161	120	-135	954	2.82	76.9	1.8	19.6
Weber	10.4	6.3	4.8	49.8	196 533	231 229	17.7	5.4	20 639	8 273	141	79 860	2.92	73.4	11.3	21.7
VERMONT	15.4	9.9	7.0	50.7	608 827	625 745	2.8	0.0	31 716	28 538	-2 432	257 252	2.34	62.5	9.2	28.5
Addison	15.8	10.1	6.7	49.9	35 974	36 824	2.4	0.6	1 668	1 612	114	14 215	2.39	67.4	9.9	25.7
Bennington	15.8	11.6	9.6	51.5	36 994	37 125	0.4	-2.2	1 747	2 293	-288	15 477	2.28	65.0	11.4	29.2
Caledonia	16.1	10.7	7.2	50.3	29 702	31 232	5.2	-1.4	1 487	1 557	-352	12 398	2.42	62.9	10.2	29.8

1. No spouse present.

Table B. States and Counties — **Population, Vital Statistics, Medicare, and Crime**

STATE County	Persons in group quarters, 2015	Daytime population, 2010–2014		Births, 2015		Deaths, 2015		Persons under 65 with no health insurance, 2014		Medicare, 2015			Serious crimes known to police,[2] 2014 Total	
		Number	Employ-ment/resi-dence ratio	Total	Rate[1]	Number	Rate[1]	Number	Percent	Total Beneficiaries	Enrolled in Original Medicare	Enrolled in Medicare Advantage	Number	Rate[3]
	32	33	34	35	36	37	38	39	40	41	42	43	44	45
TEXAS—Cont'd														
Tom Green	5 510	113 598	1.00	1 583	13.5	996	8.5	19 549	20.5	19 539	15 723	3 816	4 603	3 938
Travis	22 930	1 198 011	1.19	16 327	14.0	5 409	4.6	190 790	18.5	103 699	75 776	27 923	45 530	3 959
Trinity	138	13 057	0.71	120	8.4	201	14.0	2 514	23.7	3 843	2 850	993	275	1 904
Tyler	2 408	19 658	0.73	222	10.4	221	10.3	3 024	20.0	4 575	3 455	1 120	267	1 239
Upshur	498	32 158	0.52	514	12.7	399	9.9	6 724	20.3	7 229	5 244	1 985	1 154	2 948
Upton	61	3 635	1.22	65	18.3	14	3.9	667	22.8	507	409	98	14	411
Uvalde	576	26 825	1.01	433	15.9	249	9.1	6 215	27.8	4 829	3 482	1 347	999	3 667
Val Verde	1 893	48 448	0.97	895	18.3	350	7.1	10 413	25.7	7 395	5 591	1 804	1 089	2 228
Van Zandt	601	44 452	0.61	617	11.6	621	11.7	9 471	22.5	10 853	8 249	2 604	957	1 863
Victoria	1 810	91 434	1.06	1 384	15.1	787	8.6	14 421	18.8	16 105	12 333	3 772	3 206	3 504
Walker	17 336	70 030	1.05	649	9.2	562	8.0	9 541	21.2	8 377	5 684	2 693	1 555	2 238
Waller	4 261	41 651	0.83	636	13.3	298	6.2	9 423	25.2	4 478	3 041	1 437	1 004	2 183
Ward	125	10 703	0.93	216	18.5	77	6.6	2 055	20.8	1 800	1 412	388	332	2 889
Washington	1 921	35 333	1.09	415	12.0	360	10.4	5 026	19.3	7 606	6 176	1 430	751	2 177
Webb	3 568	259 769	1.00	5 611	20.9	1 240	4.6	74 755	31.2	26 912	20 866	6 046	11 100	4 153
Wharton	427	38 959	0.88	534	12.9	373	9.0	8 390	24.4	7 217	5 778	1 439	1 011	2 437
Wheeler	39	6 819	1.48	72	12.7	62	10.9	1 182	25.1	1 050	922	128	88	1 496
Wichita	12 711	136 765	1.08	1 760	13.3	1 284	9.7	17 720	17.2	23 617	20 248	3 369	5 317	4 079
Wilbarger	634	13 485	1.04	158	12.2	132	10.2	2 374	22.5	2 530	1 970	560	343	2 611
Willacy	3 290	21 357	0.87	318	14.5	169	7.7	4 031	25.5	3 180	2 028	1 152	984	4 471
Williamson	5 389	396 838	0.73	6 377	12.8	2 355	4.7	57 157	13.3	56 851	39 711	17 140	9 248	1 901
Wilson	532	34 349	0.49	543	11.6	371	7.9	7 101	18.1	6 285	4 107	2 178	722	1 557
Winkler	97	6 060	0.86	135	17.1	37	4.7	1 466	21.4	1 003	818	185	91	1 167
Wise	1 063	54 989	0.80	792	12.7	549	8.8	10 628	20.5	8 913	6 577	2 336	768	1 242
Wood	1 601	39 309	0.80	417	9.7	600	13.9	6 813	22.4	12 761	9 630	3 131	941	2 204
Yoakum	59	8 571	1.15	195	23.1	43	5.1	1 718	23.6	1 091	939	152	117	1 404
Young	284	18 352	1.00	231	12.6	227	12.4	3 509	24.0	4 065	3 739	326	373	2 024
Zapata	30	13 736	0.90	266	18.5	101	7.0	3 678	29.3	1 704	1 445	259	117	803
Zavala	411	11 446	0.87	212	17.4	83	6.8	2 460	24.0	1 882	1 132	750	NA	NA
UTAH	46 968	2 858 121	1.00	51 516	17.3	15 582	5.2	360 274	13.8	314 742	197 730	117 012	91 057	3 094
Beaver	32	6 557	1.02	104	16.2	50	7.8	877	15.9	1 033	829	204	119	2 141
Box Elder	337	48 259	0.89	863	16.7	338	6.5	5 224	11.6	6 907	4 302	2 605	1 096	2 281
Cache	3 977	115 171	0.99	2 344	19.6	492	4.1	13 174	12.6	10 686	5 651	5 035	1 507	1 275
Carbon	481	21 255	1.02	285	13.9	181	8.8	2 397	14.0	3 716	3 357	359	658	3 411
Daggett	63	713	1.00	11	9.9	4	3.6	104	12.8	201	152	49	9	784
Davis	3 099	286 227	0.78	5 914	17.8	1 549	4.7	28 668	9.6	30 529	19 190	11 339	5 822	1 781
Duchesne	297	20 241	1.11	430	20.9	122	5.9	3 109	17.4	2 534	1 918	616	626	3 006
Emery	43	10 669	0.96	139	13.2	82	7.8	1 238	13.7	1 728	1 405	323	121	1 128
Garfield	175	5 039	0.97	58	11.6	30	6.0	656	16.9	1 007	973	34	NA	NA
Grand	143	9 675	1.07	126	13.3	65	6.9	1 418	18.1	1 638	1 600	38	262	2 787
Iron	853	45 645	0.94	810	16.9	261	5.5	7 421	18.2	6 691	4 811	1 880	1 202	2 554
Juab	122	9 428	0.78	181	17.2	87	8.3	1 372	15.0	1 323	1 263	60	253	2 432
Kane	247	7 640	1.13	82	11.4	68	9.5	775	14.2	1 646	1 573	73	79	1 081
Millard	122	12 487	0.98	190	15.1	86	6.8	1 964	18.8	1 969	1 916	53	277	2 175
Morgan	0	7 811	0.47	172	15.9	37	3.4	829	8.8	1 224	797	427	14	135
Piute	37	1 764	0.77	14	9.3	8	5.3	239	22.4	378	336	42	7	465
Rich	1	2 288	1.00	32	13.9	10	4.3	278	14.8	369	287	82	39	1 693
Salt Lake	15 502	1 140 046	1.15	18 114	16.5	6 103	5.5	144 179	14.8	112 828	62 357	50 471	52 799	4 823
San Juan	367	14 969	1.01	256	16.5	110	7.1	2 624	20.2	1 660	1 628	32	216	1 434
Sanpete	2 674	26 486	0.83	387	13.5	152	5.3	4 162	18.6	3 829	3 681	148	313	1 244
Sevier	301	21 247	1.05	310	14.8	190	9.1	2 843	16.5	3 554	3 447	107	581	2 776
Summit	116	41 518	1.18	421	10.7	141	3.6	4 818	13.7	4 011	2 642	1 369	747	1 909
Tooele	354	52 049	0.69	998	16.0	303	4.9	6 594	11.8	5 682	4 166	1 516	1 766	2 870
Uintah	255	35 303	1.05	762	20.3	208	5.6	5 484	16.5	3 287	2 362	925	736	2 016
Utah	12 467	519 186	0.91	11 936	21.0	2 097	3.7	61 947	12.1	42 619	24 882	17 737	9 431	1 678
Wasatch	249	21 535	0.65	462	16.2	120	4.2	4 396	17.7	3 603	2 195	1 408	250	917
Washington	1 917	144 396	0.99	2 264	14.7	1 140	7.4	23 476	19.6	28 422	19 626	8 796	2 749	1 860
Wayne	9	2 803	1.05	29	10.7	24	8.9	368	16.8	517	496	21	10	364
Weber	2 728	227 714	0.92	3 822	15.8	1 524	6.3	29 640	14.0	31 151	19 888	11 263	7 110	2 951
VERMONT	25 439	625 047	1.00	5 981	9.5	5 295	8.5	30 387	6.1	123 699	113 459	10 240	10 173	1 624
Addison	2 854	33 802	0.84	324	8.7	314	8.5	1 818	6.4	6 466	5 781	685	445	1 210
Bennington	1 472	38 743	1.12	328	9.0	444	12.2	1 787	6.5	8 591	7 866	725	590	1 615
Caledonia	1 327	29 558	0.89	279	9.0	267	8.7	1 607	6.6	6 281	5 790	491	427	1 371

1. Per 1,000 estimated resident population.   2. Data for serious crimes have not been adjusted for underreporting; this may affect comparability between geographic areas and over time.
3. Per 100,000 population estimated by the FBI.

Table B. States and Counties — Crime, Education, Money Income, and Poverty

STATE County	Rate[2] Violent	Rate[2] Property	Enrollment[3] Total	Enrollment Percent private	Attainment[4] (percent) High school graduate or less	Attainment Bachelor's degree or more	Local government expenditures,[5] 2012–2013 Total current spending (mil dol)	Current spending per student (dollars)	Per capita income[6] (dollars)	Median income (dollars)	Mean income (dollars)	Percent with income of $200,000 or more	Median household income (dollars)	Percent below poverty level All persons	Children under 18 years	Children 5 to 17 years in families
	46	47	48	49	50	51	52	53	54	55	56	57	58	59	60	61
TEXAS—Cont'd																
Tom Green	298	3 640	28 904	8.1	48.5	21.5	153.1	8 568	24 443	45 114	62 472	2.8	45 261	15.6	21.3	20.9
Travis	355	3 604	306 832	13.1	29.6	45.2	1 355.7	9 261	33 943	59 620	85 746	7.7	61 779	16.7	23.1	21.5
Trinity	201	1 703	2 722	3.6	61.4	10.8	22.5	9 591	19 874	35 223	48 516	1.2	36 645	19.9	31.3	28.7
Tyler	227	1 012	4 217	7.8	57.0	11.6	33.6	9 420	20 675	41 630	53 678	0.8	40 442	19.3	26.3	25.4
Upshur	330	2 619	9 490	6.7	51.4	14.3	63.2	8 876	22 917	46 834	61 435	2.5	46 346	14.6	23.5	22.1
Upton	29	382	854	4.0	59.7	11.0	12.1	15 233	23 383	50 982	65 979	2.7	55 918	14.3	18.9	18.3
Uvalde	316	3 351	8 099	4.1	52.9	15.3	52.5	8 814	17 654	37 078	51 055	1.8	37 933	22.1	34.2	32.9
Val Verde	133	2 095	12 933	6.1	60.2	16.3	87.1	8 184	19 024	42 735	57 016	1.8	41 437	22.2	31.4	30.0
Van Zandt	189	1 674	11 889	11.5	54.8	14.9	80.0	8 224	22 707	42 579	58 120	2.1	43 377	15.9	22.9	21.4
Victoria	445	3 059	22 360	12.2	49.6	16.8	129.9	8 368	25 216	50 663	67 446	3.1	51 003	15.8	24.3	22.8
Walker	380	1 858	20 587	6.6	52.0	18.4	66.8	9 232	16 571	38 903	54 710	1.8	39 984	26.3	27.9	26.4
Waller	359	1 824	15 271	16.0	54.9	18.4	81.0	8 657	22 645	50 939	68 217	3.4	50 589	16.1	23.0	22.1
Ward	374	2 515	2 618	3.7	58.5	12.8	20.0	8 786	23 887	45 938	62 708	3.4	53 244	14.0	19.1	18.6
Washington	273	1 905	7 739	7.8	48.4	23.1	45.1	8 467	23 727	49 236	61 721	2.4	55 139	15.0	21.7	21.4
Webb	403	3 750	88 549	4.5	58.7	17.0	557.4	8 189	14 852	38 679	53 183	1.9	37 935	32.3	42.3	39.8
Wharton	460	1 976	9 972	6.3	59.0	13.8	70.6	8 618	20 782	41 992	55 325	1.7	44 110	16.8	24.4	22.6
Wheeler	68	1 428	1 172	6.6	49.2	16.9	15.3	13 047	27 816	54 382	69 328	2.9	52 548	12.0	17.3	16.0
Wichita	372	3 707	33 768	8.2	46.6	20.8	175.0	8 218	23 006	44 854	60 427	2.3	43 379	19.3	29.1	25.7
Wilbarger	175	2 436	3 249	7.3	49.3	17.6	21.5	8 787	20 370	41 901	50 360	0.4	39 377	15.8	23.9	23.4
Willacy	809	3 662	5 714	3.5	70.5	9.2	49.2	10 738	11 693	27 627	39 733	0.5	29 782	38.8	45.9	43.6
Williamson	156	1 745	130 640	13.2	28.3	38.6	837.0	7 933	31 709	72 118	87 680	5.5	73 098	7.8	10.0	8.8
Wilson	149	1 409	11 619	10.8	49.8	18.5	72.0	8 433	28 411	65 760	79 132	3.7	62 752	11.0	15.1	13.8
Winkler	205	962	1 861	5.1	58.9	11.1	21.9	12 417	22 885	52 938	62 800	1.7	55 493	13.5	17.4	16.3
Wise	150	1 091	14 695	6.6	52.7	15.9	83.1	9 215	27 087	56 338	75 193	3.4	59 904	10.0	15.3	14.7
Wood	192	2 012	8 551	10.8	50.8	17.9	53.8	8 603	23 658	44 376	59 177	2.5	42 753	15.4	25.1	23.4
Yoakum	168	1 236	2 297	8.3	58.9	15.8	22.5	10 523	23 103	50 167	68 404	3.2	60 738	11.4	14.8	14.6
Young	201	1 823	3 992	9.3	56.6	17.6	31.1	8 821	25 859	41 589	63 533	2.2	41 872	16.4	24.3	22.6
Zapata	96	707	4 132	2.2	68.5	9.6	33.3	9 257	16 026	30 758	46 543	1.5	33 291	32.6	44.8	42.1
Zavala	NA	NA	3 417	1.1	66.2	8.5	25.6	10 025	13 595	27 253	39 632	1.3	26 336	31.0	41.0	40.3
UTAH	216	2 878	932 268	14.0	32.2	30.6	3 768.0	6 555	24 312	59 846	75 204	3.9	60 943	11.8	13.4	12.7
Beaver	54	2 087	1 913	3.1	44.9	18.2	13.0	8 324	20 405	50 685	59 741	1.2	50 818	9.8	13.0	12.0
Box Elder	112	2 169	15 401	8.3	40.3	21.6	72.1	6 448	22 150	57 336	68 058	1.9	56 313	11.6	15.1	13.6
Cache	57	1 218	45 565	6.8	29.3	35.9	139.4	6 261	20 195	50 367	64 156	2.5	51 735	14.2	12.8	12.3
Carbon	124	3 286	5 811	5.7	41.5	13.0	30.2	8 498	20 691	46 366	54 714	0.3	47 340	15.7	19.0	18.1
Daggett	87	697	127	29.9	48.1	19.3	3.1	14 389	24 369	47 188	58 783	2.2	53 006	8.3	10.9	10.0
Davis	101	1 680	105 526	9.0	26.1	34.6	441.4	6 289	26 309	70 388	84 570	4.4	70 797	7.2	8.3	8.1
Duchesne	423	2 584	5 368	6.4	48.2	15.4	34.6	7 061	24 162	60 700	70 141	2.4	61 976	11.6	12.2	11.8
Emery	177	951	2 744	5.4	43.3	12.3	23.2	9 713	20 274	50 653	59 606	0.7	49 709	12.9	17.2	15.1
Garfield	NA	NA	1 286	4.0	39.7	21.4	9.2	9 161	20 975	44 914	57 350	1.7	45 666	12.2	18.0	16.7
Grand	149	2 638	1 896	12.7	35.2	23.2	13.8	9 378	23 894	44 239	54 213	1.8	43 344	15.0	21.8	21.3
Iron	270	2 284	16 284	6.1	34.1	27.9	59.9	6 880	17 946	42 305	53 041	1.7	43 615	22.1	25.6	22.1
Juab	77	2 355	3 389	4.5	44.3	16.3	18.3	7 160	18 503	56 976	61 928	1.5	55 204	11.4	15.3	14.6
Kane	260	821	1 648	10.6	32.9	25.6	12.6	10 174	24 152	51 213	59 920	2.3	48 456	11.8	16.7	15.9
Millard	259	1 916	3 436	2.9	42.1	19.2	26.4	9 036	20 310	51 117	59 177	0.5	52 623	12.9	18.3	17.3
Morgan	19	116	3 274	15.1	27.9	34.5	15.1	5 839	28 193	79 304	96 406	8.7	82 597	4.6	4.8	4.5
Piute	0	465	563	10.1	54.0	17.4	4.4	12 590	16 780	33 250	43 730	0.2	37 730	18.7	34.1	28.0
Rich	87	1 607	667	11.7	44.0	16.1	6.3	13 072	23 018	50 573	75 137	2.6	56 772	10.3	14.1	13.1
Salt Lake	350	4 472	319 039	13.1	33.7	31.3	1 290.6	6 906	26 747	61 446	78 807	4.8	62 536	11.9	15.1	14.4
San Juan	106	1 328	4 610	5.9	49.3	18.8	33.6	10 586	15 531	41 411	51 096	0.8	40 590	29.2	30.5	26.9
Sanpete	64	1 181	9 968	12.5	36.9	20.3	45.5	7 948	17 519	48 305	60 427	2.5	44 644	17.1	19.8	18.9
Sevier	81	2 695	6 190	5.5	43.8	16.2	32.4	6 685	19 121	46 327	54 646	1.0	48 622	12.1	17.0	14.6
Summit	138	1 771	10 146	14.9	22.7	50.1	71.8	10 205	45 461	89 886	126 253	16.8	92 560	6.8	7.9	7.3
Tooele	228	2 642	19 846	11.4	40.7	20.6	91.8	6 454	22 423	63 077	71 955	2.0	64 193	8.1	10.5	9.7
Uintah	129	1 888	10 038	12.3	48.2	16.6	50.0	6 674	24 572	62 363	74 962	3.8	65 489	9.6	11.3	10.9
Utah	74	1 604	215 868	24.6	32.4	36.9	696.8	5 893	20 973	60 830	75 507	3.5	60 957	12.6	11.0	10.0
Wasatch	92	825	7 689	10.8	28.7	34.4	42.4	7 420	26 145	65 582	82 085	5.5	65 207	7.1	9.8	9.1
Washington	135	1 725	44 152	10.4	32.8	27.1	182.0	6 673	21 771	49 498	63 408	2.7	50 169	12.9	18.1	17.3
Wayne	36	327	767	5.0	31.2	26.5	5.3	9 558	19 950	43 393	55 253	1.0	42 366	14.1	22.9	21.6
Weber	254	2 698	69 057	8.4	39.4	23.2	303.1	6 950	23 430	56 216	67 922	2.4	59 293	12.3	15.4	14.3
VERMONT	99	1 524	152 182	19.9	38.9	35.2	1 531.5	16 377	29 535	54 447	70 524	3.6	54 153	12.0	15.4	14.1
Addison	95	1 115	9 842	34.3	40.3	35.4	85.7	17 642	29 295	59 274	73 372	3.6	59 089	9.5	12.5	10.7
Bennington	134	1 481	8 533	27.6	40.1	32.0	84.6	16 369	29 647	49 303	68 862	3.9	44 674	14.4	19.2	17.6
Caledonia	106	1 265	6 977	19.7	46.6	25.8	77.9	18 305	23 568	45 089	57 251	1.6	45 029	13.9	19.0	17.5

1. Data for serious crimes have not been adjusted for underreporting; this may affect comparability between geographic areas and over time.   2. Per 100,000 population estimated by the FBI.
3. All persons 3 years old and over enrolled in nursery school through college.   4. Persons 25 years old and over.   5. Elementary and secondary education expenditures.
6. Based on population estimated by the American Community Survey, 2010–2014.

Table B. States and Counties — **Personal Income**

| STATE County | Personal income, 2014 | | | | | | | | | | Earnings, 2014 | | |
	Total (mil dol)	Percent change, 2013–2014	Per capita¹ Dollars	Per capita¹ Rank	Wages and salaries (mil dol)	Supplements to wages and salaries; employer contributions (mil dol) Pension and insurance	Supplements... Government social insurance	Proprietors' income (mil dol)	Dividends, interest, and rent (mil dol)	Personal transfer receipts (mil dol)	Total (mil dol)	Contributions for government social insurance (mil dol) From employee and self-employed	Contributions... From employer
	62	63	64	65	66	67	68	69	70	71	72	73	74
TEXAS—Cont'd													
Tom Green	4 911	5.2	42 114	941	2 087	365	149	584	1 024	918	3 185	165	149
Travis	62 329	6.2	54 145	230	39 854	5 194	2 614	7 784	14 474	5 498	55 446	2 740	2 614
Trinity	452	3.2	31 769	2 478	80	15	5	24	62	171	124	11	5
Tyler	647	5.2	30 191	2 692	145	33	9	32	85	209	218	15	9
Upshur	1 430	5.5	35 427	1 872	287	55	19	113	155	358	475	30	19
Upton	209	12.0	60 551	124	135	21	8	30	30	28	193	9	8
Uvalde	924	3.5	34 086	2 103	332	69	23	86	184	266	510	28	23
Val Verde	1 617	4.5	33 017	2 276	731	174	59	124	252	374	1 089	57	59
Van Zandt	1 767	4.6	33 402	2 214	362	64	25	116	229	499	566	38	25
Victoria	4 319	6.5	47 419	504	2 010	283	134	688	695	761	3 115	162	134
Walker	1 782	4.9	25 534	3 044	928	230	53	101	350	433	1 311	61	53
Waller	1 596	6.1	34 078	2 105	786	124	51	77	210	301	1 037	54	51
Ward	559	10.3	48 094	474	304	38	19	76	60	84	437	23	19
Washington	1 700	5.7	49 365	419	622	106	40	270	364	353	1 038	54	40
Webb	7 561	4.3	28 355	2 890	3 499	656	243	963	1 039	1 766	5 360	270	243
Wharton	1 683	2.4	40 869	1 079	618	98	41	225	233	369	982	49	41
Wheeler	298	10.6	52 127	291	113	18	7	56	86	55	194	9	7
Wichita	5 373	3.5	40 593	1 108	2 351	447	173	835	1 018	1 120	3 806	190	173
Wilbarger	507	2.1	39 075	1 311	241	55	15	46	75	134	357	18	15
Willacy	558	14.4	25 480	3 048	142	28	10	98	49	215	277	13	10
Williamson	19 050	7.8	38 938	1 328	7 864	967	512	1 125	2 564	2 369	10 468	580	512
Wilson	1 824	6.1	39 301	1 282	277	53	18	91	265	333	438	27	18
Winkler	316	9.8	40 441	1 125	173	24	11	26	40	56	235	12	11
Wise	2 594	5.8	42 087	944	1 168	165	76	395	343	420	1 804	94	76
Wood	1 444	6.7	33 703	2 160	353	66	25	111	239	515	556	40	25
Yoakum	369	0.4	44 554	711	261	36	17	75	38	55	389	19	17
Young	945	5.8	51 473	314	306	53	20	287	160	188	666	32	20
Zapata	459	3.4	32 037	2 432	280	39	18	58	50	106	395	21	18
Zavala	294	4.7	23 952	3 080	97	20	8	13	44	115	138	8	8
UTAH	110 842	4.5	37 664	X	60 628	9 991	4 797	10 395	19 749	15 113	85 811	4 989	4 797
Beaver	237	3.3	36 622	1 665	109	20	9	37	34	45	175	8	9
Box Elder	1 659	4.9	32 208	2 416	747	123	61	132	241	279	1 063	64	61
Cache	3 601	4.6	30 428	2 662	1 842	391	147	321	631	554	2 702	152	147
Carbon	699	2.1	33 837	2 142	367	66	30	43	99	171	506	32	30
Daggett	56	1.2	50 523	357	14	4	1	22	9	7	41	2	1
Davis	12 782	5.0	38 770	1 354	5 211	1 024	429	990	1 992	1 448	7 654	433	429
Duchesne	807	6.2	39 574	1 239	507	81	37	88	110	105	713	41	37
Emery	326	2.8	30 676	2 631	174	35	14	16	44	72	238	15	14
Garfield	165	2.9	32 829	2 308	70	15	7	13	35	33	105	6	7
Grand	385	3.3	40 844	1 084	169	29	15	66	96	67	279	16	15
Iron	1 266	5.9	26 774	2 995	546	118	43	110	225	312	818	48	43
Juab	313	6.1	29 871	2 736	121	22	10	21	35	64	174	10	10
Kane	253	6.0	34 943	1 946	105	19	9	25	51	57	158	10	9
Millard	411	1.6	32 608	2 352	190	41	14	50	64	81	295	15	14
Morgan	457	6.3	43 111	834	82	14	6	34	73	44	136	8	6
Piute	38	2.7	25 456	3 051	8	2	1	4	7	13	14	1	1
Rich	90	8.8	39 190	1 297	23	5	2	21	21	13	51	2	2
Salt Lake	46 437	4.1	42 535	895	32 291	5 003	2 513	4 916	8 481	5 765	44 722	2 584	2 513
San Juan	354	-1.5	23 244	3 094	155	35	20	20	63	92	222	13	12
Sanpete	725	4.0	25 458	3 050	228	57	18	100	117	172	403	22	18
Sevier	619	3.1	29 793	2 744	284	56	23	55	97	147	417	25	23
Summit	3 784	4.6	96 766	9	1 038	127	86	387	1 310	168	1 638	92	86
Tooele	1 934	4.4	31 398	2 539	716	123	56	60	232	277	955	58	56
Uintah	1 277	5.2	34 629	1 994	782	112	59	91	187	153	1 045	61	59
Utah	18 105	4.9	32 274	2 405	8 660	1 356	686	1 868	2 751	2 353	12 571	727	686
Wasatch	1 070	6.8	38 624	1 373	286	47	23	57	223	112	412	25	23
Washington	4 507	5.9	29 659	2 764	1 904	320	158	366	988	1 098	2 748	183	158
Wayne	82	8.4	30 208	2 689	31	7	3	8	17	19	48	3	3
Weber	8 402	4.0	34 938	1 947	3 968	740	324	476	1 516	1 392	5 508	330	324
VERMONT	29 090	3.5	46 428	X	13 653	2 445	1 142	2 368	5 517	6 030	19 608	1 267	1 142
Addison	1 629	4.5	44 016	760	633	109	53	193	306	289	987	61	53
Bennington	1 672	3.5	45 874	609	719	124	63	137	406	386	1 043	72	63
Caledonia	1 161	3.6	37 471	1 529	435	86	38	125	187	294	684	47	38

1. Based on the resident population estimated as of July 1 of the year shown.

Table B. States and Counties — Earnings, Social Security, and Housing

STATE County	Earnings, 2014 (cont.) Percent by selected industries									Social Security beneficiaries, December 2014		Supplemental Security Income recipients, December 2014	Housing units, 2015	
	Farm	Mining	Construction	Manufacturing	Information: professional, scientific, technical services	Retail trade	Finance, insurance, real estate and leasing	Health care and social assistance	Government	Number	Rate[1]		Total	Percent change, 2010–2014
	75	76	77	78	79	80	81	82	83	84	85	86	87	88
TEXAS—Cont'd														
Tom Green	1.2	8.9	5.5	10.9	5.1	7.1	5.3	13.6	22.4	21 310	182	2 970	48 276	3.7
Travis	0.0	2.4	6.0	8.4	21.1	5.2	9.9	8.5	16.5	116 825	101	17 982	486 517	10.3
Trinity	-1.1	D	7.2	10.6	D	6.7	4.0	D	24.2	4 355	306	642	8 768	0.6
Tyler	2.1	2.0	3.7	6.1	3.2	9.4	D	6.5	38.9	5 240	245	662	10 624	0.4
Upshur	4.1	5.4	12.0	4.5	14.4	6.0	4.3	7.2	18.4	8 905	221	1 122	16 792	1.1
Upton	2.7	47.4	7.0	0.0	D	D	D	D	15.6	600	173	81	1 550	0.3
Uvalde	2.2	2.0	5.5	4.7	4.2	10.4	4.3	D	32.3	5 020	184	1 114	11 024	2.0
Val Verde	0.8	D	3.4	7.6	2.0	9.2	3.5	9.3	45.2	8 385	171	2 314	18 880	1.2
Van Zandt	6.0	2.1	12.8	7.9	4.3	9.1	4.2	7.3	19.8	12 490	236	1 228	22 995	0.8
Victoria	0.3	19.0	7.1	8.2	4.1	10.1	5.1	13.1	11.6	17 140	188	2 619	36 845	4.0
Walker	0.5	1.0	3.9	5.7	3.8	7.2	2.9	7.8	55.9	9 315	133	1 379	25 260	5.0
Waller	2.2	4.9	9.9	28.1	3.4	5.2	2.3	2.9	21.2	5 905	126	918	16 238	2.5
Ward	0.0	43.5	6.8	2.6	5.0	4.3	5.1	1.6	10.1	2 025	174	299	4 751	1.2
Washington	0.7	6.1	7.1	29.3	4.2	7.3	6.7	6.1	15.6	7 730	225	959	15 792	1.8
Webb	0.2	8.3	3.0	0.7	4.0	8.2	3.8	10.5	27.1	31 500	118	12 614	79 708	8.5
Wharton	11.6	13.0	5.2	9.5	2.8	8.4	5.0	7.4	14.5	8 190	199	1 169	17 439	1.8
Wheeler	11.9	29.2	D	D	4.0	4.8	2.7	2.3	15.3	1 170	206	76	2 714	-0.6
Wichita	-0.1	15.6	3.8	9.6	4.6	7.0	4.9	12.9	25.1	24 535	185	4 040	56 106	1.0
Wilbarger	0.9	5.6	2.4	19.9	2.8	10.2	3.4	3.1	34.2	2 805	217	406	6 269	-0.8
Willacy	26.9	D	2.4	0.4	D	5.6	3.1	6.7	22.8	3 715	170	1 346	7 208	2.4
Williamson	0.1	1.2	8.6	14.6	9.6	8.1	6.9	8.9	11.9	63 060	129	4 332	180 968	11.2
Wilson	2.3	8.2	12.4	4.2	4.9	13.6	3.3	7.3	26.4	7 795	168	717	17 055	1.7
Winkler	0.4	40.2	D	D	D	3.2	2.2	D	14.2	1 185	152	224	3 006	-0.7
Wise	0.7	28.3	9.2	9.1	D	6.1	2.8	D	12.9	11 020	178	801	24 032	1.1
Wood	6.4	4.1	7.6	12.8	5.7	10.6	5.6	D	17.1	14 010	326	1 041	20 984	0.6
Yoakum	3.1	46.1	10.3	2.0	D	2.4	2.0	D	11.0	1 285	154	136	3 015	1.2
Young	0.2	38.2	4.5	15.5	3.2	4.7	4.4	4.9	10.4	4 385	239	517	8 687	0.8
Zapata	-0.8	46.8	10.3	1.2	0.8	D	2.4	2.0	17.2	2 000	140	634	6 241	0.6
Zavala	4.3	1.6	5.2	8.7	D	4.8	3.0	9.1	27.9	2 185	180	820	4 316	0.8
UTAH	0.7	1.8	7.3	10.1	12.1	7.6	8.8	8.6	17.1	365 730	124	31 212	1 038 003	6.0
Beaver	28.5	9.1	3.7	3.0	0.3	5.5	D	2.5	20.6	1 130	175	70	2 936	1.0
Box Elder	4.5	0.6	6.8	37.1	D	5.7	2.6	6.2	12.9	8 100	157	534	18 223	5.2
Cache	2.0	D	5.2	24.3	D	6.9	4.6	10.5	21.5	12 680	107	870	39 745	7.4
Carbon	0.6	D	6.5	4.5	2.6	9.1	2.4	D	19.9	4 375	212	481	9 655	1.1
Daggett	2.8	D	11.4	D	D	D	D	3.1	30.4	240	214	0	1 156	1.2
Davis	0.2	1.2	9.6	11.0	10.5	6.7	5.0	7.8	29.4	36 690	111	2 424	104 982	7.6
Duchesne	4.4	34.8	8.8	1.7	3.1	4.7	1.9	D	14.8	2 905	143	292	9 907	4.4
Emery	2.9	D	15.9	0.5	D	5.0	D	D	17.6	2 140	201	130	4 494	0.1
Garfield	5.8	D	3.2	1.6	D	5.4	1.7	D	29.2	1 020	203	30	3 851	3.4
Grand	0.4	D	7.8	0.7	3.6	10.4	4.3	6.4	19.6	1 805	191	140	5 120	6.3
Iron	3.9	1.4	5.4	9.7	3.4	8.3	7.6	9.6	27.3	7 460	158	655	20 283	3.1
Juab	5.2	2.2	10.1	24.8	D	4.1	2.0	D	18.7	1 620	155	125	3 587	2.4
Kane	1.7	D	D	3.8	2.5	6.2	9.8	2.7	24.4	1 920	265	71	5 867	0.9
Millard	17.4	2.8	2.0	5.3	D	5.0	D	D	18.5	2 355	188	125	4 942	0.1
Morgan	5.3	1.0	24.0	10.8	D	3.8	3.8	D	15.9	1 365	129	41	3 382	12.5
Piute	19.9	0.0	D	0.0	D	D	D	D	44.7	455	306	21	918	2.1
Rich	35.0	D	7.6	D	D	3.0	D	D	21.2	395	172	11	2 932	3.4
Salt Lake	0.0	1.1	6.3	9.0	13.4	7.8	11.7	7.8	15.2	131 495	120	13 522	380 749	4.6
San Juan	3.4	11.2	5.4	2.2	D	3.1	1.5	16.1	37.4	2 140	140	613	5 841	1.8
Sanpete	13.7	1.4	5.9	8.6	D	5.8	3.3	6.9	30.1	4 670	165	327	10 520	1.4
Sevier	6.3	8.4	4.0	5.1	3.7	10.0	2.6	D	20.1	4 165	200	308	8 536	1.0
Summit	0.6	1.4	8.2	3.8	9.9	8.3	15.9	5.7	9.4	4 475	114	113	27 473	3.5
Tooele	1.3	1.1	7.6	11.8	D	5.3	2.1	6.2	28.1	7 095	115	687	20 700	6.4
Uintah	1.7	31.6	7.7	0.9	4.3	5.5	4.5	4.2	16.1	4 305	116	343	13 462	12.5
Utah	0.7	0.3	9.2	9.9	19.1	7.9	5.6	9.4	12.1	51 910	92	4 181	162 545	9.5
Wasatch	0.6	D	17.7	4.1	9.5	8.2	5.2	7.7	20.0	3 235	116	101	12 023	13.7
Washington	0.1	0.4	10.8	5.1	6.4	10.2	6.9	16.9	15.3	32 200	212	1 286	63 947	10.8
Wayne	13.4	D	14.1	0.5	D	4.2	D	D	30.0	630	232	20	1 631	2.5
Weber	0.4	0.1	6.7	16.1	5.3	7.8	7.2	12.5	22.0	32 755	136	3 683	88 596	2.8
VERMONT	1.6	0.2	7.1	11.2	9.1	7.6	5.8	14.2	19.5	140 634	224	15 783	326 894	1.4
Addison	8.2	0.3	7.7	14.5	D	8.5	3.3	12.5	11.7	7 625	206	615	17 000	1.4
Bennington	0.4	D	6.6	14.8	D	10.8	5.5	16.1	13.7	9 885	271	1 190	20 925	0.0
Caledonia	1.9	D	9.9	12.2	6.2	9.5	3.7	14.8	18.5	7 490	242	1 012	16 039	0.6

1. Per 1,000 resident population estimated as of July 1 of the year shown.

Table B. States and Counties — Housing, Labor Force, and Employment

STATE County	Housing units, 2010–2014								Civilian labor force, 2015				Civilian employment,[6] 2010–2014		
	Occupied units										Unemployment			Percent	
		Owner-occupied				Renter-occupied									
				Median owner cost as a percent of income											
	Total	Percent	Median value[1]	With a mortgage	Without a mortgage[2]	Median rent[3]	Median rent as a percent of income[2]	Sub-standard units[4] (percent)	Total	Percent change, 2014–2015	Total	Rate[5]	Total	Management, business, science and arts	Construction, production, and maintenance occupations
	89	90	91	92	93	94	95	96	97	98	99	100	101	102	103

TEXAS—Cont'd															
Tom Green	42 361	62.7	102 300	20.8	11.6	737	29.6	4.3	54 485	-0.3	2 249	4.1	50 187	30.8	25.1
Travis	419 496	51.6	224 600	23.2	12.5	1 022	30.8	4.8	658 215	2.2	21 530	3.3	577 855	45.5	14.6
Trinity	5 078	80.5	80 600	22.1	15.2	633	29.4	3.9	5 467	-1.0	326	6.0	4 946	24.9	22.6
Tyler	8 154	84.1	77 800	19.4	11.2	655	26.5	5.4	7 372	-2.7	522	7.1	7 169	25.1	31.3
Upshur	14 219	79.6	89 900	19.6	11.0	710	24.5	5.2	18 047	-2.8	952	5.3	16 602	26.7	33.1
Upton	1 183	72.5	55 000	16.8	10.0	646	18.3	6.2	1 785	-4.8	69	3.9	1 403	26.6	39.1
Uvalde	8 622	70.2	72 000	22.3	12.6	649	30.2	8.7	11 679	0.0	593	5.1	10 711	27.7	29.9
Val Verde	15 055	66.2	92 700	21.3	12.5	697	27.7	7.5	19 479	0.5	1 186	6.1	18 907	25.0	26.6
Van Zandt	18 903	78.0	100 800	21.7	12.9	694	32.2	3.5	24 198	1.3	1 094	4.5	21 283	28.3	30.3
Victoria	32 207	65.3	116 100	21.0	11.7	783	30.1	4.1	45 958	-0.6	1 907	4.1	41 031	27.1	28.1
Walker	20 681	57.6	117 600	20.6	12.1	779	37.6	1.9	22 861	-1.3	1 168	5.1	22 124	31.6	16.9
Waller	13 655	69.4	134 400	23.6	11.7	791	30.7	7.0	21 351	0.2	1 033	4.8	18 944	29.1	26.5
Ward	3 916	71.8	68 700	14.2	11.5	602	20.1	3.2	5 959	0.6	256	4.3	4 644	21.4	39.6
Washington	11 917	73.7	141 700	22.8	12.0	791	26.4	2.3	15 355	-2.2	739	4.8	14 447	31.5	28.3
Webb	68 502	62.5	107 400	26.1	14.2	745	34.6	16.7	112 415	1.1	5 328	4.7	97 303	25.3	23.4
Wharton	14 492	67.4	96 900	21.4	12.8	679	27.1	4.4	21 239	-1.5	944	4.4	18 454	25.4	33.1
Wheeler	2 281	74.0	79 100	19.8	10.0	662	21.8	4.6	2 829	-8.2	111	3.9	2 625	29.6	35.8
Wichita	47 818	62.3	89 200	21.8	12.9	737	28.3	3.1	55 745	-1.3	2 407	4.3	55 360	32.6	22.5
Wilbarger	5 253	65.4	67 100	19.4	12.4	590	25.3	4.8	5 114	-3.4	250	4.9	6 006	27.2	26.7
Willacy	5 461	79.7	51 700	22.9	13.8	526	34.3	9.3	6 763	-5.7	885	13.1	5 504	24.8	24.2
Williamson	158 283	68.1	185 700	22.4	11.8	1 054	28.0	2.8	260 653	2.1	9 003	3.5	223 864	45.0	15.1
Wilson	15 598	83.9	151 600	21.7	11.2	794	24.7	4.6	22 836	1.3	870	3.8	20 618	32.5	28.4
Winkler	2 659	79.0	45 200	14.5	10.0	604	15.5	3.2	3 105	-5.5	178	5.7	3 226	23.5	41.0
Wise	20 694	78.5	122 400	22.0	12.0	877	27.6	3.4	28 652	0.6	1 331	4.6	27 016	27.7	31.2
Wood	16 076	80.7	105 900	23.7	12.4	727	28.7	3.1	16 732	-0.2	893	5.3	15 598	29.6	27.5
Yoakum	2 594	75.7	71 300	17.3	10.0	631	25.2	8.3	4 046	-5.8	152	3.8	3 571	26.0	44.1
Young	7 268	71.5	82 800	17.9	11.9	641	25.9	2.8	8 442	-2.6	367	4.3	8 302	27.2	30.2
Zapata	4 424	79.1	54 000	22.0	11.0	431	30.7	14.0	6 227	-10.2	475	7.6	5 178	20.2	35.6
Zavala	3 556	72.0	42 400	22.7	13.1	459	36.4	8.7	3 870	-0.7	429	11.1	4 451	25.5	31.8
UTAH	896 194	69.7	212 500	23.5	10.0	875	29.4	4.0	1 464 406	2.3	51 932	3.5	1 299 818	36.6	21.4
Beaver	2 163	76.1	144 200	20.4	10.0	689	32.2	5.5	3 152	6.0	118	3.7	2 708	27.2	32.1
Box Elder	16 223	77.6	166 200	22.1	10.0	653	23.9	2.4	24 184	3.0	876	3.6	21 464	30.8	33.1
Cache	35 505	65.3	189 300	23.3	10.0	680	29.3	3.8	60 230	2.0	1 797	3.0	53 585	37.1	23.8
Carbon	7 834	69.9	123 000	20.1	10.0	594	26.3	2.4	8 782	0.7	492	5.6	9 115	25.8	30.1
Daggett	276	79.3	202 500	18.6	12.8	975	23.6	0.4	475	10.0	22	4.6	207	32.9	27.1
Davis	96 711	77.6	222 600	22.5	10.0	897	28.3	2.6	160 089	2.4	5 317	3.3	143 762	40.8	18.9
Duchesne	6 738	75.2	172 300	21.2	10.0	803	27.0	4.5	8 823	-8.1	647	7.3	7 789	29.1	39.3
Emery	3 628	81.3	125 600	18.6	10.0	620	23.6	3.2	4 443	-4.0	265	6.0	4 277	23.3	41.3
Garfield	1 815	78.5	156 600	23.0	10.0	644	19.1	3.6	2 782	2.1	241	8.7	2 139	29.5	23.2
Grand	3 822	66.2	220 500	24.4	10.0	801	31.5	3.8	5 622	1.5	335	6.0	4 692	25.9	21.2
Iron	15 135	62.9	165 400	25.4	10.0	665	31.3	3.6	20 397	2.1	890	4.4	18 852	33.1	23.3
Juab	3 066	80.8	164 000	22.2	10.0	782	22.2	5.0	5 010	4.2	193	3.9	4 384	24.4	31.5
Kane	2 925	78.0	168 200	22.0	10.0	896	25.3	4.6	3 640	1.9	160	4.4	3 222	34.4	20.0
Millard	4 210	75.3	130 300	20.4	10.0	580	24.1	5.1	6 147	2.8	215	3.5	5 424	23.7	38.6
Morgan	2 941	86.6	265 400	23.4	10.0	819	28.9	1.4	4 820	2.5	149	3.1	4 049	42.2	26.4
Piute	557	86.4	142 800	22.2	11.7	625	30.0	3.1	466	1.3	30	6.4	694	40.9	17.3
Rich	627	82.1	163 400	22.5	10.0	632	33.3	1.3	1 062	5.3	38	3.6	780	31.0	37.3
Salt Lake	348 110	66.6	231 200	23.7	10.0	922	30.0	4.4	587 026	1.7	19 529	3.3	521 190	37.0	20.3
San Juan	4 038	79.3	137 100	22.7	10.0	578	22.8	12.9	5 700	1.4	442	7.8	4 763	33.3	26.7
Sanpete	7 945	74.2	165 000	22.9	10.0	635	24.3	4.3	11 498	3.6	466	4.1	10 082	35.0	27.8
Sevier	7 112	77.3	148 300	22.9	10.0	709	25.3	4.2	9 545	2.7	419	4.4	8 322	26.2	30.5
Summit	13 425	76.4	496 800	24.3	10.0	1 218	26.1	2.3	23 128	2.4	752	3.3	19 997	44.4	15.1
Tooele	18 400	76.5	175 300	22.9	10.0	819	26.1	3.0	29 388	1.4	1 199	4.1	25 634	32.8	26.8
Uintah	11 048	75.2	187 400	21.8	10.0	964	23.7	5.0	15 381	-4.1	1 015	6.6	14 951	28.3	33.7
Utah	145 469	67.3	222 300	23.9	10.0	882	30.9	4.5	266 078	4.0	8 484	3.2	231 830	40.1	17.7
Wasatch	7 752	74.3	304 300	26.0	10.0	1 025	31.1	3.4	13 229	3.8	450	3.4	11 486	35.9	20.9
Washington	47 905	69.1	209 500	27.7	10.0	943	31.9	4.0	63 906	3.6	2 535	4.0	55 216	30.8	21.5
Wayne	954	85.1	180 300	23.2	10.0	563	23.2	3.2	1 424	2.6	127	8.9	1 283	31.6	24.0
Weber	79 860	71.3	169 200	23.2	10.0	795	28.7	3.1	117 979	2.4	4 729	4.0	107 921	31.7	26.5
VERMONT	257 252	70.9	216 200	24.9	16.7	889	31.2	2.0	344 407	-1.0	12 581	3.7	325 336	39.9	20.8
Addison	14 215	74.4	235 200	25.7	17.7	882	28.9	1.9	20 708	-1.2	757	3.7	19 378	39.9	25.0
Bennington	15 477	70.2	210 600	26.5	17.5	872	32.3	2.5	18 381	-1.8	798	4.3	17 888	34.7	22.4
Caledonia	12 398	73.4	161 800	24.6	17.4	693	32.9	3.7	14 913	-2.5	718	4.8	14 898	34.6	24.5

1. Specified owner-occupied units.   2. A value of 10.0 represents 10 percent or less; a value of 50.0 represents 50 percent or more.   3. Specified renter-occupied units.
4. Overcrowded or lacking complete plumbing facilities.   5. Percent of civilian labor force.   6. Persons 16 years old and over.

Table B. States and Counties — Nonfarm Employment and Agriculture

	Private nonfarm establishments, employment and payroll, 2014									Agriculture, 2012			
		Employment						Annual payroll		Farms			
												Percent with:	
STATE County	Number of establish-ments	Total	Health care and social assistance	Manufac-turing	Retail trade	Finance and insurance	Professional, scientific, and technical services	Total (mil dol)	Average per employee (dollars)	Number	Fewer than 50 acres	500 acres or more	Farm operators whose principal occu-pation is farming (percent)
	104	105	106	107	108	109	110	111	112	113	114	115	116

TEXAS—Cont'd

Tom Green	2 785	40 348	7 944	3 010	6 463	1 613	1 317	1 489	36 908	1 203	44.1	20.3	40.1
Travis	32 217	544 038	62 232	28 188	60 013	25 150	64 470	30 069	55 270	1 132	51.7	8.0	42.7
Trinity	176	1 661	324	182	272	D	39	51	30 788	604	32.0	6.6	39.6
Tyler	269	2 554	588	D	844	87	54	69	26 987	727	46.9	4.4	41.8
Upshur	476	4 622	598	341	797	234	435	154	33 240	1 754	46.9	3.5	33.2
Upton	84	1 361	D	NA	76	D	D	85	62 558	101	8.9	68.3	47.5
Uvalde	625	6 958	1 521	380	1 530	257	220	195	27 975	640	17.7	33.9	49.8
Val Verde	758	10 463	3 184	402	2 160	472	197	253	24 182	421	40.9	35.2	42.5
Van Zandt	852	8 218	1 008	724	1 458	250	296	278	33 844	2 915	49.6	5.0	43.6
Victoria	2 400	35 087	6 794	2 061	6 002	917	1 072	1 577	44 947	1 533	41.6	12.1	41.6
Walker	947	11 736	2 017	994	2 520	386	522	358	30 474	1 560	55.5	6.7	43.3
Waller	717	11 289	1 036	3 329	1 000	D	316	541	47 948	1 927	30.1	5.6	41.7
Ward	310	4 072	215	D	322	D	81	254	62 314	93	30.1	33.3	26.9
Washington	891	12 678	1 589	3 319	2 085	806	333	440	34 690	2 697	42.7	4.2	35.8
Webb	5 123	73 755	14 961	604	13 723	2 598	1 952	2 147	29 105	696	15.1	48.6	48.6
Wharton	990	11 317	1 678	1 642	2 054	427	262	414	36 595	1 553	31.6	21.6	51.6
Wheeler	198	1 849	283	D	253	D	D	66	35 465	551	8.3	39.2	37.0
Wichita	3 165	46 183	11 356	4 619	7 679	1 864	1 506	1 585	34 328	639	40.2	15.5	38.3
Wilbarger	289	3 470	418	D	D	119	70	116	33 324	424	18.6	33.0	43.6
Willacy	196	2 486	437	D	D	85	D	71	28 526	321	47.0	26.2	50.2
Williamson	9 252	136 393	18 406	8 867	23 315	7 831	12 128	6 389	46 840	2 542	48.3	9.3	43.2
Wilson	641	6 176	1 168	323	1 370	D	192	200	32 330	2 444	38.1	7.2	38.4
Winkler	195	1 678	D	D	228	58	D	109	64 824	43	30.2	60.5	32.6
Wise	1 284	19 652	2 680	1 869	2 257	390	291	949	48 284	3 095	54.2	6.4	37.6
Wood	801	7 915	1 184	910	1 426	331	D	258	32 559	1 465	44.6	4.9	47.4
Yoakum	187	2 760	D	145	260	77	D	167	60 560	339	5.0	58.1	50.1
Young	592	5 865	1 102	897	860	254	121	228	38 841	795	21.0	25.5	39.4
Zapata	163	2 082	233	D	287	88	12	82	39 481	449	9.4	49.9	49.4
Zavala	107	1 972	D	D	215	58	D	63	31 982	287	7.3	54.7	46.7
UTAH	73 375	1 148 251	128 811	114 537	142 367	60 036	91 966	47 913	41 727	18 027	57.9	12.3	38.5
Beaver	162	1 586	D	D	414	D	14	47	29 785	277	43.3	20.9	66.1
Box Elder	1 038	16 753	1 467	D	1 721	290	225	788	47 020	1 235	45.6	21.6	41.0
Cache	3 109	39 326	5 428	11 132	5 788	1 270	2 911	1 244	31 635	1 217	51.5	10.4	39.9
Carbon	497	6 530	915	410	1 102	D	107	270	41 298	319	63.3	13.8	46.7
Daggett	19	D	NA	NA	D	NA	D	3	D	51	37.3	21.6	31.4
Davis	6 667	77 365	9 838	9 727	13 706	2 433	8 039	2 824	36 496	493	79.9	2.4	32.9
Duchesne	759	7 840	D	270	813	115	233	391	49 887	1 058	39.0	13.7	35.4
Emery	184	2 355	160	D	468	53	94	125	53 124	587	48.9	12.4	42.9
Garfield	157	1 251	D	D	106	17	D	37	29 875	279	42.3	12.2	43.0
Grand	459	3 814	D	D	716	66	133	110	28 968	81	60.5	13.6	51.9
Iron	1 237	11 133	1 792	1 409	2 082	438	374	333	29 881	509	39.3	24.6	45.0
Juab	191	2 097	D	466	283	D	322	70	33 190	353	33.1	22.1	28.3
Kane	251	2 186	196	D	370	D	25	71	32 504	183	33.3	24.6	39.9
Millard	238	2 901	244	554	567	62	D	124	42 583	728	29.3	30.2	49.9
Morgan	236	1 498	198	D	151	D	92	60	40 272	301	59.8	10.6	37.5
Piute	25	77	D	NA	23	D	NA	1	18 351	123	23.6	15.4	54.5
Rich	82	389	D	D	D	D	D	13	33 738	158	29.1	54.4	61.4
Salt Lake	30 279	549 047	59 822	47 301	59 196	41 046	44 982	25 837	47 058	630	89.8	3.0	29.2
San Juan	261	2 556	656	D	313	64	22	78	30 626	746	53.8	22.8	54.7
Sanpete	415	4 672	859	683	932	148	D	126	27 074	901	52.5	13.1	38.5
Sevier	514	6 276	782	D	1 346	133	117	203	32 324	674	60.8	6.4	38.9
Summit	2 218	25 620	1 177	D	4 096	1 198	1 087	847	33 065	618	62.0	11.2	33.0
Tooele	793	10 957	1 301	1 676	1 841	169	1 324	421	38 452	476	60.1	14.5	31.3
Uintah	1 178	11 267	705	341	1 750	193	555	573	50 868	1 231	55.5	8.0	32.8
Utah	11 735	178 352	21 941	17 453	24 228	5 211	12 642	6 961	39 027	2 462	78.9	3.8	30.5
Wasatch	822	5 572	543	231	1 017	159	457	186	33 326	450	76.9	5.1	32.4
Washington	4 381	42 838	7 620	2 444	8 210	1 415	1 878	1 340	31 273	579	63.0	13.1	43.5
Wayne	82	503	D	D	105	D	D	16	31 165	187	29.4	10.2	48.1
Weber	5 005	77 436	10 714	11 941	10 971	3 888	6 804	2 762	35 662	1 121	79.8	3.1	36.4
VERMONT	21 041	261 058	46 691	29 823	38 530	9 034	18 079	10 180	38 994	7 338	39.2	7.3	51.5
Addison	1 152	13 300	2 071	1 487	1 897	330	397	495	37 194	814	37.0	14.7	60.6
Bennington	1 385	15 173	2 900	2 802	2 979	319	355	539	35 502	305	48.9	3.9	46.6
Caledonia	925	8 801	1 770	1 370	1 616	298	288	318	36 186	560	38.8	5.7	47.1

Table B. States and Counties — **Agriculture**

STATE County	Land in farms — Acreage (1,000) [117]	Percent change, 2007–2012 [118]	Average size of farm [119]	Total irrigated (1,000) [120]	Total cropland (1,000) [121]	Value of land and buildings (dollars) Average per farm [122]	Average per acre [123]	Value of machinery and equipment, average per farm (dollars) [124]	Value of products sold Total (mil dol) [125]	Average per farm (dollars) [126]	Percent from: Crops [127]	Live-stock and poultry products [128]	Percent of farms with sales of: $10,000 or more [129]	$100,000 or more [130]	Government payments Total ($1,000) [131]	Percent of farms [132]
TEXAS—Cont'd																
Tom Green	957	3.6	795	31.1	168.2	906 863	1 140	87 951	131.4	109 257	24.8	75.2	26.9	9.4	5 161	25.4
Travis	253	-3.7	223	1.8	61.2	856 591	3 837	55 964	41.7	36 809	82.0	18.0	24.6	6.6	1 130	16.8
Trinity	111	2.1	184	0.2	17.9	427 030	2 318	57 775	7.1	11 672	24.1	75.9	31.1	1.3	161	7.3
Tyler	91	7.6	125	0.6	16.4	364 713	2 924	58 297	19.1	26 333	74.7	25.3	21.7	1.1	43	2.9
Upshur	202	2.1	115	0.4	43.1	330 283	2 863	43 263	60.6	34 526	7.6	92.4	21.8	3.2	298	2.7
Upton	686	8.2	6 794	8.9	46.1	3 991 644	587	142 505	12.7	125 584	63.6	36.4	54.5	34.7	1 495	41.6
Uvalde	977	-1.3	1 527	49.5	139.8	3 052 314	1 999	102 739	112.5	175 742	55.0	45.0	33.6	14.1	2 447	28.1
Val Verde	1 497	0.2	3 556	0.4	8.1	2 028 570	570	39 625	10.7	25 297	3.8	96.2	20.9	6.9	1 146	10.0
Van Zandt	371	-10.9	127	2.4	100.6	405 667	3 191	47 770	94.3	32 360	50.1	49.9	25.7	3.2	887	2.9
Victoria	438	-11.3	286	3.3	80.2	654 921	2 293	54 768	47.6	31 020	58.4	41.6	27.5	4.3	2 451	18.2
Walker	281	25.2	180	0.5	38.6	598 604	3 329	52 780	34.5	22 124	53.8	46.2	16.9	2.1	533	2.8
Waller	315	16.2	163	10.1	79.9	1 020 860	6 245	64 387	91.7	47 575	76.8	23.2	25.1	4.5	2 172	14.7
Ward	392	-9.5	4 211	0.2	5.9	1 560 022	370	53 290	1.8	19 054	6.5	93.5	19.4	3.2	214	18.3
Washington	369	9.0	137	1.4	89.4	758 889	5 549	51 747	45.7	16 955	24.9	75.1	25.9	1.9	914	8.4
Webb	2 098	13.1	3 015	2.6	25.2	3 265 045	1 083	57 487	30.3	43 476	2.8	97.2	31.2	7.0	1 169	14.1
Wharton	661	7.3	425	71.6	391.6	1 080 889	2 541	159 701	373.6	240 591	72.5	27.5	49.5	22.0	13 724	52.9
Wheeler	519	-11.0	942	11.2	99.6	773 481	821	83 860	111.2	201 826	8.2	91.8	40.8	10.2	2 651	61.0
Wichita	367	10.9	574	3.0	117.1	684 844	1 193	80 674	37.9	59 362	51.6	48.4	35.1	9.5	2 069	33.5
Wilbarger	587	-4.3	1 385	15.7	196.6	1 384 455	1 000	143 679	47.2	111 425	66.5	33.5	50.2	18.9	3 593	71.9
Willacy	336	-0.6	1 047	21.1	192.1	1 913 025	1 827	165 358	82.6	257 215	94.9	5.1	40.8	23.1	3 370	60.7
Williamson	559	3.1	220	1.3	211.6	853 775	3 019	61 058	129.6	51 002	57.8	42.2	25.5	6.7	3 659	26.2
Wilson	440	-5.9	180	12.4	103.3	537 404	2 987	50 097	102.1	41 775	27.3	72.7	27.5	3.0	1 988	20.7
Winkler	533	0.1	12 406	D	D	4 500 116	363	95 000	3.4	79 907	D	D	41.9	18.6	D	7.0
Wise	487	10.0	157	2.8	114.3	600 404	3 815	52 997	49.9	16 112	32.9	67.1	23.1	2.6	1 079	7.5
Wood	227	-2.8	155	1.6	52.5	442 703	2 853	57 063	105.9	72 270	6.2	93.8	27.2	5.3	267	3.3
Yoakum	488	10.1	1 441	90.4	265.9	1 166 307	809	247 257	80.0	236 012	91.6	8.4	47.2	32.4	7 563	81.7
Young	524	-0.7	659	0.2	97.8	911 345	1 384	68 309	23.7	29 801	33.8	66.2	33.8	5.2	1 385	30.1
Zapata	563	22.6	1 254	1.8	13.0	1 465 744	1 169	50 205	11.8	26 238	38.7	61.3	32.7	4.2	932	17.4
Zavala	693	-7.9	2 414	29.4	96.0	3 705 300	1 535	109 195	72.7	253 359	39.9	60.1	32.8	18.5	1 427	31.4
UTAH	10 974	-1.1	609	1 104.3	1 645.9	888 886	1 460	84 528	1 816.1	100 746	31.6	68.4	37.2	11.0	23 898	15.4
Beaver	190	20.0	686	37.6	37.1	1 370 004	1 997	140 502	288.5	1 041 520	7.5	92.5	57.8	33.6	419	31.4
Box Elder	1 171	-11.3	948	102.9	328.6	1 140 029	1 203	129 594	169.5	137 284	45.0	55.0	47.4	21.0	7 453	40.5
Cache	269	6.7	221	76.3	137.2	778 555	3 529	96 619	142.9	117 407	26.3	73.7	43.9	14.9	2 456	33.7
Carbon	241	11.6	754	11.1	20.9	918 621	1 218	59 596	9.0	28 248	27.0	73.0	31.3	5.3	239	5.6
Daggett	D	D	D	7.3	6.9	824 255	D	91 882	2.3	45 529	33.5	66.5	45.1	13.7	44	7.8
Davis	55	11.6	112	13.8	13.0	723 596	6 484	66 773	36.8	74 564	85.9	14.1	29.8	8.3	178	7.3
Duchesne	1 089	1.1	1 029	100.9	78.2	856 720	833	92 628	57.1	53 992	33.2	66.8	47.0	11.2	455	8.4
Emery	156	-23.7	266	51.7	41.6	452 336	1 700	65 775	14.1	23 978	36.2	63.8	37.8	6.0	306	16.7
Garfield	92	11.8	328	19.6	17.6	746 086	2 274	57 297	12.0	43 165	30.0	70.0	47.7	8.2	113	7.9
Grand	D	D	D	4.2	6.3	1 571 889	D	100 469	3.9	47 815	58.5	41.5	45.7	14.8	28	11.1
Iron	532	8.2	1 046	61.6	77.6	1 973 149	1 886	141 428	136.7	268 658	39.1	60.9	47.9	21.2	714	12.8
Juab	243	-6.7	688	20.5	47.9	825 640	1 200	86 938	28.4	80 331	40.7	59.3	45.6	11.6	997	35.4
Kane	125	10.6	685	4.0	4.5	966 694	1 410	50 333	4.7	25 590	16.8	83.2	43.2	2.7	214	10.4
Millard	577	1.9	793	115.2	151.6	1 114 356	1 405	200 816	180.6	248 110	41.4	58.6	64.3	27.6	2 312	38.3
Morgan	229	-24.1	760	9.0	15.8	1 196 671	1 575	63 116	20.4	67 648	16.7	83.3	36.5	12.6	71	10.0
Piute	38	-10.7	308	13.9	15.0	901 667	2 931	124 073	16.9	137 797	10.9	89.1	52.8	15.4	101	11.4
Rich	409	12.6	2 591	66.0	77.2	2 606 139	1 006	155 513	32.8	207 753	13.6	86.4	65.2	40.5	597	18.4
Salt Lake	78	-27.3	124	6.8	13.5	586 952	4 731	55 016	21.5	34 160	65.3	34.7	21.3	5.9	80	2.4
San Juan	1 609	4.0	2 157	4.3	113.0	805 649	374	43 488	13.4	17 906	32.6	67.4	16.6	5.2	1 543	23.9
Sanpete	284	-8.7	316	68.9	74.9	679 514	2 153	95 179	147.4	163 604	14.8	85.2	41.6	15.0	1 682	15.5
Sevier	122	-34.1	181	40.2	44.6	548 010	3 019	79 190	63.0	93 399	31.6	68.4	37.1	10.5	452	12.9
Summit	270	-34.9	437	20.8	25.2	996 972	2 281	51 511	24.2	39 079	13.0	87.0	34.0	7.0	154	2.4
Tooele	347	37.2	729	23.0	40.2	870 779	1 194	80 141	40.4	84 845	28.2	71.8	33.8	8.6	170	6.9
Uintah	D	D	D	69.0	62.5	930 444	D	75 442	46.6	37 877	45.7	54.3	33.5	6.3	653	6.6
Utah	343	-0.7	139	75.2	109.5	742 896	5 331	68 401	222.6	90 427	44.1	55.9	29.4	6.2	1 123	7.6
Wasatch	149	126.3	332	12.4	17.4	1 266 053	3 818	53 662	12.2	27 069	26.0	74.0	21.3	3.6	200	3.1
Washington	148	-15.0	256	14.8	20.2	934 487	3 656	50 485	12.6	21 843	51.1	48.9	29.2	5.5	210	7.8
Wayne	42	-6.3	227	15.7	15.3	914 588	4 037	78 561	15.7	84 144	19.3	80.7	62.6	14.4	500	35.3
Weber	117	10.5	105	37.7	32.9	609 955	5 823	60 135	39.9	35 568	41.9	58.1	23.5	4.4	436	8.0
VERMONT	1 252	1.5	171	3.6	488.3	546 627	3 205	86 935	776.1	105 765	22.9	77.1	40.6	15.1	13 930	21.3
Addison	208	11.1	256	0.3	126.8	779 307	3 044	130 227	185.5	227 928	15.3	84.7	47.1	21.4	3 796	32.7
Bennington	41	13.1	136	0.3	11.2	566 646	4 176	81 639	15.1	49 420	52.4	47.6	34.1	7.5	261	10.5
Caledonia	82	-0.1	146	0.1	29.1	464 918	3 182	76 234	37.2	66 509	18.1	81.9	40.4	13.6	628	15.7

Table B. States and Counties — Water Use, Wholesale Trade, Retail Trade, and Real Estate

STATE County	Water use, 2010		Wholesale trade,[1] 2012				Retail trade,[2] 2012				Real estate and rental and leasing,[2] 2012			
	Total water withdrawn (mil gal/day)	Gallons withdrawn per person per day	Number of establishments	Number of employees	Sales (mil dol)	Annual payroll (mil dol)	Number of establishments	Number of employees	Sales (mil dol)	Annual payroll (mil dol)	Number of establishments	Number of employees	Receipts (mil dol)	Annual payroll (mil dol)
	133	134	135	136	137	138	139	140	141	142	143	144	145	146
TEXAS—Cont'd														
Tom Green	55.9	507	113	D	D	D	418	5 963	1 821.7	149.8	134	595	92.7	16.5
Travis	293.3	286	1 166	21 735	56 614.8	1 470.9	3 469	54 094	15 583.7	1 443.3	1 771	10 798	2 455.1	539.0
Trinity	2.2	152	3	D	D	D	38	291	62.0	4.9	2	D	D	D
Tyler	5.1	236	7	47	39.7	3.6	53	531	115.8	10.0	4	21	1.0	0.2
Upshur	23.6	600	11	103	54.1	3.7	76	763	203.4	16.6	10	15	2.6	0.4
Upton	21.9	6 513	6	D	D	D	8	73	22.3	1.4	1	D	D	D
Uvalde	55.7	2 109	29	D	D	D	105	1 249	424.2	27.6	32	97	15.5	2.9
Val Verde	13.1	268	24	D	D	D	148	2 019	583.5	44.1	35	122	17.5	2.8
Van Zandt	11.3	216	29	263	72.3	11.3	147	1 406	430.7	31.2	29	83	6.2	1.4
Victoria	65.0	748	112	1 703	1 247.7	91.4	382	5 501	1 657.7	141.3	127	D	D	D
Walker	12.3	181	25	D	D	D	165	2 397	759.7	51.0	57	D	D	D
Waller	26.9	623	51	1 043	684.4	47.2	90	934	303.5	21.3	23	104	10.7	2.4
Ward	18.9	1 776	8	116	36.6	4.6	30	359	105.4	7.5	10	151	55.2	16.0
Washington	6.7	198	35	508	516.6	24.2	140	1 945	569.2	46.4	48	160	47.0	8.9
Webb	43.5	174	357	2 839	2 410.1	97.0	784	12 356	3 217.6	257.8	199	692	132.4	22.0
Wharton	223.6	5 416	49	890	572.2	37.2	163	1 999	563.8	49.1	39	168	29.4	7.5
Wheeler	17.9	3 303	9	D	D	D	33	239	71.6	5.1	6	8	1.1	0.2
Wichita	71.1	540	147	1 191	660.1	55.3	502	7 397	1 991.0	166.2	162	807	167.8	29.9
Wilbarger	34.8	2 567	12	D	D	D	48	664	254.6	14.3	10	22	2.7	0.6
Willacy	41.7	1 883	7	D	D	D	32	420	118.4	9.4	9	17	3.5	0.4
Williamson	64.1	152	306	D	D	D	1 277	21 844	8 585.0	593.3	408	1 550	348.9	65.5
Wilson	21.5	501	19	D	D	D	73	1 151	452.4	25.3	15	28	4.9	0.7
Winkler	14.5	2 032	7	D	D	D	20	195	53.6	4.4	7	D	D	D
Wise	68.4	1 157	57	609	658.0	31.9	154	2 174	757.1	62.1	46	291	61.3	13.8
Wood	53.0	1 262	31	257	169.8	7.6	129	1 345	393.7	33.4	30	133	31.0	4.9
Yoakum	211.9	26 888	11	135	43.6	8.9	28	211	61.6	5.2	6	D	D	D
Young	58.0	3 126	28	D	D	D	68	827	215.5	18.4	20	51	43.4	2.1
Zapata	7.4	527	1	D	D	D	32	263	75.7	5.3	4	26	5.7	0.7
Zavala	39.5	3 381	2	D	D	D	17	181	45.6	3.8	NA	NA	NA	NA
UTAH	4 463.8	1 615	3 015	43 523	30 927.9	2 364.4	9 095	133 535	38 024.5	3 334.9	4 446	16 197	3 226.1	604.8
Beaver	101.3	15 274	1	D	D	D	38	383	115.5	6.6	1	D	D	D
Box Elder	405.3	8 109	32	D	D	D	134	1 605	482.7	33.4	41	43	6.4	0.9
Cache	289.5	2 570	109	D	D	D	402	5 469	1 154.2	108.7	181	483	69.1	16.5
Carbon	41.3	1 929	30	D	D	D	86	1 084	311.3	26.0	15	57	17.9	1.9
Daggett	19.0	17 951	NA	NA	NA	NA	3	D	D	D	2	D	D	D
Davis	84.1	274	241	2 363	1 300.8	94.8	827	12 937	3 448.8	309.8	396	1 002	220.0	35.1
Duchesne	328.3	17 641	18	198	90.3	8.2	66	758	264.9	18.2	34	116	76.8	6.9
Emery	130.6	11 894	5	D	D	D	36	478	105.1	10.2	NA	NA	NA	NA
Garfield	64.5	12 477	4	D	D	D	23	116	29.9	2.2	2	D	D	D
Grand	17.1	1 857	13	D	D	D	79	678	170.1	16.0	31	131	14.0	2.7
Iron	210.1	4 551	33	261	246.0	9.7	172	1 892	567.8	43.3	72	165	28.7	4.8
Juab	56.1	5 478	9	62	36.3	2.2	33	313	114.5	5.0	2	D	D	D
Kane	17.6	2 466	4	7	1.3	0.2	41	337	77.1	6.4	16	26	3.6	0.7
Millard	291.1	23 281	13	D	D	D	61	549	122.1	9.1	3	4	0.3	0.1
Morgan	36.0	3 802	4	D	D	D	26	213	52.1	4.6	9	15	1.9	0.3
Piute	46.6	29 929	1	D	D	D	7	D	D	D	NA	NA	NA	NA
Rich	143.9	63 556	1	D	D	D	10	49	9.6	0.7	10	23	5.1	1.1
Salt Lake	410.8	399	1 653	27 748	19 734.9	1 640.3	3 395	55 808	17 178.4	1 536.0	1 931	8 980	1 927.6	378.3
San Juan	29.1	1 975	4	D	D	D	36	291	68.7	4.7	2	D	D	D
Sanpete	181.7	6 532	9	45	35.0	1.2	80	861	169.5	15.8	15	42	4.6	0.7
Sevier	143.9	6 916	13	90	211.9	3.4	88	1 255	331.8	29.2	14	85	17.7	2.9
Summit	70.9	1 952	43	551	378.7	32.0	295	4 105	1 013.6	101.5	245	900	124.1	27.6
Tooele	186.0	3 194	13	63	31.9	2.9	104	1 688	496.8	37.1	30	76	10.3	1.6
Uintah	274.6	8 426	45	D	D	D	135	1 575	503.2	43.4	79	453	104.1	21.8
Utah	366.1	709	368	5 770	3 112.6	298.4	1 520	22 096	6 039.4	529.6	684	D	D	D
Wasatch	56.3	2 391	17	35	11.0	1.0	88	1 021	267.4	20.7	44	105	27.3	3.4
Washington	122.2	885	149	1 284	1 514.7	47.4	574	7 375	1 900.8	168.4	306	702	95.2	18.7
Wayne	69.8	25 133	NA	NA	NA	NA	15	104	32.1	1.9	1	D	D	D
Weber	270.2	1 169	183	2 924	2 655.6	129.1	721	10 462	2 991.6	245.8	280	905	130.9	24.9
VERMONT	430.5	688	696	9 464	6 450.1	464.4	3 509	38 910	9 933.8	967.1	741	3 092	509.9	103.6
Addison	7.5	203	31	D	D	D	184	1 886	536.9	51.6	37	94	11.0	2.4
Bennington	5.3	142	27	D	D	D	271	3 051	806.2	79.8	53	222	29.9	6.7
Caledonia	4.0	128	29	D	D	D	173	1 687	451.4	43.1	30	D	D	D

1. Merchant wholesalers, except manufacturers' sales branches and offices.   2. Employer establishments.

Table B. States and Counties — Professional Services, Manufacturing, and Accommodation and Food Services

STATE County	Professional, scientific, and technical services, 2012				Manufacturing, 2012				Accommodation and food services, 2012			
	Number of establish-ments	Number of employees	Receipts (mil dol)	Annual payroll (mil dol)	Number of establish-ments	Number of employees	Receipts (mil dol)	Annual payroll (mil dol)	Number of establish-ments	Number of employees	Sales (mil dol)	Annual payroll (mil dol)
	147	148	149	150	151	152	153	154	155	156	157	158
TEXAS—Cont'd												
Tom Green	209	1 358	159.0	58.5	101	3 434	D	135.1	230	D	D	D
Travis	5 624	59 846	12 138.9	4 870.9	788	23 903	12 281.9	1 501.1	2 731	59 496	3 726.8	1 033.0
Trinity	11	42	3.3	1.0	9	158	79.9	8.8	15	223	14.7	3.2
Tyler	23	50	6.0	1.6	13	71	D	2.7	21	218	9.6	2.4
Upshur	51	446	47.0	16.6	23	285	113.3	13.4	37	D	D	D
Upton	3	D	D	D	NA	NA	NA	NA	11	D	D	D
Uvalde	41	D	D	D	17	409	149.5	12.1	80	1 063	58.1	13.3
Val Verde	45	D	D	D	22	321	D	11.0	94	1 647	77.8	19.8
Van Zandt	63	258	33.9	11.9	35	690	142.8	37.9	77	975	44.8	13.7
Victoria	159	874	115.1	41.1	73	2 021	D	D	188	3 593	187.0	49.2
Walker	90	473	42.9	14.2	41	761	352.7	37.3	103	1 875	92.1	24.8
Waller	62	490	72.7	40.2	70	2 744	919.4	160.1	46	647	33.2	7.8
Ward	18	62	7.4	2.6	4	38	D	2.1	28	326	22.3	5.0
Washington	59	339	48.1	13.8	45	2 967	883.6	128.4	86	1 084	54.9	14.8
Webb	317	1 803	186.1	58.6	69	635	339.6	22.0	389	8 216	423.7	106.2
Wharton	59	267	31.5	9.6	40	1 513	400.8	55.0	68	948	47.5	12.8
Wheeler	17	102	13.7	5.1	NA	NA	NA	NA	23	284	19.7	3.9
Wichita	235	D	D	D	129	4 885	1 400.8	230.7	271	D	D	D
Wilbarger	17	D	D	D	11	D	D	D	38	484	20.8	5.1
Willacy	10	D	D	D	3	12	D	D	23	253	13.1	2.9
Williamson	1 118	7 490	1 158.6	451.6	299	7 485	1 886.3	386.1	793	15 477	817.0	224.2
Wilson	37	166	22.8	11.9	24	327	121.9	15.2	62	763	36.8	9.6
Winkler	12	18	4.1	0.7	NA	NA	NA	NA	10	D	D	D
Wise	85	289	40.3	11.2	75	1 892	550.2	94.0	105	1 568	75.9	19.4
Wood	73	643	28.0	12.5	38	822	575.7	35.6	76	864	40.6	11.3
Yoakum	7	14	1.7	0.4	7	98	D	4.8	24	168	8.1	1.8
Young	34	102	13.7	5.2	22	881	252.2	42.5	42	474	21.9	6.0
Zapata	4	D	D	D	NA	NA	NA	NA	19	D	D	D
Zavala	7	27	1.0	0.2	3	D	D	D	17	200	8.8	2.1
UTAH	9 009	76 345	10 555.1	3 909.0	3 163	108 264	50 046.4	5 762.6	5 108	95 933	4 789.3	1 362.9
Beaver	5	11	1.0	0.2	6	79	D	2.9	29	244	12.0	3.1
Box Elder	53	213	23.6	7.1	72	6 206	D	469.2	69	1 174	47.5	14.8
Cache	368	2 487	245.2	87.2	207	10 515	4 516.6	434.4	162	2 969	125.1	33.8
Carbon	29	108	14.5	4.2	21	426	121.5	19.0	37	640	25.6	7.3
Daggett	1	D	D	D	NA	NA	NA	NA	7	64	5.1	1.5
Davis	868	6 369	974.4	320.4	265	9 506	5 982.0	459.4	420	8 178	350.5	96.9
Duchesne	50	168	27.0	6.9	22	209	D	9.9	33	396	21.7	4.8
Emery	14	149	7.8	3.5	4	17	D	0.9	20	192	8.2	2.0
Garfield	9	D	D	D	5	21	2.1	0.6	51	556	62.9	15.6
Grand	30	148	12.7	4.2	6	71	D	3.8	90	1 513	86.7	24.9
Iron	107	425	59.4	15.5	65	1 273	656.4	54.4	101	1 475	64.3	17.2
Juab	18	313	34.2	17.0	12	364	136.4	13.2	21	203	7.9	2.3
Kane	17	20	2.4	0.5	5	73	D	D	52	564	47.9	12.7
Millard	10	88	6.3	3.2	12	485	D	24.0	29	308	12.4	3.2
Morgan	23	86	7.8	2.6	12	143	D	9.2	8	111	4.5	1.7
Piute	NA	NA	NA	NA	NA	NA	NA	NA	5	22	0.8	0.3
Rich	6	10	1.3	0.5	NA	NA	NA	NA	14	79	9.5	2.7
Salt Lake	4 145	D	D	D	1 360	46 402	22 060.4	2 669.6	2 080	41 574	2 170.9	634.1
San Juan	13	23	1.6	0.7	7	230	D	10.8	52	744	65.0	14.3
Sanpete	22	92	7.2	2.3	25	657	174.7	22.5	36	390	10.5	3.1
Sevier	32	109	11.0	4.7	20	202	45.1	8.3	52	725	26.9	7.4
Summit	339	900	218.6	55.3	39	465	D	24.3	169	5 803	323.2	103.6
Tooele	68	D	D	D	34	1 705	884.3	92.3	69	1 028	46.4	12.4
Uintah	102	542	73.3	25.3	33	309	52.1	12.8	68	1 079	57.5	13.1
Utah	1 636	16 643	1 707.6	639.2	513	15 599	5 945.7	794.0	688	13 046	569.4	159.2
Wasatch	109	337	45.5	13.7	33	204	41.5	7.6	56	1 066	63.1	16.8
Washington	433	D	D	D	133	1 838	415.3	76.1	307	5 140	282.3	74.4
Wayne	3	D	D	D	4	D	1.7	D	25	157	12.8	2.4
Weber	499	4 180	401.7	195.7	247	11 260	4 799.0	540.7	358	6 493	268.6	77.3
VERMONT	2 113	15 948	1 782.0	739.9	1 013	31 487	9 315.5	1 594.3	1 920	31 365	1 564.3	494.0
Addison	123	D	D	D	57	1 472	D	82.1	86	873	55.2	18.8
Bennington	125	409	43.7	16.2	69	2 472	764.5	108.4	143	1 821	95.0	33.9
Caledonia	70	D	D	D	57	1 361	256.5	61.5	72	661	37.7	10.2

1. Establishment subject to federal tax.

Table B. States and Counties — Health Care and Social Assistance, Other Services, Nonemployer Businesses, and Residential Construction

STATE County	Health care and social assistance, 2012				Other services, 2012				Nonemployer businesses, 2014		Value of residential construction authorized by building permits, 2015	
	Number of establish-ments	Number of employees	Receipts (mil dol)	Annual payroll (mil dol)	Number of establish-ments	Number of employees	Receipts (mil dol)	Annual payroll (mil dol)	Number	Receipts (mil dol)	New Construction ($1,000)	Number of housing units
	159	160	161	162	163	164	165	166	167	168	169	170
TEXAS—Cont'd												
Tom Green	269	D	D	D	210	D	D	D	8 372	371.9	46 508	236
Travis	2 969	57 586	6 996.8	2 731.1	2 084	18 611	2 448.4	703.7	110 302	6 131.2	2 102 535	13 824
Trinity	22	320	24.4	9.7	17	64	4.1	0.8	976	32.5	36	1
Tyler	23	523	33.6	15.3	13	D	D	D	1 167	48.8	823	9
Upshur	35	634	40.6	17.7	24	95	8.2	2.5	2 796	133.4	280	6
Upton	5	D	D	D	NA	NA	NA	NA	280	19.5	120	1
Uvalde	73	1 731	130.7	45.8	33	D	D	D	2 573	124.2	2 535	28
Val Verde	92	2 819	89.9	45.2	47	255	15.1	4.4	2 828	96.1	12 422	79
Van Zandt	68	1 201	72.1	33.4	56	272	27.4	7.2	4 298	189.7	2 355	17
Victoria	304	6 591	679.7	274.5	151	1 165	162.8	46.8	6 234	297.1	20 794	136
Walker	97	2 179	180.2	75.2	54	297	23.6	6.1	3 906	151.7	33 544	158
Waller	38	D	D	D	43	195	25.2	5.7	3 494	183.2	11 574	170
Ward	12	229	15.9	8.7	13	168	21.6	6.8	682	39.9	4 203	40
Washington	98	1 906	98.3	43.0	53	212	17.4	5.1	3 027	148.8	12 698	131
Webb	536	14 678	926.2	373.6	203	1 129	101.1	27.1	23 755	1 143.0	201 418	1 848
Wharton	67	2 374	131.4	51.3	71	274	18.5	5.0	3 197	131.6	14 342	71
Wheeler	13	271	17.8	7.4	12	D	D	D	557	27.0	70	1
Wichita	391	10 832	1 051.7	391.7	225	1 212	118.8	31.1	7 820	385.7	17 063	72
Wilbarger	34	513	34.2	15.1	26	D	D	D	726	24.5	571	2
Willacy	33	547	27.1	12.8	12	39	2.4	0.5	1 317	44.1	8 866	134
Williamson	982	16 410	1 861.9	721.8	608	4 107	378.7	122.0	38 266	1 717.8	1 105 889	5 525
Wilson	55	1 158	69.5	29.3	46	140	11.8	2.7	3 383	175.6	14 136	96
Winkler	6	86	8.0	3.0	7	65	13.7	2.5	543	32.8	0	0
Wise	113	D	D	D	66	D	D	D	5 141	303.8	17 572	82
Wood	86	1 421	99.9	43.5	47	186	16.5	4.3	3 491	178.4	934	23
Yoakum	10	D	D	D	9	37	6.5	1.9	490	23.6	1 911	12
Young	58	1 032	77.3	31.7	37	147	13.3	3.6	2 058	133.4	1 590	12
Zapata	18	264	9.1	4.1	5	D	D	D	1 539	61.7	NA	NA
Zavala	12	D	D	D	2	D	D	D	857	24.5	976	5
UTAH	7 285	126 175	14 521.9	5 020.8	4 259	26 026	2 544.5	723.2	209 643	9 598.5	3 851 184	18 297
Beaver	21	D	D	D	10	26	3.6	0.8	447	14.1	4 808	23
Box Elder	116	D	D	D	66	D	D	D	3 042	112.8	47 192	236
Cache	348	5 106	494.3	161.6	172	810	60.7	17.8	8 132	307.1	80 871	562
Carbon	71	862	100.7	28.9	44	D	D	D	1 040	33.5	7 604	22
Daggett	NA	NA	NA	NA	NA	NA	NA	NA	97	4.6	1 031	4
Davis	667	9 466	888.6	340.7	395	2 471	182.9	54.0	22 055	972.1	379 915	1 721
Duchesne	50	D	D	D	34	D	D	D	1 456	68.8	20 319	99
Emery	17	D	D	D	15	D	D	D	579	15.7	3 183	16
Garfield	6	D	D	D	3	D	D	D	452	12.7	289	3
Grand	25	287	37.5	12.4	22	D	D	D	1 033	46.4	17 288	84
Iron	138	1 641	130.9	43.9	74	343	24.8	6.5	3 473	115.3	45 998	241
Juab	22	415	44.2	14.5	7	19	1.6	0.5	693	33.0	17 079	65
Kane	12	268	18.3	8.2	16	D	D	D	678	23.3	955	9
Millard	21	D	D	D	17	D	D	D	762	30.2	6 227	35
Morgan	21	D	D	D	8	D	D	D	959	37.7	34 806	110
Piute	1	D	D	D	1	D	D	D	115	6.2	3 159	16
Rich	2	D	D	D	6	D	D	D	229	9.0	10 764	47
Salt Lake	2 933	60 445	7 609.2	2 669.6	1 872	12 731	1 328.0	396.5	79 310	3 952.1	1 153 510	6 274
San Juan	34	701	76.0	28.2	11	D	D	D	769	23.6	3 432	22
Sanpete	47	856	58.7	23.0	25	D	D	D	1 740	72.3	6 839	45
Sevier	58	804	71.3	24.1	29	D	D	D	1 395	57.4	14 514	90
Summit	134	D	D	D	106	769	115.4	27.0	5 850	386.7	100 946	247
Tooele	92	1 267	125.5	45.5	58	239	20.9	5.5	2 794	91.8	99 417	481
Uintah	63	D	D	D	73	436	60.3	13.7	1 819	84.2	23 631	85
Utah	1 197	20 831	2 184.1	761.6	627	3 379	271.1	73.4	42 173	1 843.2	1 010 031	4 484
Wasatch	58	D	D	D	38	D	D	D	2 637	128.8	242 856	552
Washington	500	7 443	830.8	271.4	188	1 043	87.9	24.3	12 570	582.8	322 679	1 658
Wayne	4	D	D	D	2	D	D	D	316	11.4	2 336	13
Weber	627	10 695	1 335.5	418.8	340	1 964	166.7	47.1	13 028	521.7	189 506	1 053
VERMONT	2 096	44 198	4 458.0	1 789.2	1 588	7 211	755.4	199.3	60 181	2 536.0	333 954	1 998
Addison	120	2 091	159.6	72.5	88	330	55.0	10.1	3 868	144.6	26 745	163
Bennington	158	2 704	274.8	116.3	97	395	30.7	7.8	3 734	156.6	9 976	40
Caledonia	94	1 732	146.3	63.4	76	234	21.2	5.7	3 001	117.6	10 933	50

Table B. States and Counties — Government Employment and Payroll, and Local Government Finances

STATE County	Government employment and payroll, 2012									Local government finances, 2012				
			March payroll (percent of total)							General revenue				
												Taxes		
													Per capita[1] (dollars)	
	Full-time equivalent employees	March payroll (dollars)	Administration, judicial, and legal	Police and Corrections	Fire Protection	Highways and transportation	Health and Welfare	Natural resources and utilities	Education and libraries	Total (mil dol)	Inter-govern-mental (mil dol)	Total (mil dol)	Total	Property
	171	172	173	174	175	176	177	178	179	180	181	182	183	184
TEXAS—Cont'd														
Tom Green	4 430	11 842 865	8.7	16.5	6.7	1.4	3.6	6.1	55.2	321.7	125.9	138.0	1 218	917
Travis	45 034	190 376 191	8.0	14.8	5.4	4.1	5.1	18.3	42.4	4 794.7	942.7	2 689.4	2 455	2 026
Trinity	657	1 816 086	6.2	7.0	0.0	3.0	19.3	2.2	60.4	42.8	22.8	13.7	954	889
Tyler	945	2 527 612	9.2	3.5	0.0	3.0	16.0	2.8	65.4	63.8	23.6	34.9	1 625	1 538
Upshur	1 527	4 228 679	4.9	8.6	0.6	1.7	0.1	2.3	81.6	91.7	43.7	38.4	961	866
Upton	396	1 316 616	8.8	8.6	0.0	3.5	31.5	4.4	42.2	64.5	4.8	53.2	16 191	16 022
Uvalde	2 058	6 807 776	3.6	5.1	0.2	1.9	25.8	2.2	60.5	171.9	70.8	36.8	1 374	1 094
Val Verde	2 194	5 580 787	14.3	6.2	5.3	3.0	2.4	6.1	61.0	177.1	111.3	44.7	918	690
Van Zandt	1 960	5 471 112	4.9	6.7	0.3	1.8	0.4	2.9	82.3	133.5	67.2	50.0	953	821
Victoria	5 364	18 189 328	3.7	10.4	3.1	1.8	31.4	3.0	46.0	455.8	105.2	155.9	1 746	1 294
Walker	1 980	6 982 834	14.0	12.7	0.8	2.6	1.0	18.0	43.7	157.3	53.4	61.8	904	699
Waller	1 643	5 642 929	7.6	7.4	0.3	2.5	0.1	3.3	77.2	129.4	49.0	69.2	1 560	1 448
Ward	559	1 720 115	12.0	13.3	0.1	4.4	3.1	7.7	57.1	58.5	9.0	35.1	3 231	2 922
Washington	2 307	7 486 978	4.8	5.4	0.9	1.6	2.0	4.0	80.0	171.2	48.3	57.0	1 671	1 323
Webb	14 741	48 977 584	5.1	9.2	5.1	3.0	3.0	3.7	70.4	1 245.0	614.2	391.8	1 512	1 216
Wharton	3 171	11 435 949	2.9	4.7	1.0	2.5	19.8	1.5	66.6	188.9	70.3	71.4	1 729	1 485
Wheeler	514	1 406 670	6.6	3.2	0.0	2.3	33.3	2.8	49.5	54.5	8.1	36.6	6 498	6 236
Wichita	5 729	18 326 731	6.5	14.8	7.0	2.9	9.1	5.0	51.8	380.0	131.8	178.0	1 353	1 020
Wilbarger	1 195	3 537 696	3.1	4.1	2.6	1.8	21.1	2.8	64.1	75.4	29.4	23.4	1 765	1 490
Willacy	988	3 020 755	5.5	5.6	0.0	2.6	0.6	4.5	80.4	77.1	48.6	20.8	941	793
Williamson	16 819	59 733 376	3.1	6.7	3.0	0.5	4.4	2.8	78.5	1 670.1	418.9	1 031.8	2 262	1 950
Wilson	1 799	5 521 367	3.9	4.2	0.0	1.3	11.3	8.0	71.0	127.9	49.4	47.4	1 067	977
Winkler	465	1 871 237	6.8	7.5	0.0	1.6	15.1	4.2	63.8	57.9	10.9	36.9	5 029	4 658
Wise	2 052	6 283 194	8.7	7.9	0.7	4.7	0.0	3.9	72.0	189.8	35.2	132.2	2 187	1 913
Wood	1 347	3 686 462	6.7	10.8	0.5	4.1	1.5	3.8	72.4	92.1	31.3	50.5	1 202	1 071
Yoakum	719	2 354 261	7.1	8.7	0.1	3.1	26.1	3.9	50.3	97.6	9.0	68.0	8 426	8 230
Young	1 189	3 441 113	4.9	6.9	1.2	1.6	33.2	3.4	47.6	89.6	22.2	26.3	1 434	1 181
Zapata	901	2 905 195	13.0	4.2	3.8	4.8	1.0	3.6	68.4	76.6	24.7	47.2	3 300	3 261
Zavala	676	1 796 547	3.7	8.4	0.0	2.9	3.4	5.7	71.6	42.2	30.7	7.7	641	557
UTAH	X	X	X	X	X	X	X	X	X	X	X	X	X	X
Beaver	339	1 182 302	5.5	2.7	0.0	0.6	31.1	8.3	50.7	51.1	10.9	13.4	2 054	1 709
Box Elder	1 701	4 888 324	8.2	9.3	0.8	3.1	2.0	5.8	69.8	163.1	71.5	66.7	1 329	1 068
Cache	3 328	10 972 734	7.5	7.4	2.7	3.6	8.3	6.1	61.3	309.3	134.5	108.6	940	578
Carbon	959	3 089 135	8.6	9.2	0.6	4.8	13.4	11.0	49.4	77.6	27.1	32.7	1 540	1 152
Daggett	101	367 263	17.3	30.4	0.1	4.2	2.7	2.2	42.0	12.0	5.2	2.8	2 550	2 139
Davis	10 391	37 610 946	5.6	7.5	2.5	1.4	4.5	5.5	72.1	900.2	374.8	329.2	1 047	745
Duchesne	667	2 048 894	10.0	11.8	0.7	5.0	1.5	5.8	63.0	84.8	40.2	33.0	1 715	1 314
Emery	466	1 718 363	11.2	10.6	0.0	4.9	2.1	8.1	62.3	62.8	21.5	29.4	2 685	2 355
Garfield	208	742 442	11.2	13.2	0.0	8.1	3.9	3.0	59.1	29.9	14.5	10.4	2 048	1 146
Grand	491	1 568 944	14.6	13.1	0.9	6.9	12.1	8.6	39.6	48.0	15.0	23.4	2 503	1 486
Iron	1 282	4 462 404	8.5	11.6	1.0	3.6	3.5	5.1	64.5	132.5	51.2	58.7	1 257	954
Juab	437	1 313 251	9.2	9.3	0.0	4.6	1.1	6.7	66.9	40.9	23.8	12.2	1 178	963
Kane	440	1 479 423	9.0	11.3	0.3	3.4	34.0	2.0	37.7	48.6	12.0	21.3	2 951	1 982
Millard	516	1 988 139	9.7	11.9	0.0	5.8	2.6	6.2	62.0	68.1	23.0	25.6	2 037	1 792
Morgan	299	975 455	9.6	3.4	0.9	2.2	0.0	4.1	79.3	26.9	11.8	11.1	1 126	946
Piute	89	242 632	8.4	6.3	0.0	5.8	1.4	1.1	68.5	7.9	5.5	1.6	1 026	813
Rich	110	395 515	10.7	7.4	1.1	3.8	1.8	4.6	67.9	13.2	5.2	6.2	2 714	2 297
Salt Lake	34 230	125 577 298	7.2	10.3	5.3	9.8	5.0	8.9	51.0	3 731.7	1 299.6	1 519.3	1 428	1 028
San Juan	708	2 586 369	5.3	6.4	0.5	6.1	20.5	1.9	57.4	84.2	52.5	14.9	994	908
Sanpete	1 157	3 481 157	6.7	6.0	0.2	1.8	18.6	4.4	59.7	95.1	43.9	20.5	734	527
Sevier	746	2 317 397	8.0	11.6	0.2	2.5	2.9	7.4	65.4	75.7	42.9	22.0	1 059	746
Summit	1 737	6 591 640	8.6	7.7	9.0	7.8	2.4	12.1	48.0	236.3	39.4	155.2	4 084	3 100
Tooele	2 049	6 240 915	9.0	10.6	1.0	2.9	5.1	6.2	64.3	202.7	99.2	53.2	888	639
Uintah	1 239	3 713 017	11.2	10.8	0.4	5.2	9.6	10.8	46.9	155.8	52.9	70.7	2 048	1 456
Utah	14 037	52 266 547	6.3	8.0	2.5	1.4	4.9	8.4	66.6	1 574.6	646.3	574.1	1 062	718
Wasatch	952	3 521 146	10.0	7.9	0.0	2.6	6.3	11.3	55.4	122.6	39.4	52.8	2 091	1 673
Washington	4 130	14 492 173	7.3	10.1	1.7	2.6	6.5	13.4	56.5	453.7	154.1	197.8	1 366	972
Wayne	114	391 098	6.2	5.1	0.5	6.5	3.8	4.8	70.9	13.2	9.5	2.6	961	721
Weber	7 494	26 228 893	6.1	11.2	4.3	1.7	7.0	6.9	60.7	668.4	249.5	273.1	1 154	796
VERMONT	X	X	X	X	X	X	X	X	X	X	X	X	X	X
Addison	1 255	4 519 763	4.3	2.9	0.0	5.3	0.9	2.2	84.0	127.5	92.7	23.2	632	604
Bennington	948	3 568 427	6.0	7.7	0.1	5.9	0.6	5.2	74.2	128.5	92.0	25.4	692	657
Caledonia	1 032	3 333 702	5.5	3.4	1.1	8.2	0.9	4.6	76.0	108.5	81.8	18.1	580	578

1. Based on the resident population estimated as of July 1 of the year shown.

Table B. States and Counties — Local Government Finances, Government Employment, and Voting

STATE County	Direct general expenditure — Total (mil dol)	Per capita[1] (dollars)	Percent of total for: Education	Health and hospitals	Police protection	Public welfare	Highways	Debt outstanding — Total (mil dol)	Per capita[1] (dollars)	Government employment, 2014 — Federal civilian	Federal military	State and local	Presidential election,[2] 2012 — Percent of vote cast: Democratic	Republican	All other
	185	186	187	188	189	190	191	192	193	194	195	196	197	198	199
TEXAS—Cont'd															
Tom Green	347.3	3 066	51.9	3.4	5.7	0.2	2.7	583.9	5 155	1 186	3 208	7 499	28.7	70.4	0.9
Travis	4 740.6	4 327	38.8	6.7	7.4	0.8	6.5	15 845.5	14 463	10 645	2 527	113 900	63.9	34.4	1.7
Trinity	41.5	2 899	53.9	9.1	1.8	0.5	4.9	18.1	1 265	27	29	613	31.7	67.4	0.9
Tyler	60.2	2 805	57.5	0.1	4.6	0.3	5.4	43.0	2 002	45	39	1 653	27.4	71.4	1.3
Upshur	91.6	2 291	72.4	0.0	4.3	0.1	3.6	89.1	2 229	57	83	1 687	25.0	74.0	1.0
Upton	68.5	20 851	78.3	16.8	0.3	0.1	0.7	15.4	4 703	0	0	514	24.1	75.0	0.9
Uvalde	177.9	6 652	45.7	29.2	4.7	0.7	3.6	95.4	3 566	237	55	2 540	47.1	52.4	0.6
Val Verde	202.3	4 154	44.6	1.1	4.3	0.6	18.1	196.2	4 027	2 116	1 442	2 778	54.5	44.9	0.7
Van Zandt	133.6	2 548	65.3	0.2	3.7	0.1	5.1	143.4	2 735	87	108	2 240	22.1	77.1	0.8
Victoria	447.8	5 016	35.0	30.9	5.7	0.0	7.0	427.6	4 790	193	192	6 254	32.8	66.4	0.7
Walker	336.2	4 914	20.8	2.8	2.4	0.0	2.2	2 119.8	30 987	130	135	12 664	38.3	60.7	1.0
Waller	122.5	2 761	63.3	0.0	5.3	0.2	5.2	201.4	4 540	59	95	4 213	46.1	53.3	0.6
Ward	50.2	4 618	39.7	22.1	5.2	0.5	5.1	27.1	2 491	14	24	796	25.0	74.0	1.0
Washington	177.9	5 218	67.6	1.5	3.7	0.2	9.5	209.7	6 151	80	67	2 978	28.1	70.8	1.2
Webb	1 204.4	4 647	58.3	1.3	6.0	0.4	1.5	1 569.6	6 056	3 314	545	18 571	71.4	28.0	0.5
Wharton	212.0	5 136	49.9	27.3	4.1	0.3	4.0	112.7	2 730	82	84	2 749	34.2	65.4	0.3
Wheeler	47.3	8 406	62.3	25.4	2.4	0.0	1.9	10.4	1 840	21	12	603	14.0	85.4	0.6
Wichita	367.1	2 790	48.2	3.9	7.6	0.8	4.0	311.8	2 370	1 851	4 743	9 369	30.2	69.0	0.8
Wilbarger	85.1	6 421	56.2	22.2	2.7	0.1	3.2	25.5	1 920	38	26	2 545	26.5	72.8	0.7
Willacy	71.7	3 250	69.9	2.0	3.8	0.0	3.5	245.2	11 115	28	39	1 236	69.5	29.7	0.8
Williamson	1 761.9	3 862	55.5	3.1	4.1	0.1	8.7	4 547.8	9 968	620	1 003	20 854	42.7	55.8	1.5
Wilson	123.3	2 779	58.0	17.0	2.5	0.0	3.5	291.4	6 568	80	95	2 239	32.8	66.6	0.6
Winkler	63.1	8 609	59.5	14.6	3.7	0.3	1.7	83.7	11 417	0	16	610	23.5	75.2	1.3
Wise	185.9	3 076	52.9	1.7	4.7	0.4	8.7	328.2	5 430	111	127	3 862	21.7	77.4	0.9
Wood	83.7	1 992	65.3	0.6	6.3	0.2	7.2	54.2	1 291	93	86	1 782	22.5	76.8	0.7
Yoakum	112.1	13 883	63.5	19.3	2.1	0.0	3.3	58.6	7 256	15	17	814	18.3	80.9	0.8
Young	85.3	4 653	35.5	36.5	4.0	0.1	3.6	63.6	3 466	37	37	1 400	17.8	81.3	0.8
Zapata	71.8	5 023	53.0	1.7	6.5	2.5	10.2	53.7	3 754	157	30	912	67.7	32.1	0.3
Zavala	39.0	3 260	64.7	0.8	4.7	0.6	3.1	27.4	2 292	11	25	877	84.2	15.4	0.4
UTAH	X	X	X	X	X	X	X	X	X	34 332	16 316	194 177	34.4	62.6	3.0
Beaver	56.0	8 618	45.5	16.6	4.4	0.1	4.4	64.4	9 900	41	28	686	21.6	75.8	2.6
Box Elder	160.8	3 204	53.7	1.5	5.9	0.0	5.0	153.6	3 061	197	222	2 523	17.4	79.9	2.7
Cache	279.8	2 422	51.7	4.7	6.0	0.3	5.2	189.4	1 640	342	501	10 362	24.9	70.5	4.6
Carbon	97.8	4 605	33.6	5.7	8.9	1.4	15.4	82.2	3 869	144	87	1 839	44.6	52.6	2.8
Daggett	10.8	9 932	41.8	0.6	12.0	0.0	4.4	7.7	7 049	56	0	156	29.8	67.7	2.5
Davis	883.2	2 797	54.5	3.5	5.9	0.7	2.9	783.9	2 482	12 286	4 841	13 878	27.5	69.7	2.8
Duchesne	87.6	4 553	62.9	1.4	3.7	0.6	5.4	67.8	3 525	69	87	1 974	15.9	81.6	2.5
Emery	55.4	5 071	43.3	1.6	9.6	0.2	10.6	197.2	18 039	57	46	830	21.9	75.5	2.6
Garfield	23.9	4 686	43.6	2.6	4.9	0.2	12.7	15.3	3 013	158	21	377	18.8	79.2	2.0
Grand	44.6	4 784	31.4	1.2	9.8	0.7	9.0	75.2	8 066	240	40	714	50.7	45.9	3.4
Iron	125.1	2 675	48.9	0.6	7.6	0.2	7.1	124.1	2 655	295	200	3 796	19.8	76.1	4.1
Juab	41.3	3 997	42.5	0.6	7.1	0.0	6.0	46.1	4 459	28	45	715	20.5	74.2	5.3
Kane	51.0	7 056	25.3	22.9	3.7	0.0	6.3	44.9	6 214	92	30	618	27.1	70.1	2.7
Millard	53.8	4 280	54.0	3.6	7.9	0.0	7.1	9.5	752	84	54	955	16.0	77.1	6.9
Morgan	30.5	3 110	65.1	1.3	3.6	0.0	3.2	31.7	3 228	12	46	435	16.6	79.6	3.9
Piute	8.4	5 526	63.5	0.9	6.3	0.0	8.4	7.6	5 012	0	0	135	17.7	79.6	2.8
Rich	11.4	5 038	56.3	0.8	5.5	2.9	8.5	10.7	4 710	12	10	190	15.3	82.6	2.1
Salt Lake	3 568.5	3 354	42.8	1.1	5.6	2.0	5.4	7 237.3	6 803	10 397	4 897	90 184	48.7	48.6	2.8
San Juan	80.3	5 367	48.8	16.3	2.8	0.1	14.7	21.4	1 432	158	64	1 406	46.9	51.4	1.7
Sanpete	90.3	3 237	50.5	20.9	4.6	0.0	3.0	121.5	4 352	74	111	2 483	18.6	76.0	5.4
Sevier	69.0	3 318	48.6	2.0	9.0	0.0	7.7	54.0	2 596	195	88	1 452	17.0	79.9	3.2
Summit	247.7	6 518	32.0	2.0	5.3	0.0	14.4	271.7	7 150	57	168	2 625	56.7	41.4	1.9
Tooele	205.1	3 426	44.3	2.1	5.5	2.9	3.0	186.1	3 109	1 294	331	2 523	33.6	63.4	2.9
Uintah	172.6	4 998	36.6	3.9	4.3	4.9	15.3	199.3	5 772	356	158	2 653	14.4	83.2	2.4
Utah	1 425.3	2 637	52.2	4.1	6.0	0.1	5.2	2 402.3	4 445	905	2 386	27 958	18.8	77.7	3.5
Wasatch	116.2	4 598	37.8	2.6	4.5	0.1	8.0	196.8	7 787	43	119	1 344	33.9	63.7	2.4
Washington	401.3	2 771	50.1	0.8	7.7	0.0	6.0	585.2	4 041	556	648	7 509	21.9	75.3	2.8
Wayne	11.3	4 138	49.8	0.3	9.5	0.0	14.9	0.8	300	82	12	173	25.5	71.5	3.0
Weber	687.2	2 904	45.7	2.1	6.6	3.6	2.8	686.2	2 900	6 096	1 065	13 684	35.0	62.5	2.5
VERMONT	X	X	X	X	X	X	X	X	X	6 700	4 537	47 122	67.5	30.4	2.1
Addison	134.4	3 658	71.2	0.1	2.3	0.1	11.8	60.1	1 636	104	250	1 737	68.6	29.5	1.9
Bennington	140.1	3 818	69.0	0.2	4.4	0.3	12.1	38.6	1 051	163	256	2 066	65.5	32.1	2.5
Caledonia	107.7	3 461	66.7	0.1	3.0	0.0	14.0	33.2	1 066	99	217	1 992	60.4	37.2	2.4

1. Based on the resident population estimated as of July 1 of the year shown.   2. © 2013 Election Data Services, Inc. All rights reserved.

Table B. States and Counties — **Land Area and Population**

STATE/ County code	CBSA code[1]	County type[2]	STATE County	Land area[3] (sq km) 2010	Population, 2015 Total persons 2015	Rank	Per square kilometer	Race alone or in combination, not Hispanic or Latino (percent) White	Black	American Indian, Alaska Native	Asian and Pacific Islander	Percent Hispanic or Latino[4]	Age (percent) Under 5 years	5 to 17 years	18 to 24 years	25 to 34 years	35 to 44 years	45 to 54 years
				1	2	3	4	5	6	7	8	9	10	11	12	13	14	15
			VERMONT—Cont'd															
50 007	15540	3	Chittenden	1 390	161 382	397	116.1	91.6	2.9	0.8	4.3	2.2	4.9	13.9	16.0	13.7	11.6	13.8
50 009	13620	9	Essex	1 719	6 163	2 744	3.6	97.3	0.7	1.3	0.7	1.3	4.3	13.3	6.3	8.3	10.6	15.5
50 011	15540	3	Franklin	1 641	48 799	1 003	29.7	96.4	1.1	2.4	0.9	1.4	6.0	17.0	7.8	12.1	13.1	15.7
50 013	15540	3	Grand Isle	212	6 861	2 686	32.4	96.3	1.1	3.1	0.9	1.8	4.6	14.3	6.9	9.8	11.2	16.1
50 015	...	8	Lamoille	1 188	25 235	1 600	21.2	96.4	1.3	1.3	0.9	1.6	5.2	16.0	9.6	12.2	13.0	14.6
50 017	17200	9	Orange	1 779	28 899	1 457	16.2	97.3	0.9	1.2	0.9	1.3	4.8	14.9	8.3	10.5	11.2	15.5
50 019	...	7	Orleans	1 796	27 100	1 530	15.1	97.0	1.1	1.4	0.7	1.3	4.9	15.3	7.4	10.9	11.5	13.8
50 021	40860	5	Rutland	2 408	59 736	869	24.8	97.0	1.0	0.8	1.0	1.3	4.6	13.7	9.5	10.6	10.5	15.1
50 023	12740	4	Washington	1 780	58 612	881	32.9	96.2	1.4	1.1	1.4	1.9	4.9	14.5	9.5	10.9	12.3	15.0
50 025	...	6	Windham	2 034	43 386	1 104	21.3	95.3	1.6	1.1	1.5	2.1	4.6	14.3	8.4	10.6	10.6	14.9
50 027	17200	7	Windsor	2 511	55 737	909	22.2	96.6	1.1	1.0	1.5	1.4	4.6	14.2	6.8	11.0	10.8	14.9
51 000	...	X	VIRGINIA	102 279	8 382 993	X	82.0	65.3	20.2	0.8	7.4	8.9	6.2	16.3	10.0	14.1	13.1	14.1
51 001	...	7	Accomack	1 164	32 973	1 358	28.3	62.4	28.3	0.9	1.1	8.9	6.0	14.9	7.3	10.7	10.3	13.5
51 003	16820	3	Albemarle	1 867	105 703	561	56.6	79.7	10.7	0.6	5.8	5.7	5.5	15.5	11.8	13.0	11.4	13.1
51 005	...	6	Alleghany	1 154	15 677	2 064	13.6	92.8	5.6	0.6	0.8	1.4	4.3	14.7	7.6	8.9	10.8	14.3
51 007	40060	1	Amelia	920	12 903	2 235	14.0	74.5	22.8	0.8	0.9	3.1	5.3	15.8	7.6	11.1	10.8	15.7
51 009	31340	3	Amherst	1 227	31 914	1 384	26.0	77.2	20.2	1.4	1.1	2.2	5.0	14.8	9.9	10.6	11.1	15.0
51 011	31340	3	Appomattox	864	15 414	2 078	17.8	78.3	21.2	0.5	0.7	1.2	6.1	15.8	7.5	11.9	11.6	13.8
51 013	47900	1	Arlington	67	229 164	284	3 420.4	65.2	9.3	0.7	12.0	15.7	6.2	11.0	7.8	27.1	16.5	12.3
51 015	44420	4	Augusta	2 505	74 314	740	29.7	92.2	4.7	0.6	0.9	2.5	4.3	15.4	7.9	11.0	11.9	15.3
51 017	...	9	Bath	1 371	4 470	2 865	3.3	93.3	5.1	0.6	0.6	1.8	3.8	12.2	7.6	9.4	10.5	16.5
51 019	31340	3	Bedford	1 968	77 724	712	39.5	88.9	7.6	0.7	1.6	2.0	4.4	16.1	7.6	9.4	11.6	15.6
51 021	...	8	Bland	927	6 561	2 713	7.1	95.5	4.1	0.4	0.4	0.7	4.0	12.8	7.0	11.7	14.3	15.2
51 023	40220	2	Botetourt	1 402	33 347	1 345	23.8	94.1	3.9	0.6	1.0	1.5	3.8	16.2	7.1	8.7	11.4	16.3
51 025	...	6	Brunswick	1 466	16 698	1 999	11.4	41.7	54.4	0.5	0.6	2.1	4.2	13.5	9.0	13.5	11.9	13.9
51 027	...	9	Buchanan	1 302	22 776	1 695	17.5	95.9	3.1	0.3	0.5	0.6	4.4	13.3	7.3	12.0	12.5	15.3
51 029	16820	8	Buckingham	1 501	17 032	1 979	11.3	62.6	35.6	0.6	0.7	2.1	5.4	13.4	8.0	13.3	13.0	15.5
51 031	31340	3	Campbell	1 305	55 086	915	42.2	81.7	15.4	0.7	1.4	2.2	4.7	15.4	8.9	12.4	12.1	14.4
51 033	40060	1	Caroline	1 366	29 984	1 431	22.0	66.2	29.4	1.5	1.7	4.2	6.7	16.7	7.4	13.7	12.9	14.3
51 035	...	6	Carroll	1 229	29 724	1 437	24.2	95.5	1.2	0.4	0.4	3.1	4.4	14.9	7.1	9.5	12.2	14.6
51 036	40060	1	Charles City	473	7 040	2 671	14.9	43.2	48.7	7.8	1.4	1.7	3.2	12.6	7.1	10.1	10.0	17.6
51 037	...	8	Charlotte	1 231	12 201	2 286	9.9	68.3	29.3	0.6	0.6	2.8	5.5	16.0	8.1	10.3	10.6	14.4
51 041	40060	1	Chesterfield	1 096	335 687	200	306.3	65.4	23.9	0.8	4.4	8.0	5.8	18.6	9.3	11.8	13.7	14.8
51 043	47900	1	Clarke	456	14 363	2 145	31.5	89.3	6.2	0.9	1.7	4.5	5.3	16.1	7.9	9.1	10.3	17.3
51 045	40220	2	Craig	853	5 211	2 819	6.1	98.2	0.7	0.3	0.5	1.0	4.5	14.9	7.5	9.0	11.7	15.5
51 047	47900	6	Culpeper	982	49 432	992	50.3	73.9	16.9	0.8	2.1	9.3	6.5	18.9	8.0	12.2	13.1	14.9
51 049	...	1	Cumberland	770	9 719	2 456	12.6	64.8	32.9	0.9	0.8	2.4	5.4	15.6	8.3	11.2	11.0	14.9
51 051	13720	9	Dickenson	856	15 115	2 089	17.7	98.3	0.6	0.3	0.3	0.9	5.2	15.4	7.5	11.5	12.7	13.8
51 053	40060	1	Dinwiddie	1 305	27 852	1 495	21.3	63.3	32.9	0.7	1.0	2.9	4.4	15.9	9.0	11.6	12.2	16.1
51 057	...	8	Essex	666	11 130	2 347	16.7	57.1	39.0	1.0	1.4	3.6	5.4	14.7	8.2	10.7	10.6	14.9
51 059	47900	1	Fairfax	1 013	1 142 234	37	1 127.6	54.8	10.2	0.6	21.1	16.4	6.7	17.1	8.3	14.2	14.6	15.1
51 061	47900	1	Fauquier	1 677	68 782	774	41.0	82.8	9.1	0.8	2.2	7.1	5.6	18.3	8.1	10.6	11.9	16.6
51 063	13980	8	Floyd	985	15 651	2 067	15.9	94.5	2.3	0.6	0.8	2.8	5.0	15.5	6.6	9.9	12.1	14.9
51 065	16820	3	Fluvanna	741	26 235	1 552	35.4	80.6	16.4	0.7	1.2	3.2	5.1	16.2	7.2	11.5	13.3	14.8
51 067	40220	2	Franklin	1 788	56 264	905	31.5	88.5	9.0	0.5	0.7	2.7	4.8	14.9	8.8	9.7	10.8	14.7
51 069	49020	3	Frederick	1 071	83 199	677	77.7	86.3	5.3	0.6	2.0	7.4	5.8	17.8	8.3	12.1	12.8	15.4
51 071	13980	3	Giles	921	16 708	1 997	18.1	96.3	2.2	0.5	0.7	1.6	5.1	15.6	7.5	10.6	12.4	14.6
51 073	47260	1	Gloucester	564	37 143	1 248	65.9	86.8	9.3	1.2	1.6	3.3	5.1	15.3	8.0	11.5	11.4	15.9
51 075	40060	1	Goochland	729	22 253	1 718	30.5	78.5	18.2	0.6	1.8	2.4	4.0	15.1	6.6	8.6	12.4	16.7
51 077	...	9	Grayson	1 145	16 012	2 038	14.0	89.0	2.6	0.5	0.3	2.8	4.7	13.3	6.8	9.2	11.4	14.7
51 079	16820	3	Greene	405	19 162	1 866	47.3	86.1	8.1	0.8	2.2	5.0	6.4	17.8	7.0	11.9	13.0	15.1
51 081	...	6	Greensville	765	11 885	2 303	15.5	38.7	60.0	0.5	0.9	2.1	5.2	12.3	8.6	14.9	14.9	15.8
51 083	...	6	Halifax	2 118	35 125	1 299	16.6	60.7	37.0	0.6	0.8	1.9	4.9	15.8	8.0	9.8	10.8	13.4
51 085	40060	1	Hanover	1 214	103 227	578	85.0	86.0	10.1	0.8	2.1	2.6	4.6	18.1	9.0	9.6	12.4	16.2
51 087	40060	1	Henrico	605	325 155	207	537.4	56.6	30.5	0.8	8.6	5.4	6.3	17.1	8.2	14.3	13.6	14.1
51 089	32300	4	Henry	990	51 881	969	52.4	71.9	22.7	0.6	0.8	5.4	5.0	14.8	7.3	10.1	11.0	15.1
51 091	...	9	Highland	1 075	2 214	3 031	2.1	97.3	0.6	0.2	0.5	1.5	3.2	10.1	6.0	7.4	8.4	13.7
51 093	47260	1	Isle of Wight	817	36 314	1 268	44.4	72.1	24.4	0.9	1.6	2.7	4.6	16.5	7.7	10.3	11.7	16.4
51 095	47260	1	James City	369	73 147	745	198.2	78.6	14.5	0.9	3.7	5.5	5.1	15.9	7.5	10.4	10.9	13.7
51 097	...	1	King and Queen	816	7 158	2 661	8.8	68.0	28.2	2.3	0.9	3.1	3.9	14.8	7.5	10.3	10.9	14.9
51 099	...	8	King George	465	25 515	1 584	54.9	76.6	18.5	1.2	2.6	4.4	6.8	19.4	8.6	12.8	13.6	15.3
51 101	40060	1	King William	710	16 269	2 025	22.9	77.9	18.4	2.1	1.4	2.5	6.1	17.4	7.7	12.6	12.7	15.4
51 103	...	9	Lancaster	345	10 965	2 360	31.8	69.9	28.5	0.5	0.9	1.6	3.8	11.2	6.0	7.5	7.6	11.7
51 105	...	8	Lee	1 128	24 742	1 616	21.9	93.6	4.3	0.8	0.5	1.8	5.1	14.2	7.1	12.8	13.5	13.7
51 107	47900	1	Loudoun	1 335	375 629	181	281.4	61.6	8.4	0.6	19.2	13.4	7.7	21.7	7.0	13.0	17.7	15.8

1. CBSA = Core Based Statistical Area. See Appendix A for explanation. See Appendix B for list of metropolitan areas with component counties.   2. County type code from the Economic Research Service of USDA Rural-Urban Continuum Codes. See Appendix A for definition.   3. Dry land or land partially or temporarily covered by water.   4. May be of any race.

Table B. States and Counties — **Population and Households**

STATE County	Population, 2014 (cont.) Age (percent) (cont.)				Population change and components of change, 2000–2015 Total persons		Percent change		Components of change, 2010–2015			Households, 2010–2014		Percent		
	55 to 64 years	65 to 74 years	75 years and over	Percent female	2000	2010	2000–2010	2010–2015	Births	Deaths	Net migration	Number	Persons per household	Family households	Female family householder[1]	One person
	16	17	18	19	20	21	22	23	24	25	26	27	28	29	30	31
VERMONT—Cont'd																
Chittenden	13.0	7.5	5.7	51.1	146 571	156 540	6.8	3.1	8 321	5 358	1 822	63 086	2.36	59.0	8.6	28.2
Essex	18.3	14.2	9.1	49.6	6 459	6 306	-2.4	-2.3	275	293	-134	2 752	2.26	63.2	10.6	30.7
Franklin	14.4	8.4	5.5	50.3	45 417	47 752	5.1	2.2	3 001	1 924	56	18 751	2.54	70.0	9.9	22.6
Grand Isle	19.1	12.3	5.6	50.2	6 901	6 970	1.0	-1.6	298	298	-60	2 981	2.34	69.6	7.6	25.2
Lamoille	14.2	9.1	6.1	50.1	23 233	24 475	5.3	3.1	1 370	1 016	410	10 121	2.39	59.2	7.0	31.0
Orange	17.3	10.9	6.7	50.3	28 226	28 936	2.5	-0.1	1 455	1 284	-171	12 135	2.32	66.7	10.1	25.7
Orleans	15.8	12.1	8.3	49.8	26 277	27 234	3.6	-0.5	1 429	1 536	18	11 214	2.35	61.9	9.7	30.9
Rutland	16.5	11.3	8.1	50.9	63 400	61 646	-2.8	-3.1	2 853	3 389	-1 314	25 635	2.28	62.9	9.1	29.3
Washington	15.8	9.9	7.1	50.6	58 039	59 526	2.6	-1.5	3 031	2 752	-1 131	24 704	2.31	62.3	9.9	29.1
Windham	17.3	11.6	7.7	51.0	44 216	44 513	0.7	-2.5	2 200	2 257	-966	19 223	2.20	59.2	7.9	31.7
Windsor	17.2	12.1	8.5	51.1	57 418	56 666	-1.3	-1.6	2 581	2 969	-436	24 560	2.25	62.5	8.8	30.1
VIRGINIA	12.5	8.2	5.6	50.8	7 078 515	8 001 045	13.0	4.8	539 449	324 842	164 981	3 041 710	2.61	67.3	12.4	26.5
Accomack	16.1	12.3	8.9	51.3	38 305	33 164	-13.4	-0.6	2 102	2 322	14	14 289	2.25	65.4	13.6	29.4
Albemarle	13.3	9.0	7.5	52.2	79 236	98 998	24.9	6.8	5 777	4 067	4 807	38 537	2.45	64.0	8.6	29.5
Alleghany	15.0	14.2	10.1	50.8	17 215	16 261	-5.5	-3.6	747	1 250	-152	6 714	2.36	65.1	8.4	30.0
Amelia	15.4	11.3	6.9	51.3	11 400	12 695	11.4	1.6	712	669	189	4 761	2.65	74.0	10.1	21.6
Amherst	14.7	11.0	7.9	52.2	31 894	32 354	1.4	-1.4	1 694	1 816	-284	12 577	2.47	67.3	14.1	28.7
Appomattox	14.3	11.3	7.7	51.5	13 705	14 975	9.3	2.9	921	803	313	5 964	2.53	75.4	12.7	21.6
Arlington	9.8	5.6	3.6	49.9	189 453	207 676	9.6	10.3	16 523	5 025	10 010	96 264	2.26	46.3	6.2	40.1
Augusta	14.8	11.5	7.9	49.4	65 615	73 736	12.4	0.8	3 416	3 596	571	28 124	2.49	73.4	9.3	22.8
Bath	15.0	14.4	10.6	49.3	5 048	4 727	-6.4	-5.4	191	304	-128	2 225	2.04	60.4	5.8	35.6
Bedford	16.0	11.9	7.5	50.7	60 371	74 871	24.0	3.8	3 941	3 934	2 779	30 122	2.49	70.8	8.9	24.7
Bland	14.8	12.3	7.7	44.7	6 871	6 824	-0.7	-3.9	236	458	-35	2 591	2.24	68.5	11.0	29.0
Botetourt	16.5	12.1	7.8	50.6	30 496	33 148	8.7	0.6	1 264	1 633	513	12 867	2.55	78.0	8.0	18.6
Brunswick	14.9	10.8	8.3	47.6	18 419	17 432	-5.4	-4.2	749	1 028	-448	5 865	2.53	68.2	18.2	28.6
Buchanan	15.7	11.9	7.5	49.1	26 978	24 095	-10.7	-5.5	1 084	1 475	-923	9 406	2.41	70.4	14.1	25.4
Buckingham	14.4	10.3	6.6	45.6	15 623	17 140	9.7	-0.6	880	816	-162	5 802	2.48	70.8	16.3	25.2
Campbell	14.0	10.5	7.7	51.3	51 078	54 851	7.4	0.4	2 904	2 666	-11	21 728	2.50	70.1	12.7	25.7
Caroline	13.0	9.4	5.7	50.9	22 121	28 558	29.1	5.0	2 144	1 329	546	10 728	2.55	75.0	16.1	19.8
Carroll	15.5	12.9	8.8	50.4	29 245	30 087	2.9	-1.2	1 296	1 884	258	12 508	2.37	68.2	10.2	28.6
Charles City	18.0	13.3	8.0	50.9	6 926	7 256	4.8	-3.0	279	439	-69	2 832	2.53	66.5	14.7	29.2
Charlotte	14.8	11.5	8.6	50.2	12 472	12 575	0.8	-3.0	723	816	-273	4 691	2.60	69.0	14.2	27.2
Chesterfield	13.2	8.2	4.6	51.8	259 903	316 231	21.7	6.2	19 908	11 093	10 330	115 005	2.78	72.3	12.2	23.5
Clarke	15.9	10.4	7.6	50.0	12 652	14 029	10.9	2.4	711	790	412	5 619	2.50	67.8	10.5	25.3
Craig	15.8	12.8	8.3	49.9	5 091	5 173	1.6	0.7	232	279	57	2 151	2.41	67.5	8.2	28.2
Culpeper	12.5	8.6	5.3	49.7	34 262	46 691	36.3	5.9	3 311	1 974	1 356	16 436	2.81	75.1	12.1	20.2
Cumberland	14.2	11.9	7.4	52.2	9 017	10 055	11.5	-3.3	565	489	-416	4 038	2.45	67.8	16.2	25.9
Dickenson	15.1	11.7	7.2	49.2	16 395	15 892	-3.1	-4.9	897	1 058	-583	6 200	2.47	69.2	10.8	28.6
Dinwiddie	14.6	10.0	6.3	51.1	24 533	28 001	14.1	-0.5	1 469	1 310	-325	9 956	2.73	71.9	16.0	23.6
Essex	15.1	12.0	8.4	52.9	9 989	11 146	11.6	-0.1	650	648	-50	4 288	2.56	62.1	10.3	31.2
Fairfax	12.5	7.1	4.4	50.5	969 749	1 081 685	11.5	5.6	78 887	25 795	9 221	391 794	2.83	71.2	9.3	22.6
Fauquier	14.0	9.2	5.8	50.5	55 139	65 275	18.4	5.4	4 027	2 738	2 057	23 162	2.86	74.4	8.4	21.0
Floyd	15.6	12.5	7.9	49.6	13 874	15 293	10.2	2.3	805	761	310	6 086	2.53	66.5	6.8	28.6
Fluvanna	13.7	10.8	7.5	54.3	20 047	25 704	28.2	2.1	1 361	1 034	168	9 787	2.52	73.1	9.5	22.8
Franklin	15.5	13.1	7.7	50.7	47 286	56 155	18.8	0.2	2 626	2 970	469	23 248	2.36	70.9	10.0	25.4
Frederick	12.8	9.0	6.2	50.2	59 209	78 308	32.3	6.2	5 009	3 104	2 967	29 184	2.71	74.3	9.5	19.3
Giles	14.3	12.2	7.8	50.8	16 657	17 286	3.8	-3.3	891	1 084	-355	7 253	2.33	68.8	12.8	26.8
Gloucester	15.2	10.6	6.9	50.7	34 780	36 858	6.0	0.8	1 910	1 881	175	14 074	2.60	73.3	10.8	22.1
Goochland	17.2	12.7	6.7	50.6	16 863	21 699	28.7	2.6	862	880	473	8 212	2.43	78.8	7.1	19.4
Grayson	16.3	13.3	10.4	51.3	17 917	15 551	-13.2	3.0	793	1 117	773	6 686	2.25	63.9	11.2	32.2
Greene	13.0	10.1	5.7	50.4	15 244	18 410	20.8	4.1	1 105	761	389	6 965	2.67	73.0	9.3	20.7
Greensville	13.2	9.2	5.9	38.8	11 560	12 243	5.9	-2.9	573	595	-378	3 397	2.42	72.5	18.2	23.3
Halifax	15.4	12.7	9.4	52.0	37 355	36 241	-3.0	-3.1	1 877	2 468	-521	14 472	2.41	64.7	14.7	33.0
Hanover	14.4	9.3	6.3	51.0	86 320	99 850	15.7	3.4	4 686	4 259	2 818	37 041	2.66	76.1	9.5	19.5
Henrico	12.5	7.7	6.1	52.8	262 300	306 979	17.0	5.9	20 909	13 269	10 488	123 821	2.52	64.6	15.3	29.5
Henry	15.0	12.2	9.5	51.8	57 930	54 143	-6.5	-4.2	2 673	3 647	-1 342	22 472	2.33	66.9	13.8	30.1
Highland	21.7	17.5	11.9	50.3	2 536	2 319	-8.6	-4.5	85	133	-62	1 067	2.12	67.5	7.9	28.2
Isle of Wight	15.5	10.6	6.7	51.3	29 728	35 270	18.6	3.0	1 704	1 807	1 089	13 519	2.61	75.8	10.2	20.1
James City	13.7	12.9	9.9	51.7	48 102	67 401	40.1	8.5	3 556	3 255	5 336	27 665	2.49	71.5	11.0	23.9
King and Queen	17.1	12.4	8.2	49.7	6 630	6 945	4.8	3.1	305	386	264	2 832	2.50	71.4	12.4	24.8
King George	11.9	7.3	4.3	49.4	16 803	23 584	40.4	8.2	1 638	781	1 024	8 315	2.92	74.8	10.9	20.0
King William	13.7	9.0	5.4	51.3	13 146	15 927	21.2	2.1	1 004	689	46	6 147	2.60	76.3	12.1	19.5
Lancaster	17.1	18.1	17.0	53.3	11 567	11 395	-1.5	-3.8	410	1 050	174	5 283	2.10	59.9	10.0	35.4
Lee	14.8	11.4	7.4	47.7	23 589	25 586	8.5	-3.3	1 274	1 521	-646	9 597	2.50	68.5	9.7	29.0
Loudoun	9.4	4.8	3.0	50.4	169 599	312 336	84.2	20.3	26 580	5 914	42 007	110 047	3.07	78.1	8.9	17.0

1. No spouse present.

Table B. States and Counties — Population, Vital Statistics, Medicare, and Crime

STATE County	Persons in group quarters, 2015	Daytime population, 2010–2014 Number	Employment/residence ratio	Births, 2015 Total	Rate[1]	Deaths, 2015 Number	Rate[1]	Persons under 65 with no health insurance, 2014 Number	Percent	Medicare, 2015 Total Beneficiaries	Enrolled in Original Medicare	Enrolled in Medicare Advantage	Serious crimes known to police,[2] 2014 Total Number	Rate[3]
	32	33	34	35	36	37	38	39	40	41	42	43	44	45
VERMONT—Cont'd														
Chittenden	9 771	173 009	1.17	1 613	10.0	1 045	6.5	6 800	5.2	19 762	18 002	1 760	3 404	2 126
Essex	16	4 962	0.52	49	8.0	60	9.8	422	9.0	1 802	1 662	140	15	242
Franklin	605	42 412	0.76	563	11.6	343	7.0	2 418	5.8	7 993	7 311	682	797	1 647
Grand Isle	0	4 814	0.42	56	8.1	50	7.2	382	6.7	1 605	1 414	191	100	1 430
Lamoille	716	24 160	0.95	251	10.0	184	7.3	1 495	7.2	9 187	8 429	758	158	627
Orange	737	23 603	0.64	278	9.6	244	8.4	1 540	6.6	5 599	5 278	321	253	876
Orleans	783	26 741	0.96	268	9.9	278	10.3	1 623	7.7	6 419	5 922	497	406	1 496
Rutland	2 338	60 379	0.98	526	8.8	618	10.3	3 019	6.5	15 296	14 166	1 130	1 036	1 724
Washington	2 415	62 255	1.09	547	9.3	506	8.6	2 382	5.1	12 439	11 429	1 010	870	1 469
Windham	1 496	46 711	1.12	430	9.9	417	9.6	2 297	6.7	9 404	8 699	705	894	2 047
Windsor	909	53 898	0.91	469	8.4	525	9.4	2 797	6.4	12 855	11 710	1 145	717	1 282
VIRGINIA	243 812	8 089 957	0.98	103 357	12.4	63 347	7.6	863 567	12.4	1 245 384	981 001	264 383	177 060	2 127
Accomack	426	32 097	0.93	369	11.2	452	13.7	4 843	18.8	8 181	6 956	1 225	550	1 659
Albemarle	6 318	110 855	1.19	1 096	10.4	827	7.9	9 575	11.7	9 462	8 155	1 307	1 960	1 884
Alleghany	281	16 366	1.04	121	7.7	262	16.6	1 511	12.7	2 095	1 555	540	207	1 281
Amelia	128	9 916	0.49	130	10.1	127	9.9	1 679	16.0	2 540	1 864	676	130	1 019
Amherst	1 501	27 132	0.65	310	9.7	363	11.3	3 672	14.8	6 679	5 560	1 119	430	1 334
Appomattox	56	12 291	0.55	180	11.7	155	10.1	1 780	14.4	2 893	2 448	445	132	862
Arlington	3 004	269 516	1.35	3 177	13.9	1 013	4.4	17 969	8.9	18 140	15 775	2 365	4 311	1 882
Augusta	2 500	67 687	0.82	581	7.8	720	9.7	7 772	13.5	9 742	8 067	1 675	917	1 238
Bath	53	4 434	0.90	41	9.1	45	10.0	462	13.5	1 382	1 198	184	40	871
Bedford	551	60 219	0.56	702	9.1	787	10.2	7 494	12.2	18 838	15 010	3 828	1 064	1 400
Bland	686	6 146	0.76	41	6.2	85	12.9	583	12.5	1 608	1 262	346	51	759
Botetourt	278	26 998	0.61	224	6.7	322	9.7	2 596	9.9	6 730	5 076	1 654	294	892
Brunswick	2 162	14 855	0.66	129	7.7	208	12.4	1 869	16.1	3 560	2 637	923	119	705
Buchanan	1 115	24 501	1.11	176	7.7	296	12.9	2 729	15.5	6 120	3 649	2 471	403	1 715
Buckingham	2 206	14 942	0.64	160	9.4	143	8.4	2 027	16.8	2 497	1 918	579	220	1 283
Campbell	468	49 098	0.77	475	8.6	505	9.2	5 997	13.4	10 022	8 268	1 754	910	1 644
Caroline	513	21 859	0.46	427	14.3	259	8.7	3 252	13.2	4 571	3 625	946	433	1 468
Carroll	337	26 327	0.71	231	7.8	368	12.4	4 086	17.6	5 778	4 856	922	409	1 370
Charles City	0	5 685	0.54	46	6.5	92	13.1	983	17.8	1 951	1 431	520	31	437
Charlotte	175	10 530	0.62	140	11.5	159	13.0	1 786	18.5	3 851	3 210	641	66	539
Chesterfield	4 425	282 861	0.74	3 890	11.6	2 219	6.6	31 073	10.9	40 962	30 655	10 307	6 803	2 058
Clarke	180	11 475	0.59	160	11.1	137	9.5	1 260	10.8	2 432	2 119	313	174	1 206
Craig	9	3 679	0.30	54	10.3	66	12.6	530	12.8	1 027	769	258	22	422
Culpeper	1 403	42 731	0.76	646	13.1	380	7.7	5 563	13.6	7 867	6 402	1 465	739	1 509
Cumberland	37	7 077	0.34	101	10.3	96	9.8	1 382	17.4	1 333	965	368	68	694
Dickenson	441	14 792	0.83	166	10.9	188	12.4	1 737	14.4	4 367	2 783	1 584	175	1 137
Dinwiddie	713	23 067	0.60	210	7.5	255	9.1	3 077	13.4	3 699	2 874	825	432	1 549
Essex	190	10 467	0.86	116	10.4	108	9.7	1 437	16.3	2 520	1 989	531	205	1 822
Fairfax	10 244	1 126 642	1.02	14 470	12.7	5 314	4.7	108 248	10.9	95 160	80 878	14 282	16 399	1 435
Fauquier	389	57 943	0.74	811	11.8	579	8.4	6 295	10.9	9 531	8 454	1 077	631	941
Floyd	85	12 634	0.61	145	9.3	149	9.5	2 017	16.3	3 204	2 460	744	153	982
Fluvanna	1 289	18 622	0.37	255	9.8	190	7.3	2 425	12.1	4 936	4 125	811	241	925
Franklin	1 443	48 546	0.68	482	8.6	592	10.5	6 784	15.6	10 075	6 941	3 134	735	1 303
Frederick	1 037	71 447	0.77	984	11.9	615	7.4	9 450	13.7	8 211	7 168	1 043	1 695	2 065
Giles	136	15 140	0.74	148	8.8	196	11.7	1 825	13.6	4 335	3 101	1 234	277	1 645
Gloucester	389	30 047	0.61	370	10.0	412	11.1	3 862	12.7	7 005	5 638	1 367	599	1 626
Goochland	1 001	23 588	1.20	163	7.4	162	7.3	1 102	6.6	3 138	2 439	699	187	866
Grayson	1 089	13 455	0.69	160	10.0	185	11.6	1 887	16.3	3 393	2 971	422	174	1 153
Greene	137	13 765	0.43	183	9.6	137	7.2	2 532	15.8	2 985	2 466	519	245	1 296
Greensville	3 430	12 493	1.17	126	10.8	120	10.2	907	13.1	D	D	D	98	830
Halifax	757	35 373	0.98	371	10.5	482	13.7	3 869	14.3	9 245	7 905	1 340	784	2 225
Hanover	1 970	91 596	0.82	902	8.8	763	7.4	7 209	8.6	20 177	15 649	4 528	1 389	1 365
Henrico	2 498	323 020	1.05	3 945	12.2	2 574	7.9	32 589	11.8	30 927	23 055	7 872	8 387	2 608
Henry	569	48 600	0.79	480	9.2	680	13.1	6 589	16.3	10 881	7 617	3 264	1 298	2 483
Highland	0	2 177	0.92	18	8.1	21	9.4	390	24.5	647	578	69	6	273
Isle of Wight	310	28 797	0.61	328	9.1	356	9.8	3 403	11.5	6 575	4 965	1 610	492	1 375
James City	1 078	66 757	0.90	755	10.4	618	8.5	5 695	10.3	4 737	4 061	676	1 139	1 596
King and Queen	0	5 045	0.39	51	7.1	83	11.6	950	16.7	1 450	1 149	301	71	990
King George	301	24 493	0.99	310	12.2	143	5.6	2 031	9.2	2 970	2 597	373	344	1 362
King William	72	12 466	0.55	187	11.5	125	7.7	1 717	12.4	2 709	2 259	450	96	595
Lancaster	185	11 761	1.11	73	6.6	199	18.1	984	13.8	4 379	3 671	708	73	658
Lee	1 771	23 160	0.70	218	8.8	307	12.4	2 965	15.9	5 785	3 798	1 987	523	2 083
Loudoun	1 347	311 251	0.84	5 225	14.1	1 279	3.5	24 699	7.4	24 470	20 255	4 215	3 697	1 030

1. Per 1,000 estimated resident population.   2.   Data for serious crimes have not been adjusted for underreporting; this may affect comparability between geographic areas and over time.
3.   Per 100,000 population estimated by the FBI.

Table B. States and Counties — Crime, Education, Money Income, and Poverty

STATE County	Serious crimes known to police, 2014 (cont.)[1] Rate[2] Violent	Property	Education — Enrollment[3] Total	Percent private	Attainment[4] (percent) High school graduate or less	Bachelor's degree or more	Local government expenditures,[5] 2012–2013 Total current spending (mil dol)	Current spending per student (dollars)	Money income, 2010–2014 — Households Per capita income[6] (dollars)	Median income (dollars)	Mean income (dollars)	Percent with income of $200,000 or more	Income and poverty, 2014 — Percent below poverty level Median household income (dollars)	All persons	Children under 18 years	Children 5 to 17 years in families
	46	47	48	49	50	51	52	53	54	55	56	57	58	59	60	61
VERMONT—Cont'd																
Chittenden	90	2 036	46 259	19.0	27.3	48.0	373.0	17 095	33 881	64 243	83 432	5.8	61 908	11.0	11.2	10.2
Essex	0	242	1 207	14.4	59.9	14.1	14.7	17 137	20 904	35 567	46 580	1.0	35 570	19.6	26.1	22.5
Franklin	130	1 517	11 133	9.9	48.8	23.2	110.8	14 232	27 879	57 159	70 475	2.8	59 184	9.1	13.8	12.8
Grand Isle	72	1 359	1 562	17.6	37.2	32.4	12.2	12 537	34 925	61 338	81 600	5.8	60 081	9.1	14.2	13.3
Lamoille	44	583	5 684	9.8	38.1	35.3	60.6	16 746	26 508	50 447	64 122	3.1	49 142	12.6	16.0	15.1
Orange	24	851	6 262	15.9	42.3	31.6	69.9	16 931	27 623	53 114	65 531	2.3	53 025	12.8	18.0	16.2
Orleans	85	1 411	5 481	11.6	53.7	21.4	69.9	17 112	23 164	41 437	53 855	1.8	42 089	16.2	22.7	21.3
Rutland	160	1 564	13 998	15.9	44.5	28.8	148.6	17 713	26 384	48 308	61 502	2.0	44 888	13.5	19.1	18.2
Washington	76	1 393	13 978	26.2	35.9	39.0	142.1	16 888	30 210	58 293	71 356	3.3	58 673	11.0	13.8	12.2
Windham	167	1 880	9 550	26.9	40.1	34.5	121.9	18 716	27 895	50 526	63 197	2.2	49 616	12.9	17.6	16.0
Windsor	93	1 189	11 716	18.8	40.1	34.3	150.7	18 616	31 740	53 610	71 874	3.9	51 513	12.1	16.4	14.5
VIRGINIA	196	1 930	2 156 878	17.0	37.1	35.8	13 945.9	10 960	33 958	64 792	88 413	8.0	64 923	11.8	15.9	15.0
Accomack	244	1 415	6 210	13.6	59.5	18.3	51.3	10 001	23 206	39 389	53 280	2.2	38 390	19.4	30.9	30.8
Albemarle	100	1 784	30 930	16.1	27.1	52.1	(7)	(7)	37 510	67 958	96 760	9.3	67 083	9.1	10.3	10.0
Alleghany	130	1 151	3 181	15.7	52.6	16.9	28.3	10 741	24 399	45 183	56 775	1.4	45 454	15.8	21.9	19.2
Amelia	71	949	2 493	9.7	54.5	15.6	15.2	8 518	25 545	55 870	68 135	2.1	51 738	12.9	18.9	18.1
Amherst	133	1 201	7 430	20.7	54.0	18.3	43.0	9 680	22 938	44 765	56 637	1.0	43 998	13.7	20.5	18.1
Appomattox	104	757	3 363	17.0	56.3	15.3	20.1	8 744	23 098	47 927	57 158	1.0	44 397	15.1	21.9	21.2
Arlington	138	1 744	46 258	29.5	15.3	72.0	439.0	19 472	62 854	105 120	136 943	19.5	107 143	8.5	11.0	11.0
Augusta	150	1 088	14 871	20.4	55.2	21.2	100.2	9 319	26 398	54 018	67 924	2.5	57 808	9.8	13.8	12.4
Bath	0	871	719	8.3	54.3	19.8	9.6	14 873	32 259	46 153	67 050	1.3	43 852	11.5	15.6	14.6
Bedford	97	1 302	17 764	19.7	44.4	26.3	(8)	(8)	28 548	56 043	70 033	3.1	55 507	9.4	13.6	11.7
Bland	119	640	1 196	8.3	55.1	14.2	8.3	9 324	19 042	43 508	48 992	0.0	42 624	14.1	17.4	15.5
Botetourt	100	792	7 571	16.9	43.8	25.4	49.3	9 933	32 266	63 011	81 917	4.6	63 646	7.8	10.6	9.3
Brunswick	136	569	3 705	15.9	60.9	13.3	22.1	11 191	17 920	37 028	49 106	1.3	37 344	21.9	31.5	27.8
Buchanan	179	1 536	4 538	10.3	65.5	8.6	38.5	11 743	18 357	29 678	43 691	0.8	32 083	23.2	31.3	30.1
Buckingham	140	1 143	3 454	14.3	67.5	11.2	21.0	9 921	17 345	38 484	51 420	0.4	38 731	22.8	27.1	26.4
Campbell	173	1 471	13 101	26.8	52.1	18.9	75.0	8 936	23 801	47 055	58 630	1.5	46 663	14.5	19.4	17.6
Caroline	136	1 333	6 135	11.9	54.9	19.3	39.9	9 198	26 403	58 417	71 866	3.0	56 099	11.0	17.3	16.8
Carroll	111	1 259	6 015	9.0	56.9	11.0	42.2	9 682	19 761	33 495	45 115	0.5	38 474	17.0	25.0	21.8
Charles City	84	352	1 300	10.8	66.0	11.8	10.5	13 723	26 053	48 088	62 314	2.2	49 768	13.1	19.1	16.7
Charlotte	204	335	2 741	6.8	58.8	15.4	23.2	11 326	18 767	34 820	44 568	1.4	36 339	20.7	30.4	29.3
Chesterfield	129	1 929	91 961	14.3	33.5	36.6	533.4	9 062	32 942	72 514	89 852	6.5	72 972	8.3	11.2	10.3
Clarke	28	1 178	3 243	25.9	37.4	32.2	21.7	10 547	38 590	75 508	96 721	10.0		8.2	10.6	9.3
Craig	38	383	1 246	13.3	58.1	13.1	7.1	10 291	22 435	46 658	55 145	0.0	46 551	12.4	21.0	19.4
Culpeper	147	1 362	11 762	15.0	49.9	21.4	73.6	9 373	28 076	65 235	79 396	3.4	62 394	11.0	15.3	14.8
Cumberland	143	551	2 303	14.1	57.2	16.4	14.1	9 922	22 922	41 484	55 969	1.2	41 409	19.0	29.3	27.1
Dickenson	162	974	3 072	8.8	62.4	10.2	24.5	10 242	17 954	33 106	42 803	0.4	32 103	21.3	27.1	24.8
Dinwiddie	265	1 283	6 212	9.1	59.4	13.7	41.1	9 242	23 766	52 328	62 366	1.5	52 288	12.1	17.7	16.2
Essex	213	1 609	2 300	8.5	58.5	13.7	16.1	10 083	21 595	42 143	53 347	1.0	48 277	14.5	24.6	25.4
Fairfax	91	1 344	304 901	20.0	21.3	59.2	2 485.0	13 756	51 137	112 102	142 474	21.0	110 507	6.7	8.7	8.4
Fauquier	54	887	17 726	19.8	36.5	34.3	127.2	11 496	41 394	92 078	115 586	11.6	89 106	7.4	9.4	8.4
Floyd	64	918	2 856	31.0	52.7	16.7	17.8	8 731	22 805	47 543	55 229	1.9	43 355	14.1	20.0	18.4
Fluvanna	77	848	6 001	16.6	42.1	29.6	34.6	9 161	30 300	64 641	79 457	3.9	64 258	7.9	10.7	9.7
Franklin	129	1 174	12 207	23.3	49.7	19.8	73.5	9 776	24 789	44 827	59 609	2.4	47 419	16.3	23.9	21.5
Frederick	122	1 943	19 935	18.7	43.8	28.2	(9)	(9)	30 764	68 719	83 072	4.8	65 485	7.7	11.5	10.7
Giles	178	1 466	3 399	12.5	55.3	17.0	23.0	9 379	24 485	45 919	57 369	2.5	45 979	13.5	18.2	16.8
Gloucester	114	1 512	8 873	15.6	42.4	22.9	66.7	9 795	29 396	60 980	74 858	2.9	58 900	9.7	15.2	14.2
Goochland	130	736	4 502	33.5	37.5	38.3	25.8	10 990	46 306	82 460	123 941	13.6	86 610	7.5	10.4	9.3
Grayson	119	1 033	2 671	3.8	61.4	10.8	21.3	11 482	18 760	28 892	41 728	0.8	31 893	19.9	29.0	26.3
Greene	116	1 180	4 160	18.0	49.4	24.5	29.8	9 926	28 727	63 739	76 024	2.3	61 762	9.6	13.8	13.7
Greensville	161	669	2 074	5.4	68.5	8.5	(10)	(10)	14 992	38 933	52 044	1.4	36 459	25.1	27.2	27.5
Halifax	199	2 027	7 797	10.5	57.5	14.6	54.9	9 610	19 777	35 093	47 094	0.9	39 079	18.0	25.3	23.9
Hanover	128	1 237	27 168	17.5	35.4	36.3	167.2	9 099	34 241	77 550	92 310	6.2	81 940	6.1	7.9	6.5
Henrico	156	2 451	81 603	16.3	33.1	39.7	449.9	8 982	33 576	61 438	82 874	6.1	62 446	11.0	17.2	15.0
Henry	230	2 253	11 212	9.3	56.1	11.5	68.3	9 152	19 538	34 344	45 290	0.8	34 842	20.5	31.3	31.4
Highland	0	273	317	30.9	61.2	19.4	3.6	17 756	26 949	44 132	56 847	2.2	38 636	14.6	21.8	20.3
Isle of Wight	157	1 219	8 480	19.2	42.0	26.1	55.1	9 900	31 247	65 910	80 046	4.1	64 350	10.2	13.7	12.2
James City	123	1 472	16 957	14.6	28.7	46.1	(11)	(11)	39 960	76 705	98 753	8.7	75 926	7.9	11.5	10.4
King and Queen	28	962	1 260	14.0	57.5	16.8	11.7	12 898	25 406	47 804	60 075	2.6	46 331	14.8	22.9	20.3
King George	115	1 247	6 430	17.9	37.0	31.8	36.0	8 454	34 995	83 071	100 011	8.2	76 206	7.5	10.5	9.7
King William	43	552	3 932	13.9	51.9	19.1	29.4	9 852	28 981	63 560	73 362	2.2	64 305	8.8	13.4	12.8
Lancaster	126	532	1 757	10.9	43.2	28.7	14.7	11 062	30 836	49 456	64 092	2.6	45 827	13.7	26.4	26.0
Lee	151	1 932	5 183	12.2	59.4	11.1	35.2	10 295	16 769	31 264	40 943	0.8	31 429	26.6	31.9	29.8
Loudoun	80	949	103 312	17.8	20.3	58.0	854.5	12 528	46 962	123 966	142 011	20.9	122 641	3.9	4.4	4.2

1. Data for serious crimes have not been adjusted for underreporting; this may affect comparability between geographic areas and over time.   2. Per 100,000 population estimated by the FBI.
3. All persons 3 years old and over enrolled in nursery school through college.   4. Persons 25 years old and over.   5. Elementary and secondary education expenditures.
6. Based on population estimated by the American Community Survey, 2010–2014.   7. Albemarle county is included with Charlottesville city.   8. Bedford county is included with Bedford city.
9. Frederick county is included with Winchester city.   10. Greensville county is included with Emporia city.   11. James City county is included with Williamsburg city.

Table B. States and Counties — **Personal Income**

STATE County	Personal income, 2014 Total (mil dol) [62]	Percent change, 2013–2014 [63]	Per capita[1] Dollars [64]	Per capita[1] Rank [65]	Wages and salaries (mil dol) [66]	Supplements to wages and salaries; employer contributions (mil dol) Pension and insurance [67]	Government social insurance [68]	Proprietors' income (mil dol) [69]	Dividends, interest, and rent (mil dol) [70]	Personal transfer receipts (mil dol) [71]	Earnings, 2014 Total (mil dol) [72]	Contributions for government social insurance (mil dol) From employee and self-employed [73]	From employer [74]
VERMONT—Cont'd													
Chittenden	8 327	3.0	51 871	300	5 208	858	424	595	1 639	1 246	7 084	440	424
Essex	211	2.0	34 424	2 043	40	11	3	26	31	59	80	7	3
Franklin	2 022	5.4	41 578	1 002	766	163	65	210	256	393	1 204	73	65
Grand Isle	349	3.6	49 865	389	40	9	4	29	73	56	82	6	4
Lamoille	1 137	4.1	45 314	648	446	78	40	106	269	210	670	44	40
Orange	1 179	4.8	40 861	1 081	300	64	25	107	196	257	497	34	25
Orleans	1 088	4.5	40 163	1 149	390	80	35	124	175	319	629	42	35
Rutland	2 747	2.3	45 726	617	1 148	218	98	130	430	889	1 594	110	98
Washington	2 893	3.1	49 043	434	1 570	286	127	203	510	624	2 186	139	127
Windham	1 930	3.3	44 145	749	948	168	81	161	403	453	1 358	90	81
Windsor	2 745	3.6	49 010	437	1 010	192	86	224	636	556	1 512	103	86
VIRGINIA	419 185	3.5	50 345	X	215 572	34 288	15 965	27 798	84 059	55 799	293 622	17 384	15 965
Accomack	1 220	2.8	36 960	1 605	490	105	37	76	259	324	709	46	37
Albemarle	(3)8 795	(3)4.5	(3)58 603	(3)149	(3)4 824	(3)895	(3)352	(3)865	(3)2 913	(3)901	(3)6 935	(3)399	(3)352
Alleghany	(4)752	(4)1.8	(4)34 787	(4)1 971	(4)341	(4)61	(4)26	(4)32	(4)124	(4)229	(4)459	(4)34	(4)26
Amelia	519	3.5	40 376	1 130	96	17	7	74	72	111	194	13	7
Amherst	1 053	3.3	32 869	2 303	335	70	25	51	166	274	481	35	25
Appomattox	513	3.2	33 553	2 184	101	25	7	27	71	137	157	13	7
Arlington	18 872	3.1	83 170	24	15 404	2 371	1 128	1 525	3 923	840	20 428	1 119	1 128
Augusta	(5)4 620	(5)3.3	(5)38 579	(5)1 380	(5)1 919	(5)348	(5)144	(5)377	(5)863	(5)985	(5)2 788	(5)182	(5)144
Bath	212	3.3	46 363	568	93	15	7	3	76	45	118	8	7
Bedford	(6)3 163	(6)4.2	(6)41 307	(6)1 027	(6)741	(6)124	(6)56	(6)186	(6)577	(6)629	(6)1 107	(6)84	(6)56
Bland	210	2.4	31 664	2 500	86	21	7	8	37	60	122	9	7
Botetourt	1 491	3.3	45 055	674	430	71	33	83	251	266	616	44	33
Brunswick	510	3.9	30 932	2 597	150	30	11	23	75	170	214	16	11
Buchanan	819	-0.1	35 459	1 865	370	64	27	120	98	278	582	43	27
Buckingham	474	3.4	28 038	2 915	129	29	9	53	73	131	220	15	9
Campbell	(7)4 614	(7)2.8	(7)34 450	(7)2 037	(7)3 182	(7)482	(7)237	(7)213	(7)837	(7)1 261	(7)4 113	(7)260	(7)237
Caroline	1 120	3.1	37 600	1 512	226	50	17	66	153	213	359	25	17
Carroll	(8)1 153	(8)4.5	(8)31 465	(8)2 530	(8)395	(8)78	(8)31	(8)74	(8)179	(8)390	(8)578	(8)44	(8)31
Charles City	280	1.8	39 938	1 188	66	12	5	19	49	60	102	8	5
Charlotte	378	1.8	30 915	2 600	97	23	7	32	67	116	160	12	7
Chesterfield	15 787	4.2	47 481	498	6 107	952	453	910	2 488	2 113	8 422	521	453
Clarke	782	3.2	54 203	227	180	28	14	42	195	96	263	17	14
Craig	177	2.9	33 756	2 152	27	6	2	8	31	45	42	4	2
Culpeper	1 959	3.8	39 847	1 199	661	118	50	130	318	324	960	61	50
Cumberland	318	3.7	32 369	2 392	44	10	3	18	50	88	76	6	3
Dickenson	431	0.6	28 182	2 903	162	31	12	20	54	184	224	19	12
Dinwiddie	(9)2 880	(9)1.0	(9)36 787	(9)1 635	(9)1 246	(9)225	(9)95	(9)72	(9)534	(9)823	(9)1 638	(9)108	(9)95
Essex	418	0.7	37 669	1 500	140	25	11	15	78	107	190	14	11
Fairfax	(10)88 180	(10)3.2	(10)75 007	(10)41	(10)54 185	(10)6 359	(10)3 743	(10)8 871	(10)19 408	(10)5 423	(10)73 157	(10)4 232	(10)3 743
Fauquier	4 230	4.0	61 982	112	1 059	166	78	283	1 033	405	1 586	99	78
Floyd	519	4.0	33 330	2 222	98	20	7	39	86	129	164	13	7
Fluvanna	968	4.8	37 095	1 586	180	37	14	23	183	184	253	20	14
Franklin	1 949	3.6	34 586	2 005	516	94	40	86	385	498	737	56	40
Frederick	(11)4 694	(11)3.9	(11)42 701	(11)881	(11)2 438	(11)398	(11)183	(11)285	(11)818	(11)712	(11)3 304	(11)201	(11)183
Giles	586	2.9	34 874	1 956	199	40	15	16	93	162	269	20	15
Gloucester	1 623	3.6	43 704	784	323	64	24	49	324	296	460	33	24
Goochland	1 873	3.7	85 363	20	1 230	128	79	148	545	191	1 585	96	79
Grayson	448	4.4	29 657	2 766	83	21	6	17	79	150	128	12	6
Greene	702	5.3	36 873	1 621	128	23	10	33	111	128	193	14	10
Greensville	(12)522	(12)3.5	(12)30 476	(12)2 653	(12)276	(12)57	(12)21	(12)20	(12)71	(12)164	(12)375	(12)24	(12)21
Halifax	1 161	3.0	32 970	2 282	457	91	35	61	197	358	644	46	35
Hanover	5 218	3.6	51 194	324	2 143	308	162	367	856	662	2 980	187	162
Henrico	16 036	3.7	49 814	391	10 138	1 316	736	867	3 165	2 071	13 057	789	736
Henry	(13)2 200	(13)3.0	(13)33 439	(13)2 207	(13)860	(13)158	(13)67	(13)94	(13)420	(13)735	(13)1 179	(13)90	(13)67
Highland	100	5.7	44 403	725	17	4	1	15	34	22	38	2	1
Isle of Wight	1 781	3.1	49 471	417	474	77	34	81	261	287	666	45	34
James City	(14)5 015	(14)4.1	(14)57 465	(14)165	(14)1 654	(14)284	(14)124	(14)319	(14)1 313	(14)720	(14)2 380	(14)152	(14)124
King and Queen	262	1.6	36 571	1 676	39	8	3	31	37	60	81	6	3
King George	1 199	4.2	47 244	512	855	205	69	80	214	139	1 210	65	69
King William	643	2.2	39 726	1 219	164	27	12	16	96	114	218	16	12
Lancaster	544	0.9	49 233	424	173	28	13	30	213	127	244	19	13
Lee	677	-0.2	27 137	2 971	162	41	13	43	98	260	259	22	13
Loudoun	24 464	5.5	67 384	72	9 877	1 265	692	956	3 143	1 167	12 789	743	692

1. Based on the resident population estimated as of July 1 of the year shown.   3. Charlottesville city is included with Albemarle county.   4. Covington city is included with Alleghany county.   5. Staunton and Waynesboro cities are included with Augusta county.   6. Bedford city is included with Bedford county.   7. Lynchburg city is included with Campbell county.   8. Galax city is included with Carroll county.   9. Petersburg and Colonial Heights cities are included with Dinwiddie county.   10. Fairfax city and Falls Church city are included with Fairfax county.   11. Winchester city is included with Frederick county.   12. Emporia city is included with Greensville county.   13. Martinsville city is included with Henry county.   14. Williamsburg city is included with James City county.

Table B. States and Counties — Earnings, Social Security, and Housing

STATE County	Earnings, 2014 (cont.) Percent by selected industries Farm 75	Mining 76	Construction 77	Manufacturing 78	Information: professional, scientific, technical services 79	Retail trade 80	Finance, insurance, real estate and leasing 81	Health care and social assistance 82	Government 83	Social Security beneficiaries, December 2014 Number 84	Rate[1] 85	Supplemental Security Income recipients, December 2014 86	Housing units, 2015 Total 87	Percent change, 2010–2014 88
VERMONT—Cont'd														
Chittenden	0.2	0.1	6.7	11.9	13.9	6.6	6.6	14.6	19.1	26 685	166	3 008	67 897	3.3
Essex	6.2	D	5.6	8.5	D	3.8	D	D	34.3	1 985	324	233	5 050	0.6
Franklin	6.4	D	5.4	16.6	D	9.7	2.2	11.6	27.5	9 890	203	1 324	22 090	2.3
Grand Isle	9.8	0.0	15.0	2.6	D	7.5	D	D	21.2	1 865	267	140	5 130	1.6
Lamoille	0.6	0.1	9.6	5.3	8.3	7.9	5.0	14.2	16.0	5 155	205	502	13 191	1.7
Orange	4.7	0.2	11.7	6.9	7.5	6.3	D	D	23.1	7 210	250	728	14 917	0.5
Orleans	6.5	D	9.2	10.9	D	8.7	4.0	15.4	20.7	7 400	273	1 032	16 717	3.4
Rutland	0.5	1.5	6.8	14.7	4.7	8.8	3.6	17.2	17.6	16 300	271	2 036	33 778	0.0
Washington	0.5	0.3	5.1	6.8	7.0	7.2	12.6	11.3	24.3	13 135	223	1 438	30 168	0.8
Windham	0.6	D	8.1	10.2	D	7.6	4.3	14.2	12.9	11 195	256	1 191	29 851	0.4
Windsor	0.5	0.2	7.6	7.5	10.5	6.3	3.9	15.2	24.1	14 815	265	1 334	34 141	0.1
VIRGINIA	0.2	0.4	5.3	5.9	20.3	5.2	7.1	8.8	23.7	1 415 661	170	155 501	3 468 829	3.1
Accomack	4.6	0.0	3.9	18.8	11.5	6.0	2.6	D	28.5	9 175	278	1 157	21 069	0.3
Albemarle	(3)0.0	(3)0.2	(3)4.4	(3)D	(3)13.2	(3)4.9	(3)7.4	(3)9.7	(3)34.3	17 935	172	843	44 258	5.1
Alleghany	(4)-0.6	(4)D	(4)6.0	(4)D	(4)D	(4)7.2	(4)D	(4)11.2	(4)18.2	4 655	293	327	8 044	-0.4
Amelia	16.1	0.0	12.3	5.6	D	9.1	D	D	14.5	3 185	249	303	5 451	1.7
Amherst	-0.2	0.0	7.2	19.7	D	7.0	2.0	D	30.7	8 135	254	841	14 102	0.9
Appomattox	-0.7	D	13.6	2.7	D	11.8	D	D	27.1	3 910	256	444	7 122	2.9
Arlington	0.0	D	1.7	0.7	30.1	1.9	7.2	3.3	32.0	18 770	83	2 183	112 529	6.7
Augusta	(5)2.2	(5)D	(5)D	(5)17.8	(5)6.9	(5)7.0	(5)3.4	(5)D	(5)17.4	17 920	242	623	32 139	3.0
Bath	0.2	0.0	6.7	1.4	8.9	1.4	2.1	11.2	16.8	1 330	292	102	3 292	0.7
Bedford	(6)0.2	(6)0.0	(6)9.7	(6)12.0	(6)D	(6)7.5	(6)D	(6)10.5	(6)14.4	19 230	249	1 154	36 114	3.7
Bland	0.0	D	3.2	35.2	D	D	D	13.0	26.6	1 805	273	124	3 264	0.0
Botetourt	0.0	D	8.5	21.6	5.2	D	3.1	6.2	13.1	8 160	246	352	14 749	1.3
Brunswick	3.6	D	5.9	7.7	D	4.7	2.5	D	24.6	4 410	263	704	8 140	-0.3
Buchanan	0.0	46.2	5.5	3.8	D	4.0	1.7	5.2	14.1	8 255	356	1 513	11 407	-1.4
Buckingham	4.2	D	9.3	2.5	3.6	5.3	2.0	10.1	32.7	3 820	226	446	7 290	0.7
Campbell	(7)0.1	(7)D	(7)D	(7)20.8	(7)11.6	(7)6.3	(7)6.4	(7)15.5	(7)10.1	13 625	247	1 102	25 517	3.0
Caroline	-1.2	D	9.3	5.2	D	4.8	2.2	D	30.4	5 870	197	485	12 046	2.7
Carroll	(8)1.2	(8)0.0	(8)D	(8)17.4	(8)4.3	(8)10.6	(8)2.9	(8)D	(8)22.0	9 095	307	652	16 633	0.2
Charles City	3.6	D	15.0	16.7	D	D	D	D	17.8	1 920	273	122	3 313	2.6
Charlotte	3.2	D	4.4	13.2	D	5.2	D	D	30.1	3 310	272	430	6 284	0.2
Chesterfield	0.0	D	8.1	9.3	10.6	8.8	7.5	10.7	16.4	55 595	167	4 202	127 895	4.4
Clarke	2.2	D	10.9	11.8	15.6	3.6	4.1	D	15.6	2 980	207	164	6 299	1.1
Craig	-2.6	0.0	8.5	D	D	6.5	7.0	9.4	29.4	1 415	270	106	2 876	2.6
Culpeper	0.6	0.4	8.5	9.0	11.3	8.4	3.6	13.4	21.5	8 785	179	822	18 298	3.6
Cumberland	18.7	0.0	7.1	8.2	D	6.8	D	D	29.6	2 550	259	234	4 670	0.9
Dickenson	-0.9	39.0	7.3	0.9	D	5.7	D	6.9	18.8	5 735	375	1 064	7 494	-1.1
Dinwiddie	(9)0.4	(9)D	(9)4.3	(9)11.1	(9)D	(9)11.8	(9)4.0	(9)D	(9)24.4	6 180	220	502	11 593	1.5
Essex	-1.9	0.0	4.9	10.0	D	13.9	7.8	19.1	15.2	3 000	271	346	5 798	0.7
Fairfax	(10)0.0	(10)0.1	(10)4.5	(10)0.7	(10)40.0	(10)7.7	(10)7.7	(10)5.9	(10)16.0	119 195	105	11 249	412 045	1.0
Fauquier	-0.3	0.3	12.8	3.1	15.8	8.0	7.2	10.6	20.8	11 290	165	579	26 451	3.2
Floyd	3.4	D	9.3	10.3	D	6.7	6.0	D	20.1	4 065	261	300	7 943	1.9
Fluvanna	-0.2	D	11.0	2.3	3.7	4.1	2.6	D	30.8	5 795	222	392	10 739	3.4
Franklin	3.4	D	9.6	18.5	3.5	8.8	3.7	D	16.7	15 205	270	1 254	29 500	0.6
Frederick	(11)0.2	(11)D	(11)D	(11)14.3	(11)D	(11)9.4	(11)5.7	(11)16.7	(11)18.2	15 250	185	868	32 775	4.6
Giles	-0.1	0.0	D	32.7	5.2	7.6	2.3	7.9	15.8	4 910	293	586	8 327	0.1
Gloucester	0.3	D	8.2	2.6	5.2	12.9	4.4	15.0	28.1	8 585	231	686	16 253	2.5
Goochland	0.1	D	5.7	1.6	D	1.6	2.0	5.0	5.0	5 055	231	239	9 012	4.7
Grayson	5.3	0.0	2.1	13.6	0.0	4.9	8.1	D	39.3	4 805	300	372	9 160	0.0
Greene	0.8	D	10.3	2.1	12.1	11.0	2.6	D	24.1	3 670	193	225	8 091	7.7
Greensville	(12)2.3	(12)D	(12)4.1	(12)22.7	(12)D	(12)5.3	(12)D	(12)15.4	(12)27.5	2 510	218	777	4 127	0.9
Halifax	2.1	D	5.6	17.9	2.4	6.4	2.4	16.1	17.2	10 630	302	1 638	18 090	0.5
Hanover	0.1	D	13.6	7.0	6.6	8.8	4.8	13.3	9.7	19 505	191	904	40 329	5.1
Henrico	0.0	D	4.7	4.1	14.5	6.3	18.2	12.9	9.6	54 145	168	7 301	135 555	2.1
Henry	(13)0.3	(13)D	(13)D	(13)21.2	(13)D	(13)10.2	(13)3.1	(13)13.7	(13)17.8	16 520	317	2 338	26 054	-0.8
Highland	27.1	0.0	8.1	3.5	D	3.5	D	D	21.6	765	340	23	1 862	1.5
Isle of Wight	1.0	0.0	4.6	24.5	D	4.5	3.5	D	13.3	7 930	220	510	15 159	3.6
James City	(14)0.0	(14)D	(14)6.5	(14)6.3	(14)D	(14)7.0	(14)D	(14)10.6	(14)22.9	18 205	252	774	32 401	7.8
King and Queen	1.4	D	10.8	6.7	D	D	D	D	18.8	1 750	244	152	3 448	1.0
King George	-0.1	D	3.1	0.3	20.2	1.8	1.7	1.5	62.8	3 525	139	248	9 865	4.1
King William	-0.4	1.4	6.5	31.9	D	14.3	D	D	18.7	3 340	207	212	6 737	3.3
Lancaster	-0.2	0.0	8.0	2.2	10.3	9.3	10.4	21.9	12.1	3 795	345	214	7 607	2.7
Lee	0.0	4.6	6.0	1.7	D	9.1	3.0	11.8	38.0	7 355	295	1 676	11 693	-0.4
Loudoun	-0.1	D	9.0	5.5	29.4	5.1	5.5	5.9	14.1	28 785	79	1 823	126 479	15.6

1. Per 1,000 resident population estimated as of July 1 of the year shown.   3. Charlottesville city is included with Albemarle county.   4. Covington city is included with Alleghany county.   5. Staunton and Waynesboro cities are included with Augusta county.   6. Bedford city is included with Bedford county.   7. Lynchburg city is included with Campbell county.   8. Galax city is included with Carroll county.   9. Petersburg and Colonial Heights cities are included with Dinwiddie county.   10. Fairfax city and Falls Church city are included with Fairfax county.   11. Winchester city is included with Frederick county.   12. Emporia city is included with Greensville county.   13. Martinsville city is included with Henry county.   14. Williamsburg city is included with James City county.

Table B. States and Counties — Housing, Labor Force, and Employment

STATE County	Housing units, 2010–2014								Civilian labor force, 2015				Civilian employment,[6] 2010–2014		
	Occupied units							Sub-stand-ard units[4] (percent)		Percent change, 2014–2015	Unemployment			Percent	
	Owner-occupied					Renter-occupied									
				Median owner cost as a percent of income											Con-struction, produc-tion, and mainte-nance occu-pations
	Total	Percent	Median value[1]	With a mort-gage	Without a mort-gage[2]	Median rent[3]	Median rent as a per-cent of income[2]		Total		Total	Rate[5]	Total	Manage-ment, business, science and arts	
	89	90	91	92	93	94	95	96	97	98	99	100	101	102	103
VERMONT—Cont'd															
Chittenden	63 086	64.8	269 500	23.8	14.2	1 066	32.4	1.3	95 254	-0.4	2 575	2.7	87 828	46.9	14.0
Essex	2 752	80.7	120 300	25.2	17.9	665	34.2	2.4	2 753	-2.0	188	6.8	2 711	28.1	33.8
Franklin	18 751	75.4	203 100	24.2	14.9	872	31.8	1.9	27 404	-0.5	1 002	3.7	25 404	34.9	27.4
Grand Isle	2 981	80.2	259 500	24.5	17.9	962	33.7	1.4	4 053	-0.5	168	4.1	3 759	37.1	21.5
Lamoille	10 121	71.2	216 800	28.3	19.1	858	29.7	2.2	13 666	-1.0	643	4.7	12 933	36.2	21.7
Orange	12 135	80.6	186 400	25.4	16.1	839	32.8	2.9	15 780	-1.0	552	3.5	15 341	39.5	22.5
Orleans	11 214	77.0	155 600	25.7	17.7	693	32.2	2.4	13 476	-1.6	776	5.8	12 169	31.7	29.7
Rutland	25 635	69.8	176 900	25.1	17.3	796	31.6	2.4	31 357	-1.4	1 370	4.4	30 148	34.4	23.7
Washington	24 704	73.0	207 100	23.8	16.7	853	30.1	1.6	34 130	-0.6	1 213	3.6	31 568	42.5	17.9
Windham	19 223	69.6	210 700	27.5	18.6	832	30.0	2.6	23 254	-1.3	855	3.7	22 566	39.8	22.4
Windsor	24 560	70.5	213 300	25.7	18.1	861	28.6	2.0	29 278	-1.6	966	3.3	28 745	38.8	22.5
VIRGINIA	3 041 710	66.7	243 500	23.2	10.8	1 108	30.0	2.4	4 240 476	-0.4	188 563	4.4	3 936 638	42.5	17.9
Accomack	14 289	70.4	152 500	23.3	12.6	715	26.2	3.7	15 972	-0.9	866	5.4	14 433	31.8	31.0
Albemarle	38 537	65.2	317 300	21.7	10.7	1 115	30.0	1.3	54 361	1.0	2 094	3.9	46 962	53.5	12.5
Alleghany	6 714	79.5	111 600	19.5	10.7	575	27.1	1.9	7 115	-1.3	362	5.1	6 740	30.3	33.0
Amelia	4 761	81.6	179 300	23.7	10.0	679	46.7	2.1	6 272	0.7	279	4.4	5 664	27.0	28.0
Amherst	12 577	74.5	149 000	22.6	10.3	687	25.9	1.6	15 544	-0.9	741	4.8	14 891	28.8	27.3
Appomattox	5 964	81.1	137 100	21.6	10.1	674	34.1	1.3	7 067	-1.1	343	4.9	6 410	29.6	31.9
Arlington	96 264	44.8	594 800	21.4	10.0	1 802	26.6	2.7	145 058	0.0	4 085	2.8	138 956	67.1	6.1
Augusta	28 124	81.1	197 600	22.8	10.6	806	27.5	1.5	36 792	-0.5	1 510	4.1	34 432	30.6	29.2
Bath	2 225	75.2	151 200	19.7	11.7	583	15.2	2.8	2 559	-1.6	104	4.1	2 309	25.7	25.5
Bedford	30 122	81.8	196 500	22.0	10.0	756	31.4	1.0	38 173	-1.1	1 696	4.4	35 551	34.1	25.6
Bland	2 591	80.2	94 100	20.8	11.0	607	24.9	2.0	2 801	-2.6	162	5.8	2 500	29.3	28.8
Botetourt	12 867	88.3	210 300	22.8	10.0	881	24.5	1.7	17 546	-1.2	733	4.2	16 084	38.1	21.2
Brunswick	5 865	73.9	104 200	24.0	13.5	662	35.5	2.1	6 323	-1.9	431	6.8	6 409	24.9	28.5
Buchanan	9 406	80.5	68 700	23.5	10.0	621	41.2	2.2	7 408	-5.5	798	10.8	7 314	22.9	36.4
Buckingham	5 802	76.4	128 300	25.5	11.0	654	30.5	1.9	6 371	0.7	372	5.8	6 052	25.5	24.0
Campbell	21 728	77.1	151 000	21.5	10.0	727	29.3	1.2	26 482	-0.9	1 259	4.8	25 464	32.8	28.9
Caroline	10 728	81.4	188 000	23.8	11.2	998	28.1	1.9	14 882	0.4	753	5.1	12 965	31.2	27.0
Carroll	12 508	78.7	106 100	24.8	11.3	528	28.9	1.5	13 099	-1.0	699	5.3	12 604	25.3	35.3
Charles City	2 832	80.5	154 600	23.8	10.8	861	31.6	1.5	3 769	1.0	197	5.2	3 240	22.0	35.0
Charlotte	4 691	72.8	97 700	25.0	12.7	570	30.7	3.5	5 242	-0.9	301	5.7	5 016	25.9	33.6
Chesterfield	115 005	76.6	219 800	22.5	10.0	1 107	29.5	1.5	179 333	0.7	7 699	4.3	160 708	42.5	17.2
Clarke	5 619	76.1	337 700	23.8	10.0	985	29.7	0.6	7 574	0.0	300	4.0	7 046	45.8	19.5
Craig	2 151	80.6	146 100	23.7	10.0	550	23.1	0.0	2 431	-1.5	134	5.5	2 200	27.2	33.5
Culpeper	16 436	73.2	243 400	24.9	10.0	1 012	31.4	2.7	23 328	-0.5	1 010	4.3	22 061	35.9	22.4
Cumberland	4 038	76.0	133 100	24.0	12.2	750	28.1	4.1	4 552	0.9	240	5.3	4 474	28.4	27.9
Dickenson	6 200	78.0	72 400	21.5	10.0	523	39.3	2.7	4 986	-4.4	502	10.1	4 935	26.3	28.8
Dinwiddie	9 956	75.0	159 300	24.1	11.5	946	27.4	1.5	13 536	0.2	723	5.3	12 440	27.0	32.0
Essex	4 288	74.3	158 100	26.0	11.9	830	30.9	1.3	5 535	-2.7	300	5.4	5 152	19.5	29.0
Fairfax	391 794	68.2	486 900	22.0	10.0	1 724	28.1	3.2	620 408	-0.3	22 063	3.6	597 975	56.1	9.9
Fauquier	23 162	79.5	351 900	23.5	10.1	1 161	28.0	1.2	35 985	-0.2	1 414	3.9	34 111	43.9	18.8
Floyd	6 086	78.7	153 700	22.0	10.0	553	18.0	2.0	8 340	0.1	332	4.0	7 420	30.8	31.9
Fluvanna	9 787	83.3	214 000	24.5	12.1	1 219	27.3	1.8	13 353	1.0	498	3.7	11 802	41.7	17.2
Franklin	23 248	77.7	163 000	23.7	10.1	668	30.0	2.2	26 923	-1.3	1 249	4.6	25 079	31.4	28.2
Frederick	29 184	77.7	223 300	22.6	11.2	1 111	27.4	2.2	44 758	0.3	1 773	4.0	39 830	39.9	22.5
Giles	7 253	75.6	107 700	19.9	10.0	600	26.4	1.9	8 069	-0.3	413	5.1	7 429	28.9	34.7
Gloucester	14 074	80.8	225 400	24.7	10.5	847	26.2	0.8	19 306	-1.0	786	4.1	17 560	31.6	26.1
Goochland	8 212	87.6	324 800	22.4	10.0	947	30.3	0.8	10 640	0.6	438	4.1	10 132	47.3	15.0
Grayson	6 686	76.0	93 200	24.6	11.1	579	28.6	0.7	6 983	-1.0	407	5.8	5 982	24.2	36.6
Greene	6 965	76.9	244 400	22.9	10.0	980	27.6	1.6	9 974	0.9	365	3.7	8 733	36.6	19.9
Greensville	3 397	73.1	100 400	23.1	14.5	728	29.2	1.7	4 169	-2.1	225	5.4	3 614	16.7	29.9
Halifax	14 472	73.1	106 100	22.2	12.3	555	33.6	1.9	15 324	-1.4	978	6.4	14 179	27.5	30.9
Hanover	37 041	82.3	257 600	22.2	10.0	1 049	29.2	1.0	56 478	0.8	2 175	3.9	51 390	44.6	16.5
Henrico	123 821	63.9	217 300	22.9	10.0	1 029	29.3	1.7	178 200	0.7	7 621	4.3	160 158	43.1	14.0
Henry	22 472	74.1	94 600	22.1	11.9	590	28.4	2.7	22 305	-2.8	1 449	6.5	21 198	25.0	31.0
Highland	1 067	85.4	181 100	25.1	10.0	470	26.3	1.7	1 356	-4.7	48	3.5	1 048	27.0	34.2
Isle of Wight	13 519	79.0	245 400	24.6	11.4	937	29.9	1.6	18 858	-1.0	863	4.6	17 082	37.2	25.4
James City	27 665	74.5	320 000	23.1	10.0	1 159	32.8	1.3	34 406	-1.0	1 482	4.3	31 177	44.4	13.5
King and Queen	2 832	74.9	173 300	23.0	10.0	878	25.3	2.6	3 653	-0.1	177	4.8	3 429	22.7	39.2
King George	8 315	73.5	280 900	22.5	10.0	1 088	25.5	2.0	12 059	-0.5	572	4.7	11 984	43.1	18.4
King William	6 147	82.2	201 400	23.9	10.0	967	32.5	1.5	8 810	0.3	371	4.2	8 072	29.5	33.7
Lancaster	5 283	75.4	222 200	27.3	11.3	869	28.7	2.2	5 102	-4.2	343	6.7	4 784	29.0	18.0
Lee	9 597	72.5	75 400	23.7	10.3	496	34.5	4.6	8 646	-2.5	625	7.2	7 898	29.1	25.7
Loudoun	110 047	76.9	443 100	23.5	10.0	1 673	28.0	2.0	196 323	-0.2	7 001	3.6	179 747	56.4	10.1

1. Specified owner-occupied units.   2. A value of 10.0 represents 10 percent or less; a value of 50.0 represents 50 percent or more.   3. Specified renter-occupied units.
4. Overcrowded or lacking complete plumbing facilities.   5. Percent of civilian labor force.   6. Persons 16 years old and over.

Table B. States and Counties — Nonfarm Employment and Agriculture

STATE County	Private nonfarm establishments, employment and payroll, 2014									Agriculture, 2012			
		Employment						Annual payroll		Farms			
												Percent with:	
	Number of establishments	Total	Health care and social assistance	Manufacturing	Retail trade	Finance and insurance	Professional, scientific, and technical services	Total (mil dol)	Average per employee (dollars)	Number	Fewer than 50 acres	500 acres or more	Farm operators whose principal occupation is farming (percent)
	104	105	106	107	108	109	110	111	112	113	114	115	116
VERMONT—Cont'd													
Chittenden	5 552	86 656	15 998	8 768	12 747	3 102	6 365	3 813	44 001	587	50.4	3.9	50.6
Essex	112	505	D	D	89	D	15	16	31 038	93	26.9	18.3	47.3
Franklin	1 009	12 403	2 808	2 663	2 207	306	259	463	37 316	736	28.3	12.1	54.5
Grand Isle	178	621	51	D	147	D	D	21	34 443	121	44.6	7.4	59.5
Lamoille	958	10 923	1 661	495	1 449	202	341	340	31 102	349	42.4	6.9	36.1
Orange	758	6 165	1 525	731	957	D	303	231	37 544	748	38.2	4.0	49.9
Orleans	775	8 059	1 753	D	1 283	218	168	262	32 458	638	31.7	9.7	60.3
Rutland	2 130	24 533	4 567	3 397	4 137	589	619	879	35 826	640	38.4	7.0	47.8
Washington	2 230	26 064	4 074	2 708	3 915	2 243	989	1 123	43 084	532	40.0	3.2	50.4
Windham	1 708	21 059	3 506	1 806	2 419	581	471	778	36 962	447	46.1	4.7	52.3
Windsor	2 016	19 747	3 929	2 240	2 688	502	1 011	772	39 116	768	42.1	4.7	48.7
VIRGINIA	195 639	3 160 539	427 084	232 965	420 574	157 131	435 023	159 145	50 354	46 030	38.6	7.7	45.1
Accomack	742	8 422	1 043	D	1 414	161	D	250	29 664	226	46.0	15.5	63.7
Albemarle	2 625	38 494	7 105	3 036	5 832	D	3 218	1 824	47 376	946	38.1	8.0	41.4
Alleghany	236	2 283	837	244	286	D	23	74	32 246	207	25.6	6.8	32.4
Amelia	266	1 815	D	178	220	37	49	54	29 878	407	30.5	9.3	44.5
Amherst	571	6 375	654	D	1 175	141	268	198	31 001	426	27.9	10.1	39.0
Appomattox	285	2 311	497	122	657	D	77	56	24 099	410	21.0	10.5	43.4
Arlington	6 347	132 820	9 390	176	9 506	3 531	41 627	10 104	76 071	6	100.0	0.0	50.0
Augusta	1 415	19 027	4 401	3 738	1 882	242	436	750	39 438	1 706	42.3	6.2	48.8
Bath	122	2 115	228	42	76	D	D	70	33 290	116	17.2	15.5	45.7
Bedford	1 357	11 809	1 128	2 398	1 817	320	674	440	37 244	1 369	34.2	5.0	42.7
Bland	78	1 374	D	D	D	13	D	57	41 596	362	23.2	9.1	44.8
Botetourt	719	9 939	772	2 359	866	188	237	392	39 454	584	33.0	6.5	46.7
Brunswick	251	2 271	208	209	345	42	36	72	31 825	312	19.6	10.3	44.6
Buchanan	423	6 380	612	243	850	D	234	287	44 923	103	46.6	2.9	33.0
Buckingham	257	1 900	D	95	288	29	85	66	34 533	391	24.0	13.0	52.9
Campbell	1 154	13 945	1 073	2 312	2 090	403	816	530	38 011	761	28.1	8.9	37.2
Caroline	386	3 699	349	268	584	D	252	127	34 260	221	38.5	12.2	45.2
Carroll	409	4 215	710	807	771	D	92	112	26 508	980	34.3	6.5	39.2
Charles City	144	1 547	D	249	120	D	24	57	36 767	79	43.0	16.5	58.2
Charlotte	229	1 806	308	426	236	D	D	51	28 074	518	26.8	11.4	42.9
Chesterfield	7 052	106 893	12 026	9 594	17 416	5 217	7 237	4 509	42 179	197	56.3	2.5	44.7
Clarke	357	2 872	432	D	237	D	149	124	43 222	477	47.2	4.4	46.5
Craig	59	345	D	D	105	27	D	9	27 136	207	27.5	9.7	51.7
Culpeper	970	12 166	2 038	1 294	2 265	216	732	482	39 620	731	45.7	8.1	40.9
Cumberland	141	930	102	D	228	17	D	24	26 001	262	30.2	11.1	52.7
Dickenson	206	2 047	332	D	420	68	D	68	33 174	147	48.3	4.8	51.7
Dinwiddie	346	4 312	291	737	489	130	D	189	43 869	383	32.6	9.1	45.4
Essex	299	3 521	D	668	862	131	88	103	29 150	98	36.7	26.5	43.9
Fairfax	30 139	581 452	53 699	6 160	50 666	30 000	190 438	43 162	74 232	148	77.7	2.0	34.5
Fauquier	1 784	17 262	2 710	960	2 804	669	1 570	717	41 562	1 258	48.2	7.8	43.6
Floyd	320	2 090	370	359	318	87	51	58	27 941	863	29.9	6.7	48.2
Fluvanna	396	2 493	227	143	352	51	D	82	32 946	303	36.0	6.6	43.2
Franklin	1 178	12 513	1 492	2 664	1 915	256	286	338	27 024	1 023	30.7	6.6	45.2
Frederick	1 488	22 730	1 733	4 471	3 622	D	714	888	39 076	681	45.1	5.9	36.9
Giles	287	3 669	614	1 030	678	73	D	147	39 939	378	27.0	5.3	40.2
Gloucester	861	7 128	1 319	266	1 983	263	276	191	26 849	136	62.5	8.8	39.0
Goochland	633	D	539	D	567	D	360	D	D	315	52.1	6.0	41.0
Grayson	158	1 749	D	774	156	D	25	47	26 901	764	34.6	7.6	44.2
Greene	328	2 413	184	D	791	D	119	70	29 075	216	34.7	4.6	50.0
Greensville	99	1 803	D	D	193	D	D	50	27 663	151	29.1	19.2	38.4
Halifax	718	9 670	1 804	D	1 436	202	141	332	34 357	935	17.9	9.7	44.0
Hanover	3 066	43 788	5 307	3 768	6 223	659	1 396	1 628	37 186	600	53.2	5.7	51.8
Henrico	9 002	164 343	22 798	5 718	22 325	22 342	13 068	8 201	49 903	117	58.1	3.4	41.9
Henry	821	11 119	895	3 013	1 513	278	291	356	31 997	290	35.2	2.8	26.2
Highland	89	390	D	D	47	D	D	9	22 918	261	14.2	22.6	51.0
Isle of Wight	637	7 236	697	2 219	887	205	289	311	42 925	213	47.4	20.7	51.2
James City	1 669	26 468	4 559	1 783	3 795	564	1 445	957	36 150	83	61.4	1.2	28.9
King and Queen	100	607	D	55	37	D	26	21	33 809	127	40.2	13.4	66.1
King George	488	6 067	288	D	738	D	2 535	328	54 026	160	40.6	8.1	38.1
King William	305	2 911	321	D	419	100	140	141	48 318	135	37.0	18.5	50.4
Lancaster	457	3 903	1 024	98	778	292	358	137	35 146	61	39.3	8.2	45.9
Lee	277	2 813	488	100	962	178	64	68	24 226	1 012	38.7	3.6	37.2
Loudoun	9 486	136 232	10 443	5 335	18 832	3 164	19 471	7 817	57 381	1 396	69.0	3.4	37.0

Table B. States and Counties — **Agriculture**

STATE County	Acreage (1,000)	Percent change, 2007–2012	Average size of farm	Total irrigated (1,000)	Total cropland (1,000)	Value of land and buildings — Average per farm	Average per acre	Value of machinery and equipment, average per farm (dollars)	Value of products sold — Total (mil dol)	Average per farm (dollars)	Crops	Live-stock and poultry products	$10,000 or more	$100,000 or more	Government payments — Total ($1,000)	Percent of farms
	117	118	119	120	121	122	123	124	125	126	127	128	129	130	131	132
VERMONT—Cont'd																
Chittenden	74	-11.8	125	0.5	25.9	538 598	4 297	75 608	42.2	71 951	47.0	53.0	40.9	12.3	609	21.8
Essex	25	-4.6	274	0.0	8.0	510 731	1 863	95 505	11.7	125 280	33.9	66.1	47.3	19.4	124	31.2
Franklin	186	3.5	253	0.6	80.2	708 868	2 801	145 685	184.4	250 497	17.1	82.9	55.8	31.4	2 937	34.2
Grand Isle	19	11.0	157	0.1	13.8	598 289	3 806	103 231	19.1	157 579	29.6	70.4	53.7	26.4	458	27.3
Lamoille	52	4.7	149	0.1	12.6	544 129	3 645	73 444	21.3	61 129	44.6	55.4	37.8	12.3	362	18.3
Orange	105	3.5	141	0.2	33.2	435 761	3 097	65 348	53.5	71 578	25.2	74.8	35.7	13.9	730	15.8
Orleans	130	0.1	204	0.2	52.5	497 260	2 432	90 815	99.3	155 655	14.4	85.6	48.6	20.5	1 342	24.3
Rutland	108	-16.9	170	0.2	36.5	460 703	2 718	73 945	30.8	48 114	33.2	66.8	36.9	10.2	1 131	25.9
Washington	67	10.4	127	0.2	21.1	508 002	4 013	70 991	27.1	50 972	25.9	74.1	35.3	8.8	535	14.5
Windham	51	0.0	114	0.5	14.0	454 076	3 998	64 159	26.4	59 116	43.0	57.0	36.9	8.5	499	17.4
Windsor	101	5.6	132	0.2	23.6	500 858	3 795	58 762	22.4	29 188	34.8	65.2	27.2	7.2	517	9.6
VIRGINIA	8 302	2.4	180	68.7	2 990.6	776 719	4 306	72 555	3 753.3	81 540	36.2	63.8	37.9	9.6	82 318	23.2
Accomack	77	-17.5	342	5.4	64.3	1 254 991	3 665	153 013	172.2	761 934	34.7	65.3	68.1	39.4	2 020	44.2
Albemarle	169	6.7	179	1.5	46.6	1 563 048	8 756	61 092	31.0	32 780	62.8	37.2	32.2	4.2	377	9.2
Alleghany	37	28.0	179	0.0	8.1	554 908	3 108	53 285	2.9	14 227	D	D	28.0	1.0	11	10.1
Amelia	88	-3.5	217	0.4	28.2	664 813	3 065	77 044	99.8	245 288	13.0	87.0	37.6	13.5	1 496	42.8
Amherst	99	11.9	232	D	19.4	846 944	3 646	60 845	9.3	21 758	35.2	64.8	35.4	2.6	175	10.6
Appomattox	96	26.9	235	0.1	28.7	668 800	2 847	63 924	12.6	30 788	35.1	64.9	42.0	7.8	367	30.0
Arlington	0	0.0	6	D	D	322 667	53 778	10 000	0.0	3 000	D	D	0.0	0.0	0	0.0
Augusta	260	-9.1	152	3.3	89.6	953 997	6 256	79 364	232.1	136 059	11.9	88.1	49.1	15.1	1 677	18.2
Bath	41	7.6	356	0.0	10.0	1 484 267	4 166	63 353	6.1	52 216	22.1	77.9	44.8	12.9	31	13.8
Bedford	207	-2.7	151	0.1	59.1	668 345	4 430	58 744	28.3	20 660	24.6	75.4	33.9	2.8	897	11.8
Bland	77	-4.1	214	D	14.1	690 022	3 225	64 199	9.3	25 785	13.1	86.9	44.2	5.2	179	18.8
Botetourt	89	1.6	153	0.1	26.2	668 360	4 370	69 147	18.7	32 027	32.4	67.6	34.1	6.0	397	15.8
Brunswick	90	3.6	288	1.3	25.2	601 074	2 088	73 490	25.7	82 349	67.1	32.9	32.7	7.7	1 243	52.9
Buchanan	10	2.4	93	D	0.8	245 175	2 642	29 864	0.5	4 651	46.3	53.7	8.7	0.0	166	23.3
Buckingham	84	8.6	215	0.0	24.5	660 348	3 077	66 338	39.9	101 997	16.2	83.8	40.9	10.2	215	19.9
Campbell	151	7.4	198	0.3	44.1	591 091	2 985	60 756	24.2	31 846	26.8	73.2	36.7	5.4	895	28.8
Caroline	56	1.5	255	2.0	37.8	1 052 570	4 128	114 928	20.4	92 172	96.6	3.4	29.9	13.1	1 149	24.9
Carroll	140	13.6	143	1.1	41.5	488 210	3 406	53 584	43.4	44 305	25.7	74.3	44.6	7.2	359	13.5
Charles City	31	13.4	395	1.4	21.4	1 482 443	3 756	221 367	23.7	299 747	D	D	40.5	24.1	744	30.4
Charlotte	149	19.0	288	0.8	41.0	654 878	2 271	58 116	21.7	41 849	51.2	48.8	40.5	7.1	1 200	34.4
Chesterfield	20	-7.3	101	0.1	6.9	539 970	5 329	73 452	6.4	32 487	59.4	40.6	18.8	6.6	259	13.7
Clarke	67	-1.4	140	0.2	27.6	1 105 929	7 880	59 356	25.9	54 333	33.1	66.9	33.5	7.3	235	10.5
Craig	47	12.0	225	0.0	9.9	714 005	3 170	76 580	4.9	23 604	26.6	73.4	43.5	2.4	106	18.4
Culpeper	126	13.5	173	0.6	58.0	1 115 272	6 450	80 141	42.8	58 534	59.9	40.1	36.3	7.3	1 059	14.5
Cumberland	57	0.6	218	0.0	15.6	782 668	3 588	66 351	44.9	171 260	8.6	91.4	37.8	11.8	377	27.9
Dickenson	15	4.9	102	0.0	2.6	303 755	2 967	43 837	0.8	5 313	21.4	78.7	16.3	0.0	72	8.8
Dinwiddie	89	13.2	233	1.2	39.0	699 723	3 003	73 689	24.8	64 747	82.3	17.7	36.3	6.3	2 425	49.3
Essex	57	6.3	579	D	38.7	1 761 745	3 045	258 112	22.8	232 418	98.5	1.5	44.9	29.6	873	48.0
Fairfax	8	11.7	53	0.1	1.4	804 507	15 156	42 581	3.4	23 243	94.0	6.0	19.6	2.7	26	6.8
Fauquier	228	2.6	181	0.4	82.2	1 439 924	7 935	73 037	53.9	42 884	40.0	60.0	32.6	6.4	865	9.9
Floyd	145	12.2	168	0.2	41.5	607 145	3 622	59 109	34.7	40 210	41.4	58.6	40.7	4.6	320	8.1
Fluvanna	47	-3.7	155	0.1	13.6	791 934	5 097	55 584	4.7	15 584	62.8	37.2	29.7	2.3	123	14.9
Franklin	165	-1.2	161	0.9	58.2	570 110	3 544	76 026	65.4	63 971	22.5	77.5	34.3	8.5	1 084	17.9
Frederick	101	2.5	148	0.2	39.7	872 966	5 903	57 128	34.3	50 389	72.5	27.5	34.4	5.4	398	5.6
Giles	66	0.1	173	0.0	12.2	458 352	2 642	53 362	8.1	21 402	20.0	80.0	35.4	5.0	55	3.2
Gloucester	20	-11.6	149	0.0	13.7	750 375	5 027	96 426	11.3	82 890	94.8	5.2	31.6	12.5	421	18.4
Goochland	50	-15.4	159	0.0	19.5	868 708	5 457	61 886	16.6	52 578	50.2	49.8	23.5	4.4	291	9.5
Grayson	132	-3.5	173	0.0	27.9	724 361	4 195	55 518	31.6	41 408	18.9	81.1	42.8	6.9	419	23.8
Greene	27	-12.0	126	0.0	7.6	868 801	6 880	62 347	9.9	45 759	15.9	84.1	34.7	4.2	40	22.7
Greensville	58	19.5	386	0.2	31.9	782 781	2 029	109 563	21.3	140 775	96.8	3.2	29.8	15.9	1 359	63.6
Halifax	212	9.2	226	2.2	61.5	520 118	2 298	77 607	36.5	39 065	63.4	36.6	35.2	7.8	3 737	53.7
Hanover	94	2.7	157	3.3	55.2	874 698	5 566	82 075	55.3	92 120	85.0	15.0	34.2	8.7	1 370	10.8
Henrico	13	-35.9	110	D	9.5	724 744	6 578	59 342	9.4	80 094	98.4	1.6	24.8	11.1	130	13.7
Henry	43	-15.4	148	0.1	9.3	400 117	2 700	50 052	D	D	D	D	27.2	2.8	177	13.1
Highland	93	21.3	357	0.0	11.6	1 205 379	3 380	69 057	30.1	115 199	4.5	95.5	61.7	18.4	252	13.4
Isle of Wight	76	3.0	355	0.7	50.0	1 262 986	3 556	165 127	45.6	214 202	72.4	27.6	49.8	22.5	1 689	51.2
James City	6	-4.9	67	0.0	3.0	585 530	8 766	72 687	D	D	D	D	36.1	1.2	94	12.0
King and Queen	42	-21.0	331	D	29.0	1 020 906	3 089	132 559	17.3	136 567	D	D	35.4	16.5	1 051	32.3
King George	24	-33.8	152	0.4	10.1	764 544	5 033	57 250	3.8	23 788	83.7	16.3	29.4	5.6	174	33.8
King William	54	16.3	397	1.1	28.6	1 481 511	3 734	107 889	16.6	123 296	84.4	15.6	32.6	17.8	735	18.5
Lancaster	11	-24.1	175	D	7.4	802 885	4 579	112 082	4.9	79 738	96.4	3.6	50.8	13.1	278	42.6
Lee	117	-0.5	116	0.1	30.4	255 115	2 202	47 907	18.2	18 026	23.8	76.2	30.8	3.3	1 007	44.5
Loudoun	135	-5.4	97	0.6	56.2	1 156 476	11 977	56 777	37.1	26 577	70.3	29.7	23.4	3.2	497	8.0

Table B. States and Counties — Water Use, Wholesale Trade, Retail Trade, and Real Estate

STATE County	Water use, 2010		Wholesale trade,[1] 2012				Retail trade,[2] 2012				Real estate and rental and leasing,[2] 2012			
	Total water withdrawn (mil gal/day)	Gallons withdrawn per person per day	Number of establishments	Number of employees	Sales (mil dol)	Annual payroll (mil dol)	Number of establishments	Number of employees	Sales (mil dol)	Annual payroll (mil dol)	Number of establishments	Number of employees	Receipts (mil dol)	Annual payroll (mil dol)
	133	134	135	136	137	138	139	140	141	142	143	144	145	146
VERMONT—Cont'd														
Chittenden	18.0	115	246	4 085	3 133.9	239.1	839	12 464	2 959.4	308.4	232	1 297	275.2	49.5
Essex	0.7	103	3	2	0.4	0.0	20	93	19.0	1.3	2	D	D	D
Franklin	7.4	156	46	794	1 257.8	32.1	195	2 139	628.6	50.7	26	74	7.4	1.8
Grand Isle	4.0	574	5	6	3.4	0.2	30	165	50.0	3.6	7	6	1.5	0.2
Lamoille	2.6	107	23	D	D	D	163	1 508	360.4	36.5	32	103	13.7	3.3
Orange	2.8	97	24	182	78.4	7.8	102	1 001	245.4	23.6	19	34	4.9	1.1
Orleans	3.8	138	23	D	D	D	147	1 285	350.3	31.3	21	94	14.2	2.7
Rutland	9.7	157	73	D	D	D	411	4 139	1 082.8	97.7	67	276	30.8	7.8
Washington	6.2	104	70	D	D	D	380	4 258	1 112.6	105.1	65	277	45.6	7.9
Windham	349.8	7 858	43	D	D	D	283	2 540	604.4	63.9	69	258	32.0	8.6
Windsor	8.9	157	53	670	276.6	32.1	311	2 694	726.3	70.5	81	265	30.9	8.7
VIRGINIA	7 648.0	956	6 232	88 353	86 613.6	4 983.1	27 415	410 918	110 002.4	10 007.9	8 862	54 246	11 758.9	2 378.3
Accomack	15.2	458	28	159	78.9	5.1	169	1 402	348.2	28.8	38	103	13.0	2.5
Albemarle	19.2	194	66	1 102	574.5	67.1	325	5 511	1 497.5	147.8	151	766	129.5	25.7
Alleghany	43.1	2 649	5	30	7.7	1.0	38	280	75.1	6.3	4	16	2.1	0.3
Amelia	7.9	623	6	D	D	D	30	227	71.1	4.9	6	7	0.5	0.1
Amherst	17.0	525	11	D	D	D	94	1 137	273.4	22.7	17	38	3.7	0.7
Appomattox	1.5	100	7	75	9.9	2.4	56	631	143.8	12.9	12	19	5.1	0.4
Arlington	0.3	1	85	1 090	935.3	88.8	613	9 610	2 608.8	265.6	404	5 188	1 493.4	219.8
Augusta	40.2	545	52	737	249.6	33.1	208	1 941	621.3	46.5	61	185	18.9	4.1
Bath	109.1	23 063	2	D	D	D	21	94	17.2	1.4	8	37	3.6	1.9
Bedford	21.6	314	45	440	265.1	17.5	166	2 056	521.2	47.4	64	111	19.0	3.4
Bland	2.9	422	7	D	D	D	12	64	33.8	1.2	2	D	D	D
Botetourt	8.7	261	37	D	D	D	85	873	321.4	18.5	19	D	D	D
Brunswick	28.4	1 629	6	45	27.1	1.6	45	326	103.6	6.3	5	D	D	D
Buchanan	0.9	36	21	231	265.3	13.2	79	834	173.0	14.5	12	29	4.8	0.9
Buckingham	2.3	136	8	D	D	D	38	293	83.0	6.0	3	D	D	D
Campbell	7.4	135	38	D	D	D	188	1 904	601.0	43.3	52	126	18.2	3.2
Caroline	9.0	314	8	D	D	D	49	655	404.2	15.5	12	24	4.3	0.5
Carroll	2.4	81	15	121	40.2	2.8	89	748	285.7	14.6	14	43	5.2	0.9
Charles City	0.9	127	8	D	D	D	10	57	14.7	2.0	6	20	3.8	0.6
Charlotte	1.5	118	9	68	29.6	2.2	32	230	56.5	4.3	5	12	0.7	0.2
Chesterfield	897.5	2 838	290	3 411	1 729.4	182.3	933	17 142	4 657.3	410.9	281	1 511	331.7	65.3
Clarke	1.9	133	9	D	D	D	35	229	81.5	4.6	17	D	D	D
Craig	3.1	588	3	D	D	D	11	110	18.6	1.7	2	D	D	D
Culpeper	5.1	109	24	448	296.8	16.5	157	2 120	550.1	52.5	43	239	31.2	9.2
Cumberland	5.9	587	1	D	D	D	34	204	40.4	3.9	3	D	D	D
Dickenson	4.8	300	7	20	5.3	0.4	44	451	102.3	9.4	4	5	0.4	0.1
Dinwiddie	2.1	76	8	D	D	D	56	541	144.9	9.8	7	52	7.5	1.8
Essex	2.0	182	7	D	D	D	60	826	236.6	20.3	10	73	7.1	2.6
Fairfax	14.9	14	750	11 158	25 177.2	930.7	2 735	50 244	14 589.5	1 418.8	1 447	10 962	2 918.3	687.9
Fauquier	6.6	101	38	445	159.7	20.1	223	2 632	920.8	75.7	77	203	34.6	8.1
Floyd	1.8	116	11	D	D	D	42	321	70.7	5.9	5	5	1.9	0.2
Fluvanna	118.8	4 625	11	117	76.0	5.4	39	308	75.3	6.3	15	20	3.6	0.7
Franklin	5.6	99	39	424	291.4	26.7	190	1 857	459.0	42.0	46	103	17.8	3.2
Frederick	16.2	206	84	D	D	D	197	3 512	1 346.1	91.3	54	143	30.4	6.0
Giles	149.0	8 619	8	D	D	D	62	694	184.0	14.8	11	22	3.1	0.7
Gloucester	3.5	95	23	87	22.7	2.9	141	1 905	496.2	45.7	43	110	11.6	2.6
Goochland	2.0	93	32	D	D	D	62	491	215.5	13.9	13	102	13.4	5.3
Grayson	1.9	123	6	D	D	D	24	161	40.5	2.8	5	3	0.8	0.1
Greene	1.7	95	9	60	14.6	2.8	52	764	183.9	16.9	9	D	D	D
Greensville	1.8	146	5	24	1.8	0.7	25	209	130.8	3.7	4	18	2.0	0.4
Halifax	18.5	510	20	244	99.2	8.8	133	1 436	358.1	30.3	21	69	12.1	1.6
Hanover	8.5	85	216	4 016	3 161.4	205.6	358	5 917	1 752.1	151.6	106	466	176.3	22.0
Henrico	31.0	101	405	7 312	7 293.9	446.7	1 277	22 637	5 519.9	538.8	447	3 659	718.5	164.4
Henry	11.4	211	44	D	D	D	167	1 715	581.5	41.4	25	110	16.1	2.9
Highland	9.3	4 020	2	D	D	D	17	44	8.6	0.6	1	D	D	D
Isle of Wight	23.9	678	16	75	51.2	3.4	104	950	246.9	16.8	29	80	11.3	2.5
James City	14.3	213	47	335	131.6	14.4	281	3 679	630.2	66.6	82	502	102.7	19.9
King and Queen	2.0	285	4	D	D	D	11	31	12.4	0.6	4	4	0.4	0.1
King George	3.9	165	8	D	D	D	54	721	232.4	15.4	16	46	8.7	1.3
King William	22.9	1 438	7	35	12.0	1.3	49	437	133.3	10.1	11	26	2.3	0.7
Lancaster	1.3	115	15	114	83.9	3.3	79	805	161.5	18.1	17	38	5.4	0.8
Lee	3.7	144	12	68	33.4	2.1	68	828	208.1	16.6	10	26	2.5	0.5
Loudoun	22.5	72	243	3 225	2 319.4	236.1	952	17 774	5 140.4	481.0	341	1 877	528.1	82.5

1. Merchant wholesalers, except manufacturers' sales branches and offices.   2. Employer establishments.

STATE County	Professional, scientific, and technical services, 2012				Manufacturing, 2012				Accommodation and food services, 2012			
	Number of establishments	Number of employees	Receipts (mil dol)	Annual payroll (mil dol)	Number of establishments	Number of employees	Receipts (mil dol)	Annual payroll (mil dol)	Number of establishments	Number of employees	Sales (mil dol)	Annual payroll (mil dol)
	147	148	149	150	151	152	153	154	155	156	157	158
VERMONT—Cont'd												
Chittenden	752	6 327	941.2	403.6	189	9 861	3 388.0	556.6	433	8 124	459.9	133.8
Essex	5	25	2.8	1.4	7	129	11.4	4.2	13	58	2.4	0.7
Franklin	62	236	26.7	11.9	55	2 770	D	132.8	88	771	44.6	13.6
Grand Isle	21	48	4.4	1.6	7	40	D	1.1	25	111	9.4	2.9
Lamoille	88	394	71.3	20.3	49	406	D	18.4	112	4 203	183.7	73.0
Orange	73	352	60.4	18.7	49	673	133.0	28.6	59	589	40.0	12.5
Orleans	48	169	16.5	6.5	41	1 108	D	36.8	68	1 446	54.1	20.4
Rutland	178	D	D	D	105	3 126	613.1	164.0	247	2 795	130.1	37.8
Washington	251	D	D	D	126	3 959	819.8	225.4	163	2 923	123.9	41.2
Windham	124	476	49.9	20.9	92	2 049	421.4	87.5	212	3 498	151.5	44.2
Windsor	193	5 011	265.8	108.4	110	2 062	442.6	86.8	199	3 492	176.8	50.9
VIRGINIA	29 368	429 690	92 775.9	36 364.7	5 101	228 197	96 389.9	11 586.1	16 832	320 514	17 795.9	4 908.6
Accomack	64	410	79.3	19.9	18	3 001	667.9	78.1	101	993	53.6	13.9
Albemarle	353	3 204	501.5	204.2	68	2 855	786.4	172.2	182	3 780	230.6	67.5
Alleghany	11	24	2.4	0.6	8	468	D	19.7	26	299	14.0	3.7
Amelia	14	46	3.1	1.0	19	247	98.4	7.6	11	93	5.0	1.1
Amherst	43	253	32.2	13.5	39	1 314	572.0	67.7	44	D	D	D
Appomattox	14	D	D	D	13	71	D	2.4	14	D	D	D
Arlington	1 829	42 070	11 167.3	4 296.3	34	220	54.1	7.4	647	17 342	1 362.4	363.6
Augusta	93	413	39.9	15.0	73	4 382	1 884.2	221.4	79	1 229	56.5	15.9
Bath	9	D	D	D	4	47	D	D	18	1 021	63.5	26.8
Bedford	135	630	76.4	23.0	51	2 512	D	151.2	73	715	28.9	8.2
Bland	2	D	D	D	8	488	D	25.5	6	46	2.3	0.6
Botetourt	63	D	D	D	30	D	812.0	114.2	49	D	D	D
Brunswick	13	36	3.3	1.0	17	217	69.1	10.5	11	D	D	D
Buchanan	35	277	20.9	7.4	10	238	91.7	13.8	22	317	15.3	4.2
Buckingham	15	100	12.9	5.2	11	116	D	3.5	7	D	D	D
Campbell	85	741	84.8	52.2	70	2 632	1 555.4	128.0	82	1 511	64.3	16.9
Caroline	30	206	19.9	8.7	17	279	76.1	10.8	30	332	18.5	4.9
Carroll	26	89	6.6	2.8	20	1 109	D	31.0	38	613	34.4	7.6
Charles City	3	D	D	D	18	292	D	10.6	4	D	D	D
Charlotte	9	40	2.3	0.8	15	419	74.8	13.3	10	91	4.5	1.3
Chesterfield	813	6 640	891.7	359.6	168	8 594	3 845.3	536.1	528	10 919	514.5	142.1
Clarke	44	113	16.4	6.6	14	706	89.8	27.0	21	D	D	D
Craig	7	D	D	D	NA	NA	NA	NA	4	D	D	D
Culpeper	92	674	96.9	31.4	39	1 382	563.6	63.6	77	1 193	59.3	14.7
Cumberland	5	D	D	D	3	D	D	D	4	44	1.4	0.4
Dickenson	11	163	8.9	3.7	6	43	D	1.9	13	D	D	D
Dinwiddie	24	64	4.1	1.7	10	652	D	D	18	270	15.4	3.6
Essex	23	93	6.4	2.7	14	609	90.7	16.7	30	459	19.6	5.8
Fairfax	8 232	197 134	48 404.9	18 643.4	357	6 199	1 408.8	349.1	2 158	39 514	2 795.4	731.2
Fauquier	267	1 590	287.5	115.2	58	872	137.8	39.7	110	2 008	108.1	29.8
Floyd	22	48	4.1	1.5	30	331	D	12.6	18	230	7.6	2.5
Fluvanna	29	71	7.6	2.0	10	89	D	3.0	22	D	D	D
Franklin	83	299	25.8	9.0	53	2 440	D	D	68	958	44.7	12.3
Frederick	114	D	D	D	84	4 514	2 537.6	220.9	129	2 381	117.5	30.6
Giles	15	264	19.2	10.1	13	994	D	60.1	35	429	18.3	4.9
Gloucester	74	283	24.2	9.8	15	181	22.1	6.5	65	934	40.4	12.1
Goochland	65	275	36.7	12.1	19	154	27.1	7.0	42	372	25.6	7.7
Grayson	11	20	2.1	0.6	17	819	D	27.4	14	110	4.4	1.4
Greene	30	336	23.7	20.0	11	48	D	1.9	27	299	14.9	4.0
Greensville	1	D	D	D	6	818	261.5	27.8	15	191	11.4	2.2
Halifax	35	157	17.6	4.9	37	1 685	573.4	73.0	62	914	36.0	10.1
Hanover	270	1 418	191.6	66.3	147	3 629	917.2	155.3	200	3 482	164.7	44.1
Henrico	1 142	11 253	1 505.7	630.6	175	5 104	1 808.2	262.6	720	16 249	832.8	238.8
Henry	33	270	13.4	6.6	69	2 885	834.7	115.5	55	1 003	41.3	10.9
Highland	5	7	0.9	0.3	NA	NA	NA	NA	5	D	D	D
Isle of Wight	60	296	30.2	11.8	15	D	D	83.1	50	766	34.1	9.8
James City	222	D	D	D	31	1 661	1 621.3	96.9	117	3 412	264.1	84.6
King and Queen	8	20	2.4	0.9	5	32	D	D	2	D	D	D
King George	108	2 415	459.4	194.9	8	82	D	3.3	37	369	21.8	5.4
King William	29	137	9.4	3.3	11	465	209.2	22.8	20	232	10.6	2.6
Lancaster	54	319	33.4	17.1	15	152	D	7.5	32	510	18.9	8.1
Lee	19	49	4.0	1.2	8	85	D	2.2	17	D	D	D
Loudoun	2 266	19 300	3 985.2	1 741.2	158	4 462	1 636.9	345.1	611	13 152	877.0	245.2

1. Establishment subject to federal tax.

Table B. States and Counties — Health Care and Social Assistance, Other Services, Nonemployer Businesses, and Residential Construction

STATE County	Health care and social assistance, 2012				Other services, 2012				Nonemployer businesses, 2014		Value of residential construction authorized by building permits, 2015	
	Number of establishments	Number of employees	Receipts (mil dol)	Annual payroll (mil dol)	Number of establishments	Number of employees	Receipts (mil dol)	Annual payroll (mil dol)	Number	Receipts (mil dol)	New Construction ($1,000)	Number of housing units
	159	160	161	162	163	164	165	166	167	168	169	170
VERMONT—Cont'd												
Chittenden	565	14 159	1 652.4	588.8	414	2 291	223.5	65.9	14 061	702.7	117 895	756
Essex	9	64	3.5	1.9	9	45	3.6	0.5	560	20.6	1 267	6
Franklin	108	D	D	D	69	264	25.9	6.1	3 659	155.3	28 309	142
Grand Isle	12	D	D	D	10	17	3.2	0.4	705	31.1	3 654	18
Lamoille	84	1 532	133.6	57.6	65	289	45.0	7.3	2 744	113.2	11 929	56
Orange	82	1 466	153.7	54.2	42	135	13.6	3.8	2 943	112.3	4 853	23
Orleans	75	1 714	152.5	67.2	69	217	18.9	4.3	2 540	106.5	23 094	303
Rutland	207	4 898	440.4	179.6	154	715	58.7	16.8	5 035	179.6	9 127	54
Washington	232	4 359	408.5	162.1	220	1 030	128.7	37.2	6 065	239.6	28 403	152
Windham	183	3 103	278.5	124.6	129	489	44.7	11.4	5 141	200.6	41 631	177
Windsor	167	3 691	436.7	204.6	146	760	82.6	21.9	6 125	255.5	16 138	58
VIRGINIA	18 774	411 108	47 705.0	18 628.8	14 726	112 430	17 079.4	4 471.2	560 597	24 548.1	4 724 305	28 469
Accomack	57	1 101	62.7	28.0	60	332	22.1	7.0	2 304	88.3	6 139	43
Albemarle	314	6 428	950.1	372.5	151	1 445	308.7	75.0	8 902	420.4	134 527	497
Alleghany	34	867	85.7	33.7	22	117	10.6	2.6	659	20.5	3 392	15
Amelia	24	369	21.6	9.9	20	D	D	D	843	28.3	7 473	34
Amherst	41	D	D	D	55	152	12.2	3.2	1 554	52.9	8 027	51
Appomattox	25	D	D	D	19	74	6.9	1.9	869	28.9	9 045	51
Arlington	484	8 987	1 450.6	465.6	642	10 355	2 577.8	721.4	18 603	927.3	143 549	652
Augusta	110	3 916	512.2	177.0	100	472	43.7	14.1	4 476	208.7	36 970	217
Bath	4	D	D	D	6	D	D	D	323	12.0	1 792	12
Bedford	103	1 295	82.4	34.3	86	366	36.6	9.5	4 644	189.2	69 647	302
Bland	7	81	7.6	3.2	6	D	D	D	284	9.8	1 384	11
Botetourt	48	D	D	D	57	D	D	D	2 311	85.5	16 642	83
Brunswick	12	189	10.4	4.7	20	D	D	D	699	25.7	2 368	16
Buchanan	43	655	53.4	23.0	26	D	D	D	788	29.5	394	2
Buckingham	15	375	17.4	11.2	16	70	7.9	2.2	737	27.9	7 526	47
Campbell	93	D	D	D	87	332	25.0	7.0	2 876	94.6	18 448	112
Caroline	19	283	18.2	9.2	30	172	15.1	3.8	1 588	53.6	18 286	77
Carroll	41	569	39.1	17.3	25	D	D	D	1 683	55.7	9 041	53
Charles City	3	D	D	D	7	D	D	D	385	13.4	2 669	14
Charlotte	23	284	13.2	7.7	17	D	D	D	656	22.2	2 731	14
Chesterfield	757	11 169	1 338.3	518.8	479	3 341	368.3	87.3	21 219	894.0	244 215	1 263
Clarke	25	D	D	D	30	79	10.1	3.0	1 316	55.4	15 505	45
Craig	5	D	D	D	3	D	D	D	294	10.3	2 050	11
Culpeper	74	2 007	204.3	84.8	75	539	47.4	17.3	3 480	159.9	51 271	216
Cumberland	10	115	3.3	2.1	9	D	D	D	526	20.4	2 709	18
Dickenson	27	402	24.7	12.2	19	D	D	D	473	13.1	525	6
Dinwiddie	26	263	15.5	6.7	32	D	D	D	1 260	49.0	6 274	60
Essex	35	623	68.4	19.7	23	D	D	D	783	31.8	2 927	18
Fairfax	2 860	52 008	6 870.2	2 622.2	1 950	17 487	2 708.3	760.6	102 475	5 262.6	292 418	2 721
Fauquier	125	2 571	274.8	114.2	128	875	82.3	28.9	5 939	303.2	64 232	200
Floyd	23	320	45.0	8.4	24	D	D	D	1 298	38.9	7 662	40
Fluvanna	22	199	11.7	5.5	22	138	9.4	3.0	1 722	55.2	19 843	99
Franklin	74	D	D	D	91	287	25.6	6.5	3 672	138.8	38 871	142
Frederick	88	1 551	114.1	45.9	104	591	55.8	17.4	5 366	206.7	137 221	669
Giles	29	500	46.1	16.5	26	D	D	D	842	29.9	3 665	19
Gloucester	69	1 282	128.1	45.2	75	323	22.5	7.2	2 403	87.4	27 670	127
Goochland	28	D	D	D	38	D	D	D	2 012	112.2	43 330	136
Grayson	17	197	11.3	4.5	9	D	D	D	1 036	29.2	4 659	24
Greene	15	D	D	D	20	103	9.2	2.5	1 332	44.0	8 984	56
Greensville	3	D	D	D	3	D	D	D	384	10.1	2 941	22
Halifax	82	1 767	159.9	73.5	50	173	16.1	3.9	1 769	61.5	9 986	61
Hanover	258	4 764	706.4	221.0	258	1 649	150.5	44.8	7 710	348.2	118 330	637
Henrico	977	24 726	2 887.9	1 138.2	635	4 883	735.9	163.0	22 206	1 004.8	184 471	1 450
Henry	55	1 005	51.9	23.4	47	257	20.5	6.3	2 374	73.7	3 807	26
Highland	5	58	3.3	1.4	9	D	D	D	253	7.0	1 347	10
Isle of Wight	50	648	44.0	21.2	64	309	29.2	9.7	2 110	79.1	33 549	329
James City	159	3 572	305.5	138.8	108	D	D	D	5 085	220.8	112 441	457
King and Queen	3	D	D	D	5	D	D	D	402	15.5	2 260	13
King George	21	321	21.3	8.8	29	D	D	D	1 394	42.0	26 946	108
King William	23	327	17.5	8.8	29	111	8.9	2.3	1 043	43.7	14 306	100
Lancaster	35	1 088	87.0	41.1	42	177	13.5	4.4	1 048	59.4	7 300	18
Lee	32	786	53.3	24.8	17	D	D	D	1 102	34.1	1 301	12
Loudoun	759	9 585	1 188.5	459.1	566	4 756	597.3	217.1	29 800	1 508.6	627 660	3 614

	Government employment and payroll, 2012									Local government finances, 2012				
					March payroll (percent of total)							General revenue		
													Taxes	
													Per capita[1] (dollars)	
STATE County	Full-time equivalent employees	March payroll (dollars)	Administration, judicial, and legal	Police and Corrections	Fire Protection	Highways and transportation	Health and Welfare	Natural resources and utilities	Education and libraries	Total (mil dol)	Inter-governmental (mil dol)	Total (mil dol)	Total	Property
	171	172	173	174	175	176	177	178	179	180	181	182	183	184
VERMONT—Cont'd														
Chittenden	6 092	25 796 817	4.3	6.7	2.8	6.4	0.8	8.4	68.8	648.3	401.0	117.0	738	613
Essex	227	673 088	8.5	1.1	0.0	5.4	1.1	1.2	82.3	22.3	16.5	3.7	588	586
Franklin	1 780	6 015 525	5.6	3.3	0.4	4.9	1.2	3.1	80.8	156.8	118.8	21.4	443	432
Grand Isle	201	726 392	10.7	0.0	0.0	6.8	2.7	2.1	76.7	25.5	17.3	7.2	1 026	1 022
Lamoille	1 075	3 560 151	5.3	4.1	0.1	5.4	1.5	5.9	77.1	94.8	63.4	20.8	832	792
Orange	1 252	3 813 072	7.2	1.2	0.1	5.8	0.2	0.5	84.5	109.1	85.0	17.9	618	616
Orleans	1 359	3 619 393	5.7	2.4	0.1	7.1	0.3	1.7	82.4	103.1	75.1	19.7	725	721
Rutland	2 343	8 318 234	5.3	3.7	1.6	7.2	0.7	4.0	76.9	234.3	164.7	46.5	764	726
Washington	2 492	8 165 965	5.6	4.3	2.3	5.1	1.2	3.5	77.0	224.6	150.4	42.0	707	701
Windham	1 877	6 583 583	5.5	4.5	2.2	6.1	1.0	3.8	75.7	202.3	137.1	44.4	1 010	989
Windsor	2 421	8 862 072	5.4	5.6	2.7	6.6	1.1	3.8	74.2	247.7	169.7	49.6	883	878
VIRGINIA	X	X	X	X	X	X	X	X	X	X	X	X	X	X
Accomack	1 352	3 776 224	8.2	7.7	0.6	0.7	9.6	1.0	70.7	104.5	55.5	39.6	1 188	876
Albemarle	3 014	10 671 438	7.3	10.3	3.1	1.0	4.5	4.6	65.3	368.6	114.7	187.5	1 833	1 375
Alleghany	689	2 172 894	9.7	10.5	0.3	0.7	8.8	8.3	59.0	58.7	31.2	19.1	1 178	989
Amelia	422	1 273 101	3.9	5.8	0.0	0.0	1.9	1.5	85.8	26.8	15.3	8.2	645	518
Amherst	989	3 067 237	5.7	5.9	0.0	0.0	5.8	6.4	73.5	75.6	42.9	26.1	807	633
Appomattox	535	1 345 618	8.3	5.6	2.3	0.0	7.7	3.3	71.1	37.2	20.5	13.3	878	716
Arlington	9 317	49 809 798	6.9	10.3	4.2	20.3	7.8	5.4	41.2	2 574.1	624.2	861.8	3 899	3 016
Augusta	2 388	6 901 173	5.3	10.5	2.9	0.7	5.8	1.4	72.4	160.8	85.2	60.8	826	604
Bath	219	806 860	8.1	6.7	0.0	0.0	0.7	2.2	80.7	19.6	4.6	14.0	3 000	2 445
Bedford	2 625	7 051 188	4.0	20.1	0.0	0.0	9.1	1.8	63.5	181.5	95.3	61.4	882	750
Bland	206	534 449	5.2	7.3	0.0	0.0	2.6	3.3	70.3	17.5	11.4	4.6	690	588
Botetourt	1 128	3 464 230	7.8	10.1	0.0	0.0	5.0	2.6	72.5	84.1	39.8	37.2	1 122	904
Brunswick	651	1 620 721	7.3	12.5	0.0	0.2	9.0	1.7	67.5	39.3	24.2	10.4	610	490
Buchanan	834	2 368 397	7.1	6.9	0.7	1.0	4.4	1.1	76.6	101.0	43.8	50.0	2 095	742
Buckingham	544	1 683 523	4.7	32.1	0.0	0.0	2.0	2.6	57.1	44.0	28.4	13.4	782	682
Campbell	1 839	5 409 816	5.0	6.0	1.2	0.4	4.4	1.8	78.6	131.1	70.6	44.2	801	613
Caroline	918	2 716 780	8.5	9.8	2.1	0.0	5.6	2.6	68.0	76.7	35.1	35.8	1 236	1 010
Carroll	1 015	2 970 573	6.2	5.3	1.8	0.4	12.0	2.7	68.4	74.0	35.3	24.9	836	659
Charles City	243	709 888	11.5	6.6	0.0	0.0	0.0	4.7	70.0	21.2	9.1	8.1	1 137	1 012
Charlotte	499	1 413 313	6.4	8.9	0.0	0.1	7.7	2.4	72.2	35.7	24.5	8.0	646	537
Chesterfield	12 105	41 117 167	7.5	9.1	5.5	0.2	7.4	4.0	62.3	1 045.1	437.5	443.8	1 370	1 103
Clarke	531	1 954 739	5.8	7.2	0.0	1.3	3.8	2.9	72.3	48.5	15.8	21.7	1 516	1 292
Craig	169	483 380	9.9	7.8	0.0	0.0	5.9	2.1	74.4	13.0	8.1	3.8	730	626
Culpeper	1 841	5 945 989	8.3	10.6	0.9	1.1	9.5	4.7	63.2	142.8	61.0	63.9	1 333	1 025
Cumberland	297	961 120	9.9	8.2	0.0	0.0	1.6	1.1	72.0	23.9	13.9	8.8	889	758
Dickenson	610	1 668 965	6.7	7.4	0.0	0.0	4.2	7.9	70.6	68.6	37.7	20.1	1 282	855
Dinwiddie	890	2 870 612	6.8	7.8	0.3	0.0	11.1	3.2	67.5	79.3	43.7	31.3	1 119	925
Essex	422	1 333 678	8.5	8.1	3.2	2.6	2.1	8.3	64.6	32.1	12.9	16.4	1 462	1 109
Fairfax	43 275	208 710 868	5.3	8.1	5.1	0.4	7.2	5.9	62.9	5 025.9	1 140.8	3 142.7	2 810	2 292
Fauquier	2 840	9 833 163	6.6	9.0	2.5	0.7	3.2	5.4	69.2	232.3	78.6	133.9	2 012	1 727
Floyd	421	1 524 813	5.3	6.1	0.0	0.0	3.6	2.2	81.6	27.7	14.4	11.9	771	609
Fluvanna	723	2 499 361	7.1	4.3	0.0	0.0	3.5	1.7	78.2	61.3	29.9	28.7	1 105	989
Franklin	1 773	5 802 144	5.5	5.8	2.1	0.7	4.3	1.4	79.1	131.8	64.9	58.9	1 044	833
Frederick	3 183	9 479 873	6.7	10.3	3.6	0.6	2.4	2.0	72.9	235.3	97.7	114.5	1 425	1 069
Giles	586	1 588 082	11.1	11.9	0.0	1.6	2.9	6.0	64.6	54.9	29.9	17.0	1 002	801
Gloucester	1 208	3 733 992	8.5	8.9	0.0	0.0	3.3	3.6	71.8	99.1	42.2	45.2	1 224	938
Goochland	541	1 850 764	13.7	7.7	3.4	0.0	1.5	3.0	67.1	56.0	13.5	37.7	1 768	1 342
Grayson	541	1 324 989	8.4	7.8	0.0	0.3	3.4	2.6	76.5	36.9	21.4	11.7	771	658
Greene	657	1 764 870	6.8	4.8	0.0	2.2	0.6	0.4	80.2	51.3	25.0	19.5	1 040	871
Greensville	571	1 743 841	9.5	15.1	0.0	0.0	1.0	4.8	67.5	48.9	30.7	8.1	686	540
Halifax	1 547	3 858 184	6.4	5.9	1.6	1.0	5.8	2.5	75.9	111.3	60.8	33.7	940	669
Hanover	4 522	15 814 948	6.9	13.8	4.2	0.4	5.6	3.8	63.1	349.4	131.9	160.0	1 590	1 262
Henrico	11 822	42 600 655	5.0	12.2	6.3	3.6	7.0	2.9	59.3	1 060.7	406.5	484.0	1 537	1 115
Henry	1 709	4 761 002	6.5	7.7	0.9	0.0	9.6	0.7	71.0	124.5	75.9	32.9	620	403
Highland	101	285 647	13.1	13.3	0.0	0.0	5.6	0.9	63.7	8.1	4.2	3.1	1 401	1 221
Isle of Wight	1 226	4 460 998	6.8	4.8	1.2	1.8	1.9	2.5	75.6	106.3	46.2	51.6	1 459	1 145
James City	3 104	11 075 839	5.4	9.6	5.6	1.6	3.8	10.2	60.5	257.6	89.5	138.2	2 003	1 605
King and Queen	300	906 918	6.2	30.6	0.0	0.0	0.5	0.0	57.6	23.5	13.1	6.2	884	787
King George	1 018	3 118 233	7.1	5.5	4.7	0.0	3.5	3.8	73.7	80.3	31.9	31.4	1 282	770
King William	608	1 988 516	5.8	6.3	0.6	0.6	2.4	1.7	79.0	49.7	22.6	23.3	1 459	1 282
Lancaster	380	818 567	17.4	17.6	0.0	0.5	6.5	2.5	53.6	32.1	11.5	18.8	1 669	1 337
Lee	981	2 345 408	5.5	6.0	0.0	0.7	1.6	1.9	83.8	61.5	44.1	13.2	519	363
Loudoun	13 775	59 560 641	6.5	6.9	4.6	0.5	5.4	3.9	70.0	1 546.7	373.1	1 012.0	3 004	2 472

1. Based on the resident population estimated as of July 1 of the year shown.

STATE County	Total (mil dol) 185	Per capita[1] (dollars) 186	Education 187	Health and hospitals 188	Police protection 189	Public welfare 190	Highways 191	Total (mil dol) 192	Per capita[1] (dollars) 193	Federal civilian 194	Federal military 195	State and local 196	Demo-cratic 197	Republi-can 198	All other 199

Header spans:
- 185–191: Local government finances, 2012 (cont.) — Direct general expenditure; 187–191 under "Percent of total for:"
- 192–193: Debt outstanding
- 194–196: Government employment, 2014
- 197–199: Presidential election,[2] 2012 — Percent of vote cast:

STATE County	Total (mil dol)	Per capita (dollars)	Educa-tion	Health and hospitals	Police protec-tion	Public welfare	High-ways	Total (mil dol)	Per capita (dollars)	Federal civilian	Federal military	State and local	Demo-cratic	Republi-can	All other
VERMONT—Cont'd															
Chittenden	643.2	4 058	61.0	0.2	5.1	0.1	5.6	564.9	3 564	2 344	1 195	14 879	71.4	26.7	1.9
Essex	23.3	3 739	69.1	0.2	1.7	0.1	14.9	1.6	258	96	45	322	55.9	41.4	2.7
Franklin	162.7	3 374	75.1	0.6	4.0	0.0	8.1	53.3	1 106	1 424	353	2 947	61.4	36.6	2.0
Grand Isle	24.7	3 541	70.6	0.0	3.4	0.1	10.5	14.7	2 098	18	51	297	63.1	34.9	2.0
Lamoille	96.7	3 874	66.5	0.9	8.2	0.2	8.6	76.2	3 054	62	179	1 597	70.4	27.7	1.9
Orange	114.2	3 950	75.9	0.6	1.8	0.1	10.2	35.3	1 220	82	206	1 954	64.6	33.2	2.2
Orleans	106.7	3 935	76.0	0.3	1.8	0.0	9.3	33.0	1 219	234	192	1 862	62.6	35.1	2.3
Rutland	244.1	4 010	70.6	0.1	3.7	0.0	7.9	67.5	1 108	291	424	4 101	61.2	36.6	2.1
Washington	229.0	3 852	62.5	0.9	3.6	0.1	11.1	117.9	1 983	252	447	7 040	69.3	28.4	2.3
Windham	233.0	5 297	58.8	0.2	2.3	0.2	13.5	108.8	2 474	148	310	2 800	73.0	24.9	2.1
Windsor	275.6	4 903	62.8	0.8	3.4	0.0	12.6	98.2	1 746	1 383	412	3 528	68.8	29.1	2.0
VIRGINIA	X	X	X	X	X	X	X	X	X	189 487	139 176	535 675	52.6	46.3	1.0
Accomack	93.0	2 789	51.9	1.1	4.4	4.8	1.7	62.8	1 884	647	270	2 231	48.7	50.1	1.2
Albemarle	356.2	3 484	49.8	9.7	4.8	4.1	0.2	444.7	4 349	[3]1 228	[3]920	[3]28 353	58.4	40.4	1.2
Alleghany	59.6	3 670	51.9	0.6	5.0	6.2	1.3	32.8	2 020	[4]64	[4]69	[4]1 563	48.2	50.4	1.4
Amelia	26.9	2 108	60.3	2.6	6.3	6.1	1.7	4.0	313	25	41	463	38.1	60.8	1.1
Amherst	71.6	2 212	62.9	0.8	7.1	6.1	0.1	27.2	840	45	98	2 699	41.5	57.6	0.9
Appomattox	35.6	2 351	57.9	1.0	6.3	6.5	0.0	34.6	2 285	47	49	768	34.6	64.3	1.1
Arlington	2 639.2	11 940	16.7	1.1	2.2	3.0	2.0	8 672.6	39 235	28 226	8 804	12 017	71.7	27.1	1.2
Augusta	170.0	2 308	65.1	0.6	3.9	8.2	0.9	103.4	1 404	[5]256	[5]378	[5]8 468	29.5	69.4	1.2
Bath	17.3	3 728	54.1	1.3	5.9	4.2	0.0	9.3	1 990	30	15	356	42.9	55.5	1.6
Bedford	182.3	2 619	49.8	0.5	3.6	8.7	0.1	152.7	2 194	[6]127	[6]245	[6]2 936	30.7	68.2	1.1
Bland	15.8	2 338	54.4	0.9	6.4	8.4	6.8	5.0	743	15	19	614	29.2	68.6	2.2
Botetourt	82.4	2 486	63.3	0.6	6.0	3.8	0.0	55.7	1 681	53	106	1 377	32.7	65.9	1.4
Brunswick	41.2	2 421	57.0	0.6	6.4	7.4	0.2	19.3	1 133	41	47	1 081	62.8	36.4	0.8
Buchanan	84.4	3 538	45.9	0.7	4.7	11.2	11.3	12.4	520	65	71	1 559	46.5	52.0	1.5
Buckingham	45.4	2 658	45.9	1.1	3.9	6.2	0.1	68.7	4 022	29	48	1 273	49.9	49.0	1.1
Campbell	128.3	2 326	59.4	5.8	4.7	7.0	2.3	58.2	1 055	[7]339	[7]440	[7]6 978	31.3	67.6	1.1
Caroline	67.8	2 338	54.8	0.4	8.4	6.1	3.4	132.8	4 584	463	114	1 205	55.4	43.5	1.1
Carroll	84.4	2 829	57.3	7.7	4.7	6.3	0.7	59.6	1 996	[8]94	[8]116	[8]2 417	32.7	65.1	2.2
Charles City	20.4	2 844	63.8	0.5	3.9	5.3	0.0	2.7	382	18	23	325	68.3	31.0	0.7
Charlotte	37.5	3 022	59.8	2.5	5.0	11.4	0.1	6.2	500	42	39	949	43.9	54.8	1.3
Chesterfield	985.4	3 043	54.6	5.0	6.6	4.1	1.2	716.3	2 212	2 892	1 101	17 817	45.8	53.3	0.8
Clarke	61.0	4 259	55.3	0.7	3.6	3.6	0.4	147.7	10 315	31	46	706	46.5	51.7	1.8
Craig	12.6	2 425	55.8	1.3	6.8	12.8	0.3	4.1	793	15	17	231	33.5	64.7	1.9
Culpeper	140.4	2 931	53.3	0.9	7.6	9.8	2.8	122.9	2 566	217	154	3 158	44.6	54.3	1.2
Cumberland	23.1	2 345	63.3	1.2	6.5	4.8	0.0	44.0	4 466	11	32	442	47.7	51.2	1.1
Dickenson	61.5	3 918	45.4	5.6	3.7	9.6	1.7	13.6	869	37	48	898	48.5	49.2	2.2
Dinwiddie	72.2	2 580	60.9	3.9	5.4	4.8	0.1	113.2	4 044	[9]228	[9]250	[9]6 299	48.4	50.6	0.9
Essex	34.5	3 071	57.7	0.0	5.0	9.0	1.4	48.6	4 329	16	35	535	54.7	44.4	1.0
Fairfax	4 854.2	4 340	51.6	4.1	4.6	6.0	2.1	5 037.1	4 503	[10]45 254	[10]9 848	[10]61 135	60.1	38.9	0.9
Fauquier	242.3	3 641	59.7	0.4	7.0	4.2	1.2	187.2	2 813	601	219	3 693	42.7	56.2	1.1
Floyd	26.9	1 751	66.1	2.5	5.5	3.9	0.0	15.6	1 013	47	51	608	39.1	59.1	1.8
Fluvanna	74.8	2 882	70.0	0.8	3.4	6.6	0.3	91.0	3 506	27	80	1 276	48.6	50.4	1.0
Franklin	130.9	2 320	61.7	0.5	4.3	7.9	1.1	36.2	641	96	177	2 370	37.9	60.7	1.5
Frederick	220.1	2 740	72.6	0.5	5.1	2.7	0.1	196.2	2 443	[11]2 024	[11]367	[11]5 962	38.6	59.9	1.5
Giles	49.2	2 909	47.4	0.4	7.2	7.5	2.9	61.0	3 603	40	54	852	40.9	57.2	1.8
Gloucester	94.6	2 564	65.7	1.1	5.1	5.2	0.1	62.6	1 698	84	119	2 149	36.0	62.9	1.1
Goochland	45.4	2 128	55.2	1.1	5.8	4.2	0.5	133.0	6 229	37	68	1 338	38.3	60.8	0.8
Grayson	35.4	2 329	60.0	0.4	6.1	6.7	0.3	38.8	2 555	31	48	1 051	34.3	62.9	2.8
Greene	53.8	2 869	65.7	0.8	5.7	5.5	1.9	57.6	3 067	33	61	814	38.4	60.3	1.3
Greensville	52.0	4 385	49.3	0.3	4.8	5.4	0.4	56.1	4 732	[12]34	[12]45	[12]1 798	63.9	35.4	0.7
Halifax	113.2	3 157	52.4	10.5	5.0	6.6	2.0	72.1	2 012	86	111	2 103	48.2	51.0	0.7
Hanover	342.5	3 403	52.1	0.4	6.9	6.6	1.7	364.1	3 617	151	324	4 715	32.8	66.4	0.8
Henrico	1 095.4	3 478	45.2	3.0	6.3	2.5	4.7	980.8	3 114	2 109	1 031	16 980	55.7	43.5	0.8
Henry	127.8	2 414	68.2	0.9	4.2	6.1	0.0	28.3	534	[13]134	[13]209	[13]3 917	44.1	54.6	1.3
Highland	7.7	3 440	49.1	2.3	7.9	4.4	7.0	0.7	311	10	0	160	38.0	59.8	2.2
Isle of Wight	103.6	2 926	49.8	4.9	5.6	3.1	1.0	149.3	4 218	87	115	1 439	42.9	56.3	0.8
James City	260.7	3 781	54.2	6.4	4.7	1.9	0.0	269.9	3 914	[14]224	[14]383	[14]8 175	44.9	54.2	0.9
King and Queen	25.3	3 591	43.8	0.8	5.0	7.9	0.0	5.0	707	0	23	275	51.8	47.6	0.6
King George	72.4	2 957	53.1	0.9	9.0	6.0	0.1	190.9	7 793	4 479	519	1 043	42.7	56.2	1.1
King William	48.1	3 007	64.8	0.3	6.0	3.6	0.6	39.7	2 483	23	52	723	39.9	59.2	0.9
Lancaster	31.1	2 771	52.2	1.4	6.6	6.9	0.5	18.4	1 636	34	35	540	46.6	52.6	0.8
Lee	59.5	2 335	64.3	1.3	5.4	10.3	0.4	7.4	290	433	75	1 146	34.9	63.1	2.0
Loudoun	1 488.4	4 418	60.1	2.4	5.3	2.4	1.9	1 679.5	4 985	3 840	1 169	18 854	53.7	45.4	0.9

1. Based on the resident population estimated as of July 1 of the year shown. 2. © 2013 Election Data Services, Inc. All rights reserved. 3. Charlottesville city is included with Albemarle county. 4. Covington city is included with Alleghany county. 5. Staunton and Waynesboro cities are included with Augusta county. 6. Bedford city is included with Bedford county. 7. Lynchburg city is included with Campbell county. 8. Galax city is included with Carroll county. 9. Petersburg and Colonial Heights cities are included with Dinwiddie county. 10. Fairfax city and Falls Church city are included with Fairfax county. 11. Winchester city is included with Frederick county. 12. Emporia city is included with Greensville county. 13. Martinsville city is included with Henry county. 14. Williamsburg city is included with James City county.

Table B. States and Counties — **Land Area and Population**

					Population, 2015			Population and population characteristics, 2014										
								Race alone or in combination, not Hispanic or Latino (percent)					Age (percent)					
STATE/ County code	CBSA code[1]	County type[2]	STATE County	Land area,[3] (sq km) 2010	Total persons 2015	Rank	Per square kilometer	White	Black	Amer- ican Indian, Alaska Native	Asian and Pacific Islander	Percent Hispanic or Latino[4]	Under 5 years	5 to 17 years	18 to 24 years	25 to 34 years	35 to 44 years	45 to 54 years
				1	2	3	4	5	6	7	8	9	10	11	12	13	14	15
			VIRGINIA—Cont'd															
51 109	...	1	Louisa	1 285	34 602	1 314	26.9	79.9	17.9	0.9	1.0	2.5	5.6	15.4	7.1	11.2	11.8	15.8
51 111	...	9	Lunenburg	1 118	12 299	2 276	11.0	61.6	34.4	0.8	0.6	4.2	4.4	14.3	7.6	11.6	12.2	14.3
51 113	...	8	Madison	831	13 134	2 225	15.8	87.8	11.0	0.9	0.9	2.1	5.0	16.0	7.7	10.0	10.7	14.7
51 115	47260	1	Mathews	223	8 862	2 524	39.7	88.1	10.1	1.1	1.2	2.1	3.7	13.2	6.6	7.7	9.2	14.3
51 117	...	7	Mecklenburg	1 620	31 081	1 409	19.2	61.7	35.6	0.8	1.3	2.7	4.8	14.3	7.2	9.7	10.6	13.8
51 119	...	8	Middlesex	337	10 606	2 386	31.5	80.0	18.5	0.9	0.8	2.2	4.1	11.5	6.3	8.8	8.6	13.9
51 121	13980	3	Montgomery	1 002	97 653	603	97.5	86.5	4.8	0.6	7.1	3.0	4.5	11.5	28.5	14.3	10.4	10.2
51 125	16820	3	Nelson	1 220	14 785	2 117	12.1	83.3	13.3	0.9	0.9	3.5	4.5	14.3	6.6	9.6	9.9	13.7
51 127	40060	1	New Kent	543	20 392	1 813	37.6	81.7	14.5	1.9	1.8	2.6	4.8	16.0	7.7	11.0	12.8	16.4
51 131	...	9	Northampton	548	12 155	2 289	22.2	55.8	35.8	0.8	1.1	8.5	5.8	14.1	7.0	10.2	9.3	12.3
51 133	...	9	Northumberland	495	12 232	2 282	24.7	71.2	25.1	0.7	0.5	3.6	3.9	12.0	5.9	7.6	7.2	12.3
51 135	...	6	Nottoway	814	15 673	2 065	19.3	56.5	39.6	0.8	0.7	4.0	6.1	14.2	8.3	13.3	11.7	14.5
51 137	...	6	Orange	883	35 385	1 292	40.1	81.3	14.3	1.0	1.8	4.3	5.8	16.1	7.5	11.3	11.7	14.3
51 139	...	6	Page	805	23 726	1 653	29.5	95.3	2.5	0.5	0.7	1.9	5.0	15.4	7.3	11.0	12.1	15.1
51 141	...	8	Patrick	1 251	18 045	1 916	14.4	91.0	6.5	0.6	0.4	2.8	4.0	14.1	6.6	8.8	11.7	15.1
51 143	19260	3	Pittsylvania	2 510	62 194	846	24.8	75.1	22.1	0.6	0.7	2.4	4.3	15.6	7.5	10.0	11.6	15.4
51 145	40060	1	Powhatan	674	28 031	1 482	41.6	84.4	13.0	0.7	0.9	2.0	3.9	15.3	8.5	10.2	13.7	17.8
51 147	...	6	Prince Edward	906	22 952	1 684	25.3	63.9	33.2	0.7	1.6	2.5	4.1	12.4	26.5	10.2	8.7	11.1
51 149	40060	1	Prince George	687	37 862	1 228	55.1	58.2	32.2	1.3	3.0	7.5	5.2	15.9	9.2	15.6	14.3	14.1
51 153	47900	1	Prince William	871	451 721	151	518.6	49.1	22.0	0.9	10.2	22.1	7.9	20.1	8.9	14.5	15.4	14.7
51 155	13980	3	Pulaski	828	34 332	1 321	41.5	92.4	6.2	0.6	0.8	1.5	4.8	13.6	7.4	10.9	12.7	14.7
51 157	47900	8	Rappahannock	690	7 378	2 642	10.7	91.0	5.6	0.8	1.1	3.4	3.7	13.9	7.1	8.6	10.1	15.2
51 159	...	9	Richmond	496	8 908	2 521	18.0	63.0	30.8	0.8	1.0	6.5	4.0	13.1	7.5	14.0	12.9	15.8
51 161	40220	2	Roanoke	649	94 409	620	145.5	88.1	6.4	0.6	3.8	2.7	4.8	16.0	8.1	10.4	12.4	14.4
51 163	...	6	Rockbridge	1 548	22 354	1 712	14.4	94.0	3.3	1.2	0.9	1.6	3.9	13.5	6.9	10.4	10.3	14.6
51 165	25500	3	Rockingham	2 199	78 593	706	35.7	91.2	2.5	0.5	1.0	6.0	5.4	17.0	9.3	11.1	11.7	13.8
51 167	...	6	Russell	1 227	27 891	1 494	22.7	97.5	1.2	0.5	0.4	1.1	5.2	14.5	7.6	11.1	12.4	14.6
51 169	28700	3	Scott	1 387	22 126	1 725	16.0	97.5	1.1	0.6	0.3	1.3	4.8	14.1	7.2	10.9	12.2	14.5
51 171	...	6	Shenandoah	1 318	43 190	1 107	32.8	90.3	2.8	0.7	1.0	6.8	5.6	15.9	7.5	11.1	11.2	14.4
51 173	...	6	Smyth	1 168	31 470	1 397	26.9	95.3	2.8	0.6	0.6	1.8	4.9	15.2	8.1	10.7	12.5	14.2
51 175	...	6	Southampton	1 552	18 109	1 911	11.7	61.3	36.3	0.8	0.7	1.3	4.4	14.6	7.6	10.2	11.3	17.8
51 177	47900	1	Spotsylvania	1 040	130 475	480	125.5	72.8	17.1	0.9	3.7	8.7	6.1	19.5	9.0	12.5	13.3	15.4
51 179	47900	1	Stafford	697	142 003	450	203.7	67.7	18.8	1.1	4.7	11.3	6.4	20.4	10.5	13.2	13.5	16.1
51 181	...	9	Surry	722	6 709	2 703	9.3	53.7	44.4	0.9	0.6	1.7	4.5	13.8	8.1	10.6	9.3	17.4
51 183	40060	1	Sussex	1 270	11 715	2 311	9.2	39.5	57.6	0.5	0.7	2.8	4.6	11.4	10.1	16.9	12.4	15.1
51 185	14140	7	Tazewell	1 344	42 899	1 116	31.9	94.7	4.0	0.5	0.9	0.9	5.0	14.6	8.2	11.2	12.6	13.6
51 187	47900	1	Warren	553	39 083	1 202	70.7	89.3	5.9	1.0	1.6	4.1	5.8	16.7	9.0	12.1	12.1	15.9
51 191	28700	3	Washington	1 453	54 591	921	37.6	96.4	1.8	0.5	0.7	1.4	4.9	14.2	8.2	10.8	12.1	14.6
51 193	...	7	Westmoreland	594	17 629	1 939	29.7	65.6	28.1	1.2	1.2	6.1	5.4	13.1	7.5	10.8	9.5	13.5
51 195	13720	7	Wise	1 044	39 718	1 181	38.0	92.8	5.8	0.5	0.6	1.2	5.4	14.6	10.2	13.5	12.9	13.3
51 197	...	6	Wythe	1 196	29 119	1 452	24.3	95.4	3.6	0.5	0.8	1.1	5.0	15.1	7.2	11.0	12.7	14.4
51 199	47260	1	York	271	67 837	785	250.3	74.8	14.1	0.9	7.1	5.8	5.3	18.8	9.5	11.4	12.3	15.4
	...		Independent cities															
51 510	47900	1	Alexandria city	39	153 511	423	3 936.2	54.2	22.5	0.8	8.2	16.5	7.5	10.2	5.9	23.6	18.3	13.5
51 515	31340	3	Bedford city	NA	NA	NA	NA	NA	NA	NA	NA	NA	NA	NA	NA	NA	NA	NA
51 520	28700	3	Bristol city	34	17 141	1 971	504.1	90.4	6.8	0.6	1.3	1.7	4.5	15.4	8.1	12.8	12.5	13.4
51 530	...	6	Buena Vista city	17	6 618	2 707	389.3	90.6	6.2	1.7	1.3	2.5	6.3	15.6	13.8	12.4	10.1	12.2
51 540	16820	3	Charlottesville city	27	46 597	1 036	1 725.8	68.6	20.1	0.7	8.6	4.9	5.7	9.9	22.7	20.6	11.3	10.2
51 550	47260	1	Chesapeake city	883	235 429	280	266.6	61.3	30.8	1.0	4.7	5.3	6.3	18.2	9.4	14.2	13.1	14.7
51 570	40060	1	Colonial Heights city	19	17 820	1 929	937.9	78.2	14.3	1.0	4.2	5.3	7.1	15.9	8.5	12.0	11.1	13.1
51 580	...	6	Covington city	14	5 658	2 787	404.1	85.3	14.4	0.9	1.1	2.5	7.1	15.4	8.3	11.4	11.4	14.4
51 590	19260	3	Danville city	111	42 082	1 126	379.1	46.1	50.1	0.6	1.6	3.4	6.9	15.4	9.2	11.9	9.9	12.5
51 595	...	6	Emporia city	18	5 496	2 803	305.3	29.7	61.9	0.4	1.4	5.4	4.2	19.6	9.2	12.2	11.5	13.2
51 600	47900	1	Fairfax city	16	24 013	1 644	1 500.8	63.2	5.9	0.8	19.1	17.2	9.0	14.5	8.4	14.2	12.6	13.7
51 610	47900	1	Falls Church city	5	13 892	2 173	2 778.4	76.5	6.0	0.8	11.8	9.6	7.3	19.4	6.7	11.9	11.2	15.5
51 620	...	6	Franklin city	21	8 490	2 557	404.3	39.9	58.7	0.8	1.4	2.4	8.8	17.4	8.3	11.5	10.1	12.4
51 630	47900	1	Fredericksburg city	27	28 118	1 481	1 041.4	62.8	24.7	0.9	4.2	10.9	7.2	13.1	20.5	16.7	12.0	11.3
51 640	...	6	Galax city	21	6 914	2 681	329.2	79.6	7.4	0.5	0.8	14.9	7.4	16.5	8.0	10.6	10.9	12.9
51 650	47260	1	Hampton city	133	136 454	463	1 026.0	42.3	50.4	1.4	3.6	5.3	6.3	15.5	12.1	15.7	11.0	13.2
51 660	25500	3	Harrisonburg city	45	52 538	951	1 167.5	70.4	8.0	0.5	5.0	18.7	5.3	10.9	34.3	15.6	9.7	8.5
51 670	40060	1	Hopewell city	27	22 378	1 710	828.8	53.0	40.1	1.0	2.0	7.2	7.5	17.8	8.8	14.1	11.5	13.1
51 678	...	6	Lexington city	6	7 262	2 649	1 210.3	84.9	10.5	0.9	4.4	3.9	3.7	8.6	45.2	8.4	6.0	6.1
51 680	31340	3	Lynchburg city	127	79 812	696	628.4	65.2	29.6	0.8	3.7	3.4	6.3	13.5	24.2	13.1	8.9	9.8
51 683	47900	1	Manassas city	26	41 764	1 130	1 606.3	47.2	15.4	0.8	7.0	34.3	8.6	18.3	9.6	16.3	14.5	13.6

1. CBSA = Core Based Statistical Area. See Appendix A for explanation. See Appendix B for list of metropolitan areas with component counties. Service of USDA Rural-Urban Continuum Codes. See Appendix A for definition. 3. Dry land or land partially or temporarily covered by water. 2. County type code from the Economic Research 4. May be of any race.

STATE County	Age (percent) (cont.) 55 to 64 years	65 to 74 years	75 years and over	Percent female	Population change and components of change, 2000–2015 — Total persons 2000	2010	Percent change 2000–2010	2010–2015	Components of change, 2010–2015 Births	Deaths	Net migration	Households, 2010–2014 Number	Persons per house-hold	Percent Family house-holds	Female family house-holder[1]	One per-son
	16	17	18	19	20	21	22	23	24	25	26	27	28	29	30	31
VIRGINIA—Cont'd																
Louisa	15.7	11.3	6.3	50.6	25 627	33 223	29.6	4.2	1 979	1 550	889	12 811	2.62	72.5	9.6	22.4
Lunenburg	16.0	11.4	8.2	47.3	13 146	12 916	-1.7	-4.8	608	788	-446	4 634	2.43	68.3	13.4	29.0
Madison	15.4	11.8	8.7	51.4	12 520	13 308	6.3	-1.3	641	659	-147	5 093	2.55	71.2	11.8	22.1
Mathews	17.0	16.3	12.0	51.7	9 207	8 976	-2.5	-1.3	300	593	208	3 792	2.32	73.2	8.8	24.2
Mecklenburg	15.8	13.7	10.1	51.6	32 380	32 727	1.1	-5.0	1 507	2 310	-869	12 857	2.36	62.7	14.3	34.4
Middlesex	17.7	17.4	11.7	50.8	9 932	10 959	10.3	-3.2	417	745	-32	4 432	2.36	67.4	8.9	29.3
Montgomery	9.7	6.4	4.6	47.9	83 629	94 412	12.9	3.4	4 702	3 139	1 764	34 803	2.48	53.9	6.9	28.1
Nelson	17.8	14.9	8.8	51.4	14 445	15 020	4.0	-1.6	703	905	21	6 381	2.31	63.4	13.2	30.0
New Kent	16.1	10.6	4.5	49.0	13 462	18 432	36.9	10.6	938	715	1 704	7 106	2.62	77.2	8.6	18.8
Northampton	16.8	13.6	10.8	51.6	13 093	12 389	-5.4	-1.9	757	1 005	7	5 237	2.28	58.0	12.9	36.1
Northumberland	16.9	20.4	13.9	50.5	12 259	12 326	0.5	-0.8	491	898	315	5 669	2.17	68.1	10.6	28.2
Nottoway	13.5	10.1	8.3	47.0	15 725	15 852	0.8	-1.1	927	1 044	-83	5 640	2.57	65.4	13.4	30.0
Orange	13.5	11.4	8.4	51.0	25 881	33 434	29.2	5.8	1 997	1 742	1 724	12 433	2.71	74.5	12.2	21.9
Page	14.3	11.4	8.3	50.4	23 177	24 055	3.8	-1.4	1 233	1 465	-105	9 526	2.49	71.1	12.5	23.8
Patrick	15.5	14.2	10.0	50.9	19 407	18 487	-4.7	-2.4	748	1 322	149	7 678	2.36	65.6	10.7	29.9
Pittsylvania	15.7	12.0	8.0	50.9	61 745	63 504	2.8	-2.1	2 814	3 662	-472	26 029	2.38	70.0	12.9	26.9
Powhatan	14.8	10.6	5.1	46.3	22 377	28 046	25.3	-0.1	1 233	1 044	-268	9 590	2.64	80.3	10.5	17.2
Prince Edward	11.7	8.1	7.3	50.9	19 720	23 360	18.5	-1.7	1 059	1 115	-349	7 604	2.45	64.6	15.8	28.0
Prince George	12.0	7.8	4.6	45.1	33 047	35 724	8.1	6.0	1 939	1 199	1 405	10 906	2.98	81.3	10.7	16.8
Prince William	10.2	5.5	2.8	50.2	280 813	401 972	43.1	12.4	35 072	8 632	23 180	134 737	3.15	77.5	11.9	17.8
Pulaski	15.3	12.7	7.9	49.9	35 127	34 859	-0.8	-1.5	1 671	2 199	70	15 125	2.23	67.2	12.7	28.1
Rappahannock	17.6	14.8	9.0	50.2	6 983	7 506	7.5	-1.7	308	376	-50	3 281	2.26	65.6	3.6	28.0
Richmond	13.1	9.8	9.7	44.5	8 809	9 254	5.1	-3.7	377	506	-218	2 800	2.56	66.1	14.3	29.1
Roanoke	14.3	10.9	8.7	52.0	85 778	92 439	7.8	2.1	4 408	4 966	2 349	38 197	2.38	67.0	9.8	29.0
Rockbridge	16.1	13.3	11.0	50.6	20 808	22 310	7.2	0.2	974	1 235	261	9 226	2.40	67.6	7.7	26.4
Rockingham	13.6	9.8	8.2	51.0	67 725	76 310	12.7	3.0	4 369	3 656	1 357	29 483	2.57	72.4	10.0	22.8
Russell	15.8	11.2	7.6	51.2	30 308	28 896	-4.7	-3.5	1 448	1 839	-580	11 037	2.54	66.9	10.1	30.0
Scott	14.8	12.2	9.2	49.9	23 403	23 172	-1.0	-4.5	1 030	1 547	-574	9 363	2.37	69.8	9.9	27.9
Shenandoah	14.0	11.5	8.7	51.2	35 075	41 993	19.7	2.9	2 451	2 364	1 101	17 246	2.44	69.5	9.7	26.2
Smyth	14.5	11.2	8.8	51.0	33 081	32 208	-2.6	-2.3	1 668	2 264	-133	12 852	2.43	68.9	12.0	27.6
Southampton	16.0	10.5	7.5	48.1	17 482	18 570	6.2	-2.5	858	1 020	-350	6 654	2.51	73.5	16.4	22.6
Spotsylvania	11.9	7.6	4.6	50.8	90 395	122 660	35.7	6.4	8 184	4 155	3 641	42 280	2.98	78.7	12.3	17.1
Stafford	10.7	5.8	3.3	49.6	92 446	128 952	39.5	10.1	9 052	3 405	7 256	42 763	3.07	81.3	11.2	15.0
Surry	17.2	11.8	7.3	50.7	6 829	7 065	3.5	-5.0	334	359	-304	2 652	2.60	71.5	15.0	23.6
Sussex	13.3	9.3	6.9	40.6	12 504	12 083	-3.4	-3.0	549	688	-238	3 261	2.06	62.0	18.6	33.1
Tazewell	15.6	11.1	8.1	50.3	44 598	45 078	1.1	-4.8	2 314	3 331	-1 155	18 306	2.35	67.6	10.5	28.7
Warren	13.7	9.0	5.6	50.1	31 584	37 431	18.5	4.4	2 460	1 856	1 017	14 324	2.61	70.8	12.4	23.8
Washington	15.0	12.0	8.2	50.7	51 103	54 870	7.4	-0.5	2 810	3 218	137	22 842	2.33	67.5	10.5	28.2
Westmoreland	16.6	13.9	9.8	51.4	16 718	17 454	4.4	1.0	996	1 037	217	6 981	2.49	62.8	12.2	32.2
Wise	14.2	9.6	6.3	48.2	40 123	41 476	3.4	-4.2	2 331	2 523	-1 558	15 517	2.44	67.4	12.6	27.4
Wythe	14.9	11.4	8.3	51.1	27 599	29 232	5.9	-0.4	1 431	1 813	297	11 984	2.42	66.6	10.8	29.7
York	12.7	8.7	5.9	50.7	56 297	65 191	15.8	4.1	3 259	2 127	1 422	23 970	2.71	78.2	11.8	18.2
Independent cities																
Alexandria city	10.9	6.3	3.8	51.6	128 283	140 006	9.1	9.6	14 420	3 868	3 155	65 916	2.20	47.6	8.1	42.7
Bedford city	NA	NA	NA	NA	6 299	NA	NA	NA	NA	NA	NA	NA	NA	NA	NA	NA
Bristol city	13.4	10.7	9.1	52.5	17 367	17 841	2.7	-3.9	851	1 254	-260	7 764	2.21	64.5	18.1	30.3
Buena Vista city	12.0	10.5	7.1	53.2	6 349	6 651	4.8	-0.5	442	371	-118	2 741	2.27	65.3	10.4	31.8
Charlottesville city	10.1	5.5	3.9	51.7	45 049	43 435	-3.6	7.3	2 913	1 368	1 619	17 604	2.37	43.6	10.4	37.0
Chesapeake city	12.4	7.2	4.7	51.0	199 184	222 209	11.6	5.9	14 782	8 655	6 961	80 388	2.76	74.9	15.5	20.9
Colonial Heights city	12.0	9.9	10.2	53.8	16 897	17 413	3.1	2.3	1 221	1 079	264	7 025	2.47	64.8	14.8	28.6
Covington city	13.1	10.9	8.0	50.6	6 303	5 954	-5.5	-5.0	353	345	-343	2 468	2.34	57.1	12.8	40.0
Danville city	14.4	10.3	9.5	53.8	48 411	43 059	-11.1	-2.3	2 819	3 570	-334	18 520	2.22	59.6	21.0	35.9
Emporia city	12.7	8.7	8.8	53.8	5 665	5 927	4.6	-7.3	328	457	-307	2 420	2.25	58.8	23.5	36.5
Fairfax city	12.3	8.4	7.1	50.7	21 498	22 542	4.9	6.5	2 003	1 007	356	8 480	2.71	65.8	9.7	21.7
Falls Church city	13.1	6.9	4.5	51.0	10 377	12 289	18.4	13.0	892	361	1 133	4 966	2.63	63.1	10.4	32.2
Franklin city	14.0	9.5	7.9	54.9	8 346	8 580	2.8	-1.0	686	609	-178	3 580	2.35	67.4	28.9	29.8
Fredericksburg city	9.2	5.7	4.4	54.5	19 279	24 023	24.6	17.0	2 196	969	2 702	9 849	2.44	55.2	18.0	35.7
Galax city	13.5	9.9	10.1	53.0	6 837	6 989	2.2	-1.1	542	522	-125	2 968	2.24	58.1	15.4	37.8
Hampton city	12.7	7.9	5.8	51.9	146 437	137 510	-6.1	-0.8	9 779	6 104	-4 606	52 700	2.51	62.8	18.2	30.9
Harrisonburg city	7.5	4.1	4.0	52.1	40 468	48 907	20.9	7.4	2 889	1 269	1 817	15 881	2.73	50.7	9.4	26.3
Hopewell city	11.5	8.7	7.0	53.3	22 354	22 591	1.1	-0.9	1 852	1 400	-692	8 774	2.53	62.1	22.8	33.5
Lexington city	7.8	6.7	7.4	44.4	6 867	7 038	2.5	3.2	275	284	196	1 727	2.09	49.6	9.3	41.3
Lynchburg city	10.0	7.1	7.0	53.2	65 269	75 608	15.8	5.6	5 478	3 985	2 644	28 424	2.38	57.0	15.5	34.7
Manassas city	10.8	5.1	3.1	49.7	35 135	37 839	7.7	10.4	3 585	925	1 244	12 274	3.29	74.7	14.5	20.3

1. No spouse present.

Table B. States and Counties — Population, Vital Statistics, Medicare, and Crime

STATE County	Persons in group quarters, 2015	Daytime population, 2010–2014 Number	Daytime population Employment/residence ratio	Births, 2015 Total	Births, 2015 Rate[1]	Deaths, 2015 Number	Deaths, 2015 Rate[1]	Persons under 65 with no health insurance, 2014 Number	Persons under 65 no health insurance Percent	Medicare, 2015 Total Beneficiaries	Medicare Enrolled in Original Medicare	Medicare Enrolled in Medicare Advantage	Serious crimes known to police,[2] 2014 Total Number	Serious crimes Rate[3]
	32	33	34	35	36	37	38	39	40	41	42	43	44	45
VIRGINIA—Cont'd														
Louisa	211	27 912	0.63	366	10.6	321	9.3	4 129	14.6	6 746	5 324	1 422	700	2 051
Lunenburg	947	10 737	0.57	109	8.8	159	12.8	1 652	18.2	2 166	1 708	458	91	731
Madison	193	10 322	0.52	130	9.9	108	8.2	1 699	16.3	2 342	1 934	408	114	865
Mathews	86	6 999	0.51	54	6.1	117	13.3	855	13.5	2 565	2 153	412	92	1 036
Mecklenburg	930	32 508	1.05	281	9.0	457	14.7	3 884	16.7	8 520	6 909	1 611	621	1 995
Middlesex	383	9 786	0.76	78	7.3	122	11.5	977	13.3	3 433	2 794	639	157	1 465
Montgomery	9 414	101 988	1.14	898	9.2	587	6.0	10 775	13.9	11 870	9 368	2 502	1 493	1 544
Nelson	102	12 807	0.68	132	8.9	139	9.4	1 886	16.7	4 609	3 832	777	189	1 281
New Kent	551	13 414	0.41	172	8.5	118	5.8	1 922	11.7	3 043	2 427	616	331	1 675
Northampton	262	12 410	1.03	146	12.0	209	17.2	1 728	19.1	3 216	2 440	776	179	1 484
Northumberland	0	10 701	0.66	84	6.9	168	13.7	1 417	17.6	3 952	3 412	540	133	1 093
Nottoway	2 216	16 822	1.18	185	11.8	203	13.0	1 718	15.4	3 421	2 632	789	297	1 884
Orange	601	28 100	0.58	390	11.1	304	8.6	3 914	14.1	8 542	7 219	1 323	439	1 254
Page	194	20 348	0.64	233	9.8	278	11.7	2 911	15.3	5 426	4 716	710	414	1 741
Patrick	263	16 709	0.76	132	7.3	231	12.7	2 300	16.7	4 999	3 589	1 410	280	1 526
Pittsylvania	1 053	51 842	0.59	503	8.1	703	11.3	7 042	14.3	10 481	8 523	1 958	502	808
Powhatan	1 439	22 161	0.54	225	8.0	222	7.9	2 532	11.6	4 960	3 806	1 154	314	1 109
Prince Edward	4 227	25 316	1.26	211	9.2	220	9.6	2 534	16.2	5 042	3 840	1 202	432	1 905
Prince George	4 605	42 771	1.39	321	8.5	234	6.2	3 169	11.3	3 538	3 037	501	410	1 088
Prince William	2 626	341 926	0.61	6 874	15.3	1 753	3.9	50 728	12.5	26 463	21 262	5 201	6 835	1 528
Pulaski	1 148	33 367	0.92	315	9.2	399	11.6	3 253	12.3	7 561	5 880	1 681	936	2 717
Rappahannock	35	6 381	0.69	46	6.2	69	9.4	926	16.6	2 197	1 985	212	39	522
Richmond	1 635	9 361	1.10	78	8.8	89	10.0	978	17.2	1 815	1 427	388	77	867
Roanoke	2 201	84 054	0.80	870	9.2	928	9.9	7 177	9.7	8 757	6 983	1 774	1 621	1 728
Rockbridge	175	19 885	0.74	158	7.1	221	9.9	2 509	14.9	2 974	2 324	650	395	1 769
Rockingham	1 583	73 873	0.91	803	10.2	718	9.2	9 637	15.4	11 978	9 753	2 225	774	991
Russell	434	26 022	0.76	290	10.4	342	12.2	3 272	14.5	7 222	4 877	2 345	439	1 560
Scott	706	19 840	0.65	191	8.6	290	13.0	2 466	14.4	6 400	3 200	3 200	353	1 567
Shenandoah	427	37 446	0.74	468	10.9	450	10.5	4 954	14.5	9 389	8 211	1 178	602	1 404
Smyth	887	31 465	0.97	319	10.1	455	14.4	3 427	13.7	8 127	6 352	1 775	573	1 817
Southampton	1 711	14 208	0.50	136	7.5	200	11.0	1 883	14.0	2 592	2 013	579	277	1 536
Spotsylvania	524	101 190	0.59	1 548	11.9	864	6.7	13 564	12.0	9 991	8 477	1 514	2 199	1 711
Stafford	3 793	108 670	0.61	1 809	12.8	676	4.8	11 396	9.3	14 545	12 747	1 798	2 362	1 703
Surry	0	6 175	0.77	67	9.9	56	8.3	746	13.6	1 319	958	361	71	1 060
Sussex	2 634	12 526	1.21	100	8.5	136	11.6	1 082	14.7	2 618	1 885	733	145	1 232
Tazewell	1 828	44 862	1.03	432	10.0	613	14.2	5 172	15.3	12 099	8 405	3 694	1 064	2 425
Warren	799	33 535	0.75	495	12.7	350	9.0	4 551	13.9	5 976	5 321	655	811	2 078
Washington	1 664	54 697	0.99	625	11.4	590	10.8	5 799	13.7	11 146	7 724	3 422	1 100	2 002
Westmoreland	70	14 426	0.57	185	10.5	203	11.6	2 308	17.3	4 253	3 569	684	262	1 483
Wise	3 028	44 096	1.24	436	10.9	461	11.6	4 540	14.6	10 494	6 855	3 639	976	2 418
Wythe	260	29 449	1.02	270	9.3	357	12.3	3 343	14.3	8 488	6 747	1 741	379	1 290
York	648	57 861	0.75	636	9.5	469	7.0	5 033	9.0	16 888	14 708	2 180	1 217	1 828
Independent cities														
Alexandria city	1 831	152 225	1.06	2 818	18.5	759	5.0	17 440	13.1	16 029	14 060	1 969	3 263	2 160
Bedford city	NA	NA	NA	NA	NA	NA	NA	NA	NA	NA	NA	NA	NA	NA
Bristol city	219	21 636	1.57	59	3.4	234	13.6	1 953	14.3	7 483	4 495	2 988	537	3 118
Buena Vista city	470	5 738	0.68	84	12.7	70	10.6	717	14.1	1 867	1 337	530	63	941
Charlottesville city	2 418	58 292	1.62	641	13.9	288	6.2	6 109	15.5	12 962	10 910	2 052	1 550	3 477
Chesapeake city	4 360	213 139	0.86	2 888	12.3	1 730	7.4	21 831	10.8	29 992	23 440	6 552	7 428	3 195
Colonial Heights city	171	19 332	1.23	316	17.9	185	10.5	1 757	12.4	4 724	3 906	818	905	5 111
Covington city	75	5 484	0.84	78	13.7	56	9.9	683	14.7	4 187	3 532	655	122	2 109
Danville city	1 564	51 536	1.56	553	13.1	645	15.3	4 743	14.3	14 839	12 335	2 504	1 965	4 577
Emporia city	246	6 717	1.51	45	8.1	71	12.8	698	15.6	2 528	1 679	849	306	5 553
Fairfax city	521	48 055	2.99	630	26.4	236	9.9	2 270	11.1	14 513	12 301	2 212	464	1 906
Falls Church city	42	16 882	1.52	221	16.1	75	5.5	552	4.6	1 999	1 703	296	239	1 733
Franklin city	129	9 681	1.36	158	18.7	83	9.8	1 012	14.4	2 910	2 295	615	NA	NA
Fredericksburg city	2 580	39 875	2.08	431	15.3	223	7.9	2 996	13.1	7 546	6 351	1 195	1 333	4 572
Galax city	377	7 941	1.33	100	14.5	90	13.0	956	17.2	4 005	3 582	423	312	4 438
Hampton city	4 665	139 065	1.03	1 830	13.3	1 210	8.8	15 219	13.3	22 829	17 180	5 649	4 790	3 507
Harrisonburg city	7 526	60 134	1.41	613	11.7	235	4.5	7 750	18.7	5 294	4 587	707	1 257	2 416
Hopewell city	237	21 196	0.87	380	17.1	272	12.2	2 769	14.8	4 879	3 807	1 072	764	3 464
Lexington city	2 733	9 716	2.25	87	12.1	40	5.6	543	15.0	3 563	3 022	541	60	833
Lynchburg city	10 763	100 140	1.68	1 177	14.9	691	8.7	7 826	13.3	17 382	14 686	2 696	2 372	3 016
Manassas city	46	43 083	1.13	766	18.4	164	3.9	7 567	19.7	13 846	11 066	2 780	866	2 031

1. Per 1,000 estimated resident population. 2. Data for serious crimes have not been adjusted for underreporting; this may affect comparability between geographic areas and over time.
3. Per 100,000 population estimated by the FBI.

Table B. States and Counties — Crime, Education, Money Income, and Poverty

STATE County	Serious crimes known to police, 2014 (cont.)[1] Rate[2] Violent	Property	Education — School enrollment and attainment, 2010-2014 Enrollment[3] (percent) Total	Percent private	Attainment[4] (percent) High school graduate or less	Bachelor's degree or more	Local government expenditures,[5] 2012-2013 Total current spending (mil dol)	Current spending per student (dollars)	Money income, 2010-2014 Per capita income[6] (dollars)	Households Median income (dollars)	Mean income (dollars)	Percent with income of $200,000 or more	Income and poverty, 2014 Median household income (dollars)	Percent below poverty level All persons	Children under 18 years	Children 5 to 17 years in families
	46	47	48	49	50	51	52	53	54	55	56	57	58	59	60	61
VIRGINIA—Cont'd																
Louisa	196	1 855	6 836	14.3	56.2	19.2	49.7	10 512	27 481	57 126	70 037	2.7	60 121	11.5	17.3	16.6
Lunenburg	169	563	2 708	12.7	62.1	12.5	16.0	10 110	18 595	37 881	49 899	1.5	37 548	22.4	28.7	25.9
Madison	76	789	2 878	16.1	53.7	23.1	18.3	9 677	26 096	51 641	66 433	3.0	52 513	12.3	18.3	16.8
Mathews	11	1 024	1 602	7.2	43.6	29.0	11.8	9 976	33 487	63 157	76 009	3.7	58 268	10.6	18.0	16.7
Mecklenburg	292	1 702	6 185	8.7	55.5	15.2	40.5	8 668	20 798	37 756	48 912	1.6	38 500	21.1	30.6	30.0
Middlesex	252	1 213	1 951	11.9	40.2	28.3	NA	NA	30 489	54 452	71 330	5.0	48 921	14.4	26.0	24.6
Montgomery	118	1 426	41 655	7.1	31.5	44.3	96.2	9 878	23 727	44 810	62 483	4.3	43 484	24.8	16.0	15.0
Nelson	61	1 220	2 906	13.1	50.3	29.0	23.8	11 965	27 958	50 131	64 737	1.9	48 076	13.4	21.5	20.0
New Kent	147	1 528	4 939	16.9	42.4	24.6	26.1	8 689	33 839	73 030	88 799	5.9	72 406	6.2	9.7	9.0
Northampton	75	1 409	2 055	21.4	55.7	20.4	20.2	11 740	23 412	34 656	53 404	3.7	36 822	21.5	33.4	32.7
Northumberland	115	978	1 948	10.5	45.9	23.6	15.0	10 200	29 602	50 774	64 710	3.1	51 422	14.3	30.4	28.4
Nottoway	355	1 529	3 318	11.7	62.9	12.2	21.7	9 251	19 208	35 911	48 687	0.3	37 996	24.3	30.9	30.7
Orange	120	1 134	7 543	16.1	47.8	24.0	47.4	9 131	28 856	63 538	75 357	3.9	59 282	10.7	15.7	14.5
Page	168	1 573	4 814	10.2	65.7	12.4	33.3	9 186	22 083	43 063	54 574	1.9	44 851	16.9	23.8	21.8
Patrick	109	1 417	3 793	5.0	57.9	11.2	24.5	9 254	18 916	34 753	43 760	0.5	34 885	21.9	31.8	28.5
Pittsylvania	79	729	14 419	12.3	55.2	14.0	80.0	8 597	21 615	42 311	51 725	0.8	44 207	14.6	20.1	18.1
Powhatan	74	1 035	6 168	15.5	40.8	28.0	41.7	9 618	31 918	75 447	91 463	6.2	75 539	7.1	9.1	8.0
Prince Edward	251	1 654	8 476	22.1	55.5	22.4	25.2	10 852	17 779	37 238	52 464	1.1	37 543	25.5	30.1	28.6
Prince George	111	976	8 947	9.8	47.9	18.5	58.7	9 133	24 521	61 071	73 674	2.5	61 792	10.5	13.0	12.1
Prince William	176	1 353	127 774	16.2	32.2	38.1	859.5	10 249	37 440	98 514	115 446	13.3	91 886	7.2	10.4	9.9
Pulaski	232	2 485	6 784	6.3	49.9	16.4	44.8	9 907	24 722	45 635	56 583	1.2	46 186	14.7	22.1	19.9
Rappahannock	67	455	1 517	17.4	40.0	32.0	11.5	12 558	37 211	59 753	85 965	6.6	62 800	9.3	16.6	15.3
Richmond	124	743	1 767	3.9	65.0	12.9	13.4	11 409	19 956	47 199	61 340	1.9	42 204	19.7	23.9	22.0
Roanoke	168	1 559	22 429	17.4	35.2	34.0	132.0	9 186	31 864	60 950	76 294	4.1	61 935	8.2	10.5	9.6
Rockbridge	130	1 639	4 025	16.9	62.6	23.5	29.5	10 494	26 391	48 550	62 614	3.2	48 497	13.0	18.5	16.5
Rockingham	101	889	18 502	21.2	55.1	23.7	(7)	(7)	27 696	53 728	72 012	2.9	55 798	11.7	16.3	14.9
Russell	160	1 400	5 523	12.8	61.6	11.9	39.9	9 058	20 117	34 768	48 433	0.6	37 378	17.9	24.6	23.0
Scott	98	1 469	4 196	8.1	61.4	11.6	33.9	8 662	21 376	36 579	50 223	1.2	36 290	20.8	26.1	23.9
Shenandoah	180	1 225	9 188	12.7	56.0	19.8	64.8	10 494	24 967	47 936	60 389	1.6	45 430	12.0	17.6	17.0
Smyth	152	1 665	6 368	7.1	59.2	14.9	45.6	9 404	22 010	37 880	51 937	1.8	37 831	19.7	26.9	24.5
Southampton	122	1 414	4 321	9.3	55.5	14.8	28.6	9 890	23 414	49 690	61 908	1.7	46 521	15.3	22.4	20.5
Spotsylvania	170	1 541	34 917	12.7	42.5	28.3	234.5	9 866	31 842	78 505	92 792	6.2	75 714	9.2	12.8	11.5
Stafford	178	1 525	40 583	13.1	31.1	37.1	266.9	9 718	37 237	98 721	112 917	12.3	92 647	5.9	7.6	7.1
Surry	209	851	1 529	22.4	51.9	18.8	15.2	16 891	24 469	51 527	60 130	0.6	48 707	12.9	20.1	19.1
Sussex	85	1 147	2 508	11.6	71.7	9.0	18.1	15 876	14 316	36 972	46 827	0.2	37 748	23.9	30.5	29.3
Tazewell	210	2 216	8 990	13.1	57.1	12.8	56.7	8 768	21 558	36 248	51 228	1.8	38 292	19.2	24.7	22.1
Warren	110	1 968	8 899	24.5	53.1	19.7	49.0	8 912	29 160	60 560	75 493	3.8	60 714	11.3	15.8	15.0
Washington	142	1 860	11 742	20.1	49.2	23.5	73.7	9 981	25 807	42 458	60 518	2.7	43 353	14.5	20.7	18.1
Westmoreland	147	1 336	3 451	6.4	58.9	16.5	25.0	10 705	25 591	48 750	59 922	1.6	48 232	15.0	27.5	27.2
Wise	206	2 212	9 009	7.1	59.9	12.8	58.1	9 515	19 970	37 357	51 036	1.5	38 528	21.9	28.9	27.7
Wythe	109	1 181	5 856	6.9	54.8	15.2	39.9	9 123	23 237	40 185	53 541	1.8	41 132	15.6	21.6	20.8
York	141	1 687	18 990	12.0	25.4	42.0	119.5	9 619	36 004	80 900	97 167	6.7	81 169	5.5	7.0	6.0
Independent cities																
Alexandria city	185	1 975	29 831	26.4	20.6	61.5	233.1	17 789	54 597	87 319	116 416	14.5	86 419	9.6	15.8	18.4
Bedford city	NA	NA	NA	NA	NA	NA	(8)92.5	(8)8 803	NA	NA	NA	NA	NA	NA	NA	NA
Bristol city	313	2 804	3 900	18.7	53.1	20.4	25.7	10 905	20 574	33 616	46 158	1.2	34 099	21.8	34.9	31.1
Buena Vista city	134	807	1 829	26.6	61.0	14.0	9.4	8 897	17 460	32 789	44 479	0.6	38 331	17.2	25.2	24.8
Charlottesville city	431	3 047	17 227	10.9	33.5	49.3	(9)224.5	(9)12 832	28 285	47 218	67 583	4.9	45 890	25.9	24.4	25.7
Chesapeake city	430	2 765	64 216	14.3	36.1	29.4	414.5	10 460	29 735	70 176	82 802	4.5	66 625	9.8	14.0	12.8
Colonial Heights city	215	4 897	4 033	5.1	49.5	19.6	33.3	11 764	28 282	52 529	68 164	2.4	52 355	11.5	18.7	19.7
Covington city	173	1 936	1 242	0.6	58.8	9.0	10.3	10 448	21 243	38 176	48 026	0.6	36 503	16.4	26.5	26.3
Danville city	447	4 129	10 455	17.1	49.9	17.2	68.8	10 811	20 569	32 173	46 759	1.7	33 646	23.6	36.6	36.7
Emporia city	526	5 026	1 347	8.0	60.8	15.0	(10)25.1	(10)9 847	18 909	30 240	43 120	1.2	33 160	26.1	41.8	37.5
Fairfax city	74	1 832	6 363	15.7	23.7	53.5	(11)	(11)	44 747	100 584	122 464	17.1	94 067	7.8	7.9	9.2
Falls Church city	130	1 602	3 872	24.5	12.1	75.1	38.9	17 101	59 861	120 500	152 424	26.1	125 635	3.2	3.3	2.9
Franklin city	NA	NA	2 462	11.0	48.0	19.8	15.7	12 436	19 754	33 133	47 381	2.1	38 583	22.5	34.7	36.3
Fredericksburg city	449	4 122	8 547	12.2	36.0	37.7	40.3	11 985	28 453	49 454	71 366	5.1	51 195	16.8	23.4	25.3
Galax city	327	4 111	1 470	4.5	58.2	12.4	13.5	10 231	20 081	30 430	45 561	0.8	33 182	22.7	34.8	35.1
Hampton city	256	3 251	38 504	22.1	37.5	23.3	211.9	9 925	25 131	49 879	61 727	1.8	47 615	15.2	21.6	21.5
Harrisonburg city	198	2 218	24 083	6.6	43.3	35.6	(7)180.3	(7)10 607	17 919	38 807	53 546	1.8	38 541	28.3	23.6	23.5
Hopewell city	381	3 083	4 830	9.0	59.6	10.9	43.0	10 223	21 041	39 156	49 932	1.1	40 122	19.5	31.3	30.7
Lexington city	69	764	4 519	20.8	39.1	44.8	4.8	9 079	15 627	36 840	54 859	4.3	40 829	24.1	16.5	14.8
Lynchburg city	472	2 545	29 066	53.7	38.3	32.3	91.2	10 630	21 236	39 391	54 856	2.4	40 065	25.0	31.7	30.8
Manassas city	326	1 705	11 480	16.4	44.3	29.1	89.8	12 343	28 646	71 215	88 657	6.2	72 510	9.8	16.4	16.6

1. Data for serious crimes have not been adjusted for underreporting; this may affect comparability between geographic areas and over time.   2. Per 100,000 population estimated by the FBI.
3. All persons 3 years old and over enrolled in nursery school through college.   4. Persons 25 years old and over.   5. Elementary and secondary education expenditures.
6. Based on population estimated by the American Community Survey, 2010–2014.   7. Rockingham county is included with Harrisonburg city.   8. Bedford county is included with Bedford city.
9. Albemarle county is included with Charlottesville city.   10. Greensville county is included with Emporia city.   11. Fairfax city is included with Fairfax county.

Table B. States and Counties — **Personal Income**

STATE County	Personal income, 2014										Earnings, 2014		
	Total (mil dol)	Percent change, 2013–2014	Per capita[1] Dollars	Per capita[1] Rank	Wages and salaries (mil dol)	Supplements to wages and salaries; employer contributions (mil dol) Pension and insurance	Supplements to wages and salaries; employer contributions (mil dol) Government social insurance	Proprietors' income (mil dol)	Dividends, interest, and rent (mil dol)	Personal transfer receipts (mil dol)	Total (mil dol)	Contributions for government social insurance (mil dol) From employee and self-employed	Contributions for government social insurance (mil dol) From employer
	62	63	64	65	66	67	68	69	70	71	72	73	74
VIRGINIA—Cont'd													
Louisa	1 596	5.8	46 478	561	452	83	33	299	201	271	867	56	33
Lunenburg	376	5.4	30 194	2 691	95	20	7	16	71	118	138	11	7
Madison	542	2.9	41 194	1 036	113	21	9	57	118	103	200	14	9
Mathews	448	3.2	50 657	349	48	10	4	42	125	94	103	9	4
Mecklenburg	1 034	2.7	33 158	2 256	393	74	30	54	205	336	551	41	30
Middlesex	454	1.7	42 417	911	116	24	9	20	134	113	169	13	9
Montgomery	(3)3 627	(3)4.4	(3)31 569	(3)2 518	(3)2 086	(3)468	(3)157	(3)176	(3)774	(3)617	(3)2 888	(3)168	(3)157
Nelson	630	4.3	42 403	912	134	28	10	25	163	146	197	16	10
New Kent	997	5.1	49 814	391	156	29	12	26	139	133	223	16	12
Northampton	436	2.3	35 987	1 781	168	31	13	17	111	136	228	16	13
Northumberland	520	4.3	42 435	907	95	18	7	25	184	152	145	13	7
Nottoway	532	2.3	34 170	2 087	210	56	17	19	96	159	303	20	17
Orange	1 373	2.1	39 190	1 297	363	65	27	24	284	287	480	35	27
Page	814	4.0	34 140	2 091	179	37	15	64	148	207	295	21	15
Patrick	534	4.4	29 257	2 801	153	33	12	30	91	180	228	19	12
Pittsylvania	(4)3 430	(4)3.1	(4)32 716	(4)2 329	(4)1 396	(4)253	(4)109	(4)167	(4)596	(4)1 080	(4)1 924	(4)138	(4)109
Powhatan	1 285	4.0	45 182	663	407	71	29	58	208	184	565	37	29
Prince Edward	618	3.4	26 793	2 993	313	65	24	11	114	185	413	27	24
Prince George	(5)2 168	(5)3.3	(5)36 423	(5)1 701	(5)1 777	(5)467	(5)155	(5)73	(5)476	(5)463	(5)2 471	(5)123	(5)155
Prince William	(6)24 171	(6)3.9	(6)48 020	(6)479	(6)7 977	(6)1 364	(6)615	(6)1 017	(6)3 603	(6)2 210	(6)10 973	(6)627	(6)615
Pulaski	1 193	3.3	34 747	1 976	550	95	44	46	191	331	736	51	44
Rappahannock	418	2.7	56 736	178	77	12	5	44	131	58	137	10	5
Richmond	275	1.7	30 872	2 606	111	25	8	10	59	70	154	10	8
Roanoke	(7)5 436	(7)3.1	(7)45 577	(7)633	(7)2 762	(7)468	(7)208	(7)351	(7)1 035	(7)945	(7)3 788	(7)240	(7)208
Rockbridge	(8)1 262	(8)3.9	(8)34 836	(8)1 962	(8)496	(8)95	(8)40	(8)59	(8)323	(8)299	(8)689	(8)48	(8)40
Rockingham	(9)4 403	(9)4.5	(9)33 703	(9)2 160	(9)2 495	(9)449	(9)185	(9)439	(9)842	(9)775	(9)3 568	(9)207	(9)185
Russell	860	1.1	30 705	2 627	281	52	22	33	119	288	388	32	22
Scott	657	2.2	29 347	2 794	166	33	13	11	104	236	224	21	13
Shenandoah	1 630	4.2	37 896	1 469	496	92	38	141	318	343	767	52	38
Smyth	992	4.5	31 425	2 536	455	93	36	44	155	313	628	44	36
Southampton	(10)883	(10)0.2	(10)33 229	(10)2 242	(10)290	(10)63	(10)21	(10)24	(10)177	(10)251	(10)398	(10)28	(10)21
Spotsylvania	(11)7 042	(11)4.1	(11)44 698	(11)704	(11)2 440	(11)380	(11)348	(11)181	(11)1 199	(11)971	(11)3 348	(11)207	(11)181
Stafford	6 778	4.7	48 414	459	2 223	428	168	145	1 080	725	2 964	171	168
Surry	262	0.8	38 596	1 378	173	41	12	12	37	57	238	14	12
Sussex	325	1.1	27 597	2 947	146	32	11	6	57	96	195	13	11
Tazewell	1 441	0.6	33 174	2 251	571	111	44	59	244	462	785	58	44
Warren	1 564	3.4	40 118	1 157	535	87	41	60	255	262	724	47	41
Washington	(12)2 916	(12)3.2	(12)40 556	(12)1 113	(12)1 195	(12)218	(12)90	(12)411	(12)634	(12)683	(12)1 914	(12)128	(12)90
Westmoreland	673	2.3	38 508	1 391	114	23	9	19	178	165	164	14	9
Wise	(13)1 266	(13)-0.3	(13)28 789	(13)2 849	(13)626	(13)129	(13)47	(13)32	(13)190	(13)488	(13)834	(13)60	(13)47
Wythe	968	3.8	33 237	2 240	400	81	31	34	149	278	547	38	31
York	(14)4 205	(14)3.3	(14)53 646	(14)248	(14)993	(14)184	(14)78	(14)178	(14)905	(14)495	(14)1 433	(14)89	(14)78
Independent cities													
Alexandria city	11 616	3.5	77 142	35	7 385	1 126	559	559	2 764	688	9 628	539	559
Bedford city	(15)	(15)	(15)	(15)	(15)	(15)	(15)	(15)	(15)	(15)	(15)	(15)	(15)
Bristol city	(12)	(12)	(12)	(12)	(12)	(12)	(12)	(12)	(12)	(12)	(12)	(12)	(12)
Buena Vista city	(8)	(8)	(8)	(8)	(8)	(8)	(8)	(8)	(8)	(8)	(8)	(8)	(8)
Charlottesville city	(16)	(16)	(16)	(16)	(16)	(16)	(16)	(16)	(16)	(16)	(16)	(16)	(16)
Chesapeake city	10 645	3.7	45 616	627	4 259	677	324	430	1 853	1 516	5 690	345	324
Colonial Heights city	(17)	(17)	(17)	(17)	(17)	(17)	(17)	(17)	(17)	(17)	(17)	(17)	(17)
Covington city	(18)	(18)	(18)	(18)	(18)	(18)	(18)	(18)	(18)	(18)	(18)	(18)	(18)
Danville city	(4)	(4)	(4)	(4)	(4)	(4)	(4)	(4)	(4)	(4)	(4)	(4)	(4)
Emporia city	(19)	(19)	(19)	(19)	(19)	(19)	(19)	(19)	(19)	(19)	(19)	(19)	(19)
Fairfax city	(20)	(20)	(20)	(20)	(20)	(20)	(20)	(20)	(20)	(20)	(20)	(20)	(20)
Falls Church city	(20)	(20)	(20)	(20)	(20)	(20)	(20)	(20)	(20)	(20)	(20)	(20)	(20)
Franklin city	(10)	(10)	(10)	(10)	(10)	(10)	(10)	(10)	(10)	(10)	(10)	(10)	(10)
Fredericksburg city	(11)	(11)	(11)	(11)	(11)	(11)	(11)	(11)	(11)	(11)	(11)	(11)	(11)
Galax city	(21)	(21)	(21)	(21)	(21)	(21)	(21)	(21)	(21)	(21)	(21)	(21)	(21)
Hampton city	5 435	2.9	39 707	1 226	3 171	699	259	153	1 147	1 152	4 281	238	259
Harrisonburg city	(9)	(9)	(9)	(9)	(9)	(9)	(9)	(9)	(9)	(9)	(9)	(9)	(9)
Hopewell city	(5)	(5)	(5)	(5)	(5)	(5)	(5)	(5)	(5)	(5)	(5)	(5)	(5)
Lexington city	(8)	(8)	(8)	(8)	(8)	(8)	(8)	(8)	(8)	(8)	(8)	(8)	(8)
Lynchburg city	(22)	(22)	(22)	(22)	(22)	(22)	(22)	(22)	(22)	(22)	(22)	(22)	(22)
Manassas city	(6)	(6)	(6)	(6)	(6)	(6)	(6)	(6)	(6)	(6)	(6)	(6)	(6)

1. Based on the resident population estimated as of July 1 of the year shown.   3. Radford city is included with Montgomery county.   4. Danville city is included with Pittsylvania county.   5. Hopewell city is included with Prince George county.   6. Manassas and Manassas Park cities are included with Prince William county.   7. Salem city is included with Roanoke county.   8. Buena Vista and Lexington cities are included with Rockbridge county.   9. Harrisonburg city is included with Rockingham county.   10. Franklin city is included with Southhampton county.   11. Fredericksburg city is included with Spotsylvania county.   12. Bristol city included with Washington county.   13. Norton city is included with Wise county.   14. Poquoson city is included with York county.   15. Bedford city is included with Bedford county.   16. Charlottesville city is included with Albemarle county.   17. Petersburg and Colonial Heights cities are included with Dinwiddie county.   18. Covington city is included with Alleghany county.   19. Emporia city is included with Greensville county.   20. Fairfax city and Falls Church city are included with Fairfax county.   21. Galax city is included with Carroll county.   22. Lynchburg city is included with Campbell county.

Table B. States and Counties — **Earnings, Social Security, and Housing**

STATE County	Earnings, 2014 (cont.) Percent by selected industries									Social Security beneficiaries, December 2014		Supplemental Security Income recipients, December 2014	Housing units, 2015	
	Farm	Mining	Construction	Manu-facturing	Information: professional, scientific, technical services	Retail trade	Finance, insurance, real estate and leasing	Health care and social assistance	Govern-ment	Number	Rate[1]		Total	Percent change, 2010–2014
	75	76	77	78	79	80	81	82	83	84	85	86	87	88
VIRGINIA—Cont'd														
Louisa	0.0	D	11.2	11.6	D	5.5	3.6	D	9.8	8 165	238	792	16 939	3.6
Lunenburg	3.4	0.0	7.3	10.7	D	5.6	D	8.0	29.7	3 525	283	532	5 930	-0.1
Madison	1.5	0.0	10.6	8.2	D	24.0	D	D	16.6	3 170	242	186	6 025	1.6
Mathews	-0.5	0.0	10.5	4.0	D	6.8	D	D	20.5	2 940	334	158	5 731	1.1
Mecklenburg	1.4	D	7.2	10.3	5.4	8.8	3.8	15.5	17.9	9 855	317	1 270	18 686	0.5
Middlesex	0.7	0.1	8.6	4.6	D	7.4	3.7	D	30.2	3 305	311	182	7 251	1.7
Montgomery	[3]0.2	[3]0.2	[3]D	[3]14.9	[3]D	[3]5.7	[3]3.8	[3]8.6	[3]39.8	13 905	143	1 189	39 365	2.0
Nelson	1.9	D	7.7	11.2	7.3	4.0	3.2	D	20.5	4 360	294	331	10 073	1.4
New Kent	0.0	0.0	26.8	3.9	4.4	6.3	2.1	10.4	24.4	4 060	203	208	8 045	10.3
Northampton	6.1	0.0	3.8	11.2	D	5.7	3.3	22.3	23.4	3 660	303	619	7 350	0.7
Northumberland	0.1	D	11.8	24.7	7.2	6.4	3.9	2.9	18.3	5 140	420	328	9 156	1.8
Nottoway	2.2	0.0	3.7	6.2	2.2	5.7	2.5	D	50.5	3 780	243	625	6 725	1.1
Orange	1.9	0.0	5.7	12.8	D	8.3	5.1	4.4	24.3	7 970	228	495	14 928	2.3
Page	13.0	0.0	7.1	10.2	D	7.6	3.3	D	23.5	6 420	269	585	11 656	0.4
Patrick	0.6	0.0	4.1	26.5	6.4	7.4	D	D	18.1	5 845	321	580	10 096	0.2
Pittsylvania	[4]2.0	[4]D	[4]D	[4]21.4	[4]3.4	[4]8.7	[4]3.3	[4]14.4	[4]18.1	17 420	279	1 615	31 416	0.4
Powhatan	0.1	D	14.6	2.7	6.9	4.0	26.5	3.2	25.4	5 665	199	243	10 551	5.1
Prince Edward	1.8	D	3.2	1.5	2.6	9.6	3.4	D	32.6	4 905	213	1 073	9 313	1.8
Prince George	[5]-0.1	[5]0.0	[5]D	[5]12.2	[5]D	[5]2.1	[5]D	[5]D	[5]62.1	6 380	170	954	12 325	2.2
Prince William	[6]0.0	[6]D	[6]D	[6]3.7	[6]D	[6]8.4	[6]3.6	[6]D	[6]30.0	40 975	92	3 821	145 848	6.4
Pulaski	0.8	D	4.2	42.1	D	7.0	1.8	D	16.3	9 535	278	842	17 264	0.2
Rappahannock	-0.7	0.0	12.2	2.1	37.3	5.3	3.4	2.4	14.3	1 930	262	109	3 964	1.7
Richmond	1.2	0.0	6.2	4.9	D	4.9	D	D	39.6	2 020	228	240	3 922	1.9
Roanoke	[7]0.0	[7]0.2	[7]17.7	[7]7.9	[7]7.9	[7]6.2	[7]7.3	[7]D	[7]16.4	21 775	232	1 187	40 746	1.7
Rockbridge	[8]0.3	[8]D	[8]5.5	[8]14.4	[8]D	[8]7.1	[8]D	[8]7.7	[8]23.3	6 065	270	332	11 284	1.2
Rockingham	[9]5.7	[9]D	[9]6.4	[9]17.6	[9]6.6	[9]6.6	[9]4.0	[9]11.7	[9]17.8	17 095	219	849	34 709	3.1
Russell	0.6	4.9	7.7	1.5	16.3	7.6	3.7	D	20.2	8 455	302	1 376	13 389	-0.7
Scott	-2.1	0.0	2.3	20.0	D	9.4	D	14.4	27.8	7 450	333	1 303	11 845	-0.6
Shenandoah	4.0	D	6.1	22.8	7.1	6.5	3.1	8.1	15.3	10 635	248	689	21 113	1.1
Smyth	2.2	D	5.7	32.1	D	5.9	1.9	9.0	25.0	9 590	304	1 291	15 319	-0.7
Southampton	[10]3.0	[10]D	[10]D	[10]6.9	[10]3.0	[10]8.6	[10]4.3	[10]17.3	[10]33.7	4 130	226	364	7 547	1.0
Spotsylvania	[11]0.5	[11]D	[11]6.8	[11]D	[11]10.9	[11]11.8	[11]5.4	[11]20.2	[11]17.5	19 165	148	1 264	46 554	2.8
Stafford	-0.1	D	6.0	1.5	11.5	5.6	D	5.7	37.8	15 175	108	1 012	47 235	7.4
Surry	1.2	0.0	4.6	D	0.0	0.4	D	D	12.4	1 690	248	156	3 517	2.0
Sussex	3.5	D	3.5	2.5	D	5.5	1.6	D	40.5	2 610	222	406	4 722	0.6
Tazewell	0.6	8.2	4.8	9.2	4.0	12.3	3.6	D	20.5	13 550	312	2 100	20 634	-0.9
Warren	-0.2	0.0	15.7	9.7	3.6	7.5	3.5	10.5	16.4	7 210	185	620	16 181	1.3
Washington	[12]0.5	[12]0.0	[12]D	[12]16.2	[12]3.9	[12]7.7	[12]3.2	[12]9.3	[12]14.7	15 685	287	1 580	25 714	0.4
Westmoreland	1.5	0.0	8.0	13.4	D	7.6	4.6	D	26.3	4 840	277	434	10 831	2.0
Wise	[13]0.2	[13]D	[13]2.6	[13]2.7	[13]6.5	[13]9.2	[13]2.6	[13]15.4	[13]28.8	12 070	302	2 388	17 792	-0.9
Wythe	1.5	1.0	4.3	23.7	3.2	10.7	3.3	11.3	22.4	8 320	286	804	14 228	1.1
York	[14]0.0	[14]D	[14]D	[14]D	[14]D	[14]8.4	[14]D	[14]D	[14]30.1	11 010	165	337	27 654	3.6
Independent cities														
Alexandria city	0.0	D	2.1	D	28.3	3.9	5.5	4.4	33.2	13 975	92	1 463	76 512	5.7
Bedford city	[15]	[15]	[15]	[15]	[15]	[15]	[15]	[15]	[15]	NA	NA	NA	NA	NA
Bristol city	[12]	[12]	[12]	[12]	[12]	[12]	[12]	[12]	[12]	5 035	290	809	8 812	-0.2
Buena Vista city	[8]	[8]	[8]	[8]	[8]	[8]	[8]	[8]	[8]	1 700	258	264	2 913	-0.9
Charlottesville city	[16]	[16]	[16]	[16]	[16]	[16]	[16]	[16]	[16]	5 870	129	969	20 423	6.4
Chesapeake city	0.1	0.1	9.7	5.9	14.3	9.0	5.7	7.0	18.9	35 765	153	3 503	88 880	6.8
Colonial Heights city	[17]	[17]	[17]	[17]	[17]	[17]	[17]	[17]	[17]	4 270	243	485	7 803	-0.4
Covington city	[18]	[18]	[18]	[18]	[18]	[18]	[18]	[18]	[18]	1 875	329	443	3 032	-1.0
Danville city	[4]	[4]	[4]	[4]	[4]	[4]	[4]	[4]	[4]	12 405	293	2 915	22 303	-0.6
Emporia city	[19]	[19]	[19]	[19]	[19]	[19]	[19]	[19]	[19]	1 345	241	36	2 616	2.0
Fairfax city	[20]	[20]	[20]	[20]	[20]	[20]	[20]	[20]	[20]	3 435	145	22	8 850	2.0
Falls Church city	[20]	[20]	[20]	[20]	[20]	[20]	[20]	[20]	[20]	1 440	107	124	6 025	10.1
Franklin city	[10]	[10]	[10]	[10]	[10]	[10]	[10]	[10]	[10]	2 265	269	629	3 878	-0.5
Fredericksburg city	[11]	[11]	[11]	[11]	[11]	[11]	[11]	[11]	[11]	3 880	137	516	11 471	10.6
Galax city	[21]	[21]	[21]	[21]	[21]	[21]	[21]	[21]	[21]	1 995	289	571	3 203	-0.8
Hampton city	0.0	0.0	D	4.9	12.0	5.1	2.4	9.2	48.4	25 735	187	3 314	60 392	1.3
Harrisonburg city	[9]	[9]	[9]	[9]	[9]	[9]	[9]	[9]	[9]	5 530	106	955	18 189	4.3
Hopewell city	[5]	[5]	[5]	[5]	[5]	[5]	[5]	[5]	[5]	4 915	222	1 070	10 324	2.0
Lexington city	[8]	[8]	[8]	[8]	[8]	[8]	[8]	[8]	[8]	1 495	209	226	2 530	-0.6
Lynchburg city	[22]	[22]	[22]	[22]	[22]	[22]	[22]	[22]	[22]	15 660	199	2 805	32 374	1.1
Manassas city	[6]	[6]	[6]	[6]	[6]	[6]	[6]	[6]	[6]	4 125	100	469	13 491	2.7

1. Per 1,000 resident population estimated as of July 1 of the year shown. 3. Radford city is included with Montgomery county. 4. Danville city is included with Pittsylvania county. 5. Hopewell city is included with Prince George county. 6. Manassas and Manassas Park cities are included with Prince William county. 7. Salem city is included with Roanoke county. 8. Buena Vista and Lexington cities are included with Rockbridge county. 9. Harrisonburg city is included with Rockingham county. 10. Franklin city is included with Southhampton county. 11. Fredericksburg city is included with Spotsylvania county. 12. Bristol city is included with Washington county. 13. Norton city is included with Wise county. 14. Poquoson city is included with York county. 15. Bedford city is included with Bedford county. 16. Charlottesville city is included with Albemarle county. 17. Petersburg and Colonial Heights cities are included with Dinwiddie county. 18. Covington city is included with Alleghany county. 19. Emporia city is included with Greensville county. 20. Fairfax city and Falls Church city are included with Fairfax county. 21. Galax city is included with Carroll county. 22. Lynchburg city is included with Campbell county.

Table B. States and Counties — Housing, Labor Force, and Employment

STATE County	Housing units, 2010–2014								Civilian labor force, 2015				Civilian employment,[6] 2010–2014		
	Occupied units							Sub-stand-ard units[4] (percent)		Percent change, 2014–2015	Unemployment			Percent	
	Owner-occupied					Renter-occupied									Manage-ment, business, science and arts	Con-struction, produc-tion, and mainte-nance occu-pations
	Total	Percent	Median value[1]	With a mort-gage	Without a mort-gage[2]	Median rent[3]	Median rent as a per-cent of income[2]		Total		Total	Rate[5]	Total		
	89	90	91	92	93	94	95	96	97	98	99	100	101	102	103
VIRGINIA—Cont'd															
Louisa	12 811	81.2	194 500	23.2	10.6	963	29.1	1.6	18 912	2.1	804	4.3	16 140	31.7	28.6
Lunenburg	4 634	74.0	104 200	23.9	11.7	708	29.9	2.4	5 313	-0.8	276	5.2	4 611	27.4	29.2
Madison	5 093	78.2	237 200	25.2	12.4	865	35.8	2.8	7 156	0.0	250	3.5	6 204	30.1	27.0
Mathews	3 792	81.3	263 700	23.5	10.0	976	32.6	1.3	4 106	-0.8	171	4.2	3 896	35.4	23.2
Mecklenburg	12 857	73.2	123 700	24.9	13.2	651	30.7	3.1	12 530	-1.0	773	6.2	12 548	29.4	24.8
Middlesex	4 432	83.3	241 600	24.5	10.0	807	28.3	1.7	4 984	-1.0	214	4.3	4 452	31.5	24.7
Montgomery	34 803	54.2	201 100	21.1	10.0	851	39.8	1.4	50 008	0.1	2 162	4.3	44 995	44.7	13.7
Nelson	6 381	73.9	198 500	24.2	10.9	658	25.1	3.9	7 442	0.3	300	4.0	6 741	36.1	23.0
New Kent	7 106	88.0	247 800	22.6	11.1	892	19.6	1.5	11 200	0.7	426	3.8	9 881	36.2	23.1
Northampton	5 237	69.9	162 500	24.1	13.8	680	28.9	2.3	6 103	0.7	374	6.1	4 966	34.1	29.8
Northumberland	5 669	83.4	241 500	25.8	11.7	717	33.6	2.7	5 463	-3.2	337	6.2	5 004	33.3	21.2
Nottoway	5 640	64.0	128 800	23.9	11.7	794	39.6	3.0	7 159	1.1	325	4.5	5 820	23.7	24.9
Orange	12 433	76.8	229 000	23.6	10.0	877	29.9	2.7	16 100	-0.9	738	4.6	14 883	34.3	27.5
Page	9 526	71.0	178 100	23.6	12.0	687	30.5	2.1	11 707	-1.4	812	6.9	10 216	26.6	28.8
Patrick	7 678	76.1	112 500	24.7	11.2	534	30.5	2.1	7 621	-1.6	418	5.5	6 867	25.2	38.1
Pittsylvania	26 029	78.5	107 800	21.9	11.7	612	28.0	2.0	30 102	-0.6	1 609	5.3	27 623	26.5	33.6
Powhatan	9 590	87.9	259 500	23.1	10.0	1 040	25.5	0.4	13 816	0.7	542	3.9	13 245	38.1	20.0
Prince Edward	7 604	66.0	155 200	23.6	10.5	741	29.9	3.6	9 798	0.3	632	6.5	8 581	29.6	22.0
Prince George	10 906	70.4	201 600	22.1	10.1	1 252	31.1	1.3	14 909	0.6	795	5.3	13 860	36.0	23.8
Prince William	134 737	71.8	323 400	23.0	10.0	1 532	30.6	3.3	231 924	-0.3	9 538	4.1	219 525	43.5	16.0
Pulaski	15 125	73.0	134 300	21.6	10.4	603	28.9	1.8	16 461	-0.3	826	5.0	15 519	28.9	30.4
Rappahannock	3 281	79.2	383 700	26.1	12.9	999	28.9	1.3	3 781	-0.8	155	4.1	3 517	37.2	19.1
Richmond	2 800	75.8	156 800	22.9	10.6	745	29.2	0.8	3 903	-1.7	178	4.6	3 010	26.5	28.6
Roanoke	38 197	75.3	194 000	22.5	10.0	857	25.9	1.2	49 551	-1.2	1 931	3.9	45 652	41.1	17.2
Rockbridge	9 226	75.1	184 200	25.7	10.5	759	29.9	1.6	9 904	0.1	492	5.0	9 918	31.8	28.4
Rockingham	29 483	76.4	197 300	23.2	10.0	795	27.5	3.0	40 219	-0.8	1 659	4.1	37 527	31.4	29.0
Russell	11 037	77.9	94 500	23.3	10.0	535	36.7	0.6	11 609	2.8	753	6.5	10 325	30.8	32.4
Scott	9 363	78.6	91 700	19.3	10.2	491	29.9	2.6	9 676	-1.5	497	5.1	8 776	24.2	32.3
Shenandoah	17 246	71.8	201 200	24.4	11.2	782	29.8	2.2	21 226	-0.4	904	4.3	19 632	27.9	32.6
Smyth	12 852	69.6	91 200	20.1	10.6	570	27.5	1.4	13 580	0.7	880	6.5	13 183	26.8	32.6
Southampton	6 654	71.8	159 200	23.6	11.7	734	28.6	1.6	9 239	1.2	372	4.0	8 487	26.1	31.8
Spotsylvania	42 280	76.2	245 600	23.4	10.0	1 322	30.5	1.3	64 130	-0.3	2 965	4.6	61 367	38.7	18.8
Stafford	42 763	76.6	300 000	22.7	10.0	1 447	31.2	1.7	66 721	-0.3	2 985	4.5	63 263	45.6	15.3
Surry	2 652	78.7	160 200	22.4	11.1	764	25.1	3.1	3 715	1.0	193	5.2	3 207	21.7	40.5
Sussex	3 261	65.1	124 500	24.3	11.1	693	34.3	3.8	4 156	0.8	281	6.8	2 843	20.5	36.3
Tazewell	18 306	73.5	89 600	21.5	12.3	578	29.4	1.0	16 620	-3.2	1 244	7.5	16 663	28.2	29.9
Warren	14 324	74.8	210 900	23.1	11.7	955	30.4	2.2	19 866	-0.6	941	4.7	18 711	31.4	27.3
Washington	22 842	77.1	134 000	21.6	11.1	610	27.9	1.3	27 234	-1.8	1 306	4.8	24 403	34.7	23.4
Westmoreland	6 981	77.1	188 100	25.5	12.0	914	29.9	2.4	8 930	-1.2	484	5.4	7 461	27.5	27.3
Wise	15 517	69.2	86 300	18.6	10.6	612	35.6	2.1	13 962	-3.7	1 158	8.3	14 214	29.9	30.6
Wythe	11 984	70.8	119 200	21.8	10.0	599	28.1	1.4	13 713	-0.8	745	5.4	12 795	27.2	30.9
York	23 970	73.5	313 100	22.6	10.0	1 343	29.6	1.1	31 651	-0.9	1 369	4.3	29 668	47.1	16.3
Independent cities															
Alexandria city	65 916	42.7	494 400	22.2	11.6	1 520	28.1	3.6	93 782	-0.1	3 094	3.3	90 696	57.9	8.6
Bedford city	NA	NA	NA	NA	NA	NA	NA	NA	NA	NA	NA	NA	NA	NA	NA
Bristol city	7 764	55.3	113 200	21.6	12.7	635	29.2	1.0	7 582	-2.2	403	5.3	7 311	28.7	19.7
Buena Vista city	2 741	64.1	120 500	26.9	10.6	646	36.5	1.2	3 169	0.1	165	5.2	2 962	17.1	35.2
Charlottesville city	17 604	41.6	283 100	21.8	13.2	1 015	31.4	1.3	24 613	1.2	909	3.7	22 541	50.5	9.6
Chesapeake city	80 388	71.7	254 900	25.8	12.4	1 163	31.0	2.1	116 597	-0.9	5 302	4.5	105 428	39.5	20.2
Colonial Heights city	7 025	64.7	176 300	23.7	10.8	903	29.5	2.0	8 772	0.4	413	4.7	7 856	33.6	19.9
Covington city	2 468	75.1	66 000	20.1	11.8	600	28.4	3.2	2 445	-1.9	148	6.1	2 310	19.6	38.1
Danville city	18 520	54.1	88 300	22.5	11.9	595	29.7	2.4	19 010	-2.6	1 393	7.3	16 356	30.4	25.2
Emporia city	2 420	39.3	114 100	27.2	14.2	669	31.7	2.3	2 247	-3.2	158	7.0	2 059	28.6	25.7
Fairfax city	8 480	70.1	462 800	21.4	10.2	1 671	33.3	2.3	13 242	-0.4	454	3.4	12 440	51.2	11.6
Falls Church city	4 966	59.1	665 400	21.2	10.4	1 673	27.9	2.5	7 797	-0.3	237	3.0	7 290	68.4	4.9
Franklin city	3 580	43.5	170 900	28.0	15.7	794	40.3	2.5	3 638	0.4	245	6.7	3 270	27.0	25.6
Fredericksburg city	9 849	36.2	317 000	21.7	10.0	1 065	32.6	1.4	13 679	-0.3	727	5.3	12 423	41.9	12.4
Galax city	2 968	59.2	108 300	24.2	11.1	531	27.0	3.7	2 966	-1.2	163	5.5	2 930	21.2	33.7
Hampton city	52 700	58.8	191 800	25.0	13.0	1 005	35.8	6.9	65 159	-1.0	3 891	6.0	60 197	32.9	21.9
Harrisonburg city	15 881	35.7	200 700	22.1	10.0	843	33.4	5.3	24 034	-1.1	1 272	5.3	23 397	32.4	21.5
Hopewell city	8 774	52.8	129 600	23.3	12.3	833	30.7	3.3	9 703	0.1	729	7.5	9 031	23.1	31.3
Lexington city	1 727	54.2	248 900	25.6	14.8	846	29.3	0.0	2 055	-1.5	154	7.5	2 079	42.9	6.2
Lynchburg city	28 424	52.1	147 900	22.9	11.9	759	33.8	1.8	35 740	-1.1	1 987	5.6	33 736	37.0	16.4
Manassas city	12 274	64.7	257 500	23.5	12.6	1 334	35.6	7.4	22 087	-0.5	913	4.1	21 056	32.0	22.2

1. Specified owner-occupied units.　2. A value of 10.0 represents 10 percent or less; a value of 50.0 represents 50 percent or more.　3. Specified renter-occupied units.
4. Overcrowded or lacking complete plumbing facilities.　5. Percent of civilian labor force.　6. Persons 16 years old and over.

Table B. States and Counties — Nonfarm Employment and Agriculture

STATE County	Number of establish-ments	Total	Health care and social assistance	Manufac-turing	Retail trade	Finance and insurance	Professional, scientific, and technical services	Total (mil dol)	Average per employee (dollars)	Number	Fewer than 50 acres	500 acres or more	Farm operators whose principal occu-pation is farming (percent)
	104	105	106	107	108	109	110	111	112	113	114	115	116
VIRGINIA—Cont'd													
Louisa	535	6 277	296	1 075	1 091	83	158	290	46 167	485	39.6	8.2	40.6
Lunenburg	175	1 735	332	501	265	65	D	49	28 469	371	20.2	9.7	46.9
Madison	272	2 719	D	281	905	D	D	86	31 524	522	36.2	10.3	49.6
Mathews	176	1 081	211	D	224	18	39	24	22 286	55	72.7	5.5	47.3
Mecklenburg	783	9 097	1 650	1 296	1 830	271	288	260	28 614	527	20.5	12.0	44.8
Middlesex	325	2 137	387	D	471	64	145	60	27 991	73	43.8	12.3	61.6
Montgomery	1 936	27 917	4 090	4 261	5 242	650	1 989	1 001	35 873	603	39.5	6.6	39.6
Nelson	370	3 174	242	411	303	55	158	84	26 421	455	29.0	5.9	36.0
New Kent	347	2 950	649	142	439	23	D	89	30 031	137	52.6	5.1	49.6
Northampton	325	2 855	819	D	474	D	60	92	32 099	147	40.8	24.5	57.1
Northumberland	329	1 685	98	331	315	67	91	55	32 705	98	39.8	27.6	64.3
Nottoway	302	3 695	D	385	619	121	120	97	26 369	356	31.2	6.5	56.2
Orange	644	6 183	446	1 022	997	131	278	232	37 583	547	35.5	7.5	47.5
Page	407	3 882	476	D	751	D	188	112	28 732	545	45.0	5.3	56.7
Patrick	285	4 131	673	1 496	545	79	63	108	26 239	566	35.5	3.7	40.6
Pittsylvania	822	8 320	1 212	1 937	947	D	177	252	30 298	1 354	25.2	10.1	56.6
Powhatan	660	4 758	283	149	764	137	247	164	34 565	250	42.0	5.2	48.4
Prince Edward	529	6 621	1 765	118	1 455	186	107	203	30 645	413	28.8	8.5	32.4
Prince George	472	9 319	358	972	876	95	770	305	32 728	167	32.9	9.6	59.3
Prince William	7 660	96 572	9 797	1 492	21 718	1 962	10 761	3 862	39 987	330	68.2	4.8	53.0
Pulaski	629	11 384	1 277	4 723	1 620	164	D	423	37 185	445	38.7	11.5	42.2
Rappahannock	184	1 043	45	47	201	18	D	34	32 821	397	46.6	7.3	51.9
Richmond	176	1 923	688	126	222	54	D	55	28 438	90	34.4	21.1	54.4
Roanoke	2 013	28 109	4 658	2 974	3 791	3 940	1 568	1 040	37 007	280	52.9	4.3	44.3
Rockbridge	424	4 438	268	D	1 276	D	95	124	27 982	833	28.3	8.5	42.4
Rockingham	1 404	26 754	4 638	6 849	1 943	361	589	1 078	40 306	1 902	43.2	2.8	54.6
Russell	459	5 656	1 190	D	918	D	D	194	34 373	995	34.8	7.1	41.5
Scott	288	3 522	586	825	691	96	D	113	32 104	1 292	33.7	3.0	41.4
Shenandoah	851	11 636	1 359	3 392	1 671	293	308	380	32 620	980	45.7	4.9	50.1
Smyth	507	9 261	2 347	2 993	1 225	181	176	296	31 985	792	40.8	9.2	41.2
Southampton	219	1 831	D	492	252	22	41	54	29 747	335	26.3	31.6	60.0
Spotsylvania	2 379	30 013	3 695	1 539	7 427	611	2 644	1 112	37 055	369	56.9	5.4	43.6
Stafford	2 180	30 776	3 676	861	4 851	D	3 927	1 247	40 523	215	62.3	1.4	41.9
Surry	75	D	9	D	D	D	D	D	D	127	43.3	21.3	50.4
Sussex	179	2 045	371	D	350	D	D	64	31 285	123	29.3	26.8	61.8
Tazewell	1 043	13 155	2 408	1 231	3 117	636	368	442	33 574	584	31.8	15.6	43.5
Warren	777	10 046	1 403	961	1 763	237	279	334	33 287	346	58.1	5.8	43.1
Washington	1 179	18 185	2 478	3 670	3 328	D	740	715	39 316	1 602	48.3	4.2	39.7
Westmoreland	318	2 466	226	603	449	84	176	64	25 811	152	18.4	21.7	50.7
Wise	745	9 110	1 556	243	2 232	238	421	302	33 141	165	49.7	6.1	32.7
Wythe	673	8 886	1 239	1 927	1 925	238	225	285	32 127	952	34.2	8.3	47.8
York	1 394	17 151	1 780	246	3 915	411	1 521	548	31 973	47	63.8	2.1	70.2
Independent cities													
Alexandria city	4 668	83 447	7 861	1 114	7 470	2 900	18 235	4 941	59 216	NA	NA	NA	NA
Bedford city	313	3 863	916	683	741	132	106	110	28 500	NA	NA	NA	NA
Bristol city	628	9 179	725	1 401	1 664	329	222	291	31 754	NA	NA	NA	NA
Buena Vista city	107	1 996	166	1 021	110	29	D	76	38 146	NA	NA	NA	NA
Charlottesville city	2 029	32 045	9 119	536	3 796	862	2 275	1 603	50 021	NA	NA	NA	NA
Chesapeake city	5 302	87 289	9 745	4 021	15 403	3 666	8 375	3 467	39 723	253	71.1	8.7	44.7
Colonial Heights city	656	9 633	1 603	D	3 534	274	382	233	24 199	NA	NA	NA	NA
Covington city	225	3 924	171	D	744	94	41	184	46 918	NA	NA	NA	NA
Danville city	1 287	23 350	5 224	4 506	4 308	890	426	757	32 400	NA	NA	NA	NA
Emporia city	240	4 112	1 174	853	610	D	68	118	28 699	NA	NA	NA	NA
Fairfax city	2 232	31 057	3 983	166	6 345	1 324	6 511	1 630	52 477	NA	NA	NA	NA
Falls Church city	851	9 166	1 786	D	1 087	179	1 445	430	46 939	NA	NA	NA	NA
Franklin city	279	3 539	1 164	34	1 054	190	126	100	28 364	NA	NA	NA	NA
Fredericksburg city	1 333	20 511	5 767	241	4 061	606	1 629	810	39 509	NA	NA	NA	NA
Galax city	290	4 956	1 426	767	1 171	119	D	142	28 691	NA	NA	NA	NA
Hampton city	2 350	39 893	7 179	2 025	6 805	1 049	3 897	1 583	39 674	NA	NA	NA	NA
Harrisonburg city	1 564	24 118	2 987	2 147	5 568	853	957	733	30 393	NA	NA	NA	NA
Hopewell city	419	6 699	1 281	D	630	121	157	355	53 019	NA	NA	NA	NA
Lexington city	282	3 788	646	D	393	95	D	140	37 023	NA	NA	NA	NA
Lynchburg city	2 191	56 785	9 732	9 105	7 957	2 768	3 194	2 372	41 772	NA	NA	NA	NA
Manassas city	1 439	21 039	3 650	3 687	2 654	443	3 254	1 230	58 483	NA	NA	NA	NA

Table B. States and Counties — **Agriculture**

STATE County	\[Land in farms\] Acreage (1,000)	Percent change, 2007–2012	Acres — Average size of farm	Total irrigated (1,000)	Total cropland (1,000)	Value of land and buildings (dollars) — Average per farm	Average per acre	Value of machinery and equipment, average per farm (dollars)	Value of products sold — Total (mil dol)	Average per farm (dollars)	Percent from: Crops	Livestock and poultry products	Percent of farms with sales of: $10,000 or more	$100,000 or more	Government payments — Total ($1,000)	Percent of farms
	117	118	119	120	121	122	123	124	125	126	127	128	129	130	131	132
VIRGINIA—Cont'd																
Louisa	80	2.2	165	0.3	30.1	946 557	5 723	61 971	14.5	29 928	46.9	53.1	36.3	6.0	784	24.5
Lunenburg	83	-0.6	223	0.4	27.7	530 593	2 380	77 668	18.5	49 846	73.2	26.8	33.7	7.3	1 085	33.4
Madison	107	4.1	205	0.1	40.1	1 294 623	6 316	74 799	29.0	55 517	39.8	60.2	51.1	9.2	389	18.2
Mathews	5	5.3	84	0.0	3.2	523 182	6 193	57 909	2.4	43 691	93.0	6.9	32.7	7.3	67	12.7
Mecklenburg	145	-7.5	276	2.8	50.8	710 928	2 575	100 488	42.9	81 395	82.5	17.5	35.9	11.6	1 229	35.5
Middlesex	19	8.3	263	0.5	13.7	1 013 082	3 855	139 068	11.3	154 233	92.5	7.5	38.4	19.2	384	39.7
Montgomery	107	20.0	178	0.3	31.6	867 716	4 878	68 212	23.7	39 315	28.2	71.8	34.7	6.6	219	12.1
Nelson	80	9.3	176	0.9	22.4	805 229	4 581	63 396	15.8	34 741	65.6	34.4	40.7	4.4	116	10.5
New Kent	20	-3.2	144	D	10.5	794 927	5 525	58 759	7.0	51 117	95.9	4.1	24.1	8.0	381	19.0
Northampton	56	-12.1	381	6.3	42.8	1 646 782	4 319	259 687	93.1	633 054	66.0	34.0	73.5	47.6	1 892	50.3
Northumberland	43	-2.5	442	0.0	33.5	1 324 908	3 001	220 061	21.4	217 929	98.3	1.7	60.2	33.7	1 104	60.2
Nottoway	62	-5.7	173	0.1	22.6	539 621	3 120	75 242	48.7	136 778	12.7	87.3	34.6	9.6	413	29.8
Orange	105	0.2	192	0.6	40.5	1 292 497	6 746	95 737	90.6	165 589	71.7	28.3	42.6	9.3	1 081	16.5
Page	71	10.5	131	1.0	28.2	466 200	3 336	84 549	141.1	258 894	4.4	95.6	51.6	25.3	472	17.2
Patrick	79	-1.1	140	0.1	22.9	515 637	2 430	80 956	86.9	64 211	42.5	57.5	38.3	10.0	3 886	36.0
Powhatan	32	7.7	128	0.1	10.6	735 120	5 729	48 592	10.0	40 036	39.1	60.9	25.2	4.0	128	16.0
Prince Edward	79	-4.1	191	0.1	19.7	612 015	3 203	58 479	16.5	39 993	11.6	88.4	29.5	4.8	641	51.6
Prince George	37	-18.2	220	0.0	19.0	922 305	4 202	102 784	10.8	64 449	91.8	8.2	34.7	11.4	903	47.9
Prince William	36	8.6	108	1.0	19.0	953 252	8 827	70 982	12.0	36 467	48.3	51.7	26.1	7.0	240	8.5
Pulaski	97	28.0	217	0.0	26.7	667 404	3 074	78 555	28.1	63 234	8.5	91.5	44.0	7.9	337	11.0
Rappahannock	63	-3.5	158	0.1	17.3	1 335 914	8 443	54 128	9.3	23 378	39.5	60.5	33.0	7.6	147	9.1
Richmond	32	-13.3	360	0.1	22.3	1 036 744	2 882	158 744	15.5	171 856	94.7	5.3	55.6	26.7	684	63.3
Roanoke	31	7.8	112	0.1	7.6	480 689	4 275	47 568	4.1	14 786	D	D	20.0	3.2	13	8.6
Rockbridge	168	21.7	202	0.1	42.1	868 321	4 296	57 385	31.8	38 148	21.9	78.1	41.3	5.3	649	14.3
Rockingham	222	-4.7	117	5.6	100.5	823 606	7 055	88 252	659.0	346 475	7.2	92.8	58.4	35.0	2 741	15.9
Russell	188	23.8	189	0.0	34.0	409 282	2 171	53 826	32.2	32 326	9.1	90.9	36.3	7.2	2 525	32.9
Scott	158	2.9	123	0.1	33.4	254 430	2 076	48 673	14.1	10 892	30.1	69.9	25.3	1.3	999	38.0
Shenandoah	134	-5.5	136	0.7	52.7	760 234	5 580	74 039	128.8	131 394	15.1	84.9	43.2	15.0	1 242	13.7
Smyth	167	30.9	210	0.0	34.3	586 822	2 789	64 580	58.0	73 184	6.6	93.4	43.4	13.8	760	38.1
Southampton	154	-4.8	459	3.2	94.3	1 224 988	2 668	183 934	79.2	236 310	84.6	15.4	53.7	31.9	6 268	75.8
Spotsylvania	42	-19.2	114	0.1	18.7	700 862	6 130	85 612	11.0	29 800	36.4	63.6	27.4	3.3	331	16.0
Stafford	15	-23.0	71	0.0	6.6	650 702	9 168	59 926	2.7	12 740	49.0	51.0	22.3	1.4	71	11.2
Surry	45	9.8	355	1.2	34.0	1 272 142	3 581	126 425	27.7	218 291	69.9	30.1	53.5	23.6	1 198	46.5
Sussex	64	-13.4	522	1.4	39.4	1 189 211	2 277	199 992	37.3	303 065	D	D	56.1	26.8	2 190	71.5
Tazewell	150	-2.3	257	0.0	29.1	569 505	2 215	63 351	27.0	46 267	7.2	92.8	42.3	10.8	572	21.2
Warren	48	0.8	139	0.0	15.8	990 098	7 138	60 844	5.7	16 572	37.4	62.6	24.6	2.6	40	3.2
Washington	192	-3.4	120	0.2	54.2	471 998	3 936	51 363	76.5	47 753	8.7	91.3	35.3	8.1	4 522	38.1
Westmoreland	59	-7.2	391	1.6	36.0	1 396 757	3 576	161 632	35.8	235 250	85.9	14.1	65.8	32.2	1 184	52.6
Wise	26	16.9	157	0.0	3.5	432 818	2 756	42 079	D	D	D	D	20.0	0.6	25	6.1
Wythe	174	9.4	183	0.1	49.5	619 529	3 386	69 486	51.4	54 034	13.0	87.0	47.7	10.7	840	20.7
York	3	116.4	60	D	D	298 723	4 991	77 489	2.4	50 830	86.9	13.1	29.8	10.6	5	6.4
Independent cities																
Alexandria city	NA	NA	NA	NA	NA	NA	NA	NA	NA	NA	NA	NA	NA	NA	NA	NA
Bedford city	NA	NA	NA	NA	NA	NA	NA	NA	NA	NA	NA	NA	NA	NA	NA	NA
Bristol city	NA	NA	NA	NA	NA	NA	NA	NA	NA	NA	NA	NA	NA	NA	NA	NA
Buena Vista city	NA	NA	NA	NA	NA	NA	NA	NA	NA	NA	NA	NA	NA	NA	NA	NA
Charlottesville city	NA	NA	NA	NA	NA	NA	NA	NA	NA	NA	NA	NA	NA	NA	NA	NA
Chesapeake city	45	-11.7	178	0.3	37.0	776 672	4 355	98 379	40.5	160 028	D	D	33.2	13.8	570	24.1
Colonial Heights city	NA	NA	NA	NA	NA	NA	NA	NA	NA	NA	NA	NA	NA	NA	NA	NA
Covington city	NA	NA	NA	NA	NA	NA	NA	NA	NA	NA	NA	NA	NA	NA	NA	NA
Danville city	NA	NA	NA	NA	NA	NA	NA	NA	NA	NA	NA	NA	NA	NA	NA	NA
Emporia city	NA	NA	NA	NA	NA	NA	NA	NA	NA	NA	NA	NA	NA	NA	NA	NA
Fairfax city	NA	NA	NA	NA	NA	NA	NA	NA	NA	NA	NA	NA	NA	NA	NA	NA
Falls Church city	NA	NA	NA	NA	NA	NA	NA	NA	NA	NA	NA	NA	NA	NA	NA	NA
Franklin city	NA	NA	NA	NA	NA	NA	NA	NA	NA	NA	NA	NA	NA	NA	NA	NA
Fredericksburg city	NA	NA	NA	NA	NA	NA	NA	NA	NA	NA	NA	NA	NA	NA	NA	NA
Galax city	NA	NA	NA	NA	NA	NA	NA	NA	NA	NA	NA	NA	NA	NA	NA	NA
Hampton city	NA	NA	NA	NA	NA	NA	NA	NA	NA	NA	NA	NA	NA	NA	NA	NA
Harrisonburg city	NA	NA	NA	NA	NA	NA	NA	NA	NA	NA	NA	NA	NA	NA	NA	NA
Hopewell city	NA	NA	NA	NA	NA	NA	NA	NA	NA	NA	NA	NA	NA	NA	NA	NA
Lexington city	NA	NA	NA	NA	NA	NA	NA	NA	NA	NA	NA	NA	NA	NA	NA	NA
Lynchburg city	NA	NA	NA	NA	NA	NA	NA	NA	NA	NA	NA	NA	NA	NA	NA	NA
Manassas city	NA	NA	NA	NA	NA	NA	NA	NA	NA	NA	NA	NA	NA	NA	NA	NA

Table B. States and Counties — Water Use, Wholesale Trade, Retail Trade, and Real Estate

STATE County	Water use, 2010 Total water withdrawn (mil gal/day)	Gallons withdrawn per person per day	Wholesale trade,[1] 2012 Number of establishments	Number of employees	Sales (mil dol)	Annual payroll (mil dol)	Retail trade,[2] 2012 Number of establishments	Number of employees	Sales (mil dol)	Annual payroll (mil dol)	Real estate and rental and leasing,[2] 2012 Number of establishments	Number of employees	Receipts (mil dol)	Annual payroll (mil dol)
	133	134	135	136	137	138	139	140	141	142	143	144	145	146
VIRGINIA—Cont'd														
Louisa	1 823.7	55 010	11	100	45.3	6.3	77	1 086	276.4	22.9	20	71	10.4	2.5
Lunenburg	5.2	406	6	112	111.2	7.3	36	250	51.3	5.0	1	D	D	D
Madison	2.5	185	13	74	16.5	2.6	40	635	186.4	15.0	4	6	1.0	0.1
Mathews	2.1	231	5	D	D	D	25	232	54.4	4.5	10	D	D	D
Mecklenburg	7.9	241	31	263	159.0	11.1	160	1 677	417.1	35.7	33	131	14.3	3.2
Middlesex	1.9	171	12	83	25.7	3.0	56	437	101.3	9.8	13	D	D	D
Montgomery	33.1	350	46	808	593.0	35.8	324	4 992	1 280.6	108.9	91	535	103.8	19.0
Nelson	5.9	395	4	D	D	D	50	299	115.1	6.3	12	D	D	D
New Kent	30.0	1 628	4	28	13.6	1.2	39	488	155.0	8.8	14	21	2.0	0.5
Northampton	4.2	335	18	160	167.1	5.2	72	543	117.9	10.4	13	43	6.8	0.8
Northumberland	4.2	340	12	69	31.4	2.6	48	352	85.3	7.6	18	39	5.2	1.6
Nottoway	2.4	149	12	98	85.2	3.4	62	607	126.6	12.9	6	14	2.0	0.4
Orange	5.6	166	7	D	D	D	107	970	311.6	24.5	23	41	6.1	1.1
Page	4.0	166	8	D	D	D	76	772	173.9	17.3	11	35	5.5	0.7
Patrick	3.4	183	6	52	21.7	1.9	54	550	204.6	11.0	6	6	0.4	0.1
Pittsylvania	7.6	119	29	771	381.0	21.7	133	868	242.8	16.8	24	86	12.8	1.9
Powhatan	4.3	153	21	156	51.0	6.3	66	550	264.2	17.5	22	67	12.0	1.9
Prince Edward	4.9	209	14	140	41.7	4.8	99	1 488	390.5	35.9	25	99	11.0	1.9
Prince George	17.4	487	24	D	D	D	73	977	260.7	22.7	19	41	9.1	0.9
Prince William	66.2	165	172	2 387	2 222.7	138.3	1 083	20 117	5 638.2	516.7	306	1 242	339.7	50.4
Pulaski	6.8	194	17	114	36.0	3.4	110	1 599	352.7	32.1	21	65	7.8	1.5
Rappahannock	0.8	110	5	22	2.4	0.6	26	150	29.3	3.6	4	D	D	D
Richmond	0.8	84	7	68	72.2	2.5	38	252	68.2	5.6	7	19	1.6	0.3
Roanoke	17.2	186	98	1 168	700.2	66.9	260	3 609	891.0	84.3	104	352	60.4	12.0
Rockbridge	5.0	226	9	53	16.5	1.5	74	1 175	360.1	25.8	13	38	3.6	0.8
Rockingham	38.0	498	56	946	626.3	48.3	206	1 871	429.8	40.3	44	568	110.4	23.9
Russell	11.5	399	14	53	30.0	2.0	81	934	233.2	20.3	13	43	3.5	1.1
Scott	2.2	94	10	D	D	D	78	709	210.5	13.5	5	11	1.5	0.3
Shenandoah	30.5	727	18	440	519.7	15.5	150	1 705	499.5	36.1	30	D	D	D
Smyth	19.8	614	16	D	D	D	114	1 202	272.0	24.0	15	43	7.1	1.4
Southampton	8.6	461	10	142	131.2	5.9	30	236	55.7	4.4	8	20	2.5	0.4
Spotsylvania	13.9	113	64	678	341.7	31.3	402	6 758	2 160.1	184.4	113	508	77.9	18.1
Stafford	13.7	106	47	D	D	D	253	4 489	1 247.9	111.3	89	298	58.1	10.2
Surry	1 908.5	270 397	1	D	D	D	12	53	14.9	1.0	3	D	D	D
Sussex	2.1	171	9	D	D	D	43	332	112.6	6.8	5	13	2.2	0.4
Tazewell	5.0	110	60	527	265.7	22.1	212	3 044	804.6	65.9	50	170	24.9	4.6
Warren	11.4	303	7	D	D	D	137	1 718	444.6	40.2	22	71	9.9	1.9
Washington	59.9	1 091	38	D	D	D	206	3 207	820.5	67.8	46	127	26.1	5.1
Westmoreland	4.8	273	16	48	31.2	1.7	45	415	109.8	8.7	12	22	2.1	0.4
Wise	5.3	127	37	345	299.7	16.4	168	2 092	500.9	45.1	23	69	7.3	1.5
Wythe	16.6	567	13	D	D	D	137	1 922	905.5	44.0	22	75	21.7	2.5
York	781.4	11 936	34	139	80.0	6.1	220	3 922	884.4	86.9	50	256	28.2	7.9
Independent cities														
Alexandria city	0.0	0	82	1 139	502.8	61.6	480	7 180	2 416.0	222.6	240	1 475	524.1	76.6
Bedford city	0.0	0	8	63	76.9	2.9	50	456	131.1	10.5	15	32	5.1	1.0
Bristol city	0.0	0	34	802	370.4	22.5	157	1 732	349.9	33.6	23	69	9.9	2.0
Buena Vista city	0.2	24	1	D	D	D	19	156	34.8	3.0	3	4	0.4	0.0
Charlottesville city	0.2	4	48	513	183.3	23.7	331	3 925	747.9	82.8	99	502	107.6	19.7
Chesapeake city	544.0	2 448	239	3 447	2 225.2	169.7	789	15 088	4 114.9	336.7	273	1 227	291.6	52.9
Colonial Heights city	0.0	1	10	53	19.7	2.0	180	3 498	763.3	65.3	27	151	31.6	4.5
Covington city	2.0	330	6	D	D	D	60	734	158.3	15.8	9	24	2.5	0.5
Danville city	7.2	168	50	545	285.2	24.5	306	4 165	965.0	87.2	64	339	48.7	9.1
Emporia city	0.0	7	3	D	D	D	52	620	136.5	13.5	11	36	4.6	0.8
Fairfax city	0.1	5	40	372	408.9	18.2	251	5 526	1 757.5	176.4	60	261	61.3	13.5
Falls Church city	0.0	2	18	D	D	D	92	1 010	310.2	35.9	35	192	71.7	9.3
Franklin city	1.1	122	7	52	28.3	1.8	63	979	228.3	21.6	11	D	D	D
Fredericksburg city	0.3	14	21	224	95.3	11.8	253	4 098	1 075.0	88.1	70	308	63.3	12.5
Galax city	1.9	275	5	69	117.5	3.0	64	1 105	259.6	24.3	13	52	9.9	1.6
Hampton city	0.3	2	71	886	344.7	39.3	436	6 791	1 512.5	148.3	114	750	117.3	23.7
Harrisonburg city	0.4	8	57	1 006	405.9	43.2	334	5 664	1 519.8	144.6	72	351	75.9	10.9
Hopewell city	130.5	5 775	11	84	26.9	3.5	73	586	164.8	13.1	22	97	20.3	3.7
Lexington city	0.0	0	NA	NA	NA	NA	44	458	92.7	9.4	17	32	4.4	1.0
Lynchburg city	0.2	2	69	877	509.0	39.0	385	7 371	1 995.2	178.2	109	447	79.9	14.5
Manassas city	0.1	2	41	D	D	D	194	2 778	895.3	86.1	52	229	64.0	11.4

1. Merchant wholesalers, except manufacturers' sales branches and offices.   2. Employer establishments.

STATE County	Professional, scientific, and technical services, 2012				Manufacturing, 2012				Accommodation and food services, 2012			
	Number of establishments	Number of employees	Receipts (mil dol)	Annual payroll (mil dol)	Number of establishments	Number of employees	Receipts (mil dol)	Annual payroll (mil dol)	Number of establishments	Number of employees	Sales (mil dol)	Annual payroll (mil dol)
	147	148	149	150	151	152	153	154	155	156	157	158
VIRGINIA—Cont'd												
Louisa	57	188	16.2	5.4	32	1 162	426.8	58.2	30	348	18.2	4.8
Lunenburg	10	44	3.9	1.1	7	429	99.4	12.9	8	D	D	D
Madison	22	51	5.4	1.6	18	250	D	8.5	18	190	9.4	2.8
Mathews	19	D	D	D	3	D	D	D	13	178	6.4	1.7
Mecklenburg	49	264	26.3	9.2	34	1 338	298.0	49.4	67	1 179	46.6	12.7
Middlesex	28	150	8.7	4.7	12	133	D	4.9	26	190	9.5	3.1
Montgomery	267	2 714	265.2	142.7	50	3 054	936.8	159.8	197	4 223	186.5	53.5
Nelson	42	140	14.7	5.5	27	268	D	9.0	20	168	6.4	1.9
New Kent	28	94	7.7	3.4	14	157	D	4.6	29	D	D	D
Northampton	21	56	4.7	1.8	9	397	D	13.8	40	476	29.0	6.9
Northumberland	21	91	20.4	4.5	21	426	D	14.9	20	134	5.7	2.0
Nottoway	19	93	6.8	2.5	12	329	104.3	12.7	27	335	12.7	3.8
Orange	74	302	52.6	14.7	18	836	230.0	34.0	58	850	36.3	10.3
Page	25	164	15.4	5.3	13	552	161.5	15.6	56	652	39.9	11.1
Patrick	18	67	3.4	1.4	35	1 342	189.2	39.9	20	163	7.0	1.7
Pittsylvania	47	149	19.3	4.8	45	1 959	615.9	82.0	38	421	15.5	4.7
Powhatan	62	249	27.4	11.1	19	99	D	D	25	494	17.1	5.4
Prince Edward	34	111	8.6	3.0	14	107	D	2.9	49	1 148	49.9	13.9
Prince George	49	695	89.4	35.1	24	839	602.9	42.3	45	668	39.3	8.8
Prince William	1 067	10 927	1 557.4	753.1	94	1 634	353.1	75.2	633	11 867	673.7	177.6
Pulaski	38	170	17.2	7.8	39	3 797	2 861.3	183.6	74	1 148	53.4	14.1
Rappahannock	29	77	9.1	3.2	7	36	D	0.9	14	D	D	D
Richmond	13	42	4.8	2.4	7	122	D	4.8	13	122	6.2	1.6
Roanoke	217	1 101	124.5	49.8	63	3 134	815.7	164.8	132	2 663	128.3	32.4
Rockbridge	28	89	7.8	2.9	20	1 203	197.6	42.3	52	802	44.3	11.9
Rockingham	76	565	75.6	32.5	88	7 047	5 397.1	323.0	91	2 128	82.7	35.7
Russell	46	634	80.9	42.0	9	345	D	10.7	38	504	19.3	5.7
Scott	22	102	10.6	3.9	9	962	486.8	37.8	24	D	D	D
Shenandoah	63	262	33.2	14.4	35	3 271	796.2	109.7	81	1 365	56.0	17.1
Smyth	37	198	14.7	6.4	40	3 129	833.0	128.8	45	727	29.0	8.1
Southampton	11	D	D	D	12	411	106.4	15.0	13	84	3.8	1.0
Spotsylvania	227	2 219	424.7	190.8	59	1 517	D	67.7	203	3 880	190.4	53.4
Stafford	318	3 786	677.6	268.6	39	768	171.1	31.7	183	3 102	161.4	40.9
Surry	7	21	1.2	0.5	3	108	D	3.7	5	39	1.6	0.4
Sussex	7	D	D	D	9	120	D	6.2	13	239	11.7	3.1
Tazewell	60	443	39.8	16.3	53	1 294	297.8	60.0	71	1 245	59.6	16.1
Warren	77	277	28.3	12.8	25	810	811.8	41.1	79	1 203	61.2	18.0
Washington	94	642	49.0	26.5	66	3 763	1 095.6	153.6	96	D	D	D
Westmoreland	30	235	14.4	8.3	9	560	167.0	12.9	31	D	D	D
Wise	58	423	38.4	18.1	26	303	D	12.4	55	1 130	42.1	12.2
Wythe	43	204	20.8	8.9	40	1 705	1 292.9	71.6	83	1 509	78.3	19.4
York	177	D	D	D	27	D	D	8.9	155	3 804	269.9	56.2
Independent cities												
Alexandria city	1 238	18 505	3 799.3	1 692.1	72	1 332	273.0	57.9	387	8 051	647.5	180.7
Bedford city	31	D	D	D	20	881	D	29.8	33	516	21.9	6.0
Bristol city	44	239	24.2	13.0	23	1 057	302.3	48.6	82	1 811	86.8	23.8
Buena Vista city	6	20	1.3	0.5	14	894	351.4	39.1	12	D	D	D
Charlottesville city	322	2 555	406.5	164.9	46	455	98.7	21.6	293	5 199	293.3	75.9
Chesapeake city	510	D	D	D	130	3 965	1 504.2	211.6	466	10 267	447.6	121.1
Colonial Heights city	50	491	21.5	8.3	8	129	D	5.4	82	2 180	99.9	27.8
Covington city	19	52	6.5	1.2	6	D	D	D	20	D	D	D
Danville city	74	522	71.0	31.7	46	4 635	1 703.0	223.7	139	2 850	120.4	33.6
Emporia city	18	79	4.7	1.9	9	850	203.7	35.3	26	586	25.1	7.2
Fairfax city	647	6 022	1 368.7	522.1	29	158	18.8	6.3	192	3 608	218.6	60.9
Falls Church city	157	1 798	352.4	136.3	17	74	16.1	3.4	119	1 098	73.5	19.1
Franklin city	20	200	12.5	6.2	6	27	8.5	1.3	28	484	20.3	5.1
Fredericksburg city	180	1 390	227.1	99.5	26	221	57.0	8.3	165	3 718	179.5	55.4
Galax city	26	138	12.8	4.4	12	719	157.9	18.6	39	540	22.7	7.1
Hampton city	279	3 711	648.1	289.6	68	2 189	508.3	114.9	250	5 380	249.0	72.2
Harrisonburg city	139	924	98.8	43.9	46	2 556	832.6	99.4	186	4 468	216.0	58.8
Hopewell city	35	184	16.8	7.5	16	1 338	1 930.8	110.8	52	728	33.5	8.2
Lexington city	29	121	10.5	3.7	5	14	D	D	52	540	34.2	9.3
Lynchburg city	200	3 395	969.0	265.2	83	8 339	2 749.6	504.3	215	5 071	216.4	61.0
Manassas city	213	3 462	612.2	285.9	32	4 012	1 365.7	366.4	109	1 587	91.4	24.7

1. Establishment subject to federal tax.

STATE County	Health care and social assistance, 2012				Other services, 2012				Nonemployer businesses, 2014		Value of residential construction authorized by building permits, 2015	
	Number of establishments	Number of employees	Receipts (mil dol)	Annual payroll (mil dol)	Number of establishments	Number of employees	Receipts (mil dol)	Annual payroll (mil dol)	Number	Receipts (mil dol)	New Construction ($1,000)	Number of housing units
	159	160	161	162	163	164	165	166	167	168	169	170
VIRGINIA—Cont'd												
Louisa	25	299	24.6	10.4	47	D	D	D	2 202	80.8	42 293	198
Lunenburg	16	326	11.3	5.5	12	D	D	D	576	19.2	3 198	20
Madison	21	286	13.8	6.7	21	D	D	D	1 153	39.6	10 275	41
Mathews	9	D	D	D	12	D	D	D	824	30.2	5 970	22
Mecklenburg	75	1 843	153.7	62.3	68	333	23.7	6.9	1 630	66.8	13 050	86
Middlesex	20	440	23.2	9.5	25	D	D	D	1 022	41.0	9 973	45
Montgomery	224	3 898	489.7	167.8	148	814	165.6	23.1	5 006	208.4	56 154	376
Nelson	20	D	D	D	21	181	13.1	4.9	1 274	49.7	13 779	59
New Kent	25	610	37.2	17.0	29	D	D	D	1 565	58.5	37 657	187
Northampton	40	942	97.8	34.3	20	D	D	D	1 014	39.3	10 302	50
Northumberland	11	84	3.1	1.6	26	D	D	D	1 124	39.5	12 353	57
Nottoway	28	959	48.7	25.9	25	D	D	D	670	17.5	3 849	33
Orange	45	389	23.9	10.0	56	373	36.9	10.8	2 343	85.7	1 650	9
Page	24	479	46.8	17.6	35	D	D	D	1 404	47.6	6 218	46
Patrick	23	673	40.5	17.4	13	D	D	D	1 029	33.7	3 825	20
Pittsylvania	52	1 120	51.6	23.3	72	281	23.5	6.5	3 058	98.6	0	0
Powhatan	27	D	D	D	57	344	24.2	7.6	1 942	93.6	41 426	171
Prince Edward	82	1 697	135.0	59.4	35	160	14.5	3.5	953	29.4	6 970	45
Prince George	25	159	18.1	8.3	32	143	12.2	4.4	1 421	45.2	11 908	68
Prince William	718	9 320	993.6	387.7	537	3 703	653.2	116.1	32 860	1 334.7	293 923	1 840
Pulaski	57	1 109	108.8	43.8	43	208	20.8	5.5	1 484	43.2	8 534	37
Rappahannock	10	D	D	D	9	D	D	D	1 020	50.4	12 352	26
Richmond	15	802	27.2	13.5	12	D	D	D	534	18.3	2 025	8
Roanoke	229	4 773	381.7	174.4	142	695	53.8	17.5	5 513	221.1	41 992	337
Rockbridge	39	356	24.2	9.8	28	D	D	D	1 542	58.2	28 006	109
Rockingham	100	4 573	496.7	202.5	104	474	42.1	13.5	5 394	227.9	70 137	343
Russell	65	1 199	97.1	41.9	27	D	D	D	1 162	34.1	2 978	17
Scott	37	679	39.4	18.5	15	D	D	D	925	25.3	2 792	27
Shenandoah	74	1 273	109.4	46.0	81	379	33.6	9.0	2 894	102.4	17 387	92
Smyth	65	1 756	143.8	66.6	35	179	18.5	4.7	1 469	50.2	3 445	18
Southampton	10	143	7.8	3.9	14	D	D	D	897	29.9	4 155	28
Spotsylvania	198	3 021	262.5	122.9	173	1 021	86.9	26.8	8 077	314.4	102 360	390
Stafford	173	3 363	287.0	118.9	199	1 195	107.4	35.2	7 996	319.9	177 427	785
Surry	4	11	0.9	0.4	2	D	D	D	315	9.3	3 369	22
Sussex	14	D	D	D	19	D	D	D	463	13.7	2 188	18
Tazewell	140	2 377	209.2	80.2	92	605	71.7	20.8	2 105	70.1	3 536	31
Warren	61	D	D	D	68	517	74.3	13.5	2 556	106.3	25 477	116
Washington	150	2 410	258.4	108.1	62	D	D	D	3 390	118.7	14 559	63
Westmoreland	18	238	13.2	6.7	27	88	4.8	1.4	1 191	37.3	13 011	72
Wise	93	1 598	125.1	46.5	53	D	D	D	1 587	45.8	1 020	6
Wythe	75	1 274	108.6	47.1	55	324	27.2	8.7	1 516	53.3	4 585	34
York	107	1 667	215.8	81.2	116	D	D	D	3 627	136.2	29 813	122
Independent cities												
Alexandria city	397	7 356	1 041.6	376.9	584	9 997	2 626.4	670.0	14 586	700.8	42 764	193
Bedford city	42	D	D	D	32	235	25.7	8.1	375	11.8	NA	NA
Bristol city	48	654	54.7	18.6	46	D	D	D	1 018	39.2	975	10
Buena Vista city	12	183	5.1	2.7	9	D	D	D	307	10.4	120	1
Charlottesville city	175	D	D	D	151	1 444	318.3	52.5	3 963	229.7	38 149	231
Chesapeake city	497	9 693	978.2	435.2	399	2 990	313.4	95.8	13 127	486.5	256 186	1 325
Colonial Heights city	108	1 746	139.9	56.8	50	357	25.0	8.8	938	40.4	653	4
Covington city	17	178	8.8	2.9	22	D	D	D	233	8.5	0	0
Danville city	194	4 803	441.4	188.5	101	535	49.2	11.2	2 380	74.1	1 279	13
Emporia city	37	1 078	80.1	34.4	18	D	D	D	283	8.6	470	8
Fairfax city	265	3 637	339.1	135.3	146	1 531	424.5	77.8	3 098	221.3	10 232	30
Falls Church city	108	D	D	D	93	588	69.5	22.6	1 393	92.4	14 499	33
Franklin city	52	1 200	105.1	39.4	26	182	12.3	3.1	433	15.3	297	3
Fredericksburg city	189	5 216	789.2	335.8	104	860	69.9	22.8	1 870	99.0	14 803	53
Galax city	45	D	D	D	24	D	D	D	407	13.2	150	1
Hampton city	265	7 739	888.7	394.2	176	1 056	87.5	25.0	6 530	184.0	10 384	162
Harrisonburg city	163	2 860	211.7	96.1	127	690	67.3	18.2	2 532	119.2	9 598	63
Hopewell city	49	1 450	144.0	60.4	38	200	16.7	5.1	816	23.0	4 087	48
Lexington city	41	669	69.2	23.4	34	229	31.0	7.4	456	17.7	726	5
Lynchburg city	268	9 339	1 046.5	427.9	173	1 161	100.6	30.6	4 015	140.5	33 142	281
Manassas city	174	3 297	418.2	176.8	141	848	93.5	26.4	3 211	148.7	19 308	137

Table B. States and Counties — Government Employment and Payroll, and Local Government Finances

| STATE County | Government employment and payroll, 2012 | | March payroll (percent of total) | | | | | | | Local government finances, 2012 — General revenue | | | | |
	Full-time equivalent employees	March payroll (dollars)	Adminis-tration, judicial, and legal	Police and Corrections	Fire Protection	Highways and transpor-tation	Health and Welfare	Natural resources and utilities	Education and libraries	Total (mil dol)	Inter-govern-mental (mil dol)	Taxes Total (mil dol)	Per capita[1] (dollars) Total	Property
	171	172	173	174	175	176	177	178	179	180	181	182	183	184
VIRGINIA—Cont'd														
Louisa	1 124	3 411 101	8.2	6.8	4.2	0.0	1.1	4.9	73.3	96.7	33.7	53.8	1 609	1 418
Lunenburg	403	1 190 954	9.0	11.5	0.0	0.0	2.3	2.4	72.9	33.1	20.6	9.9	790	676
Madison	403	1 326 277	10.7	6.4	0.0	0.0	5.8	0.3	69.8	34.3	15.7	16.2	1 227	1 036
Mathews	358	848 780	8.9	7.2	0.0	0.0	5.4	0.0	74.9	23.0	9.7	12.1	1 364	1 166
Mecklenburg	1 375	3 603 811	7.0	12.8	0.2	1.1	10.7	2.6	62.8	94.5	47.2	37.6	1 185	856
Middlesex	280	843 355	10.1	15.3	0.0	0.0	3.5	0.8	70.3	25.5	8.9	15.3	1 409	1 212
Montgomery	2 699	8 781 181	9.0	11.9	0.5	4.6	2.7	5.5	61.5	255.0	103.6	112.5	1 182	829
Nelson	457	1 391 646	8.9	4.1	0.0	0.0	1.6	0.5	80.1	45.2	17.7	23.6	1 590	1 346
New Kent	638	2 123 526	10.3	8.3	5.3	0.3	4.1	7.3	63.1	52.7	21.7	26.8	1 400	1 195
Northampton	850	3 278 000	5.0	9.0	0.0	20.1	6.5	3.2	55.2	101.7	23.0	21.3	1 740	1 417
Northumberland	358	1 244 110	8.2	7.7	0.0	0.0	4.8	0.9	77.1	28.9	10.2	17.4	1 407	1 269
Nottoway	548	1 646 561	8.1	8.7	0.0	2.8	5.9	4.4	67.2	39.4	23.9	10.3	650	454
Orange	1 173	3 380 570	7.0	14.3	3.2	1.7	2.2	2.9	67.7	89.1	37.1	42.7	1 247	997
Page	878	2 456 816	8.1	13.4	0.0	0.6	1.8	3.8	71.0	65.3	32.2	27.2	1 138	890
Patrick	695	1 689 450	5.6	12.0	0.0	0.0	4.5	0.8	75.3	43.9	24.0	14.5	784	617
Pittsylvania	1 563	4 924 209	5.8	7.5	0.1	0.5	1.4	1.2	80.6	127.9	84.1	37.6	599	478
Powhatan	855	2 784 066	7.2	7.7	0.5	0.0	3.4	1.3	77.9	69.7	28.5	38.3	1 361	1 230
Prince Edward	701	2 116 144	10.4	10.6	0.3	3.1	2.0	3.4	66.4	54.6	29.8	19.8	852	490
Prince George	1 519	5 308 620	5.9	28.6	0.9	0.0	2.5	1.5	58.6	118.9	72.6	36.1	976	765
Prince William	15 485	68 447 361	3.7	8.8	4.5	3.3	4.4	3.5	69.0	1 578.6	659.7	752.7	1 749	1 412
Pulaski	1 288	4 175 730	6.1	8.3	0.9	1.1	3.6	5.9	68.5	117.9	56.3	35.2	1 013	707
Rappahannock	256	760 848	9.7	11.1	0.0	0.0	6.5	0.8	68.9	20.6	4.6	14.7	1 978	1 804
Richmond	326	1 099 371	6.8	32.6	0.0	0.0	0.6	2.6	56.3	32.9	20.4	9.1	1 002	790
Roanoke	3 729	13 158 244	7.7	7.6	6.2	0.3	4.8	9.4	62.7	353.7	116.0	158.3	1 704	1 275
Rockbridge	661	1 852 653	7.0	8.7	0.0	0.3	5.5	2.1	74.0	71.1	30.7	29.1	1 299	943
Rockingham	2 706	8 346 966	7.1	8.4	3.0	0.8	4.8	4.5	70.2	227.8	108.4	83.5	1 079	895
Russell	1 094	4 018 658	3.7	6.4	0.2	1.1	0.2	2.5	83.0	73.8	48.1	20.2	710	482
Scott	721	2 170 415	5.9	6.0	0.0	0.8	3.3	2.2	79.1	62.5	41.3	16.4	722	496
Shenandoah	1 504	4 472 709	7.1	9.2	3.6	1.5	4.6	6.2	65.6	123.4	60.3	48.9	1 149	882
Smyth	1 259	3 570 921	6.6	8.1	0.4	1.0	11.3	5.6	65.4	92.2	58.8	22.8	718	494
Southampton	717	2 092 925	8.4	10.2	0.0	0.2	6.0	3.3	70.4	53.2	26.3	21.4	1 162	1 013
Spotsylvania	3 637	13 506 224	7.0	5.7	4.9	0.0	3.5	3.8	72.0	382.7	163.4	188.0	1 496	1 158
Stafford	4 475	17 648 377	6.1	5.1	2.8	0.2	2.7	4.7	77.1	448.6	192.3	213.9	1 592	1 307
Surry	386	1 034 084	6.2	6.4	0.0	0.0	0.8	3.6	77.4	29.5	7.5	21.1	3 078	2 927
Sussex	423	1 312 782	12.9	14.1	0.0	0.2	7.5	2.3	61.1	40.7	22.0	10.1	843	685
Tazewell	1 644	4 416 984	7.8	8.5	0.4	2.1	7.4	4.0	67.6	142.1	75.0	40.0	903	580
Warren	1 201	3 547 039	8.8	13.4	0.9	2.4	2.5	5.2	65.3	103.2	45.3	48.1	1 264	942
Washington	2 294	6 382 778	4.2	19.7	0.0	2.6	2.7	7.4	62.3	154.9	83.7	51.1	926	645
Westmoreland	590	1 733 294	11.3	10.8	0.0	0.5	7.2	2.7	66.0	47.8	21.1	21.6	1 230	999
Wise	1 524	4 814 554	7.6	7.5	0.1	1.5	2.6	6.1	72.2	146.0	82.3	52.0	1 271	712
Wythe	1 424	3 649 638	5.6	26.2	0.3	2.6	1.1	5.5	55.4	100.6	52.2	30.2	1 032	628
York	2 630	9 095 299	7.9	5.3	7.7	0.0	3.3	2.6	66.6	226.0	92.7	107.0	1 618	1 182
Independent cities														
Alexandria city	5 221	27 072 935	10.0	12.5	7.7	2.6	11.9	7.2	44.7	658.7	76.2	498.6	3 408	2 503
Bedford city	151	496 858	12.0	19.7	1.8	11.7	7.9	19.2	15.0	21.6	9.7	7.6	1 271	841
Bristol city	765	2 448 312	7.6	15.4	6.1	3.8	8.9	3.5	53.6	72.5	36.3	26.8	1 519	788
Buena Vista city	329	965 276	10.8	5.3	0.0	3.3	1.3	7.0	71.5	22.5	12.2	6.9	1 023	765
Charlottesville city	2 284	8 528 975	9.8	5.8	3.3	6.0	4.6	8.3	55.8	212.5	76.7	93.0	2 116	1 314
Chesapeake city	11 013	41 054 055	4.1	9.2	5.0	1.7	24.6	3.7	49.6	1 127.4	370.1	422.6	1 850	1 301
Colonial Heights city	802	3 016 516	7.0	9.3	9.1	2.9	0.6	5.1	64.2	74.5	26.0	40.1	2 297	1 225
Covington city	279	921 554	6.6	10.3	0.0	0.0	7.9	9.3	65.9	26.1	10.0	11.0	1 904	1 291
Danville city	2 451	7 816 325	9.2	11.3	5.7	3.0	4.1	10.7	51.6	173.3	85.4	50.7	1 180	635
Emporia city	121	358 410	26.1	32.7	0.8	10.3	9.0	14.9	0.0	22.4	7.1	10.4	1 814	786
Fairfax city	414	2 320 342	17.7	23.1	21.4	10.9	3.8	13.9	0.0	121.0	20.6	87.1	3 711	2 469
Falls Church city	720	3 347 248	12.1	9.0	0.2	2.9	0.5	11.6	62.0	84.9	11.0	58.9	4 454	3 374
Franklin city	602	1 874 981	4.7	34.1	3.4	2.6	4.5	7.4	40.0	43.1	23.9	11.8	1 389	766
Fredericksburg city	1 610	5 694 248	7.8	27.8	4.3	5.6	3.2	3.1	44.2	149.0	48.1	67.8	2 483	1 244
Galax city	414	1 172 160	3.5	10.4	0.0	4.3	9.1	11.5	57.5	25.9	13.1	8.9	1 283	595
Hampton city	6 125	20 173 326	6.9	11.1	6.0	1.0	6.7	5.9	61.4	526.3	220.7	218.7	1 599	1 068
Harrisonburg city	1 474	5 157 943	4.1	7.6	6.7	5.8	3.6	11.7	53.6	162.1	48.7	63.4	1 244	631
Hopewell city	1 107	3 758 446	8.1	8.6	4.7	2.5	4.1	11.7	58.7	102.8	47.0	32.3	1 448	1 059
Lexington city	273	881 406	8.8	24.4	4.0	7.7	2.1	13.4	30.0	22.6	6.6	7.8	1 109	687
Lynchburg city	3 057	9 313 489	8.7	9.6	8.0	2.9	7.1	8.5	52.5	265.1	109.0	117.5	1 524	905
Manassas city	1 551	7 149 920	5.0	8.7	4.1	2.5	2.9	8.2	67.1	180.9	61.7	83.5	2 055	1 564

1. Based on the resident population estimated as of July 1 of the year shown.

STATE County	Local government finances, 2012 (cont.) Direct general expenditure Total (mil dol) 185	Per capita¹ (dollars) 186	Percent of total for: Education 187	Health and hospitals 188	Police protection 189	Public welfare 190	Highways 191	Debt outstanding Total (mil dol) 192	Per capita¹ (dollars) 193	Government employment, 2014 Federal civilian 194	Federal military 195	State and local 196	Presidential election,² 2012 Percent of vote cast: Democratic 197	Republican 198	All other 199
VIRGINIA—Cont'd															
Louisa	99.6	2 980	58.3	1.2	5.3	6.6	0.3	25.5	763	51	110	1 554	45.5	53.3	1.3
Lunenburg	35.6	2 826	62.6	1.1	5.0	6.7	2.1	26.9	2 134	20	37	761	47.8	51.3	0.8
Madison	32.1	2 431	58.6	4.5	8.2	11.2	0.0	15.3	1 157	64	42	546	42.7	56.1	1.2
Mathews	20.3	2 283	58.0	0.8	7.8	7.9	0.7	9.8	1 108	20	64	360	35.6	63.5	0.9
Mecklenburg	89.8	2 829	48.3	6.5	7.0	4.6	2.7	33.6	1 059	118	98	1 806	47.3	51.8	0.9
Middlesex	23.8	2 198	52.5	2.0	5.6	6.1	0.0	22.7	2 100	18	33	1 004	39.8	59.0	1.2
Montgomery	258.1	2 711	48.5	0.4	8.4	3.5	4.9	475.3	4 993	(3)337	(3)396	(3)17 239	51.7	46.8	1.5
Nelson	40.8	2 750	59.8	0.5	7.1	4.4	0.7	45.5	3 068	50	48	679	54.0	44.8	1.2
New Kent	49.4	2 579	54.5	1.0	4.6	4.2	0.0	60.4	3 152	39	63	917	35.0	63.9	1.1
Northampton	81.1	6 632	27.6	1.0	3.1	3.3	15.7	159.5	13 045	35	62	929	57.7	41.2	1.1
Northumberland	27.3	2 213	57.8	1.2	7.1	6.9	1.7	42.0	3 401	28	40	450	44.7	54.6	0.7
Nottoway	38.9	2 460	57.3	0.4	7.7	6.1	2.3	16.5	1 044	335	58	2 436	48.8	50.1	1.1
Orange	87.3	2 548	55.7	0.6	6.4	3.0	2.0	124.0	3 620	51	111	2 196	45.0	53.8	1.2
Page	66.1	2 765	55.3	0.9	7.9	5.0	2.0	77.1	3 228	190	76	1 131	40.8	58.1	1.1
Patrick	36.7	1 989	67.6	1.0	5.6	2.7	0.2	44.5	2 411	44	58	813	33.7	64.4	1.9
Pittsylvania	127.3	2 026	65.4	0.5	5.2	7.6	0.3	112.9	1 797	(4)204	(4)331	(4)6 531	37.5	61.5	0.9
Powhatan	65.5	2 328	65.3	0.3	6.2	5.1	0.0	103.3	3 675	48	85	2 379	29.3	69.8	0.9
Prince Edward	54.4	2 342	50.0	0.5	7.0	7.1	5.6	67.7	2 914	66	61	2 288	54.3	44.5	1.2
Prince George	134.6	3 644	45.1	2.0	4.5	2.6	0.3	173.0	4 684	(5)5 283	(5)8 481	(5)3 096	44.5	54.7	0.8
Prince William	1 678.9	3 902	57.5	1.9	5.9	2.5	1.6	1 440.8	3 349	(6)7 639	(6)8 281	(6)23 259	57.5	41.6	0.9
Pulaski	110.5	3 181	43.4	0.7	5.8	9.2	2.0	71.9	2 069	37	107	2 424	39.3	58.9	1.8
Rappahannock	21.0	2 817	57.1	0.7	5.0	4.4	0.0	10.8	1 446	19	24	318	47.8	50.6	1.7
Richmond	32.3	3 565	42.0	0.6	4.9	5.4	0.1	11.6	1 280	32	26	1 080	43.2	55.9	0.9
Roanoke	397.1	4 275	42.0	6.5	5.5	3.6	0.2	497.3	5 353	(7)2 274	(7)372	(7)6 800	38.9	60.0	1.2
Rockbridge	69.2	3 088	45.1	10.9	3.4	9.5	0.0	67.1	2 995	(8)93	(8)148	(8)2 655	42.6	56.2	1.1
Rockingham	234.6	3 031	52.1	2.8	3.5	11.4	1.3	200.1	2 585	(9)338	(9)398	(9)10 771	31.4	67.4	1.2
Russell	71.0	2 495	57.5	0.7	4.1	8.4	6.4	22.5	790	65	89	1 345	42.9	55.6	1.5
Scott	60.2	2 640	60.3	0.7	6.9	7.1	1.4	30.5	1 339	56	70	1 139	27.6	70.7	1.7
Shenandoah	116.2	2 729	54.8	0.6	6.7	6.1	3.0	146.9	3 449	124	137	2 024	36.0	62.5	1.6
Smyth	94.6	2 984	50.5	0.9	6.6	10.5	2.3	141.0	4 444	76	99	2 874	34.5	63.5	2.0
Southampton	56.0	3 044	56.1	0.8	3.6	3.8	0.2	67.3	3 657	(10)70	(10)80	(10)2 519	48.5	50.5	0.9
Spotsylvania	378.7	3 013	60.7	0.4	4.3	4.3	2.1	483.9	3 850	(11)365	(11)499	(11)9 516	46.0	52.9	1.0
Stafford	443.1	3 298	62.9	0.3	5.0	3.4	1.5	601.1	4 474	4 271	1 059	6 247	46.4	52.7	0.9
Surry	27.8	4 061	61.1	1.2	4.9	7.5	0.0	16.2	2 369	10	22	513	60.7	38.5	0.8
Sussex	39.1	3 269	58.6	0.5	7.2	7.5	0.1	26.7	2 229	52	29	1 316	61.6	37.8	0.7
Tazewell	136.7	3 088	44.7	17.2	6.0	6.5	4.1	52.5	1 186	70	134	3 383	32.8	65.7	1.5
Warren	120.1	3 155	38.6	12.5	13.4	5.4	1.5	214.6	5 637	175	123	1 798	43.4	55.1	1.6
Washington	172.4	3 125	41.6	10.5	5.9	3.9	1.1	101.3	1 835	(12)213	(12)229	(12)4 729	32.9	65.6	1.5
Westmoreland	49.6	2 832	53.8	0.8	8.0	6.1	1.5	23.2	1 322	49	56	830	54.6	44.4	1.0
Wise	142.7	3 487	49.3	6.0	6.1	9.8	4.4	186.8	4 565	(13)223	(13)132	(13)4 207	35.3	63.0	1.6
Wythe	103.2	3 530	39.8	0.1	5.8	6.6	2.0	150.9	5 159	87	93	2 352	32.9	65.7	1.4
York	226.9	3 430	55.6	0.6	4.0	2.9	0.0	176.3	2 665	(14)1 005	(14)1 760	(14)3 603	40.4	58.5	1.1
Independent cities															
Alexandria city	692.1	4 731	34.7	6.0	9.7	6.4	3.7	714.3	4 882	14 782	1 370	8 288	71.7	27.3	1.0
Bedford city	20.8	3 494	28.9	2.1	12.2	1.0	12.3	31.1	5 208	(15)	(15)	(15)	44.2	54.8	1.1
Bristol city	80.9	4 578	41.9	3.1	10.9	5.1	11.6	60.4	3 418	(12)	(12)	(12)	36.2	62.2	1.6
Buena Vista city	21.2	3 164	51.2	2.1	6.2	6.2	4.2	43.1	6 424	(8)	(8)	(8)	45.7	52.9	1.4
Charlottesville city	227.5	5 176	31.3	8.0	7.2	11.1	6.4	151.8	3 454	(16)	(16)	(16)	78.4	20.3	1.3
Chesapeake city	1 112.4	4 870	42.2	24.6	3.6	2.6	4.4	886.9	3 883	1 122	1 628	14 756	50.2	48.9	0.8
Colonial Heights city	69.5	3 974	51.8	0.0	5.3	0.6	4.6	61.6	3 526	(17)	(17)	(17)	29.0	69.6	1.4
Covington city	33.2	5 752	46.0	0.3	7.1	5.4	4.1	55.3	9 583	(18)	(18)	(18)	55.4	43.3	1.3
Danville city	179.2	4 169	41.3	2.3	5.5	4.2	5.7	156.0	3 628	(4)	(4)	(4)	59.1	40.0	0.8
Emporia city	22.3	3 882	17.9	1.2	14.0	1.4	4.2	14.6	2 551	(19)	(19)	(19)	65.0	34.3	0.7
Fairfax city	112.7	4 804	34.1	0.9	9.6	1.5	4.8	321.3	13 695	(20)	(20)	(20)	57.7	41.2	1.2
Falls Church city	76.6	5 787	47.6	0.3	8.2	2.3	6.9	97.9	7 399	(20)	(20)	(20)	69.6	29.2	1.3
Franklin city	51.8	6 072	32.0	0.5	5.3	3.8	4.2	22.8	2 673	(10)	(10)	(10)	63.7	35.6	0.7
Fredericksburg city	158.1	5 789	24.4	0.5	4.5	4.2	4.1	451.1	16 521	(11)	(11)	(11)	63.6	35.3	1.1
Galax city	28.7	4 153	45.2	0.7	8.9	5.8	7.1	10.9	1 575	(21)	(21)	(21)	43.8	54.8	1.4
Hampton city	524.9	3 836	44.8	0.8	5.1	5.6	1.2	438.4	3 204	7 220	7 815	9 109	69.1	30.1	0.8
Harrisonburg city	165.9	3 255	39.0	0.7	4.7	1.8	11.4	529.2	10 380	(9)	(9)	(9)	57.5	41.2	1.2
Hopewell city	116.0	5 192	43.8	0.5	4.4	5.9	3.4	114.6	5 128	(5)	(5)	(5)	55.5	43.6	0.9
Lexington city	28.1	4 013	24.4	2.6	5.2	2.6	4.3	34.5	4 926	(8)	(8)	(8)	62.2	36.9	0.9
Lynchburg city	262.8	3 408	36.6	0.8	6.5	7.2	2.8	337.4	4 375	(22)	(22)	(22)	47.4	51.4	1.3
Manassas city	169.8	4 182	54.0	2.2	7.8	0.7	6.2	130.5	3 213	(6)	(6)	(6)	55.2	43.8	1.0

1. Based on the resident population estimated as of July 1 of the year shown.   2. © 2013 Election Data Services, Inc. All rights reserved.   3. Radford city is included with Montgomery county.   4. Danville city is included with Pittsylvania county.   5. Hopewell city is included with Prince George county.   6. Manassas and Manassas Park cities are included with Prince William county.   7. Salem city is included with Roanoke county.   8. Buena Vista and Lexington cities are included with Rockbridge county.   9. Harrisonburg city is included with Rockingham county.   10. Franklin city is included with Southampton county.   11. Fredericksburg city is included with Spotsylvania county.   12. Bristol city is included with Washington county.   13. Norton city is included with Wise county.   14. Poquoson city is included with York county.   15. Bedford city is included with Bedford county.   16. Charlottesville city is included with Albemarle county.   17. Petersburg and Colonial Heights cities are included with Dinwiddie county.   18. Covington city is included with Alleghany county.   19. Emporia city is included with Greensville county.   20. Fairfax city and Falls Church city are included with Fairfax county.   21. Galax city is included with Carroll county.   22. Lynchburg city is included with Campbell county.

Table B. States and Counties — **Land Area and Population**

STATE/ County code	CBSA code[1]	County type[2]	STATE County	Land area,[3] (sq km) 2010	Total persons 2015	Rank	Per square kilometer	White	Black	American Indian, Alaska Native	Asian and Pacific Islander	Percent Hispanic or Latino[4]	Under 5 years	5 to 17 years	18 to 24 years	25 to 34 years	35 to 44 years	45 to 54 years
				1	2	3	4	5	6	7	8	9	10	11	12	13	14	15
			VIRGINIA—Cont'd															
51 685	47900	1	Manassas Park city	7	15 726	2 060	2 246.6	39.2	13.9	0.9	10.7	34.1	5.1	19.8	8.1	18.7	17.1	14.4
51 690	32300	4	Martinsville city	28	13 645	2 193	487.3	49.9	46.4	0.6	1.2	4.9	7.5	15.8	7.4	11.0	10.7	13.8
51 700	47260	1	Newport News city	178	182 385	354	1 024.6	48.0	41.7	1.3	4.6	8.5	7.3	16.2	12.9	17.0	11.6	12.4
51 710	47260	1	Norfolk city	140	246 393	271	1 760.0	46.4	43.0	1.3	5.1	7.4	6.9	13.4	18.6	19.0	11.0	10.9
51 720	13720	7	Norton city	19	3 939	2 907	207.3	88.5	8.1	0.8	1.8	3.3	5.6	17.3	9.5	14.2	11.8	12.7
51 730	40060	1	Petersburg city	59	32 477	1 374	550.5	17.6	78.8	0.9	1.8	4.4	8.4	13.7	10.7	14.3	9.9	14.0
51 735	47260	1	Poquoson city	40	12 059	2 295	301.5	93.8	1.7	0.7	3.1	2.3	3.6	18.2	8.6	9.3	11.9	16.3
51 740	47260	1	Portsmouth city	87	96 201	613	1 105.8	41.4	54.1	1.2	2.2	4.0	7.6	15.9	10.3	16.4	11.4	12.4
51 750	13980	3	Radford city	26	17 403	1 954	669.3	86.4	10.5	0.6	3.0	3.3	3.8	9.5	41.8	12.3	8.5	8.1
51 760	40060	1	Richmond city	155	220 289	296	1 421.2	41.8	50.1	0.8	3.2	6.6	6.3	12.1	13.9	20.8	11.4	12.0
51 770	40220	2	Roanoke city	110	99 897	593	908.2	62.8	30.1	0.7	2.8	5.9	7.2	14.9	8.5	15.4	12.5	13.3
51 775	40220	2	Salem city	37	25 432	1 590	687.4	88.0	8.1	0.7	2.3	3.2	5.3	14.6	13.6	11.6	10.8	13.1
51 790	44420	4	Staunton city	52	24 416	1 629	469.5	84.1	13.6	0.8	1.8	2.8	5.8	13.1	10.3	13.1	11.3	12.4
51 800	47260	1	Suffolk city	1 036	88 161	653	85.1	51.5	43.4	0.8	2.6	3.7	6.4	18.5	8.3	13.2	13.2	15.0
51 810	47260	1	Virginia Beach city	645	452 745	150	701.9	65.9	20.7	1.0	8.5	7.7	6.7	16.2	10.3	16.7	12.8	13.5
51 820	44420	4	Waynesboro city	39	21 491	1 755	551.1	81.2	13.2	0.9	1.6	7.0	7.5	16.3	7.8	14.1	11.8	12.5
51 830	47260	1	Williamsburg city	23	15 052	2 094	654.4	71.0	15.4	0.8	7.6	7.0	3.2	7.3	37.6	12.5	6.9	7.7
51 840	49020	3	Winchester city	24	27 284	1 519	1 136.8	70.3	12.8	0.7	3.1	16.5	6.7	15.8	11.1	14.5	12.0	13.1
53 000	...	X	WASHINGTON	172 119	7 170 351	X	41.7	73.8	4.9	2.5	10.8	12.2	6.3	16.4	9.5	14.5	13.0	13.4
53 001	36830	6	Adams	4 986	19 254	1 862	3.9	36.3	0.6	0.7	1.2	61.9	10.6	24.7	10.4	12.0	11.8	10.6
53 003	30300	3	Asotin	1 648	22 105	1 726	13.4	93.2	1.2	2.5	1.7	3.6	5.4	15.6	7.6	11.6	10.7	12.8
53 005	28420	3	Benton	4 404	190 309	342	43.2	74.4	2.1	1.6	3.9	20.4	7.2	19.4	9.0	13.5	12.0	12.8
53 007	48300	3	Chelan	7 564	75 644	729	10.0	70.1	0.8	1.6	1.7	27.4	6.8	17.4	8.6	12.0	11.1	12.6
53 009	38820	5	Clallam	4 502	73 486	742	16.3	86.6	1.5	6.6	3.1	5.8	4.7	13.0	7.0	10.6	9.5	11.6
53 011	38900	1	Clark	1 629	459 495	149	282.1	83.3	3.0	1.8	7.1	8.7	6.3	18.9	8.3	12.7	13.5	13.7
53 013	47460	6	Columbia	2 250	3 944	2 906	1.8	91.0	1.3	2.0	1.6	6.3	3.7	15.3	6.3	8.8	9.5	13.4
53 015	31020	3	Cowlitz	2 953	103 468	575	35.0	87.4	1.4	3.0	2.8	8.4	5.8	17.2	8.2	11.3	11.6	13.4
53 017	48300	3	Douglas	4 712	40 534	1 163	8.6	67.3	0.8	1.6	1.6	30.3	6.9	19.3	8.5	12.1	11.8	12.7
53 019	...	9	Ferry	5 706	7 582	2 629	1.3	78.1	1.5	19.0	1.8	4.2	4.6	14.0	8.5	9.2	9.7	13.0
53 021	28420	3	Franklin	3 217	88 807	648	27.6	43.5	2.5	1.0	2.7	51.8	10.0	23.5	9.8	16.1	13.4	10.4
53 023	...	8	Garfield	1 841	2 219	3 029	1.2	93.2	0.6	1.0	2.3	4.5	4.2	15.6	6.2	9.1	10.2	12.1
53 025	34180	4	Grant	6 940	93 259	626	13.4	57.4	1.3	1.7	1.6	40.0	8.6	21.6	10.0	13.0	11.8	11.4
53 027	10140	4	Grays Harbor	4 926	71 122	760	14.4	82.7	1.8	6.1	2.7	9.8	5.6	15.4	7.8	11.8	11.5	13.3
53 029	36020	4	Island	540	80 593	693	149.2	84.1	3.7	2.0	7.4	7.1	5.5	13.3	9.2	12.6	9.8	11.8
53 031	...	6	Jefferson	4 672	30 466	1 421	6.5	91.3	1.5	3.7	3.0	3.7	3.3	10.1	5.5	8.3	8.6	11.8
53 033	42660	1	King	5 479	2 117 125	13	386.4	66.1	7.7	1.7	19.7	9.4	6.2	14.8	8.7	17.0	14.9	14.0
53 035	14740	3	Kitsap	1 023	260 131	259	254.3	82.1	4.0	2.9	9.2	7.2	5.7	15.2	10.5	13.5	11.2	13.5
53 037	21260	6	Kittitas	5 950	43 269	1 106	7.3	86.4	1.5	2.0	3.6	8.8	5.0	13.1	22.5	11.8	9.8	10.9
53 039	...	6	Klickitat	4 847	21 026	1 771	4.3	84.0	0.7	3.7	1.6	12.3	5.1	15.3	6.8	9.5	11.6	13.3
53 041	16500	4	Lewis	6 223	75 882	725	12.2	86.9	1.2	2.8	2.0	9.7	5.8	16.1	8.1	11.2	11.2	13.1
53 043	...	8	Lincoln	5 984	10 321	2 406	1.7	93.9	1.0	3.2	1.4	3.1	4.7	17.0	6.2	8.3	9.9	12.6
53 045	43220	6	Mason	2 485	61 023	859	24.6	84.8	1.9	5.2	3.0	8.9	5.4	13.9	7.6	11.4	11.0	13.0
53 047	...	6	Okanogan	13 644	41 516	1 136	3.0	68.7	1.0	12.3	1.4	19.0	6.4	17.0	7.4	10.5	10.9	12.2
53 049	...	7	Pacific	2 416	20 848	1 783	8.6	85.5	1.0	4.5	3.1	9.0	4.6	12.4	6.2	9.1	9.3	12.2
53 051	44060	8	Pend Oreille	3 626	13 088	2 227	3.6	91.4	1.1	5.2	1.5	3.6	4.6	15.4	6.8	7.9	9.6	13.7
53 053	42660	1	Pierce	4 324	843 954	67	195.2	73.6	9.2	2.6	11.0	10.2	6.9	17.1	9.9	15.0	12.8	13.5
53 055	...	9	San Juan	450	16 252	2 027	36.1	91.4	0.9	1.8	2.2	5.9	3.0	11.2	5.4	7.8	9.1	13.2
53 057	34580	3	Skagit	4 484	121 846	508	27.2	77.5	1.2	2.8	3.1	17.8	6.1	16.4	8.3	12.2	11.4	12.6
53 059	38900	1	Skamania	4 288	11 339	2 334	2.6	90.5	1.2	3.0	2.0	6.0	4.5	16.3	6.7	10.0	11.8	15.4
53 061	42660	1	Snohomish	5 406	772 501	81	142.9	75.6	3.9	2.2	12.8	9.7	6.2	17.0	8.7	14.4	13.8	14.8
53 063	44060	2	Spokane	4 568	490 945	142	107.5	88.7	2.9	2.6	4.1	5.2	6.1	16.3	10.4	14.4	11.9	12.9
53 065	44060	6	Stevens	6 417	43 791	1 095	6.8	89.9	1.0	7.3	1.7	3.5	5.1	17.0	7.2	8.4	10.5	13.4
53 067	36500	3	Thurston	1 870	269 536	252	144.1	80.4	4.5	2.7	9.0	8.4	6.1	16.1	8.9	14.3	12.9	13.0
53 069	...	8	Wahkiakum	682	4 042	2 899	5.9	93.4	1.2	2.8	2.1	3.4	3.6	13.7	5.8	7.2	8.6	12.8
53 071	47460	4	Walla Walla	3 290	60 338	865	18.3	74.3	2.3	1.5	2.8	21.2	5.8	15.9	13.8	12.3	11.2	11.9
53 073	13380	3	Whatcom	5 457	212 284	308	38.9	82.8	1.8	3.8	6.2	8.9	5.5	14.7	15.1	12.6	11.5	12.2
53 075	39420	4	Whitman	5 592	48 177	1 016	8.6	83.3	3.0	1.5	10.1	5.6	4.7	10.5	36.7	13.5	7.9	8.2
53 077	49420	3	Yakima	11 125	248 830	270	22.4	46.6	1.2	4.6	1.8	47.7	8.4	21.4	10.1	13.0	11.9	11.6
54 000	...	X	WEST VIRGINIA	62 259	1 844 128	X	29.6	94.0	4.4	0.7	1.1	1.5	5.5	15.0	9.2	11.8	12.4	13.6
54 001	...	7	Barbour	883	16 704	1 998	18.9	97.8	1.6	1.2	0.5	0.8	5.3	15.5	11.1	10.4	11.7	13.5
54 003	25180	3	Berkeley	832	111 901	542	134.5	87.6	8.8	0.7	1.6	3.9	6.2	17.9	7.7	13.6	13.7	14.6
54 005	16620	2	Boone	1 299	23 372	1 664	18.0	98.5	1.0	0.4	0.2	0.5	5.7	16.7	7.3	10.4	14.0	13.4
54 007	...	8	Braxton	1 323	14 415	2 137	10.9	98.2	1.1	0.7	0.5	0.7	5.8	14.7	7.5	10.7	11.7	14.0

1. CBSA = Core Based Statistical Area. See Appendix A for explanation. See Appendix B for list of metropolitan areas with component counties.   2. County type code from the Economic Research Service of USDA Rural-Urban Continuum Codes. See Appendix A for definition.   3. Dry land or land partially or temporarily covered by water.   4. May be of any race.

Table B. States and Counties — **Population and Households**

	Population, 2014 (cont.)				Population change and components of change, 2000–2015							Households, 2010–2014				
	Age (percent) (cont.)				Total persons		Percent change		Components of change, 2010–2015					Percent		
STATE County	55 to 64 years	65 to 74 years	75 years and over	Percent female	2000	2010	2000–2010	2010–2015	Births	Deaths	Net migration	Number	Persons per house-hold	Family house-holds	Female family house-holder[1]	One per-son
	16	17	18	19	20	21	22	23	24	25	26	27	28	29	30	31
VIRGINIA—Cont'd																
Manassas Park city	9.3	4.7	2.8	49.1	10 290	14 241	38.4	10.4	988	184	608	4 526	3.31	72.8	14.3	23.8
Martinsville city	13.3	10.6	9.9	54.0	15 416	13 821	-10.3	-1.3	1 006	1 137	-95	5 974	2.23	55.5	19.8	41.4
Newport News city	11.0	6.6	5.1	51.6	180 150	180 911	0.4	0.8	15 097	7 466	-6 061	68 987	2.51	62.3	17.8	31.5
Norfolk city	10.3	5.6	4.4	47.8	234 403	242 831	3.6	1.5	19 636	10 135	-5 750	86 397	2.56	57.9	18.2	32.6
Norton city	14.2	8.0	6.8	52.7	3 904	3 951	1.2	-0.3	270	198	-86	1 655	2.39	53.5	19.8	37.3
Petersburg city	13.7	8.5	6.7	53.8	33 740	32 420	-3.9	0.2	3 007	2 162	-804	12 515	2.52	57.5	25.4	35.2
Poquoson city	13.8	10.8	7.5	50.5	11 566	12 157	5.1	-0.8	464	518	-46	4 627	2.60	75.8	10.1	21.0
Portsmouth city	12.2	7.6	6.3	52.0	100 565	95 535	-5.0	0.7	8 159	5 429	-1 945	36 764	2.52	64.4	21.8	30.4
Radford city	8.0	4.2	3.6	52.5	15 859	16 408	3.5	6.1	729	455	730	5 333	2.63	46.0	11.8	33.1
Richmond city	12.1	6.4	5.0	52.3	197 790	204 175	3.2	7.9	15 135	10 063	11 073	85 913	2.33	47.0	18.6	41.4
Roanoke city	13.3	8.2	6.7	52.3	94 911	96 919	2.1	3.1	7 693	6 197	1 480	42 549	2.25	55.9	16.9	37.4
Salem city	13.8	9.3	7.8	52.2	24 747	24 848	0.4	2.4	1 273	1 524	756	9 953	2.32	62.3	13.0	32.1
Staunton city	13.4	11.0	9.6	55.0	23 853	23 746	-0.4	2.8	1 497	1 736	910	10 503	2.17	56.3	12.6	37.7
Suffolk city	12.4	7.8	5.1	51.7	63 677	84 596	32.9	4.2	5 830	3 845	1 497	30 798	2.75	73.4	17.0	22.6
Virginia Beach city	11.5	7.2	5.1	50.8	425 257	437 966	3.0	3.4	32 149	15 293	-2 170	165 296	2.63	69.0	13.9	23.9
Waynesboro city	12.5	9.5	7.8	52.6	19 520	21 020	7.7	2.2	1 576	1 254	82	8 878	2.37	63.0	16.9	32.2
Williamsburg city	8.9	8.7	7.0	53.5	11 998	13 673	14.0	10.1	512	557	1 300	4 365	2.32	50.7	10.1	40.0
Winchester city	12.0	7.9	6.7	50.4	23 585	26 201	11.1	4.1	1 899	1 401	574	10 692	2.44	57.3	13.2	33.2
WASHINGTON	12.9	8.4	5.7	50.0	5 894 121	6 724 543	14.1	6.6	459 178	268 172	251 442	2 645 396	2.55	64.5	10.3	27.8
Adams	9.8	5.8	4.4	49.1	16 428	18 728	14.0	2.8	2 156	616	-990	5 827	3.20	77.6	12.7	19.2
Asotin	15.4	11.6	9.2	51.8	20 551	21 623	5.2	2.2	1 273	1 219	446	9 405	2.30	62.9	11.7	32.5
Benton	12.7	8.0	5.4	49.8	142 475	175 177	23.0	8.6	13 498	6 658	7 951	66 625	2.71	69.2	10.9	25.9
Chelan	14.0	9.8	7.6	50.1	66 616	72 456	8.8	4.4	4 902	3 467	1 641	27 183	2.67	67.8	10.0	26.8
Clallam	16.9	15.2	11.6	50.3	64 525	71 404	10.7	2.9	3 513	4 906	3 266	30 963	2.28	60.1	8.5	31.6
Clark	12.7	8.5	5.2	50.5	345 238	425 363	23.2	8.0	28 545	16 396	21 085	160 492	2.71	69.4	11.1	24.1
Columbia	16.3	15.4	11.3	50.0	4 064	4 078	0.3	-3.3	181	260	-48	1 706	2.31	66.6	14.4	25.6
Cowlitz	14.5	10.8	7.3	50.4	92 948	102 410	10.2	1.0	6 230	5 530	227	39 765	2.54	66.1	11.6	27.5
Douglas	12.8	9.4	6.5	49.6	32 603	38 431	17.9	5.5	2 733	1 602	982	14 140	2.75	75.0	10.7	19.2
Ferry	18.8	14.7	7.6	48.3	7 260	7 551	4.0	0.4	368	442	121	3 112	2.37	64.7	10.7	30.9
Franklin	9.0	4.9	3.0	48.1	49 347	78 163	58.4	13.6	8 751	1 951	3 687	24 207	3.41	77.0	16.0	18.1
Garfield	18.0	12.6	11.9	50.9	2 397	2 266	-5.5	-2.1	102	134	-8	906	2.42	69.0	4.4	27.6
Grant	10.8	7.5	5.1	49.5	74 698	89 120	19.3	4.6	8 130	3 477	-269	30 233	2.99	72.5	12.5	23.1
Grays Harbor	15.6	11.5	7.4	48.7	67 194	72 797	8.3	-2.3	4 139	4 222	-1 536	27 318	2.51	64.0	11.0	29.3
Island	15.2	13.7	8.7	50.1	71 558	78 506	9.7	2.7	4 691	3 390	636	32 820	2.35	68.4	7.7	26.3
Jefferson	20.6	20.2	11.7	50.7	25 953	29 872	15.1	2.0	1 029	1 795	1 314	13 535	2.15	59.2	6.8	34.0
King	12.3	7.1	5.1	50.0	1 737 034	1 931 256	11.2	9.6	131 314	65 250	120 791	808 729	2.44	59.2	9.0	31.2
Kitsap	14.4	10.0	6.1	49.1	231 969	251 133	8.3	3.6	15 499	10 766	3 820	97 993	2.51	66.9	9.7	26.4
Kittitas	12.3	9.0	5.6	49.7	33 362	40 909	22.6	5.8	2 140	1 485	1 721	16 753	2.34	56.5	7.7	29.5
Klickitat	17.3	13.5	7.7	49.4	19 161	20 318	6.0	3.5	1 104	952	595	7 959	2.57	68.4	8.0	25.2
Lewis	14.7	11.6	8.2	50.0	68 600	75 455	10.0	0.6	4 608	4 275	-1	29 450	2.52	67.1	10.3	27.1
Lincoln	17.4	13.6	10.2	49.7	10 184	10 570	3.8	-2.4	513	592	-144	4 445	2.31	65.4	5.6	29.0
Mason	16.4	13.0	8.3	48.4	49 405	60 699	22.9	0.5	3 287	3 284	480	23 099	2.57	65.6	8.1	27.0
Okanogan	15.8	12.2	7.7	49.5	39 564	41 120	3.9	1.0	2 826	2 231	-179	16 401	2.44	66.1	9.5	27.9
Pacific	18.4	16.9	11.0	49.8	20 984	20 920	-0.3	-0.3	1 011	1 582	476	9 143	2.23	61.7	8.4	32.4
Pend Oreille	18.7	15.2	8.0	48.9	11 732	13 001	10.8	0.7	592	765	291	5 532	2.32	67.4	11.3	26.2
Pierce	12.2	7.5	5.1	50.3	700 820	795 229	13.5	6.1	58 983	31 608	20 669	301 364	2.64	66.6	12.0	26.6
San Juan	20.9	19.0	10.4	51.9	14 077	15 769	12.0	3.1	470	686	691	7 611	2.06	62.2	8.8	30.4
Skagit	14.3	10.9	7.8	50.4	102 979	116 901	13.5	4.2	7 601	5 861	3 033	45 309	2.57	68.5	11.2	25.0
Skamania	17.9	11.3	6.1	49.3	9 872	11 066	12.1	2.5	521	402	191	4 433	2.51	64.6	8.3	30.1
Snohomish	13.1	7.3	4.8	49.7	606 024	713 330	17.7	8.3	48 790	25 557	34 922	271 514	2.67	68.0	10.2	25.0
Spokane	13.1	8.6	6.2	50.3	417 939	471 221	12.7	4.2	31 318	21 890	9 867	188 126	2.45	63.5	11.1	28.9
Stevens	17.8	13.2	7.5	50.0	40 066	43 531	8.6	0.6	2 326	2 261	253	17 626	2.45	69.6	8.4	25.2
Thurston	13.6	9.2	6.0	50.9	207 355	252 264	21.7	6.8	16 252	10 468	11 409	101 530	2.52	66.4	11.1	26.4
Wahkiakum	17.6	19.9	10.8	50.5	3 824	3 978	4.0	1.6	159	242	167	1 716	2.29	68.4	6.3	29.3
Walla Walla	12.6	8.7	7.8	49.1	55 180	58 781	6.5	2.6	3 574	2 869	756	21 698	2.50	63.0	10.2	31.9
Whatcom	12.9	9.3	6.2	50.4	166 814	201 140	20.6	5.5	11 960	7 900	7 041	79 837	2.50	62.4	9.8	27.1
Whitman	8.5	5.7	4.3	48.9	40 740	44 776	9.9	7.6	2 359	1 325	2 345	17 174	2.30	48.7	6.7	30.7
Yakima	10.8	7.4	5.4	49.9	222 581	243 231	9.3	2.3	21 730	9 856	-6 257	79 717	3.04	72.5	15.5	22.4
WEST VIRGINIA	14.6	10.3	7.4	50.6	1 808 344	1 853 011	2.5	-0.5	108 647	114 205	-1 907	742 359	2.43	64.9	11.3	29.9
Barbour	14.1	10.7	7.6	51.1	15 557	16 589	6.6	0.7	889	991	229	6 179	2.63	69.1	10.5	27.1
Berkeley	12.8	8.6	4.7	50.7	75 905	104 172	37.2	7.4	7 204	4 774	5 205	40 614	2.62	71.0	13.6	23.9
Boone	15.8	10.2	6.6	50.3	25 535	24 627	-3.6	-5.1	1 465	1 611	-1 079	9 602	2.51	72.3	12.8	24.3
Braxton	15.7	11.9	8.1	49.7	14 702	14 519	-1.2	-0.7	822	882	-39	5 652	2.48	66.6	8.4	29.3

1. No spouse present.

Table B. States and Counties — Population, Vital Statistics, Medicare, and Crime

STATE County	Persons in group quarters, 2015	Daytime population, 2010–2014 Number	Employment/ residence ratio	Births, 2015 Total	Rate[1]	Deaths, 2015 Number	Rate[1]	Persons under 65 with no health insurance, 2014 Number	Percent	Medicare, 2015 Total Beneficiaries	Enrolled in Original Medicare	Enrolled in Medicare Advantage	Serious crimes known to police,[2] 2014 Total Number	Rate[3]
	32	33	34	35	36	37	38	39	40	41	42	43	44	45
VIRGINIA—Cont'd														
Manassas Park city	6	10 214	0.40	19	1.2	36	2.3	2 884	20.7	D	D	D	177	1 065
Martinsville city	377	17 057	1.69	219	16.1	205	15.1	1 538	14.3	8 389	6 208	2 181	437	3 175
Newport News city	8 598	202 412	1.24	2 895	15.9	1 456	8.0	20 213	13.1	25 782	18 636	7 146	6 334	3 473
Norfolk city	33 409	307 066	1.51	3 755	15.2	2 023	8.2	28 510	15.0	29 368	20 665	8 703	10 981	4 444
Norton city	68	4 268	1.15	49	12.3	26	6.5	432	12.6	1 526	1 040	486	210	5 211
Petersburg city	1 058	34 876	1.20	746	23.1	445	13.8	4 163	15.2	8 123	6 080	2 043	1 036	3 183
Poquoson city	51	8 851	0.45	93	7.7	94	7.8	839	8.5	1 407	1 231	176	103	851
Portsmouth city	2 971	105 588	1.23	1 543	16.1	1 031	10.7	10 929	13.6	16 398	11 578	4 820	5 451	5 653
Radford city	3 155	17 138	1.02	166	9.5	69	4.0	1 624	12.3	3 066	2 358	708	477	2 744
Richmond city	13 518	278 612	1.68	2 902	13.3	1 995	9.1	33 530	18.4	54 023	35 606	18 417	9 690	4 471
Roanoke city	2 137	124 059	1.58	1 505	15.1	1 140	11.4	14 648	17.5	30 040	21 467	8 573	4 476	4 524
Salem city	1 941	36 239	1.92	272	10.7	291	11.5	2 319	12.0	7 909	6 302	1 607	530	2 085
Staunton city	1 281	25 213	1.10	312	12.8	293	12.0	2 492	13.5	8 991	7 738	1 253	623	2 543
Suffolk city	1 102	76 409	0.77	1 131	12.9	752	8.6	8 003	10.7	13 662	10 143	3 519	2 485	2 890
Virginia Beach city	9 471	413 189	0.86	6 068	13.4	3 070	6.8	43 525	11.2	59 328	48 461	10 867	10 532	2 335
Waynesboro city	192	21 278	1.01	332	15.6	210	9.8	2 399	13.6	6 913	5 735	1 178	688	3 227
Williamsburg city	4 445	22 619	2.38	75	5.0	96	6.4	1 082	13.4	6 303	5 476	827	205	1 323
Winchester city	883	39 613	2.03	340	12.4	251	9.2	4 110	18.1	10 278	9 007	1 271	1 171	4 261
WASHINGTON	140 994	6 852 840	0.99	88 782	12.5	53 174	7.5	630 600	10.6	1 098 715	739 717	358 998	281 842	3 991
Adams	162	19 047	1.01	399	20.8	116	6.0	3 100	18.2	1 557	1 333	224	771	4 010
Asotin	174	19 581	0.73	241	10.9	240	10.8	1 841	10.5	5 426	4 515	911	701	3 142
Benton	1 426	184 152	1.03	2 590	13.7	1 309	6.9	17 443	10.9	28 303	24 054	4 249	4 849	2 588
Chelan	928	78 799	1.16	922	12.3	667	8.9	8 133	13.4	11 040	8 884	2 156	1 689	2 264
Clallam	1 892	71 154	0.97	677	9.3	958	13.1	6 883	13.3	22 429	20 336	2 093	2 222	3 051
Clark	3 435	394 121	0.77	5 530	12.2	3 345	7.4	39 693	10.3	70 906	31 144	39 762	10 389	2 308
Columbia	75	4 012	0.99	36	9.1	44	11.1	340	11.7	1 085	1 047	38	127	3 151
Cowlitz	1 207	100 697	0.96	1 184	11.5	1 066	10.4	9 314	11.2	21 186	11 177	10 009	3 982	3 897
Douglas	190	32 867	0.64	516	12.8	300	7.5	5 417	16.3	10 757	8 474	2 283	814	2 041
Ferry	252	7 505	0.94	74	9.7	77	10.1	977	16.5	1 603	1 525	78	52	675
Franklin	2 902	80 470	0.88	1 640	18.6	405	4.6	13 566	17.5	7 807	6 831	976	1 862	2 091
Garfield	36	2 132	0.88	21	9.5	18	8.1	146	8.8	617	600	17	40	1 768
Grant	1 242	92 914	1.04	1 500	16.1	635	6.8	13 384	16.7	13 987	11 702	2 285	3 963	4 341
Grays Harbor	2 700	69 978	0.93	755	10.6	807	11.4	7 920	14.4	16 805	15 366	1 439	2 174	3 135
Island	1 670	70 183	0.75	896	11.2	651	8.1	5 997	10.0	18 928	13 087	5 841	1 124	1 439
Jefferson	631	29 541	0.96	201	6.6	338	11.1	2 201	10.9	9 999	9 335	664	843	2 787
King	38 070	2 170 037	1.16	25 678	12.2	12 964	6.2	155 814	8.7	264 388	164 731	99 657	100 616	4 834
Kitsap	8 931	243 170	0.91	2 937	11.4	2 184	8.5	17 077	8.3	44 139	34 459	9 680	7 909	3 093
Kittitas	2 162	39 975	0.91	412	9.6	262	6.1	4 162	12.2	6 550	6 034	516	1 186	2 814
Klickitat	198	20 120	0.93	206	9.8	186	8.9	2 428	14.8	4 892	4 544	348	290	1 375
Lewis	928	73 478	0.93	853	11.3	801	10.6	7 759	13.0	18 106	12 367	5 739	2 135	2 886
Lincoln	94	10 062	0.92	96	9.3	108	10.5	804	10.3	2 725	2 594	131	170	1 654
Mason	2 329	55 527	0.76	604	9.9	610	10.0	6 077	13.4	13 808	10 972	2 836	2 201	3 626
Okanogan	640	41 530	1.02	514	12.4	449	10.8	6 097	18.6	9 232	8 392	840	970	2 345
Pacific	273	20 241	0.94	189	9.1	312	15.1	2 157	14.7	6 590	6 341	249	428	2 089
Pend Oreille	98	12 433	0.87	117	9.0	144	11.1	1 176	11.8	3 263	2 852	411	388	2 999
Pierce	16 581	770 293	0.88	11 533	13.8	6 508	7.8	76 792	10.8	122 333	84 288	38 045	35 442	4 272
San Juan	187	15 827	1.00	100	6.2	126	7.8	1 655	14.8	4 573	3 460	1 113	164	1 027
Skagit	1 626	119 807	1.03	1 444	11.9	1 158	9.6	13 110	13.5	25 481	17 322	8 159	4 588	3 829
Skamania	25	9 289	0.58	98	8.6	81	7.1	946	10.1	1 589	1 403	186	121	1 064
Snohomish	10 376	660 403	0.79	9 683	12.6	5 222	6.8	64 756	9.8	95 354	49 868	45 486	27 604	3 663
Spokane	14 487	485 804	1.04	6 065	12.4	4 298	8.8	38 486	9.6	86 571	55 305	31 266	29 502	6 103
Stevens	266	39 806	0.76	458	10.5	444	10.2	4 559	13.2	9 530	8 132	1 398	900	2 064
Thurston	4 041	245 644	0.88	3 136	11.7	2 048	7.6	21 306	9.6	46 216	29 686	16 530	7 956	2 991
Wahkiakum	48	3 796	0.83	29	7.2	43	10.6	342	12.1	1 249	935	314	37	907
Walla Walla	4 778	62 312	1.11	684	11.4	579	9.6	6 181	13.5	11 149	9 724	1 425	2 267	3 781
Whatcom	5 863	201 524	0.97	2 293	10.9	1 488	7.1	20 324	11.9	36 244	22 704	13 540	7 219	3 462
Whitman	6 573	48 753	1.14	455	9.6	238	5.0	3 416	9.5	4 961	4 770	191	870	1 871
Yakima	3 498	245 856	0.99	4 016	16.2	1 945	7.8	38 821	18.3	37 337	29 424	7 913	8 831	3 549
WEST VIRGINIA	48 188	1 837 235	0.98	20 764	11.2	21 704	11.8	156 077	10.6	406 377	290 946	115 431	43 236	2 337
Barbour	767	14 366	0.61	159	9.5	190	11.4	1 505	11.6	3 482	2 675	807	NA	NA
Berkeley	855	90 459	0.65	1 426	12.8	950	8.5	10 245	10.8	17 744	14 120	3 624	2 041	1 864
Boone	131	25 389	1.15	271	11.5	292	12.4	1 854	9.5	5 096	3 518	1 578	407	1 789
Braxton	335	14 025	0.91	151	10.5	175	12.1	1 341	11.9	2 963	2 026	937	101	840

1. Per 1,000 estimated resident population.　　2. Data for serious crimes have not been adjusted for underreporting; this may affect comparability between geographic areas and over time.
3. Per 100,000 population estimated by the FBI.

Table B. States and Counties — Crime, Education, Money Income, and Poverty

STATE County	Serious crimes known to police, 2014 (cont.)[1] Rate[2] Violent	Property	Education — Enrollment[3] Total	Percent private	Attainment[4] (percent) High school graduate or less	Bachelor's degree or more	Local government expenditures,[5] 2012–2013 Total current spending (mil dol)	Current spending per student (dollars)	Money income, 2010–2014 Per capita income[6] (dollars)	Households Median income (dollars)	Mean income (dollars)	Percent with income of $200,000 or more	Income and poverty, 2014 Median household income (dollars)	Percent below poverty level All persons	Children under 18 years	Children 5 to 17 years in families
	46	47	48	49	50	51	52	53	54	55	56	57	58	59	60	61
VIRGINIA—Cont'd																
Manassas Park city	150	915	3 978	12.1	44.3	26.3	31.6	10 132	28 054	73 460	86 033	4.9	73 065	8.9	14.7	13.0
Martinsville city	356	2 819	3 337	12.3	52.1	16.6	23.9	10 514	19 663	27 746	44 269	1.7	29 971	23.8	35.4	36.3
Newport News city	429	3 044	51 661	14.4	39.3	24.1	308.1	10 345	25 408	51 000	63 502	2.4	48 440	16.7	25.8	26.1
Norfolk city	520	3 924	68 689	11.8	40.3	25.6	349.6	10 639	24 252	44 150	59 861	2.5	42 567	23.4	31.7	33.1
Norton city	298	4 913	983	5.4	42.6	20.5	7.3	8 230	22 715	36 148	54 211	1.8	31 620	21.6	32.9	30.7
Petersburg city	593	2 590	6 322	10.1	57.4	14.9	47.8	10 771	18 535	33 927	43 421	0.5	32 749	25.8	37.5	42.4
Poquoson city	91	760	3 303	11.0	32.3	35.8	20.5	9 415	38 295	83 460	100 253	7.8	84 213	5.9	6.9	5.7
Portsmouth city	610	5 043	25 264	13.8	46.5	19.5	154.3	10 116	23 219	46 239	57 080	1.7	43 045	18.3	28.3	29.3
Radford city	598	2 146	9 835	5.1	33.4	34.9	14.8	9 443	15 509	30 284	44 166	1.2	34 267	32.4	20.6	19.8
Richmond city	583	3 887	56 013	19.1	40.7	35.4	307.9	13 019	27 860	41 331	64 040	4.2	42 074	25.0	38.9	40.7
Roanoke city	344	4 180	21 267	13.0	47.0	24.1	156.2	11 728	23 565	39 530	52 819	1.7	40 735	20.4	33.0	31.6
Salem city	114	1 971	7 027	25.9	38.5	30.7	40.1	10 420	27 559	50 590	66 625	4.1	54 195	10.2	13.9	13.5
Staunton city	127	2 416	5 399	29.1	44.2	31.5	30.3	11 245	25 255	39 982	56 256	2.2	42 552	16.5	25.6	25.0
Suffolk city	272	2 618	24 773	20.8	40.9	26.1	138.7	9 620	30 021	66 822	80 883	4.6	60 735	13.6	20.2	18.3
Virginia Beach city	148	2 187	119 503	17.2	29.3	33.5	746.5	10 625	32 477	67 001	84 615	5.0	67 676	8.6	12.4	11.7
Waynesboro city	155	3 072	4 714	9.9	53.7	19.0	31.9	9 832	21 515	45 499	51 610	1.1	44 843	14.6	24.9	25.7
Williamsburg city	161	1 162	6 985	4.2	27.1	48.6	(7)120.0	(7)10 885	23 686	48 057	70 384	5.1	46 954	20.1	24.4	23.8
Winchester city	313	3 948	6 753	23.0	47.2	28.1	(8)185.8	(8)10 683	26 624	44 731	65 500	4.3	44 537	13.4	21.7	21.9
WASHINGTON	285	3 706	1 716 547	14.9	33.3	32.3	10 226.1	9 672	31 233	60 294	79 195	5.2	61 358	13.2	17.5	16.0
Adams	291	3 719	5 107	5.5	60.4	13.5	46.0	10 188	17 398	44 533	54 461	0.8	47 423	19.0	27.1	24.7
Asotin	238	2 904	5 110	8.7	42.4	18.5	33.3	10 040	24 836	42 689	56 805	2.0	44 055	16.3	24.2	21.5
Benton	193	2 395	47 504	10.1	35.5	29.2	301.2	8 894	29 060	60 589	77 597	4.6	58 750	14.6	21.3	19.0
Chelan	135	2 128	17 549	10.1	46.3	24.0	131.2	10 047	25 619	50 876	66 348	3.0	49 174	14.0	20.2	19.2
Clallam	255	2 796	13 937	12.1	35.9	24.5	95.0	8 974	26 325	47 008	58 684	1.9	47 185	16.2	26.2	22.3
Clark	209	2 099	116 026	12.6	34.7	26.5	716.7	9 204	28 206	59 551	75 224	3.9	61 747	9.9	13.6	12.8
Columbia	0	3 151	764	12.8	37.9	20.4	5.7	11 654	23 558	41 071	55 111	2.0	45 465	15.5	25.7	22.0
Cowlitz	250	3 648	23 507	10.2	42.7	15.6	156.7	9 254	24 042	46 571	59 506	1.8	44 235	20.6	26.8	23.1
Douglas	85	1 956	9 889	6.8	47.3	17.3	75.5	9 746	23 116	53 235	63 563	1.9	51 151	15.5	24.4	22.7
Ferry	117	558	1 580	11.5	45.0	15.7	13.0	13 068	20 646	37 542	47 751	0.8	39 992	22.4	29.1	25.9
Franklin	234	1 858	24 837	8.5	54.5	15.4	170.4	9 342	19 982	56 719	65 800	2.3	55 006	17.3	24.9	22.4
Garfield	88	1 679	484	2.3	34.4	21.9	4.1	12 542	24 767	50 915	58 696	1.3	46 404	14.2	20.7	17.4
Grant	289	4 052	24 168	7.7	51.7	15.5	180.4	9 661	19 844	46 772	57 646	1.9	50 388	15.8	20.9	20.0
Grays Harbor	274	2 861	15 441	6.6	44.8	15.6	113.0	10 896	22 190	43 379	55 589	1.4	43 205	19.6	28.6	26.3
Island	102	1 336	16 035	17.2	28.9	31.7	70.5	8 691	31 563	59 107	74 252	3.3	59 358	10.3	15.4	14.7
Jefferson	291	2 496	4 562	14.1	27.8	37.3	29.3	10 066	28 607	47 202	61 332	3.4	50 964	14.1	24.5	21.8
King	334	4 500	485 006	19.2	24.6	47.1	2 509.6	10 005	40 656	73 035	98 867	9.7	75 738	11.3	13.6	12.8
Kitsap	267	2 827	59 086	13.9	29.3	30.0	356.6	9 822	31 901	62 473	79 076	4.2	61 898	11.2	14.4	12.2
Kittitas	109	2 705	14 076	9.1	36.7	34.0	46.6	9 577	23 754	45 406	57 405	1.7	48 127	18.6	18.7	17.6
Klickitat	71	1 304	4 275	13.1	43.0	20.6	34.5	10 706	22 716	46 368	56 292	1.5	49 348	14.6	22.6	20.9
Lewis	207	2 679	16 845	12.8	45.4	14.1	116.7	9 807	22 094	42 917	54 817	1.0	44 243	17.1	24.5	22.3
Lincoln	68	1 585	2 169	8.7	41.1	19.3	27.8	13 725	25 512	47 161	60 121	2.0	49 955	12.5	17.7	15.7
Mason	232	3 394	11 681	7.6	42.3	17.9	78.9	9 896	23 965	49 538	60 077	1.6	52 313	15.6	23.6	22.4
Okanogan	174	2 171	8 601	13.9	48.9	17.0	80.0	8 613	21 483	39 665	51 382	1.3	37 782	23.2	31.5	29.5
Pacific	156	1 933	3 628	5.0	44.5	16.5	34.1	10 346	23 224	39 418	51 628	1.7	40 189	17.8	28.8	28.0
Pend Oreille	62	2 938	2 601	18.3	42.6	16.6	18.2	11 175	21 758	40 070	50 168	1.6	42 579	22.3	33.1	30.2
Pierce	432	3 840	205 088	15.3	38.4	24.2	1 252.4	9 826	28 571	59 711	74 259	3.6	60 397	13.1	17.5	16.2
San Juan	44	983	2 523	22.6	22.4	45.2	20.1	11 048	38 556	54 331	80 038	6.2	54 721	12.7	19.6	16.7
Skagit	206	3 622	26 622	12.7	37.5	24.5	197.5	10 426	27 598	54 917	69 480	2.7	51 395	15.7	23.2	19.8
Skamania	106	959	2 183	16.1	38.4	21.4	12.1	10 076	28 705	50 986	68 006	3.4	52 673	12.6	20.1	17.5
Snohomish	183	3 480	182 923	14.0	32.9	29.3	1 214.7	9 426	31 782	69 443	83 440	4.8	71 890	9.9	13.1	11.5
Spokane	345	5 758	124 302	18.5	32.7	28.6	719.6	9 851	26 125	50 432	64 630	2.9	50 083	16.3	20.5	18.2
Stevens	99	1 965	9 722	12.4	42.2	17.6	69.8	10 854	22 035	42 111	53 816	1.3	43 823	19.3	28.2	24.5
Thurston	228	2 764	64 390	13.6	29.6	32.9	385.2	9 472	29 909	62 286	74 481	3.3	61 653	11.9	15.6	13.7
Wahkiakum	25	883	759	9.5	42.5	13.9	4.4	10 112	23 215	44 500	51 802	1.0	51 022	13.9	26.7	24.3
Walla Walla	217	3 565	16 475	27.2	34.7	26.5	89.8	9 945	23 656	47 854	62 749	2.3	49 819	15.7	20.8	19.1
Whatcom	188	3 274	57 126	12.7	31.7	32.4	253.3	9 366	26 671	53 025	66 422	2.5	53 733	15.7	17.7	16.4
Whitman	179	1 693	23 580	4.3	22.8	47.8	52.8	11 632	21 086	35 578	55 077	3.4	41 837	28.4	16.7	14.6
Yakima	244	3 305	66 386	8.3	55.3	15.9	509.4	9 783	19 861	43 956	58 548	2.0	44 342	20.5	30.3	28.0
WEST VIRGINIA	302	2 035	416 089	10.4	56.5	18.7	3 183.4	11 132	23 237	41 576	55 976	2.0	41 030	18.3	25.0	23.1
Barbour	NA	NA	4 064	23.4	65.8	12.3	25.3	10 346	17 909	36 351	45 474	0.6	35 615	21.5	28.4	26.1
Berkeley	155	1 709	26 424	13.4	51.4	20.3	191.3	10 527	26 516	55 100	68 643	2.2	56 737	13.2	19.4	18.6
Boone	229	1 560	4 941	4.8	69.9	9.1	59.3	13 099	22 400	42 740	55 831	1.6	37 625	22.1	28.4	25.1
Braxton	233	607	2 668	7.7	69.8	10.8	22.5	10 420	18 537	31 984	45 163	0.8	33 817	22.2	30.6	29.5

1. Data for serious crimes have not been adjusted for underreporting; this may affect comparability between geographic areas and over time. 2. Per 100,000 population estimated by the FBI.
3. All persons 3 years old and over enrolled in nursery school through college. 4. Persons 25 years old and over. 5. Elementary and secondary education expenditures.
6. Based on population estimated by the American Community Survey, 2010–2014. 7. James city county is included with Williamsburg city. 8. Frederick county is included with Winchester city.

Table B. States and Counties — **Personal Income**

	Personal income, 2014										Earnings, 2014		
STATE County	Total (mil dol)	Percent change, 2013–2014	Per capita[1] Dollars	Per capita[1] Rank	Wages and salaries (mil dol)	Supplements to wages and salaries; employer contributions (mil dol) Pension and insurance	Government social insurance	Proprietors' income (mil dol)	Dividends, interest, and rent (mil dol)	Personal transfer receipts (mil dol)	Total (mil dol)	Contributions for government social insurance (mil dol) From employee and self-employed	From employer
	62	63	64	65	66	67	68	69	70	71	72	73	74

VIRGINIA—Cont'd													
Manassas Park city	(3)	(3)	(3)	(3)	(3)	(3)	(3)	(3)	(3)	(3)	(3)	(3)	(3)
Martinsville city	(4)	(4)	(4)	(4)	(4)	(4)	(4)	(4)	(4)	(4)	(4)	(4)	(4)
Newport News city	7 046	2.9	38 509	1 390	5 677	1 118	435	232	1 462	1 348	7 463	413	435
Norfolk city	9 440	2.7	38 463	1 400	9 974	2 204	842	635	2 381	1 761	13 654	687	842
Norton city	(5)	(5)	(5)	(5)	(5)	(5)	(5)	(5)	(5)	(5)	(5)	(5)	(5)
Petersburg city	(6)	(6)	(6)	(6)	(6)	(6)	(6)	(6)	(6)	(6)	(6)	(6)	(6)
Poquoson city	(7)	(7)	(7)	(7)	(7)	(7)	(7)	(7)	(7)	(7)	(7)	(7)	(7)
Portsmouth city	3 728	2.6	38 836	1 344	2 769	722	233	174	761	880	3 898	207	233
Radford city	(8)	(8)	(8)	(8)	(8)	(8)	(8)	(8)	(8)	(8)	(8)	(8)	(8)
Richmond city	10 194	3.5	46 794	536	9 026	1 532	650	894	2 732	1 758	12 101	693	650
Roanoke city	3 916	3.1	39 385	1 265	3 250	507	258	251	856	954	4 267	262	258
Salem city	(9)	(9)	(9)	(9)	(9)	(9)	(9)	(9)	(9)	(9)	(9)	(9)	(9)
Staunton city	(10)	(10)	(10)	(10)	(10)	(10)	(10)	(10)	(10)	(10)	(10)	(10)	(10)
Suffolk city	3 940	3.6	45 390	643	1 416	233	106	153	670	674	1 908	119	106
Virginia Beach city	23 073	3.2	51 161	326	8 650	1 570	678	1 636	5 418	2 942	12 534	717	678
Waynesboro city	(10)	(10)	(10)	(10)	(10)	(10)	(10)	(10)	(10)	(10)	(10)	(10)	(10)
Williamsburg city	(11)	(11)	(11)	(11)	(11)	(11)	(11)	(11)	(11)	(11)	(11)	(11)	(11)
Winchester city	(12)	(12)	(12)	(12)	(12)	(12)	(12)	(12)	(12)	(12)	(12)	(12)	(12)
WASHINGTON	350 322	5.8	49 610	X	181 978	26 012	15 742	25 979	72 149	55 427	249 711	14 578	15 742
Adams	717	0.6	37 405	1 537	276	48	28	96	159	163	448	21	28
Asotin	877	5.0	39 503	1 249	208	38	20	60	182	251	325	24	20
Benton	7 638	3.4	40 956	1 068	4 244	578	396	611	1 216	1 437	5 829	336	396
Chelan	3 189	5.9	42 754	876	1 608	259	162	263	716	712	1 383	98	85
Clallam	2 866	4.9	39 416	1 262	898	179	85	221	777	846	1 383	98	85
Clark	19 462	6.0	43 153	831	7 029	1 062	651	1 168	3 669	3 448	9 910	621	651
Columbia	170	0.3	42 568	893	51	11	5	20	33	48	87	5	5
Cowlitz	3 895	5.3	38 135	1 435	1 762	267	170	265	615	1 091	2 465	162	170
Douglas	1 325	4.3	33 279	2 228	388	68	38	25	267	318	520	32	38
Ferry	235	6.4	30 680	2 629	70	17	6	10	47	87	103	7	6
Franklin	2 742	4.8	31 228	2 553	1 249	211	129	294	348	602	1 883	96	129
Garfield	87	-1.1	39 436	1 256	32	9	3	3	19	25	47	3	3
Grant	3 208	3.3	34 438	2 040	1 479	266	149	327	507	793	2 220	109	149
Grays Harbor	2 431	6.4	34 326	2 058	902	164	87	110	426	800	1 263	86	87
Island	3 695	5.7	46 608	552	987	247	97	159	1 113	753	1 490	89	97
Jefferson	1 309	4.9	43 311	811	307	62	29	55	445	368	452	36	29
King	143 261	6.1	68 877	64	93 140	10 831	7 445	13 332	32 471	13 476	124 748	7 200	7 445
Kitsap	11 838	5.7	46 573	554	4 680	1 076	438	480	3 011	2 057	6 675	376	438
Kittitas	1 606	4.1	37 761	1 488	537	108	52	113	376	327	811	48	52
Klickitat	951	4.6	45 694	630	328	52	32	129	192	239	541	33	32
Lewis	2 725	6.6	36 276	1 728	992	172	97	155	464	830	1 416	94	97
Lincoln	429	-3.4	41 877	964	111	26	10	50	95	113	198	11	10
Mason	2 169	6.0	35 732	1 815	572	113	53	83	459	624	822	60	53
Okanogan	1 551	6.3	37 562	1 516	556	112	55	160	318	456	883	52	55
Pacific	810	5.9	39 374	1 268	236	49	23	34	173	279	341	25	23
Pend Oreille	435	5.9	33 530	2 193	131	28	12	10	89	154	181	13	12
Pierce	36 283	6.3	43 613	792	15 767	2 847	1 503	2 304	6 521	6 806	22 421	1 273	1 503
San Juan	958	4.7	59 831	136	200	32	20	65	517	154	316	23	20
Skagit	5 155	6.1	42 829	869	2 167	386	208	285	1 153	1 145	3 046	185	208
Skamania	420	5.7	36 999	1 602	81	16	8	11	90	96	115	8	8
Snohomish	34 156	6.6	44 967	679	16 101	2 414	1 392	1 338	5 133	4 970	21 245	1 261	1 392
Spokane	18 921	5.2	39 067	1 312	9 875	1 552	924	1 038	3 661	4 340	13 388	817	924
Stevens	1 444	6.1	33 088	2 265	393	76	38	60	267	471	567	42	38
Thurston	11 430	6.0	42 994	850	4 973	933	446	611	2 264	2 213	6 964	412	446
Wahkiakum	145	6.7	35 534	1 850	28	6	3	7	37	49	45	4	3
Walla Walla	2 373	3.6	39 648	1 232	1 121	206	105	180	500	534	1 611	89	105
Whatcom	8 509	4.3	40 840	1 085	3 747	638	354	735	1 826	1 661	5 473	325	354
Whitman	1 587	0.3	33 883	2 132	812	215	70	128	348	285	1 225	63	70
Yakima	9 321	6.5	37 630	1 506	3 941	639	400	984	1 645	2 407	5 964	310	400
WEST VIRGINIA	66 857	2.6	36 132	X	30 081	5 387	2 428	4 564	9 493	18 371	42 461	2 824	2 428
Barbour	498	3.2	29 702	2 760	130	25	10	32	57	155	197	15	10
Berkeley	3 960	4.0	35 836	1 801	1 349	285	114	194	471	749	1 942	123	114
Boone	748	0.9	31 526	2 523	356	57	27	40	70	255	481	34	27
Braxton	410	1.2	28 315	2 894	132	26	11	27	56	136	195	15	11

1. Based on the resident population estimated as of July 1 of the year shown.   3. Manassas and Manassas Park cities are included with Prince William county.   4. Martinsville city is included with Henry county.   5. Norton city is included with Wise county.   6. Petersburg and Colonial Heights cities are included with Dinwiddie county.   7. Poquoson city is included with York county.   8. Radford city is included with Montgomery county.   9. Salem city is included with Roanoke county.   10. Staunton and Waynesboro cities are included with Augusta county.   11. Williamsburg city is included with James City county.   12. Winchester city is included with Frederick county.

Table B. States and Counties — Earnings, Social Security, and Housing

STATE County	Earnings, 2014 (cont.) Percent by selected industries									Social Security beneficiaries, December 2014		Supplemental Security Income recipients, December 2014	Housing units, 2015	
	Farm	Mining	Construction	Manufacturing	Information: professional, scientific, technical services	Retail trade	Finance, insurance, real estate and leasing	Health care and social assistance	Government	Number	Rate[1]		Total	Percent change, 2010–2014
	75	76	77	78	79	80	81	82	83	84	85	86	87	88
VIRGINIA—Cont'd														
Manassas Park city	(3)	(3)	(3)	(3)	(3)	(3)	(3)	(3)	(3)	1 185	75	11	4 906	0.2
Martinsville city	(4)	(4)	(4)	(4)	(4)	(4)	(4)	(4)	(4)	4 325	319	50	7 149	-0.8
Newport News city	0.0	D	2.7	33.0	7.3	4.2	3.2	9.6	25.3	28 385	156	4 742	77 589	1.7
Norfolk city	0.0	D	2.1	3.0	9.2	2.8	5.5	10.3	48.1	33 450	136	7 569	97 123	2.2
Norton city	(5)	(5)	(5)	(5)	(5)	(5)	(5)	(5)	(5)	1 320	328	420	1 936	-0.4
Petersburg city	(6)	(6)	(6)	(6)	(6)	(6)	(6)	(6)	(6)	7 520	233	2 432	16 423	0.6
Poquoson city	(7)	(7)	(7)	(7)	(7)	(7)	(7)	(7)	(7)	2 440	203	64	4 765	0.8
Portsmouth city	0.0	0.0	4.4	3.2	3.7	2.4	1.5	10.3	59.5	18 610	194	3 867	41 142	0.8
Radford city	(8)	(8)	(8)	(8)	(8)	(8)	(8)	(8)	(8)	2 370	136	383	6 558	2.1
Richmond city	0.0	D	3.4	4.1	15.8	2.3	8.2	12.6	27.2	34 180	158	7 082	100 393	2.1
Roanoke city	0.0	D	D	6.1	7.7	6.8	7.3	23.4	13.2	21 440	215	4 669	47 329	-0.1
Salem city	(9)	(9)	(9)	(9)	(9)	(9)	(9)	(9)	(9)	6 060	239	556	10 871	0.2
Staunton city	(10)	(10)	(10)	(10)	(10)	(10)	(10)	(10)	(10)	6 420	263	773	11 864	1.1
Suffolk city	0.9	D	4.6	8.5	17.1	6.0	3.4	12.7	24.5	15 695	181	2 285	35 481	7.4
Virginia Beach city	0.0	D	7.2	2.9	11.6	6.3	12.1	11.0	28.0	67 670	150	5 393	183 119	2.9
Waynesboro city	(10)	(10)	(10)	(10)	(10)	(10)	(10)	(10)	(10)	5 395	255	715	10 059	3.5
Williamsburg city	(11)	(11)	(11)	(11)	(11)	(11)	(11)	(11)	(11)	2 340	158	14	5 224	6.3
Winchester city	(12)	(12)	(12)	(12)	(12)	(12)	(12)	(12)	(12)	5 350	195	732	11 916	0.4
WASHINGTON	1.3	0.1	6.0	11.1	17.0	6.9	6.1	10.0	18.8	1 230 039	174	151 262	2 991 484	3.7
Adams	21.1	0.0	2.1	15.1	1.4	5.1	1.7	D	19.1	2 520	131	337	6 322	1.3
Asotin	0.4	D	9.7	7.1	4.6	12.9	4.5	D	19.5	6 240	281	715	9 851	-0.2
Benton	4.0	D	6.9	5.6	19.4	6.1	3.5	10.5	17.7	32 150	172	3 750	73 065	6.5
Chelan	7.1	D	6.9	6.4	4.7	7.5	3.7	17.8	19.9	16 280	218	1 468	36 452	2.8
Clallam	0.1	0.1	5.7	6.7	4.5	9.1	3.0	8.7	36.6	24 190	333	1 926	35 868	0.8
Clark	0.2	D	8.5	9.7	D	7.0	6.2	14.5	17.7	79 615	177	8 449	174 688	4.3
Columbia	22.3	D	3.9	3.3	1.8	4.2	1.8	D	34.2	1 295	326	158	2 119	-0.8
Cowlitz	0.2	0.8	12.8	23.2	3.3	6.6	3.0	12.5	15.1	25 400	248	3 785	43 566	0.3
Douglas	13.9	0.0	6.2	5.5	6.3	9.4	2.4	7.1	29.8	7 415	186	588	16 330	2.0
Ferry	0.7	D	D	D	D	5.4	1.5	D	52.0	2 245	293	268	4 405	0.0
Franklin	13.3	D	6.9	9.0	2.1	6.7	2.1	6.8	20.7	9 465	108	1 797	26 688	9.3
Garfield	6.6	0.0	D	0.0	D	5.3	0.0	1.0	65.0	690	312	36	1 221	-1.0
Grant	19.5	D	4.2	14.2	2.3	5.7	2.4	5.3	26.0	15 380	166	2 166	35 633	1.6
Grays Harbor	0.4	D	5.6	15.0	4.1	8.6	3.5	10.6	30.5	18 925	267	2 993	35 297	0.4
Island	0.3	D	5.0	3.2	4.6	6.4	2.6	5.2	57.2	20 630	260	1 028	40 850	1.5
Jefferson	0.4	D	7.8	9.3	7.4	7.8	4.2	7.5	33.6	11 260	373	634	18 021	1.4
King	0.0	0.0	5.4	9.3	27.1	7.0	7.3	8.0	11.8	279 905	134	38 641	893 157	4.9
Kitsap	0.0	0.1	4.9	2.1	7.3	6.0	3.1	10.7	52.9	48 630	191	5 139	109 690	2.2
Kittitas	4.2	D	10.1	3.6	4.8	8.3	3.6	6.1	35.1	7 805	183	550	22 775	4.1
Klickitat	7.1	D	4.5	6.3	16.0	2.8	2.6	3.0	18.9	5 735	275	631	9 999	2.2
Lewis	4.4	0.7	5.0	16.1	3.2	9.4	2.4	13.3	21.1	20 545	273	2 679	34 143	0.3
Lincoln	17.5	0.0	6.5	1.2	4.7	4.5	1.8	D	34.5	3 025	295	257	5 849	1.3
Mason	0.6	D	4.9	14.2	3.0	7.9	3.2	5.4	41.7	16 585	273	1 547	32 642	0.4
Okanogan	8.8	2.3	5.0	3.1	5.2	9.0	4.6	7.4	32.6	10 665	258	1 312	22 526	1.3
Pacific	2.4	0.5	6.2	11.6	2.8	6.4	4.1	D	36.3	7 475	364	673	15 745	1.3
Pend Oreille	0.6	D	4.3	12.5	3.4	4.0	1.6	D	52.3	3 925	303	514	8 029	1.2
Pierce	0.1	0.1	7.2	6.5	4.7	6.4	5.2	15.0	33.0	140 200	169	19 588	336 357	3.4
San Juan	0.3	D	14.7	D	D	9.1	5.6	5.8	16.3	4 915	307	127	13 806	3.7
Skagit	3.2	0.1	9.3	16.5	5.2	9.0	4.9	8.3	23.5	27 880	232	2 470	52 214	1.4
Skamania	-0.8	D	6.3	14.2	D	5.4	1.6	D	35.8	2 505	221	198	5 667	0.7
Snohomish	0.2	0.1	7.0	34.4	7.8	6.4	5.6	8.4	14.9	112 575	148	12 233	300 455	4.8
Spokane	0.1	0.1	6.0	7.7	7.9	7.6	8.4	17.2	19.7	95 040	196	14 081	208 296	3.4
Stevens	0.6	D	4.8	16.1	3.6	7.7	2.5	13.7	28.9	12 505	287	1 435	21 149	0.0
Thurston	0.7	0.0	5.1	3.2	6.1	6.7	4.5	12.6	39.7	53 820	202	5 195	112 553	4.0
Wahkiakum	4.0	0.0	9.1	4.7	6.8	3.2	2.6	D	30.3	1 470	362	94	2 073	0.3
Walla Walla	9.6	D	3.8	15.0	4.2	5.6	3.9	15.4	24.4	12 200	204	1 374	24 036	2.5
Whatcom	3.4	0.2	8.5	14.2	7.6	8.3	5.1	11.9	18.9	40 555	195	4 468	93 247	2.8
Whitman	4.8	D	2.3	16.2	2.3	4.4	1.7	6.0	48.9	5 595	119	416	20 131	4.2
Yakima	15.7	0.1	4.6	8.2	3.1	6.6	3.0	13.9	18.3	42 785	173	7 542	86 569	1.3
WEST VIRGINIA	0.0	8.1	6.7	8.5	7.4	6.9	4.6	15.0	20.9	464 823	251	77 715	885 475	0.4
Barbour	-0.2	D	10.3	D	D	5.5	2.8	D	18.9	4 185	250	811	7 853	0.1
Berkeley	0.2	D	5.6	4.8	8.9	6.3	3.7	13.1	36.6	20 905	189	2 258	46 797	4.5
Boone	0.0	42.0	1.3	0.8	D	4.7	D	D	18.6	6 610	279	1 295	11 012	-0.5
Braxton	0.2	2.9	8.8	11.8	3.0	13.2	2.8	14.4	21.8	3 575	247	760	7 363	-0.7

1. Per 1,000 resident population estimated as of July 1 of the year shown. 3. Manassas and Manassas Park cities are included with Prince William county. 4. Martinsville city is included with Henry county. 5. Norton city is included with Wise county. 6. Petersburg and Colonial Heights cities are included with Dinwiddie county. 7. Poquoson city is included with York county. 8. Radford city is included with Montgomery county. 9. Salem city is included with Roanoke county. 10. Staunton and Waynesboro cities are included with Augusta county. 11. Williamsburg city is included with James City county. 12. Winchester city is included with Frederick county.

Table B. States and Counties — Housing, Labor Force, and Employment

STATE County	Occupied units Total	Percent	Owner-occupied Median value[1]	With a mortgage	Without a mortgage[2]	Renter-occupied Median rent[3]	Median rent as a percent of income[2]	Sub-standard units[4] (percent)	Civilian labor force, 2015 Total	Percent change, 2014–2015	Unemployment Total	Rate[5]	Civilian employment,[6] 2010–2014 Total	Percent Management, business, science and arts	Construction, production, and maintenance occupations
	89	90	91	92	93	94	95	96	97	98	99	100	101	102	103
VIRGINIA—Cont'd															
Manassas Park city	4 526	63.9	222 300	26.7	14.2	1 474	24.9	2.3	8 166	-0.3	342	4.2	7 909	32.4	25.2
Martinsville city	5 974	55.0	85 800	23.1	15.0	593	36.4	1.4	5 384	-3.1	473	8.8	4 900	24.5	30.9
Newport News city	68 987	50.6	194 600	24.4	12.5	975	30.3	2.8	90 051	-1.1	4 866	5.4	82 525	33.0	21.7
Norfolk city	86 397	43.7	196 700	27.7	14.0	965	33.7	3.0	111 318	-1.0	6 211	5.6	101 648	31.5	23.3
Norton city	1 655	53.1	89 900	25.1	10.0	532	28.2	2.2	1 754	-3.3	122	7.0	1 795	30.0	16.9
Petersburg city	12 515	44.6	114 100	25.0	13.1	845	35.0	2.6	13 811	-0.2	1 247	9.0	12 125	25.9	22.7
Poquoson city	4 627	81.3	304 200	23.1	13.1	1 223	27.2	0.3	6 263	-0.9	240	3.8	5 845	49.2	15.6
Portsmouth city	36 764	55.8	173 700	27.6	15.8	967	33.3	2.9	44 656	-1.3	2 781	6.2	40 770	30.4	24.8
Radford city	5 333	47.2	148 400	21.4	12.5	743	44.6	0.0	8 487	-0.2	478	5.6	6 809	33.5	14.4
Richmond city	85 913	42.7	195 000	25.7	15.0	893	33.1	3.4	113 384	0.5	5 888	5.2	101 637	39.6	15.2
Roanoke city	42 549	54.5	135 600	24.1	13.6	719	29.4	2.5	49 475	-1.6	2 404	4.9	45 784	31.7	22.4
Salem city	9 953	67.4	172 400	22.7	12.1	833	29.5	2.1	13 001	-1.3	570	4.4	12 306	37.3	15.7
Staunton city	10 503	57.9	167 700	23.1	12.2	742	36.0	3.6	11 992	-0.8	527	4.4	11 276	37.3	18.8
Suffolk city	30 798	71.6	240 200	25.6	11.9	1 022	32.6	2.3	42 106	-1.0	2 089	5.0	39 211	38.9	22.7
Virginia Beach city	165 296	64.1	263 200	25.8	11.9	1 239	31.5	1.5	230 434	-0.9	9 869	4.3	213 788	39.7	17.0
Waynesboro city	8 878	57.5	161 300	24.5	13.2	785	32.4	1.9	10 047	-0.6	477	4.7	9 276	29.8	22.4
Williamsburg city	4 365	46.3	305 000	26.3	10.0	1 063	33.8	1.3	6 572	-1.4	417	6.3	6 037	42.6	10.6
Winchester city	10 692	47.7	219 700	23.2	13.0	919	34.6	4.0	14 519	0.2	630	4.3	12 605	31.4	20.9
WASHINGTON	2 645 398	62.7	257 200	24.9	12.0	995	30.3	3.4	3 544 243	1.5	200 251	5.7	3 194 382	38.7	20.8
Adams	5 827	64.8	139 200	25.1	10.0	669	27.7	13.2	8 665	2.3	590	6.8	7 649	23.9	47.3
Asotin	9 405	67.1	170 000	23.8	10.9	681	29.9	3.2	9 727	0.3	457	4.7	9 162	31.4	22.7
Benton	66 625	68.0	179 800	19.5	10.0	822	28.8	3.5	91 650	1.9	6 026	6.6	81 934	38.0	23.9
Chelan	27 183	65.1	247 800	25.3	10.9	785	26.9	4.4	42 983	3.1	2 347	5.5	32 428	29.1	31.3
Clallam	30 963	69.5	220 400	26.0	11.3	832	32.6	2.2	26 842	0.5	2 146	8.0	27 230	30.2	23.5
Clark	160 492	64.9	228 400	25.0	11.5	963	30.4	3.1	213 480	2.1	13 572	6.4	195 031	35.1	23.1
Columbia	1 706	75.0	147 800	26.6	12.8	704	42.5	3.5	1 721	-1.1	110	6.4	1 601	34.2	21.2
Cowlitz	39 765	66.1	175 200	24.6	12.2	758	35.7	3.0	44 276	1.6	3 359	7.6	39 500	27.2	30.5
Douglas	14 140	71.9	200 800	24.3	10.9	782	27.0	8.3	19 808	2.0	1 241	6.3	17 656	24.2	38.0
Ferry	3 112	70.8	161 500	27.5	10.4	559	27.3	5.7	2 469	0.9	251	10.2	2 491	32.0	34.4
Franklin	24 207	67.1	163 900	22.2	10.0	782	28.5	11.3	38 952	2.5	2 915	7.5	35 435	24.2	39.9
Garfield	906	75.2	140 300	22.1	10.7	651	19.2	2.9	927	-3.4	57	6.1	985	37.3	19.1
Grant	30 233	60.1	160 600	23.3	10.3	695	26.1	6.8	45 494	1.4	3 223	7.1	37 523	26.0	39.1
Grays Harbor	27 318	69.0	158 500	24.8	11.5	732	29.5	3.5	26 909	-1.0	2 408	8.9	26 084	25.5	27.1
Island	32 820	68.5	287 600	26.6	12.0	1 076	29.5	1.4	31 880	0.6	1 924	6.0	31 781	35.4	22.7
Jefferson	13 535	74.7	282 400	28.1	13.5	870	33.8	2.7	11 171	-0.1	791	7.1	11 175	32.0	20.5
King	808 729	57.5	376 200	24.8	12.8	1 161	29.1	3.3	1 177 297	1.4	52 307	4.4	1 050 186	48.5	14.4
Kitsap	97 993	66.9	259 000	24.9	11.5	1 043	31.1	2.2	115 211	1.5	6 315	5.5	107 330	38.0	20.3
Kittitas	16 753	57.3	246 000	26.1	11.8	809	38.8	3.5	20 817	3.2	1 279	6.1	19 282	34.1	22.1
Klickitat	7 959	68.6	197 500	27.3	10.2	791	30.1	4.8	9 447	-1.4	675	7.1	7 931	32.2	29.4
Lewis	29 450	67.8	178 200	24.8	12.0	782	32.0	3.8	31 115	2.0	2 588	8.3	28 856	24.4	31.7
Lincoln	4 445	78.6	142 000	22.5	11.1	621	24.0	2.9	4 882	-3.3	282	5.8	4 267	34.7	28.1
Mason	23 099	78.2	204 800	27.1	11.1	896	34.8	3.5	23 303	0.8	1 783	7.7	21 958	26.9	27.8
Okanogan	16 401	68.3	162 600	22.8	10.5	626	29.5	7.8	21 150	-0.9	1 459	6.9	16 319	30.9	28.7
Pacific	9 143	72.9	158 400	23.9	13.6	701	30.1	2.2	7 880	0.4	719	9.1	7 478	27.5	30.8
Pend Oreille	5 532	74.7	180 100	24.9	11.1	812	33.1	3.5	4 624	1.1	437	9.5	4 146	31.9	27.8
Pierce	301 364	61.2	233 800	26.1	12.8	1 021	31.4	3.1	391 963	1.8	24 827	6.3	357 268	33.4	23.2
San Juan	7 611	72.0	467 000	29.9	11.3	954	31.5	6.1	7 675	-0.1	368	4.8	7 677	37.1	20.9
Skagit	45 309	67.1	254 900	26.5	12.7	961	32.9	5.0	56 856	0.7	3 791	6.7	50 599	31.3	26.1
Skamania	4 433	72.6	237 500	25.7	11.8	708	28.1	3.7	5 016	1.4	364	7.3	4 659	36.5	27.0
Snohomish	271 514	66.5	287 500	26.6	12.8	1 128	30.1	3.1	401 742	1.3	19 401	4.8	358 749	37.2	21.5
Spokane	188 126	63.4	182 000	23.6	11.1	780	31.9	1.8	227 976	1.2	14 639	6.4	211 284	35.4	18.8
Stevens	17 626	76.5	171 900	26.3	11.1	670	31.4	4.2	17 594	1.2	1 541	8.8	16 355	31.1	28.2
Thurston	101 530	64.9	241 300	25.2	11.6	1 056	29.4	2.6	125 603	1.9	7 425	5.9	117 307	39.9	17.7
Wahkiakum	1 716	76.9	187 900	22.6	10.7	613	50.0	1.6	1 268	-0.5	115	9.1	1 291	28.0	38.9
Walla Walla	21 698	62.7	193 900	23.5	12.1	709	29.8	3.5	28 157	-1.0	1 632	5.8	26 043	34.1	22.1
Whatcom	79 837	62.6	273 000	25.8	12.2	919	33.6	2.4	102 918	1.6	6 110	5.9	96 727	34.6	21.2
Whitman	17 174	45.0	179 700	20.9	10.0	695	46.1	0.8	22 743	2.7	1 061	4.7	20 878	46.6	13.4
Yakima	79 717	61.8	157 900	23.9	11.5	771	32.1	8.2	122 052	2.1	9 716	8.0	100 127	24.9	36.0
WEST VIRGINIA	742 359	73.0	100 200	19.4	10.0	630	29.1	1.9	785 056	-0.6	52 907	6.7	753 227	31.5	25.3
Barbour	6 179	75.7	86 600	20.2	10.0	533	29.9	1.2	6 910	1.1	509	7.4	6 151	22.1	30.4
Berkeley	40 614	74.7	162 400	23.0	10.0	874	29.8	2.9	52 550	-0.2	2 631	5.0	48 741	31.8	26.1
Boone	9 602	75.3	77 400	18.8	10.0	569	30.4	3.1	8 332	-1.3	801	9.6	8 073	27.9	31.6
Braxton	5 652	75.4	81 800	16.8	10.0	491	30.4	3.2	5 449	4.0	489	9.0	5 144	24.1	30.3

1. Specified owner-occupied units. 2. A value of 10.0 represents 10 percent or less; a value of 50.0 represents 50 percent or more. 3. Specified renter-occupied units.
4. Overcrowded or lacking complete plumbing facilities. 5. Percent of civilian labor force. 6. Persons 16 years old and over.

STATE County	Private nonfarm establishments, employment and payroll, 2014									Agriculture, 2012			
		Employment						Annual payroll		Farms			
												Percent with:	
	Number of establishments	Total	Health care and social assistance	Manufacturing	Retail trade	Finance and insurance	Professional, scientific, and technical services	Total (mil dol)	Average per employee (dollars)	Number	Fewer than 50 acres	500 acres or more	Farm operators whose principal occupation is farming (percent)
	104	105	106	107	108	109	110	111	112	113	114	115	116
VIRGINIA—Cont'd													
Manassas Park city	322	3 102	105	D	228	26	122	140	45 057	NA	NA	NA	NA
Martinsville city	549	9 275	2 210	D	1 567	225	218	278	30 011	NA	NA	NA	NA
Newport News city	3 737	88 776	13 782	D	10 204	1 706	5 017	4 311	48 555	NA	NA	NA	NA
Norfolk city	5 349	107 411	19 016	6 714	12 160	4 798	10 805	4 796	44 651	NA	NA	NA	NA
Norton city	237	5 331	1 319	D	819	D	173	212	39 801	NA	NA	NA	NA
Petersburg city	716	14 120	6 034	D	1 376	212	152	490	34 668	NA	NA	NA	NA
Poquoson city	204	1 281	159	D	309	D	65	33	25 415	NA	NA	NA	NA
Portsmouth city	1 658	27 251	7 456	1 733	3 070	557	1 316	1 035	37 968	NA	NA	NA	NA
Radford city	303	4 370	619	1 246	563	142	195	154	35 317	NA	NA	NA	NA
Richmond city	6 046	121 294	27 573	5 271	9 043	10 482	12 459	6 518	53 738	NA	NA	NA	NA
Roanoke city	3 133	66 295	13 888	4 360	9 985	3 315	3 309	2 750	41 479	NA	NA	NA	NA
Salem city	963	18 633	D	3 249	2 105	616	531	849	45 568	NA	NA	NA	NA
Staunton city	761	10 609	2 991	492	1 935	361	289	297	28 011	NA	NA	NA	NA
Suffolk city	1 520	20 546	4 367	1 848	3 523	864	968	788	38 370	308	57.8	10.7	56.2
Virginia Beach city	10 815	151 195	18 623	5 912	22 713	10 617	16 779	5 762	38 110	187	64.7	7.0	48.1
Waynesboro city	603	9 458	818	1 728	2 197	D	276	319	33 693	NA	NA	NA	NA
Williamsburg city	528	9 100	672	22	1 833	180	130	256	28 092	NA	NA	NA	NA
Winchester city	1 319	23 756	6 842	1 949	4 263	617	988	937	39 460	NA	NA	NA	NA
WASHINGTON	179 012	2 528 874	384 476	257 814	322 099	99 671	195 908	141 278	55 866	37 249	63.2	11.0	47.4
Adams	353	4 319	D	D	645	91	47	166	38 327	713	17.8	46.6	54.8
Asotin	440	4 613	962	348	1 122	178	260	154	33 338	185	35.1	40.0	60.5
Benton	4 088	60 614	10 279	4 189	9 754	1 662	6 870	2 960	48 838	1 509	76.0	7.8	44.8
Chelan	2 441	26 785	5 523	1 799	4 318	706	1 070	1 118	41 744	890	72.2	2.9	55.7
Clallam	2 054	17 007	3 781	1 291	3 463	514	688	574	33 752	536	79.7	0.6	45.9
Clark	9 881	119 895	21 121	13 338	16 602	4 590	8 318	5 521	46 045	1 929	86.3	0.5	35.4
Columbia	130	781	174	D	118	27	28	27	34 905	308	23.1	37.7	42.5
Cowlitz	2 119	30 038	5 444	6 402	4 681	821	679	1 377	45 831	492	72.4	2.8	46.7
Douglas	695	6 152	896	363	1 509	196	171	202	32 789	849	43.0	25.9	55.9
Ferry	141	1 027	D	D	148	D	D	59	57 195	255	27.8	16.1	52.2
Franklin	1 445	18 597	1 902	2 813	3 055	367	450	727	39 071	883	37.5	27.2	62.7
Garfield	47	327	D	NA	D	D	D	11	32 630	211	15.6	51.2	56.9
Grant	1 758	20 230	2 816	4 046	3 272	534	436	783	38 725	1 552	31.2	25.9	66.6
Grays Harbor	1 634	15 544	2 774	1 916	2 881	D	417	590	37 978	557	63.9	4.7	44.7
Island	1 694	11 618	2 559	686	2 200	421	572	386	33 209	377	80.6	0.8	46.7
Jefferson	1 022	6 767	1 485	741	1 054	149	259	228	33 711	221	64.7	0.9	49.3
King	65 314	1 096 927	138 634	84 258	104 586	43 769	100 989	78 431	71 501	1 837	90.5	0.4	44.3
Kitsap	5 607	55 893	12 375	1 939	10 964	1 859	3 976	2 039	36 477	706	94.9	0.1	44.6
Kittitas	1 167	10 513	1 558	660	1 609	213	260	336	31 989	1 006	66.4	6.7	48.9
Klickitat	535	3 601	552	D	359	79	245	141	39 250	760	44.5	22.8	51.7
Lewis	1 817	18 564	3 260	3 025	3 609	411	557	679	36 587	1 647	63.8	2.1	41.0
Lincoln	255	1 639	D	D	308	D	105	65	39 479	897	16.7	48.6	54.3
Mason	1 002	9 445	1 855	953	1 605	299	251	334	35 314	377	83.8	1.9	40.6
Okanogan	1 089	8 206	1 612	497	1 836	229	D	252	30 680	1 449	52.3	11.5	48.5
Pacific	566	3 860	653	601	566	165	D	121	31 258	330	61.8	6.1	45.8
Pend Oreille	217	1 581	D	D	226	50	72	65	40 980	288	45.5	4.2	37.8
Pierce	16 609	241 294	48 915	17 858	34 400	10 219	9 462	10 128	41 974	1 478	85.3	0.3	47.0
San Juan	982	4 250	362	163	636	142	230	156	36 608	274	73.0	1.5	52.9
Skagit	3 361	39 626	7 269	5 804	6 911	1 585	1 590	1 663	41 971	1 074	73.0	4.4	48.0
Skamania	198	1 416	153	D	144	22	D	43	30 258	144	75.0	0.0	45.8
Snohomish	17 509	236 257	28 464	59 996	34 915	8 933	11 051	11 682	49 447	1 438	82.3	1.2	35.5
Spokane	12 389	176 491	34 275	14 869	26 186	11 228	9 166	7 415	42 011	2 501	59.7	9.2	41.5
Stevens	843	6 664	1 493	1 036	1 180	D	218	242	36 302	1 148	44.3	11.1	46.7
Thurston	5 923	66 373	13 204	2 642	12 391	2 681	4 689	2 561	38 578	1 336	79.3	2.0	30.7
Wahkiakum	86	411	D	D	48	D	15	14	33 569	109	50.5	1.8	50.5
Walla Walla	1 364	18 974	3 865	D	2 219	D	511	692	36 453	943	53.0	24.0	48.4
Whatcom	6 279	71 947	9 416	9 493	11 589	2 322	3 435	2 883	40 068	1 702	74.7	2.5	45.4
Whitman	839	9 630	1 867	D	1 324	223	303	374	38 843	1 195	21.5	45.4	59.5
Yakima	4 653	63 154	12 743	8 059	9 611	1 593	1 905	2 379	37 673	3 143	73.9	5.5	51.9
WEST VIRGINIA	37 354	575 228	132 829	49 589	85 753	18 006	26 406	22 100	38 420	21 489	28.3	5.8	42.6
Barbour	237	3 264	819	126	345	75	106	78	23 854	513	22.4	6.0	41.1
Berkeley	1 577	24 189	5 719	2 414	4 133	587	1 101	878	36 285	676	57.5	3.7	34.5
Boone	284	5 485	779	51	707	127	97	286	52 053	19	21.1	0.0	73.7
Braxton	262	3 722	918	D	585	82	51	134	36 130	386	16.6	12.2	50.3

Table B. States and Counties — **Agriculture**

STATE County	Land in farms Acreage (1,000) [117]	Percent change, 2007–2012 [118]	Acres Average size of farm [119]	Total irrigated (1,000) [120]	Total cropland (1,000) [121]	Value of land and buildings (dollars) Average per farm [122]	Average per acre [123]	Value of machinery and equipment, average per farm (dollars) [124]	Value of products sold Total (mil dol) [125]	Average per farm (dollars) [126]	Percent from: Crops [127]	Live-stock and poultry products [128]	Percent of farms with sales of: $10,000 or more [129]	$100,000 or more [130]	Government payments Total ($1,000) [131]	Percent of farms [132]
VIRGINIA—Cont'd																
Manassas Park city	NA	NA	NA	NA	NA	NA	NA	NA	NA	NA	NA	NA	NA	NA	NA	NA
Martinsville city	NA	NA	NA	NA	NA	NA	NA	NA	NA	NA	NA	NA	NA	NA	NA	NA
Newport News city	NA	NA	NA	NA	NA	NA	NA	NA	NA	NA	NA	NA	NA	NA	NA	NA
Norfolk city	NA	NA	NA	NA	NA	NA	NA	NA	NA	NA	NA	NA	NA	NA	NA	NA
Norton city	NA	NA	NA	NA	NA	NA	NA	NA	NA	NA	NA	NA	NA	NA	NA	NA
Petersburg city	NA	NA	NA	NA	NA	NA	NA	NA	NA	NA	NA	NA	NA	NA	NA	NA
Poquoson city	NA	NA	NA	NA	NA	NA	NA	NA	NA	NA	NA	NA	NA	NA	NA	NA
Portsmouth city	NA	NA	NA	NA	NA	NA	NA	NA	NA	NA	NA	NA	NA	NA	NA	NA
Radford city	NA	NA	NA	NA	NA	NA	NA	NA	NA	NA	NA	NA	NA	NA	NA	NA
Richmond city	NA	NA	NA	NA	NA	NA	NA	NA	NA	NA	NA	NA	NA	NA	NA	NA
Roanoke city	NA	NA	NA	NA	NA	NA	NA	NA	NA	NA	NA	NA	NA	NA	NA	NA
Salem city	NA	NA	NA	NA	NA	NA	NA	NA	NA	NA	NA	NA	NA	NA	NA	NA
Staunton city	NA	NA	NA	NA	NA	NA	NA	NA	NA	NA	NA	NA	NA	NA	NA	NA
Suffolk city	69	-3.0	225	0.4	50.9	1 016 494	4 521	155 899	62.5	202 760	94.4	5.6	37.3	15.6	2 466	47.4
Virginia Beach city	26	-1.8	140	0.2	21.2	744 428	5 317	93 203	17.7	94 631	95.0	5.0	36.9	13.9	373	23.0
Waynesboro city	NA	NA	NA	NA	NA	NA	NA	NA	NA	NA	NA	NA	NA	NA	NA	NA
Williamsburg city	NA	NA	NA	NA	NA	NA	NA	NA	NA	NA	NA	NA	NA	NA	NA	NA
Winchester city	NA	NA	NA	NA	NA	NA	NA	NA	NA	NA	NA	NA	NA	NA	NA	NA
WASHINGTON	14 748	-1.5	396	1 633.6	7 526.7	910 249	2 299	98 588	9 120.7	244 859	71.2	28.8	34.2	16.4	159 269	19.4
Adams	1 037	-5.6	1 454	127.0	815.0	1 790 387	1 231	252 728	430.2	603 303	79.0	21.0	50.5	39.4	15 567	68.2
Asotin	263	-3.9	1 423	0.5	84.3	1 210 465	851	103 357	20.5	110 854	79.9	20.2	40.5	25.4	2 504	49.2
Benton	704	11.2	466	197.3	519.1	1 276 306	2 738	127 966	923.2	611 771	D	D	34.5	15.0	6 225	10.9
Chelan	76	-19.2	85	22.8	31.5	746 306	8 760	64 446	206.5	231 999	98.2	1.8	65.6	33.7	658	7.0
Clallam	24	3.6	44	4.2	8.1	549 722	12 464	36 032	10.6	19 866	38.8	61.1	16.6	3.9	47	2.2
Clark	75	-4.6	39	3.7	29.0	490 328	12 652	38 798	50.9	26 367	37.1	62.9	16.4	2.6	293	2.4
Columbia	297	-5.1	966	4.1	184.5	1 038 701	1 076	177 896	57.7	187 442	93.4	6.6	39.3	24.0	5 273	73.4
Cowlitz	39	27.1	79	7.6	18.6	689 236	8 693	67 535	28.8	58 482	D	D	19.5	6.9	44	1.6
Douglas	814	-7.8	959	18.3	545.4	976 847	1 019	130 582	199.0	234 442	98.4	1.6	55.2	35.7	12 940	48.5
Ferry	792	5.7	3 107	2.8	19.4	1 320 859	425	55 478	5.3	20 906	54.0	46.0	28.2	7.5	159	13.3
Franklin	625	2.6	708	207.2	452.2	2 071 813	2 927	302 318	740.0	838 068	68.0	32.0	60.6	46.2	8 142	38.7
Garfield	308	0.1	1 462	0.8	187.5	1 384 441	947	153 076	48.2	228 474	92.0	8.0	50.7	37.0	4 878	80.6
Grant	964	-11.4	621	428.2	720.0	2 128 600	3 428	291 085	1 762.3	1 135 499	75.6	24.4	63.0	47.1	11 429	38.5
Grays Harbor	119	0.1	214	8.6	22.8	450 820	2 102	66 575	31.4	56 289	53.3	46.7	22.6	6.8	186	5.4
Island	15	-13.8	40	1.6	7.4	575 838	14 236	41 111	11.5	30 416	28.6	71.4	24.1	3.4	56	4.2
Jefferson	16	22.3	70	1.2	4.2	643 059	9 136	36 900	7.7	34 647	22.7	77.3	33.0	7.2	94	9.0
King	47	-5.2	25	4.1	19.7	545 036	21 432	39 027	120.7	65 732	36.4	63.6	22.8	4.6	791	4.0
Kitsap	10	-34.2	14	0.5	2.5	377 215	26 446	27 010	5.3	7 513	70.0	30.0	14.3	1.4	30	2.5
Kittitas	183	-4.2	182	66.9	68.3	804 841	4 421	77 593	68.9	68 500	68.4	31.6	35.5	12.2	875	10.3
Klickitat	551	-8.3	725	21.7	192.3	1 033 424	1 425	83 599	72.4	95 246	80.3	19.7	31.6	11.4	4 275	37.8
Lewis	133	1.0	81	8.2	54.3	507 676	6 294	48 523	132.3	80 345	22.0	78.0	24.0	6.3	879	6.8
Lincoln	1 115	2.3	1 243	34.7	808.5	1 383 491	1 113	173 996	183.2	204 285	94.7	5.3	46.5	33.8	20 307	77.6
Mason	24	-5.7	63	0.8	4.8	522 432	8 295	40 891	40.8	108 247	6.2	93.8	24.7	8.8	57	2.1
Okanogan	1 205	0.0	832	51.7	129.2	1 103 226	1 326	73 568	287.1	198 150	87.0	13.0	42.1	21.0	2 383	9.5
Pacific	52	-15.5	158	2.5	13.0	546 279	3 456	60 573	36.8	111 461	20.2	79.8	43.3	16.1	305	9.4
Pend Oreille	44	-20.8	151	0.9	15.3	462 514	3 054	45 521	4.0	13 729	58.5	41.5	15.3	2.4	27	2.8
Pierce	49	3.8	33	2.8	11.5	476 152	14 222	35 548	90.9	61 524	26.3	73.7	17.9	3.0	96	1.3
San Juan	16	-27.0	57	0.3	5.5	756 471	13 228	28 427	4.2	15 493	60.8	39.2	33.9	2.9	41	3.6
Skagit	107	-1.8	99	19.2	66.8	752 365	7 585	118 998	272.3	253 515	73.8	26.2	29.1	12.2	1 442	11.1
Skamania	6	18.3	45	0.4	1.3	456 965	10 166	36 611	5.5	38 458	27.7	72.3	25.0	6.9	0	0.0
Snohomish	71	-7.8	49	5.3	29.1	791 114	16 054	40 122	139.5	97 000	45.3	54.7	21.8	6.5	620	4.9
Spokane	537	-14.2	215	10.3	369.6	611 087	2 844	72 631	149.8	59 880	88.7	11.3	25.6	9.3	7 355	24.7
Stevens	527	-0.7	459	6.7	88.8	722 020	1 572	49 637	36.3	31 660	47.9	52.1	32.3	7.3	926	12.6
Thurston	77	-4.9	57	5.3	23.1	498 439	8 689	40 468	122.4	91 634	39.9	60.1	19.5	5.2	267	2.4
Wahkiakum	10	-20.5	88	0.0	2.7	411 376	4 692	38 826	3.5	31 991	8.3	91.7	31.2	7.3	92	11.9
Walla Walla	645	-5.5	684	91.1	565.8	1 426 922	2 086	175 634	437.4	463 795	D	D	42.2	23.5	12 372	45.2
Whatcom	116	12.9	68	35.5	78.7	786 343	11 554	80 437	357.3	209 937	33.5	66.5	31.2	15.5	3 425	17.6
Whitman	1 275	0.3	1 067	4.3	1 020.0	1 490 631	1 397	214 180	370.8	310 294	95.0	5.0	50.5	40.4	28 405	77.9
Yakima	1 780	8.0	566	224.4	306.9	1 021 212	1 803	118 874	1 645.5	523 548	65.0	35.0	45.7	22.4	5 804	11.5
WEST VIRGINIA	3 607	-2.5	168	2.1	804.0	413 407	2 463	50 020	806.8	37 544	17.2	82.8	25.3	4.0	7 034	10.2
Barbour	85	-6.9	165	0.0	19.2	323 021	1 955	52 060	6.6	12 930	17.5	82.5	28.8	1.9	109	8.2
Berkeley	70	-6.7	104	0.1	33.3	596 855	5 757	53 351	30.5	45 185	78.5	21.5	25.7	4.7	374	14.5
Boone	2	-2.9	117	0.0	0.1	203 895	1 736	26 526	0.0	2 526	43.8	56.3	5.3	0.0	D	10.5
Braxton	89	11.9	230	0.0	14.7	376 614	1 635	40 829	4.9	12 586	20.0	80.0	27.7	1.3	147	9.3

STATE County	Water use, 2010		Wholesale trade,[1] 2012				Retail trade,[2] 2012				Real estate and rental and leasing,[2] 2012			
	Total water withdrawn (mil gal/day)	Gallons withdrawn per person per day	Number of establishments	Number of employees	Sales (mil dol)	Annual payroll (mil dol)	Number of establishments	Number of employees	Sales (mil dol)	Annual payroll (mil dol)	Number of establishments	Number of employees	Receipts (mil dol)	Annual payroll (mil dol)
	133	134	135	136	137	138	139	140	141	142	143	144	145	146
VIRGINIA—Cont'd														
Manassas Park city	0.0	1	23	281	170.8	17.1	31	240	124.7	7.5	9	33	7.3	1.3
Martinsville city	0.0	0	16	D	D	D	111	1 578	317.8	34.4	31	104	14.3	2.3
Newport News city	28.6	158	110	1 438	851.3	72.7	686	9 879	2 480.8	229.7	254	1 672	276.5	60.3
Norfolk city	1.0	4	209	3 287	3 195.3	161.6	867	12 440	2 683.2	281.6	291	2 496	430.8	127.7
Norton city	0.8	200	8	123	78.3	7.1	48	786	219.7	19.3	11	42	5.0	1.0
Petersburg city	0.1	3	21	570	560.1	16.2	145	1 426	334.5	33.0	32	223	27.2	5.8
Poquoson city	0.0	0	4	D	D	D	28	305	63.8	6.1	12	20	3.2	0.6
Portsmouth city	1.4	15	48	688	249.5	32.0	273	3 081	699.5	71.1	71	332	52.6	9.7
Radford city	2.1	128	8	51	84.6	2.3	39	537	105.8	11.8	21	83	12.5	2.5
Richmond city	65.6	321	269	3 767	3 288.5	201.3	808	8 666	1 955.2	206.1	258	1 539	304.3	67.1
Roanoke city	5.3	54	180	2 727	1 398.0	130.3	535	9 912	2 461.0	230.1	155	950	141.8	31.0
Salem city	4.6	187	77	1 567	1 228.3	89.3	145	1 995	507.8	48.3	35	176	50.4	7.2
Staunton city	0.2	10	22	200	76.0	7.1	134	1 862	432.7	42.6	43	D	D	D
Suffolk city	82.8	979	54	961	666.0	49.8	226	3 536	958.9	79.1	67	243	37.5	8.1
Virginia Beach city	1.7	4	391	6 893	8 187.6	477.1	1 500	22 723	5 671.5	521.6	649	6 165	902.5	210.7
Waynesboro city	6.0	286	16	253	113.3	12.7	123	2 123	474.3	45.2	30	D	D	D
Williamsburg city	1.0	70	7	49	31.9	3.2	119	1 931	348.7	37.9	24	D	D	D
Winchester city	0.1	4	39	677	286.8	26.1	283	4 126	888.5	94.4	59	260	56.4	8.0
WASHINGTON	4 955.8	737	7 733	103 307	83 313.4	5 789.8	21 588	307 089	118 924.0	8 722.5	9 913	45 209	9 695.5	1 895.1
Adams	217.3	11 602	26	D	D	D	51	548	157.8	13.1	10	21	3.4	0.4
Asotin	4.9	227	13	D	D	D	59	1 094	285.9	30.3	21	143	11.8	3.1
Benton	415.5	2 372	109	999	1 230.3	44.5	583	9 216	2 463.5	222.7	244	1 004	179.4	30.2
Chelan	68.6	947	89	2 118	1 018.7	76.5	379	4 154	1 004.5	106.7	118	399	51.9	11.3
Clallam	21.0	294	38	D	D	D	287	3 476	812.0	92.1	87	246	35.3	7.0
Clark	134.1	315	414	4 410	4 395.4	253.2	1 011	15 547	4 276.5	419.9	465	D	D	D
Columbia	8.4	2 048	18	D	D	D	18	111	30.5	2.6	7	12	0.8	0.2
Cowlitz	146.6	1 431	85	1 036	2 021.4	53.2	333	4 644	1 188.3	113.8	104	337	50.7	8.5
Douglas	35.2	915	38	D	D	D	98	1 547	430.0	40.2	27	76	11.1	2.2
Ferry	6.3	837	1	D	D	D	27	167	45.4	3.8	6	20	0.7	0.3
Franklin	479.3	6 132	113	1 513	1 741.6	67.8	189	2 719	918.9	84.7	56	240	41.0	7.1
Garfield	3.0	1 337	9	D	D	D	11	55	10.4	1.0	NA	NA	NA	NA
Grant	1 074.9	12 061	117	D	D	D	287	3 160	825.6	77.4	81	203	28.2	5.1
Grays Harbor	34.3	471	52	D	D	D	264	2 871	761.5	73.3	82	246	24.5	5.6
Island	9.0	115	36	145	57.5	6.3	212	2 181	456.3	52.5	82	238	36.8	6.6
Jefferson	5.6	187	20	D	D	D	144	1 012	209.9	26.0	49	116	14.5	2.6
King	259.7	134	3 235	49 268	42 092.5	3 183.4	6 524	97 959	61 598.2	3 159.8	4 186	23 233	5 825.0	1 180.7
Kitsap	32.1	128	147	953	407.9	43.7	731	10 343	2 674.2	276.3	338	979	198.5	32.7
Kittitas	132.0	3 227	41	442	398.7	23.6	159	1 646	516.0	39.0	54	140	25.6	4.1
Klickitat	40.6	1 997	16	D	D	D	47	330	64.5	7.0	21	23	3.6	0.4
Lewis	39.2	519	60	D	D	D	314	3 521	912.2	87.0	75	251	34.4	7.7
Lincoln	32.3	3 057	27	D	D	D	46	292	106.9	8.1	5	6	0.5	0.1
Mason	43.8	722	33	D	D	D	134	1 557	404.3	40.4	44	233	17.6	5.1
Okanogan	98.7	2 400	39	D	D	D	199	1 836	447.0	44.5	60	154	11.5	2.3
Pacific	9.2	441	6	D	D	D	89	555	107.9	14.2	22	52	4.5	1.0
Pend Oreille	4.0	308	4	D	D	D	32	249	58.3	5.0	7	14	0.8	0.2
Pierce	197.2	248	686	9 171	7 705.6	449.9	2 154	33 111	10 114.4	944.9	947	4 673	837.6	158.6
San Juan	1.8	113	14	61	12.7	2.0	111	608	150.6	19.6	52	92	12.9	2.0
Skagit	45.3	388	104	1 277	793.5	58.2	553	6 801	1 999.2	186.8	158	467	81.8	14.4
Skamania	23.1	2 083	5	24	10.7	1.0	21	134	25.2	2.7	3	D	D	D
Snohomish	201.9	283	731	7 287	5 652.7	407.7	2 184	32 776	9 130.8	903.2	863	3 131	710.2	122.0
Spokane	185.1	393	561	8 334	4 946.9	400.8	1 617	24 749	6 560.8	668.0	614	3 053	518.3	102.2
Stevens	29.9	688	21	D	D	D	128	1 214	283.2	27.5	23	76	12.1	2.0
Thurston	52.3	207	169	1 824	1 252.0	90.8	769	12 317	3 330.8	324.6	325	994	202.1	31.3
Wahkiakum	0.7	173	2	D	D	D	9	51	10.1	1.0	6	9	0.4	0.1
Walla Walla	160.2	2 725	70	D	D	D	183	2 322	555.5	56.5	55	175	22.2	5.0
Whatcom	85.5	425	289	D	D	D	818	11 310	3 103.6	272.4	317	1 131	230.9	34.3
Whitman	8.9	199	61	D	D	D	100	1 331	333.6	28.0	50	194	21.5	4.6
Yakima	608.4	2 501	234	4 373	3 335.1	198.3	713	9 575	2 560.2	246.1	249	974	132.0	26.7
WEST VIRGINIA	3 533.0	1 907	1 334	16 906	14 295.4	761.9	6 393	85 305	22 637.9	1 908.5	1 405	6 011	1 255.8	203.8
Barbour	2.1	128	4	8	1.3	0.2	37	378	89.6	7.0	6	13	0.8	0.3
Berkeley	28.8	276	40	840	709.5	39.3	247	3 879	939.2	82.4	67	264	32.9	6.6
Boone	3.0	123	10	D	D	D	63	790	227.4	17.7	5	D	D	D
Braxton	2.3	160	8	59	23.3	2.1	67	572	171.1	13.5	8	26	3.4	0.6

1. Merchant wholesalers, except manufacturers' sales branches and offices.　2. Employer establishments.

Professional Services, Manufacturing, and Accommodation and Food Services

STATE County	Professional, scientific, and technical services, 2012				Manufacturing, 2012				Accommodation and food services, 2012			
	Number of establishments	Number of employees	Receipts (mil dol)	Annual payroll (mil dol)	Number of establishments	Number of employees	Receipts (mil dol)	Annual payroll (mil dol)	Number of establishments	Number of employees	Sales (mil dol)	Annual payroll (mil dol)
	147	148	149	150	151	152	153	154	155	156	157	158
VIRGINIA—Cont'd												
Manassas Park city	23	153	18.2	10.3	12	237	29.6	8.1	14	89	5.6	1.8
Martinsville city	48	241	21.6	8.9	24	1 041	192.7	33.0	46	718	28.8	7.8
Newport News city	364	4 971	762.0	292.6	91	26 503	5 578.9	1 558.5	386	6 621	323.8	87.6
Norfolk city	708	12 065	2 415.0	1 025.2	130	6 866	1 812.5	328.2	593	11 264	547.1	148.4
Norton city	21	173	12.9	5.7	8	585	109.8	22.2	24	D	D	D
Petersburg city	36	175	20.5	8.0	28	1 646	D	91.0	79	885	39.1	10.2
Poquoson city	22	85	7.2	3.1	3	D	1.0	D	21	278	10.0	2.9
Portsmouth city	147	D	D	D	56	2 196	447.1	97.6	172	2 624	107.1	29.3
Radford city	25	196	20.1	7.9	18	2 794	712.0	149.8	49	934	36.0	9.3
Richmond city	856	10 406	2 522.3	894.5	187	5 882	16 885.9	386.3	618	11 470	576.5	184.1
Roanoke city	328	2 920	390.6	170.1	100	3 869	1 629.7	174.8	320	6 509	308.1	94.4
Salem city	75	552	66.4	24.2	61	3 558	1 335.7	199.7	92	1 825	75.6	22.7
Staunton city	52	295	30.7	11.9	23	430	87.3	19.1	80	1 433	59.5	18.2
Suffolk city	123	D	D	D	46	1 996	1 521.0	103.6	147	2 477	122.9	30.6
Virginia Beach city	1 395	17 405	3 911.2	1 197.5	207	5 616	1 954.2	255.1	1 153	21 910	1 202.7	324.3
Waynesboro city	42	761	21.7	43.4	28	1 856	465.5	79.5	68	1 330	67.9	18.2
Williamsburg city	39	154	12.5	4.6	3	D	1.0	0.3	143	4 043	217.5	71.5
Winchester city	131	1 122	98.6	47.9	23	2 197	866.2	117.6	130	2 518	119.1	33.1
WASHINGTON	20 047	167 512	28 283.6	11 976.5	6 992	248 192	131 530.6	14 461.8	16 333	234 145	14 297.3	4 159.7
Adams	13	D	D	D	10	1 243	D	43.2	37	341	18.7	4.6
Asotin	32	1 182	19.7	11.9	25	277	50.5	10.1	40	581	25.2	8.5
Benton	436	8 899	1 654.5	668.2	144	3 990	1 828.0	217.8	375	5 996	311.6	88.4
Chelan	181	886	100.9	38.8	89	1 702	572.6	83.5	289	3 364	197.2	61.8
Clallam	170	850	77.1	33.7	82	1 215	372.2	57.4	224	2 050	113.3	33.5
Clark	1 141	7 197	1 005.6	364.9	409	11 562	D	630.8	721	10 524	550.7	163.9
Columbia	8	21	1.1	0.5	6	57	D	2.7	12	62	3.2	0.8
Cowlitz	140	830	86.5	34.9	116	5 722	3 264.5	385.6	215	2 796	124.2	39.2
Douglas	36	184	15.3	6.5	20	304	62.4	16.1	52	810	36.1	11.4
Ferry	7	D	D	D	6	141	D	5.2	17	D	D	D
Franklin	75	442	46.6	19.0	53	2 774	993.7	109.3	117	1 740	94.2	26.1
Garfield	4	D	D	D	NA	NA	NA	NA	6	12	0.3	0.1
Grant	101	406	40.6	14.5	73	4 074	1 458.5	182.3	189	1 935	117.2	29.7
Grays Harbor	91	427	43.9	18.6	84	2 580	874.2	121.2	232	1 902	104.2	29.5
Island	181	D	D	D	65	705	125.7	25.7	159	D	D	D
Jefferson	108	256	25.2	10.1	70	676	D	30.2	108	939	44.9	14.4
King	9 676	97 576	18 749.2	7 992.6	2 233	79 631	D	4 816.6	5 861	93 388	6 223.8	1 864.5
Kitsap	710	D	D	D	161	1 817	328.2	80.7	468	7 138	426.0	124.0
Kittitas	66	252	23.1	8.9	29	640	D	15.5	161	1 990	101.4	35.4
Klickitat	61	298	59.5	11.4	33	638	139.0	26.9	50	298	20.8	5.7
Lewis	118	D	D	D	123	3 270	1 238.1	139.7	188	1 842	93.6	26.6
Lincoln	11	D	D	D	8	36	D	1.5	24	D	D	D
Mason	73	D	D	D	47	942	268.5	40.2	95	D	D	D
Okanogan	76	227	23.8	6.6	35	354	123.7	12.4	124	1 031	54.8	16.6
Pacific	38	104	10.4	4.0	32	566	154.9	21.2	110	698	46.1	11.6
Pend Oreille	15	D	D	D	10	298	D	19.5	27	176	8.7	2.6
Pierce	1 427	9 464	1 043.4	546.3	566	16 027	4 461.0	796.5	1 553	22 535	1 363.0	368.8
San Juan	96	230	35.7	12.2	37	207	D	7.2	100	699	67.8	21.8
Skagit	300	D	D	D	174	5 269	11 529.4	295.7	330	4 195	291.5	79.1
Skamania	17	55	8.5	4.1	16	192	D	8.9	25	517	32.9	10.2
Snohomish	1 548	10 150	1 514.0	712.6	785	60 156	D	4 264.2	1 550	19 757	1 168.5	324.6
Spokane	1 259	D	D	D	512	13 940	3 943.1	660.3	1 057	17 949	1 062.6	299.7
Stevens	63	208	18.1	7.3	44	987	282.2	43.8	87	567	28.4	7.9
Thurston	593	D	D	D	168	2 883	910.5	123.8	533	7 785	419.2	120.5
Wahkiakum	7	D	D	D	6	D	D	D	7	D	D	D
Walla Walla	109	438	44.8	17.1	131	3 394	D	156.8	135	1 936	92.7	27.6
Whatcom	685	D	D	D	330	9 613	14 932.2	552.3	509	8 282	492.9	140.6
Whitman	56	D	D	D	27	2 136	D	128.4	130	1 463	62.1	17.1
Yakima	319	2 023	193.3	80.5	232	8 152	2 622.2	327.3	416	5 364	281.5	79.8
WEST VIRGINIA	2 974	24 816	3 104.8	1 143.4	1 245	48 686	24 553.1	2 603.9	3 629	66 302	4 036.3	975.9
Barbour	16	116	8.6	3.2	10	101	28.6	D	24	D	D	D
Berkeley	136	963	133.6	48.4	41	2 210	866.6	98.0	171	2 660	127.5	36.5
Boone	18	D	D	D	4	34	D	1.1	20	D	D	D
Braxton	12	50	4.5	1.5	12	258	148.2	12.2	27	D	D	D

1. Establishment subject to federal tax.

STATE County	Health care and social assistance, 2012				Other services, 2012				Nonemployer businesses, 2014		Value of residential construction authorized by building permits, 2015	
	Number of establish-ments	Number of employees	Receipts (mil dol)	Annual payroll (mil dol)	Number of establish-ments	Number of employees	Receipts (mil dol)	Annual payroll (mil dol)	Number	Receipts (mil dol)	New Construction ($1,000)	Number of housing units
	159	160	161	162	163	164	165	166	167	168	169	170
VIRGINIA—Cont'd												
Manassas Park city	5	D	D	D	52	D	D	D	1 199	48.9	1 864	10
Martinsville city	109	2 135	205.5	80.8	46	231	20.6	4.7	768	30.9	335	2
Newport News city	390	13 476	1 546.8	651.1	289	1 963	210.3	60.0	8 665	298.8	25 033	512
Norfolk city	533	18 651	2 391.6	900.9	374	3 245	443.7	110.7	11 851	474.8	80 752	931
Norton city	52	1 379	141.0	51.2	15	D	D	D	240	7.3	155	1
Petersburg city	126	4 740	437.7	175.4	74	554	43.2	14.7	1 260	42.6	4 631	85
Poquoson city	14	204	12.6	5.3	26	D	D	D	781	34.3	4 546	18
Portsmouth city	207	7 793	815.7	310.9	148	1 100	134.6	38.1	4 598	129.6	12 830	94
Radford city	39	507	40.4	17.4	29	D	D	D	638	30.2	375	4
Richmond city	597	25 804	3 769.4	1 303.8	516	3 904	445.6	125.1	14 624	639.5	52 933	523
Roanoke city	314	12 451	1 582.3	615.0	250	2 083	159.3	47.5	5 532	254.4	21 498	155
Salem city	114	5 223	737.8	266.3	101	563	33.6	12.8	1 398	61.0	6 794	35
Staunton city	86	2 194	154.1	74.3	85	436	38.3	11.3	1 537	60.5	3 628	27
Suffolk city	177	4 087	494.9	192.3	94	593	43.3	13.3	4 915	180.7	85 380	798
Virginia Beach city	997	18 362	1 959.4	814.7	829	4 778	618.6	119.9	28 677	1 377.1	175 889	1 493
Waynesboro city	48	875	66.9	24.1	52	364	39.4	11.5	1 020	42.9	5 546	43
Williamsburg city	44	D	D	D	29	276	33.3	12.4	845	42.3	4 676	20
Winchester city	261	6 460	885.3	355.8	85	506	36.7	10.9	2 039	118.3	2 968	13
WASHINGTON	19 833	374 227	43 966.9	17 833.2	12 425	69 976	13 185.2	2 203.3	430 670	21 011.2	8 518 859	40 374
Adams	27	716	64.2	30.7	28	D	D	D	702	41.5	14 669	163
Asotin	54	995	99.1	36.8	23	D	D	D	1 109	42.3	5 832	31
Benton	544	9 802	1 108.3	436.7	250	1 506	120.3	39.1	8 570	368.5	274 880	1 068
Chelan	221	5 233	642.6	288.8	162	571	67.6	15.7	4 569	201.7	75 980	372
Clallam	273	4 062	329.7	146.7	148	D	D	D	4 449	160.6	45 552	217
Clark	1 075	20 893	2 251.1	1 011.9	682	D	D	D	27 629	1 392.2	671 144	3 472
Columbia	11	164	11.9	5.8	8	D	D	D	214	6.9	1 342	10
Cowlitz	240	5 444	567.0	232.1	148	D	D	D	4 207	175.8	34 769	178
Douglas	64	1 042	59.3	25.6	43	149	12.1	3.3	1 619	58.6	41 535	221
Ferry	13	165	12.4	4.7	8	D	D	D	366	11.0	1 731	16
Franklin	118	1 737	201.5	83.8	95	462	41.3	11.1	3 196	156.9	104 480	396
Garfield	4	D	D	D	1	D	D	D	138	5.1	0	0
Grant	146	2 710	255.6	104.2	125	D	D	D	3 634	179.4	69 577	467
Grays Harbor	202	2 882	263.9	107.1	104	D	D	D	3 070	121.8	34 474	178
Island	172	2 326	228.3	94.4	96	401	28.1	9.1	5 747	222.8	73 733	281
Jefferson	108	1 370	127.3	54.3	88	D	D	D	3 130	110.6	28 371	156
King	7 309	135 353	17 719.2	7 109.5	4 537	29 268	9 324.7	1 074.5	159 920	8 904.9	3 766 558	18 537
Kitsap	685	11 861	1 272.8	484.3	382	1 789	149.7	48.6	14 142	608.4	244 718	918
Kittitas	96	1 613	114.9	48.7	76	D	D	D	2 519	109.6	74 497	295
Klickitat	40	599	63.7	26.3	33	103	7.3	2.2	1 412	59.2	20 455	120
Lewis	202	3 432	350.3	140.9	116	D	D	D	3 478	136.7	18 029	129
Lincoln	16	441	42.4	19.2	11	D	D	D	667	25.2	5 710	33
Mason	94	1 658	161.5	65.4	80	D	D	D	2 793	99.6	43 758	111
Okanogan	116	1 704	143.8	64.2	68	D	D	D	2 252	93.0	24 288	166
Pacific	44	618	55.6	23.5	39	D	D	D	1 371	66.3	10 171	62
Pend Oreille	19	D	D	D	15	32	4.9	0.8	697	21.5	12 487	47
Pierce	1 915	43 245	5 369.3	2 118.8	1 328	8 133	760.7	241.0	40 709	1 896.1	731 311	2 897
San Juan	61	352	26.5	10.4	62	D	D	D	2 587	114.5	24 074	100
Skagit	330	7 152	700.3	296.6	252	1 128	106.0	31.3	7 548	357.7	87 559	438
Skamania	15	128	6.6	3.0	11	22	2.2	0.5	648	23.6	10 915	47
Snohomish	1 770	28 491	2 931.5	1 217.9	1 223	6 446	572.5	178.0	42 881	1 952.7	849 895	3 574
Spokane	1 497	33 772	3 968.0	1 576.7	813	4 742	415.5	126.4	28 477	1 264.4	466 926	2 617
Stevens	82	1 627	128.4	54.5	60	D	D	D	2 522	94.2	15 640	74
Thurston	790	13 079	1 584.8	619.1	483	2 769	331.1	98.1	14 338	610.0	238 139	1 020
Wahkiakum	7	D	D	D	2	D	D	D	305	11.1	3 312	15
Walla Walla	160	4 194	443.5	198.7	80	D	D	D	3 095	121.3	47 378	204
Whatcom	659	9 901	1 026.2	422.5	404	2 282	239.2	70.4	14 710	696.7	219 961	1 144
Whitman	97	D	D	D	60	D	D	D	2 033	69.5	35 339	205
Yakima	557	12 903	1 431.4	574.7	281	1 449	130.9	34.3	9 217	419.4	89 672	395
WEST VIRGINIA	4 939	129 075	12 259.4	4 824.5	2 661	16 583	1 773.3	443.6	89 044	3 391.5	417 183	2 814
Barbour	31	842	43.7	18.2	17	D	D	D	656	18.1	1 600	25
Berkeley	197	5 667	629.5	296.9	116	635	55.2	15.7	5 597	219.1	113 015	658
Boone	37	835	45.1	22.0	23	D	D	D	735	19.1	2 325	16
Braxton	19	842	48.3	17.5	17	D	D	D	585	19.9	1 854	19

Government Employment and Payroll, and Local Government Finances

	Government employment and payroll, 2012									Local government finances, 2012				
			March payroll (percent of total)							General revenue				
													Taxes	
													Per capita[1] (dollars)	
STATE County	Full-time equivalent employees	March payroll (dollars)	Adminis- tration, judicial, and legal	Police and Corrections	Fire Protection	Highways and transpor- tation	Health and Welfare	Natural resources and utilities	Education and libraries	Total (mil dol)	Inter- govern- mental (mil dol)	Total (mil dol)	Total	Property
	171	172	173	174	175	176	177	178	179	180	181	182	183	184
VIRGINIA—Cont'd														
Manassas Park city.........	547	2 174 966	6.3	8.6	5.6	0.7	1.8	6.3	67.3	58.7	24.8	25.4	1 608	1 293
Martinsville city..............	769	2 241 998	9.4	13.6	4.4	3.9	2.0	9.5	54.3	58.0	32.0	15.8	1 148	628
Newport News city.........	8 482	34 753 223	6.1	10.1	4.5	2.1	4.5	9.1	62.7	786.5	332.1	322.2	1 783	1 269
Norfolk city	14 612	55 628 038	4.8	10.3	4.2	8.7	8.6	7.9	54.2	1 422.2	577.3	416.3	1 694	1 029
Norton city......................	226	662 054	8.5	13.0	0.5	4.4	8.7	6.7	55.1	22.2	11.9	7.7	1 884	632
Petersburg city	1 476	4 759 064	5.8	19.4	8.6	4.3	5.8	7.7	45.6	126.3	70.3	45.2	1 415	1 044
Poquoson city	447	1 474 638	7.0	6.8	6.8	3.3	0.8	2.3	70.5	38.2	15.0	19.1	1 576	1 340
Portsmouth city	4 358	16 114 476	6.2	15.8	6.6	0.8	6.9	6.3	55.4	449.4	234.6	161.2	1 671	1 219
Radford city....................	450	1 533 350	9.5	10.2	2.3	3.6	4.7	13.6	53.1	37.9	20.4	11.1	664	455
Richmond city	8 977	34 059 020	8.8	19.1	5.9	2.9	6.0	10.3	41.5	1 102.8	456.7	412.6	1 962	1 249
Roanoke city	3 900	14 209 461	8.0	12.7	8.2	3.3	6.2	4.1	55.6	398.1	176.5	172.9	1 774	1 086
Salem city......................	1 239	4 093 202	12.6	9.6	6.7	6.7	2.4	12.1	49.5	108.5	42.3	49.5	1 982	1 301
Staunton city	1 131	3 120 624	7.9	23.4	4.4	2.5	1.7	5.3	51.1	82.8	39.3	32.3	1 349	839
Suffolk city.....................	3 558	11 946 187	10.3	7.7	9.6	2.9	4.4	6.4	58.0	305.1	145.8	134.5	1 579	1 162
Virginia Beach city	19 058	68 439 433	3.5	9.0	3.4	0.3	6.4	12.4	57.0	1 816.6	615.1	810.1	1 812	1 218
Waynesboro city	795	2 593 698	8.5	8.2	4.6	3.4	1.3	8.3	60.2	77.5	33.4	33.2	1 574	946
Williamsburg city	407	1 404 121	11.0	37.6	9.6	3.3	4.2	10.1	21.2	46.8	11.2	29.9	1 971	766
Winchester city..............	1 491	5 190 139	6.6	22.4	6.4	2.6	4.2	6.7	49.4	137.9	46.7	61.6	2 292	1 298
WASHINGTON	X	X	X	X	X	X	X	X	X	X	X	X	X	X
Adams	1 040	3 937 847	5.7	6.6	0.8	5.5	21.8	10.0	47.7	141.3	72.5	24.1	1 269	906
Asotin	728	2 891 078	6.7	8.1	3.6	6.7	12.3	6.0	54.9	69.3	39.9	19.3	881	674
Benton	7 559	41 657 634	4.9	6.8	3.2	4.4	13.0	32.6	34.0	876.0	367.1	242.6	1 330	745
Chelan...........................	3 427	16 843 859	4.7	6.8	2.3	5.4	9.3	32.8	36.9	368.1	151.3	114.2	1 550	1 003
Clallam	3 439	16 962 339	5.9	7.8	3.5	5.4	38.0	11.5	26.0	416.5	135.2	89.7	1 249	834
Clark	11 478	56 406 570	6.0	8.5	5.1	6.1	1.9	9.2	59.4	1 575.0	717.2	576.6	1 316	967
Columbia	318	1 186 883	10.8	5.9	1.0	8.9	38.0	7.4	25.7	32.7	11.4	6.7	1 687	1 352
Cowlitz..........................	3 301	15 112 407	7.8	11.6	3.0	7.2	3.7	14.2	51.3	420.9	170.2	127.1	1 246	848
Douglas	1 297	6 128 626	5.0	6.0	1.5	6.7	0.5	26.3	52.5	145.0	88.5	39.7	1 008	759
Ferry..............................	420	1 474 156	7.4	5.9	0.4	5.7	31.9	8.5	39.8	44.5	24.8	5.0	651	505
Franklin	2 593	11 637 558	6.0	7.6	3.3	4.6	0.0	14.4	62.8	318.4	176.1	82.9	965	615
Garfield..........................	229	842 190	7.7	6.5	0.9	9.8	47.5	1.7	24.6	29.1	16.3	3.5	1 591	960
Grant	4 837	22 986 238	4.1	5.2	1.2	2.7	20.7	28.8	35.5	555.0	232.9	128.7	1 403	1 005
Grays Harbor	2 841	12 751 235	7.3	9.1	6.2	10.1	5.9	14.9	44.7	305.6	124.6	95.4	1 330	817
Island............................	2 321	11 320 614	5.9	5.9	5.9	8.0	32.6	3.6	36.8	280.9	92.9	87.2	1 101	776
Jefferson	1 311	6 130 951	7.9	5.4	5.8	9.2	41.3	2.8	26.6	158.5	38.9	46.4	1 556	1 102
King	65 821	388 288 446	8.0	10.3	5.9	13.1	13.5	13.9	33.3	12 411.3	3 474.5	5 105.6	2 543	1 381
Kitsap	6 732	32 797 634	7.2	7.7	9.1	6.6	1.0	9.5	56.8	1 053.2	532.7	344.8	1 352	960
Kittitas	1 664	7 365 807	8.8	8.2	3.6	3.8	32.4	9.0	32.4	197.1	81.5	58.9	1 412	1 006
Klickitat	1 119	4 905 212	5.9	6.8	0.4	4.5	31.9	13.1	35.6	136.0	44.1	27.2	1 316	1 015
Lewis	2 603	11 808 449	7.8	9.5	3.2	6.0	10.1	11.8	47.1	268.0	123.6	81.1	1 072	750
Lincoln	806	3 420 386	7.1	4.6	0.1	8.4	38.7	1.4	38.6	95.2	44.6	15.2	1 458	1 199
Mason	2 164	10 240 656	6.6	6.6	4.0	5.9	26.0	11.1	37.8	268.3	97.3	72.6	1 193	869
Okanogan......................	1 848	8 014 386	6.5	8.2	0.5	3.7	30.9	10.5	38.5	228.9	90.9	42.6	1 031	722
Pacific	1 032	5 269 056	8.5	7.3	3.7	6.5	27.8	11.0	33.1	126.6	42.8	31.2	1 518	1 146
Pend Oreille	786	3 517 534	6.4	5.1	0.4	3.4	34.6	21.7	26.3	81.4	36.0	10.4	799	627
Pierce............................	23 934	131 701 698	8.7	9.5	9.2	8.4	2.7	12.1	47.1	3 300.2	1 329.7	1 234.7	1 521	1 076
San Juan........................	551	2 448 595	14.0	7.8	3.9	9.0	9.8	11.9	39.1	76.6	25.1	34.7	2 196	1 573
Skagit	5 963	27 675 332	5.4	5.4	2.0	4.5	41.5	4.7	33.8	852.8	275.6	199.6	1 688	1 157
Skamania	390	1 668 143	14.8	12.9	0.3	6.4	8.7	12.8	38.8	36.0	22.6	8.7	781	588
Snohomish	19 389	108 720 406	6.9	9.4	6.5	8.0	5.4	13.4	47.9	2 865.2	1 091.9	1 077.6	1 470	1 030
Spokane	13 368	67 439 060	9.4	11.5	7.6	7.3	3.7	7.0	51.9	1 818.7	806.0	639.3	1 344	862
Stevens	1 254	5 040 095	8.1	7.4	1.3	6.3	7.8	4.7	61.9	143.8	97.8	31.2	717	541
Thurston	7 290	36 403 899	10.9	9.6	5.9	9.3	2.0	8.9	51.8	946.4	372.7	391.6	1 516	997
Wahkiakum	161	658 898	16.0	9.8	0.1	7.0	7.0	12.6	31.8	27.2	18.9	3.6	909	651
Walla Walla	1 801	7 900 373	8.1	11.4	5.9	6.2	5.5	3.9	55.3	236.4	107.1	76.1	1 281	877
Whatcom	5 120	25 193 563	10.0	10.9	7.5	8.7	1.8	7.1	50.4	696.1	261.3	292.4	1 424	871
Whitman	1 636	7 215 336	5.6	5.7	3.5	8.0	37.2	2.3	36.4	210.9	64.2	44.8	961	644
Yakima	8 019	34 900 911	7.0	10.7	3.2	2.8	3.3	5.9	66.0	970.4	601.4	232.4	941	607
WEST VIRGINIA.........	X	X	X	X	X	X	X	X	X	X	X	X	X	X
Barbour	525	1 593 938	6.5	3.2	0.0	1.0	6.3	5.7	74.1	35.3	22.1	6.7	408	324
Berkeley	3 583	11 743 879	4.1	3.5	2.1	0.6	1.2	4.4	82.8	263.0	125.8	97.1	907	806
Boone............................	1 129	3 935 149	4.3	3.0	1.1	0.8	17.5	1.2	69.9	102.4	38.1	37.4	1 528	1 483
Braxton..........................	464	1 418 168	6.8	3.5	5.0	0.8	1.9	4.6	76.8	34.7	20.6	7.6	528	481

1. Based on the resident population estimated as of July 1 of the year shown.

STATE County	Total (mil dol) 185	Per capita[1] (dollars) 186	Education 187	Health and hospitals 188	Police protection 189	Public welfare 190	Highways 191	Total (mil dol) 192	Per capita[1] (dollars) 193	Federal civilian 194	Federal military 195	State and local 196	Democratic 197	Republican 198	All other 199
VIRGINIA—Cont'd															
Manassas Park city	60.1	3 803	52.0	0.2	7.5	2.3	0.9	123.4	7 811	(3)	(3)	(3)	59.5	39.5	1.0
Martinsville city	59.6	4 339	42.2	0.5	6.3	0.5	5.7	35.1	2 555	(4)	(4)	(4)	63.5	35.4	1.1
Newport News city	820.9	4 542	41.6	8.3	5.6	5.0	3.9	1 041.2	5 761	5 506	6 712	11 341	63.9	35.3	0.8
Norfolk city	1 457.9	5 932	43.5	5.0	4.7	5.2	3.6	2 294.3	9 335	14 325	41 727	20 889	71.0	28.1	0.9
Norton city	20.8	5 109	39.7	0.5	9.9	6.6	7.9	19.6	4 823	(5)	(5)	(5)	49.1	49.2	1.7
Petersburg city	134.0	4 190	38.8	1.0	8.8	11.1	4.6	60.3	1 887	(6)	(6)	(6)	88.6	10.2	1.2
Poquoson city	38.6	3 191	55.1	1.5	6.4	1.1	7.3	56.8	4 694	(7)	(7)	(7)	24.7	74.0	1.2
Portsmouth city	543.5	5 633	31.4	2.0	6.5	4.7	1.3	647.6	6 713	12 947	6 631	5 487	69.3	30.0	0.8
Radford city	44.5	2 667	45.2	0.5	8.1	5.6	5.3	28.4	1 701	(8)	(8)	(8)	54.0	44.5	1.5
Richmond city	1 081.3	5 141	30.1	4.3	8.5	1.5	3.8	1 910.6	9 085	5 169	1 204	37 444	79.1	20.0	0.9
Roanoke city	391.0	4 011	38.2	0.8	5.9	14.8	3.4	597.7	6 132	1 533	340	7 037	61.2	37.8	1.1
Salem city	120.6	4 828	38.5	0.7	5.3	1.5	4.9	167.0	6 689	(9)	(9)	(9)	41.6	57.1	1.2
Staunton city	94.0	3 928	32.9	8.4	5.8	5.6	5.2	98.6	4 122	(10)	(10)	(10)	50.6	48.4	1.1
Suffolk city	324.3	3 808	45.2	0.2	6.3	4.4	6.8	654.0	7 677	994	459	4 792	56.2	43.0	0.7
Virginia Beach city	2 062.0	4 613	40.8	2.6	4.3	3.3	4.2	2 582.9	5 778	6 319	18 284	22 881	49.1	49.8	1.0
Waynesboro city	75.1	3 556	42.8	0.6	5.0	4.9	6.7	92.3	4 374	(10)	(10)	(10)	44.1	54.3	1.6
Williamsburg city	53.2	3 510	14.0	0.9	7.4	3.7	3.5	32.4	2 134	(11)	(11)	(11)	63.8	34.7	1.6
Winchester city	131.6	4 897	37.2	0.9	5.5	5.5	4.3	337.1	12 539	(12)	(12)	(12)	52.0	46.7	1.3
WASHINGTON	X	X	X	X	X	X	X	X	X	71 470	76 552	470 808	57.7	40.5	1.9
Adams	135.7	7 140	46.3	18.1	2.6	0.0	5.7	62.9	3 309	34	53	1 529	31.9	66.3	1.7
Asotin	68.8	3 142	46.9	7.4	5.3	0.0	7.3	21.9	1 003	45	61	1 153	42.3	55.7	1.9
Benton	835.7	4 582	38.0	28.0	4.0	0.0	3.3	6 728.4	36 888	755	524	11 819	36.1	62.2	1.8
Chelan	345.4	4 688	41.8	14.6	4.2	0.0	5.4	1 594.5	21 638	594	204	5 913	43.1	55.1	1.8
Clallam	403.3	5 612	25.3	39.7	3.3	0.0	3.6	172.3	2 398	430	511	6 922	50.5	47.2	2.2
Clark	1 525.7	3 481	51.0	3.7	4.0	0.5	5.8	2 123.7	4 845	3 198	1 288	20 811	52.2	46.1	1.7
Columbia	29.1	7 286	21.7	37.4	4.2	0.0	7.5	17.2	4 300	74	11	424	30.8	67.3	1.9
Cowlitz	424.6	4 163	38.6	3.9	5.4	0.0	4.9	609.4	5 974	222	280	5 563	54.4	43.2	2.4
Douglas	142.5	3 622	59.9	8.3	5.1	0.0	6.7	350.0	8 893	236	109	1 896	38.5	59.8	1.7
Ferry	39.2	5 090	46.3	22.7	2.6	0.0	9.2	9.5	1 236	153	20	750	41.9	54.7	3.4
Franklin	294.3	3 429	60.6	1.4	3.9	0.0	4.7	315.8	3 679	459	235	5 542	37.4	61.1	1.5
Garfield	32.0	14 354	37.5	23.0	2.9	0.0	17.9	7.7	3 442	128	0	340	28.0	70.5	1.5
Grant	519.5	5 664	37.4	28.7	3.4	0.6	4.6	1 451.0	15 819	746	254	7 467	35.0	62.5	2.5
Grays Harbor	303.0	4 227	38.5	9.5	5.7	0.2	6.2	405.8	5 660	185	225	6 038	56.0	41.5	2.5
Island	257.0	3 246	28.7	33.0	3.3	0.2	7.4	171.2	2 163	1 369	5 879	3 131	52.3	46.1	1.6
Jefferson	155.4	5 205	19.1	39.9	3.6	0.3	5.2	145.8	4 885	166	93	2 066	66.3	31.7	2.0
King	11 212.0	5 585	28.9	12.4	5.0	1.2	5.5	22 389.4	11 153	20 214	6 922	148 725	70.3	28.2	1.5
Kitsap	1 054.5	4 135	42.3	4.6	3.5	0.0	3.5	748.5	2 935	17 026	10 799	12 668	55.2	42.9	1.9
Kittitas	186.9	4 485	26.5	30.6	4.7	0.0	6.5	110.8	2 658	140	122	4 254	44.9	53.0	2.1
Klickitat	118.4	5 721	34.2	32.3	3.9	0.0	8.0	215.9	10 431	94	57	1 557	48.8	48.6	2.5
Lewis	254.6	3 367	47.6	10.3	5.3	0.0	6.3	343.9	4 547	223	205	4 768	39.3	58.4	2.3
Lincoln	96.3	9 226	34.5	30.0	2.8	0.0	10.9	34.2	3 279	61	28	1 241	34.0	63.6	2.4
Mason	257.4	4 232	32.2	26.8	3.0	0.0	4.3	295.3	4 854	70	161	5 452	53.2	44.5	2.3
Okanogan	207.5	5 027	35.7	32.4	4.0	0.1	3.7	126.1	3 056	421	112	4 297	45.1	52.2	2.7
Pacific	123.7	6 010	30.5	32.4	3.3	0.0	4.1	113.3	5 509	62	159	1 767	55.7	41.6	2.6
Pend Oreille	75.9	5 850	25.2	33.2	3.2	0.1	6.9	158.1	12 178	103	36	1 370	39.1	56.7	4.2
Pierce	3 273.5	4 033	43.7	2.1	5.8	0.6	5.6	4 565.2	5 624	11 842	34 688	44 873	55.2	43.0	1.8
San Juan	74.8	4 726	30.2	8.5	3.4	0.3	9.8	34.2	2 159	58	44	764	70.0	28.1	1.9
Skagit	797.6	6 747	26.4	43.2	2.9	0.1	3.4	556.4	4 706	368	328	10 635	53.8	44.2	2.1
Skamania	41.2	3 682	35.3	7.8	6.4	0.2	7.2	16.3	1 455	119	31	498	51.3	46.0	2.7
Snohomish	2 730.6	3 725	42.2	8.8	4.8	0.6	4.4	3 753.7	5 121	2 118	6 335	35 499	58.5	39.6	2.0
Spokane	1 872.4	3 936	45.5	5.1	5.4	0.2	4.0	1 560.2	3 280	4 505	4 167	30 329	48.2	49.3	2.5
Stevens	148.2	3 405	61.9	5.5	3.5	0.0	7.0	45.9	1 055	334	120	2 551	38.0	58.8	3.2
Thurston	952.8	3 688	42.4	5.4	4.0	0.0	7.1	917.5	3 552	867	771	35 152	59.9	38.2	1.9
Wahkiakum	25.9	6 484	20.6	41.0	3.8	0.0	7.9	4.8	1 207	15	11	254	48.9	48.2	3.0
Walla Walla	228.3	3 844	45.7	5.8	5.9	0.0	7.1	249.9	4 207	1 211	155	4 465	40.8	57.4	1.9
Whatcom	644.4	3 139	42.5	4.3	6.1	0.0	5.7	595.5	2 901	1 376	624	13 814	58.0	40.1	1.9
Whitman	199.6	4 282	27.1	40.8	3.9	0.3	4.7	87.2	1 870	223	123	8 762	51.6	46.1	2.4
Yakima	1 052.2	4 260	60.9	3.2	4.2	0.8	4.9	606.3	2 455	1 226	801	15 749	43.9	54.4	1.7
WEST VIRGINIA	X	X	X	X	X	X	X	X	X	23 430	9 192	124 136	42.6	55.7	1.7
Barbour	38.2	2 315	63.0	3.6	3.6	0.0	1.0	23.1	1 402	36	78	699	38.8	59.1	2.1
Berkeley	274.3	2 561	76.5	0.5	4.5	0.0	0.7	319.3	2 981	3 896	596	4 862	42.9	55.9	1.2
Boone	117.1	4 784	50.3	15.4	4.9	0.2	0.5	11.7	479	71	115	1 628	54.1	43.4	2.5
Braxton	39.8	2 754	58.6	1.2	2.1	0.0	0.5	106.5	7 361	61	69	881	50.0	48.6	1.4

1. Based on the resident population estimated as of July 1 of the year shown.   2. © 2013 Election Data Services, Inc. All rights reserved.   3. Manassas and Manassas Park cities are included with Prince William county.   4. Martinsville city is included with Henry county.   5. Norton city is included with Wise county.   6. Petersburg and Colonial Heights cities are included with Dinwiddie county.   7. Poquoson city is included with York county.   8. Radford city is included with Montgomery county.   9. Salem city is included with Roanoke county.   10. Staunton and Waynesboro cities are included with Augusta county.   11. Williamsburg city is included with James City county.   12. Winchester city is included with Frederick county.

Table B. States and Counties — **Land Area and Population**

STATE/County code	CBSA code[1]	County type[2]	STATE County	Land area[3] (sq km) 2010	Total persons 2015	Rank	Per square kilometer	White	Black	American Indian, Alaska Native	Asian and Pacific Islander	Percent Hispanic or Latino[4]	Under 5 years	5 to 17 years	18 to 24 years	25 to 34 years	35 to 44 years	45 to 54 years
				1	2	3	4	5	6	7	8	9	10	11	12	13	14	15
			WEST VIRGINIA—Cont'd															
54 009	48260	3	Brooke	231	23 350	1 667	101.1	97.1	2.1	0.5	0.7	0.8	3.8	13.9	10.1	9.3	11.5	13.6
54 011	26580	2	Cabell	728	96 844	610	133.0	92.5	6.2	0.8	1.6	1.4	6.1	14.0	13.3	12.9	11.8	12.0
54 013	...	8	Calhoun	723	7 470	2 638	10.3	97.8	0.7	0.7	0.5	1.1	4.9	14.1	6.6	10.7	11.8	14.8
54 015	16620	2	Clay	886	8 910	2 520	10.1	98.9	0.7	0.8	0.3	0.5	6.5	16.3	7.2	9.7	12.3	14.0
54 017	17220	9	Doddridge	828	8 176	2 587	9.9	99.6	2.4	0.8	0.4	0.7	4.0	13.7	9.9	11.3	13.0	15.6
54 019	13220	6	Fayette	1 713	44 997	1 071	26.3	93.6	5.3	0.7	0.4	1.1	5.9	14.7	7.6	11.2	12.7	13.5
54 021	...	9	Gilmer	877	8 518	2 555	9.7	81.2	12.8	1.1	1.2	6.3	4.0	9.7	15.1	15.7	14.8	13.7
54 023	...	6	Grant	1 236	11 766	2 307	9.5	97.3	1.2	0.5	0.3	1.3	5.2	14.7	7.1	9.8	11.7	14.5
54 025	...	7	Greenbrier	2 641	35 516	1 287	13.4	94.9	3.7	0.8	0.7	1.4	5.4	14.1	7.3	11.0	11.2	14.0
54 027	49020	3	Hampshire	1 658	23 353	1 666	14.1	97.1	1.7	0.7	0.5	1.3	4.6	15.5	7.4	10.0	12.1	15.1
54 029	48260	3	Hancock	214	29 815	1 434	139.3	95.9	3.4	0.6	0.5	1.2	4.9	14.9	6.9	10.2	12.2	14.3
54 031	...	8	Hardy	1 508	13 852	2 178	9.2	92.5	3.2	0.7	0.9	3.6	5.1	15.1	7.2	10.3	12.4	15.0
54 033	17220	5	Harrison	1 077	68 714	775	63.8	95.7	2.5	0.8	0.9	1.6	5.8	15.6	7.6	12.2	12.4	14.1
54 035	...	6	Jackson	1 203	29 237	1 447	24.3	98.0	0.9	0.6	0.5	0.8	5.4	16.4	7.5	10.8	12.3	14.0
54 037	47900	1	Jefferson	543	56 482	903	104.0	85.8	7.8	0.9	2.4	5.5	5.4	17.5	9.1	11.6	13.3	15.6
54 039	16620	2	Kanawha	2 335	188 332	343	80.7	90.1	8.8	0.8	1.6	1.1	5.6	14.9	7.9	12.2	12.4	13.5
54 041	...	7	Lewis	997	16 448	2 009	16.5	97.6	1.1	0.7	0.6	1.0	5.7	14.7	7.4	11.1	12.7	14.4
54 043	26580	3	Lincoln	1 132	21 415	1 758	18.9	98.6	0.5	0.5	0.3	0.7	5.9	16.6	7.3	10.9	13.1	14.3
54 045	30880	6	Logan	1 175	34 707	1 311	29.5	96.9	2.4	0.5	0.4	0.9	5.9	14.7	7.7	11.1	13.9	12.9
54 047	...	7	McDowell	1 382	19 835	1 842	14.4	90.7	9.7	0.7	0.3	0.6	6.3	14.3	7.3	10.9	12.6	13.7
54 049	21900	4	Marion	800	56 925	897	71.2	94.4	4.4	0.7	0.8	1.2	5.8	14.1	11.4	11.4	12.3	12.7
54 051	48540	3	Marshall	791	31 978	1 383	40.4	98.0	1.2	0.6	0.6	1.0	5.3	14.8	7.6	10.8	12.0	13.9
54 053	38580	6	Mason	1 116	27 037	1 532	24.2	97.6	1.4	0.7	0.5	0.6	5.3	15.9	7.4	11.2	12.4	13.8
54 055	14140	3	Mercer	1 085	61 164	855	56.4	92.1	7.2	0.7	0.8	1.0	6.4	14.6	8.9	11.3	12.0	12.5
54 057	19060	3	Mineral	849	27 451	1 513	32.3	95.4	3.9	0.5	0.6	0.9	5.3	14.8	9.5	10.5	11.7	14.1
54 059	...	6	Mingo	1 096	25 292	1 598	23.1	97.1	2.5	0.5	0.5	0.6	6.4	15.7	7.4	11.9	13.2	14.1
54 061	34060	3	Monongalia	933	104 236	570	111.7	91.2	4.8	0.6	3.8	2.0	5.0	11.0	23.4	17.3	11.3	10.6
54 063	...	8	Monroe	1 224	13 506	2 202	11.0	98.2	1.2	1.0	0.4	0.8	5.4	15.5	6.7	9.7	11.5	13.8
54 065	...	3	Morgan	593	17 524	1 946	29.6	96.9	1.3	1.0	0.7	1.2	4.1	15.0	6.9	9.4	11.8	15.6
54 067	...	6	Nicholas	1 675	25 594	1 578	15.3	98.3	0.6	1.2	0.6	0.7	5.8	15.0	7.8	10.5	12.2	13.8
54 069	48540	3	Ohio	274	43 066	1 110	157.2	94.6	4.9	0.6	1.2	1.1	5.5	13.7	10.8	11.1	10.9	12.9
54 071	...	8	Pendleton	1 803	7 229	2 653	4.0	97.1	2.9	0.9	0.5	1.1	4.6	13.2	7.9	9.5	9.9	13.9
54 073	...	3	Pleasants	337	7 674	2 619	22.8	96.3	1.7	0.8	0.3	0.9	4.6	14.8	8.4	11.3	13.2	15.3
54 075	...	9	Pocahontas	2 435	8 607	2 545	3.5	96.9	1.3	1.0	0.4	1.5	4.9	12.5	6.5	10.5	11.2	14.7
54 077	34060	3	Preston	1 680	33 940	1 329	20.2	97.0	1.6	0.6	0.4	0.9	4.9	14.4	7.3	13.4	13.2	14.5
54 079	26580	2	Putnam	895	56 848	898	63.5	96.5	1.6	0.6	1.2	1.1	5.4	17.5	6.9	11.2	13.7	14.4
54 081	13220	4	Raleigh	1 568	77 510	713	49.4	89.3	9.0	0.9	1.3	1.5	6.2	15.0	7.7	12.4	13.3	12.3
54 083	21180	3	Randolph	2 693	29 126	1 451	10.8	97.5	1.9	0.7	0.6	0.8	5.3	13.9	8.7	11.8	11.8	14.1
54 085	...	8	Ritchie	1 171	9 982	2 436	8.5	98.6	0.6	0.6	0.3	0.7	4.7	15.6	7.4	9.7	11.8	14.8
54 087	...	6	Roane	1 252	14 435	2 135	11.5	98.5	0.8	0.7	0.6	0.9	5.7	16.2	7.1	9.8	12.4	13.8
54 089	...	7	Summers	934	13 239	2 221	14.2	93.4	5.7	1.1	0.5	1.8	4.1	13.0	6.4	11.3	13.0	14.3
54 091	17220	6	Taylor	447	16 912	1 984	37.8	97.3	1.6	0.7	0.6	0.9	5.4	15.2	7.2	12.3	12.9	14.6
54 093	...	9	Tucker	1 085	6 966	2 679	6.4	98.0	0.7	0.6	0.3	0.8	4.1	12.9	7.5	9.9	11.4	15.6
54 095	...	6	Tyler	664	8 975	2 514	13.5	98.9	0.5	0.6	0.3	0.7	4.6	15.5	7.5	9.1	11.9	14.7
54 097	...	7	Upshur	919	24 758	1 614	26.9	97.5	1.4	0.6	0.6	1.2	5.6	15.0	11.5	11.2	11.4	13.1
54 099	26580	2	Wayne	1 310	40 971	1 152	31.3	97.9	0.8	0.7	0.6	0.7	4.9	16.3	7.9	11.1	13.0	14.1
54 101	...	9	Webster	1 433	8 755	2 533	6.1	98.8	0.8	0.7	0.5	0.6	5.6	14.3	7.1	9.5	11.9	13.8
54 103	...	6	Wetzel	927	15 816	2 053	17.1	98.4	0.8	0.5	0.6	0.7	5.3	14.8	7.7	10.0	11.4	14.5
54 105	37620	3	Wirt	602	5 880	2 765	9.8	98.6	0.9	0.8	0.3	0.7	5.4	15.6	7.3	9.7	11.8	16.1
54 107	37620	3	Wood	949	86 452	665	91.1	96.6	2.0	0.7	0.9	1.0	5.4	15.6	7.8	11.6	12.2	14.4
54 109	...	7	Wyoming	1 294	22 151	1 722	17.1	98.8	1.1	0.7	0.3	0.5	5.3	16.1	7.4	10.2	13.4	13.3
55 000		X	**WISCONSIN**	140 268	5 771 337	X	41.1	83.6	7.1	1.4	3.1	6.5	5.9	16.7	9.8	12.7	12.0	14.2
55 001	...	8	Adams	1 672	20 148	1 826	12.1	91.7	3.5	1.4	0.8	3.9	3.7	11.2	5.7	9.9	9.9	14.4
55 003	...	7	Ashland	2 707	15 843	2 051	5.9	86.2	1.0	13.0	0.9	2.4	6.2	16.5	9.6	11.0	10.5	13.9
55 005	...	6	Barron	2 234	45 563	1 059	20.4	95.0	1.4	1.3	1.0	2.4	6.0	15.7	7.5	10.8	11.1	13.9
55 007	...	8	Bayfield	3 828	14 977	2 099	3.9	87.9	1.0	11.6	0.8	1.5	4.4	13.7	6.0	8.3	9.2	14.6
55 009	24580	2	Brown	1 372	258 718	261	188.6	84.0	3.2	3.2	3.6	8.0	6.7	17.6	9.4	13.8	12.5	14.4
55 011	...	8	Buffalo	1 740	13 192	2 222	7.6	96.9	0.7	0.6	0.5	1.9	5.2	15.9	7.1	10.4	10.6	15.1
55 013	...	8	Burnett	2 129	15 159	2 088	7.1	92.9	1.2	5.9	0.8	1.6	4.5	13.6	6.2	8.1	9.0	14.2
55 015	11540	3	Calumet	824	49 762	983	60.4	92.6	1.1	0.8	2.8	4.0	6.2	19.2	7.5	10.9	13.6	16.1
55 017	20740	3	Chippewa	2 612	63 531	829	24.3	95.0	1.9	0.8	1.8	1.6	5.7	17.0	7.3	12.8	12.3	14.7
55 019	...	8	Clark	3 133	34 445	1 317	11.0	94.3	0.7	0.8	0.7	4.2	8.2	21.2	7.6	10.2	10.7	13.1
55 021	31540	2	Columbia	1 983	56 743	899	28.6	94.5	1.8	0.9	1.0	3.0	5.4	17.0	7.2	11.6	12.8	15.3
55 023	...	7	Crawford	1 478	16 391	2 018	11.1	96.1	2.3	0.6	0.8	1.1	5.0	16.0	7.5	10.5	10.2	14.3
55 025	31540	2	Dane	3 101	523 643	128	168.9	82.6	6.3	0.7	6.3	6.2	6.0	15.1	13.7	15.7	12.9	12.8

1. CBSA = Core Based Statistical Area. See Appendix A for explanation. See Appendix B for list of metropolitan areas with component counties. 2. County type code from the Economic Research Service of USDA Rural-Urban Continuum Codes. See Appendix A for definition. 3. Dry land or land partially or temporarily covered by water. 4. May be of any race.

Table B. States and Counties — Population and Households

STATE County	55 to 64 years (16)	65 to 74 years (17)	75 years and over (18)	Percent female (19)	2000 (20)	2010 (21)	2000–2010 (22)	2010–2015 (23)	Births (24)	Deaths (25)	Net migration (26)	Number (27)	Persons per household (28)	Family households (29)	Female family householder[1] (30)	One person (31)
WEST VIRGINIA—Cont'd																
Brooke	16.2	11.4	10.1	51.0	25 447	24 071	-5.4	-3.0	957	1 717	35	10 086	2.26	65.0	12.0	30.9
Cabell	13.0	9.4	7.6	51.3	96 784	96 316	-0.5	0.5	6 300	5 952	442	40 220	2.31	58.9	13.7	33.6
Calhoun	16.4	12.1	8.7	49.8	7 582	7 627	0.6	-2.1	437	471	-115	3 112	2.43	68.0	12.7	27.6
Clay	14.9	11.4	7.6	49.9	10 330	9 386	-9.1	-5.1	575	562	-508	3 486	2.62	71.4	8.0	22.1
Doddridge	15.6	10.5	6.4	45.2	7 403	8 198	10.7	-0.3	345	414	27	2 761	2.81	68.2	10.4	27.7
Fayette	15.7	10.7	8.0	49.6	47 579	46 039	-3.2	-2.3	2 938	3 419	-554	17 566	2.49	67.8	14.2	27.6
Gilmer	12.0	7.8	7.1	39.9	7 160	8 697	21.5	-2.1	372	380	-174	2 645	2.49	61.3	7.6	29.7
Grant	14.9	13.2	8.9	50.3	11 299	11 937	5.6	-1.4	625	669	-162	4 256	2.75	68.6	7.2	25.5
Greenbrier	15.6	12.3	9.0	51.1	34 453	35 480	3.0	0.1	1 940	2 493	573	15 246	2.29	63.9	10.6	31.2
Hampshire	15.4	12.6	7.2	49.3	20 203	23 964	18.6	-2.5	1 189	1 341	-414	10 628	2.17	43.2	8.0	54.3
Hancock	16.3	10.8	9.4	51.6	32 667	30 675	-6.1	-2.8	1 468	2 080	-211	12 970	2.32	65.5	11.0	30.4
Hardy	15.0	12.0	7.7	49.7	12 669	14 025	10.7	-1.2	745	764	-195	5 169	2.68	63.8	8.1	32.4
Harrison	14.3	10.1	7.8	51.1	68 652	69 108	0.7	-0.6	4 293	4 520	-25	27 755	2.46	65.0	11.7	31.0
Jackson	14.5	10.3	8.8	50.7	28 000	29 211	4.3	0.1	1 727	1 780	120	11 242	2.58	69.0	11.5	26.9
Jefferson	13.4	9.1	5.0	50.8	42 190	53 488	26.8	5.6	3 232	2 301	2 012	20 126	2.64	70.9	10.9	22.6
Kanawha	15.5	10.2	8.0	51.8	200 073	193 058	-3.5	-2.4	11 518	12 774	-3 097	82 531	2.29	61.7	12.7	32.8
Lewis	14.5	11.4	8.1	50.6	16 919	16 372	-3.2	0.5	1 071	1 131	148	6 476	2.49	68.0	11.3	26.9
Lincoln	14.7	10.3	6.9	50.3	22 108	21 720	-1.8	-1.4	1 435	1 462	-301	8 128	2.65	69.2	11.2	28.1
Logan	16.5	10.3	6.9	50.4	37 710	36 745	-2.6	-5.5	2 279	2 739	-1 598	14 444	2.46	70.2	12.5	24.9
McDowell	16.9	10.6	7.5	50.6	27 329	22 111	-19.1	-10.3	1 421	1 894	-1 806	8 386	2.41	64.9	14.1	30.2
Marion	14.3	10.2	7.9	50.8	56 598	56 418	-0.3	0.9	3 543	3 402	457	22 596	2.45	65.1	11.6	29.1
Marshall	16.1	11.3	8.3	50.7	35 519	33 107	-6.8	-3.4	1 680	2 134	-611	13 847	2.33	66.6	9.2	27.5
Mason	15.3	10.9	7.9	51.9	25 957	27 326	5.3	-1.1	1 488	1 710	-109	10 729	2.47	69.7	14.0	26.2
Mercer	15.1	10.9	8.4	52.1	62 980	62 267	-1.1	-1.8	3 975	4 699	-378	25 590	2.38	64.8	12.3	30.5
Mineral	14.2	12.0	7.8	50.4	27 078	28 212	4.2	-2.7	1 549	1 736	-545	11 148	2.44	55.6	10.6	41.8
Mingo	15.7	9.8	5.7	50.7	28 253	26 834	-5.0	-5.7	1 773	1 910	-1 351	10 836	2.41	70.3	12.6	26.4
Monongalia	10.7	6.3	4.5	48.6	81 866	96 189	17.5	8.4	5 571	3 395	5 880	36 857	2.53	52.8	8.1	34.6
Monroe	15.0	13.5	9.0	50.6	14 583	13 500	-7.4	0.0	678	863	247	5 719	2.35	72.0	13.8	24.3
Morgan	16.4	12.3	8.7	50.4	14 943	17 541	17.4	-0.1	766	1 116	357	7 358	2.35	52.1	6.1	42.6
Nicholas	15.7	11.5	7.7	50.7	26 562	26 233	-1.2	-2.4	1 535	1 780	-415	10 686	2.43	71.1	8.8	24.8
Ohio	15.5	10.0	9.5	52.1	47 427	44 442	-6.3	-3.1	2 473	3 030	-654	18 582	2.24	58.7	11.8	36.8
Pendleton	16.5	12.8	11.8	48.7	8 196	7 695	-6.1	-6.1	386	477	-375	3 199	2.30	63.6	6.5	30.9
Pleasants	14.1	10.9	7.4	46.4	7 514	7 605	1.2	0.9	394	471	131	2 822	2.49	70.3	8.8	24.1
Pocahontas	17.3	13.5	8.9	48.4	9 131	8 722	-4.5	-1.3	475	555	-29	3 719	2.25	64.6	6.2	29.2
Preston	14.8	10.2	7.1	48.5	29 334	33 520	14.3	1.3	1 857	1 794	393	12 610	2.50	70.3	7.9	24.4
Putnam	14.3	9.9	6.6	50.8	51 589	55 508	7.6	2.4	3 153	2 851	948	21 453	2.62	73.4	10.4	22.6
Raleigh	14.8	10.5	7.7	49.3	79 220	78 862	-0.5	-1.7	4 989	5 315	-946	31 164	2.41	67.4	12.1	28.0
Randolph	14.4	11.9	8.1	48.3	28 262	29 405	4.0	-0.9	1 610	1 914	29	11 351	2.41	67.1	9.9	29.6
Ritchie	15.8	11.8	8.4	50.3	10 343	10 449	1.0	-4.5	490	665	-238	4 023	2.52	64.8	9.4	31.8
Roane	15.8	11.4	7.9	50.4	15 446	14 926	-3.4	-3.3	817	968	-313	5 902	2.48	65.1	10.5	30.0
Summers	16.8	11.9	9.2	55.2	12 999	13 927	7.1	-4.9	581	944	-261	5 560	2.25	66.5	8.6	31.2
Taylor	14.8	10.3	7.4	49.3	16 089	16 890	5.0	0.1	935	1 026	132	6 801	2.42	69.4	13.6	26.5
Tucker	15.9	13.2	9.5	49.4	7 321	7 141	-2.5	-2.5	362	505	-34	2 969	2.30	65.3	5.4	30.6
Tyler	16.6	11.5	8.7	50.5	9 592	9 211	-4.0	-2.6	480	619	-102	3 750	2.40	67.7	10.3	28.5
Upshur	14.0	10.8	7.4	50.4	23 404	24 254	3.6	2.1	1 454	1 378	422	8 937	2.60	69.0	9.2	26.3
Wayne	14.4	10.7	7.8	51.2	42 903	42 484	-1.0	-3.6	2 221	2 495	-1 228	16 757	2.48	64.9	12.8	31.3
Webster	16.4	13.0	8.4	50.6	9 719	9 154	-5.8	-4.4	534	640	-318	3 854	2.32	70.2	12.0	25.6
Wetzel	14.9	12.1	9.3	50.6	17 693	16 580	-6.3	-4.6	883	1 195	-455	6 734	2.41	66.5	11.1	30.0
Wirt	15.8	11.7	6.6	49.5	5 873	5 717	-2.7	2.9	318	290	134	2 425	2.40	67.1	12.0	23.8
Wood	14.4	10.8	7.8	51.6	87 986	86 956	-1.2	-0.6	5 220	5 404	-155	35 900	2.39	64.2	10.4	31.3
Wyoming	16.8	10.9	6.7	50.5	25 708	23 801	-7.4	-6.9	1 210	1 803	-1 033	9 201	2.51	70.1	9.7	26.7
WISCONSIN	13.6	8.4	6.8	50.3	5 363 675	5 687 289	6.0	1.5	353 372	254 683	-14 210	2 293 250	2.43	64.1	10.1	29.0
Adams	18.2	16.6	10.5	46.4	18 643	20 875	12.0	-3.5	699	1 312	-100	7 829	2.46	65.1	6.6	29.7
Ashland	14.9	9.9	7.6	49.7	16 866	16 157	-4.2	-1.9	936	965	-267	6 741	2.29	59.2	10.0	34.2
Barron	14.9	11.3	8.9	50.2	44 963	45 870	2.0	-0.7	2 722	2 599	-401	19 029	2.37	66.8	8.8	27.7
Bayfield	20.0	14.9	8.9	48.9	15 013	15 014	0.0	-0.2	652	817	128	6 949	2.15	63.0	6.7	30.8
Brown	12.6	7.3	5.8	50.4	226 778	248 007	9.4	4.3	17 867	9 402	2 279	99 705	2.46	65.2	10.3	28.0
Buffalo	15.5	11.0	9.1	49.3	13 804	13 587	-1.6	-2.9	731	691	-423	5 783	2.29	65.7	8.2	29.7
Burnett	18.1	15.4	10.8	48.9	15 674	15 457	-1.4	-1.9	687	883	0	7 288	2.09	63.9	7.9	29.2
Calumet	13.2	7.5	5.8	49.9	40 631	48 971	20.5	1.6	2 940	1 699	-457	18 606	2.65	73.5	6.6	21.5
Chippewa	14.0	9.1	7.2	48.1	55 195	62 505	13.2	1.6	3 781	2 810	80	24 643	2.47	67.1	7.9	27.2
Clark	13.0	8.2	7.8	49.5	33 557	34 691	3.4	-0.7	2 990	1 740	-1 471	12 882	2.64	69.7	8.1	25.7
Columbia	14.6	9.2	6.9	49.2	52 468	56 833	8.3	-0.2	3 143	2 740	-545	22 571	2.44	67.5	8.9	27.0
Crawford	15.8	11.9	8.7	48.6	17 243	16 644	-3.5	-1.5	870	913	-207	6 607	2.39	63.2	7.5	32.0
Dane	12.0	7.0	5.0	50.4	426 526	488 075	14.4	7.3	32 290	15 998	18 688	208 749	2.34	58.1	8.4	30.8

1. No spouse present.

Table B. States and Counties — Population, Vital Statistics, Medicare, and Crime

STATE County	Persons in group quarters, 2015	Daytime population, 2010–2014 Number	Employ-ment/ resi-dence ratio	Births, 2015 Total	Rate[1]	Deaths, 2015 Number	Rate[1]	Persons under 65 with no health insurance, 2014 Number	Percent	Medicare, 2015 Total Beneficiaries	Enrolled in Original Medicare	Enrolled in Medicare Advantage	Serious crimes known to police,[2] 2014 Total Number	Rate[3]
	32	33	34	35	36	37	38	39	40	41	42	43	44	45
WEST VIRGINIA—Cont'd														
Brooke	873	22 043	0.82	172	7.3	314	13.4	1 595	9.0	4 810	3 020	1 790	191	845
Cabell	3 900	109 011	1.31	1 222	12.6	1 090	11.3	7 656	9.9	23 281	16 145	7 136	1 797	1 850
Calhoun	22	7 078	0.79	88	11.7	79	10.5	715	12.0	1 753	1 409	344	NA	NA
Clay	74	8 212	0.66	94	10.5	107	12.0	849	11.7	2 573	1 727	846	NA	NA
Doddridge	649	6 983	0.55	64	7.8	69	8.4	647	10.6	1 069	775	294	NA	NA
Fayette	1 843	42 493	0.79	552	12.2	671	14.9	4 132	11.7	11 019	7 862	3 157	1 027	2 466
Gilmer	2 097	8 835	1.05	74	8.7	72	8.5	628	12.1	1 416	999	417	NA	NA
Grant	126	11 322	0.90	115	9.8	116	9.9	1 030	11.4	3 801	3 003	798	70	780
Greenbrier	614	36 992	1.10	358	10.1	481	13.6	3 253	11.8	8 736	6 797	1 939	405	1 187
Hampshire	482	19 557	0.53	232	9.9	241	10.3	2 354	12.8	4 861	3 916	945	194	846
Hancock	226	29 255	0.91	256	8.5	415	13.9	2 318	9.7	7 981	5 977	2 004	337	1 160
Hardy	58	14 069	1.02	138	9.9	156	11.2	1 421	12.8	2 956	2 310	646	145	1 067
Harrison	884	75 952	1.24	844	12.3	865	12.6	5 932	10.6	15 829	11 773	4 056	NA	NA
Jackson	180	27 211	0.81	332	11.4	339	11.6	2 455	10.5	6 991	5 281	1 710	208	824
Jefferson	1 293	47 392	0.72	636	11.3	459	8.2	4 602	9.9	8 604	6 819	1 785	787	1 557
Kanawha	3 114	211 812	1.24	2 215	11.7	2 432	12.9	14 865	9.7	44 669	29 650	15 019	8 347	4 539
Lewis	248	17 090	1.11	211	12.8	233	14.2	1 377	10.6	4 247	2 890	1 357	167	1 016
Lincoln	76	17 850	0.47	274	12.7	288	13.4	2 086	11.7	5 005	3 369	1 636	NA	NA
Logan	633	37 681	1.13	426	12.2	485	13.9	3 171	11.0	9 538	6 447	3 091	650	1 996
McDowell	240	21 962	1.14	266	13.3	338	16.8	2 293	13.9	6 077	4 157	1 920	238	1 419
Marion	1 310	52 496	0.83	694	12.2	673	11.8	4 681	10.3	12 979	9 096	3 883	560	1 119
Marshall	447	31 150	0.88	318	9.9	386	12.0	2 341	9.2	6 247	3 571	2 676	571	1 938
Mason	691	25 263	0.79	272	10.0	331	12.2	2 189	10.3	5 990	4 632	1 358	417	1 695
Mercer	1 111	61 698	0.98	736	12.0	877	14.3	5 798	11.8	16 491	12 101	4 390	928	1 535
Mineral	690	25 125	0.73	299	10.9	336	12.2	2 084	9.7	5 426	4 642	784	474	1 822
Mingo	85	25 304	0.88	310	12.2	360	14.1	2 472	11.4	6 699	4 667	2 032	293	1 232
Monongalia	6 791	111 500	1.23	1 115	10.8	657	6.3	8 225	9.7	11 641	7 773	3 868	2 025	2 079
Monroe	57	11 115	0.53	115	8.5	150	11.1	1 356	12.9	3 891	3 005	886	101	751
Morgan	123	14 282	0.51	153	8.7	215	12.3	1 621	11.8	3 811	3 158	653	218	1 333
Nicholas	162	25 703	0.96	278	10.8	337	13.1	2 320	11.2	6 538	4 278	2 260	563	2 363
Ohio	2 492	53 886	1.50	464	10.8	580	13.4	2 892	8.8	11 245	6 392	4 853	1 201	2 815
Pendleton	141	6 796	0.76	74	10.2	66	9.1	708	13.0	1 975	1 536	439	NA	NA
Pleasants	671	7 709	1.04	90	11.7	75	9.7	460	8.1	1 546	1 095	451	NA	NA
Pocahontas	318	8 651	0.98	94	10.9	110	12.7	807	12.5	2 129	1 645	484	58	764
Preston	2 371	28 863	0.64	363	10.7	340	10.0	2 878	11.2	6 637	4 941	1 696	260	841
Putnam	249	51 631	0.81	615	10.8	565	9.9	3 829	8.2	10 127	6 759	3 368	1 067	1 913
Raleigh	3 635	81 080	1.08	910	11.7	1 037	13.3	6 571	10.8	18 439	13 667	4 772	3 161	4 098
Randolph	2 281	30 154	1.06	301	10.3	365	12.5	2 267	10.5	7 230	5 638	1 592	325	1 107
Ritchie	106	10 391	1.05	92	9.2	139	13.9	1 052	13.2	2 502	1 917	585	104	1 170
Roane	98	13 131	0.65	152	10.5	175	12.1	1 502	12.7	3 482	2 485	997	191	1 311
Summers	1 210	11 839	0.59	99	7.5	148	11.1	1 101	11.6	2 965	2 227	738	181	1 346
Taylor	511	13 610	0.50	176	10.4	183	10.8	1 390	10.2	3 044	2 390	654	33	195
Tucker	147	6 662	0.89	76	10.9	109	15.7	570	10.8	1 648	1 116	532	NA	NA
Tyler	67	8 186	0.73	97	10.7	107	11.9	726	10.1	1 838	1 258	580	66	813
Upshur	1 219	24 506	1.00	281	11.4	266	10.8	2 224	11.7	5 088	3 416	1 672	310	1 254
Wayne	246	37 652	0.73	426	10.4	496	12.1	3 865	11.6	6 983	4 961	2 022	795	2 112
Webster	58	8 264	0.75	101	11.5	113	12.9	840	12.1	2 368	1 621	747	NA	NA
Wetzel	124	17 239	1.17	170	10.7	229	14.4	1 314	10.5	4 572	2 828	1 744	NA	NA
Wirt	0	4 448	0.38	59	10.1	44	7.5	511	10.7	1 499	1 143	356	144	2 428
Wood	1 001	89 568	1.08	1 047	12.1	1 033	11.9	7 050	10.1	21 300	16 742	4 558	1 820	2 110
Wyoming	56	22 294	0.86	211	9.4	345	15.4	2 109	11.3	5 546	3 581	1 965	512	2 482
WISCONSIN	148 192	5 677 916	0.98	66 859	11.6	47 984	8.3	407 618	8.6	1 010 994	629 226	381 768	136 952	2 379
Adams	1 251	17 615	0.60	136	6.7	247	12.2	1 306	9.7	3 470	2 703	767	449	2 202
Ashland	594	17 116	1.15	175	11.0	175	11.0	1 440	11.3	3 802	2 577	1 225	432	2 703
Barron	600	45 933	1.01	493	10.8	455	10.0	3 563	9.9	10 891	7 027	3 864	207	555
Bayfield	101	13 068	0.71	121	8.1	170	11.4	1 335	11.8	3 529	2 372	1 157	170	1 119
Brown	6 545	272 039	1.15	3 404	13.2	1 736	6.7	19 396	8.9	40 472	20 291	20 181	4 332	1 812
Buffalo	111	11 018	0.65	138	10.5	118	8.9	988	9.4	3 038	2 358	680	111	834
Burnett	134	14 300	0.82	121	7.9	162	10.6	1 285	11.5	4 256	2 858	1 398	502	3 278
Calumet	190	37 773	0.55	523	10.5	335	6.7	2 482	5.8	4 746	1 629	3 117	551	1 107
Chippewa	2 608	59 121	0.87	693	10.9	565	8.9	4 152	8.2	11 594	7 942	3 652	920	1 453
Clark	492	32 085	0.84	558	16.2	310	9.0	5 690	19.9	6 359	3 173	3 186	193	558
Columbia	1 461	49 338	0.75	592	10.4	518	9.1	3 259	7.0	12 064	8 593	3 471	688	1 418
Crawford	775	16 851	1.04	172	10.5	164	10.0	1 122	9.1	3 368	2 213	1 155	270	1 652
Dane	12 861	538 759	1.13	6 240	12.0	3 096	6.0	31 735	7.2	67 053	50 819	16 234	12 261	2 447

1. Per 1,000 estimated resident population.   2. Data for serious crimes have not been adjusted for underreporting; this may affect comparability between geographic areas and over time.
3. Per 100,000 population estimated by the FBI.

Table B. States and Counties — Crime, Education, Money Income, and Poverty

STATE County	Serious crimes known to police, 2014 (cont.)[1] Rate[2] Violent	Property	Education — School enrollment and attainment, 2010–2014 — Enrollment[3] Total	Percent private	Attainment[4] (percent) High school graduate or less	Bachelor's degree or more	Local government expenditures,[5] 2012–2013 Total current spending (mil dol)	Current spending per student (dollars)	Money income, 2010–2014 Per capita income[6] (dollars)	Households Median income (dollars)	Mean income (dollars)	Percent with income of $200,000 or more	Income and poverty, 2014 Percent below poverty level Median household income (dollars)	All persons	Children under 18 years	Children 5 to 17 years in families
	46	47	48	49	50	51	52	53	54	55	56	57	58	59	60	61
WEST VIRGINIA—Cont'd																
Brooke	53	792	5 328	18.7	54.2	17.1	38.1	11 425	23 310	44 067	55 024	1.4	43 572	15.1	22.5	18.8
Cabell	55	1 796	25 217	10.8	46.5	26.4	143.4	11 046	23 595	37 716	54 522	2.7	34 887	21.9	27.0	26.4
Calhoun	NA	NA	1 521	4.2	74.0	8.9	11.1	10 288	18 181	31 017	41 211	0.2	32 162	21.8	29.8	26.4
Clay	NA	NA	2 037	0.8	73.8	9.4	22.5	10 915	16 487	32 933	41 608	0.4	32 961	25.1	35.9	34.5
Doddridge	NA	NA	1 577	4.4	66.2	12.7	16.6	14 276	18 552	40 329	47 740	0.9	41 838	17.4	24.9	21.8
Fayette	279	2 188	9 222	13.4	64.0	11.8	76.9	11 191	18 928	34 914	46 235	1.1	36 739	21.4	31.4	28.4
Gilmer	NA	NA	2 318	18.5	57.9	16.6	10.8	11 410	17 175	35 625	49 462	0.9	32 705	28.9	28.2	27.5
Grant	189	591	2 359	3.9	70.5	12.6	18.9	10 264	19 696	41 600	48 383	0.7	41 039	17.0	25.5	23.5
Greenbrier	108	1 079	7 285	9.0	59.2	18.2	60.2	11 517	22 913	40 256	52 374	2.3	36 996	21.1	28.5	27.3
Hampshire	227	619	5 078	9.1	75.2	8.7	36.1	10 320	17 652	26 828	36 715	0.2	35 980	21.2	29.5	25.7
Hancock	120	1 040	6 304	10.1	56.4	16.8	47.0	11 188	23 947	39 342	55 102	2.0	48 178	12.9	21.0	18.9
Hardy	390	677	2 672	8.4	69.3	12.2	22.7	9 661	20 977	36 465	49 908	0.9	41 010	15.3	24.5	23.1
Harrison	NA	NA	14 631	9.6	52.8	20.2	143.9	13 158	24 021	43 130	57 464	2.1	42 121	13.9	18.5	16.8
Jackson	214	610	6 284	8.1	56.1	16.2	54.4	10 947	22 870	40 733	56 770	2.8	41 121	16.7	24.7	23.0
Jefferson	154	1 403	14 451	12.7	45.1	28.3	100.1	11 171	29 861	66 205	79 869	4.6	66 950	10.2	13.1	11.9
Kanawha	562	3 977	40 054	13.5	49.6	24.9	319.1	11 176	27 913	46 583	63 744	3.4	43 936	16.8	25.8	25.0
Lewis	73	943	3 053	10.7	62.6	14.9	28.7	10 917	20 587	38 006	50 436	1.7	40 568	20.0	28.1	24.5
Lincoln	NA	NA	4 046	3.1	66.9	9.1	44.0	11 783	18 824	35 623	47 243	0.5	34 295	24.4	32.0	28.6
Logan	547	1 449	6 935	4.4	65.0	8.5	69.2	10 762	20 644	37 312	51 011	1.2	36 437	20.2	28.4	26.9
McDowell	352	1 067	3 492	4.1	78.3	5.8	50.1	14 178	14 813	23 607	36 425	0.5	24 707	34.9	46.2	41.0
Marion	210	910	12 982	9.8	53.5	20.9	90.1	11 123	23 870	43 085	56 955	1.7	43 729	17.9	23.3	21.4
Marshall	210	1 728	7 102	10.9	58.3	15.9	59.2	12 615	24 419	41 978	57 428	1.8	43 356	15.2	20.7	19.8
Mason	126	1 569	5 792	7.1	62.7	10.1	47.9	11 087	19 969	38 297	48 371	0.7	35 799	20.6	28.0	25.9
Mercer	246	1 289	13 831	10.8	55.8	19.0	105.3	10 888	20 833	35 678	49 101	1.1	35 046	20.5	31.0	30.6
Mineral	234	1 587	5 989	8.2	64.1	12.8	49.0	11 535	19 055	30 713	42 810	0.3	40 012	16.1	22.2	20.4
Mingo	315	916	5 365	4.2	68.1	10.5	54.6	12 295	20 222	34 495	48 495	1.0	29 839	28.1	36.9	33.8
Monongalia	246	1 833	36 904	5.6	39.3	38.8	123.5	11 197	26 109	46 166	64 758	4.0	43 835	22.5	17.3	15.5
Monroe	97	654	2 554	6.4	68.5	13.8	19.8	10 673	20 041	38 239	47 520	0.5	36 351	19.3	29.0	24.5
Morgan	465	869	3 212	8.9	62.5	16.5	28.6	11 107	22 770	37 406	50 988	1.0	44 446	13.0	20.6	18.1
Nicholas	772	1 591	5 239	4.6	64.8	13.6	46.7	11 567	22 674	38 755	57 383	3.0	36 375	19.6	26.7	25.6
Ohio	588	2 227	10 564	20.8	44.9	28.6	67.8	12 368	26 370	40 342	60 278	2.6	40 195	18.4	25.9	22.9
Pendleton	NA	NA	1 293	7.8	64.9	14.0	13.4	13 286	21 486	36 052	48 709	1.2	38 204	16.7	25.8	23.8
Pleasants	NA	NA	1 499	4.7	59.4	13.3	16.1	12 916	22 308	43 831	58 010	1.1	44 801	16.5	21.8	19.0
Pocahontas	158	606	1 447	5.9	63.2	15.8	14.7	12 992	21 120	34 761	47 819	1.4	34 341	17.6	27.5	26.5
Preston	165	676	6 074	9.3	64.7	12.9	45.1	9 859	21 237	45 806	54 303	0.8	41 420	17.6	23.0	20.5
Putnam	448	1 465	12 756	11.1	47.1	23.9	108.2	11 049	28 493	55 939	71 823	3.4	59 472	10.0	13.2	11.9
Raleigh	450	3 648	16 434	14.5	56.7	18.2	139.1	11 056	22 384	41 152	55 083	1.6	40 270	17.7	25.0	23.8
Randolph	249	858	5 810	16.8	64.5	18.1	47.3	11 072	20 464	40 146	50 911	1.1	37 468	20.8	27.5	26.6
Ritchie	68	1 103	2 077	7.0	66.6	10.4	17.6	11 389	18 717	39 118	44 903	0.4	46 383	17.7	25.7	23.2
Roane	206	1 105	2 910	4.7	71.0	10.3	25.1	10 222	18 124	30 104	43 497	1.0	33 041	23.1	30.0	27.6
Summers	119	1 227	2 504	7.8	60.7	13.0	16.9	10 794	19 181	35 040	44 993	0.4	32 456	25.8	34.4	31.6
Taylor	24	171	3 422	9.0	61.5	15.8	25.4	10 528	21 266	39 933	52 287	1.5	40 305	16.8	22.9	21.0
Tucker	NA	NA	1 223	6.9	63.6	13.8	12.8	12 417	21 014	38 663	47 770	0.2	36 466	17.1	24.9	24.4
Tyler	185	628	1 785	4.8	64.2	10.0	17.4	12 677	20 900	39 974	49 836	0.9	41 019	15.8	23.6	21.0
Upshur	32	1 222	5 740	23.1	65.1	15.8	41.1	10 668	19 537	39 188	50 304	1.3	38 387	19.7	27.3	24.2
Wayne	136	1 977	9 682	3.7	62.2	12.6	78.9	10 506	19 910	37 491	47 495	0.9	37 242	20.0	28.0	26.1
Webster	NA	NA	1 538	4.9	72.3	9.1	16.3	10 893	17 423	28 907	40 887	0.3	29 331	26.1	39.6	36.4
Wetzel	NA	NA	3 113	5.2	65.8	10.2	34.2	12 128	20 996	38 066	49 817	0.8	40 013	18.5	26.8	23.7
Wirt	270	2 159	1 134	4.1	60.9	10.9	11.1	10 772	23 240	37 117	54 394	2.4	38 600	20.3	29.5	27.7
Wood	196	1 914	19 460	11.2	48.2	18.7	149.9	11 238	24 528	42 471	57 482	2.0	41 932	17.2	27.4	24.2
Wyoming	911	1 570	4 693	5.6	71.0	9.0	48.7	11 405	18 729	34 620	46 267	0.7	34 419	22.8	30.5	27.0
WISCONSIN	290	2 088	1 490 311	16.8	41.6	27.4	9 685.4	11 071	27 907	52 738	68 319	3.1	52 632	13.2	18.4	16.7
Adams	177	2 026	3 417	9.7	56.3	12.6	19.8	11 808	22 639	45 366	54 913	1.6	42 063	17.8	28.9	26.6
Ashland	282	2 422	3 706	21.8	44.4	22.3	30.8	11 658	21 159	39 172	49 569	1.0	41 294	14.9	23.9	20.4
Barron	32	523	9 510	9.7	51.8	16.6	90.6	11 566	23 547	44 709	55 925	1.5	46 375	13.7	21.2	19.6
Bayfield	178	941	2 863	11.1	37.4	28.3	22.7	14 975	25 919	45 158	56 242	1.5	44 395	13.6	23.9	21.4
Brown	258	1 554	67 971	15.4	41.2	27.5	452.1	10 439	27 734	53 254	69 272	3.4	54 141	12.0	16.6	14.4
Buffalo	68	766	2 940	11.6	51.6	17.7	22.9	15 207	25 007	48 585	58 021	1.4	50 998	10.5	15.3	14.2
Burnett	222	3 056	2 844	11.8	50.0	16.8	28.2	11 270	23 542	40 722	50 724	1.2	41 810	16.5	26.5	21.7
Calumet	119	988	13 088	15.4	41.9	28.0	39.3	10 084	29 406	66 250	77 654	3.1	68 430	5.9	7.9	7.0
Chippewa	134	1 319	14 172	10.5	47.2	19.2	94.7	10 724	25 097	51 428	62 130	1.7	52 485	10.7	15.6	13.6
Clark	23	535	7 649	23.2	62.4	11.7	54.0	10 903	21 005	43 515	54 937	1.9	45 316	16.0	23.9	22.3
Columbia	150	1 267	13 408	12.0	43.1	22.2	94.7	10 693	28 655	58 703	70 689	2.6	59 020	8.8	12.4	10.6
Crawford	116	1 536	3 728	15.2	52.9	15.3	33.7	12 184	22 801	43 638	53 505	1.4	43 562	14.7	22.4	21.3
Dane	229	2 218	148 238	12.0	24.5	47.6	851.4	11 439	33 895	62 303	80 625	5.0	61 937	13.4	14.3	13.0

1. Data for serious crimes have not been adjusted for underreporting; this may affect comparability between geographic areas and over time.   2. Per 100,000 population estimated by the FBI.
3. All persons 3 years old and over enrolled in nursery school through college.   4. Persons 25 years old and over.   5. Elementary and secondary education expenditures.
6. Based on population estimated by the American Community Survey, 2010–2014.

Table B. States and Counties — Personal Income

STATE County	Personal income, 2014 Total (mil dol)	Percent change, 2013–2014	Per capita[1] Dollars	Per capita[1] Rank	Wages and salaries (mil dol)	Supplements to wages and salaries; employer contributions (mil dol) — Pension and insurance	Supplements — Government social insurance	Proprietors' income (mil dol)	Dividends, interest, and rent (mil dol)	Personal transfer receipts (mil dol)	Earnings, 2014 Total (mil dol)	Contributions for government social insurance (mil dol) — From employee and self-employed	Contributions — From employer
	62	63	64	65	66	67	68	69	70	71	72	73	74
WEST VIRGINIA—Cont'd													
Brooke	852	3.1	36 225	1 741	322	59	26	78	118	234	485	34	26
Cabell	3 640	2.4	37 481	1 527	2 257	382	187	234	588	1 008	3 060	194	187
Calhoun	214	7.0	28 424	2 883	77	13	6	12	23	81	108	9	6
Clay	246	0.8	27 555	2 952	49	10	4	11	26	93	75	7	4
Doddridge	174	-1.2	20 757	3 109	67	11	5	19	32	43	102	8	5
Fayette	1 368	0.3	30 314	2 675	424	82	34	83	160	509	623	47	34
Gilmer	228	5.0	26 457	3 009	98	25	8	16	44	69	147	9	8
Grant	372	3.5	31 789	2 474	162	32	14	31	57	120	239	16	14
Greenbrier	1 240	2.4	34 966	1 941	506	86	44	131	196	396	767	53	44
Hampshire	703	2.5	29 944	2 723	135	29	11	42	98	193	217	18	11
Hancock	1 078	2.6	35 814	1 803	396	76	33	19	136	317	524	38	33
Hardy	397	2.5	28 548	2 876	185	38	17	22	60	110	263	17	17
Harrison	2 960	4.1	43 048	840	1 751	325	140	319	445	669	2 535	156	140
Jackson	977	2.3	33 560	2 182	309	54	25	65	118	279	453	33	25
Jefferson	2 460	3.7	44 160	748	632	111	53	108	356	452	905	58	53
Kanawha	8 377	2.5	44 039	759	4 991	832	391	962	1 322	2 132	7 176	448	391
Lewis	602	3.0	36 695	1 647	372	56	28	46	91	162	502	33	28
Lincoln	584	2.9	27 096	2 975	129	22	10	11	58	201	172	16	10
Logan	1 182	0.9	33 446	2 206	482	80	38	24	135	453	623	46	38
McDowell	553	-2.9	27 024	2 979	249	48	20	11	68	260	327	26	20
Marion	2 201	2.6	38 756	1 358	905	150	72	145	290	545	1 271	86	72
Marshall	1 297	5.5	40 005	1 175	628	103	47	190	164	308	967	63	47
Mason	774	1.1	28 654	2 870	253	53	20	25	86	273	351	26	20
Mercer	2 072	1.0	33 542	2 188	775	141	67	122	284	784	1 104	81	67
Mineral	982	3.2	35 599	1 840	315	64	27	40	121	288	446	32	27
Mingo	769	-6.7	29 896	2 731	328	55	28	19	97	308	430	33	28
Monongalia	4 174	4.0	40 343	1 134	2 733	505	208	298	673	712	3 745	216	208
Monroe	388	4.3	28 577	2 874	77	19	6	22	50	133	125	11	6
Morgan	562	3.4	32 212	2 415	97	19	8	27	86	176	150	13	8
Nicholas	841	2.0	32 557	2 361	301	54	25	59	118	289	439	33	25
Ohio	1 933	3.7	44 621	707	1 193	198	95	40	417	478	1 527	97	95
Pendleton	254	2.4	34 519	2 024	58	13	5	20	47	79	96	7	5
Pleasants	295	5.6	38 707	1 363	153	31	11	24	34	93	219	14	11
Pocahontas	292	5.0	33 690	2 162	97	19	9	26	50	116	151	11	9
Preston	1 108	3.1	32 802	2 311	317	67	27	66	134	288	477	34	27
Putnam	2 337	2.2	41 160	1 045	1 034	152	85	153	281	445	1 424	93	85
Raleigh	2 831	0.9	36 180	1 748	1 390	243	113	220	399	880	1 965	131	113
Randolph	942	2.1	32 022	2 435	395	77	34	69	139	320	575	39	34
Ritchie	313	4.4	31 314	2 545	151	26	12	19	46	104	209	15	12
Roane	450	1.8	30 672	2 632	119	22	10	25	57	151	176	15	10
Summers	358	0.6	26 714	2 999	81	16	8	8	51	159	112	11	8
Taylor	587	3.5	34 375	2 050	142	26	12	15	74	148	195	15	12
Tucker	220	4.7	31 818	2 461	98	18	8	13	35	79	136	10	8
Tyler	286	2.7	31 415	2 537	109	23	8	8	45	86	148	11	8
Upshur	771	1.9	31 182	2 557	308	54	26	71	105	209	459	32	26
Wayne	1 224	2.3	29 767	2 748	412	91	34	84	138	364	620	45	34
Webster	236	0.8	26 692	3 000	82	16	7	9	35	97	114	10	7
Wetzel	522	2.2	32 672	2 341	158	30	13	13	89	184	214	17	13
Wirt	157	0.7	26 888	2 989	19	4	2	6	20	48	31	4	2
Wood	3 200	4.3	37 104	1 584	1 559	294	127	180	482	900	2 160	143	127
Wyoming	654	-1.1	28 962	2 835	238	41	19	11	62	249	308	25	19
WISCONSIN	254 405	3.7	44 186	X	129 574	24 311	10 242	18 560	45 104	44 028	182 687	11 103	10 242
Adams	770	2.0	38 097	1 444	165	40	14	135	120	225	353	26	14
Ashland	552	2.5	34 292	2 066	306	74	25	47	94	159	452	28	25
Barron	1 998	5.7	43 948	765	854	185	69	178	422	427	1 286	79	69
Bayfield	599	2.6	39 945	1 185	123	37	10	40	141	152	210	16	10
Brown	11 731	4.0	45 704	621	7 368	1 292	571	1 044	2 104	1 642	10 275	609	571
Buffalo	592	3.5	44 893	685	151	36	12	101	96	113	300	19	12
Burnett	582	3.3	37 966	1 460	159	44	13	54	115	174	270	20	13
Calumet	2 193	4.2	44 305	733	517	101	43	213	317	265	874	53	43
Chippewa	2 597	5.4	40 924	1 069	968	201	79	296	378	506	1 544	95	79
Clark	1 271	7.5	36 917	1 612	416	94	34	258	201	256	801	42	34
Columbia	2 457	1.5	43 393	806	875	189	73	217	418	407	1 355	85	73
Crawford	607	3.9	37 047	1 594	270	58	23	55	111	151	405	26	23
Dane	26 600	3.2	51 523	310	16 515	3 299	1 260	1 716	5 270	3 046	22 791	1 310	1 260

1. Based on the resident population estimated as of July 1 of the year shown.

Table B. States and Counties — Earnings, Social Security, and Housing

STATE County	Earnings, 2014 (cont.) Percent by selected industries									Social Security beneficiaries, December 2014		Supplemental Security Income recipients, December 2014	Housing units, 2015	
	Farm	Mining	Construction	Manu-facturing	Infor-mation: professional, scientific, technical services	Retail trade	Finance, insur-ance, real estate and leasing	Health care and social assistance	Govern-ment	Number	Rate[1]		Total	Percent change, 2010–2014
	75	76	77	78	79	80	81	82	83	84	85	86	87	88
WEST VIRGINIA—Cont'd														
Brooke	0.0	D	D	28.3	1.9	7.0	2.4	D	9.7	6 635	282	536	10 884	-0.8
Cabell	0.0	2.1	5.5	11.2	6.1	7.9	4.4	25.9	16.3	21 975	227	3 807	46 485	0.7
Calhoun	-1.2	D	44.4	0.5	2.1	4.0	D	D	14.3	2 250	299	549	3 949	-0.4
Clay	0.1	D	9.8	2.2	D	6.8	D	14.2	32.1	2 940	329	734	4 570	0.0
Doddridge	-1.3	35.8	D	D	D	8.1	3.3	4.7	25.4	1 140	140	203	3 912	-0.8
Fayette	-0.1	9.4	4.4	8.8	4.0	9.3	2.6	D	26.8	12 250	271	2 414	21 494	-0.6
Gilmer	2.7	D	7.1	5.3	3.4	3.1	D	D	44.0	1 720	202	335	3 482	0.9
Grant	-0.2	D	18.1	6.5	D	5.4	3.3	D	19.8	3 245	277	397	6 518	2.4
Greenbrier	1.6	9.3	4.0	5.4	4.4	8.8	2.9	18.3	17.0	9 590	270	1 208	19 134	0.8
Hampshire	-0.5	D	9.7	4.4	D	7.5	5.6	D	30.0	5 670	242	720	13 806	0.9
Hancock	0.0	D	D	38.9	4.4	4.5	4.0	6.9	13.5	8 325	277	935	14 412	-0.9
Hardy	2.0	0.0	3.0	D	3.2	6.9	3.4	D	14.9	3 790	272	440	8 151	0.9
Harrison	-0.2	8.3	8.7	4.7	10.0	6.4	4.2	12.6	24.3	17 860	259	2 856	31 580	0.4
Jackson	-0.1	1.8	6.9	26.5	5.5	8.8	4.4	D	16.3	8 070	277	1 298	13 251	-0.4
Jefferson	1.4	D	5.2	6.4	10.3	6.1	3.9	6.9	27.0	10 070	181	817	22 717	3.1
Kanawha	0.0	5.2	6.1	4.4	D	5.7	8.2	17.9	18.3	49 520	260	7 418	92 494	-0.1
Lewis	0.1	38.6	6.1	1.5	1.3	5.4	3.3	9.4	14.5	4 605	280	880	7 907	-0.6
Lincoln	0.0	D	16.7	0.3	4.3	5.7	1.3	10.3	25.0	6 285	291	1 899	9 799	-0.9
Logan	0.0	D	2.1	4.5	5.5	9.5	2.2	D	18.3	9 805	278	2 274	16 696	-0.3
McDowell	0.0	34.7	3.6	0.3	D	5.5	1.9	D	32.3	6 415	316	2 589	11 157	-1.4
Marion	-0.2	D	6.9	5.0	9.2	7.9	4.9	9.3	18.2	13 900	244	2 053	26 316	-0.6
Marshall	-0.6	29.9	5.4	17.2	4.3	4.8	2.2	7.6	9.7	8 360	259	916	15 801	-0.7
Mason	2.1	0.5	D	11.8	2.9	5.5	2.9	D	21.6	7 245	267	1 306	12 929	-0.6
Mercer	0.2	2.7	4.9	5.2	5.0	10.5	3.6	17.6	24.4	17 700	287	3 783	29 787	-1.1
Mineral	-0.3	0.3	5.9	30.6	10.8	7.2	4.7	D	18.6	6 960	252	744	13 102	0.5
Mingo	0.0	41.3	2.3	4.2	3.3	3.4	2.1	7.7	15.6	7 240	282	2 457	12 623	-0.6
Monongalia	-0.1	2.5	6.2	9.7	8.4	5.0	3.4	18.9	26.6	14 145	137	1 733	44 545	3.0
Monroe	-0.6	0.0	9.6	23.1	D	3.7	D	7.2	36.8	4 415	326	656	7 562	-0.5
Morgan	-0.2	D	D	8.9	4.0	8.1	5.0	16.5	23.2	4 790	274	357	9 858	1.1
Nicholas	0.2	13.7	3.3	10.5	4.2	14.1	2.0	D	22.6	8 120	316	1 361	12 984	-0.6
Ohio	-0.1	D	D	4.1	11.0	7.7	5.5	22.8	13.6	11 065	256	1 394	21 088	-0.4
Pendleton	7.2	D	D	D	3.9	6.6	D	D	33.4	2 280	313	206	5 171	0.8
Pleasants	0.0	D	13.5	19.4	D	3.0	D	5.7	13.8	1 920	249	251	3 372	-0.5
Pocahontas	0.9	D	5.2	8.4	D	6.9	4.0	D	26.4	2 690	310	316	8 833	-0.2
Preston	-0.8	0.7	20.6	7.2	D	6.3	3.1	D	34.6	7 810	230	1 176	15 031	-0.4
Putnam	0.2	0.3	16.6	12.3	6.5	6.0	7.9	7.8	9.8	12 710	224	1 125	23 883	1.9
Raleigh	0.0	16.2	5.0	2.8	6.2	8.8	3.0	17.5	19.4	22 335	286	3 895	36 013	0.2
Randolph	0.2	3.9	5.3	10.4	3.3	9.4	4.4	D	19.8	7 410	253	1 255	14 174	-0.1
Ritchie	-1.0	28.0	11.0	22.1	5.6	5.2	2.8	D	11.4	3 110	311	530	5 812	-0.5
Roane	-1.6	D	12.0	5.6	3.5	9.9	5.8	D	17.5	4 330	296	993	7 395	0.6
Summers	-1.4	0.0	6.3	0.8	D	7.2	3.7	D	28.6	3 285	247	798	7 668	-0.2
Taylor	-0.9	D	6.1	D	D	9.7	D	D	27.6	3 565	209	669	7 502	-0.5
Tucker	0.6	D	D	10.4	D	4.3	4.7	8.5	20.8	2 080	299	217	5 359	0.2
Tyler	-0.4	4.7	3.2	41.3	D	3.6	D	9.7	18.9	2 350	259	295	4 984	-0.3
Upshur	-0.1	7.5	11.5	9.5	5.3	10.3	3.2	D	14.5	5 900	239	1 074	11 239	1.3
Wayne	0.0	D	4.7	7.5	2.9	4.8	1.2	D	35.7	11 630	282	3 142	19 196	-0.2
Webster	-0.1	D	1.5	8.2	D	4.2	D	8.1	26.6	2 730	309	710	5 401	-0.5
Wetzel	-0.3	D	13.8	3.0	D	13.1	3.6	D	26.5	4 505	282	780	8 142	-0.4
Wirt	-1.3	6.5	9.7	D	D	7.7	D	11.1	41.7	1 465	251	382	3 237	0.2
Wood	-0.1	1.3	7.2	12.5	5.2	9.6	6.7	15.5	20.5	23 680	274	3 717	40 260	0.1
Wyoming	-0.1	40.6	2.7	1.5	4.7	5.8	1.3	D	20.2	7 665	340	1 991	10 785	-1.6
WISCONSIN	2.0	0.2	5.4	18.7	7.9	6.0	7.4	12.3	15.1	1 153 149	200	117 679	2 657 231	1.3
Adams	7.2	0.0	6.7	6.8	D	5.8	D	6.1	21.7	7 145	354	564	17 394	-0.2
Ashland	1.3	0.0	8.3	13.4	3.8	7.3	2.9	D	25.4	4 025	250	432	9 603	-0.5
Barron	5.6	2.0	5.1	23.1	2.5	7.9	2.9	14.9	17.3	11 850	260	927	23 731	0.5
Bayfield	2.5	0.0	9.0	D	D	7.4	3.5	D	37.3	4 770	319	248	13 162	1.3
Brown	1.5	0.1	5.3	17.4	7.4	5.4	9.0	12.8	11.9	45 260	176	4 707	107 992	3.5
Buffalo	9.0	D	6.7	4.1	D	11.4	3.7	D	16.8	3 300	250	198	6 698	0.5
Burnett	2.3	D	7.6	20.8	2.9	7.1	2.3	D	29.5	5 370	351	270	15 454	1.2
Calumet	8.8	D	7.2	28.1	D	6.5	6.0	D	10.2	8 625	174	243	20 192	2.5
Chippewa	5.3	1.5	8.2	23.1	3.4	9.7	2.3	10.9	14.8	13 905	219	1 151	27 829	2.4
Clark	21.3	D	7.8	20.3	1.5	5.7	D	D	13.9	7 125	207	573	15 032	-0.3
Columbia	2.9	D	6.7	26.1	2.8	6.4	2.8	10.7	16.4	12 040	213	562	26 287	0.6
Crawford	5.2	D	3.8	24.1	D	16.1	2.6	D	15.2	4 495	274	329	8 835	0.4
Dane	0.7	0.1	5.5	8.1	15.9	5.1	9.5	9.3	23.6	77 840	151	7 408	225 514	4.4

1. Per 1,000 resident population estimated as of July 1 of the year shown.

Table B. States and Counties — Housing, Labor Force, and Employment

STATE County	Total [89]	Percent [90]	Median value[1] [91]	With a mortgage [92]	Without a mortgage[2] [93]	Median rent[3] [94]	Median rent as a percent of income[2] [95]	Substandard units[4] (percent) [96]	Total [97]	Percent change, 2014–2015 [98]	Total [99]	Rate[5] [100]	Total [101]	Management, business, science and arts [102]	Construction, production, and maintenance occupations [103]
WEST VIRGINIA—Cont'd															
Brooke	10 086	74.4	84 300	16.6	10.0	580	25.5	2.3	10 151	0.2	743	7.3	10 031	29.1	26.6
Cabell	40 220	60.6	109 600	20.2	10.0	647	31.8	1.4	41 710	-1.2	2 243	5.4	40 360	37.2	15.3
Calhoun	3 112	79.2	69 500	18.2	10.0	500	40.9	1.7	2 772	-4.7	346	12.5	2 543	23.3	39.0
Clay	3 486	84.7	77 100	22.4	10.0	490	33.6	1.9	3 297	-0.8	368	11.2	3 035	26.0	36.1
Doddridge	2 761	84.7	89 000	20.1	10.0	537	28.2	1.1	3 638	-0.1	209	5.7	2 859	22.7	40.1
Fayette	17 566	77.8	74 700	19.5	10.7	571	28.2	1.8	16 354	-1.7	1 398	8.5	15 617	25.2	26.5
Gilmer	2 645	76.4	74 400	16.3	10.0	545	29.6	2.0	2 730	-0.6	214	7.8	2 952	30.5	25.0
Grant	4 256	77.0	121 100	22.5	10.2	583	24.2	0.4	5 747	-1.3	437	7.6	5 020	20.7	41.8
Greenbrier	15 246	74.1	100 200	20.9	10.0	639	30.0	2.2	15 350	1.2	1 005	6.5	14 341	31.7	26.6
Hampshire	10 628	51.5	117 600	24.3	11.1	513	28.8	1.8	9 714	3.1	539	5.5	8 943	17.3	40.8
Hancock	12 970	74.2	84 200	18.3	10.2	623	28.7	0.9	13 106	-0.4	1 019	7.8	13 253	27.7	29.5
Hardy	5 169	76.5	123 200	23.6	10.0	558	26.4	1.8	5 431	1.3	409	7.5	6 174	19.0	43.0
Harrison	27 755	74.2	93 600	18.0	10.0	644	29.3	2.1	31 687	-0.6	2 013	6.4	29 611	32.0	24.2
Jackson	11 242	77.2	106 100	18.3	10.0	558	28.6	3.4	11 962	0.9	858	7.2	10 683	29.3	28.8
Jefferson	20 126	76.1	204 900	23.0	10.8	887	30.6	1.9	27 597	2.4	1 133	4.1	26 557	39.9	18.6
Kanawha	82 531	70.4	101 300	18.7	10.0	688	25.9	1.4	87 425	-1.6	5 209	6.0	86 300	37.0	18.0
Lewis	6 476	71.2	94 800	17.7	10.0	537	27.2	2.6	7 006	-2.6	577	8.2	6 458	25.3	29.5
Lincoln	8 128	77.2	78 300	18.2	10.0	548	33.0	2.6	7 459	-1.1	720	9.7	7 149	23.6	32.4
Logan	14 444	75.2	80 500	19.6	10.0	555	28.0	1.5	11 485	-3.7	1 304	11.4	11 956	25.8	33.9
McDowell	8 386	77.9	38 100	18.8	11.0	502	39.0	3.1	5 320	-8.0	692	13.0	4 830	23.5	32.3
Marion	22 596	77.3	94 600	17.6	10.9	675	29.9	2.0	26 043	-1.7	1 791	6.9	25 485	31.3	25.9
Marshall	13 847	77.2	88 800	18.3	10.1	545	25.3	1.1	14 218	-0.4	1 199	8.4	13 457	27.6	28.5
Mason	10 729	81.0	81 000	19.8	10.0	493	29.6	2.1	9 966	-1.8	851	8.5	9 407	26.0	34.2
Mercer	25 590	72.9	84 100	19.7	10.1	580	31.0	1.2	21 955	-1.3	1 606	7.3	23 454	29.4	22.4
Mineral	11 148	58.0	118 300	19.9	10.3	522	30.5	1.2	11 653	-1.3	847	7.3	10 622	25.3	33.1
Mingo	10 836	76.6	68 000	19.5	10.0	556	27.0	2.9	7 265	-6.0	955	13.1	8 184	28.6	36.8
Monongalia	36 857	57.3	161 500	17.8	10.0	735	32.9	2.0	50 908	1.0	2 389	4.7	48 460	41.7	17.1
Monroe	5 719	81.1	103 600	19.5	10.0	571	25.8	3.3	5 752	3.2	320	5.6	5 326	27.7	33.8
Morgan	7 358	66.1	160 700	23.9	12.4	704	27.3	1.7	7 417	0.0	411	5.5	6 713	29.2	33.2
Nicholas	10 686	79.5	75 400	19.4	10.0	543	28.5	2.7	9 879	-2.0	903	9.1	9 889	23.8	32.7
Ohio	18 582	68.2	102 500	18.4	10.0	558	30.6	1.5	20 757	-1.3	1 165	5.6	20 444	33.2	20.1
Pendleton	3 199	76.5	89 200	19.7	10.0	683	23.5	2.3	3 580	2.7	168	4.7	2 996	23.6	36.4
Pleasants	2 822	84.2	99 600	17.6	10.0	523	27.0	1.6	2 998	0.6	255	8.5	2 859	29.2	32.4
Pocahontas	3 719	80.9	107 400	21.2	10.0	538	27.9	2.6	3 598	1.5	296	8.2	3 622	30.8	29.2
Preston	12 610	79.6	107 800	19.3	10.2	584	26.8	1.6	14 788	2.0	913	6.2	13 955	25.0	33.8
Putnam	21 453	83.0	146 800	18.7	10.0	744	27.2	0.8	25 693	-1.0	1 425	5.5	25 281	38.0	18.8
Raleigh	31 164	73.1	97 700	18.7	10.4	642	25.9	1.1	30 683	-1.9	2 254	7.3	29 295	30.3	24.8
Randolph	11 351	75.2	98 600	20.8	10.0	546	30.8	2.2	11 949	1.0	840	7.0	11 619	27.5	24.8
Ritchie	4 023	78.9	69 400	20.0	10.0	554	26.9	0.9	4 481	-2.7	315	7.0	3 714	25.1	35.3
Roane	5 902	75.8	82 800	19.9	10.0	487	31.0	2.0	5 247	-0.9	603	11.5	4 738	26.0	31.3
Summers	5 560	78.9	82 500	19.7	10.0	493	27.5	3.3	4 555	1.4	320	7.0	4 735	28.4	33.8
Taylor	6 801	77.4	87 900	19.4	10.8	523	26.5	1.1	7 748	-0.1	466	6.0	6 836	31.0	30.6
Tucker	2 969	81.0	104 200	20.9	10.8	529	23.1	1.5	3 419	1.5	210	6.1	3 010	30.5	30.5
Tyler	3 750	79.9	80 900	17.6	10.0	484	30.6	1.9	3 647	1.0	342	9.4	3 320	21.8	31.8
Upshur	8 937	77.0	100 100	19.9	10.0	566	25.9	2.1	9 694	1.3	778	8.0	9 494	29.7	30.9
Wayne	16 757	77.7	84 200	19.1	10.0	576	34.6	1.9	15 743	-0.9	1 109	7.0	15 130	29.4	25.1
Webster	3 854	74.9	65 100	22.6	10.0	460	34.0	1.5	3 454	0.2	265	7.7	3 044	16.5	38.7
Wetzel	6 734	78.3	83 000	16.0	10.0	509	35.0	1.8	7 193	-1.2	721	10.0	5 616	22.7	35.8
Wirt	2 425	82.4	74 500	17.2	10.0	481	24.1	2.9	2 278	0.4	234	10.3	2 217	25.6	39.0
Wood	35 900	72.3	106 100	19.5	10.0	613	31.2	1.7	37 554	-0.9	2 339	6.2	36 874	32.1	23.2
Wyoming	9 201	80.4	60 400	16.9	10.0	520	27.2	3.6	7 759	-2.6	751	9.7	6 650	26.3	35.1
WISCONSIN	2 293 250	67.7	165 900	23.2	13.7	772	29.3	2.1	3 095 384	0.3	142 583	4.6	2 852 018	34.3	25.2
Adams	7 829	85.0	133 100	25.3	15.8	718	29.6	1.6	8 338	-0.8	614	7.4	7 586	22.6	32.3
Ashland	6 741	74.1	107 400	22.8	14.8	588	28.2	3.7	8 020	-0.6	505	6.3	7 352	28.6	28.8
Barron	19 029	74.1	135 600	24.6	14.1	642	27.4	1.8	24 516	1.7	1 239	5.1	22 161	27.5	34.7
Bayfield	6 949	82.9	158 300	24.7	14.9	563	26.1	3.0	7 510	-0.6	632	8.4	6 873	33.9	26.1
Brown	99 705	65.8	158 600	22.0	12.9	708	27.3	2.6	139 236	0.4	5 712	4.1	127 662	33.3	24.7
Buffalo	5 783	75.0	142 300	24.2	14.3	638	27.5	2.4	6 518	0.7	325	5.0	6 909	31.5	34.6
Burnett	7 288	80.7	146 900	27.8	14.7	645	29.2	2.7	7 264	-1.6	517	7.1	6 369	26.0	31.2
Calumet	18 606	81.9	165 700	20.7	12.5	678	25.5	1.6	27 488	1.1	987	3.6	26 373	34.4	29.5
Chippewa	24 643	72.0	147 300	22.4	12.3	710	28.1	1.9	33 273	0.5	1 582	4.8	30 794	29.7	32.1
Clark	12 882	77.3	110 800	23.1	13.5	585	25.2	5.1	17 481	2.9	772	4.4	15 525	27.6	39.1
Columbia	22 571	74.7	174 500	24.0	13.5	749	26.9	1.5	31 626	1.2	1 386	4.4	29 473	31.5	28.5
Crawford	6 607	74.6	120 100	22.9	14.5	572	28.7	2.4	7 951	-0.6	469	5.9	7 656	24.9	34.2
Dane	208 749	58.8	229 000	23.5	12.4	912	30.3	2.2	309 956	1.2	9 944	3.2	281 116	48.3	13.9

1. Specified owner-occupied units. 2. A value of 10.0 represents 10 percent or less; a value of 50.0 represents 50 percent or more. 3. Specified renter-occupied units.
4. Overcrowded or lacking complete plumbing facilities. 5. Percent of civilian labor force. 6. Persons 16 years old and over.

STATE County	Number of establishments	Total	Health care and social assistance	Manufacturing	Retail trade	Finance and insurance	Professional, scientific, and technical services	Total (mil dol)	Average per employee (dollars)	Number	Fewer than 50 acres	500 acres or more	Farm operators whose principal occupation is farming (percent)
	104	105	106	107	108	109	110	111	112	113	114	115	116
WEST VIRGINIA—Cont'd													
Brooke	394	7 204	2 153	1 607	861	125	88	265	36 816	96	29.2	8.3	45.8
Cabell	2 456	47 298	13 525	4 448	7 075	1 307	1 922	1 753	37 059	383	33.2	2.9	31.6
Calhoun	110	985	D	32	122	D	D	44	44 249	227	16.7	8.8	35.7
Clay	90	880	D	D	134	D	D	26	29 825	114	20.2	3.5	34.2
Doddridge	67	D	D	D	128	D	D	D	D	352	19.6	5.4	49.4
Fayette	754	9 744	2 014	588	1 560	D	167	438	44 942	232	39.7	1.3	40.1
Gilmer	129	1 214	247	D	154	D	64	37	30 190	235	9.4	11.1	46.4
Grant	240	2 541	777	252	349	95	D	95	37 526	486	24.5	12.1	45.7
Greenbrier	936	10 827	2 855	743	2 019	D	277	350	32 366	819	29.9	10.4	40.2
Hampshire	329	2 618	802	176	472	183	D	72	27 647	798	40.6	8.8	43.4
Hancock	579	9 955	1 179	3 132	939	285	425	326	32 794	96	47.9	1.0	30.2
Hardy	259	4 707	463	2 558	588	191	50	132	28 120	494	33.8	13.4	52.8
Harrison	1 835	28 754	7 029	1 631	4 940	580	1 784	1 220	42 425	778	26.2	4.4	34.8
Jackson	503	6 994	1 158	1 477	1 210	211	295	274	39 124	732	24.2	3.6	41.7
Jefferson	832	13 462	1 169	798	1 904	D	373	421	31 271	501	51.7	5.6	50.7
Kanawha	5 077	86 782	19 488	3 339	11 450	4 842	5 864	3 575	41 195	210	34.8	1.0	41.0
Lewis	384	5 476	D	D	1 059	110	46	214	39 079	476	20.6	5.5	42.9
Lincoln	200	1 963	D	D	328	D	D	64	32 356	149	14.8	4.0	47.7
Logan	636	10 033	1 947	593	1 755	D	268	436	43 476	11	54.5	9.1	45.5
McDowell	268	2 840	842	D	616	D	D	94	33 251	11	72.7	9.1	54.5
Marion	1 213	17 722	3 096	1 028	2 338	499	1 144	705	39 808	557	34.1	0.9	53.5
Marshall	509	9 456	1 642	465	1 278	D	360	417	44 093	682	23.3	1.6	43.5
Mason	319	3 882	989	D	621	D	74	162	41 827	875	26.2	4.0	38.9
Mercer	1 261	17 873	4 732	1 189	3 195	473	598	582	32 571	400	30.8	3.5	40.8
Mineral	455	6 074	1 301	D	968	130	D	239	39 343	429	34.3	7.5	33.3
Mingo	402	3 813	D	D	373	174	366	132	34 505	20	70.0	10.0	55.0
Monongalia	2 296	44 406	14 213	3 937	6 039	827	2 286	1 813	40 820	458	26.4	2.6	34.3
Monroe	172	1 356	316	D	107	47	D	46	34 147	796	27.4	7.8	41.7
Morgan	228	1 991	540	D	389	84	D	60	30 359	196	42.9	2.0	46.9
Nicholas	574	6 577	1 729	782	1 508	D	168	203	30 818	393	31.3	5.1	52.2
Ohio	1 426	27 325	7 027	1 291	3 346	D	1 787	989	36 185	197	26.4	5.1	38.1
Pendleton	132	1 176	329	137	185	D	D	37	31 315	556	17.3	16.2	51.8
Pleasants	121	2 032	D	462	158	79	47	95	46 944	150	27.3	5.3	44.0
Pocahontas	204	3 013	411	D	334	48	D	68	22 426	389	18.5	14.7	44.7
Preston	523	4 970	1 157	486	813	164	110	168	33 779	1 084	26.2	3.6	46.1
Putnam	1 224	18 208	1 842	2 226	2 315	477	742	818	44 930	544	28.9	1.5	41.9
Raleigh	1 854	28 628	7 165	1 058	5 059	515	913	1 052	36 764	332	44.9	2.4	51.5
Randolph	683	9 370	2 776	1 249	1 453	251	203	271	28 873	405	27.7	10.9	44.2
Ritchie	210	2 427	D	D	268	78	60	101	41 731	428	17.5	7.7	42.1
Roane	234	2 542	D	236	606	93	D	90	35 355	575	15.5	7.1	45.2
Summers	160	1 392	428	D	D	45	D	39	27 989	345	21.4	3.8	43.5
Taylor	231	2 401	606	D	457	35	D	93	38 916	404	36.4	4.2	40.1
Tucker	179	2 334	289	D	236	45	D	56	24 073	162	20.4	9.9	52.5
Tyler	104	1 814	538	D	130	D	D	78	43 173	286	18.9	5.2	44.1
Upshur	536	6 305	1 542	718	760	124	217	219	34 740	456	27.9	4.8	42.3
Wayne	519	7 203	D	713	1 096	D	149	304	42 203	197	21.8	4.6	39.1
Webster	142	1 156	443	150	167	D	11	36	31 545	70	28.6	0.0	44.3
Wetzel	355	4 471	865	D	918	123	182	172	38 581	249	13.7	2.0	44.6
Wirt	52	386	D	D	79	D	7	8	21 262	217	19.4	6.0	37.3
Wood	2 059	32 898	7 312	2 658	6 246	1 002	920	1 146	34 831	816	30.3	1.3	34.1
Wyoming	292	3 713	729	64	634	80	62	175	47 034	27	33.3	3.7	33.3
WISCONSIN	138 221	2 450 254	388 018	443 111	305 703	136 126	102 960	106 791	43 584	69 754	32.2	8.8	49.8
Adams	330	3 241	450	410	469	53	63	92	28 500	313	19.8	16.6	55.3
Ashland	507	6 535	1 568	1 105	943	202	156	236	36 136	187	23.5	13.4	35.3
Barron	1 283	15 917	2 613	4 821	3 041	505	294	576	36 214	1 322	25.3	11.0	54.5
Bayfield	431	2 233	298	181	376	85	D	60	26 693	352	27.3	9.9	51.4
Brown	6 349	140 949	19 548	25 574	15 335	D	5 318	6 178	43 834	1 111	52.7	6.0	54.3
Buffalo	313	2 815	265	288	286	139	83	97	34 302	1 061	20.3	14.8	49.8
Burnett	390	3 229	671	755	558	D	92	104	32 244	406	27.1	10.6	42.9
Calumet	881	12 758	1 225	3 370	1 750	672	217	494	38 686	719	36.7	9.2	53.3
Chippewa	1 569	21 488	3 309	5 767	3 703	376	525	777	36 146	1 757	29.5	9.6	47.2
Clark	724	8 419	983	3 200	956	D	159	286	33 955	2 317	23.3	7.1	64.7
Columbia	1 401	18 969	2 512	4 475	2 984	401	477	657	34 644	1 564	39.5	9.6	52.9
Crawford	395	5 984	928	1 467	993	D	376	189	31 553	1 105	24.1	6.9	43.5
Dane	13 590	267 697	45 566	23 620	31 147	23 131	20 711	13 168	49 189	2 749	43.0	7.8	47.3

STATE County	Acreage (1,000) 117	Percent change, 2007–2012 118	Average size of farm 119	Total irrigated (1,000) 120	Total cropland (1,000) 121	Average per farm 122	Average per acre 123	Value of machinery and equipment, average per farm (dollars) 124	Total (mil dol) 125	Average per farm (dollars) 126	Crops 127	Live-stock and poultry products 128	$10,000 or more 129	$100,000 or more 130	Total ($1,000) 131	Percent of farms 132
WEST VIRGINIA—Cont'd																
Brooke	15	-4.5	153	D	4.3	298 448	1 948	68 323	1.4	14 406	20.4	79.5	30.2	3.1	D	3.1
Cabell	42	-10.9	111	0.0	6.3	332 266	2 998	42 608	2.0	5 198	50.3	49.7	9.4	0.5	60	16.2
Calhoun	49	-11.7	218	0.0	7.4	331 432	1 521	38 423	2.1	9 326	17.9	82.1	17.2	2.6	40	6.6
Clay	20	0.6	176	D	2.2	329 789	1 873	34 000	0.5	4 570	30.3	69.7	10.5	0.0	37	6.1
Doddridge	65	-19.6	186	D	10.0	349 517	1 882	41 406	2.3	6 452	33.7	66.3	15.3	0.3	50	4.3
Fayette	23	-13.2	100	0.0	6.1	245 427	2 458	43 509	1.7	7 478	41.5	58.5	18.1	0.9	66	7.3
Gilmer	70	9.9	300	0.0	11.7	440 783	1 472	55 600	8.8	37 634	4.4	95.6	25.1	3.0	139	10.2
Grant	112	3.2	231	0.0	21.3	549 519	2 377	44 138	51.3	105 498	2.4	97.6	37.2	11.7	253	19.1
Greenbrier	190	7.4	232	0.0	35.7	658 885	2 837	71 835	76.8	93 722	2.8	97.2	37.6	8.5	461	15.4
Hampshire	142	10.0	178	0.1	34.8	641 143	3 601	51 271	39.2	49 102	19.3	80.7	26.2	5.5	227	16.9
Hancock	9	-7.9	93	D	3.1	271 469	2 932	59 625	0.6	6 750	53.1	46.9	13.5	1.0	2	5.2
Hardy	155	15.6	314	0.0	29.2	891 816	2 837	87 621	189.0	382 530	2.7	97.3	46.6	27.7	336	15.4
Harrison	117	4.8	150	0.0	25.7	318 695	2 119	45 731	9.5	12 264	25.2	74.8	20.3	2.1	71	3.3
Jackson	105	-19.1	143	0.0	25.8	315 790	2 207	42 680	7.4	10 067	28.8	71.2	20.8	1.2	256	8.9
Jefferson	67	-7.1	134	0.3	41.4	918 731	6 874	74 527	35.5	70 920	45.0	55.0	36.7	9.6	852	24.8
Kanawha	26	9.5	124	0.0	4.1	268 152	2 165	31 386	1.3	6 310	33.3	66.7	18.6	0.5	25	8.1
Lewis	82	-10.5	173	D	16.2	341 069	1 969	42 935	7.0	14 735	14.0	86.0	35.1	1.5	73	3.6
Lincoln	26	-20.8	172	0.0	3.3	348 013	2 021	38 450	0.9	6 087	37.6	62.4	12.8	1.3	63	24.8
Logan	1	-40.3	76	D	0.0	147 273	1 949	34 455	0.1	5 364	89.8	10.2	18.2	0.0	0	0.0
McDowell	1	-29.7	95	0.0	0.2	227 091	2 400	47 091	D	D	D	D	9.1	9.1	0	0.0
Marion	53	-8.0	96	0.0	12.7	206 381	2 155	42 246	2.4	4 370	39.1	60.9	11.8	0.0	49	3.6
Marshall	86	-10.3	126	0.0	22.8	277 150	2 199	46 801	3.3	4 890	40.9	59.1	11.9	0.0	121	7.6
Mason	139	5.0	159	0.3	39.7	335 312	2 114	52 757	34.1	38 965	74.1	25.9	24.1	4.6	465	17.5
Mercer	52	-4.0	129	0.0	9.7	287 660	2 222	45 280	3.9	9 790	33.2	66.8	19.8	1.8	34	2.8
Mineral	76	-2.3	178	0.1	16.7	533 772	3 006	49 399	22.2	51 849	6.9	93.1	22.6	5.6	257	11.7
Mingo	2	-49.2	102	0.0	0.1	143 850	1 417	23 300	0.1	5 300	D	D	10.0	0.0	0	0.0
Monongalia	58	-2.1	127	0.0	14.9	391 255	3 090	48 055	4.0	8 784	27.8	72.2	21.8	0.9	165	6.1
Monroe	145	8.9	182	0.0	29.2	414 754	2 283	52 758	31.4	39 447	9.5	90.5	36.8	7.5	426	15.8
Morgan	18	-18.1	94	0.1	7.8	419 311	4 470	39 770	3.0	15 408	77.2	22.8	19.4	3.1	86	6.6
Nicholas	58	13.2	148	0.0	13.6	377 216	2 552	42 771	4.6	11 649	16.8	83.2	22.9	2.0	37	8.7
Ohio	30	-2.4	153	D	11.9	353 061	2 312	80 888	3.5	17 660	20.5	79.5	28.4	5.6	64	24.4
Pendleton	170	0.1	306	D	24.4	711 710	2 326	68 344	118.8	213 608	2.4	97.6	58.6	21.0	207	17.1
Pleasants	21	-16.6	143	D	4.1	277 013	1 933	55 173	D	D	D	D	14.7	2.7	D	1.3
Pocahontas	118	-2.8	305	0.0	18.7	670 208	2 201	61 131	9.3	23 779	11.3	88.7	40.1	4.4	174	21.9
Preston	161	5.5	148	0.1	44.9	365 799	2 467	55 455	18.2	16 749	28.1	71.9	31.5	2.8	222	8.4
Putnam	60	-9.7	110	0.1	12.2	281 868	2 556	39 509	10.1	18 603	83.1	16.9	14.3	1.1	85	9.6
Raleigh	37	-15.1	111	0.0	8.1	276 123	2 487	47 337	3.0	9 036	24.6	75.4	17.2	0.9	47	6.0
Randolph	94	-9.9	232	D	19.8	422 042	1 815	54 812	9.4	23 173	21.8	78.2	35.1	3.2	147	9.9
Ritchie	89	-2.3	207	0.0	17.6	331 741	1 599	54 668	7.6	17 776	15.1	84.9	21.7	1.2	57	4.0
Roane	111	-5.7	193	D	21.6	330 957	1 716	42 193	5.6	9 781	26.2	73.8	23.1	0.7	209	9.6
Summers	58	-2.8	168	0.0	10.9	369 194	2 198	42 614	5.0	14 365	25.7	74.3	25.2	3.5	45	6.7
Taylor	49	-8.7	122	0.0	10.4	301 597	2 481	50 545	3.7	9 228	19.2	80.8	18.1	1.5	131	4.2
Tucker	34	-2.7	210	D	6.7	641 191	3 059	47 975	2.2	13 580	22.6	77.4	29.0	1.9	37	9.9
Tyler	48	1.4	169	0.0	11.5	309 413	1 836	41 035	2.2	7 829	35.1	64.9	26.2	0.3	34	7.0
Upshur	68	-3.4	150	0.0	15.0	348 270	2 320	46 175	6.8	14 925	18.8	81.3	24.6	2.6	48	3.9
Wayne	30	-24.2	153	0.0	3.7	288 345	1 880	36 102	1.0	5 183	40.7	59.2	12.2	1.0	24	4.1
Webster	8	-31.2	113	0.0	1.8	248 500	2 194	25 086	0.3	4 743	62.7	37.3	15.7	0.0	D	2.9
Wetzel	38	-26.5	153	D	7.6	279 361	1 826	34 867	1.2	4 727	43.9	56.1	6.8	0.4	45	4.4
Wirt	38	-7.8	175	D	7.7	287 650	1 642	42 065	2.2	10 286	28.8	71.2	20.3	1.4	55	8.8
Wood	88	-1.3	108	0.0	21.8	251 165	2 333	34 237	6.1	7 496	30.9	69.1	14.0	0.2	102	3.4
Wyoming	3	-26.5	110	D	0.5	227 889	2 072	42 407	0.1	2 556	15.9	84.1	3.7	0.0	0	0.0
WISCONSIN	14 569	-4.1	209	421.7	9 911.0	819 551	3 924	129 561	11 744.5	168 370	39.2	60.8	52.3	24.6	237 304	55.8
Adams	118	2.6	378	44.3	87.5	1 467 256	3 879	173 677	105.7	337 601	88.5	11.5	52.4	23.0	882	54.3
Ashland	46	-17.3	245	0.0	21.2	450 973	1 841	83 807	12.0	64 364	20.9	79.1	42.2	8.0	214	18.2
Barron	310	-4.5	234	11.7	202.9	655 775	2 799	148 573	343.1	259 503	29.1	70.9	58.5	29.0	4 643	59.5
Bayfield	72	-19.6	204	0.1	36.3	414 466	2 031	70 830	13.9	39 528	35.3	64.7	34.9	10.8	267	19.6
Brown	181	-3.2	163	0.5	151.3	884 833	5 425	149 589	307.5	276 792	17.4	82.6	52.8	27.2	3 585	48.7
Buffalo	305	-0.6	288	4.6	162.7	968 225	3 365	147 399	225.8	212 814	32.1	67.9	58.9	30.3	4 876	68.7
Burnett	84	-13.1	206	0.2	44.4	506 421	2 459	84 613	37.2	91 626	38.8	61.2	39.7	13.5	661	42.4
Calumet	142	-6.1	198	0.0	120.9	1 092 981	5 520	172 268	213.2	296 527	25.5	74.5	64.4	33.1	3 196	64.0
Chippewa	385	8.8	219	5.7	249.9	597 028	2 727	114 201	253.2	144 107	38.1	61.9	51.5	24.6	5 088	54.5
Clark	458	4.1	198	0.6	310.9	618 184	3 126	119 200	401.9	173 441	22.9	77.1	64.2	38.2	5 774	38.1
Columbia	308	-2.6	197	1.6	234.1	993 045	5 043	129 485	214.3	137 021	55.7	44.3	51.0	20.5	5 783	51.3
Crawford	217	-9.1	196	0.2	98.4	530 437	2 706	78 187	74.9	67 783	50.3	49.7	48.1	15.3	2 373	61.3
Dane	504	-5.8	183	4.6	396.3	1 111 346	6 057	145 729	471.6	171 553	39.1	60.9	50.5	23.2	12 023	62.2

Table B. States and Counties — Water Use, Wholesale Trade, Retail Trade, and Real Estate

STATE County	Water use, 2010		Wholesale trade,[1] 2012				Retail trade,[2] 2012				Real estate and rental and leasing,[2] 2012			
	Total water withdrawn (mil gal/day)	Gallons withdrawn per person per day	Number of establishments	Number of employees	Sales (mil dol)	Annual payroll (mil dol)	Number of establishments	Number of employees	Sales (mil dol)	Annual payroll (mil dol)	Number of establishments	Number of employees	Receipts (mil dol)	Annual payroll (mil dol)
	133	134	135	136	137	138	139	140	141	142	143	144	145	146
WEST VIRGINIA—Cont'd														
Brooke	12.5	518	13	D	D	D	63	931	236.8	20.4	2	D	D	D
Cabell	29.3	304	106	1 754	873.6	82.4	439	6 687	1 570.9	145.2	97	362	69.0	12.4
Calhoun	0.8	106	NA	NA	NA	NA	19	128	27.3	2.4	3	6	0.5	0.1
Clay	1.1	121	1	D	D	D	17	134	45.7	2.7	1	D	D	D
Doddridge	1.1	135	1	D	D	D	10	90	22.8	1.4	1	D	D	D
Fayette	7.8	169	25	D	D	D	134	1 683	413.8	37.0	21	56	8.6	1.2
Gilmer	2.9	331	4	D	D	D	22	157	38.3	3.2	2	D	D	D
Grant	1 120.9	93 903	2	D	D	D	38	377	115.2	7.7	5	10	0.9	0.2
Greenbrier	8.9	250	17	D	D	D	173	2 029	543.4	47.6	42	118	23.3	3.7
Hampshire	2.6	110	6	D	D	D	57	480	123.6	9.6	14	29	3.6	0.8
Hancock	78.7	2 565	13	154	105.9	4.9	93	1 000	235.3	19.2	22	D	D	D
Hardy	16.4	1 172	4	D	D	D	45	599	133.3	12.2	7	20	2.2	0.4
Harrison	55.4	802	74	867	381.8	37.0	327	4 727	1 314.7	104.5	62	508	161.0	24.8
Jackson	4.1	139	18	254	191.4	9.9	96	1 138	348.2	25.9	14	49	24.9	2.1
Jefferson	9.9	184	14	58	51.0	2.8	142	1 866	451.4	40.8	43	117	18.0	3.4
Kanawha	590.8	3 060	256	3 709	2 518.9	183.3	760	11 292	3 186.6	274.2	238	1 208	278.6	42.3
Lewis	2.5	151	14	116	109.9	5.8	75	1 063	301.2	23.6	9	39	5.2	0.8
Lincoln	1.9	88	3	D	D	D	38	312	80.3	6.5	2	D	D	D
Logan	9.4	256	34	411	138.2	18.1	118	1 726	551.2	42.6	20	86	9.3	2.4
McDowell	3.6	162	5	D	D	D	53	650	131.2	12.7	6	29	17.9	3.1
Marion	16.4	291	44	D	D	D	189	2 291	743.2	55.4	35	128	24.0	4.4
Marshall	433.9	13 105	16	D	D	D	85	1 224	344.7	27.3	7	D	D	D
Mason	643.1	23 536	5	D	D	D	54	575	143.9	11.9	14	51	6.1	1.2
Mercer	10.2	163	52	590	355.8	28.1	251	3 183	929.1	78.2	38	126	61.9	4.6
Mineral	4.3	153	12	D	D	D	71	999	237.3	20.4	15	37	4.7	0.8
Mingo	6.6	246	14	197	55.0	8.2	62	445	119.7	11.2	15	D	D	D
Monongalia	115.4	1 199	56	401	340.9	14.5	382	6 325	1 608.6	129.8	132	D	D	D
Monroe	3.1	230	6	16	3.6	0.4	31	145	26.6	2.7	3	4	0.6	0.1
Morgan	4.4	249	3	D	D	D	48	397	90.3	8.2	10	29	3.4	0.6
Nicholas	4.8	185	17	149	59.3	6.3	109	1 505	432.5	34.7	18	46	9.0	1.5
Ohio	10.5	236	72	D	D	D	201	3 486	896.0	79.7	56	D	D	D
Pendleton	9.7	1 257	3	D	D	D	24	204	37.2	3.5	2	D	D	D
Pleasants	67.7	8 899	NA	NA	NA	NA	16	168	45.7	3.7	2	D	D	D
Pocahontas	5.7	649	1	D	D	D	33	327	75.7	6.0	11	47	6.2	1.0
Preston	7.9	236	15	85	33.3	2.9	94	854	234.5	16.9	20	D	D	D
Putnam	47.7	859	74	D	D	D	174	2 359	748.5	55.8	57	316	112.1	18.1
Raleigh	12.3	156	96	D	D	D	346	5 057	1 452.4	124.3	74	287	50.0	9.8
Randolph	13.6	461	24	238	368.9	8.9	142	1 477	352.7	32.6	21	100	14.7	3.3
Ritchie	1.6	154	5	D	D	D	34	288	73.2	5.6	4	8	0.5	0.1
Roane	2.3	151	9	78	50.8	2.2	41	513	132.6	11.3	10	22	1.8	0.4
Summers	5.7	406	6	D	D	D	29	259	68.4	5.6	3	6	0.5	0.1
Taylor	2.3	134	7	D	D	D	33	448	110.9	10.3	2	D	D	D
Tucker	1.5	210	1	D	D	D	28	223	50.1	4.8	10	52	3.8	1.1
Tyler	13.5	1 468	NA	NA	NA	NA	21	139	44.1	2.7	1	D	D	D
Upshur	5.0	205	12	154	171.6	6.6	82	874	264.2	20.4	19	65	8.8	1.7
Wayne	13.0	305	15	252	140.5	11.4	107	1 048	254.9	20.8	19	D	D	D
Webster	3.5	387	3	D	D	D	21	153	42.9	3.2	3	D	D	D
Wetzel	4.0	242	12	93	27.6	2.4	77	879	208.7	18.7	13	34	4.4	1.0
Wirt	0.5	93	1	D	D	D	13	77	19.8	1.2	1	D	D	D
Wood	63.3	728	76	699	332.7	27.9	390	6 018	1 396.6	129.2	84	332	68.8	10.4
Wyoming	2.9	124	5	D	D	D	72	677	154.3	12.6	9	28	3.1	0.7
WISCONSIN	6 157.6	1 083	5 990	97 040	77 066.9	5 253.6	19 272	296 956	78 201.8	6 835.0	4 509	23 762	4 358.9	801.1
Adams	50.9	2 436	6	32	10.3	0.8	44	454	192.3	11.7	13	41	4.8	1.1
Ashland	35.1	2 169	11	90	33.7	3.2	87	897	214.2	20.0	9	38	2.7	0.5
Barron	11.6	253	41	319	166.0	11.3	220	3 033	713.3	67.7	33	80	12.8	2.0
Bayfield	10.7	713	8	D	D	D	69	391	84.5	6.6	9	18	2.1	0.3
Brown	312.8	1 261	329	6 081	4 360.8	321.1	864	14 521	3 686.2	322.1	203	1 407	203.8	43.4
Buffalo	344.1	25 322	9	117	62.3	5.9	46	281	77.8	5.6	10	24	2.5	0.3
Burnett	2.7	177	4	D	D	D	63	588	121.0	10.8	15	18	4.3	0.5
Calumet	5.9	119	44	498	222.9	22.9	109	1 796	418.6	37.0	13	50	3.1	0.8
Chippewa	19.3	310	62	671	408.4	24.9	213	3 500	1 064.9	82.6	34	95	13.8	2.5
Clark	6.1	174	41	331	256.0	16.9	99	820	260.6	18.1	7	15	1.7	0.3
Columbia	29.0	510	46	494	342.4	23.0	197	3 292	795.2	76.2	41	D	D	D
Crawford	3.4	204	11	D	D	D	78	1 034	216.6	22.0	8	21	2.1	0.3
Dane	72.2	148	597	11 599	8 106.6	613.2	1 687	29 330	8 516.2	743.4	620	4 076	952.3	158.3

1. Merchant wholesalers, except manufacturers' sales branches and offices.   2. Employer establishments.

Professional Services, Manufacturing, and Accommodation and Food Services

STATE County	Professional, scientific, and technical services, 2012				Manufacturing, 2012				Accommodation and food services, 2012			
	Number of establish- ments	Number of employees	Receipts (mil dol)	Annual payroll (mil dol)	Number of establish- ments	Number of employees	Receipts (mil dol)	Annual payroll (mil dol)	Number of establish- ments	Number of employees	Sales (mil dol)	Annual payroll (mil dol)
	147	148	149	150	151	152	153	154	155	156	157	158
WEST VIRGINIA—Cont'd												
Brooke	21	D	D	D	22	1 800	1 641.4	102.4	55	D	D	D
Cabell	202	2 070	204.9	77.5	90	4 818	2 345.2	298.5	269	4 968	237.4	64.9
Calhoun	5	21	1.8	0.6	6	33	D	0.7	4	22	1.1	0.4
Clay	2	D	D	D	4	43	D	2.4	5	D	D	D
Doddridge	1	D	D	D	NA	NA	NA	NA	3	D	D	D
Fayette	50	222	25.1	9.9	31	583	275.0	31.0	73	989	58.6	16.9
Gilmer	8	55	5.4	2.0	5	214	D	6.4	11	D	D	D
Grant	12	58	4.2	1.6	7	221	68.9	8.8	21	D	D	D
Greenbrier	75	295	24.0	7.7	35	774	D	30.8	88	2 455	190.7	67.3
Hampshire	24	D	D	D	12	153	66.0	7.7	35	310	18.7	5.2
Hancock	47	487	36.2	13.1	20	2 689	D	136.6	79	D	D	D
Hardy	15	48	4.4	1.3	11	2 575	D	71.4	28	309	13.9	3.9
Harrison	139	1 674	270.5	99.6	52	1 752	D	D	155	3 196	155.3	41.2
Jackson	43	236	29.9	11.9	15	1 188	D	78.3	52	852	39.1	10.4
Jefferson	84	360	48.6	18.6	17	816	206.7	35.2	127	D	D	D
Kanawha	565	5 965	884.4	340.3	121	2 985	2 196.6	185.5	458	9 306	552.9	145.9
Lewis	15	56	5.5	1.6	15	124	D	4.6	37	596	34.3	11.0
Lincoln	9	71	8.0	2.6	4	11	2.2	0.5	15	D	D	D
Logan	39	246	17.7	7.5	36	734	157.8	31.1	62	979	48.3	12.7
McDowell	13	D	D	D	4	26	D	0.8	22	D	D	D
Marion	119	1 060	130.7	59.5	50	1 154	469.5	50.6	113	2 043	93.7	23.7
Marshall	33	173	15.7	5.5	19	473	D	24.3	60	792	32.4	8.5
Mason	25	87	9.1	3.0	19	696	D	41.2	33	344	14.2	4.2
Mercer	92	639	71.4	20.2	57	1 246	241.5	50.6	106	2 177	100.9	27.6
Mineral	27	195	11.2	4.5	16	1 821	D	117.3	50	D	D	D
Mingo	47	D	D	D	13	173	D	4.2	31	322	11.2	3.4
Monongalia	205	2 723	394.9	120.9	53	3 668	2 034.3	256.4	281	5 885	253.5	70.4
Monroe	9	30	2.2	0.6	5	411	D	19.0	11	D	D	D
Morgan	13	79	13.2	6.3	6	140	D	D	27	D	D	D
Nicholas	45	246	14.7	7.7	25	709	212.9	30.6	59	844	36.9	10.3
Ohio	154	1 777	215.8	80.0	42	1 520	337.5	55.6	135	2 984	226.7	45.3
Pendleton	5	D	D	D	5	127	D	5.3	11	D	D	D
Pleasants	4	D	D	D	8	565	305.6	32.5	12	D	D	D
Pocahontas	6	D	D	D	6	261	38.1	7.9	24	1 360	51.4	16.8
Preston	29	111	10.4	3.8	25	465	147.1	17.4	36	280	13.6	3.4
Putnam	105	1 037	117.0	42.1	41	1 989	1 948.4	115.1	91	1 535	74.3	19.6
Raleigh	123	864	107.0	41.2	60	1 058	278.6	48.3	149	3 189	177.8	48.3
Randolph	49	226	17.8	6.8	24	1 069	189.4	37.2	54	776	38.4	10.6
Ritchie	14	51	3.8	1.6	13	741	D	31.8	17	D	D	D
Roane	16	46	4.2	1.4	16	226	45.2	8.1	13	D	D	D
Summers	11	70	6.8	2.5	7	19	3.1	0.7	19	247	9.6	2.5
Taylor	10	D	D	D	8	D	D	D	26	D	D	D
Tucker	7	D	D	D	15	224	D	9.9	32	D	D	D
Tyler	8	19	1.4	0.3	4	514	D	46.2	6	D	D	D
Upshur	37	228	15.8	6.4	18	665	285.3	32.5	48	644	30.0	8.5
Wayne	22	158	17.4	5.7	26	523	446.1	26.7	52	D	D	D
Webster	5	D	D	D	7	114	D	3.1	11	D	D	D
Wetzel	19	117	8.9	3.3	10	850	D	70.5	42	606	28.2	6.6
Wirt	4	D	D	D	4	D	D	2.2	8	D	D	D
Wood	161	986	105.9	42.2	59	D	2 261.9	205.7	210	4 070	181.8	53.1
Wyoming	19	55	4.5	1.4	9	51	D	2.5	21	D	D	D
WISCONSIN	11 301	99 162	15 135.0	5 738.3	8 995	436 777	177 728.9	21 879.3	14 137	221 567	10 303.3	2 764.3
Adams	15	57	4.6	1.6	12	377	D	18.3	60	1 117	55.1	17.9
Ashland	29	161	15.2	7.2	23	1 107	219.8	51.9	62	588	28.9	7.9
Barron	66	317	28.2	12.4	92	4 865	1 520.7	199.1	137	1 474	59.1	15.8
Bayfield	9	28	2.0	1.3	21	170	D	5.5	90	515	31.8	9.0
Brown	526	4 885	709.5	255.6	442	24 628	11 068.4	1 230.8	593	11 889	479.2	141.4
Buffalo	18	63	4.8	1.3	20	386	303.2	17.7	41	286	10.5	2.6
Burnett	22	62	7.1	2.3	25	790	286.6	34.5	65	456	20.9	5.8
Calumet	64	206	18.6	7.8	71	3 827	1 616.8	174.4	95	1 502	47.0	12.7
Chippewa	86	383	48.5	17.9	125	5 030	1 930.5	237.5	165	1 801	70.0	17.0
Clark	33	165	13.4	5.1	77	3 513	2 021.0	136.7	57	508	17.8	4.9
Columbia	80	465	41.3	15.9	94	4 732	2 530.5	220.7	167	3 440	158.0	45.2
Crawford	21	227	10.0	4.7	24	1 534	1 054.2	66.7	55	638	27.6	7.0
Dane	1 741	19 907	3 387.5	1 313.8	521	23 154	7 205.3	1 210.9	1 265	24 284	1 111.2	316.1

1. Establishment subject to federal tax.

Table B. States and Counties — **Health Care and Social Assistance, Other Services, Nonemployer Businesses, and Residential Construction**

STATE County	Health care and social assistance, 2012				Other services, 2012				Nonemployer businesses, 2014		Value of residential construction authorized by building permits, 2015	
	Number of establishments	Number of employees	Receipts (mil dol)	Annual payroll (mil dol)	Number of establishments	Number of employees	Receipts (mil dol)	Annual payroll (mil dol)	Number	Receipts (mil dol)	New Construction ($1,000)	Number of housing units
	159	160	161	162	163	164	165	166	167	168	169	170
WEST VIRGINIA—Cont'd												
Brooke	65	1 959	171.3	66.2	32	165	9.7	3.2	961	37.5	2 989	13
Cabell	372	12 905	1 426.9	570.0	170	1 053	161.2	32.3	4 772	179.1	14 843	95
Calhoun	9	294	17.0	10.0	5	D	D	D	523	12.4	NA	NA
Clay	12	283	10.6	5.2	5	D	D	D	351	11.1	500	11
Doddridge	11	176	4.2	2.4	2	D	D	D	246	9.2	0	0
Fayette	105	2 040	162.6	65.2	56	372	37.0	9.1	1 701	56.9	4 255	32
Gilmer	13	255	14.2	7.1	9	32	2.6	0.6	397	10.8	2 940	27
Grant	28	738	45.9	19.5	19	D	D	D	678	25.2	5 421	79
Greenbrier	145	3 028	238.4	101.2	55	291	26.7	7.9	2 183	87.3	18 666	54
Hampshire	34	752	52.1	21.9	26	107	9.1	2.3	1 362	53.3	10 406	92
Hancock	75	1 251	73.4	31.6	46	198	13.8	3.4	1 294	43.5	5 136	27
Hardy	30	451	28.4	12.1	19	54	5.6	0.9	846	25.4	4 690	34
Harrison	237	6 341	666.5	275.1	134	D	D	D	3 837	164.9	16 624	81
Jackson	62	1 111	71.6	30.1	27	D	D	D	1 504	58.4	81	2
Jefferson	77	1 217	103.1	41.8	72	541	76.6	15.1	3 507	134.1	57 797	304
Kanawha	746	18 799	2 083.3	768.4	388	D	D	D	9 298	388.1	27 921	256
Lewis	35	1 261	112.6	42.7	30	103	8.6	2.2	888	33.1	197	3
Lincoln	18	D	D	D	15	66	4.4	1.3	782	24.8	1 677	13
Logan	96	1 880	186.3	68.7	60	486	87.4	15.9	1 161	44.4	146	1
McDowell	34	867	58.5	21.8	19	D	D	D	528	14.1	964	15
Marion	163	2 878	259.9	99.2	107	761	59.1	20.2	2 638	91.3	3 348	35
Marshall	79	D	D	D	42	208	16.0	4.2	1 188	37.0	432	4
Mason	38	1 034	93.9	37.5	28	111	9.7	2.5	924	28.8	290	1
Mercer	244	4 629	432.9	161.6	94	831	81.3	25.1	3 006	121.6	726	4
Mineral	64	1 382	70.4	28.4	41	180	14.1	3.8	1 404	46.6	6 556	35
Mingo	48	686	71.0	23.7	21	211	19.8	6.8	891	29.5	0	0
Monongalia	233	13 029	1 513.8	539.2	143	1 104	170.3	29.1	5 347	256.3	8 617	165
Monroe	19	338	18.5	7.2	8	29	1.9	0.5	760	27.3	0	0
Morgan	20	558	44.9	16.3	22	66	4.4	1.1	1 127	42.5	6 169	40
Nicholas	58	1 626	100.1	47.2	35	168	19.3	5.1	1 194	43.8	0	0
Ohio	234	D	D	D	125	1 074	117.3	28.9	2 502	111.7	13 263	59
Pendleton	17	325	18.4	7.9	11	49	5.6	1.3	494	15.4	2 193	21
Pleasants	15	497	21.0	8.8	7	D	D	D	318	11.0	1 125	6
Pocahontas	20	415	24.2	9.9	17	104	7.1	1.8	582	21.8	180	3
Preston	62	1 149	68.3	30.3	34	212	20.4	5.2	1 627	63.3	130	1
Putnam	120	D	D	D	64	418	51.5	12.8	2 943	119.0	23 240	143
Raleigh	284	7 414	735.3	289.5	112	796	87.8	23.4	3 576	131.9	13 374	68
Randolph	107	2 872	183.3	82.9	44	217	19.9	5.5	1 469	46.2	433	6
Ritchie	18	208	11.7	5.3	11	D	D	D	718	27.4	3 413	29
Roane	22	665	48.6	20.5	8	D	D	D	903	31.2	0	0
Summers	20	426	33.6	12.7	14	D	D	D	489	14.8	3 333	22
Taylor	27	552	47.1	17.7	23	D	D	D	720	21.2	175	3
Tucker	10	284	12.8	6.4	11	101	9.8	2.5	391	12.4	0	0
Tyler	12	544	26.7	13.1	16	53	2.7	0.8	364	8.6	1 176	7
Upshur	77	1 626	100.5	53.6	30	124	11.7	2.5	1 239	52.2	11 950	91
Wayne	72	2 462	312.9	122.2	32	150	14.5	4.2	1 531	49.6	1 325	16
Webster	13	462	25.8	12.5	2	D	D	D	334	10.9	0	0
Wetzel	41	717	52.7	19.7	32	152	9.5	2.6	575	15.6	1 050	19
Wirt	5	73	4.1	1.5	2	D	D	D	290	8.7	4 169	52
Wood	282	7 096	635.4	247.0	150	859	83.5	20.6	4 313	182.9	16 192	125
Wyoming	27	778	36.1	17.6	13	D	D	D	795	21.2	277	2
WISCONSIN	14 659	386 141	40 680.6	16 257.6	10 210	62 054	6 406.7	1 732.2	339 963	15 612.6	3 078 382	16 793
Adams	30	454	31.0	12.0	25	121	10.9	3.4	1 056	45.5	11 779	60
Ashland	62	1 629	143.1	62.5	36	121	9.1	2.7	1 101	43.0	1 221	9
Barron	127	2 646	282.3	112.2	96	316	27.8	7.1	3 132	136.5	19 629	142
Bayfield	21	248	12.4	6.7	24	41	5.2	1.4	1 529	60.0	13 215	75
Brown	593	19 588	2 446.2	907.0	433	2 833	241.9	67.9	13 339	671.5	152 599	882
Buffalo	23	293	14.0	6.3	19	D	D	D	1 039	48.9	4 849	41
Burnett	30	587	34.7	16.6	22	63	6.4	1.4	1 141	44.4	13 840	70
Calumet	79	1 175	95.3	37.3	58	261	18.5	5.1	2 442	98.2	40 796	274
Chippewa	175	3 185	260.2	110.4	101	545	58.6	15.3	3 956	195.9	43 753	267
Clark	61	904	54.5	26.0	62	D	D	D	2 234	131.1	4 730	36
Columbia	132	2 563	206.1	91.7	91	398	37.1	9.9	3 669	163.9	33 600	175
Crawford	48	1 129	74.6	35.1	34	107	9.5	2.4	1 062	43.2	5 483	37
Dane	1 217	43 351	5 188.2	2 019.6	1 094	8 233	1 237.6	280.6	36 290	1 775.0	616 349	3 197

		Government employment and payroll, 2012								Local government finances, 2012				
			March payroll (percent of total)							General revenue				
													Taxes	
													Per capita[1] (dollars)	
STATE County	Full-time equivalent employees	March payroll (dollars)	Adminis-tration, judicial, and legal	Police and Corrections	Fire Protection	Highways and transpor-tation	Health and Welfare	Natural resources and utilities	Education and libraries	Total (mil dol)	Inter-govern-mental (mil dol)	Total (mil dol)	Total	Property
	171	172	173	174	175	176	177	178	179	180	181	182	183	184
WEST VIRGINIA— Cont'd														
Brooke	700	2 209 915	5.0	5.9	0.0	2.9	3.5	5.7	73.7	55.0	24.1	20.4	854	747
Cabell	2 866	9 646 891	2.5	7.4	3.4	4.5	2.0	4.8	70.4	298.6	122.6	110.8	1 142	895
Calhoun	235	856 049	5.0	1.6	0.0	0.1	2.0	2.3	88.7	15.2	10.3	3.4	451	395
Clay	380	1 124 468	6.3	1.8	0.0	0.0	5.2	2.2	84.1	27.4	19.9	4.1	442	430
Doddridge	298	898 174	6.8	2.9	0.0	0.0	5.3	2.4	82.0	22.4	10.1	9.7	1 188	1 164
Fayette	1 528	4 553 455	4.1	5.0	0.3	1.5	1.0	5.1	80.2	107.2	57.1	37.1	808	664
Gilmer	243	631 014	10.3	2.7	0.0	0.5	1.7	3.3	80.9	15.5	7.0	5.8	665	612
Grant	680	2 034 759	3.4	1.7	0.0	3.5	45.2	3.2	40.6	59.3	13.0	10.1	852	816
Greenbrier	1 170	3 506 733	7.6	5.7	0.3	0.6	1.5	5.0	78.7	105.9	52.9	33.6	939	809
Hampshire	737	2 045 370	7.4	3.3	0.0	0.4	2.4	3.6	80.9	45.1	25.8	14.3	602	574
Hancock	1 042	3 202 337	5.3	8.5	2.6	2.7	1.3	6.7	66.6	87.7	34.1	29.9	986	818
Hardy	415	1 314 488	8.0	4.5	0.0	1.3	3.9	3.7	78.2	29.6	15.9	10.0	724	691
Harrison	2 683	9 099 926	6.8	6.1	3.8	3.1	1.3	6.8	71.1	209.4	84.1	90.4	1 308	979
Jackson	990	3 308 041	4.4	4.8	0.0	0.8	4.8	4.0	80.4	73.7	39.2	26.2	895	804
Jefferson	1 638	5 678 847	10.1	5.7	0.0	0.8	0.7	3.3	76.3	146.5	52.8	59.7	1 096	978
Kanawha	6 718	23 530 157	5.6	7.2	4.5	3.9	6.5	3.5	65.5	605.2	237.9	258.2	1 344	860
Lewis	544	1 762 505	8.2	4.5	0.7	0.9	5.8	2.3	77.1	39.7	21.5	16.2	990	848
Lincoln	667	2 364 650	4.5	2.3	0.0	1.6	1.0	3.2	85.7	53.6	38.2	11.4	526	507
Logan	1 162	3 939 889	5.9	3.5	0.7	0.2	1.5	5.1	81.4	91.3	48.4	36.2	1 001	949
McDowell	898	2 888 117	9.6	3.1	0.0	0.2	2.7	2.7	81.5	73.1	34.6	20.5	959	873
Marion	1 717	5 814 952	5.2	6.4	2.4	3.4	0.7	6.1	74.1	167.3	77.9	56.2	991	827
Marshall	1 141	3 323 871	5.8	8.5	0.5	1.2	2.2	5.2	75.5	112.7	45.9	46.4	1 420	1 271
Mason	808	2 759 625	5.8	3.8	1.1	0.5	1.8	4.4	81.7	67.3	31.9	24.3	894	820
Mercer	2 791	9 567 647	3.0	2.7	1.1	1.6	34.9	3.3	53.2	241.4	83.0	39.7	634	442
Mineral	785	2 765 305	6.5	4.1	0.0	1.4	1.0	5.1	80.1	68.4	36.1	19.1	682	591
Mingo	985	3 045 535	7.8	3.4	0.6	0.0	0.8	5.9	81.3	90.1	46.0	25.0	959	895
Monongalia	2 739	8 098 611	6.5	7.5	2.5	4.8	3.8	8.2	63.2	216.0	81.0	90.9	906	711
Monroe	414	1 100 622	5.2	1.8	0.0	0.0	1.4	2.7	86.0	27.7	19.5	5.8	431	417
Morgan	518	1 614 401	8.1	3.1	0.0	0.2	3.5	2.2	81.4	35.9	14.8	15.4	884	845
Nicholas	1 289	3 992 571	5.3	3.7	0.0	1.2	46.4	3.6	39.7	111.9	37.5	19.6	748	569
Ohio	2 026	6 205 898	4.8	7.0	5.8	5.4	1.5	21.6	51.3	195.9	55.2	71.7	1 626	865
Pendleton	226	700 064	8.4	1.3	0.0	0.8	2.2	3.9	80.7	15.5	10.2	4.1	537	478
Pleasants	324	1 102 661	10.6	2.5	0.0	0.4	3.5	3.5	79.3	32.6	11.4	12.9	1 701	1 664
Pocahontas	405	1 184 054	6.2	3.0	0.0	0.0	30.8	3.2	53.8	31.5	10.0	9.0	1 038	857
Preston	940	2 685 410	7.1	3.2	0.9	1.2	1.0	4.1	82.2	66.4	36.1	18.3	541	504
Putnam	1 860	6 184 199	4.2	3.8	0.1	0.5	2.8	5.9	81.7	150.7	66.0	58.4	1 035	970
Raleigh	2 440	7 917 866	5.4	5.4	1.7	1.5	2.8	5.6	75.8	223.2	112.9	76.2	964	750
Randolph	999	2 905 572	3.8	2.3	0.5	0.9	3.4	6.7	80.2	72.1	40.5	17.4	593	462
Ritchie	297	909 321	8.7	3.8	0.0	1.0	0.1	2.4	84.1	24.5	12.7	8.6	838	761
Roane	376	1 154 052	6.1	3.9	0.0	1.0	2.1	6.9	79.1	31.0	21.0	6.6	447	384
Summers	287	926 192	9.8	3.8	1.5	1.2	2.4	1.1	80.2	23.4	14.8	6.1	443	343
Taylor	364	895 244	5.7	4.2	1.5	2.1	4.6	11.1	66.9	51.2	18.8	11.0	648	459
Tucker	275	825 484	9.3	1.5	0.0	1.3	7.1	3.8	69.5	25.7	10.2	7.0	1 003	837
Tyler	484	1 507 476	5.2	4.0	0.0	1.0	29.5	1.8	58.1	30.4	11.4	7.0	778	752
Upshur	769	2 460 649	3.9	3.4	0.6	1.2	4.6	5.0	78.3	57.1	29.8	16.0	654	566
Wayne	1 363	3 245 672	6.1	5.2	0.0	0.5	1.6	4.5	81.4	101.8	63.8	27.0	648	573
Webster	358	989 930	7.5	2.5	2.2	1.0	1.1	6.1	78.1	23.4	16.4	3.8	420	365
Wetzel	861	2 789 337	4.5	3.5	0.0	0.7	30.1	6.0	54.4	69.9	21.7	17.0	1 038	859
Wirt	221	579 537	5.0	1.0	0.0	0.0	0.0	1.9	92.1	12.0	8.3	2.5	428	408
Wood	2 923	9 783 040	4.6	5.6	2.1	2.8	2.7	6.6	73.9	223.4	105.4	75.1	866	645
Wyoming	818	2 431 168	7.1	3.1	0.0	0.1	2.6	2.9	82.3	59.6	32.3	21.1	906	862
WISCONSIN	X	X	X	X	X	X	X	X	X	X	X	X	X	X
Adams	752	2 398 694	11.0	12.5	0.7	11.1	19.9	3.2	40.0	75.0	26.6	36.5	1 766	1 664
Ashland	751	2 545 721	7.6	8.1	4.1	10.6	10.7	7.0	49.8	79.8	47.9	22.4	1 398	1 298
Barron	1 838	6 618 589	8.0	8.4	1.3	6.3	10.3	4.0	60.6	190.4	84.2	79.1	1 729	1 625
Bayfield	707	2 315 340	13.5	8.9	0.8	14.7	14.5	4.4	42.0	70.7	26.8	33.0	2 186	2 071
Brown	9 417	41 301 919	3.9	9.3	3.3	3.0	7.6	3.8	67.8	1 182.5	506.0	459.7	1 817	1 685
Buffalo	479	1 597 741	7.7	7.1	0.2	11.0	7.2	3.7	62.0	50.4	28.0	18.4	1 378	1 318
Burnett	687	2 258 798	11.7	9.6	0.3	13.5	8.5	4.2	51.0	63.0	23.4	33.2	2 157	2 077
Calumet	1 110	4 057 590	8.1	8.8	0.2	5.3	10.0	4.7	61.8	111.1	46.0	47.5	956	941
Chippewa	1 941	7 086 033	6.6	8.6	2.6	10.3	6.3	4.1	60.8	196.6	102.1	74.2	1 179	1 086
Clark	1 398	4 771 022	6.3	8.0	0.1	9.4	23.0	4.1	48.3	140.3	73.6	38.4	1 115	1 055
Columbia	2 325	8 247 107	8.1	9.2	0.4	3.5	8.2	3.5	65.9	255.2	98.3	121.8	2 154	2 025
Crawford	593	1 975 908	11.0	8.6	0.2	10.4	5.2	3.1	60.2	77.0	46.6	24.3	1 469	1 348
Dane	19 136	83 118 268	5.7	10.6	3.0	6.3	5.9	6.9	59.9	2 389.4	787.6	1 194.7	2 373	2 225

1. Based on the resident population estimated as of July 1 of the year shown.

	Local government finances, 2012 (cont.)									Government employment, 2014			Presidential election,[2] 2012		
	Direct general expenditure							Debt outstanding					Percent of vote cast:		
			Percent of total for:												
STATE County	Total (mil dol)	Per capita[1] (dollars)	Education	Health and hospitals	Police protection	Public welfare	Highways	Total (mil dol)	Per capita[1] (dollars)	Federal civilian	Federal military	State and local	Democratic	Republican	All other
	185	186	187	188	189	190	191	192	193	194	195	196	197	198	199
WEST VIRGINIA—Cont'd															
Brooke	57.1	2 394	62.3	1.0	9.7	0.1	2.8	99.9	4 186	32	111	924	47.9	50.3	1.8
Cabell	294.4	3 035	46.5	1.1	6.6	0.4	1.3	141.0	1 454	939	578	7 279	44.2	54.3	1.5
Calhoun	16.5	2 170	67.3	0.0	4.6	0.1	0.1	13.0	1 714	16	37	284	40.9	56.2	2.9
Clay	29.0	3 117	78.1	4.6	7.4	0.0	0.0	1.2	128	14	43	464	43.5	53.8	2.7
Doddridge	22.0	2 695	75.1	2.0	2.2	0.0	0.2	8.1	994	11	37	519	24.4	73.5	2.2
Fayette	113.9	2 482	68.7	0.5	5.7	0.0	1.6	47.9	1 045	274	218	2 946	47.7	50.4	1.9
Gilmer	17.4	1 988	61.7	1.3	6.6	0.0	0.4	4.5	516	337	32	648	39.8	57.3	2.9
Grant	59.2	5 007	30.0	52.8	2.8	0.0	0.1	13.9	1 177	48	57	892	23.6	75.1	1.3
Greenbrier	128.0	3 574	63.2	0.6	4.9	0.1	1.0	116.1	3 241	90	171	2 281	42.8	55.1	2.1
Hampshire	52.8	2 229	71.4	1.4	6.3	0.0	0.5	31.5	1 328	40	112	1 323	35.7	62.6	1.7
Hancock	95.4	3 148	57.0	1.9	5.9	0.4	3.5	88.0	2 903	56	146	1 312	41.6	56.9	1.5
Hardy	30.9	2 227	67.5	1.2	3.9	0.1	1.5	61.4	4 426	49	68	778	35.2	62.4	2.4
Harrison	213.8	3 092	57.6	0.7	4.7	0.0	3.1	154.5	2 234	3 990	334	3 821	42.6	55.9	1.5
Jackson	77.4	2 647	65.9	3.3	6.4	0.0	0.9	34.3	1 172	76	142	1 260	39.7	58.4	1.9
Jefferson	165.6	3 037	64.7	0.4	7.7	0.0	1.5	64.5	1 183	799	266	3 037	51.8	47.0	1.1
Kanawha	630.4	3 280	49.5	0.7	6.4	0.0	3.1	316.3	1 646	2 088	954	20 016	49.2	49.6	1.1
Lewis	44.9	2 740	61.9	2.9	2.7	0.3	0.8	5.9	361	54	79	1 389	31.9	65.6	2.5
Lincoln	56.1	2 593	81.6	0.7	1.6	0.1	0.0	11.6	535	36	105	790	44.3	53.2	2.5
Logan	90.2	2 493	72.3	0.9	1.5	0.0	1.1	10.2	281	106	170	2 096	43.6	54.4	2.0
McDowell	77.6	3 641	65.1	0.4	3.6	0.0	1.0	12.9	606	391	98	1 662	53.3	44.8	1.8
Marion	168.8	2 978	58.1	1.2	4.9	0.0	1.1	273.1	4 819	208	272	4 152	49.2	48.7	2.1
Marshall	98.2	3 004	56.7	2.0	5.2	0.2	2.1	187.9	5 751	48	156	1 736	42.8	55.4	1.8
Mason	71.4	2 625	63.5	7.2	3.0	0.1	1.4	29.8	1 097	106	129	1 390	42.3	55.2	2.5
Mercer	244.7	3 914	40.5	39.9	4.2	0.0	1.0	92.7	1 483	178	297	4 819	35.4	63.0	1.6
Mineral	67.8	2 426	67.5	0.9	6.0	0.1	1.0	39.5	1 413	91	132	1 501	32.5	66.0	1.6
Mingo	98.5	3 774	63.6	0.6	2.1	0.1	1.1	29.5	1 128	70	126	1 290	43.0	55.0	2.0
Monongalia	226.2	2 254	54.5	2.7	5.6	0.4	2.1	196.0	1 954	1 216	484	15 506	51.1	47.3	1.6
Monroe	25.2	1 875	79.9	0.7	5.6	0.1	0.8	11.1	828	211	66	466	36.1	60.9	2.9
Morgan	37.8	2 162	73.4	1.3	6.3	0.0	0.5	22.3	1 279	28	85	732	37.4	60.9	1.7
Nicholas	110.3	4 207	42.1	40.3	4.8	0.0	1.0	40.6	1 546	97	126	1 683	46.5	51.3	2.1
Ohio	204.2	4 634	34.0	0.9	7.3	0.2	3.3	309.3	7 017	388	201	3 705	44.0	54.7	1.3
Pendleton	16.3	2 160	74.5	2.0	1.0	0.0	0.2	4.2	549	93	140	339	38.6	59.9	1.5
Pleasants	31.1	4 098	51.5	1.1	2.8	1.2	0.9	168.6	22 201	10	34	641	38.4	59.6	2.1
Pocahontas	32.3	3 712	42.6	29.0	6.8	0.3	0.3	7.5	861	57	41	779	42.5	55.2	2.3
Preston	67.7	2 001	71.9	0.8	3.4	0.0	0.8	71.7	2 120	869	154	1 578	35.6	62.1	2.3
Putnam	187.6	3 324	75.3	0.9	5.2	0.0	0.4	178.8	3 168	197	278	2 079	37.7	61.2	1.1
Raleigh	227.9	2 884	60.0	0.6	7.4	0.1	1.6	109.6	1 387	1 793	389	3 763	36.2	62.1	1.7
Randolph	78.4	2 667	59.6	0.4	4.2	0.1	1.6	33.1	1 126	170	133	1 949	41.9	55.9	2.2
Ritchie	26.4	2 577	64.5	8.2	3.8	0.1	1.0	5.0	492	27	49	500	25.9	72.3	1.7
Roane	32.6	2 218	76.9	1.3	2.2	0.0	1.1	10.7	731	26	71	596	45.1	52.9	2.0
Summers	26.4	1 922	59.2	1.1	4.3	0.0	1.2	7.1	514	45	59	727	43.1	54.4	2.5
Taylor	50.1	2 947	47.3	30.5	3.2	0.0	2.7	25.2	1 485	46	81	1 066	39.7	58.1	2.2
Tucker	25.6	3 656	47.4	5.2	1.8	0.0	0.6	6.1	873	47	33	574	36.7	60.5	2.7
Tyler	31.5	3 490	53.3	28.3	3.8	0.0	0.6	14.5	1 606	17	44	526	33.2	64.6	2.3
Upshur	57.5	2 351	66.4	0.5	2.2	0.1	1.6	23.7	969	121	115	1 172	32.6	65.9	1.5
Wayne	99.1	2 380	75.7	1.2	4.2	0.1	0.6	56.7	1 362	1 406	202	1 711	39.8	58.0	2.2
Webster	23.6	2 613	67.1	0.1	6.5	0.0	0.6	2.3	257	14	43	559	50.8	45.3	3.9
Wetzel	76.4	4 650	43.1	35.0	3.3	0.0	1.3	24.0	1 459	32	78	1 125	45.6	51.8	2.6
Wirt	12.5	2 133	82.9	0.0	0.1	0.0	0.6	1.6	280	13	29	251	33.6	64.3	2.1
Wood	223.9	2 582	63.1	0.1	5.4	0.0	4.0	189.9	2 190	2 189	419	4 337	34.9	63.6	1.5
Wyoming	60.0	2 578	76.4	0.9	3.5	0.1	0.4	21.2	910	107	110	1 093	36.3	61.4	2.3
WISCONSIN	X	X	X	X	X	X	X	X	X	28 740	16 403	389 488	56.2	42.3	1.5
Adams	74.9	3 623	28.9	10.0	7.1	4.2	20.2	54.3	2 624	302	52	872	58.1	39.8	2.1
Ashland	80.3	5 021	41.4	3.1	6.4	7.4	11.1	35.5	2 221	155	43	1 939	67.9	30.7	1.4
Barron	194.8	4 259	48.2	0.6	5.4	8.5	14.2	109.9	2 402	134	124	3 917	52.8	45.7	1.5
Bayfield	74.2	4 916	33.4	7.0	4.7	0.1	19.4	43.1	2 852	118	56	1 401	63.1	35.5	1.4
Brown	1 202.2	4 751	49.8	5.5	6.3	4.1	6.6	1 130.3	4 467	1 133	730	17 423	53.9	44.8	1.3
Buffalo	53.1	3 982	48.0	1.8	3.5	5.5	22.8	23.0	1 723	161	36	676	56.4	41.8	1.8
Burnett	66.0	4 292	45.3	5.0	4.3	3.4	18.5	34.6	2 248	28	42	1 660	49.9	48.3	1.7
Calumet	110.0	2 217	42.6	3.7	6.9	6.6	12.0	109.5	2 206	105	137	1 337	50.2	48.1	1.7
Chippewa	206.5	3 282	53.4	4.8	4.8	2.5	14.8	127.7	2 030	192	170	3 369	53.7	44.6	1.7
Clark	143.7	4 173	42.9	4.9	4.0	14.6	11.4	69.7	2 024	111	94	1 946	52.5	45.0	2.5
Columbia	257.0	4 546	51.3	1.4	5.7	6.8	11.3	215.7	3 815	172	153	3 566	56.9	41.7	1.4
Crawford	74.8	4 519	39.3	3.0	5.3	4.1	18.5	47.8	2 889	64	43	1 025	62.5	35.5	2.1
Dane	2 429.4	4 825	46.4	1.9	6.1	8.3	5.9	2 890.1	5 740	5 085	1 485	74 108	72.8	25.8	1.4

1. Based on the resident population estimated as of July 1 of the year shown.   2.

Table B. States and Counties — **Land Area and Population**

STATE/ County code	CBSA code[1]	County type[2]	STATE County	Land area,[3] (sq km) 2010	Total persons 2015	Rank	Per square kilometer	White	Black	American Indian, Alaska Native	Asian and Pacific Islander	Percent Hispanic or Latino[4]	Under 5 years	5 to 17 years	18 to 24 years	25 to 34 years	35 to 44 years	45 to 54 years
				1	2	3	4	5	6	7	8	9	10	11	12	13	14	15
			WISCONSIN—Cont'd															
55 027	13180	4	Dodge	2 268	88 502	649	39.0	91.3	3.3	0.7	0.9	4.6	4.9	15.9	8.0	12.6	12.6	15.8
55 029	...	6	Door	1 248	27 554	1 508	22.1	95.7	1.0	1.0	0.7	2.7	3.9	12.9	6.2	8.7	9.6	13.7
55 031	20260	2	Douglas	3 378	43 601	1 100	12.9	94.4	2.0	3.4	1.4	1.4	5.3	15.3	9.1	13.0	11.7	14.3
55 033	32860	6	Dunn	2 202	44 497	1 083	20.2	94.2	1.1	0.8	3.3	1.8	5.1	14.9	18.8	11.5	10.7	12.2
55 035	20740	3	Eau Claire	1 652	102 105	588	61.8	92.4	1.7	0.9	4.3	2.3	5.8	14.7	17.1	13.8	10.8	11.9
55 037	27020	9	Florence	1 264	4 464	2 866	3.5	97.8	0.7	1.3	0.9	1.0	3.5	11.6	5.7	8.0	9.1	17.3
55 039	22540	3	Fond du Lac	1 864	101 973	589	54.7	91.7	2.0	0.8	1.6	4.9	5.6	16.3	8.9	11.9	11.8	14.6
55 041	...	9	Forest	2 626	9 057	2 507	3.4	83.0	1.7	15.2	0.9	2.0	5.8	14.8	8.9	9.6	10.1	13.2
55 043	38420	6	Grant	2 970	52 250	956	17.6	96.2	1.6	0.5	1.1	1.4	5.3	15.1	18.2	10.8	9.6	11.9
55 045	31540	6	Green	1 512	37 186	1 247	24.6	95.5	1.1	0.5	1.0	2.9	5.6	17.5	7.2	10.4	12.6	15.1
55 047	...	6	Green Lake	905	18 856	1 879	20.8	93.8	0.8	0.7	0.8	4.6	5.5	17.5	6.4	9.7	10.4	14.1
55 049	31540	2	Iowa	1 975	23 813	1 649	12.1	97.0	0.9	0.5	0.9	1.8	5.9	17.3	7.0	10.8	11.7	15.2
55 051	...	9	Iron	1 964	5 794	2 775	3.0	97.6	0.7	1.6	0.5	1.0	3.8	12.1	5.5	7.8	9.4	14.8
55 053	...	6	Jackson	2 558	20 554	1 801	8.0	87.8	2.6	7.1	0.9	3.3	6.2	16.2	7.7	11.9	11.8	14.6
55 055	48020	4	Jefferson	1 441	84 559	670	58.7	91.1	1.2	0.6	1.2	6.9	5.5	16.9	9.7	11.8	12.6	14.8
55 057	...	7	Juneau	1 986	26 224	1 553	13.2	93.2	2.6	1.8	0.8	2.9	5.5	14.9	6.9	11.2	11.9	15.7
55 059	16980	1	Kenosha	704	168 437	380	239.3	78.6	7.9	0.8	2.2	12.6	5.9	18.2	9.9	12.7	12.9	15.3
55 061	24580	2	Kewaunee	887	20 366	1 814	23.0	96.5	0.7	0.9	0.7	2.3	5.3	16.7	7.1	10.1	11.8	15.2
55 063	29100	3	La Crosse	1 170	118 212	522	101.0	92.0	2.2	0.8	5.1	1.7	5.4	14.9	16.1	13.0	10.9	12.3
55 065	...	8	Lafayette	1 641	16 829	1 989	10.3	95.3	0.6	0.5	0.6	3.8	6.4	18.5	8.3	10.9	10.4	14.3
55 067	...	6	Langlade	2 255	19 223	1 863	8.5	96.2	1.2	1.6	0.6	1.9	5.0	15.0	7.0	9.1	10.2	15.2
55 069	32980	6	Lincoln	2 277	27 980	1 486	12.3	97.3	1.7	0.9	0.8	1.5	4.5	15.9	7.2	9.3	11.1	16.1
55 071	31820	4	Manitowoc	1 526	79 806	697	52.3	92.5	1.0	0.9	3.0	3.5	5.2	16.0	7.6	10.5	11.2	15.4
55 073	48140	3	Marathon	4 001	135 868	467	34.0	90.6	1.3	0.8	6.2	2.6	6.1	17.3	8.1	12.0	12.1	14.8
55 075	31940	6	Marinette	3 624	40 884	1 157	11.3	96.9	0.8	1.2	0.9	1.5	4.7	14.8	7.3	9.9	10.2	14.8
55 077	...	8	Marquette	1 180	15 075	2 092	12.8	95.6	0.8	1.0	0.8	2.9	5.0	14.7	5.9	9.3	10.0	15.5
55 078	43020	8	Menominee	926	4 573	2 861	4.9	14.0	1.3	78.8	2.4	5.3	10.9	21.9	9.9	10.9	9.7	13.0
55 079	33340	1	Milwaukee	625	957 735	49	1 532.4	54.8	27.6	1.2	4.4	14.2	7.2	17.2	10.2	16.3	12.6	12.5
55 081	...	6	Monroe	2 333	45 549	1 060	19.5	92.6	1.9	1.6	1.2	4.0	6.8	18.5	7.4	12.0	11.5	14.1
55 083	24580	2	Oconto	2 585	37 435	1 241	14.5	96.1	0.5	1.8	0.6	1.7	4.8	15.9	6.8	9.6	11.5	16.6
55 085	...	7	Oneida	2 883	35 567	1 286	12.3	96.8	0.7	1.7	0.8	1.4	4.6	12.7	6.6	9.4	9.7	15.1
55 087	11540	3	Outagamie	1 651	183 245	353	111.0	89.7	1.8	2.1	3.9	4.1	6.3	17.8	9.0	13.3	12.7	15.1
55 089	33340	1	Ozaukee	604	87 850	655	145.4	93.3	1.8	0.5	2.7	2.7	5.0	17.0	8.7	9.6	11.2	15.6
55 091	...	8	Pepin	601	7 290	2 646	12.1	97.3	0.6	0.6	0.5	1.4	5.2	16.6	7.1	9.4	10.3	14.3
55 093	33460	1	Pierce	1 486	40 889	1 155	27.5	96.2	1.1	0.9	1.3	1.9	5.3	16.0	16.7	11.0	11.3	13.9
55 095	...	6	Polk	2 367	43 441	1 103	18.4	96.3	0.7	1.4	0.8	1.7	5.1	16.7	7.1	9.8	11.7	15.4
55 097	44620	4	Portage	2 074	70 408	767	33.9	93.0	1.2	0.7	3.3	3.0	5.0	14.7	17.1	11.9	10.6	13.1
55 099	...	9	Price	3 249	13 645	2 193	4.2	96.3	0.7	1.1	1.3	1.6	3.9	13.8	6.3	7.6	10.2	15.6
55 101	39540	3	Racine	861	195 080	335	226.6	74.9	12.3	0.8	1.6	12.5	6.2	17.7	8.4	12.0	12.1	15.1
55 103	...	6	Richland	1 518	17 495	1 947	11.5	96.0	1.0	0.6	0.8	2.4	5.4	16.9	7.9	9.9	10.9	13.3
55 105	27500	3	Rock	1 860	161 448	396	86.8	85.4	6.0	0.7	1.6	8.2	6.0	17.8	8.7	12.3	12.5	14.2
55 107	...	6	Rusk	2 366	14 124	2 157	6.0	96.6	0.9	1.0	0.7	1.7	5.3	15.8	6.8	8.5	10.0	14.2
55 109	33460	1	St. Croix	1 871	87 513	660	46.8	95.5	1.2	0.7	1.5	2.2	6.2	19.7	7.2	12.2	14.2	15.3
55 111	12660	4	Sauk	2 152	63 642	826	29.6	92.6	1.2	1.5	1.0	4.9	6.0	17.0	7.5	12.2	12.1	14.2
55 113	...	9	Sawyer	3 256	16 376	2 020	5.0	80.5	1.0	18.9	0.6	2.1	5.5	14.4	6.6	8.7	9.9	13.8
55 115	43020	6	Shawano	2 313	41 304	1 144	17.9	89.2	0.7	8.8	0.8	2.6	5.4	16.5	7.3	10.3	11.1	15.2
55 117	43100	3	Sheboygan	1 324	115 569	532	87.3	86.8	2.3	0.7	5.5	6.0	5.6	17.2	8.3	11.5	11.9	15.0
55 119	...	6	Taylor	2 525	20 455	1 810	8.1	97.1	0.5	0.5	0.6	1.8	5.8	17.9	6.8	9.9	11.5	15.0
55 121	...	8	Trempealeau	1 898	29 550	1 439	15.6	91.9	0.7	0.5	0.8	6.8	6.8	17.5	7.5	10.9	11.9	14.4
55 123	...	6	Vernon	2 050	30 506	1 420	14.9	97.4	0.8	0.6	0.6	1.6	7.2	18.7	7.0	9.6	10.5	13.6
55 125	...	9	Vilas	2 219	21 387	1 760	9.6	86.8	0.7	11.5	0.7	1.9	4.1	12.7	6.0	7.4	8.7	14.3
55 127	48580	4	Walworth	1 438	102 804	580	71.5	86.6	1.5	0.6	1.3	11.1	5.1	16.8	12.9	10.6	11.5	14.1
55 129	...	6	Washburn	2 065	15 552	2 072	7.5	96.4	0.7	2.2	0.8	1.6	5.0	14.6	6.0	8.9	9.9	14.2
55 131	33340	1	Washington	1 116	133 674	472	119.8	94.1	1.5	0.5	1.6	3.0	5.3	17.7	7.2	10.7	12.5	16.6
55 133	33340	1	Waukesha	1 423	396 488	174	278.6	90.5	1.8	0.5	3.8	4.6	5.1	17.2	7.7	10.5	12.1	15.8
55 135	...	6	Waupaca	1 937	51 945	962	26.8	95.6	0.7	1.0	0.7	3.0	5.2	16.0	7.4	10.1	11.4	15.4
55 137	...	8	Waushara	1 622	24 033	1 643	14.8	90.6	2.3	0.9	0.6	6.4	4.8	13.9	6.6	9.7	10.6	15.4
55 139	36780	3	Winnebago	1 125	169 546	378	150.7	90.9	2.6	1.0	3.2	3.9	5.6	15.2	12.5	13.1	11.9	14.0
55 141	49220	4	Wood	2 054	73 435	743	35.8	94.0	1.1	1.0	2.2	2.7	5.7	16.1	7.6	11.1	11.0	15.0
56 000	...	X	WYOMING	251 470	586 107	X	2.3	85.6	1.8	2.9	1.5	9.8	6.5	17.1	9.8	14.1	12.0	12.6
56 001	29660	4	Albany	11 069	37 956	1 223	3.4	84.9	2.0	1.3	4.1	9.3	5.2	11.3	28.0	16.5	9.6	9.1
56 003	...	9	Big Horn	8 125	12 022	2 296	1.5	88.8	1.1	1.5	0.7	9.1	6.5	18.7	7.7	10.4	10.7	12.4
56 005	23940	5	Campbell	12 439	49 220	994	4.0	89.5	1.1	1.9	1.2	8.2	8.0	20.0	8.9	16.8	13.3	13.1
56 007	...	7	Carbon	20 455	15 559	2 071	0.8	79.3	1.7	1.6	1.3	17.3	6.2	17.6	8.0	14.9	12.1	12.9
56 009	...	6	Converse	11 020	14 236	2 153	1.3	89.3	1.1	1.6	0.9	7.7	6.9	17.7	8.0	12.9	12.1	14.0

1. CBSA = Core Based Statistical Area. See Appendix A for explanation. See Appendix B for list of metropolitan areas with component counties.   2. County type code from the Economic Research Service of USDA Rural-Urban Continuum Codes. See Appendix A for definition.   3. Dry land or land partially or temporarily covered by water.   4. May be of any race.

STATE County	55 to 64 years (16)	65 to 74 years (17)	75 years and over (18)	Percent female (19)	2000 (20)	2010 (21)	2000–2010 (22)	2010–2015 (23)	Births (24)	Deaths (25)	Net migration (26)	Number (27)	Persons per household (28)	Family households (29)	Female family householder[1] (30)	One person (31)
WISCONSIN—Cont'd																
Dodge	14.0	8.5	7.8	47.3	85 897	88 761	3.3	-0.3	4 467	4 536	-300	32 979	2.53	66.7	8.0	28.8
Door	18.5	15.3	11.1	50.8	27 961	27 785	-0.6	-0.8	1 077	1 664	311	13 154	2.08	63.1	5.7	30.5
Douglas	15.0	9.3	7.0	50.1	43 287	44 159	2.0	-1.3	2 311	2 206	-620	18 598	2.28	61.6	10.6	32.5
Dunn	12.2	8.3	6.4	49.6	39 858	43 857	10.0	1.5	2 402	1 607	-266	16 460	2.47	64.3	7.8	25.7
Eau Claire	12.0	7.8	6.3	50.7	93 142	98 885	6.2	3.3	6 217	4 039	1 125	40 072	2.40	58.8	8.1	30.5
Florence	19.0	15.0	10.8	48.6	5 088	4 423	-13.1	0.9	138	256	129	1 844	2.39	71.7	6.8	23.2
Fond du Lac	14.3	8.9	7.7	50.8	97 296	101 633	4.5	0.3	5 818	4 848	-533	41 290	2.38	67.1	9.1	27.7
Forest	15.9	12.1	9.7	49.0	10 024	9 304	-7.2	-2.7	579	578	-225	3 717	2.40	67.0	9.4	28.6
Grant	12.7	8.3	8.1	47.8	49 597	51 208	3.2	2.0	2 835	2 514	725	19 472	2.43	62.5	6.7	27.7
Green	14.7	9.3	7.6	50.4	33 647	36 842	9.5	0.9	2 047	1 775	-26	14 748	2.48	68.3	8.0	25.9
Green Lake	15.6	11.4	9.4	49.7	19 105	19 051	-0.3	-1.0	1 071	1 175	-90	7 898	2.38	67.3	8.2	28.9
Iowa	15.4	9.5	7.2	50.1	22 780	23 687	4.0	0.5	1 405	1 048	-313	9 656	2.44	67.8	6.7	26.1
Iron	18.4	14.9	13.3	49.9	6 861	5 916	-13.8	-2.1	201	434	107	2 958	1.96	60.0	7.6	34.0
Jackson	14.0	10.1	7.5	46.4	19 100	20 441	7.0	0.6	1 282	1 023	-119	8 038	2.39	65.0	10.0	28.8
Jefferson	13.7	8.7	6.3	50.1	74 021	83 681	13.1	1.0	4 714	3 277	-422	32 267	2.50	67.1	9.3	26.2
Juneau	14.8	10.9	8.1	47.0	24 316	26 664	9.7	-1.7	1 410	1 424	-359	10 074	2.50	65.9	9.3	28.8
Kenosha	12.6	7.0	5.5	50.6	149 577	166 426	11.3	1.2	10 415	7 052	-1 299	62 573	2.60	66.5	13.5	26.6
Kewaunee	14.8	10.1	8.8	49.3	20 187	20 574	1.9	-1.0	1 027	960	-266	8 125	2.50	67.8	5.4	27.7
La Crosse	12.5	7.9	6.8	51.0	107 120	114 638	7.0	3.1	6 641	5 038	1 882	46 303	2.40	60.5	8.5	28.6
Lafayette	14.8	8.5	8.0	49.3	16 137	16 836	4.3	0.0	1 101	686	-431	6 612	2.53	69.7	7.3	25.9
Langlade	16.2	11.9	10.4	49.6	20 740	19 977	-3.7	-3.8	1 022	1 221	-605	8 742	2.22	62.3	8.4	30.7
Lincoln	16.1	10.6	9.2	49.2	29 641	28 743	-3.0	-2.7	1 399	1 679	-450	12 483	2.23	66.1	6.8	27.3
Manitowoc	15.6	9.9	8.7	50.1	82 887	81 442	-1.7	-2.0	4 332	4 306	-1 662	33 917	2.35	64.2	6.9	30.8
Marathon	13.7	8.6	7.3	49.7	125 834	134 063	6.5	1.3	8 456	5 921	-908	53 392	2.49	67.7	8.5	26.9
Marinette	16.5	12.1	9.6	49.8	43 384	41 749	-3.8	-2.1	1 985	2 567	-217	18 419	2.19	61.2	7.4	34.1
Marquette	17.2	12.9	9.7	49.2	15 832	15 404	-2.7	-2.1	805	892	-213	6 322	2.38	67.8	7.1	26.9
Menominee	11.1	8.2	4.4	50.7	4 562	4 232	-7.2	8.1	519	222	42	1 238	3.49	72.9	23.0	20.5
Milwaukee	11.8	6.5	5.7	51.7	940 164	947 736	0.8	1.1	73 815	42 602	-19 534	381 446	2.44	57.1	17.0	34.9
Monroe	13.9	9.0	6.7	49.6	40 899	44 675	9.2	2.0	3 231	2 137	-231	17 727	2.50	67.0	9.7	27.5
Oconto	16.3	10.9	7.6	49.8	35 634	37 660	5.7	-0.6	1 870	1 790	-232	15 441	2.41	70.1	6.3	24.4
Oneida	18.0	13.4	10.5	49.9	36 776	35 998	-2.1	-1.2	1 586	2 305	296	15 519	2.26	64.0	5.6	31.4
Outagamie	12.7	7.4	5.7	50.2	160 971	176 695	9.8	3.7	12 001	6 603	1 127	70 144	2.51	67.6	8.7	26.2
Ozaukee	15.5	9.7	7.8	50.9	82 317	86 395	5.0	1.7	4 213	3 718	944	34 319	2.50	70.3	7.4	25.3
Pepin	16.4	10.9	9.8	50.0	7 213	7 469	3.5	-2.4	409	386	-223	3 027	2.39	67.1	5.2	28.2
Pierce	13.2	7.3	5.2	50.4	36 804	41 019	11.5	-0.3	2 038	1 312	-867	15 198	2.51	67.1	7.6	22.5
Polk	15.6	10.5	7.9	49.5	41 319	44 205	7.0	-1.7	2 268	2 196	-836	18 225	2.37	68.2	9.0	26.2
Portage	13.1	8.2	6.4	49.8	67 182	70 019	4.2	0.6	3 658	2 715	-540	27 954	2.39	62.4	7.4	27.6
Price	18.6	13.1	10.9	49.3	15 822	14 159	-10.5	-3.6	568	888	-177	6 654	2.05	63.9	5.6	31.2
Racine	13.8	8.3	6.5	50.5	188 831	195 428	3.5	-0.2	12 624	8 830	-4 011	75 078	2.53	65.8	11.9	28.4
Richland	16.2	10.1	9.5	49.7	17 924	18 021	0.5	-2.9	957	898	-566	7 489	2.33	67.1	7.9	29.0
Rock	13.3	8.3	6.8	50.9	152 307	160 331	5.3	0.7	10 178	7 489	-1 580	63 385	2.48	66.5	12.7	27.1
Rusk	16.7	11.8	10.3	49.8	15 347	14 755	-3.9	-4.3	743	926	-392	6 306	2.26	66.5	9.3	28.3
St. Croix	12.9	7.3	4.9	50.1	63 155	84 345	33.6	3.8	5 627	2 874	347	32 199	2.63	73.8	9.4	20.8
Sauk	13.9	9.4	7.6	50.3	55 225	61 976	12.2	2.7	4 023	3 011	523	25 400	2.43	65.7	9.7	27.7
Sawyer	17.8	14.1	9.3	49.3	16 196	16 557	2.2	-1.1	879	1 039	21	7 439	2.17	66.5	11.6	27.1
Shawano	14.4	10.9	8.9	50.0	40 664	41 955	3.2	-1.6	2 286	2 353	-601	17 019	2.41	68.3	8.9	26.5
Sheboygan	14.4	8.8	7.4	49.8	112 646	115 507	2.5	0.1	6 645	5 547	-1 165	46 433	2.41	66.0	8.8	28.2
Taylor	14.9	9.2	9.1	49.1	19 680	20 689	5.1	-1.1	1 177	936	-539	8 784	2.32	65.9	8.0	28.3
Trempealeau	14.0	9.0	8.0	49.6	27 010	28 816	6.7	2.5	2 069	1 412	130	11 776	2.44	67.3	8.9	27.2
Vernon	15.0	9.9	8.5	50.2	28 056	29 771	6.1	2.5	2 197	1 524	-18	11 815	2.51	67.0	7.6	27.5
Vilas	17.7	16.8	12.3	49.5	21 033	21 430	1.9	-0.2	950	1 489	563	10 552	2.00	61.6	7.6	32.5
Walworth	13.6	8.8	6.5	50.0	93 759	102 228	9.0	0.6	5 435	4 675	-245	39 846	2.51	66.8	9.6	25.4
Washburn	17.5	14.0	9.9	50.4	16 036	15 911	-0.8	-2.3	810	1 072	-110	7 259	2.14	63.0	8.3	31.4
Washington	14.3	8.8	6.9	50.3	117 493	131 885	12.2	1.4	7 013	5 466	137	52 554	2.50	72.3	7.9	22.8
Waukesha	15.0	9.0	7.4	50.9	360 767	389 938	8.1	1.7	19 928	16 577	2 761	153 882	2.52	70.5	6.7	24.7
Waupaca	15.1	10.2	9.3	49.7	51 731	52 410	1.3	-0.9	2 737	3 672	450	21 262	2.38	67.3	8.5	27.2
Waushara	16.5	12.9	9.6	47.3	23 154	24 496	5.8	-1.9	1 204	1 367	-233	9 786	2.37	66.0	6.3	29.2
Winnebago	12.9	7.8	6.9	49.7	156 763	166 994	6.5	1.5	9 868	7 442	34	68 484	2.33	60.2	8.5	31.1
Wood	14.9	9.7	8.9	50.6	75 555	74 749	-1.1	-1.8	4 381	3 915	-1 744	32 115	2.28	63.6	7.9	31.0
WYOMING	13.8	8.3	5.7	49.0	493 782	563 767	14.2	4.0	39 862	23 752	6 061	225 514	2.49	65.3	8.8	27.7
Albany	10.5	6.0	3.8	47.7	32 014	36 299	13.4	4.6	2 212	972	425	15 440	2.26	48.4	5.3	31.6
Big Horn	14.4	11.2	8.0	49.7	11 461	11 668	1.8	3.0	739	703	304	4 363	2.66	67.6	6.0	29.2
Campbell	12.8	4.8	2.4	48.0	33 698	46 133	36.9	6.7	3 940	1 319	438	17 316	2.71	70.7	8.7	21.7
Carbon	14.5	8.6	5.2	45.6	15 639	15 885	1.6	-2.1	1 072	645	-726	6 161	2.42	65.5	9.1	26.8
Converse	14.2	8.3	5.8	49.0	12 052	13 833	14.8	2.9	1 005	627	51	5 721	2.43	64.9	7.8	31.8

1. No spouse present.

Table B. States and Counties — **Population, Vital Statistics, Medicare, and Crime**

STATE County	Persons in group quarters, 2015	Daytime population, 2010–2014 Number	Employ-ment/resi-dence ratio	Births, 2015 Total	Rate¹	Deaths, 2015 Number	Rate¹	Persons under 65 with no health insurance, 2014 Number	Percent	Medicare, 2015 Total Beneficiaries	Enrolled in Original Medicare	Enrolled in Medicare Advantage	Serious crimes known to police,² 2014 Total Number	Rate³
	32	33	34	35	36	37	38	39	40	41	42	43	44	45
WISCONSIN—Cont'd														
Dodge	6 276	82 336	0.85	868	9.8	869	9.8	5 242	7.6	11 668	7 906	3 762	1 186	1 343
Door	340	27 070	0.94	202	7.3	334	12.1	1 817	9.0	7 833	5 813	2 020	308	1 102
Douglas	1 350	40 464	0.84	419	9.6	391	9.0	3 038	8.6	9 584	5 866	3 718	2 116	4 829
Dunn	3 289	40 688	0.85	459	10.3	306	6.9	2 611	7.5	6 787	4 486	2 301	810	1 833
Eau Claire	4 769	106 844	1.12	1 209	11.9	753	7.4	7 116	8.6	19 863	14 707	5 156	2 169	2 124
Florence	54	3 740	0.61	27	6.1	39	8.7	363	11.0	931	692	239	107	2 351
Fond du Lac	3 469	97 187	0.91	1 101	10.8	880	8.6	6 167	7.5	20 348	10 784	9 564	1 801	1 768
Forest	360	8 918	0.92	116	12.8	100	11.0	959	13.7	2 442	1 641	801	123	1 354
Grant	5 062	47 546	0.85	555	10.7	482	9.3	4 123	10.5	10 903	6 949	3 954	623	1 266
Green	357	34 481	0.87	374	10.1	333	9.0	2 512	8.2	6 834	5 627	1 207	509	1 370
Green Lake	192	17 879	0.87	204	10.8	230	12.2	1 591	10.8	4 533	2 171	2 362	330	1 742
Iowa	201	22 856	0.93	255	10.7	185	7.8	1 578	8.0	3 955	2 589	1 366	250	1 051
Iron	93	5 454	0.81	39	6.7	75	12.8	452	10.7	1 693	1 007	686	98	1 665
Jackson	1 318	19 703	0.91	248	12.0	175	8.5	1 902	12.0	3 636	2 160	1 476	365	1 764
Jefferson	3 445	74 219	0.77	874	10.3	648	7.7	5 413	7.8	14 754	10 430	4 324	1 269	1 608
Juneau	1 667	25 045	0.87	256	9.7	240	9.1	2 065	10.2	5 803	4 569	1 234	389	1 467
Kenosha	4 385	148 314	0.75	1 987	11.8	1 326	7.9	12 303	8.6	24 003	18 046	5 957	3 750	2 231
Kewaunee	173	18 354	0.78	191	9.4	186	9.1	1 229	7.4	4 089	2 179	1 910	200	976
La Crosse	5 785	125 287	1.14	1 246	10.6	944	8.0	6 568	6.9	20 136	11 300	8 836	2 559	2 183
Lafayette	99	13 981	0.66	225	13.4	133	7.9	1 845	13.2	2 949	2 076	873	168	1 015
Langlade	239	19 215	0.94	184	9.5	228	11.8	1 485	10.0	4 813	2 851	1 962	554	2 842
Lincoln	628	25 965	0.81	258	9.2	303	10.8	1 844	8.3	7 256	4 339	2 917	NA	NA
Manitowoc	1 040	77 190	0.91	807	10.1	814	10.2	4 991	7.7	17 356	10 062	7 294	1 594	1 980
Marathon	1 624	137 104	1.03	1 590	11.7	1 064	7.8	8 307	7.3	23 101	12 974	10 127	1 906	1 424
Marinette	718	42 718	1.07	366	8.9	449	10.9	2 707	8.5	11 668	7 498	4 170	694	1 669
Marquette	147	12 924	0.66	153	10.2	159	10.6	1 240	10.7	4 570	3 149	1 421	203	1 342
Menominee	40	5 267	1.63	108	23.7	55	12.1	534	13.9	639	461	178	33	761
Milwaukee	24 181	989 481	1.08	13 932	14.5	7 990	8.3	91 000	11.1	141 092	88 210	52 882	48 786	5 092
Monroe	788	46 640	1.07	608	13.4	397	8.7	3 775	10.0	7 453	4 880	2 573	630	1 401
Oconto	282	28 912	0.54	361	9.6	359	9.6	2 605	8.6	7 225	3 626	3 599	NA	NA
Oneida	541	36 454	1.04	291	8.2	441	12.4	2 254	8.4	11 188	7 653	3 535	616	1 729
Outagamie	3 000	183 429	1.05	2 297	12.6	1 257	6.9	10 983	7.1	31 356	12 877	18 479	3 201	1 766
Ozaukee	2 046	82 182	0.89	802	9.1	723	8.2	3 712	5.3	16 301	10 448	5 853	797	913
Pepin	125	6 555	0.77	74	10.1	88	12.0	540	9.4	1 657	1 265	392	74	1 008
Pierce	2 498	29 906	0.50	366	8.9	256	6.3	2 307	6.9	6 836	4 031	2 805	604	1 475
Polk	426	39 215	0.78	438	10.1	426	9.8	3 356	9.6	8 493	5 096	3 397	573	1 323
Portage	3 578	70 668	1.01	675	9.6	501	7.1	4 454	7.8	10 980	6 547	4 433	1 068	1 515
Price	177	14 216	1.05	107	7.8	156	11.4	945	9.2	3 843	2 388	1 455	200	1 457
Racine	4 787	182 311	0.86	2 380	12.2	1 618	8.3	15 323	9.5	36 899	23 651	13 248	4 833	2 479
Richland	345	16 494	0.84	187	10.6	172	9.8	1 432	10.2	3 377	2 781	596	81	459
Rock	2 709	148 984	0.84	1 966	12.2	1 408	8.7	12 011	8.9	29 682	20 055	9 627	4 401	2 735
Rusk	160	14 210	0.96	142	10.0	169	11.9	1 230	11.1	3 356	1 997	1 359	195	1 362
St. Croix	807	74 095	0.75	1 067	12.2	557	6.4	4 450	5.9	10 908	6 254	4 654	1 176	1 406
Sauk	767	65 401	1.08	767	12.1	577	9.1	5 499	10.5	11 537	7 076	4 461	1 635	2 576
Sawyer	312	16 985	1.07	162	9.9	199	12.1	1 601	13.0	4 200	2 889	1 311	234	1 418
Shawano	743	36 861	0.76	427	10.3	404	9.8	3 598	10.9	8 528	3 894	4 634	570	1 371
Sheboygan	2 825	115 859	1.01	1 219	10.6	1 027	8.9	7 662	8.1	21 663	12 693	8 970	2 162	1 883
Taylor	209	19 894	0.93	225	11.0	177	8.6	1 718	10.3	3 474	1 898	1 576	198	961
Trempealeau	450	29 056	0.99	396	13.4	261	8.8	2 294	9.5	6 093	3 706	2 387	238	799
Vernon	355	27 398	0.79	418	13.7	305	10.0	3 251	13.3	6 115	2 971	3 144	289	1 038
Vilas	205	21 246	0.99	182	8.5	281	13.1	2 024	13.5	6 928	4 985	1 943	235	1 100
Walworth	2 626	96 807	0.88	1 011	9.8	894	8.7	9 172	10.8	16 694	13 328	3 366	1 694	1 642
Washburn	204	15 560	0.97	152	9.7	193	12.4	1 192	10.1	5 993	3 934	2 059	324	2 073
Washington	1 148	116 100	0.77	1 336	10.0	1 066	8.0	6 226	5.6	23 280	14 796	8 484	1 805	1 595
Waukesha	5 419	418 931	1.13	3 791	9.4	3 253	8.2	15 907	4.9	73 331	46 885	26 446	4 860	1 369
Waupaca	1 584	49 402	0.89	524	10.1	691	13.3	3 291	7.9	13 006	6 041	6 965	1 005	1 923
Waushara	1 222	21 269	0.69	230	9.5	241	10.0	2 001	11.4	5 386	2 832	2 554	317	1 305
Winnebago	8 035	178 996	1.13	1 847	10.9	1 410	8.3	9 756	7.1	28 254	13 041	15 213	3 126	1 837
Wood	795	78 434	1.12	792	10.8	735	10.0	4 294	7.2	19 077	9 611	9 466	1 308	1 773
WYOMING	14 143	581 944	1.02	7 695	13.1	4 606	7.9	69 582	14.2	89 707	85 729	3 978	12 619	2 160
Albany	2 241	36 783	0.98	428	11.3	174	4.6	4 252	13.4	3 891	3 638	253	962	2 568
Big Horn	183	11 712	0.98	144	12.0	122	10.2	1 775	18.7	2 365	2 319	46	74	692
Campbell	422	51 632	1.16	737	15.1	286	5.9	5 025	11.3	3 868	3 814	54	1 283	2 650
Carbon	788	15 393	0.95	224	14.3	133	8.5	2 088	16.2	2 407	2 272	135	279	1 835
Converse	103	13 923	0.99	206	14.5	117	8.2	1 455	12.1	2 114	2 087	27	300	2 089

1. Per 1,000 estimated resident population.   2. Data for serious crimes have not been adjusted for underreporting; this may affect comparability between geographic areas and over time.
3. Per 100,000 population estimated by the FBI.

Table B. States and Counties — Crime, Education, Money Income, and Poverty

STATE County	Serious crimes known to police, 2014 (cont.)[1] Rate[2] Violent	Property	Enrollment[3] Total	Percent private	Attainment[4] (percent) High school graduate or less	Bachelor's degree or more	Local government expenditures,[5] 2012–2013 Total current spending (mil dol)	Current spending per student (dollars)	Per capita income[6] (dollars)	Households Median income (dollars)	Mean income (dollars)	Percent with income of $200,000 or more	Income and poverty, 2014 Median household income (dollars)	Percent below poverty level All persons	Children under 18 years	Children 5 to 17 years in families
	46	47	48	49	50	51	52	53	54	55	56	57	58	59	60	61
WISCONSIN—Cont'd																
Dodge	74	1 270	19 596	18.4	52.0	15.7	119.2	10 975	24 864	53 189	63 248	1.6	54 359	9.9	13.6	12.2
Door	43	1 059	4 871	9.7	40.5	29.4	44.8	12 537	30 216	50 078	64 445	3.1	49 717	11.0	16.5	15.0
Douglas	194	4 635	10 759	9.1	39.4	21.9	70.0	10 800	24 821	44 956	56 856	1.4	46 475	13.9	20.9	18.9
Dunn	156	1 677	14 741	6.4	42.9	25.3	63.0	10 296	23 324	49 897	60 424	1.5	52 224	13.9	16.4	15.1
Eau Claire	130	1 994	31 094	10.4	33.8	31.1	156.7	11 008	25 808	48 209	63 209	2.4	48 102	14.4	15.1	14.2
Florence	66	2 285	854	4.9	50.3	15.4	6.6	15 656	24 690	49 703	57 980	1.4	44 562	12.8	19.5	17.6
Fond du Lac	200	1 568	24 308	22.3	48.0	20.9	146.4	10 908	27 158	54 529	66 159	1.9	52 149	9.9	13.6	12.6
Forest	198	1 155	1 921	7.5	54.5	14.2	20.5	12 692	20 890	40 331	49 761	0.8	41 418	17.0	25.7	24.2
Grant	122	1 144	15 083	11.1	48.4	20.2	82.7	11 739	22 343	47 266	57 075	1.4	46 972	15.0	19.0	17.8
Green	89	1 281	8 821	8.0	47.4	20.9	65.2	11 238	27 575	54 868	67 600	2.3	53 328	8.7	11.7	10.0
Green Lake	53	1 689	3 954	17.5	54.7	17.3	34.1	10 708	25 486	46 502	60 954	2.0	51 175	11.3	19.9	17.5
Iowa	135	917	5 493	12.6	43.2	23.2	43.2	12 240	27 052	54 390	66 528	2.4	58 419	8.9	12.6	11.5
Iron	119	1 546	957	6.1	43.9	20.6	10.4	13 610	25 053	41 900	50 904	1.1	39 408	15.6	23.7	22.1
Jackson	82	1 682	4 105	7.6	56.4	13.9	34.4	10 839	22 169	44 699	55 437	1.8	47 985	14.0	20.8	19.8
Jefferson	117	1 491	22 627	18.2	45.3	23.3	149.9	10 954	26 349	54 522	67 041	2.4	56 365	10.6	13.7	12.7
Juneau	219	1 248	5 616	11.8	56.8	12.4	43.8	11 691	22 439	45 135	55 602	1.4	45 158	13.1	20.8	19.3
Kenosha	207	2 024	46 654	14.0	44.0	24.3	326.7	11 024	26 560	54 653	68 882	3.1	53 945	15.4	22.4	19.3
Kewaunee	44	932	4 595	12.4	54.2	14.4	37.8	10 727	25 651	53 023	63 360	1.9	56 160	8.9	11.5	10.3
La Crosse	124	2 060	35 894	14.5	34.3	30.8	191.4	11 985	26 719	50 769	65 828	2.7	49 790	12.6	12.2	10.9
Lafayette	72	942	3 852	11.5	53.0	17.3	33.1	11 752	24 370	50 154	61 477	2.0	52 260	11.7	18.5	18.2
Langlade	67	2 776	4 053	19.2	56.0	13.5	36.3	11 658	23 081	40 994	51 648	1.2	40 968	15.9	23.4	20.7
Lincoln	NA	NA	6 176	15.0	51.6	15.2	48.6	10 453	25 371	49 189	59 070	1.4	48 881	10.9	16.9	15.4
Manitowoc	156	1 823	18 340	19.9	49.9	19.6	117.0	10 719	26 085	48 629	60 762	1.6	48 430	10.8	15.3	14.2
Marathon	96	1 328	33 532	13.2	46.8	23.0	219.9	11 071	27 723	53 779	68 945	2.4	54 400	9.9	14.8	13.2
Marinette	41	1 628	9 120	13.4	53.1	13.9	67.6	10 841	23 751	41 364	52 310	1.3	43 701	13.4	19.7	17.4
Marquette	13	1 329	2 911	12.3	56.3	13.0	20.5	11 278	23 914	46 875	56 664	0.9	43 661	13.0	22.3	20.9
Menominee	0	761	1 238	5.5	50.6	16.5	15.9	20 015	15 201	37 740	49 289	0.3	36 774	29.1	44.2	45.2
Milwaukee	1 002	4 089	271 062	25.5	42.4	28.7	1 637.9	12 389	24 622	43 385	59 527	2.4	42 946	22.0	32.2	31.1
Monroe	131	1 270	10 682	13.5	50.9	17.5	76.3	10 830	23 406	49 752	58 785	1.3	52 978	14.4	23.1	22.1
Oconto	NA	NA	8 040	7.5	53.8	15.4	48.7	11 212	26 230	51 695	63 026	1.5	52 776	10.5	14.8	13.3
Oneida	205	1 524	6 757	14.5	41.2	24.4	58.7	13 477	26 352	45 736	58 828	1.9	49 040	12.6	18.5	17.1
Outagamie	144	1 622	47 062	16.8	41.0	26.9	346.6	10 210	28 441	58 421	71 244	2.7	59 377	10.0	12.5	11.6
Ozaukee	56	857	23 371	25.1	26.2	46.4	139.3	10 833	42 537	75 643	105 954	10.3	77 364	5.0	5.7	5.0
Pepin	109	899	1 568	18.6	52.2	17.1	15.4	13 112	24 945	49 321	59 129	2.0	53 828	12.1	19.9	18.2
Pierce	76	1 399	13 365	9.3	39.2	26.3	78.6	10 516	28 559	61 613	75 785	3.0	68 471	10.8	10.6	8.8
Polk	235	1 087	9 771	8.1	47.4	19.2	84.7	11 227	26 356	49 679	62 584	2.1	52 411	11.2	15.2	13.0
Portage	99	1 416	21 552	8.0	42.2	28.3	95.1	10 026	25 462	50 837	62 649	2.2	52 075	15.4	14.9	11.9
Price	87	1 369	2 542	12.3	52.2	16.1	24.0	11 693	24 535	43 581	52 213	1.2	42 659	13.0	20.1	17.7
Racine	200	2 279	50 168	18.8	43.9	23.4	330.7	11 143	27 732	55 055	70 116	3.0	54 782	13.1	18.8	17.5
Richland	17	442	4 009	19.2	51.2	16.7	19.7	11 420	23 691	44 785	56 328	1.5	44 026	13.5	21.6	19.4
Rock	232	2 503	40 804	13.5	48.5	20.0	306.9	11 026	24 715	49 645	61 661	1.8	51 237	14.9	23.7	20.9
Rusk	133	1 229	2 817	14.0	57.3	14.2	25.9	12 938	21 475	38 728	48 938	0.9	39 999	16.9	29.6	25.7
St. Croix	62	1 344	22 944	12.9	33.2	32.4	141.5	9 883	33 035	70 313	86 876	5.3	75 920	4.9	6.3	5.8
Sauk	95	2 482	14 631	11.7	47.0	21.9	130.1	10 900	25 709	50 982	62 073	1.7	50 243	11.9	17.4	15.9
Sawyer	188	1 230	3 213	9.5	43.2	22.1	27.0	11 945	24 423	40 658	54 719	2.1	40 701	17.0	28.7	26.3
Shawano	63	1 308	9 247	13.0	55.8	15.1	60.6	10 808	23 843	46 903	57 575	1.8	47 841	11.2	17.5	15.7
Sheboygan	162	1 721	28 270	17.4	46.5	22.5	210.0	10 803	26 580	53 029	65 123	2.0	55 335	9.1	13.2	11.4
Taylor	87	873	4 668	13.9	59.2	13.8	33.4	10 986	23 742	45 424	56 297	2.0	48 683	11.7	18.0	16.5
Trempealeau	57	742	6 474	8.9	51.7	18.1	64.1	10 972	25 490	49 493	62 401	1.8	50 266	12.2	16.7	15.7
Vernon	79	959	6 824	23.4	49.9	20.1	40.2	11 352	23 968	47 075	60 506	1.9	46 943	18.0	30.0	29.6
Vilas	47	1 054	4 006	8.2	41.4	24.9	41.5	15 314	26 016	40 501	53 586	1.8	41 211	14.8	23.6	21.9
Walworth	73	1 569	28 538	10.1	42.3	26.5	183.3	11 299	27 321	53 998	69 163	2.9	52 852	13.7	16.2	14.3
Washburn	218	1 856	2 961	10.9	47.5	20.5	32.2	12 310	25 313	41 749	55 195	1.8	42 079	13.4	21.8	20.0
Washington	79	1 516	32 449	20.8	37.8	27.9	207.6	10 359	33 173	67 650	82 753	4.5	69 346	5.9	7.3	6.4
Waukesha	67	1 302	100 586	23.3	28.8	41.0	678.3	10 747	38 151	76 319	96 033	7.7	76 584	5.8	7.3	6.1
Waupaca	140	1 783	11 493	13.9	53.8	16.5	98.3	10 976	26 816	52 007	63 784	1.7	52 850	10.4	15.6	14.4
Waushara	91	1 214	4 790	14.3	54.4	15.2	31.3	11 459	23 195	43 982	56 046	1.4	46 835	13.9	22.1	21.2
Winnebago	172	1 665	44 008	11.6	42.3	26.1	232.2	10 204	27 295	51 949	66 155	2.5	52 711	12.1	15.5	14.1
Wood	34	1 739	16 940	14.0	47.8	18.9	144.8	11 516	26 302	48 241	60 321	1.8	51 003	11.3	17.3	15.5
WYOMING	195	1 965	147 086	9.4	37.1	25.1	1 445.3	15 700	29 381	58 252	72 367	3.2	58 291	11.2	13.7	12.2
Albany	152	2 416	16 458	8.0	20.2	48.8	61.1	16 376	24 401	42 298	57 747	2.5	42 838	24.0	15.2	14.3
Big Horn	122	571	2 991	3.5	42.5	20.0	41.8	17 146	24 960	52 432	62 373	2.3	50 437	10.7	14.6	13.5
Campbell	174	2 477	12 202	8.3	44.7	19.2	129.9	14 923	34 342	78 609	91 231	4.8	79 358	7.1	9.2	8.5
Carbon	303	1 532	3 509	9.3	46.6	17.2	44.1	17 597	26 673	56 933	66 461	1.6	58 225	12.3	14.0	12.2
Converse	272	1 818	3 116	11.4	43.4	19.6	39.0	16 117	30 380	61 820	72 676	2.7	63 166	9.3	12.5	11.3

1. Data for serious crimes have not been adjusted for underreporting; this may affect comparability between geographic areas and over time.   2. Per 100,000 population estimated by the FBI.
3. All persons 3 years old and over enrolled in nursery school through college.   4. Persons 25 years old and over.   5. Elementary and secondary education expenditures.
6. Based on population estimated by the American Community Survey, 2010–2014.

STATE County	Personal income, 2014										Earnings, 2014		
	Total (mil dol)	Percent change, 2013–2014	Per capita[1] Dollars	Per capita[1] Rank	Wages and salaries (mil dol)	Supplements to wages and salaries; employer contributions (mil dol) Pension and insurance	Government social insurance	Proprietors' income (mil dol)	Dividends, interest, and rent (mil dol)	Personal transfer receipts (mil dol)	Total (mil dol)	Contributions for government social insurance (mil dol) From employee and self-employed	From employer
	62	63	64	65	66	67	68	69	70	71	72	73	74
WISCONSIN—Cont'd													
Dodge	3 527	3.5	39 816	1 204	1 527	299	126	399	521	615	2 351	144	126
Door	1 396	2.8	50 276	368	461	98	41	109	402	275	709	47	41
Douglas	1 604	4.0	36 697	1 646	703	152	62	63	244	420	980	66	62
Dunn	1 579	5.6	35 640	1 835	711	166	58	121	248	333	1 056	63	58
Eau Claire	4 349	4.3	42 818	870	2 516	484	197	356	851	742	3 553	215	197
Florence	180	3.8	40 094	1 161	27	8	2	3	37	47	41	4	2
Fond du Lac	4 318	4.6	42 434	908	2 040	386	168	339	674	780	2 932	177	168
Forest	316	4.2	34 585	2 006	112	33	9	31	61	99	185	12	9
Grant	1 982	2.5	38 237	1 427	712	190	56	274	327	384	1 232	70	56
Green	1 603	1.5	43 254	819	604	132	49	162	281	262	946	55	49
Green Lake	820	2.1	43 544	795	265	57	22	72	180	163	416	28	22
Iowa	1 010	3.6	42 374	916	418	79	36	121	178	159	653	37	36
Iron	278	5.2	46 905	528	57	14	5	53	59	74	129	9	5
Jackson	847	5.4	40 994	1 061	371	84	29	99	155	165	583	34	29
Jefferson	3 333	3.2	39 495	1 250	1 354	286	109	251	478	599	2 001	124	109
Juneau	957	4.0	36 256	1 730	364	88	29	82	137	230	563	34	29
Kenosha	6 680	3.5	39 748	1 217	2 468	487	199	425	896	1 215	3 580	227	199
Kewaunee	862	6.0	42 152	937	288	63	23	107	132	150	479	24	23
La Crosse	4 993	3.9	42 314	925	3 030	594	246	287	950	865	4 158	251	246
Lafayette	705	-4.1	41 818	968	148	37	12	145	118	116	342	16	12
Langlade	764	3.1	39 355	1 273	270	59	22	97	129	202	448	29	22
Lincoln	1 097	4.1	38 486	1 397	444	94	36	70	161	263	645	43	36
Manitowoc	3 408	4.7	42 519	898	1 516	296	123	252	545	661	2 187	133	123
Marathon	5 831	5.5	42 941	852	3 180	582	251	521	917	936	4 534	272	251
Marinette	1 635	3.9	39 593	1 237	801	167	65	123	266	426	1 155	74	65
Marquette	533	2.5	35 432	1 870	127	31	11	35	90	148	204	15	11
Menominee	(3)117	(3)3.0	(3)25 919	(3)3 033	(3)73	(3)31	(3)5	(3)1	(3)18	(3)44	(3)111	(3)6	(3)5
Milwaukee	39 697	3.2	41 507	1 009	25 938	4 443	2 014	3 182	6 628	8 751	35 576	2 153	2 014
Monroe	1 637	4.3	36 074	1 772	818	192	69	130	299	334	1 209	70	69
Oconto	1 486	2.5	39 713	1 222	307	78	26	116	215	312	527	36	26
Oneida	1 603	3.6	45 061	673	681	130	54	143	332	384	1 008	68	54
Outagamie	7 947	4.1	43 665	789	4 909	849	396	537	1 212	1 091	6 692	402	396
Ozaukee	6 221	3.6	71 126	55	1 930	346	150	291	1 585	602	2 717	170	150
Pepin	304	5.0	41 395	1 021	85	19	7	19	52	73	129	9	7
Pierce	1 644	5.1	40 129	1 155	393	116	31	104	262	251	644	39	31
Polk	1 729	5.5	39 807	1 207	616	137	51	85	304	373	889	58	51
Portage	2 785	3.8	39 519	1 245	1 487	296	120	186	471	509	2 089	124	120
Price	540	4.7	39 454	1 252	220	49	18	34	97	150	322	21	18
Racine	8 079	3.2	41 398	1 020	3 610	693	279	280	1 337	1 581	4 862	308	279
Richland	671	4.9	37 994	1 454	233	59	19	85	102	158	396	22	19
Rock	6 240	1.9	38 713	1 362	2 839	543	230	273	1 109	1 271	3 885	249	230
Rusk	479	6.3	33 424	2 211	184	48	16	41	76	142	289	18	16
St. Croix	3 916	5.7	45 139	667	1 322	260	107	179	566	492	1 869	115	107
Sauk	2 582	3.2	40 745	1 095	1 388	263	115	238	451	464	2 004	123	115
Sawyer	644	1.8	39 154	1 304	234	57	19	47	148	187	358	25	19
Shawano	1 535	4.0	36 916	1 613	454	105	37	164	236	347	761	48	37
Sheboygan	5 341	4.9	46 328	573	2 764	486	220	584	980	818	4 054	247	220
Taylor	704	4.3	34 260	2 069	301	64	26	82	115	152	473	28	26
Trempealeau	1 207	4.6	40 910	1 071	587	117	47	55	211	238	807	49	47
Vernon	1 079	3.7	35 532	1 852	315	75	25	114	167	236	528	32	25
Vilas	908	6.1	42 455	902	248	60	21	72	263	263	401	31	21
Walworth	4 198	3.4	40 546	1 114	1 612	357	133	258	822	722	2 361	145	133
Washburn	633	3.6	40 337	1 135	206	51	17	36	133	192	311	22	17
Washington	6 471	3.7	48 564	454	2 434	431	193	286	1 087	867	3 344	211	193
Waukesha	24 080	3.5	60 945	117	12 871	1 978	1 010	1 390	4 745	2 691	17 249	1 057	1 010
Waupaca	2 136	4.5	41 031	1 057	789	174	64	98	373	493	1 125	73	64
Waushara	887	1.9	36 693	1 648	216	55	18	63	157	215	352	24	18
Winnebago	6 865	3.5	40 498	1 120	4 610	805	357	335	1 253	1 140	6 108	373	357
Wood	2 886	4.2	39 202	1 296	1 696	325	133	105	477	635	2 258	141	133
WYOMING	31 885	5.6	54 584	X	14 413	2 401	1 408	3 193	9 397	3 900	21 415	1 219	1 408
Albany	1 432	4.0	37 870	1 474	655	164	65	75	365	207	960	52	65
Big Horn	436	3.5	36 508	1 685	198	40	20	31	74	89	289	18	20
Campbell	2 353	6.5	48 691	450	1 791	242	167	199	361	212	2 399	137	167
Carbon	777	7.3	48 991	439	379	84	39	45	173	101	548	31	39
Converse	726	8.9	51 512	311	361	60	35	52	118	97	507	30	35

1. Based on the resident population estimated as of July 1 of the year shown.　　3. Menominee county included with Shawano county.

Table B. States and Counties — Earnings, Social Security, and Housing

STATE County	Earnings, 2014 (cont.) Percent by selected industries									Social Security beneficiaries, December 2014		Supplemental Security Income recipients, December 2014	Housing units, 2015	
	Farm	Mining	Construction	Manufacturing	Information: professional, scientific, technical services	Retail trade	Finance, insurance, real estate and leasing	Health care and social assistance	Government	Number	Rate[1]		Total	Percent change, 2010–2014
	75	76	77	78	79	80	81	82	83	84	85	86	87	88
WISCONSIN—Cont'd														
Dodge	3.4	D	13.7	27.8	2.9	5.1	2.1	9.6	14.1	17 785	201	818	37 414	1.1
Door	3.3	D	7.4	19.4	D	10.0	5.4	11.6	15.6	9 035	326	277	24 427	1.9
Douglas	0.1	D	9.2	11.4	3.0	6.6	2.8	7.6	21.2	9 515	218	1 179	22 901	0.3
Dunn	6.4	D	4.9	19.0	4.0	5.4	3.1	10.6	24.8	9 495	214	700	18 092	0.7
Eau Claire	0.5	D	5.8	9.6	5.7	7.3	7.0	22.5	16.1	19 335	190	1 999	43 193	2.5
Florence	0.8	0.0	7.0	20.6	D	D	5.3	6.0	34.3	1 405	315	62	4 822	0.9
Fond du Lac	5.2	0.7	7.2	26.2	4.3	6.3	4.3	12.6	12.7	21 155	207	1 483	44 620	1.6
Forest	0.3	D	3.5	7.6	D	4.4	2.3	D	54.5	2 830	310	236	9 075	1.2
Grant	12.7	D	5.0	12.5	D	6.3	4.4	8.2	26.4	10 875	210	799	21 815	1.1
Green	7.0	D	3.9	21.5	D	13.0	2.8	13.1	13.4	7 885	213	445	15 851	0.0
Green Lake	4.0	1.2	9.0	18.2	D	6.0	5.4	14.8	15.4	5 040	268	308	10 630	0.1
Iowa	11.9	D	5.6	9.8	2.2	29.4	2.4	D	12.7	5 045	212	326	10 771	0.5
Iron	1.3	D	9.3	26.8	D	7.3	D	11.3	18.3	2 140	362	139	6 024	0.4
Jackson	8.6	D	16.1	10.7	1.2	4.4	2.2	D	23.5	4 580	222	408	9 775	0.6
Jefferson	2.2	D	6.4	32.1	4.4	6.4	3.8	8.7	12.7	16 690	198	969	35 313	0.5
Juneau	7.2	0.0	3.7	24.5	1.2	5.7	2.5	D	27.2	6 635	252	605	14 825	1.1
Kenosha	0.4	D	4.3	16.0	4.8	7.6	3.0	13.2	18.5	29 430	175	3 683	69 711	0.6
Kewaunee	25.0	D	4.8	22.2	D	3.6	2.4	D	14.7	4 630	227	200	9 344	0.4
La Crosse	0.4	D	5.2	12.7	5.0	6.1	6.4	21.6	15.6	22 020	187	2 201	49 443	2.2
Lafayette	35.1	D	4.7	13.4	D	3.2	D	2.3	17.4	3 580	213	209	7 216	-0.2
Langlade	6.8	D	5.6	18.4	2.3	14.0	4.3	D	14.8	5 700	294	442	12 435	0.6
Lincoln	1.5	D	6.0	26.0	1.6	6.8	12.4	8.1	17.2	7 650	272	472	16 902	0.7
Manitowoc	6.5	0.2	5.7	30.3	2.7	5.2	2.5	10.6	12.2	19 750	246	1 371	37 207	0.0
Marathon	3.3	0.2	5.0	22.1	5.6	7.1	9.5	15.3	11.3	27 475	203	2 096	58 613	1.5
Marinette	3.2	D	4.8	37.7	2.3	6.6	2.8	D	11.7	12 235	297	828	30 384	0.0
Marquette	11.4	0.0	2.9	31.9	2.5	5.0	3.2	D	21.1	4 615	308	303	9 859	-0.4
Menominee	[3]0.0	[3]0.0	[3]0.3	[3]D	[3]D	[3]D	[3]D	[3]0.5	[3]95.5	885	195	225	2 265	0.5
Milwaukee	0.0	0.1	2.8	13.1	10.2	4.6	10.5	15.0	13.2	161 290	168	43 037	416 951	-0.3
Monroe	4.8	2.1	5.3	18.3	D	5.3	2.5	7.0	29.6	9 080	200	847	19 578	0.9
Oconto	9.9	D	6.5	21.7	D	7.0	2.3	D	21.0	9 560	255	630	23 751	0.3
Oneida	0.9	0.0	7.8	10.4	4.5	13.4	4.9	21.2	15.3	11 190	315	592	30 507	1.3
Outagamie	1.1	0.1	8.4	21.3	7.1	6.2	8.0	11.6	11.7	32 255	177	2 526	75 693	3.5
Ozaukee	0.9	D	4.3	25.9	9.8	5.6	9.2	12.7	9.5	18 135	207	508	36 930	1.8
Pepin	9.5	0.0	8.6	5.8	D	7.7	4.2	10.9	19.6	2 240	305	122	3 624	1.3
Pierce	6.4	D	5.3	13.5	3.2	4.5	3.5	4.5	37.2	6 940	170	394	16 328	1.2
Polk	3.4	0.9	4.4	23.1	D	6.3	3.4	17.1	18.3	10 865	250	658	24 307	0.2
Portage	4.1	D	3.0	12.6	4.5	7.1	18.9	10.1	17.1	13 585	193	879	30 421	1.2
Price	4.3	D	1.7	39.6	5.7	5.3	2.5	10.4	15.8	4 395	321	297	11 199	0.7
Racine	0.3	0.1	4.7	35.8	4.2	5.7	4.2	12.0	14.0	40 735	209	5 321	82 323	0.2
Richland	12.7	D	5.1	23.7	1.7	7.5	2.3	11.4	20.3	4 500	255	442	8 878	0.1
Rock	1.6	0.3	5.5	17.4	5.4	6.9	3.3	15.8	15.6	34 315	212	3 904	68 313	-0.2
Rusk	7.9	D	2.5	28.7	D	5.7	2.3	D	22.2	4 050	282	367	9 032	1.7
St. Croix	1.9	0.0	6.7	23.1	6.3	7.7	4.5	12.8	14.8	13 875	160	614	34 932	2.8
Sauk	2.7	D	10.1	18.4	4.3	8.3	4.5	10.7	15.8	13 800	218	907	29 910	0.7
Sawyer	1.6	D	6.4	10.9	4.2	9.8	5.1	D	28.8	5 350	326	369	16 274	1.9
Shawano	11.6	0.0	5.0	17.4	D	6.7	3.1	10.1	19.1	10 385	250	717	20 701	-0.1
Sheboygan	1.8	D	4.7	41.0	3.1	5.6	6.1	11.4	9.3	24 485	212	1 787	50 589	-0.3
Taylor	10.6	D	5.7	23.6	D	5.9	3.2	9.6	12.2	4 450	216	260	10 606	0.2
Trempealeau	4.1	D	3.0	44.9	2.1	4.1	2.5	D	16.5	6 210	210	421	12 864	1.9
Vernon	14.0	0.0	4.6	7.3	3.6	6.7	4.5	D	18.9	6 910	228	568	13 822	0.8
Vilas	1.0	D	8.8	3.5	2.3	7.8	3.5	6.9	30.6	8 850	414	432	25 535	1.7
Walworth	2.1	D	4.7	24.7	3.6	6.6	3.7	7.5	21.9	19 885	192	1 249	51 792	0.5
Washburn	2.4	D	2.5	19.6	D	10.4	2.4	D	26.3	5 315	339	393	13 085	0.8
Washington	1.2	0.2	5.2	29.8	4.6	6.9	6.9	11.0	10.9	26 280	197	902	55 759	1.9
Waukesha	0.1	0.2	7.4	21.2	11.0	6.0	9.5	9.8	7.3	80 025	202	2 884	163 376	1.6
Waupaca	4.6	D	4.0	37.2	3.5	6.0	2.9	9.5	18.3	13 415	258	876	25 480	0.3
Waushara	11.4	D	5.8	15.1	D	6.1	2.5	D	24.0	6 980	289	396	14 910	0.4
Winnebago	0.5	D	6.0	30.5	7.1	4.7	5.1	9.6	12.6	32 875	194	2 473	74 551	1.7
Wood	2.1	D	4.8	17.8	8.0	5.5	2.8	21.8	14.4	17 940	244	1 512	34 560	1.4
WYOMING	1.6	17.7	9.1	3.9	5.5	5.5	5.1	6.8	23.7	101 296	173	6 786	269 448	2.9
Albany	3.0	0.7	4.6	2.0	7.6	5.8	4.9	8.0	49.7	4 400	116	299	18 777	4.7
Big Horn	3.5	16.9	8.1	6.3	D	3.9	2.8	D	31.6	2 695	226	153	5 363	-0.3
Campbell	0.2	40.3	9.1	2.0	3.2	4.0	2.3	2.6	14.9	4 985	103	306	19 759	4.2
Carbon	2.3	5.1	12.8	D	3.5	5.3	2.5	D	25.0	2 610	165	160	8 580	0.0
Converse	1.3	28.0	11.3	2.5	3.0	3.5	2.9	D	21.9	2 410	170	133	6 534	2.0

1. Per 1,000 resident population estimated as of July 1 of the year shown.   3. Menominee county included with Shawano county.

Table B. States and Counties — Housing, Labor Force, and Employment

	Housing units, 2010–2014								Civilian labor force, 2015				Civilian employment,[6] 2010–2014		
	Occupied units										Unemployment			Percent	
		Owner-occupied				Renter-occupied									
				Median owner cost as a percent of income											Con-struction, produc-tion, and mainte-nance occu-pations
STATE County	Total	Percent	Median value[1]	With a mort-gage	Without a mort-gage[2]	Median rent[3]	Median rent as a per-cent of income[2]	Sub-stand-ard units[4] (percent)	Total	Percent change, 2014–2015	Total	Rate[5]	Total	Manage-ment, business, science and arts	
	89	90	91	92	93	94	95	96	97	98	99	100	101	102	103

STATE County	89	90	91	92	93	94	95	96	97	98	99	100	101	102	103
WISCONSIN—Cont'd															
Dodge	32 979	73.5	152 900	24.2	14.4	759	26.9	1.6	47 535	-0.1	2 129	4.5	42 867	27.1	35.8
Door	13 154	77.9	192 900	25.1	14.2	697	27.7	1.2	15 503	0.7	1 049	6.8	13 198	30.0	24.9
Douglas	18 598	67.9	130 500	22.7	13.2	691	31.1	2.2	23 275	-1.3	1 177	5.1	21 266	30.2	23.3
Dunn	16 460	67.2	154 900	23.7	13.5	732	27.8	2.2	23 693	0.1	1 081	4.6	22 270	30.2	28.0
Eau Claire	40 072	62.1	149 300	21.8	13.0	725	31.0	2.0	58 136	0.1	2 245	3.9	53 993	33.6	21.1
Florence	1 844	85.7	142 600	24.6	13.3	572	24.1	1.8	2 226	0.9	152	6.8	1 927	27.4	32.1
Fond du Lac	41 290	71.0	146 300	22.5	13.2	695	26.7	1.9	57 286	0.2	2 354	4.1	52 643	28.8	33.3
Forest	3 717	77.1	122 200	24.5	13.6	470	22.6	2.9	4 035	0.1	304	7.5	3 648	28.3	31.9
Grant	19 472	70.8	129 500	22.2	13.0	662	28.3	2.9	28 199	1.5	1 239	4.4	25 841	29.5	30.9
Green	14 748	74.2	157 400	23.3	15.4	684	27.5	1.2	21 252	1.8	812	3.8	19 509	31.1	30.7
Green Lake	7 898	75.2	138 400	22.8	13.2	586	25.7	2.5	10 103	0.4	547	5.4	9 024	25.1	36.5
Iowa	9 656	75.6	161 300	24.5	14.8	700	26.5	1.5	13 844	2.0	588	4.2	12 479	32.6	27.5
Iron	2 958	80.2	105 600	22.8	13.7	506	28.7	3.4	2 666	-0.7	236	8.9	2 501	27.7	28.9
Jackson	8 038	73.0	124 800	24.6	15.0	605	26.8	3.6	10 355	1.3	504	4.9	9 164	26.3	31.9
Jefferson	32 267	71.4	174 600	24.1	14.6	761	27.6	1.4	45 644	-0.5	1 950	4.3	43 639	30.1	29.0
Juneau	10 074	76.5	116 400	25.2	14.6	688	28.1	2.9	13 566	1.2	709	5.2	11 732	24.1	30.9
Kenosha	62 573	66.9	163 800	24.4	14.8	851	32.4	2.3	87 432	0.3	4 509	5.2	78 293	33.4	24.5
Kewaunee	8 125	80.8	145 600	23.4	14.3	622	28.1	1.9	11 014	1.4	450	4.1	10 206	28.9	37.4
La Crosse	46 303	64.8	154 500	21.6	12.8	741	29.3	1.7	66 728	-0.1	2 600	3.9	61 875	35.0	22.3
Lafayette	6 612	77.6	122 800	24.4	14.2	628	23.9	2.1	9 740	3.5	363	3.7	8 686	29.9	34.6
Langlade	8 742	77.0	109 900	22.3	13.1	596	31.0	3.7	9 526	-0.6	588	6.2	8 944	25.4	33.2
Lincoln	12 483	76.2	131 800	22.0	13.4	614	24.5	1.9	15 382	-0.1	793	5.2	13 844	24.7	34.1
Manitowoc	33 917	75.8	124 900	21.9	13.5	604	26.1	1.5	42 020	-1.4	2 139	5.1	40 666	26.7	35.0
Marathon	53 392	73.5	142 900	21.8	12.6	690	28.7	1.7	73 833	0.8	3 000	4.1	69 743	32.9	28.2
Marinette	18 419	77.3	107 100	22.7	14.0	594	29.2	1.7	20 851	-1.3	1 231	5.9	18 600	23.6	38.6
Marquette	6 322	80.6	139 500	25.0	15.3	728	24.2	2.5	7 452	1.6	464	6.2	6 884	23.1	37.7
Menominee	1 238	73.8	91 100	17.5	12.5	506	19.9	9.0	1 589	-0.8	157	9.9	1 418	28.3	23.3
Milwaukee	381 446	50.7	154 400	24.7	15.5	802	32.6	3.0	477 696	-0.4	27 915	5.8	438 689	35.1	21.0
Monroe	17 727	66.9	135 600	22.8	13.0	759	25.5	4.0	23 088	2.3	1 031	4.5	20 944	28.6	31.7
Oconto	15 441	83.4	149 900	23.6	13.9	610	28.5	1.7	20 492	0.6	1 064	5.2	18 891	27.5	36.6
Oneida	15 519	83.1	162 000	24.5	14.8	742	32.6	0.7	18 554	-1.3	1 096	5.9	16 684	29.7	24.7
Outagamie	70 144	71.6	156 200	22.2	12.9	727	25.3	2.0	101 958	0.5	4 081	4.0	94 662	32.8	27.5
Ozaukee	34 319	76.9	247 300	21.9	12.7	820	26.4	0.5	48 136	0.3	1 794	3.7	44 944	46.5	16.7
Pepin	3 027	80.3	133 000	24.1	14.7	580	28.0	2.3	4 113	1.9	175	4.3	3 648	31.6	31.1
Pierce	15 198	72.9	187 400	23.5	13.7	760	29.8	1.5	24 426	1.6	963	3.9	22 521	30.3	29.6
Polk	18 225	77.6	155 500	26.6	14.8	720	28.0	1.8	24 694	0.9	1 209	4.9	21 038	29.0	33.5
Portage	27 954	68.3	147 600	21.8	11.9	664	29.7	1.6	39 748	1.0	1 843	4.6	35 983	30.9	24.9
Price	6 654	78.7	116 900	23.7	14.3	576	27.1	1.9	6 822	0.5	311	4.6	6 685	27.5	38.1
Racine	75 078	69.8	167 300	23.5	14.5	783	30.3	1.8	99 446	-0.5	5 650	5.7	90 567	32.9	27.2
Richland	7 489	74.0	123 900	23.8	13.6	608	28.8	3.9	9 262	-0.6	397	4.3	8 442	27.7	35.8
Rock	63 385	69.8	131 500	23.5	13.0	744	30.4	2.0	83 596	1.4	4 370	5.2	75 359	28.9	30.2
Rusk	6 306	77.6	102 600	25.3	14.0	654	28.4	3.3	7 065	0.8	394	5.6	6 446	23.5	39.1
St. Croix	32 199	77.4	205 700	22.7	12.0	881	28.2	2.2	48 903	1.1	1 880	3.8	45 355	37.6	23.5
Sauk	25 400	68.8	168 200	23.5	14.2	737	29.4	2.2	35 233	0.6	1 468	4.2	32 811	27.6	27.9
Sawyer	7 439	75.0	159 200	24.7	13.4	646	30.3	3.7	7 896	-0.9	627	7.9	7 084	29.9	24.0
Shawano	17 019	76.3	130 600	23.5	14.5	616	25.5	1.3	21 438	0.5	1 056	4.9	20 018	27.5	32.1
Sheboygan	46 433	71.2	150 800	22.2	13.9	660	25.6	1.7	61 368	0.1	2 338	3.8	58 747	29.2	32.2
Taylor	8 784	77.1	127 400	24.0	13.9	557	27.5	2.6	10 828	1.6	479	4.4	10 095	29.1	41.5
Trempealeau	11 776	72.8	137 200	22.8	14.6	644	25.4	2.7	16 621	0.4	660	4.0	14 918	30.1	36.5
Vernon	11 815	78.3	139 800	23.6	13.7	626	27.3	6.4	15 449	2.5	643	4.2	13 387	30.9	31.7
Vilas	10 552	76.6	193 500	27.6	15.2	676	30.3	1.5	9 973	-1.2	713	7.1	8 948	30.8	22.1
Walworth	39 846	68.0	191 400	25.4	14.3	820	30.0	2.6	56 684	-0.7	2 701	4.8	52 183	29.8	27.5
Washburn	7 259	78.1	142 200	24.9	14.3	644	28.0	2.2	7 959	0.2	436	5.5	6 794	29.0	29.7
Washington	52 554	78.0	217 900	23.4	13.6	833	26.6	0.9	75 988	0.2	2 879	3.8	71 182	35.4	25.9
Waukesha	153 882	76.8	249 900	22.6	13.3	925	28.0	1.3	221 126	0.1	8 502	3.8	206 915	43.5	17.3
Waupaca	21 262	75.8	136 100	22.7	14.4	672	24.0	1.6	27 215	-0.5	1 275	4.7	25 525	25.2	37.7
Waushara	9 786	81.6	138 100	24.3	14.5	659	30.2	2.0	11 534	-0.9	733	6.4	10 327	24.3	36.9
Winnebago	68 484	65.9	142 100	21.9	13.3	673	26.7	1.4	91 499	-0.2	3 937	4.3	85 353	29.7	27.4
Wood	32 115	74.7	120 000	20.8	12.2	613	28.4	1.3	34 506	-0.9	1 909	5.5	36 164	30.1	30.4
WYOMING	225 514	69.3	189 300	21.1	10.0	778	25.7	2.5	306 016	-0.3	12 752	4.2	291 552	32.8	28.1
Albany	15 440	50.1	205 300	22.3	10.0	727	38.5	2.1	20 883	1.7	637	3.1	19 833	45.1	16.3
Big Horn	4 363	75.1	137 000	21.2	10.0	593	20.5	2.8	5 596	0.1	242	4.3	5 277	33.0	31.7
Campbell	17 316	74.1	206 500	19.3	10.0	921	25.4	3.3	25 930	-1.4	987	3.8	26 028	25.3	39.1
Carbon	6 161	69.7	140 900	19.6	10.0	811	22.3	2.6	8 619	2.0	309	3.6	7 984	27.3	35.4
Converse	5 721	73.7	187 200	20.0	10.6	628	22.1	3.3	8 370	0.2	300	3.6	7 386	27.9	37.0

1. Specified owner-occupied units.   2. A value of 10.0 represents 10 percent or less; a value of 50.0 represents 50 percent or more.   3. Specified renter-occupied units.
4. Overcrowded or lacking complete plumbing facilities.   5. Percent of civilian labor force.   6. Persons 16 years old and over.

Table B. States and Counties — Nonfarm Employment and Agriculture

STATE County	Private nonfarm establishments, employment and payroll, 2014									Agriculture, 2012			
	Number of establishments	Employment						Annual payroll		Farms			
		Total	Health care and social assistance	Manufacturing	Retail trade	Finance and insurance	Professional, scientific, and technical services	Total (mil dol)	Average per employee (dollars)	Number	Percent with:		Farm operators whose principal occupation is farming (percent)
											Fewer than 50 acres	500 acres or more	
	104	105	106	107	108	109	110	111	112	113	114	115	116
WISCONSIN—Cont'd													
Dodge	1 717	31 088	4 155	9 854	3 323	674	501	1 468	47 235	2 012	36.9	9.7	47.5
Door	1 285	9 714	1 545	1 596	1 710	349	226	333	34 309	803	40.6	6.2	45.0
Douglas	1 018	13 400	2 040	1 534	2 040	354	389	523	39 009	364	29.4	5.8	42.0
Dunn	901	13 803	2 571	2 626	1 787	470	407	506	36 689	1 404	24.0	12.0	45.4
Eau Claire	2 679	49 935	11 002	4 911	7 054	2 743	2 027	1 827	36 595	1 313	31.7	4.0	42.3
Florence	103	589	D	123	D	D	D	15	24 920	90	31.1	0.0	38.9
Fond du Lac	2 339	42 213	6 327	8 847	5 772	1 649	1 488	1 581	37 447	1 399	31.9	10.7	59.0
Forest	244	1 635	222	318	261	D	78	46	28 201	127	21.3	9.4	54.3
Grant	1 211	13 659	2 194	2 266	2 547	661	481	450	32 932	2 436	25.6	10.7	53.8
Green	943	13 024	2 028	3 610	1 605	346	301	484	37 132	1 545	42.0	7.4	45.8
Green Lake	480	5 473	966	1 200	936	282	70	200	36 544	608	26.8	13.2	48.4
Iowa	558	8 627	1 014	1 012	D	188	122	329	38 089	1 588	25.8	9.9	47.2
Iron	207	1 393	311	158	237	D	26	36	25 602	61	34.4	8.2	32.8
Jackson	430	6 364	D	693	815	187	D	278	43 608	864	23.0	11.5	49.4
Jefferson	1 910	29 525	4 014	9 468	4 036	640	656	1 107	37 506	1 225	39.7	6.9	46.1
Juneau	545	6 384	1 092	2 159	1 003	D	D	227	35 550	827	29.7	8.1	39.4
Kenosha	3 060	49 250	8 311	6 939	9 553	917	1 329	1 879	38 153	359	51.5	11.1	46.8
Kewaunee	455	5 179	434	1 888	602	D	D	203	39 219	734	27.9	9.4	49.7
La Crosse	3 008	61 229	10 891	7 222	8 905	3 157	1 858	2 316	37 822	748	23.7	10.0	46.9
Lafayette	358	2 930	251	692	399	147	56	87	29 701	1 252	28.9	13.1	57.1
Langlade	554	6 407	991	1 519	1 280	D	114	219	34 107	396	24.2	14.6	56.3
Lincoln	670	8 672	943	2 463	1 346	D	118	315	36 357	449	28.1	6.2	48.8
Manitowoc	1 774	30 080	4 418	10 481	3 611	791	539	1 225	40 739	1 224	39.1	7.9	47.7
Marathon	3 243	62 652	10 183	15 907	9 567	3 714	1 905	2 530	40 387	2 266	23.2	7.5	55.0
Marinette	1 086	16 245	2 735	6 269	2 066	400	285	619	38 079	535	31.2	11.8	51.6
Marquette	291	3 614	330	1 339	291	D	67	116	32 106	478	28.0	9.2	52.1
Menominee	24	D	D	D	46	NA	D	D	D	5	60.0	0.0	0.0
Milwaukee	19 407	447 390	89 206	46 104	43 505	34 822	22 291	22 610	50 539	82	76.8	2.4	59.8
Monroe	950	15 392	D	3 590	1 909	426	504	601	39 023	1 926	25.7	6.1	44.3
Oconto	777	6 968	1 569	2 123	952	D	141	223	31 955	929	35.1	9.1	48.1
Oneida	1 320	13 598	3 187	1 292	3 541	307	330	469	34 478	150	43.3	9.3	28.0
Outagamie	4 914	97 883	11 828	19 242	12 678	5 048	3 637	4 249	43 412	1 170	38.7	10.7	56.0
Ozaukee	2 752	38 167	5 360	8 950	4 854	2 134	2 528	1 628	42 651	416	38.5	7.0	53.4
Pepin	222	1 766	344	141	244	82	D	62	35 082	459	22.9	10.0	47.3
Pierce	781	6 695	982	1 240	998	291	179	218	32 515	1 259	31.6	7.8	52.2
Polk	1 113	12 048	2 342	3 621	1 865	264	355	399	33 100	1 313	30.1	8.1	47.8
Portage	1 616	28 992	D	3 692	3 923	4 633	981	1 096	37 811	969	27.1	11.8	51.2
Price	414	4 546	856	1 904	581	142	86	162	35 725	472	26.1	7.8	47.2
Racine	3 986	68 267	11 126	16 231	8 820	2 093	1 898	3 062	44 849	575	51.0	8.2	45.6
Richland	373	4 691	D	1 411	890	153	D	153	32 537	1 260	27.9	6.4	44.4
Rock	3 236	54 808	9 106	10 099	8 592	1 307	1 184	2 231	40 706	1 509	44.1	10.3	50.0
Rusk	311	4 416	847	1 669	636	109	61	138	31 211	529	16.8	10.0	62.9
St. Croix	2 167	28 474	4 077	5 552	4 357	870	1 351	1 043	36 639	1 417	39.0	8.0	41.6
Sauk	1 772	30 071	3 709	5 361	4 040	896	1 002	1 101	36 626	1 665	29.1	8.2	51.2
Sawyer	642	4 922	776	625	940	179	149	161	32 683	172	26.7	11.0	47.1
Shawano	866	10 141	1 436	2 205	1 484	272	192	329	32 424	1 278	26.7	8.1	54.4
Sheboygan	2 635	51 649	6 333	17 040	6 027	2 002	1 272	2 088	40 435	986	42.4	10.1	52.7
Taylor	478	6 918	1 080	2 465	901	288	119	232	33 574	967	25.9	8.8	52.7
Trempealeau	651	13 058	1 160	7 255	1 034	297	231	484	37 098	1 436	26.5	9.5	48.7
Vernon	622	6 860	1 846	825	1 136	D	162	213	31 021	2 228	31.7	4.2	49.2
Vilas	930	5 387	520	302	993	203	99	153	28 324	47	59.6	6.4	40.4
Walworth	2 610	34 056	4 068	8 654	4 584	769	1 003	1 183	34 737	870	45.3	11.1	51.8
Washburn	511	4 389	991	1 016	730	126	198	118	26 825	405	27.4	7.4	39.8
Washington	3 189	50 892	6 164	14 623	7 083	2 066	1 787	2 055	40 372	712	43.3	8.6	51.4
Waukesha	12 391	228 213	26 399	43 605	24 882	12 913	13 231	11 173	48 960	557	54.0	7.7	51.2
Waupaca	1 211	16 213	2 601	5 792	2 381	504	289	574	35 375	1 145	30.0	7.9	49.8
Waushara	465	4 640	769	934	710	121	170	133	28 561	592	27.2	9.6	44.6
Winnebago	3 490	81 908	12 116	19 561	8 700	3 402	2 893	3 887	47 458	1 117	48.5	6.0	39.2
Wood	1 765	34 611	9 553	5 860	4 249	1 300	508	1 511	43 666	1 067	27.8	9.3	56.7
WYOMING	20 807	219 857	31 867	10 051	31 749	6 670	10 164	10 376	47 192	11 736	28.8	36.3	49.8
Albany	1 024	10 074	2 107	366	1 852	472	800	320	31 779	448	26.8	45.5	40.4
Big Horn	307	2 726	D	D	402	89	D	110	40 241	627	32.1	26.6	54.4
Campbell	1 475	22 903	1 697	615	2 786	D	723	1 392	60 795	744	30.4	44.9	36.4
Carbon	537	4 164	580	D	667	D	D	186	44 786	319	16.3	59.9	60.2
Converse	489	5 079	D	306	427	D	126	268	52 694	410	18.3	51.7	57.8

Table B. States and Counties — **Agriculture**

STATE County	Acreage (1,000) [117]	Percent change, 2007–2012 [118]	Average size of farm [119]	Total irrigated (1,000) [120]	Total cropland (1,000) [121]	Average per farm [122]	Average per acre [123]	Value of machinery and equipment, average per farm (dollars) [124]	Total (mil dol) [125]	Average per farm (dollars) [126]	Crops [127]	Livestock and poultry products [128]	$10,000 or more [129]	$100,000 or more [130]	Total ($1,000) [131]	Percent of farms [132]
WISCONSIN—Cont'd																
Dodge	402	-2.6	200	0.8	332.6	1 069 970	5 355	169 021	373.5	185 612	45.8	54.2	57.6	30.2	7 872	58.2
Door	132	-1.9	164	0.9	94.3	668 813	4 070	99 567	82.6	102 905	46.1	53.9	45.0	16.4	1 826	50.7
Douglas	71	-2.9	194	0.1	29.1	336 918	1 738	55 228	7.8	21 434	52.1	48.0	25.0	5.5	74	4.9
Dunn	372	-2.7	265	36.3	252.5	879 304	3 316	141 909	263.2	187 452	48.9	51.1	52.4	23.5	4 915	59.5
Eau Claire	204	-0.8	155	3.1	128.8	465 939	3 003	79 664	113.3	86 287	49.6	50.4	43.0	15.2	3 239	52.9
Florence	13	-33.9	149	0.0	4.9	463 544	3 115	43 489	1.0	11 067	D	D	24.4	1.1	28	26.7
Fond du Lac	316	-6.0	226	2.1	262.1	1 128 100	5 001	182 828	412.3	294 743	26.9	73.1	62.2	37.8	7 648	74.2
Forest	30	-10.5	238	D	10.3	490 488	2 059	82 496	2.9	22 449	62.0	38.0	28.3	3.1	33	15.7
Grant	588	-3.8	241	1.3	361.3	1 004 051	4 163	147 729	404.8	166 171	31.9	68.1	58.2	31.1	11 713	70.4
Green	302	-1.5	196	3.4	238.6	855 977	4 375	130 524	200.3	129 669	36.3	63.7	47.4	25.6	6 293	61.5
Green Lake	155	8.3	254	4.6	119.9	1 155 334	4 544	166 630	102.5	168 615	59.6	40.4	58.7	26.5	1 945	55.6
Iowa	351	-3.9	221	4.6	198.2	881 751	3 991	116 704	195.3	123 008	29.9	70.1	47.4	22.0	7 074	74.4
Iron	10	1.0	167	0.2	4.9	386 016	2 307	91 934	5.6	91 967	D	D	24.6	8.2	63	13.1
Jackson	240	0.4	278	7.2	139.3	859 022	3 093	155 612	169.6	196 263	53.2	46.8	54.5	27.0	3 186	60.1
Jefferson	228	-6.7	186	9.5	181.8	964 365	5 184	134 604	256.1	209 024	42.4	57.6	53.2	22.7	4 367	68.7
Juneau	180	-0.6	218	7.4	108.8	670 272	3 079	129 543	124.8	150 871	62.5	37.5	45.2	17.0	2 210	56.5
Kenosha	77	-9.1	213	0.2	68.1	1 075 507	5 038	145 295	68.9	191 827	70.1	29.9	51.3	28.4	1 592	46.8
Kewaunee	177	0.7	241	0.2	144.7	1 047 736	4 351	177 185	276.6	376 865	21.3	78.7	59.3	34.3	4 137	72.6
La Crosse	159	-4.0	212	1.0	86.9	709 759	3 345	118 472	86.5	115 671	44.7	55.3	53.5	21.4	2 565	62.7
Lafayette	369	7.6	294	0.2	276.1	1 440 604	4 895	191 424	287.3	229 493	34.4	65.6	62.1	35.8	8 268	73.6
Langlade	114	-7.3	288	19.7	73.1	796 227	2 769	178 447	103.9	262 381	58.4	41.6	51.8	28.0	1 114	48.0
Lincoln	77	-11.4	171	0.2	38.2	422 924	2 471	75 920	29.9	66 588	33.6	66.3	41.0	10.9	415	26.9
Manitowoc	231	-7.1	189	1.1	186.9	995 194	5 279	142 426	343.8	280 845	21.8	78.2	52.9	29.5	5 698	64.4
Marathon	479	-2.4	211	6.2	320.1	616 429	2 916	136 874	391.1	172 605	24.8	75.2	61.9	32.7	6 615	48.5
Marinette	132	-8.5	247	2.8	84.7	749 350	3 035	124 665	101.4	189 608	28.7	71.3	44.5	22.2	1 557	41.7
Marquette	120	-11.6	251	8.5	84.2	862 079	3 429	127 736	69.7	145 774	54.9	45.1	43.1	15.7	1 410	45.6
Menominee	1	76.4	112	0.0	0.4	144 200	1 285	29 200	0.0	4 200	0.0	100.0	0.0	0.0	D	20.0
Milwaukee	5	-16.4	56	0.1	3.5	526 354	9 459	56 915	7.6	92 878	99.6	0.4	57.3	19.5	64	19.5
Monroe	338	-3.8	175	4.3	173.2	562 429	3 206	98 238	202.0	104 903	45.4	54.6	50.4	17.2	4 423	50.9
Oconto	189	-8.0	204	1.2	141.0	667 081	3 272	114 002	165.9	178 589	39.2	60.8	48.2	26.5	2 856	54.6
Oneida	35	-10.8	233	3.0	12.1	975 653	4 190	86 700	20.2	134 973	84.8	15.2	30.7	12.7	D	12.0
Outagamie	251	1.3	214	0.4	210.1	1 129 579	5 271	174 059	302.2	258 319	34.9	65.1	60.2	37.2	5 994	65.0
Ozaukee	65	-8.1	156	0.3	51.7	876 038	5 608	110 024	64.7	155 505	37.4	62.6	55.5	25.7	1 218	51.0
Pepin	104	-4.4	226	3.6	63.0	741 634	3 286	130 987	71.7	156 288	38.8	61.2	58.4	27.5	1 966	69.7
Pierce	246	-9.3	195	0.5	166.3	773 024	3 957	130 292	178.7	141 902	52.8	47.2	50.8	25.3	4 639	62.0
Polk	256	-11.4	195	1.5	159.9	555 723	2 851	93 011	167.0	127 214	40.5	59.5	42.3	18.3	3 252	51.0
Portage	279	-1.0	288	92.5	201.4	946 737	3 292	203 829	295.1	304 528	71.8	28.2	53.3	23.3	2 782	52.0
Price	92	-9.9	196	D	39.4	371 648	1 901	65 871	31.6	66 892	22.8	77.2	38.3	10.6	537	25.0
Racine	110	-8.7	191	1.9	92.6	1 042 289	5 450	127 732	94.8	164 887	77.6	22.4	50.3	21.7	1 972	50.6
Richland	228	-10.2	181	1.7	111.8	544 504	3 011	83 011	115.5	91 628	28.2	71.8	41.9	14.6	2 969	63.1
Rock	354	2.7	234	16.2	303.7	1 294 782	5 523	154 109	274.4	181 858	60.4	39.6	49.8	23.5	7 892	68.2
Rusk	134	-16.8	253	0.1	70.1	514 170	2 036	104 786	64.2	121 367	28.4	71.6	58.6	24.8	1 236	47.6
St. Croix	268	-13.2	189	8.3	196.1	793 838	4 202	115 975	214.3	151 251	50.1	49.9	49.4	20.5	4 492	59.6
Sauk	333	-7.3	200	19.7	209.8	775 477	3 881	132 189	207.1	124 356	34.4	65.6	49.4	22.3	5 597	57.4
Sawyer	44	-7.5	253	1.0	21.9	580 750	2 293	124 134	25.3	147 145	40.0	60.0	48.3	20.3	552	32.0
Shawano	261	-3.9	204	0.3	183.5	734 011	3 592	133 984	254.1	198 858	26.0	74.0	61.4	33.6	4 470	61.8
Sheboygan	190	-0.8	193	0.2	155.9	1 011 178	5 243	162 747	242.1	245 507	27.1	72.9	59.2	29.8	3 790	51.4
Taylor	217	-10.7	224	0.1	120.0	491 262	2 189	102 087	136.5	141 155	24.7	75.3	51.3	26.1	2 265	43.2
Trempealeau	323	-5.3	225	7.9	197.8	719 451	3 197	124 753	268.9	187 243	32.6	67.4	52.3	24.4	4 772	67.7
Vernon	346	-3.1	155	0.5	181.5	512 496	3 301	76 915	221.4	99 359	32.2	67.8	52.4	16.3	3 703	46.0
Vilas	7	-30.8	146	1.0	2.8	783 574	5 352	94 830	10.2	216 894	95.6	4.4	40.4	17.0	42	21.3
Walworth	188	-13.7	216	2.8	163.9	1 323 506	6 134	154 289	168.6	193 830	46.9	53.1	53.8	23.8	4 539	60.2
Washburn	87	-14.2	216	0.8	38.2	535 677	2 483	81 933	32.5	80 294	48.1	51.9	36.0	12.3	494	33.6
Washington	133	2.8	187	0.5	107.3	1 093 001	5 832	165 548	122.7	172 313	39.9	60.1	55.3	25.8	2 609	48.0
Waukesha	92	6.5	166	1.3	75.6	1 080 562	6 527	104 210	55.1	98 860	75.9	24.1	40.6	16.9	1 587	33.9
Waupaca	215	-8.1	188	7.0	141.5	722 332	3 841	120 088	160.0	139 767	31.6	68.4	50.8	22.7	4 066	53.5
Waushara	145	-2.5	245	39.9	108.7	848 429	3 459	129 704	134.1	226 603	77.6	22.4	50.7	19.4	1 156	40.4
Winnebago	156	-5.2	139	0.4	126.2	585 332	4 204	97 747	126.6	113 315	41.3	58.7	41.5	20.1	3 245	54.3
Wood	223	0.3	209	6.2	132.9	656 817	3 147	127 231	160.3	150 256	53.2	46.8	59.0	26.1	2 887	48.2
WYOMING	30 364	0.6	2 587	1 435.7	2 418.9	1 759 200	680	114 212	1 689.4	143 952	26.0	74.0	48.8	23.5	28 146	23.9
Albany	1 964	5.8	4 385	94.4	120.4	2 466 013	562	99 815	93.4	208 509	8.6	91.4	48.0	23.2	473	8.5
Big Horn	303	-30.9	483	108.7	99.2	736 719	1 527	116 603	88.8	141 684	59.7	40.3	48.5	23.0	900	32.7
Campbell	2 878	22.7	3 868	1.8	140.7	2 239 153	579	94 640	67.2	90 269	5.3	94.7	41.4	18.7	2 305	20.6
Carbon	2 374	9.3	7 442	165.5	126.4	4 187 091	563	144 317	78.6	246 326	14.3	85.7	56.4	37.0	362	6.0
Converse	2 447	3.4	5 969	31.9	60.9	2 256 332	378	125 300	48.6	118 507	12.7	87.3	57.1	27.3	1 303	15.9

Table B. States and Counties — Water Use, Wholesale Trade, Retail Trade, and Real Estate

STATE County	Water use, 2010		Wholesale trade,[1] 2012				Retail trade,[2] 2012				Real estate and rental and leasing,[2] 2012			
	Total water withdrawn (mil gal/day)	Gallons withdrawn per person per day	Number of establishments	Number of employees	Sales (mil dol)	Annual payroll (mil dol)	Number of establishments	Number of employees	Sales (mil dol)	Annual payroll (mil dol)	Number of establishments	Number of employees	Receipts (mil dol)	Annual payroll (mil dol)
	133	134	135	136	137	138	139	140	141	142	143	144	145	146
WISCONSIN—Cont'd														
Dodge	12.3	138	71	978	474.7	40.7	234	3 189	833.0	69.8	40	100	18.3	2.9
Door	5.1	183	25	144	62.9	6.0	259	1 682	414.1	40.8	46	188	20.7	4.4
Douglas	7.0	159	44	701	840.6	33.1	150	1 993	577.7	48.7	37	110	14.9	2.5
Dunn	19.2	437	36	D	D	D	113	1 755	440.6	35.2	29	D	D	D
Eau Claire	13.9	141	95	1 601	1 013.6	69.6	402	6 995	1 658.9	143.1	107	564	77.4	16.0
Florence	0.2	43	5	D	D	D	11	61	19.9	1.2	2	D	D	D
Fond du Lac	14.4	142	111	1 541	1 372.0	74.4	354	5 462	1 402.4	130.0	64	235	37.7	6.0
Forest	0.8	89	4	D	D	D	33	276	72.2	5.3	5	13	0.8	0.2
Grant	136.9	2 673	61	481	213.7	17.9	191	2 379	657.0	51.2	49	118	16.7	3.8
Green	7.5	203	41	699	269.3	29.2	150	2 325	1 003.2	71.1	25	D	D	D
Green Lake	11.8	620	14	87	77.4	4.4	71	952	253.1	21.9	13	45	3.9	0.8
Iowa	7.8	330	25	280	252.3	13.7	89	3 980	1 426.1	151.6	9	D	D	D
Iron	2.1	357	9	91	21.3	2.3	30	232	54.3	4.9	8	D	D	D
Jackson	18.0	882	15	174	97.9	5.6	66	784	327.5	16.8	7	15	1.6	0.2
Jefferson	17.3	207	66	1 356	793.8	55.6	273	3 891	911.0	77.6	60	219	33.6	6.6
Juneau	19.1	718	17	205	110.5	5.8	92	1 030	335.5	20.9	11	21	6.8	0.4
Kenosha	30.2	181	101	1 639	1 779.7	86.5	491	8 523	2 134.1	213.6	115	460	73.0	11.2
Kewaunee	550.9	26 778	12	151	75.3	5.0	65	561	146.3	11.7	7	7	0.8	0.2
La Crosse	34.9	304	121	2 592	6 131.4	115.3	421	8 393	1 891.1	173.4	121	791	99.3	20.6
Lafayette	3.4	201	20	260	187.3	9.4	50	433	119.5	8.0	6	D	D	D
Langlade	22.3	1 115	26	352	450.3	17.7	89	1 310	428.7	31.0	13	32	3.3	0.6
Lincoln	14.1	491	21	328	143.7	13.0	111	1 222	308.7	26.0	14	68	7.3	2.1
Manitowoc	787.1	9 664	68	837	497.0	38.1	254	3 473	848.6	76.0	43	D	D	D
Marathon	126.8	946	180	2 955	1 276.6	126.2	472	9 545	2 572.4	208.5	83	412	79.2	11.9
Marinette	15.5	370	22	D	D	D	181	2 109	532.5	43.8	17	D	D	D
Marquette	6.4	414	8	D	D	D	35	319	70.9	5.2	8	D	D	D
Menominee	0.5	121	NA	NA	NA	NA	5	29	6.6	0.4	NA	NA	NA	NA
Milwaukee	1 753.0	1 850	848	17 873	12 445.3	1 263.2	2 724	41 381	10 427.9	945.7	795	5 063	1 085.5	208.1
Monroe	44.0	984	36	538	510.0	28.7	150	1 865	575.3	40.8	31	106	10.0	2.9
Oconto	6.4	170	23	143	54.9	5.4	100	872	261.1	19.8	23	71	4.9	1.2
Oneida	17.2	479	29	359	171.1	17.6	221	3 450	959.5	84.1	59	178	26.6	4.5
Outagamie	67.2	380	273	4 591	7 397.7	236.8	729	12 738	3 277.8	277.5	138	859	160.7	27.8
Ozaukee	473.9	5 485	150	1 479	1 677.6	75.9	303	4 642	1 228.0	108.0	94	312	59.5	10.0
Pepin	3.2	432	12	154	145.0	6.5	41	246	80.2	6.1	3	3	1.8	0.2
Pierce	5.7	139	18	D	D	D	102	984	256.5	19.3	23	D	D	D
Polk	9.6	218	37	465	183.9	20.1	165	1 889	452.0	38.6	36	59	7.8	1.2
Portage	79.6	1 137	70	D	D	D	230	3 758	933.9	79.2	45	188	21.4	4.3
Price	15.4	1 085	19	122	63.5	6.6	73	536	126.4	11.4	11	25	2.8	0.6
Racine	28.6	146	170	2 243	1 702.5	118.6	591	8 542	2 182.0	181.6	100	327	58.9	9.7
Richland	3.8	213	13	74	50.3	2.3	66	878	200.3	17.1	12	37	6.8	1.1
Rock	28.3	176	149	3 035	3 225.1	155.1	502	8 396	2 215.2	208.2	101	400	148.1	18.7
Rusk	3.6	241	6	101	18.9	3.6	52	595	145.3	12.0	5	11	0.6	0.2
St. Croix	17.3	205	99	1 072	1 907.3	55.0	263	3 935	1 107.7	90.4	64	D	D	D
Sauk	16.4	264	54	1 341	929.1	66.9	322	3 971	990.8	84.9	59	255	45.0	9.5
Sawyer	4.3	258	14	159	61.0	5.7	103	946	238.1	22.3	27	63	8.7	1.3
Shawano	12.2	291	38	1 219	498.6	54.1	122	1 441	397.1	30.9	13	43	5.0	1.0
Sheboygan	328.5	2 844	86	1 002	593.9	47.9	395	6 124	1 400.0	133.5	73	298	58.2	10.4
Taylor	2.5	123	9	82	36.0	3.2	76	838	238.3	17.1	9	26	3.4	0.4
Trempealeau	7.6	262	32	253	163.6	9.8	105	1 163	322.8	26.2	7	D	D	D
Vernon	101.9	3 421	18	D	D	D	98	1 138	320.4	25.7	18	29	2.2	0.5
Vilas	6.5	305	11	123	68.3	4.8	151	989	269.1	23.0	22	70	7.4	1.6
Walworth	13.0	127	107	1 395	1 544.6	67.7	358	4 521	1 234.4	106.2	88	350	54.8	10.4
Washburn	4.4	277	10	62	17.2	2.4	78	828	196.0	16.4	18	39	4.2	0.9
Washington	13.3	101	167	2 850	2 053.3	159.7	369	7 039	1 813.6	152.1	75	223	35.6	6.4
Waukesha	40.1	103	816	12 343	6 986.1	744.7	1 299	24 751	6 616.8	600.8	390	3 505	456.2	119.2
Waupaca	11.1	211	35	429	286.6	14.2	191	2 247	541.6	50.7	33	150	15.6	3.3
Waushara	40.3	1 643	19	154	100.6	6.9	73	706	219.5	13.9	11	19	2.6	0.5
Winnebago	35.3	211	136	D	D	D	473	7 892	2 064.9	174.5	113	576	219.2	19.9
Wood	174.4	2 333	59	913	626.2	46.6	279	4 815	1 101.7	105.6	59	210	37.8	4.6
WYOMING	4 701.5	8 342	709	7 003	5 597.9	398.7	2 681	30 088	9 446.0	796.0	1 076	4 546	1 259.1	215.6
Albany	189.3	5 215	23	115	132.8	4.6	141	1 729	479.6	36.8	53	147	22.5	3.2
Big Horn	392.8	33 664	10	57	43.7	2.3	47	403	90.7	8.4	9	15	2.1	0.4
Campbell	121.4	2 632	76	1 403	758.3	81.2	184	2 533	896.0	74.8	76	304	86.9	11.5
Carbon	375.7	23 651	4	D	D	D	86	683	305.5	17.3	25	83	25.0	2.5
Converse	156.1	11 284	9	45	19.3	1.9	57	486	141.5	9.6	21	55	6.1	0.9

1. Merchant wholesalers, except manufacturers' sales branches and offices.   2. Employer establishments.

Table B. States and Counties — Professional Services, Manufacturing, and Accommodation and Food Services

STATE County	Professional, scientific, and technical services, 2012				Manufacturing, 2012				Accommodation and food services, 2012			
	Number of establishments	Number of employees	Receipts (mil dol)	Annual payroll (mil dol)	Number of establishments	Number of employees	Receipts (mil dol)	Annual payroll (mil dol)	Number of establishments	Number of employees	Sales (mil dol)	Annual payroll (mil dol)
	147	148	149	150	151	152	153	154	155	156	157	158
WISCONSIN—Cont'd												
Dodge	78	467	52.4	19.0	148	10 011	3 727.6	462.8	155	1 801	69.5	18.2
Door	74	237	28.7	9.4	56	1 968	416.7	88.3	238	1 999	147.6	36.9
Douglas	72	343	37.1	15.0	46	1 222	D	78.5	157	1 906	72.1	19.7
Dunn	66	388	38.5	16.9	58	2 369	1 528.6	118.7	89	1 222	42.9	11.9
Eau Claire	179	1 706	203.6	84.9	84	4 938	1 690.9	207.0	275	5 130	206.6	58.5
Florence	7	11	0.5	0.2	9	112	D	3.8	26	154	6.4	1.4
Fond du Lac	154	1 337	154.4	76.3	144	9 140	3 989.9	407.6	240	3 872	140.8	39.8
Forest	10	91	11.2	3.5	19	223	D	7.6	36	D	D	D
Grant	64	518	59.4	26.7	67	2 315	965.2	101.1	122	1 205	47.1	11.7
Green	57	280	73.7	13.7	82	2 934	1 420.7	131.1	84	966	37.9	10.2
Green Lake	22	76	6.8	2.3	37	1 335	390.1	53.5	50	538	21.9	7.5
Iowa	39	128	12.4	4.8	37	846	1 335.1	32.8	51	525	23.3	6.8
Iron	8	28	2.5	0.8	16	191	D	6.3	54	D	D	D
Jackson	22	93	6.0	2.5	29	921	499.5	47.3	59	661	27.9	7.1
Jefferson	129	672	92.1	24.4	152	8 385	3 842.9	415.5	186	2 126	88.3	22.0
Juneau	17	51	4.3	1.7	50	2 136	719.2	92.2	76	604	26.8	6.7
Kenosha	223	1 212	123.1	50.9	168	5 704	2 370.3	260.6	362	5 510	237.8	66.8
Kewaunee	27	135	13.2	5.4	37	1 771	466.7	81.3	50	518	15.4	4.2
La Crosse	250	1 855	177.7	85.7	157	6 805	1 941.7	266.0	330	6 383	243.7	72.1
Lafayette	16	55	6.2	2.0	23	681	270.2	22.8	36	D	D	D
Langlade	22	110	6.5	4.6	47	1 494	330.2	57.0	59	583	26.1	7.0
Lincoln	32	111	7.3	3.4	50	2 329	772.4	103.1	90	681	27.6	7.0
Manitowoc	103	646	92.8	23.7	179	9 968	3 138.3	457.1	174	2 443	87.7	24.9
Marathon	225	1 943	284.9	113.9	238	14 472	4 306.0	654.1	305	4 458	180.7	51.8
Marinette	49	243	22.8	11.0	90	6 302	1 889.6	300.4	161	1 398	61.1	15.5
Marquette	17	54	6.2	1.5	21	1 325	D	53.5	40	282	13.4	3.0
Menominee	3	D	D	D	NA	NA	NA	NA	3	D	D	D
Milwaukee	1 955	23 788	3 849.6	1 598.9	991	48 963	19 176.2	2 974.2	1 900	36 303	1 831.0	496.0
Monroe	72	545	48.6	19.5	59	3 937	1 364.2	163.2	112	1 540	60.0	16.6
Oconto	47	159	14.4	5.2	56	1 897	522.3	72.7	98	669	29.1	7.2
Oneida	81	363	51.2	12.4	46	1 397	330.5	69.2	186	1 503	82.0	22.2
Outagamie	385	3 279	499.0	179.5	357	17 963	7 208.5	888.2	453	8 198	330.0	91.7
Ozaukee	336	2 169	353.2	112.6	206	8 663	2 762.9	473.0	207	3 307	134.8	38.9
Pepin	15	43	4.9	1.6	13	140	D	5.4	28	D	D	D
Pierce	66	177	22.6	7.2	47	1 250	516.5	57.4	99	994	38.2	10.3
Polk	84	352	46.2	12.6	105	3 117	995.3	133.7	118	1 108	42.2	11.0
Portage	100	892	84.9	35.0	75	3 912	1 383.0	165.0	204	2 827	112.4	31.4
Price	20	83	5.2	2.0	44	1 973	502.0	85.5	48	319	11.8	3.1
Racine	310	1 967	234.8	91.7	325	15 444	8 100.1	844.4	382	5 974	251.7	70.5
Richland	18	60	3.6	1.3	30	1 545	682.1	61.8	29	333	11.3	2.9
Rock	208	1 172	129.3	49.5	224	8 850	4 474.2	421.3	363	5 355	236.2	63.7
Rusk	12	59	3.3	1.2	27	1 579	423.5	48.3	29	210	8.9	2.2
St. Croix	221	1 273	228.3	68.9	161	5 838	1 307.7	269.4	184	2 922	122.9	33.9
Sauk	120	982	118.6	49.3	94	5 001	1 669.5	223.1	238	7 576	542.6	133.3
Sawyer	41	136	21.1	5.1	46	561	256.7	27.1	115	1 022	67.2	19.5
Shawano	36	D	D	D	66	D	633.2	84.7	115	D	D	D
Sheboygan	179	1 240	207.9	65.8	230	16 716	7 346.2	825.1	269	4 151	188.8	53.4
Taylor	18	116	10.2	3.8	45	2 483	817.6	85.0	43	495	13.0	5.1
Trempealeau	38	195	15.3	5.9	58	6 418	1 786.7	248.4	81	649	25.4	6.6
Vernon	42	170	11.0	4.6	33	981	275.8	40.7	53	626	19.5	5.8
Vilas	37	91	13.8	3.0	28	257	39.0	8.7	207	1 941	126.0	34.1
Walworth	192	1 000	135.9	43.3	207	7 974	2 705.8	384.6	298	6 109	288.1	81.2
Washburn	28	193	25.2	8.0	29	969	198.9	28.4	81	505	25.0	6.7
Washington	222	1 643	278.9	95.9	318	13 257	3 740.7	676.5	248	4 147	165.4	43.7
Waukesha	1 328	13 383	2 265.1	822.6	950	43 232	15 221.2	2 481.1	824	16 092	725.2	202.0
Waupaca	62	309	29.2	10.8	89	5 784	2 587.2	277.4	151	1 621	64.5	17.6
Waushara	17	153	8.9	3.4	27	873	369.5	33.4	68	582	24.8	6.1
Winnebago	247	2 575	514.5	134.8	300	23 892	11 476.5	1 321.6	367	5 963	234.6	65.3
Wood	89	589	69.7	25.6	117	5 757	2 482.4	285.9	179	1 972	78.6	21.2
WYOMING	2 141	9 134	1 297.4	467.0	553	10 094	10 783.8	630.6	1 799	27 580	1 644.8	468.7
Albany	116	832	115.7	41.0	31	341	D	16.1	113	2 074	79.6	23.3
Big Horn	23	67	6.9	2.2	16	185	D	8.5	27	D	D	D
Campbell	113	757	97.8	37.2	35	632	267.8	38.4	105	1 678	95.1	26.6
Carbon	36	126	14.5	4.5	9	390	D	D	83	718	47.7	13.2
Converse	32	108	13.0	5.0	16	129	D	7.1	45	D	D	D

1. Establishment subject to federal tax.

STATE County	Health care and social assistance, 2012				Other services, 2012				Nonemployer businesses, 2014		Value of residential construction authorized by building permits, 2015	
	Number of establishments	Number of employees	Receipts (mil dol)	Annual payroll (mil dol)	Number of establishments	Number of employees	Receipts (mil dol)	Annual payroll (mil dol)	Number	Receipts (mil dol)	New Construction ($1,000)	Number of housing units
	159	160	161	162	163	164	165	166	167	168	169	170
WISCONSIN—Cont'd												
Dodge	205	4 611	437.1	170.0	133	452	39.3	10.9	4 506	198.9	27 161	137
Door	78	1 630	131.8	61.6	98	472	53.9	11.6	2 816	113.7	44 117	229
Douglas	114	2 066	129.1	51.7	77	590	36.4	12.2	2 128	86.8	11 901	83
Dunn	92	2 779	170.5	76.9	71	301	23.1	7.1	2 528	112.2	20 774	187
Eau Claire	364	11 109	1 261.7	552.5	201	1 283	103.5	29.9	5 822	290.8	63 371	410
Florence	3	D	D	D	7	11	1.6	0.3	347	14.0	1 334	16
Fond du Lac	281	5 764	758.8	248.8	191	1 245	114.4	31.3	4 902	232.6	35 945	195
Forest	17	294	10.6	5.9	14	25	2.8	0.8	732	35.5	5 517	32
Grant	113	2 435	145.0	65.9	114	399	45.3	9.6	3 254	137.8	22 172	155
Green	71	2 048	206.9	91.7	77	286	27.5	6.7	2 549	113.1	15 243	71
Green Lake	48	1 111	101.2	44.7	33	108	8.8	3.1	1 341	59.2	7 905	25
Iowa	53	1 116	83.5	36.3	36	117	12.1	2.8	1 938	78.5	12 131	55
Iron	13	321	12.6	7.3	8	D	D	D	503	22.4	5 700	30
Jackson	48	1 012	82.3	37.1	27	D	D	D	1 156	53.8	5 560	40
Jefferson	229	4 021	395.0	134.6	139	607	53.3	15.0	4 947	223.7	40 007	242
Juneau	52	1 138	105.4	43.9	48	184	24.0	5.5	1 455	68.8	15 830	82
Kenosha	415	8 620	831.7	339.9	241	1 485	101.2	31.0	8 477	368.0	64 729	288
Kewaunee	37	495	21.2	10.9	28	61	7.4	1.4	1 241	47.9	8 532	31
La Crosse	282	11 223	1 472.4	520.9	233	1 679	148.1	44.8	6 352	266.2	65 496	454
Lafayette	23	232	19.5	6.2	29	D	D	D	1 346	66.6	7 113	42
Langlade	45	984	114.5	40.4	47	164	13.1	4.1	1 250	52.7	8 135	41
Lincoln	60	D	D	D	59	242	18.3	5.1	1 747	72.2	11 609	97
Manitowoc	175	4 731	382.0	176.8	130	553	54.3	12.0	3 954	166.8	17 424	117
Marathon	367	10 123	1 133.0	459.7	221	1 313	138.5	37.7	7 809	385.1	47 880	241
Marinette	117	2 875	251.2	109.4	77	322	27.1	7.6	2 290	99.2	14 014	95
Marquette	24	273	10.0	4.9	28	D	D	D	1 026	38.7	1 268	8
Menominee	1	D	D	D	3	15	1.0	0.4	99	3.1	1 824	9
Milwaukee	2 847	86 674	9 866.4	3 872.0	1 476	11 203	1 438.2	368.4	47 239	1 930.1	184 362	1 269
Monroe	83	2 640	255.6	138.7	73	427	28.9	8.7	2 573	118.9	15 643	108
Oconto	71	1 578	111.1	46.5	44	125	12.0	2.9	2 259	102.6	16 253	105
Oneida	139	2 895	335.8	115.0	98	387	32.7	8.9	2 951	117.1	34 902	228
Outagamie	464	11 090	1 289.6	521.0	361	2 827	247.8	73.7	9 773	486.4	131 480	845
Ozaukee	289	5 256	623.2	242.1	183	1 178	81.0	27.0	6 732	358.5	59 420	170
Pepin	15	286	26.7	9.3	18	D	D	D	570	25.9	3 070	17
Pierce	63	909	53.8	23.5	60	203	20.9	4.6	2 732	121.6	25 751	123
Polk	99	2 477	227.0	88.9	79	246	18.9	5.3	3 286	131.3	21 281	103
Portage	154	3 797	385.8	155.9	119	759	72.6	19.6	3 661	196.0	36 284	249
Price	43	890	55.9	26.2	29	81	6.2	1.8	1 089	41.2	7 332	51
Racine	459	10 588	764.4	335.7	317	1 839	140.4	44.5	9 539	386.2	54 673	217
Richland	48	898	71.3	31.4	25	D	D	D	1 174	58.6	5 519	31
Rock	320	9 667	1 120.9	438.4	268	1 417	105.0	30.8	8 127	338.5	45 107	216
Rusk	34	780	62.4	27.9	20	D	D	D	981	41.7	12 623	68
St. Croix	189	4 427	353.4	151.4	148	696	56.8	15.7	6 285	274.7	75 229	349
Sauk	144	3 910	340.6	147.5	129	541	50.6	16.3	4 425	213.1	38 449	168
Sawyer	39	832	71.5	28.7	40	168	15.1	3.9	1 557	64.3	15 678	101
Shawano	79	D	D	D	61	233	20.2	5.4	2 454	111.4	7 833	48
Sheboygan	299	6 483	597.2	247.8	202	992	67.4	19.5	5 604	231.6	28 883	123
Taylor	49	1 017	81.1	35.5	39	92	6.9	1.9	1 408	74.3	5 823	45
Trempealeau	53	1 344	86.0	38.7	40	110	11.2	2.8	2 001	90.6	17 237	122
Vernon	66	1 768	131.7	55.8	38	97	8.0	1.6	2 455	100.0	12 185	81
Vilas	51	519	46.7	16.1	59	216	15.1	4.5	2 389	99.1	41 233	224
Walworth	219	4 385	342.3	133.0	192	877	80.9	20.6	6 900	321.8	62 849	224
Washburn	49	992	59.8	26.2	37	131	9.6	2.7	1 433	55.4	14 821	73
Washington	263	6 231	482.2	208.8	265	1 450	113.4	34.6	8 212	396.7	95 902	444
Waukesha	1 333	25 812	2 722.5	1 122.9	812	6 537	634.5	206.3	26 872	1 521.9	303 465	1 165
Waupaca	114	2 577	198.7	73.5	91	322	30.0	7.9	3 043	128.2	15 208	115
Waushara	42	806	46.1	20.3	32	D	D	D	1 550	75.3	9 886	53
Winnebago	439	13 580	1 272.0	555.0	257	2 279	221.0	68.1	8 275	363.1	106 564	710
Wood	178	9 523	1 234.5	493.6	133	798	64.2	17.6	3 909	171.2	28 905	271
WYOMING	1 898	31 340	3 291.5	1 361.9	1 373	6 655	884.6	214.9	47 576	2 367.4	607 666	1 903
Albany	127	2 241	178.2	80.9	87	433	33.9	9.7	2 542	83.3	22 705	142
Big Horn	21	373	23.9	12.2	19	48	4.0	0.9	900	29.2	1 885	9
Campbell	97	1 738	264.5	91.6	132	989	146.5	41.5	3 373	167.7	42 655	109
Carbon	49	642	51.4	22.1	37	130	15.8	3.5	1 056	44.8	6 539	34
Converse	29	568	67.3	25.4	37	119	12.6	2.8	1 073	57.0	6 944	40

Table B. States and Counties — Government Employment and Payroll, and Local Government Finances

	Government employment and payroll, 2012									Local government finances, 2012				
			March payroll (percent of total)							General revenue				
												Taxes		
													Per capita[1] (dollars)	
STATE County	Full-time equivalent employees	March payroll (dollars)	Administration, judicial, and legal	Police and Corrections	Fire Protection	Highways and transportation	Health and Welfare	Natural resources and utilities	Education and libraries	Total (mil dol)	Inter-governmental (mil dol)	Total (mil dol)	Total	Property
	171	172	173	174	175	176	177	178	179	180	181	182	183	184
WISCONSIN—Cont'd														
Dodge	2 529	9 541 340	7.2	13.4	1.1	6.9	16.7	4.2	48.9	269.1	119.0	102.8	1 162	1 082
Door	1 091	4 311 224	10.3	10.3	2.4	7.1	11.5	5.3	51.6	140.6	38.4	81.9	2 946	2 757
Douglas	2 164	7 766 579	6.6	9.7	2.6	4.7	3.9	4.3	66.9	239.4	102.3	103.0	2 352	2 221
Dunn	1 509	5 639 405	7.9	8.3	2.6	8.0	16.0	4.0	50.9	163.0	74.1	60.7	1 377	1 302
Eau Claire	3 593	14 808 173	5.9	7.8	3.1	4.5	5.6	4.3	67.1	406.0	166.9	179.3	1 781	1 647
Florence	185	612 638	17.1	13.9	0.2	11.3	10.7	4.5	42.3	20.9	8.4	9.9	2 211	2 114
Fond du Lac	3 703	15 389 801	4.9	9.2	2.4	4.4	10.7	3.5	63.8	424.7	174.4	182.3	1 790	1 688
Forest	493	1 528 680	11.1	10.4	0.1	9.6	6.8	1.9	59.2	43.8	19.4	21.0	2 284	2 224
Grant	2 070	7 484 129	5.4	5.9	0.1	7.1	11.1	4.5	64.9	195.5	97.7	59.2	1 159	1 089
Green	1 522	5 434 245	4.8	8.5	0.3	10.0	14.6	4.1	57.2	147.1	64.1	57.3	1 551	1 465
Green Lake	764	2 599 596	7.3	12.4	0.1	5.7	12.4	4.5	56.6	82.2	28.8	43.6	2 290	2 188
Iowa	1 004	3 519 446	8.0	6.3	0.3	11.9	9.5	4.0	59.0	96.3	43.2	39.1	1 641	1 551
Iron	343	1 294 139	9.8	10.2	0.3	17.8	25.1	5.0	30.4	30.8	12.7	13.2	2 218	2 077
Jackson	903	2 811 059	8.8	7.7	0.2	16.9	6.6	2.7	55.8	82.1	42.1	26.7	1 304	1 221
Jefferson	2 850	11 172 911	7.2	10.2	3.2	5.1	9.1	5.9	58.7	312.5	124.7	137.1	1 622	1 528
Juneau	1 087	3 617 443	10.2	11.0	0.2	10.0	8.0	7.6	51.7	107.4	51.9	43.2	1 624	1 536
Kenosha	6 796	30 615 896	4.1	10.1	3.6	2.9	5.4	4.3	68.6	855.8	363.2	367.3	2 187	2 088
Kewaunee	848	3 565 289	8.2	10.2	0.1	10.8	12.1	3.4	53.7	87.1	41.2	29.7	1 440	1 419
La Crosse	4 828	18 746 528	5.8	8.4	2.7	4.3	18.1	4.4	55.5	639.3	314.3	218.1	1 873	1 730
Lafayette	850	2 868 337	5.6	5.1	0.3	8.3	23.6	4.4	52.0	87.8	38.3	24.8	1 472	1 414
Langlade	760	2 800 264	10.3	8.9	3.8	7.9	3.0	5.0	60.4	84.0	40.2	32.5	1 656	1 556
Lincoln	1 136	4 470 314	7.0	8.8	2.5	7.1	16.7	4.1	52.4	126.6	51.7	46.2	1 628	1 550
Manitowoc	2 832	11 154 230	5.9	8.4	4.1	9.0	10.6	8.0	52.8	283.3	138.4	103.3	1 281	1 252
Marathon	5 721	22 517 091	4.6	6.0	1.9	5.6	19.3	2.6	59.4	701.3	346.1	232.0	1 722	1 622
Marinette	1 554	5 323 156	6.8	9.6	2.0	8.0	9.0	6.7	56.8	164.4	77.1	65.5	1 576	1 476
Marquette	499	1 734 369	8.4	12.2	0.1	8.1	10.6	1.6	56.1	50.8	18.7	27.4	1 805	1 741
Menominee	308	1 058 752	4.7	7.1	0.5	4.3	17.3	0.5	64.4	30.1	23.2	5.7	1 306	1 299
Milwaukee	34 086	166 779 941	5.4	14.8	5.3	4.3	9.0	4.7	53.9	5 067.2	2 122.5	1 803.2	1 888	1 733
Monroe	1 770	5 806 833	5.3	7.6	0.2	6.8	15.8	3.7	59.6	171.3	88.6	56.7	1 258	1 152
Oconto	1 242	4 597 591	8.0	8.3	1.4	7.3	18.7	4.2	50.7	129.3	64.1	50.5	1 349	1 293
Oneida	1 507	5 601 172	7.6	9.0	2.1	9.2	4.7	4.2	61.9	177.2	45.0	110.8	3 102	2 972
Outagamie	6 670	30 535 826	4.5	7.0	2.4	3.0	7.4	3.1	70.7	783.6	353.3	271.9	1 521	1 483
Ozaukee	2 849	10 891 062	5.8	12.2	1.1	5.8	11.9	5.0	57.3	314.5	88.3	173.0	1 993	1 870
Pepin	383	1 190 672	6.0	7.9	0.0	9.8	16.0	3.3	54.8	32.7	15.7	13.8	1 862	1 799
Pierce	1 550	5 604 968	7.8	8.1	0.6	7.2	7.5	3.9	64.3	161.3	69.8	71.2	1 743	1 678
Polk	1 872	6 676 347	6.7	6.6	0.1	8.1	13.3	2.7	61.5	182.9	73.8	81.7	1 873	1 795
Portage	2 267	8 603 550	8.0	9.1	2.6	7.5	10.8	4.0	57.1	239.8	105.3	94.6	1 343	1 237
Price	681	1 985 878	8.8	8.8	0.2	14.3	8.2	2.4	55.9	60.2	26.4	26.8	1 934	1 859
Racine	6 208	25 453 020	4.3	13.6	5.6	3.5	5.9	4.0	61.9	757.1	345.7	302.7	1 554	1 513
Richland	693	2 209 583	6.2	8.6	0.0	9.2	22.4	9.3	43.6	68.8	31.9	17.8	999	928
Rock	6 252	25 471 665	5.9	9.6	3.9	4.4	7.9	4.5	62.6	723.4	387.9	249.8	1 557	1 471
Rusk	655	2 410 554	18.7	7.8	0.0	7.6	8.7	4.6	51.6	86.0	34.2	18.5	1 293	1 209
St. Croix	2 777	10 535 818	8.9	8.5	0.6	5.0	10.3	3.3	61.9	287.9	124.7	126.4	1 483	1 393
Sauk	2 740	9 073 443	5.8	14.7	0.2	6.1	14.5	4.3	52.3	342.6	171.4	136.3	2 178	1 826
Sawyer	647	2 033 247	11.4	10.0	0.3	11.0	9.7	2.2	53.1	68.2	23.3	37.0	2 229	2 110
Shawano	1 508	5 334 917	7.7	11.2	0.3	6.9	9.6	4.4	58.3	146.4	73.0	52.6	1 264	1 190
Sheboygan	4 469	19 622 392	8.8	8.8	2.1	5.2	8.0	3.0	63.5	489.1	213.6	207.1	1 801	1 746
Taylor	791	2 632 338	8.6	8.5	0.1	7.8	13.4	3.7	56.2	77.9	42.6	26.0	1 270	1 206
Trempealeau	1 609	5 095 842	6.3	7.1	0.0	5.3	19.8	4.5	56.5	151.2	71.4	42.1	1 437	1 369
Vernon	1 200	3 885 090	13.0	10.1	0.0	9.9	7.7	3.8	53.3	116.3	57.2	38.4	1 270	1 203
Vilas	838	2 943 859	11.7	11.7	1.3	12.5	6.2	4.2	50.1	90.0	23.9	58.7	2 751	2 602
Walworth	3 935	15 369 324	8.6	14.6	5.1	5.4	7.1	4.6	53.9	432.3	127.0	247.7	2 409	2 279
Washburn	809	2 970 221	6.5	8.7	0.0	6.2	26.7	4.1	45.5	75.6	23.6	43.2	2 729	2 639
Washington	3 924	16 777 954	5.5	11.3	2.0	3.5	11.1	4.9	60.4	533.8	224.7	238.1	1 795	1 685
Waukesha	12 148	56 004 430	5.2	10.5	3.1	3.9	3.5	4.4	68.1	1 501.6	376.8	897.3	2 287	2 229
Waupaca	2 041	7 209 482	6.6	9.8	1.0	6.0	8.5	3.2	64.1	213.4	94.7	87.0	1 668	1 589
Waushara	768	2 669 797	12.8	9.7	0.0	7.3	14.0	2.2	51.2	79.8	31.6	38.3	1 565	1 495
Winnebago	5 300	21 156 305	4.4	11.7	4.6	5.5	11.2	7.1	54.5	697.9	338.4	249.0	1 475	1 436
Wood	3 170	12 767 826	6.1	9.1	3.2	5.9	6.1	3.5	65.8	337.6	146.1	136.7	1 837	1 741
WYOMING	X	X	X	X	X	X	X	X	X	X	X	X	X	X
Albany	2 004	7 113 079	5.9	6.8	3.8	1.8	26.8	5.7	48.8	203.8	74.7	35.3	948	550
Big Horn	940	3 298 694	4.9	6.2	0.2	2.2	30.5	4.5	51.0	99.0	52.6	18.8	1 595	1 308
Campbell	3 518	15 943 966	6.3	7.1	1.0	2.6	31.3	5.6	43.0	513.4	102.2	227.8	4 757	4 113
Carbon	1 195	4 095 546	7.4	9.7	1.4	3.4	23.3	5.9	44.5	136.5	41.4	57.8	3 691	2 846
Converse	1 098	4 194 426	4.6	6.9	0.0	1.8	33.4	4.4	47.4	123.9	29.5	48.7	3 477	2 778

1. Based on the resident population estimated as of July 1 of the year shown.

STATE County	Total (mil dol)	Per capita¹ (dollars)	Education	Health and hospitals	Police protection	Public welfare	Highways	Total (mil dol)	Per capita¹ (dollars)	Federal civilian	Federal military	State and local	Democratic	Republican	All other
	185	186	187	188	189	190	191	192	193	194	195	196	197	198	199
WISCONSIN—Cont'd															
Dodge	312.6	3 536	31.9	3.5	7.1	19.1	11.6	247.2	2 795	177	229	5 067	44.8	53.7	1.5
Door	143.6	5 161	33.0	8.5	5.0	3.5	16.6	112.6	4 047	77	145	1 784	58.0	40.7	1.3
Douglas	245.2	5 600	52.1	1.4	5.6	3.7	10.6	236.8	5 408	170	120	3 207	65.8	32.6	1.7
Dunn	163.3	3 704	41.6	2.5	5.7	12.3	12.7	105.8	2 402	92	114	4 584	56.6	41.6	1.8
Eau Claire	470.2	4 671	54.2	3.8	7.3	3.4	9.5	361.0	3 586	347	269	8 596	60.3	38.1	1.6
Florence	21.2	4 727	37.2	8.9	7.2	0.6	19.4	5.9	1 314	13	12	258	42.2	56.3	1.5
Fond du Lac	449.6	4 415	51.8	7.3	5.2	3.9	9.0	580.9	5 704	202	274	5 408	44.8	53.8	1.3
Forest	45.1	4 904	47.2	2.3	5.4	5.0	13.7	7.9	854	100	24	1 701	57.1	41.9	1.0
Grant	214.5	4 199	52.3	3.3	4.2	7.2	12.4	147.8	2 894	148	131	5 627	61.2	37.3	1.6
Green	151.7	4 109	48.0	2.6	6.1	10.5	13.8	103.5	2 805	79	102	2 058	62.1	36.3	1.6
Green Lake	81.9	4 301	48.2	3.2	6.9	5.3	9.5	68.9	3 620	56	52	1 092	41.9	56.6	1.5
Iowa	95.1	3 993	48.5	1.0	5.7	8.7	15.3	45.1	1 896	77	66	1 326	66.7	32.0	1.3
Iron	31.8	5 354	32.4	7.4	7.7	0.5	21.4	22.9	3 853	17	16	357	55.8	42.7	1.6
Jackson	85.1	4 152	52.3	2.5	4.5	6.0	13.4	40.6	1 983	50	54	2 491	60.2	38.4	1.4
Jefferson	322.8	3 820	49.7	5.1	6.2	5.7	8.1	312.0	3 693	174	225	3 939	49.7	48.9	1.4
Juneau	108.2	4 063	46.9	4.1	5.3	3.2	12.3	117.9	4 426	254	92	1 997	53.7	44.6	1.7
Kenosha	850.4	5 064	53.7	3.4	6.5	6.9	5.1	759.4	4 522	257	482	9 345	58.2	40.1	1.7
Kewaunee	102.8	4 983	40.7	9.0	4.0	5.5	16.5	50.3	2 438	68	56	1 157	54.7	43.7	1.6
La Crosse	639.1	5 488	42.3	2.8	3.9	23.8	4.9	409.7	3 518	462	317	9 931	60.9	37.5	1.6
Lafayette	90.2	5 355	43.0	14.6	2.7	11.4	12.9	33.1	1 965	54	47	1 021	60.4	38.1	1.5
Langlade	87.8	4 467	47.1	4.3	4.7	3.7	13.7	55.1	2 802	43	53	1 077	49.8	48.8	1.3
Lincoln	128.6	4 529	40.0	5.5	5.8	12.3	13.4	69.0	2 431	60	77	1 708	55.2	42.7	2.1
Manitowoc	296.5	3 675	42.9	1.3	6.2	6.4	9.3	337.8	4 187	189	244	3 818	52.9	45.3	1.8
Marathon	710.6	5 274	41.9	10.2	3.9	18.8	7.9	440.9	3 273	453	374	7 508	53.5	44.7	1.8
Marinette	165.7	3 988	44.3	5.4	5.8	7.1	14.3	116.0	2 790	139	117	2 125	52.7	45.8	1.6
Marquette	54.9	3 612	43.4	5.5	7.6	3.4	17.9	23.8	1 566	52	41	702	51.8	46.6	1.6
Menominee	30.7	7 067	60.2	0.0	5.9	18.3	5.8	5.7	1 309	(3)0	(3)12	(3)2 105	86.8	12.8	0.4
Milwaukee	5 034.7	5 271	40.9	10.3	8.2	1.9	4.9	6 485.7	6 790	9 384	2 931	51 528	67.3	31.4	1.2
Monroe	165.6	3 672	50.0	1.1	5.0	10.2	11.3	105.8	2 346	2 458	252	2 475	53.2	45.2	1.5
Oconto	134.4	3 590	40.5	9.2	4.7	5.0	18.4	80.7	2 154	92	103	1 837	52.3	46.2	1.5
Oneida	201.2	5 634	52.6	2.8	6.1	3.2	10.2	98.0	2 743	184	97	2 025	54.3	43.9	1.8
Outagamie	855.9	4 786	56.0	2.4	5.0	4.7	8.6	649.4	3 632	564	529	10 505	54.9	43.3	1.7
Ozaukee	321.3	3 701	46.5	2.6	7.4	7.0	10.8	290.2	3 342	146	238	3 575	38.6	60.3	1.2
Pepin	34.1	4 609	48.2	4.5	4.1	3.3	20.4	10.3	1 392	35	20	472	55.7	42.9	1.4
Pierce	163.8	4 014	51.4	3.3	5.2	3.2	16.2	140.8	3 451	86	107	4 210	53.4	44.4	2.2
Polk	186.0	4 265	50.3	5.5	4.6	6.5	13.2	178.6	4 095	132	119	2 645	48.0	49.8	2.1
Portage	238.8	3 391	43.8	5.1	6.1	6.5	12.7	142.9	2 029	170	191	5 986	63.0	35.0	2.0
Price	60.0	4 326	45.1	2.0	5.7	8.2	16.4	25.8	1 862	76	37	875	55.6	42.2	2.1
Racine	764.1	3 923	45.5	3.8	9.7	5.3	7.3	710.7	3 648	332	529	8 548	53.1	45.7	1.3
Richland	68.5	3 844	34.6	2.0	4.7	20.1	12.9	25.0	1 405	60	48	1 353	59.7	39.0	1.3
Rock	729.2	4 546	49.6	7.4	6.2	7.1	5.3	614.8	3 833	288	441	8 591	63.8	34.6	1.6
Rusk	90.1	6 292	32.1	22.9	3.9	8.8	12.1	51.6	3 603	46	39	1 059	53.0	44.7	2.3
St. Croix	287.7	3 375	50.6	2.2	5.7	8.2	13.4	288.4	3 383	154	239	4 365	47.2	51.0	1.8
Sauk	331.0	5 288	35.3	5.0	4.8	22.8	8.1	211.8	3 384	150	175	5 493	60.8	37.8	1.5
Sawyer	72.4	4 365	38.2	6.1	5.3	7.8	21.4	22.8	1 377	79	45	1 869	52.4	46.2	1.3
Shawano	157.1	3 776	42.7	6.0	5.5	4.6	17.3	107.1	2 575	113	113	2 722	51.1	47.5	1.5
Sheboygan	492.9	4 286	55.2	3.6	5.7	6.1	8.2	375.9	3 269	203	329	5 567	48.9	49.6	1.5
Taylor	77.2	3 770	44.9	3.6	5.2	8.1	16.4	38.0	1 857	59	56	954	48.8	49.1	2.1
Trempealeau	154.8	5 283	44.9	1.8	4.6	18.1	10.5	112.0	3 824	114	80	2 236	62.5	36.1	1.4
Vernon	117.6	3 887	43.6	1.7	3.8	13.5	14.5	68.6	2 265	119	83	1 764	60.1	38.1	1.7
Vilas	84.7	3 971	43.9	2.5	7.8	5.4	13.1	52.1	2 443	68	59	2 139	47.2	51.3	1.5
Walworth	423.9	4 121	48.5	3.3	9.0	4.8	9.2	448.4	4 360	187	279	8 230	47.9	50.5	1.5
Washburn	75.7	4 781	45.6	1.7	4.0	5.9	18.7	56.9	3 597	87	43	1 280	51.5	47.2	1.3
Washington	537.2	4 049	42.6	2.9	6.1	19.2	7.1	398.2	3 001	257	368	5 238	34.6	64.1	1.3
Waukesha	1 525.8	3 890	54.5	2.7	7.1	2.3	6.8	1 282.0	3 268	754	1 084	17 010	36.6	62.3	1.0
Waupaca	217.6	4 174	48.6	2.1	6.1	7.4	12.8	224.2	4 301	128	140	3 442	50.8	47.9	1.3
Waushara	86.2	3 523	39.0	3.9	8.2	9.2	13.7	34.2	1 400	44	64	1 341	49.5	48.7	1.8
Winnebago	708.5	4 197	35.6	2.5	5.6	20.8	8.3	688.0	4 076	401	453	11 933	54.9	43.3	1.8
Wood	353.7	4 752	52.5	6.5	5.5	4.9	9.8	274.0	3 681	194	202	4 993	55.6	42.5	1.9
WYOMING	X	X	X	X	X	X	X	X	X	7 363	6 072	62 052	32.5	64.8	2.7
Albany	193.6	5 194	32.5	30.5	5.1	0.3	6.1	57.2	1 535	165	203	7 916	50.5	46.4	3.1
Big Horn	99.3	8 416	44.8	21.5	3.8	0.1	2.7	33.3	2 823	103	64	1 395	20.9	76.2	3.0
Campbell	532.9	11 131	37.0	22.6	3.1	1.5	5.4	188.2	3 931	89	260	4 870	18.3	79.7	2.0
Carbon	136.8	8 731	40.1	19.3	4.0	0.4	2.9	63.8	4 069	197	82	1 816	34.1	63.2	2.7
Converse	125.0	8 921	39.9	31.1	4.0	0.2	6.5	11.6	826	68	76	1 496	21.4	76.3	2.3

1. Based on the resident population estimated as of July 1 of the year shown.   2. © 2013 Election Data Services, Inc. All rights reserved.   3. Menominee county included with Shawano county.

Table B. States and Counties — **Land Area and Population**

STATE/ County code	CBSA code[1]	County type[2]	STATE County	Land area,[3] (sq km) 2010	Total persons 2015	Rank	Per square kilometer	White	Black	American Indian, Alaska Native	Asian and Pacific Islander	Percent Hispanic or Latino[4]	Under 5 years	5 to 17 years	18 to 24 years	25 to 34 years	35 to 44 years	45 to 54 years
				1	2	3	4	5	6	7	8	9	10	11	12	13	14	15
			WYOMING—Cont'd															
56 011	...	9	Crook	7 393	7 444	2 639	1.0	95.1	1.2	1.5	0.7	2.5	6.6	16.9	7.2	10.7	10.0	13.8
56 013	40180	7	Fremont	23 786	40 315	1 169	1.7	72.6	0.9	21.3	1.0	6.7	7.5	18.1	8.3	12.8	10.7	12.2
56 015	...	7	Goshen	5 764	13 383	2 212	2.3	87.1	1.3	1.2	1.0	10.4	5.6	14.5	10.1	11.6	10.6	12.6
56 017	...	7	Hot Springs	5 191	4 741	2 850	0.9	93.7	1.1	2.1	0.9	4.0	4.4	16.4	5.8	10.0	9.6	12.3
56 019	...	7	Johnson	10 759	8 585	2 547	0.8	92.7	1.1	1.7	1.2	4.8	5.8	16.2	6.7	11.1	11.0	12.4
56 021	16940	3	Laramie	6 956	97 121	608	14.0	80.6	3.8	1.4	2.0	14.2	6.5	17.0	9.9	14.3	11.9	12.9
56 023	...	7	Lincoln	10 557	18 722	1 884	1.8	93.5	1.0	1.3	0.7	4.5	6.6	20.4	6.9	10.9	12.6	12.7
56 025	16220	3	Natrona	13 831	82 178	682	5.9	88.5	2.2	1.6	1.4	8.1	6.8	17.1	9.3	15.5	12.4	12.5
56 027	...	9	Niobrara	6 801	2 542	3 003	0.4	92.2	1.7	2.3	0.8	2.5	4.7	11.9	6.8	14.3	12.3	12.3
56 029	...	7	Park	17 980	29 228	1 448	1.6	91.2	1.3	1.4	1.3	5.8	5.5	15.0	8.7	11.4	10.4	12.8
56 031	...	7	Platte	5 398	8 812	2 528	1.6	90.4	0.9	1.2	1.0	8.1	4.9	15.5	6.9	10.0	9.9	13.8
56 033	43260	7	Sheridan	6 537	30 009	1 429	4.6	92.9	1.1	1.9	1.4	4.2	5.6	15.9	8.1	11.6	11.8	12.7
56 035	...	9	Sublette	12 656	9 899	2 442	0.8	88.8	1.5	1.4	1.6	8.1	5.8	18.2	6.8	13.1	14.0	15.0
56 037	40540	5	Sweetwater	27 005	44 626	1 079	1.7	81.3	1.7	1.5	1.4	15.8	7.3	19.7	9.1	15.8	13.2	12.3
56 039	27220	7	Teton	10 348	23 125	1 679	2.2	82.1	1.3	1.0	1.8	15.2	5.7	13.3	6.3	19.3	15.9	13.5
56 041	21740	7	Uinta	5 390	20 822	1 787	3.9	88.8	1.1	1.4	1.1	9.2	7.6	22.2	7.9	13.1	12.6	11.9
56 043	...	7	Washakie	5 798	8 328	2 571	1.4	84.0	1.2	1.4	0.9	13.9	5.5	18.4	6.6	10.7	11.3	12.8
56 045	...	7	Weston	6 211	7 234	2 651	1.2	93.5	1.1	2.4	0.8	4.2	6.5	15.1	7.5	12.2	11.5	13.6

1. CBSA = Core Based Statistical Area. See Appendix A for explanation. See Appendix B for list of metropolitan areas with component counties.   2. County type code from the Economic Research Service of USDA Rural-Urban Continuum Codes. See Appendix A for definition.   3. Dry land or land partially or temporarily covered by water.   4. May be of any race.

Table B. States and Counties — **Population and Households**

STATE County	Population, 2014 (cont.) Age (percent) (cont.) 55 to 64 years	65 to 74 years	75 years and over	Percent female	Population change and components of change, 2000–2015 Total persons 2000	2010	Percent change 2000–2010	2010–2015	Components of change, 2010–2015 Births	Deaths	Net migration	Households, 2010–2014 Number	Persons per house-hold	Family house-holds	Percent Female family house-holder[1]	One per-son
	16	17	18	19	20	21	22	23	24	25	26	27	28	29	30	31
WYOMING—Cont'd																
Crook	16.8	11.0	7.0	49.5	5 887	7 083	20.3	5.1	516	321	193	2 974	2.39	72.3	7.3	24.5
Fremont	14.3	9.4	6.8	50.0	35 804	40 123	12.1	0.5	3 149	2 286	-690	15 290	2.61	66.0	10.8	27.9
Goshen	14.6	11.5	9.0	47.9	12 538	13 247	5.7	1.0	739	718	96	5 370	2.35	65.0	7.2	31.4
Hot Springs	18.0	12.7	10.9	50.3	4 882	4 812	-1.4	-1.5	270	352	16	2 218	2.12	60.4	5.9	35.7
Johnson	16.2	12.0	8.6	49.4	7 075	8 569	21.1	0.2	497	414	-90	3 785	2.25	63.1	5.0	32.8
Laramie	13.1	8.2	6.0	49.6	81 607	91 881	12.6	5.7	6 656	3 976	2 566	37 364	2.48	66.4	10.5	27.6
Lincoln	15.1	9.4	5.3	49.3	14 573	18 106	24.2	3.4	1 292	625	-48	6 584	2.75	74.7	6.2	21.1
Natrona	13.4	7.2	5.7	49.5	66 533	75 450	13.4	8.9	5 867	3 635	4 437	31 790	2.42	64.5	10.5	28.3
Niobrara	16.6	11.1	10.1	54.3	2 407	2 484	3.2	2.3	121	118	65	1 015	2.21	56.4	4.8	35.5
Park	16.1	11.7	8.3	50.1	25 786	28 205	9.4	3.6	1 636	1 382	748	11 751	2.37	65.3	8.4	28.9
Platte	16.3	13.1	9.6	49.1	8 807	8 667	-1.6	1.7	453	513	220	3 690	2.33	64.5	11.9	32.6
Sheridan	16.0	10.7	7.5	50.0	26 560	29 116	9.6	3.1	1 767	1 581	609	12 568	2.27	63.6	6.4	30.8
Sublette	14.5	8.3	4.3	46.3	5 920	10 247	73.1	-3.4	688	241	-827	3 540	2.82	77.1	6.1	20.1
Sweetwater	13.0	6.1	3.4	48.1	37 613	43 806	16.5	1.9	3 308	1 404	-1 043	16 687	2.63	69.1	8.9	24.8
Teton	13.7	8.0	4.3	48.2	18 251	21 294	16.7	8.6	1 344	399	870	7 873	2.69	61.4	6.3	25.3
Uinta	13.7	7.1	4.0	49.6	19 742	21 118	7.0	-1.4	1 656	706	-1 270	7 557	2.75	71.7	13.5	23.6
Washakie	14.6	11.1	9.0	49.3	8 289	8 533	2.9	-2.4	505	444	-249	3 461	2.39	65.0	8.8	30.5
Weston	15.7	9.8	8.2	47.4	6 644	7 208	8.5	0.4	430	371	-34	2 996	2.27	61.7	6.0	35.8

1. No spouse present.

Table B. States and Counties — **Population, Vital Statistics, Medicare, and Crime**

STATE County	Persons in group quarters, 2015	Daytime population, 2010-2014 Number	Daytime population, 2010-2014 Employ-ment/ resi-dence ratio	Births, 2015 Total	Births, 2015 Rate[1]	Deaths, 2015 Number	Deaths, 2015 Rate[1]	Persons under 65 with no health insurance, 2014 Number	Persons under 65 with no health insurance, 2014 Percent	Medicare, 2015 Total Beneficiaries	Medicare, 2015 Enrolled in Original Medicare	Medicare, 2015 Enrolled in Medicare Advantage	Serious crimes known to police,[2] 2014 Total Number	Serious crimes known to police,[2] 2014 Total Rate[3]
	32	33	34	35	36	37	38	39	40	41	42	43	44	45
WYOMING—Cont'd														
Crook	34	6 242	0.75	105	14.3	56	7.6	860	14.5	1 294	1 218	76	90	1 256
Fremont	871	40 434	0.98	583	14.4	466	11.5	6 735	20.3	7 373	6 733	640	853	2 082
Goshen	1 158	13 128	0.93	154	11.5	142	10.6	1 686	17.4	2 820	2 783	37	212	1 560
Hot Springs	86	4 733	0.96	49	10.3	73	15.3	638	17.5	1 294	1 272	22	39	807
Johnson	71	7 957	0.86	92	10.7	77	9.0	993	14.7	1 787	1 760	27	165	1 920
Laramie	1 957	96 867	1.05	1 263	13.0	776	8.0	9 515	11.7	15 821	15 140	681	2 495	2 593
Lincoln	71	16 783	0.83	248	13.3	116	6.2	2 360	15.0	2 917	2 813	104	176	1 020
Natrona	1 721	79 412	1.02	1 194	14.6	706	8.6	9 969	14.3	12 006	11 421	585	2 102	2 565
Niobrara	248	2 505	1.01	25	9.9	18	7.1	292	17.2	541	530	11	NA	NA
Park	866	28 846	1.01	313	10.7	253	8.7	3 490	15.5	6 437	6 326	111	497	1 696
Platte	100	8 815	1.02	90	10.2	91	10.3	1 004	14.9	2 097	2 053	44	164	1 877
Sheridan	1 023	28 707	0.94	338	11.3	318	10.6	3 308	13.9	6 086	5 771	315	499	1 673
Sublette	550	11 170	1.19	128	12.8	51	5.1	1 142	13.1	1 166	1 135	31	86	865
Sweetwater	672	46 649	1.09	620	13.8	262	5.9	5 626	14.0	5 130	4 897	233	954	2 101
Teton	267	25 111	1.24	269	11.7	76	3.3	3 009	15.0	2 705	2 562	143	NA	NA
Uinta	254	20 105	0.91	316	15.1	137	6.6	2 408	13.1	2 525	2 225	300	432	2 292
Washakie	140	8 670	1.06	90	10.8	79	9.5	1 105	16.9	1 697	1 679	18	63	750
Weston	317	6 367	0.77	79	11.0	77	10.7	847	15.1	1 366	1 281	85	87	1 445

1. Per 1,000 estimated resident population.   2. Data for serious crimes have not been adjusted for underreporting; this may affect comparability between geographic areas and over time.
3. Per 100,000 population estimated by the FBI.

Table B. States and Counties — **Crime, Education, Money Income, and Poverty**

STATE County	Serious crimes known to police, 2014 (cont.)[1] Rate[2]		Education						Money income, 2010–2014				Income and poverty, 2014			
			School enrollment and attainment, 2010–2014				Local government expenditures,[5] 2012–2013			Households				Percent below poverty level		
			Enrollment[3]		Attainment[4] (percent)											
	Violent	Property	Total	Per-cent private	High school grad-uate or less	Bach-elor's degree or more	Total current spending (mil dol)	Current spend-ing per student (dollars)	Per capita income[6] (dollars)	Median income (dollars)	Mean income (dollars)	Percent with income of $200,000 or more	Median house-hold income (dollars)	All per-sons	Children under 18 years	Children 5 to 17 years in families
	46	47	48	49	50	51	52	53	54	55	56	57	58	59	60	61
WYOMING—Cont'd																
Crook	195	1 061	1 539	10.7	39.5	21.6	20.4	18 935	31 183	58 795	73 954	3.7	59 701	8.4	11.3	10.7
Fremont	142	1 941	9 914	8.7	39.1	21.5	128.5	19 033	24 431	51 749	62 630	1.9	48 624	14.0	20.2	18.4
Goshen	309	1 251	3 121	15.4	41.0	21.5	31.0	18 009	24 900	45 287	60 394	1.2	45 721	14.3	19.0	17.3
Hot Springs	41	766	1 000	8.7	42.0	19.5	12.0	18 464	27 548	45 385	59 388	2.6	44 427	10.9	16.7	14.2
Johnson	128	1 792	1 842	13.6	39.0	27.0	22.0	17 080	28 062	56 708	64 047	1.3	51 434	9.7	11.7	10.5
Laramie	160	2 433	24 252	9.5	33.6	26.8	218.6	15 257	29 375	58 324	72 015	2.9	57 192	10.8	14.2	12.8
Lincoln	87	933	4 675	7.1	38.2	20.1	50.7	16 048	28 077	66 530	75 533	3.2	63 575	9.0	12.2	10.8
Natrona	184	2 380	19 291	9.5	36.4	21.3	180.8	13 823	30 265	56 769	73 021	4.1	57 427	10.4	13.6	12.1
Niobrara	NA	NA	440	10.0	36.6	21.4	11.4	11 668	25 867	39 567	59 703	3.7	45 251	14.7	18.2	16.6
Park	201	1 494	6 604	7.0	35.3	28.3	61.8	15 542	28 870	56 318	67 802	2.4	55 354	10.8	15.7	14.2
Platte	137	1 740	1 703	12.1	38.8	19.2	23.9	19 318	25 302	41 299	55 468	0.5	49 713	13.0	19.3	15.2
Sheridan	151	1 522	6 633	13.9	32.2	28.9	67.0	15 684	29 656	56 015	68 432	3.2	54 716	9.9	13.1	11.6
Sublette	101	765	2 364	4.4	36.3	23.6	32.9	19 991	33 532	78 578	86 355	1.6	77 222	6.8	7.5	6.6
Sweetwater	295	1 806	11 749	10.4	45.3	18.1	115.2	14 100	30 500	69 448	79 437	2.9	72 604	9.8	11.9	10.3
Teton	NA	NA	4 200	15.3	23.5	51.9	43.8	17 596	43 628	73 572	110 785	10.8	75 348	7.7	9.5	8.7
Uinta	48	2 245	5 908	6.0	43.9	18.7	64.6	14 776	25 778	56 158	68 728	3.1	56 800	10.0	12.6	10.5
Washakie	83	667	1 966	10.5	42.5	21.2	25.8	17 104	26 922	45 696	63 543	2.9	50 802	12.6	16.2	14.6
Weston	183	1 262	1 609	13.2	43.7	16.8	19.2	18 420	29 091	53 920	66 972	2.9	55 520	13.2	18.4	18.1

1. Data for serious crimes have not been adjusted for underreporting; this may affect comparability between geographic areas and over time.   2. Per 100,000 population estimated by the FBI.
3. All persons 3 years old and over enrolled in nursery school through college.   4. Persons 25 years old and over.   5. Elementary and secondary education expenditures.
6. Based on population estimated by the American Community Survey, 2010–2014.

STATE County	Personal income, 2014										Earnings, 2014		
			Per capita[1]			Supplements to wages and salaries; employer contributions (mil dol)						Contributions for government social insurance (mil dol)	
	Total (mil dol)	Percent change, 2013–2014	Dollars	Rank	Wages and salaries (mil dol)	Pension and insurance	Government social insurance	Proprietors' income (mil dol)	Dividends, interest, and rent (mil dol)	Personal transfer receipts (mil dol)	Total (mil dol)	From employee and self-employed	From employer
	62	63	64	65	66	67	68	69	70	71	72	73	74
WYOMING—Cont'd													
Crook	337	9.6	46 529	557	104	20	10	37	88	46	172	10	10
Fremont	1 668	2.8	40 970	1 065	741	140	72	88	387	334	1 041	63	72
Goshen	549	4.6	40 640	1 104	177	38	18	60	114	111	293	17	18
Hot Springs	218	4.7	45 227	655	87	16	8	18	44	51	129	8	8
Johnson	398	9.4	46 439	563	149	28	15	58	104	61	250	14	15
Laramie	4 745	3.9	49 225	426	2 376	478	245	296	1 131	725	3 394	190	245
Lincoln	747	4.3	40 217	1 146	271	56	26	60	198	116	414	24	26
Natrona	4 888	6.5	59 890	134	2 343	292	219	730	1 210	536	3 584	206	219
Niobrara	121	13.0	49 300	421	42	10	4	21	26	23	77	4	4
Park	1 381	4.0	47 625	492	589	107	59	117	408	238	871	53	59
Platte	393	7.4	44 713	702	174	35	19	57	76	80	286	16	19
Sheridan	1 569	5.8	52 239	286	580	105	62	132	492	229	879	53	62
Sublette	519	4.7	51 579	309	322	45	28	66	151	45	461	26	28
Sweetwater	2 514	3.4	55 855	201	1 523	217	136	556	288	239	2 432	134	136
Teton	4 460	8.8	194 485	1	873	100	95	281	3 295	110	1 349	74	95
Uinta	886	0.9	42 395	914	412	71	40	56	148	133	579	34	40
Washakie	350	3.9	42 004	951	166	30	17	23	86	64	236	14	17
Weston	420	9.0	58 314	154	100	24	10	133	61	53	266	13	10

1. Based on the resident population estimated as of July 1 of the year shown.

STATE County	Earnings, 2014 (cont.)									Social Security beneficiaries, December 2014			Housing units, 2015	
	Percent by selected industries											Supplemental Security Income recipients, December 2014		
	Farm	Mining	Construction	Manu-facturing	Infor-mation: professional, scientific, technical services	Retail trade	Finance, insur-ance, real estate and leasing	Health care and social assistance	Govern-ment	Number	Rate[1]		Total	Percent change, 2010–2014
	75	76	77	78	79	80	81	82	83	84	85	86	87	88
WYOMING—Cont'd														
Crook	7.5	14.8	11.0	8.1	2.2	5.3	2.7	D	24.7	1 485	204	37	3 567	-0.8
Fremont	2.2	10.6	6.3	1.2	5.1	6.8	5.2	D	35.2	8 495	209	865	17 685	-0.6
Goshen	14.2	0.3	4.5	4.6	3.9	4.8	3.9	13.9	31.4	3 070	227	231	5 936	-0.6
Hot Springs	3.2	D	D	2.3	D	D	2.5	9.6	26.7	1 465	306	94	2 542	-1.5
Johnson	7.6	7.1	22.9	0.7	5.5	4.5	5.6	D	27.6	2 010	235	49	4 530	-0.5
Laramie	1.3	1.5	7.6	3.5	7.2	6.2	5.7	7.7	39.8	17 105	177	1 533	41 955	3.7
Lincoln	2.0	18.2	11.3	1.8	5.3	6.2	4.0	3.2	28.6	3 415	184	150	9 058	1.3
Natrona	0.3	20.2	9.6	4.5	5.2	5.7	5.7	12.0	12.1	13 640	167	1 186	36 067	6.7
Niobrara	18.7	8.4	D	D	D	D	4.1	D	36.5	610	241	29	1 334	-0.3
Park	1.1	7.5	10.6	3.8	6.0	7.6	4.2	10.4	27.6	7 140	245	277	14 010	3.3
Platte	12.0	D	12.9	1.2	2.1	6.0	3.4	5.7	19.1	2 315	264	95	4 711	0.9
Sheridan	1.4	3.2	10.9	3.1	7.1	7.5	5.9	8.6	28.9	6 540	218	299	14 440	3.6
Sublette	2.6	38.2	14.3	0.4	3.6	3.9	3.6	D	17.1	1 380	137	42	5 879	1.9
Sweetwater	0.2	46.3	6.0	6.7	2.4	3.7	3.3	2.6	12.9	6 040	134	375	19 245	2.7
Teton	0.3	D	10.8	1.0	12.6	7.0	14.4	4.4	13.6	2 850	124	54	13 395	4.5
Uinta	0.6	11.7	13.7	3.6	8.2	6.4	3.7	D	22.7	3 125	150	276	8 788	0.9
Washakie	3.1	7.2	8.3	12.2	5.0	5.8	4.4	D	23.2	1 935	233	88	3 804	-0.8
Weston	5.3	19.9	16.0	5.3	3.4	5.7	6.8	D	18.6	1 575	219	55	3 489	-1.2

1. Per 1,000 resident population estimated as of July 1 of the year shown.

Table B. States and Counties — Housing, Labor Force, and Employment

STATE County	Housing units, 2010–2014								Civilian labor force, 2015				Civilian employment,[6] 2010–2014		
	Occupied units										Unemployment			Percent	
			Owner-occupied			Renter-occupied									
				Median owner cost as a percent of income											Con-struction, produc-tion, and mainte-nance occu-pations
	Total	Percent	Median value[1]	With a mort-gage	Without a mort-gage[2]	Median rent[3]	Median rent as a per-cent of income[2]	Sub-stand-ard units[4] (percent)	Total	Percent change, 2014–2015	Total	Rate[5]	Total	Manage-ment, business, science and arts	
	89	90	91	92	93	94	95	96	97	98	99	100	101	102	103
WYOMING—Cont'd															
Crook........................	2 974	78.6	188 100	19.1	10.0	726	15.4	2.5	3 711	-0.2	127	3.4	3 722	33.4	34.7
Fremont.....................	15 290	71.8	183 700	22.1	10.0	683	25.7	4.5	20 379	-1.1	1 106	5.4	18 352	34.3	23.8
Goshen......................	5 370	75.0	147 600	20.2	10.6	672	26.1	1.0	7 199	0.6	230	3.2	6 411	32.3	30.2
Hot Springs	2 218	73.0	147 600	21.9	10.0	628	21.5	2.1	2 409	-3.3	98	4.1	2 246	36.2	24.1
Johnson.....................	3 785	74.2	225 400	20.1	12.6	792	23.3	1.0	4 218	-6.0	203	4.8	4 548	37.5	26.0
Laramie.....................	37 364	68.1	186 600	21.7	10.0	783	27.0	1.3	48 910	0.1	1 888	3.9	45 964	36.7	22.4
Lincoln......................	6 584	82.4	194 700	22.2	10.0	792	23.8	3.2	8 419	2.0	389	4.6	8 534	31.1	31.2
Natrona.....................	31 790	67.9	183 100	20.9	10.0	831	26.2	1.9	42 894	-1.3	2 053	4.8	40 974	29.4	27.5
Niobrara....................	1 015	62.8	135 900	23.5	11.2	600	24.4	0.1	1 318	-2.7	38	2.9	1 179	41.1	22.2
Park..........................	11 751	72.3	213 200	21.5	11.4	673	20.2	1.3	15 875	0.6	664	4.2	15 270	31.0	23.2
Platte........................	3 690	76.9	147 200	23.3	11.5	580	28.2	0.6	4 977	3.9	189	3.8	4 030	32.1	27.0
Sheridan....................	12 568	69.9	219 400	22.4	10.6	757	26.3	2.5	15 988	0.3	663	4.1	14 386	37.2	26.0
Sublette.....................	3 540	73.1	284 400	20.8	10.0	1 180	22.1	2.7	4 617	-5.4	236	5.1	5 411	40.8	36.3
Sweetwater................	16 687	70.6	183 400	19.0	10.0	908	22.5	3.4	22 886	-1.9	1 053	4.6	22 956	24.7	39.0
Teton........................	7 873	59.0	675 000	23.7	10.0	1 108	29.2	5.7	14 771	2.1	558	3.8	13 843	39.5	16.3
Uinta.........................	7 557	70.4	174 800	21.2	10.0	675	24.2	2.8	9 745	-1.6	475	4.9	9 941	29.8	32.0
Washakie...................	3 461	68.9	158 700	21.9	12.6	578	21.3	2.6	4 322	0.9	174	4.0	3 875	27.7	35.8
Weston......................	2 996	75.6	160 600	21.3	10.0	735	20.0	4.7	3 980	0.0	133	3.3	3 402	30.6	38.0

1. Specified owner-occupied units.   2. A value of 10.0 represents 10 percent or less; a value of 50.0 represents 50 percent or more.   3. Specified renter-occupied units.
4. Overcrowded or lacking complete plumbing facilities.   5. Percent of civilian labor force.   6. Persons 16 years old and over.

STATE County	Number of establishments	Total	Health care and social assistance	Manufacturing	Retail trade	Finance and insurance	Professional, scientific, and technical services	Total (mil dol)	Average per employee (dollars)	Number	Fewer than 50 acres	500 acres or more	Farm operators whose principal occupation is farming (percent)
	104	105	106	107	108	109	110	111	112	113	114	115	116
WYOMING—Cont'd													
Crook	231	1 559	195	D	168	D	D	71	45 486	482	10.4	58.5	61.8
Fremont	1 364	11 890	1 969	291	2 154	306	473	479	40 326	1 363	37.0	20.4	55.0
Goshen	346	3 079	708	300	447	134	126	92	29 874	790	15.4	43.0	59.6
Hot Springs	176	1 657	415	D	167	D	49	63	37 883	178	32.6	31.5	42.7
Johnson	413	2 324	D	64	355	144	167	86	36 864	358	19.0	53.4	51.7
Laramie	3 056	34 481	6 608	1 257	6 099	1 753	2 414	1 409	40 859	1 116	33.5	31.2	37.3
Lincoln	630	4 033	691	275	624	115	104	190	47 155	608	41.0	20.1	46.4
Natrona	2 982	36 040	5 766	1 656	5 167	976	1 791	1 766	49 012	397	31.5	33.5	49.4
Niobrara	89	434	62	D	127	D	D	13	30 724	234	6.0	82.5	80.8
Park	1 176	9 892	D	540	1 622	309	389	404	40 796	860	37.4	18.8	47.4
Platte	267	2 288	327	132	446	105	51	93	40 660	505	18.2	46.9	59.4
Sheridan	1 126	10 473	2 199	455	1 681	D	676	386	36 816	702	36.3	31.8	45.9
Sublette	436	3 629	191	D	302	D	120	282	77 689	398	32.4	41.5	51.5
Sweetwater	1 338	17 350	1 275	1 894	2 505	318	539	1 000	57 625	255	27.8	36.9	30.6
Teton	2 005	16 495	1 235	142	1 959	D	849	670	40 634	154	50.6	12.3	41.6
Uinta	596	8 542	1 352	218	1 116	D	315	423	49 497	315	28.9	33.3	44.1
Washakie	366	2 846	774	276	363	96	130	106	37 104	209	39.2	35.4	52.6
Weston	224	1 744	353	D	312	54	27	65	37 370	264	7.2	50.4	51.1

Table B. States and Counties — **Agriculture**

Agriculture, 2012 (cont.)

STATE County	Land in farms — Acreage (1,000)	Percent change, 2007–2012	Average size of farm	Total irrigated (1,000)	Total cropland (1,000)	Value of land and buildings (dollars) Average per farm	Average per acre	Value of machinery and equipment, average per farm (dollars)	Value of products sold Total (mil dol)	Average per farm (dollars)	Percent from: Crops	Live-stock and poultry products	Percent of farms with sales of: $10,000 or more	$100,000 or more	Government payments Total ($1,000)	Percent of farms
	117	118	119	120	121	122	123	124	125	126	127	128	129	130	131	132
WYOMING—Cont'd																
Crook	1 587	1.1	3 292	7.8	151.3	2 920 595	887	130 118	67.1	139 137	8.6	91.4	57.3	26.8	1 205	43.2
Fremont	1 710	-5.0	1 255	157.1	168.0	1 091 768	870	103 492	102.5	75 189	49.8	50.2	45.3	21.4	2 052	17.2
Goshen	1 370	0.1	1 735	109.2	241.5	1 346 967	777	141 356	246.6	312 103	26.8	73.2	58.1	33.3	4 662	55.6
Hot Springs	517	-5.4	2 906	12.6	28.1	2 030 427	699	84 197	16.4	92 388	12.7	87.3	49.4	17.4	361	10.7
Johnson	2 036	4.6	5 686	40.0	59.8	3 452 782	607	119 444	51.7	144 441	8.9	91.1	57.8	32.4	750	14.5
Laramie	1 676	-0.9	1 502	59.3	338.1	1 079 159	719	110 585	190.7	170 918	24.4	75.6	37.0	17.6	4 938	32.7
Lincoln	344	0.3	565	72.7	98.5	1 017 597	1 800	87 056	40.8	67 153	30.7	69.3	45.6	19.9	732	27.8
Natrona	1 691	-22.5	4 259	28.9	43.3	2 656 418	624	133 912	42.9	108 118	16.5	83.5	49.6	23.7	634	11.3
Niobrara	1 359	-6.2	5 807	14.6	75.4	3 112 043	536	122 726	45.3	193 684	18.0	82.0	78.6	49.6	1 331	39.7
Park	813	-7.8	946	110.3	109.9	1 324 298	1 401	105 421	100.3	116 611	63.4	36.6	42.8	18.3	1 271	27.1
Platte	1 224	-6.4	2 424	72.2	147.9	1 743 954	719	178 135	130.4	258 151	23.3	76.7	61.0	32.3	2 397	40.0
Sheridan	1 305	6.6	1 859	49.8	74.6	1 532 138	824	87 229	59.8	85 190	16.5	83.5	46.0	17.1	537	10.5
Sublette	778	29.7	1 954	143.1	122.6	2 626 852	1 345	104 369	54.2	136 116	14.5	85.5	43.5	24.6	373	5.5
Sweetwater	1 665	12.0	6 531	28.4	36.0	1 321 392	202	106 012	21.1	82 894	35.2	64.8	49.8	14.9	250	16.5
Teton	40	-24.1	261	14.7	10.5	829 494	3 181	69 526	9.0	58 675	24.2	75.8	34.4	7.1	16	1.9
Uinta	650	-12.5	2 064	70.1	68.7	1 518 038	735	99 092	29.9	94 816	10.2	89.8	53.7	21.6	88	3.8
Washakie	341	-27.3	1 633	38.4	39.9	1 450 273	888	172 411	51.9	248 153	51.2	48.8	57.9	29.7	451	20.6
Weston	1 290	-2.9	4 888	4.2	57.0	2 282 818	467	132 371	52.2	197 833	4.3	95.7	45.5	26.9	757	27.3

Table B. States and Counties — **Water Use, Wholesale Trade, Retail Trade, and Real Estate**

STATE County	Water use, 2010		Wholesale trade,[1] 2012				Retail trade,[2] 2012				Real estate and rental and leasing,[2] 2012			
	Total water withdrawn (mil gal/day)	Gallons withdrawn per person per day	Number of establishments	Number of employees	Sales (mil dol)	Annual payroll (mil dol)	Number of establishments	Number of employees	Sales (mil dol)	Annual payroll (mil dol)	Number of establishments	Number of employees	Receipts (mil dol)	Annual payroll (mil dol)
	133	134	135	136	137	138	139	140	141	142	143	144	145	146
WYOMING—Cont'd														
Crook	50.5	7 124	8	D	D	D	26	160	39.6	3.4	8	D	D	D
Fremont	510.0	12 711	42	D	D	D	165	2 096	581.8	53.8	71	459	130.6	27.0
Goshen	395.2	29 829	20	156	69.8	5.8	51	402	107.4	8.7	14	25	3.5	0.6
Hot Springs	78.3	16 268	4	30	13.1	2.3	26	195	48.2	3.0	6	D	D	D
Johnson	118.4	13 814	6	27	8.6	0.7	52	359	91.4	8.1	17	46	4.8	1.5
Laramie	236.4	2 577	121	1 105	722.2	67.0	370	5 513	1 896.2	161.3	142	461	99.5	16.5
Lincoln	204.3	11 282	8	55	17.8	1.7	79	659	180.6	13.3	13	17	2.2	0.4
Natrona	172.3	2 283	163	1 890	2 052.7	115.2	363	4 796	1 487.5	132.1	166	1 281	502.0	79.4
Niobrara	68.9	27 738	2	D	D	D	13	110	28.8	2.3	5	3	1.7	0.2
Park	305.0	10 813	40	270	227.9	12.3	185	1 523	417.5	37.1	57	117	15.1	2.3
Platte	350.2	40 404	5	28	22.0	0.8	35	371	87.5	8.0	11	44	15.2	2.2
Sheridan	198.2	6 808	34	187	84.7	6.8	151	1 559	475.9	42.5	60	204	28.6	5.9
Sublette	167.1	16 311	8	46	41.6	2.7	41	401	94.7	9.7	31	151	27.9	6.4
Sweetwater	169.0	3 859	61	D	D	D	199	2 461	921.4	69.9	85	377	115.4	21.0
Teton	31.2	1 466	32	D	D	D	241	1 929	512.6	55.6	146	527	128.8	26.0
Uinta	217.9	10 316	20	216	153.9	11.3	92	1 119	389.9	24.3	39	148	29.8	5.1
Washakie	165.5	19 393	8	42	15.8	1.3	46	334	95.4	10.0	17	D	D	D
Weston	27.9	3 869	5	40	27.6	1.7	31	267	76.5	6.1	4	6	1.1	0.2

1. Merchant wholesalers, except manufacturers' sales branches and offices.   2. Employer establishments.

STATE County	Professional, scientific, and technical services, 2012				Manufacturing, 2012				Accommodation and food services, 2012			
	Number of establishments	Number of employees	Receipts (mil dol)	Annual payroll (mil dol)	Number of establishments	Number of employees	Receipts (mil dol)	Annual payroll (mil dol)	Number of establishments	Number of employees	Sales (mil dol)	Annual payroll (mil dol)
	147	148	149	150	151	152	153	154	155	156	157	158
WYOMING—Cont'd												
Crook	14	30	4.0	1.1	7	139	D	5.4	27	156	8.5	1.9
Fremont	129	494	66.2	25.4	35	246	57.0	10.4	128	1 373	66.1	18.5
Goshen	24	158	8.4	4.3	12	308	D	9.9	30	320	15.9	3.8
Hot Springs	15	49	4.2	1.7	4	32	8.0	2.1	26	D	D	D
Johnson	49	149	18.1	6.6	12	64	D	2.8	42	403	23.3	7.2
Laramie	458	1 860	279.8	99.7	67	1 190	2 549.8	76.8	207	3 980	224.8	59.8
Lincoln	62	106	12.6	4.0	18	371	D	22.2	60	406	18.0	4.4
Natrona	278	1 537	222.4	83.2	83	2 428	1 780.3	163.0	200	3 814	198.2	57.4
Niobrara	5	9	0.7	0.1	3	D	1.4	D	13	95	5.1	1.2
Park	99	338	36.9	14.6	44	410	90.4	18.5	124	1 891	170.9	49.7
Platte	16	51	6.2	1.3	14	64	10.8	2.3	36	346	21.3	4.1
Sheridan	127	675	92.3	31.2	28	383	102.3	19.3	92	1 213	68.7	19.2
Sublette	54	139	20.1	6.7	9	31	D	1.5	40	358	24.4	6.9
Sweetwater	121	493	90.2	31.7	35	1 772	1 575.5	148.7	113	1 771	128.9	28.1
Teton	268	744	139.3	46.8	34	254	34.1	8.0	186	4 598	344.0	114.7
Uinta	54	285	33.8	13.8	24	233	204.2	9.8	48	875	35.5	9.9
Washakie	37	104	11.9	4.1	14	387	187.5	18.5	32	284	11.6	3.2
Weston	11	23	2.4	0.7	3	D	D	D	22	190	9.4	2.4

1. Establishment subject to federal tax.

Table B. States and Counties — **Health Care and Social Assistance, Other Services, Nonemployer Businesses, and Residential Construction**

STATE County	Health care and social assistance, 2012				Other services, 2012				Nonemployer businesses, 2014		Value of residential construction authorized by building permits, 2015	
	Number of establish-ments	Number of employees	Receipts (mil dol)	Annual payroll (mil dol)	Number of establish-ments	Number of employees	Receipts (mil dol)	Annual payroll (mil dol)	Number	Receipts (mil dol)	New Construction ($1,000)	Number of housing units
	159	160	161	162	163	164	165	166	167	168	169	170
WYOMING—Cont'd												
Crook	15	D	D	D	9	D	D	D	717	32.2	1 314	5
Fremont	161	1 985	181.5	72.1	82	349	37.2	9.5	2 965	117.2	3 323	19
Goshen	27	803	60.5	25.6	28	89	9.3	2.3	946	36.9	1 176	4
Hot Springs	19	395	34.2	15.5	14	58	3.9	1.1	400	13.9	0	0
Johnson	32	375	32.1	13.2	22	104	7.6	2.8	1 118	54.1	5 250	19
Laramie	323	6 700	647.9	305.2	189	943	93.6	27.1	7 327	450.5	75 787	440
Lincoln	56	643	58.5	24.1	38	77	9.9	2.2	1 861	78.9	28 986	105
Natrona	305	5 141	687.2	266.3	207	1 333	227.6	49.8	5 861	331.0	56 822	271
Niobrara	7	D	D	D	7	28	6.7	1.3	255	11.6	625	11
Park	116	1 399	146.3	55.5	70	248	24.9	6.5	3 025	129.0	35 548	143
Platte	22	325	27.7	10.9	13	50	3.7	0.9	773	28.9	4 646	23
Sheridan	128	2 705	302.2	125.1	74	334	31.1	8.6	2 716	112.6	32 200	133
Sublette	23	207	13.3	6.8	32	162	25.1	6.3	1 003	48.6	8 461	30
Sweetwater	104	1 285	150.2	51.2	88	464	58.7	16.1	2 176	101.0	20 853	84
Teton	117	1 120	158.9	60.5	113	450	109.0	17.0	4 838	320.6	242 843	236
Uinta	67	1 265	110.3	53.9	35	D	D	D	1 379	69.3	7 857	35
Washakie	29	787	51.6	23.0	28	94	9.7	1.8	668	23.8	970	5
Weston	24	352	25.3	10.5	12	38	3.1	0.8	604	25.2	277	6

Table B. States and Counties — Government Employment and Payroll, and Local Government Finances

STATE County	Government employment and payroll, 2012									Local government finances, 2012				
	Full-time equivalent employees	March payroll (dollars)	March payroll (percent of total)							General revenue				
			Adminis-tration, judicial, and legal	Police and Corrections	Fire Protection	Highways and transpor-tation	Health and Welfare	Natural resources and utilities	Education and libraries	Total (mil dol)	Inter-govern-mental (mil dol)	Taxes		
												Total (mil dol)	Per capita[1] (dollars) Total	Property
	171	172	173	174	175	176	177	178	179	180	181	182	183	184
WYOMING—Cont'd														
Crook	486	1 567 725	9.6	7.3	0.1	2.9	16.3	2.3	60.3	47.3	23.8	13.5	1 893	1 459
Fremont	2 549	9 152 411	3.7	7.9	0.4	2.1	3.0	9.4	71.6	264.6	168.1	62.0	1 509	1 270
Goshen	800	2 841 581	5.6	7.0	0.0	2.4	1.3	5.3	77.7	86.6	58.5	10.5	773	552
Hot Springs	363	1 248 475	7.7	7.2	0.0	3.0	30.6	3.5	46.8	44.5	12.8	14.8	3 062	2 366
Johnson	670	2 461 238	5.8	13.9	1.0	2.9	30.1	3.1	42.7	83.0	14.4	44.9	5 208	4 585
Laramie	6 173	27 578 286	2.8	4.6	1.9	1.8	39.8	1.5	46.1	796.0	292.8	103.3	1 094	589
Lincoln	1 211	4 847 475	5.1	5.7	0.0	2.9	30.1	3.4	50.4	146.8	60.4	43.1	2 402	2 075
Natrona	3 954	15 321 295	4.4	7.8	3.5	2.3	2.0	5.1	72.5	442.5	254.7	108.8	1 384	938
Niobrara	300	1 035 735	7.3	4.9	0.0	2.2	34.2	5.3	43.5	21.1	9.3	5.8	2 352	1 687
Park	2 084	8 399 901	4.2	4.7	0.4	2.6	27.2	5.2	52.8	238.1	92.8	47.9	1 668	1 494
Platte	543	2 168 168	5.1	7.9	0.2	2.2	1.5	6.3	74.9	46.5	26.6	13.3	1 519	995
Sheridan	2 207	8 719 701	3.2	4.7	1.0	2.3	30.0	3.0	54.6	234.1	106.6	40.1	1 354	946
Sublette	677	2 840 346	8.1	15.4	0.0	10.5	11.9	4.2	49.3	142.2	33.5	91.3	8 805	8 657
Sweetwater	2 985	12 809 450	6.0	8.4	2.4	2.6	20.2	5.8	52.6	382.6	116.8	165.8	3 662	2 797
Teton	1 475	6 340 874	5.4	7.3	1.5	7.9	37.5	5.7	32.3	225.0	41.2	80.1	3 695	2 344
Uinta	1 240	4 518 508	5.8	7.1	0.8	2.5	1.9	5.2	73.2	117.5	70.3	38.1	1 811	1 505
Washakie	459	1 506 233	5.8	5.8	0.7	2.9	2.6	6.0	75.1	45.2	28.7	12.2	1 442	998
Weston	521	1 865 375	4.5	8.0	0.4	2.9	23.8	5.3	54.7	44.2	22.9	9.7	1 375	1 062

1. Based on the resident population estimated as of July 1 of the year shown.

Table B. States and Counties — **Local Government Finances, Government Employment, and Voting**

STATE County	Local government finances, 2012 (cont.)									Government employment, 2014			Presidential election,[2] 2012		
	Direct general expenditure							Debt outstanding					Percent of vote cast:		
			Percent of total for:												
	Total (mil dol)	Per capita[1] (dollars)	Educa-tion	Health and hospitals	Police protec-tion	Public welfare	High-ways	Total (mil dol)	Per capita[1] (dollars)	Federal civilian	Federal military	State and local	Demo-cratic	Republi-can	All other
	185	186	187	188	189	190	191	192	193	194	195	196	197	198	199
WYOMING—Cont'd															
Crook	47.5	6 641	47.4	16.7	4.3	0.1	7.7	3.6	504	85	39	628	16.6	80.6	2.8
Fremont	258.8	6 295	73.2	1.1	4.0	0.4	3.3	31.2	759	483	216	5 322	34.2	63.0	2.8
Goshen	86.2	6 325	66.3	1.5	3.7	0.9	7.3	10.3	756	79	67	1 412	31.0	66.7	2.3
Hot Springs	44.9	9 306	33.3	31.7	3.7	0.0	5.2	4.5	931	13	26	553	24.3	72.0	3.7
Johnson	95.5	11 080	33.0	26.7	3.3	0.5	6.3	14.7	1 711	124	46	867	20.9	76.6	2.6
Laramie	781.4	8 270	37.0	40.5	2.5	0.2	3.1	132.4	1 401	2 567	3 485	11 386	38.6	59.0	2.4
Lincoln	144.3	8 033	47.9	26.3	3.6	0.1	4.8	60.9	3 388	111	100	1 663	21.3	75.7	3.0
Natrona	436.0	5 546	59.1	0.4	4.8	0.7	4.1	147.1	1 871	638	433	5 169	31.5	65.8	2.7
Niobrara	27.9	11 371	45.7	24.9	4.4	0.1	4.6	111.4	45 347	13	12	446	18.9	78.7	2.5
Park	277.9	9 682	41.4	36.2	2.5	0.0	2.9	79.0	2 754	775	152	2 801	25.1	72.3	2.6
Platte	48.9	5 582	54.4	2.9	7.4	0.1	4.1	8.7	993	111	47	827	30.9	65.8	3.3
Sheridan	252.8	8 543	49.0	26.5	2.5	0.0	5.2	33.2	1 121	752	157	2 686	29.8	67.9	2.3
Sublette	154.1	14 868	43.1	8.2	4.0	1.8	11.0	9.5	919	124	51	947	21.5	76.1	2.4
Sweetwater	389.7	8 609	48.2	17.5	5.5	0.3	4.3	69.5	1 536	217	240	4 312	34.5	62.0	3.5
Teton	218.0	10 059	24.1	34.3	3.8	0.0	2.4	92.9	4 287	416	123	1 939	60.7	37.1	2.3
Uinta	121.7	5 787	64.9	0.8	5.8	0.9	4.8	14.0	665	67	112	2 098	27.6	68.7	3.6
Washakie	52.1	6 153	68.3	0.8	4.1	0.4	3.0	12.8	1 512	115	44	743	25.5	72.3	2.2
Weston	48.0	6 780	47.5	21.6	4.2	0.6	10.3	2.0	286	51	37	760	19.4	77.2	3.4

1. Based on the resident population estimated as of July 1 of the year shown.   2. © 2013 Election Data Services, Inc. All rights reserved.

Metropolitan Areas

(For explanation of symbols, see page viii)

Page

Part C—Metropolitan Areas

Metropolitan Area Highlights and Rankings

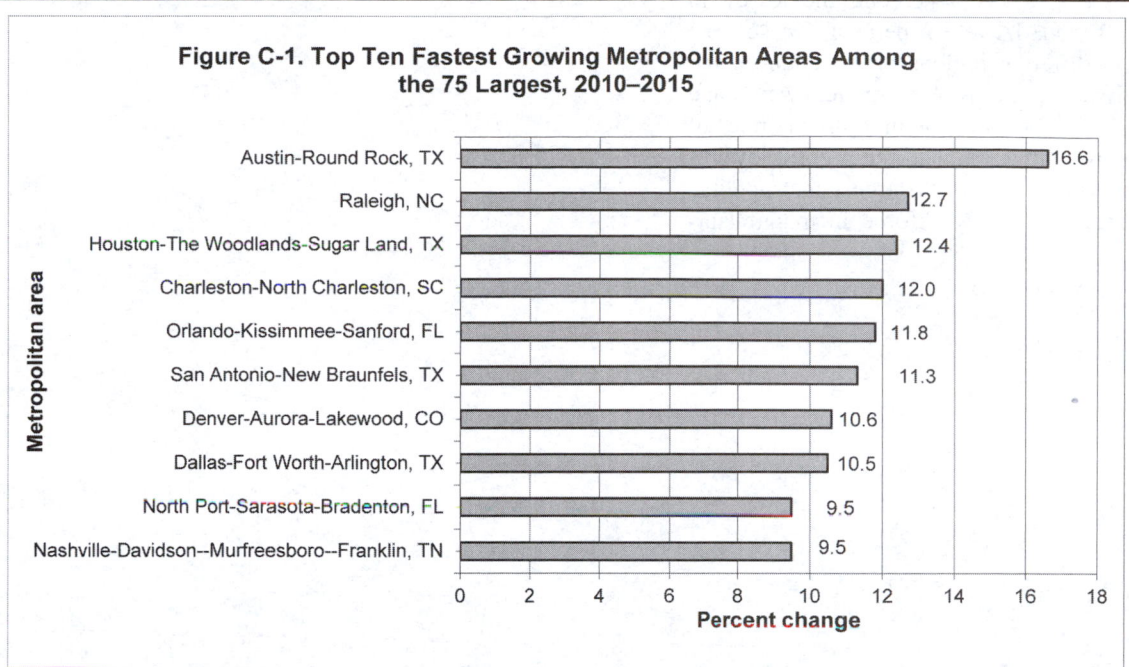

Figure C-1. Top Ten Fastest Growing Metropolitan Areas Among the 75 Largest, 2010–2015

Metropolitan area	Percent change
Austin-Round Rock, TX	16.6
Raleigh, NC	12.7
Houston-The Woodlands-Sugar Land, TX	12.4
Charleston-North Charleston, SC	12.0
Orlando-Kissimmee-Sanford, FL	11.8
San Antonio-New Braunfels, TX	11.3
Denver-Aurora-Lakewood, CO	10.6
Dallas-Fort Worth-Arlington, TX	10.5
North Port-Sarasota-Bradenton, FL	9.5
Nashville-Davidson--Murfreesboro--Franklin, TN	9.5

In 2015, 85.5 percent of Americans lived in metropolitan areas, but these metropolitan areas made up a mere 28 percent of the nation's land area. After nearly a decade of research and development, the Office of Management and Budget (OMB) first established new rules for defining metropolitan areas and issued a completely new list after the 2000 census. This scheme defines a variety of areas called "Core Based Statistical Areas" (CBSAs). Along with the new definition of metropolitan areas, OMB defined a new type of area—called a micropolitan area—that defines the many American communities with population clusters that are too small to meet the 50,000 minimum that defines a metropolitan area. Appendix C lists these micropolitan areas as of February 2013 but, because of size constraints, *County and City Extra* continues to include only metropolitan area data in Table C. In 2013, the Census Bureau released data for new metropolitan and micropolitan areas based on the 2010 census. This edition of *County and City Extra* uses these 2013 metropolitan area delineations. Most of the data producers are now releasing data for the new metropolitan areas. For a few data sources, the counties have been aggregated to the new areas.

With over 20 million people, the New York metropolitan area was the largest, followed by Los Angeles with a population of over 13 million. Chicago ranked third with 9.5 million people. Another 11 metropolitan areas had more than 4 million residents (Dallas, Houston, Washington, Philadelphia, Miami, Atlanta, Boston, San Francisco, Phoenix, Riverside, and Detroit), while 39 other metropolitan areas had between 1 million and 4 million people. Fifty-six percent of the U.S. population lived in these 53 metropolitan areas with one million or more residents.

One hundred and twenty one metropolitan areas grew by 5 percent or more between 2010 and 2015. The Villages, FL had the highest growth rate, increasing by 27.3 percent to a 2015 population of 118,891 residents. Among the 75 largest metropolitan areas, Austin-Round Rock-San Marcos, TX had the largest increase at 16.6 percent followed by Raleigh, NC at 12.7 percent. Four of the most populous metropolitan areas lost population since 2010—Pittsburgh, PA, Hartford-West Hartford-East Hartford, CT, New Haven-Milford, CT and Cleveland-Elyria, OH).

Among metropolitan areas, New York and Los Angeles shared the top spots for density as well as for total population. With 1,062.3 persons per square kilometer, Los Angeles-Long Beach-Anaheim, CA was the most densely populated metropolitan area in the country. At the other extreme, three of the largest metropolitan areas had fewer than 50 persons per square kilometer. All three of these had large land areas and were located in western states (Albuquerque, NM; Bakersfield, CA; and Tucson, AZ).

In 2015, 10 metropolitan areas had an unemployment rate at 10 percent or higher. In contrast, 131 metropolitan areas had an unemployment rate at 10 percent or higher in 2010. Topping the list are El Centro, CA and Yuma, AZ, two metropolitan areas with large agricultural workforces and unemployment rates at 24.0 percent and 21.8 percent respectively. Eight of the 10 metropolitan areas with the highest unemployment were in California. Among the 75 most populous metropolitan areas, Fresno and Bakersfield, CA were the two MSAs with unemployment rates above 10 percent. One hundred and forty-nine metropolitan areas had unemployment rates below 5 percent in 2015. Many of them were relatively small areas. Fargo, ND-MN and Ames, IA had the lowest unemployment rate among all metropolitan areas at 2.4 percent followed by Sioux Falls, SD and Bismark, ND at 2.6 percent. Nine of the 75 largest metropolitan areas had unemployment rates below 4 percent, the lowest in Omaha-Council Bluffs, NE-IA at 3.2 percent. These were metropolitan areas in different regions of the country, and with different employment patterns. Among them was Grand Rapids-Wyoming, MI with an unemployment rate of 3.7 percent. This metropolitan area had the highest level of manufacturing employment of the 75 largest metropolitan areas, with 22.1 percent of the workforce in manufacturing industries.

75 Largest Metropolitan Areas by 2015 Population
Selected Rankings

Population, 2015			Total land area, 2010			
Popu-lation rank	Metropolitan area	Population [col 2]	Popu-lation rank	Land area rank	Metropolitan area	Land area (square kilometers) [col 1]
1	New York-Newark-Jersey City, NY-NJ-PA	20 182 305	13	1	Riverside-San Bernardino-Ontario, CA	70 612
2	Los Angeles-Long Beach-Anaheim, CA	13 340 068	12	2	Phoenix-Mesa-Scottsdale, AZ	37 725
3	Chicago-Naperville-Elgin, IL-IN-WI	9 551 031	60	3	Albuquerque, NM	24 042
4	Dallas-Fort Worth-Arlington, TX	7 102 796	4	4	Dallas-Fort Worth-Arlington, TX	24 029
5	Houston-The Woodlands-Sugar Land, TX	6 656 947	53	5	Tucson, AZ	23 794
6	Washington-Arlington-Alexandria, DC-VA-MD-WV	6 097 684	9	6	Atlanta-Sandy Springs-Roswell, GA	22 498
7	Philadelphia-Camden-Wilmington, PA-NJ-DE-MD	6 069 875	19	7	Denver-Aurora-Lakewood, CO	21 616
8	Miami-Fort Lauderdale-West Palm Beach, FL	6 012 331	1	8	New York-Newark-Jersey City, NY-NJ-PA	21 480
9	Atlanta-Sandy Springs-Roswell, GA	5 710 795	5	9	Houston-The Woodlands-Sugar Land, TX	21 388
10	Boston-Cambridge-Newton, MA-NH	4 774 321	61	10	Bakersfield, CA	21 062
11	San Francisco-Oakland-Hayward, CA	4 656 132	29	11	Las Vegas-Henderson-Paradise, NV	20 439
12	Phoenix-Mesa-Scottsdale, AZ	4 574 531	20	12	St. Louis, MO-IL	20 366
13	Riverside-San Bernardino-Ontario, CA	4 489 159	48	13	Salt Lake City, UT	19 901
14	Detroit-Warren-Dearborn, MI	4 302 043	16	14	Minneapolis-St. Paul-Bloomington, MN	19 779
15	Seattle-Tacoma-Bellevue, WA	3 733 580	25	15	San Antonio-New Braunfels, TX	18 941
16	Minneapolis-St. Paul-Bloomington, MN	3 524 583	30	16	Kansas City, MO-KS	18 793
17	San Diego-Carlsbad, CA	3 299 521	3	17	Chicago-Naperville-Elgin, IL-IN-WI	18 639
18	Tampa-St. Petersburg-Clearwater, FL	2 975 225	23	18	Portland-Vancouver-Hillsboro, OR-WA	17 311
19	Denver-Aurora-Lakewood, CO	2 814 330	36	19	Nashville-Davidson—Murfreesboro—Franklin, TN	16 320
20	St. Louis, MO-IL	2 811 588	55	20	Tulsa, OK	16 237
21	Baltimore-Columbia-Towson, MD	2 797 407	6	21	Washington-Arlington-Alexandria, DC-VA-MD-WV	16 172
22	Charlotte-Concord-Gastonia, NC-SC	2 426 363	56	22	Fresno, CA	15 431
23	Portland-Vancouver-Hillsboro, OR-WA	2 389 228	15	23	Seattle-Tacoma-Bellevue, WA	15 209
24	Orlando-Kissimmee-Sanford, FL	2 387 138	68	24	El Paso, TX	14 462
25	San Antonio-New Braunfels, TX	2 384 075	41	25	Oklahoma City, OK	14 274
26	Pittsburgh, PA	2 353 045	26	26	Pittsburgh, PA	13 679
27	Sacramento—Roseville—Arden-Arcade, CA	2 274 194	49	27	Birmingham-Hoover, AL	13 673
28	Cincinnati, OH-KY-IN	2 157 719	27	28	Sacramento—Roseville—Arden-Arcade, CA	13 193
29	Las Vegas-Henderson-Paradise, NV	2 114 801	8	29	Miami-Fort Lauderdale-West Palm Beach, FL	13 150
30	Kansas City, MO-KS	2 087 471	22	30	Charlotte-Concord-Gastonia, NC-SC	13 123
31	Cleveland-Elyria, OH	2 060 810	42	31	Memphis, TN-MS-AR	12 909
32	Columbus, OH	2 021 632	2	32	Los Angeles-Long Beach-Anaheim, CA	12 558
33	Austin-Round Rock, TX	2 000 860	32	33	Columbus, OH	12 423
34	Indianapolis-Carmel-Anderson, IN	1 988 817	7	34	Philadelphia-Camden-Wilmington, PA-NJ-DE-MD	11 919
35	San Jose-Sunnyvale-Santa Clara, CA	1 976 836	45	35	Richmond, VA	11 852
36	Nashville-Davidson—Murfreesboro—Franklin, TN	1 830 345	59	36	Omaha-Council Bluffs, NE-IA	11 266
37	Virginia Beach-Norfolk-Newport News, VA-NC	1 724 876	34	37	Indianapolis-Carmel-Anderson, IN	11 153
38	Providence-Warwick, RI-MA	1 613 070	33	38	Austin-Round Rock, TX	10 929
39	Milwaukee-Waukesha-West Allis, WI	1 575 747	17	39	San Diego-Carlsbad, CA	10 895
40	Jacksonville, FL	1 449 481	28	40	Cincinnati, OH-KY-IN	10 797
41	Oklahoma City, OK	1 358 452	70	41	Baton Rouge, LA	10 429
42	Memphis, TN-MS-AR	1 344 127	14	42	Detroit-Warren-Dearborn, MI	10 070
43	Louisville/Jefferson County, KY-IN	1 278 413	71	43	Columbia, SC	9 590
44	Raleigh, NC	1 273 568	43	44	Louisville/Jefferson County, KY-IN	9 267
45	Richmond, VA	1 271 334	64	45	Knoxville, TN	9 066
46	New Orleans-Metairie, LA	1 262 888	10	46	Boston-Cambridge-Newton, MA-NH	9 033
47	Hartford-West Hartford-East Hartford, CT	1 211 324	24	47	Orlando-Kissimmee-Sanford, FL	9 009
48	Salt Lake City, UT	1 170 266	51	48	Rochester, NY	8 459
49	Birmingham-Hoover, AL	1 145 647	46	49	New Orleans-Metairie, LA	8 294
50	Buffalo-Cheektowaga-Niagara Falls, NY	1 135 230	40	50	Jacksonville, FL	8 291
51	Rochester, NY	1 081 954	62	51	Albany-Schenectady-Troy, NY	7 283
52	Grand Rapids-Wyoming, MI	1 038 583	63	52	Greenville-Anderson-Mauldin, SC	7 021
53	Tucson, AZ	1 010 025	37	53	Virginia Beach-Norfolk-Newport News, VA-NC	6 969
54	Urban Honolulu, HI	998 714	35	54	San Jose-Sunnyvale-Santa Clara, CA	6 938
55	Tulsa, OK	981 005	52	55	Grand Rapids-Wyoming, MI	6 913
56	Fresno, CA	974 861	21	56	Baltimore-Columbia-Towson, MD	6 738
57	Bridgeport-Stamford-Norwalk, CT	948 053	75	57	Charleston-North Charleston, SC	6 704
58	Worcester, MA-CT	935 536	18	58	Tampa-St. Petersburg-Clearwater, FL	6 509
59	Omaha-Council Bluffs, NE-IA	915 312	11	59	San Francisco-Oakland-Hayward, CA	6 398
60	Albuquerque, NM	907 301	44	60	Raleigh, NC	5 485
61	Bakersfield, CA	882 176	58	61	Worcester, MA-CT	5 241
62	Albany-Schenectady-Troy, NY	881 830	31	62	Cleveland-Elyria, OH	5 172
63	Greenville-Anderson-Mauldin, SC	874 869	74	63	Greensboro-High Point, NC	5 164
64	Knoxville, TN	861 424	66	64	Oxnard-Thousand Oaks-Ventura, CA	4 774
65	New Haven-Milford, CT	859 470	38	65	Providence-Warwick, RI-MA	4 111
66	Oxnard-Thousand Oaks-Ventura, CA	850 536	67	66	McAllen-Edinburg-Mission, TX	4 069
67	McAllen-Edinburg-Mission, TX	842 304	50	67	Buffalo-Cheektowaga-Niagara Falls, NY	4 054
68	El Paso, TX	838 972	47	68	Hartford-West Hartford-East Hartford, CT	3 922
69	Allentown-Bethlehem-Easton, PA-NJ	832 327	39	69	Milwaukee-Waukesha-West Allis, WI	3 768
70	Baton Rouge, LA	830 480	69	70	Allentown-Bethlehem-Easton, PA-NJ	3 763
71	Columbia, SC	810 068	73	71	North Port-Sarasota-Bradenton, FL	3 364
72	Dayton, OH	800 909	72	72	Dayton, OH	3 320
73	North Port-Sarasota-Bradenton, FL	768 918	57	73	Bridgeport-Stamford-Norwalk, CT	1 618
74	Greensboro-High Point, NC	752 157	65	74	New Haven-Milford, CT	1 566
75	Charleston-North Charleston, SC	744 526	54	75	Urban Honolulu, HI	1 556

75 Largest Metropolitan Areas by 2015 Population
Selected Rankings

	Population density, 2015				Percent population change, 2010 – 2015		
Popu-lation rank	Density rank	Metropolitan area	Density (per square kilometer) [col 4]	Popu-lation rank	Percent change rank	Metropolitan area	Percent change [col 23]
2	1	Los Angeles-Long Beach-Anaheim, CA	1 062.3	33	1	Austin-Round Rock, TX	16.6
1	2	New York-Newark-Jersey City, NY-NJ-PA	939.6	44	2	Raleigh, NC	12.7
11	3	San Francisco-Oakland-Hayward, CA	727.7	5	3	Houston-The Woodlands-Sugar Land, TX	12.4
54	4	Urban Honolulu, HI	641.8	75	4	Charleston-North Charleston, SC	12.0
57	5	Bridgeport-Stamford-Norwalk, CT	585.9	24	5	Orlando-Kissimmee-Sanford, FL	11.8
65	6	New Haven-Milford, CT	548.8	25	6	San Antonio-New Braunfels, TX	11.3
10	7	Boston-Cambridge-Newton, MA-NH	528.5	19	7	Denver-Aurora-Lakewood, CO	10.6
3	8	Chicago-Naperville-Elgin, IL-IN-WI	512.4	4	8	Dallas-Fort Worth-Arlington, TX	10.5
7	9	Philadelphia-Camden-Wilmington, PA-NJ-DE-MD	509.3	36	9	Nashville-Davidson—Murfreesboro—Franklin, TN	9.5
8	10	Miami-Fort Lauderdale-West Palm Beach, FL	457.2	73	9	North Port-Sarasota-Bradenton, FL	9.5
18	11	Tampa-St. Petersburg-Clearwater, FL	457.1	22	11	Charlotte-Concord-Gastonia, NC-SC	9.4
14	12	Detroit-Warren-Dearborn, MI	427.2	12	12	Phoenix-Mesa-Scottsdale, AZ	9.1
39	13	Milwaukee-Waukesha-West Allis, WI	418.2	67	13	McAllen-Edinburg-Mission, TX	8.7
21	14	Baltimore-Columbia-Towson, MD	415.2	15	14	Seattle-Tacoma-Bellevue, WA	8.5
31	15	Cleveland-Elyria, OH	398.5	29	15	Las Vegas-Henderson-Paradise, NV	8.4
38	16	Providence-Warwick, RI-MA	392.4	41	15	Oklahoma City, OK	8.4
6	17	Washington-Arlington-Alexandria, DC-VA-MD-WV	377.1	6	17	Washington-Arlington-Alexandria, DC-VA-MD-WV	8.2
5	18	Houston-The Woodlands-Sugar Land, TX	311.2	8	18	Miami-Fort Lauderdale-West Palm Beach, FL	8.0
47	19	Hartford-West Hartford-East Hartford, CT	308.9	9	18	Atlanta-Sandy Springs-Roswell, GA	8.0
17	20	San Diego-Carlsbad, CA	302.8	40	20	Jacksonville, FL	7.7
4	21	Dallas-Fort Worth-Arlington, TX	295.6	35	21	San Jose-Sunnyvale-Santa Clara, CA	7.6
35	22	San Jose-Sunnyvale-Santa Clara, CA	284.9	48	21	Salt Lake City, UT	7.6
50	23	Buffalo-Cheektowaga-Niagara Falls, NY	280.0	11	23	San Francisco-Oakland-Hayward, CA	7.4
24	24	Orlando-Kissimmee-Sanford, FL	265.0	23	24	Portland-Vancouver-Hillsboro, OR-WA	7.3
9	25	Atlanta-Sandy Springs-Roswell, GA	253.8	18	25	Tampa-St. Petersburg-Clearwater, FL	6.9
37	26	Virginia Beach-Norfolk-Newport News, VA-NC	247.5	17	26	San Diego-Carlsbad, CA	6.6
15	27	Seattle-Tacoma-Bellevue, WA	245.5	13	27	Riverside-San Bernardino-Ontario, CA	6.3
72	28	Dayton, OH	241.2	32	27	Columbus, OH	6.3
44	29	Raleigh, NC	232.2	63	29	Greenville-Anderson-Mauldin, SC	6.2
73	30	North Port-Sarasota-Bradenton, FL	228.6	46	30	New Orleans-Metairie, LA	6.1
69	31	Allentown-Bethlehem-Easton, PA-NJ	221.2	27	31	Sacramento—Roseville—Arden-Arcade, CA	5.8
67	32	McAllen-Edinburg-Mission, TX	207.0	59	31	Omaha-Council Bluffs, NE-IA	5.8
28	33	Cincinnati, OH-KY-IN	199.8	71	33	Columbia, SC	5.5
22	34	Charlotte-Concord-Gastonia, NC-SC	184.9	34	34	Indianapolis-Carmel-Anderson, IN	5.3
33	35	Austin-Round Rock, TX	183.1	16	35	Minneapolis-St. Paul-Bloomington, MN	5.2
58	36	Worcester, MA-CT	178.5	45	35	Richmond, VA	5.2
34	37	Indianapolis-Carmel-Anderson, IN	178.3	61	37	Bakersfield, CA	5.1
16	38	Minneapolis-St. Paul-Bloomington, MN	178.2	52	38	Grand Rapids-Wyoming, MI	5.0
66	38	Oxnard-Thousand Oaks-Ventura, CA	178.2	10	39	Boston-Cambridge-Newton, MA-NH	4.9
40	40	Jacksonville, FL	174.8	54	40	Urban Honolulu, HI	4.8
27	41	Sacramento—Roseville—Arden-Arcade, CA	172.4	56	40	Fresno, CA	4.8
26	42	Pittsburgh, PA	172.0	55	42	Tulsa, OK	4.6
32	43	Columbus, OH	162.7	68	43	El Paso, TX	4.3
46	44	New Orleans-Metairie, LA	152.3	2	44	Los Angeles-Long Beach-Anaheim, CA	4.0
52	45	Grand Rapids-Wyoming, MI	150.2	30	45	Kansas City, MO-KS	3.9
74	46	Greensboro-High Point, NC	145.7	74	45	Greensboro-High Point, NC	3.9
20	47	St. Louis, MO-IL	138.1	43	47	Louisville/Jefferson County, KY-IN	3.5
23	48	Portland-Vancouver-Hillsboro, OR-WA	138.0	70	47	Baton Rouge, LA	3.5
43	48	Louisville/Jefferson County, KY-IN	138.0	57	49	Bridgeport-Stamford-Norwalk, CT	3.4
19	50	Denver-Aurora-Lakewood, CO	130.2	66	50	Oxnard-Thousand Oaks-Ventura, CA	3.3
51	51	Rochester, NY	127.9	21	51	Baltimore-Columbia-Towson, MD	3.2
25	52	San Antonio-New Braunfels, TX	125.9	1	52	New York-Newark-Jersey City, NY-NJ-PA	3.1
63	53	Greenville-Anderson-Mauldin, SC	124.6	53	53	Tucson, AZ	3.0
12	54	Phoenix-Mesa-Scottsdale, AZ	121.3	37	54	Virginia Beach-Norfolk-Newport News, VA-NC	2.9
62	55	Albany-Schenectady-Troy, NY	121.1	64	55	Knoxville, TN	2.8
36	56	Nashville-Davidson—Murfreesboro—Franklin, TN	112.2	60	56	Albuquerque, NM	2.3
30	57	Kansas City, MO-KS	111.1	28	57	Cincinnati, OH-KY-IN	2.0
75	57	Charleston-North Charleston, SC	111.1	58	57	Worcester, MA-CT	2.0
45	59	Richmond, VA	107.3	7	59	Philadelphia-Camden-Wilmington, PA-NJ-DE-MD	1.8
42	60	Memphis, TN-MS-AR	104.1	49	60	Birmingham-Hoover, AL	1.6
29	61	Las Vegas-Henderson-Paradise, NV	103.5	42	61	Memphis, TN-MS-AR	1.5
41	62	Oklahoma City, OK	95.2	39	62	Milwaukee-Waukesha-West Allis, WI	1.3
64	63	Knoxville, TN	95.0	62	62	Albany-Schenectady-Troy, NY	1.3
71	64	Columbia, SC	84.5	69	62	Allentown-Bethlehem-Easton, PA-NJ	1.3
49	65	Birmingham-Hoover, AL	83.8	3	65	Chicago-Naperville-Elgin, IL-IN-WI	0.9
59	66	Omaha-Council Bluffs, NE-IA	81.2	20	65	St. Louis, MO-IL	0.9
70	67	Baton Rouge, LA	79.6	38	67	Providence-Warwick, RI-MA	0.7
13	68	Riverside-San Bernardino-Ontario, CA	63.6	51	68	Rochester, NY	0.2
56	69	Fresno, CA	63.2	72	68	Dayton, OH	0.2
55	70	Tulsa, OK	60.4	14	70	Detroit-Warren-Dearborn, MI	0.1
48	71	Salt Lake City, UT	58.8	50	71	Buffalo-Cheektowaga-Niagara Falls, NY	0.0
68	72	El Paso, TX	58.0	26	72	Pittsburgh, PA	-0.1
53	73	Tucson, AZ	42.4	47	72	Hartford-West Hartford-East Hartford, CT	-0.1
61	74	Bakersfield, CA	41.9	65	74	New Haven-Milford, CT	-0.3
60	75	Albuquerque, NM	37.7	31	75	Cleveland-Elyria, OH	-0.8

75 Largest Metropolitan Areas by 2015 Population
Selected Rankings

Population rank	White rank	Metropolitan area	Percent White [col 5]	Population rank	Black rank	Metropolitan area	Percent Black [col 6]
		Percent White, not Hispanic or Latino, alone or in combination, 2014				**Percent Black, not Hispanic or Latino, alone or in combination, 2014**	
64	1	Knoxville, TN	88.9	42	1	Memphis, TN-MS-AR	47.1
26	2	Pittsburgh, PA	87.6	70	2	Baton Rouge, LA	36.3
62	3	Albany-Schenectady-Troy, NY	83.1	46	3	New Orleans-Metairie, LA	35.2
28	4	Cincinnati, OH-KY-IN	82.3	71	4	Columbia, SC	34.3
52	5	Grand Rapids-Wyoming, MI	81.5	9	5	Atlanta-Sandy Springs-Roswell, GA	33.9
58	6	Worcester, MA-CT	80.9	37	6	Virginia Beach-Norfolk-Newport News, VA-NC	31.9
38	7	Providence-Warwick, RI-MA	79.8	45	7	Richmond, VA	31.0
50	7	Buffalo-Cheektowaga-Niagara Falls, NY	79.8	21	8	Baltimore-Columbia-Towson, MD	29.9
73	9	North Port-Sarasota-Bradenton, FL	79.5	49	9	Birmingham-Hoover, AL	29.3
16	10	Minneapolis-St. Paul-Bloomington, MN	79.4	75	10	Charleston-North Charleston, SC	27.6
59	11	Omaha-Council Bluffs, NE-IA	79.3	74	11	Greensboro-High Point, NC	27.3
72	11	Dayton, OH	79.3	6	12	Washington-Arlington-Alexandria, DC-VA-MD-WV	26.3
43	13	Louisville/Jefferson County, KY-IN	79.1	14	13	Detroit-Warren-Dearborn, MI	23.4
51	14	Rochester, NY	78.9	22	14	Charlotte-Concord-Gastonia, NC-SC	23.2
23	15	Portland-Vancouver-Hillsboro, OR-WA	78.0	40	15	Jacksonville, FL	22.3
32	16	Columbus, OH	77.1	7	16	Philadelphia-Camden-Wilmington, PA-NJ-DE-MD	21.5
69	16	Allentown-Bethlehem-Easton, PA-NJ	77.1	44	17	Raleigh, NC	21.0
20	18	St. Louis, MO-IL	76.0	8	18	Miami-Fort Lauderdale-West Palm Beach, FL	20.9
34	19	Indianapolis-Carmel-Anderson, IN	75.8	31	18	Cleveland-Elyria, OH	20.9
30	20	Kansas City, MO-KS	75.4	20	20	St. Louis, MO-IL	19.3
48	21	Salt Lake City, UT	75.0	39	21	Milwaukee-Waukesha-West Allis, WI	17.5
36	22	Nashville-Davidson—Murfreesboro—Franklin, TN	74.9	63	21	Greenville-Anderson-Mauldin, SC	17.5
63	23	Greenville-Anderson-Mauldin, SC	74.8	5	23	Houston-The Woodlands-Sugar Land, TX	17.4
10	24	Boston-Cambridge-Newton, MA-NH	74.3	3	24	Chicago-Naperville-Elgin, IL-IN-WI	17.3
31	25	Cleveland-Elyria, OH	72.3	72	25	Dayton, OH	17.0
55	26	Tulsa, OK	71.8	1	26	New York-Newark-Jersey City, NY-NJ-PA	16.7
47	27	Hartford-West Hartford-East Hartford, CT	70.6	24	27	Orlando-Kissimmee-Sanford, FL	16.4
15	28	Seattle-Tacoma-Bellevue, WA	69.8	32	28	Columbus, OH	16.3
41	28	Oklahoma City, OK	69.8	36	29	Nashville-Davidson—Murfreesboro—Franklin, TN	16.2
39	30	Milwaukee-Waukesha-West Allis, WI	69.2	34	30	Indianapolis-Carmel-Anderson, IN	16.0
14	31	Detroit-Warren-Dearborn, MI	68.9	4	31	Dallas-Fort Worth-Arlington, TX	15.9
19	32	Denver-Aurora-Lakewood, CO	66.9	43	32	Louisville/Jefferson County, KY-IN	15.4
18	33	Tampa-St. Petersburg-Clearwater, FL	66.8	30	33	Kansas City, MO-KS	13.6
65	34	New Haven-Milford, CT	66.4	28	34	Cincinnati, OH-KY-IN	13.3
40	35	Jacksonville, FL	66.3	65	34	New Haven-Milford, CT	13.3
75	36	Charleston-North Charleston, SC	65.5	50	36	Buffalo-Cheektowaga-Niagara Falls, NY	13.0
49	37	Birmingham-Hoover, AL	65.2	18	37	Tampa-St. Petersburg-Clearwater, FL	12.5
57	38	Bridgeport-Stamford-Norwalk, CT	64.9	51	38	Rochester, NY	12.1
7	39	Philadelphia-Camden-Wilmington, PA-NJ-DE-MD	64.7	29	39	Las Vegas-Henderson-Paradise, NV	11.9
22	40	Charlotte-Concord-Gastonia, NC-SC	64.3	41	39	Oklahoma City, OK	11.9
44	41	Raleigh, NC	63.9	47	41	Hartford-West Hartford-East Hartford, CT	11.5
74	42	Greensboro-High Point, NC	61.6	57	42	Bridgeport-Stamford-Norwalk, CT	11.3
21	43	Baltimore-Columbia-Towson, MD	60.0	55	43	Tulsa, OK	9.6
45	43	Richmond, VA	60.0	26	44	Pittsburgh, PA	9.4
12	45	Phoenix-Mesa-Scottsdale, AZ	58.9	16	45	Minneapolis-St. Paul-Bloomington, MN	9.0
71	46	Columbia, SC	58.8	59	46	Omaha-Council Bluffs, NE-IA	8.9
37	47	Virginia Beach-Norfolk-Newport News, VA-NC	58.7	62	46	Albany-Schenectady-Troy, NY	8.9
70	48	Baton Rouge, LA	58.1	11	48	San Francisco-Oakland-Hayward, CA	8.7
27	49	Sacramento—Roseville—Arden-Arcade, CA	57.3	27	49	Sacramento—Roseville—Arden-Arcade, CA	8.4
3	50	Chicago-Naperville-Elgin, IL-IN-WI	55.0	10	50	Boston-Cambridge-Newton, MA-NH	8.2
33	50	Austin-Round Rock, TX	55.0	13	51	Riverside-San Bernardino-Ontario, CA	8.0
53	50	Tucson, AZ	55.0	33	52	Austin-Round Rock, TX	7.8
46	53	New Orleans-Metairie, LA	53.6	52	53	Grand Rapids-Wyoming, MI	7.6
24	54	Orlando-Kissimmee-Sanford, FL	51.5	2	54	Los Angeles-Long Beach-Anaheim, CA	7.2
9	55	Atlanta-Sandy Springs-Roswell, GA	50.6	15	54	Seattle-Tacoma-Bellevue, WA	7.2
4	56	Dallas-Fort Worth-Arlington, TX	49.8	73	54	North Port-Sarasota-Bradenton, FL	7.2
17	57	San Diego-Carlsbad, CA	49.4	25	57	San Antonio-New Braunfels, TX	7.0
6	58	Washington-Arlington-Alexandria, DC-VA-MD-WV	49.2	64	58	Knoxville, TN	6.6
1	59	New York-Newark-Jersey City, NY-NJ-PA	48.8	19	59	Denver-Aurora-Lakewood, CO	6.3
66	60	Oxnard-Thousand Oaks-Ventura, CA	48.7	38	60	Providence-Warwick, RI-MA	6.1
29	61	Las Vegas-Henderson-Paradise, NV	48.1	61	61	Bakersfield, CA	5.9
42	62	Memphis, TN-MS-AR	46.0	12	62	Phoenix-Mesa-Scottsdale, AZ	5.8
11	63	San Francisco-Oakland-Hayward, CA	44.1	17	63	San Diego-Carlsbad, CA	5.7
60	64	Albuquerque, NM	42.2	69	64	Allentown-Bethlehem-Easton, PA-NJ	5.6
5	65	Houston-The Woodlands-Sugar Land, TX	39.0	56	65	Fresno, CA	5.3
61	66	Bakersfield, CA	37.8	58	66	Worcester, MA-CT	4.7
25	67	San Antonio-New Braunfels, TX	36.1	53	67	Tucson, AZ	4.1
13	68	Riverside-San Bernardino-Ontario, CA	36.0	54	68	Urban Honolulu, HI	3.9
35	68	San Jose-Sunnyvale-Santa Clara, CA	36.0	23	69	Portland-Vancouver-Hillsboro, OR-WA	3.7
8	70	Miami-Fort Lauderdale-West Palm Beach, FL	33.5	68	70	El Paso, TX	3.5
54	71	Urban Honolulu, HI	32.7	35	71	San Jose-Sunnyvale-Santa Clara, CA	2.9
56	72	Fresno, CA	32.5	60	71	Albuquerque, NM	2.9
2	73	Los Angeles-Long Beach-Anaheim, CA	32.3	66	73	Oxnard-Thousand Oaks-Ventura, CA	2.2
68	74	El Paso, TX	14.0	48	74	Salt Lake City, UT	2.1
67	75	McAllen-Edinburg-Mission, TX	7.3	67	75	McAllen-Edinburg-Mission, TX	0.5

75 Largest Metropolitan Areas by 2015 Population
Selected Rankings

Percent American Indian, Alaska Native, alone or in combination, 2014

Population rank	American Indian Alaska native rank	Metropolitan area	Percent American Indian, Alaska Native [col 7]
55	1	Tulsa, OK	12.8
41	2	Oklahoma City, OK	6.7
60	3	Albuquerque, NM	5.9
53	4	Tucson, AZ	3.1
12	5	Phoenix-Mesa-Scottsdale, AZ	2.5
15	6	Seattle-Tacoma-Bellevue, WA	2.0
23	7	Portland-Vancouver-Hillsboro, OR-WA	1.7
27	8	Sacramento—Roseville—Arden-Arcade, CA	1.5
54	8	Urban Honolulu, HI	1.5
16	10	Minneapolis-St. Paul-Bloomington, MN	1.3
61	10	Bakersfield, CA	1.3
30	12	Kansas City, MO-KS	1.2
56	12	Fresno, CA	1.2
19	14	Denver-Aurora-Lakewood, CO	1.1
37	14	Virginia Beach-Norfolk-Newport News, VA-NC	1.1
48	14	Salt Lake City, UT	1.1
13	17	Riverside-San Bernardino-Ontario, CA	1.0
17	17	San Diego-Carlsbad, CA	1.0
29	17	Las Vegas-Henderson-Paradise, NV	1.0
50	17	Buffalo-Cheektowaga-Niagara Falls, NY	1.0
59	17	Omaha-Council Bluffs, NE-IA	1.0
74	17	Greensboro-High Point, NC	1.0
4	23	Dallas-Fort Worth-Arlington, TX	0.9
14	23	Detroit-Warren-Dearborn, MI	0.9
22	23	Charlotte-Concord-Gastonia, NC-SC	0.9
38	23	Providence-Warwick, RI-MA	0.9
39	23	Milwaukee-Waukesha-West Allis, WI	0.9
44	23	Raleigh, NC	0.9
45	23	Richmond, VA	0.9
52	23	Grand Rapids-Wyoming, MI	0.9
64	23	Knoxville, TN	0.9
66	23	Oxnard-Thousand Oaks-Ventura, CA	0.9
75	23	Charleston-North Charleston, SC	0.9
6	34	Washington-Arlington-Alexandria, DC-VA-MD-WV	0.8
11	34	San Francisco-Oakland-Hayward, CA	0.8
21	34	Baltimore-Columbia-Towson, MD	0.8
32	34	Columbus, OH	0.8
33	34	Austin-Round Rock, TX	0.8
40	34	Jacksonville, FL	0.8
46	34	New Orleans-Metairie, LA	0.8
71	34	Columbia, SC	0.8
72	34	Dayton, OH	0.8
9	43	Atlanta-Sandy Springs-Roswell, GA	0.7
18	43	Tampa-St. Petersburg-Clearwater, FL	0.7
20	43	St. Louis, MO-IL	0.7
35	43	San Jose-Sunnyvale-Santa Clara, CA	0.7
36	43	Nashville-Davidson—Murfreesboro—Franklin, TN	0.7
43	43	Louisville/Jefferson County, KY-IN	0.7
49	43	Birmingham-Hoover, AL	0.7
2	50	Los Angeles-Long Beach-Anaheim, CA	0.6
5	50	Houston-The Woodlands-Sugar Land, TX	0.6
7	50	Philadelphia-Camden-Wilmington, PA-NJ-DE-MD	0.6
24	50	Orlando-Kissimmee-Sanford, FL	0.6
25	50	San Antonio-New Braunfels, TX	0.6
28	50	Cincinnati, OH-KY-IN	0.6
31	50	Cleveland-Elyria, OH	0.6
34	50	Indianapolis-Carmel-Anderson, IN	0.6
42	50	Memphis, TN-MS-AR	0.6
47	50	Hartford-West Hartford-East Hartford, CT	0.6
51	50	Rochester, NY	0.6
58	50	Worcester, MA-CT	0.6
62	50	Albany-Schenectady-Troy, NY	0.6
63	50	Greenville-Anderson-Mauldin, SC	0.6
65	50	New Haven-Milford, CT	0.6
70	50	Baton Rouge, LA	0.6
73	50	North Port-Sarasota-Bradenton, FL	0.6
1	67	New York-Newark-Jersey City, NY-NJ-PA	0.5
3	67	Chicago-Naperville-Elgin, IL-IN-WI	0.5
10	67	Boston-Cambridge-Newton, MA-NH	0.5
26	67	Pittsburgh, PA	0.5
68	67	El Paso, TX	0.5
57	72	Bridgeport-Stamford-Norwalk, CT	0.4
69	72	Allentown-Bethlehem-Easton, PA-NJ	0.4
8	74	Miami-Fort Lauderdale-West Palm Beach, FL	0.3
67	75	McAllen-Edinburg-Mission, TX	0.1

Percent Asian and Pacific Islander, alone or in combination, 2014

Population rank	Asian and Pacific Islander rank	Metropolitan area	Percent Asian and Pacific Islander [col 8]
54	1	Urban Honolulu, HI	76.8
35	2	San Jose-Sunnyvale-Santa Clara, CA	36.0
11	3	San Francisco-Oakland-Hayward, CA	28.5
2	4	Los Angeles-Long Beach-Anaheim, CA	17.1
15	5	Seattle-Tacoma-Bellevue, WA	16.3
27	6	Sacramento—Roseville—Arden-Arcade, CA	16.1
17	7	San Diego-Carlsbad, CA	14.1
29	8	Las Vegas-Henderson-Paradise, NV	12.5
1	9	New York-Newark-Jersey City, NY-NJ-PA	11.7
6	10	Washington-Arlington-Alexandria, DC-VA-MD-WV	11.5
56	11	Fresno, CA	11.0
66	12	Oxnard-Thousand Oaks-Ventura, CA	8.8
23	13	Portland-Vancouver-Hillsboro, OR-WA	8.7
10	14	Boston-Cambridge-Newton, MA-NH	8.3
5	15	Houston-The Woodlands-Sugar Land, TX	8.0
13	15	Riverside-San Bernardino-Ontario, CA	8.0
16	17	Minneapolis-St. Paul-Bloomington, MN	7.3
3	18	Chicago-Naperville-Elgin, IL-IN-WI	7.0
4	19	Dallas-Fort Worth-Arlington, TX	6.9
48	20	Salt Lake City, UT	6.4
7	21	Philadelphia-Camden-Wilmington, PA-NJ-DE-MD	6.3
21	21	Baltimore-Columbia-Towson, MD	6.3
33	21	Austin-Round Rock, TX	6.3
9	24	Atlanta-Sandy Springs-Roswell, GA	6.2
57	25	Bridgeport-Stamford-Norwalk, CT	6.1
44	26	Raleigh, NC	6.0
61	27	Bakersfield, CA	5.4
37	28	Virginia Beach-Norfolk-Newport News, VA-NC	5.3
24	29	Orlando-Kissimmee-Sanford, FL	5.2
47	29	Hartford-West Hartford-East Hartford, CT	5.2
19	31	Denver-Aurora-Lakewood, CO	5.1
40	32	Jacksonville, FL	4.9
12	33	Phoenix-Mesa-Scottsdale, AZ	4.8
58	33	Worcester, MA-CT	4.8
62	33	Albany-Schenectady-Troy, NY	4.8
14	36	Detroit-Warren-Dearborn, MI	4.6
65	36	New Haven-Milford, CT	4.6
45	38	Richmond, VA	4.5
32	39	Columbus, OH	4.3
18	40	Tampa-St. Petersburg-Clearwater, FL	4.1
41	41	Oklahoma City, OK	4.0
39	42	Milwaukee-Waukesha-West Allis, WI	3.9
74	42	Greensboro-High Point, NC	3.9
22	44	Charlotte-Concord-Gastonia, NC-SC	3.8
53	44	Tucson, AZ	3.8
38	46	Providence-Warwick, RI-MA	3.6
30	47	Kansas City, MO-KS	3.5
51	48	Rochester, NY	3.4
69	48	Allentown-Bethlehem-Easton, PA-NJ	3.4
46	50	New Orleans-Metairie, LA	3.3
50	50	Buffalo-Cheektowaga-Niagara Falls, NY	3.3
34	52	Indianapolis-Carmel-Anderson, IN	3.2
59	52	Omaha-Council Bluffs, NE-IA	3.2
8	54	Miami-Fort Lauderdale-West Palm Beach, FL	3.1
20	54	St. Louis, MO-IL	3.1
36	54	Nashville-Davidson—Murfreesboro—Franklin, TN	3.1
25	57	San Antonio-New Braunfels, TX	3.0
52	57	Grand Rapids-Wyoming, MI	3.0
60	59	Albuquerque, NM	2.9
28	60	Cincinnati, OH-KY-IN	2.8
72	60	Dayton, OH	2.8
31	62	Cleveland-Elyria, OH	2.7
55	62	Tulsa, OK	2.7
26	64	Pittsburgh, PA	2.6
71	64	Columbia, SC	2.6
75	64	Charleston-North Charleston, SC	2.6
42	67	Memphis, TN-MS-AR	2.5
70	67	Baton Rouge, LA	2.5
43	69	Louisville/Jefferson County, KY-IN	2.4
73	70	North Port-Sarasota-Bradenton, FL	2.2
63	71	Greenville-Anderson-Mauldin, SC	2.1
64	72	Knoxville, TN	1.9
49	73	Birmingham-Hoover, AL	1.7
68	74	El Paso, TX	1.6
67	75	McAllen-Edinburg-Mission, TX	1.1

75 Largest Metropolitan Areas by 2015 Population
Selected Rankings

Percent Hispanic or Latino,[1] 2014				Percent under 18 years old, 2014			
Population rank	Hispanic or Latino rank	Metropolitan area	Percent Hispanic or Latino [col 9]	Population rank	Under 18 years old rank	Metropolitan area	Percent Under 18 years old [cols 10 and 11]
67	1	McAllen-Edinburg-Mission, TX	91.1	67	1	McAllen-Edinburg-Mission, TX	33.6
68	2	El Paso, TX	81.0	61	2	Bakersfield, CA	29.5
25	3	San Antonio-New Braunfels, TX	54.5	56	3	Fresno, CA	28.9
56	4	Fresno, CA	52.0	48	4	Salt Lake City, UT	28.7
61	5	Bakersfield, CA	51.6	68	5	El Paso, TX	28.2
13	6	Riverside-San Bernardino-Ontario, CA	49.5	5	6	Houston-The Woodlands-Sugar Land, TX	27.0
60	7	Albuquerque, NM	48.0	4	7	Dallas-Fort Worth-Arlington, TX	26.7
2	8	Los Angeles-Long Beach-Anaheim, CA	45.1	13	7	Riverside-San Bernardino-Ontario, CA	26.7
8	9	Miami-Fort Lauderdale-West Palm Beach, FL	43.2	25	9	San Antonio-New Braunfels, TX	25.8
66	10	Oxnard-Thousand Oaks-Ventura, CA	42.0	59	9	Omaha-Council Bluffs, NE-IA	25.8
5	11	Houston-The Woodlands-Sugar Land, TX	36.3	42	11	Memphis, TN-MS-AR	25.5
53	12	Tucson, AZ	36.1	9	12	Atlanta-Sandy Springs-Roswell, GA	25.4
17	13	San Diego-Carlsbad, CA	33.2	34	13	Indianapolis-Carmel-Anderson, IN	25.2
33	14	Austin-Round Rock, TX	32.0	44	13	Raleigh, NC	25.2
29	15	Las Vegas-Henderson-Paradise, NV	30.3	55	15	Tulsa, OK	25.1
12	16	Phoenix-Mesa-Scottsdale, AZ	30.2	12	16	Phoenix-Mesa-Scottsdale, AZ	25.0
4	17	Dallas-Fort Worth-Arlington, TX	28.2	30	17	Kansas City, MO-KS	24.9
24	18	Orlando-Kissimmee-Sanford, FL	27.9	41	17	Oklahoma City, OK	24.9
35	19	San Jose-Sunnyvale-Santa Clara, CA	27.5	52	17	Grand Rapids-Wyoming, MI	24.9
1	20	New York-Newark-Jersey City, NY-NJ-PA	23.8	22	20	Charlotte-Concord-Gastonia, NC-SC	24.6
19	21	Denver-Aurora-Lakewood, CO	22.8	33	21	Austin-Round Rock, TX	24.2
11	22	San Francisco-Oakland-Hayward, CA	21.9	66	21	Oxnard-Thousand Oaks-Ventura, CA	24.2
3	23	Chicago-Naperville-Elgin, IL-IN-WI	21.7	16	23	Minneapolis-St. Paul-Bloomington, MN	24.1
27	24	Sacramento—Roseville—Arden-Arcade, CA	21.0	28	23	Cincinnati, OH-KY-IN	24.1
57	25	Bridgeport-Stamford-Norwalk, CT	18.7	32	23	Columbus, OH	24.1
18	26	Tampa-St. Petersburg-Clearwater, FL	17.7	3	26	Chicago-Naperville-Elgin, IL-IN-WI	23.8
48	27	Salt Lake City, UT	17.5	29	26	Las Vegas-Henderson-Paradise, NV	23.8
65	28	New Haven-Milford, CT	16.8	70	26	Baton Rouge, LA	23.8
6	29	Washington-Arlington-Alexandria, DC-VA-MD-WV	15.1	19	29	Denver-Aurora-Lakewood, CO	23.7
69	30	Allentown-Bethlehem-Easton, PA-NJ	15.0	36	29	Nashville-Davidson—Murfreesboro—Franklin, TN	23.7
47	31	Hartford-West Hartford-East Hartford, CT	14.0	39	29	Milwaukee-Waukesha-West Allis, WI	23.7
41	32	Oklahoma City, OK	12.4	27	32	Sacramento—Roseville—Arden-Arcade, CA	23.6
73	33	North Port-Sarasota-Bradenton, FL	12.0	57	32	Bridgeport-Stamford-Norwalk, CT	23.6
38	34	Providence-Warwick, RI-MA	11.6	6	34	Washington-Arlington-Alexandria, DC-VA-MD-WV	23.3
23	35	Portland-Vancouver-Hillsboro, OR-WA	11.5	35	34	San Jose-Sunnyvale-Santa Clara, CA	23.3
9	36	Atlanta-Sandy Springs-Roswell, GA	10.5	49	34	Birmingham-Hoover, AL	23.3
58	36	Worcester, MA-CT	10.5	60	34	Albuquerque, NM	23.3
44	38	Raleigh, NC	10.4	43	38	Louisville/Jefferson County, KY-IN	23.1
10	39	Boston-Cambridge-Newton, MA-NH	10.2	14	39	Detroit-Warren-Dearborn, MI	23.0
39	39	Milwaukee-Waukesha-West Allis, WI	10.2	40	40	Jacksonville, FL	22.9
59	41	Omaha-Council Bluffs, NE-IA	9.8	2	41	Los Angeles-Long Beach-Anaheim, CA	22.8
22	42	Charlotte-Concord-Gastonia, NC-SC	9.7	63	41	Greenville-Anderson-Mauldin, SC	22.8
15	43	Seattle-Tacoma-Bellevue, WA	9.6	20	43	St. Louis, MO-IL	22.7
54	44	Urban Honolulu, HI	9.5	71	43	Columbia, SC	22.7
52	45	Grand Rapids-Wyoming, MI	9.1	74	43	Greensboro-High Point, NC	22.7
55	45	Tulsa, OK	9.1	23	46	Portland-Vancouver-Hillsboro, OR-WA	22.5
7	47	Philadelphia-Camden-Wilmington, PA-NJ-DE-MD	8.8	37	46	Virginia Beach-Norfolk-Newport News, VA-NC	22.5
30	48	Kansas City, MO-KS	8.7	46	46	New Orleans-Metairie, LA	22.5
46	49	New Orleans-Metairie, LA	8.5	75	46	Charleston-North Charleston, SC	22.5
74	50	Greensboro-High Point, NC	8.1	17	50	San Diego-Carlsbad, CA	22.4
40	51	Jacksonville, FL	7.9	24	50	Orlando-Kissimmee-Sanford, FL	22.4
36	52	Nashville-Davidson—Murfreesboro—Franklin, TN	6.9	7	52	Philadelphia-Camden-Wilmington, PA-NJ-DE-MD	22.3
51	53	Rochester, NY	6.8	45	52	Richmond, VA	22.3
63	54	Greenville-Anderson-Mauldin, SC	6.5	21	54	Baltimore-Columbia-Towson, MD	22.2
34	55	Indianapolis-Carmel-Anderson, IN	6.4	72	54	Dayton, OH	22.2
37	56	Virginia Beach-Norfolk-Newport News, VA-NC	6.3	15	56	Seattle-Tacoma-Bellevue, WA	22.1
45	57	Richmond, VA	5.8	1	57	New York-Newark-Jersey City, NY-NJ-PA	22.0
16	58	Minneapolis-St. Paul-Bloomington, MN	5.6	31	58	Cleveland-Elyria, OH	21.9
71	59	Columbia, SC	5.4	53	59	Tucson, AZ	21.8
21	60	Baltimore-Columbia-Towson, MD	5.3	58	59	Worcester, MA-CT	21.8
31	60	Cleveland-Elyria, OH	5.3	54	61	Urban Honolulu, HI	21.5
75	60	Charleston-North Charleston, SC	5.3	69	61	Allentown-Bethlehem-Easton, PA-NJ	21.5
42	63	Memphis, TN-MS-AR	5.2	51	63	Rochester, NY	21.3
62	64	Albany-Schenectady-Troy, NY	4.9	64	64	Knoxville, TN	21.2
50	65	Buffalo-Cheektowaga-Niagara Falls, NY	4.6	65	65	New Haven-Milford, CT	21.1
43	66	Louisville/Jefferson County, KY-IN	4.3	47	66	Hartford-West Hartford-East Hartford, CT	21.0
49	66	Birmingham-Hoover, AL	4.3	8	67	Miami-Fort Lauderdale-West Palm Beach, FL	20.7
14	68	Detroit-Warren-Dearborn, MI	4.2	50	67	Buffalo-Cheektowaga-Niagara Falls, NY	20.7
32	69	Columbus, OH	3.8	10	69	Boston-Cambridge-Newton, MA-NH	20.6
70	70	Baton Rouge, LA	3.7	18	70	Tampa-St. Petersburg-Clearwater, FL	20.5
64	71	Knoxville, TN	3.5	38	70	Providence-Warwick, RI-MA	20.5
28	72	Cincinnati, OH-KY-IN	3.0	11	72	San Francisco-Oakland-Hayward, CA	20.4
20	73	St. Louis, MO-IL	2.9	62	73	Albany-Schenectady-Troy, NY	20.3
72	74	Dayton, OH	2.5	26	74	Pittsburgh, PA	19.3
26	75	Pittsburgh, PA	1.6	73	75	North Port-Sarasota-Bradenton, FL	17.1

75 Largest Metropolitan Areas by 2015 Population
Selected Rankings

Percent 65 years old and over, 2014				Percent female-headed family households, 2014			
Population rank	65 years old and over rank	Metropolitan area	Percent 65 years old and over [cols 17 + 18]	Population rank	Female households rank	Metropolitan area	Percent female households [col 30]
73	1	North Port-Sarasota-Bradenton, FL	30.0	67	1	McAllen-Edinburg-Mission, TX	21.8
18	2	Tampa-St. Petersburg-Clearwater, FL	18.7	42	2	Memphis, TN-MS-AR	19.7
26	3	Pittsburgh, PA	18.3	68	3	El Paso, TX	19.3
53	4	Tucson, AZ	17.7	56	4	Fresno, CA	18.2
8	5	Miami-Fort Lauderdale-West Palm Beach, FL	17.0	61	5	Bakersfield, CA	16.5
64	6	Knoxville, TN	16.8	8	6	Miami-Fort Lauderdale-West Palm Beach, FL	15.9
69	6	Allentown-Bethlehem-Easton, PA-NJ	16.8	46	6	New Orleans-Metairie, LA	15.9
50	8	Buffalo-Cheektowaga-Niagara Falls, NY	16.7	25	8	San Antonio-New Braunfels, TX	15.7
31	9	Cleveland-Elyria, OH	16.6	49	9	Birmingham-Hoover, AL	15.5
72	10	Dayton, OH	16.5	9	10	Atlanta-Sandy Springs-Roswell, GA	15.4
51	11	Rochester, NY	15.9	37	10	Virginia Beach-Norfolk-Newport News, VA-NC	15.4
54	12	Urban Honolulu, HI	15.8	71	10	Columbia, SC	15.4
38	13	Providence-Warwick, RI-MA	15.7	1	13	New York-Newark-Jersey City, NY-NJ-PA	15.3
47	13	Hartford-West Hartford-East Hartford, CT	15.7	70	13	Baton Rouge, LA	15.3
62	15	Albany-Schenectady-Troy, NY	15.6	2	15	Los Angeles-Long Beach-Anaheim, CA	15.2
65	15	New Haven-Milford, CT	15.6	21	16	Baltimore-Columbia-Towson, MD	14.9
63	17	Greenville-Anderson-Mauldin, SC	15.2	13	17	Riverside-San Bernardino-Ontario, CA	14.8
20	18	St. Louis, MO-IL	14.8	75	17	Charleston-North Charleston, SC	14.8
74	18	Greensboro-High Point, NC	14.8	74	19	Greensboro-High Point, NC	14.7
14	20	Detroit-Warren-Dearborn, MI	14.7	14	20	Detroit-Warren-Dearborn, MI	14.5
7	21	Philadelphia-Camden-Wilmington, PA-NJ-DE-MD	14.5	45	20	Richmond, VA	14.5
49	21	Birmingham-Hoover, AL	14.5	31	22	Cleveland-Elyria, OH	14.4
60	21	Albuquerque, NM	14.5	38	22	Providence-Warwick, RI-MA	14.4
10	24	Boston-Cambridge-Newton, MA-NH	14.4	40	22	Jacksonville, FL	14.4
43	24	Louisville/Jefferson County, KY-IN	14.4	60	25	Albuquerque, NM	14.3
57	26	Bridgeport-Stamford-Norwalk, CT	14.3	7	26	Philadelphia-Camden-Wilmington, PA-NJ-DE-MD	14.2
12	27	Phoenix-Mesa-Scottsdale, AZ	14.2	4	27	Dallas-Fort Worth-Arlington, TX	14.0
40	27	Jacksonville, FL	14.2	5	27	Houston-The Woodlands-Sugar Land, TX	14.0
55	27	Tulsa, OK	14.2	22	29	Charlotte-Concord-Gastonia, NC-SC	13.9
58	27	Worcester, MA-CT	14.2	50	29	Buffalo-Cheektowaga-Niagara Falls, NY	13.9
1	31	New York-Newark-Jersey City, NY-NJ-PA	14.1	39	31	Milwaukee-Waukesha-West Allis, WI	13.7
21	31	Baltimore-Columbia-Towson, MD	14.1	72	31	Dayton, OH	13.7
11	33	San Francisco-Oakland-Hayward, CA	14.0	43	33	Louisville/Jefferson County, KY-IN	13.6
27	33	Sacramento—Roseville—Arden-Arcade, CA	14.0	29	34	Las Vegas-Henderson-Paradise, NV	13.5
39	35	Milwaukee-Waukesha-West Allis, WI	13.9	3	35	Chicago-Naperville-Elgin, IL-IN-WI	13.4
24	36	Orlando-Kissimmee-Sanford, FL	13.8	34	35	Indianapolis-Carmel-Anderson, IN	13.4
45	36	Richmond, VA	13.8	36	35	Nashville-Davidson—Murfreesboro—Franklin, TN	13.4
46	38	New Orleans-Metairie, LA	13.7	47	35	Hartford-West Hartford-East Hartford, CT	13.4
28	39	Cincinnati, OH-KY-IN	13.6	27	39	Sacramento—Roseville—Arden-Arcade, CA	13.2
66	39	Oxnard-Thousand Oaks-Ventura, CA	13.6	32	39	Columbus, OH	13.2
23	41	Portland-Vancouver-Hillsboro, OR-WA	13.3	53	39	Tucson, AZ	13.2
29	41	Las Vegas-Henderson-Paradise, NV	13.3	24	42	Orlando-Kissimmee-Sanford, FL	13.1
30	41	Kansas City, MO-KS	13.3	20	43	St. Louis, MO-IL	13.0
71	41	Columbia, SC	13.3	51	44	Rochester, NY	12.8
75	41	Charleston-North Charleston, SC	13.3	55	44	Tulsa, OK	12.8
37	46	Virginia Beach-Norfolk-Newport News, VA-NC	13.0	57	44	Bridgeport-Stamford-Norwalk, CT	12.8
52	46	Grand Rapids-Wyoming, MI	13.0	54	47	Urban Honolulu, HI	12.7
3	48	Chicago-Naperville-Elgin, IL-IN-WI	12.8	6	48	Washington-Arlington-Alexandria, DC-VA-MD-WV	12.6
17	49	San Diego-Carlsbad, CA	12.7	63	48	Greenville-Anderson-Mauldin, SC	12.6
41	49	Oklahoma City, OK	12.7	66	48	Oxnard-Thousand Oaks-Ventura, CA	12.6
2	51	Los Angeles-Long Beach-Anaheim, CA	12.4	41	51	Oklahoma City, OK	12.5
22	51	Charlotte-Concord-Gastonia, NC-SC	12.4	12	52	Phoenix-Mesa-Scottsdale, AZ	12.4
34	51	Indianapolis-Carmel-Anderson, IN	12.4	28	53	Cincinnati, OH-KY-IN	12.3
16	54	Minneapolis-St. Paul-Bloomington, MN	12.3	44	53	Raleigh, NC	12.3
59	54	Omaha-Council Bluffs, NE-IA	12.3	58	53	Worcester, MA-CT	12.3
70	54	Baton Rouge, LA	12.3	17	56	San Diego-Carlsbad, CA	12.2
15	57	Seattle-Tacoma-Bellevue, WA	12.2	18	56	Tampa-St. Petersburg-Clearwater, FL	12.2
35	57	San Jose-Sunnyvale-Santa Clara, CA	12.2	65	58	New Haven-Milford, CT	12.0
25	59	San Antonio-New Braunfels, TX	12.1	69	59	Allentown-Bethlehem-Easton, PA-NJ	11.9
36	59	Nashville-Davidson—Murfreesboro—Franklin, TN	12.1	10	60	Boston-Cambridge-Newton, MA-NH	11.8
42	59	Memphis, TN-MS-AR	12.1	62	61	Albany-Schenectady-Troy, NY	11.6
32	62	Columbus, OH	12.0	30	62	Kansas City, MO-KS	11.5
13	63	Riverside-San Bernardino-Ontario, CA	11.9	52	62	Grand Rapids-Wyoming, MI	11.5
19	64	Denver-Aurora-Lakewood, CO	11.7	59	64	Omaha-Council Bluffs, NE-IA	11.2
6	65	Washington-Arlington-Alexandria, DC-VA-MD-WV	11.3	26	65	Pittsburgh, PA	11.1
68	65	El Paso, TX	11.3	11	66	San Francisco-Oakland-Hayward, CA	10.8
56	67	Fresno, CA	11.2	33	66	Austin-Round Rock, TX	10.8
9	68	Atlanta-Sandy Springs-Roswell, GA	10.8	64	66	Knoxville, TN	10.8
44	69	Raleigh, NC	10.6	19	69	Denver-Aurora-Lakewood, CO	10.7
67	70	McAllen-Edinburg-Mission, TX	10.4	35	69	San Jose-Sunnyvale-Santa Clara, CA	10.7
4	71	Dallas-Fort Worth-Arlington, TX	10.3	23	71	Portland-Vancouver-Hillsboro, OR-WA	10.6
61	72	Bakersfield, CA	9.9	48	71	Salt Lake City, UT	10.6
5	73	Houston-The Woodlands-Sugar Land, TX	9.8	16	73	Minneapolis-St. Paul-Bloomington, MN	10.0
48	74	Salt Lake City, UT	9.6	15	74	Seattle-Tacoma-Bellevue, WA	9.6
33	75	Austin-Round Rock, TX	9.5	73	75	North Port-Sarasota-Bradenton, FL	9.0

75 Largest Metropolitan Areas by 2015 Population
Selected Rankings

Birth rate, 2015				Percent under 65 who have no health insurance, 2014			
Population rank	Birth rate rank	Metropolitan area	Births (per 1,000 population) [col 36]	Population rank	No health insurance rank	Metropolitan area	Percent with no health insurance [col 40]
67	1	McAllen-Edinburg-Mission, TX	19.3	67	1	McAllen-Edinburg-Mission, TX	33.8
56	2	Fresno, CA	16.4	68	2	El Paso, TX	25.0
61	2	Bakersfield, CA	16.4	8	3	Miami-Fort Lauderdale-West Palm Beach, FL	23.1
48	4	Salt Lake City, UT	16.3	5	4	Houston-The Woodlands-Sugar Land, TX	21.6
68	4	El Paso, TX	16.3	73	5	North Port-Sarasota-Bradenton, FL	20.4
5	6	Houston-The Woodlands-Sugar Land, TX	14.8	4	6	Dallas-Fort Worth-Arlington, TX	20.1
59	7	Omaha-Council Bluffs, NE-IA	14.5	24	7	Orlando-Kissimmee-Sanford, FL	19.5
41	8	Oklahoma City, OK	14.3	25	8	San Antonio-New Braunfels, TX	18.5
4	9	Dallas-Fort Worth-Arlington, TX	14.1	18	9	Tampa-St. Petersburg-Clearwater, FL	17.9
25	10	San Antonio-New Braunfels, TX	14.0	29	10	Las Vegas-Henderson-Paradise, NV	17.8
42	10	Memphis, TN-MS-AR	14.0	9	11	Atlanta-Sandy Springs-Roswell, GA	17.6
32	12	Columbus, OH	13.8	33	11	Austin-Round Rock, TX	17.6
54	12	Urban Honolulu, HI	13.8	46	13	New Orleans-Metairie, LA	17.3
13	14	Riverside-San Bernardino-Ontario, CA	13.7	55	14	Tulsa, OK	17.0
55	15	Tulsa, OK	13.6	41	15	Oklahoma City, OK	16.6
17	16	San Diego-Carlsbad, CA	13.5	2	16	Los Angeles-Long Beach-Anaheim, CA	16.4
34	16	Indianapolis-Carmel-Anderson, IN	13.5	53	17	Tucson, AZ	16.0
70	16	Baton Rouge, LA	13.5	13	18	Riverside-San Bernardino-Ontario, CA	15.9
52	19	Grand Rapids-Wyoming, MI	13.4	63	19	Greenville-Anderson-Mauldin, SC	15.8
6	20	Washington-Arlington-Alexandria, DC-VA-MD-WV	13.3	12	20	Phoenix-Mesa-Scottsdale, AZ	15.5
33	20	Austin-Round Rock, TX	13.3	56	21	Fresno, CA	15.4
12	22	Phoenix-Mesa-Scottsdale, AZ	13.2	70	22	Baton Rouge, LA	15.3
16	22	Minneapolis-St. Paul-Bloomington, MN	13.2	60	23	Albuquerque, NM	15.2
30	22	Kansas City, MO-KS	13.2	74	23	Greensboro-High Point, NC	15.2
36	22	Nashville-Davidson—Murfreesboro—Franklin, TN	13.2	40	25	Jacksonville, FL	15.0
37	22	Virginia Beach-Norfolk-Newport News, VA-NC	13.2	75	25	Charleston-North Charleston, SC	15.0
9	27	Atlanta-Sandy Springs-Roswell, GA	12.8	22	27	Charlotte-Concord-Gastonia, NC-SC	14.8
75	27	Charleston-North Charleston, SC	12.8	42	28	Memphis, TN-MS-AR	14.7
19	29	Denver-Aurora-Lakewood, CO	12.7	48	28	Salt Lake City, UT	14.7
29	29	Las Vegas-Henderson-Paradise, NV	12.7	71	30	Columbia, SC	14.6
46	29	New Orleans-Metairie, LA	12.7	61	31	Bakersfield, CA	14.5
2	32	Los Angeles-Long Beach-Anaheim, CA	12.6	36	32	Nashville-Davidson—Murfreesboro—Franklin, TN	13.5
15	32	Seattle-Tacoma-Bellevue, WA	12.6	17	33	San Diego-Carlsbad, CA	13.4
39	32	Milwaukee-Waukesha-West Allis, WI	12.6	34	34	Indianapolis-Carmel-Anderson, IN	13.1
28	35	Cincinnati, OH-KY-IN	12.5	64	34	Knoxville, TN	13.1
40	35	Jacksonville, FL	12.5	66	34	Oxnard-Thousand Oaks-Ventura, CA	13.1
43	35	Louisville/Jefferson County, KY-IN	12.5	44	37	Raleigh, NC	12.9
66	35	Oxnard-Thousand Oaks-Ventura, CA	12.5	49	37	Birmingham-Hoover, AL	12.9
1	39	New York-Newark-Jersey City, NY-NJ-PA	12.4	45	39	Richmond, VA	12.7
3	39	Chicago-Naperville-Elgin, IL-IN-WI	12.4	3	40	Chicago-Naperville-Elgin, IL-IN-WI	12.3
22	39	Charlotte-Concord-Gastonia, NC-SC	12.4	37	41	Virginia Beach-Norfolk-Newport News, VA-NC	12.1
49	39	Birmingham-Hoover, AL	12.4	1	42	New York-Newark-Jersey City, NY-NJ-PA	11.8
35	43	San Jose-Sunnyvale-Santa Clara, CA	12.3	30	43	Kansas City, MO-KS	11.7
44	43	Raleigh, NC	12.3	19	44	Denver-Aurora-Lakewood, CO	11.6
27	45	Sacramento—Roseville—Arden-Arcade, CA	12.2	27	45	Sacramento—Roseville—Arden-Arcade, CA	10.9
21	46	Baltimore-Columbia-Towson, MD	12.1	20	46	St. Louis, MO-IL	10.7
63	46	Greenville-Anderson-Mauldin, SC	12.1	23	47	Portland-Vancouver-Hillsboro, OR-WA	10.6
72	46	Dayton, OH	12.1	57	48	Bridgeport-Stamford-Norwalk, CT	10.5
20	49	St. Louis, MO-IL	12.0	69	48	Allentown-Bethlehem-Easton, PA-NJ	10.5
24	50	Orlando-Kissimmee-Sanford, FL	11.9	14	50	Detroit-Warren-Dearborn, MI	10.3
53	50	Tucson, AZ	11.9	72	50	Dayton, OH	10.3
7	52	Philadelphia-Camden-Wilmington, PA-NJ-DE-MD	11.8	6	52	Washington-Arlington-Alexandria, DC-VA-MD-WV	10.2
14	52	Detroit-Warren-Dearborn, MI	11.8	43	52	Louisville/Jefferson County, KY-IN	10.2
23	52	Portland-Vancouver-Hillsboro, OR-WA	11.8	7	54	Philadelphia-Camden-Wilmington, PA-NJ-DE-MD	10.0
45	52	Richmond, VA	11.8	59	54	Omaha-Council Bluffs, NE-IA	10.0
71	56	Columbia, SC	11.6	32	56	Columbus, OH	9.9
74	56	Greensboro-High Point, NC	11.6	52	56	Grand Rapids-Wyoming, MI	9.9
60	58	Albuquerque, NM	11.5	11	58	San Francisco-Oakland-Hayward, CA	9.5
8	59	Miami-Fort Lauderdale-West Palm Beach, FL	11.4	31	58	Cleveland-Elyria, OH	9.5
11	59	San Francisco-Oakland-Hayward, CA	11.4	15	60	Seattle-Tacoma-Bellevue, WA	9.4
31	59	Cleveland-Elyria, OH	11.4	28	61	Cincinnati, OH-KY-IN	9.3
10	62	Boston-Cambridge-Newton, MA-NH	11.0	39	62	Milwaukee-Waukesha-West Allis, WI	8.8
51	63	Rochester, NY	10.9	35	63	San Jose-Sunnyvale-Santa Clara, CA	8.6
18	64	Tampa-St. Petersburg-Clearwater, FL	10.8	26	64	Pittsburgh, PA	8.3
50	64	Buffalo-Cheektowaga-Niagara Falls, NY	10.8	65	65	New Haven-Milford, CT	8.0
64	64	Knoxville, TN	10.8	21	66	Baltimore-Columbia-Towson, MD	7.5
57	67	Bridgeport-Stamford-Norwalk, CT	10.6	51	67	Rochester, NY	7.3
58	67	Worcester, MA-CT	10.6	38	68	Providence-Warwick, RI-MA	7.1
69	69	Allentown-Bethlehem-Easton, PA-NJ	10.5	50	69	Buffalo-Cheektowaga-Niagara Falls, NY	6.9
38	70	Providence-Warwick, RI-MA	10.4	62	70	Albany-Schenectady-Troy, NY	6.8
62	70	Albany-Schenectady-Troy, NY	10.4	16	71	Minneapolis-St. Paul-Bloomington, MN	6.5
65	70	New Haven-Milford, CT	10.4	47	71	Hartford-West Hartford-East Hartford, CT	6.5
26	73	Pittsburgh, PA	10.3	54	73	Urban Honolulu, HI	5.5
47	74	Hartford-West Hartford-East Hartford, CT	9.8	10	74	Boston-Cambridge-Newton, MA-NH	4.2
73	75	North Port-Sarasota-Bradenton, FL	8.4	58	75	Worcester, MA-CT	4.0

75 Largest Metropolitan Areas by 2015 Population
Selected Rankings

	Percent college graduates (bachelor's degree or more), 2014				Median household income, 2014		
Population rank	Percent college graduates rank	Metropolitan area	Percent college graduates [col 51]	Population rank	Median income rank	Metropolitan area	Median income (dollars) [col 55]
6	1	Washington-Arlington-Alexandria, DC-VA-MD-WV	49.3	57	1	Bridgeport-Stamford-Norwalk, CT	142 190
35	2	San Jose-Sunnyvale-Santa Clara, CA	47.5	35	2	San Jose-Sunnyvale-Santa Clara, CA	128 682
57	3	Bridgeport-Stamford-Norwalk, CT	46.7	11	3	San Francisco-Oakland-Hayward, CA	117 134
11	4	San Francisco-Oakland-Hayward, CA	45.9	6	4	Washington-Arlington-Alexandria, DC-VA-MD-WV	117 085
10	5	Boston-Cambridge-Newton, MA-NH	45.2	10	5	Boston-Cambridge-Newton, MA-NH	104 657
44	6	Raleigh, NC	43.4	66	6	Oxnard-Thousand Oaks-Ventura, CA	98 741
33	7	Austin-Round Rock, TX	41.5	1	7	New York-Newark-Jersey City, NY-NJ-PA	98 451
19	8	Denver-Aurora-Lakewood, CO	40.8	15	8	Seattle-Tacoma-Bellevue, WA	93 389
16	9	Minneapolis-St. Paul-Bloomington, MN	40.0	21	9	Baltimore-Columbia-Towson, MD	92 935
15	10	Seattle-Tacoma-Bellevue, WA	39.4	47	10	Hartford-West Hartford-East Hartford, CT	92 151
1	11	New York-Newark-Jersey City, NY-NJ-PA	37.9	54	11	Urban Honolulu, HI	91 428
21	12	Baltimore-Columbia-Towson, MD	37.7	16	12	Minneapolis-St. Paul-Bloomington, MN	91 246
47	13	Hartford-West Hartford-East Hartford, CT	37.5	19	13	Denver-Aurora-Lakewood, CO	89 498
17	14	San Diego-Carlsbad, CA	37.1	17	14	San Diego-Carlsbad, CA	89 137
3	15	Chicago-Naperville-Elgin, IL-IN-WI	36.1	2	15	Los Angeles-Long Beach-Anaheim, CA	88 098
9	16	Atlanta-Sandy Springs-Roswell, GA	35.8	7	16	Philadelphia-Camden-Wilmington, PA-NJ-DE-MD	86 635
23	17	Portland-Vancouver-Hillsboro, OR-WA	35.7	5	17	Houston-The Woodlands-Sugar Land, TX	86 296
62	18	Albany-Schenectady-Troy, NY	35.4	33	18	Austin-Round Rock, TX	85 806
7	19	Philadelphia-Camden-Wilmington, PA-NJ-DE-MD	35.3	3	19	Chicago-Naperville-Elgin, IL-IN-WI	85 507
30	20	Kansas City, MO-KS	34.7	44	20	Raleigh, NC	84 855
32	20	Columbus, OH	34.7	4	21	Dallas-Fort Worth-Arlington, TX	83 408
65	22	New Haven-Milford, CT	34.5	58	22	Worcester, MA-CT	83 321
59	23	Omaha-Council Bluffs, NE-IA	34.3	65	23	New Haven-Milford, CT	82 661
45	24	Richmond, VA	33.8	48	24	Salt Lake City, UT	82 403
39	25	Milwaukee-Waukesha-West Allis, WI	33.7	27	25	Sacramento—Roseville—Arden-Arcade, CA	81 519
58	26	Worcester, MA-CT	33.2	45	26	Richmond, VA	80 968
75	27	Charleston-North Charleston, SC	33.0	62	27	Albany-Schenectady-Troy, NY	79 446
22	28	Charlotte-Concord-Gastonia, NC-SC	32.9	23	28	Portland-Vancouver-Hillsboro, OR-WA	79 375
54	29	Urban Honolulu, HI	32.6	9	29	Atlanta-Sandy Springs-Roswell, GA	79 085
4	30	Dallas-Fort Worth-Arlington, TX	32.4	69	30	Allentown-Bethlehem-Easton, PA-NJ	77 183
20	31	St. Louis, MO-IL	32.3	30	31	Kansas City, MO-KS	76 444
51	32	Rochester, NY	32.2	32	32	Columbus, OH	76 201
2	33	Los Angeles-Long Beach-Anaheim, CA	32.1	38	33	Providence-Warwick, RI-MA	76 189
36	33	Nashville-Davidson—Murfreesboro—Franklin, TN	32.1	22	34	Charlotte-Concord-Gastonia, NC-SC	75 943
26	35	Pittsburgh, PA	31.7	20	35	St. Louis, MO-IL	75 223
71	35	Columbia, SC	31.7	75	36	Charleston-North Charleston, SC	74 299
34	37	Indianapolis-Carmel-Anderson, IN	31.6	36	37	Nashville-Davidson—Murfreesboro—Franklin, TN	74 288
66	37	Oxnard-Thousand Oaks-Ventura, CA	31.6	28	38	Cincinnati, OH-KY-IN	74 251
28	39	Cincinnati, OH-KY-IN	31.4	37	39	Virginia Beach-Norfolk-Newport News, VA-NC	73 919
73	39	North Port-Sarasota-Bradenton, FL	31.4	39	40	Milwaukee-Waukesha-West Allis, WI	73 894
27	41	Sacramento—Roseville—Arden-Arcade, CA	31.3	59	41	Omaha-Council Bluffs, NE-IA	73 754
48	41	Salt Lake City, UT	31.3	73	42	North Port-Sarasota-Bradenton, FL	73 484
52	43	Grand Rapids-Wyoming, MI	31.1	12	43	Phoenix-Mesa-Scottsdale, AZ	72 867
5	44	Houston-The Woodlands-Sugar Land, TX	31.0	8	44	Miami-Fort Lauderdale-West Palm Beach, FL	72 349
53	45	Tucson, AZ	30.8	14	45	Detroit-Warren-Dearborn, MI	71 997
60	46	Albuquerque, NM	30.5	26	46	Pittsburgh, PA	71 459
37	47	Virginia Beach-Norfolk-Newport News, VA-NC	29.6	41	47	Oklahoma City, OK	71 449
50	47	Buffalo-Cheektowaga-Niagara Falls, NY	29.6	25	48	San Antonio-New Braunfels, TX	71 260
31	49	Cleveland-Elyria, OH	29.5	34	49	Indianapolis-Carmel-Anderson, IN	71 103
8	50	Miami-Fort Lauderdale-West Palm Beach, FL	29.4	13	50	Riverside-San Bernardino-Ontario, CA	71 067
14	50	Detroit-Warren-Dearborn, MI	29.4	46	51	New Orleans-Metairie, LA	70 159
12	52	Phoenix-Mesa-Scottsdale, AZ	29.0	40	52	Jacksonville, FL	70 042
46	53	New Orleans-Metairie, LA	28.9	52	53	Grand Rapids-Wyoming, MI	69 886
38	54	Providence-Warwick, RI-MA	28.8	70	54	Baton Rouge, LA	69 747
24	55	Orlando-Kissimmee-Sanford, FL	28.7	51	55	Rochester, NY	68 915
41	56	Oklahoma City, OK	28.6	43	56	Louisville/Jefferson County, KY-IN	68 897
49	57	Birmingham-Hoover, AL	28.2	55	57	Tulsa, OK	68 277
43	58	Louisville/Jefferson County, KY-IN	27.6	31	58	Cleveland-Elyria, OH	68 252
64	58	Knoxville, TN	27.6	24	59	Orlando-Kissimmee-Sanford, FL	67 825
18	60	Tampa-St. Petersburg-Clearwater, FL	27.5	50	60	Buffalo-Cheektowaga-Niagara Falls, NY	67 381
40	60	Jacksonville, FL	27.5	29	61	Las Vegas-Henderson-Paradise, NV	66 603
70	62	Baton Rouge, LA	27.3	71	62	Columbia, SC	65 966
72	62	Dayton, OH	27.3	61	63	Bakersfield, CA	65 772
74	64	Greensboro-High Point, NC	27.2	18	64	Tampa-St. Petersburg-Clearwater, FL	65 646
63	65	Greenville-Anderson-Mauldin, SC	26.8	49	65	Birmingham-Hoover, AL	65 478
55	66	Tulsa, OK	26.5	42	66	Memphis, TN-MS-AR	65 233
42	67	Memphis, TN-MS-AR	26.4	60	67	Albuquerque, NM	65 138
69	67	Allentown-Bethlehem-Easton, PA-NJ	26.4	64	68	Knoxville, TN	64 318
25	69	San Antonio-New Braunfels, TX	26.3	53	69	Tucson, AZ	64 136
29	70	Las Vegas-Henderson-Paradise, NV	22.7	72	70	Dayton, OH	63 087
68	71	El Paso, TX	21.0	56	71	Fresno, CA	62 536
13	72	Riverside-San Bernardino-Ontario, CA	19.9	63	72	Greenville-Anderson-Mauldin, SC	61 659
56	73	Fresno, CA	19.7	74	73	Greensboro-High Point, NC	59 977
67	74	McAllen-Edinburg-Mission, TX	17.9	68	74	El Paso, TX	54 484
61	75	Bakersfield, CA	15.4	67	75	McAllen-Edinburg-Mission, TX	49 841

75 Largest Metropolitan Areas by 2015 Population
Selected Rankings

Percent of population below the poverty level, 2014				Percent of children under 18 years old below the poverty level, 2014			
Popu-lation rank	Poverty rate rank	Metropolitan area	Poverty rate [col 59]	Popu-lation rank	Poverty rate rank	Metropolitan area	Poverty rate [col 60]
67	1	McAllen-Edinburg-Mission, TX	34.0	67	1	McAllen-Edinburg-Mission, TX	46.5
56	2	Fresno, CA	27.7	56	2	Fresno, CA	38.9
61	3	Bakersfield, CA	24.8	61	3	Bakersfield, CA	33.6
68	4	El Paso, TX	23.4	68	4	El Paso, TX	32.0
42	5	Memphis, TN-MS-AR	20.3	42	5	Memphis, TN-MS-AR	30.8
60	6	Albuquerque, NM	19.2	46	6	New Orleans-Metairie, LA	27.0
53	7	Tucson, AZ	18.9	72	7	Dayton, OH	26.7
13	8	Riverside-San Bernardino-Ontario, CA	18.7	74	8	Greensboro-High Point, NC	26.4
46	9	New Orleans-Metairie, LA	18.1	53	9	Tucson, AZ	26.2
49	10	Birmingham-Hoover, AL	17.5	13	10	Riverside-San Bernardino-Ontario, CA	26.0
2	11	Los Angeles-Long Beach-Anaheim, CA	17.3	49	11	Birmingham-Hoover, AL	25.3
64	11	Knoxville, TN	17.3	60	11	Albuquerque, NM	25.3
72	11	Dayton, OH	17.3	12	13	Phoenix-Mesa-Scottsdale, AZ	24.7
74	11	Greensboro-High Point, NC	17.3	2	14	Los Angeles-Long Beach-Anaheim, CA	24.6
8	15	Miami-Fort Lauderdale-West Palm Beach, FL	17.2	64	14	Knoxville, TN	24.6
12	15	Phoenix-Mesa-Scottsdale, AZ	17.2	25	16	San Antonio-New Braunfels, TX	24.2
70	17	Baton Rouge, LA	17.0	31	16	Cleveland-Elyria, OH	24.2
24	18	Orlando-Kissimmee-Sanford, FL	16.7	8	18	Miami-Fort Lauderdale-West Palm Beach, FL	23.8
25	18	San Antonio-New Braunfels, TX	16.7	14	19	Detroit-Warren-Dearborn, MI	23.7
63	20	Greenville-Anderson-Mauldin, SC	16.5	24	20	Orlando-Kissimmee-Sanford, FL	23.6
27	21	Sacramento—Roseville—Arden-Arcade, CA	16.4	39	21	Milwaukee-Waukesha-West Allis, WI	22.9
14	22	Detroit-Warren-Dearborn, MI	16.1	75	21	Charleston-North Charleston, SC	22.9
31	23	Cleveland-Elyria, OH	15.9	9	23	Atlanta-Sandy Springs-Roswell, GA	22.8
18	24	Tampa-St. Petersburg-Clearwater, FL	15.8	63	24	Greenville-Anderson-Mauldin, SC	22.7
71	24	Columbia, SC	15.8	40	25	Jacksonville, FL	22.6
9	26	Atlanta-Sandy Springs-Roswell, GA	15.5	29	26	Las Vegas-Henderson-Paradise, NV	22.4
39	27	Milwaukee-Waukesha-West Allis, WI	15.4	5	27	Houston-The Woodlands-Sugar Land, TX	22.2
40	27	Jacksonville, FL	15.4	18	27	Tampa-St. Petersburg-Clearwater, FL	22.2
5	29	Houston-The Woodlands-Sugar Land, TX	15.3	71	27	Columbia, SC	22.2
41	29	Oklahoma City, OK	15.3	50	30	Buffalo-Cheektowaga-Niagara Falls, NY	22.0
22	31	Charlotte-Concord-Gastonia, NC-SC	15.2	70	31	Baton Rouge, LA	21.8
29	31	Las Vegas-Henderson-Paradise, NV	15.2	4	32	Dallas-Fort Worth-Arlington, TX	21.6
33	33	Austin-Round Rock, TX	15.1	36	32	Nashville-Davidson—Murfreesboro—Franklin, TN	21.6
36	33	Nashville-Davidson—Murfreesboro—Franklin, TN	15.1	51	34	Rochester, NY	21.5
75	33	Charleston-North Charleston, SC	15.1	22	35	Charlotte-Concord-Gastonia, NC-SC	21.3
4	36	Dallas-Fort Worth-Arlington, TX	14.8	34	36	Indianapolis-Carmel-Anderson, IN	21.2
34	36	Indianapolis-Carmel-Anderson, IN	14.8	41	37	Oklahoma City, OK	21.0
50	36	Buffalo-Cheektowaga-Niagara Falls, NY	14.8	55	38	Tulsa, OK	20.8
17	39	San Diego-Carlsbad, CA	14.7	27	39	Sacramento—Roseville—Arden-Arcade, CA	20.7
1	40	New York-Newark-Jersey City, NY-NJ-PA	14.6	43	40	Louisville/Jefferson County, KY-IN	20.5
32	41	Columbus, OH	14.5	1	41	New York-Newark-Jersey City, NY-NJ-PA	20.4
43	41	Louisville/Jefferson County, KY-IN	14.5	32	42	Columbus, OH	20.2
55	43	Tulsa, OK	14.4	3	43	Chicago-Naperville-Elgin, IL-IN-WI	20.1
51	44	Rochester, NY	14.1	33	44	Austin-Round Rock, TX	19.9
28	45	Cincinnati, OH-KY-IN	14.0	45	44	Richmond, VA	19.9
3	46	Chicago-Naperville-Elgin, IL-IN-WI	13.9	28	46	Cincinnati, OH-KY-IN	19.7
52	47	Grand Rapids-Wyoming, MI	13.8	73	47	North Port-Sarasota-Bradenton, FL	19.4
23	48	Portland-Vancouver-Hillsboro, OR-WA	13.6	17	48	San Diego-Carlsbad, CA	18.9
38	48	Providence-Warwick, RI-MA	13.6	38	48	Providence-Warwick, RI-MA	18.9
7	50	Philadelphia-Camden-Wilmington, PA-NJ-DE-MD	13.4	7	50	Philadelphia-Camden-Wilmington, PA-NJ-DE-MD	18.6
65	51	New Haven-Milford, CT	13.1	20	51	St. Louis, MO-IL	18.4
20	52	St. Louis, MO-IL	13.0	65	52	New Haven-Milford, CT	18.3
45	53	Richmond, VA	12.8	30	53	Kansas City, MO-KS	17.9
30	54	Kansas City, MO-KS	12.6	52	54	Grand Rapids-Wyoming, MI	17.8
26	55	Pittsburgh, PA	12.4	37	55	Virginia Beach-Norfolk-Newport News, VA-NC	17.7
37	55	Virginia Beach-Norfolk-Newport News, VA-NC	12.4	26	56	Pittsburgh, PA	17.5
44	57	Raleigh, NC	12.2	23	57	Portland-Vancouver-Hillsboro, OR-WA	17.3
73	58	North Port-Sarasota-Bradenton, FL	12.0	62	58	Albany-Schenectady-Troy, NY	17.1
62	59	Albany-Schenectady-Troy, NY	11.7	69	59	Allentown-Bethlehem-Easton, PA-NJ	16.8
48	60	Salt Lake City, UT	11.4	44	60	Raleigh, NC	16.0
15	61	Seattle-Tacoma-Bellevue, WA	11.3	47	61	Hartford-West Hartford-East Hartford, CT	15.7
59	61	Omaha-Council Bluffs, NE-IA	11.3	66	62	Oxnard-Thousand Oaks-Ventura, CA	15.5
66	61	Oxnard-Thousand Oaks-Ventura, CA	11.3	48	63	Salt Lake City, UT	15.0
58	64	Worcester, MA-CT	11.2	19	64	Denver-Aurora-Lakewood, CO	14.7
69	64	Allentown-Bethlehem-Easton, PA-NJ	11.2	58	64	Worcester, MA-CT	14.7
21	66	Baltimore-Columbia-Towson, MD	11.1	59	66	Omaha-Council Bluffs, NE-IA	14.6
47	66	Hartford-West Hartford-East Hartford, CT	11.1	15	67	Seattle-Tacoma-Bellevue, WA	14.4
11	68	San Francisco-Oakland-Hayward, CA	10.9	21	68	Baltimore-Columbia-Towson, MD	14.3
19	69	Denver-Aurora-Lakewood, CO	10.7	16	69	Minneapolis-St. Paul-Bloomington, MN	13.6
10	70	Boston-Cambridge-Newton, MA-NH	10.6	10	70	Boston-Cambridge-Newton, MA-NH	13.5
16	71	Minneapolis-St. Paul-Bloomington, MN	10.3	11	71	San Francisco-Oakland-Hayward, CA	12.9
54	72	Urban Honolulu, HI	9.7	54	72	Urban Honolulu, HI	12.7
57	73	Bridgeport-Stamford-Norwalk, CT	8.9	57	73	Bridgeport-Stamford-Norwalk, CT	11.5
6	74	Washington-Arlington-Alexandria, DC-VA-MD-WV	8.7	6	74	Washington-Arlington-Alexandria, DC-VA-MD-WV	11.1
35	74	San Jose-Sunnyvale-Santa Clara, CA	8.7	35	75	San Jose-Sunnyvale-Santa Clara, CA	9.4

75 Largest Metropolitan Areas by 2015 Population
Selected Rankings

	Median value of owner-occupied housing units, 2014				Mean gross rent of renter-occupied housing units, 2014		
Popu-lation rank	Median value rank	Metropolitan area	Median value (dollars) [col 91]	Popu-lation rank	Median gross rent	Metropolitan area	Mean rent (dollars) [col 94]
35	1	San Jose-Sunnyvale-Santa Clara, CA	735 400	35	1	San Jose-Sunnyvale-Santa Clara, CA	1 779
11	2	San Francisco-Oakland-Hayward, CA	657 300	54	2	Urban Honolulu, HI	1 602
54	3	Urban Honolulu, HI	590 600	6	3	Washington-Arlington-Alexandria, DC-VA-MD-WV	1 525
2	4	Los Angeles-Long Beach-Anaheim, CA	494 900	11	4	San Francisco-Oakland-Hayward, CA	1 519
66	5	Oxnard-Thousand Oaks-Ventura, CA	483 100	66	5	Oxnard-Thousand Oaks-Ventura, CA	1 505
17	6	San Diego-Carlsbad, CA	457 300	57	6	Bridgeport-Stamford-Norwalk, CT	1 382
57	7	Bridgeport-Stamford-Norwalk, CT	408 900	17	7	San Diego-Carlsbad, CA	1 373
1	8	New York-Newark-Jersey City, NY-NJ-PA	396 700	2	8	Los Angeles-Long Beach-Anaheim, CA	1 309
6	9	Washington-Arlington-Alexandria, DC-VA-MD-WV	386 900	1	9	New York-Newark-Jersey City, NY-NJ-PA	1 281
10	10	Boston-Cambridge-Newton, MA-NH	375 200	10	10	Boston-Cambridge-Newton, MA-NH	1 247
15	11	Seattle-Tacoma-Bellevue, WA	334 700	15	11	Seattle-Tacoma-Bellevue, WA	1 179
27	12	Sacramento—Roseville—Arden-Arcade, CA	314 400	21	12	Baltimore-Columbia-Towson, MD	1 166
21	13	Baltimore-Columbia-Towson, MD	279 900	13	13	Riverside-San Bernardino-Ontario, CA	1 159
23	14	Portland-Vancouver-Hillsboro, OR-WA	277 100	8	14	Miami-Fort Lauderdale-West Palm Beach, FL	1 146
19	15	Denver-Aurora-Lakewood, CO	276 800	19	15	Denver-Aurora-Lakewood, CO	1 078
13	16	Riverside-San Bernardino-Ontario, CA	272 200	33	16	Austin-Round Rock, TX	1 063
38	17	Providence-Warwick, RI-MA	249 700	37	17	Virginia Beach-Norfolk-Newport News, VA-NC	1 059
58	18	Worcester, MA-CT	244 400	65	17	New Haven-Milford, CT	1 059
47	19	Hartford-West Hartford-East Hartford, CT	243 100	27	19	Sacramento—Roseville—Arden-Arcade, CA	1 057
65	20	New Haven-Milford, CT	242 700	24	20	Orlando-Kissimmee-Sanford, FL	1 035
48	21	Salt Lake City, UT	237 900	7	21	Philadelphia-Camden-Wilmington, PA-NJ-DE-MD	1 020
7	22	Philadelphia-Camden-Wilmington, PA-NJ-DE-MD	234 400	45	22	Richmond, VA	1 011
37	23	Virginia Beach-Norfolk-Newport News, VA-NC	232 300	23	23	Portland-Vancouver-Hillsboro, OR-WA	1 009
33	24	Austin-Round Rock, TX	217 900	73	24	North Port-Sarasota-Bradenton, FL	1 007
16	25	Minneapolis-St. Paul-Bloomington, MN	216 400	47	25	Hartford-West Hartford-East Hartford, CT	999
45	26	Richmond, VA	213 900	3	26	Chicago-Naperville-Elgin, IL-IN-WI	990
44	27	Raleigh, NC	212 900	75	27	Charleston-North Charleston, SC	986
3	28	Chicago-Naperville-Elgin, IL-IN-WI	211 800	9	28	Atlanta-Sandy Springs-Roswell, GA	982
8	29	Miami-Fort Lauderdale-West Palm Beach, FL	210 000	29	29	Las Vegas-Henderson-Paradise, NV	981
56	30	Fresno, CA	204 700	12	30	Phoenix-Mesa-Scottsdale, AZ	969
12	31	Phoenix-Mesa-Scottsdale, AZ	197 900	40	31	Jacksonville, FL	966
62	32	Albany-Schenectady-Troy, NY	196 900	18	32	Tampa-St. Petersburg-Clearwater, FL	957
69	33	Allentown-Bethlehem-Easton, PA-NJ	195 900	4	33	Dallas-Fort Worth-Arlington, TX	949
39	34	Milwaukee-Waukesha-West Allis, WI	190 400	69	34	Allentown-Bethlehem-Easton, PA-NJ	945
75	35	Charleston-North Charleston, SC	189 700	16	35	Minneapolis-St. Paul-Bloomington, MN	938
29	36	Las Vegas-Henderson-Paradise, NV	188 700	44	35	Raleigh, NC	938
73	37	North Port-Sarasota-Bradenton, FL	183 300	5	37	Houston-The Woodlands-Sugar Land, TX	937
61	38	Bakersfield, CA	183 100	48	38	Salt Lake City, UT	932
36	39	Nashville-Davidson—Murfreesboro—Franklin, TN	177 600	58	38	Worcester, MA-CT	932
46	40	New Orleans-Metairie, LA	174 200	62	40	Albany-Schenectady-Troy, NY	931
60	41	Albuquerque, NM	173 700	46	41	New Orleans-Metairie, LA	903
9	42	Atlanta-Sandy Springs-Roswell, GA	170 300	25	42	San Antonio-New Braunfels, TX	899
22	43	Charlotte-Concord-Gastonia, NC-SC	169 400	56	43	Fresno, CA	891
24	44	Orlando-Kissimmee-Sanford, FL	162 700	38	44	Providence-Warwick, RI-MA	890
32	45	Columbus, OH	160 800	22	45	Charlotte-Concord-Gastonia, NC-SC	884
4	46	Dallas-Fort Worth-Arlington, TX	160 600	36	46	Nashville-Davidson—Murfreesboro—Franklin, TN	881
30	47	Kansas City, MO-KS	160 400	61	47	Bakersfield, CA	870
40	48	Jacksonville, FL	159 100	71	48	Columbia, SC	857
53	49	Tucson, AZ	158 400	14	49	Detroit-Warren-Dearborn, MI	853
70	50	Baton Rouge, LA	157 500	42	50	Memphis, TN-MS-AR	851
20	51	St. Louis, MO-IL	156 100	30	51	Kansas City, MO-KS	850
5	52	Houston-The Woodlands-Sugar Land, TX	153 200	32	52	Columbus, OH	847
28	53	Cincinnati, OH-KY-IN	152 100	39	53	Milwaukee-Waukesha-West Allis, WI	836
64	54	Knoxville, TN	151 900	59	54	Omaha-Council Bluffs, NE-IA	830
43	55	Louisville/Jefferson County, KY-IN	151 300	70	54	Baton Rouge, LA	830
18	56	Tampa-St. Petersburg-Clearwater, FL	149 500	34	56	Indianapolis-Carmel-Anderson, IN	818
59	57	Omaha-Council Bluffs, NE-IA	147 300	20	57	St. Louis, MO-IL	817
49	58	Birmingham-Hoover, AL	145 500	53	58	Tucson, AZ	814
52	59	Grand Rapids-Wyoming, MI	144 300	60	58	Albuquerque, NM	814
25	60	San Antonio-New Braunfels, TX	143 900	51	60	Rochester, NY	800
34	61	Indianapolis-Carmel-Anderson, IN	141 500	49	61	Birmingham-Hoover, AL	797
71	62	Columbia, SC	140 800	52	62	Grand Rapids-Wyoming, MI	794
63	63	Greenville-Anderson-Mauldin, SC	139 400	41	63	Oklahoma City, OK	782
41	64	Oklahoma City, OK	139 200	55	64	Tulsa, OK	775
74	65	Greensboro-High Point, NC	138 600	72	65	Dayton, OH	754
31	66	Cleveland-Elyria, OH	137 800	74	66	Greensboro-High Point, NC	753
14	67	Detroit-Warren-Dearborn, MI	136 400	31	67	Cleveland-Elyria, OH	752
26	68	Pittsburgh, PA	134 700	28	68	Cincinnati, OH-KY-IN	751
51	69	Rochester, NY	133 400	26	69	Pittsburgh, PA	743
55	70	Tulsa, OK	133 100	43	70	Louisville/Jefferson County, KY-IN	741
42	71	Memphis, TN-MS-AR	132 900	50	71	Buffalo-Cheektowaga-Niagara Falls, NY	739
50	72	Buffalo-Cheektowaga-Niagara Falls, NY	125 400	68	71	El Paso, TX	739
72	73	Dayton, OH	120 200	64	73	Knoxville, TN	738
68	74	El Paso, TX	114 700	63	74	Greenville-Anderson-Mauldin, SC	736
67	75	McAllen-Edinburg-Mission, TX	79 400	67	75	McAllen-Edinburg-Mission, TX	668

75 Largest Metropolitan Areas by 2015 Population
Selected Rankings

	Unemployment rate, 2015				Percent of Votes for Barack Obama, 2012		
Population rank	Unemployment rate rank	Metropolitan area	Unemployment rate [col 100]	Population Rank	Vote for Obama rank	Metropolitan area	Percent of votes for Obama [col 197]
56	1	Fresno, CA	10.2	11	1	San Francisco-Oakland-Hayward, CA	75.4
61	1	Bakersfield, CA	10.2	67	2	McAllen-Edinburg-Mission, TX	70.4
67	3	McAllen-Edinburg-Mission, TX	7.9	35	3	San Jose-Sunnyvale-Santa Clara, CA	69.8
29	4	Las Vegas-Henderson-Paradise, NV	6.8	54	4	Urban Honolulu, HI	68.9
13	5	Riverside-San Bernardino-Ontario, CA	6.6	6	5	Washington-Arlington-Alexandria, DC-VA-MD-WV	67.3
42	6	Memphis, TN-MS-AR	6.5	68	6	El Paso, TX	65.4
2	7	Los Angeles-Long Beach-Anaheim, CA	6.2	1	7	New York-Newark-Jersey City, NY-NJ-PA	64.8
14	7	Detroit-Warren-Dearborn, MI	6.2	7	8	Philadelphia-Camden-Wilmington, PA-NJ-DE-MD	64.0
60	7	Albuquerque, NM	6.2	3	9	Chicago-Naperville-Elgin, IL-IN-WI	63.8
38	10	Providence-Warwick, RI-MA	6.1	15	10	Seattle-Tacoma-Bellevue, WA	63.6
65	10	New Haven-Milford, CT	6.1	2	11	Los Angeles-Long Beach-Anaheim, CA	63.4
46	12	New Orleans-Metairie, LA	6.0	8	12	Miami-Fort Lauderdale-West Palm Beach, FL	62.6
27	13	Sacramento—Roseville—Arden-Arcade, CA	5.9	31	13	Cleveland-Elyria, OH	61.5
74	13	Greensboro-High Point, NC	5.9	38	13	Providence-Warwick, RI-MA	61.5
3	15	Chicago-Naperville-Elgin, IL-IN-WI	5.8	47	15	Hartford-West Hartford-East Hartford, CT	60.7
66	16	Oxnard-Thousand Oaks-Ventura, CA	5.7	65	15	New Haven-Milford, CT	60.7
9	17	Atlanta-Sandy Springs-Roswell, GA	5.6	10	17	Boston-Cambridge-Newton, MA-NH	60.1
47	17	Hartford-West Hartford-East Hartford, CT	5.6	23	18	Portland-Vancouver-Hillsboro, OR-WA	60.0
50	17	Buffalo-Cheektowaga-Niagara Falls, NY	5.6	14	19	Detroit-Warren-Dearborn, MI	59.5
53	17	Tucson, AZ	5.6	21	20	Baltimore-Columbia-Towson, MD	57.8
8	21	Miami-Fort Lauderdale-West Palm Beach, FL	5.5	62	21	Albany-Schenectady-Troy, NY	57.0
22	21	Charlotte-Concord-Gastonia, NC-SC	5.5	29	22	Las Vegas-Henderson-Paradise, NV	56.4
49	21	Birmingham-Hoover, AL	5.5	50	23	Buffalo-Cheektowaga-Niagara Falls, NY	55.9
71	21	Columbia, SC	5.5	42	24	Memphis, TN-MS-AR	55.7
21	25	Baltimore-Columbia-Towson, MD	5.4	19	25	Denver-Aurora-Lakewood, CO	55.5
58	25	Worcester, MA-CT	5.4	57	26	Bridgeport-Stamford-Norwalk, CT	54.9
64	25	Knoxville, TN	5.4	37	27	Virginia Beach-Norfolk-Newport News, VA-NC	54.8
70	25	Baton Rouge, LA	5.4	16	28	Minneapolis-St. Paul-Bloomington, MN	54.7
1	29	New York-Newark-Jersey City, NY-NJ-PA	5.3	51	29	Rochester, NY	54.4
7	29	Philadelphia-Camden-Wilmington, PA-NJ-DE-MD	5.3	60	30	Albuquerque, NM	54.0
12	29	Phoenix-Mesa-Scottsdale, AZ	5.3	58	31	Worcester, MA-CT	53.9
23	29	Portland-Vancouver-Hillsboro, OR-WA	5.3	24	32	Orlando-Kissimmee-Sanford, FL	53.4
57	29	Bridgeport-Stamford-Norwalk, CT	5.3	27	33	Sacramento—Roseville—Arden-Arcade, CA	53.1
63	29	Greenville-Anderson-Mauldin, SC	5.3	32	34	Columbus, OH	52.7
17	35	San Diego-Carlsbad, CA	5.2	17	35	San Diego-Carlsbad, CA	52.6
40	35	Jacksonville, FL	5.2	20	35	St. Louis, MO-IL	52.6
51	35	Rochester, NY	5.2	53	35	Tucson, AZ	52.6
68	35	El Paso, TX	5.2	66	38	Oxnard-Thousand Oaks-Ventura, CA	52.3
69	35	Allentown-Bethlehem-Easton, PA-NJ	5.2	39	39	Milwaukee-Waukesha-West Allis, WI	52.1
18	40	Tampa-St. Petersburg-Clearwater, FL	5.1	44	39	Raleigh, NC	52.1
20	40	St. Louis, MO-IL	5.1	45	41	Richmond, VA	52.0
26	40	Pittsburgh, PA	5.1	33	42	Austin-Round Rock, TX	51.9
75	40	Charleston-North Charleston, SC	5.1	13	43	Riverside-San Bernardino-Ontario, CA	51.0
24	44	Orlando-Kissimmee-Sanford, FL	5.0	18	43	Tampa-St. Petersburg-Clearwater, FL	51.0
39	44	Milwaukee-Waukesha-West Allis, WI	5.0	69	45	Allentown-Bethlehem-Easton, PA-NJ	50.6
73	44	North Port-Sarasota-Bradenton, FL	5.0	71	46	Columbia, SC	50.2
15	47	Seattle-Tacoma-Bellevue, WA	4.9	56	47	Fresno, CA	49.9
37	47	Virginia Beach-Norfolk-Newport News, VA-NC	4.9	74	48	Greensboro-High Point, NC	49.8
30	49	Kansas City, MO-KS	4.8	9	49	Atlanta-Sandy Springs-Roswell, GA	49.6
31	49	Cleveland-Elyria, OH	4.8	46	50	New Orleans-Metairie, LA	49.2
44	49	Raleigh, NC	4.8	26	51	Pittsburgh, PA	48.8
72	49	Dayton, OH	4.8	43	52	Louisville/Jefferson County, KY-IN	48.1
43	53	Louisville/Jefferson County, KY-IN	4.7	30	53	Kansas City, MO-KS	47.9
5	54	Houston-The Woodlands-Sugar Land, TX	4.6	22	54	Charlotte-Concord-Gastonia, NC-SC	47.2
36	54	Nashville-Davidson—Murfreesboro—Franklin, TN	4.6	75	55	Charleston-North Charleston, SC	46.5
45	54	Richmond, VA	4.6	72	56	Dayton, OH	46.2
28	57	Cincinnati, OH-KY-IN	4.5	25	57	San Antonio-New Braunfels, TX	45.3
34	57	Indianapolis-Carmel-Anderson, IN	4.5	34	58	Indianapolis-Carmel-Anderson, IN	45.2
62	57	Albany-Schenectady-Troy, NY	4.5	73	59	North Port-Sarasota-Bradenton, FL	44.8
6	60	Washington-Arlington-Alexandria, DC-VA-MD-WV	4.4	59	60	Omaha-Council Bluffs, NE-IA	44.0
10	60	Boston-Cambridge-Newton, MA-NH	4.4	5	61	Houston-The Woodlands-Sugar Land, TX	43.6
11	62	San Francisco-Oakland-Hayward, CA	4.3	12	62	Phoenix-Mesa-Scottsdale, AZ	43.5
35	62	San Jose-Sunnyvale-Santa Clara, CA	4.3	70	63	Baton Rouge, LA	43.0
55	64	Tulsa, OK	4.2	4	64	Dallas-Fort Worth-Arlington, TX	41.9
4	65	Dallas-Fort Worth-Arlington, TX	4.1	52	65	Grand Rapids-Wyoming, MI	41.5
32	65	Columbus, OH	4.1	28	66	Cincinnati, OH-KY-IN	41.4
25	67	San Antonio-New Braunfels, TX	3.8	36	67	Nashville-Davidson—Murfreesboro—Franklin, TN	41.0
19	68	Denver-Aurora-Lakewood, CO	3.7	61	68	Bakersfield, CA	40.4
41	68	Oklahoma City, OK	3.7	40	69	Jacksonville, FL	40.0
52	68	Grand Rapids-Wyoming, MI	3.7	49	70	Birmingham-Hoover, AL	39.3
16	71	Minneapolis-St. Paul-Bloomington, MN	3.4	48	71	Salt Lake City, UT	37.6
33	71	Austin-Round Rock, TX	3.4	41	72	Oklahoma City, OK	36.5
48	71	Salt Lake City, UT	3.4	55	73	Tulsa, OK	33.9
54	71	Urban Honolulu, HI	3.4	63	74	Greenville-Anderson-Mauldin, SC	33.3
59	75	Omaha-Council Bluffs, NE-IA	3.2	64	75	Knoxville, TN	31.2

75 Largest Metropolitan Areas by 2015 Population
Selected Rankings

Employment in manufacturing as a percent of total nonfarm employment, 2014				Employment in professional, scientific, and technical services as a percent of total nonfarm employment, 2014			
Population rank	Manufacturing rank	Metropolitan area	Percent employed in manufacturing [col 107/col 105]	Population rank	Professional services rank	Metropolitan area	Percent employed in services [col 110/col 105]
52	1	Grand Rapids-Wyoming, MI	22.1	6	1	Washington-Arlington-Alexandria, DC-VA-MD-WV	20.9
74	2	Greensboro-High Point, NC	16.7	35	2	San Jose-Sunnyvale-Santa Clara, CA	13.6
63	3	Greenville-Anderson-Mauldin, SC	15.5	11	3	San Francisco-Oakland-Hayward, CA	11.6
39	4	Milwaukee-Waukesha-West Allis, WI	14.8	21	4	Baltimore-Columbia-Towson, MD	11.2
55	5	Tulsa, OK	13.8	17	5	San Diego-Carlsbad, CA	11.1
72	6	Dayton, OH	13.3	33	6	Austin-Round Rock, TX	10.6
31	7	Cleveland-Elyria, OH	13.2	44	6	Raleigh, NC	10.6
14	8	Detroit-Warren-Dearborn, MI	12.8	14	8	Detroit-Warren-Dearborn, MI	9.8
43	9	Louisville/Jefferson County, KY-IN	12.5	10	9	Boston-Cambridge-Newton, MA-NH	9.7
51	10	Rochester, NY	12.3	2	10	Los Angeles-Long Beach-Anaheim, CA	9.6
58	11	Worcester, MA-CT	11.8	19	11	Denver-Aurora-Lakewood, CO	9.3
23	12	Portland-Vancouver-Hillsboro, OR-WA	11.2	1	12	New York-Newark-Jersey City, NY-NJ-PA	9.0
50	12	Buffalo-Cheektowaga-Niagara Falls, NY	11.2	57	13	Bridgeport-Stamford-Norwalk, CT	8.8
69	14	Allentown-Bethlehem-Easton, PA-NJ	11.0	66	13	Oxnard-Thousand Oaks-Ventura, CA	8.8
47	15	Hartford-West Hartford-East Hartford, CT	10.9	9	15	Atlanta-Sandy Springs-Roswell, GA	8.6
28	16	Cincinnati, OH-KY-IN	10.7	37	15	Virginia Beach-Norfolk-Newport News, VA-NC	8.6
64	17	Knoxville, TN	10.5	18	17	Tampa-St. Petersburg-Clearwater, FL	8.5
38	18	Providence-Warwick, RI-MA	10.4	5	18	Houston-The Woodlands-Sugar Land, TX	8.4
15	19	Seattle-Tacoma-Bellevue, WA	10.3	30	18	Kansas City, MO-KS	8.4
16	20	Minneapolis-St. Paul-Bloomington, MN	10.2	48	20	Salt Lake City, UT	8.3
66	21	Oxnard-Thousand Oaks-Ventura, CA	9.7	3	21	Chicago-Naperville-Elgin, IL-IN-WI	8.1
75	21	Charleston-North Charleston, SC	9.7	7	21	Philadelphia-Camden-Wilmington, PA-NJ-DE-MD	8.1
37	23	Virginia Beach-Norfolk-Newport News, VA-NC	9.6	62	21	Albany-Schenectady-Troy, NY	8.1
65	23	New Haven-Milford, CT	9.6	75	24	Charleston-North Charleston, SC	8.0
3	25	Chicago-Naperville-Elgin, IL-IN-WI	9.5	4	25	Dallas-Fort Worth-Arlington, TX	7.7
22	25	Charlotte-Concord-Gastonia, NC-SC	9.5	15	25	Seattle-Tacoma-Bellevue, WA	7.7
56	25	Fresno, CA	9.5	8	27	Miami-Fort Lauderdale-West Palm Beach, FL	7.5
2	28	Los Angeles-Long Beach-Anaheim, CA	9.4	60	27	Albuquerque, NM	7.5
71	28	Columbia, SC	9.4	23	29	Portland-Vancouver-Hillsboro, OR-WA	7.4
5	30	Houston-The Woodlands-Sugar Land, TX	9.0	27	29	Sacramento—Roseville—Arden-Arcade, CA	7.4
35	30	San Jose-Sunnyvale-Santa Clara, CA	9.0	64	31	Knoxville, TN	7.2
13	32	Riverside-San Bernardino-Ontario, CA	8.7	72	31	Dayton, OH	7.2
48	32	Salt Lake City, UT	8.7	45	33	Richmond, VA	7.1
30	34	Kansas City, MO-KS	8.5	12	34	Phoenix-Mesa-Scottsdale, AZ	7.0
34	34	Indianapolis-Carmel-Anderson, IN	8.5	20	34	St. Louis, MO-IL	7.0
36	34	Nashville-Davidson—Murfreesboro—Franklin, TN	8.5	46	34	New Orleans-Metairie, LA	7.0
49	34	Birmingham-Hoover, AL	8.5	16	37	Minneapolis-St. Paul-Bloomington, MN	6.9
20	38	St. Louis, MO-IL	8.4	26	37	Pittsburgh, PA	6.9
4	39	Dallas-Fort Worth-Arlington, TX	8.3	34	39	Indianapolis-Carmel-Anderson, IN	6.8
26	40	Pittsburgh, PA	8.2	47	39	Hartford-West Hartford-East Hartford, CT	6.8
17	41	San Diego-Carlsbad, CA	8.1	61	41	Bakersfield, CA	6.7
57	41	Bridgeport-Stamford-Norwalk, CT	8.1	70	41	Baton Rouge, LA	6.7
59	43	Omaha-Council Bluffs, NE-IA	7.9	24	43	Orlando-Kissimmee-Sanford, FL	6.4
32	44	Columbus, OH	7.5	41	43	Oklahoma City, OK	6.4
53	44	Tucson, AZ	7.5	50	43	Buffalo-Cheektowaga-Niagara Falls, NY	6.4
70	46	Baton Rouge, LA	7.3	28	46	Cincinnati, OH-KY-IN	6.3
42	47	Memphis, TN-MS-AR	7.1	36	46	Nashville-Davidson—Murfreesboro—Franklin, TN	6.3
7	48	Philadelphia-Camden-Wilmington, PA-NJ-DE-MD	6.7	40	46	Jacksonville, FL	6.3
12	49	Phoenix-Mesa-Scottsdale, AZ	6.5	59	46	Omaha-Council Bluffs, NE-IA	6.3
73	50	North Port-Sarasota-Bradenton, FL	6.4	22	50	Charlotte-Concord-Gastonia, NC-SC	6.2
9	51	Atlanta-Sandy Springs-Roswell, GA	6.3	32	50	Columbus, OH	6.2
10	51	Boston-Cambridge-Newton, MA-NH	6.3	25	52	San Antonio-New Braunfels, TX	5.9
62	51	Albany-Schenectady-Troy, NY	6.3	51	52	Rochester, NY	5.9
41	54	Oklahoma City, OK	6.2	73	52	North Port-Sarasota-Bradenton, FL	5.9
68	54	El Paso, TX	6.2	55	55	Tulsa, OK	5.8
45	56	Richmond, VA	6.1	63	55	Greenville-Anderson-Mauldin, SC	5.8
61	56	Bakersfield, CA	6.1	58	57	Worcester, MA-CT	5.6
46	58	New Orleans-Metairie, LA	5.9	31	58	Cleveland-Elyria, OH	5.5
11	59	San Francisco-Oakland-Hayward, CA	5.7	53	58	Tucson, AZ	5.5
33	59	Austin-Round Rock, TX	5.7	71	58	Columbia, SC	5.5
60	61	Albuquerque, NM	5.6	29	61	Las Vegas-Henderson-Paradise, NV	5.3
25	62	San Antonio-New Braunfels, TX	5.5	43	61	Louisville/Jefferson County, KY-IN	5.3
18	63	Tampa-St. Petersburg-Clearwater, FL	5.2	54	61	Urban Honolulu, HI	5.3
27	64	Sacramento—Roseville—Arden-Arcade, CA	4.9	39	64	Milwaukee-Waukesha-West Allis, WI	5.2
19	65	Denver-Aurora-Lakewood, CO	4.8	49	65	Birmingham-Hoover, AL	4.9
40	65	Jacksonville, FL	4.8	38	66	Providence-Warwick, RI-MA	4.5
44	65	Raleigh, NC	4.8	56	66	Fresno, CA	4.5
21	68	Baltimore-Columbia-Towson, MD	4.6	65	66	New Haven-Milford, CT	4.5
1	69	New York-Newark-Jersey City, NY-NJ-PA	4.2	68	69	El Paso, TX	4.3
24	70	Orlando-Kissimmee-Sanford, FL	3.8	52	70	Grand Rapids-Wyoming, MI	4.0
67	71	McAllen-Edinburg-Mission, TX	3.3	69	70	Allentown-Bethlehem-Easton, PA-NJ	4.0
8	72	Miami-Fort Lauderdale-West Palm Beach, FL	3.2	74	70	Greensboro-High Point, NC	4.0
54	73	Urban Honolulu, HI	2.6	42	73	Memphis, TN-MS-AR	3.5
29	74	Las Vegas-Henderson-Paradise, NV	2.4	13	74	Riverside-San Bernardino-Ontario, CA	3.3
6	75	Washington-Arlington-Alexandria, DC-VA-MD-WV	1.9	67	75	McAllen-Edinburg-Mission, TX	3.2

75 Largest Metropolitan Areas by 2015 Population
Selected Rankings

Per capita local government taxes, 2012				Violent crime rate, 2014 (violent crimes known to police)			
Population rank	Local taxes rank	Metropolitan area	Local per capita taxes (dollars) [col 183]	Population rank	Crime rate rank	Metropolitan area	Crime rate (per 100,000 population) [col 46]
1	1	New York-Newark-Jersey City, NY-NJ-PA	4 280	42	1	Memphis, TN-MS-AR	1 104
57	2	Bridgeport-Stamford-Norwalk, CT	3 419	29	2	Las Vegas-Henderson-Paradise, NV	743
6	3	Washington-Arlington-Alexandria, DC-VA-MD-WV	3 255	60	3	Albuquerque, NM	732
3	4	Chicago-Naperville-Elgin, IL-IN-WI	2 701	34	4	Indianapolis-Carmel-Anderson, IN	715
11	5	San Francisco-Oakland-Hayward, CA	2 658	39	5	Milwaukee-Waukesha-West Allis, WI	659
62	6	Albany-Schenectady-Troy, NY	2 620	36	6	Nashville-Davidson—Murfreesboro—Franklin, TN	614
35	7	San Jose-Sunnyvale-Santa Clara, CA	2 585	49	7	Birmingham-Hoover, AL	590
47	8	Hartford-West Hartford-East Hartford, CT	2 512	21	8	Baltimore-Columbia-Towson, MD	584
51	9	Rochester, NY	2 381	71	9	Columbia, SC	581
31	10	Cleveland-Elyria, OH	2 378	5	10	Houston-The Woodlands-Sugar Land, TX	568
10	11	Boston-Cambridge-Newton, MA-NH	2 362	63	11	Greenville-Anderson-Mauldin, SC	538
65	12	New Haven-Milford, CT	2 358	14	12	Detroit-Warren-Dearborn, MI	534
7	13	Philadelphia-Camden-Wilmington, PA-NJ-DE-MD	2 356	24	13	Orlando-Kissimmee-Sanford, FL	531
50	14	Buffalo-Cheektowaga-Niagara Falls, NY	2 326	40	14	Jacksonville, FL	528
32	15	Columbus, OH	2 274	46	15	New Orleans-Metairie, LA	522
33	16	Austin-Round Rock, TX	2 267	8	16	Miami-Fort Lauderdale-West Palm Beach, FL	520
19	17	Denver-Aurora-Lakewood, CO	2 240	70	17	Baton Rouge, LA	514
21	18	Baltimore-Columbia-Towson, MD	2 145	61	18	Bakersfield, CA	510
4	19	Dallas-Fort Worth-Arlington, TX	2 139	11	19	San Francisco-Oakland-Hayward, CA	498
8	20	Miami-Fort Lauderdale-West Palm Beach, FL	2 106	30	20	Kansas City, MO-KS	486
69	20	Allentown-Bethlehem-Easton, PA-NJ	2 106	56	21	Fresno, CA	471
15	22	Seattle-Tacoma-Bellevue, WA	2 088	55	22	Tulsa, OK	467
5	23	Houston-The Woodlands-Sugar Land, TX	2 087	41	23	Oklahoma City, OK	466
30	24	Kansas City, MO-KS	2 040	7	24	Philadelphia-Camden-Wilmington, PA-NJ-DE-MD	460
59	25	Omaha-Council Bluffs, NE-IA	2 037	53	25	Tucson, AZ	443
38	26	Providence-Warwick, RI-MA	2 018	20	26	St. Louis, MO-IL	440
46	27	New Orleans-Metairie, LA	1 991	50	27	Buffalo-Cheektowaga-Niagara Falls, NY	431
39	28	Milwaukee-Waukesha-West Allis, WI	1 986	58	28	Worcester, MA-CT	419
2	29	Los Angeles-Long Beach-Anaheim, CA	1 870	27	29	Sacramento—Roseville—Arden-Arcade, CA	411
72	30	Dayton, OH	1 861	9	30	Atlanta-Sandy Springs-Roswell, GA	407
20	31	St. Louis, MO-IL	1 841	25	31	San Antonio-New Braunfels, TX	402
17	32	San Diego-Carlsbad, CA	1 791	43	31	Louisville/Jefferson County, KY-IN	402
28	33	Cincinnati, OH-KY-IN	1 786	73	31	North Port-Sarasota-Bradenton, FL	402
26	34	Pittsburgh, PA	1 785	31	34	Cleveland-Elyria, OH	395
23	35	Portland-Vancouver-Hillsboro, OR-WA	1 774	22	35	Charlotte-Concord-Gastonia, NC-SC	392
70	36	Baton Rouge, LA	1 760	64	36	Knoxville, TN	387
9	37	Atlanta-Sandy Springs-Roswell, GA	1 744	75	36	Charleston-North Charleston, SC	387
37	38	Virginia Beach-Norfolk-Newport News, VA-NC	1 733	3	38	Chicago-Naperville-Elgin, IL-IN-WI	382
75	39	Charleston-North Charleston, SC	1 730	1	39	New York-Newark-Jersey City, NY-NJ-PA	372
73	40	North Port-Sarasota-Bradenton, FL	1 684	18	39	Tampa-St. Petersburg-Clearwater, FL	372
25	41	San Antonio-New Braunfels, TX	1 669	2	41	Los Angeles-Long Beach-Anaheim, CA	369
66	42	Oxnard-Thousand Oaks-Ventura, CA	1 650	12	41	Phoenix-Mesa-Scottsdale, AZ	369
58	43	Worcester, MA-CT	1 628	59	43	Omaha-Council Bluffs, NE-IA	365
24	44	Orlando-Kissimmee-Sanford, FL	1 583	68	44	El Paso, TX	363
16	45	Minneapolis-St. Paul-Bloomington, MN	1 558	48	45	Salt Lake City, UT	344
42	46	Memphis, TN-MS-AR	1 555	10	46	Boston-Cambridge-Newton, MA-NH	333
45	47	Richmond, VA	1 521	65	46	New Haven-Milford, CT	333
27	48	Sacramento—Roseville—Arden-Arcade, CA	1 504	4	48	Dallas-Fort Worth-Arlington, TX	332
22	49	Charlotte-Concord-Gastonia, NC-SC	1 487	19	48	Denver-Aurora-Lakewood, CO	332
49	50	Birmingham-Hoover, AL	1 483	38	50	Providence-Warwick, RI-MA	329
12	51	Phoenix-Mesa-Scottsdale, AZ	1 447	67	50	McAllen-Edinburg-Mission, TX	329
36	52	Nashville-Davidson—Murfreesboro—Franklin, TN	1 445	13	52	Riverside-San Bernardino-Ontario, CA	327
40	52	Jacksonville, FL	1 445	15	53	Seattle-Tacoma-Bellevue, WA	325
53	54	Tucson, AZ	1 438	17	53	San Diego-Carlsbad, CA	325
34	55	Indianapolis-Carmel-Anderson, IN	1 402	74	55	Greensboro-High Point, NC	321
48	56	Salt Lake City, UT	1 399	6	56	Washington-Arlington-Alexandria, DC-VA-MD-WV	317
71	57	Columbia, SC	1 385	52	57	Grand Rapids-Wyoming, MI	315
18	58	Tampa-St. Petersburg-Clearwater, FL	1 381	37	58	Virginia Beach-Norfolk-Newport News, VA-NC	309
14	59	Detroit-Warren-Dearborn, MI	1 374	32	59	Columbus, OH	308
29	60	Las Vegas-Henderson-Paradise, NV	1 367	26	60	Pittsburgh, PA	291
61	61	Bakersfield, CA	1 365	33	60	Austin-Round Rock, TX	291
54	62	Urban Honolulu, HI	1 348	72	62	Dayton, OH	279
44	63	Raleigh, NC	1 332	62	63	Albany-Schenectady-Troy, NY	274
41	64	Oklahoma City, OK	1 331	23	64	Portland-Vancouver-Hillsboro, OR-WA	272
13	65	Riverside-San Bernardino-Ontario, CA	1 326	51	65	Rochester, NY	266
68	66	El Paso, TX	1 321	28	66	Cincinnati, OH-KY-IN	263
55	67	Tulsa, OK	1 319	16	67	Minneapolis-St. Paul-Bloomington, MN	261
43	68	Louisville/Jefferson County, KY-IN	1 265	47	68	Hartford-West Hartford-East Hartford, CT	253
74	69	Greensboro-High Point, NC	1 262	35	69	San Jose-Sunnyvale-Santa Clara, CA	250
60	70	Albuquerque, NM	1 208	57	70	Bridgeport-Stamford-Norwalk, CT	246
64	71	Knoxville, TN	1 191	45	71	Richmond, VA	231
52	72	Grand Rapids-Wyoming, MI	1 159	66	72	Oxnard-Thousand Oaks-Ventura, CA	223
56	73	Fresno, CA	1 131	69	73	Allentown-Bethlehem-Easton, PA-NJ	185
67	74	McAllen-Edinburg-Mission, TX	1 071	44	74	Raleigh, NC	136
63	75	Greenville-Anderson-Mauldin, SC	978	54	75	Urban Honolulu, HI	72

All Metropolitan Areas
Selected Rankings

	Nonemployer businesses, 2014				Value of residential construction authorized by building permits, 2015		
Popu-lation rank	Non-employer business	Metropolitan area	Non-employer business [col 167]	Popu-lation rank	New Construc-tion rank	Metropolitan area	New Construc-tion [col 169]
1	1	New York-Newark-Jersey City, NY-NJ-PA	1 836 538	1	1	New York-Newark-Jersey City, NY-NJ-PA	11 996 315
2	2	Los Angeles-Long Beach-Anaheim, CA	1 282 607	4	2	Dallas-Fort Worth-Arlington, TX	10 566 289
8	3	Miami-Fort Lauderdale-West Palm Beach, FL	837 150	5	3	Houston-The Woodlands-Sugar Land, TX	8 566 381
3	4	Chicago-Naperville-Elgin, IL-IN-WI	764 074	2	4	Los Angeles-Long Beach-Anaheim, CA	7 348 035
4	5	Dallas-Fort Worth-Arlington, TX	598 286	12	5	Phoenix-Mesa-Scottsdale, AZ	5 565 485
5	6	Houston-The Woodlands-Sugar Land, TX	552 918	15	6	Seattle-Tacoma-Bellevue, WA	5 347 764
9	7	Atlanta-Sandy Springs-Roswell, GA	545 604	9	7	Atlanta-Sandy Springs-Roswell, GA	5 318 834
6	8	Washington-Arlington-Alexandria, DC-VA-MD-WV	514 453	8	8	Miami-Fort Lauderdale-West Palm Beach, FL	4 498 201
11	9	San Francisco-Oakland-Hayward, CA	420 932	6	9	Washington-Arlington-Alexandria, DC-VA-MD-WV	3 788 184
7	10	Philadelphia-Camden-Wilmington, PA-NJ-DE-MD	399 535	19	10	Denver-Aurora-Lakewood, CO	3 740 467
10	11	Boston-Cambridge-Newton, MA-NH	368 828	33	11	Austin-Round Rock, TX	3 669 933
14	12	Detroit-Warren-Dearborn, MI	331 356	24	12	Orlando-Kissimmee-Sanford, FL	3 667 980
12	13	Phoenix-Mesa-Scottsdale, AZ	304 623	22	13	Charlotte-Concord-Gastonia, NC-SC	3 650 576
13	14	Riverside-San Bernardino-Ontario, CA	297 808	11	14	San Francisco-Oakland-Hayward, CA	3 642 107
16	15	Minneapolis-St. Paul-Bloomington, MN	261 376	18	15	Tampa-St. Petersburg-Clearwater, FL	3 625 527
17	16	San Diego-Carlsbad, CA	258 892	3	16	Chicago-Naperville-Elgin, IL-IN-WI	3 581 960
15	17	Seattle-Tacoma-Bellevue, WA	243 510	36	17	Nashville-Davidson—Murfreesboro—Franklin, TN	3 472 438
19	18	Denver-Aurora-Lakewood, CO	241 294	10	18	Boston-Cambridge-Newton, MA-NH	3 259 037
18	19	Tampa-St. Petersburg-Clearwater, FL	234 807	16	19	Minneapolis-St. Paul-Bloomington, MN	2 861 363
24	20	Orlando-Kissimmee-Sanford, FL	209 712	23	20	Portland-Vancouver-Hillsboro, OR-WA	2 713 034
21	21	Baltimore-Columbia-Towson, MD	207 015	13	21	Riverside-San Bernardino-Ontario, CA	2 150 630
22	22	Charlotte-Concord-Gastonia, NC-SC	181 309	17	22	San Diego-Carlsbad, CA	2 100 214
20	23	St. Louis, MO-IL	180 726	44	23	Raleigh, NC	2 092 616
33	24	Austin-Round Rock, TX	172 337	40	24	Jacksonville, FL	2 057 108
25	25	San Antonio-New Braunfels, TX	167 199	7	25	Philadelphia-Camden-Wilmington, PA-NJ-DE-MD	1 925 338
23	26	Portland-Vancouver-Hillsboro, OR-WA	166 824	34	26	Indianapolis-Carmel-Anderson, IN	1 906 999
27	27	Sacramento—Roseville—Arden-Arcade, CA	157 923	27	27	Sacramento—Roseville—Arden-Arcade, CA	1 699 421
36	28	Nashville-Davidson—Murfreesboro—Franklin, TN	157 709	14	28	Detroit-Warren-Dearborn, MI	1 676 030
29	29	Las Vegas-Henderson-Paradise, NV	148 576	30	29	Kansas City, MO-KS	1 674 508
31	30	Cleveland-Elyria, OH	146 268	20	30	St. Louis, MO-IL	1 636 355
32	31	Columbus, OH	145 717	73	31	North Port-Sarasota-Bradenton, FL	1 601 753
26	32	Pittsburgh, PA	141 732	25	32	San Antonio-New Braunfels, TX	1 555 440
30	33	Kansas City, MO-KS	140 249	29	33	Las Vegas-Henderson-Paradise, NV	1 407 544
28	34	Cincinnati, OH-KY-IN	138 744	35	34	San Jose-Sunnyvale-Santa Clara, CA	1 385 172
35	35	San Jose-Sunnyvale-Santa Clara, CA	138 424	32	35	Columbus, OH	1 366 663
34	36	Indianapolis-Carmel-Anderson, IN	134 985	75	36	Charleston-North Charleston, SC	1 347 644
46	37	New Orleans-Metairie, LA	114 656	21	37	Baltimore-Columbia-Towson, MD	1 339 099
42	38	Memphis, TN-MS-AR	108 249	41	38	Oklahoma City, OK	1 285 543
38	39	Providence-Warwick, RI-MA	106 897	48	39	Salt Lake City, UT	1 252 926
41	40	Oklahoma City, OK	104 667	63	40	Greenville-Anderson-Mauldin, SC	1 095 345
40	41	Jacksonville, FL	104 142	26	41	Pittsburgh, PA	1 073 130
37	42	Virginia Beach-Norfolk-Newport News, VA-NC	96 593	37	42	Virginia Beach-Norfolk-Newport News, VA-NC	955 424
44	43	Raleigh, NC	96 376	54	43	Urban Honolulu, HI	914 918
57	44	Bridgeport-Stamford-Norwalk, CT	90 880	28	44	Cincinnati, OH-KY-IN	890 580
39	45	Milwaukee-Waukesha-West Allis, WI	89 055	45	45	Richmond, VA	794 838
43	46	Louisville/Jefferson County, KY-IN	84 203	52	46	Grand Rapids-Wyoming, MI	769 219
48	47	Salt Lake City, UT	82 104	71	47	Columbia, SC	756 610
45	48	Richmond, VA	81 295	70	48	Baton Rouge, LA	731 562
47	49	Hartford-West Hartford-East Hartford, CT	80 646	57	49	Bridgeport-Stamford-Norwalk, CT	726 201
49	50	Birmingham-Hoover, AL	79 484	49	50	Birmingham-Hoover, AL	704 038
55	51	Tulsa, OK	70 971	55	51	Tulsa, OK	686 767
52	52	Grand Rapids-Wyoming, MI	70 811	59	52	Omaha-Council Bluffs, NE-IA	677 404
67	53	McAllen-Edinburg-Mission, TX	68 931	43	53	Louisville/Jefferson County, KY-IN	667 795
73	54	North Port-Sarasota-Bradenton, FL	68 249	53	54	Tucson, AZ	659 557
66	55	Oxnard-Thousand Oaks-Ventura, CA	66 566	31	55	Cleveland-Elyria, OH	658 337
51	56	Rochester, NY	63 536	39	56	Milwaukee-Waukesha-West Allis, WI	643 149
53	57	Tucson, AZ	63 004	67	57	McAllen-Edinburg-Mission, TX	620 741
54	58	Urban Honolulu, HI	62 867	68	58	El Paso, TX	603 056
70	59	Baton Rouge, LA	62 757	42	59	Memphis, TN-MS-AR	597 911
64	60	Knoxville, TN	60 382	62	60	Albany-Schenectady-Troy, NY	591 439
65	61	New Haven-Milford, CT	58 579	56	61	Fresno, CA	581 775
63	62	Greenville-Anderson-Mauldin, SC	58 206	46	62	New Orleans-Metairie, LA	538 281
59	63	Omaha-Council Bluffs, NE-IA	57 461	64	63	Knoxville, TN	535 911
58	64	Worcester, MA-CT	57 363	61	64	Bakersfield, CA	473 930
50	65	Buffalo-Cheektowaga-Niagara Falls, NY	56 155	74	65	Greensboro-High Point, NC	466 533
68	66	El Paso, TX	55 383	60	66	Albuquerque, NM	439 471
75	67	Charleston-North Charleston, SC	55 082	51	67	Rochester, NY	409 886
74	68	Greensboro-High Point, NC	53 762	38	68	Providence-Warwick, RI-MA	358 971
62	69	Albany-Schenectady-Troy, NY	52 286	66	69	Oxnard-Thousand Oaks-Ventura, CA	350 485
60	70	Albuquerque, NM	51 801	50	70	Buffalo-Cheektowaga-Niagara Falls, NY	330 564
71	71	Columbia, SC	51 576	58	71	Worcester, MA-CT	265 350
56	72	Fresno, CA	50 231	72	72	Dayton, OH	253 730
69	73	Allentown-Bethlehem-Easton, PA-NJ	49 600	47	73	Hartford-West Hartford-East Hartford, CT	253 151
72	74	Dayton, OH	48 044	69	74	Allentown-Bethlehem-Easton, PA-NJ	236 634
61	75	Bakersfield, CA	44 623	65	75	New Haven-Milford, CT	146 364

75 Metropolitan Areas with Highest Agricultural Sales
Selected rankings

	Value of agricultural products sold, 2012			Number of farms, 2012		
Value of sales rank	Metropolitan area	Value of sales (millions of dollars) [col 125]	Value of sales rank	Number of farms rank	Metropolitan area	Number of farms [col 113]
1	Fresno, CA	4 973.0	56	1	Dallas-Fort Worth-Arlington, TX	29 659
2	Visalia-Porterville, CA	4 017.1	9	2	Minneapolis-St. Paul-Bloomington, MN	13 251
3	Bakersfield, CA	3 999.0	51	3	Kansas City, MO-KS	12 757
4	Salinas, CA	2 979.7	26	4	St. Louis, MO-IL	11 270
5	Merced, CA	2 967.5	35	5	Portland-Vancouver-Hillsboro, OR-WA	10 838
6	Stockton-Lodi, CA	2 250.2	28	6	Columbus, OH	8 198
7	Modesto, CA	2 228.1	32	7	Madison, WI	7 446
8	Chicago-Naperville-Elgin, IL-IN-WI	2 187.2	8	8	Chicago-Naperville-Elgin, IL-IN-WI	6 841
9	Minneapolis-St. Paul-Bloomington, MN	2 169.8	24	9	Fayetteville-Springdale-Rogers, AR-M	6 835
10	Phoenix-Mesa-Scottsdale, AZ	1 931.2	25	10	Philadelphia-Camden-Wilmington, PA-N	6 543
11	El Centro, CA	1 888.6	36	11	Indianapolis-Carmel-Anderson, IN	6 205
12	Greeley, CO	1 860.7	16	12	Omaha-Council Bluffs, NE-IA	6 055
13	Hanford-Corcoran, CA	1 829.2	58	13	San Diego-Carlsbad, CA	5 732
14	Kennewick-Richland, WA	1 663.2	1	14	Fresno, CA	5 683
15	Miami-Fort Lauderdale-West Palm Beac	1 650.7	21	15	Lancaster, PA	5 657
16	Omaha-Council Bluffs, NE-IA	1 649.3	49	16	Wichita, KS	5 345
17	Yakima, WA	1 645.5	33	17	Boise City, ID	5 077
18	Riverside-San Bernardino-Ontario, CA	1 621.2	42	18	Sacramento—Roseville—Arden-Arcade,	5 076
19	Madera, CA	1 602.8	15	19	Miami-Fort Lauderdale-West Palm Beac	4 978
20	Salisbury, MD-DE	1 575.7	2	20	Visalia-Porterville, CA	4 931
21	Lancaster, PA	1 475.0	48	21	Des Moines-West Des Moines, IA	4 898
22	Sioux City, IA-NE-SD	1 460.1	30	22	Grand Rapids-Wyoming, MI	4 680
23	Oxnard-Thousand Oaks-Ventura, CA	1 440.1	38	23	St. Cloud, MN	4 459
24	Fayetteville-Springdale-Rogers, AR-M	1 356.1	44	24	Rochester, NY	4 268
25	Philadelphia-Camden-Wilmington, PA-N	1 264.9	31	25	Rochester, MN	4 233
26	St. Louis, MO-IL	1 235.6	18	26	Riverside-San Bernardino-Ontario, CA	4 198
27	Grand Island, NE	1 227.8	64	27	Jackson, MS	4 186
28	Columbus, OH	1 180.0	7	28	Modesto, CA	4 143
29	Santa Maria-Santa Barbara, CA	1 177.9	61	29	Memphis, TN-MS-AR	3 934
30	Grand Rapids-Wyoming, MI	1 120.3	57	30	Salem, OR	3 710
31	Rochester, MN	1 111.6	46	31	Cedar Rapids, IA	3 678
32	Madison, WI	1 081.6	22	32	Sioux City, IA-NE-SD	3 644
33	Boise City, ID	1 071.7	43	33	Peoria, IL	3 605
34	Grand Forks, ND-MN	1 023.3	6	34	Stockton-Lodi, CA	3 580
35	Portland-Vancouver-Hillsboro, OR-WA	1 008.7	39	35	Santa Rosa, CA	3 579
36	Indianapolis-Carmel-Anderson, IN	985.1	12	36	Greeley, CO	3 525
37	Yuma, AZ	985.0	41	37	Davenport-Moline-Rock Island, IA-IL	3 513
38	St. Cloud, MN	976.0	53	38	Sioux Falls, SD	3 418
39	Santa Rosa, CA	974.4	10	39	Phoenix-Mesa-Scottsdale, AZ	3 417
40	Fargo, ND-MN	965.2	17	40	Yakima, WA	3 143
41	Davenport-Moline-Rock Island, IA-IL	964.4	73	41	Orlando-Kissimmee-Sanford, FL	3 123
42	Sacramento—Roseville—Arden-Arcade,	961.8	66	42	Columbia, SC	3 085
43	Peoria, IL	960.8	55	43	Green Bay, WI	2 774
44	Rochester, NY	930.7	60	44	San Luis Obispo-Paso Robles-Arroyo G	2 666
45	Waterloo-Cedar Falls, IA	921.7	45	45	Waterloo-Cedar Falls, IA	2 643
46	Cedar Rapids, IA	918.4	5	46	Merced, CA	2 486
47	Mankato-North Mankato, MN	892.1	52	47	Iowa City, IA	2 481
48	Des Moines-West Des Moines, IA	891.6	14	48	Kennewick-Richland, WA	2 392
49	Wichita, KS	864.4	20	49	Salisbury, MD-DE	2 384
50	Champaign-Urbana, IL	802.9	69	50	Bismarck, ND	2 367
51	Kansas City, MO-KS	785.7	27	51	Grand Island, NE	2 339
52	Iowa City, IA	785.1	34	52	Grand Forks, ND-MN	2 292
53	Sioux Falls, SD	781.7	50	53	Champaign-Urbana, IL	2 284
54	Amarillo, TX	776.4	59	54	Yuba City, CA	2 153
55	Green Bay, WI	750.0	23	55	Oxnard-Thousand Oaks-Ventura, CA	2 150
56	Dallas-Fort Worth-Arlington, TX	743.8	71	56	Chico, CA	2 056
57	Salem, OR	742.7	75	57	Reading, PA	2 039
58	San Diego-Carlsbad, CA	726.0	63	58	Bloomington, IL	2 000
59	Yuba City, CA	701.6	54	59	Amarillo, TX	1 976
60	San Luis Obispo-Paso Robles-Arroyo G	665.0	3	60	Bakersfield, CA	1 938
61	Memphis, TN-MS-AR	661.4	62	61	Harrisonburg, VA	1 902
62	Harrisonburg, VA	659.0	47	62	Mankato-North Mankato, MN	1 834
63	Bloomington, IL	655.9	40	63	Fargo, ND-MN	1 772
64	Jackson, MS	633.0	74	64	Napa, CA	1 685
65	Lafayette-West Lafayette, IN	583.0	29	65	Santa Maria-Santa Barbara, CA	1 597
66	Columbia, SC	578.6	65	66	Lafayette-West Lafayette, IN	1 574
67	Goldsboro, NC	577.2	19	67	Madera, CA	1 507
68	Santa Cruz-Watsonville, CA	565.8	4	68	Salinas, CA	1 179
69	Bismarck, ND	553.1	13	69	Hanford-Corcoran, CA	1 056
70	Jonesboro, AR	549.0	72	70	Pine Bluff, AR	1 032
71	Chico, CA	541.3	70	71	Jonesboro, AR	980
72	Pine Bluff, AR	540.5	68	72	Santa Cruz-Watsonville, CA	667
73	Orlando-Kissimmee-Sanford, FL	539.8	67	73	Goldsboro, NC	563
74	Napa, CA	536.1	37	74	Yuma, AZ	562
75	Reading, PA	528.7	11	75	El Centro, CA	421

75 Metropolitan Areas with Highest Agricultural Sales
Selected rankings

Land in farms, 2012				Average value of agricultural land and buildings per acre, 2012			
Value of sales rank	Land in farms rank	Metropolitan area	Land in farms (1,000 acres) [col 117]	Value of sales rank	Value per Acre rank	Metropolitan area	Value per acre (1,000 acres) [col 123]
56	1	Dallas-Fort Worth-Arlington, TX	4 075	74	1	Napa, CA	21 801
69	2	Bismarck, ND	3 139	58	2	San Diego-Carlsbad, CA	17 964
51	3	Kansas City, MO-KS	3 124	23	3	Oxnard-Thousand Oaks-Ventura, CA	15 621
26	4	St. Louis, MO-IL	2 912	39	4	Santa Rosa, CA	14 620
54	5	Amarillo, TX	2 889	21	5	Lancaster, PA	12 529
49	6	Wichita, KS	2 856	68	6	Santa Cruz-Watsonville, CA	12 390
9	7	Minneapolis-St. Paul-Bloomington, MN	2 598	18	7	Riverside-San Bernardino-Ontario, CA	10 807
16	8	Omaha-Council Bluffs, NE-IA	2 373	25	8	Philadelphia-Camden-Wilmington, PA-N	10 682
3	9	Bakersfield, CA	2 330	35	9	Portland-Vancouver-Hillsboro, OR-WA	10 520
8	10	Chicago-Naperville-Elgin, IL-IN-WI	2 232	6	10	Stockton-Lodi, CA	10 090
12	11	Greeley, CO	1 956	15	11	Miami-Fort Lauderdale-West Palm Beac	9 911
34	12	Grand Forks, ND-MN	1 911	7	12	Modesto, CA	9 636
17	13	Yakima, WA	1 780	75	13	Reading, PA	8 859
28	14	Columbus, OH	1 746	1	14	Fresno, CA	8 286
22	15	Sioux City, IA-NE-SD	1 733	50	15	Champaign-Urbana, IL	8 014
1	16	Fresno, CA	1 721	63	16	Bloomington, IL	7 961
40	17	Fargo, ND-MN	1 718	45	17	Waterloo-Cedar Falls, IA	7 913
36	18	Indianapolis-Carmel-Anderson, IN	1 689	5	18	Merced, CA	7 737
10	19	Phoenix-Mesa-Scottsdale, AZ	1 651	19	19	Madera, CA	7 614
61	20	Memphis, TN-MS-AR	1 573	71	20	Chico, CA	7 599
53	21	Sioux Falls, SD	1 521	2	21	Visalia-Porterville, CA	7 535
32	22	Madison, WI	1 466	29	22	Santa Maria-Santa Barbara, CA	7 365
33	23	Boise City, ID	1 376	57	23	Salem, OR	7 337
48	24	Des Moines-West Des Moines, IA	1 371	43	24	Peoria, IL	7 332
60	25	San Luis Obispo-Paso Robles-Arroyo G	1 339	8	25	Chicago-Naperville-Elgin, IL-IN-WI	7 285
14	26	Kennewick-Richland, WA	1 329	37	26	Yuma, AZ	7 220
43	27	Peoria, IL	1 288	62	27	Harrisonburg, VA	7 055
4	28	Salinas, CA	1 268	11	28	El Centro, CA	7 002
2	29	Visalia-Porterville, CA	1 239	20	29	Salisbury, MD-DE	6 943
50	30	Champaign-Urbana, IL	1 184	46	30	Cedar Rapids, IA	6 910
27	31	Grand Island, NE	1 181	42	31	Sacramento—Roseville—Arden-Arcade,	6 892
31	32	Rochester, MN	1 158	41	32	Davenport-Moline-Rock Island, IA-IL	6 834
64	33	Jackson, MS	1 156	65	33	Lafayette-West Lafayette, IN	6 657
41	34	Davenport-Moline-Rock Island, IA-IL	1 101	52	34	Iowa City, IA	6 496
46	35	Cedar Rapids, IA	1 075	47	35	Mankato-North Mankato, MN	6 445
24	36	Fayetteville-Springdale-Rogers, AR-M	1 073	59	36	Yuba City, CA	6 343
5	37	Merced, CA	979	16	37	Omaha-Council Bluffs, NE-IA	6 064
38	38	St. Cloud, MN	946	13	38	Hanford-Corcoran, CA	6 031
42	39	Sacramento—Roseville—Arden-Arcade,	927	48	39	Des Moines-West Des Moines, IA	5 875
44	39	Rochester, NY	927	22	40	Sioux City, IA-NE-SD	5 823
63	41	Bloomington, IL	888	36	41	Indianapolis-Carmel-Anderson, IN	5 724
45	42	Waterloo-Cedar Falls, IA	886	73	42	Orlando-Kissimmee-Sanford, FL	5 374
73	43	Orlando-Kissimmee-Sanford, FL	853	26	43	St. Louis, MO-IL	5 260
6	44	Stockton-Lodi, CA	787	9	44	Minneapolis-St. Paul-Bloomington, MN	5 180
7	45	Modesto, CA	768	31	45	Rochester, MN	5 117
30	46	Grand Rapids-Wyoming, MI	746	32	46	Madison, WI	5 002
70	47	Jonesboro, AR	723	28	47	Columbus, OH	4 928
29	48	Santa Maria-Santa Barbara, CA	701	4	48	Salinas, CA	4 893
65	49	Lafayette-West Lafayette, IN	679	53	49	Sioux Falls, SD	4 792
13	50	Hanford-Corcoran, CA	674	30	50	Grand Rapids-Wyoming, MI	4 790
19	51	Madera, CA	654	27	51	Grand Island, NE	4 451
25	52	Philadelphia-Camden-Wilmington, PA-N	653	3	52	Bakersfield, CA	4 435
47	53	Mankato-North Mankato, MN	651	55	53	Green Bay, WI	4 333
35	54	Portland-Vancouver-Hillsboro, OR-WA	644	56	54	Dallas-Fort Worth-Arlington, TX	4 260
52	55	Iowa City, IA	643	60	55	San Luis Obispo-Paso Robles-Arroyo G	4 212
15	56	Miami-Fort Lauderdale-West Palm Beac	610	67	56	Goldsboro, NC	4 124
39	57	Santa Rosa, CA	590	38	57	St. Cloud, MN	3 808
59	58	Yuba City, CA	563	24	58	Fayetteville-Springdale-Rogers, AR-M	3 541
55	59	Green Bay, WI	547	10	59	Phoenix-Mesa-Scottsdale, AZ	3 326
66	60	Columbia, SC	522	66	60	Columbia, SC	3 177
20	61	Salisbury, MD-DE	520	70	61	Jonesboro, AR	3 134
72	62	Pine Bluff, AR	519	40	62	Fargo, ND-MN	3 097
11	63	El Centro, CA	516	51	63	Kansas City, MO-KS	3 062
21	64	Lancaster, PA	439	44	64	Rochester, NY	3 055
57	65	Salem, OR	431	72	65	Pine Bluff, AR	2 912
18	66	Riverside-San Bernardino-Ontario, CA	421	14	66	Kennewick-Richland, WA	2 827
71	67	Chico, CA	381	33	67	Boise City, ID	2 809
23	68	Oxnard-Thousand Oaks-Ventura, CA	281	61	68	Memphis, TN-MS-AR	2 682
74	69	Napa, CA	253	34	69	Grand Forks, ND-MN	2 559
75	70	Reading, PA	234	64	70	Jackson, MS	2 409
58	71	San Diego-Carlsbad, CA	222	12	71	Greeley, CO	1 979
62	71	Harrisonburg, VA	222	49	72	Wichita, KS	1 907
37	73	Yuma, AZ	215	17	73	Yakima, WA	1 803
67	74	Goldsboro, NC	191	69	74	Bismarck, ND	1 116
68	75	Santa Cruz-Watsonville, CA	100	54	75	Amarillo, TX	788

Table C. Metropolitan Areas — **Land Area and Population**

CBSA/DIV code[1]	Area name	Land area,[2] 2010 (sq km)	Population 2015			Population characteristics, 2014										
						Race alone or in combination, not Hispanic or Latino (percent)					Age (percent)					
			Total persons	Rank	Per square kilometer	White	Black	American Indian, Alaska Native	Asian and Pacific Islander	Percent Hispanic or Latino[3]	Under 5 years	5 to 17 years	18 to 24 years	25 to 34 years	35 to 44 years	45 to 54 years
		1	2	3	4	5	6	7	8	9	10	11	12	13	14	15

1. CBSA = Core Based Statistical Area. DIV = Metropolitan Division. See Appendix A for explanation. See Appendix B for list of metropolitan areas identified by type.   2. Dry land or land partially or temporarily covered by water.   3. May be of any race.

Table C. Metropolitan Areas — **Population and Households**

Area name	Population, 2014 (cont.)				Population change and components of change, 2000–2015							Households, 2014				
	Age (percent) (cont.)				Total persons		Percent change		Components of change, 2010–2015						Percent		
	55 to 64 years	65 to 74 years	75 years and over	Percent female	2000	2010	2000–2010	2010–2015	Births	Deaths	Net migration	Number	Persons per household	Family households	Female family householder[1]	One person
	16	17	18	19	20	21	22	23	24	25	26	27	28	29	30	31

1. No spouse present.

Table C. Metropolitan Areas — **Population, Vital Statistics, Medicare, and Crime**

Area name	Daytime population, 2014			Births, 2015		Deaths, 2015		Persons under 65 with no health insurance 2014		Medicare, 2015			Serious crimes known to police,[2] 2014	
													Total	
	Persons in group quarters, 2015	Number	Employment/ residence ratio	Total	Rate[1]	Number	Rate[1]	Number	Percent	Total Beneficiaries	Enrolled in Original Medicare	Enrolled in Medicare Advantage	Number	Rate[3]
	32	33	34	35	36	37	38	39	40	41	42	43	44	45

1. Per 1,000 estimated resident population.   2. Data for serious crimes have not been adjusted for underreporting; this may affect comparability between geographic areas and over time.
3. Per 100,000 population estimated by the FBI.

Table C. Metropolitan Areas — **Crime, Education, Money Income, and Poverty**

Area name	Serious crimes known to police, 2014 (cont.)[1]		Education						Income and Poverty, 2014							
	Rate[2]		School enrollment and attainment, 2014				Local government expenditures,[5] 2012–2013							Percent below poverty level		
			Enrollment[3]		Attainment[4] (percent)								Percent of households with income of less than $25,000	Percent of households with income of $200,000 or more			
	Violent	Property	Total	Percent private	High school graduate or less	Bachelor's degree or more	Total current expenditures (mil dol)	Current expenditures per student (dollars)	Per capita income[6] (dollars)	Mean household income (dollars)	Median household income			All persons	Children under 18 years	Age 65 years and older
	46	47	48	49	50	51	52	53	54	55	56	57	58	59	60	61

1. Data for serious crimes have not been adjusted for underreporting; this may affect comparability between geographic areas and over time.   2. Per 100,000 population estimated by the FBI.
3. All persons 3 years old and over enrolled in nursery school through college.   4. Persons 25 years old and over.   5. Elementary and secondary education expenditures.   6. Based on resident population estimated in the 2014 American Community Survey.

Table C. Metropolitan Areas — **Personal Income**

	Personal income, 2014										Earnings, 2014		
	Total (mil dol)	Percent change 2013–2014	Per capita[1]		Wages and salaries (mil dol)	Supplements to wages and salaries; employer contributions (mil dol)		Proprietors' income (mil dol)	Dividends, interest, and rent (mil dol)	Personal transfer receipts (mil dol)	Total (mil dol)	Contributions for government social insurance (mil dol)	
Area name			Dollars	Rank		Pension and insurance	Government social insurance					From employee and self-employed	From employer
	62	63	64	65	66	67	68	69	70	71	72	73	74

1. Based on the resident population estimated as of July 1 of the year shown.

Table C. Metropolitan Areas — **Earnings, Social Security, and Housing**

	Earnings, 2014 (cont.)									Social Security beneficiaries, December 2014			Housing units, 2015	
	Percent by selected industries											Supplemental Security Income recipients, December 2014		
Area name	Farm	Mining	Construction	Manufacturing	Information, professional, scientific, technical services	Retail trade	Finance, insurance, real estate, rental and leasing	Health care and social assistance	Government	Number	Rate[1]		Total	Percent change, 2000–2015
	75	76	77	78	79	80	81	82	83	84	85	86	87	88

1. Per 1,000 resident population estimated as of July 1, 2011 of the year shown.

Table C. Metropolitan Areas — **Housing, Labor Force, and Employment**

	Housing units, 2014								Civilian labor force, 2015				Civilian employment[5], 2014		
	Occupied units										Unemployment			Percent	
			Owner-occupied				Renter-occupied								
				Median owner cost as a percent of income											
Area name	Total	Percent	Median value[1]	With a mortgage	Without a mortgage[2]	Median rent[3]	Median rent as a percent of income	Percent with a computer	Total	Percent change, 2013–2014	Total	Rate[4]	Total employed	Management, professional, and related occupations	Construction, production, and related occupations
	89	90	91	92	93	94	95	96	97	98	99	100	101	102	103

1. Specified owner-occupied units.   2. A value of 10.0 represents 10 percent or less.   3. Specified renter-occupied units.   4. Percent of civilian labor force.
5. Persons 16 years old and over.

Table C. Metropolitan Areas — **Nonfarm Employment and Agriculture**

	Private nonfarm establishments, employment and payroll, 2014									Agriculture, 2012			
		Employment						Annual payroll		Farms			
											Percent with:		
Area name	Number of establishments	Total	Health care and social assistance	Manufacturing	Retail trade	Finance and insurance	Professional, scientific, and technical services	Total (mil dol)	Average per employee (dollars)	Number	Fewer than 50 acres	500 acres or more	Farm operators whose principal occupation is farming (percent)
	104	105	106	107	108	109	110	111	112	113	114	115	116

Table C. Metropolitan Areas — **Agriculture**

Area name	Agriculture, 2012 (cont.)															
	Land in farms					Value of land and buildings (dollars)			Value of products sold					Percent of farms with sales of:		Government payments	
			Acres								Percent from:						
	Acreage (1,000)	Percent change, 2007–2012	Average size of farm	Total irrigated (1,000)	Total cropland (1,000)	Average per farm	Average per acre	Value of machinery and equipment, average per farm (dollars)	Total (mil dol)	Average per farm (dollars)	Crops	Live-stock and poultry products	$10,000 or more	$100,000 or more	Total ($1,000)	Percent of farms
	117	118	119	120	121	122	123	124	125	126	127	128	129	130	131	132

Table C. Metropolitan Areas — **Water Use, Wholesale Trade, Retail Trade, and Real Estate**

Area name	Water use, 2010		Wholesale trade,[1] 2012				Retail trade, 2012				Real estate and rental and leasing, 2012			
	Total water withdrawn (mil gal/day)	Gallons withdrawn per person per day	Number of establish-ments	Number of employees	Sales (mil dol)	Annual payroll (mil dol)	Number of establish-ments	Number of employees	Sales (mil dol)	Annual payroll (mil dol)	Number of establish-ments	Number of employees	Receipts (mil dol)	Annual payroll (mil dol)
	133	134	135	136	137	138	139	140	141	142	143	144	145	146

1. Merchant wholesalers, except manufacturers' sales branches and offices.

Table C. Metropolitan Areas — **Professional Services, Manufacturing, and Accommodation and Food Services**

Area name	Professional, scientific, and technical services, 2012				Manufacturing, 2012				Accommodation and food services, 2012			
	Number of establish-ments	Number of employees	Sales (mil dol)	Annual payroll (mil dol)	Number of establish-ments	Number of employees	Sales (mil dol)	Annual payroll (mil dol)	Number of establish-ments	Number of employees	Sales (mil dol)	Annual payroll (mil dol)
	147	148	149	150	151	152	153	154	155	156	157	158

Table C. Metropolitan Areas — **Health Care and Social Assistance, Other Services, Nonemployer Business and Residential Construction**

Area name	Health care and social assistance, 2012				Other services, 2012				Nonemployer business, 2014		Value of residential construction authorized by building permits, 2015	
	Number of establish-ments	Number of employees	Receipts (mil dol)	Annual payroll (mil dol)	Number of establish-ments	Number of employees	Receipts (mil dol)	Annual payroll (mil dol)	Number	Receipts (mil dol)	New construc-tion ($1,000)	Number of housing units
	159	160	161	162	163	164	165	166	167	168	169	170

Table C. Metropolitan Areas — **Government Employment and Payroll and Local Government Finances**

Area name	Government employment and payroll, 2012										Local government finances, 2012				
			March payroll (percent of total)								General revenue				
														Taxes	
															Per capita[1] (dollars)	
	Full-time equivalent employees	March Payroll (dollars)	Administration, judicial, and legal	Police and corrections	Fire protection	Highways and transportation	Health and welfare	Natural resources and utilities	Education and libraries	Total (mil dol)	Intergovernmental (mil dol)	Total (mil dol)	Total	Property
	171	172	173	174	175	176	177	178	179	180	181	182	183	184

1. Based on the resident population estimated as of July 1 of the year shown.

Table C. Metropolitan Areas — **Local Government Finances, Government Employment, and Voting**

Area name	Local government finances, 2012 (cont.)									Government employment, 2014			Presidential election,[2] 2012		
	Direct general expenditure							Debt outstanding					Percent of vote cast:		
			Percent of total for:												
	Total (mil dol)	Per capita[1] (dollars)	Education	Health and hospitals	Police protection	Public welfare	Highways	Total (mil dol)	Per capita[1] (dollars)	Federal civilian	Federal military	State and local	Democratic	Republican	All other
	185	186	187	188	189	190	191	192	193	194	195	196	197	198	199

1. Based on the resident population estimated as of July 1 of the year shown.   2. © 2013 Election Data Services, Inc. All rights reserved.

Table C. Metropolitan Areas — **Land Area and Population**

CBSA/DIV code[1]	Area name	Land area[2] 2010 (sq km)	Total persons	Rank	Per square kilometer	White	Black	American Indian, Alaska Native	Asian and Pacific Islander	Percent Hispanic or Latino[3]	Under 5 years	5 to 17 years	18 to 24 years	25 to 34 years	35 to 44 years	45 to 54 years
		1	2	3	4	5	6	7	8	9	10	11	12	13	14	15
10180	Abilene, TX	7 105	169 578	243	23.9	67.9	8.1	0.9	2.2	22.9	6.9	16.8	13.6	14.4	11.1	11.8
10420	Akron, OH	2 331	704 243	78	302.1	82.9	13.5	0.7	3.1	1.9	5.4	15.7	10.7	12.3	11.7	14.1
10500	Albany, GA	5 005	153 526	267	30.7	43.1	53.4	0.6	1.5	2.6	6.9	17.8	10.8	13.1	12.0	12.8
10540	Albany, OR	5 931	120 547	320	20.3	88.8	0.9	2.6	2.1	8.4	6.2	17.0	8.2	12.7	11.9	12.7
10580	Albany-Schenectady-Troy, NY	7 283	881 830	62	121.1	83.1	8.9	0.6	4.8	4.9	5.3	15.0	11.4	12.6	11.9	14.5
10740	Albuquerque, NM	24 042	907 301	60	37.7	42.2	2.9	5.9	2.9	48.0	6.2	17.1	9.3	14.3	12.4	13.2
10780	Alexandria, LA	5 079	154 484	265	30.4	65.2	30.3	1.5	1.7	3.1	6.6	18.1	9.0	13.6	12.2	13.3
10900	Allentown-Bethlehem-Easton, PA-NJ	3 763	832 327	69	221.2	77.1	5.6	0.4	3.4	15.0	5.3	16.2	9.2	11.9	12.1	14.8
11020	Altoona, PA	1 362	125 593	313	92.2	96.1	2.6	0.4	1.0	1.2	5.5	15.0	8.9	11.4	11.9	13.6
11100	Amarillo, TX	13 338	262 056	182	19.6	62.6	6.6	1.0	3.4	27.4	7.4	18.5	9.9	14.9	12.5	12.3
11180	Ames, IA	1 484	96 021	362	64.7	85.6	3.2	0.5	7.6	3.1	4.9	12.3	30.6	13.3	9.3	9.2
11260	Anchorage, AK	68 149	399 790	134	5.9	70.8	6.3	11.2	11.5	7.9	7.3	18.2	11.2	16.6	12.5	13.1
11460	Ann Arbor, MI	1 828	358 880	147	196.3	73.8	14.1	1.0	10.0	4.4	5.3	14.5	18.1	14.1	11.7	12.6
11500	Anniston-Oxford-Jacksonville, AL	1 569	115 620	334	73.7	74.2	21.6	1.0	1.3	3.5	5.7	16.4	9.8	12.9	12.1	13.4
11540	Appleton, WI	2 475	233 007	194	94.1	90.3	1.6	1.8	3.6	4.0	6.3	18.1	8.7	12.8	12.9	15.3
11700	Asheville, NC	5 265	446 840	116	84.9	87.1	5.4	1.0	1.5	6.8	5.1	14.3	7.9	12.0	12.4	13.4
12020	Athens-Clarke County, GA	2 654	203 189	218	76.6	67.9	20.7	0.5	4.2	8.3	5.6	14.7	20.0	14.2	11.9	11.3
12060	Atlanta-Sandy Springs-Roswell, GA	22 498	5 710 795	9	253.8	50.6	33.9	0.7	6.2	10.5	6.6	18.8	9.4	13.9	14.7	14.5
12100	Atlantic City-Hammonton, NJ	1 439	274 219	173	190.6	58.2	15.7	0.6	8.9	18.5	6.1	16.1	9.6	11.9	11.9	14.9
12220	Auburn-Opelika, AL	1 574	156 993	260	99.7	68.9	24.0	0.7	3.8	3.9	5.8	15.8	19.4	14.6	12.3	11.8
12260	Augusta-Richmond County, GA-SC	9 015	590 146	92	65.5	57.3	36.2	0.9	2.8	5.1	6.4	17.3	9.9	13.9	12.0	13.4
12420	Austin-Round Rock, TX	10 929	2 000 860	33	183.1	55.0	7.8	0.8	6.3	32.0	6.7	17.5	10.2	17.3	15.4	12.9
12540	Bakersfield, CA	21 062	882 176	61	41.9	37.8	5.9	1.3	5.4	51.6	8.4	21.1	11.1	15.0	12.5	12.1
12580	Baltimore-Columbia-Towson, MD	6 738	2 797 407	21	415.2	60.0	29.9	0.8	6.3	5.3	6.1	16.1	9.4	14.4	12.5	14.5
12620	Bangor, ME	8 799	152 692	268	17.4	95.5	1.3	2.0	1.5	1.3	4.8	13.9	11.3	13.1	11.3	14.6
12700	Barnstable Town, MA	1 020	214 333	204	210.1	92.9	3.1	1.2	1.9	2.7	3.9	12.0	7.1	8.7	9.1	14.2
12940	Baton Rouge, LA	10 429	830 480	70	79.6	58.1	36.3	0.6	2.5	3.7	6.5	17.3	11.9	14.5	12.5	12.9
12980	Battle Creek, MI	1 829	134 314	298	73.4	81.8	12.6	1.4	2.5	4.8	6.1	17.1	9.3	11.9	11.8	13.7
13020	Bay City, MI	1 146	105 659	343	92.2	92.1	2.6	1.1	1.0	5.0	5.2	15.8	8.3	11.8	11.6	14.1
13140	Beaumont-Port Arthur, TX	7 859	408 419	131	52.0	58.7	24.6	0.8	3.0	14.0	6.7	17.3	9.6	13.8	12.3	13.4
13220	Beckley, WV	3 281	122 507	316	37.3	90.9	7.6	0.8	1.0	1.3	6.1	14.9	7.7	12.0	13.1	12.7
13380	Bellingham, WA	5 457	212 284	209	38.9	82.8	1.8	3.8	6.2	8.9	5.5	14.7	15.1	12.6	11.5	12.2
13460	Bend-Redmond, OR	7 817	175 268	235	22.4	89.8	0.8	1.7	2.1	7.8	5.3	16.1	7.1	12.3	13.1	13.1
13740	Billings, MT	15 170	168 283	247	11.1	89.9	1.3	5.0	1.3	5.1	6.3	16.9	8.4	13.5	12.0	13.0
13780	Binghamton, NY	3 171	246 020	189	77.6	88.5	5.3	0.7	4.2	3.4	5.1	15.0	12.9	11.2	10.4	13.9
13820	Birmingham-Hoover, AL	13 673	1 145 647	49	83.8	65.2	29.3	0.7	1.7	4.3	6.3	17.0	8.7	13.6	13.1	13.6
13900	Bismarck, ND	13 923	129 517	304	9.3	89.6	1.5	7.4	1.0	2.1	6.9	16.5	9.7	14.7	12.0	12.9
13980	Blacksburg-Christiansburg-Radford, VA	3 762	181 747	228	48.3	89.2	5.1	0.6	4.4	2.6	4.6	12.4	22.0	12.7	10.9	11.6
14010	Bloomington, IL	4 095	189 413	225	46.3	83.4	8.1	0.5	5.5	4.6	6.1	16.0	17.3	12.7	12.2	12.5
14020	Bloomington, IN	2 020	165 577	252	82.0	87.8	3.8	0.7	6.6	3.1	4.5	12.3	25.2	14.1	10.2	10.7
14100	Bloomsburg-Berwick, PA	1 588	85 229	368	53.7	94.2	2.2	0.4	1.8	2.6	4.9	13.7	14.6	11.0	10.7	13.4
14260	Boise City, ID	30 473	676 909	81	22.2	83.0	1.4	1.3	3.3	13.2	6.7	19.8	8.9	13.9	13.4	12.8
14460	Boston-Cambridge-Newton, MA-NH	9 033	4 774 321	10	528.5	74.3	8.2	0.5	8.3	10.2	5.5	15.1	10.2	14.6	12.7	14.7
14460	Boston, MA Div 14454	2 884	1 984 537	X	688.1	68.5	13.5	0.6	8.2	10.8	5.5	14.7	11.0	15.9	12.6	14.1
14460	Cambridge-Newton-Framingham, MA Div 15764	3 394	2 361 182	X	695.7	75.6	5.0	0.4	9.5	11.1	5.6	15.4	9.6	14.1	12.9	14.9
14460	Rockingham County-Strafford County, NH 40484	2 755	428 602	X	155.6	94.1	1.3	0.7	2.9	2.5	4.7	15.6	10.3	11.3	12.1	16.5
14500	Boulder, CO	1 881	319 372	156	169.8	80.2	1.4	0.9	5.8	13.8	5.0	15.2	15.2	13.2	13.0	13.5
14540	Bowling Green, KY	4 183	168 436	246	40.3	85.8	8.0	0.6	2.8	4.3	6.1	16.3	14.3	13.1	12.3	12.6
14740	Bremerton-Silverdale, WA	1 023	260 131	184	254.3	82.1	4.0	2.9	9.2	7.2	5.7	15.2	10.5	13.5	11.2	13.5
14860	Bridgeport-Stamford-Norwalk, CT	1 618	948 053	57	585.9	64.9	11.3	0.4	6.1	18.7	5.7	17.9	8.8	11.7	13.0	15.7
15180	Brownsville-Harlingen, TX	2 307	422 156	126	183.0	10.1	0.5	0.2	0.8	88.7	8.7	22.9	10.7	12.1	12.6	11.0
15260	Brunswick, GA	3 332	116 003	333	34.8	69.7	24.4	0.8	1.6	5.2	6.0	16.9	8.2	11.6	11.9	13.7
15380	Buffalo-Cheektowaga-Niagara Falls, NY	4 054	1 135 230	50	280.0	79.8	13.0	1.0	3.3	4.6	5.4	15.3	9.9	13.2	11.2	14.3
15500	Burlington, NC	1 098	158 276	259	144.1	66.8	19.7	0.8	1.9	12.1	5.8	17.1	9.9	11.9	12.5	14.2
15540	Burlington-South Burlington, VT	3 243	217 042	202	66.9	92.9	2.5	1.2	3.4	2.0	5.1	14.6	13.9	13.2	11.9	14.3
15680	California-Lexington Park, MD	925	111 413	337	120.4	77.9	15.7	0.8	4.0	4.7	6.6	18.3	9.7	13.9	12.4	15.5
15940	Canton-Massillon, OH	2 512	402 976	133	160.4	89.8	8.7	0.8	1.2	1.9	5.4	16.5	8.9	11.5	11.6	13.9
15980	Cape Coral-Fort Myers, FL	2 032	701 982	79	345.5	70.3	8.8	0.5	2.1	19.6	4.9	13.8	7.4	10.7	10.6	12.3
16020	Cape Girardeau, MO-IL	3 708	97 534	357	26.3	87.8	9.9	0.8	1.6	2.1	5.9	15.9	13.4	12.1	11.2	12.8
16060	Carbondale-Marion, IL	2 601	126 828	310	48.8	84.9	10.1	0.8	3.0	3.3	5.5	14.6	15.4	13.7	11.4	12.0
16180	Carson City, NV	375	54 521	381	145.4	70.7	2.4	2.9	3.3	22.9	5.2	15.3	8.4	12.1	11.4	14.0
16220	Casper, WY	13 831	82 178	375	5.9	88.5	2.2	1.6	1.4	8.1	6.8	17.1	9.3	15.5	12.4	12.5

1. CBSA = Core Based Statistical Area. DIV = Metropolitan Division. See Appendix A for explanation. See Appendix B for list of metropolitan areas identified by type.　2. Dry land or land partially or temporarily covered by water.　3. May be of any race.

Table C. Metropolitan Areas — **Population and Households**

Area name	Population, 2014 (cont.) Age (percent) (cont.)				Population change and components of change, 2000–2015							Households, 2014				
					Total persons		Percent change		Components of change, 2010–2015					Percent		
	55 to 64 years	65 to 74 years	75 years and over	Percent female	2000	2010	2000–2010	2010–2015	Births	Deaths	Net migration	Number	Persons per house-hold	Family house-holds	Female family house-holder[1]	One person
	16	17	18	19	20	21	22	23	24	25	26	27	28	29	30	31
Abilene, TX	11.1	7.8	6.7	49.4	160 245	165 252	3.1	2.6	12 227	8 483	531	59 932	2.56	69.1	12.6	24.8
Akron, OH	14.1	8.8	7.0	51.4	694 960	703 207	1.2	0.1	40 031	36 174	-1 982	283 364	2.43	62.6	13.3	30.7
Albany, GA	12.7	8.2	5.6	52.5	157 833	157 500	-0.2	-2.5	11 412	7 395	-7 985	57 795	2.54	67.9	22.3	27.1
Albany, OR	13.9	10.1	7.2	50.5	103 069	116 672	13.2	3.3	7 582	6 130	2 237	45 907	2.57	68.4	11.6	25.4
Albany-Schenectady-Troy, NY	13.7	8.8	6.8	51.1	825 875	870 716	5.4	1.3	48 015	40 345	4 462	347 291	2.44	60.0	11.6	31.5
Albuquerque, NM	12.9	8.6	5.9	50.8	729 649	887 075	21.6	2.3	56 632	36 066	-402	342 552	2.61	63.9	14.3	30.1
Alexandria, LA	12.4	8.5	6.3	50.6	145 035	153 922	6.1	0.4	10 690	8 343	-1 671	53 802	2.73	69.8	14.8	26.7
Allentown-Bethlehem-Easton, PA-NJ	13.7	9.1	7.7	51.1	740 395	821 303	10.9	1.3	45 117	40 975	6 917	315 376	2.56	67.2	11.9	26.7
Altoona, PA	14.7	10.2	9.1	51.2	129 144	127 078	-1.6	-1.2	7 207	8 477	-485	49 678	2.47	63.9	10.7	29.7
Amarillo, TX	11.8	7.2	5.6	49.8	228 707	251 933	10.2	4.0	20 104	11 692	1 632	95 667	2.63	68.1	15.4	27.3
Ames, IA	9.7	5.7	5.0	48.1	79 981	89 542	12.0	7.2	5 020	2 489	4 023	35 880	2.36	51.1	5.0	28.5
Anchorage, AK	12.0	6.0	3.0	48.3	319 605	380 821	19.2	5.0	31 968	11 100	-1 758	135 449	2.87	68.0	10.6	23.4
Ann Arbor, MI	11.7	7.2	4.8	50.7	322 895	345 066	6.9	4.0	19 637	11 191	5 342	137 240	2.46	58.0	9.8	29.8
Anniston-Oxford-Jacksonville, AL	13.6	9.3	6.6	51.8	112 249	118 586	5.6	-2.5	7 055	7 209	-2 686	46 087	2.45	68.8	16.7	25.8
Appleton, WI	12.8	7.4	5.8	50.1	201 602	225 666	11.9	3.3	14 941	8 302	670	90 046	2.53	68.3	8.9	24.3
Asheville, NC	14.3	11.7	8.9	51.8	369 171	424 860	15.1	5.2	23 166	24 369	21 899	182 129	2.37	61.0	8.3	33.2
Athens-Clarke County, GA	10.6	7.1	4.7	51.7	166 079	192 541	15.9	5.5	11 656	6 877	5 546	71 814	2.59	57.2	11.1	29.5
Atlanta-Sandy Springs-Roswell, GA	11.3	6.8	4.0	51.5	4 263 438	5 286 727	24.0	8.0	381 487	176 264	215 011	1 981 447	2.79	67.7	15.4	26.5
Atlantic City-Hammonton, NJ	13.8	9.1	6.7	51.6	252 552	274 549	8.7	-0.1	17 369	13 523	-4 110	101 937	2.64	66.2	16.9	27.1
Auburn-Opelika, AL	10.0	6.4	3.9	50.7	115 092	140 296	21.9	11.9	9 295	4 979	12 044	57 880	2.57	63.6	17.0	26.2
Augusta-Richmond County, GA-SC	13.0	8.6	5.6	51.2	508 032	564 873	11.2	4.5	38 755	26 840	12 642	208 479	2.72	67.1	16.5	29.0
Austin-Round Rock, TX	10.4	5.9	3.6	50.0	1 249 763	1 716 313	37.3	16.6	134 107	46 718	192 904	703 976	2.70	61.6	10.8	28.2
Bakersfield, CA	10.0	5.9	4.0	48.7	661 645	839 631	26.9	5.1	75 269	29 397	-2 440	261 135	3.22	75.8	16.5	19.3
Baltimore-Columbia-Towson, MD	12.9	8.1	6.0	51.8	2 552 994	2 710 575	6.2	3.2	176 761	123 513	35 502	1 032 604	2.63	65.1	14.9	28.0
Bangor, ME	14.6	9.3	7.3	50.6	144 919	153 920	6.2	-0.8	7 770	7 908	-1 202	61 218	2.39	59.7	10.3	31.4
Barnstable Town, MA	17.1	15.2	12.6	52.4	222 230	215 888	-2.9	-0.7	8 293	14 792	4 731	95 697	2.22	59.5	7.7	35.4
Baton Rouge, LA	12.0	7.5	4.8	51.0	705 973	802 500	13.7	3.5	57 960	34 022	4 151	305 096	2.63	66.6	15.3	27.2
Battle Creek, MI	13.7	9.0	7.4	51.2	137 985	136 148	-1.3	-1.3	8 784	7 612	-2 924	52 385	2.50	63.0	14.0	31.7
Bay City, MI	15.0	10.2	8.1	50.7	110 157	107 771	-2.2	-2.0	5 644	6 069	-1 626	42 706	2.45	64.1	13.3	29.6
Beaumont-Port Arthur, TX	12.7	7.9	6.3	49.4	400 162	403 190	0.8	1.3	28 440	20 914	-2 132	152 806	2.53	66.6	17.2	29.9
Beckley, WV	15.2	10.6	7.8	49.8	126 799	124 901	-1.5	-1.9	7 927	8 734	-1 500	49 335	2.39	68.8	13.5	27.0
Bellingham, WA	12.9	9.3	6.2	50.4	166 814	201 140	20.6	5.5	11 960	7 900	7 041	81 973	2.47	61.8	8.7	26.5
Bend-Redmond, OR	14.8	11.5	6.8	50.7	115 367	157 733	36.7	11.1	9 073	6 954	15 127	66 218	2.55	67.6	7.5	25.5
Billings, MT	14.0	8.8	7.0	50.9	139 946	158 934	13.6	5.9	10 941	7 762	6 088	66 824	2.45	60.9	8.7	32.0
Binghamton, NY	13.9	9.2	8.4	50.7	252 320	251 723	-0.2	-2.3	13 521	13 176	-5 876	99 298	2.38	61.7	11.9	31.2
Birmingham-Hoover, AL	13.1	8.4	6.1	51.9	1 052 238	1 128 056	7.2	1.6	75 977	59 676	1 718	439 531	2.54	66.8	15.5	28.7
Bismarck, ND	13.0	7.7	6.6	50.0	100 828	114 778	13.8	12.8	9 220	5 168	10 341	53 813	2.28	63.9	9.8	27.4
Blacksburg-Christiansburg-Radford, VA	11.5	8.4	5.7	49.1	165 146	178 258	7.9	2.0	8 798	7 638	2 519	67 185	2.49	54.4	5.7	33.0
Bloomington, IL	11.3	6.7	5.3	51.2	167 231	186 133	11.3	1.8	12 032	6 837	-1 871	72 551	2.50	61.1	9.6	28.5
Bloomington, IN	10.8	7.0	5.1	50.1	142 349	159 542	12.1	3.8	7 979	5 721	3 787	61 929	2.40	53.5	9.5	30.8
Bloomsburg-Berwick, PA	14.0	9.5	8.2	51.8	82 387	85 563	3.9	-0.4	4 307	4 628	-44	33 873	2.38	64.9	10.7	25.4
Boise City, ID	11.6	7.8	5.1	50.1	464 840	616 561	32.6	9.8	45 056	21 927	36 353	240 402	2.73	68.0	9.4	26.0
Boston-Cambridge-Newton, MA-NH	12.8	8.0	6.4	51.5	4 391 344	4 552 412	3.7	4.9	273 057	183 337	137 505	1 777 817	2.57	62.9	11.8	28.6
Boston, MA Div 14454	12.3	7.8	6.2	51.7	1 812 937	1 887 745	4.1	5.1	115 223	76 329	59 737	738 496	2.56	60.2	13.5	30.3
Cambridge-Newton-Framingham, MA Div 15764	12.9	8.0	6.5	51.4	2 188 815	2 246 301	2.6	5.1	137 534	90 820	71 440	873 442	2.59	64.4	10.9	27.8
Rockingham County-Strafford County, NH 40484	14.7	8.8	6.0	50.7	389 592	418 366	7.4	2.4	20 300	16 188	6 328	165 879	2.50	66.7	9.2	25.2
Boulder, CO	12.6	7.4	4.9	49.8	269 814	294 571	9.2	8.4	15 535	8 580	17 624	123 690	2.45	59.4	8.1	27.2
Bowling Green, KY	11.8	8.1	5.4	50.9	134 976	158 599	17.5	6.2	10 724	7 229	6 353	61 834	2.56	67.6	10.9	25.9
Bremerton-Silverdale, WA	14.4	10.0	6.1	49.1	231 969	251 133	8.3	3.6	15 499	10 766	3 820	95 249	2.60	68.5	9.3	25.8
Bridgeport-Stamford-Norwalk, CT	12.9	7.7	6.6	51.2	882 567	916 850	3.9	3.4	53 486	34 170	13 815	338 421	2.74	69.6	12.8	25.4
Brownsville-Harlingen, TX	9.6	6.9	5.5	51.7	335 227	406 219	21.2	3.9	39 172	12 855	-10 664	121 009	3.44	79.5	24.0	18.3
Brunswick, GA	14.0	10.9	6.8	52.1	93 044	112 368	20.8	3.2	6 940	5 725	2 273	43 618	2.54	66.4	14.3	28.4
Buffalo-Cheektowaga-Niagara Falls, NY	14.1	8.9	7.8	51.6	1 170 111	1 135 551	-3.0	0.0	63 696	62 713	962	470 564	2.35	59.8	13.9	33.9
Burlington, NC	12.5	9.0	7.1	52.3	130 800	151 241	15.6	4.7	9 271	8 046	5 558	62 799	2.41	62.9	14.8	31.1
Burlington-South Burlington, VT	13.5	7.9	5.6	50.9	198 889	211 262	6.2	2.7	11 620	7 580	1 818	85 222	2.41	62.1	9.4	26.6
California-Lexington Park, MD	11.7	7.2	4.8	50.2	86 211	105 151	22.0	6.0	7 454	3 888	2 524	39 179	2.75	70.4	11.3	23.6
Canton-Massillon, OH	14.5	9.8	8.0	51.4	406 934	404 420	-0.6	-0.4	23 348	22 678	-1 654	159 604	2.47	66.7	12.2	27.9
Cape Coral-Fort Myers, FL	14.0	15.0	11.3	51.0	440 888	618 754	40.3	13.5	33 534	33 097	81 946	263 295	2.54	64.4	12.0	29.4
Cape Girardeau, MO-IL	12.9	8.7	7.3	51.3	90 312	96 275	6.6	1.3	6 116	4 974	121	37 842	2.48	62.7	9.8	31.3
Carbondale-Marion, IL	12.1	8.8	6.7	50.1	120 908	126 580	4.7	0.2	7 579	6 313	-1 040	50 423	2.38	61.7	11.0	29.6
Carson City, NV	14.4	10.9	8.3	48.9	52 457	55 274	5.4	-1.4	2 992	3 450	-430	21 228	2.48	60.4	12.3	32.2
Casper, WY	13.4	7.2	5.7	49.5	66 533	75 450	13.4	8.9	5 867	3 635	4 437	33 323	2.39	61.2	9.0	32.9

1. No spouse present.

Table C. Metropolitan Areas — Population, Vital Statistics, Medicare, and Crime

Area name	Daytime population, 2014: Persons in group quarters, 2015	Daytime population, 2014: Number	Daytime population, 2014: Employment/residence ratio	Births, 2015: Total	Births, 2015: Rate[1]	Deaths, 2015: Number	Deaths, 2015: Rate[1]	Persons under 65 with no health insurance 2014: Number	Persons under 65 with no health insurance 2014: Percent	Medicare, 2015: Total Beneficiaries	Medicare, 2015: Enrolled in Original Medicare	Medicare, 2015: Enrolled in Medicare Advantage	Serious crimes known to police[2] 2014 Total: Number	Serious crimes known to police[2] 2014 Total: Rate[3]
	32	33	34	35	36	37	38	39	40	41	42	43	44	45
Abilene, TX	10 131	165 990	0.99	2 344	13.8	1 669	9.8	26 082	19.2	28 422	22 574	5 848	6 884	4 069
Akron, OH	18 232	704 611	1.00	7 651	10.9	6 967	9.9	54 528	9.4	121 655	60 163	61 492	19 601	3 004
Albany, GA	5 318	152 238	0.99	2 085	13.6	1 427	9.3	23 190	18.0	25 927	18 440	7 487	7 193	4 726
Albany, OR	1 191	117 776	0.97	1 440	11.9	1 247	10.3	10 106	10.3	26 375	12 646	13 729	4 028	3 364
Albany-Schenectady-Troy, NY	32 974	896 832	1.04	9 128	10.4	7 784	8.8	48 872	6.8	154 097	86 763	67 334	22 003	2 497
Albuquerque, NM	14 863	901 459	0.99	10 478	11.5	7 290	8.0	115 271	15.2	141 184	65 939	75 245	44 988	4 981
Alexandria, LA	7 452	154 862	1.00	2 037	13.2	1 555	10.1	20 777	16.5	29 377	24 798	4 579	7 957	5 284
Allentown-Bethlehem-Easton, PA-NJ	22 362	792 355	0.91	8 718	10.5	7 760	9.3	70 634	10.5	159 213	115 297	43 916	17 658	2 132
Altoona, PA	3 751	132 054	1.11	1 377	11.0	1 627	13.0	9 419	9.4	29 903	14 423	15 480	2 368	1 878
Amarillo, TX	10 068	259 993	0.99	3 881	14.8	2 188	8.3	43 948	20.1	36 950	29 264	7 686	11 558	4 420
Ames, IA	11 329	96 016	1.04	968	10.1	491	5.1	5 364	7.2	11 641	10 287	1 354	1 647	1 903
Anchorage, AK	10 685	394 389	0.98	6 211	15.5	2 228	5.6	60 657	17.1	39 262	38 743	519	14 136	4 692
Ann Arbor, MI	17 890	389 378	1.18	3 709	10.3	2 193	6.1	22 780	7.7	47 474	33 428	14 046	7 632	2 139
Anniston-Oxford-Jacksonville, AL	2 804	115 824	1.00	1 335	11.5	1 395	12.1	13 543	14.2	26 839	22 473	4 366	4 615	3 965
Appleton, WI	3 190	222 575	0.93	2 820	12.1	1 592	6.8	13 465	6.8	36 102	14 506	21 596	3 752	1 624
Asheville, NC	11 123	448 733	1.03	4 497	10.1	4 790	10.7	53 686	15.6	103 526	76 030	27 496	10 990	2 507
Athens-Clarke County, GA	12 240	196 338	0.99	2 184	10.7	1 322	6.5	30 367	18.4	28 099	20 373	7 726	6 304	3 175
Atlanta-Sandy Springs-Roswell, GA	83 916	5 628 887	1.01	73 242	12.8	36 005	6.3	866 307	17.6	660 203	423 651	236 552	210 035	3 757
Atlantic City-Hammonton, NJ	6 215	275 376	1.00	3 167	11.5	2 678	9.8	34 377	15.1	48 514	43 093	5 421	9 170	3 315
Auburn-Opelika, AL	4 940	145 274	0.87	1 900	12.1	989	6.3	17 961	13.4	17 786	15 044	2 742	4 155	2 704
Augusta-Richmond County, GA-SC	17 692	584 366	1.01	7 410	12.6	5 268	8.9	75 185	15.5	96 354	67 369	28 985	14 158	2 446
Austin-Round Rock, TX	42 149	1 944 610	1.00	26 572	13.3	9 618	4.8	301 989	17.6	197 769	142 595	55 174	61 284	3 167
Bakersfield, CA	32 500	879 078	1.01	14 429	16.4	5 830	6.6	109 766	14.5	98 896	60 031	38 865	32 748	3 744
Baltimore-Columbia-Towson, MD	70 294	2 759 468	0.98	33 719	12.1	24 763	8.9	176 511	7.5	408 706	364 193	44 513	93 199	3 340
Bangor, ME	7 502	153 849	1.01	1 483	9.7	1 506	9.9	17 410	14.3	32 937	25 599	7 338	3 585	2 337
Barnstable Town, MA	3 962	212 105	0.97	1 526	7.1	2 801	13.1	6 234	4.1	66 532	58 903	7 629	5 243	2 434
Baton Rouge, LA	25 636	833 311	1.02	11 251	13.5	6 716	8.1	106 994	15.3	116 682	61 074	55 608	32 228	3 920
Battle Creek, MI	4 011	141 623	1.12	1 705	12.7	1 367	10.2	10 886	9.9	28 256	22 455	5 801	4 563	3 383
Bay City, MI	1 437	97 317	0.80	1 026	9.7	1 132	10.7	7 671	8.9	23 914	17 238	6 676	2 436	2 283
Beaumont-Port Arthur, TX	17 831	406 305	1.01	5 530	13.5	4 057	9.9	68 436	20.6	69 393	44 878	24 515	14 148	3 467
Beckley, WV	5 478	122 564	0.98	1 462	11.9	1 708	13.9	10 703	11.2	29 458	21 529	7 929	4 188	3 526
Bellingham, WA	5 863	206 120	0.98	2 293	10.8	1 488	7.0	20 324	11.9	36 244	22 704	13 540	7 219	3 462
Bend-Redmond, OR	1 217	169 208	0.98	1 822	10.4	1 343	7.7	16 562	12.0	35 277	24 038	11 239	4 379	2 595
Billings, MT	3 837	167 870	1.00	2 074	12.3	1 452	8.6	20 818	15.1	28 958	22 700	6 258	6 379	3 814
Binghamton, NY	11 301	245 376	0.98	2 603	10.6	2 520	10.2	13 942	7.1	52 299	32 901	19 398	6 892	2 787
Birmingham-Hoover, AL	24 505	1 145 621	1.00	14 199	12.4	11 526	10.1	123 126	12.9	205 723	117 453	88 270	41 803	4 137
Bismarck, ND	4 162	NA	NA	1 854	14.3	992	7.7	8 497	8.1	19 963	15 512	4 451	2 895	2 290
Blacksburg-Christiansburg-Radford, VA	13 938	181 721	1.01	1 672	9.2	1 400	7.7	19 494	13.6	30 036	23 167	6 869	3 336	1 844
Bloomington, IL	10 842	193 673	1.05	2 225	11.7	1 350	7.1	10 426	6.6	25 999	18 071	7 928	3 780	2 011
Bloomington, IN	15 343	168 698	1.06	1 519	9.2	1 081	6.5	18 333	14.1	22 211	17 968	4 243	4 188	2 932
Bloomsburg-Berwick, PA	5 150	90 789	1.13	788	9.2	903	10.6	6 141	9.3	18 134	10 112	8 022	1 407	1 651
Boise City, ID	14 618	664 033	0.99	8 704	12.9	4 257	6.3	82 707	14.6	97 412	49 580	47 832	13 451	2 029
Boston-Cambridge-Newton, MA-NH	167 614	4 892 700	1.07	52 663	11.0	36 126	7.6	166 074	4.2	719 076	568 365	150 711	94 798	2 048
Boston, MA Div 14454	80 337	X	X	22 212	11.2	15 176	7.6	63 776	3.9	286 784	226 583	60 201	45 762	2 430
Cambridge-Newton-Framingham, MA Div 15764	75 622	X	X	26 476	11.2	17 810	7.5	66 927	3.4	360 307	275 400	84 907	40 834	1 751
Rockingham County-Strafford County, NH 40484	11 655	X	X	3 975	9.3	3 140	7.3	35 371	10.0	71 985	66 382	5 603	8 202	1 985
Boulder, CO	10 887	343 310	1.18	2 933	9.2	1 755	5.5	26 315	9.9	44 977	26 021	18 956	6 581	2 617
Bowling Green, KY	7 068	167 912	1.03	2 147	12.7	1 382	8.2	15 956	11.6	27 834	21 366	6 468	4 118	2 497
Bremerton-Silverdale, WA	8 931	242 434	0.90	2 937	11.3	2 184	8.4	17 077	8.3	44 139	34 459	9 680	7 909	3 093
Bridgeport-Stamford-Norwalk, CT	20 233	953 504	1.02	10 078	10.6	6 604	7.0	83 782	10.5	133 598	100 888	32 710	17 221	1 857
Brownsville-Harlingen, TX	3 845	416 159	0.97	7 403	17.5	2 556	6.1	119 223	32.8	53 597	32 424	21 173	15 087	3 569
Brunswick, GA	1 389	113 646	1.02	1 322	11.4	1 123	9.7	17 736	18.9	21 591	15 863	5 728	5 151	4 573
Buffalo-Cheektowaga-Niagara Falls, NY	32 433	1 144 904	1.02	12 289	10.8	11 848	10.4	64 087	6.0	221 581	89 107	132 474	34 654	3 052
Burlington, NC	4 599	148 162	0.89	1 784	11.3	1 535	9.7	21 046	16.5	29 566	13 707	15 859	4 880	3 140
Burlington-South Burlington, VT	10 376	222 578	1.06	2 232	10.3	1 438	6.6	9 600	5.4	29 360	26 727	2 633	4 301	1 996
California-Lexington Park, MD	2 799	105 363	0.91	1 422	12.8	784	7.0	6 006	6.4	13 475	13 213	262	2 474	2 232
Canton-Massillon, OH	9 487	394 726	0.95	4 550	11.3	4 262	10.6	28 556	8.8	85 229	41 191	44 038	11 465	3 116
Cape Coral-Fort Myers, FL	8 479	661 196	0.93	6 583	9.4	6 808	9.7	115 883	23.5	155 944	105 636	50 308	15 855	2 342
Cape Girardeau, MO-IL	4 127	99 661	1.05	1 174	12.0	922	9.5	9 998	12.7	18 506	16 760	1 746	3 056	3 125
Carbondale-Marion, IL	5 985	129 597	1.05	1 447	11.4	1 192	9.4	10 385	10.1	22 516	18 183	4 333	2 917	2 381
Carson City, NV	2 747	NA	NA	583	10.7	631	11.6	6 766	16.3	13 494	12 014	1 480	1 035	1 906
Casper, WY	1 721	NA	NA	1 194	14.5	706	8.6	9 969	14.3	12 006	11 421	585	2 102	2 565

1. Per 1,000 estimated resident population.   2. Data for serious crimes have not been adjusted for underreporting; this may affect comparability between geographic areas and over time.
3. Per 100,000 population estimated by the FBI.

Table C. Metropolitan Areas — Crime, Education, Money Income, and Poverty

Area name	Serious crimes known to police, 2014 (cont.)[1] Rate[2] Violent	Property	Enrollment[3] Total	Percent private	High school graduate or less	Bachelor's degree or more	Local government expenditures,[5] 2012–2013 Total current expenditures (mil dol)	Current expenditures per student (dollars)	Per capita income[6] (dollars)	Mean household income (dollars)	Median household income	Percent of households with income of less than $25,000	Percent of households with income of $200,000 or more	All persons	Children under 18 years	Age 65 years and older
	46	47	48	49	50	51	52	53	54	55	56	57	58	59	60	61
Abilene, TX	400	3 668	43 512	23.0	45.0	21.6	247.0	8 732	23 132	61 532	44 303	25.2	3.0	16.5	20.6	12.3
Akron, OH	282	2 721	180 102	13.3	41.8	29.9	1 111.2	11 692	28 113	67 821	50 538	24.0	3.6	13.3	19.5	6.3
Albany, GA.........................	635	4 091	47 359	8.0	47.7	19.0	246.8	9 020	20 069	51 306	39 071	34.7	1.3	25.3	40.7	14.7
Albany, OR.........................	109	3 255	28 156	10.4	41.1	20.5	197.8	8 945	22 132	55 665	43 428	25.2	1.4	20.3	31.2	7.7
Albany-Schenectady-Troy, NY	274	2 224	215 439	22.8	35.2	35.4	2 025.5	17 228	32 354	79 446	62 265	18.6	4.4	11.7	17.1	6.0
Albuquerque, NM................	732	4 249	243 752	13.4	37.0	30.5	1 129.2	8 561	25 731	65 138	47 581	27.1	3.6	19.2	25.3	13.3
Alexandria, LA....................	823	4 462	38 368	13.0	54.0	16.9	249.2	9 109	20 720	55 290	40 209	32.7	1.6	19.6	22.8	14.4
Allentown-Bethlehem-Easton, PA-NJ	185	1 947	199 011	25.3	45.7	26.4	1 756.2	14 927	30 062	77 183	60 320	19.2	4.8	11.2	16.8	6.7
Altoona, PA.........................	235	1 643	25 287	15.0	56.2	20.0	229.4	13 023	23 456	57 033	44 019	28.9	2.1	14.8	19.3	10.5
Amarillo, TX........................	563	3 857	70 494	7.9	39.3	22.7	425.9	8 634	26 334	70 037	51 280	23.2	2.8	14.8	20.2	7.9
Ames, IA............................	127	1 776	41 132	2.5	23.5	47.9	105.8	9 640	25 376	64 148	46 091	29.2	4.4	22.5	10.2	2.3
Anchorage, AK....................	865	3 827	107 599	14.6	32.9	29.7	1 031.2	15 481	34 285	94 657	75 682	12.9	7.2	9.9	15.4	4.7
Ann Arbor, MI.....................	288	1 851	123 044	11.3	20.7	53.0	462.8	12 094	35 267	87 399	62 845	18.2	6.9	14.5	13.8	5.7
Anniston-Oxford-Jacksonville, AL	618	3 348	28 605	9.7	47.8	18.8	164.3	9 010	21 750	52 858	41 428	32.2	1.8	20.6	27.6	14.3
Appleton, WI.......................	138	1 485	61 609	14.6	41.1	27.3	385.9	10 197	29 023	73 343	60 106	16.0	3.0	9.7	13.1	4.3
Asheville, NC	205	2 302	98 348	16.1	34.6	32.6	467.5	8 686	26 464	61 044	46 917	25.3	2.2	12.6	16.8	6.5
Athens-Clarke County, GA ...	300	2 875	68 618	11.9	38.3	35.9	278.4	10 555	21 593	57 531	41 761	33.5	2.6	29.0	34.8	9.8
Atlanta-Sandy Springs-Roswell, GA	407	3 350	1 586 300	15.9	36.4	35.8	8 619.3	9 135	29 170	79 085	56 166	20.5	6.1	15.5	22.8	9.3
Atlantic City-Hammonton, NJ	384	2 931	66 574	10.0	47.6	24.8	833.0	18 329	27 885	72 116	55 313	22.8	4.7	15.5	25.3	7.6
Auburn-Opelika, AL.............	241	2 463	54 649	8.2	36.8	31.7	193.4	8 989	25 204	63 553	39 932	33.6	4.0	27.7	33.4	8.8
Augusta-Richmond County, GA-SC............................	201	2 244	150 632	13.1	45.1	25.4	842.2	8 905	23 484	61 743	46 689	27.8	2.4	18.9	30.0	9.2
Austin-Round Rock, TX	291	2 876	544 642	12.4	30.7	41.5	2 621.6	8 599	32 549	85 806	63 603	18.6	7.2	15.1	19.9	7.1
Bakersfield, CA...................	510	3 234	254 661	8.8	53.2	15.4	1 708.5	9 682	20 488	65 772	47 644	26.6	2.9	24.8	33.6	13.8
Baltimore-Columbia-Towson, MD..................	584	2 757	722 736	20.3	36.6	37.7	5 404.6	13 724	35 596	92 935	71 501	16.9	8.1	11.1	14.3	8.1
Bangor, ME.........................	77	2 260	40 023	11.5	42.7	25.1	262.5	11 775	23 475	55 570	42 242	32.1	2.3	19.0	26.3	8.2
Barnstable Town, MA	431	2 003	40 510	14.4	26.6	44.3	400.2	16 305	40 188	88 287	65 384	18.8	5.7	7.7	10.4	5.6
Baton Rouge, LA	514	3 406	220 583	17.8	45.7	27.3	1 235.7	10 553	26 783	69 747	52 091	25.3	4.0	17.0	21.8	11.4
Battle Creek, MI	548	2 835	32 011	11.2	45.5	20.7	239.7	12 695	23 171	57 708	46 088	25.0	2.3	14.8	22.2	7.7
Bay City, MI	284	1 999	25 409	8.9	47.6	18.8	155.3	11 226	26 385	63 340	46 844	25.9	2.4	17.5	27.7	9.1
Beaumont-Port Arthur, TX	494	2 973	91 644	7.5	52.2	16.6	616.2	8 953	23 687	60 289	42 494	30.3	2.3	18.6	28.5	10.7
Beckley, WV........................	390	3 136	26 487	14.0	57.4	17.4	215.9	11 104	22 292	54 495	39 498	32.2	2.2	17.4	26.7	7.0
Bellingham, WA	188	3 274	57 980	13.2	32.9	32.6	253.3	9 366	26 616	66 744	53 665	23.8	3.3	16.1	19.1	8.6
Bend-Redmond, OR	181	2 414	36 613	15.7	31.0	30.4	235.4	9 490	28 938	71 797	52 006	19.9	4.2	13.1	14.8	9.1
Billings, MT	327	3 487	39 229	12.5	39.8	28.0	231.7	9 529	29 843	72 605	51 111	23.3	5.3	12.2	15.7	8.2
Binghamton, NY...................	259	2 528	61 003	8.9	42.0	26.0	600.3	17 025	25 682	62 800	48 188	25.8	2.7	15.6	20.9	7.1
Birmingham-Hoover, AL........	590	3 546	278 605	15.1	41.9	28.2	1 634.1	9 209	25 945	65 478	47 046	27.0	3.3	17.5	25.3	10.2
Bismarck, ND	236	2 053	29 077	21.0	34.9	32.2	187.1	11 032	34 571	83 092	63 356	16.3	6.3	9.8	10.8	9.1
Blacksburg-Christiansburg-Radford, VA	187	1 657	66 766	7.1	39.1	33.2	196.6	9 676	22 862	57 499	43 709	29.5	2.4	23.1	16.1	9.1
Bloomington, IL...................	272	1 739	59 469	13.9	33.0	41.9	305.0	10 901	29 568	74 022	57 592	19.9	3.3	14.4	11.7	6.8
Bloomington, IN	286	2 645	65 557	9.1	34.5	41.9	157.0	9 691	24 145	61 799	44 963	27.9	3.7	24.1	19.8	5.2
Bloomsburg-Berwick, PA	206	1 444	21 636	9.5	54.5	23.9	111.9	12 913	25 223	63 931	49 670	24.0	2.9	13.2	15.9	5.4
Boise City, ID.....................	230	1 799	181 556	14.1	35.1	29.4	708.8	6 488	25 927	69 597	51 826	21.8	4.4	13.9	17.8	8.9
Boston-Cambridge-Newton, MA-NH	333	1 715	1 231 871	28.9	32.4	45.2	9 990.1	15 660	40 593	104 657	75 667	18.0	11.2	10.6	13.5	8.8
Boston, MA Div 14454........	470	1 960	523 339	33.9	33.9	43.6	4 123.3	16 112	39 388	101 165	71 530	20.2	10.8	12.7	16.5	9.9
Cambridge-Newton-Framingham, MA Div 15764	254	1 497	603 816	26.9	30.9	48.0	5 033.5	15 764	42 123	109 337	79 516	16.8	12.3	9.5	11.4	8.9
Rockingham County-Strafford County, NH 40484	158	1 827	104 716	15.1	33.6	37.5	833.2	13 285	37 757	95 563	72 861	13.9	7.8	7.7	11.2	3.3
Boulder, CO	246	2 372	93 813	13.4	18.9	58.0	521.1	8 769	38 765	95 996	71 540	17.4	9.3	14.1	16.2	7.0
Bowling Green, KY	162	2 335	46 789	6.9	51.7	21.4	212.0	8 283	22 073	58 042	47 277	26.3	1.1	18.6	22.9	10.4
Bremerton-Silverdale, WA	267	2 827	55 894	11.4	28.9	32.0	356.6	9 822	32 340	80 368	61 794	19.3	5.6	11.0	14.1	9.6
Bridgeport-Stamford-Norwalk, CT	246	1 611	257 939	25.3	32.4	46.7	2 503.2	17 442	52 284	142 190	85 925	15.1	19.2	8.9	11.5	7.6
Brownsville-Harlingen, TX.....	259	3 310	127 007	2.9	59.1	17.4	912.1	9 142	14 770	47 427	32 093	40.8	1.0	35.2	48.8	23.2
Brunswick, GA	420	4 153	26 641	12.8	42.3	23.4	164.6	9 150	24 209	60 468	46 268	28.1	2.9	20.2	29.0	7.5
Buffalo-Cheektowaga-Niagara Falls, NY	431	2 620	272 187	16.9	39.3	29.6	2 597.1	17 446	28 680	67 381	50 074	25.3	3.2	14.8	22.0	9.1
Burlington, NC	372	2 768	38 855	24.9	45.2	20.5	181.0	7 914	23 179	55 895	39 576	30.4	1.6	18.3	25.3	11.4
Burlington-South Burlington, VT	98	1 897	56 620	18.7	32.9	41.7	496.0	16 221	32 065	80 053	61 947	17.9	4.6	10.4	11.2	5.6
California-Lexington Park, MD	237	1 995	29 437	12.0	39.9	28.9	217.6	12 469	36 628	98 619	86 417	13.6	8.5	7.5	10.5	6.7
Canton-Massillon, OH	302	2 814	98 529	18.7	48.3	21.3	606.1	10 096	25 261	62 048	47 729	24.2	2.6	14.6	21.0	8.8
Cape Coral-Fort Myers, FL...	340	2 002	137 882	11.4	44.1	26.5	756.4	8 819	28 190	67 172	49 055	24.0	3.8	16.3	26.8	7.7
Cape Girardeau, MO-IL	400	2 725	25 630	8.6	47.9	25.6	112.4	8 659	22 394	55 606	44 347	31.1	1.8	21.3	29.6	9.9
Carbondale-Marion, IL	238	2 144	39 639	4.3	36.3	28.6	194.0	10 928	24 044	58 936	41 174	31.6	2.1	22.8	25.7	9.4
Carson City, NV..................	295	1 611	13 888	8.5	43.2	23.0	82.4	10 502	23 967	58 475	43 850	25.6	1.7	22.4	37.6	10.7
Casper, WY........................	184	2 380	18 851	8.9	33.2	21.0	180.8	13 823	30 967	83 179	56 392	19.2	2.9	9.3	12.1	4.9

1. Data for serious crimes have not been adjusted for underreporting; this may affect comparability between geographic areas and over time. 2. Per 100,000 population estimated by the FBI. 3. All persons 3 years old and over enrolled in nursery school through college. 4. Persons 25 years old and over. 5. Elementary and secondary education expenditures. 6. Based on resident population estimated in the 2014 American Community Survey.

Table C. Metropolitan Areas — **Personal Income**

Area name	Personal income, 2014										Earnings, 2014		
			Per capita[1]			Supplements to wages and salaries; employer contributions (mil dol)						Contributions for government social insurance (mil dol)	
	Total (mil dol)	Percent change 2013–2014	Dollars	Rank	Wages and salaries (mil dol)	Pension and insurance	Government social insurance	Proprietors' income (mil dol)	Dividends, interest, and rent (mil dol)	Personal transfer receipts (mil dol)	Total (mil dol)	From employee and self-employed	From employer
	62	63	64	65	66	67	68	69	70	71	72	73	74
Abilene, TX	6 780	4.9	40 215	179	2 991	523	216	875	1 195	1 409	4 604	237	216
Akron, OH	30 564	3.7	43 426	109	15 572	2 790	1 129	2 119	4 580	5 832	21 610	1 233	1 129
Albany, GA	5 220	1.2	33 692	341	2 489	515	178	284	847	1 368	3 467	202	178
Albany, OR...........................	4 087	6.2	34 239	327	1 734	272	164	177	633	1 263	2 347	161	164
Albany-Schenectady-Troy, NY	43 902	3.2	49 879	39	23 021	5 911	1 961	2 886	7 071	7 623	33 779	1 746	1 961
Albuquerque, NM	33 782	4.2	37 345	251	17 269	2 890	1 394	1 841	5 980	7 161	23 394	1 492	1 394
Alexandria, LA	5 993	1.9	38 695	212	2 606	512	169	528	1 027	1 557	3 815	210	169
Allentown-Bethlehem-Easton, PA-NJ	37 503	4.8	45 193	88	17 076	3 050	1 368	2 221	5 833	7 193	23 716	1 446	1 368
Altoona, PA	4 829	3.4	38 336	224	2 382	510	209	295	744	1 321	3 396	212	209
Amarillo, TX	10 788	5.6	41 510	152	5 132	793	355	1 633	1 590	1 810	7 912	403	355
Ames, IA	3 574	4.6	37 990	235	2 076	491	155	334	795	468	3 056	173	155
Anchorage, AK....................	22 789	5.6	57 131	15	11 137	2 289	876	2 096	3 723	3 309	16 397	875	876
Ann Arbor, MI......................	17 260	4.4	48 365	53	10 316	2 208	758	844	3 460	2 258	14 125	802	758
Anniston-Oxford-Jacksonville, AL	3 797	3.2	32 753	358	1 739	362	133	237	670	1 082	2 472	160	133
Appleton, WI	10 140	4.1	43 801	102	5 426	950	439	751	1 530	1 356	7 566	455	439
Asheville, NC	16 131	4.6	36 470	271	7 190	1 248	562	964	3 524	4 026	9 964	662	562
Athens-Clarke County, GA ...	6 650	5.2	33 414	348	3 524	837	238	476	1 286	1 274	5 075	270	238
Atlanta-Sandy Springs-Roswell, GA	244 066	5.6	43 472	108	142 550	20 501	9 812	20 067	38 795	33 206	192 930	11 129	9 812
Atlantic City-Hammonton, NJ	11 927	3.7	43 336	114	6 059	1 128	505	1 123	1 936	2 630	8 815	530	505
Auburn-Opelika, AL..............	5 100	5.5	33 064	351	2 047	396	154	333	864	899	2 930	179	154
Augusta-Richmond County, GA-SC	21 079	3.6	36 117	290	10 473	2 116	791	1 090	3 525	4 780	14 470	843	791
Austin-Round Rock, TX	91 386	6.7	47 026	64	50 884	6 704	3 342	9 821	18 563	9 678	70 751	3 580	3 342
Bakersfield, CA	31 629	3.8	36 165	288	15 468	3 367	1 087	3 911	4 333	5 945	23 833	1 275	1 087
Baltimore-Columbia-Towson, MD..................	149 573	3.7	53 690	22	80 247	13 917	6 026	10 586	27 197	23 256	110 776	6 447	6 026
Bangor, ME	5 510	2.4	35 914	295	2 845	519	206	387	761	1 446	3 958	256	206
Barnstable Town, MA	12 872	4.2	59 892	10	4 274	786	324	1 046	3 570	2 490	6 430	382	324
Baton Rouge, LA	34 876	3.7	42 249	135	19 604	3 365	1 213	2 941	5 399	5 755	27 122	1 422	1 213
Battle Creek, MI	4 732	2.6	35 084	315	2 850	482	217	163	734	1 291	3 712	236	217
Bay City, MI	3 867	3.6	36 419	274	1 561	278	122	159	567	1 107	2 120	147	122
Beaumont-Port Arthur, TX	16 117	6.8	39 752	192	8 561	1 439	595	1 227	2 133	3 720	11 822	649	595
Beckley, WV	4 199	0.7	34 034	336	1 814	325	147	303	559	1 389	2 588	178	147
Bellingham, WA	8 509	4.3	40 840	167	3 747	638	354	735	1 826	1 661	5 473	325	354
Bend-Redmond, OR	7 101	7.0	41 675	150	2 855	418	270	758	1 810	1 519	4 301	289	270
Billings, MT	7 110	4.3	42 606	130	3 729	540	340	594	1 372	1 177	5 203	341	340
Binghamton, NY	9 407	1.4	38 050	233	4 260	1 194	369	602	1 372	2 289	6 425	358	369
Birmingham-Hoover, AL........	50 619	4.6	44 256	96	25 277	3 857	1 842	5 830	8 587	9 331	36 805	2 295	1 842
Bismarck, ND	6 352	5.8	50 173	37	3 532	474	285	446	1 207	873	4 737	291	285
Blacksburg-Christiansburg-Radford, VA	5 925	4.0	32 627	360	2 933	623	224	277	1 144	1 239	4 057	253	224
Bloomington, IL	8 197	-1.4	43 064	120	5 140	866	337	605	1 238	1 057	6 947	371	337
Bloomington, IN	5 533	4.3	33 675	342	2 833	634	210	266	1 143	1 021	3 943	234	210
Bloomsburg-Berwick, PA	3 447	2.5	40 189	180	1 980	413	149	331	489	758	2 873	169	149
Boise City, ID	25 242	5.4	37 991	234	12 512	1 744	1 072	2 756	4 927	4 276	18 083	1 151	1 072
Boston-Cambridge-Newton, MA-NH	304 329	4.7	64 311	6	182 453	24 872	12 326	27 358	59 517	37 679	247 009	13 542	12 326
Boston, MA Div 14454........	128 544	4.6	65 366	X	86 730	12 044	5 692	13 795	24 940	17 219	118 260	6 346	5 692
Cambridge-Newton-Framingham, MA Div 15764	152 144	4.6	65 035	X	85 511	11 325	5 925	11 528	30 708	17 525	114 290	6 309	5 925
Rockingham County-Strafford County, NH 40484	23 641	5.1	55 465	X	10 212	1 503	709	2 036	3 869	2 934	14 459	888	709
Boulder, CO	18 370	5.6	58 627	13	10 852	1 386	747	1 448	4 920	1 644	14 432	794	747
Bowling Green, KY	5 569	4.8	33 600	346	2 731	525	213	498	746	1 329	3 967	243	213
Bremerton-Silverdale, WA	11 838	5.7	46 573	72	4 680	1 076	438	480	3 011	2 057	6 675	376	438
Bridgeport-Stamford-Norwalk, CT	93 304	4.9	98 688	1	37 394	4 977	2 256	11 213	24 371	7 248	55 840	3 101	2 256
Brownsville-Harlingen, TX.....	10 599	4.2	25 211	380	4 476	905	320	836	1 310	3 415	6 537	357	320
Brunswick, GA	3 926	3.0	34 194	328	1 647	346	118	175	931	931	2 286	141	118
Buffalo-Cheektowaga-Niagara Falls, NY	49 631	3.0	43 676	105	24 514	5 737	2 124	3 420	7 139	10 779	35 964	1 945	2 124
Burlington, NC	5 422	4.3	34 801	320	2 323	383	184	325	825	1 245	3 215	213	184
Burlington-South Burlington, VT	10 698	3.5	49 490	43	6 013	1 030	492	834	1 967	1 694	8 370	519	492
California-Lexington Park, MD	5 545	3.7	50 234	36	3 046	635	240	225	997	714	4 145	229	240
Canton-Massillon, OH	16 185	3.9	40 069	185	7 138	1 293	546	1 308	2 287	3 713	10 285	617	546
Cape Coral-Fort Myers, FL...	28 705	5.9	42 243	136	10 145	1 572	735	2 008	10 022	6 275	14 460	992	735
Cape Girardeau, MO-IL	3 673	2.9	37 507	247	1 783	328	129	382	617	807	2 622	155	129
Carbondale-Marion, IL	4 560	1.5	35 992	293	2 289	576	155	272	786	1 008	3 293	171	155
Carson City, NV	2 238	5.8	41 046	164	1 294	376	77	228	476	491	1 975	92	77
Casper, WY	4 888	6.5	59 890	11	2 343	292	219	730	1 210	536	3 584	206	219

1. Based on the resident population estimated as of July 1 of the year shown.

Table C. Metropolitan Areas — Earnings, Social Security, and Housing

Area name	Earnings, 2014 (cont.) — Percent by selected industries									Social Security beneficiaries, December 2014		Supplemental Security Income recipients, December 2014	Housing units, 2015	
	Farm	Mining	Construction	Manufacturing	Information, professional, scientific, technical services	Retail trade	Finance, insurance, real estate, rental and leasing	Health care and social assistance	Government	Number	Rate[1]		Total	Percent change, 2000–2015
	75	76	77	78	79	80	81	82	83	84	85	86	87	88
Abilene, TX	0.5	10.3	7.4	3.4	5.8	6.8	6.2	12.7	22.8	31 130	185	4 617	70 931	1.7
Akron, OH	0.0	0.2	5.2	14.1	8.3	6.6	5.9	14.0	14.4	136 290	193	16 954	313 488	0.3
Albany, GA	2.9	D	D	D	D	6.5	D	15.7	25.8	30 840	199	7 163	66 489	0.5
Albany, OR	2.2	D	6.7	23.0	3.2	7.0	2.9	11.2	16.7	27 605	231	3 300	49 164	0.7
Albany-Schenectady-Troy, NY	0.2	0.4	6.2	7.0	12.5	5.6	7.4	11.0	29.4	178 205	202	19 976	398 546	1.3
Albuquerque, NM	0.3	0.2	6.2	5.8	D	6.8	6.1	12.3	26.0	165 640	183	23 804	381 626	1.9
Alexandria, LA	1.0	D	9.4	8.1	D	7.7	D	D	23.6	32 085	207	7 851	66 402	2.8
Allentown-Bethlehem-Easton, PA-NJ	0.2	D	D	12.0	8.1	6.2	5.6	16.2	12.8	179 040	216	19 420	345 227	0.9
Altoona, PA	1.4	0.4	4.9	13.8	6.1	8.2	3.1	19.6	16.6	30 445	242	4 841	56 011	-0.5
Amarillo, TX	2.5	D	D	11.9	D	7.5	5.8	D	15.4	40 750	156	4 504	107 873	4.3
Ames, IA	1.2	D	6.8	15.9	7.0	4.7	3.1	7.0	39.3	12 210	128	646	38 569	4.8
Anchorage, AK	0.0	5.2	8.3	1.1	12.2	6.0	5.3	12.5	26.6	46 240	116	7 399	156 278	1.2
Ann Arbor, MI	0.1	0.0	2.4	8.8	16.4	4.3	4.4	11.0	36.5	54 985	154	5 451	150 075	1.7
Anniston-Oxford-Jacksonville, AL	1.1	D	2.8	15.0	4.5	8.2	3.2	10.2	31.9	29 195	252	4 829	53 326	0.1
Appleton, WI	2.0	D	8.2	22.1	D	6.3	7.8	D	11.5	40 880	177	2 769	95 885	3.3
Asheville, NC	0.8	0.1	5.6	13.1	D	8.6	5.1	D	16.1	113 890	258	10 204	218 117	2.1
Athens-Clarke County, GA	3.5	0.2	3.6	9.7	D	6.4	6.4	14.4	33.0	32 085	161	4 688	83 878	2.6
Atlanta-Sandy Springs-Roswell, GA	0.2	D	D	6.8	18.5	5.8	D	8.9	12.0	789 130	141	111 322	2 239 194	3.0
Atlantic City-Hammonton, NJ	0.7	D	6.5	D	6.2	7.1	3.8	15.1	23.8	56 410	205	6 891	127 865	1.0
Auburn-Opelika, AL	0.4	0.1	5.2	12.5	5.1	7.3	4.4	6.6	34.5	23 600	153	3 419	66 382	6.4
Augusta-Richmond County, GA-SC	0.4	D	6.0	D	8.3	6.1	4.2	10.8	29.2	114 305	196	16 945	251 168	3.9
Austin-Round Rock, TX	0.0	2.2	6.8	9.3	18.4	6.0	9.1	8.6	16.2	224 195	115	27 432	784 346	11.0
Bakersfield, CA	7.4	9.8	6.4	5.0	5.4	5.6	3.7	7.9	22.7	114 465	131	34 191	293 574	3.2
Baltimore-Columbia-Towson, MD	0.1	D	D	4.6	15.5	5.0	8.5	12.4	23.3	465 735	167	68 234	1 155 341	2.0
Bangor, ME	0.4	D	5.3	5.0	5.3	9.7	4.2	22.6	20.6	35 935	234	5 489	74 331	0.6
Barnstable Town, MA	0.1	0.1	10.1	2.5	9.4	9.5	6.7	16.9	19.8	69 375	323	3 336	162 118	1.1
Baton Rouge, LA	0.2	0.6	15.0	11.9	9.7	5.8	D	10.2	17.2	133 410	162	25 414	345 301	4.7
Battle Creek, MI	0.6	D	3.6	20.9	D	5.0	2.0	13.4	21.8	31 855	236	4 941	60 602	-0.7
Bay City, MI	0.8	0.1	3.8	13.2	12.8	8.1	3.6	17.8	18.4	28 345	267	3 279	47 973	-0.5
Beaumont-Port Arthur, TX	-0.1	D	13.3	23.3	D	6.9	D	9.8	13.0	78 270	193	13 648	175 558	3.6
Beckley, WV	-0.1	14.6	4.8	4.2	5.7	8.9	2.9	D	21.2	34 585	280	6 309	57 507	-0.1
Bellingham, WA	3.4	0.2	8.5	14.2	7.6	8.3	5.1	11.9	18.9	40 555	195	4 468	93 247	2.8
Bend-Redmond, OR	0.0	0.1	10.2	6.2	11.8	8.9	7.1	18.0	14.2	39 350	231	2 254	83 873	4.7
Billings, MT	1.0	D	D	D	D	D	D	D	12.4	31 980	192	2 625	74 482	5.1
Binghamton, NY	0.3	0.2	5.4	15.6	D	6.7	4.1	14.6	26.3	58 225	235	7 928	111 802	-0.9
Birmingham-Hoover, AL	0.3	0.9	8.3	7.7	D	6.0	11.7	12.9	13.9	243 350	213	37 087	509 664	1.9
Bismarck, ND	0.7	D	9.2	D	9.0	7.3	D	16.8	19.7	21 920	173	1 382	57 904	15.7
Blacksburg-Christiansburg-Radford, VA	0.4	0.2	5.0	20.8	D	6.1	3.4	8.5	33.2	34 785	192	3 300	79 457	1.4
Bloomington, IL	2.4	D	3.6	5.0	D	4.8	21.1	D	15.3	28 440	149	2 000	79 033	2.4
Bloomington, IN	0.3	0.4	4.6	14.7	D	5.7	4.2	D	31.4	25 850	157	2 213	70 493	1.9
Bloomsburg-Berwick, PA	0.8	D	5.4	11.5	D	5.3	5.2	D	15.0	20 065	234	2 016	37 642	0.5
Boise City, ID	1.8	D	7.0	13.1	D	8.4	D	D	15.1	113 125	170	12 102	260 390	5.8
Boston-Cambridge-Newton, MA-NH	0.1	0.1	4.8	8.0	21.1	4.3	13.7	12.4	11.1	788 115	166	108 152	1 917 255	1.8
Boston, MA Div 14454	0.0	D	4.4	3.3	18.1	3.9	21.0	14.8	12.1	316 345	161	55 000	804 241	2.3
Cambridge-Newton-Framingham, MA Div 15764	0.1	0.1	5.0	12.5	25.4	4.1	6.5	10.2	10.1	387 590	165	48 672	930 960	1.3
Rockingham County-Strafford County, NH 40484	0.1	0.1	6.9	10.7	12.5	8.8	10.2	10.0	11.9	84 180	197	4 480	182 054	2.0
Boulder, CO	0.1	0.5	3.8	12.2	31.1	4.9	5.4	9.3	14.6	41 290	132	2 528	132 457	4.2
Bowling Green, KY	1.8	D	D	D	D	8.7	D	12.4	17.3	31 415	189	5 556	71 928	4.4
Bremerton-Silverdale, WA	0.0	0.1	4.9	2.1	7.3	6.0	3.1	10.7	52.9	48 630	191	5 139	109 690	2.2
Bridgeport-Stamford-Norwalk, CT	0.0	0.1	4.2	9.2	14.2	5.2	26.9	8.5	7.5	148 140	157	12 136	366 122	1.4
Brownsville-Harlingen, TX	0.7	0.2	3.8	5.2	3.9	9.4	4.2	20.6	28.3	61 070	145	23 087	147 492	3.9
Brunswick, GA	0.1	D	4.9	D	5.3	8.0	4.1	7.7	33.4	24 930	217	2 883	59 222	2.1
Buffalo-Cheektowaga-Niagara Falls, NY	0.3	D	4.5	12.1	8.6	6.2	7.5	12.6	22.2	256 205	225	33 546	520 981	0.4
Burlington, NC	0.3	0.1	5.7	16.4	4.3	7.9	5.2	21.3	11.3	32 665	209	3 369	68 493	2.8
Burlington-South Burlington, VT	1.2	D	6.6	12.5	D	7.1	5.9	D	20.3	38 440	178	4 472	95 117	3.0
California-Lexington Park, MD	0.0	D	4.1	0.7	25.7	3.8	1.5	6.2	45.7	14 925	135	1 586	43 625	5.7
Canton-Massillon, OH	0.6	2.5	6.9	19.9	5.6	6.8	6.0	15.9	12.3	91 245	226	10 179	179 318	0.2
Cape Coral-Fort Myers, FL	0.3	0.2	8.2	3.1	10.2	9.8	6.4	12.1	19.4	172 795	254	12 730	379 018	2.1
Cape Girardeau, MO-IL	1.7	0.2	D	11.0	D	7.9	D	D	15.4	21 045	216	2 571	42 912	1.0
Carbondale-Marion, IL	1.1	3.4	5.0	5.9	4.3	6.8	5.0	16.2	36.5	24 425	193	3 167	59 550	1.0
Carson City, NV	0.2	D	3.6	9.0	5.5	6.9	4.8	14.4	37.9	12 610	231	990	23 445	-0.4
Casper, WY	0.3	20.2	9.6	4.5	5.2	5.7	5.7	12.0	12.1	13 640	167	1 186	36 067	6.7

1. Per 1,000 resident population estimated as of July 1, 2011 of the year shown.

Table C. Metropolitan Areas — Housing, Labor Force, and Employment

Area name	Housing units, 2014								Civilian labor force, 2015				Civilian employment⁵, 2014		
	Occupied units										Unemployment			Percent	
	Owner-occupied					Renter-occupied									
				Median owner cost as a percent of income											
	Total	Percent	Median value¹	With a mortgage	Without a mortgage²	Median rent³	Median rent as a percent of income	Percent with a computer	Total	Percent change, 2013–2014	Total	Rate⁴	Total employed	Management, professional, and related occupations	Construction, production, and related occupations
	89	90	91	92	93	94	95	96	97	98	99	100	101	102	103
Abilene, TX	59 932	61.5	98 900	19.7	12.1	814	31.2	86.9	75 160	-1.2	2 918	3.9	73 410	29.0	26.1
Akron, OH	283 364	65.7	134 700	20.6	12.0	756	29.0	86.3	359 928	0.2	17 722	4.9	347 452	36.8	20.8
Albany, GA	57 795	54.0	104 400	19.5	11.7	712	32.7	77.6	65 508	-1.5	4 561	7.0	59 482	29.7	25.8
Albany, OR	45 907	66.8	167 400	22.1	13.0	842	35.4	88.8	54 608	0.9	3 760	6.9	48 173	28.7	29.1
Albany-Schenectady-Troy, NY	347 291	64.0	196 900	22.0	13.3	931	28.3	88.0	449 051	0.7	20 323	4.5	442 927	43.0	16.6
Albuquerque, NM	342 552	65.6	173 700	22.6	10.0	814	32.2	83.6	413 907	-0.2	25 644	6.2	401 350	39.7	17.6
Alexandria, LA	53 802	63.5	120 700	19.7	10.0	758	30.4	77.1	67 099	0.6	4 350	6.5	57 907	30.5	25.0
Allentown-Bethlehem-Easton, PA-NJ	315 376	69.9	195 900	23.3	15.6	945	32.0	84.8	429 733	0.7	22 433	5.2	404 235	33.2	23.9
Altoona, PA	49 678	71.5	112 500	19.7	13.3	645	29.5	76.7	61 018	0.2	3 053	5.0	58 115	29.4	26.2
Amarillo, TX	95 667	64.3	121 800	19.5	10.8	801	28.3	82.5	130 021	-0.6	4 067	3.1	126 380	32.5	22.5
Ames, IA	35 880	51.8	167 000	18.8	10.0	797	35.9	94.4	57 365	1.3	1 377	2.4	51 244	47.5	17.4
Anchorage, AK	135 449	62.4	272 700	21.9	10.0	1 234	31.4	94.8	203 081	-0.1	11 420	5.6	194 941	37.2	23.0
Ann Arbor, MI	137 240	60.2	212 400	19.6	11.7	981	31.1	92.4	189 852	0.9	6 701	3.5	179 686	53.0	12.9
Anniston-Oxford-Jacksonville, AL	46 087	68.8	106 500	21.0	10.0	598	33.0	82.4	46 051	-2.5	3 214	7.0	48 114	28.9	30.4
Appleton, WI	90 046	71.0	158 500	20.4	12.3	714	24.5	89.1	129 446	0.7	5 068	3.9	124 032	31.8	28.6
Asheville, NC	182 129	67.1	183 200	22.0	10.9	807	30.2	84.0	219 079	2.4	10 085	4.6	202 727	35.4	22.6
Athens-Clarke County, GA	71 814	51.4	153 200	19.6	10.0	815	36.3	85.2	93 471	0.7	5 119	5.5	86 392	43.0	18.7
Atlanta-Sandy Springs-Roswell, GA	1 981 447	62.4	170 300	21.4	10.3	982	31.1	89.8	2 836 326	1.0	158 458	5.6	2 654 680	40.0	18.9
Atlantic City-Hammonton, NJ	101 937	66.7	217 000	28.5	16.5	1 018	35.6	84.5	127 666	-3.8	11 962	9.4	129 393	31.1	16.5
Auburn-Opelika, AL	57 880	58.0	156 000	21.5	10.0	748	43.0	85.5	71 548	0.2	3 660	5.1	68 479	39.0	20.8
Augusta-Richmond County, GA-SC	208 479	66.6	132 100	20.5	11.2	754	30.8	81.7	256 201	0.2	16 187	6.3	238 378	33.6	22.4
Austin-Round Rock, TX	703 976	57.1	217 900	21.9	12.6	1 063	30.1	91.1	1 069 773	2.1	36 048	3.4	999 617	44.1	15.8
Bakersfield, CA	261 135	56.6	183 100	23.9	11.4	870	31.9	80.3	393 764	-0.3	40 212	10.2	328 210	26.4	34.6
Baltimore-Columbia-Towson, MD	1 032 604	65.5	279 900	22.6	11.3	1 166	30.6	87.7	1 472 177	0.7	79 478	5.4	1 384 210	45.3	15.2
Bangor, ME	61 218	68.5	135 500	21.2	14.4	706	33.9	82.9	76 643	-3.0	3 649	4.8	71 558	36.1	19.9
Barnstable Town, MA	95 697	79.4	359 700	26.5	15.0	1 054	31.0	88.0	111 332	-0.2	7 011	6.3	104 476	41.4	15.9
Baton Rouge, LA	305 096	65.6	157 500	19.7	10.0	830	30.7	83.9	421 898	1.6	22 770	5.4	387 732	34.4	23.6
Battle Creek, MI	52 385	71.2	95 800	21.4	13.8	734	29.3	79.8	64 682	0.5	3 159	4.9	56 162	27.5	31.6
Bay City, MI	42 706	78.5	104 600	20.2	13.1	647	32.3	80.1	52 570	-1.5	2 902	5.5	45 622	30.5	24.9
Beaumont-Port Arthur, TX	152 806	66.7	93 900	21.9	11.4	757	29.3	73.7	176 632	-1.3	11 852	6.7	166 332	29.9	28.6
Beckley, WV	49 335	76.6	93 600	18.5	10.0	648	27.1	78.2	47 037	-1.8	3 652	7.8	45 905	27.4	22.9
Bellingham, WA	81 973	62.5	273 500	25.6	12.0	936	35.9	89.5	102 918	1.6	6 110	5.9	99 061	35.8	21.2
Bend-Redmond, OR	66 218	65.6	257 200	25.5	11.4	945	32.5	91.9	84 185	3.8	5 024	6.0	79 420	36.4	20.9
Billings, MT	66 824	68.1	195 500	22.0	10.8	771	27.1	85.4	87 832	2.4	2 885	3.3	86 048	32.9	25.7
Binghamton, NY	99 298	66.7	113 600	21.0	13.7	732	33.0	84.9	110 454	-1.4	6 582	6.0	111 784	36.5	19.6
Birmingham-Hoover, AL	439 531	67.5	145 500	21.7	11.5	797	30.9	81.6	531 231	-0.9	29 231	5.5	509 071	35.6	22.3
Bismarck, ND	53 813	69.2	203 300	19.1	10.0	741	24.4	86.9	67 337	2.4	1 739	2.6	67 426	39.7	20.2
Blacksburg-Christiansburg-Radford, VA	67 185	61.1	164 800	21.7	10.8	782	32.2	80.3	91 365	0.0	4 211	4.6	82 510	39.3	18.2
Bloomington, IL	72 551	64.7	157 800	19.4	11.2	751	27.6	88.0	99 036	0.1	4 873	4.9	98 890	41.7	14.8
Bloomington, IN	61 929	57.7	155 400	19.8	10.0	834	36.8	89.4	76 540	-0.6	3 850	5.0	79 469	44.5	18.5
Bloomsburg-Berwick, PA	33 873	71.9	147 100	20.9	13.1	748	31.0	80.0	43 034	-1.0	2 240	5.2	38 494	31.9	26.8
Boise City, ID	240 402	67.3	173 200	21.0	10.0	828	28.2	89.5	324 068	2.3	13 105	4.0	304 049	37.3	21.0
Boston-Cambridge-Newton, MA-NH	1 777 817	61.2	375 200	23.2	14.4	1 247	30.1	88.7	2 564 753	0.6	113 599	4.4	2 491 650	47.4	14.4
Boston, MA Div 14454	738 496	57.2	377 800	23.5	14.4	1 288	30.8	87.8	1 052 776	0.6	49 260	4.7	1 023 697	45.7	13.5
Cambridge-Newton-Framingham, MA Div 15764	873 442	62.3	400 200	22.8	14.0	1 254	29.6	89.1	1 263 377	0.6	55 659	4.4	1 235 281	49.8	14.1
Rockingham County-Strafford County, NH 40484	165 879	72.8	264 300	23.8	16.4	1 026	29.9	91.1	248 600	0.7	8 680	3.5	232 672	41.4	20.0
Boulder, CO	123 690	61.2	383 100	21.2	10.0	1 204	33.5	94.8	176 726	-0.2	5 599	3.2	168 639	51.4	11.9
Bowling Green, KY	61 834	61.9	124 900	19.9	10.0	685	27.3	79.8	75 913	-2.7	3 704	4.9	75 105	29.7	30.2
Bremerton-Silverdale, WA	95 249	65.3	255 200	23.3	11.5	1 028	31.5	92.5	115 211	1.5	6 315	5.5	108 617	38.4	20.1
Bridgeport-Stamford-Norwalk, CT	338 421	67.2	408 900	24.7	16.6	1 382	32.6	90.0	479 044	0.5	25 273	5.3	471 048	44.5	14.1
Brownsville-Harlingen, TX	121 009	66.9	76 200	23.8	12.1	653	33.4	64.7	164 295	-1.2	11 692	7.1	150 394	27.4	21.6
Brunswick, GA	43 618	65.2	128 900	23.7	10.8	805	27.7	84.7	50 101	0.5	3 114	6.2	48 182	28.6	23.1
Buffalo-Cheektowaga-Niagara Falls, NY	470 564	66.4	125 400	20.0	13.4	739	29.9	81.9	550 798	-0.1	30 681	5.6	544 689	37.1	19.1
Burlington, NC	62 799	65.4	133 700	22.1	13.0	770	32.0	82.6	77 083	0.5	4 123	5.3	71 695	32.1	24.7
Burlington-South Burlington, VT	85 222	67.1	254 400	22.9	14.0	1 149	31.8	90.8	126 711	-0.4	3 745	3.0	119 255	44.8	18.2
California-Lexington Park, MD	39 179	69.2	291 300	20.8	12.6	1 236	28.4	89.0	54 498	0.7	2 701	5.0	53 934	42.9	20.9
Canton-Massillon, OH	159 604	68.2	123 600	20.0	11.3	683	27.3	82.9	200 293	-0.8	10 635	5.3	189 978	31.6	25.4
Cape Coral-Fort Myers, FL	263 295	67.0	163 400	24.4	12.7	940	30.8	86.7	319 967	2.8	16 084	5.0	278 917	31.3	18.5
Cape Girardeau, MO-IL	37 842	68.7	129 100	21.5	11.4	673	28.4	79.0	49 351	0.8	2 306	4.7	45 291	32.1	23.0
Carbondale-Marion, IL	50 423	61.5	107 300	19.4	11.0	670	30.7	82.8	60 747	1.2	3 619	6.0	54 690	37.6	16.4
Carson City, NV	21 228	57.9	199 400	21.9	11.8	738	30.8	84.0	25 103	-0.1	1 821	7.3	24 340	33.0	17.9
Casper, WY	33 323	62.9	206 600	20.6	10.4	849	24.2	86.2	42 894	-1.3	2 053	4.8	43 966	28.4	29.7

1. Specified owner-occupied units.　2. A value of 10.0 represents 10 percent or less.　3. Specified renter-occupied units.　4. Percent of civilian labor force.
5. Persons 16 years old and over.

Table C. Metropolitan Areas — **Nonfarm Employment and Agriculture**

Area name		Private nonfarm establishments, employment and payroll, 2014								Agriculture, 2012			
			Employment					Annual payroll		Farms			
											Percent with:		
	Number of establishments	Total	Health care and social assistance	Manufacturing	Retail trade	Finance and insurance	Professional, scientific, and technical services	Total (mil dol)	Average per employee (dollars)	Number	Fewer than 50 acres	500 acres or more	Farm operators whose principal occupation is farming (percent)
	104	105	106	107	108	109	110	111	112	113	114	115	116
Abilene, TX	3 858	57 611	12 194	2 436	8 835	2 946	1 875	1 995	34 636	3 155	27.5	20.3	39.8
Akron, OH	16 419	291 083	51 724	39 596	38 042	10 946	17 109	12 756	43 821	1 151	60.7	2.6	42.5
Albany, GA..........................	3 169	46 393	9 308	4 089	7 966	1 480	2 476	1 628	35 100	1 198	26.8	25.6	51.3
Albany, OR..........................	2 441	33 472	5 027	7 038	4 770	1 071	859	1 239	37 011	2 083	64.8	6.7	48.7
Albany-Schenectady-Troy, NY	21 201	340 468	65 547	21 323	48 422	20 087	27 732	15 236	44 749	2 273	36.8	5.7	55.3
Albuquerque, NM.................	18 571	279 897	54 184	15 685	42 058	11 704	20 918	10 716	38 285	4 231	70.2	11.9	45.3
Alexandria, LA.....................	3 320	49 751	14 237	3 938	7 946	1 612	1 919	1 840	36 990	1 091	50.4	9.6	45.6
Allentown-Bethlehem-Easton, PA-NJ	18 280	308 398	59 738	33 897	43 353	11 168	12 267	14 251	46 208	1 963	61.2	4.5	50.2
Altoona, PA	3 174	50 319	9 880	7 011	8 885	1 651	1 825	1 719	34 164	525	35.8	5.9	58.5
Amarillo, TX	6 279	94 941	18 543	11 347	15 249	4 406	3 032	3 528	37 165	1 976	22.8	38.7	41.6
Ames, IA.............................	2 003	31 660	5 246	5 112	5 092	732	1 249	1 213	38 315	966	42.8	20.9	49.1
Anchorage, AK.....................	10 799	164 797	28 252	2 037	18 836	5 392	15 597	9 950	60 378	291	56.7	5.8	56.4
Ann Arbor, MI	8 049	142 761	D	12 749	16 897	3 913	13 688	7 389	51 755	1 236	55.3	6.9	48.8
Anniston-Oxford-Jacksonville, AL	2 309	35 096	6 106	5 854	6 129	912	1 013	1 137	32 401	592	45.4	3.5	46.1
Appleton, WI	5 795	110 641	13 053	22 612	14 428	5 720	3 854	4 743	42 867	1 889	38.0	10.1	54.9
Asheville, NC	11 745	156 217	34 061	19 231	25 953	3 869	5 811	5 672	36 307	2 844	60.2	1.6	46.2
Athens-Clarke County, GA ...	4 475	58 608	11 748	6 195	9 484	1 599	2 333	2 054	35 041	1 616	44.1	3.8	45.4
Atlanta-Sandy Springs-Roswell, GA	134 212	2 178 578	244 292	137 589	259 255	111 258	187 507	114 276	52 454	7 760	52.7	3.4	47.1
Atlantic City-Hammonton, NJ	6 365	110 726	17 978	1 492	16 780	2 751	4 383	3 981	35 949	402	69.4	2.2	61.4
Auburn-Opelika, AL..............	2 576	39 528	5 721	6 520	6 702	1 012	1 363	1 224	30 971	315	32.7	7.6	37.1
Augusta-Richmond County, GA-SC..............................	10 318	179 942	35 180	21 068	25 338	4 536	10 453	7 324	40 704	2 510	43.7	8.4	37.1
Austin-Round Rock, TX	46 884	745 697	89 664	42 592	98 831	34 508	78 996	38 585	51 744	8 819	46.4	7.9	42.5
Bakersfield, CA	12 480	192 765	29 321	11 663	30 011	5 985	12 845	8 555	44 382	1 938	40.6	26.6	63.2
Baltimore-Columbia-Towson, MD....................	66 213	1 123 100	197 903	51 726	142 698	51 978	125 802	57 923	51 574	3 518	57.8	6.3	45.2
Bangor, ME..........................	4 138	57 535	14 011	3 445	11 094	1 902	1 773	2 025	35 192	677	36.9	7.7	51.7
Barnstable Town, MA	8 390	72 254	16 114	2 084	14 572	2 181	4 641	3 134	43 378	333	91.9	0.0	58.0
Baton Rouge, LA	17 862	338 772	46 527	24 732	43 311	14 911	22 727	16 455	48 572	2 686	48.6	11.1	41.9
Battle Creek, MI	2 617	61 843	19 006	13 013	6 127	974	2 212	2 725	44 067	1 023	35.1	10.8	45.7
Bay City, MI	2 234	30 512	7 125	3 480	5 474	915	1 435	1 142	37 420	766	36.9	14.6	54.4
Beaumont-Port Arthur, TX ...	7 908	129 190	19 185	20 976	19 939	3 241	5 709	6 408	49 603	2 545	62.5	8.0	39.3
Beckley, WV.........................	2 608	38 372	9 179	1 646	6 619	755	1 080	1 490	38 841	564	42.7	2.0	46.8
Bellingham, WA	6 279	71 947	9 416	9 493	11 589	2 322	3 435	2 883	40 068	1 702	74.7	2.5	45.4
Bend-Redmond, OR	6 260	56 454	9 972	4 230	9 835	1 870	2 788	2 144	37 978	1 283	78.9	3.0	44.0
Billings, MT	5 965	71 014	14 000	3 420	11 343	3 737	3 552	2 953	41 576	2 213	37.5	28.2	51.1
Binghamton, NY...................	5 075	82 583	16 188	8 631	13 060	2 992	6 557	3 276	39 669	1 099	28.7	5.8	51.4
Birmingham-Hoover, AL.......	25 260	445 333	67 238	37 771	57 776	34 241	22 020	20 854	46 829	3 790	43.5	4.7	44.9
Bismarck, ND.......................	3 912	58 623	12 720	2 043	8 811	2 481	3 720	2 722	46 428	2 367	19.9	43.7	50.3
Blacksburg-Christiansburg-Radford, VA	3 475	49 430	6 970	11 619	8 421	1 116	2 569	1 784	36 092	2 289	33.6	7.4	43.5
Bloomington, IL....................	4 035	81 138	9 183	4 449	10 060	21 239	2 758	4 103	50 571	2 000	33.3	27.9	55.6
Bloomington, IN	3 173	51 752	9 307	8 064	7 613	1 562	2 070	1 902	36 746	1 011	43.5	5.5	39.1
Bloomsburg-Berwick, PA	1 842	37 443	11 392	5 829	4 136	D	1 291	1 745	46 596	1 403	39.2	3.6	41.6
Boise City, ID	16 914	234 236	39 143	21 336	31 560	10 869	17 035	9 928	42 383	5 077	68.9	8.0	48.3
Boston-Cambridge-Newton, MA-NH	125 686	2 363 791	434 898	149 577	260 184	151 707	229 073	153 529	64 950	3 363	72.9	1.0	51.7
Boston, MA Div 14454........	NA	NA	NA	NA	NA	NA	NA	NA	NA	1 090	75.3	1.7	51.9
Cambridge-Newton-Framingham, MA Div 15764	NA	NA	NA	NA	NA	NA	NA	NA	NA	1 261	76.8	0.5	54.0
Rockingham County-Strafford County, NH 40484	NA	NA	NA	NA	NA	NA	NA	NA	NA	1 012	65.6	0.9	48.7
Boulder, CO	11 932	145 558	19 729	14 554	17 389	3 414	27 024	8 918	61 265	855	72.0	4.3	44.9
Bowling Green, KY	3 502	55 872	9 259	9 736	8 109	1 791	1 944	2 039	36 500	4 063	37.3	5.2	37.4
Bremerton-Silverdale, WA	5 607	55 893	12 375	1 939	10 964	1 859	3 976	2 039	36 477	706	94.9	0.1	44.6
Bridgeport-Stamford-Norwalk, CT	27 022	408 854	65 138	33 195	50 234	39 358	35 959	31 864	77 935	439	82.2	1.6	57.9
Brownsville-Harlingen, TX.....	6 312	100 798	31 505	4 656	18 218	3 266	3 413	2 660	26 393	1 305	66.3	11.5	45.4
Brunswick, GA	2 807	33 005	4 899	2 347	5 600	856	947	1 093	33 113	324	56.2	3.7	47.8
Buffalo-Cheektowaga-Niagara Falls, NY.................	27 077	474 220	83 488	52 971	65 597	29 802	30 529	19 705	41 553	1 804	46.1	5.9	55.5
Burlington, NC......................	3 138	51 102	8 405	8 439	8 950	1 512	1 284	1 809	35 395	732	42.5	4.6	41.7
Burlington-South Burlington, VT	6 739	99 680	18 857	11 476	15 101	3 429	6 669	4 297	43 109	1 444	38.6	8.4	53.3
California-Lexington Park, MD..................................	1 925	28 959	4 224	308	4 563	482	8 638	1 436	49 587	632	48.3	3.3	53.6
Canton-Massillon, OH..........	8 684	143 440	28 599	26 051	20 813	6 151	4 305	5 313	37 039	1 901	47.2	4.1	44.3
Cape Coral-Fort Myers, FL...	16 857	193 523	34 032	4 649	37 239	5 488	10 246	7 063	36 496	844	79.5	4.5	48.1
Cape Girardeau, MO-IL	2 697	40 531	10 529	4 243	6 590	1 078	1 238	1 414	34 890	2 071	24.4	11.8	46.4
Carbondale-Marion, IL	2 923	39 025	9 313	3 358	7 579	1 924	1 291	1 343	34 401	1 485	39.5	8.6	40.9
Carson City, NV	1 930	20 718	3 645	2 917	3 289	1 004	1 141	887	42 823	21	81.0	4.8	47.6
Casper, WY..........................	2 982	36 040	5 766	1 656	5 167	976	1 791	1 766	49 012	397	31.5	33.5	49.4

Table C. Metropolitan Areas — **Agriculture**

	Agriculture, 2012 (cont.)															
	Land in farms					Value of land and buildings (dollars)			Value of products sold				Percent of farms with sales of:		Government payments	
			Acres								Percent from:					
Area name	Acreage (1,000)	Percent change, 2007–2012	Average size of farm	Total irrigated (1,000)	Total cropland (1,000)	Average per farm	Average per acre	Value of machinery and equipment, average per farm (dollars)	Total (mil dol)	Average per farm (dollars)	Crops	Live-stock and poultry products	$10,000 or more	$100,000 or more	Total ($1,000)	Percent of farms
	117	118	119	120	121	122	123	124	125	126	127	128	129	130	131	132
Abilene, TX	1 705	1.2	540	5.4	548.0	675 529	1 250	64 184	110.8	35 122	41.5	58.5	27.1	5.7	11 170	39.2
Akron, OH	100	2.0	87	0.6	68.4	497 519	5 734	73 795	55.0	47 754	76.4	23.6	32.8	7.7	730	15.8
Albany, GA	667	-1.6	557	133.4	343.6	1 500 641	2 694	179 389	412.2	344 040	D	D	40.2	26.3	14 085	67.6
Albany, OR	331	-12.0	159	28.7	227.5	769 891	4 840	89 696	241.2	115 812	77.1	22.9	31.3	11.7	882	6.8
Albany-Schenectady-Troy, NY	349	3.8	154	2.1	195.0	515 614	3 356	92 574	222.7	97 955	43.5	56.5	44.1	12.2	2 936	21.7
Albuquerque, NM	3 835	22.5	906	62.8	101.5	520 688	574	45 045	143.0	33 799	34.8	65.2	16.8	3.0	4 887	10.8
Alexandria, LA	259	13.1	237	21.5	149.1	585 570	2 467	92 173	140.1	128 375	87.5	12.5	39.2	14.7	4 367	22.2
Allentown-Bethlehem-Easton, PA-NJ	235	-5.0	120	3.0	178.6	1 046 204	8 721	96 891	234.9	119 650	69.2	30.8	41.4	13.2	2 510	23.3
Altoona, PA	90	3.1	172	0.3	63.3	783 611	4 565	106 916	107.7	205 145	16.2	83.8	54.1	29.0	1 416	32.6
Amarillo, TX	2 889	-6.3	1 462	76.3	812.6	1 152 791	788	110 223	776.4	392 933	10.2	89.8	35.3	15.3	17 080	54.4
Ames, IA	306	-13.1	317	0.4	279.4	2 482 983	7 838	205 934	292.8	303 082	79.6	20.4	60.0	37.3	6 566	73.5
Anchorage, AK	36	-5.2	125	1.3	17.1	879 979	7 039	92 491	30.0	103 158	47.3	52.7	46.0	14.8	354	17.5
Ann Arbor, MI	170	2.0	138	3.6	133.5	701 358	5 095	92 338	87.8	71 004	77.0	23.0	42.5	14.6	3 466	31.7
Anniston-Oxford-Jacksonville, AL	81	6.6	137	0.9	21.4	418 128	3 046	61 630	92.4	156 052	11.8	88.2	30.1	7.3	406	17.4
Appleton, WI	393	-1.5	208	0.5	330.9	1 115 648	5 361	173 377	515.4	272 862	31.0	69.0	61.8	35.6	9 190	64.6
Asheville, NC	212	-8.8	75	4.9	54.9	530 540	7 101	45 581	136.0	47 831	76.2	23.8	23.8	5.0	4 540	21.5
Athens-Clarke County, GA	206	-7.3	128	3.1	51.5	642 869	5 039	60 082	508.8	314 880	D	D	40.8	20.5	1 712	22.3
Atlanta-Sandy Springs-Roswell, GA	856	-11.2	110	D	215.3	543 881	4 933	53 993	D	D	D	89.5	28.3	9.1	4 842	13.1
Atlantic City-Hammonton, NJ	29	-2.9	73	11.3	18.9	903 438	12 320	135 682	125.4	312 040	98.2	1.8	51.7	25.4	247	8.2
Auburn-Opelika, AL	59	-6.6	187	0.9	12.2	707 330	3 775	71 403	D	D	D	D	32.4	4.8	692	19.0
Augusta-Richmond County, GA-SC	486	-7.1	194	35.2	183.2	584 162	3 018	74 457	284.3	113 255	D	D	27.8	8.0	5 008	22.2
Austin-Round Rock, TX	1 754	0.4	199	7.7	419.3	808 944	4 067	50 217	284.5	32 265	49.0	51.0	22.8	4.2	8 012	15.2
Bakersfield, CA	2 330	-1.3	1 202	730.0	899.4	5 332 548	4 435	332 960	3 999.0	2 063 462	80.8	19.2	62.0	43.8	5 306	15.5
Baltimore-Columbia-Towson, MD	491	-2.0	140	18.6	347.9	1 191 135	8 534	104 999	452.4	128 582	71.1	28.9	36.1	15.2	9 885	34.4
Bangor, ME	113	-1.4	167	2.3	35.6	336 186	2 015	63 316	50.2	74 084	32.3	67.7	33.4	9.0	1 044	13.3
Barnstable Town, MA	5	-10.6	14	1.2	1.5	500 691	35 657	50 009	19.1	57 438	50.8	49.2	40.5	11.4	358	7.5
Baton Rouge, LA	778	11.7	290	9.9	343.2	876 897	3 026	117 136	323.6	120 465	81.1	18.9	34.9	8.5	4 656	17.8
Battle Creek, MI	225	-1.4	220	10.7	175.6	807 980	3 676	117 543	133.0	130 044	64.6	35.4	43.4	17.5	3 618	47.7
Bay City, MI	194	4.0	253	6.3	174.5	1 015 918	4 017	198 977	165.3	215 789	95.1	4.9	58.6	31.9	2 628	68.0
Beaumont-Port Arthur, TX	534	-2.4	210	24.5	151.1	428 972	2 044	65 018	D	D	61.3	D	20.2	3.9	D	7.7
Beckley, WV	60	-14.3	106	0.1	14.3	263 496	2 476	45 762	4.7	8 395	30.8	69.2	17.6	0.9	113	6.6
Bellingham, WA	116	12.9	68	35.5	78.7	786 343	11 554	80 437	357.3	209 937	33.5	66.5	31.2	15.5	3 425	17.6
Bend-Redmond, OR	131	1.3	102	34.0	28.9	716 430	7 015	52 158	20.6	16 033	54.1	45.9	22.1	2.4	241	3.4
Billings, MT	3 168	2.8	1 431	153.0	623.2	1 177 360	822	103 667	315.1	142 371	29.9	70.1	43.6	18.2	7 886	34.5
Binghamton, NY	188	-3.0	171	0.8	88.8	383 313	2 246	75 197	67.5	61 384	27.2	72.8	38.1	10.1	1 882	27.6
Birmingham-Hoover, AL	513	-2.6	135	2.7	128.0	458 537	3 386	57 174	D	D	D	85.7	31.0	7.8	2 312	11.9
Bismarck, ND	3 139	-0.4	1 326	D	1 364.8	1 479 235	1 116	191 431	553.1	233 661	65.8	34.2	59.5	31.8	14 391	59.9
Blacksburg-Christiansburg-Radford, VA	414	15.3	181	0.6	112.1	662 932	3 664	64 339	94.6	41 344	26.5	73.5	38.9	5.9	931	8.9
Bloomington, IL	888	1.5	444	1.7	836.5	3 533 991	7 961	280 254	655.9	327 951	88.7	11.3	65.4	44.9	16 405	79.7
Bloomington, IN	148	4.9	147	0.2	90.1	573 007	3 907	66 578	36.5	36 101	77.0	23.0	28.7	6.9	2 291	40.3
Bloomsburg-Berwick, PA	166	-3.8	118	0.8	114.7	580 503	4 899	80 597	121.8	86 797	63.4	36.6	41.8	15.0	2 766	44.8
Boise City, ID	1 376	9.6	271	450.6	446.8	761 085	2 809	98 357	1 071.7	211 086	40.0	60.0	38.2	14.9	5 503	19.9
Boston-Cambridge-Newton, MA-NH	191	4.6	57	D	D	712 383	12 555	55 708	253.6	75 420	84.7	15.3	34.7	10.3	D	8.9
Boston, MA Div 14454	74	19.8	67	D	D	891 116	13 214	60 695	120.7	110 755	90.5	9.5	43.8	17.3	D	10.9
Cambridge-Newton-Framingham, MA Div 15764	51	-18.0	40	2.3	19.9	798 193	19 881	52 883	101.7	80 665	85.3	14.7	33.8	9.3	689	7.1
Rockingham County-Strafford County, NH 40484	67	12.4	66	0.6	16.6	412 952	6 267	53 856	31.2	30 825	59.9	40.1	26.1	4.1	647	8.9
Boulder, CO	133	-3.4	155	30.1	39.2	888 591	5 715	49 384	33.9	39 629	D	D	22.8	5.8	474	12.0
Bowling Green, KY	630	-10.3	155	0.9	296.1	450 659	2 907	60 060	230.6	56 745	43.0	57.0	32.9	7.2	12 288	43.1
Bremerton-Silverdale, WA	10	-34.2	14	0.5	2.5	377 215	26 446	27 010	5.3	7 513	70.0	30.0	14.3	1.4	30	2.5
Bridgeport-Stamford-Norwalk, CT	54	36.4	123	0.3	5.0	1 492 513	12 145	68 132	34.8	79 317	60.1	39.9	35.3	7.5	160	5.5
Brownsville-Harlingen, TX	310	-11.4	237	112.3	209.2	697 056	2 937	84 762	160.4	122 916	91.9	8.1	32.1	13.3	4 851	45.4
Brunswick, GA	44	9.4	136	1.1	8.7	388 679	2 857	67 997	11.6	35 846	55.8	44.2	34.9	5.6	164	18.2
Buffalo-Cheektowaga-Niagara Falls, NY	285	-2.2	158	4.8	212.4	415 481	2 625	122 739	255.8	141 808	53.9	46.1	43.5	15.7	3 547	25.3
Burlington, NC	84	-4.9	114	0.9	31.8	538 171	4 715	60 452	32.9	44 986	46.8	53.2	30.3	9.2	470	17.5
Burlington-South Burlington, VT	279	-0.6	193	1.2	119.8	630 386	3 264	113 641	245.7	170 130	23.2	76.8	49.6	23.2	4 004	28.6
California-Lexington Park, MD	67	-2.3	106	0.7	41.2	700 921	6 603	80 758	21.8	34 494	87.4	12.6	42.6	6.6	783	30.1
Canton-Massillon, OH	242	-5.1	127	0.9	163.8	601 600	4 726	95 972	169.9	89 370	50.8	49.2	43.9	14.1	2 682	27.0
Cape Coral-Fort Myers, FL	87	1.6	103	13.6	22.8	979 161	9 485	53 895	105.9	125 478	95.8	4.2	32.8	7.3	61	1.7
Cape Girardeau, MO-IL	516	-7.6	249	23.3	288.5	677 065	2 720	76 665	135.0	65 193	69.5	30.5	45.0	10.6	5 488	50.7
Carbondale-Marion, IL	318	-0.3	214	1.5	245.1	874 978	4 091	111 110	89.9	60 533	84.5	15.5	29.9	10.2	4 275	53.7
Carson City, NV	D	D	D	D	D	665 048	D	108 429	5.8	275 476	D	D	23.8	19.0	0	0.0
Casper, WY	1 691	-22.5	4 259	28.9	43.3	2 656 418	624	133 912	42.9	108 118	16.5	83.5	49.6	23.7	634	11.3

Table C. Metropolitan Areas — **Water Use, Wholesale Trade, Retail Trade, and Real Estate**

Area name	Water use, 2010		Wholesale trade,[1] 2012				Retail trade, 2012				Real estate and rental and leasing, 2012			
	Total water withdrawn (mil gal/day)	Gallons withdrawn per person per day	Number of establishments	Number of employees	Sales (mil dol)	Annual payroll (mil dol)	Number of establishments	Number of employees	Sales (mil dol)	Annual payroll (mil dol)	Number of establishments	Number of employees	Receipts (mil dol)	Annual payroll (mil dol)
	133	134	135	136	137	138	139	140	141	142	143	144	145	146
Abilene, TX	21.8	132	176	1 943	2 557.2	95.4	635	8 371	2 538.9	202.1	180	928	155.6	28.5
Akron, OH	74.8	106	959	16 088	10 045.5	927.1	2 193	36 505	10 384.1	905.1	581	3 191	582.1	118.3
Albany, GA	207.0	1 316	166	2 133	1 897.2	109.2	661	7 757	1 874.7	166.1	173	654	113.5	20.4
Albany, OR	122.6	1 051	110	1 396	1 066.7	61.3	343	4 753	1 181.6	112.6	112	360	48.5	10.2
Albany-Schenectady-Troy, NY	321.9	370	768	10 035	9 506.1	543.4	3 028	46 426	12 455.2	1 118.7	852	4 632	1 021.3	171.6
Albuquerque, NM	433.7	489	858	10 480	5 775.8	508.1	2 448	39 437	11 245.8	996.7	1 062	4 578	876.4	161.5
Alexandria, LA	553.2	3 594	125	1 550	829.5	59.6	611	7 996	2 294.7	193.6	139	605	92.0	18.4
Allentown-Bethlehem-Easton, PA-NJ	369.3	450	772	D	D	D	2 695	41 717	11 314.2	976.6	587	2 615	648.7	95.6
Altoona, PA	22.8	179	119	1 832	2 258.4	80.7	561	8 383	2 286.7	189.4	87	349	72.9	11.3
Amarillo, TX	123.5	490	260	D	D	D	938	13 922	4 425.5	331.7	311	1 431	287.9	48.9
Ames, IA	12.5	140	74	D	D	D	288	4 708	1 084.2	98.5	97	465	75.5	16.1
Anchorage, AK	80.0	210	376	5 526	3 282.6	311.4	1 104	18 668	6 005.9	551.5	458	2 584	669.6	118.4
Ann Arbor, MI	34.8	101	276	3 580	4 695.9	221.8	1 106	16 577	4 461.1	411.4	306	2 409	727.2	115.9
Anniston-Oxford-Jacksonville, AL	29.3	247	97	1 792	1 808.8	73.6	477	5 954	1 463.5	134.1	73	299	48.9	8.0
Appleton, WI	73.0	324	317	5 089	7 620.6	259.7	838	14 534	3 696.4	314.4	151	909	163.8	28.6
Asheville, NC	424.0	998	417	3 984	2 143.2	168.3	1 837	23 933	6 137.5	569.6	585	1 756	316.6	56.7
Athens-Clarke County, GA	27.9	145	148	2 155	2 079.7	100.6	698	9 141	2 257.6	195.6	262	1 199	223.1	41.9
Atlanta-Sandy Springs-Roswell, GA	727.7	138	6 996	107 280	102 221.8	6 641.1	16 888	246 883	69 477.9	6 136.7	6 808	39 825	11 502.2	2 232.5
Atlantic City-Hammonton, NJ	60.1	219	188	D	D	D	1 227	16 099	4 292.7	394.9	227	1 383	351.1	52.0
Auburn-Opelika, AL	18.2	130	75	613	504.3	28.3	477	6 450	1 632.1	141.6	113	544	81.0	16.0
Augusta-Richmond County, GA-SC	436.2	772	357	3 678	1 952.8	163.5	1 851	25 118	6 639.8	563.7	437	1 920	386.4	62.5
Austin-Round Rock, TX	622.0	362	1 641	32 902	77 904.9	2 642.0	5 621	89 835	27 852.9	2 331.3	2 421	13 215	2 998.0	631.2
Bakersfield, CA	2 159.9	2 572	582	7 990	6 987.9	447.4	1 867	27 918	8 640.6	700.7	634	3 492	733.6	141.3
Baltimore-Columbia-Towson, MD	1 090.7	402	2 653	43 211	33 873.6	2 572.3	8 871	136 209	36 505.4	3 449.0	2 795	19 455	6 677.9	965.9
Bangor, ME	58.4	379	162	1 794	955.4	82.3	735	10 931	3 203.1	249.6	172	692	123.3	22.9
Barnstable Town, MA	60.8	282	178	1 152	563.1	57.0	1 503	14 395	3 856.9	401.4	331	1 361	260.5	53.1
Baton Rouge, LA	1 239.1	1 544	845	10 959	7 974.1	590.2	2 873	41 392	11 292.1	987.8	756	4 551	944.6	171.3
Battle Creek, MI	28.1	206	94	D	D	D	488	5 858	1 702.3	133.4	87	373	53.9	10.5
Bay City, MI	608.3	5 644	87	D	D	D	419	5 526	1 303.0	124.5	65	212	29.3	4.7
Beaumont-Port Arthur, TX	666.7	1 654	332	D	D	D	1 448	19 217	5 663.9	474.7	349	2 085	437.8	84.0
Beckley, WV	20.1	161	121	1 426	797.4	63.4	480	6 740	1 866.3	161.3	95	343	58.6	10.9
Bellingham, WA	85.5	425	289	D	D	D	818	11 310	3 103.6	272.4	317	1 131	230.9	34.3
Bend-Redmond, OR	157.5	998	215	1 262	794.9	57.1	755	9 365	2 476.6	244.0	388	1 252	186.1	40.0
Billings, MT	877.3	5 520	322	4 747	3 237.2	233.6	785	10 572	3 334.4	283.3	295	944	166.8	30.7
Binghamton, NY	53.6	213	221	4 201	3 365.7	177.8	851	12 657	3 114.1	278.6	172	857	183.5	28.1
Birmingham-Hoover, AL	1 815.0	1 609	1 513	21 833	21 530.8	1 180.9	4 281	55 841	15 249.7	1 379.9	996	8 182	1 597.3	354.4
Bismarck, ND	501.2	4 367	167	2 362	2 105.2	126.5	482	8 216	2 621.2	219.6	175	522	124.1	17.1
Blacksburg-Christiansburg-Radford, VA	192.7	1 081	90	1 056	758.2	44.7	577	8 143	1 993.7	173.5	149	710	129.1	23.9
Bloomington, IL	781.5	4 199	196	2 867	9 734.4	185.1	632	10 111	2 662.2	218.4	152	748	151.6	23.1
Bloomington, IN	20.8	130	92	D	D	D	496	7 814	1 773.2	154.5	170	872	153.9	27.8
Bloomsburg-Berwick, PA	29.3	342	59	568	308.6	21.9	290	4 075	1 072.1	84.0	49	223	36.9	7.0
Boise City, ID	2 865.1	4 647	717	9 901	8 538.3	497.1	1 977	28 218	8 072.2	735.4	879	3 055	510.1	96.5
Boston-Cambridge-Newton, MA-NH	2 405.3	528	5 066	88 499	106 488.4	6 697.2	16 564	252 652	67 308.1	6 697.1	4 796	35 738	12 052.3	2 087.3
Boston, MA Div 14454	663.8	352	2 008	33 191	36 166.3	2 246.6	6 851	101 678	27 541.6	2 754.3	2 231	19 179	5 940.4	1 278.7
Cambridge-Newton-Framingham, MA Div 15764	851.4	379	2 486	47 467	61 732.6	3 937.2	7 741	118 530	31 382.5	3 150.4	2 169	14 713	5 717.1	730.1
Rockingham County-Strafford County, NH 40484	890.2	2 128	572	7 841	8 589.5	513.4	1 972	32 444	8 384.0	792.4	396	1 846	394.9	78.5
Boulder, CO	231.6	786	392	D	D	D	1 174	16 623	4 498.3	478.9	648	1 954	434.3	74.5
Bowling Green, KY	26.0	164	146	2 040	2 960.5	92.7	612	7 922	1 892.4	170.4	138	455	86.7	13.4
Bremerton-Silverdale, WA	32.1	128	147	953	407.9	43.7	731	10 343	2 674.2	276.3	338	979	198.5	32.7
Bridgeport-Stamford-Norwalk, CT	494.3	539	1 190	18 611	130 674.8	1 622.4	3 459	49 401	15 166.5	1 553.9	1 077	6 971	1 808.6	418.1
Brownsville-Harlingen, TX	281.5	693	317	D	D	D	1 119	16 624	4 124.8	353.2	312	1 338	185.5	32.2
Brunswick, GA	67.9	604	74	557	307.6	22.2	550	5 299	1 579.2	123.8	151	526	71.9	16.6
Buffalo-Cheektowaga-Niagara Falls, NY	850.2	749	1 177	20 641	20 849.6	1 106.2	4 078	62 656	14 627.6	1 352.0	929	6 446	944.0	207.0
Burlington, NC	23.9	158	143	1 642	627.2	70.0	624	8 756	2 108.4	178.0	119	607	142.0	24.4
Burlington-South Burlington, VT	29.4	139	297	4 885	4 395.2	271.4	1 064	14 768	3 638.0	362.7	265	1 377	284.2	51.6
California-Lexington Park, MD	7.9	75	39	397	189.5	17.6	294	4 835	1 227.0	109.5	83	312	94.7	11.4
Canton-Massillon, OH	48.2	119	346	D	D	D	1 326	20 654	5 535.1	470.3	296	1 352	222.3	43.0
Cape Coral-Fort Myers, FL	746.6	1 207	585	5 144	2 481.0	232.6	2 517	34 453	9 445.3	850.6	1 218	3 992	856.4	135.9
Cape Girardeau, MO-IL	52.7	548	147	1 565	935.9	65.4	468	6 306	1 709.0	140.0	117	357	56.4	9.7
Carbondale-Marion, IL	287.2	2 269	86	962	442.8	38.2	496	7 467	2 124.6	170.2	128	537	79.1	12.7
Carson City, NV	17.0	307	89	519	276.4	25.2	212	3 139	918.2	92.6	111	304	51.7	9.5
Casper, WY	172.3	2 283	163	1 890	2 052.7	115.2	363	4 796	1 487.5	132.1	166	1 281	502.0	79.4

1. Merchant wholesalers, except manufacturers' sales branches and offices.

Table C. Metropolitan Areas — Professional Services, Manufacturing, and Accommodation and Food Services

Area name	Professional, scientific, and technical services, 2012				Manufacturing, 2012				Accommodation and food services, 2012			
	Number of establishments	Number of employees	Sales (mil dol)	Annual payroll (mil dol)	Number of establishments	Number of employees	Sales (mil dol)	Annual payroll (mil dol)	Number of establishments	Number of employees	Sales (mil dol)	Annual payroll (mil dol)
	147	148	149	150	151	152	153	154	155	156	157	158
Abilene, TX	299	1 868	194.5	76.5	116	2 406	992.5	98.2	336	6 732	316.9	88.9
Akron, OH	1 724	D	D	D	1 081	37 550	12 567.9	1 871.0	1 499	26 419	1 225.2	330.6
Albany, GA	275	D	D	D	94	4 213	3 493.7	214.9	265	4 706	212.9	55.7
Albany, OR	164	802	84.8	27.8	181	6 318	2 253.6	355.2	216	2 796	130.4	35.5
Albany-Schenectady-Troy, NY	2 313	26 033	4 405.1	1 717.2	595	20 698	8 060.7	1 223.8	2 284	31 820	1 736.9	489.3
Albuquerque, NM	2 521	19 811	3 610.6	1 150.8	673	16 378	18 058.5	841.3	1 667	37 340	1 989.1	578.5
Alexandria, LA	291	2 261	243.0	96.9	83	4 158	3 339.5	228.1	242	4 406	219.3	59.1
Allentown-Bethlehem-Easton, PA-NJ	1 634	D	D	D	869	32 882	16 436.0	1 734.7	1 774	27 527	1 808.3	436.2
Altoona, PA	221	1 789	208.3	74.8	135	6 943	2 115.6	298.8	280	4 634	199.4	56.5
Amarillo, TX	528	4 274	538.8	182.4	202	12 867	D	784.6	570	11 176	558.8	151.3
Ames, IA	203	1 114	118.0	53.3	77	4 821	2 787.2	256.8	229	4 269	172.6	48.0
Anchorage, AK	1 306	14 431	2 646.4	1 004.2	227	2 272	533.7	104.8	988	16 739	1 241.7	373.4
Ann Arbor, MI	1 284	13 390	2 329.9	928.1	332	13 232	5 419.9	725.8	766	14 879	764.9	216.3
Anniston-Oxford-Jacksonville, AL	167	1 140	137.1	43.1	114	5 957	2 713.2	256.9	212	4 673	199.1	53.0
Appleton, WI	449	3 485	517.6	187.4	428	21 791	8 825.3	1 062.6	548	9 700	377.0	104.3
Asheville, NC	1 233	5 652	612.7	253.5	461	21 831	6 553.6	987.3	1 127	20 288	1 165.0	336.4
Athens-Clarke County, GA	490	D	D	D	138	5 949	2 145.1	259.3	423	7 878	354.2	96.4
Atlanta-Sandy Springs-Roswell, GA	20 920	192 024	36 037.1	13 725.0	3 762	131 702	60 486.1	6 477.2	10 694	208 494	11 868.4	3 260.4
Atlantic City-Hammonton, NJ	579	D	D	D	96	1 730	285.4	72.3	860	46 661	4 008.5	1 282.5
Auburn-Opelika, AL	202	1 474	138.0	55.1	111	5 903	2 386.1	248.4	323	5 947	271.6	70.4
Augusta-Richmond County, GA-SC	996	10 922	2 764.6	797.1	318	21 316	13 266.7	1 143.5	960	18 609	852.8	232.8
Austin-Round Rock, TX	7 256	69 730	13 548.4	5 417.0	1 301	36 984	15 784.9	2 157.4	4 053	85 096	5 071.2	1 406.8
Bakersfield, CA	1 204	11 757	1 641.3	637.3	391	12 257	6 890.7	558.2	1 278	19 829	1 092.2	284.0
Baltimore-Columbia-Towson, MD	9 506	117 982	27 098.7	9 886.3	1 631	53 494	22 199.6	3 275.5	5 570	101 810	6 089.2	1 659.1
Bangor, ME	328	1 831	179.4	84.5	134	3 749	977.7	164.0	315	5 639	313.9	86.7
Barnstable Town, MA	733	4 806	932.9	341.7	187	2 157	478.6	119.4	1 143	13 117	1 000.4	291.5
Baton Rouge, LA	2 138	19 451	3 087.2	1 126.7	600	24 133	84 643.9	1 778.4	1 507	31 681	1 626.7	447.9
Battle Creek, MI	191	1 058	93.0	55.5	148	11 179	5 445.1	599.3	280	6 023	471.2	104.3
Bay City, MI	152	1 360	111.0	57.1	123	3 650	1 149.4	190.6	233	4 039	172.0	47.6
Beaumont-Port Arthur, TX	660	6 726	1 077.1	423.5	306	19 149	87 422.5	1 568.3	696	13 367	637.8	171.8
Beckley, WV	173	1 086	132.0	51.1	91	1 641	553.6	79.4	222	4 178	236.4	65.2
Bellingham, WA	685	D	D	D	330	9 613	14 932.2	552.3	509	8 282	492.9	140.6
Bend-Redmond, OR	708	2 631	332.0	120.7	279	3 672	801.8	165.8	498	7 635	435.6	133.5
Billings, MT	633	3 693	634.7	205.6	194	3 225	6 885.5	187.0	459	8 438	477.5	128.8
Binghamton, NY	367	6 531	973.4	425.8	217	8 946	2 639.1	451.7	611	8 814	423.6	115.1
Birmingham-Hoover, AL	2 690	22 265	3 914.9	1 383.4	950	36 531	14 836.4	1 827.0	2 010	38 797	2 033.2	578.4
Bismarck, ND	374	3 124	490.9	182.4	110	1 833	2 998.6	96.0	234	6 184	336.0	92.0
Blacksburg-Christiansburg-Radford, VA	367	3 392	325.8	170.0	150	10 969	5 682.6	565.9	373	6 964	301.9	84.2
Bloomington, IL	386	2 942	289.8	127.8	106	4 393	1 771.6	220.2	417	8 625	412.8	114.3
Bloomington, IN	311	2 082	246.1	100.7	121	7 695	1 717.9	331.8	386	8 168	348.3	95.8
Bloomsburg-Berwick, PA	129	1 126	188.9	47.4	91	5 908	1 754.0	238.8	198	3 192	148.0	39.5
Boise City, ID	1 928	13 673	1 947.4	772.0	589	22 032	7 099.3	1 212.2	1 277	21 430	964.4	276.0
Boston-Cambridge-Newton, MA-NH	17 311	225 723	55 357.8	21 911.7	4 533	156 284	58 110.8	10 067.9	11 697	202 244	13 543.1	3 886.6
Boston, MA Div 14454	7 073	89 222	22 948.5	8 531.9	1 450	39 895	17 097.4	2 241.3	5 103	100 153	7 073.7	2 041.1
Cambridge-Newton-Framingham, MA Div 15764	8 954	126 579	31 082.5	12 822.1	2 521	97 905	35 508.6	6 773.6	5 459	84 611	5 476.4	1 556.1
Rockingham County-Strafford County, NH 40484	1 284	9 922	1 326.8	557.7	562	18 483	5 504.8	1 052.9	1 135	17 480	993.0	289.4
Boulder, CO	2 679	27 395	4 767.9	2 011.5	536	14 305	5 061.5	998.4	866	15 855	842.2	252.2
Bowling Green, KY	234	2 203	185.8	65.7	139	8 810	5 362.6	440.2	302	6 331	297.6	79.1
Bremerton-Silverdale, WA	710	D	D	D	161	1 817	328.2	80.7	468	7 138	426.0	124.0
Bridgeport-Stamford-Norwalk, CT	3 481	40 694	8 738.6	3 975.9	837	35 507	13 412.5	2 338.2	2 266	30 574	2 153.3	604.6
Brownsville-Harlingen, TX	488	2 359	258.4	81.1	204	4 414	1 709.6	D	660	12 582	635.1	171.7
Brunswick, GA	292	912	121.5	41.1	69	2 197	1 010.8	131.0	298	7 042	409.6	125.3
Buffalo-Cheektowaga-Niagara Falls, NY	2 463	30 722	3 833.2	1 742.2	1 281	50 593	18 970.4	2 713.2	2 800	50 984	2 927.8	734.8
Burlington, NC	218	1 375	133.0	55.8	200	9 268	3 138.4	399.3	293	5 761	254.4	71.8
Burlington-South Burlington, VT	835	6 611	972.3	417.1	251	12 671	4 891.5	690.5	546	9 006	513.9	150.4
California-Lexington Park, MD	309	8 327	1 654.0	640.7	28	225	D	9.6	184	3 670	166.6	48.1
Canton-Massillon, OH	700	D	D	D	546	24 034	12 551.6	1 116.3	810	14 329	648.0	180.0
Cape Coral-Fort Myers, FL	1 893	12 312	2 202.7	844.3	366	4 010	812.8	165.1	1 189	25 851	1 346.6	402.6
Cape Girardeau, MO-IL	172	D	D	D	113	3 999	D	193.2	192	4 338	177.5	50.6
Carbondale-Marion, IL	229	1 325	133.9	48.4	81	2 421	971.3	104.4	288	5 651	235.2	66.8
Carson City, NV	295	1 180	170.1	60.0	122	2 798	634.0	162.7	159	2 740	133.4	41.2
Casper, WY	278	1 537	222.4	83.2	83	2 428	1 780.3	163.0	200	3 814	198.2	57.4

Table C. Metropolitan Areas — Health Care and Social Assistance, Other Services, Nonemployer Business and Residential Construction

Area name	Health care and social assistance, 2012				Other services, 2012				Nonemployer business, 2014		Value of residential construction authorized by building permits, 2015	
	Number of establishments	Number of employees	Receipts (mil dol)	Annual payroll (mil dol)	Number of establishments	Number of employees	Receipts (mil dol)	Annual payroll (mil dol)	Number	Receipts (mil dol)	New construction ($1,000)	Number of housing units
	159	160	161	162	163	164	165	166	167	168	169	170
Abilene, TX	420	12 633	1 064.8	421.7	248	1 857	152.3	42.3	12 310	593.8	81 096	535
Akron, OH	1 786	51 155	5 068.1	2 050.0	1 311	8 916	974.1	243.0	47 511	2 059.4	209 694	967
Albany, GA	382	9 907	968.2	368.4	222	1 234	112.6	30.5	11 549	356.7	23 405	203
Albany, OR	216	4 660	422.3	174.0	142	D	D	D	5 783	241.1	80 934	365
Albany-Schenectady-Troy, NY	2 412	64 310	6 091.5	2 533.7	1 611	10 243	1 081.3	347.0	52 286	2 367.4	591 439	3 623
Albuquerque, NM	2 205	54 420	5 690.4	2 313.8	1 276	8 132	814.0	238.6	51 801	2 055.0	439 471	2 295
Alexandria, LA	523	14 367	1 529.4	560.2	209	1 068	107.6	28.5	8 844	403.8	47 213	289
Allentown-Bethlehem-Easton, PA-NJ	2 401	61 400	6 250.5	2 499.5	1 579	9 010	803.1	234.6	49 600	2 306.7	236 634	1 356
Altoona, PA	438	11 356	1 149.5	472.4	283	1 573	118.4	36.7	6 089	289.5	24 723	117
Amarillo, TX	705	17 438	1 952.4	701.1	411	2 866	350.5	85.9	19 119	962.6	175 163	880
Ames, IA	192	4 855	513.2	206.0	146	1 000	136.1	27.5	5 358	227.5	97 639	555
Anchorage, AK	1 432	29 237	4 067.7	1 509.4	703	4 435	578.7	152.7	27 259	1 363.5	482 982	1 767
Ann Arbor, MI	964	36 873	4 710.2	2 219.2	537	3 891	489.6	143.2	28 506	1 242.6	104 778	420
Anniston-Oxford-Jacksonville, AL	273	5 785	573.5	221.0	177	785	80.2	23.3	6 546	233.9	9 098	61
Appleton, WI	543	12 265	1 384.9	558.4	419	3 088	266.3	78.8	12 215	584.5	172 276	1 119
Asheville, NC	1 307	30 548	3 452.0	1 394.1	737	3 776	386.7	106.2	40 767	1 617.7	484 452	2 161
Athens-Clarke County, GA	602	10 408	1 274.7	512.7	271	1 723	235.1	52.1	14 924	573.7	183 401	1 159
Atlanta-Sandy Springs-Roswell, GA	13 077	230 926	28 008.1	10 487.2	8 560	59 105	7 668.8	1 894.6	545 604	22 150.9	5 318 834	30 342
Atlantic City-Hammonton, NJ	846	17 487	1 969.3	780.4	563	3 588	293.9	85.2	16 335	801.3	112 218	710
Auburn-Opelika, AL	235	5 923	541.5	218.4	172	787	72.8	18.6	9 606	420.9	240 681	838
Augusta-Richmond County, GA-SC	1 277	35 811	4 187.5	1 602.4	658	3 832	374.8	102.8	36 663	1 301.3	509 232	3 035
Austin-Round Rock, TX	4 433	83 036	9 710.8	3 783.2	3 006	24 324	2 984.0	872.5	172 337	8 956.4	3 669 933	22 370
Bakersfield, CA	1 550	27 833	3 675.0	1 265.4	835	5 099	567.8	153.6	44 623	2 196.1	473 930	2 200
Baltimore-Columbia-Towson, MD	7 428	200 484	23 846.6	9 213.0	4 781	37 448	4 255.3	1 233.4	207 015	9 046.0	1 339 099	8 264
Bangor, ME	547	14 740	1 570.2	624.9	273	1 395	142.7	36.9	9 243	363.0	74 118	555
Barnstable Town, MA	811	15 781	1 766.8	730.5	590	3 176	320.4	95.6	25 490	1 313.5	198 776	572
Baton Rouge, LA	1 918	48 310	4 807.8	1 827.7	1 261	11 145	1 308.9	452.0	62 757	2 656.6	731 562	3 569
Battle Creek, MI	323	9 313	966.4	421.9	208	1 173	448.4	41.7	6 605	228.3	9 584	59
Bay City, MI	329	7 152	682.5	261.2	190	928	70.8	21.3	5 499	200.1	17 296	147
Beaumont-Port Arthur, TX	1 025	20 354	1 951.3	701.4	504	3 670	393.6	111.7	24 373	1 028.0	183 850	1 132
Beckley, WV	389	9 454	898.0	354.7	168	1 168	124.8	32.5	5 277	188.8	17 629	100
Bellingham, WA	659	9 901	1 026.2	422.5	404	2 282	239.2	70.4	14 710	696.7	219 961	1 144
Bend-Redmond, OR	608	9 398	1 114.0	442.5	329	1 526	156.8	41.9	16 143	828.6	473 441	2 227
Billings, MT	592	12 939	1 549.9	590.1	389	2 186	239.0	59.9	12 666	638.8	296 135	1 764
Binghamton, NY	503	15 897	1 582.1	639.3	406	2 142	171.4	48.5	12 828	525.9	38 405	249
Birmingham-Hoover, AL	2 524	70 853	8 979.9	3 315.2	1 607	12 325	1 613.1	398.1	79 484	3 501.7	704 038	3 733
Bismarck, ND	340	12 237	1 180.9	537.1	316	1 975	246.8	63.0	9 644	558.3	182 833	1 082
Blacksburg-Christiansburg-Radford, VA	372	6 334	730.0	254.0	270	1 359	225.8	39.1	9 268	350.6	76 389	476
Bloomington, IL	399	9 128	1 008.2	385.5	286	2 409	221.6	77.3	10 289	415.5	50 704	396
Bloomington, IN	352	9 328	950.4	366.4	231	1 973	270.3	56.9	10 403	409.4	76 768	395
Bloomsburg-Berwick, PA	264	11 077	1 817.3	664.3	149	727	110.5	18.4	4 243	182.7	36 166	190
Boise City, ID	1 829	37 600	3 759.2	1 594.1	1 010	5 254	477.6	141.0	49 095	2 160.2	1 109 579	5 499
Boston-Cambridge-Newton, MA-NH	13 000	422 688	48 286.9	20 807.5	10 259	72 079	8 446.7	2 368.1	368 828	20 718.0	3 259 037	15 036
Boston, MA Div 14454	5 263	214 091	25 294.2	10 889.4	4 533	34 135	4 287.4	1 114.9	144 710	8 417.1	1 801 155	7 937
Cambridge-Newton-Framingham, MA Div 15764	6 569	186 471	20 460.6	8 918.9	4 846	33 113	3 711.6	1 116.2	190 360	10 284.6	1 199 963	5 745
Rockingham County-Strafford County, NH 40484	1 168	22 126	2 532.1	999.2	880	4 831	447.8	137.0	33 758	2 016.4	257 919	1 354
Boulder, CO	1 332	18 386	2 129.6	841.9	717	4 415	670.1	176.7	37 760	1 966.9	354 113	1 249
Bowling Green, KY	444	8 799	924.0	349.4	242	1 169	98.7	28.3	11 793	603.8	140 418	1 147
Bremerton-Silverdale, WA	685	11 861	1 272.8	484.3	382	1 789	149.7	48.6	14 142	608.4	244 718	918
Bridgeport-Stamford-Norwalk, CT	2 827	63 963	8 087.6	3 291.8	2 103	13 041	1 654.3	420.8	90 880	6 355.3	726 201	2 598
Brownsville-Harlingen, TX	1 003	31 018	1 911.3	844.7	402	2 159	163.6	44.6	30 897	1 207.3	143 131	1 285
Brunswick, GA	291	5 206	657.2	240.4	169	806	89.7	19.1	8 530	358.1	136 363	535
Buffalo-Cheektowaga-Niagara Falls, NY	3 187	85 040	8 321.9	3 500.3	2 093	12 616	1 168.9	314.5	56 155	2 476.2	330 564	1 677
Burlington, NC	379	8 367	801.9	369.4	190	1 097	100.7	29.2	9 624	350.5	122 046	1 032
Burlington-South Burlington, VT	685	16 844	1 869.8	685.4	493	2 572	252.7	72.4	18 425	889.1	149 858	916
California-Lexington Park, MD	179	4 110	379.9	172.2	142	865	80.7	30.1	6 742	245.3	229 921	1 282
Canton-Massillon, OH	1 035	28 763	2 497.1	1 107.4	740	4 994	477.5	135.2	25 572	1 058.7	105 900	558
Cape Coral-Fort Myers, FL	1 488	26 009	3 362.1	1 226.1	1 209	6 696	580.1	164.2	61 657	2 964.1	1 380 982	6 879
Cape Girardeau, MO-IL	345	11 469	1 176.6	468.0	181	864	84.3	21.1	6 419	263.3	34 859	179
Carbondale-Marion, IL	371	9 440	1 194.8	410.7	186	915	94.1	22.5	7 463	255.5	13 853	137
Carson City, NV	224	3 744	510.8	182.9	126	660	62.8	19.0	4 902	408.2	9 311	43
Casper, WY	305	5 141	687.2	266.3	207	1 333	227.6	49.8	5 861	331.0	56 822	271

Table C. Metropolitan Areas — Government Employment and Payroll and Local Government Finances

Area name	Government employment and payroll, 2012									Local government finances, 2012				
			March payroll (percent of total)							General revenue				
												Taxes		
													Per capita[1] (dollars)	
	Full-time equivalent employees	March Payroll (dollars)	Administration, judicial, and legal	Police and corrections	Fire protection	Highways and transportation	Health and welfare	Natural resources and utilities	Education and libraries	Total (mil dol)	Inter-governmental (mil dol)	Total (mil dol)	Total	Property
	171	172	173	174	175	176	177	178	179	180	181	182	183	184
Abilene, TX	6 849	21 021 831	5.9	11.8	4.6	1.9	9.1	4.7	60.5	518.5	218.5	216.8	1 298	958
Akron, OH	26 841	107 374 120	7.1	9.8	5.3	5.1	11.5	6.3	53.1	3 076.7	1 096.1	1 324.2	1 886	1 236
Albany, GA	7 162	21 657 598	7.9	10.7	4.5	3.1	5.4	7.1	58.2	562.0	254.3	209.6	1 331	844
Albany, OR	3 984	16 207 525	6.1	11.2	5.6	4.0	5.1	4.9	61.9	447.9	223.4	146.4	1 237	1 133
Albany-Schenectady-Troy, NY	36 516	166 624 101	5.4	11.1	2.5	4.0	8.5	3.7	63.1	4 760.1	1 679.6	2 291.7	2 620	1 927
Albuquerque, NM	30 074	112 231 236	6.2	14.9	5.8	5.5	4.5	5.9	55.8	3 116.0	1 545.5	1 089.1	1 208	691
Alexandria, LA	6 219	18 920 106	10.2	14.7	7.3	3.5	1.6	5.7	54.5	537.9	262.7	207.5	1 343	529
Allentown-Bethlehem-Easton, PA-NJ	28 544	125 365 734	7.1	11.0	1.6	3.5	8.4	4.3	62.3	3 830.4	1 426.8	1 741.8	2 106	1 770
Altoona, PA	4 030	13 533 958	4.8	8.4	2.3	5.0	8.5	7.0	62.6	402.4	214.5	126.2	993	707
Amarillo, TX	11 385	38 289 774	6.0	11.5	5.0	2.8	5.4	3.4	64.4	911.4	355.4	389.8	1 513	1 141
Ames, IA	2 892	10 932 541	7.4	7.6	2.9	7.7	10.1	9.9	52.8	476.0	102.3	138.3	1 518	1 219
Anchorage, AK	12 850	64 974 760	5.2	7.0	5.6	4.8	2.6	8.4	65.2	1 699.8	812.1	683.6	1 741	1 513
Ann Arbor, MI	9 997	45 620 706	8.5	10.1	3.0	4.2	5.2	5.4	62.0	1 472.6	631.4	577.8	1 646	1 596
Anniston-Oxford-Jacksonville, AL	5 708	17 129 463	3.6	6.8	2.8	2.8	32.2	7.0	43.2	507.7	169.3	112.4	958	366
Appleton, WI	7 780	34 593 416	4.9	7.3	2.2	3.3	7.7	3.3	69.6	894.7	399.3	319.4	1 398	1 365
Asheville, NC	17 505	58 826 655	4.2	7.0	2.1	1.1	24.6	5.0	53.1	1 741.6	575.9	513.1	1 187	868
Athens-Clarke County, GA	7 394	23 449 444	6.9	10.8	3.3	3.2	5.2	6.6	61.6	987.4	199.2	256.9	1 308	933
Atlanta-Sandy Springs-Roswell, GA	203 403	731 570 783	7.2	9.5	4.1	4.5	5.7	5.0	62.5	20 074.6	5 922.8	9 520.7	1 744	1 190
Atlantic City-Hammonton, NJ.	14 001	71 971 044	5.3	13.7	4.7	1.7	5.3	3.8	63.4	1 749.6	507.4	1 016.6	3 691	3 639
Auburn-Opelika, AL	6 506	23 295 526	2.9	5.8	2.5	1.6	40.7	4.1	41.4	640.1	158.1	164.2	1 115	594
Augusta-Richmond County, GA-SC	20 099	65 183 308	7.2	9.6	2.7	2.9	4.2	5.7	66.1	1 739.1	746.8	669.1	1 162	761
Austin-Round Rock, TX	73 039	288 365 719	6.7	12.6	4.5	3.0	4.9	13.3	53.3	7 348.5	1 653.0	4 159.1	2 267	1 895
Bakersfield, CA	32 191	158 787 344	5.1	10.1	4.5	2.2	16.0	4.2	56.8	6 098.2	2 797.6	1 169.0	1 365	1 151
Baltimore-Columbia-Towson, MD	99 896	465 911 722	4.8	11.2	4.8	2.5	4.4	5.4	65.0	11 911.4	4 396.6	5 905.6	2 145	1 222
Bangor, ME	5 352	18 128 721	5.6	7.8	5.2	7.6	1.3	6.1	64.9	466.9	185.2	205.7	1 338	1 324
Barnstable Town, MA	7 548	35 968 725	7.2	11.5	10.0	4.2	3.5	6.4	53.6	1 003.5	207.7	645.0	2 994	2 809
Baton Rouge, LA	30 360	102 896 811	8.5	10.0	4.5	3.6	6.5	7.1	57.0	3 050.2	1 092.8	1 434.7	1 760	767
Battle Creek, MI	4 008	16 572 500	10.0	11.0	3.1	3.3	5.9	4.4	61.4	671.0	371.6	175.1	1 296	1 142
Bay City, MI	4 027	15 471 429	6.7	5.7	2.4	4.8	13.5	5.1	61.1	536.8	284.0	123.7	1 157	1 137
Beaumont-Port Arthur, TX	17 005	59 961 656	6.9	13.5	4.6	3.6	4.5	7.9	57.9	1 621.0	485.7	770.1	1 905	1 584
Beckley, WV	3 968	12 471 321	4.9	5.2	1.2	1.5	2.1	5.4	77.4	330.4	170.0	113.2	907	718
Bellingham, WA	5 120	25 193 563	10.0	10.9	7.5	8.7	1.8	7.1	50.4	696.1	261.3	292.4	1 424	871
Bend-Redmond, OR	4 773	21 188 503	8.1	12.1	5.4	2.6	5.0	7.0	55.3	649.0	217.1	283.8	1 749	1 579
Billings, MT	5 275	20 966 552	5.5	8.5	4.5	5.0	8.4	5.9	55.7	507.5	191.1	179.3	1 101	1 025
Binghamton, NY	11 995	45 564 792	4.9	8.0	2.3	4.3	9.9	2.6	66.0	1 446.5	620.9	619.4	2 492	1 689
Birmingham-Hoover, AL	41 677	145 061 797	5.5	12.3	6.2	3.5	6.2	8.1	54.6	3 941.4	1 461.0	1 685.8	1 483	659
Bismarck, ND	3 791	13 709 939	4.6	8.1	3.4	4.7	6.7	8.1	61.8	473.7	232.8	141.1	1 176	966
Blacksburg-Christiansburg-Radford, VA	5 444	17 603 156	8.2	10.4	0.7	3.0	3.2	6.1	64.4	493.5	224.5	187.6	1 048	749
Bloomington, IL	7 152	27 482 356	6.5	10.1	4.3	4.2	7.4	5.2	60.3	732.2	198.8	386.9	2 050	1 720
Bloomington, IN	4 067	13 951 012	10.1	10.5	4.9	5.1	2.9	7.9	58.1	391.1	166.8	163.4	1 006	789
Bloomsburg-Berwick, PA	2 432	8 805 660	6.5	10.1	0.0	3.5	1.8	3.7	73.5	290.1	113.0	109.7	1 287	914
Boise City, ID	19 235	61 842 070	8.7	13.8	5.3	3.5	3.2	5.5	58.0	1 734.2	757.9	596.2	935	874
Boston-Cambridge-Newton, MA-NH	153 708	758 103 739	4.2	10.4	7.6	2.3	4.2	5.6	63.4	20 238.4	6 374.7	10 961.5	2 362	2 272
Boston, MA Div 14454	62 159	318 038 206	3.6	12.1	8.7	2.3	3.8	6.0	61.6	8 478.9	2 834.2	4 659.2	2 419	2 297
Cambridge-Newton-Framingham, MA Div 15764	76 602	380 709 237	4.6	9.0	6.9	2.4	4.4	5.7	64.4	10 119.6	3 073.3	5 273.3	2 300	2 225
Rockingham County-Strafford County, NH 40484.	14 947	59 356 296	4.6	10.5	5.5	2.5	4.3	3.2	67.3	1 639.9	467.1	1 028.9	2 439	2 409
Boulder, CO	11 666	48 102 144	8.2	10.8	5.0	2.7	5.3	10.3	53.3	1 374.3	334.5	816.3	2 674	1 840
Bowling Green, KY	5 785	16 747 663	3.0	7.9	3.3	1.9	4.2	9.0	67.7	397.4	175.4	150.8	930	466
Bremerton-Silverdale, WA	6 732	32 797 634	7.2	7.7	9.1	6.6	1.0	9.5	56.8	1 053.2	532.7	344.8	1 352	960
Bridgeport-Stamford-Norwalk, CT	32 029	179 963 079	3.5	9.1	5.1	3.1	3.2	3.7	70.6	4 597.7	963.2	3 193.1	3 419	3 370
Brownsville-Harlingen, TX	21 552	67 816 703	3.9	8.4	2.8	2.4	1.6	5.2	74.0	1 662.8	982.8	420.5	1 012	795
Brunswick, GA	6 136	22 282 830	5.0	6.9	2.5	1.3	40.1	3.5	40.2	600.6	116.0	196.4	1 731	1 127
Buffalo-Cheektowaga-Niagara Falls, NY	44 201	202 514 083	3.8	12.1	3.3	3.0	5.4	4.9	65.5	6 495.4	2 759.6	2 637.8	2 326	1 539
Burlington, NC	1 005 835	17 822 770	4.1	10.8	2.8	1.7	7.8	5.8	64.0	420.3	210.4	147.7	960	694
Burlington-South Burlington, VT	8 073	32 538 734	4.7	5.9	2.3	6.1	0.9	7.3	71.2	830.6	537.1	145.5	681	585
California-Lexington Park, MD	3 187	14 069 480	5.9	10.5	0.0	2.3	1.5	4.3	73.2	356.5	125.4	191.8	1 760	923
Canton-Massillon, OH	12 345	44 734 873	4.8	6.7	4.6	4.4	2.5	5.9	70.3	1 381.0	667.7	493.7	1 224	920
Cape Coral-Fort Myers, FL	29 739	118 190 826	4.0	7.9	5.4	3.4	39.4	4.7	33.6	3 672.5	586.2	1 065.4	1 651	1 448
Cape Girardeau, MO-IL	3 276	8 670 805	6.6	8.7	4.7	6.8	1.2	9.4	60.9	259.7	107.2	113.5	1 169	651
Carbondale-Marion, IL	4 224	14 371 667	6.4	9.2	3.2	3.8	4.1	6.6	65.5	411.6	200.9	146.7	1 158	929
Carson City, NV	1 396	6 652 347	9.5	13.4	7.3	4.2	3.5	6.4	53.3	189.1	96.1	54.9	1 001	717
Casper, WY	3 954	15 321 295	4.4	7.8	3.5	2.3	2.0	5.1	72.5	442.5	254.7	108.8	1 384	938

1. Based on the resident population estimated as of July 1 of the year shown.

Area name	Local government finances, 2012 (cont.) Direct general expenditure		Percent of total for:					Debt outstanding		Government employment, 2014			Presidential election,[2] 2012 Percent of vote cast:		
	Total (mil dol)	Per capita[1] (dollars)	Educa-tion	Health and hospitals	Police protec-tion	Public welfare	High-ways	Total (mil dol)	Per capita[1] (dollars)	Federal civilian	Federal military	State and local	Demo-cratic	Republi-can	All other
	185	186	187	188	189	190	191	192	193	194	195	196	197	198	199
Abilene, TX	488.6	2 927	54.4	6.6	7.0	0.5	3.1	339.1	2 031	1 135	4 577	11 306	21.7	76.9	1.4
Akron, OH	2 952.8	4 205	42.5	10.2	5.2	4.1	3.5	4 519.2	6 435	2 305	1 808	44 793	56.0	42.5	1.5
Albany, GA	576.8	3 665	46.3	10.0	6.0	0.1	3.2	314.8	2 000	2 923	760	10 255	53.6	45.9	0.6
Albany, OR	449.1	3 794	51.6	3.6	6.2	0.4	4.4	449.9	3 801	318	321	5 950	39.6	56.3	4.1
Albany-Schenectady-Troy, NY	4 877.2	5 576	47.3	3.9	3.9	11.4	4.6	4 658.9	5 327	6 430	3 263	93 405	57.0	41.0	2.0
Albuquerque, NM	2 976.7	3 301	50.0	1.6	8.3	1.5	5.0	4 360.6	4 836	14 340	5 775	65 986	54.0	41.0	5.0
Alexandria, LA	559.7	3 624	51.4	0.1	8.2	0.1	5.0	528.4	3 421	2 999	680	10 593	32.2	66.4	1.4
Allentown-Bethlehem-Easton, PA-NJ	4 050.8	4 897	50.0	3.0	3.6	9.9	3.0	7 000.9	8 464	2 241	2 117	38 147	50.6	48.1	1.4
Altoona, PA	409.0	3 217	49.0	3.1	3.0	8.6	3.9	474.2	3 730	983	328	7 613	32.4	66.3	1.3
Amarillo, TX	915.3	3 553	53.8	4.6	5.9	0.0	2.6	933.7	3 625	2 114	670	18 053	18.8	79.8	1.4
Ames, IA	440.2	4 830	30.3	42.8	3.2	0.5	3.7	391.5	4 295	998	356	18 839	55.6	41.7	2.7
Anchorage, AK	1 661.6	4 233	54.5	2.2	8.1	0.0	6.1	2 262.7	5 764	8 682	14 591	25 094	NA	NA	NA
Ann Arbor, MI	1 495.8	4 262	46.0	12.6	6.5	0.9	4.9	2 033.3	5 794	3 943	622	69 842	67.3	31.4	1.3
Anniston-Oxford-Jacksonville, AL	517.7	4 414	32.7	36.2	5.9	0.0	3.9	358.0	3 052	3 912	575	8 286	33.5	65.3	1.2
Appleton, WI	965.9	4 228	54.4	2.6	5.2	4.9	9.0	758.9	3 322	669	666	11 842	47.2	51.2	1.6
Asheville, NC	1 591.2	3 680	36.5	20.8	7.4	7.0	1.7	929.8	2 150	3 356	1 136	22 887	48.4	49.8	1.8
Athens-Clarke County, GA	1 058.7	5 390	28.8	41.0	3.3	0.2	2.0	748.8	3 812	1 238	613	25 924	45.5	52.6	2.0
Atlanta-Sandy Springs-Roswell, GA	19 663.2	3 603	49.2	7.0	6.1	0.9	3.6	35 894.1	6 577	44 942	16 723	271 889	49.6	49.2	1.2
Atlantic City-Hammonton, NJ	1 718.6	6 240	52.7	0.6	6.1	2.1	1.7	1 314.6	4 773	2 608	919	20 990	58.0	41.1	0.9
Auburn-Opelika, AL	638.8	4 338	33.9	39.7	4.1	0.0	2.6	782.4	5 313	285	727	17 024	39.2	59.1	1.7
Augusta-Richmond County, GA-SC	1 747.7	3 035	52.5	4.4	5.9	0.3	3.6	1 584.4	2 751	8 836	12 730	39 357	45.3	53.7	1.1
Austin-Round Rock, TX	7 452.3	4 063	43.6	5.9	6.4	0.6	7.0	22 572.2	12 306	11 894	4 171	152 135	51.9	44.8	3.3
Bakersfield, CA	5 683.5	6 638	55.4	8.5	3.6	6.7	3.0	3 571.0	4 171	9 728	3 889	48 902	40.4	57.2	2.4
Baltimore-Columbia-Towson, MD	12 715.1	4 618	49.6	1.9	6.8	0.5	4.0	11 152.6	4 051	79 818	25 713	169 614	57.8	39.8	2.4
Bangor, ME	527.2	3 429	48.1	1.1	3.8	0.2	4.2	409.3	2 662	1 172	495	13 083	50.2	47.3	2.5
Barnstable Town, MA	1 041.6	4 835	45.9	1.1	5.3	0.2	3.5	892.5	4 143	1 684	1 183	13 276	53.2	45.4	1.4
Baton Rouge, LA	3 383.6	4 150	44.3	5.0	6.4	0.2	4.9	3 940.9	4 834	2 756	3 833	68 293	43.0	55.4	1.6
Battle Creek, MI	680.5	5 037	45.5	17.6	4.3	2.6	5.4	473.1	3 502	2 906	285	7 801	50.2	48.6	1.2
Bay City, MI	521.5	4 877	44.7	20.6	3.3	4.5	4.2	246.5	2 305	245	238	5 591	52.2	46.7	1.1
Beaumont-Port Arthur, TX	1 598.1	3 954	44.3	3.2	7.1	0.5	5.0	5 940.9	14 699	2 061	1 029	22 820	38.6	60.5	0.9
Beckley, WV	341.8	2 737	62.9	0.6	6.8	0.1	1.6	157.5	1 261	2 067	607	6 709	30.7	67.5	1.8
Bellingham, WA	644.4	3 139	42.5	4.3	6.1	0.0	5.7	595.5	2 901	1 376	624	13 814	55.4	41.4	3.1
Bend-Redmond, OR	663.5	4 089	49.1	3.5	7.4	0.4	5.0	1 093.2	6 736	871	459	7 610	45.1	51.8	3.0
Billings, MT	545.0	3 346	48.4	6.7	5.9	0.2	6.4	248.2	1 524	1 776	832	7 742	38.1	59.1	2.8
Binghamton, NY	1 497.1	6 024	49.5	3.4	2.7	11.2	4.5	1 460.3	5 875	679	392	20 967	49.5	48.4	2.2
Birmingham-Hoover, AL	3 959.1	3 483	45.9	4.8	7.2	0.1	4.3	8 903.8	7 833	8 740	5 496	69 393	39.3	59.6	1.1
Bismarck, ND	438.5	3 652	44.7	1.5	5.4	1.8	11.0	308.2	2 567	1 383	823	13 512	33.4	63.5	3.1
Blacksburg-Christiansburg-Radford, VA	489.3	2 734	47.9	0.6	7.5	5.4	3.8	652.1	3 644	461	608	21 123	43.8	53.5	2.8
Bloomington, IL	735.9	3 900	45.5	3.6	4.9	1.2	5.6	815.8	4 323	537	368	15 706	42.7	55.2	2.1
Bloomington, IN	330.0	2 032	47.5	1.0	4.6	0.4	4.3	424.9	2 617	316	520	22 110	55.5	42.2	2.3
Bloomsburg-Berwick, PA	287.0	3 367	58.3	0.0	2.7	3.0	4.5	1 108.2	13 001	178	217	6 615	41.8	56.5	1.7
Boise City, ID	1 619.0	2 538	42.6	1.3	9.7	0.9	6.7	1 042.0	1 633	5 962	2 445	37 912	38.6	58.3	3.1
Boston-Cambridge-Newton, MA-NH	19 978.0	4 305	50.4	5.7	5.4	0.8	2.6	12 543.9	2 703	35 442	14 766	268 653	60.1	38.2	1.7
Boston, MA Div 14454	8 442.8	4 384	47.1	3.7	6.6	0.7	2.2	5 428.2	2 818	18 954	6 058	128 350	61.9	36.5	1.6
Cambridge-Newton-Framingham, MA Div 15764	9 961.0	4 344	52.0	8.3	4.3	0.2	2.7	6 297.2	2 746	15 173	7 048	115 456	60.9	37.3	1.8
Rockingham County-Strafford County, NH 40484	1 574.2	3 731	58.3	0.3	6.2	4.9	4.0	818.5	1 940	1 315	1 660	24 847	49.6	48.9	1.5
Boulder, CO	1 414.6	4 633	43.6	2.5	8.2	2.3	4.6	1 940.0	6 354	1 977	887	30 712	69.7	27.8	2.5
Bowling Green, KY	401.0	2 472	50.4	4.6	5.8	0.1	3.9	1 131.7	6 976	646	517	11 537	35.0	63.4	1.5
Bremerton-Silverdale, WA	1 054.5	4 135	42.3	4.6	3.5	0.0	3.5	748.5	2 935	17 026	10 799	12 668	54.5	42.8	2.6
Bridgeport-Stamford-Norwalk, CT	4 616.9	4 944	50.9	1.2	6.6	1.0	3.1	4 013.1	4 297	2 809	1 902	45 058	54.9	44.2	0.9
Brownsville-Harlingen, TX	1 613.4	3 883	61.9	0.8	4.4	0.5	3.7	1 801.3	4 335	3 224	969	27 511	65.0	33.9	1.1
Brunswick, GA	608.7	5 365	32.5	39.7	4.6	0.1	2.6	370.2	3 264	1 721	390	8 352	34.6	64.4	1.0
Buffalo-Cheektowaga-Niagara Falls, NY	6 848.3	6 038	44.7	9.1	3.7	9.2	3.7	6 125.0	5 400	9 190	2 101	78 401	55.9	42.3	1.7
Burlington, NC	427.7	2 779	50.9	3.4	8.3	5.8	1.6	182.0	1 183	216	377	6 833	42.3	56.7	1.1
Burlington-South Burlington, VT	830.6	3 887	64.1	0.3	4.8	0.1	6.2	632.9	2 962	3 786	1 599	18 123	67.5	30.1	2.4
California-Lexington Park, MD	331.8	3 045	62.8	2.2	6.2	0.9	2.7	197.3	1 810	8 977	2 451	4 656	41.2	56.0	2.8
Canton-Massillon, OH	1 338.5	3 318	54.8	4.8	5.6	5.1	5.6	461.4	1 144	972	1 054	19 039	48.8	49.2	2.0
Cape Coral-Fort Myers, FL	3 730.8	5 782	25.4	32.3	4.8	0.5	3.9	5 119.6	7 934	2 526	1 334	36 328	41.4	57.9	0.7
Cape Girardeau, MO-IL	263.0	2 098	55.0	0.5	5.3	0.1	9.3	203.7	2 098	434	337	6 858	28.9	69.3	1.8
Carbondale-Marion, IL	466.0	3 677	59.1	1.7	5.1	2.0	4.7	325.9	2 572	1 840	255	16 104	45.1	52.2	2.7
Carson City, NV	205.0	3 738	48.3	2.1	8.1	1.2	5.3	391.1	7 131	517	147	8 778	44.1	53.1	2.7
Casper, WY	436.0	5 546	59.1	0.4	4.8	0.7	4.1	147.1	1 871	638	433	5 169	27.7	68.4	4.0

1. Based on the resident population estimated as of July 1 of the year shown.   2. © 2013 Election Data Services, Inc. All rights reserved.

Table C. Metropolitan Areas — **Land Area and Population**

CBSA/ DIV code[1]	Area name	Land area,[2] 2010 (sq km)	Total persons	Rank	Per square kilometer	White	Black	American Indian, Alaska Native	Asian and Pacific Islander	Percent Hispanic or Latino[3]	Under 5 years	5 to 17 years	18 to 24 years	25 to 34 years	35 to 44 years	45 to 54 years
		1	2	3	4	5	6	7	8	9	10	11	12	13	14	15
16300	Cedar Rapids, IA	5 203	266 040	179	51.1	91.3	5.0	0.6	2.5	2.7	6.2	17.5	9.2	13.1	12.6	13.9
16540	Chambersburg-Waynesboro, PA	2 000	153 638	266	76.8	90.4	4.3	0.5	1.4	5.0	6.1	16.9	7.8	11.7	12.2	13.9
16580	Champaign-Urbana, IL	4 976	238 984	191	48.0	74.5	12.1	0.5	10.0	5.2	5.5	14.1	21.2	14.4	10.8	10.8
16620	Charleston, WV	4 520	220 614	200	48.8	91.3	7.7	0.8	1.4	1.0	5.7	15.1	7.8	11.9	12.5	13.5
16700	Charleston-North Charleston, SC	6 704	744 526	75	111.1	65.5	27.6	0.9	2.6	5.3	6.4	16.1	9.8	15.9	12.8	13.4
16740	Charlotte-Concord-Gastonia, NC-SC	13 123	2 426 363	22	184.9	64.3	23.2	0.9	3.8	9.7	6.4	18.2	9.0	13.6	14.5	14.4
16820	Charlottesville, VA	5 761	229 514	196	39.8	77.1	15.1	0.7	4.8	4.8	5.5	14.4	12.4	14.1	11.7	13.1
16860	Chattanooga, TN-GA	5 411	547 776	101	101.2	80.2	14.5	0.8	2.0	4.1	5.8	15.9	9.2	12.9	12.8	13.7
16940	Cheyenne, WY	6 956	97 121	360	14.0	80.6	3.8	1.4	2.0	14.2	6.5	17.0	9.9	14.3	11.9	12.9
16980	Chicago-Naperville-Elgin, IL-IN-WI	18 639	9 551 031	3	512.4	55.0	17.3	0.5	7.0	21.7	6.3	17.5	9.5	14.3	13.5	13.9
16980	Chicago-Naperville-Arlington Heights, IL Div 16974	8 939	7 340 454	X	821.2	51.9	19.3	0.4	7.8	22.0	6.3	17.0	9.3	15.1	13.7	13.8
16980	Elgin, IL Div 20994	2 982	635 199	X	213.0	62.6	6.3	0.4	4.2	28.0	6.5	19.6	10.9	12.4	13.5	13.9
16980	Gary, IN Div 23844	4 865	703 031	X	144.5	65.3	18.5	0.6	1.7	15.2	6.0	18.0	9.1	12.2	12.6	13.7
16980	Lake County-Kenosha County, IL-WI Div 29404	1 853	872 347	X	470.8	67.5	7.6	0.5	6.8	19.4	5.9	19.2	10.1	11.3	13.0	15.4
17020	Chico, CA	4 238	225 411	197	53.2	76.7	2.4	3.0	6.2	15.5	5.4	14.8	15.8	12.0	10.3	11.4
17140	Cincinnati, OH-KY-IN	10 797	2 157 719	28	199.8	82.3	13.3	0.6	2.8	3.0	6.4	17.7	9.5	13.2	12.5	14.1
17300	Clarksville, TN-KY	4 397	281 021	166	63.9	69.7	20.6	1.2	3.6	8.7	8.8	18.3	12.7	17.9	12.4	10.9
17420	Cleveland, TN	1 977	120 864	319	61.1	89.6	4.7	0.9	1.3	4.9	5.5	16.7	9.8	12.1	12.9	14.1
17460	Cleveland-Elyria, OH	5 172	2 060 810	31	398.5	72.3	20.9	0.6	2.7	5.3	5.6	16.3	8.8	12.2	11.9	14.3
17660	Coeur d'Alene, ID	3 222	150 346	273	46.7	93.2	0.7	2.2	1.8	4.3	6.1	17.6	8.3	12.4	11.9	13.1
17780	College Station-Bryan, TX ...	5 439	249 156	187	45.8	54.5	12.1	0.6	5.4	24.1	6.2	14.7	25.3	15.0	10.4	9.8
17820	Colorado Springs, CO	6 951	697 856	80	100.4	74.2	7.5	1.5	4.8	15.9	6.8	18.0	11.4	14.9	12.3	13.1
17860	Columbia, MO	1 775	174 974	236	98.6	82.3	10.8	1.0	5.3	3.2	6.0	14.5	20.6	15.4	11.4	11.0
17900	Columbia, SC	9 590	810 068	71	84.5	58.8	34.3	0.8	2.6	5.4	6.0	16.7	12.1	13.7	12.6	13.3
17980	Columbus, GA-AL	5 014	313 749	160	62.6	50.3	41.2	1.0	2.9	6.9	7.3	16.8	11.5	15.7	12.4	12.4
18020	Columbus, IN	1 054	81 162	376	77.0	85.9	2.8	0.6	5.7	6.4	6.6	17.7	8.4	13.5	13.2	13.3
18140	Columbus, OH	12 423	2 021 632	32	162.7	77.1	16.3	0.8	4.3	3.8	6.7	17.4	9.5	15.3	13.6	13.6
18580	Corpus Christi, TX	4 621	452 422	114	97.9	35.2	3.5	0.6	2.2	59.4	6.7	18.5	10.0	14.1	12.2	12.5
18700	Corvallis, OR	1 751	87 572	366	50.0	85.0	1.6	1.6	8.0	7.0	4.1	12.7	22.6	12.9	9.9	10.6
18880	Crestview-Fort Walton Beach-Destin, FL	5 096	262 172	181	51.4	80.1	9.9	1.4	4.4	7.9	6.4	15.3	9.3	15.0	11.6	13.5
19060	Cumberland, MD-WV	1 948	99 979	351	51.3	90.7	7.8	0.5	1.1	1.4	4.9	13.4	11.9	12.0	11.7	13.5
19100	Dallas-Fort Worth-Arlington, TX	24 029	7 102 796	4	295.6	49.8	15.9	0.9	6.9	28.2	7.1	19.6	9.3	14.7	14.4	13.8
19100	Dallas-Plano-Irving, TX Div 19124	13 661	4 707 151	X	344.6	46.7	16.9	0.8	7.7	29.4	7.2	19.6	9.4	14.9	14.8	13.8
19100	Fort Worth-Arlington, TX Div 23104	10 368	2 395 645	X	231.1	56.0	13.9	0.9	5.2	25.8	7.1	19.6	9.3	14.2	13.6	13.8
19140	Dalton, GA	1 644	143 781	286	87.5	67.5	3.6	0.6	1.4	28.0	6.9	19.6	9.5	13.0	13.4	13.7
19180	Danville, IL	2 327	79 282	378	34.1	81.0	14.5	0.6	1.2	4.7	6.7	17.3	8.5	11.6	11.7	13.1
19300	Daphne-Fairhope-Foley, AL	4 118	203 709	216	49.5	84.5	10.0	1.4	1.3	4.6	5.6	16.6	7.7	11.4	12.5	13.8
19340	Davenport-Moline-Rock Island, IA-IL	5 880	383 606	137	65.2	82.1	8.4	0.7	2.5	8.3	6.2	16.9	8.6	12.7	12.1	13.4
19380	Dayton, OH	3 320	800 909	72	241.2	79.3	17.0	0.8	2.8	2.5	6.0	16.2	9.9	12.9	11.5	13.5
19460	Decatur, AL	3 289	152 680	269	46.4	78.8	12.8	3.3	0.9	6.7	5.9	16.9	8.3	12.1	12.6	14.8
19500	Decatur, IL	1 504	107 303	341	71.3	79.4	18.7	0.6	1.7	2.1	6.2	16.2	9.3	11.7	11.5	12.8
19660	Deltona-Daytona Beach-Ormond Beach, FL	4 109	623 279	89	151.7	75.4	11.2	0.7	2.4	11.8	4.6	13.5	8.2	10.6	10.5	13.4
19740	Denver-Aurora-Lakewood, CO	21 616	2 814 330	19	130.2	66.9	6.3	1.1	5.1	22.8	6.4	17.3	8.4	16.0	14.5	13.6
19780	Des Moines-West Des Moines, IA	7 469	622 899	90	83.4	83.7	6.1	0.6	4.3	7.1	7.2	18.4	8.6	15.1	13.6	13.4
19820	Detroit-Warren-Dearborn, MI	10 070	4 302 043	14	427.2	68.9	23.4	0.9	4.6	4.2	5.9	17.1	9.0	12.2	12.7	14.7
19820	Detroit-Dearborn-Livonia, MI Div 19804	1 585	1 759 335	X	1 110.0	51.8	40.0	1.0	3.7	5.7	6.5	17.6	9.8	12.7	12.5	13.8
19820	Warren-Troy-Farmington Hills, MI Div 47664	8 485	2 542 708	X	299.7	80.8	11.7	0.9	5.2	3.2	5.4	16.7	8.4	11.9	12.8	15.4
20020	Dothan, AL	4 445	148 171	280	33.3	71.9	24.3	1.1	1.1	3.3	6.1	17.1	8.0	12.3	12.6	13.5
20100	Dover, DE	1 518	173 533	237	114.3	65.9	26.1	1.3	3.2	6.9	6.5	17.1	10.8	13.4	11.5	13.3
20220	Dubuque, IA	1 576	97 125	359	61.6	92.9	3.6	0.5	2.0	2.2	6.1	17.0	10.2	12.8	10.8	13.5
20260	Duluth, MN-WI	21 790	279 601	168	12.8	93.4	2.3	3.8	1.5	1.5	5.3	14.7	11.5	12.1	11.1	13.4
20500	Durham-Chapel Hill, NC	4 555	552 493	98	121.3	56.3	27.9	0.9	5.5	11.3	6.0	15.3	11.9	14.9	13.4	13.0
20700	East Stroudsburg, PA	1 575	166 397	250	105.6	69.4	13.9	0.8	2.9	14.5	4.5	16.8	10.9	10.2	11.4	16.5
20740	Eau Claire, WI	4 264	165 636	251	38.8	93.4	1.8	0.9	3.3	2.0	5.8	15.6	13.3	13.4	11.4	12.9
20940	El Centro, CA	10 817	180 191	229	16.7	12.8	2.7	1.0	1.7	82.2	8.3	20.2	11.0	14.1	12.1	12.0
21060	Elizabethtown-Fort Knox, KY	3 082	148 604	278	48.2	82.4	11.2	1.1	2.9	5.2	6.5	18.3	9.8	13.6	12.9	14.1
21140	Elkhart-Goshen, IN	1 200	203 474	217	169.6	77.8	7.0	0.7	1.5	15.1	7.5	20.4	9.0	12.6	12.5	12.9
21300	Elmira, NY	1 055	87 071	367	82.5	89.2	8.1	0.7	2.0	2.9	5.1	15.8	9.2	12.2	11.5	14.2
21340	El Paso, TX	14 462	838 972	68	58.0	14.0	3.5	0.5	1.6	81.0	8.1	20.1	11.8	14.2	12.5	11.8
21500	Erie, PA	2 070	278 045	170	134.3	87.2	8.4	0.5	1.8	3.8	5.8	16.1	10.7	12.9	11.3	13.4
21660	Eugene, OR	11 793	362 895	144	30.8	86.6	1.7	2.7	4.6	8.3	4.9	14.2	13.2	12.5	11.5	12.2
21780	Evansville, IN-KY	3 794	315 693	158	83.2	89.4	8.1	0.6	1.7	2.2	6.2	16.6	9.4	13.1	11.8	13.5

1. CBSA = Core Based Statistical Area. DIV = Metropolitan Division. See Appendix A for explanation. See Appendix B for list of metropolitan areas identified by type.   2. Dry land or land partially or temporarily covered by water.   3. May be of any race.

Table C. Metropolitan Areas — **Population and Households**

Area name	Population, 2014 (cont.) Age (percent) (cont.)				Population change and components of change, 2000–2015							Households, 2014				
					Total persons		Percent change		Components of change, 2010–2015				Percent			
	55 to 64 years	65 to 74 years	75 years and over	Percent female	2000	2010	2000–2010	2010–2015	Births	Deaths	Net migration	Number	Persons per household	Family households	Female family householder[1]	One person
	16	17	18	19	20	21	22	23	24	25	26	27	28	29	30	31
Cedar Rapids, IA	12.7	8.1	6.8	50.4	237 230	257 940	8.7	3.1	16 991	10 816	2 024	106 799	2.41	66.7	9.1	27.1
Chambersburg-Waynesboro, PA	13.2	10.0	8.2	51.0	129 313	149 618	15.7	2.7	9 793	7 518	1 533	58 565	2.57	67.4	10.5	28.7
Champaign-Urbana, IL	11.1	6.6	5.5	50.1	210 275	231 889	10.3	3.1	14 203	8 374	1 314	94 306	2.36	54.9	10.1	33.6
Charleston, WV	15.5	10.2	7.8	51.6	235 938	227 071	-3.8	-2.8	13 558	14 947	-4 684	93 385	2.35	64.9	14.2	29.2
Charleston-North Charleston, SC	12.4	8.3	5.0	51.1	549 033	664 643	21.1	12.0	48 410	26 820	55 450	276 509	2.57	65.6	14.8	27.3
Charlotte-Concord-Gastonia, NC-SC	11.6	7.6	4.8	51.4	1 717 372	2 217 248	29.1	9.4	154 704	89 506	140 115	883 281	2.66	67.0	13.9	27.0
Charlottesville, VA	13.0	9.1	6.7	51.7	189 644	218 707	15.3	4.9	12 739	8 951	6 842	87 139	2.45	63.3	10.9	27.4
Chattanooga, TN-GA	13.5	9.5	6.8	51.5	476 531	528 145	10.8	3.7	32 754	27 435	14 286	207 829	2.54	66.2	14.0	28.3
Cheyenne, WY	13.1	8.2	6.0	49.6	81 607	91 881	12.6	5.7	6 656	3 976	2 566	38 705	2.44	65.0	9.7	29.3
Chicago-Naperville-Elgin, IL-IN-WI	12.3	7.3	5.5	51.1	9 098 316	9 461 537	4.0	0.9	633 992	358 796	-175 204	3 442 174	2.73	66.0	13.4	27.9
Chicago-Naperville-Arlington Heights, IL Div 16974	12.1	7.2	5.5	51.3	7 135 324	7 263 098	1.8	1.1	495 088	275 762	-131 279	2 668 895	2.71	64.5	13.5	29.1
Elgin, IL Div 20994	11.4	6.9	4.7	50.3	493 088	620 466	25.8	2.4	42 507	19 322	-9 397	209 315	2.97	72.3	12.1	21.9
Gary, IN Div 23844	13.6	8.3	6.3	51.3	675 971	708 138	4.8	-0.7	43 857	34 270	-14 034	261 698	2.65	69.4	16.0	25.9
Lake County-Kenosha County, IL-WI Div 29404	12.8	7.1	5.2	50.2	793 933	869 835	9.6	0.3	52 540	29 442	-20 494	302 266	2.81	72.4	11.2	22.8
Chico, CA	13.2	9.5	7.5	50.5	203 171	220 000	8.3	2.5	12 767	11 856	4 237	85 366	2.57	56.8	10.6	31.6
Cincinnati, OH-KY-IN	13.0	7.8	5.8	51.1	1 994 830	2 114 755	6.0	2.0	143 253	96 465	-2 131	829 142	2.54	64.2	12.3	29.2
Clarksville, TN-KY	9.2	5.9	4.0	49.4	219 630	260 610	18.7	7.8	26 069	9 873	3 700	97 747	2.76	72.3	13.2	22.3
Cleveland, TN	12.6	9.8	6.5	51.2	104 015	115 788	11.3	4.4	7 050	6 120	3 993	44 048	2.63	68.4	10.8	28.4
Cleveland-Elyria, OH	14.3	9.0	7.6	51.8	2 148 143	2 077 246	-3.3	-0.8	122 513	109 967	-27 711	848 493	2.38	61.0	14.4	33.4
Coeur d'Alene, ID	13.7	10.2	6.8	50.6	108 685	138 494	27.4	8.6	9 076	6 502	9 123	56 177	2.59	67.4	11.0	26.4
College Station-Bryan, TX	8.9	5.5	4.2	49.5	184 885	228 660	23.7	9.0	15 991	6 789	10 996	89 858	2.50	54.6	12.2	28.3
Colorado Springs, CO	11.7	7.1	4.6	49.5	537 484	645 611	20.1	8.1	49 460	21 423	23 500	255 330	2.62	69.0	11.4	24.9
Columbia, MO	10.6	6.1	4.4	51.6	135 454	162 642	20.1	7.6	11 190	5 291	6 360	67 198	2.43	59.2	10.4	27.5
Columbia, SC	12.4	8.1	5.2	51.3	647 158	767 477	18.6	5.5	49 461	33 207	25 578	298 600	2.56	63.9	15.4	29.7
Columbus, GA-AL	11.4	7.2	5.2	50.1	281 768	295 531	4.9	6.2	24 439	14 165	7 484	113 195	2.66	66.2	19.1	28.4
Columbus, IN	12.4	8.5	6.4	50.1	71 435	76 786	7.5	5.7	5 551	3 700	2 604	31 827	2.49	66.3	10.7	29.2
Columbus, OH	11.9	7.1	4.9	50.8	1 675 013	1 902 015	13.6	6.3	142 078	76 770	55 111	764 395	2.54	64.0	13.2	28.6
Corpus Christi, TX	12.1	8.1	5.9	50.6	403 280	428 188	6.2	5.7	31 787	19 294	11 880	160 869	2.71	68.7	15.1	25.0
Corvallis, OR	12.8	8.3	6.0	49.9	78 153	85 581	9.5	2.3	3 807	2 872	980	33 904	2.38	53.2	5.3	28.1
Crestview-Fort Walton Beach-Destin, FL	12.9	9.3	6.7	49.2	211 099	235 865	11.7	11.2	17 794	11 255	19 163	95 662	2.62	65.6	9.9	28.5
Cumberland, MD-WV	13.3	10.8	8.6	48.5	102 008	103 299	1.3	-3.2	5 122	6 449	-1 835	40 318	2.29	61.7	11.5	32.4
Dallas-Fort Worth-Arlington, TX	10.8	6.3	4.0	50.8	5 204 126	6 426 214	23.5	10.5	510 606	209 291	372 601	2 445 239	2.81	69.2	14.0	24.9
Dallas-Plano-Irving, TX Div 19124	10.6	6.0	3.8	50.8	3 445 899	4 230 031	22.8	11.3	339 420	130 628	267 888	1 618 859	2.81	69.1	14.1	24.9
Fort Worth-Arlington, TX Div 23104	11.3	6.7	4.4	50.9	1 758 227	2 196 183	24.9	9.1	171 186	78 663	104 713	826 380	2.81	69.4	13.8	25.1
Dalton, GA	11.1	7.8	5.1	50.3	120 031	142 227	18.5	1.1	9 998	5 906	-2 607	50 238	2.82	74.1	11.5	20.7
Danville, IL	13.7	9.6	7.8	50.3	83 919	81 625	-2.7	-2.9	5 629	4 863	-2 968	31 338	2.46	61.4	13.5	32.4
Daphne-Fairhope-Foley, AL	13.8	11.2	7.4	51.2	140 415	182 265	29.8	11.8	11 382	10 174	19 436	71 307	2.76	66.0	9.5	31.0
Davenport-Moline-Rock Island, IA-IL	13.7	9.1	7.3	50.8	376 019	379 690	1.0	1.0	25 016	18 955	-1 727	153 602	2.43	62.5	11.2	31.5
Dayton, OH	13.5	9.1	7.4	51.5	805 816	799 216	-0.8	0.2	50 543	42 325	-5 898	327 610	2.37	61.5	13.7	33.4
Decatur, AL	13.3	9.6	6.5	50.9	145 867	153 825	5.5	-0.7	9 333	8 458	-1 925	58 351	2.59	68.9	12.3	28.3
Decatur, IL	14.4	9.6	8.3	52.2	114 706	110 768	-3.4	-3.1	7 082	6 141	-4 207	44 063	2.37	62.2	13.3	33.0
Deltona-Daytona Beach-Ormond Beach, FL	15.0	13.4	10.7	51.4	493 175	590 293	19.7	5.6	28 888	39 504	42 799	237 527	2.53	63.9	11.1	28.8
Denver-Aurora-Lakewood, CO	12.1	7.1	4.6	50.2	2 179 240	2 543 600	16.7	10.6	183 019	85 274	169 823	1 054 371	2.58	63.4	10.7	28.5
Des Moines-West Des Moines, IA	11.6	7.0	5.2	50.8	481 394	569 633	18.3	9.4	45 668	22 077	29 159	235 515	2.55	66.2	9.9	26.5
Detroit-Warren-Dearborn, MI	13.8	8.3	6.4	51.5	4 452 557	4 296 313	-3.5	0.1	264 327	208 862	-47 620	1 654 584	2.57	64.6	14.5	30.4
Detroit-Dearborn-Livonia, MI Div 19804	13.3	7.7	6.1	51.9	2 061 162	1 820 641	-11.7	-3.4	123 577	93 702	-89 890	661 414	2.64	62.5	19.3	32.7
Warren-Troy-Farmington Hills, MI Div 47664	14.1	8.8	6.6	51.1	2 391 395	2 475 672	3.5	2.7	140 750	115 160	42 270	993 170	2.52	66.0	11.3	28.8
Dothan, AL	13.3	10.0	7.2	51.9	130 861	145 639	11.3	1.7	9 246	8 386	1 665	55 998	2.62	66.6	15.8	29.0
Dover, DE	11.9	9.3	6.3	51.8	126 697	162 349	28.1	6.9	11 447	7 682	7 173	61 270	2.72	70.3	16.4	23.2
Dubuque, IA	13.4	8.4	7.8	50.6	89 143	93 653	5.1	3.7	6 293	4 598	1 744	38 824	2.37	69.3	9.1	24.3
Duluth, MN-WI	15.1	9.3	7.6	49.5	275 486	279 771	1.6	-0.1	15 020	14 892	115	116 768	2.29	61.1	9.1	32.3
Durham-Chapel Hill, NC	12.3	7.8	5.4	52.1	426 493	506 631	18.8	9.1	34 537	18 906	29 255	213 163	2.43	60.1	13.5	31.1
East Stroudsburg, PA	14.8	9.2	5.9	50.6	138 687	169 842	22.5	-2.0	7 487	7 159	-3 585	54 404	3.02	73.5	13.0	21.2
Eau Claire, WI	12.7	8.3	6.6	49.7	148 337	161 390	8.8	2.6	9 998	6 849	1 205	65 392	2.42	61.9	7.0	28.4
El Centro, CA	10.2	6.5	5.5	48.9	142 361	174 528	22.6	3.2	16 150	5 040	-5 747	43 635	3.89	77.7	19.9	20.0
Elizabethtown-Fort Knox, KY	12.1	7.5	5.3	50.1	133 896	148 351	10.8	0.2	10 756	6 517	-4 256	54 612	2.71	68.3	11.0	27.4
Elkhart-Goshen, IN	11.7	7.4	5.9	50.5	182 791	197 561	8.1	3.0	15 789	8 279	-1 498	70 636	2.81	71.6	13.9	22.5
Elmira, NY	14.1	9.2	7.8	50.4	91 070	88 842	-2.4	-2.0	5 176	4 809	-2 066	34 617	2.40	64.9	12.7	26.4
El Paso, TX	10.0	6.2	5.1	51.0	682 966	804 123	17.7	4.3	72 178	25 746	-11 748	256 548	3.20	74.3	19.3	22.2
Erie, PA	14.0	8.6	7.2	50.7	280 843	280 566	-0.1	-0.9	16 756	14 534	-4 356	108 655	2.45	64.9	13.3	28.3
Eugene, OR	14.2	10.2	7.2	50.9	322 959	351 715	8.9	3.2	18 637	17 367	9 570	145 732	2.40	58.6	11.0	28.8
Evansville, IN-KY	13.9	8.7	6.9	51.3	296 195	311 552	5.2	1.3	19 872	16 454	1 017	125 439	2.44	64.1	11.4	29.9

1. No spouse present.

Table C. Metropolitan Areas — **Population, Vital Statistics, Medicare, and Crime**

Area name	Persons in group quarters, 2015	Daytime population, 2014 Number	Employ-ment/residence ratio	Births, 2015 Total	Rate[1]	Deaths, 2015 Number	Rate[1]	Persons under 65 with no health insurance 2014 Number	Percent	Medicare, 2015 Total Benefici-aries	Enrolled in Original Medicare	Enrolled in Medicare Advantage	Serious crimes known to police,[2] 2014 Total Number	Rate[3]
	32	33	34	35	36	37	38	39	40	41	42	43	44	45
Cedar Rapids, IA	6 617	266 443	1.02	3 265	12.3	2 082	7.8	12 355	5.6	43 890	32 280	11 610	6 786	2 595
Chambersburg-Waynesboro, PA...........	2 560	145 779	0.90	1 850	12.0	1 529	10.0	15 281	12.3	30 378	22 930	7 448	3 321	2 176
Champaign-Urbana, IL..........	16 707	242 988	1.04	2 750	11.5	1 630	6.8	17 757	9.2	31 013	16 806	14 207	6 554	2 821
Charleston, WV......................	3 319	244 349	1.23	2 580	11.7	2 831	12.8	17 568	9.8	52 338	34 895	17 443	8 831	4 274
Charleston-North Charleston, SC.............................	15 875	730 451	1.01	9 542	12.8	5 475	7.4	92 490	15.0	109 813	87 286	22 527	23 688	3 274
Charlotte-Concord-Gastonia, NC-SC..................................	35 923	2 399 096	1.02	30 069	12.4	17 883	7.4	303 581	14.8	344 262	238 283	105 979	75 601	3 212
Charlottesville, VA................	12 470	233 266	1.05	2 467	10.7	1 724	7.5	24 554	13.6	37 451	31 406	6 045	4 405	1 954
Chattanooga, TN-GA	13 422	549 441	1.03	6 281	11.5	5 355	9.8	63 672	14.3	102 746	67 959	34 787	26 726	4 890
Cheyenne, WY	1 957	99 168	1.06	1 263	13.0	776	8.0	9 515	11.7	15 821	15 140	681	2 495	2 593
Chicago-Naperville-Elgin, IL-IN-WI...........................	161 178	9 588 344	1.01	118 637	12.4	70 522	7.4	1 007 365	12.3	1 276 214	996 766	279 448	236 496	2 525
Chicago-Naperville-Arlington Heights, IL Div 16974	115 033	X	X	92 559	12.6	54 201	7.4	790 229	12.5	962 531	738 650	223 881	191 275	2 641
Elgin, IL Div 20994	12 859	X	X	7 965	12.5	3 868	6.1	63 773	11.6	81 958	63 296	18 662	9 755	1 584
Gary, IN Div 23844	10 927	X	X	8 230	11.7	6 708	9.5	81 425	13.8	118 514	99 872	18 642	19 681	3 075
Lake County-Kenosha County, IL-WI Div 29404.....................	22 359	X	X	9 883	11.3	5 745	6.6	71 938	9.7	113 211	94 948	18 263	15 785	1 821
Chico, CA...........................	5 420	226 905	1.03	2 485	11.0	2 296	10.2	23 914	13.1	45 377	44 306	1 071	7 309	3 265
Cincinnati, OH-KY-IN	48 349	2 159 522	1.01	27 011	12.5	18 900	8.8	169 079	9.3	337 306	198 895	138 411	64 200	3 174
Clarksville, TN-KY	8 893	281 086	1.01	5 049	18.0	1 923	6.8	27 984	11.6	34 158	26 359	7 799	8 209	2 982
Cleveland, TN	3 053	116 210	0.94	1 410	11.7	1 193	9.9	15 260	15.6	24 688	15 799	8 889	4 691	3 925
Cleveland-Elyria, OH	43 730	2 110 429	1.05	23 481	11.4	20 507	10.0	160 928	9.5	373 544	219 925	153 619	47 693	2 778
Coeur d'Alene, ID	1 488	139 919	0.88	1 781	11.8	1 284	8.5	19 135	15.8	30 012	20 592	9 420	4 328	2 951
College Station-Bryan, TX ..	14 485	242 140	1.02	3 155	12.7	1 372	5.5	41 305	20.1	25 548	20 175	5 373	6 729	2 799
Colorado Springs, CO	18 019	684 271	0.99	9 631	13.8	4 376	6.3	60 286	10.2	88 812	60 452	28 360	22 584	3 276
Columbia, MO	9 012	179 471	1.08	2 193	12.5	1 021	5.8	17 744	12.1	21 650	18 293	3 357	5 735	3 316
Columbia, SC.......................	34 518	808 367	1.02	9 414	11.6	6 536	8.1	96 883	14.6	121 131	95 144	25 987	31 494	3 933
Columbus, GA-AL	12 921	322 789	1.07	4 582	14.6	2 840	9.1	44 704	16.9	50 468	35 882	14 586	17 594	5 513
Columbus, IN	1 147	87 589	1.18	1 102	13.6	674	8.3	9 160	13.6	15 152	12 312	2 840	2 664	3 316
Columbus, OH	50 350	2 020 371	1.03	27 839	13.8	15 132	7.5	169 901	9.9	268 214	144 297	123 917	64 315	3 442
Corpus Christi, TX	7 207	442 173	0.99	6 335	14.0	3 657	8.1	78 576	20.7	70 342	35 981	34 361	20 985	4 668
Corvallis, OR	4 467	88 085	1.04	693	7.9	566	6.5	7 031	10.1	11 544	6 036	5 508	2 620	3 004
Crestview-Fort Walton Beach-Destin, FL	6 324	269 544	1.10	3 591	13.7	2 276	8.7	37 214	17.7	45 200	38 367	6 833	7 270	2 801
Cumberland, MD-WV	8 287	101 819	1.03	957	9.6	1 230	12.3	6 038	8.2	22 416	20 766	1 650	3 054	3 075
Dallas-Fort Worth-Arlington, TX	82 284	6 973 527	1.01	99 906	14.1	42 514	6.0	1 239 787	20.1	770 465	509 315	261 150	212 467	3 058
Dallas-Plano-Irving, 19124...	53 841	X	X	66 389	14.1	26 742	5.7	832 874	20.3	489 358	341 087	148 271	133 575	2 906
Fort Worth-Arlington, TX Div 23104	28 443	X	X	33 517	14.0	15 772	6.6	406 913	19.7	281 107	168 228	112 879	78 892	3 354
Dalton, GA	1 369	147 143	1.07	1 881	13.1	1 139	7.9	29 388	23.8	22 355	18 463	3 892	4 111	2 932
Danville, IL	2 979	78 547	0.96	1 063	13.4	911	11.5	5 617	8.8	17 093	10 132	6 961	3 240	4 120
Daphne-Fairhope-Foley, AL..	2 309	186 158	0.84	2 240	11.0	1 992	9.8	25 892	16.1	42 444	28 071	14 373	4 227	2 189
Davenport-Moline-Rock Island, IA-IL....................	9 026	387 198	1.03	4 733	12.3	3 514	9.2	26 725	8.5	71 060	55 496	15 564	10 400	2 845
Dayton, OH	24 500	819 347	1.05	9 672	12.1	8 077	10.1	66 789	10.3	148 248	80 042	68 206	27 405	3 487
Decatur, AL.........................	2 356	145 560	0.88	1 745	11.4	1 586	10.4	20 417	16.1	31 088	26 925	4 163	3 792	2 504
Decatur, IL...........................	4 130	114 429	1.13	1 316	12.3	1 143	10.7	7 108	8.2	22 944	18 097	4 847	3 039	2 793
Deltona-Daytona Beach-Ormond Beach, FL	14 086	577 646	0.87	5 583	9.0	7 731	12.4	94 778	20.9	157 451	87 191	70 260	19 947	3 290
Denver-Aurora-Lakewood, CO....................................	33 884	2 749 088	1.00	35 808	12.7	17 313	6.2	278 350	11.6	329 298	155 885	173 413	81 271	2 956
Des Moines-West Des Moines, IA......................	12 357	624 993	1.04	9 027	14.5	4 327	6.9	34 909	6.6	83 798	67 629	16 169	17 232	2 833
Detroit-Warren-Dearborn, MI	48 556	4 316 170	1.01	50 851	11.8	40 060	9.3	375 256	10.3	748 289	500 458	247 831	117 769	2 745
Detroit-Dearborn-Livonia, MI Div 19804.......................	22 874	X	X	23 586	13.4	17 736	10.1	183 978	12.2	308 568	204 160	104 408	75 016	4 268
Warren-Troy-Farmington Hills, MI Div 47664	25 682	X	X	27 265	10.7	22 324	8.8	191 278	9.0	439 721	296 298	143 423	42 753	1 688
Dothan, AL..........................	1 845	149 398	1.02	1 714	11.6	1 618	10.9	17 385	14.3	31 099	26 532	4 567	3 613	2 446
Dover, DE	4 665	163 013	0.88	2 196	12.7	1 585	9.1	13 073	9.2	29 976	27 486	2 490	5 424	3 160
Dubuque, IA	4 349	104 646	1.16	1 240	12.8	878	9.0	4 763	6.1	18 614	10 728	7 886	1 908	1 980
Duluth, MN-WI	12 628	283 744	1.03	2 830	10.1	2 749	9.8	16 025	7.2	58 559	30 250	28 309	9 449	3 371
Durham-Chapel Hill, NC	23 429	585 007	1.17	6 627	12.0	3 758	6.8	64 507	14.3	73 117	48 379	24 738	19 974	3 681
East Stroudsburg, PA	4 371	153 986	0.83	1 424	8.6	1 458	8.8	16 177	11.7	28 423	22 860	5 563	4 401	2 644
Eau Claire, WI.....................	7 377	166 020	1.01	1 902	11.5	1 318	8.0	11 268	8.4	31 457	22 649	8 808	3 089	1 867
El Centro, CA......................	8 914	178 664	0.99	3 127	17.4	967	5.4	23 763	16.0	24 351	20 676	3 675	6 119	3 577
Elizabethtown-Fort Knox, KY	3 786	145 322	0.91	2 042	13.7	1 254	8.4	11 228	8.7	25 341	21 076	4 265	2 173	1 429
Elkhart-Goshen, IN	3 758	228 215	1.28	3 028	14.9	1 557	7.7	33 286	19.3	30 909	22 017	8 892	5 051	2 507
Elmira, NY...........................	4 569	89 804	1.06	920	10.6	921	10.6	4 457	6.5	18 519	12 408	6 111	2 151	2 430
El Paso, TX..........................	16 108	839 014	1.01	13 650	16.3	5 127	6.1	181 444	25.0	108 795	53 058	55 737	20 124	2 386
Erie, PA..............................	12 863	283 848	1.04	3 155	11.3	2 718	9.8	24 067	10.7	53 380	28 053	25 327	6 587	2 351
Eugene, OR	7 815	358 446	1.00	3 636	10.0	3 344	9.2	34 733	12.0	71 163	33 865	37 298	NA	NA
Evansville, IN-KY	9 557	318 594	1.02	3 756	11.9	3 165	10.0	28 623	11.0	59 097	43 075	16 022	11 210	3 557

1. Per 1,000 estimated resident population.   2. Data for serious crimes have not been adjusted for underreporting; this may affect comparability between geographic areas and over time.
3. Per 100,000 population estimated by the FBI.

Area name	Serious crimes known to police, 2014 (cont.)[1] Rate[2] Violent	Property	Education — Enrollment[3] Total	Percent private	Attainment[4] (percent) High school graduate or less	Bachelor's degree or more	Local government expenditures,[5] 2012–2013 Total current expenditures (mil dol)	Current expenditures per student (dollars)	Income and Poverty, 2014 Per capita income[6] (dollars)	Mean household income (dollars)	Median household income	Percent of households with income of less than $25,000	Percent of households with income of $200,000 or more	Percent below poverty level All persons	Children under 18 years	Age 65 years and older
	46	47	48	49	50	51	52	53	54	55	56	57	58	59	60	61
Cedar Rapids, IA	193	2 402	66 797	17.2	34.4	30.6	481.2	11 096	32 195	78 842	61 865	19.8	4.4	9.2	11.9	5.1
Chambersburg-Waynesboro, PA	149	2 027	33 241	16.3	58.0	17.7	250.5	10 985	23 916	60 256	49 487	21.3	1.7	12.9	19.4	7.8
Champaign-Urbana, IL	444	2 377	88 142	6.0	30.8	38.9	356.9	11 705	26 556	65 529	48 063	27.4	3.8	22.1	26.3	7.0
Charleston, WV	528	3 745	45 372	11.9	55.2	21.3	400.8	11 408	25 193	59 235	42 761	28.5	2.7	17.9	27.8	7.7
Charleston-North Charleston, SC	387	2 888	187 509	16.0	35.5	33.0	1 007.6	9 928	29 303	74 299	53 572	22.1	4.9	15.1	22.9	8.1
Charlotte-Concord-Gastonia, NC-SC	392	2 819	628 357	15.5	36.3	32.9	3 032.1	8 196	29 193	75 943	53 549	22.2	5.4	15.2	21.3	9.0
Charlottesville, VA	165	1 789	65 147	15.7	37.9	39.9	333.8	11 758	31 428	80 138	58 189	22.6	6.7	14.2	10.2	8.2
Chattanooga, TN-GA	592	4 298	127 464	19.9	43.6	25.1	644.3	8 671	24 863	62 267	46 600	26.7	2.5	15.9	22.4	8.1
Cheyenne, WY	160	2 433	23 703	10.4	31.9	30.7	218.6	15 257	28 934	70 617	57 551	21.8	2.6	10.9	12.3	4.3
Chicago-Naperville-Elgin, IL-IN-WI	382	2 143	2 539 057	20.1	37.0	36.1	20 132.2	12 876	31 885	85 507	61 598	20.2	7.0	13.9	20.1	8.8
.Chicago-Naperville-Arlington Heights, IL Div 16974	430	2 211	1 926 827	21.2	36.3	37.2	15 188.1	13 270	31 950	84 857	61 086	20.7	7.0	14.4	20.8	9.8
.Elgin, IL Div 20994	174	1 410	184 653	14.8	39.2	32.5	1 569.6	11 244	30 743	89 597	69 537	16.0	7.2	11.3	16.0	4.4
.Gary, IN Div 23844	350	2 724	183 091	17.2	47.0	21.8	1 084.2	9 612	25 733	67 139	52 461	22.0	2.5	15.2	23.9	6.5
.Lake County-Kenosha County, IL-WI Div 29404	160	1 661	244 486	17.1	33.8	40.8	2 290.3	13 749	37 129	104 322	72 151	16.5	11.5	10.7	14.9	6.1
Chico, CA	303	2 962	64 557	7.6	35.2	27.1	306.8	9 812	25 842	64 663	42 365	32.1	3.8	22.3	23.8	9.0
Cincinnati, OH-KY-IN	263	2 911	554 845	18.4	40.5	31.4	3 354.1	10 996	29 317	74 251	55 729	22.8	4.8	14.0	19.7	7.6
Clarksville, TN-KY	463	2 519	78 044	14.1	41.4	21.6	347.3	8 231	21 609	58 273	45 130	25.0	1.7	15.7	18.8	7.3
Cleveland, TN	495	3 430	28 929	22.5	53.6	19.4	141.0	7 617	23 853	61 327	41 176	29.5	2.7	19.1	25.7	10.8
Cleveland-Elyria, OH	395	2 383	500 961	21.7	40.6	29.5	3 529.6	13 202	28 785	68 252	49 889	26.1	4.0	15.9	24.2	8.9
Coeur d'Alene, ID	279	2 672	35 467	14.0	36.1	22.1	136.4	6 501	26 677	67 950	48 776	20.0	3.9	12.0	16.9	8.4
College Station-Bryan, TX	292	2 506	95 137	5.9	40.1	33.7	286.9	8 728	23 569	61 162	42 116	30.8	3.2	26.3	27.1	10.4
Colorado Springs, CO	382	2 893	196 351	13.7	27.7	36.2	934.9	8 160	29 376	76 509	59 411	19.3	4.6	12.0	15.1	6.6
Columbia, MO	342	2 974	62 041	13.2	27.7	44.7	220.1	9 502	25 928	64 774	50 085	25.9	2.9	20.7	19.1	6.4
Columbia, SC	581	3 352	220 188	16.3	38.6	31.7	1 323.5	10 816	26 038	65 966	50 091	24.4	3.1	15.8	22.2	7.1
Columbus, GA-AL	434	5 079	82 007	10.7	43.1	23.9	476.1	9 526	23 354	59 190	42 669	28.0	2.7	19.3	28.0	11.0
Columbus, IN	110	3 206	19 390	16.1	46.2	30.4	112.6	9 142	27 667	67 650	53 002	21.8	3.1	12.7	18.1	6.7
Columbus, OH	308	3 134	535 282	17.0	37.6	34.7	3 458.3	12 150	29 950	76 201	56 371	21.4	5.0	14.5	20.2	7.7
Corpus Christi, TX	588	4 079	109 884	7.0	47.7	20.1	676.6	8 522	26 427	70 503	52 050	23.8	3.3	15.5	20.2	13.5
Corvallis, OR	127	2 877	31 846	3.8	20.1	53.5	81.2	9 368	28 257	70 582	52 486	26.6	4.0	20.4	7.3	6.6
Crestview-Fort Walton Beach-Destin, FL	391	2 410	60 190	11.2	36.4	29.8	324.9	8 642	28 293	71 389	53 679	20.6	3.9	13.3	22.6	7.1
Cumberland, MD-WV	264	2 811	24 463	11.5	57.2	15.5	176.8	13 420	20 585	51 108	38 580	31.8	0.9	17.8	18.8	10.0
Dallas-Fort Worth-Arlington, TX	332	2 726	1 915 794	12.8	38.6	32.4	9 993.2	8 068	30 325	83 408	59 530	19.6	6.6	14.8	21.6	8.1
Dallas-Plano-Irving, 19124	320	2 586	1 278 600	12.5	37.9	34.5	6 682.2	8 094	31 190	85 881	60 231	19.4	7.3	14.9	21.6	8.6
Fort Worth-Arlington, TX Div 23104	356	2 998	637 194	13.4	40.1	28.4	3 311.0	8 018	28 629	78 564	58 132	20.0	5.4	14.8	21.6	7.4
Dalton, GA	218	2 714	35 080	4.3	63.6	13.9	245.8	8 644	20 451	57 880	41 034	30.5	2.5	21.6	31.5	11.7
Danville, IL	598	3 523	17 849	5.8	54.2	13.8	146.8	10 877	21 933	54 361	41 690	31.6	1.4	18.7	25.8	6.7
Daphne-Fairhope-Foley, AL	189	2 000	45 836	13.1	36.5	30.5	243.6	8 279	26 721	66 013	48 461	25.5	4.0	12.7	17.5	10.9
Davenport-Moline-Rock Island, IA-IL	366	2 479	91 784	16.8	40.3	25.7	656.4	10 565	26 968	65 258	51 410	22.0	2.7	13.5	18.5	9.4
Dayton, OH	279	3 208	209 581	20.1	38.9	27.3	1 251.5	11 800	26 555	63 087	46 697	27.5	2.8	17.3	26.7	8.7
Decatur, AL	156	2 349	36 225	6.3	52.5	16.9	228.6	9 376	23 223	58 085	44 600	26.3	1.6	14.1	20.4	9.1
Decatur, IL	364	2 429	25 230	22.4	43.7	24.2	211.2	12 747	26 459	63 140	47 574	26.7	2.1	15.4	24.5	7.2
Deltona-Daytona Beach-Ormond Beach, FL	402	2 887	125 332	16.2	46.0	22.2	594.0	8 029	23 504	56 396	42 468	27.6	2.0	16.4	25.1	8.3
Denver-Aurora-Lakewood, CO	332	2 624	702 600	14.0	30.7	40.8	3 911.3	8 857	35 256	89 498	66 870	16.2	7.3	10.8	14.7	6.8
Des Moines-West Des Moines, IA	323	2 510	159 353	18.9	33.0	36.1	1 068.5	10 248	32 621	83 213	62 446	17.1	5.4	12.0	17.1	7.6
Detroit-Warren-Dearborn, MI	534	2 211	1 088 916	12.9	38.3	29.4	6 622.4	11 295	28 527	71 997	52 462	23.9	4.6	16.1	23.7	9.1
Detroit-Dearborn-Livonia, MI Div 19804	995	3 273	457 056	11.2	45.7	22.1	2 525.1	11 693	22 529	57 551	41 435	32.2	2.6	24.0	35.5	12.4
Warren-Troy-Farmington Hills, MI Div 47664	214	1 474	631 860	14.1	33.5	34.3	4 097.4	11 063	32 708	81 617	61 488	18.4	5.9	10.7	14.7	7.1
Dothan, AL	291	2 155	33 887	12.2	52.5	17.3	186.6	8 342	21 450	53 968	38 300	33.5	2.1	20.2	31.9	10.5
Dover, DE	422	2 377	49 273	16.7	45.1	24.2	306.6	13 046	25 751	68 479	55 227	20.0	1.9	13.4	19.4	7.6
Dubuque, IA	177	1 803	24 863	32.1	43.1	28.8	144.7	9 945	26 066	65 924	56 129	20.3	1.8	12.2	16.2	12.8
Duluth, MN-WI	223	3 148	69 198	12.0	37.7	26.6	401.1	11 162	26 839	62 843	50 275	24.9	2.6	16.2	20.6	7.0
Durham-Chapel Hill, NC	426	3 255	155 904	21.0	30.3	44.8	674.5	10 163	31 477	78 110	51 988	23.4	6.6	16.3	20.0	8.2
East Stroudsburg, PA	218	2 426	42 880	12.5	47.3	23.5	435.0	15 532	25 081	71 199	63 118	18.5	3.3	13.4	21.6	6.6
Eau Claire, WI	132	1 736	43 899	7.6	38.8	26.4	251.4	10 899	25 891	64 089	48 873	23.5	2.4	12.6	11.4	6.4
El Centro, CA	341	3 236	51 224	4.1	54.8	14.8	354.7	9 692	16 226	58 528	39 290	35.3	3.0	23.7	30.1	17.3
Elizabethtown-Fort Knox, KY	97	1 332	40 704	10.5	44.1	21.9	212.3	8 617	23 964	63 083	49 649	21.8	2.1	13.3	19.8	10.1
Elkhart-Goshen, IN	357	2 149	50 484	13.2	55.8	18.1	347.2	9 626	21 959	60 416	49 937	22.0	2.3	14.3	21.1	4.1
Elmira, NY	186	2 243	19 152	14.4	43.3	25.3	180.4	14 937	26 159	65 626	50 232	25.4	3.4	18.7	28.4	12.1
El Paso, TX	363	2 024	256 369	6.8	49.7	21.0	1 529.6	8 572	18 214	54 484	40 133	31.1	2.0	23.4	32.0	20.5
Erie, PA	228	2 114	69 425	24.7	49.0	28.0	502.3	13 085	24 996	62 404	45 560	26.5	2.7	16.3	22.7	8.6
Eugene, OR	NA	NA	96 176	8.8	33.4	29.0	443.9	9 761	24 878	59 717	44 877	27.4	2.4	18.4	17.7	9.2
Evansville, IN-KY	293	3 264	78 834	16.9	44.0	23.8	428.0	9 695	25 867	62 889	46 547	25.6	2.7	16.0	24.7	8.4

1. Data for serious crimes have not been adjusted for underreporting; this may affect comparability between geographic areas and over time.   2. Per 100,000 population estimated by the FBI.   3. All persons 3 years old and over enrolled in nursery school through college.   4. Persons 25 years old and over.   5. Elementary and secondary education expenditures.   6. Based on resident population estimated in the 2014 American Community Survey.

Table C. Metropolitan Areas — **Personal Income**

Area name	Personal income, 2014 Total (mil dol)	Percent change 2013–2014	Per capita[1] Dollars	Per capita Rank	Wages and salaries (mil dol)	Supplements to wages and salaries; employer contributions (mil dol) Pension and insurance	Government social insurance	Proprietors' income (mil dol)	Dividends, interest, and rent (mil dol)	Personal transfer receipts (mil dol)	Earnings, 2014 Total (mil dol)	Contributions for government social insurance (mil dol) From employee and self-employed	From employer
	62	63	64	65	66	67	68	69	70	71	72	73	74
Cedar Rapids, IA	12 233	3.6	46 356	73	6 948	1 092	531	883	2 150	1 860	9 455	581	531
Chambersburg-Waynesboro, PA	6 111	4.0	39 972	187	2 378	488	203	438	986	1 267	3 507	211	203
Champaign-Urbana, IL	9 309	2.7	39 237	204	4 903	1 206	310	647	1 785	1 316	7 067	328	310
Charleston, WV	9 371	2.3	42 046	141	5 396	900	422	1 014	1 418	2 479	7 731	489	422
Charleston-North Charleston, SC	30 057	5.5	41 305	159	15 378	2 561	1 169	2 586	5 744	5 191	21 695	1 299	1 169
Charlotte-Concord-Gastonia, NC-SC	100 985	6.1	42 425	132	59 769	8 409	4 454	8 364	14 819	16 057	80 997	4 874	4 454
Charlottesville, VA	11 569	4.5	50 971	28	5 395	1 011	394	999	3 444	1 490	7 799	464	394
Chattanooga, TN-GA	21 379	4.0	39 260	201	10 571	1 785	757	2 214	3 261	4 561	15 326	932	757
Cheyenne, WY	4 745	3.9	49 225	45	2 376	478	245	296	1 131	725	3 394	190	245
Chicago-Naperville-Elgin, IL-IN-WI	484 322	3.3	50 690	30	272 088	40 545	19 086	37 811	90 101	68 043	369 530	20 778	19 086
.Chicago-Naperville-Arlington Heights, IL Div 16974	377 190	3.3	51 363	X	220 303	32 071	15 458	32 351	70 416	53 448	300 183	16 805	15 458
.Elgin, IL Div 20994	26 262	3.3	41 503	X	11 687	2 192	842	1 201	3 889	3 494	15 922	862	842
.Gary, IN Div 23844	28 121	3.4	39 891	X	12 511	2 050	939	1 720	3 756	5 850	17 220	1 095	939
.Lake County-Kenosha County, IL-WI Div 29404	52 750	3.5	60 406	X	27 588	4 232	1 847	2 539	12 041	5 250	36 205	2 016	1 847
Chico, CA	8 298	3.0	37 005	260	3 104	724	224	795	1 568	2 217	4 847	303	224
Cincinnati, OH-KY-IN	98 613	4.5	45 878	82	53 994	8 510	3 930	7 470	16 737	16 380	73 903	4 297	3 930
Clarksville, TN-KY	10 650	1.7	38 259	226	5 121	1 255	451	763	1 957	2 028	7 589	376	451
Cleveland, TN	4 602	4.5	38 441	222	1 751	314	130	806	602	1 021	3 001	181	130
Cleveland-Elyria, OH	96 907	3.7	46 960	65	53 447	8 916	3 923	8 397	16 156	18 309	74 683	4 263	3 923
Coeur d'Alene, ID	5 400	5.0	36 656	269	2 060	332	191	367	1 135	1 143	2 950	204	191
College Station-Bryan, TX	8 270	6.3	34 044	335	4 222	822	265	700	1 522	1 288	6 008	283	265
Colorado Springs, CO	28 830	4.7	41 971	142	14 820	2 600	1 172	1 300	5 959	4 832	19 892	1 052	1 172
Columbia, MO	7 154	2.9	41 418	153	3 985	915	270	459	1 317	1 077	5 629	295	270
Columbia, SC	30 795	4.5	38 469	217	16 818	2 949	1 271	1 974	4 750	6 045	23 013	1 392	1 271
Columbus, GA-AL	11 519	3.3	36 683	267	6 347	1 384	494	618	2 624	2 602	8 843	478	494
Columbus, IN	3 540	3.5	44 129	98	2 565	395	189	297	552	593	3 447	208	189
Columbus, OH	89 559	4.2	44 902	92	51 982	9 188	3 615	7 247	12 537	14 159	72 032	3 833	3 615
Corpus Christi, TX	18 803	4.9	41 961	143	9 319	1 515	661	2 834	2 986	3 755	14 328	737	661
Corvallis, OR	3 427	4.4	39 698	193	1 760	339	148	259	827	513	2 507	152	148
Crestview-Fort Walton Beach-Destin, FL	11 599	4.3	44 950	91	5 533	1 102	451	551	3 394	2 087	7 637	425	451
Cumberland, MD-WV	3 604	3.4	35 849	299	1 524	330	128	150	580	1 138	2 133	143	128
Dallas-Fort Worth-Arlington, TX	344 280	5.9	49 506	42	190 144	23 579	12 964	53 151	54 073	39 569	279 838	14 222	12 964
Dallas-Plano-Irving, 19124	237 227	6.0	51 525	X	139 525	16 553	9 416	38 346	37 982	25 163	203 840	10 307	9 416
Fort Worth-Arlington, TX Div 23104	107 053	5.7	45 550	X	50 619	7 026	3 548	14 805	16 091	14 405	75 997	3 915	3 548
Dalton, GA	4 385	3.9	30 676	371	2 767	480	209	460	664	1 003	3 916	229	209
Danville, IL	2 791	-1.0	35 009	317	1 223	263	92	227	417	729	1 805	105	92
Daphne-Fairhope-Foley, AL	7 812	5.4	39 040	207	2 364	375	181	527	1 519	1 669	3 446	242	181
Davenport-Moline-Rock Island, IA-IL	16 735	1.9	43 690	103	8 837	1 506	647	1 204	3 069	3 047	12 195	726	647
Dayton, OH	33 144	3.7	41 386	155	17 718	3 378	1 342	2 104	5 747	6 965	24 542	1 388	1 342
Decatur, AL	5 269	3.0	34 418	324	2 299	405	169	357	784	1 301	3 231	213	169
Decatur, IL	4 704	1.5	43 413	110	2 666	456	193	409	775	990	3 724	216	193
Deltona-Daytona Beach-Ormond Beach, FL	22 061	5.2	36 169	286	7 088	1 145	526	578	5 188	6 196	9 337	702	526
Denver-Aurora-Lakewood, CO	148 684	6.7	53 983	21	83 427	10 532	5 837	18 495	27 101	16 503	118 291	6 602	5 837
Des Moines-West Des Moines, IA	29 842	5.6	48 797	50	17 806	2 587	1 333	2 745	4 888	3 862	24 472	1 482	1 333
Detroit-Warren-Dearborn, MI	191 199	4.1	44 500	95	105 011	14 400	8 010	15 303	29 678	38 250	142 724	9 020	8 010
Detroit-Dearborn-Livonia, MI Div 19804	65 022	3.6	36 844	X	41 200	5 891	3 110	4 547	9 221	18 375	54 748	3 468	3 110
Warren-Troy-Farmington Hills, MI Div 47664	126 177	4.4	49 837	X	63 811	8 509	4 901	10 755	20 457	19 875	87 976	5 553	4 901
Dothan, AL	5 342	3.2	36 070	292	2 197	392	166	432	876	1 370	3 186	208	166
Dover, DE	6 555	4.8	38 114	231	2 936	699	234	588	979	1 558	4 458	244	234
Dubuque, IA	4 160	4.1	43 167	118	2 439	388	191	327	822	720	3 345	212	191
Duluth, MN-WI	11 255	4.2	40 166	182	5 574	987	449	673	1 833	2 779	7 684	495	449
Durham-Chapel Hill, NC	24 892	4.5	45 867	83	18 120	2 841	1 282	1 928	4 863	3 655	24 171	1 409	1 282
East Stroudsburg, PA	6 037	4.2	36 297	281	2 269	537	192	282	835	1 306	3 280	200	192
Eau Claire, WI	6 946	4.7	42 090	139	3 483	686	277	651	1 229	1 248	5 097	310	277
El Centro, CA	5 802	3.8	32 398	362	2 382	712	171	872	710	1 475	4 137	196	171
Elizabethtown-Fort Knox, KY	5 605	2.9	36 974	261	2 623	643	222	436	1 013	1 256	3 923	218	222
Elkhart-Goshen, IN	7 542	6.0	37 344	252	5 494	914	435	711	1 138	1 403	7 553	450	435
Elmira, NY	3 407	2.6	38 820	210	1 696	425	147	187	433	862	2 454	136	147
El Paso, TX	26 606	3.6	31 799	368	12 657	2 645	956	2 649	4 026	5 995	18 906	951	956
Erie, PA	10 637	2.0	38 200	228	5 280	1 123	431	536	1 712	2 658	7 371	446	431
Eugene, OR	13 393	5.3	37 374	249	6 077	996	557	989	2 697	3 293	8 619	573	557
Evansville, IN-KY	12 848	4.2	40 768	169	6 768	1 151	517	1 112	2 086	2 636	9 548	594	517

1. Based on the resident population estimated as of July 1 of the year shown.

Table C. Metropolitan Areas — Earnings, Social Security, and Housing

Area name	Earnings, 2014 (cont.) Percent by selected industries									Social Security beneficiaries, December 2014		Housing units, 2015		
	Farm	Mining	Construction	Manufacturing	Information, professional, scientific, technical services	Retail trade	Finance, insurance, real estate, rental and leasing	Health care and social assistance	Government	Number	Rate[1]	Supplemental Security Income recipients, December 2014	Total	Percent change, 2000–2015
	75	76	77	78	79	80	81	82	83	84	85	86	87	88
Cedar Rapids, IA	1.5	0.1	7.1	21.5	8.7	6.9	10.1	D	11.0	49 765	189	4 235	115 320	2.7
Chambersburg-Waynesboro, PA	4.6	0.1	4.6	19.2	4.6	6.9	3.2	14.9	17.3	34 990	229	2 553	64 325	1.7
Champaign-Urbana, IL	3.7	D	3.9	7.0	D	4.9	4.4	D	38.1	33 260	140	3 392	104 152	3.0
Charleston, WV	0.0	D	5.9	4.2	D	5.7	D	D	18.5	59 070	265	9 447	108 076	-0.2
Charleston-North Charleston, SC	0.1	0.1	6.2	10.6	12.1	7.2	7.1	9.7	23.4	127 875	176	13 444	318 456	6.7
Charlotte-Concord-Gastonia, NC-SC	0.4	0.1	5.9	9.4	D	6.3	13.7	D	12.1	397 730	167	42 586	989 531	5.7
Charlottesville, VA	0.2	D	5.0	D	12.5	5.0	6.9	9.5	33.5	41 450	183	3 206	100 874	4.7
Chattanooga, TN-GA	0.4	0.1	D	14.2	D	7.1	D	D	17.6	118 420	218	13 895	240 080	2.4
Cheyenne, WY	1.3	1.5	7.6	3.5	7.2	6.2	5.7	7.7	39.8	17 105	177	1 533	41 955	3.7
Chicago-Naperville-Elgin, IL-IN-WI	0.1	0.1	5.0	10.5	D	5.0	10.9	9.7	12.6	1 447 820	151	207 337	3 812 136	0.4
.Chicago-Naperville-Arlington Heights, IL Div 16974	0.0	0.1	4.9	8.1	17.2	4.6	12.1	9.6	12.1	1 092 925	149	174 154	2 956 521	0.2
.Elgin, IL Div 20994	0.3	D	7.2	16.1	8.1	6.1	5.2	11.2	20.3	85 920	136	6 096	225 916	1.2
.Gary, IN Div 23844	1.1	D	9.1	22.7	4.6	7.1	3.6	14.4	10.8	139 260	197	15 516	297 657	1.2
.Lake County-Kenosha County, IL-WI Div 29404	0.1	0.0	3.6	21.6	9.6	7.1	6.2	7.3	13.9	129 715	149	11 571	332 042	0.8
Chico, CA	5.9	0.1	5.6	5.0	6.7	8.7	5.2	19.4	22.3	49 965	223	11 615	98 035	2.3
Cincinnati, OH-KY-IN	0.1	0.1	5.3	12.6	D	5.4	9.3	12.3	11.7	380 245	177	48 705	922 108	1.2
Clarksville, TN-KY	0.6	0.3	4.9	8.5	4.3	5.2	3.3	D	51.4	41 025	148	6 243	115 905	8.0
Cleveland, TN	2.2	0.1	5.7	20.6	D	6.6	D	D	10.7	28 375	237	3 182	51 364	4.0
Cleveland-Elyria, OH	0.1	D	4.6	13.7	10.7	5.2	9.6	13.9	13.7	413 980	201	63 474	957 499	0.2
Coeur d'Alene, ID	0.1	1.0	8.1	8.9	6.8	10.8	6.8	12.6	21.8	34 135	232	2 647	67 028	6.1
College Station-Bryan, TX	1.0	6.1	6.9	5.5	D	7.3	4.4	D	34.1	28 495	117	4 660	102 735	8.1
Colorado Springs, CO	0.0	D	5.5	D	15.9	6.3	6.1	9.1	33.5	102 010	149	8 867	281 862	6.2
Columbia, MO	0.5	0.1	5.1	4.4	8.1	7.3	7.1	10.9	37.0	24 680	143	2 772	74 436	7.0
Columbia, SC	0.3	0.1	4.9	9.3	9.6	6.3	D	9.6	25.5	143 730	180	16 198	345 117	4.1
Columbus, GA-AL	0.3	0.2	4.1	8.0	D	5.2	D	10.2	37.1	57 495	183	10 288	132 443	3.3
Columbus, IN	1.2	D	3.3	47.0	4.9	5.2	4.0	6.4	9.1	15 990	199	1 245	33 727	1.9
Columbus, OH	0.3	0.4	4.9	7.8	11.7	5.9	11.0	10.5	18.3	301 650	151	45 173	845 562	3.0
Corpus Christi, TX	0.8	D	12.4	7.7	5.8	5.9	4.5	D	17.0	79 220	177	16 106	190 999	4.4
Corvallis, OR	1.5	0.1	3.0	11.8	11.3	5.3	2.9	14.7	31.3	14 610	169	1 000	37 695	4.0
Crestview-Fort Walton Beach-Destin, FL	0.2	0.1	4.7	3.6	10.5	7.0	5.9	7.7	40.4	52 330	203	4 332	144 245	4.9
Cumberland, MD-WV	0.0	0.5	4.2	13.5	D	7.3	3.9	D	26.5	24 360	242	3 041	46 257	-0.2
Dallas-Fort Worth-Arlington, TX	0.1	5.7	6.6	9.1	14.0	5.5	11.4	D	10.1	872 100	125	130 192	2 686 705	6.3
Dallas-Plano-Irving, 19124	0.0	4.7	6.3	8.0	16.4	5.2	12.8	9.2	9.5	549 210	119	88 214	1 777 642	7.2
Fort Worth-Arlington, TX Div 23104	0.1	0.0	7.2	12.1	7.5	6.2	7.9	9.2	11.6	322 890	137	41 978	909 063	4.4
Dalton, GA	1.3	D	2.4	38.1	D	6.9	2.0	D	10.5	26 280	184	3 700	55 369	-0.9
Danville, IL	5.3	D	2.7	20.4	2.1	6.4	5.0	9.4	21.5	18 700	234	2 819	35 940	-1.0
Daphne-Fairhope-Foley, AL	0.6	0.2	8.4	6.9	5.4	13.9	7.2	12.4	14.4	48 780	244	3 462	108 564	4.3
Davenport-Moline-Rock Island, IA-IL	1.2	D	6.0	15.2	D	6.9	5.5	10.8	15.9	78 195	204	7 510	168 600	0.9
Dayton, OH	0.2	0.0	4.3	12.0	D	5.5	6.2	15.0	22.9	161 355	201	20 520	367 933	0.2
Decatur, AL	2.3	D	7.3	31.8	D	6.8	3.9	D	14.4	36 595	239	4 872	66 743	0.5
Decatur, IL	2.1	0.1	6.5	31.7	4.9	5.0	3.7	11.9	10.5	24 855	229	3 257	50 298	-0.4
Deltona-Daytona Beach-Ormond Beach, FL	0.4	D	5.6	7.8	7.4	10.2	5.6	18.1	16.4	175 495	288	13 806	307 011	1.4
Denver-Aurora-Lakewood, CO	0.1	5.8	6.1	5.1	D	4.8	D	8.3	12.2	368 530	134	36 598	1 132 228	4.9
Des Moines-West Des Moines, IA	0.9	0.1	7.9	6.0	9.9	5.5	D	10.3	12.6	96 020	157	8 920	258 050	7.4
Detroit-Warren-Dearborn, MI	0.1	D	4.7	15.9	D	5.6	7.5	11.9	10.4	863 165	201	133 775	1 895 743	0.5
Detroit-Dearborn-Livonia, MI Div 19804	0.0	0.3	4.0	14.8	D	4.4	5.7	13.6	12.8	355 660	201	85 261	814 328	-0.9
Warren-Troy-Farmington Hills, MI Div 47664	0.1	0.1	5.1	16.5	17.4	6.4	8.6	10.8	9.0	507 505	200	48 514	1 081 415	1.6
Dothan, AL	3.0	D	6.3	8.1	4.8	10.1	4.2	D	18.6	37 280	252	6 093	68 298	2.1
Dover, DE	3.3	D	5.4	D	4.8	7.9	6.0	11.9	36.8	36 125	210	3 769	68 692	5.1
Dubuque, IA	2.2	D	5.7	19.9	8.4	6.6	8.7	14.1	8.2	20 045	208	1 576	40 588	4.2
Duluth, MN-WI	0.1	6.3	6.9	6.9	5.9	6.9	4.5	20.2	19.6	63 310	226	7 068	142 131	0.4
Durham-Chapel Hill, NC	0.4	0.0	2.6	16.6	14.7	3.7	7.5	13.8	19.6	87 725	161	9 730	235 645	5.8
East Stroudsburg, PA	0.1	0.1	4.3	14.5	4.0	8.5	3.3	12.2	28.1	34 140	204	3 027	80 720	0.4
Eau Claire, WI	1.9	D	6.6	13.7	5.0	8.0	5.6	19.0	15.7	33 240	201	3 150	71 022	2.4
El Centro, CA	17.4	D	3.2	2.5	2.1	7.2	2.4	5.4	37.2	29 695	166	10 510	57 216	2.0
Elizabethtown-Fort Knox, KY	0.1	0.2	3.8	12.4	D	5.8	3.7	D	45.1	28 730	189	4 287	64 547	5.5
Elkhart-Goshen, IN	1.5	D	3.2	49.1	2.8	4.4	2.6	8.1	6.1	35 190	174	3 150	78 030	0.3
Elmira, NY	0.1	3.1	5.0	15.1	3.6	6.8	5.3	15.0	25.3	21 310	244	3 196	38 340	-0.1
El Paso, TX	0.1	D	D	D	D	7.5	D	10.1	36.2	122 035	145	30 053	290 975	7.0
Erie, PA	0.3	0.2	4.1	21.6	4.9	6.8	8.0	17.0	16.6	61 595	221	11 420	120 094	0.8
Eugene, OR	0.7	0.2	5.5	11.1	8.4	8.6	5.6	15.9	19.9	79 785	223	9 089	159 288	2.0
Evansville, IN-KY	1.3	2.9	8.8	20.0	D	6.4	3.6	15.8	9.6	67 395	214	7 390	140 561	1.3

1. Per 1,000 resident population estimated as of July 1, 2011 of the year shown.

Table C. Metropolitan Areas — **Housing, Labor Force, and Employment**

Area name	Housing units, 2014								Civilian labor force, 2015		Unemployment		Civilian employment[5], 2014		
	Occupied units													Percent	
		Owner-occupied				Renter-occupied									
				Median owner cost as a percent of income			Median rent as a percent of income	Percent with a computer		Percent change, 2013–2014				Management, professional, and related occupations	Construction, production, and related occupations
	Total	Percent	Median value[1]	With a mortgage	Without a mortgage[2]	Median rent[3]			Total		Total	Rate[4]	Total employed		
	89	90	91	92	93	94	95	96	97	98	99	100	101	102	103
Cedar Rapids, IA	106 799	75.1	149 600	19.4	11.8	695	26.1	87.2	144 526	-0.7	5 426	3.8	138 945	37.2	23.3
Chambersburg-Waynesboro, PA	58 565	68.2	165 100	21.8	11.6	809	27.4	78.7	77 739	1.7	3 723	4.8	70 617	29.5	29.9
Champaign-Urbana, IL	94 306	58.4	139 400	19.4	11.3	784	32.5	88.3	119 357	0.7	6 229	5.2	119 371	42.6	16.8
Charleston, WV	93 385	69.9	97 800	18.5	10.0	699	25.7	79.6	99 054	-1.6	6 378	6.4	91 854	36.4	19.0
Charleston-North Charleston, SC	276 509	64.0	189 700	23.1	12.1	986	32.2	87.7	361 515	2.5	18 526	5.1	349 358	37.5	19.5
Charlotte-Concord-Gastonia, NC-SC	883 281	64.6	169 400	20.3	11.0	884	29.1	87.5	1 235 300	2.7	67 511	5.5	1 143 533	37.9	20.8
Charlottesville, VA	87 139	61.4	261 800	22.0	10.6	1 040	31.4	87.0	116 114	1.0	4 538	3.9	106 989	46.0	15.1
Chattanooga, TN-GA	207 829	66.4	145 700	20.4	10.6	751	29.4	81.2	253 594	1.0	14 093	5.6	250 974	34.2	23.0
Cheyenne, WY	38 705	68.0	201 200	21.9	10.6	834	27.9	90.5	48 910	0.1	1 888	3.9	47 850	38.6	22.2
Chicago-Naperville-Elgin, IL-IN-WI	3 442 174	64.0	211 800	23.8	14.4	990	31.0	86.4	4 888 023	0.0	285 428	5.8	4 617 002	38.3	20.1
.Chicago-Naperville-Arlington Heights, IL Div 16974	2 668 895	61.8	221 900	24.3	14.8	1 001	31.0	85.8	3 772 665	-0.1	220 752	5.9	3 564 166	39.0	19.5
.Elgin, IL Div 20994	209 315	70.1	208 300	23.6	13.2	1 005	31.6	90.6	322 262	0.5	18 625	5.8	314 725	34.5	22.6
.Gary, IN Div 23844	261 698	71.3	143 800	20.3	11.6	823	30.1	85.2	337 557	-0.1	21 470	6.4	315 867	31.3	27.0
.Lake County-Kenosha County, IL-WI Div 29404	302 266	72.7	219 900	23.2	14.7	1 018	30.9	90.0	455 539	0.3	24 581	5.4	422 244	41.0	17.6
Chico, CA	85 366	59.3	225 400	25.0	10.7	887	38.2	86.7	101 731	-0.1	7 334	7.2	91 759	34.1	19.4
Cincinnati, OH-KY-IN	829 142	65.2	152 100	20.1	11.6	751	28.8	85.5	1 072 143	-0.3	48 406	4.5	1 041 322	38.5	20.4
Clarksville, TN-KY	97 747	56.8	137 100	20.5	10.0	816	30.5	83.7	108 713	0.1	6 586	6.1	103 031	31.7	24.1
Cleveland, TN	44 048	68.0	132 900	21.3	10.3	744	26.8	76.1	56 372	-0.7	3 134	5.6	50 676	28.1	31.0
Cleveland-Elyria, OH	848 493	64.4	137 800	21.2	12.8	752	30.7	83.4	1 025 539	-0.9	49 618	4.8	979 179	38.3	19.9
Coeur d'Alene, ID	56 177	66.3	192 100	23.8	10.2	792	25.0	86.9	71 896	1.8	3 582	5.0	65 274	29.1	27.3
College Station-Bryan, TX	89 858	47.7	149 600	22.0	11.6	853	33.5	88.2	120 844	1.5	4 279	3.5	113 615	37.8	20.8
Colorado Springs, CO	255 330	63.9	225 200	22.6	10.0	978	31.0	91.8	319 535	-0.1	14 713	4.6	305 729	40.1	17.4
Columbia, MO	67 198	55.5	170 700	19.6	10.0	802	31.6	93.1	100 284	2.5	3 491	3.5	93 405	42.2	12.7
Columbia, SC	298 600	66.3	140 800	20.7	10.7	857	30.6	84.4	396 021	1.9	21 640	5.5	377 334	36.1	20.0
Columbus, GA-AL	113 195	52.6	142 000	22.8	12.4	810	30.1	82.2	124 454	-2.0	8 570	6.9	131 333	32.2	21.9
Columbus, IN	31 827	69.8	132 400	19.6	14.1	810	24.4	80.5	43 649	2.4	1 559	3.6	40 270	36.9	28.4
Columbus, OH	764 395	60.7	160 800	20.5	12.3	847	28.6	87.7	1 038 547	1.0	42 907	4.1	1 003 744	41.4	18.2
Corpus Christi, TX	160 869	60.3	112 500	20.1	11.3	891	30.5	84.5	207 775	-0.6	10 733	5.2	204 281	30.3	27.0
Corvallis, OR	33 904	54.6	265 800	20.7	11.1	893	36.8	95.1	45 171	1.8	1 945	4.3	40 265	48.2	14.5
Crestview-Fort Walton Beach-Destin, FL	95 662	65.4	187 700	22.9	10.0	1 008	30.0	86.7	119 866	0.0	5 419	4.5	114 166	35.5	18.7
Cumberland, MD-WV	40 318	63.5	121 500	19.6	13.4	581	31.8	70.1	44 385	-1.6	3 158	7.1	39 753	26.4	24.9
Dallas-Fort Worth-Arlington, TX	2 445 239	59.2	160 600	21.6	12.0	949	29.4	88.8	3 584 196	1.4	145 674	4.1	3 412 127	38.1	21.1
Dallas-Plano-Irving, 19124	1 618 859	57.6	170 400	21.5	12.1	958	29.2	88.7	2 400 143	2.0	96 025	4.0	2 290 224	39.2	20.1
Fort Worth-Arlington, TX Div 23104	826 380	62.4	143 900	21.8	11.8	927	29.9	89.1	1 184 053	0.3	49 649	4.2	1 121 903	35.7	23.1
Dalton, GA	50 238	64.1	109 500	19.1	10.0	649	30.3	77.4	60 505	-0.2	4 003	6.6	64 403	18.1	46.7
Danville, IL	31 338	65.6	76 400	19.2	10.0	625	28.3	68.3	35 642	0.0	2 542	7.1	32 374	27.7	32.1
Daphne-Fairhope-Foley, AL	71 307	72.4	180 100	24.1	11.0	857	30.9	83.2	87 316	1.1	4 791	5.5	87 303	34.1	20.4
Davenport-Moline-Rock Island, IA-IL	153 602	69.7	126 800	19.6	12.4	685	26.5	80.7	192 696	-1.1	10 773	5.6	183 270	31.3	25.9
Dayton, OH	327 610	62.6	120 200	20.7	12.8	754	30.9	84.0	381 765	0.2	18 294	4.8	364 814	36.1	22.0
Decatur, AL	58 351	71.9	112 800	20.9	10.0	602	27.5	78.5	68 970	-1.6	4 280	6.2	65 844	28.7	34.6
Decatur, IL	44 063	71.2	95 100	17.9	11.7	613	27.7	81.8	50 593	-0.7	3 588	7.1	49 285	33.1	22.1
Deltona-Daytona Beach-Ormond Beach, FL	237 527	71.1	141 400	25.7	12.3	944	37.5	86.9	282 822	0.4	16 400	5.8	245 022	30.7	21.0
Denver-Aurora-Lakewood, CO	1 054 371	62.3	276 800	21.6	10.0	1 078	29.9	91.6	1 504 945	0.7	55 456	3.7	1 456 813	42.2	17.6
Des Moines-West Des Moines, IA	235 515	68.4	164 400	19.2	12.1	816	26.3	89.9	339 509	0.2	11 794	3.5	328 538	40.3	18.7
Detroit-Warren-Dearborn, MI	1 654 584	68.0	136 400	20.7	13.3	853	31.5	85.4	1 998 430	-0.6	124 239	6.2	1 939 406	37.4	21.3
Detroit-Dearborn-Livonia, MI Div 19804	661 414	61.5	84 900	21.7	14.1	788	34.8	81.5	750 854	-1.5	54 821	7.3	714 905	31.1	24.6
Warren-Troy-Farmington Hills, MI Div 47664	993 170	72.4	164 400	20.2	12.7	905	28.8	88.1	1 247 576	-0.1	69 418	5.6	1 224 501	41.1	19.4
Dothan, AL	55 998	68.4	106 300	19.8	10.8	669	29.6	76.3	62 284	-0.7	3 854	6.2	60 068	29.0	28.0
Dover, DE	61 270	67.2	205 300	23.1	11.2	1 025	30.7	87.2	76 887	2.2	4 149	5.4	78 047	33.1	24.0
Dubuque, IA	38 824	72.6	147 200	19.3	10.5	698	32.4	86.8	55 729	0.3	1 997	3.6	51 855	31.5	26.0
Duluth, MN-WI	116 768	71.7	140 100	20.8	12.6	724	31.0	83.2	142 600	-0.9	7 139	5.0	133 719	34.2	22.6
Durham-Chapel Hill, NC	213 163	58.6	199 200	20.7	10.0	908	30.6	88.7	281 198	2.1	14 015	5.0	262 124	47.9	15.8
East Stroudsburg, PA	54 404	78.0	167 800	26.4	19.0	1 169	32.1	88.6	80 651	1.1	5 046	6.3	73 771	33.8	22.2
Eau Claire, WI	65 392	62.7	150 400	20.8	13.8	750	27.6	87.0	91 409	0.3	3 827	4.2	87 820	33.5	27.1
El Centro, CA	43 635	56.7	156 000	24.9	12.2	775	33.3	79.8	78 910	0.3	18 945	24.0	57 497	25.1	26.8
Elizabethtown-Fort Knox, KY	54 612	65.9	136 500	19.1	10.0	762	27.7	84.5	63 537	-1.5	3 316	5.2	66 172	31.1	27.3
Elkhart-Goshen, IN	70 636	68.6	125 900	18.5	11.6	714	28.7	79.2	104 616	2.4	4 021	3.8	94 609	26.2	37.0
Elmira, NY	34 617	68.6	111 800	18.7	11.1	778	33.5	85.9	37 960	-0.8	2 247	5.9	37 388	35.4	21.6
El Paso, TX	256 548	61.5	114 700	23.3	11.1	739	29.7	77.3	344 725	-0.3	18 025	5.2	330 707	29.1	21.7
Erie, PA	108 655	66.3	124 400	20.6	12.5	694	29.5	84.5	134 873	0.2	7 185	5.3	127 150	34.4	21.1
Eugene, OR	145 732	59.1	214 700	24.7	12.3	870	34.4	89.7	171 388	1.2	10 194	5.9	163 371	33.5	21.4
Evansville, IN-KY	125 439	67.6	127 600	20.4	10.9	726	31.4	84.4	158 056	0.0	6 761	4.3	150 919	32.0	27.5

1. Specified owner-occupied units. 2. A value of 10.0 represents 10 percent or less. 3. Specified renter-occupied units. 4. Percent of civilian labor force.
5. Persons 16 years old and over.

Table C. Metropolitan Areas — **Nonfarm Employment and Agriculture**

Area name	Private nonfarm establishments, employment and payroll, 2014									Agriculture, 2012			
		Employment						Annual payroll		Farms			
											Percent with:		
	Number of establishments	Total	Health care and social assistance	Manufacturing	Retail trade	Finance and insurance	Professional, scientific, and technical services	Total (mil dol)	Average per employee (dollars)	Number	Fewer than 50 acres	500 acres or more	Farm operators whose principal occupation is farming (percent)
	104	105	106	107	108	109	110	111	112	113	114	115	116
Cedar Rapids, IA	6 445	125 754	17 140	18 020	16 159	9 953	5 910	5 729	45 554	3 678	32.5	19.9	55.6
Chambersburg-Waynesboro, PA	3 017	48 464	7 774	8 579	7 428	1 139	1 748	1 767	36 461	1 596	35.9	6.3	60.8
Champaign-Urbana, IL	4 844	75 108	D	8 008	11 518	3 231	3 117	2 845	37 883	2 284	28.5	32.7	56.8
Charleston, WV	5 451	93 147	20 613	3 421	12 291	5 004	5 967	3 887	41 727	343	29.2	1.7	40.5
Charleston-North Charleston, SC	17 270	256 192	34 812	24 829	38 411	7 948	20 379	10 657	41 597	1 143	56.3	7.0	45.2
Charlotte-Concord-Gastonia, NC-SC	56 408	954 262	124 847	90 178	114 411	77 011	58 805	47 874	50 169	7 328	50.8	4.6	44.6
Charlottesville, VA	6 005	80 519	17 192	4 278	11 362	4 026	5 947	3 728	46 304	2 311	33.3	8.0	43.4
Chattanooga, TN-GA	11 112	213 139	30 410	33 733	26 405	12 685	8 203	8 118	38 087	2 018	44.2	5.0	43.8
Cheyenne, WY	3 056	34 481	6 608	1 257	6 099	1 753	2 414	1 409	40 859	1 116	33.5	31.2	37.3
Chicago-Naperville-Elgin, IL-IN-WI	241 284	4 079 228	587 572	388 104	449 672	253 911	329 265	224 870	55 126	6 841	47.6	18.3	56.1
.Chicago-Naperville-Arlington Heights, IL Div 16974	NA	NA	NA	NA	NA	NA	NA	NA	NA	2 789	48.8	16.7	58.6
.Elgin, IL Div 20994	NA	NA	NA	NA	NA	NA	NA	NA	NA	1 470	40.2	22.6	63.2
.Gary, IN Div 23844	NA	NA	NA	NA	NA	NA	NA	NA	NA	1 874	45.0	21.5	48.8
.Lake County-Kenosha County, IL-WI Div 29404	NA	NA	NA	NA	NA	NA	NA	NA	NA	708	65.4	7.8	51.4
Chico, CA	4 637	57 562	13 656	4 477	10 411	2 300	2 557	2 018	35 059	2 056	66.8	7.0	59.4
Cincinnati, OH-KY-IN	45 633	896 336	141 539	96 059	105 305	58 239	56 250	43 206	48 203	9 242	46.3	4.5	40.7
Clarksville, TN-KY	4 276	66 687	10 923	11 680	12 221	2 059	2 434	2 151	32 249	2 359	31.5	9.6	41.3
Cleveland, TN	2 104	40 238	5 374	7 810	5 664	1 871	737	1 466	36 445	1 062	49.4	4.8	44.9
Cleveland-Elyria, OH	51 260	914 102	177 784	120 988	101 669	52 677	50 356	43 385	47 462	2 975	59.3	3.6	49.1
Coeur d'Alene, ID	4 366	46 988	9 025	4 980	8 612	2 091	2 914	1 660	35 334	824	58.4	6.7	48.1
College Station-Bryan, TX	4 698	67 251	9 815	5 561	11 376	1 762	3 203	2 340	34 795	4 361	35.0	10.1	44.6
Colorado Springs, CO	16 965	229 344	33 848	11 174	31 302	10 626	21 220	9 894	43 139	1 329	45.4	17.6	48.5
Columbia, MO	4 517	73 688	16 855	3 909	12 273	6 869	3 941	2 688	36 482	1 171	39.5	8.6	38.3
Columbia, SC	16 848	279 659	44 116	26 315	37 883	22 636	15 307	11 112	39 734	3 085	44.1	7.2	42.0
Columbus, GA-AL	5 621	97 888	17 901	11 166	13 999	D	2 881	3 523	35 995	770	32.2	13.1	42.2
Columbus, IN	1 796	44 983	4 598	11 771	4 762	988	3 401	2 094	46 552	623	44.1	14.4	44.8
Columbus, OH	40 850	826 924	141 122	62 190	98 181	74 492	51 085	39 163	47 360	8 198	47.4	9.9	43.1
Corpus Christi, TX	9 463	159 813	29 983	11 431	22 283	4 349	7 096	6 638	41 538	1 555	45.8	20.6	38.6
Corvallis, OR	2 103	24 947	5 706	1 892	3 515	603	2 283	1 025	41 071	886	71.4	5.6	46.3
Crestview-Fort Walton Beach-Destin, FL	7 071	75 717	11 030	D	16 340	2 562	6 490	2 645	34 933	1 147	46.7	5.8	41.9
Cumberland, MD-WV	2 030	30 983	7 266	4 218	4 828	952	1 708	1 050	33 876	720	32.9	5.3	37.2
Dallas-Fort Worth-Arlington, TX	152 400	2 869 738	356 355	238 757	330 741	201 088	222 056	152 299	53 071	29 659	61.7	4.8	35.8
Dallas-Plano-Irving, 19124	NA	NA	NA	NA	NA	NA	NA	NA	NA	16 257	61.9	4.6	35.6
Fort Worth-Arlington, TX Div 23104	NA	NA	NA	NA	NA	NA	NA	NA	NA	13 402	61.5	4.9	36.1
Dalton, GA	2 541	54 075	4 765	19 989	5 503	819	1 931	2 061	38 113	698	46.7	3.2	44.6
Danville, IL	1 451	24 259	5 288	4 771	3 765	1 232	429	941	38 805	956	36.6	29.5	54.5
Daphne-Fairhope-Foley, AL	4 969	56 531	6 953	4 052	13 471	1 596	1 856	1 749	30 943	989	52.6	8.1	45.8
Davenport-Moline-Rock Island, IA-IL	8 960	159 530	24 252	25 068	21 850	5 996	6 222	6 890	43 192	3 513	34.0	19.0	55.7
Dayton, OH	16 598	310 429	61 201	41 372	40 198	13 030	22 269	13 169	42 421	2 638	59.4	8.7	41.3
Decatur, AL	2 963	46 068	6 434	11 929	6 387	1 502	1 614	1 847	40 103	2 788	42.7	4.1	42.7
Decatur, IL	2 434	46 164	7 916	7 130	5 672	1 637	1 214	1 902	41 208	674	35.9	29.5	59.1
Deltona-Daytona Beach-Ormond Beach, FL	14 071	153 420	30 413	9 141	28 404	5 187	7 111	5 107	33 286	1 481	78.8	3.4	55.0
Denver-Aurora-Lakewood, CO	78 126	1 174 056	145 590	56 271	133 927	69 329	109 335	64 723	55 128	4 856	52.4	14.4	43.8
Des Moines-West Des Moines, IA	15 320	297 427	39 811	19 451	38 523	46 919	17 211	14 204	47 757	4 898	41.1	16.0	44.2
Detroit-Warren-Dearborn, MI	97 940	1 658 435	261 341	211 506	201 655	78 557	162 799	85 606	51 618	4 242	56.9	5.8	54.0
Detroit-Dearborn-Livonia, MI Div 19804	NA	NA	NA	NA	NA	NA	NA	NA	NA	287	77.7	1.4	59.9
Warren-Troy-Farmington Hills, MI Div 47664	NA	NA	NA	NA	NA	NA	NA	NA	NA	3 955	55.3	6.1	53.5
Dothan, AL	3 394	48 817	10 318	5 313	9 035	1 407	1 318	1 741	35 668	2 331	31.5	12.2	43.5
Dover, DE	3 263	49 311	9 676	4 449	9 130	1 675	2 271	1 903	38 583	863	54.5	9.0	56.8
Dubuque, IA	2 779	53 990	7 804	9 073	7 241	3 527	2 856	2 129	39 439	1 462	28.3	10.3	52.5
Duluth, MN-WI	7 001	108 003	28 909	7 140	15 646	4 087	3 976	4 283	39 658	1 550	25.4	6.1	41.0
Durham-Chapel Hill, NC	12 116	233 692	44 551	16 795	24 469	10 196	29 648	13 164	56 330	2 410	48.6	4.0	46.7
East Stroudsburg, PA	3 350	45 985	6 674	D	9 468	966	2 836	1 728	37 576	283	53.0	2.5	55.1
Eau Claire, WI	4 248	71 423	14 311	10 678	10 757	3 119	2 552	2 604	36 460	3 070	30.4	7.2	45.1
El Centro, CA	2 465	32 849	4 764	3 647	8 461	D	780	1 003	30 535	421	29.7	40.6	69.4
Elizabethtown-Fort Knox, KY	2 904	40 169	8 234	6 470	6 519	1 715	1 729	1 372	34 145	2 831	44.0	5.5	44.5
Elkhart-Goshen, IN	4 825	117 990	10 537	60 478	9 119	1 960	1 964	4 917	41 671	1 724	62.8	3.9	38.3
Elmira, NY	1 810	31 795	6 662	5 197	5 340	994	721	1 249	39 287	372	27.2	4.3	53.8
El Paso, TX	13 907	223 804	41 360	13 804	38 176	6 556	9 631	6 976	31 170	824	67.7	17.0	43.9
Erie, PA	6 176	112 761	23 617	20 045	15 859	D	3 702	4 258	37 759	1 422	41.2	4.1	48.7
Eugene, OR	9 558	120 985	22 831	13 417	19 364	5 359	5 244	4 496	37 163	2 660	73.9	2.9	44.5
Evansville, IN-KY	7 539	140 148	25 721	21 428	17 250	5 609	4 929	5 762	41 115	1 527	41.5	19.9	48.6

Table C. Metropolitan Areas — **Agriculture**

Area name	Land in farms					Value of land and buildings (dollars)		Value of machinery and equipment, average per farm (dollars)	Value of products sold				Percent of farms with sales of:		Government payments	
	Acreage (1,000)	Percent change, 2007–2012	Acres			Average per farm	Average per acre		Total (mil dol)	Average per farm (dollars)	Percent from:		$10,000 or more	$100,000 or more	Total ($1,000)	Percent of farms
			Average size of farm	Total irrigated (1,000)	Total cropland (1,000)						Crops	Live-stock and poultry products				
	117	118	119	120	121	122	123	124	125	126	127	128	129	130	131	132
Cedar Rapids, IA	1 075	1.4	292	0.4	930.0	2 020 529	6 910	203 111	918.4	249 694	69.5	30.5	63.3	38.3	28 988	76.7
Chambersburg-Waynesboro, PA	265	9.0	166	2.8	201.8	1 101 504	6 646	133 634	413.8	259 277	21.6	78.4	66.3	40.4	4 302	34.1
Champaign-Urbana, IL	1 184	8.8	518	19.6	1 140.6	4 153 230	8 014	311 067	802.9	351 514	92.5	7.5	73.2	50.6	21 102	84.3
Charleston, WV	48	5.0	141	D	6.4	285 079	2 024	31 985	1.9	5 522	32.7	67.3	15.2	0.3	D	7.6
Charleston-North Charleston, SC	185	16.1	162	4.0	62.8	651 877	4 027	59 942	D	D	D	52.2	27.9	7.1	1 317	18.1
Charlotte-Concord-Gastonia, NC-SC	939	2.4	128	5.0	437.2	717 330	5 599	71 406	D	D	D	D	31.1	10.8	D	13.6
Charlottesville, VA	407	4.8	176	2.5	114.7	1 095 125	6 216	61 828	101.3	43 836	40.3	59.7	35.3	5.0	871	13.3
Chattanooga, TN-GA	267	2.2	132	D	94.7	532 958	4 035	67 110	213.6	105 852	10.7	89.3	31.1	9.0	1 684	11.3
Cheyenne, WY	1 676	-0.9	1 502	59.3	338.1	1 079 159	719	110 585	190.7	170 918	24.4	75.6	37.0	17.6	4 938	32.7
Chicago-Naperville-Elgin, IL-IN-WI	2 232	-2.6	326	D	2 069.2	2 377 211	7 285	210 709	2 187.2	319 717	75.5	24.5	57.9	36.1	44 738	55.3
.Chicago-Naperville-Arlington Heights, IL Div 16974	831	-0.5	298	D	776.8	2 382 011	7 995	200 859	604.2	216 622	89.5	10.5	58.1	33.3	14 208	51.8
.Elgin, IL Div 20994	566	0.6	385	5.1	537.8	3 142 503	8 157	253 384	671.1	456 510	74.7	25.3	66.4	48.0	16 157	63.7
.Gary, IN Div 23844	728	-5.9	389	45.5	664.5	2 295 203	5 904	227 225	807.7	430 977	66.3	33.7	55.1	36.6	12 509	64.2
.Lake County-Kenosha County, IL-WI Div 29404	107	-10.3	151	0.7	90.1	986 410	6 547	117 194	104.3	147 323	70.9	29.1	47.2	21.6	1 864	28.2
Chico, CA	381	1.9	185	199.7	227.3	1 408 199	7 599	135 591	541.3	263 266	97.3	2.7	59.7	26.2	9 386	13.7
Cincinnati, OH-KY-IN	1 216	-5.6	132	D	698.5	582 601	4 427	73 512	418.6	45 298	82.2	17.8	31.2	7.8	14 347	34.1
Clarksville, TN-KY	637	0.5	270	5.5	401.2	958 646	3 552	104 747	280.3	118 814	80.1	19.9	43.1	15.8	9 847	46.5
Cleveland, TN	122	-4.6	115	0.2	44.8	593 111	5 157	61 272	153.7	144 771	6.4	93.6	31.5	12.4	397	9.4
Cleveland-Elyria, OH	304	3.1	102	4.4	217.0	614 628	6 011	86 924	375.3	126 146	83.2	16.8	42.2	13.4	3 173	19.7
Coeur d'Alene, ID	124	-5.1	151	13.8	64.3	624 138	4 139	57 726	23.7	28 750	83.8	16.2	19.5	4.1	1 075	20.1
College Station-Bryan, TX	1 102	0.9	253	46.6	231.0	736 281	2 914	63 936	321.5	73 722	24.9	75.1	32.1	5.4	5 786	11.1
Colorado Springs, CO	720	4.4	542	8.3	57.0	696 877	1 287	43 971	45.2	33 977	46.2	53.8	23.9	4.8	1 334	10.2
Columbia, MO	241	-7.0	206	5.3	144.4	749 119	3 644	69 631	52.2	44 565	66.0	34.0	34.9	8.1	1 837	31.0
Columbia, SC	522	3.0	169	D	198.1	537 771	3 177	78 787	578.6	187 568	26.8	73.2	29.9	11.0	4 185	19.8
Columbus, GA-AL	206	-3.8	267	5.7	51.8	724 603	2 715	63 508	58.6	76 142	D	D	25.8	6.0	1 166	26.8
Columbus, IN	172	3.2	275	13.5	153.4	1 619 191	5 878	151 406	95.6	153 387	89.5	10.5	54.9	27.1	4 647	63.7
Columbus, OH	1 746	5.0	213	2.9	1 448.9	1 049 293	4 928	131 542	1 180.0	143 942	76.3	23.7	42.8	18.9	28 755	43.7
Corpus Christi, TX	938	0.9	603	6.0	612.9	949 925	1 575	166 062	172.2	110 713	85.3	14.8	31.6	12.9	9 227	35.0
Corvallis, OR	124	8.2	140	11.3	68.2	830 059	5 932	68 867	103.3	116 597	78.2	21.8	28.6	10.4	486	6.4
Crestview-Fort Walton Beach-Destin, FL	209	8.7	183	1.5	49.3	565 418	3 097	49 066	38.8	33 870	49.0	51.0	22.1	5.3	1 802	27.6
Cumberland, MD-WV	112	-1.9	156	0.1	28.5	493 965	3 163	50 556	25.4	35 232	13.4	86.6	25.8	3.8	510	19.7
Dallas-Fort Worth-Arlington, TX	4 075	10.8	137	29.3	1 275.6	585 215	4 260	50 241	743.8	25 077	46.4	53.6	19.6	2.8	10 166	7.2
Dallas-Plano-Irving, 19124 TX Div	2 203	9.1	136	18.2	853.9	558 320	4 120	49 299	483.1	29 718	53.6	46.4	19.4	2.9	7 646	9.0
Fort Worth-Arlington, TX Div 23104	1 872	12.9	140	11.1	421.7	617 838	4 424	51 384	260.7	19 449	33.3	66.7	19.9	2.7	2 520	4.9
Dalton, GA	86	4.1	123	0.6	29.3	560 004	4 542	73 451	222.9	319 338	5.8	94.2	37.8	17.3	358	11.6
Danville, IL	434	-5.0	454	0.2	409.5	3 200 276	7 043	259 283	283.6	296 653	95.7	4.3	60.4	41.8	7 122	76.2
Daphne-Fairhope-Foley, AL	192	1.3	194	7.7	100.9	773 980	3 980	107 905	135.6	137 070	85.3	14.7	35.2	11.7	2 649	26.7
Davenport-Moline-Rock Island, IA-IL	1 101	-10.0	313	21.3	970.1	2 141 963	6 834	206 181	964.4	274 514	77.8	22.2	59.6	39.0	28 824	74.8
Dayton, OH	454	-3.5	172	4.2	394.2	1 006 136	5 845	111 095	282.7	107 154	89.5	10.5	44.1	17.8	6 976	51.1
Decatur, AL	396	3.2	142	5.0	167.3	471 748	3 318	68 907	301.3	108 081	23.3	76.7	32.3	11.8	6 226	31.2
Decatur, IL	337	15.8	499	0.0	321.7	3 911 432	7 833	294 921	211.3	313 540	95.7	4.3	66.0	42.7	5 762	80.1
Deltona-Daytona Beach-Ormond Beach, FL	150	5.6	101	12.9	28.8	564 216	5 584	45 579	128.4	86 726	90.0	10.0	35.0	9.6	D	7.6
Denver-Aurora-Lakewood, CO	2 490	-8.7	513	D	923.4	890 955	1 737	67 853	D	D	D	D	24.4	6.5	D	17.4
Des Moines-West Des Moines, IA	1 371	-3.9	280	D	1 079.5	1 644 653	5 875	143 481	891.6	182 028	70.5	29.5	49.3	22.9	32 090	65.6
Detroit-Warren-Dearborn, MI	557	2.2	131	7.3	437.7	626 459	4 770	106 037	399.2	94 113	83.9	16.1	41.1	14.6	6 302	21.4
Detroit-Dearborn-Livonia, MI Div 19804	16	-9.6	55	0.3	10.9	408 840	7 442	80 902	26.5	92 456	98.2	1.8	36.9	8.4	102	9.4
Warren-Troy-Farmington Hills, MI Div 47664	541	2.6	137	7.0	426.9	642 251	4 692	107 860	372.7	94 233	82.9	17.1	41.4	15.1	6 200	22.3
Dothan, AL	587	-0.7	252	20.0	263.4	586 922	2 332	93 694	342.7	147 028	44.1	55.9	34.8	15.3	13 121	60.3
Dover, DE	172	-0.9	200	31.8	147.4	1 596 656	7 999	121 074	277.7	321 816	D	D	53.3	29.8	2 550	37.2
Dubuque, IA	291	-6.2	199	0.0	224.3	1 214 544	6 093	172 274	387.8	265 260	31.0	69.0	67.5	39.7	11 080	81.2
Duluth, MN-WI	290	-9.1	187	D	131.9	345 245	1 843	52 513	35.8	23 111	54.9	45.1	34.8	3.6	D	7.3
Durham-Chapel Hill, NC	285	-1.5	118	5.1	104.5	611 832	5 181	58 915	245.0	101 639	28.0	72.0	35.7	9.9	2 245	21.0
East Stroudsburg, PA	26	-9.2	94	0.1	13.0	735 583	7 861	71 198	11.0	38 777	66.8	33.2	35.7	8.5	174	15.5
Eau Claire, WI	588	5.3	192	8.7	378.7	540 963	2 823	99 430	366.5	119 378	41.7	58.3	47.9	20.6	8 327	53.8
El Centro, CA	516	20.7	1 225	455.0	487.9	8 577 865	7 002	745 304	1 888.6	4 486 078	69.4	30.6	84.3	66.7	2 788	29.5
Elizabethtown-Fort Knox, KY	434	-7.4	153	0.9	245.1	523 605	3 412	77 721	136.4	48 180	66.5	33.5	36.8	7.3	4 749	44.3
Elkhart-Goshen, IN	173	5.8	100	25.5	140.2	808 782	8 067	83 012	296.8	172 178	28.0	72.0	51.8	27.4	2 785	20.1
Elmira, NY	58	-10.8	156	0.2	28.1	376 065	2 407	75 599	16.0	43 143	41.2	58.8	28.5	8.6	482	22.8
El Paso, TX	2 461	1.4	2 986	43.0	101.6	2 030 155	680	101 518	80.0	97 103	80.4	19.6	33.7	12.0	2 091	14.7
Erie, PA	169	-2.6	119	0.9	96.2	407 705	3 438	75 158	91.7	64 469	76.5	23.5	41.5	12.8	1 693	20.5
Eugene, OR	220	-10.6	83	19.3	100.0	563 427	6 824	49 734	142.5	53 574	74.6	25.4	23.5	5.6	575	5.1
Evansville, IN-KY	581	-0.1	380	D	524.8	1 668 276	4 386	228 634	294.2	192 650	90.1	9.9	51.7	27.9	10 066	67.8

Area name	Water use, 2010		Wholesale trade,¹ 2012				Retail trade, 2012				Real estate and rental and leasing, 2012			
	Total water withdrawn (mil gal/day)	Gallons withdrawn per person per day	Number of establishments	Number of employees	Sales (mil dol)	Annual payroll (mil dol)	Number of establishments	Number of employees	Sales (mil dol)	Annual payroll (mil dol)	Number of establishments	Number of employees	Receipts (mil dol)	Annual payroll (mil dol)
	133	134	135	136	137	138	139	140	141	142	143	144	145	146
Cedar Rapids, IA	153.4	595	364	5 483	4 229.0	284.7	882	16 193	4 949.8	393.1	239	1 022	210.4	36.0
Chambersburg-Waynesboro, PA	19.1	127	108	D	D	D	486	7 106	1 809.5	157.6	87	328	54.9	10.4
Champaign-Urbana, IL	42.0	181	235	3 501	3 586.0	161.9	724	11 239	2 735.2	241.0	213	3 033	562.6	119.0
Charleston, WV	595.0	2 620	267	3 771	2 568.6	186.0	840	12 216	3 459.6	294.5	244	1 220	279.9	42.5
Charleston-North Charleston, SC	658.6	991	692	7 954	6 339.0	417.6	2 628	35 904	9 411.5	849.2	929	4 326	796.6	155.8
Charlotte-Concord-Gastonia, NC-SC	4 214.7	1 901	3 185	46 227	33 695.9	2 696.6	7 467	107 892	29 996.8	2 541.1	2 704	13 096	2 885.5	646.3
Charlottesville, VA	148.2	678	146	1 853	868.8	100.8	835	11 100	2 702.8	266.0	289	1 356	248.1	48.0
Chattanooga, TN-GA	1 991.2	3 770	543	6 354	3 413.3	305.2	1 932	25 651	6 903.8	613.2	445	2 309	453.4	103.9
Cheyenne, WY	236.4	2 577	121	1 105	722.2	67.0	370	5 513	1 896.2	161.3	142	461	99.5	16.5
Chicago-Naperville-Elgin, IL-IN-WI	7 722.8	816	12 340	204 598	231 996.5	13 565.0	28 181	437 310	127 688.0	11 090.7	9 629	64 763	21 668.7	3 443.4
.Chicago-Naperville-Arlington Heights, IL Div 16974	4 602.2	634	9 720	158 870	187 061.2	10 316.5	21 489	331 143	93 728.7	8 416.8	7 713	55 585	19 420.2	3 045.0
.Elgin, IL Div 20994	76.2	123	801	9 957	9 982.0	598.8	1 767	27 240	6 733.8	599.9	508	2 492	684.0	97.9
.Gary, IN Div 23844	2 357.1	3 329	612	6 761	6 918.2	335.4	2 125	32 702	10 190.7	748.4	548	2 840	496.9	96.3
.Lake County-Kenosha County, IL-WI Div 29404	687.4	790	1 207	29 010	28 035.2	2 314.3	2 800	46 225	17 034.7	1 325.6	860	3 846	1 067.6	204.2
Chico, CA	715.3	3 252	148	D	D	D	725	9 231	2 576.9	240.4	234	1 160	147.6	28.3
Cincinnati, OH-KY-IN	1 580.1	747	2 292	43 770	51 641.2	2 634.6	6 428	104 296	30 586.2	2 564.2	1 911	11 621	2 614.7	482.8
Clarksville, TN-KY	46.0	176	147	1 921	1 653.1	79.5	828	11 849	3 261.3	284.6	211	958	146.6	29.3
Cleveland, TN	23.6	204	65	D	D	D	409	5 046	1 419.3	118.8	66	294	38.3	8.6
Cleveland-Elyria, OH	1 768.5	851	2 840	42 048	26 946.9	2 259.0	6 674	97 427	25 943.9	2 303.9	2 111	16 590	5 313.5	765.5
Coeur d'Alene, ID	56.5	408	132	D	D	D	574	7 996	2 501.7	207.0	201	623	122.6	19.1
College Station-Bryan, TX	531.0	2 322	160	1 805	1 275.7	91.1	736	10 830	3 113.8	233.7	244	1 352	271.6	46.2
Colorado Springs, CO	123.7	192	442	4 431	2 576.6	248.6	2 025	29 505	8 137.0	775.0	1 074	3 427	669.1	122.3
Columbia, MO	18.7	115	135	1 461	631.4	73.2	627	11 563	3 741.0	287.7	227	920	160.6	28.8
Columbia, SC	1 216.5	1 585	762	11 901	8 591.9	627.6	2 616	36 865	9 747.3	839.7	701	4 198	985.9	181.5
Columbus, GA-AL	95.8	325	182	2 405	1 716.5	95.0	1 034	13 671	3 475.8	300.0	289	1 615	285.7	59.6
Columbus, IN	18.2	237	77	998	774.4	52.7	306	4 701	1 113.1	99.4	72	303	57.0	9.4
Columbus, OH	294.4	155	1 746	30 642	33 473.9	1 742.1	5 592	97 309	31 432.9	2 571.3	1 937	11 638	3 033.5	480.4
Corpus Christi, TX	247.1	577	407	D	D	D	1 351	20 248	6 139.4	495.5	504	3 109	706.8	138.3
Corvallis, OR	38.8	454	44	346	452.5	22.6	262	3 455	731.0	82.5	105	453	53.3	10.2
Crestview-Fort Walton Beach-Destin, FL	40.1	170	184	1 624	883.8	79.2	1 194	14 773	3 704.0	346.5	528	2 300	404.8	86.3
Cumberland, MD-WV	46.5	450	57	596	234.7	25.5	359	4 853	1 160.1	102.0	67	236	34.0	6.4
Dallas-Fort Worth-Arlington, TX	3 374.1	525	7 562	130 067	150 841.7	8 112.6	19 506	305 066	97 494.7	8 162.1	7 462	57 356	12 829.3	2 748.1
Dallas-Plano-Irving, 19124	902.2	213	5 279	92 203	118 378.4	5 990.3	12 725	199 722	63 747.3	5 406.4	5 314	43 570	9 887.9	2 154.9
Fort Worth-Arlington, TX Div 23104	2 471.9	1 126	2 283	37 864	32 463.3	2 122.4	6 781	105 344	33 747.3	2 755.7	2 148	13 786	2 941.5	593.2
Dalton, GA	26.4	186	217	3 003	1 320.0	120.1	525	5 401	1 500.4	123.7	75	349	133.7	13.2
Danville, IL	14.0	171	77	1 788	3 136.5	84.3	255	3 401	850.3	74.3	45	158	28.7	4.5
Daphne-Fairhope-Foley, AL	64.4	353	175	1 868	1 118.2	84.1	950	12 072	3 145.8	280.0	292	1 760	250.3	53.8
Davenport-Moline-Rock Island, IA-IL	1 271.5	3 349	496	7 650	7 471.4	414.1	1 314	21 284	5 530.5	501.3	326	1 311	309.0	42.9
Dayton, OH	173.3	217	684	9 796	17 365.8	533.2	2 487	39 751	9 851.3	905.5	735	3 939	665.2	133.2
Decatur, AL	196.5	1 277	164	2 144	1 455.9	91.4	583	6 300	1 891.5	144.5	87	351	78.8	12.7
Decatur, IL	39.4	356	112	D	D	D	395	5 724	1 494.2	133.7	88	471	105.2	13.8
Deltona-Daytona Beach-Ormond Beach, FL	251.7	426	474	3 222	1 725.6	154.7	2 104	26 736	6 941.6	642.5	792	2 866	478.1	88.2
Denver-Aurora-Lakewood, CO	748.1	294	3 311	48 922	53 628.2	3 061.7	8 302	123 338	35 076.0	3 331.1	4 455	20 864	5 461.1	959.7
Des Moines-West Des Moines, IA	71.5	126	795	12 805	10 596.6	699.5	1 966	35 339	9 452.9	842.5	654	3 714	759.0	160.6
Detroit-Warren-Dearborn, MI	3 379.8	787	4 655	66 120	60 968.3	4 010.0	15 127	194 583	54 637.0	4 845.5	3 605	25 561	8 298.0	1 035.2
Detroit-Dearborn-Livonia, MI Div 19804	1 797.3	987	1 483	23 525	25 358.3	1 417.5	6 091	65 409	17 409.4	1 539.9	1 070	6 044	4 464.6	225.3
Warren-Troy-Farmington Hills, MI Div 47664	1 582.5	639	3 172	42 595	35 609.9	2 592.5	9 036	129 174	37 227.6	3 305.6	2 535	19 517	3 833.4	810.0
Dothan, AL	132.0	906	196	2 986	8 979.2	154.7	716	8 675	2 426.0	204.9	110	440	74.7	16.4
Dover, DE	43.3	267	94	D	D	D	561	8 856	2 690.8	214.1	127	459	92.2	17.0
Dubuque, IA	40.5	432	158	2 353	2 083.1	107.4	442	7 157	1 659.1	149.1	110	381	72.4	12.2
Duluth, MN-WI	376.0	1 344	267	3 351	2 368.2	158.6	1 168	15 179	3 937.6	340.4	260	1 098	180.2	30.4
Durham-Chapel Hill, NC	1 319.2	2 616	355	9 817	7 270.2	1 042.0	1 626	23 631	5 748.8	553.7	503	2 351	485.6	94.3
East Stroudsburg, PA	33.1	195	97	D	D	D	634	8 710	2 140.4	187.8	123	507	86.8	15.2
Eau Claire, WI	33.3	206	157	2 272	1 422.0	94.5	615	10 495	2 723.8	225.7	141	659	91.2	18.5
El Centro, CA	1 169.2	6 699	197	1 801	1 599.1	72.5	446	7 322	1 676.9	160.3	119	574	92.6	15.9
Elizabethtown-Fort Knox, KY	27.6	186	74	D	D	D	501	6 618	1 900.3	154.9	129	543	68.2	12.9
Elkhart-Goshen, IN	33.0	167	340	5 803	3 329.9	249.5	678	8 754	2 440.4	206.9	157	768	134.5	25.4
Elmira, NY	9.8	111	85	1 193	765.0	51.5	350	5 044	1 174.8	115.8	84	382	106.6	17.0
El Paso, TX	397.4	494	952	D	D	D	2 332	34 975	9 192.0	754.1	699	3 143	617.3	108.0
Erie, PA	49.4	176	264	3 127	1 242.5	145.7	958	15 221	3 752.8	326.4	182	1 042	158.5	32.3
Eugene, OR	224.2	637	384	4 860	2 852.0	229.0	1 270	18 265	4 291.5	449.9	505	2 115	314.3	58.4
Evansville, IN-KY	826.3	2 652	366	5 873	3 818.1	346.7	1 154	17 133	4 570.3	396.7	289	1 954	297.2	54.7

1. Merchant wholesalers, except manufacturers' sales branches and offices.

Table C. Metropolitan Areas — **Professional Services, Manufacturing, and Accommodation and Food Services**

Area name	Professional, scientific, and technical services, 2012				Manufacturing, 2012				Accommodation and food services, 2012			
	Number of establishments	Number of employees	Sales (mil dol)	Annual payroll (mil dol)	Number of establishments	Number of employees	Sales (mil dol)	Annual payroll (mil dol)	Number of establishments	Number of employees	Sales (mil dol)	Annual payroll (mil dol)
	147	148	149	150	151	152	153	154	155	156	157	158
Cedar Rapids, IA	564	5 682	747.4	328.4	265	19 213	10 486.4	1 348.3	570	9 449	410.9	119.2
Chambersburg-Waynesboro, PA	223	2 067	234.8	100.3	196	8 182	3 180.0	403.9	270	D	D	D
Champaign-Urbana, IL	485	2 967	381.1	144.2	162	7 807	3 700.2	345.5	579	10 454	459.4	126.4
Charleston, WV	585	6 079	898.7	344.1	129	3 062	2 207.6	188.9	483	9 649	568.7	150.6
Charleston-North Charleston, SC	2 001	18 874	3 340.8	1 296.0	465	23 529	13 956.2	1 379.1	1 616	34 059	1 968.3	543.8
Charlotte-Concord-Gastonia, NC-SC	6 214	58 864	10 186.8	3 891.2	2 340	86 773	36 489.5	4 175.6	4 465	87 966	4 719.8	1 269.1
Charlottesville, VA	791	6 406	967.0	401.8	173	3 830	977.5	211.2	551	9 857	561.8	153.9
Chattanooga, TN-GA	942	D	D	D	557	32 303	14 940.6	1 610.2	1 056	21 292	1 089.7	306.5
Cheyenne, WY	458	1 860	279.8	99.7	67	1 190	2 549.8	76.8	207	3 980	224.8	59.8
Chicago-Naperville-Elgin, IL-IN-WI	33 178	323 636	64 623.4	26 279.3	10 473	383 870	194 249.9	21 208.1	19 708	355 344	22 899.9	6 279.1
.Chicago-Naperville-Arlington Heights, IL Div 16974	26 911	277 996	58 343.8	23 040.6	8 005	274 717	127 047.1	14 762.8	15 390	281 814	18 925.7	5 214.3
.Elgin, IL Div 20994	1 690	10 006	1 667.7	598.1	909	33 826	11 678.1	1 702.8	1 064	18 219	856.3	243.1
.Gary, IN Div 23844	1 302	8 302	1 004.9	369.3	545	34 450	41 108.4	2 531.9	1 394	25 099	1 480.8	349.3
.Lake County-Kenosha County, IL-WI Div 29404	3 275	27 332	3 606.9	2 271.3	1 014	40 878	14 416.3	2 210.6	1 860	30 212	1 637.1	472.3
Chico, CA	424	2 394	388.0	97.2	177	4 126	1 341.1	168.3	397	7 091	350.5	96.4
Cincinnati, OH-KY-IN	D	D	D	D	2 239	100 872	47 994.7	5 697.6	4 151	88 347	4 798.4	1 274.3
Clarksville, TN-KY	297	2 668	337.7	120.4	155	10 702	4 287.4	484.5	470	8 759	408.6	113.4
Cleveland, TN	150	867	78.4	32.6	122	8 069	5 718.3	345.2	196	3 834	177.5	47.1
Cleveland-Elyria, OH	5 775	50 835	7 976.9	3 175.2	3 358	120 600	43 530.2	6 669.9	4 461	79 070	3 864.1	1 065.2
Coeur d'Alene, ID	442	D	D	D	241	4 011	D	170.2	362	D	D	D
College Station-Bryan, TX	441	2 877	539.8	139.6	123	4 903	1 180.0	198.2	502	10 084	476.3	129.7
Colorado Springs, CO	2 505	20 151	3 041.6	1 280.6	479	10 471	3 382.5	562.2	1 371	28 383	1 554.0	427.2
Columbia, MO	414	3 570	424.0	156.7	99	3 994	2 042.1	173.3	419	9 006	373.2	104.7
Columbia, SC	1 911	16 971	2 745.8	1 045.8	516	24 989	13 694.4	1 250.5	1 500	29 589	1 391.3	385.3
Columbus, GA-AL	463	3 050	359.1	133.7	186	11 255	3 755.5	471.4	562	12 474	617.9	173.3
Columbus, IN	159	3 550	299.0	234.7	142	11 663	5 636.4	553.6	201	4 243	198.6	54.2
Columbus, OH	4 702	50 668	8 800.6	3 360.9	1 411	60 169	33 070.4	3 129.4	4 071	81 490	4 087.9	1 162.2
Corpus Christi, TX	927	6 378	928.0	338.3	238	10 950	44 697.1	775.4	1 048	20 133	1 046.4	279.9
Corvallis, OR	284	1 996	332.6	125.1	93	1 613	412.7	71.4	209	3 087	142.8	41.6
Crestview-Fort Walton Beach-Destin, FL	811	6 485	975.9	407.7	113	2 832	572.2	139.7	666	16 040	940.1	278.4
Cumberland, MD-WV	123	681	53.9	22.8	68	4 367	1 470.3	236.5	231	D	D	D
Dallas-Fort Worth-Arlington, TX	19 150	210 153	39 787.8	15 548.4	5 481	225 780	109 647.6	12 308.6	12 577	263 818	15 353.0	4 225.5
Dallas-Plano-Irving, 19124	14 206	168 149	33 185.1	13 176.9	3 512	145 699	61 179.9	7 948.5	8 449	176 054	10 381.6	2 902.0
Fort Worth-Arlington, TX Div 23104	4 944	42 004	6 602.7	2 371.5	1 969	80 081	48 467.8	4 360.1	4 128	87 764	4 971.4	1 323.5
Dalton, GA	188	D	D	D	330	17 966	7 111.9	668.8	213	3 781	196.4	50.1
Danville, IL	84	428	46.7	16.6	96	5 168	2 353.2	256.1	143	2 161	86.0	25.4
Daphne-Fairhope-Foley, AL	450	1 899	211.5	86.2	146	3 780	1 438.8	166.8	462	10 726	560.6	161.1
Davenport-Moline-Rock Island, IA-IL	776	5 712	1 007.7	280.0	402	24 533	16 677.3	1 289.9	872	15 809	832.3	208.7
Dayton, OH	1 717	21 824	3 582.6	1 420.6	1 048	40 297	13 041.0	2 179.3	1 611	32 811	1 508.4	428.8
Decatur, AL	230	1 483	167.8	69.3	202	12 048	10 543.3	718.5	243	4 370	197.9	54.9
Decatur, IL	157	1 216	142.7	54.0	109	8 240	13 379.3	435.3	225	4 331	189.8	55.6
Deltona-Daytona Beach-Ormond Beach, FL	1 510	7 316	886.3	301.5	380	8 224	2 024.2	367.4	1 156	22 876	1 134.5	341.5
Denver-Aurora-Lakewood, CO	12 927	108 529	22 675.3	8 365.9	2 237	52 525	24 861.3	2 880.5	5 846	115 312	7 069.5	2 014.3
Des Moines-West Des Moines, IA	1 686	15 965	2 633.1	966.8	427	19 669	11 785.8	953.5	1 354	24 834	1 211.0	348.2
Detroit-Warren-Dearborn, MI	11 419	163 997	24 342.5	12 026.3	5 353	199 394	110 685.0	11 620.7	8 168	153 118	8 567.2	2 275.4
Detroit-Dearborn-Livonia, MI Div 19804	2 848	46 825	7 135.0	3 444.6	1 483	71 526	56 638.5	4 413.5	3 184	61 446	4 238.8	1 050.2
Warren-Troy-Farmington Hills, MI Div 47664	8 571	117 172	17 207.5	8 581.7	3 870	127 869	54 046.5	7 207.2	4 984	91 672	4 328.4	1 225.2
Dothan, AL	261	1 359	162.4	59.6	132	4 834	1 646.4	182.8	280	5 084	231.9	61.9
Dover, DE	278	D	D	D	74	4 797	1 930.8	218.9	272	6 183	475.8	101.1
Dubuque, IA	166	2 956	450.9	147.7	144	8 498	6 036.4	434.6	242	4 456	169.5	49.8
Duluth, MN-WI	510	D	D	D	286	6 999	12 135.4	375.2	754	12 463	632.6	155.0
Durham-Chapel Hill, NC	1 838	35 056	6 112.3	2 966.1	350	15 118	10 445.6	957.9	1 179	22 267	1 248.1	344.0
East Stroudsburg, PA	306	D	D	D	111	4 449	D	358.1	387	8 392	724.8	155.1
Eau Claire, WI	265	2 089	252.1	102.8	209	9 968	3 621.4	444.4	440	6 931	276.6	75.5
El Centro, CA	179	787	79.1	30.4	50	2 218	1 466.0	95.4	258	3 516	182.6	47.9
Elizabethtown-Fort Knox, KY	270	1 809	184.5	69.0	88	5 679	2 366.8	262.1	229	5 034	220.3	61.7
Elkhart-Goshen, IN	313	2 004	220.2	81.0	795	53 705	14 833.3	2 288.0	348	6 500	280.7	75.8
Elmira, NY	111	774	83.5	36.1	85	5 495	1 247.0	278.8	202	3 534	154.5	43.3
El Paso, TX	1 202	D	D	D	505	13 129	D	543.2	1 481	28 757	1 385.5	375.5
Erie, PA	412	3 028	375.8	135.3	476	21 490	9 437.7	1 179.0	630	10 877	485.4	128.2
Eugene, OR	948	5 301	583.9	226.2	529	12 345	4 039.3	581.3	937	13 627	711.8	203.7
Evansville, IN-KY	640	5 050	D	228.1	398	20 872	15 137.5	1 118.6	656	14 254	694.8	185.7

Area name	Health care and social assistance, 2012				Other services, 2012				Nonemployer business, 2014		Value of residential construction authorized by building permits, 2015	
	Number of establishments	Number of employees	Receipts (mil dol)	Annual payroll (mil dol)	Number of establishments	Number of employees	Receipts (mil dol)	Annual payroll (mil dol)	Number	Receipts (mil dol)	New construction ($1,000)	Number of housing units
	159	160	161	162	163	164	165	166	167	168	169	170
Cedar Rapids, IA	663	16 556	1 557.5	658.3	469	2 866	281.8	83.6	16 225	696.4	114 844	1 073
Chambersburg-Waynesboro, PA..........	305	8 178	820.5	349.3	287	1 558	131.5	32.7	8 944	380.5	44 392	231
Champaign-Urbana, IL.........	420	13 306	1 770.8	610.5	317	2 293	414.2	69.0	13 884	512.8	166 840	1 235
Charleston, WV	795	19 917	2 139.0	795.7	416	3 070	299.4	91.1	10 384	418.4	30 745	283
Charleston-North Charleston, SC	1 669	35 964	4 763.9	1 578.2	1 120	7 240	733.9	205.1	55 082	2 563.5	1 347 644	6 590
Charlotte-Concord-Gastonia, NC-SC.........................	5 167	113 438	13 463.8	5 178.0	3 490	22 305	2 609.7	674.3	181 309	7 775.1	3 650 576	19 543
Charlottesville, VA...............	561	16 296	2 372.6	999.2	381	3 381	666.6	140.0	17 930	826.9	222 809	989
Chattanooga, TN-GA	1 275	31 220	3 602.0	1 420.4	716	5 022	569.2	149.4	37 255	1 732.5	325 005	2 093
Cheyenne, WY	323	6 700	647.9	305.2	189	943	93.6	27.1	7 327	450.5	75 787	440
Chicago-Naperville-Elgin, IL-IN-WI	25 714	569 844	63 927.3	24 944.8	17 586	132 350	17 826.4	4 831.8	764 074	34 675.4	3 581 960	15 813
.Chicago-Naperville-Arlington Heights, IL Div 16974	20 277	459 774	51 473.0	20 190.9	13 870	107 796	15 518.3	4 150.1	623 184	28 078.9	2 617 262	11 596
.Elgin, IL Div 20994	1 382	26 345	2 910.1	1 147.8	968	6 879	664.2	187.5	38 789	1 662.6	310 994	1 589
.Gary, IN Div 23844	1 691	41 436	4 686.3	1 716.8	1 231	8 564	814.5	239.1	39 982	1 577.3	371 563	1 697
.Lake County-Kenosha County, IL-WI Div 29404	2 364	42 289	4 858.0	1 889.3	1 517	9 111	829.4	255.1	62 119	3 356.6	282 141	931
Chico, CA	716	12 868	1 434.5	560.2	321	2 158	190.0	56.0	13 232	620.0	124 758	621
Cincinnati, OH-KY-IN	4 831	134 554	15 421.0	6 374.0	3 255	24 339	2 431.1	681.1	138 744	6 182.1	890 580	4 661
Clarksville, TN-KY	510	10 678	986.1	367.7	285	1 577	129.3	36.8	13 435	610.8	168 081	1 342
Cleveland, TN	248	5 054	653.8	200.8	102	873	73.0	21.8	7 935	380.0	92 346	732
Cleveland-Elyria, OH	5 423	173 697	17 969.1	7 747.1	3 895	26 763	2 784.6	775.0	146 268	6 616.4	658 337	2 938
Coeur d'Alene, ID	509	8 630	806.2	308.4	236	D	D	D	11 422	484.2	278 541	1 414
College Station-Bryan, TX ...	433	8 794	1 080.7	395.8	316	2 193	405.2	62.8	15 354	718.1	267 154	1 712
Colorado Springs, CO	1 955	31 286	3 300.0	1 327.9	1 128	8 548	1 816.7	326.1	49 543	1 989.9	1 172 684	3 665
Columbia, MO	602	16 725	2 033.5	699.4	327	1 985	187.4	53.2	11 136	539.2	260 589	1 433
Columbia, SC	1 637	42 874	4 546.9	1 828.4	1 224	8 398	794.5	241.2	51 576	2 105.7	756 610	4 642
Columbus, GA-AL	691	16 540	1 625.9	635.9	404	2 693	259.9	74.2	19 431	642.4	180 085	1 244
Columbus, IN	221	4 824	512.8	203.1	111	692	82.5	19.7	4 229	166.8	52 630	233
Columbus, OH	4 677	133 376	14 049.2	5 491.7	2 808	23 334	3 073.2	774.6	145 717	6 633.0	1 366 663	7 555
Corpus Christi, TX	1 186	30 414	2 800.7	1 049.3	633	4 993	581.9	158.7	30 676	1 392.3	341 240	2 153
Corvallis, OR	271	5 258	588.1	258.8	147	891	153.8	30.3	5 696	229.3	39 562	142
Crestview-Fort Walton Beach-Destin, FL	658	11 275	1 378.0	474.1	435	2 145	198.0	56.5	22 109	1 203.2	704 606	2 027
Cumberland, MD-WV	314	7 665	686.5	263.5	180	960	72.1	20.7	4 455	163.9	11 149	84
Dallas-Fort Worth-Arlington, TX	17 015	331 041	40 730.9	15 173.9	8 560	70 090	8 772.4	2 385.7	598 286	31 345.9	10 566 289	57 146
Dallas-Plano-Irving, 19124...	11 734	226 936	28 266.9	10 701.7	5 677	47 622	6 382.3	1 735.2	404 173	21 934.9	8 346 357	46 785
Fort Worth-Arlington, TX Div 23104	5 281	104 105	12 464.0	4 472.2	2 883	22 468	2 390.1	650.5	194 113	9 411.0	2 219 932	10 361
Dalton, GA	225	4 744	525.2	198.0	141	958	85.2	28.7	7 844	369.0	26 263	159
Danville, IL	143	4 736	514.4	235.4	121	540	47.4	13.3	4 329	139.3	1 340	10
Daphne-Fairhope-Foley, AL..	444	7 029	622.5	265.3	269	1 203	110.5	31.9	17 301	835.2	361 390	2 203
Davenport-Moline-Rock Island, IA-IL....................	1 010	22 953	2 081.4	893.8	684	4 209	364.7	106.2	20 834	834.1	122 637	751
Dayton, OH	2 004	59 132	6 556.8	2 598.1	1 242	8 387	863.6	206.1	48 044	1 906.1	253 730	980
Decatur, AL.........................	376	6 469	541.2	207.7	180	1 060	103.0	29.5	9 599	370.0	20 930	139
Decatur, IL	291	8 193	886.2	332.1	176	1 170	239.1	37.3	5 940	184.8	11 023	47
Deltona-Daytona Beach-Ormond Beach, FL	1 542	28 190	3 112.5	1 157.7	1 150	5 517	584.5	186.5	48 003	2 022.8	619 221	2 047
Denver-Aurora-Lakewood, CO	7 163	130 863	15 988.2	6 540.4	5 189	35 432	4 395.4	1 161.3	241 294	11 938.9	3 740 467	18 326
Des Moines-West Des Moines, IA	1 414	39 163	4 078.1	1 844.6	1 143	8 007	992.9	271.6	43 094	2 093.7	1 170 252	5 707
Detroit-Warren-Dearborn, MI	12 474	254 643	28 793.7	11 432.0	6 992	44 589	4 734.0	1 273.7	331 356	14 330.6	1 676 030	7 304
Detroit-Dearborn-Livonia, MI Div 19804	4 091	101 848	12 420.4	4 712.3	2 645	16 865	1 763.8	497.5	126 525	3 945.3	353 058	1 774
Warren-Troy-Farmington Hills, MI Div 47664	8 383	152 795	16 373.3	6 719.7	4 347	27 724	2 970.2	776.2	204 831	10 385.3	1 322 973	5 530
Dothan, AL..........................	375	10 243	1 127.1	486.2	221	D	D	D	9 751	409.2	71 989	327
Dover, DE	398	9 405	990.6	379.5	233	1 325	105.5	32.0	9 359	536.4	144 720	1 061
Dubuque, IA	271	7 806	702.0	318.7	201	1 157	109.4	28.1	6 251	277.6	55 045	255
Duluth, MN-WI	931	28 824	2 484.4	1 168.0	525	3 338	297.5	76.6	15 641	599.7	136 743	841
Durham-Chapel Hill, NC	1 373	42 120	5 452.9	1 974.5	755	6 461	1 033.8	248.0	42 170	1 631.6	706 692	4 411
East Stroudsburg, PA	393	7 031	643.1	276.0	309	1 571	115.7	37.0	10 218	466.0	35 527	152
Eau Claire, WI	539	14 294	1 521.9	662.8	302	1 828	162.1	45.1	9 778	486.7	107 123	677
El Centro, CA	268	4 536	511.1	182.9	142	608	53.4	16.5	9 772	319.7	44 451	293
Elizabethtown-Fort Knox, KY	398	8 120	728.7	319.5	182	1 053	95.6	24.0	7 919	304.4	49 735	308
Elkhart-Goshen, IN	362	10 105	1 160.8	413.6	336	2 069	261.0	61.1	12 645	545.5	65 196	309
Elmira, NY	211	6 421	621.6	294.0	128	670	57.3	15.6	3 893	141.6	20 143	78
El Paso, TX.........................	1 525	41 470	4 304.3	1 488.3	910	5 676	464.5	129.4	55 383	2 386.5	603 056	4 491
Erie, PA..............................	850	24 899	2 216.5	923.1	563	3 591	322.7	80.2	13 951	595.0	43 855	267
Eugene, OR	1 135	20 576	2 247.4	828.6	611	3 480	443.9	97.7	22 905	982.8	157 338	721
Evansville, IN-KY	852	24 213	2 658.0	999.2	548	3 988	441.5	121.4	17 076	688.2	116 267	763

1. Establishments subject to federal tax.

Table C. Metropolitan Areas — Government Employment and Payroll and Local Government Finances

Area name	Government employment and payroll, 2012		March payroll (percent of total)							Local government finances, 2012				
										General revenue			Taxes	
														Per capita[1] (dollars)
	Full-time equivalent employees	March Payroll (dollars)	Administration, judicial, and legal	Police and corrections	Fire protection	Highways and transportation	Health and welfare	Natural resources and utilities	Education and libraries	Total (mil dol)	Inter-governmental (mil dol)	Total (mil dol)	Total	Property
	171	172	173	174	175	176	177	178	179	180	181	182	183	184
Cedar Rapids, IA	10 705	42 251 213	4.0	6.0	2.5	6.3	2.3	4.9	72.2	1 343.4	584.3	503.5	1 924	1 486
Chambersburg-Waynesboro, PA	3 820	13 644 359	7.7	8.8	1.7	2.3	9.1	6.1	63.5	415.1	130.8	191.4	1 265	978
Champaign-Urbana, IL	8 553	32 026 460	5.7	8.9	3.4	7.5	6.1	5.5	61.1	891.5	342.7	404.0	1 728	1 506
Charleston, WV	8 227	28 589 774	5.5	6.5	3.8	3.3	7.9	3.1	66.9	735.0	295.9	299.7	1 326	910
Charleston-North Charleston, SC	22 813	76 849 945	8.2	12.8	6.2	2.8	3.9	8.3	55.3	2 449.1	759.7	1 206.4	1 730	1 171
Charlotte-Concord-Gastonia, NC-SC	106 366	436 927 670	3.6	7.0	2.3	1.5	39.9	4.1	40.2	12 067.6	3 110.9	3 416.0	1 487	1 141
Charlottesville, VA	7 679	26 539 813	8.0	9.0	2.3	2.5	3.9	4.9	64.7	782.8	292.5	365.6	1 641	1 221
Chattanooga, TN-GA	19 778	70 912 137	6.7	7.6	2.9	3.3	31.0	10.3	37.0	2 452.8	620.7	669.9	1 245	910
Cheyenne, WY	6 173	27 578 286	2.8	4.6	1.9	1.8	39.8	1.5	46.1	796.0	292.8	103.3	1 094	589
Chicago-Naperville-Elgin, IL-IN-WI	358 119	1 755 095 339	5.6	15.8	4.2	6.1	4.0	6.3	56.6	49 995.8	16 211.6	25 716.1	2 701	2 261
.Chicago-Naperville-Arlington Heights, IL Div 16974	272 297	1 388 594 555	5.4	17.5	4.2	7.0	4.3	6.3	54.0	39 231.9	12 680.6	19 977.9	2 730	2 208
.Elgin, IL Div 20994	25 482	114 832 272	5.3	10.3	5.2	2.2	1.5	6.6	67.5	3 172.7	934.1	1 826.9	2 913	2 670
.Gary, IN Div 23844	25 614	86 646 440	8.5	10.0	3.9	4.2	3.6	7.3	60.8	3 048.3	1 320.8	1 243.6	1 759	1 670
.Lake County-Kenosha County, IL-WI Div 29404	34 726	165 022 072	5.5	8.7	3.9	2.4	4.0	6.2	68.5	4 542.9	1 276.0	2 667.7	3 066	2 896
Chico, CA	8 734	37 694 370	6.4	9.6	2.6	2.0	12.6	5.9	58.9	1 079.1	643.7	243.0	1 097	878
Cincinnati, OH-KY-IN	72 643	287 857 130	6.6	10.8	6.5	4.5	6.9	6.8	56.1	8 861.6	3 178.0	3 802.3	1 786	1 197
Clarksville, TN-KY	8 620	27 138 883	4.3	10.6	3.8	3.1	6.5	6.8	62.4	701.2	298.6	267.5	975	569
Cleveland, TN	4 049	11 684 208	5.5	10.1	5.8	3.7	9.5	2.4	62.1	282.7	134.8	92.6	786	497
Cleveland-Elyria, OH	92 435	406 449 865	6.4	10.2	4.7	5.9	15.2	7.7	48.3	11 282.4	3 960.2	4 907.0	2 378	1 483
Coeur d'Alene, ID	6 580	25 436 541	6.0	8.3	3.6	2.4	37.6	3.3	38.1	678.7	158.8	148.1	1 040	972
College Station-Bryan, TX	8 862	27 409 320	8.4	12.4	4.3	4.5	3.2	11.0	51.4	682.0	173.0	393.1	1 676	1 379
Colorado Springs, CO	25 178	98 225 856	5.3	9.9	3.8	2.2	15.3	15.2	45.7	2 631.8	836.0	850.3	1 272	745
Columbia, MO	6 008	20 052 275	7.9	5.3	3.3	2.8	2.7	11.3	63.5	497.3	161.0	228.2	1 354	805
Columbia, SC	33 084	120 753 751	4.2	6.5	2.3	1.0	25.0	4.6	54.7	3 250.3	958.1	1 087.0	1 385	1 204
Columbus, GA-AL	13 084	41 360 235	6.9	10.8	4.0	2.6	6.1	6.8	60.6	1 009.9	422.9	376.5	1 213	848
Columbus, IN	4 371	15 688 309	3.2	6.6	2.9	1.3	44.5	3.1	37.7	469.7	111.3	106.7	1 348	1 076
Columbus, OH	70 274	306 173 279	9.4	10.4	7.0	4.4	8.1	5.2	53.9	9 594.0	3 610.3	4 421.2	2 274	1 428
Corpus Christi, TX	19 396	62 362 670	4.9	10.1	3.6	4.7	4.1	5.7	63.6	1 651.1	548.8	775.1	1 773	1 396
Corvallis, OR	1 834	7 923 562	9.3	13.4	6.2	3.8	7.4	9.4	45.7	259.6	93.0	115.4	1 335	1 185
Crestview-Fort Walton Beach-Destin, FL	8 719	30 209 052	6.5	11.1	6.5	3.5	2.3	6.1	60.8	813.5	261.8	380.6	1 537	1 209
Cumberland, MD-WV	3 611	14 623 810	4.0	5.7	1.6	3.1	0.5	6.1	76.2	340.7	169.2	105.4	1 034	723
Dallas-Fort Worth-Arlington, TX	263 325	1 034 080 549	5.5	11.1	4.7	4.3	9.8	4.8	58.2	28 591.5	7 248.4	14 334.2	2 139	1 724
Dallas-Plano-Irving, 19124	172 608	694 884 179	5.0	10.6	4.8	5.5	10.3	4.8	57.3	19 625.6	4 888.2	9 734.9	2 199	1 766
Fort Worth-Arlington, TX Div 23104	90 717	339 196 370	6.6	12.1	4.4	1.7	8.6	4.7	60.2	8 965.9	2 360.2	4 599.3	2 022	1 644
Dalton, GA	5 343	18 100 335	4.0	6.7	3.7	3.2	5.9	9.7	65.2	440.0	199.5	149.2	1 045	674
Danville, IL	3 642	12 242 579	7.0	7.8	2.7	3.5	3.6	4.2	67.9	289.5	151.8	91.4	1 132	940
Daphne-Fairhope-Foley, AL	7 374	22 581 577	7.4	8.0	2.9	4.3	20.7	5.6	47.7	640.7	189.9	231.1	1 211	537
Davenport-Moline-Rock Island, IA-IL	14 533	58 873 005	5.4	9.2	3.4	4.7	5.9	5.6	64.3	1 610.6	616.3	675.0	1 764	1 489
Dayton, OH	31 140	126 902 617	7.8	9.6	4.5	5.3	8.1	7.6	55.4	3 577.2	1 408.5	1 490.6	1 861	1 242
Decatur, AL	6 083	20 609 391	3.2	7.4	2.8	2.6	21.3	8.4	53.1	589.6	255.2	134.1	870	438
Decatur, IL	4 204	17 133 160	5.9	11.8	4.5	3.0	2.0	8.2	63.3	407.1	180.7	163.9	1 488	1 260
Deltona-Daytona Beach-Ormond Beach, FL	23 653	83 363 572	6.3	11.3	4.7	2.1	21.7	6.5	45.3	2 404.0	575.9	895.2	1 504	1 170
Denver-Aurora-Lakewood, CO	95 098	432 423 959	6.6	12.7	5.6	6.2	10.7	9.5	46.7	13 355.6	3 846.7	5 924.4	2 240	1 358
Des Moines-West Des Moines, IA	22 853	93 893 961	5.5	8.0	3.0	4.3	8.9	5.3	63.7	2 778.1	968.6	1 212.2	2 058	1 784
Detroit-Warren-Dearborn, MI	115 282	533 695 857	7.4	12.9	5.0	4.6	2.5	4.5	60.8	18 679.3	8 819.4	5 896.0	1 374	1 225
Detroit-Dearborn-Livonia, MI Div 19804	52 078	243 918 311	7.3	16.2	6.7	6.5	2.2	6.4	52.0	9 260.6	4 384.4	2 686.6	1 499	1 195
Warren-Troy-Farmington Hills, MI Div 47664	63 204	289 777 546	7.4	10.1	3.5	3.0	2.7	2.9	68.2	9 418.7	4 435.0	3 209.5	1 284	1 246
Dothan, AL	7 365	24 527 281	3.9	6.4	3.0	2.7	40.1	5.5	36.7	730.7	179.2	156.0	1 057	387
Dover, DE	4 210	17 226 252	4.7	6.0	0.1	0.6	1.6	5.6	79.4	494.8	323.1	88.0	525	459
Dubuque, IA	3 261	12 486 456	6.7	9.6	3.9	7.2	5.0	6.0	60.6	400.9	169.8	165.8	1 743	1 320
Duluth, MN-WI	11 586	52 151 960	6.8	9.8	2.9	6.5	13.3	7.0	48.7	1 488.3	728.3	373.6	1 337	1 215
Durham-Chapel Hill, NC	18 475	63 324 374	5.8	6.4	1.4	2.2	10.3	6.8	63.0	1 793.6	701.9	824.7	1 577	1 277
East Stroudsburg, PA	5 957	25 067 544	5.7	4.3	0.0	5.4	1.6	1.5	80.9	719.0	225.3	441.5	2 616	2 404
Eau Claire, WI	5 534	21 894 206	6.1	8.1	3.0	6.4	5.8	4.3	65.0	602.6	268.9	253.5	1 549	1 431
El Centro, CA	10 122	49 143 599	4.2	6.0	1.7	1.1	19.5	16.2	45.5	1 293.3	740.8	180.2	1 019	733
Elizabethtown-Fort Knox, KY	6 654	21 761 001	1.7	4.2	1.5	1.3	37.6	3.5	49.3	547.6	189.2	112.2	746	448
Elkhart-Goshen, IN	6 985	24 411 992	5.4	8.4	4.1	2.5	1.6	3.6	73.6	630.5	315.1	218.4	1 094	907
Elmira, NY	3 853	14 858 297	5.0	9.7	2.9	4.0	13.2	3.8	59.7	476.3	219.3	175.3	1 971	1 236
El Paso, TX	38 548	140 371 856	4.5	10.4	3.7	3.1	8.1	3.1	65.5	3 358.7	1 620.5	1 097.5	1 321	1 022
Erie, PA	8 523	32 472 819	5.3	9.7	2.6	5.6	3.9	6.0	65.7	1 197.6	616.5	364.0	1 297	1 046
Eugene, OR	11 647	50 155 119	7.2	10.9	5.2	6.9	4.1	11.4	48.1	1 390.4	585.1	463.2	1 306	1 120
Evansville, IN-KY	10 347	34 710 256	6.8	10.9	4.5	3.9	1.7	8.5	62.2	995.2	463.1	341.3	1 089	857

1. Based on the resident population estimated as of July 1 of the year shown.

Table C. Metropolitan Areas — Local Government Finances, Government Employment, and Voting

Area name	Local government finances, 2012 (cont.) Direct general expenditure Total (mil dol)	Per capita[1] (dollars)	Percent of total for: Education	Health and hospitals	Police protection	Public welfare	Highways	Debt outstanding Total (mil dol)	Per capita[1] (dollars)	Government employment, 2014 Federal civilian	Federal military	State and local	Presidential election,[2] 2012 Percent of vote cast: Democratic	Republican	All other
	185	186	187	188	189	190	191	192	193	194	195	196	197	198	199
Cedar Rapids, IA	1 498.7	5 725	47.4	3.1	3.7	1.0	5.5	1 735.1	6 629	1 132	1 022	15 416	56.7	41.5	1.9
Chambersburg-Waynesboro, PA	452.7	2 992	54.1	4.1	1.9	5.5	4.8	619.1	4 092	2 271	409	5 968	30.1	68.6	1.3
Champaign-Urbana, IL	941.0	4 025	49.1	2.4	5.0	2.5	6.1	728.3	3 115	1 318	480	37 037	49.0	48.3	2.7
Charleston, WV	776.4	3 436	50.7	3.1	6.2	0.1	2.6	329.2	1 457	2 173	1 112	22 108	41.8	56.3	1.8
Charleston-North Charleston, SC	2 212.6	3 173	45.5	1.1	9.5	0.2	4.7	5 523.5	7 920	10 117	13 110	50 961	46.5	51.8	1.6
Charlotte-Concord-Gastonia, NC-SC	11 496.9	5 006	29.1	35.1	5.3	2.9	2.0	12 295.6	5 354	9 730	6 513	137 693	47.2	51.6	1.2
Charlottesville, VA	798.6	3 583	47.8	6.8	5.5	6.6	2.1	859.4	3 856	1 367	1 157	32 395	56.0	42.3	1.7
Chattanooga, TN-GA	2 273.9	4 228	31.4	31.0	4.8	0.8	2.7	1 828.1	3 399	5 980	1 706	30 069	36.6	61.6	1.7
Cheyenne, WY	781.4	8 270	37.0	40.5	2.5	0.2	3.1	132.4	1 401	2 567	3 485	11 386	36.2	60.5	3.3
Chicago-Naperville-Elgin, IL-IN-WI	48 512.9	5 095	44.9	3.1	7.1	1.3	4.3	81 674.3	8 577	53 967	31 187	506 744	63.8	34.8	1.5
Chicago-Naperville-Ar Heights, IL Div 16974	38 566.5	5 270	42.7	3.4	7.4	1.3	4.3	70 331.4	9 610	44 544	15 142	384 945	66.5	32.0	1.5
Elgin, IL Div 20994	3 112.0	4 962	53.7	0.6	6.3	0.5	5.5	4 822.0	7 688	1 791	1 257	42 060	50.1	48.2	1.8
Gary, IN Div 23844	2 464.8	3 487	47.7	2.5	4.8	0.9	2.2	2 682.0	3 795	1 870	2 241	33 810	59.7	38.9	1.4
Lake County-Kenosha County, IL-WI Div 29404	4 369.5	5 022	56.1	2.3	6.1	1.8	4.4	3 838.9	4 412	5 762	12 547	45 929	53.9	44.7	1.4
Chico, CA	1 098.2	4 957	46.2	6.8	4.4	11.8	3.6	480.5	2 169	542	342	14 609	47.0	49.0	4.0
Cincinnati, OH-KY-IN	9 065.0	4 259	41.6	5.6	6.4	3.8	4.1	13 076.8	6 143	15 860	5 934	111 105	41.4	57.1	1.6
Clarksville, TN-KY	654.4	2 385	56.0	3.0	7.0	0.1	4.1	4 800.5	17 498	5 762	30 552	13 303	41.4	57.2	1.4
Cleveland, TN	268.7	2 281	54.1	7.7	7.1	0.1	5.2	242.0	2 054	274	371	5 536	23.5	75.0	1.4
Cleveland-Elyria, OH	11 203.3	5 429	41.3	12.0	5.9	3.4	4.1	14 162.1	6 863	17 747	5 731	114 069	61.5	37.2	1.2
Coeur d'Alene, ID	637.0	4 475	29.8	40.2	5.8	0.4	3.9	121.1	851	561	529	9 849	31.5	65.8	2.7
College Station-Bryan, TX	708.6	3 022	50.7	1.9	5.8	0.4	5.6	1 389.0	5 923	816	540	36 925	31.5	66.4	2.0
Colorado Springs, CO	2 586.9	3 871	37.1	21.4	6.1	2.0	8.1	4 453.6	6 663	12 635	39 303	37 335	38.3	59.2	2.6
Columbia, MO	580.4	3 444	44.8	3.1	4.3	0.2	6.2	2 592.5	15 382	2 466	588	28 559	50.2	47.1	2.7
Columbia, SC	3 328.6	4 242	44.0	20.7	4.0	0.1	1.1	7 155.9	9 119	9 940	12 097	71 549	50.2	48.5	1.4
Columbus, GA-AL	1 107.4	3 566	50.3	6.1	5.6	1.9	4.1	1 051.1	3 385	6 851	22 294	17 747	54.1	45.1	0.7
Columbus, IN	465.6	5 883	32.7	40.9	1.8	0.5	0.9	364.3	4 603	162	256	6 073	36.2	61.7	2.1
Columbus, OH	9 248.5	4 757	41.8	5.3	5.8	5.4	4.5	10 699.7	5 504	13 847	5 542	153 661	52.7	45.7	1.6
Corpus Christi, TX	1 702.5	3 895	49.7	4.7	6.4	0.2	3.7	3 153.1	7 214	6 306	4 648	26 461	44.8	53.9	1.3
Corvallis, OR	259.2	2 999	46.3	7.4	9.6	0.0	4.2	233.8	2 705	508	254	10 581	62.0	33.5	4.5
Crestview-Fort Walton Beach-Destin, FL	907.3	3 663	47.7	3.2	7.3	0.3	4.4	501.5	2 025	8 309	16 789	10 863	24.4	74.3	1.2
Cumberland, MD-WV	335.7	3 292	62.0	0.8	3.9	0.5	4.1	213.3	2 092	600	340	7 641	31.0	66.3	2.6
Dallas-Fort Worth-Arlington, TX	28 447.6	4 245	42.1	11.3	5.7	0.4	4.3	75 576.3	11 278	44 213	16 531	355 897	41.9	56.7	1.4
Dallas-Plano-Irving, 19124	19 555.5	4 418	41.1	11.5	5.2	0.5	4.4	53 566.2	12 101	29 204	10 386	242 952	44.5	54.2	1.4
Fort Worth-Arlington, Div 23104	8 892.1	3 910	44.2	11.0	6.7	0.1	4.1	22 010.2	9 677	15 009	6 145	112 945	37.0	61.6	1.4
Dalton, GA	487.6	3 416	54.9	8.7	3.9	0.4	4.8	143.3	1 004	235	408	6 793	25.6	72.9	1.5
Danville, IL	308.3	3 819	46.4	0.7	6.4	3.5	6.3	102.1	1 265	1 488	155	4 309	42.5	55.7	1.8
Daphne-Fairhope-Foley, AL	700.0	3 669	34.5	19.2	6.1	0.1	7.7	911.0	4 775	327	906	8 660	21.6	77.2	1.2
Davenport-Moline-Rock Island, IA-IL	1 675.1	4 378	48.5	5.0	5.5	1.5	4.6	1 215.2	3 176	5 759	1 516	20 434	56.7	41.8	1.5
Dayton, OH	3 712.9	4 635	47.4	3.3	6.4	7.2	5.2	3 143.4	3 924	18 149	7 353	43 089	46.2	52.1	1.7
Decatur, AL	670.1	4 345	54.9	16.9	4.4	0.3	3.3	924.8	5 996	407	691	8 091	29.1	69.6	1.3
Decatur, IL	452.8	4 112	52.8	2.0	7.8	0.1	8.1	462.5	4 200	318	219	5 467	46.6	51.8	1.7
Deltona-Daytona Beach-Ormond Beach, FL	2 484.9	4 174	30.8	22.3	7.3	0.4	3.9	3 027.1	5 085	1 279	1 190	21 552	48.4	50.7	1.0
Denver-Aurora-Lakewood, CO	12 432.0	4 700	33.7	6.3	6.2	4.2	4.8	24 877.2	9 405	27 863	9 941	167 184	55.5	42.2	2.2
Des Moines-West Des Moines, IA	3 004.6	5 101	48.5	8.3	4.2	1.2	5.5	3 647.7	6 193	6 208	2 521	36 876	53.3	44.9	1.8
Detroit-Warren-Dearborn, MI	19 021.2	4 432	43.4	5.7	6.5	3.0	3.8	31 478.0	7 334	27 462	8 221	162 894	59.5	39.5	0.9
Detroit-Dearborn-Livo Div 19804	9 500.3	5 300	36.3	3.3	7.0	5.2	2.9	21 084.6	11 764	13 897	3 395	74 054	73.0	26.2	0.8
Warren-Troy-Farmingto Hills, MI Div 47664	9 520.9	3 809	50.5	8.0	6.0	0.9	4.7	10 393.4	4 158	13 565	4 826	88 840	50.9	48.1	1.0
Dothan, AL	704.8	4 774	29.3	42.3	4.1	0.1	4.1	485.5	3 289	401	700	10 255	28.2	71.0	0.8
Dover, DE	527.3	3 145	73.4	1.1	4.4	0.0	1.5	478.7	2 856	1 728	4 389	17 564	51.7	46.8	1.5
Dubuque, IA	405.9	4 268	37.6	4.5	4.7	2.0	7.0	372.4	3 916	253	382	4 480	56.5	41.8	1.7
Duluth, MN-WI	1 639.0	5 865	37.0	6.4	5.3	6.4	9.4	1 391.0	4 977	1 642	1 074	23 449	63.5	34.0	2.5
Durham-Chapel Hill, NC	1 919.0	3 670	40.5	5.6	8.2	5.6	2.1	1 899.7	3 633	6 366	1 491	58 356	69.0	29.7	1.3
East Stroudsburg, PA	739.9	4 384	67.9	0.1	3.0	3.9	2.5	1 201.0	7 115	3 396	464	8 412	56.0	42.7	1.3
Eau Claire, WI	676.7	4 137	54.0	4.1	6.5	3.1	11.1	488.8	2 988	539	439	11 965	53.5	45.0	1.5
El Centro, CA	1 172.3	6 625	40.7	23.6	4.1	7.5	2.9	1 408.8	7 962	2 356	412	15 111	65.2	33.1	1.7
Elizabethtown-Fort Knox, KY	515.1	3 425	39.9	37.7	2.7	0.0	2.2	447.0	2 972	6 074	6 991	8 909	37.7	60.6	1.7
Elkhart-Goshen, IN	609.8	3 055	58.2	1.0	3.9	0.2	3.5	758.8	3 801	248	640	8 430	36.0	62.5	1.6
Elmira, NY	467.0	5 252	42.9	3.0	3.0	18.1	8.9	490.6	5 518	210	136	6 050	48.1	50.4	1.5
El Paso, TX	3 277.0	3 945	52.3	15.5	5.0	0.4	1.0	4 036.3	4 859	12 853	28 240	54 267	65.4	33.3	1.3
Erie, PA	1 203.4	4 288	44.0	5.6	2.7	14.2	3.5	1 705.3	6 076	1 522	758	15 847	57.4	41.3	1.3
Eugene, OR	1 390.2	3 921	44.2	5.1	6.9	2.2	4.3	1 580.1	4 457	1 586	1 038	23 241	59.7	36.4	3.9
Evansville, IN-KY	984.8	3 142	43.4	0.7	5.9	0.3	3.2	1 444.5	4 609	1 247	991	15 457	41.6	56.7	1.8

1. Based on the resident population estimated as of July 1 of the year shown. 2. © 2013 Election Data Services, Inc. All rights reserved.

Table C. Metropolitan Areas — **Land Area and Population**

CBSA/ DIV code[1]	Area name	Land area,[2] 2010 (sq km)	Population 2015			Population characteristics, 2014											
						Race alone or in combination, not Hispanic or Latino (percent)					Age (percent)						
			Total persons	Rank	Per square kilometer	White	Black	American Indian, Alaska Native	Asian and Pacific Islander	Percent Hispanic or Latino[3]	Under 5 years	5 to 17 years	18 to 24 years	25 to 34 years	35 to 44 years	45 to 54 years	
		1	2	3	4	5	6	7	8	9	10	11	12	13	14	15
21820	Fairbanks, AK	19 006	99 631	353	5.2	76.5	6.3	10.3	5.3	7.7	7.7	16.4	14.8	18.7	11.8	11.4
22020	Fargo, ND-MN	7 278	233 836	192	32.1	90.4	3.7	2.0	2.9	2.9	6.9	15.6	16.1	16.2	12.0	11.3
22140	Farmington, NM	14 279	118 737	325	8.3	42.2	1.1	38.0	0.9	19.5	7.3	20.0	9.2	14.0	11.9	12.2
22180	Fayetteville, NC	2 701	376 509	141	139.4	47.6	37.8	3.5	4.0	11.2	8.3	17.9	12.1	17.1	12.1	11.8
22220	Fayetteville-Springdale-Rogers, AR-MO	8 193	513 559	105	62.7	76.4	2.9	2.6	4.7	15.6	7.2	18.9	11.0	14.7	13.4	12.3
22380	Flagstaff, AZ	48 223	139 097	291	2.9	56.9	2.0	26.9	2.8	13.9	6.1	15.8	19.7	13.4	10.8	11.4
22420	Flint, MI	1 650	410 849	129	249.0	74.6	21.8	1.3	1.5	3.2	6.0	17.4	9.2	11.6	12.2	14.1
22500	Florence, SC	3 525	206 448	212	58.6	54.7	42.2	0.7	1.4	2.2	6.3	17.6	9.4	12.0	12.4	13.4
22520	Florence-Muscle Shoals, AL	3 264	146 950	283	45.0	83.9	13.2	1.0	0.9	2.5	5.4	15.6	10.6	11.4	11.6	13.4
22540	Fond du Lac, WI	1 864	101 973	350	54.7	91.7	2.0	0.8	1.6	4.9	5.6	16.3	8.9	11.9	11.8	14.6
22660	Fort Collins, CO	6 724	333 577	152	49.6	85.1	1.4	1.1	3.1	11.1	5.4	15.1	14.7	13.9	12.1	11.9
22900	Fort Smith, AR-OK	8 774	280 241	167	31.9	77.4	4.8	9.7	3.0	9.3	6.3	18.1	8.8	12.5	12.3	13.7
23060	Fort Wayne, IN	3 524	429 820	125	122.0	80.1	11.7	0.8	3.5	6.5	7.1	18.9	9.2	13.0	12.5	13.1
23420	Fresno, CA	15 431	974 861	56	63.2	32.5	5.3	1.2	11.0	52.0	8.3	20.6	11.0	14.8	12.1	11.8
23460	Gadsden, AL	1 386	103 057	347	74.4	79.8	16.0	1.0	1.0	3.7	5.7	16.3	8.7	11.7	12.7	13.7
23540	Gainesville, FL	3 172	277 163	172	87.4	66.2	20.2	0.7	6.5	8.8	5.6	12.6	21.7	14.7	10.3	10.7
23580	Gainesville, GA	1 017	193 535	223	190.3	63.0	8.0	0.6	2.2	27.5	6.9	19.6	9.4	13.0	13.2	13.4
23900	Gettysburg, PA	1 343	102 295	349	76.2	90.6	2.2	0.5	1.2	6.6	5.1	15.6	9.8	10.5	11.4	15.0
24020	Glens Falls, NY	4 398	126 918	308	28.9	94.6	2.5	0.7	1.0	2.4	4.8	14.6	8.3	11.5	11.7	15.5
24140	Goldsboro, NC	1 432	124 132	315	86.7	56.0	32.1	0.9	2.0	11.1	6.8	17.3	10.4	13.2	11.9	13.1
24220	Grand Forks, ND-MN	8 825	102 449	348	11.6	88.6	3.3	3.2	2.7	4.5	6.6	14.7	18.8	14.1	10.0	11.1
24260	Grand Island, NE	5 552	85 066	369	15.3	77.3	2.1	0.7	1.3	19.6	7.1	18.9	8.6	12.3	12.1	13.2
24300	Grand Junction, CO	8 622	148 513	279	17.2	83.7	1.2	1.4	1.5	14.1	6.3	16.1	10.2	13.3	11.2	12.2
24340	Grand Rapids-Wyoming, MI	6 913	1 038 583	52	150.2	81.5	7.6	0.9	3.0	9.1	6.7	18.2	10.6	13.8	12.1	13.4
24420	Grants Pass, OR	4 247	84 745	370	20.0	90.1	0.9	2.9	1.9	7.0	4.9	14.6	7.0	9.8	10.1	12.6
24500	Great Falls, MT	6 988	82 278	374	11.8	89.0	2.4	6.1	1.9	4.1	6.7	15.8	10.5	13.8	10.5	12.4
24540	Greeley, CO	10 327	285 174	164	27.6	68.3	1.4	1.2	2.1	29.0	7.3	19.7	10.0	14.3	13.4	12.8
24580	Green Bay, WI	4 844	316 519	157	65.3	86.2	2.7	2.9	3.0	6.9	6.4	17.3	8.9	13.1	12.3	14.7
24660	Greensboro-High Point, NC	5 164	752 157	74	145.7	61.6	27.3	1.0	3.9	8.1	5.9	16.8	10.1	12.7	12.9	14.1
24780	Greenville, NC	1 689	175 842	234	104.1	57.7	35.2	0.7	2.4	5.9	6.1	15.8	18.4	13.8	12.0	11.6
24860	Greenville-Anderson-Mauldin, SC	7 021	874 869	63	124.6	74.8	17.5	0.6	2.1	6.5	6.1	16.7	10.5	12.6	12.6	13.7
25060	Gulfport-Biloxi-Pascagoula, MS	4 586	389 255	136	84.9	70.5	22.1	1.0	3.2	5.2	6.4	17.6	9.5	13.6	12.5	13.6
25180	Hagerstown-Martinsburg, MD-WV	2 018	261 486	183	129.6	85.1	10.7	0.7	2.0	4.1	6.0	17.1	8.1	13.2	13.2	14.8
25220	Hammond, LA	2 049	128 755	305	62.8	65.0	30.6	0.8	1.0	3.9	7.2	17.6	11.3	14.4	11.8	12.4
25260	Hanford-Corcoran, CA	3 599	150 965	271	41.9	35.6	6.9	1.4	5.2	53.2	7.9	19.6	11.5	16.7	13.6	12.4
25420	Harrisburg-Carlisle, PA	4 201	565 006	96	134.5	80.7	11.2	0.6	4.0	5.6	5.8	15.7	9.1	13.1	12.2	14.1
25500	Harrisonburg, VA	2 244	131 131	301	58.4	82.9	4.7	0.5	2.6	11.1	5.4	14.6	19.4	12.9	10.9	11.7
25540	Hartford-West Hartford-East Hartford, CT	3 922	1 211 324	47	308.9	70.6	11.5	0.6	5.2	14.0	5.1	15.9	10.2	12.4	12.0	15.0
25620	Hattiesburg, MS	4 171	148 839	276	35.7	67.1	29.6	0.6	1.4	2.8	6.8	17.4	12.9	14.8	12.5	12.1
25860	Hickory-Lenoir-Morganton, NC	4 240	362 510	145	85.5	83.2	7.8	0.6	3.2	6.8	5.3	16.3	8.7	10.9	12.7	15.0
25940	Hilton Head Island-Bluffton-Beaufort, NC	3 190	207 413	211	65.0	65.1	22.7	0.6	1.8	11.8	5.8	14.3	9.7	12.1	10.8	11.2
25980	Hinesville, GA	2 306	80 198	377	34.8	48.7	38.1	1.2	3.8	12.0	10.5	18.2	14.1	19.1	11.4	10.4
26140	Homosassa Springs, FL	1 507	141 058	289	93.6	90.0	3.5	0.9	1.9	5.2	3.8	11.2	5.7	7.6	8.1	12.2
26300	Hot Springs, AR	1 755	97 177	358	55.4	84.9	9.3	1.5	1.2	5.3	5.7	15.2	7.7	11.2	11.2	12.9
26380	Houma-Thibodaux, LA	5 957	212 297	208	35.6	73.4	17.3	5.1	1.4	4.7	6.7	18.0	9.5	14.4	11.9	14.3
26420	Houston-The Woodlands-Sugar Land, TX	21 388	6 656 947	5	311.2	39.0	17.4	0.6	8.0	36.3	7.4	19.6	9.6	15.1	14.3	13.1
26580	Huntington-Ashland, WV-KY-OH	6 545	361 580	146	55.2	95.5	3.2	0.7	1.0	1.1	5.6	15.9	9.1	11.8	12.7	13.6
26620	Huntsville, AL	3 526	444 752	118	126.1	69.9	22.9	1.5	3.1	4.9	5.8	16.8	9.4	13.6	12.7	15.3
26820	Idaho Falls, ID	13 445	139 747	290	10.4	86.0	0.9	1.2	1.5	12.0	8.8	23.1	8.3	13.7	12.0	11.2
26900	Indianapolis-Carmel-Anderson, IN	11 153	1 988 817	34	178.3	75.8	16.0	0.6	3.2	6.4	6.8	18.4	8.9	14.2	13.5	13.9
26980	Iowa City, IA	3 063	166 498	249	54.4	83.8	5.9	0.6	6.0	5.5	6.2	14.7	19.0	15.8	11.5	11.0
27060	Ithaca, NY	1 229	104 926	344	85.4	80.5	5.0	0.8	11.9	4.7	4.2	11.2	27.8	12.7	9.8	10.7
27100	Jackson, MI	1 817	159 494	257	87.8	87.3	9.7	1.0	1.2	3.4	5.5	16.6	9.4	11.8	12.2	14.5
27140	Jackson, MS	12 041	578 777	94	48.1	47.6	49.0	0.4	1.4	2.3	6.6	18.4	9.9	14.2	12.9	13.0
27180	Jackson, TN	2 871	129 682	303	45.2	64.1	31.5	0.5	1.3	4.1	6.3	16.8	11.3	12.2	11.8	13.3
27260	Jacksonville, FL	8 291	1 449 481	40	174.8	66.3	22.3	0.8	4.9	7.9	6.2	16.7	9.1	14.2	12.7	14.1
27340	Jacksonville, NC	1 975	186 311	227	94.3	70.8	16.8	1.4	3.8	12.2	9.8	15.5	21.5	18.9	10.0	8.4
27500	Janesville-Beloit, WI	1 860	161 448	255	86.8	85.4	6.0	0.7	1.6	8.2	6.0	17.8	8.7	12.3	12.5	14.2
27620	Jefferson City, MO	5 822	151 145	270	26.0	88.4	8.6	0.9	1.3	2.5	6.0	16.8	9.7	13.2	12.6	14.2
27740	Johnson City, TN	2 212	200 648	219	90.7	93.1	3.8	0.7	1.3	2.9	5.1	14.5	10.8	11.9	12.3	13.8
27780	Johnstown, PA	1 783	136 411	295	76.5	94.5	4.3	0.3	0.9	1.5	4.9	14.4	9.2	10.4	11.3	13.6
27860	Jonesboro, AR	3 796	128 394	306	33.8	81.2	13.9	0.8	1.3	4.3	6.8	17.9	11.0	14.5	12.5	12.3

1. CBSA = Core Based Statistical Area. DIV = Metropolitan Division. See Appendix A for explanation. See Appendix B for list of metropolitan areas identified by type. 2. Dry land or land partially or temporarily covered by water. 3. May be of any race.

Table C. Metropolitan Areas — **Population and Households**

Area name	55 to 64 years	65 to 74 years	75 years and over	Percent female	2000	2010	2000–2010	2010–2015	Births	Deaths	Net migration	Number	Persons per house-hold	Family house-holds	Female family house-holder[1]	One person
	16	17	18	19	20	21	22	23	24	25	26	27	28	29	30	31
Fairbanks, AK	11.2	5.4	2.5	45.9	82 840	97 581	17.8	2.1	8 969	2 411	-4 546	35 692	2.67	66.3	8.8	24.6
Fargo, ND-MN	10.8	6.0	5.3	49.7	174 367	208 777	19.7	12.0	16 762	7 314	15 192	92 345	2.37	57.3	8.9	33.0
Farmington, NM	12.4	7.4	5.6	50.6	113 801	130 045	14.3	-8.7	9 862	4 866	-16 381	40 378	3.02	72.8	17.1	23.2
Fayetteville, NC	10.2	6.3	4.2	51.0	336 609	366 383	8.8	2.8	34 895	13 911	-11 417	140 204	2.61	65.1	15.7	29.5
Fayetteville-Springdale-Rogers, AR-MO	10.3	7.1	5.0	50.2	347 045	463 207	33.5	10.9	37 079	17 868	30 385	182 570	2.70	67.3	10.1	25.4
Flagstaff, AZ	11.8	7.0	4.0	50.8	116 320	134 437	15.6	3.5	8 997	3 933	-477	46 919	2.70	65.1	13.6	23.1
Flint, MI	13.9	8.8	6.8	51.8	436 141	425 790	-2.4	-3.5	26 341	22 440	-18 632	167 096	2.44	64.6	16.7	29.3
Florence, SC	13.6	9.4	6.1	53.1	193 155	205 571	6.4	0.4	13 477	11 898	-531	77 815	2.60	69.8	20.4	26.3
Florence-Muscle Shoals, AL	13.8	10.4	7.9	52.0	142 950	147 137	2.9	-0.1	8 057	9 146	1 070	61 239	2.37	66.0	14.0	29.9
Fond du Lac, WI	14.3	8.9	7.7	50.8	97 296	101 633	4.5	0.3	5 818	4 848	-533	41 938	2.35	64.9	8.2	28.7
Fort Collins, CO	12.9	8.4	5.6	50.2	251 494	299 630	19.1	11.3	17 937	10 268	25 303	125 165	2.51	61.9	7.9	26.6
Fort Smith, AR-OK	12.8	9.2	6.3	50.7	255 399	280 515	9.8	-0.1	18 310	15 295	-3 309	106 099	2.60	70.5	13.2	26.1
Fort Wayne, IN	12.7	7.7	5.9	51.1	390 156	416 254	6.7	3.3	31 019	18 272	1 125	163 139	2.57	67.5	13.0	28.2
Fresno, CA	10.2	6.4	4.8	50.1	799 407	930 452	16.4	4.8	83 845	33 956	-5 826	297 993	3.18	72.6	18.2	21.5
Gadsden, AL	13.8	10.2	7.1	51.6	103 459	104 427	0.9	-1.3	6 162	7 291	-210	39 714	2.57	67.6	12.1	29.0
Gainesville, FL	11.5	7.5	5.4	51.5	232 392	264 274	13.7	4.9	16 101	10 254	6 813	103 619	2.46	54.4	11.2	32.8
Gainesville, GA	10.9	8.1	5.5	50.1	139 277	179 684	29.0	7.7	13 258	6 894	7 160	63 383	2.98	73.7	12.6	20.8
Gettysburg, PA	14.5	10.3	8.0	50.7	91 292	101 417	11.1	0.9	5 385	4 983	202	38 748	2.52	72.9	9.6	23.1
Glens Falls, NY	15.1	10.7	7.8	49.6	124 345	128 921	3.7	-1.6	6 433	6 608	-1 642	49 937	2.47	65.5	11.9	27.9
Goldsboro, NC	12.7	8.3	6.2	50.8	113 329	122 623	8.2	1.2	8 988	5 944	-1 505	46 281	2.63	68.1	19.2	28.3
Grand Forks, ND-MN	11.5	7.0	6.0	48.9	97 478	98 461	1.0	4.1	7 222	4 244	925	41 882	2.28	58.4	7.9	31.4
Grand Island, NE	12.5	8.1	7.3	49.7	77 708	81 850	5.3	3.9	6 345	3 853	736	32 187	2.58	65.3	11.2	27.7
Grand Junction, CO	13.7	9.4	7.5	50.3	116 255	146 723	26.2	1.2	9 653	7 148	-856	59 703	2.42	61.6	10.8	29.5
Grand Rapids-Wyoming, MI	12.3	7.3	5.7	50.6	930 670	988 940	6.3	5.0	71 624	37 886	15 943	375 683	2.67	69.2	11.5	24.1
Grants Pass, OR	16.1	14.3	10.6	51.2	75 726	82 713	9.2	2.5	4 335	6 047	3 687	33 486	2.46	62.0	12.9	29.8
Great Falls, MT	13.3	9.1	7.8	49.6	80 357	81 327	1.2	1.2	6 223	4 187	-1 085	34 018	2.34	60.8	11.3	33.2
Greeley, CO	11.5	6.8	4.3	49.6	180 926	252 831	39.7	12.8	20 309	8 092	19 457	96 803	2.81	72.6	10.9	20.6
Green Bay, WI	13.2	7.9	6.2	50.2	282 599	306 241	8.4	3.4	20 764	12 152	1 781	124 899	2.46	66.1	9.4	26.9
Greensboro-High Point, NC	12.7	8.6	6.2	52.0	643 430	723 798	12.5	3.9	45 437	33 740	16 597	289 450	2.51	63.5	14.7	31.1
Greenville, NC	11.0	6.7	4.6	52.8	133 798	168 148	25.7	4.6	11 192	6 187	2 731	68 412	2.47	62.6	16.8	24.8
Greenville-Anderson-Mauldin, SC	12.6	9.0	6.2	51.3	725 680	824 107	13.6	6.2	54 507	40 589	35 326	324 282	2.59	66.1	12.6	28.2
Gulfport-Biloxi-Pascagoula, MS	12.7	8.4	5.7	50.6	363 988	370 787	1.9	5.0	25 538	18 386	11 066	146 693	2.59	64.9	16.4	28.3
Hagerstown-Martinsburg, MD-WV	12.8	8.6	6.1	49.7	207 828	251 602	21.1	3.9	16 319	12 560	5 881	95 920	2.62	68.3	13.3	26.5
Hammond, LA	12.4	8.0	4.9	51.5	100 588	121 101	20.4	6.3	9 982	6 051	3 574	45 786	2.70	67.6	18.5	27.5
Hanford-Corcoran, CA	9.2	5.3	3.8	44.8	129 461	152 982	18.2	-1.3	12 779	4 234	-10 754	41 596	3.21	77.6	20.2	16.2
Harrisburg-Carlisle, PA	13.9	9.0	7.1	51.0	509 074	549 473	7.9	2.8	34 328	26 489	8 070	226 058	2.39	63.3	10.9	29.7
Harrisonburg, VA	11.2	7.5	6.5	51.5	108 193	125 217	15.7	4.7	7 258	4 925	3 174	47 052	2.58	64.4	11.4	24.6
Hartford-West Hartford-East Hartford, CT	13.7	8.6	7.1	51.2	1 148 618	1 212 387	5.6	-0.1	63 398	53 924	-8 800	467 615	2.49	65.4	13.4	28.8
Hattiesburg, MS	10.9	7.4	5.2	52.0	123 812	142 857	15.4	4.2	10 543	6 433	1 648	52 610	2.76	68.0	19.6	26.0
Hickory-Lenoir-Morganton, NC	13.8	10.4	7.0	50.5	341 851	365 492	6.9	-0.8	19 801	20 039	-2 924	131 741	2.70	68.9	14.0	26.2
Hilton Head Island-Bluffton-Beaufort, NC	13.2	14.3	8.7	50.5	141 615	187 010	32.1	10.9	12 552	8 488	15 819	74 717	2.64	65.2	10.6	30.8
Hinesville, GA	8.7	5.0	2.6	49.0	71 914	77 917	8.3	2.9	8 778	2 083	-4 783	28 069	2.86	72.7	16.7	22.5
Homosassa Springs, FL	16.1	19.2	16.0	51.6	118 085	141 236	19.6	-0.1	5 440	12 586	6 775	60 315	2.28	65.3	9.6	30.7
Hot Springs, AR	14.4	12.2	9.5	51.7	88 068	96 000	9.0	1.2	5 784	7 056	2 640	39 045	2.44	62.1	13.6	31.4
Houma-Thibodaux, LA	12.1	7.7	5.4	50.6	194 477	208 176	7.0	2.0	15 200	9 708	-1 250	74 539	2.79	69.9	17.1	24.9
Houston-The Woodlands-Sugar Land, TX	11.1	6.1	3.7	50.3	4 693 161	5 920 493	26.2	12.4	494 164	187 291	428 160	2 226 123	2.88	69.4	14.0	25.1
Huntington-Ashland, WV-KY-OH	13.9	10.0	7.4	51.0	362 346	364 930	0.7	-0.9	21 823	21 651	-3 076	146 108	2.43	64.7	12.4	30.5
Huntsville, AL	12.6	7.9	5.8	50.9	342 376	417 593	22.0	6.5	26 782	18 160	17 775	172 409	2.49	67.0	12.1	28.4
Idaho Falls, ID	10.8	7.0	5.1	50.2	104 576	133 337	27.5	4.8	12 767	4 841	-1 569	45 712	2.99	74.3	9.5	21.8
Indianapolis-Carmel-Anderson, IN	12.0	7.2	5.2	51.1	1 658 462	1 888 082	13.8	5.3	140 019	80 570	42 037	744 765	2.60	64.8	13.4	28.7
Iowa City, IA	10.8	6.3	4.8	50.3	131 676	152 586	15.9	9.1	10 961	4 630	7 436	64 409	2.42	58.1	8.9	28.5
Ithaca, NY	11.2	7.2	5.1	50.7	96 501	101 594	5.3	3.3	4 636	3 382	2 081	38 120	2.39	51.2	8.2	34.5
Jackson, MI	14.0	9.0	7.0	48.8	158 422	160 248	1.2	-0.5	9 339	8 320	-1 677	61 686	2.44	65.2	13.5	28.6
Jackson, MS	12.3	7.4	5.3	52.0	525 346	567 645	8.1	2.0	40 066	26 175	-2 593	206 952	2.68	69.1	19.6	26.8
Jackson, TN	12.9	8.8	6.6	52.6	121 909	130 009	6.6	-0.3	8 525	6 597	-2 252	49 095	2.55	67.9	15.9	26.1
Jacksonville, FL	12.9	8.5	5.7	51.3	1 122 750	1 345 596	19.8	7.7	92 777	61 089	70 439	528 993	2.63	65.6	14.4	28.2
Jacksonville, NC	7.4	5.0	3.5	45.4	150 355	177 772	18.2	4.8	22 825	4 861	-9 895	61 873	2.81	69.5	11.6	26.2
Janesville-Beloit, WI	13.3	8.3	6.8	50.9	152 307	160 331	5.3	0.7	10 178	7 489	-1 580	63 037	2.51	65.4	13.8	28.2
Jefferson City, MO	13.1	8.2	6.1	49.0	140 052	149 807	7.0	0.9	9 482	6 543	-1 500	55 887	2.50	64.8	12.2	29.7
Johnson City, TN	13.6	10.6	7.5	51.0	181 607	198 716	9.4	1.0	10 626	11 666	2 774	84 847	2.29	64.9	11.7	28.3
Johnstown, PA	15.8	10.5	9.9	50.8	152 598	143 674	-5.8	-5.1	6 965	9 484	-4 651	57 004	2.27	65.8	12.4	31.0
Jonesboro, AR	11.2	8.0	5.7	51.3	107 762	121 026	12.3	6.1	9 012	6 348	4 536	48 043	2.56	66.9	15.3	27.8

1. No spouse present.

Table C. Metropolitan Areas — **Population, Vital Statistics, Medicare, and Crime**

Area name	Persons in group quarters, 2015	Daytime population, 2014 Number	Employment/ residence ratio	Births, 2015 Total	Rate[1]	Deaths, 2015 Number	Rate[1]	Persons under 65 with no health insurance 2014 Number	Percent	Medicare, 2015 Total Beneficiaries	Enrolled in Original Medicare	Enrolled in Medicare Advantage	Serious crimes known to police[2] 2014 Total Number	Rate[3]
	32	33	34	35	36	37	38	39	40	41	42	43	44	45
Fairbanks, AK	4 777	NA	NA	1 707	17.1	463	4.6	14 472	16.6	7 955	7 856	99	NA	NA
Fargo, ND-MN....................	9 051	232 589	1.03	3 353	14.3	1 440	6.2	14 910	7.7	28 214	19 970	8 244	5 491	2 410
Farmington, NM	1 746	123 914	1.00	1 826	15.4	986	8.3	20 607	19.4	17 228	16 350	878	3 155	2 518
Fayetteville, NC.................	8 557	395 232	1.10	6 535	17.4	2 751	7.3	45 852	13.9	51 286	38 638	12 648	18 498	4 862
Fayetteville-Springdale-Rogers, AR-MO..........	10 559	503 200	1.00	7 152	13.9	3 441	6.7	68 587	15.9	70 868	50 218	20 650	10 917	2 587
Flagstaff, AZ.....................	11 174	136 310	0.98	1 691	12.2	812	5.8	21 211	18.8	19 750	16 583	3 167	4 877	3 529
Flint, MI..........................	5 982	397 164	0.90	4 965	12.1	4 332	10.5	30 107	8.7	86 632	56 063	30 569	13 935	3 374
Florence, SC	4 650	210 815	1.04	2 529	12.3	2 277	11.0	26 471	15.4	41 289	34 709	6 580	9 281	4 504
Florence-Muscle Shoals, AL.	2 547	145 568	0.97	1 531	10.4	1 714	11.7	15 974	13.5	33 713	29 340	4 373	4 561	3 100
Fond du Lac, WI	3 469	97 182	0.91	1 101	10.8	880	8.6	6 167	7.5	20 348	10 784	9 564	1 801	1 768
Fort Collins, CO	8 933	311 584	0.92	3 543	10.6	2 016	6.0	27 958	10.3	47 105	33 356	13 749	7 548	2 345
Fort Smith, AR-OK..............	5 018	275 742	0.97	3 597	12.8	2 991	10.7	41 126	17.7	55 427	40 244	15 183	9 990	3 581
Fort Wayne, IN..................	7 020	433 895	1.03	5 844	13.6	3 503	8.1	51 655	14.2	68 160	37 376	30 784	11 143	2 761
Fresno, CA.......................	17 885	966 757	1.00	16 002	16.4	6 807	7.0	129 986	15.4	114 896	76 689	38 207	37 082	3 837
Gadsden, AL	2 085	99 605	0.91	1 168	11.3	1 449	14.1	12 311	14.6	24 259	17 947	6 312	4 647	4 475
Gainesville, FL..................	14 315	285 661	1.11	3 087	11.1	2 051	7.4	38 170	16.9	41 616	33 608	8 008	9 313	3 411
Gainesville, GA.................	2 908	195 219	1.05	2 535	13.1	1 480	7.6	35 062	21.6	28 640	20 414	8 226	4 071	2 139
Gettysburg, PA..................	3 963	87 386	0.70	1 044	10.2	945	9.2	8 141	10.2	18 706	12 721	5 985	1 224	1 205
Glens Falls, NY	3 847	123 039	0.92	1 214	9.6	1 268	10.0	8 058	8.0	28 667	17 324	11 343	1 939	1 509
Goldsboro, NC	2 976	124 621	1.00	1 698	13.7	1 235	9.9	17 397	16.7	22 485	18 082	4 403	4 608	3 764
Grand Forks, ND-MN..........	5 460	102 729	1.02	1 404	13.7	778	7.6	7 281	8.7	15 276	10 782	4 494	2 449	2 410
Grand Island, NE	1 513	86 664	1.05	1 273	15.0	711	8.4	9 671	13.7	14 940	13 733	1 207	2 763	3 532
Grand Junction, CO	4 209	144 690	0.95	1 816	12.2	1 379	9.3	15 547	13.0	27 273	16 415	10 858	4 393	2 955
Grand Rapids-Wyoming, MI .	23 245	1 050 290	1.05	13 916	13.4	7 368	7.1	86 793	9.9	162 365	79 178	83 187	21 473	2 106
Grants Pass, OR................	1 542	83 482	1.00	867	10.2	1 103	13.0	7 481	12.0	23 456	14 051	9 405	2 896	3 457
Great Falls, MT	2 526	NA	NA	1 177	14.3	748	9.1	10 399	15.6	16 221	12 327	3 894	2 942	3 554
Greeley, CO	4 692	261 514	0.88	4 041	14.2	1 634	5.7	29 259	12.1	31 275	21 516	9 759	6 203	2 261
Green Bay, WI	7 000	323 129	1.05	3 956	12.5	2 281	7.2	23 230	8.8	51 786	26 096	25 690	4 664	1 767
Greensboro-High Point, NC..	18 853	775 546	1.09	8 736	11.6	6 788	9.0	94 723	15.2	133 509	64 058	69 451	25 199	3 380
Greenville, NC..................	6 467	177 992	1.03	2 128	12.1	1 256	7.1	21 566	14.4	25 402	21 368	4 034	6 114	3 532
Greenville-Anderson-Mauldin, SC	23 923	865 535	1.01	10 604	12.1	7 913	9.0	112 035	15.8	157 914	107 088	50 826	37 580	4 363
Gulfport-Biloxi-Pascagoula, MS................................	7 012	393 438	1.04	4 923	12.6	3 467	8.9	58 465	18.0	65 348	51 722	13 626	14 048	3 973
Hagerstown-Martinsburg, MD-WV	9 092	246 041	0.88	3 157	12.1	2 436	9.3	19 944	9.3	44 514	38 042	6 472	5 756	2 215
Hammond, LA	3 654	114 590	0.76	1 965	15.3	1 224	9.5	19 394	18.0	21 532	14 770	6 762	7 591	6 096
Hanford-Corcoran, CA	16 752	151 904	1.03	2 420	16.0	823	5.5	17 130	14.3	14 529	12 533	1 996	4 171	2 754
Harrisburg-Carlisle, PA	19 995	607 485	1.17	6 607	11.7	5 019	8.9	44 262	9.7	103 852	55 995	47 857	11 999	2 145
Harrisonburg, VA	9 109	135 193	1.07	1 416	10.8	953	7.3	17 387	16.7	17 272	14 340	2 932	2 031	1 560
Hartford-West Hartford-East Hartford, CT	47 422	1 243 256	1.05	11 913	9.8	10 321	8.5	64 245	6.5	202 765	141 948	60 817	25 563	2 495
Hattiesburg, MS	3 659	150 838	1.02	1 979	13.3	1 197	8.0	20 873	16.5	24 893	20 258	4 635	NA	NA
Hickory-Lenoir-Morganton, NC................................	7 213	358 778	0.97	3 736	10.3	3 843	10.6	47 935	16.2	75 018	50 763	24 255	10 636	2 938
Hilton Head Island-Bluffton-Beaufort, NC	6 371	203 229	1.00	2 429	11.7	1 705	8.2	27 047	18.1	45 048	36 848	8 200	6 389	3 163
Hinesville, GA	2 795	82 883	1.00	1 695	21.1	405	5.1	11 609	15.8	6 542	4 868	1 674	2 413	2 945
Homosassa Springs, FL	2 247	NA	NA	1 031	7.3	2 497	17.7	16 556	18.6	46 663	32 012	14 651	2 868	2 096
Hot Springs, AR	2 173	98 743	1.04	1 059	10.9	1 285	13.2	11 458	15.2	30 753	24 021	6 732	NA	NA
Houma-Thibodaux, LA	3 107	220 140	1.10	3 000	14.1	1 871	8.8	33 973	18.8	34 115	27 276	6 839	6 561	3 118
Houston-The Woodlands-Sugar Land, TX	81 815	6 519 268	1.01	98 397	14.8	38 553	5.8	1 244 181	21.6	664 275	401 450	262 825	243 686	3 776
Huntington-Ashland, WV-KY-OH........................	7 866	355 141	0.94	4 188	11.6	4 156	11.5	28 860	9.8	80 171	57 851	22 320	6 922	2 049
Huntsville, AL	10 594	462 325	1.10	5 200	11.7	3 644	8.2	47 651	12.9	69 070	57 287	11 783	16 049	3 646
Idaho Falls, ID...................	1 371	139 259	1.01	2 349	16.8	908	6.5	17 075	14.2	19 569	15 155	4 414	2 667	1 920
Indianapolis-Carmel-Anderson, IN	39 173	1 980 669	1.01	26 847	13.5	15 399	7.7	221 808	13.1	282 820	206 313	76 507	70 311	4 117
Iowa City, IA.....................	8 326	171 375	1.08	2 135	12.8	889	5.3	9 601	6.9	18 970	16 272	2 698	3 390	2 072
Ithaca, NY	13 249	115 076	1.22	842	8.0	604	5.8	6 391	8.1	13 671	10 563	3 108	2 611	2 504
Jackson, MI	9 268	153 774	0.91	1 734	10.9	1 575	9.9	11 840	9.4	31 686	23 779	7 907	4 054	2 559
Jackson, MS	21 589	585 341	1.04	7 527	13.0	5 137	8.9	72 291	14.9	89 411	68 873	20 538	16 194	3 424
Jackson, TN	5 913	142 451	1.22	1 617	12.5	1 259	9.7	14 160	13.5	24 207	19 582	4 625	5 117	3 902
Jacksonville, FL.................	27 852	1 423 195	1.01	18 104	12.5	12 358	8.5	178 884	15.0	229 617	164 587	65 030	52 727	3 719
Jacksonville, NC................	13 405	188 008	1.00	4 348	23.3	995	5.3	17 953	11.5	19 140	16 505	2 635	NA	NA
Janesville-Beloit, WI...........	2 709	151 613	0.88	1 966	12.2	1 408	8.7	12 011	8.9	29 682	20 055	9 627	4 401	2 735
Jefferson City, MO.............	10 662	154 290	1.06	1 826	12.1	1 278	8.4	15 491	13.0	25 885	22 470	3 415	3 302	2 190
Johnson City, TN...............	5 565	198 499	0.96	1 982	9.9	2 196	10.9	22 603	14.1	44 403	23 840	20 563	5 569	2 757
Johnstown, PA...................	6 431	133 195	0.92	1 270	9.3	1 748	12.8	9 275	8.9	34 368	12 439	21 929	2 707	1 937
Jonesboro, AR	4 194	129 128	1.04	1 727	13.5	1 249	9.7	14 269	13.5	23 354	19 323	4 031	4 926	3 968

1. Per 1,000 estimated resident population. 2. Data for serious crimes have not been adjusted for underreporting; this may affect comparability between geographic areas and over time.
3. Per 100,000 population estimated by the FBI.

Table C. Metropolitan Areas — Crime, Education, Money Income, and Poverty

Area name	Serious crimes known to police, 2014 (cont.)[1] Rate[2] Violent	Property	School enrollment and attainment, 2014 Enrollment[3] Total	Percent private	Attainment[4] (percent) High school graduate or less	Bachelor's degree or more	Local government expenditures,[5] 2012–2013 Total current expenditures (mil dol)	Current expenditures per student (dollars)	Per capita income[6] (dollars)	Mean household income (dollars)	Median household income	Percent of households with income of less than $25,000	Percent of households with income of $200,000 or more	Percent below poverty level All persons	Children under 18 years	Age 65 years and older
	46	47	48	49	50	51	52	53	54	55	56	57	58	59	60	61
Fairbanks, AK	NA	NA	29 928	9.0	27.6	34.4	275.6	17 384	33 599	88 618	69 820	12.6	6.5	9.9	9.5	2.7
Fargo, ND-MN	253	2 156	66 546	12.9	28.9	36.7	330.6	10 720	31 236	75 239	53 867	19.9	5.0	12.5	14.5	7.3
Farmington, NM	535	1 983	33 912	9.1	48.9	16.0	211.3	8 814	22 609	66 347	48 773	27.0	3.3	22.0	33.8	10.9
Fayetteville, NC	459	4 404	109 888	18.0	36.1	22.4	500.3	8 157	22 606	57 120	42 181	26.9	1.8	17.8	26.0	10.7
Fayetteville-Springdale-Rogers, AR-MO	323	2 263	134 956	9.4	46.7	27.9	760.1	9 067	26 491	71 207	50 128	24.0	4.3	16.2	19.9	11.0
Flagstaff, AZ	346	3 183	47 615	6.2	31.8	35.2	134.3	7 962	23 867	68 483	49 757	24.8	4.3	22.1	25.3	11.9
Flint, MI	654	2 720	101 244	9.1	41.9	20.3	699.6	10 792	23 253	56 725	41 682	30.2	2.1	21.5	33.9	7.4
Florence, SC	472	4 031	53 915	12.2	51.9	19.7	308.5	9 206	21 281	55 165	40 139	32.6	1.9	21.1	30.4	14.8
Florence-Muscle Shoals, AL	338	2 762	33 330	9.7	49.2	21.7	199.4	9 342	23 277	54 674	41 597	31.9	1.4	18.1	26.5	9.3
Fond du Lac, WI	200	1 568	24 200	24.1	46.4	21.4	146.4	10 908	27 655	65 731	51 717	19.9	1.7	9.7	13.9	6.0
Fort Collins, CO	190	2 156	99 614	9.3	24.9	42.7	379.0	8 405	30 626	76 841	56 575	19.7	4.2	13.2	11.8	6.1
Fort Smith, AR-OK	432	3 148	69 257	10.4	54.2	16.6	431.1	8 610	21 934	55 791	39 207	32.7	2.2	23.4	34.2	12.5
Fort Wayne, IN	237	2 524	116 285	22.4	41.5	26.8	577.7	9 191	25 408	64 858	49 405	23.3	2.9	14.6	21.1	6.2
Fresno, CA	471	3 367	286 339	7.2	49.6	19.7	1 841.6	9 403	20 170	62 536	43 423	28.6	3.0	27.7	38.9	14.4
Gadsden, AL	490	3 985	23 035	10.6	49.2	16.7	132.2	8 058	20 810	51 863	40 529	34.8	1.2	18.4	29.9	9.5
Gainesville, FL	552	2 859	92 643	10.0	31.7	39.2	267.6	8 803	25 408	63 509	45 353	31.5	4.1	22.2	21.0	9.6
Gainesville, GA	173	1 965	51 276	8.8	48.7	23.8	290.9	8 521	23 769	69 276	52 519	19.7	3.6	16.6	25.0	9.6
Gettysburg, PA	103	1 102	24 087	26.5	55.4	22.6	276.2	20 032	28 862	75 196	61 543	17.5	3.8	11.4	15.7	4.2
Glens Falls, NY	115	1 394	25 867	10.3	47.8	23.0	320.5	17 446	26 944	66 041	51 880	23.6	3.1	14.6	22.8	6.7
Goldsboro, NC	372	3 392	32 153	14.3	49.0	20.2	153.4	7 765	19 382	49 457	35 966	30.4	1.5	25.5	43.6	12.2
Grand Forks, ND-MN	214	2 197	30 338	6.6	33.9	28.0	156.4	11 387	27 245	65 357	49 691	29.1	3.4	18.9	24.2	6.8
Grand Island, NE	210	3 322	20 301	12.1	45.3	17.9	178.1	11 522	25 587	63 543	49 742	23.9	2.8	14.8	18.7	13.0
Grand Junction, CO	346	2 609	36 949	11.0	40.6	25.1	174.7	7 802	26 910	63 273	50 174	23.8	2.1	16.9	22.7	7.5
Grand Rapids-Wyoming, MI	315	1 791	282 267	19.3	37.9	31.1	1 677.8	10 931	26 200	69 886	54 372	20.4	3.5	13.8	17.8	7.1
Grants Pass, OR	222	3 235	NA	NA	42.4	17.1	99.3	9 292	22 500	55 069	36 870	31.1	2.6	19.6	34.1	6.2
Great Falls, MT	249	3 305	19 063	11.4	36.2	27.7	109.4	9 502	24 352	56 345	42 170	28.8	1.6	13.3	14.0	7.0
Greeley, CO	285	1 976	77 722	12.1	39.7	25.7	325.5	8 426	27 678	77 486	62 083	15.3	3.8	9.8	10.5	5.7
Green Bay, WI	240	1 527	77 726	13.1	42.7	25.9	538.6	10 524	26 728	66 173	53 208	20.6	2.5	11.9	17.4	7.5
Greensboro-High Point, NC	321	3 060	190 860	12.4	43.2	27.2	972.4	8 739	24 300	59 977	42 565	27.3	2.7	17.3	26.4	8.8
Greenville, NC	416	3 116	59 194	7.1	35.0	29.1	197.0	8 282	23 026	58 535	41 632	32.1	2.5	23.5	25.4	10.0
Greenville-Anderson-Mauldin, SC	538	3 826	218 957	18.8	44.3	26.8	1 095.7	8 387	24 536	61 659	44 783	28.1	2.8	16.5	22.7	7.6
Gulfport-Biloxi-Pascagoula, MS	216	3 758	99 609	13.1	42.4	22.1	517.5	8 485	22 141	55 149	43 906	27.7	1.5	16.7	20.5	10.2
Hagerstown-Martinsburg, MD-WV	250	1 965	63 590	14.4	50.0	20.9	473.0	11 659	27 075	70 639	56 537	20.0	2.8	13.9	21.4	7.3
Hammond, LA	789	5 308	35 908	10.9	57.4	19.6	176.4	8 892	21 410	55 825	40 689	31.4	1.3	21.6	30.9	15.8
Hanford-Corcoran, CA	460	2 295	45 111	5.5	52.9	11.5	255.8	8 888	17 378	60 030	42 784	28.6	1.8	26.6	38.5	11.8
Harrisburg-Carlisle, PA	239	1 906	128 041	20.6	45.7	29.9	913.7	13 575	30 764	74 852	57 742	19.3	4.1	11.1	16.6	5.1
Harrisonburg, VA	140	1 421	42 005	12.5	49.3	28.1	180.3	10 607	23 790	63 386	51 136	22.9	3.3	19.3	20.2	8.2
Hartford-West Hartford-East Hartford, CT	253	2 242	313 275	17.2	37.1	37.5	3 002.5	16 972	36 615	92 151	68 532	18.2	8.1	11.1	15.7	8.0
Hattiesburg, MS	NA	NA	44 863	11.8	38.7	26.6	201.2	8 544	21 494	56 642	42 028	33.2	2.5	20.6	24.4	7.0
Hickory-Lenoir-Morganton, NC	194	2 744	83 314	10.9	50.4	18.1	462.7	8 286	20 910	53 719	41 106	30.0	1.6	18.9	28.4	12.5
Hilton Head Island-Bluffton-Beaufort, NC	443	2 720	42 509	17.5	34.5	35.0	266.0	11 393	29 978	74 055	52 691	20.0	5.9	14.1	30.2	5.1
Hinesville, GA	336	2 609	22 230	10.7	44.2	16.0	120.4	9 206	18 452	50 641	43 331	25.0	0.4	15.6	21.3	11.5
Homosassa Springs, FL	355	1 741	21 861	9.3	52.1	17.6	136.2	8 895	23 159	51 701	35 671	33.7	2.3	21.2	38.1	10.4
Hot Springs, AR	NA	NA	20 774	6.3	46.8	22.1	141.5	9 550	24 118	57 529	41 032	32.6	2.7	18.9	24.0	6.8
Houma-Thibodaux, LA	242	2 875	51 596	14.1	63.5	14.6	306.4	9 210	23 092	61 796	45 104	27.1	2.9	20.9	30.3	8.4
Houston-The Woodlands-Sugar Land, TX	568	3 209	1 829 867	11.2	40.9	31.0	9 374.1	7 944	30 689	86 296	60 072	20.2	8.0	15.3	22.2	10.4
Huntington-Ashland, WV-KY-OH	163	1 886	84 319	7.5	51.2	19.8	623.1	10 817	22 555	53 940	40 830	32.6	1.7	18.2	24.1	9.9
Huntsville, AL	476	3 170	113 388	13.9	34.6	35.2	594.7	9 188	31 077	77 477	56 453	22.4	5.0	14.4	20.4	10.4
Idaho Falls, ID	154	1 766	39 935	12.7	39.0	25.6	164.5	5 917	23 880	70 371	50 208	23.0	3.7	15.1	20.2	8.2
Indianapolis-Carmel-Anderson, IN	715	3 402	516 130	17.0	39.8	31.6	2 946.3	9 676	27 598	71 103	52 268	22.0	4.2	14.8	21.2	6.0
Iowa City, IA	260	1 812	59 437	8.4	24.5	48.8	202.3	9 947	34 448	85 522	59 791	23.0	6.5	16.0	8.0	7.3
Ithaca, NY	123	2 381	41 489	60.2	24.6	52.4	209.0	19 154	28 648	74 339	52 885	23.0	5.4	19.8	18.1	3.9
Jackson, MI	414	2 145	39 272	15.5	44.6	20.4	257.0	11 350	23 575	59 811	45 371	27.0	2.5	15.0	25.4	6.6
Jackson, MS	402	3 022	162 783	20.3	37.5	29.4	749.9	8 053	25 096	67 303	46 967	26.8	3.5	18.5	25.6	12.8
Jackson, TN	759	3 143	33 189	28.0	49.0	23.6	155.7	8 092	21 141	53 911	40 338	31.2	1.9	21.1	29.1	9.1
Jacksonville, FL	528	3 191	353 190	19.7	38.9	27.5	1 724.7	8 235	27 439	70 042	51 117	22.2	3.9	15.4	22.6	9.1
Jacksonville, NC	NA	NA	51 354	9.9	36.9	19.3	198.2	7 762	22 359	59 652	47 581	23.6	1.6	13.2	15.6	6.8
Janesville-Beloit, WI	232	2 503	40 071	14.9	48.3	21.4	306.9	11 026	26 250	65 389	50 610	19.7	2.2	15.6	26.3	6.8
Jefferson City, MO	236	1 954	35 857	24.9	48.6	25.4	176.4	8 646	24 238	63 109	51 329	21.8	1.1	13.9	21.8	7.1
Johnson City, TN	288	2 469	49 113	12.0	47.4	26.2	222.0	8 031	23 396	54 505	38 813	33.2	2.5	19.8	26.4	9.2
Johnstown, PA	173	1 764	30 784	19.9	55.7	20.3	228.6	12 404	24 607	58 493	43 224	29.0	2.3	15.4	26.5	8.3
Jonesboro, AR	412	3 557	34 279	4.4	46.1	21.2	190.3	8 684	22 313	56 550	40 751	30.6	3.7	23.5	38.1	7.9

1. Data for serious crimes have not been adjusted for underreporting; this may affect comparability between geographic areas and over time.   2. Per 100,000 population estimated by the FBI.
3. All persons 3 years old and over enrolled in nursery school through college.   4. Persons 25 years old and over.   5. Elementary and secondary education expenditures.   6. Based on resident population estimated in the 2014 American Community Survey.

Table C. Metropolitan Areas — **Personal Income**

Area name	Personal income, 2014 Total (mil dol)	Percent change 2013–2014	Per capita[1] Dollars	Per capita[1] Rank	Wages and salaries (mil dol)	Supplements to wages and salaries; employer contributions (mil dol) Pension and insurance	Government social insurance	Proprietors' income (mil dol)	Dividends, interest, and rent (mil dol)	Personal transfer receipts (mil dol)	Earnings, 2014 Total (mil dol)	Contributions for government social insurance (mil dol) From employee and self-employed	From employer
	62	63	64	65	66	67	68	69	70	71	72	73	74
Fairbanks, AK	5 146	4.0	51 792	26	2 520	648	203	270	944	806	3 641	175	203
Fargo, ND-MN...................	11 167	4.3	48 914	48	6 234	838	494	1 191	2 267	1 370	8 757	532	494
Farmington, NM	4 481	5.0	36 197	285	2 453	404	185	271	585	939	3 313	206	185
Fayetteville, NC.................	13 753	3.3	36 390	275	8 589	2 177	764	655	3 174	3 220	12 184	596	764
Fayetteville-Springdale-Rogers, AR-MO...................	25 427	4.9	50 686	31	11 019	1 472	805	1 522	9 422	3 161	14 819	917	805
Flagstaff, AZ.....................	5 400	5.3	39 220	205	2 571	548	190	315	1 108	1 026	3 623	207	190
Flint, MI	14 401	3.3	34 878	319	5 979	1 022	470	827	1 946	4 386	8 299	573	470
Florence, SC.....................	7 292	2.9	35 220	312	3 697	616	275	430	1 014	1 955	5 018	327	275
Florence-Muscle Shoals, AL.	5 047	4.2	34 185	331	2 089	379	161	335	848	1 334	2 965	202	161
Fond du Lac, WI	4 318	4.6	42 434	131	2 040	386	168	339	674	780	2 932	177	168
Fort Collins, CO	14 127	6.7	43 584	106	7 027	1 041	487	914	3 016	1 967	9 469	523	487
Fort Smith, AR-OK..............	9 478	4.0	33 900	337	4 371	698	348	921	1 456	2 529	6 338	411	348
Fort Wayne, IN..................	16 864	4.6	39 477	197	9 071	1 498	694	1 418	2 715	3 217	12 682	788	694
Fresno, CA	34 568	3.6	35 785	300	15 198	3 455	1 119	3 638	5 438	8 271	23 410	1 292	1 119
Gadsden, AL	3 455	4.3	33 374	349	1 299	227	100	272	484	1 056	1 898	134	100
Gainesville, FL...................	10 515	5.0	38 462	219	5 852	1 243	418	480	2 060	1 979	7 992	451	418
Gainesville, GA.................	6 770	5.1	35 491	305	3 551	615	236	519	1 062	1 283	4 920	292	236
Gettysburg, PA..................	4 351	3.5	42 776	128	1 352	279	115	330	709	807	2 075	127	115
Glens Falls, NY.................	5 181	3.2	40 684	171	2 241	577	201	320	773	1 183	3 338	183	201
Goldsboro, NC	4 378	3.2	35 181	313	1 849	405	149	324	722	1 088	2 726	152	149
Grand Forks, ND-MN...........	4 433	0.8	43 532	107	2 337	395	194	365	880	739	3 290	187	194
Grand Island, NE...............	3 447	1.2	40 673	172	1 692	305	126	456	619	589	2 579	149	126
Grand Junction, CO	5 645	5.0	38 074	232	2 669	390	201	444	1 054	1 113	3 703	222	201
Grand Rapids-Wyoming, MI .	44 317	5.2	43 123	119	23 545	3 677	1 830	3 359	9 721	7 065	32 411	1 984	1 830
Grants Pass, OR................	2 807	5.7	33 577	347	860	138	83	194	556	1 025	1 275	101	83
Great Falls, MT	3 389	4.1	41 163	163	1 565	286	148	287	753	670	2 286	145	148
Greeley, CO	10 736	7.7	38 664	214	4 895	680	358	1 134	1 424	1 587	7 067	385	358
Green Bay, WI	14 079	4.0	44 761	93	7 963	1 432	619	1 266	2 451	2 104	11 281	669	619
Greensboro-High Point, NC..	28 208	4.6	37 782	239	15 971	2 530	1 237	1 912	4 684	5 866	21 649	1 344	1 237
Greenville, NC...................	6 209	4.1	35 410	307	3 288	669	236	342	1 035	1 356	4 535	264	236
Greenville-Anderson-Mauldin, SC..........................	32 198	5.3	37 333	253	17 124	2 603	1 305	1 988	4 689	6 905	23 019	1 485	1 305
Gulfport-Biloxi-Pascagoula, MS..............................	13 385	3.0	34 664	322	7 238	1 329	567	829	2 564	3 093	9 963	619	567
Hagerstown-Martinsburg, MD-WV	9 926	3.7	38 166	229	4 258	814	339	467	1 437	2 056	5 878	366	339
Hammond, LA	4 344	3.6	34 192	330	1 697	338	96	279	529	1 146	2 411	130	96
Hanford-Corcoran, CA	4 864	7.3	32 371	363	2 119	612	155	661	763	1 001	3 547	158	155
Harrisburg-Carlisle, PA	25 813	3.4	46 024	80	16 452	3 347	1 308	1 782	4 203	4 651	22 889	1 301	1 308
Harrisonburg, VA	4 403	4.5	33 703	340	2 495	449	185	439	842	775	3 568	207	185
Hartford-West Hartford-East Hartford, CT	68 095	4.0	56 078	16	39 843	6 720	2 816	5 755	10 811	10 431	55 135	3 011	2 816
Hattiesburg, MS	4 874	3.3	32 787	356	2 348	387	175	461	837	1 170	3 372	217	175
Hickory-Lenoir-Morganton, NC..............................	12 210	4.5	33 647	344	5 632	1 017	454	833	1 877	3 136	7 937	519	454
Hilton Head Island-Bluffton-Beaufort, NC	8 774	4.5	43 215	116	3 247	587	265	571	2 805	1 785	4 670	297	265
Hinesville, GA...................	2 496	3.2	30 322	375	1 803	540	165	51	622	500	2 559	107	165
Homosassa Springs, FL	4 766	3.2	34 194	328	1 249	214	92	177	1 211	1 814	1 731	160	92
Hot Springs, AR	3 525	4.3	36 218	284	1 331	203	107	213	716	1 072	1 854	138	107
Houma-Thibodaux, LA	10 400	4.2	49 209	46	5 735	831	357	1 439	1 526	1 535	8 363	454	357
Houston-The Woodlands-Sugar Land, TX	355 790	6.7	54 820	19	193 622	23 045	12 376	66 266	53 650	37 225	295 309	14 700	12 376
Huntington-Ashland, WV-KY-OH...........................	12 816	2.6	35 273	310	5 906	1 050	480	689	1 648	3 645	8 125	541	480
Huntsville, AL....................	18 993	4.1	43 059	121	11 932	1 998	917	1 010	3 491	3 090	15 857	945	917
Idaho Falls, ID..................	5 088	2.7	36 798	264	2 481	321	218	791	980	870	3 811	238	218
Indianapolis-Carmel-Anderson, IN	86 769	3.9	44 017	99	48 960	7 636	3 648	7 696	13 041	14 277	67 940	4 121	3 648
Iowa City, IA.....................	7 484	4.3	45 535	85	4 188	1 019	316	626	1 540	856	6 148	333	316
Ithaca, NY	3 945	3.1	37 686	241	2 471	503	219	253	728	635	3 445	176	219
Jackson, MI......................	5 509	2.9	34 490	323	2 564	478	200	248	803	1 426	3 490	227	200
Jackson, MS	23 844	3.3	41 284	161	11 786	1 822	866	3 053	3 887	4 716	17 527	1 099	866
Jackson, TN	4 735	1.5	36 359	276	2 577	490	187	585	638	1 179	3 839	227	187
Jacksonville, FL	61 609	4.9	43 413	110	32 114	4 674	2 354	3 263	13 026	11 163	42 405	2 577	2 354
Jacksonville, NC................	8 355	2.0	44 538	94	4 305	1 218	406	277	1 816	1 237	6 206	264	406
Janesville-Beloit, WI...........	6 240	1.9	38 713	211	2 839	543	230	273	1 109	1 271	3 885	249	230
Jefferson City, MO.............	5 803	3.1	38 463	218	3 071	736	211	457	957	1 105	4 475	240	211
Johnson City, TN	6 989	2.6	34 757	321	2 981	586	217	520	1 006	1 906	4 304	278	217
Johnstown, PA	5 170	2.1	37 536	246	2 100	466	185	290	782	1 570	3 041	202	185
Jonesboro, AR	4 186	2.4	33 024	353	2 029	321	162	487	526	1 123	2 998	191	162

1. Based on the resident population estimated as of July 1 of the year shown.

Table C. Metropolitan Areas — **Earnings, Social Security, and Housing**

Area name	Farm	Mining	Construction	Manufacturing	Information, professional, scientific, technical services	Retail trade	Finance, insurance, real estate, rental and leasing	Health care and social assistance	Government	Number	Rate[1]	Supplemental Security Income recipients, December 2014	Total	Percent change, 2000–2015
	75	76	77	78	79	80	81	82	83	84	85	86	87	88
Fairbanks, AK	0.1	4.7	8.7	1.4	4.2	5.7	D	9.6	45.8	10 010	101	1 081	41 616	-0.4
Fargo, ND-MN	0.9	D	8.6	7.6	10.1	7.2	11.7	12.7	13.5	31 895	140	2 870	103 693	12.8
Farmington, NM	1.1	23.5	7.6	2.4	2.5	7.2	3.2	11.1	20.5	20 860	168	4 019	49 661	0.6
Fayetteville, NC	0.7	D	3.3	4.8	D	4.7	2.3	D	61.5	60 165	159	11 233	164 591	7.1
Fayetteville-Springdale-Rogers, AR-MO	2.6	0.2	4.6	9.5	6.4	6.0	4.6	8.8	12.1	84 275	168	9 076	207 938	4.9
Flagstaff, AZ	0.2	0.3	3.8	10.4	3.4	6.9	3.3	16.5	33.2	18 765	136	2 667	64 446	1.8
Flint, MI	0.3	0.0	4.7	12.0	9.6	8.3	6.1	18.1	17.2	97 225	235	17 113	190 887	-0.7
Florence, SC	0.3	D	3.7	16.1	6.4	7.7	10.5	12.4	17.9	46 690	226	8 936	89 425	0.5
Florence-Muscle Shoals, AL.	1.4	D	7.5	19.0	3.5	10.1	4.8	12.1	20.4	38 545	261	4 919	70 684	1.6
Fond du Lac, WI	5.2	0.7	7.2	26.2	4.3	6.3	4.3	12.6	12.7	21 155	207	1 483	44 620	1.6
Fort Collins, CO	0.5	0.7	8.7	13.4	13.1	6.6	4.8	8.9	22.2	51 960	160	2 617	140 892	6.2
Fort Smith, AR-OK	2.6	5.0	5.0	16.2	5.6	6.8	4.8	D	15.3	66 055	236	10 684	123 514	2.2
Fort Wayne, IN	1.1	D	5.7	20.4	6.8	6.1	7.9	16.6	9.5	79 905	187	8 510	181 519	1.9
Fresno, CA	6.7	0.2	4.9	6.2	6.1	6.5	6.4	13.6	22.6	130 440	135	43 366	325 996	3.3
Gadsden, AL	0.8	0.2	5.0	15.7	3.8	8.4	4.8	21.8	14.7	28 785	278	4 865	47 510	0.1
Gainesville, FL	1.0	D	3.3	4.3	7.3	5.6	5.6	D	39.3	45 170	165	6 868	121 823	1.5
Gainesville, GA	0.6	D	5.5	20.9	4.2	6.7	4.7	15.4	12.4	32 355	170	3 029	70 107	1.9
Gettysburg, PA	4.5	D	7.4	19.5	5.3	6.6	3.9	D	15.4	23 235	228	1 113	41 462	1.6
Glens Falls, NY	2.2	0.4	6.8	13.4	D	7.9	4.0	13.0	24.1	32 855	258	3 209	68 208	0.9
Goldsboro, NC	8.0	D	3.7	12.2	3.5	6.8	3.3	11.6	32.1	25 645	206	4 554	53 290	0.6
Grand Forks, ND-MN	5.0	0.5	7.2	6.5	5.1	8.5	4.5	D	27.0	16 705	164	1 343	46 961	6.8
Grand Island, NE	8.2	D	6.5	17.9	3.7	7.5	4.8	10.3	15.4	15 835	187	1 207	35 196	3.0
Grand Junction, CO	0.7	10.3	8.2	4.5	6.5	7.7	5.8	14.3	16.4	30 075	203	2 453	64 247	2.6
Grand Rapids-Wyoming, MI .	1.0	D	5.1	24.0	D	6.2	6.7	D	10.3	185 590	180	20 394	410 654	1.5
Grants Pass, OR	0.6	D	5.7	11.3	4.3	11.5	5.6	19.6	15.6	26 400	316	2 775	38 136	0.4
Great Falls, MT	1.1	0.1	7.1	3.3	6.3	8.3	6.2	16.5	27.5	17 635	214	1 902	37 932	1.8
Greeley, CO	5.4	12.7	13.0	10.2	3.8	5.6	4.7	7.1	11.8	38 130	138	3 431	102 603	6.6
Green Bay, WI	2.9	0.1	5.4	17.8	D	5.4	8.4	12.3	12.4	59 450	189	5 537	141 087	2.8
Greensboro-High Point, NC..	0.6	D	5.0	17.5	D	6.4	8.5	11.5	12.0	149 970	201	17 947	329 921	2.2
Greenville, NC	2.0	D	4.0	10.6	4.5	7.0	4.5	12.2	35.9	28 745	164	5 997	77 332	3.1
Greenville-Anderson-Mauldin, SC	0.1	0.1	6.1	17.1	10.2	6.8	6.2	D	15.0	184 895	214	18 626	372 546	2.9
Gulfport-Biloxi-Pascagoula, MS	0.0	0.3	7.0	17.6	5.8	6.1	3.9	D	29.1	78 150	202	10 839	176 197	5.4
Hagerstown-Martinsburg, MD-WV	1.0	D	5.2	9.7	6.3	8.9	8.9	14.5	22.7	51 680	199	5 667	108 141	2.4
Hammond, LA	0.5	0.5	5.1	5.9	4.4	10.2	11.2	11.4	25.9	23 460	185	5 986	53 138	6.1
Hanford-Corcoran, CA	16.8	0.0	2.1	8.6	2.3	4.5	2.1	8.5	41.6	17 225	115	4 612	45 253	3.2
Harrisburg-Carlisle, PA	0.8	D	4.3	7.4	8.6	4.7	9.4	14.0	21.8	114 460	204	11 003	246 295	2.3
Harrisonburg, VA	5.7	D	6.4	17.6	6.6	6.6	4.0	11.7	17.8	22 625	174	1 804	52 898	3.5
Hartford-West Hartford-East Hartford, CT	0.1	D	4.9	11.9	11.6	5.2	17.2	12.2	15.8	228 335	188	23 421	508 930	0.4
Hattiesburg, MS	0.7	1.1	5.5	7.1	D	9.6	D	17.5	24.1	27 205	184	4 884	62 545	1.1
Hickory-Lenoir-Morganton, NC	1.2	0.0	3.7	26.8	4.0	7.2	2.9	12.2	15.6	86 255	238	7 482	162 293	-0.2
Hilton Head Island-Bluffton-Beaufort, NC	0.2	0.1	7.4	1.2	D	9.4	7.9	9.2	31.2	49 700	246	2 685	106 364	2.9
Hinesville, GA	0.2	D	D	D	D	2.4	1.5	1.7	76.5	8 795	107	1 449	33 712	2.9
Homosassa Springs, FL	0.1	0.2	7.7	1.1	6.5	12.5	4.1	23.4	14.8	56 635	407	3 228	77 726	-0.4
Hot Springs, AR	0.4	0.8	6.3	7.4	6.2	11.2	7.0	22.6	14.4	29 430	303	3 924	50 538	0.0
Houma-Thibodaux, LA	0.2	11.7	6.3	11.6	4.4	4.8	5.2	6.8	9.0	39 655	188	8 113	84 850	2.9
Houston-The Woodlands-Sugar Land, TX	0.0	14.1	8.4	9.8	D	4.4	6.6	6.6	8.9	763 745	118	139 778	2 501 900	9.0
Huntington-Ashland, WV-KY-OH	0.0	3.0	9.0	11.6	D	7.0	4.2	D	16.8	89 510	246	17 619	164 657	0.1
Huntsville, AL	0.4	0.0	4.0	12.2	23.7	5.5	3.0	6.8	29.3	79 270	180	9 036	192 458	6.1
Idaho Falls, ID	3.3	0.1	6.0	5.6	24.1	8.3	4.3	D	10.8	22 665	164	2 547	51 308	3.0
Indianapolis-Carmel-Anderson, IN	0.6	0.1	6.2	12.9	D	6.0	D	D	12.2	333 995	169	36 554	842 432	3.2
Iowa City, IA	3.1	0.2	4.8	7.2	6.3	5.5	4.0	6.9	42.9	22 195	135	1 993	69 357	5.9
Ithaca, NY	0.8	1.3	2.2	8.0	7.5	5.2	3.5	D	15.0	15 470	148	1 500	42 272	1.4
Jackson, MI	0.2	0.2	3.9	19.9	5.1	6.7	3.5	14.5	15.6	36 200	227	4 603	69 016	-0.6
Jackson, MS	1.2	D	5.6	7.1	8.8	6.7	8.9	12.4	20.9	107 915	187	20 800	239 263	2.8
Jackson, TN	0.4	D	D	17.4	D	8.0	4.6	12.5	21.7	28 575	220	4 224	56 214	1.7
Jacksonville, FL	0.1	0.1	5.0	5.5	11.9	6.6	13.1	D	15.5	260 735	183	31 492	622 262	4.0
Jacksonville, NC	1.5	D	3.0	0.8	2.1	4.3	1.8	3.0	74.3	23 285	126	2 927	76 926	12.8
Janesville-Beloit, WI	1.6	0.3	5.5	17.4	5.4	6.9	3.3	15.8	15.6	34 135	212	3 904	68 313	-0.2
Jefferson City, MO	3.2	D	6.1	7.4	7.2	6.0	4.8	9.0	33.7	30 855	205	2 505	64 115	0.9
Johnson City, TN	0.3	0.1	5.4	11.2	D	8.3	5.9	D	22.3	51 065	255	6 156	96 065	2.4
Johnstown, PA	0.2	1.1	4.4	8.2	7.9	7.8	6.0	22.2	17.8	38 270	278	5 113	65 126	-0.8
Jonesboro, AR	4.5	0.1	6.5	12.7	3.9	7.6	4.6	20.3	15.8	26 450	209	5 642	54 908	6.7

1. Per 1,000 resident population estimated as of July 1, 2011 of the year shown.

Table C. Metropolitan Areas — Housing, Labor Force, and Employment

Area name	Housing units, 2014								Civilian labor force, 2015		Unemployment		Civilian employment[5], 2014	Percent	
	Occupied units														
	Owner-occupied				Renter-occupied										
				Median owner cost as a percent of income			Median rent as a percent of income	Percent with a computer		Percent change, 2013–2014				Management, professional, and related occupations	Construction, production, and related occupations
	Total	Percent	Median value[1]	With a mortgage	Without a mortgage[2]	Median rent[3]			Total		Total	Rate[4]	Total employed		
	89	90	91	92	93	94	95	96	97	98	99	100	101	102	103
Fairbanks, AK	35 692	56.5	237 400	24.6	11.6	1 232	33.3	92.6	46 486	-0.8	2 527	5.4	46 305	38.4	22.8
Fargo, ND-MN	92 345	58.4	171 300	19.0	10.9	715	27.7	86.6	130 873	2.1	3 193	2.4	129 419	37.6	21.9
Farmington, NM	40 378	70.1	151 500	21.1	10.0	748	24.7	68.2	55 257	0.4	3 893	7.0	50 525	28.4	26.6
Fayetteville, NC	140 204	53.2	125 900	22.1	13.0	857	31.5	86.4	145 827	-0.6	10 879	7.5	140 376	32.3	22.5
Fayetteville-Springdale-Rogers, AR-MO	182 570	61.7	152 300	18.5	10.0	731	26.8	85.8	253 105	5.2	9 584	3.8	236 965	35.6	23.4
Flagstaff, AZ	46 919	60.4	227 500	22.6	10.0	969	31.7	84.8	73 041	1.4	4 786	6.6	64 328	35.5	16.9
Flint, MI	167 096	65.7	93 800	21.9	14.0	721	34.6	80.5	182 886	-1.1	10 653	5.8	159 125	30.8	25.6
Florence, SC	77 815	67.5	108 700	19.9	10.0	664	31.1	75.1	95 466	1.2	6 524	6.8	84 893	32.0	22.8
Florence-Muscle Shoals, AL	61 239	68.4	110 700	20.2	10.3	637	33.0	74.8	66 300	-1.8	4 828	7.3	61 946	30.5	26.7
Fond du Lac, WI	41 938	70.9	141 600	21.8	12.9	716	28.2	84.9	57 286	0.2	2 354	4.1	52 730	30.0	30.7
Fort Collins, CO	125 165	63.1	269 700	22.3	10.0	1 022	34.1	92.6	180 306	1.3	5 942	3.3	166 820	40.4	15.9
Fort Smith, AR-OK	106 099	68.7	106 700	19.9	10.7	639	31.1	76.4	121 212	1.7	6 684	5.5	116 657	29.0	29.7
Fort Wayne, IN	163 139	70.7	115 200	19.2	10.0	658	28.0	85.3	210 126	1.8	9 372	4.5	205 200	32.5	26.1
Fresno, CA	297 993	51.2	204 700	24.3	10.2	891	35.3	83.4	444 168	0.8	45 262	10.2	380 001	28.0	29.6
Gadsden, AL	39 714	68.2	99 700	22.2	12.3	668	29.6	79.3	43 203	-1.2	2 644	6.1	43 010	33.2	27.0
Gainesville, FL	103 619	54.2	155 100	20.8	11.3	875	32.4	85.8	136 632	0.1	6 273	4.6	121 201	45.2	10.6
Gainesville, GA	63 383	68.0	156 400	22.6	10.0	846	28.3	83.4	92 277	2.4	4 383	4.7	88 311	27.2	33.9
Gettysburg, PA	38 748	75.1	190 700	21.7	13.7	869	28.9	85.5	55 038	-0.1	2 241	4.1	49 317	30.1	29.0
Glens Falls, NY	49 937	72.1	160 100	23.1	14.3	810	33.1	85.4	61 203	0.4	3 291	5.4	58 131	31.2	26.3
Goldsboro, NC	46 281	57.9	105 700	23.4	13.1	703	29.6	81.3	53 947	0.3	3 291	6.1	49 740	27.7	32.6
Grand Forks, ND-MN	41 882	58.0	149 300	18.8	11.1	768	32.7	87.8	54 843	1.1	1 630	3.0	53 041	34.7	20.0
Grand Island, NE	32 187	66.5	122 400	21.0	11.4	649	27.9	79.9	43 894	-1.8	1 651	3.8	43 041	28.6	30.8
Grand Junction, CO	59 703	65.3	198 000	21.9	10.0	837	33.4	87.0	72 039	-2.0	3 997	5.5	69 582	30.9	28.1
Grand Rapids-Wyoming, MI	375 683	71.1	144 300	20.0	11.4	794	30.2	87.1	555 088	1.7	20 370	3.7	505 988	35.0	26.5
Grants Pass, OR	33 486	65.4	213 100	27.2	13.3	820	36.0	84.5	33 162	1.1	2 605	7.9	29 696	30.1	23.7
Great Falls, MT	34 018	63.8	160 900	20.6	11.7	610	26.7	81.3	38 888	0.9	1 553	4.0	37 134	36.5	20.3
Greeley, CO	96 803	71.1	212 000	22.6	10.0	898	29.0	90.0	147 984	1.3	5 670	3.8	137 247	31.5	28.5
Green Bay, WI	124 899	68.1	155 200	21.1	12.5	692	27.5	85.3	170 742	0.5	7 226	4.2	159 520	33.5	26.3
Greensboro-High Point, NC	289 450	61.7	138 600	22.1	11.1	753	30.9	79.1	364 824	1.2	21 596	5.9	343 110	33.5	24.5
Greenville, NC	68 412	50.5	126 400	21.8	12.3	772	33.9	86.0	87 628	0.4	5 339	6.1	80 513	35.8	17.0
Greenville-Anderson-Mauldin, SC	324 282	67.6	139 400	20.0	10.0	736	30.5	79.9	415 467	2.4	21 870	5.3	389 284	34.7	24.0
Gulfport-Biloxi-Pascagoula, MS	146 693	62.6	128 800	23.2	11.0	799	31.6	80.0	163 808	0.8	10 665	6.5	160 498	28.6	23.6
Hagerstown-Martinsburg, MD-WV	95 920	69.2	182 300	21.7	11.8	826	27.9	83.9	128 895	-0.2	7 048	5.5	116 405	33.4	24.8
Hammond, LA	45 786	67.3	131 700	23.6	10.0	747	31.7	83.6	54 029	0.2	3 870	7.2	52 748	28.0	28.5
Hanford-Corcoran, CA	41 596	51.4	169 200	23.8	11.7	855	32.4	81.4	58 354	1.0	6 120	10.5	49 372	22.2	34.3
Harrisburg-Carlisle, PA	226 058	68.0	171 100	20.9	11.7	836	30.4	84.4	293 252	1.4	12 348	4.2	278 760	37.8	21.3
Harrisonburg, VA	47 052	58.2	205 500	21.1	10.0	830	29.2	82.2	64 253	-0.9	2 931	4.6	66 727	34.0	22.5
Hartford-West Hartford-East Hartford, CT	467 615	66.6	243 100	23.0	14.8	999	30.5	87.4	649 443	0.1	36 153	5.6	616 483	43.8	17.3
Hattiesburg, MS	52 610	65.7	134 600	21.6	12.6	763	31.1	83.3	66 575	3.5	3 886	5.8	61 733	32.0	23.8
Hickory-Lenoir-Morganton, NC	131 741	69.4	124 800	20.0	10.2	652	29.8	77.0	167 395	0.4	9 538	5.7	155 514	26.1	33.0
Hilton Head Island-Bluffton-Beaufort, NC	74 717	69.4	257 000	25.4	12.4	1 016	30.2	86.8	83 077	3.0	4 478	5.4	83 105	31.1	19.9
Hinesville, GA	28 069	48.5	107 700	22.0	11.6	1 000	32.8	87.6	32 006	-1.0	1 992	6.2	29 101	29.1	25.0
Homosassa Springs, FL	60 315	79.8	116 300	23.9	12.5	761	36.6	83.9	47 739	-1.3	3 552	7.4	42 987	27.9	22.8
Hot Springs, AR	39 045	67.2	124 800	20.7	10.0	680	34.2	80.4	40 046	0.2	2 268	5.7	39 405	28.6	21.7
Houma-Thibodaux, LA	74 539	69.3	137 300	20.9	10.0	839	29.1	80.9	99 998	-3.4	5 632	5.6	90 695	25.0	35.2
Houston-The Woodlands-Sugar Land, TX	2 226 123	59.1	153 200	20.8	11.0	937	28.9	86.9	3 252 943	0.4	149 965	4.6	3 112 384	36.9	23.1
Huntington-Ashland, WV-KY-OH	146 108	69.1	106 700	20.1	10.0	665	29.4	79.6	147 778	-2.0	9 291	6.3	145 194	34.6	20.6
Huntsville, AL	172 409	69.5	165 900	18.6	10.0	718	30.6	85.6	209 345	-0.2	11 465	5.5	204 755	43.0	18.9
Idaho Falls, ID	45 712	74.1	155 800	20.3	10.0	710	28.8	87.2	65 172	3.0	2 248	3.4	58 604	32.4	27.2
Indianapolis-Carmel-Anderson, IN	744 765	64.6	141 500	19.5	10.5	818	30.8	86.7	1 008 205	1.6	45 398	4.5	951 436	37.8	21.4
Iowa City, IA	64 409	63.2	193 500	19.9	10.0	911	37.4	92.4	96 342	0.0	2 557	2.7	87 835	45.3	15.1
Ithaca, NY	38 120	54.7	182 100	20.6	12.7	995	33.6	88.9	55 371	0.9	2 255	4.1	47 837	52.1	9.6
Jackson, MI	61 686	75.5	109 400	21.2	12.5	703	31.8	81.8	73 043	-0.4	3 719	5.1	66 457	28.8	26.1
Jackson, MS	206 952	68.1	135 400	21.4	11.2	805	31.3	80.8	267 233	2.7	14 464	5.4	255 646	37.1	21.7
Jackson, TN	49 095	64.3	108 200	23.6	11.6	759	34.5	81.7	61 636	-0.1	3 769	6.1	55 850	29.1	25.4
Jacksonville, FL	528 993	62.2	159 100	22.1	10.5	966	33.0	87.1	724 881	1.0	38 021	5.2	638 491	35.7	18.4
Jacksonville, NC	61 873	54.7	156 800	24.1	11.1	911	30.2	89.6	63 959	0.1	3 856	6.0	63 979	31.7	20.6
Janesville-Beloit, WI	63 037	67.3	135 100	21.3	12.2	767	28.1	84.7	83 596	1.4	4 370	5.2	79 395	28.9	31.0
Jefferson City, MO	55 887	72.5	145 500	21.1	10.0	589	26.4	80.6	76 650	0.6	3 259	4.3	68 175	34.5	24.1
Johnson City, TN	84 847	68.3	129 600	21.1	10.3	682	34.3	80.2	88 392	-0.6	5 452	6.2	86 540	34.2	22.0
Johnstown, PA	57 004	73.6	88 800	18.4	12.7	551	25.6	77.3	62 363	-0.9	3 981	6.4	58 547	33.5	22.3
Jonesboro, AR	48 043	60.0	117 000	19.0	10.9	660	31.5	81.8	60 852	3.1	2 906	4.8	55 172	30.7	24.7

1. Specified owner-occupied units. 2. A value of 10.0 represents 10 percent or less. 3. Specified renter-occupied units. 4. Percent of civilian labor force.
5. Persons 16 years old and over.

Table C. Metropolitan Areas — **Nonfarm Employment and Agriculture**

Area name	Private nonfarm establishments, employment and payroll, 2014									Agriculture, 2012			
	Number of establishments	Employment						Annual payroll		Farms			Farm operators whose principal occupation is farming (percent)
		Total	Health care and social assistance	Manufacturing	Retail trade	Finance and insurance	Professional, scientific, and technical services	Total (mil dol)	Average per employee (dollars)	Number	Percent with:		
											Fewer than 50 acres	500 acres or more	
	104	105	106	107	108	109	110	111	112	113	114	115	116
Fairbanks, AK	2 471	27 435	5 399	626	4 952	750	1 181	1 399	50 978	217	39.2	20.7	47.9
Fargo, ND-MN	6 559	117 483	21 278	9 617	15 908	8 364	6 294	4 927	41 941	1 772	20.8	42.4	60.1
Farmington, NM	2 793	39 206	6 667	1 685	6 257	1 015	1 314	1 843	47 002	2 628	61.7	20.8	54.2
Fayetteville, NC	6 106	97 552	20 360	8 270	17 422	2 003	5 192	3 206	32 869	591	43.3	11.7	48.6
Fayetteville-Springdale-Rogers, AR-MO	11 125	193 752	22 987	26 030	24 789	5 193	10 696	9 332	48 165	6 835	37.1	5.7	46.8
Flagstaff, AZ	3 522	47 538	7 822	D	7 735	783	1 607	1 762	37 071	2 239	92.0	3.8	72.5
Flint, MI	7 716	115 459	26 791	9 999	19 642	4 145	3 658	4 474	38 750	835	58.6	6.2	50.1
Florence, SC	4 142	73 195	15 405	9 419	10 972	4 653	2 688	2 777	37 940	1 017	34.7	14.5	45.0
Florence-Muscle Shoals, AL.	3 197	46 611	7 267	9 819	8 365	1 626	1 112	1 515	32 503	2 153	43.9	6.4	42.2
Fond du Lac, WI	2 339	42 213	6 327	8 847	5 772	1 649	1 488	1 581	37 447	1 399	31.9	10.7	59.0
Fort Collins, CO	10 031	116 753	18 786	11 069	17 918	3 915	10 941	5 209	44 612	1 625	60.7	8.5	46.5
Fort Smith, AR-OK	5 829	96 280	18 194	18 011	12 717	2 753	2 284	3 465	35 992	4 703	36.8	6.9	45.2
Fort Wayne, IN	10 382	187 136	34 580	32 611	23 278	9 032	5 972	7 421	39 657	3 071	52.7	9.9	42.5
Fresno, CA	16 119	244 494	41 610	23 173	35 917	8 706	11 094	9 626	39 371	5 683	59.7	11.2	59.6
Gadsden, AL	1 995	28 573	7 134	4 750	4 465	1 027	602	935	32 723	853	51.1	2.9	40.3
Gainesville, FL	6 155	86 989	23 252	3 114	13 523	4 126	5 081	3 328	38 263	2 243	68.8	5.0	42.9
Gainesville, GA	4 040	66 547	10 260	17 916	7 902	2 000	1 688	2 833	42 564	622	59.0	2.3	51.3
Gettysburg, PA	1 930	28 076	4 479	5 462	3 426	552	1 156	1 001	35 648	1 188	48.2	6.3	50.9
Glens Falls, NY	3 355	41 649	8 332	6 738	7 801	1 370	1 098	1 597	38 352	968	34.7	10.2	55.5
Goldsboro, NC	2 145	33 742	7 284	6 061	5 888	1 135	730	1 115	33 048	563	40.1	18.1	60.9
Grand Forks, ND-MN	2 697	42 548	9 316	4 283	7 442	1 262	1 849	1 525	35 834	2 292	11.9	36.6	58.9
Grand Island, NE	2 518	35 599	5 142	8 257	5 839	1 509	785	1 262	35 457	2 339	26.5	34.1	62.0
Grand Junction, CO	4 427	50 695	9 581	2 539	8 288	1 797	2 313	2 142	42 259	2 264	75.4	5.4	48.6
Grand Rapids-Wyoming, MI .	23 512	457 413	62 914	100 876	47 374	17 374	18 349	19 139	41 841	4 680	49.2	6.5	49.6
Grants Pass, OR	1 906	20 344	4 525	2 609	4 234	659	533	653	32 096	617	76.3	0.6	55.8
Great Falls, MT	2 420	29 900	6 609	867	5 275	1 643	1 143	982	32 847	1 105	36.0	29.3	47.8
Greeley, CO	5 637	77 367	8 424	11 820	9 238	3 634	2 571	3 647	47 142	3 525	35.5	19.6	49.8
Green Bay, WI	7 581	153 096	21 551	29 585	16 889	D	5 608	6 604	43 137	2 774	40.3	8.0	51.0
Greensboro-High Point, NC..	17 400	316 549	44 602	52 963	35 773	14 429	12 593	12 982	41 010	3 350	49.0	3.5	46.6
Greenville, NC	3 533	57 990	15 688	5 319	8 604	2 044	2 003	2 062	35 563	391	34.8	21.5	59.3
Greenville-Anderson-Mauldin, SC	18 851	318 675	39 853	49 237	40 400	10 041	18 529	12 418	38 967	4 152	55.1	2.7	36.6
Gulfport-Biloxi-Pascagoula, MS	7 039	123 516	20 070	D	18 036	3 757	5 746	4 922	39 845	988	59.6	2.0	39.9
Hagerstown-Martinsburg, MD-WV	5 012	83 845	16 186	8 475	14 305	7 239	2 859	3 041	36 270	1 536	51.2	4.6	43.0
Hammond, LA	2 307	34 530	8 718	2 322	6 433	2 073	1 014	1 224	35 458	1 070	52.1	3.0	44.1
Hanford-Corcoran, CA	1 589	23 624	4 752	4 186	4 129	505	487	842	35 626	1 056	51.2	18.6	66.0
Harrisburg-Carlisle, PA	13 300	263 396	50 781	17 236	32 528	19 887	15 625	11 986	45 504	3 115	43.4	3.7	50.2
Harrisonburg, VA	2 968	50 872	7 625	8 996	7 511	1 214	1 546	1 811	35 606	1 902	43.2	2.8	54.6
Hartford-West Hartford-East Hartford, CT	29 110	536 262	103 107	58 432	64 728	52 418	36 280	29 994	55 932	1 995	71.1	1.6	44.9
Hattiesburg, MS	3 291	49 475	11 348	3 846	9 755	1 681	1 775	1 743	35 236	1 093	43.8	4.0	39.5
Hickory-Lenoir-Morganton, NC	7 325	124 874	19 641	37 076	16 228	2 201	2 707	4 497	36 015	2 198	56.5	2.6	47.5
Hilton Head Island-Bluffton-Beaufort, NC	5 516	58 645	8 554	782	11 341	2 834	3 181	1 967	33 538	252	49.6	19.4	51.2
Hinesville, GA	886	12 444	2 075	1 979	2 029	370	665	468	37 583	113	39.8	7.1	41.6
Homosassa Springs, FL	2 632	26 262	8 364	236	5 452	D	830	871	33 183	559	73.9	3.4	49.7
Hot Springs, AR	2 648	32 870	7 991	2 294	6 076	967	1 549	1 015	30 879	361	49.3	2.5	55.4
Houma-Thibodaux, LA	4 825	83 844	11 333	9 584	11 319	2 072	3 520	4 273	50 966	596	44.5	12.1	43.6
Houston-The Woodlands-Sugar Land, TX	132 729	2 507 620	316 656	225 396	282 797	94 280	211 665	155 430	61 983	15 026	56.9	7.3	38.6
Huntington-Ashland, WV-KY-OH	7 097	112 452	28 237	11 405	17 310	3 124	3 950	4 435	39 436	2 683	28.7	2.6	39.7
Huntsville, AL	9 451	170 407	24 698	19 311	22 415	4 050	34 568	8 002	46 959	2 263	44.1	7.4	47.9
Idaho Falls, ID	3 830	49 134	8 373	3 627	8 195	1 289	D	1 894	38 556	1 883	49.7	19.3	44.7
Indianapolis-Carmel-Anderson, IN	45 350	854 861	132 441	72 611	96 576	42 589	58 160	39 471	46 172	6 205	54.5	14.8	46.0
Iowa City, IA	3 922	67 175	17 472	6 386	10 089	2 462	2 428	2 617	38 955	2 481	33.2	15.9	51.9
Ithaca, NY	2 361	47 972	5 631	2 569	5 111	1 078	2 332	1 767	36 842	558	43.9	6.8	50.5
Jackson, MI	2 905	48 179	9 518	8 773	7 310	1 292	2 724	2 109	43 784	1 073	48.7	7.7	45.4
Jackson, MS	13 095	214 422	47 683	17 463	30 284	11 495	10 146	8 614	40 173	4 186	30.1	12.6	43.3
Jackson, TN	3 006	56 058	12 698	9 693	7 873	1 449	1 378	2 004	35 752	1 352	32.8	10.4	40.5
Jacksonville, FL	35 227	528 075	78 689	25 235	71 242	48 955	33 134	23 831	45 129	1 768	74.4	3.8	46.2
Jacksonville, NC	2 757	34 547	5 210	1 078	8 097	1 013	1 840	946	27 394	347	48.4	7.2	54.2
Janesville-Beloit, WI	3 236	54 808	9 106	10 099	8 592	1 307	1 184	2 231	40 706	1 509	44.1	10.3	50.0
Jefferson City, MO	3 619	50 402	9 229	5 366	7 416	2 369	2 089	1 872	37 138	4 676	23.1	9.0	39.7
Johnson City, TN	3 758	63 725	16 318	7 089	10 940	3 148	3 153	2 252	35 332	1 898	54.8	1.9	45.2
Johnstown, PA	3 286	47 647	12 045	4 518	6 896	2 073	2 695	1 646	34 546	551	33.4	5.6	37.4
Jonesboro, AR	2 797	43 048	10 268	6 313	7 578	1 205	947	1 478	34 336	980	31.9	39.2	57.8

Table C. Metropolitan Areas — **Agriculture**

Area name	Land in farms — Acreage (1,000) [117]	Percent change, 2007–2012 [118]	Acres — Average size of farm [119]	Total irrigated (1,000) [120]	Total cropland (1,000) [121]	Value of land and buildings (dollars) — Average per farm [122]	Average per acre [123]	Value of machinery and equipment, average per farm (dollars) [124]	Value of products sold — Total (mil dol) [125]	Average per farm (dollars) [126]	Percent from: Crops [127]	Livestock and poultry products [128]	Percent of farms with sales of: $10,000 or more [129]	$100,000 or more [130]	Government payments — Total ($1,000) [131]	Percent of farms [132]
Fairbanks, AK	100	-10.1	459	1.0	61.4	580 382	1 264	94 359	9.1	42 120	84.8	15.2	42.4	10.6	1 354	30.9
Fargo, ND-MN	1 718	4.0	970	19.2	1 599.8	3 003 294	3 097	390 421	965.2	544 686	94.1	5.9	65.4	48.4	22 932	77.1
Farmington, NM	2 580	58.2	982	85.9	115.6	341 496	348	41 084	71.3	27 135	88.9	11.1	13.3	1.2	1 023	14.0
Fayetteville, NC	141	-5.2	238	4.1	85.1	752 283	3 155	117 093	201.6	341 140	33.5	66.5	41.5	19.6	1 876	40.4
Fayetteville-Springdale-Rogers, AR-MO	1 073	3.0	157	2.0	278.5	555 647	3 541	64 923	1 356.1	198 410	1.4	98.6	44.7	13.9	6 743	15.3
Flagstaff, AZ	5 816	-4.7	2 597	1.9	8.3	543 406	209	23 731	25.8	11 528	9.1	90.9	9.6	1.4	987	23.0
Flint, MI	123	-4.6	148	1.5	102.6	570 910	3 867	107 984	91.3	109 389	88.7	11.3	38.4	12.9	2 131	32.2
Florence, SC	333	0.5	327	9.1	208.0	768 491	2 348	125 798	183.2	180 155	70.2	29.8	39.1	17.2	5 109	48.9
Florence-Muscle Shoals, AL	364	2.2	169	4.0	165.6	491 966	2 907	64 124	139.4	64 748	55.0	45.0	31.2	7.4	4 969	33.6
Fond du Lac, WI	316	-6.0	226	2.1	262.1	1 128 100	5 001	182 828	412.3	294 743	26.9	73.1	62.2	37.8	7 648	74.2
Fort Collins, CO	450	-8.0	277	52.5	106.4	854 599	3 083	72 401	128.6	79 167	44.6	55.4	28.8	7.6	1 061	11.2
Fort Smith, AR-OK	854	-7.3	182	13.9	251.1	405 541	2 233	56 091	507.6	107 930	11.2	88.8	35.2	9.0	4 858	15.0
Fort Wayne, IN	611	4.3	199	2.7	550.8	1 191 722	5 987	120 572	498.0	162 173	73.6	26.4	52.0	24.7	12 089	58.8
Fresno, CA	1 721	5.2	303	968.7	1 153.4	2 509 484	8 286	161 509	4 973.0	875 073	74.4	25.6	71.9	41.9	10 149	9.0
Gadsden, AL	86	-8.6	101	0.1	19.5	359 368	3 559	51 635	83.7	98 161	6.5	93.5	27.8	8.2	450	11.8
Gainesville, FL	272	11.5	121	23.3	102.5	575 798	4 750	53 346	189.9	84 661	51.3	48.7	30.4	6.6	1 400	7.7
Gainesville, GA	52	-9.3	84	0.1	12.3	686 416	8 212	68 188	166.3	267 434	2.1	97.9	34.9	19.8	115	8.2
Gettysburg, PA	171	-1.9	144	2.2	125.6	898 623	6 232	113 572	201.7	169 817	56.5	43.5	48.6	19.2	1 818	28.5
Glens Falls, NY	199	-5.9	205	0.7	103.4	514 006	2 501	104 877	D	D	D	D	50.3	19.8	D	25.2
Goldsboro, NC	191	9.1	340	4.8	146.8	1 400 607	4 124	199 504	577.2	1 025 265	27.4	72.6	61.5	44.8	2 943	56.5
Grand Forks, ND-MN	1 911	-0.7	834	28.3	1 740.6	2 134 497	2 559	375 743	1 023.3	446 464	95.7	4.3	55.9	39.2	28 960	87.6
Grand Island, NE	1 181	0.6	505	726.0	901.2	2 248 299	4 451	272 145	1 227.8	524 935	63.4	36.6	71.4	50.1	18 245	71.1
Grand Junction, CO	387	3.9	171	75.3	71.4	575 360	3 367	51 431	84.6	37 360	48.1	51.9	25.7	6.1	821	7.1
Grand Rapids-Wyoming, MI	746	-0.7	159	88.2	559.1	763 593	4 790	120 642	1 120.3	239 375	60.9	39.1	44.8	18.7	10 536	31.0
Grants Pass, OR	28	-25.1	46	9.0	8.4	460 319	10 052	35 806	18.8	30 481	D	D	25.0	4.7	129	2.9
Great Falls, MT	1 255	-9.1	1 136	33.4	427.7	1 197 706	1 055	96 719	111.1	100 568	48.2	51.8	40.9	16.2	5 952	51.5
Greeley, CO	1 956	-6.3	555	299.9	850.2	1 098 289	1 979	146 652	1 860.7	527 863	20.1	79.9	42.8	20.2	15 649	39.7
Green Bay, WI	547	-3.7	197	1.9	437.0	855 013	4 333	144 973	750.0	270 384	23.7	76.3	53.0	28.8	10 578	57.0
Greensboro-High Point, NC	360	-0.3	107	6.0	135.9	527 298	4 910	60 005	327.4	97 730	24.8	75.2	30.5	10.7	2 649	17.5
Greenville, NC	172	0.2	439	3.6	131.7	1 397 719	3 181	233 246	215.9	552 194	51.5	48.5	60.1	38.9	3 877	57.3
Greenville-Anderson-Mauldin, SC	400	-6.4	96	3.7	115.1	441 917	4 592	45 588	128.7	30 999	D	D	20.6	3.1	2 211	9.5
Gulfport-Biloxi-Pascagoula, MS	87	-17.2	88	0.3	24.7	396 775	4 504	47 253	20.6	20 805	D	D	22.6	2.4	515	9.5
Hagerstown-Martinsburg, MD-WV	200	5.6	130	1.0	118.5	767 295	5 902	89 473	138.2	89 995	50.2	49.8	38.0	15.6	1 452	21.0
Hammond, LA	107	-13.8	100	0.7	36.3	410 570	4 117	54 967	45.7	42 694	40.2	59.8	29.1	7.2	790	17.3
Hanford-Corcoran, CA	674	-1.0	638	407.4	501.5	3 847 243	6 031	340 454	1 829.2	1 732 231	46.7	53.3	68.3	45.1	7 901	36.4
Harrisburg-Carlisle, PA	419	7.2	135	2.6	260.9	795 107	5 906	98 039	458.3	147 142	25.3	74.7	52.9	24.6	4 537	30.3
Harrisonburg, VA	222	-4.7	117	5.6	100.5	823 606	7 055	88 252	659.0	346 475	7.2	92.8	58.4	35.0	2 741	15.9
Hartford-West Hartford-East Hartford, CT	126	15.0	63	6.0	52.0	750 128	11 887	66 721	222.4	111 456	87.0	13.0	31.4	8.9	1 294	7.6
Hattiesburg, MS	150	-5.8	138	1.5	35.1	458 851	3 335	65 786	67.7	61 954	19.7	80.3	32.2	6.5	1 676	24.4
Hickory-Lenoir-Morganton, NC	192	2.0	87	3.5	75.0	487 357	5 573	57 925	318.1	144 744	16.2	83.8	34.3	14.5	839	9.2
Hilton Head Island-Bluffton-Beaufort, NC	111	9.1	440	D	15.2	1 305 794	2 970	85 413	D	D	D	14.2	29.4	6.0	111	13.9
Hinesville, GA	16	-26.8	146	D	3.4	339 894	2 330	48 301	11.8	104 841	7.2	92.8	32.7	7.1	143	31.0
Homosassa Springs, FL	41	1.3	73	0.7	7.3	480 195	6 621	29 451	14.1	25 190	54.9	45.1	17.7	3.4	146	3.6
Hot Springs, AR	36	-9.6	99	0.3	8.4	364 504	3 688	43 119	24.1	66 756	18.6	81.4	24.7	5.3	93	8.9
Houma-Thibodaux, LA	251	-11.8	421	1.0	73.9	919 569	2 183	127 193	95.1	159 572	61.9	38.1	39.8	8.7	146	4.5
Houston-The Woodlands-Sugar Land, TX	2 677	2.4	178	73.1	765.7	699 599	3 927	58 371	D	D	67.9	D	24.8	4.1	18 927	11.1
Huntington-Ashland, WV-KY-OH	323	-13.2	121	0.4	64.8	274 665	2 279	44 660	25.8	9 618	63.1	36.9	14.9	0.9	931	18.0
Huntsville, AL	456	4.5	202	18.2	271.4	787 164	3 906	96 602	206.9	91 443	72.1	27.9	33.9	9.6	6 761	34.3
Idaho Falls, ID	857	-4.7	455	367.6	538.5	1 055 110	2 318	147 762	500.6	265 869	65.4	34.6	48.1	23.4	8 915	45.0
Indianapolis-Carmel-Anderson, IN	1 689	7.5	272	13.4	1 525.2	1 558 263	5 724	150 794	985.1	158 753	D	D	44.8	22.9	28 897	50.0
Iowa City, IA	643	-0.6	259	0.4	549.7	1 683 794	6 496	164 372	785.1	316 441	43.6	56.4	59.0	36.6	21 083	71.5
Ithaca, NY	91	-16.5	163	0.3	54.4	448 507	2 757	113 717	67.4	120 772	33.7	66.3	43.7	16.1	900	25.8
Jackson, MI	183	0.4	171	3.9	136.0	652 247	3 822	85 794	78.2	72 866	69.2	30.8	36.4	12.0	4 210	32.1
Jackson, MS	1 156	-5.8	276	46.8	400.9	665 400	2 409	73 821	633.0	151 223	33.9	66.1	29.3	10.4	17 513	39.4
Jackson, TN	357	-10.2	264	12.6	258.1	669 964	2 534	100 337	138.2	102 192	93.9	6.1	33.9	12.1	5 638	60.1
Jacksonville, FL	186	16.2	105	13.8	38.5	565 515	5 383	56 509	117.4	66 417	77.0	23.0	20.4	3.5	D	3.5
Jacksonville, NC	58	4.4	166	1.5	38.4	634 349	3 819	115 625	187.7	540 928	15.6	84.4	46.4	30.5	1 001	38.3
Janesville-Beloit, WI	354	2.7	234	16.2	303.7	1 294 782	5 523	154 109	274.4	181 858	60.4	39.6	49.8	23.5	7 892	68.2
Jefferson City, MO	1 011	-3.2	216	8.8	410.6	590 339	2 731	71 559	375.4	80 288	19.9	80.1	49.5	9.2	6 757	35.2
Johnson City, TN	157	-3.2	83	D	63.6	504 477	6 084	61 423	D	D	31.1	D	26.3	4.5	483	19.3
Johnstown, PA	77	-12.6	140	0.1	45.4	457 327	3 277	82 508	32.6	59 240	55.5	44.5	42.3	8.5	775	31.9
Jonesboro, AR	723	6.7	738	581.6	684.0	2 311 689	3 134	359 641	549.0	560 225	99.4	0.6	60.0	44.9	25 872	68.1

Area name	Water use, 2010		Wholesale trade,[1] 2012				Retail trade, 2012				Real estate and rental and leasing, 2012			
	Total water withdrawn (mil gal/day)	Gallons withdrawn per person per day	Number of establishments	Number of employees	Sales (mil dol)	Annual payroll (mil dol)	Number of establishments	Number of employees	Sales (mil dol)	Annual payroll (mil dol)	Number of establishments	Number of employees	Receipts (mil dol)	Annual payroll (mil dol)
	133	134	135	136	137	138	139	140	141	142	143	144	145	146
Fairbanks, AK	53.6	549	69	666	413.5	36.5	301	4 758	1 732.5	153.1	144	661	159.6	33.2
Fargo, ND-MN	23.8	114	401	6 920	6 673.0	383.0	805	15 182	4 455.4	360.4	318	1 876	322.0	68.5
Farmington, NM	343.7	2 643	156	1 412	663.0	73.8	450	6 210	1 801.6	157.4	107	750	205.0	36.8
Fayetteville, NC	71.9	196	173	2 711	1 078.4	106.5	1 128	16 393	4 631.9	382.0	345	1 903	368.3	63.2
Fayetteville-Springdale-Rogers, AR-MO	414.0	894	484	5 216	4 145.6	273.4	1 522	22 576	6 183.1	524.0	498	3 276	367.4	100.3
Flagstaff, AZ	52.2	388	95	738	439.3	33.8	590	7 337	1 896.5	164.8	188	667	137.3	28.1
Flint, MI	13.4	31	272	3 969	3 673.6	218.5	1 459	19 368	5 307.9	444.9	318	1 843	255.8	57.1
Florence, SC	259.6	1 263	231	3 085	2 445.4	130.8	936	10 523	2 686.2	224.1	167	657	150.8	22.3
Florence-Muscle Shoals, AL.	1 361.8	9 255	154	2 097	1 235.0	71.4	647	7 749	2 202.1	181.0	127	522	70.0	14.0
Fond du Lac, WI	14.4	142	111	1 541	1 372.0	74.4	354	5 462	1 402.4	130.0	64	235	37.7	6.0
Fort Collins, CO	412.9	1 378	295	4 294	5 143.6	368.5	1 244	17 307	4 341.3	414.2	526	2 112	307.0	71.4
Fort Smith, AR-OK	72.5	258	291	3 410	2 259.1	145.2	990	12 490	3 264.4	271.3	246	1 167	176.1	37.3
Fort Wayne, IN	60.2	145	556	9 321	14 090.5	435.5	1 465	22 309	5 772.6	520.2	428	2 005	385.3	70.5
Fresno, CA	2 813.2	3 024	819	12 981	9 266.3	663.0	2 421	32 954	9 117.8	836.0	769	4 299	715.1	139.6
Gadsden, AL	146.3	1 401	82	837	549.9	31.2	392	4 675	1 236.5	96.1	62	367	57.2	10.5
Gainesville, FL	62.9	238	205	1 896	1 356.0	92.7	958	13 245	3 261.2	286.8	325	1 727	232.5	52.3
Gainesville, GA	100.2	558	235	3 265	9 022.6	173.1	579	7 640	2 231.9	193.5	164	450	116.5	17.1
Gettysburg, PA	20.2	199	61	D	D	D	333	3 231	801.2	74.4	47	210	35.8	7.0
Glens Falls, NY	86.8	673	89	D	D	D	633	8 195	2 047.9	191.9	91	286	49.8	10.0
Goldsboro, NC	34.3	280	95	1 822	1 244.8	74.4	464	5 709	1 557.5	125.8	63	257	29.3	7.1
Grand Forks, ND-MN	30.6	311	136	1 704	2 175.4	85.6	423	7 237	1 893.8	159.3	88	554	89.2	15.8
Grand Island, NE	555.2	6 783	144	1 833	1 868.6	92.9	397	5 589	1 497.8	123.6	89	315	58.5	10.2
Grand Junction, CO	754.7	5 144	219	2 076	876.5	96.2	604	7 966	2 173.3	202.6	263	889	170.7	33.7
Grand Rapids-Wyoming, MI .	1 010.0	1 021	1 336	26 242	20 615.3	1 444.6	3 218	44 758	12 253.0	1 107.9	882	4 947	859.4	175.3
Grants Pass, OR	30.2	365	49	D	D	D	312	4 150	987.9	105.1	106	354	44.8	8.5
Great Falls, MT	166.9	2 052	112	D	D	D	352	4 859	1 359.7	117.4	121	349	62.1	9.8
Greeley, CO	462.1	1 828	246	3 166	5 349.2	157.4	620	8 154	2 707.6	228.7	212	870	149.0	31.5
Green Bay, WI	870.1	2 841	364	6 375	4 491.1	331.5	1 029	15 954	4 093.6	353.6	233	1 485	209.4	44.7
Greensboro-High Point, NC..	222.8	308	1 157	16 682	15 345.7	893.5	2 570	34 286	8 953.9	831.4	791	4 726	773.8	181.8
Greenville, NC	28.8	171	144	1 597	1 028.7	69.5	633	8 597	2 354.8	193.0	176	681	115.5	22.7
Greenville-Anderson-Mauldin, SC	364.5	442	976	12 422	13 210.8	659.6	2 958	39 157	10 145.3	912.0	747	3 498	980.5	137.0
Gulfport-Biloxi-Pascagoula, MS	686.9	1 853	236	2 165	911.0	90.8	1 357	17 028	4 425.8	382.2	375	1 614	270.2	50.4
Hagerstown-Martinsburg, MD-WV	87.6	348	177	2 757	2 513.7	128.2	859	13 123	3 396.8	290.0	208	1 019	249.3	36.1
Hammond, LA	20.1	166	86	1 701	1 300.4	68.5	438	6 290	1 769.7	144.7	94	498	86.5	18.5
Hanford-Corcoran, CA	1 298.9	8 490	69	684	746.6	36.3	285	3 961	1 032.0	92.2	97	371	71.0	9.9
Harrisburg-Carlisle, PA	137.3	250	500	9 590	9 403.2	521.2	1 973	32 462	9 074.5	750.1	450	2 997	825.2	157.6
Harrisonburg, VA	38.5	307	113	1 952	1 032.2	91.5	540	7 535	1 949.6	185.0	116	919	186.3	34.8
Hartford-West Hartford-East Hartford, CT	350.3	289	1 192	21 837	17 564.8	1 261.3	4 166	63 342	17 268.0	1 593.2	1 082	6 148	1 269.1	270.7
Hattiesburg, MS	53.0	371	126	1 168	747.6	46.2	683	9 522	4 784.0	198.8	156	594	111.0	19.8
Hickory-Lenoir-Morganton, NC	1 139.5	3 118	367	6 273	4 530.1	282.7	1 317	15 617	4 183.6	353.0	305	817	163.8	23.6
Hilton Head Island-Bluffton-Beaufort, NC	53.6	287	140	728	442.4	34.0	838	10 505	2 665.3	243.6	397	1 787	280.7	66.0
Hinesville, GA	18.8	241	12	217	151.6	12.1	183	1 990	580.2	42.0	51	187	24.9	5.6
Homosassa Springs, FL	1 201.2	8 505	80	D	D	D	455	5 122	1 421.0	121.8	172	415	54.4	10.4
Hot Springs, AR	17.6	183	79	D	D	D	513	5 877	1 564.0	133.8	133	439	65.0	13.0
Houma-Thibodaux, LA	49.5	238	257	2 970	1 943.9	160.2	793	11 090	2 895.0	256.2	233	2 023	530.3	113.4
Houston-The Woodlands-Sugar Land, TX	2 798.0	473	8 019	117 487	362 243.5	7 813.0	17 508	263 099	83 979.5	6 764.3	6 497	44 896	10 828.1	2 163.8
Huntington-Ashland, WV-KY-OH	159.4	437	292	4 395	3 127.7	208.0	1 237	16 832	4 430.6	367.6	258	1 265	264.5	49.3
Huntsville, AL	2 823.4	6 761	376	4 558	4 101.6	240.2	1 577	21 457	5 735.1	514.5	461	1 872	370.6	66.3
Idaho Falls, ID	2 282.8	17 130	197	2 401	3 208.9	103.3	534	7 307	2 094.6	168.7	147	485	83.3	14.3
Indianapolis-Carmel-Anderson, IN	611.0	324	2 120	36 502	30 286.1	2 075.0	5 917	94 488	28 311.3	2 293.9	2 162	15 619	3 839.4	666.0
Iowa City, IA	42.5	279	127	1 695	1 284.8	74.3	612	9 834	2 117.8	218.0	146	560	132.6	21.1
Ithaca, NY	232.7	2 291	36	454	259.0	21.6	349	5 071	1 112.0	105.5	112	609	121.6	20.5
Jackson, MI	20.3	127	137	D	D	D	526	7 003	1 841.7	163.5	99	567	82.0	15.5
Jackson, MS	156.4	276	676	9 658	9 533.7	490.2	2 142	28 676	7 644.0	665.5	622	3 434	612.3	131.5
Jackson, TN	22.8	175	164	1 795	1 196.1	83.2	565	7 756	2 114.1	177.4	117	573	93.4	17.4
Jacksonville, FL	880.8	655	1 447	21 814	21 129.8	1 212.3	4 889	66 146	18 318.6	1 632.2	1 787	9 036	2 200.0	383.6
Jacksonville, NC	32.3	182	50	304	139.1	11.9	545	7 716	2 213.0	177.9	187	664	127.0	20.7
Janesville-Beloit, WI	28.3	176	149	3 035	3 225.1	155.1	502	8 396	2 215.2	208.2	101	400	148.1	18.7
Jefferson City, MO	104.5	697	115	2 595	1 154.4	77.3	531	7 253	1 924.3	158.9	100	344	54.1	9.2
Johnson City, TN	49.6	250	138	1 477	871.3	57.2	688	10 457	2 572.3	220.8	143	668	103.6	20.3
Johnstown, PA	27.1	189	115	1 365	664.9	51.0	561	6 927	1 733.8	148.6	86	408	48.3	12.2
Jonesboro, AR	1 360.0	11 237	153	1 899	1 854.8	94.1	524	7 142	1 858.9	156.2	124	509	83.2	13.9

1. Merchant wholesalers, except manufacturers' sales branches and offices.

Table C. Metropolitan Areas — Professional Services, Manufacturing, and Accommodation and Food Services

Area name	Professional, scientific, and technical services, 2012				Manufacturing, 2012				Accommodation and food services, 2012			
	Number of establishments	Number of employees	Sales (mil dol)	Annual payroll (mil dol)	Number of establishments	Number of employees	Sales (mil dol)	Annual payroll (mil dol)	Number of establishments	Number of employees	Sales (mil dol)	Annual payroll (mil dol)
	147	148	149	150	151	152	153	154	155	156	157	158
Fairbanks, AK	237	1 683	293.4	86.5	67	641	1 941.2	36.2	213	3 092	255.3	66.4
Fargo, ND-MN	558	D	D	D	224	9 398	3 860.5	D	469	11 495	515.6	151.1
Farmington, NM	256	D	D	D	85	1 318	268.6	62.8	197	4 253	201.8	56.3
Fayetteville, NC	577	6 813	911.9	374.1	115	8 193	5 481.1	379.5	657	13 928	645.9	177.0
Fayetteville-Springdale-Rogers, AR-MO	1 226	9 359	1 413.8	541.7	409	25 466	7 229.0	917.4	950	17 956	786.9	224.0
Flagstaff, AZ	331	1 584	178.5	65.3	90	4 025	2 181.3	312.0	545	11 436	765.7	191.8
Flint, MI	639	3 544	370.3	143.2	273	10 675	9 418.1	684.4	704	13 207	563.9	157.4
Florence, SC	268	2 684	294.3	112.7	148	8 952	4 326.5	479.5	384	6 611	325.8	85.6
Florence-Muscle Shoals, AL.	246	1 071	110.4	40.5	181	7 761	3 325.2	322.7	268	5 455	231.8	66.1
Fond du Lac, WI	154	1 337	154.4	76.3	144	9 140	3 989.9	407.6	240	3 872	140.8	39.8
Fort Collins, CO	1 493	8 727	1 031.1	450.9	403	10 163	4 275.7	642.6	847	14 821	756.5	218.0
Fort Smith, AR-OK	534	2 168	304.8	80.0	298	18 435	6 525.7	709.7	458	8 769	433.6	117.5
Fort Wayne, IN	950	5 721	757.5	266.1	621	32 052	19 526.4	1 658.4	817	16 688	703.1	204.7
Fresno, CA	1 522	10 531	1 367.8	474.3	585	25 269	8 658.3	1 052.9	1 450	24 100	1 226.2	333.9
Gadsden, AL	130	1 250	82.2	35.5	96	4 715	1 355.8	194.1	172	3 231	153.0	40.0
Gainesville, FL	841	4 713	553.2	221.0	158	3 270	1 135.7	169.8	578	11 837	553.1	148.7
Gainesville, GA	402	D	D	D	225	17 020	7 629.2	647.1	283	4 742	298.3	67.4
Gettysburg, PA	126	D	D	D	113	5 745	2 148.7	240.8	222	3 521	185.7	53.0
Glens Falls, NY	229	1 111	141.8	49.2	163	6 709	2 135.1	358.7	540	4 750	344.1	95.6
Goldsboro, NC	147	816	76.0	27.4	83	5 833	1 691.3	243.8	186	3 284	161.7	42.0
Grand Forks, ND-MN	178	D	D	D	89	3 692	1 778.5	142.3	257	5 362	226.3	67.4
Grand Island, NE	143	767	90.3	30.2	114	7 947	7 126.4	313.9	198	2 852	128.6	36.5
Grand Junction, CO	561	2 529	289.0	119.8	159	2 388	520.6	95.1	300	6 052	282.6	88.8
Grand Rapids-Wyoming, MI	2 215	17 189	2 524.8	982.1	1 735	94 665	30 246.9	4 672.9	1 735	34 865	1 559.5	448.7
Grants Pass, OR	140	563	40.6	13.5	106	2 190	434.8	89.6	199	2 483	124.5	35.8
Great Falls, MT	202	1 159	131.8	50.3	62	964	955.3	45.0	240	3 887	194.7	51.5
Greeley, CO	533	2 362	311.5	113.7	284	11 102	5 991.4	485.8	400	5 794	273.9	76.2
Green Bay, WI	600	5 179	737.1	266.2	535	28 296	12 057.4	1 384.8	741	13 076	523.8	152.8
Greensboro-High Point, NC.	1 717	D	D	D	1 019	53 589	35 757.7	2 468.5	1 494	28 185	1 408.2	385.3
Greenville, NC	311	1 893	247.9	84.4	87	4 905	2 160.8	248.8	362	8 055	357.6	96.7
Greenville-Anderson-Mauldin, SC	2 010	17 391	2 409.8	1 004.5	942	47 115	18 292.1	2 151.2	1 775	31 297	1 515.6	410.8
Gulfport-Biloxi-Pascagoula, MS	692	6 021	792.9	312.5	215	19 150	20 839.8	1 341.7	789	23 827	1 832.9	459.6
Hagerstown-Martinsburg, MD-WV	370	2 689	324.2	120.5	168	7 822	3 601.7	405.2	461	7 743	386.2	110.3
Hammond, LA	208	889	93.5	33.6	79	2 389	681.2	84.4	213	4 285	185.8	50.9
Hanford-Corcoran, CA	85	461	51.0	18.4	60	4 380	2 904.0	180.5	172	2 824	378.6	42.6
Harrisburg-Carlisle, PA	1 411	15 758	2 357.2	1 010.5	408	15 894	7 108.0	779.4	1 256	22 385	1 204.4	333.9
Harrisonburg, VA	215	1 489	174.5	76.4	134	9 603	6 229.7	422.4	277	6 596	298.7	94.5
Hartford-West Hartford-East Hartford, CT	2 801	30 314	5 830.7	2 201.0	1 638	69 502	21 474.5	4 621.6	2 685	42 030	2 453.9	706.2
Hattiesburg, MS	309	1 777	214.9	80.2	91	4 070	1 202.2	170.7	313	6 850	301.0	82.8
Hickory-Lenoir-Morganton, NC	548	2 538	742.2	102.2	727	37 686	10 405.1	1 403.5	624	10 992	481.6	134.1
Hilton Head Island-Bluffton-Beaufort, NC	579	2 999	352.7	150.2	90	713	128.5	27.5	555	11 189	688.9	202.0
Hinesville, GA	76	776	65.5	25.7	19	1 737	767.7	83.4	105	1 680	81.6	19.0
Homosassa Springs, FL	254	891	106.3	35.8	44	203	35.8	7.2	191	2 362	114.6	32.2
Hot Springs, AR	217	1 160	91.1	40.4	90	2 180	476.9	95.1	274	5 162	218.0	63.4
Houma-Thibodaux, LA	447	4 432	492.2	211.9	202	8 876	2 402.4	462.9	394	7 792	410.5	113.8
Houston-The Woodlands-Sugar Land, TX	16 999	221 829	49 233.9	19 369.0	5 365	214 702	290 261.2	13 767.5	10 981	226 927	13 340.3	3 592.4
Huntington-Ashland, WV-KY-OH	507	4 535	452.5	174.0	246	11 611	19 017.6	716.9	649	11 746	561.3	151.9
Huntsville, AL	1 442	33 281	7 765.6	2 691.5	344	20 108	8 833.7	1 121.3	828	16 350	810.1	224.6
Idaho Falls, ID	406	8 460	1 379.8	585.5	158	3 193	845.8	117.1	280	4 757	207.9	59.7
Indianapolis-Carmel-Anderson, IN	5 276	48 613	7 960.5	3 183.3	1 704	72 434	41 533.8	3 938.9	3 983	84 075	4 306.3	1 207.4
Iowa City, IA	328	2 127	314.1	96.7	125	6 061	3 799.2	276.4	419	8 252	436.6	114.4
Ithaca, NY	274	2 312	356.6	124.1	93	2 766	861.1	150.4	334	4 408	231.7	65.4
Jackson, MI	217	2 504	367.1	180.4	268	8 414	2 621.3	409.3	275	4 788	201.5	57.3
Jackson, MS	1 412	9 876	1 571.9	566.0	355	15 987	8 597.5	793.7	1 096	20 707	1 050.9	273.8
Jackson, TN	194	1 874	138.2	72.2	135	9 352	4 578.7	437.0	256	5 191	242.5	68.8
Jacksonville, FL	4 523	35 397	6 308.6	2 429.5	803	25 439	11 888.7	1 444.0	2 849	55 538	2 999.8	853.5
Jacksonville, NC	246	1 748	198.1	69.5	40	1 049	271.0	34.2	347	6 640	353.1	86.9
Janesville-Beloit, WI	208	1 172	129.3	49.5	224	8 850	4 474.2	421.3	363	5 355	236.2	63.7
Jefferson City, MO	290	1 937	279.3	93.1	147	5 562	3 774.8	238.7	279	4 545	185.2	54.0
Johnson City, TN	273	2 908	232.5	106.2	170	7 241	2 132.8	309.7	380	7 891	343.0	100.3
Johnstown, PA	228	3 359	380.3	168.2	127	5 232	1 798.8	241.6	300	4 070	179.0	47.8
Jonesboro, AR	188	916	129.1	47.1	120	5 910	2 325.7	245.4	248	4 784	213.7	57.5

Area name	Health care and social assistance, 2012				Other services, 2012				Nonemployer business, 2014		Value of residential construction authorized by building permits, 2015	
	Number of establishments	Number of employees	Receipts (mil dol)	Annual payroll (mil dol)	Number of establishments	Number of employees	Receipts (mil dol)	Annual payroll (mil dol)	Number	Receipts (mil dol)	New construction ($1,000)	Number of housing units
	159	160	161	162	163	164	165	166	167	168	169	170
Fairbanks, AK	290	5 748	746.9	305.5	185	842	88.8	25.6	5 461	242.6	2 189	7
Fargo, ND-MN	606	19 302	2 096.3	901.9	485	3 040	316.3	82.2	15 672	841.9	417 615	2 719
Farmington, NM	275	6 819	682.5	291.7	226	1 571	164.1	54.5	5 266	245.0	28 033	118
Fayetteville, NC	843	21 330	2 156.0	978.9	441	2 504	229.0	61.4	19 450	700.6	250 778	1 386
Fayetteville-Springdale-Rogers, AR-MO	1 084	22 894	2 307.6	908.9	596	3 738	472.9	101.8	34 167	1 500.1	796 083	3 793
Flagstaff, AZ	381	6 995	1 040.7	354.3	230	1 307	105.8	32.7	8 753	353.5	91 572	566
Flint, MI	1 294	25 418	2 787.5	1 148.7	562	3 406	376.2	91.1	28 368	973.6	81 603	413
Florence, SC	450	15 888	1 783.9	668.8	275	1 693	165.6	40.0	12 361	452.8	58 639	424
Florence-Muscle Shoals, AL.	382	6 957	731.4	269.8	186	D	D	D	10 076	422.5	31 539	338
Fond du Lac, WI	281	5 764	758.8	248.8	191	1 245	114.4	31.3	4 902	232.6	35 945	195
Fort Collins, CO	1 021	18 142	1 988.2	783.2	658	3 536	374.1	96.2	29 905	1 342.9	569 560	2 434
Fort Smith, AR-OK	681	18 011	1 641.2	658.4	341	1 645	141.9	40.0	17 887	842.3	74 677	466
Fort Wayne, IN	1 069	31 129	3 035.1	1 282.7	791	5 195	491.7	147.2	26 853	1 052.5	269 387	1 355
Fresno, CA	2 204	42 281	5 325.6	1 997.0	1 000	7 367	747.6	200.1	50 231	2 465.3	581 775	2 322
Gadsden, AL	316	7 433	701.9	303.4	125	632	98.9	19.0	7 162	317.8	11 147	83
Gainesville, FL	757	22 437	2 752.6	1 043.5	392	2 664	465.2	93.2	18 165	699.9	149 017	1 214
Gainesville, GA	443	9 275	1 297.8	493.4	246	1 193	123.8	32.4	14 384	637.9	158 694	946
Gettysburg, PA	182	4 634	448.2	167.1	150	909	75.1	19.8	6 475	266.9	50 501	240
Glens Falls, NY	388	8 109	665.2	305.5	218	1 088	112.7	33.7	8 482	373.4	61 200	381
Goldsboro, NC	254	6 896	606.6	265.8	142	939	69.3	20.3	6 089	232.5	39 671	248
Grand Forks, ND-MN	250	9 377	823.3	372.6	204	1 128	126.4	27.2	6 116	280.9	80 974	529
Grand Island, NE	231	5 479	552.8	199.0	202	1 161	111.3	25.6	5 748	249.3	47 379	300
Grand Junction, CO	426	10 176	1 029.0	427.2	293	1 883	182.6	47.8	11 180	513.3	115 142	486
Grand Rapids-Wyoming, MI .	2 285	64 137	6 540.1	2 608.2	1 690	11 582	1 100.9	313.1	70 811	3 329.7	769 219	3 672
Grants Pass, OR	269	4 376	418.5	151.1	103	D	D	D	5 702	233.1	45 516	237
Great Falls, MT	262	6 363	711.9	269.1	155	871	76.6	21.7	4 743	203.2	50 884	226
Greeley, CO	435	7 951	893.1	325.4	329	1 537	175.9	44.5	20 025	972.0	680 955	3 186
Green Bay, WI	701	21 661	2 578.4	964.5	505	3 019	261.3	72.2	16 839	822.0	177 384	1 018
Greensboro-High Point, NC..	1 697	41 710	4 164.2	1 648.4	1 095	6 325	947.5	185.8	53 762	2 229.9	466 533	2 212
Greenville, NC	510	16 075	1 880.0	681.9	183	1 104	93.9	25.1	10 300	387.1	73 208	538
Greenville-Anderson-Mauldin, SC	1 770	35 622	3 666.0	1 530.0	1 138	9 603	1 165.4	351.8	58 206	2 516.5	1 095 345	5 896
Gulfport-Biloxi-Pascagoula, MS	789	18 643	2 454.1	1 001.3	462	2 663	247.4	73.3	26 411	1 036.3	257 190	1 712
Hagerstown-Martinsburg, MD-WV	637	15 877	1 685.9	725.3	377	2 229	191.8	54.1	14 035	582.1	172 511	978
Hammond, LA	301	8 143	655.2	261.4	149	966	98.1	25.5	9 468	350.3	89 632	627
Hanford-Corcoran, CA	231	4 770	587.8	203.5	94	382	37.4	9.9	4 370	193.0	100 953	591
Harrisburg-Carlisle, PA	1 562	42 982	3 882.5	1 598.3	1 285	9 158	1 124.9	310.5	33 948	1 596.3	275 580	1 615
Harrisonburg, VA	263	7 433	708.4	298.6	231	1 164	109.4	31.6	7 926	347.2	79 735	406
Hartford-West Hartford-East Hartford, CT	3 543	99 706	10 449.5	4 596.2	2 462	15 615	1 759.3	537.5	80 646	4 384.3	253 151	1 582
Hattiesburg, MS	368	11 108	1 237.7	562.0	168	943	83.1	22.5	10 334	450.9	9 789	212
Hickory-Lenoir-Morganton, NC	744	19 423	1 882.9	733.3	437	2 380	199.7	55.8	22 914	948.6	140 085	805
Hilton Head Island-Bluffton-Beaufort, NC	470	6 794	751.1	249.6	351	2 862	258.7	86.0	16 540	865.7	651 957	2 102
Hinesville, GA	81	2 055	251.1	101.6	68	435	32.7	9.5	3 519	108.3	63 274	545
Homosassa Springs, FL	390	7 932	819.7	307.1	212	744	53.2	15.5	8 882	345.3	86 746	378
Hot Springs, AR	319	7 374	717.5	275.4	161	766	53.3	16.2	7 836	319.5	9 869	59
Houma-Thibodaux, LA	478	11 115	1 181.6	466.8	285	2 135	304.2	92.7	14 907	729.8	145 201	663
Houston-The Woodlands-Sugar Land, TX	14 336	290 976	35 675.8	13 099.0	7 926	72 280	8 932.1	2 623.8	552 918	28 708.6	8 566 381	56 901
Huntington-Ashland, WV-KY-OH	1 054	28 659	3 170.0	1 241.0	457	3 096	360.0	96.4	17 192	631.1	46 692	291
Huntsville, AL	1 053	23 925	2 645.2	1 060.2	556	4 015	617.2	140.6	28 985	1 152.0	358 830	2 607
Idaho Falls, ID	577	8 114	865.6	297.5	194	892	91.4	22.7	10 275	460.7	112 599	862
Indianapolis-Carmel-Anderson, IN	4 724	131 895	15 661.0	6 100.5	3 192	26 908	4 270.6	900.2	134 985	5 742.5	1 906 999	8 735
Iowa City, IA	450	16 991	2 046.3	803.8	270	1 667	207.7	46.4	10 862	516.8	206 947	1 327
Ithaca, NY	271	5 283	483.0	199.8	152	966	122.9	23.9	7 371	274.4	40 961	279
Jackson, MI	351	9 060	936.8	409.4	210	1 361	129.7	37.1	8 815	320.8	23 822	117
Jackson, MS	1 446	44 764	4 786.6	1 894.4	853	5 442	604.1	185.0	48 431	2 103.7	361 513	1 569
Jackson, TN	370	12 812	1 231.3	510.1	151	812	66.4	20.5	8 501	371.9	36 272	214
Jacksonville, FL	3 685	74 724	9 238.6	3 315.2	2 369	13 420	2 219.4	438.7	104 142	4 264.4	2 057 108	9 671
Jacksonville, NC	257	5 765	491.7	197.5	210	1 172	89.9	26.6	8 866	325.8	113 726	894
Janesville-Beloit, WI	320	9 667	1 120.9	438.4	268	1 417	105.0	30.8	8 127	338.5	45 107	216
Jefferson City, MO	370	9 486	874.8	358.5	325	1 760	200.3	59.5	8 961	366.5	25 056	270
Johnson City, TN	458	16 539	1 833.8	815.0	234	1 347	100.5	32.1	12 024	504.0	96 914	689
Johnstown, PA	540	11 708	1 047.3	444.7	312	1 690	133.9	34.2	6 180	249.2	12 406	47
Jonesboro, AR	405	9 349	958.7	378.4	151	D	D	D	8 774	404.7	64 282	482

1. Establishments subject to federal tax.

	Government employment and payroll, 2012									Local government finances, 2012				
			March payroll (percent of total)							General revenue				
												Taxes		
													Per capita[1] (dollars)	
Area name	Full-time equivalent employees	March Payroll (dollars)	Adminis-tration, judicial, and legal	Police and corrections	Fire protection	Highways and transporta-tion	Health and welfare	Natural resources and utilities	Education and libraries	Total (mil dol)	Inter-govern-mental (mil dol)	Total (mil dol)	Total	Property
	171	172	173	174	175	176	177	178	179	180	181	182	183	184
Fairbanks, AK	2 949	14 833 210	7.9	3.4	2.6	2.4	1.8	5.3	75.9	380.0	201.2	148.5	1 481	1 335
Fargo, ND-MN	6 888	27 847 634	5.1	9.5	2.7	4.4	9.5	7.5	60.2	969.4	445.6	298.8	1 381	1 058
Farmington, NM	5 857	21 149 302	4.2	11.0	2.6	2.0	1.9	8.4	68.4	491.8	290.9	126.9	987	702
Fayetteville, NC	20 611	71 938 105	1.4	6.0	1.8	0.8	38.1	3.6	42.6	1 147.7	620.9	372.5	995	717
Fayetteville-Springdale-Rogers, AR-MO	15 951	51 196 846	5.5	9.4	4.3	3.2	1.0	5.4	70.1	1 400.1	793.7	404.4	839	367
Flagstaff, AZ	4 575	17 536 070	11.8	13.5	9.2	3.5	4.5	6.4	48.1	469.7	159.1	223.4	1 643	979
Flint, MI	15 234	64 330 939	5.5	5.9	1.4	3.5	24.1	3.5	55.1	2 005.4	1 056.8	353.2	844	786
Florence, SC	6 966	21 627 471	5.6	9.2	1.9	2.7	6.2	5.3	67.5	538.5	250.7	178.7	867	649
Florence-Muscle Shoals, AL	5 882	19 596 410	3.1	6.8	3.3	3.2	20.6	13.8	47.1	488.1	192.2	137.3	934	418
Fond du Lac, WI	3 703	15 389 801	4.9	9.2	2.4	4.4	10.7	3.5	63.8	424.7	174.4	182.3	1 790	1 688
Fort Collins, CO	10 782	47 317 101	8.8	11.5	1.1	2.8	7.5	18.4	46.2	1 178.8	292.6	577.8	1 861	1 211
Fort Smith, AR-OK	9 950	33 824 806	6.1	6.9	2.1	3.1	5.0	11.1	65.4	795.9	453.2	202.5	722	305
Fort Wayne, IN	12 482	46 187 211	6.4	12.8	3.8	4.6	1.3	5.6	63.8	1 286.9	601.6	479.3	1 137	913
Fresno, CA	34 954	165 436 346	4.1	10.3	2.1	3.3	9.7	4.5	65.0	5 127.4	3 047.2	1 071.6	1 131	789
Gadsden, AL	3 980	11 900 349	4.3	10.5	6.2	3.7	6.9	8.4	56.6	284.1	137.1	99.7	955	293
Gainesville, FL	10 035	36 051 916	10.0	15.5	4.4	4.8	3.2	11.5	46.9	897.9	290.9	376.2	1 402	1 085
Gainesville, GA	6 523	22 620 107	6.4	9.1	7.3	1.6	4.4	4.9	65.4	563.5	217.3	266.2	1 436	890
Gettysburg, PA	2 548	9 790 732	7.8	9.5	0.9	2.6	2.1	3.4	73.2	374.0	165.8	167.3	1 648	1 256
Glens Falls, NY	6 698	24 733 643	6.0	8.2	0.4	6.9	8.7	2.7	65.0	745.4	272.2	360.1	2 803	2 155
Goldsboro, NC	5 237	14 176 474	3.0	6.2	2.1	1.3	9.2	6.0	66.2	346.7	199.6	101.5	817	585
Grand Forks, ND-MN	4 147	14 917 010	5.7	8.3	2.6	5.2	15.5	10.4	50.1	471.6	218.9	130.8	1 323	1 063
Grand Island, NE	4 036	14 835 732	5.6	6.7	2.9	4.0	6.4	15.9	57.5	355.7	117.9	148.0	1 773	1 410
Grand Junction, CO	5 197	18 735 519	8.2	13.3	5.0	4.1	7.0	9.6	48.8	498.4	180.8	228.0	1 542	966
Grand Rapids-Wyoming, MI	26 602	112 436 599	7.9	9.0	2.5	4.3	3.1	4.9	66.6	3 718.2	1 877.6	1 165.3	1 159	1 055
Grants Pass, OR	2 192	8 995 230	6.6	12.9	2.5	3.4	1.3	3.1	68.4	243.6	119.9	70.8	854	781
Great Falls, MT	2 704	9 771 107	6.8	13.0	3.8	5.6	3.7	6.9	59.0	238.3	103.2	77.2	944	913
Greeley, CO	8 663	35 763 495	8.2	17.4	4.0	5.2	6.6	11.0	45.5	919.9	308.8	411.9	1 562	1 194
Green Bay, WI	11 507	49 464 799	4.6	9.3	2.9	4.0	8.9	3.8	65.2	1 398.9	611.3	539.9	1 735	1 620
Greensboro-High Point, NC	26 780	99 652 358	4.7	9.7	3.6	2.0	7.2	5.5	64.4	2 394.5	1 098.1	928.6	1 262	995
Greenville, NC	6 107	20 619 861	3.8	8.9	3.2	2.0	4.2	10.9	60.2	555.7	265.7	167.7	972	677
Greenville-Anderson-Mauldin, SC	32 635	116 071 503	4.0	6.4	3.0	1.4	33.6	5.1	45.4	3 592.7	858.8	824.2	978	830
Gulfport-Biloxi-Pascagoula, MS	18 635	68 245 147	4.0	7.4	3.9	3.0	36.0	3.0	41.5	2 388.7	948.4	466.4	1 229	1 099
Hagerstown-Martinsburg, MD-WV	8 853	33 633 765	4.2	5.9	2.5	1.9	0.9	6.7	76.6	810.6	360.1	325.5	1 270	912
Hammond, LA	6 393	23 444 209	4.2	6.0	1.2	1.7	46.4	1.8	37.5	621.2	213.8	128.9	1 044	366
Hanford-Corcoran, CA	4 882	22 137 016	6.6	11.1	2.5	1.2	11.7	3.6	60.7	623.0	383.4	130.2	860	727
Harrisburg-Carlisle, PA	18 305	73 828 976	7.2	11.2	0.6	3.9	3.7	5.0	66.8	2 496.2	893.1	1 022.1	1 845	1 338
Harrisonburg, VA	4 180	13 504 909	5.9	8.1	4.4	2.7	4.3	7.2	63.8	389.9	157.1	146.9	1 145	791
Hartford-West Hartford-East Hartford, CT	41 889	212 590 921	3.4	7.9	3.6	2.6	3.3	4.5	73.1	5 466.8	1 915.2	3 050.0	2 512	2 484
Hattiesburg, MS	9 029	27 151 166	3.5	4.9	2.0	2.5	47.7	1.9	36.9	819.4	196.1	154.2	1 050	973
Hickory-Lenoir-Morganton, NC	15 251	50 474 252	3.6	5.9	2.0	1.2	24.3	3.5	56.8	1 280.9	597.8	326.4	898	671
Hilton Head Island-Bluffton-Beaufort, NC	6 425	25 024 387	7.0	9.7	6.6	1.7	25.2	3.9	43.8	837.8	157.8	429.0	2 213	1 771
Hinesville, GA	3 104	9 754 876	5.6	9.3	1.5	1.2	15.4	1.8	61.7	272.2	113.4	80.9	993	612
Homosassa Springs, FL	3 890	11 674 757	8.6	11.3	0.1	3.6	5.4	3.4	65.1	322.4	98.7	162.1	1 163	1 064
Hot Springs, AR	2 929	9 379 603	4.7	8.8	4.0	3.5	3.4	5.5	68.3	270.5	155.0	62.1	640	262
Houma-Thibodaux, LA	10 111	34 879 997	4.6	9.7	0.6	2.6	31.8	4.0	45.8	1 130.5	411.7	323.8	1 550	688
Houston-The Woodlands-Sugar Land, TX	234 372	897 703 915	4.7	10.8	3.1	4.2	7.4	3.2	64.5	25 851.7	7 434.4	12 890.3	2 087	1 738
Huntington-Ashland, WV-KY-OH	12 579	40 423 670	4.4	6.3	2.0	2.6	4.4	5.0	73.1	1 054.7	525.7	330.6	907	701
Huntsville, AL	20 024	74 872 202	3.7	6.3	3.0	2.8	37.7	7.5	35.8	2 192.6	900.1	428.1	994	510
Idaho Falls, ID	4 554	14 040 874	6.5	10.1	4.5	3.7	7.6	7.0	58.6	341.3	174.7	100.7	740	715
Indianapolis-Carmel-Anderson, IN	70 652	276 197 106	4.2	7.9	5.6	1.8	17.0	11.3	51.5	8 491.1	3 269.0	2 704.9	1 402	1 025
Iowa City, IA	3 919	16 365 120	7.2	7.7	1.2	4.7	10.4	5.1	60.1	620.3	195.2	302.5	1 912	1 555
Ithaca, NY	4 530	19 870 493	5.0	6.2	2.8	4.4	7.3	3.5	68.0	531.9	184.0	252.8	2 465	1 857
Jackson, MI	4 304	17 626 740	7.6	8.1	2.4	4.2	3.5	3.4	69.5	585.1	325.3	139.2	868	809
Jackson, MS	21 103	60 140 323	6.0	10.4	4.8	2.9	1.9	4.3	69.2	1 733.1	846.9	586.9	1 017	965
Jackson, TN	8 999	31 890 237	2.6	6.7	2.4	1.5	58.7	4.5	23.0	995.9	160.4	156.2	1 197	685
Jacksonville, FL	42 905	156 841 760	5.8	13.6	6.1	2.2	1.4	6.6	57.0	4 877.5	1 516.3	1 990.7	1 445	1 051
Jacksonville, NC	5 873	18 455 158	3.9	7.0	1.9	1.2	10.7	4.8	66.2	585.4	209.5	152.5	832	536
Janesville-Beloit, WI	6 252	25 471 665	5.9	9.6	3.9	4.4	7.9	4.5	62.6	723.4	387.9	249.8	1 557	1 471
Jefferson City, MO	4 566	13 402 962	7.4	8.2	3.3	4.3	4.8	6.3	65.4	359.6	122.3	173.3	1 154	721
Johnson City, TN	6 906	20 205 200	5.5	9.0	2.8	6.4	4.7	12.5	56.6	469.5	191.0	177.3	884	595
Johnstown, PA	4 484	15 273 184	8.2	8.3	1.4	5.9	5.7	6.0	63.9	555.1	293.7	143.3	1 012	781
Jonesboro, AR	4 524	13 523 979	4.9	9.6	2.5	3.7	1.1	9.1	68.6	354.5	215.8	87.8	708	311

1. Based on the resident population estimated as of July 1 of the year shown.

Table C. Metropolitan Areas — Local Government Finances, Government Employment, and Voting

	Local government finances, 2012 (cont.)									Government employment, 2014			Presidential election,[2] 2012		
	Direct general expenditure							Debt outstanding					Percent of vote cast:		
				Percent of total for:											
Area name	Total (mil dol)	Per capita[1] (dollars)	Educa- tion	Health and hospitals	Police protec- tion	Public welfare	High- ways	Total (mil dol)	Per capita[1] (dollars)	Federal civilian	Federal military	State and local	Demo- cratic	Republi- can	All other
	185	186	187	188	189	190	191	192	193	194	195	196	197	198	199
Fairbanks, AK	342.4	3 415	63.0	1.6	2.3	0.0	6.2	170.2	1 698	2 879	8 350	8 452	NA	NA	NA
Fargo, ND-MN	990.1	4 577	37.7	0.6	5.3	4.1	12.4	1 641.6	7 589	2 387	1 316	16 533	48.6	48.4	3.0
Farmington, NM	551.0	4 287	55.6	3.3	6.3	1.2	4.3	2 140.3	16 652	1 496	321	9 843	34.3	62.4	3.3
Fayetteville, NC	1 203.8	3 214	51.4	3.6	7.6	6.4	1.2	604.8	1 615	14 379	48 344	25 291	59.3	39.7	1.0
Fayetteville-Springdale-Rog- ers, AR-MO	1 387.0	2 876	60.9	0.3	5.5	0.0	4.9	2 146.7	4 452	2 545	2 203	28 167	33.4	63.6	3.0
Flagstaff, AZ	457.2	3 361	35.9	3.4	6.5	1.6	7.6	377.9	2 779	2 738	296	16 059	56.6	41.0	2.4
Flint, MI	2 064.7	4 935	41.9	28.1	3.5	1.1	3.3	995.9	2 380	1 041	691	19 784	63.6	35.4	1.1
Florence, SC	530.6	2 575	60.9	4.4	6.7	0.2	1.8	374.1	1 815	723	862	15 458	49.9	49.2	0.9
Florence-Muscle Shoals, AL.	484.2	3 294	44.6	19.9	4.8	0.1	5.0	444.4	3 023	1 074	667	8 944	35.8	62.6	1.6
Fond du Lac, WI	449.6	4 415	51.8	7.3	5.2	3.9	9.0	580.9	5 704	202	274	5 408	41.9	56.8	1.3
Fort Collins, CO	1 080.2	3 479	37.9	4.5	6.4	3.0	9.0	1 388.6	4 472	2 429	868	32 314	51.5	45.7	2.8
Fort Smith, AR-OK	802.3	2 860	58.0	2.8	5.0	0.2	6.3	1 030.6	3 674	1 335	1 233	16 437	28.7	69.5	1.8
Fort Wayne, IN	1 126.6	2 673	51.6	0.6	6.1	0.3	3.5	1 205.7	2 861	1 980	1 387	19 600	38.8	59.5	1.6
Fresno, CA	5 031.5	5 308	44.7	7.0	5.6	10.3	3.4	3 847.5	4 059	9 875	1 617	56 254	49.9	48.1	2.0
Gadsden, AL	278.9	2 672	46.7	1.9	11.2	0.2	4.8	218.9	2 097	303	464	5 117	30.0	68.3	1.6
Gainesville, FL	944.7	3 522	39.3	3.8	8.2	1.7	4.8	1 953.5	7 283	4 507	581	39 050	55.8	42.6	1.6
Gainesville, GA	566.0	3 053	55.8	6.1	4.5	0.8	2.5	1 522.9	8 213	458	542	9 917	21.2	77.4	1.4
Gettysburg, PA	458.0	4 513	68.9	3.6	1.4	3.2	2.7	405.6	3 997	708	262	3 441	35.5	63.0	1.4
Glens Falls, NY	755.6	5 881	49.4	4.6	2.6	10.7	7.9	575.7	4 481	314	203	9 492	50.1	47.9	1.9
Goldsboro, NC	344.7	2 774	55.1	4.8	6.3	6.3	1.4	151.3	1 217	1 213	4 580	8 125	45.4	53.8	0.8
Grand Forks, ND-MN	433.5	4 384	39.7	1.2	4.5	5.2	9.0	875.4	8 852	1 137	2 104	12 422	46.5	50.7	2.8
Grand Island, NE	357.6	4 284	52.8	8.0	4.1	0.3	5.6	317.1	3 799	755	308	6 081	32.3	65.6	2.2
Grand Junction, CO	517.8	3 502	35.4	1.7	13.1	5.6	9.4	476.5	3 223	1 459	398	8 275	32.7	65.1	2.2
Grand Rapids-Wyoming, MI .	3 715.2	3 694	53.0	6.3	4.2	1.7	4.7	5 263.1	5 234	3 345	1 821	44 465	41.5	57.3	1.2
Grants Pass, OR	253.3	3 055	59.6	2.9	7.1	0.1	5.0	145.0	1 748	264	222	2 748	37.2	58.8	4.0
Great Falls, MT	242.5	2 968	53.0	1.0	9.7	1.4	5.2	90.0	1 101	1 627	3 544	4 052	44.1	53.1	2.9
Greeley, CO	839.9	3 185	42.6	1.2	7.3	4.0	6.6	868.6	3 294	591	727	15 640	42.3	55.0	2.6
Green Bay, WI	1 439.4	4 627	48.3	6.1	6.0	4.3	8.4	1 261.2	4 054	1 293	889	20 417	47.9	50.9	1.2
Greensboro-High Point, NC..	2 532.1	3 440	46.9	4.0	7.4	4.8	2.6	2 453.8	3 334	4 223	1 864	40 181	49.8	49.1	1.1
Greenville, NC	557.6	3 232	46.8	1.8	9.9	5.2	2.1	400.7	2 322	595	458	24 323	53.1	45.9	1.0
Greenville-Anderson-Maul- din, SC	3 672.8	4 358	32.8	39.0	3.5	0.2	1.5	5 469.6	6 489	2 455	3 529	54 006	33.3	65.0	1.7
Gulfport-Biloxi-Pascagoula, MS	2 433.4	6 411	24.7	32.2	3.8	0.1	4.4	1 537.8	4 051	8 853	10 393	23 616	33.0	65.7	1.2
Hagerstown-Martinsburg, MD-WV	838.7	3 272	65.4	0.7	4.2	0.3	3.3	710.6	2 773	4 488	1 057	13 313	39.3	58.3	2.4
Hammond, LA	692.4	5 610	29.5	47.0	3.7	0.0	2.7	361.5	2 929	344	561	9 980	35.4	63.1	1.6
Hanford-Corcoran, CA	602.9	3 983	45.9	6.6	4.9	9.6	2.9	261.9	1 730	1 102	5 123	12 294	41.3	56.2	2.4
Harrisburg-Carlisle, PA	2 716.3	4 903	51.9	3.9	3.3	8.1	2.6	3 833.1	6 919	7 102	2 270	53 556	45.3	53.3	1.4
Harrisonburg, VA	400.5	3 120	46.7	1.9	4.0	7.4	5.5	729.3	5 681	338	398	10 771	37.1	60.9	2.0
Hartford-West Hartford-East Hartford, CT	5 447.0	4 485	58.0	0.9	5.6	0.7	4.2	3 350.1	2 759	6 127	2 453	94 751	60.7	38.1	1.2
Hattiesburg, MS	821.7	5 598	26.1	51.6	3.1	0.0	4.2	543.5	3 703	792	1 215	13 876	33.4	65.4	1.2
Hickory-Lenoir-Morganton, NC	1 270.8	3 495	44.3	23.2	5.0	6.0	1.2	476.3	1 310	674	884	22 700	33.7	64.7	1.6
Hilton Head Island-Bluffton- Beaufort, NC	819.4	4 226	33.8	18.0	6.2	1.1	2.3	1 530.6	7 895	2 363	9 972	8 865	42.7	56.2	1.0
Hinesville, GA	286.7	3 516	55.3	16.9	4.8	0.2	3.0	89.3	1 095	3 920	16 769	3 865	59.6	39.4	1.0
Homosassa Springs, FL	362.7	2 602	47.4	5.5	9.1	2.5	6.6	493.5	3 541	213	280	4 171	38.5	60.4	1.1
Hot Springs, AR	268.9	2 775	57.5	0.3	5.6	0.0	3.6	344.1	3 551	490	429	4 128	33.9	63.9	2.2
Houma-Thibodaux, LA	1 104.3	5 286	31.2	30.4	4.8	0.4	2.8	502.1	2 403	393	1 009	11 832	26.6	71.4	2.0
Houston-The Woodlands- Sugar Land, TX	25 345.7	4 103	45.4	8.8	5.5	0.2	5.0	71 316.9	11 545	27 821	14 719	341 251	43.6	55.2	1.3
Huntington-Ashland, WV- KY-OH	1 087.6	2 982	60.9	2.7	4.7	1.1	2.2	804.6	2 206	3 179	1 585	19 481	38.4	59.6	1.9
Huntsville, AL	2 106.9	4 891	33.3	37.0	3.8	0.1	2.7	2 214.6	5 141	19 912	2 765	29 410	37.6	60.8	1.5
Idaho Falls, ID	346.6	2 547	46.8	2.7	7.1	0.3	4.8	344.6	2 532	856	518	6 606	20.5	77.3	2.2
Indianapolis-Carmel-Ander- son, IN	8 480.2	4 396	36.1	22.7	4.0	0.2	1.7	17 097.1	8 863	16 427	6 738	113 468	45.2	52.9	1.9
Iowa City, IA	652.2	4 122	35.8	7.3	3.9	0.8	6.6	863.6	5 458	1 994	660	35 102	64.1	33.6	2.2
Ithaca, NY	541.1	5 276	48.3	4.4	2.7	8.0	5.5	696.7	6 794	267	169	5 981	68.7	28.0	3.2
Jackson, MI	586.0	3 655	54.4	10.1	2.6	3.6	6.4	539.6	3 366	325	256	7 351	46.5	52.3	1.2
Jackson, MS	1 812.3	3 142	55.0	1.6	6.1	0.3	7.0	2 027.9	3 516	6 597	3 417	53 398	50.7	48.5	0.8
Jackson, TN	966.4	7 408	17.5	58.3	3.3	0.1	2.4	1 066.4	8 174	480	398	13 487	41.2	57.9	0.9
Jacksonville, FL	4 951.5	3 594	40.9	2.0	9.1	1.2	4.9	13 946.9	10 122	16 986	14 864	57 288	40.0	59.1	0.9
Jacksonville, NC	563.2	3 073	38.6	24.7	6.7	6.5	1.0	439.4	2 398	7 015	45 767	8 053	35.9	62.7	1.4
Janesville-Beloit, WI	729.2	4 546	49.6	7.4	6.2	7.1	5.3	614.8	3 833	288	441	8 591	61.0	37.8	1.2
Jefferson City, MO	363.3	2 419	52.7	3.5	8.9	0.0	8.7	294.3	1 960	832	508	24 960	30.8	67.4	1.8
Johnson City, TN	497.7	2 480	48.2	7.3	6.4	0.4	5.3	765.4	3 814	2 746	656	12 908	27.8	70.4	1.8
Johnstown, PA	571.5	4 037	49.2	3.2	5.7	14.0	3.6	641.5	4 531	1 036	378	7 021	40.1	58.1	1.8
Jonesboro, AR	344.4	2 776	59.5	0.3	5.9	0.1	5.2	518.7	4 182	377	555	8 823	32.9	64.5	2.6

1. Based on the resident population estimated as of July 1 of the year shown.   2. © 2013 Election Data Services, Inc. All rights reserved.

Table C. Metropolitan Areas — **Land Area and Population**

CBSA/DIV code[1]	Area name	Land area,[2] 2010 (sq km)	Total persons	Rank	Per square kilometer	White	Black	American Indian, Alaska Native	Asian and Pacific Islander	Percent Hispanic or Latino[3]	Under 5 years	5 to 17 years	18 to 24 years	25 to 34 years	35 to 44 years	45 to 54 years
		1	2	3	4	5	6	7	8	9	10	11	12	13	14	15
27900	Joplin, MO	3 272	177 211	233	54.2	88.2	2.6	3.3	2.1	6.7	6.9	18.3	9.2	13.2	12.2	12.8
27980	Kahului-Wailuku-Lahaina, HI	3 039	164 726	253	54.2	44.6	1.6	1.8	66.5	10.9	6.2	16.1	7.6	13.5	13.1	14.1
28020	Kalamazoo-Portage, MI	3 028	335 340	151	110.7	81.8	11.1	1.3	2.8	6.1	6.0	16.5	14.4	12.5	11.4	12.4
28100	Kankakee, IL	1 752	110 879	339	63.3	73.7	16.0	0.5	1.4	9.8	6.0	18.1	10.4	12.0	12.1	13.5
28140	Kansas City, MO-KS	18 793	2 087 471	30	111.1	75.4	13.6	1.2	3.5	8.7	6.7	18.2	8.3	14.1	13.2	13.7
28420	Kennewick-Richland, WA	7 621	279 116	169	36.6	64.5	2.2	1.4	3.5	30.5	8.1	20.7	9.2	14.3	12.4	12.0
28660	Killeen-Temple, TX	7 293	431 032	124	59.1	54.1	21.1	1.2	4.8	22.3	8.3	18.7	12.0	17.4	12.9	11.4
28700	Kingsport-Bristol-Bristol, TN-VA	5 206	307 120	162	59.0	95.5	2.6	0.7	0.8	1.6	5.0	14.9	7.9	10.7	12.3	14.5
28740	Kingston, NY	2 912	180 143	230	61.9	81.9	6.9	0.8	2.7	9.7	4.5	14.0	9.9	11.9	12.0	15.4
28940	Knoxville, TN	9 066	861 424	64	95.0	88.9	6.6	0.9	1.9	3.5	5.5	15.7	10.2	12.1	12.4	13.9
29020	Kokomo, IN	759	82 556	373	108.8	88.6	8.6	0.9	1.6	3.1	6.1	16.9	8.2	11.3	11.8	13.9
29100	La Crosse-Onalaska, WI-MN	2 600	136 985	294	52.7	92.8	2.0	0.7	4.5	1.6	5.4	15.1	14.9	12.6	10.9	12.6
29180	Lafayette, LA	8 829	490 488	108	55.6	69.2	25.6	0.7	2.0	3.7	6.9	18.2	9.7	14.9	12.2	13.3
29200	Lafayette-West Lafayette, IN	3 311	214 363	203	64.7	81.6	4.9	0.6	6.9	7.5	6.1	15.1	21.9	13.8	10.8	10.8
29340	Lake Charles, LA	6 083	205 605	213	33.8	70.8	25.3	1.0	1.7	3.1	6.8	18.1	9.7	14.1	11.8	13.0
29420	Lake Havasu City-Kingman, AZ	34 476	204 737	214	5.9	79.6	1.6	2.9	1.9	15.8	4.6	14.1	6.8	9.8	9.4	12.5
29460	Lakeland-Winter Haven, FL	4 656	650 092	84	139.6	63.4	15.5	0.7	2.3	19.6	5.9	17.0	8.7	12.3	11.7	12.6
29540	Lancaster, PA	2 444	536 624	103	219.6	84.4	4.3	0.4	2.5	9.8	6.6	17.6	9.4	12.6	11.5	13.3
29620	Lansing-East Lansing, MI	4 397	472 276	110	107.4	79.7	10.4	1.2	5.1	6.5	5.6	15.6	15.8	13.0	11.2	12.6
29700	Laredo, TX	8 706	269 721	176	31.0	3.8	0.3	0.1	0.6	95.1	10.0	24.0	11.6	13.4	13.2	11.1
29740	Las Cruces, NM	9 861	214 295	205	21.7	29.6	1.8	1.2	1.5	66.7	7.2	18.2	14.9	12.6	10.7	11.3
29820	Las Vegas-Henderson-Paradise, NV	20 439	2 114 801	29	103.5	48.1	11.9	1.0	12.5	30.3	6.4	17.4	9.0	14.7	14.1	13.5
29940	Lawrence, KS	1 181	118 053	326	100.0	82.9	5.7	3.5	5.7	5.8	5.2	13.7	24.1	15.3	11.2	10.2
30020	Lawton, OK	4 408	130 644	302	29.6	62.7	18.5	7.8	4.5	12.3	7.3	16.9	13.1	16.6	12.2	11.9
30140	Lebanon, PA	937	137 067	293	146.3	85.4	2.5	0.4	1.6	11.4	6.2	16.7	8.5	11.4	11.8	13.6
30300	Lewiston, ID-WA	3 845	62 153	380	16.2	90.9	1.0	5.1	1.7	3.7	5.9	15.5	8.6	12.2	10.9	12.9
30340	Lewiston-Auburn, ME	1 212	107 233	342	88.5	93.4	4.6	1.1	1.3	1.7	6.1	15.9	8.8	12.3	12.2	14.8
30460	Lexington-Fayette, KY	3 804	500 535	107	131.6	80.0	12.2	0.6	3.3	5.9	6.3	16.0	12.5	14.2	13.4	13.2
30620	Lima, OH	1 042	104 425	345	100.2	84.0	14.1	0.7	1.2	2.8	6.1	17.2	10.6	11.9	11.6	13.0
30700	Lincoln, NE	3 649	323 578	154	88.7	85.4	4.7	1.1	4.5	6.3	6.7	16.4	15.2	14.1	12.0	11.6
30780	Little Rock-North Little Rock-Conway, AR	10 580	731 612	76	69.2	69.9	23.6	1.1	2.2	5.1	6.7	17.3	9.7	14.5	12.9	12.9
30860	Logan, UT-ID	4 736	133 857	299	28.3	86.2	0.9	1.0	3.4	10.1	9.1	22.2	17.8	13.9	11.2	8.6
30980	Longview, TX	4 611	217 781	201	47.2	65.9	18.0	1.0	1.3	15.7	7.1	17.7	9.6	13.2	12.0	12.8
31020	Longview, WA	2 953	103 468	346	35.0	87.4	1.4	3.0	2.8	8.4	5.8	17.2	8.2	11.3	11.6	13.4
31080	Los Angeles-Long Beach-Anaheim, CA	12 558	13 340 068	2	1 062.3	32.3	7.2	0.6	17.1	45.1	6.3	16.5	10.4	15.2	13.8	13.9
31080	Anaheim-Santa Ana-Irvine, CA Div 11244	2 048	3 169 776	X	1 547.7	44.2	2.0	0.6	21.4	34.4	6.1	16.8	10.0	14.1	13.6	14.6
31080	Los Angeles-Long Beach-Glendale, CA Div 31084	10 510	10 170 292	X	967.7	28.5	8.8	0.6	15.8	48.4	6.4	16.4	10.5	15.6	13.9	13.7
31140	Louisville/Jefferson County, KY-IN	9 267	1 278 413	43	138.0	79.1	15.4	0.7	2.4	4.3	6.2	16.9	8.6	13.5	13.0	14.2
31180	Lubbock, TX	6 962	311 154	161	44.7	55.6	7.3	0.7	2.6	34.6	6.8	17.5	16.9	14.5	11.0	11.0
31340	Lynchburg, VA	5 491	259 950	185	47.3	78.1	18.3	0.8	2.1	2.4	5.3	15.0	13.2	11.5	10.8	13.4
31420	Macon, GA	4 461	230 096	195	51.6	51.2	44.7	0.6	1.9	2.8	6.5	17.7	9.8	12.6	11.9	13.4
31460	Madera, CA	5 535	154 998	263	28.0	37.1	3.7	1.9	2.7	56.1	7.5	20.1	10.2	13.8	12.5	12.1
31540	Madison, WI	8 571	641 385	87	74.8	85.0	5.4	0.7	5.3	5.6	5.9	15.5	12.5	14.8	12.8	13.3
31700	Manchester-Nashua, NH	2 269	406 678	132	179.2	87.8	2.8	0.6	4.4	6.0	5.4	16.3	8.9	12.7	12.8	16.2
31740	Manhattan, KS	3 757	98 545	356	26.2	83.1	6.5	1.3	5.0	7.5	7.2	13.1	26.9	17.6	9.5	8.1
31860	Mankato-North Mankato, MN	3 099	99 134	355	32.0	90.8	3.7	0.6	2.6	3.5	5.6	14.8	18.5	14.3	10.5	11.3
31900	Mansfield, OH	1 283	121 707	318	94.9	88.0	10.5	0.7	1.0	1.7	5.7	16.1	8.7	11.9	12.0	13.6
32580	McAllen-Edinburg-Mission, TX	4 069	842 304	67	207.0	7.3	0.5	0.1	1.1	91.1	9.7	23.9	11.1	13.2	13.0	10.6
32780	Medford, OR	7 209	212 567	207	29.5	84.7	1.2	2.4	2.5	12.0	5.7	15.3	8.2	12.0	11.3	12.5
32820	Memphis, TN-MS-AR	12 909	1 344 127	42	104.1	46.0	47.1	0.6	2.5	5.2	7.0	18.5	9.9	13.7	13.0	13.4
32900	Merced, CA	5 012	268 455	178	53.6	31.1	3.8	0.9	8.6	57.6	8.1	21.9	11.9	14.1	12.3	11.8
33100	Miami-Fort Lauderdale-West Palm Beach, FL	13 150	6 012 331	8	457.2	33.5	20.9	0.3	3.1	43.2	5.7	15.0	8.8	13.4	13.4	14.7
33100	Fort Lauderdale-Pompano Beach-Deerfield Beach, FL	3 133	1 896 425	X	605.3	40.9	28.3	0.5	4.5	27.5	5.8	15.7	8.5	13.5	13.4	15.0
33100	Miami-Miami Beach-Kendall, FL Div 33124	4 915	2 693 117	X	547.9	15.3	17.0	0.2	2.0	66.0	5.8	14.8	9.3	14.2	14.2	14.9
33100	West Palm Beach-Boca Raton-Delray Beach, FL Div 48	5 102	1 422 789	X	278.9	58.3	18.5	0.4	3.3	20.7	5.1	14.4	8.0	11.7	11.7	13.7
33140	Michigan City-La Porte, IN	1 550	110 884	338	71.5	81.7	12.3	0.7	0.9	6.1	5.9	16.1	8.6	13.0	12.6	14.0
33220	Midland, MI	1 337	83 632	372	62.6	93.2	1.8	0.9	2.8	2.5	5.2	16.7	9.2	11.7	11.7	15.2
33260	Midland, TX	4 702	166 718	248	35.5	49.6	6.4	0.8	1.8	42.5	8.4	19.3	10.2	16.8	12.0	11.9
33340	Milwaukee-Waukesha-West Allis, WI	3 768	1 575 747	39	418.2	69.2	17.5	0.9	3.9	10.2	6.4	17.3	9.3	14.0	12.4	13.9
33460	Minneapolis-St. Paul-Bloomington, MN	19 779	3 524 583	16	178.2	79.4	9.0	1.3	7.3	5.6	6.6	17.5	8.8	14.8	13.1	14.4
33540	Missoula, MT	6 717	114 181	336	17.0	92.1	1.0	4.0	2.4	3.1	5.4	14.0	15.6	15.2	11.8	11.6
33660	Mobile, AL	3 184	415 395	127	130.5	59.1	35.8	1.4	2.4	2.8	6.7	17.4	9.7	13.5	12.1	13.2

1. CBSA = Core Based Statistical Area. DIV = Metropolitan Division. See Appendix A for explanation. See Appendix B for list of metropolitan areas identified by type.   2. Dry land or land partially or temporarily covered by water.   3. May be of any race.

Table C. Metropolitan Areas — Population and Households

Area name	55 to 64 years	65 to 74 years	75 years and over	Percent female	Total persons 2000	Total persons 2010	Percent change 2000–2010	Percent change 2010–2015	Births	Deaths	Net migration	Number	Persons per household	Family households	Female family householder[1]	One person
	16	17	18	19	20	21	22	23	24	25	26	27	28	29	30	31
Joplin, MO	12.3	8.5	6.6	50.9	157 322	175 516	11.6	1.0	12 841	9 187	-2 111	66 564	2.59	65.9	11.3	27.3
Kahului-Wailuku-Lahaina, HI	14.2	9.2	5.9	49.7	128 241	154 925	20.8	6.3	10 707	5 995	5 060	54 355	2.95	68.3	13.1	22.7
Kalamazoo-Portage, MI	12.6	8.0	6.1	50.9	314 866	326 592	3.7	2.7	21 323	14 438	1 883	128 755	2.52	62.5	11.6	27.4
Kankakee, IL	12.9	8.3	6.6	50.9	103 833	113 449	9.3	-2.3	7 110	5 627	-4 105	40 732	2.60	67.9	15.5	24.3
Kansas City, MO-KS	12.5	7.6	5.7	51.0	1 811 254	2 009 338	10.9	3.9	145 098	85 074	18 666	800 035	2.55	64.3	11.5	29.8
Kennewick-Richland, WA	11.5	7.0	4.6	49.3	191 822	253 340	32.1	10.2	22 249	8 609	11 638	93 357	2.90	71.7	14.4	24.4
Killeen-Temple, TX	9.2	6.0	4.1	50.1	330 714	405 303	22.6	6.3	39 785	13 207	-1 479	145 055	2.76	70.6	13.6	24.6
Kingsport-Bristol-Bristol, TN-VA	14.6	11.7	8.4	51.2	298 484	309 542	3.7	-0.8	15 779	19 828	1 685	130 044	2.33	65.6	11.5	30.6
Kingston, NY	15.0	10.0	7.4	50.2	177 749	182 531	2.7	-1.3	8 562	8 495	-2 337	69 522	2.43	61.4	10.8	32.0
Knoxville, TN	13.4	9.9	6.9	51.2	748 259	837 579	11.9	2.8	48 897	46 029	20 379	336 174	2.49	64.7	10.8	29.4
Kokomo, IN	13.7	10.2	7.8	51.7	84 964	82 752	-2.6	-0.2	5 182	4 782	-590	34 026	2.41	67.5	13.8	28.2
La Crosse-Onalaska, WI-MN	13.0	8.2	7.2	50.9	126 838	133 665	5.4	2.5	7 636	5 920	1 496	54 762	2.39	61.2	7.7	27.4
Lafayette, LA	12.3	7.2	5.2	51.1	425 020	466 750	9.8	5.1	35 682	21 055	9 013	178 319	2.68	64.9	15.3	28.6
Lafayette-West Lafayette, IN	10.3	6.4	4.9	49.0	178 541	201 798	13.0	6.2	13 396	7 119	6 507	77 266	2.54	59.2	10.8	28.0
Lake Charles, LA	12.8	8.0	5.8	51.2	193 568	199 629	3.1	3.0	14 560	10 175	1 809	76 395	2.62	66.6	14.8	28.6
Lake Havasu City-Kingman, AZ	15.9	15.9	11.0	49.7	155 032	200 186	29.1	2.3	9 767	13 594	7 699	81 292	2.47	64.3	10.7	27.4
Lakeland-Winter Haven, FL	12.4	11.1	8.4	51.0	483 924	602 095	24.4	8.0	38 488	32 068	40 367	218 286	2.85	68.9	13.7	25.7
Lancaster, PA	12.8	8.6	7.8	51.1	470 658	519 448	10.4	3.3	37 164	24 537	4 010	194 764	2.67	69.7	10.1	23.6
Lansing-East Lansing, MI	12.7	7.9	5.6	51.2	447 728	464 032	3.6	1.8	27 466	18 577	-659	183 357	2.45	60.3	11.3	30.1
Laredo, TX	8.1	5.0	3.6	51.2	193 117	250 304	29.6	7.8	28 941	6 465	-2 935	70 418	3.74	82.1	24.3	15.0
Las Cruces, NM	11.0	8.0	6.1	50.8	174 682	209 241	19.8	2.4	16 207	7 771	-3 594	75 530	2.76	65.8	14.3	27.4
Las Vegas-Henderson-Paradise, NV	11.5	8.3	5.0	50.7	1 375 765	1 951 269	41.8	8.4	139 109	75 710	96 780	731 322	2.80	63.0	13.5	24.4
Lawrence, KS	10.0	5.9	4.4	50.1	99 962	110 826	10.9	6.5	6 484	3 251	3 976	45 224	2.38	53.0	8.9	33.4
Lawton, OK	10.6	6.4	4.9	48.1	121 610	130 291	7.1	0.3	10 923	5 556	-5 105	43 648	2.80	66.8	15.2	27.8
Lebanon, PA	13.4	9.8	8.6	50.9	120 327	133 577	11.0	2.6	8 500	7 504	2 347	51 234	2.60	68.6	11.8	27.8
Lewiston, ID-WA	14.3	10.6	9.0	51.0	57 961	60 888	5.0	2.1	3 770	3 749	1 297	25 932	2.35	59.5	13.6	32.4
Lewiston-Auburn, ME	13.9	9.0	6.9	50.9	103 793	107 702	3.8	-0.4	6 801	5 354	-1 896	44 267	2.36	58.9	10.8	32.1
Lexington-Fayette, KY	12.0	7.4	5.2	51.0	408 326	472 099	15.6	6.0	32 906	18 959	14 605	196 716	2.43	61.1	12.5	28.6
Lima, OH	13.6	8.6	7.3	49.6	108 473	106 331	-2.0	-1.8	6 738	5 623	-2 976	39 412	2.56	66.1	14.3	28.5
Lincoln, NE	11.6	7.0	5.4	49.9	266 787	302 157	13.3	7.1	22 320	10 990	9 770	125 923	2.43	61.6	11.7	29.1
Little Rock-North Little Rock-Conway, AR	12.2	8.2	5.6	51.5	610 518	699 823	14.6	4.5	51 384	32 900	13 198	273 841	2.61	65.3	14.0	29.5
Logan, UT-ID	8.0	5.1	4.0	50.0	102 720	125 442	22.1	6.7	13 635	3 072	-2 262	40 017	3.18	76.5	7.5	15.6
Longview, TX	12.6	8.3	6.6	50.0	194 042	214 384	10.5	1.6	15 974	11 523	-999	78 567	2.64	69.3	14.0	27.2
Longview, WA	14.5	10.8	7.3	50.4	92 948	102 410	10.2	1.0	6 230	5 530	227	40 036	2.52	63.2	15.4	30.3
Los Angeles-Long Beach-Anaheim, CA	11.4	6.9	5.5	50.7	12 365 627	12 828 966	3.7	4.0	882 218	414 345	54 525	4 287 974	3.04	68.2	15.2	24.4
Anaheim-Santa Ana-Irvine, CA Div 11244	11.7	7.4	5.8	50.6	2 846 289	3 010 266	5.8	5.3	198 487	97 434	58 490	1 018 862	3.05	72.5	12.6	21.0
Los Angeles-Long Beach-Glendale, CA Div 31084	11.3	6.8	5.4	50.7	9 519 338	9 818 700	3.1	3.6	683 731	316 911	-3 965	3 269 112	3.04	66.9	16.0	25.5
Louisville/Jefferson County, KY-IN	13.3	8.4	6.0	51.2	1 121 109	1 235 710	10.2	3.5	82 854	60 850	21 756	493 973	2.51	63.6	13.6	30.2
Lubbock, TX	10.4	6.6	5.4	50.6	256 250	290 805	13.5	7.0	22 182	12 625	10 396	115 322	2.55	63.7	13.7	27.2
Lynchburg, VA	13.4	10.0	7.4	51.8	228 616	252 659	10.5	2.9	14 938	13 204	5 441	98 399	2.49	66.0	12.9	28.3
Macon, GA	13.2	8.8	6.1	52.1	222 368	232 293	4.5	-0.9	15 994	12 413	-5 935	84 688	2.66	66.0	19.7	30.2
Madera, CA	11.0	7.6	5.2	51.9	123 109	150 865	22.5	2.7	12 400	5 396	-2 625	42 895	3.41	77.5	15.9	20.4
Madison, WI	12.5	7.4	5.4	50.3	535 421	605 437	13.1	5.9	38 885	21 561	17 804	259 371	2.38	60.4	8.6	29.4
Manchester-Nashua, NH	13.8	8.1	5.8	50.4	380 841	400 721	5.2	1.5	22 839	15 656	-1 179	153 482	2.59	67.1	11.1	24.4
Manhattan, KS	8.5	5.0	4.2	47.4	81 052	92 735	14.4	6.3	7 485	2 562	696	34 452	2.57	59.4	8.1	28.8
Mankato-North Mankato, MN	11.7	7.0	6.2	49.7	85 712	96 740	12.9	2.5	5 959	3 529	-30	37 736	2.43	61.9	10.6	27.4
Mansfield, OH	14.0	9.8	8.3	49.2	128 852	124 475	-3.4	-2.2	7 345	7 123	-2 961	47 378	2.42	65.1	11.2	29.6
McAllen-Edinburg-Mission, TX	8.1	5.8	4.6	51.2	569 463	774 774	36.1	8.7	84 955	20 499	2 143	226 000	3.63	83.0	21.8	14.4
Medford, OR	14.9	11.6	8.6	51.4	181 269	203 206	12.1	4.6	12 227	11 636	8 380	83 131	2.48	64.3	12.0	29.1
Memphis, TN-MS-AR	12.3	7.3	4.8	52.1	1 213 230	1 324 829	9.2	1.5	99 039	58 560	-20 849	493 329	2.68	66.3	19.7	28.0
Merced, CA	9.6	6.0	4.4	49.5	210 554	255 798	21.5	4.9	22 292	8 441	-893	79 255	3.28	78.0	19.2	17.7
Miami-Fort Lauderdale-West Palm Beach, FL	12.2	8.8	8.2	51.5	5 007 564	5 566 299	11.2	8.0	350 163	247 883	338 296	2 047 325	2.86	65.0	15.9	28.6
Fort Lauderdale-Pompano Beach-Deerfield Beach, FL	12.7	8.3	7.0	51.4	1 623 018	1 748 148	7.7	8.5	112 725	76 811	112 114	665 192	2.78	63.8	15.7	29.5
Miami-Miami Beach-Kendall, FL Div 33124	11.6	8.1	7.1	51.4	2 253 362	2 498 017	10.9	7.8	163 446	99 443	128 596	843 887	3.10	68.4	18.5	26.1
West Palm Beach-Boca Raton-Delray Beach, FL Div 48	12.7	10.9	11.8	51.6	1 131 184	1 320 134	16.7	7.8	73 992	71 629	97 586	538 246	2.56	61.3	12.2	31.3
Michigan City-La Porte, IN	14.0	9.3	6.5	48.2	110 106	111 467	1.2	-0.5	6 913	5 989	-1 367	42 068	2.44	68.2	11.8	25.0
Midland, MI	14.0	8.7	7.7	50.8	82 874	83 629	0.9	0.0	4 467	3 662	-811	33 579	2.45	68.8	8.7	25.1
Midland, TX	11.3	5.4	4.8	49.8	120 755	141 674	17.3	17.7	13 926	5 558	16 583	55 814	2.89	70.0	12.5	25.2
Milwaukee-Waukesha-West Allis, WI	13.0	7.5	6.4	51.3	1 500 741	1 555 954	3.7	1.3	104 969	68 363	-15 692	626 248	2.46	62.9	13.7	30.6
Minneapolis-St. Paul-Bloomington, MN	12.5	7.1	5.2	50.5	3 031 918	3 348 857	10.5	5.2	239 665	113 801	51 228	1 337 263	2.57	64.2	10.0	28.3
Missoula, MT	12.8	8.3	5.3	49.7	95 802	109 299	14.1	4.5	6 518	4 251	2 558	46 407	2.35	55.4	7.3	32.5
Mobile, AL	12.9	8.6	6.0	52.2	399 843	413 143	3.3	0.5	29 262	22 178	-4 688	153 450	2.63	68.0	18.1	27.9

1. No spouse present.

Table C. Metropolitan Areas — Population, Vital Statistics, Medicare, and Crime

Area name	Persons in group quarters, 2015	Daytime population, 2014 Number	Daytime population, 2014 Employment/residence ratio	Births, 2015 Total	Births, 2015 Rate[1]	Deaths, 2015 Number	Deaths, 2015 Rate[1]	Persons under 65 with no health insurance 2014 Number	Persons under 65 with no health insurance 2014 Percent	Medicare, 2015 Total Beneficiaries	Medicare, 2015 Enrolled in Original Medicare	Medicare, 2015 Enrolled in Medicare Advantage	Serious crimes known to police,[2] 2014 Total Number	Serious crimes known to police,[2] 2014 Total Rate[3]
	32	33	34	35	36	37	38	39	40	41	42	43	44	45
Joplin, MO	3 360	182 032	1.07	2 425	13.7	1 693	9.6	25 492	17.3	32 532	24 942	7 590	8 073	4 606
Kahului-Wailuku-Lahaina, HI	2 790	NA	NA	2 091	12.7	1 270	7.7	10 200	7.4	22 817	10 303	12 514	6 309	3 889
Kalamazoo-Portage, MI	9 385	335 902	1.01	4 096	12.2	2 853	8.5	27 061	9.7	58 773	39 305	19 468	9 965	2 985
Kankakee, IL	5 161	108 685	0.95	1 329	12.0	1 099	9.9	8 749	9.6	19 764	15 918	3 846	2 999	3 053
Kansas City, MO-KS	31 196	2 085 699	1.02	27 584	13.2	16 513	7.9	207 460	11.7	309 380	213 608	95 772	71 856	3 514
Kennewick-Richland, WA	4 328	274 127	1.00	4 230	15.2	1 714	6.1	31 009	13.1	36 110	30 885	5 225	6 711	2 428
Killeen-Temple, TX	19 948	425 818	1.00	7 597	17.6	2 584	6.0	56 327	15.5	50 964	35 157	15 807	13 305	3 115
Kingsport-Bristol-Bristol, TN-VA	5 677	311 425	1.02	2 994	9.7	3 693	12.0	33 535	13.8	79 261	38 370	40 891	8 851	2 868
Kingston, NY	11 651	168 988	0.86	1 602	8.9	1 641	9.1	13 094	9.2	34 540	26 004	8 536	3 267	1 806
Knoxville, TN	19 464	868 077	1.03	9 312	10.8	8 847	10.3	91 344	13.1	171 503	98 391	73 112	28 957	3 493
Kokomo, IN	1 280	86 475	1.10	977	11.8	918	11.1	8 728	13.0	18 969	16 445	2 524	2 466	3 017
La Crosse-Onalaska, WI-MN	6 042	143 807	1.10	1 449	10.6	1 125	8.2	7 499	6.8	24 171	13 478	10 693	2 643	1 944
Lafayette, LA	8 397	486 460	1.01	7 126	14.5	4 194	8.6	70 160	16.8	72 380	63 790	8 590	16 699	3 640
Lafayette-West Lafayette, IN	14 686	216 589	1.05	2 565	12.0	1 349	6.3	25 116	14.4	26 580	21 660	4 920	5 219	2 854
Lake Charles, LA	3 819	212 598	1.10	2 832	13.8	1 959	9.5	29 585	17.1	34 760	29 258	5 502	10 134	5 000
Lake Havasu City-Kingman, AZ	4 832	192 113	0.83	1 854	9.1	2 789	13.6	28 091	19.5	54 715	38 928	15 787	6 743	3 364
Lakeland-Winter Haven, FL	12 617	613 442	0.91	7 596	11.7	6 409	9.9	97 953	19.6	123 864	64 669	59 195	19 500	3 080
Lancaster, PA	12 782	521 129	0.95	7 247	13.5	4 816	9.0	58 557	13.4	96 072	59 597	36 475	9 261	1 741
Lansing-East Lansing, MI	20 405	484 990	1.07	5 271	11.2	3 592	7.6	34 491	8.9	76 388	54 778	21 610	10 655	2 287
Laredo, TX	3 568	264 957	0.98	5 611	20.8	1 240	4.6	74 755	31.2	26 912	20 866	6 046	11 100	4 153
Las Cruces, NM	4 576	202 092	0.87	2 925	13.6	1 498	7.0	33 147	18.5	33 714	22 546	11 168	7 132	3 337
Las Vegas-Henderson-Paradise, NV	23 123	2 077 151	1.01	26 841	12.7	15 447	7.3	315 827	17.8	269 825	157 271	112 554	72 994	3 532
Lawrence, KS	8 793	110 801	0.90	1 247	10.6	617	5.2	10 862	11.3	14 614	12 667	1 947	2 521	2 190
Lawton, OK	10 368	131 315	1.00	2 036	15.6	1 119	8.6	17 126	16.1	18 259	17 272	987	5 778	4 408
Lebanon, PA	3 614	125 859	0.83	1 595	11.6	1 435	10.5	12 097	11.1	27 565	16 486	11 079	2 350	1 729
Lewiston, ID-WA	1 140	63 012	1.03	724	11.6	683	11.0	6 213	12.6	14 998	11 835	3 163	1 996	3 185
Lewiston-Auburn, ME	2 781	106 209	0.98	1 233	11.5	1 006	9.4	10 497	12.0	22 766	16 850	5 916	2 474	2 297
Lexington-Fayette, KY	17 087	513 862	1.08	6 380	12.7	3 629	7.3	43 979	10.6	70 500	47 426	23 074	18 542	3 752
Lima, OH	5 929	113 082	1.18	1 282	12.3	1 057	10.1	8 343	10.0	19 926	14 592	5 334	3 862	3 672
Lincoln, NE	16 398	323 392	1.02	4 242	13.1	2 070	6.4	26 146	9.9	43 017	38 704	4 313	10 592	3 360
Little Rock-North Little Rock-Conway, AR	15 495	741 456	1.04	9 708	13.3	6 307	8.6	74 552	12.1	117 242	96 237	21 005	36 769	5 041
Logan, UT-ID	4 079	129 744	0.98	2 539	19.0	578	4.3	14 939	12.9	12 609	7 529	5 080	1 649	1 257
Longview, TX	9 583	225 164	1.08	3 011	13.8	2 192	10.1	37 721	21.4	40 097	30 219	9 878	7 872	3 660
Longview, WA	1 207	102 992	1.02	1 184	11.4	1 066	10.3	9 314	11.2	21 186	11 177	10 009	3 982	3 897
Los Angeles-Long Beach-Anaheim, CA	222 579	13 484 333	1.04	167 846	12.6	83 692	6.3	1 879 423	16.4	1 625 311	730 152	895 159	321 229	2 419
Anaheim-Santa Ana-Irvine, CA Div 11244	43 952	X	X	37 776	11.9	19 480	6.1	360 533	13.4	411 226	200 569	210 657	61 011	1 933
Los Angeles-Long Beach-Glendale, CA Div 31084	178 627	X	X	130 070	12.8	64 212	6.3	1 518 890	17.4	1 214 085	529 583	684 502	260 218	2 571
Louisville/Jefferson County, KY-IN	26 582	1 283 017	1.03	15 977	12.5	11 581	9.1	108 492	10.2	217 824	155 974	61 850	46 200	3 749
Lubbock, TX	12 457	302 266	0.98	4 414	14.2	2 545	8.2	49 129	19.0	41 923	28 420	13 503	14 239	4 691
Lynchburg, VA	13 339	251 431	0.95	2 844	10.9	2 501	9.6	26 769	13.2	55 814	45 972	9 842	4 908	1 906
Macon, GA	8 192	240 716	1.08	2 934	12.8	2 475	10.8	31 876	16.8	41 442	27 237	14 205	NA	NA
Madera, CA	7 810	153 897	0.99	2 412	15.6	980	6.3	22 004	17.4	21 597	14 319	7 278	4 268	2 780
Madison, WI	14 880	659 984	1.08	7 461	11.6	4 132	6.4	39 084	7.2	89 906	67 628	22 278	13 708	2 245
Manchester-Nashua, NH	7 964	387 857	0.92	4 302	10.6	3 097	7.6	35 777	10.4	64 761	58 805	5 956	9 289	2 360
Manhattan, KS	9 374	96 769	0.97	1 335	13.5	510	5.2	7 999	9.9	10 002	9 229	773	1 707	1 718
Mankato-North Mankato, MN	6 954	101 235	1.05	1 123	11.3	673	6.8	4 840	6.1	15 758	7 676	8 082	2 344	2 364
Mansfield, OH	7 404	124 926	1.06	1 398	11.5	1 359	11.2	10 250	10.9	26 802	19 621	7 181	5 689	4 880
McAllen-Edinburg-Mission, TX	7 305	820 258	0.96	16 293	19.3	4 221	5.0	247 930	33.8	87 337	55 678	31 659	30 676	3 689
Medford, OR	3 572	210 049	1.00	2 361	11.1	2 181	10.3	21 410	12.9	48 594	32 093	16 501	9 061	4 300
Memphis, TN-MS-AR	24 149	1 356 202	1.02	18 780	14.0	11 559	8.6	170 698	14.7	191 588	142 674	48 914	67 711	5 394
Merced, CA	6 438	249 782	0.83	4 219	15.7	1 658	6.2	34 486	14.9	30 478	27 717	2 761	8 611	3 233
Miami-Fort Lauderdale-West Palm Beach, FL	78 084	5 949 413	1.01	68 332	11.4	49 960	8.3	1 118 448	23.1	963 100	434 428	528 672	235 037	3 958
Fort Lauderdale-Pompano Beach-Deerfield Beach, FL	16 179	X	X	22 161	11.7	15 213	8.0	326 737	20.8	271 704	117 911	153 793	64 848	3 457
Miami-Miami Beach-Kendall, FL Div 33124	41 107	X	X	31 534	11.7	20 313	7.5	566 562	25.5	407 629	142 187	265 442	122 865	4 606
West Palm Beach-Boca Raton-Delray Beach, FL Div 48	20 798	X	X	14 637	10.3	14 434	10.1	225 149	21.2	283 767	174 330	109 437	47 324	3 391
Michigan City-La Porte, IN	6 521	108 984	0.95	1 320	11.9	1 169	10.5	11 814	13.5	20 421	17 893	2 528	2 473	2 427
Midland, MI	1 274	84 619	1.03	840	10.0	702	8.4	5 819	8.5	15 312	10 338	4 974	1 148	1 366
Midland, TX	1 695	180 303	1.20	2 942	17.6	1 072	6.4	27 468	19.1	16 790	13 581	3 209	4 701	2 902
Milwaukee-Waukesha-West Allis, WI	32 794	1 609 781	1.05	19 861	12.6	13 032	8.3	116 845	8.8	254 004	160 339	93 665	56 248	3 716
Minneapolis-St. Paul-Bloomington, MN	64 815	3 511 314	1.01	46 378	13.2	22 208	6.3	196 545	6.5	466 959	191 399	275 560	95 940	2 751
Missoula, MT	3 636	115 143	1.04	1 280	11.2	816	7.1	14 557	15.4	18 070	15 015	3 055	3 636	3 228
Mobile, AL	7 507	423 935	1.05	5 585	13.4	4 343	10.5	52 191	14.9	74 616	41 524	33 092	18 673	4 505

1. Per 1,000 estimated resident population.　　2. Data for serious crimes have not been adjusted for underreporting; this may affect comparability between geographic areas and over time.
3. Per 100,000 population estimated by the FBI.

Table C. Metropolitan Areas — Crime, Education, Money Income, and Poverty

Area name	Serious crimes known to police, 2014 (cont.)[1] Rate[2] Violent	Property	Education: School enrollment and attainment, 2014 — Enrollment[3] Total	Percent private	High school graduate or less	Bachelor's degree or more	Local government expenditures,[5] 2012–2013 Total current expenditures (mil dol)	Current expenditures per student (dollars)	Income and Poverty, 2014 Per capita income[6] (dollars)	Mean household income (dollars)	Median household income	Percent of households with income of less than $25,000	Percent of households with income of $200,000 or more	Percent below poverty level All persons	Children under 18 years	Age 65 years and older
	46	47	48	49	50	51	52	53	54	55	56	57	58	59	60	61
Joplin, MO	329	4 276	44 676	15.9	49.2	19.8	239.2	7 965	22 463	57 331	42 705	27.4	1.7	17.5	20.6	11.0
Kahului-Wailuku-Lahaina, HI	314	3 575	34 093	16.9	41.1	25.3	NA	NA	29 797	85 391	66 987	16.3	4.8	13.2	18.0	10.0
Kalamazoo-Portage, MI	457	2 529	97 418	9.1	33.5	31.5	549.5	11 189	24 610	62 592	45 721	25.5	3.0	18.7	20.9	7.2
Kankakee, IL	329	2 724	28 784	25.2	44.6	20.7	204.9	10 598	26 033	69 795	58 378	20.4	3.0	13.7	18.9	10.9
Kansas City, MO-KS	486	3 028	533 928	17.6	34.8	34.7	3 206.7	9 668	30 369	76 444	56 994	20.7	4.8	12.6	17.9	7.7
Kennewick-Richland, WA	206	2 222	75 708	8.7	39.1	25.1	471.6	9 051	26 161	74 014	58 020	20.6	4.8	16.3	25.7	8.4
Killeen-Temple, TX	343	2 773	125 666	10.2	36.7	21.4	653.4	7 999	23 478	64 328	50 478	21.3	3.0	13.9	19.7	6.6
Kingsport-Bristol-Bristol, TN-VA	323	2 545	63 840	12.9	50.6	21.1	390.1	8 888	23 311	54 473	39 213	31.9	1.8	18.2	28.4	10.6
Kingston, NY	183	1 622	40 107	16.1	39.8	30.6	527.3	21 935	30 870	77 260	58 093	22.2	5.5	13.3	15.2	10.5
Knoxville, TN	387	3 105	197 269	16.1	45.5	27.6	987.4	8 042	26 054	64 318	45 151	28.5	3.4	17.3	24.6	9.4
Kokomo, IN	225	2 792	20 174	9.5	47.9	18.4	128.0	9 608	24 373	58 810	47 159	25.9	1.8	18.2	24.2	6.7
La Crosse-Onalaska, WI-MN	116	1 827	38 455	12.5	34.2	29.9	237.4	11 378	27 153	66 200	50 568	19.5	2.6	11.8	6.0	6.1
Lafayette, LA	439	3 201	123 814	20.0	52.2	21.5	690.4	9 543	26 423	68 632	48 668	27.0	4.2	16.3	21.0	11.7
Lafayette-West Lafayette, IN	232	2 622	76 099	9.6	36.9	33.4	243.3	9 325	22 900	60 364	46 109	28.3	2.1	22.3	21.9	4.7
Lake Charles, LA	544	4 456	52 006	13.6	50.2	20.3	349.4	10 417	23 626	59 811	46 336	29.5	2.2	18.2	26.4	11.3
Lake Havasu City-Kingman, AZ	202	3 162	38 819	17.4	50.4	12.9	131.8	6 291	20 450	48 224	37 674	29.9	1.0	20.6	30.5	8.5
Lakeland-Winter Haven, FL	349	2 732	150 620	16.2	52.6	19.7	888.4	9 165	20 706	55 591	42 780	26.8	1.6	18.1	27.3	10.9
Lancaster, PA	165	1 577	125 408	25.4	53.2	26.6	949.3	13 988	27 697	73 993	57 403	17.8	3.7	10.4	14.5	7.3
Lansing-East Lansing, MI	412	1 875	149 449	11.1	31.7	32.5	732.3	11 283	26 754	66 339	49 697	23.6	3.4	16.1	18.5	6.5
Laredo, TX	403	3 750	88 134	6.4	60.4	17.4	557.4	8 189	15 286	54 237	38 312	36.0	2.0	33.4	44.0	29.7
Las Cruces, NM	286	3 051	70 800	5.3	41.7	30.6	353.6	8 696	20 245	55 113	39 502	33.3	2.7	29.6	43.2	13.7
Las Vegas-Henderson-Paradise, NV	743	2 790	508 000	12.5	43.9	22.7	2 555.2	8 066	25 326	66 603	51 214	22.1	3.2	15.2	22.4	8.7
Lawrence, KS	203	1 986	43 494	10.9	23.3	50.9	137.2	9 243	25 134	61 426	48 565	27.9	3.1	20.5	16.5	5.7
Lawton, OK	705	3 703	37 533	6.4	42.6	21.2	181.9	7 643	23 444	63 314	47 584	26.3	2.0	18.2	23.1	11.1
Lebanon, PA	149	1 580	29 464	25.2	56.3	20.6	221.1	11 553	26 122	67 312	54 068	17.4	1.4	10.3	16.7	5.8
Lewiston, ID-WA	185	3 000	14 287	10.9	40.5	21.3	81.6	9 258	25 136	57 646	44 937	27.3	1.4	14.8	15.5	9.7
Lewiston-Auburn, ME	141	2 156	25 163	16.3	47.0	22.9	196.7	11 599	24 433	58 079	48 007	27.1	0.9	15.6	23.0	10.3
Lexington-Fayette, KY	263	3 488	135 201	16.8	36.9	35.0	686.8	9 887	27 727	68 443	50 270	25.5	4.2	18.2	24.6	7.6
Lima, OH	386	3 286	27 823	15.5	52.2	14.2	161.7	11 172	21 635	54 997	42 701	31.1	1.7	17.8	24.2	8.6
Lincoln, NE	303	3 057	94 854	13.8	30.9	35.6	472.8	10 623	27 500	68 621	52 046	21.4	3.2	14.0	17.2	4.3
Little Rock-North Little Rock-Conway, AR	688	4 354	190 592	14.3	39.6	28.6	1 037.1	9 669	25 737	64 467	48 330	23.8	2.7	14.0	19.1	5.8
Logan, UT-ID	54	1 203	51 881	5.5	30.5	32.6	156.1	6 152	19 280	62 120	51 497	21.5	1.9	14.5	11.9	6.1
Longview, TX	387	3 273	53 214	9.8	47.8	17.5	345.1	8 798	23 962	63 709	49 500	26.4	2.5	16.2	25.1	9.1
Longview, WA	250	3 648	22 942	6.2	42.4	14.7	156.7	9 254	23 421	56 224	42 223	29.4	1.4	22.5	31.4	11.0
Los Angeles-Long Beach-Anaheim, CA	369	2 050	3 593 473	15.1	40.9	32.1	20 050.7	9 722	29 918	88 098	60 514	21.1	8.1	17.3	24.6	12.6
Anaheim-Santa Ana-Irvine, CA Div 11244	198	1 735	864 459	14.7	33.0	38.0	4 361.7	8 692	34 886	104 121	76 306	14.8	11.2	12.8	17.9	8.8
Los Angeles-Long Beach-Glendale, CA Div 31084	422	2 149	2 729 014	15.3	43.4	30.3	15 689.0	10 053	28 373	83 104	55 746	23.1	7.2	18.7	26.7	13.9
Louisville/Jefferson County, KY-IN	402	3 346	308 600	20.4	41.8	27.6	1 864.8	10 216	27 910	68 897	50 932	24.3	3.9	14.5	20.5	8.5
Lubbock, TX	741	3 950	99 056	9.4	41.8	27.0	440.5	8 785	25 084	65 186	45 825	26.1	4.2	17.6	18.4	9.9
Lynchburg, VA	233	1 673	68 587	35.5	43.7	27.2	321.7	9 403	24 160	60 884	47 567	25.9	2.1	15.9	21.4	7.7
Macon, GA	NA	NA	59 200	18.5	51.9	23.2	354.2	9 602	22 308	58 587	38 146	34.1	3.1	24.3	35.3	14.1
Madera, CA	578	2 201	41 913	5.8	55.6	12.2	269.6	8 845	17 601	58 507	42 433	28.0	2.0	22.2	30.7	11.5
Madison, WI	211	2 035	174 644	11.7	26.6	44.7	1 054.6	11 386	32 839	79 257	60 903	18.2	4.9	12.7	14.8	6.0
Manchester-Nashua, NH	272	2 088	98 137	23.6	36.5	35.1	721.9	12 670	35 255	90 207	71 422	14.7	7.1	8.7	12.0	5.6
Manhattan, KS	235	1 482	36 748	6.4	24.3	45.8	112.6	9 878	25 269	66 594	50 323	27.3	3.9	19.6	15.3	4.3
Mankato-North Mankato, MN	180	2 184	31 567	17.7	34.2	31.0	139.9	11 111	27 774	70 536	54 055	21.0	4.5	16.3	14.6	7.8
Mansfield, OH	218	4 662	28 816	17.9	53.8	17.1	200.6	13 157	21 373	54 501	41 548	28.9	1.4	15.1	20.9	9.1
McAllen-Edinburg-Mission, TX	329	3 360	270 396	7.6	60.2	17.9	1 868.5	9 112	14 422	49 841	34 801	38.5	1.3	34.0	46.5	24.3
Medford, OR	319	3 981	46 446	9.1	39.0	26.8	279.8	9 729	24 902	59 978	44 918	25.5	2.2	18.1	26.3	7.4
Memphis, TN-MS-AR	1 104	4 291	359 947	17.8	43.8	26.4	1 995.9	8 816	24 837	65 233	45 844	28.4	3.7	20.3	30.8	10.7
Merced, CA	558	2 675	81 078	4.4	56.2	13.9	540.7	9 596	18 585	59 701	44 084	26.2	2.4	25.2	38.1	10.6
Miami-Fort Lauderdale-West Palm Beach, FL	520	3 438	1 448 410	19.9	42.9	29.4	7 059.4	8 891	27 126	72 349	48 458	26.5	5.2	17.2	23.8	14.8
Fort Lauderdale-Pompano Beach-Deerfield Beach, FL	409	3 048	472 692	20.3	40.2	30.5	2 183.4	8 390	27 820	72 409	51 608	24.0	4.8	14.4	19.7	11.9
Miami-Miami Beach-Kendall, FL Div 33124	633	3 973	663 015	20.0	47.3	26.6	3 183.4	8 986	23 651	67 125	42 926	30.6	4.7	20.4	27.7	20.9
West Palm Beach-Boca Raton-Delray Beach, FL Div 48	452	2 939	312 703	19.4	38.3	33.0	1 692.7	9 429	32 819	80 466	52 203	23.0	6.7	14.8	21.9	9.6
Michigan City-La Porte, IN	143	2 283	24 854	14.2	48.5	18.3	178.6	10 209	22 835	61 052	45 744	21.9	2.5	19.4	36.2	7.9
Midland, MI	125	1 241	19 830	14.6	36.3	29.7	126.4	10 591	29 065	70 677	49 194	21.1	4.8	11.7	13.2	7.7
Midland, TX	322	2 580	41 788	15.0	42.0	25.5	224.5	8 544	35 856	100 541	77 574	15.7	10.6	7.8	6.5	5.8
Milwaukee-Waukesha-West Allis, WI	659	3 057	415 287	24.7	36.6	33.7	2 663.0	11 669	30 206	73 894	53 164	23.6	4.7	15.4	22.9	8.0
Minneapolis-St. Paul-Bloomington, MN	261	2 489	914 273	17.3	29.0	40.0	6 126.2	11 758	35 652	91 246	69 111	16.2	7.4	10.3	13.6	6.6
Missoula, MT	274	2 954	29 740	9.8	26.5	40.9	136.0	10 192	28 103	65 380	44 289	26.0	4.2	15.4	10.3	7.6
Mobile, AL	510	3 994	101 338	20.3	47.8	21.0	563.8	8 881	22 854	59 047	43 642	30.0	2.2	19.3	28.9	11.5

1. Data for serious crimes have not been adjusted for underreporting; this may affect comparability between geographic areas and over time.   2. Per 100,000 population estimated by the FBI.
3. All persons 3 years old and over enrolled in nursery school through college.   4. Persons 25 years old and over.   5. Elementary and secondary education expenditures.   6. Based on resident population estimated in the 2014 American Community Survey.

Table C. Metropolitan Areas — **Personal Income**

| | Personal income, 2014 | | | | | | | | | | Earnings, 2014 | | |
| | | | Per capita[1] | | | Supplements to wages and salaries; employer contributions (mil dol) | | | | | | Contributions for government social insurance (mil dol) | |
Area name	Total (mil dol)	Percent change 2013–2014	Dollars	Rank	Wages and salaries (mil dol)	Pension and insurance	Government social insurance	Proprietors' income (mil dol)	Dividends, interest, and rent (mil dol)	Personal transfer receipts (mil dol)	Total (mil dol)	From employee and self-employed	From employer
	62	63	64	65	66	67	68	69	70	71	72	73	74
Joplin, MO	6 059	3.0	34 400	325	3 081	558	226	477	932	1 399	4 342	260	226
Kahului-Wailuku-Lahaina, HI	6 433	5.7	39 439	199	3 165	532	248	535	1 357	1 110	4 480	274	248
Kalamazoo-Portage, MI	13 221	3.5	39 583	194	6 505	1 148	501	699	2 455	2 662	8 853	546	501
Kankakee, IL	3 971	0.7	35 657	303	1 821	361	135	168	535	940	2 485	142	135
Kansas City, MO-KS	95 932	3.8	46 319	75	53 840	7 833	4 022	9 233	15 854	14 374	74 929	4 475	4 022
Kennewick-Richland, WA	10 380	3.8	37 842	238	5 492	789	524	906	1 564	2 038	7 712	432	524
Killeen-Temple, TX	16 577	2.4	39 017	208	8 087	1 841	661	977	3 086	3 172	11 566	537	661
Kingsport-Bristol-Bristol, TN-VA	11 064	2.6	35 912	296	5 081	908	363	864	1 824	3 072	7 216	489	363
Kingston, NY	7 515	4.2	41 648	151	2 486	751	221	383	1 256	1 740	3 841	215	221
Knoxville, TN	33 901	3.7	39 530	196	17 178	2 665	1 219	3 681	5 200	7 243	24 743	1 523	1 219
Kokomo, IN	2 965	3.4	35 728	301	1 888	295	146	137	427	813	2 466	161	146
La Crosse-Onalaska, WI-MN	5 833	3.8	42 653	129	3 193	629	260	362	1 093	1 021	4 444	270	260
Lafayette, LA	21 848	4.1	45 049	89	11 296	1 588	712	3 395	3 431	3 443	16 992	918	712
Lafayette-West Lafayette, IN	7 250	3.6	34 246	326	4 101	785	304	594	1 192	1 224	5 784	335	304
Lake Charles, LA	8 179	7.1	40 116	183	4 764	858	304	640	1 283	1 564	6 567	356	304
Lake Havasu City-Kingman, AZ	5 634	4.4	27 704	379	1 755	309	133	306	936	1 995	2 503	203	133
Lakeland-Winter Haven, FL	20 722	4.8	32 652	359	8 705	1 385	630	1 098	3 888	5 672	11 818	804	630
Lancaster, PA	22 246	4.6	41 712	149	10 133	1 822	832	2 582	3 824	4 139	15 369	892	832
Lansing-East Lansing, MI	17 246	3.6	36 659	268	9 561	1 840	721	1 085	2 680	3 503	13 207	800	721
Laredo, TX	7 561	4.3	28 355	378	3 499	656	243	963	1 039	1 766	5 360	270	243
Las Cruces, NM	6 537	5.0	30 593	373	2 779	579	225	490	1 100	1 809	4 074	255	225
Las Vegas-Henderson-Paradise, NV	81 821	5.9	39 533	195	42 091	6 930	3 167	5 795	17 219	13 268	57 983	3 333	3 167
Lawrence, KS	4 277	3.9	36 686	266	1 891	366	148	223	822	624	2 628	157	148
Lawton, OK	4 901	1.8	37 360	250	2 425	572	209	274	925	1 007	3 480	173	209
Lebanon, PA	5 595	3.6	41 034	165	1 974	453	167	436	865	1 171	3 030	180	167
Lewiston, ID-WA	2 347	3.6	37 729	240	1 058	168	94	160	472	602	1 481	102	94
Lewiston-Auburn, ME	3 900	3.0	36 300	280	2 045	322	155	271	487	1 029	2 793	186	155
Lexington-Fayette, KY	20 870	4.6	42 231	137	11 923	2 191	905	1 759	3 689	3 542	16 778	976	905
Lima, OH	3 799	2.9	36 169	286	2 197	428	167	294	514	931	3 086	177	167
Lincoln, NE	13 842	3.9	43 399	112	7 664	1 378	567	1 004	2 702	1 941	10 613	635	567
Little Rock-North Little Rock-Conway, AR	29 840	3.3	40 925	166	16 047	2 472	1 242	2 255	5 101	6 104	22 016	1 384	1 242
Logan, UT-ID	3 991	4.8	30 379	374	1 944	413	157	370	688	627	2 884	162	157
Longview, TX	9 500	4.5	43 684	104	4 903	658	345	1 451	1 299	1 904	7 357	393	345
Longview, WA	3 895	5.3	38 135	230	1 762	267	170	265	615	1 091	2 465	162	170
Los Angeles-Long Beach-Anaheim, CA	673 074	4.5	50 751	29	348 925	57 306	24 329	74 660	138 698	103 883	505 220	29 569	24 329
Anaheim-Santa Ana-Irvine, CA Div 11244	173 306	4.5	55 096	X	91 763	13 918	6 559	18 496	36 152	19 856	130 736	7 681	6 559
Los Angeles-Long Beach-Glendale, CA Div 31084	499 768	4.5	49 400	X	257 162	43 387	17 770	56 164	102 545	84 027	374 483	21 888	17 770
Louisville/Jefferson County, KY-IN	54 592	4.7	42 996	123	29 326	4 547	2 255	4 270	9 115	10 382	40 398	2 513	2 255
Lubbock, TX	11 442	3.7	37 434	248	5 642	947	375	1 222	1 735	2 208	8 186	418	375
Lynchburg, VA	9 343	3.4	36 237	283	4 360	697	326	476	1 650	2 301	5 858	392	326
Macon, GA	8 361	3.3	36 282	282	4 224	767	301	560	1 406	2 072	5 851	355	301
Madera, CA	5 107	2.7	33 042	352	1 951	487	139	979	740	1 115	3 556	171	139
Madison, WI	31 670	3.0	49 969	38	18 412	3 699	1 418	2 216	6 147	3 874	25 746	1 488	1 418
Manchester-Nashua, NH	22 438	5.0	55 378	17	11 937	1 662	819	1 803	4 228	2 870	16 221	983	819
Manhattan, KS	3 795	1.7	38 692	213	1 553	313	120	187	815	466	2 173	125	120
Mankato-North Mankato, MN	4 073	3.0	41 358	158	2 152	381	169	464	760	691	3 168	181	169
Mansfield, OH	4 168	3.7	34 180	332	1 999	411	153	210	607	1 118	2 773	163	153
McAllen-Edinburg-Mission, TX	19 741	4.9	23 753	381	8 229	1 593	567	2 602	2 075	5 854	12 991	672	567
Medford, OR	7 915	5.8	37 637	242	3 273	511	308	679	1 724	2 106	4 771	326	308
Memphis, TN-MS-AR	56 328	2.4	41 935	145	30 547	4 414	2 122	6 503	7 823	10 410	43 586	2 567	2 122
Merced, CA	9 020	4.5	33 865	338	2 949	790	209	1 579	1 222	2 216	5 526	257	209
Miami-Fort Lauderdale-West Palm Beach, FL	285 961	5.0	48 224	55	127 890	17 357	8 978	22 445	83 819	47 995	176 670	11 047	8 978
Fort Lauderdale-Pompano Beach-Deerfield Beach, FL	80 906	5.2	43 283	X	39 465	5 347	2 811	5 350	18 032	13 275	52 974	3 276	2 811
Miami-Miami Beach-Kendall, FL Div 33124	111 529	5.0	41 883	X	57 785	8 094	4 066	11 094	24 748	22 515	81 039	5 033	4 066
West Palm Beach-Boca Raton-Delray Beach, FL Div 48	93 526	4.9	66 914	X	30 640	3 916	2 101	6 001	41 039	12 204	42 657	2 739	2 101
Michigan City-La Porte, IN	3 999	3.3	35 882	298	1 698	298	133	251	585	925	2 379	153	133
Midland, MI	3 850	4.0	46 151	77	2 161	335	150	163	679	683	2 810	176	150
Midland, TX	15 300	9.5	94 863	2	6 664	747	420	5 524	2 224	893	13 355	602	420
Milwaukee-Waukesha-West Allis, WI	76 470	3.4	48 638	51	43 173	7 198	3 367	5 147	14 044	12 911	58 886	3 591	3 367
Minneapolis-St. Paul-Bloomington, MN	185 825	4.9	53 166	23	108 897	15 033	8 149	14 338	33 107	24 836	146 417	8 802	8 149
Missoula, MT	4 330	4.2	38 422	223	2 257	365	211	322	1 111	756	3 154	205	211
Mobile, AL	14 542	4.1	35 031	316	7 903	1 291	593	1 243	2 352	3 557	11 029	701	593

1. Based on the resident population estimated as of July 1 of the year shown.

Table C. Metropolitan Areas — Earnings, Social Security, and Housing

Area name	Earnings, 2014 (cont.) — Percent by selected industries									Social Security beneficiaries, December 2014		Supplemental Security Income recipients, December 2014	Housing units, 2015	
	Farm	Mining	Construction	Manufacturing	Information, professional, scientific, technical services	Retail trade	Finance, insurance, real estate, rental and leasing	Health care and social assistance	Government	Number	Rate[1]		Total	Percent change, 2000–2015
	75	76	77	78	79	80	81	82	83	84	85	86	87	88
Joplin, MO	3.0	D	5.2	17.5	4.0	8.4	3.9	15.0	12.1	37 410	212	4 587	76 046	1.4
Kahului-Wailuku-Lahaina, HI	2.2	D	7.9	1.5	4.2	8.4	5.9	7.0	17.9	27 790	170	2 093	71 835	1.9
Kalamazoo-Portage, MI	1.5	D	5.0	20.7	5.8	6.0	7.7	13.9	15.9	66 325	199	8 577	147 152	0.2
Kankakee, IL	2.7	D	4.0	19.5	D	7.4	4.7	17.2	16.7	22 205	199	2 723	45 185	-0.1
Kansas City, MO-KS	0.4	0.2	6.0	8.3	D	5.6	D	10.6	14.3	353 160	171	34 540	891 296	2.2
Kennewick-Richland, WA	6.3	0.0	6.9	6.5	15.2	6.3	3.2	9.6	18.4	41 615	152	5 547	99 753	7.2
Killeen-Temple, TX	0.1	D	6.4	3.9	D	5.6	3.1	11.6	50.4	61 110	144	9 283	171 106	7.4
Kingsport-Bristol-Bristol, TN-VA	0.0	D	D	24.8	D	7.2	D	D	12.9	90 055	293	10 630	147 405	0.3
Kingston, NY	0.6	0.2	5.1	5.7	5.6	9.0	4.5	12.6	34.3	40 605	225	4 255	83 801	0.2
Knoxville, TN	0.1	D	D	10.7	13.0	7.5	6.6	13.4	15.2	194 470	227	23 042	388 913	2.0
Kokomo, IN	0.9	D	3.1	45.3	3.2	6.1	3.2	12.6	10.0	20 995	254	2 242	38 747	0.2
La Crosse-Onalaska, WI-MN	1.2	D	5.5	12.5	D	6.1	6.1	20.8	15.9	26 320	193	2 418	58 098	1.9
Lafayette, LA	0.7	18.6	7.4	9.7	8.0	6.1	8.0	10.8	9.2	84 305	174	15 857	204 102	4.2
Lafayette-West Lafayette, IN	3.1	D	4.1	D	D	5.4	4.7	12.0	25.3	31 270	147	2 481	88 162	4.3
Lake Charles, LA	0.4	1.2	19.9	17.3	D	D	3.7	11.1	12.9	38 855	191	6 442	90 806	6.0
Lake Havasu City-Kingman, AZ	0.4	1.5	5.0	6.3	4.6	12.6	5.3	21.0	18.8	62 965	310	4 685	112 867	1.8
Lakeland-Winter Haven, FL	0.9	0.7	5.4	9.3	5.4	8.9	8.0	14.0	14.1	148 405	234	20 892	284 342	1.1
Lancaster, PA	3.7	0.2	10.1	16.3	7.1	7.0	6.5	13.5	9.8	107 425	201	9 957	207 090	2.0
Lansing-East Lansing, MI	0.9	0.3	4.5	11.8	7.1	5.2	9.7	11.7	27.6	86 970	185	10 185	200 375	0.7
Laredo, TX	0.2	8.3	3.0	0.7	4.0	8.2	3.8	10.5	27.1	31 500	118	12 614	79 708	8.5
Las Cruces, NM	3.4	0.0	5.4	3.8	8.3	6.2	3.7	14.7	33.8	37 595	176	8 076	84 646	3.9
Las Vegas-Henderson-Paradise, NV	0.0	0.1	6.5	2.7	8.7	7.4	6.1	8.8	15.7	320 495	155	38 973	871 807	3.7
Lawrence, KS	0.8	0.6	5.4	9.1	10.0	6.6	4.3	7.1	35.3	15 545	133	1 345	48 540	3.9
Lawton, OK	1.1	D	3.8	8.1	D	5.9	3.8	5.3	53.5	20 900	159	3 363	54 703	1.8
Lebanon, PA	5.1	D	4.9	17.6	5.1	7.2	2.9	13.2	20.7	31 400	231	2 472	56 464	1.6
Lewiston, ID-WA	-0.1	D	5.7	18.2	4.3	8.9	7.4	D	19.3	16 750	270	1 766	27 278	-0.1
Lewiston-Auburn, ME	1.3	D	6.9	11.2	6.8	8.0	6.3	21.2	11.2	25 220	235	4 103	49 105	0.0
Lexington-Fayette, KY	0.5	1.3	6.0	14.6	9.8	6.4	4.9	9.8	21.5	81 380	164	11 691	216 459	3.5
Lima, OH	0.8	0.1	4.8	24.4	3.8	6.9	3.5	18.2	13.1	21 960	209	3 200	44 799	-0.4
Lincoln, NE	1.5	D	5.7	9.0	8.8	6.0	9.9	D	21.4	47 530	149	4 935	133 554	4.5
Little Rock-North Little Rock-Conway, AR	0.4	0.9	6.0	6.1	D	7.4	D	12.2	23.2	143 215	196	24 756	320 011	4.3
Logan, UT-ID	3.3	D	5.3	23.1	D	7.0	4.5	D	21.5	14 915	114	1 037	44 421	6.9
Longview, TX	0.7	17.3	11.3	10.0	D	6.8	4.4	10.3	8.5	42 765	197	6 980	89 818	2.9
Longview, WA	0.2	0.8	12.8	23.2	3.3	6.6	3.0	12.5	15.1	25 400	248	3 785	43 566	0.3
Los Angeles-Long Beach-Anaheim, CA	0.0	0.6	4.1	9.0	19.1	5.6	10.4	9.4	14.0	1 698 150	128	498 253	4 585 126	2.0
Anaheim-Santa Ana-Irvine, CA Div 11244	0.0	0.3	6.5	11.6	14.8	5.8	13.8	8.5	10.8	423 770	135	74 855	1 080 987	3.1
Los Angeles-Long Beach-Glendale, CA Div 31084	0.0	0.7	3.2	8.0	20.6	5.5	9.2	9.8	15.1	1 274 380	126	423 398	3 504 139	1.7
Louisville/Jefferson County, KY-IN	0.3	0.1	D	D	9.2	5.4	D	13.5	13.1	250 835	197	35 941	551 210	2.0
Lubbock, TX	0.5	D	D	D	D	9.0	7.6	15.2	23.7	46 545	152	7 050	128 688	6.7
Lynchburg, VA	0.1	D	D	18.5	D	6.7	D	13.7	13.0	60 560	235	6 346	115 229	2.4
Macon, GA	1.0	0.8	D	D	7.6	D	D	19.1	15.0	48 950	212	9 683	102 241	0.6
Madera, CA	21.7	D	3.4	9.9	2.7	4.7	1.9	13.3	21.8	24 215	157	4 804	50 084	1.9
Madison, WI	1.3	0.2	5.5	9.5	D	6.1	8.7	D	22.6	102 810	162	8 741	278 423	3.6
Manchester-Nashua, NH	0.0	0.0	5.7	14.6	15.9	8.0	11.4	11.1	10.1	76 450	189	7 134	168 074	1.2
Manhattan, KS	1.8	0.5	6.6	8.0	6.0	7.1	5.2	D	35.5	11 120	114	737	39 371	6.9
Mankato-North Mankato, MN	6.2	D	5.2	16.6	D	6.9	4.1	D	16.8	16 430	166	1 329	40 650	4.0
Mansfield, OH	1.5	0.0	5.9	22.0	4.5	8.0	4.2	14.0	18.1	28 610	235	3 438	54 199	-0.7
McAllen-Edinburg-Mission, TX	0.7	2.7	5.3	3.1	4.2	10.3	4.5	18.9	25.1	101 130	122	42 814	264 604	6.6
Medford, OR	0.8	0.1	7.1	9.4	6.4	10.4	4.9	18.5	15.6	53 595	255	4 670	92 844	2.1
Memphis, TN-MS-AR	0.3	0.0	5.4	9.8	5.8	D	D	12.0	14.4	229 480	171	47 377	566 162	2.0
Merced, CA	22.6	D	3.4	10.9	2.2	5.6	2.6	8.3	24.5	35 880	135	11 320	84 322	0.7
Miami-Fort Lauderdale-West Palm Beach, FL	0.3	0.1	4.7	3.4	13.9	7.7	11.1	11.5	13.6	1 013 750	171	226 904	2 508 205	1.8
Fort Lauderdale-Pompano Beach-Deerfield Beach, FL	0.0	0.1	5.6	3.7	14.1	8.4	9.6	10.1	14.6	302 775	162	44 368	818 623	1.0
Miami-Miami Beach-Kendall, FL Div 33124	0.3	0.1	4.1	3.0	13.8	7.5	11.0	11.6	14.2	407 735	153	159 102	1 010 556	2.1
West Palm Beach-Boca Raton-Delray Beach, FL Div 48	0.5	0.3	5.0	3.7	13.7	7.2	13.2	13.2	11.4	303 240	217	23 434	679 026	2.2
Michigan City-La Porte, IN	2.5	D	8.3	21.2	3.1	6.9	3.8	13.9	15.0	24 165	216	2 201	48 782	0.7
Midland, MI	0.2	D	6.2	24.3	4.6	4.3	3.0	11.7	8.3	18 625	223	1 627	36 465	1.4
Midland, TX	0.1	56.2	D	D	D	3.2	D	2.7	4.8	19 380	120	2 372	61 377	9.2
Milwaukee-Waukesha-West Allis, WI	0.1	D	4.3	17.0	10.1	5.2	10.0	13.1	11.2	285 730	182	47 331	673 016	0.5
Minneapolis-St. Paul-Bloomington, MN	0.2	0.1	5.0	11.9	D	5.0	12.5	D	12.0	529 530	151	60 844	1 425 849	2.8
Missoula, MT	-0.1	D	6.2	3.5	D	8.9	6.5	18.0	20.0	20 035	178	2 132	51 869	3.5
Mobile, AL	0.3	0.8	7.0	14.8	8.8	6.7	6.4	11.6	15.2	88 830	214	15 331	182 025	2.1

1. Per 1,000 resident population estimated as of July 1, 2011 of the year shown.

Table C. Metropolitan Areas — **Housing, Labor Force, and Employment**

Area name	Housing units, 2014								Civilian labor force, 2015		Unemployment		Civilian employment[5], 2014		
	Occupied units													Percent	
	Owner-occupied				Renter-occupied										
				Median owner cost as a percent of income			Median rent as a percent of income	Percent with a computer		Percent change, 2013–2014				Management, professional, and related occupations	Construction, production, and related occupations
	Total	Percent	Median value[1]	With a mortgage	Without a mortgage[2]	Median rent[3]			Total		Total	Rate[4]	Total employed		
	89	90	91	92	93	94	95	96	97	98	99	100	101	102	103
Joplin, MO.............	66 564	67.1	109 300	20.2	11.2	709	29.5	79.0	87 769	1.7	3 804	4.3	82 706	30.2	28.2
Kahului-Wailuku-Lahaina, HI	54 355	56.9	534 300	28.7	10.0	1 237	30.3	85.8	84 233	1.9	3 164	3.8	81 247	29.5	20.6
Kalamazoo-Portage, MI	128 755	64.7	132 000	20.1	12.7	711	30.6	87.0	165 663	0.9	7 511	4.5	157 697	35.1	23.3
Kankakee, IL	40 732	69.0	136 700	21.7	12.0	850	28.8	85.4	55 211	-1.0	3 763	6.8	51 591	30.5	28.0
Kansas City, MO-KS	800 035	64.6	160 400	20.5	12.2	850	28.6	87.1	1 121 621	2.0	53 595	4.8	1 018 734	39.0	19.2
Kennewick-Richland, WA......	93 357	66.4	185 800	20.2	10.0	859	31.0	83.4	130 602	2.1	8 941	6.8	122 030	34.5	27.9
Killeen-Temple, TX	145 055	54.6	123 100	20.3	11.6	871	27.5	89.1	169 589	0.6	7 943	4.7	167 080	32.2	21.1
Kingsport-Bristol-Bristol, TN-VA	130 044	73.6	120 100	20.9	10.9	579	28.7	77.0	137 222	-1.5	7 860	5.7	127 611	31.5	23.3
Kingston, NY	69 522	68.8	217 100	26.5	17.5	1 012	37.1	85.0	88 438	0.3	4 339	4.9	84 877	39.1	18.5
Knoxville, TN	336 174	69.8	151 900	21.6	10.2	738	29.7	81.1	405 227	0.7	21 750	5.4	378 406	35.8	21.9
Kokomo, IN	34 026	65.4	101 500	18.5	10.0	687	25.7	82.4	36 934	0.0	1 844	5.0	35 846	26.4	33.9
La Crosse-Onalaska, WI-MN	54 762	67.3	157 000	21.6	12.4	761	29.8	86.7	77 256	0.1	3 005	3.9	73 019	36.8	23.7
Lafayette, LA	178 319	66.5	132 000	18.0	10.0	754	28.7	80.6	228 600	-2.2	14 384	6.3	230 239	29.7	27.3
Lafayette-West Lafayette, IN	77 266	57.3	136 300	19.2	10.0	800	35.9	88.1	107 381	1.6	4 517	4.2	97 657	37.7	23.7
Lake Charles, LA	76 395	67.1	114 800	18.9	10.0	792	31.7	82.6	102 160	3.9	5 448	5.3	87 549	28.6	26.9
Lake Havasu City-Kingman, AZ	81 292	67.2	120 200	26.6	10.2	769	28.0	82.1	79 310	1.2	6 363	8.0	66 530	26.7	23.1
Lakeland-Winter Haven, FL..	218 286	68.5	105 400	23.5	11.6	876	32.5	80.4	279 903	0.2	17 349	6.2	251 168	31.5	25.6
Lancaster, PA	194 764	67.8	188 100	21.4	12.6	894	29.5	82.1	275 869	1.3	10 997	4.0	265 900	32.9	28.3
Lansing-East Lansing, MI	183 357	64.1	129 100	20.6	12.7	783	31.0	89.0	242 918	0.4	10 391	4.3	224 986	39.0	19.3
Laredo, TX	70 418	61.2	108 600	24.4	13.1	749	37.7	72.1	112 415	1.1	5 328	4.7	100 864	25.4	23.5
Las Cruces, NM	75 530	61.2	135 600	23.3	10.0	731	31.7	82.1	93 179	-0.3	6 868	7.4	89 861	32.2	20.4
Las Vegas-Henderson-Paradise, NV	731 322	50.3	188 700	23.3	10.1	981	29.9	88.0	1 047 528	2.2	71 265	6.8	949 624	26.2	16.5
Lawrence, KS.....................	45 224	52.6	175 700	21.5	11.9	841	32.3	91.5	65 273	0.8	2 411	3.7	60 409	45.5	13.6
Lawton, OK	43 648	56.6	117 200	20.6	10.0	801	26.7	85.5	53 127	1.9	2 228	4.2	49 449	34.8	21.7
Lebanon, PA	51 234	69.4	168 100	21.9	12.6	775	25.7	82.8	70 133	0.1	3 071	4.4	64 072	29.2	27.1
Lewiston, ID-WA	25 932	66.1	163 200	22.4	10.6	684	25.8	85.1	30 473	1.3	1 222	4.0	28 151	32.0	22.4
Lewiston-Auburn, ME...........	44 267	65.5	153 800	22.5	13.9	702	30.8	83.3	54 566	-2.4	2 259	4.1	53 972	32.3	22.2
Lexington-Fayette, KY	196 716	57.7	162 900	19.8	10.1	755	29.5	87.6	254 913	-1.7	10 396	4.1	247 953	39.9	20.6
Lima, OH	39 412	66.3	98 800	20.0	12.5	612	31.5	82.5	48 106	-0.5	2 326	4.8	46 730	22.8	33.5
Lincoln, NE.......................	125 923	60.7	150 300	19.8	11.9	751	28.7	90.0	177 288	0.0	4 647	2.6	172 284	38.9	19.9
Little Rock-North Little Rock-Conway, AR.................	273 841	63.1	137 600	19.9	10.1	763	28.7	83.7	346 926	2.0	16 148	4.7	335 933	37.5	19.4
Logan, UT-ID	40 017	65.5	191 700	21.7	10.0	671	30.1	92.8	66 786	2.0	1 999	3.0	58 296	36.9	26.9
Longview, TX	78 567	68.1	113 300	20.1	10.2	777	30.3	80.2	100 907	-2.9	5 019	5.0	93 787	28.4	30.2
Longview, WA	40 036	63.3	165 400	24.2	11.1	738	33.8	83.6	44 276	1.6	3 359	7.6	38 474	27.7	31.3
Los Angeles-Long Beach-Anaheim, CA	4 287 974	48.3	494 900	27.6	11.1	1 309	35.1	88.2	6 608 778	0.1	408 367	6.2	6 286 841	37.0	19.6
Anaheim-Santa Ana-Irvine, CA Div 11244	1 018 862	57.4	591 800	26.3	10.5	1 572	33.9	92.4	1 597 071	1.2	71 507	4.5	1 542 361	40.5	16.5
Los Angeles-Long Beach-Glendale, CA Div 31084	3 269 112	45.5	464 400	28.1	11.3	1 239	35.5	86.9	5 011 707	-0.3	336 860	6.7	4 744 480	35.9	20.6
Louisville/Jefferson County, KY-IN	493 973	66.3	151 300	20.1	11.2	741	28.5	82.7	623 267	-1.0	29 471	4.7	610 480	35.3	24.8
Lubbock, TX	115 322	56.3	111 200	22.6	11.5	817	31.0	86.7	153 745	0.3	5 317	3.5	150 281	33.9	20.5
Lynchburg, VA	98 399	70.7	164 400	20.2	10.0	787	29.5	77.7	123 006	-1.0	6 026	4.9	120 104	33.5	25.9
Macon, GA........................	84 688	60.6	109 600	22.4	11.2	741	34.7	77.2	103 239	-0.8	6 542	6.3	90 793	33.6	20.0
Madera, CA.......................	42 895	61.3	201 100	25.4	11.5	929	34.0	81.6	60 566	-2.6	6 357	10.5	55 983	21.5	36.3
Madison, WI	259 371	60.0	221 100	22.2	13.1	895	29.4	91.2	376 678	1.3	12 730	3.4	351 765	46.2	16.4
Manchester-Nashua, NH	153 482	66.4	244 700	23.9	15.5	1 086	31.2	91.5	228 523	0.1	8 232	3.6	219 266	39.9	18.6
Manhattan, KS	34 452	50.3	177 200	20.2	10.0	879	35.2	91.2	50 089	2.9	1 675	3.3	46 460	43.5	19.2
Mankato-North Mankato, MN	37 736	65.3	169 600	21.3	11.2	813	29.0	86.4	59 195	1.2	1 690	2.9	54 933	35.4	18.3
Mansfield, OH	47 378	68.8	100 400	20.7	12.8	625	29.6	78.5	53 647	-1.6	2 986	5.6	49 413	29.0	30.8
McAllen-Edinburg-Mission, TX	226 000	68.0	79 400	23.8	13.2	668	35.4	77.5	331 632	-0.1	26 299	7.9	302 524	27.3	23.0
Medford, OR	83 131	62.2	222 900	24.7	13.5	885	33.3	88.8	97 648	1.0	6 751	6.9	89 016	32.3	22.4
Memphis, TN-MS-AR............	493 399	60.5	132 900	22.4	12.1	851	33.4	81.1	614 498	0.3	39 766	6.5	606 338	33.1	24.5
Merced, CA.......................	79 255	49.8	173 000	25.6	10.0	858	31.1	83.7	115 086	0.1	13 063	11.4	101 101	24.3	37.3
Miami-Fort Lauderdale-West Palm Beach, FL.............	2 047 325	59.6	210 000	27.4	14.9	1 146	37.6	85.6	3 020 429	0.7	166 830	5.5	2 796 169	33.3	18.1
Fort Lauderdale-Pompano Beach-Deerfield Beach, FL...............................	665 192	61.8	200 900	27.6	16.0	1 194	35.4	87.8	992 392	0.3	49 980	5.0	916 222	34.7	16.8
Miami-Miami Beach-Kendall, FL Div 33124	843 887	52.7	216 000	28.6	14.4	1 111	39.5	83.0	1 334 402	0.8	81 983	6.1	1 240 549	31.5	19.8
West Palm Beach-Boca Raton-Delray Beach, FL Div 48.....................	538 246	67.5	211 200	25.1	14.7	1 155	36.5	87.0	693 635	1.0	34 867	5.0	639 398	35.0	16.5
Michigan City-La Porte, IN....	42 068	69.1	128 300	20.1	11.4	712	29.6	86.0	48 522	-0.8	3 033	6.3	46 750	28.1	32.9
Midland, MI	33 579	74.6	126 200	20.3	12.3	713	31.9	83.7	41 702	-0.3	1 941	4.7	38 086	40.0	20.2
Midland, TX.......................	55 814	66.3	165 600	19.0	10.0	1 210	24.9	88.6	91 038	-2.8	3 143	3.5	85 583	36.0	29.1
Milwaukee-Waukesha-West Allis, WI	626 248	59.6	190 400	22.5	14.1	836	31.4	85.1	822 946	-0.1	41 090	5.0	779 629	39.5	20.4
Minneapolis-St. Paul-Bloomington, MN	1 337 263	69.9	216 400	20.8	11.0	938	29.5	90.3	1 938 857	0.8	66 767	3.4	1 883 341	43.6	17.6
Missoula, MT	46 407	58.4	246 800	23.4	13.4	745	32.9	91.3	61 143	1.3	2 365	3.9	61 099	39.1	16.3
Mobile, AL	153 450	65.2	120 700	21.4	10.5	822	33.5	77.4	183 097	-1.2	12 811	7.0	171 194	30.9	25.4

1. Specified owner-occupied units.   2. A value of 10.0 represents 10 percent or less.   3. Specified renter-occupied units.   4. Percent of civilian labor force.
5. Persons 16 years old and over.

Table C. Metropolitan Areas — **Nonfarm Employment and Agriculture**

Area name	Private nonfarm establishments, employment and payroll, 2014									Agriculture, 2012			
	Number of establishments	Employment						Annual payroll		Farms			Farm operators whose principal occupation is farming (percent)
		Total	Health care and social assistance	Manufacturing	Retail trade	Finance and insurance	Professional, scientific, and technical services	Total (mil dol)	Average per employee (dollars)	Number	Percent with: Fewer than 50 acres	Percent with: 500 acres or more	
	104	105	106	107	108	109	110	111	112	113	114	115	116
Joplin, MO..................	3 980	68 025	12 599	11 566	9 947	1 671	1 930	2 473	36 352	2 877	35.9	6.1	39.6
Kahului-Wailuku-Lahaina, HI	4 500	63 431	6 018	1 198	9 674	935	1 497	2 300	36 253	1 128	89.0	3.5	54.0
Kalamazoo-Portage, MI	6 783	119 742	20 746	18 693	15 636	6 031	5 437	5 292	44 193	1 847	52.1	6.2	51.4
Kankakee, IL.................	2 360	36 792	7 355	5 599	5 724	1 495	761	1 328	36 103	818	33.7	24.4	56.8
Kansas City, MO-KS.........	51 485	908 323	135 050	77 520	109 688	60 161	76 500	43 793	48 213	12 757	35.5	10.8	42.8
Kennewick-Richland, WA.....	5 533	79 211	12 181	7 002	12 809	2 029	7 320	3 687	46 545	2 392	61.8	14.9	51.4
Killeen-Temple, TX	6 022	101 153	26 348	7 079	16 427	3 909	4 052	3 655	36 130	4 858	42.7	11.4	38.9
Kingsport-Bristol-Bristol, TN-VA	5 988	104 930	17 909	24 721	15 356	3 058	3 039	4 223	40 241	5 405	45.3	2.7	40.6
Kingston, NY.................	4 727	45 384	9 193	3 514	8 986	2 024	1 595	1 529	33 688	486	48.4	5.1	67.3
Knoxville, TN..............	17 489	319 576	49 739	33 618	45 138	14 570	23 130	13 274	41 536	5 613	46.9	1.8	42.6
Kokomo, IN.................	1 742	31 758	5 413	9 768	4 963	690	685	1 340	42 203	476	40.8	15.5	57.4
La Crosse-Onalaska, WI-MN	3 440	65 254	11 939	7 678	9 520	3 268	1 962	2 429	37 218	1 668	18.8	10.7	47.8
Lafayette, LA................	13 350	198 883	32 425	16 224	26 738	5 520	11 313	9 299	46 758	3 276	53.8	10.9	47.0
Lafayette-West Lafayette, IN	3 975	69 505	9 778	17 256	9 564	2 875	2 562	2 718	39 111	1 574	42.7	22.9	48.7
Lake Charles, LA	4 532	73 507	13 607	9 094	10 920	2 131	4 452	3 146	42 795	1 244	44.3	12.4	35.4
Lake Havasu City-Kingman, AZ	3 630	40 695	8 585	2 853	9 255	1 009	945	1 336	32 841	335	59.1	23.9	51.3
Lakeland-Winter Haven, FL..	11 021	171 305	27 107	14 418	24 889	11 348	5 774	6 558	38 285	2 415	64.4	7.2	45.3
Lancaster, PA...............	12 414	220 898	35 953	33 882	30 338	7 163	10 311	8 931	40 430	5 657	44.1	1.3	72.2
Lansing-East Lansing, MI	9 486	160 216	27 725	17 357	21 489	12 774	7 617	6 682	41 704	3 235	46.2	9.9	49.0
Laredo, TX..................	5 123	73 755	14 961	604	13 723	2 598	1 952	2 147	29 105	696	15.1	48.6	48.6
Las Cruces, NM..............	3 546	50 861	13 190	2 371	8 034	1 649	5 064	1 594	31 337	2 184	85.6	4.5	37.7
Las Vegas-Henderson-Paradise, NV	42 031	797 871	76 305	18 913	104 745	25 280	41 981	31 099	38 977	252	78.6	2.0	46.8
Lawrence, KS.................	2 675	38 850	6 227	3 370	6 188	1 029	1 695	1 182	30 424	945	38.5	9.7	35.8
Lawton, OK.................	2 237	33 026	6 228	3 538	5 777	1 724	968	1 101	33 332	1 607	19.1	27.8	46.2
Lebanon, PA................	2 641	44 254	8 264	9 055	6 853	950	1 133	1 589	35 898	1 219	48.2	2.3	58.9
Lewiston, ID-WA	1 546	21 337	3 937	4 046	3 662	1 405	804	774	36 269	615	39.5	33.0	54.6
Lewiston-Auburn, ME..........	2 667	44 283	9 590	5 082	6 087	3 155	2 122	1 681	37 968	463	51.6	5.0	56.4
Lexington-Fayette, KY	12 195	216 411	34 889	26 571	27 538	6 394	15 122	8 863	40 954	4 727	44.1	7.6	46.4
Lima, OH...................	2 436	44 435	10 922	7 274	5 956	1 180	905	1 747	39 321	904	38.8	11.8	42.9
Lincoln, NE.................	8 556	134 985	24 434	12 800	18 610	10 286	8 560	5 238	38 803	2 828	46.0	17.8	38.7
Little Rock-North Little Rock-Conway, AR................	17 632	274 359	54 054	21 103	38 484	15 053	14 414	11 362	41 414	3 534	40.0	9.0	42.9
Logan, UT-ID	3 380	41 306	5 755	11 438	6 290	1 344	2 959	1 300	31 484	2 051	46.9	14.0	41.4
Longview, TX................	5 408	84 869	12 574	11 547	11 759	2 924	3 719	3 607	42 496	3 671	42.6	5.3	35.3
Longview, WA................	2 119	30 038	5 444	6 402	4 681	821	679	1 377	45 831	492	72.4	2.8	46.7
Los Angeles-Long Beach-Anaheim, CA................	349 938	5 354 029	665 406	501 325	564 969	243 111	513 826	280 218	52 338	1 606	88.2	3.3	60.2
Anaheim-Santa Ana-Irvine, CA Div 11244	NA	NA	NA	NA	NA	NA	NA	NA	NA	312	85.3	4.8	58.7
Los Angeles-Long Beach-Glendale, CA Div 31084	NA	NA	NA	NA	NA	NA	NA	NA	NA	1 294	88.9	2.9	60.6
Louisville/Jefferson County, KY-IN	28 932	540 954	82 857	67 856	60 670	33 153	28 539	23 332	43 131	7 555	48.0	4.9	43.3
Lubbock, TX..................	7 196	112 158	23 194	5 324	18 437	5 789	4 159	3 846	34 290	2 002	23.9	35.5	50.1
Lynchburg, VA	5 871	95 088	14 000	15 889	14 437	3 845	5 135	3 705	38 967	2 966	29.9	7.5	40.9
Macon, GA..................	5 122	83 900	16 887	5 409	11 857	9 038	3 095	3 039	36 227	734	38.4	6.7	44.0
Madera, CA.................	1 918	25 722	5 811	3 725	3 598	454	482	1 001	38 910	1 507	44.8	14.3	57.9
Madison, WI.................	16 492	308 317	51 120	32 717	39 817	24 066	21 611	14 637	47 474	7 446	38.4	8.5	48.1
Manchester-Nashua, NH	10 889	180 527	28 859	26 505	28 018	10 330	10 772	9 693	53 691	688	64.0	1.5	50.0
Manhattan, KS................	2 176	28 976	4 710	2 061	6 171	1 083	1 251	902	31 129	1 383	23.1	23.4	43.5
Mankato-North Mankato, MN	2 573	47 621	10 525	7 650	7 097	1 200	1 549	1 701	35 730	1 834	25.5	21.8	57.4
Mansfield, OH................	2 613	43 022	7 686	8 362	6 302	1 022	928	1 449	33 678	1 010	37.2	5.0	52.0
McAllen-Edinburg-Mission, TX	11 780	181 601	55 588	6 008	37 203	6 329	5 750	4 974	27 389	2 161	57.9	14.7	51.4
Medford, OR.................	5 951	67 428	12 986	6 196	11 771	2 248	2 222	2 447	36 285	1 722	72.1	2.4	56.2
Memphis, TN-MS-AR...........	25 224	523 501	80 471	37 266	63 767	18 215	18 249	23 620	45 119	3 934	32.7	15.3	44.0
Merced, CA.................	2 903	42 083	6 738	9 390	8 069	992	795	1 520	36 124	2 486	56.7	12.8	64.5
Miami-Fort Lauderdale-West Palm Beach, FL	184 069	2 052 560	302 910	66 640	317 567	100 158	154 855	92 919	45 270	4 978	92.1	1.9	55.8
Fort Lauderdale-Pompano Beach-Deerfield Beach, FL..	NA	NA	NA	NA	NA	NA	NA	NA	NA	615	93.7	1.3	50.1
Miami-Miami Beach-Kendall, FL Div 33124	NA	NA	NA	NA	NA	NA	NA	NA	NA	2 954	92.8	1.2	56.5
West Palm Beach-Boca Raton-Delray Beach, FL Div 48................	NA	NA	NA	NA	NA	NA	NA	NA	NA	1 409	90.0	3.5	56.7
Michigan City-La Porte, IN....	2 290	33 509	5 349	7 092	5 824	794	930	1 206	35 998	731	43.8	17.1	51.4
Midland, MI	1 908	34 973	6 145	6 005	4 163	1 064	891	2 304	65 880	555	47.9	7.0	46.7
Midland, TX.................	5 250	88 906	6 976	3 118	9 440	2 062	4 652	6 053	68 087	954	32.8	29.6	38.5
Milwaukee-Waukesha-West Allis, WI..................	37 739	764 662	127 129	113 282	80 324	51 935	39 837	37 466	48 997	1 767	47.1	7.6	52.2
Minneapolis-St. Paul-Bloomington, MN	93 843	1 753 004	275 110	178 365	184 468	120 511	121 098	94 918	54 146	13 251	40.4	9.2	49.4
Missoula, MT.................	4 225	49 006	10 261	1 612	8 140	1 941	3 528	1 680	34 273	637	58.4	10.0	38.3
Mobile, AL..................	8 492	142 481	19 403	16 571	20 370	5 400	8 911	5 650	39 654	698	60.9	4.4	48.6

Table C. Metropolitan Areas — **Agriculture**

Table C. Metropolitan Areas — **Agriculture**

Agriculture, 2012 (cont.)

Area name	Land in farms — Acreage (1,000)	Land in farms — Percent change, 2007–2012	Acres — Average size of farm	Acres — Total irrigated (1,000)	Acres — Total cropland (1,000)	Value of land and buildings (dollars) — Average per farm	Value of land and buildings (dollars) — Average per acre	Value of machinery and equipment, average per farm (dollars)	Value of products sold — Total (mil dol)	Value of products sold — Average per farm (dollars)	Percent from: Crops	Percent from: Live-stock and poultry products	Percent of farms with sales of: $10,000 or more	Percent of farms with sales of: $100,000 or more	Government payments — Total ($1,000)	Government payments — Percent of farms
	117	118	119	120	121	122	123	124	125	126	127	128	129	130	131	132
Joplin, MO	494	-2.0	172	3.8	221.1	422 288	2 457	61 142	352.0	122 343	13.5	86.5	43.1	9.2	3 356	26.2
Kahului-Wailuku-Lahaina, HI	229	1.6	203	41.5	49.6	1 998 207	9 836	53 229	188.1	166 755	96.5	3.5	37.1	7.1	558	10.5
Kalamazoo-Portage, MI	319	-3.5	173	73.1	237.9	782 997	4 538	138 933	438.6	237 484	81.1	18.9	47.4	18.5	4 898	23.6
Kankakee, IL	343	-11.2	419	14.6	327.9	2 769 373	6 612	264 800	287.5	351 460	90.2	9.8	71.8	48.5	5 827	76.5
Kansas City, MO-KS	3 124	-5.1	245	D	1 916.0	749 999	3 062	83 462	785.7	61 589	68.9	31.1	41.2	10.1	34 070	44.7
Kennewick-Richland, WA	1 329	7.0	555	404.5	971.3	1 569 965	2 827	192 328	1 663.2	695 308	D	D	44.1	26.5	14 367	21.2
Killeen-Temple, TX	1 329	-0.5	274	3.7	306.5	727 280	2 658	57 979	169.6	34 905	45.8	54.2	25.2	4.0	3 614	15.2
Kingsport-Bristol-Bristol, TN-VA	569	-2.9	105	0.5	161.6	374 389	3 558	48 349	126.4	23 393	15.2	84.8	26.1	3.5	6 226	30.7
Kingston, NY	71	-5.3	147	4.2	26.1	738 835	5 042	103 237	55.9	115 019	83.0	17.0	43.0	12.6	328	10.1
Knoxville, TN	538	-6.7	96	1.6	194.1	495 626	5 174	57 244	158.2	28 176	56.8	43.2	22.7	2.2	1 294	13.0
Kokomo, IN	144	-11.1	303	D	134.5	1 924 391	6 353	182 880	140.4	294 874	81.1	18.9	68.1	37.2	2 993	67.0
La Crosse-Onalaska, WI-MN	388	-5.3	233	1.1	216.2	792 875	3 409	126 932	232.8	139 555	48.7	51.3	56.6	25.2	7 429	71.6
Lafayette, LA	761	-3.1	232	152.3	537.5	627 401	2 702	115 382	440.9	134 575	84.1	15.9	32.9	11.7	14 740	39.4
Lafayette-West Lafayette, IN	679	-0.4	431	D	638.6	2 869 720	6 657	239 864	583.0	370 363	75.3	24.7	57.4	39.8	12 438	64.2
Lake Charles, LA	573	-1.8	461	27.4	141.2	1 029 838	2 235	77 753	52.3	42 007	60.6	39.4	27.3	6.2	3 549	22.7
Lake Havasu City-Kingman, AZ	1 244	45.0	3 714	20.8	29.1	1 792 487	483	75 743	30.2	90 102	68.9	31.1	33.7	11.9	1 242	11.3
Lakeland-Winter Haven, FL	521	-5.1	216	79.9	125.1	1 182 091	5 480	64 954	350.3	145 042	90.2	9.8	48.1	18.3	419	1.4
Lancaster, PA	439	3.3	78	6.1	332.0	973 388	12 529	101 987	1 475.0	260 731	17.7	82.3	74.2	48.4	5 843	18.4
Lansing-East Lansing, MI	668	-1.8	206	7.4	549.2	837 223	4 057	126 959	513.0	158 584	63.2	36.8	46.4	19.6	9 730	43.6
Laredo, TX	2 098	13.1	3 015	2.6	25.2	3 265 045	1 083	57 487	30.3	43 476	2.8	97.2	31.2	7.0	1 169	14.1
Las Cruces, NM	660	12.0	302	76.3	93.8	540 877	1 790	75 238	351.0	160 729	47.5	52.5	23.9	8.1	1 453	9.5
Las Vegas-Henderson-Paradise, NV	16	-82.3	62	3.7	4.4	347 790	5 611	66 325	6.8	27 083	48.2	51.8	33.7	4.4	34	3.6
Lawrence, KS	211	-4.5	223	3.3	127.3	636 186	2 854	82 519	43.9	46 436	66.2	33.8	37.7	8.4	2 332	46.9
Lawton, OK	863	-0.2	537	0.8	322.6	678 021	1 263	80 981	111.8	69 573	41.7	58.3	46.7	14.1	8 694	54.8
Lebanon, PA	121	7.0	100	1.5	97.4	1 052 028	10 562	122 164	348.9	286 245	13.1	86.9	64.1	37.6	2 250	26.6
Lewiston, ID-WA	585	-6.7	952	1.3	265.7	1 245 914	1 309	136 184	101.7	165 337	87.2	12.8	44.4	26.0	7 534	54.0
Lewiston-Auburn, ME	59	16.9	128	0.8	22.0	329 181	2 564	72 955	53.8	116 266	22.1	77.9	32.8	8.0	445	15.6
Lexington-Fayette, KY	759	-6.0	161	3.1	281.9	895 506	5 577	77 863	459.8	97 273	19.6	80.4	42.7	11.0	7 009	31.4
Lima, OH	183	-2.2	203	D	163.0	1 070 715	5 284	144 872	144.1	159 393	76.2	23.8	61.7	30.3	3 593	74.4
Lincoln, NE	844	11.9	298	151.4	696.9	1 423 260	4 770	156 127	486.3	171 957	68.0	32.0	48.6	23.8	15 528	63.6
Little Rock-North Little Rock-Conway, AR	788	-2.6	223	233.1	424.9	654 503	2 936	91 716	348.0	98 485	68.6	31.4	33.2	7.8	16 332	22.1
Logan, UT-ID	531	11.5	259	137.5	278.0	718 986	2 776	105 031	249.0	121 400	24.9	75.1	44.4	16.3	5 876	39.8
Longview, TX	525	-3.6	143	1.2	98.9	371 975	2 602	49 545	139.5	37 992	18.1	81.9	22.0	2.9	634	2.3
Longview, WA	39	27.1	79	7.6	18.6	689 236	8 693	67 535	28.8	58 482	D	D	19.5	6.9	44	1.6
Los Angeles-Long Beach-Anaheim, CA	152	-22.3	95	47.7	74.7	1 534 556	16 194	50 774	351.6	218 935	94.1	5.9	35.6	12.9	290	3.4
Anaheim-Santa Ana-Irvine, CA Div 11244	60	-30.8	194	8.1	15.2	4 237 538	21 854	70 968	158.5	508 055	99.0	1.0	41.3	18.3	43	4.8
Los Angeles-Long Beach-Glendale, CA Div 31084	92	-15.5	71	39.7	59.6	882 832	12 459	45 905	193.1	149 225	90.1	9.9	34.2	11.6	247	3.1
Louisville/Jefferson County, KY-IN	1 068	-8.0	141	D	607.7	573 173	4 054	69 317	410.6	54 342	60.1	39.9	33.6	7.7	13 211	37.0
Lubbock, TX	1 533	-1.9	766	338.8	1 130.1	915 687	1 196	206 678	314.0	156 835	72.9	27.1	45.8	27.4	28 253	73.9
Lynchburg, VA	552	6.9	186	D	151.2	674 238	3 620	60 278	74.4	25 088	28.4	71.6	35.9	4.1	2 334	18.5
Macon, GA	145	-14.1	197	10.1	46.0	599 775	3 039	77 030	120.5	164 170	31.4	68.6	28.5	10.6	1 459	19.1
Madera, CA	654	-3.8	434	292.3	304.2	3 302 033	7 614	182 022	1 602.8	1 063 547	77.4	22.6	70.2	46.8	2 400	11.4
Madison, WI	1 466	-3.8	197	14.2	1 067.2	984 545	5 002	132 972	1 081.6	145 256	40.2	59.8	49.3	22.9	31 173	62.4
Manchester-Nashua, NH	48	-5.0	69	0.7	11.1	450 385	6 495	52 282	22.5	32 759	69.8	30.2	22.8	7.0	261	6.8
Manhattan, KS	628	-5.0	454	26.0	264.3	853 839	1 881	103 492	171.4	123 929	51.7	48.3	54.2	19.6	4 125	59.9
Mankato-North Mankato, MN	651	-5.6	355	1.7	588.8	2 286 660	6 445	257 171	892.1	486 398	49.3	50.7	71.0	49.7	13 782	82.1
Mansfield, OH	161	9.6	159	0.1	120.3	789 172	4 962	110 557	128.7	127 408	51.7	48.3	55.0	29.5	1 806	32.5
McAllen-Edinburg-Mission, TX	795	10.0	368	183.6	465.6	1 117 900	3 038	115 296	452.8	209 517	91.7	8.3	33.2	14.2	9 106	20.0
Medford, OR	214	-12.3	124	36.5	32.8	582 023	4 682	40 415	64.1	37 240	57.6	42.4	25.7	3.4	252	3.8
Memphis, TN-MS-AR	1 573	-0.6	400	D	1 086.1	1 072 560	2 682	131 704	661.4	168 123	D	D	32.2	13.4	26 335	44.6
Merced, CA	979	-6.0	394	468.2	522.6	3 045 778	7 737	236 454	2 967.5	1 193 694	42.9	57.1	76.0	45.7	9 528	20.2
Miami-Fort Lauderdale-West Palm Beach, FL	610	1.4	122	409.8	509.9	1 213 970	9 911	83 861	1 650.7	331 597	98.0	2.0	52.0	15.2	8 726	7.1
Fort Lauderdale-Pompano Beach-Deerfield Beach, FL	14	65.9	24	1.8	4.3	540 185	22 916	31 886	47.4	77 099	91.2	8.8	41.0	8.6	246	2.9
Miami-Miami Beach-Kendall, FL Div 33124	81	21.3	28	45.2	64.9	699 727	25 423	47 644	604.2	204 549	98.0	2.0	58.5	16.0	6 944	8.5
West Palm Beach-Boca Raton-Delray Beach, FL Div 48	514	-2.2	365	362.7	440.7	2 586 187	7 090	182 476	999.0	709 041	98.3	1.7	43.2	16.2	1 536	6.0
Michigan City-La Porte, IN	228	-11.0	312	54.4	209.3	1 896 432	6 084	188 253	223.1	305 215	80.5	19.5	55.7	33.8	4 036	58.4
Midland, MI	90	-1.2	161	1.0	69.5	580 838	3 600	98 339	70.1	126 285	67.9	32.1	39.1	14.1	2 310	44.3
Midland, TX	858	-6.2	899	27.9	342.0	1 097 884	1 221	116 852	37.5	39 285	78.2	21.8	21.3	8.8	7 024	48.4
Milwaukee-Waukesha-West Allis, WI	295	0.9	167	2.2	238.1	1 011 705	6 056	128 100	250.1	141 516	49.0	51.0	50.8	22.7	5 478	43.0
Minneapolis-St. Paul-Bloomington, MN	2 598	-1.6	196	105.7	2 044.9	1 015 662	5 180	136 564	2 169.8	163 748	66.3	33.7	52.7	22.9	43 747	54.6
Missoula, MT	247	-12.3	388	16.8	19.9	1 074 215	2 769	40 830	13.6	21 355	29.8	70.2	22.1	4.6	395	9.4
Mobile, AL	89	-21.9	127	2.8	36.6	516 701	4 062	78 354	84.7	121 289	90.7	9.3	33.2	8.5	796	12.2

Table C. Metropolitan Areas — Water Use, Wholesale Trade, Retail Trade, and Real Estate

Area name	Water use, 2010		Wholesale trade,[1] 2012				Retail trade, 2012				Real estate and rental and leasing, 2012			
	Total water withdrawn (mil gal/day)	Gallons withdrawn per person per day	Number of establishments	Number of employees	Sales (mil dol)	Annual payroll (mil dol)	Number of establishments	Number of employees	Sales (mil dol)	Annual payroll (mil dol)	Number of establishments	Number of employees	Receipts (mil dol)	Annual payroll (mil dol)
	133	134	135	136	137	138	139	140	141	142	143	144	145	146
Joplin, MO	40.5	231	184	2 895	2 647.0	118.9	710	9 859	2 841.3	215.3	143	583	86.0	14.9
Kahului-Wailuku-Lahaina, HI	278.1	1 795	140	1 141	714.6	50.4	759	9 174	2 461.0	258.2	306	2 022	454.4	70.8
Kalamazoo-Portage, MI	218.7	670	287	D	D	D	1 115	14 993	3 764.0	338.3	242	2 430	239.0	73.5
Kankakee, IL	26.8	236	119	2 196	1 443.3	95.0	370	5 548	1 463.3	120.0	95	371	70.9	10.6
Kansas City, MO-KS	1 626.1	809	2 529	42 419	52 860.3	2 756.7	6 294	104 436	29 998.3	2 579.3	2 430	13 232	3 092.0	568.9
Kennewick-Richland, WA	894.8	3 532	222	2 512	2 971.9	112.3	772	11 935	3 382.4	307.4	300	1 244	220.5	37.3
Killeen-Temple, TX	80.7	199	143	2 717	3 687.0	139.5	1 093	15 406	4 328.6	344.5	350	1 640	241.7	55.4
Kingsport-Bristol-Bristol, TN-VA	929.6	3 003	275	3 317	1 816.0	121.0	1 101	15 030	3 779.9	327.2	208	741	126.5	23.1
Kingston, NY	458.2	2 511	159	1 504	810.4	71.3	733	8 606	2 324.9	211.8	195	732	116.6	22.0
Knoxville, TN	699.1	835	867	12 090	8 194.7	621.5	2 923	44 783	11 873.6	1 086.3	791	4 105	764.5	149.0
Kokomo, IN	17.5	212	62	559	512.7	31.6	328	4 927	1 193.3	104.0	71	311	50.4	8.9
La Crosse-Onalaska, WI-MN	37.3	279	137	2 724	6 239.4	119.7	491	9 017	2 027.3	185.4	125	801	101.7	20.9
Lafayette, LA	436.2	935	708	10 557	5 896.8	547.1	1 856	25 397	7 064.9	625.9	688	6 875	2 269.2	460.8
Lafayette-West Lafayette, IN	39.9	198	142	1 637	1 256.9	69.6	611	9 409	2 378.7	200.9	181	892	148.2	30.0
Lake Charles, LA	250.2	1 254	199	2 196	1 971.0	102.7	772	10 240	3 155.4	241.0	216	1 018	235.6	41.5
Lake Havasu City-Kingman, AZ	121.2	605	114	816	391.1	30.5	593	8 918	2 712.7	211.4	199	628	83.2	15.6
Lakeland-Winter Haven, FL	298.7	496	544	8 056	10 601.3	394.0	1 756	22 988	6 495.3	558.8	651	2 928	510.6	93.1
Lancaster, PA	78.2	151	582	10 776	8 764.0	496.7	1 917	29 783	6 899.6	669.6	342	2 009	396.6	79.1
Lansing-East Lansing, MI	239.1	515	327	5 044	7 143.8	236.0	1 416	20 926	5 462.7	475.9	385	2 530	349.8	88.0
Laredo, TX	43.5	174	357	2 839	2 410.1	97.0	784	12 356	3 217.6	257.8	199	692	132.4	22.0
Las Cruces, NM	397.2	1 899	102	D	D	D	496	7 916	1 965.4	167.7	209	690	116.6	18.9
Las Vegas-Henderson-Paradise, NV	486.6	249	1 630	16 747	11 597.1	958.8	5 712	95 369	27 971.7	2 531.6	2 794	17 855	3 700.3	647.4
Lawrence, KS	19.1	172	71	610	282.9	24.6	373	6 066	1 354.2	122.6	157	761	97.7	20.9
Lawton, OK	32.1	247	64	D	D	D	424	5 410	1 444.7	119.5	126	519	90.6	16.5
Lebanon, PA	14.6	109	99	2 679	3 913.7	112.7	431	6 597	1 695.7	158.6	70	309	40.5	7.8
Lewiston, ID-WA	133.2	2 188	55	613	497.2	26.3	259	3 343	968.8	87.2	60	280	37.3	7.6
Lewiston-Auburn, ME	15.3	142	102	1 236	473.9	54.6	439	6 018	1 818.1	138.5	111	376	62.9	11.6
Lexington-Fayette, KY	183.8	389	473	9 899	9 127.9	669.6	1 734	27 528	7 438.5	652.4	554	2 474	505.0	85.7
Lima, OH	34.6	325	124	2 287	1 388.8	91.6	417	6 072	1 641.5	134.3	85	376	55.2	11.0
Lincoln, NE	73.2	242	305	4 427	3 667.9	183.4	1 063	17 686	4 428.3	398.8	353	1 726	257.6	56.7
Little Rock-North Little Rock-Conway, AR	619.6	885	868	12 971	9 583.7	658.8	2 605	37 471	10 847.9	901.3	836	4 140	765.8	147.3
Logan, UT-ID	513.5	4 094	119	978	613.1	37.7	447	5 980	1 270.6	118.4	190	D	D	D
Longview, TX	1 708.9	7 972	290	3 950	2 602.1	209.8	866	11 363	3 285.3	283.8	231	1 303	427.0	65.6
Longview, WA	146.6	1 431	85	1 036	2 021.4	53.2	333	4 644	1 188.3	113.8	104	337	50.7	8.5
Los Angeles-Long Beach-Anaheim, CA	3 829.4	298	27 704	317 329	297 600.8	18 082.1	37 817	528 453	166 583.0	14 835.1	19 194	120 995	38 846.0	6 397.2
Anaheim-Santa Ana-Irvine, CA Div 11244	765.4	254	6 434	79 685	97 796.0	5 200.7	9 390	143 012	45 193.6	4 135.3	5 320	38 952	9 259.7	1 921.2
Los Angeles-Long Beach-Glendale, CA Div 31084	3 064.0	312	21 270	237 644	199 804.8	12 881.4	28 427	385 441	121 389.4	10 699.7	13 874	82 043	29 586.3	4 476.1
Louisville/Jefferson County, KY-IN	1 008.9	816	1 322	19 345	15 452.9	992.4	4 011	59 405	16 279.7	1 413.5	1 250	8 356	3 099.2	326.1
Lubbock, TX	260.9	897	389	D	D	D	1 073	16 669	4 850.9	409.5	399	D	D	D
Lynchburg, VA	47.7	189	178	2 025	1 098.8	87.6	939	13 555	3 665.7	315.0	269	773	131.2	23.3
Macon, GA	131.1	565	224	2 679	1 666.2	128.0	980	11 588	2 932.4	260.9	225	969	179.2	32.4
Madera, CA	748.7	4 963	76	815	508.9	37.8	326	3 455	1 012.9	84.3	75	336	38.4	8.5
Madison, WI	116.5	192	709	13 072	8 970.5	679.2	2 123	38 927	11 740.7	1 042.3	695	4 410	992.1	164.6
Manchester-Nashua, NH	55.1	137	537	6 822	4 749.3	470.5	1 584	26 984	7 724.7	700.9	387	2 697	565.9	123.8
Manhattan, KS	46.0	496	56	725	307.1	30.8	353	6 208	1 242.8	130.0	129	511	74.1	13.2
Mankato-North Mankato, MN	41.1	425	123	1 798	1 325.4	85.2	395	6 930	1 645.7	151.2	104	692	75.5	16.9
Mansfield, OH	17.0	137	104	1 993	939.2	78.9	438	6 528	1 501.2	139.9	102	417	49.2	9.1
McAllen-Edinburg-Mission, TX	470.2	607	841	D	D	D	2 219	33 566	9 296.8	733.9	497	2 209	445.0	61.9
Medford, OR	392.4	1 931	206	1 771	828.4	76.8	865	11 223	3 202.7	297.5	306	1 043	164.1	26.3
Memphis, TN-MS-AR	1 088.0	821	1 435	28 963	41 205.9	1 583.6	4 178	61 787	26 311.6	1 598.5	1 125	7 663	1 573.2	327.6
Merced, CA	1 494.7	5 843	112	1 635	2 260.2	71.2	528	7 497	1 959.5	173.3	152	532	79.1	14.6
Miami-Fort Lauderdale-West Palm Beach, FL	2 446.7	440	14 077	109 773	124 749.4	5 674.1	22 695	290 852	90 104.2	7 832.7	10 475	48 690	11 005.1	1 996.5
Fort Lauderdale-Pompano Beach-Deerfield Beach, FL	1 279.1	732	3 902	33 141	33 606.6	1 781.8	7 070	97 344	32 042.9	2 675.4	3 237	17 682	3 934.9	701.7
Miami-Miami Beach-Kendall, FL Div 33124	461.0	185	8 242	61 377	78 985.4	3 003.6	10 389	123 883	38 361.2	3 252.7	4 776	19 563	4 936.4	811.9
West Palm Beach-Boca Raton-Delray Beach, FL Div 48	706.5	535	1 933	15 255	12 157.3	888.7	5 236	69 625	19 700.1	1 904.6	2 462	11 445	2 133.8	482.9
Michigan City-La Porte, IN	44.0	395	100	1 161	694.9	46.8	457	5 845	1 367.8	116.2	84	367	95.2	10.6
Midland, MI	10.6	127	44	297	703.7	16.7	314	4 050	1 015.7	88.4	63	257	36.8	8.4
Midland, TX	73.9	521	272	D	D	D	515	7 607	3 019.3	221.5	267	1 505	491.4	79.1
Milwaukee-Waukesha-West Allis, WI	2 280.3	1 466	1 981	34 545	23 162.4	2 243.4	4 695	77 813	20 086.4	1 806.6	1 354	9 103	1 636.8	343.6
Minneapolis-St. Paul-Bloomington, MN	1 762.8	526	4 390	77 536	72 483.1	5 723.3	10 525	179 498	51 537.1	4 494.9	4 636	27 832	6 835.8	1 224.7
Missoula, MT	85.6	783	151	1 838	1 220.7	81.5	570	7 931	2 044.0	180.0	206	918	130.6	29.7
Mobile, AL	1 096.7	2 656	499	6 116	3 680.0	283.8	1 454	19 204	5 102.6	454.7	410	2 125	419.1	83.2

1. Merchant wholesalers, except manufacturers' sales branches and offices.

Table C. Metropolitan Areas

Professional Services, Manufacturing, and Accommodation and Food Services

Area name	Professional, scientific, and technical services, 2012				Manufacturing, 2012				Accommodation and food services, 2012			
	Number of establishments	Number of employees	Sales (mil dol)	Annual payroll (mil dol)	Number of establishments	Number of employees	Sales (mil dol)	Annual payroll (mil dol)	Number of establishments	Number of employees	Sales (mil dol)	Annual payroll (mil dol)
	147	148	149	150	151	152	153	154	155	156	157	158
Joplin, MO	250	D	D	D	243	11 659	4 282.8	486.5	358	6 644	297.2	81.6
Kahului-Wailuku-Lahaina, HI	390	1 381	186.4	67.0	99	997	D	41.1	499	19 943	2 307.5	625.7
Kalamazoo-Portage, MI	621	5 037	771.8	268.6	398	18 339	8 609.7	1 051.9	695	13 630	575.0	173.0
Kankakee, IL	152	735	64.1	24.5	100	4 889	4 842.8	269.7	219	3 675	160.3	47.4
Kansas City, MO-KS	6 155	69 705	13 938.8	5 014.4	1 744	74 320	40 520.9	4 025.8	3 910	82 476	4 552.6	1 254.3
Kennewick-Richland, WA	511	9 341	1 701.1	687.2	197	6 764	2 821.7	327.1	492	7 736	405.8	114.5
Killeen-Temple, TX	474	4 383	504.2	203.8	180	6 556	2 110.1	268.1	697	13 241	632.5	170.8
Kingsport-Bristol-Bristol, TN-VA	460	2 948	327.7	135.9	282	24 543	9 574.3	1 421.8	586	10 841	488.5	140.0
Kingston, NY	443	1 601	189.3	69.1	170	3 518	D	170.2	546	6 655	367.3	117.4
Knoxville, TN	1 691	21 671	2 523.0	1 399.6	727	33 148	13 060.5	1 823.5	1 507	32 820	1 566.1	466.9
Kokomo, IN	114	631	61.2	22.6	70	7 671	D	593.4	186	3 866	159.9	46.1
La Crosse-Onalaska, WI-MN	274	1 949	185.4	88.2	179	7 092	1 996.6	277.2	365	6 575	252.0	74.4
Lafayette, LA	1 761	10 784	1 848.4	631.0	582	19 339	9 405.7	1 128.7	969	19 563	1 026.7	290.3
Lafayette-West Lafayette, IN	331	2 418	345.0	108.9	161	16 598	13 028.7	935.4	446	8 493	383.2	104.9
Lake Charles, LA	432	5 212	479.4	222.9	128	8 620	44 186.6	688.2	358	10 817	984.6	210.8
Lake Havasu City-Kingman, AZ	239	931	72.4	30.8	133	2 566	D	109.5	382	5 787	256.7	74.3
Lakeland-Winter Haven, FL	1 036	6 724	768.7	300.4	401	14 200	9 822.2	681.0	788	15 188	797.9	220.1
Lancaster, PA	957	12 486	1 249.1	1 037.2	856	33 212	13 655.7	1 638.7	998	17 833	878.4	246.9
Lansing-East Lansing, MI	1 051	7 399	1 210.3	408.7	341	17 312	16 198.9	1 002.6	913	17 000	708.1	201.7
Laredo, TX	317	1 803	186.1	58.6	69	635	339.6	22.0	389	8 216	423.7	106.2
Las Cruces, NM	339	D	D	D	128	2 520	D	87.1	319	6 813	285.2	80.7
Las Vegas-Henderson-Paradise, NV	5 645	35 253	5 825.0	2 128.2	894	17 390	5 673.8	782.0	4 050	250 601	24 283.8	7 612.3
Lawrence, KS	292	D	D	D	69	3 079	1 217.3	136.1	301	6 511	261.1	72.2
Lawton, OK	168	1 143	115.7	50.2	49	3 495	1 354.6	D	234	4 927	223.2	66.8
Lebanon, PA	197	1 083	151.2	48.6	205	8 099	2 743.8	336.5	232	3 320	146.1	40.5
Lewiston, ID-WA	112	D	D	D	60	3 067	1 175.1	144.0	139	2 677	133.7	38.7
Lewiston-Auburn, ME	183	1 652	359.2	80.1	150	5 205	1 886.9	251.6	209	3 021	153.3	44.5
Lexington-Fayette, KY	1 384	12 042	1 702.3	653.5	423	25 017	17 174.3	1 286.4	1 051	23 086	1 191.8	340.1
Lima, OH	164	952	75.8	33.0	124	7 318	15 270.4	448.1	234	4 521	211.3	54.3
Lincoln, NE	871	9 241	1 313.8	464.2	255	13 208	6 540.1	653.7	702	13 936	616.8	161.3
Little Rock-North Little Rock-Conway, AR	2 012	12 058	1 911.2	627.2	540	21 045	9 263.0	990.1	1 461	29 034	1 362.2	386.9
Logan, UT-ID	385	2 538	251.4	88.6	226	10 761	4 556.5	443.1	178	3 173	130.7	35.4
Longview, TX	508	3 998	554.5	213.9	233	10 657	4 029.0	552.1	426	8 138	374.1	105.1
Longview, WA	140	830	86.5	34.9	116	5 722	3 264.5	385.6	215	2 796	124.2	39.2
Los Angeles-Long Beach-Anaheim, CA	45 444	633 648	90 371.7	35 143.8	17 461	509 552	211 129.0	28 731.8	27 439	499 255	32 015.8	8 990.4
Anaheim-Santa Ana-Irvine, CA Div 11244	14 120	112 581	24 110.2	8 899.6	4 701	150 020	47 299.4	8 879.0	7 141	143 519	9 050.6	2 599.9
Los Angeles-Long Beach-Glendale, CA Div 31084	31 324	521 067	66 261.5	26 244.3	12 760	359 532	163 829.6	19 852.8	20 298	355 736	22 965.1	6 390.6
Louisville/Jefferson County, KY-IN	3 045	26 012	3 734.3	1 286.6	1 223	65 362	37 466.2	3 253.0	2 382	56 076	2 984.5	793.9
Lubbock, TX	640	3 878	483.4	176.3	246	5 075	1 586.2	219.0	638	14 366	721.2	191.8
Lynchburg, VA	508	5 203	1 175.9	359.6	276	15 749	6 265.7	883.3	461	8 653	367.3	101.8
Macon, GA	467	2 857	365.3	128.7	154	5 041	1 729.2	234.4	470	8 864	394.7	109.9
Madera, CA	116	493	66.9	21.6	92	3 298	1 441.1	168.0	193	2 461	150.1	37.1
Madison, WI	1 917	20 780	3 515.0	1 348.2	734	31 666	12 491.6	1 595.6	1 567	29 215	1 330.4	378.2
Manchester-Nashua, NH	1 335	10 986	1 721.0	737.1	554	25 287	7 450.8	1 732.0	897	14 781	762.2	229.8
Manhattan, KS	198	D	D	D	60	1 847	472.0	93.5	201	4 325	164.5	46.5
Mankato-North Mankato, MN	189	1 540	173.9	77.6	138	7 573	4 903.6	321.6	208	4 343	170.1	46.8
Mansfield, OH	187	925	113.1	36.0	168	8 064	3 122.7	385.9	239	4 556	190.1	54.1
McAllen-Edinburg-Mission, TX	886	5 381	566.0	169.6	268	5 713	1 675.4	216.0	1 014	19 468	985.9	247.1
Medford, OR	506	D	D	D	308	5 370	1 624.6	217.4	586	7 381	382.2	112.5
Memphis, TN-MS-AR	2 112	19 494	2 687.2	1 117.7	846	34 515	26 369.2	1 846.8	2 239	55 258	3 253.0	858.2
Merced, CA	142	791	67.1	26.2	116	9 973	4 435.6	405.4	298	4 585	232.9	60.2
Miami-Fort Lauderdale-West Palm Beach, FL	28 955	142 450	26 210.5	9 220.5	4 452	63 174	16 753.9	2 987.1	11 402	234 634	16 293.0	4 445.0
Fort Lauderdale-Pompano Beach-Deerfield Beach, FL	9 583	46 815	8 286.6	2 833.0	1 454	21 057	6 010.6	1 054.7	3 685	72 428	5 129.2	1 322.2
Miami-Miami Beach-Kendall, FL Div 33124	12 008	58 711	11 734.8	4 018.8	2 070	30 387	7 192.9	1 318.2	5 052	104 467	7 696.6	2 078.4
West Palm Beach-Boca Raton-Delray Beach, FL Div 48	7 364	36 924	6 189.1	2 368.7	928	11 731	3 550.4	614.2	2 665	57 739	3 467.3	1 044.3
Michigan City-La Porte, IN	158	1 069	85.0	40.4	172	7 589	2 644.0	350.5	235	4 992	357.0	78.7
Midland, MI	154	785	87.9	34.9	62	6 241	3 591.1	466.1	138	2 861	136.2	40.7
Midland, TX	499	4 739	1 006.1	267.4	143	3 296	1 324.8	165.8	304	6 675	477.6	109.6
Milwaukee-Waukesha-West Allis, WI	3 841	40 983	6 746.8	2 630.0	2 465	114 114	40 901.0	6 604.8	3 179	59 849	2 856.5	780.7
Minneapolis-St. Paul-Bloomington, MN	13 160	111 963	20 342.0	8 273.1	4 641	176 842	71 530.0	10 348.0	6 596	144 111	7 830.5	2 217.4
Missoula, MT	501	2 865	325.4	137.2	102	1 351	310.6	49.1	342	6 106	317.4	84.0
Mobile, AL	850	9 039	1 175.1	474.0	343	16 063	10 562.7	886.3	671	13 684	617.9	167.9

Area name	Health care and social assistance, 2012				Other services, 2012				Nonemployer business, 2014		Value of residential construction authorized by building permits, 2015	
	Number of establishments	Number of employees	Receipts (mil dol)	Annual payroll (mil dol)	Number of establishments	Number of employees	Receipts (mil dol)	Annual payroll (mil dol)	Number	Receipts (mil dol)	New construction ($1,000)	Number of housing units
	159	160	161	162	163	164	165	166	167	168	169	170
Joplin, MO	474	12 922	1 236.6	588.5	288	1 496	119.0	35.0	10 233	426.1	51 271	531
Kahului-Wailuku-Lahaina, HI	393	6 138	741.5	308.2	383	2 185	238.1	62.0	15 867	759.9	139 665	502
Kalamazoo-Portage, MI	760	21 248	2 457.4	946.4	516	3 367	414.5	97.6	20 714	848.1	147 963	623
Kankakee, IL	311	7 349	753.9	294.5	180	956	100.3	25.1	6 215	210.1	16 974	89
Kansas City, MO-KS	5 421	133 626	15 085.9	5 992.9	3 361	22 120	3 219.6	701.1	140 249	6 389.8	1 674 508	8 954
Kennewick-Richland, WA	662	11 539	1 309.8	520.5	345	1 968	161.5	50.3	11 766	525.4	379 360	1 464
Killeen-Temple, TX	606	24 367	2 965.3	1 295.4	506	3 411	248.4	84.7	20 359	852.2	347 981	2 310
Kingsport-Bristol-Bristol, TN-VA	733	17 517	1 976.4	754.1	387	2 119	527.7	56.8	18 008	684.1	89 009	705
Kingston, NY	514	8 991	741.4	312.4	322	1 229	114.9	28.6	16 206	675.8	72 158	307
Knoxville, TN	1 987	53 573	5 749.5	2 129.1	1 162	8 068	755.7	251.4	60 382	2 857.9	535 911	3 060
Kokomo, IN	221	5 417	456.4	182.6	129	922	68.2	18.9	4 247	148.9	48 462	441
La Crosse-Onalaska, WI-MN	327	12 270	1 508.1	539.7	274	1 785	157.9	46.8	7 783	331.2	73 116	497
Lafayette, LA	1 533	32 257	3 120.9	1 178.7	715	5 199	674.7	168.1	41 572	2 047.7	462 704	2 483
Lafayette-West Lafayette, IN	424	11 181	1 217.2	433.2	276	1 907	218.4	49.4	10 790	450.8	107 139	527
Lake Charles, LA	521	12 330	1 209.9	457.2	244	1 617	178.0	51.1	13 544	625.5	173 910	1 034
Lake Havasu City-Kingman, AZ	478	8 222	995.0	364.2	290	1 394	110.3	29.4	10 449	450.3	128 018	636
Lakeland-Winter Haven, FL	1 048	27 066	3 015.2	1 109.8	673	3 366	328.5	94.6	40 327	1 524.1	584 385	3 039
Lancaster, PA	1 110	34 977	3 387.5	1 411.1	1 031	6 339	588.6	161.3	40 764	2 115.6	214 161	1 154
Lansing-East Lansing, MI	1 155	27 524	2 988.8	1 167.0	817	6 682	808.3	240.6	31 030	1 332.9	208 230	1 056
Laredo, TX	536	14 678	926.2	373.6	203	1 129	101.1	27.1	23 755	1 143.0	201 418	1 848
Las Cruces, NM	496	12 122	1 010.7	418.4	234	1 124	86.4	26.3	12 134	457.5	150 247	760
Las Vegas-Henderson-Paradise, NV	4 426	75 019	9 714.9	3 493.8	2 344	17 926	1 602.8	476.8	148 576	7 394.1	1 407 544	10 605
Lawrence, KS	289	6 580	545.8	211.1	181	1 423	230.7	37.2	7 861	317.6	126 050	839
Lawton, OK	282	6 960	709.7	273.2	141	846	70.7	21.3	5 131	212.1	17 910	100
Lebanon, PA	279	8 165	772.4	341.9	233	1 086	110.1	27.5	8 107	366.2	60 062	384
Lewiston, ID-WA	192	4 024	440.3	159.8	108	561	39.4	12.2	3 243	124.0	23 031	139
Lewiston-Auburn, ME	385	9 531	947.5	402.8	211	1 024	84.6	23.5	6 117	280.0	16 167	74
Lexington-Fayette, KY	1 524	34 868	4 154.5	1 607.9	792	5 378	821.8	163.5	34 656	1 593.7	282 492	2 206
Lima, OH	307	11 307	1 256.5	501.7	197	1 264	92.0	25.5	5 457	208.5	16 101	77
Lincoln, NE	1 007	23 965	2 418.6	963.5	705	4 286	593.7	134.2	21 477	823.1	381 786	2 548
Little Rock-North Little Rock-Conway, AR	2 067	52 656	5 908.8	2 359.2	1 178	8 198	1 001.5	238.3	50 264	2 208.4	329 407	2 699
Logan, UT-ID	373	5 431	519.3	170.7	191	D	D	D	9 137	345.1	91 104	614
Longview, TX	543	12 575	1 468.4	479.6	311	2 349	288.1	91.0	15 127	775.0	39 693	248
Longview, WA	240	5 444	567.0	232.1	148	D	D	D	4 207	175.8	34 769	178
Los Angeles-Long Beach-Anaheim, CA	40 695	651 603	87 943.5	31 496.0	20 823	146 211	17 344.3	4 317.7	1 282 607	68 658.5	7 348 035	34 034
Anaheim-Santa Ana-Irvine, CA Div 11244	10 873	152 659	20 682.2	7 379.9	4 980	35 537	3 782.2	1 039.3	291 516	16 869.7	2 227 919	10 771
Los Angeles-Long Beach-Glendale, CA Div 31084	29 822	498 944	67 261.3	24 116.1	15 843	110 674	13 562.1	3 278.3	991 091	51 788.7	5 120 116	23 263
Louisville/Jefferson County, KY-IN	3 410	86 187	9 206.9	3 559.7	1 965	16 301	1 665.5	481.2	84 203	3 726.2	667 795	3 979
Lubbock, TX	864	22 490	2 538.0	873.1	472	3 502	313.4	94.4	21 212	1 081.7	307 133	1 856
Lynchburg, VA	572	13 913	1 313.6	539.9	452	2 320	207.0	60.3	14 333	517.9	138 310	797
Macon, GA	642	16 370	1 869.5	686.3	318	1 831	220.9	58.8	17 926	601.9	54 100	317
Madera, CA	204	5 871	761.0	321.0	112	489	45.2	11.8	7 108	330.4	57 569	211
Madison, WI	1 473	49 078	5 684.6	2 239.3	1 298	9 034	1 314.3	300.0	44 446	2 130.5	677 323	3 498
Manchester-Nashua, NH	1 094	28 561	3 089.1	1 339.9	824	5 516	490.3	160.3	28 189	1 609.6	171 801	921
Manhattan, KS	230	4 249	391.3	142.5	172	1 252	223.3	48.7	4 938	210.3	97 683	496
Mankato-North Mankato, MN	301	11 383	823.6	416.8	186	1 230	262.3	31.3	6 148	257.9	101 626	808
Mansfield, OH	316	7 570	674.5	274.6	209	1 186	108.4	25.3	6 809	277.5	15 906	62
McAllen-Edinburg-Mission, TX	2 048	54 356	3 479.0	1 471.2	571	3 701	350.3	84.2	68 931	2 671.8	620 741	4 306
Medford, OR	674	12 116	1 443.8	510.7	315	1 836	157.3	51.0	16 447	734.1	159 429	717
Memphis, TN-MS-AR	2 948	80 010	9 324.5	3 561.1	1 557	12 365	2 119.0	414.4	108 249	4 084.2	597 911	3 951
Merced, CA	427	6 718	788.1	302.8	183	895	72.4	26.3	10 703	513.2	50 806	232
Miami-Fort Lauderdale-West Palm Beach, FL	20 622	297 739	39 497.8	13 743.7	12 231	68 020	7 193.6	1 854.5	837 150	36 413.2	4 498 201	23 450
Fort Lauderdale-Pompano Beach-Deerfield Beach, FL	6 273	89 756	12 193.7	4 272.6	4 124	21 448	2 245.9	602.5	239 667	10 096.9	807 553	5 452
Miami-Miami Beach-Kendall, FL Div 33124	9 030	132 886	17 547.4	6 100.1	4 903	28 561	3 116.7	758.0	435 368	18 064.5	2 331 082	12 617
West Palm Beach-Boca Raton-Delray Beach, FL Div 48	5 319	75 097	9 756.7	3 371.0	3 204	18 011	1 831.0	493.9	162 115	8 251.7	1 359 567	5 381
Michigan City-La Porte, IN	228	5 626	611.2	208.3	194	1 090	79.0	22.5	5 826	204.4	39 741	159
Midland, MI	239	6 268	682.2	242.8	147	882	113.0	23.2	4 922	187.4	23 111	130
Midland, TX	405	7 331	829.3	304.4	272	2 159	340.6	74.2	16 389	1 292.8	205 018	1 030
Milwaukee-Waukesha-West Allis, WI	4 732	123 973	13 694.3	5 445.8	2 736	20 368	2 267.0	636.2	89 055	4 207.2	643 149	3 048
Minneapolis-St. Paul-Bloomington, MN	9 429	270 065	26 555.5	11 497.3	6 672	51 085	5 701.2	1 543.4	261 376	12 229.7	2 861 363	11 673
Missoula, MT	489	9 292	965.9	351.1	287	1 889	258.2	56.0	9 678	444.9	47 913	574
Mobile, AL	734	21 863	2 397.2	927.8	570	3 577	334.8	96.2	29 747	1 106.6	144 552	907

1. Establishments subject to federal tax.

Table C. Metropolitan Areas — Government Employment and Payroll and Local Government Finances

	Government employment and payroll, 2012									Local government finances, 2012				
			March payroll (percent of total)							General revenue				
												Taxes		
													Per capita¹ (dollars)	
Area name	Full-time equivalent employees	March Payroll (dollars)	Adminis-tration, judicial, and legal	Police and corrections	Fire protection	Highways and transporta-tion	Health and welfare	Natural resources and utilities	Education and libraries	Total (mil dol)	Inter-govern-mental (mil dol)	Total (mil dol)	Total	Property
	171	172	173	174	175	176	177	178	179	180	181	182	183	184
Joplin, MO....................	6 292	18 337 340	4.7	8.3	3.6	3.0	2.0	3.3	74.4	510.9	199.2	185.7	1 065	527
Kahului-Wailuku-Lahaina, HI..	2 328	11 762 934	19.0	23.7	16.4	6.9	6.2	25.4	0.0	252.6	23.1	224.7	1 419	1 316
Kalamazoo-Portage, MI	9 976	43 436 306	7.0	10.5	12.8	2.9	6.0	3.3	56.6	1 340.8	705.4	408.5	1 238	1 210
Kankakee, IL..................	4 413	16 356 166	7.8	13.5	3.6	3.7	1.5	3.4	65.4	441.9	208.0	169.2	1 496	1 433
Kansas City, MO-KS............	86 196	339 122 341	5.7	9.8	5.2	3.5	13.8	6.1	54.6	9 183.3	2 533.9	4 159.3	2 040	1 219
Kennewick-Richland, WA.......	10 152	53 295 192	5.2	7.0	3.2	4.4	10.2	28.7	40.3	1 194.4	543.2	325.4	1 213	704
Killeen-Temple, TX............	19 513	61 961 488	4.6	8.5	3.2	1.8	4.0	4.2	72.6	1 379.2	598.6	457.1	1 087	854
Kingsport-Bristol-Bristol, TN-VA........................	11 566	36 313 120	5.1	10.8	2.2	3.5	5.1	5.7	66.0	805.9	377.3	312.3	1 011	695
Kingston, NY	8 282	38 442 668	5.7	7.7	1.3	4.8	8.8	1.7	68.0	1 095.2	330.4	630.3	3 467	2 848
Knoxville, TN.................	29 145	97 687 242	5.6	9.5	2.6	3.1	10.2	13.4	54.2	2 517.0	845.0	1 010.5	1 191	718
Kokomo, IN	4 091	15 459 399	5.0	6.2	3.5	2.0	35.8	3.0	42.2	435.8	136.7	118.7	1 433	1 170
La Crosse-Onalaska, WI-MN .	5 559	21 504 753	6.0	8.2	2.4	4.3	16.8	4.2	57.0	720.4	365.8	237.4	1 755	1 630
Lafayette, LA.................	17 787	55 296 831	6.7	12.0	3.2	3.4	8.4	8.0	57.3	1 668.5	663.9	685.1	1 444	587
Lafayette-West Lafayette, IN .	5 636	18 225 886	7.4	11.9	4.8	5.8	2.8	5.4	60.9	552.8	259.3	207.6	1 006	798
Lake Charles, LA	9 670	30 588 485	5.1	13.5	3.3	5.8	7.9	5.3	57.2	1 055.7	360.2	475.0	2 361	1 046
Lake Havasu City-Kingman, AZ.........................	5 613	20 393 845	13.0	13.4	11.7	4.5	2.0	5.6	47.4	538.5	183.2	229.9	1 131	849
Lakeland-Winter Haven, FL ...	22 910	75 047 946	7.9	12.5	4.2	2.1	2.6	10.6	56.6	1 844.2	710.5	644.8	1 047	726
Lancaster, PA.................	12 622	54 624 168	5.9	11.7	0.8	2.8	3.4	3.5	70.9	1 833.2	668.6	843.7	1 601	1 327
Lansing-East Lansing, MI	15 249	64 035 635	8.2	8.0	3.0	4.4	9.2	6.8	56.5	1 895.2	923.3	587.0	1 260	1 174
Laredo, TX...................	14 741	48 977 584	5.1	9.2	5.1	3.0	3.0	3.7	70.4	1 245.0	614.2	391.8	1 512	1 216
Las Cruces, NM	7 916	26 726 295	5.8	10.4	2.7	2.6	2.1	5.9	66.7	732.8	425.3	209.7	978	447
Las Vegas-Henderson-Para-dise, NV	51 796	300 546 553	8.1	16.4	5.9	3.4	8.6	10.1	45.3	8 606.7	3 678.4	2 735.1	1 367	869
Lawrence, KS	4 535	18 551 008	5.6	11.2	5.0	2.9	33.2	7.9	33.4	537.2	114.0	188.6	1 671	1 239
Lawton, OK	6 503	22 717 032	3.8	5.7	3.0	2.2	36.2	3.3	45.2	523.3	171.6	106.3	802	354
Lebanon, PA	4 116	14 939 586	6.1	9.0	1.7	2.8	9.0	5.5	65.4	485.8	160.6	191.5	1 416	1 136
Lewiston, ID-WA	2 076	7 939 079	7.0	11.4	5.6	6.0	7.0	7.6	51.8	188.3	89.3	64.0	1 042	932
Lewiston-Auburn, ME..........	3 959	13 779 680	4.1	8.3	4.8	4.2	2.0	5.1	70.2	355.6	153.6	163.3	1 517	1 507
Lexington-Fayette, KY.........	16 579	58 038 313	4.2	11.6	6.9	2.1	7.1	4.3	61.5	1 418.6	398.6	746.8	1 540	758
Lima, OH	4 029	14 917 726	8.3	9.1	4.8	3.4	9.8	5.8	55.9	394.8	197.5	125.6	1 195	774
Lincoln, NE	11 413	48 128 898	5.2	7.7	3.8	4.5	4.1	11.5	61.4	1 034.8	326.0	505.1	1 628	1 186
Little Rock-North Little Rock-Conway, AR.................	24 915	82 533 612	5.8	10.8	5.3	3.7	2.5	8.9	61.2	2 303.6	1 228.7	601.7	838	423
Logan, UT-ID.................	3 888	12 693 319	7.2	7.0	2.3	3.6	11.8	5.5	59.8	338.7	155.8	113.9	888	560
Longview, TX	9 132	29 631 047	5.5	10.9	3.9	2.0	4.4	4.8	66.6	721.4	245.0	370.6	1 710	1 319
Longview, WA	3 301	15 112 407	7.8	11.6	3.0	7.2	3.7	14.2	51.3	420.9	170.2	127.1	1 246	848
Los Angeles-Long Beach-Anaheim, CA...............	471 707	2 757 691 350	8.8	12.1	4.7	5.2	12.5	8.6	45.7	77 422.5	34 902.2	24 415.1	1 870	1 275
Anaheim-Santa Ana-Irvine, CA Div 11244...............	85 251	527 595 855	5.4	11.0	4.8	3.1	7.4	5.7	58.4	14 543.9	5 867.6	5 580.4	1 806	1 406
Los Angeles-Long Beach-Glendale, CA Div 31084..	386 456	2 230 095 495	9.6	12.3	4.7	5.7	13.7	9.3	42.7	62 878.6	29 034.6	18 834.7	1 891	1 234
Louisville/Jefferson County, KY-IN......................	45 148	162 939 795	3.7	9.1	3.7	3.4	14.2	6.3	58.2	4 084.7	1 333.6	1 583.1	1 265	787
Lubbock, TX..................	13 751	49 840 306	4.7	10.3	4.2	1.2	27.8	5.7	45.1	1 319.2	362.2	422.7	1 420	1 113
Lynchburg, VA................	9 196	26 684 206	6.4	11.2	3.2	1.3	7.0	5.1	63.4	712.1	348.1	270.1	1 058	752
Macon, GA...................	9 317	31 505 415	6.5	10.3	4.0	2.8	5.6	5.3	64.2	803.6	331.4	347.0	1 491	1 002
Madera, CA	4 578	20 019 402	8.1	8.1	0.2	2.2	10.1	5.2	64.4	627.3	366.3	154.2	1 013	706
Madison, WI	23 987	100 319 066	5.9	10.2	2.5	6.5	6.7	6.3	60.2	2 887.9	993.2	1 412.8	2 276	2 136
Manchester-Nashua, NH........	13 991	56 054 764	4.1	10.8	6.0	4.5	3.9	3.8	65.8	1 458.9	470.6	808.2	2 006	1 981
Manhattan, KS	3 088	9 783 062	8.5	11.2	3.9	5.6	3.6	7.1	58.8	275.9	79.3	146.5	1 497	1 108
Mankato-North Mankato, MN .	3 049	12 248 005	8.1	9.4	1.0	5.0	10.7	5.9	57.5	419.6	200.3	109.1	1 113	999
Mansfield, OH	5 091	18 513 991	8.5	9.4	5.0	4.1	11.2	8.3	52.0	473.0	237.7	163.9	1 336	864
McAllen-Edinburg-Mission, TX........................	39 042	129 583 687	3.7	6.7	1.7	1.6	2.9	3.9	78.6	3 159.2	1 926.2	864.1	1 071	868
Medford, OR.................	4 931	20 369 335	9.1	14.6	6.5	6.1	5.2	6.8	50.0	668.0	291.3	260.8	1 263	1 068
Memphis, TN-MS-AR	53 881	181 275 652	6.8	14.3	6.6	4.1	9.1	12.2	45.2	5 455.9	2 056.3	2 087.0	1 555	1 086
Merced, CA	10 959	49 202 192	6.5	7.6	1.6	1.1	10.0	6.7	63.4	1 305.5	840.8	219.3	836	680
Miami-Fort Lauderdale-West Palm Beach, FL	222 370	1 025 593 818	5.5	14.7	6.9	4.6	20.6	7.6	34.5	30 329.9	7 063.4	12 134.4	2 106	1 662
Fort Lauderdale-Pompano Beach-Deerfield Beach, FL........................	73 864	331 154 408	5.1	13.2	6.2	3.7	29.6	6.0	33.6	9 918.0	2 186.8	3 161.3	1 742	1 392
Miami-Miami Beach-Kendall, FL Div 33124...............	102 308	498 941 928	4.9	14.9	6.0	5.9	20.8	6.6	32.3	14 058.6	3 695.7	5 524.1	2 132	1 564
West Palm Beach-Boca Raton-Delray Beach, FL Div 48....................	46 198	195 497 482	7.6	16.4	10.2	2.6	5.1	13.1	41.6	6 353.4	1 180.9	3 449.0	2 542	2 211
Michigan City-La Porte, IN.....	4 264	12 639 630	5.9	11.9	4.3	3.5	3.5	6.6	63.1	369.8	180.5	137.0	1 231	1 055
Midland, MI..................	2 175	9 622 686	11.4	7.8	3.3	4.0	3.3	5.7	62.5	271.7	113.5	103.5	1 235	1 220
Midland, TX..................	7 075	27 853 270	5.2	7.7	3.9	1.9	29.9	1.6	47.9	800.8	131.1	362.9	2 393	1 787
Milwaukee-Waukesha-West Allis, WI....................	53 007	250 453 387	5.4	13.5	4.4	4.2	8.1	4.6	57.7	7 417.1	2 812.4	3 111.6	1 986	1 860
Minneapolis-St. Paul-Bloomington, MN	104 532	577 809 573	7.1	9.9	1.7	3.7	7.6	5.5	63.0	15 990.0	6 976.7	5 332.5	1 558	1 450
Missoula, MT	3 035	11 623 602	8.8	11.6	6.2	6.3	5.7	3.6	55.2	333.0	140.7	131.9	1 189	1 156
Mobile, AL	15 334	47 151 677	5.5	11.5	5.1	4.9	9.2	7.3	53.7	1 405.0	626.1	561.4	1 356	491

1. Based on the resident population estimated as of July 1 of the year shown.

Area name	Total (mil dol)	Per capita[1] (dollars)	Education	Health and hospitals	Police protection	Public welfare	Highways	Total (mil dol)	Per capita[1] (dollars)	Federal civilian	Federal military	State and local	Democratic	Republican	All other
	185	186	187	188	189	190	191	192	193	194	195	196	197	198	199
Joplin, MO	524.5	3 009	58.0	8.8	4.8	0.2	5.1	349.6	2 005	440	621	9 523	27.4	70.5	2.2
Kahului-Wailuku-Lahaina, HI	264.1	1 668	0.0	0.0	15.8	6.0	2.7	281.6	1 779	826	1 160	8 993	74.1	23.8	2.1
Kalamazoo-Portage, MI	1 323.6	4 011	48.7	15.6	6.2	1.0	5.0	1 469.4	4 452	873	555	18 965	54.7	44.1	1.2
Kankakee, IL	442.3	3 912	52.1	0.7	6.1	0.1	5.9	327.2	2 894	229	215	6 017	47.5	50.8	1.7
Kansas City, MO-KS	8 722.0	4 278	43.2	9.9	7.0	0.6	5.4	16 793.0	8 237	26 646	11 578	123 112	47.9	50.2	1.9
Kennewick-Richland, WA	1 130.0	4 213	43.9	21.1	4.0	0.0	3.7	7 044.2	26 261	1 214	759	17 361	35.8	61.8	2.4
Killeen-Temple, TX	1 411.2	3 357	57.9	3.8	4.8	0.5	5.9	2 196.8	5 226	10 456	40 282	26 470	38.3	60.4	1.3
Kingsport-Bristol-Bristol, TN-VA	860.9	2 786	50.0	3.8	6.6	1.8	4.1	782.5	2 532	895	969	15 636	26.4	72.0	1.6
Kingston, NY	1 119.8	6 160	51.1	2.0	2.8	12.1	5.4	695.1	3 823	451	292	13 178	60.3	37.4	2.3
Knoxville, TN	2 428.1	2 862	44.3	9.6	6.5	0.1	3.1	4 983.9	5 875	5 445	2 761	53 235	31.2	67.0	1.8
Kokomo, IN	406.5	4 907	32.7	36.7	3.9	0.3	1.8	200.3	2 417	220	264	5 037	41.7	56.0	2.3
La Crosse-Onalaska, WI-MN	720.8	5 328	43.6	2.8	4.0	21.7	5.6	467.2	3 453	531	385	11 045	56.8	41.5	1.7
Lafayette, LA	1 702.8	3 589	44.6	7.6	6.9	0.4	5.4	2 036.0	4 292	1 347	2 210	23 981	31.3	67.1	1.6
Lafayette-West Lafayette, IN	486.9	2 359	51.4	0.5	5.8	0.7	6.1	413.5	2 003	548	679	24 562	44.6	52.8	2.5
Lake Charles, LA	995.9	4 950	38.4	7.2	6.5	0.4	6.8	2 332.0	11 591	549	1 005	13 914	33.7	64.5	1.9
Lake Havasu City-Kingman, AZ	555.1	2 730	33.9	2.7	6.9	0.1	8.7	627.7	3 087	463	444	7 370	27.9	70.2	1.9
Lakeland-Winter Haven, FL	1 992.7	3 234	48.6	3.2	8.2	1.6	5.5	2 776.3	4 506	1 017	1 242	26 220	46.1	52.9	1.0
Lancaster, PA	2 018.4	3 831	55.1	5.4	4.3	5.1	3.3	3 447.0	6 543	1 222	1 397	19 367	39.8	58.7	1.5
Lansing-East Lansing, MI	1 885.3	4 048	47.2	10.6	4.5	3.4	4.3	2 304.1	4 947	1 934	933	47 049	57.2	41.5	1.3
Laredo, TX	1 204.4	4 647	58.3	1.3	6.0	0.4	1.5	1 569.6	6 056	3 314	545	18 571	76.6	22.6	0.9
Las Cruces, NM	719.6	3 356	57.5	1.3	6.7	1.9	4.1	440.1	2 052	3 640	557	16 817	55.9	41.1	3.0
Las Vegas-Henderson-Paradise, NV	9 171.7	4 584	29.1	8.3	9.6	2.7	7.2	21 727.8	10 860	12 366	15 709	83 157	56.4	41.8	1.8
Lawrence, KS	474.7	4 206	28.6	35.1	4.9	0.0	3.3	544.9	4 828	424	479	15 168	61.0	36.3	2.8
Lawton, OK	533.8	4 027	37.6	38.9	4.3	0.0	3.4	253.8	1 915	4 190	11 472	10 927	40.4	59.6	0.0
Lebanon, PA	507.4	3 752	47.7	2.2	2.9	15.0	5.1	705.4	5 215	2 962	358	5 216	35.2	63.4	1.4
Lewiston, ID-WA	188.3	3 065	43.4	3.1	7.2	0.1	7.4	47.1	767	246	204	5 131	39.1	58.4	2.5
Lewiston-Auburn, ME	348.5	3 239	53.0	0.2	4.0	0.4	5.6	353.5	3 285	257	348	5 139	54.8	42.1	3.1
Lexington-Fayette, KY	1 363.2	2 811	49.9	3.2	5.3	0.7	2.2	2 544.8	5 247	4 433	1 584	45 798	43.8	54.0	2.2
Lima, OH	385.4	3 665	49.5	5.4	6.9	4.3	6.7	180.7	1 719	326	258	5 819	37.1	61.2	1.7
Lincoln, NE	1 130.3	3 642	53.2	1.9	4.3	0.9	6.9	2 872.1	9 255	3 136	1 164	31 086	47.7	50.0	2.3
Little Rock-North Little Rock-Conway, AR	2 292.8	3 195	53.1	2.7	6.0	0.0	4.2	3 061.0	4 265	9 541	8 226	61 216	43.2	54.5	2.3
Logan, UT-ID	308.4	2 404	52.6	4.4	6.1	0.3	5.4	194.5	1 516	375	548	11 323	13.7	84.0	2.3
Longview, TX	736.4	3 399	58.8	4.2	5.0	0.0	4.6	1 187.1	5 479	467	431	11 233	26.4	72.7	0.9
Longview, WA	424.6	4 163	38.6	3.9	5.4	0.0	4.9	609.4	5 974	222	280	5 563	50.9	46.5	2.6
Los Angeles-Long Beach-Anaheim, CA	74 228.5	5 687	36.2	9.6	7.8	8.4	3.3	106 636.6	8 170	58 257	23 106	645 974	63.4	34.1	2.5
Anaheim-Santa Ana-Irvine, CA Div 11244	13 915.7	4 503	41.4	2.9	7.7	7.3	4.5	22 316.3	7 222	11 042	5 359	136 230	45.6	51.9	2.5
Los Angeles-Long Beach-Glendale, CA Div 31084	60 312.8	6 054	35.0	11.1	7.8	8.7	3.1	84 320.3	8 464	47 215	17 747	509 744	69.7	27.8	2.5
Louisville/Jefferson County, KY-IN	4 180.4	3 341	44.5	11.9	4.0	0.3	2.5	7 079.6	5 658	8 698	4 229	68 846	48.1	50.3	1.6
Lubbock, TX	1 388.9	4 666	35.4	31.5	4.7	0.1	2.3	2 311.9	7 767	1 308	663	28 076	28.9	69.6	1.6
Lynchburg, VA	701.3	2 747	47.7	1.7	5.7	7.2	1.9	641.2	2 511	558	832	13 381	34.6	63.8	1.6
Macon, GA	816.9	3 510	46.8	7.0	6.4	0.3	2.9	577.8	2 483	1 121	658	13 606	51.4	47.8	0.8
Madera, CA	649.2	4 265	45.6	3.7	3.9	8.8	6.2	475.5	3 124	322	227	9 642	40.2	57.3	2.5
Madison, WI	2 933.1	4 725	47.0	1.8	6.0	8.3	7.1	3 254.4	5 243	5 413	1 806	81 058	68.9	29.7	1.4
Manchester-Nashua, NH	1 496.1	3 713	52.0	0.6	6.1	3.8	4.7	1 157.0	2 872	3 870	1 362	17 741	49.7	48.6	1.6
Manhattan, KS	320.7	3 279	52.2	2.1	6.0	0.0	6.6	601.2	6 146	500	403	12 537	37.0	60.0	3.0
Mankato-North Mankato, MN	409.8	4 181	36.2	5.3	4.8	5.7	13.5	455.8	4 650	288	374	8 097	52.9	43.9	3.2
Mansfield, OH	480.9	3 920	52.3	8.7	5.0	4.8	5.5	209.0	1 703	587	298	7 257	39.3	58.7	2.0
McAllen-Edinburg-Mission, TX	3 161.8	3 920	67.1	2.0	3.8	0.5	2.9	3 738.4	4 635	3 891	1 752	51 385	70.4	28.6	1.0
Medford, OR	678.0	3 285	42.6	5.3	8.6	0.0	6.1	887.0	4 297	1 720	562	8 732	45.8	50.5	3.7
Memphis, TN-MS-AR	5 764.4	4 296	46.3	6.7	8.6	0.9	2.8	6 748.2	5 030	14 390	5 883	71 167	55.7	43.5	0.9
Merced, CA	1 403.1	5 349	48.6	3.6	4.1	10.0	2.7	901.0	3 435	757	403	16 796	53.2	44.4	2.4
Miami-Fort Lauderdale-West Palm Beach, FL	31 257.3	5 424	25.8	15.2	8.8	2.5	2.0	39 629.0	6 877	33 245	14 043	267 128	62.6	36.9	0.5
Fort Lauderdale-Pompano Beach-Deerfield Beach, FL	10 214.0	5 627	24.6	26.3	10.2	1.2	1.4	8 639.5	4 760	NA	NA	NA	67.2	32.3	0.5
Miami-Miami Beach-Kendall, FL Div 33124	14 468.1	5 584	25.8	12.2	7.5	3.5	2.2	23 549.3	9 089	19 667	7 330	118 785	61.6	37.9	0.4
West Palm Beach-Boca Raton-Delray Beach, FL Div 48	6 575.2	4 847	27.6	4.7	9.3	2.5	2.5	7 440.3	5 485	6 611	2 756	54 621	58.2	41.2	0.6
Michigan City-La Porte, IN	330.9	2 974	53.0	1.0	4.1	0.3	2.3	311.4	2 799	172	355	6 671	55.2	42.6	2.2
Midland, MI	272.5	3 250	51.0	2.8	4.1	2.1	7.6	318.6	3 800	138	139	3 353	41.8	57.3	0.9
Midland, TX	864.5	5 700	32.3	45.1	3.2	0.0	1.2	654.6	4 316	526	330	8 739	18.5	80.2	1.4
Milwaukee-Waukesha-West Allis, WI	7 419.0	4 735	44.0	7.8	7.8	3.4	5.7	8 456.0	5 396	10 541	4 621	77 351	52.1	46.9	1.0
Minneapolis-St. Paul-Bloomington, MN	16 677.1	4 873	39.7	6.9	5.5	5.4	7.0	24 523.9	7 166	20 330	13 008	224 508	54.7	43.0	2.3
Missoula, MT	338.7	3 052	44.0	5.5	7.0	0.8	5.2	188.8	1 701	1 315	537	9 376	57.4	39.6	3.0
Mobile, AL	1 433.8	3 464	41.2	6.0	6.8	0.5	8.3	1 386.2	3 349	2 589	2 748	23 477	45.0	54.2	0.8

1. Based on the resident population estimated as of July 1 of the year shown.   2. © 2013 Election Data Services, Inc. All rights reserved.

Table C. Metropolitan Areas — **Land Area and Population**

CBSA/ DIV code[1]	Area name	Land area,[2] 2010 (sq km)	Total persons	Rank	Per square kilometer	White	Black	American Indian, Alaska Native	Asian and Pacific Islander	Percent Hispanic or Latino[3]	Under 5 years	5 to 17 years	18 to 24 years	25 to 34 years	35 to 44 years	45 to 54 years
		1	2	3	4	5	6	7	8	9	10	11	12	13	14	15
33700	Modesto, CA	3 872	538 388	102	139.0	46.6	3.3	1.3	7.6	44.1	7.3	20.1	10.2	14.0	12.5	12.8
33740	Monroe, LA	3 852	179 238	232	46.5	60.7	36.3	0.6	1.2	2.4	6.9	18.2	10.1	13.8	12.0	12.6
33780	Monroe, MI	1 423	149 568	275	105.1	93.3	3.0	0.9	1.0	3.4	5.4	17.1	8.4	11.0	12.1	15.3
33860	Montgomery, AL	7 027	373 792	142	53.2	51.0	44.2	0.7	2.4	3.1	6.5	17.4	10.1	13.9	12.9	13.3
34060	Morgantown, WV	2 613	138 176	292	52.9	92.6	4.0	0.6	3.0	1.8	5.0	11.8	19.4	16.3	11.7	11.6
34100	Morristown, TN	1 127	116 642	330	103.5	88.2	4.0	0.7	1.1	7.5	5.7	16.5	8.7	11.1	12.5	14.3
34580	Mount Vernon-Anacortes, WA	4 484	121 846	317	27.2	77.5	1.2	2.8	3.1	17.8	6.1	16.4	8.3	12.2	11.4	12.6
34620	Muncie, IN	1 016	116 852	329	115.0	89.2	8.2	0.7	1.8	2.1	5.1	13.8	20.1	11.0	10.4	11.9
34740	Muskegon, MI	1 293	172 790	239	133.6	79.1	15.6	1.6	1.0	5.3	6.1	17.6	9.0	12.5	11.9	13.9
34820	Myrtle Beach-Conway-North Myrtle Beach, NC-SC	5 131	431 964	123	84.2	80.0	13.6	1.1	1.5	5.7	5.0	13.7	7.6	11.5	11.4	12.8
34900	Napa, CA	1 938	142 456	288	73.5	55.8	2.5	1.1	9.4	33.7	5.4	16.4	9.1	12.4	12.7	13.8
34940	Naples-Immokalee-Marco Island, FL	5 176	357 305	148	69.0	65.1	7.1	0.4	1.8	26.8	4.8	13.5	7.0	9.9	10.2	12.2
34980	Nashville-Davidson—Murfreesboro—Franklin, TN	16 320	1 830 345	36	112.2	74.9	16.2	0.7	3.1	6.9	6.4	17.3	9.7	14.8	13.8	13.8
35100	New Bern, NC	3 927	126 245	312	32.1	68.8	23.1	1.1	3.0	6.5	6.5	15.1	12.2	12.9	10.4	11.6
35300	New Haven-Milford, CT	1 566	859 470	65	548.8	66.4	13.3	0.6	4.6	16.8	5.3	15.8	10.2	13.1	12.1	14.7
35380	New Orleans-Metairie, LA	8 294	1 262 888	46	152.3	53.6	35.2	0.8	3.3	8.5	6.2	16.3	9.0	15.2	12.5	13.7
35620	New York-Newark-Jersey City, NY-NJ-PA	21 480	20 182 305	1	939.6	48.8	16.7	0.5	11.7	23.8	6.2	15.8	9.3	14.6	13.3	14.3
35620	Dutchess County-Putnam County, NY Div 20524	2 658	394 796	X	148.5	76.3	8.9	0.5	4.2	12.0	4.7	15.8	10.7	10.9	12.0	16.6
35620	Nassau County-Suffolk County, NY Div 35004	3 099	2 862 937	X	923.8	67.0	9.7	0.4	7.0	17.2	5.4	16.8	9.2	11.3	12.4	15.8
35620	Newark, NJ-PA Div 35084	6 430	2 511 493	X	390.6	54.2	19.8	0.4	8.1	19.1	5.9	17.3	8.7	11.9	13.4	15.9
35620	New York-Jersey City-White Plains, NY-NJ Div 35614	9 293	14 413 079	X	1 551.0	43.5	17.8	0.5	13.5	26.3	6.5	15.4	9.4	15.8	13.6	13.7
35660	Niles-Benton Harbor, MI	1 470	154 636	264	105.2	77.2	16.2	1.2	2.5	5.1	6.0	16.4	8.7	11.2	11.5	13.9
35840	North Port-Sarasota-Bradenton, FL	3 364	768 918	73	228.6	79.5	7.2	0.6	2.2	12.0	4.4	12.7	6.6	9.2	9.7	12.6
35980	Norwich-New London, CT	1 722	271 863	175	157.9	79.0	7.3	1.8	5.4	10.0	5.1	15.2	10.5	12.7	11.6	14.9
36100	Ocala, FL	4 104	343 254	149	83.6	73.6	13.2	0.8	2.0	12.0	4.9	13.9	7.2	10.2	9.9	12.3
36140	Ocean City, NJ	651	94 727	363	145.5	87.1	5.2	0.5	1.5	7.3	4.9	13.0	8.3	10.2	9.4	14.0
36220	Odessa, TX	2 325	159 436	258	68.6	36.7	4.6	0.8	1.2	57.3	9.0	20.8	11.0	16.2	12.0	11.4
36260	Ogden-Clearfield, UT	18 725	642 850	86	34.3	84.0	1.7	0.9	3.3	12.2	8.6	23.2	9.4	14.6	13.4	10.9
36420	Oklahoma City, OK	14 274	1 358 452	41	95.2	69.8	11.9	6.7	4.0	12.4	7.1	17.8	10.4	15.0	12.7	12.5
36500	Olympia-Tumwater, WA	1 870	269 536	177	144.1	80.4	4.5	2.7	9.0	8.4	6.1	16.1	8.9	14.3	12.9	13.0
36540	Omaha-Council Bluffs, NE-IA	11 266	915 312	59	81.2	79.3	8.9	1.0	3.2	9.8	7.3	18.5	9.0	14.9	12.9	13.2
36740	Orlando-Kissimmee-Sanford, FL	9 009	2 387 138	24	265.0	51.5	16.4	0.6	5.2	27.9	5.9	16.5	10.2	14.8	13.5	13.8
36780	Oshkosh-Neenah, WI	1 125	169 546	244	150.7	90.9	2.6	1.0	3.2	3.9	5.6	15.2	12.5	13.1	11.9	14.0
36980	Owensboro, KY	2 327	117 463	328	50.5	92.2	5.5	0.4	1.1	2.6	6.6	17.7	8.4	12.0	12.1	13.7
37100	Oxnard-Thousand Oaks-Ventura, CA	4 774	850 536	66	178.2	48.7	2.2	0.9	8.8	42.0	6.4	17.8	10.0	13.0	12.6	14.2
37340	Palm Bay-Melbourne-Titusville, FL	2 631	568 088	95	215.9	77.7	11.1	0.9	3.3	9.3	4.6	14.0	7.8	10.7	10.3	14.7
37460	Panama City, FL	3 425	197 506	220	57.7	79.9	12.7	1.5	3.3	5.7	6.0	15.1	8.9	14.1	12.2	14.3
37620	Parkersburg-Vienna, WV	1 551	92 332	365	59.5	96.7	1.9	0.7	0.9	1.0	5.4	15.6	7.8	11.4	12.2	14.5
37860	Pensacola-Ferry Pass-Brent, FL	4 320	478 043	109	110.7	74.2	18.0	1.6	4.2	5.4	5.9	15.5	11.5	13.8	11.4	13.6
37900	Peoria, IL	6 400	378 018	139	59.1	84.9	10.5	0.6	2.7	3.4	6.5	17.0	8.8	12.9	12.3	13.1
37980	Philadelphia-Camden-Wilmington, PA-NJ-DE-MD	11 919	6 069 875	7	509.3	64.7	21.5	0.6	6.3	8.8	6.0	16.3	9.6	13.9	12.4	14.3
37980	Camden, NJ Div 15804	3 475	1 252 628	X	360.5	68.5	16.9	0.6	5.5	10.4	5.7	16.9	8.9	12.7	12.7	15.1
37980	Montgomery County-Bucks County-Chester County, PA	4 760	1 962 570	X	412.3	82.0	7.4	0.4	6.4	5.4	5.4	16.8	8.3	11.7	12.4	15.4
37980	Philadelphia, PA Div 37964	823	2 131 336	X	2 589.7	46.0	37.1	0.7	7.3	11.0	6.8	15.5	11.1	16.7	12.1	12.7
37980	Wilmington, DE-MD-NJ Div 48864	2 861	723 341	X	252.8	66.4	21.7	0.7	4.8	8.5	6.0	16.4	9.8	13.7	12.4	14.6
38060	Phoenix-Mesa-Scottsdale, AZ	37 725	4 574 531	12	121.3	58.9	5.8	2.5	4.8	30.2	6.6	18.4	9.5	14.1	13.3	12.8
38220	Pine Bluff, AR	5 257	93 696	364	17.8	48.9	48.3	0.9	1.0	2.2	5.9	16.7	10.1	13.2	12.0	13.6
38300	Pittsburgh, PA	13 679	2 353 045	26	172.0	87.6	9.4	0.5	2.6	1.6	5.1	14.2	8.7	13.0	11.5	14.2
38340	Pittsfield, MA	2 400	127 828	307	53.3	91.5	3.9	0.6	2.0	4.1	4.4	13.6	9.7	10.4	10.5	14.8
38540	Pocatello, ID	2 880	83 744	371	29.1	86.6	1.2	3.6	2.4	8.0	7.3	19.4	10.6	15.5	11.8	10.8
38860	Portland-South Portland, ME	5 386	526 295	104	97.7	94.3	2.4	0.9	2.3	1.8	4.9	14.8	8.4	12.1	12.2	15.4
38900	Portland-Vancouver-Hillsboro, OR-WA	17 311	2 389 228	23	138.0	78.0	3.7	1.7	8.7	11.5	6.0	16.5	8.4	15.0	14.5	13.5
38940	Port St. Lucie, FL	2 889	454 846	113	157.4	67.5	15.3	0.6	2.2	16.0	4.8	14.6	7.3	10.3	10.7	13.5
39140	Prescott, AZ	21 040	222 255	199	10.6	82.4	1.2	2.4	1.7	14.2	4.1	13.3	6.8	9.0	9.0	12.1
39300	Providence-Warwick, RI-MA	4 111	1 613 070	38	392.4	79.8	6.1	0.9	3.6	11.6	5.2	15.3	10.6	12.8	12.1	14.8
39340	Provo-Orem, UT	13 975	585 799	93	41.9	85.3	0.9	0.9	3.9	11.1	10.1	24.7	16.5	14.3	12.2	8.3
39380	Pueblo, CO	6 180	163 591	254	26.5	54.1	2.2	1.3	1.3	42.5	6.0	17.2	9.6	12.3	11.6	12.7
39460	Punta Gorda, FL	1 762	173 115	238	98.2	85.9	6.3	0.7	1.9	6.7	3.1	9.9	5.5	7.3	7.9	11.8
39540	Racine, WI	861	195 080	221	226.6	74.9	12.3	0.8	1.6	12.5	6.2	17.7	8.4	12.0	12.1	15.1
39580	Raleigh, NC	5 485	1 273 568	44	232.2	63.9	21.0	0.9	6.0	10.4	6.5	18.7	9.2	14.1	15.4	14.6
39660	Rapid City, SD	20 214	144 134	285	7.1	85.2	2.2	9.4	1.8	4.6	6.7	16.9	9.2	13.7	11.2	12.5
39740	Reading, PA	2 218	415 271	128	187.2	75.3	5.1	0.4	1.8	18.6	5.9	17.0	9.9	11.9	11.9	14.5

1. CBSA = Core Based Statistical Area. DIV = Metropolitan Division. See Appendix A for explanation. See Appendix B for list of metropolitan areas identified by type. 2. Dry land or land partially or temporarily covered by water. 3. May be of any race.

Table C. Metropolitan Areas — **Population and Households**

Area name	Population, 2014 (cont.) Age (percent) (cont.) 55 to 64 years	65 to 74 years	75 years and over	Percent female	Population change and components of change, 2000–2015 Total persons 2000	2010	Percent change 2000–2010	2010–2015	Components of change, 2010–2015 Births	Deaths	Net migration	Households, 2014 Number	Persons per household	Percent Family households	Female family householder[1]	One person
	16	17	18	19	20	21	22	23	24	25	26	27	28	29	30	31
Modesto, CA	11.0	6.9	5.2	50.5	446 997	514 451	15.1	4.7	40 301	20 041	3 253	169 038	3.12	73.7	15.0	20.0
Monroe, LA	12.3	7.9	6.1	51.9	170 053	176 502	3.8	1.6	13 334	9 130	-1 531	66 596	2.51	69.1	20.2	26.6
Monroe, MI	15.0	9.1	6.6	50.6	145 945	152 021	4.2	-1.6	8 146	7 211	-3 420	57 879	2.57	70.2	9.8	25.6
Montgomery, AL.................	12.2	8.0	5.7	52.2	346 528	374 529	8.1	-0.2	25 272	17 952	-8 232	142 432	2.55	66.2	19.3	28.9
Morgantown, WV	11.8	7.2	5.2	48.5	111 200	129 709	16.6	6.5	7 428	5 189	6 273	49 804	2.58	57.1	7.9	31.3
Morristown, TN..................	13.0	11.0	7.3	51.1	102 422	114 111	11.4	2.2	6 815	6 724	2 337	45 581	2.48	69.9	12.9	27.2
Mount Vernon-Anacortes, WA	14.3	10.9	7.8	50.4	102 979	116 901	13.5	4.2	7 601	5 861	3 033	45 447	2.61	65.7	8.6	26.7
Muncie, IN.........................	11.6	8.8	7.1	51.9	118 769	117 671	-0.9	-0.7	6 640	6 220	-1 119	45 207	2.43	59.2	12.0	30.1
Muskegon, MI	13.9	8.6	6.5	50.3	170 200	172 188	1.2	0.3	11 180	8 723	-1 960	64 646	2.57	66.7	14.8	28.7
Myrtle Beach-Conway-North Myrtle Beach, NC-SC	15.6	14.8	7.6	51.5	269 772	376 722	39.6	14.7	21 658	21 439	54 080	174 999	2.37	63.7	11.9	29.7
Napa, CA	13.4	9.4	7.4	50.3	124 279	136 530	9.9	4.3	7 810	6 354	4 354	50 516	2.72	70.3	10.4	23.8
Naples-Immokalee-Marco Island, FL	13.1	15.4	14.0	50.8	251 377	321 520	27.9	11.1	16 903	15 853	34 572	133 162	2.59	68.7	8.6	26.1
Nashville-Davidson—Murfreesboro—Franklin, TN	12.1	7.3	4.8	51.2	1 381 287	1 670 896	21.0	9.5	121 373	69 564	105 958	674 665	2.60	66.2	13.4	27.2
New Bern, NC....................	13.0	10.5	7.8	49.3	114 751	126 802	10.5	-0.4	9 302	6 639	-3 580	49 335	2.50	64.9	11.2	30.0
New Haven-Milford, CT	13.3	8.5	7.1	51.8	824 008	862 474	4.7	-0.3	47 416	39 802	-9 854	326 050	2.55	60.6	12.0	33.9
New Orleans-Metairie, LA.....	13.4	8.1	5.6	51.6	1 337 726	1 189 863	-11.1	6.1	82 050	56 035	45 886	474 715	2.59	61.5	15.9	32.4
New York-Newark-Jersey City, NY-NJ-PA	12.3	7.8	6.3	51.6	18 944 519	19 566 387	3.3	3.1	1 317 457	746 154	73 211	7 152 760	2.75	66.0	15.3	27.9
Dutchess County-Putnam County, NY Div 20524...	14.1	8.7	6.6	50.2	375 895	397 198	5.7	-0.6	18 567	16 145	-4 838	138 424	2.71	68.6	9.5	25.7
Nassau County-Suffolk County, NY Div 35004...	13.4	8.6	7.2	51.1	2 753 913	2 833 053	2.9	1.1	157 818	119 453	-4 763	933 455	3.01	75.1	11.7	20.7
Newark, NJ-PA Div 35084....	13.0	7.8	6.1	51.3	2 396 333	2 469 792	3.1	1.7	147 831	96 150	-7 255	882 527	2.79	69.0	14.1	26.6
New York-Jersey City-White Plains, NY-NJ Div 35614	11.9	7.6	6.2	51.9	13 418 378	13 866 344	3.3	3.9	993 241	514 406	90 067	5 198 354	2.70	63.8	16.3	29.5
Niles-Benton Harbor, MI	14.4	9.9	8.0	51.2	162 453	156 817	-3.5	-1.4	9 810	8 651	-3 263	62 984	2.38	66.8	12.9	28.5
North Port-Sarasota-Bradenton, FL..............................	14.8	15.7	14.3	52.0	589 959	702 268	19.0	9.5	33 088	45 636	77 820	313 576	2.36	63.7	9.0	29.7
Norwich-New London, CT.....	13.9	9.1	6.9	49.9	259 088	274 046	5.8	-0.8	14 404	12 229	-4 063	105 504	2.47	64.0	12.7	30.1
Ocala, FL	13.7	15.6	12.3	52.0	258 916	331 304	28.0	3.6	17 540	23 794	17 207	132 275	2.49	63.0	11.2	30.8
Ocean City, NJ...................	16.3	13.5	10.5	51.2	102 326	97 265	-4.9	-2.6	4 690	6 758	-279	40 779	2.27	63.8	11.8	30.9
Odessa, TX........................	10.0	5.4	4.1	49.6	121 123	137 133	13.2	16.3	14 509	6 096	13 854	50 724	3.00	70.4	14.1	23.9
Ogden-Clearfield, UT	9.7	5.8	4.4	49.7	485 401	597 159	23.0	7.7	56 593	18 312	7 361	199 206	3.14	78.1	9.6	18.0
Oklahoma City, OK.............	11.8	7.4	5.3	50.7	1 095 421	1 252 992	14.4	8.4	99 964	58 057	62 378	499 878	2.60	65.2	12.5	28.1
Olympia-Tumwater, WA.......	13.6	9.2	6.0	50.9	207 355	252 264	21.7	6.8	16 252	10 468	11 409	103 319	2.53	65.4	11.9	27.2
Omaha-Council Bluffs, NE-IA	11.9	7.0	5.3	50.5	767 041	865 356	12.8	5.8	69 281	33 673	15 351	346 283	2.56	64.9	11.2	28.5
Orlando-Kissimmee-Sanford, FL	11.5	8.0	5.8	51.1	1 644 561	2 134 405	29.8	11.8	142 721	82 186	189 354	800 299	2.85	65.6	13.1	27.1
Oshkosh-Neenah, WI............	12.9	7.8	6.9	49.7	156 763	166 994	6.5	1.5	9 868	7 442	34	69 417	2.33	62.3	9.5	28.2
Owensboro, KY...................	13.3	9.1	7.1	51.2	109 875	114 754	4.4	2.4	8 068	6 241	868	46 540	2.43	69.8	12.2	25.6
Oxnard-Thousand Oaks-Ventura, CA............................	12.5	7.7	5.9	50.5	753 197	823 387	9.3	3.3	55 951	28 088	-1 072	269 869	3.09	73.9	12.6	20.7
Palm Bay-Melbourne-Titusville, FL	15.2	12.1	10.5	51.2	476 230	543 378	14.1	4.5	26 746	33 680	30 354	225 226	2.45	63.8	12.0	30.2
Panama City, FL	13.2	9.4	6.9	49.4	161 549	184 715	14.3	6.9	12 448	9 983	9 738	71 161	2.63	66.6	10.5	28.6
Parkersburg-Vienna, WV......	14.5	10.8	7.7	51.4	93 859	92 673	-1.3	-0.4	5 538	5 694	-21	38 667	2.37	61.7	9.7	32.8
Pensacola-Ferry Pass-Brent, FL	12.9	9.0	6.3	49.7	412 153	448 991	8.9	6.5	29 907	23 266	21 708	171 179	2.62	63.5	12.5	29.1
Peoria, IL...........................	13.3	8.8	7.4	51.1	366 899	379 186	3.3	-0.3	25 614	19 608	-6 928	149 515	2.48	65.2	11.8	29.4
Philadelphia-Camden-Wilmington, PA-NJ-DE-MD.	13.0	8.0	6.5	51.7	5 687 147	5 965 379	4.9	1.8	379 426	279 211	8 078	2 230 807	2.64	64.5	14.2	29.5
Camden, NJ Div 15804	13.3	8.2	6.4	51.3	1 186 999	1 250 694	5.4	0.2	73 475	56 559	-14 381	457 793	2.68	69.3	14.1	25.4
Montgomery County-Bucks County-Chester County, PA	14.1	8.7	7.3	51.1	1 781 233	1 924 285	8.0	2.0	106 720	87 166	18 084	727 685	2.63	69.2	9.3	25.1
Philadelphia, PA Div 37964..	11.9	7.1	6.0	52.5	2 068 414	2 084 732	0.8	2.2	154 714	104 311	-330	782 436	2.62	57.1	19.0	36.2
Wilmington, DE-MD-NJ Div 48864	13.0	8.1	6.0	51.4	650 501	705 668	8.5	2.5	44 517	31 175	4 705	262 893	2.66	65.5	13.4	28.5
Phoenix-Mesa-Scottsdale, AZ	11.1	8.3	5.9	50.3	3 251 876	4 193 127	28.9	9.1	310 615	156 248	220 111	1 590 240	2.77	65.4	12.4	27.1
Pine Bluff, AR	13.4	8.7	6.5	49.1	107 341	100 258	-6.6	-6.5	6 077	5 508	-7 062	35 978	2.39	63.2	18.9	34.4
Pittsburgh, PA	15.0	9.6	8.7	51.4	2 431 087	2 356 283	-3.1	-0.1	125 987	141 833	15 854	991 951	2.31	61.3	11.1	32.7
Pittsfield, MA	15.8	11.3	9.5	51.6	134 953	131 272	-2.7	-2.6	5 865	7 434	-1 754	54 706	2.23	57.0	11.4	36.4
Pocatello, ID......................	11.7	7.5	5.3	50.2	75 565	82 839	9.6	1.1	6 906	3 441	-2 544	30 240	2.69	69.2	12.8	23.8
Portland-South Portland, ME	15.1	9.9	7.4	51.4	487 568	514 100	5.4	2.4	26 324	24 252	9 426	215 232	2.38	63.7	10.0	27.4
Portland-Vancouver-Hillsboro, OR-WA	12.8	8.0	5.3	50.6	1 927 881	2 226 011	15.5	7.3	146 121	84 914	99 139	894 801	2.58	63.9	10.6	27.2
Port St. Lucie, FL...............	13.9	13.1	11.8	50.9	319 426	424 107	32.8	7.2	22 002	24 546	32 613	171 289	2.55	64.2	10.3	29.5
Prescott, AZ	17.6	16.7	11.4	51.1	167 517	211 015	26.0	5.3	9 717	14 129	15 180	90 584	2.37	64.1	10.1	28.7
Providence-Warwick, RI-MA.	13.4	8.6	7.1	51.5	1 582 997	1 601 216	1.2	0.7	87 599	76 676	1 766	622 555	2.49	64.3	14.4	28.7
Provo-Orem, UT.................	6.6	4.2	3.0	49.6	376 774	526 886	39.8	11.2	63 888	11 354	6 216	154 567	3.62	81.9	8.1	12.3
Pueblo, CO	13.5	9.5	7.6	50.7	141 472	159 063	12.4	2.8	9 975	8 609	3 038	63 385	2.48	66.4	16.1	27.6
Punta Gorda, FL.................	16.7	20.4	17.3	51.3	141 627	159 991	13.0	8.2	5 336	12 323	19 957	75 234	2.19	63.7	7.6	32.0
Racine, WI	13.8	8.3	6.5	50.5	188 831	195 428	3.5	-0.2	12 624	8 830	-4 011	75 876	2.51	67.7	13.4	26.3
Raleigh, NC.......................	11.0	6.6	4.0	51.2	797 071	1 130 491	41.8	12.7	80 989	34 365	94 090	457 547	2.66	68.0	12.3	25.7
Rapid City, SD...................	14.1	8.9	6.8	49.4	120 093	134 609	12.1	7.1	10 217	5 582	4 784	56 274	2.47	66.3	9.9	27.5
Reading, PA.......................	13.1	8.6	7.3	50.8	373 638	411 572	10.2	0.9	25 594	19 438	-1 904	152 908	2.61	71.2	12.7	23.8

1. No spouse present.

Table C. Metropolitan Areas — Population, Vital Statistics, Medicare, and Crime

Area name	Persons in group quarters, 2015	Daytime population, 2014 Number	Employment/ residence ratio	Births, 2015 Total	Rate[1]	Deaths, 2015 Number	Rate[1]	Persons under 65 with no health insurance 2014 Number	Percent	Medicare, 2015 Total Beneficiaries	Enrolled in Original Medicare	Enrolled in Medicare Advantage	Serious crimes known to police,[2] 2014 Total Number	Rate[3]
	32	33	34	35	36	37	38	39	40	41	42	43	44	45
Modesto, CA	6 477	515 815	0.92	7 736	14.4	3 826	7.1	59 158	12.8	74 092	40 342	33 750	21 385	4 027
Monroe, LA	6 034	180 125	1.02	2 531	14.1	1 800	10.0	25 615	17.2	30 119	23 728	6 391	11 512	6 624
Monroe, MI	1 462	130 725	0.72	1 516	10.1	1 341	9.0	9 760	7.8	27 742	19 076	8 666	2 847	1 947
Montgomery, AL	15 210	383 052	1.05	4 765	12.7	3 468	9.3	39 870	12.9	64 910	44 993	19 917	14 790	3 999
Morgantown, WV	9 162	141 856	1.08	1 478	10.7	997	7.2	11 103	10.0	18 278	12 714	5 564	2 285	1 781
Morristown, TN	2 722	114 297	0.97	1 282	11.0	1 308	11.2	14 479	15.6	27 844	15 942	11 902	3 580	3 092
Mount Vernon-Anacortes, WA	1 626	121 101	1.01	1 444	11.9	1 158	9.5	13 110	13.5	25 481	17 322	8 159	4 588	3 829
Muncie, IN	9 138	118 423	1.03	1 277	10.9	1 160	9.9	13 378	14.8	22 915	19 059	3 856	3 820	3 250
Muskegon, MI	6 496	164 229	0.88	2 129	12.3	1 665	9.6	14 362	10.2	35 642	21 352	14 290	6 907	4 041
Myrtle Beach-Conway-North Myrtle Beach, NC-SC	3 917	407 625	0.94	4 258	9.9	4 408	10.2	64 560	20.1	103 272	84 664	18 608	19 514	4 754
Napa, CA	5 043	149 791	1.12	1 495	10.5	1 251	8.8	14 365	12.5	25 269	14 797	10 472	2 919	2 055
Naples-Immokalee-Marco Island, FL	4 546	358 983	1.07	3 293	9.2	3 276	9.2	64 436	26.5	81 936	64 638	17 298	5 985	1 726
Nashville-Davidson—Murfreesboro—Franklin, TN	40 107	1 813 864	1.02	24 090	13.2	13 748	7.5	207 290	13.5	253 114	149 678	103 436	56 914	3 190
New Bern, NC	5 783	127 374	0.99	1 678	13.3	1 268	10.0	14 673	14.8	27 658	24 708	2 950	3 229	2 728
New Haven-Milford, CT	29 707	842 619	0.95	8 968	10.4	7 596	8.8	56 146	8.0	142 496	98 806	43 690	24 314	3 009
New Orleans-Metairie, LA	19 828	1 277 404	1.04	15 987	12.7	11 091	8.8	183 783	17.3	196 602	91 644	104 958	46 920	3 752
New York-Newark-Jersey City, NY-NJ-PA	415 846	20 212 356	1.01	249 610	12.4	147 174	7.3	2 000 835	11.8	2 872 497	1 987 626	884 871	377 851	1 883
Dutchess County-Putnam County, NY Div 20524	21 966	X	X	3 440	8.7	3 199	8.1	25 250	7.9	66 925	53 505	13 420	5 582	1 418
Nassau County-Suffolk County, NY Div 35004	49 609	X	X	29 681	10.4	23 253	8.1	190 078	8.0	476 323	356 695	119 628	43 631	1 526
Newark, NJ-PA Div 35084	49 098	X	X	27 618	11.0	18 726	7.5	265 076	12.5	346 267	286 613	59 654	47 882	1 910
New York-Jersey City-White Plains, NY-NJ Div 35614	295 173	X	X	188 871	13.1	101 996	7.1	1 520 431	12.5	1 982 982	1 290 813	692 169	280 756	1 963
Niles-Benton Harbor, MI	3 536	151 971	0.95	1 876	12.1	1 624	10.5	15 178	12.1	36 289	27 080	9 209	3 541	2 345
North Port-Sarasota-Bradenton, FL	10 439	746 757	0.99	6 472	8.4	9 176	11.9	105 561	20.4	208 753	148 097	60 656	21 816	2 925
Norwich-New London, CT	12 059	274 926	1.01	2 715	10.0	2 387	8.8	15 152	6.9	47 759	38 563	9 196	NA	NA
Ocala, FL	9 329	327 634	0.90	3 405	9.9	4 560	13.3	50 481	21.4	100 704	60 910	39 794	8 346	2 444
Ocean City, NJ	2 611	97 889	1.06	842	8.9	1 281	13.5	8 575	12.0	24 928	22 024	2 904	3 765	3 934
Odessa, TX	2 439	155 326	1.02	3 070	19.3	1 196	7.5	30 970	22.6	17 973	14 398	3 575	7 375	4 797
Ogden-Clearfield, UT	6 164	583 144	0.83	10 771	16.8	3 448	5.4	64 361	11.4	69 811	44 177	25 634	14 042	2 243
Oklahoma City, OK	31 692	1 342 719	1.01	19 434	14.3	11 048	8.1	189 606	16.6	189 973	146 999	42 974	51 242	3 833
Olympia-Tumwater, WA	4 041	250 247	0.88	3 136	11.6	2 048	7.6	21 306	9.6	46 216	29 686	16 530	7 956	2 991
Omaha-Council Bluffs, NE-IA	17 965	908 075	1.01	13 307	14.5	6 423	7.0	77 872	10.0	125 665	97 735	27 930	31 601	3 501
Orlando-Kissimmee-Sanford, FL	45 943	2 376 659	1.05	28 323	11.9	16 848	7.1	383 512	19.5	397 803	232 163	165 640	86 516	3 746
Oshkosh-Neenah, WI	8 035	180 915	1.13	1 847	10.9	1 410	8.3	9 756	7.1	28 254	13 041	15 213	3 126	1 837
Owensboro, KY	2 783	118 829	1.05	1 534	13.1	1 186	10.1	7 333	7.7	24 613	19 472	5 141	2 956	2 527
Oxnard-Thousand Oaks-Ventura, CA	11 129	807 750	0.90	10 605	12.5	5 682	6.7	94 627	13.1	121 707	81 912	39 795	18 702	2 206
Palm Bay-Melbourne-Titusville, FL	6 874	546 777	0.96	5 232	9.2	6 653	11.7	75 213	17.7	134 101	84 910	49 191	17 253	3 098
Panama City, FL	7 230	193 741	1.02	2 453	12.4	2 019	10.2	29 363	18.7	39 001	31 707	7 294	8 401	4 335
Parkersburg-Vienna, WV	1 001	94 682	1.05	1 106	12.0	1 077	11.7	7 561	10.2	22 799	17 885	4 914	1 964	2 130
Pensacola-Ferry Pass-Brent, FL	26 010	460 056	0.93	5 716	12.0	4 661	9.8	58 578	15.6	88 830	63 987	24 843	16 540	3 484
Peoria, IL	8 983	385 258	1.03	4 869	12.9	3 728	9.9	24 072	7.7	69 748	48 949	20 799	9 871	2 697
Philadelphia-Camden-Wilmington, PA-NJ-DE-MD.	169 007	6 025 549	0.99	71 412	11.8	54 414	9.0	504 587	10.0	960 788	668 614	292 174	168 972	2 792
Camden, NJ Div 15804	25 063	X	X	13 842	11.1	11 000	8.8	103 324	9.8	201 972	161 514	40 458	29 595	2 355
Montgomery County-Bucks County-Chester County, PA	43 405	X	X	20 221	10.3	17 149	8.7	116 105	7.2	324 510	223 177	101 333	32 164	1 647
Philadelphia, PA Div 37964	79 733	X	X	29 019	13.6	20 162	9.5	233 561	13.1	322 241	184 205	138 036	82 502	3 889
Wilmington, DE-MD-NJ Div 48864	20 806	X	X	8 330	11.5	6 103	8.4	51 597	8.6	112 065	99 718	12 347	24 711	3 424
Phoenix-Mesa-Scottsdale, AZ	87 030	4 479 249	0.99	60 296	13.2	31 720	6.9	582 858	15.5	613 550	334 193	279 357	148 820	3 324
Pine Bluff, AR	8 827	92 193	0.91	1 130	12.1	1 031	11.0	8 428	11.7	18 924	14 677	4 247	4 166	4 399
Pittsburgh, PA	63 373	2 366 771	1.01	24 336	10.3	27 124	11.5	155 031	8.3	485 877	162 733	323 144	49 484	2 106
Pittsfield, MA	6 056	129 769	1.02	1 078	8.4	1 365	10.7	3 928	4.0	30 898	29 347	1 551	2 911	2 446
Pocatello, ID	2 006	81 742	0.95	1 266	15.1	638	7.6	9 638	13.6	13 298	8 684	4 614	2 131	2 540
Portland-South Portland, ME	12 637	520 782	0.99	5 152	9.8	4 790	9.1	45 151	10.6	103 937	78 264	25 673	11 106	2 127
Portland-Vancouver-Hillsboro, OR-WA	39 374	2 349 836	1.00	28 258	11.8	16 853	7.1	212 425	10.6	338 610	136 357	202 253	70 330	3 300
Port St. Lucie, FL	7 131	418 852	0.85	4 258	9.4	4 989	11.0	67 804	20.7	103 457	69 607	33 850	10 070	2 263
Prescott, AZ	3 777	214 819	0.95	1 914	8.6	2 726	12.3	28 098	18.1	61 698	43 516	18 182	NA	NA
Providence-Warwick, RI-MA	58 070	1 548 081	0.92	16 698	10.4	14 610	9.1	93 729	7.1	292 451	200 092	92 359	39 662	2 463
Provo-Orem, UT	12 589	548 596	0.90	12 117	20.7	2 184	3.7	63 319	12.2	43 942	26 145	17 797	9 684	1 692
Pueblo, CO	4 482	160 346	0.98	1 911	11.7	1 694	10.4	15 017	11.5	32 217	20 467	11 750	9 275	5 695
Punta Gorda, FL	3 190	161 493	0.88	1 027	5.9	2 478	14.3	21 264	20.7	52 587	36 303	16 284	3 208	1 918
Racine, WI	4 787	185 075	0.89	2 380	12.2	1 618	8.3	15 323	9.5	36 899	23 651	13 248	4 833	2 479
Raleigh, NC	24 209	1 232 192	0.98	15 702	12.3	7 043	5.5	139 775	12.9	150 642	103 348	47 294	19 881	1 615
Rapid City, SD	3 617	142 568	0.98	1 974	13.7	1 105	7.7	14 841	12.6	26 574	21 615	4 959	4 101	2 863
Reading, PA	11 846	394 057	0.90	4 908	11.8	3 682	8.9	39 628	11.7	74 096	46 747	27 349	8 699	2 102

1. Per 1,000 estimated resident population. 2. Data for serious crimes have not been adjusted for underreporting; this may affect comparability between geographic areas and over time.
3. Per 100,000 population estimated by the FBI.

Table C. Metropolitan Areas — Crime, Education, Money Income, and Poverty

Area name	Serious crimes known to police, 2014 (cont.)[1] Rate[2] Violent	Property	Education — School enrollment and attainment, 2014 Enrollment[3] Total	Percent private	Attainment[4] (percent) High school grad-uate or less	Bach-elor's degree or more	Local government expenditures,[5] 2012–2013 Total current expendi-tures (mil dol)	Current expendi-tures per student (dollars)	Income and Poverty, 2014 Per capita income[6] (dollars)	Mean house-hold income (dollars)	Median household income	Percent of households with income of less than $25,000	Percent of house-holds with in-come of $200,000 or more	Percent below poverty level All persons	Children under 18 years	Age 65 years and older
	46	47	48	49	50	51	52	53	54	55	56	57	58	59	60	61
Modesto, CA	532	3 495	154 323	7.8	48.9	17.0	996.5	9 467	21 609	65 663	51 084	23.4	2.9	18.0	23.7	10.8
Monroe, LA	1 255	5 369	43 959	12.0	50.8	23.5	310.0	9 987	21 956	57 503	41 175	33.9	3.3	24.6	38.3	12.9
Monroe, MI	224	1 723	35 751	10.2	46.2	17.3	245.8	10 550	27 726	69 949	57 275	19.5	2.7	9.7	13.3	3.7
Montgomery, AL	393	3 607	94 630	21.9	44.6	27.8	464.8	8 296	24 007	60 854	47 159	27.3	2.4	19.6	28.0	9.2
Morgantown, WV	227	1 554	42 348	7.1	46.5	31.7	168.6	10 804	23 961	60 041	41 924	30.4	3.2	23.5	20.1	8.0
Morristown, TN	383	2 708	24 867	12.2	56.9	19.1	131.6	7 390	21 016	52 194	38 542	33.6	1.3	22.3	33.2	9.8
Mount Vernon-Anacortes, WA	206	3 622	27 822	12.3	37.3	27.4	197.5	10 426	27 752	70 529	50 558	25.9	4.3	16.6	26.7	7.3
Muncie, IN	281	2 970	38 065	6.5	43.6	25.4	148.2	9 741	21 582	53 982	39 323	28.9	2.1	21.9	25.0	8.9
Muskegon, MI	443	3 597	43 220	7.5	46.5	18.4	294.0	10 921	20 613	53 889	42 600	30.1	1.8	20.3	26.9	7.7
Myrtle Beach-Conway-North Myrtle Beach, NC-SC	426	4 328	81 239	11.2	43.8	24.2	524.5	10 003	24 998	57 483	43 993	25.1	2.1	17.4	31.2	7.5
Napa, CA	376	1 679	34 106	15.6	36.3	33.7	216.5	10 447	37 731	101 798	74 123	14.8	10.8	8.3	9.6	7.2
Naples-Immokalee-Marco Island, FL	260	1 466	63 871	13.2	40.5	34.8	445.8	10 182	38 317	95 772	58 026	16.5	8.8	14.5	27.9	6.0
Nashville-Davidson—Mur-freesboro—Franklin, TN	614	2 576	456 477	21.2	40.4	32.1	2 233.5	8 311	29 061	74 288	52 640	21.7	4.8	15.1	21.6	8.3
New Bern, NC	240	2 488	27 216	15.9	41.5	21.9	150.0	8 529	22 255	54 320	42 819	25.5	1.8	16.5	29.4	7.5
New Haven-Milford, CT	333	2 676	223 687	23.6	41.5	34.5	2 073.6	16 895	32 895	82 661	60 391	21.9	6.7	13.1	18.3	8.5
New Orleans-Metairie, LA	522	3 230	311 951	30.7	42.8	28.9	1 650.8	12 304	28 122	70 159	46 784	27.5	4.8	18.1	27.0	12.4
New York-Newark-Jersey City, NY-NJ-PA	372	1 511	5 039 443	23.0	39.8	37.9	57 989.5	21 284	36 323	98 451	67 066	20.9	10.4	14.6	20.4	12.2
Dutchess County-Putnam County, NY Div 20524	175	1 243	103 676	25.0	35.2	35.8	1 190.0	20 431	35 513	97 480	77 279	15.1	8.5	8.8	10.9	5.6
Nassau County-Suffolk County, NY Div 35004	137	1 389	726 486	19.7	36.5	38.4	10 471.1	23 199	40 267	119 495	91 770	12.0	14.2	7.0	9.3	5.3
Newark, NJ-PA Div 35084	316	1 594	650 587	17.3	36.6	40.5	7 719.1	19 848	40 124	109 756	76 038	16.5	13.6	10.1	13.7	8.5
New York-Jersey City-White Plains, NY-NJ Div 35614	434	1 528	3 558 694	24.6	41.2	37.5	38 609.4	21 144	34 892	92 779	61 335	23.4	9.2	17.1	24.2	14.6
Niles-Benton Harbor, MI	390	1 955	37 944	23.5	39.8	26.9	262.7	11 019	25 264	61 549	44 031	26.3	3.2	17.4	25.3	7.9
North Port-Sarasota-Braden-ton, FL	402	2 523	136 583	15.3	39.2	31.4	819.9	9 396	32 075	73 484	52 077	22.4	4.8	12.0	19.4	6.7
Norwich-New London, CT	NA	NA	64 065	17.1	39.9	32.0	618.5	17 545	34 287	84 800	66 148	17.8	5.8	11.3	19.3	6.4
Ocala, FL	415	2 028	65 578	18.6	50.8	17.1	350.4	8 344	21 915	52 197	39 958	27.5	1.7	17.4	27.9	8.2
Ocean City, NJ	239	3 694	18 990	12.7	48.2	26.3	257.1	19 903	35 004	82 259	56 899	20.5	5.8	13.5	19.9	10.2
Odessa, TX	911	3 886	41 489	11.4	53.2	16.8	219.9	7 418	27 364	80 661	58 701	20.5	6.1	10.0	13.7	14.1
Ogden-Clearfield, UT	159	2 083	201 737	9.3	30.7	29.9	831.7	6 520	25 303	78 156	64 301	15.4	3.9	9.5	11.3	6.7
Oklahoma City, OK	466	3 367	360 020	12.2	38.9	28.6	1 614.8	7 286	27 714	71 449	52 416	22.0	4.4	15.3	21.0	6.1
Olympia-Tumwater, WA	228	2 764	63 522	12.1	27.8	33.9	385.2	9 472	30 441	75 523	61 609	17.0	4.1	12.0	16.1	9.9
Omaha-Council Bluffs, NE-IA	365	3 136	246 766	16.4	33.8	34.3	1 615.4	10 835	28 814	73 754	57 527	19.1	3.8	11.3	14.6	6.7
Orlando-Kissimmee-Sanford, FL	531	3 214	619 517	16.8	38.6	28.7	2 794.8	8 091	25 156	67 825	48 270	24.3	4.0	16.7	23.6	10.2
Oshkosh-Neenah, WI	172	1 665	43 126	12.9	40.5	26.3	232.2	10 204	27 557	66 818	52 387	21.6	2.9	12.4	17.4	6.8
Owensboro, KY	129	2 398	28 208	14.9	50.3	20.1	181.2	9 236	22 613	56 423	41 827	26.2	2.7	14.9	22.5	8.8
Oxnard-Thousand Oaks-Ven-tura, CA	223	1 983	224 871	14.0	35.8	31.6	1 248.7	8 813	32 686	98 741	75 449	13.9	9.7	11.3	15.5	8.5
Palm Bay-Melbourne-Titus-ville, FL	493	2 605	117 316	15.6	38.0	27.2	568.2	7 977	27 847	64 550	47 907	24.8	3.3	14.4	21.8	7.7
Panama City, FL	500	3 835	42 066	15.7	43.5	21.2	227.8	7 975	25 156	63 059	44 638	25.7	3.3	14.7	19.3	10.6
Parkersburg-Vienna, WV	201	1 929	20 645	10.0	49.3	19.9	161.1	11 204	23 604	54 325	41 793	30.1	1.5	17.9	29.8	8.7
Pensacola-Ferry Pass-Brent, FL	503	2 981	120 985	19.0	38.4	26.0	543.5	8 166	26 032	67 129	50 003	21.7	3.0	12.5	17.2	6.3
Peoria, IL	323	2 373	95 036	23.5	37.7	29.4	644.9	10 725	29 630	72 746	56 186	20.1	3.9	12.6	17.8	7.1
Philadelphia-Camden-Wil-mington, PA-NJ-DE-MD	460	2 332	1 535 009	26.0	40.8	35.3	13 258.8	17 304	33 196	86 635	62 171	20.6	7.3	13.4	18.6	8.9
Camden, NJ Div 15804	276	2 079	319 171	17.6	40.3	33.0	3 522.0	17 773	34 380	91 662	72 489	17.1	7.3	9.7	13.8	7.7
Montgomery County-Bucks County-Chester County, PA	126	1 521	483 157	26.0	32.5	44.7	4 319.7	16 555	41 012	107 689	80 209	12.9	11.4	7.0	9.0	5.3
Philadelphia, PA Div 37964	861	3 027	551 451	33.0	48.8	28.8	4 038.1	18 940	26 006	65 718	43 819	30.4	4.1	22.1	31.1	13.9
Wilmington, DE-MD-NJ Div 48864	501	2 923	181 230	19.6	41.9	32.0	1 379.1	14 681	31 104	81 857	63 446	18.6	5.8	11.9	16.1	8.2
Phoenix-Mesa-Scottsdale, AZ	369	2 955	1 185 153	11.5	37.2	29.0	4 660.5	7 210	27 069	72 867	53 365	21.9	4.7	17.2	24.7	8.6
Pine Bluff, AR	694	3 706	23 244	15.3	59.6	14.8	152.1	10 021	19 745	50 078	33 838	39.0	1.7	26.2	44.4	8.9
Pittsburgh, PA	291	1 814	513 068	21.0	42.2	31.7	4 241.6	14 342	30 780	71 459	52 293	24.2	4.3	12.4	17.5	7.8
Pittsfield, MA	309	2 136	28 431	22.5	40.4	31.1	275.5	16 468	30 879	69 452	50 211	26.9	4.7	12.4	20.7	7.1
Pocatello, ID	223	2 317	25 338	5.1	34.9	26.8	89.6	6 374	21 898	59 314	44 018	26.6	2.3	16.9	18.9	5.7
Portland-South Portland, ME	127	2 000	119 143	19.0	33.3	38.6	918.2	12 837	33 873	80 803	59 573	19.1	5.4	11.0	14.0	7.3
Portland-Vancouver-Hills-boro, OR-WA	272	3 027	581 728	17.4	30.6	35.7	3 279.9	9 632	31 155	79 375	60 248	19.2	5.3	13.6	17.3	8.3
Port St. Lucie, FL	299	1 964	97 349	12.2	44.9	21.6	495.0	8 487	27 523	67 310	47 483	25.4	3.9	15.3	24.7	6.5
Prescott, AZ	NA	NA	44 984	13.8	36.2	25.5	139.2	6 708	26 018	60 018	44 255	26.0	3.0	15.5	21.7	8.5
Providence-Warwick, RI-MA	329	2 133	400 492	22.3	44.8	28.8	3 214.2	15 008	30 278	76 189	55 836	23.5	5.4	13.6	18.9	10.2
Provo-Orem, UT	74	1 617	226 141	23.5	24.1	37.1	715.0	5 919	21 085	76 285	60 890	16.2	3.4	12.5	11.0	4.8
Pueblo, CO	577	5 119	41 536	8.1	38.1	23.6	210.6	7 852	22 188	54 852	41 047	29.6	1.8	18.8	24.7	11.1
Punta Gorda, FL	176	1 741	23 231	11.3	43.6	21.2	146.4	8 952	26 542	57 316	43 039	27.0	2.3	10.7	15.7	6.8
Racine, WI	200	2 279	49 039	20.5	42.7	24.0	330.7	11 143	26 950	68 354	54 525	21.1	3.1	12.8	16.3	8.0
Raleigh, NC	136	1 479	352 423	17.1	28.4	43.4	1 519.4	7 858	32 107	84 855	62 313	18.0	6.4	12.2	16.0	7.1
Rapid City, SD	392	2 472	35 491	13.3	35.8	26.8	175.5	8 333	26 333	64 263	49 808	21.2	2.9	11.9	16.0	7.6
Reading, PA	328	1 774	101 027	17.1	54.0	23.1	944.1	13 729	26 153	69 160	56 059	21.7	3.1	14.7	22.4	7.8

1. Data for serious crimes have not been adjusted for underreporting; this may affect comparability between geographic areas and over time.   2. Per 100,000 population estimated by the FBI.
3. All persons 3 years old and over enrolled in nursery school through college.   4. Persons 25 years old and over.   5. Elementary and secondary education expenditures.   6. Based on resident population estimated in the 2014 American Community Survey.

Table C. Metropolitan Areas — **Personal Income**

Area name	Personal income, 2014 Total (mil dol)	Percent change 2013–2014	Per capita Dollars	Per capita Rank	Wages and salaries (mil dol)	Supplements to wages and salaries; employer contributions (mil dol) Pension and insurance	Government social insurance	Proprietors' income (mil dol)	Dividends, interest, and rent (mil dol)	Personal transfer receipts (mil dol)	Earnings, 2014 Total (mil dol)	Contributions for government social insurance (mil dol) From employee and self-employed	From employer
	62	63	64	65	66	67	68	69	70	71	72	73	74
Modesto, CA	19 341	5.1	36 356	277	7 793	1 636	575	1 943	2 845	4 272	11 947	683	575
Monroe, LA	6 515	2.3	36 425	273	3 053	544	194	703	1 035	1 526	4 495	246	194
Monroe, MI	5 886	3.8	39 284	200	1 997	335	152	276	727	1 242	2 759	188	152
Montgomery, AL	14 633	3.4	39 215	206	7 341	1 376	561	1 221	2 658	3 127	10 498	633	561
Morgantown, WV	5 282	3.8	38 487	216	3 050	573	235	363	807	1 000	4 221	250	235
Morristown, TN	3 656	3.4	31 593	369	1 662	297	120	275	477	1 081	2 353	156	120
Mount Vernon-Anacortes, WA	5 155	6.1	42 829	127	2 167	386	208	285	1 153	1 145	3 046	185	208
Muncie, IN	3 739	2.8	31 933	367	1 818	349	140	236	595	1 071	2 543	166	140
Muskegon, MI	5 662	4.6	32 856	355	2 588	452	205	304	790	1 632	3 548	236	205
Myrtle Beach-Conway-North Myrtle Beach, NC-SC	13 747	6.3	32 913	354	5 269	856	426	975	2 602	4 128	7 526	538	426
Napa, CA	7 735	4.5	54 596	20	3 779	774	278	773	1 911	1 084	5 604	315	278
Naples-Immokalee-Marco Island, FL	25 764	4.9	73 869	4	6 389	802	445	1 272	14 236	3 010	8 908	596	445
Nashville-Davidson—Murfreesboro—Franklin, TN	84 957	5.4	47 392	58	44 429	6 222	3 070	15 949	11 301	12 147	69 670	3 971	3 070
New Bern, NC	5 005	3.3	39 242	203	2 347	560	197	278	1 065	1 192	3 382	189	197
New Haven-Milford, CT	43 288	4.2	50 261	35	20 391	3 584	1 562	3 384	7 490	8 070	28 921	1 621	1 562
New Orleans-Metairie, LA	57 937	4.0	46 282	76	28 949	4 650	1 860	6 979	11 410	9 361	42 438	2 297	1 860
New York-Newark-Jersey City, NY-NJ-PA	1 234 506	4.6	61 440	9	659 997	104 139	47 133	120 424	242 606	185 456	931 692	50 683	47 133
Dutchess County-Putnam County, NY Div 20524	19 601	4.2	49 489	X	7 029	1 643	601	902	3 073	3 263	10 175	556	601
Nassau County-Suffolk County, NY Div 35004	185 274	4.4	64 745	X	72 688	14 489	6 017	14 423	34 617	25 644	107 617	5 692	6 017
Newark, NJ-PA Div 35084	167 002	4.9	66 584	X	82 310	12 697	5 958	15 132	30 996	19 550	116 097	6 746	5 958
New York-Jersey City-White Plains, NY-NJ Div 35614	862 629	4.5	60 210	X	497 970	75 310	34 556	89 967	173 921	137 000	697 802	37 688	34 556
Niles-Benton Harbor, MI	6 227	4.7	40 113	184	2 894	554	223	328	1 003	1 487	4 000	254	223
North Port-Sarasota-Bradenton, FL	35 879	5.2	47 921	56	11 890	1 667	854	2 186	13 272	7 505	16 597	1 168	854
Norwich-New London, CT	13 758	3.6	50 271	34	6 899	1 451	500	791	2 647	2 317	9 641	508	500
Ocala, FL	11 047	4.2	32 571	361	3 729	622	275	410	2 494	3 815	5 036	402	275
Ocean City, NJ	4 940	3.7	51 812	25	1 591	345	145	462	1 259	1 140	2 542	168	145
Odessa, TX	7 244	11.4	47 069	63	4 684	525	307	778	693	913	6 294	330	307
Ogden-Clearfield, UT	23 300	4.7	36 851	263	10 008	1 901	821	1 632	3 822	3 162	14 361	834	821
Oklahoma City, OK	62 394	4.9	46 675	69	30 376	4 964	2 276	10 334	10 329	9 331	47 950	2 515	2 276
Olympia-Tumwater, WA	11 430	6.0	42 994	124	4 973	933	446	611	2 264	2 213	6 964	412	446
Omaha-Council Bluffs, NE-IA	44 154	3.8	48 821	49	23 457	3 711	1 770	4 955	8 422	5 964	33 892	2 043	1 770
Orlando-Kissimmee-Sanford, FL	86 134	5.9	37 104	257	51 432	6 880	3 661	4 736	14 037	16 859	66 709	4 079	3 661
Oshkosh-Neenah, WI	6 865	3.5	40 498	175	4 610	805	357	335	1 253	1 140	6 108	373	357
Owensboro, KY	4 574	3.6	39 259	202	2 121	373	163	460	709	1 095	3 116	192	163
Oxnard-Thousand Oaks-Ventura, CA	42 651	4.2	50 405	33	17 921	3 235	1 258	3 068	8 575	5 714	25 482	1 478	1 258
Palm Bay-Melbourne-Titusville, FL	21 647	3.5	38 872	209	9 555	1 471	700	855	4 598	5 457	12 581	840	700
Panama City, FL	7 329	5.9	37 596	244	3 423	620	265	360	1 565	1 703	4 668	286	265
Parkersburg-Vienna, WV	3 357	4.1	36 456	272	1 577	298	128	186	501	948	2 190	147	128
Pensacola-Ferry Pass-Brent, FL	17 526	3.7	36 969	262	7 644	1 431	592	548	3 629	4 012	10 216	622	592
Peoria, IL	16 680	0.5	43 889	100	9 613	1 500	693	851	2 814	2 876	12 657	725	693
Philadelphia-Camden-Wilmington, PA-NJ-DE-MD	332 426	4.0	54 936	18	166 181	26 826	12 758	33 781	59 007	54 540	239 546	13 852	12 758
Camden, NJ Div 15804	61 691	3.8	49 285	X	26 759	4 877	2 216	4 003	9 001	10 841	37 855	2 295	2 216
Montgomery County-Bucks County-Chester County, PA	138 029	4.1	70 555	X	64 317	9 300	4 804	13 923	29 156	15 207	92 344	5 294	4 804
Philadelphia, PA Div 37964	97 634	3.9	45 983	X	54 496	9 243	4 230	12 771	15 190	22 497	80 740	4 629	4 230
Wilmington, DE-MD-NJ Div 48864	35 072	4.2	48 720	X	20 609	3 406	1 508	3 083	5 660	5 996	28 607	1 634	1 508
Phoenix-Mesa-Scottsdale, AZ	178 871	5.1	39 846	189	95 818	13 495	6 845	14 721	30 902	31 260	130 880	7 962	6 845
Pine Bluff, AR	2 935	0.5	30 986	370	1 384	257	112	238	377	905	1 992	126	112
Pittsburgh, PA	116 265	3.0	49 349	44	60 530	10 132	4 743	10 565	18 515	22 464	85 969	5 165	4 743
Pittsfield, MA	6 109	3.2	47 458	57	2 732	502	203	457	1 205	1 492	3 894	225	203
Pocatello, ID	2 672	3.6	32 063	365	1 210	222	114	152	428	629	1 698	112	114
Portland-South Portland, ME	24 449	3.6	46 697	68	12 694	1 967	943	1 690	4 499	4 298	17 294	1 114	943
Portland-Vancouver-Hillsboro, OR-WA	107 537	5.5	45 794	84	59 771	7 781	5 147	7 696	20 117	16 726	80 394	4 995	5 147
Port St. Lucie, FL	19 987	5.1	44 974	90	5 477	876	399	783	6 659	4 264	7 535	539	399
Prescott, AZ	7 172	5.3	32 774	357	2 257	398	167	282	1 884	2 309	3 103	247	167
Providence-Warwick, RI-MA	75 870	4.7	47 143	61	35 058	5 913	2 774	5 240	12 069	15 837	48 985	3 107	2 774
Provo-Orem, UT	18 418	4.9	32 230	364	8 781	1 379	696	1 889	2 786	2 417	12 746	738	696
Pueblo, CO	5 450	5.5	33 666	343	2 490	394	190	284	876	1 591	3 359	208	190
Punta Gorda, FL	6 124	5.6	36 350	278	1 697	266	126	309	1 756	2 063	2 398	203	126
Racine, WI	8 079	3.2	41 398	154	3 610	693	279	280	1 337	1 581	4 862	308	279
Raleigh, NC	57 967	5.2	46 636	70	30 156	4 417	2 247	3 630	9 310	6 898	40 449	2 390	2 247
Rapid City, SD	6 077	5.4	42 309	134	2 747	500	212	567	1 466	1 076	4 026	244	212
Reading, PA	17 729	3.8	42 856	126	8 081	1 596	657	1 284	2 744	3 620	11 619	685	657

1. Based on the resident population estimated as of July 1 of the year shown.

Table C. Metropolitan Areas — Earnings, Social Security, and Housing

Area name	Earnings, 2014 (cont.) Percent by selected industries									Social Security beneficiaries, December 2014		Supplemental Security Income recipients, December 2014	Housing units, 2015	
	Farm	Mining	Construction	Manufacturing	Information, professional, scientific, technical services	Retail trade	Finance, insurance, real estate, rental and leasing	Health care and social assistance	Government	Number	Rate[1]		Total	Percent change, 2000–2015
	75	76	77	78	79	80	81	82	83	84	85	86	87	88
Modesto, CA	8.7	0.0	4.8	13.4	4.0	7.4	4.5	16.0	18.1	83 850	158	22 345	180 704	0.7
Monroe, LA	1.1	0.5	5.6	9.7	D	8.3	8.6	17.4	15.7	33 625	188	7 858	78 410	3.4
Monroe, MI	1.3	D	8.7	16.4	D	7.0	3.0	9.2	13.1	33 720	225	2 595	63 654	1.1
Montgomery, AL	1.2	0.1	5.8	12.4	D	6.3	D	10.3	28.0	75 830	203	14 686	165 497	2.4
Morgantown, WV	-0.2	2.3	7.8	9.4	D	5.2	3.3	D	27.5	21 955	160	2 909	59 576	2.1
Morristown, TN	0.5	D	D	27.2	D	8.1	3.5	D	14.2	30 125	260	3 558	50 696	0.5
Mount Vernon-Anacortes, WA	3.2	0.1	9.3	16.5	5.2	9.0	4.9	8.3	23.5	27 880	232	2 470	52 214	1.4
Muncie, IN	0.8	D	4.1	10.7	7.1	8.2	6.0	19.0	22.8	25 775	220	3 061	52 489	0.3
Muskegon, MI	1.0	D	4.8	26.3	3.9	9.9	3.8	17.3	14.7	41 200	239	6 406	73 331	-0.3
Myrtle Beach-Conway-North Myrtle Beach, NC-SC	0.8	D	7.7	3.7	D	11.1	11.1	11.1	16.4	121 180	290	8 320	279 196	6.0
Napa, CA	2.4	D	6.9	19.5	6.2	5.2	6.0	10.2	16.3	26 435	187	2 387	55 472	1.3
Naples-Immokalee-Marco Island, FL	1.3	0.5	9.8	2.6	9.4	9.4	11.2	14.2	10.6	85 895	247	3 982	206 375	4.6
Nashville-Davidson—Murfreesboro—Franklin, TN	0.1	0.2	6.0	8.0	12.1	6.0	D	20.6	10.2	294 110	164	32 760	744 320	5.9
New Bern, NC	2.3	D	3.6	6.9	D	5.5	D	9.1	49.8	29 505	232	3 225	58 470	1.9
New Haven-Milford, CT	0.1	0.1	5.7	9.3	10.5	6.2	6.5	15.9	15.0	160 930	187	19 800	362 679	0.2
New Orleans-Metairie, LA	0.0	5.4	7.4	7.9	D	5.7	7.2	9.6	14.4	222 650	178	45 123	555 843	1.7
New York-Newark-Jersey City, NY-NJ-PA	0.0	D	4.4	D	D	5.0	19.0	10.3	14.1	3 207 905	160	603 451	7 892 416	1.4
Dutchess County-Putnam County, NY Div 20524	0.1	D	6.6	10.8	D	6.5	4.4	15.6	25.8	76 805	194	6 241	157 569	0.5
Nassau County-Suffolk County, NY Div 35004	0.1	D	6.6	5.7	12.4	7.1	9.6	14.4	19.8	541 110	189	37 498	1 037 488	-0.1
Newark, NJ-PA Div 35084	0.0	0.1	0.0	9.5	18.1	5.3	9.9	9.3	14.0	403 130	161	50 895	984 251	0.9
New York-Jersey City-White Plains, NY-NJ Div 35614	0.0	D	4.0	2.7	19.3	4.6	22.2	9.8	13.1	2 186 860	153	508 817	5 713 108	1.8
Niles-Benton Harbor, MI	1.3	0.2	4.0	30.2	3.9	5.5	3.9	11.2	14.3	37 255	240	5 020	76 793	-0.2
North Port-Sarasota-Bradenton, FL	0.9	0.1	7.8	6.1	11.1	9.7	8.3	16.4	11.3	218 015	291	10 718	414 742	3.4
Norwich-New London, CT	0.6	0.1	5.0	18.3	8.0	5.9	2.8	11.5	28.3	53 905	198	4 082	121 637	0.5
Ocala, FL	-0.3	0.1	6.2	8.9	6.5	11.1	5.4	19.1	17.2	110 610	327	9 350	163 808	-0.1
Ocean City, NJ	0.2	0.1	10.2	D	4.8	10.2	6.5	11.8	27.7	27 985	293	1 812	99 010	0.7
Odessa, TX	0.0	22.6	11.7	8.1	4.1	5.8	5.6	5.1	9.7	19 355	125	3 521	57 025	7.5
Ogden-Clearfield, UT	0.6	0.8	8.4	14.9	D	7.0	5.7	D	25.2	78 910	125	6 682	215 183	5.4
Oklahoma City, OK	0.3	D	5.5	6.1	D	6.1	6.6	D	18.7	220 865	165	27 254	564 440	4.7
Olympia-Tumwater, WA	0.7	0.0	5.1	3.2	6.1	6.7	4.5	12.6	39.7	53 820	202	5 195	112 553	4.0
Omaha-Council Bluffs, NE-IA	1.1	0.3	8.2	7.3	D	5.7	10.4	10.9	14.2	140 715	155	14 560	377 871	4.3
Orlando-Kissimmee-Sanford, FL	0.3	0.1	5.6	4.6	12.9	7.6	9.4	11.5	11.8	402 615	173	58 345	988 892	4.9
Oshkosh-Neenah, WI	0.5	D	6.0	30.5	7.1	4.7	5.1	9.6	12.6	32 875	194	2 473	74 551	1.7
Owensboro, KY	4.7	0.7	6.1	22.8	D	6.6	D	14.7	12.3	27 730	238	4 396	50 749	2.6
Oxnard-Thousand Oaks-Ventura, CA	3.9	1.8	4.7	15.6	9.6	6.7	9.0	9.0	17.2	130 995	155	16 583	285 880	1.5
Palm Bay-Melbourne-Titusville, FL	0.1	0.0	4.6	15.8	11.7	7.5	4.3	14.0	17.9	150 235	270	11 594	273 096	1.2
Panama City, FL	0.0	0.1	5.4	5.5	8.0	8.9	6.3	D	27.4	42 150	217	5 232	109 942	1.1
Parkersburg-Vienna, WV	-0.1	1.4	7.2	D	D	9.5	D	15.5	20.8	25 145	272	4 099	43 497	0.1
Pensacola-Ferry Pass-Brent, FL	0.1	0.2	5.1	4.5	8.7	7.4	6.9	14.9	30.1	101 520	215	12 616	207 629	3.1
Peoria, IL	1.3	D	5.7	25.7	D	5.0	D	14.7	11.4	77 420	204	7 277	166 098	1.1
Philadelphia-Camden-Wilmington, PA-NJ-DE-MD.	0.2	D	D	D	18.0	5.2	11.4	13.1	12.8	1 095 775	181	183 625	2 455 432	0.9
Camden, NJ Div 15804	0.3	0.0	6.1	8.1	10.2	7.8	7.5	14.1	19.4	239 205	191	27 118	496 585	1.3
Montgomery County-Bucks County-Chester County, PA	0.3	0.3	7.4	9.4	18.7	5.6	12.5	11.4	7.8	365 830	187	20 069	772 551	1.1
Philadelphia, PA Div 37964	0.0	D	2.9	4.4	21.1	3.5	9.8	15.0	15.1	360 775	170	122 939	894 462	0.2
Wilmington, DE-MD-NJ Div 48864	0.3	D	4.5	D	16.9	4.9	17.4	12.1	13.3	129 965	180	13 499	291 834	2.0
Phoenix-Mesa-Scottsdale, AZ	0.5	0.4	6.1	8.2	10.9	7.7	11.8	11.7	13.0	713 540	159	67 362	1 859 996	3.4
Pine Bluff, AR	7.2	D	3.3	17.5	D	6.3	D	D	28.0	20 880	220	5 357	42 149	0.5
Pittsburgh, PA	0.1	3.4	6.3	8.4	12.7	5.4	8.7	13.6	11.2	550 595	233	68 652	1 107 452	0.5
Pittsfield, MA	0.1	0.1	6.9	9.9	8.6	7.7	7.5	18.9	15.0	33 980	264	4 076	68 397	-0.2
Pocatello, ID	1.0	D	4.9	7.7	5.6	8.2	6.8	15.9	26.1	13 960	167	1 867	33 457	0.8
Portland-South Portland, ME	0.1	D	5.8	D	10.5	7.1	10.2	14.7	16.0	114 710	219	10 118	267 081	1.7
Portland-Vancouver-Hillsboro, OR-WA	0.6	0.1	6.2	13.9	D	5.8	7.2	D	13.8	383 105	163	44 345	959 565	3.7
Port St. Lucie, FL	0.9	D	6.0	5.2	8.8	10.2	5.7	16.9	16.5	117 005	263	8 408	217 310	1.0
Prescott, AZ	0.3	D	6.8	6.5	4.6	10.0	4.8	16.0	21.7	72 670	332	3 733	113 083	2.4
Providence-Warwick, RI-MA	0.1	D	5.5	D	10.2	6.4	8.3	15.0	16.6	334 620	208	52 431	694 206	0.0
Provo-Orem, UT	0.8	0.3	9.2	10.1	D	7.8	5.5	D	12.2	53 530	94	4 306	166 132	9.4
Pueblo, CO	0.3	0.2	7.6	11.4	6.1	8.1	3.1	19.8	21.1	34 920	216	6 287	70 142	0.9
Punta Gorda, FL	2.1	0.2	6.8	1.5	7.0	12.7	5.8	23.9	15.8	62 695	372	2 698	101 775	1.1
Racine, WI	0.3	0.1	4.7	35.8	4.2	5.7	4.2	12.0	14.0	40 735	209	5 321	82 323	0.2
Raleigh, NC	0.5	D	6.8	8.2	D	6.1	7.7	9.1	15.1	170 570	137	17 733	509 636	9.3
Rapid City, SD	2.1	D	8.1	4.0	D	8.0	6.7	D	24.0	30 155	210	2 394	63 745	5.2
Reading, PA	1.7	0.1	6.2	19.1	7.3	7.0	5.2	13.3	14.0	85 070	205	10 643	164 904	0.1

1. Per 1,000 resident population estimated as of July 1, 2011 of the year shown.

Table C. Metropolitan Areas — Housing, Labor Force, and Employment

Area name	Housing units, 2014 Occupied units Owner-occupied Total	Percent	Median value[1]	Median owner cost as a percent of income With a mortgage	Without a mortgage[2]	Renter-occupied Median rent[3]	Median rent as a percent of income	Percent with a computer	Civilian labor force, 2015 Total	Percent change, 2013–2014	Unemployment Total	Rate[4]	Civilian employment[5], 2014 Total employed	Percent Management, professional, and related occupations	Construction, production, and related occupations
	89	90	91	92	93	94	95	96	97	98	99	100	101	102	103
Modesto, CA	169 038	55.3	216 000	23.8	10.2	959	33.6	86.0	242 710	0.3	23 073	9.5	210 302	26.5	33.6
Monroe, LA	66 596	63.4	122 800	19.0	10.0	687	32.7	75.4	81 813	0.2	5 406	6.6	73 424	30.4	24.7
Monroe, MI	57 879	78.8	140 500	21.3	11.4	742	31.3	85.9	76 732	0.4	3 345	4.4	68 791	29.4	33.1
Montgomery, AL	142 432	64.8	134 000	21.3	10.2	817	28.8	82.8	168 786	-1.3	9 994	5.9	160 650	35.4	22.0
Morgantown, WV	49 804	64.2	137 400	17.7	10.0	758	35.7	85.2	65 696	1.2	3 302	5.0	60 487	40.6	19.9
Morristown, TN	45 581	67.9	131 100	20.9	12.0	660	31.1	77.7	49 733	0.4	3 199	6.4	46 382	28.8	34.1
Mount Vernon-Anacortes, WA	45 447	66.3	258 500	26.3	12.8	917	33.4	85.7	56 856	0.7	3 791	6.7	51 476	29.2	27.7
Muncie, IN	45 207	65.2	88 300	19.4	11.1	680	34.8	87.7	54 475	1.6	3 087	5.7	54 162	32.5	23.6
Muskegon, MI	64 646	74.6	96 200	21.0	12.2	659	32.5	82.4	77 763	0.3	4 319	5.6	68 884	29.6	29.4
Myrtle Beach-Conway-North Myrtle Beach, NC-SC	174 999	70.6	162 000	25.4	11.4	821	29.9	87.0	184 985	1.9	13 092	7.1	183 925	28.3	19.9
Napa, CA	50 516	63.3	511 800	24.9	11.2	1 450	34.3	90.2	74 752	1.2	3 442	4.6	69 374	35.1	21.6
Naples-Immokalee-Marco Island, FL	133 162	71.6	273 100	26.1	11.3	1 084	33.3	89.3	162 124	1.0	8 447	5.2	144 750	30.4	21.9
Nashville-Davidson—Murfreesboro—Franklin, TN	674 665	64.5	177 600	21.9	10.0	881	30.4	86.5	934 338	1.8	43 150	4.6	892 106	37.1	21.3
New Bern, NC	49 335	63.9	146 700	25.7	13.7	803	28.6	82.4	51 352	1.1	3 125	6.1	49 771	36.4	24.0
New Haven-Milford, CT	326 050	62.1	242 700	24.6	17.9	1 059	34.1	83.6	454 396	-0.2	27 907	6.1	418 153	41.4	18.4
New Orleans-Metairie, LA.....	474 715	61.2	174 200	23.3	10.7	903	33.1	79.9	603 674	0.7	36 072	6.0	582 103	36.2	19.7
New York-Newark-Jersey City, NY-NJ-PA	7 152 760	50.7	396 700	27.1	16.6	1 281	32.5	86.4	10 073 374	1.1	532 499	5.3	9 678 171	41.0	16.1
Dutchess County-Putnam County, NY Div 20524..	138 424	70.7	291 200	27.2	16.6	1 161	32.5	90.0	194 132	0.6	8 769	4.5	198 654	39.7	17.5
Nassau County-Suffolk County, NY Div 35004....	933 455	79.2	400 200	27.8	18.9	1 622	36.3	90.3	1 472 173	1.2	67 221	4.6	1 413 483	40.7	16.8
Newark, NJ-PA Div 35084....	882 527	62.5	361 600	25.8	17.0	1 177	31.6	87.9	1 262 102	0.2	68 811	5.5	1 250 203	42.6	16.8
New York-Jersey City-White Plains, NY-NJ Div 35614	5 198 354	43.0	413 200	27.2	15.5	1 279	32.4	85.4	7 144 967	1.2	387 698	5.4	6 815 831	40.9	15.7
Niles-Benton Harbor, MI	62 984	68.3	141 600	19.9	12.5	682	32.3	81.8	74 150	0.5	3 694	5.0	70 955	33.0	27.2
North Port-Sarasota-Bradenton, FL...........................	313 576	70.1	183 300	23.0	12.3	1 007	32.3	88.7	343 357	2.1	17 042	5.0	307 072	33.7	17.3
Norwich-New London, CT.....	105 504	66.8	234 900	23.6	13.6	1 003	29.0	87.5	136 630	-0.3	7 939	5.8	136 304	38.7	18.1
Ocala, FL	132 275	76.0	101 300	23.6	12.0	811	28.2	80.4	131 147	-0.6	8 358	6.4	121 979	26.0	19.9
Ocean City, NJ...................	40 779	76.0	296 800	27.2	19.4	1 099	38.0	85.1	48 896	0.2	5 307	10.9	42 481	31.9	17.9
Odessa, TX	50 724	62.9	123 700	19.9	10.0	1 049	26.1	87.8	79 869	-3.0	3 682	4.6	71 779	25.5	37.1
Ogden-Clearfield, UT...........	199 206	74.5	206 100	21.8	10.0	847	27.6	92.5	307 072	2.5	11 071	3.6	288 449	37.0	22.1
Oklahoma City, OK.............	499 878	63.2	139 200	20.1	10.5	782	28.3	86.6	668 199	2.7	24 707	3.7	634 967	36.9	22.0
Olympia-Tumwater, WA	103 319	60.3	244 100	22.9	10.7	1 108	29.2	89.6	125 603	1.9	7 425	5.9	123 121	42.4	17.7
Omaha-Council Bluffs, NE-IA......................................	346 283	65.0	147 300	20.8	12.1	830	27.8	86.1	477 954	0.3	15 379	3.2	468 767	38.0	19.3
Orlando-Kissimmee-Sanford, FL...................	800 299	59.7	162 700	23.9	11.8	1 035	34.0	87.8	1 223 514	1.4	61 540	5.0	1 086 088	35.4	16.1
Oshkosh-Neenah, WI...........	69 417	64.0	142 300	21.4	13.3	706	27.6	83.1	91 499	-0.2	3 937	4.3	89 519	28.7	28.4
Owensboro, KY	46 540	66.6	117 100	19.0	10.3	644	32.8	82.3	52 664	-2.9	2 500	4.7	50 281	31.0	28.5
Oxnard-Thousand Oaks-Ventura, CA........................	269 869	63.1	483 100	27.0	10.0	1 505	34.0	90.0	429 784	-0.7	24 435	5.7	401 648	37.2	21.8
Palm Bay-Melbourne-Titusville, FL..........................	225 226	69.3	149 400	23.1	11.5	924	32.2	88.2	257 684	-0.3	15 122	5.9	229 441	39.5	16.5
Panama City, FL.................	71 161	63.1	161 800	22.7	12.4	923	33.2	85.4	93 702	-0.2	5 047	5.4	80 061	31.3	22.3
Parkersburg-Vienna, WV	38 667	69.9	102 500	17.8	10.0	629	29.9	82.1	39 832	-0.8	2 573	6.5	39 577	30.1	24.1
Pensacola-Ferry Pass-Brent, FL......................................	171 179	63.0	134 800	22.4	11.0	919	29.2	87.9	213 181	0.1	11 259	5.3	201 475	35.2	18.8
Peoria, IL...........................	149 515	71.6	131 600	19.5	10.7	708	26.5	84.1	186 547	-0.9	12 100	6.5	178 071	38.1	21.5
Philadelphia-Camden-Wilmington, PA-NJ-DE-MD.	2 230 807	67.0	234 400	23.1	14.6	1 020	32.3	85.9	3 059 036	1.2	161 303	5.3	2 903 048	41.9	16.7
Camden, NJ Div 15804	457 793	72.6	214 800	23.7	17.2	1 073	32.3	87.7	637 382	1.1	36 990	5.8	615 635	40.9	17.6
Montgomery County-Bucks County-Chester County, PA	727 685	73.6	303 400	22.6	13.8	1 161	30.5	90.2	1 056 108	1.1	43 257	4.1	1 021 666	46.7	15.7
Philadelphia, PA Div 37964 ..	782 436	56.7	165 100	23.9	14.7	942	34.1	81.6	988 102	0.8	61 742	6.2	919 670	37.5	16.5
Wilmington, DE-MD-NJ Div 48864	262 893	69.2	234 000	22.0	12.7	1 012	30.0	83.5	377 444	2.8	19 314	5.1	346 077	41.4	19.0
Phoenix-Mesa-Scottsdale, AZ	1 590 240	59.6	197 900	21.3	10.3	969	29.8	86.6	2 165 131	2.5	113 890	5.3	2 000 722	36.2	18.6
Pine Bluff, AR	35 978	65.6	80 200	20.9	10.7	611	31.8	74.6	36 709	-0.3	2 572	7.0	34 931	30.7	27.7
Pittsburgh, PA	991 951	69.3	134 700	19.7	12.2	743	28.1	82.0	1 213 284	0.3	62 419	5.1	1 146 908	39.7	19.1
Pittsfield, MA	54 706	67.6	202 100	22.5	12.9	716	29.6	84.7	65 608	-0.5	3 658	5.6	64 714	36.6	18.0
Pocatello, ID......................	30 240	70.6	139 600	20.1	10.0	639	27.8	87.3	42 141	1.3	1 673	4.0	37 054	33.3	22.6
Portland-South Portland, ME	215 232	70.5	238 700	23.5	14.0	916	30.5	89.2	283 514	-1.6	10 211	3.6	278 375	40.6	17.7
Portland-Vancouver-Hillsboro, OR-WA	894 801	59.5	277 100	23.3	11.9	1 009	31.9	91.7	1 224 063	2.0	64 603	5.3	1 152 179	40.5	19.4
Port St. Lucie, FL................	171 289	75.6	151 800	25.7	13.3	1 050	36.4	85.9	201 248	0.8	11 861	5.9	179 975	33.0	17.8
Prescott, AZ	90 584	71.4	192 700	24.4	10.6	864	31.5	86.5	97 545	2.1	5 434	5.6	78 725	32.1	22.3
Providence-Warwick, RI-MA..	622 555	59.6	249 700	24.4	15.0	890	30.6	83.5	842 619	-0.1	51 268	6.1	795 418	35.6	20.2
Provo-Orem, UT..................	154 567	67.4	237 600	22.8	10.0	881	29.3	95.6	271 088	4.0	8 677	3.2	253 240	39.7	19.5
Pueblo, CO	63 385	65.3	137 500	23.3	11.4	750	32.5	84.3	71 996	-0.9	4 069	5.7	65 373	33.4	20.9
Punta Gorda, FL.................	75 234	79.2	146 300	25.4	13.0	849	36.2	86.5	67 559	0.8	3 967	5.9	58 030	30.6	19.9
Racine, WI	75 876	68.5	164 400	22.7	14.1	806	29.1	82.2	99 446	-0.5	5 650	5.7	92 157	32.9	26.4
Raleigh, NC	457 547	64.4	212 900	19.7	10.0	938	29.6	91.9	656 759	3.2	31 339	4.8	631 161	45.9	14.3
Rapid City, SD	56 274	67.4	165 200	22.3	12.9	779	27.3	85.2	71 553	0.3	2 353	3.3	73 135	32.5	21.9
Reading, PA.......................	152 908	70.1	168 600	22.6	13.8	864	33.0	82.1	213 249	1.1	10 151	4.8	198 117	31.4	28.8

1. Specified owner-occupied units.   2. A value of 10.0 represents 10 percent or less.   3. Specified renter-occupied units.   4. Percent of civilian labor force.
5. Persons 16 years old and over.

Table C. Metropolitan Areas — Nonfarm Employment and Agriculture

Area name	Private nonfarm establishments, employment and payroll, 2014									Agriculture, 2012			
	Number of establish-ments	Employment						Annual payroll		Farms			
		Total	Health care and social assistance	Manufac-turing	Retail trade	Finance and insurance	Professional, scientific, and technical services	Total (mil dol)	Average per employee (dollars)	Number	Percent with:		Farm operators whose principal occu-pation is farming (percent)
											Fewer than 50 acres	500 acres or more	
	104	105	106	107	108	109	110	111	112	113	114	115	116
Modesto, CA	8 544	132 417	23 286	19 300	22 628	3 314	5 416	5 466	41 277	4 143	68.8	5.9	59.1
Monroe, LA	4 552	66 676	15 228	5 967	10 245	4 152	2 844	2 343	35 146	863	40.0	6.7	44.5
Monroe, MI	2 260	36 169	5 418	6 868	5 019	871	1 091	1 550	42 856	1 144	53.0	10.9	46.3
Montgomery, AL	7 626	130 334	20 296	17 797	18 182	4 939	6 661	5 018	38 501	1 985	33.0	15.7	47.5
Morgantown, WV	2 819	49 376	15 370	4 423	6 852	991	2 396	1 981	40 111	1 542	26.3	3.3	42.6
Morristown, TN	1 923	37 218	5 212	10 704	5 669	780	442	1 284	34 497	1 550	47.2	1.6	45.5
Mount Vernon-Anacortes, WA	3 361	39 626	7 269	5 804	6 911	1 585	1 590	1 663	41 971	1 074	73.0	4.4	48.0
Muncie, IN	2 322	38 419	8 997	4 306	6 157	3 020	1 472	1 314	34 199	610	49.5	13.3	54.8
Muskegon, MI	3 153	52 027	10 904	12 286	8 006	1 055	1 431	2 009	38 614	514	56.6	4.9	48.4
Myrtle Beach-Conway-North Myrtle Beach, NC-SC	10 592	123 205	14 607	4 025	26 715	4 133	3 819	3 668	29 775	1 192	46.0	9.2	48.9
Napa, CA	4 075	60 882	10 383	11 304	6 861	1 412	1 829	2 933	48 174	1 685	71.9	5.3	34.9
Naples-Immokalee-Marco Island, FL	11 003	114 225	16 666	2 900	20 412	3 854	4 907	4 690	41 057	319	74.0	10.3	43.9
Nashville-Davidson—Mur-freesboro—Franklin, TN	40 484	774 736	125 230	66 153	89 657	41 560	49 169	36 576	47 211	13 301	39.9	4.5	41.6
New Bern, NC	2 521	30 794	7 033	3 265	5 253	889	1 841	1 103	35 821	506	41.3	17.2	61.3
New Haven-Milford, CT	19 467	338 587	73 535	32 597	42 717	12 527	15 224	16 614	49 068	695	77.3	1.2	43.0
New Orleans-Metairie, LA	30 049	490 361	72 310	28 770	60 613	19 636	34 239	23 114	47 137	1 027	65.4	7.4	45.2
New York-Newark-Jersey City, NY-NJ-PA	569 055	8 040 243	1 440 938	336 736	935 456	568 360	727 334	544 649	67 740	6 758	68.3	2.9	50.9
Dutchess County-Putnam County, NY Div 20524	NA	NA	NA	NA	NA	NA	NA	NA	NA	750	47.2	6.9	53.9
Nassau County-Suffolk County, NY Div 35004	NA	NA	NA	NA	NA	NA	NA	NA	NA	659	72.1	1.5	67.4
Newark, NJ-PA Div 35084	NA	NA	NA	NA	NA	NA	NA	NA	NA	3 169	71.7	2.1	43.4
New York-Jersey City-White Plains, NY-NJ Div 35614	NA	NA	NA	NA	NA	NA	NA	NA	NA	2 180	69.6	3.0	55.9
Niles-Benton Harbor, MI	3 543	53 366	9 144	8 773	6 966	1 262	1 932	2 273	42 584	1 063	57.9	7.0	51.0
North Port-Sarasota-Braden-ton, FL	21 306	221 630	42 206	14 162	40 577	8 007	12 994	8 298	37 440	972	65.3	8.8	43.7
Norwich-New London, CT	5 732	102 281	17 339	D	14 579	2 066	7 461	4 882	47 734	949	64.0	1.3	48.6
Ocala, FL	6 842	76 032	15 900	6 089	15 479	2 020	3 665	2 586	34 011	3 870	76.7	2.2	49.5
Ocean City, NJ	3 788	25 547	4 538	471	6 499	1 048	1 033	986	38 581	152	75.7	1.3	48.0
Odessa, TX	3 686	63 283	7 049	4 672	8 387	1 403	1 690	3 539	55 926	264	70.5	14.4	28.8
Ogden-Clearfield, UT	12 946	173 052	22 217	28 970	26 549	6 662	15 160	6 433	37 174	3 150	64.5	11.0	37.7
Oklahoma City, OK	34 769	502 066	79 303	31 006	66 860	23 098	32 000	22 142	44 102	9 797	35.7	12.4	43.2
Olympia-Tumwater, WA	5 923	66 373	13 204	2 642	12 391	2 681	4 689	2 561	38 578	1 336	79.3	2.0	30.7
Omaha-Council Bluffs, NE-IA	22 855	402 263	59 735	31 596	54 094	38 885	25 516	18 341	45 594	6 055	35.4	26.4	56.8
Orlando-Kissimmee-Sanford, FL	58 984	959 387	112 704	36 400	138 384	37 903	61 007	38 710	40 349	3 123	76.1	4.8	47.9
Oshkosh-Neenah, WI	3 490	81 908	12 116	19 561	8 700	3 402	2 893	3 887	47 458	1 117	48.5	6.0	39.2
Owensboro, KY	2 533	46 605	8 373	7 553	6 549	3 258	1 939	1 743	37 398	1 600	41.6	11.8	46.0
Oxnard-Thousand Oaks-Ven-tura, CA	20 251	251 566	34 844	24 280	38 761	12 799	22 262	12 826	50 984	2 150	78.0	5.2	48.7
Palm Bay-Melbourne-Titus-ville, FL	13 348	166 056	29 270	17 305	27 329	5 656	11 772	6 804	40 976	513	80.3	5.1	38.8
Panama City, FL	4 744	62 727	10 398	4 790	11 256	1 674	3 474	2 060	32 839	149	64.4	3.4	45.0
Parkersburg-Vienna, WV	2 111	33 284	7 390	2 778	6 325	1 018	927	1 154	34 673	1 033	28.0	2.3	34.8
Pensacola-Ferry Pass-Brent, FL	9 185	122 512	24 152	5 243	20 285	7 013	8 470	4 517	36 869	1 395	64.1	5.7	42.3
Peoria, IL	8 465	161 541	29 452	17 079	19 656	6 103	6 347	8 050	49 831	3 605	32.5	22.3	52.8
Philadelphia-Camden-Wil-mington, PA-NJ-DE-MD	145 269	2 550 162	465 181	171 896	306 480	170 018	207 039	139 916	54 865	6 543	65.1	3.9	54.8
Camden, NJ Div 15804	NA	NA	NA	NA	NA	NA	NA	NA	NA	1 597	72.5	3.7	51.6
Montgomery County-Bucks County-Chester County, PA	NA	NA	NA	NA	NA	NA	NA	NA	NA	3 153	64.2	2.3	57.2
Philadelphia, PA Div 37964	NA	NA	NA	NA	NA	NA	NA	NA	NA	98	68.4	0.0	48.0
Wilmington, DE-MD-NJ Div 48864	NA	NA	NA	NA	NA	NA	NA	NA	NA	1 695	59.6	7.4	53.7
Phoenix-Mesa-Scottsdale, AZ	90 849	1 574 007	216 628	101 772	207 184	114 961	109 667	72 328	45 952	3 417	76.9	10.4	54.2
Pine Bluff, AR	1 590	22 935	4 559	5 411	3 635	D	398	791	34 471	1 032	32.0	19.6	54,9
Pittsburgh, PA	59 644	1 092 675	201 024	89 196	127 444	58 064	75 867	51 895	47 493	7 048	37.1	3.0	45.3
Pittsfield, MA	3 900	52 802	11 587	4 764	8 755	1 997	D	2 192	41 507	525	49.9	4.4	51.0
Pocatello, ID	1 943	25 273	4 970	1 693	4 580	2 754	1 389	765	30 274	819	46.6	16.1	42.6
Portland-South Portland, ME	17 349	225 199	44 939	20 915	33 840	14 523	13 174	9 930	44 096	1 726	56.6	2.8	50.2
Portland-Vancouver-Hills-boro, OR-WA	65 127	941 033	135 502	105 533	111 677	43 628	69 176	48 488	51 527	10 838	79.1	1.9	42.3
Port St. Lucie, FL	10 324	107 781	20 312	5 472	22 990	2 980	5 482	3 875	35 951	993	64.7	13.1	54.0
Prescott, AZ	5 647	55 932	12 415	3 227	10 259	1 315	1 752	1 871	33 444	940	69.9	13.1	64.1
Providence-Warwick, RI-MA	40 615	610 632	127 299	63 405	83 010	31 402	27 657	27 550	45 117	1 960	72.3	0.8	49.5
Provo-Orem, UT	11 926	180 449	22 369	17 919	24 511	5 249	12 964	7 030	38 960	2 815	73.2	6.1	30.3
Pueblo, CO	3 014	47 148	12 634	4 136	7 914	1 154	1 595	1 757	37 269	894	38.9	21.3	52.3
Punta Gorda, FL	3 704	35 818	8 475	492	8 669	1 074	1 380	1 119	31 235	284	61.3	12.0	51.1
Racine, WI	3 986	68 267	11 126	16 231	8 820	2 093	1 898	3 062	44 849	575	51.0	8.2	45.6
Raleigh, NC	30 759	472 872	62 496	22 827	64 143	23 391	49 978	23 498	49 692	2 500	50.5	6.7	45.9
Rapid City, SD	4 705	54 622	10 817	3 157	9 721	3 641	2 033	2 006	36 734	1 936	24.9	42.6	54.8
Reading, PA	8 274	149 151	24 997	30 352	20 609	5 627	6 357	6 527	43 764	2 039	47.8	3.5	61.4

Table C. Metropolitan Areas — **Agriculture**

Area name	Land in farms Acreage (1,000)	Percent change, 2007–2012	Acres Average size of farm	Total irrigated (1,000)	Total cropland (1,000)	Value of land and buildings (dollars) Average per farm	Average per acre	Value of machinery and equipment, average per farm (dollars)	Value of products sold Total (mil dol)	Average per farm (dollars)	Percent from: Crops	Live-stock and poultry products	Percent of farms with sales of: $10,000 or more	$100,000 or more	Government payments Total ($1,000)	Percent of farms
	117	118	119	120	121	122	123	124	125	126	127	128	129	130	131	132
Modesto, CA	768	-2.7	185	320.8	340.9	1 786 289	9 636	117 810	2 228.1	537 807	47.7	52.3	66.5	33.9	7 049	10.7
Monroe, LA	156	2.0	180	12.2	64.3	525 813	2 913	73 651	142.0	164 531	20.0	80.0	34.8	12.4	2 099	17.8
Monroe, MI	215	3.2	188	9.8	196.2	853 688	4 553	135 682	173.9	152 008	95.5	4.5	54.6	20.3	3 653	50.8
Montgomery, AL	640	2.6	322	10.1	172.7	753 146	2 337	72 061	200.1	100 782	D	D	36.2	8.4	4 011	25.6
Morgantown, WV	219	3.4	142	0.1	59.8	373 360	2 633	53 257	22.2	14 383	28.0	72.0	28.7	2.2	387	7.7
Morristown, TN	154	-9.7	100	D	65.1	510 717	5 127	57 306	59.8	38 562	26.4	73.6	27.5	3.4	754	15.3
Mount Vernon-Anacortes, WA	107	-1.8	99	19.2	66.8	752 365	7 585	118 998	272.3	253 515	73.8	26.2	29.1	12.2	1 442	11.1
Muncie, IN	175	13.5	287	0.0	160.4	1 522 762	5 300	152 951	125.6	205 836	93.2	6.8	52.1	26.9	3 980	67.4
Muskegon, MI	74	-6.8	144	9.5	49.0	741 080	5 130	95 333	76.0	147 860	61.6	38.4	38.9	15.6	658	21.8
Myrtle Beach-Conway-North Myrtle Beach, NC-SC	223	7.4	187	6.8	135.5	613 356	3 278	93 415	159.5	133 816	67.5	32.5	32.0	13.7	2 576	41.3
Napa, CA	253	13.5	150	54.6	63.0	3 278 130	21 801	85 134	536.1	318 188	97.8	2.2	74.5	34.1	85	1.1
Naples-Immokalee-Marco Island, FL	124	12.4	387	26.4	66.9	1 736 727	4 482	151 806	202.8	635 583	98.1	1.9	36.4	14.7	207	2.8
Nashville-Davidson—Murfreesboro—Franklin, TN	1 868	-3.1	140	6.1	733.8	592 188	4 217	60 620	D	D	D	D	28.9	4.6	7 865	17.8
New Bern, NC	177	-5.0	349	4.4	136.2	1 010 889	2 893	192 399	276.9	547 283	D	D	49.4	31.8	4 482	57.7
New Haven-Milford, CT	42	-7.4	61	1.3	14.1	764 679	12 561	56 881	84.6	121 755	91.7	8.3	31.9	10.1	383	7.3
New Orleans-Metairie, LA	230	-15.3	224	D	68.4	635 817	2 843	75 303	77.8	75 785	71.4	28.6	33.7	7.6	D	6.3
New York-Newark-Jersey City, NY-NJ-PA	D	D	D	D	D	D	D	D	D	D	D	D	39.5	13.2	D	9.8
Dutchess County-Putnam County, NY Div 20524	118	9.6	158	D	47.2	820 965	5 201	92 353	52.3	69 704	55.5	44.5	47.2	16.4	451	10.0
Nassau County-Suffolk County, NY Div 35004	39	8.3	59	11.9	23.5	713 168	12 158	131 416	246.1	373 389	84.3	15.7	62.4	31.1	790	6.5
Newark, NJ-PA Div 35084	235	-3.4	74	2.8	117.1	1 055 516	14 250	59 764	144.7	45 663	D	D	27.8	6.2	D	8.4
New York-Jersey City-White Plains, NY-NJ Div 35614	D	D	D	10.2	D	D	D	D	D	D	D	D	46.8	16.9	D	12.8
Niles-Benton Harbor, MI	156	-7.5	147	18.1	126.1	822 736	5 591	123 913	161.5	151 968	90.3	9.7	51.6	20.6	3 303	29.4
North Port-Sarasota-Bradenton, FL	267	-6.9	274	52.1	75.1	1 468 749	5 356	94 934	323.5	332 798	89.0	11.0	38.4	12.4	395	1.3
Norwich-New London, CT	65	2.8	69	0.8	22.8	709 299	10 330	47 891	118.3	124 690	43.2	56.8	26.9	6.7	537	9.2
Ocala, FL	321	20.6	83	13.2	69.8	776 909	9 353	37 481	188.2	48 624	23.3	76.7	27.8	8.2	483	2.1
Ocean City, NJ	7	-7.8	48	2.2	4.3	557 868	11 534	51 809	8.0	52 809	93.4	6.6	40.1	10.5	D	2.0
Odessa, TX	429	1.2	1 624	0.8	3.6	786 019	484	48 008	2.2	8 296	28.9	71.1	16.3	1.5	211	5.3
Ogden-Clearfield, UT	1 572	-11.5	499	163.5	390.3	891 628	1 787	88 691	266.5	84 616	48.0	52.0	35.1	12.3	8 138	20.8
Oklahoma City, OK	2 466	-7.5	252	31.6	839.6	492 117	1 955	64 720	451.1	46 043	32.4	67.6	32.8	6.8	13 028	25.7
Olympia-Tumwater, WA	77	-4.9	57	5.3	23.1	498 439	8 689	40 468	122.4	91 634	39.9	60.1	19.5	5.2	267	2.4
Omaha-Council Bluffs, NE-IA	2 373	9.9	392	D	2 092.0	2 376 608	6 064	217 610	1 649.3	272 378	74.2	25.8	60.6	39.0	40 234	69.0
Orlando-Kissimmee-Sanford, FL	853	-9.2	273	55.0	81.9	1 468 380	5 374	45 570	539.8	172 845	88.9	11.1	37.6	14.1	632	1.6
Oshkosh-Neenah, WI	156	-5.2	139	0.4	126.2	585 332	4 204	97 747	126.6	113 315	41.3	58.7	41.5	20.1	3 245	54.3
Owensboro, KY	414	-10.9	259	11.3	310.1	959 871	3 711	135 426	370.2	231 353	49.6	50.4	43.7	18.8	6 252	57.9
Oxnard-Thousand Oaks-Ventura, CA	281	8.5	131	87.1	101.1	2 041 990	15 621	94 136	1 440.1	669 829	99.3	0.7	65.1	24.7	154	2.0
Palm Bay-Melbourne-Titusville, FL	146	-12.3	286	13.4	19.3	1 545 698	5 414	45 433	46.0	89 651	77.2	22.8	36.8	6.6	142	2.1
Panama City, FL	15	-12.4	101	D	3.2	494 671	4 886	36 826	3.6	24 436	63.6	36.4	18.8	2.0	D	7.4
Parkersburg-Vienna, WV	126	-3.3	122	D	29.5	258 830	2 124	35 881	8.3	8 082	30.4	69.6	15.3	0.5	157	4.5
Pensacola-Ferry Pass-Brent, FL	172	13.2	123	7.1	109.7	508 622	4 120	72 795	105.3	75 502	92.7	7.3	24.9	9.5	3 971	27.7
Peoria, IL	1 288	2.9	357	D	1 149.9	2 619 353	7 332	215 209	960.8	266 524	87.7	12.3	62.8	41.4	25 748	76.4
Philadelphia-Camden-Wilmington, PA-NJ-DE-MD	653	-3.8	100	51.0	456.1	1 066 581	10 682	100 412	1 264.9	193 316	D	D	43.9	18.2	D	16.8
Camden, NJ Div 15804	146	3.6	92	24.7	89.0	960 535	10 485	93 126	204.6	128 112	95.0	5.0	39.6	14.6	2 659	12.4
Montgomery County-Bucks County-Chester County, PA	259	-8.9	82	2.9	173.7	1 068 407	12 992	94 153	748.8	237 474	80.2	19.8	47.1	20.3	2 503	14.3
Philadelphia, PA Div 37964	5	8.4	51	0.1	1.3	797 133	15 593	51 439	10.5	107 643	98.7	1.3	36.7	7.1	D	2.0
Wilmington, DE-MD-NJ Div 48864	243	-2.4	143	23.3	192.1	1 178 678	8 232	121 753	301.0	177 561	D	D	42.4	18.3	4 693	26.5
Phoenix-Mesa-Scottsdale, AZ	1 651	7.7	483	416.5	525.1	1 606 626	3 326	134 243	1 931.2	565 178	39.5	60.5	37.0	18.4	14 937	14.7
Pine Bluff, AR	519	-0.3	503	D	421.0	1 463 373	2 912	248 855	540.5	523 758	58.2	41.8	49.1	33.6	18 108	53.1
Pittsburgh, PA	818	-6.7	116	2.4	409.7	491 395	4 235	76 477	231.1	32 792	59.1	40.9	34.4	6.1	5 514	18.6
Pittsfield, MA	62	-7.1	117	0.2	18.4	824 924	7 024	51 476	22.5	42 796	45.1	54.9	29.5	6.7	268	9.3
Pocatello, ID	295	-8.3	360	52.6	164.1	651 077	1 807	83 179	54.3	66 267	66.6	33.4	29.4	9.2	3 067	37.0
Portland-South Portland, ME	147	13.6	85	2.1	44.1	404 259	4 737	57 375	D	D	D	D	32.4	6.8	994	7.0
Portland-Vancouver-Hillsboro, OR-WA	644	-2.7	59	75.1	340.4	624 772	10 520	59 443	1 008.7	93 072	D	D	27.6	7.6	5 384	7.7
Port St. Lucie, FL	334	18.2	337	94.1	110.4	1 858 422	5 518	72 106	333.5	335 878	77.8	22.2	42.8	17.1	1 270	5.5
Prescott, AZ	825	29.0	877	7.6	10.7	1 382 518	1 576	51 250	41.6	44 285	25.5	74.5	32.2	12.0	141	3.2
Providence-Warwick, RI-MA	D	D	D	5.6	34.5	757 972	D	54 363	97.3	49 648	81.1	18.9	35.9	8.7	D	14.3
Provo-Orem, UT	586	-3.3	208	95.6	157.4	753 272	3 619	70 725	251.0	89 161	43.7	56.3	31.4	6.9	2 120	11.0
Pueblo, CO	895	-1.7	1 001	18.6	88.5	735 098	734	62 169	51.1	57 149	35.4	64.6	27.2	8.1	2 223	20.6
Punta Gorda, FL	217	30.8	765	13.7	18.4	3 875 556	5 067	65 965	103.4	364 088	91.8	8.2	38.0	13.0	92	1.8
Racine, WI	110	-8.7	191	1.9	92.6	1 042 289	5 450	127 732	94.8	164 887	77.6	22.4	50.3	21.7	1 972	50.6
Raleigh, NC	396	1.0	158	10.6	237.5	902 766	5 700	94 320	411.9	164 756	65.9	34.1	35.6	14.4	6 265	34.1
Rapid City, SD	3 730	-6.6	1 927	12.9	619.5	1 464 500	760	105 970	208.2	107 542	27.8	72.2	56.0	24.1	9 162	33.6
Reading, PA	234	5.2	115	1.6	182.3	1 015 554	8 859	120 253	528.7	259 299	42.6	57.4	58.5	30.2	3 646	28.3

Area name	Water use, 2010		Wholesale trade,[1] 2012				Retail trade, 2012				Real estate and rental and leasing, 2012			
	Total water withdrawn (mil gal/day)	Gallons withdrawn per person per day	Number of establishments	Number of employees	Sales (mil dol)	Annual payroll (mil dol)	Number of establishments	Number of employees	Sales (mil dol)	Annual payroll (mil dol)	Number of establishments	Number of employees	Receipts (mil dol)	Annual payroll (mil dol)
	133	134	135	136	137	138	139	140	141	142	143	144	145	146
Modesto, CA	1 642.7	3 193	405	6 087	5 295.1	313.6	1 374	20 970	5 933.6	527.1	433	2 141	387.9	73.2
Monroe, LA	72.2	409	187	2 190	1 793.0	96.6	776	9 812	2 528.4	220.3	190	1 154	229.3	38.1
Monroe, MI	1 830.0	12 038	89	D	D	D	377	4 977	1 471.2	110.5	78	306	43.8	7.9
Montgomery, AL	113.7	303	360	5 844	4 361.6	272.4	1 322	17 359	4 678.9	421.7	309	2 146	377.1	72.4
Morgantown, WV	123.3	950	71	486	374.3	17.4	476	7 179	1 843.1	146.7	152	799	128.8	22.1
Morristown, TN	18.2	160	68	943	1 100.5	45.5	391	5 674	1 619.1	131.9	79	297	62.0	8.9
Mount Vernon-Anacortes, WA	45.3	388	104	1 277	793.5	58.2	553	6 801	1 999.2	186.8	158	467	81.8	14.4
Muncie, IN	15.6	132	92	894	805.8	32.1	428	6 189	1 519.9	131.9	95	447	90.7	16.5
Muskegon, MI	271.7	1 578	121	D	D	D	552	7 597	1 919.4	171.2	91	457	71.7	14.8
Myrtle Beach-Conway-North Myrtle Beach, NC-SC	1 525.6	4 050	307	2 149	971.4	87.0	2 037	25 110	6 365.9	556.0	718	5 052	591.6	151.2
Napa, CA	96.9	710	167	D	D	D	524	6 318	1 699.0	184.2	207	1 026	160.4	38.2
Naples-Immokalee-Marco Island, FL	256.9	799	306	2 417	2 306.5	163.1	1 418	18 924	5 304.1	511.0	907	2 610	546.6	109.8
Nashville-Davidson—Murfreesboro—Franklin, TN	891.7	534	1 760	32 450	48 065.9	1 851.8	6 018	85 291	23 831.1	2 149.6	1 756	10 598	2 557.2	478.8
New Bern, NC	44.8	353	91	803	1 408.6	30.5	461	4 882	1 347.4	115.1	111	376	46.1	10.7
New Haven-Milford, CT	113.5	132	922	14 185	11 237.2	821.2	2 901	41 925	11 567.5	1 100.7	673	5 378	2 008.0	220.2
New Orleans-Metairie, LA	4 541.9	3 817	1 411	19 692	33 417.9	1 064.1	4 480	57 986	16 445.2	1 503.7	1 222	7 682	1 793.8	319.7
New York-Newark-Jersey City, NY-NJ-PA	7 105.0	363	33 908	412 171	507 384.4	28 173.7	78 193	896 588	270 758.2	25 968.1	33 390	178 052	65 022.2	9 852.3
Dutchess County-Putnam County, NY Div 20524	84.5	213	315	2 814	4 858.3	181.1	1 375	17 192	4 744.9	429.7	414	1 533	280.2	53.6
Nassau County-Suffolk County, NY Div 35004	1 136.2	401	5 694	66 586	60 342.0	4 120.9	12 669	156 986	47 799.0	4 388.8	4 008	16 099	4 922.6	835.9
Newark, NJ-PA Div 35084	410.6	166	3 527	58 817	76 074.4	4 651.1	8 600	112 874	36 178.3	3 107.7	2 541	16 253	5 851.7	899.5
New York-Jersey City-White Plains, NY-NJ Div 35614	5 473.7	395	24 372	283 954	366 109.6	19 220.6	55 549	609 536	182 036.0	18 042.0	26 427	144 167	53 967.8	8 063.3
Niles-Benton Harbor, MI	2 019.0	12 875	133	D	D	D	587	6 783	1 681.1	147.2	152	614	78.3	19.5
North Port-Sarasota-Bradenton, FL	157.8	225	751	6 092	3 496.9	283.0	2 832	37 299	9 942.8	926.9	1 301	4 688	1 068.6	180.5
Norwich-New London, CT	2 249.8	8 209	150	D	D	D	1 023	14 372	3 679.3	364.3	204	765	182.6	32.0
Ocala, FL	65.4	197	277	3 157	1 719.3	143.3	1 152	14 430	4 263.6	353.9	338	1 382	211.8	41.3
Ocean City, NJ	79.6	818	60	D	D	D	669	5 803	1 639.4	166.2	218	681	148.7	26.0
Odessa, TX	60.2	439	298	4 659	3 608.8	330.5	451	7 286	2 711.7	218.7	176	1 482	604.9	101.9
Ogden-Clearfield, UT	795.6	1 332	460	5 797	4 437.8	247.6	1 708	25 217	6 975.2	593.7	726	1 965	359.1	61.2
Oklahoma City, OK	263.1	210	1 472	21 416	45 661.6	1 219.0	4 318	61 357	19 131.2	1 578.5	1 713	9 151	2 064.4	407.4
Olympia-Tumwater, WA	52.3	207	169	1 824	1 252.0	90.8	769	12 317	3 330.8	324.6	325	994	202.1	31.3
Omaha-Council Bluffs, NE-IA	1 570.7	1 815	1 139	16 116	19 466.9	866.4	2 705	51 093	14 650.4	1 227.3	1 015	6 759	1 210.3	292.0
Orlando-Kissimmee-Sanford, FL	509.9	239	2 582	28 410	24 271.6	1 413.0	8 166	124 686	37 046.0	3 002.2	3 691	27 653	6 908.9	1 046.4
Oshkosh-Neenah, WI	35.3	211	136	D	D	D	473	7 892	2 064.9	174.5	113	576	219.2	19.9
Owensboro, KY	577.6	5 034	108	1 392	1 267.3	60.1	456	6 229	1 547.9	141.1	85	591	102.2	19.5
Oxnard-Thousand Oaks-Ventura, CA	719.5	874	985	D	D	D	2 562	37 012	11 194.2	1 011.0	1 008	4 568	983.6	196.5
Palm Bay-Melbourne-Titusville, FL	251.4	463	451	3 962	1 846.5	195.7	1 955	24 885	6 527.5	606.1	642	2 056	340.7	66.7
Panama City, FL	303.6	1 644	163	1 472	522.2	63.9	857	10 636	2 805.1	256.9	291	1 460	213.3	40.8
Parkersburg-Vienna, WV	63.8	689	77	D	D	D	403	6 095	1 416.4	130.3	85	D	D	D
Pensacola-Ferry Pass-Brent, FL	337.9	753	330	2 953	1 719.6	124.7	1 477	19 315	5 356.2	468.5	489	1 781	340.3	56.9
Peoria, IL	648.5	1 710	401	6 169	4 946.2	296.2	1 290	19 211	5 010.7	456.4	312	1 335	266.4	43.7
Philadelphia-Camden-Wilmington, PA-NJ-DE-MD	5 352.0	897	6 714	103 885	112 303.8	6 892.7	19 892	297 081	85 570.3	7 755.5	5 229	36 509	13 076.4	1 908.7
Camden, NJ Div 15804	239.2	191	1 360	25 642	36 358.5	1 498.0	4 112	63 959	17 767.4	1 638.0	933	7 228	1 743.9	381.8
Montgomery County-Bucks County-Chester County, PA	488.6	254	3 100	47 014	49 846.9	3 504.5	7 186	122 083	38 696.3	3 449.9	1 977	13 567	3 404.4	703.1
Philadelphia, PA Div 37964	1 157.1	555	1 569	23 901	18 664.2	1 509.3	6 206	74 456	18 710.1	1 767.7	1 488	11 801	2 727.4	613.2
Wilmington, DE-MD-NJ Div 48864	3 467.2	4 913	685	7 328	7 434.2	380.9	2 388	36 583	10 396.5	899.8	831	3 913	5 200.6	210.6
Phoenix-Mesa-Scottsdale, AZ	3 083.7	735	4 058	59 578	61 626.6	3 549.5	10 899	191 751	59 671.8	5 115.0	5 578	30 399	7 712.9	1 367.6
Pine Bluff, AR	576.3	5 748	65	D	D	D	329	3 719	914.8	82.4	70	229	39.7	6.6
Pittsburgh, PA	1 712.7	727	2 561	37 959	42 687.8	2 075.7	8 271	126 114	34 250.1	2 907.5	2 034	12 564	2 998.5	548.8
Pittsfield, MA	24.3	185	105	1 242	455.0	58.0	711	8 482	1 916.5	201.7	108	715	99.5	23.1
Pocatello, ID	168.1	2 029	80	D	D	D	299	4 330	1 155.3	95.7	80	221	31.5	5.2
Portland-South Portland, ME	114.0	222	622	7 227	6 787.0	367.3	2 457	32 974	8 665.6	788.1	768	3 495	647.7	132.3
Portland-Vancouver-Hillsboro, OR-WA	733.4	329	3 035	44 671	40 137.7	2 629.7	7 084	105 037	29 004.4	2 832.2	3 353	17 891	3 578.8	700.3
Port St. Lucie, FL	1 302.5	3 071	352	D	D	D	1 438	21 908	6 262.8	600.4	519	2 333	386.7	80.6
Prescott, AZ	92.3	437	163	1 385	880.4	59.1	787	9 854	2 504.3	233.3	341	941	153.0	27.7
Providence-Warwick, RI-MA	1 257.6	786	1 675	26 253	31 686.2	1 626.5	5 987	81 494	20 467.4	2 020.3	1 476	6 997	1 413.5	271.7
Provo-Orem, UT	422.2	801	377	5 832	3 148.9	300.7	1 553	22 409	6 153.9	534.7	686	1 871	339.0	53.7
Pueblo, CO	288.9	1 816	85	D	D	D	508	7 551	1 952.8	183.4	143	585	105.1	17.7
Punta Gorda, FL	58.8	367	94	D	D	D	558	8 000	2 091.3	185.9	232	680	113.1	19.1
Racine, WI	28.6	146	170	2 243	1 702.5	118.6	591	8 542	2 182.0	181.6	100	327	58.9	9.7
Raleigh, NC	153.6	136	1 212	19 573	19 650.4	1 474.6	3 838	59 857	16 847.3	1 453.3	1 439	7 825	1 764.6	407.5
Rapid City, SD	74.5	554	180	1 944	1 287.9	86.1	683	9 154	2 529.9	219.6	192	645	115.1	18.0
Reading, PA	57.1	139	354	6 912	4 277.4	362.2	1 256	20 219	5 719.4	494.3	246	1 249	213.0	41.4

1. Merchant wholesalers, except manufacturers' sales branches and offices.

Table C. Metropolitan Areas — **Professional Services, Manufacturing, and Accommodation and Food Services**

Area name	Professional, scientific, and technical services, 2012				Manufacturing, 2012				Accommodation and food services, 2012			
	Number of establishments	Number of employees	Sales (mil dol)	Annual payroll (mil dol)	Number of establishments	Number of employees	Sales (mil dol)	Annual payroll (mil dol)	Number of establishments	Number of employees	Sales (mil dol)	Annual payroll (mil dol)
	147	148	149	150	151	152	153	154	155	156	157	158
Modesto, CA	649	5 111	507.5	196.0	395	19 963	11 703.6	1 007.8	813	13 611	705.7	192.6
Monroe, LA	449	2 737	379.1	125.2	136	6 067	2 438.8	286.3	310	6 524	298.1	81.5
Monroe, MI	147	828	129.9	40.6	128	6 591	2 976.5	351.3	259	4 280	179.9	49.6
Montgomery, AL	756	6 906	1 421.8	433.6	287	17 367	14 627.6	896.5	671	13 503	636.6	174.8
Morgantown, WV	234	2 834	405.3	124.7	78	4 133	2 181.4	273.8	317	6 165	267.1	73.8
Morristown, TN	110	438	48.8	14.1	144	10 205	4 224.1	418.1	178	3 065	152.3	40.6
Mount Vernon-Anacortes, WA	300	D	D	D	174	5 269	11 529.4	295.7	330	4 195	291.5	79.1
Muncie, IN	163	1 522	240.5	63.4	130	4 205	1 591.3	191.2	211	4 417	172.7	49.6
Muskegon, MI	223	1 513	182.5	65.7	259	12 483	3 727.0	608.0	335	5 450	236.1	67.6
Myrtle Beach-Conway-North Myrtle Beach, NC-SC	866	3 696	400.6	143.7	216	4 213	2 742.7	222.8	1 489	29 339	1 897.5	499.8
Napa, CA	395	1 801	280.5	101.5	431	10 837	4 623.5	622.5	375	10 466	774.1	247.7
Naples-Immokalee-Marco Island, FL	1 342	4 810	784.7	270.4	197	2 722	607.5	130.0	763	19 624	1 406.5	404.2
Nashville-Davidson—Murfreesboro—Franklin, TN	3 785	38 289	6 215.8	2 520.0	1 488	61 378	28 947.4	2 916.1	3 530	76 659	4 275.8	1 250.6
New Bern, NC	250	1 884	220.7	97.0	85	3 535	1 308.0	164.3	234	4 207	198.3	54.1
New Haven-Milford, CT	1 907	16 222	2 461.1	1 216.8	1 151	31 792	10 818.1	1 879.2	1 969	26 342	1 487.2	411.3
New Orleans-Metairie, LA	3 884	31 419	5 507.7	2 078.7	742	34 170	104 969.4	2 377.1	3 217	69 067	4 502.4	1 259.1
New York-Newark-Jersey City, NY-NJ-PA	69 819	710 316	163 194.8	61 316.7	16 232	346 950	134 229.9	19 621.2	48 312	634 388	49 193.7	13 558.1
Dutchess County-Putnam County, NY Div 20524	1 086	5 256	833.3	299.0	285	10 022	2 790.6	742.5	979	10 711	599.9	162.2
Nassau County-Suffolk County, NY Div 35004	12 457	87 339	13 447.4	5 200.1	3 110	68 546	21 084.1	3 694.2	7 107	89 642	5 929.2	1 628.8
Newark, NJ-PA Div 35084	9 067	112 684	22 364.6	9 712.9	2 448	70 600	38 127.3	4 797.5	5 475	72 580	4 728.5	1 272.8
New York-Jersey City-White Plains, NY-NJ Div 35614	47 209	505 037	126 549.4	46 104.7	10 389	197 783	72 228.0	10 387.1	34 751	461 455	37 936.1	10 494.2
Niles-Benton Harbor, MI	284	2 149	201.0	108.3	289	8 330	1 962.8	388.9	365	5 323	241.7	69.4
North Port-Sarasota-Bradenton, FL	2 703	20 704	1 945.0	841.3	591	13 680	3 538.1	670.9	1 446	26 437	1 429.1	419.4
Norwich-New London, CT	529	8 100	666.1	862.0	172	12 435	4 693.7	950.2	698	28 347	3 023.8	748.7
Ocala, FL	669	3 676	415.5	157.2	178	4 806	1 471.2	212.9	437	7 369	375.2	102.5
Ocean City, NJ	214	D	D	D	66	615	98.2	21.5	903	5 888	593.0	160.0
Odessa, TX	227	1 832	205.4	80.1	251	4 756	1 706.3	265.7	261	6 150	389.0	94.0
Ogden-Clearfield, UT	1 443	10 848	1 407.6	525.8	596	27 115	14 050.6	1 478.6	855	15 956	671.2	190.6
Oklahoma City, OK	4 132	27 776	4 052.7	1 582.9	1 050	31 032	11 209.0	1 338.6	2 685	57 866	2 741.9	749.8
Olympia-Tumwater, WA	593	D	D	D	168	2 883	910.5	123.8	533	7 785	419.2	120.5
Omaha-Council Bluffs, NE-IA	2 342	59 415	3 755.6	2 966.2	656	30 185	17 651.7	1 361.4	1 901	36 416	1 866.7	512.8
Orlando-Kissimmee-Sanford, FL	7 816	58 862	8 811.8	3 756.9	1 337	32 960	11 209.7	1 917.5	4 484	138 873	10 349.4	2 695.0
Oshkosh-Neenah, WI	247	2 575	514.5	134.8	300	23 892	11 476.5	1 321.6	367	5 963	234.6	65.3
Owensboro, KY	169	1 563	105.3	44.8	125	6 938	5 391.9	357.4	193	4 448	191.8	55.3
Oxnard-Thousand Oaks-Ventura, CA	2 634	22 377	3 185.4	2 063.2	867	23 166	8 334.0	1 295.4	1 598	27 725	1 597.4	442.6
Palm Bay-Melbourne-Titusville, FL	1 669	13 893	2 433.6	981.2	407	19 152	5 441.9	1 311.3	1 042	18 994	902.6	257.7
Panama City, FL	434	3 465	493.8	184.2	110	3 904	1 482.5	197.5	497	10 318	581.6	165.7
Parkersburg-Vienna, WV	165	D	D	D	63	2 882	D	207.9	218	D	D	D
Pensacola-Ferry Pass-Brent, FL	1 063	9 010	1 234.8	486.1	229	4 433	2 552.0	262.3	747	14 767	744.0	203.9
Peoria, IL	676	6 718	865.5	374.9	331	19 563	13 708.7	1 081.5	870	15 632	778.2	212.7
Philadelphia-Camden-Wilmington, PA-NJ-DE-MD	18 064	199 353	37 881.9	16 087.3	5 115	172 790	99 584.5	10 453.8	12 771	198 333	11 474.3	3 164.3
Camden, NJ Div 15804	3 281	D	D	D	967	34 775	D	2 101.0	2 395	36 821	1 967.4	525.4
Montgomery County-Bucks County-Chester County, PA	8 266	83 896	15 163.1	6 634.4	2 565	82 694	30 889.5	4 823.6	4 218	66 585	3 705.4	1 043.4
Philadelphia, PA Div 37964	4 370	59 242	12 848.3	5 152.2	1 132	35 487	27 083.4	2 173.3	4 774	69 816	4 429.8	1 218.4
Wilmington, DE-MD-NJ Div 48864	2 147	D	D	D	451	19 834	D	1 356.0	1 384	25 111	1 371.7	377.1
Phoenix-Mesa-Scottsdale, AZ	11 812	91 918	15 658.8	5 865.3	3 000	94 061	36 827.5	5 560.6	7 121	165 154	9 456.3	2 745.4
Pine Bluff, AR	87	594	66.7	28.3	70	5 532	2 226.6	243.5	134	2 365	93.0	23.1
Pittsburgh, PA	5 871	81 204	15 404.9	5 698.3	2 506	90 107	38 416.1	4 812.4	5 374	92 549	4 548.1	1 266.2
Pittsfield, MA	338	2 688	397.7	162.8	151	5 275	1 288.9	310.7	522	7 006	418.7	124.2
Pocatello, ID	165	1 277	84.2	40.3	44	1 633	916.3	67.7	197	3 199	135.5	37.2
Portland-South Portland, ME	1 923	13 183	2 086.5	801.2	662	21 142	6 501.6	1 099.6	1 823	24 102	1 457.2	436.0
Portland-Vancouver-Hillsboro, OR-WA	8 099	68 556	9 720.6	5 233.3	3 058	D	D	D	5 743	86 242	4 870.0	1 428.9
Port St. Lucie, FL	1 211	5 244	685.0	246.3	296	4 883	1 709.0	237.3	724	12 867	642.0	182.8
Prescott, AZ	522	1 748	190.9	74.3	184	2 765	706.9	130.8	548	8 223	407.5	130.8
Providence-Warwick, RI-MA	4 042	27 215	4 161.4	1 605.4	2 183	66 543	19 277.2	3 628.5	4 214	63 818	3 450.4	982.0
Provo-Orem, UT	1 654	16 956	1 741.7	656.3	525	15 963	6 082.1	807.2	709	13 249	577.3	161.5
Pueblo, CO	238	1 744	435.3	157.3	90	4 221	2 333.3	216.8	356	5 698	236.0	67.8
Punta Gorda, FL	381	1 295	138.5	50.5	69	402	90.4	14.6	261	4 804	219.2	61.7
Racine, WI	310	1 967	234.8	91.7	325	15 444	8 100.1	844.4	382	5 974	251.7	70.5
Raleigh, NC	4 656	41 942	7 437.7	3 117.2	738	21 629	17 865.0	1 146.8	2 415	47 908	2 436.0	675.1
Rapid City, SD	372	2 151	243.7	83.2	164	2 383	570.3	95.4	480	7 455	426.6	117.1
Reading, PA	703	D	D	D	498	29 439	10 905.1	1 547.9	754	12 294	548.8	155.6

Area name	Health care and social assistance, 2012				Other services, 2012				Nonemployer business, 2014		Value of residential construction authorized by building permits, 2015	
	Number of establishments	Number of employees	Receipts (mil dol)	Annual payroll (mil dol)	Number of establishments	Number of employees	Receipts (mil dol)	Annual payroll (mil dol)	Number	Receipts (mil dol)	New construction ($1,000)	Number of housing units
	159	160	161	162	163	164	165	166	167	168	169	170
Modesto, CA	1 075	24 257	3 635.0	1 274.8	604	3 817	371.6	118.9	26 685	1 347.0	93 426	413
Monroe, LA	661	14 936	1 407.9	504.3	243	1 568	144.3	42.1	14 238	571.1	123 585	605
Monroe, MI	282	5 347	457.9	193.6	156	727	67.6	17.0	8 394	356.9	49 920	291
Montgomery, AL	875	20 240	2 062.6	869.8	569	3 906	468.3	130.1	24 550	1 018.1	177 300	1 099
Morgantown, WV	295	14 178	1 582.2	569.5	177	1 316	190.7	34.3	6 974	319.6	8 747	166
Morristown, TN	230	5 680	491.1	189.8	114	526	42.4	12.9	6 667	280.5	44 487	188
Mount Vernon-Anacortes, WA	330	7 152	700.3	296.6	252	1 128	106.0	31.3	7 548	357.7	87 559	438
Muncie, IN	313	9 158	873.1	318.7	174	1 043	105.9	26.2	5 510	206.6	10 089	46
Muskegon, MI	369	11 494	982.3	483.8	250	1 315	120.8	29.6	9 409	339.1	45 234	241
Myrtle Beach-Conway-North Myrtle Beach, NC-SC	878	14 479	1 600.7	571.0	623	3 183	324.9	77.9	32 729	1 451.5	1 167 044	6 154
Napa, CA	404	10 222	1 360.7	553.3	241	1 359	127.7	40.0	11 740	722.3	56 035	172
Naples-Immokalee-Marco Island, FL	995	16 310	2 089.4	772.0	850	5 209	474.4	138.1	36 864	2 165.4	1 275 698	4 060
Nashville-Davidson—Murfreesboro—Franklin, TN	4 208	109 447	13 584.2	5 158.9	2 507	19 844	2 180.7	640.4	157 709	8 192.7	3 472 438	18 291
New Bern, NC	293	8 064	806.0	330.9	167	832	70.7	18.5	7 255	276.0	54 987	435
New Haven-Milford, CT	2 408	73 162	7 788.2	3 238.4	1 717	9 881	977.8	297.8	58 579	3 051.3	146 364	1 161
New Orleans-Metairie, LA	3 205	67 442	7 698.1	2 899.3	1 850	12 712	1 868.6	426.7	114 656	5 234.2	538 281	2 495
New York-Newark-Jersey City, NY-NJ-PA	60 802	1 438 772	161 273.4	66 480.3	48 848	291 897	42 605.8	10 194.7	1 836 538	99 777.3	11 996 315	86 424
Dutchess County-Putnam County, NY Div 20524	1 162	23 662	2 563.7	1 086.5	824	3 627	397.2	105.5	30 013	1 418.4	86 845	351
Nassau County-Suffolk County, NY Div 35004	10 507	207 080	23 582.4	10 013.4	8 013	40 426	4 189.4	1 107.1	262 027	16 014.8	1 083 964	2 304
Newark, NJ-PA Div 35084	7 795	155 717	17 765.9	7 176.8	5 410	35 343	3 614.8	1 051.8	198 815	11 914.5	974 652	9 929
New York-Jersey City-White Plains, NY-NJ Div 35614	41 338	1 052 313	117 361.3	48 203.6	34 601	212 501	34 404.4	7 930.2	1 345 683	70 429.5	9 850 854	73 840
Niles-Benton Harbor, MI	399	9 410	816.5	329.2	251	1 199	116.0	32.2	9 818	380.6	58 833	208
North Port-Sarasota-Bradenton, FL	2 393	40 770	4 488.5	1 669.2	1 448	7 481	648.2	176.8	68 249	3 418.5	1 601 753	7 141
Norwich-New London, CT	734	17 357	1 728.0	751.2	459	2 498	274.7	61.9	16 099	780.0	108 515	531
Ocala, FL	878	15 494	1 874.0	674.9	455	2 315	196.6	54.0	23 622	978.3	195 638	1 055
Ocean City, NJ	278	4 767	443.7	186.8	296	1 237	96.3	32.4	8 029	461.3	181 526	614
Odessa, TX	293	7 384	823.7	297.6	250	2 276	340.1	83.5	11 204	728.6	111 046	612
Ogden-Clearfield, UT	1 431	21 624	2 361.9	801.8	809	4 688	374.1	106.9	39 084	1 644.3	651 418	3 120
Oklahoma City, OK	4 134	76 535	9 611.3	3 270.6	2 067	13 049	1 632.8	381.5	104 667	5 213.2	1 285 543	6 004
Olympia-Tumwater, WA	790	13 079	1 584.8	619.1	483	2 769	331.1	98.1	14 338	610.0	238 139	1 020
Omaha-Council Bluffs, NE-IA	2 439	61 248	6 795.6	2 552.5	1 603	10 653	1 536.4	314.5	57 461	2 591.8	677 404	4 157
Orlando-Kissimmee-Sanford, FL	5 726	108 835	13 809.2	4 884.8	3 592	23 294	2 405.8	635.2	209 712	8 235.2	3 667 980	20 474
Oshkosh-Neenah, WI	439	13 580	1 272.0	555.0	257	2 279	221.0	68.1	8 275	363.1	106 564	710
Owensboro, KY	348	7 891	759.3	301.6	167	1 100	83.1	25.8	6 483	269.2	33 245	243
Oxnard-Thousand Oaks-Ventura, CA	2 557	32 438	3 987.6	1 434.5	1 176	7 150	763.3	188.6	66 566	3 590.0	350 485	1 433
Palm Bay-Melbourne-Titusville, FL	1 522	31 218	3 727.6	1 387.7	958	4 563	372.7	117.7	41 106	1 616.9	557 448	1 918
Panama City, FL	515	10 051	1 078.2	412.5	321	1 936	160.6	43.4	14 398	688.0	246 368	988
Parkersburg-Vienna, WV	287	7 169	639.4	248.5	152	D	D	D	4 603	191.6	20 361	177
Pensacola-Ferry Pass-Brent, FL	1 019	24 040	2 905.3	1 091.4	594	3 417	307.7	88.5	31 324	1 289.2	378 541	2 634
Peoria, IL	840	30 651	3 197.1	1 286.0	613	6 256	590.3	251.2	19 543	734.6	116 071	502
Philadelphia-Camden-Wilmington, PA-NJ-DE-MD	17 408	463 943	51 028.6	20 690.6	11 378	74 202	9 462.5	2 309.9	399 535	21 222.7	1 925 338	12 317
Camden, NJ Div 15804	3 439	76 614	8 247.2	3 369.2	2 200	13 271	1 065.6	334.8	71 336	3 821.4	280 607	2 670
Montgomery County-Bucks County-Chester County, PA	6 477	145 503	15 158.5	6 213.8	4 374	28 315	4 325.0	894.6	160 369	9 568.7	697 892	3 767
Philadelphia, PA Div 37964	5 528	191 974	21 925.2	8 572.2	3 609	24 712	3 271.7	844.7	124 905	5 231.8	771 888	4 015
Wilmington, DE-MD-NJ Div 48864	1 964	49 852	5 697.8	2 535.4	1 195	7 904	800.2	235.9	42 925	2 600.9	174 951	1 865
Phoenix-Mesa-Scottsdale, AZ	11 231	207 257	24 523.2	9 574.2	5 505	43 914	4 609.6	1 279.1	304 623	14 734.7	5 565 485	22 402
Pine Bluff, AR	237	4 827	429.9	173.6	105	530	49.1	15.8	4 758	160.9	3 726	31
Pittsburgh, PA	7 942	190 828	18 711.4	7 858.7	5 155	32 089	3 524.7	897.4	141 732	6 586.1	1 073 130	5 264
Pittsfield, MA	438	11 415	1 091.4	488.4	278	1 675	144.1	39.5	10 121	445.3	58 072	214
Pocatello, ID	335	3 819	314.1	115.4	120	591	61.6	15.7	5 008	188.0	23 503	190
Portland-South Portland, ME	2 038	44 844	4 350.3	1 882.7	1 164	6 448	701.2	179.9	47 172	2 251.7	385 898	1 980
Portland-Vancouver-Hillsboro, OR-WA	7 272	132 399	16 118.5	6 283.0	4 277	25 065	3 122.2	806.2	166 824	8 191.5	2 713 034	13 967
Port St. Lucie, FL	1 191	18 821	2 288.4	829.9	761	3 811	330.2	96.8	38 009	1 679.4	381 546	1 601
Prescott, AZ	759	11 555	1 245.1	517.8	364	1 717	142.9	41.0	18 322	751.4	292 110	1 377
Providence-Warwick, RI-MA	4 650	123 284	11 708.9	5 129.5	3 361	18 660	1 923.7	529.5	106 897	4 877.1	358 971	1 818
Provo-Orem, UT	1 219	21 246	2 228.3	776.1	634	3 398	272.7	73.9	42 866	1 876.2	1 027 110	4 549
Pueblo, CO	419	11 404	1 063.1	458.0	238	1 222	93.1	28.2	8 095	305.1	46 258	282
Punta Gorda, FL	485	8 927	1 119.6	401.0	297	1 326	113.0	33.0	12 454	571.3	246 218	1 129
Racine, WI	459	10 588	764.4	335.7	317	1 839	140.4	44.5	9 539	386.2	54 673	217
Raleigh, NC	3 069	53 424	5 654.4	2 278.0	1 959	13 792	1 557.4	446.6	96 376	4 339.2	2 092 616	11 987
Rapid City, SD	408	11 766	1 318.5	509.7	334	1 801	220.7	45.4	11 014	502.6	128 759	798
Reading, PA	827	25 605	2 588.9	1 067.0	767	4 046	363.5	101.5	24 160	1 132.4	74 107	416

1. Establishments subject to federal tax.

Table C. Metropolitan Areas — Government Employment and Payroll and Local Government Finances

		Government employment and payroll, 2012								Local government finances, 2012				
			March payroll (percent of total)							General revenue				
												Taxes		
													Per capita[1] (dollars)	
Area name	Full-time equivalent employees	March Payroll (dollars)	Administration, judicial, and legal	Police and corrections	Fire protection	Highways and transportation	Health and welfare	Natural resources and utilities	Education and libraries	Total (mil dol)	Inter-governmental (mil dol)	Total (mil dol)	Total	Property
	171	172	173	174	175	176	177	178	179	180	181	182	183	184
Modesto, CA	19 446	94 702 481	5.9	8.3	2.5	1.6	11.8	9.4	58.2	2 696.4	1 547.9	554.1	1 062	825
Monroe, LA	8 044	23 625 209	7.1	11.1	3.2	2.1	4.4	5.4	65.9	699.4	335.0	289.5	1 628	585
Monroe, MI	3 882	16 268 085	7.1	8.4	1.4	3.3	1.1	4.8	72.4	475.7	225.8	166.5	1 102	1 074
Montgomery, AL	12 833	40 413 140	4.7	13.6	5.4	3.2	3.3	7.9	56.9	1 415.6	468.2	359.9	954	325
Morgantown, WV	3 679	10 784 021	6.6	6.4	2.1	3.9	3.1	7.2	67.9	282.4	117.1	109.2	814	659
Morristown, TN	3 406	10 523 184	5.5	8.9	3.2	3.2	3.1	11.3	62.6	288.5	121.7	106.7	928	541
Mount Vernon-Anacortes, WA	5 963	27 675 332	5.4	5.4	2.0	4.5	41.5	4.7	33.8	852.8	275.6	199.6	1 688	1 157
Muncie, IN	3 335	10 832 587	6.2	9.0	3.6	4.7	3.7	4.2	64.9	345.4	171.1	109.1	930	778
Muskegon, MI	5 428	21 789 876	7.5	7.4	2.5	3.3	9.1	3.1	65.4	721.5	413.6	168.4	989	913
Myrtle Beach-Conway-North Myrtle Beach, NC-SC	13 720	47 691 925	8.0	11.3	4.0	2.9	7.2	7.6	55.9	1 554.9	373.0	787.2	1 995	1 260
Napa, CA	5 012	27 819 123	11.8	13.2	3.0	2.1	9.4	6.0	49.6	811.6	274.6	367.8	2 645	2 138
Naples-Immokalee-Marco Island, FL	9 918	41 162 175	6.9	15.7	6.7	3.5	4.2	9.1	52.0	1 300.6	231.7	737.4	2 218	2 006
Nashville-Davidson—Murfreesboro—Franklin, TN .	62 367	213 611 379	6.4	10.6	4.9	2.3	11.3	9.7	53.1	5 944.5	1 864.0	2 495.0	1 445	925
New Bern, NC	6 791	24 592 380	3.3	4.8	1.6	1.2	45.2	4.1	38.0	754.9	290.2	112.7	880	654
New Haven-Milford, CT	28 448	140 929 161	3.5	10.1	6.3	2.6	2.7	5.4	68.7	3 790.8	1 443.5	2 034.2	2 358	2 333
New Orleans-Metairie, LA	43 957	168 084 037	8.4	14.9	3.0	2.9	22.4	8.9	37.2	7 012.5	2 504.9	2 443.4	1 991	986
New York-Newark-Jersey City, NY-NJ-PA	859 136	4 981 795 701	4.0	15.9	3.9	8.2	12.0	4.2	49.2	158 755.3	48 519.4	84 882.7	4 280	2 827
Dutchess County-Putnam County, NY Div 20524	15 834	82 439 707	5.8	9.6	2.2	4.0	5.7	1.6	70.0	2 303.5	678.0	1 388.4	3 498	2 873
Nassau County-Suffolk County, NY Div 35004	123 812	732 874 581	4.1	11.7	0.9	2.5	7.4	3.2	68.6	20 978.5	5 325.7	13 527.4	4 749	3 856
Newark, NJ-PA Div 35084	95 852	533 906 989	5.6	13.8	3.9	2.5	4.8	4.3	63.1	13 124.9	3 533.4	8 066.3	3 241	3 160
New York-Jersey City-White Plains, NY-NJ Div 35614	623 638	3 632 574 424	3.8	17.2	4.5	10.3	14.2	4.4	42.7	122 348.4	38 982.3	61 900.6	4 391	2 559
Niles-Benton Harbor, MI	4 813	18 604 576	9.6	10.9	2.0	2.9	2.9	4.5	64.6	601.1	301.4	200.9	1 288	1 264
North Port-Sarasota-Bradenton, FL	26 901	101 649 100	7.7	11.2	6.0	3.4	20.0	5.4	43.7	3 172.2	626.1	1 212.8	1 684	1 368
Norwich-New London, CT	8 967	42 369 410	4.4	7.7	3.8	3.8	2.3	8.0	68.3	1 101.6	386.5	598.5	2 183	2 159
Ocala, FL	10 760	33 096 942	6.2	11.8	9.0	0.5	2.5	5.9	63.0	875.9	312.2	296.0	883	746
Ocean City, NJ	5 885	27 086 618	8.8	13.8	3.3	3.6	9.4	7.3	49.4	701.1	152.6	449.5	4 667	4 561
Odessa, TX	6 915	26 339 816	4.0	7.3	3.2	1.3	27.3	2.1	53.3	690.5	140.4	269.5	1 867	1 389
Ogden-Clearfield, UT	19 885	69 703 618	6.0	9.0	3.0	1.6	5.2	6.0	67.8	1 758.6	707.7	680.0	1 110	794
Oklahoma City, OK	43 376	150 970 463	5.1	11.2	7.5	3.0	11.2	5.1	56.1	4 132.3	1 264.1	1 725.9	1 331	666
Olympia-Tumwater, WA	7 290	36 403 899	10.9	9.6	5.9	9.3	2.0	8.9	51.8	946.4	372.7	391.6	1 516	997
Omaha-Council Bluffs, NE-IA	36 524	145 002 288	4.4	9.9	3.3	3.6	4.1	18.6	55.0	3 737.9	1 239.7	1 804.1	2 037	1 532
Orlando-Kissimmee-Sanford, FL	79 591	284 688 968	6.3	14.2	7.2	4.2	4.2	8.8	52.4	8 588.1	2 537.2	3 519.5	1 583	1 131
Oshkosh-Neenah, WI	5 300	21 156 305	4.4	11.7	4.6	5.5	11.2	7.1	54.5	697.9	338.4	249.0	1 475	1 436
Owensboro, KY	5 043	15 494 560	4.3	6.6	2.9	2.8	6.8	13.2	62.0	421.7	154.4	115.6	996	570
Oxnard-Thousand Oaks-Ventura, CA	27 714	159 457 912	10.1	10.8	4.6	3.0	13.0	7.6	49.2	4 630.9	2 005.3	1 379.1	1 650	1 378
Palm Bay-Melbourne-Titusville, FL	19 755	66 076 682	7.5	12.3	7.0	4.4	7.8	7.9	52.0	1 764.4	557.0	634.8	1 160	923
Panama City, FL	8 675	32 038 863	3.7	6.7	2.4	3.9	34.3	5.0	42.7	881.5	209.8	288.2	1 536	1 098
Parkersburg-Vienna, WV	3 144	10 362 577	4.7	5.3	2.0	2.6	2.6	6.3	74.9	235.4	113.7	77.6	838	630
Pensacola-Ferry Pass-Brent, FL	14 772	47 095 540	7.2	13.2	2.2	2.6	3.7	6.5	62.2	1 288.3	501.5	467.6	1 014	750
Peoria, IL	13 803	52 130 853	6.3	10.3	3.9	4.6	3.2	6.6	63.1	1 517.9	612.5	635.6	1 671	1 435
Philadelphia-Camden-Wilmington, PA-NJ-DE-MD	205 195	1 004 418 815	6.6	13.0	2.3	7.2	5.0	5.0	59.4	31 396.9	12 075.3	14 182.1	2 356	1 683
Camden, NJ Div 15804	50 866	263 407 426	3.8	10.2	2.3	2.9	4.8	3.0	70.8	6 825.7	2 374.5	3 161.2	2 520	2 481
Montgomery County-Bucks County-Chester County, PA	55 254	262 211 582	6.4	11.3	0.4	2.9	4.5	3.7	69.4	8 269.3	2 143.8	4 825.6	2 485	2 076
Philadelphia, PA Div 37964	78 984	387 798 667	9.0	16.8	3.9	13.9	6.0	7.3	42.1	13 846.4	6 463.2	5 279.8	2 504	1 061
Wilmington, DE-MD-NJ Div 48864	20 091	91 001 140	5.5	9.7	1.2	2.8	2.8	4.4	71.6	2 455.5	1 093.8	915.5	1 283	1 049
Phoenix-Mesa-Scottsdale, AZ	139 712	587 672 336	8.5	13.3	5.3	2.9	6.2	12.0	50.6	15 082.4	5 190.2	6 265.2	1 447	928
Pine Bluff, AR	3 495	9 830 121	6.5	12.0	3.9	3.6	1.5	2.1	68.3	261.9	169.1	57.9	594	257
Pittsburgh, PA	76 232	322 348 429	6.5	11.1	1.8	8.6	5.9	6.4	58.3	10 916.6	4 733.0	4 213.3	1 785	1 286
Pittsfield, MA	4 790	19 230 480	4.3	8.5	3.3	5.5	1.3	4.1	71.5	506.3	218.2	246.7	1 897	1 828
Pocatello, ID	2 618	8 746 568	9.9	14.1	5.7	4.0	6.0	6.6	51.4	238.0	114.9	73.0	871	828
Portland-South Portland, ME .	19 117	71 307 958	5.3	8.8	5.0	4.0	3.6	6.3	65.4	1 897.9	500.0	1 074.0	2 073	2 046
Portland-Vancouver-Hillsboro, OR-WA	70 641	332 827 613	7.2	11.0	5.2	8.1	4.4	8.5	51.7	10 118.9	3 858.3	4 062.9	1 774	1 375
Port St. Lucie, FL	15 221	57 466 642	7.0	15.0	8.7	2.3	1.8	6.2	55.9	1 562.3	448.2	714.5	1 651	1 400
Prescott, AZ	6 155	23 081 009	10.4	13.4	9.4	4.0	2.1	5.5	45.2	648.3	201.2	335.8	1 579	1 029
Providence-Warwick, RI-MA	47 209	226 744 364	3.5	10.7	8.1	2.2	1.2	5.2	67.9	6 092.6	2 097.6	3 232.0	2 018	1 964
Provo-Orem, UT	14 474	53 579 798	6.4	8.0	2.5	1.5	4.8	8.4	66.6	1 615.5	670.1	586.2	1 064	722
Pueblo, CO	5 698	21 434 409	5.8	12.3	11.0	3.0	6.6	9.0	49.7	552.8	247.0	223.3	1 388	895
Punta Gorda, FL	4 654	16 650 878	13.2	15.5	8.9	5.6	2.0	7.8	45.5	559.2	101.1	264.1	1 626	1 290
Racine, WI	6 208	25 453 020	4.3	13.6	5.6	3.5	5.9	4.0	61.9	757.1	345.7	302.7	1 554	1 513
Raleigh, NC	40 839	150 997 987	3.4	8.5	3.1	3.1	10.3	5.9	61.8	4 020.3	1 569.5	1 583.3	1 332	1 007
Rapid City, SD	5 051	15 769 374	6.1	10.9	1.5	3.1	2.5	4.6	66.3	484.3	139.9	245.5	1 773	1 269
Reading, PA	14 566	69 528 665	6.1	16.3	5.1	2.6	4.7	5.3	58.7	2 039.3	792.5	835.6	2 021	1 642

1. Based on the resident population estimated as of July 1 of the year shown.

Table C. Metropolitan Areas — Local Government Finances, Government Employment, and Voting

Area name	Local government finances, 2012 (cont.) Direct general expenditure — Total (mil dol)	Per capita[1] (dollars)	Percent of total for: Education	Health and hospitals	Police protection	Public welfare	Highways	Debt outstanding Total (mil dol)	Per capita[1] (dollars)	Government employment, 2014 Federal civilian	Federal military	State and local	Presidential election,[2] 2012 Percent of vote cast: Democratic	Republican	All other
	185	186	187	188	189	190	191	192	193	194	195	196	197	198	199
Modesto, CA	2 792.3	5 352	50.1	6.9	4.9	10.2	3.4	4 496.8	8 619	818	819	25 891	50.0	47.3	2.7
Monroe, LA	748.1	4 208	53.1	2.8	5.8	0.1	2.9	495.7	2 788	523	787	11 174	37.5	61.2	1.3
Monroe, MI	515.6	3 414	53.6	6.7	3.7	0.2	9.1	557.6	3 691	219	252	5 304	49.8	48.9	1.3
Montgomery, AL	1 403.7	3 722	34.2	33.5	5.6	0.3	2.9	1 403.6	3 722	6 280	4 239	33 764	49.8	49.5	0.7
Morgantown, WV	293.9	2 191	58.5	2.3	5.1	0.3	1.8	267.7	1 996	2 085	638	17 084	39.3	58.0	2.7
Morristown, TN	294.2	2 560	53.3	1.8	5.5	4.4	4.6	336.9	2 932	284	363	5 886	25.2	73.3	1.5
Mount Vernon-Anacortes, WA	797.6	6 747	26.4	43.2	2.9	0.1	3.4	556.4	4 706	368	328	10 635	51.9	45.4	2.7
Muncie, IN	323.3	2 755	48.4	0.8	3.9	0.5	2.7	191.9	1 635	281	352	10 587	50.4	47.3	2.4
Muskegon, MI	746.4	4 386	51.2	13.2	3.2	3.6	4.5	688.6	4 046	335	306	7 308	58.3	40.5	1.1
Myrtle Beach-Conway-North Myrtle Beach, NC-SC	1 496.4	3 793	37.4	11.8	6.6	1.4	4.4	2 146.9	5 441	1 005	1 572	20 065	35.9	63.0	1.2
Napa, CA	821.7	5 909	37.5	5.9	7.5	4.2	4.0	746.0	5 365	215	212	9 716	63.0	34.3	2.8
Naples-Immokalee-Marco Island, FL	1 313.8	3 952	37.5	3.0	12.1	0.6	6.0	2 257.5	6 791	628	651	12 032	34.7	64.7	0.6
Nashville-Davidson—Murfreesboro—Franklin, TN	5 917.9	3 427	40.3	11.8	6.7	0.7	3.2	9 772.4	5 660	12 375	6 027	93 980	41.0	57.4	1.5
New Bern, NC	730.7	5 704	24.7	49.9	4.0	4.0	0.8	197.3	1 540	5 404	9 062	8 440	40.9	58.1	1.0
New Haven-Milford, CT	4 427.8	5 132	58.4	0.6	4.3	0.3	2.5	3 649.0	4 229	5 335	1 921	44 838	60.7	38.3	1.0
New Orleans-Metairie, LA	6 862.8	5 593	28.3	16.1	5.5	1.0	4.4	9 273.5	7 557	11 764	8 588	69 918	49.2	48.9	2.0
New York-Newark-Jersey City, NY-NJ-PA	155 295.2	7 831	37.1	7.8	6.1	10.2	2.3	228 317.6	11 513	111 514	43 152	1 162 270	64.8	34.2	1.0
Dutchess County-Putnam County, NY Div 20524	2 273.0	5 726	57.0	3.2	3.6	6.6	4.3	1 817.8	4 580	1 324	609	23 152	50.6	47.8	1.6
Nassau County-Suffolk County, NY Div 35004	22 106.9	7 761	50.8	5.4	7.0	5.6	3.2	19 089.0	6 701	16 614	5 258	166 529	52.2	46.7	1.1
Newark, NJ-PA Div 35084	13 275.6	5 334	50.9	2.5	6.4	2.0	2.6	11 054.8	4 442	18 346	5 212	158 507	58.9	40.1	1.0
New York-Jersey City-White Plains, NY-NJ Div 35614	117 639.8	8 345	32.6	8.9	6.0	12.1	2.1	196 356.0	13 928	75 230	32 073	814 082	69.7	29.3	1.0
Niles-Benton Harbor, MI	618.7	3 965	53.9	7.1	5.5	1.4	5.2	398.2	2 551	312	278	9 140	46.2	52.7	1.1
North Port-Sarasota-Bradenton, FL	3 246.3	4 509	31.7	19.9	6.6	0.3	4.4	3 286.5	4 564	1 915	1 480	24 328	44.8	54.3	0.9
Norwich-New London, CT	1 142.0	4 165	60.1	0.7	5.5	0.6	6.1	911.5	3 324	2 510	7 050	29 671	58.3	40.1	1.6
Ocala, FL	879.1	2 623	48.9	2.0	7.6	0.7	6.3	732.6	2 186	673	626	13 955	41.4	57.7	0.9
Ocean City, NJ	808.9	8 400	33.8	1.5	5.3	4.4	4.9	673.4	6 992	446	1 029	8 317	45.2	53.8	1.0
Odessa, TX	691.3	4 790	36.3	40.0	3.5	0.0	2.4	385.4	2 670	164	314	9 348	25.0	73.8	1.2
Ogden-Clearfield, UT	1 761.7	2 877	51.2	2.7	6.1	1.8	3.1	1 655.4	2 703	18 591	6 174	30 520	20.0	78.0	2.1
Oklahoma City, OK	3 850.3	2 970	45.9	9.2	8.1	0.1	5.6	3 940.9	3 039	27 031	10 934	94 754	36.5	63.5	0.0
Olympia-Tumwater, WA	952.8	3 688	42.4	5.4	4.0	0.0	7.1	917.5	3 552	867	771	35 152	58.3	38.8	2.9
Omaha-Council Bluffs, NE-IA	3 646.7	4 118	52.0	2.7	5.1	0.7	4.4	7 717.4	8 714	9 418	9 130	53 514	44.0	54.0	2.0
Orlando-Kissimmee-Sanford, FL	8 694.5	3 910	39.3	3.5	7.5	0.8	5.5	14 655.7	6 591	12 593	4 645	101 861	53.4	45.7	0.9
Oshkosh-Neenah, WI	708.5	4 197	35.6	2.5	5.6	20.8	8.3	688.0	4 076	401	453	11 933	51.0	47.2	1.8
Owensboro, KY	454.5	3 917	36.1	5.3	3.4	0.1	3.3	1 881.3	16 214	294	384	6 445	38.6	59.5	1.9
Oxnard-Thousand Oaks-Ventura, CA	4 471.8	5 349	38.6	13.1	7.5	4.6	3.5	3 011.8	3 603	6 917	5 055	35 902	52.3	45.3	2.5
Palm Bay-Melbourne-Titusville, FL	1 830.9	3 345	36.4	11.6	7.9	0.4	4.3	1 872.2	3 421	6 157	2 836	22 388	43.1	55.8	1.1
Panama City, FL	987.2	5 261	32.4	23.6	6.5	0.0	4.6	937.7	4 998	3 620	4 199	9 855	27.7	71.1	1.2
Parkersburg-Vienna, WV	236.3	2 554	64.2	0.1	5.1	0.0	3.8	191.5	2 070	2 202	448	4 588	33.0	65.3	1.7
Pensacola-Ferry Pass-Brent, FL	1 512.8	3 280	44.3	2.8	7.1	0.2	4.4	3 484.8	7 556	6 558	13 664	20 898	33.7	65.2	1.1
Peoria, IL	1 492.8	3 924	48.0	1.3	5.9	1.7	6.8	1 259.9	3 312	2 240	823	19 547	44.2	53.9	1.9
Philadelphia-Camden-Wilmington, PA-NJ-DE-MD	30 309.1	5 036	49.1	6.0	5.4	5.2	2.6	44 541.2	7 400	51 314	23 396	291 736	64.0	34.9	1.1
Camden, NJ Div 15804	6 604.3	5 265	56.5	2.6	4.4	2.8	3.3	7 416.2	5 912	8 064	7 720	73 893	61.4	37.5	1.1
Montgomery County-Buc County-Chester County, PA	8 574.7	4 415	57.3	2.4	4.9	5.8	3.8	11 320.4	5 829	6 029	5 313	77 723	52.6	46.3	1.1
Philadelphia, PA Div	12 546.9	5 950	37.7	11.3	5.9	7.0	1.3	23 338.7	11 068	32 019	6 667	96 954	77.9	21.2	0.8
Wilmington, DE-MD-NJ 48864	2 583.2	3 620	58.6	1.0	6.6	0.5	3.1	2 465.8	3 456	5 202	3 696	43 166	61.2	37.2	1.6
Phoenix-Mesa-Scottsdale, AZ	15 046.5	3 475	42.0	5.1	8.3	1.5	4.0	29 018.4	6 702	21 469	13 724	211 214	43.5	54.7	1.8
Pine Bluff, AR	262.8	2 696	61.5	0.1	6.9	0.1	4.7	246.8	2 533	1 556	411	8 508	57.4	40.8	1.8
Pittsburgh, PA	10 894.8	4 615	46.7	6.2	3.8	6.8	3.4	20 628.3	8 738	17 618	6 636	101 533	48.8	50.0	1.2
Pittsfield, MA	629.4	4 841	60.3	0.5	3.2	0.3	5.9	274.5	2 111	367	318	8 318	75.7	22.1	2.2
Pocatello, ID	221.0	2 637	41.2	2.7	8.1	1.0	5.5	54.8	654	529	296	7 682	37.5	59.6	2.9
Portland-South Portland, ME	1 867.4	3 604	49.3	0.7	4.6	1.6	5.8	1 662.8	3 209	7 943	4 170	28 362	59.9	37.6	2.4
Portland-Vancouver-Hillsboro, OR-WA	9 964.4	4 352	40.1	4.1	5.7	2.0	5.7	15 721.1	6 866	17 865	6 785	118 656	60.0	36.6	3.3
Port St. Lucie, FL	1 660.8	3 838	40.0	3.2	8.5	1.4	5.4	2 747.3	6 349	1 000	901	17 399	47.5	51.7	0.7
Prescott, AZ	653.7	3 074	36.5	2.1	7.2	1.8	9.0	725.7	3 413	1 410	491	9 187	33.8	64.3	1.9
Providence-Warwick, RI-MA	5 907.2	3 689	56.8	0.5	6.6	0.5	2.8	4 257.8	2 659	11 338	8 716	82 166	61.5	36.5	2.0
Provo-Orem, UT	1 466.7	2 663	52.0	4.0	6.1	0.1	5.2	2 448.4	4 445	933	2 431	28 673	9.8	88.3	2.0
Pueblo, CO	566.4	3 521	40.3	1.5	6.6	5.3	3.7	456.3	2 837	1 034	438	11 451	55.8	41.9	2.3
Punta Gorda, FL	563.6	3 470	33.1	3.8	11.0	1.5	11.1	628.4	3 868	323	314	5 408	42.4	56.7	0.9
Racine, WI	764.1	3 923	45.5	3.8	9.7	5.3	7.3	710.7	3 648	332	529	8 548	51.3	47.7	1.0
Raleigh, NC	4 137.2	3 481	42.6	8.6	6.0	3.5	1.9	9 884.5	8 316	5 449	3 574	89 336	52.1	46.4	1.5
Rapid City, SD	516.0	3 719	46.0	1.5	5.8	0.4	9.0	476.3	3 433	3 047	4 026	8 158	32.4	65.0	2.6
Reading, PA	2 024.3	4 896	54.5	3.4	4.1	7.2	2.8	3 478.7	8 413	911	1 080	21 684	48.7	49.7	1.5

1. Based on the resident population estimated as of July 1 of the year shown. 2. © 2013 Election Data Services, Inc. All rights reserved.

Table C. Metropolitan Areas — **Land Area and Population**

CBSA/ DIV code[1]	Area name	Land area,[2] 2010 (sq km)	Total persons	Rank	Per square kilometer	White	Black	American Indian, Alaska Native	Asian and Pacific Islander	Percent Hispanic or Latino[3]	Under 5 years	5 to 17 years	18 to 24 years	25 to 34 years	35 to 44 years	45 to 54 years
			Population 2015			**Population characteristics, 2014**										
						Race alone or in combination, not Hispanic or Latino (percent)					Age (percent)					
		1	2	3	4	5	6	7	8	9	10	11	12	13	14	15
39820	Redding, CA	9 778	179 533	231	18.4	84.2	1.8	4.1	4.3	9.4	5.8	15.8	8.4	12.3	10.6	13.1
39900	Reno, NV	17 004	450 890	115	26.5	66.7	3.0	2.0	7.7	23.4	6.0	16.3	9.6	14.3	12.2	13.6
40060	Richmond, VA	11 852	1 271 334	45	107.3	60.0	31.0	0.9	4.5	5.8	5.9	16.4	9.6	14.0	12.9	14.3
40140	Riverside-San Bernardino-Ontario, CA	70 612	4 489 159	13	63.6	36.0	8.0	1.0	8.0	49.5	7.0	19.7	10.9	14.0	12.8	13.0
40220	Roanoke, VA	4 839	314 560	159	65.0	80.9	14.2	0.6	2.4	3.6	5.5	15.3	8.7	11.8	11.9	14.2
40340	Rochester, MN	6 416	213 873	206	33.3	87.1	4.8	0.5	5.2	4.1	6.8	17.8	7.6	13.7	12.4	13.7
40380	Rochester, NY	8 459	1 081 954	51	127.9	78.9	12.1	0.6	3.4	6.8	5.5	15.8	10.7	12.8	11.3	14.4
40420	Rockford, IL	2 057	340 663	150	165.6	73.2	12.0	0.6	2.9	13.4	6.1	18.1	8.7	11.9	12.5	14.1
40580	Rocky Mount, NC	2 709	148 069	281	54.7	47.3	46.4	1.0	1.0	5.7	6.0	17.0	9.0	11.2	11.8	14.0
40660	Rome, GA	1 321	96 504	361	73.1	73.6	15.2	0.6	1.7	10.3	6.1	17.3	10.5	12.4	12.4	13.2
40900	Sacramento—Roseville—Arden-Arcade, CA	13 193	2 274 194	27	172.4	57.3	8.4	1.5	16.1	21.0	6.2	17.4	10.0	13.9	12.7	13.5
40980	Saginaw, MI	2 072	193 307	224	93.3	71.5	19.7	0.8	1.6	8.1	5.8	16.2	10.4	11.5	11.2	13.5
41060	St. Cloud, MN	4 536	194 418	222	42.9	91.2	4.3	0.7	2.5	2.8	6.3	16.8	14.2	13.3	11.2	13.0
41100	St. George, UT	6 284	155 602	262	24.8	86.7	0.9	1.6	2.6	10.0	7.3	21.1	8.8	12.4	10.9	9.4
41140	St. Joseph, MO-KS	4 288	126 880	309	29.6	88.0	6.6	1.0	1.4	4.9	6.2	16.1	9.7	13.8	12.3	13.7
41180	St. Louis, MO-IL	20 366	2 811 588	20	138.1	76.0	19.3	0.7	3.1	2.9	6.0	16.7	8.9	13.5	12.3	14.1
41420	Salem, OR	4 981	410 091	130	82.3	71.8	1.6	2.3	3.9	23.3	6.6	18.4	10.3	13.0	12.3	12.2
41500	Salinas, CA	8 497	433 898	122	51.1	33.0	3.2	0.9	7.9	57.4	7.7	18.7	10.6	14.8	13.0	12.2
41540	Salisbury, MD-DE	5 435	395 300	135	72.7	73.1	18.9	0.9	2.1	7.1	5.5	14.3	10.0	10.9	10.4	13.1
41620	Salt Lake City, UT	19 901	1 170 266	48	58.8	75.0	2.1	1.1	6.4	17.5	8.1	20.6	9.7	16.5	14.2	11.4
41660	San Angelo, TX	6 666	119 659	323	18.0	56.4	4.4	0.8	1.8	37.8	6.8	16.8	12.6	15.4	10.7	11.5
41700	San Antonio-New Braunfels, TX	18 941	2 384 075	25	125.9	36.1	7.0	0.6	3.0	54.5	6.9	18.9	10.3	14.7	13.1	12.8
41740	San Diego-Carlsbad, CA	10 895	3 299 521	17	302.8	49.4	5.7	1.0	14.1	33.2	6.6	15.8	11.2	16.1	13.2	13.1
41860	San Francisco-Oakland-Hayward, CA	6 398	4 656 132	11	727.7	44.1	8.7	0.8	28.5	21.9	5.7	14.7	8.4	15.7	14.6	14.4
41860	Oakland-Hayward-Berkeley, CA Div 36084	3 768	2 764 960	X	733.8	41.3	11.5	0.9	26.8	23.7	6.0	16.3	9.0	14.6	14.3	14.4
41860	San Francisco-Redwood City-South San Francisco, CA	1 282	1 629 951	X	1 271.4	43.7	4.7	0.7	34.5	20.0	5.3	11.9	7.7	18.7	15.3	14.1
41860	San Rafael, CA Div 42034	1 348	261 221	X	193.8	75.0	3.3	0.8	8.2	16.0	4.8	15.6	6.4	9.1	13.0	16.1
41940	San Jose-Sunnyvale-Santa Clara, CA	6 938	1 976 836	35	284.9	36.0	2.9	0.7	36.0	27.5	6.5	16.8	8.8	15.1	14.9	14.4
42020	San Luis Obispo-Paso Robles-Arroyo Grande, CA	8 543	281 401	165	32.9	71.8	2.4	1.3	5.1	22.0	4.8	13.3	15.7	11.7	10.6	12.2
42100	Santa Cruz-Watsonville, CA	1 153	274 146	174	237.8	60.9	1.6	1.2	6.3	33.3	5.6	14.5	15.4	12.0	11.9	13.1
42140	Santa Fe, NM	4 945	148 686	277	30.1	44.2	1.0	3.1	1.7	51.3	4.8	14.6	7.7	11.3	11.8	13.8
42200	Santa Maria-Santa Barbara, CA	7 084	444 769	117	62.8	47.8	2.3	1.0	6.7	44.4	6.4	16.0	16.1	13.2	11.4	11.8
42220	Santa Rosa, CA	4 081	502 146	106	123.0	67.2	2.2	1.6	5.9	26.1	5.3	15.3	8.9	13.0	12.1	13.9
42340	Savannah, GA	3 470	379 199	138	109.3	58.1	34.4	0.7	3.2	5.7	6.9	16.6	11.2	15.8	12.6	12.5
42540	Scranton—Wilkes-Barre—Hazleton, PA	4 524	558 166	97	123.4	87.6	3.7	0.4	1.9	7.6	5.1	14.7	9.3	12.1	11.6	14.2
42660	Seattle-Tacoma-Bellevue, WA	15 209	3 733 580	15	245.5	69.8	7.2	2.0	16.3	9.6	6.3	15.8	9.0	16.0	14.2	14.1
42660	Seattle-Bellevue-Everett, WA Div 42644	10 885	2 889 626	X	265.5	68.7	6.7	1.8	17.9	9.5	6.2	15.4	8.7	16.3	14.6	14.3
42660	Tacoma-Lakewood, WA Div 45104	4 324	843 954	X	195.2	73.6	9.2	2.6	11.0	10.2	6.9	17.1	9.9	15.0	12.8	13.5
42680	Sebastian-Vero Beach, FL	1 302	147 919	282	113.6	77.3	9.5	0.6	1.9	11.9	4.4	13.2	6.8	9.0	9.2	12.6
42700	Sebring, FL	2 633	99 491	354	37.8	70.0	10.3	0.9	1.8	18.5	4.7	13.1	6.5	9.2	8.7	10.7
43100	Sheboygan, WI	1 324	115 569	335	87.3	86.8	2.3	0.7	5.5	6.0	5.6	17.2	8.3	11.5	11.9	15.0
43300	Sherman-Denison, TX	2 416	125 467	314	51.9	78.9	6.8	2.4	1.6	12.6	6.1	17.6	9.0	11.8	11.5	13.5
43340	Shreveport-Bossier City, LA	8 255	443 708	119	53.8	55.9	39.4	1.0	1.8	3.7	7.1	17.3	9.3	14.2	12.1	12.6
43420	Sierra Vista-Douglas, AZ	15 969	126 427	311	7.9	58.3	4.8	1.6	3.5	34.6	6.5	15.9	8.8	12.8	10.6	12.0
43580	Sioux City, IA-NE-SD	7 606	169 069	245	22.2	78.9	3.1	2.0	2.8	15.1	7.0	19.1	9.4	12.2	11.8	12.9
43620	Sioux Falls, SD	6 671	251 854	186	37.8	88.7	4.5	2.7	2.2	4.1	7.7	18.2	8.9	15.4	12.8	12.9
43780	South Bend-Mishawaka, IN-MI	2 455	320 098	155	130.4	78.5	13.0	1.1	2.6	7.4	6.2	17.4	10.6	12.5	11.8	13.1
43900	Spartanburg, SC	3 425	325 079	153	94.9	70.0	22.5	0.6	2.5	5.9	6.2	17.3	9.7	12.3	12.5	13.9
44060	Spokane-Spokane Valley, WA	14 611	547 824	100	37.5	88.9	2.7	3.1	3.9	5.0	6.0	16.4	10.1	13.8	11.7	13.0
44100	Springfield, IL	3 063	211 156	210	68.9	84.2	13.0	0.6	2.3	2.1	6.0	17.0	8.4	12.7	12.2	14.1
44140	Springfield, MA	2 964	631 982	88	213.2	71.3	7.3	0.6	3.6	18.6	5.3	15.4	14.1	12.0	11.1	13.7
44180	Springfield, MO	7 788	456 456	112	58.6	92.5	3.2	1.5	2.0	3.1	6.2	16.5	12.1	13.3	11.9	12.6
44220	Springfield, OH	1 029	135 959	296	132.1	87.0	10.6	0.9	1.2	3.1	5.9	17.0	8.8	11.4	11.4	13.6
44300	State College, PA	2 875	160 580	256	55.9	87.3	4.1	0.4	6.3	2.8	4.1	11.3	26.0	13.6	10.4	11.4
44420	Staunton-Waynesboro, VA	2 596	120 221	322	46.3	88.6	8.0	0.7	1.2	3.3	5.2	15.1	8.4	12.0	11.8	14.2
44700	Stockton-Lodi, CA	3 604	726 106	77	201.5	36.7	8.0	1.2	17.3	40.5	7.3	20.5	10.3	13.5	12.8	12.9
44940	Sumter, SC	1 723	107 480	340	62.4	47.7	47.4	0.8	2.0	3.8	7.1	17.5	11.1	13.4	11.3	12.9
45060	Syracuse, NY	6 177	660 458	82	106.9	84.4	9.3	1.2	3.4	3.9	5.6	16.1	11.2	12.6	11.2	14.6
45220	Tallahassee, FL	6 184	377 924	140	61.1	57.8	33.6	0.8	3.3	6.4	5.3	14.2	19.4	13.8	11.3	11.8
45300	Tampa-St. Petersburg-Clearwater, FL	6 509	2 975 225	18	457.1	66.8	12.5	0.7	4.1	17.7	5.4	15.1	8.3	12.7	12.4	14.1
45460	Terre Haute, IN	3 794	171 019	240	45.1	91.0	6.2	0.7	1.8	2.1	5.8	15.4	12.8	12.4	12.1	12.9
45500	Texarkana, TX-AR	5 291	149 769	274	28.3	68.5	24.9	1.5	1.2	5.7	6.5	17.2	8.8	13.2	12.8	13.3

1. CBSA = Core Based Statistical Area. DIV = Metropolitan Division. See Appendix A for explanation. See Appendix B for list of metropolitan areas identified by type. 2. Dry land or land partially or temporarily covered by water. 3. May be of any race.

Table C. Metropolitan Areas — **Population and Households**

Area name	Population, 2014 (cont.) Age (percent) (cont.) 55 to 64 years	65 to 74 years	75 years and over	Percent female	Population change and components of change, 2000–2015 Total persons 2000	Total persons 2010	Percent change 2000–2010	Percent change 2010–2015	Components of change, 2010–2015 Births	Deaths	Net migration	Households, 2014 Number	Persons per house-hold	Family house-holds Percent	Female family house-holder[1] Percent	One person Percent
	16	17	18	19	20	21	22	23	24	25	26	27	28	29	30	31
Redding, CA......................	14.7	11.2	8.0	51.0	163 256	177 223	8.6	1.3	11 128	10 984	1 787	68 542	2.57	62.0	10.9	31.5
Reno, NV	13.3	9.3	5.4	49.7	342 885	425 437	24.1	6.0	28 393	18 641	15 010	168 863	2.60	60.9	10.2	30.6
Richmond, VA	13.1	8.2	5.6	51.7	1 055 683	1 208 080	14.4	5.2	77 847	52 287	36 940	474 003	2.58	65.5	14.5	28.7
Riverside-San Bernardino-Ontario, CA	10.7	6.9	5.0	50.3	3 254 821	4 224 972	29.8	6.3	320 572	146 986	86 701	1 317 650	3.30	74.4	14.8	20.3
Roanoke, VA	14.4	10.5	7.7	51.7	288 309	308 682	7.1	1.9	17 496	17 569	5 624	129 528	2.35	64.6	12.4	30.7
Rochester, MN	13.0	8.0	7.0	50.8	184 740	206 877	12.0	3.4	15 272	7 774	-686	83 812	2.50	70.1	10.0	24.1
Rochester, NY	13.6	8.9	7.0	51.3	1 062 452	1 079 695	1.6	0.2	61 717	49 991	-9 207	428 750	2.43	60.9	12.8	32.1
Rockford, IL......................	13.1	8.7	6.6	51.0	320 204	349 431	9.1	-2.5	21 850	16 092	-14 334	133 136	2.54	63.4	13.5	30.1
Rocky Mount, NC..............	14.3	9.7	6.9	52.5	143 026	152 390	6.5	-2.8	9 155	8 285	-5 241	58 714	2.49	67.0	17.7	28.3
Rome, GA	12.4	8.9	6.8	51.5	90 565	96 317	6.4	0.2	6 228	5 308	-673	36 177	2.54	68.2	14.8	26.6
Sacramento—Roseville—Arden-Arcade, CA...........	12.4	8.0	6.0	51.0	1 796 857	2 149 143	19.6	5.8	144 413	84 888	63 264	797 624	2.76	66.6	13.2	25.9
Saginaw, MI	14.1	9.6	7.7	51.5	210 039	200 169	-4.7	-3.4	12 013	10 677	-8 039	78 000	2.42	64.5	14.6	29.9
St. Cloud, MN	11.7	7.2	6.3	49.7	167 392	189 093	13.0	2.8	13 144	6 614	-1 071	72 884	2.51	65.0	10.5	25.0
St. George, UT..................	10.7	10.8	8.8	50.5	90 354	138 115	52.9	12.7	11 792	5 878	11 397	49 468	3.03	77.4	7.2	19.0
St. Joseph, MO-KS............	12.9	8.4	6.9	48.5	122 336	127 329	4.1	-0.4	8 151	6 830	-1 725	46 526	2.56	61.6	12.3	32.6
St. Louis, MO-IL...............	13.5	8.2	6.6	51.6	2 675 343	2 787 748	4.2	0.9	179 251	132 062	-22 381	1 096 200	2.51	64.4	13.0	30.2
Salem, OR	12.3	8.6	6.3	50.4	347 214	390 738	12.5	5.0	27 656	17 144	8 423	141 971	2.77	67.6	13.0	25.8
Salinas, CA	11.0	6.7	5.2	49.0	401 762	415 057	3.3	4.5	35 039	12 593	-3 146	123 920	3.34	72.5	14.7	22.1
Salisbury, MD-DE	14.6	12.7	8.5	51.3	312 572	373 764	19.6	5.8	21 846	21 029	20 330	151 227	2.49	67.4	13.0	27.0
Salt Lake City, UT.............	10.0	5.7	3.9	49.8	939 122	1 087 799	15.8	7.6	99 896	33 174	16 801	376 913	3.03	71.1	10.6	22.6
San Angelo, TX.................	11.7	7.8	6.7	50.3	105 781	111 823	5.7	7.0	8 205	5 254	4 961	43 143	2.61	60.5	10.5	34.1
San Antonio-New Braunfels, TX	11.0	7.1	5.0	50.7	1 711 703	2 142 518	25.2	11.3	167 339	81 866	152 107	786 460	2.91	68.2	15.7	26.0
San Diego-Carlsbad, CA	11.4	7.1	5.6	49.8	2 813 833	3 095 308	10.0	6.6	231 748	107 677	78 523	1 100 858	2.88	67.6	12.2	23.6
San Francisco-Oakland-Hayward, CA	12.6	7.9	6.1	50.7	4 123 740	4 335 560	5.1	7.4	272 905	154 181	207 569	1 665 925	2.71	63.1	10.8	27.6
Oakland-Hayward-Berkeley, CA Div 36084.........	12.4	7.6	5.6	51.1	2 392 557	2 559 458	7.0	8.0	166 442	89 062	130 125	951 537	2.81	68.5	12.2	23.9
San Francisco-Redwood City-South San Francisco, CA .	12.5	7.9	6.7	49.9	1 483 894	1 523 693	2.7	7.0	94 242	55 299	70 400	610 879	2.59	55.4	9.1	32.2
San Rafael, CA Div 42034 .	15.5	11.3	8.1	51.2	247 289	252 409	2.1	3.5	12 221	9 820	7 044	103 509	2.45	59.5	7.5	33.8
San Jose-Sunnyvale-Santa Clara, CA ...	11.3	6.8	5.4	49.7	1 735 819	1 836 941	5.8	7.6	128 416	52 271	67 029	639 301	3.00	71.7	10.7	21.4
San Luis Obispo-Paso Robles-Arroyo Grande, CA......	14.1	10.0	7.5	49.1	246 681	269 593	9.3	4.4	14 003	11 754	9 089	102 645	2.56	62.7	8.5	27.2
Santa Cruz-Watsonville, CA .	14.0	8.3	5.2	50.4	255 602	262 362	2.6	4.5	16 009	9 215	4 827	96 127	2.70	64.1	11.7	25.6
Santa Fe, NM....................	16.4	12.6	7.1	51.3	129 292	144 171	11.5	3.1	7 188	5 586	2 689	60 565	2.40	58.5	9.6	33.0
Santa Maria-Santa Barbara, CA	11.2	7.4	6.6	49.9	399 347	423 939	6.2	4.9	30 292	15 534	5 940	142 912	2.95	64.2	12.6	25.1
Santa Rosa, CA	14.7	9.9	6.8	51.0	458 614	483 880	5.5	3.8	27 027	20 958	11 478	190 875	2.58	63.7	10.2	28.7
Savannah, GA	11.5	7.7	5.2	51.4	293 000	347 621	18.6	9.1	26 860	15 055	19 131	135 708	2.65	64.3	14.4	28.0
Scranton--Wilkes-Barre--Hazleton, PA	14.1	10.0	8.8	51.0	560 625	563 630	0.5	-1.0	29 680	36 353	1 903	220 225	2.44	62.3	11.8	32.4
Seattle-Tacoma-Bellevue, WA	12.4	7.2	5.0	50.0	3 043 878	3 439 815	13.0	8.5	239 087	122 415	176 382	1 406 259	2.57	62.6	9.6	28.6
Seattle-Bellevue-Everett, WA Div 42644	12.5	7.2	5.0	50.0	2 343 058	2 644 586	12.9	9.3	180 104	90 807	155 713	1 103 871	2.53	61.9	9.1	29.0
Tacoma-Lakewood, WA Div 45104....................	12.2	7.5	5.1	50.3	700 820	795 229	13.5	6.1	58 983	31 608	20 669	302 388	2.69	65.2	11.5	27.4
Sebastian-Vero Beach, FL....	14.8	15.3	14.8	52.0	112 947	138 028	22.2	7.2	6 624	9 673	12 758	55 618	2.58	63.4	9.8	31.5
Sebring, FL	13.4	16.9	16.9	51.5	87 366	98 786	13.1	0.7	4 716	7 621	3 525	39 288	2.46	64.5	10.8	31.1
Sheboygan, WI	14.4	8.8	7.4	49.8	112 646	115 507	2.5	0.1	6 645	5 547	-1 165	46 504	2.42	66.6	8.6	28.7
Sherman-Denison, TX	13.4	9.8	7.2	51.2	110 595	120 873	9.3	3.8	7 888	6 955	3 638	46 621	2.60	70.5	13.4	23.9
Shreveport-Bossier City, LA .	12.7	8.2	6.4	51.8	417 796	439 811	5.3	0.9	33 826	23 303	-6 454	167 018	2.61	63.3	18.2	32.4
Sierra Vista-Douglas, AZ ...	13.5	11.6	8.3	49.2	117 755	131 357	11.6	-3.8	8 722	6 416	-7 351	47 653	2.50	66.9	11.6	29.0
Sioux City, IA-NE-SD...........	12.8	8.0	6.6	50.3	167 902	168 563	0.4	0.3	12 757	7 743	-4 255	64 369	2.57	67.7	10.5	27.2
Sioux Falls, SD	11.9	6.9	5.4	49.9	187 093	228 264	22.0	10.3	19 990	8 713	11 912	94 764	2.55	63.6	10.2	29.7
South Bend-Mishawaka, IN-MI	13.4	8.4	6.7	51.3	316 663	319 215	0.8	0.3	21 107	15 680	-4 220	121 857	2.52	66.2	13.4	28.4
Spartanburg, SC	12.8	9.2	6.2	51.6	283 672	313 268	10.4	3.8	20 406	16 759	8 044	121 860	2.57	69.2	16.3	26.8
Spokane-Spokane Valley, WA	13.6	9.1	6.3	50.3	469 737	527 753	12.4	3.8	34 236	24 916	10 411	209 867	2.50	65.1	11.5	28.1
Springfield, IL...................	14.0	8.8	6.9	52.0	201 437	210 170	4.3	0.5	12 926	10 705	-1 090	88 468	2.34	60.4	11.3	31.4
Springfield, MA	13.3	8.4	6.8	52.2	608 479	621 705	2.2	1.7	34 111	28 729	5 542	235 074	2.52	62.6	16.4	30.2
Springfield, MO	12.1	8.6	6.7	51.0	368 374	436 713	18.6	4.5	29 715	20 860	10 401	179 069	2.43	64.0	10.4	28.2
Springfield, OH	14.0	10.0	7.9	51.5	144 742	138 333	-4.4	-1.7	8 393	8 695	-2 034	55 199	2.42	66.4	15.5	29.7
State College, PA	10.7	6.9	5.6	47.6	135 758	153 981	13.4	4.3	6 759	4 959	4 868	57 583	2.47	58.2	6.0	28.1
Staunton-Waynesboro, VA ...	14.1	11.0	8.2	51.1	108 988	118 502	8.7	1.5	6 489	6 586	1 563	48 754	2.37	66.3	10.9	27.6
Stockton-Lodi, CA..............	10.9	6.8	4.9	50.2	563 598	685 308	21.6	6.0	53 135	26 076	13 029	221 874	3.16	72.8	15.9	20.6
Sumter, SC	12.2	8.3	6.2	51.8	104 646	107 463	2.7	0.0	7 939	5 353	-2 608	39 936	2.64	68.2	19.6	29.3
Syracuse, NY....................	13.6	8.4	6.8	51.3	650 154	662 589	1.9	-0.3	38 566	30 189	-9 891	257 052	2.46	62.7	13.5	30.1
Tallahassee, FL	11.8	7.5	4.8	51.3	320 304	368 770	15.1	2.5	21 231	13 538	1 216	144 333	2.44	56.3	13.4	30.5
Tampa-St. Petersburg-Clearwater, FL..........	13.3	10.3	8.3	51.6	2 395 997	2 783 514	16.2	6.9	164 235	154 187	176 744	1 149 735	2.49	60.3	12.2	31.7
Terre Haute, IN	13.0	8.8	6.7	49.2	170 943	172 422	0.9	-0.8	10 503	9 813	-2 128	65 313	2.43	66.0	13.7	27.6
Texarkana, TX-AR..............	12.5	9.2	6.6	50.0	143 377	149 195	4.1	0.4	10 293	8 164	-1 416	54 860	2.57	66.5	16.5	28.9

1. No spouse present.

Table C. Metropolitan Areas — Population, Vital Statistics, Medicare, and Crime

Area name	Daytime population, 2014 — Persons in group quarters, 2015	Daytime population, 2014 — Number	Daytime population, 2014 — Employment/residence ratio	Births, 2015 — Total	Births, 2015 — Rate[1]	Deaths, 2015 — Number	Deaths, 2015 — Rate[1]	Persons under 65 with no health insurance 2014 — Number	Persons under 65 with no health insurance 2014 — Percent	Medicare, 2015 — Total Beneficiaries	Medicare, 2015 — Enrolled in Original Medicare	Medicare, 2015 — Enrolled in Medicare Advantage	Serious crimes known to police[2] 2014, Total — Number	Serious crimes known to police[2] 2014, Total — Rate[3]
	32	33	34	35	36	37	38	39	40	41	42	43	44	45
Redding, CA	2 764	179 377	0.99	2 162	12.0	2 085	11.6	19 409	13.5	42 520	39 831	2 689	6 980	3 869
Reno, NV	5 298	441 752	0.99	5 515	12.2	3 638	8.1	58 780	15.7	71 899	49 281	22 618	12 175	2 737
Richmond, VA	35 533	1 267 753	1.01	15 062	11.8	10 183	8.0	133 605	12.7	196 582	144 405	52 177	31 483	2 507
Riverside-San Bernardino-Ontario, CA	72 464	4 207 632	0.87	61 645	13.7	29 877	6.7	610 217	15.9	539 770	199 579	340 191	130 753	2 945
Roanoke, VA	8 009	326 713	1.09	3 407	10.8	3 339	10.6	34 054	13.6	64 538	47 538	17 000	7 678	2 455
Rochester, MN	3 411	220 009	1.07	2 923	13.7	1 484	6.9	10 669	6.0	34 582	19 051	15 531	3 248	1 522
Rochester, NY	40 938	1 089 490	1.01	11 741	10.9	9 451	8.7	64 065	7.3	202 202	70 167	132 035	27 279	2 512
Rockford, IL	5 026	338 341	0.97	4 066	11.9	2 999	8.8	31 035	10.8	60 793	43 496	17 297	11 971	3 503
Rocky Mount, NC	3 115	148 527	0.99	1 690	11.4	1 608	10.9	18 472	15.1	31 114	25 281	5 833	5 053	3 437
Rome, GA	3 990	99 206	1.08	1 158	12.0	1 032	10.7	14 824	19.1	19 066	14 454	4 612	4 392	4 576
Sacramento—Roseville—Arden-Arcade, CA	36 518	2 239 252	0.99	27 670	12.2	16 962	7.5	207 088	10.9	333 887	172 590	161 297	64 748	2 886
Saginaw, MI	7 134	207 801	1.16	2 266	11.7	2 055	10.6	14 692	9.4	43 062	29 694	13 368	5 135	2 621
St. Cloud, MN	8 822	201 668	1.09	2 534	13.0	1 218	6.3	10 161	6.4	33 614	15 032	18 582	4 798	2 497
St. George, UT	1 917	151 069	0.98	2 264	14.5	1 140	7.3	23 476	19.6	28 422	19 626	8 796	2 749	1 860
St. Joseph, MO-KS	8 646	129 583	1.03	1 498	11.8	1 220	9.6	13 571	13.5	22 290	20 424	1 866	5 556	4 339
St. Louis, MO-IL	55 135	2 816 176	1.01	33 866	12.0	25 761	9.2	252 194	10.7	473 230	305 211	168 019	80 890	2 944
Salem, OR	12 640	397 673	0.96	5 301	12.9	3 335	8.1	43 466	13.1	69 132	27 387	41 745	13 696	3 387
Salinas, CA	17 453	428 229	0.98	6 618	15.3	2 484	5.7	63 127	17.4	52 792	51 449	1 343	12 410	2 857
Salisbury, MD-DE	13 733	381 944	0.95	4 141	10.5	4 306	10.9	32 806	11.1	90 420	86 071	4 349	14 174	3 642
Salt Lake City, UT	15 856	1 226 477	1.13	19 112	16.3	6 406	5.5	150 773	14.7	118 510	66 523	51 987	54 565	4 719
San Angelo, TX	5 510	118 542	1.00	1 602	13.4	1 004	8.4	19 743	20.4	19 808	15 953	3 855	4 649	3 923
San Antonio-New Braunfels, TX	50 240	2 314 635	0.99	33 288	14.0	16 358	6.9	370 313	18.5	322 418	193 244	129 174	106 461	4 578
San Diego-Carlsbad, CA	106 429	3 292 342	1.02	44 561	13.5	21 580	6.5	370 758	13.4	422 056	197 811	224 245	69 635	2 138
San Francisco-Oakland-Hayward, CA	88 316	4 650 691	1.03	52 913	11.4	31 080	6.7	368 321	9.5	634 261	329 081	305 180	177 382	3 868
Oakland-Hayward-Berkeley, CA Div 36084	47 536	X	X	32 530	11.8	18 163	6.6	225 346	9.7	354 696	175 767	178 929	103 858	3 825
San Francisco-Redwood City-South San Francisco, CA	32 433	X	X	18 093	11.1	11 055	6.8	125 276	9.2	230 233	123 465	106 768	68 505	4 258
San Rafael, CA Div 42034	8 347	X	X	2 290	8.8	1 862	7.1	17 699	8.7	49 332	29 849	19 483	5 019	1 922
San Jose-Sunnyvale-Santa Clara, CA	31 291	2 071 146	1.12	24 394	12.3	10 773	5.4	144 784	8.6	227 444	132 334	95 110	48 692	2 497
San Luis Obispo-Paso Robles-Arroyo Grande, CA	15 751	278 773	1.00	2 734	9.7	2 249	8.0	29 235	13.6	52 415	45 873	6 542	6 860	2 453
Santa Cruz-Watsonville, CA	13 426	259 520	0.90	2 934	10.7	1 836	6.7	29 000	12.9	39 658	35 826	3 832	9 260	3 398
Santa Fe, NM	2 627	150 537	1.03	1 323	8.9	1 064	7.2	23 172	19.9	30 450	20 708	9 742	4 483	3 033
Santa Maria-Santa Barbara, CA	19 094	452 410	1.06	5 883	13.2	3 045	6.8	56 050	15.5	65 551	55 232	10 319	10 382	2 354
Santa Rosa, CA	10 424	482 427	0.93	5 116	10.2	4 174	8.3	52 536	12.8	87 780	50 364	37 416	10 404	2 079
Savannah, GA	14 611	377 355	1.03	5 241	13.8	3 012	7.9	54 546	17.5	54 271	36 163	18 108	12 589	3 387
Scranton—Wilkes-Barre—Hazleton, PA	20 702	564 675	1.02	5 686	10.2	6 807	12.2	46 135	10.5	121 136	88 081	33 055	12 814	2 294
Seattle-Tacoma-Bellevue, WA	65 027	3 718 455	1.03	46 894	12.6	24 694	6.6	297 362	9.4	482 075	298 887	183 188	163 662	4 466
Seattle-Bellevue-Everett, WA Div 42644	48 446	X	X	35 361	12.2	18 186	6.3	220 570	9.0	359 742	214 599	145 143	128 220	4 523
Tacoma-Lakewood, WA Div 45104	16 581	X	X	11 533	13.7	6 508	7.7	76 792	10.8	122 333	84 288	38 045	35 442	4 272
Sebastian-Vero Beach, FL	1 322	143 918	0.98	1 264	8.5	1 989	13.4	22 887	22.8	42 698	32 838	9 860	3 579	2 484
Sebring, FL	1 733	97 278	0.97	893	9.0	1 419	14.3	16 123	25.1	30 160	21 543	8 617	2 841	3 182
Sheboygan, WI	2 825	115 591	1.01	1 219	10.5	1 027	8.9	7 662	8.1	21 663	12 693	8 970	2 162	1 883
Sherman-Denison, TX	2 180	117 813	0.89	1 533	12.2	1 284	10.2	21 994	21.8	25 470	20 248	5 222	2 961	2 417
Shreveport-Bossier City, LA	10 072	449 183	1.02	6 294	14.2	4 449	10.0	59 987	16.1	75 932	61 616	14 316	17 617	3 976
Sierra Vista-Douglas, AZ	5 052	127 526	1.00	1 580	12.5	1 203	9.5	13 788	14.2	26 770	17 935	8 835	2 473	2 314
Sioux City, IA-NE-SD	3 377	168 689	1.00	2 395	14.2	1 406	8.3	15 492	11.0	28 625	22 233	6 392	4 867	2 926
Sioux Falls, SD	7 023	251 241	1.02	3 876	15.4	1 657	6.6	19 051	8.9	36 485	28 207	8 278	6 476	2 616
South Bend-Mishawaka, IN-MI	11 840	312 565	0.95	4 103	12.8	2 922	9.1	36 693	14.1	53 181	36 920	16 261	9 890	3 166
Spartanburg, SC	8 710	329 246	1.06	3 904	12.0	3 238	10.0	43 016	16.2	67 370	42 645	24 725	11 008	3 421
Spokane-Spokane Valley, WA	14 851	547 117	1.02	6 640	12.1	4 886	8.9	44 221	9.9	99 364	66 289	33 075	30 790	5 703
Springfield, IL	4 066	223 186	1.12	2 403	11.4	2 176	10.3	13 440	7.6	38 820	24 086	14 734	8 834	4 388
Springfield, MA	38 797	615 906	0.95	6 443	10.2	5 417	8.6	20 637	4.1	115 815	78 131	37 684	18 801	3 053
Springfield, MO	14 456	457 696	1.04	5 734	12.6	4 053	8.9	54 057	14.6	85 130	48 363	36 767	20 129	4 452
Springfield, OH	2 861	126 615	0.83	1 571	11.6	1 633	12.0	11 922	10.8	28 539	14 360	14 179	6 145	4 539
State College, PA	19 633	165 229	1.09	1 286	8.0	991	6.2	11 322	9.4	20 708	10 430	10 278	1 970	1 265
Staunton-Waynesboro, VA	3 973	113 478	0.89	1 225	10.2	1 223	10.2	12 663	13.5	25 646	21 540	4 106	2 228	1 859
Stockton-Lodi, CA	14 857	682 925	0.88	10 044	13.8	5 171	7.1	81 653	13.2	91 477	55 998	35 479	30 438	4 271
Sumter, SC	2 799	111 047	1.08	1 495	13.9	1 046	9.7	15 054	16.8	20 030	16 325	3 705	4 780	4 395
Syracuse, NY	26 683	668 847	1.02	7 262	11.0	5 693	8.6	39 670	7.4	119 692	76 969	42 723	16 807	2 536
Tallahassee, FL	23 135	380 688	1.03	4 033	10.7	2 607	6.9	45 236	14.7	51 025	26 842	24 183	16 349	4 341
Tampa-St. Petersburg-Clearwater, FL	50 444	2 908 372	0.99	32 114	10.4	30 912	10.4	418 479	17.9	574 517	291 234	283 283	88 473	3 036
Terre Haute, IN	12 305	174 085	1.03	1 992	11.6	1 791	10.5	19 253	14.4	33 219	28 862	4 357	NA	NA
Texarkana, TX-AR	7 846	150 404	1.05	1 931	12.9	1 554	10.4	19 338	16.2	28 819	23 009	5 810	6 928	4 609

1. Per 1,000 estimated resident population.   2. Data for serious crimes have not been adjusted for underreporting; this may affect comparability between geographic areas and over time.
3. Per 100,000 population estimated by the FBI.

Table C. Metropolitan Areas — Crime, Education, Money Income, and Poverty

Area name	Serious crimes known to police, 2014 (cont.)[1] — Rate[2] Violent	Property	School enrollment and attainment, 2014 — Enrollment[3] Total	Percent private	Attainment[4] (percent) High school grad-uate or less	Bach-elor's degree or more	Local government expenditures,[5] 2012–2013 Total current expendi-tures (mil dol)	Current expendi-tures per student (dollars)	Per capita income[6] (dollars)	Mean house-hold income (dollars)	Median household income	Percent of households with income of less than $25,000	Percent of house-holds with in-come of $200,000 or more	Percent below poverty level All persons	Children under 18 years	Age 65 years and older
	46	47	48	49	50	51	52	53	54	55	56	57	58	59	60	61
Redding, CA......................	707	3 162	43 837	17.0	32.9	20.8	276.2	10 161	24 373	59 773	43 706	28.4	2.4	13.8	13.7	6.8
Reno, NV...........................	374	2 363	114 519	9.5	38.2	28.9	552.9	8 453	27 833	70 250	52 728	23.6	3.8	15.5	18.8	7.6
Richmond, VA....................	231	2 276	321 053	15.4	38.1	33.8	1 888.9	9 737	31 741	80 968	60 936	18.3	5.6	12.8	19.9	6.5
Riverside-San Bernardino-Ontario, CA................	327	2 617	1 301 312	11.8	46.9	19.9	7 170.7	8 564	22 310	71 067	54 586	22.9	3.8	18.7	26.0	10.9
Roanoke, VA......................	203	2 252	71 389	20.7	42.7	27.1	458.3	10 249	27 714	65 405	51 318	23.3	3.3	14.3	23.1	7.6
Rochester, MN...................	141	1 381	54 981	13.3	30.7	35.9	335.1	10 050	34 356	86 340	66 214	14.2	5.4	9.5	13.4	5.8
Rochester, NY....................	266	2 247	270 811	21.2	38.3	32.2	2 776.0	17 900	28 487	68 915	51 086	23.1	3.3	14.1	21.5	6.3
Rockford, IL.......................	668	2 836	89 455	18.4	45.5	22.5	645.1	11 345	25 455	63 554	48 385	25.6	2.5	16.3	25.0	7.7
Rocky Mount, NC...............	457	2 980	36 937	9.8	55.0	15.4	215.2	9 107	21 084	53 270	40 407	35.1	1.9	20.3	28.1	11.5
Rome, GA..........................	349	4 227	24 461	21.6	52.5	21.0	163.8	10 091	22 761	59 934	41 752	30.0	3.8	20.8	26.1	11.7
Sacramento—Roseville—Arden-Arcade, CA...	411	2 475	616 535	11.7	33.2	31.3	3 138.7	8 787	29 955	81 519	60 015	20.9	5.9	16.4	20.7	9.2
Saginaw, MI.......................	659	1 962	49 731	11.1	44.5	22.2	299.4	11 025	23 442	57 427	44 931	26.3	1.9	16.6	22.5	6.7
St. Cloud, MN....................	179	2 319	55 308	16.9	36.3	27.4	306.5	10 309	26 353	67 544	55 390	21.1	3.1	14.6	14.9	12.2
St. George, UT...................	135	1 725	46 307	9.2	29.3	25.4	182.0	6 673	20 552	61 268	49 981	20.9	2.5	12.0	15.0	7.1
St. Joseph, MO-KS............	345	3 994	31 226	19.3	48.5	19.2	171.6	9 434	23 148	59 860	47 402	27.8	2.2	16.6	27.3	9.9
St. Louis, MO-IL................	440	2 504	710 664	24.1	36.0	32.3	4 505.0	11 103	30 293	75 223	55 535	21.3	4.6	13.0	18.4	7.4
Salem, OR.........................	234	3 154	107 371	13.8	42.1	23.7	645.5	9 787	22 492	61 123	49 508	23.8	2.0	16.7	22.5	9.2
Salinas, CA........................	422	2 435	120 354	8.0	51.3	23.1	734.8	9 999	25 712	83 375	57 864	18.2	6.9	17.2	26.6	9.7
Salisbury, MD-DE..............	412	3 229	91 647	9.4	47.1	25.4	733.9	14 014	28 643	71 776	54 128	20.5	4.0	14.0	20.9	6.9
Salt Lake City, UT.............	344	4 375	340 145	12.5	33.8	31.3	1 382.4	6 874	27 900	82 403	62 642	16.1	5.6	11.4	15.0	6.9
San Angelo, TX..................	294	3 628	29 843	11.1	47.4	21.3	156.9	8 639	28 682	74 835	45 284	25.9	5.1	15.1	18.7	12.1
San Antonio-New Braunfels, TX	402	4 176	648 076	12.7	41.8	26.3	3 379.2	8 226	25 546	71 260	52 689	23.2	4.2	16.7	24.2	9.9
San Diego-Carlsbad, CA	325	1 813	866 106	15.4	32.2	37.1	4 493.3	9 033	31 770	89 137	66 192	17.9	8.1	14.7	18.9	9.5
San Francisco-Oakland-Hay-ward, CA.....................	498	3 370	1 125 067	19.7	28.5	45.9	5 594.7	9 771	43 924	117 134	83 222	15.6	14.5	10.9	12.9	8.6
Oakland-Hayward-Berke-ley, CA Div 36084..........	516	3 309	709 926	15.6	31.0	41.5	3 538.8	9 083	38 269	106 428	78 190	15.8	11.6	11.7	14.2	8.6
San Francisco-Redwood City-South San Fran-cisco, CA....................	521	3 737	354 046	27.0	25.9	51.3	1 678.4	11 104	50 907	128 712	91 949	15.7	17.8	9.8	10.5	9.4
San Rafael, CA Div 42034 .	174	1 748	61 095	23.9	20.3	55.2	377.6	11 849	59 824	147 223	95 749	13.2	21.9	8.8	10.5	5.1
San Jose-Sunnyvale-Santa Clara, CA.....................	250	2 247	527 241	19.5	28.7	47.5	2 695.2	9 476	43 597	128 682	96 481	12.1	18.2	8.7	9.4	9.3
San Luis Obispo-Paso Robles-Arroyo Grande, CA...............................	421	2 032	76 808	8.4	29.6	33.9	324.7	9 366	31 746	83 940	63 474	19.1	6.0	14.8	15.5	6.1
Santa Cruz-Watsonville, CA .	418	2 980	77 734	9.9	30.2	39.5	399.3	9 881	33 911	93 276	65 368	19.8	9.2	16.8	21.0	7.4
Santa Fe, NM.....................	267	2 766	31 581	14.3	36.0	39.3	146.9	9 052	32 050	74 490	52 809	22.4	4.6	14.2	20.8	6.3
Santa Maria-Santa Barbara, CA...............................	293	2 060	134 493	10.2	38.0	32.0	640.6	9 585	29 833	88 181	63 833	18.8	7.5	18.0	24.5	6.5
Santa Rosa, CA.................	364	1 715	122 190	12.8	31.8	34.8	674.3	9 575	35 771	91 481	67 771	17.1	7.6	11.3	12.8	7.9
Savannah, GA....................	341	3 046	105 670	19.7	38.4	31.2	497.8	8 869	26 229	68 497	51 809	22.6	3.9	15.3	23.1	7.4
Scranton—Wilkes-Barre—Hazleton, PA.................	229	2 065	124 231	25.2	48.9	23.8	957.2	12 664	24 846	60 056	45 257	27.5	2.2	15.5	22.7	8.7
Seattle-Tacoma-Bellevue, WA..............................	325	4 141	878 197	16.8	28.5	39.4	4 976.7	9 813	36 854	93 389	71 273	16.0	8.2	11.3	14.4	8.7
Seattle-Bellevue-Everett, WA Div 42644...............	294	4 229	672 933	17.6	25.9	43.5	3 724.3	9 808	39 222	98 412	74 743	15.2	9.5	10.8	13.5	8.9
Tacoma-Lakewood, WA Div 45104...................	432	3 840	205 264	14.5	37.8	24.6	1 252.4	9 826	28 771	75 054	60 496	19.0	3.7	12.9	17.2	8.2
Sebastian-Vero Beach, FL...	282	2 202	29 024	18.1	40.4	27.2	144.9	8 047	30 705	73 194	46 238	24.5	5.1	15.1	24.6	8.7
Sebring, FL........................	308	2 874	NA	NA	51.5	17.8	103.3	8 558	20 953	48 774	36 120	32.1	1.7	18.1	26.3	9.6
Sheboygan, WI	162	1 721	26 262	14.5	45.8	21.7	210.0	10 803	27 353	66 561	54 042	19.8	1.9	8.1	11.6	4.3
Sherman-Denison, TX	272	2 145	29 879	10.1	44.9	22.2	184.2	8 670	24 838	64 054	52 058	26.2	2.0	15.3	22.6	8.2
Shreveport-Bossier City, LA .	517	3 459	110 432	12.2	48.1	21.8	791.0	10 599	24 028	59 470	42 157	31.9	2.9	21.4	32.7	10.5
Sierra Vista-Douglas, AZ	283	2 032	31 104	11.8	35.1	24.8	125.5	7 181	23 507	58 383	45 688	28.4	2.8	18.4	24.6	13.8
Sioux City, IA-NE-SD...........	247	2 679	42 515	14.1	48.8	21.1	333.7	10 921	24 610	63 311	49 981	24.4	2.7	13.0	19.6	8.5
Sioux Falls, SD..................	331	2 285	64 357	16.3	35.0	32.6	309.5	7 745	29 600	74 650	58 849	17.6	3.6	9.7	11.8	9.6
South Bend-Mishawaka, IN-MI...............................	325	2 842	86 917	27.5	42.3	26.6	456.1	10 173	24 769	63 221	46 610	25.9	3.1	16.7	26.9	6.8
Spartanburg, SC	392	3 028	79 668	18.3	46.0	21.8	492.5	9 653	22 211	56 521	43 161	28.5	1.9	17.8	28.2	9.5
Spokane-Spokane Valley, WA..............................	319	5 384	138 201	14.4	33.5	27.3	807.7	9 957	25 642	64 095	49 320	24.9	2.7	16.9	21.3	9.2
Springfield, IL....................	796	3 592	52 859	13.5	38.6	31.3	378.6	11 696	30 937	73 208	55 021	23.9	4.2	15.8	24.6	6.0
Springfield, MA..................	511	2 542	179 940	17.8	41.0	31.1	1 365.9	15 500	27 070	69 221	50 916	25.8	4.2	17.4	23.8	10.2
Springfield, MO.................	536	3 916	122 120	16.4	41.9	26.4	553.0	8 205	22 670	55 604	41 248	28.7	2.3	18.8	23.8	8.2
Springfield, OH..................	369	4 171	30 919	16.8	49.7	16.5	217.1	10 699	22 687	54 611	41 729	28.6	1.6	18.4	27.1	7.0
State College, PA...............	82	1 184	57 140	9.2	37.4	40.1	193.1	14 954	24 965	65 970	51 367	25.7	3.5	18.6	9.7	6.3
Staunton-Waynesboro, VA ...	146	1 713	23 511	22.5	46.8	25.6	162.5	9 730	25 865	62 505	52 603	23.9	2.3	11.7	16.8	6.8
Stockton-Lodi, CA..............	750	3 521	206 195	12.1	50.4	18.3	1 189.0	8 545	23 028	70 979	51 659	25.7	4.1	20.9	28.3	10.1
Sumter, SC........................	647	3 748	31 088	18.5	51.5	16.7	143.8	8 563	18 350	47 624	36 633	36.0	0.6	24.1	32.9	18.4
Syracuse, NY.....................	285	2 251	171 763	23.3	39.1	30.8	1 710.3	16 863	27 627	68 355	51 915	23.2	3.8	16.5	25.5	8.1
Tallahassee, FL..................	679	3 662	127 949	12.2	35.0	36.4	403.4	8 852	24 289	61 698	44 242	27.3	2.8	22.8	25.0	11.4
Tampa-St. Petersburg-Clear-water, FL.....................	372	2 664	664 532	15.9	40.9	27.5	3 377.9	8 586	27 173	65 646	46 876	25.4	3.7	15.8	22.2	10.5
Terre Haute, IN..................	NA	NA	46 027	13.0	50.2	18.2	240.2	9 434	21 389	55 268	41 953	29.0	1.7	18.0	24.0	8.0
Texarkana, TX-AR	532	4 076	35 216	7.9	50.5	15.7	236.1	8 845	20 867	53 630	40 773	30.2	1.4	20.0	31.8	8.9

1. Data for serious crimes have not been adjusted for underreporting; this may affect comparability between geographic areas and over time.   2. Per 100,000 population estimated by the FBI.
3. All persons 3 years old and over enrolled in nursery school through college.   4. Persons 25 years old and over.   5. Elementary and secondary education expenditures.   6. Based on resident population estimated in the 2014 American Community Survey.

Table C. Metropolitan Areas — **Personal Income**

Area name	Personal income, 2014										Earnings, 2014		
	Total (mil dol)	Percent change 2013–2014	Per capita¹ Dollars	Rank	Wages and salaries (mil dol)	Supplements to wages and salaries; employer contributions (mil dol) Pension and insurance	Government social insurance	Proprietors' income (mil dol)	Dividends, interest, and rent (mil dol)	Personal transfer receipts (mil dol)	Total (mil dol)	Contributions for government social insurance (mil dol) From employee and self-employed	From employer
	62	63	64	65	66	67	68	69	70	71	72	73	74
Redding, CA	6 815	4.6	37 905	237	2 608	603	191	546	1 282	2 108	3 948	263	191
Reno, NV	20 477	5.6	46 120	78	9 373	1 763	680	1 303	5 705	3 008	13 120	744	680
Richmond, VA	59 326	3.6	47 083	62	32 928	5 164	2 423	3 594	11 571	8 993	44 109	2 644	2 423
Riverside-San Bernardino-Ontario, CA	147 727	4.8	33 258	350	59 397	12 892	4 363	9 814	22 502	30 600	86 467	5 237	4 363
Roanoke, VA	12 969	3.2	41 383	156	6 984	1 145	541	779	2 557	2 708	9 450	606	541
Rochester, MN	9 918	4.0	46 611	71	5 907	834	443	703	1 576	1 521	7 886	468	443
Rochester, NY	47 494	2.7	43 838	101	23 810	5 253	2 044	4 184	6 538	9 847	35 291	1 896	2 044
Rockford, IL	13 092	2.2	38 234	227	6 796	1 188	513	672	1 936	2 711	9 169	538	513
Rocky Mount, NC	5 306	3.8	35 544	304	2 268	443	177	298	832	1 483	3 186	202	177
Rome, GA	3 238	3.9	33 705	339	1 634	306	118	220	511	874	2 278	140	118
Sacramento—Roseville—Arden-Arcade, CA	105 154	4.2	46 852	67	52 593	12 578	3 436	7 601	17 985	18 484	76 207	4 081	3 436
Saginaw, MI	6 640	3.4	34 050	334	3 623	617	287	362	958	2 006	4 889	323	287
St. Cloud, MN	7 773	5.1	40 396	178	4 295	724	348	743	1 236	1 458	6 110	358	348
St. George, UT	4 507	5.9	29 659	376	1 904	320	158	366	988	1 098	2 748	183	158
St. Joseph, MO-KS	4 544	2.4	35 662	302	2 357	439	172	414	707	1 049	3 382	198	172
St. Louis, MO-IL	132 989	3.5	47 391	59	70 018	10 876	5 027	9 261	27 064	22 006	95 182	5 641	5 027
Salem, OR	14 286	6.7	35 360	308	6 637	1 249	594	1 066	2 413	3 699	9 546	598	594
Salinas, CA	19 889	3.7	46 109	79	8 549	1 877	644	2 587	4 542	2 947	13 656	682	644
Salisbury, MD-DE	15 899	5.0	40 774	168	5 874	1 190	468	1 482	3 108	4 098	9 014	547	468
Salt Lake City, UT	48 371	4.1	41 940	144	33 007	5 126	2 568	4 976	8 713	6 042	45 677	2 642	2 568
San Angelo, TX	5 007	5.2	42 365	133	2 142	372	152	597	1 048	929	3 263	169	152
San Antonio-New Braunfels, TX	96 341	5.8	41 372	157	46 069	7 294	3 272	10 896	16 885	16 661	67 531	3 479	3 272
San Diego-Carlsbad, CA	167 931	4.4	51 459	27	87 582	16 051	6 296	13 690	36 218	23 539	123 619	6 979	6 296
San Francisco-Oakland-Hayward, CA	332 445	6.1	72 364	5	183 857	25 676	11 361	28 006	75 066	33 135	248 900	14 333	11 361
Oakland-Hayward-Berkeley, CA Div 36084	161 481	6.3	59 319	X	72 894	12 013	5 014	11 092	30 102	20 061	101 012	5 900	5 014
San Francisco-Redwood City-South San Francisco, CA	145 247	5.9	90 157	X	103 482	12 490	5 848	14 350	36 345	11 138	136 170	7 730	5 848
San Rafael, CA Div 42034	25 717	5.4	98 626	X	7 482	1 173	500	2 564	8 619	1 937	11 718	702	500
San Jose-Sunnyvale-Santa Clara, CA	144 291	6.1	73 887	3	109 721	11 079	6 088	8 007	28 685	11 960	134 895	7 870	6 088
San Luis Obispo-Paso Robles-Arroyo Grande, CA	12 823	3.9	45 947	81	4 994	1 163	353	1 321	3 192	1 993	7 830	460	353
Santa Cruz-Watsonville, CA	14 210	5.6	52 280	24	4 744	985	332	1 424	3 242	1 885	7 485	430	332
Santa Fe, NM	7 155	4.4	48 291	54	2 816	503	213	449	2 149	1 215	3 980	259	213
Santa Maria-Santa Barbara, CA	22 264	4.0	50 523	32	10 086	2 007	716	2 220	6 702	2 890	15 029	832	716
Santa Rosa, CA	24 607	5.7	49 185	47	9 739	1 842	711	2 404	5 800	3 747	14 696	895	711
Savannah, GA	15 131	3.8	40 599	174	7 676	1 380	561	799	2 723	2 714	10 416	597	561
Scranton—Wilkes-Barre—Hazleton, PA	22 486	3.4	40 177	181	10 435	2 119	883	1 413	3 648	5 562	14 850	919	883
Seattle-Tacoma-Bellevue, WA	213 700	6.2	58 205	14	125 009	16 091	10 340	16 974	44 126	25 252	168 414	9 734	10 340
Seattle-Bellevue-Everett, WA Div 42644	177 417	6.2	62 481	X	109 242	13 245	8 837	14 670	37 604	18 446	145 993	8 461	8 837
Tacoma-Lakewood, WA Div 45104	36 283	6.3	43 613	X	15 767	2 847	1 503	2 304	6 521	6 806	22 421	1 273	1 503
Sebastian-Vero Beach, FL	9 140	5.1	63 140	7	2 099	299	153	332	4 310	1 547	2 884	209	153
Sebring, FL	3 011	3.2	30 650	372	942	169	71	145	644	1 151	1 327	104	71
Sheboygan, WI	5 341	4.9	46 328	74	2 764	486	220	584	980	818	4 054	247	220
Sherman-Denison, TX	4 575	4.7	37 034	258	1 875	284	133	288	678	1 171	2 580	152	133
Shreveport-Bossier City, LA	18 589	2.6	41 760	147	8 314	1 535	558	2 374	3 615	3 767	12 781	678	558
Sierra Vista-Douglas, AZ	4 680	1.9	36 720	265	1 849	437	150	185	941	1 426	2 621	157	150
Sioux City, IA-NE-SD	7 456	1.8	44 170	97	3 589	614	278	1 047	1 281	1 195	5 528	320	278
Sioux Falls, SD	12 068	3.6	48 592	52	6 524	946	476	1 515	2 388	1 463	9 461	573	476
South Bend-Mishawaka, IN-MI	12 740	5.3	39 909	188	5 670	965	439	1 230	2 072	2 551	8 304	525	439
Spartanburg, SC	11 538	4.7	35 897	297	6 173	958	467	895	1 968	2 709	8 493	553	467
Spokane-Spokane Valley, WA	20 801	5.3	38 452	220	10 398	1 656	974	1 108	4 017	4 965	14 136	872	974
Springfield, IL	8 925	1.8	42 185	138	4 853	967	333	604	1 656	1 587	6 758	360	333
Springfield, MA	27 160	3.2	43 172	117	12 667	2 578	897	1 358	3 906	6 915	17 501	935	897
Springfield, MO	16 251	4.3	35 931	294	7 969	1 394	589	1 540	2 749	3 547	11 492	705	589
Springfield, OH	4 995	3.7	36 580	270	1 948	379	147	281	721	1 374	2 755	171	147
State College, PA	6 345	4.3	39 973	186	3 455	1 349	270	506	1 151	993	5 580	278	270
Staunton-Waynesboro, VA	4 620	3.3	38 579	215	1 919	348	144	377	863	985	2 788	182	144
Stockton-Lodi, CA	25 859	5.7	36 136	289	9 918	2 136	734	2 318	3 741	6 129	15 107	877	734
Sumter, SC	3 893	2.9	36 077	291	1 825	395	153	179	670	994	2 552	149	153
Syracuse, NY	27 617	2.8	41 751	148	14 133	3 382	1 213	1 857	3 795	5 880	20 585	1 090	1 213
Tallahassee, FL	13 647	4.8	36 319	279	7 223	1 544	512	721	2 507	2 511	10 000	574	512
Tampa-St. Petersburg-Clearwater, FL	120 401	4.9	41 296	160	60 255	8 726	4 320	7 107	22 965	26 016	80 408	5 113	4 320
Terre Haute, IN	5 763	1.6	33 608	345	2 739	526	213	400	891	1 541	3 878	245	213
Texarkana, TX-AR	5 100	3.4	34 175	333	2 336	415	172	429	835	1 338	3 352	199	172

1. Based on the resident population estimated as of July 1 of the year shown.

Table C. Metropolitan Areas — **Earnings, Social Security, and Housing**

Area name	Farm	Mining	Construction	Manufacturing	Information, professional, scientific, technical services	Retail trade	Finance, insurance, real estate, rental and leasing	Health care and social assistance	Government	Social Security beneficiaries, December 2014 — Number	Rate[1]	Supplemental Security Income recipients, December 2014	Housing units, 2015 — Total	Percent change, 2000–2015
	75	76	77	78	79	80	81	82	83	84	85	86	87	88
Redding, CA	0.9	D	6.1	3.8	6.4	9.7	5.7	18.7	24.9	48 200	268	10 178	78 101	1.0
Reno, NV	0.1	D	6.7	7.0	D	D	D	D	17.5	80 350	181	6 927	190 961	2.2
Richmond, VA	0.1	D	6.1	11.7	D	11.9	11.5	19.7	224 395	178	27 150	522 517	3.0
Riverside-San Bernardino-Ontario, CA	0.5	0.3	7.4	7.3	5.4	8.4	5.1	11.7	25.1	623 700	141	135 673	1 538 450	2.5
Roanoke, VA	0.3	D	5.5	D	D	D	6.7	17.6	14.8	74 055	236	8 124	146 071	0.8
Rochester, MN	3.1	0.1	4.8	11.7	4.1	5.0	3.0	D	9.7	38 215	180	2 795	90 316	2.4
Rochester, NY	0.9	D	5.9	13.1	12.0	5.7	5.7	12.3	18.2	233 345	215	32 087	475 773	1.5
Rockford, IL	0.2	D	5.0	26.4	4.6	6.8	5.5	15.4	12.9	69 795	204	7 745	145 395	-0.4
Rocky Mount, NC	3.6	0.1	5.2	21.3	D	8.1	3.7	D	17.9	35 400	237	6 608	67 083	-0.1
Rome, GA	1.1	D	2.4	17.3	D	7.5	4.0	23.7	14.9	21 700	226	3 362	40 410	-0.3
Sacramento—Roseville—Arden-Arcade, CA	0.4	0.1	5.5	4.6	10.8	5.7	5.7	11.2	34.3	369 930	165	82 063	889 022	2.0
Saginaw, MI	0.6	0.2	4.0	19.4	6.7	7.3	5.7	18.0	15.0	49 015	251	8 545	86 822	0.0
St. Cloud, MN	4.2	0.2	8.6	14.3	6.0	7.3	6.8	16.6	14.2	32 890	171	2 732	79 798	2.2
St. George, UT	0.1	0.4	10.8	5.1	6.4	10.2	6.9	16.9	15.3	32 200	212	1 286	63 947	10.8
St. Joseph, MO-KS	3.1	0.1	6.0	23.1	D	6.6	4.9	13.7	15.9	25 390	199	2 939	53 563	-0.1
St. Louis, MO-IL	0.4	D	D	11.0	12.2	5.5	8.7	12.2	13.0	540 555	193	60 643	1 241 161	1.3
Salem, OR	3.0	D	6.4	6.5	D	6.7	4.8	15.7	30.9	78 845	195	8 576	154 633	2.2
Salinas, CA	12.5	0.3	3.5	2.6	5.6	5.4	4.1	7.5	25.3	59 520	138	9 256	140 470	1.0
Salisbury, MD-DE	6.0	0.0	6.8	9.0	5.2	9.7	5.8	15.6	17.5	99 425	255	7 059	240 770	4.2
Salt Lake City, UT	0.0	1.1	6.3	9.0	D	7.7	11.5	7.8	15.5	138 590	120	14 209	401 449	4.7
San Angelo, TX	1.3	10.1	D	D	D	6.9	D	D	22.0	21 640	183	2 989	49 133	3.6
San Antonio-New Braunfels, TX	0.1	D	7.3	4.9	9.5	6.8	11.0	10.4	21.3	369 075	158	63 621	872 477	4.1
San Diego-Carlsbad, CA	0.3	D	4.9	8.3	17.5	5.2	8.7	8.4	24.2	464 905	142	85 337	1 194 415	2.5
San Francisco-Oakland-Hayward, CA	0.1	D	4.8	6.5	26.4	4.6	11.3	8.1	13.5	660 540	144	139 336	1 782 303	2.3
Oakland-Hayward-Berkeley, CA Div 36084	0.1	0.5	6.4	9.5	16.8	5.6	6.8	11.7	16.0	380 145	140	79 478	1 004 570	2.2
San Francisco-Redwood City-South San Francisco, CA	0.0	0.1	3.5	4.5	34.3	3.6	14.5	5.3	11.6	230 455	143	56 234	665 041	2.6
San Rafael, CA Div 42034	0.3	D	5.7	4.0	18.5	7.0	13.6	10.8	13.6	49 940	192	3 624	112 692	1.3
San Jose-Sunnyvale-Santa Clara, CA	0.2	D	3.1	22.9	D	4.0	4.8	6.6	7.1	234 120	120	49 115	678 844	4.5
San Luis Obispo-Paso Robles-Arroyo Grande, CA	3.2	0.2	8.3	6.2	8.3	7.9	6.2	10.7	22.6	55 820	200	4 951	120 137	2.4
Santa Cruz-Watsonville, CA	5.0	D	8.9	7.7	8.1	6.8	5.1	13.1	21.3	43 020	159	6 107	105 530	1.0
Santa Fe, NM	0.0	1.4	4.5	1.1	8.9	8.9	9.9	13.7	30.7	34 465	233	2 872	71 873	0.8
Santa Maria-Santa Barbara, CA	4.8	1.7	4.6	7.4	13.5	6.1	5.7	10.3	21.9	70 420	160	9 306	155 163	1.5
Santa Rosa, CA	2.2	0.2	7.7	12.4	9.5	7.6	6.6	13.6	15.5	94 015	188	9 652	207 891	1.6
Savannah, GA	0.1	D	4.2	16.8	D	6.8	4.6	D	19.7	62 060	167	8 368	157 902	4.5
Scranton—Wilkes-Barre—Hazleton, PA	0.2	0.9	5.3	11.7	D	7.6	6.7	D	15.3	139 485	249	17 556	259 895	0.4
Seattle-Tacoma-Bellevue, WA	0.1	0.0	5.8	12.1	21.7	6.8	6.8	9.0	15.0	532 680	145	70 462	1 529 969	4.6
Seattle-Bellevue-Everett, WA Div 42644	0.1	0.0	5.6	13.0	24.3	6.9	7.0	8.0	12.3	392 480	138	50 874	1 193 612	4.9
Tacoma-Lakewood, WA Div 45104	0.1	0.1	7.2	6.5	4.7	6.4	5.2	15.0	33.0	140 200	169	19 588	336 357	3.4
Sebastian-Vero Beach, FL	1.8	0.2	6.0	4.9	9.9	10.4	8.4	17.7	11.9	46 020	318	2 387	77 900	2.0
Sebring, FL	7.6	0.0	3.2	2.5	4.8	10.8	3.8	22.3	17.8	32 655	333	2 729	54 822	-1.0
Sheboygan, WI	1.8	D	4.7	41.0	3.1	5.6	6.1	11.4	9.3	24 485	212	1 787	50 589	-0.3
Sherman-Denison, TX	0.4	1.1	9.2	15.4	4.5	8.2	7.1	18.0	13.5	27 225	221	3 052	54 653	1.7
Shreveport-Bossier City, LA	0.1	10.2	D	D	5.3	7.4	5.6	14.5	20.8	85 480	192	19 891	200 169	3.7
Sierra Vista-Douglas, AZ	1.7	0.2	3.0	1.1	9.1	6.4	2.6	7.4	51.6	30 525	240	3 085	60 620	2.7
Sioux City, IA-NE-SD	8.1	D	D	D	D	6.2	5.0	11.2	11.7	31 550	187	2 620	69 537	1.3
Sioux Falls, SD	1.8	D	6.1	D	D	7.6	D	D	9.3	41 745	168	3 322	103 807	8.3
South Bend-Mishawaka, IN-MI	0.5	D	4.7	15.8	8.6	6.1	5.7	D	10.3	63 455	199	6 962	141 700	0.7
Spartanburg, SC	0.2	D	5.2	26.0	5.2	6.4	4.7	D	15.8	73 635	229	8 189	139 330	1.9
Spokane-Spokane Valley, WA	0.1	D	6.0	8.1	7.7	7.6	8.1	D	20.5	111 470	206	16 030	237 474	3.0
Springfield, IL	1.6	D	4.8	3.0	8.5	5.9	8.3	D	26.0	43 570	206	4 782	96 455	0.9
Springfield, MA	0.0	0.1	5.3	9.1	D	6.3	8.4	18.0	22.9	128 240	203	33 231	255 006	0.1
Springfield, MO	0.8	D	D	9.1	8.8	8.1	6.7	17.0	14.5	94 430	209	10 142	198 901	3.4
Springfield, OH	0.6	0.3	3.9	15.7	3.9	6.7	9.1	14.2	15.9	30 660	225	4 055	61 102	-0.5
State College, PA	0.6	1.2	4.3	5.1	8.0	5.1	3.7	9.8	49.8	23 405	147	1 588	65 478	3.5
Staunton-Waynesboro, VA	2.2	D	D	17.8	6.9	7.0	3.4	D	17.4	29 735	248	2 111	54 062	2.7
Stockton-Lodi, CA	6.0	0.1	5.4	8.6	4.1	7.1	5.4	12.2	21.0	104 650	146	29 669	238 571	2.1
Sumter, SC	0.7	0.0	6.0	15.4	4.3	5.6	2.6	11.2	36.9	22 720	210	4 268	47 183	2.5
Syracuse, NY	0.6	D	5.1	9.6	9.6	6.4	6.7	12.4	22.4	137 685	208	18 886	290 392	0.9
Tallahassee, FL	0.6	D	3.8	2.0	D	6.2	5.7	D	39.1	60 105	160	9 902	166 456	2.1
Tampa-St. Petersburg-Clearwater, FL	0.2	0.1	4.7	5.6	14.6	7.8	11.3	13.7	14.0	645 440	221	77 540	1 385 058	2.4
Terre Haute, IN	2.2	2.9	6.1	19.5	D	6.9	D	D	17.6	37 375	218	4 560	74 638	0.7
Texarkana, TX-AR	1.7	D	5.2	11.6	D	7.8	6.3	D	23.6	32 355	217	6 708	65 106	1.4

1. Per 1,000 resident population estimated as of July 1, 2011 of the year shown.

Table C. Metropolitan Areas — Housing, Labor Force, and Employment

Area name	Housing units, 2014								Civilian labor force, 2015				Civilian employment[5], 2014		
	Occupied units									Unemployment				Percent	
			Owner-occupied			Renter-occupied									
				Median owner cost as a percent of income											
	Total	Percent	Median value[1]	With a mortgage	Without a mortgage[2]	Median rent[3]	Median rent as a percent of income	Percent with a computer	Total	Percent change, 2013–2014	Total	Rate[4]	Total employed	Management, professional, and related occupations	Construction, production, and related occupations
	89	90	91	92	93	94	95	96	97	98	99	100	101	102	103
Redding, CA	68 542	61.5	226 900	25.3	13.0	916	35.7	83.9	74 858	-0.6	5 842	7.8	71 645	32.7	19.5
Reno, NV	168 863	57.5	232 700	23.7	11.0	879	29.8	86.6	230 111	1.9	14 382	6.3	211 139	33.7	19.7
Richmond, VA	474 003	64.7	213 900	21.4	10.0	1 011	30.1	86.9	661 671	0.6	30 577	4.6	627 743	40.5	18.4
Riverside-San Bernardino-Ontario, CA	1 317 650	60.9	272 200	26.4	12.5	1 159	35.6	87.5	1 961 819	1.8	129 493	6.6	1 784 861	28.7	25.7
Roanoke, VA	129 528	67.0	172 100	21.4	10.7	807	27.2	82.2	158 927	-1.4	7 021	4.4	149 380	35.4	22.0
Rochester, MN	83 812	75.5	170 200	20.0	10.0	830	27.9	88.3	118 535	0.9	3 808	3.2	111 923	45.8	19.8
Rochester, NY	428 750	67.0	133 400	21.3	14.0	800	32.8	83.5	525 622	0.0	27 353	5.2	520 934	39.9	18.2
Rockford, IL	133 136	65.6	112 600	20.7	12.7	727	29.3	84.0	168 616	-0.1	11 813	7.0	157 710	30.5	28.1
Rocky Mount, NC	58 714	63.3	103 900	23.1	13.6	679	32.6	74.9	67 015	-0.5	5 440	8.1	61 238	30.3	27.0
Rome, GA	36 177	56.5	132 200	19.3	12.0	653	31.0	81.0	42 787	-1.1	2 812	6.6	40 990	28.0	27.1
Sacramento—Roseville—Arden-Arcade, CA	797 624	58.6	314 400	24.3	10.5	1 057	33.0	90.5	1 060 164	0.9	62 073	5.9	986 403	39.4	16.4
Saginaw, MI	78 000	74.0	89 700	22.1	11.9	700	31.0	79.1	89 015	-0.6	4 856	5.5	83 287	32.8	19.9
St. Cloud, MN	72 884	70.8	162 900	22.1	11.2	696	28.7	87.1	110 552	0.7	4 157	3.8	102 830	32.4	25.6
St. George, UT	49 468	68.7	221 800	24.4	10.2	928	32.8	91.1	63 906	3.6	2 535	4.0	59 386	29.1	22.2
St. Joseph, MO-KS	46 526	66.8	113 900	20.2	12.0	682	26.4	80.0	66 285	1.2	3 006	4.5	57 803	27.7	25.5
St. Louis, MO-IL	1 096 200	68.7	156 100	20.3	12.0	817	29.6	84.4	1 481 428	1.6	74 872	5.1	1 347 860	39.5	18.4
Salem, OR	141 971	60.4	190 800	24.2	11.9	782	32.0	85.4	188 764	2.1	11 377	6.0	171 718	32.6	24.1
Salinas, CA	123 920	50.9	391 200	27.4	11.5	1 233	33.2	81.2	221 383	1.1	17 875	8.1	175 290	27.5	31.7
Salisbury, MD-DE	151 227	72.6	203 700	22.9	11.8	1 013	31.3	84.6	184 118	2.4	11 860	6.4	176 123	31.3	23.3
Salt Lake City, UT	376 913	66.3	237 900	22.0	10.0	932	28.4	92.0	616 414	1.7	20 728	3.4	575 462	37.1	20.9
San Angelo, TX	43 143	60.9	97 800	18.9	10.5	789	31.9	78.8	55 306	-0.3	2 279	4.1	52 533	32.9	27.1
San Antonio-New Braunfels, TX	786 460	61.4	143 900	21.6	11.4	899	29.7	85.2	1 099 596	1.0	42 059	3.8	1 064 103	34.5	21.0
San Diego-Carlsbad, CA	1 100 858	52.2	457 300	26.7	11.0	1 373	33.4	91.4	1 563 836	0.9	81 308	5.2	1 500 994	41.7	16.4
San Francisco-Oakland-Hayward, CA	1 665 925	53.2	657 300	25.1	10.1	1 519	29.8	91.3	2 505 850	2.0	106 594	4.3	2 349 040	47.7	13.7
Oakland-Hayward-Berkeley, CA Div 36084	951 537	56.7	542 800	24.9	10.1	1 407	31.3	91.6	1 374 757	1.4	66 663	4.8	1 322 282	45.5	15.5
San Francisco-Redwood City-South San Francisco, CA	610 879	46.4	841 800	25.6	10.0	1 674	27.9	90.5	989 970	3.0	34 932	3.5	891 830	50.6	11.2
San Rafael, CA Div 42034	103 509	61.6	862 800	25.0	11.8	1 741	32.3	92.7	141 123	1.1	4 999	3.5	134 928	51.1	12.5
San Jose-Sunnyvale-Santa Clara, CA	639 301	56.3	735 400	25.1	10.0	1 779	29.7	93.3	1 048 170	2.3	44 586	4.3	976 328	50.0	15.5
San Luis Obispo-Paso Robles-Arroyo Grande, CA	102 645	59.6	459 900	27.2	10.0	1 219	33.8	89.6	143 293	1.6	6 648	4.6	123 934	36.4	19.2
Santa Cruz-Watsonville, CA	96 127	56.6	615 200	27.5	12.4	1 477	38.0	90.3	144 248	0.8	10 816	7.5	132 323	41.2	19.5
Santa Fe, NM	60 565	68.1	269 300	25.5	10.9	945	30.3	82.3	71 658	0.1	3 891	5.4	69 686	42.1	16.4
Santa Maria-Santa Barbara, CA	142 912	52.2	476 400	26.0	12.1	1 395	34.4	86.7	220 001	0.4	11 608	5.3	205 838	34.7	20.7
Santa Rosa, CA	190 875	58.4	469 400	25.1	11.3	1 374	32.6	91.2	260 344	1.1	11 680	4.5	248 279	38.1	20.2
Savannah, GA	135 708	58.9	165 400	21.7	12.0	939	30.4	88.9	175 755	1.3	9 795	5.6	167 752	34.9	22.5
Scranton—Wilkes-Barre—Hazleton, PA	220 225	68.4	131 900	21.3	14.7	729	28.9	79.2	278 915	-0.3	16 826	6.0	253 597	32.8	25.0
Seattle-Tacoma-Bellevue, WA	1 406 259	59.3	334 700	23.5	12.1	1 179	29.5	91.9	1 971 002	1.4	96 535	4.9	1 859 133	44.1	17.6
Seattle-Bellevue-Everett, WA Div 42644	1 103 871	59.1	369 800	23.4	12.0	1 219	29.1	92.7	1 579 039	1.4	71 708	4.5	1 486 463	46.6	15.9
Tacoma-Lakewood, WA Div 45104	302 388	59.9	237 100	23.9	12.3	1 034	31.3	89.2	391 963	1.8	24 827	6.3	372 670	34.1	24.0
Sebastian-Vero Beach, FL	55 618	73.1	167 800	23.4	12.0	924	36.6	84.9	61 307	-1.0	4 140	6.8	55 496	32.4	19.3
Sebring, FL	39 288	76.3	80 800	25.1	10.7	645	34.2	79.2	35 272	-1.8	2 602	7.4	31 616	27.4	20.2
Sheboygan, WI	46 504	70.8	143 700	21.6	13.6	665	24.4	83.9	61 368	0.1	2 338	3.8	60 977	30.0	32.9
Sherman-Denison, TX	46 621	67.6	109 100	20.7	14.3	800	28.3	82.9	60 503	0.3	2 422	4.0	55 196	32.8	27.2
Shreveport-Bossier City, LA	167 018	61.8	127 000	20.1	10.1	797	30.4	76.4	195 684	-0.5	13 356	6.8	186 515	33.5	22.8
Sierra Vista-Douglas, AZ	47 653	67.1	144 800	19.4	10.0	783	29.0	84.6	50 040	-1.6	3 715	7.4	43 452	36.3	15.7
Sioux City, IA-NE-SD	64 369	68.8	117 600	19.2	11.2	655	27.1	81.9	92 977	0.2	3 260	3.5	86 009	29.4	30.0
Sioux Falls, SD	94 764	67.2	162 900	19.8	10.0	710	25.9	87.4	144 580	1.8	3 805	2.6	140 175	37.3	20.5
South Bend-Mishawaka, IN-MI	121 857	69.2	113 800	19.4	10.2	713	29.3	83.1	155 200	1.6	7 703	5.0	150 813	32.4	25.3
Spartanburg, SC	121 860	66.7	115 200	20.4	10.0	698	30.1	81.7	150 795	1.9	8 863	5.9	141 945	30.3	32.1
Spokane-Spokane Valley, WA	209 867	63.4	181 600	22.8	10.4	806	31.1	87.4	250 194	1.2	16 617	6.6	234 103	33.7	20.8
Springfield, IL	88 468	68.3	131 600	19.0	10.0	740	31.0	85.8	111 709	0.3	5 857	5.2	103 145	40.7	16.3
Springfield, MA	235 074	60.1	214 300	22.8	15.3	869	32.0	82.8	307 893	-0.2	18 802	6.1	298 046	38.0	18.0
Springfield, MO	179 069	63.2	130 700	20.6	10.8	686	31.7	83.1	233 488	2.7	10 101	4.3	205 262	35.3	21.0
Springfield, OH	55 199	63.9	100 800	20.2	11.9	659	30.2	81.6	64 200	-1.2	3 207	5.0	60 274	27.8	30.1
State College, PA	57 583	59.8	198 500	21.2	10.7	911	36.0	89.4	77 888	0.4	2 969	3.8	74 442	45.5	16.5
Staunton-Waynesboro, VA	48 754	71.0	181 800	22.7	11.0	826	32.8	77.9	58 831	-0.6	2 514	4.3	59 058	32.5	28.6
Stockton-Lodi, CA	221 874	53.5	250 800	25.2	11.4	1 027	34.3	83.6	316 903	1.0	28 127	8.9	289 829	27.9	29.9
Sumter, SC	39 936	66.7	111 100	23.4	13.6	714	33.0	78.2	44 413	0.3	3 047	6.9	39 278	26.1	30.0
Syracuse, NY	257 052	67.3	126 900	20.8	13.3	765	30.3	85.6	312 827	-0.3	17 010	5.4	305 661	37.7	19.3
Tallahassee, FL	144 333	54.9	167 000	22.0	10.7	899	34.2	88.5	186 294	-1.4	9 624	5.2	173 407	42.2	12.7
Tampa-St. Petersburg-Clearwater, FL	1 149 735	62.9	149 500	23.4	12.5	957	31.9	85.6	1 447 077	0.6	74 158	5.1	1 303 358	36.5	17.4
Terre Haute, IN	65 313	66.0	89 000	18.5	12.7	666	29.3	80.7	77 277	-0.7	4 697	6.1	73 868	29.8	28.9
Texarkana, TX-AR	54 860	64.7	99 300	21.2	10.0	689	33.4	76.7	64 636	0.5	3 248	5.0	58 034	27.6	29.4

1. Specified owner-occupied units. 2. A value of 10.0 represents 10 percent or less. 3. Specified renter-occupied units. 4. Percent of civilian labor force.
5. Persons 16 years old and over.

Table C. Metropolitan Areas — Nonfarm Employment and Agriculture

Area name	Private nonfarm establishments, employment and payroll, 2014									Agriculture, 2012			
	Number of establishments	Employment						Annual payroll		Farms			
		Total	Health care and social assistance	Manufacturing	Retail trade	Finance and insurance	Professional, scientific, and technical services	Total (mil dol)	Average per employee (dollars)	Number	Fewer than 50 acres	500 acres or more	Farm operators whose principal occupation is farming (percent)
	104	105	106	107	108	109	110	111	112	113	114	115	116
Redding, CA......................	4 114	47 366	9 875	1 986	9 230	2 029	2 292	1 748	36 912	1 544	72.9	6.1	44.9
Reno, NV............................	11 742	173 723	22 361	14 654	22 587	5 717	10 111	7 419	42 708	485	69.7	7.0	43.5
Richmond, VA.....................	30 695	517 420	80 180	31 431	65 375	47 837	36 902	24 574	47 493	3 131	43.1	8.6	48.2
Riverside-San Bernardino-Ontario, CA......................	68 525	1 069 244	153 807	93 412	174 387	24 808	35 684	41 108	38 446	4 198	86.0	3.0	51.5
Roanoke, VA.......................	8 065	135 834	25 567	15 620	18 767	8 342	5 942	5 379	39 598	2 094	34.0	6.6	46.1
Rochester, MN....................	5 140	98 888	21 227	8 065	12 553	2 343	D	4 605	46 569	4 233	29.7	14.5	53.4
Rochester, NY.....................	24 531	433 909	79 519	53 451	59 002	14 784	25 512	18 334	42 254	4 268	38.0	9.1	61.0
Rockford, IL........................	7 309	132 384	21 512	32 906	16 144	4 056	4 910	5 453	41 191	1 286	47.4	13.6	47.5
Rocky Mount, NC................	2 787	47 893	8 441	10 136	6 710	1 602	1 016	1 736	36 256	702	37.9	16.7	54.8
Rome, GA...........................	1 942	33 947	7 575	5 951	4 565	815	722	1 236	36 412	559	44.4	3.6	36.5
Sacramento—Roseville—Arden-Arcade, CA..........	46 077	669 449	110 856	32 941	94 679	39 721	49 289	32 791	48 982	5 076	71.7	6.4	50.7
Saginaw, MI........................	4 368	77 998	17 749	10 595	13 184	2 705	2 310	2 933	37 606	1 318	41.0	12.1	48.9
St. Cloud, MN.....................	5 288	95 502	19 756	15 087	13 332	3 993	2 635	3 800	39 792	4 459	24.5	8.3	54.6
St. George, UT....................	4 381	42 838	7 620	2 444	8 210	1 415	1 878	1 340	31 273	579	63.0	13.1	43.5
St. Joseph, MO-KS..............	2 959	47 077	9 006	10 464	6 422	2 125	1 054	1 846	39 212	2 838	26.1	14.6	44.1
St. Louis, MO-IL..................	73 306	1 201 903	187 254	100 938	143 460	66 678	84 064	57 684	47 994	11 270	35.8	13.6	43.9
Salem, OR..........................	9 096	111 414	21 430	11 411	17 599	3 504	4 238	3 905	35 048	3 710	70.5	5.4	48.7
Salinas, CA........................	8 420	102 790	15 249	6 750	16 669	2 851	6 981	4 397	42 780	1 179	42.0	26.4	61.7
Salisbury, MD-DE...............	10 364	121 303	23 507	13 168	23 663	3 659	3 969	4 283	35 308	2 384	51.8	10.4	63.4
Salt Lake City, UT...............	31 072	560 004	61 123	48 977	61 037	41 215	46 306	26 258	46 890	1 106	77.0	8.0	30.1
San Angelo, TX...................	2 850	40 957	7 961	3 010	6 476	1 626	1 328	1 532	37 411	1 358	41.6	23.9	40.5
San Antonio-New Braunfels, TX...................................	43 171	798 637	125 070	43 978	104 790	61 378	46 738	33 995	42 566	14 598	41.6	10.4	40.4
San Diego-Carlsbad, CA	79 958	1 202 583	155 350	97 352	150 619	51 279	133 602	61 752	51 349	5 732	91.6	0.9	47.6
San Francisco-Oakland-Hayward, CA	124 273	1 969 853	249 087	112 200	204 455	114 718	228 511	156 908	79 655	1 717	61.4	13.6	53.2
Oakland-Hayward-Berkeley, CA Div 36084..........	NA	NA	NA	NA	NA	NA	NA	NA	NA	1 054	67.6	9.8	50.6
San Francisco-Redwood City-South San Francisco, CA........................	NA	NA	NA	NA	NA	NA	NA	NA	NA	340	62.4	6.2	56.5
San Rafael, CA Div 42034 .	NA	NA	NA	NA	NA	NA	NA	NA	NA	323	39.9	34.1	58.5
San Jose-Sunnyvale-Santa Clara, CA..........................	47 951	973 967	103 778	87 807	85 136	25 576	132 495	101 719	104 438	1 631	66.8	12.4	56.9
San Luis Obispo-Paso Robles-Arroyo Grande, CA....................................	8 028	89 509	15 590	6 081	14 744	2 309	4 788	3 510	39 213	2 666	55.8	12.2	47.0
Santa Cruz-Watsonville, CA .	6 830	72 301	12 651	4 671	11 946	2 105	4 001	3 144	43 481	667	73.8	4.6	62.1
Santa Fe, NM.....................	4 711	45 219	8 071	754	9 657	1 718	2 345	1 784	39 456	715	67.0	13.4	43.6
Santa Maria-Santa Barbara, CA....................................	11 296	141 785	20 431	13 874	20 023	4 146	9 657	6 827	48 152	1 597	63.9	11.3	51.7
Santa Rosa, CA..................	13 523	158 918	24 148	18 874	24 838	5 600	9 335	7 389	46 494	3 579	71.3	6.0	51.3
Savannah, GA.....................	8 717	139 798	20 741	17 163	19 628	3 073	5 683	5 667	40 534	281	50.9	9.3	43.1
Scranton—Wilkes-Barre—Hazleton, PA....................	13 208	238 759	49 803	27 610	32 595	10 724	9 664	8 958	37 518	1 367	32.8	2.9	44.0
Seattle-Tacoma-Bellevue, WA.................................	99 432	1 574 478	216 013	162 112	173 901	62 921	121 502	100 241	63 666	4 753	86.4	0.6	42.5
Seattle-Bellevue-Everett, WA Div 42644...............	NA	NA	NA	NA	NA	NA	NA	NA	NA	3 275	86.9	0.7	40.5
Tacoma-Lakewood, WA Div 45104.....................	NA	NA	NA	NA	NA	NA	NA	NA	NA	1 478	85.3	0.3	47.0
Sebastian-Vero Beach, FL....	4 058	40 165	8 151	1 773	8 704	1 275	1 649	1 453	36 170	461	73.1	7.2	49.0
Sebring, FL	1 833	19 520	5 582	720	4 351	568	596	580	29 723	969	64.3	11.0	49.3
Sheboygan, WI	2 635	51 649	6 333	17 040	6 027	2 002	1 272	2 088	40 435	986	42.4	10.1	52.7
Sherman-Denison, TX	2 517	39 698	8 412	7 088	6 320	1 909	926	1 335	33 629	2 562	50.8	5.6	44.1
Shreveport-Bossier City, LA .	9 980	160 556	33 125	9 749	23 903	4 695	6 681	5 962	37 132	2 202	45.9	7.6	49.0
Sierra Vista-Douglas, AZ	2 222	26 487	4 766	342	5 419	548	3 616	889	33 577	1 093	43.8	22.4	56.1
Sioux City, IA-NE-SD..........	4 394	76 646	11 558	14 689	10 193	3 189	1 537	2 778	36 250	3 644	26.2	30.3	61.9
Sioux Falls, SD	7 302	133 393	D	14 202	17 318	14 057	4 874	5 618	42 117	3 418	32.9	28.4	53.1
South Bend-Mishawaka, IN-MI....................................	6 465	123 813	20 037	16 963	15 888	4 031	5 085	4 632	37 409	1 489	48.6	10.8	47.1
Spartanburg, SC	6 575	128 014	15 348	28 724	14 861	2 203	4 903	5 308	41 466	1 602	53.6	2.4	42.1
Spokane-Spokane Valley, WA.................................	13 449	184 736	36 121	16 194	27 592	11 496	9 456	7 721	41 796	3 937	54.2	9.4	42.8
Springfield, IL.....................	5 233	84 441	21 069	2 745	12 606	6 457	4 423	3 363	39 832	1 461	40.4	21.7	52.1
Springfield, MA....................	13 217	225 499	59 134	22 727	30 933	10 425	8 724	9 208	40 835	1 381	62.6	1.2	46.8
Springfield, MO...................	11 601	175 052	33 724	15 493	24 485	8 520	8 416	6 418	36 665	7 459	37.1	6.4	45.1
Springfield, OH...................	2 321	40 253	7 429	5 879	5 628	3 026	1 273	1 399	34 746	785	53.2	11.3	49.6
State College, PA...............	3 290	45 984	8 657	3 989	8 015	1 281	3 096	1 715	37 296	1 192	40.1	4.8	57.4
Staunton-Waynesboro, VA ...	2 779	39 094	8 210	5 958	6 014	989	1 001	1 366	34 947	1 706	42.3	6.2	48.8
Stockton-Lodi, CA...............	10 825	168 367	26 839	18 597	25 445	6 303	4 459	6 916	41 079	3 580	63.5	8.3	59.0
Sumter, SC	1 777	31 005	5 325	5 492	4 455	794	1 120	1 025	33 010	515	44.3	14.2	45.8
Syracuse, NY......................	15 392	258 096	48 096	23 701	36 582	12 702	17 023	10 757	41 677	2 176	34.1	8.5	56.1
Tallahassee, FL	8 771	108 416	20 088	2 949	18 779	4 767	11 333	4 145	38 235	1 474	59.2	5.7	39.4
Tampa-St. Petersburg-Clearwater, FL........................	72 931	1 038 508	168 560	53 874	145 000	75 224	88 594	44 948	43 281	4 448	78.6	3.0	51.6
Terre Haute, IN...................	3 563	59 126	10 738	11 889	8 780	1 475	1 334	2 144	36 265	1 732	43.6	18.7	46.1
Texarkana, TX-AR	3 075	46 704	8 280	5 855	8 293	1 832	1 132	1 622	34 722	2 592	38.7	9.6	42.6

Table C. Metropolitan Areas — **Agriculture**

Area name	Land in farms					Value of land and buildings (dollars)		Value of machinery and equipment, average per farm (dollars)	Value of products sold				Percent of farms with sales of:		Government payments	
			Acres								Percent from:					
	Acreage (1,000)	Percent change, 2007–2012	Average size of farm	Total irrigated (1,000)	Total cropland (1,000)	Average per farm	Average per acre		Total (mil dol)	Average per farm (dollars)	Crops	Live-stock and poultry products	$10,000 or more	$100,000 or more	Total ($1,000)	Percent of farms
	117	118	119	120	121	122	123	124	125	126	127	128	129	130	131	132
Redding, CA	376	-3.7	244	38.2	36.9	682 565	2 801	36 550	65.6	42 501	36.6	63.4	26.2	4.8	420	4.6
Reno, NV	443	-8.9	913	D	D	749 691	821	52 786	D	D	D	D	27.4	6.6	75	3.9
Richmond, VA	649	-1.9	207	D	325.5	853 057	4 118	85 962	338.0	107 947	D	D	32.0	10.1	12 201	26.8
Riverside-San Bernardino-Ontario, CA	421	-51.5	100	167.7	257.1	1 084 366	10 807	78 134	1 621.2	386 179	50.1	49.9	47.9	14.7	3 038	4.5
Roanoke, VA	332	2.0	159	1.1	102.0	599 779	3 783	70 357	93.2	44 495	D	33.2	6.5	1 600	16.1
Rochester, MN	1 158	-7.6	274	D	906.6	1 399 848	5 117	185 604	1 111.6	262 609	59.8	40.2	63.1	35.0	23 694	71.1
Rochester, NY	927	-6.2	217	9.2	701.3	663 751	3 055	158 475	930.7	218 057	61.4	38.6	56.4	29.8	11 479	29.3
Rockford, IL	318	-1.0	247	1.4	286.5	1 617 918	6 550	156 317	205.4	159 703	83.9	16.1	48.3	27.9	8 500	57.8
Rocky Mount, NC	267	-8.9	381	11.9	181.9	1 238 600	3 253	197 288	340.4	484 865	61.8	38.2	49.1	32.2	4 184	58.5
Rome, GA	70	-17.1	126	0.8	19.6	489 283	3 898	54 420	77.0	137 828	6.9	93.1	29.3	8.6	616	19.7
Sacramento—Roseville—Arden-Arcade, CA	927	-11.5	183	343.4	457.4	1 259 225	6 892	84 057	961.8	189 475	D	D	39.7	14.6	10 256	9.9
Saginaw, MI	310	-4.5	235	2.3	274.5	896 656	3 816	144 832	243.6	184 855	91.7	8.3	55.8	27.6	6 093	71.6
St. Cloud, MN	946	5.8	212	63.5	722.7	808 127	3 808	165 913	976.0	218 883	34.3	65.7	66.3	35.3	19 180	71.8
St. George, UT	148	-15.0	256	14.8	20.2	934 487	3 656	50 485	12.6	21 843	51.1	48.9	29.2	5.5	210	7.8
St. Joseph, MO-KS	810	-14.3	285	D	576.3	947 085	3 320	103 711	265.9	93 709	82.2	17.8	51.1	17.0	14 038	67.9
St. Louis, MO-IL	2 912	-0.9	258	14.1	2 232.2	1 359 070	5 260	137 402	1 235.6	109 636	73.4	26.6	46.7	19.4	42 877	56.7
Salem, OR	431	-9.1	116	105.3	314.8	852 208	7 337	116 718	742.7	200 189	80.7	19.3	38.6	16.2	2 495	11.7
Salinas, CA	1 268	-4.5	1 076	263.8	358.3	5 263 068	4 893	396 806	2 979.7	2 527 341	98.5	1.5	59.6	35.4	635	7.0
Salisbury, MD-DE	520	-2.4	218	105.7	399.5	1 515 910	6 943	176 840	1 575.7	660 933	24.2	75.8	66.0	48.9	11 071	48.2
Salt Lake City, UT	425	18.0	384	29.8	53.7	709 106	1 845	65 829	61.9	55 974	41.1	58.9	26.7	7.1	250	4.3
San Angelo, TX	1 453	-6.1	1 070	31.8	179.0	1 146 386	1 071	85 947	138.9	102 282	24.0	76.0	29.2	9.4	6 065	25.5
San Antonio-New Braunfels, TX	3 642	3.0	249	102.6	629.7	791 780	3 174	49 698	D	D	D	55.8	22.7	3.3	11 155	13.4
San Diego-Carlsbad, CA	222	-27.1	39	45.2	68.2	694 313	17 964	34 672	726.0	126 657	89.3	10.7	42.9	9.1	451	1.7
San Francisco-Oakland-Hayward, CA	525	-3.2	305	42.7	89.8	2 135 551	6 991	67 439	D	D	D	D	48.0	16.4	1 746	6.8
Oakland-Hayward-Berkeley, CA Div 36084	305	-13.1	290	36.2	66.9	1 951 273	6 733	66 327	146.9	139 355	83.9	16.1	43.0	11.7	281	4.7
San Francisco-Redwood City-South San Francisco, CA	48	-15.6	142	2.8	8.5	1 604 941	11 328	69 188	D	D	D	D	48.2	14.4	182	4.1
San Rafael, CA Div 42034	171	28.2	529	3.7	14.4	3 295 415	6 229	69 226	91.8	284 238	9.3	90.7	64.1	34.1	1 283	16.4
San Jose-Sunnyvale-Santa Clara, CA	834	-5.2	511	37.0	76.9	2 000 239	3 911	78 560	407.9	250 068	88.1	11.9	47.1	15.1	194	3.6
San Luis Obispo-Paso Robles-Arroyo Grande, CA	1 339	-2.2	502	81.6	255.4	2 115 410	4 212	92 222	665.0	249 431	92.9	7.1	52.2	19.1	3 488	9.0
Santa Cruz-Watsonville, CA	100	110.5	150	28.9	41.1	1 857 240	12 390	113 943	565.8	848 328	96.9	3.1	59.2	28.0	D	0.1
Santa Fe, NM	718	26.0	1 004	8.9	13.1	848 969	846	39 010	12.8	17 869	75.1	24.9	15.0	2.7	394	5.7
Santa Maria-Santa Barbara, CA	701	-3.6	439	96.7	132.3	3 233 061	7 365	125 663	1 177.9	737 581	95.8	4.2	58.8	29.4	554	1.5
Santa Rosa, CA	590	11.1	165	75.0	130.6	2 409 158	14 620	78 965	974.4	272 253	62.2	37.8	60.3	24.3	2 615	4.1
Savannah, GA	59	-8.5	212	D	23.3	629 249	2 972	99 313	D	D	105.4	D	32.0	9.6	D	25.6
Scranton—Wilkes-Barre—Hazleton, PA	162	-11.9	119	0.5	82.9	519 072	4 369	72 280	48.8	35 732	71.8	28.2	32.1	8.2	1 730	32.5
Seattle-Tacoma-Bellevue, WA	167	-3.9	35	12.3	60.3	598 066	17 015	38 276	351.7	73 883	37.3	62.7	20.9	4.7	1 507	3.5
Seattle-Bellevue-Everett, WA Div 42644	118	-6.8	36	9.5	48.7	653 085	18 191	39 507	260.2	79 461	41.2	58.8	22.3	5.4	1 411	4.4
Tacoma-Lakewood, WA Div 45104	49	3.8	33	2.8	11.5	476 152	14 222	35 548	90.9	61 524	26.3	73.7	17.9	3.0	96	1.3
Sebastian-Vero Beach, FL	162	3.3	352	57.6	54.8	1 359 020	3 856	54 672	144.9	314 419	92.2	7.8	49.7	18.4	809	4.1
Sebring, FL	490	2.9	506	61.8	84.0	1 484 852	2 937	82 911	273.4	282 121	72.6	27.4	41.4	21.4	609	2.2
Sheboygan, WI	190	-0.8	193	0.2	155.9	1 011 178	5 243	162 747	242.1	245 507	27.1	72.9	59.2	29.8	3 790	51.4
Sherman-Denison, TX	431	7.7	168	3.5	176.4	632 363	3 757	58 110	91.9	35 889	72.7	27.3	24.6	4.3	1 948	14.2
Shreveport-Bossier City, LA	438	-7.2	199	D	127.3	581 894	2 927	75 391	96.1	43 622	61.7	38.3	27.8	5.2	4 003	11.5
Sierra Vista-Douglas, AZ	917	11.2	839	65.5	123.3	1 175 308	1 401	81 234	150.0	137 235	D	D	37.6	13.3	2 594	16.9
Sioux City, IA-NE-SD	1 733	4.6	476	102.0	1 485.9	2 768 921	5 823	252 868	1 460.1	400 692	50.7	49.3	70.1	45.3	32 806	77.9
Sioux Falls, SD	1 521	2.1	445	D	1 281.2	2 132 173	4 792	221 113	781.7	228 689	59.5	40.5	61.6	35.5	22 368	70.5
South Bend-Mishawaka, IN-MI	341	-7.7	229	85.2	284.3	1 128 461	4 932	144 874	310.7	208 639	74.9	25.1	45.5	22.1	5 134	51.0
Spartanburg, SC	149	-4.0	93	2.0	46.7	380 610	4 088	39 334	49.9	31 150	43.0	57.0	20.0	2.2	1 136	9.2
Spokane-Spokane Valley, WA	1 108	-8.6	281	17.9	473.7	632 566	2 247	63 943	190.1	48 275	80.3	19.7	26.8	8.2	8 308	19.6
Springfield, IL	672	-2.2	460	5.3	615.7	3 274 998	7 122	262 928	442.9	303 152	94.0	6.0	51.0	34.3	12 337	73.8
Springfield, MA	93	3.4	67	1.7	32.6	521 085	7 767	50 067	72.8	52 742	74.9	25.1	28.8	8.6	1 162	10.7
Springfield, MO	1 216	-3.9	163	2.2	367.2	435 524	2 671	46 051	274.8	36 841	11.5	88.5	41.9	6.8	3 665	10.0
Springfield, OH	174	-1.7	222	1.6	149.8	1 141 031	5 138	147 288	145.1	184 896	80.4	19.6	45.1	23.8	2 754	47.6
State College, PA	162	9.1	136	1.1	84.9	736 207	5 416	86 739	91.6	76 830	34.3	65.7	47.2	20.0	1 985	30.3
Staunton-Waynesboro, VA	260	-9.1	152	3.3	89.6	953 997	6 256	79 364	232.1	136 059	11.9	88.1	49.1	15.1	1 677	18.2
Stockton-Lodi, CA	787	6.7	220	485.4	517.9	2 218 140	10 090	145 302	2 250.2	628 536	73.7	26.3	73.5	39.3	5 508	9.4
Sumter, SC	176	14.7	342	8.9	69.5	792 967	2 320	105 033	130.5	253 379	36.9	63.1	27.2	10.9	1 870	57.3
Syracuse, NY	432	-1.6	199	2.7	258.2	481 316	2 425	122 464	317.4	145 856	32.1	67.9	47.7	19.0	4 474	26.8
Tallahassee, FL	293	-6.7	198	7.2	46.2	899 716	4 533	43 945	108.8	73 841	D	D	25.0	4.1	761	14.9
Tampa-St. Petersburg-Clearwater, FL	449	5.2	101	35.5	116.5	824 501	8 159	47 987	482.9	108 574	75.8	24.2	31.0	8.7	1 670	2.4
Terre Haute, IN	569	-3.3	329	D	489.0	1 408 309	4 286	168 128	261.3	150 886	84.3	15.7	46.0	24.4	9 160	68.2
Texarkana, TX-AR	609	0.4	235	21.4	223.1	475 867	2 027	61 443	188.1	72 558	30.0	70.0	34.1	7.9	3 271	16.9

Area name	Water use, 2010		Wholesale trade,[1] 2012				Retail trade, 2012				Real estate and rental and leasing, 2012			
	Total water withdrawn (mil gal/day)	Gallons withdrawn per person per day	Number of establish-ments	Number of employees	Sales (mil dol)	Annual payroll (mil dol)	Number of establish-ments	Number of employees	Sales (mil dol)	Annual payroll (mil dol)	Number of establish-ments	Number of employees	Receipts (mil dol)	Annual payroll (mil dol)
	133	134	135	136	137	138	139	140	141	142	143	144	145	146
Redding, CA..........................	239.0	1 349	158	1 437	1 023.9	59.8	647	8 980	2 507.1	241.4	207	765	121.4	22.1
Reno, NV	134.9	317	584	8 064	6 401.9	414.6	1 411	21 644	6 173.0	580.9	672	3 245	1 049.1	124.3
Richmond, VA	1 231.6	1 019	1 349	21 390	20 135.9	1 158.4	4 251	64 627	16 923.0	1 530.7	1 288	8 019	1 667.1	345.4
Riverside-San Bernardino-Ontario, CA	1 758.7	416	4 061	55 568	49 713.0	2 646.5	9 744	160 809	49 439.3	4 142.4	3 608	16 254	3 307.2	620.1
Roanoke, VA	44.4	144	434	6 455	3 944.5	340.1	1 226	18 356	4 658.8	424.8	361	1 693	283.0	57.0
Rochester, MN	48.4	234	171	2 237	1 675.9	108.3	823	12 429	2 948.5	271.3	194	803	149.2	24.0
Rochester, NY	714.6	662	1 041	13 319	7 667.8	692.4	3 549	57 373	13 433.0	1 266.8	1 069	7 229	1 212.2	257.3
Rockford, IL	41.5	119	364	4 362	2 903.0	219.4	1 094	15 667	4 147.5	358.1	236	1 573	178.9	45.3
Rocky Mount, NC	35.9	235	128	2 404	2 899.8	109.2	551	6 475	1 606.6	140.2	126	464	73.5	14.7
Rome, GA	474.7	4 928	74	812	691.5	33.8	386	3 986	1 022.4	89.3	76	252	41.7	8.2
Sacramento—Roseville—Arden-Arcade, CA.........	1 708.2	795	1 768	24 256	30 299.6	1 354.9	5 715	89 921	25 231.7	2 423.6	2 832	14 883	2 682.4	598.9
Saginaw, MI	22.3	111	181	1 975	1 264.9	96.7	870	12 210	2 913.3	262.8	132	602	101.1	16.3
St. Cloud, MN	58.0	307	225	4 802	2 975.1	220.1	790	12 674	3 428.2	287.7	196	900	146.3	25.1
St. George, UT	122.2	885	149	1 284	1 514.7	47.4	574	7 375	1 900.8	168.4	306	702	95.2	18.7
St. Joseph, MO-KS...............	99.5	781	133	2 102	1 983.2	91.9	440	6 469	1 627.6	140.6	124	D	D	D
St. Louis, MO-IL....................	3 444.4	1 236	3 234	52 073	56 278.9	2 936.0	9 170	140 597	44 947.4	3 614.6	2 904	17 590	3 989.1	764.2
Salem, OR	324.1	829	293	3 958	3 290.9	187.9	1 228	17 043	4 222.9	413.9	476	2 158	289.1	61.7
Salinas, CA	545.5	1 314	346	4 574	5 775.2	278.9	1 316	16 335	4 457.4	437.2	444	1 873	436.3	69.6
Salisbury, MD-DE	311.4	833	321	3 198	3 074.0	154.2	1 959	22 278	5 698.2	523.9	562	2 528	400.9	85.4
Salt Lake City, UT.................	596.8	549	1 666	27 811	19 766.8	1 643.3	3 499	57 496	17 675.2	1 573.1	1 961	9 056	1 937.9	379.9
San Angelo, TX.....................	59.6	533	115	D	D	D	422	5 980	1 823.3	150.0	134	595	92.7	16.5
San Antonio-New Braunfels, TX	1 571.4	733	1 816	D	D	D	5 984	96 472	32 018.0	2 399.0	2 102	15 075	3 359.6	662.5
San Diego-Carlsbad, CA	2 818.2	910	3 883	59 227	35 937.4	4 055.0	9 219	138 929	39 786.1	3 787.5	5 401	28 321	7 895.7	1 308.8
San Francisco-Oakland-Hayward, CA	787.0	182	5 594	81 370	73 423.7	5 831.6	13 370	195 011	63 799.7	6 071.0	6 785	40 566	14 041.3	2 383.1
Oakland-Hayward-Berkeley, CA Div 36084....	557.6	218	3 119	51 504	44 467.8	3 551.0	6 703	102 866	32 748.9	3 008.4	3 226	16 093	4 354.7	794.9
San Francisco-Redwood City-South San Francisco, CA...........................	186.6	122	2 116	27 086	27 091.4	2 099.8	5 614	77 447	25 963.3	2 517.8	2 970	22 018	8 228.1	1 419.5
San Rafael, CA Div 42034 .	42.9	170	359	2 780	1 864.6	180.8	1 053	14 698	5 087.5	544.8	589	2 455	1 458.6	168.7
San Jose-Sunnyvale-Santa Clara, CA	383.7	209	2 349	84 942	92 134.3	10 863.8	5 032	85 434	40 681.9	3 247.2	2 479	12 943	4 484.6	767.8
San Luis Obispo-Paso Robles-Arroyo Grande, CA	2 579.1	9 565	289	D	D	D	1 177	13 992	3 624.0	361.5	430	1 552	278.4	52.2
Santa Cruz-Watsonville, CA .	66.4	253	266	5 614	5 898.2	297.2	887	11 120	4 368.0	294.7	363	1 271	264.1	41.8
Santa Fe, NM........................	49.8	345	111	867	773.2	37.4	813	8 981	2 324.5	250.1	280	933	181.8	36.9
Santa Maria-Santa Barbara, CA	264.3	623	406	5 325	3 475.6	397.1	1 509	18 781	4 853.8	501.5	691	3 047	570.7	113.7
Santa Rosa, CA	259.5	536	593	8 047	4 443.2	557.8	1 768	23 032	6 016.3	655.8	679	2 824	631.1	103.4
Savannah, GA.......................	404.3	1 163	348	4 265	6 501.3	216.0	1 407	18 108	4 967.3	427.7	445	1 954	404.7	63.4
Scranton—Wilkes-Barre—Hazleton, PA.....................	150.5	267	569	9 845	7 916.9	425.6	2 277	32 708	11 676.8	720.0	357	1 640	353.7	57.2
Seattle-Tacoma-Bellevue, WA	658.8	192	4 652	65 726	55 450.8	4 041.0	10 862	163 846	80 843.3	5 007.9	5 996	31 037	7 372.8	1 461.3
Seattle-Bellevue-Everett, WA Div 42644............	461.6	175	3 966	56 555	47 745.2	3 591.1	8 708	130 735	70 728.9	4 063.0	5 049	26 364	6 535.2	1 302.6
Tacoma-Lakewood, WA Div 45104.................	197.2	248	686	9 171	7 705.6	449.9	2 154	33 111	10 114.4	944.9	947	4 673	837.6	158.6
Sebastian-Vero Beach, FL....	154.5	1 119	125	D	D	D	659	7 958	1 881.3	189.1	231	1 213	162.3	36.9
Sebring, FL	107.8	1 091	57	D	D	D	316	4 292	1 112.5	100.2	87	264	51.2	7.5
Sheboygan, WI	328.5	2 844	86	1 002	593.9	47.9	395	6 124	1 400.0	133.5	73	298	58.2	10.4
Sherman-Denison, TX	22.3	185	100	905	906.6	36.6	417	5 685	1 620.2	137.9	109	327	48.9	8.6
Shreveport-Bossier City, LA .	206.3	469	487	7 141	6 959.9	343.2	1 641	22 553	6 759.2	557.8	462	3 206	620.0	123.9
Sierra Vista-Douglas, AZ	238.4	1 815	47	269	133.9	10.1	408	5 266	1 267.3	115.2	113	424	57.1	11.4
Sioux City, IA-NE-SD...........	1 055.6	6 263	242	3 529	4 024.5	168.6	652	9 729	2 409.8	203.7	143	679	87.2	18.3
Sioux Falls, SD	45.5	200	440	6 274	4 859.6	319.5	981	16 468	4 854.0	385.7	293	1 511	299.3	56.7
South Bend-Mishawaka, IN-MI	68.2	214	352	4 687	3 447.2	229.0	1 027	15 578	4 032.2	362.8	246	1 281	213.2	42.5
Spartanburg, SC	46.7	149	428	5 915	5 383.9	301.5	1 168	14 364	4 162.4	333.6	241	1 133	188.7	40.3
Spokane-Spokane Valley, WA	219.0	415	586	D	D	D	1 777	26 212	6 902.3	700.5	644	3 143	531.3	104.3
Springfield, IL	325.6	1 549	206	3 433	3 525.5	155.9	785	12 269	3 205.4	283.0	215	849	154.4	25.7
Springfield, MA	176.6	284	470	8 257	7 835.9	436.2	2 119	30 551	7 502.9	727.9	478	2 274	569.0	81.5
Springfield, MO	249.7	572	527	8 382	5 528.0	354.2	1 646	24 111	6 492.0	552.8	520	2 647	375.5	75.4
Springfield, OH	25.8	187	88	2 274	2 697.8	111.4	403	5 708	1 541.5	128.0	95	468	56.8	12.5
State College, PA	45.4	295	90	873	538.9	42.5	481	7 570	1 748.7	155.7	133	1 036	255.5	34.7
Staunton-Waynesboro, VA ...	46.4	391	90	1 190	438.9	52.9	465	5 926	1 528.2	134.3	134	424	45.0	11.2
Stockton-Lodi, CA.................	1 753.4	2 559	515	9 279	11 713.5	495.7	1 602	24 097	7 059.5	616.4	572	2 655	464.7	97.2
Sumter, SC	23.5	219	69	635	342.0	28.8	398	4 416	1 096.8	85.4	78	258	28.9	6.4
Syracuse, NY	1 098.7	1 658	685	11 688	17 632.5	597.7	2 257	36 012	8 919.9	802.6	700	4 109	704.0	159.0
Tallahassee, FL	68.0	185	285	D	D	D	1 227	17 445	4 073.0	382.0	438	2 112	295.1	62.2
Tampa-St. Petersburg-Clearwater, FL............................	4 151.3	1 492	3 244	40 574	34 352.8	2 027.1	9 767	136 584	39 880.0	3 530.2	3 941	17 281	3 803.9	672.2
Terre Haute, IN.....................	1 382.6	8 019	135	D	D	D	635	8 698	2 233.2	180.8	116	570	93.5	18.9
Texarkana, TX-AR	136.7	917	132	1 974	2 955.7	87.5	577	7 946	2 151.3	185.7	131	589	110.1	20.1

1. Merchant wholesalers, except manufacturers' sales branches and offices.

Table C. Metropolitan Areas — **Professional Services, Manufacturing, and Accommodation and Food Services**

Area name	Professional, scientific, and technical services, 2012				Manufacturing, 2012				Accommodation and food services, 2012			
	Number of establishments	Number of employees	Sales (mil dol)	Annual payroll (mil dol)	Number of establishments	Number of employees	Sales (mil dol)	Annual payroll (mil dol)	Number of establishments	Number of employees	Sales (mil dol)	Annual payroll (mil dol)
	147	148	149	150	151	152	153	154	155	156	157	158
Redding, CA	358	D	D	D	147	1 990	511.9	93.7	376	5 421	285.5	76.7
Reno, NV	1 625	9 036	1 435.9	540.1	448	14 065	6 444.7	843.5	987	28 209	1 870.1	583.2
Richmond, VA	3 513	32 374	5 370.9	2 052.1	889	29 624	27 862.1	1 722.4	2 516	48 940	2 419.9	696.4
Riverside-San Bernardino-Ontario, CA	5 671	33 151	4 350.9	1 587.8	3 261	88 341	32 728.6	4 043.2	6 476	128 108	8 088.9	2 150.4
Roanoke, VA	773	5 088	632.5	261.7	309	15 342	5 067.6	743.0	665	12 830	592.8	172.4
Rochester, MN	368	11 211	1 098.1	677.9	194	12 474	4 784.7	741.7	493	8 963	441.5	124.4
Rochester, NY	2 481	24 105	3 556.2	1 390.8	1 326	56 345	20 527.1	3 110.6	2 383	36 363	1 740.8	499.6
Rockford, IL	667	4 418	717.0	220.8	678	32 643	14 051.7	1 895.8	635	10 964	531.9	147.7
Rocky Mount, NC	201	1 066	109.1	42.5	119	9 582	4 213.2	455.8	244	4 714	204.8	56.0
Rome, GA	186	809	104.1	35.0	100	5 567	3 615.6	265.3	183	3 593	163.4	46.9
Sacramento—Roseville—Arden-Arcade, CA	5 860	50 049	10 506.0	3 539.0	1 348	32 798	10 949.4	1 820.9	4 221	76 566	4 851.1	1 263.4
Saginaw, MI	318	2 226	299.2	109.3	206	11 249	4 523.3	653.2	368	7 829	373.8	97.6
St. Cloud, MN	359	D	D	D	318	14 205	4 221.1	604.2	419	7 450	311.7	84.8
St. George, UT	433	D	D	D	133	1 838	415.3	76.1	307	5 140	282.3	74.4
St. Joseph, MO-KS	184	1 131	128.8	54.6	110	12 749	7 338.7	492.7	223	D	D	D
St. Louis, MO-IL	7 187	83 135	14 035.8	5 306.9	2 641	99 727	61 153.6	6 113.4	6 026	120 774	6 396.3	1 759.0
Salem, OR	781	4 222	484.6	183.1	412	10 956	2 965.0	415.7	809	12 587	746.7	203.9
Salinas, CA	806	7 448	847.3	338.0	263	6 078	2 258.9	252.3	979	17 786	1 328.8	378.0
Salisbury, MD-DE	742	D	D	D	263	12 888	5 301.6	483.0	1 263	18 991	1 296.5	358.3
Salt Lake City, UT	4 213	40 353	6 437.6	2 413.6	1 394	48 107	22 944.7	2 761.9	2 149	42 602	2 217.2	646.5
San Angelo, TX	213	1 362	159.7	58.6	102	D	1 276.3	D	231	4 761	237.4	64.7
San Antonio-New Braunfels, TX	4 713	44 402	7 158.5	2 719.4	1 207	40 835	18 863.7	1 918.7	4 448	101 868	5 687.6	1 548.8
San Diego-Carlsbad, CA	12 528	134 334	24 111.3	9 099.2	2 891	97 346	33 320.5	6 196.1	6 880	147 457	10 403.8	2 857.4
San Francisco-Oakland-Hayward, CA	19 772	214 269	59 734.6	20 918.1	3 931	110 944	80 170.9	8 312.6	12 156	197 200	14 277.7	4 118.8
Oakland-Hayward-Berkeley, CA Div 36084	8 734	87 351	19 476.4	7 526.8	2 386	78 796	D	5 592.8	5 436	79 002	4 852.4	1 340.7
San Francisco-Redwood City-South San Francisco, CA	9 294	117 823	38 220.9	12 693.3	1 326	30 213	D	2 627.2	5 969	106 620	8 695.6	2 552.5
San Rafael, CA Div 42034	1 744	9 095	2 037.3	698.0	219	1 935	D	92.7	751	11 578	729.7	225.6
San Jose-Sunnyvale-Santa Clara, CA	8 465	125 608	30 165.3	13 558.7	2 447	103 203	42 041.7	9 264.8	4 487	73 416	4 859.1	1 349.7
San Luis Obispo-Paso Robles-Arroyo Grande, CA	868	4 914	673.1	269.5	382	6 107	2 854.0	285.7	865	14 254	824.8	229.5
Santa Cruz-Watsonville, CA	880	4 268	603.0	249.2	293	4 479	1 213.4	219.2	678	10 032	586.0	168.6
Santa Fe, NM	625	2 604	356.9	151.5	138	719	131.0	27.5	421	9 049	592.4	179.9
Santa Maria-Santa Barbara, CA	1 347	9 785	1 751.7	654.0	458	13 896	4 157.6	851.5	1 087	20 623	1 428.9	400.1
Santa Rosa, CA	1 514	9 140	1 244.4	524.0	821	19 324	6 131.7	1 085.2	1 192	17 606	1 058.7	301.8
Savannah, GA	833	6 360	692.4	274.9	208	15 862	10 027.5	1 138.9	1 033	19 741	1 097.8	296.2
Scranton—Wilkes-Barre—Hazleton, PA	1 111	8 480	925.1	352.4	581	27 852	12 229.0	1 255.8	1 390	20 178	960.9	249.9
Seattle-Tacoma-Bellevue, WA	12 651	117 190	21 306.5	9 251.6	3 584	155 814	77 904.1	9 877.4	8 964	135 680	8 755.3	2 557.9
Seattle-Bellevue-Everett, WA Div 42644	11 224	107 726	20 263.1	8 705.3	3 018	139 787	73 443.1	9 080.9	7 411	113 145	7 392.3	2 189.1
Tacoma-Lakewood, WA Div 45104	1 427	9 464	1 043.4	546.3	566	16 027	4 461.0	796.5	1 553	22 535	1 363.0	368.8
Sebastian-Vero Beach, FL	454	1 601	229.1	84.3	84	1 487	D	68.7	250	4 351	225.1	66.2
Sebring, FL	132	602	57.5	18.4	44	570	214.0	22.7	147	2 331	110.6	30.7
Sheboygan, WI	179	1 240	207.9	65.8	230	16 716	7 346.2	825.1	269	4 151	188.8	53.4
Sherman-Denison, TX	227	844	99.0	32.7	112	6 886	2 574.9	288.3	224	4 305	200.2	57.1
Shreveport-Bossier City, LA	894	5 650	756.8	265.3	294	9 906	7 610.9	533.8	821	21 991	1 491.1	349.4
Sierra Vista-Douglas, AZ	217	4 592	586.7	254.7	43	279	141.0	14.2	277	3 875	173.4	48.4
Sioux City, IA-NE-SD	306	1 520	178.5	67.1	183	15 637	10 083.3	584.0	411	6 796	312.3	86.0
Sioux Falls, SD	587	D	D	D	260	13 256	4 720.2	584.5	535	11 487	535.9	159.1
South Bend-Mishawaka, IN-MI	563	5 073	1 374.8	279.6	435	16 080	7 230.4	829.5	624	11 677	516.5	147.6
Spartanburg, SC	474	4 904	698.1	265.2	425	25 455	15 562.6	1 351.9	586	10 544	498.9	134.0
Spokane-Spokane Valley, WA	1 337	D	D	D	566	15 225	D	723.6	1 171	18 692	1 099.7	310.1
Springfield, IL	542	4 460	556.4	227.4	114	2 858	688.9	140.1	544	9 678	444.7	130.5
Springfield, MA	1 214	8 727	1 111.4	446.2	717	23 526	7 355.7	1 240.8	1 312	20 253	978.6	276.9
Springfield, MO	1 042	7 464	1 131.2	410.6	477	14 338	5 202.5	607.4	938	17 836	761.9	224.2
Springfield, OH	166	1 172	141.2	58.3	158	6 116	2 832.4	275.0	235	4 288	197.0	53.2
State College, PA	365	3 204	432.1	191.2	145	3 960	1 053.5	181.9	311	6 352	289.0	79.7
Staunton-Waynesboro, VA	187	1 469	92.3	70.3	124	6 667	2 437.0	320.0	227	3 992	183.9	52.3
Stockton-Lodi, CA	780	4 463	491.1	190.0	517	18 703	9 212.4	879.0	997	15 422	808.6	211.0
Sumter, SC	126	714	75.8	23.2	71	5 524	1 817.5	214.6	158	2 951	127.0	34.9
Syracuse, NY	1 435	14 683	2 187.0	815.3	579	23 640	10 592.6	1 283.4	1 600	24 414	1 158.4	330.5
Tallahassee, FL	1 454	D	D	D	141	2 861	D	138.7	755	D	D	D
Tampa-St. Petersburg-Clearwater, FL	10 447	85 745	12 902.8	5 325.3	2 121	51 778	18 823.8	2 583.0	5 275	100 640	6 300.5	1 646.5
Terre Haute, IN	257	1 453	145.3	54.2	174	12 457	5 125.1	604.5	385	6 822	291.4	82.5
Texarkana, TX-AR	208	1 126	118.7	38.6	99	5 410	2 601.2	308.5	270	5 616	260.2	74.3

Area name	Health care and social assistance, 2012				Other services, 2012				Nonemployer business, 2014		Value of residential construction authorized by building permits, 2015	
	Number of establishments	Number of employees	Receipts (mil dol)	Annual payroll (mil dol)	Number of establishments	Number of employees	Receipts (mil dol)	Annual payroll (mil dol)	Number	Receipts (mil dol)	New construction ($1,000)	Number of housing units
	159	160	161	162	163	164	165	166	167	168	169	170
Redding, CA........................	634	10 525	1 324.6	469.3	296	1 658	162.7	48.2	11 727	536.3	72 774	375
Reno, NV............................	1 191	23 356	3 028.7	1 167.9	731	4 788	675.8	142.5	30 264	1 693.9	586 535	2 787
Richmond, VA.....................	3 086	77 601	9 636.5	3 570.9	2 343	16 581	1 941.2	497.6	81 295	3 503.5	794 838	4 875
Riverside-San Bernardino-Ontario, CA......................	7 983	147 321	19 611.4	7 140.3	4 688	30 021	2 676.3	788.6	297 808	12 751.2	2 150 630	9 926
Roanoke, VA.......................	784	24 402	2 855.7	1 119.8	644	3 814	287.1	88.7	18 720	771.0	127 847	763
Rochester, MN....................	549	22 061	2 524.6	908.0	368	2 406	208.4	59.1	14 238	627.4	297 720	1 776
Rochester, NY.....................	2 645	78 759	7 020.1	3 004.4	1 691	9 959	979.4	264.8	63 536	2 855.2	409 886	2 652
Rockford, IL........................	738	20 948	2 479.1	953.1	601	3 558	336.6	91.8	21 401	776.1	19 067	134
Rocky Mount, NC................	348	6 552	552.6	216.7	184	D	D	D	8 078	286.2	41 751	263
Rome, GA...........................	281	8 058	1 049.2	412.6	104	831	64.9	19.5	6 910	237.4	18 298	93
Sacramento—Roseville—Arden-Arcade, CA.........	5 224	109 282	17 012.0	6 397.8	3 327	24 372	2 889.2	797.2	157 923	7 665.0	1 699 421	6 184
Saginaw, MI........................	582	17 262	1 766.5	712.8	328	1 943	161.3	45.2	10 952	395.1	49 680	382
St. Cloud, MN.....................	497	18 050	1 736.2	799.1	438	2 932	286.2	73.2	12 902	609.1	141 229	858
St. George, UT....................	500	7 443	830.8	271.4	188	1 043	87.9	24.3	12 570	582.8	322 679	1 658
St. Joseph, MO-KS..............	380	8 613	902.6	367.8	208	1 294	140.0	39.2	6 429	250.5	27 471	211
St. Louis, MO-IL..................	8 729	185 365	18 992.4	7 415.9	4 924	33 886	3 497.5	1 037.4	180 726	7 863.7	1 636 355	7 698
Salem, OR..........................	1 162	19 987	1 955.5	833.3	571	2 726	241.4	74.3	20 121	904.0	273 869	1 297
Salinas, CA.........................	994	14 898	2 151.0	838.2	560	3 765	457.6	111.7	24 494	1 355.6	120 923	587
Salisbury, MD-DE................	1 062	22 506	2 375.2	963.4	711	4 120	359.8	107.3	27 937	1 342.0	446 363	3 031
Salt Lake City, UT...............	3 025	61 712	7 734.6	2 715.1	1 930	12 970	1 348.9	402.0	82 104	4 044.0	1 252 926	6 755
San Angelo, TX...................	270	6 877	701.7	303.3	213	1 158	130.1	31.8	8 579	386.6	46 508	236
San Antonio-New Braunfels, TX...................................	5 165	124 245	13 302.5	4 824.4	3 055	21 342	1 912.9	575.5	167 199	7 907.2	1 555 440	7 824
San Diego-Carlsbad, CA	8 522	151 783	21 337.8	7 872.6	5 193	41 437	4 080.6	1 179.4	258 892	13 057.6	2 100 214	9 883
San Francisco-Oakland-Hayward, CA.......................	13 665	244 910	38 656.8	14 517.2	8 720	66 357	12 726.2	2 535.8	420 932	24 359.9	3 642 107	13 386
Oakland-Hayward-Berkeley, CA Div 36084..........	7 150	133 199	21 211.7	7 813.2	4 276	30 323	3 881.3	1 077.8	219 990	11 485.6	1 930 112	7 711
San Francisco-Redwood City-South San Francisco, CA..........................	5 398	95 851	15 342.8	5 855.6	3 801	31 495	8 261.0	1 298.0	163 080	10 114.6	1 596 884	5 285
San Rafael, CA Div 42034 .	1 117	15 860	2 102.3	848.3	643	4 539	583.8	160.1	37 862	2 759.7	115 112	390
San Jose-Sunnyvale-Santa Clara, CA..........................	5 506	100 436	17 164.2	6 157.0	3 076	21 108	3 516.2	733.7	138 424	8 146.6	1 385 172	5 788
San Luis Obispo-Paso Robles-Arroyo Grande, CA...................................	1 010	14 086	1 580.5	650.0	430	2 668	216.9	60.5	24 487	1 264.6	239 542	821
Santa Cruz-Watsonville, CA .	893	12 989	1 689.9	622.3	451	2 973	328.1	98.5	24 427	1 233.0	60 519	335
Santa Fe, NM......................	513	8 697	961.0	384.4	335	1 892	268.6	66.4	16 248	750.3	26 627	110
Santa Maria-Santa Barbara, CA...................................	1 360	20 279	2 637.3	949.2	725	4 544	933.5	142.1	33 354	1 904.0	299 793	1 082
Santa Rosa, CA...................	1 462	23 222	3 156.2	1 198.4	853	4 845	494.1	146.9	45 205	2 326.8	146 363	621
Savannah, GA.....................	830	20 161	2 442.9	911.6	498	3 921	368.3	118.2	25 814	1 119.5	479 980	2 407
Scranton—Wilkes-Barre—Hazleton, PA.................	1 764	43 487	4 120.7	1 722.2	1 012	5 221	498.0	131.3	30 263	1 468.2	183 263	831
Seattle-Tacoma-Bellevue, WA..................................	10 994	207 089	26 020.0	10 446.3	7 088	43 847	10 657.9	1 493.5	243 510	12 753.6	5 347 764	25 008
Seattle-Bellevue-Everett, WA Div 42644...............	9 079	163 844	20 650.8	8 327.4	5 760	35 714	9 897.2	1 252.5	202 801	10 857.5	4 616 454	22 111
Tacoma-Lakewood, WA Div 45104.....................	1 915	43 245	5 369.3	2 118.8	1 328	8 133	760.7	241.0	40 709	1 896.1	731 311	2 897
Sebastian-Vero Beach, FL....	466	7 828	886.2	333.8	280	1 395	124.5	34.6	12 995	734.4	339 050	873
Sebring, FL.........................	325	5 021	576.5	194.8	134	504	37.4	9.1	5 835	232.1	33 229	162
Sheboygan, WI....................	299	6 483	597.2	247.8	202	992	67.4	19.5	5 604	231.6	28 883	123
Sherman-Denison, TX	381	9 105	809.1	337.4	139	834	81.0	27.5	9 538	445.1	44 351	340
Shreveport-Bossier City, LA .	1 150	35 588	3 413.9	1 334.0	581	3 848	379.2	103.9	33 091	1 449.7	212 775	1 107
Sierra Vista-Douglas, AZ	273	4 896	408.9	167.4	150	684	53.1	16.1	6 582	195.1	30 980	215
Sioux City, IA-NE-SD...........	487	11 259	1 083.6	409.5	317	2 057	192.8	55.5	10 223	489.1	98 750	510
Sioux Falls, SD	636	24 272	2 615.5	1 082.9	478	2 699	293.8	76.5	18 598	993.6	301 195	1 926
South Bend-Mishawaka, IN-MI....................................	704	18 666	2 226.8	752.1	517	3 460	318.4	91.6	18 750	734.3	101 738	524
Spartanburg, SC	613	11 037	1 165.9	495.2	443	3 072	334.2	82.5	19 591	864.2	240 082	1 418
Spokane-Spokane Valley, WA..................................	1 598	D	D	D	888	D	D	D	31 696	1 380.1	495 053	2 738
Springfield, IL.....................	457	20 585	2 565.9	894.3	490	3 383	422.4	126.1	13 178	489.7	73 312	383
Springfield, MA...................	1 596	55 768	4 697.9	2 118.5	1 110	7 289	661.2	187.6	36 809	1 709.5	95 284	458
Springfield, MO	1 095	33 457	3 330.3	1 366.5	815	5 245	457.3	131.9	33 306	1 459.2	299 972	2 223
Springfield, OH...................	313	10 029	912.0	334.8	212	1 363	134.3	40.5	6 748	257.9	16 571	63
State College, PA................	363	7 882	767.4	316.6	249	1 471	131.7	37.0	9 489	454.0	91 172	389
Staunton-Waynesboro, VA ...	244	6 985	733.2	275.4	237	1 272	121.3	36.9	7 033	312.1	46 144	287
Stockton-Lodi, CA...............	1 361	27 052	3 447.7	1 264.8	841	5 038	445.0	135.0	35 974	1 848.6	550 282	2 431
Sumter, SC.........................	188	5 504	471.1	184.1	130	996	77.4	27.8	6 153	209.8	27 545	217
Syracuse, NY.......................	1 666	46 313	5 000.1	1 985.0	1 157	7 013	701.6	199.0	37 297	1 625.6	164 133	1 194
Tallahassee, FL...................	851	19 656	2 074.4	853.0	692	4 701	687.4	176.0	26 099	1 001.4	150 690	896
Tampa-St. Petersburg-Clearwater, FL......................	8 585	162 388	21 286.9	7 571.4	4 856	28 790	2 982.5	812.9	234 807	10 329.7	3 625 527	15 653
Terre Haute, IN...................	458	10 665	1 309.9	409.5	262	1 677	144.4	39.2	8 082	292.2	27 411	215
Texarkana, TX-AR	370	8 528	889.6	333.1	212	1 253	110.7	32.9	8 341	359.6	23 539	333

1. Establishments subject to federal tax.

Table C. Metropolitan Areas — Government Employment and Payroll and Local Government Finances

Area name	Government employment and payroll, 2012									Local government finances, 2012				
			March payroll (percent of total)							General revenue				
												Taxes		
													Per capita[1] (dollars)	
	Full-time equivalent employees	March Payroll (dollars)	Administration, judicial, and legal	Police and corrections	Fire protection	Highways and transportation	Health and welfare	Natural resources and utilities	Education and libraries	Total (mil dol)	Inter-govern-mental (mil dol)	Total (mil dol)	Total	Property
	171	172	173	174	175	176	177	178	179	180	181	182	183	184
Redding, CA	6 528	30 533 939	6.7	8.7	2.8	3.4	15.6	9.0	52.2	922.9	498.8	217.9	1 220	1 000
Reno, NV	13 611	57 292 494	10.4	14.1	5.7	4.2	4.2	8.4	50.4	1 736.5	755.1	608.1	1 402	1 025
Richmond, VA	47 868	168 064 481	7.1	13.2	5.2	1.8	6.2	5.1	57.6	4 453.2	1 860.0	1 873.9	1 521	1 127
Riverside-San Bernardino-Ontario, CA	137 986	750 815 862	7.1	10.8	3.0	2.2	12.9	6.4	55.7	22 872.7	12 544.1	5 769.7	1 326	1 022
Roanoke, VA	11 938	41 210 661	8.0	9.5	5.8	2.0	5.0	6.0	62.2	1 089.3	447.6	480.6	1 550	1 087
Rochester, MN	6 278	37 136 188	6.6	8.4	1.8	3.7	9.6	6.9	60.3	935.5	426.1	273.1	1 303	1 205
Rochester, NY	48 625	209 834 432	4.8	9.5	2.6	3.2	6.4	4.2	67.9	6 041.6	2 624.6	2 577.1	2 381	1 781
Rockford, IL	11 902	48 299 662	5.1	11.8	5.6	3.5	3.6	7.1	62.7	1 352.3	558.5	615.0	1 777	1 610
Rocky Mount, NC	8 741	30 617 673	3.2	6.0	2.3	1.7	32.7	6.1	46.8	725.6	291.0	136.9	903	699
Rome, GA	3 631	12 476 709	5.7	9.3	4.2	4.2	1.7	5.5	67.7	620.3	284.0	151.4	1 574	957
Sacramento—Roseville—Arden-Arcade, CA	74 788	405 371 174	6.2	12.5	5.4	3.7	8.2	11.7	48.6	11 604.0	5 395.4	3 303.5	1 504	1 115
Saginaw, MI	5 686	21 466 345	8.3	8.5	2.2	2.7	9.8	4.8	61.7	786.5	475.8	154.2	777	684
St. Cloud, MN	5 890	30 573 727	7.4	9.3	1.2	4.2	13.3	3.7	58.2	806.5	393.2	236.4	1 241	1 100
St. George, UT	4 130	14 492 173	7.3	10.1	1.7	2.6	6.5	13.4	56.5	453.7	154.1	197.8	1 366	972
St. Joseph, MO-KS	4 475	13 492 001	5.7	7.9	3.9	3.6	2.8	5.1	69.9	408.2	157.7	172.1	1 346	855
St. Louis, MO-IL	99 216	391 779 336	5.2	10.7	5.1	5.6	2.8	5.2	63.6	10 918.1	3 849.2	5 146.2	1 841	1 249
Salem, OR	13 276	58 238 836	5.8	9.3	3.5	3.1	4.0	3.9	68.1	1 449.9	756.3	442.2	1 116	1 009
Salinas, CA	16 674	95 953 296	5.6	9.2	2.7	3.8	28.8	5.1	41.4	3 062.0	1 376.2	682.3	1 599	1 199
Salisbury, MD-DE	12 705	51 865 541	5.6	9.0	1.0	1.9	3.6	5.9	70.9	1 432.6	624.3	557.2	1 459	1 077
Salt Lake City, UT	36 279	131 818 213	7.3	10.3	5.1	9.5	5.0	8.7	51.6	3 934.4	1 398.7	1 572.5	1 399	1 008
San Angelo, TX	4 541	12 163 357	8.9	16.3	6.6	1.5	3.5	6.2	55.4	335.7	127.3	150.0	1 306	1 006
San Antonio-New Braunfels, TX	94 742	356 044 474	4.4	8.7	3.2	3.7	9.8	10.5	58.5	8 697.5	3 005.2	3 729.5	1 669	1 358
San Diego-Carlsbad, CA	97 178	529 647 292	9.3	10.8	3.9	3.4	11.1	7.0	52.0	16 495.7	6 780.5	5 691.2	1 791	1 381
San Francisco-Oakland-Hayward, CA	155 343	998 941 828	7.6	12.2	5.4	11.0	17.4	9.2	35.0	32 009.2	10 425.4	11 842.8	2 658	1 820
Oakland-Hayward-Berkeley, CA Div 36084	87 214	540 452 372	5.4	11.4	5.0	8.5	17.1	9.7	40.0	17 465.2	6 071.1	5 674.3	2 154	1 538
San Francisco-Redwood City-South San Francisco, CA	59 585	406 735 774	10.1	13.4	5.7	15.2	18.9	8.4	27.1	13 022.2	4 026.7	5 343.5	3 414	2 179
San Rafael, CA Div 42034	8 544	51 753 682	10.8	11.2	8.5	4.2	8.9	10.4	44.3	1 521.9	327.6	825.0	3 222	2 533
San Jose-Sunnyvale-Santa Clara, CA	61 998	413 816 866	7.6	10.1	4.9	4.9	20.6	6.4	42.8	13 018.5	4 094.2	4 897.7	2 585	1 941
San Luis Obispo-Paso Robles-Arroyo Grande, CA	8 194	48 094 004	7.2	11.4	2.8	2.5	6.9	6.4	57.6	1 189.7	435.4	547.8	1 994	1 615
Santa Cruz-Watsonville, CA	9 292	50 504 116	8.1	10.1	3.9	7.3	13.5	7.9	47.1	1 432.9	632.4	483.8	1 813	1 441
Santa Fe, NM	4 848	18 022 225	9.3	12.0	6.4	3.8	4.1	9.6	48.1	527.4	253.9	199.3	1 361	807
Santa Maria-Santa Barbara, CA	15 712	89 085 924	7.3	11.4	5.3	3.7	14.4	7.2	48.4	2 761.9	960.5	877.6	2 035	1 531
Santa Rosa, CA	16 072	90 178 192	9.5	12.6	3.9	2.6	12.9	7.2	47.9	2 545.8	918.8	972.6	1 978	1 555
Savannah, GA	13 962	46 151 027	10.0	13.9	3.6	3.3	6.0	6.9	53.1	1 947.0	409.1	744.0	2 056	1 229
Scranton—Wilkes-Barre—Hazleton, PA	16 712	64 672 766	7.6	11.9	3.2	3.8	5.2	5.6	61.4	1 935.2	804.6	806.0	1 430	1 072
Seattle-Tacoma-Bellevue, WA	109 144	628 710 550	8.0	10.0	6.7	11.2	9.8	13.4	38.7	18 576.7	5 896.1	7 417.8	2 088	1 239
Seattle-Bellevue-Everett, WA Div 42644	85 210	497 008 852	7.8	10.1	6.0	12.0	11.7	13.8	36.5	15 276.4	4 566.4	6 183.2	2 256	1 287
Tacoma-Lakewood, WA Div 45104	23 934	131 701 698	8.7	9.5	9.2	8.4	2.7	12.1	47.1	3 300.2	1 329.7	1 234.7	1 521	1 076
Sebastian-Vero Beach, FL	4 188	14 858 891	4.7	16.3	4.8	5.0	5.1	12.6	48.7	445.1	88.8	266.5	1 896	1 553
Sebring, FL	3 358	10 445 615	8.2	12.8	2.4	5.5	3.7	6.4	56.9	264.2	111.3	100.2	1 021	799
Sheboygan, WI	4 469	19 622 392	8.8	8.8	2.1	5.2	8.0	3.0	63.5	489.1	213.6	207.1	1 801	1 746
Sherman-Denison, TX	5 248	18 290 717	5.6	9.2	3.5	2.7	4.2	4.8	69.0	414.8	144.6	188.3	1 544	1 271
Shreveport-Bossier City, LA	18 558	60 559 700	6.4	15.5	6.0	2.9	2.1	5.0	60.8	1 909.4	657.9	985.4	2 204	997
Sierra Vista-Douglas, AZ	4 879	16 984 358	11.7	10.2	5.2	2.9	3.0	3.3	61.1	397.9	175.5	144.2	1 092	821
Sioux City, IA-NE-SD	7 016	27 062 681	5.1	8.4	2.6	4.9	5.3	5.2	67.0	775.3	326.0	295.7	1 751	1 347
Sioux Falls, SD	7 176	25 345 869	6.6	9.8	3.7	4.0	2.2	5.5	66.9	751.2	210.8	404.9	1 707	1 166
South Bend-Mishawaka, IN-MI	10 955	36 623 695	5.5	11.4	6.3	4.0	1.2	6.4	63.3	1 211.4	523.3	434.1	1 362	1 022
Spartanburg, SC	15 589	60 744 767	3.4	5.1	1.5	0.6	46.5	4.0	38.2	1 645.4	411.5	361.9	1 142	1 015
Spokane-Spokane Valley, WA	15 408	75 996 689	9.2	11.0	6.8	7.0	5.4	7.5	51.4	2 043.9	939.8	680.9	1 279	830
Springfield, IL	9 009	38 285 598	5.0	9.2	3.6	4.6	2.0	19.1	56.1	823.8	336.6	347.9	1 641	1 427
Springfield, MA	24 505	106 805 892	3.3	9.5	6.2	2.5	1.8	7.6	67.7	2 499.8	1 290.8	947.8	1 515	1 471
Springfield, MO	15 530	53 052 304	4.5	7.1	2.8	3.8	8.8	10.0	56.5	1 328.3	481.9	530.1	1 192	662
Springfield, OH	5 386	19 627 638	7.6	10.0	4.2	2.3	8.2	4.4	57.6	501.3	270.1	168.3	1 227	774
State College, PA	3 965	14 048 206	7.5	8.6	0.0	7.9	9.9	5.8	58.3	455.2	154.4	216.4	1 394	1 018
Staunton-Waynesboro, VA	4 314	12 615 495	6.6	13.2	3.6	1.7	3.9	3.8	64.6	321.2	157.8	126.3	1 064	712
Stockton-Lodi, CA	23 911	123 453 125	6.5	12.7	3.3	2.6	14.7	5.0	53.3	3 894.7	2 276.8	855.2	1 217	851
Sumter, SC	6 341	17 021 292	4.2	6.1	1.7	1.8	1.6	3.3	80.4	271.8	124.5	114.5	1 060	719
Syracuse, NY	30 026	133 886 154	3.8	8.2	2.5	4.4	6.3	4.1	69.2	3 812.8	1 691.2	1 541.0	2 332	1 687
Tallahassee, FL	14 377	48 690 908	8.9	11.4	3.1	5.3	3.7	13.3	50.6	1 358.3	476.8	458.3	1 221	865
Tampa-St. Petersburg-Clearwater, FL	98 152	350 589 348	7.0	15.7	5.6	4.0	2.8	8.5	53.8	9 943.4	3 586.7	3 926.4	1 381	1 060
Terre Haute, IN	5 719	18 131 023	7.8	8.7	4.1	4.4	5.0	5.4	63.3	562.1	284.5	168.7	978	782
Texarkana, TX-AR	6 292	19 132 215	5.6	9.2	3.4	2.8	3.9	5.8	68.2	458.1	217.9	156.0	1 042	715

1. Based on the resident population estimated as of July 1 of the year shown.

Area name	Total (mil dol)	Per capita[1] (dollars)	Education	Health and hospitals	Police protection	Public welfare	Highways	Total (mil dol)	Per capita[1] (dollars)	Federal civilian	Federal military	State and local	Democratic	Republican	All other
	185	186	187	188	189	190	191	192	193	194	195	196	197	198	199
Redding, CA	906.1	5 074	43.3	8.1	5.8	10.6	4.0	544.3	3 048	1 300	317	11 334	33.8	63.0	3.2
Reno, NV	1 700.3	3 919	35.7	1.0	6.7	4.2	3.4	4 528.8	10 439	3 488	1 290	24 046	50.7	47.2	2.1
Richmond, VA	4 393.3	3 566	45.4	3.2	6.9	3.5	2.9	4 997.3	4 056	16 537	12 866	95 017	52.0	46.6	1.4
Riverside-San Bernardino-Ontario, CA	23 480.7	5 398	39.0	11.9	6.3	7.3	4.9	24 738.9	5 687	20 389	22 596	216 266	51.0	46.7	2.3
Roanoke, VA	1 134.6	3 659	44.3	2.7	5.5	7.8	1.9	1 358.0	4 379	3 971	1 012	17 815	41.6	56.1	2.3
Rochester, MN	953.0	4 547	35.9	2.2	5.0	7.4	11.0	3 142.1	14 990	991	771	10 888	49.4	47.9	2.7
Rochester, NY	6 147.1	5 680	50.8	4.1	3.8	11.1	4.2	4 984.9	4 606	4 622	1 795	70 548	54.4	43.7	1.8
Rockford, IL	1 291.0	3 731	51.6	1.6	7.8	2.7	5.4	877.0	2 534	899	708	16 168	51.0	47.2	1.8
Rocky Mount, NC	764.0	5 037	34.6	34.0	5.2	5.1	1.5	144.7	954	383	364	10 075	56.5	42.9	0.6
Rome, GA	658.4	6 846	27.4	47.2	2.2	0.1	2.6	238.0	2 474	206	267	5 577	29.4	69.2	1.4
Sacramento—Roseville—Arden-Arcade, CA	11 753.9	5 351	35.4	5.1	5.1	7.8	5.9	20 700.4	9 424	13 627	4 207	233 707	53.1	44.2	2.7
Saginaw, MI	801.9	4 043	42.8	14.5	5.8	0.7	5.8	494.0	2 490	1 419	330	9 485	55.5	43.6	1.0
St. Cloud, MN	798.0	4 189	41.0	7.6	5.1	5.3	11.0	1 171.2	6 149	2 253	680	11 243	42.5	54.9	2.6
St. George, UT	401.3	2 771	50.1	0.8	7.7	0.0	6.0	585.2	4 041	556	648	7 509	15.4	82.8	1.8
St. Joseph, MO-KS	361.2	2 824	56.2	2.3	8.0	0.6	5.5	644.5	5 038	604	433	9 517	39.8	57.8	2.4
St. Louis, MO-IL	11 016.7	3 940	50.5	2.4	7.4	0.6	5.2	13 307.4	4 760	28 304	13 697	140 125	52.6	45.7	1.7
Salem, OR	1 466.0	3 699	55.7	4.1	5.3	0.2	4.7	2 202.9	5 558	1 323	1 068	37 388	46.7	50.1	3.2
Salinas, CA	2 904.3	6 806	36.5	22.7	4.6	5.4	2.6	1 444.4	3 385	5 284	6 040	25 259	67.1	30.3	2.6
Salisbury, MD-DE	1 397.6	3 660	55.9	1.9	6.1	1.0	2.5	1 055.9	2 765	1 042	1 884	22 324	43.8	54.7	1.5
Salt Lake City, UT	3 773.6	3 358	42.9	1.2	5.6	2.1	5.3	7 423.5	6 606	11 691	5 228	92 707	37.6	59.4	3.1
San Angelo, TX	359.0	3 125	52.5	3.3	5.7	0.2	2.7	590.0	5 137	1 189	3 211	7 620	25.1	73.4	1.5
San Antonio-New Braunfels, TX	8 877.6	3 974	45.3	13.6	5.3	1.8	3.0	21 467.3	9 609	34 632	33 941	127 496	45.3	53.3	1.4
San Diego-Carlsbad, CA	16 846.0	5 302	37.0	9.8	5.3	6.9	2.9	27 732.0	8 729	46 225	99 789	182 955	52.6	45.0	2.4
San Francisco-Oakland-Hayward, CA	31 954.0	7 172	25.5	16.6	5.8	5.5	3.3	56 702.8	12 726	32 363	9 284	270 394	75.4	21.8	2.8
Oakland-Hayward-Berkeley, CA Div 36084	18 716.4	7 105	26.5	15.3	5.6	5.5	3.2	31 762.2	12 057	13 935	5 741	141 266	73.6	23.7	2.8
San Francisco-Redwood City-South San Francisco, CA	11 668.6	7 455	22.7	19.9	6.1	5.8	3.5	22 636.4	14 463	17 674	2 952	114 867	78.5	18.5	3.0
San Rafael, CA Div 42034	1 569.1	6 127	34.5	6.9	6.2	4.1	3.1	2 304.2	8 998	754	591	14 261	74.1	23.1	2.8
San Jose-Sunnyvale-Santa Clara, CA	12 193.4	6 437	32.5	22.1	5.1	5.2	2.2	18 023.9	9 514	10 053	3 402	79 550	69.8	27.5	2.7
San Luis Obispo-Paso Robles-Arroyo Grande, CA	1 206.8	4 391	38.5	5.9	6.2	8.2	3.9	850.7	3 096	543	544	20 187	48.8	47.7	3.5
Santa Cruz-Watsonville, CA	1 415.2	5 305	36.6	6.6	6.3	8.5	2.3	1 074.8	4 029	535	404	17 817	75.6	20.0	4.4
Santa Fe, NM	578.2	3 950	45.8	1.3	6.0	2.2	3.5	916.2	6 259	956	385	16 196	73.5	22.4	4.1
Santa Maria-Santa Barbara, CA	2 786.6	6 462	32.4	18.7	5.7	6.7	3.0	1 346.9	3 123	3 704	3 333	30 922	57.6	39.6	2.8
Santa Rosa, CA	2 601.9	5 290	35.4	10.3	6.3	6.4	5.0	2 547.1	5 179	1 394	1 401	26 595	71.1	25.3	3.6
Savannah, GA	1 874.0	5 178	31.0	28.9	9.3	0.3	2.3	889.2	2 457	2 816	6 130	20 213	48.3	50.7	1.1
Scranton—Wilkes-Barre—Hazleton, PA	2 105.8	3 736	51.8	0.4	3.4	5.0	4.2	2 409.6	4 275	4 119	1 475	25 928	56.0	42.7	1.3
Seattle-Tacoma-Bellevue, WA	17 216.0	4 847	33.8	9.8	5.1	1.0	5.3	30 708.3	8 645	34 174	47 945	229 097	63.6	34.0	2.4
Seattle-Bellevue-Everett, WA Div 42644	13 942.5	5 088	31.5	11.7	5.0	1.1	5.2	26 143.1	9 540	22 332	13 257	184 224	66.0	31.5	2.4
Tacoma-Lakewood, WA Div 45104	3 273.5	4 033	43.7	2.1	5.8	0.6	5.6	4 565.2	5 624	11 842	34 688	44 873	54.4	43.3	2.3
Sebastian-Vero Beach, FL	470.0	3 343	38.2	4.8	9.4	0.8	8.2	436.2	3 103	336	271	4 684	38.5	60.8	0.7
Sebring, FL	276.6	2 818	46.6	3.7	7.8	0.6	6.0	143.0	1 457	252	182	3 745	38.0	61.1	0.9
Sheboygan, WI	492.9	4 286	55.2	3.6	5.7	6.1	8.2	375.9	3 269	203	329	5 567	44.6	54.4	1.1
Sherman-Denison, TX	423.3	3 471	54.8	3.3	5.1	0.0	6.0	717.6	5 885	319	252	6 106	25.2	73.2	1.6
Shreveport-Bossier City, LA	1 871.4	4 185	49.7	1.4	7.4	0.2	3.7	1 823.7	4 078	4 882	7 382	27 034	43.5	55.4	1.2
Sierra Vista-Douglas, AZ	407.1	3 082	44.0	3.5	12.3	4.9	7.3	161.6	1 223	5 260	4 453	6 441	37.8	60.2	2.0
Sioux City, IA-NE-SD	799.7	4 734	53.5	7.0	4.5	1.1	5.7	754.0	4 464	926	683	9 990	44.4	53.7	1.8
Sioux Falls, SD	772.0	3 254	47.6	1.5	5.3	0.5	10.0	951.0	4 008	2 592	1 520	10 505	42.7	55.4	2.0
South Bend-Mishawaka, IN-MI	1 028.2	3 227	51.4	1.7	4.7	1.1	3.4	1 041.8	3 270	962	1 009	14 591	49.6	49.0	1.4
Spartanburg, SC	1 655.8	5 223	33.7	46.8	3.0	0.4	1.0	1 083.5	3 418	559	1 292	21 161	38.6	60.1	1.3
Spokane-Spokane Valley, WA	2 096.5	3 939	45.9	6.2	5.2	0.2	4.3	1 764.2	3 315	4 942	4 323	34 250	44.6	52.6	2.8
Springfield, IL	869.8	4 103	52.8	1.5	7.5	0.9	4.5	2 540.3	11 983	1 790	465	19 334	44.0	53.9	2.1
Springfield, MA	2 618.5	4 185	57.6	0.6	4.8	0.6	3.1	1 821.1	2 910	5 226	1 722	47 737	64.2	33.6	2.2
Springfield, MO	1 305.4	2 936	50.3	8.6	6.8	0.8	6.6	1 931.0	4 343	2 344	1 524	25 860	33.1	64.8	2.1
Springfield, OH	474.6	3 459	49.3	5.8	5.9	6.2	3.3	206.0	1 502	552	348	6 482	48.8	49.6	1.6
State College, PA	453.5	2 923	51.0	2.2	3.5	7.9	6.1	486.7	3 136	450	453	47 555	49.1	48.8	2.1
Staunton-Waynesboro, VA	339.0	2 856	51.3	2.7	4.7	6.7	3.4	294.4	2 480	256	378	8 468	35.4	62.8	1.8
Stockton-Lodi, CA	3 717.2	5 291	40.5	9.2	5.9	8.8	3.5	3 309.2	4 710	3 143	1 160	33 472	55.8	42.0	2.2
Sumter, SC	256.2	2 371	55.2	1.2	7.1	0.3	2.5	245.3	2 270	1 286	5 791	5 446	58.3	40.7	0.9
Syracuse, NY	4 111.0	6 220	49.2	3.2	3.0	9.8	5.1	4 285.9	6 485	4 751	1 177	49 682	57.6	40.6	1.8
Tallahassee, FL	1 372.1	3 655	40.1	1.3	7.9	0.1	7.2	4 333.3	11 544	1 952	757	58 890	59.9	39.1	1.0
Tampa-St. Petersburg-Clearwater, FL	10 477.2	3 685	38.4	3.3	8.7	2.4	4.2	11 252.6	3 958	22 230	12 275	124 159	51.0	47.9	1.1
Terre Haute, IN	504.6	2 925	50.6	6.3	3.2	0.5	3.2	559.6	3 244	1 260	535	11 167	44.8	53.1	2.1
Texarkana, TX-AR	437.3	2 921	59.2	2.4	5.9	1.0	4.9	430.1	2 873	3 934	443	9 203	29.2	69.7	1.2

1. Based on the resident population estimated as of July 1 of the year shown.   2. © 2013 Election Data Services, Inc. All rights reserved.

Table C. Metropolitan Areas — **Land Area and Population**

CBSA/ DIV code[1]	Area name	Land area,[2] 2010 (sq km)	Population 2015 Total persons	Rank	Per square kilometer	White	Black	American Indian, Alaska Native	Asian and Pacific Islander	Percent Hispanic or Latino[3]	Under 5 years	5 to 17 years	18 to 24 years	25 to 34 years	35 to 44 years	45 to 54 years
		1	2	3	4	5	6	7	8	9	10	11	12	13	14	15
45540	The Villages, FL..............	1 417	118 891	324	83.9	85.6	8.2	0.7	1.0	5.7	2.0	5.4	3.4	5.9	6.5	7.5
45780	Toledo, OH	3 532	605 956	91	171.6	77.4	15.6	0.7	2.1	6.5	6.1	16.6	11.5	13.1	11.8	13.1
45820	Topeka, KS	8 372	233 791	193	27.9	81.4	8.0	2.5	1.7	9.6	6.5	17.8	8.3	12.2	11.4	13.4
45940	Trenton, NJ	582	371 398	143	638.1	53.1	20.4	0.5	11.2	16.6	5.9	16.0	11.2	12.5	13.3	14.7
46060	Tucson, AZ	23 794	1 010 025	53	42.4	55.0	4.1	3.1	3.8	36.1	5.9	15.9	12.2	12.3	11.4	11.9
46140	Tulsa, OK	16 237	981 005	55	60.4	71.8	9.6	12.8	2.7	9.1	6.9	18.2	9.0	13.6	12.5	13.1
46220	Tuscaloosa, AL	7 374	239 908	190	32.5	61.8	33.8	0.6	1.6	3.2	5.9	15.2	17.5	13.7	11.6	11.7
46340	Tyler, TX	2 387	222 936	198	93.4	61.6	18.0	0.7	1.9	18.6	7.0	17.9	10.2	13.4	11.8	12.2
46520	Urban Honolulu, HI	1 556	998 714	54	641.8	32.7	3.9	1.5	76.8	9.5	6.5	15.0	10.5	15.7	12.5	12.3
46540	Utica-Rome, NY	6 796	295 600	163	43.5	86.9	5.9	0.6	3.5	4.6	5.7	15.6	9.8	11.9	11.2	14.3
46660	Valdosta, GA	4 117	142 875	287	34.7	57.7	34.9	0.8	2.2	6.1	7.2	17.5	16.3	14.2	11.3	11.5
46700	Vallejo-Fairfield, CA	2 128	436 092	121	204.9	43.7	15.8	1.4	19.3	25.7	6.0	16.9	9.8	14.2	12.3	14.0
47020	Victoria, TX	4 492	99 913	352	22.2	48.0	6.4	0.6	1.4	44.5	7.1	18.5	9.4	13.7	11.5	12.2
47220	Vineland-Bridgeton, NJ........	1 253	155 854	261	124.4	49.5	20.3	1.4	1.8	29.3	6.8	17.0	8.8	14.8	13.6	13.7
47260	Virginia Beach-Norfolk-New-port News, VA-NC	6 969	1 724 876	37	247.5	58.7	31.9	1.1	5.3	6.3	6.4	16.1	11.6	15.5	12.0	13.4
47300	Visalia-Porterville, CA	12 495	450 863	111	36.8	31.6	1.7	1.2	4.2	63.1	8.9	22.7	10.7	14.0	12.3	11.4
47380	Waco, TX	4 669	262 813	180	56.3	58.3	15.6	0.7	1.9	25.0	7.1	17.5	14.7	12.9	11.1	11.8
47460	Walla Walla, WA	5 540	64 282	379	11.6	75.3	2.2	1.6	2.7	20.3	5.7	15.9	13.3	12.1	11.1	12.0
47580	Warner Robins, GA	2 007	188 149	226	93.7	58.6	33.2	0.9	3.3	6.5	6.7	18.2	10.5	14.3	12.5	14.0
47900	Washington-Arlington-Alexandria, DC-VA-MD-WV.	16 172	6 097 684	6	377.1	49.2	26.3	0.8	11.5	15.1	6.7	16.6	9.1	15.5	14.4	14.6
47900	Silver Spring-Frederick-Rockville, MD Div 43524...................	2 982	1 285 438	X	431.1	53.9	17.0	0.6	14.4	16.7	6.4	17.2	8.0	13.3	13.8	14.9
47900	Washington-Arlington-Alexandria, DC-VA-MD-WV Div 4	13 190	4 812 246	X	364.8	48.0	28.8	0.8	10.8	14.6	6.8	16.4	9.4	16.1	14.6	14.5
47940	Waterloo-Cedar Falls, IA	3 893	170 612	242	43.8	87.4	8.2	0.5	2.3	3.5	6.0	15.7	14.8	12.6	10.9	11.7
48060	Watertown-Fort Drum, NY ...	3 286	117 635	327	35.8	84.4	7.0	1.0	2.8	7.3	8.7	16.1	13.0	17.0	11.5	11.4
48140	Wausau, WI	4 001	135 868	297	34.0	90.6	1.3	0.8	6.2	2.6	6.1	17.3	8.1	12.0	12.1	14.8
48260	Weirton-Steubenville, WV-OH	1 503	120 512	321	80.2	94.2	5.0	0.6	0.7	1.2	4.6	14.6	9.1	10.2	11.5	13.8
48300	Wenatchee, WA	12 276	116 178	331	9.5	69.1	0.8	1.6	1.7	28.4	6.8	18.1	8.6	12.0	11.3	12.6
48540	Wheeling, WV-OH	2 443	144 198	284	59.0	95.2	4.1	0.6	0.8	1.0	5.2	14.2	8.9	11.6	11.6	13.6
48620	Wichita, KS	12 982	644 610	85	49.7	75.5	8.9	2.0	4.3	12.3	7.3	18.9	9.5	13.7	11.2	12.7
48660	Wichita Falls, TX..............	6 785	150 780	272	22.2	71.0	9.8	1.4	2.7	16.7	6.3	16.3	12.8	14.4	11.2	12.3
48700	Williamsport, PA	3 182	116 048	332	36.5	92.5	5.7	0.5	0.9	2.0	5.6	15.1	9.9	12.7	11.1	13.7
48900	Wilmington, NC	2 749	277 969	171	101.1	77.9	15.5	1.0	1.9	5.6	5.3	14.7	12.0	13.0	12.8	13.1
49020	Winchester, VA-WV	2 753	133 836	300	48.6	84.9	6.2	0.6	2.0	8.2	5.8	17.0	8.7	12.2	12.5	14.9
49180	Winston-Salem, NC	5 202	659 330	83	126.7	70.5	18.3	0.8	2.0	10.0	5.8	17.2	9.1	11.7	12.6	14.5
49340	Worcester, MA-CT	5 241	935 536	58	178.5	80.9	4.7	0.6	4.8	10.5	5.5	16.3	10.0	12.3	12.6	15.6
49420	Yakima, WA	11 125	248 830	188	22.4	46.6	1.2	4.6	1.8	47.7	8.4	21.4	10.1	13.0	11.9	11.6
49620	York-Hanover, PA.............	2 342	442 867	120	189.1	86.3	6.5	0.5	1.8	6.5	5.7	16.7	8.4	12.0	12.5	15.0
49660	Youngstown-Warren-Boardman, OH-PA	4 409	549 885	99	124.7	85.2	11.8	0.6	1.0	3.1	5.1	15.5	8.8	10.9	11.3	13.8
49700	Yuba City, CA.................	3 196	170 955	241	53.5	55.0	3.6	2.6	14.2	28.8	7.3	19.7	9.9	14.4	11.9	12.4
49740	Yuma, AZ......................	14 281	204 275	215	14.3	33.9	2.3	1.4	1.9	61.6	7.5	18.7	11.8	13.1	10.9	11.0

1. CBSA = Core Based Statistical Area. DIV = Metropolitan Division. See Appendix A for explanation. See Appendix B for list of metropolitan areas identified by type.   2. Dry land or land partially or temporarily covered by water.   3. May be of any race.

Table C. Metropolitan Areas — **Population and Households**

Area name	55 to 64 years	65 to 74 years	75 years and over	Percent female	2000	2010	2000–2010	2010–2015	Births	Deaths	Net migration	Number	Persons per house-hold	Family house-holds	Female family house-holder[1]	One person
	16	17	18	19	20	21	22	23	24	25	26	27	28	29	30	31
The Villages, FL..................	16.4	33.9	19.0	49.3	53 345	93 420	75.1	27.3	2 414	7 193	30 145	50 209	2.09	68.1	5.0	24.7
Toledo, OH..........................	13.4	8.1	6.4	51.3	618 203	610 001	-1.3	-0.7	39 559	30 171	-13 542	242 952	2.43	60.6	12.8	31.8
Topeka, KS..........................	14.0	9.1	7.3	51.1	224 551	233 868	4.1	0.0	15 911	11 847	-4 031	92 799	2.46	66.8	11.2	27.6
Trenton, NJ..........................	12.7	7.6	6.2	51.0	350 761	367 508	4.8	1.1	22 442	14 970	-3 182	131 564	2.69	67.6	12.8	27.5
Tucson, AZ...........................	12.6	10.0	7.7	50.8	843 746	980 263	16.2	3.0	62 878	46 603	12 769	389 737	2.50	60.9	13.2	31.1
Tulsa, OK.............................	12.5	8.2	6.0	51.0	859 532	937 528	9.1	4.6	69 784	47 411	20 540	375 790	2.55	66.3	12.8	28.3
Tuscaloosa, AL	11.7	7.3	5.3	51.7	203 009	230 159	13.4	4.2	14 892	10 925	5 647	80 582	2.80	66.7	15.9	28.5
Tyler, TX	12.0	8.6	6.9	51.7	174 706	209 721	20.0	6.3	15 984	10 232	7 184	77 469	2.76	68.7	13.8	27.1
Urban Honolulu, HI	11.6	8.4	7.4	49.2	876 156	953 207	8.8	4.8	71 809	39 221	13 834	309 002	3.09	70.7	12.7	23.2
Utica-Rome, NY	13.8	9.5	8.3	50.3	299 896	299 376	-0.2	-1.3	17 397	16 513	-4 315	116 231	2.43	63.1	13.1	29.6
Valdosta, GA.........................	10.2	7.1	4.8	51.0	119 560	139 665	16.8	2.3	10 829	5 923	-2 066	49 067	2.83	67.4	15.6	25.6
Vallejo-Fairfield, CA	13.2	8.1	5.5	50.3	394 542	413 344	4.8	5.5	27 379	15 911	10 833	145 313	2.90	73.3	16.7	21.3
Victoria, TX	12.6	8.5	6.5	50.8	91 016	94 003	3.3	6.3	7 239	4 359	3 027	35 523	2.76	71.4	12.8	24.7
Vineland-Bridgeton, NJ........	11.7	7.7	5.9	48.4	146 438	156 898	7.1	-0.7	10 987	7 512	-4 179	50 593	2.86	69.4	22.4	24.4
Virginia Beach-Norfolk-New-port News, VA-NC	12.0	7.6	5.4	50.8	1 580 057	1 676 817	6.1	2.9	118 953	69 371	-1 722	637 189	2.59	67.5	15.4	26.5
Visalia-Porterville, CA	9.6	6.0	4.4	49.9	368 021	442 182	20.2	4.0	41 223	14 923	-8 155	132 742	3.41	77.6	16.3	16.8
Waco, TX	11.3	7.4	6.2	51.3	232 093	252 772	8.9	4.0	19 298	11 480	2 380	93 166	2.70	66.3	13.4	28.2
Walla Walla, WA	12.8	9.2	8.0	49.2	59 244	62 859	6.1	2.3	3 755	3 129	708	23 296	2.50	64.4	10.3	30.7
Warner Robins, GA...............	11.6	7.3	5.1	51.7	144 021	179 605	24.7	4.8	12 818	7 251	2 578	67 667	2.68	69.8	15.6	26.1
Washington-Arlington-Alex-andria, DC-VA-MD-WV..	11.7	6.8	4.5	51.2	4 837 428	5 636 406	16.5	8.2	422 676	171 606	211 921	2 154 147	2.75	65.3	12.6	27.4
Silver Spring-Frederick-Rockville, MD Div 43524......	12.8	7.6	5.9	51.6	1 068 618	1 205 191	12.8	6.7	83 461	39 103	36 650	453 938	2.78	69.4	11.6	24.5
Washington-Arlington-Alex-andria, DC-VA-MD-WV Div 4..	11.5	6.6	4.1	51.0	3 768 810	4 431 215	17.6	8.6	339 215	132 503	175 271	1 700 209	2.74	64.2	12.8	28.2
Waterloo-Cedar Falls, IA	12.7	8.3	7.4	51.0	163 706	167 819	2.5	1.7	10 945	7 918	-112	67 957	2.40	61.9	10.8	30.6
Watertown-Fort Drum, NY	10.1	7.0	5.2	47.7	111 738	116 232	4.0	1.2	11 491	4 703	-5 617	43 516	2.59	66.7	10.6	26.5
Wausau, WI	13.7	8.6	7.3	49.7	125 834	134 063	6.5	1.3	8 456	5 921	-908	54 739	2.45	67.6	8.6	28.2
Weirton-Steubenville, WV-OH..........................	16.0	10.8	9.3	51.4	132 008	124 455	-5.7	-3.2	5 874	8 788	-797	51 058	2.39	66.9	13.1	28.3
Wenatchee, WA....................	13.6	9.7	7.2	49.9	99 219	110 887	11.8	4.8	7 635	5 069	2 623	41 500	2.72	66.8	10.1	26.8
Wheeling, WV-OH.................	15.7	10.4	8.8	50.3	153 172	147 949	-3.4	-2.5	7 839	9 802	-1 455	58 775	2.35	63.6	11.2	30.1
Wichita, KS	12.5	7.4	6.1	50.4	579 839	630 919	8.8	2.2	48 845	28 739	-6 560	240 230	2.62	66.3	11.4	29.2
Wichita Falls, TX..................	12.2	7.8	6.7	48.6	151 524	151 476	0.0	-0.5	10 201	7 781	-3 157	54 196	2.51	62.5	11.8	31.7
Williamsport, PA...................	14.2	9.4	8.1	50.8	120 044	116 108	-3.3	-0.1	6 722	6 541	-162	45 742	2.42	64.3	12.2	30.3
Wilmington, NC	13.0	9.6	6.5	51.6	201 389	254 884	26.6	9.1	14 908	11 555	19 017	110 993	2.38	59.8	10.9	30.5
Winchester, VA-WV	13.1	9.4	6.5	50.1	102 997	128 473	24.7	4.2	8 097	5 846	3 127	51 140	2.57	66.4	11.7	29.0
Winston-Salem, NC	13.2	9.2	6.7	51.8	569 207	640 577	12.5	2.9	39 237	31 611	10 701	256 999	2.50	65.1	13.2	29.4
Worcester, MA-CT................	13.5	8.0	6.2	50.7	860 054	916 976	6.6	2.0	51 932	40 044	7 194	344 496	2.60	67.4	12.3	26.4
Yakima, WA	10.8	7.4	5.4	49.9	222 581	243 231	9.3	2.3	21 730	9 856	-6 257	79 700	3.06	72.4	15.9	22.5
York-Hanover, PA.................	13.7	9.1	6.8	50.5	381 751	434 998	13.9	1.8	26 031	19 839	2 062	169 212	2.55	70.2	10.3	24.0
Youngstown-Warren-Board-man, OH-PA	15.2	10.2	9.1	51.2	602 964	565 804	-6.2	-2.8	29 566	36 271	-8 422	228 797	2.33	63.3	14.7	32.0
Yuba City, CA	11.3	7.6	5.6	49.8	139 149	166 892	19.9	2.4	13 227	6 695	-2 546	57 366	2.92	74.1	14.0	20.9
Yuma, AZ	9.7	9.2	8.2	48.8	160 026	195 750	22.3	4.4	16 490	7 305	-1 204	70 593	2.80	76.9	10.7	18.4

1. No spouse present.

Table C. Metropolitan Areas — **Population, Vital Statistics, Medicare, and Crime**

Area name	Daytime population, 2014 Persons in group quarters, 2015	Number	Employ-ment/residence ratio	Births, 2015 Total	Rate[1]	Deaths, 2015 Number	Rate[1]	Persons under 65 with no health insurance 2014 Number	Percent	Medicare, 2015 Total Benefici-aries	Enrolled in Original Medicare	Enrolled in Medicare Advantage	Serious crimes known to police,[2] 2014 Total Number	Rate[3]
	32	33	34	35	36	37	38	39	40	41	42	43	44	45
The Villages, FL..................	8 431	120 281	1.26	484	4.1	1 560	13.1	7 378	16.1	17 306	11 202	6 104	1 302	1 178
Toledo, OH........................	17 264	625 328	1.06	7 572	12.5	5 798	9.6	46 758	9.3	103 621	61 806	41 815	14 235	2 496
Topeka, KS	5 050	234 262	1.00	2 971	12.7	2 247	9.6	21 764	11.4	45 418	41 079	4 339	8 687	3 748
Trenton, NJ.......................	19 420	421 813	1.29	4 157	11.2	2 870	7.7	35 429	11.7	59 008	48 867	10 141	7 866	2 117
Tucson, AZ........................	25 522	1 001 161	0.99	12 048	11.9	9 251	9.2	129 021	16.0	183 450	94 188	89 262	49 303	4 894
Tulsa, OK	15 543	973 781	1.01	13 299	13.6	9 281	9.5	138 909	17.0	155 824	108 433	47 391	34 728	3 587
Tuscaloosa, AL	13 265	240 253	1.04	2 877	12.0	2 158	9.0	24 486	12.5	39 568	34 846	4 722	8 177	3 682
Tyler, TX	5 059	223 889	1.05	3 147	14.1	1 965	8.8	39 070	21.5	40 238	30 782	9 456	7 096	3 269
Urban Honolulu, HI	36 280	993 465	1.00	13 789	13.8	8 010	8.0	44 203	5.5	150 496	69 069	81 427	11 193	1 126
Utica-Rome, NY	14 408	293 456	0.98	3 298	11.2	3 093	10.5	18 515	7.9	61 233	39 396	21 837	6 996	2 385
Valdosta, GA.....................	5 772	145 774	1.05	2 027	14.2	1 187	8.3	23 749	19.8	20 467	15 422	5 045	5 542	3 864
Vallejo-Fairfield, CA	11 109	380 007	0.73	5 450	12.5	3 270	7.5	37 143	10.3	61 654	30 448	31 206	15 562	3 620
Victoria, TX	1 903	99 395	1.00	1 448	14.5	849	8.5	15 382	18.7	17 439	13 410	4 029	3 321	3 352
Vineland-Bridgeton, NJ	12 013	156 792	0.99	1 929	12.4	1 397	9.0	18 876	15.1	26 583	22 108	4 475	6 931	4 397
Virginia Beach-Norfolk-Newport News, VA-NC	71 836	1 726 462	1.01	22 782	13.2	13 760	8.0	173 504	12.1	249 167	193 776	55 391	52 249	3 067
Visalia-Porterville, CA	4 956	452 116	0.96	7 751	16.9	2 908	6.3	67 762	16.7	52 948	45 628	7 320	13 301	2 895
Waco, TX	11 291	266 753	1.04	3 761	14.3	2 204	8.4	45 571	21.2	40 572	27 913	12 659	8 909	3 471
Walla Walla, WA	4 853	66 432	1.10	720	11.2	623	9.7	6 521	13.4	12 234	10 771	1 463	2 394	3 742
Warner Robins, GA..............	3 736	182 694	0.95	2 414	12.8	1 485	7.9	24 893	15.5	28 291	22 441	5 850	7 978	4 364
Washington-Arlington-Alexandria, DC-VA-MD-WV ..	106 500	6 185 612	1.05	81 094	13.3	34 998	5.7	537 693	10.2	D	D	D	146 420	2 430
Silver Spring-Frederick-Rockville, MD Div 43524	13 523	X	X	15 920	12.4	7 615	5.9	102 451	9.4	151 574	134 427	17 147	22 815	1 792
Washington-Arlington-Alexandria, DC-VA-MD-WV Div 4..........................	92 977	X	X	65 174	13.5	27 383	5.7	435 242	10.5	D	D	D	123 605	2 600
Waterloo-Cedar Falls, IA	7 379	175 585	1.06	2 119	12.4	1 492	8.7	9 644	7.0	31 137	27 035	4 102	4 891	2 873
Watertown-Fort Drum, NY	6 165	121 858	1.05	2 195	18.7	919	7.8	8 096	8.2	18 337	13 671	4 666	2 563	2 180
Wausau, WI	1 624	138 085	1.03	1 590	11.7	1 064	7.8	8 307	7.3	23 101	12 974	10 127	1 906	1 424
Weirton-Steubenville, WV-OH.......................	3 436	117 910	0.85	1 121	9.3	1 672	13.9	8 930	9.5	29 498	19 564	9 934	NA	NA
Wenatchee, WA..................	1 118	112 649	0.96	1 438	12.4	967	8.3	13 550	14.4	21 797	17 358	4 439	2 503	2 186
Wheeling, WV-OH...............	6 775	148 933	1.06	1 502	10.4	1 778	12.3	10 604	9.5	31 547	16 911	14 636	2 453	1 864
Wichita, KS	11 513	643 870	1.01	9 146	14.2	5 506	8.5	68 826	12.6	98 884	80 680	18 204	26 377	4 146
Wichita Falls, TX................	12 835	151 580	1.00	1 937	12.8	1 460	9.7	20 763	17.6	26 533	22 732	3 801	5 529	3 785
Williamsport, PA.................	5 480	119 087	1.05	1 283	11.1	1 297	11.2	10 027	10.9	24 558	16 219	8 339	2 479	2 121
Wilmington, NC	7 940	279 290	1.05	2 889	10.4	2 316	8.3	33 081	14.9	50 280	41 605	8 675	10 287	3 810
Winchester, VA-WV	2 402	132 802	0.98	1 556	11.6	1 107	8.3	15 914	14.5	23 350	20 091	3 259	3 060	2 310
Winston-Salem, NC	13 492	629 806	0.91	7 427	11.3	6 038	9.2	82 980	15.4	120 095	52 593	67 502	25 542	3 929
Worcester, MA-CT	33 826	867 867	0.86	9 884	10.6	7 773	8.3	31 006	4.0	151 739	91 633	60 106	19 400	2 289
Yakima, WA	3 498	245 735	0.98	4 016	16.1	1 945	7.8	38 821	18.3	37 337	29 424	7 913	8 831	3 549
York-Hanover, PA...............	8 741	405 036	0.83	4 993	11.3	3 832	8.7	30 937	8.5	79 644	50 927	28 717	8 253	1 877
Youngstown-Warren-Boardman, OH-PA	18 538	544 612	0.96	5 697	10.4	6 834	12.4	45 742	10.6	124 093	63 376	60 717	15 558	2 932
Yuba City, CA	2 077	164 014	0.91	2 522	14.8	1 237	7.2	21 067	14.4	25 825	24 588	1 237	5 111	3 006
Yuma, AZ..........................	9 082	200 868	0.97	3 107	15.2	1 493	7.3	30 961	19.4	28 653	21 773	6 880	6 006	2 946

1. Per 1,000 estimated resident population.   2. Data for serious crimes have not been adjusted for underreporting; this may affect comparability between geographic areas and over time.
3. Per 100,000 population estimated by the FBI.

Table C. Metropolitan Areas — Crime, Education, Money Income, and Poverty

Area name	Serious crimes known to police, 2014 (cont.)[1] Rate[2] Violent	Property	Enrollment[3] Total	Percent private	Attainment[4] (percent) High school graduate or less	Bachelor's degree or more	Local government expenditures,[5] 2012–2013 Total current expenditures (mil dol)	Current expenditures per student (dollars)	Per capita income[6] (dollars)	Mean household income (dollars)	Median household income	Percent of households with income of less than $25,000	Percent of households with income of $200,000 or more	Percent below poverty level All persons	Children under 18 years	Age 65 years and older
	46	47	48	49	50	51	52	53	54	55	56	57	58	59	60	61
The Villages, FL	188	990	NA	NA	42.3	27.7	68.5	8 569	30 468	68 217	50 942	20.3	3.4	9.3	23.5	4.8
Toledo, OH	586	1 910	165 581	15.9	41.2	27.4	1 015.6	13 299	26 680	64 591	45 603	28.7	3.2	18.8	25.2	8.2
Topeka, KS	364	3 383	58 739	12.3	40.8	27.1	390.7	10 206	27 247	67 679	54 388	21.1	2.2	13.4	17.8	7.8
Trenton, NJ	343	1 774	102 311	24.0	36.9	41.0	1 078.0	18 652	38 159	105 163	74 961	17.8	12.3	11.9	16.8	9.7
Tucson, AZ	443	4 451	266 400	10.6	35.0	30.8	1 033.5	8 133	25 738	64 136	45 856	26.9	3.5	18.9	26.2	9.0
Tulsa, OK	467	3 121	245 266	15.7	41.5	26.5	1 243.0	7 628	27 140	68 277	50 740	23.1	3.6	14.4	20.8	7.8
Tuscaloosa, AL	386	3 296	66 590	9.3	47.2	25.1	299.3	8 935	22 156	59 548	44 143	30.7	2.7	19.0	24.8	11.4
Tyler, TX	342	2 927	59 497	13.6	43.2	25.7	272.8	8 242	23 320	62 654	43 958	29.1	3.4	19.0	27.6	10.6
Urban Honolulu, HI	72	1 054	245 663	23.7	35.2	32.6	2 199.3	11 903	30 744	91 428	74 634	13.9	6.9	9.7	12.7	7.5
Utica-Rome, NY	269	2 116	66 932	10.5	45.2	22.2	703.6	16 179	25 265	62 087	47 736	26.5	2.2	17.5	29.1	6.9
Valdosta, GA	295	3 569	46 288	6.8	45.3	21.9	201.1	8 676	20 243	55 610	36 340	32.4	2.8	26.0	37.1	11.0
Vallejo-Fairfield, CA	491	3 129	112 936	11.8	35.0	24.9	544.6	8 255	28 948	83 626	67 999	17.3	5.2	12.3	17.2	6.1
Victoria, TX	427	2 925	24 705	10.2	48.3	18.9	143.7	8 506	27 160	72 405	50 107	21.9	4.3	16.7	29.2	8.7
Vineland-Bridgeton, NJ	511	3 886	37 980	9.0	62.1	12.5	504.4	18 695	21 131	60 626	45 339	26.6	2.3	19.8	30.8	7.0
Virginia Beach-Norfolk-Newport News, VA-NC	309	2 757	463 337	16.1	35.5	29.6	2 771.7	10 325	28 755	73 919	58 871	19.5	4.0	12.4	17.7	8.4
Visalia-Porterville, CA	414	2 481	138 816	5.1	58.5	12.3	974.8	9 752	17 760	58 417	42 611	29.1	2.7	28.6	38.0	14.9
Waco, TX	387	3 084	75 962	21.2	46.5	21.2	404.8	9 020	21 402	57 873	43 184	30.9	2.4	19.7	29.4	6.2
Walla Walla, WA	203	3 539	18 244	32.7	33.7	26.7	95.4	10 032	24 193	64 196	50 737	21.7	2.4	13.8	14.7	6.6
Warner Robins, GA	341	4 023	54 895	12.7	43.0	23.9	309.7	9 443	22 422	60 224	46 773	27.3	1.9	20.1	27.3	6.5
Washington-Arlington-Alexandria, DC-VA-MD-WV	317	2 113	1 610 910	20.8	28.2	49.3	11 908.0	13 655	43 371	117 085	91 193	11.5	14.4	8.7	11.1	7.1
Silver Spring-Frederick-Rockville, MD Div 43524	184	1 608	343 352	21.4	24.0	55.0	2 755.2	14 560	45 861	125 265	94 463	10.2	15.9	6.8	8.0	6.4
Washington-Arlington-Alexandria, DC-VA-MD-WV Div 4	352	2 248	1 267 558	20.7	29.4	47.8	9 152.8	13 404	42 704	114 901	90 534	11.9	14.0	9.2	12.0	7.3
Waterloo-Cedar Falls, IA	480	2 393	47 461	13.8	38.6	27.3	306.7	11 585	26 918	65 200	52 991	21.7	2.6	12.9	15.1	4.6
Watertown-Fort Drum, NY	185	1 994	28 962	18.5	41.2	22.0	276.6	14 686	24 054	62 125	51 086	20.5	2.7	14.4	20.0	5.9
Wausau, WI	96	1 328	33 098	13.4	43.8	25.2	219.9	11 071	27 568	67 505	53 300	21.2	2.4	9.4	14.6	3.5
Weirton-Steubenville, WV-OH	NA	NA	28 583	21.7	51.2	17.1	184.4	10 999	23 074	55 134	44 582	29.5	1.2	16.9	29.0	7.0
Wenatchee, WA	118	2 068	28 053	9.4	43.6	24.2	206.7	9 935	25 113	66 177	50 986	22.4	2.5	14.3	18.7	11.9
Wheeling, WV-OH	291	1 573	28 567	9.9	51.9	19.3	209.1	11 158	23 547	55 858	40 929	30.5	1.7	16.3	25.7	7.8
Wichita, KS	531	3 615	175 135	16.8	37.7	29.4	1 063.0	9 623	26 445	68 786	52 231	22.1	3.4	13.9	19.2	7.9
Wichita Falls, TX	348	3 438	38 100	8.0	45.8	21.5	208.3	8 405	22 806	60 088	43 804	28.5	2.6	19.2	30.6	9.3
Williamsport, PA	218	1 903	25 914	14.5	50.9	21.4	222.2	13 719	23 963	58 593	45 161	26.9	1.9	17.1	27.0	7.5
Wilmington, NC	408	3 402	71 061	10.3	33.0	34.9	292.5	8 456	28 809	69 355	48 469	26.2	5.1	17.9	22.7	6.2
Winchester, VA-WV	180	2 130	30 218	16.6	51.8	25.1	221.9	10 622	27 827	70 426	52 568	22.8	3.6	10.3	11.2	9.9
Winston-Salem, NC	402	3 526	164 370	17.0	44.9	25.2	820.7	8 263	24 008	59 055	43 665	27.9	2.4	18.8	27.6	8.7
Worcester, MA-CT	419	1 870	237 552	18.3	40.2	33.2	2 059.4	14 419	31 792	83 321	64 556	19.6	6.1	11.2	14.7	9.4
Yakima, WA	244	3 305	67 303	9.4	57.7	14.5	509.4	9 783	20 000	59 405	44 648	23.4	2.4	20.3	30.4	8.9
York-Hanover, PA	206	1 671	104 161	19.8	52.5	23.7	849.3	13 141	28 702	73 379	58 587	19.7	2.9	10.2	15.2	7.4
Youngstown-Warren-Boardman, OH-PA	246	2 687	123 450	17.1	53.0	20.4	967.1	12 831	23 383	55 386	42 228	28.7	1.7	17.2	28.7	7.0
Yuba City, CA	360	2 646	47 840	11.7	46.9	16.7	303.5	8 686	22 031	63 704	48 115	24.1	2.4	17.8	21.9	15.3
Yuma, AZ	370	2 576	54 731	8.0	56.3	13.5	207.3	5 941	19 235	54 402	40 008	31.4	1.8	22.4	28.6	16.2

1. Data for serious crimes have not been adjusted for underreporting; this may affect comparability between geographic areas and over time.   2. Per 100,000 population estimated by the FBI.
3. All persons 3 years old and over enrolled in nursery school through college.   4. Persons 25 years old and over.   5. Elementary and secondary education expenditures.   6. Based on resident population estimated in the 2014 American Community Survey.

Table C. Metropolitan Areas — **Personal Income**

Area name	Personal income, 2014										Earnings, 2014		
	Total (mil dol)	Percent change 2013–2014	Per capita[1] Dollars	Rank	Wages and salaries (mil dol)	Supplements to wages and salaries; employer contributions (mil dol) Pension and insurance	Government social insurance	Proprietors' income (mil dol)	Dividends, interest, and rent (mil dol)	Personal transfer receipts (mil dol)	Total (mil dol)	Contributions for government social insurance (mil dol) From employee and self-employed	From employer
	62	63	64	65	66	67	68	69	70	71	72	73	74
The Villages, FL..............	4 295	8.5	37 558	245	1 063	189	78	93	1 140	1 842	1 422	150	78
Toledo, OH............................	24 684	4.1	40 635	173	13 585	2 499	1 019	2 075	3 395	5 330	19 178	1 070	1 019
Topeka, KS	9 519	2.2	40 720	170	4 960	820	388	517	1 594	1 980	6 686	425	388
Trenton, NJ	22 246	4.6	59 875	12	15 137	2 495	1 123	1 582	4 297	3 115	20 337	1 166	1 123
Tucson, AZ............................	37 199	4.0	37 031	259	16 863	3 047	1 229	1 950	7 946	8 849	23 090	1 458	1 229
Tulsa, OK.............................	48 274	4.8	49 807	40	21 530	3 176	1 640	9 478	8 880	7 233	35 824	1 882	1 640
Tuscaloosa, AL	8 321	4.0	34 999	318	4 307	767	319	678	1 407	1 878	6 071	375	319
Tyler, TX	9 465	4.9	43 249	115	4 376	637	303	1 689	1 589	1 829	7 005	366	303
Urban Honolulu, HI	49 313	4.4	49 722	41	25 610	5 464	2 135	3 134	10 130	7 063	36 344	2 065	2 135
Utica-Rome, NY	11 251	1.2	37 932	236	4 940	1 449	433	680	1 596	2 932	7 501	411	433
Valdosta, GA........................	4 583	3.3	31 975	366	2 190	517	165	284	814	1 071	3 155	172	165
Vallejo-Fairfield, CA	18 139	6.2	42 073	140	7 579	1 603	536	856	3 020	3 277	10 574	630	536
Victoria, TX	4 623	6.6	46 870	66	2 075	295	138	700	759	828	3 208	168	138
Vineland-Bridgeton, NJ	5 582	3.6	35 468	306	2 736	604	233	434	778	1 538	4 008	243	233
Virginia Beach-Norfolk-Newport News, VA-NC	77 723	3.2	45 276	87	39 700	7 894	3 165	4 156	16 823	12 437	54 915	3 084	3 165
Visalia-Porterville, CA	16 147	6.3	35 240	311	5 670	1 450	410	2 811	2 159	3 749	10 340	491	410
Waco, TX	9 204	4.8	35 340	309	4 720	769	330	762	1 454	2 047	6 580	359	330
Walla Walla, WA	2 542	3.3	39 830	190	1 172	217	109	200	533	583	1 698	94	109
Warner Robins, GA..............	6 969	3.7	37 165	256	3 363	870	261	271	1 263	1 391	4 766	256	261
Washington-Arlington-Alexandria, DC-VA-MD-WV ..	379 974	3.7	62 975	8	228 059	37 077	16 657	32 125	73 962	34 083	313 918	17 410	16 657
Silver Spring-Frederick-Rockville, MD Div 43524	88 526	3.9	69 480	X	39 489	6 310	2 873	9 750	18 980	7 357	58 422	3 328	2 873
Washington-Arlington-Alexandria, DC-VA-MD-WV Div 4.............................	291 448	3.7	61 233	X	188 570	30 767	13 784	22 375	54 982	26 726	255 497	14 082	13 784
Waterloo-Cedar Falls, IA	7 002	2.5	41 192	162	3 954	675	303	521	1 245	1 320	5 453	335	303
Watertown-Fort Drum, NY	5 167	1.5	43 384	113	2 666	834	256	300	980	929	4 056	180	256
Wausau, WI	5 831	5.5	42 941	125	3 180	582	251	521	917	936	4 534	272	251
Weirton-Steubenville, WV-OH.........................	4 265	2.7	35 150	314	1 596	316	129	221	547	1 291	2 261	153	129
Wenatchee, WA	4 514	5.4	39 457	198	1 996	327	200	288	983	1 029	2 811	162	200
Wheeling, WV-OH.................	5 868	4.6	40 410	177	2 857	489	214	455	922	1 441	4 016	255	214
Wichita, KS	29 039	2.3	45 297	86	13 829	2 140	1 079	3 272	6 838	4 430	20 319	1 247	1 079
Wichita Falls, TX	6 349	4.1	41 895	146	2 504	474	183	1 088	1 149	1 281	4 250	211	183
Williamsport, PA...................	4 633	4.0	39 766	191	2 377	502	194	257	739	1 043	3 329	202	194
Wilmington, NC	10 433	4.4	38 278	225	4 983	842	377	960	2 231	2 180	7 162	441	377
Winchester, VA-WV	5 397	3.7	40 456	176	2 572	427	195	327	916	904	3 521	219	195
Winston-Salem, NC	25 180	4.6	38 443	221	12 008	1 860	931	1 829	4 126	5 306	16 629	1 063	931
Worcester, MA-CT	43 918	4.2	47 200	60	19 255	3 508	1 383	2 381	6 011	7 770	26 527	1 449	1 383
Yakima, WA	9 321	6.5	37 630	243	3 941	639	400	984	1 645	2 407	5 964	310	400
York-Hanover, PA	18 969	3.3	43 037	122	8 007	1 527	660	839	2 884	3 560	11 033	672	660
Youngstown-Warren-Boardman, OH-PA	20 563	3.1	37 166	255	8 828	1 709	692	1 524	3 103	5 717	12 754	794	692
Yuba City, CA	6 314	2.8	37 180	254	2 202	583	166	639	993	1 557	3 589	199	166
Yuma, AZ..............................	5 842	0.1	28 742	377	2 617	551	213	488	928	1 441	3 869	212	213

1. Based on the resident population estimated as of July 1 of the year shown.

Table C. Metropolitan Areas — **Earnings, Social Security, and Housing**

Area name	Earnings, 2014 (cont.) Percent by selected industries									Social Security beneficiaries, December 2014		Supplemental Security Income recipients, December 2014	Housing units, 2015	
	Farm	Mining	Construction	Manufacturing	Information, professional, scientific, technical services	Retail trade	Finance, insurance, real estate, rental and leasing	Health care and social assistance	Government	Number	Rate[1]		Total	Percent change, 2000–2015
	75	76	77	78	79	80	81	82	83	84	85	86	87	88
The Villages, FL	1.4	0.6	11.1	5.5	D	8.8	5.1	14.2	22.9	61 425	539	1 588	66 850	26.1
Toledo, OH	0.4	D	6.4	19.6	D	6.3	5.4	15.0	15.8	114 320	188	19 815	273 761	0.1
Topeka, KS	0.9	0.8	D	7.0	D	5.0	D	14.6	24.4	50 235	215	5 809	104 297	0.5
Trenton, NJ	0.0	D	3.0	5.9	20.7	4.1	10.9	9.5	19.5	65 715	177	9 623	144 487	0.9
Tucson, AZ	0.2	1.3	4.5	10.0	9.7	6.8	5.5	14.7	25.6	202 670	202	20 237	452 040	2.5
Tulsa, OK	0.4	D	7.2	12.2	8.1	5.6	D	10.1	8.6	183 700	189	21 856	425 016	3.7
Tuscaloosa, AL	1.4	4.4	4.9	18.6	D	6.1	4.0	8.8	26.5	48 970	206	9 329	106 135	4.0
Tyler, TX	0.4	16.2	4.7	6.8	7.6	8.0	5.6	20.2	11.2	42 925	195	5 549	88 852	1.8
Urban Honolulu, HI	0.2	0.1	7.0	1.9	8.0	5.3	6.5	9.9	34.2	168 315	170	16 642	344 108	2.1
Utica-Rome, NY	1.1	0.1	3.7	9.8	5.6	7.3	7.0	14.7	32.7	70 870	239	9 925	137 184	-0.3
Valdosta, GA	1.6	D	6.1	7.8	D	8.1	4.8	D	35.9	24 575	171	4 872	59 395	3.4
Vallejo-Fairfield, CA	1.0	0.3	7.8	14.3	4.0	6.8	5.5	15.9	26.0	71 210	165	12 762	155 625	1.9
Victoria, TX	0.1	18.8	7.1	8.0	D	10.0	5.1	D	12.0	18 870	191	2 819	40 565	3.7
Vineland-Bridgeton, NJ	1.8	0.3	5.8	14.2	2.9	6.9	2.7	14.6	28.1	30 520	194	5 737	56 360	0.9
Virginia Beach-Norfolk-Newport News, VA-NC	0.1	D	D	D	9.9	5.2	6.2	9.8	35.0	286 155	167	33 848	711 353	3.4
Visalia-Porterville, CA	20.1	0.1	3.6	8.0	3.2	6.6	3.5	6.3	23.0	62 080	136	19 398	146 520	3.4
Waco, TX	0.7	D	7.2	17.0	D	6.4	D	10.4	16.8	46 315	178	8 103	106 383	3.4
Walla Walla, WA	10.2	D	3.8	14.4	4.1	5.5	3.8	D	24.9	13 495	212	1 532	26 155	2.2
Warner Robins, GA	0.7	D	D	D	D	6.0	2.3	D	53.2	30 960	165	5 100	77 562	4.1
Washington-Arlington-Alexandria, DC-VA-MD-WV	0.0	D	D	1.6	D	3.7	D	6.7	27.8	702 746	116	86 989	2 324 126	4.0
Silver Spring-Frederick-Rockville, MD Div 43524	0.1	D	D	3.5	23.1	4.7	D	8.9	21.5	165 985	130	16 111	483 741	3.8
Washington-Arlington-Alexandria, DC-VA-MD-WV Div 4	0.0	0.0	D	1.2	27.3	3.5	5.7	6.2	29.3	536 761	113	70 878	1 840 385	4.0
Waterloo-Cedar Falls, IA	2.7	0.1	5.5	25.1	D	6.2	7.1	11.7	15.4	34 275	202	3 523	72 824	2.1
Watertown-Fort Drum, NY	2.4	0.1	4.5	4.0	2.5	5.9	2.0	8.8	59.0	21 280	179	2 724	59 123	2.0
Wausau, WI	3.3	0.2	5.0	22.1	5.6	7.1	9.5	15.3	11.3	27 475	203	2 096	58 613	1.5
Weirton-Steubenville, WV-OH	0.1	D	D	19.1	3.4	6.9	3.2	17.6	13.3	32 770	270	4 168	57 779	-1.0
Wenatchee, WA	8.4	D	6.8	6.2	5.0	7.9	3.4	15.8	21.7	23 695	207	2 056	52 782	2.5
Wheeling, WV-OH	-0.1	D	D	7.1	D	7.8	6.1	14.6	13.0	36 205	250	4 426	68 961	-0.8
Wichita, KS	0.6	4.6	5.7	22.9	D	5.9	4.5	11.6	13.2	113 340	177	12 696	271 000	1.6
Wichita Falls, TX	1.1	D	3.9	8.9	4.4	6.7	4.6	D	23.8	28 905	190	4 325	65 401	0.9
Williamsport, PA	0.5	7.3	5.9	16.1	5.0	6.4	4.6	13.9	18.4	27 080	232	3 381	52 671	0.3
Wilmington, NC	0.9	D	7.2	9.3	D	8.9	7.1	D	19.6	55 080	202	5 518	134 649	5.1
Winchester, VA-WV	0.1	D	D	13.7	D	9.3	5.7	D	18.9	26 270	197	2 320	58 497	2.8
Winston-Salem, NC	0.6	0.1	4.5	13.0	D	7.0	D	D	10.7	138 655	212	13 890	292 303	1.8
Worcester, MA-CT	0.1	D	D	14.0	9.3	6.3	6.6	16.3	17.6	171 155	184	25 069	379 267	0.9
Yakima, WA	15.7	0.1	4.6	8.2	3.1	6.6	3.0	13.9	18.3	42 785	173	7 542	86 569	1.3
York-Hanover, PA	0.4	0.3	8.2	19.7	6.9	6.5	4.3	13.5	14.6	92 080	209	8 688	181 068	1.3
Youngstown-Warren-Boardman, OH-PA	0.2	0.7	5.5	18.0	4.3	8.0	6.6	15.5	15.2	140 245	253	19 083	258 212	-0.6
Yuba City, CA	7.1	0.5	4.4	3.9	3.7	6.6	3.8	12.0	36.6	29 595	175	8 281	62 393	1.5
Yuma, AZ	9.0	0.1	3.8	2.8	5.3	7.2	3.2	11.0	33.1	33 820	166	4 280	90 485	3.0

1. Per 1,000 resident population estimated as of July 1, 2011 of the year shown.

Table C. Metropolitan Areas — **Housing, Labor Force, and Employment**

Area name	Housing units, 2014								Civilian labor force, 2015		Unemployment		Civilian employment[5], 2014		
	Total	Percent	Owner-occupied			Renter-occupied		Percent with a computer	Total	Percent change, 2013–2014	Total	Rate[4]	Total employed	Percent	
			Median value[1]	Median owner cost as a percent of income		Median rent[3]	Median rent as a percent of income							Management, professional, and related occupations	Construction, production, and related occupations
				With a mortgage	Without a mortgage[2]										
	89	90	91	92	93	94	95	96	97	98	99	100	101	102	103
The Villages, FL..................	50 209	89.2	224 200	25.1	10.4	731	33.8	86.8	28 583	0.9	2 130	7.5	24 289	26.4	20.0
Toledo, OH............................	242 952	62.7	117 200	20.3	12.7	679	29.4	85.7	301 153	0.2	15 206	5.0	285 803	34.2	24.1
Topeka, KS	92 799	69.0	120 700	19.6	12.1	745	28.0	84.1	121 135	-0.3	5 188	4.3	111 229	36.0	23.9
Trenton, NJ	131 564	63.5	272 000	24.7	14.4	1 142	32.2	86.8	199 062	2.1	9 611	4.8	180 308	45.7	14.4
Tucson, AZ	389 737	60.1	158 400	21.7	10.7	814	31.5	87.8	464 150	0.4	25 787	5.6	430 957	35.6	17.1
Tulsa, OK	375 790	65.3	133 100	20.1	10.9	775	26.9	85.4	476 532	2.3	20 166	4.2	462 532	35.9	23.3
Tuscaloosa, AL	80 582	64.4	145 100	20.9	11.0	789	32.5	77.9	111 973	1.0	6 354	5.7	99 521	32.6	27.6
Tyler, TX	77 469	61.9	147 000	21.8	13.2	825	30.8	85.5	102 736	0.5	4 648	4.5	94 937	33.3	25.0
Urban Honolulu, HI	309 002	54.4	590 600	26.5	10.0	1 602	35.1	88.8	468 885	1.3	15 920	3.4	464 504	36.0	17.0
Utica-Rome, NY	116 231	65.9	110 100	21.8	13.3	713	29.7	82.4	131 965	-0.2	7 371	5.6	132 595	34.8	21.2
Valdosta, GA	49 067	57.2	110 900	23.2	10.0	719	29.6	84.2	62 718	-0.1	3 734	6.0	56 448	29.8	24.8
Vallejo-Fairfield, CA	145 313	57.9	304 100	24.3	10.0	1 293	31.2	89.6	206 604	1.3	12 650	6.1	192 886	32.6	22.1
Victoria, TX	35 523	67.2	122 600	19.1	10.7	807	32.1	78.7	49 508	-0.6	2 062	4.2	47 704	24.9	31.5
Vineland-Bridgeton, NJ	50 593	61.9	166 000	25.8	16.9	946	34.8	74.5	67 387	-0.1	5 846	8.7	65 588	22.6	29.5
Virginia Beach-Norfolk-New-port News, VA-NC	637 189	59.9	232 300	23.8	11.2	1 059	32.1	89.0	839 466	-1.0	41 373	4.9	783 689	36.3	20.7
Visalia-Porterville, CA	132 742	57.2	170 300	25.7	10.2	829	31.4	73.7	203 392	2.1	23 721	11.7	175 877	21.9	39.8
Waco, TX	93 166	59.1	113 400	23.6	12.6	767	32.4	80.9	118 946	-0.4	4 897	4.1	114 633	30.9	25.7
Walla Walla, WA	23 296	69.0	190 800	23.7	11.8	757	29.1	89.0	29 878	-1.0	1 742	5.8	28 949	35.5	22.2
Warner Robins, GA..............	67 667	63.3	133 000	21.5	10.5	809	28.1	79.8	80 533	-1.2	4 941	6.1	75 145	32.5	22.3
Washington-Arlington-Alex-andria, DC-VA-MD-WV ..	2 154 147	62.7	386 900	22.3	10.0	1 525	29.9	92.3	3 287 741	0.5	146 204	4.4	3 175 406	51.5	12.8
Silver Spring-Frederick-Rockville, MD Div 43524	453 938	67.1	418 400	22.5	10.0	1 579	30.8	93.7	678 582	0.9	27 644	4.1	672 778	54.4	11.7
Washington-Arlington-Alex-andria, DC-VA-MD-WV Div 4	1 700 209	61.5	378 700	22.3	10.0	1 510	29.7	92.0	2 609 159	0.5	118 560	4.5	2 502 628	50.8	13.1
Waterloo-Cedar Falls, IA	67 957	68.9	137 500	19.0	11.9	707	28.7	81.5	91 256	-1.9	3 902	4.3	88 487	34.7	26.3
Watertown-Fort Drum, NY	43 516	54.6	147 900	22.0	11.8	951	27.5	88.8	46 610	-0.2	3 144	6.7	44 644	35.4	17.3
Wausau, WI	54 739	75.6	145 600	20.8	13.6	663	27.0	85.4	73 833	0.8	3 000	4.1	71 550	32.2	28.9
Weirton-Steubenville, WV-OH..................................	51 058	67.7	87 700	19.1	11.2	590	27.5	78.3	52 809	-0.5	3 954	7.5	53 099	29.3	25.1
Wenatchee, WA	41 500	69.6	227 600	23.2	10.9	753	26.5	87.0	62 791	2.7	3 588	5.7	50 356	28.4	32.7
Wheeling, WV-OH.................	58 775	71.5	95 800	17.5	10.5	651	28.8	78.5	66 273	-1.3	4 346	6.6	62 433	27.4	26.6
Wichita, KS	240 230	65.7	127 600	20.4	11.7	739	28.5	83.4	312 386	0.4	14 658	4.7	301 198	36.2	24.7
Wichita Falls, TX..................	54 196	66.2	90 300	21.1	12.2	713	29.4	81.7	64 860	-1.4	2 811	4.3	64 939	32.7	21.1
Williamsport, PA...................	45 742	68.9	144 100	20.6	13.7	741	33.8	80.0	60 975	-0.8	3 574	5.9	53 696	30.6	23.9
Wilmington, NC	110 993	61.4	209 000	23.5	13.8	879	34.3	86.4	139 010	2.5	7 629	5.5	130 993	37.2	19.2
Winchester, VA-WV	51 140	66.6	205 300	21.3	12.5	873	28.4	73.5	68 991	0.6	2 942	4.3	64 461	35.5	24.6
Winston-Salem, NC	256 999	66.1	138 400	21.7	10.9	701	29.9	81.6	317 805	1.2	17 332	5.5	287 359	34.3	24.9
Worcester, MA-CT................	344 496	64.6	244 400	23.0	14.2	932	30.2	87.2	488 301	0.0	26 423	5.4	472 687	40.1	19.0
Yakima, WA	79 700	64.7	156 700	24.6	11.5	793	29.7	77.0	122 052	2.1	9 716	8.0	102 976	22.9	40.0
York-Hanover, PA.................	169 212	75.0	167 000	22.7	14.1	856	32.4	83.6	232 848	1.0	10 718	4.6	220 362	33.2	27.2
Youngstown-Warren-Board-man, OH-PA	228 797	70.2	100 000	19.7	12.2	626	29.2	78.8	251 809	-0.7	15 276	6.1	243 101	29.6	26.9
Yuba City, CA	57 366	57.8	187 900	24.2	11.6	886	29.3	88.6	72 961	0.5	7 424	10.2	64 950	30.1	26.5
Yuma, AZ..............................	70 593	66.1	108 900	23.1	10.0	851	29.2	78.0	93 702	0.4	20 446	21.8	75 232	22.9	29.8

1. Specified owner-occupied units.　2. A value of 10.0 represents 10 percent or less.　3. Specified renter-occupied units.　4. Percent of civilian labor force.
5. Persons 16 years old and over.

Table C. Metropolitan Areas — **Nonfarm Employment and Agriculture**

Area name	Private nonfarm establishments, employment and payroll, 2014									Agriculture, 2012			
		Employment						Annual payroll		Farms			
											Percent with:		
	Number of establishments	Total	Health care and social assistance	Manufacturing	Retail trade	Finance and insurance	Professional, scientific, and technical services	Total (mil dol)	Average per employee (dollars)	Number	Fewer than 50 acres	500 acres or more	Farm operators whose principal occupation is farming (percent)
	104	105	106	107	108	109	110	111	112	113	114	115	116
The Villages, FL..................	1 334	18 994	3 773	1 168	3 179	657	595	697	36 689	1 367	70.1	4.0	34.7
Toledo, OH..........................	13 313	262 741	45 427	37 608	31 727	7 154	12 173	10 657	40 560	2 246	43.9	13.4	45.9
Topeka, KS	5 166	85 311	20 389	7 042	10 874	5 840	4 729	3 388	39 718	4 507	27.3	16.6	39.9
Trenton, NJ	9 627	182 255	30 928	6 902	19 591	15 405	22 196	12 049	66 109	272	71.0	2.9	46.0
Tucson, AZ	19 931	303 841	56 150	22 642	46 061	12 657	16 638	11 769	38 734	855	79.4	9.4	49.0
Tulsa, OK	24 173	398 738	59 714	55 077	47 602	17 062	23 120	18 621	46 699	9 103	39.4	11.1	37.6
Tuscaloosa, AL	4 454	78 365	12 780	14 242	10 836	2 005	2 378	3 108	39 666	1 386	33.4	11.8	44.3
Tyler, TX	5 734	90 521	22 096	7 023	12 389	5 104	4 664	3 719	41 087	2 961	54.8	3.0	45.3
Urban Honolulu, HI	21 195	354 302	50 939	9 191	47 643	16 519	18 858	14 993	42 317	999	90.6	2.1	66.3
Utica-Rome, NY	6 035	101 751	22 045	12 469	14 275	6 803	3 679	3 640	35 775	1 753	23.8	8.1	57.8
Valdosta, GA	3 025	42 666	8 251	3 607	7 086	1 125	1 228	1 293	30 315	901	43.4	13.7	47.7
Vallejo-Fairfield, CA	6 745	105 212	22 806	9 915	18 994	4 207	3 353	4 979	47 326	860	62.9	11.7	53.7
Victoria, TX	2 524	35 847	6 909	2 134	6 117	934	1 098	1 608	44 844	2 708	35.7	14.3	42.8
Vineland-Bridgeton, NJ	2 883	44 491	10 481	7 377	7 281	1 190	1 017	1 664	37 406	583	61.7	5.3	55.2
Virginia Beach-Norfolk-Newport News, VA-NC	36 925	597 243	89 907	57 222	87 956	25 068	51 072	24 246	40 597	1 546	57.2	11.5	48.3
Visalia-Porterville, CA	6 165	90 454	15 643	12 427	15 856	2 939	2 553	3 313	36 632	4 931	61.2	8.4	58.3
Waco, TX	5 248	101 733	17 543	14 068	12 362	4 740	2 539	3 583	35 218	4 541	47.3	7.9	42.8
Walla Walla, WA	1 494	19 755	4 039	3 467	2 337	769	539	719	36 392	1 251	45.6	27.3	46.9
Warner Robins, GA	3 014	43 911	7 778	5 890	8 288	1 206	4 173	1 448	32 971	592	50.2	13.3	42.4
Washington-Arlington-Alexandria, DC-VA-MD-WV ..	147 986	2 545 212	303 657	47 741	273 215	101 233	532 039	160 657	63 121	9 020	55.6	5.5	44.4
Silver Spring-Frederick-Rockville, MD Div 43524	NA	NA	NA	NA	NA	NA	NA	NA	NA	1 848	54.5	5.7	46.0
Washington-Arlington-Alexandria, DC-VA-MD-WV Div 4.............................	NA	NA	NA	NA	NA	NA	NA	NA	NA	7 172	55.9	5.4	43.9
Waterloo-Cedar Falls, IA	4 126	81 935	17 282	16 190	10 488	3 639	3 974	3 078	37 566	2 643	33.6	21.2	53.4
Watertown-Fort Drum, NY	2 435	29 831	6 176	2 305	6 975	739	898	1 027	34 441	876	20.5	17.2	57.4
Wausau, WI	3 243	62 652	10 183	15 907	9 567	3 714	1 905	2 530	40 387	2 266	23.2	7.5	55.0
Weirton-Steubenville, WV-OH.........................	2 245	36 182	7 878	5 976	4 855	775	809	1 243	34 364	685	29.5	4.2	39.0
Wenatchee, WA	3 136	32 937	6 419	2 162	5 827	902	1 241	1 320	40 072	1 739	58.0	14.1	55.8
Wheeling, WV-OH................	3 406	56 037	12 889	2 616	8 807	2 198	2 714	2 047	36 529	1 579	25.4	3.5	42.2
Wichita, KS	14 605	261 043	41 509	52 248	33 288	10 451	11 286	11 386	43 616	5 345	27.9	25.2	45.7
Wichita Falls, TX	3 495	48 534	11 800	4 772	8 007	1 912	1 600	1 670	34 410	2 031	24.1	25.8	42.8
Williamsport, PA..................	2 826	46 628	8 577	7 926	7 682	1 521	1 606	1 773	38 027	1 207	32.4	3.7	44.0
Wilmington, NC	7 902	95 866	17 401	4 994	16 359	2 960	6 369	3 757	39 193	385	54.3	7.0	50.1
Winchester, VA-WV	3 136	49 104	9 377	6 596	8 357	2 161	1 789	1 898	38 652	1 479	42.7	7.4	40.4
Winston-Salem, NC	12 966	224 191	40 478	28 209	28 789	11 373	8 595	9 782	43 631	4 242	53.3	2.0	47.5
Worcester, MA-CT	19 713	313 932	69 065	37 054	44 301	15 400	17 731	14 426	45 951	2 252	63.7	1.6	45.8
Yakima, WA	4 653	63 154	12 743	8 059	9 611	1 593	1 905	2 379	37 673	3 143	73.9	5.5	51.9
York-Hanover, PA	8 611	159 950	23 402	31 617	22 290	3 651	5 392	6 407	40 057	2 171	56.6	4.4	48.9
Youngstown-Warren-Boardman, OH-PA	12 447	202 884	42 915	31 461	29 512	5 585	5 951	7 436	36 650	2 651	38.1	4.1	46.4
Yuba City, CA	2 498	29 333	5 768	1 960	5 736	952	1 216	1 102	37 584	2 153	55.4	12.7	56.9
Yuma, AZ	2 907	41 082	6 544	3 453	8 194	1 149	1 373	1 274	31 011	562	64.4	14.4	54.8

Table C. Metropolitan Areas — **Agriculture**

Area name	Land in farms		Acres			Value of land and buildings (dollars)		Value of machinery and equipment, average per farm (dollars)	Value of products sold		Percent from:		Percent of farms with sales of:		Government payments	
	Acreage (1,000)	Percent change, 2007–2012	Average size of farm	Total irrigated (1,000)	Total cropland (1,000)	Average per farm	Average per acre		Total (mil dol)	Average per farm (dollars)	Crops	Livestock and poultry products	$10,000 or more	$100,000 or more	Total ($1,000)	Percent of farms
	117	118	119	120	121	122	123	124	125	126	127	128	129	130	131	132
The Villages, FL	183	14.7	134	3.1	20.7	717 143	5 350	45 931	42.1	30 773	58.9	41.1	19.3	5.3	164	2.9
Toledo, OH	526	0.8	234	2.9	491.5	1 339 764	5 717	160 193	469.6	209 092	80.6	19.4	61.5	34.6	10 688	72.1
Topeka, KS	1 606	-4.5	356	30.4	746.2	645 650	1 812	88 309	290.6	64 475	54.1	45.9	44.2	12.8	13 372	51.5
Trenton, NJ	20	-9.1	73	1.1	12.4	1 474 301	20 310	59 195	19.7	72 533	83.1	16.9	43.0	11.0	310	14.3
Tucson, AZ	D	D	D	32.4	36.7	1 651 870	D	64 622	97.3	113 786	76.8	23.2	31.2	10.3	1 085	5.3
Tulsa, OK	2 757	-8.9	303	12.2	525.7	487 549	1 610	48 596	320.1	35 165	20.5	79.5	31.0	5.0	10 260	18.1
Tuscaloosa, AL	349	-15.0	252	D	79.8	579 205	2 299	70 007	203.4	146 773	D	D	35.1	12.3	1 801	22.9
Tyler, TX	302	0.0	102	2.5	77.1	386 589	3 786	43 300	76.8	25 934	77.5	22.5	18.6	2.6	189	1.8
Urban Honolulu, HI	69	14.5	69	10.8	22.2	1 396 597	20 171	56 908	161.5	161 650	90.0	10.0	54.6	12.7	283	6.1
Utica-Rome, NY	345	4.0	197	0.3	195.1	387 175	1 965	102 671	183.6	104 752	32.6	67.4	52.0	21.4	3 569	31.7
Valdosta, GA	268	-17.4	298	37.0	127.0	994 700	3 343	118 135	172.8	191 747	73.9	26.1	35.2	14.1	4 463	47.7
Vallejo-Fairfield, CA	407	13.6	473	130.9	169.6	2 631 010	5 558	146 770	307.4	357 463	79.0	21.0	53.1	22.7	1 911	15.7
Victoria, TX	933	-3.2	344	4.1	113.1	748 694	2 174	54 903	67.0	24 741	47.2	52.8	28.4	4.1	3 202	14.4
Vineland-Bridgeton, NJ	65	-7.1	111	19.3	49.7	889 362	8 035	130 184	170.4	292 216	97.2	2.8	50.9	22.1	520	14.9
Virginia Beach-Norfolk-Newport News, VA-NC	348	-3.4	225	5.6	D	954 757	4 240	128 940	D	D	D	D	39.2	17.0	7 172	37.0
Visalia-Porterville, CA	1 239	6.0	251	557.4	677.5	1 893 271	7 535	144 666	4 017.1	814 657	41.6	58.4	70.2	36.6	12 174	13.5
Waco, TX	936	-4.0	206	8.6	418.3	479 933	2 328	62 287	318.4	70 112	40.8	59.2	26.8	6.6	8 368	20.6
Walla Walla, WA	943	-5.3	753	95.2	750.3	1 331 341	1 767	176 191	495.1	395 756	D	D	41.5	23.7	17 645	52.1
Warner Robins, GA	145	1.2	245	33.2	89.1	763 294	3 110	139 532	129.7	219 166	72.7	27.3	30.7	14.9	2 575	34.1
Washington-Arlington-Alexandria, DC-VA-MD-WV	1 192	-2.8	132	D	D	1 082 771	8 191	74 808	479.4	53 150	D	D	31.3	7.8	9 447	15.6
Silver Spring-Frederick-Rockville, MD Div 43524	245	-9.2	133	2.4	172.7	1 095 421	8 262	106 409	198.8	107 576	58.6	41.4	37.6	15.7	3 896	28.8
Washington-Arlington-Alexandria, DC-VA-MD-WV Div 4	947	-1.0	132	D	D	1 079 511	8 173	66 666	280.6	39 126	D	D	29.7	5.7	5 551	12.2
Waterloo-Cedar Falls, IA	886	5.4	335	0.8	817.5	2 653 546	7 913	260 785	921.7	348 721	69.2	30.8	66.5	46.6	23 091	81.8
Watertown-Fort Drum, NY	291	10.9	332	0.3	173.5	544 535	1 640	133 429	183.6	209 551	24.7	75.3	51.6	24.1	2 974	31.5
Wausau, WI	479	-2.4	211	6.2	320.1	616 429	2 916	136 874	391.1	172 605	24.8	75.2	61.9	32.7	6 615	48.5
Weirton-Steubenville, WV-OH	92	-2.7	134	D	33.3	354 781	2 643	67 448	9.9	14 394	44.8	55.2	27.9	3.1	D	15.5
Wenatchee, WA	890	-8.9	512	41.1	577.0	858 859	1 678	96 734	405.5	233 192	98.3	1.7	60.6	34.7	13 598	27.3
Wheeling, WV-OH	229	-10.3	145	D	69.6	403 551	2 779	56 892	26.9	17 067	24.1	75.9	25.3	2.5	798	10.6
Wichita, KS	2 856	-1.3	534	147.5	1 911.4	1 018 921	1 907	140 007	864.4	161 729	63.3	36.7	54.3	23.6	25 429	62.2
Wichita Falls, TX	1 541	2.7	759	4.8	332.0	968 725	1 277	78 397	194.6	95 797	23.0	77.0	45.3	14.2	6 647	35.8
Williamsport, PA	158	-1.2	131	0.6	79.7	559 934	4 265	73 065	72.2	59 819	53.8	46.2	41.6	13.2	2 246	39.1
Wilmington, NC	59	-11.1	152	1.8	31.7	719 145	4 720	86 745	178.9	464 691	21.8	78.2	41.3	24.4	1 612	31.2
Winchester, VA-WV	243	6.7	164	0.3	74.5	747 885	4 556	53 968	73.5	49 694	44.1	55.9	30.0	5.5	625	11.7
Winston-Salem, NC	379	-5.4	89	2.1	174.8	500 191	5 592	54 495	252.2	59 444	37.1	62.9	26.1	6.9	3 083	19.6
Worcester, MA-CT	160	-3.9	71	1.8	52.3	619 520	8 716	50 890	101.7	45 155	56.7	43.3	27.4	7.0	1 949	9.0
Yakima, WA	1 780	8.0	566	224.4	306.9	1 021 212	1 803	118 874	1 645.5	523 548	65.0	35.0	45.7	22.4	5 804	11.5
York-Hanover, PA	262	-10.4	121	0.8	195.0	910 957	7 547	87 005	234.1	107 814	62.9	37.1	45.3	16.5	2 746	22.2
Youngstown-Warren-Boardman, OH-PA	352	-2.5	133	1.2	229.7	523 104	3 940	102 994	214.6	80 935	58.1	41.9	46.8	15.9	3 340	30.7
Yuba City, CA	563	8.1	261	326.8	365.6	1 658 114	6 343	168 077	701.6	325 882	93.5	6.5	66.0	35.1	14 667	22.8
Yuma, AZ	215	2.0	382	181.4	200.1	2 758 098	7 220	372 064	985.0	1 752 685	D	D	61.7	28.5	1 815	17.1

Table C. Metropolitan Areas — Water Use, Wholesale Trade, Retail Trade, and Real Estate

Area name	Water use, 2010		Wholesale trade,[1] 2012				Retail trade, 2012				Real estate and rental and leasing, 2012			
	Total water withdrawn (mil gal/day)	Gallons withdrawn per person per day	Number of establishments	Number of employees	Sales (mil dol)	Annual payroll (mil dol)	Number of establishments	Number of employees	Sales (mil dol)	Annual payroll (mil dol)	Number of establishments	Number of employees	Receipts (mil dol)	Annual payroll (mil dol)
	133	134	135	136	137	138	139	140	141	142	143	144	145	146
The Villages, FL.................	32.0	342	45	D	D	D	217	2 840	908.8	62.1	79	176	25.6	5.7
Toledo, OH.......................	701.5	1 150	649	9 697	7 499.0	479.7	2 001	31 636	8 224.9	732.7	547	3 285	2 664.1	183.5
Topeka, KS......................	47.9	205	192	2 204	1 496.3	107.9	801	10 823	2 632.3	233.1	218	946	138.5	27.3
Trenton, NJ	477.6	1 303	354	D	D	D	1 305	18 794	5 127.4	477.9	347	1 934	729.3	91.8
Tucson, AZ......................	305.4	312	703	6 172	3 099.3	269.6	2 770	43 642	11 377.2	1 094.8	1 250	6 042	973.5	205.5
Tulsa, OK........................	387.7	414	1 210	16 787	15 854.1	976.9	3 066	44 465	12 865.2	1 081.7	1 097	6 653	1 083.1	261.7
Tuscaloosa, AL	65.7	285	160	1 774	1 240.0	86.6	835	10 366	2 796.3	233.7	192	1 511	166.7	45.0
Tyler, TX	30.8	147	215	D	D	D	829	11 883	3 388.9	293.6	281	1 477	301.0	61.6
Urban Honolulu, HI	799.2	838	1 167	13 446	8 052.8	596.9	2 889	46 165	13 036.4	1 233.1	1 219	7 213	2 553.5	340.7
Utica-Rome, NY	48.2	161	205	2 626	1 249.6	116.1	1 017	13 905	3 556.1	308.4	204	799	126.9	22.4
Valdosta, GA	41.3	296	128	1 261	1 438.4	48.5	563	6 439	1 880.1	142.3	142	1 467	107.4	26.5
Vallejo-Fairfield, CA	452.8	1 095	249	4 165	2 803.7	215.6	1 060	17 610	5 106.6	469.9	381	1 629	389.2	59.2
Victoria, TX	456.6	4 858	115	1 716	1 251.0	91.8	397	5 629	1 698.7	143.3	129	1 057	604.9	59.8
Vineland-Bridgeton, NJ........	58.9	375	152	3 223	2 422.4	133.6	512	7 201	2 049.0	175.0	120	471	96.2	15.8
Virginia Beach-Norfolk-Newport News, VA-NC	1 494.4	891	1 282	18 502	16 160.5	1 040.2	5 848	87 532	21 164.8	1 960.2	2 017	14 556	2 348.7	549.1
Visalia-Porterville, CA	2 600.3	5 881	325	4 564	3 890.5	191.8	1 044	14 210	3 903.5	340.6	306	1 421	249.0	40.9
Waco, TX	84.6	335	248	D	D	D	898	11 518	3 321.4	258.7	228	1 531	290.6	64.7
Walla Walla, WA	168.5	2 681	88	673	602.4	25.8	201	2 433	586.0	59.1	62	187	23.0	5.2
Warner Robins, GA..............	62.6	348	73	D	D	D	581	7 789	2 146.6	179.0	151	519	81.0	14.4
Washington-Arlington-Alexandria, DC-VA-MD-WV..	6 238.9	1 107	3 527	49 567	57 941.8	3 388.0	16 124	264 471	74 306.7	7 157.0	6 881	53 448	15 623.8	3 069.8
Silver Spring-Frederick-Rockville, MD Div 43524	778.5	646	875	11 325	11 642.7	792.1	3 438	58 054	16 973.9	1 633.0	1 570	13 206	4 741.5	869.1
Washington-Arlington-Alexandria, DC-VA-MD-WV Div 4	5 460.4	1 232	2 652	38 242	46 299.2	2 595.9	12 686	206 417	57 332.8	5 524.0	5 311	40 242	10 882.3	2 200.7
Waterloo-Cedar Falls, IA	43.2	257	197	3 210	2 774.7	154.0	639	10 445	2 555.7	225.1	164	706	141.0	22.9
Watertown-Fort Drum, NY	24.2	208	67	870	345.2	34.7	476	6 849	1 937.9	161.4	119	588	103.9	17.8
Wausau, WI	126.8	946	180	2 955	1 276.6	126.2	472	9 545	2 572.4	208.5	83	412	79.2	11.9
Weirton-Steubenville, WV-OH............................	1 825.2	14 665	71	D	D	D	372	5 013	1 195.3	105.3	67	306	35.9	8.4
Wenatchee, WA	103.7	935	127	D	D	D	477	5 701	1 434.5	146.9	145	475	63.0	13.5
Wheeling, WV-OH...............	623.9	4 217	126	D	D	D	585	8 547	2 283.3	189.1	117	601	84.5	16.8
Wichita, KS	185.4	294	727	9 369	9 027.7	524.5	2 115	31 655	8 362.2	740.0	650	4 202	610.9	138.1
Wichita Falls, TX	83.4	551	163	1 255	715.2	58.5	544	7 725	2 105.4	174.4	170	822	169.1	30.2
Williamsport, PA................	16.0	138	108	2 110	1 271.2	82.6	503	7 404	1 878.1	154.7	89	618	120.0	24.4
Wilmington, NC	55.0	216	315	2 837	1 368.8	136.0	1 174	14 996	4 258.4	367.1	425	2 314	395.5	86.3
Winchester, VA-WV	18.9	147	129	D	D	D	537	8 118	2 358.1	195.3	127	432	90.4	14.8
Winston-Salem, NC	1 381.9	2 157	608	8 614	5 513.2	389.1	2 151	27 365	7 696.4	651.1	530	2 200	739.1	77.4
Worcester, MA-CT	316.8	346	827	12 550	7 416.0	685.2	2 928	43 798	12 212.7	1 080.8	643	2 883	651.1	124.6
Yakima, WA	608.4	2 501	234	4 373	3 335.1	198.3	713	9 575	2 560.2	246.1	249	974	132.0	26.7
York-Hanover, PA	2 641.2	6 072	359	6 685	4 340.8	301.4	1 297	21 024	5 192.4	463.9	258	1 470	263.7	51.8
Youngstown-Warren-Boardman, OH-PA	214.8	380	538	7 293	4 748.0	345.2	2 094	29 036	7 127.0	610.9	384	3 946	486.5	114.2
Yuba City, CA	983.7	5 894	96	D	D	D	414	5 557	1 459.7	136.6	134	559	68.5	14.4
Yuma, AZ	1 161.4	5 933	137	2 433	1 439.8	102.5	449	7 408	1 996.0	171.9	159	639	91.9	18.0

1. Merchant wholesalers, except manufacturers' sales branches and offices.

Table C. Metropolitan Areas —

Professional Services, Manufacturing, and Accommodation and Food Services

Area name	Professional, scientific, and technical services, 2012				Manufacturing, 2012				Accommodation and food services, 2012			
	Number of establish-ments	Number of employees	Sales (mil dol)	Annual payroll (mil dol)	Number of establish-ments	Number of employees	Sales (mil dol)	Annual payroll (mil dol)	Number of establish-ments	Number of employees	Sales (mil dol)	Annual payroll (mil dol)
	147	148	149	150	151	152	153	154	155	156	157	158
The Villages, FL..................	128	500	53.9	21.0	36	942	461.9	40.7	106	2 464	117.2	35.9
Toledo, OH...........................	1 127	D	D	D	732	35 417	35 387.1	2 068.8	1 420	26 503	1 122.3	320.8
Topeka, KS	517	D	D	D	131	5 986	2 893.2	270.6	434	D	D	D
Trenton, NJ	1 591	21 394	5 318.1	2 127.7	246	7 070	2 220.3	378.2	812	11 894	731.4	201.0
Tucson, AZ..........................	2 531	16 514	2 241.1	940.0	640	24 297	8 686.6	1 906.7	1 787	42 311	2 154.7	637.4
Tulsa, OK	2 808	D	D	D	1 317	52 150	24 817.4	2 774.6	1 901	37 592	1 899.4	537.9
Tuscaloosa, AL	357	2 263	328.8	102.3	172	12 576	14 491.5	745.1	418	9 331	443.6	113.5
Tyler, TX	596	4 265	689.9	244.8	189	6 739	5 066.1	318.0	405	9 236	427.1	124.3
Urban Honolulu, HI	2 399	18 234	2 895.1	1 105.4	544	9 076	D	370.8	2 355	57 486	5 273.2	1 333.0
Utica-Rome, NY	469	3 829	573.9	215.9	296	12 368	4 147.5	581.4	727	12 339	862.6	219.5
Valdosta, GA	239	1 235	144.3	51.3	103	3 263	2 683.6	142.3	322	5 907	255.2	68.6
Vallejo-Fairfield, CA	547	3 258	415.3	150.6	259	9 266	11 412.2	558.9	711	11 129	625.6	163.2
Victoria, TX	173	899	118.4	42.6	77	2 090	2 172.9	136.0	204	3 702	192.7	50.8
Vineland-Bridgeton, NJ........	207	D	D	D	162	8 055	2 812.0	351.2	265	3 555	173.7	43.6
Virginia Beach-Norfolk-New-port News, VA-NC	4 187	51 649	9 454.7	3 521.0	847	54 304	15 652.6	2 873.8	3 805	74 606	3 885.1	1 062.9
Visalia-Porterville, CA	407	D	D	D	237	11 412	8 362.4	538.0	568	8 540	451.9	118.1
Waco, TX	377	2 607	337.8	140.5	240	14 284	6 478.1	682.2	502	9 682	475.4	130.6
Walla Walla, WA	117	459	46.0	17.6	137	3 450	1 773.2	159.6	147	1 998	95.8	28.4
Warner Robins, GA..............	312	3 445	450.1	174.3	85	5 334	2 785.0	216.8	343	6 719	310.2	80.9
Washington-Arlington-Alex-andria, DC-VA-MD-WV .. Silver Spring-Frederick-Rockville, MD Div 43524	30 747	517 949	125 259.6	49 288.9	2 091	49 219	15 671.4	3 030.8	12 138	247 606	17 932.2	4 868.0
Silver Spring-Frederick-Rockville, MD Div 43524	6 546	80 941	15 488.5	7 179.1	544	14 259	5 408.7	974.0	2 259	39 978	2 529.6	701.8
Washington-Arlington-Alex-andria, DC-VA-MD-WV Div 4	24 201	437 008	109 771.1	42 109.9	1 547	34 961	10 262.7	2 056.8	9 879	207 628	15 402.6	4 166.1
Waterloo-Cedar Falls, IA	280	3 998	310.2	210.6	213	15 285	10 703.1	762.0	370	7 330	342.8	91.2
Watertown-Fort Drum, NY	142	1 092	115.9	45.4	66	2 247	770.5	102.6	335	4 117	198.8	57.0
Wausau, WI	225	1 943	284.9	113.9	238	14 472	4 306.0	654.1	305	4 458	180.7	51.8
Weirton-Steubenville, WV-OH.	155	D	D	D	77	5 822	3 877.9	314.9	276	4 415	375.3	63.3
Wenatchee, WA...................	217	1 070	116.2	45.4	109	2 005	635.0	99.6	341	4 174	233.2	73.2
Wheeling, WV-OH................	268	2 501	287.4	105.6	106	2 887	981.8	117.4	322	6 150	371.3	85.2
Wichita, KS	1 350	11 334	1 676.4	603.6	687	46 169	23 736.2	2 589.4	1 320	25 323	1 163.6	321.8
Wichita Falls, TX	250	1 551	212.3	72.3	142	5 114	1 434.9	238.1	286	D	D	D
Williamsport, PA..................	200	2 151	184.5	74.5	160	8 162	3 186.7	371.5	296	4 696	237.9	62.6
Wilmington, NC	937	5 852	1 090.5	295.5	207	5 268	2 640.9	349.5	746	13 951	673.8	185.5
Winchester, VA-WV	269	1 885	178.2	85.7	119	6 864	3 469.8	346.3	294	5 209	255.3	68.9
Winston-Salem, NC	1 288	8 118	1 077.1	446.8	671	26 926	18 915.9	1 212.5	1 133	20 985	989.5	278.5
Worcester, MA-CT	1 945	D	D	D	1 132	40 227	12 621.8	2 273.0	1 956	27 526	1 425.5	400.0
Yakima, WA	319	2 023	193.3	80.5	232	8 152	2 622.2	327.3	416	5 364	281.5	79.8
York-Hanover, PA	705	5 671	635.2	279.4	568	31 890	11 489.4	1 602.6	791	13 391	593.3	165.9
Youngstown-Warren-Board-man, OH-PA	917	5 807	560.3	218.3	730	31 925	14 956.5	1 845.3	1 140	24 546	1 101.8	309.3
Yuba City, CA	204	978	118.4	46.1	100	2 091	650.7	99.0	224	3 374	171.4	44.9
Yuma, AZ.............................	221	1 364	132.3	68.0	68	2 084	884.3	79.8	329	5 736	307.5	76.2

Area name	Health care and social assistance, 2012				Other services, 2012				Nonemployer business, 2014		Value of residential construction authorized by building permits, 2015	
	Number of establish-ments	Number of employees	Receipts (mil dol)	Annual payroll (mil dol)	Number of establish-ments	Number of employees	Receipts (mil dol)	Annual payroll (mil dol)	Number	Receipts (mil dol)	New construc-tion ($1,000)	Number of housing units
	159	160	161	162	163	164	165	166	167	168	169	170
The Villages, FL	146	2 956	381.2	123.8	64	304	22.2	6.7	5 834	225.8	451 041	1 568
Toledo, OH	1 611	45 338	4 689.0	1 918.0	1 012	6 823	597.0	174.5	35 212	1 512.4	159 965	715
Topeka, KS	609	19 147	1 803.3	791.6	449	3 859	347.5	108.9	13 270	542.8	69 566	388
Trenton, NJ	1 165	28 970	2 981.0	1 326.6	815	6 403	1 245.5	239.1	23 914	1 386.6	107 634	896
Tucson, AZ	2 777	56 539	6 617.5	2 441.8	1 483	10 691	1 008.6	281.2	63 004	2 471.7	659 557	2 428
Tulsa, OK	2 640	57 324	6 459.5	2 399.4	1 479	9 217	1 253.9	281.4	70 971	3 464.3	686 767	3 774
Tuscaloosa, AL	479	14 351	1 485.8	644.6	259	1 660	154.9	43.1	13 237	586.2	153 932	747
Tyler, TX	640	21 211	2 527.9	969.6	347	2 613	252.8	87.5	17 750	926.3	132 119	470
Urban Honolulu, HI	2 520	50 049	6 302.6	2 481.0	2 012	14 967	1 522.4	411.8	62 867	3 082.6	914 918	3 833
Utica-Rome, NY	724	21 377	1 820.7	801.3	501	4 229	251.1	82.6	15 416	608.9	45 012	246
Valdosta, GA	400	8 078	828.5	305.9	174	1 111	78.5	22.0	8 519	407.2	99 506	627
Vallejo-Fairfield, CA	861	21 490	3 241.8	1 204.0	552	3 228	326.8	102.6	22 666	922.5	314 903	1 434
Victoria, TX	314	6 698	684.2	276.3	158	1 175	163.1	46.9	6 827	325.5	20 944	139
Vineland-Bridgeton, NJ	417	8 593	872.1	338.7	240	1 253	97.1	27.3	5 985	274.6	26 226	237
Virginia Beach-Norfolk-New-port News, VA-NC	3 558	88 360	9 916.7	4 051.8	2 792	18 235	2 070.9	534.5	96 593	3 874.8	955 424	6 722
Visalia-Porterville, CA	836	15 488	1 610.2	632.1	383	2 114	219.4	60.0	20 036	946.7	257 548	1 275
Waco, TX	574	17 072	1 527.0	641.3	379	2 408	236.0	65.4	15 574	713.5	210 042	1 507
Walla Walla, WA	171	4 358	455.3	204.5	88	D	D	D	3 309	128.2	48 719	214
Warner Robins, GA	351	7 250	654.0	264.3	181	983	79.5	22.9	11 830	378.2	162 813	1 048
Washington-Arlington-Alex-andria, DC-VA-MD-WV	15 282	295 912	36 062.8	14 351.2	12 704	147 087	35 947.3	8 469.9	514 453	23 498.0	3 788 184	23 007
Silver Spring-Frederick-Rockville, MD Div 43524	4 197	73 187	8 433.4	3 585.4	2 317	21 946	4 674.0	1 095.5	126 269	6 289.2	691 413	3 383
Washington-Arlington-Alex-andria, DC-VA-MD-WV Div 4	11 085	222 725	27 629.4	10 765.8	10 387	125 141	31 273.3	7 374.5	388 184	17 208.8	3 096 771	19 624
Waterloo-Cedar Falls, IA	446	12 695	1 142.7	482.3	309	1 779	161.8	43.2	9 757	443.7	75 952	414
Watertown-Fort Drum, NY	277	6 183	536.8	247.5	187	912	83.3	21.0	5 031	194.0	17 368	147
Wausau, WI	367	10 123	1 133.0	459.7	221	1 313	138.5	37.7	7 809	385.1	47 880	241
Weirton-Steubenville, WV-OH	295	7 787	682.8	262.3	179	953	64.5	18.5	5 241	185.3	9 693	48
Wenatchee, WA	285	6 275	701.9	314.4	205	720	79.7	19.0	6 188	260.3	117 516	593
Wheeling, WV-OH	521	12 959	1 076.5	427.5	291	1 936	174.3	45.2	6 988	288.7	18 669	115
Wichita, KS	1 710	42 014	4 111.4	1 693.2	983	6 533	748.0	191.4	39 788	1 760.8	347 591	2 021
Wichita Falls, TX	414	11 201	1 080.1	404.4	242	1 300	124.4	32.5	9 487	475.4	18 504	80
Williamsport, PA	287	8 233	825.8	345.7	240	1 546	152.8	35.4	6 190	282.6	37 055	159
Wilmington, NC	845	13 790	1 374.7	550.2	495	2 759	244.2	70.6	23 465	1 081.8	400 184	2 358
Winchester, VA-WV	383	8 763	1 051.5	423.6	215	1 204	101.6	30.6	8 767	378.3	150 594	774
Winston-Salem, NC	1 155	39 069	3 997.0	1 523.5	848	4 224	485.5	115.3	44 652	1 720.8	322 838	2 044
Worcester, MA-CT	2 274	67 479	6 940.7	3 070.9	1 518	8 318	808.2	227.2	57 363	2 801.4	265 350	1 385
Yakima, WA	557	12 903	1 431.4	574.7	281	1 449	130.9	34.3	9 217	419.4	89 672	395
York-Hanover, PA	924	24 161	2 604.4	1 031.9	783	5 242	651.3	139.7	25 586	1 187.3	137 570	778
Youngstown-Warren-Board-man, OH-PA	1 755	40 695	3 681.2	1 454.5	946	5 527	442.5	117.9	34 481	1 442.5	63 149	311
Yuba City, CA	329	5 566	789.3	253.2	155	724	67.1	20.7	8 675	471.0	72 217	371
Yuma, AZ	359	7 092	794.1	282.4	194	1 099	77.8	25.0	8 669	331.9	117 304	768

1. Establishments subject to federal tax.

Table C. Metropolitan Areas

Table C. Metropolitan Areas — Government Employment and Payroll and Local Government Finances

Area name	Government employment and payroll, 2012									Local government finances, 2012				
			March payroll (percent of total)							General revenue				
												Taxes		
													Per capita[1] (dollars)	
	Full-time equivalent employees	March Payroll (dollars)	Administration, judicial, and legal	Police and corrections	Fire protection	Highways and transportation	Health and welfare	Natural resources and utilities	Education and libraries	Total (mil dol)	Inter-governmental (mil dol)	Total (mil dol)	Total	Property
	171	172	173	174	175	176	177	178	179	180	181	182	183	184
The Villages, FL....................	1 509	4 669 736	4.3	3.1	1.1	6.4	1.4	4.3	72.3	251.5	43.7	105.9	1 042	834
Toledo, OH..........................	20 923	85 663 164	9.0	10.9	7.2	4.7	9.5	5.3	52.3	2 794.2	1 171.7	1 080.1	1 774	1 098
Topeka, KS	10 897	35 463 350	4.3	10.3	3.4	3.2	2.7	5.2	70.1	954.7	354.8	369.2	1 574	1 171
Trenton, NJ	15 352	84 285 619	4.4	12.4	3.3	2.0	4.4	4.9	64.8	2 164.5	711.0	1 168.1	3 172	3 117
Tucson, AZ	31 634	115 785 276	10.5	14.5	6.6	3.5	2.2	7.1	52.9	3 257.1	1 214.5	1 427.3	1 438	1 057
Tulsa, OK	33 451	106 348 173	5.8	9.5	5.7	4.2	2.6	6.1	63.2	2 858.0	992.1	1 256.0	1 319	714
Tuscaloosa, AL	11 519	40 376 521	3.7	7.3	3.3	3.6	45.3	3.8	32.1	1 108.1	293.7	229.4	983	397
Tyler, TX.............................	8 764	29 028 100	7.6	10.8	2.8	1.5	6.8	3.6	65.8	648.3	207.0	325.4	1 515	1 170
Urban Honolulu, HI	9 304	47 881 176	14.1	35.4	14.0	2.6	6.8	20.8	0.0	2 232.4	331.8	1 316.4	1 348	833
Utica-Rome, NY	13 622	60 609 793	5.4	11.3	5.5	6.7	5.6	4.7	59.5	1 597.5	779.4	603.1	2 024	1 388
Valdosta, GA	7 094	22 829 566	3.5	7.5	1.9	1.7	36.8	2.6	44.7	654.5	164.9	169.0	1 171	661
Vallejo-Fairfield, CA	14 386	72 410 858	7.6	13.9	3.4	2.8	9.9	7.1	53.4	1 896.3	937.5	594.6	1 413	1 051
Victoria, TX.........................	5 691	19 191 140	4.0	10.2	2.9	1.9	29.7	3.0	47.2	483.0	112.9	173.9	1 800	1 367
Vineland-Bridgeton, NJ	7 697	36 180 326	5.2	9.1	0.8	1.2	4.3	5.3	72.5	886.9	544.0	234.1	1 483	1 435
Virginia Beach-Norfolk-New-port News, VA-NC	78 042	285 080 100	5.2	9.8	4.7	2.6	8.9	7.9	57.4	7 361.3	2 849.8	2 945.6	1 733	1 190
Visalia-Porterville, CA	21 502	97 324 423	4.7	7.2	1.7	1.1	30.4	3.5	50.1	3 132.9	1 499.7	450.9	998	665
Waco, TX	11 156	37 341 296	5.7	11.3	3.0	2.0	4.2	8.5	64.1	1 218.5	462.8	380.3	1 484	1 179
Walla Walla, WA	2 119	9 087 256	8.5	10.7	5.3	6.5	9.7	4.4	51.5	269.2	118.5	82.8	1 307	907
Warner Robins, GA...............	6 945	22 535 113	5.6	9.7	2.9	2.1	4.2	3.2	70.2	591.5	229.4	253.3	1 365	800
Washington-Arlington-Alexan-dria, DC-VA-MD-WV	238 082	1 225 240 040	6.3	10.4	4.1	8.1	7.2	5.9	54.7	35 371.1	10 257.7	19 074.9	3 255	1 833
Silver Spring-Frederick-Rockville, MD Div 43524	49 143	284 578 074	3.5	7.4	4.0	2.8	6.0	9.5	65.7	6 273.9	1 440.7	3 712.4	2 984	1 415
Washington-Arlington-Alex-andria, DC-VA-MD-WV Div 4.......................	188 939	940 661 966	7.1	11.3	4.2	9.7	7.5	4.8	51.4	29 097.2	8 817.0	15 362.6	3 328	1 946
Waterloo-Cedar Falls, IA.......	5 986	22 105 854	5.2	9.3	3.5	4.9	8.6	9.6	56.3	779.9	309.2	283.0	1 677	1 331
Watertown-Fort Drum, NY	5 239	20 682 670	6.0	6.1	2.2	6.7	6.7	3.0	66.9	631.5	312.9	217.3	1 807	1 154
Wausau, WI.........................	5 721	22 517 091	4.6	6.0	1.9	5.6	19.3	2.6	59.4	701.3	346.1	232.0	1 722	1 622
Weirton-Steubenville, WV-OH	4 496	13 800 652	7.0	10.6	2.3	5.5	8.0	7.2	56.9	422.2	201.3	126.9	1 036	755
Wenatchee, WA	4 724	22 972 485	4.8	6.6	2.1	5.8	6.9	31.1	41.1	513.2	239.9	153.9	1 361	918
Wheeling, WV-OH.................	5 774	18 658 082	6.6	9.0	3.0	7.2	6.7	13.1	53.0	499.7	202.4	181.6	1 241	837
Wichita, KS..........................	24 964	87 029 872	6.0	10.7	4.3	3.5	5.1	4.4	64.0	2 420.1	936.4	884.7	1 391	1 088
Wichita Falls, TX	6 724	21 253 583	6.4	13.3	6.1	3.0	9.1	5.3	54.1	453.8	154.7	207.0	1 372	1 062
Williamsport, PA...................	3 615	14 906 594	7.7	7.9	1.8	4.3	2.7	6.0	68.7	451.3	198.0	155.7	1 329	953
Wilmington, NC	13 583	50 754 541	2.9	7.0	2.4	1.1	45.2	4.5	33.4	1 618.1	350.1	385.0	1 461	1 059
Winchester, VA-WV	5 411	16 715 382	6.8	13.2	4.1	1.2	2.9	3.6	66.6	418.3	170.3	190.4	1 454	1 027
Winston-Salem, NC...............	1 023 990	75 606 649	4.5	8.8	4.0	1.2	8.6	5.0	65.1	1 918.0	964.0	681.2	1 052	828
Worcester, MA-CT	32 279	147 826 569	3.6	7.7	4.7	3.3	1.4	4.3	74.0	3 495.3	1 632.4	1 503.7	1 628	1 589
Yakima, WA	8 019	34 900 911	7.0	10.7	3.2	2.8	3.3	5.9	66.0	970.4	601.4	232.4	941	607
York-Hanover, PA	12 293	50 416 660	6.7	12.2	1.5	2.7	6.3	3.6	64.5	1 771.5	572.5	787.5	1 799	1 467
Youngstown-Warren-Board-man, OH-PA	20 254	71 750 350	7.4	10.2	3.8	3.6	7.7	6.8	59.4	1 994.8	1 016.8	698.5	1 251	866
Yuba City, CA	6 669	32 864 622	7.3	8.3	2.0	2.2	10.3	3.3	64.0	941.7	532.4	189.6	1 129	918
Yuma, AZ	7 924	25 609 990	12.0	12.1	3.1	2.2	2.4	7.3	59.9	638.9	314.0	221.6	1 108	716

1. Based on the resident population estimated as of July 1 of the year shown.

Area name	Total (mil dol)	Per capita[1] (dollars)	Education	Health and hospitals	Police protection	Public welfare	Highways	Total (mil dol)	Per capita[1] (dollars)	Federal civilian	Federal military	State and local	Democratic	Republican	All other
	Local government finances, 2012 (cont.)									Government employment, 2014			Presidential election,[2] 2012		
	Direct general expenditure							Debt outstanding					Percent of vote cast:		
				Percent of total for:											
	185	186	187	188	189	190	191	192	193	194	195	196	197	198	199
The Villages, FL	263.4	2 592	27.3	1.6	6.0	0.5	7.8	594.1	5 846	1 603	200	2 951	32.3	67.2	0.5
Toledo, OH	2 631.6	4 323	42.5	7.5	6.3	6.1	4.2	2 796.0	4 593	2 195	1 639	41 936	60.4	37.7	1.9
Topeka, KS	921.3	3 928	54.3	2.2	6.2	0.2	4.0	1 441.3	6 144	3 649	1 218	24 029	44.9	52.7	2.4
Trenton, NJ	2 145.5	5 825	52.3	0.9	5.3	4.3	1.4	1 928.9	5 237	2 362	741	39 569	68.0	30.8	1.2
Tucson, AZ	3 531.8	3 559	37.0	3.1	9.1	2.7	5.3	5 788.9	5 833	12 480	8 418	68 064	52.6	45.7	1.6
Tulsa, OK	2 829.0	2 972	48.0	4.0	5.9	0.6	8.2	3 865.4	4 061	4 596	3 731	49 764	33.9	66.1	0.0
Tuscaloosa, AL	1 116.2	4 783	30.5	41.4	4.7	0.0	5.1	682.1	2 923	1 897	1 043	23 854	43.2	55.7	1.1
Tyler, TX	645.1	3 003	55.0	5.1	5.6	0.2	3.4	1 145.0	5 330	642	478	12 851	27.0	72.0	1.0
Urban Honolulu, HI	1 596.7	1 635	0.0	1.5	15.2	0.0	7.8	5 300.0	5 428	30 393	54 206	68 530	68.9	29.8	1.3
Utica-Rome, NY	1 653.0	5 546	53.3	2.7	2.8	10.6	6.2	1 633.5	5 480	2 346	507	28 066	46.4	51.8	1.8
Valdosta, GA	724.2	5 017	28.8	47.7	4.1	0.7	2.5	413.2	2 862	1 145	4 817	11 738	43.8	55.3	0.8
Vallejo-Fairfield, CA	1 873.8	4 454	35.1	6.1	9.3	7.8	4.2	1 624.0	3 860	3 726	7 106	20 051	63.5	34.2	2.3
Victoria, TX	470.7	4 872	36.4	29.6	5.8	0.0	7.0	443.6	4 591	211	207	6 700	30.7	68.0	1.2
Vineland-Bridgeton, NJ	880.4	5 580	60.1	2.7	3.8	3.4	2.5	354.4	2 246	646	295	12 989	61.6	37.4	1.0
Virginia Beach-Norfolk-Newport News, VA-NC	7 765.7	4 568	42.7	6.6	4.8	4.0	3.4	9 372.3	5 513	49 914	85 788	106 674	54.8	43.7	1.4
Visalia-Porterville, CA	3 186.6	7 050	39.0	24.4	3.2	8.0	4.7	1 380.8	3 055	1 051	705	29 899	41.3	56.3	2.4
Waco, TX	1 187.0	4 631	42.3	2.5	5.0	0.6	1.8	11 603.4	45 270	3 037	606	15 419	34.7	64.1	1.2
Walla Walla, WA	257.4	4 061	43.0	9.4	5.8	0.0	7.2	267.1	4 213	1 285	166	4 889	38.0	59.3	2.7
Warner Robins, GA	571.7	3 082	54.7	6.0	6.4	0.1	5.0	263.3	1 419	15 249	4 138	12 057	41.1	57.9	1.0
Washington-Arlington-Alexandria, DC-VA-MD-WV	35 473.9	6 053	40.6	3.4	5.3	10.4	3.3	44 210.4	7 544	383 728	65 636	320 516	67.3	31.1	1.6
Silver Spring-Frederick-Rockville, MD Div 43524	6 498.3	5 222	51.5	1.7	5.2	3.2	3.5	7 084.9	5 694	50 498	9 812	54 583	66.1	31.8	2.2
Washington-Arlington-Alexandria, DC-VA-MD-WV Div 4	28 975.7	6 277	38.1	3.8	5.3	12.0	3.3	37 125.5	8 043	333 230	55 824	265 933	67.6	30.9	1.5
Waterloo-Cedar Falls, IA	855.9	5 072	49.6	11.0	4.2	0.3	7.5	561.2	3 325	625	669	14 057	56.3	42.1	1.6
Watertown-Fort Drum, NY	631.0	5 247	49.6	3.4	2.6	9.2	6.9	554.7	4 612	3 184	16 970	8 352	47.9	50.8	1.4
Wausau, WI	710.6	5 274	41.9	10.2	3.9	18.8	7.9	440.9	3 273	453	374	7 508	46.3	52.4	1.3
Weirton-Steubenville, WV-OH	426.7	3 482	51.2	4.9	6.0	2.5	5.9	341.9	2 790	251	426	5 363	44.1	53.8	2.1
Wenatchee, WA	488.0	4 317	47.1	12.8	4.5	0.0	5.8	1 944.4	17 202	830	313	7 809	38.7	59.0	2.3
Wheeling, WV-OH	488.4	3 335	43.9	3.2	5.0	2.6	4.4	552.7	3 775	597	527	9 270	40.8	57.2	2.1
Wichita, KS	2 506.2	3 940	49.5	4.3	5.3	0.1	5.5	6 729.7	10 580	4 928	5 456	36 449	37.4	60.2	2.4
Wichita Falls, TX	440.1	2 918	47.9	5.2	7.0	0.7	4.4	688.7	4 566	1 897	4 847	10 367	23.5	75.0	1.5
Williamsport, PA	560.5	4 783	43.8	0.0	2.2	3.1	4.4	997.6	8 514	359	300	8 996	32.7	65.9	1.4
Wilmington, NC	1 610.9	6 115	23.7	45.2	4.9	2.9	1.0	1 660.3	6 303	976	876	21 265	45.5	53.1	1.4
Winchester, VA-WV	404.5	3 090	60.9	0.7	5.4	3.3	1.5	564.7	4 314	2 064	479	7 285	36.7	61.0	2.3
Winston-Salem, NC	2 021.7	3 121	49.9	5.3	7.8	4.7	1.7	1 785.1	2 756	1 983	1 631	30 246	42.3	56.4	1.2
Worcester, MA-CT	3 721.4	4 029	62.3	0.4	3.9	0.2	3.5	2 671.4	2 892	3 241	2 249	57 145	53.9	44.1	2.0
Yakima, WA	1 052.2	4 260	60.9	3.2	4.2	0.8	4.9	606.3	2 455	1 226	801	15 749	43.2	54.9	2.0
York-Hanover, PA	1 790.5	4 089	47.4	3.5	3.3	9.2	2.6	2 454.1	5 605	3 989	1 325	16 248	38.7	59.9	1.4
Youngstown-Warren-Boardman, OH-PA	2 023.9	3 626	53.2	5.1	6.2	4.2	4.0	1 224.6	2 194	1 929	1 457	28 054	59.5	39.0	1.5
Yuba City, CA	962.8	5 733	49.2	5.2	4.2	8.2	2.8	640.8	3 816	1 440	4 910	9 837	39.2	58.0	2.8
Yuma, AZ	616.3	3 081	47.8	2.1	6.0	2.5	4.6	668.5	3 342	3 601	4 138	11 115	43.0	55.7	1.3

1. Based on the resident population estimated as of July 1 of the year shown.   2. © 2013 Election Data Services, Inc. All rights reserved.

Cities of 25,000 or More

(For explanation of symbols, see page viii)

Page

Part D—Cities of 25,000 or More

City Highlights and Rankings

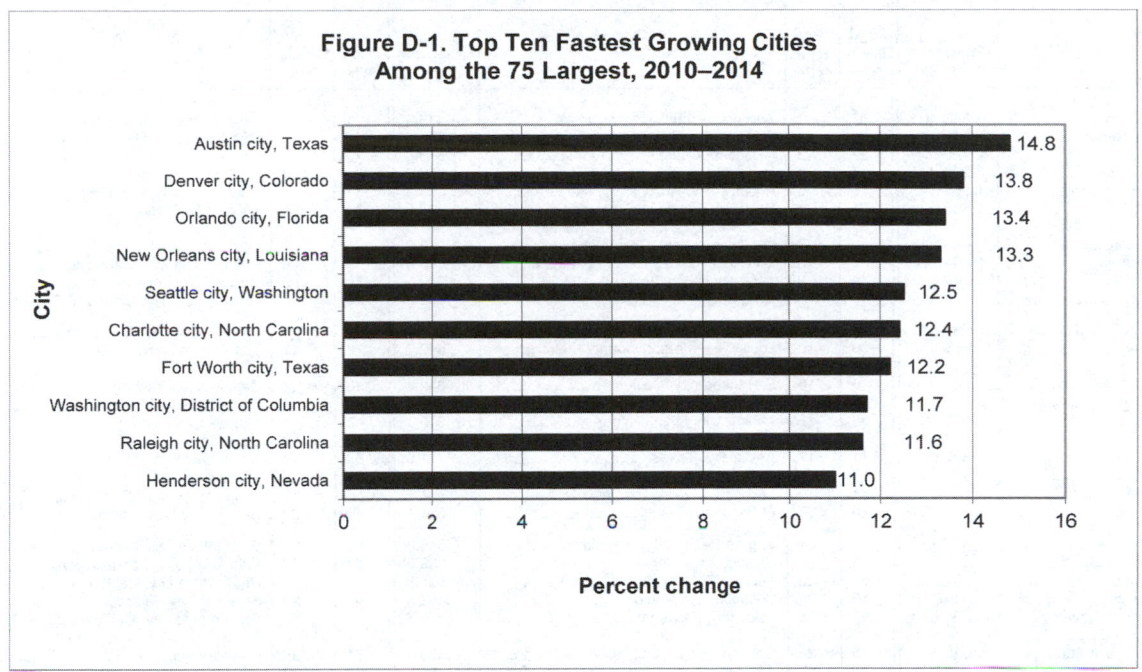

Figure D-1. Top Ten Fastest Growing Cities Among the 75 Largest, 2010–2014

City	Percent change
Austin city, Texas	14.8
Denver city, Colorado	13.8
Orlando city, Florida	13.4
New Orleans city, Louisiana	13.3
Seattle city, Washington	12.5
Charlotte city, North Carolina	12.4
Fort Worth city, Texas	12.2
Washington city, District of Columbia	11.7
Raleigh city, North Carolina	11.6
Henderson city, Nevada	11.0

In 2015, 10 cities had more than 1 million residents, led by New York City with over 8.5 million people, Los Angeles with nearly 4.0 million people, and Chicago with 2.7 million people. California had 14 cities among the nation's 75 most populous, as well as 4 among the top 15 (Los Angeles, San Diego, San Jose, and San Francisco). Texas had 9 cities in the top 75, and also had 4 among the top 15 (Houston, San Antonio, Dallas, and Austin).

Among the largest cities, 44 had growth rates equaling 5 percent or higher from 2010 to 2015 and fourteen had growth rates exceeding 10 percent. Many of these cities were in the south. Austin, TX had the highest growth rate at 14.8 percent. Texas had two cities in the top ten (Austin and Fort Worth), as did North Carolina (Charlotte, Raleigh).Fifty-one of the largest cities equaled or exceeded the U.S. growth rate of 4.1 percent.

Among the 75 largest cities, five lost population between 2010 and 2015. Detroit lost more than 5 percent of its population while Cleveland and Toledo each lost more than 2 percent of their populations. Though New Orleans lost 29.1 percent of its population between 2000 and 2010, it actually grew by nearly two-thirds between 2006 and 2010, after losing more than half of its population after Hurricane Katrina in 2005. It was the fourth fastest growing city from 2010 to 2015, but its 2015 population is still more than 65,000 short of its pre-Katrina total.

Among all cities of 25,000 or more, 32 cities had unemployment rates of 10 percent or more, significantly lower than five years earlier, when 555 cities had an unemployment rate of 10 percent or more. Fourteen of the twenty-five cities with the highest unemployment rates were located in California, three were in Michigan, two each were in Arizona, Illinois, and New Jersey while Texas and Connecticut each had one. Among the largest cities, Detroit, MI had the highest unemployment rate at 12.4 percent followed by Fresno, CA at 11.1 percent while Austin, TX and Lincoln, NE had the lowest unemployment rates at 3.0 percent and 2.5 percent respectively. Among all cities, 351 had unemployment

rates of 4.0 percent or lower. Four of the ten cities with the lowest unemployment rates were in North Dakota and four were in Iowa

While the 2010 census provides updated counts of the population and basic demographic characteristics, updated information on social and economic characteristics is now obtained through the ongoing American Community Survey (ACS). For states, counties, and metropolitan areas, the official intercensal estimates are provided by age, sex, race, and Hispanic origin through the Population Estimates Program. Estimates of these demographic characteristics are not included for cities through the Population Estimates Program, but are available through the ACS. This book includes ACS 5-year estimates for 2010–2014, including data on education, income, housing characteristics, and more.

Among the largest cities, San Jose, San Francisco, and Washington, DC were in the top five for both median income and median housing value. Plano, TX ranked second for median household income, but its median housing value ranked only 22nd among the large cities. New York city ranked 4th for median housing value, but its median household income ranked 25th among large cities. San Francisco tops the ranking with an estimated median housing value of $765,700. Detroit had the lowest median housing value among the large cities, at $45,100.

In the 2010–2014 time period, there were 19 of the largest cities where 10 percent or more of the residents had moved there during the previous year. This may result from population growth: Denver, CO had one of the highest growth rates in recent years as well as one of the highest proportions of people who had moved there in the past year. Other cities have large shifts because of student or military population groups: Pittsburgh, PA lost .4 percent of its population from 2010 to 2015 but 11.8 percent of its population were new residents in the 2010–2014 time period, reflecting the 17.4 percent of residents who were between the ages of 18 and 24, well above the 9.9 percent national average.

75 Largest Cities by 2015 Population
Selected rankings

Population, 2014			Land area, 2010				Population density, 2014			
Population rank	City	Population [col 2]	Population rank	Land area rank	City	Land area (square kilometers) [col 1]	Population rank	Density rank	City	Density (per square kilometer) [col 4]
1	New York city, New York	8 550 405	65	1	Anchorage municipality, Alaska	4 415.1	1	1	New York city, New York	10 909
2	Los Angeles city, California	3 971 883	12	2	Jacksonville city, Florida	1 934.7	13	2	San Francisco city, California	7 124
3	Chicago city, Illinois	2 720 546	27	3	Oklahoma City city, Oklahoma	1 570.6	75	3	Jersey City city, New Jersey	6 900
4	Houston city, Texas	2 296 224	4	4	Houston city, Texas	1 552.9	23	4	Boston city, Massachusetts	5 337
5	Philadelphia city, Pennsylvania	1 567 442	6	5	Phoenix city, Arizona	1 338.3	57	5	Santa Ana city, California	4 751
6	Phoenix city, Arizona	1 563 025	25	6	Nashville-Davidson metro gov, Tennessee	1 230.6	44	6	Miami city, Florida	4 747
7	San Antonio city, Texas	1 469 845	2	7	Los Angeles city, California	1 213.9	3	7	Chicago city, Illinois	4 614
8	San Diego city, California	1 394 928	7	8	San Antonio city, Texas	1 193.8	5	8	Philadelphia city, Pennsylvania	4 513
9	Dallas city, Texas	1 300 092	14	9	Indianapolis city, Indiana	949.1	70	9	Newark city, New Jersey	4 504
10	San Jose city, California	1 026 908	9	10	Dallas city, Texas	881.9	22	10	Washington city, District of Columbia	4 252
11	Austin city, Texas	931 830	16	11	Fort Worth city, Texas	880.1	37	11	Long Beach city, California	3 639
12	Jacksonville city, Florida	868 031	30	12	Louisville/Jefferson County metro gov, Kentucky	842.4	2	12	Los Angeles city, California	3 272
13	San Francisco city, California	864 816	8	13	San Diego city, California	842.2	18	13	Seattle city, Washington	3 148
14	Indianapolis city, Indiana	853 173	24	14	Memphis city, Tennessee	816.0	29	14	Baltimore city, Maryland	2 967
15	Columbus city, Ohio	850 106	36	15	Kansas City city, Missouri	815.7	46	15	Minneapolis city, Minnesota	2 940
16	Fort Worth city, Texas	833 319	1	16	New York city, New York	783.8	45	16	Oakland city, California	2 902
17	Charlotte city, North Carolina	827 097	11	17	Austin city, Texas	771.6	56	17	Anaheim city, California	2 717
18	Seattle city, Washington	684 451	17	18	Charlotte city, North Carolina	771.0	31	18	Milwaukee city, Wisconsin	2 410
19	Denver city, Colorado	682 545	61	19	Lexington-Fayette urban county, Kentucky	734.7	55	19	Urban Honolulu CDP, Hawaii	2 250
20	El Paso city, Texas	681 124	20	20	El Paso city, Texas	661.1	10	20	San Jose city, California	2 246
21	Detroit city, Michigan	677 116	41	21	Virginia Beach city, Virginia	645.0	64	21	St. Paul city, Minnesota	2 235
22	Washington city, District of Columbia	672 228	3	22	Chicago city, Illinois	589.6	63	22	Pittsburgh city, Pennsylvania	2 123
23	Boston city, Massachusetts	667 137	33	23	Tucson city, Arizona	587.2	74	23	Chula Vista city, California	2 068
24	Memphis city, Tennessee	655 770	15	24	Columbus city, Ohio	562.5	60	24	St. Louis city, Missouri	1 969
25	Nashville-Davidson metro gov, Tennessee	654 610	47	25	Tulsa city, Oklahoma	509.6	35	25	Sacramento city, California	1 935
26	Portland city, Oregon	632 309	40	26	Colorado Springs city, Colorado	503.9	51	26	Cleveland city, Ohio	1 929
27	Oklahoma City city, Oklahoma	631 346	32	27	Albuquerque city, New Mexico	486.2	62	27	Stockton city, California	1 914
28	Las Vegas city, Nevada	623 747	10	28	San Jose city, California	457.2	21	28	Detroit city, Michigan	1 884
29	Baltimore city, Maryland	621 849	49	29	New Orleans city, Louisiana	438.8	26	29	Portland city, Oregon	1 830
30	Louisville/Jefferson County metro gov, Kentucky	615 366	58	30	Corpus Christi city, Texas	416.0	34	30	Fresno city, California	1 793
31	Milwaukee city, Wisconsin	600 155	48	31	Wichita city, Kansas	412.6	28	31	Las Vegas city, Nevada	1 773
32	Albuquerque city, New Mexico	559 121	54	32	Aurora city, Colorado	400.8	19	32	Denver city, Colorado	1 722
33	Tucson city, Arizona	531 641	19	33	Denver city, Colorado	396.3	8	33	San Diego city, California	1 656
34	Fresno city, California	520 052	42	34	Raleigh city, North Carolina	370.1	50	34	Arlington city, Texas	1 563
35	Sacramento city, California	490 712	52	35	Bakersfield city, California	368.2	59	35	Riverside city, California	1 534
36	Kansas City city, Missouri	475 378	21	36	Detroit city, Michigan	359.4	69	36	Plano city, Texas	1 529
37	Long Beach city, California	474 140	38	37	Mesa city, Arizona	353.4	15	37	Columbus city, Ohio	1 511
38	Mesa city, Arizona	471 825	28	38	Las Vegas city, Nevada	351.8	4	38	Houston city, Texas	1 479
39	Atlanta city, Georgia	463 878	5	39	Philadelphia city, Pennsylvania	347.3	66	38	Cincinnati city, Ohio	1 479
40	Colorado Springs city, Colorado	456 568	26	40	Portland city, Oregon	345.6	9	40	Dallas city, Texas	1 474
41	Virginia Beach city, Virginia	452 745	39	41	Atlanta city, Georgia	344.9	43	41	Omaha city, Nebraska	1 348
42	Raleigh city, North Carolina	451 066	43	42	Omaha city, Nebraska	329.2	39	42	Atlanta city, Georgia	1 345
43	Omaha city, Nebraska	443 885	68	43	Greensboro city, North Carolina	327.7	71	43	Toledo city, Ohio	1 339
44	Miami city, Florida	441 003	53	44	Tampa city, Florida	293.7	38	44	Mesa city, Arizona	1 335
45	Oakland city, California	419 267	34	45	Fresno city, California	290.0	53	45	Tampa city, Florida	1 257
46	Minneapolis city, Minnesota	410 939	67	46	Henderson city, Nevada	279.0	7	46	San Antonio city, Texas	1 231
47	Tulsa city, Oklahoma	403 505	73	47	Orlando city, Florida	265.2	42	47	Raleigh city, North Carolina	1 219
48	Wichita city, Kansas	389 965	35	48	Sacramento city, California	253.6	11	48	Austin city, Texas	1 208
49	New Orleans city, Louisiana	389 617	31	49	Milwaukee city, Wisconsin	249.0	72	49	Lincoln city, Nebraska	1 202
50	Arlington city, Texas	388 125	50	50	Arlington city, Texas	248.3	6	50	Phoenix city, Arizona	1 168
51	Cleveland city, Ohio	388 072	72	51	Lincoln city, Nebraska	230.8	32	51	Albuquerque city, New Mexico	1 150
52	Bakersfield city, California	373 640	18	52	Seattle city, Washington	217.4	17	52	Charlotte city, North Carolina	1 073
53	Tampa city, Florida	369 075	59	53	Riverside city, California	210.2	20	53	El Paso city, Texas	1 030
54	Aurora city, Colorado	359 407	29	54	Baltimore city, Maryland	209.6	67	54	Henderson city, Nevada	1 024
55	Urban Honolulu CDP, Hawaii	352 769	71	55	Toledo city, Ohio	209.0	73	55	Orlando city, Florida	1 022
56	Anaheim city, California	350 742	66	56	Cincinnati city, Ohio	201.9	52	56	Bakersfield city, California	1 015
57	Santa Ana city, California	335 400	51	57	Cleveland city, Ohio	201.2	16	57	Fort Worth city, Texas	947
58	Corpus Christi city, Texas	324 074	69	58	Plano city, Texas	185.4	48	58	Wichita city, Kansas	945
59	Riverside city, California	322 424	60	59	St. Louis city, Missouri	160.3	14	59	Indianapolis city, Indiana	911
60	St. Louis city, Missouri	315 685	62	60	Stockton city, California	159.7	40	60	Colorado Springs city, Colorado	906
61	Lexington-Fayette urban county, Kentucky	314 488	22	61	Washington city, District of Columbia	158.1	33	61	Tucson city, Arizona	905
62	Stockton city, California	305 658	55	62	Urban Honolulu CDP, Hawaii	156.8	54	62	Aurora city, Colorado	897
63	Pittsburgh city, Pennsylvania	304 391	45	63	Oakland city, California	144.5	49	63	New Orleans city, Louisiana	888
64	St. Paul city, Minnesota	300 851	63	64	Pittsburgh city, Pennsylvania	143.4	68	64	Greensboro city, North Carolina	871
65	Anchorage municipality, Alaska	298 695	46	65	Minneapolis city, Minnesota	139.8	24	65	Memphis city, Tennessee	804
66	Cincinnati city, Ohio	298 550	64	66	St. Paul city, Minnesota	134.6	47	66	Tulsa city, Oklahoma	792
67	Henderson city, Nevada	285 667	37	67	Long Beach city, California	130.3	58	67	Corpus Christi city, Texas	779
68	Greensboro city, North Carolina	285 342	56	68	Anaheim city, California	129.1	30	68	Louisville/Jefferson County metro gov, Kentucky	730
69	Plano city, Texas	283 558	74	69	Chula Vista city, California	128.5	41	69	Virginia Beach city, Virginia	702
70	Newark city, New Jersey	281 944	23	70	Boston city, Massachusetts	125.0	36	70	Kansas City city, Missouri	583
71	Toledo city, Ohio	279 789	13	71	San Francisco city, California	121.4	25	71	Nashville-Davidson metro gov, Tennessee	532
72	Lincoln city, Nebraska	277 348	44	72	Miami city, Florida	92.9	12	72	Jacksonville city, Florida	449
73	Orlando city, Florida	270 934	57	73	Santa Ana city, California	70.6	61	73	Lexington-Fayette urban county, Kentucky	428
74	Chula Vista city, California	265 757	70	74	Newark city, New Jersey	62.6	27	74	Oklahoma City city, Oklahoma	402
75	Jersey City city, New Jersey	264 290	75	75	Jersey City city, New Jersey	38.3	65	75	Anchorage municipality, Alaska	68

75 Largest Cities by 2015 Population
Selected rankings

	Percent population change, 2010–2014				Percent White, alone or in combination, 2010–2014				Percent Black, alone or in combination, 2010–2014		
Population rank	Percent change rank	City	Percent change [col 26]	Population rank	White rank	City	Percent White [col 5]	Population rank	Black rank	City	Percent Black [col 6]
11	1	Austin city, Texas	14.8	72	1	Lincoln city, Nebraska	89.5	21	1	Detroit city, Michigan	82.5
19	2	Denver city, Colorado	13.8	58	2	Corpus Christi city, Texas	87.0	29	2	Baltimore city, Maryland	64.6
73	3	Orlando city, Florida	13.4	38	3	Mesa city, Arizona	86.7	24	3	Memphis city, Tennessee	63.9
49	4	New Orleans city, Louisiana	13.3	20	4	El Paso city, Texas	84.6	49	4	New Orleans city, Louisiana	60.5
18	5	Seattle city, Washington	12.5	40	5	Colorado Springs city, Colorado	84.1	51	5	Cleveland city, Ohio	54.3
17	6	Charlotte city, North Carolina	12.4	67	6	Henderson city, Nevada	81.7	39	6	Atlanta city, Georgia	54.0
16	7	Fort Worth city, Texas	12.2	26	7	Portland city, Oregon	81.4	70	7	Newark city, New Jersey	53.9
22	8	Washington city, District of Columbia	11.7	43	8	Omaha city, Nebraska	79.5	22	8	Washington city, District of Columbia	50.7
42	9	Raleigh city, North Carolina	11.6	7	9	San Antonio city, Texas	79.3	60	9	St. Louis city, Missouri	49.5
67	10	Henderson city, Nevada	11.0	48	10	Wichita city, Kansas	79.1	66	10	Cincinnati city, Ohio	45.6
7	11	San Antonio city, Texas	10.7	61	11	Lexington-Fayette urban county, Kentucky	78.5	5	11	Philadelphia city, Pennsylvania	44.7
54	11	Aurora city, Colorado	10.7	6	12	Phoenix city, Arizona	78.2	68	12	Greensboro city, North Carolina	42.6
39	13	Atlanta city, Georgia	10.4	33	12	Tucson city, Arizona	78.2	31	13	Milwaukee city, Wisconsin	41.5
44	13	Miami city, Florida	10.4	19	14	Denver city, Colorado	77.5	17	14	Charlotte city, North Carolina	36.6
53	15	Tampa city, Florida	9.9	11	15	Austin city, Texas	77.2	3	15	Chicago city, Illinois	32.8
40	16	Colorado Springs city, Colorado	9.4	44	16	Miami city, Florida	75.9	12	16	Jacksonville city, Florida	32.2
69	17	Plano city, Texas	9.1	30	17	Louisville/Jefferson County metro gov, Kentucky	75.7	36	17	Kansas City city, Missouri	31.1
74	18	Chula Vista city, California	9.0	18	18	Seattle city, Washington	74.9	15	18	Columbus city, Ohio	30.4
4	19	Houston city, Texas	8.9	32	18	Albuquerque city, New Mexico	74.9	42	19	Raleigh city, North Carolina	30.0
27	19	Oklahoma City city, Oklahoma	8.9	65	20	Anchorage municipality, Alaska	73.5	71	20	Toledo city, Ohio	29.7
9	21	Dallas city, Texas	8.5	27	21	Oklahoma City city, Oklahoma	72.9	73	20	Orlando city, Florida	29.7
25	21	Nashville-Davidson metro gov, Tennessee	8.5	47	22	Tulsa city, Oklahoma	72.0	14	22	Indianapolis city, Indiana	29.3
26	23	Portland city, Oregon	8.3	74	22	Chula Vista city, California	72.0	45	23	Oakland city, California	29.0
6	24	Phoenix city, Arizona	8.0	41	24	Virginia Beach city, Virginia	71.8	25	24	Nashville-Davidson metro gov, Tennessee	28.8
23	24	Boston city, Massachusetts	8.0	69	25	Plano city, Texas	71.5	23	25	Boston city, Massachusetts	28.2
10	26	San Jose city, California	7.8	52	26	Bakersfield city, California	70.8	53	26	Tampa city, Florida	27.5
15	26	Columbus city, Ohio	7.8	59	26	Riverside city, California	70.8	75	27	Jersey City city, New Jersey	26.9
52	28	Bakersfield city, California	7.5	46	28	Minneapolis city, Minnesota	70.5	63	28	Pittsburgh city, Pennsylvania	26.6
13	29	San Francisco city, California	7.4	28	29	Las Vegas city, Nevada	69.2	1	29	New York city, New York	26.3
46	29	Minneapolis city, Minnesota	7.4	63	29	Pittsburgh city, Pennsylvania	69.2	9	30	Dallas city, Texas	25.5
45	31	Oakland city, California	7.3	71	31	Toledo city, Ohio	68.8	4	31	Houston city, Texas	23.9
72	31	Lincoln city, Nebraska	7.3	56	32	Anaheim city, California	68.6	30	32	Louisville/Jefferson County metro gov, Kentucky	22.6
8	33	San Diego city, California	7.2	54	33	Aurora city, Colorado	68.5	41	33	Virginia Beach city, Virginia	21.7
38	33	Mesa city, Arizona	7.2	50	34	Arlington city, Texas	68.3	50	34	Arlington city, Texas	20.8
28	35	Las Vegas city, Nevada	6.7	8	35	San Diego city, California	68.2	46	35	Minneapolis city, Minnesota	20.6
75	35	Jersey City city, New Jersey	6.7	16	36	Fort Worth city, Texas	67.8	44	36	Miami city, Florida	20.3
61	37	Lexington-Fayette urban county, Kentucky	6.3	53	37	Tampa city, Florida	65.8	16	37	Fort Worth city, Texas	20.1
50	38	Arlington city, Texas	6.2	15	38	Columbus city, Ohio	65.0	54	38	Aurora city, Colorado	18.6
58	38	Corpus Christi city, Texas	6.2	14	39	Indianapolis city, Indiana	64.7	64	39	St. Paul city, Minnesota	18.2
59	40	Riverside city, California	6.1	64	40	St. Paul city, Minnesota	64.3	47	40	Tulsa city, Oklahoma	17.9
68	40	Greensboro city, North Carolina	6.1	25	41	Nashville-Davidson metro gov, Tennessee	64.1	27	41	Oklahoma City city, Oklahoma	17.0
12	42	Jacksonville city, Florida	5.6	12	42	Jacksonville city, Florida	63.0	35	42	Sacramento city, California	16.4
64	43	St. Paul city, Minnesota	5.5	42	43	Raleigh city, North Carolina	62.7	61	43	Lexington-Fayette urban county, Kentucky	16.2
35	44	Sacramento city, California	5.2	36	44	Kansas City city, Missouri	62.5	37	44	Long Beach city, California	15.3
20	45	El Paso city, Texas	4.9	73	45	Orlando city, Florida	61.1	43	45	Omaha city, Nebraska	14.5
34	46	Fresno city, California	4.8	9	46	Dallas city, Texas	59.9	62	46	Stockton city, California	14.1
62	46	Stockton city, California	4.8	4	47	Houston city, Texas	59.3	48	47	Wichita city, Kansas	13.6
2	48	Los Angeles city, California	4.7	37	48	Long Beach city, California	58.5	28	48	Las Vegas city, Nevada	13.1
1	49	New York city, New York	4.6	23	49	Boston city, Massachusetts	57.2	19	49	Denver city, Colorado	11.1
55	49	Urban Honolulu CDP, Hawaii	4.6	2	50	Los Angeles city, California	55.4	2	50	Los Angeles city, California	10.2
56	51	Anaheim city, California	4.3	35	50	Sacramento city, California	55.4	52	51	Bakersfield city, California	9.6
14	52	Indianapolis city, Indiana	4.0	34	52	Fresno city, California	55.2	34	52	Fresno city, California	9.2
36	53	Kansas City city, Missouri	3.4	17	53	Charlotte city, North Carolina	54.1	11	53	Austin city, Texas	9.0
41	53	Virginia Beach city, Virginia	3.4	13	54	San Francisco city, California	53.2	18	53	Seattle city, Washington	9.0
57	55	Santa Ana city, California	3.3	66	55	Cincinnati city, Ohio	52.9	69	55	Plano city, Texas	8.4
47	56	Tulsa city, Oklahoma	3.0	68	56	Greensboro city, North Carolina	51.3	65	56	Anchorage municipality, Alaska	8.3
43	57	Omaha city, Nebraska	2.8	3	57	Chicago city, Illinois	50.1	40	57	Colorado Springs city, Colorado	8.1
5	58	Philadelphia city, Pennsylvania	2.7	62	57	Stockton city, California	50.1	8	58	San Diego city, California	8.0
37	59	Long Beach city, California	2.6	31	59	Milwaukee city, Wisconsin	49.9	6	59	Phoenix city, Arizona	7.9
65	60	Anchorage municipality, Alaska	2.4	10	60	San Jose city, California	49.2	7	60	San Antonio city, Texas	7.8
32	61	Albuquerque city, New Mexico	2.3	57	61	Santa Ana city, California	48.6	59	60	Riverside city, California	7.8
33	62	Tucson city, Arizona	2.1	60	62	St. Louis city, Missouri	47.7	26	62	Portland city, Oregon	7.5
48	63	Wichita city, Kansas	2.0	1	63	New York city, New York	45.8	67	63	Henderson city, Nevada	7.0
70	64	Newark city, New Jersey	1.7	45	64	Oakland city, California	44.1	13	64	San Francisco city, California	6.7
3	65	Chicago city, Illinois	0.9	5	65	Philadelphia city, Pennsylvania	43.5	33	65	Tucson city, Arizona	6.3
31	65	Milwaukee city, Wisconsin	0.9	51	66	Cleveland city, Ohio	42.9	74	66	Chula Vista city, California	6.0
24	67	Memphis city, Tennessee	0.6	22	67	Washington city, District of Columbia	42.1	72	67	Lincoln city, Nebraska	5.5
66	68	Cincinnati city, Ohio	0.5	39	68	Atlanta city, Georgia	41.2	58	68	Corpus Christi city, Texas	5.1
29	69	Baltimore city, Maryland	0.1	75	69	Jersey City city, New Jersey	36.9	38	69	Mesa city, Arizona	4.5
30	70	Louisville/Jefferson County metro gov, Kentucky	0.0	49	70	New Orleans city, Louisiana	35.4	32	70	Albuquerque city, New Mexico	4.4
63	71	Pittsburgh city, Pennsylvania	-0.4	29	71	Baltimore city, Maryland	31.9	20	71	El Paso city, Texas	4.1
60	72	St. Louis city, Missouri	-1.2	24	72	Memphis city, Tennessee	31.7	10	72	San Jose city, California	4.0
51	73	Cleveland city, Ohio	-2.2	55	73	Urban Honolulu CDP, Hawaii	30.3	55	73	Urban Honolulu CDP, Hawaii	3.3
71	74	Toledo city, Ohio	-2.6	70	74	Newark city, New Jersey	28.4	56	74	Anaheim city, California	3.0
21	75	Detroit city, Michigan	-5.1	21	75	Detroit city, Michigan	14.0	57	75	Santa Ana city, California	1.5

75 Largest Cities by 2015 Population
Selected rankings

Percent American Indian, Alaska Native, 2011–2013

Population rank	American Indian, Alaska Native rank	City	Percent American Indian, Alaska Native [col 7]
65	1	Anchorage municipality, Alaska	12.3
47	2	Tulsa city, Oklahoma	9.5
27	3	Oklahoma City city, Oklahoma	7.7
32	4	Albuquerque city, New Mexico	5.5
33	5	Tucson city, Arizona	3.8
37	6	Long Beach city, California	3.5
62	7	Stockton city, California	3.3
46	8	Minneapolis city, Minnesota	3.0
38	9	Mesa city, Arizona	2.9
6	10	Phoenix city, Arizona	2.8
48	11	Wichita city, Kansas	2.7
64	12	St. Paul city, Minnesota	2.6
34	13	Fresno city, California	2.5
35	13	Sacramento city, California	2.5
54	13	Aurora city, Colorado	2.5
26	16	Portland city, Oregon	2.4
52	16	Bakersfield city, California	2.4
59	16	Riverside city, California	2.4
19	19	Denver city, Colorado	2.3
18	20	Seattle city, Washington	2.2
45	20	Oakland city, California	2.2
40	22	Colorado Springs city, Colorado	2.0
31	23	Milwaukee city, Wisconsin	1.8
43	23	Omaha city, Nebraska	1.8
55	23	Urban Honolulu CDP, Hawaii	1.8
8	26	San Diego city, California	1.6
36	26	Kansas City city, Missouri	1.6
10	28	San Jose city, California	1.5
70	28	Newark city, New Jersey	1.5
72	28	Lincoln city, Nebraska	1.5
7	31	San Antonio city, Texas	1.4
16	31	Fort Worth city, Texas	1.4
28	31	Las Vegas city, Nevada	1.4
53	31	Tampa city, Florida	1.4
2	35	Los Angeles city, California	1.3
11	36	Austin city, Texas	1.2
15	36	Columbus city, Ohio	1.2
17	36	Charlotte city, North Carolina	1.2
41	36	Virginia Beach city, Virginia	1.2
63	36	Pittsburgh city, Pennsylvania	1.2
71	36	Toledo city, Ohio	1.2
9	42	Dallas city, Texas	1.1
13	42	San Francisco city, California	1.1
21	42	Detroit city, Michigan	1.1
29	42	Baltimore city, Maryland	1.1
50	42	Arlington city, Texas	1.1
51	42	Cleveland city, Ohio	1.1
58	42	Corpus Christi city, Texas	1.1
68	42	Greensboro city, North Carolina	1.1
74	42	Chula Vista city, California	1.1
5	51	Philadelphia city, Pennsylvania	1.0
20	51	El Paso city, Texas	1.0
56	51	Anaheim city, California	1.0
60	51	St. Louis city, Missouri	1.0
66	51	Cincinnati city, Ohio	1.0
67	51	Henderson city, Nevada	1.0
69	51	Plano city, Texas	1.0
1	58	New York city, New York	0.9
4	58	Houston city, Texas	0.9
12	58	Jacksonville city, Florida	0.9
14	58	Indianapolis city, Indiana	0.9
22	58	Washington city, District of Columbia	0.9
23	58	Boston city, Massachusetts	0.9
61	58	Lexington-Fayette urban county, Kentucky	0.9
25	65	Nashville-Davidson metro gov, Tennessee	0.8
30	65	Louisville/Jefferson County metro gov, Kentucky	0.8
39	65	Atlanta city, Georgia	0.8
42	65	Raleigh city, North Carolina	0.8
49	65	New Orleans city, Louisiana	0.8
57	65	Santa Ana city, California	0.8
75	65	Jersey City city, New Jersey	0.8
3	72	Chicago city, Illinois	0.7
24	72	Memphis city, Tennessee	0.7
73	72	Orlando city, Florida	0.7
44	75	Miami city, Florida	0.3

Percent Asian and Pacific Islander, 2011–2013

Population rank	Asian and Pacific Islander rank	City	Percent Asian and Pacific Islander [col 8]
55	1	Urban Honolulu CDP, Hawaii	67.1
13	2	San Francisco city, California	36.3
10	3	San Jose city, California	35.8
75	4	Jersey City city, New Jersey	26.1
62	5	Stockton city, California	24.4
35	6	Sacramento city, California	21.5
69	7	Plano city, Texas	19.6
8	8	San Diego city, California	19.0
45	9	Oakland city, California	18.9
56	10	Anaheim city, California	17.3
74	10	Chula Vista city, California	17.3
18	12	Seattle city, Washington	17.2
64	13	St. Paul city, Minnesota	16.9
37	14	Long Beach city, California	15.0
34	15	Fresno city, California	14.6
1	16	New York city, New York	14.3
2	17	Los Angeles city, California	12.9
57	18	Santa Ana city, California	11.0
65	18	Anchorage municipality, Alaska	11.0
23	20	Boston city, Massachusetts	10.1
67	21	Henderson city, Nevada	9.8
26	22	Portland city, Oregon	9.3
59	23	Riverside city, California	8.5
28	24	Las Vegas city, Nevada	8.3
41	25	Virginia Beach city, Virginia	8.1
50	26	Arlington city, Texas	7.8
52	26	Bakersfield city, California	7.8
11	28	Austin city, Texas	7.6
5	29	Philadelphia city, Pennsylvania	7.3
4	30	Houston city, Texas	7.0
46	31	Minneapolis city, Minnesota	6.9
3	32	Chicago city, Illinois	6.5
54	33	Aurora city, Colorado	6.3
17	34	Charlotte city, North Carolina	6.2
48	35	Wichita city, Kansas	5.6
63	35	Pittsburgh city, Pennsylvania	5.6
12	37	Jacksonville city, Florida	5.5
15	38	Columbus city, Ohio	5.2
42	39	Raleigh city, North Carolina	5.0
27	40	Oklahoma City city, Oklahoma	4.9
40	41	Colorado Springs city, Colorado	4.8
22	42	Washington city, District of Columbia	4.7
53	42	Tampa city, Florida	4.7
72	42	Lincoln city, Nebraska	4.7
16	45	Fort Worth city, Texas	4.6
19	46	Denver city, Colorado	4.5
68	46	Greensboro city, North Carolina	4.5
39	48	Atlanta city, Georgia	4.4
73	48	Orlando city, Florida	4.4
6	50	Phoenix city, Arizona	4.2
31	50	Milwaukee city, Wisconsin	4.2
61	52	Lexington-Fayette urban county, Kentucky	4.1
32	53	Albuquerque city, New Mexico	3.9
33	53	Tucson city, Arizona	3.9
25	55	Nashville-Davidson metro gov, Tennessee	3.8
60	56	St. Louis city, Missouri	3.6
9	57	Dallas city, Texas	3.4
43	57	Omaha city, Nebraska	3.4
49	59	New Orleans city, Louisiana	3.3
7	60	San Antonio city, Texas	3.1
36	60	Kansas City city, Missouri	3.1
47	60	Tulsa city, Oklahoma	3.1
29	63	Baltimore city, Maryland	3.0
30	64	Louisville/Jefferson County metro gov, Kentucky	2.9
14	65	Indianapolis city, Indiana	2.8
38	66	Mesa city, Arizona	2.7
58	67	Corpus Christi city, Texas	2.4
66	67	Cincinnati city, Ohio	2.4
51	69	Cleveland city, Ohio	2.2
70	69	Newark city, New Jersey	2.2
24	71	Memphis city, Tennessee	2.1
20	72	El Paso city, Texas	1.9
71	73	Toledo city, Ohio	1.7
21	74	Detroit city, Michigan	1.5
44	75	Miami city, Florida	1.1

Percent Hispanic or Latino,[1] 2011–2013

Population rank	Hispanic or Latino rank	City	Percent Hispanic or Latino [col 10]
20	1	El Paso city, Texas	79.7
57	2	Santa Ana city, California	78.6
44	3	Miami city, Florida	70.7
7	4	San Antonio city, Texas	63.3
58	5	Corpus Christi city, Texas	60.8
74	6	Chula Vista city, California	58.4
56	7	Anaheim city, California	52.8
59	8	Riverside city, California	51.5
2	9	Los Angeles city, California	48.6
34	10	Fresno city, California	48.0
32	11	Albuquerque city, New Mexico	47.3
52	12	Bakersfield city, California	46.9
4	13	Houston city, Texas	43.9
33	14	Tucson city, Arizona	42.2
9	15	Dallas city, Texas	41.7
37	15	Long Beach city, California	41.7
62	17	Stockton city, California	41.3
6	18	Phoenix city, Arizona	40.5
11	19	Austin city, Texas	34.8
70	19	Newark city, New Jersey	34.8
16	21	Fort Worth city, Texas	34.2
10	22	San Jose city, California	33.1
28	23	Las Vegas city, Nevada	32.2
19	24	Denver city, Colorado	31.2
8	25	San Diego city, California	29.5
3	26	Chicago city, Illinois	28.9
54	26	Aurora city, Colorado	28.9
1	28	New York city, New York	28.8
50	29	Arlington city, Texas	28.7
35	30	Sacramento city, California	27.6
75	31	Jersey City city, New Jersey	27.4
38	32	Mesa city, Arizona	26.8
73	32	Orlando city, Florida	26.8
45	34	Oakland city, California	25.9
53	35	Tampa city, Florida	23.3
23	36	Boston city, Massachusetts	18.4
27	37	Oklahoma City city, Oklahoma	18.0
31	38	Milwaukee city, Wisconsin	17.7
40	39	Colorado Springs city, Colorado	17.0
48	40	Wichita city, Kansas	15.7
13	41	San Francisco city, California	15.3
67	42	Henderson city, Nevada	14.9
47	43	Tulsa city, Oklahoma	14.8
69	44	Plano city, Texas	14.7
17	45	Charlotte city, North Carolina	13.4
43	46	Omaha city, Nebraska	13.3
5	47	Philadelphia city, Pennsylvania	13.0
42	48	Raleigh city, North Carolina	10.9
36	49	Kansas City city, Missouri	10.1
51	50	Cleveland city, Ohio	10.0
22	51	Washington city, District of Columbia	9.9
25	52	Nashville-Davidson metro gov, Tennessee	9.8
46	52	Minneapolis city, Minnesota	9.8
14	54	Indianapolis city, Indiana	9.6
26	54	Portland city, Oregon	9.6
64	56	St. Paul city, Minnesota	9.5
65	57	Anchorage municipality, Alaska	8.3
12	58	Jacksonville city, Florida	8.2
71	59	Toledo city, Ohio	7.6
68	60	Greensboro city, North Carolina	7.4
21	61	Detroit city, Michigan	7.3
41	62	Virginia Beach city, Virginia	7.2
61	63	Lexington-Fayette urban county, Kentucky	6.8
72	64	Lincoln city, Nebraska	6.7
24	65	Memphis city, Tennessee	6.5
18	66	Seattle city, Washington	6.4
55	67	Urban Honolulu CDP, Hawaii	5.9
15	68	Columbus city, Ohio	5.7
39	69	Atlanta city, Georgia	5.6
49	70	New Orleans city, Louisiana	5.4
30	71	Louisville/Jefferson County metro gov, Kentucky	4.6
29	72	Baltimore city, Maryland	4.5
60	73	St. Louis city, Missouri	3.7
66	74	Cincinnati city, Ohio	3.0
63	75	Pittsburgh city, Pennsylvania	2.7

75 Largest Cities by 2015 Population
Selected rankings

Percent under 18 years old, 2010–2014				Percent 65 years old and over, 2010–2014				Percent high school graduate or less, 2010–2014			
Population rank	Under 18 years old rank	City	Percent under 18 years old [col 12 and 13]	Population rank	65 years old and over rank	City	Percent 65 years old and over [col 19 and 20]	Population rank	Percent high school graduate or less rank	City	Percent high school graduate or less [col 40]
52	1	Bakersfield city, California	30.6	55	1	Urban Honolulu CDP, Hawaii	17.9	57	1	Santa Ana city, California	67.9
62	2	Stockton city, California	29.9	67	2	Henderson city, Nevada	16.4	70	2	Newark city, New Jersey	63.9
34	3	Fresno city, California	29.6	44	3	Miami city, Florida	15.9	44	3	Miami city, Florida	57.7
57	4	Santa Ana city, California	29.3	38	4	Mesa city, Arizona	15.2	51	4	Cleveland city, Ohio	55.6
16	5	Fort Worth city, Texas	29.0	13	5	San Francisco city, California	13.9	21	5	Detroit city, Michigan	54.6
20	6	El Paso city, Texas	28.1	63	5	Pittsburgh city, Pennsylvania	13.9	5	6	Philadelphia city, Pennsylvania	52.9
6	7	Phoenix city, Arizona	27.1	28	7	Las Vegas city, Nevada	13.2	62	7	Stockton city, California	49.6
50	8	Arlington city, Texas	27.0	30	7	Louisville/Jefferson County metro gov, Kentucky	13.2	71	8	Toledo city, Ohio	49.1
54	9	Aurora city, Colorado	26.8	32	9	Albuquerque city, New Mexico	12.9	29	9	Baltimore city, Maryland	48.8
31	10	Milwaukee city, Wisconsin	26.7	47	10	Tulsa city, Oklahoma	12.8	31	10	Milwaukee city, Wisconsin	48.4
74	11	Chula Vista city, California	26.6	71	10	Toledo city, Ohio	12.7	34	11	Fresno city, California	48.2
48	12	Wichita city, Kansas	26.3	1	12	New York city, New York	12.5	56	12	Anaheim city, California	48.0
7	13	San Antonio city, Texas	26.2	33	12	Tucson city, Arizona	12.5	9	13	Dallas city, Texas	47.8
56	14	Anaheim city, California	26.1	51	14	Cleveland city, Ohio	12.4	20	14	El Paso city, Texas	46.8
59	14	Riverside city, California	26.1	5	15	Philadelphia city, Pennsylvania	12.3	4	15	Houston city, Texas	46.5
9	16	Dallas city, Texas	25.8	58	15	Corpus Christi city, Texas	12.3	59	16	Riverside city, California	46.3
27	17	Oklahoma City city, Oklahoma	25.7	21	17	Detroit city, Michigan	12.2	28	17	Las Vegas city, Nevada	46.2
70	18	Newark city, New Jersey	25.6	68	18	Greensboro city, North Carolina	12.0	24	18	Memphis city, Tennessee	46.1
21	19	Detroit city, Michigan	25.5	29	19	Baltimore city, Maryland	11.9	58	18	Corpus Christi city, Texas	46.1
58	19	Corpus Christi city, Texas	25.5	48	19	Wichita city, Kansas	11.9	52	20	Bakersfield city, California	45.0
4	21	Houston city, Texas	25.4	12	21	Jacksonville city, Florida	11.7	2	21	Los Angeles city, California	44.6
65	22	Anchorage municipality, Alaska	25.3	43	21	Omaha city, Nebraska	11.7	1	22	New York city, New York	44.4
69	22	Plano city, Texas	25.3	36	23	Kansas City city, Missouri	11.6	7	22	San Antonio city, Texas	44.4
24	24	Memphis city, Tennessee	25.2	45	23	Oakland city, California	11.6	14	24	Indianapolis city, Indiana	44.3
64	24	St. Paul city, Minnesota	25.2	20	25	El Paso city, Texas	11.5	16	25	Fort Worth city, Texas	44.2
17	26	Charlotte city, North Carolina	25.0	35	26	Sacramento city, California	11.4	6	26	Phoenix city, Arizona	43.1
38	27	Mesa city, Arizona	24.9	41	26	Virginia Beach city, Virginia	11.4	3	27	Chicago city, Illinois	41.6
43	27	Omaha city, Nebraska	24.9	49	26	New Orleans city, Louisiana	11.4	12	28	Jacksonville city, Florida	41.3
14	29	Indianapolis city, Indiana	24.8	8	29	San Diego city, California	11.3	66	29	Cincinnati city, Ohio	41.1
28	30	Las Vegas city, Nevada	24.6	18	29	Seattle city, Washington	11.3	60	30	St. Louis city, Missouri	41.0
37	31	Long Beach city, California	24.5	22	29	Washington city, District of Columbia	11.3	27	31	Oklahoma City city, Oklahoma	40.4
40	31	Colorado Springs city, Colorado	24.5	40	29	Colorado Springs city, Colorado	11.3	53	32	Tampa city, Florida	40.3
47	31	Tulsa city, Oklahoma	24.5	53	29	Tampa city, Florida	11.3	33	33	Tucson city, Arizona	39.8
10	34	San Jose city, California	24.0	72	29	Lincoln city, Nebraska	11.3	38	34	Mesa city, Arizona	39.4
35	34	Sacramento city, California	24.0	27	35	Oklahoma City city, Oklahoma	11.2	30	35	Louisville/Jefferson County metro gov, Kentucky	39.3
36	36	Kansas City city, Missouri	23.6	66	35	Cincinnati city, Ohio	11.2	48	35	Wichita city, Kansas	39.3
32	37	Albuquerque city, New Mexico	23.5	7	37	San Antonio city, Texas	11.0	37	37	Long Beach city, California	39.2
12	38	Jacksonville city, Florida	23.4	26	37	Portland city, Oregon	11.0	49	37	New Orleans city, Louisiana	39.2
30	38	Louisville/Jefferson County metro gov, Kentucky	23.4	60	37	St. Louis city, Missouri	11.0	54	39	Aurora city, Colorado	38.9
41	38	Virginia Beach city, Virginia	23.4	61	37	Lexington-Fayette urban county, Kentucky	11.0	74	39	Chula Vista city, California	38.9
71	41	Toledo city, Ohio	23.3	2	41	Los Angeles city, California	10.9	50	41	Arlington city, Texas	38.8
15	42	Columbus city, Ohio	23.1	10	41	San Jose city, California	10.9	47	42	Tulsa city, Oklahoma	38.6
51	42	Cleveland city, Ohio	23.1	14	43	Indianapolis city, Indiana	10.8	75	43	Jersey City city, New Jersey	38.4
42	44	Raleigh city, North Carolina	22.9	3	44	Chicago city, Illinois	10.7	36	44	Kansas City city, Missouri	38.1
72	45	Lincoln city, Nebraska	22.7	62	44	Stockton city, California	10.7	63	44	Pittsburgh city, Pennsylvania	38.1
3	46	Chicago city, Illinois	22.4	19	46	Denver city, Colorado	10.6	35	46	Sacramento city, California	37.9
5	47	Philadelphia city, Pennsylvania	22.3	24	46	Memphis city, Tennessee	10.6	15	47	Columbus city, Ohio	37.8
2	48	Los Angeles city, California	22.2	74	46	Chula Vista city, California	10.6	25	48	Nashville-Davidson metro gov, Tennessee	37.7
68	48	Greensboro city, North Carolina	22.2	23	49	Boston city, Massachusetts	10.5	23	49	Boston city, Massachusetts	37.1
73	48	Orlando city, Florida	22.2	25	50	Nashville-Davidson metro gov, Tennessee	10.4	55	50	Urban Honolulu CDP, Hawaii	36.5
33	51	Tucson city, Arizona	22.1	69	51	Plano city, Texas	10.3	73	51	Orlando city, Florida	36.4
66	51	Cincinnati city, Ohio	22.1	56	52	Anaheim city, California	10.1	45	52	Oakland city, California	36.2
67	51	Henderson city, Nevada	22.1	39	53	Atlanta city, Georgia	10.0	10	53	San Jose city, California	35.7
11	54	Austin city, Texas	21.7	37	54	Long Beach city, California	9.9	64	54	St. Paul city, Minnesota	35.5
25	54	Nashville-Davidson metro gov, Tennessee	21.7	75	55	Jersey City city, New Jersey	9.8	43	55	Omaha city, Nebraska	35.2
53	56	Tampa city, Florida	21.6	34	56	Fresno city, California	9.7	68	56	Greensboro city, North Carolina	34.8
8	57	San Diego city, California	21.5	54	56	Aurora city, Colorado	9.7	32	57	Albuquerque city, New Mexico	34.2
1	58	New York city, New York	21.4	73	56	Orlando city, Florida	9.7	67	58	Henderson city, Nevada	33.8
19	59	Denver city, Colorado	21.1	59	59	Riverside city, California	9.6	19	59	Denver city, Colorado	32.6
29	59	Baltimore city, Maryland	21.1	4	60	Houston city, Texas	9.5	61	60	Lexington-Fayette urban county, Kentucky	31.9
61	59	Lexington-Fayette urban county, Kentucky	21.1	31	61	Milwaukee city, Wisconsin	9.3	17	61	Charlotte city, North Carolina	31.3
45	62	Oakland city, California	21.0	9	62	Dallas city, Texas	9.1	39	61	Atlanta city, Georgia	31.3
46	63	New Orleans city, Louisiana	20.8	64	62	St. Paul city, Minnesota	9.1	65	63	Anchorage municipality, Alaska	30.8
60	64	St. Louis city, Missouri	20.6	6	64	Phoenix city, Arizona	9.0	72	64	Lincoln city, Nebraska	29.8
75	65	Jersey City city, New Jersey	20.5	15	65	Columbus city, Ohio	8.9	22	65	Washington city, District of Columbia	29.7
46	66	Minneapolis city, Minnesota	20.3	17	65	Charlotte city, North Carolina	8.9	11	66	Austin city, Texas	29.5
44	67	Miami city, Florida	18.7	42	67	Raleigh city, North Carolina	8.8	41	67	Virginia Beach city, Virginia	29.3
26	68	Portland city, Oregon	18.6	50	67	Arlington city, Texas	8.8	8	68	San Diego city, California	29.0
39	69	Atlanta city, Georgia	18.5	52	67	Bakersfield city, California	8.8	46	69	Minneapolis city, Minnesota	28.1
55	70	Urban Honolulu CDP, Hawaii	17.8	16	67	Fort Worth city, Texas	8.5	40	70	Colorado Springs city, Colorado	27.8
22	71	Washington city, District of Columbia	17.0	70	70	Newark city, New Jersey	8.5	13	71	San Francisco city, California	26.4
23	72	Boston city, Massachusetts	16.7	46	72	Minneapolis city, Minnesota	8.4	26	72	Portland city, Oregon	26.1
63	73	Pittsburgh city, Pennsylvania	16.1	65	73	Anchorage municipality, Alaska	8.2	42	73	Raleigh city, North Carolina	25.4
18	74	Seattle city, Washington	15.8	11	74	Austin city, Texas	7.3	69	74	Plano city, Texas	19.7
13	75	San Francisco city, California	13.4	57	75	Santa Ana city, California	7.2	18	75	Seattle city, Washington	18.1

75 Largest Cities by 2015 Population
Selected rankings

\<-- Percent college graduates (bachelor's degree or more), 2010–2014 --\>				\<-- Percent female-headed family households, 2010–2014 --\>				\<-- Percent of households composed of one person, 2010–2014 --\>			
Population rank	Percent college graduate rank	City	Percent college graduates [col 41]	Population rank	Female households rank	City	Percent female households [col 29]	Population rank	One-person household rank	City	Percent one-person households [col 30]
18	1	Seattle city, Washington	57.9	70	1	Newark city, New Jersey	29.1	39	1	Atlanta city, Georgia	46.4
69	2	Plano city, Texas	54.6	21	2	Detroit city, Michigan	29.0	22	2	Washington city, District of Columbia	45.1
22	3	Washington city, District of Columbia	53.4	24	3	Memphis city, Tennessee	24.2	60	3	St. Louis city, Missouri	44.2
13	4	San Francisco city, California	52.9	51	4	Cleveland city, Ohio	24.1	66	4	Cincinnati city, Ohio	43.7
42	5	Raleigh city, North Carolina	47.6	29	5	Baltimore city, Maryland	22.9	51	5	Cleveland city, Ohio	41.6
39	6	Atlanta city, Georgia	47.1	31	6	Milwaukee city, Wisconsin	22.2	63	6	Pittsburgh city, Pennsylvania	41.2
46	7	Minneapolis city, Minnesota	47.0	62	7	Stockton city, California	20.9	18	7	Seattle city, Washington	41.1
11	8	Austin city, Texas	46.0	5	8	Philadelphia city, Pennsylvania	20.6	46	8	Minneapolis city, Minnesota	40.3
23	9	Boston city, Massachusetts	44.6	20	9	El Paso city, Texas	19.8	49	9	New Orleans city, Louisiana	40.2
26	10	Portland city, Oregon	44.4	34	10	Fresno city, California	19.7	19	10	Denver city, Colorado	40.1
19	11	Denver city, Colorado	43.7	49	11	New Orleans city, Louisiana	19.6	5	11	Philadelphia city, Pennsylvania	39.5
75	12	Jersey City city, New Jersey	42.5	71	12	Toledo city, Ohio	19.3	29	12	Baltimore city, Maryland	39.0
8	13	San Diego city, California	42.3	66	13	Cincinnati city, Ohio	19.0	13	13	San Francisco city, California	38.2
17	14	Charlotte city, North Carolina	40.7	57	14	Santa Ana city, California	18.7	21	14	Detroit city, Michigan	38.1
61	15	Lexington-Fayette urban county, Kentucky	40.2	1	15	New York city, New York	18.5	23	15	Boston city, Massachusetts	37.4
45	16	Oakland city, California	38.6	60	16	St. Louis city, Missouri	18.1	73	16	Orlando city, Florida	36.8
64	16	St. Paul city, Minnesota	38.6	7	17	San Antonio city, Texas	17.7	36	17	Kansas City city, Missouri	36.7
10	18	San Jose city, California	38.2	44	17	Miami city, Florida	17.7	44	18	Miami city, Florida	36.5
63	19	Pittsburgh city, Pennsylvania	37.2	58	17	Corpus Christi city, Texas	17.7	53	18	Tampa city, Florida	36.5
25	20	Nashville-Davidson metro gov, Tennessee	36.5	75	20	Jersey City city, New Jersey	17.6	71	20	Toledo city, Ohio	36.4
40	21	Colorado Springs city, Colorado	36.3	3	21	Chicago city, Illinois	17.1	3	21	Chicago city, Illinois	36.2
68	21	Greensboro city, North Carolina	36.3	73	22	Orlando city, Florida	17.0	15	22	Columbus city, Ohio	35.8
72	23	Lincoln city, Nebraska	36.2	14	23	Indianapolis city, Indiana	16.9	33	23	Tucson city, Arizona	35.5
55	24	Urban Honolulu CDP, Hawaii	35.2	23	23	Boston city, Massachusetts	16.9	25	24	Nashville-Davidson metro gov, Tennessee	35.4
1	25	New York city, New York	35.0	52	23	Bakersfield city, California	16.9	64	25	St. Paul city, Minnesota	35.3
3	26	Chicago city, Illinois	34.9	37	26	Long Beach city, California	16.7	45	26	Oakland city, California	35.1
49	27	New Orleans city, Louisiana	34.4	68	27	Greensboro city, North Carolina	16.6	47	26	Tulsa city, Oklahoma	35.1
43	28	Omaha city, Nebraska	33.8	4	28	Houston city, Texas	16.3	31	28	Milwaukee city, Wisconsin	35.0
53	29	Tampa city, Florida	33.7	9	28	Dallas city, Texas	16.3	24	29	Memphis city, Tennessee	34.5
41	30	Virginia Beach city, Virginia	33.5	12	30	Jacksonville city, Florida	16.2	26	29	Portland city, Oregon	34.5
15	31	Columbus city, Ohio	33.4	15	31	Columbus city, Ohio	16.1	68	29	Greensboro city, North Carolina	34.5
73	31	Orlando city, Florida	33.4	16	31	Fort Worth city, Texas	16.1	9	32	Dallas city, Texas	34.4
32	33	Albuquerque city, New Mexico	33.2	53	33	Tampa city, Florida	16.0	14	33	Indianapolis city, Indiana	34.1
65	34	Anchorage municipality, Alaska	32.9	17	34	Charlotte city, North Carolina	15.8	11	34	Austin city, Texas	34.0
66	35	Cincinnati city, Ohio	32.3	36	35	Kansas City city, Missouri	15.6	42	35	Raleigh city, North Carolina	33.9
36	36	Kansas City city, Missouri	31.6	74	35	Chula Vista city, California	15.6	55	36	Urban Honolulu CDP, Hawaii	33.3
2	37	Los Angeles city, California	31.5	22	37	Washington city, District of Columbia	15.5	30	37	Louisville/Jefferson County metro gov, Kentucky	33.0
30	38	Louisville/Jefferson County metro gov, Kentucky	30.8	35	37	Sacramento city, California	15.5	43	37	Omaha city, Nebraska	33.0
67	39	Henderson city, Nevada	30.7	50	37	Arlington city, Texas	15.5	32	39	Albuquerque city, New Mexico	32.7
60	40	St. Louis city, Missouri	30.4	56	37	Anaheim city, California	15.5	61	40	Lexington-Fayette urban county, Kentucky	32.6
47	41	Tulsa city, Oklahoma	30.1	2	41	Los Angeles city, California	15.4	1	41	New York city, New York	32.5
4	42	Houston city, Texas	29.8	6	41	Phoenix city, Arizona	15.4	48	41	Wichita city, Kansas	32.5
9	43	Dallas city, Texas	29.7	33	41	Tucson city, Arizona	15.4	35	43	Sacramento city, California	32.3
35	44	Sacramento city, California	29.3	39	41	Atlanta city, Georgia	15.4	4	44	Houston city, Texas	32.2
37	45	Long Beach city, California	29.0	47	41	Tulsa city, Oklahoma	15.4	17	45	Charlotte city, North Carolina	31.2
50	46	Arlington city, Texas	28.9	45	46	Oakland city, California	15.3	12	46	Jacksonville city, Florida	30.8
48	47	Wichita city, Kansas	28.8	28	47	Las Vegas city, Nevada	15.1	27	47	Oklahoma City city, Oklahoma	30.7
27	48	Oklahoma City city, Oklahoma	28.5	54	47	Aurora city, Colorado	15.1	72	47	Lincoln city, Nebraska	30.7
14	49	Indianapolis city, Indiana	27.7	59	47	Riverside city, California	15.1	37	49	Long Beach city, California	30.4
29	49	Baltimore city, Maryland	27.7	30	50	Louisville/Jefferson County metro gov, Kentucky	14.7	2	50	Los Angeles city, California	30.1
74	51	Chula Vista city, California	27.4	25	51	Nashville-Davidson metro gov, Tennessee	14.6	70	50	Newark city, New Jersey	30.1
54	52	Aurora city, Colorado	27.1	64	51	St. Paul city, Minnesota	14.6	40	52	Colorado Springs city, Colorado	29.4
16	53	Fort Worth city, Texas	26.7	32	53	Albuquerque city, New Mexico	14.4	75	53	Jersey City city, New Jersey	29.3
6	54	Phoenix city, Arizona	26.5	63	54	Pittsburgh city, Pennsylvania	14.3	6	54	Phoenix city, Arizona	28.7
12	55	Jacksonville city, Florida	25.5	42	55	Raleigh city, North Carolina	14.0	8	55	San Diego city, California	28.6
33	56	Tucson city, Arizona	25.0	41	56	Virginia Beach city, Virginia	13.9	7	56	San Antonio city, Texas	28.3
7	57	San Antonio city, Texas	24.9	43	57	Omaha city, Nebraska	13.7	28	56	Las Vegas city, Nevada	28.3
56	58	Anaheim city, California	24.8	27	58	Oklahoma City city, Oklahoma	13.4	38	58	Mesa city, Arizona	27.8
24	59	Memphis city, Tennessee	24.7	48	59	Wichita city, Kansas	12.9	54	59	Aurora city, Colorado	27.7
5	60	Philadelphia city, Pennsylvania	24.5	38	60	Mesa city, Arizona	12.5	16	60	Fort Worth city, Texas	27.2
38	61	Mesa city, Arizona	24.3	10	61	San Jose city, California	12.4	67	61	Henderson city, Nevada	26.1
44	62	Miami city, Florida	23.5	61	61	Lexington-Fayette urban county, Kentucky	12.4	50	62	Arlington city, Texas	26.0
31	63	Milwaukee city, Wisconsin	22.8	40	63	Colorado Springs city, Colorado	12.0	58	63	Corpus Christi city, Texas	25.0
20	64	El Paso city, Texas	22.7	65	63	Anchorage municipality, Alaska	12.0	65	63	Anchorage municipality, Alaska	25.0
59	65	Riverside city, California	22.1	8	65	San Diego city, California	11.8	69	65	Plano city, Texas	24.4
28	66	Las Vegas city, Nevada	21.6	11	65	Austin city, Texas	11.8	41	66	Virginia Beach city, Virginia	23.9
58	67	Corpus Christi city, Texas	21.2	55	65	Urban Honolulu CDP, Hawaii	11.8	20	67	El Paso city, Texas	23.1
52	68	Bakersfield city, California	20.7	46	68	Minneapolis city, Minnesota	11.4	34	68	Fresno city, California	22.9
34	69	Fresno city, California	20.1	67	68	Henderson city, Nevada	11.4	62	69	Stockton city, California	21.3
71	70	Toledo city, Ohio	17.7	19	70	Denver city, Colorado	10.4	59	70	Riverside city, California	21.1
62	71	Stockton city, California	17.4	72	70	Lincoln city, Nebraska	10.4	10	71	San Jose city, California	19.7
51	72	Cleveland city, Ohio	15.2	69	72	Plano city, Texas	10.1	52	72	Bakersfield city, California	19.5
70	73	Newark city, New Jersey	13.3	26	73	Portland city, Oregon	9.9	74	73	Chula Vista city, California	18.8
21	74	Detroit city, Michigan	13.1	13	74	San Francisco city, California	8.6	56	74	Anaheim city, California	17.9
57	75	Santa Ana city, California	11.8	18	75	Seattle city, Washington	6.9	57	75	Santa Ana city, California	13.3

75 Largest Cities by 2015 Population
Selected rankings

Median household income, 2010–2014				Median value of owner-occupied housing units, 2010–2014				Median gross rent of renter-occupied housing units, 2010–2014			
Population rank	Median income rank	City	Median income (dollars) [col 43]	Population rank	Median value rank	City	Median value (dollars) [col 52]	Population rank	Median rent rank	City	Median rent (dollars) [col 56]
10	1	San Jose city, California	83 787	13	1	San Francisco city, California	765 700	13	1	San Francisco city, California	1 533
69	2	Plano city, Texas	82 944	10	2	San Jose city, California	579 500	10	2	San Jose city, California	1 528
13	3	San Francisco city, California	78 378	55	3	Urban Honolulu CDP, Hawaii	565 000	56	3	Anaheim city, California	1 362
65	4	Anchorage municipality, Alaska	78 121	1	4	New York city, New York	490 700	8	4	San Diego city, California	1 359
22	5	Washington city, District of Columbia	69 235	22	5	Washington city, District of Columbia	454 500	57	5	Santa Ana city, California	1 307
18	6	Seattle city, Washington	67 365	2	6	Los Angeles city, California	453 800	22	6	Washington city, District of Columbia	1 302
41	7	Virginia Beach city, Virginia	67 001	8	7	San Diego city, California	448 000	74	6	Chula Vista city, California	1 302
74	8	Chula Vista city, California	66 110	18	8	Seattle city, Washington	437 400	23	8	Boston city, Massachusetts	1 298
8	9	San Diego city, California	65 753	45	9	Oakland city, California	435 000	55	9	Urban Honolulu CDP, Hawaii	1 297
67	10	Henderson city, Nevada	63 830	37	10	Long Beach city, California	419 400	41	10	Virginia Beach city, Virginia	1 239
55	11	Urban Honolulu CDP, Hawaii	60 548	56	11	Anaheim city, California	413 800	1	11	New York city, New York	1 234
56	12	Anaheim city, California	59 707	23	12	Boston city, Massachusetts	379 500	2	12	Los Angeles city, California	1 194
75	13	Jersey City city, New Jersey	58 907	74	13	Chula Vista city, California	359 500	75	13	Jersey City city, New Jersey	1 187
52	14	Bakersfield city, California	56 842	57	14	Santa Ana city, California	343 000	65	14	Anchorage municipality, Alaska	1 172
59	15	Riverside city, California	56 089	75	15	Jersey City city, New Jersey	323 800	59	15	Riverside city, California	1 158
11	16	Austin city, Texas	55 216	65	16	Anchorage municipality, Alaska	286 600	67	16	Henderson city, Nevada	1 155
42	17	Raleigh city, North Carolina	54 581	26	17	Portland city, Oregon	285 300	18	17	Seattle city, Washington	1 131
23	18	Boston city, Massachusetts	54 485	41	18	Virginia Beach city, Virginia	263 200	37	18	Long Beach city, California	1 118
40	19	Colorado Springs city, Colorado	54 228	19	19	Denver city, Colorado	257 500	69	19	Plano city, Texas	1 115
17	20	Charlotte city, North Carolina	53 274	59	20	Riverside city, California	242 100	45	20	Oakland city, California	1 114
26	21	Portland city, Oregon	53 230	70	21	Newark city, New Jersey	229 600	11	21	Austin city, Texas	1 012
50	22	Arlington city, Texas	53 055	35	22	Sacramento city, California	228 400	35	22	Sacramento city, California	1 008
45	23	Oakland city, California	52 962	11	23	Austin city, Texas	227 800	73	23	Orlando city, Florida	999
37	24	Long Beach city, California	52 944	3	24	Chicago city, Illinois	225 700	52	24	Bakersfield city, California	985
1	25	New York city, New York	52 737	69	25	Plano city, Texas	222 800	28	25	Las Vegas city, Nevada	983
57	26	Santa Ana city, California	52 519	44	26	Miami city, Florida	211 400	54	25	Aurora city, Colorado	983
16	27	Fort Worth city, Texas	52 492	40	27	Colorado Springs city, Colorado	208 600	70	27	Newark city, New Jersey	978
54	28	Aurora city, Colorado	52 275	67	28	Henderson city, Nevada	207 500	39	28	Atlanta city, Georgia	969
19	29	Denver city, Colorado	51 800	42	29	Raleigh city, North Carolina	205 200	3	29	Chicago city, Illinois	963
28	30	Las Vegas city, Nevada	50 903	46	29	Minneapolis city, Minnesota	205 200	44	30	Miami city, Florida	958
46	31	Minneapolis city, Minnesota	50 767	39	31	Atlanta city, Georgia	205 000	62	30	Stockton city, California	958
35	32	Sacramento city, California	50 013	32	32	Albuquerque city, New Mexico	185 100	53	32	Tampa city, Florida	956
72	33	Lincoln city, Nebraska	49 794	52	33	Bakersfield city, California	184 800	26	33	Portland city, Oregon	945
2	34	Los Angeles city, California	49 682	49	34	New Orleans city, Louisiana	184 100	29	34	Baltimore city, Maryland	944
58	35	Corpus Christi city, Texas	49 675	54	35	Aurora city, Colorado	179 300	12	35	Jacksonville city, Florida	932
43	36	Omaha city, Nebraska	48 751	34	36	Fresno city, California	175 600	49	36	New Orleans city, Louisiana	927
61	37	Lexington-Fayette urban county, Kentucky	48 667	64	37	St. Paul city, Minnesota	175 000	5	37	Philadelphia city, Pennsylvania	915
38	38	Mesa city, Arizona	48 259	17	38	Charlotte city, North Carolina	170 200	42	38	Raleigh city, North Carolina	914
64	39	St. Paul city, Minnesota	48 258	25	39	Nashville-Davidson metro gov, Tennessee	167 400	19	39	Denver city, Colorado	913
3	40	Chicago city, Illinois	47 831	62	40	Stockton city, California	166 800	17	40	Charlotte city, North Carolina	902
30	41	Louisville/Jefferson County metro gov, Kentucky	47 692	61	41	Lexington-Fayette urban county, Kentucky	166 000	34	41	Fresno city, California	890
25	42	Nashville-Davidson metro gov, Tennessee	47 434	28	42	Las Vegas city, Nevada	161 600	40	42	Colorado Springs city, Colorado	888
32	43	Albuquerque city, New Mexico	47 413	73	43	Orlando city, Florida	158 600	16	43	Fort Worth city, Texas	878
27	44	Oklahoma City city, Oklahoma	47 004	53	44	Tampa city, Florida	157 500	6	44	Phoenix city, Arizona	876
6	45	Phoenix city, Arizona	46 881	6	45	Phoenix city, Arizona	155 900	38	45	Mesa city, Arizona	875
12	46	Jacksonville city, Florida	46 768	29	46	Baltimore city, Maryland	155 000	58	46	Corpus Christi city, Texas	872
39	47	Atlanta city, Georgia	46 439	38	47	Mesa city, Arizona	150 800	4	47	Houston city, Texas	862
7	48	San Antonio city, Texas	46 317	30	48	Louisville/Jefferson County metro gov, Kentucky	149 900	50	48	Arlington city, Texas	861
48	49	Wichita city, Kansas	45 907	68	49	Greensboro city, North Carolina	147 500	25	49	Nashville-Davidson metro gov, Tennessee	859
4	50	Houston city, Texas	45 728	72	50	Lincoln city, Nebraska	144 900	46	50	Minneapolis city, Minnesota	854
36	51	Kansas City city, Missouri	45 376	5	51	Philadelphia city, Pennsylvania	143 200	9	51	Dallas city, Texas	852
62	52	Stockton city, California	45 347	12	52	Jacksonville city, Florida	138 500	7	52	San Antonio city, Texas	840
15	53	Columbus city, Ohio	44 774	27	53	Oklahoma City city, Oklahoma	135 200	24	53	Memphis city, Tennessee	831
53	54	Tampa city, Florida	43 740	43	54	Omaha city, Nebraska	134 700	64	54	St. Paul city, Minnesota	823
9	55	Dallas city, Texas	43 359	36	55	Kansas City city, Missouri	133 600	15	55	Columbus city, Ohio	822
14	56	Indianapolis city, Indiana	42 169	33	56	Tucson city, Arizona	133 500	32	56	Albuquerque city, New Mexico	798
20	57	El Paso city, Texas	42 037	9	57	Dallas city, Texas	130 900	43	57	Omaha city, Nebraska	797
47	58	Tulsa city, Oklahoma	41 957	50	58	Arlington city, Texas	129 800	36	58	Kansas City city, Missouri	796
73	59	Orlando city, Florida	41 901	15	59	Columbus city, Ohio	128 900	63	59	Pittsburgh city, Pennsylvania	794
29	60	Baltimore city, Maryland	41 819	4	60	Houston city, Texas	125 400	14	60	Indianapolis city, Indiana	784
68	61	Greensboro city, North Carolina	41 518	47	61	Tulsa city, Oklahoma	123 100	31	60	Milwaukee city, Wisconsin	784
34	62	Fresno city, California	41 455	16	62	Fort Worth city, Texas	122 100	61	62	Lexington-Fayette urban county, Kentucky	766
63	63	Pittsburgh city, Pennsylvania	40 009	66	63	Cincinnati city, Ohio	121 900	27	63	Oklahoma City city, Oklahoma	763
5	64	Philadelphia city, Pennsylvania	37 460	31	64	Milwaukee city, Wisconsin	121 600	21	64	Detroit city, Michigan	756
33	65	Tucson city, Arizona	37 149	60	65	St. Louis city, Missouri	118 600	68	65	Greensboro city, North Carolina	751
24	66	Memphis city, Tennessee	37 099	48	66	Wichita city, Kansas	118 400	33	66	Tucson city, Arizona	750
49	67	New Orleans city, Louisiana	36 964	20	67	El Paso city, Texas	117 800	20	67	El Paso city, Texas	747
31	68	Milwaukee city, Wisconsin	35 489	14	68	Indianapolis city, Indiana	117 600	60	68	St. Louis city, Missouri	742
60	69	St. Louis city, Missouri	34 800	7	69	San Antonio city, Texas	114 600	47	69	Tulsa city, Oklahoma	738
70	70	Newark city, New Jersey	34 012	58	70	Corpus Christi city, Texas	113 700	30	70	Louisville/Jefferson County metro gov, Kentucky	734
66	71	Cincinnati city, Ohio	34 002	24	71	Memphis city, Tennessee	95 400	72	71	Lincoln city, Nebraska	727
71	72	Toledo city, Ohio	33 485	63	72	Pittsburgh city, Pennsylvania	91 500	48	72	Wichita city, Kansas	708
44	73	Miami city, Florida	30 858	71	73	Toledo city, Ohio	80 600	51	73	Cleveland city, Ohio	661
51	74	Cleveland city, Ohio	26 179	51	74	Cleveland city, Ohio	73 100	66	74	Cincinnati city, Ohio	653
21	75	Detroit city, Michigan	26 095	21	75	Detroit city, Michigan	45 100	71	75	Toledo city, Ohio	638

75 Largest Cities by 2015 Population
Selected rankings

Percent of population below the poverty level, 2010–2014

Population rank	Poverty rate rank	City	Poverty rate [col 46]
21	1	Detroit city, Michigan	34.8
51	2	Cleveland city, Ohio	31.1
70	3	Newark city, New Jersey	26.9
31	4	Milwaukee city, Wisconsin	25.3
66	5	Cincinnati city, Ohio	25.1
44	6	Miami city, Florida	25.0
34	7	Fresno city, California	24.9
49	8	New Orleans city, Louisiana	22.7
71	8	Toledo city, Ohio	22.7
24	10	Memphis city, Tennessee	22.6
60	11	St. Louis city, Missouri	22.0
62	12	Stockton city, California	21.4
5	13	Philadelphia city, Pennsylvania	21.2
9	14	Dallas city, Texas	20.6
39	15	Atlanta city, Georgia	19.9
4	16	Houston city, Texas	19.6
29	17	Baltimore city, Maryland	19.5
57	17	Santa Ana city, California	19.5
3	19	Chicago city, Illinois	18.7
33	20	Tucson city, Arizona	18.6
6	21	Phoenix city, Arizona	18.5
20	21	El Paso city, Texas	18.5
2	23	Los Angeles city, California	18.2
35	24	Sacramento city, California	17.7
1	25	New York city, New York	17.5
64	25	St. Paul city, Minnesota	17.5
15	27	Columbus city, Ohio	17.4
23	28	Boston city, Massachusetts	17.1
53	29	Tampa city, Florida	17.0
14	30	Indianapolis city, Indiana	16.9
45	31	Oakland city, California	16.8
37	32	Long Beach city, California	16.5
52	32	Bakersfield city, California	16.5
63	34	Pittsburgh city, Pennsylvania	16.2
75	34	Jersey City city, New Jersey	16.2
46	36	Minneapolis city, Minnesota	16.1
47	36	Tulsa city, Oklahoma	16.1
7	38	San Antonio city, Texas	16.0
73	39	Orlando city, Florida	15.6
16	40	Fort Worth city, Texas	15.2
32	41	Albuquerque city, New Mexico	14.8
36	41	Kansas City city, Missouri	14.8
68	43	Greensboro city, North Carolina	14.6
59	44	Riverside city, California	14.4
22	45	Washington city, District of Columbia	14.3
25	46	Nashville-Davidson metro gov, Tennessee	14.2
27	47	Oklahoma City city, Oklahoma	14.1
56	48	Anaheim city, California	14.0
12	49	Jacksonville city, Florida	13.7
17	49	Charlotte city, North Carolina	13.7
19	49	Denver city, Colorado	13.7
58	49	Corpus Christi city, Texas	13.7
50	53	Arlington city, Texas	13.5
11	54	Austin city, Texas	13.3
28	55	Las Vegas city, Nevada	13.2
48	56	Wichita city, Kansas	13.0
38	57	Mesa city, Arizona	12.5
30	58	Louisville/Jefferson County metro gov, Kentucky	12.3
54	58	Aurora city, Colorado	12.3
43	60	Omaha city, Nebraska	12.2
61	60	Lexington-Fayette urban county, Kentucky	12.2
26	62	Portland city, Oregon	12.1
42	63	Raleigh city, North Carolina	11.8
8	64	San Diego city, California	11.2
72	65	Lincoln city, Nebraska	10.3
74	66	Chula Vista city, California	10.1
40	67	Colorado Springs city, Colorado	9.9
10	68	San Jose city, California	8.3
13	69	San Francisco city, California	7.8
55	70	Urban Honolulu CDP, Hawaii	7.7
18	71	Seattle city, Washington	7.6
67	72	Henderson city, Nevada	7.2
41	73	Virginia Beach city, Virginia	6.6
65	74	Anchorage municipality, Alaska	5.6
69	75	Plano city, Texas	5.4

Unemployment rate, 2014

Population rank	Unemployment rate rank	City	Unemployment rate [col 64]
21	1	Detroit city, Michigan	12.4
34	2	Fresno city, California	11.1
62	3	Stockton city, California	9.6
52	4	Bakersfield city, California	9.1
70	5	Newark city, New Jersey	8.8
29	6	Baltimore city, Maryland	7.7
37	7	Long Beach city, California	7.4
24	8	Memphis city, Tennessee	7.3
2	9	Los Angeles city, California	7.1
28	10	Las Vegas city, Nevada	7.0
5	11	Philadelphia city, Pennsylvania	6.9
22	11	Washington city, District of Columbia	6.9
31	13	Milwaukee city, Wisconsin	6.7
67	13	Henderson city, Nevada	6.7
49	15	New Orleans city, Louisiana	6.5
74	15	Chula Vista city, California	6.5
3	17	Chicago city, Illinois	6.4
35	17	Sacramento city, California	6.4
59	17	Riverside city, California	6.4
39	20	Atlanta city, Georgia	6.3
51	20	Cleveland city, Ohio	6.3
44	22	Miami city, Florida	6.1
60	22	St. Louis city, Missouri	6.1
33	24	Tucson city, Arizona	5.9
45	24	Oakland city, California	5.9
71	26	Toledo city, Ohio	5.8
1	27	New York city, New York	5.7
32	27	Albuquerque city, New Mexico	5.7
56	27	Anaheim city, California	5.7
68	27	Greensboro city, North Carolina	5.7
12	31	Jacksonville city, Florida	5.6
36	32	Kansas City city, Missouri	5.5
6	33	Phoenix city, Arizona	5.4
75	34	Jersey City city, New Jersey	5.3
38	35	Mesa city, Arizona	5.2
53	35	Tampa city, Florida	5.2
57	35	Santa Ana city, California	5.2
63	38	Pittsburgh city, Pennsylvania	5.1
14	39	Indianapolis city, Indiana	5.0
48	39	Wichita city, Kansas	5.0
65	39	Anchorage municipality, Alaska	5.0
66	39	Cincinnati city, Ohio	5.0
8	43	San Diego city, California	4.9
17	43	Charlotte city, North Carolina	4.9
30	43	Louisville/Jefferson County metro gov, Kentucky	4.9
20	46	El Paso city, Texas	4.8
26	46	Portland city, Oregon	4.8
58	48	Corpus Christi city, Texas	4.7
10	49	San Jose city, California	4.6
23	49	Boston city, Massachusetts	4.6
42	49	Raleigh city, North Carolina	4.6
73	49	Orlando city, Florida	4.6
25	53	Nashville-Davidson metro gov, Tennessee	4.5
40	53	Colorado Springs city, Colorado	4.5
4	55	Houston city, Texas	4.3
41	55	Virginia Beach city, Virginia	4.3
16	57	Fort Worth city, Texas	4.2
54	57	Aurora city, Colorado	4.2
9	59	Dallas city, Texas	4.1
15	59	Columbus city, Ohio	4.1
18	59	Seattle city, Washington	4.1
50	62	Arlington city, Texas	4.0
47	63	Tulsa city, Oklahoma	3.9
61	63	Lexington-Fayette urban county, Kentucky	3.9
7	65	San Antonio city, Texas	3.7
19	65	Denver city, Colorado	3.7
64	65	St. Paul city, Minnesota	3.7
69	65	Plano city, Texas	3.7
13	69	San Francisco city, California	3.6
27	70	Oklahoma City city, Oklahoma	3.5
46	71	Minneapolis city, Minnesota	3.3
43	72	Omaha city, Nebraska	3.1
11	73	Austin city, Texas	3.0
72	74	Lincoln city, Nebraska	2.5
55	75	Urban Honolulu CDP, Hawaii	NA

Percent change in civilian labor force, 2013–2014

Population rank	Percent change rank	City	Percent change [col 62]
42	1	Raleigh city, North Carolina	3.4
17	2	Charlotte city, North Carolina	3.2
13	3	San Francisco city, California	3.1
22	4	Washington city, District of Columbia	2.7
36	5	Kansas City city, Missouri	2.6
27	6	Oklahoma City city, Oklahoma	2.5
38	6	Mesa city, Arizona	2.5
6	8	Phoenix city, Arizona	2.4
10	9	San Jose city, California	2.2
11	9	Austin city, Texas	2.2
28	9	Las Vegas city, Nevada	2.2
67	12	Henderson city, Nevada	2.1
69	12	Plano city, Texas	2.1
47	14	Tulsa city, Oklahoma	2.0
9	15	Dallas city, Texas	1.9
25	15	Nashville-Davidson metro gov, Tennessee	1.9
26	15	Portland city, Oregon	1.9
59	15	Riverside city, California	1.9
60	19	St. Louis city, Missouri	1.6
68	19	Greensboro city, North Carolina	1.6
18	21	Seattle city, Washington	1.5
73	21	Orlando city, Florida	1.5
1	23	New York city, New York	1.3
14	24	Indianapolis city, Indiana	1.2
45	24	Oakland city, California	1.2
7	26	San Antonio city, Texas	1.0
8	26	San Diego city, California	1.0
12	26	Jacksonville city, Florida	1.0
15	26	Columbus city, Ohio	1.0
57	26	Santa Ana city, California	1.0
56	31	Anaheim city, California	0.9
5	32	Philadelphia city, Pennsylvania	0.8
35	32	Sacramento city, California	0.8
53	32	Tampa city, Florida	0.8
62	32	Stockton city, California	0.8
64	32	St. Paul city, Minnesota	0.8
75	32	Jersey City city, New Jersey	0.8
19	38	Denver city, Colorado	0.7
23	38	Boston city, Massachusetts	0.7
39	38	Atlanta city, Georgia	0.7
46	38	Minneapolis city, Minnesota	0.7
34	42	Fresno city, California	0.6
49	42	New Orleans city, Louisiana	0.6
74	42	Chula Vista city, California	0.6
44	45	Miami city, Florida	0.5
29	46	Baltimore city, Maryland	0.4
54	46	Aurora city, Colorado	0.4
4	48	Houston city, Texas	0.3
16	48	Fort Worth city, Texas	0.3
33	48	Tucson city, Arizona	0.3
43	48	Omaha city, Nebraska	0.3
48	48	Wichita city, Kansas	0.3
63	53	Pittsburgh city, Pennsylvania	0.2
66	53	Cincinnati city, Ohio	0.2
50	55	Arlington city, Texas	0.1
71	55	Toledo city, Ohio	0.1
40	57	Colorado Springs city, Colorado	0.0
55	57	Urban Honolulu CDP, Hawaii	0.0
3	59	Chicago city, Illinois	-0.1
32	59	Albuquerque city, New Mexico	-0.1
65	59	Anchorage municipality, Alaska	-0.1
72	59	Lincoln city, Nebraska	-0.1
20	63	El Paso city, Texas	-0.2
52	63	Bakersfield city, California	-0.2
2	65	Los Angeles city, California	-0.4
37	65	Long Beach city, California	-0.4
24	67	Memphis city, Tennessee	-0.5
70	67	Newark city, New Jersey	-0.5
31	69	Milwaukee city, Wisconsin	-0.6
58	70	Corpus Christi city, Texas	-0.8
41	71	Virginia Beach city, Virginia	-0.9
51	72	Cleveland city, Ohio	-1.3
61	73	Lexington-Fayette urban county, Kentucky	-1.7
30	74	Louisville/Jefferson County metro gov, Kentucky	-1.9
21	75	Detroit city, Michigan	-3.3

75 Largest Cities by 2015 Population
Selected rankings

		Per capita local government taxes, 2012				Per capita city government debt outstanding, 2012				Violent crime rate, 2014 (violent crimes known to police)	
Population rank	Local taxes rank	City	Local per capita taxes (dollars) [col 121]	Population rank	Debt rank	City	Debt per capita (dollars) [col 138]	Population rank	Violent crime rate rank	City	Violent crimes (per 100,000) population) [col 37]
22	1	Washington city, District of Columbia	9 344	22	1	Washington city, District of Columbia	17 761	21	1	Detroit city, Michigan	1 990
1	2	New York city, New York	5 077	39	2	Atlanta city, Georgia	16 770	24	2	Memphis city, Tennessee	1 744
13	3	San Francisco city, California	3 430	13	3	San Francisco city, California	15 759	45	3	Oakland city, California	1 685
23	4	Boston city, Massachusetts	2 844	1	4	New York city, New York	15 714	60	4	St. Louis city, Missouri	1 679
5	5	Philadelphia city, Pennsylvania	2 089	12	5	Jacksonville city, Florida	12 465	31	5	Milwaukee city, Wisconsin	1 485
29	6	Baltimore city, Maryland	1 989	21	6	Detroit city, Michigan	11 720	29	6	Baltimore city, Maryland	1 339
25	7	Nashville-Davidson metro gov, Tennessee	1 952	19	7	Denver city, Colorado	11 106	51	6	Cleveland city, Ohio	1 339
65	8	Anchorage municipality, Alaska	1 830	48	8	Wichita city, Kansas	9 003	62	8	Stockton city, California	1 331
41	9	Virginia Beach city, Virginia	1 817	46	9	Minneapolis city, Minnesota	8 754	36	9	Kansas City city, Missouri	1 258
19	10	Denver city, Colorado	1 748	25	10	Nashville-Davidson metro gov, Tennessee	7 828	14	10	Indianapolis city, Indiana	1 255
60	11	St. Louis city, Missouri	1 706	3	11	Chicago city, Illinois	7 811	39	11	Atlanta city, Georgia	1 227
36	12	Kansas City city, Missouri	1 599	14	12	Indianapolis city, Indiana	7 191	22	12	Washington city, District of Columbia	1 185
18	13	Seattle city, Washington	1 438	18	13	Seattle city, Washington	6 556	25	13	Nashville-Davidson metro gov, Tennessee	1 125
45	14	Oakland city, California	1 420	51	14	Cleveland city, Ohio	6 465	71	14	Toledo city, Ohio	1 091
66	15	Cincinnati city, Ohio	1 400	4	15	Houston city, Texas	6 459	70	15	Newark city, New Jersey	1 078
49	16	New Orleans city, Louisiana	1 349	11	16	Austin city, Texas	6 438	44	16	Miami city, Florida	1 060
39	17	Atlanta city, Georgia	1 173	9	17	Dallas city, Texas	6 389	5	17	Philadelphia city, Pennsylvania	1 021
46	18	Minneapolis city, Minnesota	1 170	7	18	San Antonio city, Texas	6 374	46	18	Minneapolis city, Minnesota	1 012
63	19	Pittsburgh city, Pennsylvania	1 166	36	19	Kansas City city, Missouri	6 347	4	19	Houston city, Texas	991
12	20	Jacksonville city, Florida	1 104	40	20	Colorado Springs city, Colorado	6 097	49	20	New Orleans city, Louisiana	974
70	21	Newark city, New Jersey	1 099	59	21	Riverside city, California	6 092	66	21	Cincinnati city, Ohio	913
21	22	Detroit city, Michigan	1 078	10	22	San Jose city, California	6 013	73	22	Orlando city, Florida	901
51	23	Cleveland city, Ohio	1 071	65	23	Anchorage municipality, Alaska	5 991	3	23	Chicago city, Illinois	886
14	24	Indianapolis city, Indiana	1 064	2	24	Los Angeles city, California	5 983	32	24	Albuquerque city, New Mexico	883
61	25	Lexington-Fayette urban county, Kentucky	1 045	60	25	St. Louis city, Missouri	5 832	65	25	Anchorage municipality, Alaska	865
26	26	Portland city, Oregon	1 016	50	26	Arlington city, Texas	5 724	28	26	Las Vegas city, Nevada	841
27	27	Oklahoma City city, Oklahoma	1 003	45	27	Oakland city, California	5 709	47	27	Tulsa city, Oklahoma	805
2	28	Los Angeles city, California	997	26	28	Portland city, Oregon	5 608	63	28	Pittsburgh city, Pennsylvania	798
44	29	Miami city, Florida	976	6	29	Phoenix city, Arizona	5 557	13	29	San Francisco city, California	795
15	30	Columbus city, Ohio	958	49	30	New Orleans city, Louisiana	5 454	27	30	Oklahoma City city, Oklahoma	774
3	31	Chicago city, Illinois	930	56	31	Anaheim city, California	5 304	48	31	Wichita city, Kansas	758
75	32	Jersey City city, New Jersey	918	37	32	Long Beach city, California	5 095	23	32	Boston city, Massachusetts	726
69	33	Plano city, Texas	907	5	33	Philadelphia city, Pennsylvania	4 985	12	33	Jacksonville city, Florida	684
43	34	Omaha city, Nebraska	903	72	34	Lincoln city, Nebraska	4 876	9	34	Dallas city, Texas	665
73	35	Orlando city, Florida	895	73	35	Orlando city, Florida	4 219	64	35	St. Paul city, Minnesota	662
4	36	Houston city, Texas	888	29	36	Baltimore city, Maryland	4 208	58	36	Corpus Christi city, Texas	656
37	37	Long Beach city, California	877	17	37	Charlotte city, North Carolina	4 165	33	37	Tucson city, Arizona	653
10	38	San Jose city, California	876	53	38	Tampa city, Florida	3 945	35	38	Sacramento city, California	615
9	39	Dallas city, Texas	872	41	39	Virginia Beach city, Virginia	3 811	18	39	Seattle city, Washington	604
47	40	Tulsa city, Oklahoma	862	24	40	Memphis city, Tennessee	3 791	19	40	Denver city, Colorado	601
8	41	San Diego city, California	838	32	41	Albuquerque city, New Mexico	3 769	1	41	New York city, New York	597
17	42	Charlotte city, North Carolina	803	58	42	Corpus Christi city, Texas	3 689	30	42	Louisville/Jefferson County metro gov, Kentucky	592
24	43	Memphis city, Tennessee	789	54	43	Aurora city, Colorado	3 582	17	43	Charlotte city, North Carolina	590
16	44	Fort Worth city, Texas	783	38	44	Mesa city, Arizona	3 305	53	44	Tampa city, Florida	582
56	45	Anaheim city, California	779	75	45	Jersey City city, New Jersey	3 300	6	45	Phoenix city, Arizona	572
53	46	Tampa city, Florida	774	61	46	Lexington-Fayette urban county, Kentucky	3 277	43	46	Omaha city, Nebraska	561
35	47	Sacramento city, California	771	47	47	Tulsa city, Oklahoma	3 179	15	47	Columbus city, Ohio	558
30	48	Louisville/Jefferson County metro gov, Kentucky	753	15	48	Columbus city, Ohio	3 153	16	47	Fort Worth city, Texas	558
68	49	Greensboro city, North Carolina	711	66	49	Cincinnati city, Ohio	3 091	7	49	San Antonio city, Texas	539
11	50	Austin city, Texas	709	16	50	Fort Worth city, Texas	3 084	2	50	Jersey City city, New Jersey	531
42	51	Raleigh city, North Carolina	679	64	51	St. Paul city, Minnesota	2 646	37	51	Los Angeles city, California	491
6	52	Phoenix city, Arizona	663	30	52	Louisville/Jefferson County metro gov, Kentucky	2 633	50	52	Long Beach city, California	489
32	52	Albuquerque city, New Mexico	663	8	53	San Diego city, California	2 563	68	53	Arlington city, Texas	484
50	54	Arlington city, Texas	644	23	54	Boston city, Massachusetts	2 454	26	54	Greensboro city, North Carolina	477
54	55	Aurora city, Colorado	638	43	55	Omaha city, Nebraska	2 411	34	55	Portland city, Oregon	473
59	56	Riverside city, California	631	42	56	Raleigh city, North Carolina	2 373	38	56	Fresno city, California	464
57	57	Santa Ana city, California	621	70	57	Newark city, New Jersey	2 366	52	57	Mesa city, Arizona	459
71	58	Toledo city, Ohio	618	63	58	Pittsburgh city, Pennsylvania	2 300	40	58	Bakersfield city, California	457
58	59	Corpus Christi city, Texas	614	35	59	Sacramento city, California	2 286	59	59	Colorado Springs city, Colorado	456
64	60	St. Paul city, Minnesota	602	20	60	El Paso city, Texas	2 270	54	60	Riverside city, California	433
20	61	El Paso city, Texas	572	33	61	Tucson city, Arizona	2 236	11	61	Aurora city, Colorado	407
62	62	Stockton city, California	544	27	62	Oklahoma City city, Oklahoma	2 199	20	62	Austin city, Texas	396
7	63	San Antonio city, Texas	534	31	63	Milwaukee city, Wisconsin	2 181	8	63	El Paso city, Texas	393
33	63	Tucson city, Arizona	534	34	64	Fresno city, California	2 099	57	64	San Diego city, California	381
34	65	Fresno city, California	529	44	65	Miami city, Florida	2 095	72	65	Santa Ana city, California	374
72	66	Lincoln city, Nebraska	516	74	66	Chula Vista city, California	2 027	61	66	Lincoln city, Nebraska	338
31	67	Milwaukee city, Wisconsin	505	62	67	Stockton city, California	1 926	10	67	Lexington-Fayette urban county, Kentucky	337
74	68	Chula Vista city, California	501	68	68	Greensboro city, North Carolina	1 603	56	68	San Jose city, California	321
40	69	Colorado Springs city, Colorado	494	69	69	Plano city, Texas	1 293	74	69	Anaheim city, California	317
67	70	Henderson city, Nevada	487	71	70	Toledo city, Ohio	1 260	67	70	Chula Vista city, California	235
48	71	Wichita city, Kansas	435	67	71	Henderson city, Nevada	1 165	69	71	Henderson city, Nevada	165
52	72	Bakersfield city, California	417	57	72	Santa Ana city, California	1 080	42	71	Plano city, Texas	165
38	73	Mesa city, Arizona	346	28	73	Las Vegas city, Nevada	1 069	41	73	Raleigh city, North Carolina	152
28	74	Las Vegas city, Nevada	336	52	74	Bakersfield city, California	966	55	74	Virginia Beach city, Virginia	148
55	75	Urban Honolulu CDP, Hawaii	NA	55	75	Urban Honolulu CDP, Hawaii	NA	75	75	Urban Honolulu CDP, Hawaii	NA

75 Largest Cities by 2015 Population
Selected rankings

Property crime rate, 2014				Full time equivalent local government employees, 2012				Local government employee payroll for March 2012			
Popu-lation rank	Property crime rate rank	City	Property crimes (per 100,000 population) [col 38]	Popu-lation rank	Govern-ment employees rank	City	Govern-ment employees [col 108]	Popu-lation rank	Govern-ment employee payroll rank	City	Government payroll (thousands of dollars) [col 109]
73	1	Orlando city, Florida	6 360	1	1	New York city, New York	404 260	1	1	New York city, New York	2 380 283 176
60	2	St. Louis city, Missouri	6 253	2	2	Los Angeles city, California	47 505	2	2	Los Angeles city, California	361 983 103
18	3	Seattle city, Washington	6 146	22	3	Washington city, District of Columbia	34 002	13	3	San Francisco city, California	217 722 943
24	4	Memphis city, Tennessee	5 995	5	4	Philadelphia city, Pennsylvania	29 409	22	4	Washington city, District of Columbia	194 813 463
33	5	Tucson city, Arizona	5 993	13	5	San Francisco city, California	28 349	3	5	Chicago city, Illinois	175 627 618
45	6	Oakland city, California	5 943	29	6	Baltimore city, Maryland	26 392	5	6	Philadelphia city, Pennsylvania	148 399 324
39	7	Atlanta city, Georgia	5 747	3	7	Chicago city, Illinois	25 630	29	7	Baltimore city, Maryland	122 552 640
66	8	Cincinnati city, Ohio	5 604	24	8	Memphis city, Tennessee	24 196	23	8	Boston city, Massachusetts	112 444 857
51	9	Cleveland city, Ohio	5 459	25	9	Nashville-Davidson metro gov, Tennessee	21 697	4	9	Houston city, Texas	99 616 057
32	10	Albuquerque city, New Mexico	5 446	4	10	Houston city, Texas	21 007	25	10	Nashville-Davidson metro gov, Tennessee	83 700 973
7	11	San Antonio city, Texas	5 418	23	11	Boston city, Massachusetts	19 230	24	11	Memphis city, Tennessee	79 305 378
13	12	San Francisco city, California	5 303	41	12	Virginia Beach city, Virginia	18 286	18	12	Seattle city, Washington	71 586 796
26	13	Portland city, Oregon	5 235	7	13	San Antonio city, Texas	15 382	7	13	San Antonio city, Texas	70 371 976
47	14	Tulsa city, Oklahoma	5 082	9	14	Dallas city, Texas	14 235	6	14	Phoenix city, Arizona	69 633 897
22	15	Washington city, District of Columbia	5 012	6	15	Phoenix city, Arizona	13 392	9	15	Dallas city, Texas	67 511 933
36	16	Kansas City city, Missouri	4 862	11	16	Austin city, Texas	12 580	11	16	Austin city, Texas	64 599 610
44	17	Miami city, Florida	4 833	21	17	Detroit city, Michigan	12 364	41	17	Virginia Beach city, Virginia	64 539 702
14	18	Indianapolis city, Indiana	4 823	14	18	Indianapolis city, Indiana	12 328	19	18	Denver city, Colorado	62 559 560
21	19	Detroit city, Michigan	4 819	19	19	Denver city, Colorado	11 914	8	19	San Diego city, California	62 476 850
46	20	Minneapolis city, Minnesota	4 728	18	20	Seattle city, Washington	10 193	21	20	Detroit city, Michigan	57 433 160
48	21	Wichita city, Kansas	4 723	12	21	Jacksonville city, Florida	10 137	65	21	Anchorage municipality, Alaska	51 971 256
29	22	Baltimore city, Maryland	4 718	65	22	Anchorage municipality, Alaska	9 819	14	22	Indianapolis city, Indiana	49 785 804
4	23	Houston city, Texas	4 694	8	23	San Diego city, California	9 425	12	23	Jacksonville city, Florida	46 960 164
31	24	Milwaukee city, Wisconsin	4 588	30	24	Louisville/Jefferson County metro gov, Kentucky	8 264	15	24	Columbus city, Ohio	42 573 757
58	25	Corpus Christi city, Texas	4 420	39	25	Atlanta city, Georgia	8 214	10	25	San Jose city, California	38 715 963
27	26	Oklahoma City city, Oklahoma	4 411	15	26	Columbus city, Ohio	8 035	40	26	Colorado Springs city, Colorado	37 084 390
62	27	Stockton city, California	4 390	17	27	Charlotte city, North Carolina	7 449	37	27	Long Beach city, California	36 050 392
43	28	Omaha city, Nebraska	4 345	51	28	Cleveland city, Ohio	7 389	26	28	Portland city, Oregon	35 656 383
15	29	Columbus city, Ohio	4 278	40	29	Colorado Springs city, Colorado	6 835	17	29	Charlotte city, North Carolina	34 348 745
49	30	New Orleans city, Louisiana	4 232	49	30	New Orleans city, Louisiana	6 570	32	30	Albuquerque city, New Mexico	33 331 138
30	31	Louisville/Jefferson County metro gov, Kentucky	4 196	16	31	Fort Worth city, Texas	6 536	51	31	Cleveland city, Ohio	33 318 506
11	32	Austin city, Texas	4 142	36	32	Kansas City city, Missouri	6 482	30	32	Louisville/Jefferson County metro gov, Kentucky	32 734 538
34	33	Fresno city, California	4 112	31	33	Milwaukee city, Wisconsin	6 455	31	33	Milwaukee city, Wisconsin	32 385 292
16	34	Fort Worth city, Texas	4 001	32	34	Albuquerque city, New Mexico	6 438	16	34	Fort Worth city, Texas	32 292 472
52	35	Bakersfield city, California	3 972	60	35	St. Louis city, Missouri	6 234	39	35	Atlanta city, Georgia	31 551 612
12	36	Jacksonville city, Florida	3 941	20	36	El Paso city, Texas	5 996	45	36	Oakland city, California	30 153 764
61	37	Lexington-Fayette urban county, Kentucky	3 912	37	37	Long Beach city, California	5 861	35	37	Sacramento city, California	29 508 935
65	38	Anchorage municipality, Alaska	3 827	26	38	Portland city, Oregon	5 804	66	38	Cincinnati city, Ohio	26 843 252
6	39	Phoenix city, Arizona	3 724	66	39	Cincinnati city, Ohio	5 222	46	39	Minneapolis city, Minnesota	26 103 507
40	40	Colorado Springs city, Colorado	3 668	10	40	San Jose city, California	5 214	49	40	New Orleans city, Louisiana	26 033 023
25	41	Nashville-Davidson metro gov, Tennessee	3 647	46	41	Minneapolis city, Minnesota	5 068	70	41	Newark city, New Jersey	25 580 741
68	42	Greensboro city, North Carolina	3 600	33	42	Tucson city, Arizona	4 691	60	42	St. Louis city, Missouri	25 364 525
9	43	Dallas city, Texas	3 589	35	43	Sacramento city, California	4 483	27	43	Oklahoma City city, Oklahoma	24 268 820
17	44	Charlotte city, North Carolina	3 567	27	44	Oklahoma City city, Oklahoma	4 418	20	44	El Paso city, Texas	23 812 936
50	45	Arlington city, Texas	3 515	53	45	Tampa city, Florida	4 247	53	45	Tampa city, Florida	22 517 912
64	46	St. Paul city, Minnesota	3 484	63	46	Pittsburgh city, Pennsylvania	4 176	33	46	Tucson city, Arizona	21 780 237
5	47	Philadelphia city, Pennsylvania	3 388	45	47	Oakland city, California	3 940	36	47	Kansas City city, Missouri	21 087 489
19	48	Denver city, Colorado	3 367	42	48	Raleigh city, North Carolina	3 936	38	48	Mesa city, Arizona	20 622 110
72	49	Lincoln city, Nebraska	3 349	47	49	Tulsa city, Oklahoma	3 932	75	49	Jersey City city, New Jersey	18 762 329
63	50	Pittsburgh city, Pennsylvania	3 213	61	50	Lexington-Fayette urban county, Kentucky	3 926	44	50	Miami city, Florida	18 642 774
3	51	Chicago city, Illinois	3 133	70	51	Newark city, New Jersey	3 857	34	51	Fresno city, California	18 551 770
35	52	Sacramento city, California	3 123	44	52	Miami city, Florida	3 807	64	52	St. Paul city, Minnesota	18 028 194
59	53	Riverside city, California	3 088	38	53	Mesa city, Arizona	3 616	28	53	Las Vegas city, Nevada	17 371 881
28	54	Las Vegas city, Nevada	2 923	34	54	Fresno city, California	3 214	47	54	Tulsa city, Oklahoma	16 951 552
70	55	Newark city, New Jersey	2 851	68	55	Greensboro city, North Carolina	3 098	63	55	Pittsburgh city, Pennsylvania	16 527 485
54	56	Aurora city, Colorado	2 839	64	56	St. Paul city, Minnesota	3 092	61	56	Lexington-Fayette urban county, Kentucky	16 180 537
38	57	Mesa city, Arizona	2 800	75	57	Jersey City city, New Jersey	2 936	42	57	Raleigh city, North Carolina	15 850 858
37	58	Long Beach city, California	2 640	48	58	Wichita city, Kansas	2 864	56	58	Anaheim city, California	15 281 363
23	59	Boston city, Massachusetts	2 639	43	59	Omaha city, Nebraska	2 835	43	59	Omaha city, Nebraska	15 258 712
10	60	San Jose city, California	2 434	73	60	Orlando city, Florida	2 773	59	60	Riverside city, California	15 114 251
53	61	Tampa city, Florida	2 428	58	61	Corpus Christi city, Texas	2 747	73	61	Orlando city, Florida	14 180 368
56	62	Anaheim city, California	2 362	57	62	Santa Ana city, California	2 711	67	62	Henderson city, Nevada	13 759 509
41	63	Virginia Beach city, Virginia	2 187	72	63	Lincoln city, Nebraska	2 609	54	63	Aurora city, Colorado	13 742 359
20	64	El Paso city, Texas	2 142	28	64	Las Vegas city, Nevada	2 582	72	64	Lincoln city, Nebraska	13 359 820
2	65	Los Angeles city, California	2 128	54	65	Aurora city, Colorado	2 579	57	65	Santa Ana city, California	12 719 386
71	66	Toledo city, Ohio	2 006	50	66	Arlington city, Texas	2 551	62	66	Stockton city, California	12 427 436
69	67	Plano city, Texas	1 983	59	67	Riverside city, California	2 260	48	67	Wichita city, Kansas	12 396 633
67	68	Henderson city, Nevada	1 978	67	68	Henderson city, Nevada	2 239	50	68	Arlington city, Texas	12 130 944
8	69	San Diego city, California	1 959	56	69	Anaheim city, California	2 214	68	69	Greensboro city, North Carolina	11 503 988
74	70	Chula Vista city, California	1 741	71	70	Toledo city, Ohio	2 146	58	70	Corpus Christi city, Texas	10 789 288
57	71	Santa Ana city, California	1 719	69	71	Plano city, Texas	2 089	69	71	Plano city, Texas	10 395 648
75	72	Jersey City city, New Jersey	1 631	62	72	Stockton city, California	2 010	71	72	Toledo city, Ohio	10 282 276
1	73	New York city, New York	1 602	52	73	Bakersfield city, California	1 424	52	73	Bakersfield city, California	8 316 644
42	74	Raleigh city, North Carolina	1 030	74	74	Chula Vista city, California	1 114	74	74	Chula Vista city, California	7 346 424
55	75	Urban Honolulu CDP, Hawaii	NA	55	75	Urban Honolulu CDP, Hawaii	NA	55	75	Urban Honolulu CDP, Hawaii	NA

Table D. Cities — **Land Area and Population**

STATE Place code	City	Population, 2015				Race alone or in combination (percent), 2010-2014						
		Land area,[1] 2010 (sq km)	Total persons	Rank	Per square kilometer	White	Black	American Indian, Alaska Native	Asian	Hawaiian Pacific Islander	Percent Hispanic or Latino[2], 2010-2014	Percent foreign born 2010–2014
		1	2	3	4	5	6	7	8	9	10	11

1. Dry land or land partially or temporarily covered by water.　　2. May be of any race.

Table D. Cities — **Population**

City	Age of population (percent), 2010-2014											Population			
												Census counts		Percent change	
	Under 5 years	5 to 17 years	18 to 24 years	25 to 34 years	35 to 44 years	45 to 54 years	55 to 64 years	65 to 74 years	75 years and over	Median age 2010-2014	Percent female 2010-2014	2000	2010	2000–2010	2010–2015
	12	13	14	15	16	17	18	19	20	21	22	23	24	25	26

Table D. Cities — **Households, Group Quarters, Crime, and Education**

City	Households, 2010-2014				Persons in group quarters, 2010				Serious crimes known to police,[2] 2014				Educational attainment, 2010–2014		
			Percent			Institutional			Total		Rate[3]			Attainment[4] (percent)	
	Number	Persons per household	Female family householder[1]	One-person	Total	Total	Persons in nursing facilities	Non-institutional	Number	Rate[3]	Violent	Property	Population age 25 and older	High school graduate or less	Bachelor's degree or more
	27	28	29	30	31	32	33	34	35	36	37	38	39	40	41

1. No spouse present.　　2. Data for serious crimes have not been adjusted for underreporting. This may affect comparability between geographic areas and over time.　　3. Per 100,000 population estimated by the FBI.　　4. Persons 25 years old and over.

Table D. Cities — **Income, Poverty, and Housing**

City	Money income, 2010–2014					Housing units, 2010			Occupied housing units 2010–2014				
	Households											Median owner costs as a percent of income	
									Owner-occupied				
	Per capita income[1] (dollars)	Median income	Percent with income of $200,000 or more	Percent with income of less than $25,000	Families with income below poverty (percent)	Total	Percent change, 2000–2010	Vacant units for sale or rent[2]	Total	Percent	Median value[3] (dollars)	With a mortgage[4]	Without a mortgage[5]
	42	43	44	45	46	47	48	49	50	51	52	53	54

1. Based on population estimated by the American Community Survey.　　2. Includes units rented or sold but not occupied.　　3. Specified owner-occupied units; $1,000,000 represents $1,000,000 or more　　4. 50.0 represents 50 percent or more.　　5. 10.0 represents 10 percent or less.

Table D. Cities — Housing, Labor Force, and Employment

City	Occupied housing units, 2010–2014 (cont.)				Migration, 2010–2014		Civilian labor force, 2015				Civilian employment[4], 2010–2014			
									Unemployment			Percent		
	Percent renter occupied	Median gross rent[1]	Median gross rent as a percent of income[2]	Percent with no vehicle available	Percent who lived in the same house one year ago	Percent who lived outside current city one year ago	Total	Percent change, 2014–2015	Total	Rate[3]	Population age 16 and older	In labor force	Civilian full-year full-time workers	Households with no workers (percent)
	55	56	57	58	59	60	61	62	63	64	65	66	67	68

1. $2,000 represents $2,000 or more. 2. 50.0 represents 50 percent or more. 3. Percent of civilian labor force. 4. Persons 16 years old and over.

Table D. Cities — Construction, Wholesale Trade, and Retail Trade

City	Value of residential construction authorized by building permits, 2015			Wholesale trade,[1] 2012				Retail trade,[2] 2012			
	New construction ($1,000)	Number of housing units	Percent single family	Number of establishments	Number of employees	Sales (mil dol)	Annual payroll (mil dol)	Number of establishments	Number of employees	Sales (mil dol)	Annual payroll (mil dol)
	69	70	71	72	73	74	75	76	77	78	79

1. Merchant wholesalers except manufacturers' sales branches and offices. 2. Establishments with payroll.

Table D. Cities — Real Estate, Professional Services, and Manufacturing

City	Real estate and rental and leasing, 2012				Professional, scientific, and technical services,[1] 2012				Manufacturing, 2012			
	Number of establishments	Number of employees	Receipts (mil dol)	Annual payroll (mil dol)	Number of establishments	Number of employees	Receipts (mil dol)	Annual payroll (mil dol)	Number of establishments	Number of employees	Receipts (mil dol)	Annual payroll (mil dol)
	80	81	82	83	84	85	86	87	88	89	90	91

1. Establishments subject to federal tax.

Table D. Cities — Accommodation and Food Services, Arts, Entertainment, and Recreation, and Health Care and Social Assistance

City	Accommodation and food services, 2012				Arts, entertainment, and recreation,[1] 2012				Health care and social assistance,[1] 2012			
	Number of establishments	Number of employees	Sales (mil dol)	Annual payroll (mil dol)	Number of establishments	Number of employees	Receipts (mil dol)	Annual payroll (mil dol)	Number of establishments	Number of employees	Receipts (mil dol)	Annual payroll (mil dol)
	92	93	94	95	96	97	98	99	100	101	102	103

1. Establishments subject to federal tax.

Table D. Cities — **Other Services and Government Employment and Payroll**

City	Other services[1], 2012				Government employment and payroll, 2012									
					Full-time equivalent employees	March payroll								
						Total (dollars)	Percent of total for:							
	Number of establish-ments	Number of employees	Receipts (mil dol)	Annual payroll (mil dol)			Adminis-tration, judicial, and legal	Police and Corrections	Fire Protection	Highways and trans-portation	Health and welfare	Natural resources and utilities	Education and libraries
	104	105	106	107	108	109	110	111	112	113	114	115	116

1. Establishments subject to federal tax.

Table D. Cities — **City Government Finances**

City	City government finances, 2012									
	General revenue							General expenditure		
		Intergovernmental		Taxes					Per capita[1] (dollars)	
					Per capita[1] (dollars)					
	Total (mil dol)	Total (mil dol)	Percent from state government	Total (mil dol)	Total	Property	Sales and gross receipts	Total (mil dol)	Total	Capital outlays
	117	118	119	120	121	122	123	124	125	126

1. Based on population estimated as of July 1 of the year shown.

Table D. Cities — **City Government Finances**

City	City government finances, 2012 (cont.)									
	General expenditure (cont.)									
	Percent of total for:									
	Public welfare	Highways	Parking facilities	Education	Health and hospitals	Police protection	Sewerage and sanitation	Parks and recreation	Housing and community development	Interest on debt
	127	128	129	130	131	132	133	134	135	136

Table D. Cities — **City Government Finances, City Government Employment, and Climate**

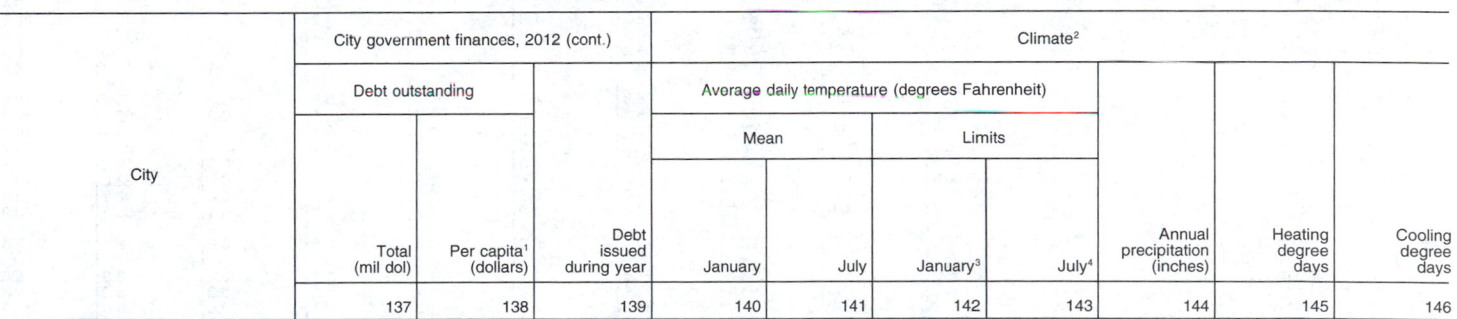

City	City government finances, 2012 (cont.)			Climate[2]						
	Debt outstanding			Average daily temperature (degrees Fahrenheit)						
				Mean		Limits				
	Total (mil dol)	Per capita[1] (dollars)	Debt issued during year	January	July	January[3]	July[4]	Annual precipitation (inches)	Heating degree days	Cooling degree days
	137	138	139	140	141	142	143	144	145	146

1. Based on the population estimated as of July 1 of the year shown.   2. Represents normal values based on the 30-year period, 1971–2000.   3. Average daily minimum.
4. Average daily maximum.

Table D. Cities — Land Area and Population

STATE Place code	City	Land area,[1] 2010 (sq km)	Population, 2015 Total persons	Rank	Per square kilometer	Race alone or in combination (percent), 2010-2014 White	Black	American Indian, Alaska Native	Asian	Hawaiian Pacific Islander	Percent Hispanic or Latino[2] 2010-2014	Percent foreign born 2010–2014
		1	2	3	4	5	6	7	8	9	10	11
00 00000	United States............	9 147 592.7	321 418 820	X	35.1	76.3	13.7	1.7	5.9	0.4	16.9	13.1
01 00000	ALABAMA	131 170.8	4 858 979	X	37.0	70.4	27.1	1.2	1.5	0.1	4.0	3.5
01 00820	Alabaster....................	64.9	32 707	1 147	504.0	77.2	13.9	0.6	0.8	0.1	11.5	8.4
01 03076	Auburn........................	150.4	62 059	584	412.6	75.0	17.4	0.5	7.0	0.2	4.0	10.0
01 05980	Bessemer....................	103.2	26 730	1 370	259.0	25.3	72.3	0.5	0.1	0.0	3.4	2.5
01 07000	Birmingham................	378.3	212 461	102	561.6	24.0	73.8	0.6	1.2	0.0	3.5	3.4
01 20104	Decatur......................	139.0	55 437	676	398.8	73.5	22.7	2.4	1.3	0.1	13.0	7.6
01 21184	Dothan.......................	231.5	68 567	510	296.2	64.2	34.2	0.9	1.5	0.1	2.8	2.6
01 24184	Enterprise..................	80.9	27 978	1 320	345.8	76.9	21.3	1.1	2.8	0.3	8.4	5.9
01 26896	Florence.....................	67.3	40 026	935	594.7	77.9	21.0	0.9	1.5	0.1	2.6	2.8
01 28696	Gadsden.....................	96.3	36 084	1 046	374.7	61.1	37.4	1.4	1.3	0.0	4.8	3.2
01 35800	Homewood..................	21.7	25 708	1 402	1 184.7	80.9	16.0	0.2	2.2	0.0	5.8	7.1
01 35896	Hoover.......................	122.2	84 848	386	694.3	74.2	15.4	0.8	6.1	0.1	7.0	8.9
01 37000	Huntsville...................	541.5	190 582	125	352.0	65.2	31.6	1.3	3.2	0.3	5.7	6.6
01 45784	Madison......................	76.7	46 962	803	612.3	77.3	15.8	1.5	7.2	0.2	4.5	7.8
01 50000	Mobile........................	360.3	194 288	123	539.2	46.5	51.7	0.7	1.5	0.0	2.7	3.2
01 51000	Montgomery................	413.3	200 602	115	485.4	37.8	58.9	0.6	2.8	0.1	3.6	4.5
01 57048	Opelika.......................	154.3	29 527	1 258	191.4	53.4	41.5	0.9	1.4	0.0	5.9	6.2
01 59472	Phenix City.................	71.9	37 570	1 002	522.5	51.9	47.5	0.7	1.5	0.2	5.5	2.5
01 62328	Prattville....................	85.1	35 420	1 067	416.2	79.4	18.1	0.6	2.1	0.0	3.6	1.9
01 77256	Tuscaloosa.................	156.0	98 332	307	630.3	53.4	44.0	0.5	2.7	0.1	3.2	4.8
01 78552	Vestavia Hills..............	50.3	34 174	1 099	679.4	90.6	3.4	0.4	5.5	0.0	1.4	6.4
02 00000	ALASKA	1 477 953.2	738 432	X	0.5	73.6	5.0	19.4	7.5	1.7	6.2	7.1
02 03000	Anchorage..................	4 415.1	298 695	65	67.7	73.5	8.3	12.3	11.0	2.9	8.3	9.7
02 24230	Fairbanks...................	82.1	32 325	1 165	393.7	73.9	11.3	12.7	6.5	1.8	10.5	7.3
02 36400	Juneau.......................	6 998.0	32 756	1 146	4.7	76.9	1.9	18.8	8.5	1.5	5.9	6.9
04 00000	ARIZONA	294 207.3	6 828 065	X	23.2	81.5	5.1	5.4	3.8	0.4	30.1	13.5
04 02830	Apache Junction.........	90.6	38 074	985	420.2	93.7	1.8	3.4	1.7	0.1	16.8	7.4
04 04720	Avondale	118.1	80 684	412	683.2	77.8	11.9	2.3	4.2	0.3	53.3	15.6
04 07940	Buckeye.....................	971.9	62 138	581	63.9	80.4	8.7	2.4	1.9	0.3	37.6	11.0
04 08220	Bullhead City.............	153.8	39 445	955	256.5	92.5	2.2	2.8	2.2	0.4	21.4	10.8
04 10530	Casa Grande..............	284.0	51 460	735	181.2	79.6	5.6	4.7	3.3	0.1	38.4	11.0
04 12000	Chandler....................	166.8	260 828	76	1 563.7	80.9	6.4	2.2	10.5	0.5	23.6	14.5
04 22220	El Mirage...................	26.0	33 935	1 105	1 305.2	81.8	6.8	2.6	2.5	0.3	47.0	15.7
04 23620	Flagstaff....................	165.4	70 320	496	425.2	77.0	3.1	12.8	3.7	1.0	18.8	7.6
04 23760	Florence	135.9	31 110	1 193	228.9	82.8	6.3	4.4	1.0	0.3	41.9	21.9
04 27400	Gilbert.......................	176.0	247 542	85	1 406.5	87.1	4.5	1.7	7.5	0.4	15.6	9.3
04 27820	Glendale....................	155.3	240 126	89	1 546.2	79.5	7.4	2.8	4.7	0.3	36.9	16.8
04 28380	Goodyear...................	495.9	79 003	427	159.3	82.1	9.6	2.5	6.0	0.4	28.4	10.8
04 37620	Kingman....................	90.2	28 912	1 279	320.5	95.2	1.8	3.8	1.6	1.5	13.3	4.8
04 39370	Lake Havasu City..........	115.1	53 553	699	465.3	95.0	1.4	0.9	1.8	0.2	12.9	6.2
04 44270	Marana......................	314.6	41 315	904	131.3	86.9	4.4	1.4	6.0	0.4	20.8	8.0
04 44410	Maricopa....................	123.0	48 602	780	395.1	78.3	12.1	2.8	4.9	0.7	21.2	9.2
04 46000	Mesa.........................	353.4	471 825	38	1 335.1	86.7	4.5	2.9	2.7	0.5	26.8	12.4
04 51600	Oro Valley.................	92.0	43 565	859	473.5	91.1	1.7	1.0	4.6	0.5	10.8	7.6
04 54050	Peoria.......................	451.7	171 237	146	379.1	89.5	4.7	1.4	5.2	0.4	19.7	9.1
04 55000	Phoenix.....................	1 338.3	1 563 025	6	1 167.9	78.2	7.9	2.8	4.2	0.4	40.5	20.2
04 57380	Prescott	107.1	41 899	893	391.2	94.6	1.2	2.6	2.1	0.0	7.5	6.2
04 57450	Prescott Valley...........	100.1	42 197	884	421.5	94.2	1.3	1.5	1.7	0.1	16.6	6.5
04 58150	Queen Creek..............	72.6	34 614	1 086	476.8	88.2	2.9	1.9	1.8	0.1	17.7	4.0
04 62140	Sahuarita...................	80.4	25 707	1 403	319.7	88.3	4.7	0.7	5.5	0.1	30.2	10.0
04 63470	San Luis.....................	83.0	31 520	1 185	379.8	95.2	1.0	1.0	0.1	0.0	95.4	45.2
04 65000	Scottsdale..................	476.4	236 839	92	497.1	91.1	2.3	1.6	5.1	0.1	9.7	10.7
04 66820	Sierra Vista...............	394.4	43 355	861	109.9	80.2	10.5	1.9	7.1	1.3	22.0	8.7
04 71510	Surprise.....................	273.9	128 422	213	468.9	89.1	6.5	1.2	2.4	0.5	18.2	8.8
04 73000	Tempe.......................	103.4	175 826	138	1 700.4	77.6	6.4	3.7	8.1	0.9	22.2	13.3
04 77000	Tucson.......................	587.2	531 641	33	905.4	78.2	6.3	3.8	3.9	0.4	42.2	14.9
04 85540	Yuma.........................	311.5	94 139	328	302.2	72.8	4.3	1.7	2.8	0.4	56.8	20.9
05 00000	ARKANSAS...............	134 771.3	2 978 204	X	22.1	80.1	16.2	1.6	1.6	0.3	6.7	4.6
05 04840	Bella Vista	114.6	27 999	1 317	244.3	97.3	1.1	1.4	1.4	0.2	3.9	3.6
05 05290	Benton.......................	57.6	34 177	1 098	593.4	90.1	8.9	1.7	1.2	0.2	5.2	2.6
05 05320	Bentonville.................	81.0	44 499	839	549.4	84.2	2.6	1.9	10.1	0.5	9.0	12.8
05 15190	Conway......................	117.4	64 980	548	553.5	80.4	16.8	1.2	2.8	0.1	5.2	4.5
05 23290	Fayetteville................	139.5	82 830	399	593.8	85.8	6.9	2.5	3.8	0.1	6.9	7.1
05 24560	Fort Smith..................	160.5	88 194	361	549.5	82.4	10.9	3.7	6.2	0.4	17.0	12.4
05 33400	Hot Springs................	90.7	35 635	1 060	392.9	72.9	19.9	1.4	1.8	0.1	8.9	6.0

1. Dry land or land partially or temporarily covered by water.   2. May be of any race.

Table D. Cities — Population

City	Under 5 years	5 to 17 years	18 to 24 years	25 to 34 years	35 to 44 years	45 to 54 years	55 to 64 years	65 to 74 years	75 years and over	Median age 2010–2014	Percent female 2010–2014	Census counts 2000	Census counts 2010	Percent change 2000–2010	Percent change 2010–2015
	12	13	14	15	16	17	18	19	20	21	22	23	24	25	26
United States............	6.4	17.1	10.0	13.5	12.9	14.1	12.3	7.6	6.1	37.4	50.8	281 421 906	308 745 538	9.7	4.1
ALABAMA	6.2	17.0	10.1	12.7	12.7	14.0	12.8	8.3	6.2	38.3	51.6	4 447 100	4 779 736	7.5	1.6
Alabaster	5.9	21.2	8.8	12.9	16.3	15.1	9.3	6.3	4.2	35.8	51.4	22 619	30 352	34.2	5.6
Auburn.......................	4.8	13.5	36.6	14.3	9.6	8.2	6.1	4.2	2.6	23.5	49.1	42 987	53 380	24.2	16.2
Bessemer...................	7.1	18.8	7.9	12.9	11.0	13.4	13.1	7.4	8.4	38.6	52.5	29 672	27 456	-7.5	-2.7
Birmingham	7.0	13.9	12.2	15.5	12.0	13.8	13.0	6.6	6.1	36.0	53.4	242 820	212 237	-12.6	0.1
Decatur......................	6.1	17.1	9.6	12.5	13.6	13.9	12.4	8.3	6.5	37.9	51.7	53 929	55 683	3.3	-0.5
Dothan.......................	6.8	16.9	8.8	13.8	12.6	13.6	12.6	8.2	6.7	38.1	52.3	57 737	65 496	13.4	4.0
Enterprise...................	7.3	19.2	8.5	14.4	15.1	12.4	10.1	6.8	6.2	35.3	50.5	21 178	26 562	25.4	5.1
Florence	5.4	13.2	16.0	12.3	10.0	11.5	13.5	9.4	8.7	37.7	55.1	36 264	39 319	8.4	1.7
Gadsden....................	7.4	14.8	9.5	13.4	11.4	13.7	13.1	8.9	7.6	39.4	52.9	38 978	36 856	-5.4	-2.2
Homewood	7.9	16.0	17.3	19.7	12.8	8.6	8.7	4.2	4.8	29.2	49.1	25 043	25 167	0.5	2.2
Hoover.......................	6.5	19.2	6.0	14.9	14.6	12.9	12.8	7.7	5.4	37.2	52.6	62 742	81 619	30.1	4.7
Huntsville...................	6.2	15.2	11.4	14.7	12.0	14.7	11.7	7.7	6.3	36.7	51.1	158 216	180 105	13.8	5.7
Madison.....................	6.1	20.4	8.9	12.9	12.6	18.5	11.7	5.4	3.4	36.7	49.5	29 329	42 938	46.4	9.4
Mobile.......................	6.7	16.4	11.4	14.0	12.0	12.8	12.4	7.7	6.5	36.1	52.2	198 915	195 111	-1.9	-0.5
Montgomery	7.2	17.8	11.8	14.5	12.3	12.5	11.5	7.0	5.4	34.2	53.2	201 568	205 764	2.1	-2.4
Opelika......................	6.6	17.1	9.9	14.1	11.8	13.7	12.9	7.6	6.4	37.2	53.1	23 498	26 477	12.7	11.7
Phenix City................	8.4	19.6	10.7	16.2	12.5	12.2	9.5	5.7	5.2	31.9	52.8	28 265	32 822	16.1	14.3
Prattville....................	6.5	19.4	9.8	12.8	14.1	15.1	9.4	7.6	5.2	36.2	52.9	24 303	33 960	39.7	4.2
Tuscaloosa	5.1	12.9	27.9	13.4	10.4	10.2	9.8	5.1	5.1	27.3	52.4	77 906	90 468	16.1	8.6
Vestavia Hills.............	6.7	19.1	5.1	12.0	13.3	14.9	13.1	6.9	8.8	41.2	52.3	24 476	34 033	39.0	0.2
ALASKA	7.5	18.3	11.0	15.2	12.6	14.3	12.6	5.6	3.0	33.5	47.8	626 932	710 231	13.3	4.0
Anchorage.................	7.5	17.8	11.6	16.4	12.9	14.0	11.7	5.2	3.0	32.7	49.1	260 283	291 826	12.1	2.4
Fairbanks...................	9.8	18.0	16.2	21.3	9.7	8.2	9.1	4.3	3.6	27.4	45.8	30 224	31 535	4.3	2.5
Juneau......................	6.2	16.8	8.8	14.2	13.6	16.5	14.9	5.8	3.1	37.4	48.1	30 711	31 275	1.8	4.7
ARIZONA	6.7	18.0	10.0	13.3	12.6	12.8	11.7	8.5	6.3	36.6	50.3	5 130 632	6 392 017	24.6	6.8
Apache Junction...........	4.8	16.0	5.5	8.3	10.8	11.7	13.8	16.2	12.9	49.2	51.7	31 814	35 840	12.7	6.2
Avondale	9.0	22.3	11.5	16.1	15.0	11.8	8.0	4.5	1.8	29.3	52.1	35 883	76 238	112.5	6.0
Buckeye.....................	7.8	21.9	9.2	16.6	14.4	11.7	9.9	6.1	2.3	32.2	47.0	6 537	50 876	678.3	22.1
Bullhead City	5.9	14.2	7.1	6.8	9.7	14.0	15.0	17.0	10.2	49.7	50.4	33 769	39 540	17.1	-0.2
Casa Grande...............	7.5	19.4	7.4	11.2	12.6	11.8	12.1	10.4	7.6	38.7	49.5	25 224	48 571	92.6	5.9
Chandler....................	7.4	19.6	9.2	14.8	15.5	14.6	10.2	5.3	3.4	34.3	50.4	176 581	236 123	33.7	10.4
El Mirage	9.4	21.9	10.3	17.2	14.1	10.8	7.4	5.6	3.3	30.8	49.3	7 609	31 797	317.9	6.7
Flagstaff.....................	6.3	13.5	28.4	15.3	10.8	9.5	9.5	4.8	2.1	25.9	50.0	52 894	65 870	24.5	6.4
Florence	1.5	8.0	8.7	19.3	16.7	15.1	10.1	14.9	5.7	42.2	28.7	17 054	25 536	49.7	4.4
Gilbert.......................	8.2	24.5	7.1	14.1	17.5	13.3	8.3	4.8	2.3	32.4	50.4	109 697	208 453	90.0	18.8
Glendale....................	7.1	19.3	11.6	14.0	13.3	13.8	11.1	5.8	4.1	33.5	50.2	218 812	226 721	3.6	6.0
Goodyear...................	6.1	20.3	7.2	15.2	15.5	12.6	10.7	8.7	3.8	36.0	52.9	18 911	65 275	245.2	21.1
Kingman.....................	6.2	15.4	6.7	13.8	9.4	16.4	11.7	11.0	9.4	43.6	51.1	20 069	28 068	39.9	3.0
Lake Havasu City.........	3.5	13.6	6.2	8.7	7.9	13.4	16.1	17.4	13.2	52.9	52.6	41 938	52 527	25.2	1.9
Marana	7.4	17.5	6.7	12.1	14.5	10.9	13.8	9.8	7.2	39.4	50.3	13 556	34 961	157.9	19.5
Maricopa....................	10.0	19.8	6.4	17.5	17.3	10.5	11.9	4.8	1.9	33.6	50.7	1 040	43 482	4 081.0	11.8
Mesa.........................	7.1	17.8	9.9	14.4	11.9	12.7	11.0	7.9	7.3	35.5	50.9	396 375	439 041	10.8	7.2
Oro Valley	3.9	14.6	7.8	7.6	8.9	13.9	15.4	16.7	11.3	50.3	53.1	29 700	41 011	38.1	6.2
Peoria	5.8	19.5	7.9	12.1	13.2	14.1	12.1	8.2	7.0	39.0	51.9	108 364	154 065	42.2	11.1
Phoenix	7.7	19.4	10.5	15.4	14.2	13.5	10.2	5.3	3.7	33.0	50.0	1 321 045	1 445 632	9.4	8.0
Prescott	1.9	9.2	9.5	8.6	7.1	11.8	17.7	16.5	17.7	55.7	51.5	33 938	39 843	17.4	5.2
Prescott Valley	7.0	17.0	8.6	13.5	9.2	10.6	13.7	11.3	9.2	40.6	52.2	23 535	38 822	65.0	8.5
Queen Creek...............	9.2	30.3	5.3	10.3	18.3	11.7	8.3	4.9	1.8	30.5	51.7	4 316	26 361	510.8	31.4
Sahuarita...................	10.9	20.2	4.9	13.2	14.2	9.7	10.5	10.4	6.0	35.5	49.9	3 242	25 259	679.1	1.8
San Luis	8.2	23.9	13.0	14.9	12.5	14.1	7.0	4.1	2.5	27.3	46.5	15 322	25 505	66.5	12.9
Scottsdale..................	4.7	13.2	7.0	13.0	12.5	14.4	14.5	11.9	8.9	44.7	51.7	202 705	217 385	7.2	8.9
Sierra Vista	6.5	18.1	13.9	14.4	10.7	10.6	10.3	8.4	7.2	33.0	51.8	37 775	43 888	16.2	-4.0
Surprise	7.3	21.5	5.3	11.7	13.8	9.9	9.5	13.1	7.8	38.3	52.0	30 848	117 517	281.0	9.3
Tempe	5.2	11.4	24.4	19.1	11.1	10.2	10.2	5.0	3.4	28.5	48.2	158 625	161 719	2.0	8.7
Tucson.......................	6.3	15.8	15.8	14.3	12.0	12.2	11.2	6.7	5.8	33.3	50.3	486 699	520 116	6.9	2.1
Yuma.........................	7.6	20.4	13.8	14.5	11.6	10.5	8.4	7.1	6.1	30.2	48.1	77 515	93 064	20.1	3.8
ARKANSAS...............	6.6	17.5	9.8	13.0	12.4	13.4	12.4	8.5	6.5	37.6	50.9	2 673 400	2 915 918	9.1	2.1
Bella Vista	5.2	12.2	4.0	8.6	12.0	11.3	13.0	17.6	16.1	52.3	52.0	16 582	26 461	59.6	5.6
Benton	7.4	19.1	8.3	14.8	13.0	13.6	10.3	7.4	6.1	35.3	52.0	21 906	30 681	40.1	12.0
Bentonville.................	7.5	19.8	8.4	16.8	16.9	14.1	9.3	3.9	3.3	33.3	48.7	19 730	35 301	78.9	26.0
Conway	6.2	16.9	21.0	16.9	11.9	9.3	9.1	4.5	4.2	27.9	50.3	43 167	58 908	36.5	10.3
Fayetteville.................	5.0	12.7	26.3	18.5	11.3	9.3	8.7	4.2	4.1	27.7	50.1	58 047	73 580	26.8	12.6
Fort Smith..................	7.6	17.3	10.0	15.0	11.8	13.6	12.0	6.6	6.0	35.0	50.3	80 268	86 209	7.4	2.2
Hot Springs	6.2	15.5	9.7	12.8	10.1	12.5	13.0	9.5	10.7	40.8	52.1	35 750	35 193	-1.6	1.3

City	Households, 2010-2014 Number	Persons per house-hold	Percent Female family house-holder[1]	Percent One-person	Persons in group quarters, 2010 Total	Institutional Total	Persons in nursing facilities	Non-institu-tional	Serious crimes known to police,[2] 2014 Total Number	Total Rate[3]	Rate[3] Violent	Rate[3] Property	Population age 25 and older	Attainment[4] (percent) High school graduate or less	Attainment[4] (percent) Bachelor's degree or more
	27	28	29	30	31	32	33	34	35	36	37	38	39	40	41
United States..............	116 211 092	2.70	13.0	27.6	7 987 323	3 993 659	1 502 264	3 993 664	94 432 120	2 962	3 660	2 596	209 056 129	41.6	29.3
ALABAMA....................	1 842 174	2.62	15.3	28.5	115 816	67 004	22 995	48 812	174 821	3 605	427	3 178	3 217 902	47.4	23.1
Alabaster....................	10 416	2.97	12.0	20.5	300	297	293	3	670	2 122	184	1 939	19 916	35.1	33.7
Auburn.......................	21 644	2.63	9.7	31.4	3 827	130	130	3 697	1 780	2 974	211	2 763	25 538	19.2	60.0
Bessemer....................	10 457	2.60	26.9	33.8	871	519	472	352	2 226	8 258	1 339	6 918	18 213	54.3	12.8
Birmingham.................	88 817	2.38	24.4	39.3	9 035	3 300	1 559	5 735	17 298	8 155	1 588	6 567	141 986	44.5	23.1
Decatur.......................	22 006	2.53	15.0	33.4	966	767	246	199	2 563	4 590	201	4 390	37 906	47.5	23.1
Dothan.......................	25 935	2.61	18.3	30.1	1 369	1 171	484	198	1 998	2 918	304	2 614	45 261	44.3	24.0
Enterprise...................	10 182	2.69	15.0	27.8	279	245	245	34	1 059	3 778	375	3 403	18 125	40.0	28.8
Florence.....................	17 617	2.26	14.2	38.0	1 701	524	370	1 177	1 678	4 170	502	3 668	25 659	44.1	26.7
Gadsden.....................	14 689	2.49	19.8	35.6	1 752	1 189	380	563	3 164	8 679	982	7 697	24 923	51.8	15.2
Homewood..................	9 306	2.73	9.3	31.4	1 864	18	0	1 846	1 101	4 251	259	3 992	14 947	20.5	59.9
Hoover.......................	32 375	2.56	9.6	27.8	408	393	361	0	2 357	2 778	116	2 663	56 833	16.8	56.0
Huntsville...................	76 959	2.39	14.3	36.8	6 786	1 924	874	4 862	10 628	5 665	782	4 883	123 617	30.3	39.1
Madison.....................	16 583	2.71	8.3	23.5	270	270	225	0	1 093	2 354	323	2 031	29 038	17.7	55.2
Mobile.......................	75 653	2.58	20.7	34.8	5 598	2 632	1 196	2 966	13 091	5 223	594	4 629	127 048	41.6	26.7
Montgomery................	79 760	2.56	22.2	32.0	6 879	2 967	1 005	3 912	10 071	5 031	522	4 508	129 404	40.8	31.4
Opelika......................	11 183	2.50	19.7	30.1	572	481	141	91	1 810	6 198	644	5 555	19 086	46.4	26.0
Phenix City.................	13 787	2.59	23.1	32.5	557	494	203	63	2 499	6 462	644	5 818	22 081	45.7	19.6
Prattville....................	12 480	2.75	12.3	27.1	398	362	181	36	1 355	3 814	228	3 586	22 009	38.9	30.2
Tuscaloosa..................	31 794	2.94	17.5	33.0	9 659	942	144	8 717	4 604	4 775	483	4 292	51 566	39.2	33.8
Vestavia Hills...............	13 637	2.50	6.8	29.8	141	138	138	3	478	1 406	65	1 341	23 578	12.2	67.1
ALASKA......................	251 678	2.89	11.2	25.5	26 352	6 458	1 626	19 894	25 018	3 396	636	2 760	460 319	35.7	27.7
Anchorage..................	105 164	2.84	12.0	25.0	8 450	2 828	1 137	5 622	14 136	4 692	865	3 827	188 115	30.8	32.9
Fairbanks...................	11 512	2.79	12.8	29.8	2 518	427	81	2 091	1 461	4 499	659	3 840	18 070	37.7	21.5
Juneau......................	12 081	2.67	11.0	25.7	887	408	57	479	1 061	3 216	573	2 643	21 948	26.8	37.8
ARIZONA....................	2 387 246	2.75	12.7	27.2	139 384	84 788	13 819	54 596	242 156	3 597	400	3 198	4 284 776	38.6	27.1
Apache Junction............	15 519	2.38	11.8	29.3	283	120	120	163	1 323	3 549	247	3 303	27 343	49.0	12.9
Avondale....................	23 030	3.38	19.4	15.4	160	146	132	14	3 797	4 778	287	4 491	45 071	47.0	18.9
Buckeye.....................	15 396	3.57	12.9	15.3	5 094	5 084	0	10	1 170	2 013	50	1 963	33 405	46.0	16.2
Bullhead City...............	16 796	2.35	13.2	30.4	166	96	93	70	1 684	4 281	206	4 075	29 307	51.5	13.1
Casa Grande...............	17 672	2.85	14.1	24.4	282	47	3	235	2 035	4 053	478	3 575	32 531	45.7	17.7
Chandler....................	86 853	2.82	11.2	23.1	546	136	94	410	6 109	2 421	185	2 236	156 264	25.8	39.7
El Mirage....................	9 888	3.30	18.2	18.7	13	0	0	13	1 071	3 216	168	3 047	18 520	48.9	14.0
Flagstaff.....................	23 239	2.90	12.7	25.1	8 076	668	114	7 408	3 295	4 742	396	4 346	35 215	25.3	42.8
Florence.....................	5 232	5.07	6.0	32.2	17 700	17 700	0	0	182	726	128	598	21 102	56.6	7.7
Gilbert.......................	71 614	3.12	11.0	16.1	304	4	0	300	3 730	1 584	90	1 494	135 259	21.3	40.3
Glendale....................	78 496	2.96	17.0	25.7	3 257	1 000	836	2 257	13 499	5 701	389	5 312	142 631	44.1	21.6
Goodyear....................	22 873	3.07	9.9	17.7	3 828	3 670	164	158	1 684	2 251	148	2 102	46 904	33.3	27.0
Kingman.....................	10 715	2.65	12.2	29.6	699	541	132	158	1 544	5 413	256	5 157	20 013	46.7	13.7
Lake Havasu City...........	22 633	2.33	9.8	26.4	201	151	142	50	1 197	2 263	166	2 097	39 934	46.2	14.5
Marana......................	13 470	2.75	9.0	17.8	520	499	0	21	1 090	2 777	51	2 726	25 070	22.7	40.1
Maricopa....................	14 481	3.13	10.3	17.5	0	0	0	0	738	1 613	175	1 439	29 319	33.4	25.6
Mesa........................	167 609	2.70	12.5	27.8	3 538	1 344	928	2 194	15 059	3 259	459	2 800	295 405	39.4	24.3
Oro Valley..................	17 364	2.39	8.3	24.3	68	63	42	5	665	1 592	36	1 556	30 682	16.6	50.8
Peoria.......................	58 203	2.75	12.0	24.2	1 227	868	826	359	3 543	2 151	148	2 003	106 982	33.9	27.5
Phoenix.....................	520 856	2.86	15.4	28.7	21 738	13 589	2 696	8 149	65 726	4 296	572	3 724	929 365	43.1	26.5
Prescott.....................	18 691	2.15	8.2	37.1	2 008	675	474	1 333	1 370	3 342	344	2 998	31 337	25.4	38.4
Prescott Valley..............	15 611	2.54	11.7	26.0	209	158	118	51	1 016	2 538	220	2 318	26 934	39.8	18.3
Queen Creek................	8 307	3.43	8.6	13.6	16	0	0	16	NA	NA	NA	NA	15 730	20.2	37.7
Sahuarita...................	9 135	2.89	8.6	17.0	63	44	44	19	402	1 478	33	1 444	16 805	24.9	35.2
San Luis....................	7 944	3.79	19.5	7.6	524	502	0	22	507	1 581	156	1 425	16 224	68.6	8.6
Scottsdale..................	100 891	2.22	7.9	33.5	1 159	686	622	473	5 663	2 469	158	2 312	169 772	17.7	53.2
Sierra Vista.................	16 911	2.68	12.3	26.1	3 037	233	217	2 804	1 396	3 092	171	2 922	28 404	25.9	31.4
Surprise.....................	44 472	2.74	10.8	21.5	274	89	80	185	2 236	1 788	110	1 679	81 636	33.1	28.3
Tempe.......................	63 523	2.63	11.7	33.2	10 188	298	280	9 890	8 843	5 208	471	4 737	96 643	26.2	41.0
Tucson......................	204 341	2.57	15.4	35.5	20 706	9 920	1 798	10 786	35 048	6 646	653	5 993	326 468	39.8	25.0
Yuma........................	32 523	2.86	13.7	20.5	5 128	3 291	308	1 837	5 223	3 397	442	2 956	54 665	48.3	16.1
ARKANSAS.................	1 132 488	2.60	13.4	27.9	78 931	47 287	18 532	31 644	113 261	3 818	480	3 338	1 949 963	50.7	20.6
Bella Vista..................	11 430	2.39	4.8	19.6	133	133	133	0	213	763	158	605	21 017	31.8	34.5
Benton.......................	11 851	2.72	15.3	25.6	493	462	289	31	1 576	4 669	376	4 292	21 276	41.0	27.3
Bentonville..................	14 209	2.71	10.5	22.5	258	179	160	79	751	1 817	150	1 667	24 507	31.3	44.4
Conway......................	23 205	2.69	12.0	30.0	4 038	1 118	372	2 920	3 265	5 031	391	4 640	34 680	33.4	36.6
Fayetteville..................	32 601	2.37	8.7	37.2	6 818	1 124	405	5 694	3 799	4 733	496	4 237	42 989	27.6	46.1
Fort Smith..................	34 542	2.52	13.9	33.1	1 930	1 083	592	847	5 339	6 068	752	5 315	56 410	49.5	20.7
Hot Springs.................	15 115	2.35	14.9	38.4	1 692	1 127	578	565	NA	NA	NA	NA	24 734	48.8	20.1

1. No spouse present.   2. Data for serious crimes have not been adjusted for underreporting. This may affect comparability between geographic areas and over time.   3. Per 100,000 population estimated by the FBI.   4. Persons 25 years old and over.

Table D. Cities — Income, Poverty, and Housing

City	Money income, 2010–2014				Housing units, 2010			Occupied housing units 2010–2014				
		Households			Families with income below poverty (percent)				Owner-occupied		Median owner costs as a percent of income	
	Per capita income[1] (dollars)	Median income	Percent with income of $200,000 or more	Percent with income of less than $25,000		Total	Percent change, 2000–2010	Vacant units for sale or rent[2]	Total	Percent	Median value[3] (dollars)	With a mortgage[4]	Without a mortgage[5]
	42	43	44	45	46	47	48	49	50	51	52	53	54
United States............	28 555	53 482	5.0	23.2	11.5	131 704 730	13.6	14 988 438	116 211 092	64.4	175 700	23.7	12.3
ALABAMA	23 936	43 511	2.6	29.8	14.6	2 171 853	10.6	288 062	1 842 174	69.2	123 800	21.7	11.4
Alabaster.................	27 625	70 173	2.9	15.2	8.5	11 295	28.3	667	10 416	83.3	164 200	21.4	10.2
Auburn....................	24 896	37 406	3.9	39.1	12.0	24 646	22.7	2 535	21 644	43.8	216 800	21.7	10.0
Bessemer................	16 716	30 369	0.5	42.6	26.2	12 369	-3.2	1 658	10 457	57.4	90 500	26.6	14.6
Birmingham..............	19 640	31 217	1.4	41.8	26.7	108 981	-2.9	19 599	88 817	48.5	86 100	26.6	14.1
Decatur..................	24 756	42 867	2.1	29.4	15.6	24 538	2.2	1 962	22 006	61.6	123 500	20.8	10.0
Dothan....................	24 847	42 026	3.3	30.6	15.4	29 274	12.6	2 429	25 935	59.3	137 700	20.5	10.0
Enterprise...............	25 916	51 692	1.9	26.1	15.9	11 616	20.2	1 103	10 182	63.1	169 600	20.2	10.0
Florence	22 991	35 632	1.9	39.2	19.4	19 299	9.1	2 032	17 617	57.5	119 200	22.2	10.5
Gadsden.................	17 981	27 922	1.5	45.5	25.0	17 672	-5.9	2 501	14 689	59.6	70 600	23.1	14.2
Homewood..............	32 160	62 431	6.7	20.4	7.9	11 385	0.5	1 293	9 306	54.1	286 300	21.3	10.2
Hoover...................	38 802	76 469	8.4	11.5	4.1	35 474	31.2	2 996	32 375	67.4	260 700	21.6	10.0
Huntsville...............	31 010	49 060	5.0	26.7	13.0	84 949	15.4	7 916	76 959	59.8	160 400	19.4	10.0
Madison.................	42 284	92 965	11.0	9.3	5.7	17 203	43.1	1 092	16 583	71.4	231 700	17.0	10.0
Mobile...................	23 509	39 241	3.1	33.9	19.6	89 127	3.5	10 168	75 653	57.1	123 600	23.8	11.9
Montgomery............	24 537	43 535	3.2	30.0	19.6	92 115	6.1	10 629	79 760	57.2	119 500	22.1	10.1
Opelika..................	25 012	39 506	2.5	32.0	17.5	11 751	14.4	1 228	11 183	60.4	148 300	21.0	10.7
Phenix City	21 014	36 225	1.3	32.5	21.1	15 198	15.0	1 955	13 787	49.3	118 600	23.4	12.3
Prattville................	26 834	57 478	2.9	19.5	7.1	13 541	40.7	830	12 480	68.4	150 100	20.1	10.0
Tuscaloosa.............	22 308	38 762	3.7	34.9	17.4	40 842	16.8	4 657	31 794	50.0	165 500	23.4	11.6
Vestavia Hills..........	51 102	81 352	14.8	13.0	3.2	14 952	40.8	965	13 637	73.3	339 000	20.6	11.2
ALASKA	33 129	71 829	5.9	14.8	7.0	306 967	17.6	48 909	251 678	63.3	246 300	22.8	10.8
Anchorage..............	36 508	78 121	8.0	11.9	5.6	113 032	12.6	5 700	105 164	59.8	286 600	22.8	10.9
Fairbanks...............	27 620	55 778	2.2	20.4	9.9	13 056	5.2	1 522	11 512	37.0	197 800	28.4	12.7
Juneau...................	38 057	84 750	7.4	9.9	4.3	13 055	6.3	868	12 081	63.7	318 000	23.1	11.0
ARIZONA	25 537	49 928	3.6	24.1	13.3	2 844 526	29.9	463 536	2 387 246	63.4	162 900	23.9	10.8
Apache Junction........	20 966	36 771	0.9	31.9	17.0	22 564	-1.0	6 990	15 519	72.7	88 000	26.7	11.7
Avondale	20 559	57 170	1.3	17.4	13.8	27 001	136.6	3 615	23 030	57.3	129 600	23.9	11.0
Buckeye.................	20 149	58 703	2.8	17.7	12.8	18 207	NA	3 783	15 396	66.4	139 400	22.9	10.0
Bullhead City	21 999	37 121	1.9	30.3	13.6	23 464	27.5	6 703	16 796	60.4	98 000	25.8	11.5
Casa Grande............	21 301	44 719	1.6	24.1	12.3	22 400	104.8	4 749	17 672	67.4	110 200	24.3	12.8
Chandler................	32 092	72 072	5.8	12.7	6.9	94 404	41.7	7 480	86 853	62.4	220 700	21.7	10.0
El Mirage...............	17 849	47 564	0.6	20.9	17.2	11 326	NA	1 910	9 888	63.1	94 800	25.1	12.4
Flagstaff................	24 702	48 120	3.6	27.4	15.0	26 254	22.5	3 418	23 239	44.9	263 000	23.6	10.0
Florence	13 286	48 503	1.4	25.2	10.8	5 224	60.5	1 894	5 232	72.8	99 600	23.0	10.0
Gilbert...................	31 546	81 485	6.4	9.5	5.3	74 907	102.2	5 535	71 614	71.3	231 100	21.9	10.0
Glendale................	21 817	46 855	2.4	26.1	17.0	90 505	13.6	11 391	78 496	55.8	141 500	23.2	11.7
Goodyear................	27 599	70 293	3.7	11.7	7.9	25 027	275.6	3 536	22 873	69.4	192 500	22.7	10.0
Kingman	22 436	42 859	1.6	28.3	15.3	12 724	48.6	1 507	10 715	62.9	106 500	22.4	11.5
Lake Havasu City........	24 136	42 718	1.6	23.7	9.3	32 327	40.6	9 159	22 633	68.5	194 800	27.1	12.4
Marana..................	33 649	74 817	5.7	9.8	3.3	14 726	160.3	1 653	13 470	75.9	210 900	22.6	10.2
Maricopa................	25 222	65 214	2.0	9.3	3.3	17 240	NA	2 881	14 481	78.0	134 600	23.6	13.4
Mesa....................	24 427	48 259	2.5	24.0	12.5	201 173	14.5	35 799	167 609	60.5	150 800	23.5	10.7
Oro Valley	39 397	74 480	6.8	12.3	3.6	20 340	45.2	2 536	17 364	74.8	276 600	21.9	10.0
Peoria...................	29 038	63 025	4.1	16.5	7.6	64 818	51.9	7 361	58 203	70.0	178 600	23.6	10.4
Phoenix..................	24 057	46 881	3.9	26.1	18.5	590 149	19.0	75 343	520 856	54.0	155 900	24.2	11.7
Prescott	29 120	45 190	2.8	28.0	8.4	22 159	27.1	3 548	18 691	65.7	265 500	27.2	12.2
Prescott Valley	21 560	42 973	1.2	26.4	11.3	17 494	84.5	2 130	15 611	60.4	164 400	25.7	10.7
Queen Creek............	30 547	83 809	8.0	8.8	7.2	8 557	NA	837	8 307	79.4	237 800	25.2	10.0
Sahuarita................	26 856	65 183	1.9	9.5	4.0	10 615	NA	1 595	9 135	80.9	181 600	23.3	11.3
San Luis	9 702	31 064	0.0	40.0	30.2	6 525	95.8	572	7 944	73.9	113 700	30.0	15.3
Scottsdale..............	51 564	72 455	13.8	15.9	5.7	124 001	18.2	22 728	100 891	66.8	376 700	23.9	11.5
Sierra Vista............	27 734	58 818	3.0	18.7	8.7	18 742	20.0	1 683	16 911	53.7	184 800	19.1	10.0
Surprise	25 609	59 094	1.6	14.9	8.2	52 586	222.5	9 314	44 472	74.1	171 700	24.0	11.0
Tempe	26 094	48 183	3.3	26.8	14.1	73 462	9.6	7 462	63 523	42.6	197 200	22.7	10.0
Tucson..................	20 437	37 149	1.2	34.5	18.6	229 762	9.5	24 372	204 341	49.6	133 500	24.3	12.3
Yuma	20 661	44 166	2.2	26.9	14.4	38 626	10.2	7 912	32 523	60.0	122 100	24.1	11.9
ARKANSAS...............	22 595	41 264	2.2	30.5	14.3	1 316 299	12.2	169 215	1 132 488	66.5	108 700	20.4	10.6
Bella Vista	31 734	62 500	3.9	12.8	2.4	13 241	49.2	1 512	11 430	87.2	151 500	19.4	10.0
Benton..................	25 794	52 341	2.3	21.1	9.7	12 902	38.9	1 068	11 851	68.9	135 700	20.9	11.6
Bentonville.............	34 811	71 461	7.0	16.7	6.2	14 693	84.9	1 440	14 209	56.5	167 800	18.1	10.0
Conway	24 785	47 126	3.1	27.0	11.4	24 402	41.2	2 003	23 205	49.8	158 500	20.0	10.0
Fayetteville.............	27 266	37 350	4.2	36.0	12.2	36 188	42.9	5 462	32 601	41.4	179 800	19.4	10.0
Fort Smith..............	23 452	36 777	3.2	34.0	20.6	37 899	7.2	3 547	34 542	54.3	113 500	20.8	10.3
Hot Springs	20 108	31 302	1.6	42.9	22.3	18 947	1.2	3 372	15 115	53.6	114 100	25.3	10.9

1. Based on population estimated by the American Community Survey.   2. Includes units rented or sold but not occupied.   3. Specified owner-occupied units; $1,000,000 represents $1,000,000 or more   4. 50.0 represents 50 percent or more.   5. 10.0 represents 10 percent or less.

Table D. Cities — Housing, Labor Force, and Employment

City	Occupied housing units, 2010–2014 (cont.)				Migration, 2010–2014		Civilian labor force, 2015		Unemployment		Civilian employment[4], 2010–2014			
	Percent renter occupied	Median gross rent[1]	Median gross rent as a percent of income[2]	Percent with no vehicle available	Percent who lived in the same house one year ago	Percent who lived outside current city one year ago	Total	Percent change, 2014–2015	Total	Rate[3]	Population age 16 and older	In labor force	Civilian full-year full-time workers	Households with no workers (percent)
	55	56	57	58	59	60	61	62	63	64	65	66	67	68
United States............	35.6	920	31.3	9.1	85.0	10.1	157 259 108	0.6	8 303 246	5.3	248 775 628	63.9	39.6	27.1
ALABAMA	30.8	715	30.9	6.5	85.0	10.4	2 146 157	-0.7	130 968	6.1	3 828 799	58.8	37.4	32.3
Alabaster................	16.7	985	27.3	1.4	88.7	9.5	16 709	-0.4	721	4.3	23 117	70.7	48.1	17.1
Auburn....................	56.2	791	44.8	5.0	64.1	19.8	28 172	0.5	1 531	5.4	48 318	59.1	29.5	26.5
Bessemer................	42.6	712	35.6	14.7	83.8	9.0	10 065	0.5	997	9.9	21 323	51.2	30.4	43.4
Birmingham............	51.5	728	35.2	14.5	78.8	9.7	91 963	-1.1	6 615	7.2	171 642	59.0	33.9	35.5
Decatur..................	38.4	606	26.7	6.7	85.5	7.3	26 293	-1.6	1 592	6.1	44 197	62.7	39.0	32.2
Dothan...................	40.7	684	29.3	7.1	84.4	7.2	29 284	-0.9	1 812	6.2	53 094	60.1	39.4	31.0
Enterprise..............	36.9	739	27.3	5.3	81.6	14.3	10 618	0.6	619	5.8	21 221	60.5	34.9	29.2
Florence.................	42.5	569	32.6	8.5	79.0	10.8	18 368	-1.9	1 226	6.7	32 727	55.9	32.3	37.1
Gadsden.................	40.4	590	31.8	11.3	81.7	9.1	13 793	-1.6	1 011	7.3	29 052	50.7	29.4	44.6
Homewood..............	45.9	923	28.1	3.7	75.7	19.0	13 934	-0.6	556	4.0	20 157	70.1	46.9	18.3
Hoover...................	32.6	977	27.6	2.9	83.1	12.1	43 587	-0.6	1 800	4.1	64 293	68.7	47.3	20.5
Huntsville..............	40.2	723	30.2	6.9	81.2	8.6	90 848	0.2	5 362	5.9	149 514	64.8	39.9	27.6
Madison.................	28.6	857	24.2	1.7	84.8	12.0	23 332	0.3	1 096	4.7	34 279	70.5	49.3	15.9
Mobile...................	42.9	764	34.0	9.6	83.4	6.6	85 466	-1.3	6 170	7.2	155 016	58.4	36.2	32.6
Montgomery............	42.8	818	32.6	8.6	77.3	8.5	91 113	-1.2	5 741	6.3	158 895	61.9	39.0	28.2
Opelika..................	39.6	685	32.6	10.5	83.5	9.6	13 679	0.4	753	5.5	22 475	60.3	39.3	28.8
Phenix City............	50.7	749	30.5	8.9	75.7	13.3	15 471	-1.3	857	5.5	27 043	63.5	38.6	28.2
Prattville...............	31.6	929	29.6	4.9	80.3	14.1	16 536	-0.5	836	5.1	26 037	65.1	43.2	25.3
Tuscaloosa.............	50.0	778	35.4	9.8	73.2	14.4	44 410	1.2	2 784	6.3	77 492	54.9	32.7	31.2
Vestavia Hills..........	26.7	1 093	32.7	6.6	88.1	9.8	17 234	-0.4	652	3.8	26 361	63.5	45.7	25.4
ALASKA	36.7	1 131	28.3	9.6	80.9	11.2	363 822	-0.6	23 595	6.5	560 680	70.8	40.2	20.2
Anchorage..............	40.2	1 172	28.9	6.0	80.3	8.0	158 216	-0.1	7 915	5.0	230 822	74.1	45.2	15.6
Fairbanks...............	63.0	1 253	33.6	10.5	64.8	24.7	12 768	-0.8	812	6.4	24 142	71.9	32.5	22.2
Juneau...................	36.3	1 169	26.2	8.5	82.2	6.6	17 308	-1.0	800	4.6	25 814	71.7	49.0	17.8
ARIZONA	36.6	905	30.5	6.9	80.9	11.3	3 152 708	1.8	193 190	6.1	5 121 781	60.1	36.9	30.1
Apache Junction...........	27.3	772	32.2	7.6	82.0	10.8	13 793	2.8	1 167	8.5	30 373	45.5	24.8	52.6
Avondale................	42.7	1 043	26.7	4.7	81.9	13.1	40 244	2.3	2 271	5.6	56 818	69.9	47.6	15.1
Buckeye.................	33.6	1 112	31.6	3.6	79.3	15.6	23 630	2.1	1 465	6.2	40 105	53.8	36.7	22.7
Bullhead City...........	39.6	779	30.2	6.7	75.6	13.2	15 692	0.9	1 208	7.7	32 874	50.0	27.0	47.1
Casa Grande..........	32.6	892	30.6	5.9	81.8	9.1	22 001	2.2	1 423	6.5	38 093	55.1	34.2	37.2
Chandler................	37.6	1 103	26.1	3.4	79.9	13.1	142 059	2.6	6 395	4.5	185 373	73.0	49.7	15.8
El Mirage...............	36.9	1 089	29.3	3.7	86.6	11.1	15 258	2.1	903	5.9	23 002	63.8	39.5	21.5
Flagstaff................	55.1	1 037	34.9	6.4	70.2	16.3	39 760	1.4	1 815	4.6	55 922	69.7	33.9	18.4
Florence.................	27.2	787	27.2	4.5	63.1	32.6	3 757	2.2	251	6.7	24 204	15.2	9.8	58.2
Gilbert...................	28.7	1 263	26.4	2.1	80.9	12.9	129 066	2.6	5 374	4.2	159 025	73.6	49.9	13.6
Glendale................	44.2	863	32.6	9.1	81.8	12.8	114 350	2.3	6 306	5.5	176 618	64.2	39.7	24.2
Goodyear................	30.6	1 183	27.5	3.4	82.9	13.2	35 399	2.6	1 918	5.4	53 221	59.6	41.1	23.9
Kingman................	37.1	825	26.6	7.3	71.5	15.4	12 395	2.2	1 007	8.1	22 990	49.4	29.4	41.8
Lake Havasu City........	31.5	853	31.1	4.9	82.2	8.4	22 769	0.6	1 712	7.5	44 671	48.5	26.4	46.5
Marana..................	24.1	1 282	26.7	2.1	80.0	14.4	20 012	0.5	876	4.4	28 170	64.8	43.5	26.9
Maricopa...............	22.0	1 232	27.1	1.0	83.7	10.6	23 281	2.4	1 279	5.5	33 011	66.3	47.0	17.7
Mesa.....................	39.5	875	31.7	7.2	79.8	11.4	224 574	2.5	11 743	5.2	353 246	61.9	38.6	30.0
Oro Valley	25.2	1 051	26.8	3.0	84.3	11.6	18 120	0.6	925	5.1	34 712	52.8	31.0	40.7
Peoria...................	30.0	1 102	30.7	5.4	85.8	9.6	84 446	2.5	4 057	4.8	124 743	64.5	42.7	26.9
Phoenix	46.0	876	31.2	9.1	79.8	8.0	754 848	2.4	40 780	5.4	1 126 981	65.8	42.3	22.4
Prescott.................	34.3	811	35.5	8.9	76.1	16.2	17 027	2.2	1 063	6.2	35 397	44.3	22.2	50.9
Prescott Valley	39.6	866	32.7	4.7	80.4	13.5	19 669	2.1	991	5.0	31 517	57.7	31.5	36.9
Queen Creek............	20.6	1 305	22.8	1.2	78.6	15.8	15 667	2.8	636	4.1	18 282	69.5	50.4	15.6
Sahuarita	19.1	1 260	27.7	1.1	84.2	9.3	11 563	0.4	575	5.0	18 639	59.5	41.1	27.5
San Luis	26.1	618	32.6	8.9	89.4	7.0	18 999	0.4	9 130	48.1	21 660	53.1	23.8	32.7
Scottsdale..............	33.2	1 132	27.4	4.5	81.1	11.7	127 319	2.7	5 458	4.3	189 999	63.9	42.0	28.4
Sierra Vista............	46.3	939	27.2	6.3	74.0	18.8	18 350	-1.3	1 164	6.3	34 938	63.9	32.8	28.9
Surprise.................	25.9	1 195	29.5	2.8	86.1	9.2	51 705	2.4	2 919	5.6	92 103	55.8	36.1	35.8
Tempe....................	57.4	941	31.2	10.4	67.0	22.1	101 068	2.6	4 898	4.8	142 212	69.3	38.8	21.8
Tucson...................	50.4	750	33.7	12.3	74.9	9.4	249 867	0.3	14 622	5.9	422 318	61.7	33.7	29.8
Yuma....................	40.0	885	31.4	6.3	76.5	12.2	42 024	0.6	5 892	14.0	69 608	61.9	34.4	29.0
ARKANSAS.............	33.5	675	29.6	6.4	83.8	10.5	1 330 099	2.0	69 484	5.2	2 315 782	59.2	38.4	31.4
Bella Vista	12.8	964	28.8	1.8	87.6	9.2	11 631	5.2	513	4.4	22 720	49.9	35.7	41.9
Benton...................	31.1	748	27.9	7.1	86.9	8.4	15 967	2.4	707	4.4	24 688	64.2	45.0	27.2
Bentonville.............	43.5	770	21.8	4.9	73.7	20.4	21 653	5.3	758	3.5	28 722	69.1	54.0	15.0
Conway.................	50.2	723	30.2	6.5	76.9	12.5	32 592	1.9	1 488	4.6	49 233	67.0	42.2	21.3
Fayetteville............	58.6	711	33.1	7.1	65.9	19.1	44 068	5.2	1 660	3.8	64 944	65.6	36.9	25.0
Fort Smith..............	45.7	620	29.1	9.0	82.6	7.9	39 911	1.2	2 000	5.0	67 798	60.3	40.2	29.4
Hot Springs	46.4	661	34.2	14.8	77.5	10.5	14 019	0.0	887	6.3	28 897	53.1	28.9	41.6

1. $2,000 represents $2,000 or more.   2. 50.0 represents 50 percent or more.   3. Percent of civilian labor force.   4. Persons 16 years old and over.

Table D. Cities — Construction, Wholesale Trade, and Retail Trade

City	Value of residential construction authorized by building permits, 2015			Wholesale trade,[1] 2012				Retail trade,[2] 2012			
	New construction ($1,000)	Number of housing units	Percent single family	Number of establishments	Number of employees	Sales (mil dol)	Annual payroll (mil dol)	Number of establishments	Number of employees	Sales (mil dol)	Annual payroll (mil dol)
	69	70	71	72	73	74	75	76	77	78	79
United States............	223 611 322	1 182 582	58.9	355 983	4 880 666	5 208 023.5	287 549.6	1 062 083	14 703 529	4 219 821.9	369 001.4
ALABAMA	2 416 774	14 054	73.0	4 600	60 332	57 746.6	2 894.7	18 211	218 531	58 565.0	5 123.1
Alabaster	33 076	109	100.0	44	579	489.1	26.3	92	1 773	388.8	39.2
Auburn........................	151 065	488	98.8	34	217	235.5	9.0	206	3 180	779.4	70.4
Bessemer	1 823	10	100.0	58	944	417.9	52.0	194	2 746	732.0	70.4
Birmingham	81 578	778	4.6	500	9 168	7 099.9	481.8	943	12 300	3 305.9	318.1
Decatur.......................	6 759	36	100.0	77	1 316	1 022.6	56.7	332	4 256	1 140.4	99.1
Dothan.......................	58 031	233	93.1	148	D	D	D	501	7 114	1 990.0	173.0
Enterprise	9 570	55	100.0	11	38	13.6	1.4	155	1 802	521.3	47.9
Florence	11 585	151	44.4	49	584	209.3	22.4	302	4 139	967.8	88.7
Gadsden.....................	584	8	100.0	39	351	293.5	14.5	229	3 037	731.2	60.6
Homewood	12 783	30	100.0	65	775	499.4	42.2	224	3 152	662.1	76.7
Hoover.......................	104 410	358	100.0	80	1 134	2 347.7	102.5	384	7 578	2 425.7	200.6
Huntsville...................	78 069	1 505	67.8	225	3 051	3 197.3	168.8	999	14 677	3 945.3	360.9
Madison	167 869	466	100.0	52	728	426.2	39.6	131	2 356	550.6	52.7
Mobile	29 708	195	35.9	353	4 191	2 717.6	205.9	968	14 109	3 661.5	339.7
Montgomery	71 147	528	49.2	274	4 739	3 703.7	214.7	874	11 871	3 163.3	294.6
Opelika	33 970	149	100.0	32	373	261.3	18.4	206	2 732	725.2	58.3
Phenix City	38 392	400	21.5	10	D	D	D	125	1 683	413.4	36.8
Prattville....................	39 749	158	100.0	19	84	33.2	2.7	152	2 669	621.9	60.7
Tuscaloosa	110 123	567	48.1	77	955	638.5	48.4	475	6 821	1 782.8	149.8
Vestavia Hills..............	62 322	360	24.4	39	220	213.9	14.5	156	1 659	396.1	43.3
ALASKA	324 596	1 298	76.4	638	7 734	5 216.3	440.9	2 508	33 721	10 474.3	977.4
Anchorage.................	232 790	834	77.7	336	5 228	3 147.7	296.6	860	15 253	4 966.8	462.2
Fairbanks...................	0	0	0.0	47	531	309.2	29.6	208	3 630	1 300.3	116.3
Juneau.......................	18 824	94	87.2	36	265	196.9	12.8	142	1 821	491.4	53.0
ARIZONA	6 985 714	28 910	77.2	5 570	73 496	69 437.3	4 144.3	17 479	286 184	84 716.5	7 367.8
Apache Junction..........	5 588	40	80.0	11	D	D	D	90	1 591	515.0	41.0
Avondale	35 240	123	100.0	15	161	73.6	8.2	113	3 480	1 360.9	107.5
Buckeye......................	269 414	1 106	100.0	15	106	71.4	4.9	50	597	260.8	14.1
Bullhead City	20 288	79	100.0	9	64	26.3	2.4	119	2 195	552.0	52.5
Casa Grande...............	20 791	89	100.0	25	403	196.3	17.9	190	3 440	896.6	75.4
Chandler.....................	561 638	2 122	54.2	228	4 007	5 269.8	257.8	658	13 607	4 225.0	382.5
El Mirage	535	3	100.0	4	36	16.5	1.3	26	498	117.5	12.0
Flagstaff.....................	56 093	396	50.5	68	554	377.7	26.2	322	5 224	1 383.9	120.5
Florence	58 220	177	100.0	1	D	D	D	12	142	39.9	3.1
Gilbert........................	363 787	1 949	93.3	143	1 264	666.2	63.7	470	9 470	2 762.7	251.0
Glendale.....................	115 884	447	24.4	118	1 188	834.2	47.7	674	12 710	3 821.3	320.8
Goodyear....................	308 803	1 194	100.0	23	D	D	D	141	3 318	788.1	74.7
Kingman	36 029	207	99.0	22	211	115.2	7.7	128	2 586	896.1	59.8
Lake Havasu City.........	55 986	291	97.3	48	223	86.2	9.0	215	2 843	914.5	71.1
Marana	190 921	633	100.0	20	108	41.2	5.1	114	2 868	865.1	73.1
Maricopa....................	72 081	322	100.0	7	16	4.6	0.6	26	729	213.8	16.1
Mesa.........................	672 148	2 693	64.8	292	3 313	2 705.3	168.9	1 315	22 342	5 819.7	549.5
Oro Valley	70 760	159	100.0	23	57	52.4	3.6	90	2 092	496.7	46.5
Peoria........................	423 582	1 599	99.4	60	289	266.3	12.7	387	8 515	2 657.7	235.0
Phoenix......................	1 105 661	4 611	49.1	1 853	30 877	31 193.7	1 638.2	3 712	60 797	18 448.4	1 620.7
Prescott	92 749	442	62.9	62	557	453.8	29.8	279	4 290	1 030.2	102.4
Prescott Valley............	94 716	421	99.0	31	430	305.1	15.7	100	1 348	360.2	32.2
Queen Creek...............	370 554	987	100.0	7	14	5.0	0.6	50	973	227.1	20.0
Sahuarita	62 766	271	100.0	3	D	D	D	23	730	192.6	16.4
San Luis	21 783	146	100.0	8	233	36.1	11.0	36	591	136.0	10.2
Scottsdale..................	308 392	733	73.7	505	4 707	4 011.1	311.5	1 218	18 728	5 848.1	574.5
Sierra Vista.................	10 971	59	100.0	12	86	25.4	2.4	160	2 810	686.5	63.9
Surprise	187 160	609	88.2	27	401	159.2	16.0	169	4 396	1 137.0	105.7
Tempe	103 478	938	24.4	436	8 635	8 373.2	562.7	755	14 805	7 231.6	431.6
Tucson.......................	120 942	560	63.9	446	4 468	2 221.8	192.0	1 883	30 599	7 878.2	774.0
Yuma	69 615	383	100.0	80	1 615	963.8	67.0	302	5 503	1 528.9	132.8
ARKANSAS.............	1 380 106	8 500	67.2	2 884	34 492	31 256.1	1 630.8	10 923	135 448	36 815.3	3 061.5
Bella Vista	18 846	68	100.0	12	20	21.6	0.9	25	307	60.7	5.8
Benton	58 885	790	20.0	23	138	130.1	5.6	127	1 859	659.5	46.2
Bentonville..................	196 364	878	55.1	86	1 135	1 338.4	79.1	119	2 488	1 024.2	68.7
Conway	30 194	138	94.2	57	618	460.6	27.8	284	4 730	1 246.1	100.9
Fayetteville.................	117 548	604	62.6	54	550	372.7	25.1	419	7 043	1 766.8	156.5
Fort Smith	38 164	170	54.1	171	2 184	1 605.2	98.1	521	7 161	1 767.6	157.2
Hot Springs	9 869	59	100.0	43	409	151.5	14.7	364	4 655	1 242.1	108.3

1. Merchant wholesalers except manufacturers' sales branches and offices. 2. Establishments with payroll.

Table D. Cities — Real Estate, Professional Services, and Manufacturing

City	Real estate and rental and leasing, 2012				Professional, scientific, and technical services,[1] 2012				Manufacturing, 2012			
	Number of establishments	Number of employees	Receipts (mil dol)	Annual payroll (mil dol)	Number of establishments	Number of employees	Receipts (mil dol)	Annual payroll (mil dol)	Number of establishments	Number of employees	Receipts (mil dol)	Annual payroll (mil dol)
	80	81	82	83	84	85	86	87	88	89	90	91
United States	354 106	1 923 770	487 655.2	85 326.0	851 542	7 997 617	1 440 060.5	566 412.5	297 191	11 214 165	5 696 729.6	593 397.0
ALABAMA	3 858	22 852	3 919.4	819.6	9 062	88 566	16 043.5	5 633.1	4 283	232 650	124 809.8	11 099.5
Alabaster	17	54	11.1	1.8	58	528	119.8	20.0	26	1 145	478.6	63.1
Auburn	54	299	45.0	8.5	125	1 074	102.4	44.3	60	3 523	D	141.7
Bessemer	27	159	26.3	6.6	72	D	D	D	41	1 549	466.6	70.1
Birmingham	281	3 076	417.2	129.1	834	D	D	D	249	10 654	4 118.4	568.2
Decatur	57	218	43.9	6.7	139	978	110.2	44.0	82	4 735	4 680.9	284.7
Dothan	94	D	D	D	192	D	D	D	78	D	1 285.1	D
Enterprise	40	198	19.6	4.1	49	425	74.3	21.0	18	844	D	32.6
Florence	77	309	47.2	9.1	134	D	D	D	53	2 616	631.6	82.3
Gadsden	39	182	34.3	5.0	99	1 065	55.2	29.2	48	3 839	1 058.2	162.3
Homewood	59	362	70.9	17.5	157	1 291	225.2	76.1	24	1 121	564.1	55.4
Hoover	95	675	274.1	36.2	281	D	D	D	25	345	49.7	13.1
Huntsville	311	D	D	D	999	28 634	6 933.7	2 324.3	173	13 598	6 213.8	771.4
Madison	56	266	48.8	8.9	150	D	D	D	32	977	D	48.4
Mobile	310	1 554	312.4	60.4	701	D	D	D	152	8 817	3 274.4	471.1
Montgomery	219	1 890	339.1	64.8	575	5 871	1 258.6	386.5	172	10 902	9 125.1	528.6
Opelika	40	149	17.8	4.0	62	D	D	D	34	2 067	D	93.7
Phenix City	34	95	16.7	2.5	46	170	16.6	4.4	31	839	1 110.6	113.0
Prattville	35	138	20.4	3.9	54	276	28.7	10.8	15	839	651.5	54.1
Tuscaloosa	124	1 192	129.1	35.8	232	1 584	260.5	78.4	53	4 454	4 234.8	221.7
Vestavia Hills	81	1 191	389.9	73.2	173	D	D	D	15	47	D	1.9
ALASKA	872	4 212	1 022.7	187.6	1 866	17 328	3 140.3	1 163.5	527	12 450	D	514.5
Anchorage	383	2 403	631.3	112.1	1 128	13 444	2 515.7	954.8	182	2 049	479.8	95.7
Fairbanks	88	468	116.2	25.1	137	D	D	D	37	239	D	10.7
Juneau	61	249	42.2	7.0	86	D	D	D	26	236	75.4	11.7
ARIZONA	8 089	40 479	9 329.7	1 693.2	16 112	119 843	19 041.9	7 272.6	4 269	131 941	51 243.5	8 193.2
Apache Junction	40	141	22.6	2.6	22	76	7.6	2.2	13	85	D	3.5
Avondale	42	118	15.7	3.1	47	197	14.8	5.4	9	29	12.9	1.5
Buckeye	19	59	9.6	2.0	37	196	32.4	10.6	11	203	D	6.4
Bullhead City	52	187	20.0	4.5	45	D	D	D	6	39	D	1.3
Casa Grande	52	198	39.6	5.6	59	D	D	D	37	1 753	1 807.3	96.5
Chandler	304	896	252.4	34.7	642	3 678	535.3	203.9	165	7 413	2 535.2	459.9
El Mirage	10	D	D	D	7	18	2.4	0.4	13	251	74.4	12.3
Flagstaff	129	450	101.0	16.3	249	D	D	D	58	3 453	2 006.0	287.8
Florence	4	D	D	D	8	23	1.4	0.8	NA	NA	NA	NA
Gilbert	292	787	170.2	33.4	533	D	D	D	118	1 887	338.2	84.8
Glendale	215	820	160.3	26.3	308	D	D	D	134	2 988	829.9	156.5
Goodyear	62	136	25.4	4.4	88	480	48.3	24.1	22	1 220	384.0	58.7
Kingman	35	94	14.4	2.6	48	D	D	D	11	133	47.4	5.1
Lake Havasu City	80	277	38.8	6.6	96	319	26.2	9.5	65	916	217.3	34.4
Marana	31	81	12.7	2.8	57	D	D	D	30	1 028	344.7	59.1
Maricopa	15	29	4.7	0.7	38	94	6.4	4.0	11	148	D	6.4
Mesa	547	2 280	456.6	72.6	1 021	5 199	668.1	255.6	245	7 319	3 353.0	583.2
Oro Valley	60	D	D	D	123	447	49.3	36.5	10	2 279	803.0	215.5
Peoria	156	621	111.0	20.1	219	D	D	D	49	874	177.8	36.4
Phoenix	1 894	13 507	2 965.5	673.8	4 848	43 895	7 794.4	2 992.6	1 338	38 642	12 978.9	2 175.5
Prescott	127	254	52.5	7.3	218	D	D	D	61	1 457	404.8	76.0
Prescott Valley	36	99	21.8	4.0	42	336	43.9	21.0	31	603	149.6	24.3
Queen Creek	24	D	D	D	52	136	13.3	4.6	5	27	D	1.3
Sahuarita	10	17	2.7	0.4	14	34	3.1	1.2	3	D	D	D
San Luis	5	D	D	D	5	D	D	D	5	D	D	D
Scottsdale	983	5 713	2 175.5	276.0	1 986	D	D	D	216	7 082	4 532.5	612.3
Sierra Vista	60	317	42.5	9.0	103	D	D	D	11	57	7.8	1.7
Surprise	63	148	31.2	4.2	81	D	D	D	19	281	143.7	8.9
Tempe	407	3 684	1 027.0	165.6	970	12 464	2 302.8	772.1	373	15 660	5 445.1	914.4
Tucson	735	3 966	628.3	129.9	1 563	10 568	1 457.1	581.5	393	6 648	1 551.5	312.7
Yuma	124	513	71.6	14.0	171	D	D	D	42	1 800	785.5	71.2
ARKANSAS	2 802	12 867	1 922.7	409.8	5 655	31 871	4 464.9	1 549.2	2 688	153 706	62 712.9	6 290.8
Bella Vista	24	D	D	D	34	65	9.3	2.6	NA	NA	NA	NA
Benton	26	53	14.9	1.3	62	250	26.1	8.8	35	561	133.7	24.4
Bentonville	67	286	68.9	14.3	225	D	D	D	21	304	135.3	12.0
Conway	94	402	98.9	17.6	168	D	D	D	54	3 479	1 156.6	168.0
Fayetteville	137	2 012	133.0	52.1	364	1 850	231.9	87.0	57	4 106	1 031.7	156.0
Fort Smith	156	813	124.2	25.5	272	D	D	D	148	13 228	4 983.3	538.8
Hot Springs	73	302	48.2	8.4	147	D	D	D	33	800	147.3	37.0

1. Establishments subject to federal tax.

Table D. Cities — Accommodation and Food Services, Arts, Entertainment, and Recreation, and Health Care and Social Assistance

City	Accommodation and food services, 2012				Arts, entertainment, and recreation,[1] 2012				Health care and social assistance,[1] 2012			
	Number of establishments	Number of employees	Sales (mil dol)	Annual payroll (mil dol)	Number of establishments	Number of employees	Receipts (mil dol)	Annual payroll (mil dol)	Number of establishments	Number of employees	Receipts (mil dol)	Annual payroll (mil dol)
	92	93	94	95	96	97	98	99	100	101	102	103
United States.............	662 489	12 007 689	708 138.6	196 103.3	99 659	1 486 462	161 690.3	50 328.5	690 525	9 542 138	1 008 744.6	409 811.9
ALABAMA	8 339	157 337	7 576.5	2 071.1	782	10 487	885.0	178.3	8 489	142 386	14 627.8	5 995.0
Alabaster	48	1 162	60.6	17.0	5	D	D	D	85	D	D	D
Auburn	198	3 581	163.3	41.4	13	D	D	D	103	D	D	D
Bessemer	95	1 734	86.8	24.2	7	89	6.5	2.0	85	D	D	D
Birmingham	564	11 239	625.3	185.7	38	570	38.8	10.9	615	12 973	1 675.5	690.7
Decatur	140	2 847	134.6	38.0	10	171	6.8	2.2	217	2 511	271.7	95.3
Dothan	223	4 538	209.2	56.1	18	D	D	D	257	D	D	D
Enterprise	73	1 202	58.3	14.4	9	D	D	D	75	D	D	D
Florence	129	3 445	141.4	42.9	10	D	D	D	183	3 575	406.3	142.1
Gadsden.......................	90	2 203	101.3	27.6	6	D	D	D	182	5 271	564.2	244.0
Homewood	117	2 294	132.3	35.5	6	D	D	D	182	5 513	800.3	271.4
Hoover	187	4 241	244.5	72.4	20	213	19.4	3.1	219	3 211	266.0	124.0
Huntsville	527	11 685	575.1	162.0	53	831	33.1	12.8	596	9 963	1 301.2	536.7
Madison	109	1 795	93.9	24.8	11	105	3.9	1.2	110	D	D	D
Mobile..........................	488	10 868	488.5	134.3	41	1 339	25.6	7.7	469	10 192	1 150.0	515.1
Montgomery	471	9 716	462.3	127.8	28	D	D	D	539	D	D	D
Opelika	98	2 049	94.4	25.6	3	D	D	D	82	D	D	D
Phenix City	67	1 285	60.2	14.6	3	D	D	D	53	D	D	D
Prattville......................	85	2 148	103.2	28.2	7	D	D	D	73	D	D	D
Tuscaloosa	284	6 941	344.2	86.9	13	157	8.5	3.2	217	D	D	D
Vestavia Hills...............	77	1 770	83.6	23.4	13	226	19.2	8.0	118	D	D	D
ALASKA	2 126	26 836	2 221.3	626.0	441	4 161	328.4	68.0	1 851	21 389	2 810.2	1 098.5
Anchorage	788	14 957	1 106.2	338.1	108	D	D	D	962	12 792	1 783.5	682.5
Fairbanks	138	2 215	177.4	46.9	31	D	D	D	165	2 316	301.7	136.0
Juneau.........................	119	1 329	81.5	24.1	27	D	D	D	92	644	90.1	33.2
ARIZONA	11 669	251 455	13 996.6	4 030.3	1 424	33 881	3 279.3	1 088.3	15 041	184 186	20 221.1	7 974.6
Apache Junction...........	45	665	28.9	7.9	4	D	D	D	48	1 078	84.4	37.2
Avondale	86	1 658	82.7	22.2	7	D	D	D	104	1 026	109.9	35.9
Buckeye.......................	46	798	35.8	9.3	4	163	5.7	2.3	16	D	D	D
Bullhead City	85	1 091	54.2	14.5	7	167	4.0	1.5	109	2 009	285.4	97.3
Casa Grande.................	114	D	D	D	7	D	D	D	144	1 810	164.5	71.2
Chandler......................	474	10 996	559.8	181.3	63	2 325	434.4	62.7	676	7 874	833.7	289.4
El Mirage	11	128	7.1	1.6	NA	NA	NA	NA	6	D	D	D
Flagstaff.......................	300	6 034	326.5	86.4	29	440	27.4	9.3	286	2 220	273.8	105.4
Florence	24	D	D	D	2	D	D	D	17	D	D	D
Gilbert..........................	287	6 139	297.6	85.7	48	1 045	48.7	14.8	619	5 146	520.0	191.9
Glendale	381	8 050	387.3	108.4	40	D	D	D	574	7 794	931.5	370.5
Goodyear	113	2 899	141.1	39.2	12	D	D	D	129	3 464	369.7	146.7
Kingman	92	1 681	74.6	21.2	5	D	D	D	103	D	D	D
Lake Havasu City.........	134	2 333	97.3	29.5	12	D	D	D	165	2 272	263.2	93.2
Marana	96	2 178	121.3	36.3	14	454	19.5	9.8	44	D	D	D
Maricopa......................	30	479	23.2	5.9	3	D	D	D	33	D	D	D
Mesa............................	733	14 688	685.3	202.1	76	1 920	85.3	29.5	1 135	14 098	1 418.9	568.5
Oro Valley	67	1 998	87.2	30.1	14	D	D	D	117	D	D	D
Peoria..........................	243	5 889	281.9	85.8	31	480	28.5	9.0	368	4 425	462.6	214.7
Phoenix	2 493	57 339	3 479.6	992.4	295	6 038	626.0	312.8	3 435	45 960	5 433.6	2 241.6
Prescott........................	154	2 390	116.7	34.9	17	163	10.3	3.5	323	3 046	292.3	110.1
Prescott Valley	75	1 112	49.3	14.8	11	241	7.4	2.9	103	1 203	95.9	41.0
Queen Creek.................	38	698	31.9	9.4	4	109	6.9	1.7	71	D	D	D
Sahuarita	19	438	15.1	4.0	2	D	D	D	19	D	D	D
San Luis	14	206	9.5	2.2	1	D	D	D	14	123	10.6	4.7
Scottsdale.....................	746	22 062	1 370.6	421.5	145	3 996	294.0	97.4	1 422	13 486	1 598.1	648.8
Sierra Vista	100	2 058	91.3	26.4	8	D	D	D	135	1 490	125.8	49.2
Surprise	140	3 145	151.8	42.8	11	210	10.9	4.1	165	1 110	119.2	43.1
Tempe..........................	563	12 672	646.1	183.9	60	1 217	267.5	181.7	507	7 866	855.5	321.6
Tucson.........................	1 214	26 136	1 235.4	350.0	117	1 487	61.4	17.9	1 485	19 878	2 194.4	824.6
Yuma...........................	227	4 641	254.2	64.1	14	D	D	D	273	D	D	D
ARKANSAS...............	5 473	95 854	4 307.3	1 182.5	563	5 927	499.0	104.3	5 936	86 999	8 540.6	3 495.8
Bella Vista	20	D	D	D	2	D	D	D	26	402	28.6	11.3
Benton.........................	62	1 080	51.2	13.5	9	53	1.6	0.5	80	1 254	91.3	43.5
Bentonville...................	123	2 365	111.2	30.2	10	119	8.0	2.2	99	1 121	120.3	44.2
Conway	172	4 248	177.6	48.5	11	D	D	D	206	2 682	239.8	96.7
Fayetteville	326	6 288	270.4	77.3	28	309	13.5	4.3	304	4 648	483.1	202.3
Fort Smith....................	245	5 188	232.1	67.2	16	D	D	D	299	6 889	843.4	335.9
Hot Springs	194	4 178	178.1	52.6	27	D	D	D	199	2 884	369.2	142.9

1. Establishments subject to federal tax.

Table D. Cities — Other Services and Government Employment and Payroll

	Other services[1], 2012				Government employment and payroll, 2012								
						March payroll							
							Percent of total for:						
City	Number of establishments	Number of employees	Receipts (mil dol)	Annual payroll (mil dol)	Full-time equivalent employees	Total (dollars)	Administration, judicial, and legal	Police and Corrections	Fire Protection	Highways and transportation	Health and welfare	Natural resources and utilities	Education and libraries
	104	105	106	107	108	109	110	111	112	113	114	115	116
United States..............	422 719	2 543 493	230 974.9	69 948.3	X	X	X	X	X	X	X	X	X
ALABAMA	5 009	31 262	3 191.9	893.0	X	X	X	X	X	X	X	X	X
Alabaster..................	36	177	12.5	3.9	226	902 906	9.2	32.9	29.4	6.0	0.0	14.0	4.0
Auburn......................	70	342	24.8	7.2	541	1 872 172	15.3	25.8	16.5	9.6	0.9	24.2	4.1
Bessemer..................	45	470	67.5	19.5	570	2 109 401	7.5	25.2	23.3	0.5	0.9	32.7	1.8
Birmingham	308	3 072	292.1	97.3	4 784	19 867 336	9.5	27.6	17.4	3.5	0.9	29.6	4.1
Decatur.....................	77	654	60.7	18.3	695	2 762 157	6.2	20.0	17.7	5.1	1.4	45.8	0.0
Dothan......................	145	D	D	D	980	3 540 917	11.7	22.1	20.0	3.1	0.8	33.9	0.0
Enterprise.................	45	236	21.2	6.5	572	1 406 470	3.3	16.3	8.9	3.8	48.7	17.5	0.8
Florence...................	70	471	30.4	9.5	814	2 966 594	5.4	16.5	13.1	6.3	0.6	51.8	0.0
Gadsden...................	51	332	33.7	10.1	813	2 569 152	8.3	19.3	20.9	8.8	0.9	30.2	2.8
Homewood	63	1 403	81.3	31.4	357	1 440 394	4.5	33.6	23.3	6.7	0.0	16.2	7.0
Hoover......................	79	450	43.0	12.5	663	3 382 691	10.6	31.1	26.9	5.3	0.7	8.2	7.7
Huntsville..................	269	2 553	476.6	101.5	2 636	11 833 638	8.9	19.0	14.5	7.2	2.2	32.4	0.0
Madison....................	54	366	30.0	9.7	374	1 553 149	16.6	30.8	22.6	2.6	0.0	24.9	0.0
Mobile......................	311	2 205	183.3	55.0	2 894	9 605 291	10.7	26.2	21.6	4.7	1.5	25.1	3.9
Montgomery..............	243	1 612	142.5	42.9	2 884	10 068 707	8.1	26.1	17.3	7.2	0.4	29.4	2.1
Opelika.....................	49	232	22.7	6.1	355	1 405 862	10.4	27.1	19.6	3.6	0.5	35.2	2.4
Phenix City	46	253	19.0	6.6	795	2 466 225	53.9	13.6	9.1	2.5	0.4	18.3	0.5
Prattville...................	44	210	18.2	5.4	328	1 108 761	10.0	29.2	32.0	3.9	0.0	16.8	0.0
Tuscaloosa................	103	1 037	83.4	26.8	1 302	4 845 351	13.7	29.6	21.7	13.7	0.3	17.3	0.0
Vestavia Hills............	55	493	33.3	12.2	264	1 136 169	7.5	27.3	44.1	1.9	0.0	6.9	5.2
ALASKA	882	4 807	495.9	152.7	X	X	X	X	X	X	X	X	X
Anchorage.................	400	2 688	261.8	87.3	9 819	51 971 256	4.5	7.8	6.6	5.5	1.4	9.1	63.8
Fairbanks..................	82	408	40.9	12.3	207	1 185 064	19.9	35.9	23.3	6.8	8.7	5.4	0.0
Juneau......................	45	202	18.7	5.3	1 960	10 163 476	5.6	5.4	3.1	7.4	27.2	8.1	43.2
ARIZONA	7 025	46 847	4 192.9	1 223.9	X	X	X	X	X	X	X	X	X
Apache Junction.........	31	165	25.8	8.4	234	1 013 473	20.4	42.8	0.0	10.1	7.9	13.1	5.7
Avondale	58	399	27.3	8.4	512	2 677 540	26.3	33.3	15.4	3.4	3.4	12.3	1.8
Buckeye....................	12	37	3.0	0.8	391	1 821 664	27.3	19.8	28.2	3.6	1.6	9.5	2.0
Bullhead City.............	36	207	15.3	4.8	298	1 290 523	21.2	44.5	0.0	12.9	1.8	11.0	0.0
Casa Grande.............	61	361	28.4	8.8	385	1 771 597	18.0	31.5	19.5	7.8	0.7	17.0	3.4
Chandler...................	257	1 995	169.0	53.6	1 623	9 363 010	16.5	33.2	15.8	6.3	4.4	16.4	3.0
El Mirage..................	13	58	3.7	1.3	144	789 368	14.2	35.0	17.6	4.7	0.0	9.4	0.0
Flagstaff....................	123	695	58.4	17.0	767	3 403 748	18.4	24.3	12.4	4.2	3.2	21.7	4.8
Florence...................	3	D	D	D	163	645 551	22.7	26.9	19.9	12.8	1.7	13.7	2.3
Gilbert......................	212	1 299	91.0	27.5	1 117	5 590 864	15.8	33.0	20.5	2.9	0.1	18.9	0.0
Glendale...................	250	1 436	143.9	40.6	1 775	9 436 681	12.7	32.7	19.8	5.2	1.8	16.0	2.7
Goodyear..................	48	281	17.3	5.6	482	2 715 439	27.9	20.6	25.2	2.4	0.0	14.0	0.0
Kingman...................	41	257	19.9	6.4	335	1 383 755	16.2	24.7	22.1	11.4	0.0	22.8	0.0
Lake Havasu City.........	117	416	37.7	9.5	484	2 122 419	13.0	26.9	20.4	11.4	0.0	20.7	0.0
Marana.....................	69	387	30.7	10.5	306	1 328 433	22.4	36.4	0.0	14.2	1.2	11.8	0.0
Maricopa...................	23	D	D	D	204	1 087 610	13.2	32.5	35.7	1.6	0.0	5.6	2.4
Mesa........................	552	3 294	272.4	78.7	3 616	20 622 110	15.1	36.5	16.1	6.6	1.6	17.7	1.6
Oro Valley	49	327	22.6	8.3	311	1 409 218	13.9	47.7	0.0	6.6	0.8	15.0	4.3
Peoria......................	157	942	72.8	23.1	1 162	6 255 922	23.5	26.8	16.6	7.4	0.0	20.3	2.2
Phoenix....................	1 631	14 684	1 515.2	403.1	13 392	69 633 897	11.5	35.6	16.7	9.5	5.0	18.7	1.5
Prescott	111	551	45.7	13.9	538	2 411 836	19.0	24.9	16.7	6.7	0.0	14.5	3.4
Prescott Valley	54	199	17.3	4.8	189	851 635	20.9	38.1	0.0	4.8	7.5	7.0	8.5
Queen Creek..............	21	101	6.9	2.3	217	1 060 750	23.5	0.0	16.7	8.1	23.4	23.1	0.0
Sahuarita..................	8	91	4.3	1.9	131	644 309	29.4	41.1	0.0	11.3	0.0	7.5	0.0
San Luis...................	3	6	0.3	0.1	233	639 318	48.6	5.8	13.3	7.7	0.0	21.5	0.0
Scottsdale.................	533	3 863	294.6	94.1	2 454	13 029 893	23.6	31.2	13.0	3.8	2.1	18.0	3.7
Sierra Vista...............	47	253	19.6	6.5	380	1 580 863	16.3	28.2	17.1	6.7	1.2	17.2	2.1
Surprise....................	87	462	30.5	9.9	738	4 192 160	14.5	25.4	22.6	5.1	6.0	22.1	0.0
Tempe......................	292	2 006	188.3	62.7	1 762	9 492 774	16.0	31.6	13.1	6.2	9.5	18.8	1.5
Tucson......................	756	4 997	423.7	128.2	4 691	21 780 237	12.6	30.8	18.8	10.4	3.2	19.2	0.0
Yuma........................	115	709	52.0	16.5	946	3 797 070	16.5	30.3	16.4	7.6	3.3	23.1	0.0
ARKANSAS...............	3 157	17 091	1 427.6	423.7	X	X	X	X	X	X	X	X	X
Bella Vista	11	D	D	D	93	498 217	10.0	35.9	53.0	1.1	0.0	0.0	0.0
Benton......................	48	216	21.4	5.5	270	875 166	13.5	25.7	22.5	4.2	2.4	27.6	0.0
Bentonville................	62	475	27.9	13.7	435	1 712 143	20.1	20.9	18.7	4.1	0.0	33.1	3.1
Conway.....................	100	535	40.7	11.2	474	1 540 085	12.3	31.7	27.5	7.8	0.0	17.9	0.0
Fayetteville................	111	661	43.6	14.9	692	2 378 996	14.3	27.3	16.7	11.7	2.3	20.9	0.0
Fort Smith.................	143	751	62.0	17.6	880	3 505 049	10.2	26.1	17.9	14.1	2.6	29.1	0.0
Hot Springs	82	454	27.2	9.5	597	2 082 915	9.8	24.7	17.9	10.7	1.2	28.2	0.0

1. Establishments subject to federal tax.

Table D. Cities — **City Government Finances**

City	City government finances, 2012									
	General revenue							General expenditure		
		Intergovernmental		Taxes					Per capita[1] (dollars)	
					Per capita[1] (dollars)					
	Total (mil dol)	Total (mil dol)	Percent from state government	Total (mil dol)	Total	Property	Sales and gross receipts	Total (mil dol)	Total	Capital outlays
	117	118	119	120	121	122	123	124	125	126
United States..............	X	X	X	X	X	X	X	X	X	X
ALABAMA	X	X	X	X	X	X	X	X	X	X
Alabaster	27.6	0.0	0.0	19.2	619	107	511	23.9	773	0
Auburn...........................	94.7	3.9	77.7	64.8	1 135	368	766	67.3	1 180	135
Bessemer	51.9	5.8	81.8	34.8	1 279	240	1 039	52.4	1 924	4
Birmingham	436.4	42.3	52.9	334.4	1 583	243	985	466.4	2 207	235
Decatur..........................	174.2	68.7	100.0	61.6	1 103	209	877	202.0	3 616	209
Dothan...........................	93.4	4.5	88.0	70.5	1 046	66	980	98.8	1 467	83
Enterprise	30.6	1.8	95.9	23.0	826	157	670	32.1	1 155	209
Florence	64.7	4.1	76.8	43.9	1 107	284	821	58.6	1 477	59
Gadsden.........................	64.3	6.9	28.4	44.2	1 206	66	731	60.4	1 647	45
Homewood	54.6	1.8	36.5	50.5	1 996	632	1 363	51.4	2 034	100
Hoover...........................	104.2	6.8	51.4	83.0	998	121	853	95.0	1 143	78
Huntsville......................	329.0	28.2	93.3	217.9	1 186	320	866	337.4	1 836	440
Madison	51.4	5.9	79.3	34.9	777	291	451	50.2	1 117	123
Mobile...........................	353.3	20.4	65.4	248.6	1 275	83	1 192	344.5	1 767	296
Montgomery	280.1	36.3	46.1	169.8	830	151	679	218.0	1 065	80
Opelika	54.6	2.4	35.3	39.9	1 425	328	810	51.4	1 834	224
Phenix City	33.7	1.9	100.0	26.0	717	165	552	36.4	1 007	213
Prattville.......................	35.5	1.0	99.2	26.5	765	71	695	28.2	814	6
Tuscaloosa	163.4	34.6	20.3	77.7	834	145	637	163.0	1 750	124
Vestavia Hills................	34.2	1.8	33.1	29.1	857	387	470	34.6	1 017	160
ALASKA	X	X	X	X	X	X	X	X	X	X
Anchorage.....................	1 296.8	572.1	91.3	546.6	1 830	1 623	208	1 251.1	4 190	417
Fairbanks......................	42.7	11.6	100.0	21.4	659	432	227	39.7	1 220	110
Juneau..........................	316.5	94.8	75.9	83.0	2 561	1 130	1 431	302.2	9 325	1 605
ARIZONA	X	X	X	X	X	X	X	X	X	X
Apache Junction...........	26.7	11.0	100.0	11.6	316	0	316	29.2	793	0
Avondale	84.4	25.7	100.0	40.9	523	67	456	73.8	945	93
Buckeye........................	61.1	12.9	69.2	27.9	512	172	339	48.2	882	7
Bullhead City	48.4	17.4	91.6	11.3	286	0	285	42.5	1 075	35
Casa Grande.................	70.3	17.3	83.1	29.4	586	128	458	77.3	1 541	234
Chandler........................	333.6	72.6	90.2	151.1	617	130	487	266.6	1 089	179
El Mirage	30.1	8.5	100.0	9.5	290	94	196	33.0	1 011	114
Flagstaff........................	130.0	35.8	90.1	54.3	801	176	624	120.0	1 768	130
Florence	23.1	8.7	80.8	6.8	254	38	210	20.6	772	122
Gilbert...........................	261.7	63.3	83.0	136.2	614	108	503	189.6	854	154
Glendale........................	324.3	103.3	81.2	145.1	625	87	538	226.0	974	13
Goodyear.......................	108.4	19.5	99.3	60.0	864	237	627	78.8	1 135	56
Kingman	39.6	14.2	100.0	12.5	439	0	439	31.4	1 108	1
Lake Havasu City..........	80.6	21.3	85.8	26.9	509	186	322	98.9	1 874	405
Marana	50.4	18.1	58.5	27.9	760	14	742	43.7	1 189	179
Maricopa.......................	36.8	14.6	100.0	19.2	428	242	187	33.5	747	45
Mesa.............................	511.1	172.3	70.6	156.6	346	32	309	601.2	1 330	186
Oro Valley	29.7	10.8	100.0	15.4	373	0	373	29.9	723	49
Peoria...........................	190.2	41.3	95.5	90.5	566	140	418	239.6	1 498	187
Phoenix	2 902.9	848.4	63.4	987.1	663	152	507	2 651.7	1 780	445
Prescott	74.7	16.1	77.8	30.5	761	71	684	77.2	1 928	429
Prescott Valley..............	38.2	14.1	87.4	14.0	357	47	310	41.2	1 051	74
Queen Creek.................	50.6	8.0	99.8	20.6	739	223	477	52.0	1 861	347
Sahuarita......................	26.6	12.6	63.4	10.0	379	11	368	22.4	852	221
San Luis	21.1	8.0	87.4	6.9	228	0	228	26.1	861	37
Scottsdale.....................	477.7	126.1	80.7	238.4	1 068	291	776	562.4	2 518	823
Sierra Vista...................	48.4	13.6	97.0	18.9	407	9	398	48.8	1 052	142
Surprise	112.2	31.8	91.0	40.3	332	56	276	106.8	880	55
Tempe	344.4	69.4	71.3	183.5	1 097	215	883	286.8	1 715	177
Tucson..........................	736.3	277.8	53.0	280.3	534	76	458	608.5	1 159	174
Yuma............................	125.5	30.9	90.5	51.1	545	108	435	125.6	1 341	167
ARKANSAS...............	X	X	X	X	X	X	X	X	X	X
Bella Vista	12.2	6.0	28.9	3.3	122	28	94	12.1	440	15
Benton	23.3	4.6	40.9	12.8	398	73	324	22.8	712	138
Bentonville....................	57.6	8.2	48.3	30.3	790	159	630	57.0	1 486	389
Conway	95.8	7.8	55.2	33.5	532	61	471	88.6	1 408	244
Fayetteville...................	107.6	24.4	45.2	48.2	626	53	572	96.7	1 256	246
Fort Smith.....................	133.9	29.8	38.6	61.3	700	146	554	126.0	1 439	456
Hot Springs	69.7	12.2	60.6	26.7	752	1	751	69.2	1 951	328

1. Based on population estimated as of July 1 of the year shown.

Table D. Cities — **City Government Finances**

	City government finances, 2012 (cont.)									
	General expenditure (cont.)									
	Percent of total for:									
City	Public welfare	Highways	Parking facilities	Education	Health and hospitals	Police protection	Sewerage and sanitation	Parks and recreation	Housing and community development	Interest on debt
	127	128	129	130	131	132	133	134	135	136
United States............	X	X	X	X	X	X	X	X	X	X
ALABAMA	X	X	X	X	X	X	X	X	X	X
Alabaster	0.0	6.5	0.0	0.0	0.0	25.9	23.2	8.6	0.0	0.0
Auburn.........................	0.0	5.6	0.0	0.0	2.5	16.6	14.8	7.9	1.4	12.2
Bessemer......................	0.0	6.1	0.0	0.0	0.0	21.1	6.2	3.2	0.0	6.0
Birmingham	0.0	12.7	1.3	0.0	0.0	16.8	0.0	4.0	1.4	4.9
Decatur........................	0.3	5.0	0.0	53.7	2.3	6.1	12.6	3.4	0.9	1.1
Dothan.........................	0.0	10.4	0.0	4.0	2.8	16.8	17.1	8.5	0.5	3.4
Enterprise	0.0	8.4	0.0	16.6	0.7	13.2	23.7	7.3	0.0	8.6
Florence	0.0	9.8	0.0	14.4	0.0	15.5	16.1	11.6	0.3	2.8
Gadsden.......................	0.0	6.2	0.0	0.0	0.0	16.2	16.8	9.0	2.3	4.3
Homewood	0.1	5.6	0.0	28.6	0.0	16.9	4.9	6.2	0.0	4.2
Hoover.........................	0.0	9.1	0.0	2.1	0.3	21.8	8.8	8.6	0.0	4.5
Huntsville....................	0.2	6.6	0.5	5.6	1.2	12.4	8.8	9.0	2.3	8.1
Madison	0.0	14.5	0.0	0.0	0.0	14.0	12.2	7.0	0.0	6.1
Mobile.........................	0.0	7.7	2.7	0.0	0.4	12.3	20.0	8.1	0.1	4.3
Montgomery	0.0	5.6	1.7	0.0	0.0	20.0	7.3	12.6	1.3	6.6
Opelika	0.0	8.4	0.0	14.7	0.6	16.6	11.9	9.8	0.5	6.3
Phenix City	0.0	1.8	0.0	5.6	0.3	16.9	14.0	10.2	0.0	3.9
Prattville.....................	0.0	0.0	0.0	0.0	0.0	22.0	13.5	6.2	0.0	8.8
Tuscaloosa...................	0.1	14.2	0.3	7.9	0.1	17.4	9.0	8.0	1.4	2.3
Vestavia Hills...............	0.0	4.8	0.0	0.7	0.5	12.9	7.4	16.4	0.0	5.5
ALASKA	X	X	X	X	X	X	X	X	X	X
Anchorage....................	0.0	5.9	0.4	53.2	2.1	9.9	5.0	1.7	0.0	2.8
Fairbanks.....................	0.0	33.1	0.6	0.0	0.0	15.6	0.0	0.0	0.0	0.5
Juneau.........................	0.0	4.5	0.0	28.1	32.3	5.7	3.6	4.3	1.4	3.0
ARIZONA	X	X	X	X	X	X	X	X	X	X
Apache Junction............	0.0	24.4	0.0	0.0	0.0	30.0	0.0	11.6	6.9	0.0
Avondale	3.8	15.7	0.0	0.0	0.0	31.7	20.3	3.4	4.4	6.6
Buckeye.......................	0.0	4.5	0.0	0.0	0.0	19.8	24.3	3.3	0.4	17.7
Bullhead City	0.0	20.8	0.0	0.0	4.2	23.1	21.7	7.4	1.4	6.7
Casa Grande.................	0.0	8.0	0.0	0.0	0.0	17.5	17.4	8.7	0.9	6.8
Chandler......................	0.0	7.7	0.0	0.0	0.0	21.8	19.2	0.9	13.7	4.7
El Mirage	0.0	8.4	0.0	0.0	1.4	31.0	25.8	3.8	0.3	1.9
Flagstaff......................	0.0	14.0	0.0	0.0	0.0	13.5	14.1	0.0	12.3	3.7
Florence	0.0	8.9	3.0	0.0	0.0	25.5	11.9	4.9	4.2	6.6
Gilbert.........................	0.0	20.7	0.0	0.0	0.0	19.1	13.1	5.3	0.8	8.4
Glendale......................	0.0	3.3	0.2	0.0	0.0	22.4	12.4	4.5	6.7	18.5
Goodyear.....................	0.0	2.1	0.0	0.0	0.0	16.8	9.8	9.8	5.8	13.2
Kingman......................	0.0	5.6	0.0	0.0	0.0	23.3	22.2	11.9	2.1	2.3
Lake Havasu City..........	0.0	6.5	0.0	0.0	0.0	11.7	38.4	6.7	0.4	10.7
Marana	0.0	15.9	0.0	0.0	0.0	23.0	2.8	3.8	0.9	10.8
Maricopa......................	0.0	3.8	0.0	0.0	0.0	20.8	0.0	6.7	29.9	3.2
Mesa...........................	0.6	10.4	0.0	0.0	0.0	26.2	11.2	7.4	3.3	6.1
Oro Valley	0.0	14.5	0.0	0.0	0.0	40.4	0.0	9.9	0.0	0.0
Peoria.........................	0.0	9.6	0.0	0.2	0.0	12.3	12.7	11.6	0.7	5.5
Phoenix	0.0	6.6	0.0	0.9	0.0	17.8	11.1	7.4	7.3	10.4
Prescott	0.0	26.8	0.1	0.0	0.0	16.5	17.0	7.8	0.3	3.3
Prescott Valley	0.0	10.3	0.0	0.0	0.0	20.4	14.9	3.7	0.0	11.3
Queen Creek	0.0	6.0	0.0	0.0	0.0	3.2	8.0	12.7	1.3	8.9
Sahuarita	0.0	27.9	0.0	0.0	0.0	23.8	7.8	5.8	0.0	11.5
San Luis	0.5	5.6	0.0	0.0	0.0	14.5	18.2	0.0	0.6	24.2
Scottsdale....................	0.0	5.4	0.0	0.0	0.0	14.2	16.1	6.3	1.5	9.3
Sierra Vista..................	0.0	26.3	0.0	0.0	0.0	32.3	13.8	9.6	2.6	2.4
Surprise	0.0	14.1	0.0	0.0	0.0	19.0	11.3	12.5	5.8	4.6
Tempe	0.0	10.3	0.0	0.0	0.0	21.8	10.9	1.8	14.8	5.2
Tucson.........................	0.0	5.0	0.0	0.0	0.0	21.9	6.7	8.0	12.2	6.0
Yuma..........................	0.0	11.8	0.0	0.0	0.6	17.9	15.0	9.1	1.2	11.1
ARKANSAS..............	X	X	X	X	X	X	X	X	X	X
Bella Vista	0.0	26.0	0.0	0.0	0.0	19.9	13.8	0.0	0.0	0.0
Benton.........................	0.0	22.3	0.0	0.0	1.5	20.7	12.3	6.4	0.0	7.0
Bentonville...................	0.0	16.9	0.0	0.0	0.0	12.6	25.2	11.3	0.2	5.6
Conway	0.0	14.7	0.0	0.0	0.4	11.7	15.7	4.1	0.0	15.9
Fayetteville..................	0.0	11.2	1.0	0.0	1.0	16.4	26.2	5.7	0.5	5.3
Fort Smith....................	0.0	13.8	0.2	0.0	0.1	12.5	25.6	2.5	1.0	8.9
Hot Springs	0.0	6.7	0.2	0.0	0.9	15.8	27.9	2.4	0.4	2.1

City	City government finances, 2012 (cont.)			Climate[2]						
	Debt outstanding			Average daily temperature (degrees Fahrenheit)						
				Mean		Limits				
	Total (mil dol)	Per capita[1] (dollars)	Debt issued during year	January	July	January[3]	July[4]	Annual precipitation (inches)	Heating degree days	Cooling degree days
	137	138	139	140	141	142	143	144	145	146
United States	X	X	X	X	X	X	X	X	X	X
ALABAMA	X	X	X	X	X	X	X	X	X	X
Alabaster	101.5	3 276	0.0	NA	NA	NA	NA	NA	NA	NA
Auburn	229.8	4 028	11.0	44.7	79.9	34.2	89.7	52.63	2 507	1 932
Bessemer	103.0	3 783	12.0	42.9	81.0	30.8	93.6	59.38	2 766	1 943
Birmingham	573.7	2 715	109.7	42.6	80.2	32.3	90.6	53.99	2 823	1 881
Decatur	508.8	9 106	6.5	38.9	79.2	29.1	90.3	55.31	3 469	1 609
Dothan	84.7	1 257	3.4	47.7	81.3	36.2	93.3	56.61	2 058	2 264
Enterprise	79.9	2 876	8.3	NA	NA	NA	NA	NA	NA	NA
Florence	116.3	2 932	59.9	39.9	80.2	30.7	90.6	55.80	3 236	1 789
Gadsden	75.3	2 052	5.0	40.3	79.8	29.9	90.5	56.10	3 220	1 716
Homewood	49.2	1 946	0.3	42.6	80.2	32.3	90.6	53.99	2 823	1 881
Hoover	108.5	1 306	58.5	42.9	81.0	30.8	93.6	59.38	2 766	1 943
Huntsville	774.8	4 216	13.8	39.8	79.5	30.7	89.4	57.51	3 262	1 671
Madison	75.1	1 672	13.3	46.6	81.8	35.5	92.7	54.77	2 194	2 252
Mobile	547.6	2 809	13.3	50.1	81.5	39.5	91.2	66.29	1 681	2 539
Montgomery	275.9	1 348	38.8	46.6	81.8	35.5	92.7	54.77	2 194	2 252
Opelika	162.2	5 790	70.3	NA	NA	NA	NA	NA	NA	NA
Phenix City	139.4	3 853	52.5	46.8	82.0	36.6	91.7	48.57	2 154	2 296
Prattville	61.2	1 766	5.6	NA	NA	NA	NA	NA	NA	NA
Tuscaloosa	198.6	2 132	1.3	42.9	80.4	32.5	90.8	54.99	2 787	1 893
Vestavia Hills	41.6	1 224	0.0	NA	NA	NA	NA	NA	NA	NA
ALASKA	X	X	X	X	X	X	X	X	X	X
Anchorage	1 789.0	5 991	62.0	15.8	58.4	9.3	65.3	16.08	10 470	3
Fairbanks	2.3	71	0.0	-9.7	62.4	-19.0	73.0	10.34	13 980	74
Juneau	193.0	5 956	14.8	25.7	56.8	20.7	64.3	58.33	8 574	0
ARIZONA	X	X	X	X	X	X	X	X	X	X
Apache Junction	10.8	294	0.0	52.7	89.5	40.0	104.3	12.29	1 542	3 443
Avondale	93.9	1 202	0.0	54.7	93.5	41.3	107.6	9.03	1 173	4 166
Buckeye	160.3	2 937	1.5	NA	NA	NA	NA	NA	NA	NA
Bullhead City	73.4	1 858	0.0	54.4	95.6	43.3	111.7	5.84	1 164	4 508
Casa Grande	119.9	2 388	14.4	52.4	90.4	37.3	105.1	9.22	1 572	3 554
Chandler	579.4	2 367	0.0	54.3	91.3	41.5	105.7	9.23	1 271	3 798
El Mirage	27.3	836	0.0	NA	NA	NA	NA	NA	NA	NA
Flagstaff	118.5	1 746	34.4	29.7	66.1	16.5	82.2	22.91	6 999	126
Florence	18.6	697	0.0	NA	NA	NA	NA	NA	NA	NA
Gilbert	479.5	2 159	37.9	54.3	91.3	41.5	105.7	9.23	1 271	3 798
Glendale	1 053.0	4 536	86.3	52.5	90.6	39.2	104.2	7.78	1 535	3 488
Goodyear	426.4	6 140	38.6	NA	NA	NA	NA	NA	NA	NA
Kingman	55.1	1 944	11.1	NA	NA	NA	NA	NA	NA	NA
Lake Havasu City	321.9	6 096	8.4	53.9	95.2	42.9	107.5	6.25	1 230	4 523
Marana	94.8	2 584	0.1	NA	NA	NA	NA	NA	NA	NA
Maricopa	19.3	430	0.0	NA	NA	NA	NA	NA	NA	NA
Mesa	1 494.6	3 305	352.1	54.3	91.3	41.5	105.7	9.23	1 271	3 798
Oro Valley	64.1	1 547	21.8	50.6	86.3	34.6	100.7	12.40	1 831	2 810
Peoria	511.6	3 199	51.7	54.7	93.5	41.3	107.6	9.03	1 173	4 166
Phoenix	8 278.0	5 557	760.6	54.2	92.8	43.4	104.2	8.29	1 125	4 189
Prescott	73.2	1 829	3.5	37.1	73.4	23.3	88.3	19.19	4 849	742
Prescott Valley	104.9	2 678	33.8	NA	NA	NA	NA	NA	NA	NA
Queen Creek	165.6	5 930	0.1	NA	NA	NA	NA	NA	NA	NA
Sahuarita	56.9	2 161	0.4	NA	NA	NA	NA	NA	NA	NA
San Luis	169.5	5 602	0.0	NA	NA	NA	NA	NA	NA	NA
Scottsdale	1 200.6	5 375	53.3	54.2	92.8	43.4	104.2	8.29	1 125	4 189
Sierra Vista	37.2	803	9.3	47.7	79.1	33.7	92.6	14.02	2 369	1 739
Surprise	37.0	305	0.0	54.7	93.5	41.3	107.6	9.03	1 173	4 166
Tempe	740.2	4 427	68.6	54.1	89.9	40.1	103.6	9.36	1 390	3 655
Tucson	1 174.4	2 236	152.8	54.0	88.5	41.9	100.5	12.00	1 333	3 501
Yuma	302.8	3 234	0.0	58.1	94.1	46.2	107.3	3.01	782	4 540
ARKANSAS	X	X	X	X	X	X	X	X	X	X
Bella Vista	0.0	0	0.0	NA	NA	NA	NA	NA	NA	NA
Benton	44.1	1 373	0.0	NA	NA	NA	NA	NA	NA	NA
Bentonville	97.5	2 541	0.0	NA	NA	NA	NA	NA	NA	NA
Conway	383.2	6 092	0.0	38.3	82.1	28.1	92.4	48.67	3 320	1 961
Fayetteville	139.6	1 813	0.0	34.3	78.9	24.2	89.1	46.02	4 166	1 439
Fort Smith	454.0	5 184	22.1	38.0	82.2	27.8	92.9	43.87	3 437	1 929
Hot Springs	68.3	1 925	1.0	40.2	82.2	29.6	94.3	57.69	3 133	1 993

1. Based on the population estimated as of July 1 of the year shown. 2. Represents normal values based on the 30-year period, 1971–2000. 3. Average daily minimum.
4. Average daily maximum.

STATE Place code	City	Land area,[1] 2010 (sq km)	Population, 2015			Race alone or in combination (percent), 2010-2014					Percent Hispanic or Latino[2] 2010-2014	Percent foreign born 2010–2014
			Total persons	Rank	Per square kilometer	White	Black	American Indian, Alaska Native	Asian	Hawaiian Pacific Islander		
		1	2	3	4	5	6	7	8	9	10	11
	ARKANSAS—Cont'd											
05 34750	Jacksonville	72.8	28 643	1 292	393.4	62.3	35.4	1.4	3.1	0.1	7.5	5.9
05 35710	Jonesboro	206.9	73 907	469	357.2	77.5	19.9	1.1	1.8	0.4	5.3	5.1
05 41000	Little Rock	308.7	197 992	118	641.4	53.4	43.0	0.8	3.6	0.1	5.8	6.8
05 50450	North Little Rock	133.4	66 504	534	498.5	57.4	41.5	0.9	1.0	0.0	7.5	4.6
05 53390	Paragould	80.8	27 900	1 323	345.3	97.3	1.9	1.1	0.2	0.1	3.0	1.4
05 55310	Pine Bluff	115.5	44 772	836	387.6	21.8	76.9	0.6	1.2	0.2	1.4	1.5
05 60410	Rogers	98.3	63 159	570	642.5	88.2	1.8	2.2	3.0	0.0	31.9	18.6
05 61670	Russellville	73.2	29 166	1 270	398.4	89.2	8.3	1.5	2.0	0.0	13.9	6.6
05 63800	Sherwood	53.4	30 517	1 224	571.5	79.9	17.8	0.8	2.0	0.1	6.7	4.3
05 66080	Springdale	108.3	77 859	433	718.9	65.4	2.8	2.0	2.5	6.9	35.4	24.2
05 68810	Texarkana	107.9	30 353	1 233	281.3	64.4	35.1	2.2	0.3	0.1	3.1	0.7
05 74540	West Memphis	73.7	25 052	1 417	339.9	33.6	66.1	0.4	0.4	0.3	0.6	0.7
06 00000	CALIFORNIA	403 466.3	39 144 818	X	97.0	65.8	7.1	1.9	15.4	0.8	38.2	27.0
06 00296	Adelanto	145.1	33 166	1 133	228.6	62.4	24.5	1.1	3.3	1.2	55.1	20.5
06 00562	Alameda	27.5	78 630	429	2 859.3	55.2	9.4	1.4	35.9	1.6	11.9	26.7
06 00884	Alhambra	19.8	85 551	381	4 320.8	26.4	1.8	0.6	53.3	0.4	35.3	50.7
06 00947	Aliso Viejo	19.4	50 195	748	2 587.4	75.6	3.4	1.4	18.9	0.5	16.5	22.5
06 02000	Anaheim	129.1	350 742	56	2 716.8	68.6	3.0	1.0	17.3	0.6	52.8	37.0
06 02252	Antioch	73.4	110 542	258	1 506.0	55.0	20.8	2.1	14.5	2.1	34.0	21.0
06 02364	Apple Valley	189.6	72 174	479	380.7	83.4	9.5	2.1	4.4	0.2	28.7	8.1
06 02462	Arcadia	28.3	58 408	636	2 063.9	33.3	1.5	0.5	60.8	0.6	12.7	48.7
06 03064	Atascadero	66.4	29 819	1 249	449.1	91.4	2.5	2.0	2.8	0.1	15.8	6.3
06 03162	Atwater	15.8	29 237	1 267	1 850.4	68.2	5.2	2.5	7.4	0.9	51.5	21.6
06 03386	Azusa	25.0	49 690	756	1 987.6	44.6	3.6	1.0	11.2	0.2	65.2	31.8
06 03526	Bakersfield	368.2	373 640	52	1 014.8	70.8	9.6	2.4	7.8	0.5	46.9	18.5
06 03666	Baldwin Park	17.2	77 071	439	4 480.9	37.0	1.7	1.7	17.2	0.2	77.9	44.7
06 03820	Banning	59.8	30 945	1 199	517.5	75.3	9.3	1.9	5.7	0.3	39.5	16.4
06 04758	Beaumont	80.1	43 811	853	547.0	72.2	6.4	2.1	11.8	0.4	37.9	18.0
06 04870	Bell	6.5	36 205	1 040	5 570.0	70.2	1.7	0.5	0.8	0.2	92.7	43.6
06 04982	Bellflower	15.8	78 441	430	4 964.6	43.9	15.4	1.1	12.0	0.5	54.2	29.2
06 04996	Bell Gardens	6.4	43 106	868	6 735.3	72.8	1.4	0.8	0.7	0.0	96.5	45.1
06 05108	Belmont	12.0	27 218	1 351	2 268.2	69.9	3.2	0.8	28.9	0.4	12.8	28.7
06 05290	Benicia	33.5	28 167	1 311	840.8	79.4	8.5	3.0	15.0	0.8	15.2	10.4
06 06000	Berkeley	27.1	120 972	225	4 463.9	67.1	10.1	1.6	23.3	0.5	10.9	20.8
06 06308	Beverly Hills	14.8	34 869	1 076	2 356.0	86.2	2.9	1.5	11.1	0.4	6.4	36.5
06 08100	Brea	31.3	41 944	891	1 340.1	75.4	1.5	0.8	21.1	1.2	27.9	21.4
06 08142	Brentwood	38.3	58 968	627	1 539.6	80.2	6.9	1.6	11.6	0.8	25.8	14.8
06 08786	Buena Park	27.3	83 270	397	3 050.2	60.3	4.7	0.6	30.8	1.2	38.1	37.7
06 08954	Burbank	44.9	105 319	282	2 345.6	78.0	3.1	1.2	14.2	0.5	25.8	35.0
06 09066	Burlingame	11.4	30 459	1 227	2 671.8	72.9	1.8	1.1	24.7	0.7	13.3	26.0
06 09710	Calexico	21.7	40 053	934	1 845.8	68.6	0.6	1.2	1.5	0.0	96.9	46.9
06 10046	Camarillo	50.6	67 608	519	1 336.1	79.8	3.2	1.2	13.2	0.5	25.5	14.6
06 10345	Campbell	15.0	41 117	910	2 741.1	75.9	3.0	1.7	19.3	0.4	20.0	22.9
06 11194	Carlsbad	97.7	113 453	244	1 161.2	88.5	1.9	1.1	9.5	0.6	14.2	14.0
06 11530	Carson	48.5	93 281	334	1 923.3	38.4	25.4	6.5	28.3	3.1	39.6	34.4
06 12048	Cathedral City	55.7	53 826	693	966.4	77.6	3.1	1.7	5.5	0.4	62.4	34.0
06 12524	Ceres	20.8	47 963	789	2 305.9	72.9	2.1	2.4	7.5	1.5	58.7	26.9
06 12552	Cerritos	22.6	49 975	752	2 211.3	24.9	7.8	0.4	63.8	0.5	12.0	45.4
06 13014	Chico	85.3	90 316	349	1 058.8	88.9	3.5	3.2	6.0	0.6	17.0	7.8
06 13210	Chino	76.8	85 595	380	1 114.5	60.9	7.2	3.7	13.4	0.6	54.7	23.0
06 13214	Chino Hills	115.7	78 309	431	676.8	55.0	4.9	1.0	34.7	0.4	28.9	29.4
06 13392	Chula Vista	128.5	265 757	74	2 068.1	72.0	6.0	1.1	17.3	0.9	58.4	30.5
06 13588	Citrus Heights	36.9	87 056	374	2 359.2	85.7	4.1	2.7	5.2	0.7	17.9	13.4
06 13756	Claremont	34.6	36 283	1 036	1 048.6	74.0	5.4	1.6	17.6	0.5	21.2	18.3
06 14218	Clovis	60.3	104 180	287	1 727.7	73.7	3.5	2.5	12.4	0.5	27.6	11.8
06 14260	Coachella	75.0	44 635	838	595.1	35.9	1.9	0.7	0.1	0.1	96.8	41.2
06 14890	Colton	39.7	54 621	685	1 375.8	61.0	9.0	2.0	4.5	0.7	72.4	25.5
06 15044	Compton	25.9	98 462	306	3 801.6	39.0	32.8	0.9	1.0	0.3	66.3	29.9
06 16000	Concord	79.1	128 667	212	1 626.6	74.3	5.5	1.7	14.2	1.7	30.1	25.8
06 16350	Corona	100.6	164 226	153	1 632.5	74.5	5.8	1.1	13.0	1.4	42.2	25.8
06 16532	Costa Mesa	40.5	113 204	245	2 795.2	68.8	2.2	0.9	11.0	0.8	35.4	24.2
06 16742	Covina	18.2	48 984	771	2 691.4	56.6	6.0	1.1	13.7	0.2	57.0	22.2
06 17568	Culver City	13.2	39 717	944	3 008.9	70.0	9.7	1.3	18.5	0.3	22.9	23.4
06 17610	Cupertino	29.2	60 572	600	2 074.4	32.9	0.6	0.6	67.1	0.4	4.7	50.3
06 17750	Cypress	17.0	49 290	766	2 899.4	61.6	3.4	1.3	34.6	0.9	18.5	28.3
06 17918	Daly City	19.9	106 562	280	5 354.9	25.9	4.3	0.9	60.3	0.8	23.2	52.3
06 17946	Dana Point	16.8	34 181	1 097	2 034.6	87.2	1.3	1.2	5.2	0.3	15.7	13.9
06 17988	Danville	46.7	44 400	841	950.7	86.7	1.3	0.5	14.1	0.4	5.8	12.6
06 18100	Davis	25.6	67 666	518	2 643.2	69.4	3.5	1.3	26.5	1.2	13.5	18.8

1. Dry land or land partially or temporarily covered by water.   2. May be of any race.

Table D. Cities — **Population**

City	Age of population (percent), 2010-2014									Median age 2010–2014	Percent female 2010–2014	Population			
	Under 5 years	5 to 17 years	18 to 24 years	25 to 34 years	35 to 44 years	45 to 54 years	55 to 64 years	65 to 74 years	75 years and over			Census counts		Percent change	
												2000	2010	2000–2010	2010–2015
	12	13	14	15	16	17	18	19	20	21	22	23	24	25	26
ARKANSAS—Cont'd															
Jacksonville	7.4	21.4	13.2	15.3	11.3	10.8	9.2	6.9	4.6	30.3	49.0	29 916	28 364	-5.2	0.9
Jonesboro	7.6	17.1	14.5	15.6	12.2	11.1	10.2	5.8	5.9	31.2	51.7	55 515	67 263	21.2	9.7
Little Rock	6.8	16.3	9.5	15.7	13.6	13.1	12.4	7.0	5.6	36.5	52.2	183 133	193 524	5.7	2.3
North Little Rock	8.4	18.2	9.2	16.6	11.5	11.5	12.8	5.9	5.9	33.7	52.0	60 433	62 304	3.1	6.6
Paragould	6.3	18.8	9.6	13.8	13.2	11.2	12.8	7.8	6.5	36.3	51.3	22 017	26 113	18.6	6.8
Pine Bluff	6.6	17.9	12.3	13.0	10.8	12.8	13.2	6.8	6.6	35.2	53.0	55 085	49 083	-10.9	-8.8
Rogers	9.3	21.7	9.8	16.7	13.4	11.6	8.4	4.9	4.0	30.6	51.0	38 829	55 964	44.1	12.8
Russellville	6.9	16.7	21.7	10.5	13.2	9.6	8.9	6.7	5.8	29.2	52.0	23 682	27 920	17.9	4.5
Sherwood	7.6	14.9	10.3	13.3	14.9	15.3	11.4	7.7	4.6	37.2	52.2	21 511	29 523	37.2	2.9
Springdale	10.6	23.4	8.8	15.9	14.8	10.0	7.8	4.6	4.1	29.9	48.9	45 798	69 797	52.4	10.0
Texarkana	7.6	16.5	8.3	14.8	12.3	13.5	12.4	7.7	6.8	37.2	50.0	26 448	29 919	13.1	1.5
West Memphis	8.6	18.7	9.8	13.5	10.9	13.0	12.3	7.8	5.5	34.7	53.2	27 666	26 245	-5.1	-4.6
CALIFORNIA	6.6	17.6	10.5	14.5	13.6	13.8	11.3	6.7	5.4	35.6	50.3	33 871 648	37 253 956	10.0	5.1
Adelanto	12.9	24.9	13.8	15.0	11.9	11.2	4.5	3.5	2.3	23.9	49.8	18 130	31 765	75.2	4.4
Alameda	5.4	15.0	6.8	14.3	14.9	16.4	13.8	7.6	5.8	40.9	50.9	72 259	73 812	2.1	6.5
Alhambra	5.1	13.2	9.6	15.8	12.8	15.7	13.3	7.3	7.1	40.7	51.7	85 804	83 089	-3.2	3.0
Aliso Viejo	8.8	18.3	6.7	14.2	19.7	17.5	7.8	4.8	2.2	36.1	51.6	40 166	47 823	19.1	4.5
Anaheim	7.5	18.6	10.8	16.0	13.8	13.4	9.8	5.5	4.6	32.9	50.1	328 014	336 265	2.5	4.3
Antioch	5.7	21.0	11.1	12.6	12.0	14.5	13.7	5.9	3.5	34.6	51.6	90 532	102 372	13.1	7.6
Apple Valley	6.5	19.4	10.3	11.4	9.9	13.1	13.4	9.0	7.0	37.8	51.2	54 239	69 135	27.5	4.4
Arcadia	3.9	17.1	7.8	10.2	13.3	18.5	12.6	8.2	8.4	43.7	52.9	53 054	56 364	6.2	3.6
Atascadero	5.5	15.7	8.7	12.5	10.9	15.7	15.6	8.0	7.4	42.6	47.8	26 411	28 310	7.2	5.3
Atwater	7.9	23.9	10.3	13.9	13.4	11.3	9.6	5.6	4.2	30.7	51.9	23 113	28 168	21.9	3.8
Azusa	5.8	17.4	21.2	15.1	12.5	11.7	8.7	4.9	2.7	28.2	50.5	44 712	46 361	3.7	7.2
Bakersfield	9.1	21.5	11.5	15.1	12.8	12.1	9.3	5.0	3.8	30.1	50.3	247 057	347 483	40.6	7.5
Baldwin Park	6.4	20.1	12.8	14.0	14.4	13.1	9.7	5.7	3.8	32.5	49.6	75 837	75 390	-0.6	2.2
Banning	5.8	12.8	9.1	13.5	9.1	11.1	10.2	12.4	16.0	44.5	52.4	23 562	29 603	25.6	4.5
Beaumont	10.1	20.4	8.0	14.2	14.7	11.8	9.7	7.7	3.2	33.6	50.9	11 384	36 877	223.9	18.8
Bell	8.6	20.5	13.4	14.0	14.7	12.3	8.7	4.4	3.4	30.0	48.3	36 664	35 477	-3.2	2.1
Bellflower	7.8	21.0	10.9	15.0	13.6	12.5	10.1	5.1	3.9	31.5	52.1	72 878	76 616	5.1	2.4
Bell Gardens	10.3	25.0	10.7	16.9	14.3	9.8	7.5	3.4	2.1	27.1	50.2	44 054	42 072	-4.5	2.5
Belmont	6.3	15.1	6.6	10.9	16.8	15.7	13.3	7.5	7.8	41.3	50.1	25 123	25 835	2.8	5.3
Benicia	5.1	18.7	6.8	11.7	10.6	17.0	16.7	9.3	4.2	42.2	52.3	26 865	26 997	0.5	4.3
Berkeley	3.8	8.7	24.5	17.3	11.5	10.2	10.7	8.0	5.3	31.8	50.9	102 743	112 580	9.6	7.5
Beverly Hills	4.9	15.2	7.5	13.4	11.5	15.7	11.2	11.1	9.5	43.1	54.8	33 784	34 109	1.0	2.2
Brea	5.9	17.4	10.7	12.4	14.9	13.9	12.2	7.0	5.7	38.4	50.3	35 410	39 282	10.9	7.0
Brentwood	6.6	23.5	7.7	9.0	17.9	14.8	8.7	6.9	4.7	36.2	48.7	23 302	51 481	120.9	14.2
Buena Park	6.2	17.6	10.7	13.6	14.0	14.7	11.4	6.9	5.0	36.2	50.9	78 282	80 530	2.9	3.3
Burbank	5.3	14.6	7.2	16.8	15.9	15.2	11.0	7.2	6.9	38.9	52.6	100 316	103 340	3.0	2.0
Burlingame	6.8	14.6	5.7	12.4	19.1	15.6	12.6	6.6	6.6	40.5	51.0	28 158	28 806	2.3	5.7
Calexico	7.4	22.5	11.2	10.6	13.0	10.6	12.4	6.1	6.2	33.4	53.1	27 109	38 572	42.3	3.8
Camarillo	6.3	17.0	8.1	12.7	13.0	14.8	11.7	7.7	8.6	39.4	51.4	57 077	65 201	14.2	3.7
Campbell	5.4	14.6	9.4	16.7	15.7	16.0	10.9	5.9	5.4	37.8	49.9	38 138	39 349	3.2	4.5
Carlsbad	5.6	17.1	6.2	11.4	14.6	16.1	13.4	7.6	8.0	41.9	49.7	78 247	105 328	34.6	7.6
Carson	6.0	15.9	11.2	13.7	12.3	14.7	11.4	8.4	6.5	37.6	51.7	89 730	91 714	2.2	1.7
Cathedral City	7.5	20.7	9.1	12.6	13.7	13.2	9.6	7.7	5.9	35.1	48.2	42 647	51 200	20.1	5.1
Ceres	8.1	21.1	12.5	15.0	13.7	11.0	9.4	4.6	4.6	30.5	50.1	34 609	45 417	31.2	4.5
Cerritos	3.6	16.4	8.4	9.2	13.5	14.7	15.1	10.5	8.5	44.3	53.3	51 488	49 041	-4.8	1.9
Chico	6.0	13.9	23.2	14.3	11.4	10.3	9.9	5.5	5.5	29.5	52.3	59 954	86 187	43.8	4.5
Chino	6.6	16.9	10.8	16.4	14.4	15.2	10.6	5.9	3.4	34.7	47.2	67 168	77 983	16.1	9.8
Chino Hills	5.3	20.6	11.5	10.1	14.2	18.6	12.0	4.7	2.9	37.1	49.8	66 787	74 799	12.0	4.7
Chula Vista	6.8	19.8	10.4	14.9	13.4	14.0	10.1	5.7	4.9	33.8	51.1	173 556	243 916	40.5	9.0
Citrus Heights	6.1	15.4	10.4	15.5	12.2	14.4	12.2	8.1	5.8	36.9	52.1	85 071	83 301	-2.1	4.6
Claremont	3.1	17.4	16.3	9.2	10.6	12.3	13.6	9.0	8.5	40.1	51.5	33 998	34 926	2.7	3.9
Clovis	6.6	21.8	10.3	12.6	13.2	14.0	10.5	6.1	4.9	34.0	52.3	68 468	95 631	39.7	8.9
Coachella	10.1	27.4	10.8	18.1	13.2	9.2	6.1	3.3	1.7	25.8	49.5	22 724	40 704	79.1	9.7
Colton	9.6	23.5	13.9	14.9	12.0	11.6	7.9	4.0	2.6	27.2	50.1	47 662	52 154	9.4	4.7
Compton	9.3	23.2	12.4	14.6	12.8	11.7	8.0	4.5	3.4	28.1	51.8	93 493	96 455	3.2	2.1
Concord	7.8	15.6	8.2	16.3	13.6	14.3	11.7	7.0	5.6	36.4	49.7	121 780	122 067	0.2	5.2
Corona	7.2	21.0	10.7	14.0	15.1	14.6	9.5	4.7	3.2	32.9	49.8	124 966	152 374	21.9	7.8
Costa Mesa	6.8	14.8	10.1	20.0	15.1	14.1	10.2	5.0	3.9	33.7	49.1	108 724	109 960	1.1	2.8
Covina	7.3	18.7	10.0	14.4	11.8	14.7	11.2	5.9	6.0	34.6	51.6	46 837	47 796	2.0	2.5
Culver City	5.8	13.9	6.4	15.8	16.5	13.0	12.6	9.2	6.9	39.9	52.1	38 816	38 883	0.2	2.1
Cupertino	6.0	21.8	4.9	8.2	18.7	17.2	10.7	6.7	5.9	40.2	51.5	50 546	58 302	15.3	3.4
Cypress	5.3	17.5	10.9	10.6	12.7	17.6	12.5	6.9	6.2	40.3	52.1	46 229	47 802	3.4	3.0
Daly City	5.8	13.5	10.2	15.9	15.0	12.6	13.3	7.7	6.1	38.3	50.1	103 621	101 123	-2.4	5.4
Dana Point	5.4	11.6	5.6	13.7	12.1	15.2	18.0	10.4	8.1	46.7	50.1	35 110	33 351	-5.0	2.7
Danville	5.8	20.9	5.4	5.9	11.0	17.3	16.7	8.7	8.4	45.6	52.4	41 715	42 039	0.8	6.1
Davis	4.3	12.8	31.6	12.8	9.8	10.8	8.9	5.0	4.0	25.7	51.4	60 308	65 622	8.8	3.1

City	Households, 2010-2014 Number	Persons per house-hold	Percent Female family house-holder[1]	Percent One-person	Persons in group quarters, 2010 Total	Institutional Total	Persons in nursing facilities	Non-institu-tional	Serious crimes known to police,[2] 2014 Total Number	Total Rate[3]	Rate[3] Violent	Property	Population age 25 and older	High school graduate or less	Bachelor's degree or more
	27	28	29	30	31	32	33	34	35	36	37	38	39	40	41
ARKANSAS—Cont'd															
Jacksonville..................	10 523	2.73	20.4	28.6	847	100	98	747	1 505	5 219	728	4 491	17 530	48.6	18.6
Jonesboro..................	26 771	2.62	16.5	27.4	3 412	1 238	800	2 174	3 578	4 930	539	4 392	42 355	40.6	29.7
Little Rock..................	78 658	2.49	16.2	36.7	4 543	2 781	1 074	1 762	17 457	8 807	1 405	7 402	130 339	32.6	38.5
North Little Rock............	25 879	2.50	18.4	35.6	870	638	583	232	3 277	4 889	639	4 250	42 685	40.9	25.9
Paragould..................	10 831	2.48	12.0	30.1	550	391	226	159	2 112	7 736	432	7 304	17 761	57.8	15.5
Pine Bluff..................	17 998	2.61	24.3	37.0	3 999	2 512	429	1 487	3 232	7 119	1 269	5 850	29 501	52.2	17.6
Rogers..................	20 289	2.91	11.9	23.4	450	312	312	138	1 998	3 270	347	2 923	35 642	48.4	27.3
Russellville..................	9 922	2.88	15.6	31.7	3 251	448	277	2 803	1 409	4 923	321	4 602	16 236	47.2	24.7
Sherwood..................	11 828	2.54	14.8	30.0	85	85	85	0	1 316	4 364	497	3 866	20 382	37.5	31.7
Springdale..................	24 340	3.03	15.6	22.3	830	678	577	152	NA	NA	NA	NA	42 163	58.9	18.8
Texarkana..................	11 825	2.54	18.5	32.6	1 468	1 251	300	217	2 041	6 797	749	6 048	20 180	52.9	13.9
West Memphis...............	9 675	2.66	30.6	29.7	608	505	206	103	1 841	7 257	1 435	5 822	16 091	59.4	11.3
CALIFORNIA...............	12 617 280	3.02	13.6	24.1	819 816	397 142	111 884	422 674	1 100 901	2 837	396	2 441	24 865 866	39.2	31.0
Adelanto..................	7 392	4.30	27.5	10.7	1 753	1 723	0	30	979	3 137	606	2 531	15 710	60.1	6.4
Alameda..................	30 346	2.50	11.7	29.3	1 496	639	639	857	1 868	2 424	188	2 236	54 864	22.7	49.2
Alhambra..................	29 061	2.90	15.7	25.0	614	482	455	132	1 911	2 250	198	2 052	60 872	41.0	32.4
Aliso Viejo..................	18 351	2.69	9.1	24.8	469	19	19	450	308	608	69	539	32 984	15.9	56.9
Anaheim..................	99 208	3.46	15.5	17.9	3 557	1 537	1 376	2 020	9 297	2 680	317	2 362	216 178	48.0	24.8
Antioch..................	32 900	3.21	17.9	18.6	664	260	229	404	5 039	4 656	784	3 872	66 039	41.7	20.2
Apple Valley..................	23 987	2.94	16.1	20.1	461	300	104	161	1 866	2 616	297	2 319	45 587	44.1	16.5
Arcadia..................	19 463	2.94	12.0	19.5	862	223	220	639	1 219	2 104	104	2 000	40 430	24.0	52.3
Atascadero..................	11 065	2.60	12.0	21.3	1 324	1 100	91	224	520	1 777	246	1 531	20 305	29.8	28.2
Atwater..................	8 672	3.31	19.7	18.6	102	71	63	31	1 206	4 164	628	3 536	16 366	53.0	13.5
Azusa..................	11 816	4.01	20.7	17.3	2 802	111	97	2 691	1 230	2 551	342	2 208	26 119	53.7	19.0
Bakersfield..................	111 988	3.20	16.9	19.5	3 395	1 301	749	2 094	16 273	4 429	457	3 972	208 447	45.0	20.7
Baldwin Park...............	17 434	4.38	21.8	8.6	406	318	276	88	1 561	2 029	285	1 744	46 465	69.7	11.3
Banning..................	11 739	2.58	13.2	30.8	1 365	1 111	177	254	747	2 433	417	2 016	21 314	53.0	15.8
Beaumont..................	12 721	3.11	11.8	19.4	474	211	137	263	1 045	2 529	172	2 357	24 770	36.3	25.4
Bell..................	8 998	3.99	22.5	12.9	579	89	89	490	935	2 593	602	1 991	20 684	74.6	6.3
Bellflower..................	23 473	3.30	22.1	21.0	739	340	329	399	1 916	2 462	376	2 085	47 345	52.5	15.5
Bell Gardens...............	9 693	4.41	23.7	9.1	424	299	299	125	818	1 898	251	1 648	23 555	81.4	4.7
Belmont..................	10 493	2.53	7.3	29.7	514	120	120	394	408	1 514	134	1 380	18 920	16.7	57.5
Benicia..................	10 788	2.54	12.7	25.2	26	0	0	26	510	1 837	94	1 743	19 048	20.4	41.1
Berkeley..................	45 569	2.54	7.6	35.3	12 849	419	237	12 430	5 533	4 699	366	4 333	71 341	12.6	70.2
Beverly Hills..................	14 606	2.36	8.8	37.9	121	0	0	121	1 182	3 398	319	3 079	25 272	18.2	60.1
Brea..................	14 153	2.86	12.9	22.1	69	0	0	69	1 177	2 846	128	2 718	27 377	24.6	40.5
Brentwood..................	17 138	3.15	11.2	15.5	146	5	5	141	1 352	2 422	183	2 239	33 898	30.3	29.1
Buena Park...............	23 223	3.54	15.4	12.6	814	261	242	553	2 247	2 694	260	2 434	53 744	40.2	29.2
Burbank..................	41 414	2.52	11.5	31.6	573	282	268	291	2 576	2 452	143	2 310	76 281	30.1	38.3
Burlingame..................	12 186	2.43	8.8	35.7	449	294	294	155	797	2 642	156	2 487	21 216	17.5	58.0
Calexico..................	9 213	4.26	25.7	12.6	100	0	0	100	1 726	4 362	243	4 119	22 866	61.8	13.3
Camarillo..................	24 270	2.72	9.3	24.9	496	341	227	155	1 037	1 565	109	1 456	45 975	24.4	40.4
Campbell..................	15 763	2.56	11.1	26.7	201	122	114	79	1 469	3 594	198	3 396	28 708	23.5	47.2
Carlsbad..................	42 516	2.57	8.5	25.6	915	456	451	459	1 935	1 723	182	1 541	76 824	15.9	53.9
Carson..................	24 729	3.74	19.3	15.9	1 303	133	49	1 170	2 455	2 644	365	2 279	61 164	42.2	24.2
Cathedral City...............	16 840	3.12	13.5	24.9	295	32	32	263	1 322	2 477	240	2 237	32 873	53.5	16.1
Ceres..................	13 110	3.55	19.3	14.9	353	60	38	293	1 729	3 686	309	3 377	27 516	62.5	9.7
Cerritos..................	15 140	3.28	10.5	12.7	104	18	18	86	1 611	3 231	172	3 058	35 349	23.0	48.9
Chico..................	34 314	2.55	11.8	32.4	3 178	587	577	2 591	3 553	4 012	384	3 628	49 528	25.5	34.9
Chino..................	20 468	3.95	14.6	16.2	7 064	6 900	3	164	2 002	2 453	228	2 225	52 684	45.8	21.4
Chino Hills..................	23 039	3.31	10.6	14.4	155	147	0	8	1 091	1 417	79	1 338	48 899	24.3	44.0
Chula Vista...............	77 062	3.28	15.6	18.8	1 736	1 080	538	656	5 136	1 976	235	1 741	158 568	38.9	27.4
Citrus Heights...............	32 889	2.57	13.9	27.8	486	182	131	304	3 080	3 592	454	3 138	58 425	38.1	18.9
Claremont..................	11 836	3.01	9.0	27.9	5 124	198	192	4 926	892	2 475	108	2 367	22 686	16.8	56.0
Clovis..................	33 555	2.94	14.2	22.0	388	258	221	130	3 280	3 257	214	3 043	60 454	31.9	29.9
Coachella..................	9 694	4.39	24.0	8.5	58	0	0	58	1 318	3 021	380	2 640	22 250	79.0	4.1
Colton..................	14 885	3.57	22.4	19.6	330	245	243	85	1 712	3 201	256	2 945	28 659	59.3	11.8
Compton..................	23 395	4.17	27.4	14.4	755	112	84	643	3 748	3 816	1 149	2 666	54 023	66.5	6.4
Concord..................	44 987	2.78	12.3	23.3	1 047	535	469	512	5 661	4 466	367	4 100	86 253	36.0	30.9
Corona..................	45 790	3.44	12.3	16.0	511	282	268	229	3 611	2 241	106	2 135	97 291	39.2	26.7
Costa Mesa..................	40 505	2.76	11.8	27.3	2 970	738	581	2 232	3 780	3 354	282	3 072	76 166	30.7	36.8
Covina..................	15 340	3.16	16.9	21.8	435	367	341	68	1 218	2 502	226	2 276	30 968	37.0	25.2
Culver City...............	16 515	2.38	10.5	35.2	311	227	227	84	1 862	4 707	427	4 279	28 861	19.0	54.0
Cupertino..................	20 643	2.90	7.2	19.7	337	276	258	61	1 066	1 760	66	1 694	40 491	9.7	75.6
Cypress..................	15 905	3.06	14.4	16.5	502	0	0	502	803	1 626	103	1 523	33 128	27.0	39.7
Daly City..................	31 008	3.35	13.8	20.4	681	408	397	273	1 879	1 779	184	1 595	73 644	35.8	33.2
Dana Point...............	14 523	2.33	8.0	30.4	241	81	77	160	534	1 559	207	1 352	25 761	17.9	48.4
Danville..................	15 685	2.73	6.6	20.7	243	187	183	56	456	1 044	39	1 005	29 216	11.3	64.2
Davis..................	24 306	2.72	7.1	25.8	2 100	277	203	1 823	1 539	2 319	127	2 193	33 825	12.3	71.0

1. No spouse present. 2. Data for serious crimes have not been adjusted for underreporting. This may affect comparability between geographic areas and over time. 3. Per 100,000 population estimated by the FBI. 4. Persons 25 years old and over.

Table D. Cities — Income, Poverty, and Housing

City	Money income, 2010–2014					Housing units, 2010			Occupied housing units 2010–2014			Median owner costs as a percent of income	
		Households			Families with income below poverty (percent)					Owner-occupied			
	Per capita income[1] (dollars)	Median income	Percent with income of $200,000 or more	Percent with income of less than $25,000		Total	Percent change, 2000–2010	Vacant units for sale or rent[2]	Total	Percent	Median value[3] (dollars)	With a mortgage[4]	Without a mortgage[5]
	42	43	44	45	46	47	48	49	50	51	52	53	54
ARKANSAS—Cont'd													
Jacksonville	20 480	40 720	1.2	25.6	14.1	12 412	4.8	1 476	10 523	52.9	112 800	22.7	11.4
Jonesboro	23 840	40 583	3.5	32.7	19.5	28 321	16.5	2 210	26 771	53.8	140 400	19.5	10.0
Little Rock	29 583	46 409	5.0	28.3	13.1	91 288	7.5	9 270	78 658	57.1	151 600	21.8	11.3
North Little Rock	23 196	40 305	1.9	30.4	15.4	29 437	6.8	2 907	25 879	53.9	118 200	20.5	10.9
Paragould	19 878	38 481	0.5	33.7	11.2	11 070	12.9	782	10 831	57.1	106 500	20.4	12.6
Pine Bluff	17 334	30 415	1.3	42.4	24.3	20 923	-6.2	2 852	17 998	55.2	72 300	21.7	13.0
Rogers	26 647	52 386	5.7	19.6	11.4	22 022	47.9	2 347	20 289	60.3	145 800	20.6	10.0
Russellville	18 942	36 360	2.1	33.7	20.6	11 124	8.9	806	9 922	52.3	130 600	22.3	10.0
Sherwood	28 434	58 300	2.3	19.7	9.5	12 924	40.5	717	11 828	67.6	144 700	19.5	10.0
Springdale	18 590	41 385	1.7	25.6	20.3	25 614	50.4	2 809	24 340	50.6	127 400	20.6	10.7
Texarkana	21 452	40 422	1.2	31.6	16.9	13 375	13.5	1 343	11 825	58.5	101 600	20.3	11.1
West Memphis	16 853	29 764	1.1	42.3	28.3	10 966	-0.5	1 131	9 675	47.1	85 100	21.2	12.1
CALIFORNIA	29 906	61 489	7.6	20.4	12.3	13 680 081	12.0	1 102 583	12 617 280	54.8	371 400	28.3	11.3
Adelanto	9 998	35 262	0.1	38.3	36.1	9 086	62.6	1 277	7 392	53.6	95 200	30.4	14.9
Alameda	42 331	76 439	11.1	15.4	7.2	32 351	2.2	2 228	30 346	47.6	628 500	25.8	10.5
Alhambra	24 971	53 195	3.4	23.8	12.2	30 915	2.8	1 698	29 061	39.9	484 100	28.9	11.5
Aliso Viejo	44 986	102 325	14.6	7.4	4.3	18 867	13.6	663	18 351	62.1	468 900	27.7	10.0
Anaheim	23 990	59 707	5.2	19.1	14.0	104 237	4.7	5 943	99 208	47.4	413 800	28.6	10.0
Antioch	25 499	65 770	4.9	17.8	10.5	34 849	15.5	2 597	32 900	61.0	240 000	28.9	10.0
Apple Valley	23 543	48 337	3.5	27.1	15.9	26 117	29.5	2 519	23 987	67.1	167 100	26.0	13.5
Arcadia	38 582	80 147	13.3	17.3	8.6	20 686	3.5	1 094	19 463	60.0	832 400	29.6	12.6
Atascadero	32 602	66 342	5.0	17.2	8.3	11 505	16.8	768	11 065	63.5	380 000	29.1	11.1
Atwater	18 663	41 619	3.7	28.8	22.4	9 771	20.8	933	8 672	49.6	134 900	23.6	11.9
Azusa	18 159	52 087	2.5	22.2	15.2	13 386	3.6	670	11 816	51.2	311 600	29.1	11.0
Bakersfield	23 786	56 842	4.2	22.7	16.5	120 725	36.9	9 593	111 988	56.9	184 800	25.0	10.3
Baldwin Park	15 419	51 189	1.8	19.5	15.4	17 736	1.8	547	17 434	58.7	292 800	32.5	10.0
Banning	20 246	39 556	0.8	28.5	15.4	12 144	24.7	1 306	11 739	66.8	160 500	28.9	14.6
Beaumont	26 627	66 775	4.8	16.6	8.3	12 908	203.1	1 107	12 721	76.5	216 300	28.9	12.4
Bell	12 031	36 496	0.1	33.0	25.8	9 217	0.0	347	8 998	28.8	282 200	36.0	11.9
Bellflower	20 213	49 360	2.6	24.1	14.7	24 897	2.9	1 246	23 473	39.5	341 700	29.6	10.0
Bell Gardens	11 460	37 103	0.4	28.4	26.4	9 986	2.0	331	9 693	22.8	280 600	31.6	10.0
Belmont	56 302	106 287	24.4	10.5	3.4	11 028	3.8	453	10 493	60.7	910 600	26.1	10.0
Benicia	43 640	89 094	10.8	11.3	3.7	11 306	7.1	620	10 788	68.2	424 000	24.1	10.0
Berkeley	42 406	65 283	12.8	25.3	7.5	49 454	5.5	3 425	45 569	41.9	719 500	25.3	10.7
Beverly Hills	81 788	87 366	21.9	18.4	7.9	16 394	3.4	1 525	14 606	40.7	1 000 000	35.9	15.1
Brea	35 245	81 857	8.4	12.4	4.9	14 785	11.4	519	14 153	61.6	530 500	27.5	10.0
Brentwood	33 357	88 697	7.2	9.5	3.7	17 523	125.6	1 029	17 138	73.5	365 300	28.5	15.3
Buena Park	24 525	68 884	5.3	16.3	9.9	24 623	3.1	937	23 223	55.7	401 000	27.7	10.1
Burbank	33 882	66 111	6.0	19.5	6.4	44 309	3.4	2 369	41 414	41.6	566 700	29.6	10.3
Burlingame	61 062	90 890	23.7	12.3	4.7	13 027	1.3	666	12 186	48.2	1 000 000	28.3	11.4
Calexico	12 960	35 233	1.2	37.1	25.4	10 651	52.5	535	9 213	51.6	154 300	29.0	12.1
Camarillo	39 689	87 120	10.8	11.5	3.5	25 702	17.2	1 198	24 270	70.1	456 500	26.2	10.1
Campbell	44 769	91 269	13.5	12.0	3.2	16 950	3.7	787	15 763	50.9	681 300	27.4	10.1
Carlsbad	44 305	87 416	14.9	15.0	8.2	44 673	32.5	3 328	42 516	62.6	626 000	27.2	10.5
Carson	23 622	71 420	4.1	16.3	8.3	26 226	3.6	794	24 729	74.7	341 200	28.8	10.0
Cathedral City	19 674	43 128	2.4	28.1	18.2	20 995	17.9	3 948	16 840	61.7	180 300	33.9	16.0
Ceres	18 575	46 132	1.4	25.5	17.7	13 673	26.6	981	13 110	58.4	154 100	29.4	11.8
Cerritos	35 460	91 487	11.4	8.4	3.2	15 859	1.6	333	15 140	80.8	596 500	26.9	10.0
Chico	24 775	42 334	2.6	30.9	13.5	37 050	52.1	2 245	34 314	43.8	263 100	24.9	11.4
Chino	23 116	72 554	4.1	14.8	8.2	21 797	21.0	1 025	20 468	69.6	337 200	29.9	10.0
Chino Hills	35 529	97 609	11.5	8.6	5.0	23 617	15.8	676	23 039	79.2	489 700	28.0	10.0
Chula Vista	25 385	66 110	4.1	18.6	10.1	79 416	33.4	3 901	77 062	58.2	359 500	30.4	10.0
Citrus Heights	24 915	51 150	1.3	20.0	10.5	35 075	0.4	2 389	32 889	55.2	191 100	28.1	10.3
Claremont	39 402	89 648	14.0	12.4	4.4	12 156	5.0	548	11 836	66.2	539 800	25.0	10.2
Clovis	28 497	63 662	5.7	18.9	11.3	35 306	40.4	1 887	33 555	60.2	247 400	25.8	12.7
Coachella	12 321	40 423	0.8	27.9	27.8	9 903	98.8	905	9 694	63.9	143 600	33.7	14.7
Colton	16 004	39 915	1.2	28.7	21.2	16 350	3.6	1 379	14 885	50.2	161 000	29.6	11.5
Compton	13 847	43 230	0.6	29.0	23.2	24 523	3.1	1 461	23 395	54.9	233 400	33.1	12.6
Concord	31 404	67 122	4.7	17.0	9.9	47 125	4.8	2 847	44 987	59.0	368 900	27.5	11.9
Corona	27 577	77 021	5.9	13.6	8.8	47 174	20.2	2 224	45 790	66.6	335 000	27.9	12.2
Costa Mesa	33 342	66 491	7.3	16.7	10.6	42 120	4.3	2 174	40 505	39.8	586 800	29.0	10.0
Covina	25 622	64 496	3.4	16.8	9.3	16 576	0.9	721	15 340	57.8	373 700	29.4	10.0
Culver City	45 792	79 292	12.1	15.0	6.4	17 491	2.1	712	16 515	55.0	618 000	29.2	11.6
Cupertino	55 867	134 872	29.7	9.6	2.9	21 027	12.4	846	20 643	63.0	1 000 000	25.9	10.0
Cypress	33 693	83 819	8.1	9.1	4.9	16 068	0.3	414	15 905	68.0	500 100	27.1	10.1
Daly City	28 753	74 489	7.0	14.3	6.3	32 588	4.3	1 498	31 008	55.2	564 000	30.5	10.0
Dana Point	51 474	84 404	15.1	12.7	6.0	15 938	1.8	1 756	14 523	57.7	710 000	29.5	11.2
Danville	65 783	140 616	29.9	6.4	2.6	15 934	3.9	514	15 685	84.3	852 400	26.3	11.0
Davis	33 646	57 454	9.8	26.9	6.2	25 869	9.6	996	24 306	44.1	532 800	22.7	10.0

1. Based on population estimated by the American Community Survey.   2. Includes units rented or sold but not occupied.   3. Specified owner-occupied units; $1,000,000 represents $1,000,000 or more   4. 50.0 represents 50 percent or more.   5. 10.0 represents 10 percent or less.

City	Occupied housing units, 2010–2014 (cont.)					Migration, 2010–2014		Civilian labor force, 2015				Civilian employment[4], 2010–2014			
										Unemployment			Percent		
	Percent renter occupied	Median gross rent[1]	Median gross rent as a percent of income[2]	Percent with no vehicle available	Percent who lived in the same house one year ago	Percent who lived outside current city one year ago	Total	Percent change, 2014–2015	Total	Rate[3]	Population age 16 and older	In labor force	Civilian full-year full-time workers	Households with no workers (percent)
	55	56	57	58	59	60	61	62	63	64	65	66	67	68
ARKANSAS—Cont'd														
Jacksonville	47.1	759	29.0	8.3	75.9	14.6	11 723	1.6	658	5.6	22 348	62.3	36.6	25.9
Jonesboro	46.2	674	33.7	8.2	71.7	11.4	35 402	3.3	1 640	4.6	54 564	62.5	37.8	29.2
Little Rock	42.9	785	30.2	7.5	83.7	6.2	95 833	2.0	4 481	4.7	154 348	65.9	43.7	26.8
North Little Rock	46.1	779	31.0	10.6	79.7	12.7	29 890	2.1	1 550	5.2	49 570	63.6	41.7	29.3
Paragould	42.9	664	29.6	4.8	78.0	8.6	12 463	2.6	685	5.5	21 016	57.6	37.8	37.8
Pine Bluff	44.8	660	34.7	9.3	83.3	6.4	17 562	-0.7	1 442	8.2	36 650	55.4	31.1	35.3
Rogers	39.7	813	24.7	3.5	81.1	10.8	32 184	5.2	1 293	4.0	43 692	68.4	49.2	17.8
Russellville	47.7	647	30.8	7.5	76.1	13.4	13 738	0.9	738	5.4	22 631	62.3	33.2	26.0
Sherwood	32.4	792	27.0	3.0	84.5	12.0	15 342	2.2	603	3.9	23 782	69.4	49.6	19.9
Springdale	49.4	702	28.0	6.8	77.4	11.1	36 829	5.2	1 309	3.6	50 935	69.2	46.3	18.9
Texarkana	41.5	705	30.8	10.2	75.7	13.0	13 652	2.5	748	5.5	23 389	59.8	40.5	32.0
West Memphis	52.9	683	36.8	15.7	80.2	7.6	10 725	1.1	746	7.0	19 360	58.0	35.4	34.6
CALIFORNIA	45.2	1 243	33.8	7.8	84.6	9.5	18 981 770	0.8	1 183 156	6.2	29 934 838	63.8	37.2	24.8
Adelanto	46.4	1 057	48.8	8.2	72.5	22.9	9 227	0.7	998	10.8	20 912	46.6	24.0	39.1
Alameda	52.4	1 375	29.3	8.7	84.0	11.1	41 274	1.6	1 687	4.1	62 037	67.9	41.6	24.1
Alhambra	60.1	1 217	33.2	8.0	86.1	10.6	45 213	0.3	1 977	4.4	70 682	62.6	40.2	20.9
Aliso Viejo	37.9	1 862	28.7	3.1	83.4	13.3	29 318	1.4	1 026	3.5	37 956	77.5	52.5	11.4
Anaheim	52.6	1 362	36.8	7.2	84.4	9.2	170 710	0.9	9 702	5.7	263 069	67.5	40.9	19.6
Antioch	39.0	1 373	36.9	6.4	81.8	9.4	50 873	0.8	3 531	6.9	81 082	64.7	36.2	23.9
Apple Valley	32.9	978	39.2	5.6	82.5	10.8	27 959	1.6	1 927	6.9	55 000	51.7	27.8	38.1
Arcadia	40.0	1 416	31.8	5.0	88.6	8.7	28 573	0.4	1 108	3.9	46 813	60.8	40.1	23.6
Atascadero	36.5	1 138	31.4	4.0	86.7	10.2	15 255	1.8	586	3.8	23 365	60.7	37.7	26.0
Atwater	50.4	905	32.3	8.8	82.7	8.9	12 317	-0.1	1 540	12.5	20 405	60.2	34.7	30.8
Azusa	48.8	1 199	36.0	7.0	83.3	12.3	23 823	0.1	1 206	5.1	37 307	64.1	36.4	18.1
Bakersfield	43.1	985	32.9	6.7	80.9	7.3	180 174	-0.2	16 430	9.1	261 667	64.3	38.5	23.1
Baldwin Park	41.3	1 213	36.0	5.8	89.9	7.3	35 274	-0.8	3 141	8.9	58 705	62.6	34.8	16.1
Banning	33.2	968	34.5	7.5	85.3	11.8	10 743	2.0	637	5.9	24 945	44.4	26.8	50.9
Beaumont	23.5	1 077	34.0	2.9	87.0	8.1	19 111	2.4	760	4.0	28 915	63.6	41.2	24.6
Bell	71.2	993	38.7	10.7	90.1	8.0	15 427	-0.9	1 407	9.1	26 401	62.1	33.5	15.6
Bellflower	60.5	1 177	35.7	7.4	88.1	8.9	35 966	-0.2	2 295	6.4	58 289	63.9	39.8	21.6
Bell Gardens	77.2	1 125	38.9	9.7	89.6	6.7	18 289	-0.5	1 418	7.8	30 240	64.1	36.5	15.7
Belmont	39.3	1 588	31.1	4.9	86.5	10.9	16 343	3.0	486	3.0	21 401	69.5	46.8	21.1
Benicia	31.8	1 369	32.6	3.2	85.9	8.6	14 807	1.9	565	3.8	21 856	67.3	41.3	23.8
Berkeley	58.1	1 338	34.3	21.2	69.9	19.5	61 518	1.7	2 347	3.8	102 800	59.5	30.1	29.6
Beverly Hills	59.3	1 908	31.0	7.9	84.5	11.8	18 406	-0.2	1 175	6.4	28 969	64.1	40.3	25.5
Brea	38.4	1 552	29.8	3.2	85.7	11.3	22 022	1.2	947	4.3	32 555	68.7	42.3	19.8
Brentwood	26.5	1 865	31.9	2.3	86.1	8.7	26 447	1.5	1 115	4.2	40 568	63.9	39.3	22.9
Buena Park	44.3	1 388	34.8	4.4	86.2	10.9	40 183	1.4	1 541	3.8	65 023	63.1	39.7	18.6
Burbank	58.4	1 394	32.6	8.6	87.5	8.5	57 859	0.0	3 182	5.5	86 235	68.2	42.4	22.3
Burlingame	51.8	1 588	27.8	6.8	84.2	12.4	17 829	3.1	472	2.6	23 394	69.2	45.4	20.0
Calexico	48.4	813	39.9	9.9	86.9	4.8	18 201	0.3	5 047	27.7	28 994	56.0	24.8	29.3
Camarillo	29.9	1 658	33.4	4.8	85.1	9.1	33 781	-0.5	1 612	4.8	52 608	64.9	40.2	28.1
Campbell	49.1	1 573	28.6	5.4	86.0	11.4	25 396	2.6	763	3.0	32 972	71.7	49.5	17.4
Carlsbad	37.4	1 714	33.9	3.5	86.1	10.5	53 965	1.0	2 538	4.7	86 826	63.5	38.7	27.9
Carson	25.3	1 388	32.7	4.3	88.3	8.3	46 710	-0.7	4 039	8.6	74 606	64.1	37.4	22.2
Cathedral City	38.3	1 145	35.7	6.6	82.4	9.1	25 066	2.1	1 370	5.5	39 442	63.3	35.4	28.7
Ceres	41.6	981	36.8	5.6	82.2	12.3	21 508	0.2	2 190	10.2	34 441	63.8	32.9	23.7
Cerritos	19.2	1 977	33.3	3.0	94.2	4.2	24 441	0.1	1 217	5.0	41 272	59.4	39.1	22.4
Chico	56.2	917	36.9	8.5	69.2	12.5	47 141	0.2	2 836	6.0	72 592	63.9	30.3	30.4
Chino	30.4	1 335	34.1	3.6	79.5	16.9	39 287	2.1	1 946	5.0	64 273	58.4	35.0	16.1
Chino Hills	20.8	1 825	32.6	2.8	89.4	7.8	41 272	2.2	1 954	4.7	59 141	69.9	43.2	13.8
Chula Vista	41.8	1 302	36.5	5.6	88.9	6.6	120 978	0.6	7 914	6.5	193 543	65.1	37.8	21.1
Citrus Heights	44.8	1 034	31.8	5.6	79.5	14.8	43 280	0.8	2 735	6.3	68 691	65.1	34.7	27.7
Claremont	33.8	1 326	31.7	7.6	83.9	12.8	16 725	-0.2	1 068	6.4	29 719	58.6	31.4	29.5
Clovis	39.8	1 067	31.6	5.8	85.2	9.8	51 219	1.1	4 045	7.9	74 783	64.1	37.9	25.9
Coachella	36.1	890	39.4	4.5	85.8	8.5	18 636	0.9	1 934	10.4	28 397	70.6	36.8	14.8
Colton	49.8	989	39.0	7.7	81.9	13.0	23 994	1.8	1 552	6.5	37 970	64.9	35.9	21.7
Compton	45.1	1 082	41.3	9.0	87.9	7.6	40 147	-1.2	4 180	10.4	70 363	61.0	33.5	25.8
Concord	41.0	1 321	33.7	6.7	85.2	8.8	66 211	1.2	3 593	5.4	99 798	67.5	38.6	22.6
Corona	33.4	1 370	35.0	3.7	89.1	7.3	79 554	2.1	4 170	5.2	118 592	67.1	42.5	14.2
Costa Mesa	60.2	1 551	32.2	4.9	83.3	11.3	65 657	1.2	2 979	4.5	90 334	74.0	45.3	17.5
Covina	42.2	1 237	33.5	4.7	85.2	13.0	24 351	-0.6	1 948	8.0	37 546	66.0	38.6	22.2
Culver City	45.0	1 649	28.8	6.6	84.6	12.9	22 510	0.2	1 112	4.9	32 351	70.2	44.2	24.1
Cupertino	37.0	2 000	23.2	3.8	83.7	12.5	29 470	2.5	988	3.4	45 410	61.7	44.0	21.0
Cypress	32.0	1 609	29.8	2.7	88.5	9.7	24 805	1.5	756	3.0	39 412	63.6	39.7	18.3
Daly City	44.8	1 599	33.9	9.2	87.7	8.6	63 932	2.7	2 660	4.2	86 481	69.5	43.2	18.8
Dana Point	42.3	1 826	33.4	3.5	81.1	13.2	18 955	1.3	794	4.2	28 545	67.3	40.6	28.2
Danville	15.7	2 000	33.0	3.8	89.5	7.6	20 566	1.6	816	4.0	32 565	63.5	41.0	23.0
Davis	55.9	1 247	43.0	8.7	67.8	18.8	34 920	1.3	1 720	4.9	56 313	60.6	29.5	25.3

1. $2,000 represents $2,000 or more. 2. 50.0 represents 50 percent or more. 3. Percent of civilian labor force. 4. Persons 16 years old and over.

Table D. Cities — Construction, Wholesale Trade, and Retail Trade

City	Value of residential construction authorized by building permits, 2015			Wholesale trade,[1] 2012				Retail trade,[2] 2012			
	New construction ($1,000)	Number of housing units	Percent single family	Number of establish-ments	Number of employees	Sales (mil dol)	Annual payroll (mil dol)	Number of establish-ments	Number of employees	Sales (mil dol)	Annual payroll (mil dol)
	69	70	71	72	73	74	75	76	77	78	79
ARKANSAS—Cont'd											
Jacksonville	5 633	43	100.0	10	84	66.9	3.8	89	1 404	396.8	36.7
Jonesboro	49 280	354	81.4	94	1 133	643.5	50.6	406	6 053	1 556.4	135.5
Little Rock	110 366	770	43.1	358	6 552	3 801.0	340.0	994	14 533	4 025.2	354.2
North Little Rock	17 266	92	100.0	196	3 234	3 898.4	185.7	417	6 092	1 557.4	138.8
Paragould	13 621	139	72.7	26	378	459.2	15.1	130	1 608	395.9	33.7
Pine Bluff	1 126	8	100.0	40	354	189.0	14.8	248	3 072	744.6	71.2
Rogers	78 567	499	79.2	60	510	619.9	30.8	297	5 130	1 162.2	114.4
Russellville	5 815	63	71.4	47	384	296.7	16.6	216	2 815	782.7	60.7
Sherwood	30 949	187	100.0	30	188	93.2	8.1	94	1 899	763.9	53.7
Springdale	74 262	312	100.0	144	1 569	1 133.8	74.0	247	3 448	1 011.1	86.8
Texarkana	5 817	43	90.7	37	D	D	D	113	1 324	416.4	29.7
West Memphis	1 084	15	60.0	38	717	1 799.2	32.4	102	1 660	617.7	35.6
CALIFORNIA	22 637 174	98 188	46.5	52 664	723 526	666 652.2	48 408.7	106 419	1 540 055	481 800.5	43 361.0
Adelanto	33 229	116	100.0	7	114	42.2	4.5	19	286	80.8	8.0
Alameda	44 833	181	65.2	63	2 252	2 887.1	218.6	155	1 956	492.2	54.1
Alhambra	37 236	273	3.3	234	999	476.8	31.3	233	3 923	1 636.6	116.7
Aliso Viejo	66 280	637	0.0	74	1 311	1 010.6	133.6	82	1 210	500.3	43.2
Anaheim	144 426	1 000	3.6	799	9 520	7 153.5	562.0	826	13 333	3 757.9	374.1
Antioch	19 900	68	100.0	23	316	276.1	18.2	216	3 781	939.3	102.9
Apple Valley	15 852	110	100.0	10	32	8.6	1.2	113	2 311	598.1	53.9
Arcadia	44 432	240	28.3	284	1 066	527.0	39.5	295	4 276	860.3	94.2
Atascadero	14 603	96	63.5	30	210	66.5	9.5	116	1 230	298.5	30.7
Atwater	505	3	100.0	8	D	D	D	74	1 314	257.5	27.3
Azusa	50 822	113	98.2	75	1 416	883.0	103.9	94	1 147	470.7	33.6
Bakersfield	367 471	1 463	95.1	274	3 933	3 693.1	216.0	960	18 130	5 263.8	454.7
Baldwin Park	3 761	21	100.0	151	860	373.8	34.0	130	2 106	535.3	52.4
Banning	0	0	0.0	11	347	72.0	10.9	58	616	176.7	16.6
Beaumont	83 965	485	100.0	9	27	3.9	0.8	57	1 297	348.8	32.0
Bell	0	0	0.0	71	1 564	1 029.1	83.9	51	458	128.5	10.8
Bellflower	5 463	25	100.0	34	226	98.4	10.3	174	1 970	551.5	53.2
Bell Gardens	6 951	23	56.5	39	474	178.2	18.6	79	1 127	321.2	30.9
Belmont	3 675	7	100.0	19	D	D	D	57	761	292.3	28.8
Benicia	350	1	100.0	66	1 134	733.7	63.0	71	844	266.6	31.0
Berkeley	51 971	304	3.9	94	1 175	565.1	82.4	497	5 449	1 341.0	164.2
Beverly Hills	57 350	75	40.0	158	778	647.5	48.2	429	5 382	2 912.3	275.0
Brea	65 021	330	32.4	263	3 865	3 321.6	215.5	321	6 133	1 260.4	134.2
Brentwood	102 073	486	100.0	14	59	18.3	2.5	142	2 263	557.2	54.7
Buena Park	37 991	176	100.0	204	3 037	2 044.9	165.9	202	3 987	1 731.1	134.4
Burbank	6 679	15	80.0	208	2 987	4 628.6	209.3	399	7 310	2 316.8	191.7
Burlingame	9 361	14	100.0	136	978	870.8	64.3	159	2 011	776.4	79.8
Calexico	8 325	51	2.0	58	403	416.3	11.7	136	1 997	432.4	40.7
Camarillo	35 709	88	100.0	147	2 132	1 157.4	130.2	313	5 248	1 526.8	133.7
Campbell	15 241	50	100.0	74	D	D	D	182	2 925	757.9	83.6
Carlsbad	91 641	251	98.4	292	5 465	3 115.2	354.2	485	7 796	2 649.1	215.9
Carson	13 322	39	74.4	337	6 718	5 893.4	352.1	210	4 267	1 398.5	148.4
Cathedral City	5 056	24	100.0	24	127	37.6	4.6	145	2 002	790.1	65.7
Ceres	6 442	35	100.0	22	335	281.9	16.9	89	1 606	443.7	38.5
Cerritos	37 669	330	0.0	254	5 230	5 454.5	329.6	233	7 278	2 479.9	213.9
Chico	76 941	521	49.1	84	831	399.3	40.8	419	6 368	1 790.7	165.7
Chino	197 565	843	47.0	457	5 476	3 872.9	265.8	266	4 563	1 188.9	105.8
Chino Hills	30 879	123	87.0	90	248	203.5	8.8	140	2 399	635.6	57.1
Chula Vista	127 565	689	13.1	299	1 793	1 406.4	77.9	616	11 228	2 744.4	273.1
Citrus Heights	4 942	21	100.0	16	58	70.0	3.3	263	4 698	1 029.7	103.2
Claremont	7 995	23	100.0	20	86	48.1	4.1	80	1 102	379.7	34.8
Clovis	239 252	899	94.8	47	190	189.9	9.0	267	5 059	1 496.3	130.8
Coachella	6 460	34	100.0	22	460	162.5	29.0	49	671	259.6	15.9
Colton	5 046	15	100.0	44	770	642.1	36.6	103	1 508	480.9	44.2
Compton	558	3	100.0	141	2 276	1 584.9	122.5	160	1 571	368.8	31.3
Concord	6 458	25	100.0	116	896	444.6	53.7	423	7 650	2 376.7	225.2
Corona	46 123	561	5.0	288	5 898	7 239.0	355.9	450	8 115	2 616.1	218.4
Costa Mesa	42 318	229	100.0	288	4 160	17 724.3	315.1	748	13 371	3 815.5	386.4
Covina	845	3	100.0	67	405	143.3	18.1	154	2 746	671.1	78.3
Culver City	3 001	8	100.0	110	2 279	1 690.9	200.3	287	5 510	1 660.3	154.5
Cupertino	44 560	179	29.1	71	1 507	1 092.5	107.8	121	D	D	D
Cypress	1 414	6	100.0	101	3 164	3 767.2	259.9	103	1 617	614.0	46.7
Daly City	52 302	164	66.5	35	D	D	D	193	3 738	885.4	91.3
Dana Point	59 369	49	100.0	51	232	155.8	12.7	102	1 042	340.4	27.3
Danville	46 917	65	96.9	44	173	167.2	10.3	124	1 610	548.1	45.5
Davis	23 566	97	81.4	16	256	495.9	21.3	124	2 061	466.0	50.5

1. Merchant wholesalers except manufacturers' sales branches and offices. 2. Establishments with payroll.

Table D. Cities — Real Estate, Professional Services, and Manufacturing

City	Real estate and rental and leasing, 2012				Professional, scientific, and technical services,[1] 2012				Manufacturing, 2012			
	Number of establishments	Number of employees	Receipts (mil dol)	Annual payroll (mil dol)	Number of establishments	Number of employees	Receipts (mil dol)	Annual payroll (mil dol)	Number of establishments	Number of employees	Receipts (mil dol)	Annual payroll (mil dol)
	80	81	82	83	84	85	86	87	88	89	90	91
ARKANSAS—Cont'd												
Jacksonville	44	170	24.3	4.4	34	191	14.4	5.0	23	543	D	27.2
Jonesboro	110	469	79.0	12.8	157	D	D	D	80	4 781	1 900.6	203.7
Little Rock	377	2 450	423.0	89.3	1 182	D	D	D	166	8 152	4 227.1	419.7
North Little Rock	89	440	89.0	13.4	175	1 435	172.4	62.8	62	1 978	D	93.1
Paragould	30	D	D	D	47	423	38.2	18.6	37	3 299	D	128.4
Pine Bluff	53	173	26.7	4.4	57	D	D	D	48	4 258	1 859.3	185.2
Rogers	83	322	65.1	13.2	216	1 644	275.6	87.7	53	5 462	1 753.7	217.3
Russellville	59	174	26.2	4.9	105	D	D	D	40	4 067	1 339.7	149.1
Sherwood	28	80	21.3	2.5	43	539	113.1	30.5	17	D	D	D
Springdale	74	254	39.7	7.5	135	D	D	D	101	7 619	2 375.8	265.0
Texarkana	27	D	D	D	41	D	D	D	26	2 303	D	D
West Memphis	30	168	20.0	5.0	37	D	D	D	25	815	469.3	31.6
CALIFORNIA	49 276	273 511	78 740.2	13 467.5	113 553	1 270 902	227 858.9	87 924.6	38 741	1 163 341	512 303.2	69 316.8
Adelanto	9	21	3.3	0.4	7	75	11.0	4.5	42	1 108	263.4	55.3
Alameda	95	382	65.5	13.6	234	2 323	614.3	222.1	50	3 006	1 130.2	274.0
Alhambra	117	396	66.2	15.1	220	D	D	D	76	1 252	307.3	64.9
Aliso Viejo	79	D	D	D	288	3 609	843.5	364.2	30	378	58.0	21.7
Anaheim	381	3 684	508.9	131.9	681	4 384	760.1	251.7	693	19 991	4 824.4	1 071.6
Antioch	60	266	43.1	7.5	92	600	103.3	28.6	22	235	125.9	12.2
Apple Valley	37	179	23.1	4.3	68	339	33.2	12.1	25	319	D	15.4
Arcadia	175	483	98.1	17.1	258	D	D	D	47	905	194.3	46.0
Atascadero	27	D	D	D	74	D	D	D	26	109	15.8	4.6
Atwater	12	32	4.9	0.6	10	27	3.0	1.0	13	368	D	18.9
Azusa	22	46	13.8	1.5	35	309	64.0	22.4	100	4 979	1 505.2	318.8
Bakersfield	343	1 907	335.7	69.5	798	D	D	D	143	2 541	646.2	110.3
Baldwin Park	22	119	17.8	4.2	31	143	12.0	4.6	85	1 533	285.7	63.8
Banning	29	216	38.8	6.0	14	145	9.5	3.7	22	326	72.9	14.2
Beaumont	24	77	10.2	1.7	19	45	4.4	1.7	14	361	102.3	15.9
Bell	12	D	D	D	16	405	45.4	18.2	30	1 711	657.2	85.4
Bellflower	78	249	48.7	10.7	60	317	17.0	6.3	33	254	46.8	11.2
Bell Gardens	10	36	10.0	0.9	10	153	14.6	5.2	50	863	156.7	32.5
Belmont	49	533	67.1	25.6	107	508	62.1	41.7	20	352	D	19.2
Benicia	43	187	47.1	8.7	98	580	92.2	36.8	70	2 579	7 511.9	195.5
Berkeley	198	744	175.2	40.0	605	3 646	692.1	295.7	152	3 744	D	241.1
Beverly Hills	481	2 312	1 293.7	155.3	1 017	5 275	1 681.6	538.7	57	348	33.9	9.2
Brea	97	536	118.4	26.9	288	D	D	D	152	5 251	1 292.7	254.2
Brentwood	55	173	40.2	6.8	84	280	36.7	12.6	17	232	D	12.3
Buena Park	57	218	40.3	6.9	110	960	135.1	50.1	109	3 966	1 990.3	204.1
Burbank	242	2 976	1 052.6	246.5	608	D	D	D	191	5 031	1 269.2	284.4
Burlingame	149	935	213.8	44.8	272	D	D	D	49	1 679	D	98.9
Calexico	24	104	9.3	1.8	42	112	12.2	3.4	12	265	D	20.8
Camarillo	87	608	111.7	28.3	299	2 498	601.1	181.4	134	4 292	1 636.8	230.4
Campbell	85	448	155.2	36.3	312	D	D	D	92	1 840	431.0	113.7
Carlsbad	314	1 571	330.6	74.0	894	D	D	D	160	12 711	4 983.1	1 024.6
Carson	64	625	453.8	62.4	101	970	159.8	40.6	230	9 808	15 329.4	624.3
Cathedral City	38	182	40.7	5.8	40	99	11.0	2.7	13	29	5.5	1.3
Ceres	30	110	24.6	4.0	25	311	34.0	14.1	21	391	90.1	16.8
Cerritos	79	226	56.8	9.6	188	D	D	D	88	2 532	509.8	111.1
Chico	137	769	88.0	18.4	291	D	D	D	71	1 549	568.6	65.1
Chino	78	289	66.4	11.5	148	1 068	130.1	42.1	220	5 480	1 465.1	232.5
Chino Hills	66	116	36.2	4.9	169	428	66.5	18.7	10	72	D	1.4
Chula Vista	241	987	217.4	34.8	357	D	D	D	126	4 237	1 363.4	330.2
Citrus Heights	79	408	46.7	11.6	122	1 252	128.6	50.2	12	31	3.2	1.0
Claremont	58	180	24.5	7.7	133	D	D	D	20	620	114.6	26.2
Clovis	79	276	49.5	7.6	155	894	88.8	35.3	42	2 866	D	131.0
Coachella	17	58	8.7	1.8	6	D	D	D	11	773	433.2	37.5
Colton	34	222	39.8	7.7	49	D	D	D	53	2 758	1 090.7	95.5
Compton	21	61	13.2	2.3	15	D	D	D	129	4 001	1 184.2	178.4
Concord	148	996	215.3	48.3	298	3 084	581.0	226.3	106	1 779	464.2	97.9
Corona	175	641	156.0	25.2	319	1 877	210.8	106.2	341	12 813	4 810.5	586.6
Costa Mesa	298	3 347	666.1	135.9	687	8 743	2 097.9	740.2	232	6 196	1 541.4	321.1
Covina	94	479	63.9	16.8	148	946	131.5	44.7	89	1 490	344.0	69.4
Culver City	107	1 251	229.6	59.8	424	D	D	D	53	1 612	367.4	84.7
Cupertino	104	401	256.0	28.6	444	2 980	1 111.0	417.2	35	927	382.1	90.2
Cypress	65	277	58.0	13.3	118	979	212.8	55.6	35	1 287	588.1	92.4
Daly City	54	273	136.9	13.2	69	291	25.2	8.4	20	283	D	7.2
Dana Point	78	163	34.4	7.8	168	548	113.1	46.1	24	155	37.3	7.0
Danville	103	379	148.2	26.7	223	956	185.9	66.9	11	125	D	5.1
Davis	116	619	75.6	21.2	205	D	D	D	22	627	D	32.0

1. Establishments subject to federal tax.

Table D. Cities — Accommodation and Food Services, Arts, Entertainment, and Recreation, and Health Care and Social Assistance

City	Accommodation and food services, 2012				Arts, entertainment, and recreation,[1] 2012				Health care and social assistance,[1] 2012			
	Number of establish-ments	Number of employees	Sales (mil dol)	Annual payroll (mil dol)	Number of establish-ments	Number of employees	Receipts (mil dol)	Annual payroll (mil dol)	Number of establish-ments	Number of employees	Receipts (mil dol)	Annual payroll (mil dol)
	92	93	94	95	96	97	98	99	100	101	102	103
ARKANSAS—Cont'd												
Jacksonville	61	1 010	44.9	12.3	5	D	D	D	51	D	D	D
Jonesboro	193	4 134	182.9	50.6	14	184	7.4	3.1	284	D	D	D
Little Rock	593	12 849	626.5	185.9	64	677	40.9	13.3	825	10 939	1 405.6	615.5
North Little Rock	227	4 536	213.5	63.3	20	D	D	D	212	2 659	322.4	127.2
Paragould	61	D	D	D	4	D	D	D	73	D	D	D
Pine Bluff	102	D	D	D	3	D	D	D	153	D	D	D
Rogers	145	3 735	169.7	52.0	9	174	11.6	4.9	164	D	D	D
Russellville	103	2 256	101.8	24.9	9	42	2.0	0.4	112	D	D	D
Sherwood	43	673	34.9	8.9	3	D	D	D	68	D	D	D
Springdale	134	2 345	106.4	30.2	12	D	D	D	139	3 900	446.2	171.2
Texarkana	69	D	D	D	5	D	D	D	50	D	D	D
West Memphis	68	1 158	65.6	15.7	5	D	D	D	66	D	D	D
CALIFORNIA	78 560	1 394 984	90 830.4	25 147.8	19 010	245 599	34 302.9	11 726.7	89 999	1 005 201	127 355.7	48 372.7
Adelanto	14	D	D	D	1	D	D	D	4	D	D	D
Alameda	208	2 505	145.4	38.8	28	566	281.4	169.8	182	2 115	251.2	88.4
Alhambra	196	3 107	170.3	46.8	15	D	D	D	265	2 672	292.9	102.2
Aliso Viejo	68	1 335	87.1	24.8	15	D	D	D	119	D	D	D
Anaheim	692	23 526	1 589.1	507.2	75	D	D	D	825	11 330	1 388.6	525.8
Antioch	129	1 981	105.6	29.7	13	D	D	D	210	D	D	D
Apple Valley	85	D	D	D	7	D	D	D	190	D	D	D
Arcadia	212	3 593	220.4	59.1	70	D	D	D	383	D	D	D
Atascadero	70	926	53.1	12.9	9	127	4.6	1.6	85	D	D	D
Atwater	35	532	27.7	6.5	3	69	3.6	1.0	23	D	D	D
Azusa	73	895	48.0	12.8	3	D	D	D	44	523	27.4	11.7
Bakersfield	675	12 835	713.4	189.0	59	2 198	85.8	29.3	973	11 550	1 564.5	498.1
Baldwin Park	85	1 201	74.2	18.5	2	D	D	D	77	D	D	D
Banning	46	751	41.3	10.1	NA	NA	NA	NA	41	653	93.4	23.7
Beaumont	45	629	33.1	10.0	4	D	D	D	41	D	D	D
Bell	54	580	35.7	8.8	1	D	D	D	30	279	20.7	8.9
Bellflower	117	1 294	72.6	18.7	8	170	7.6	2.4	143	D	D	D
Bell Gardens	53	669	50.4	10.7	2	D	D	D	26	526	40.3	15.0
Belmont	62	716	58.0	13.2	5	D	D	D	47	D	D	D
Benicia	60	767	40.2	10.6	6	112	8.9	1.7	51	D	D	D
Berkeley	437	6 068	383.7	114.8	62	836	131.8	27.2	401	3 197	463.0	188.7
Beverly Hills	200	8 518	782.3	248.1	857	3 764	1 868.9	804.7	1 091	5 921	1 249.2	360.7
Brea	160	4 045	232.7	69.9	18	221	20.7	4.9	158	D	D	D
Brentwood	102	1 623	88.8	23.1	10	D	D	D	98	D	D	D
Buena Park	185	2 924	183.6	46.4	13	D	D	D	161	1 619	170.0	58.5
Burbank	325	6 840	532.9	130.3	308	D	D	D	467	D	D	D
Burlingame	145	4 340	387.8	115.5	18	216	19.1	4.6	179	2 136	426.2	133.0
Calexico	53	852	44.7	11.6	2	D	D	D	16	115	12.0	4.3
Camarillo	165	3 099	173.5	47.2	21	379	23.1	7.4	236	2 256	202.5	78.3
Campbell	133	2 474	150.8	42.2	19	D	D	D	193	D	D	D
Carlsbad	251	7 216	468.8	154.5	59	2 435	246.6	49.3	290	3 598	496.5	180.1
Carson	158	2 289	144.2	34.6	17	D	D	D	146	1 327	109.9	42.4
Cathedral City	85	1 365	67.0	19.6	10	D	D	D	53	462	29.2	13.1
Ceres	58	1 188	52.0	13.4	4	54	5.6	0.7	39	345	34.5	12.9
Cerritos	146	D	D	D	10	D	D	D	196	2 163	236.9	89.7
Chico	247	4 730	213.1	60.4	23	556	19.7	6.3	374	3 766	383.8	139.8
Chino	149	2 564	127.7	36.8	26	441	22.0	7.2	190	2 297	255.9	84.2
Chino Hills	116	2 267	114.5	33.9	13	324	19.0	6.0	108	661	71.1	23.0
Chula Vista	385	6 198	357.9	96.7	35	829	66.2	15.1	506	4 450	514.8	213.8
Citrus Heights	126	2 343	113.2	32.5	18	D	D	D	148	1 507	122.3	49.4
Claremont	97	1 667	90.5	24.3	11	D	D	D	141	1 336	118.8	48.2
Clovis	197	3 352	167.2	46.2	16	D	D	D	187	D	D	D
Coachella	46	753	35.2	8.2	1	D	D	D	10	D	D	D
Colton	85	1 150	58.0	15.2	4	D	D	D	79	D	D	D
Compton	94	1 207	77.6	18.5	4	D	D	D	62	527	41.3	17.7
Concord	247	3 850	229.6	61.7	30	714	40.8	12.1	333	3 810	420.7	163.9
Corona	276	4 993	261.4	70.9	29	D	D	D	315	3 204	333.1	119.1
Costa Mesa	422	8 168	530.6	147.9	54	581	50.5	12.4	344	3 573	343.0	121.0
Covina	114	1 803	98.7	26.0	10	D	D	D	199	2 636	265.1	113.9
Culver City	183	3 434	231.9	63.6	129	626	172.6	43.9	181	5 143	367.4	142.9
Cupertino	150	2 728	168.4	45.5	15	203	12.8	3.5	184	D	D	D
Cypress	105	1 460	88.3	23.2	26	393	30.3	10.6	114	1 648	166.5	66.6
Daly City	145	2 549	165.7	42.9	11	D	D	D	241	D	D	D
Dana Point	111	3 674	299.2	94.4	21	D	D	D	97	613	66.3	23.1
Danville	96	1 576	85.1	25.8	18	330	35.2	9.5	132	1 097	114.6	45.2
Davis	182	D	D	D	17	266	9.0	3.2	118	1 483	229.0	63.5

1. Establishments subject to federal tax.

City	Other services[1], 2012				Government employment and payroll, 2012								
						March payroll							
							Percent of total for:						
	Number of establish-ments	Number of employees	Receipts (mil dol)	Annual payroll (mil dol)	Full-time equivalent employees	Total (dollars)	Adminis-tration, judicial, and legal	Police and Corrections	Fire Protection	Highways and trans-portation	Health and welfare	Natural resources and utilities	Education and libraries
	104	105	106	107	108	109	110	111	112	113	114	115	116
ARKANSAS—Cont'd													
Jacksonville	24	124	8.6	2.6	351	1 152 915	9.7	28.8	19.4	4.2	5.3	27.7	0.0
Jonesboro	90	653	67.9	19.3	689	2 345 837	8.5	24.7	13.3	9.8	1.2	42.4	0.0
Little Rock	291	2 215	176.7	54.2	2 851	11 721 278	7.5	27.1	19.0	8.2	12.4	20.1	0.0
North Little Rock	118	1 132	69.5	23.3	971	3 614 112	10.1	25.8	20.1	6.7	0.9	29.4	2.5
Paragould	34	D	D	D	282	995 938	7.4	13.5	10.1	7.0	0.0	34.9	0.0
Pine Bluff	56	D	D	D	430	1 262 555	9.4	40.1	30.3	11.6	2.7	0.0	0.0
Rogers	64	326	28.7	7.6	478	1 723 247	11.6	29.5	25.6	5.5	1.0	18.2	4.6
Russellville	62	350	23.9	8.9	247	826 281	6.7	26.5	27.2	7.8	0.0	20.1	0.0
Sherwood	41	196	17.8	5.0	260	794 982	19.0	40.7	0.0	5.0	4.1	26.7	0.1
Springdale	87	778	60.4	21.5	584	1 997 062	10.3	28.7	23.9	6.6	1.7	21.9	3.3
Texarkana	34	D	D	D	237	974 321	9.2	47.4	27.7	4.9	2.8	2.3	0.0
West Memphis	37	D	D	D	383	1 214 605	9.2	23.7	21.2	5.8	0.8	25.0	1.3
CALIFORNIA	46 852	299 033	29 320.9	8 446.1	X	X	X	X	X	X	X	X	X
Adelanto	5	D	D	D	122	519 045	17.9	63.0	0.0	6.8	0.0	11.6	0.0
Alameda	104	556	42.8	12.8	658	4 669 134	6.4	25.2	22.5	8.7	5.7	19.2	3.1
Alhambra	97	427	40.9	11.2	423	2 729 610	8.0	33.5	27.5	3.8	4.0	18.8	4.5
Aliso Viejo	41	D	D	D	20	114 486	83.1	0.0	0.0	0.0	0.0	16.9	0.0
Anaheim	354	2 718	252.4	74.3	2 214	15 281 363	10.2	31.2	18.4	2.6	1.6	22.9	1.9
Antioch	88	506	37.6	12.3	306	1 931 728	10.7	57.2	0.0	6.0	2.1	20.9	0.0
Apple Valley	38	261	13.8	6.6	115	584 392	38.7	9.0	0.0	3.2	20.4	28.7	0.0
Arcadia	97	448	32.9	10.0	327	2 164 149	7.3	33.8	24.4	10.7	0.9	4.2	5.7
Atascadero	31	126	12.9	3.7	131	738 888	19.1	30.8	22.5	9.0	0.0	14.3	0.0
Atwater	19	88	7.8	1.8	124	673 870	13.1	42.2	13.9	5.5	4.6	18.3	0.0
Azusa	61	287	23.1	6.8	312	2 003 992	16.2	36.1	0.0	4.3	3.4	34.3	3.5
Bakersfield	360	2 420	249.6	70.7	1 424	8 316 644	6.2	38.5	18.9	8.6	0.9	17.6	0.0
Baldwin Park	35	125	13.5	3.8	227	1 307 981	10.1	58.7	0.0	11.0	9.8	10.4	0.0
Banning	24	139	11.8	4.4	195	1 176 594	19.1	35.3	0.3	9.9	1.7	30.2	0.0
Beaumont	41	189	16.1	4.3	168	910 677	6.3	58.6	0.8	7.4	3.3	11.9	0.0
Bell	24	190	12.3	4.4	208	970 721	15.5	65.9	0.0	1.2	2.2	15.3	0.0
Bellflower	120	540	54.4	14.6	135	560 110	32.9	10.6	0.0	29.1	9.0	18.3	0.0
Bell Gardens	35	341	26.4	8.6	195	974 379	15.1	53.7	0.0	4.2	3.0	14.3	0.0
Belmont	51	D	D	D	110	851 441	1.4	33.4	0.0	4.3	7.0	30.3	0.0
Benicia	57	552	58.2	25.0	293	1 695 705	13.1	23.5	18.0	3.4	0.0	29.9	7.0
Berkeley	184	1 327	101.2	57.4	1 669	13 806 771	10.8	38.3	13.0	4.5	13.4	11.2	4.6
Beverly Hills	286	1 965	162.3	48.7	680	6 033 141	8.8	32.8	21.5	1.8	6.2	14.5	3.8
Brea	82	920	94.9	35.4	435	2 822 410	14.6	42.7	17.3	2.4	1.3	14.0	0.0
Brentwood	74	455	37.4	12.5	277	2 032 978	16.0	33.4	0.0	3.6	6.7	27.5	0.0
Buena Park	76	D	D	D	314	1 712 183	10.2	51.5	0.0	9.3	10.0	14.8	0.0
Burbank	249	2 438	233.0	94.4	1 339	10 789 444	10.5	20.6	13.7	5.7	4.5	35.6	3.0
Burlingame	116	720	62.3	18.2	257	2 033 098	7.4	25.4	24.0	8.9	0.0	20.2	9.2
Calexico	14	D	D	D	180	959 584	5.6	39.4	18.0	0.4	3.6	18.6	2.2
Camarillo	100	687	46.9	15.2	150	1 175 192	38.2	4.5	0.0	28.2	1.2	24.7	0.0
Campbell	176	1 133	97.9	32.0	194	1 441 718	19.7	44.4	0.0	5.3	0.4	13.4	0.0
Carlsbad	145	1 476	146.1	43.5	776	4 824 420	15.7	25.6	15.4	11.2	1.9	15.0	9.2
Carson	96	716	83.4	24.7	510	2 517 774	28.5	6.7	0.0	15.0	7.7	26.1	0.0
Cathedral City	80	514	39.8	11.8	175	1 230 278	13.0	52.3	30.1	4.1	0.0	0.6	0.0
Ceres	43	562	63.2	34.2	182	1 207 924	11.0	48.7	18.9	7.5	0.0	8.8	0.0
Cerritos	58	521	37.0	16.0	300	1 151 269	17.9	4.7	0.0	2.1	2.0	12.8	8.8
Chico	143	775	76.5	23.2	388	2 759 409	11.9	39.0	24.3	7.0	1.6	8.0	0.0
Chino	127	1 343	98.7	42.2	425	2 145 199	12.8	49.4	0.0	3.6	12.3	20.9	0.0
Chino Hills	55	285	14.7	4.4	182	1 001 156	45.8	0.0	0.0	13.9	0.0	34.0	0.0
Chula Vista	207	1 602	108.9	37.2	1 114	7 346 424	14.6	37.1	17.1	15.8	1.2	10.8	2.8
Citrus Heights	80	443	53.8	12.3	204	1 278 252	11.3	69.4	0.0	6.6	1.3	2.7	0.0
Claremont	34	142	8.7	2.6	169	958 849	29.8	43.5	0.0	0.0	0.0	26.7	0.0
Clovis	111	729	59.0	17.3	505	2 897 575	9.7	32.5	16.7	12.7	3.2	20.0	0.0
Coachella	13	D	D	D	79	428 436	23.4	3.0	0.0	9.0	11.1	39.1	0.0
Colton	48	489	60.2	13.4	360	2 494 835	14.1	29.0	19.7	3.6	3.4	18.7	1.8
Compton	60	552	35.1	14.2	329	1 870 002	18.8	5.9	37.1	8.5	3.7	15.6	0.0
Concord	206	1 154	132.7	40.1	443	2 858 330	14.9	60.6	0.0	9.1	1.2	10.7	0.0
Corona	219	1 374	108.4	31.0	692	4 620 304	10.2	34.8	23.7	7.6	2.3	16.8	2.3
Costa Mesa	316	1 916	167.0	46.4	499	4 282 210	13.5	43.0	28.9	5.5	1.1	5.7	0.0
Covina	104	497	48.3	13.9	187	1 234 035	14.5	55.3	0.0	3.8	3.1	11.5	0.0
Culver City	130	1 050	82.8	22.7	409	1 848 474	11.4	41.4	12.9	4.7	9.6	15.5	0.0
Cupertino	66	268	25.6	7.0	154	1 132 814	34.4	0.0	0.0	21.5	0.0	26.3	0.0
Cypress	64	663	99.0	34.4	171	1 179 800	19.6	48.1	0.0	5.4	0.7	14.5	0.0
Daly City	83	D	D	D	560	4 065 527	12.0	29.6	20.8	3.3	3.1	19.2	3.3
Dana Point	60	358	91.5	9.6	66	459 856	20.0	0.0	0.0	25.3	33.8	14.3	0.0
Danville	46	239	14.8	4.5	101	575 902	34.0	3.2	0.0	27.3	0.0	27.4	0.0
Davis	65	350	29.0	8.9	423	2 817 726	14.4	26.2	16.3	3.9	5.3	24.3	0.0

1. Establishments subject to federal tax.

City	General revenue							General expenditure		
	Intergovernmental			Taxes					Per capita[1] (dollars)	
					Per capita[1] (dollars)					
	Total (mil dol)	Total (mil dol)	Percent from state government	Total (mil dol)	Total	Property	Sales and gross receipts	Total (mil dol)	Total	Capital outlays
	117	118	119	120	121	122	123	124	125	126
ARKANSAS—Cont'd										
Jacksonville	66.7	10.5	44.6	9.9	344	27	317	75.1	2 619	339
Jonesboro	78.3	23.6	30.3	30.7	435	65	371	71.4	1 014	147
Little Rock	376.0	98.2	37.1	121.4	617	247	370	369.8	1 881	297
North Little Rock	90.5	26.5	30.0	39.2	606	159	447	97.5	1 506	165
Paragould	29.1	6.0	40.6	7.3	270	31	239	27.7	1 027	152
Pine Bluff	45.8	15.6	31.1	17.4	370	78	293	42.9	915	56
Rogers	66.9	18.0	35.4	33.4	565	89	476	49.1	832	178
Russellville	28.8	7.4	31.7	14.0	492	24	468	23.4	820	49
Sherwood	26.4	11.3	17.7	7.8	261	19	243	26.0	868	128
Springdale	72.7	20.3	30.2	29.9	406	72	333	53.9	732	67
Texarkana	31.4	6.9	34.8	13.5	449	104	344	26.4	879	33
West Memphis	33.0	8.5	26.7	13.1	507	50	458	32.5	1 262	139
CALIFORNIA	X	X	X	X	X	X	X	X	X	X
Adelanto	12.0	0.9	64.5	6.2	197	83	105	18.3	586	65
Alameda	117.1	11.9	69.1	72.8	961	544	346	118.5	1 564	250
Alhambra	94.9	11.0	57.2	48.2	570	309	260	85.5	1 012	77
Aliso Viejo	19.0	1.4	100.0	14.0	283	134	120	22.2	448	112
Anaheim	697.7	119.6	21.0	267.6	779	340	436	658.5	1 917	451
Antioch	69.2	16.1	79.1	35.4	336	194	139	57.9	550	87
Apple Valley	55.7	5.3	91.3	27.5	389	258	118	55.8	790	105
Arcadia	68.8	2.9	73.3	48.5	848	441	400	64.5	1 130	99
Atascadero	31.8	7.6	92.3	15.9	555	349	188	28.1	978	301
Atwater	26.6	3.9	48.1	8.3	291	192	93	49.2	1 714	675
Azusa	58.3	7.2	30.8	36.3	767	353	363	55.0	1 161	37
Bakersfield	360.1	84.2	69.9	149.4	417	223	192	382.6	1 069	301
Baldwin Park	50.2	15.9	46.5	25.1	328	172	153	43.8	572	46
Banning	33.1	4.9	90.4	13.0	427	251	175	30.4	1 003	237
Beaumont	83.3	0.7	100.0	14.4	366	160	203	79.5	2 017	1 172
Bell	29.7	1.8	72.8	16.9	471	317	154	30.0	835	223
Bellflower	32.9	3.7	60.2	25.4	328	163	163	34.3	442	71
Bell Gardens	36.8	3.6	71.1	22.7	531	201	329	31.1	726	78
Belmont	43.6	2.2	83.1	25.6	965	712	247	44.8	1 687	160
Benicia	43.3	1.4	100.0	29.1	1 061	603	453	46.0	1 679	414
Berkeley	293.3	31.1	90.2	147.9	1 281	526	494	300.7	2 605	242
Beverly Hills	261.2	5.5	72.9	142.7	4 124	1 370	2 727	226.1	6 532	1 003
Brea	90.0	3.5	86.5	56.2	1 395	893	497	87.6	2 176	593
Brentwood	78.8	1.8	100.0	33.7	628	397	152	88.6	1 654	238
Buena Park	87.0	7.0	64.8	64.8	788	449	336	105.8	1 285	278
Burbank	265.6	36.3	55.0	147.7	1 412	849	560	282.4	2 701	443
Burlingame	72.1	2.7	100.0	42.6	1 436	445	977	70.0	2 356	686
Calexico	34.0	6.5	59.4	15.9	405	203	194	33.5	852	103
Camarillo	73.4	5.0	40.6	40.7	617	335	278	73.6	1 117	261
Campbell	46.2	3.4	53.9	33.2	823	390	428	49.3	1 222	160
Carlsbad	179.5	13.2	50.3	112.9	1 033	528	496	160.2	1 465	200
Carson	105.5	19.8	56.9	74.0	799	340	456	135.1	1 459	403
Cathedral City	70.1	6.3	64.9	52.7	1 002	695	304	69.7	1 324	144
Ceres	34.3	3.7	83.6	18.9	406	213	188	38.7	834	89
Cerritos	96.9	2.0	89.7	65.5	1 320	774	541	96.8	1 950	141
Chico	99.3	7.9	55.7	69.9	799	467	330	91.9	1 050	275
Chino	102.9	7.3	90.6	54.2	677	425	248	109.3	1 365	144
Chino Hills	60.2	3.8	89.2	21.6	283	154	126	65.7	861	137
Chula Vista	240.2	25.5	80.3	126.8	501	240	258	247.0	976	73
Citrus Heights	52.7	10.0	85.5	32.4	382	164	216	48.9	578	136
Claremont	35.2	1.7	82.5	23.2	653	293	356	34.7	978	122
Clovis	110.7	10.2	67.2	46.4	470	218	249	105.9	1 074	201
Coachella	37.8	11.0	71.9	18.0	421	228	167	49.1	1 150	551
Colton	50.0	6.2	92.7	27.9	524	332	190	44.1	829	84
Compton	98.6	17.9	28.9	54.6	558	319	236	114.4	1 170	108
Concord	120.0	9.6	80.8	70.7	566	241	321	128.3	1 026	86
Corona	225.6	16.4	78.9	106.2	672	397	245	219.2	1 388	272
Costa Mesa	117.6	9.7	76.3	92.1	823	381	439	111.9	1 001	113
Covina	49.3	4.1	69.9	32.6	672	369	300	49.1	1 013	132
Culver City	173.5	27.4	43.4	99.6	2 528	1 144	1 336	143.8	3 651	482
Cupertino	60.4	2.0	89.4	42.9	716	306	399	59.2	989	78
Cypress	43.8	2.7	66.2	33.4	683	409	270	44.8	917	226
Daly City	103.9	12.0	48.5	57.4	551	324	225	112.7	1 082	108
Dana Point	29.3	1.6	100.0	25.1	740	287	445	31.5	929	121
Danville	35.0	6.4	100.0	21.8	508	306	190	34.7	809	181
Davis	96.8	18.9	87.5	47.1	714	397	221	90.4	1 372	150

1. Based on population estimated as of July 1 of the year shown.

City	City government finances, 2012 (cont.)									
	General expenditure (cont.)									
	Percent of total for:									
	Public welfare	Highways	Parking facilities	Education	Health and hospitals	Police protection	Sewerage and sanitation	Parks and recreation	Housing and community development	Interest on debt
	127	128	129	130	131	132	133	134	135	136
ARKANSAS—Cont'd										
Jacksonville	0.0	4.8	0.0	0.0	51.2	10.2	15.6	3.1	0.4	2.2
Jonesboro	0.0	12.4	0.0	0.0	1.1	17.0	17.2	3.4	0.5	15.4
Little Rock	0.0	4.7	0.2	0.0	5.8	15.0	12.9	10.2	2.6	6.0
North Little Rock	0.0	6.2	0.0	0.0	0.4	18.6	16.6	6.3	3.6	5.9
Paragould	0.2	9.6	0.0	0.0	0.5	10.6	23.1	6.0	0.0	2.5
Pine Bluff	0.5	10.5	0.0	0.0	0.1	24.5	18.2	6.0	4.3	1.9
Rogers	0.0	9.9	0.0	0.0	0.8	17.6	15.7	9.0	0.0	5.8
Russellville	0.0	20.6	0.0	0.0	1.1	18.7	18.5	6.1	0.0	0.0
Sherwood	0.0	20.6	0.0	0.0	1.0	23.1	14.0	13.5	0.0	1.2
Springdale	0.0	8.2	0.0	0.0	1.0	20.7	17.2	4.4	1.2	9.5
Texarkana	0.0	5.7	0.0	0.0	1.2	28.6	21.0	1.4	0.8	3.8
West Memphis	0.0	13.7	0.0	0.0	0.5	20.8	16.6	4.2	2.0	3.0
CALIFORNIA	X	X	X	X	X	X	X	X	X	X
Adelanto	0.0	9.8	0.0	0.0	1.4	25.8	0.0	4.3	9.3	0.0
Alameda	0.0	8.5	0.8	0.0	14.8	22.2	8.2	11.0	6.1	3.5
Alhambra	0.0	9.2	2.7	0.0	0.1	28.1	12.5	7.4	4.9	4.2
Aliso Viejo	0.0	15.3	0.0	0.0	1.0	28.2	0.0	7.9	0.5	9.0
Anaheim	0.0	8.5	0.0	0.0	0.1	16.5	8.2	12.1	18.0	10.6
Antioch	0.0	16.1	0.0	0.0	2.4	43.6	4.2	9.6	8.8	3.6
Apple Valley	0.0	8.4	0.0	0.0	2.9	19.9	23.3	8.7	11.7	5.3
Arcadia	0.0	9.9	0.0	0.0	6.9	25.6	2.2	4.2	3.1	1.5
Atascadero	0.0	7.5	0.0	0.0	0.0	21.1	6.6	9.2	20.1	4.0
Atwater	0.0	2.7	0.0	0.0	0.0	14.1	51.3	3.5	5.4	8.0
Azusa	0.0	3.3	0.0	0.0	1.2	30.7	8.1	6.3	8.1	11.6
Bakersfield	0.0	10.0	0.0	0.0	0.0	17.9	17.4	6.8	2.6	3.6
Baldwin Park	0.0	15.9	0.0	0.0	0.0	41.3	0.6	8.7	17.9	3.9
Banning	0.0	11.9	0.0	0.0	0.3	24.5	18.5	2.1	18.5	4.9
Beaumont	0.0	3.8	0.0	0.0	0.6	12.7	7.1	4.6	0.6	0.5
Bell	0.0	6.8	0.0	0.0	0.0	22.5	4.9	3.5	21.8	9.1
Bellflower	0.0	31.2	0.0	0.0	0.0	30.7	0.0	6.3	6.8	6.6
Bell Gardens	0.0	13.1	0.0	0.0	0.0	42.3	7.6	15.9	3.0	3.7
Belmont	0.0	9.5	0.0	0.0	0.0	21.4	17.5	8.4	8.9	2.3
Benicia	0.0	7.0	0.0	0.0	0.0	19.3	14.2	10.6	0.2	3.1
Berkeley	0.0	7.4	2.4	0.0	11.4	18.1	14.2	5.9	6.0	1.9
Beverly Hills	0.0	5.7	21.3	0.0	4.9	17.9	10.5	9.5	0.1	1.7
Brea	0.0	14.6	0.0	0.0	4.1	30.3	6.4	10.8	11.8	1.2
Brentwood	0.0	14.0	0.0	0.0	0.0	18.8	17.9	12.0	9.8	9.7
Buena Park	0.0	12.0	0.0	0.0	0.3	20.3	3.1	4.7	23.0	5.3
Burbank	0.0	7.2	0.3	0.0	4.6	15.9	9.3	5.7	14.2	5.8
Burlingame	0.0	24.2	2.0	0.0	0.0	13.4	14.4	8.0	0.0	2.4
Calexico	0.0	6.0	0.0	0.0	0.9	30.5	16.3	3.8	10.3	0.4
Camarillo	0.0	24.2	0.0	0.0	0.3	20.3	17.6	0.9	6.1	5.0
Campbell	0.0	13.9	0.0	0.0	0.0	26.2	0.0	12.0	10.3	3.4
Carlsbad	0.0	8.7	0.0	0.0	8.2	17.9	8.5	13.4	4.7	1.6
Carson	0.0	13.8	1.0	0.0	0.1	16.4	0.1	13.3	26.3	7.1
Cathedral City	0.0	9.7	0.0	0.0	4.2	22.1	0.6	1.4	22.4	15.6
Ceres	0.0	8.7	0.0	0.0	1.2	28.2	19.7	5.0	9.7	5.6
Cerritos	0.0	10.6	0.0	0.0	0.3	14.0	3.4	14.7	6.5	8.1
Chico	0.0	17.5	1.9	0.0	0.3	23.6	6.6	3.2	11.8	6.1
Chino	0.0	13.4	0.0	0.0	0.0	25.6	18.7	5.2	15.2	6.1
Chino Hills	0.0	20.8	0.0	0.0	0.0	17.3	14.6	6.5	0.4	6.1
Chula Vista	0.0	10.6	0.1	0.0	0.9	20.6	17.6	9.9	2.7	7.6
Citrus Heights	0.0	22.4	0.0	0.0	1.3	38.7	1.2	0.1	14.3	2.1
Claremont	0.0	12.7	0.0	0.0	0.8	28.4	15.5	9.0	4.2	2.9
Clovis	0.0	10.8	0.0	0.0	0.7	21.2	28.1	5.4	3.1	2.4
Coachella	0.0	33.0	0.0	0.0	0.4	12.4	16.2	10.2	4.8	5.7
Colton	0.0	6.2	0.0	0.0	1.3	23.1	11.2	3.9	8.2	9.8
Compton	0.0	8.3	0.0	0.0	0.0	15.0	9.0	2.9	15.0	1.3
Concord	0.0	12.7	0.0	0.0	0.0	33.4	16.2	6.9	3.5	2.3
Corona	0.0	4.4	0.1	0.0	0.5	18.5	23.8	3.9	7.9	9.2
Costa Mesa	0.0	8.7	0.0	0.0	1.0	33.4	0.0	6.1	2.3	2.0
Covina	0.0	5.4	0.2	0.0	0.7	30.8	3.6	5.8	13.9	6.1
Culver City	0.0	5.6	0.2	0.0	3.7	19.6	11.6	4.8	13.5	6.5
Cupertino	0.0	11.9	0.0	0.0	0.3	28.1	2.6	25.6	1.8	3.2
Cypress	0.0	21.7	0.0	0.0	0.5	31.3	3.4	13.1	11.8	1.7
Daly City	0.0	10.1	0.0	0.0	0.5	24.9	20.5	8.8	1.7	0.4
Dana Point	0.0	24.9	0.0	0.0	1.0	30.4	0.0	14.2	0.0	1.4
Danville	0.0	21.8	0.0	0.0	1.0	21.0	0.0	21.4	0.4	1.5
Davis	0.0	8.9	0.0	0.0	0.0	16.4	20.0	26.2	3.7	2.4

Table D. Cities — **City Government Finances, City Government Employment, and Climate**

	City government finances, 2012 (cont.)			Climate[2]						
	Debt outstanding			Average daily temperature (degrees Fahrenheit)						
				Mean		Limits				
City	Total (mil dol)	Per capita[1] (dollars)	Debt issued during year	January	July	January[3]	July[4]	Annual precipitation (inches)	Heating degree days	Cooling degree days
	137	138	139	140	141	142	143	144	145	146

City	137	138	139	140	141	142	143	144	145	146
ARKANSAS—Cont'd										
Jacksonville	28.9	1 008	1.9	38.2	79.9	27.4	91.1	50.56	3 470	1 699
Jonesboro	298.0	4 230	2.9	35.6	81.6	25.8	92.3	46.18	3 737	1 858
Little Rock	511.4	2 601	23.9	40.1	82.4	30.8	92.8	50.93	3 084	2 086
North Little Rock	204.0	3 152	19.6	40.1	82.4	30.8	92.8	50.93	3 084	2 086
Paragould	25.8	953	7.4	NA	NA	NA	NA	NA	NA	NA
Pine Bluff	29.1	619	9.6	40.8	82.4	31.5	92.4	52.48	2 935	2 099
Rogers	160.5	2 718	85.8	32.9	77.5	22.0	88.8	46.92	4 483	1 269
Russellville	0.0	0	0.0	NA	NA	NA	NA	NA	NA	NA
Sherwood	8.3	277	0.0	NA	NA	NA	NA	NA	NA	NA
Springdale	110.5	1 501	0.0	34.3	78.9	24.2	89.1	46.02	4 166	1 439
Texarkana	34.1	1 136	0.0	44.3	82.7	35.6	92.7	47.38	2 421	2 280
West Memphis	31.2	1 214	0.0	37.5	81.5	28.5	90.9	52.80	3 417	1 903
CALIFORNIA	X	X	X	X	X	X	X	X	X	X
Adelanto	0.0	0	0.0	NA	NA	NA	NA	NA	NA	NA
Alameda	152.6	2 014	3.6	50.9	64.9	44.7	72.7	22.94	2 400	377
Alhambra	70.5	834	0.0	56.3	75.6	42.6	89.0	18.56	1 295	1 575
Aliso Viejo	34.0	686	0.0	56.7	72.4	47.2	82.3	14.03	1 465	1 183
Anaheim	1 822.5	5 304	0.0	56.9	73.2	45.2	84.0	11.23	1 286	1 294
Antioch	41.8	397	0.0	45.7	74.4	37.8	90.7	13.33	2 714	1 179
Apple Valley	63.0	893	0.0	45.5	80.0	31.4	99.1	6.20	2 929	1 735
Arcadia	40.4	707	0.0	56.3	75.6	42.6	89.0	18.56	1 295	1 575
Atascadero	27.6	962	0.0	47.3	71.6	33.1	91.3	14.71	2 932	785
Atwater	93.3	3 253	0.0	NA	NA	NA	NA	NA	NA	NA
Azusa	235.4	4 970	0.0	54.6	73.8	41.5	88.7	16.96	1 727	1 191
Bakersfield	345.9	966	49.8	47.8	83.1	39.3	96.9	6.49	2 120	2 286
Baldwin Park	66.8	873	0.0	56.3	75.6	42.6	89.0	18.56	1 295	1 575
Banning	48.2	1 591	0.0	NA	NA	NA	NA	NA	NA	NA
Beaumont	9.6	244	0.4	NA	NA	NA	NA	NA	NA	NA
Bell	55.7	1 550	0.0	58.8	76.6	47.9	88.9	14.44	949	1 837
Bellflower	31.8	410	0.0	57.0	73.8	46.0	82.9	12.94	1 211	1 186
Bell Gardens	36.7	856	0.0	58.8	76.6	47.9	88.9	14.44	949	1 837
Belmont	38.8	1 460	0.0	48.1	69.7	36.4	88.2	28.71	2 769	569
Benicia	55.1	2 008	4.3	46.3	71.2	38.8	87.4	19.58	2 757	786
Berkeley	188.8	1 635	0.0	50.0	62.8	43.6	70.4	25.40	2 857	142
Beverly Hills	142.3	4 111	0.0	57.9	69.5	49.4	76.9	18.68	1 379	893
Brea	39.1	971	0.0	56.9	73.2	45.2	84.0	11.23	1 286	1 294
Brentwood	194.1	3 622	22.4	NA	NA	NA	NA	NA	NA	NA
Buena Park	115.5	1 403	0.0	57.0	73.8	46.0	82.9	12.94	1 211	1 186
Burbank	463.3	4 430	9.8	54.8	75.5	42.0	88.9	17.49	1 575	1 455
Burlingame	33.1	1 114	0.0	50.0	62.7	42.9	70.5	23.35	2 720	184
Calexico	2.8	71	0.0	55.8	91.4	41.3	107.0	2.96	1 080	3 952
Camarillo	90.1	1 367	7.6	55.7	66.0	45.3	74.0	13.61	1 961	389
Campbell	28.0	694	0.1	48.7	70.3	38.8	85.4	22.64	2 641	613
Carlsbad	65.0	594	0.2	54.7	67.6	45.4	72.1	11.13	2 009	505
Carson	217.3	2 347	0.0	56.3	69.4	46.2	77.6	14.79	1 526	742
Cathedral City	271.4	5 160	0.3	57.3	92.1	44.2	108.2	5.23	951	4 224
Ceres	50.3	1 083	0.0	47.2	77.7	40.1	93.6	13.12	2 358	1 570
Cerritos	153.8	3 099	0.0	57.0	73.8	46.0	82.9	12.94	1 211	1 186
Chico	163.2	1 865	0.8	44.5	76.9	35.2	93.0	26.23	2 945	1 334
Chino	211.8	2 645	12.9	54.6	73.8	41.5	88.7	16.96	1 727	1 191
Chino Hills	127.2	1 667	0.0	56.9	73.2	45.2	84.0	11.23	1 286	1 294
Chula Vista	512.8	2 027	4.0	57.3	70.1	46.1	76.1	9.95	1 321	862
Citrus Heights	28.5	337	0.0	46.9	77.7	39.2	94.8	24.61	2 532	1 528
Claremont	26.2	739	0.0	54.6	73.8	41.5	88.7	16.96	1 727	1 191
Clovis	232.4	2 358	0.0	46.0	81.4	38.4	96.6	11.23	2 447	1 963
Coachella	94.7	2 219	2.4	NA	NA	NA	NA	NA	NA	NA
Colton	96.4	1 813	0.0	54.4	79.6	41.8	96.0	16.43	1 599	1 937
Compton	73.6	752	0.0	57.0	73.8	46.0	82.9	12.94	1 211	1 186
Concord	63.7	510	0.0	46.3	71.2	38.8	87.4	19.58	2 757	786
Corona	346.1	2 191	25.3	54.7	75.9	41.5	92.0	12.00	1 599	1 534
Costa Mesa	38.8	347	0.0	55.9	67.3	48.2	71.4	11.65	1 719	543
Covina	86.2	1 779	2.3	54.6	73.8	41.5	88.7	16.96	1 727	1 191
Culver City	206.5	5 244	0.0	56.7	70.8	46.1	80.0	13.32	1 344	959
Cupertino	43.9	734	43.9	48.7	70.3	38.8	85.4	22.64	2 641	613
Cypress	8.8	181	0.0	57.0	73.8	46.0	82.9	12.94	1 211	1 186
Daly City	45.3	435	0.0	50.6	57.3	44.6	61.1	19.77	3 665	17
Dana Point	8.2	241	0.0	55.4	68.7	43.9	77.3	13.56	1 756	666
Danville	12.9	300	0.0	47.5	72.4	39.3	85.2	23.96	3 267	983
Davis	55.0	835	0.0	45.2	74.3	37.1	92.7	19.05	2 853	1 127

1. Based on the population estimated as of July 1 of the year shown.   2. Represents normal values based on the 30-year period, 1971–2000.   3. Average daily minimum.
4. Average daily maximum.

Table D. Cities — **Land Area and Population**

STATE Place code	City	Land area,[1] 2010 (sq km)	Population, 2015 Total persons	Rank	Per square kilometer	Race alone or in combination (percent), 2010-2014 White	Black	American Indian, Alaska Native	Asian	Hawaiian Pacific Islander	Percent Hispanic or Latino[2], 2010-2014	Percent foreign born 2010-2014
		1	2	3	4	5	6	7	8	9	10	11
	CALIFORNIA—Cont'd											
06 18394	Delano	37.0	52 733	707	1 425.2	69.6	5.5	1.5	14.7	0.3	73.4	37.9
06 18996	Desert Hot Springs	61.2	28 335	1 301	463.0	62.8	7.9	2.6	3.8	0.9	56.4	24.0
06 19192	Diamond Bar	38.5	56 897	652	1 477.8	35.7	4.7	0.8	53.4	1.2	20.5	42.1
06 19766	Downey	32.1	114 219	243	3 558.2	63.3	4.3	0.8	7.9	0.3	71.8	34.9
06 20018	Dublin	38.6	57 721	642	1 495.4	55.7	8.1	1.2	35.9	0.7	12.8	28.7
06 20956	East Palo Alto	6.5	29 662	1 256	4 563.4	48.8	15.6	1.5	4.1	12.1	62.0	41.1
06 21712	El Cajon	37.4	103 679	290	2 772.2	80.2	7.6	2.2	7.3	2.3	29.2	29.6
06 21782	El Centro	28.7	43 956	851	1 531.6	69.4	2.9	2.1	3.6	0.3	82.4	34.0
06 22020	Elk Grove	109.3	166 913	149	1 527.1	51.7	13.9	1.7	31.8	2.8	17.8	22.9
06 22230	El Monte	24.8	116 732	235	4 706.9	51.1	0.8	0.9	28.7	0.4	66.0	50.6
06 22300	El Paso de Robles (Paso Robles)	49.5	31 580	1 183	638.0	81.9	4.0	1.8	2.9	0.1	38.3	18.1
06 22678	Encinitas	48.7	62 930	571	1 292.2	91.2	0.7	0.8	6.6	0.3	13.9	13.2
06 22804	Escondido	95.3	151 451	170	1 589.2	83.6	3.0	1.2	7.0	0.6	48.8	28.3
06 23042	Eureka	24.3	27 017	1 357	1 111.8	85.5	3.3	7.7	7.3	0.7	9.6	7.5
06 23182	Fairfield	96.8	112 970	249	1 167.0	52.9	17.6	1.8	19.4	2.3	27.3	21.5
06 24638	Folsom	56.8	76 375	444	1 344.6	74.1	6.8	1.1	17.1	1.1	11.8	15.3
06 24680	Fontana	109.9	207 460	107	1 887.7	57.3	11.1	1.6	7.8	1.0	66.7	29.3
06 25338	Foster City	9.7	33 477	1 122	3 451.2	50.0	3.2	0.4	49.7	0.7	5.5	43.1
06 25380	Fountain Valley	23.4	56 987	650	2 435.3	56.8	1.8	0.7	37.2	0.6	15.1	30.5
06 26000	Fremont	200.6	232 206	96	1 157.6	34.2	4.8	1.3	56.0	1.2	14.1	44.0
06 27000	Fresno	290.0	520 052	34	1 793.3	55.2	9.2	2.5	14.6	0.5	48.0	21.1
06 28000	Fullerton	57.9	140 847	185	2 432.6	58.1	3.1	1.3	26.2	0.6	34.8	31.2
06 28168	Gardena	15.1	60 447	604	4 003.1	26.7	26.3	1.3	28.2	1.2	36.0	33.0
06 29000	Garden Grove	46.5	175 393	140	3 771.9	46.1	1.6	1.0	40.0	1.2	36.4	43.9
06 29504	Gilroy	41.8	53 231	703	1 273.5	73.2	2.6	1.2	7.7	0.8	59.0	25.3
06 30000	Glendale	78.9	201 020	113	2 547.8	76.9	1.8	0.9	18.0	0.4	17.4	54.9
06 30014	Glendora	50.2	52 009	726	1 036.0	80.8	3.5	1.3	9.3	0.3	29.9	15.8
06 30378	Goleta	20.5	30 944	1 200	1 509.5	73.2	1.3	2.1	11.5	0.4	38.3	22.9
06 31960	Hanford	43.0	55 659	668	1 294.4	82.7	5.9	1.6	5.3	0.2	47.0	15.4
06 32548	Hawthorne	15.8	88 451	360	5 598.2	52.0	31.0	5.5	7.7	1.1	53.6	33.8
06 33000	Hayward	117.4	158 289	160	1 348.3	44.2	13.9	1.9	26.6	3.5	40.6	38.1
06 33182	Hemet	72.1	83 861	393	1 163.1	76.2	9.5	2.2	3.9	0.2	37.6	15.1
06 33434	Hesperia	189.3	93 295	333	492.8	78.1	8.3	2.8	2.4	0.4	49.3	14.2
06 33588	Highland	48.6	54 854	683	1 128.7	60.5	12.7	1.9	9.6	0.4	48.9	21.1
06 34120	Hollister	18.9	37 462	1 008	1 982.1	84.7	1.6	1.9	4.7	0.8	68.2	24.3
06 36000	Huntington Beach	69.3	201 899	111	2 913.4	80.5	1.6	1.3	13.1	0.8	19.2	16.9
06 36056	Huntington Park	7.8	59 430	618	7 619.2	70.3	0.8	0.6	1.1	0.3	97.5	50.4
06 36294	Imperial Beach	10.8	27 408	1 344	2 537.8	76.9	6.6	2.2	10.9	1.5	50.0	20.5
06 36448	Indio	75.6	87 533	368	1 157.8	85.6	3.2	1.6	3.4	0.3	69.0	27.9
06 36546	Inglewood	23.5	111 666	254	4 751.7	30.6	44.5	1.5	1.9	0.7	50.7	28.3
06 36770	Irvine	171.2	256 927	81	1 500.7	55.5	2.8	0.7	42.6	0.5	9.9	36.6
06 39220	Laguna Hills	17.3	31 748	1 180	1 835.1	72.3	3.1	1.0	16.8	0.9	18.6	26.4
06 39248	Laguna Niguel	38.4	65 806	541	1 713.7	82.2	3.2	1.0	12.1	0.3	15.8	21.0
06 39290	La Habra	19.1	62 131	582	3 252.9	63.4	2.0	1.4	10.0	0.2	60.4	27.0
06 39486	Lake Elsinore	93.8	61 981	585	660.8	64.0	4.7	0.7	6.8	1.5	50.5	21.9
06 39496	Lake Forest	46.1	82 492	401	1 789.4	71.1	2.7	1.3	17.2	0.9	24.0	23.3
06 39892	Lakewood	24.4	81 611	407	3 344.7	58.1	8.2	1.9	19.3	1.9	33.2	21.5
06 40004	La Mesa	23.5	60 089	609	2 557.0	79.0	10.9	1.9	8.3	1.0	25.7	14.6
06 40032	La Mirada	20.3	49 520	761	2 439.4	60.3	3.0	1.5	21.0	0.3	40.4	24.2
06 40130	Lancaster	244.2	161 103	157	659.7	66.3	23.4	1.8	5.5	0.7	37.7	13.6
06 40340	La Puente	9.0	40 745	918	4 527.2	55.9	2.0	1.5	10.5	0.3	85.6	40.7
06 40354	La Quinta	91.0	40 476	926	444.8	85.9	3.4	0.8	4.3	0.3	33.1	13.6
06 40830	La Verne	21.8	32 681	1 149	1 499.1	79.1	4.8	2.0	10.7	0.5	32.5	14.8
06 40886	Lawndale	5.1	33 430	1 126	6 554.9	63.2	11.2	6.3	11.9	0.6	65.6	40.1
06 41124	Lemon Grove	10.1	26 709	1 371	2 644.5	62.8	11.5	2.3	7.8	1.3	44.6	19.5
06 41474	Lincoln	52.1	46 474	815	892.0	87.3	1.9	1.8	7.5	0.7	18.6	12.6
06 41992	Livermore	65.2	88 126	364	1 351.6	84.9	2.6	1.3	12.7	0.7	20.0	17.3
06 42202	Lodi	35.3	64 596	554	1 829.9	83.4	1.7	7.5	9.5	0.7	36.3	20.3
06 42524	Lompoc	30.0	44 164	847	1 472.1	71.2	7.5	2.6	5.9	1.7	53.2	21.8
06 43000	Long Beach	130.3	474 140	37	3 638.8	58.5	15.3	3.5	15.0	1.5	41.7	26.1
06 43280	Los Altos	16.8	30 671	1 215	1 825.7	74.5	0.7	0.3	28.6	0.2	3.6	23.3
06 44000	Los Angeles	1 213.9	3 971 883	2	3 272.0	55.4	10.2	1.3	12.9	0.4	48.6	38.6
06 44028	Los Banos	25.9	37 457	1 009	1 446.2	80.1	4.2	1.4	3.4	0.2	69.6	24.8
06 44112	Los Gatos	28.7	30 705	1 212	1 069.9	84.0	2.1	1.1	14.7	0.3	5.2	18.1
06 44574	Lynwood	12.5	71 969	480	5 759.1	41.7	8.9	0.9	0.9	0.0	88.8	40.3
06 45022	Madera	40.9	64 208	559	1 569.9	83.2	3.9	1.7	3.9	0.2	77.7	32.0
06 45400	Manhattan Beach	10.2	35 818	1 057	3 511.6	87.8	1.5	0.7	12.6	0.3	8.3	11.4
06 45484	Manteca	45.9	75 448	453	1 643.7	74.8	4.7	2.2	9.8	1.5	39.9	15.4
06 46114	Martinez	31.4	38 137	983	1 214.6	84.5	4.1	2.5	10.0	0.7	16.4	11.7
06 46492	Maywood	3.1	27 888	1 324	8 996.1	81.0	0.6	0.3	0.3	0.1	97.9	46.1
06 46842	Menifee	120.4	87 174	371	724.0	77.9	7.1	1.6	6.6	0.7	33.6	13.9

1. Dry land or land partially or temporarily covered by water.   2. May be of any race.

Table D. Cities — **Population**

City	Under 5 years (12)	5 to 17 years (13)	18 to 24 years (14)	25 to 34 years (15)	35 to 44 years (16)	45 to 54 years (17)	55 to 64 years (18)	65 to 74 years (19)	75 years and over (20)	Median age 2010–2014 (21)	Percent female 2010–2014 (22)	2000 (23)	2010 (24)	2000–2010 (25)	2010–2015 (26)
CALIFORNIA—Cont'd															
Delano	8.6	20.6	13.4	17.4	15.0	10.7	7.7	3.7	2.9	28.5	42.2	38 824	53 041	36.6	-0.6
Desert Hot Springs	8.0	22.7	10.2	13.8	14.3	12.4	8.5	6.2	3.8	32.5	48.0	16 582	25 938	56.4	4.8
Diamond Bar	4.0	17.2	9.3	13.4	13.1	16.1	14.5	7.9	4.6	41.0	52.4	56 287	55 544	-1.3	2.4
Downey	7.5	18.0	11.7	15.2	14.6	12.1	10.2	5.9	4.7	33.4	51.0	107 323	111 772	4.1	2.2
Dublin	7.6	16.4	7.3	16.6	18.8	16.3	8.8	5.9	2.3	36.3	50.4	29 973	46 036	53.6	25.4
East Palo Alto	9.1	21.8	11.6	19.7	12.3	11.0	8.6	3.6	2.3	29.2	52.6	29 506	28 155	-4.6	5.4
El Cajon	7.7	18.4	11.9	15.9	11.5	13.3	10.1	5.7	5.4	32.5	50.9	94 869	99 478	4.9	4.2
El Centro	8.9	21.2	12.2	14.8	11.8	10.7	11.0	5.4	3.9	29.8	51.4	37 835	42 598	12.6	3.2
Elk Grove	6.1	23.8	8.6	12.1	14.7	14.7	10.4	5.5	4.1	34.6	50.7	59 984	153 015	155.1	9.1
El Monte	7.1	17.9	9.7	15.8	14.2	13.0	10.6	6.6	5.2	34.7	50.4	115 965	113 475	-2.1	2.9
El Paso de Robles (Paso Robles)	7.6	18.2	8.4	14.9	13.8	12.9	11.5	5.8	7.0	35.5	51.7	24 297	29 793	22.6	6.0
Encinitas	6.8	14.4	6.5	13.8	14.1	14.9	15.0	8.1	6.5	41.3	50.7	58 014	59 518	2.6	5.7
Escondido	8.3	18.2	11.3	15.8	13.5	12.7	9.9	4.9	5.3	32.9	50.8	133 559	143 911	7.8	5.2
Eureka	5.7	13.4	13.1	16.8	9.6	14.0	13.6	7.1	6.7	35.7	49.1	26 128	27 191	4.1	-0.6
Fairfield	7.0	18.0	12.0	15.1	12.7	14.0	10.1	5.8	5.3	33.5	51.0	96 178	105 321	9.5	7.2
Folsom	6.6	18.4	7.7	12.6	17.3	15.9	11.5	5.3	4.6	37.7	45.7	51 884	72 203	39.2	5.8
Fontana	7.8	23.2	11.8	15.4	14.6	12.4	8.3	3.9	2.5	29.5	50.2	128 929	196 069	52.1	5.6
Foster City	6.1	15.5	4.9	13.3	18.0	12.5	13.8	9.2	6.7	40.8	51.1	28 803	30 567	6.1	9.5
Fountain Valley	4.5	14.7	8.9	11.6	12.7	16.3	12.9	10.2	8.2	43.3	50.2	54 978	55 313	0.6	2.9
Fremont	6.8	17.5	7.2	14.8	16.8	14.8	11.3	6.1	4.7	37.0	50.7	203 413	214 089	5.2	8.5
Fresno	9.0	20.6	12.1	15.9	11.8	11.5	9.5	5.4	4.3	29.8	50.7	427 652	494 665	15.7	4.8
Fullerton	6.6	16.8	12.2	16.2	12.8	13.5	9.9	5.9	6.1	33.8	51.4	126 003	135 161	7.3	4.1
Gardena	6.3	15.2	8.7	14.5	12.2	15.3	12.1	7.2	8.4	39.4	51.5	57 746	58 829	1.9	2.8
Garden Grove	5.8	18.8	10.6	13.0	14.4	14.5	11.4	6.5	5.1	36.3	49.5	165 196	170 883	3.4	2.6
Gilroy	8.3	21.3	9.5	13.7	15.5	13.1	9.6	5.5	3.4	33.1	50.2	41 464	48 821	17.7	9.1
Glendale	5.5	13.5	8.3	14.2	14.8	14.0	13.5	7.9	8.2	40.8	52.3	194 973	191 719	-1.7	4.8
Glendora	3.7	18.5	10.2	11.0	11.9	16.2	14.0	7.4	7.1	40.3	50.6	49 415	50 073	1.3	3.9
Goleta	5.2	15.6	16.8	13.0	11.1	13.0	10.9	6.9	7.5	34.6	50.8	55 204	29 888	-45.9	3.5
Hanford	7.6	23.5	9.4	14.9	12.7	11.3	10.3	5.7	4.8	30.9	51.3	41 686	53 967	29.5	2.9
Hawthorne	7.2	20.2	11.5	18.2	14.1	12.3	9.1	4.9	2.5	30.8	51.7	84 112	84 293	0.2	4.9
Hayward	6.7	16.3	10.8	16.5	13.6	13.8	11.2	5.9	5.2	34.8	51.4	140 030	144 186	3.0	9.6
Hemet	6.1	18.9	8.7	11.8	10.0	11.3	10.5	11.1	11.7	39.5	51.8	58 812	78 657	33.7	6.6
Hesperia	7.3	23.0	9.8	14.2	12.2	13.8	9.8	6.2	3.8	32.0	49.0	62 582	90 173	44.1	3.5
Highland	7.4	24.5	11.6	13.0	13.1	13.8	9.4	4.4	2.7	29.3	51.0	44 605	53 104	19.1	3.3
Hollister	8.1	21.8	9.9	15.3	13.5	13.3	10.3	4.4	3.4	31.8	50.5	34 413	34 928	1.5	7.3
Huntington Beach	4.9	14.8	8.8	13.7	13.6	16.1	12.6	8.9	6.6	41.1	50.9	189 594	189 992	0.2	5.7
Huntington Park	9.1	20.7	12.9	16.1	14.3	10.8	9.4	3.9	2.7	29.6	50.7	61 348	58 114	-5.3	2.3
Imperial Beach	8.0	18.6	13.6	17.7	10.6	12.9	9.7	3.7	5.4	30.0	49.4	26 992	26 324	-2.5	4.1
Indio	8.0	21.5	8.7	13.8	13.4	10.7	10.3	8.5	5.3	33.7	50.5	49 116	76 036	54.8	10.6
Inglewood	7.4	18.9	9.3	16.2	13.4	13.4	11.3	6.2	3.9	33.8	52.7	112 580	109 673	-2.6	1.8
Irvine	5.3	16.6	13.6	15.8	15.5	13.6	9.9	5.6	3.9	34.2	50.8	143 072	212 375	48.4	21.2
Laguna Hills	4.4	15.0	9.3	13.0	13.0	14.2	16.3	7.8	6.8	41.7	51.7	31 178	30 344	-2.7	4.9
Laguna Niguel	5.9	15.8	8.4	10.4	12.9	16.7	16.7	8.2	5.0	42.8	51.8	61 891	62 979	1.8	4.5
La Habra	7.4	18.3	10.2	16.7	12.7	13.6	10.3	5.1	5.8	33.4	51.2	58 974	60 239	2.1	3.1
Lake Elsinore	8.2	24.7	10.4	14.1	14.9	11.9	9.6	4.0	2.3	29.1	50.4	28 928	51 821	79.1	17.3
Lake Forest	5.5	17.7	8.4	13.1	15.0	17.3	12.3	6.5	4.1	38.5	50.7	58 707	77 264	31.6	6.5
Lakewood	6.4	17.7	9.2	12.0	14.4	15.3	13.5	5.6	5.8	38.6	52.2	79 345	80 048	0.9	1.9
La Mesa	7.0	13.7	10.4	17.1	12.8	12.7	12.0	6.2	8.2	36.5	52.4	54 749	57 065	4.2	5.3
La Mirada	5.3	15.7	14.2	12.2	10.7	13.5	12.1	8.6	7.6	38.2	50.7	46 783	48 527	3.7	2.0
Lancaster	8.3	20.8	11.0	13.6	13.7	13.1	10.6	5.2	3.6	32.2	49.1	118 718	156 633	31.9	2.8
La Puente	8.0	18.8	11.1	15.7	13.8	13.8	9.4	5.4	4.1	32.9	51.4	41 063	39 816	-3.0	2.3
La Quinta	5.4	17.0	6.4	9.0	10.3	12.9	15.2	16.3	7.5	46.2	51.8	23 694	37 467	58.1	8.0
La Verne	4.8	16.1	10.8	10.6	10.5	14.8	13.5	10.3	8.5	43.0	51.4	31 638	31 063	-1.8	5.2
Lawndale	8.1	20.4	10.2	16.5	14.9	13.5	8.2	4.5	3.7	32.1	50.0	31 711	32 769	3.3	2.0
Lemon Grove	5.3	19.4	11.0	12.2	12.4	14.7	13.9	6.1	5.1	36.8	50.3	24 918	25 320	1.6	5.5
Lincoln	6.5	16.3	5.2	10.9	14.3	10.1	10.5	15.0	11.2	42.1	52.6	11 205	42 819	282.1	8.6
Livermore	6.9	17.4	8.1	13.3	13.8	17.1	12.0	6.3	5.1	38.1	49.7	73 345	80 968	10.4	8.7
Lodi	7.0	20.8	10.3	12.0	12.6	13.3	10.6	6.9	6.8	35.0	51.1	56 999	62 134	9.0	4.0
Lompoc	9.3	19.0	10.9	14.7	13.5	12.4	10.5	5.5	4.2	31.8	47.8	41 103	42 434	3.2	4.1
Long Beach	7.0	17.5	11.6	15.3	14.5	13.5	10.7	5.6	4.3	34.0	50.7	461 522	462 257	0.2	2.6
Los Altos	5.7	20.6	3.5	5.2	13.8	16.7	14.3	9.4	10.4	45.8	50.8	27 693	28 976	4.6	5.8
Los Angeles	6.5	15.7	11.3	17.1	14.8	13.3	10.5	5.9	5.0	34.6	50.3	3 694 820	3 792 621	2.6	4.7
Los Banos	8.7	24.0	11.1	12.8	13.1	11.6	8.7	6.4	3.8	30.3	51.1	25 869	35 972	39.1	4.1
Los Gatos	4.1	18.8	5.5	7.6	13.0	18.8	14.1	9.7	8.4	45.4	51.4	28 592	29 413	2.9	4.3
Lynwood	9.1	24.9	12.1	14.0	15.7	10.5	7.1	3.7	2.9	27.7	51.4	69 845	69 772	-0.1	3.2
Madera	10.0	24.3	11.7	14.7	13.4	10.7	7.2	4.7	3.4	27.2	48.8	43 207	61 416	42.1	4.5
Manhattan Beach	5.2	19.1	4.4	11.1	15.5	17.8	13.0	7.3	6.8	41.5	51.7	33 852	35 135	3.8	1.9
Manteca	8.0	20.9	9.5	13.6	13.2	12.7	11.4	6.2	4.6	33.5	51.4	49 258	67 096	36.2	12.1
Martinez	4.4	14.3	7.8	12.3	12.8	17.2	16.8	9.2	5.2	44.1	51.5	35 866	35 824	-0.1	5.8
Maywood	9.5	24.0	13.4	14.0	14.7	10.9	7.4	3.8	2.4	27.2	50.3	28 083	27 395	-2.4	1.8
Menifee	6.7	17.6	8.8	13.6	11.7	11.5	10.6	10.3	9.1	37.5	51.0	NA	77 519	NA	12.5

Table D. Cities — Households, Group Quarters, Crime, and Education

City	Households, 2010-2014				Persons in group quarters, 2010				Serious crimes known to police,[2] 2014				Educational attainment, 2010–2014		
			Percent			Institutional			Total		Rate[3]			Attainment[4] (percent)	
	Number	Persons per household	Female family householder[1]	One-person	Total	Total	Persons in nursing facilities	Non-institutional	Number	Rate[3]	Violent	Property	Population age 25 and older	High school graduate or less	Bachelor's degree or more
	27	28	29	30	31	32	33	34	35	36	37	38	39	40	41
CALIFORNIA—Cont'd															
Delano	10 549	5.01	21.4	10.3	10 897	10 719	189	178	1 701	3 257	412	2 845	30 775	73.5	7.0
Desert Hot Springs	9 164	3.02	18.1	25.8	118	0	0	118	1 328	4 728	598	4 130	16 459	57.5	13.0
Diamond Bar	17 266	3.26	13.2	11.5	129	27	22	102	771	1 361	86	1 274	39 253	25.0	47.9
Downey	33 169	3.41	19.6	17.0	683	561	534	122	3 178	2 798	247	2 550	72 377	49.1	21.3
Dublin	16 476	3.02	7.8	21.0	5 774	5 682	0	92	868	1 614	130	1 483	34 580	22.3	52.2
East Palo Alto	6 940	4.17	16.8	17.9	154	4	0	150	698	2 376	422	1 954	16 469	60.1	16.0
El Cajon	32 088	3.17	18.2	21.7	2 482	1 350	1 339	1 132	2 579	2 508	318	2 190	63 397	49.9	18.2
El Centro	12 752	3.39	20.6	20.4	816	520	98	296	2 262	5 196	384	4 813	25 781	52.1	16.8
Elk Grove	48 737	3.25	14.6	15.9	669	209	133	460	3 694	2 267	382	1 885	98 306	28.0	35.0
El Monte	29 793	3.87	19.9	13.5	1 080	763	618	317	2 546	2 191	287	1 904	74 326	70.1	11.3
El Paso de Robles (Paso Robles)	11 356	2.69	11.6	22.2	169	5	0	164	913	2 934	402	2 532	20 126	38.2	22.6
Encinitas	23 208	2.63	7.0	24.9	528	405	405	123	1 012	1 630	168	1 463	44 424	18.1	56.7
Escondido	44 798	3.29	13.8	19.9	2 119	786	657	1 333	3 538	2 361	342	2 020	92 238	47.9	21.6
Eureka	10 758	2.51	13.0	36.8	1 883	449	8	1 434	2 321	8 647	540	8 106	18 443	39.9	23.6
Fairfield	34 674	3.11	14.1	19.4	2 489	1 268	332	1 221	4 392	3 982	471	3 511	68 336	39.3	23.2
Folsom	25 111	2.92	8.3	24.6	6 960	6 772	96	188	1 384	1 887	108	1 780	50 124	25.2	45.7
Fontana	49 438	4.07	18.3	10.8	444	228	194	216	4 420	2 161	347	1 814	116 354	53.9	16.0
Foster City	12 188	2.61	8.1	23.9	109	57	57	52	380	1 157	43	1 115	23 388	14.3	63.0
Fountain Valley	18 777	3.01	12.2	18.4	437	180	160	257	1 109	1 945	151	1 794	40 736	27.3	38.2
Fremont	71 575	3.10	9.4	16.3	1 651	682	662	969	4 194	1 843	125	1 718	152 672	27.3	51.7
Fresno	160 172	3.16	19.7	22.9	8 867	4 552	1 825	4 315	23 483	4 576	464	4 112	295 046	48.2	20.1
Fullerton	44 406	3.11	12.9	20.2	3 077	759	629	2 318	3 545	2 534	242	2 292	88 749	32.5	37.1
Gardena	20 658	2.89	18.2	27.8	794	672	631	122	1 665	2 764	458	2 306	41 038	45.9	23.7
Garden Grove	46 453	3.74	16.9	15.1	1 941	707	624	1 234	3 504	1 990	231	1 759	112 986	50.1	19.2
Gilroy	14 922	3.40	16.4	14.8	806	164	128	642	1 683	3 211	376	2 835	30 537	41.9	26.2
Glendale	71 132	2.75	13.2	25.8	1 429	1 206	1 181	223	3 259	1 654	94	1 559	142 832	34.7	37.9
Glendora	16 608	3.06	14.0	19.6	765	573	519	192	1 307	2 548	129	2 419	34 123	30.4	31.2
Goleta	10 375	2.92	11.6	26.5	201	178	170	23	457	1 490	114	1 376	19 159	30.0	41.3
Hanford	17 200	3.17	16.0	19.0	899	616	296	283	2 162	3 944	556	3 387	32 790	45.1	17.6
Hawthorne	29 145	2.95	22.7	27.2	539	331	311	208	3 246	3 745	759	2 986	53 018	50.0	19.1
Hayward	45 972	3.25	16.6	20.5	2 724	770	723	1 954	5 478	3 573	395	3 178	98 405	46.2	24.3
Hemet	30 585	2.65	15.4	31.8	614	459	421	155	3 787	4 595	522	4 073	53 992	52.8	12.1
Hesperia	26 203	3.50	17.0	16.6	28	6	6	22	2 599	2 807	320	2 487	53 141	55.3	9.6
Highland	15 111	3.58	18.3	15.3	172	96	96	76	1 565	2 868	469	2 399	31 229	49.6	19.3
Hollister	10 188	3.54	16.0	14.4	115	106	102	9	634	1 715	368	1 347	21 555	52.8	15.2
Huntington Beach	74 235	2.64	11.3	24.9	890	403	391	487	4 629	2 324	196	2 128	139 726	24.2	40.9
Huntington Park	14 637	4.02	25.5	12.3	255	7	0	248	2 215	3 750	692	3 058	33 842	79.0	5.8
Imperial Beach	8 649	3.11	17.0	25.0	619	0	0	619	528	1 939	411	1 528	16 115	43.5	16.0
Indio	25 281	3.26	13.8	20.6	949	584	135	365	2 676	3 165	551	2 614	50 485	54.4	16.4
Inglewood	36 309	3.06	24.6	27.6	1 502	515	405	987	3 523	3 146	699	2 446	70 826	49.2	17.4
Irvine	83 321	2.76	9.9	23.8	6 556	588	55	5 968	3 165	1 303	49	1 253	148 012	12.3	65.6
Laguna Hills	10 261	3.00	9.6	20.1	369	136	136	233	486	1 566	145	1 421	21 903	25.7	44.8
Laguna Niguel	24 538	2.62	8.3	23.5	248	0	0	248	627	964	112	852	45 605	15.7	54.5
La Habra	18 832	3.26	14.1	20.0	340	171	167	169	1 154	1 862	169	1 693	39 366	45.8	22.0
Lake Elsinore	14 846	3.79	14.6	12.8	432	208	0	224	1 790	3 051	218	2 833	32 181	47.8	16.1
Lake Forest	26 772	2.95	10.1	21.0	515	216	216	299	786	986	130	855	53 253	23.9	44.1
Lakewood	26 339	3.07	15.4	20.3	109	0	0	109	1 939	2 383	248	2 134	53 980	35.0	27.3
La Mesa	23 566	2.47	12.2	32.5	657	533	512	124	1 792	3 037	353	2 685	40 325	27.9	34.7
La Mirada	14 346	3.42	11.1	18.1	2 857	271	271	2 586	724	1 469	181	1 289	31 995	34.3	29.4
Lancaster	47 872	3.32	17.9	22.1	8 259	6 775	486	1 484	4 552	2 842	556	2 285	95 967	48.8	15.4
La Puente	9 002	4.48	20.4	10.5	43	0	0	43	576	1 419	335	1 084	24 384	70.3	9.0
La Quinta	14 977	2.59	9.6	22.0	57	7	7	50	1 411	3 549	219	3 331	27 546	28.5	34.9
La Verne	10 993	2.87	12.1	22.2	676	175	104	501	866	2 701	143	2 557	21 573	26.4	36.3
Lawndale	9 597	3.45	18.4	19.3	175	17	0	158	555	1 665	471	1 194	20 305	55.3	15.8
Lemon Grove	8 396	3.09	15.2	25.7	346	146	129	200	641	2 434	475	1 960	16 757	49.8	14.8
Lincoln	16 938	2.62	7.8	21.9	115	85	85	30	480	1 048	37	1 011	31 775	26.0	32.6
Livermore	29 956	2.80	9.6	20.2	510	121	121	389	1 737	2 016	274	1 742	57 143	26.5	39.5
Lodi	21 988	2.87	12.8	25.5	677	490	470	187	2 385	3 750	456	3 294	38 973	47.1	18.4
Lompoc	13 359	3.22	17.2	25.5	3 656	3 557	163	99	1 007	2 299	349	1 949	26 360	52.9	14.3
Long Beach	163 232	2.87	16.7	30.4	8 277	2 956	2 370	5 321	14 742	3 129	489	2 640	301 023	39.2	29.0
Los Altos	10 982	2.71	5.7	20.3	227	193	193	34	329	1 087	23	1 064	21 031	6.1	79.0
Los Angeles	1 329 372	2.91	15.4	30.1	84 601	26 415	13 845	58 186	102 310	2 619	491	2 128	2 568 460	44.6	31.5
Los Banos	10 303	3.55	18.4	14.8	181	78	78	103	1 033	2 791	359	2 432	21 003	62.6	10.2
Los Gatos	12 425	2.43	6.6	28.8	350	258	238	92	639	2 087	75	2 012	22 074	9.6	68.0
Lynwood	15 206	4.66	24.0	10.9	2 652	2 203	370	449	1 825	2 541	558	1 983	39 631	75.5	5.5
Madera	16 446	3.80	23.9	17.1	591	173	173	418	2 101	3 309	654	2 655	33 938	63.1	9.3
Manhattan Beach	13 951	2.55	5.9	27.1	28	0	0	28	915	2 551	103	2 448	25 257	9.0	74.2
Manteca	22 396	3.16	14.0	17.0	495	345	341	150	2 276	3 115	241	2 875	43 661	49.7	15.1
Martinez	14 192	2.60	10.8	26.8	1 296	1 061	268	235	1 047	2 798	195	2 603	26 620	24.8	37.3
Maywood	6 287	4.41	23.6	10.9	119	119	119	0	338	1 214	316	898	14 885	80.8	4.4
Menifee	26 955	3.03	10.6	23.1	188	107	106	81	1 608	1 895	126	1 769	54 294	41.8	17.3

1. No spouse present.   2. Data for serious crimes have not been adjusted for underreporting. This may affect comparability between geographic areas and over time.   3. Per 100,000 population estimated by the FBI.   4. Persons 25 years old and over.

Table D. Cities — Income, Poverty, and Housing

City	Money income, 2010–2014					Housing units, 2010			Occupied housing units 2010–2014			Median owner costs as a percent of income	
			Households							Owner-occupied			
	Per capita income[1] (dollars)	Median income	Percent with income of $200,000 or more	Percent with income of less than $25,000	Families with income below poverty (percent)	Total	Percent change, 2000–2010	Vacant units for sale or rent[2]	Total	Percent	Median value[3] (dollars)	With a mortgage[4]	Without a mortgage[5]
	42	43	44	45	46	47	48	49	50	51	52	53	54
CALIFORNIA—Cont'd													
Delano	10 455	36 244	0.4	30.3	28.1	10 713	21.0	453	10 549	55.3	143 500	30.2	13.3
Desert Hot Springs	14 466	33 575	0.7	35.1	29.4	10 902	55.2	2 252	9 164	44.3	125 500	29.0	13.5
Diamond Bar	34 539	90 901	10.4	8.8	4.7	18 455	2.8	575	17 266	79.2	533 700	28.4	11.5
Downey	23 216	60 374	4.4	16.5	9.6	35 601	2.4	1 665	33 169	50.6	413 400	31.3	10.0
Dublin	44 679	114 699	16.4	6.5	2.1	15 782	59.6	869	16 476	62.9	588 100	27.7	10.0
East Palo Alto	18 527	52 716	3.8	18.3	13.4	7 819	10.8	879	6 940	36.9	386 100	30.6	16.4
El Cajon	20 430	45 957	2.6	29.5	21.7	35 850	1.9	1 716	32 088	38.6	333 700	27.4	12.1
El Centro	18 463	41 677	2.2	33.9	20.3	14 476	17.8	1 368	12 752	49.7	147 100	24.7	10.7
Elk Grove	29 695	79 051	6.5	12.4	8.0	50 634	167.9	2 707	48 737	71.2	269 600	26.5	10.5
El Monte	15 010	38 906	1.2	29.3	21.2	29 069	4.8	1 255	29 793	40.3	349 000	32.5	11.0
El Paso de Robles (Paso Robles)	28 358	59 978	3.3	15.7	11.0	11 426	30.1	593	11 356	54.8	350 400	28.5	13.6
Encinitas	48 067	92 564	15.8	14.4	5.3	25 740	7.8	1 658	23 208	65.4	720 800	27.7	10.8
Escondido	21 684	49 409	3.7	23.4	15.5	48 044	6.8	2 560	44 798	49.0	335 900	29.3	12.6
Eureka	21 151	38 007	0.9	33.5	12.8	11 891	2.6	741	10 758	45.5	240 900	28.0	10.0
Fairfield	27 110	66 190	4.8	16.6	9.8	37 184	16.7	2 700	34 674	56.9	262 400	28.1	10.0
Folsom	38 472	100 163	10.3	9.0	2.0	26 109	45.5	1 158	25 111	68.0	393 600	24.5	11.6
Fontana	19 685	64 995	3.1	16.3	13.9	51 857	44.5	2 741	49 438	65.6	253 700	29.1	10.0
Foster City	55 318	114 651	23.0	7.7	2.2	12 458	3.7	442	12 188	58.6	850 800	26.1	12.3
Fountain Valley	34 382	82 532	8.3	12.9	4.5	19 164	3.7	516	18 777	70.7	605 000	27.2	10.0
Fremont	40 815	103 591	15.9	9.4	4.1	73 989	6.5	2 985	71 575	63.2	614 500	25.0	10.0
Fresno	19 226	41 455	2.5	31.7	24.9	171 288	15.0	12 939	160 172	47.4	175 600	26.5	11.2
Fullerton	29 733	65 909	7.5	19.3	11.8	47 869	7.0	2 478	44 406	53.1	492 800	28.8	10.0
Gardena	23 230	47 856	3.0	24.8	12.0	21 472	2.1	914	20 658	50.2	341 900	33.1	10.1
Garden Grove	21 241	59 360	3.8	20.2	13.5	47 755	2.0	1 718	46 453	56.0	406 800	28.8	10.0
Gilroy	29 559	81 056	8.5	16.4	11.3	14 854	22.1	679	14 922	58.4	458 500	28.3	10.4
Glendale	29 264	52 451	6.5	26.1	11.6	76 269	3.5	4 000	71 132	36.2	598 600	31.3	11.5
Glendora	32 090	74 169	7.7	13.4	7.0	17 778	3.5	637	16 608	68.7	454 200	29.3	10.9
Goleta	33 469	75 766	8.4	14.0	3.2	11 473	-43.6	570	10 375	54.6	616 500	30.1	10.0
Hanford	22 307	53 543	2.4	23.1	18.7	18 493	25.4	1 001	17 200	57.2	171 600	24.5	10.4
Hawthorne	20 445	44 384	2.2	24.7	16.5	29 869	1.0	1 383	29 145	25.5	387 300	32.7	10.0
Hayward	25 770	62 691	5.7	18.6	11.3	48 296	5.1	2 931	45 972	52.5	339 700	28.8	10.7
Hemet	18 284	33 932	1.1	38.0	20.4	35 305	19.8	5 213	30 585	58.2	117 000	28.5	15.0
Hesperia	16 584	44 472	1.4	28.0	18.6	29 004	36.2	2 573	26 203	63.3	148 700	26.9	11.4
Highland	21 578	53 385	4.2	21.6	17.1	16 578	10.9	1 107	15 111	63.3	250 700	26.0	11.8
Hollister	22 516	66 045	2.8	17.7	11.0	10 401	4.5	541	10 188	56.8	300 700	30.0	12.1
Huntington Beach	42 680	82 554	11.1	12.3	6.1	78 003	2.9	3 718	74 235	59.1	628 600	27.6	10.0
Huntington Park	12 088	34 777	0.5	35.9	29.1	15 151	-1.2	554	14 637	25.6	287 900	36.2	10.0
Imperial Beach	19 896	48 117	1.1	23.6	13.6	9 882	1.5	770	8 649	33.4	342 600	28.5	10.0
Indio	20 674	47 922	2.4	26.6	17.0	28 971	71.4	5 593	25 281	65.1	196 400	30.8	13.2
Inglewood	19 837	42 249	1.5	28.3	18.9	38 429	-0.5	2 040	36 309	35.7	325 000	33.9	12.0
Irvine	43 456	91 999	15.0	14.4	6.8	83 899	56.2	4 921	83 321	49.2	662 200	26.6	10.0
Laguna Hills	43 958	91 460	15.6	10.0	4.2	11 054	-2.5	577	10 261	70.2	580 800	28.5	10.0
Laguna Niguel	51 750	98 957	19.0	9.6	3.9	25 312	5.9	1 080	24 538	71.8	668 900	28.3	10.4
La Habra	25 646	61 364	4.7	17.5	11.9	19 924	2.0	947	18 832	56.3	378 800	28.0	10.1
Lake Elsinore	21 016	63 303	1.4	16.1	11.3	16 253	70.6	1 465	14 846	65.2	218 200	27.5	12.7
Lake Forest	38 760	92 781	11.1	9.3	4.4	27 088	31.6	864	26 772	70.3	507 600	25.7	10.0
Lakewood	29 981	79 113	4.8	11.2	5.0	27 470	0.7	927	26 339	71.2	415 600	27.6	10.0
La Mesa	30 728	54 630	3.5	19.5	8.9	26 167	5.1	1 655	23 566	43.9	379 000	27.7	10.5
La Mirada	29 467	81 178	6.6	14.5	5.0	15 092	1.9	411	14 346	78.3	409 800	27.4	10.0
Lancaster	19 703	49 057	2.2	26.7	19.5	51 835	24.4	4 843	47 872	58.3	160 100	27.8	13.4
La Puente	15 509	54 660	0.9	18.8	13.4	9 761	1.0	310	9 002	56.2	293 500	32.2	10.0
La Quinta	39 021	71 074	9.1	16.0	6.1	23 489	99.7	8 669	14 977	70.6	343 200	29.1	15.7
La Verne	34 778	75 662	8.4	16.7	6.2	11 886	3.5	425	10 993	73.3	443 200	26.4	11.9
Lawndale	18 145	48 376	1.6	23.5	14.6	10 151	2.8	470	9 597	33.4	365 000	32.4	13.1
Lemon Grove	21 915	52 339	0.9	21.6	13.0	8 868	1.2	434	8 396	54.1	295 200	30.0	11.4
Lincoln	32 182	70 870	3.2	14.1	6.5	17 457	322.6	978	16 938	78.0	328 300	30.7	12.7
Livermore	42 594	99 683	14.8	10.2	3.4	30 342	14.3	1 208	29 956	69.9	490 700	26.0	10.0
Lodi	23 648	48 662	3.4	25.7	15.0	23 792	11.2	1 695	21 988	53.0	228 400	26.1	12.7
Lompoc	20 151	47 908	2.1	24.4	18.7	14 416	5.8	1 061	13 359	44.7	227 500	27.3	10.3
Long Beach	27 014	52 944	4.9	24.3	16.5	176 032	2.5	12 501	163 232	40.2	419 400	28.5	10.0
Los Altos	84 705	157 500	40.3	7.4	1.8	11 204	4.4	459	10 982	84.8	1 000 000	25.8	10.6
Los Angeles	28 320	49 682	6.7	27.1	18.2	1 413 995	5.7	95 827	1 329 372	37.2	453 800	32.5	13.2
Los Banos	17 160	45 665	2.1	26.7	21.0	11 375	40.9	1 116	10 303	52.9	152 200	27.5	12.6
Los Gatos	72 050	122 860	28.8	8.3	3.3	13 050	5.2	695	12 425	63.9	1 000 000	26.8	10.0
Lynwood	12 580	41 930	0.7	27.6	23.9	15 271	1.8	597	15 206	44.1	278 300	34.4	11.6
Madera	14 460	42 027	0.6	28.9	24.0	17 049	34.7	1 111	16 446	47.8	147 400	29.2	10.0
Manhattan Beach	81 787	142 071	34.2	7.1	2.5	14 929	-1.1	891	13 951	68.5	1 000 000	25.6	10.0
Manteca	23 806	62 032	2.2	16.8	9.2	23 132	36.9	1 514	22 396	60.0	217 900	28.2	12.1
Martinez	39 701	85 736	9.3	11.2	5.0	14 976	2.3	689	14 192	65.5	407 600	26.1	10.1
Maywood	11 656	36 492	0.1	34.0	29.4	6 766	1.0	207	6 287	25.8	284 100	32.7	10.0
Menifee	23 165	56 671	2.2	18.8	8.5	30 269	NA	2 808	26 955	75.1	198 800	29.0	14.1

1. Based on population estimated by the American Community Survey.   2. Includes units rented or sold but not occupied.   3. Specified owner-occupied units; $1,000,000 represents $1,000,000 or more.   4. 50.0 represents 50 percent or more.   5. 10.0 represents 10 percent or less.

Table D. Cities — Housing, Labor Force, and Employment

City	Occupied housing units, 2010–2014 (cont.)				Migration, 2010–2014		Civilian labor force, 2015				Civilian employment[4], 2010–2014			
									Unemployment			Percent		
	Percent renter occupied	Median gross rent[1]	Median gross rent as a percent of income[2]	Percent with no vehicle available	Percent who lived in the same house one year ago	Percent who lived outside current city one year ago	Total	Percent change, 2014–2015	Total	Rate[3]	Population age 16 and older	In labor force	Civilian full-year full-time workers	Households with no workers (percent)
	55	56	57	58	59	60	61	62	63	64	65	66	67	68
CALIFORNIA—Cont'd														
Delano	44.7	770	33.1	6.0	79.1	12.8	19 413	-0.3	2 373	12.2	39 278	48.5	23.3	20.4
Desert Hot Springs	55.7	905	40.9	8.9	78.2	11.4	11 191	1.5	894	8.0	19 753	59.2	29.0	32.0
Diamond Bar	20.8	1 804	31.9	2.4	88.7	8.5	29 579	0.3	1 268	4.3	46 706	63.9	41.1	15.8
Downey	49.4	1 225	34.1	5.0	89.5	6.8	56 935	-0.1	3 393	6.0	87 945	66.2	41.8	18.8
Dublin	37.1	1 885	26.3	3.5	78.5	18.0	27 948	1.9	823	2.9	39 474	65.8	44.6	13.5
East Palo Alto	63.1	1 393	37.9	6.2	84.9	11.9	15 001	2.4	810	5.4	21 537	69.9	37.9	15.1
El Cajon	61.4	1 096	38.6	9.0	80.5	13.1	46 269	0.3	3 454	7.5	78 675	62.4	32.3	27.3
El Centro	50.3	744	33.6	10.8	80.7	7.0	21 250	0.3	4 756	22.4	32 080	59.6	30.7	29.3
Elk Grove	28.8	1 480	32.7	3.0	84.0	8.9	78 375	1.2	3 620	4.6	118 529	67.0	42.1	18.6
El Monte	59.7	1 081	40.8	9.7	92.0	5.1	52 165	-0.7	4 336	8.3	89 826	60.0	36.9	19.0
El Paso de Robles (Paso Robles)	45.2	1 138	29.6	3.2	80.9	10.8	16 546	1.5	861	5.2	23 454	67.9	41.5	22.3
Encinitas	34.6	1 737	31.5	3.1	87.1	9.2	33 090	1.2	1 393	4.2	49 797	66.1	40.2	23.3
Escondido	51.0	1 193	38.2	6.8	85.6	7.0	69 273	0.9	3 610	5.2	113 102	62.4	36.3	24.5
Eureka	54.5	829	35.6	12.5	76.2	12.8	12 819	-0.1	705	5.5	22 636	61.5	32.3	32.1
Fairfield	43.1	1 304	32.4	5.4	80.8	10.0	51 865	1.4	2 858	5.5	83 782	66.1	36.1	23.2
Folsom	32.0	1 416	25.6	3.7	84.1	11.1	35 627	1.4	1 387	3.9	57 632	61.9	39.7	20.3
Fontana	34.4	1 135	36.5	3.9	86.0	8.6	94 873	1.6	6 656	7.0	147 141	66.3	38.1	14.9
Foster City	41.4	2 000	25.9	3.2	81.8	12.6	18 864	3.0	590	3.1	25 721	66.5	45.0	19.6
Fountain Valley	29.3	1 630	35.4	5.5	89.5	8.1	28 857	1.2	1 269	4.4	46 825	62.3	38.9	25.3
Fremont	36.8	1 663	25.9	4.2	87.2	7.7	116 577	1.7	4 324	3.7	173 315	66.5	45.1	27.5
Fresno	52.6	890	37.0	11.5	80.8	6.3	237 792	0.6	26 295	11.1	372 071	61.9	32.8	29.0
Fullerton	46.9	1 342	35.5	5.5	79.9	13.8	70 649	1.1	3 590	5.1	110 014	65.0	36.8	22.2
Gardena	49.8	1 137	34.7	7.5	87.7	10.4	30 024	-0.3	2 013	6.7	47 668	63.4	40.2	24.6
Garden Grove	44.0	1 337	35.8	5.5	89.1	7.5	83 461	0.9	4 649	5.6	137 177	63.9	38.1	19.2
Gilroy	41.6	1 367	34.9	5.9	84.6	8.4	27 201	2.0	1 483	5.5	37 229	70.4	40.3	17.9
Glendale	63.8	1 304	39.0	12.1	87.2	8.2	101 119	-0.2	6 581	6.5	163 554	62.1	35.9	25.7
Glendora	31.3	1 442	32.5	4.0	88.9	8.6	25 198	0.0	1 442	5.7	40 726	62.9	36.7	24.3
Goleta	45.4	1 588	29.4	5.7	79.2	18.0	17 398	0.8	545	3.1	25 087	67.4	41.4	23.9
Hanford	42.8	934	30.8	7.7	82.1	7.8	24 736	1.2	2 345	9.5	39 982	62.5	38.0	26.3
Hawthorne	74.5	1 045	33.7	8.8	83.9	10.6	43 894	-0.1	2 641	6.0	65 067	68.5	41.3	17.1
Hayward	47.5	1 312	34.5	7.0	85.3	9.8	77 667	1.0	5 155	6.6	118 717	68.0	39.1	21.8
Hemet	41.8	937	42.0	11.6	77.7	13.6	28 887	1.2	2 688	9.3	63 178	48.5	22.9	50.1
Hesperia	36.7	1 046	38.5	6.1	84.9	9.6	34 923	1.2	3 076	8.8	67 041	55.2	30.1	30.4
Highland	36.7	977	37.1	5.9	85.2	10.3	23 828	2.0	1 342	5.6	39 428	62.2	35.7	23.1
Hollister	43.2	1 284	35.7	3.5	81.5	7.2	18 650	1.4	1 440	7.7	26 370	70.8	37.3	19.6
Huntington Beach	40.9	1 595	31.4	4.1	87.2	7.6	108 746	1.2	4 695	4.3	161 839	67.5	41.0	22.8
Huntington Park	74.4	934	39.1	17.1	88.9	7.2	27 193	-0.8	2 405	8.8	42 897	65.8	36.3	15.9
Imperial Beach	66.6	1 194	34.0	9.4	79.0	16.0	12 242	0.2	984	8.0	20 198	64.0	33.3	24.7
Indio	34.9	998	36.5	6.3	81.5	9.1	37 896	1.7	2 757	7.3	60 626	62.6	34.3	28.9
Inglewood	64.3	1 097	37.6	9.3	88.0	8.8	53 617	-0.8	4 741	8.8	85 369	67.1	37.7	25.6
Irvine	50.8	1 863	30.4	3.7	78.1	14.5	128 682	1.5	4 305	3.3	184 586	65.6	42.5	18.7
Laguna Hills	29.8	1 808	31.7	3.7	85.2	13.0	16 985	1.3	694	4.1	25 298	68.6	43.7	18.3
Laguna Niguel	28.2	1 818	34.4	2.8	86.8	10.6	35 047	1.3	1 436	4.1	52 619	68.7	43.3	19.0
La Habra	43.7	1 303	35.7	5.3	86.2	8.4	31 054	1.1	1 580	5.1	47 363	66.9	41.1	20.3
Lake Elsinore	34.8	1 237	33.5	4.1	82.3	12.0	26 941	1.7	1 930	7.2	39 961	67.0	38.1	16.6
Lake Forest	29.7	1 681	31.4	2.9	88.5	9.0	45 539	1.5	1 449	3.2	62 646	72.9	48.1	14.4
Lakewood	28.8	1 524	32.5	3.6	88.7	9.0	42 371	0.1	2 194	5.2	64 380	67.3	44.1	19.3
La Mesa	56.1	1 259	34.2	9.3	77.7	17.4	30 625	0.9	1 612	5.3	47 817	65.9	39.8	27.7
La Mirada	21.7	1 563	33.6	3.2	90.3	7.6	23 754	0.2	1 122	4.7	40 296	59.4	36.9	25.6
Lancaster	41.7	1 075	35.6	7.3	87.8	7.5	63 800	-0.5	4 797	7.5	118 339	54.4	35.8	28.4
La Puente	43.8	1 185	33.5	5.9	89.1	8.2	18 897	-0.1	1 119	5.9	30 136	63.9	40.0	16.1
La Quinta	29.4	1 373	31.9	4.0	87.8	8.3	17 733	2.4	752	4.2	31 544	54.6	29.1	37.5
La Verne	26.7	1 366	32.4	6.5	87.2	10.1	15 581	0.1	800	5.1	25 697	60.3	35.6	30.7
Lawndale	66.6	1 326	35.0	5.5	88.1	8.7	16 645	-0.2	1 069	6.4	24 863	69.8	40.8	17.0
Lemon Grove	45.9	1 152	36.4	7.7	90.6	7.8	12 502	0.5	855	6.8	20 169	64.0	38.1	26.7
Lincoln	22.0	1 525	31.8	2.2	88.7	8.8	18 503	0.8	1 020	5.5	35 133	53.3	31.8	42.3
Livermore	30.1	1 492	30.2	4.0	88.5	7.1	46 637	1.8	1 502	3.2	66 224	71.0	45.5	18.7
Lodi	47.0	1 002	34.5	8.3	81.9	6.9	29 040	1.1	2 421	8.3	47 502	62.5	33.1	27.6
Lompoc	55.3	966	33.0	9.5	79.4	10.1	18 295	0.2	1 263	6.9	32 531	58.9	34.1	26.3
Long Beach	59.8	1 118	33.7	11.0	82.6	8.2	238 845	-0.4	17 568	7.4	368 742	66.5	38.7	23.2
Los Altos	15.2	2 000	25.1	2.7	90.9	8.2	14 348	2.6	387	2.7	23 022	58.5	38.4	27.8
Los Angeles	62.8	1 194	36.7	13.3	85.4	5.5	2 011 069	-0.4	143 154	7.1	3 103 574	66.3	38.5	23.4
Los Banos	47.1	1 087	36.6	5.8	81.2	9.4	15 849	0.1	1 839	11.6	25 787	60.5	29.0	26.5
Los Gatos	36.1	1 779	26.3	2.7	86.0	10.4	15 803	2.6	443	2.8	24 327	62.6	41.2	23.2
Lynwood	55.9	1 044	40.6	7.8	90.2	7.7	28 764	-0.7	2 386	8.3	51 565	59.8	35.6	16.5
Madera	52.2	904	32.0	11.2	89.1	4.3	26 198	-2.5	2 373	9.1	43 596	59.3	28.5	39.4
Manhattan Beach	31.5	1 987	24.3	1.8	88.9	7.5	19 031	0.7	523	2.7	27 774	67.4	46.7	21.1
Manteca	40.0	1 196	33.1	4.0	83.5	10.4	35 141	1.0	3 141	8.9	52 346	67.0	38.2	22.4
Martinez	34.5	1 446	30.8	2.9	86.5	9.8	20 417	1.4	918	4.5	30 409	68.4	40.9	20.4
Maywood	74.2	1 002	39.0	13.2	90.7	6.8	12 496	-0.3	873	7.0	19 494	66.1	40.3	14.4
Menifee	24.9	1 352	37.9	4.1	83.0	12.1	36 407	1.5	2 865	7.9	63 835	57.6	32.0	35.6

1. $2,000 represents $2,000 or more. 2. 50.0 represents 50 percent or more. 3. Percent of civilian labor force. 4. Persons 16 years old and over.

Table D. Cities — Construction, Wholesale Trade, and Retail Trade

City	Value of residential construction authorized by building permits, 2015			Wholesale trade,[1] 2012				Retail trade,[2] 2012			
	New construction ($1,000)	Number of housing units	Percent single family	Number of establishments	Number of employees	Sales (mil dol)	Annual payroll (mil dol)	Number of establishments	Number of employees	Sales (mil dol)	Annual payroll (mil dol)
	69	70	71	72	73	74	75	76	77	78	79
CALIFORNIA—Cont'd											
Delano	394	4	100.0	20	180	189.0	7.9	80	1 045	277.3	26.3
Desert Hot Springs	4 041	26	100.0	1	D	D	D	40	549	144.4	13.1
Diamond Bar	32 745	126	90.5	249	634	1 359.9	29.2	113	1 062	311.6	23.4
Downey	10 205	27	66.7	97	813	338.5	37.5	275	4 421	1 163.8	107.2
Dublin	260 688	908	58.3	64	323	222.6	20.3	175	3 862	1 329.0	124.1
East Palo Alto	15 794	53	100.0	5	D	D	D	24	926	270.5	24.8
El Cajon	21 872	105	100.0	134	1 080	556.8	49.7	445	6 280	1 756.0	158.4
El Centro	9 394	96	12.5	53	433	294.8	15.8	200	4 172	925.9	91.7
Elk Grove	135 881	665	100.0	42	347	83.9	18.9	280	5 913	1 823.8	173.9
El Monte	9 702	39	100.0	294	1 887	808.8	71.4	274	3 254	1 676.8	111.8
El Paso de Robles (Paso Robles)	28 764	153	39.9	47	328	129.7	14.1	151	2 429	625.2	61.4
Encinitas	39 926	142	100.0	96	462	212.1	24.3	282	3 927	1 119.7	110.9
Escondido	24 184	162	12.3	132	1 165	545.8	54.2	541	9 202	2 786.0	263.2
Eureka	4 543	59	15.3	42	388	134.3	15.8	233	3 186	971.3	84.0
Fairfield	134 577	671	57.1	69	1 393	869.7	72.1	311	5 307	1 398.6	133.8
Folsom	72 475	246	100.0	44	374	788.8	36.4	282	5 534	1 639.5	151.0
Fontana	124 577	513	88.9	145	3 620	1 811.5	165.0	321	5 905	2 145.1	171.5
Foster City	86 346	346	7.5	60	D	D	D	31	876	305.0	25.3
Fountain Valley	1 059	4	100.0	105	1 076	657.1	60.4	221	3 205	1 298.6	88.7
Fremont	100 935	458	45.0	458	9 470	13 487.4	720.4	411	7 229	2 617.9	231.1
Fresno	253 934	994	84.9	514	7 741	5 459.8	388.1	1 539	22 005	5 960.2	555.9
Fullerton	53 965	370	10.8	236	2 434	2 539.6	141.5	374	5 211	1 516.4	130.8
Gardena	8 734	57	57.9	164	1 540	642.6	63.2	177	2 197	754.0	66.5
Garden Grove	24 107	265	7.5	232	2 465	1 239.7	113.3	402	5 005	1 656.2	134.7
Gilroy	188 853	679	61.4	41	D	D	D	313	5 155	1 191.9	111.9
Glendale	85 450	698	1.3	254	1 911	1 386.6	97.1	731	11 330	3 138.2	300.7
Glendora	38 957	113	79.6	34	362	162.9	25.1	131	2 471	688.2	64.0
Goleta	437	3	100.0	52	999	620.2	95.5	127	2 317	727.7	66.4
Hanford	65 881	327	65.7	26	325	191.2	18.5	168	2 905	741.6	67.5
Hawthorne	13 537	132	3.8	67	1 209	480.3	56.2	183	3 443	1 382.2	101.6
Hayward	101 706	301	100.0	457	6 380	4 546.4	386.7	399	5 840	1 765.7	162.5
Hemet	21 014	91	100.0	21	124	69.1	4.0	203	3 658	845.5	93.6
Hesperia	18 628	100	100.0	42	186	231.4	7.7	173	2 101	615.5	45.9
Highland	2 004	8	100.0	14	D	D	D	59	836	234.9	21.1
Hollister	32 718	121	100.0	20	212	72.2	10.3	88	1 192	318.2	32.5
Huntington Beach	50 405	179	73.2	403	4 714	10 353.7	291.2	556	8 069	2 505.6	233.2
Huntington Park	0	0	0.0	55	740	399.3	28.5	182	2 196	622.7	55.4
Imperial Beach	2 353	19	21.1	6	9	3.3	0.3	30	224	45.3	4.4
Indio	59 771	273	100.0	35	373	166.7	15.3	162	2 624	862.9	79.5
Inglewood	1 063	4	50.0	81	2 277	977.4	76.3	257	3 440	1 219.9	85.6
Irvine	847 085	4 660	28.6	986	18 431	30 339.3	1 395.5	593	9 845	4 254.4	363.2
Laguna Hills	1 155	2	100.0	94	623	282.3	41.9	186	2 324	452.6	51.3
Laguna Niguel	5 818	6	66.7	63	264	95.4	11.1	133	2 959	1 254.0	107.5
La Habra	6 017	20	100.0	72	416	247.9	22.0	173	3 158	912.1	78.9
Lake Elsinore	87 439	452	100.0	37	272	79.4	10.4	157	2 732	784.9	69.5
Lake Forest	110 480	493	59.0	187	3 004	1 741.4	213.4	205	3 212	1 068.1	116.0
Lakewood	23 459	94	76.6	32	142	38.9	5.3	228	4 820	1 104.4	106.2
La Mesa	5 555	26	88.5	23	192	66.6	8.5	229	3 846	1 070.3	101.9
La Mirada	9 297	37	100.0	125	3 047	2 257.2	185.6	88	1 375	391.9	40.2
Lancaster	28 537	95	100.0	68	867	887.2	30.5	300	4 983	1 562.3	132.5
La Puente	0	0	0.0	24	110	40.7	3.6	92	1 111	243.8	25.7
La Quinta	46 210	189	91.5	17	33	34.7	3.3	93	2 204	637.4	57.4
La Verne	2 081	5	100.0	66	691	527.1	37.9	74	1 298	355.7	27.2
Lawndale	337	2	100.0	15	111	39.2	4.8	87	774	208.4	19.2
Lemon Grove	20 932	75	100.0	9	46	16.7	2.8	77	1 227	411.6	35.5
Lincoln	74 946	233	100.0	16	151	55.5	6.3	52	975	268.0	24.8
Livermore	104 413	420	79.5	162	3 292	2 192.9	228.9	281	3 560	1 212.0	126.4
Lodi	5 451	20	100.0	39	265	639.3	14.3	209	3 353	974.6	93.3
Lompoc	8 123	45	95.6	9	51	12.6	2.2	111	1 395	371.9	35.3
Long Beach	19 056	152	13.2	318	4 469	6 962.3	284.9	957	13 033	3 783.9	334.5
Los Altos	35 503	46	91.3	17	D	D	D	102	D	D	D
Los Angeles	3 371 663	16 013	11.5	8 552	83 938	63 834.9	4 787.1	11 359	133 706	40 156.9	3 735.0
Los Banos	8 412	43	90.7	11	131	122.9	4.9	74	1 197	270.5	26.6
Los Gatos	42 194	31	87.1	28	D	D	D	176	D	D	D
Lynwood	1 515	7	0.0	39	580	312.5	28.8	118	1 386	322.3	27.6
Madera	38 580	145	100.0	22	250	213.0	14.2	173	2 163	556.1	50.7
Manhattan Beach	70 757	106	94.3	40	D	D	D	178	2 924	772.1	69.1
Manteca	86 915	494	100.0	26	393	225.1	13.9	177	3 440	824.0	85.3
Martinez	10 674	54	100.0	23	D	D	D	57	1 031	309.8	32.5
Maywood	418	2	100.0	20	432	233.0	20.4	54	472	107.1	9.3
Menifee	110 314	408	100.0	14	57	39.8	2.4	87	1 672	417.3	37.9

1. Merchant wholesalers except manufacturers' sales branches and offices. 2. Establishments with payroll.

City	Real estate and rental and leasing, 2012				Professional, scientific, and technical services,[1] 2012				Manufacturing, 2012			
	Number of establish-ments	Number of employees	Receipts (mil dol)	Annual payroll (mil dol)	Number of establish-ments	Number of employees	Receipts (mil dol)	Annual payroll (mil dol)	Number of establish-ments	Number of employees	Receipts (mil dol)	Annual payroll (mil dol)
	80	81	82	83	84	85	86	87	88	89	90	91
CALIFORNIA—Cont'd												
Delano......................	19	69	10.6	1.6	20	D	D	D	11	85	38.3	2.9
Desert Hot Springs.........	10	D	D	D	8	215	4.4	2.9	NA	NA	NA	NA
Diamond Bar..............	98	D	D	D	234	D	D	D	14	231	D	9.9
Downey..................	153	1 051	130.9	28.1	145	D	D	D	79	1 968	1 037.0	95.1
Dublin...................	55	214	73.4	10.1	190	1 452	291.3	124.2	18	1 281	509.7	118.6
East Palo Alto	20	92	48.2	4.5	19	D	D	D	6	D	D	D
El Cajon..................	158	625	90.8	20.7	199	2 323	151.5	60.1	162	4 472	D	242.7
El Centro..................	46	207	45.5	6.7	90	D	D	D	16	204	D	7.7
Elk Grove	110	427	68.7	12.9	198	D	D	D	30	532	111.0	22.4
El Monte	72	390	52.0	11.1	105	D	D	D	142	2 558	515.5	113.7
El Paso de Robles (Paso Robles)	55	178	26.8	5.3	77	273	31.3	12.1	67	2 175	524.6	101.9
Encinitas.................	181	428	86.5	19.1	525	1 658	350.3	110.8	41	186	48.2	10.7
Escondido................	180	937	862.9	53.1	337	1 810	230.1	84.0	165	2 794	D	125.1
Eureka...................	61	263	46.4	8.4	103	D	D	D	29	541	109.6	19.1
Fairfield..................	99	406	106.4	15.0	156	D	D	D	60	2 638	1 718.9	152.8
Folsom...................	103	489	95.5	17.6	327	D	D	D	26	674	198.9	49.2
Fontana	88	538	131.0	25.1	89	411	34.7	10.0	105	4 084	1 574.6	197.3
Foster City................	50	352	119.1	24.9	151	2 145	485.6	210.3	11	817	D	D
Fountain Valley	106	346	80.4	15.6	231	D	D	D	86	2 752	2 318.1	165.1
Fremont..................	240	1 052	392.8	54.1	1 047	13 204	2 603.7	1 153.9	328	18 254	5 194.0	1 594.2
Fresno...................	506	3 269	512.4	105.4	1 121	D	D	D	335	12 295	4 367.7	522.7
Fullerton..................	172	684	123.9	23.6	378	3 338	471.3	246.0	195	6 326	2 032.2	315.5
Gardena..................	54	332	27.1	7.8	69	364	27.2	10.6	224	4 643	891.1	222.1
Garden Grove	138	495	125.3	19.1	244	D	D	D	272	7 436	1 533.1	355.2
Gilroy....................	40	136	48.6	4.7	73	382	51.8	19.1	54	1 346	498.9	68.7
Glendale.................	310	2 740	1 391.5	162.4	888	D	D	D	198	4 473	842.3	237.4
Glendora.................	63	256	46.6	7.8	114	692	77.5	31.3	41	827	363.0	37.9
Goleta...................	52	278	43.8	9.9	158	D	D	D	109	5 347	1 857.5	408.2
Hanford..................	50	200	34.3	4.8	52	268	30.2	10.9	29	894	D	35.3
Hawthorne................	64	427	74.0	13.7	72	514	87.5	23.5	67	3 043	D	209.5
Hayward..................	171	1 330	279.1	57.6	262	D	D	D	315	10 345	4 108.1	608.5
Hemet...................	74	345	51.8	8.1	75	333	33.7	11.6	21	748	169.0	36.2
Hesperia.................	54	187	31.5	5.6	51	450	30.8	8.0	53	392	55.4	16.2
Highland.................	20	57	10.4	1.4	24	113	16.3	3.4	9	168	D	5.8
Hollister	32	81	20.9	2.8	46	147	15.6	4.6	38	1 274	341.6	D
Huntington Beach..........	319	1 411	311.7	62.6	769	D	D	D	320	12 880	D	1 221.6
Huntington Park	21	104	13.7	2.4	26	240	16.0	6.1	100	2 565	441.3	99.1
Imperial Beach	20	D	D	D	21	88	9.2	2.5	NA	NA	NA	NA
Indio....................	45	232	38.4	7.8	73	D	D	D	25	329	48.7	13.1
Inglewood................	65	939	147.2	31.8	73	D	D	D	68	2 175	D	99.3
Irvine....................	647	10 154	2 790.0	512.7	2 768	D	D	D	427	27 718	11 089.1	1 999.5
Laguna Hills..............	93	631	88.9	28.8	335	1 852	279.2	119.9	49	426	74.9	20.6
Laguna Niguel.............	108	446	112.4	22.8	298	872	138.3	41.2	24	209	D	12.2
La Habra	48	128	33.4	3.9	80	381	47.0	13.4	57	829	168.9	38.3
Lake Elsinore	39	103	20.6	3.6	55	235	35.7	8.0	65	790	113.3	31.5
Lake Forest	115	1 051	165.2	49.8	412	3 461	683.1	298.9	96	5 765	1 446.9	283.3
Lakewood................	36	147	28.9	4.4	67	367	30.4	11.8	10	238	D	8.7
La Mesa.................	133	884	104.7	26.8	229	1 068	128.8	51.4	21	115	18.7	4.0
La Mirada	56	501	98.5	23.4	67	355	47.1	17.3	58	2 267	590.8	93.1
Lancaster................	132	545	134.8	19.0	149	D	D	D	57	983	219.7	36.2
La Puente................	19	62	10.5	2.0	15	239	32.2	16.5	13	105	9.3	2.6
La Quinta................	87	190	44.5	7.5	89	339	65.4	25.8	4	6	1.1	0.3
La Verne.................	34	153	21.1	4.6	72	290	37.7	11.8	55	1 093	204.7	53.5
Lawndale................	22	295	59.8	9.2	43	D	D	D	18	239	D	10.5
Lemon Grove	16	71	22.3	1.9	23	119	6.7	2.7	9	81	16.3	3.8
Lincoln...................	38	86	18.0	2.4	44	216	18.0	6.8	10	601	176.9	30.1
Livermore................	99	525	173.9	24.0	204	D	D	D	132	3 690	1 339.4	234.4
Lodi.....................	77	403	39.7	10.1	104	656	71.3	25.7	80	2 124	561.9	81.6
Lompoc..................	31	146	18.8	4.1	35	D	D	D	23	573	108.4	25.5
Long Beach..............	502	3 660	2 647.9	266.4	1 036	7 701	1 489.9	485.4	234	8 027	4 464.4	758.2
Los Altos	98	304	114.2	21.0	275	D	D	D	23	189	30.0	12.6
Los Angeles	5 948	36 498	14 628.8	2 035.5	14 376	134 211	30 105.0	10 658.0	5 034	101 103	43 502.5	4 752.3
Los Banos	23	59	8.4	1.2	18	86	7.9	3.3	9	553	D	26.3
Los Gatos................	105	366	123.7	18.9	277	1 637	303.1	122.9	32	488	169.9	36.6
Lynwood.................	16	100	10.7	4.5	15	96	7.2	2.2	51	1 057	236.6	42.3
Madera	35	148	19.2	4.0	38	D	D	D	35	1 055	445.4	51.3
Manhattan Beach..........	127	430	272.3	23.1	308	1 384	312.1	121.5	19	82	D	2.9
Manteca..................	56	231	50.5	9.3	54	319	23.7	9.4	22	972	D	57.2
Martinez.................	41	171	35.4	5.8	78	D	D	D	18	907	D	111.5
Maywood.................	3	4	0.2	0.0	4	D	D	D	16	228	D	6.9
Menifee..................	50	242	36.5	6.8	52	174	13.4	3.8	16	266	61.8	11.7

1. Establishments subject to federal tax.

Table D. Cities — Accommodation and Food Services, Arts, Entertainment, and Recreation, and Health Care and Social Assistance

City	Accommodation and food services, 2012				Arts, entertainment, and recreation,[1] 2012				Health care and social assistance,[1] 2012			
	Number of establishments	Number of employees	Sales (mil dol)	Annual payroll (mil dol)	Number of establishments	Number of employees	Receipts (mil dol)	Annual payroll (mil dol)	Number of establishments	Number of employees	Receipts (mil dol)	Annual payroll (mil dol)
	92	93	94	95	96	97	98	99	100	101	102	103
CALIFORNIA—Cont'd												
Delano	43	432	23.3	5.2	2	D	D	D	66	D	D	D
Desert Hot Springs	36	353	19.2	4.8	2	D	D	D	11	61	4.0	1.5
Diamond Bar	123	1 370	75.1	23.4	6	114	7.9	2.0	165	1 273	115.1	42.3
Downey	213	4 046	247.7	66.5	12	D	D	D	278	5 105	739.3	295.8
Dublin	141	2 588	181.4	45.7	15	D	D	D	117	1 174	151.5	51.5
East Palo Alto	14	660	46.3	16.6	2	D	D	D	12	D	D	D
El Cajon	236	3 169	173.6	44.6	13	189	15.1	2.8	205	3 958	345.4	143.9
El Centro	116	1 870	97.1	25.8	5	D	D	D	121	925	100.5	38.7
Elk Grove	206	3 919	212.5	57.4	16	D	D	D	275	2 744	414.4	112.2
El Monte	164	1 488	91.3	20.8	4	D	D	D	147	1 988	157.8	60.8
El Paso de Robles (Paso Robles)	114	2 080	119.4	31.2	13	D	D	D	71	736	45.7	15.7
Encinitas	214	4 943	277.9	78.7	46	366	24.4	7.6	362	2 859	347.1	124.7
Escondido	263	4 164	233.7	60.5	24	D	D	D	313	3 443	351.6	138.1
Eureka	135	1 649	92.7	25.5	12	186	5.8	2.1	108	1 163	110.5	46.1
Fairfield	211	3 101	190.2	46.8	18	D	D	D	219	2 316	348.6	100.5
Folsom	180	3 470	169.3	49.0	22	490	21.7	6.2	231	D	D	D
Fontana	219	3 451	188.4	48.0	18	D	D	D	159	D	D	D
Foster City	59	1 120	80.5	22.4	3	D	D	D	76	D	D	D
Fountain Valley	146	2 203	128.3	34.6	21	D	D	D	377	D	D	D
Fremont	381	5 412	331.7	87.2	32	722	36.4	11.3	577	6 977	1 074.4	399.9
Fresno	927	16 854	841.3	233.1	77	2 455	94.6	31.0	1 397	17 786	2 161.5	877.0
Fullerton	323	5 151	293.1	76.7	26	399	28.0	7.4	374	D	D	D
Gardena	202	2 258	130.3	33.5	7	D	D	D	137	2 174	270.4	96.6
Garden Grove	396	6 025	389.7	98.0	23	D	D	D	456	4 760	527.1	180.1
Gilroy	127	2 168	124.6	31.7	8	D	D	D	116	D	D	D
Glendale	403	6 449	400.5	111.6	163	755	117.6	36.7	968	8 146	871.9	316.1
Glendora	88	1 402	74.6	20.7	16	D	D	D	192	D	D	D
Goleta	102	1 752	104.7	27.1	4	145	6.5	2.2	112	1 339	152.1	57.9
Hanford	91	1 597	84.0	21.8	5	109	3.3	0.6	147	1 349	140.9	50.6
Hawthorne	124	1 650	108.8	25.2	14	222	16.5	4.3	125	1 950	189.7	72.8
Hayward	297	3 731	225.0	55.7	16	308	15.4	7.9	231	4 468	704.8	308.2
Hemet	144	2 179	112.1	32.1	10	D	D	D	213	2 976	305.8	105.1
Hesperia	104	1 773	88.6	23.7	6	D	D	D	77	700	70.2	24.3
Highland	56	753	43.6	11.0	3	D	D	D	49	D	D	D
Hollister	53	645	35.5	8.8	6	D	D	D	59	D	D	D
Huntington Beach	441	8 517	534.8	151.5	67	754	58.6	12.8	609	4 641	531.3	204.7
Huntington Park	99	1 374	82.7	20.6	2	D	D	D	125	1 294	152.6	47.9
Imperial Beach	33	351	20.6	4.8	3	D	D	D	19	367	27.3	11.4
Indio	106	2 965	229.2	63.3	21	D	D	D	114	1 760	238.1	80.6
Inglewood	168	2 570	145.5	38.5	32	1 156	168.8	33.9	237	3 724	505.3	167.9
Irvine	606	14 173	907.9	244.5	234	8 490	501.7	114.6	954	8 749	1 347.3	422.5
Laguna Hills	94	1 905	103.5	30.4	9	D	D	D	334	D	D	D
Laguna Niguel	119	1 929	110.3	29.0	25	D	D	D	215	1 500	138.1	58.8
La Habra	136	1 866	102.6	28.6	5	D	D	D	99	D	D	D
Lake Elsinore	98	1 432	77.8	21.6	9	D	D	D	57	297	31.1	11.4
Lake Forest	181	2 897	173.1	46.3	27	359	26.9	7.2	189	4 891	328.9	178.3
Lakewood	156	3 191	169.1	46.4	10	205	16.5	3.7	159	2 002	319.3	106.1
La Mesa	167	3 198	172.3	52.7	13	D	D	D	322	D	D	D
La Mirada	98	1 486	85.4	21.3	10	D	D	D	104	1 392	127.6	49.9
Lancaster	205	3 762	184.0	47.1	13	D	D	D	365	5 673	790.7	256.4
La Puente	68	734	41.5	10.1	1	D	D	D	52	352	27.9	9.6
La Quinta	73	3 254	207.1	67.1	17	498	37.2	13.8	71	389	46.6	18.3
La Verne	78	1 240	64.9	18.0	12	195	12.3	3.5	62	427	37.8	13.3
Lawndale	46	610	38.0	9.2	4	11	4.2	0.8	60	294	29.4	10.6
Lemon Grove	48	643	35.3	8.8	3	38	1.3	0.5	31	622	44.5	17.3
Lincoln	50	D	D	D	7	D	D	D	71	D	D	D
Livermore	180	2 541	153.7	42.3	23	D	D	D	150	1 658	225.7	78.3
Lodi	127	1 893	98.6	26.8	9	266	12.6	3.7	176	D	D	D
Lompoc	82	1 055	62.9	16.2	2	D	D	D	57	D	D	D
Long Beach	877	16 971	984.1	276.1	94	1 467	109.3	28.3	1 053	12 915	1 473.7	546.7
Los Altos	85	1 252	84.0	26.0	14	D	D	D	136	1 133	165.0	54.6
Los Angeles	8 009	138 886	9 295.6	2 593.6	7 686	31 974	9 416.1	3 866.7	9 711	109 130	13 605.4	4 917.1
Los Banos	57	804	43.0	11.4	2	D	D	D	41	273	29.1	10.2
Los Gatos	124	2 447	145.9	46.4	16	D	D	D	296	2 222	320.7	125.2
Lynwood	79	1 053	64.6	14.9	NA	NA	NA	NA	110	D	D	D
Madera	79	1 081	57.8	13.4	6	75	3.4	0.9	105	D	D	D
Manhattan Beach	154	3 688	247.0	75.6	73	281	48.9	19.8	187	D	D	D
Manteca	117	1 839	103.7	26.1	10	323	18.4	5.9	103	D	D	D
Martinez	79	753	43.4	10.9	6	D	D	D	41	D	D	D
Maywood	39	425	24.1	6.0	NA	NA	NA	NA	22	D	D	D
Menifee	67	1 348	75.4	21.6	8	D	D	D	87	1 573	128.0	50.8

1. Establishments subject to federal tax.

City	Other services[1], 2012					Government employment and payroll, 2012							
							March payroll						
									Percent of total for:				
	Number of establishments	Number of employees	Receipts (mil dol)	Annual payroll (mil dol)	Full-time equivalent employees	Total (dollars)	Administration, judicial, and legal	Police and Corrections	Fire Protection	Highways and transportation	Health and welfare	Natural resources and utilities	Education and libraries
	104	105	106	107	108	109	110	111	112	113	114	115	116
CALIFORNIA—Cont'd													
Delano	21	58	7.4	1.3	220	881 307	8.4	41.4	0.0	13.6	3.9	30.6	0.0
Desert Hot Springs	17	47	3.1	0.8	73	440 127	17.0	60.5	0.0	11.0	10.1	1.4	0.0
Diamond Bar	54	D	D	D	72	380 697	40.0	0.0	0.0	16.5	10.9	32.6	0.0
Downey	126	702	60.2	15.2	505	3 402 608	8.6	42.0	25.6	4.8	1.5	12.4	2.5
Dublin	83	D	D	D	106	716 632	36.7	5.5	0.8	23.0	3.5	24.9	0.0
East Palo Alto	11	D	D	D	112	1 036 706	21.8	57.6	0.0	11.0	9.5	0.0	0.0
El Cajon	171	1 183	130.3	31.8	443	2 609 521	7.2	42.2	14.7	6.2	11.0	13.4	0.0
El Centro	52	239	21.3	6.3	964	4 003 786	4.7	10.9	5.9	2.3	69.2	5.8	0.5
Elk Grove	137	707	57.1	16.3	280	1 987 037	15.1	76.6	0.0	2.4	1.4	1.1	0.0
El Monte	132	434	49.1	10.7	336	2 338 846	6.8	63.2	0.0	15.0	2.5	12.4	0.0
El Paso de Robles (Paso Robles)	43	247	23.8	6.5	164	981 684	11.7	27.8	19.1	3.0	4.3	20.5	2.9
Encinitas	141	825	67.4	21.3	242	1 673 551	30.3	0.0	25.3	14.3	0.8	20.7	0.0
Escondido	225	1 215	123.8	34.8	1 133	10 074 411	16.4	29.3	13.9	7.9	0.9	24.7	3.3
Eureka	73	461	45.5	12.5	282	1 300 511	8.5	31.6	18.8	2.4	4.7	21.0	0.0
Fairfield	121	906	97.2	32.5	645	3 404 101	10.9	36.3	15.3	11.5	3.2	11.0	0.0
Folsom	97	764	50.8	16.0	483	3 244 300	14.2	23.2	21.7	8.2	0.0	28.9	1.6
Fontana	170	945	83.8	23.5	767	4 073 819	10.2	49.0	0.0	8.3	6.6	23.2	0.0
Foster City	20	D	D	D	192	1 556 154	16.6	27.7	24.1	6.3	0.0	25.3	0.0
Fountain Valley	84	562	47.6	14.9	232	1 801 733	11.7	37.6	26.9	4.9	0.9	10.1	0.0
Fremont	276	1 983	276.4	67.3	881	7 171 062	20.6	30.1	20.1	9.2	7.6	8.2	0.0
Fresno	536	3 750	381.1	106.9	3 214	18 551 770	10.2	39.0	13.4	20.0	0.0	15.9	0.0
Fullerton	185	884	110.0	26.1	676	4 122 933	7.6	39.6	18.4	6.3	5.0	12.8	3.4
Gardena	124	780	69.3	20.9	419	2 062 110	7.9	42.6	0.0	28.2	6.3	8.7	0.0
Garden Grove	216	884	78.3	21.3	657	4 420 328	10.0	44.2	22.5	0.7	7.8	7.6	0.0
Gilroy	82	713	68.2	19.1	258	1 936 702	13.1	41.6	20.3	4.9	2.7	13.4	0.0
Glendale	308	2 190	165.1	65.5	1 864	13 741 087	17.0	23.8	18.6	3.2	4.9	27.1	3.1
Glendora	78	D	D	D	321	1 582 591	10.6	43.7	0.0	11.9	6.9	19.8	7.2
Goleta	48	D	D	D	47	334 846	63.8	0.0	0.0	23.1	5.9	7.2	0.0
Hanford	43	192	17.7	4.8	259	1 321 734	9.8	38.2	13.4	8.8	0.0	24.1	0.0
Hawthorne	97	369	35.3	7.5	283	1 907 186	16.2	40.8	0.0	5.5	2.8	5.5	0.0
Hayward	202	1 576	223.3	52.6	761	6 582 512	8.9	39.0	24.1	6.2	3.7	9.7	2.7
Hemet	88	384	31.1	8.2	409	2 543 919	11.5	33.8	20.3	7.4	2.2	11.7	3.6
Hesperia	83	355	37.7	10.1	127	669 050	29.0	0.1	0.0	16.7	15.9	0.0	0.0
Highland	29	147	9.2	2.7	38	273 354	31.6	0.0	0.0	15.6	10.8	4.6	0.0
Hollister	50	D	D	D	131	912 911	12.2	25.2	24.4	4.8	4.9	18.9	0.0
Huntington Beach	309	1 944	159.4	52.3	1 071	7 579 599	14.4	34.3	23.5	5.3	1.3	14.6	2.6
Huntington Park	49	417	37.5	10.0	208	1 200 684	11.4	67.5	0.0	5.5	5.1	6.0	0.0
Imperial Beach	23	100	6.1	1.9	82	452 081	44.4	0.0	17.6	4.4	3.2	9.8	0.0
Indio	59	314	27.8	7.7	253	1 534 809	8.8	49.5	0.0	12.9	5.9	15.1	0.0
Inglewood	122	934	85.6	23.8	724	3 812 741	19.1	49.5	0.0	10.8	5.9	11.8	2.9
Irvine	293	2 511	248.1	68.7	977	6 075 973	20.0	39.1	0.0	10.5	2.9	13.8	0.0
Laguna Hills	68	390	33.7	10.7	40	246 065	39.8	0.0	0.0	13.2	20.3	26.7	0.0
Laguna Niguel	92	520	41.6	11.9	79	590 935	24.7	1.6	0.0	17.2	21.8	28.0	0.0
La Habra	95	531	47.0	10.7	325	1 702 615	11.2	45.6	0.0	0.0	0.0	0.0	0.0
Lake Elsinore	66	351	29.9	8.7	66	784 724	0.4	0.0	0.0	8.2	0.0	11.8	0.0
Lake Forest	111	695	85.9	20.7	79	477 565	58.7	1.2	0.0	5.1	13.9	21.1	0.0
Lakewood	76	D	D	D	255	1 549 892	26.5	6.5	0.0	16.3	2.1	41.0	0.0
La Mesa	106	820	54.6	17.8	283	1 642 547	12.9	41.7	20.9	5.6	2.7	10.2	0.0
La Mirada	33	141	6.3	2.0	142	702 597	25.1	9.5	0.0	0.0	9.3	25.7	0.0
Lancaster	167	864	78.2	22.3	338	1 643 288	21.1	3.3	0.0	28.3	10.6	32.5	0.0
La Puente	35	121	7.6	2.2	44	173 692	49.1	0.0	0.0	14.7	2.7	17.6	0.0
La Quinta	39	168	10.1	2.9	94	580 882	30.3	0.0	0.0	26.7	22.0	0.0	0.0
La Verne	38	215	12.2	3.4	200	1 245 972	16.1	41.5	26.1	2.8	0.0	10.1	0.0
Lawndale	65	299	25.9	6.0	72	370 627	35.6	0.0	0.0	27.9	0.0	17.4	0.0
Lemon Grove	44	150	11.9	3.3	50	320 723	14.9	0.0	50.2	14.0	7.5	6.0	0.0
Lincoln	34	D	D	D	204	1 072 286	18.7	28.4	11.2	10.5	9.3	10.6	1.8
Livermore	109	D	D	D	431	3 325 675	14.6	36.7	0.0	16.4	4.9	18.3	6.5
Lodi	100	559	54.0	15.2	481	2 698 469	10.3	27.2	16.3	7.0	1.8	29.2	2.7
Lompoc	37	D	D	D	391	1 833 592	11.8	26.5	9.3	5.4	0.4	32.9	2.7
Long Beach	514	3 723	492.5	110.7	5 861	36 050 392	7.5	28.9	14.8	19.5	6.1	12.6	1.4
Los Altos	51	D	D	D	127	885 014	8.2	40.0	0.0	11.6	3.4	17.8	0.0
Los Angeles	5 383	33 721	2 988.4	814.2	47 505	361 983 103	11.8	27.5	11.6	12.8	4.2	30.5	1.2
Los Banos	22	100	7.8	2.4	285	749 390	11.4	40.2	15.6	5.1	2.2	19.0	0.0
Los Gatos	88	419	37.6	11.5	148	1 210 153	16.6	44.9	0.0	10.6	7.2	6.5	7.5
Lynwood	52	296	21.9	5.7	230	916 329	42.8	2.5	0.0	20.8	5.6	28.3	0.0
Madera	43	202	19.6	4.9	274	1 196 996	16.2	35.6	0.0	9.9	12.2	22.5	0.0
Manhattan Beach	76	594	37.8	12.1	381	1 720 027	11.4	41.4	12.9	4.7	9.6	15.5	0.0
Manteca	76	307	28.1	6.9	345	2 165 170	13.0	35.1	16.6	6.2	1.2	25.5	0.0
Martinez	41	166	22.5	5.1	52	324 363	4.1	88.0	0.0	0.0	4.6	1.4	0.0
Maywood	27	98	6.0	1.9	18	66 828	51.7	0.0	0.0	0.0	5.9	31.7	0.0
Menifee	43	233	27.6	5.1	23	165 702	68.9	0.0	0.0	10.5	13.6	0.0	0.0

1. Establishments subject to federal tax.

Table D. Cities — **City Government Finances**

	City government finances, 2012									
	General revenue							General expenditure		
		Intergovernmental			Taxes				Per capita[1] (dollars)	
						Per capita[1] (dollars)					
City	Total (mil dol)	Total (mil dol)	Percent from state government	Total (mil dol)	Total	Property	Sales and gross receipts	Total (mil dol)	Total	Capital outlays
	117	118	119	120	121	122	123	124	125	126

City	117	118	119	120	121	122	123	124	125	126
CALIFORNIA—Cont'd										
Delano....................	32.5	6.6	92.1	16.4	313	163	105	31.3	597	53
Desert Hot Springs........	20.2	3.1	33.2	12.4	446	214	213	27.4	988	219
Diamond Bar	24.3	2.3	77.9	16.9	300	165	128	31.6	561	189
Downey	89.0	11.9	58.4	53.0	468	227	239	98.0	866	54
Dublin	67.1	3.0	97.7	50.4	1 032	529	415	63.3	1 298	122
East Palo Alto	36.0	3.8	90.2	24.9	858	568	285	31.6	1 090	142
El Cajon.....................	103.0	8.1	84.7	70.6	695	308	385	103.4	1 017	157
El Centro	182.9	11.7	52.8	25.2	582	256	318	173.8	4 019	507
Elk Grove	117.6	21.2	77.7	55.8	352	138	210	116.8	737	118
El Monte	92.1	16.0	67.9	64.7	561	290	268	92.7	803	118
El Paso de Robles (Paso Robles)	46.5	6.6	62.1	30.0	983	513	466	43.1	1 414	272
Encinitas.....................	74.3	4.1	60.5	49.4	809	584	217	77.2	1 265	265
Escondido....................	143.3	14.3	60.1	78.5	531	315	209	135.9	919	78
Eureka	46.5	7.0	68.0	27.9	1 036	386	648	49.7	1 845	324
Fairfield......................	135.2	23.7	86.3	87.3	811	437	371	120.8	1 122	219
Folsom........................	106.2	4.7	81.7	61.5	840	482	272	106.9	1 459	214
Fontana	243.1	25.3	66.9	150.7	748	563	182	241.4	1 198	265
Foster City..................	51.6	1.9	100.0	38.7	1 203	920	277	53.2	1 654	65
Fountain Valley	51.8	4.2	91.1	35.6	630	394	227	53.9	954	197
Fremont......................	214.4	29.7	64.9	141.4	637	367	230	244.1	1 100	468
Fresno........................	632.4	127.3	42.9	267.5	529	240	287	528.7	1 045	197
Fullerton	151.4	23.8	80.4	79.9	576	371	202	188.8	1 362	506
Gardena......................	78.5	10.8	48.9	56.0	938	205	564	63.5	1 065	158
Garden Grove	143.3	12.1	44.0	78.1	448	263	183	176.5	1 012	138
Gilroy.........................	73.7	6.7	42.5	38.7	762	281	360	72.6	1 432	389
Glendale......................	315.9	29.1	55.9	145.8	748	379	366	334.4	1 717	239
Glendora.....................	41.0	5.3	97.4	28.1	553	361	190	34.8	685	69
Goleta........................	31.1	4.4	87.8	22.0	727	257	426	33.8	1 118	384
Hanford......................	41.5	3.7	86.5	19.3	355	224	123	40.0	736	127
Hawthorne...................	103.1	37.8	12.8	48.4	564	260	302	99.8	1 163	96
Hayward......................	216.5	39.7	29.1	108.3	724	336	353	190.5	1 273	255
Hemet........................	71.2	3.5	72.5	44.9	552	243	299	68.8	846	126
Hesperia.....................	73.7	15.0	93.8	44.5	483	317	165	101.5	1 103	350
Highland	29.3	5.5	73.6	17.0	315	231	64	34.1	631	199
Hollister	49.1	1.4	100.0	27.1	753	551	186	40.2	1 115	356
Huntington Beach..........	237.1	14.8	87.5	142.7	732	378	348	245.0	1 257	137
Huntington Park	53.9	9.0	53.2	35.6	605	397	207	47.0	799	63
Imperial Beach	31.4	1.9	89.6	17.2	640	488	150	27.2	1 012	70
Indio..........................	79.4	8.3	78.1	47.6	577	315	258	80.9	980	123
Inglewood....................	168.9	42.5	51.9	97.4	874	422	400	161.6	1 451	100
Irvine.........................	221.8	16.6	67.8	150.8	656	245	405	296.0	1 289	255
Laguna Hills	26.8	8.5	93.2	16.2	524	301	209	23.6	764	235
Laguna Niguel..............	38.2	3.2	97.6	31.8	495	300	189	40.3	626	203
La Habra	54.3	8.3	81.6	32.0	521	283	239	52.1	847	84
Lake Elsinore	62.9	4.4	97.8	38.1	682	451	180	70.3	1 261	194
Lake Forest	48.6	4.3	66.7	38.8	491	253	234	69.4	879	338
Lakewood	58.5	5.6	92.9	38.4	474	248	223	55.1	680	68
La Mesa	60.0	3.3	82.3	42.5	729	333	392	58.2	999	181
La Mirada	53.4	5.0	48.8	36.5	744	494	247	62.4	1 271	395
Lancaster.....................	155.7	14.4	70.0	98.7	621	395	225	158.8	999	170
La Puente....................	17.0	3.2	83.5	10.1	251	139	110	16.8	417	64
La Quinta	92.3	4.4	99.5	69.5	1 801	1 413	377	79.1	2 049	214
La Verne......................	36.0	1.3	97.5	23.8	756	457	290	35.3	1 123	55
Lawndale.....................	21.9	4.6	43.6	15.6	470	264	205	22.6	682	195
Lemon Grove	23.6	3.5	40.3	12.9	495	317	176	23.1	888	142
Lincoln	39.4	1.9	82.7	16.0	363	218	137	39.2	887	142
Livermore	144.6	12.8	81.4	70.9	848	452	391	146.1	1 746	314
Lodi...........................	74.4	14.8	61.1	37.4	591	232	358	65.7	1 040	203
Lompoc.......................	49.0	7.6	70.8	20.7	479	244	198	57.4	1 329	168
Long Beach..................	1 850.9	195.5	44.1	411.4	877	543	331	1 760.6	3 753	846
Los Altos	38.7	1.3	98.4	24.5	820	464	333	41.7	1 397	179
Los Angeles	9 274.5	847.5	41.5	3 849.3	997	441	528	8 678.1	2 247	524
Los Banos	30.8	1.2	94.3	16.0	437	268	87	30.9	844	146
Los Gatos	39.5	1.7	100.0	30.5	1 010	550	425	44.6	1 477	382
Lynwood......................	48.4	7.5	65.9	33.0	465	265	191	48.6	685	116
Madera.......................	61.9	6.4	52.4	35.7	571	205	290	58.8	939	220
Manhattan Beach..........	64.9	2.0	100.0	40.2	1 132	649	468	68.9	1 939	189
Manteca......................	96.8	11.6	80.0	40.6	571	382	177	94.8	1 335	419
Martinez......................	24.4	2.4	100.0	18.2	493	310	179	24.1	653	42
Maywood.....................	11.1	1.5	55.8	8.9	321	203	117	10.0	361	22
Menifee.......................	33.2	8.6	100.0	19.8	243	138	102	27.8	341	43

1. Based on population estimated as of July 1 of the year shown.

City	Public welfare	Highways	Parking facilities	Education	Health and hospitals	Police protection	Sewerage and sanitation	Parks and recreation	Housing and community development	Interest on debt
				City government finances, 2012 (cont.)						
				General expenditure (cont.)						
				Percent of total for:						
	127	128	129	130	131	132	133	134	135	136
CALIFORNIA—Cont'd										
Delano	0.0	7.9	0.1	0.0	0.7	35.9	16.1	5.8	6.3	4.8
Desert Hot Springs	0.0	19.3	0.0	0.0	1.2	32.8	0.0	2.7	15.7	5.8
Diamond Bar	0.0	11.3	0.0	0.0	0.4	17.3	1.0	17.5	2.2	2.7
Downey	0.0	10.4	0.0	0.0	3.3	29.8	2.0	12.8	8.4	2.2
Dublin	0.0	9.9	0.0	0.0	0.9	23.6	5.1	13.7	4.2	0.4
East Palo Alto	0.0	15.7	0.0	0.0	0.0	32.7	8.2	3.9	9.5	7.2
El Cajon	0.0	7.2	0.0	0.0	4.9	29.0	15.2	4.3	14.7	2.9
El Centro	0.0	3.7	0.0	0.0	71.3	5.1	5.8	1.4	1.4	2.7
Elk Grove	0.0	20.1	0.0	0.0	0.7	26.4	11.1	0.6	15.2	3.0
El Monte	0.0	8.9	0.1	0.0	0.1	24.2	0.0	3.9	14.8	4.7
El Paso de Robles (Paso Robles)	0.0	14.0	0.0	0.0	0.0	18.5	11.1	8.4	4.2	5.6
Encinitas	0.0	11.1	0.0	0.0	1.4	14.8	5.7	11.7	3.2	0.4
Escondido	0.0	9.0	0.0	0.0	1.1	26.8	15.4	5.9	4.7	6.9
Eureka	0.0	7.4	0.3	0.0	0.2	21.6	17.7	5.2	11.4	6.1
Fairfield	0.0	22.4	0.0	0.0	0.9	26.9	0.0	8.9	8.3	6.3
Folsom	0.0	7.4	0.0	0.0	0.6	18.0	10.0	10.4	7.7	6.6
Fontana	0.0	16.0	0.0	0.0	0.0	21.8	4.9	5.1	16.6	14.1
Foster City	0.0	4.8	0.0	0.0	0.0	17.3	12.1	18.0	5.0	0.0
Fountain Valley	0.0	16.9	0.0	0.0	5.8	26.6	8.8	7.4	11.0	1.2
Fremont	0.1	18.2	0.0	0.0	4.6	27.3	2.1	6.1	8.7	3.7
Fresno	0.0	9.2	0.9	0.0	1.8	27.9	21.5	4.8	2.7	8.1
Fullerton	0.0	19.9	0.0	0.0	3.1	19.1	8.1	6.3	16.0	3.9
Gardena	0.0	12.4	0.0	0.0	3.2	33.0	1.6	5.6	7.1	2.4
Garden Grove	0.0	9.7	0.0	0.0	3.7	26.6	4.0	4.9	25.2	3.8
Gilroy	0.0	3.9	0.0	0.0	0.1	23.5	11.0	1.2	31.3	2.7
Glendale	0.0	6.5	1.9	0.0	0.2	20.8	9.9	5.1	16.0	1.2
Glendora	0.0	7.3	0.0	0.0	0.3	38.7	0.0	9.5	14.0	4.6
Goleta	0.0	35.2	0.0	0.0	1.4	19.9	0.0	7.5	6.3	2.1
Hanford	0.0	14.3	0.0	0.0	1.1	20.5	28.6	8.9	2.1	3.4
Hawthorne	0.0	13.4	0.0	0.0	0.0	30.2	0.7	1.5	12.0	4.8
Hayward	0.0	22.7	0.0	0.0	1.1	29.9	8.1	0.9	3.9	2.6
Hemet	0.0	13.6	0.0	0.0	0.3	23.8	21.6	1.1	10.9	0.9
Hesperia	0.0	18.2	0.0	0.0	1.8	12.4	0.0	0.0	33.4	8.9
Highland	0.0	33.6	0.0	0.0	3.7	20.5	0.0	3.0	9.1	8.3
Hollister	0.0	9.2	0.0	0.0	1.5	15.8	30.4	3.1	12.4	4.5
Huntington Beach	0.0	12.4	1.3	0.0	1.9	28.9	8.3	6.7	4.8	2.2
Huntington Park	0.0	8.1	1.2	0.0	5.3	33.4	0.8	4.2	12.8	4.9
Imperial Beach	0.0	9.3	0.0	0.0	0.7	26.9	16.9	5.6	13.1	5.9
Indio	0.0	11.9	0.0	0.0	5.2	25.3	0.2	5.0	15.5	8.5
Inglewood	0.0	9.8	0.2	0.0	1.6	19.3	8.5	5.2	14.3	7.4
Irvine	0.0	25.6	0.0	0.0	1.6	18.7	0.0	21.6	1.9	12.6
Laguna Hills	0.0	25.2	0.0	0.0	0.3	27.3	0.0	23.3	0.3	2.6
Laguna Niguel	0.0	23.9	0.0	0.0	0.8	23.4	0.0	17.7	0.2	0.0
La Habra	0.0	8.8	0.0	0.0	1.8	30.7	10.8	10.5	12.4	2.9
Lake Elsinore	0.0	5.0	0.0	0.0	0.7	12.7	0.0	16.1	15.7	24.3
Lake Forest	0.0	38.6	0.0	0.0	0.2	18.1	0.0	16.3	6.7	0.7
Lakewood	0.0	18.5	0.0	0.0	0.5	20.7	12.1	21.5	3.7	3.9
La Mesa	0.0	19.6	0.3	0.0	0.9	25.3	16.9	6.5	1.6	2.5
La Mirada	0.0	37.1	0.0	0.0	0.1	12.1	0.0	18.7	14.6	3.8
Lancaster	0.0	12.1	0.0	0.0	0.4	17.3	0.0	6.5	26.8	11.9
La Puente	0.0	11.0	0.0	0.0	1.7	27.8	3.9	17.2	8.0	4.3
La Quinta	0.0	10.7	0.0	0.0	0.5	15.3	0.0	8.3	24.6	17.5
La Verne	0.0	8.7	0.0	0.0	5.5	33.7	3.3	6.8	15.6	2.9
Lawndale	0.0	12.3	0.0	0.0	0.6	20.2	0.2	10.8	29.6	4.8
Lemon Grove	0.0	4.3	0.0	0.0	0.7	19.3	17.8	3.7	15.4	4.9
Lincoln	0.0	14.1	0.0	0.0	0.0	13.0	24.9	4.2	2.1	3.8
Livermore	0.0	17.3	0.0	0.0	0.4	17.7	12.7	1.7	2.3	2.6
Lodi	0.0	12.3	0.0	0.0	0.6	24.8	16.8	7.4	2.4	0.1
Lompoc	0.0	9.5	0.0	0.0	0.6	34.0	20.4	5.7	8.5	1.8
Long Beach	0.0	3.4	0.0	0.0	3.0	11.4	5.2	7.6	7.6	4.6
Los Altos	0.0	14.1	0.0	0.0	0.8	22.9	12.7	6.1	2.6	0.2
Los Angeles	0.0	8.1	0.4	0.0	2.6	19.6	8.6	4.5	4.2	6.1
Los Banos	0.0	9.9	0.0	0.0	0.3	24.6	26.0	13.3	5.1	2.8
Los Gatos	0.0	12.1	0.0	0.0	0.3	26.6	0.3	7.1	9.0	2.5
Lynwood	0.0	22.5	0.0	0.0	1.0	16.7	1.5	5.8	13.5	1.6
Madera	0.0	25.5	0.1	0.0	1.7	16.8	19.2	6.0	4.6	5.3
Manhattan Beach	0.0	10.0	4.3	0.0	4.5	30.5	9.0	13.7	0.0	1.3
Manteca	0.0	16.3	0.0	0.0	0.3	15.0	25.2	6.9	13.6	4.5
Martinez	0.0	10.7	1.3	0.0	0.0	41.2	0.0	13.9	0.1	3.6
Maywood	0.0	11.2	0.0	0.0	0.0	39.4	0.0	6.2	4.2	10.1
Menifee	0.0	9.1	0.0	0.0	1.3	31.9	0.0	0.0	6.7	0.3

City	City government finances, 2012 (cont.)			Climate[2]						
	Debt outstanding			Average daily temperature (degrees Fahrenheit)						
				Mean		Limits				
	Total (mil dol)	Per capita[1] (dollars)	Debt issued during year	January	July	January[3]	July[4]	Annual precipitation (inches)	Heating degree days	Cooling degree days
	137	138	139	140	141	142	143	144	145	146
CALIFORNIA—Cont'd										
Delano	62.8	1 196	0.0	46.6	81.1	36.5	99.0	7.34	2 434	1 990
Desert Hot Springs	12.2	440	6.2	NA	NA	NA	NA	NA	NA	NA
Diamond Bar	0.0	0	12.0	54.6	73.8	41.5	88.7	16.96	1 727	1 191
Downey	63.1	558	1.5	57.0	73.8	46.0	82.9	12.94	1 211	1 186
Dublin	6.2	127	0.0	47.2	72.0	37.4	89.1	14.82	2 755	858
East Palo Alto	47.6	1 643	0.0	49.0	68.0	40.4	78.8	15.71	2 584	452
El Cajon	68.2	671	0.1	54.9	74.7	41.6	87.0	11.96	1 560	1 371
El Centro	100.3	2 320	0.0	55.8	91.4	41.3	107.0	2.96	1 080	3 852
Elk Grove	95.6	603	0.0	46.3	75.4	38.8	92.4	17.93	2 666	1 248
El Monte	168.9	1 465	13.3	56.3	75.6	42.6	89.0	18.56	1 295	1 575
El Paso de Robles (Paso Robles)	54.4	1 784	6.4	NA	NA	NA	NA	NA	NA	NA
Encinitas	40.7	667	0.0	55.5	75.1	42.5	88.6	15.10	1 464	1 436
Escondido	191.9	1 298	11.4	55.5	75.1	42.5	88.6	15.10	1 464	1 436
Eureka	109.2	4 052	9.4	47.9	58.1	40.8	63.3	38.10	4 430	7
Fairfield	271.5	2 523	10.5	46.1	72.6	37.5	88.8	23.46	2 649	975
Folsom	237.5	3 241	15.0	46.9	77.7	39.2	94.8	24.61	2 532	1 528
Fontana	677.9	3 364	0.8	56.6	78.3	45.3	95.0	14.77	1 364	1 901
Foster City	0.0	0	0.0	48.4	68.0	39.1	80.8	20.16	2 764	422
Fountain Valley	9.7	171	0.0	58.0	72.9	46.6	87.7	13.84	1 153	1 299
Fremont	313.6	1 414	53.3	49.8	78.3	42.0	78.3	14.85	2 367	530
Fresno	1 062.2	2 099	0.0	46.0	81.4	38.4	96.6	11.23	2 447	1 963
Fullerton	195.2	1 408	0.0	56.9	73.2	45.2	84.0	11.23	1 286	1 294
Gardena	24.8	415	0.0	56.3	69.4	46.2	77.6	14.79	1 526	742
Garden Grove	179.2	1 028	6.7	58.0	72.9	46.6	87.7	13.84	1 153	1 299
Gilroy	54.9	1 083	0.0	49.7	72.0	39.4	88.3	20.60	2 278	913
Glendale	322.6	1 656	38.3	54.8	75.5	42.0	88.9	17.49	1 575	1 455
Glendora	46.8	921	0.0	54.6	73.8	41.5	88.7	16.96	1 727	1 191
Goleta	15.7	518	0.0	53.1	67.0	40.8	76.7	16.93	2 121	482
Hanford	43.0	792	0.0	44.7	79.6	35.7	95.9	8.58	2 749	1 724
Hawthorne	104.9	1 223	0.0	57.1	69.3	48.6	75.3	13.15	1 274	679
Hayward	196.8	1 315	0.0	49.7	64.6	41.7	75.2	26.30	2 810	261
Hemet	13.7	168	0.0	52.4	79.9	38.4	97.8	12.55	1 914	1 903
Hesperia	168.7	1 834	0.0	45.5	80.0	31.4	99.1	6.20	2 929	1 735
Highland	73.8	1 364	0.0	54.4	79.6	41.8	96.0	16.43	1 599	1 937
Hollister	43.7	1 213	0.0	49.5	66.6	37.8	80.9	13.61	2 724	405
Huntington Beach	257.9	1 323	36.3	55.9	67.3	48.2	71.4	11.65	1 719	543
Huntington Park	42.4	720	0.0	58.3	74.2	48.5	83.8	15.14	928	1 506
Imperial Beach	40.1	1 493	0.0	57.3	70.1	46.1	76.1	9.95	1 321	862
Indio	184.2	2 232	0.0	56.8	92.8	42.0	107.1	3.15	903	4 388
Inglewood	277.3	2 489	30.8	57.1	69.3	48.6	75.3	13.15	1 274	679
Irvine	1 400.1	6 096	270.1	54.5	72.1	41.4	83.8	13.87	1 794	1 102
Laguna Hills	15.6	507	0.0	56.7	72.4	47.2	82.3	14.03	1 465	1 183
Laguna Niguel	0.0	0	0.0	55.4	68.7	43.9	77.3	13.56	1 756	666
La Habra	55.8	908	0.0	56.9	73.2	45.2	84.0	11.23	1 286	1 294
Lake Elsinore	410.2	7 355	1.5	52.2	79.6	38.3	98.1	12.09	1 924	1 874
Lake Forest	18.8	238	11.0	56.7	72.4	47.2	82.3	14.03	1 465	1 183
Lakewood	42.5	525	0.0	57.0	73.8	46.0	82.9	12.94	1 211	1 186
La Mesa	46.3	795	0.9	57.1	73.0	45.7	83.6	13.75	1 313	1 261
La Mirada	92.9	1 893	1.9	58.8	76.6	47.9	88.9	14.44	949	1 837
Lancaster	431.7	2 716	0.0	43.9	80.8	31.0	95.5	7.40	3 241	1 733
La Puente	9.5	236	0.0	58.8	76.6	47.9	88.9	14.44	949	1 837
La Quinta	324.4	8 401	0.0	NA	NA	NA	NA	NA	NA	NA
La Verne	19.4	618	0.0	54.6	73.8	41.5	88.7	16.96	1 727	1 191
Lawndale	21.1	635	0.0	57.1	69.3	48.6	75.3	13.15	1 274	679
Lemon Grove	26.5	1 021	0.0	NA	NA	NA	NA	NA	NA	NA
Lincoln	35.5	801	0.0	NA	NA	NA	NA	NA	NA	NA
Livermore	175.1	2 093	0.0	47.2	72.0	37.4	89.1	14.82	2 755	858
Lodi	0.2	4	0.0	46.1	73.8	37.5	91.1	18.22	2 710	1 057
Lompoc	54.1	1 253	0.0	53.7	64.5	41.4	75.4	15.85	2 250	322
Long Beach	2 390.0	5 095	112.4	57.0	73.8	46.0	82.9	12.94	1 211	1 186
Los Altos	1.9	62	0.0	49.0	68.0	40.4	78.8	15.71	2 584	452
Los Angeles	23 104.2	5 983	2 268.6	58.3	74.2	48.5	83.8	15.14	928	1 506
Los Banos	28.4	774	0.0	45.9	78.1	36.8	94.6	9.95	2 570	1 547
Los Gatos	23.8	789	0.0	48.7	70.3	38.8	85.4	22.64	2 641	613
Lynwood	30.0	423	0.0	58.3	74.2	48.5	83.8	15.14	928	1 506
Madera	114.1	1 823	0.0	45.7	79.6	37.2	96.5	11.94	2 670	1 706
Manhattan Beach	37.6	1 058	0.0	57.1	69.3	48.6	75.3	13.15	1 274	679
Manteca	214.3	3 017	1.7	46.0	77.3	38.1	93.8	13.84	2 563	1 456
Martinez	29.2	790	18.7	46.3	71.2	38.8	87.4	19.58	2 757	786
Maywood	0.0	0	0.0	58.3	74.2	48.5	83.8	15.14	928	1 506
Menifee	20.0	246	20.0	NA	NA	NA	NA	NA	NA	NA

1. Based on the population estimated as of July 1 of the year shown.   2. Represents normal values based on the 30-year period, 1971–2000.   3. Average daily minimum.
4. Average daily maximum.

STATE Place code	City	Land area,[1] 2010 (sq km)	Population, 2015				Race alone or in combination (percent), 2010-2014					Percent Hispanic or Latino[2], 2010-2014	Percent foreign born 2010–2014
			Total persons	Rank	Per square kilometer	White	Black	American Indian, Alaska Native	Asian	Hawaiian Pacific Islander			
		1	2	3	4	5	6	7	8	9		10	11
	CALIFORNIA—Cont'd												
06 46870	Menlo Park	25.4	33 449	1 125	1 316.9	76.6	6.0	0.6	13.7	2.1		15.9	23.6
06 46898	Merced	60.4	82 436	402	1 364.8	60.5	6.7	2.0	13.9	0.3		48.8	21.4
06 47766	Milpitas	35.2	77 604	436	2 204.7	23.6	3.5	1.1	66.3	1.7		16.6	50.7
06 48256	Mission Viejo	45.9	97 156	311	2 116.7	85.3	2.2	0.8	11.2	0.5		16.0	19.3
06 48354	Modesto	95.5	211 266	103	2 212.2	76.4	5.4	2.6	9.2	1.5		37.2	17.5
06 48648	Monrovia	35.2	37 463	1 007	1 064.3	63.0	7.6	1.1	15.7	0.7		38.8	25.1
06 48788	Montclair	14.3	38 690	968	2 705.6	44.2	4.9	1.4	10.7	1.2		68.5	34.5
06 48816	Montebello	21.6	63 921	562	2 959.3	68.6	1.6	1.4	13.6	0.2		76.1	36.8
06 48872	Monterey	21.9	28 338	1 300	1 294.0	83.9	4.3	1.3	10.2	0.4		17.0	18.8
06 48914	Monterey Park	19.9	61 468	588	3 088.8	20.6	0.7	0.9	64.6	0.9		30.7	53.8
06 49138	Moorpark	32.6	36 104	1 045	1 107.5	80.7	1.4	0.8	8.4	0.6		29.8	17.4
06 49270	Moreno Valley	132.8	204 198	109	1 537.6	56.5	19.5	1.4	7.0	0.8		55.5	24.5
06 49278	Morgan Hill	33.4	42 948	869	1 285.9	72.1	3.6	1.3	14.8	0.8		33.0	19.5
06 49670	Mountain View	31.1	80 435	414	2 586.3	64.9	2.8	0.9	30.5	0.7		20.9	37.2
06 50076	Murrieta	87.0	109 830	263	1 262.4	73.0	9.7	2.0	12.0	1.4		26.6	13.4
06 50258	Napa	46.2	80 434	415	1 741.0	85.4	1.2	1.6	3.2	0.5		38.9	23.4
06 50398	National City	18.9	61 060	592	3 230.7	60.6	6.4	1.0	19.9	0.6		65.1	40.7
06 50916	Newark	35.9	45 336	829	1 262.8	44.3	5.2	1.4	32.9	2.0		33.1	34.6
06 51182	Newport Beach	61.7	87 127	372	1 412.1	88.7	0.9	1.0	9.1	0.4		8.2	13.6
06 51560	Norco	36.2	26 289	1 387	726.2	78.1	7.3	3.1	5.8	0.6		29.9	13.1
06 52526	Norwalk	25.1	107 140	277	4 268.5	56.0	4.9	1.7	13.8	0.3		70.3	35.2
06 52582	Novato	71.1	55 530	672	781.0	82.2	3.8	1.2	7.4	0.2		19.6	19.3
06 53000	Oakland	144.5	419 267	45	2 901.5	44.1	29.0	2.2	18.9	1.0		25.9	27.1
06 53070	Oakley	41.1	39 813	941	968.7	72.4	9.3	4.0	10.9	0.8		36.9	17.3
06 53322	Oceanside	106.8	175 691	139	1 645.0	73.1	6.7	1.7	9.0	1.9		35.8	20.0
06 53896	Ontario	129.4	171 214	147	1 323.1	60.2	7.3	2.1	6.0	0.5		70.2	30.2
06 53980	Orange	64.2	140 992	184	2 196.1	68.0	1.9	1.2	13.6	0.4		39.4	25.7
06 54652	Oxnard	69.7	207 254	108	2 973.5	77.5	3.6	2.0	9.0	0.5		74.4	36.9
06 54806	Pacifica	32.8	39 260	958	1 197.0	71.0	4.7	1.4	24.7	1.7		17.7	20.0
06 55156	Palmdale	274.4	158 351	159	577.1	45.7	15.5	1.8	5.7	0.3		56.6	25.8
06 55184	Palm Desert	69.4	51 869	727	747.4	86.0	1.7	1.1	7.1	1.2		24.9	18.8
06 55254	Palm Springs	243.8	47 371	801	194.3	82.0	5.9	1.8	5.9	0.5		26.2	21.5
06 55282	Palo Alto	61.9	66 853	530	1 080.4	66.3	2.1	0.4	33.0	0.3		7.8	32.2
06 55520	Paradise	47.4	26 476	1 381	558.6	96.6	1.1	2.7	2.5	0.9		6.7	3.9
06 55618	Paramount	12.3	55 412	677	4 505.0	45.0	10.9	1.3	3.5	1.1		79.9	37.6
06 56000	Pasadena	59.5	142 250	183	2 390.8	65.2	12.3	0.9	16.9	0.3		33.6	30.5
06 56700	Perris	81.3	74 971	456	922.2	42.1	11.7	1.3	4.2	0.2		73.7	27.9
06 56784	Petaluma	37.3	60 438	605	1 620.3	83.2	1.5	1.5	6.2	0.4		23.4	18.2
06 56924	Pico Rivera	21.5	64 218	558	2 986.9	51.7	1.4	1.2	3.4	0.2		90.9	32.9
06 57456	Pittsburg	44.6	69 424	501	1 556.6	40.4	21.0	2.1	19.3	2.9		40.2	31.6
06 57526	Placentia	17.0	52 495	714	3 087.9	77.7	2.1	0.8	18.0	0.4		37.7	25.8
06 57764	Pleasant Hill	18.3	34 810	1 078	1 902.2	81.7	2.7	1.2	16.9	0.8		14.3	19.0
06 57792	Pleasanton	62.5	79 510	425	1 272.2	69.0	3.2	0.4	29.1	0.4		11.0	25.1
06 58072	Pomona	59.4	153 266	167	2 580.2	65.4	8.2	1.5	10.2	0.4		69.4	34.2
06 58240	Porterville	45.6	56 058	661	1 229.3	82.9	1.4	2.9	6.7	0.3		64.6	20.9
06 58520	Poway	101.2	50 157	750	495.6	82.9	2.8	2.0	16.0	0.3		16.3	16.0
06 59444	Rancho Cordova	86.8	71 017	494	818.2	68.3	13.2	2.2	14.3	2.3		20.1	24.3
06 59451	Rancho Cucamonga	103.2	175 236	141	1 698.0	69.6	10.7	1.7	14.7	0.7		36.1	20.5
06 59514	Rancho Palos Verdes	34.9	42 732	875	1 224.4	66.0	3.8	1.2	31.4	0.6		7.8	26.5
06 59587	Rancho Santa Margarita	33.6	49 324	765	1 468.0	82.5	1.8	0.6	12.7	0.6		18.7	17.4
06 59920	Redding	154.5	91 582	345	592.8	89.9	2.3	4.4	5.1	0.3		8.6	5.2
06 59962	Redlands	93.6	71 035	492	758.9	77.5	6.6	1.1	9.2	0.9		30.0	13.9
06 60018	Redondo Beach	16.1	68 166	513	4 233.9	78.4	4.1	1.2	16.3	0.6		17.9	18.4
06 60102	Redwood City	50.3	85 288	383	1 695.6	73.0	2.8	1.2	14.1	1.0		40.5	31.9
06 60466	Rialto	57.9	103 132	292	1 781.2	63.4	16.4	1.5	3.0	0.5		71.6	27.2
06 60620	Richmond	77.9	109 708	265	1 408.3	46.0	26.5	2.0	16.1	1.2		40.6	32.4
06 60704	Ridgecrest	53.8	28 780	1 286	534.9	81.0	6.4	2.0	8.2	1.8		14.9	10.2
06 62000	Riverside	210.2	322 424	59	1 533.9	70.8	7.8	2.4	8.5	0.6		51.5	22.9
06 62364	Rocklin	50.6	61 213	589	1 209.7	85.9	3.0	2.1	12.0	0.9		12.2	10.1
06 62546	Rohnert Park	18.1	42 407	881	2 342.9	81.2	3.2	3.1	8.3	1.4		24.7	15.3
06 62896	Rosemead	13.4	54 908	682	4 097.6	23.7	0.3	0.7	62.3	0.8		32.2	57.0
06 62938	Roseville	93.8	130 269	205	1 388.8	84.2	2.3	1.6	11.8	0.7		14.2	12.5
06 64000	Sacramento	253.6	490 712	35	1 935.0	55.4	16.4	2.5	21.5	2.3		27.6	22.1
06 64224	Salinas	60.0	157 380	161	2 623.0	76.7	2.0	1.3	8.3	0.4		75.4	37.2
06 65000	San Bernardino	153.3	216 108	100	1 409.7	58.5	16.2	2.6	5.8	0.6		61.2	23.0
06 65028	San Bruno	14.2	43 185	865	3 041.2	56.8	3.8	2.7	29.0	3.7		30.0	36.0
06 65042	San Buenaventura (Ventura)	56.1	109 708	265	1 955.6	84.9	2.5	1.9	4.9	0.5		32.7	14.5
06 65070	San Carlos	14.3	29 931	1 247	2 093.1	83.6	2.2	0.8	14.9	0.9		10.7	18.8
06 65084	San Clemente	48.5	65 526	543	1 351.1	85.8	1.2	1.3	5.8	1.4		19.3	11.2
06 66000	San Diego	842.2	1 394 928	8	1 656.3	68.2	8.0	1.6	19.0	0.8		29.5	26.3
06 66070	San Dimas	39.0	34 630	1 084	887.9	72.2	5.4	1.6	16.2	0.8		30.0	19.9

1. Dry land or land partially or temporarily covered by water. 2. May be of any race.

Table D. Cities — **Population**

City	Age of population (percent), 2010-2014									Median age 2010–2014	Percent female 2010–2014	Population Census counts		Percent change	
	Under 5 years	5 to 17 years	18 to 24 years	25 to 34 years	35 to 44 years	45 to 54 years	55 to 64 years	65 to 74 years	75 years and over			2000	2010	2000–2010	2010–2015
	12	13	14	15	16	17	18	19	20	21	22	23	24	25	26
CALIFORNIA—Cont'd															
Menlo Park	6.8	18.0	6.2	14.3	15.3	14.5	11.4	7.5	6.0	38.3	52.5	30 785	32 026	4.0	4.4
Merced	9.5	21.9	12.5	14.8	12.3	10.5	9.2	5.4	3.9	28.7	51.0	63 893	78 958	23.6	4.4
Milpitas	6.3	14.8	8.4	16.6	15.7	16.1	11.6	6.4	4.1	37.0	49.1	62 698	66 790	6.5	16.1
Mission Viejo	5.0	16.2	9.3	9.3	12.2	17.1	14.9	8.4	7.5	43.7	51.0	93 102	93 305	0.2	4.3
Modesto	7.4	18.6	11.2	14.1	11.8	13.8	11.2	6.5	5.4	33.9	51.6	188 856	201 165	6.5	4.0
Monrovia	8.6	14.4	7.8	16.3	13.5	15.5	12.1	7.2	4.6	37.3	50.9	36 929	36 590	-0.9	2.4
Montclair	6.9	19.8	13.1	13.2	13.7	14.6	9.5	5.4	3.9	32.3	48.3	33 049	36 664	10.9	5.5
Montebello	7.0	15.6	10.3	14.7	13.1	12.4	11.7	7.7	7.5	36.9	50.9	62 150	62 500	0.6	2.3
Monterey	5.6	11.7	9.7	19.1	12.9	11.3	11.9	8.5	9.3	37.8	49.5	29 674	27 810	-6.3	3.7
Monterey Park	4.9	12.8	9.4	13.4	12.7	15.1	13.3	8.3	10.1	42.5	51.0	60 051	60 269	0.4	2.0
Moorpark	5.8	20.6	9.6	11.6	13.5	18.2	11.7	5.9	3.0	37.5	50.9	31 415	34 421	9.6	4.9
Moreno Valley	7.6	22.3	12.5	14.8	13.3	12.1	10.1	4.4	2.9	29.4	51.5	142 381	193 365	35.8	5.6
Morgan Hill	6.9	18.9	8.5	11.2	14.8	17.0	12.3	6.2	4.3	38.4	52.9	33 556	37 882	12.9	13.4
Mountain View	6.7	14.1	7.0	20.4	17.0	13.5	10.5	6.0	4.8	35.8	48.1	70 708	74 066	4.7	8.7
Murrieta	7.0	22.0	9.5	13.1	14.0	13.8	10.0	5.6	5.0	33.6	52.3	44 282	103 466	133.7	6.2
Napa	6.8	17.3	8.8	14.9	12.1	13.7	12.5	7.3	6.5	36.8	50.6	72 585	76 915	6.0	4.5
National City	6.1	17.9	15.4	14.5	14.0	11.8	9.6	5.3	5.5	32.0	49.7	54 260	58 582	8.0	4.2
Newark	5.4	16.4	7.9	14.3	15.8	17.6	11.0	5.8	5.7	39.0	50.1	42 471	42 573	0.2	6.5
Newport Beach	4.0	14.2	7.9	12.7	13.2	14.8	14.3	10.2	8.8	43.9	49.6	70 032	85 186	21.6	2.2
Norco	4.3	16.5	10.3	13.6	13.8	18.1	11.5	6.1	5.7	39.3	43.6	24 157	27 063	12.0	-2.9
Norwalk	7.0	19.4	12.4	13.9	14.2	13.5	9.1	6.1	4.5	32.9	50.5	103 298	105 549	2.2	1.5
Novato	5.8	16.5	5.5	9.5	13.7	17.0	15.6	9.0	7.4	44.1	51.4	47 630	51 904	9.0	7.0
Oakland	6.5	14.5	9.1	17.7	15.5	13.0	12.1	6.5	5.1	36.4	51.4	399 484	390 724	-2.2	7.3
Oakley	6.8	22.0	9.3	13.3	15.1	15.0	10.3	5.0	3.1	34.0	50.1	25 619	35 432	38.3	12.4
Oceanside	6.4	16.1	10.9	14.7	13.7	13.4	11.7	6.9	6.1	36.1	48.8	161 029	167 086	3.8	5.2
Ontario	7.5	20.3	11.8	15.8	14.4	13.2	9.2	4.3	3.6	31.8	51.9	158 007	163 924	3.7	4.4
Orange	6.0	15.4	12.9	14.5	14.8	14.7	10.2	6.4	5.0	35.7	49.9	128 821	136 416	5.9	3.3
Oxnard	8.6	19.7	12.1	16.2	13.5	11.8	9.4	5.0	3.8	30.5	49.1	170 358	197 899	16.2	4.7
Pacifica	4.6	15.5	8.4	11.8	14.5	16.3	15.7	8.0	5.2	41.7	52.4	38 390	37 234	-3.0	5.3
Palmdale	9.1	23.3	11.7	12.4	13.1	14.2	8.6	4.4	3.2	29.0	50.6	116 670	152 750	30.9	3.7
Palm Desert	4.4	12.2	7.7	9.7	9.0	11.2	13.9	14.9	17.0	50.8	53.9	41 155	48 445	17.7	7.1
Palm Springs	3.4	9.7	5.6	9.2	9.9	17.3	18.2	14.0	12.8	52.3	43.3	42 807	44 552	4.1	6.4
Palo Alto	4.8	18.0	6.0	13.1	12.9	15.8	11.8	8.7	9.0	41.6	50.9	58 598	64 403	9.9	3.8
Paradise	3.5	12.0	10.6	8.1	10.1	13.3	17.9	11.3	13.1	49.7	49.6	26 408	26 218	-0.7	1.0
Paramount	7.4	24.2	12.0	13.9	16.2	12.1	7.5	4.7	2.0	29.6	50.5	55 266	54 098	-2.1	2.4
Pasadena	5.4	12.8	10.0	18.6	14.5	13.1	11.3	7.1	7.2	36.8	50.6	133 936	137 122	2.4	3.7
Perris	8.3	27.6	11.9	14.4	13.6	12.0	7.2	3.2	1.9	26.5	51.7	36 189	68 386	89.0	9.6
Petaluma	6.7	18.0	6.4	12.9	12.6	15.7	14.1	8.1	5.6	40.6	52.5	54 548	57 941	6.2	4.3
Pico Rivera	6.6	17.8	10.6	14.1	13.5	13.5	10.7	6.8	6.4	35.9	51.0	63 428	62 942	-0.8	2.0
Pittsburg	7.5	18.3	11.5	15.8	13.8	13.0	10.4	5.5	4.2	33.0	51.7	56 769	63 264	11.4	9.7
Placentia	6.5	17.8	9.7	13.4	14.0	14.1	11.2	7.7	5.6	36.8	50.3	46 488	50 533	8.7	3.1
Pleasant Hill	4.8	13.3	9.9	12.6	13.9	16.3	14.2	7.6	7.3	42.6	53.6	32 837	33 152	1.0	5.1
Pleasanton	5.0	21.1	7.1	8.8	14.5	18.8	12.0	7.7	5.1	41.3	50.1	63 654	70 285	10.4	13.1
Pomona	7.5	19.7	14.2	14.9	13.2	12.5	9.5	4.7	3.8	30.4	50.4	149 473	149 058	-0.3	2.8
Porterville	10.2	22.8	10.7	14.0	12.2	11.1	8.1	6.1	4.8	29.3	50.3	39 615	54 165	36.7	3.5
Poway	6.4	16.6	9.9	10.7	13.4	16.0	13.6	8.1	5.4	40.2	51.0	48 044	47 811	-0.5	4.9
Rancho Cordova	8.5	16.5	8.9	16.4	13.9	13.0	11.2	6.3	5.4	34.9	51.5	55 060	64 776	17.6	9.6
Rancho Cucamonga	6.1	18.5	10.5	14.3	15.4	14.6	11.1	5.5	4.0	35.3	49.9	127 743	165 269	29.4	6.0
Rancho Palos Verdes	3.6	19.0	4.6	6.2	10.4	17.3	14.4	11.5	12.9	49.2	52.0	41 145	41 643	1.2	2.6
Rancho Santa Margarita	5.9	21.0	8.6	12.3	14.7	20.2	10.7	3.8	2.8	36.5	50.1	47 214	47 853	1.4	3.1
Redding	5.9	16.6	11.0	13.3	10.7	12.9	12.4	8.8	8.4	38.0	50.4	80 865	89 861	11.1	1.9
Redlands	6.4	18.1	10.9	12.2	11.7	13.5	13.2	7.5	6.5	36.8	51.9	63 591	68 747	8.1	3.4
Redondo Beach	6.8	14.3	5.0	14.7	18.8	17.9	11.2	6.4	4.7	40.5	52.1	63 261	66 748	5.5	2.1
Redwood City	7.1	16.9	6.6	16.7	15.3	15.0	10.5	7.0	4.9	37.1	49.7	75 402	76 815	1.9	11.0
Rialto	8.9	23.0	12.8	13.4	12.9	12.7	8.5	4.5	3.2	28.4	49.9	91 873	99 171	7.9	4.0
Richmond	7.6	16.7	9.7	16.3	14.5	12.7	11.7	6.6	4.2	34.8	51.2	99 216	103 701	4.5	5.8
Ridgecrest	6.3	22.2	9.1	13.4	11.4	13.0	11.2	7.1	6.2	34.3	49.8	24 927	27 616	10.8	4.2
Riverside	7.0	19.1	15.6	14.0	12.7	13.1	9.0	5.1	4.5	30.8	50.3	255 166	303 871	19.1	6.1
Rocklin	5.8	21.6	8.4	12.7	14.8	14.9	10.9	5.6	5.3	35.9	51.5	36 330	56 974	56.8	7.4
Rohnert Park	5.9	12.2	18.3	15.3	11.9	15.0	11.7	5.0	4.8	33.7	53.8	42 236	40 971	-3.0	3.9
Rosemead	4.9	16.5	8.5	12.5	14.4	16.0	12.9	8.0	6.2	39.9	51.1	53 505	53 764	0.5	2.1
Roseville	6.6	18.9	8.4	13.3	13.6	14.4	11.3	6.9	6.6	37.5	52.8	79 921	118 788	48.6	9.8
Sacramento	7.1	16.9	11.0	16.5	13.1	12.6	11.3	6.1	5.3	34.0	51.4	407 018	466 488	14.6	5.2
Salinas	9.4	21.9	11.2	16.8	14.0	11.1	8.2	4.1	3.3	29.4	48.9	151 060	150 441	-0.4	4.6
San Bernardino	8.3	22.3	12.9	15.1	11.6	12.1	9.5	4.8	3.3	29.1	50.4	185 401	209 924	13.2	2.9
San Bruno	6.4	14.0	8.0	18.3	12.6	16.5	12.0	6.1	6.1	37.0	49.8	40 165	41 114	2.4	5.2
San Buenaventura (Ventura)	5.7	15.2	9.3	13.1	13.4	15.2	13.3	7.5	7.3	40.3	50.6	100 916	106 433	5.5	2.3
San Carlos	6.2	17.3	4.8	9.5	15.6	17.8	13.7	7.8	7.3	43.1	51.6	27 718	28 406	2.5	5.4
San Clemente	6.5	19.3	6.9	10.0	15.1	14.8	13.0	8.6	5.7	40.1	50.9	49 936	63 522	27.2	3.2
San Diego	6.4	15.1	12.6	17.9	13.5	13.0	10.3	6.2	5.1	33.6	49.6	1 223 400	1 307 402	6.9	7.2
San Dimas	4.7	15.0	10.7	12.4	11.3	16.0	14.3	8.7	6.9	41.3	51.9	34 980	33 371	-4.6	3.8

City	Households, 2010-2014				Persons in group quarters, 2010				Serious crimes known to police,[2] 2014				Educational attainment, 2010-2014		
	Number	Persons per house-hold	Female family house-holder[1]	One-person	Total	Total	Persons in nursing facilities	Non-institu-tional	Number	Rate[3]	Violent	Property	Population age 25 and older	High school graduate or less	Bachelor's degree or more
	27	28	29	30	31	32	33	34	35	36	37	38	39	40	41
CALIFORNIA—Cont'd															
Menlo Park	12 397	2.65	6.8	28.3	845	246	236	599	617	1 852	156	1 696	22 985	14.7	70.9
Merced	24 950	3.23	21.0	22.2	1 080	588	343	492	3 202	3 924	699	3 225	44 906	48.3	16.5
Milpitas	19 973	3.47	10.6	15.9	2 698	2 594	34	104	2 243	3 178	159	3 020	48 870	32.4	41.4
Mission Viejo	33 640	2.83	7.8	19.5	942	83	66	859	935	963	73	890	66 851	21.7	45.6
Modesto	70 310	2.93	16.8	24.1	2 955	1 766	1 169	1 189	10 891	5 292	864	4 428	130 823	46.6	18.4
Monrovia	13 032	2.84	11.3	24.9	156	95	76	61	765	2 055	126	1 929	25 471	31.8	36.4
Montclair	10 336	3.65	19.9	18.1	396	181	181	215	1 716	4 475	548	3 927	23 263	60.9	12.5
Montebello	19 674	3.22	21.7	22.6	400	361	350	39	1 583	2 484	210	2 273	42 476	58.1	17.6
Monterey	12 527	2.24	6.1	38.0	2 503	293	293	2 210	1 137	3 988	403	3 584	20 468	21.5	46.9
Monterey Park	18 875	3.23	18.3	16.5	230	189	186	41	1 130	1 844	148	1 695	44 793	46.9	28.9
Moorpark	10 634	3.29	9.8	12.3	0	0	0	0	316	895	110	785	22 358	27.8	37.3
Moreno Valley	50 650	3.93	21.9	12.2	554	83	27	471	6 994	3 447	288	3 159	113 095	52.5	14.4
Morgan Hill	12 879	3.10	12.6	15.1	386	222	144	164	677	1 628	156	1 472	25 652	30.4	37.7
Mountain View	32 432	2.37	7.6	33.5	265	120	107	145	1 764	2 240	198	2 042	55 661	17.9	64.1
Murrieta	32 568	3.26	11.2	17.6	429	138	56	291	1 526	1 408	63	1 345	64 430	29.8	28.8
Napa	28 476	2.76	11.6	25.3	1 237	669	343	568	1 564	1 966	313	1 653	52 660	40.7	28.2
National City	15 523	3.84	22.7	19.1	5 752	411	411	5 341	1 856	3 087	444	2 643	36 297	56.0	12.7
Newark	13 474	3.24	12.9	16.5	145	0	0	145	1 080	2 429	245	2 184	30 858	42.8	28.9
Newport Beach	38 451	2.25	6.5	33.9	402	251	221	151	1 989	2 266	124	2 142	64 502	11.6	64.5
Norco	7 027	3.86	9.5	17.7	4 397	4 322	0	75	688	2 554	171	2 384	18 783	46.3	17.3
Norwalk	27 132	3.92	18.3	13.5	1 615	1 300	474	315	2 317	2 169	296	1 873	66 644	54.7	15.2
Novato	20 890	2.56	8.9	28.4	626	177	175	449	850	1 552	146	1 406	38 699	24.5	44.1
Oakland	155 918	2.58	15.3	35.1	8 138	2 463	1 349	5 675	31 277	7 629	1 685	5 943	281 250	36.2	38.6
Oakley	11 136	3.36	14.2	15.6	103	28	6	75	514	1 323	116	1 207	23 108	46.4	15.5
Oceanside	59 144	2.90	11.8	24.1	936	134	91	802	4 636	2 663	374	2 288	112 959	37.6	25.4
Ontario	45 680	3.65	18.2	19.7	758	347	347	411	5 085	3 022	256	2 766	99 631	57.2	13.2
Orange	42 754	3.25	13.1	19.7	6 253	3 666	299	2 587	2 383	1 693	101	1 592	90 342	36.0	34.3
Oxnard	50 291	4.01	18.1	14.0	1 434	502	465	932	7 266	3 559	433	3 126	120 094	56.5	15.9
Pacifica	14 168	2.70	11.3	25.5	182	118	115	64	729	1 873	234	1 639	27 341	22.5	40.7
Palmdale	42 012	3.71	18.7	14.5	199	41	0	158	4 059	2 566	531	2 035	87 101	50.5	15.5
Palm Desert	23 636	2.11	8.8	39.2	308	210	210	98	2 318	4 548	275	4 273	38 037	29.8	34.5
Palm Springs	22 906	2.00	7.7	44.3	539	196	190	343	3 017	6 465	632	5 833	37 372	32.8	34.3
Palo Alto	26 420	2.50	7.3	28.6	583	378	323	205	1 358	2 022	88	1 934	47 070	8.4	80.3
Paradise	10 917	2.40	10.2	34.8	408	269	246	139	568	2 159	198	1 962	19 440	34.8	23.3
Paramount	13 732	3.99	23.9	15.0	310	283	283	27	1 647	2 984	433	2 551	30 731	70.3	7.7
Pasadena	54 092	2.57	10.7	34.0	3 493	1 021	890	2 472	3 863	2 752	281	2 471	99 736	27.8	49.1
Perris	16 242	4.39	23.9	7.8	240	100	71	140	2 085	2 847	246	2 602	37 628	64.2	8.2
Petaluma	21 538	2.74	10.9	25.5	724	363	363	361	1 274	2 130	334	1 796	40 948	31.4	36.4
Pico Rivera	16 464	3.87	18.4	15.7	454	415	415	39	1 635	2 556	430	2 126	40 444	62.6	11.3
Pittsburg	19 629	3.35	18.4	18.0	291	138	123	153	2 537	3 758	259	3 499	41 599	46.5	18.2
Placentia	15 778	3.29	13.2	16.5	337	84	73	253	814	1 550	156	1 394	33 766	33.2	35.6
Pleasant Hill	13 774	2.46	7.7	32.3	463	312	291	151	1 798	5 232	175	5 058	24 174	17.9	51.5
Pleasanton	25 222	2.90	8.6	16.7	456	136	129	320	1 305	1 739	81	1 657	48 566	17.5	57.8
Pomona	38 894	3.89	19.3	16.1	4 138	1 356	1 166	2 782	5 180	3 410	512	2 899	88 385	58.1	16.5
Porterville	16 060	3.42	18.2	18.0	1 147	940	931	207	1 362	2 459	285	2 174	31 195	58.5	10.7
Poway	15 936	3.08	9.9	15.3	550	266	260	284	506	1 016	141	876	32 650	22.8	46.1
Rancho Cordova	23 908	2.81	18.2	23.9	325	155	143	170	1 949	2 840	444	2 395	43 649	36.0	25.3
Rancho Cucamonga	55 410	3.07	13.4	20.7	3 124	2 988	73	136	3 951	2 288	164	2 124	110 749	29.8	31.5
Rancho Palos Verdes	15 852	2.67	8.6	20.9	340	27	27	313	496	1 163	56	1 107	30 999	11.9	64.8
Rancho Santa Margarita	16 559	2.94	9.9	18.8	2	0	0	2	230	464	54	410	30 748	19.0	49.1
Redding	34 818	2.61	13.0	30.2	2 020	882	543	1 138	4 534	4 959	667	4 292	60 837	34.5	23.2
Redlands	23 923	2.92	11.5	26.6	2 368	512	485	1 856	2 984	4 245	209	4 036	44 326	30.0	38.6
Redondo Beach	27 929	2.42	8.7	30.9	431	64	64	367	1 605	2 358	232	2 126	49 601	15.5	56.8
Redwood City	28 129	2.83	11.1	27.5	1 547	1 139	53	408	1 922	2 348	237	2 111	54 305	33.0	41.3
Rialto	24 810	4.09	19.2	14.0	447	193	153	254	2 482	2 421	320	2 101	55 881	60.4	10.0
Richmond	36 413	2.92	20.9	27.7	1 583	913	172	670	5 124	4 724	777	3 947	69 874	44.5	25.6
Ridgecrest	10 948	2.58	10.5	31.9	196	87	87	109	588	2 040	409	1 630	18 180	32.3	28.9
Riverside	90 690	3.45	15.1	21.1	11 549	2 624	1 153	8 925	11 248	3 521	433	3 088	184 929	46.3	22.1
Rocklin	21 276	2.77	11.3	21.3	637	181	176	456	1 089	1 804	83	1 721	37 894	20.7	39.6
Rohnert Park	15 832	2.61	12.1	30.5	397	6	6	391	895	2 155	385	1 770	26 376	35.8	23.6
Rosemead	14 604	3.73	16.7	13.1	413	278	208	135	1 333	2 435	269	2 166	38 314	62.1	15.8
Roseville	45 657	2.72	10.7	25.1	847	369	361	478	3 263	2 530	150	2 380	81 912	23.9	36.7
Sacramento	177 578	2.68	15.5	32.3	8 314	4 046	1 367	4 268	18 046	3 738	615	3 123	309 062	37.9	29.3
Salinas	40 441	3.81	19.1	16.9	2 465	1 807	531	658	6 224	3 967	635	3 331	88 341	61.7	12.6
San Bernardino	57 577	3.70	24.4	19.6	7 325	4 247	878	3 078	11 367	5 297	992	4 305	120 291	60.1	11.7
San Bruno	14 669	2.87	11.7	26.5	398	82	72	316	1 164	2 720	257	2 463	30 152	32.6	35.0
San Buenaventura (Ventura)	41 306	2.63	12.8	29.2	2 493	1 738	293	755	4 143	3 792	253	3 540	74 636	29.3	33.6
San Carlos	11 570	2.52	8.0	27.5	91	12	12	79	NA	NA	NA	NA	20 861	14.5	61.1
San Clemente	24 126	2.68	8.3	23.7	273	28	0	245	756	1 156	106	1 051	43 566	17.4	46.3
San Diego	479 079	2.80	11.8	28.6	51 956	7 050	2 902	44 906	32 026	2 340	381	1 959	888 185	29.0	42.3
San Dimas	11 840	2.86	11.5	24.0	540	220	128	320	700	2 062	203	1 858	23 464	26.9	35.8

1. No spouse present.   2. Data for serious crimes have not been adjusted for underreporting. This may affect comparability between geographic areas and over time.   3. Per 100,000 population estimated by the FBI.   4. Persons 25 years old and over.

Table D. Cities — Income, Poverty, and Housing

City	Money income, 2010–2014					Housing units, 2010			Occupied housing units 2010–2014				
	Per capita income[1] (dollars)	Households			Families with income below poverty (percent)	Total	Percent change, 2000–2010	Vacant units for sale or rent[2]	Total	Owner-occupied		Median owner costs as a percent of income	
		Median income	Percent with income of $200,000 or more	Percent with income of less than $25,000						Percent	Median value[3] (dollars)	With a mortgage[4]	Without a mortgage[5]
	42	43	44	45	46	47	48	49	50	51	52	53	54
CALIFORNIA—Cont'd													
Menlo Park	69 802	115 650	29.5	7.4	3.5	13 085	2.7	738	12 397	55.9	1 000 000	26.6	10.0
Merced	17 623	38 917	1.3	32.8	25.3	27 446	27.4	2 547	24 950	42.2	148 100	24.7	11.1
Milpitas	34 237	99 072	13.4	11.4	5.6	19 806	14.0	622	19 973	64.7	547 100	26.9	10.0
Mission Viejo	41 513	98 157	12.9	9.6	3.3	34 228	4.0	1 020	33 640	77.3	560 100	27.2	10.0
Modesto	23 034	47 607	3.3	25.8	16.7	75 044	11.5	5 937	70 310	53.8	171 200	26.2	11.4
Monrovia	34 668	72 034	7.8	17.4	7.2	14 473	3.9	711	13 032	49.2	542 200	28.2	10.0
Montclair	17 881	48 767	1.9	22.5	14.7	9 911	8.0	388	10 336	60.1	254 400	29.4	10.7
Montebello	20 972	47 562	2.4	25.1	10.9	19 768	1.8	756	19 674	46.1	384 400	29.9	11.1
Monterey	36 812	64 772	5.4	18.5	3.9	13 584	1.2	1 400	12 527	34.0	615 900	27.9	10.0
Monterey Park	24 637	54 821	5.0	23.9	11.8	20 850	3.3	887	18 875	52.0	485 400	31.3	10.0
Moorpark	37 016	99 353	14.4	7.6	4.1	10 738	18.1	254	10 634	75.3	532 000	27.4	11.6
Moreno Valley	17 874	54 229	2.1	19.8	17.0	55 559	34.0	3 967	50 650	60.5	188 100	29.4	10.3
Morgan Hill	40 972	96 232	16.9	14.2	7.7	12 859	15.7	533	12 879	71.4	587 900	27.1	12.3
Mountain View	56 156	100 028	20.0	13.0	5.6	33 881	4.5	1 924	32 432	41.3	807 100	23.2	11.0
Murrieta	28 719	74 401	6.7	12.2	6.7	35 294	136.5	2 545	32 568	67.9	287 700	28.9	12.2
Napa	31 185	64 058	6.2	18.1	8.0	30 149	8.6	1 983	28 476	55.2	412 600	28.3	11.8
National City	17 143	39 517	1.0	32.4	21.3	16 762	8.0	1 260	15 523	31.9	272 700	30.3	10.0
Newark	31 825	86 521	7.5	11.3	5.6	13 414	2.0	442	13 474	69.0	455 500	27.1	10.0
Newport Beach	78 012	107 991	26.2	12.8	5.0	44 193	18.4	5 442	38 451	55.4	1 000 000	30.1	11.0
Norco	27 702	85 142	9.3	10.0	4.6	7 322	17.7	299	7 027	77.6	393 200	29.2	10.2
Norwalk	19 584	60 523	1.8	17.5	11.5	28 083	1.9	953	27 132	65.3	320 900	29.5	10.0
Novato	44 724	76 609	12.2	15.1	5.5	21 158	11.5	879	20 890	65.4	554 400	30.0	12.5
Oakland	32 566	52 962	7.5	26.5	16.8	169 710	7.7	15 919	155 918	39.8	435 000	28.7	12.3
Oakley	27 993	78 597	3.9	15.0	7.3	11 484	44.0	757	11 136	74.7	249 200	27.1	11.9
Oceanside	27 009	58 385	4.5	18.6	10.5	64 435	8.3	5 197	59 144	56.3	350 600	28.9	11.8
Ontario	18 601	54 156	1.7	18.9	14.8	47 449	5.2	2 518	45 680	54.7	255 400	30.7	11.0
Orange	31 330	77 086	9.8	13.9	8.8	45 111	8.0	1 744	42 754	57.8	515 000	27.2	10.0
Oxnard	20 651	62 349	3.9	16.2	13.0	52 772	16.8	2 975	50 291	55.0	332 600	29.1	10.3
Pacifica	44 886	96 875	13.7	9.9	3.1	14 523	1.9	556	14 168	67.2	613 700	27.8	10.0
Palmdale	19 438	54 921	2.7	23.0	18.0	46 544	25.3	3 592	42 012	64.3	173 700	28.5	12.8
Palm Desert	39 275	52 053	6.5	21.2	7.7	37 073	32.1	13 956	23 636	62.8	299 500	30.3	16.9
Palm Springs	36 126	45 497	5.3	29.0	13.5	34 794	12.3	12 048	22 906	57.8	265 400	29.5	17.7
Palo Alto	75 257	126 771	32.0	10.6	3.9	28 216	7.9	1 723	26 420	54.7	1 000 000	25.3	10.0
Paradise	24 573	41 482	1.6	29.6	9.5	12 981	5.4	1 088	10 917	71.2	201 800	27.7	14.6
Paramount	14 168	43 784	0.6	25.2	22.5	14 571	-0.4	690	13 732	38.3	253 900	33.9	10.2
Pasadena	41 268	70 845	11.3	19.4	8.7	59 551	10.0	4 281	54 092	43.9	614 400	27.5	12.1
Perris	13 516	48 591	0.6	25.1	23.2	17 906	70.5	1 541	16 242	64.1	164 400	32.9	10.7
Petaluma	35 239	80 590	8.1	15.1	6.8	22 736	11.8	999	21 538	65.6	438 100	26.4	10.8
Pico Rivera	18 643	56 576	1.5	18.8	11.6	17 109	1.8	543	16 464	67.7	328 500	30.1	10.2
Pittsburg	23 330	60 376	3.7	21.9	14.6	21 126	14.9	1 599	19 629	57.5	228 600	28.6	10.6
Placentia	30 218	79 275	8.2	13.5	7.7	16 872	9.4	507	15 778	66.1	514 000	28.1	11.1
Pleasant Hill	43 580	81 556	10.6	13.9	4.3	14 321	2.0	613	13 774	57.5	513 000	26.1	10.0
Pleasanton	50 972	123 608	22.5	8.4	3.3	26 053	8.6	808	25 222	69.5	732 100	25.2	10.0
Pomona	17 041	48 993	1.6	24.0	18.4	40 685	2.7	2 208	38 894	52.6	264 800	31.8	11.9
Porterville	17 330	41 267	1.9	30.4	23.6	16 734	31.4	1 090	16 060	57.4	146 300	26.5	12.7
Poway	40 681	96 315	13.4	10.6	4.0	16 715	5.6	587	15 936	75.5	501 600	25.4	11.3
Rancho Cordova	24 462	53 563	2.4	20.2	12.9	25 479	18.5	2 031	23 908	54.3	195 600	26.4	10.0
Rancho Cucamonga	31 528	77 061	7.4	12.8	6.1	56 618	34.1	2 235	55 410	63.9	365 100	27.6	12.0
Rancho Palos Verdes	57 201	120 697	24.0	8.6	3.3	16 179	3.3	618	15 852	79.7	952 400	25.1	10.0
Rancho Santa Margarita	42 768	104 952	13.7	8.2	3.0	17 260	3.7	595	16 559	72.2	537 100	27.6	13.8
Redding	23 893	43 773	2.8	27.9	12.0	38 679	14.5	2 549	34 818	53.3	221 800	26.4	13.8
Redlands	31 745	67 112	7.9	18.4	8.9	26 634	7.1	1 870	23 923	59.1	297 100	24.7	10.0
Redondo Beach	52 775	103 064	16.0	11.8	3.2	30 609	3.6	1 598	27 929	50.7	720 600	28.0	10.0
Redwood City	42 063	81 955	15.8	12.7	5.5	29 167	0.8	1 210	28 129	52.1	795 000	28.3	12.2
Rialto	16 206	50 277	1.5	21.4	17.5	27 203	5.4	2 001	24 810	62.8	184 900	30.0	11.3
Richmond	25 769	54 857	4.8	23.1	14.6	39 328	8.8	3 235	36 413	49.4	271 300	29.0	10.0
Ridgecrest	27 954	61 480	2.3	18.6	8.3	11 915	4.8	1 134	10 948	60.4	176 200	19.3	10.0
Riverside	22 212	56 089	4.2	21.9	14.4	98 444	14.4	6 512	90 690	55.4	242 100	27.5	10.0
Rocklin	35 200	79 274	7.6	14.4	6.6	22 010	52.4	1 210	21 276	65.7	336 900	26.2	12.5
Rohnert Park	27 021	57 557	1.9	21.4	7.1	16 551	4.6	743	15 832	51.1	308 300	29.1	13.2
Rosemead	17 129	44 524	1.7	27.3	17.6	14 805	3.4	558	14 604	47.5	430 800	36.0	10.0
Roseville	34 514	76 712	6.9	14.7	6.0	47 757	49.3	2 698	45 657	64.6	317 800	24.9	12.3
Sacramento	26 060	50 013	3.6	26.4	17.7	190 911	16.5	16 287	177 578	47.6	228 400	26.7	10.0
Salinas	17 810	49 728	1.8	21.9	18.0	42 651	7.7	2 264	40 441	42.6	262 000	29.8	10.0
San Bernardino	14 759	38 774	1.3	34.3	28.2	65 401	3.1	6 118	57 577	48.9	151 400	28.3	12.3
San Bruno	35 866	81 420	8.8	11.0	5.0	15 356	2.7	655	14 669	55.6	602 300	29.8	10.5
San Buenaventura (Ventura)	33 180	66 485	5.8	17.9	7.3	42 827	7.5	2 389	41 306	54.3	428 600	27.3	10.0
San Carlos	62 548	125 747	26.7	7.5	2.2	12 018	3.6	494	11 570	70.3	939 600	26.3	11.6
San Clemente	48 063	91 749	16.6	10.4	5.7	25 966	25.7	2 060	24 126	64.6	728 000	30.2	10.0
San Diego	33 789	65 753	8.0	19.0	11.2	516 033	9.9	32 941	479 079	47.5	448 000	27.8	10.0
San Dimas	35 345	78 911	9.9	14.3	3.7	12 506	-0.6	476	11 840	71.6	433 100	26.8	12.3

1. Based on population estimated by the American Community Survey.　　2. Includes units rented or sold but not occupied.　　3. Specified owner-occupied units; $1,000,000 represents $1,000,000 or more.　　4. 50.0 represents 50 percent or more.　　5. 10.0 represents 10 percent or less.

City	Occupied housing units, 2010–2014 (cont.)				Migration, 2010–2014		Civilian labor force, 2015				Civilian employment[4], 2010–2014			
									Unemployment			Percent		
	Percent renter occupied	Median gross rent[1]	Median gross rent as a percent of income[2]	Percent with no vehicle available	Percent who lived in the same house one year ago	Percent who lived outside current city one year ago	Total	Percent change, 2014–2015	Total	Rate[3]	Population age 16 and older	In labor force	Civilian full-year full-time workers	Households with no workers (percent)
	55	56	57	58	59	60	61	62	63	64	65	66	67	68
CALIFORNIA—Cont'd														
Menlo Park	44.1	1 831	26.1	5.6	84.8	13.1	18 777	3.1	503	2.7	25 354	67.6	45.1	21.1
Merced	57.8	830	33.9	10.8	78.3	8.8	34 665	0.2	3 715	10.7	58 025	60.6	31.2	30.5
Milpitas	35.3	1 803	29.0	4.6	84.8	10.9	38 929	2.3	1 519	3.9	55 965	65.3	42.5	17.7
Mission Viejo	22.7	1 900	34.4	3.8	88.4	8.7	50 581	1.3	2 117	4.2	77 718	66.4	42.6	22.0
Modesto	46.2	1 013	35.8	8.1	80.6	9.0	95 752	0.3	8 914	9.3	158 473	61.2	32.2	29.8
Monrovia	50.8	1 311	30.7	4.5	85.9	11.3	20 728	0.1	1 069	5.2	29 189	72.8	44.7	17.4
Montclair	39.9	1 097	36.5	8.4	90.2	8.3	18 450	2.0	1 008	5.5	29 063	62.2	38.7	18.8
Montebello	53.9	1 139	36.4	11.0	91.1	6.8	28 593	0.0	1 643	5.7	50 562	57.1	39.5	27.6
Monterey	66.0	1 423	31.7	6.6	75.1	20.4	15 690	1.4	906	5.8	23 895	64.5	34.2	29.5
Monterey Park	48.0	1 253	35.2	8.6	90.2	7.0	29 266	-0.1	1 748	6.0	51 272	58.1	36.4	26.5
Moorpark	24.7	1 726	37.3	2.0	89.8	7.4	19 291	-0.4	852	4.4	27 154	72.0	45.7	12.4
Moreno Valley	39.5	1 283	38.2	4.8	81.4	9.5	91 645	1.7	6 573	7.2	145 623	63.7	34.5	19.1
Morgan Hill	28.6	1 663	35.0	3.0	88.4	8.3	22 518	2.2	1 036	4.6	30 551	68.8	39.5	18.6
Mountain View	58.7	1 688	25.4	6.3	81.1	15.4	49 656	2.5	1 573	3.2	62 415	74.0	50.7	17.5
Murrieta	32.1	1 541	34.0	2.5	79.3	15.2	51 869	2.1	2 793	5.4	78 663	66.0	38.8	21.9
Napa	44.8	1 342	33.3	6.4	85.2	6.2	42 498	1.2	2 074	4.9	62 035	68.1	38.3	25.3
National City	68.1	995	35.0	12.3	88.6	8.3	24 698	0.6	1 630	6.6	47 040	62.6	30.5	25.8
Newark	31.0	1 570	30.4	3.9	90.8	7.4	23 568	1.6	955	4.1	35 111	66.8	44.7	33.1
Newport Beach	44.6	1 966	29.5	3.4	81.9	12.1	45 811	1.4	1 691	3.7	72 988	63.2	39.5	27.5
Norco	22.4	1 825	32.4	4.3	87.2	10.8	11 609	2.1	625	5.4	22 052	53.4	31.9	20.7
Norwalk	34.7	1 318	34.5	6.3	91.5	5.3	50 452	-0.3	3 470	6.9	82 271	62.6	40.1	18.1
Novato	34.6	1 669	34.3	4.6	86.3	9.5	29 446	1.1	1 026	3.5	42 871	66.2	37.8	26.6
Oakland	60.2	1 114	32.6	17.7	83.0	8.7	211 094	1.2	12 401	5.9	327 145	66.3	36.8	27.3
Oakley	25.3	1 427	35.8	4.3	90.7	8.3	18 953	1.0	1 184	6.2	28 206	67.7	40.5	17.5
Oceanside	43.7	1 393	35.6	5.0	83.2	10.2	82 322	0.9	4 397	5.3	136 737	64.2	35.6	28.2
Ontario	45.3	1 248	35.8	4.5	86.0	9.3	82 020	1.7	5 320	6.5	125 911	66.8	37.7	18.0
Orange	42.2	1 498	34.1	4.3	84.4	10.7	72 234	1.3	3 049	4.2	111 441	66.1	40.6	17.3
Oxnard	45.0	1 332	35.3	5.0	88.3	4.7	100 289	-0.7	6 209	6.2	150 464	69.0	39.3	18.7
Pacifica	32.8	1 806	28.3	3.4	90.9	6.8	23 966	3.0	753	3.1	31 163	70.5	46.6	18.9
Palmdale	35.7	1 172	40.7	6.0	84.2	8.5	64 323	-0.8	5 791	9.0	111 788	59.6	33.9	21.9
Palm Desert	37.2	1 137	31.3	6.9	81.0	15.1	23 156	2.3	1 107	4.8	42 433	53.8	29.6	42.7
Palm Springs	42.2	963	35.9	8.3	81.1	11.4	21 811	2.1	1 200	5.5	40 942	53.7	29.7	43.9
Palo Alto	45.3	2 000	26.5	6.1	81.6	14.2	35 285	2.6	1 005	2.8	52 686	64.2	43.1	25.7
Paradise	28.8	899	36.7	6.0	84.0	7.4	11 212	0.1	702	6.3	22 304	49.6	25.6	45.4
Paramount	61.7	1 179	37.0	7.0	88.0	8.5	24 845	-0.6	1 955	7.9	40 041	62.8	36.9	17.9
Pasadena	56.1	1 375	30.9	10.5	82.7	12.3	77 163	-0.1	4 609	6.0	115 712	66.9	41.7	24.8
Perris	35.9	1 240	38.7	3.9	85.1	8.7	29 354	1.1	2 868	9.8	49 543	64.2	31.4	18.3
Petaluma	34.4	1 479	31.3	4.8	86.7	8.0	32 852	1.3	1 138	3.5	46 474	69.3	40.1	21.7
Pico Rivera	32.3	1 235	35.9	7.5	90.0	7.4	30 138	-0.1	1 864	6.2	49 388	62.0	38.2	21.0
Pittsburg	42.5	1 327	36.7	6.4	82.4	11.2	32 932	1.1	1 975	6.0	50 787	66.0	35.5	21.3
Placentia	33.9	1 544	33.9	4.0	86.2	10.7	26 333	1.1	1 330	5.1	40 621	66.1	39.4	20.6
Pleasant Hill	42.5	1 533	31.7	8.1	83.4	14.3	18 062	1.5	753	4.2	28 246	64.3	40.1	26.0
Pleasanton	30.5	1 742	27.8	3.0	87.1	9.1	38 988	1.7	1 431	3.7	56 211	66.7	43.8	19.0
Pomona	47.4	1 134	38.4	7.2	83.5	10.5	67 529	-0.5	5 071	7.5	114 475	60.8	33.3	21.0
Porterville	42.6	783	32.1	6.2	86.9	5.0	23 581	2.0	2 852	12.1	38 489	60.1	33.1	28.2
Poway	24.5	1 476	32.0	4.9	90.2	6.9	25 602	1.4	856	3.3	38 863	65.9	41.2	19.8
Rancho Cordova	45.7	964	32.1	6.6	78.4	12.8	33 468	0.7	2 224	6.6	51 677	67.2	39.3	24.1
Rancho Cucamonga	36.1	1 454	33.4	4.0	83.1	11.7	92 601	2.2	4 439	4.8	134 252	68.6	41.1	19.0
Rancho Palos Verdes	20.3	2 000	34.1	3.3	91.2	7.0	19 107	0.6	618	3.2	34 308	55.4	35.4	31.5
Rancho Santa Margarita	27.8	1 686	32.2	3.1	86.8	9.1	27 850	1.6	722	2.6	36 876	75.3	50.3	11.7
Redding	46.7	961	37.2	9.1	77.7	11.0	39 885	-0.4	2 857	7.2	72 650	56.5	29.5	37.9
Redlands	40.9	1 128	31.2	4.7	85.4	10.8	34 043	2.5	1 270	3.7	54 770	60.1	37.7	25.6
Redondo Beach	49.3	1 719	28.0	3.9	84.8	10.7	40 283	0.3	1 664	4.1	54 627	74.0	48.7	19.0
Redwood City	47.9	1 588	32.1	5.8	87.8	8.0	48 230	3.0	1 494	3.1	61 752	71.4	45.7	19.1
Rialto	37.2	1 088	36.5	5.7	83.7	10.2	44 186	1.4	3 399	7.7	72 779	63.2	33.7	20.3
Richmond	50.6	1 190	33.7	9.7	82.4	11.9	53 106	1.1	3 066	5.8	83 372	65.8	37.1	25.5
Ridgecrest	39.6	859	26.9	6.2	81.4	7.0	14 372	-0.2	987	6.9	21 536	64.6	39.4	26.8
Riverside	44.6	1 158	36.7	5.9	82.4	9.4	148 381	1.9	9 539	6.4	242 023	62.5	34.6	23.5
Rocklin	34.3	1 360	32.5	3.9	83.8	11.9	30 208	-0.9	1 542	5.1	44 808	67.7	40.2	23.2
Rohnert Park	48.9	1 294	36.9	6.2	81.4	12.4	23 233	1.0	1 081	4.7	34 472	68.1	35.3	24.7
Rosemead	52.5	1 175	43.6	7.7	92.3	5.4	25 395	-0.5	1 967	7.7	44 928	58.8	34.6	20.8
Roseville	35.4	1 283	31.6	4.3	83.4	9.4	64 206	1.0	3 056	4.8	95 933	65.6	40.9	25.9
Sacramento	52.4	1 008	33.4	10.8	78.8	10.2	228 230	0.8	14 494	6.4	373 374	63.7	36.0	29.1
Salinas	57.4	1 137	34.5	5.8	87.3	3.9	80 197	1.0	6 827	8.5	110 507	63.9	34.5	20.9
San Bernardino	51.1	944	39.6	11.4	79.5	11.0	83 773	1.3	6 889	8.2	155 030	56.9	29.7	29.8
San Bruno	44.4	1 685	29.4	4.5	90.0	7.6	26 438	3.0	871	3.3	34 681	71.4	44.9	18.5
San Buenaventura (Ventura)	45.7	1 391	32.4	6.3	85.1	7.8	56 910	-0.7	3 276	5.8	87 120	65.6	39.2	26.6
San Carlos	29.7	1 668	28.1	3.4	89.6	8.5	17 164	2.9	577	3.4	22 883	71.3	44.9	19.3
San Clemente	35.4	1 686	36.1	2.9	84.7	9.2	31 854	1.4	1 180	3.7	50 259	65.0	38.2	23.6
San Diego	52.5	1 359	32.4	7.4	81.8	8.5	702 525	1.0	34 729	4.9	1 088 580	67.6	39.8	21.8
San Dimas	28.4	1 504	32.1	6.1	84.7	13.3	17 744	0.1	940	5.3	28 188	61.7	39.4	25.9

1. $2,000 represents $2,000 or more.　　2. 50.0 represents 50 percent or more.　　3. Percent of civilian labor force.　　4. Persons 16 years old and over.

Table D. Cities — Construction, Wholesale Trade, and Retail Trade

City	Value of residential construction authorized by building permits, 2015			Wholesale trade,[1] 2012				Retail trade,[2] 2012			
	New construction ($1,000)	Number of housing units	Percent single family	Number of establishments	Number of employees	Sales (mil dol)	Annual payroll (mil dol)	Number of establishments	Number of employees	Sales (mil dol)	Annual payroll (mil dol)
	69	70	71	72	73	74	75	76	77	78	79
CALIFORNIA—Cont'd											
Menlo Park	59 155	255	19.2	33	468	410.3	40.2	122	1 502	438.2	48.9
Merced	14 217	56	100.0	37	742	1 669.5	35.7	227	3 728	945.6	89.5
Milpitas	79 332	247	37.2	143	4 902	4 031.6	568.9	307	5 295	1 132.7	119.5
Mission Viejo	0	0	0.0	107	576	268.8	39.3	356	6 275	1 726.5	159.4
Modesto	3 635	17	100.0	113	1 977	2 459.5	99.8	683	10 639	2 347.6	237.2
Monrovia	2 040	5	100.0	89	709	545.3	34.5	109	1 951	779.4	62.0
Montclair	12 249	59	49.2	82	593	226.0	23.9	243	4 021	1 003.5	93.6
Montebello	0	0	0.0	114	1 826	1 166.8	90.1	203	3 498	817.9	76.0
Monterey	6 064	35	8.6	36	382	1 264.0	28.0	199	2 265	464.5	59.9
Monterey Park	15 446	58	89.7	207	1 082	878.6	44.2	202	1 671	399.6	34.6
Moorpark	72 534	183	100.0	53	774	411.4	40.9	55	890	227.3	22.6
Moreno Valley	43 638	132	100.0	30	663	544.9	23.8	311	5 600	1 696.8	136.7
Morgan Hill	109 174	516	49.0	58	1 873	1 259.4	115.3	105	D	D	D
Mountain View	57 287	279	27.6	106	2 330	2 021.6	246.3	244	4 078	1 222.6	126.3
Murrieta	78 758	471	38.6	97	667	425.6	30.9	218	3 873	1 082.7	97.5
Napa	27 410	100	98.0	69	437	309.9	24.7	315	4 374	1 128.4	125.6
National City	15 582	77	9.1	87	1 198	702.7	55.7	304	5 393	1 395.9	140.2
Newark	52 288	170	57.1	61	1 443	788.0	61.8	168	2 856	684.3	69.8
Newport Beach	98 140	146	67.8	190	1 183	976.1	98.6	441	6 409	2 885.4	252.0
Norco	0	0	0.0	27	469	175.8	13.5	86	1 093	337.4	28.9
Norwalk	1 065	6	33.3	88	639	469.4	29.8	178	3 078	1 101.5	88.1
Novato	50 002	287	36.2	73	579	450.4	38.8	162	2 538	834.3	80.7
Oakland	188 655	866	12.6	376	4 921	3 620.2	263.0	1 014	10 458	3 029.1	311.7
Oakley	78 654	235	100.0	9	D	D	D	38	366	124.8	10.8
Oceanside	22 092	88	40.9	149	1 476	696.8	75.4	389	6 742	1 677.8	166.9
Ontario	78 379	534	54.5	681	11 341	14 205.7	557.2	579	13 650	4 833.5	378.2
Orange	26 010	267	2.6	333	3 442	4 940.7	176.7	558	7 821	2 152.9	207.9
Oxnard	76 096	532	16.7	183	3 805	5 873.6	213.8	430	6 729	2 363.1	194.0
Pacifica	2 873	8	50.0	7	D	D	D	61	699	194.3	16.8
Palmdale	22 625	102	98.0	28	128	87.5	4.2	299	6 423	1 557.0	144.8
Palm Desert	52 857	134	79.9	74	389	215.3	17.5	453	6 199	2 309.1	160.9
Palm Springs	41 719	121	100.0	35	535	309.8	27.3	184	2 480	733.1	66.8
Palo Alto	132 480	307	35.5	76	D	D	D	317	5 759	2 461.0	261.4
Paradise	32 829	35	100.0	6	D	D	D	77	791	190.8	19.4
Paramount	348	2	100.0	212	1 709	989.1	73.8	110	1 202	326.9	30.2
Pasadena	91 046	510	5.1	163	1 382	2 271.6	79.9	594	9 409	2 700.9	256.4
Perris	23 124	240	58.8	20	265	204.0	12.6	92	2 151	609.3	52.9
Petaluma	13 790	56	100.0	101	2 055	1 396.4	198.1	262	3 233	875.4	96.3
Pico Rivera	941	4	100.0	84	1 923	1 419.8	97.3	113	2 571	1 480.3	55.9
Pittsburg	68 221	383	65.5	32	324	185.9	19.2	99	2 084	524.4	53.0
Placentia	13 094	53	81.1	108	923	329.5	51.3	96	1 099	356.1	33.2
Pleasant Hill	1 160	3	100.0	29	172	112.4	8.8	146	2 490	607.5	56.9
Pleasanton	191 920	1 052	8.9	135	5 394	2 651.3	430.8	330	6 278	1 662.3	190.3
Pomona	21 882	176	7.4	301	3 224	2 099.4	139.4	293	3 308	845.7	76.5
Porterville	13 026	58	100.0	24	127	42.0	5.9	147	2 231	513.7	52.2
Poway	6 618	11	100.0	96	2 136	1 103.5	131.1	144	2 679	969.9	77.4
Rancho Cordova	109 438	403	100.0	173	2 537	1 593.6	179.2	218	3 332	929.1	91.9
Rancho Cucamonga	109 126	410	100.0	322	3 710	3 866.2	174.8	436	8 160	2 025.3	192.2
Rancho Palos Verdes	6 178	28	100.0	53	163	209.1	8.4	46	388	128.2	10.0
Rancho Santa Margarita	0	0	0.0	59	550	364.4	30.7	72	1 504	540.6	43.3
Redding	46 425	245	78.0	115	1 223	918.6	51.6	444	7 061	1 974.7	192.8
Redlands	15 508	82	70.7	56	495	190.5	19.2	240	4 676	2 221.1	118.9
Redondo Beach	46 875	143	100.0	64	311	156.2	15.0	274	3 969	869.7	94.8
Redwood City	32 684	127	40.2	65	1 049	1 124.1	110.9	204	4 486	1 656.7	172.2
Rialto	2 682	24	0.0	54	698	739.7	34.3	152	2 173	541.9	52.3
Richmond	18 292	90	84.4	99	1 431	1 476.7	83.3	238	3 600	1 092.5	105.9
Ridgecrest	3 007	21	100.0	4	D	D	D	82	1 246	272.4	28.2
Riverside	74 304	446	49.8	293	4 399	2 747.6	223.9	829	13 943	4 127.4	385.4
Rocklin	139 462	606	62.7	65	1 562	785.8	86.0	149	1 824	616.0	59.6
Rohnert Park	22 836	101	20.8	41	692	299.9	40.5	106	2 088	637.6	57.9
Rosemead	8 435	29	100.0	107	450	245.6	13.5	172	1 583	460.9	34.2
Roseville	272 466	967	100.0	108	1 597	1 587.0	90.0	588	13 555	4 159.6	380.2
Sacramento	205 030	1 187	36.9	488	7 125	9 800.4	381.3	1 200	18 042	4 363.3	447.7
Salinas	19 278	94	48.9	123	1 861	1 717.4	124.3	428	6 955	1 928.3	175.7
San Bernardino	7 767	38	100.0	128	2 392	2 145.2	102.9	526	8 518	2 610.4	216.6
San Bruno	4 230	9	100.0	36	798	1 046.6	96.4	149	2 508	528.7	59.6
San Buenaventura (Ventura)	34 337	260	11.5	167	1 531	762.2	83.3	517	6 814	1 824.7	183.5
San Carlos	8 164	18	38.9	103	885	488.8	52.5	142	1 828	490.1	55.9
San Clemente	66 136	127	92.1	162	1 826	810.7	119.4	204	2 501	670.2	68.7
San Diego	1 210 768	6 185	21.4	1 823	35 353	24 027.1	2 803.8	4 119	61 044	17 869.3	1 740.7
San Dimas	2 126	7	100.0	75	704	304.0	36.4	112	1 792	538.4	45.5

1. Merchant wholesalers except manufacturers' sales branches and offices. 2. Establishments with payroll.

Table D. Cities — Real Estate, Professional Services, and Manufacturing

City	Real estate and rental and leasing, 2012				Professional, scientific, and technical services,[1] 2012				Manufacturing, 2012			
	Number of establishments	Number of employees	Receipts (mil dol)	Annual payroll (mil dol)	Number of establishments	Number of employees	Receipts (mil dol)	Annual payroll (mil dol)	Number of establishments	Number of employees	Receipts (mil dol)	Annual payroll (mil dol)
	80	81	82	83	84	85	86	87	88	89	90	91
CALIFORNIA—Cont'd												
Menlo Park	84	374	119.4	18.4	336	D	D	D	56	2 390	D	199.1
Merced	69	322	48.1	10.2	84	D	D	D	28	1 234	273.9	55.5
Milpitas	72	394	207.8	18.2	265	D	D	D	157	8 969	4 539.3	968.4
Mission Viejo	161	775	177.2	37.0	469	D	D	D	51	440	275.1	26.6
Modesto	207	925	194.6	31.8	390	D	D	D	91	7 104	D	441.5
Monrovia	58	202	32.3	8.1	152	2 436	594.7	198.6	94	2 885	719.6	171.7
Montclair	32	179	97.5	13.0	25	217	12.4	5.8	85	938	121.3	31.4
Montebello	55	309	76.9	14.6	66	375	41.1	12.3	71	2 433	753.8	101.7
Monterey	88	312	64.7	10.7	238	D	D	D	44	717	116.9	37.5
Monterey Park	89	296	53.3	13.6	158	D	D	D	42	593	89.3	24.3
Moorpark	35	137	22.6	4.9	94	313	49.0	17.9	52	1 349	398.3	73.8
Moreno Valley	73	312	60.1	8.9	85	509	32.6	12.4	23	802	233.3	32.3
Morgan Hill	65	232	49.9	8.0	142	2 207	183.8	71.9	79	3 047	933.8	193.4
Mountain View	121	668	151.4	33.2	584	17 005	3 739.2	1 721.2	121	3 230	825.0	231.9
Murrieta	118	326	62.7	12.5	206	873	98.4	34.8	63	609	108.9	27.0
Napa	101	472	90.9	17.1	210	957	151.4	55.6	110	1 899	1 079.0	127.4
National City	50	288	51.0	10.6	46	473	44.5	15.9	70	1 045	D	44.2
Newark	42	132	46.2	5.3	132	1 882	561.3	168.0	67	2 348	806.2	148.0
Newport Beach	698	4 870	1 633.4	354.5	1 244	8 075	1 727.4	632.4	86	3 739	547.2	180.8
Norco	38	108	19.4	3.4	75	1 221	142.0	76.0	33	449	71.6	20.6
Norwalk	44	194	45.2	6.9	66	D	D	D	52	698	174.2	28.2
Novato	105	D	D	D	233	D	D	D	52	557	D	30.2
Oakland	482	2 716	672.7	126.2	1 414	10 188	2 035.0	834.8	333	6 555	1 744.2	314.1
Oakley	18	78	18.0	4.3	25	102	8.8	2.9	7	201	D	7.6
Oceanside	157	562	121.3	19.3	310	2 326	256.5	95.6	164	4 715	1 537.3	221.0
Ontario	182	1 205	368.5	65.3	256	D	D	D	391	11 003	4 490.4	494.1
Orange	259	1 787	400.2	84.1	713	D	D	D	287	6 122	1 980.3	301.4
Oxnard	139	694	144.8	27.4	213	D	D	D	172	6 057	3 144.4	359.9
Pacifica	28	64	12.5	2.5	72	272	30.5	9.7	9	139	D	4.1
Palmdale	102	326	51.4	8.5	95	D	D	D	35	4 686	D	D
Palm Desert	144	713	131.3	32.2	260	862	140.2	41.9	40	196	23.4	6.1
Palm Springs	123	573	120.2	20.7	191	664	110.6	32.3	27	624	242.9	23.3
Palo Alto	197	1 214	562.6	101.1	838	11 477	3 506.9	1 646.9	81	6 683	2 798.4	597.1
Paradise	25	204	30.2	4.3	34	107	9.0	2.7	16	85	D	3.3
Paramount	33	192	28.8	4.7	38	384	35.3	13.8	205	4 348	1 996.3	204.6
Pasadena	322	1 704	320.0	64.2	1 212	D	D	D	89	1 016	172.5	47.9
Perris	32	110	24.5	4.8	29	133	17.0	5.7	39	1 034	166.0	34.9
Petaluma	70	347	64.0	10.8	207	D	D	D	100	3 106	1 069.6	156.8
Pico Rivera	34	214	58.7	11.8	30	229	21.4	8.1	60	1 446	433.3	59.6
Pittsburg	25	231	75.7	11.2	49	310	27.6	12.1	40	2 175	D	149.4
Placentia	61	362	68.3	14.1	112	377	65.9	17.6	108	3 097	757.0	153.9
Pleasant Hill	46	233	67.3	15.2	135	779	143.3	53.2	17	78	D	3.3
Pleasanton	176	748	218.6	40.7	553	7 366	1 220.2	707.5	78	1 560	836.9	109.3
Pomona	76	475	141.3	21.1	112	D	D	D	212	4 462	991.4	202.3
Porterville	33	115	18.6	2.8	45	185	15.3	4.3	16	868	312.0	29.4
Poway	89	353	53.1	11.5	252	1 442	304.0	99.7	117	9 014	3 400.3	652.7
Rancho Cordova	108	532	79.7	20.4	235	D	D	D	115	4 676	1 083.4	329.7
Rancho Cucamonga	177	1 031	236.0	40.9	400	D	D	D	246	8 056	3 331.7	401.0
Rancho Palos Verdes	66	D	D	D	138	585	104.4	49.0	11	63	D	2.8
Rancho Santa Margarita	65	148	49.0	8.1	191	1 525	234.9	55.4	42	2 892	682.8	202.3
Redding	148	550	85.4	16.5	280	D	D	D	83	757	162.0	32.5
Redlands	72	293	56.3	9.5	209	1 046	152.6	48.7	58	1 140	305.6	39.5
Redondo Beach	111	309	43.9	9.7	329	D	D	D	35	183	D	5.2
Redwood City	129	628	222.9	26.3	444	7 705	2 124.6	913.7	75	1 834	660.3	107.8
Rialto	48	204	31.0	6.1	32	208	16.6	7.5	70	1 567	410.5	74.0
Richmond	72	370	107.6	14.4	139	1 720	313.7	150.6	118	3 925	11 604.0	268.8
Ridgecrest	25	141	20.6	3.7	53	1 267	142.5	65.6	4	22	D	0.5
Riverside	341	1 685	308.8	59.2	625	4 385	630.9	250.0	264	9 041	2 802.9	410.9
Rocklin	104	407	79.5	18.3	170	1 185	267.0	79.6	45	916	173.2	47.1
Rohnert Park	49	248	58.1	11.3	67	424	45.2	16.6	38	791	240.4	44.1
Rosemead	28	70	15.0	1.6	78	389	35.5	12.1	53	670	D	19.8
Roseville	238	1 902	349.5	82.7	494	8 360	3 354.9	878.1	69	1 325	296.8	77.5
Sacramento	573	3 255	622.2	160.8	1 775	16 337	3 011.6	1 134.8	322	7 890	3 149.8	404.4
Salinas	116	586	141.3	22.3	226	D	D	D	77	2 255	903.1	105.0
San Bernardino	125	514	93.1	16.8	239	D	D	D	122	2 811	929.3	118.4
San Bruno	44	156	67.8	7.6	82	1 002	379.3	116.3	13	D	D	D
San Buenaventura (Ventura)	190	1 046	207.7	39.3	467	D	D	D	157	2 717	517.2	119.4
San Carlos	55	277	74.1	14.6	205	D	D	D	90	1 460	D	88.4
San Clemente	138	386	87.7	17.1	381	D	D	D	99	1 448	314.0	72.1
San Diego	2 764	17 178	4 869.5	851.4	7 387	100 220	18 660.6	7 260.6	1 137	41 655	14 667.0	2 613.2
San Dimas	55	535	66.7	16.9	135	1 890	352.9	135.7	71	1 267	D	61.9

1. Establishments subject to federal tax.

Table D. Cities — Accommodation and Food Services, Arts, Entertainment, and Recreation, and Health Care and Social Assistance

City	Accommodation and food services, 2012				Arts, entertainment, and recreation,[1] 2012				Health care and social assistance,[1] 2012			
	Number of establishments	Number of employees	Sales (mil dol)	Annual payroll (mil dol)	Number of establishments	Number of employees	Receipts (mil dol)	Annual payroll (mil dol)	Number of establishments	Number of employees	Receipts (mil dol)	Annual payroll (mil dol)
	92	93	94	95	96	97	98	99	100	101	102	103
CALIFORNIA—Cont'd												
Menlo Park	104	1 790	139.2	43.6	17	D	D	D	136	988	157.7	64.5
Merced	131	2 340	107.7	28.6	11	113	7.0	1.8	245	2 514	266.6	96.1
Milpitas	282	4 613	320.4	86.0	21	D	D	D	210	2 097	351.1	107.7
Mission Viejo	193	3 372	184.2	53.7	26	D	D	D	466	D	D	D
Modesto	394	7 262	391.0	107.5	30	469	32.2	6.4	580	10 528	1 492.8	561.7
Monrovia	108	1 787	109.3	29.1	15	D	D	D	83	1 573	150.0	63.4
Montclair	83	1 650	82.2	23.8	7	D	D	D	96	1 960	168.3	59.6
Montebello	130	1 741	101.4	26.2	6	D	D	D	171	D	D	D
Monterey	212	5 518	416.3	131.8	22	D	D	D	280	D	D	D
Monterey Park	177	2 613	149.0	40.7	8	D	D	D	262	3 352	515.5	164.7
Moorpark	41	835	48.9	14.1	11	62	4.5	1.3	40	659	51.7	22.4
Moreno Valley	213	3 468	191.9	49.7	11	137	6.3	1.7	206	D	D	D
Morgan Hill	113	1 457	89.8	23.6	9	D	D	D	96	D	D	D
Mountain View	314	4 218	296.3	90.7	19	487	228.8	14.2	302	D	D	D
Murrieta	148	2 672	135.9	36.2	33	475	27.1	7.9	256	3 678	504.8	176.8
Napa	205	3 698	270.3	79.2	18	330	12.8	4.0	225	2 573	344.6	136.0
National City	169	2 512	145.8	35.9	7	D	D	D	148	2 719	229.2	83.2
Newark	162	2 273	149.0	39.7	7	D	D	D	73	D	D	D
Newport Beach	369	11 543	805.0	251.5	95	954	123.4	41.8	887	D	D	D
Norco	72	1 532	221.1	22.5	7	D	D	D	39	D	D	D
Norwalk	138	1 902	110.9	29.2	7	198	10.0	2.5	135	D	D	D
Novato	122	1 804	98.9	28.4	19	289	14.5	5.1	150	1 781	258.6	94.9
Oakland	967	13 126	833.7	237.5	66	2 500	383.9	195.8	837	10 763	1 560.7	744.1
Oakley	25	D	D	D	3	D	D	D	24	D	D	D
Oceanside	306	5 216	354.8	87.9	32	826	47.6	13.6	290	2 490	295.4	117.0
Ontario	332	6 564	383.2	104.6	19	D	D	D	186	D	D	D
Orange	398	6 959	424.2	114.0	36	358	25.4	5.6	597	8 280	979.2	407.1
Oxnard	282	4 397	264.2	68.2	28	414	25.9	6.5	373	3 719	448.7	170.8
Pacifica	67	633	43.7	11.5	6	D	D	D	47	D	D	D
Palmdale	206	4 388	228.8	62.4	12	D	D	D	176	1 715	185.6	59.5
Palm Desert	194	5 547	365.5	109.1	37	1 326	97.5	32.4	226	2 038	226.0	76.2
Palm Springs	262	6 904	411.2	124.8	27	1 116	216.2	34.6	239	4 434	735.1	243.8
Palo Alto	280	6 048	422.3	131.5	31	530	36.4	12.6	329	D	D	D
Paradise	40	D	D	D	6	D	D	D	87	D	D	D
Paramount	73	683	41.0	9.9	2	D	D	D	78	1 276	153.4	58.7
Pasadena	473	9 619	617.4	184.7	150	954	136.2	50.7	873	10 536	1 619.4	533.6
Perris	68	1 017	55.9	14.7	4	D	D	D	34	498	47.0	17.2
Petaluma	162	2 080	125.4	33.8	29	659	49.4	12.6	165	2 145	253.5	83.3
Pico Rivera	118	1 627	105.0	26.5	4	D	D	D	74	931	85.5	31.9
Pittsburg	84	1 394	73.9	19.6	4	76	3.8	1.0	65	693	54.3	24.0
Placentia	91	1 268	74.5	19.3	7	D	D	D	125	2 113	211.4	91.8
Pleasant Hill	93	1 540	106.1	28.9	14	204	10.2	4.5	114	1 550	164.1	57.1
Pleasanton	240	3 856	247.7	70.1	37	D	D	D	273	3 240	621.3	164.5
Pomona	195	2 940	169.5	48.4	12	D	D	D	272	3 383	335.7	125.5
Porterville	81	1 268	60.0	14.8	4	D	D	D	126	D	D	D
Poway	105	1 280	69.7	20.1	24	D	D	D	148	D	D	D
Rancho Cordova	144	2 383	136.5	37.8	15	D	D	D	98	3 006	767.2	253.0
Rancho Cucamonga	312	7 074	366.2	105.5	31	299	42.0	6.4	386	4 315	417.1	156.3
Rancho Palos Verdes	38	1 388	127.9	38.1	12	D	D	D	120	D	D	D
Rancho Santa Margarita	83	1 423	76.4	22.1	16	D	D	D	83	D	D	D
Redding	254	4 374	228.7	62.0	25	D	D	D	465	6 274	676.0	257.0
Redlands	174	3 257	163.8	44.1	13	194	12.7	4.7	289	3 092	466.2	151.4
Redondo Beach	212	4 099	247.5	78.7	42	D	D	D	204	1 310	193.7	70.3
Redwood City	216	2 841	205.9	55.3	30	799	45.3	13.2	273	D	D	D
Rialto	89	1 287	71.8	18.0	6	98	17.2	3.3	87	733	63.4	25.8
Richmond	123	1 053	72.7	18.7	16	D	D	D	118	2 201	345.6	138.1
Ridgecrest	60	939	45.2	12.0	6	61	1.4	0.4	56	D	D	D
Riverside	535	9 620	516.6	142.1	52	723	46.2	12.7	761	12 615	1 758.6	662.6
Rocklin	80	1 274	65.2	19.0	13	D	D	D	137	D	D	D
Rohnert Park	87	1 698	95.0	27.2	12	D	D	D	69	556	81.6	20.8
Rosemead	157	2 023	112.0	29.5	6	155	9.1	2.8	127	1 343	141.6	46.4
Roseville	365	7 478	394.2	113.6	37	766	43.4	11.9	450	D	D	D
Sacramento	1 093	20 289	1 145.7	327.5	90	2 682	303.0	111.5	1 052	15 968	2 608.6	1 092.1
Salinas	253	3 746	221.3	57.4	11	D	D	D	276	2 941	365.6	148.3
San Bernardino	342	5 741	303.7	82.1	25	D	D	D	364	5 388	522.1	207.2
San Bruno	129	1 868	119.7	33.7	9	D	D	D	104	1 117	171.6	55.4
San Buenaventura (Ventura)	327	5 534	319.0	91.8	47	731	45.3	12.4	440	4 394	516.3	195.0
San Carlos	116	1 498	104.4	27.0	15	86	7.5	1.4	94	646	67.7	25.3
San Clemente	162	2 475	136.2	36.7	34	D	D	D	201	D	D	D
San Diego	3 527	80 688	5 590.8	1 561.3	403	8 652	1 213.2	467.7	3 572	40 873	5 882.8	2 308.0
San Dimas	77	1 183	71.5	19.0	16	D	D	D	101	1 648	157.6	61.0

1. Establishments subject to federal tax.

Table D. Cities — Other Services and Government Employment and Payroll

City	Other services[1], 2012				Government employment and payroll, 2012								
					Full-time equivalent employees	March payroll							
						Total (dollars)	Percent of total for:						
	Number of establishments	Number of employees	Receipts (mil dol)	Annual payroll (mil dol)			Administration, judicial, and legal	Police and Corrections	Fire Protection	Highways and transportation	Health and welfare	Natural resources and utilities	Education and libraries
	104	105	106	107	108	109	110	111	112	113	114	115	116
CALIFORNIA—Cont'd													
Menlo Park	62	D	D	D	265	1 760 354	14.1	39.6	0.0	11.5	2.4	17.6	6.2
Merced	59	326	26.8	8.3	442	2 547 548	11.6	31.0	16.4	3.0	2.2	22.9	0.0
Milpitas	108	1 035	201.8	34.8	391	3 312 573	25.8	33.3	22.1	4.4	1.1	10.0	0.0
Mission Viejo	169	1 052	91.3	28.5	180	959 036	31.7	0.0	0.0	15.3	6.3	22.8	18.2
Modesto	237	1 355	141.6	35.1	1 217	6 592 366	14.4	32.0	18.1	7.5	1.5	23.8	0.0
Monrovia	67	392	51.0	11.7	256	1 668 764	17.2	33.0	27.7	1.5	3.1	13.2	3.5
Montclair	73	398	35.7	9.4	251	1 296 597	25.0	33.8	17.4	1.8	13.1	5.5	0.0
Montebello	81	611	42.8	10.4	486	2 561 705	6.5	30.7	19.8	32.0	1.1	6.0	0.0
Monterey	57	547	34.6	13.1	506	3 399 804	0.1	18.1	19.6	2.7	1.3	10.8	4.3
Monterey Park	81	333	32.7	7.0	327	1 888 775	11.2	36.1	23.6	5.9	0.0	17.1	5.2
Moorpark	25	126	12.5	3.2	67	465 036	35.0	0.0	0.0	14.4	20.2	30.4	0.0
Moreno Valley	121	474	34.7	10.2	743	3 360 444	15.3	2.0	2.4	17.1	12.4	15.5	1.9
Morgan Hill	68	347	34.4	9.8	182	1 516 788	12.8	39.9	0.0	2.3	1.1	25.1	0.0
Mountain View	137	800	84.5	25.9	600	5 229 873	11.3	28.6	21.6	9.3	5.2	17.2	4.4
Murrieta	142	925	70.6	22.7	339	2 066 931	19.5	46.2	23.2	0.5	0.0	6.5	3.4
Napa	119	638	58.5	17.7	431	3 308 340	12.4	30.1	19.6	7.4	8.5	18.7	0.0
National City	104	512	41.9	13.0	361	2 077 359	8.6	42.0	20.4	3.0	4.5	9.8	7.3
Newark	63	D	D	D	169	764 266	14.7	51.1	0.0	5.4	1.7	15.4	0.0
Newport Beach	205	1 435	107.2	31.2	797	6 997 470	14.3	26.3	21.3	6.9	1.1	16.5	4.6
Norco	62	303	27.3	8.0	81	317 544	33.7	2.4	2.2	9.4	11.1	25.1	0.0
Norwalk	72	363	35.5	10.3	339	1 671 145	18.7	10.3	0.0	35.5	8.6	18.6	0.0
Novato	87	853	75.5	28.5	190	1 241 125	11.4	43.9	0.0	18.8	2.5	18.0	0.0
Oakland	594	3 810	392.7	119.0	3 940	30 153 764	10.1	31.4	20.4	17.1	7.7	5.5	3.1
Oakley	23	58	7.1	1.9	26	121 823	56.5	10.1	0.0	3.7	0.0	20.3	0.0
Oceanside	178	1 117	103.6	31.0	950	5 925 758	16.2	36.9	16.2	3.6	4.4	18.2	2.3
Ontario	177	2 305	216.1	68.5	1 078	8 143 877	8.3	39.1	22.6	0.5	2.8	14.8	2.5
Orange	279	2 345	198.3	65.4	662	5 240 608	10.8	40.5	25.9	5.9	1.0	10.0	3.4
Oxnard	159	939	94.1	25.7	1 267	7 972 661	9.1	36.5	12.3	4.2	8.3	23.4	2.6
Pacifica	29	D	D	D	186	1 351 528	12.4	28.8	17.8	10.7	2.1	16.8	2.6
Palmdale	89	433	30.0	9.6	315	1 381 568	13.7	8.9	0.0	20.8	15.6	20.9	2.9
Palm Desert	117	624	45.2	14.4	122	957 854	30.8	0.0	0.0	28.3	24.5	7.0	0.0
Palm Springs	80	514	32.2	10.3	513	3 307 054	15.7	33.0	17.9	11.3	2.5	5.4	3.1
Palo Alto	104	1 104	97.7	36.6	921	7 610 093	16.4	17.4	16.0	3.9	0.9	38.7	3.0
Paradise	41	123	12.7	3.3	88	528 134	9.9	38.1	34.1	5.6	8.4	2.9	0.0
Paramount	67	609	74.6	24.1	210	830 396	17.7	15.7	0.0	19.4	8.9	20.4	0.0
Pasadena	333	2 438	363.4	87.9	1 821	13 044 662	12.2	21.1	13.6	1.9	4.8	27.1	0.2
Perris	32	156	23.1	4.6	76	396 603	36.6	0.0	0.0	22.9	32.0	8.5	0.0
Petaluma	106	599	49.6	15.6	301	2 362 449	10.3	35.7	22.9	9.0	1.1	20.1	0.0
Pico Rivera	68	535	59.8	17.1	288	1 134 401	19.4	0.0	0.0	28.7	11.6	40.3	0.0
Pittsburg	44	530	53.6	17.1	267	1 784 475	10.5	44.3	0.0	7.0	2.9	12.6	0.0
Placentia	63	401	47.0	11.9	175	1 008 861	10.4	58.5	0.0	7.4	1.7	17.6	0.0
Pleasant Hill	55	410	36.4	10.9	125	907 055	21.9	52.8	0.0	22.8	2.3	0.0	0.0
Pleasanton	135	1 000	105.4	37.9	509	4 073 003	13.7	23.1	30.7	5.5	2.2	14.7	4.4
Pomona	133	729	74.7	22.6	630	2 988 643	8.4	51.9	0.0	5.9	6.3	15.1	2.8
Porterville	35	165	14.0	5.3	323	1 445 053	12.8	29.5	14.5	7.6	0.7	28.3	2.8
Poway	88	592	49.4	15.7	291	1 821 500	20.9	0.0	28.9	10.0	4.0	27.1	0.0
Rancho Cordova	81	482	53.1	16.4	67	438 835	46.2	0.0	0.0	25.2	6.1	0.0	0.0
Rancho Cucamonga	215	1 149	89.7	27.4	639	3 536 504	13.7	0.0	32.8	6.4	4.3	31.3	5.3
Rancho Palos Verdes	20	103	5.8	1.7	69	423 058	29.0	0.0	0.0	13.7	0.0	30.2	0.0
Rancho Santa Margarita	52	288	21.8	5.6	27	142 356	100.0	0.0	0.0	0.0	0.0	0.0	0.0
Redding	185	1 012	97.6	30.5	747	5 047 088	9.6	20.1	14.2	8.9	1.6	42.2	0.0
Redlands	110	567	48.6	15.6	429	2 798 020	10.0	32.4	23.6	5.8	1.1	19.2	3.1
Redondo Beach	123	745	68.2	17.6	980	23 723 684	11.5	36.3	24.3	11.4	4.1	9.3	3.2
Redwood City	122	D	D	D	543	4 492 820	13.2	30.5	20.6	0.0	1.1	19.6	6.0
Rialto	61	322	37.7	10.1	357	2 259 378	9.8	38.9	27.3	6.1	4.1	10.2	0.0
Richmond	88	448	49.5	16.7	843	5 538 248	8.5	38.6	12.2	3.0	6.2	8.4	4.2
Ridgecrest	29	124	10.7	3.1	106	565 833	18.2	47.9	0.0	13.3	4.0	14.5	0.0
Riverside	366	2 248	213.7	58.3	2 260	15 114 251	6.2	28.2	15.6	5.5	4.5	29.8	1.6
Rocklin	72	487	38.0	11.3	287	1 697 873	10.7	35.7	20.8	8.4	6.6	17.7	0.0
Rohnert Park	55	337	34.1	9.8	176	1 106 615	17.8	57.7	0.0	0.0	1.6	22.9	0.0
Rosemead	91	245	22.4	5.1	102	521 909	25.8	14.7	0.0	10.3	10.6	24.2	0.0
Roseville	179	1 842	231.3	58.3	1 160	7 733 037	12.9	18.3	15.7	2.8	2.2	35.9	2.0
Sacramento	612	3 879	358.6	106.5	4 483	29 508 935	6.7	46.8	16.2	10.8	3.9	15.6	0.0
Salinas	164	962	110.0	28.5	553	3 536 035	7.9	43.0	21.0	11.8	4.5	3.6	5.1
San Bernardino	202	974	78.5	24.7	1 527	9 251 817	6.8	36.8	22.6	1.2	6.6	19.6	1.2
San Bruno	96	679	64.5	18.7	262	1 918 097	12.9	28.0	20.2	5.7	0.5	17.9	6.2
San Buenaventura (Ventura)	197	993	93.1	27.9	659	4 241 287	13.8	29.9	21.1	8.7	1.1	23.0	0.0
San Carlos	83	914	67.7	24.1	99	739 930	23.5	27.1	4.5	4.5	27.8		0.0
San Clemente	88	489	39.8	11.5	220	909 552	22.8	0.0	0.0	23.9	7.3	44.4	0.0
San Diego	1 994	16 826	1 333.9	457.3	9 425	62 476 850	19.9	28.7	13.9	2.4	0.3	25.5	2.3
San Dimas	50	D	D	D	106	558 552	25.6	0.0	0.0	20.9	21.8	31.7	0.0

1. Establishments subject to federal tax.

Table D. Cities — **City Government Finances**

City	City government finances, 2012									
	General revenue							General expenditure		
		Intergovernmental		Taxes					Per capita[1] (dollars)	
					Per capita[1] (dollars)					
	Total (mil dol)	Total (mil dol)	Percent from state government	Total (mil dol)	Total	Property	Sales and gross receipts	Total (mil dol)	Total	Capital outlays
	117	118	119	120	121	122	123	124	125	126
CALIFORNIA—Cont'd										
Menlo Park	57.5	3.5	90.3	37.8	1 149	690	444	61.2	1 859	334
Merced	96.3	17.9	51.3	32.3	401	192	205	102.4	1 271	255
Milpitas	117.5	7.2	69.9	80.2	1 162	727	430	122.5	1 776	418
Mission Viejo	74.4	7.3	60.1	55.9	588	365	219	78.4	825	168
Modesto	229.0	48.3	51.3	90.4	440	167	270	226.5	1 101	147
Monrovia	51.2	2.2	84.3	38.6	1 042	714	321	56.5	1 525	198
Montclair	47.1	5.3	94.7	33.5	892	526	363	50.6	1 346	152
Montebello	97.7	20.3	71.7	57.3	904	479	394	66.8	1 053	70
Monterey	96.6	3.5	87.7	44.7	1 575	505	1 065	99.9	3 520	328
Monterey Park	60.2	3.6	69.4	41.1	674	471	200	56.7	929	44
Moorpark	30.0	1.5	80.3	17.5	500	296	187	35.7	1 021	81
Moreno Valley	147.5	17.1	68.1	88.6	446	252	192	166.7	838	157
Morgan Hill	67.3	2.7	96.6	37.9	960	628	229	61.1	1 548	436
Mountain View	174.0	5.3	63.1	102.5	1 337	778	411	183.3	2 392	549
Murrieta	80.7	26.1	46.3	39.0	366	220	142	83.1	780	255
Napa	110.6	18.2	18.2	57.4	732	363	365	117.8	1 502	144
National City	79.9	19.2	23.1	47.7	801	407	387	70.4	1 183	258
Newark	41.0	2.5	91.0	33.4	766	334	424	40.3	924	81
Newport Beach	200.4	9.9	61.5	127.8	1 472	878	579	233.0	2 684	829
Norco	33.0	2.3	44.5	21.6	787	582	187	36.0	1 314	451
Norwalk	85.6	27.5	48.8	49.4	464	166	296	67.8	637	38
Novato	49.0	2.3	100.0	35.6	669	475	189	48.6	913	211
Oakland	1 343.3	204.3	54.6	570.6	1 420	810	448	1 312.4	3 266	765
Oakley	29.3	2.8	84.6	16.7	447	271	122	25.9	696	242
Oceanside	233.9	38.0	49.7	106.3	620	416	200	212.9	1 241	113
Ontario	317.2	21.8	84.9	172.3	1 031	570	459	290.2	1 736	274
Orange	142.3	16.7	75.8	101.3	726	444	279	160.6	1 151	284
Oxnard	312.9	40.3	93.9	115.8	575	339	234	320.7	1 592	328
Pacifica	41.0	2.7	100.0	20.9	544	352	188	44.4	1 157	119
Palmdale	135.7	21.8	54.2	85.7	550	380	156	117.3	753	85
Palm Desert	168.1	3.9	64.2	125.5	2 515	1 931	574	156.3	3 132	538
Palm Springs	141.9	13.2	18.3	76.2	1 662	780	860	157.5	3 436	660
Palo Alto	217.5	3.5	57.6	84.1	1 269	530	666	250.9	3 789	623
Paradise	16.8	4.1	95.7	11.0	420	262	156	14.4	551	19
Paramount	37.4	3.7	65.3	29.9	546	300	244	36.2	660	87
Pasadena	411.2	38.8	79.2	194.6	1 402	638	686	403.1	2 905	429
Perris	49.1	3.7	86.4	26.8	376	223	151	54.9	770	150
Petaluma	90.6	5.2	59.0	46.6	792	514	263	83.8	1 424	233
Pico Rivera	61.1	23.1	28.9	26.9	422	222	200	71.3	1 118	307
Pittsburg	89.1	17.2	34.3	46.4	708	555	146	101.3	1 544	207
Placentia	41.3	4.4	89.2	26.6	512	274	225	39.0	750	113
Pleasant Hill	28.8	3.6	100.0	22.5	664	309	316	29.7	877	199
Pleasanton	134.8	6.1	84.2	81.3	1 125	737	334	130.6	1 807	174
Pomona	196.5	41.6	62.7	104.5	692	386	299	201.6	1 334	134
Porterville	49.1	8.8	73.5	21.3	387	135	246	51.3	933	177
Poway	88.7	1.8	88.7	67.5	1 375	1 096	258	85.0	1 731	191
Rancho Cordova	68.7	14.0	40.7	44.1	660	234	422	65.9	985	308
Rancho Cucamonga	230.6	19.5	59.9	162.0	950	784	163	207.7	1 218	193
Rancho Palos Verdes	29.2	1.6	88.9	24.4	577	282	294	28.5	673	66
Rancho Santa Margarita	16.9	2.4	90.6	13.9	285	143	138	17.3	354	60
Redding	182.1	39.5	29.9	57.9	638	314	302	162.8	1 795	572
Redlands	93.8	3.7	75.1	56.2	805	451	352	85.8	1 228	162
Redondo Beach	117.9	8.1	72.6	58.6	867	423	419	113.6	1 680	108
Redwood City	145.3	7.3	85.5	81.5	1 028	589	431	149.2	1 881	250
Rialto	107.1	8.8	38.5	65.0	639	365	273	111.4	1 095	208
Richmond	254.5	35.4	49.7	151.0	1 416	681	645	274.3	2 573	398
Ridgecrest	21.9	1.1	90.4	15.8	556	343	211	20.8	736	131
Riverside	410.7	63.1	60.7	197.7	631	327	295	486.0	1 551	356
Rocklin	52.5	5.7	74.5	32.4	549	319	184	53.8	911	89
Rohnert Park	59.0	3.3	100.0	32.1	780	488	289	57.7	1 402	280
Rosemead	34.4	2.8	59.2	25.5	469	313	155	32.2	592	173
Roseville	251.3	19.4	55.2	91.7	738	331	402	243.4	1 960	236
Sacramento	884.8	128.8	66.1	366.7	771	418	342	806.3	1 695	296
Salinas	117.7	16.6	57.5	82.1	532	198	333	122.6	794	103
San Bernardino	250.9	21.3	61.3	132.6	621	311	305	230.8	1 081	128
San Bruno	58.6	3.4	100.0	29.7	704	334	342	51.8	1 228	135
San Buenaventura (Ventura)	132.2	9.8	64.9	71.9	662	319	341	135.5	1 247	155
San Carlos	46.8	1.0	100.0	27.3	933	565	359	38.4	1 315	156
San Clemente	74.5	6.4	93.0	44.4	685	501	177	82.7	1 276	289
San Diego	2 616.7	370.0	40.2	1 122.2	838	439	397	2 361.5	1 763	396
San Dimas	30.5	1.5	86.2	23.3	690	367	317	33.2	982	105

1. Based on population estimated as of July 1 of the year shown.

Table D. Cities — City Government Finances

City	Public welfare	Highways	Parking facilities	Education	Health and hospitals	Police protection	Sewerage and sanitation	Parks and recreation	Housing and community development	Interest on debt
	127	128	129	130	131	132	133	134	135	136
CALIFORNIA—Cont'd										
Menlo Park	0.0	9.7	2.0	0.0	0.0	23.7	0.7	24.5	5.2	7.1
Merced	0.0	14.7	0.0	0.0	0.2	17.9	21.6	4.9	8.8	3.6
Milpitas	0.0	8.7	0.0	0.0	10.6	17.8	7.2	5.0	24.5	5.9
Mission Viejo	0.0	22.7	0.0	0.0	2.2	20.0	0.0	20.2	7.8	1.5
Modesto	0.0	11.8	0.5	0.3	0.4	20.9	16.0	9.7	4.4	2.0
Monrovia	0.0	4.3	0.0	0.0	3.4	33.5	2.0	4.6	10.1	7.2
Montclair	0.0	8.2	0.0	0.0	8.2	20.5	7.9	8.1	24.7	6.2
Montebello	0.0	6.7	0.0	0.0	0.3	27.9	5.1	15.8	5.7	8.2
Monterey	0.0	11.5	6.8	0.0	0.0	12.8	1.9	15.4	6.0	0.7
Monterey Park	0.0	6.8	0.0	0.0	1.2	26.8	11.0	5.8	9.8	4.7
Moorpark	0.0	11.6	0.0	0.0	1.1	18.2	0.9	12.0	18.3	2.7
Moreno Valley	0.0	19.1	0.0	0.0	1.3	26.1	0.0	9.0	14.2	3.7
Morgan Hill	0.0	10.4	0.0	0.0	0.0	18.6	10.0	10.1	21.8	3.2
Mountain View	0.0	4.2	0.1	0.0	0.0	16.0	15.2	21.1	2.5	1.5
Murrieta	0.0	30.4	0.0	0.0	0.0	29.4	0.0	11.0	5.8	4.3
Napa	0.0	15.7	0.4	0.0	2.6	16.9	17.1	6.9	13.2	1.1
National City	0.0	3.6	0.0	0.0	1.7	30.9	9.9	3.5	23.8	4.2
Newark	0.0	12.0	0.0	0.0	0.6	32.5	0.4	11.1	0.5	1.2
Newport Beach	0.0	13.8	0.0	0.0	2.6	17.7	1.5	10.0	0.0	3.5
Norco	0.0	9.4	0.0	0.0	5.5	12.6	18.0	6.1	16.3	12.3
Norwalk	0.0	12.1	0.7	0.0	7.3	19.7	0.0	10.0	18.0	8.9
Novato	0.0	12.8	0.0	0.0	1.2	25.4	0.0	19.0	6.7	9.6
Oakland	0.0	3.5	0.7	0.0	5.4	14.9	3.4	3.6	9.4	7.2
Oakley	0.0	20.6	0.0	0.0	0.7	28.9	0.0	14.6	12.4	5.7
Oceanside	0.0	7.9	0.8	0.0	0.1	22.7	19.9	6.2	10.5	3.6
Ontario	0.0	7.4	0.0	0.0	0.4	24.6	11.6	5.0	10.1	4.7
Orange	0.0	11.8	0.0	0.0	6.7	23.1	3.8	11.6	10.8	2.7
Oxnard	0.0	12.2	0.3	0.0	0.0	21.3	22.0	10.3	4.4	7.3
Pacifica	0.0	14.4	0.0	0.0	1.7	20.3	20.0	8.3	0.5	4.7
Palmdale	0.0	15.6	0.0	0.0	0.7	16.8	2.5	12.1	20.8	10.5
Palm Desert	0.0	10.2	0.0	0.0	2.6	10.4	0.0	10.7	38.1	11.7
Palm Springs	0.0	15.8	0.3	0.0	0.8	12.8	3.7	14.0	5.4	3.7
Palo Alto	0.0	4.4	0.1	2.9	0.3	13.8	24.8	13.4	0.2	1.9
Paradise	0.0	15.3	0.0	0.0	1.1	27.0	4.7	0.2	1.9	7.0
Paramount	0.0	18.4	0.0	0.0	0.0	29.4	0.0	12.7	10.6	4.9
Pasadena	0.0	6.9	2.7	0.0	4.4	15.8	4.9	10.1	6.4	3.9
Perris	0.0	14.3	0.0	0.0	0.8	20.1	3.8	3.3	23.1	17.7
Petaluma	0.0	9.4	0.0	0.0	1.0	18.2	19.3	5.4	15.3	10.8
Pico Rivera	0.0	35.5	0.0	0.0	0.0	14.1	0.0	10.4	18.0	0.0
Pittsburg	0.0	7.8	0.0	0.0	0.4	18.5	2.0	3.9	33.7	17.9
Placentia	0.0	16.3	0.0	0.0	0.3	28.1	8.9	5.7	6.5	3.6
Pleasant Hill	0.0	29.3	0.0	0.0	0.6	35.4	0.8	0.0	9.2	2.4
Pleasanton	0.0	10.4	0.0	0.0	0.2	18.3	10.1	17.9	1.6	2.7
Pomona	0.0	15.1	0.0	0.0	0.0	20.1	6.5	1.6	23.4	13.4
Porterville	0.0	8.0	0.1	0.0	0.2	15.8	24.2	9.3	3.5	6.2
Poway	0.0	11.2	0.0	0.0	0.4	12.3	9.1	7.3	12.9	15.2
Rancho Cordova	0.0	34.1	0.0	0.0	0.7	24.0	0.0	1.0	7.5	1.7
Rancho Cucamonga	0.0	11.8	0.0	1.1	1.4	12.6	1.6	3.3	19.8	13.7
Rancho Palos Verdes	0.0	21.5	0.0	0.0	0.7	14.0	1.6	11.5	1.2	3.6
Rancho Santa Margarita	0.0	22.7	0.0	0.0	2.1	43.6	0.0	5.7	0.0	3.1
Redding	0.0	8.9	0.0	0.0	0.4	15.2	34.2	5.3	9.1	2.7
Redlands	0.0	5.8	0.0	0.0	5.2	24.9	19.0	6.7	5.8	3.4
Redondo Beach	0.0	6.3	0.0	0.0	4.0	24.5	5.8	5.0	14.1	1.4
Redwood City	0.0	12.8	1.2	0.0	0.5	20.3	14.1	6.2	5.9	3.2
Rialto	0.0	8.0	0.0	0.4	4.0	23.1	8.6	5.0	18.0	8.2
Richmond	0.0	11.3	0.0	0.0	0.5	23.5	3.7	1.7	15.8	7.2
Ridgecrest	0.0	9.8	0.0	0.0	0.0	30.5	5.8	8.8	15.7	7.3
Riverside	0.0	11.4	1.0	0.0	0.1	18.0	8.8	5.0	13.1	6.9
Rocklin	0.0	10.2	0.0	0.0	0.0	21.7	0.0	12.6	9.7	4.8
Rohnert Park	0.0	4.3	0.0	0.0	1.7	17.8	25.1	6.1	17.1	5.0
Rosemead	0.0	5.7	0.0	0.0	0.9	20.7	0.0	7.6	18.2	4.3
Roseville	0.0	11.4	0.0	0.0	0.0	12.0	14.3	9.5	4.3	15.7
Sacramento	0.0	18.4	1.9	0.0	2.2	16.9	15.2	7.8	3.6	5.8
Salinas	0.0	8.9	1.2	0.0	3.6	33.3	3.9	3.8	3.4	1.3
San Bernardino	0.0	5.3	0.0	0.0	1.1	29.7	15.7	3.3	9.8	1.9
San Bruno	0.0	6.9	0.0	0.0	0.0	23.1	16.6	12.8	1.6	0.9
San Buenaventura (Ventura)	0.0	11.6	0.5	0.0	0.2	22.4	15.1	9.0	2.0	3.7
San Carlos	0.0	9.3	0.2	0.0	0.0	18.2	15.9	9.3	3.0	2.2
San Clemente	0.0	8.3	0.0	0.0	3.0	14.5	11.0	25.3	3.1	1.1
San Diego	0.0	9.7	0.1	0.0	0.6	12.7	12.6	9.9	19.7	6.2
San Dimas	0.0	13.5	0.1	0.0	0.4	15.5	0.1	11.6	10.1	3.7

Table D. Cities — City Government Finances, City Government Employment, and Climate

City	City government finances, 2012 (cont.)			Climate[2]						
	Debt outstanding		Debt issued during year	Average daily temperature (degrees Fahrenheit)				Annual precipitation (inches)	Heating degree days	Cooling degree days
				Mean		Limits				
	Total (mil dol)	Per capita[1] (dollars)		January	July	January[3]	July[4]			
	137	138	139	140	141	142	143	144	145	146
CALIFORNIA—Cont'd										
Menlo Park	89.8	2 729	9.8	49.0	68.0	40.4	78.8	15.71	2 584	452
Merced	93.3	1 159	0.0	46.3	78.6	37.5	96.5	12.50	2 602	1 578
Milpitas	171.2	2 482	0.0	50.5	70.9	41.7	84.3	15.08	2 171	811
Mission Viejo	47.5	500	0.0	56.7	72.4	47.2	82.3	14.03	1 465	1 183
Modesto	441.0	2 144	52.8	47.2	77.7	40.1	93.6	13.12	2 358	1 570
Monrovia	103.5	2 796	0.0	56.1	75.3	44.3	89.4	21.09	1 398	1 558
Montclair	77.9	2 073	0.0	54.6	73.8	41.5	88.7	16.96	1 727	1 191
Montebello	88.0	1 388	0.0	58.8	76.6	47.9	88.9	14.44	949	1 837
Monterey	14.8	521	0.0	51.6	60.2	43.4	68.1	20.35	3 092	74
Monterey Park	83.1	1 363	0.0	56.3	75.6	42.6	89.0	18.56	1 295	1 575
Moorpark	27.6	788	0.0	54.7	68.3	41.2	80.7	18.41	1 911	602
Moreno Valley	91.6	461	0.0	54.2	77.4	42.0	93.5	10.67	1 674	1 697
Morgan Hill	124.6	3 156	0.0	43.5	70.7	37.5	78.2	23.73	4 566	747
Mountain View	83.5	1 090	39.4	49.0	68.0	40.4	78.8	15.71	2 584	452
Murrieta	90.8	852	0.0	52.2	79.6	38.3	98.1	12.09	1 924	1 874
Napa	95.7	1 221	0.0	47.9	68.6	39.2	82.6	26.46	2 689	529
National City	84.5	1 419	0.0	57.3	70.1	46.1	76.1	9.95	1 321	862
Newark	11.4	261	9.7	49.8	68.0	42.0	78.3	14.85	2 367	530
Newport Beach	270.0	3 110	2.6	55.9	67.3	48.2	71.4	11.65	1 719	543
Norco	136.8	4 999	0.0	NA	NA	NA	NA	NA	NA	NA
Norwalk	142.9	1 342	2.1	57.0	73.8	46.0	82.9	12.94	1 211	1 186
Novato	141.1	2 647	0.0	48.8	67.7	41.3	80.9	34.29	2 621	451
Oakland	2 294.4	5 709	429.5	50.9	64.9	44.7	72.7	22.94	2 400	377
Oakley	39.5	1 060	0.0	45.7	74.4	37.8	90.7	13.33	2 714	1 179
Oceanside	200.5	1 168	7.7	54.7	67.6	45.4	72.1	11.13	2 009	505
Ontario	212.5	1 271	0.9	54.6	73.8	41.5	88.7	16.96	1 727	1 191
Orange	107.1	768	3.0	58.0	72.9	46.6	82.7	13.84	1 153	1 299
Oxnard	484.3	2 404	9.3	55.6	65.9	45.5	72.7	15.62	1 936	403
Pacifica	52.3	1 363	0.0	49.4	62.8	42.9	71.1	20.11	2 862	142
Palmdale	251.2	1 614	2.2	46.6	81.7	34.3	97.5	7.36	2 704	1 998
Palm Desert	450.5	9 024	1.0	56.8	92.8	42.0	107.1	3.15	903	4 388
Palm Springs	165.5	3 611	68.9	57.3	92.1	44.2	108.2	5.23	951	4 224
Palo Alto	142.0	2 144	17.2	49.0	68.0	40.4	78.8	15.71	2 584	452
Paradise	14.9	568	0.0	45.7	77.8	37.7	91.7	56.20	3 145	1 464
Paramount	69.2	1 262	0.0	57.0	73.8	46.0	82.9	12.94	1 211	1 186
Pasadena	766.2	5 522	88.3	56.1	75.3	44.3	89.4	21.09	1 398	1 558
Perris	262.8	3 686	0.0	51.2	78.3	36.1	97.8	11.40	2 123	1 710
Petaluma	244.3	4 153	12.9	48.4	67.3	38.9	82.7	25.85	2 741	385
Pico Rivera	49.9	784	0.0	58.3	74.2	48.5	83.8	15.14	928	1 506
Pittsburg	474.6	7 230	0.0	45.7	74.4	37.8	90.7	13.33	2 714	1 179
Placentia	28.8	554	0.0	58.0	72.9	46.6	82.7	13.84	1 153	1 299
Pleasant Hill	21.7	641	0.0	46.3	71.2	38.8	87.4	19.58	2 757	786
Pleasanton	82.6	1 143	0.0	47.2	72.0	37.4	89.1	14.82	2 755	858
Pomona	411.1	2 721	0.0	54.6	73.8	41.5	88.7	16.96	1 727	1 191
Porterville	72.6	1 321	0.1	48.7	82.8	39.4	98.1	11.49	2 053	2 246
Poway	246.1	5 010	0.2	55.3	70.9	43.5	80.8	11.97	1 808	979
Rancho Cordova	23.3	349	0.0	48.2	77.4	41.3	93.8	19.87	2 226	1 597
Rancho Cucamonga	503.8	2 954	0.4	56.6	78.3	45.3	95.0	14.77	1 364	1 901
Rancho Palos Verdes	24.4	575	0.3	56.3	69.4	46.2	77.6	14.79	1 526	742
Rancho Santa Margarita	11.4	233	0.0	56.7	72.4	47.2	82.3	14.03	1 465	1 183
Redding	140.7	1 552	25.2	45.5	81.3	35.5	98.5	33.52	2 961	1 741
Redlands	63.1	903	0.0	52.9	78.0	40.4	94.4	13.62	1 904	1 714
Redondo Beach	53.3	789	0.0	57.1	69.3	48.6	75.3	13.15	1 274	679
Redwood City	164.1	2 069	10.0	48.4	68.0	39.1	80.8	20.16	2 764	422
Rialto	226.0	2 222	0.0	54.4	79.6	41.8	96.0	16.43	1 599	1 937
Richmond	657.3	6 165	25.9	50.0	62.7	42.9	70.5	23.35	2 720	184
Ridgecrest	40.5	1 430	0.0	NA	NA	NA	NA	NA	NA	NA
Riverside	1 908.6	6 092	61.7	55.3	78.7	42.7	94.1	10.22	1 475	1 863
Rocklin	85.0	1 439	11.8	46.9	77.7	39.2	94.8	24.61	2 532	1 528
Rohnert Park	71.7	1 743	0.0	48.7	67.6	39.5	82.2	31.01	2 694	526
Rosemead	43.5	799	0.0	56.3	75.6	42.6	89.0	18.56	1 295	1 575
Roseville	1 069.1	8 607	0.0	46.9	77.7	39.2	94.8	24.61	2 532	1 528
Sacramento	1 087.3	2 286	1.8	46.3	75.4	38.8	92.4	17.93	2 666	1 248
Salinas	42.6	276	18.0	51.2	63.2	41.3	71.3	12.91	2 770	210
San Bernardino	121.7	570	0.0	54.4	79.6	41.8	96.0	16.43	1 599	1 937
San Bruno	11.6	274	0.0	49.4	62.8	42.9	71.1	20.11	2 862	142
San Buenaventura (Ventura)	122.9	1 132	23.5	55.6	65.9	45.5	72.7	15.62	1 936	403
San Carlos	24.3	832	0.0	48.4	68.0	39.1	80.8	20.16	2 764	422
San Clemente	18.2	280	5.0	55.4	68.7	43.9	77.3	13.56	1 756	666
San Diego	3 433.7	2 563	465.2	57.8	70.9	49.7	75.8	10.77	1 063	866
San Dimas	19.7	582	0.0	54.6	73.8	41.5	88.7	16.96	1 727	1 191

1. Based on the population estimated as of July 1 of the year shown. 2. Represents normal values based on the 30-year period, 1971–2000. 3. Average daily minimum. 4. Average daily maximum.

Table D. Cities — **Land Area and Population**

STATE Place code	City	Population, 2015				Race alone or in combination (percent), 2010-2014						
		Land area,[1] 2010 (sq km)	Total persons	Rank	Per square kilometer	White	Black	American Indian, Alaska Native	Asian	Hawaiian Pacific Islander	Percent Hispanic or Latino[2], 2010-2014	Percent foreign born 2010-2014
		1	2	3	4	5	6	7	8	9	10	11
	CALIFORNIA—Cont'd											
06 67000	San Francisco	121.4	864 816	13	7 123.7	53.2	6.7	1.1	36.3	0.8	15.3	35.5
06 67042	San Gabriel	10.7	40 424	929	3 777.9	24.6	1.0	0.6	61.4	0.3	26.4	54.6
06 67112	San Jacinto	66.6	46 951	805	705.0	65.6	8.0	3.4	5.1	0.8	52.2	22.0
06 68000	San Jose	457.2	1 026 908	10	2 246.1	49.2	4.0	1.5	35.8	0.9	33.1	38.7
06 68028	San Juan Capistrano	36.6	36 454	1 031	996.0	73.3	0.8	1.5	4.0	0.4	37.2	25.9
06 68084	San Leandro	34.6	90 712	347	2 621.7	46.8	13.2	2.5	34.6	1.7	28.0	35.4
06 68154	San Luis Obispo	33.1	47 339	802	1 430.2	87.0	3.3	1.3	8.3	0.2	16.8	10.0
06 68196	San Marcos	63.1	92 931	337	1 472.8	78.7	3.4	1.1	11.3	0.9	35.0	23.4
06 68252	San Mateo	31.4	103 536	291	3 297.3	68.5	2.9	1.2	22.4	2.6	26.2	32.7
06 68294	San Pablo	6.8	30 407	1 230	4 471.6	56.4	17.9	2.3	15.4	0.5	55.0	41.1
06 68364	San Rafael	42.7	59 162	622	1 385.5	73.0	3.9	0.9	8.2	0.5	28.9	28.2
06 68378	San Ramon	46.8	76 134	446	1 626.8	53.9	3.1	0.9	44.4	0.9	8.6	32.1
06 69000	Santa Ana	70.6	335 400	57	4 750.7	48.6	1.5	0.8	11.0	0.3	78.6	47.3
06 69070	Santa Barbara	50.4	91 842	344	1 822.3	78.0	2.2	1.3	4.5	0.4	40.4	25.9
06 69084	Santa Clara	47.7	126 215	218	2 646.0	49.8	4.2	0.9	41.9	1.1	19.1	41.0
06 69088	Santa Clarita	136.5	182 371	133	1 336.1	79.1	4.0	2.5	11.7	0.6	31.4	20.2
06 69112	Santa Cruz	33.0	64 220	557	1 946.1	83.2	3.0	1.7	10.9	0.8	20.9	13.3
06 69196	Santa Maria	58.9	105 093	284	1 784.3	72.6	2.4	1.5	6.0	0.5	71.5	34.3
06 70000	Santa Monica	21.8	93 220	336	4 276.1	83.8	5.0	1.6	11.7	0.4	14.5	22.8
06 70042	Santa Paula	11.9	30 546	1 223	2 566.9	75.3	0.4	2.3	1.8	0.2	78.8	29.4
06 70098	Santa Rosa	107.0	174 972	143	1 635.3	79.2	3.4	3.4	6.9	1.1	30.4	18.8
06 70224	Santee	42.1	57 787	641	1 372.6	90.0	3.8	2.7	7.1	1.5	17.8	8.2
06 70280	Saratoga	32.1	30 968	1 198	964.7	53.5	0.5	0.4	48.2	0.1	3.3	37.9
06 70742	Seaside	23.9	34 533	1 090	1 444.9	61.6	10.7	3.2	12.6	2.2	43.0	31.6
06 72016	Simi Valley	107.4	126 788	217	1 180.5	81.6	1.8	1.9	11.2	0.6	24.4	19.1
06 72520	Soledad	11.4	25 003	1 419	2 193.2	72.6	11.6	4.1	3.6	0.3	72.8	31.6
06 73080	South Gate	18.7	96 401	315	5 155.1	50.1	1.3	0.7	1.0	0.2	95.6	43.8
06 73220	South Pasadena	8.8	26 151	1 393	2 971.7	60.2	3.7	1.4	34.4	1.0	21.4	28.3
06 73262	South San Francisco	23.7	67 271	523	2 838.4	41.6	3.8	1.3	41.2	3.2	34.0	41.6
06 73962	Stanton	8.2	38 872	964	4 740.5	52.9	3.1	1.4	25.8	0.9	49.7	43.6
06 75000	Stockton	159.7	305 658	62	1 914.0	50.1	14.1	3.3	24.4	1.4	41.3	26.2
06 75630	Suisun City	10.6	29 492	1 260	2 782.3	41.0	24.7	2.2	24.0	2.9	25.1	21.7
06 77000	Sunnyvale	57.0	151 754	169	2 662.4	51.3	2.6	0.8	43.9	0.9	18.0	44.6
06 78120	Temecula	78.1	112 011	252	1 434.2	77.7	5.3	3.1	13.2	1.0	24.1	15.3
06 78148	Temple City	10.4	36 365	1 032	3 496.6	28.5	0.9	0.4	58.6	0.4	21.2	47.2
06 78582	Thousand Oaks	142.5	129 339	209	907.6	82.8	1.8	0.8	12.0	0.4	17.0	18.8
06 80000	Torrance	53.0	148 475	174	2 801.4	56.8	4.1	1.3	37.9	0.9	16.3	28.9
06 80238	Tracy	57.0	87 075	373	1 527.6	66.6	8.6	3.1	18.8	2.5	39.0	24.8
06 80644	Tulare	54.2	62 315	579	1 149.7	84.5	4.4	2.2	3.3	0.5	57.7	20.1
06 80812	Turlock	43.8	72 292	477	1 650.5	84.2	2.9	1.6	7.5	1.0	36.6	24.1
06 80854	Tustin	28.7	80 583	413	2 807.8	55.7	3.3	1.0	22.1	0.9	41.4	36.5
06 80994	Twentynine Palms	153.2	26 025	1 397	169.9	78.1	10.0	2.1	5.3	1.8	22.6	5.5
06 81204	Union City	50.4	74 494	461	1 478.1	26.0	7.1	1.9	56.2	2.7	22.0	46.0
06 81344	Upland	40.5	76 443	443	1 887.5	65.2	7.0	1.8	10.9	0.4	38.4	18.6
06 81554	Vacaville	73.5	96 803	312	1 317.0	71.9	11.4	1.8	9.8	1.2	23.6	12.9
06 81666	Vallejo	79.4	121 253	224	1 527.1	46.4	24.1	1.7	28.0	1.8	24.2	28.3
06 82590	Victorville	189.5	122 225	222	645.0	64.2	17.6	1.7	6.0	0.7	52.1	18.1
06 82954	Visalia	93.9	130 104	207	1 385.6	83.2	3.7	2.2	6.6	0.8	47.5	13.8
06 82996	Vista	48.4	100 890	297	2 084.5	82.6	3.4	1.1	7.0	1.0	47.7	25.9
06 83332	Walnut	23.3	30 237	1 237	1 297.7	25.7	3.3	0.7	66.4	0.7	19.5	48.4
06 83346	Walnut Creek	51.2	68 910	506	1 345.9	83.2	2.3	0.8	15.5	0.3	10.1	22.4
06 83542	Wasco	24.4	26 279	1 388	1 077.0	79.8	7.8	1.3	1.5	0.2	77.3	29.1
06 83668	Watsonville	17.3	53 628	698	3 099.9	70.6	0.6	1.3	3.8	0.3	80.8	39.3
06 84200	West Covina	41.6	108 484	270	2 607.8	40.0	6.1	1.0	28.2	0.5	54.7	34.5
06 84410	West Hollywood	4.9	36 222	1 037	7 392.2	84.8	4.1	1.9	7.3	0.5	12.7	26.5
06 84550	Westminster	26.0	92 114	342	3 542.8	41.4	1.4	1.1	49.2	0.7	22.8	45.8
06 84816	West Sacramento	55.5	52 721	708	949.9	70.2	6.5	3.4	13.7	3.2	31.9	22.9
06 85292	Whittier	37.9	87 438	369	2 307.1	60.5	1.5	1.4	5.1	0.3	66.9	18.1
06 85446	Wildomar	61.4	35 632	1 061	580.3	72.1	6.4	1.7	4.8	2.0	40.0	19.0
06 85922	Windsor	18.8	27 464	1 340	1 460.9	80.6	0.7	4.1	5.0	0.3	28.3	14.9
06 86328	Woodland	39.6	58 567	633	1 479.0	73.8	1.9	2.9	7.7	0.4	47.7	21.9
06 86832	Yorba Linda	50.5	67 973	515	1 346.0	79.2	1.5	1.7	19.8	0.7	17.0	18.0
06 86972	Yuba City	37.8	66 941	528	1 770.9	69.3	4.2	3.0	21.3	1.2	28.2	25.0
06 87042	Yucaipa	72.2	53 328	702	738.6	85.1	2.3	1.7	2.7	1.1	30.9	9.6
08 00000	COLORADO	268 431.3	5 456 574	X	20.3	87.0	5.1	2.1	3.9	0.3	20.9	9.8
08 03455	Arvada	91.0	115 368	239	1 267.8	93.5	1.1	1.4	2.8	0.2	13.9	5.0
08 04000	Aurora	400.8	359 407	54	896.7	68.5	18.6	2.5	6.3	0.4	28.9	20.2
08 07850	Boulder	63.9	107 349	276	1 680.0	91.4	1.7	1.2	6.2	0.3	8.9	10.4
08 08675	Brighton	51.8	37 585	1 001	725.6	88.3	2.2	1.7	2.2	0.8	40.3	13.3
08 09280	Broomfield	85.6	65 065	545	760.1	90.4	1.7	1.5	7.5	0.1	11.6	9.2

1. Dry land or land partially or temporarily covered by water.   2. May be of any race.

Table D. Cities — Population

City	Age of population (percent), 2010-2014											Population			
	Under 5 years	5 to 17 years	18 to 24 years	25 to 34 years	35 to 44 years	45 to 54 years	55 to 64 years	65 to 74 years	75 years and over	Median age 2010–2014	Percent female 2010–2014	Census counts		Percent change	
												2000	2010	2000–2010	2010–2015
	12	13	14	15	16	17	18	19	20	21	22	23	24	25	26
CALIFORNIA—Cont'd															
San Francisco	4.5	8.9	8.4	21.9	16.4	13.7	12.2	7.1	6.8	38.6	49.1	776 733	805 235	3.7	7.4
San Gabriel	3.7	14.2	8.0	12.8	15.2	16.7	13.6	8.0	7.7	42.4	51.7	39 804	39 718	-0.2	2.0
San Jacinto	9.0	21.8	11.0	12.7	14.5	11.6	8.7	5.7	5.0	31.3	50.8	23 779	44 199	85.9	6.2
San Jose	6.8	17.2	9.3	15.2	15.4	14.3	10.8	6.0	4.9	35.8	49.7	894 943	945 942	5.7	7.8
San Juan Capistrano	6.0	18.0	8.5	8.9	11.6	13.5	16.5	8.0	8.9	42.5	50.6	33 826	34 593	2.3	5.0
San Leandro	5.0	16.0	8.3	12.6	14.6	16.1	13.9	6.8	6.7	40.7	49.8	79 452	84 950	6.9	6.8
San Luis Obispo	3.3	8.6	36.9	13.5	8.0	9.0	8.9	5.2	6.5	25.5	47.0	44 174	45 119	2.1	4.8
San Marcos	6.2	19.2	9.7	13.9	17.4	13.0	9.3	5.7	5.5	35.6	52.5	54 977	83 781	52.4	11.1
San Mateo	6.7	13.6	7.5	15.2	16.7	13.8	11.5	7.1	7.9	39.1	50.9	92 482	97 207	5.1	6.5
San Pablo	6.9	18.8	12.8	14.8	13.0	14.3	9.1	4.9	5.4	32.2	50.9	30 215	29 139	-3.6	4.4
San Rafael	6.8	14.0	8.2	13.1	13.8	14.2	12.8	8.4	8.7	40.8	50.7	56 063	57 713	2.9	2.5
San Ramon	6.2	24.0	5.3	9.7	19.9	17.6	9.8	4.4	3.1	37.4	51.3	44 722	72 148	61.3	5.4
Santa Ana	8.3	21.0	12.6	16.1	15.0	12.2	7.5	4.2	3.0	29.5	49.8	337 977	324 528	-4.0	3.3
Santa Barbara	6.4	12.8	13.6	16.7	12.0	12.3	12.1	6.9	7.2	35.4	50.3	92 325	88 410	-4.2	3.9
Santa Clara	8.1	14.3	10.1	18.8	17.2	12.8	9.0	5.3	4.4	34.4	49.8	102 361	116 468	13.8	8.3
Santa Clarita	6.1	19.5	9.8	12.6	13.6	15.7	12.3	6.4	4.1	36.8	50.2	151 088	176 320	16.7	3.4
Santa Cruz	4.3	10.4	30.1	12.7	11.4	11.1	11.0	5.2	4.0	29.0	50.4	54 593	59 946	9.8	7.1
Santa Maria	8.5	22.4	12.3	15.6	12.2	11.8	7.5	4.7	5.0	29.3	49.0	77 423	99 553	28.6	5.5
Santa Monica	4.6	9.5	8.6	19.3	15.9	14.9	11.8	7.9	7.6	40.1	51.8	84 084	89 736	6.7	3.9
Santa Paula	7.8	22.0	12.1	11.9	14.7	12.2	8.4	5.5	5.4	32.3	47.7	28 598	29 321	2.5	4.2
Santa Rosa	6.1	17.3	9.1	13.9	13.1	14.1	12.7	7.0	6.7	37.8	50.2	147 595	167 815	13.7	4.3
Santee	6.5	18.1	9.5	14.1	14.1	16.6	10.6	6.1	4.4	36.1	53.0	52 975	53 413	0.8	8.2
Saratoga	2.9	21.4	4.6	4.7	12.2	19.4	15.0	10.2	9.6	47.3	51.3	29 843	29 926	0.3	3.3
Seaside	9.1	17.7	11.7	16.7	15.5	10.8	10.0	4.6	4.1	31.8	53.1	31 696	33 025	4.2	4.6
Simi Valley	6.2	17.9	8.6	12.0	13.8	16.4	12.7	7.6	4.7	38.9	51.4	111 351	124 237	11.6	2.1
Soledad	6.4	13.7	10.0	16.7	20.3	18.0	9.5	3.2	2.0	36.6	29.5	11 263	25 738	128.5	-2.9
South Gate	7.7	20.7	12.2	16.0	13.8	12.1	9.2	4.9	3.3	30.5	49.8	96 375	94 396	-2.1	2.1
South Pasadena	5.5	18.1	7.0	14.3	14.5	15.6	12.8	7.2	5.1	39.1	52.0	24 292	25 619	5.5	2.1
South San Francisco	6.8	15.7	8.4	14.3	12.9	15.4	12.3	7.6	6.6	38.2	50.3	60 552	63 632	5.1	5.7
Stanton	6.9	19.7	10.1	15.0	13.9	13.4	10.6	5.0	5.2	33.7	51.2	37 403	38 186	2.1	2.8
Stockton	8.3	21.6	11.7	14.1	12.3	11.4	10.0	6.1	4.6	30.7	51.3	243 771	291 707	19.7	4.8
Suisun City	6.9	23.2	8.3	15.1	13.1	14.1	11.0	5.5	2.8	32.6	49.5	26 118	28 111	7.6	4.9
Sunnyvale	8.3	14.0	6.9	20.4	15.6	13.6	9.8	6.1	5.2	35.2	48.8	131 760	140 081	6.3	8.4
Temecula	6.2	24.0	10.0	10.3	15.0	16.1	10.1	4.9	3.4	34.2	51.6	57 716	100 097	73.4	11.8
Temple City	5.0	17.3	6.9	10.2	15.0	15.7	14.0	7.8	7.9	41.9	53.0	33 377	35 558	6.5	2.3
Thousand Oaks	4.4	19.2	8.4	10.1	12.4	16.2	13.5	8.5	7.2	42.0	51.3	117 005	126 683	8.3	2.2
Torrance	5.4	15.7	8.0	11.6	14.2	17.5	11.7	7.9	8.0	41.8	52.4	137 946	145 438	5.4	2.1
Tracy	7.7	22.3	9.4	12.4	15.4	15.5	9.5	5.1	2.8	33.9	48.2	56 929	82 922	45.7	4.8
Tulare	9.3	22.2	11.7	14.4	12.4	11.3	9.6	5.0	4.2	30.1	51.6	43 994	59 278	34.7	5.1
Turlock	7.1	20.2	10.6	14.7	13.5	10.7	11.2	6.4	5.7	33.0	50.3	55 810	68 549	22.8	5.5
Tustin	7.8	18.4	10.1	16.7	15.4	13.5	9.3	4.6	4.2	33.4	51.2	67 504	75 540	11.9	7.0
Twentynine Palms	13.7	11.6	27.4	19.3	9.2	6.2	6.9	3.5	2.3	24.2	48.4	14 764	25 048	69.7	3.9
Union City	7.2	16.3	9.3	14.7	14.7	13.3	11.9	7.1	5.4	36.3	50.8	66 869	69 516	4.0	7.1
Upland	6.4	17.7	10.0	13.7	13.0	14.5	11.2	7.8	5.6	36.4	53.3	68 393	73 732	7.8	3.7
Vacaville	5.8	16.9	10.2	14.1	13.4	16.2	11.7	6.9	4.9	38.0	46.8	88 625	92 428	4.3	4.7
Vallejo	6.4	14.9	10.0	13.5	12.0	14.6	15.7	7.1	5.8	39.1	51.7	116 760	115 942	-0.7	4.6
Victorville	8.7	24.5	10.9	14.8	14.0	11.2	8.1	4.8	3.0	29.2	51.5	64 029	115 903	81.0	5.4
Visalia	8.7	20.7	9.7	15.4	12.7	12.9	9.3	6.3	4.4	31.8	51.2	91 565	124 442	35.9	4.5
Vista	6.5	15.7	11.1	17.9	15.4	13.5	9.6	5.0	5.3	34.5	50.1	89 857	93 834	4.4	7.5
Walnut	3.3	16.6	10.5	10.5	11.5	17.0	17.1	8.8	4.7	43.0	50.7	30 004	29 172	-2.8	3.7
Walnut Creek	4.4	12.9	6.2	11.1	12.3	14.7	11.9	12.1	14.5	46.9	53.9	64 296	64 173	-0.2	7.4
Wasco	8.9	18.4	13.6	19.6	14.9	11.5	7.7	2.4	3.0	29.3	37.3	21 263	25 545	20.1	2.8
Watsonville	9.6	21.7	12.9	13.4	13.7	11.6	8.4	4.3	4.4	28.9	50.4	44 265	51 199	15.7	4.7
West Covina	5.9	17.5	10.7	14.6	12.7	13.5	12.1	6.5	6.4	35.9	51.5	105 080	106 098	1.0	2.2
West Hollywood	1.2	2.1	5.5	30.6	17.4	18.0	10.2	7.4	7.6	40.9	43.3	35 716	34 399	-3.7	5.3
Westminster	5.5	16.8	9.6	12.6	13.5	14.8	11.9	8.0	7.3	39.6	51.1	88 207	89 701	1.7	2.8
West Sacramento	7.0	18.9	10.6	16.5	13.9	12.9	8.5	6.6	5.0	33.4	50.5	31 615	48 744	54.2	8.2
Whittier	7.0	18.0	11.4	13.8	13.4	14.3	10.0	5.2	6.8	34.9	51.5	83 680	85 331	2.0	2.5
Wildomar	7.0	20.6	9.7	12.7	13.5	12.6	13.5	5.7	4.8	35.1	48.2	14 064	32 176	128.8	10.6
Windsor	6.2	20.2	9.4	10.0	12.9	16.3	11.4	7.0	6.5	37.9	50.3	22 744	26 801	17.8	2.5
Woodland	7.2	18.9	10.1	13.4	13.5	13.1	11.5	6.5	5.8	35.3	50.8	49 151	55 468	12.9	5.6
Yorba Linda	5.5	17.7	8.6	9.4	12.0	18.4	14.5	7.9	6.0	42.8	50.9	58 918	64 234	9.0	5.9
Yuba City	7.0	19.4	11.3	13.3	12.5	12.8	10.4	7.0	6.2	34.0	50.0	36 758	64 925	76.6	2.0
Yucaipa	6.2	19.6	9.7	11.6	12.8	13.1	12.6	8.1	6.3	37.5	51.0	41 207	51 367	24.7	3.8
COLORADO	6.5	17.3	9.8	14.7	13.7	13.9	12.4	6.9	4.9	36.2	49.8	4 301 261	5 029 196	16.9	8.5
Arvada	5.6	17.0	8.1	12.4	12.9	15.3	14.2	8.0	6.4	40.2	51.5	102 153	106 433	4.2	8.3
Aurora	8.0	18.8	9.8	15.9	14.2	12.7	11.0	5.8	3.9	33.4	51.0	276 393	325 078	17.6	10.7
Boulder	3.9	10.5	30.3	15.0	10.7	10.5	9.4	5.4	4.3	27.8	49.9	94 673	97 385	2.9	10.1
Brighton	7.4	23.2	9.1	15.0	15.4	11.8	10.0	4.8	3.3	32.5	50.9	20 905	33 352	59.5	11.3
Broomfield	6.5	19.0	8.1	16.0	15.3	13.6	10.3	6.5	4.6	35.3	50.7	38 272	55 889	46.0	16.5

Table D. Cities — **Households, Group Quarters, Crime, and Education**

City	Households, 2010-2014				Persons in group quarters, 2010				Serious crimes known to police,[2] 2014				Educational attainment, 2010–2014		
			Percent			Institutional			Total		Rate[3]			Attainment[4] (percent)	
	Number	Persons per house-hold	Female family house-holder[1]	One-person	Total	Total	Persons in nursing facilities	Non-institu-tional	Number	Rate[3]	Violent	Property	Population age 25 and older	High school graduate or less	Bachelor's degree or more
	27	28	29	30	31	32	33	34	35	36	37	38	39	40	41
CALIFORNIA—Cont'd															
San Francisco	348 832	2.38	8.6	38.2	24 264	5 362	2 942	18 902	51 854	6 098	795	5 303	647 337	26.4	52.9
San Gabriel	12 051	3.33	15.3	19.1	452	418	395	34	638	1 579	205	1 373	29 391	47.4	30.3
San Jacinto	13 269	3.43	15.6	19.5	228	59	43	169	1 976	4 276	219	4 057	26 656	54.7	11.6
San Jose	310 584	3.18	12.4	19.7	13 322	3 780	2 190	9 542	27 819	2 755	321	2 434	657 583	35.7	38.2
San Juan Capistrano	11 671	3.05	10.6	21.1	87	0	0	87	445	1 232	172	1 060	23 987	35.0	34.7
San Leandro	31 226	2.79	13.4	26.5	650	368	364	282	4 126	4 652	416	4 236	61 623	44.4	27.7
San Luis Obispo	17 855	2.57	7.2	31.5	1 182	215	206	967	1 679	3 597	514	3 083	22 965	20.0	49.6
San Marcos	28 428	3.09	12.3	20.1	844	108	108	736	1 482	1 632	216	1 416	56 420	36.5	29.4
San Mateo	38 011	2.63	10.0	29.4	1 316	341	306	975	2 174	2 130	225	1 904	72 341	27.6	45.4
San Pablo	8 967	3.29	21.6	19.6	441	373	373	68	1 403	4 703	808	3 895	18 362	61.5	12.5
San Rafael	22 907	2.56	10.6	31.7	2 119	805	497	1 314	1 857	3 132	326	2 806	42 439	28.7	44.6
San Ramon	25 215	2.93	6.0	18.6	75	23	0	52	771	1 027	31	997	47 904	11.3	65.0
Santa Ana	74 437	4.45	18.7	13.3	4 658	3 243	895	1 415	7 044	2 094	374	1 719	192 736	67.9	11.8
Santa Barbara	34 522	2.60	10.0	32.5	1 627	455	375	1 172	2 691	2 961	332	2 628	61 037	29.9	43.1
Santa Clara	42 751	2.80	9.5	25.7	3 196	336	318	2 860	3 430	2 832	134	2 698	80 049	23.0	53.9
Santa Clarita	59 314	3.02	12.4	19.9	1 410	129	111	1 281	2 744	1 326	148	1 178	115 624	30.5	32.0
Santa Cruz	21 015	2.95	9.1	31.8	8 289	379	2	7 910	3 794	5 980	826	5 154	34 220	21.3	49.4
Santa Maria	27 541	3.68	16.6	18.6	1 007	419	263	588	3 484	3 386	427	2 960	58 046	60.0	13.0
Santa Monica	46 536	1.97	7.6	48.4	2 126	827	783	1 299	3 364	3 611	363	3 248	71 542	14.4	65.0
Santa Paula	8 630	3.48	15.5	18.8	133	89	89	44	532	1 758	281	1 477	17 709	56.7	13.9
Santa Rosa	63 213	2.70	11.7	29.2	3 410	1 713	830	1 697	4 486	2 593	368	2 226	115 253	34.8	30.4
Santee	19 173	2.89	14.7	21.6	966	889	274	77	924	1 629	229	1 399	36 571	33.2	24.6
Saratoga	10 704	2.86	5.5	14.2	199	165	161	34	307	986	61	925	22 052	6.9	77.6
Seaside	10 185	3.31	15.0	20.9	1 127	0	0	1 127	623	1 814	338	1 476	20 560	47.9	22.9
Simi Valley	41 803	3.01	11.4	17.8	660	178	123	482	1 758	1 389	111	1 278	84 518	30.7	32.2
Soledad	3 735	6.96	16.5	7.8	10 103	10 103	55	0	285	1 104	205	899	17 849	72.6	3.7
South Gate	23 386	4.08	22.5	11.7	88	72	72	16	3 193	3 327	527	2 800	56 949	73.3	6.9
South Pasadena	10 394	2.49	11.2	31.8	163	155	151	8	505	1 939	115	1 824	18 388	14.2	60.4
South San Francisco	21 470	3.05	11.7	21.8	579	51	18	528	1 430	2 141	234	1 907	46 496	38.0	30.7
Stanton	11 586	3.32	18.0	20.5	350	258	240	92	808	2 083	320	1 763	24 442	55.3	17.6
Stockton	91 304	3.26	20.9	21.3	5 734	1 838	1 558	3 896	17 136	5 721	1 331	4 390	175 869	49.6	17.4
Suisun City	8 684	3.30	18.9	15.7	44	17	5	27	674	2 325	235	2 091	18 046	33.9	19.8
Sunnyvale	54 267	2.69	7.8	24.4	849	469	457	380	2 523	1 689	112	1 577	102 920	20.6	59.3
Temecula	32 233	3.26	12.0	15.1	129	8	0	121	2 635	2 433	92	2 341	63 116	28.9	30.9
Temple City	11 393	3.16	13.5	18.0	422	393	388	29	473	1 304	124	1 180	25 586	35.8	37.6
Thousand Oaks	45 849	2.79	9.0	22.3	1 742	352	348	1 390	1 727	1 337	99	1 238	87 539	22.2	48.7
Torrance	55 279	2.66	11.6	25.9	1 146	640	578	506	2 778	1 877	105	1 773	104 623	24.5	45.3
Tracy	24 480	3.45	11.9	13.5	316	247	245	69	2 391	2 810	152	2 659	50 271	43.2	22.1
Tulare	18 064	3.36	16.1	16.5	278	216	216	62	2 511	4 077	742	3 335	34 522	58.6	10.7
Turlock	23 606	2.96	15.0	21.2	1 207	520	445	687	2 882	4 071	526	3 546	43 473	47.0	23.0
Tustin	25 517	3.05	13.7	21.9	520	180	150	340	1 488	1 882	167	1 715	50 430	35.0	38.6
Twentynine Palms	8 217	3.12	15.6	24.5	3 347	0	0	3 347	363	1 400	239	1 161	11 975	41.7	20.7
Union City	20 529	3.49	12.6	15.0	518	96	75	422	1 809	2 469	283	2 186	49 338	39.2	35.0
Upland	27 017	2.78	15.8	25.3	682	377	359	305	2 335	3 081	224	2 857	50 176	33.8	29.8
Vacaville	31 224	3.01	14.7	25.1	8 022	7 989	171	33	2 855	3 015	283	2 732	63 006	36.5	22.5
Vallejo	40 848	2.89	19.1	25.2	1 663	533	483	1 130	5 911	4 946	865	4 081	80 475	38.0	23.5
Victorville	31 440	3.80	22.0	15.5	5 103	4 762	294	341	5 016	4 101	525	3 576	67 041	52.7	10.5
Visalia	41 554	3.05	16.6	21.5	1 326	720	408	606	4 280	3 331	377	2 954	76 637	41.4	21.9
Vista	30 662	3.14	12.7	20.8	2 045	1 384	588	661	2 026	2 075	348	1 727	62 910	47.6	18.7
Walnut	8 421	3.54	10.2	8.5	34	12	10	22	323	1 067	96	971	20 712	20.6	51.5
Walnut Creek	30 328	2.17	6.0	37.6	1 002	826	826	176	2 513	3 720	110	3 610	51 060	13.2	61.9
Wasco	5 264	4.91	21.7	12.7	5 720	5 710	0	10	NA	NA	NA	NA	15 117	76.5	3.7
Watsonville	14 148	3.68	18.0	18.2	528	206	201	322	1 754	3 323	502	2 821	29 521	64.8	10.5
West Covina	31 042	3.46	18.4	15.8	674	323	299	351	3 057	2 827	208	2 619	70 392	41.7	26.6
West Hollywood	21 808	1.61	4.1	60.2	109	0	0	109	1 592	4 484	752	3 732	31 458	15.6	59.9
Westminster	27 195	3.36	14.2	17.4	670	289	197	381	2 404	2 607	210	2 397	62 638	49.2	21.4
West Sacramento	17 571	2.84	12.6	24.8	338	92	82	246	1 557	3 105	522	2 582	32 005	42.0	25.0
Whittier	27 449	3.15	16.8	22.0	1 635	552	434	1 083	2 486	2 859	275	2 584	55 331	40.0	24.3
Wildomar	9 814	3.42	12.4	14.7	42	4	4	38	589	1 736	115	1 621	20 866	43.5	15.6
Windsor	9 435	2.87	8.8	21.1	51	0	0	51	340	1 243	314	929	17 832	34.2	30.2
Woodland	19 348	2.91	12.9	23.3	985	829	323	156	2 054	3 613	524	3 089	35 713	45.5	23.6
Yorba Linda	21 583	3.07	8.2	13.6	190	93	93	97	747	1 103	66	1 037	44 734	17.1	49.4
Yuba City	21 557	3.02	15.0	22.6	580	455	247	125	1 922	2 933	340	2 593	40 787	45.3	18.9
Yucaipa	17 834	2.94	12.6	21.1	554	327	242	227	1 049	1 987	134	1 852	34 207	39.7	19.7
COLORADO	1 998 314	2.60	10.3	28.0	115 878	61 591	18 079	54 287	152 064	2 839	309	2 530	3 453 403	31.6	37.5
Arvada	43 779	2.51	10.4	27.0	506	343	314	163	2 835	2 509	150	2 359	76 315	30.0	36.4
Aurora	123 344	2.75	15.1	27.7	2 556	1 850	1 145	706	11 393	3 246	407	2 839	215 799	38.9	27.1
Boulder	41 687	2.45	5.7	33.5	8 105	1 080	531	7 025	3 025	2 901	235	2 666	57 419	11.7	71.5
Brighton	10 895	3.21	15.7	21.3	1 546	1 518	197	28	1 280	3 537	370	3 167	21 511	48.0	18.5
Broomfield	22 651	2.61	7.6	25.8	282	279	207	3	1 071	1 765	51	1 714	39 477	20.4	49.5

1. No spouse present.   2. Data for serious crimes have not been adjusted for underreporting. This may affect comparability between geographic areas and over time.   3. Per 100,000 population estimated by the FBI.   4. Persons 25 years old and over.

Table D. Cities — Income, Poverty, and Housing

City	Per capita income[1] (dollars)	Median income	Percent with income of $200,000 or more	Percent with income of less than $25,000	Families with income below poverty (percent)	Total	Percent change, 2000–2010	Vacant units for sale or rent[2]	Total	Percent	Median value[3] (dollars)	With a mortgage[4]	Without a mortgage[5]
	42	43	44	45	46	47	48	49	50	51	52	53	54
CALIFORNIA—Cont'd													
San Francisco	49 986	78 378	15.0	20.4	7.8	376 942	8.8	31 131	348 832	36.6	765 700	28.4	10.4
San Gabriel	25 047	56 238	5.8	19.2	11.2	13 237	3.0	695	12 051	49.6	574 600	28.9	11.4
San Jacinto	17 350	46 714	0.8	26.9	14.9	14 977	58.7	1 825	13 269	67.2	139 800	28.5	13.2
San Jose	34 992	83 787	13.0	14.5	8.3	314 038	11.5	12 672	310 584	57.4	579 500	27.5	10.0
San Juan Capistrano	37 917	72 568	12.3	15.5	10.6	11 940	5.3	546	11 671	73.4	497 500	31.7	13.3
San Leandro	29 442	64 279	4.8	17.3	7.9	32 419	3.6	1 702	31 226	55.4	372 600	28.1	10.0
San Luis Obispo	26 377	44 894	4.8	31.9	9.1	20 553	6.3	1 360	17 855	36.4	519 200	26.7	10.0
San Marcos	24 789	56 139	4.6	22.0	13.1	28 641	51.5	1 439	28 428	59.5	378 800	31.8	14.1
San Mateo	46 782	90 087	15.0	10.7	3.9	40 014	4.7	1 781	38 011	53.0	736 600	27.9	10.9
San Pablo	16 874	42 746	0.5	29.7	18.2	9 571	2.5	810	8 967	42.4	183 300	30.6	12.0
San Rafael	46 075	75 668	14.4	17.8	8.6	24 011	4.6	1 247	22 907	52.7	691 400	26.8	10.9
San Ramon	51 569	129 062	25.3	5.2	2.8	26 222	50.5	938	25 215	68.5	722 700	26.2	10.4
Santa Ana	16 345	52 519	2.4	20.0	19.5	76 896	3.3	3 722	74 437	45.4	343 000	31.3	10.0
Santa Barbara	37 692	65 916	9.6	18.8	9.7	37 820	1.7	2 371	34 522	40.0	837 200	28.4	11.9
Santa Clara	41 222	93 840	13.9	12.2	5.0	45 147	14.0	2 126	42 751	44.9	633 600	25.8	10.0
Santa Clarita	33 879	83 178	8.9	12.4	6.4	62 055	18.3	2 548	59 314	69.0	376 700	27.9	12.5
Santa Cruz	29 177	61 533	7.6	24.0	9.7	23 316	8.6	1 659	21 015	43.3	645 600	27.7	10.5
Santa Maria	18 509	50 753	1.9	22.8	17.6	28 294	24.0	1 386	27 541	50.2	252 200	28.0	12.1
Santa Monica	58 252	74 534	13.8	19.9	5.2	50 912	6.4	3 995	46 536	27.1	1 000 000	27.5	12.1
Santa Paula	20 303	53 692	3.4	25.5	15.9	8 749	4.5	402	8 630	57.4	306 100	29.1	10.5
Santa Rosa	29 890	60 758	5.2	18.3	9.0	67 396	17.2	3 806	63 213	53.5	370 100	27.9	11.9
Santee	30 531	74 213	3.6	12.5	5.7	20 048	6.6	742	19 173	69.9	336 300	27.6	12.7
Saratoga	77 667	167 917	43.5	7.0	2.0	11 123	4.3	389	10 704	86.4	1 000 000	26.3	10.0
Seaside	21 548	52 538	2.4	19.4	14.7	10 872	-1.2	779	10 185	38.1	343 800	29.7	10.2
Simi Valley	37 279	89 595	10.9	10.0	4.8	42 506	13.9	1 269	41 803	73.1	438 700	27.2	10.6
Soledad	9 701	46 010	3.6	21.6	19.3	3 876	52.4	212	3 735	56.1	199 400	31.5	10.0
South Gate	14 256	43 526	0.8	25.1	19.8	24 160	-0.5	882	23 386	47.1	297 200	35.2	10.4
South Pasadena	46 649	80 479	13.4	12.4	4.6	11 118	2.5	651	10 394	43.5	832 200	27.0	10.0
South San Francisco	32 269	78 101	9.1	15.0	4.8	21 814	8.2	876	21 470	59.7	589 100	28.8	10.6
Stanton	18 870	45 842	1.9	22.7	17.7	11 283	3.1	458	11 586	48.7	281 700	30.0	14.8
Stockton	19 927	45 347	2.8	28.8	21.4	99 637	21.3	9 032	91 304	49.6	166 800	27.3	10.7
Suisun City	25 809	71 306	4.0	14.8	9.4	9 454	16.0	536	8 684	62.0	215 800	26.1	10.0
Sunnyvale	48 203	103 257	17.8	10.4	4.8	55 791	3.8	2 407	54 267	47.0	748 700	23.5	10.0
Temecula	28 630	78 535	5.0	12.4	6.8	34 004	78.8	2 223	32 233	65.7	311 100	28.3	12.5
Temple City	27 403	63 803	6.8	20.6	8.8	12 117	3.5	511	11 393	66.0	591 500	31.3	11.0
Thousand Oaks	46 231	99 115	17.4	12.2	5.1	47 497	10.6	1 661	45 849	71.4	601 500	27.4	11.3
Torrance	36 876	78 286	8.1	14.3	4.9	58 377	4.3	2 376	55 279	55.6	622 800	27.9	10.0
Tracy	26 121	74 748	3.9	12.2	7.2	25 963	43.9	1 632	24 480	63.6	273 300	27.3	11.5
Tulare	18 336	46 387	1.6	25.9	18.0	18 863	32.6	1 143	18 064	58.0	157 000	24.8	12.9
Turlock	22 847	51 594	2.8	23.4	12.6	24 627	29.3	1 855	23 606	53.1	197 700	26.0	12.1
Tustin	31 392	71 105	9.1	14.8	9.5	26 476	3.9	1 273	25 517	50.2	501 500	29.3	10.0
Twentynine Palms	20 510	40 890	1.0	26.6	12.8	9 431	38.9	1 336	8 217	31.9	124 100	23.9	10.7
Union City	30 158	82 564	9.2	12.6	6.0	21 258	12.7	825	20 529	65.1	484 300	27.5	10.9
Upland	29 064	61 551	5.2	20.5	10.9	27 355	7.4	1 532	27 017	56.9	412 700	28.1	10.0
Vacaville	30 111	74 207	6.4	13.8	7.8	32 814	14.4	1 722	31 224	60.5	275 100	26.1	10.0
Vallejo	25 945	58 472	3.6	22.8	14.4	44 433	7.9	3 874	40 848	57.2	222 100	27.6	10.2
Victorville	15 873	47 142	0.8	27.7	22.0	36 655	61.8	4 097	31 440	58.8	135 600	27.0	13.9
Visalia	22 885	52 262	3.1	23.7	16.2	44 205	34.8	2 856	41 554	60.1	172 800	26.7	10.8
Vista	21 161	47 782	2.2	22.1	12.4	30 986	3.5	1 669	30 662	49.2	346 200	31.9	13.1
Walnut	35 064	100 934	13.4	9.8	4.8	8 753	4.3	220	8 421	85.7	635 000	28.3	10.6
Walnut Creek	51 998	80 399	13.4	13.0	3.5	32 681	3.8	2 238	30 328	64.6	591 700	26.6	16.4
Wasco	10 931	39 273	0.4	33.9	29.1	5 477	28.2	346	5 264	51.3	120 900	25.3	12.9
Watsonville	17 377	46 691	1.6	25.9	17.0	14 089	19.7	561	14 148	41.3	325 500	30.6	11.2
West Covina	24 944	67 069	4.2	14.5	7.7	32 705	2.2	1 109	31 042	64.6	385 400	29.5	10.0
West Hollywood	54 352	56 025	7.9	25.3	6.8	24 588	2.0	2 077	21 808	22.1	595 200	28.4	16.0
Westminster	22 821	53 660	4.1	22.9	15.0	27 650	2.7	1 486	27 195	52.7	455 200	29.8	11.2
West Sacramento	25 081	53 307	2.7	26.3	15.6	18 681	54.1	1 260	17 571	53.8	248 000	25.9	10.0
Whittier	27 632	65 583	5.3	18.1	10.2	29 591	1.9	1 318	27 449	57.4	421 900	28.3	10.0
Wildomar	22 380	60 816	2.4	17.1	10.3	10 806	128.0	814	9 814	71.3	226 900	30.7	10.2
Windsor	33 615	81 442	7.1	11.3	1.9	9 549	23.4	579	9 435	74.4	385 700	28.1	14.9
Woodland	25 149	54 532	3.0	21.7	10.9	19 806	15.8	1 085	19 348	56.0	254 200	26.7	10.2
Yorba Linda	47 852	115 994	20.5	7.3	1.9	22 305	14.2	729	21 583	84.1	687 300	27.4	10.7
Yuba City	23 038	50 494	2.8	24.5	14.9	23 174	66.6	1 624	21 557	55.6	188 500	25.8	12.1
Yucaipa	26 103	58 506	4.3	21.4	12.8	19 642	21.9	1 411	17 834	71.6	219 600	28.5	13.7
COLORADO	31 674	59 448	5.5	19.6	8.8	2 212 898	22.4	240 030	1 998 314	64.8	239 400	23.5	10.1
Arvada	34 312	69 550	5.6	14.9	6.0	44 427	12.1	1 726	43 779	73.5	245 300	23.0	10.1
Aurora	24 732	52 275	2.5	20.3	12.3	131 040	20.1	9 139	123 344	57.3	179 300	24.3	10.3
Boulder	37 406	58 062	9.6	25.8	6.4	43 479	6.6	2 177	41 687	48.0	499 200	23.3	10.2
Brighton	23 950	60 319	2.1	15.8	8.2	11 387	63.0	599	10 895	68.0	191 100	24.8	10.0
Broomfield	38 706	80 430	8.6	13.0	4.3	22 646	57.8	1 232	22 651	69.6	284 100	21.7	10.0

1. Based on population estimated by the American Community Survey. 2. Includes units rented or sold but not occupied. 3. Specified owner-occupied units; $1,000,000 represents $1,000,000 or more. 4. 50.0 represents 50 percent or more. 5. 10.0 represents 10 percent or less.

Table D. Cities — Housing, Labor Force, and Employment

City	Occupied housing units, 2010–2014 (cont.)				Migration, 2010–2014		Civilian labor force, 2015				Civilian employment[4], 2010–2014		
									Unemployment			Percent	
	Percent renter occupied	Median gross rent[1]	Median gross rent as a percent of income[2]	Percent with no vehicle available	Percent who lived in the same house one year ago	Percent who lived outside current city one year ago	Total	Percent change, 2014–2015	Total	Rate[3]	Population age 16 and older	In labor force	Civilian full-year full-time workers	Households with no workers (percent)
	55	56	57	58	59	60	61	62	63	64	65	66	67	68
CALIFORNIA—Cont'd														
San Francisco	63.4	1 533	28.1	30.4	84.4	7.8	548 004	3.1	19 930	3.6	729 309	69.3	44.0	24.3
San Gabriel	50.4	1 277	36.2	7.1	88.2	8.7	20 797	0.4	852	4.1	33 738	62.4	38.9	17.4
San Jacinto	32.8	985	35.9	6.8	82.1	14.2	18 326	1.0	1 841	10.0	33 145	58.3	28.4	34.5
San Jose	42.6	1 528	31.8	5.5	86.0	6.4	543 476	2.2	25 261	4.6	774 214	67.8	41.8	18.1
San Juan Capistrano	26.6	1 753	42.3	5.4	87.1	8.6	17 494	1.1	867	5.0	27 991	64.6	36.6	27.1
San Leandro	44.6	1 260	29.9	7.5	88.1	7.0	46 941	1.4	2 402	5.1	71 289	67.3	41.4	23.2
San Luis Obispo	63.6	1 275	45.5	7.9	63.2	18.0	26 120	1.5	1 282	4.9	40 915	60.5	28.3	28.3
San Marcos	40.5	1 306	34.0	3.5	88.6	8.0	40 816	1.2	1 662	4.1	67 593	59.3	35.7	28.5
San Mateo	47.0	1 710	29.3	6.0	84.6	10.1	62 588	3.0	2 052	3.3	81 795	70.9	45.2	21.3
San Pablo	57.6	1 076	36.8	13.7	84.1	10.6	13 954	0.7	1 078	7.7	22 715	64.8	32.6	26.4
San Rafael	47.3	1 489	35.4	9.7	84.2	10.6	33 011	1.1	1 219	3.7	48 127	67.1	39.0	27.0
San Ramon	31.5	1 754	29.1	3.2	86.1	11.1	39 500	1.7	1 322	3.3	54 089	72.0	49.5	12.4
Santa Ana	54.6	1 307	37.2	6.7	87.0	5.7	159 825	1.0	8 234	5.2	245 074	67.4	40.0	13.6
Santa Barbara	60.0	1 517	33.7	10.0	79.5	10.7	51 755	0.6	2 176	4.2	74 415	68.1	40.0	25.8
Santa Clara	55.1	1 686	27.4	5.0	82.0	14.2	66 869	2.4	2 500	3.7	95 132	67.6	45.1	18.7
Santa Clarita	31.0	1 581	32.9	4.8	84.2	9.6	95 578	-0.1	5 874	6.1	139 044	68.7	40.7	19.8
Santa Cruz	56.7	1 547	41.0	8.3	72.6	18.3	33 572	0.9	2 243	6.7	54 463	61.1	27.6	25.2
Santa Maria	49.8	1 160	35.1	7.8	83.2	5.8	48 335	0.2	3 094	6.4	73 239	66.3	37.8	22.8
Santa Monica	72.9	1 583	29.5	10.4	80.5	14.4	55 828	0.0	3 183	5.7	80 289	70.8	41.9	26.7
Santa Paula	42.6	1 128	38.9	8.8	86.6	6.0	14 059	-1.0	1 039	7.4	21 860	65.6	36.9	24.2
Santa Rosa	46.5	1 286	33.7	6.6	82.1	8.1	89 330	0.9	4 467	5.0	135 055	66.1	35.5	27.0
Santee	30.1	1 355	29.9	3.3	86.2	10.8	29 077	0.9	1 480	5.1	43 355	67.6	42.8	22.4
Saratoga	13.6	2 000	27.5	2.8	90.3	8.6	14 712	2.6	434	2.9	24 532	57.9	37.7	27.4
Seaside	61.9	1 478	36.1	6.8	81.0	14.0	18 440	1.1	1 529	8.3	25 433	68.6	34.5	17.0
Simi Valley	26.9	1 711	32.7	3.8	88.3	5.3	69 435	-0.5	3 473	5.0	99 848	70.0	43.0	19.4
Soledad	43.9	1 126	40.4	4.3	78.2	16.4	7 941	0.7	890	11.2	20 885	33.1	19.0	20.3
South Gate	52.9	993	38.7	7.9	88.3	7.7	43 532	-0.8	3 824	8.8	72 155	63.7	35.9	16.8
South Pasadena	56.5	1 394	27.3	3.7	85.1	12.1	14 744	0.2	699	4.7	20 513	70.8	46.5	19.0
South San Francisco	40.3	1 521	31.6	8.2	90.0	7.4	38 532	2.9	1 394	3.6	53 396	67.8	43.4	22.6
Stanton	51.3	1 272	39.0	8.8	88.1	9.2	18 946	0.9	1 120	5.9	29 592	65.3	37.3	20.1
Stockton	50.4	958	37.0	9.8	79.4	7.3	129 064	0.8	12 372	9.6	220 637	60.4	31.7	29.8
Suisun City	38.0	1 506	33.7	5.0	81.3	14.8	14 400	1.5	768	5.3	21 556	68.8	39.2	19.9
Sunnyvale	53.0	1 692	23.2	4.6	82.2	13.1	85 186	2.4	3 174	3.7	115 316	69.9	47.3	17.3
Temecula	34.3	1 522	34.3	3.2	82.2	12.8	51 692	2.2	2 503	4.8	77 881	66.2	38.2	19.7
Temple City	34.0	1 316	39.6	4.1	89.3	8.5	17 768	0.3	777	4.4	29 400	60.0	38.1	23.2
Thousand Oaks	28.6	1 845	33.5	4.3	86.7	8.7	67 345	-0.6	3 728	5.5	102 221	66.5	39.4	23.9
Torrance	44.4	1 466	29.8	5.0	87.6	7.8	77 512	0.2	3 628	4.7	120 031	64.8	40.8	25.0
Tracy	36.4	1 413	30.4	4.1	84.6	8.0	41 965	1.3	3 142	7.5	61 151	69.5	39.4	16.6
Tulare	42.0	923	33.5	6.8	85.5	5.0	27 710	2.3	2 735	9.9	42 982	61.6	38.5	24.5
Turlock	46.9	965	33.7	8.5	80.0	9.1	33 936	0.5	2 887	8.5	53 487	63.7	35.5	27.1
Tustin	49.8	1 514	35.3	4.1	81.7	13.5	43 030	1.3	1 797	4.2	60 196	72.1	45.1	15.4
Twentynine Palms	68.1	940	31.3	8.4	57.7	27.9	6 830	1.3	571	8.4	19 595	69.0	20.0	26.0
Union City	34.9	1 513	31.1	6.6	90.8	7.1	36 745	1.6	1 573	4.3	57 153	65.1	41.6	30.8
Upland	43.1	1 188	36.6	5.1	84.2	11.5	38 140	2.2	1 813	4.8	59 976	63.9	39.4	24.0
Vacaville	39.5	1 390	30.7	5.1	83.0	8.8	44 748	1.6	2 185	4.9	75 033	62.3	35.8	22.2
Vallejo	42.8	1 208	36.1	8.0	82.7	8.7	58 341	0.8	4 849	8.3	95 197	63.4	34.7	28.6
Victorville	41.2	1 106	38.7	6.2	82.2	11.2	44 661	1.6	3 094	6.9	84 362	53.3	31.1	28.0
Visalia	39.9	952	33.2	8.5	82.7	7.3	61 820	2.4	5 821	9.4	93 771	63.5	37.3	26.1
Vista	50.8	1 239	37.4	3.6	88.2	8.1	43 628	1.0	2 018	4.6	76 430	60.0	35.5	26.8
Walnut	14.3	2 000	36.2	1.5	91.7	7.1	15 685	0.2	753	4.8	24 828	62.2	40.9	18.1
Walnut Creek	35.4	1 479	28.9	8.0	83.2	13.4	33 437	1.7	1 146	3.4	56 257	58.7	35.8	36.0
Wasco	48.7	678	29.1	13.0	72.3	20.0	8 556	-0.3	1 155	13.5	19 554	43.8	22.8	25.5
Watsonville	58.7	1 203	36.0	9.3	90.5	4.4	25 508	0.4	2 462	9.7	38 085	66.6	33.6	21.1
West Covina	35.4	1 371	34.5	4.8	85.9	10.8	53 733	-0.6	4 419	8.2	85 311	65.2	38.3	21.5
West Hollywood	77.9	1 389	32.0	13.5	79.7	17.2	25 571	0.0	1 423	5.6	33 580	77.0	47.3	25.0
Westminster	47.3	1 356	38.6	5.9	86.3	10.5	42 974	0.8	2 654	6.2	74 143	61.1	34.7	24.3
West Sacramento	46.2	917	34.3	9.0	81.7	9.9	25 478	0.8	1 898	7.4	38 095	65.3	38.6	26.9
Whittier	42.6	1 216	33.4	6.5	89.2	7.5	43 002	0.1	2 274	5.3	68 043	63.9	39.9	23.0
Wildomar	28.7	1 454	35.5	3.1	84.5	12.2	NA	NA	NA	NA	25 240	65.7	35.3	22.2
Windsor	25.6	1 763	30.9	4.9	88.9	5.6	14 066	1.2	543	3.9	20 989	67.7	41.4	25.0
Woodland	44.0	944	32.1	7.7	83.9	7.5	29 302	0.9	1 993	6.8	43 719	64.6	38.9	25.6
Yorba Linda	15.9	1 709	37.2	3.5	89.2	7.4	34 859	1.3	1 367	3.9	52 114	67.9	43.0	18.7
Yuba City	44.4	913	32.4	6.8	83.8	6.9	31 049	0.5	3 574	11.5	49 647	61.4	32.6	29.3
Yucaipa	28.4	1 100	31.2	4.5	86.4	8.2	24 785	1.7	1 630	6.6	40 883	60.7	33.9	29.7
COLORADO	35.2	969	30.8	5.7	80.6	12.9	2 828 529	0.5	109 831	3.9	4 094 922	68.7	42.4	22.8
Arvada	26.5	1 020	29.8	4.2	84.9	10.9	62 746	0.8	2 243	3.6	88 203	70.9	46.7	23.3
Aurora	42.7	983	33.5	6.8	76.9	12.4	181 481	0.4	7 579	4.2	256 947	71.3	43.6	20.2
Boulder	52.0	1 203	40.0	9.1	62.7	21.5	60 364	-0.2	1 869	3.1	89 519	67.4	33.5	23.0
Brighton	32.0	1 012	29.5	5.2	85.8	10.8	17 905	1.1	861	4.8	25 552	65.9	42.6	18.4
Broomfield	30.4	1 248	27.9	4.0	82.1	14.5	34 673	1.0	1 157	3.3	45 531	71.5	49.5	20.0

1. $2,000 represents $2,000 or more. 2. 50.0 represents 50 percent or more. 3. Percent of civilian labor force. 4. Persons 16 years old and over.

Table D. Cities — Construction, Wholesale Trade, and Retail Trade

City	Value of residential construction authorized by building permits, 2015			Wholesale trade,[1] 2012				Retail trade,[2] 2012			
	New construction ($1,000)	Number of housing units	Percent single family	Number of establishments	Number of employees	Sales (mil dol)	Annual payroll (mil dol)	Number of establishments	Number of employees	Sales (mil dol)	Annual payroll (mil dol)
	69	70	71	72	73	74	75	76	77	78	79
CALIFORNIA—Cont'd											
San Francisco	1 041 273	3 665	1.7	1 066	12 056	11 121.7	850.7	3 573	43 378	14 632.7	1 455.0
San Gabriel	34 465	120	63.3	128	479	219.8	15.3	211	1 577	473.4	36.5
San Jacinto	17 500	113	100.0	13	59	27.0	2.1	50	861	214.3	22.6
San Jose	318 079	2 019	7.7	1 023	42 254	49 902.3	5 435.8	2 297	40 525	14 982.0	1 850.7
San Juan Capistrano	22 635	48	0.0	62	339	254.3	19.5	128	1 795	714.4	61.3
San Leandro	0	0	0.0	249	3 095	1 784.4	179.0	305	5 619	4 342.8	158.5
San Luis Obispo	37 904	151	100.0	83	1 001	442.4	42.4	365	4 892	1 390.7	134.8
San Marcos	84 038	602	15.1	133	1 494	606.3	65.6	246	4 005	1 194.8	115.7
San Mateo	71 851	416	26.9	87	839	586.3	61.8	378	6 587	1 817.9	200.3
San Pablo	9 238	37	100.0	8	30	11.4	1.0	77	947	227.9	22.5
San Rafael	15 296	27	100.0	124	1 151	763.5	73.0	344	5 031	1 757.0	185.3
San Ramon	9 585	60	11.7	98	1 095	2 125.6	86.1	117	2 015	671.5	64.0
Santa Ana	80 507	541	7.2	555	6 699	3 284.1	352.4	822	11 680	3 169.4	309.8
Santa Barbara	54 670	180	16.7	110	1 641	832.1	115.2	531	6 881	1 537.8	181.2
Santa Clara	45 455	251	46.6	378	12 811	10 163.3	1 455.7	352	5 045	2 126.5	215.2
Santa Clarita	118 545	409	78.7	198	3 225	7 495.9	181.0	535	9 774	2 781.7	257.4
Santa Cruz	18 900	57	100.0	59	1 181	594.5	70.1	255	3 098	773.2	81.7
Santa Maria	119 687	437	35.5	109	1 108	692.5	54.8	367	5 362	1 561.2	144.1
Santa Monica	34 740	66	77.3	159	1 317	675.4	71.4	682	10 986	4 981.6	451.1
Santa Paula	604	2	100.0	16	D	D	D	55	705	193.2	17.9
Santa Rosa	27 783	123	80.5	166	1 963	1 002.8	113.8	654	10 479	2 817.5	292.1
Santee	16 862	116	21.6	46	410	152.7	18.9	123	2 861	750.0	73.1
Saratoga	10 779	9	100.0	25	D	D	D	34	D	D	D
Seaside	0	0	0.0	13	D	D	D	98	1 427	526.3	48.7
Simi Valley	33 055	103	100.0	144	1 371	847.5	70.8	413	5 841	1 672.1	145.6
Soledad	342	2	100.0	7	70	55.4	4.4	27	259	79.1	6.4
South Gate	437	6	100.0	79	1 000	650.4	41.1	165	2 220	686.4	53.4
South Pasadena	2 322	6	100.0	36	130	159.3	7.6	56	720	196.3	19.3
South San Francisco	6 042	35	0.0	330	5 622	4 819.0	441.5	187	3 063	1 133.4	96.8
Stanton	7 688	33	100.0	28	D	D	D	104	1 162	386.5	30.1
Stockton	71 466	410	38.3	239	4 944	5 746.4	249.4	695	10 893	3 295.0	277.1
Suisun City	0	0	0.0	5	D	D	D	31	316	79.6	7.7
Sunnyvale	168 635	859	22.0	210	13 280	9 873.2	2 070.1	279	5 005	1 693.0	148.4
Temecula	39 682	179	79.9	150	2 522	2 074.4	101.5	439	8 208	2 541.9	214.3
Temple City	40 912	117	100.0	91	352	104.0	8.8	99	1 152	299.8	27.6
Thousand Oaks	38 411	121	32.2	158	2 474	5 097.7	275.4	545	9 016	2 880.6	267.4
Torrance	4 371	15	80.0	607	5 653	9 142.9	349.4	663	11 780	3 783.7	319.2
Tracy	116 648	584	33.0	62	1 275	2 123.1	88.6	235	3 772	1 041.6	93.5
Tulare	49 273	278	100.0	50	515	233.8	23.8	181	2 794	808.1	63.7
Turlock	14 761	58	100.0	64	696	377.1	35.5	209	3 514	956.6	86.3
Tustin	46 050	169	62.1	192	2 126	1 489.7	157.5	282	6 234	2 205.6	177.2
Twentynine Palms	781	5	100.0	4	17	9.3	0.6	31	312	75.0	7.1
Union City	47 895	290	16.2	139	3 705	2 980.9	306.2	107	2 198	621.1	62.9
Upland	17 790	67	100.0	120	664	276.2	25.2	240	3 685	882.0	91.3
Vacaville	117 252	425	86.8	36	332	320.6	15.6	323	5 699	1 586.2	136.8
Vallejo	7 194	27	100.0	28	794	434.0	36.2	233	3 910	1 147.5	114.0
Victorville	22 803	83	100.0	32	241	314.6	8.8	318	6 108	1 710.9	154.4
Visalia	150 816	650	84.9	126	1 321	1 749.7	69.2	396	6 664	1 873.7	166.6
Vista	67 859	408	28.9	201	3 510	1 611.1	184.4	252	4 089	1 219.6	106.9
Walnut	5 287	16	100.0	229	925	557.6	37.6	105	1 008	232.5	20.0
Walnut Creek	19 402	70	42.9	68	595	1 067.3	50.8	308	6 753	1 972.8	221.6
Wasco	8 280	72	100.0	3	D	D	D	41	426	98.5	8.5
Watsonville	7 124	78	50.0	54	1 108	941.3	57.4	146	2 398	2 233.3	65.5
West Covina	31 154	101	100.0	88	433	203.6	17.9	292	5 618	1 476.3	137.6
West Hollywood	114 616	584	1.9	103	527	222.6	29.4	331	3 472	1 179.9	115.1
Westminster	24 104	82	87.8	118	533	307.3	24.1	453	5 841	1 466.4	145.4
West Sacramento	18 386	61	96.7	140	3 579	5 481.1	185.2	124	2 110	547.8	55.1
Whittier	12 727	85	0.0	71	342	114.4	12.0	200	2 993	619.8	66.5
Wildomar	37 936	113	100.0	8	31	5.8	0.7	39	377	110.5	10.6
Windsor	4 736	37	2.7	23	441	297.5	22.1	52	1 077	263.2	30.4
Woodland	46 381	153	100.0	77	829	565.9	44.8	154	2 515	703.3	66.7
Yorba Linda	79 430	275	74.9	124	1 029	775.1	74.6	114	1 557	565.2	46.0
Yuba City	13 045	49	91.8	44	372	199.2	19.4	247	4 003	1 015.1	97.0
Yucaipa	226	1	100.0	15	62	22.7	2.0	89	995	271.5	24.6
COLORADO	7 532 619	31 871	62.8	5 733	75 717	77 035.0	4 762.1	18 474	245 704	67 815.2	6 508.6
Arvada	202 957	732	100.0	83	880	498.7	59.0	259	3 832	1 145.4	99.5
Aurora	248 057	986	100.0	230	5 173	6 512.0	258.0	908	15 374	4 095.7	376.0
Boulder	91 348	243	52.3	187	3 538	1 572.6	297.4	574	8 079	2 002.7	229.8
Brighton	59 206	209	100.0	25	462	250.7	24.9	100	2 136	683.4	52.2
Broomfield	145 059	447	90.2	52	D	D	D	261	4 606	1 000.2	101.7

1. Merchant wholesalers except manufacturers' sales branches and offices. 2. Establishments with payroll.

City	Real estate and rental and leasing, 2012				Professional, scientific, and technical services,[1] 2012				Manufacturing, 2012			
	Number of establish-ments	Number of employees	Receipts (mil dol)	Annual payroll (mil dol)	Number of establish-ments	Number of employees	Receipts (mil dol)	Annual payroll (mil dol)	Number of establish-ments	Number of employees	Receipts (mil dol)	Annual payroll (mil dol)
	80	81	82	83	84	85	86	87	88	89	90	91
CALIFORNIA—Cont'd												
San Francisco	1 828	15 000	6 000.9	1 071.1	6 233	82 644	28 932.6	8 880.3	693	7 506	D	327.6
San Gabriel	81	209	44.7	6.0	144	483	49.4	15.3	43	389	56.0	13.7
San Jacinto	22	63	13.8	1.3	15	126	8.9	4.2	30	354	45.2	12.2
San Jose	1 045	5 858	1 734.1	314.5	2 961	39 395	9 252.2	4 203.2	897	32 421	15 126.0	2 545.5
San Juan Capistrano	74	237	68.9	14.0	219	993	197.0	63.5	28	792	272.1	51.3
San Leandro	129	905	283.7	43.6	123	D	D	D	182	4 777	1 833.5	233.7
San Luis Obispo	137	693	116.7	25.1	338	D	D	D	73	1 170	219.2	52.4
San Marcos	103	377	79.4	15.8	233	D	D	D	157	4 276	D	204.5
San Mateo	182	789	420.2	55.7	532	D	D	D	46	601	D	36.6
San Pablo	17	59	11.9	1.6	12	95	8.0	3.1	10	50	D	2.1
San Rafael	161	794	806.7	46.0	493	D	D	D	76	632	157.8	32.1
San Ramon	131	D	D	D	523	7 408	2 010.9	642.3	27	302	D	18.1
Santa Ana	316	2 685	564.8	123.4	1 013	D	D	D	771	19 771	5 177.3	938.8
Santa Barbara	287	1 101	228.5	47.7	647	D	D	D	96	998	197.0	51.4
Santa Clara	177	1 396	691.0	107.1	920	D	D	D	508	15 935	4 524.8	1 286.2
Santa Clarita	233	1 129	228.7	48.7	511	D	D	D	231	8 930	2 137.1	549.9
Santa Cruz	87	286	75.5	8.3	283	D	D	D	90	1 324	346.2	64.2
Santa Maria	100	522	89.8	17.0	147	D	D	D	89	2 996	790.2	118.9
Santa Monica	418	3 011	1 488.6	234.2	1 162	8 835	2 052.7	791.5	88	807	172.9	38.0
Santa Paula	22	111	32.5	6.0	21	146	17.4	6.0	23	433	81.8	19.2
Santa Rosa	254	1 131	247.9	41.8	608	4 438	446.1	232.5	153	4 862	1 036.0	344.0
Santee	58	270	38.3	8.6	72	D	D	D	84	1 353	D	65.9
Saratoga	85	219	79.9	14.2	167	D	D	D	14	252	D	24.7
Seaside	12	66	11.0	2.0	18	D	D	D	10	85	3.7	1.5
Simi Valley	118	557	168.5	25.9	369	2 804	537.5	176.7	130	3 504	833.5	189.1
Soledad	12	45	5.3	1.0	4	32	1.6	0.7	4	73	D	2.8
South Gate	41	202	45.9	8.1	28	402	45.0	18.4	121	4 380	1 778.1	206.4
South Pasadena	58	D	D	D	141	D	D	D	13	86	D	3.0
South San Francisco	76	666	132.1	27.1	187	D	D	D	111	10 909	D	1 501.6
Stanton	19	84	24.1	3.2	31	D	D	D	63	702	101.6	31.4
Stockton	253	1 338	218.7	48.2	370	D	D	D	166	5 937	2 921.8	277.1
Suisun City	10	23	4.0	0.9	18	89	8.0	3.0	7	22	3.1	0.6
Sunnyvale	153	960	227.4	45.3	804	18 744	5 191.0	1 991.2	225	25 088	10 930.7	2 976.8
Temecula	184	706	142.9	26.4	368	D	D	D	125	5 024	3 482.1	298.6
Temple City	41	D	D	D	76	235	26.3	7.7	24	149	14.3	4.1
Thousand Oaks	279	971	217.6	50.5	807	D	D	D	124	3 346	1 238.8	239.2
Torrance	343	1 992	374.5	76.2	879	D	D	D	248	12 560	11 915.2	799.0
Tracy	76	181	51.3	7.4	106	D	D	D	52	2 358	1 110.0	110.2
Tulare	46	149	26.3	3.7	47	322	46.6	16.0	27	1 940	2 387.4	99.7
Turlock	58	280	33.7	7.1	74	D	D	D	71	2 986	1 675.0	122.7
Tustin	172	853	210.1	42.1	549	D	D	D	98	3 270	679.2	193.1
Twentynine Palms	11	77	17.9	2.8	15	D	D	D	NA	NA	NA	NA
Union City	40	162	39.3	7.5	109	D	D	D	81	3 879	1 033.7	226.9
Upland	102	876	99.4	49.3	209	1 306	185.3	64.5	95	981	198.4	46.1
Vacaville	106	542	123.2	18.1	114	632	67.7	26.4	44	2 425	D	138.6
Vallejo	73	300	80.3	10.0	95	D	D	D	32	356	D	16.1
Victorville	88	465	57.7	12.2	103	D	D	D	18	1 222	665.7	49.7
Visalia	131	834	120.0	25.9	245	D	D	D	67	2 417	1 355.8	121.5
Vista	138	738	172.1	27.4	230	1 448	254.4	77.5	178	7 380	2 754.2	405.5
Walnut	56	D	D	D	107	340	55.3	13.1	30	318	84.6	17.4
Walnut Creek	224	1 209	285.4	68.5	691	6 364	1 516.1	549.4	32	591	D	33.9
Wasco	14	37	6.6	1.1	4	20	2.4	0.5	6	104	D	5.8
Watsonville	60	256	46.9	8.8	72	D	D	D	57	1 381	353.8	59.3
West Covina	82	421	55.4	14.7	144	D	D	D	16	632	104.1	35.0
West Hollywood	146	820	248.1	40.6	398	2 286	623.2	201.7	36	225	31.0	8.4
Westminster	93	300	81.0	12.0	145	635	68.8	25.2	93	775	106.4	30.0
West Sacramento	77	604	123.5	25.4	83	D	D	D	64	3 118	D	165.9
Whittier	102	338	57.2	9.6	166	755	83.9	25.8	47	732	223.4	31.7
Wildomar	15	123	9.5	2.7	23	D	D	D	8	75	D	4.6
Windsor	23	160	41.9	4.6	57	335	82.2	13.8	26	570	122.3	31.5
Woodland	60	300	55.2	10.6	81	D	D	D	57	2 002	D	92.5
Yorba Linda	102	293	60.3	12.2	246	D	D	D	54	1 386	714.1	106.8
Yuba City	78	420	47.8	10.8	103	484	48.6	18.0	43	1 144	457.9	62.2
Yucaipa	45	152	21.2	4.8	59	175	19.2	5.3	20	326	39.2	12.4
COLORADO	9 295	38 706	8 482.5	1 569.6	23 761	175 448	32 686.8	12 537.0	4 898	114 632	50 447.1	6 230.1
Arvada	125	276	48.7	9.2	382	1 535	215.1	79.5	110	2 139	615.1	128.0
Aurora	298	1 233	267.5	46.2	635	D	D	D	122	2 400	644.1	118.3
Boulder	316	1 091	258.0	42.8	1 346	D	D	D	216	7 153	2 744.6	521.0
Brighton	34	114	13.8	3.3	50	D	D	D	22	697	222.2	38.9
Broomfield	96	313	77.1	11.4	323	D	D	D	82	3 087	3 918.4	188.5

1. Establishments subject to federal tax.

Table D. Cities — Accommodation and Food Services, Arts, Entertainment, and Recreation, and Health Care and Social Assistance

City	Accommodation and food services, 2012				Arts, entertainment, and recreation,[1] 2012				Health care and social assistance,[1] 2012			
	Number of establish-ments	Number of employees	Sales (mil dol)	Annual payroll (mil dol)	Number of establish-ments	Number of employees	Receipts (mil dol)	Annual payroll (mil dol)	Number of establish-ments	Number of employees	Receipts (mil dol)	Annual payroll (mil dol)
	92	93	94	95	96	97	98	99	100	101	102	103
CALIFORNIA—Cont'd												
San Francisco	4 059	73 417	6 142.7	1 841.6	320	6 226	1 006.9	402.9	2 413	18 874	2 647.7	1 112.5
San Gabriel	176	1 866	105.8	26.5	3	D	D	D	209	D	D	D
San Jacinto	40	628	27.2	6.9	NA	NA	NA	NA	31	234	22.6	8.2
San Jose	1 916	31 023	1 919.1	523.7	141	4 615	413.7	177.4	2 175	24 468	3 274.0	1 300.7
San Juan Capistrano	73	1 257	72.0	21.1	15	325	32.8	6.9	115	1 172	106.9	43.2
San Leandro	191	2 329	146.2	37.7	12	D	D	D	240	3 538	346.0	150.9
San Luis Obispo	218	4 125	220.9	62.5	12	164	6.9	2.3	302	3 655	493.7	183.6
San Marcos	169	2 973	180.6	46.5	17	D	D	D	135	1 504	166.4	68.7
San Mateo	313	4 808	325.1	89.5	29	D	D	D	417	4 045	533.1	182.6
San Pablo	60	739	38.6	9.7	1	D	D	D	29	D	D	D
San Rafael	224	2 841	163.4	47.3	63	352	83.8	17.7	235	3 214	429.2	221.2
San Ramon	148	2 324	159.8	41.1	19	520	27.8	8.6	273	2 624	416.2	140.8
Santa Ana	542	7 493	462.8	121.3	25	226	31.1	6.2	708	9 016	1 138.6	464.2
Santa Barbara	421	8 143	494.4	143.1	62	721	53.2	16.6	469	3 762	656.2	216.6
Santa Clara	400	7 151	581.1	157.9	31	2 308	382.4	216.1	211	D	D	D
Santa Clarita	327	6 766	351.4	98.9	117	1 303	86.4	30.6	468	4 669	577.5	213.6
Santa Cruz	256	4 446	253.9	74.7	24	906	59.8	21.6	173	1 586	166.8	71.0
Santa Maria	178	2 596	144.9	39.6	14	249	11.8	3.8	274	2 403	258.2	98.4
Santa Monica	454	12 289	947.7	276.5	677	1 752	660.2	254.2	841	5 314	753.0	267.1
Santa Paula	42	D	D	D	5	29	1.6	0.4	36	257	29.5	11.9
Santa Rosa	389	5 764	355.0	95.6	52	826	50.3	22.4	579	8 031	1 158.3	525.6
Santee	108	1 620	85.1	24.6	12	D	D	D	70	450	42.3	16.6
Saratoga	64	883	58.5	15.6	6	78	7.1	2.7	102	D	D	D
Seaside	71	1 005	65.6	17.6	2	D	D	D	15	D	D	D
Simi Valley	251	3 984	230.6	59.4	45	D	D	D	324	2 835	295.7	109.2
Soledad	21	D	D	D	NA	NA	NA	NA	7	42	9.1	2.3
South Gate	108	1 192	74.4	17.5	6	D	D	D	75	841	82.5	28.5
South Pasadena	61	882	45.7	13.4	39	D	D	D	106	717	73.8	27.1
South San Francisco	204	3 673	316.2	82.3	17	D	D	D	162	2 570	353.5	192.7
Stanton	82	924	52.9	13.0	6	D	D	D	31	D	D	D
Stockton	424	6 912	366.5	95.4	34	716	47.6	17.9	587	9 180	993.6	391.5
Suisun City	31	426	23.3	5.9	4	D	D	D	17	54	5.3	2.1
Sunnyvale	346	4 781	349.1	86.3	34	D	D	D	390	3 554	486.8	163.1
Temecula	281	9 653	965.6	240.6	28	697	33.3	9.3	311	2 408	227.9	86.7
Temple City	64	836	47.4	11.5	4	8	1.6	0.3	95	D	D	D
Thousand Oaks	317	6 760	378.5	109.1	96	684	71.5	26.4	636	6 430	1 012.7	325.7
Torrance	419	8 055	498.1	139.8	55	D	D	D	1 030	9 696	1 168.6	428.5
Tracy	137	2 191	111.1	28.9	16	D	D	D	158	D	D	D
Tulare	80	1 403	74.5	19.3	7	D	D	D	100	D	D	D
Turlock	146	2 528	128.2	35.1	14	D	D	D	154	1 477	166.6	56.7
Tustin	232	4 167	224.8	65.2	20	D	D	D	346	3 588	605.0	147.8
Twentynine Palms	49	661	48.0	9.9	3	D	D	D	12	D	D	D
Union City	113	1 771	95.5	26.3	7	D	D	D	116	1 019	90.2	38.7
Upland	145	D	D	D	23	D	D	D	346	D	D	D
Vacaville	168	3 293	173.1	48.6	16	411	22.5	5.3	167	2 305	379.6	145.5
Vallejo	167	2 623	147.9	38.4	17	1 257	78.4	21.8	214	4 353	620.0	337.9
Victorville	175	3 245	167.9	46.5	12	D	D	D	199	3 415	365.9	130.7
Visalia	234	4 245	216.8	60.7	11	293	17.9	3.9	349	3 648	417.3	160.1
Vista	171	2 150	114.0	29.2	10	288	22.6	6.6	207	2 342	240.7	88.8
Walnut	48	539	29.1	7.5	6	D	D	D	87	702	41.8	19.2
Walnut Creek	202	4 358	259.1	78.0	28	363	25.0	7.5	442	D	D	D
Wasco	28	D	D	D	1	D	D	D	13	D	D	D
Watsonville	90	1 218	72.9	17.9	6	D	D	D	139	2 047	245.2	88.9
West Covina	196	3 421	184.5	48.2	11	D	D	D	314	D	D	D
West Hollywood	229	7 741	543.1	166.4	482	D	D	D	248	1 104	177.3	57.1
Westminster	245	2 672	144.5	39.6	14	D	D	D	281	2 520	273.5	96.0
West Sacramento	91	D	D	D	9	D	D	D	67	D	D	D
Whittier	177	2 662	149.2	42.8	10	D	D	D	295	D	D	D
Wildomar	31	402	22.3	5.8	7	D	D	D	53	1 307	161.0	68.4
Windsor	52	D	D	D	5	89	4.1	1.4	37	230	17.3	6.3
Woodland	104	D	D	D	9	124	3.6	1.1	85	1 376	153.3	86.4
Yorba Linda	92	1 710	83.5	24.6	25	D	D	D	167	D	D	D
Yuba City	124	2 121	110.6	28.1	14	D	D	D	196	D	D	D
Yucaipa	55	764	39.2	10.6	11	D	D	D	83	D	D	D
COLORADO	12 744	240 484	13 617.7	3 994.6	1 950	41 585	3 048.6	1 082.5	12 701	140 738	14 693.2	6 167.1
Arvada	186	3 172	160.0	45.6	24	225	9.3	2.8	216	2 393	194.0	72.0
Aurora	577	10 728	567.1	162.5	44	760	41.5	13.5	575	7 897	607.0	279.9
Boulder	429	8 834	501.9	149.9	102	970	50.4	16.4	579	4 074	429.0	172.7
Brighton	83	1 338	72.1	19.3	7	D	D	D	76	D	D	D
Broomfield	143	2 944	169.6	54.7	20	D	D	D	135	1 542	167.0	62.6

1. Establishments subject to federal tax.

Table D. Cities — Other Services and Government Employment and Payroll

City	Other services[1], 2012				Government employment and payroll, 2012								
					Full-time equivalent employees	March payroll							
						Total (dollars)	Percent of total for:						
	Number of establishments	Number of employees	Receipts (mil dol)	Annual payroll (mil dol)			Administration, judicial, and legal	Police and Corrections	Fire Protection	Highways and transportation	Health and welfare	Natural resources and utilities	Education and libraries
	104	105	106	107	108	109	110	111	112	113	114	115	116
CALIFORNIA—Cont'd													
San Francisco	1 603	10 876	1 109.6	320.2	28 349	217 722 943	13.9	17.4	7.3	22.7	24.7	11.1	2.1
San Gabriel	96	408	39.5	11.3	191	1 327 334	11.3	38.5	24.6	6.9	3.8	11.2	0.0
San Jacinto	34	D	D	D	65	267 518	30.0	0.0	0.0	10.8	18.2	28.6	0.0
San Jose	1 175	6 748	929.6	202.4	5 214	38 715 963	8.8	33.1	18.0	9.9	1.0	14.9	3.3
San Juan Capistrano	48	217	27.5	7.0	115	698 016	51.1	0.6	0.0	8.3	1.4	33.4	0.0
San Leandro	163	1 027	148.8	32.8	375	2 465 492	13.1	40.7	0.0	11.7	4.5	15.4	7.2
San Luis Obispo	106	523	45.2	13.0	406	3 104 703	10.0	27.1	17.3	3.8	5.5	22.1	0.0
San Marcos	120	713	60.9	18.7	279	1 870 622	14.4	0.0	37.4	21.7	5.6	15.9	0.0
San Mateo	203	D	D	D	610	5 077 524	8.5	28.2	20.6	5.7	5.0	23.9	4.0
San Pablo	34	189	13.0	3.7	74	394 492	49.3	1.6	0.0	13.4	12.2	22.1	0.0
San Rafael	194	1 244	151.0	45.2	864	2 915 776	12.5	26.3	32.7	4.3	0.0	17.6	4.1
San Ramon	112	897	75.3	23.7	279	2 017 589	12.1	37.5	0.0	31.3	1.9	13.4	0.0
Santa Ana	390	2 175	232.8	64.4	2 711	12 719 386	0.7	3.5	1.9	0.5	0.5	0.5	0.1
Santa Barbara	186	1 179	94.1	27.8	1 156	7 284 111	11.3	26.7	14.2	12.8	3.2	19.5	2.7
Santa Clara	235	1 567	145.2	45.6	961	8 545 138	10.4	22.6	18.9	6.8	0.8	30.5	3.6
Santa Clarita	255	1 689	176.5	43.8	434	2 697 699	16.1	0.0	0.0	6.2	6.5	35.1	0.0
Santa Cruz	86	701	70.7	23.5	774	4 763 881	12.0	20.2	14.4	4.6	2.0	33.9	8.6
Santa Maria	115	781	97.3	22.6	497	2 980 086	10.3	35.8	13.6	5.8	5.2	22.7	3.8
Santa Monica	353	2 604	175.5	57.6	2 163	15 220 898	14.3	23.8	11.2	20.8	3.2	14.6	3.3
Santa Paula	27	65	7.4	1.7	110	646 323	13.8	38.3	18.1	4.2	7.2	16.1	0.0
Santa Rosa	252	1 669	155.6	51.2	1 213	8 220 156	11.3	23.5	16.6	10.0	2.3	23.5	0.0
Santee	91	554	55.8	16.7	148	1 012 079	28.3	0.6	51.2	9.9	1.2	8.9	0.0
Saratoga	30	141	14.2	3.4	58	435 826	25.2	0.0	0.0	22.5	22.1	14.1	0.0
Seaside	49	196	21.9	5.6	158	994 460	9.5	41.0	20.0	8.9	0.9	6.0	0.0
Simi Valley	155	1 140	145.1	27.9	592	3 356 138	14.7	32.1	0.0	21.1	15.4	16.6	0.0
Soledad	4	16	1.4	0.3	45	264 288	21.2	60.5	0.0	1.9	0.0	16.4	0.0
South Gate	76	242	20.4	4.9	318	1 634 468	11.2	44.3	0.0	17.0	9.3	18.2	0.0
South Pasadena	40	185	13.1	3.6	168	950 670	11.5	35.7	20.9	5.1	8.3	7.4	9.4
South San Francisco	114	1 365	141.2	47.8	497	3 574 682	9.0	29.5	25.0	5.7	0.7	17.9	6.9
Stanton	52	290	23.7	6.8	38	219 326	37.8	0.0	0.0	18.7	21.0	22.5	0.0
Stockton	289	1 996	163.5	53.9	2 010	12 427 436	7.5	55.8	14.5	0.7	2.3	9.7	2.3
Suisun City	26	82	7.1	2.2	85	454 879	15.9	38.0	4.6	17.0	8.7	8.9	0.0
Sunnyvale	167	956	108.4	37.1	870	7 456 793	9.7	27.3	18.0	7.5	4.3	20.3	3.7
Temecula	183	1 029	84.1	22.4	200	1 117 348	29.5	0.5	0.7	25.3	14.8	29.0	0.0
Temple City	57	216	18.4	4.3	75	319 507	42.5	0.0	0.0	0.0	0.0	25.4	0.0
Thousand Oaks	209	1 193	114.8	31.6	440	2 648 993	26.5	1.5	0.0	28.8	2.2	20.8	12.0
Torrance	244	1 814	167.6	51.1	1 361	10 031 057	10.8	31.2	18.3	15.1	4.3	10.6	3.4
Tracy	100	467	54.4	18.3	420	2 906 444	11.9	31.9	22.5	6.6	1.4	20.4	0.0
Tulare	53	314	42.3	11.1	347	1 781 358	7.7	33.8	16.3	2.3	3.5	23.6	2.6
Turlock	89	557	53.2	15.3	394	2 010 112	13.5	34.3	14.7	8.6	2.6	22.0	0.0
Tustin	115	974	97.2	28.4	338	2 566 292	15.4	48.7	0.0	14.6	2.0	11.4	0.0
Twentynine Palms	17	95	7.7	2.4	26	143 616	18.5	18.8	0.0	23.3	0.0	39.5	0.0
Union City	68	618	95.8	22.4	252	1 774 885	14.0	49.2	0.0	3.0	5.2	19.0	0.0
Upland	130	575	53.8	14.8	892	4 437 479	3.7	19.6	11.3	3.4	2.6	5.7	1.6
Vacaville	115	578	46.5	13.3	584	4 121 808	12.2	30.0	19.8	13.3	4.5	20.2	0.0
Vallejo	105	454	43.4	12.4	573	3 266 338	8.6	32.1	16.0	8.2	5.4	28.1	0.0
Victorville	89	506	48.5	13.3	340	1 783 174	43.6	0.0	0.0	23.9	2.4	30.1	0.0
Visalia	159	989	95.7	27.0	612	3 335 649	7.1	37.8	15.7	9.2	6.0	23.1	0.0
Vista	114	744	73.7	22.1	290	1 741 746	25.7	0.0	39.6	9.1	5.0	16.8	0.0
Walnut	49	269	24.4	7.7	52	276 966	49.6	0.0	0.0	21.7	8.9	19.8	0.0
Walnut Creek	154	2 209	191.8	80.2	389	2 700 536	16.3	37.1	0.0	5.7	0.7	23.8	0.0
Wasco	12	D	D	D	60	270 885	30.6	0.0	0.0	10.8	0.0	46.4	0.0
Watsonville	64	225	22.2	6.1	373	2 335 983	9.1	27.3	13.3	4.5	1.8	31.8	5.7
West Covina	85	472	27.2	8.0	445	2 840 481	9.7	46.0	25.6	12.3	2.3	4.1	0.0
West Hollywood	167	1 186	102.6	24.5	216	1 683 338	37.7	0.0	0.0	20.8	29.7	11.7	0.0
Westminster	142	768	59.5	22.1	290	1 903 418	13.5	58.3	0.0	6.1	4.4	8.3	0.0
West Sacramento	87	674	95.2	28.0	402	3 250 336	14.1	25.4	25.1	1.9	6.5	14.5	0.0
Whittier	107	517	43.8	12.2	478	2 572 894	10.2	44.2	0.0	4.8	6.2	21.3	5.7
Wildomar	17	D	D	D	12	48 677	78.0	0.0	0.0	0.0	0.0	0.0	0.0
Windsor	24	D	D	D	98	584 900	39.6	0.0	0.0	13.3	0.0	47.2	0.0
Woodland	72	394	32.9	9.0	304	1 839 421	7.6	32.0	20.0	4.8	13.1	16.1	2.4
Yorba Linda	77	517	47.3	14.9	130	661 872	25.1	0.0	0.0	10.0	1.5	30.7	18.9
Yuba City	80	502	45.5	14.6	299	1 719 010	11.1	33.5	26.1	7.0	0.0	20.2	0.0
Yucaipa	42	177	13.9	3.4	44	165 657	7.8	0.0	0.0	38.1	0.0	54.1	0.0
COLORADO	7 918	46 005	3 942.1	1 242.3	X	X	X	X	X	X	X	X	X
Arvada	164	824	65.2	20.3	661	3 647 076	20.5	35.5	0.0	9.8	4.4	22.2	0.0
Aurora	396	2 655	208.3	66.3	2 579	13 742 359	13.6	38.9	14.9	4.2	2.6	20.7	1.4
Boulder	215	1 177	93.8	31.3	1 108	6 200 124	15.9	23.9	11.2	6.6	1.6	26.0	4.7
Brighton	47	213	22.1	5.8	297	2 531 155	9.4	15.0	0.0	3.0	57.8	11.9	0.0
Broomfield	92	520	39.4	13.2	687	3 465 198	16.4	35.0	0.0	2.4	18.0	19.6	3.9

1. Establishments subject to federal tax.

Table D. Cities — **City Government Finances**

City	General revenue — Total (mil dol)	Intergovernmental Total (mil dol)	Intergovernmental Percent from state government	Taxes Total (mil dol)	Taxes Per capita¹ Total	Taxes Per capita¹ Property	Taxes Sales and gross receipts	General expenditure Total (mil dol)	Per capita¹ Total	Capital outlays
	117	118	119	120	121	122	123	124	125	126
CALIFORNIA—Cont'd										
San Francisco	7 274.1	2 355.9	68.6	2 846.2	3 430	1 747	885	5 704.0	6 875	846
San Gabriel	37.1	3.0	81.2	25.2	626	356	258	40.2	999	177
San Jacinto	28.1	1.5	100.0	14.5	318	213	92	31.0	681	34
San Jose	1 721.1	116.7	56.0	863.4	876	456	363	1 428.0	1 449	178
San Juan Capistrano	47.2	4.4	76.8	30.4	856	577	270	40.6	1 144	265
San Leandro	123.0	8.3	72.0	88.5	1 016	465	517	121.7	1 398	127
San Luis Obispo	81.4	6.3	56.0	48.1	1 049	330	716	76.5	1 668	350
San Marcos	121.3	7.6	84.2	76.6	879	491	384	132.6	1 523	283
San Mateo	145.7	11.0	62.3	86.7	867	454	370	148.4	1 483	264
San Pablo	44.1	1.8	97.0	39.1	1 326	549	776	38.0	1 291	386
San Rafael	85.9	4.1	86.9	52.8	903	369	506	87.5	1 496	47
San Ramon	74.2	3.7	100.0	41.1	557	343	208	75.1	1 017	190
Santa Ana	440.5	127.5	23.8	205.9	621	334	285	391.8	1 181	145
Santa Barbara	246.8	36.0	63.6	102.8	1 149	512	631	228.4	2 550	530
Santa Clara	280.5	11.7	71.5	124.3	1 039	577	456	212.3	1 776	110
Santa Clarita	152.4	24.6	54.9	80.2	448	205	233	145.6	814	191
Santa Cruz	132.1	4.8	59.8	60.6	977	437	528	145.4	2 345	279
Santa Maria	117.0	16.8	78.0	58.2	574	182	391	112.6	1 111	201
Santa Monica	560.2	57.7	51.4	332.1	3 618	1 337	2 095	538.6	5 867	1 727
Santa Paula	29.3	4.2	87.4	12.9	428	275	94	23.2	771	142
Santa Rosa	262.1	24.5	59.6	119.5	702	255	435	250.3	1 470	305
Santee	44.7	2.6	60.7	34.2	616	379	155	49.1	885	180
Saratoga	20.9	1.1	97.2	15.0	490	306	160	22.6	736	169
Seaside	27.0	2.8	39.4	22.4	662	372	288	30.5	899	206
Simi Valley	96.1	10.2	52.4	62.4	497	300	194	92.5	736	103
Soledad	15.7	1.0	97.1	6.1	229	125	103	14.9	563	43
South Gate	80.6	17.7	38.8	36.7	383	216	166	67.6	707	121
South Pasadena	28.7	3.5	84.1	19.0	731	429	296	28.2	1 089	148
South San Francisco	128.4	5.4	89.0	77.6	1 179	732	371	122.6	1 863	259
Stanton	32.9	2.6	78.3	26.3	682	496	169	38.1	989	253
Stockton	381.7	98.9	79.6	161.7	544	215	325	384.7	1 293	244
Suisun City	27.1	4.4	39.6	13.1	458	385	71	30.3	1 061	113
Sunnyvale	274.8	32.4	34.0	112.9	770	377	386	274.4	1 871	145
Temecula	113.3	14.0	33.6	69.7	665	351	310	129.7	1 238	371
Temple City	15.4	1.3	81.7	11.0	305	164	133	14.2	393	12
Thousand Oaks	143.2	11.9	64.9	84.5	660	350	305	145.4	1 135	190
Torrance	261.0	41.4	39.9	155.5	1 056	365	677	234.0	1 589	118
Tracy	114.6	11.3	53.2	47.1	556	256	297	128.6	1 519	332
Tulare	97.1	4.2	71.5	38.5	632	245	375	90.8	1 492	464
Turlock	69.6	5.8	56.0	34.6	496	222	216	83.2	1 193	431
Tustin	77.0	3.6	66.8	51.5	661	437	220	77.9	1 001	98
Twentynine Palms	11.2	1.2	85.8	9.5	370	226	143	12.3	477	86
Union City	85.1	5.7	83.5	61.0	850	562	282	92.0	1 283	294
Upland	71.1	4.5	65.1	37.7	502	337	159	74.2	987	59
Vacaville	153.8	33.0	26.6	79.6	848	575	270	156.0	1 662	571
Vallejo	195.2	49.6	22.5	64.7	549	229	308	152.7	1 295	112
Victorville	115.4	9.5	68.3	53.9	448	251	195	130.1	1 082	123
Visalia	157.6	23.1	61.9	68.5	540	218	320	143.8	1 134	282
Vista	132.0	9.1	80.1	57.8	601	345	252	117.1	1 217	321
Walnut	21.5	1.3	82.0	13.1	436	322	106	20.0	668	25
Walnut Creek	70.1	2.6	97.1	45.9	699	317	354	80.4	1 224	103
Wasco	13.5	2.6	29.2	5.5	217	145	72	13.2	517	75
Watsonville	67.3	6.4	30.2	31.1	599	394	194	72.0	1 387	113
West Covina	102.2	8.7	74.3	63.9	594	395	196	91.9	854	133
West Hollywood	88.9	5.0	44.0	55.8	1 601	602	980	93.6	2 685	485
Westminster	91.7	10.4	70.7	68.6	750	538	210	114.0	1 245	487
West Sacramento	140.9	23.6	64.6	66.7	1 344	812	401	129.2	2 601	822
Whittier	79.8	8.9	72.4	41.7	483	250	231	82.4	954	94
Wildomar	9.4	3.2	100.0	5.9	177	97	62	9.3	280	7
Windsor	23.5	2.8	29.7	16.3	603	373	188	23.2	859	257
Woodland	72.5	12.3	93.9	44.7	793	310	482	78.0	1 385	376
Yorba Linda	62.1	4.6	47.2	35.0	526	382	138	79.9	1 201	263
Yuba City	54.9	5.2	89.4	33.0	508	270	193	59.0	910	163
Yucaipa	28.1	0.9	94.5	20.9	398	293	82	29.1	554	111
COLORADO	X	X	X	X	X	X	X	X	X	X
Arvada	132.6	21.2	32.5	67.8	619	84	534	119.2	1 086	160
Aurora	380.8	48.7	50.2	216.5	638	102	536	400.3	1 180	162
Boulder	219.5	16.4	84.1	150.1	1 471	286	1 185	210.4	2 063	39
Brighton	32.9	3.4	84.3	21.9	624	53	567	24.3	691	69
Broomfield	149.9	15.4	40.7	113.5	1 924	654	1 161	109.7	1 860	53

1. Based on population estimated as of July 1 of the year shown.

City	City government finances, 2012 (cont.)									
	General expenditure (cont.)									
	Percent of total for:									
	Public welfare	Highways	Parking facilities	Education	Health and hospitals	Police protection	Sewerage and sanitation	Parks and recreation	Housing and community development	Interest on debt
	127	128	129	130	131	132	133	134	135	136
CALIFORNIA—Cont'd										
San Francisco	8.5	4.4	2.4	0.0	30.2	6.6	4.7	4.3	4.2	7.1
San Gabriel	0.0	12.3	0.0	0.0	0.0	30.1	0.2	11.5	3.0	0.2
San Jacinto	0.0	13.6	0.0	0.0	0.0	28.1	10.6	3.1	13.0	4.6
San Jose	0.0	6.0	0.5	0.0	0.1	17.6	18.1	6.3	3.6	18.3
San Juan Capistrano	0.0	12.0	0.0	0.0	1.3	17.5	6.8	9.2	9.6	7.7
San Leandro................	0.0	9.1	0.2	0.0	1.1	22.2	6.5	5.1	9.9	2.9
San Luis Obispo...........	0.0	16.3	3.7	0.0	0.0	20.2	13.2	9.3	2.1	2.5
San Marcos	0.0	12.9	0.0	0.0	3.2	11.1	0.0	7.4	24.5	11.5
San Mateo	0.0	10.7	1.3	0.0	1.3	19.6	17.8	9.7	2.9	4.2
San Pablo....................	0.0	22.7	0.0	0.0	0.4	36.6	0.0	6.8	8.3	9.8
San Rafael	0.0	8.4	3.3	0.0	6.9	21.6	0.0	11.4	2.3	2.2
San Ramon	0.0	11.3	0.0	0.0	0.0	21.4	0.0	20.7	7.9	7.1
Santa Ana	0.0	9.8	1.0	0.0	2.9	30.3	5.4	5.0	15.2	5.2
Santa Barbara..............	0.0	12.0	2.9	0.0	0.2	15.2	15.9	8.4	3.7	1.3
Santa Clara	0.0	9.0	0.6	0.0	2.0	19.7	16.4	8.4	2.4	4.7
Santa Clarita	0.0	30.6	0.0	0.0	0.1	13.0	0.3	12.7	3.7	3.5
Santa Cruz	0.0	6.8	2.2	0.0	1.0	27.5	18.8	8.9	8.5	2.8
Santa Maria	0.0	11.1	0.0	0.0	0.0	18.5	25.1	6.9	0.4	3.7
Santa Monica	0.0	6.8	0.2	0.0	3.3	13.7	7.2	9.9	25.8	2.8
Santa Paula	0.0	10.9	0.0	0.0	0.8	23.3	14.7	14.4	4.7	6.1
Santa Rosa	0.0	11.5	1.9	0.0	0.9	17.4	23.0	7.1	3.3	7.1
Santee........................	0.0	15.5	0.0	0.0	6.2	21.7	0.0	3.5	17.3	4.1
Saratoga.....................	0.0	23.5	0.0	0.0	3.2	18.0	0.0	18.8	0.4	2.4
Seaside	0.0	9.8	0.0	0.0	0.6	36.9	0.0	8.6	10.5	5.0
Simi Valley	0.0	9.2	0.0	0.0	1.4	30.9	17.3	1.0	10.4	3.5
Soledad	0.0	13.2	0.0	0.0	1.3	25.1	31.6	3.9	2.2	2.7
South Gate..................	0.0	24.1	0.0	0.0	0.1	28.3	7.2	6.6	3.6	9.8
South Pasadena...........	0.0	13.6	0.1	0.0	1.0	25.7	4.3	10.7	1.7	0.0
South San Francisco.....	0.0	19.1	0.7	0.0	6.2	17.3	14.3	8.2	4.4	5.1
Stanton	0.0	6.3	0.0	0.0	0.2	22.4	1.8	5.3	35.3	8.9
Stockton	0.0	9.4	0.6	0.0	0.6	24.6	11.6	5.1	6.1	5.1
Suisun City	0.0	7.8	0.0	0.0	0.0	16.2	0.0	6.2	22.0	8.1
Sunnyvale....................	0.0	8.6	0.5	0.3	0.5	11.3	28.1	8.2	2.4	1.5
Temecula.....................	0.0	19.9	0.0	0.0	0.2	17.4	4.7	15.3	10.4	3.5
Temple City.................	0.0	9.2	1.0	0.0	1.7	23.9	0.2	13.7	6.8	1.8
Thousand Oaks...........	0.0	22.4	0.0	0.0	0.5	17.9	13.0	6.9	8.4	2.8
Torrance	0.0	12.5	0.0	0.0	4.5	28.2	6.5	8.3	2.8	3.0
Tracy	0.0	6.2	0.0	0.0	0.4	16.6	24.2	12.4	3.8	5.1
Tulare........................	0.0	20.9	0.0	0.0	1.3	13.0	23.7	3.4	6.2	11.6
Turlock........................	0.0	9.9	0.0	0.0	0.5	33.2	16.6	4.4	11.0	1.6
Tustin.........................	0.0	13.4	0.0	0.0	0.0	29.4	0.0	4.0	8.8	9.1
Twentynine Palms........	0.0	17.8	0.0	0.0	5.0	25.2	0.0	13.8	5.5	4.2
Union City...................	0.0	8.6	0.0	0.0	0.6	22.1	0.8	13.1	17.7	7.7
Upland........................	0.0	9.8	0.0	0.0	1.4	22.4	19.7	2.8	10.4	2.3
Vacaville	0.0	6.6	0.0	0.0	4.4	17.0	29.3	4.9	18.9	3.8
Vallejo........................	0.0	10.3	0.0	0.0	0.4	22.0	15.1	0.9	18.2	3.0
Victorville	0.0	6.3	0.0	0.0	0.4	13.7	19.3	5.0	2.1	11.3
Visalia........................	0.0	12.5	0.0	0.0	0.0	19.7	23.2	7.4	2.8	1.1
Vista	0.0	9.8	0.0	0.0	3.8	15.0	17.2	7.4	9.0	7.5
Walnut	0.0	20.0	0.0	0.0	0.6	30.8	0.0	17.0	5.4	5.1
Walnut Creek	0.0	11.1	4.4	0.0	0.0	23.7	0.0	30.1	1.5	0.3
Wasco........................	0.0	17.2	0.0	0.0	1.0	28.0	26.1	0.0	8.4	1.4
Watsonville	0.0	7.2	0.0	0.0	1.0	19.7	25.5	4.2	6.2	0.5
West Covina................	0.0	14.3	0.4	0.0	2.6	31.7	0.0	5.3	5.0	7.9
West Hollywood	0.0	10.7	3.8	0.0	7.0	16.4	2.5	5.8	5.8	3.5
Westminster................	0.0	7.6	0.0	0.0	0.9	22.8	0.0	3.0	44.5	5.1
West Sacramento.........	0.0	18.1	0.0	0.0	0.3	13.0	10.0	6.8	11.0	8.6
Whittier	0.0	9.9	0.0	0.0	0.0	33.8	13.2	11.2	4.0	4.8
Wildomar	0.0	21.2	0.0	0.0	2.4	22.8	0.0	0.9	0.0	0.0
Windsor	0.0	20.4	0.0	0.0	1.0	24.7	0.0	3.9	13.1	4.1
Woodland	0.0	17.7	0.0	0.0	0.0	19.0	12.1	6.1	4.4	3.6
Yorba Linda.................	0.0	25.6	0.0	0.0	0.0	14.8	6.4	14.1	10.6	6.2
Yuba City....................	0.0	6.1	0.0	0.0	0.8	23.5	22.2	5.7	6.5	1.7
Yucaipa	0.0	24.1	0.0	0.0	4.3	22.0	0.0	13.1	11.5	2.4
COLORADO.............	X	X	X	X	X	X	X	X	X	X
Arvada........................	0.0	15.3	0.0	0.0	0.0	19.8	10.3	18.6	8.4	1.3
Aurora........................	0.0	13.0	0.0	0.0	0.0	21.5	14.3	11.3	2.9	2.2
Boulder.......................	0.0	17.2	3.0	0.0	0.0	21.6	5.5	19.0	9.4	2.5
Brighton	0.0	11.9	0.0	0.0	0.0	22.3	16.7	14.5	0.0	7.4
Broomfield	10.4	8.0	0.0	0.0	1.6	14.4	5.1	12.8	0.0	12.6

Table D. Cities — **City Government Finances, City Government Employment, and Climate**

	City government finances, 2012 (cont.)			Climate[2]						
	Debt outstanding			Average daily temperature (degrees Fahrenheit)						
				Mean		Limits				
City	Total (mil dol)	Per capita[1] (dollars)	Debt issued during year	January	July	January[3]	July[4]	Annual precipitation (inches)	Heating degree days	Cooling degree days
	137	138	139	140	141	142	143	144	145	146

CALIFORNIA—Cont'd										
San Francisco	13 075.2	15 759	3 426.5	52.3	61.3	46.4	68.2	22.28	2 597	163
San Gabriel	3.0	74	3.3	56.3	75.6	42.6	89.0	18.56	1 295	1 575
San Jacinto	24.5	538	0.0	NA	NA	NA	NA	NA	NA	NA
San Jose	5 924.6	6 013	690.9	50.5	70.9	41.7	84.3	15.08	2 171	811
San Juan Capistrano	68.5	1 928	0.0	55.4	68.7	43.9	77.3	13.56	1 756	666
San Leandro	78.3	899	0.0	50.0	62.8	43.6	70.4	25.40	2 857	142
San Luis Obispo	65.5	1 429	0.0	53.3	66.5	41.9	80.3	24.36	2 138	476
San Marcos	501.2	5 755	0.0	56.4	71.6	45.1	82.2	13.69	1 514	1 047
San Mateo	159.9	1 599	0.0	48.4	68.0	39.1	80.8	20.16	2 764	422
San Pablo	81.2	2 754	0.2	48.8	67.7	41.3	80.9	34.29	2 621	451
San Rafael	46.5	794	0.1	48.8	67.7	41.3	80.9	34.29	2 621	451
San Ramon	108.0	1 464	11.6	47.2	72.0	37.4	89.1	14.82	2 755	858
Santa Ana	358.1	1 080	0.0	58.0	72.9	46.6	87.7	13.84	1 153	1 299
Santa Barbara	112.5	1 257	1.5	53.1	67.0	40.8	76.7	16.93	2 121	482
Santa Clara	388.8	3 251	0.0	50.5	70.9	41.7	84.3	15.08	2 171	811
Santa Clarita	94.2	526	0.0	50.3	74.1	36.1	94.2	13.96	2 502	1 139
Santa Cruz	79.2	1 278	0.0	50.6	63.7	40.2	74.8	30.67	2 836	162
Santa Maria	66.7	658	51.7	51.6	63.5	39.3	73.5	14.01	2 783	121
Santa Monica	353.1	3 846	20.3	57.0	65.5	50.2	68.8	13.27	1 810	429
Santa Paula	69.0	2 299	0.0	54.7	68.3	41.2	80.7	18.41	1 911	602
Santa Rosa	483.1	2 836	59.1	48.7	67.6	39.5	82.2	31.01	2 694	526
Santee	52.7	950	3.0	57.1	73.0	45.7	83.6	13.75	1 313	1 261
Saratoga	12.0	391	12.0	50.5	70.9	41.7	84.3	15.08	2 171	811
Seaside	39.4	1 164	0.0	51.6	60.2	43.4	68.1	20.35	3 092	74
Simi Valley	147.8	1 177	0.0	53.7	76.0	39.5	95.0	17.79	1 822	1 485
Soledad	45.3	1 710	0.0	NA	NA	NA	NA	NA	NA	NA
South Gate	167.3	1 750	0.0	58.3	74.2	48.5	83.8	15.14	928	1 506
South Pasadena	7.3	280	0.0	NA	NA	NA	NA	NA	NA	NA
South San Francisco	146.4	2 225	0.0	49.4	62.8	42.9	71.1	20.11	2 862	142
Stanton	76.1	1 975	0.0	58.0	72.9	46.6	87.7	13.84	1 153	1 299
Stockton	572.9	1 926	0.1	46.0	77.3	38.1	93.8	13.84	2 563	1 456
Suisun City	69.5	2 431	0.5	46.1	72.6	37.5	88.8	23.46	2 649	975
Sunnyvale	125.4	855	0.0	50.5	70.9	41.7	84.3	15.08	2 171	811
Temecula	96.6	922	0.0	51.2	78.3	36.1	97.8	11.40	2 123	1 710
Temple City	6.3	174	0.0	56.3	75.6	42.6	89.0	18.56	1 295	1 575
Thousand Oaks	133.2	1 040	0.0	53.7	76.0	39.5	95.0	17.79	1 822	1 485
Torrance	148.8	1 010	0.0	56.3	69.4	46.2	77.6	14.79	1 526	742
Tracy	222.9	2 633	0.0	47.1	76.4	38.5	92.5	12.51	2 421	1 470
Tulare	200.3	3 290	0.0	45.8	79.3	37.4	93.8	11.03	2 588	1 685
Turlock	69.6	997	0.0	46.4	77.6	39.0	93.3	12.43	2 519	1 506
Tustin	193.5	2 486	8.9	54.5	72.1	41.4	83.8	13.87	1 794	1 102
Twentynine Palms	11.0	429	0.0	50.0	88.4	36.1	105.8	4.57	1 910	3 064
Union City	178.1	2 483	0.0	49.8	68.0	42.0	78.3	14.85	2 367	530
Upland	41.7	555	0.0	54.6	73.8	41.5	88.7	16.96	1 727	1 191
Vacaville	190.4	2 028	31.2	47.2	77.3	38.8	95.8	24.55	2 410	1 498
Vallejo	192.2	1 630	0.0	46.3	71.2	38.8	87.4	19.58	2 757	786
Victorville	370.9	3 084	0.0	45.5	80.0	31.4	99.1	6.20	2 929	1 735
Visalia	31.2	246	0.0	45.8	79.3	37.4	93.8	11.03	2 588	1 685
Vista	245.6	2 552	0.0	56.4	71.6	45.1	82.2	13.69	1 514	1 047
Walnut	28.7	956	0.0	54.6	73.8	41.5	88.7	16.96	1 727	1 191
Walnut Creek	4.9	74	0.2	47.5	72.4	39.3	85.2	23.96	3 267	983
Wasco	4.4	173	0.0	NA	NA	NA	NA	NA	NA	NA
Watsonville	36.2	698	0.0	49.7	62.4	38.7	72.0	23.25	3 080	123
West Covina	181.9	1 691	8.9	56.3	75.6	42.6	89.0	18.56	1 295	1 575
West Hollywood	100.2	2 875	0.0	58.3	74.2	48.5	83.8	15.14	928	1 506
Westminster	142.2	1 553	0.0	58.0	72.9	46.6	82.7	13.84	1 153	1 299
West Sacramento	368.8	7 425	94.7	46.3	75.4	38.8	92.4	17.93	2 666	1 248
Whittier	98.6	1 142	7.7	56.3	75.6	42.6	89.0	18.56	1 295	1 575
Wildomar	0.0	0	0.0	NA	NA	NA	NA	NA	NA	NA
Windsor	27.1	1 000	12.5	NA	NA	NA	NA	NA	NA	NA
Woodland	111.4	1 977	5.9	45.7	76.4	37.6	94.0	20.78	2 683	1 417
Yorba Linda	117.7	1 769	2.7	56.9	73.2	45.2	84.0	11.23	1 286	1 294
Yuba City	63.6	980	0.0	46.3	78.9	37.8	96.3	22.07	2 488	1 687
Yucaipa	35.9	684	0.0	52.9	78.0	40.4	94.4	13.62	1 904	1 714
COLORADO	X	X	X	X	X	X	X	X	X	X
Arvada	120.5	1 098	0.0	31.2	71.5	15.6	88.3	18.17	5 988	496
Aurora	1 215.3	3 582	2.6	29.2	73.4	15.2	88.0	15.81	6 128	696
Boulder	155.7	1 527	18.5	32.5	71.6	19.2	87.2	19.93	5 687	552
Brighton	76.1	2 167	0.0	NA	NA	NA	NA	NA	NA	NA
Broomfield	293.0	4 968	0.0	32.5	71.6	19.2	87.2	19.93	5 687	552

1. Based on the population estimated as of July 1 of the year shown.   2. Represents normal values based on the 30-year period, 1971–2000.   3. Average daily minimum.   4. Average daily maximum.

Table D. Cities — Land Area and Population

STATE Place code	City	Land area,[1] 2010 (sq km)	Population, 2015 Total persons	Rank	Per square kilometer	Race alone or in combination (percent), 2010-2014 White	Black	American Indian, Alaska Native	Asian	Hawaiian Pacific Islander	Percent Hispanic or Latino[2], 2010-2014	Percent foreign born 2010-2014
		1	2	3	4	5	6	7	8	9	10	11
	COLORADO—Cont'd											
08 12415	Castle Rock	87.5	55 591	669	635.3	95.7	1.9	1.5	2.3	0.4	11.5	5.9
08 12815	Centennial	74.4	109 741	264	1 475.0	90.3	3.0	1.3	5.6	0.2	7.5	8.7
08 16000	Colorado Springs	503.9	456 568	40	906.1	84.1	8.1	2.0	4.8	0.6	17.0	8.2
08 16495	Commerce City	88.8	53 696	696	604.7	83.0	4.0	2.6	3.9	0.4	45.5	15.7
08 20000	Denver	396.3	682 545	19	1 722.3	77.5	11.1	2.3	4.5	0.2	31.2	16.0
08 24785	Englewood	17.0	33 082	1 137	1 946.0	88.6	3.3	1.8	2.7	0.2	17.3	9.3
08 27425	Fort Collins	140.6	161 175	156	1 146.3	92.2	2.3	1.8	4.4	0.3	11.4	6.4
08 27865	Fountain	62.1	27 767	1 329	447.1	82.8	13.4	3.7	5.6	0.7	16.4	5.2
08 31660	Grand Junction	99.0	60 358	606	609.7	93.2	1.6	2.1	1.9	0.6	15.1	3.9
08 32155	Greeley	120.6	100 883	298	836.5	83.6	2.8	2.0	1.9	0.3	35.6	10.6
08 43000	Lakewood	111.1	152 597	168	1 373.5	91.3	2.6	2.5	3.9	0.4	22.4	8.5
08 45255	Littleton	33.6	46 368	817	1 380.0	94.0	1.6	0.9	2.9	0.4	11.9	7.6
08 45970	Longmont	67.8	92 088	343	1 358.2	86.6	1.8	2.3	3.9	0.1	25.9	13.4
08 46465	Loveland	87.0	75 182	455	864.2	93.5	1.2	1.5	2.4	0.3	10.5	4.1
08 54330	Northglenn	19.2	39 197	961	2 041.5	89.8	2.2	2.2	3.9	0.1	30.9	9.3
08 57630	Parker	53.0	49 550	760	934.9	94.5	2.3	1.5	4.3	0.4	7.6	5.0
08 62000	Pueblo	138.9	109 412	267	787.7	78.2	3.8	5.1	1.3	0.2	50.7	4.7
08 77290	Thornton	90.2	133 451	196	1 479.5	87.4	2.4	1.7	5.9	0.4	31.7	11.6
08 83835	Westminster	81.7	113 130	247	1 384.7	88.0	2.8	2.4	6.5	0.2	21.7	10.5
08 84440	Wheat Ridge	24.1	31 192	1 192	1 294.3	94.5	0.7	1.9	2.4	0.3	22.4	6.4
09 00000	CONNECTICUT	12 541.6	3 590 886	X	286.3	79.9	11.6	0.9	4.7	0.1	14.3	13.7
09 08000	Bridgeport	41.4	147 629	178	3 565.9	43.7	38.2	0.8	4.3	0.1	38.9	27.7
09 08420	Bristol	68.4	60 452	602	883.8	91.7	4.8	0.8	2.5	0.2	10.7	10.0
09 18430	Danbury	108.5	84 657	387	780.2	68.0	9.2	1.0	6.4	0.1	27.1	32.0
09 37000	Hartford	45.0	124 006	220	2 755.7	39.1	41.7	1.6	3.2	0.2	43.6	22.2
09 46450	Meriden	61.6	59 988	610	973.8	77.9	11.9	1.1	2.1	0.4	28.2	9.5
09 47290	Middletown	106.2	46 756	810	440.3	80.4	15.9	1.2	5.2	0.1	9.1	11.0
09 47500	Milford	56.7	52 087	725	918.6	91.3	2.4	0.6	5.6	0.0	5.3	9.6
09 49880	Naugatuck	42.2	31 538	1 184	747.3	89.9	6.7	0.5	3.3	0.0	9.9	12.1
09 50370	New Britain	34.7	72 808	475	2 098.2	69.0	12.8	0.7	3.6	0.3	38.1	19.5
09 52000	New Haven	48.4	130 322	204	2 692.6	46.3	37.2	1.0	5.6	0.1	26.0	15.8
09 52280	New London	14.5	27 179	1 352	1 874.4	64.4	20.7	1.1	4.2	0.3	29.3	15.4
09 55990	Norwalk	59.2	88 485	357	1 494.7	74.6	16.6	0.7	5.9	0.2	21.9	24.4
09 56200	Norwich	72.7	39 899	937	548.8	74.6	16.5	4.7	9.2	0.8	14.1	15.5
09 68100	Shelton	79.3	41 296	905	520.8	94.4	1.2	0.3	3.7	0.0	5.5	10.7
09 73000	Stamford	97.5	128 874	211	1 321.8	62.1	14.8	0.3	9.1	0.0	27.0	34.4
09 76500	Torrington	103.0	34 906	1 075	338.9	91.8	4.0	0.8	3.7	0.1	8.6	9.4
09 80000	Waterbury	73.9	108 802	269	1 472.3	64.9	22.8	1.5	2.5	0.1	34.2	14.5
09 82800	West Haven	27.8	54 927	681	1 975.8	67.9	24.0	1.4	4.3	0.1	19.3	15.4
10 00000	DELAWARE	5 046.7	945 934	X	187.4	72.0	23.2	1.0	4.0	0.1	8.6	8.4
10 21200	Dover	60.0	37 522	1 004	625.4	51.0	46.8	3.0	2.7	0.4	8.3	6.3
10 50670	Newark	23.8	33 817	1 111	1 420.9	81.7	10.5	0.7	8.0	0.0	5.4	10.5
10 77580	Wilmington	28.2	71 948	482	2 551.3	38.1	57.3	0.7	1.3	0.1	13.6	7.0
11 00000	DISTRICT OF COLUMBIA	158.1	672 228	X	4 251.9	42.1	50.7	0.9	4.7	0.1	9.9	14.0
11 50000	Washington	158.1	672 228	22	4 251.9	42.1	50.7	0.9	4.7	0.1	9.9	14.0
12 00000	FLORIDA	138 887.5	20 271 272	X	146.0	78.1	17.2	0.8	3.2	0.2	23.3	19.6
12 00950	Altamonte Springs	23.3	43 159	867	1 852.3	81.0	15.6	0.6	3.4	0.3	23.4	14.9
12 01700	Apopka	80.9	48 382	784	598.0	66.8	23.3	0.8	4.9	0.6	27.1	19.8
12 02681	Aventura	6.9	37 649	999	5 456.4	94.4	3.7	0.3	1.2	0.1	35.6	46.4
12 07300	Boca Raton	76.0	93 235	335	1 226.8	89.5	5.5	0.6	3.2	0.1	12.2	19.5
12 07525	Bonita Springs	100.0	51 704	730	517.0	90.7	2.3	1.2	1.7	0.0	27.5	23.6
12 07875	Boynton Beach	41.9	73 966	468	1 765.3	62.7	33.5	0.4	2.6	0.1	12.2	24.7
12 07950	Bradenton	36.7	54 437	688	1 483.3	77.3	18.3	0.4	1.2	0.1	18.8	13.6
12 10275	Cape Coral	273.7	175 229	142	640.2	91.3	5.0	0.7	2.0	0.0	18.6	14.2
12 11050	Casselberry	18.1	27 056	1 356	1 494.8	85.5	9.2	1.3	3.4	0.0	22.4	10.9
12 12875	Clearwater	66.2	113 003	248	1 707.0	84.6	11.7	0.7	3.1	0.2	13.2	14.4
12 12925	Clermont	35.3	32 390	1 162	917.6	74.5	16.3	0.7	5.9	0.1	22.6	13.0
12 13275	Coconut Creek	30.7	59 302	620	1 931.7	78.2	14.8	0.2	5.5	0.4	23.4	26.8
12 14125	Cooper City	20.8	35 364	1 068	1 700.2	85.0	8.1	0.6	7.8	0.0	27.2	22.8
12 14250	Coral Gables	33.5	51 117	743	1 525.9	92.5	4.3	0.3	3.3	0.0	53.8	37.3
12 14400	Coral Springs	61.6	129 485	208	2 102.0	70.2	22.0	1.0	5.1	0.2	24.5	27.5
12 15968	Cutler Bay	25.5	44 865	834	1 759.4	80.6	14.4	0.3	2.2	0.0	51.4	36.1
12 16335	Dania Beach	21.0	31 446	1 187	1 497.4	69.6	25.2	0.5	2.3	0.3	21.8	26.9
12 16475	Davie	90.4	100 882	299	1 116.0	80.1	11.2	0.6	5.7	0.2	32.1	27.1
12 16525	Daytona Beach	151.3	64 736	551	427.9	59.5	35.4	1.1	3.3	0.1	7.7	8.9

1. Dry land or land partially or temporarily covered by water.   2. May be of any race.

Table D. Cities — **Population**

City	Age of population (percent), 2010-2014									Median age 2010–2014	Percent female 2010–2014	Population			
												Census counts		Percent change	
	Under 5 years	5 to 17 years	18 to 24 years	25 to 34 years	35 to 44 years	45 to 54 years	55 to 64 years	65 to 74 years	75 years and over			2000	2010	2000–2010	2010–2015
	12	13	14	15	16	17	18	19	20	21	22	23	24	25	26
COLORADO—Cont'd															
Castle Rock	8.7	21.9	6.6	12.4	18.3	14.2	10.2	5.1	2.5	35.2	50.4	20 224	48 231	138.5	15.2
Centennial	5.6	18.4	6.8	11.8	13.3	16.3	14.3	8.3	5.2	40.8	50.7	NA	100 377	NA	8.5
Colorado Springs	7.1	17.4	11.2	15.3	12.4	13.8	11.3	6.4	4.9	34.0	50.4	360 890	416 427	15.4	9.4
Commerce City	10.3	22.8	6.5	16.9	16.1	10.7	10.2	4.0	2.5	31.7	50.5	20 991	45 913	118.7	16.9
Denver	7.0	14.1	9.3	21.5	15.3	11.7	10.5	5.8	4.8	34.0	50.0	554 636	600 158	8.2	13.8
Englewood	6.0	12.1	9.3	18.7	13.9	15.2	12.5	5.9	6.4	37.6	48.9	31 727	30 255	-4.6	9.3
Fort Collins	5.5	13.9	22.3	16.4	11.5	11.7	9.8	5.0	4.0	29.7	50.5	118 652	143 986	21.4	11.7
Fountain	9.3	23.6	7.6	17.7	14.5	13.4	7.1	4.3	2.5	29.5	52.2	15 197	25 846	70.1	7.3
Grand Junction	6.6	15.5	13.0	14.5	11.4	11.3	12.1	7.4	8.1	35.3	50.6	41 986	58 566	39.5	2.3
Greeley	6.8	17.8	17.0	14.3	12.8	10.2	10.0	5.8	5.2	30.5	50.4	76 930	92 889	20.7	8.6
Lakewood	6.0	13.9	9.3	15.2	13.2	13.3	13.9	8.2	6.9	38.8	49.8	144 126	142 980	-0.8	6.7
Littleton	6.0	15.5	8.3	12.9	13.1	14.5	13.8	8.3	7.5	40.8	51.9	40 340	41 737	3.5	11.0
Longmont	7.1	18.1	9.1	13.9	13.9	14.2	11.9	6.8	5.0	36.4	49.1	71 093	86 270	21.3	6.7
Loveland	6.6	17.3	7.6	14.5	12.8	13.2	12.6	8.1	7.3	38.0	51.2	50 608	66 859	32.1	12.5
Northglenn	6.3	16.9	11.2	18.7	12.8	11.6	10.3	6.4	5.8	32.7	48.8	31 575	35 789	13.3	9.6
Parker	6.7	24.5	7.5	12.3	19.2	15.8	8.1	4.2	1.8	34.2	49.6	23 558	45 297	92.3	9.4
Pueblo	6.6	16.8	10.2	13.3	12.1	12.6	13.0	7.4	8.1	37.8	50.9	102 121	106 595	4.4	2.7
Thornton	8.3	21.4	9.2	15.5	15.3	13.6	8.9	4.7	3.1	32.2	49.7	82 384	118 772	44.2	12.3
Westminster	6.7	16.9	8.5	17.0	14.3	14.7	11.7	5.9	4.3	35.6	50.4	100 940	106 114	5.1	6.6
Wheat Ridge	5.5	13.9	8.0	14.1	13.7	14.1	13.6	8.1	9.1	42.3	53.0	32 913	30 166	-8.3	3.3
CONNECTICUT	5.4	16.7	9.5	12.1	12.7	15.7	13.1	7.8	7.0	40.3	51.3	3 405 565	3 574 097	4.9	0.5
Bridgeport	7.0	18.4	11.8	17.1	13.5	12.8	9.7	5.1	4.6	32.2	51.7	139 529	144 229	3.4	2.4
Bristol	4.9	15.7	7.8	12.5	13.2	16.0	13.3	7.9	8.6	42.4	50.3	60 062	60 477	0.7	0.0
Danbury	5.9	13.9	10.7	16.3	15.8	13.9	11.3	6.7	5.6	36.6	51.0	74 848	80 893	8.1	4.6
Hartford	6.8	18.6	16.2	16.5	11.5	11.7	9.3	5.3	4.1	29.8	51.1	121 578	124 775	2.6	-0.6
Meriden	6.7	14.2	8.0	15.0	13.7	13.9	14.2	7.7	6.6	39.1	50.6	58 244	60 868	4.5	-1.4
Middletown	4.2	13.6	14.4	15.0	12.2	14.4	12.2	7.3	6.6	37.2	52.8	43 167	47 648	10.4	-1.9
Milford	4.8	14.5	6.7	11.2	13.7	14.8	18.8	13.4	8.9	44.4	51.3	52 305	51 271	1.3	1.6
Naugatuck	5.8	16.1	10.5	14.1	11.6	16.2	13.2	6.6	5.9	38.2	48.9	30 989	31 862	2.8	-1.1
New Britain	6.1	17.2	13.2	15.0	11.3	13.4	11.1	6.2	6.5	34.0	53.9	71 538	73 206	2.3	-0.5
New Haven	6.1	16.0	15.7	20.3	12.0	10.6	8.5	5.5	5.2	30.4	52.8	123 626	129 779	5.0	0.3
New London	5.2	14.3	21.2	15.0	12.0	13.5	8.7	5.7	4.5	30.9	53.6	25 671	27 620	7.6	-1.6
Norwalk	6.3	12.3	7.8	15.5	14.9	15.0	14.0	7.4	6.7	41.1	50.5	82 951	85 603	3.2	3.3
Norwich	7.1	15.8	9.5	16.1	11.6	15.0	11.4	6.4	6.9	35.9	50.9	36 117	40 493	12.1	-1.5
Shelton	3.9	15.3	8.5	10.3	11.5	18.6	13.1	10.0	8.9	45.3	53.1	38 101	39 559	3.8	4.4
Stamford	7.1	14.8	8.3	17.2	14.6	14.0	10.9	6.6	6.3	36.6	50.7	117 083	122 643	4.7	5.1
Torrington	5.5	13.6	7.2	11.2	11.5	18.2	14.9	9.6	8.5	45.8	51.2	35 202	36 383	3.4	-4.1
Waterbury	7.7	17.4	10.4	14.5	13.5	13.5	11.0	6.3	5.6	35.0	51.8	107 271	110 366	2.9	-1.4
West Haven	6.4	15.6	13.5	12.3	13.3	13.7	13.0	6.9	5.3	36.8	52.8	52 360	55 564	6.1	-1.1
DELAWARE	6.1	16.2	10.1	12.7	12.2	14.5	12.9	8.8	6.5	39.1	51.6	783 600	897 934	14.6	5.3
Dover	6.3	14.4	20.5	14.9	10.7	11.2	8.7	6.4	6.9	29.8	52.8	32 135	36 047	12.2	4.4
Newark	2.8	8.3	44.2	11.2	7.0	7.6	8.5	5.0	5.4	22.5	54.1	28 547	31 454	10.2	7.3
Wilmington	7.5	16.6	9.8	17.2	13.2	13.6	10.4	6.6	5.1	34.1	53.5	72 664	70 851	-2.5	1.5
DISTRICT OF COLUMBIA	6.1	10.9	13.0	22.2	13.7	12.0	10.7	6.2	5.1	33.7	52.7	572 059	601 723	5.2	11.7
Washington	6.1	10.9	13.0	22.2	13.7	12.0	10.7	6.2	5.1	33.7	52.7	572 059	601 723	5.2	11.7
FLORIDA	5.6	15.2	9.2	12.4	12.5	14.2	12.8	9.8	8.4	41.2	51.1	15 982 378	18 801 310	17.6	7.8
Altamonte Springs	5.8	13.1	7.5	17.7	14.2	14.4	12.3	9.3	5.6	39.3	54.1	41 200	41 496	0.7	4.0
Apopka	7.3	19.4	9.3	12.1	16.4	12.8	12.3	5.8	4.6	36.7	50.4	26 642	41 542	55.9	16.1
Aventura	5.9	13.4	2.0	11.5	15.4	12.7	10.7	14.0	14.3	46.0	53.2	25 267	35 762	41.5	5.3
Boca Raton	3.7	14.0	11.1	9.6	10.8	15.0	14.0	10.6	11.2	45.7	50.3	74 764	84 392	12.9	10.5
Bonita Springs	3.5	10.7	6.4	12.2	9.6	11.0	14.4	17.8	14.2	52.0	51.5	32 797	43 914	33.9	18.1
Boynton Beach	5.3	13.6	7.9	13.9	12.5	13.6	11.8	8.3	13.0	42.8	53.2	60 389	68 217	13.0	8.4
Bradenton	6.0	14.5	7.8	13.3	12.1	10.7	12.3	10.2	13.0	42.0	52.3	49 504	49 546	0.1	10.5
Cape Coral	5.7	17.6	6.7	10.3	12.3	14.5	14.1	10.9	7.8	43.0	51.1	102 286	154 305	50.9	13.6
Casselberry	6.1	12.1	9.6	16.2	13.6	17.3	11.4	8.2	5.5	40.2	51.3	22 629	26 241	16.0	3.0
Clearwater	6.0	13.4	7.6	12.5	11.6	15.1	13.1	9.5	11.3	44.0	52.2	108 787	107 685	-1.0	4.0
Clermont	6.2	20.4	6.9	8.3	15.4	10.8	11.5	12.3	8.2	40.6	50.5	9 333	28 742	208.0	12.7
Coconut Creek	6.2	16.0	8.1	13.1	15.0	13.2	10.2	7.3	11.0	39.5	51.7	43 566	52 909	21.4	12.0
Cooper City	5.2	19.6	8.6	12.8	11.5	16.8	14.8	6.3	4.4	38.5	50.8	27 939	28 547	2.2	23.9
Coral Gables	4.8	11.7	15.4	11.2	13.4	14.2	12.5	10.1	6.7	41.4	51.0	42 249	46 780	10.7	9.3
Coral Springs	7.0	19.5	10.5	11.4	15.3	15.9	11.5	5.6	3.3	36.2	51.6	117 549	121 096	3.0	6.9
Cutler Bay	6.4	17.9	8.7	16.9	13.1	17.0	9.0	6.2	4.9	35.1	48.5	NA	40 286	NA	11.4
Dania Beach	6.5	14.2	9.5	13.9	12.4	14.7	14.4	9.2	5.1	39.7	51.8	20 061	29 639	47.7	6.1
Davie	5.7	16.8	11.5	13.0	12.8	16.7	11.5	7.2	4.8	36.9	52.0	75 720	91 992	21.5	9.7
Daytona Beach	5.4	9.9	16.3	14.2	9.9	12.9	13.2	9.2	9.0	39.9	50.8	64 112	61 005	-4.8	6.1

Table D. Cities — Households, Group Quarters, Crime, and Education

City	Households, 2010-2014				Persons in group quarters, 2010				Serious crimes known to police,[2] 2014				Educational attainment, 2010–2014		
			Percent			Institutional			Total		Rate[3]			Attainment[4] (percent)	
	Number	Persons per house-hold	Female family house-holder[1]	One-person	Total	Total	Persons in nursing facilities	Non-institu-tional	Number	Rate[3]	Violent	Property	Population age 25 and older	High school graduate or less	Bachelor's degree or more
	27	28	29	30	31	32	33	34	35	36	37	38	39	40	41
COLORADO—Cont'd															
Castle Rock	17 767	2.92	9.1	17.1	460	390	108	70	452	833	76	758	32 444	21.8	46.6
Centennial	38 423	2.71	8.9	20.1	1 701	1 559	307	142	1 440	1 340	132	1 208	71 763	17.1	54.0
Colorado Springs	170 273	2.55	12.0	29.4	7 629	3 467	1 657	4 162	18 348	4 124	456	3 668	279 531	27.8	36.3
Commerce City	14 581	3.35	13.7	17.7	351	191	191	160	1 832	3 610	398	3 212	28 824	50.2	20.6
Denver	271 054	2.34	10.4	40.1	15 981	6 518	2 333	9 463	26 407	3 969	601	3 367	441 119	32.6	43.7
Englewood	14 231	2.20	12.9	40.9	291	238	238	53	1 833	5 762	201	5 561	22 437	36.4	33.2
Fort Collins	57 146	2.62	8.1	26.1	7 085	1 437	514	5 648	4 104	2 665	209	2 456	86 682	18.0	51.6
Fountain	9 144	2.94	14.6	18.3	0	0	0	0	773	2 804	301	2 503	15 738	31.0	22.6
Grand Junction	24 343	2.45	10.8	32.7	2 884	1 077	395	1 807	2 820	4 702	477	4 225	38 618	36.3	29.5
Greeley	33 533	2.85	13.3	26.3	4 853	1 627	627	3 226	3 780	3 881	496	3 385	55 871	42.2	25.6
Lakewood	62 283	2.34	11.5	34.2	2 171	1 552	1 064	619	7 558	5 099	481	4 618	102 538	32.6	36.0
Littleton	19 031	2.30	9.0	35.8	491	448	313	43	1 023	2 280	89	2 191	31 006	23.5	44.6
Longmont	33 859	2.62	12.6	25.6	639	498	482	141	2 376	2 616	344	2 273	57 871	33.1	37.1
Loveland	29 227	2.40	9.9	28.2	510	416	414	94	2 121	2 927	233	2 694	48 326	30.4	34.0
Northglenn	13 945	2.66	11.9	30.5	129	129	129	0	1 130	2 981	314	2 667	24 697	46.5	18.1
Parker	16 282	2.92	7.3	19.2	28	0	0	28	677	1 370	134	1 236	28 891	16.5	51.6
Pueblo	43 371	2.48	16.2	35.4	4 045	3 050	1 444	995	7 980	7 349	819	6 530	71 759	44.0	19.4
Thornton	41 632	3.00	11.9	20.2	462	430	430	32	4 090	3 160	255	2 905	77 017	40.7	26.6
Westminster	41 821	2.61	10.9	26.3	467	448	348	19	3 528	3 147	234	2 913	73 529	32.9	34.6
Wheat Ridge	13 895	2.21	11.0	37.6	554	434	381	120	1 182	3 801	312	3 489	22 936	36.9	33.9
CONNECTICUT	1 356 206	2.65	13.0	27.9	118 152	49 370	26 371	68 782	77 592	2 157	237	1 920	2 455 577	38.1	37.0
Bridgeport	50 034	2.93	25.8	28.8	4 838	1 960	759	2 878	5 623	3 804	905	2 899	92 205	57.8	16.5
Bristol	25 194	2.40	12.9	32.2	849	637	611	212	1 580	2 608	120	2 487	43 135	47.7	23.7
Danbury	29 046	2.85	12.0	27.0	3 953	1 904	538	2 049	1 505	1 786	178	1 608	56 858	47.8	30.5
Hartford	45 801	2.73	31.4	34.9	8 951	2 194	777	6 757	6 660	5 330	1 105	4 226	73 543	60.4	15.0
Meriden	24 018	2.52	15.9	29.4	955	688	660	267	1 595	2 643	300	2 343	42 964	52.5	18.8
Middletown	19 419	2.44	14.0	35.3	3 731	998	552	2 733	940	1 989	169	1 820	32 218	37.6	35.8
Milford	21 199	2.50	9.1	29.7	472	355	344	117	1 422	2 672	66	2 606	39 014	34.0	39.9
Naugatuck	12 157	2.61	11.8	27.3	267	236	236	31	645	2 037	85	1 951	21 883	45.4	24.5
New Britain	27 820	2.63	21.8	32.1	3 194	790	557	2 404	2 439	3 347	441	2 907	46 634	57.7	18.4
New Haven	49 945	2.61	21.1	39.7	11 220	1 774	768	9 446	6 653	5 083	1 089	3 994	81 199	47.0	33.6
New London	10 224	2.69	16.8	38.7	3 713	225	225	3 488	1 012	3 677	596	3 081	16 573	52.1	21.1
Norwalk	35 450	2.46	11.8	33.8	797	461	405	336	1 864	2 113	298	1 815	63 756	35.5	41.1
Norwich	16 331	2.47	15.2	34.0	514	219	205	295	1 001	2 484	380	2 104	27 610	49.5	20.1
Shelton	15 186	2.67	10.0	25.6	502	446	442	56	414	1 001	56	946	29 230	35.7	37.8
Stamford	46 418	2.70	12.3	28.6	1 280	662	653	618	2 373	1 863	243	1 619	87 421	34.0	45.8
Torrington	14 820	2.41	11.3	33.1	838	611	559	227	681	1 922	124	1 798	26 263	51.8	20.8
Waterbury	40 960	2.68	23.2	31.8	1 938	1 149	886	789	4 999	4 566	373	4 193	70 744	56.7	16.0
West Haven	20 463	2.70	18.7	32.4	2 857	458	362	2 399	1 665	3 032	264	2 768	36 124	49.2	21.2
DELAWARE	339 046	2.70	13.9	26.6	24 413	11 673	4 591	12 740	32 476	3 471	489	2 982	620 886	43.5	29.4
Dover	12 680	2.90	19.6	34.1	3 745	569	340	3 176	2 112	5 606	637	4 969	21 529	41.3	28.4
Newark	9 691	3.33	7.0	29.2	7 128	0	0	7 128	850	2 590	317	2 273	14 740	23.5	53.8
Wilmington	29 085	2.45	23.3	39.5	3 226	2 324	531	902	4 941	6 890	1 636	5 254	47 763	51.4	25.6
DISTRICT OF COLUM-BIA	267 415	2.37	15.5	45.1	40 021	7 339	3 064	32 682	42 346	6 427	1 244	5 182	442 721	29.7	53.4
Washington	267 415	2.37	15.5	45.1	40 021	7 339	3 064	32 682	40 837	6 198	1 185	5 012	442 721	29.7	53.4
FLORIDA	7 217 508	2.68	13.2	29.0	421 709	254 506	73 372	167 203	786 967	3 956	540	3 415	13 561 596	43.2	26.8
Altamonte Springs	16 481	2.54	13.3	40.1	448	444	444	4	1 503	3 553	364	3 189	31 475	32.5	33.9
Apopka	14 819	3.00	16.3	17.7	178	118	118	60	1 676	3 599	363	3 236	28 900	39.2	27.0
Aventura	18 102	2.04	8.3	41.8	96	96	96	0	2 055	5 475	202	5 272	29 063	25.0	50.9
Boca Raton	36 507	2.42	8.2	32.7	3 444	430	415	3 014	2 233	2 468	185	2 283	63 549	21.8	52.1
Bonita Springs	18 761	2.47	6.1	28.5	157	12	0	145	NA	NA	NA	NA	36 424	41.2	31.2
Boynton Beach	28 493	2.47	13.6	36.9	1 000	649	630	351	3 257	4 536	526	4 010	50 826	42.2	25.2
Bradenton	20 483	2.48	14.0	36.2	1 757	1 074	966	683	2 347	4 483	646	3 838	35 999	51.1	20.5
Cape Coral	57 643	2.81	12.0	22.2	445	350	307	95	3 513	2 082	143	1 939	114 548	46.2	21.1
Casselberry	10 496	2.53	12.0	37.4	51	12	5	39	1 235	4 635	499	4 136	19 035	38.5	23.7
Clearwater	47 015	2.32	13.5	38.4	3 584	1 011	1 000	2 573	4 924	4 473	582	3 891	80 135	40.6	27.9
Clermont	10 678	2.77	11.3	19.3	199	177	177	22	950	3 131	224	2 907	19 709	32.3	27.6
Coconut Creek	22 067	2.52	11.4	33.6	146	138	65	8	1 353	2 342	147	2 195	38 943	36.4	33.9
Cooper City	10 508	3.05	13.3	14.5	40	0	0	40	482	1 351	118	1 233	21 190	24.6	41.8
Coral Gables	17 599	2.80	6.6	30.8	4 540	1	0	4 539	2 063	4 100	151	3 949	32 765	15.9	62.1
Coral Springs	40 554	3.09	18.2	17.2	359	227	222	132	2 684	2 098	159	1 939	79 570	31.1	35.1
Cutler Bay	12 873	3.31	17.0	20.3	338	245	199	93	1 973	4 476	288	4 188	28 139	37.5	30.3
Dania Beach	11 986	2.55	17.5	34.7	329	294	87	35	1 344	4 336	494	3 842	21 428	48.3	21.3
Davie	33 170	2.89	14.7	23.5	1 355	86	50	1 269	3 464	3 534	262	3 272	63 516	35.3	33.0
Daytona Beach	25 775	2.40	14.1	42.7	5 048	1 094	1 059	3 954	4 778	7 629	1 284	6 345	42 285	47.7	19.4

1. No spouse present. 2. Data for serious crimes have not been adjusted for underreporting. This may affect comparability between geographic areas and over time. 3. Per 100,000 population estimated by the FBI. 4. Persons 25 years old and over.

Table D. Cities — Income, Poverty, and Housing

City	Money income, 2010–2014					Housing units, 2010			Occupied housing units 2010–2014				
	Per capita income[1] (dollars)	Households			Families with income below poverty (percent)	Total	Percent change, 2000–2010	Vacant units for sale or rent[2]		Owner-occupied		Median owner costs as a percent of income	
		Median income	Percent with income of $200,000 or more	Percent with income of less than $25,000					Total	Percent	Median value[3] (dollars)	With a mortgage[4]	Without a mortgage[5]
	42	43	44	45	46	47	48	49	50	51	52	53	54
COLORADO—Cont'd													
Castle Rock	35 779	86 563	8.3	10.0	4.6	17 626	135.5	938	17 767	76.0	283 700	22.8	10.9
Centennial	41 356	90 090	10.9	8.7	3.5	38 779	NA	1 330	38 423	83.1	296 800	21.9	10.0
Colorado Springs	29 355	54 228	3.9	21.6	9.9	179 607	20.7	11 819	170 273	58.8	208 600	23.3	10.0
Commerce City	22 889	64 672	2.8	15.5	11.3	15 452	123.7	973	14 581	71.9	187 300	25.2	11.7
Denver	34 423	51 800	6.4	24.5	13.7	285 797	13.7	22 690	271 054	49.7	257 500	22.9	10.4
Englewood	28 814	46 776	2.4	25.5	13.5	15 478	4.0	1 103	14 231	48.9	216 800	24.1	11.3
Fort Collins	28 921	53 775	4.2	23.9	7.5	60 503	26.7	2 674	57 146	54.6	253 200	22.8	10.0
Fountain	23 501	56 687	1.2	16.1	8.4	9 371	80.1	647	9 144	63.3	178 800	23.5	10.0
Grand Junction	25 899	44 887	2.3	27.3	12.8	26 170	38.7	1 859	24 343	59.6	208 900	24.1	10.4
Greeley	22 354	47 342	1.8	26.8	14.4	36 323	25.9	2 896	33 533	56.2	168 400	22.8	10.0
Lakewood	31 689	56 134	3.8	20.1	9.0	65 758	5.3	3 772	62 283	57.9	242 200	23.5	10.2
Littleton	36 577	62 683	6.3	21.4	5.9	19 434	7.1	1 122	19 031	61.1	271 000	22.7	10.0
Longmont	29 884	60 218	4.5	19.2	11.5	35 008	27.6	1 756	33 859	61.9	243 900	21.7	10.0
Loveland	28 705	55 580	2.2	20.1	6.7	28 557	40.5	1 404	29 227	63.5	218 200	23.2	10.0
Northglenn	25 008	53 616	1.8	19.2	9.0	14 274	17.5	782	13 945	59.1	185 300	24.4	12.1
Parker	36 763	98 170	8.5	8.0	3.1	16 533	97.8	616	16 282	79.6	288 400	22.4	10.0
Pueblo	20 450	34 889	1.1	36.0	18.0	47 593	10.4	4 303	43 371	57.3	113 300	24.2	12.7
Thornton	26 782	66 160	3.3	12.4	7.1	43 230	46.6	1 871	41 632	69.0	210 600	23.7	10.6
Westminster	31 694	66 300	4.3	14.2	7.8	43 968	11.4	1 927	41 821	63.5	225 300	22.9	10.0
Wheat Ridge	29 798	49 003	2.3	24.6	10.3	14 868	-0.7	892	13 895	53.9	242 600	22.6	10.0
CONNECTICUT	38 480	69 899	9.4	18.0	7.5	1 487 891	7.4	116 804	1 356 206	67.3	274 500	25.3	16.7
Bridgeport	20 442	41 204	2.2	33.1	20.4	57 012	4.9	5 757	50 034	41.1	176 000	31.8	23.4
Bristol	31 365	60 208	3.2	19.5	7.2	27 011	3.4	1 691	25 194	66.9	199 000	25.0	17.7
Danbury	31 411	65 981	5.9	18.1	8.4	31 154	9.2	2 247	29 046	60.3	295 600	28.0	17.2
Hartford	16 813	29 313	1.2	44.8	31.3	51 822	2.3	6 698	45 801	23.5	163 600	31.1	17.7
Meriden	27 483	53 401	2.1	20.8	11.0	25 892	5.1	1 915	24 018	60.9	184 300	26.8	16.0
Middletown	34 226	61 373	5.5	18.9	9.9	21 223	7.7	1 360	19 419	53.1	231 700	23.9	14.6
Milford	40 797	80 743	9.8	14.8	3.1	23 074	5.1	1 366	21 199	77.3	304 200	25.0	18.8
Naugatuck	30 491	58 641	3.4	19.2	7.8	13 061	5.8	722	12 157	66.5	192 500	25.1	19.9
New Britain	21 070	40 515	1.4	32.4	18.3	31 226	0.2	3 068	27 820	40.3	162 100	27.3	18.0
New Haven	23 796	37 508	3.3	36.0	22.3	54 967	3.8	6 090	49 945	29.5	199 200	28.9	16.7
New London	21 754	41 230	2.2	33.8	21.8	11 840	2.4	1 467	10 224	36.3	186 700	28.0	15.7
Norwalk	43 778	76 051	11.3	15.8	5.9	35 415	4.9	2 198	35 450	62.1	406 600	29.6	18.8
Norwich	27 111	49 695	2.4	24.3	12.2	18 659	12.4	2 060	16 331	52.2	183 200	25.6	17.8
Shelton	41 189	88 369	9.2	11.3	4.1	16 146	9.8	821	15 186	79.9	348 200	26.0	16.7
Stamford	46 074	77 221	16.3	15.3	6.9	50 573	6.9	3 216	46 418	54.8	506 000	27.8	17.3
Torrington	28 368	55 460	1.8	22.1	6.6	16 761	3.8	1 518	14 820	67.2	172 800	26.2	18.7
Waterbury	21 251	41 136	1.5	33.4	20.5	47 991	2.5	5 230	40 960	46.7	140 700	28.5	21.4
West Haven	25 718	49 993	2.7	23.0	10.3	22 446	0.5	1 334	20 463	54.5	210 300	31.2	23.0
DELAWARE	30 191	60 231	4.9	18.7	8.2	405 885	18.3	63 588	339 046	71.6	232 900	23.5	11.1
Dover	22 013	45 660	1.7	27.0	15.2	15 024	12.5	1 253	12 680	51.4	181 600	24.5	11.6
Newark	23 675	53 125	5.6	29.1	5.3	10 475	12.5	641	9 691	55.0	272 700	21.6	10.0
Wilmington	25 686	38 979	3.5	34.2	22.6	32 820	2.1	4 205	29 085	46.4	171 400	24.2	13.7
DISTRICT OF COLUMBIA	46 502	69 235	12.8	22.2	14.3	296 719	8.0	30 012	267 415	41.6	454 500	22.9	10.9
Washington	46 502	69 235	12.8	22.2	14.3	296 719	8.0	30 012	267 415	41.6	454 500	22.9	10.9
FLORIDA	26 499	47 212	3.9	25.7	12.2	8 989 580	23.1	1 568 778	7 217 508	66.1	156 200	26.9	13.3
Altamonte Springs	27 236	50 013	2.2	20.5	7.8	22 088	9.5	2 962	16 481	49.0	134 800	26.9	15.0
Apopka	25 895	57 925	4.2	20.1	14.7	15 707	55.9	1 347	14 819	76.3	156 000	26.8	10.9
Aventura	46 137	59 657	9.8	23.7	9.7	26 120	30.5	8 228	18 102	67.8	288 200	35.1	24.5
Boca Raton	48 918	71 867	14.0	15.6	5.4	44 539	18.3	7 761	36 507	68.9	354 800	27.5	14.9
Bonita Springs	38 366	53 530	7.5	20.6	12.2	31 716	35.2	11 699	18 761	74.2	234 700	27.8	13.5
Boynton Beach	26 557	44 973	2.5	25.9	13.1	36 289	18.6	7 185	28 493	64.3	136 900	28.1	15.0
Bradenton	22 121	40 592	1.4	29.6	14.4	26 767	7.3	5 362	20 483	53.2	126 100	25.8	14.2
Cape Coral	24 001	49 841	2.4	21.4	10.5	78 948	72.7	18 181	57 643	69.4	146 300	28.0	14.5
Casselberry	24 667	41 950	1.7	27.1	8.6	12 708	22.5	1 278	10 496	61.8	108 200	28.1	13.5
Clearwater	28 500	43 306	3.7	29.0	11.1	59 156	4.3	11 518	47 015	59.1	153 900	27.9	16.0
Clermont	25 029	55 336	1.7	19.3	10.5	12 730	NA	1 514	10 678	70.9	176 900	25.0	11.8
Coconut Creek	28 217	53 316	2.5	19.3	6.7	25 926	17.1	3 172	22 067	65.4	139 400	26.5	21.1
Cooper City	37 680	91 285	11.9	7.8	3.8	9 912	7.4	284	10 508	85.9	290 900	27.3	12.9
Coral Gables	56 721	93 590	22.5	16.3	3.9	20 266	13.9	2 320	17 599	64.2	621 800	26.3	14.1
Coral Springs	30 282	66 271	6.8	14.8	8.4	45 433	10.0	3 619	40 554	62.9	269 600	28.3	12.9
Cutler Bay	24 418	62 130	4.1	17.9	8.2	14 620	NA	1 282	12 873	74.9	179 700	29.1	12.8
Dania Beach	23 302	40 222	1.5	33.5	22.1	15 671	44.1	2 794	11 986	54.1	155 600	29.1	16.2
Davie	30 340	58 924	6.9	20.7	8.6	37 306	19.6	2 991	33 170	72.0	200 800	27.1	16.3
Daytona Beach	18 378	28 164	1.0	44.3	21.3	33 920	1.6	6 606	25 775	46.8	113 000	28.5	14.3

1. Based on population estimated by the American Community Survey. 2. Includes units rented or sold but not occupied. 3. Specified owner-occupied units; $1,000,000 represents $1,000,000 or more. 4. 50.0 represents 50 percent or more. 5. 10.0 represents 10 percent or less.

Table D. Cities — Housing, Labor Force, and Employment

City	Occupied housing units, 2010–2014 (cont.) Percent renter occupied	Median gross rent[1]	Median gross rent as a percent of income[2]	Percent with no vehicle available	Migration, 2010–2014 Percent who lived in the same house one year ago	Percent who lived outside current city one year ago	Civilian labor force, 2015 Total	Percent change, 2014–2015	Unemployment Total	Rate[3]	Civilian employment[4], 2010–2014 Population age 16 and older	Percent In labor force	Civilian full-year full-time workers	Households with no workers (percent)
	55	56	57	58	59	60	61	62	63	64	65	66	67	68
COLORADO—Cont'd														
Castle Rock	24.0	1 219	31.4	2.3	80.7	11.2	29 412	0.9	944	3.2	37 336	74.8	49.8	14.3
Centennial	16.9	1 344	28.6	2.3	87.0	11.5	60 106	0.7	2 178	3.6	82 012	70.4	46.3	17.8
Colorado Springs	41.2	888	30.3	5.9	75.9	11.9	216 813	0.0	9 809	4.5	339 065	68.2	39.3	23.5
Commerce City	28.1	982	30.0	4.5	85.4	11.6	25 708	0.7	1 182	4.6	33 670	71.1	47.3	14.9
Denver	50.3	913	29.9	11.7	77.0	12.2	373 109	0.7	13 818	3.7	511 703	71.0	45.7	23.4
Englewood	51.1	863	30.0	10.8	77.4	18.6	19 222	0.9	745	3.9	25 894	72.4	43.7	24.7
Fort Collins	45.4	1 036	35.2	5.3	70.6	15.2	90 292	1.3	2 848	3.2	123 514	69.8	36.6	20.4
Fountain	36.7	1 180	33.7	3.0	76.8	20.4	11 518	0.1	642	5.6	18 675	68.4	43.0	20.0
Grand Junction	40.4	846	33.0	9.3	72.0	16.6	29 197	-2.1	1 879	6.4	47 358	62.9	35.6	33.0
Greeley	43.8	764	31.4	7.1	73.7	15.0	49 507	1.2	2 079	4.2	74 345	64.2	37.4	25.7
Lakewood	42.1	963	30.7	6.8	80.2	13.6	80 817	0.6	3 143	3.9	119 545	68.1	43.6	25.8
Littleton	38.9	937	30.8	7.0	80.2	15.3	23 772	0.8	857	3.6	35 847	67.5	44.2	26.5
Longmont	38.1	992	32.2	5.3	79.7	10.3	47 861	-0.3	1 758	3.7	68 416	70.5	41.7	21.4
Loveland	36.5	962	30.7	5.1	83.4	10.5	38 788	1.4	1 485	3.8	55 717	67.4	42.8	25.6
Northglenn	40.9	986	32.1	6.8	82.9	15.0	20 491	0.4	895	4.4	29 278	70.7	44.5	23.9
Parker	20.4	1 219	27.7	1.7	84.1	10.7	28 088	0.9	921	3.3	33 596	78.6	55.3	11.4
Pueblo	42.7	725	34.3	11.7	79.2	7.8	46 365	-1.2	2 865	6.2	85 075	56.5	31.8	37.2
Thornton	31.0	1 106	31.1	4.0	85.2	10.7	70 132	0.6	2 798	4.0	91 798	74.0	49.1	15.0
Westminster	36.5	1 072	29.4	4.3	83.4	12.7	62 838	0.7	2 383	3.8	85 838	73.4	47.8	19.4
Wheat Ridge	46.1	847	32.1	8.5	81.0	16.0	16 360	0.5	718	4.4	25 626	65.4	42.0	29.7
CONNECTICUT	32.7	1 069	31.9	9.1	87.8	8.7	1 888 001	0.1	106 484	5.6	2 895 925	67.8	40.7	25.3
Bridgeport	58.9	1 098	37.4	21.1	81.4	7.2	71 198	-0.3	6 187	8.7	113 555	68.6	35.5	28.2
Bristol	33.1	904	28.8	6.7	89.2	5.4	32 899	0.1	2 127	6.5	49 249	68.7	42.6	29.3
Danbury	39.7	1 269	31.4	8.9	85.8	8.6	46 733	0.6	2 142	4.6	67 471	72.6	42.3	20.8
Hartford	76.5	887	36.2	35.7	77.7	10.4	54 053	-0.9	5 689	10.4	97 295	62.0	30.0	35.3
Meriden	39.1	956	32.2	10.1	87.1	6.0	32 161	-0.6	2 293	7.1	49 668	66.0	41.2	28.2
Middletown	46.9	1 027	28.9	9.7	82.2	11.5	26 094	0.0	1 464	5.6	39 789	67.6	41.3	24.3
Milford	22.7	1 410	32.5	5.6	89.6	6.2	29 771	0.6	1 466	4.9	43 812	69.0	43.6	25.5
Naugatuck	33.5	988	30.0	6.3	91.1	5.8	17 260	-0.7	1 132	6.6	25 526	70.2	41.4	26.7
New Britain	59.7	890	32.0	17.4	83.6	8.1	36 627	-0.4	2 975	8.1	58 012	66.9	36.8	29.6
New Haven	70.5	1 097	36.4	28.5	80.7	10.2	64 181	-0.7	4 797	7.5	104 766	64.8	33.5	31.6
New London	63.7	884	33.4	20.1	73.8	16.4	12 055	-1.0	997	8.3	23 091	67.1	33.0	29.4
Norwalk	37.9	1 371	30.3	9.7	89.5	6.3	50 227	0.7	2 426	4.8	72 289	73.1	46.3	21.7
Norwich	47.8	933	30.5	12.7	84.5	9.6	20 361	-0.7	1 472	7.2	32 073	69.8	40.4	27.3
Shelton	20.1	1 147	25.8	4.7	90.8	6.4	22 102	0.4	1 183	5.4	33 627	67.7	42.9	23.9
Stamford	45.2	1 566	32.5	11.0	87.1	6.9	69 283	0.6	3 221	4.6	100 922	73.4	44.7	20.0
Torrington	32.8	865	29.7	9.0	89.0	4.8	19 799	-0.1	1 227	6.2	29 645	66.5	39.8	29.7
Waterbury	53.3	904	35.2	19.3	85.8	6.0	50 929	-1.2	4 745	9.3	85 512	62.4	34.5	33.0
West Haven	45.5	1 081	35.2	12.2	86.2	8.2	29 975	-0.5	2 038	6.8	44 484	69.7	40.0	25.7
DELAWARE	28.4	1 012	30.6	6.4	86.6	11.5	467 472	3.1	22 894	4.9	734 886	63.8	40.5	27.0
Dover	48.6	929	32.3	12.4	75.8	17.1	15 727	2.0	1 067	6.8	29 486	59.8	32.1	29.9
Newark	45.0	1 030	40.0	9.1	63.0	26.8	16 004	3.3	767	4.8	29 133	51.0	23.6	28.1
Wilmington	53.6	909	33.5	23.3	79.5	11.4	34 174	3.3	2 371	6.9	56 023	62.9	37.5	31.7
DISTRICT OF COLUMBIA	58.4	1 302	29.6	36.2	80.0	9.6	388 388	2.7	26 844	6.9	536 771	68.5	45.7	25.0
Washington	58.4	1 302	29.6	36.2	80.0	9.6	388 388	2.7	26 844	6.9	536 771	68.5	45.7	25.0
FLORIDA	33.9	998	34.7	7.1	83.7	12.3	9 675 328	0.7	522 064	5.4	15 817 611	59.5	36.4	32.6
Altamonte Springs	51.0	979	29.1	4.5	82.2	12.7	24 683	1.5	1 176	4.8	35 522	69.4	45.4	20.5
Apopka	23.7	1 027	34.2	4.2	89.2	8.3	24 979	1.5	1 099	4.4	34 521	67.5	44.1	20.4
Aventura	32.2	1 600	35.7	8.0	82.3	13.9	16 895	1.6	925	5.5	30 991	53.4	36.2	38.7
Boca Raton	31.1	1 418	36.6	4.6	81.6	12.3	48 940	1.3	1 986	4.1	75 349	62.2	36.2	30.5
Bonita Springs	25.8	1 082	32.9	3.0	83.8	10.2	22 352	3.1	1 051	4.7	40 132	47.2	26.0	49.5
Boynton Beach	35.7	1 230	38.0	7.5	83.7	12.1	36 804	1.1	1 793	4.9	58 855	63.1	37.0	34.7
Bradenton	46.8	897	36.1	8.6	78.4	13.0	24 837	2.2	1 276	5.1	41 587	56.1	34.2	40.4
Cape Coral	30.6	1 061	32.9	3.9	81.4	10.2	83 963	2.8	4 269	5.1	129 526	59.5	34.9	33.5
Casselberry	38.2	954	34.2	4.1	86.4	9.5	14 606	1.3	707	4.8	21 835	64.7	41.8	28.6
Clearwater	40.9	957	35.0	11.8	83.5	11.8	55 896	0.9	2 657	4.8	91 134	59.5	38.6	35.8
Clermont	29.1	1 095	38.6	4.4	85.5	11.1	14 176	1.4	694	4.9	23 001	57.7	35.0	34.6
Coconut Creek	34.6	1 321	32.3	6.1	82.5	13.3	31 579	0.6	1 448	4.6	44 827	67.0	41.9	28.8
Cooper City	14.1	1 724	28.3	1.3	90.7	8.4	19 762	0.7	818	4.1	25 034	73.4	45.9	13.8
Coral Gables	35.8	1 319	33.4	5.0	79.5	16.1	26 580	1.4	1 260	4.7	41 706	60.5	40.7	21.9
Coral Springs	37.1	1 295	34.0	5.0	83.0	10.5	71 014	0.6	3 500	4.9	97 198	73.6	44.7	13.6
Cutler Bay	25.1	1 231	32.3	5.4	88.4	9.9	23 322	1.4	1 353	5.8	33 349	66.3	46.6	18.9
Dania Beach	45.9	1 129	40.8	8.4	79.8	16.5	16 071	0.7	804	5.0	24 724	66.6	37.3	28.4
Davie	28.0	1 198	36.7	4.8	83.1	13.4	55 103	0.6	2 347	4.3	76 532	68.8	43.1	20.5
Daytona Beach	53.2	762	37.9	16.5	80.4	13.3	29 161	0.4	1 938	6.6	53 374	49.9	26.7	43.4

1. $2,000 represents $2,000 or more.   2. 50.0 represents 50 percent or more.   3. Percent of civilian labor force.   4. Persons 16 years old and over.

Table D. Cities — Construction, Wholesale Trade, and Retail Trade

City	Value of residential construction authorized by building permits, 2015			Wholesale trade,[1] 2012				Retail trade,[2] 2012			
	New construction ($1,000)	Number of housing units	Percent single family	Number of establish-ments	Number of employees	Sales (mil dol)	Annual payroll (mil dol)	Number of establish-ments	Number of employees	Sales (mil dol)	Annual payroll (mil dol)
	69	70	71	72	73	74	75	76	77	78	79
COLORADO—Cont'd											
Castle Rock	227 916	933	87.7	30	D	D	D	189	2 800	698.3	61.0
Centennial	12 274	38	100.0	189	3 340	12 326.3	261.0	264	4 771	1 842.4	159.3
Colorado Springs	NA	NA	NA	325	3 638	2 062.8	210.3	1 621	24 923	6 966.7	660.4
Commerce City	54 855	345	86.7	140	2 530	1 915.3	128.8	105	1 333	468.0	39.3
Denver	1 265 944	7 901	23.4	1 175	17 997	14 625.8	1 090.1	2 282	26 469	7 111.4	725.7
Englewood	54 277	482	7.5	100	1 489	754.3	84.5	203	2 525	876.6	72.2
Fort Collins	193 841	976	52.5	108	D	D	D	617	9 667	2 309.8	229.5
Fountain	NA	NA	NA	3	D	D	D	37	1 021	283.6	25.7
Grand Junction	NA	NA	NA	167	1 556	706.3	70.9	477	6 718	1 749.6	171.6
Greeley	126 909	941	54.5	77	1 110	790.0	51.2	291	4 986	1 379.5	132.7
Lakewood	138 086	653	38.1	129	930	1 069.2	68.6	669	10 547	2 528.7	263.6
Littleton	42 459	289	27.0	60	901	833.2	60.7	244	4 098	1 390.7	138.9
Longmont	128 286	411	74.7	69	775	427.5	52.2	270	3 932	1 137.4	105.0
Loveland	156 669	693	67.0	79	1 202	484.9	57.9	320	5 233	1 401.1	123.9
Northglenn	0	0	0.0	18	201	47.2	6.8	105	1 817	584.0	62.9
Parker	155 880	728	44.6	30	228	190.4	17.6	153	2 728	837.5	71.6
Pueblo	NA	NA	NA	58	704	341.3	29.7	406	6 473	1 653.1	157.5
Thornton	225 269	1 022	49.4	29	213	116.7	16.9	189	4 625	1 326.7	126.4
Westminster	49 670	171	98.2	72	1 572	1 733.1	183.3	322	6 329	1 552.3	145.2
Wheat Ridge	17 174	58	72.4	68	680	274.3	35.3	163	2 222	659.2	63.2
CONNECTICUT	1 282 308	6 077	40.1	3 675	58 814	161 962.2	3 934.4	12 597	182 528	51 632.5	4 974.5
Bridgeport	17 456	119	12.6	138	D	D	D	266	3 050	900.7	93.0
Bristol	3 144	30	83.3	38	342	180.9	16.3	170	2 867	824.5	75.6
Danbury	84 811	551	12.5	109	1 316	1 349.4	85.0	454	8 144	2 283.3	221.8
Hartford	638	6	66.7	112	2 244	1 317.7	107.6	357	3 053	1 813.7	100.6
Meriden	0	0	0.0	38	306	165.0	15.1	228	3 081	750.7	68.0
Middletown	22 639	123	24.4	44	1 087	800.9	65.3	120	1 690	457.4	45.7
Milford	24 917	358	7.8	98	1 476	792.5	87.7	323	5 819	1 667.1	149.2
Naugatuck	2 794	18	100.0	21	480	331.4	29.1	66	1 031	320.9	28.6
New Britain	722	6	100.0	39	402	179.8	21.3	146	1 691	553.7	45.6
New Haven	26 886	262	3.1	74	D	D	D	322	3 135	835.6	84.8
New London	6 786	41	100.0	13	D	D	D	101	1 343	463.7	42.2
Norwalk	51 020	350	7.1	129	2 445	1 940.3	142.7	343	5 913	1 719.0	217.9
Norwich	1 529	4	100.0	20	571	381.6	38.9	125	2 053	477.6	45.9
Shelton	19 134	191	20.4	56	D	D	D	90	1 821	831.5	65.7
Stamford	117 584	639	5.6	213	5 498	109 632.9	713.5	482	6 199	1 626.0	178.9
Torrington	623	4	100.0	32	D	D	D	159	2 832	931.4	75.3
Waterbury	5 564	71	85.9	80	803	519.7	46.1	425	6 035	1 620.9	152.8
West Haven	1 940	22	81.8	60	1 248	626.2	70.0	110	1 361	351.0	35.7
DELAWARE	641 676	5 221	81.2	835	7 653	5 628.9	385.9	3 616	51 711	14 456.0	1 270.1
Dover	35 433	247	24.7	38	296	114.7	13.2	205	3 883	1 005.0	85.7
Newark	2 563	19	100.0	41	195	117.5	9.5	176	2 877	921.4	81.8
Wilmington	3 109	123	20.3	114	878	767.7	50.7	303	2 882	862.8	84.2
DISTRICT OF COLUMBIA	495 021	4 956	5.1	335	3 415	2 591.9	260.6	1 710	19 780	4 439.9	525.2
Washington	495 021	4 956	5.1	335	3 415	2 591.9	260.6	1 710	19 780	4 439.9	525.2
FLORIDA	23 439 129	109 924	61.6	27 109	252 418	252 626.6	12 867.6	71 189	947 877	273 867.1	24 033.5
Altamonte Springs	2 895	16	18.8	77	1 929	423.7	42.2	342	5 824	1 363.3	127.9
Apopka	103 949	318	100.0	67	724	226.1	26.4	155	2 058	625.8	49.2
Aventura	15 158	160	0.0	142	476	1 807.9	35.5	375	9 146	2 197.9	206.7
Boca Raton	195 644	975	13.4	379	4 030	4 550.7	313.9	652	9 944	2 534.2	293.6
Bonita Springs	310 876	1 146	44.6	43	525	373.7	28.1	187	2 067	484.2	48.9
Boynton Beach	78 802	564	6.9	105	828	627.9	48.3	377	5 602	1 279.4	120.7
Bradenton	50 325	241	48.1	43	288	161.6	13.6	265	3 701	1 102.0	95.9
Cape Coral	294 089	1 090	100.0	100	294	140.4	12.3	404	6 381	1 692.8	150.1
Casselberry	150	1	100.0	26	111	53.1	4.2	128	2 264	478.2	52.0
Clearwater	33 607	222	18.9	143	1 373	633.3	75.8	647	9 790	2 790.5	261.7
Clermont	60 188	326	98.8	21	82	58.2	2.4	147	2 818	733.0	63.3
Coconut Creek	4 800	45	100.0	58	237	221.5	12.6	153	3 213	1 345.4	118.9
Cooper City	2 552	10	100.0	39	D	D	D	81	1 450	346.6	38.9
Coral Gables	45 362	48	100.0	180	1 576	9 268.1	128.7	297	4 154	1 556.6	152.6
Coral Springs	20 505	181	0.6	239	1 345	632.7	62.3	455	7 810	2 066.6	197.0
Cutler Bay	1 665	13	100.0	28	116	26.7	3.2	165	2 223	546.1	50.3
Dania Beach	870	5	100.0	129	857	529.1	39.0	183	1 613	510.5	45.7
Davie	25 249	406	12.1	262	1 782	688.4	76.7	405	5 802	2 050.3	170.3
Daytona Beach	48 949	285	49.5	79	627	253.7	26.3	461	6 387	1 687.6	152.6

1. Merchant wholesalers except manufacturers' sales branches and offices. 2. Establishments with payroll.

City	Real estate and rental and leasing, 2012				Professional, scientific, and technical services,[1] 2012				Manufacturing, 2012			
	Number of establish-ments	Number of employees	Receipts (mil dol)	Annual payroll (mil dol)	Number of establish-ments	Number of employees	Receipts (mil dol)	Annual payroll (mil dol)	Number of establish-ments	Number of employees	Receipts (mil dol)	Annual payroll (mil dol)
	80	81	82	83	84	85	86	87	88	89	90	91
COLORADO—Cont'd												
Castle Rock	78	202	39.4	6.8	195	D	D	D	16	221	D	9.5
Centennial	250	998	354.1	53.2	695	3 802	1 019.8	274.6	69	1 750	667.5	112.4
Colorado Springs	845	2 875	545.3	102.9	1 907	D	D	D	351	8 351	2 236.8	473.5
Commerce City	48	531	114.8	20.7	43	293	229.5	19.6	87	2 851	5 446.3	164.6
Denver	1 451	9 373	2 723.8	488.3	4 273	D	D	D	759	17 032	5 343.9	761.4
Englewood	87	377	113.3	18.9	161	D	D	D	128	2 688	522.0	118.8
Fort Collins	298	1 258	173.5	40.5	877	6 219	736.6	343.1	109	5 760	3 156.6	361.8
Fountain	9	47	2.8	0.9	20	97	3.4	1.2	7	145	D	7.6
Grand Junction	195	663	143.5	26.7	365	D	D	D	93	1 938	382.8	78.8
Greeley	119	518	73.6	16.7	181	D	D	D	53	4 235	3 090.6	145.1
Lakewood	251	791	145.6	27.9	823	D	D	D	99	1 112	270.9	51.5
Littleton	89	410	52.1	12.4	346	4 994	1 110.9	517.6	32	4 492	1 698.0	414.4
Longmont	121	362	80.1	12.2	379	4 846	752.7	392.9	118	2 180	599.1	141.3
Loveland	110	577	74.2	19.1	260	1 265	144.6	54.4	99	2 619	756.9	199.0
Northglenn	31	107	18.8	3.5	59	256	22.9	8.6	26	425	100.2	19.9
Parker	71	118	30.1	4.5	220	687	102.7	36.3	27	399	D	15.2
Pueblo	108	523	83.1	15.4	185	D	D	D	54	1 733	821.0	72.1
Thornton	81	487	118.9	13.9	171	1 048	124.5	45.4	16	250	D	12.9
Westminster	157	568	114.5	20.7	378	D	D	D	53	747	270.3	42.9
Wheat Ridge	53	272	40.7	9.7	189	D	D	D	42	1 007	293.8	54.2
CONNECTICUT	3 219	19 778	5 349.5	958.4	9 176	96 768	17 863.9	8 316.7	4 350	163 847	55 160.1	10 546.2
Bridgeport	94	406	79.7	15.6	208	D	D	D	139	3 274	1 063.3	168.4
Bristol	40	151	31.1	5.5	67	302	40.4	15.8	130	2 827	663.8	148.5
Danbury	84	1 711	327.0	105.0	226	2 662	597.8	264.5	93	5 623	2 084.0	376.1
Hartford	164	1 337	270.0	66.6	392	5 588	1 361.1	488.4	68	1 013	207.6	44.6
Meriden	44	505	47.4	17.8	76	760	108.3	45.2	66	2 433	940.2	173.9
Middletown	39	248	37.7	10.2	108	D	D	D	52	3 583	2 078.3	231.1
Milford	51	D	D	D	178	2 832	268.5	104.6	151	3 305	1 532.1	214.8
Naugatuck	14	D	D	D	32	213	24.5	9.7	47	1 168	386.1	61.1
New Britain	40	184	44.2	6.2	84	D	D	D	94	2 959	758.3	165.2
New Haven	128	751	151.1	31.4	365	2 957	599.6	267.5	70	2 250	510.5	114.6
New London	24	147	24.3	5.7	96	D	D	D	15	212	D	9.0
Norwalk	95	327	81.0	15.6	340	3 538	837.7	299.1	100	1 733	404.2	120.5
Norwich	35	D	D	D	63	894	118.3	54.5	25	699	132.4	35.9
Shelton	38	605	89.0	23.4	140	1 681	394.2	141.0	64	2 951	1 302.9	191.0
Stamford	217	1 369	456.5	114.3	641	D	D	D	104	1 959	495.4	106.4
Torrington	25	102	14.1	3.6	61	463	74.5	35.4	65	1 870	422.2	92.3
Waterbury	72	293	70.0	10.1	146	D	D	D	153	3 206	956.8	157.0
West Haven	43	132	39.5	5.1	61	D	D	D	49	1 411	382.6	73.7
DELAWARE	1 111	5 402	5 471.2	264.9	2 536	D	D	D	573	26 355	22 597.4	1 393.2
Dover	75	286	50.3	10.6	159	D	D	D	19	1 518	940.3	91.7
Newark	49	192	409.9	5.4	115	D	D	D	25	932	276.4	66.4
Wilmington	204	805	1 802.6	35.2	585	D	D	D	66	999	D	53.8
DISTRICT OF COLUMBIA	1 112	10 103	3 213.9	673.7	4 831	89 224	29 796.2	10 549.2	113	1 361	309.8	61.5
Washington	1 112	10 103	3 213.9	673.7	4 831	89 224	29 796.2	10 549.2	113	1 361	309.8	61.5
FLORIDA	29 845	139 955	30 560.1	5 337.4	70 617	436 764	69 653.4	26 855.4	12 890	277 089	96 924.1	14 270.0
Altamonte Springs	109	1 328	141.9	42.8	293	1 495	158.6	57.3	40	307	45.4	11.9
Apopka	34	90	19.6	2.6	96	354	38.7	13.1	27	360	88.0	15.1
Aventura	206	737	136.8	26.3	362	944	181.4	59.5	13	149	D	4.4
Boca Raton	432	3 486	519.2	170.9	1 457	D	D	D	153	2 052	451.1	113.8
Bonita Springs	119	399	75.8	18.8	198	962	183.2	56.3	24	146	19.5	4.6
Boynton Beach	116	610	108.0	20.3	353	1 510	207.6	76.2	64	735	153.3	33.8
Bradenton	79	390	70.6	10.9	220	D	D	D	30	1 819	995.3	132.5
Cape Coral	292	534	104.5	17.6	348	D	D	D	85	548	84.2	25.4
Casselberry	46	329	40.6	10.9	89	414	34.4	11.9	26	298	39.2	12.5
Clearwater	280	1 132	166.8	39.4	694	D	D	D	97	1 674	319.2	64.9
Clermont	83	205	38.0	6.0	105	340	36.5	12.6	9	65	7.3	1.0
Coconut Creek	46	1 730	603.7	81.4	166	725	108.1	29.6	14	216	67.0	7.5
Cooper City	42	91	15.9	2.6	180	404	60.8	17.0	7	21	2.2	0.7
Coral Gables	359	1 144	331.7	54.6	1 505	D	D	D	28	447	D	25.9
Coral Springs	217	765	177.5	30.6	752	2 530	355.4	106.9	59	775	197.7	40.5
Cutler Bay	28	68	8.8	1.8	72	344	18.6	6.2	4	9	D	0.3
Dania Beach	58	301	83.0	16.7	137	D	D	D	44	696	136.0	31.9
Davie	196	604	147.1	24.9	538	D	D	D	88	1 879	924.1	130.4
Daytona Beach	143	667	137.5	25.6	312	D	D	D	63	1 532	376.6	82.0

1. Establishments subject to federal tax.

Table D. Cities — **Accommodation and Food Services, Arts, Entertainment, and Recreation, and Health Care and Social Assistance**

City	Accommodation and food services, 2012				Arts, entertainment, and recreation,[1] 2012				Health care and social assistance,[1] 2012			
	Number of establish-ments	Number of employees	Sales (mil dol)	Annual payroll (mil dol)	Number of establish-ments	Number of employees	Receipts (mil dol)	Annual payroll (mil dol)	Number of establish-ments	Number of employees	Receipts (mil dol)	Annual payroll (mil dol)
	92	93	94	95	96	97	98	99	100	101	102	103
COLORADO—Cont'd												
Castle Rock	103	1 843	88.7	26.4	16	D	D	D	107	D	D	D
Centennial	207	3 322	186.9	57.4	34	D	D	D	365	2 886	309.3	118.6
Colorado Springs	1 040	23 240	1 274.8	344.7	133	1 678	92.3	27.7	1 477	15 806	1 630.5	678.0
Commerce City	58	926	47.2	11.4	2	D	D	D	26	D	D	D
Denver	1 982	42 906	2 884.9	823.2	235	5 851	687.1	309.6	1 695	25 982	3 209.7	1 299.9
Englewood	95	1 448	75.2	21.7	8	D	D	D	206	D	D	D
Fort Collins	427	8 329	374.5	113.7	66	910	47.5	15.0	546	6 422	677.3	306.6
Fountain	45	967	37.6	9.6	1	D	D	D	22	155	15.1	5.9
Grand Junction	211	4 578	218.7	67.6	20	321	12.9	3.7	309	D	D	D
Greeley	184	3 501	157.6	47.0	23	216	6.4	2.1	222	2 645	241.0	98.5
Lakewood	378	7 456	385.9	117.3	44	641	29.8	9.3	487	7 651	747.3	321.9
Littleton	135	D	D	D	20	D	D	D	215	2 503	244.6	108.5
Longmont	187	3 623	177.6	53.6	26	167	8.5	2.1	250	2 606	228.9	107.6
Loveland	194	4 019	189.3	53.5	30	159	8.5	2.6	224	2 558	257.2	104.5
Northglenn	45	922	46.2	14.4	8	239	10.1	2.7	53	D	D	D
Parker	106	2 252	101.4	32.7	16	287	16.5	5.5	160	1 259	131.5	51.3
Pueblo	286	4 992	205.1	60.2	20	D	D	D	319	D	D	D
Thornton	164	3 197	178.1	48.7	23	D	D	D	155	2 057	211.7	89.3
Westminster	231	5 395	292.5	86.3	29	610	30.4	9.2	246	2 827	313.2	146.7
Wheat Ridge	91	1 347	68.7	20.1	16	83	5.2	1.5	168	D	D	D
CONNECTICUT	8 263	134 546	9 542.1	2 590.8	1 160	14 862	1 538.5	418.5	7 876	131 732	13 333.4	6 058.8
Bridgeport	227	2 202	148.4	36.4	23	366	29.6	6.3	217	4 554	524.5	261.5
Bristol	108	1 222	70.9	19.2	13	381	32.1	8.0	101	1 854	157.9	72.5
Danbury	211	3 531	226.6	63.2	19	226	14.3	4.5	216	D	D	D
Hartford	326	4 429	297.2	82.4	13	201	38.9	6.7	237	5 215	831.5	439.4
Meriden	116	1 292	67.8	17.0	4	D	D	D	98	1 770	163.6	80.8
Middletown	110	1 311	86.4	24.9	8	58	5.2	1.2	116	2 661	282.4	126.8
Milford	172	2 632	141.5	39.4	20	296	17.6	7.4	139	2 189	248.7	116.0
Naugatuck	51	474	23.7	5.8	3	D	D	D	36	728	49.5	25.3
New Britain	91	1 195	66.5	18.1	8	66	9.3	1.4	104	1 728	213.0	93.8
New Haven	337	4 119	284.4	75.6	24	D	D	D	269	4 257	438.6	190.6
New London	89	1 217	68.1	20.3	11	32	2.6	0.9	84	D	D	D
Norwalk	251	2 845	219.3	61.1	54	916	118.8	42.0	192	2 678	308.7	141.5
Norwich	93	D	D	D	7	D	D	D	114	2 071	199.2	89.0
Shelton	112	1 915	117.2	36.3	10	118	9.5	2.6	105	2 312	243.7	118.4
Stamford	389	5 995	451.2	133.7	52	1 193	404.4	75.7	351	4 135	495.2	221.6
Torrington	79	959	55.1	14.4	13	91	5.9	1.4	112	1 801	182.1	71.6
Waterbury	231	3 063	158.2	43.5	11	99	6.2	1.4	230	4 952	513.4	234.8
West Haven	110	1 471	86.4	22.4	4	D	D	D	59	D	D	D
DELAWARE	1 987	35 609	2 148.4	566.7	302	5 087	490.5	148.6	1 964	30 400	3 173.7	1 434.8
Dover	151	4 280	387.3	78.2	17	D	D	D	188	3 325	290.5	129.7
Newark	133	3 183	177.0	45.9	10	143	6.6	1.8	133	D	D	D
Wilmington	197	2 964	169.2	48.2	28	243	17.8	5.4	258	3 681	330.2	137.8
DISTRICT OF COLUMBIA	2 371	60 370	5 101.6	1 504.8	210	5 103	778.3	327.3	1 353	24 356	2 870.9	1 203.4
Washington	2 371	60 370	5 101.6	1 504.8	210	5 103	778.3	327.3	1 353	24 356	2 870.9	1 203.4
FLORIDA	37 118	786 082	49 817.9	13 598.2	6 594	136 273	14 212.0	4 120.2	51 567	614 004	76 785.9	27 914.4
Altamonte Springs	140	3 730	196.0	61.3	21	D	D	D	244	D	D	D
Apopka	67	D	D	D	8	131	6.8	2.5	69	658	84.0	38.9
Aventura	109	3 319	244.7	73.0	23	168	12.3	3.3	291	D	D	D
Boca Raton	362	10 342	697.3	208.7	89	728	54.8	14.7	726	6 025	893.3	349.7
Bonita Springs	116	D	D	D	31	876	58.0	19.2	115	975	135.0	47.5
Boynton Beach	197	4 235	220.6	63.8	26	D	D	D	340	D	D	D
Bradenton	134	2 396	122.9	35.8	25	191	14.9	6.3	291	7 453	892.2	318.4
Cape Coral	212	3 797	181.0	52.6	35	238	17.4	3.5	270	2 503	346.7	110.5
Casselberry	70	873	46.2	11.5	10	85	4.3	1.5	63	D	D	D
Clearwater	346	7 252	482.0	130.8	54	917	45.3	10.5	468	5 606	706.4	279.5
Clermont	91	1 932	93.6	26.1	16	D	D	D	151	D	D	D
Coconut Creek	80	1 383	69.2	18.3	21	D	D	D	101	D	D	D
Cooper City	49	687	33.2	9.0	13	D	D	D	132	D	D	D
Coral Gables	246	5 972	363.6	117.6	51	321	44.2	14.9	528	D	D	D
Coral Springs	275	4 612	264.7	71.0	75	551	40.1	9.7	469	D	D	D
Cutler Bay	66	D	D	D	8	63	3.5	0.8	64	D	D	D
Dania Beach	83	1 723	129.3	31.1	24	D	D	D	45	D	D	D
Davie	195	D	D	D	48	D	D	D	252	D	D	D
Daytona Beach	256	5 862	321.0	91.6	38	D	D	D	237	4 513	412.7	178.0

1. Establishments subject to federal tax.

Table D. Cities — **Other Services and Government Employment and Payroll**

City	Other services[1], 2012				Government employment and payroll, 2012								
					Full-time equivalent employees	March payroll							
							Percent of total for:						
	Number of establishments	Number of employees	Receipts (mil dol)	Annual payroll (mil dol)		Total (dollars)	Adminis-tration, judicial, and legal	Police and Corrections	Fire Protection	Highways and trans-portation	Health and welfare	Natural resources and utilities	Education and libraries
	104	105	106	107	108	109	110	111	112	113	114	115	116
COLORADO—Cont'd													
Castle Rock..............	98	511	34.5	11.9	454	2 257 316	12.3	18.0	21.0	7.0	3.2	27.7	0.0
Centennial	167	809	75.5	22.6	56	312 389	97.1	0.0	0.0	0.0	0.0	0.0	0.0
Colorado Springs	703	4 195	357.7	115.6	6 835	37 084 390	4.0	14.0	7.5	3.0	35.7	34.0	0.0
Commerce City	90	712	87.2	22.8	331	1 840 907	22.9	42.5	0.0	11.7	8.4	14.5	0.0
Denver......................	1 071	8 716	708.5	244.9	11 914	62 559 560	13.5	28.4	10.9	11.0	11.2	19.1	2.3
Englewood..............	118	799	76.5	27.1	496	2 612 051	12.2	19.8	16.5	5.4	2.5	32.9	2.4
Fort Collins..............	247	1 400	92.3	31.1	1 475	7 276 841	19.4	25.1	0.0	10.9	0.5	39.9	0.0
Fountain	15	61	5.4	1.2	195	852 760	16.1	9.5	14.2	2.6	3.5	38.5	0.0
Grand Junction..............	187	1 438	129.5	36.6	684	3 402 863	13.8	30.4	21.4	6.4	0.5	21.7	0.0
Greeley......................	117	634	55.5	16.1	980	4 950 974	9.9	28.6	15.1	7.5	1.4	32.8	0.0
Lakewood..............	250	1 404	103.2	35.4	1 014	5 146 071	18.0	47.7	0.0	3.7	1.4	18.8	0.0
Littleton	105	756	64.3	24.2	427	2 523 624	11.4	21.4	46.3	4.8	4.3	5.3	4.2
Longmont	150	783	56.9	19.1	895	4 775 325	12.8	26.4	13.8	4.3	4.2	29.7	3.4
Loveland..............	134	851	75.9	24.6	677	3 104 613	23.9	23.9	13.3	6.0	0.0	25.8	3.5
Northglenn..............	48	237	18.5	5.9	323	4 495 142	20.4	39.8	0.0	2.3	0.0	30.8	0.0
Parker......................	122	772	57.9	17.7	295	1 383 773	22.2	35.4	0.0	13.3	0.0	22.5	0.0
Pueblo......................	142	832	57.8	18.7	859	4 316 626	8.8	33.4	18.2	8.7	0.5	28.3	0.0
Thornton...................	101	778	51.3	20.7	842	4 836 932	20.0	27.9	10.2	10.4	4.4	24.7	0.0
Westminster	135	894	56.6	20.4	992	5 125 430	12.9	29.5	16.6	4.2	3.5	24.3	3.3
Wheat Ridge	109	562	56.1	16.5	198	835 164	27.5	56.8	0.0	15.6	0.0	0.0	0.0
CONNECTICUT	5 816	34 073	3 031.0	960.6	X	X	X	X	X	X	X	X	X
Bridgeport..............	153	654	68.5	19.9	4 248	23 926 290	4.5	12.4	5.7	0.9	3.3	1.9	70.6
Bristol......................	76	373	31.9	9.4	1 756	9 163 919	3.3	10.9	5.8	2.6	1.2	5.4	69.3
Danbury..............	159	986	86.8	26.3	1 817	10 016 152	3.5	11.0	8.0	3.2	1.8	2.8	68.2
Hartford...................	214	1 242	113.2	33.1	5 207	24 306 797	2.8	9.1	6.3	1.0	3.8	0.9	76.1
Meriden..............	67	388	30.1	9.1	1 673	9 260 984	3.4	12.3	8.7	1.1	3.7	5.2	65.5
Middletown	77	441	48.9	14.4	1 621	8 623 913	3.5	13.7	9.7	2.6	6.4	5.0	55.8
Milford......................	126	752	61.9	20.0	2 207	11 763 788	2.2	6.1	6.4	1.6	1.9	2.6	77.1
Naugatuck..............	36	134	12.9	3.6	976	4 533 881	3.1	10.0	5.6	1.8	1.8	2.7	73.9
New Britain..............	74	358	28.8	9.3	2 064	11 112 239	2.6	10.0	9.5	2.3	1.6	6.1	66.2
New Haven..............	170	901	83.8	27.2	4 808	23 846 140	3.9	13.4	10.0	1.1	2.8	3.0	65.4
New London	53	336	24.9	8.5	789	3 869 245	5.6	17.4	11.4	1.4	2.1	4.5	54.9
Norwalk..............	178	1 009	93.6	30.5	2 837	13 813 488	4.1	12.3	8.1	3.0	1.2	1.8	68.2
Norwich	59	459	28.3	10.5	984	5 092 687	3.2	11.7	7.1	3.7	4.1	20.9	47.0
Shelton..............	69	379	25.9	8.9	952	5 269 099	4.2	8.4	0.5	4.0	2.3	3.1	77.5
Stamford..............	251	1 622	134.5	42.7	3 375	22 400 736	3.9	13.4	9.4	1.1	5.3	3.3	60.5
Torrington	69	433	30.9	10.6	923	4 776 132	2.9	12.2	7.3	3.8	3.3	2.6	66.3
Waterbury..............	144	916	93.7	26.2	3 875	18 570 027	3.9	12.3	7.5	1.2	2.6	5.2	67.1
West Haven..............	74	338	35.7	10.1	1 404	6 641 617	4.9	17.7	4.6	4.7	2.6	0.6	64.8
DELAWARE	1 190	7 668	617.2	207.1	X	X	X	X	X	X	X	X	X
Dover.......................	59	509	30.1	11.0	348	1 666 145	16.3	43.4	1.4	2.0	1.1	25.4	3.3
Newark	53	290	15.9	6.3	258	1 304 591	12.9	41.6	0.4	3.6	4.4	29.6	0.0
Wilmington...............	116	825	80.0	23.8	1 254	5 779 211	16.3	41.1	15.0	4.0	5.1	11.7	0.0
DISTRICT OF COLUMBIA...............	940	7 719	633.3	194.1	X	X	X	X	X	X	X	X	X
Washington	940	7 719	633.3	194.1	34 002	194 813 463	15.0	19.3	5.8	2.2	15.5	8.1	25.7
FLORIDA...................	27 843	145 010	12 202.5	3 616.4	X	X	X	X	X	X	X	X	X
Altamonte Springs........	107	D	D	D	387	1 562 231	12.2	35.2	0.0	2.6	0.0	35.5	1.2
Apopka.....................	58	268	18.9	5.7	391	1 780 824	13.9	31.5	26.1	2.1	0.0	17.9	0.0
Aventura....................	79	867	43.0	16.3	366	1 349 401	17.9	28.7	27.3	9.0	0.5	15.5	0.0
Boca Raton...............	314	1 584	114.4	35.2	1 418	6 984 386	9.9	26.8	24.4	3.6	0.1	27.8	2.2
Bonita Springs...........	86	306	19.6	6.8	55	213 459	44.7	0.0	0.0	0.0	0.0	11.7	0.0
Boynton Beach...........	159	1 102	75.5	26.0	747	4 117 701	10.9	32.9	22.3	0.2	0.5	25.1	2.4
Bradenton.................	83	288	22.5	6.3	434	1 525 511	8.1	37.6	20.9	3.9	0.5	24.1	0.0
Cape Coral...............	227	1 016	67.2	21.0	1 360	5 329 766	17.8	25.1	19.0	5.1	0.4	27.7	0.0
Casselberry	63	237	16.4	4.8	217	833 769	18.9	28.6	21.7	6.1	0.0	23.7	0.0
Clearwater................	197	921	75.6	21.2	1 653	6 760 407	11.2	29.1	14.6	5.7	0.6	28.3	3.3
Clermont...................	64	393	27.0	9.0	262	960 550	4.5	26.8	25.5	20.2	0.0	23.0	0.0
Coconut Creek............	70	365	23.8	7.0	330	1 913 611	28.0	41.4	1.7	4.0	0.0	17.4	0.0
Cooper City	48	326	25.4	9.0	138	525 375	17.6	0.0	0.0	0.0	0.0	48.0	0.0
Coral Gables	131	897	65.6	19.8	793	4 845 710	17.3	32.6	27.2	4.5	0.5	12.9	0.0
Coral Springs	235	860	68.5	19.5	845	4 451 797	13.6	41.1	25.3	2.0	0.0	11.7	0.0
Cutler Bay	37	155	13.9	4.3	47	173 292	50.2	1.3	0.0	11.8	0.0	32.6	0.0
Dania Beach..............	93	1 143	60.0	18.5	113	516 841	46.4	0.0	0.0	4.7	3.0	37.2	0.0
Davie.......................	230	1 116	121.6	32.4	617	4 513 053	8.3	40.2	31.1	7.0	1.3	8.4	0.0
Daytona Beach............	122	572	38.3	13.6	1 046	4 375 710	11.9	39.3	11.4	5.1	1.4	26.4	0.0

1. Establishments subject to federal tax.

Table D. Cities — **City Government Finances**

City	City government finances, 2012									
	General revenue								General expenditure		
	Intergovernmental			Taxes					Per capita[1] (dollars)		
					Per capita[1] (dollars)						
	Total (mil dol)	Total (mil dol)	Percent from state government	Total (mil dol)	Total	Property	Sales and gross receipts	Total (mil dol)	Total	Capital outlays
	117	118	119	120	121	122	123	124	125	126
COLORADO—Cont'd										
Castle Rock..................	72.3	4.3	100.0	39.3	764	86	677	61.6	1 198	135
Centennial	67.4	9.9	66.5	52.6	505	129	376	66.6	640	152
Colorado Springs	1 020.1	65.7	31.6	214.4	494	52	442	968.4	2 233	239
Commerce City	59.2	2.8	60.8	47.8	984	138	846	61.0	1 256	0
Denver........................	2 940.6	477.1	60.5	1 107.9	1 748	610	1 138	2 623.4	4 139	261
Englewood...................	60.4	3.3	42.3	31.3	1 002	139	864	53.0	1 698	1
Fort Collins	238.1	30.8	16.5	125.6	843	119	724	233.7	1 569	354
Fountain	12.7	1.1	60.7	10.1	374	74	300	26.4	981	22
Grand Junction.............	114.1	18.2	45.4	60.4	1 009	214	795	130.2	2 176	564
Greeley	114.2	13.2	62.0	60.1	630	105	514	99.4	1 042	109
Lakewood....................	155.5	22.9	36.1	96.4	663	105	514	144.6	994	114
Littleton......................	70.6	17.6	14.5	32.8	749	95	655	75.6	1 725	102
Longmont	98.1	6.6	75.4	57.7	650	161	388	98.8	1 114	42
Loveland.....................	115.2	11.2	96.5	59.5	847	268	579	109.1	1 554	315
Northglenn	32.1	4.4	67.4	19.9	539	82	457	33.8	914	210
Parker........................	53.8	8.3	22.1	33.0	699	35	636	55.5	1 175	321
Pueblo	152.7	29.0	69.9	79.2	734	146	589	141.8	1 315	332
Thornton	147.1	14.0	41.5	89.2	717	95	617	134.0	1 078	204
Westminster................	153.4	13.5	40.6	99.8	914	126	788	145.3	1 330	246
Wheat Ridge	30.8	2.8	58.9	23.1	752	27	726	32.0	1 043	219
CONNECTICUT	X	X	X	X	X	X	X	X	X	X
Bridgeport...................	693.1	370.2	98.3	277.5	1 888	1 865	23	743.6	5 058	849
Bristol	263.8	119.3	95.5	120.4	1 987	1 939	38	318.7	5 258	1 671
Danbury......................	280.7	82.5	95.8	171.7	2 074	2 030	44	248.5	3 001	199
Hartford......................	809.1	477.2	84.9	283.3	2 262	2 204	49	793.7	6 336	712
Meriden	212.7	85.0	99.7	110.3	1 819	1 801	2	226.8	3 739	412
Middletown	189.7	68.5	99.3	101.5	2 142	2 129	12	158.3	3 339	308
Milford........................	203.4	27.7	97.5	162.8	3 160	3 130	13	206.1	4 000	448
Naugatuck	113.1	38.6	96.7	67.3	2 115	2 091	21	123.1	3 870	120
New Britain..................	264.0	124.4	97.4	111.2	1 521	1 505	16	274.7	3 758	394
New Haven...................	723.5	431.0	93.9	232.5	1 776	1 722	46	1 130.4	8 633	3 741
New London	123.5	69.0	97.3	39.7	1 438	1 415	23	112.6	4 081	298
Norwalk	353.8	52.6	97.8	263.8	3 023	2 994	29	360.1	4 125	476
Norwich	159.1	79.8	97.7	64.1	1 584	1 562	13	163.0	4 029	489
Shelton	121.4	15.0	88.2	99.0	2 457	2 415	42	115.7	2 872	166
Stamford.....................	535.4	50.2	94.1	426.4	3 408	3 340	47	551.6	4 408	402
Torrington	128.3	39.4	97.2	77.2	2 158	2 136	0	121.9	3 409	87
Waterbury....................	498.5	253.0	94.0	220.5	2 006	1 989	11	626.2	5 696	845
West Haven.................	172.1	67.7	99.0	89.3	1 617	1 606	11	169.2	3 062	287
DELAWARE	X	X	X	X	X	X	X	X	X	X
Dover.........................	42.7	9.6	91.3	15.8	426	298	91	55.8	1 506	400
Newark	23.4	3.3	100.0	8.4	258	155	72	32.7	1 010	108
Wilmington..................	193.4	38.2	53.3	110.5	1 550	547	108	166.5	2 334	116
DISTRICT OF COLUMBIA..............	X	X	X	X	X	X	X	X	X	X
Washington	10 710.4	3 077.7	0.0	5 933.8	9 344	2 957	2 601	11 199.3	17 636	2 228
FLORIDA...................	X	X	X	X	X	X	X	X	X	X
Altamonte Springs........	42.8	3.7	94.1	21.6	515	214	300	30.6	731	144
Apopka.......................	48.2	9.5	80.2	19.4	437	163	273	45.1	1 012	64
Aventura	42.7	11.2	85.4	25.0	671	315	355	38.3	1 028	79
Boca Raton.................	195.4	30.0	30.6	109.3	1 242	718	524	210.8	2 397	278
Bonita Springs.............	18.8	4.9	87.3	11.2	243	125	118	17.6	382	76
Boynton Beach.............	116.4	15.6	61.0	50.6	721	474	247	120.3	1 714	146
Bradenton	58.2	10.3	29.0	24.6	488	329	158	58.4	1 157	9
Cape Coral.................	245.7	47.7	80.3	92.3	572	430	143	240.6	1 492	184
Casselberry................	34.0	7.5	31.2	12.8	484	228	256	41.1	1 552	195
Clearwater..................	200.9	27.4	47.6	81.7	751	363	387	194.0	1 782	189
Clermont.....................	32.1	6.1	87.7	12.5	423	203	221	30.7	1 043	125
Coconut Creek	61.2	5.4	70.6	29.6	537	289	249	52.9	959	77
Cooper City	35.4	2.6	92.2	17.7	547	292	255	32.2	994	12
Coral Gables	158.0	11.2	62.7	97.1	1 954	1 350	604	127.4	2 564	171
Coral Springs	123.2	15.5	67.5	65.4	521	261	253	133.1	1 060	84
Cutler Bay	23.2	9.8	41.7	11.1	260	99	161	26.0	611	269
Dania Beach...............	52.7	10.5	66.3	24.3	793	518	275	52.7	1 718	156
Davie	104.7	13.7	53.9	70.6	738	407	331	98.2	1 027	73
Daytona Beach............	124.9	15.8	46.5	44.7	724	392	332	118.4	1 915	146

1. Based on population estimated as of July 1 of the year shown.

City	City government finances, 2012 (cont.)									
	General expenditure (cont.)									
	Percent of total for:									
	Public welfare	Highways	Parking facilities	Education	Health and hospitals	Police protection	Sewerage and sanitation	Parks and recreation	Housing and community development	Interest on debt
	127	128	129	130	131	132	133	134	135	136
COLORADO—Cont'd										
Castle Rock..............	0.0	16.9	0.0	0.0	0.0	12.1	16.6	16.7	0.0	4.0
Centennial	0.0	26.3	0.0	0.0	0.0	29.9	0.0	9.5	5.1	0.2
Colorado Springs	0.0	8.7	0.2	0.0	53.3	9.2	3.9	2.2	0.5	2.8
Commerce City	0.0	7.9	0.0	0.0	0.0	23.6	3.0	10.5	3.7	7.1
Denver........................	6.4	5.9	0.0	0.0	2.0	8.6	3.3	7.4	4.4	11.0
Englewood..................	0.0	6.9	0.0	0.0	0.0	19.6	18.4	14.4	2.6	5.1
Fort Collins	0.0	22.5	0.0	0.0	0.0	13.6	7.0	20.8	0.0	1.9
Fountain	0.0	4.7	0.0	0.0	0.8	19.5	0.0	3.1	0.3	0.0
Grand Junction.............	0.0	12.8	0.3	0.0	0.0	27.0	12.8	14.2	1.8	5.2
Greeley.......................	0.0	6.4	0.3	0.0	0.0	27.1	11.9	13.9	4.4	3.0
Lakewood....................	0.0	10.8	0.0	0.0	0.9	27.9	2.2	12.3	1.2	1.7
Littleton......................	0.4	8.2	0.0	0.0	0.0	14.2	10.6	3.0	0.1	2.6
Longmont	0.0	1.0	0.2	0.0	0.0	22.5	18.0	19.4	5.9	2.3
Loveland	0.0	11.3	0.0	0.0	0.0	15.0	10.4	11.8	13.3	0.5
Northglenn...................	1.3	36.3	0.0	0.0	0.0	21.1	7.6	18.5	0.7	0.0
Parker........................	0.0	15.6	0.0	0.0	0.0	16.9	2.2	37.3	2.0	5.8
Pueblo	0.0	5.5	0.8	0.0	0.0	18.6	20.0	6.8	11.0	1.6
Thornton......................	0.0	19.8	0.0	0.0	0.0	19.1	12.4	16.7	1.5	2.1
Westminster	0.0	5.0	0.0	0.0	0.0	13.9	6.9	14.9	9.1	4.9
Wheat Ridge	0.0	14.0	0.0	0.0	0.0	32.8	6.3	20.9	0.0	0.3
CONNECTICUT	X	X	X	X	X	X	X	X	X	X
Bridgeport....................	0.4	1.9	0.3	44.8	0.5	12.4	5.2	0.8	1.2	5.5
Bristol.........................	0.0	5.0	0.0	63.2	2.8	4.2	3.8	1.2	0.3	0.8
Danbury......................	0.2	4.2	0.5	53.7	1.2	6.5	3.4	2.5	0.2	2.4
Hartford	1.6	3.6	0.1	58.0	1.8	8.2	0.4	0.2	8.4	1.9
Meriden	0.6	1.9	0.1	57.5	1.4	5.2	4.0	0.9	0.4	1.6
Middletown	0.1	2.3	0.3	50.9	0.6	8.1	3.9	1.7	0.3	1.8
Milford........................	0.5	1.5	0.0	54.6	1.2	4.9	13.6	0.5	0.4	1.1
Naugatuck....................	0.2	2.0	0.0	56.2	0.8	4.8	6.3	1.1	0.0	3.5
New Britain...................	0.1	4.1	0.0	51.5	0.6	12.7	4.6	3.5	1.1	5.1
New Haven...................	0.0	1.2	1.6	66.9	0.3	3.3	1.0	0.5	1.0	1.6
New London	0.0	9.3	0.5	48.4	0.2	11.0	4.0	8.9	1.6	1.9
Norwalk	0.0	4.6	1.3	50.9	0.6	5.2	5.7	3.8	0.4	3.4
Norwich	1.6	10.4	0.2	52.7	0.0	7.4	10.4	1.5	1.0	0.7
Shelton	0.0	2.6	0.0	60.5	2.6	4.5	4.5	1.7	0.1	2.3
Stamford	2.7	1.6	0.6	47.9	4.0	10.2	4.2	0.6	0.6	3.4
Torrington	0.0	4.5	0.0	56.8	5.0	6.7	4.0	1.2	0.2	1.8
Waterbury....................	0.6	1.7	0.0	58.3	0.5	4.8	4.0	0.7	1.1	4.5
West Haven..................	0.2	3.3	0.0	53.9	0.9	7.6	10.9	1.1	0.5	4.1
DELAWARE	X	X	X	X	X	X	X	X	X	X
Dover..........................	0.0	4.4	0.0	0.0	0.1	25.4	18.7	1.5	0.7	0.2
Newark........................	0.0	8.2	2.2	0.0	0.0	30.5	22.1	7.9	1.1	0.3
Wilmington...................	0.0	5.8	4.3	0.0	0.0	30.6	10.4	4.8	6.2	3.2
DISTRICT OF COLUMBIA..............	X	X	X	X	X	X	X	X	X	X
Washington	25.6	4.7	0.2	21.2	6.0	5.0	5.3	1.8	4.9	4.5
FLORIDA...................	X	X	X	X	X	X	X	X	X	X
Altamonte Springs........	0.0	19.8	0.0	0.0	0.0	30.9	9.3	11.4	0.0	0.1
Apopka	0.0	5.4	0.0	0.0	8.7	26.1	18.4	5.7	0.0	1.3
Aventura	0.0	8.4	0.0	17.8	0.0	41.5	0.0	7.7	0.0	3.2
Boca Raton	0.0	5.0	0.0	0.0	0.0	17.6	14.0	17.3	0.2	1.6
Bonita Springs..............	0.0	31.5	0.0	0.0	1.0	9.5	0.0	12.6	1.6	7.3
Boynton Beach.............	0.0	1.9	0.0	0.0	0.0	21.9	20.0	8.6	0.3	2.3
Bradenton....................	0.0	3.5	1.4	0.0	0.0	22.9	24.5	5.3	9.3	1.9
Cape Coral	0.0	10.9	0.0	10.4	0.0	15.1	5.4	7.0	3.0	4.8
Casselberry	0.0	6.3	0.0	0.0	0.1	13.0	22.3	3.0	0.0	1.2
Clearwater...................	0.1	6.4	2.0	0.0	3.0	19.9	21.2	14.6	0.6	1.4
Clermont......................	0.0	3.8	0.0	0.0	0.0	20.7	33.3	12.1	0.0	0.5
Coconut Creek	0.0	3.4	0.0	0.0	0.0	29.3	2.2	9.1	1.0	1.9
Cooper City	0.0	2.4	0.1	0.0	0.0	31.4	17.8	9.4	0.0	0.4
Coral Gables	0.0	4.8	3.5	0.0	0.0	29.1	12.4	6.3	0.5	1.9
Coral Springs	0.0	4.5	0.0	0.0	6.2	37.8	6.6	11.4	0.0	1.5
Cutler Bay	0.0	2.3	0.0	0.0	0.0	30.8	0.0	32.3	0.0	3.8
Dania Beach.................	0.0	4.0	2.3	0.0	0.0	19.8	10.2	6.8	0.0	1.4
Davie..........................	0.0	8.0	0.0	0.0	0.0	36.2	0.0	7.4	2.6	3.2
Daytona Beach.............	0.0	11.2	0.0	0.0	0.0	29.4	13.1	11.5	1.8	3.5

Table D. Cities — City Government Finances, City Government Employment, and Climate

City	City government finances, 2012 (cont.) Debt outstanding		Debt issued during year	Climate[2] Average daily temperature (degrees Fahrenheit) Mean		Limits		Annual precipitation (inches)	Heating degree days	Cooling degree days
	Total (mil dol)	Per capita[1] (dollars)		January	July	January[3]	July[4]			
	137	138	139	140	141	142	143	144	145	146
COLORADO—Cont'd										
Castle Rock	110.8	2 154	0.0	NA	NA	NA	NA	NA	NA	NA
Centennial	2.8	27	0.0	NA	NA	NA	NA	NA	NA	NA
Colorado Springs	2 643.8	6 097	167.5	28.1	69.6	14.5	84.4	17.40	6 480	404
Commerce City	182.6	3 760	0.1	NA	NA	NA	NA	NA	NA	NA
Denver	7 039.4	11 106	660.3	31.2	71.5	15.6	88.3	18.17	5 988	496
Englewood	89.9	2 879	0.3	28.2	70.2	12.7	85.8	17.06	6 773	435
Fort Collins	216.4	1 453	11.2	28.2	71.5	14.5	86.2	13.98	6 256	524
Fountain	29.0	1 078	9.0	NA	NA	NA	NA	NA	NA	NA
Grand Junction	74.2	1 241	0.0	27.4	77.5	16.8	91.9	9.06	5 489	1 098
Greeley	155.4	1 629	0.0	27.8	74.0	15.6	88.7	14.22	5 980	759
Lakewood	74.1	509	0.0	28.2	70.2	12.7	85.8	17.06	6 773	435
Littleton	52.5	1 198	2.4	28.2	70.2	12.7	85.8	17.06	6 773	435
Longmont	86.1	971	2.5	27.1	72.2	12.0	88.9	14.15	6 415	587
Loveland	5.0	71	0.0	28.2	71.5	14.5	86.2	13.98	6 256	524
Northglenn	9.0	244	0.0	30.0	72.0	16.2	87.9	13.25	6 074	590
Parker	55.9	1 184	0.0	NA	NA	NA	NA	NA	NA	NA
Pueblo	144.1	1 337	15.5	30.8	77.0	14.7	93.8	12.60	5 346	997
Thornton	191.4	1 539	0.0	30.0	72.0	16.2	87.9	13.25	6 074	590
Westminster	297.6	2 724	5.2	29.2	73.4	15.2	88.0	15.81	6 128	696
Wheat Ridge	2.7	86	0.0	31.2	71.5	15.6	88.3	18.17	5 988	496
CONNECTICUT	X	X	X	X	X	X	X	X	X	X
Bridgeport	742.4	5 050	77.6	29.9	74.0	22.9	81.9	44.15	5 466	789
Bristol	95.9	1 582	23.9	23.4	70.5	12.6	83.3	51.03	6 825	395
Danbury	169.5	2 047	37.8	26.5	72.5	17.6	83.9	51.77	6 159	597
Hartford	413.5	3 301	78.1	25.9	73.6	16.3	83.8	44.29	6 121	654
Meriden	121.0	1 994	1.8	28.3	73.4	20.3	84.2	52.35	5 791	669
Middletown	145.6	3 071	0.0	29.9	74.0	22.9	81.9	44.15	5 466	789
Milford	167.9	3 259	24.1	29.9	74.0	22.9	81.9	44.15	5 466	789
Naugatuck	75.9	2 387	0.0	29.9	74.0	22.9	81.9	44.15	5 466	789
New Britain	280.1	3 831	34.0	28.3	73.4	20.3	84.2	52.35	5 791	669
New Haven	585.6	4 473	50.6	25.9	72.5	16.9	82.8	52.73	6 271	558
New London	63.6	2 305	6.8	28.9	71.8	20.0	80.7	48.72	5 799	511
Norwalk	269.9	3 093	45.1	27.8	73.4	18.8	84.2	48.38	5 854	652
Norwich	48.2	1 190	17.7	27.6	73.2	17.3	83.8	52.78	5 916	627
Shelton	84.7	2 103	22.7	29.9	74.0	22.9	81.9	44.15	5 466	789
Stamford	448.3	3 582	64.9	28.7	73.5	19.2	85.4	52.79	5 582	692
Torrington	36.3	1 015	0.0	23.6	69.5	13.9	80.7	54.59	6 839	323
Waterbury	472.8	4 301	67.1	25.9	72.5	16.9	82.8	52.73	6 271	558
West Haven	122.2	2 213	51.1	25.9	72.5	16.9	82.8	52.73	6 271	558
DELAWARE	X	X	X	X	X	X	X	X	X	X
Dover	41.3	1 115	4.1	35.3	77.8	26.9	87.4	46.28	4 212	1 262
Newark	13.6	418	12.7	32.5	76.4	23.5	87.6	45.35	4 746	1 047
Wilmington	353.0	4 950	53.2	31.5	76.6	23.7	86.0	42.81	4 888	1 125
DISTRICT OF COLUMBIA	X	X	X	X	X	X	X	X	X	X
Washington	11 278.8	17 761	1 642.8	34.9	79.2	27.3	88.3	39.35	4 055	1 531
FLORIDA	X	X	X	X	X	X	X	X	X	X
Altamonte Springs	0.0	0	0.0	58.7	81.5	47.0	91.9	51.31	799	3 017
Apopka	33.4	751	0.0	58.7	81.5	47.0	91.9	51.31	799	3 017
Aventura	32.5	872	6.8	67.9	82.7	62.6	87.0	46.60	141	4 090
Boca Raton	139.0	1 580	0.0	67.2	83.3	57.8	91.8	57.27	219	4 241
Bonita Springs	24.3	526	0.0	64.3	82.0	53.4	91.2	51.90	316	3 646
Boynton Beach	126.0	1 795	0.0	66.2	82.5	57.3	90.1	61.39	246	3 999
Bradenton	34.5	683	0.0	61.6	81.9	50.9	91.3	54.12	538	3 327
Cape Coral	907.6	5 629	196.0	62.7	81.3	50.3	91.3	50.07	427	3 287
Casselberry	20.3	766	9.1	NA	NA	NA	NA	NA	NA	NA
Clearwater	247.9	2 276	47.0	61.3	82.5	52.4	89.7	44.77	591	3 482
Clermont	19.7	668	0.0	NA	NA	NA	NA	NA	NA	NA
Coconut Creek	22.8	413	0.0	67.2	83.3	57.8	91.8	57.27	219	4 241
Cooper City	6.1	189	1.5	67.5	82.6	59.2	89.8	64.19	167	4 120
Coral Gables	79.3	1 596	50.7	67.9	82.7	62.6	87.0	46.60	141	4 090
Coral Springs	71.6	570	8.8	67.2	83.3	57.8	91.8	57.27	219	4 241
Cutler Bay	18.6	437	3.6	NA	NA	NA	NA	NA	NA	NA
Dania Beach	30.3	988	3.6	NA	NA	NA	NA	NA	NA	NA
Davie	144.9	1 515	20.0	66.2	82.5	57.3	90.1	61.39	246	3 999
Daytona Beach	154.8	2 505	36.2	57.1	81.2	44.5	91.2	57.03	954	2 819

1. Based on the population estimated as of July 1 of the year shown. 2. Represents normal values based on the 30-year period, 1971–2000. 3. Average daily minimum.
4. Average daily maximum.

Table D. Cities — **Land Area and Population**

STATE Place code	City	Land area,[1] 2010 (sq km)	Total persons	Rank	Per square kilometer	White	Black	American Indian, Alaska Native	Asian	Hawaiian Pacific Islander	Percent Hispanic or Latino[2], 2010-2014	Percent foreign born 2010–2014
			Population, 2015			Race alone or in combination (percent), 2010-2014						
		1	2	3	4	5	6	7	8	9	10	11
	FLORIDA—Cont'd											
12 16725	Deerfield Beach............	39.1	79 768	424	2 040.1	71.7	26.1	0.6	2.0	0.1	17.0	31.6
12 16875	DeLand.........................	45.6	30 195	1 239	662.2	75.9	16.9	0.3	4.2	0.1	14.8	8.7
12 17100	Delray Beach................	40.9	66 255	538	1 619.9	65.5	28.7	0.6	2.4	0.0	11.4	23.0
12 17200	Deltona........................	97.2	88 474	359	910.2	80.7	11.8	1.7	1.3	0.1	30.7	9.6
12 17935	Doral...........................	35.9	56 035	662	1 560.9	92.4	2.3	0.5	4.6	0.0	79.7	62.4
12 18575	Dunedin.......................	26.8	36 164	1 042	1 349.4	93.8	3.6	0.8	2.1	0.1	7.1	10.0
12 24000	Fort Lauderdale............	90.0	178 590	136	1 984.3	64.2	32.5	0.6	1.9	0.3	15.6	22.8
12 24125	Fort Myers...................	103.5	74 013	467	715.1	62.9	31.1	0.6	2.2	0.1	20.5	16.3
12 24300	Fort Pierce...................	53.3	44 484	840	834.6	57.2	38.2	0.3	0.5	0.0	21.3	19.0
12 25175	Gainesville..................	158.8	130 128	206	819.4	68.0	24.9	0.8	8.0	0.2	10.1	11.7
12 27322	Greenacres..................	15.0	39 676	945	2 645.1	75.7	20.3	1.0	4.0	0.5	40.9	36.0
12 28452	Hallandale Beach	10.9	39 488	950	3 622.8	76.9	19.9	0.8	2.3	0.2	32.3	45.7
12 30000	Hialeah........................	55.6	237 069	90	4 263.8	95.1	2.6	0.2	0.4	0.0	95.6	73.0
12 32000	Hollywood....................	70.9	149 728	172	2 111.8	75.8	19.7	0.6	3.4	0.2	31.5	32.8
12 32275	Homestead...................	39.2	66 498	535	1 696.4	76.0	21.1	0.5	2.7	0.1	59.8	36.0
12 35000	Jacksonville.................	1 934.7	868 031	12	448.7	63.0	32.2	0.9	5.5	0.2	8.2	9.7
12 35875	Jupiter.........................	55.6	62 707	573	1 127.8	94.8	1.2	0.8	3.1	0.0	12.4	13.5
12 36950	Kissimmee...................	54.9	69 152	505	1 259.6	74.8	13.9	0.5	3.3	0.2	62.1	26.9
12 38250	Lakeland......................	169.1	104 401	286	617.4	76.2	21.2	0.8	2.3	0.1	14.1	8.7
12 39075	Lake Worth...................	15.2	37 498	1 005	2 467.0	75.9	21.7	1.1	0.9	0.3	41.1	36.0
12 39425	Largo...........................	45.6	81 000	411	1 776.3	89.6	7.9	0.9	3.3	0.3	12.6	12.2
12 39525	Lauderdale Lakes..........	9.5	34 796	1 080	3 662.7	13.5	84.1	0.7	2.1	0.1	6.6	47.5
12 39550	Lauderhill....................	22.1	71 579	486	3 238.9	18.0	79.1	0.6	2.4	0.3	8.7	35.5
12 43125	Margate........................	22.9	57 234	645	2 499.3	64.7	27.7	0.5	5.9	0.1	22.3	33.1
12 43975	Melbourne...................	87.7	80 127	419	913.6	85.8	12.3	1.3	3.8	0.1	8.3	10.1
12 45000	Miami...........................	92.9	441 003	44	4 747.1	75.9	20.3	0.3	1.1	0.1	70.7	57.6
12 45025	Miami Beach.................	19.8	92 312	341	4 662.2	78.6	5.4	0.4	2.1	0.1	53.5	52.2
12 45060	Miami Gardens............	47.2	113 187	246	2 398.0	21.0	76.6	0.4	1.0	0.2	24.2	29.8
12 45100	Miami Lakes.................	14.6	30 972	1 197	2 121.4	93.9	3.9	0.1	2.2	0.0	82.0	49.7
12 45975	Miramar.......................	76.5	137 132	190	1 792.6	42.8	48.0	0.2	7.4	0.1	36.9	43.9
12 49425	North Lauderdale	11.9	43 703	856	3 672.5	37.5	56.8	1.2	4.2	0.3	24.6	43.6
12 49450	North Miami..................	21.8	62 435	576	2 864.0	34.2	59.7	0.3	3.1	0.5	26.8	49.1
12 49475	North Miami Beach	12.5	43 971	850	3 517.7	50.0	45.4	0.3	3.8	0.1	33.1	50.4
12 49675	North Port....................	257.9	62 345	578	241.7	88.3	10.5	0.4	1.5	0.1	7.7	11.8
12 50575	Oakland Park	19.3	44 319	843	2 296.3	67.4	27.6	1.3	3.4	0.1	28.0	32.3
12 50750	Ocala...........................	116.1	58 218	637	501.4	72.1	23.2	1.3	4.4	0.4	12.5	6.4
12 51075	Ocoee..........................	38.1	43 608	858	1 144.6	64.4	23.4	0.9	5.2	0.0	19.5	18.4
12 53000	Orlando........................	265.2	270 934	73	1 021.6	61.1	29.7	0.7	4.4	0.2	26.8	18.3
12 53150	Ormond Beach..............	82.7	40 970	913	495.4	90.3	5.7	0.3	4.3	0.0	3.9	8.6
12 53575	Oviedo.........................	39.4	38 551	970	978.5	84.3	9.3	0.7	5.9	0.1	19.5	11.8
12 54000	Palm Bay......................	170.2	107 888	274	633.9	77.1	19.3	1.1	2.6	0.3	15.7	12.8
12 54075	Palm Beach Gardens....	142.7	52 923	706	370.9	88.2	7.1	0.8	4.3	1.0	10.2	15.1
12 54200	Palm Coast...................	232.8	82 893	398	356.1	81.0	14.2	0.4	3.3	0.1	11.0	14.9
12 54700	Panama City.................	75.8	38 286	979	505.1	77.5	20.6	2.0	4.5	0.2	7.4	5.8
12 55775	Pembroke Pines............	85.8	166 611	151	1 941.9	68.7	21.8	0.9	6.3	0.1	43.7	35.3
12 55925	Pensacola....................	58.4	53 193	704	910.8	69.6	28.1	1.4	4.0	0.1	4.5	6.2
12 56975	Pinellas Park	40.2	51 617	733	1 284.0	86.0	5.9	1.0	7.7	0.0	12.0	14.5
12 57425	Plantation	56.3	92 560	339	1 644.0	72.3	22.1	0.3	5.0	0.2	22.0	26.8
12 57550	Plant City....................	70.4	37 406	1 010	531.3	74.8	16.1	0.4	1.2	0.1	29.2	15.2
12 58050	Pompano Beach............	62.2	107 762	275	1 732.5	65.8	31.4	0.6	1.8	0.3	17.9	25.1
12 58575	Port Orange.................	69.1	59 866	613	866.4	92.6	4.8	1.1	2.2	0.1	4.2	6.7
12 58715	Port St. Lucie	295.1	179 413	134	608.0	76.0	19.4	1.0	2.9	0.2	19.4	16.9
12 60975	Riviera Beach...............	22.1	34 005	1 103	1 538.7	31.2	66.3	0.4	2.8	0.1	9.0	16.8
12 62100	Royal Palm Beach	29.0	37 633	1 000	1 297.7	71.9	23.8	0.1	3.4	0.1	21.6	19.3
12 62625	St. Cloud.....................	46.0	45 298	830	984.7	87.1	9.1	0.3	3.8	0.0	30.5	10.9
12 63000	St. Petersburg..............	159.9	257 083	80	1 607.8	71.3	25.4	0.6	4.1	0.3	6.9	10.5
12 63650	Sanford........................	59.5	58 111	638	976.7	65.9	30.6	0.6	3.5	0.6	20.6	10.2
12 64175	Sarasota......................	38.0	55 118	680	1 450.5	82.9	15.3	1.0	1.7	0.1	18.4	17.4
12 69700	Sunrise.......................	46.9	92 700	338	1 976.5	60.2	33.2	0.8	4.7	0.1	27.7	35.8
12 70600	Tallahassee..................	259.6	189 907	126	731.5	58.9	36.7	0.7	4.4	0.1	6.6	7.7
12 70675	Tamarac.......................	30.1	64 681	552	2 148.9	70.1	26.2	0.5	2.2	0.3	27.1	32.9
12 71000	Tampa..........................	293.7	369 075	53	1 256.6	65.8	27.5	1.4	4.7	0.3	23.3	15.4
12 71900	Titusville.....................	76.1	45 393	827	596.5	79.7	17.6	1.0	2.7	0.2	6.3	5.4
12 75812	Wellington...................	116.3	62 560	575	537.9	81.4	13.8	0.5	4.9	0.0	19.0	21.5
12 76582	Weston........................	65.2	69 959	498	1 073.0	87.5	5.6	0.7	4.8	0.0	47.8	39.9
12 76600	West Palm Beach	143.2	106 779	278	745.7	62.3	32.0	0.6	2.8	0.1	23.8	26.4
12 78250	Winter Garden..............	39.9	40 356	931	1 011.4	68.0	19.3	0.8	5.2	0.1	23.9	15.9
12 78275	Winter Haven...............	81.1	37 689	998	464.7	68.9	28.5	0.8	2.4	0.1	13.5	10.8
12 78300	Winter Park..................	22.5	29 943	1 245	1 330.8	86.5	8.8	0.9	3.6	0.4	9.5	9.0
12 78325	Winter Springs..............	38.0	34 789	1 082	915.5	89.6	6.2	1.0	2.8	0.3	20.5	10.9

1. Dry land or land partially or temporarily covered by water.   2. May be of any race.

Table D. Cities — **Population**

City	Age of population (percent), 2010-2014											Population			
												Census counts		Percent change	
	Under 5 years	5 to 17 years	18 to 24 years	25 to 34 years	35 to 44 years	45 to 54 years	55 to 64 years	65 to 74 years	75 years and over	Median age 2010–2014	Percent female 2010–2014	2000	2010	2000–2010	2010–2015
	12	13	14	15	16	17	18	19	20	21	22	23	24	25	26
FLORIDA—Cont'd															
Deerfield Beach	5.4	14.1	6.5	13.7	12.4	13.4	11.6	10.5	12.3	42.9	52.0	64 583	75 018	16.2	6.3
DeLand	4.8	17.3	13.8	8.6	14.0	11.1	10.1	10.1	10.2	38.7	51.8	20 904	27 031	29.3	12.0
Delray Beach	4.4	10.7	7.1	13.5	10.9	14.2	14.8	11.2	13.2	47.4	53.3	60 020	60 522	0.8	9.3
Deltona	6.1	17.9	9.4	12.5	12.3	14.5	13.1	7.8	6.5	38.6	50.6	69 543	85 182	22.5	3.9
Doral	9.4	20.3	7.7	15.9	18.7	14.4	7.5	4.1	2.1	33.2	52.9	20 438	45 704	123.6	22.6
Dunedin	5.5	11.7	4.7	12.0	8.1	12.9	16.3	14.3	14.5	51.9	55.4	35 691	35 321	-1.0	2.3
Fort Lauderdale	4.9	12.7	7.5	15.4	12.9	16.4	14.5	8.9	6.8	42.5	47.4	152 397	165 521	8.6	7.9
Fort Myers	5.5	14.8	8.7	13.5	13.8	12.8	12.6	10.4	7.9	40.3	48.9	48 208	62 298	29.2	19.0
Fort Pierce	9.0	15.6	11.0	13.6	10.2	10.8	13.3	8.8	7.7	35.6	51.7	37 516	41 590	10.9	6.1
Gainesville	4.5	8.2	36.9	16.4	8.4	8.0	9.1	4.2	4.2	25.1	52.0	95 447	124 354	30.3	4.5
Greenacres	6.5	18.5	9.3	14.3	16.1	12.3	8.9	7.6	6.5	35.8	51.8	27 569	37 573	36.3	5.6
Hallandale Beach	5.1	9.5	5.0	13.5	14.0	12.9	14.4	12.7	12.9	46.9	52.8	34 282	37 113	8.3	6.4
Hialeah	5.2	13.5	9.8	11.4	14.7	15.8	10.1	9.8	9.7	42.0	52.4	226 419	224 669	-0.8	5.5
Hollywood	5.7	15.2	7.8	12.6	13.9	16.0	13.1	8.3	7.3	41.8	50.8	139 357	140 768	1.0	6.4
Homestead	7.9	21.1	9.4	18.1	15.0	12.8	7.7	5.5	2.5	32.0	49.0	31 909	60 512	89.6	9.9
Jacksonville	7.0	16.4	10.3	15.4	13.1	14.1	12.0	6.8	4.9	35.7	51.5	735 617	821 784	11.7	5.6
Jupiter	4.9	14.6	4.6	12.4	11.6	15.5	14.5	11.2	10.7	46.0	51.3	39 328	55 156	40.2	13.5
Kissimmee	7.4	18.9	11.3	14.8	13.2	15.3	8.5	6.5	4.0	32.7	50.7	47 814	59 682	24.8	16.0
Lakeland	6.2	15.3	11.5	12.2	11.0	11.7	12.0	10.5	9.7	39.9	52.6	78 452	97 422	24.2	7.2
Lake Worth	7.1	15.8	8.9	17.4	12.6	15.2	10.1	6.7	6.2	35.5	46.7	35 133	34 910	-0.6	7.4
Largo	3.5	11.7	7.5	11.7	12.1	14.7	13.5	12.6	12.7	47.8	51.5	69 371	77 648	11.9	2.4
Lauderdale Lakes	7.6	17.1	9.7	13.2	10.4	13.0	12.8	9.0	7.2	38.5	56.6	31 705	32 593	2.8	6.6
Lauderhill	7.3	17.2	11.3	13.4	12.3	14.8	11.1	7.4	5.2	35.5	54.2	57 585	66 887	16.2	6.9
Margate	5.1	13.8	8.2	12.1	13.7	14.5	13.2	10.8	8.7	43.3	52.0	53 909	53 284	-1.2	7.4
Melbourne	4.7	11.9	9.8	13.0	9.9	15.9	13.4	10.3	11.2	45.6	51.6	71 382	76 068	6.6	5.1
Miami	6.3	12.4	8.6	16.7	14.8	14.2	11.2	7.9	8.0	39.0	50.0	362 470	399 457	10.2	10.4
Miami Beach	6.6	10.1	6.7	18.2	17.9	14.5	10.4	7.5	8.0	39.5	47.6	87 933	87 779	-0.2	5.2
Miami Gardens	6.3	17.7	11.9	14.5	12.9	13.3	11.8	6.6	5.0	34.7	53.3	NA	107 167	NA	5.6
Miami Lakes	6.5	16.0	8.5	13.2	14.1	16.2	10.9	7.8	6.8	38.9	53.1	22 676	29 361	29.5	5.5
Miramar	5.9	20.4	9.8	14.2	15.9	15.4	10.6	3.9	4.0	34.9	51.9	72 739	122 041	67.8	12.4
North Lauderdale	10.0	20.0	12.4	16.3	13.7	13.0	8.7	3.9	2.0	29.5	51.3	32 264	41 023	27.1	6.4
North Miami	5.7	16.8	12.7	13.1	15.7	14.3	11.2	6.1	4.3	36.2	50.9	59 880	58 786	-1.8	4.8
North Miami Beach	4.8	17.1	10.1	15.8	14.2	12.8	12.2	7.2	5.7	36.8	50.5	40 786	41 523	1.8	5.9
North Port	5.2	18.3	7.8	8.9	12.0	12.9	14.2	13.1	7.6	43.2	51.0	22 797	57 357	151.6	8.7
Oakland Park	8.6	13.1	8.2	15.2	14.2	15.8	13.8	7.1	4.1	38.7	47.4	30 966	41 363	33.6	7.1
Ocala	7.4	16.2	10.0	14.2	12.2	12.1	11.0	8.5	8.5	36.1	51.7	45 943	56 315	22.6	3.4
Ocoee	6.9	20.6	10.4	12.2	18.4	14.6	7.1	5.4	4.3	34.8	51.2	24 391	35 579	45.9	22.0
Orlando	7.3	14.9	11.4	19.5	14.9	12.8	9.4	5.4	4.3	32.9	51.8	185 951	238 300	28.2	13.4
Ormond Beach	3.8	12.4	7.2	9.0	11.3	12.5	14.9	13.4	15.4	50.1	52.3	36 301	38 137	5.1	4.4
Oviedo	5.7	21.7	8.7	13.8	14.1	17.5	11.0	4.5	3.0	35.0	51.1	26 316	33 342	26.7	15.2
Palm Bay	5.9	16.9	8.2	11.4	11.1	16.3	13.6	9.3	7.3	41.8	54.2	79 413	103 190	29.9	4.5
Palm Beach Gardens	4.1	12.0	5.0	11.0	12.4	14.5	13.6	14.2	13.1	48.7	53.4	35 058	48 452	38.2	9.0
Palm Coast	4.7	15.4	7.4	8.6	12.1	11.5	14.7	15.3	10.4	46.9	52.9	32 732	75 180	129.7	10.2
Panama City	6.7	16.6	10.0	12.9	11.9	14.4	10.6	8.1	8.6	38.1	52.4	36 417	36 484	0.2	7.8
Pembroke Pines	5.3	16.6	8.6	13.0	13.5	15.9	11.7	7.1	8.3	40.0	52.5	137 427	154 750	12.6	8.2
Pensacola	5.4	13.6	9.8	14.0	11.5	14.8	13.1	9.5	8.2	41.2	51.5	56 255	51 923	-7.7	2.4
Pinellas Park	5.0	12.5	7.1	12.8	12.5	15.1	15.1	11.7	8.3	45.1	49.0	45 658	49 079	7.5	4.8
Plantation	5.4	15.5	7.3	14.6	13.9	16.3	13.3	7.6	6.1	40.9	51.6	82 934	84 955	2.4	9.1
Plant City	7.4	19.7	7.7	14.1	13.7	14.7	11.1	7.1	4.5	35.9	51.6	29 915	34 721	16.1	7.8
Pompano Beach	6.3	12.3	8.9	14.5	13.0	14.6	12.4	7.8	10.1	41.2	48.6	78 191	99 845	27.7	7.9
Port Orange	4.4	13.5	7.4	9.1	10.2	15.8	14.6	11.9	11.9	49.1	52.6	45 823	56 048	22.3	5.8
Port St. Lucie	5.8	19.1	7.8	11.4	13.3	14.4	11.8	9.0	7.4	39.9	50.8	88 769	164 603	85.4	8.9
Riviera Beach	7.6	15.4	10.4	12.5	14.2	13.8	12.6	7.1	6.4	38.8	52.3	29 884	32 488	8.7	4.7
Royal Palm Beach	5.1	21.3	8.8	10.3	13.4	15.9	13.1	7.2	4.8	37.5	52.4	21 523	34 140	58.6	10.2
St. Cloud	8.9	17.1	8.3	14.5	13.7	13.9	11.0	8.1	4.6	36.0	51.3	20 074	35 183	75.3	24.7
St. Petersburg	5.1	13.9	9.0	13.0	12.7	15.6	14.3	8.6	7.7	41.9	52.1	248 232	244 769	-1.4	4.8
Sanford	7.5	19.6	10.1	15.9	14.7	12.8	9.4	6.2	3.9	32.9	52.1	38 291	53 570	39.9	8.2
Sarasota	4.9	10.8	9.0	12.5	12.0	14.4	12.9	11.2	12.2	45.6	51.2	52 715	51 917	-1.5	5.9
Sunrise	6.6	14.3	8.8	14.2	13.4	14.8	12.1	7.1	8.6	39.3	55.0	85 779	84 439	-1.6	9.9
Tallahassee	5.1	11.8	30.5	16.4	9.9	9.2	8.6	4.5	4.1	26.1	52.1	150 624	181 376	20.4	4.7
Tamarac	4.0	14.0	5.6	11.7	14.5	13.1	11.9	11.6	13.6	45.2	55.5	55 588	60 427	8.7	6.9
Tampa	6.1	15.5	12.3	15.9	13.6	14.3	11.0	6.0	5.3	35.2	51.1	303 447	335 709	10.6	9.9
Titusville	5.3	13.6	9.2	10.2	13.5	13.2	12.9	10.5	11.6	43.8	52.5	40 670	43 761	7.6	3.8
Wellington	5.2	21.6	8.6	8.2	14.2	17.1	12.5	8.0	4.7	40.4	52.4	38 216	56 508	47.9	10.3
Weston	4.8	25.3	7.8	7.5	15.0	19.6	11.3	5.3	3.4	38.6	50.8	49 286	65 333	32.6	7.1
West Palm Beach	5.8	12.6	10.7	15.4	12.3	13.3	12.3	8.8	8.7	39.5	50.9	82 103	99 919	21.7	6.4
Winter Garden	7.3	20.3	8.0	14.5	15.5	16.8	8.6	4.8	4.2	34.6	52.3	14 351	34 568	140.9	16.5
Winter Haven	5.5	14.2	7.4	10.0	12.4	13.5	12.1	13.0	12.0	45.9	54.2	26 487	33 874	27.9	11.3
Winter Park	5.4	14.0	13.7	11.3	8.8	13.2	14.9	9.0	9.8	42.1	51.2	24 090	27 852	15.6	7.5
Winter Springs	4.2	16.9	9.3	12.9	12.6	14.5	14.5	8.7	6.4	39.2	50.6	31 666	33 282	5.1	4.5

Table D. Cities — **Households, Group Quarters, Crime, and Education**

City	Households, 2010-2014 Number	Persons per house-hold	Percent Female family house-holder[1]	Percent One-person	Persons in group quarters, 2010 Total	Institutional Total	Persons in nursing facilities	Non-institu-tional	Serious crimes known to police,[2] 2014 Total Number	Total Rate[3]	Rate[3] Violent	Rate[3] Property	Population age 25 and older	Attainment[4] (percent) High school graduate or less	Attainment[4] (percent) Bachelor's degree or more
	27	28	29	30	31	32	33	34	35	36	37	38	39	40	41
FLORIDA—Cont'd															
Deerfield Beach	31 667	2.44	14.0	37.3	1 046	863	229	183	2 442	3 100	468	2 632	56 707	50.8	23.0
DeLand	10 079	2.77	12.5	35.0	2 377	595	587	1 782	1 424	4 988	501	4 487	17 926	44.8	22.8
Delray Beach	26 554	2.37	10.9	38.4	1 114	584	539	530	3 165	4 875	665	4 210	47 696	37.8	33.7
Deltona	28 949	2.96	14.3	20.9	166	127	127	39	NA	NA	NA	NA	57 363	51.8	14.9
Doral	14 507	3.40	14.5	13.9	6	0	0	6	2 142	4 171	140	4 031	30 482	23.5	53.7
Dunedin	16 548	2.15	9.0	39.4	385	344	338	41	794	2 219	268	1 951	28 381	37.6	29.0
Fort Lauderdale	73 279	2.34	11.2	42.0	3 418	1 861	324	1 557	10 278	5 905	773	5 132	128 260	39.6	33.9
Fort Myers	23 847	2.77	18.0	35.4	3 236	2 520	598	716	2 945	4 224	1 103	3 121	46 009	49.2	23.9
Fort Pierce	16 283	2.63	20.3	34.8	577	455	314	122	2 620	6 044	1 061	4 983	27 639	59.2	13.9
Gainesville	47 420	2.67	11.5	37.8	12 493	1 796	748	10 697	5 397	4 210	637	3 573	63 691	29.2	42.6
Greenacres	13 296	2.89	18.9	27.5	51	5	5	46	1 788	4 590	680	3 909	25 558	51.3	18.9
Hallandale Beach	18 042	2.12	11.9	42.3	101	0	0	101	1 766	4 528	615	3 913	30 004	42.2	29.1
Hialeah	68 878	3.37	19.7	20.5	1 493	727	700	766	7 318	3 108	332	2 776	168 100	66.4	13.2
Hollywood	55 823	2.60	14.1	33.0	1 203	608	476	595	7 116	4 811	494	4 317	104 273	43.7	26.8
Homestead	19 269	3.29	21.6	23.0	450	227	223	223	3 825	5 890	1 327	4 563	37 908	56.7	15.7
Jacksonville	315 619	2.65	16.2	30.8	19 747	8 158	3 155	11 589	39 585	4 624	684	3 941	555 271	41.3	25.5
Jupiter	24 257	2.38	8.0	30.9	393	131	131	262	1 175	1 990	213	1 777	43 857	29.5	44.0
Kissimmee	20 616	3.07	21.8	21.8	595	317	54	278	3 261	4 895	668	4 227	40 483	52.8	14.6
Lakeland	39 497	2.53	13.7	35.1	4 126	1 140	1 094	2 986	5 738	5 657	447	5 211	67 529	46.9	24.7
Lake Worth	11 824	3.04	16.0	30.9	618	518	409	100	2 401	6 622	1 147	5 475	23 826	57.2	19.7
Largo	35 683	2.20	10.7	39.4	1 026	941	836	85	3 214	4 094	431	3 664	60 090	48.4	20.1
Lauderdale Lakes	11 328	2.98	27.5	27.8	392	387	363	5	1 771	5 148	773	4 375	22 300	59.4	13.1
Lauderhill	23 265	2.97	28.0	27.6	592	225	225	367	2 932	4 159	654	3 505	44 633	50.6	18.9
Margate	20 891	2.63	15.3	32.5	169	6	6	163	1 027	1 835	225	1 609	40 019	49.9	20.6
Melbourne	33 083	2.33	12.0	38.2	2 125	746	713	1 379	3 713	4 773	785	3 987	56 017	41.9	24.5
Miami	152 525	2.73	17.7	36.5	8 161	5 133	1 526	3 028	24 867	5 893	1 060	4 833	303 201	57.7	23.5
Miami Beach	43 650	2.08	9.2	47.5	1 026	534	473	492	10 316	11 241	973	10 268	70 697	34.1	43.2
Miami Gardens	31 365	3.53	30.2	22.7	1 367	64	11	1 303	5 260	4 681	655	4 026	71 358	57.4	14.6
Miami Lakes	9 741	3.12	13.3	22.4	28	0	0	28	688	2 230	68	2 162	20 997	34.1	31.8
Miramar	37 439	3.43	22.9	15.7	87	24	11	63	3 167	2 393	315	2 078	81 913	34.0	31.0
North Lauderdale	12 047	3.52	26.3	17.0	31	0	0	31	1 291	2 991	426	2 564	25 663	61.9	13.5
North Miami	18 038	3.37	23.0	27.8	1 640	539	539	1 101	3 383	5 501	938	4 563	39 007	52.2	19.5
North Miami Beach	14 065	3.06	18.2	29.2	236	151	148	85	1 991	4 561	843	3 718	29 193	48.3	20.0
North Port	22 622	2.59	9.1	24.9	119	100	100	19	995	1 668	173	1 495	41 465	46.7	16.4
Oakland Park	17 031	2.51	16.1	37.3	205	19	0	186	2 019	4 615	519	4 096	30 665	44.8	21.1
Ocala	21 922	2.60	16.7	35.9	3 281	2 856	922	425	3 363	5 824	623	5 201	37 715	44.4	22.2
Ocoee	12 049	3.18	14.9	18.4	287	225	225	62	1 549	3 870	345	3 525	24 434	39.9	29.4
Orlando	102 570	2.44	17.0	36.8	3 294	1 227	1 009	2 067	18 855	7 261	901	6 360	167 292	36.4	33.4
Ormond Beach	15 550	2.48	8.8	30.0	458	434	434	24	1 721	4 438	428	4 010	29 280	34.2	31.3
Oviedo	10 012	3.56	9.6	14.1	103	94	94	9	517	1 380	149	1 230	22 010	23.8	42.6
Palm Bay	37 249	2.80	15.1	24.1	430	331	320	99	2 826	2 684	570	2 114	71 650	47.8	17.0
Palm Beach Gardens	22 675	2.21	8.7	34.6	235	205	154	30	1 523	2 974	148	2 826	39 369	24.0	46.9
Palm Coast	27 466	2.83	8.7	22.3	319	282	144	37	NA	NA	NA	NA	56 456	44.0	21.5
Panama City	14 781	2.46	14.9	34.2	2 782	2 453	553	329	2 924	7 859	922	6 937	25 177	44.7	20.8
Pembroke Pines	56 308	2.84	14.8	26.4	1 397	1 187	125	210	4 052	2 465	169	2 297	110 588	34.2	32.5
Pensacola	22 062	2.38	14.6	38.1	727	284	224	443	2 763	5 226	705	4 520	36 616	33.4	33.0
Pinellas Park	20 911	2.39	10.9	36.2	1 165	510	337	655	3 156	6 285	456	5 829	36 963	51.1	17.3
Plantation	33 521	2.64	15.0	27.0	363	307	304	56	3 067	3 350	341	3 009	63 125	28.0	40.2
Plant City	12 329	2.91	17.5	25.3	185	118	118	67	1 617	4 439	464	3 975	22 550	54.8	18.2
Pompano Beach	41 138	2.51	14.4	38.9	4 267	3 680	415	587	5 437	5 152	824	4 329	75 082	50.7	23.1
Port Orange	23 941	2.39	9.7	30.8	167	118	102	49	1 168	2 036	56	1 981	42 912	42.1	25.2
Port St. Lucie	59 101	2.86	13.4	21.6	711	330	322	381	2 741	1 589	141	1 449	115 287	46.3	19.0
Riviera Beach	11 950	2.77	22.0	31.8	323	134	134	189	1 954	5 842	1 190	4 652	21 903	49.6	21.9
Royal Palm Beach	11 188	3.17	16.5	17.5	236	229	119	7	984	2 671	269	2 402	22 721	38.7	26.1
St. Cloud	13 102	3.03	17.1	22.7	448	375	349	73	1 001	2 377	325	2 052	26 373	48.7	17.5
St. Petersburg	105 071	2.36	13.6	38.0	6 607	2 719	2 364	3 888	16 319	6 508	865	5 643	179 580	39.2	30.0
Sanford	18 267	3.03	18.8	31.5	1 531	996	180	535	3 437	6 072	804	5 268	35 620	44.3	21.8
Sarasota	22 773	2.33	12.7	39.3	3 582	1 632	738	1 950	2 894	5 397	666	4 731	39 236	42.6	30.7
Sunrise	31 343	2.82	16.8	27.3	578	506	496	72	3 331	3 639	303	3 336	61 659	42.8	25.9
Tallahassee	74 108	2.50	13.8	33.1	14 623	3 231	718	11 392	10 838	5 778	937	4 841	97 505	24.1	47.5
Tamarac	27 011	2.31	16.2	37.1	261	234	234	27	1 432	2 245	277	1 967	48 058	44.2	25.1
Tampa	139 337	2.50	16.0	36.5	12 282	2 138	876	10 144	10 750	3 010	582	2 428	229 907	40.3	33.7
Titusville	18 438	2.39	14.4	31.8	473	344	344	129	1 714	3 868	603	3 266	32 015	42.7	20.7
Wellington	19 770	2.99	10.5	15.9	2	0	0	2	1 312	2 148	167	1 981	38 754	25.2	42.9
Weston	21 317	3.17	11.8	12.9	0	0	0	0	425	615	65	550	41 904	16.0	57.9
West Palm Beach	41 411	2.47	14.9	37.9	2 943	1 196	1 093	1 747	5 637	5 471	824	4 647	72 553	40.6	31.2
Winter Garden	12 213	3.02	11.0	20.6	497	483	483	14	1 276	3 318	424	2 894	23 705	34.1	35.7
Winter Haven	13 907	2.52	15.1	33.4	598	491	490	107	1 575	4 383	623	3 760	24 370	50.1	16.9
Winter Park	11 747	2.45	6.9	37.7	1 609	338	338	1 271	1 185	4 013	274	3 739	19 551	20.7	54.2
Winter Springs	11 214	3.00	11.0	24.5	31	31	0	0	432	1 270	185	1 085	23 113	32.9	35.5

1. No spouse present.   2. Data for serious crimes have not been adjusted for underreporting. This may affect comparability between geographic areas and over time.   3. Per 100,000 population estimated by the FBI.   4. Persons 25 years old and over.

Table D. Cities — Income, Poverty, and Housing

City	Money income, 2010–2014					Housing units, 2010			Occupied housing units 2010–2014			Median owner costs as a percent of income	
	Households									Owner-occupied			
	Per capita income[1] (dollars)	Median income	Percent with income of $200,000 or more	Percent with income of less than $25,000	Families with income below poverty (percent)	Total	Percent change, 2000–2010	Vacant units for sale or rent[2]	Total	Percent	Median value[3] (dollars)	With a mortgage[4]	Without a mortgage[5]
	42	43	44	45	46	47	48	49	50	51	52	53	54
FLORIDA—Cont'd													
Deerfield Beach	23 743	38 209	2.0	32.8	17.0	42 671	14.3	9 301	31 667	62.8	106 100	32.6	18.8
DeLand	20 626	37 417	1.8	31.4	15.1	12 610	35.6	1 864	10 079	55.4	142 300	26.3	14.5
Delray Beach	34 339	50 833	5.8	24.2	12.9	34 156	7.9	6 963	26 554	63.9	176 900	29.8	16.1
Deltona	19 370	44 046	0.9	25.8	12.6	34 089	28.4	3 866	28 949	78.0	108 600	27.9	13.0
Doral	27 904	72 623	7.5	14.5	9.8	17 785	89.4	2 541	14 507	54.6	296 400	29.8	14.0
Dunedin	29 891	46 310	2.7	27.6	5.8	21 113	5.0	3 495	16 548	62.5	151 500	27.1	16.6
Fort Lauderdale	36 405	48 898	7.2	26.4	16.0	93 159	15.3	18 373	73 279	52.9	243 600	29.2	16.2
Fort Myers	23 096	37 360	3.6	34.0	20.4	35 138	60.9	10 170	23 847	47.1	138 500	25.0	12.7
Fort Pierce	16 479	25 976	1.9	48.4	31.8	21 357	24.1	5 507	16 283	45.3	85 400	30.2	16.5
Gainesville	19 615	32 108	2.2	40.8	18.3	57 576	43.5	6 547	47 420	38.0	145 700	23.0	11.8
Greenacres	19 732	43 235	1.3	26.8	15.8	17 249	21.0	2 865	13 296	65.1	99 800	28.8	15.8
Hallandale Beach	25 048	33 838	2.4	38.1	16.5	27 057	7.8	8 756	18 042	56.3	144 700	32.7	22.5
Hialeah	14 148	29 959	0.5	42.5	23.1	74 067	2.6	2 862	68 878	48.5	152 700	34.4	16.5
Hollywood	26 118	46 419	3.6	26.4	12.8	71 070	3.9	12 632	55 823	59.9	172 800	30.4	15.4
Homestead	17 231	40 250	1.7	32.3	26.8	23 419	111.0	4 423	19 269	41.2	110 700	26.2	13.7
Jacksonville	25 496	46 768	3.0	26.1	13.7	366 273	18.6	43 167	315 619	60.3	138 500	25.0	12.2
Jupiter	45 595	70 240	10.3	15.7	5.9	29 825	41.7	5 905	24 257	72.5	268 800	27.2	13.3
Kissimmee	16 943	35 452	1.2	32.2	21.9	26 275	33.6	5 549	20 616	44.0	112 900	28.9	13.3
Lakeland	22 449	39 238	1.9	29.9	14.4	48 218	23.3	7 460	39 497	55.3	109 700	23.7	13.3
Lake Worth	18 768	37 036	1.5	34.3	25.5	16 473	3.6	3 515	11 824	49.0	131 600	30.3	14.6
Largo	26 635	39 722	1.8	29.3	10.6	46 859	16.4	8 837	35 683	56.2	90 000	24.5	14.6
Lauderdale Lakes	15 362	33 070	0.5	38.2	20.9	15 000	4.5	3 109	11 328	58.8	87 000	38.3	18.6
Lauderhill	17 940	37 691	0.6	31.5	19.7	29 519	15.0	4 693	23 265	57.5	97 700	32.9	18.3
Margate	22 530	42 599	1.7	27.0	11.1	24 863	0.5	3 380	20 891	76.3	118 600	31.1	16.8
Melbourne	24 355	40 400	1.8	30.4	12.3	38 955	15.7	4 915	33 083	60.2	113 400	25.3	13.2
Miami	21 724	30 858	3.7	42.3	25.0	183 994	23.9	25 677	152 525	31.6	211 400	35.2	16.2
Miami Beach	43 243	42 547	8.4	32.3	12.9	67 499	13.0	20 331	43 650	35.9	341 000	29.5	20.7
Miami Gardens	16 731	39 545	1.0	31.9	19.1	34 284	NA	2 065	31 365	66.7	129 200	34.7	13.4
Miami Lakes	28 006	65 269	6.5	18.3	8.3	10 698	18.8	2 874	9 741	65.3	298 500	31.6	13.8
Miramar	24 895	64 987	4.2	14.1	8.5	40 294	55.6	2 874	37 439	74.2	194 000	32.5	13.2
North Lauderdale	15 860	42 610	0.3	25.1	18.3	14 709	28.1	1 732	12 047	55.0	102 500	32.6	16.0
North Miami	18 154	36 776	2.3	35.2	24.4	22 110	-0.7	2 835	18 038	49.0	146 300	34.5	15.2
North Miami Beach	18 581	38 130	1.3	32.0	18.9	16 402	7.1	1 990	14 065	54.3	142 600	33.0	16.0
North Port	24 241	50 855	1.7	22.0	8.3	27 986	170.2	5 555	22 622	73.5	123 500	24.1	12.6
Oakland Park	24 615	45 137	1.6	25.9	16.9	20 076	38.1	2 577	17 031	55.3	150 600	29.7	13.2
Ocala	22 399	37 442	3.6	34.5	17.7	26 764	29.8	3 661	21 922	52.8	118 900	25.7	13.8
Ocoee	25 386	62 487	3.6	13.3	9.0	12 802	53.8	1 010	12 049	74.4	171 500	26.6	12.0
Orlando	25 664	41 901	3.3	29.2	15.6	121 254	36.8	18 733	102 570	37.4	158 600	27.1	13.9
Ormond Beach	31 821	49 000	5.0	23.4	8.1	19 576	12.8	2 514	15 550	77.8	166 300	25.9	13.1
Oviedo	28 457	82 259	5.8	9.1	5.0	11 720	28.9	595	10 012	80.3	222 900	23.7	10.5
Palm Bay	20 458	43 064	1.1	25.7	12.6	45 220	37.3	5 738	37 249	73.5	101 800	26.2	10.8
Palm Beach Gardens	50 600	67 102	12.5	15.2	3.8	27 663	52.6	4 859	22 675	71.2	284 600	26.5	14.7
Palm Coast	22 335	47 634	1.8	22.9	11.2	35 058	132.0	5 253	27 466	79.4	158 800	28.7	12.5
Panama City	22 431	37 453	2.1	34.0	17.1	17 438	5.5	2 646	14 781	49.1	133 800	23.6	13.6
Pembroke Pines	28 498	61 539	3.7	20.0	6.5	61 703	11.6	4 830	56 308	73.1	202 800	28.3	19.0
Pensacola	28 844	46 424	3.6	26.6	10.6	26 848	-0.3	3 256	22 062	59.5	144 100	23.7	12.8
Pinellas Park	22 887	41 877	0.8	27.0	10.1	23 458	7.5	2 835	20 911	65.9	108 200	26.6	15.2
Plantation	35 524	66 886	7.0	14.8	7.4	37 587	7.1	3 397	33 521	66.4	236 900	27.2	13.8
Plant City	22 429	45 794	2.4	25.2	14.8	13 732	16.5	1 493	12 329	56.9	127 700	24.5	11.5
Pompano Beach	24 829	40 534	2.9	31.5	18.2	55 885	25.9	13 703	41 138	55.5	154 900	30.1	15.3
Port Orange	26 003	44 981	2.8	24.9	6.9	27 972	34.2	3 131	23 941	75.1	138 400	26.0	13.3
Port St. Lucie	23 240	48 898	2.1	21.9	12.0	70 877	92.0	9 975	59 101	77.8	131 700	28.5	13.6
Riviera Beach	23 652	38 300	2.7	31.6	19.4	17 124	19.4	4 744	11 950	55.2	128 900	29.2	13.5
Royal Palm Beach	26 299	66 620	3.7	15.8	6.6	12 854	58.1	1 298	11 188	79.7	184 400	26.2	12.3
St. Cloud	20 522	48 911	1.4	24.3	13.3	14 544	68.6	1 979	13 102	69.6	117 000	26.7	14.4
St. Petersburg	28 670	45 483	3.6	26.9	11.9	129 401	3.9	20 586	105 071	58.7	140 100	26.7	13.9
Sanford	18 298	39 776	0.6	30.8	17.8	23 061	49.0	2 943	18 267	56.6	104 400	28.1	12.0
Sarasota	29 969	41 670	5.1	31.1	15.6	29 151	8.2	6 009	22 773	53.2	157 700	29.9	14.6
Sunrise	23 915	49 370	1.8	24.9	9.7	37 609	5.5	5 116	31 343	69.6	137 300	29.6	20.0
Tallahassee	23 942	39 407	3.0	34.6	16.1	84 248	23.2	9 433	74 108	40.6	176 900	23.3	10.9
Tamarac	24 938	43 250	1.5	27.1	8.1	32 794	10.3	4 379	27 011	72.6	116 600	29.8	18.4
Tampa	29 704	43 740	5.8	30.6	17.0	157 130	15.8	21 175	139 337	49.6	157 500	25.2	12.1
Titusville	23 221	40 420	1.5	29.0	15.3	22 729	18.2	3 712	18 438	65.9	91 600	24.6	11.1
Wellington	36 106	81 481	9.7	10.9	5.9	22 685	54.2	3 026	19 770	79.4	293 900	27.1	13.8
Weston	40 452	91 613	15.6	10.9	6.1	24 394	28.9	3 174	21 317	72.3	382 900	27.5	15.3
West Palm Beach	29 882	45 027	4.8	26.7	15.1	54 179	34.1	11 267	41 411	50.5	173 000	30.6	14.9
Winter Garden	26 602	58 355	4.8	17.4	5.9	13 260	128.8	1 385	12 213	71.0	194 500	27.4	12.2
Winter Haven	21 448	36 602	1.7	34.3	15.4	17 037	22.3	2 714	13 907	58.5	100 300	27.3	13.0
Winter Park	49 449	56 995	15.0	23.9	6.6	13 626	18.2	1 398	11 747	63.1	308 600	23.8	13.7
Winter Springs	31 258	64 038	6.8	15.2	8.2	14 052	14.3	951	11 214	77.9	202 600	24.6	11.5

1. Based on population estimated by the American Community Survey.   2. Includes units rented or sold but not occupied.   3. Specified owner-occupied units; $1,000,000 represents $1,000,000 or more   4. 50.0 represents 50 percent or more.   5. 10.0 represents 10 percent or less.

Table D. Cities — Housing, Labor Force, and Employment

City	Occupied housing units, 2010–2014 (cont.)				Migration, 2010–2014		Civilian labor force, 2015				Civilian employment[4], 2010–2014			
									Unemployment			Percent		
	Percent renter occupied	Median gross rent[1]	Median gross rent as a percent of income[2]	Percent with no vehicle available	Percent who lived in the same house one year ago	Percent who lived outside current city one year ago	Total	Percent change, 2014–2015	Total	Rate[3]	Population age 16 and older	In labor force	Civilian full-year full-time workers	Households with no workers (percent)
	55	56	57	58	59	60	61	62	63	64	65	66	67	68
FLORIDA—Cont'd														
Deerfield Beach............	37.2	1 155	36.1	10.3	81.1	14.8	39 620	0.5	1 881	4.7	64 273	60.4	36.8	35.8
DeLand.......................	44.6	949	40.2	11.2	81.2	15.3	12 694	1.0	759	6.0	22 335	49.0	29.6	41.5
Delray Beach...............	36.1	1 258	34.4	8.0	84.2	11.5	34 217	0.9	1 618	4.7	54 160	62.0	36.1	35.0
Deltona......................	22.0	1 075	36.9	3.8	89.8	7.6	42 612	0.4	2 604	6.1	67 109	58.2	37.4	31.1
Doral.........................	45.4	1 712	34.6	2.0	80.5	13.0	27 706	1.6	1 283	4.6	35 714	67.6	50.2	11.0
Dunedin......................	37.5	980	31.9	9.7	84.0	11.0	17 939	0.8	863	4.8	30 581	57.9	36.2	40.7
Fort Lauderdale.............	47.1	1 065	34.8	10.1	79.3	12.7	93 954	0.4	4 569	4.9	144 273	65.5	39.3	29.6
Fort Myers..................	52.9	810	34.5	12.0	74.5	16.7	31 262	2.8	1 609	5.1	53 467	53.1	29.8	38.0
Fort Pierce.................	54.7	790	46.1	17.7	84.9	9.7	18 097	-0.8	1 599	8.8	33 057	52.7	26.0	43.8
Gainesville.................	62.0	851	39.3	12.2	65.9	18.4	64 769	0.2	3 062	4.7	112 466	56.7	28.5	29.7
Greenacres..................	34.9	1 131	36.6	5.6	84.0	13.6	20 902	1.2	841	4.0	30 395	68.2	42.1	27.5
Hallandale Beach...........	43.7	1 080	39.3	12.5	78.8	15.4	18 100	-0.3	1 066	5.9	33 136	57.2	33.5	41.2
Hialeah......................	51.5	1 002	45.1	12.8	93.6	3.2	113 045	1.2	7 561	6.7	195 785	58.3	37.0	29.4
Hollywood...................	40.1	1 036	37.4	8.2	82.8	11.1	77 996	0.2	4 032	5.2	119 105	66.2	39.5	27.2
Homestead..................	58.8	1 064	41.6	15.2	77.0	13.5	29 866	1.4	1 890	6.3	45 563	65.8	39.9	21.8
Jacksonville................	39.7	932	33.5	8.5	80.9	6.4	438 602	1.0	24 450	5.6	662 541	65.8	40.3	26.3
Jupiter......................	27.5	1 407	33.7	4.7	87.3	8.8	32 252	1.5	1 257	3.9	47 742	63.3	41.9	30.8
Kissimmee...................	56.0	938	40.9	8.8	85.6	10.4	35 030	1.5	1 966	5.6	49 228	66.4	38.7	22.2
Lakeland.....................	44.7	868	33.0	10.0	79.3	12.1	44 436	0.4	2 564	5.8	81 173	54.7	32.7	38.0
Lake Worth..................	51.0	953	39.1	13.5	77.9	12.0	19 015	1.1	908	4.8	28 551	72.0	39.8	26.9
Largo........................	43.8	909	32.8	11.4	79.0	16.5	38 874	0.8	1 816	4.7	67 070	58.0	36.0	40.5
Lauderdale Lakes..........	41.2	986	42.5	15.5	85.9	12.1	16 779	0.1	956	5.7	26 469	68.2	33.3	29.5
Lauderhill..................	42.5	990	40.6	12.0	82.1	13.1	35 157	0.5	1 981	5.6	54 324	66.9	35.9	27.3
Margate......................	23.7	1 166	36.5	9.5	86.7	11.4	29 291	0.2	1 531	5.2	45 630	65.2	37.4	30.2
Melbourne...................	39.8	833	32.7	7.1	83.3	12.0	37 016	-0.2	2 163	5.8	65 529	57.3	34.1	37.3
Miami........................	68.4	958	39.8	20.8	83.7	7.9	213 376	0.5	12 956	6.1	346 830	61.5	38.6	30.5
Miami Beach................	64.1	1 115	36.0	26.6	74.9	14.1	55 960	1.3	2 590	4.6	78 042	68.1	46.0	26.8
Miami Gardens..............	33.3	1 069	45.0	8.3	91.5	5.9	53 259	-0.7	4 551	8.5	87 371	62.8	37.4	25.3
Miami Lakes	34.7	1 356	36.4	4.2	93.7	5.0	16 012	1.5	854	5.3	24 215	63.0	44.6	20.5
Miramar.....................	25.8	1 448	37.9	2.8	88.1	8.5	73 737	0.0	3 529	4.8	98 882	72.5	47.2	10.6
North Lauderdale	45.0	1 198	39.6	6.8	80.9	15.1	23 026	-0.1	1 101	4.8	32 161	72.4	42.2	16.4
North Miami................	51.0	971	45.5	12.1	84.5	12.1	30 542	-1.5	2 190	7.2	48 884	64.0	37.7	21.9
North Miami Beach	45.7	974	41.0	12.6	87.4	9.1	22 573	-0.1	1 451	6.4	34 729	66.1	40.1	23.6
North Port..................	26.5	945	28.5	4.0	84.8	9.0	26 823	2.1	1 462	5.5	47 964	55.7	35.3	37.9
Oakland Park	44.7	1 076	37.1	8.5	79.0	16.3	25 364	0.5	1 109	4.4	34 619	75.0	43.2	21.4
Ocala........................	47.2	808	34.2	11.1	75.4	14.6	24 541	-0.6	1 414	5.8	44 544	56.8	34.1	36.5
Ocoee........................	25.6	1 165	29.2	4.5	86.5	11.4	23 232	1.8	955	4.1	28 748	71.6	45.9	18.4
Orlando......................	62.6	999	34.3	8.7	72.7	15.5	154 078	1.5	7 071	4.6	200 764	72.6	44.8	21.2
Ormond Beach..............	22.2	981	37.0	5.7	89.7	8.1	18 097	0.6	915	5.1	33 007	48.7	28.5	43.7
Oviedo.......................	19.7	1 321	32.5	1.1	88.7	9.8	20 631	1.6	840	4.1	26 698	71.0	44.6	13.5
Palm Bay....................	26.5	929	38.1	4.2	85.0	8.9	49 611	-0.6	3 021	6.1	83 866	58.7	34.4	32.2
Palm Beach Gardens....	28.8	1 403	31.2	4.5	84.2	12.1	27 077	1.4	1 022	3.8	43 200	58.9	38.6	34.8
Palm Coast.................	20.6	1 083	32.8	4.0	88.7	6.6	34 590	0.5	2 128	6.2	63 900	48.4	29.1	43.2
Panama City................	50.9	842	34.3	12.2	75.8	14.2	17 282	-0.3	1 030	6.0	29 215	59.4	33.8	33.7
Pembroke Pines............	26.9	1 411	36.8	7.3	86.1	9.8	87 880	0.3	4 051	4.6	128 266	66.6	43.0	25.3
Pensacola...................	40.5	847	30.2	9.5	80.9	11.7	27 058	0.1	1 258	4.6	43 436	64.2	38.9	31.6
Pinellas Park	34.1	944	32.3	9.2	87.9	9.3	25 392	0.8	1 076	4.2	42 043	59.2	38.4	34.6
Plantation..................	33.6	1 397	30.7	3.8	82.8	13.1	52 490	0.4	2 237	4.3	71 878	69.2	46.2	19.5
Plant City..................	43.1	864	32.0	5.5	82.5	9.6	18 766	0.8	925	4.9	26 913	65.9	42.1	25.7
Pompano Beach...........	44.5	1 075	40.5	11.8	79.4	14.1	50 240	0.5	2 593	5.2	85 759	58.1	34.9	36.7
Port Orange................	24.9	991	30.8	3.7	85.8	10.9	29 415	0.5	1 380	4.7	48 605	53.4	32.4	39.3
Port St. Lucie..............	22.2	1 173	37.3	3.7	83.2	9.7	83 457	0.7	4 370	5.2	133 550	61.8	36.4	31.8
Riviera Beach...............	44.8	1 038	43.2	11.6	85.4	8.6	15 878	0.5	910	5.7	26 350	65.0	36.7	30.4
Royal Palm Beach	20.3	1 376	33.5	3.1	87.9	8.3	20 116	1.4	855	4.3	27 453	68.4	45.7	17.8
St. Cloud....................	30.4	1 110	31.6	6.0	84.2	11.4	20 880	1.8	965	4.6	30 823	63.0	38.2	28.6
St. Petersburg	41.3	927	32.9	10.3	82.9	8.9	135 754	0.6	6 277	4.6	207 208	64.5	40.8	29.5
Sanford......................	43.4	938	36.9	7.6	83.5	11.2	27 144	1.2	1 508	5.6	42 391	62.7	34.9	26.9
Sarasota.....................	46.8	920	32.3	12.5	77.5	13.7	27 020	2.0	1 218	4.5	45 250	58.1	32.7	37.4
Sunrise......................	30.4	1 238	32.6	8.5	85.8	11.3	50 467	0.5	2 545	5.0	71 475	68.6	42.8	25.3
Tallahassee.................	59.4	921	39.2	8.4	65.1	15.7	97 468	-1.3	5 028	5.2	156 854	65.6	34.7	25.1
Tamarac.....................	27.4	1 150	34.5	8.2	81.1	15.5	33 334	0.2	1 749	5.2	53 440	61.0	36.7	35.3
Tampa........................	50.4	956	33.4	11.3	78.6	11.3	186 819	0.8	9 645	5.2	280 239	65.0	40.7	27.0
Titusville....................	34.1	825	33.8	8.7	81.1	10.1	20 023	0.0	1 244	6.2	36 567	54.7	32.3	41.4
Wellington..................	20.6	1 440	34.1	2.2	86.6	10.5	32 723	1.2	1 344	4.1	45 991	67.0	44.0	19.4
Weston	27.7	1 886	30.2	2.2	83.9	10.4	35 452	0.6	1 470	4.1	49 397	67.5	42.9	15.3
West Palm Beach	49.5	1 056	34.5	10.1	78.9	12.7	55 688	1.2	2 591	4.7	84 522	64.0	39.5	29.2
Winter Garden.............	29.0	969	34.5	3.5	86.6	9.0	20 146	1.9	832	4.1	27 677	69.5	46.8	17.0
Winter Haven	41.5	811	34.8	11.8	81.6	12.9	15 388	0.7	959	6.2	28 456	53.4	30.1	42.5
Winter Park.................	36.9	1 042	32.8	10.1	81.6	14.7	14 288	1.9	658	4.6	23 935	55.4	36.2	34.6
Winter Springs..............	22.1	1 086	30.6	2.1	87.1	10.8	18 624	1.6	859	4.6	27 293	67.7	39.4	20.8

1. $2,000 represents $2,000 or more.   2. 50.0 represents 50 percent or more.   3. Percent of civilian labor force.   4. Persons 16 years old and over.

Table D. Cities — Construction, Wholesale Trade, and Retail Trade

City	Value of residential construction authorized by building permits, 2015			Wholesale trade,[1] 2012				Retail trade,[2] 2012			
	New construction ($1,000)	Number of housing units	Percent single family	Number of establishments	Number of employees	Sales (mil dol)	Annual payroll (mil dol)	Number of establishments	Number of employees	Sales (mil dol)	Annual payroll (mil dol)
	69	70	71	72	73	74	75	76	77	78	79
FLORIDA—Cont'd											
Deerfield Beach............	3 221	10	100.0	218	2 314	10 619.2	148.1	298	3 593	1 084.7	99.1
DeLand........................	121 450	347	100.0	45	209	116.2	10.7	175	2 527	752.9	66.0
Delray Beach...............	77 269	363	35.5	112	564	548.9	32.4	380	4 553	1 576.5	139.0
Deltona......................	18 223	48	100.0	10	D	D	D	97	1 566	368.2	35.7
Doral.........................	167 863	802	70.8	1 540	13 960	31 206.3	805.1	445	6 595	2 137.1	195.8
Dunedin......................	1 036	4	100.0	29	265	114.0	8.9	123	1 010	233.2	25.7
Fort Lauderdale...........	66 287	128	96.9	571	5 787	4 332.2	299.5	1 161	12 021	4 045.3	367.8
Fort Myers..................	247 659	1 229	73.6	167	2 206	1 030.4	96.2	688	9 914	2 678.6	251.3
Fort Pierce.................	7 613	26	73.1	35	360	225.0	16.8	220	2 803	919.2	77.6
Gainesville..................	25 420	355	20.0	135	1 457	1 010.0	67.6	547	8 426	2 169.4	189.1
Greenacres..................	5 180	26	100.0	27	108	35.5	5.1	94	1 481	469.2	42.6
Hallandale Beach.........	3 486	19	42.1	80	429	248.2	20.4	137	1 858	437.1	44.0
Hialeah......................	16 402	126	59.5	515	3 886	1 380.5	132.7	1 060	10 595	2 456.0	240.2
Hollywood...................	224 945	1 112	3.5	285	2 279	1 521.9	131.5	573	6 316	1 916.1	159.0
Homestead..................	112 997	672	62.2	41	288	179.1	11.0	182	2 386	656.3	51.3
Jacksonville................	698 352	4 258	55.2	1 075	18 668	18 797.6	1 056.4	3 011	43 471	12 498.4	1 114.5
Jupiter.......................	80 737	284	78.5	100	669	352.8	36.1	257	2 886	673.8	77.3
Kissimmee..................	74 858	365	93.4	49	D	D	D	366	4 823	1 248.2	107.1
Lakeland.....................	66 019	251	96.8	156	2 930	7 572.0	187.5	559	8 370	2 282.0	200.0
Lake Worth..................	5 691	39	100.0	43	331	126.8	21.2	120	888	256.9	24.5
Largo.........................	201 167	891	92.0	102	D	D	D	330	4 311	1 033.1	112.4
Lauderdale Lakes..........	0	0	0.0	20	102	33.4	2.8	73	1 072	253.1	26.1
Lauderhill...................	1 870	19	100.0	41	D	D	D	198	1 478	364.1	37.0
Margate	12 612	285	1.1	62	411	354.4	17.4	171	2 476	889.2	78.1
Melbourne	54 830	157	100.0	102	1 461	820.5	80.6	464	6 067	1 626.6	155.3
Miami........................	1 158 081	6 490	1.5	1 440	8 474	7 906.8	371.9	2 398	21 175	6 476.3	551.4
Miami Beach	103 603	84	89.3	151	415	275.6	19.3	561	5 912	1 556.8	145.4
Miami Gardens.............	14 118	124	95.2	180	3 106	2 120.4	149.9	302	4 416	1 685.6	138.4
Miami Lakes	2 403	5	100.0	113	1 305	835.1	68.0	72	1 372	559.3	49.3
Miramar	35 611	405	14.3	198	2 748	2 686.5	197.4	198	3 297	1 659.5	96.3
North Lauderdale	0	0	0.0	7	D	D	D	70	961	241.1	24.2
North Miami................	3 842	9	100.0	76	364	210.0	18.5	188	1 749	462.3	46.5
North Miami Beach	6 761	48	100.0	57	156	76.7	6.6	191	2 470	1 125.3	69.9
North Port..................	212 874	851	100.0	23	133	41.1	3.9	80	1 454	375.3	35.2
Oakland Park	1 265	9	100.0	114	811	360.5	49.2	252	2 047	654.6	55.5
Ocala.........................	25 741	110	100.0	166	2 285	1 310.3	109.1	631	9 325	2 756.9	228.6
Ocoee........................	61 223	370	35.1	32	632	675.2	40.5	160	2 639	564.9	54.3
Orlando......................	485 663	2 586	32.9	634	8 653	5 585.7	443.6	1 580	27 103	8 359.0	641.1
Ormond Beach.............	45 192	138	100.0	44	767	287.7	31.1	195	2 299	579.6	55.4
Oviedo........................	57 894	172	100.0	31	D	D	D	148	2 331	405.9	44.8
Palm Bay....................	77 747	323	100.0	32	202	71.9	8.4	170	2 500	736.5	63.0
Palm Beach Gardens...	89 706	261	64.8	68	341	138.0	14.8	348	6 747	1 555.8	167.7
Palm Coast.................	101 957	355	100.0	36	100	27.0	3.2	140	2 406	588.2	58.2
Panama City...............	7 000	19	100.0	68	765	247.4	31.0	338	4 441	1 199.2	113.9
Pembroke Pines...........	50 029	419	18.9	202	702	334.8	32.1	577	10 690	3 250.8	264.3
Pensacola...................	11 346	47	100.0	67	641	246.2	27.8	418	6 109	1 366.9	130.7
Pinellas Park	16 006	106	43.4	166	2 065	728.0	83.2	284	3 773	1 371.7	103.5
Plantation	15 037	55	36.4	120	490	277.2	31.8	348	5 590	1 724.9	134.2
Plant City...................	24 798	250	48.0	79	1 769	1 236.6	70.7	157	2 140	698.8	53.4
Pompano Beach...........	59 195	922	26.9	454	6 291	4 882.2	310.0	624	8 020	4 203.6	258.0
Port Orange................	42 927	130	100.0	34	D	D	D	164	2 608	585.4	58.6
Port St. Lucie	141 155	1 014	77.2	81	489	148.1	19.5	334	8 054	2 257.6	240.5
Riviera Beach..............	4 682	8	100.0	102	2 211	1 640.8	133.5	106	878	354.3	29.7
Royal Palm Beach	12 008	36	100.0	32	184	124.2	7.4	154	3 525	975.5	88.3
St. Cloud....................	206 948	740	100.0	12	D	D	D	127	1 765	490.8	41.8
St. Petersburg	194 657	1 325	22.6	187	2 580	1 218.2	128.5	905	13 444	4 893.4	361.6
Sanford......................	16 640	57	100.0	88	1 374	538.6	64.0	358	5 781	1 758.4	148.0
Sarasota.....................	174 932	728	15.9	88	651	303.2	32.0	505	5 274	1 363.5	141.3
Sunrise......................	34 857	427	2.3	262	2 458	1 729.8	140.2	544	10 882	2 776.1	241.5
Tallahassee	63 467	460	65.4	176	1 987	1 622.5	155.3	854	13 278	3 039.5	290.5
Tamarac.....................	26 055	259	96.9	60	1 056	609.3	50.8	131	2 294	530.4	78.0
Tampa........................	569 326	3 155	33.2	646	9 863	9 457.0	490.2	1 878	24 934	7 449.8	673.5
Titusville	20 157	82	100.0	21	236	100.8	11.2	168	2 468	612.6	59.0
Wellington..................	53 809	336	10.1	78	239	386.9	12.4	243	3 279	570.2	69.5
Weston	451	2	100.0	279	1 712	2 552.4	102.4	134	2 210	864.1	70.8
West Palm Beach	44 426	268	63.1	146	1 663	1 282.1	90.9	535	8 040	2 939.5	248.0
Winter Garden.............	225 554	537	100.0	41	446	359.2	15.9	158	2 483	603.2	53.6
Winter Haven	56 315	354	100.0	45	1 427	534.7	34.0	201	2 939	801.8	72.5
Winter Park	43 577	88	100.0	52	335	233.1	16.8	232	2 936	816.0	80.3
Winter Springs.............	66 309	218	100.0	28	125	30.6	5.5	43	453	182.0	13.4

1. Merchant wholesalers except manufacturers' sales branches and offices. 2. Establishments with payroll.

Table D. Cities — **Real Estate, Professional Services, and Manufacturing**

City	Real estate and rental and leasing, 2012				Professional, scientific, and technical services,[1] 2012				Manufacturing, 2012			
	Number of establishments	Number of employees	Receipts (mil dol)	Annual payroll (mil dol)	Number of establishments	Number of employees	Receipts (mil dol)	Annual payroll (mil dol)	Number of establishments	Number of employees	Receipts (mil dol)	Annual payroll (mil dol)
	80	81	82	83	84	85	86	87	88	89	90	91
FLORIDA—Cont'd												
Deerfield Beach	122	846	131.8	33.0	338	2 736	400.9	136.7	107	2 166	751.5	109.1
DeLand	56	207	30.3	5.3	131	573	65.2	21.3	57	1 798	358.7	76.5
Delray Beach	152	673	85.9	19.7	467	1 971	299.1	98.3	73	585	136.6	21.5
Deltona	18	24	3.5	0.6	67	193	17.8	5.4	3	D	D	D
Doral	212	1 180	264.7	49.9	560	D	D	D	127	2 765	533.1	112.8
Dunedin	42	87	23.3	4.0	154	544	91.0	26.6	18	234	D	11.1
Fort Lauderdale	708	3 644	1 279.5	186.4	2 319	14 924	2 716.3	1 134.6	282	3 899	975.0	177.2
Fort Myers	212	1 133	239.2	40.0	486	6 661	1 451.1	576.0	93	1 720	396.6	75.2
Fort Pierce	61	221	41.6	7.7	137	D	D	D	26	495	108.8	21.3
Gainesville	201	1 076	156.0	32.4	472	2 740	317.7	130.2	86	1 558	587.6	82.4
Greenacres	22	55	23.2	2.4	96	629	52.3	17.5	4	56	D	1.4
Hallandale Beach	92	188	43.0	7.3	183	663	109.6	34.7	34	334	52.9	11.4
Hialeah	250	682	126.3	20.8	348	1 631	208.5	68.1	436	4 833	837.4	174.1
Hollywood	297	3 294	231.6	94.1	905	3 385	541.2	200.0	96	1 125	249.1	44.8
Homestead	43	141	17.7	3.4	80	344	33.6	13.4	19	221	D	8.6
Jacksonville	1 093	6 806	1 758.4	308.0	2 865	28 566	5 420.9	2 114.3	579	21 616	10 146.3	1 252.8
Jupiter	160	862	98.9	30.5	452	D	D	D	57	777	D	68.0
Kissimmee	147	584	102.0	15.8	177	811	73.7	22.8	28	125	D	4.2
Lakeland	194	1 027	197.6	34.5	357	D	D	D	82	3 922	1 614.7	155.8
Lake Worth	43	88	31.0	3.3	120	D	D	D	45	244	36.8	9.1
Largo	115	569	108.6	20.9	220	2 075	310.6	103.4	107	2 541	531.7	128.3
Lauderdale Lakes	20	282	50.3	10.1	28	D	D	D	8	32	2.3	0.6
Lauderhill	56	635	134.3	22.4	98	342	46.2	12.8	19	158	D	5.5
Margate	51	171	34.4	4.5	133	648	71.1	23.4	30	154	14.8	5.1
Melbourne	170	628	103.9	19.7	399	3 608	775.2	251.9	96	5 615	2 026.1	392.0
Miami	1 169	4 273	1 121.7	207.2	3 517	D	D	D	343	3 948	887.3	142.4
Miami Beach	457	1 556	402.9	70.2	661	D	D	D	29	99	13.4	2.9
Miami Gardens	69	266	70.9	9.7	78	335	30.7	18.5	68	1 871	338.3	79.1
Miami Lakes	85	607	137.0	28.8	270	1 165	271.1	70.2	24	2 155	578.1	148.6
Miramar	72	466	80.6	15.6	270	D	D	D	33	825	209.5	37.4
North Lauderdale	18	70	25.2	2.4	40	D	D	D	11	44		1.5
North Miami	90	276	54.4	9.5	158	521	84.3	25.4	27	468	51.4	17.4
North Miami Beach	72	239	34.3	9.2	213	734	97.9	31.4	23	247	D	12.8
North Port	29	50	6.0	2.0	62	137	13.0	4.1	12	247	D	9.7
Oakland Park	96	430	59.5	12.9	220	D	D	D	103	724	157.5	34.1
Ocala	171	897	130.2	27.8	383	1 854	216.2	81.0	105	3 819	1 196.5	169.6
Ocoee	30	241	37.3	8.6	92	412	38.8	12.8	13	192	D	4.7
Orlando	762	7 122	2 384.5	297.4	2 017	D	D	D	253	11 032	4 157.9	783.3
Ormond Beach	74	338	53.8	11.0	172	654	98.2	30.8	40	820	116.8	32.7
Oviedo	66	186	41.7	5.7	140	D	D	D	13	44	D	1.7
Palm Bay	54	143	24.5	4.2	99	D	D	D	39	8 936	2 317.2	672.1
Palm Beach Gardens	138	730	253.4	36.1	499	D	D	D	24	489	D	39.2
Palm Coast	98	D	D	D	128	288	42.8	12.6	21	428	D	20.4
Panama City	98	488	90.8	15.9	199	D	D	D	39	1 448	739.4	92.9
Pembroke Pines	159	506	135.3	19.8	563	1 725	276.4	78.8	46	249	44.4	9.8
Pensacola	122	590	114.5	18.9	450	D	D	D	49	766	361.0	41.0
Pinellas Park	67	263	56.7	11.4	167	D	D	D	238	7 383	2 189.6	333.8
Plantation	198	1 034	102.6	38.4	723	D	D	D	41	268	29.7	10.0
Plant City	46	146	41.2	4.9	91	D	D	D	49	1 795	748.9	76.0
Pompano Beach	228	930	191.6	35.6	471	1 768	287.0	89.9	250	5 908	1 497.3	326.0
Port Orange	94	362	53.1	10.2	120	901	112.2	36.9	18	210	28.5	7.4
Port St. Lucie	139	353	59.0	10.1	277	D	D	D	48	840	332.3	38.3
Riviera Beach	44	312	36.6	10.6	49	464	52.6	14.6	69	1 424	463.1	63.0
Royal Palm Beach	23	38	10.3	1.6	117	547	59.2	26.1	5	15	D	0.6
St. Cloud	43	132	15.4	2.8	53	163	14.0	4.5	15	163	D	7.1
St. Petersburg	347	1 614	298.8	58.1	1 158	11 396	1 508.6	594.7	148	4 906	1 377.7	262.0
Sanford	70	417	107.4	13.6	128	D	D	D	59	1 596	652.5	69.0
Sarasota	242	768	190.2	30.9	622	D	D	D	57	552	D	30.1
Sunrise	122	492	115.4	20.6	364	2 464	366.1	135.5	71	495	165.2	25.8
Tallahassee	331	1 808	256.7	54.4	1 158	D	D	D	77	1 297	382.7	66.0
Tamarac	63	250	47.5	7.7	166	553	71.6	28.5	20	370	52.6	15.1
Tampa	856	5 003	1 353.4	236.3	2 675	31 236	6 007.1	2 573.3	303	5 894	2 751.2	266.4
Titusville	35	121	19.4	3.1	95	565	76.9	27.8	37	433	43.6	15.4
Wellington	117	203	54.6	8.9	319	776	116.3	37.7	22	191	D	5.8
Weston	165	346	86.0	13.6	485	1 320	1 009.4	95.4	20	153	D	5.0
West Palm Beach	260	1 144	229.8	51.3	1 119	D	D	D	103	1 822	343.3	103.7
Winter Garden	63	199	43.3	7.2	110	377	39.9	14.1	26	470	186.1	17.1
Winter Haven	59	305	69.0	10.4	120	497	56.7	24.6	28	513	293.4	26.9
Winter Park	134	416	89.2	15.7	476	2 577	409.0	162.9	32	185	D	7.5
Winter Springs	42	D	D	D	101	230	27.4	10.9	13	82	12.8	3.0

1. Establishments subject to federal tax.

Table D. Cities — Accommodation and Food Services, Arts, Entertainment, and Recreation, and Health Care and Social Assistance

City	Accommodation and food services, 2012				Arts, entertainment, and recreation,[1] 2012				Health care and social assistance,[1] 2012			
	Number of establishments	Number of employees	Sales (mil dol)	Annual payroll (mil dol)	Number of establishments	Number of employees	Receipts (mil dol)	Annual payroll (mil dol)	Number of establishments	Number of employees	Receipts (mil dol)	Annual payroll (mil dol)
	92	93	94	95	96	97	98	99	100	101	102	103
FLORIDA—Cont'd												
Deerfield Beach	155	2 717	163.2	44.0	38	241	25.1	6.5	168	D	D	D
DeLand	94	1 414	61.1	17.5	13	123	6.2	2.2	120	1 769	166.1	69.1
Delray Beach	211	4 061	273.6	79.2	49	255	28.5	6.0	383	4 546	761.1	220.0
Deltona	40	500	25.4	5.7	7	D	D	D	84	805	65.8	24.4
Doral	228	3 851	320.6	83.4	41	D	D	D	211	1 991	219.2	60.8
Dunedin	100	1 271	62.0	16.6	10	34	2.2	0.6	116	D	D	D
Fort Lauderdale	710	20 279	1 934.4	464.8	144	962	172.8	31.6	863	12 461	1 320.6	599.4
Fort Myers	282	5 994	305.0	89.8	33	1 294	66.5	24.3	374	5 692	734.2	298.9
Fort Pierce	126	2 222	105.7	30.7	11	241	26.7	8.7	161	3 140	489.6	153.0
Gainesville	380	8 375	391.2	105.3	43	854	29.3	8.4	379	6 465	967.8	305.0
Greenacres	58	939	46.3	12.2	11	56	2.6	0.7	84	622	60.8	18.0
Hallandale Beach	85	2 230	121.5	35.0	31	D	D	D	148	D	D	D
Hialeah	347	3 876	238.1	61.1	35	180	14.7	3.0	784	9 203	1 171.2	341.0
Hollywood	330	5 683	427.6	115.8	88	1 142	170.7	30.4	544	D	D	D
Homestead	93	1 813	102.5	26.2	8	D	D	D	148	1 687	165.8	54.6
Jacksonville	1 765	33 931	1 820.0	501.7	204	4 730	435.0	228.5	2 029	D	D	D
Jupiter	151	3 307	179.7	61.8	45	1 168	82.3	31.5	326	D	D	D
Kissimmee	209	5 035	345.2	88.3	19	D	D	D	284	4 309	608.9	218.7
Lakeland	246	5 649	294.2	83.3	19	348	16.8	6.2	352	7 330	896.2	289.6
Lake Worth	63	683	38.8	11.2	15	D	D	D	73	1 043	105.6	40.2
Largo	183	2 788	146.3	39.2	30	D	D	D	242	7 076	803.8	308.4
Lauderdale Lakes	35	391	24.5	6.3	NA	NA	NA	NA	86	1 412	256.4	72.5
Lauderhill	82	944	61.7	14.2	15	D	D	D	127	D	D	D
Margate	98	D	D	D	13	168	7.8	2.5	159	2 272	365.7	109.6
Melbourne	213	4 009	194.2	58.9	27	D	D	D	408	7 860	928.5	375.3
Miami	1 267	26 462	1 914.9	527.4	207	3 993	846.1	359.3	1 679	17 673	2 388.6	733.1
Miami Beach	626	23 117	2 085.9	568.7	114	639	135.8	30.7	404	2 235	306.7	113.0
Miami Gardens	100	1 628	91.0	22.0	22	D	D	D	144	1 173	127.5	45.6
Miami Lakes	54	1 634	101.3	26.2	16	D	D	D	197	D	D	D
Miramar	118	1 660	95.1	23.5	25	D	D	D	223	1 967	419.1	91.0
North Lauderdale	28	364	20.1	5.1	6	23	15.7	1.3	44	D	D	D
North Miami	104	1 478	83.9	21.4	18	113	14.5	2.4	129	2 233	175.9	88.9
North Miami Beach	124	1 833	98.1	26.6	16	280	9.5	1.9	212	D	D	D
North Port	38	682	30.9	9.3	5	D	D	D	44	529	51.6	15.8
Oakland Park	100	1 691	90.7	26.4	14	D	D	D	149	D	D	D
Ocala	251	5 431	277.0	76.1	17	D	D	D	535	8 831	1 199.2	423.3
Ocoee	77	904	48.0	13.4	17	D	D	D	104	D	D	D
Orlando	999	26 376	1 938.1	473.7	144	16 398	2 187.0	457.1	879	11 319	1 616.4	697.7
Ormond Beach	118	2 321	112.8	33.4	28	339	19.2	6.3	226	D	D	D
Oviedo	62	1 202	54.4	15.1	14	115	5.7	1.5	123	D	D	D
Palm Bay	108	1 820	81.1	22.2	15	D	D	D	131	1 612	113.2	50.2
Palm Beach Gardens	143	4 820	235.6	85.0	40	D	D	D	319	3 706	535.7	163.4
Palm Coast	91	D	D	D	17	D	D	D	148	D	D	D
Panama City	167	3 198	158.1	45.4	18	D	D	D	294	6 840	827.5	314.0
Pembroke Pines	285	5 958	330.2	92.6	57	500	31.2	6.7	576	D	D	D
Pensacola	212	5 204	250.7	75.2	15	709	16.7	5.1	343	6 294	856.9	350.2
Pinellas Park	106	1 876	134.8	38.0	13	122	8.7	2.1	136	1 898	203.6	78.2
Plantation	188	3 356	218.5	56.0	51	405	26.1	7.4	586	6 332	923.7	328.2
Plant City	76	D	D	D	6	D	D	D	122	D	D	D
Pompano Beach	249	3 807	258.2	69.0	50	1 455	129.3	42.4	295	3 416	395.6	135.1
Port Orange	103	2 310	99.2	30.7	20	D	D	D	133	D	D	D
Port St. Lucie	204	3 628	180.6	48.3	36	D	D	D	370	5 191	645.7	223.1
Riviera Beach	39	836	62.1	13.2	10	289	18.8	5.1	41	D	D	D
Royal Palm Beach	95	1 883	101.7	28.4	14	140	6.0	2.1	121	1 020	115.9	46.0
St. Cloud	61	1 042	46.1	13.8	5	D	D	D	72	D	D	D
St. Petersburg	525	9 116	540.4	147.3	72	1 850	212.6	143.0	799	8 081	1 079.9	424.7
Sanford	119	2 238	104.8	30.3	15	D	D	D	118	1 977	292.3	101.4
Sarasota	286	6 049	377.5	110.2	41	843	33.5	11.3	449	4 964	632.8	228.5
Sunrise	187	4 135	217.4	61.9	38	D	D	D	260	3 931	557.9	269.7
Tallahassee	588	13 051	593.0	160.9	56	691	72.6	14.7	576	D	D	D
Tamarac	63	926	55.1	12.4	20	187	11.5	3.3	216	3 052	340.0	122.6
Tampa	1 087	25 033	1 655.4	420.6	152	5 489	847.6	350.2	1 345	16 190	2 907.9	955.1
Titusville	95	1 730	81.8	23.1	6	120	6.0	2.0	141	D	D	D
Wellington	105	2 479	107.4	33.3	64	D	D	D	245	D	D	D
Weston	97	2 066	122.1	35.9	26	D	D	D	258	D	D	D
West Palm Beach	356	6 424	390.8	105.9	52	1 061	115.7	33.7	543	8 828	1 360.8	428.4
Winter Garden	62	D	D	D	23	D	D	D	82	938	79.0	29.9
Winter Haven	119	1 878	90.7	26.6	12	D	D	D	163	D	D	D
Winter Park	153	3 518	183.9	59.3	38	D	D	D	307	3 291	428.3	170.9
Winter Springs	36	497	19.9	7.0	19	D	D	D	40	D	D	D

1. Establishments subject to federal tax.

City	Other services[1], 2012				Government employment and payroll, 2012								
					Full-time equivalent employees	March payroll							
						Total (dollars)	Percent of total for:						
	Number of establishments	Number of employees	Receipts (mil dol)	Annual payroll (mil dol)			Administration, judicial, and legal	Police and Corrections	Fire Protection	Highways and transportation	Health and welfare	Natural resources and utilities	Education and libraries
	104	105	106	107	108	109	110	111	112	113	114	115	116
FLORIDA—Cont'd													
Deerfield Beach	154	534	48.1	11.9	608	3 242 063	11.8	0.0	36.3	1.9	4.4	33.5	0.0
DeLand	75	321	23.6	7.6	339	1 192 527	21.8	28.4	14.3	9.1	0.0	23.5	0.0
Delray Beach	180	854	61.4	17.8	762	3 820 363	10.4	30.3	26.8	3.3	0.8	22.2	0.0
Deltona	34	111	6.8	1.9	304	1 105 426	18.7	0.0	34.0	5.8	0.9	31.1	0.0
Doral	141	1 116	195.1	39.7	269	1 347 474	13.6	55.1	0.0	6.7	0.0	8.2	0.0
Dunedin	62	216	14.1	5.4	343	1 392 549	13.9	0.0	21.1	7.5	1.6	43.2	5.9
Fort Lauderdale	617	3 575	397.5	120.8	2 346	13 506 065	10.3	32.6	25.0	0.5	4.6	19.2	0.0
Fort Myers	248	1 391	112.7	34.8	902	3 718 361	15.0	32.5	18.3	2.3	1.3	27.1	0.0
Fort Pierce	78	337	24.3	8.8	620	2 494 232	7.9	24.2	0.0	3.9	1.4	41.0	0.0
Gainesville	188	1 011	72.3	24.6	2 090	9 866 610	13.9	18.0	9.1	12.0	1.5	36.0	0.0
Greenacres	45	127	9.8	3.0	180	934 096	15.0	34.9	33.1	2.2	0.0	2.1	0.0
Hallandale Beach	98	469	33.8	11.8	437	2 597 020	14.5	36.5	23.5	4.3	3.1	15.3	0.0
Hialeah	410	1 449	138.7	34.8	1 644	7 468 317	8.8	33.3	26.1	4.7	2.0	17.7	4.4
Hollywood	256	1 597	140.4	43.2	1 340	7 260 474	10.2	35.7	23.9	4.1	2.7	17.3	0.0
Homestead	51	169	12.9	3.3	375	2 068 115	10.3	44.1	0.0	4.5	0.9	33.5	0.0
Jacksonville	1 274	7 216	656.4	208.6	10 137	46 960 164	11.8	32.9	13.5	4.4	2.3	13.0	2.0
Jupiter	154	899	68.0	26.5	368	1 870 904	18.7	37.5	0.0	8.8	0.2	23.5	0.0
Kissimmee	109	409	27.9	7.1	912	3 901 999	9.5	20.8	12.3	5.7	0.0	51.1	0.0
Lakeland	135	802	69.7	22.6	2 156	10 065 334	11.3	18.9	7.3	4.3	2.7	48.5	1.5
Lake Worth	66	303	22.4	6.9	267	1 224 227	13.4	0.0	0.0	3.3	7.0	68.8	1.3
Largo	167	822	61.4	18.5	823	3 637 673	0.0	25.8	22.2	6.2	1.2	25.5	3.2
Lauderdale Lakes	26	93	10.1	2.1	79	272 557	39.0	0.0	0.0	5.4	19.3	16.1	0.0
Lauderhill	91	328	27.4	7.0	410	2 557 908	13.6	36.5	29.7	0.9	1.2	14.4	0.0
Margate	101	343	34.4	7.5	486	2 719 607	9.8	35.2	29.2	0.0	0.8	18.8	0.0
Melbourne	173	963	67.9	26.7	870	3 653 445	13.0	26.1	21.7	11.7	0.9	24.0	0.0
Miami	815	4 921	337.4	100.8	3 807	18 642 774	9.5	38.6	27.3	0.0	1.0	10.5	0.0
Miami Beach	201	1 617	138.3	31.8	1 861	12 515 293	9.7	37.2	16.1	3.6	1.8	12.8	0.0
Miami Gardens	70	347	28.4	7.8	499	2 715 980	13.8	61.9	0.0	4.0	1.2	10.9	0.0
Miami Lakes	42	596	33.0	12.2	31	181 241	72.9	0.0	0.0	4.7	0.0	22.4	0.0
Miramar	102	488	48.4	15.7	758	4 183 683	11.9	34.2	25.2	4.0	4.9	19.8	0.0
North Lauderdale	29	148	16.0	4.7	153	612 914	14.4	0.0	35.9	6.8	9.5	24.3	0.0
North Miami	96	627	34.0	10.9	424	1 773 052	15.3	47.6	0.0	2.6	1.4	24.9	1.4
North Miami Beach	78	383	28.4	8.4	481	2 472 451	13.4	37.7	0.0	7.0	0.3	17.7	1.3
North Port	38	124	11.1	3.5	511	2 449 083	12.2	24.5	20.8	13.4	0.8	17.6	0.0
Oakland Park	163	497	61.2	13.6	238	1 116 830	16.6	0.0	36.2	5.5	0.7	31.5	2.1
Ocala	186	1 226	89.7	29.7	961	3 935 258	12.7	25.3	17.5	2.8	1.6	37.3	0.0
Ocoee	56	321	19.2	6.5	332	1 430 323	11.3	31.2	19.8	7.4	8.7	21.6	0.0
Orlando	540	4 699	341.4	120.0	2 773	14 180 368	10.1	36.7	27.1	2.9	0.6	17.8	0.0
Ormond Beach	72	368	21.4	7.0	333	1 242 053	17.4	24.9	18.0	7.1	0.0	25.6	0.0
Oviedo	54	224	14.5	4.1	281	1 140 501	10.0	30.2	24.7	5.4	5.6	24.1	0.0
Palm Bay	89	348	28.7	9.3	738	2 860 974	8.8	34.4	22.7	12.9	2.8	18.3	0.0
Palm Beach Gardens	103	689	49.4	17.3	497	2 744 921	6.6	31.5	34.9	3.9	0.0	13.0	0.0
Palm Coast	58	222	15.1	4.1	367	1 477 520	33.5	0.4	16.8	0.0	0.0	49.3	0.0
Panama City	85	526	40.6	11.7	560	1 720 128	8.5	23.2	16.5	21.6	2.5	23.8	0.0
Pembroke Pines	180	882	72.7	21.1	811	4 498 652	8.1	38.2	36.8	0.0	0.5	11.6	0.0
Pensacola	116	886	68.1	20.8	835	3 072 149	10.7	26.9	15.4	10.9	2.2	25.7	4.6
Pinellas Park	135	807	86.2	25.7	495	2 118 077	13.5	29.2	22.2	4.8	5.1	17.7	4.0
Plantation	174	912	96.6	27.0	805	3 820 829	9.6	44.3	2.6	5.4	9.5	17.4	1.1
Plant City	52	319	26.0	8.6	501	1 604 248	10.1	22.3	11.9	11.1	2.3	30.0	3.2
Pompano Beach	268	1 609	151.4	45.6	750	3 541 060	16.9	0.0	31.9	13.8	1.8	23.5	0.0
Port Orange	84	382	25.9	7.6	401	1 524 545	16.2	27.0	16.3	4.0	8.0	26.5	0.0
Port St. Lucie	151	676	48.4	14.7	947	4 712 445	20.9	40.2	0.0	10.1	2.4	19.5	0.0
Riviera Beach	67	390	47.2	14.7	471	2 072 288	16.7	31.0	21.2	5.6	2.0	15.3	1.1
Royal Palm Beach	60	401	25.2	7.5	102	467 299	20.4	0.0	0.0	30.5	0.0	29.3	0.0
St. Cloud	42	183	11.5	3.7	437	1 502 512	12.4	20.0	15.5	4.7	0.0	25.9	0.0
St. Petersburg	399	1 874	149.2	46.8	3 700	17 064 309	4.8	45.6	11.2	0.8	1.0	27.0	1.2
Sanford	99	498	30.5	11.1	571	2 356 239	8.5	26.8	18.3	14.9	0.6	25.6	0.0
Sarasota	176	1 055	66.7	21.9	650	3 097 398	13.3	41.0	0.0	3.7	1.8	26.4	0.0
Sunrise	125	556	39.2	11.0	946	5 498 554	12.5	33.9	21.2	2.4	0.9	25.6	0.0
Tallahassee	317	2 012	143.4	46.5	3 027	13 645 644	13.9	19.4	10.3	12.4	2.1	36.5	0.0
Tamarac	58	193	15.6	4.2	364	1 617 407	25.5	0.0	24.3	8.4	1.2	29.4	0.0
Tampa	787	5 615	363.3	119.3	4 247	22 517 912	11.0	35.8	17.2	4.0	2.4	25.2	0.0
Titusville	72	353	28.7	9.0	452	1 810 027	17.0	25.5	15.5	4.3	0.7	33.4	0.0
Wellington	83	454	38.0	12.5	322	1 314 469	22.1	0.0	0.0	3.5	0.0	40.8	0.0
Weston	88	469	30.5	8.7	10	117 886	74.7	0.0	0.0	0.0	0.0	25.3	0.0
West Palm Beach	237	1 177	88.5	27.3	1 355	7 409 659	10.2	30.9	19.4	4.7	1.3	25.2	2.2
Winter Garden	45	318	31.2	9.7	272	1 145 114	16.2	35.8	18.5	3.2	0.0	17.7	0.0
Winter Haven	60	247	20.2	5.6	460	1 697 693	17.7	25.5	18.1	2.2	0.0	25.4	2.8
Winter Park	115	579	36.5	12.4	506	2 395 109	10.5	24.5	19.9	4.4	0.8	35.0	0.0
Winter Springs	26	98	6.0	1.7	207	765 305	16.8	45.2	0.0	0.0	0.0	34.3	0.0

1. Establishments subject to federal tax.

Table D. Cities — City Government Finances

City	City government finances, 2012 General revenue Total (mil dol) 117	Intergovernmental Total (mil dol) 118	Intergovernmental Percent from state government 119	Taxes Total (mil dol) 120	Taxes Per capita¹ (dollars) Total 121	Taxes Per capita¹ (dollars) Property 122	Taxes Sales and gross receipts 123	General expenditure Total (mil dol) 124	General expenditure Per capita¹ (dollars) Total 125	General expenditure Capital outlays 126
FLORIDA—Cont'd										
Deerfield Beach	110.6	11.2	65.6	51.7	667	441	223	119.1	1 535	67
DeLand	35.7	3.0	61.4	17.0	614	289	325	31.5	1 139	109
Delray Beach	122.1	11.8	68.8	77.5	1 240	937	301	117.6	1 882	71
Deltona	54.5	13.8	48.2	29.8	348	137	212	53.3	623	113
Doral	55.0	5.7	60.4	41.1	848	410	438	61.9	1 277	597
Dunedin	36.4	4.4	84.4	17.5	493	184	309	42.1	1 185	73
Fort Lauderdale	351.8	52.9	32.9	172.6	1 007	601	406	357.5	2 086	178
Fort Myers	148.2	15.3	59.3	61.9	943	526	416	154.4	2 352	195
Fort Pierce	68.9	10.3	85.1	26.0	609	360	249	79.2	1 855	305
Gainesville	206.3	24.2	47.3	64.4	510	212	298	208.2	1 648	273
Greenacres	21.6	4.0	80.4	13.4	347	173	174	20.5	533	30
Hallandale Beach	73.9	8.7	37.1	31.8	827	546	281	76.5	1 992	86
Hialeah	219.5	58.6	43.0	103.2	442	208	234	207.3	887	63
Hollywood	276.4	29.3	52.2	122.9	843	565	278	276.3	1 896	231
Homestead	81.0	20.4	49.7	25.1	395	226	168	68.8	1 081	164
Jacksonville	1 946.9	245.5	61.0	924.4	1 104	595	506	1 888.1	2 255	340
Jupiter	55.9	5.9	86.7	35.6	621	347	274	60.5	1 056	189
Kissimmee	69.7	20.4	62.5	27.9	438	199	239	82.5	1 296	259
Lakeland	186.5	38.4	30.2	50.0	502	262	240	203.7	2 048	303
Lake Worth	47.4	10.9	39.7	14.0	389	189	201	55.1	1 538	116
Largo	106.7	10.7	72.0	39.5	505	186	318	110.7	1 416	238
Lauderdale Lakes	26.2	4.3	77.6	11.9	352	170	182	26.8	792	44
Lauderhill	67.1	12.7	52.9	27.3	394	187	208	71.1	1 026	65
Margate	70.3	9.0	65.1	33.0	598	364	233	69.8	1 266	200
Melbourne	117.4	17.7	39.8	45.0	584	287	297	113.2	1 469	76
Miami	722.3	172.2	31.3	406.9	976	638	338	740.7	1 777	262
Miami Beach	529.5	21.7	43.5	328.2	3 597	1 276	2 320	497.2	5 448	572
Miami Gardens	83.2	27.7	43.3	41.1	368	176	192	85.3	765	86
Miami Lakes	18.1	3.9	79.9	12.9	422	185	237	19.4	635	118
Miramar	143.9	25.7	45.7	72.6	562	324	239	135.3	1 048	75
North Lauderdale	36.7	5.7	71.1	13.9	327	169	158	33.0	775	30
North Miami	74.3	14.3	45.8	30.1	493	287	206	78.4	1 282	99
North Miami Beach	69.4	10.5	84.8	22.9	528	290	238	79.6	1 838	147
North Port	74.1	8.3	65.2	22.7	389	138	251	78.1	1 339	244
Oakland Park	60.8	8.4	54.6	23.5	546	294	252	60.3	1 403	122
Ocala	118.1	16.3	79.4	40.2	707	380	327	106.1	1 865	168
Ocoee	39.5	8.6	94.4	16.4	428	253	175	40.9	1 066	54
Orlando	675.7	172.7	30.5	223.8	895	417	478	644.8	2 578	124
Ormond Beach	49.2	7.5	40.8	21.3	554	253	301	51.7	1 346	298
Oviedo	37.7	4.2	64.8	18.8	531	271	260	40.7	1 151	91
Palm Bay	95.5	22.5	37.8	43.8	421	236	184	96.4	925	142
Palm Beach Gardens	72.5	6.7	77.4	55.9	1 116	914	202	73.8	1 475	130
Palm Coast	61.9	7.9	63.6	23.7	306	196	111	75.5	974	151
Panama City	60.3	8.8	82.6	27.9	771	279	492	64.4	1 779	119
Pembroke Pines	252.5	67.1	81.6	92.9	581	321	260	310.7	1 942	78
Pensacola	126.4	46.1	16.9	42.4	804	266	538	157.0	2 977	968
Pinellas Park	65.8	7.8	64.1	31.4	631	274	357	68.5	1 377	108
Plantation	103.5	13.9	50.3	55.4	628	333	295	108.1	1 225	75
Plant City	47.9	7.5	73.4	20.0	554	231	323	40.6	1 128	97
Pompano Beach	157.1	12.7	50.4	84.6	819	496	323	202.4	1 959	236
Port Orange	65.3	6.6	74.6	25.0	440	215	225	62.8	1 105	37
Port St. Lucie	168.3	26.2	39.2	71.3	422	209	214	184.5	1 092	286
Riviera Beach	85.9	14.2	26.9	47.7	1 438	1 016	422	92.1	2 775	315
Royal Palm Beach	21.1	5.0	54.1	11.9	338	100	237	26.3	747	203
St. Cloud	51.0	4.2	78.7	15.3	386	160	226	64.8	1 632	228
St. Petersburg	377.4	80.5	33.2	139.7	565	303	262	403.2	1 630	142
Sanford	92.0	18.1	67.1	32.7	597	311	286	78.2	1 427	372
Sarasota	157.9	32.8	32.3	54.1	1 023	523	501	163.4	3 091	774
Sunrise	184.3	17.8	52.4	62.2	698	352	347	170.9	1 920	274
Tallahassee	339.4	52.0	38.9	105.7	565	184	381	370.9	1 983	425
Tamarac	73.4	11.5	50.2	31.8	507	261	245	68.8	1 097	20
Tampa	643.2	135.9	37.9	270.1	774	350	424	634.2	1 817	201
Titusville	55.0	7.1	79.7	25.9	589	263	326	44.4	1 010	129
Wellington	61.9	10.3	59.9	28.2	481	219	261	61.6	1 048	256
Weston	90.1	5.2	88.6	38.6	569	177	392	83.3	1 228	132
West Palm Beach	226.7	39.5	30.6	109.6	1 069	714	355	255.4	2 491	117
Winter Garden	39.8	5.5	93.8	20.7	560	226	334	40.6	1 096	279
Winter Haven	52.2	3.8	56.0	20.8	594	282	312	58.7	1 677	299
Winter Park	63.4	8.3	60.7	29.5	1 019	622	397	65.0	2 246	474
Winter Springs	27.7	4.0	89.0	13.1	389	125	264	26.4	786	144

1. Based on population estimated as of July 1 of the year shown.

Table D. Cities — **City Government Finances**

City		City government finances, 2012 (cont.)								
		General expenditure (cont.)								
		Percent of total for:								
	Public welfare	Highways	Parking facilities	Education	Health and hospitals	Police protection	Sewerage and sanitation	Parks and recreation	Housing and community development	Interest on debt
	127	128	129	130	131	132	133	134	135	136
FLORIDA—Cont'd										
Deerfield Beach	2.1	2.3	1.5	0.0	0.0	18.0	25.4	5.7	0.3	1.7
DeLand	0.0	8.4	0.0	0.0	0.0	21.9	18.8	9.0	1.4	1.9
Delray Beach	0.0	3.6	0.7	0.0	0.0	25.3	3.7	15.4	1.8	2.5
Deltona	0.0	8.7	0.0	0.0	0.0	17.3	17.9	5.0	6.3	2.0
Doral	0.0	13.4	0.0	0.0	0.0	19.6	0.0	27.0	0.0	2.4
Dunedin	0.0	7.2	0.0	0.0	0.0	9.4	14.6	15.8	0.0	0.9
Fort Lauderdale	0.0	3.4	3.0	0.0	0.0	27.5	5.4	11.4	4.4	0.7
Fort Myers	0.0	10.3	0.7	0.0	0.0	19.9	24.4	9.3	1.3	3.9
Fort Pierce	0.0	4.7	0.0	0.0	0.0	14.8	34.2	10.9	6.0	5.4
Gainesville	0.7	8.6	0.2	0.0	0.1	18.0	17.1	7.9	3.6	7.8
Greenacres	0.0	8.7	0.0	0.0	0.0	35.2	5.1	6.4	0.0	0.9
Hallandale Beach	1.2	1.0	0.0	0.0	0.0	25.2	20.9	3.0	3.1	1.7
Hialeah	0.0	4.5	0.0	0.0	0.0	23.0	17.8	7.3	2.2	2.2
Hollywood	0.0	2.8	2.4	0.0	0.0	25.1	19.0	7.2	1.2	3.5
Homestead	1.6	5.0	0.0	0.0	0.0	28.2	30.0	12.4	6.6	0.8
Jacksonville	2.5	7.5	0.2	0.0	3.3	15.9	10.3	4.6	0.7	8.6
Jupiter	0.0	10.0	0.0	0.0	0.0	32.3	4.8	3.6	0.0	2.5
Kissimmee	0.0	15.8	0.0	0.0	0.0	21.3	9.0	13.5	1.1	1.6
Lakeland	0.0	11.1	0.4	0.0	0.0	17.3	14.6	14.0	3.0	1.7
Lake Worth	0.0	2.8	0.2	0.0	0.0	27.6	23.1	9.1	0.0	0.7
Largo	0.0	3.0	0.0	0.0	0.0	17.3	27.9	13.2	2.4	0.4
Lauderdale Lakes	0.0	1.7	0.0	0.0	9.4	27.5	7.2	4.2	0.0	4.7
Lauderhill	0.0	1.7	0.0	0.0	6.5	22.9	6.6	4.3	3.2	4.5
Margate	0.0	3.6	0.0	0.0	0.0	27.0	14.4	4.2	3.5	3.0
Melbourne	0.0	12.5	0.2	0.0	0.0	16.1	13.2	8.2	2.2	0.5
Miami	0.2	9.5	3.7	0.0	0.0	18.5	3.2	14.9	5.4	5.4
Miami Beach	0.4	3.6	6.2	0.0	3.2	17.9	10.5	14.6	4.3	2.3
Miami Gardens	0.0	6.2	0.0	0.0	0.0	36.6	0.0	14.2	6.2	5.6
Miami Lakes	0.0	8.4	0.0	0.0	0.0	33.7	0.0	12.1	0.0	1.3
Miramar	0.0	5.5	0.0	0.0	0.0	29.7	6.2	8.7	0.9	3.6
North Lauderdale	0.0	3.0	0.0	0.0	0.0	26.0	17.3	11.7	2.6	1.3
North Miami	0.0	9.0	0.0	0.0	0.0	28.7	22.0	7.0	7.1	2.4
North Miami Beach	0.0	1.7	0.0	0.0	0.0	31.6	17.5	6.7	2.7	2.4
North Port	0.6	22.2	0.0	0.0	0.0	16.2	17.0	6.4	0.0	0.6
Oakland Park	0.0	6.0	0.0	0.0	0.0	20.6	19.4	7.9	0.0	1.9
Ocala	0.3	12.3	0.0	0.0	0.0	20.5	21.8	6.8	1.2	1.9
Ocoee	0.0	8.8	0.0	0.0	0.0	20.3	13.9	5.3	0.0	3.7
Orlando	0.0	6.8	2.6	0.0	1.0	19.2	13.7	12.9	1.7	7.0
Ormond Beach	0.0	9.6	0.0	0.0	0.0	14.8	20.0	21.6	0.0	0.6
Oviedo	0.0	31.0	0.0	0.0	0.0	16.7	17.4	8.4	0.0	3.0
Palm Bay	0.0	10.3	0.0	0.0	0.0	21.3	19.2	3.6	3.9	4.7
Palm Beach Gardens	0.0	1.7	0.0	0.0	0.0	30.2	0.0	12.4	0.0	1.4
Palm Coast	0.0	16.0	0.0	0.0	0.0	3.5	36.5	6.2	0.0	1.3
Panama City	0.0	8.9	0.0	0.0	0.0	14.5	8.1	9.2	1.3	0.7
Pembroke Pines	0.5	1.7	0.0	0.0	0.0	15.3	12.6	5.8	3.4	5.5
Pensacola	0.0	3.8	0.3	0.0	0.0	13.4	4.1	25.3	10.0	4.8
Pinellas Park	0.0	6.9	0.0	0.0	4.5	20.1	24.8	8.4	0.0	0.7
Plantation	0.0	2.8	0.0	0.0	7.5	32.2	15.5	12.9	1.7	1.6
Plant City	0.0	8.8	0.0	0.0	0.0	19.8	27.0	8.6	1.2	1.3
Pompano Beach	0.0	2.1	0.0	0.0	7.0	18.5	11.1	7.3	1.9	0.6
Port Orange	0.0	8.8	0.0	0.0	0.0	18.5	37.4	7.4	0.7	2.5
Port St. Lucie	0.0	24.4	0.0	0.0	0.7	19.0	7.9	6.5	2.6	16.5
Riviera Beach	0.2	7.4	0.0	0.0	0.0	18.1	17.9	6.3	0.2	1.0
Royal Palm Beach	0.0	11.4	0.0	0.0	0.0	27.6	0.0	26.9	0.0	0.6
St. Cloud	0.0	25.8	0.0	0.0	3.0	12.6	26.0	4.3	0.2	6.7
St. Petersburg	0.0	9.3	1.1	0.0	3.1	22.0	21.3	14.7	2.3	1.5
Sanford	0.7	8.9	0.0	0.0	0.0	15.9	18.1	5.9	1.9	2.5
Sarasota	0.0	7.1	0.7	0.0	0.0	17.6	23.5	19.7	10.7	3.1
Sunrise	0.0	3.6	0.0	0.0	0.0	29.4	25.2	8.3	0.6	0.8
Tallahassee	0.0	15.1	0.0	0.0	0.0	13.2	31.4	5.6	1.8	2.3
Tamarac	0.0	6.9	0.0	0.0	0.0	17.5	11.9	5.4	1.8	1.9
Tampa	0.0	8.7	2.2	0.0	0.0	23.8	21.2	8.9	5.4	4.1
Titusville	0.0	4.6	0.0	0.0	0.0	24.8	18.5	2.8	7.4	1.2
Wellington	0.0	15.3	0.0	0.0	0.0	12.1	9.3	6.6	0.0	1.2
Weston	0.0	0.8	0.0	0.0	0.0	12.7	18.5	6.4	1.7	0.6
West Palm Beach	0.0	4.1	1.6	0.0	0.7	18.7	24.9	7.1	2.6	4.0
Winter Garden	0.1	13.7	0.2	0.0	0.0	17.5	15.8	18.6	0.0	2.5
Winter Haven	1.2	4.2	2.4	0.0	0.0	17.1	25.7	14.3	0.4	3.8
Winter Park	0.0	2.8	0.0	0.0	0.0	17.7	13.9	8.8	0.0	2.4
Winter Springs	0.0	10.9	0.0	0.0	0.0	28.7	22.0	7.4	0.0	2.2

Table D. Cities — City Government Finances, City Government Employment, and Climate

	City government finances, 2012 (cont.)			Climate[2]						
	Debt outstanding			Average daily temperature (degrees Fahrenheit)						
				Mean		Limits				
City	Total (mil dol)	Per capita[1] (dollars)	Debt issued during year	January	July	January[3]	July[4]	Annual precipitation (inches)	Heating degree days	Cooling degree days
	137	138	139	140	141	142	143	144	145	146
FLORIDA—Cont'd										
Deerfield Beach	72.1	929	0.0	67.2	83.3	57.8	91.8	57.27	219	4 241
DeLand	33.4	1 206	9.3	NA	NA	NA	NA	NA	NA	NA
Delray Beach	86.4	1 383	5.4	66.2	82.5	57.3	90.1	61.39	246	3 999
Deltona	97.2	1 137	0.3	57.1	81.2	44.5	91.2	57.03	954	2 819
Doral	26.4	544	0.0	NA	NA	NA	NA	NA	NA	NA
Dunedin	35.3	995	0.0	60.9	82.5	50.2	91.3	52.42	623	3 414
Fort Lauderdale	587.6	3 429	67.9	67.5	82.6	59.2	89.8	64.19	167	4 120
Fort Myers	377.2	5 747	15.1	64.9	83.0	54.5	91.7	54.19	302	3 957
Fort Pierce	216.8	5 076	1.1	62.6	81.7	50.7	91.5	53.50	477	3 430
Gainesville	1 189.9	9 418	161.7	54.4	81.1	41.8	92.4	49.56	1 249	2 608
Greenacres	4.0	105	0.0	66.2	82.5	57.3	90.1	61.39	246	3 999
Hallandale Beach	31.5	819	0.0	68.1	83.7	59.6	90.9	58.53	149	4 361
Hialeah	169.3	725	81.6	67.9	82.7	62.6	87.0	46.60	141	4 090
Hollywood	379.0	2 602	4.3	67.5	82.6	59.2	89.8	64.19	167	4 120
Homestead	18.5	291	0.0	67.0	81.8	56.2	90.6	55.55	238	3 923
Jacksonville	10 439.0	12 465	630.5	54.5	82.5	42.6	92.7	51.88	1 222	2 810
Jupiter	66.9	1 167	0.0	66.2	82.5	57.3	90.1	61.39	246	3 999
Kissimmee	457.1	7 175	151.7	59.7	81.8	47.7	91.6	48.01	694	3 111
Lakeland	951.3	9 565	203.4	62.5	84.0	51.1	94.6	49.13	487	3 886
Lake Worth	74.3	2 072	6.8	65.1	81.1	52.5	91.3	58.44	273	3 438
Largo	31.5	403	14.0	61.3	82.5	52.4	89.7	44.77	591	3 482
Lauderdale Lakes	28.4	838	0.0	67.2	83.3	57.8	91.8	57.27	219	4 241
Lauderhill	118.7	1 711	18.3	67.5	82.6	59.2	89.8	64.19	167	4 120
Margate	53.5	971	0.0	67.2	83.3	57.8	91.8	57.27	219	4 241
Melbourne	132.5	1 720	1.5	60.9	81.2	50.0	90.5	48.29	595	3 186
Miami	873.2	2 095	120.6	68.1	83.7	59.6	90.9	58.53	149	4 361
Miami Beach	465.1	5 097	56.6	68.1	83.7	59.6	90.9	58.53	149	4 361
Miami Gardens	111.4	999	55.0	NA	NA	NA	NA	NA	NA	NA
Miami Lakes	7.5	246	7.3	NA	NA	NA	NA	NA	NA	NA
Miramar	182.5	1 414	0.0	68.1	83.7	59.6	90.9	58.53	149	4 361
North Lauderdale	8.6	203	0.0	67.5	82.6	59.2	89.8	64.19	167	4 120
North Miami	21.9	359	0.0	68.1	83.7	59.6	90.9	58.53	149	4 361
North Miami Beach	111.2	2 568	18.3	68.1	83.7	59.6	90.9	58.53	149	4 361
North Port	54.0	925	17.5	NA	NA	NA	NA	NA	NA	NA
Oakland Park	38.9	904	18.2	67.5	82.6	59.2	89.8	64.19	167	4 120
Ocala	201.6	3 544	13.9	58.1	81.7	45.7	92.2	49.68	902	2 971
Ocoee	54.8	1 428	2.1	NA	NA	NA	NA	NA	NA	NA
Orlando	1 055.4	4 219	67.0	60.9	82.4	49.9	92.2	48.35	580	3 428
Ormond Beach	54.1	1 408	5.6	60.9	82.4	49.9	92.2	48.35	580	3 428
Oviedo	79.7	2 256	1.3	58.7	81.5	47.0	91.9	51.31	799	3 017
Palm Bay	157.8	1 514	5.5	60.9	81.2	50.0	90.5	48.29	595	3 186
Palm Beach Gardens	25.8	515	4.4	66.2	82.5	57.3	90.1	61.39	246	3 999
Palm Coast	176.4	2 276	2.2	57.4	82.8	46.4	92.0	49.79	909	3 193
Panama City	35.5	980	0.0	50.3	80.0	38.7	89.0	64.76	1 810	2 174
Pembroke Pines	388.8	2 430	12.3	67.5	82.6	59.2	89.8	64.19	167	4 120
Pensacola	213.6	4 050	0.0	52.0	82.6	42.7	90.7	64.28	1 498	2 650
Pinellas Park	31.8	640	0.0	61.7	83.4	54.0	90.2	49.58	548	3 718
Plantation	39.9	452	2.8	67.5	82.6	59.2	89.8	64.19	167	4 120
Plant City	68.0	1 886	0.0	61.1	81.5	49.8	90.8	51.17	625	3 261
Pompano Beach	88.3	855	28.1	67.2	83.3	57.8	91.8	57.27	219	4 241
Port Orange	156.3	2 751	13.3	57.1	81.2	44.5	91.2	57.03	954	2 819
Port St. Lucie	1 015.1	6 008	42.9	64.5	81.8	54.7	89.5	59.53	315	3 600
Riviera Beach	67.2	2 025	26.5	66.2	82.5	57.3	90.1	61.39	246	3 999
Royal Palm Beach	20.5	582	20.5	NA	NA	NA	NA	NA	NA	NA
St. Cloud	123.7	3 114	57.6	NA	NA	NA	NA	NA	NA	NA
St. Petersburg	562.7	2 275	53.9	61.7	83.4	54.0	90.2	49.58	548	3 718
Sanford	79.7	1 455	6.1	58.7	81.5	47.0	91.9	51.31	799	3 017
Sarasota	156.6	2 962	30.9	61.7	83.4	54.0	90.2	49.58	548	3 718
Sunrise	298.7	3 356	9.6	67.5	82.6	59.2	89.8	64.19	167	4 120
Tallahassee	1 263.4	6 754	173.5	51.8	82.4	39.7	92.0	63.21	1 604	2 551
Tamarac	60.4	963	23.3	67.2	83.3	57.8	91.8	57.27	219	4 241
Tampa	1 377.0	3 945	202.8	61.3	82.5	52.4	89.7	44.77	591	3 482
Titusville	56.5	1 285	3.6	59.9	82.4	49.5	91.4	52.79	677	3 300
Wellington	22.8	388	0.0	66.2	82.5	57.3	90.1	61.39	246	3 999
Weston	12.6	186	0.0	67.5	82.6	59.2	89.8	64.19	167	4 120
West Palm Beach	437.5	4 267	0.0	66.2	82.5	57.3	90.1	61.39	246	3 999
Winter Garden	22.0	596	0.0	NA	NA	NA	NA	NA	NA	NA
Winter Haven	89.2	2 549	27.3	62.3	82.3	51.0	92.5	50.22	538	3 551
Winter Park	187.9	6 488	28.7	NA	NA	NA	NA	NA	NA	NA
Winter Springs	34.5	1 028	14.4	60.9	82.4	49.9	92.2	48.35	580	3 428

1. Based on the population estimated as of July 1 of the year shown. 2. Represents normal values based on the 30-year period, 1971–2000. 3. Average daily minimum.
4. Average daily maximum.

Table D. Cities — **Land Area and Population**

STATE Place code	City	Land area,[1] 2010 (sq km)	Population, 2015			Race alone or in combination (percent), 2010-2014						
			Total persons	Rank	Per square kilometer	White	Black	American Indian, Alaska Native	Asian	Hawaiian Pacific Islander	Percent Hispanic or Latino[2], 2010-2014	Percent foreign born 2010–2014
		1	2	3	4	5	6	7	8	9	10	11
13 00000	GEORGIA..............	148 959.2	10 214 860	X	68.6	62.1	32.0	0.8	4.0	0.1	9.1	9.7
13 01052	Albany	142.8	74 843	458	524.1	26.4	72.1	0.5	1.4	0.2	2.5	2.5
13 01696	Alpharetta	69.7	63 693	564	913.8	72.0	12.5	0.7	16.8	0.3	8.2	22.0
13 03436	Athens-Clarke County ...	301.4	122 604	221	406.8	67.1	27.6	0.5	5.1	0.1	10.6	10.1
13 04000	Atlanta	344.9	463 878	39	1 345.0	41.2	54.0	0.8	4.4	0.1	5.6	7.6
13 04200	Augusta-Richmond County	783.4	197 182	121	251.7	41.6	56.5	0.9	2.4	0.4	4.4	3.6
13 19000	Columbus	560.4	200 579	116	357.9	49.1	47.1	1.1	3.3	0.2	7.1	5.5
13 21380	Dalton........................	53.2	33 853	1 110	636.3	81.9	10.0	0.8	3.0	0.6	46.3	27.7
13 23900	Douglasville	58.2	32 897	1 143	565.2	35.9	60.4	0.5	2.7	0.0	6.6	8.0
13 24600	Duluth	25.9	29 193	1 269	1 127.1	47.1	23.1	0.9	25.1	0.0	10.2	28.6
13 24768	Dunwoody	33.5	48 733	778	1 454.7	72.2	12.1	0.9	14.6	0.1	9.8	21.3
13 25720	East Point	38.0	35 467	1 066	933.3	16.0	76.6	1.5	1.4	0.1	12.6	8.9
13 31908	Gainesville	82.7	38 712	967	468.1	67.7	17.0	1.2	4.3	0.0	40.5	25.5
13 38964	Hinesville	52.8	33 398	1 127	632.5	44.8	48.8	0.7	4.1	0.7	13.1	7.2
13 42425	Johns Creek	79.6	83 335	394	1 046.9	64.8	12.0	0.5	24.0	0.2	5.5	25.4
13 43192	Kennesaw	24.5	33 584	1 119	1 370.8	66.2	26.7	0.5	5.3	0.0	13.2	15.9
13 44340	LaGrange	102.3	30 695	1 213	300.0	44.7	51.0	0.6	2.9	0.0	5.8	7.2
13 45488	Lawrenceville..............	34.7	30 493	1 225	878.8	46.5	37.0	1.0	6.6	0.2	21.3	26.7
13 49000	Macon	645.6	153 515	165	237.8	44.9	53.4	0.6	2.1	0.2	3.1	3.7
13 49756	Marietta	59.8	59 067	624	987.7	56.0	34.3	0.6	3.8	0.0	18.4	20.5
13 51670	Milton	99.8	37 547	1 003	376.2	78.7	11.1	0.2	11.1	0.3	7.6	16.8
13 55020	Newnan	47.4	37 291	1 013	786.7	67.3	29.4	0.5	3.2	0.0	11.4	9.2
13 59724	Peachtree City	63.6	35 240	1 070	554.1	85.0	9.0	0.5	6.1	0.1	7.9	11.7
13 66668	Rome	80.1	36 323	1 035	453.5	59.1	29.4	1.8	2.3	0.1	16.0	10.8
13 67284	Roswell......................	105.5	94 501	325	895.7	79.6	13.4	0.8	6.0	0.1	13.8	18.8
13 68516	Sandy Springs..............	97.5	105 330	281	1 080.3	69.1	22.9	0.6	7.5	0.1	12.9	18.7
13 69000	Savannah	267.2	145 674	180	545.2	41.9	55.3	0.6	2.5	0.3	4.9	6.0
13 71492	Smyrna	39.8	56 146	659	1 410.7	54.3	33.0	0.5	7.2	0.1	14.4	16.8
13 73256	Statesboro	35.0	30 721	1 210	877.7	54.4	42.9	0.6	3.0	0.2	2.8	4.4
13 73704	Stockbridge	34.5	28 202	1 308	817.4	29.9	59.7	1.0	10.7	0.0	8.1	14.6
13 78800	Valdosta	92.8	55 724	667	600.5	45.2	52.7	0.8	2.5	0.1	5.0	5.0
13 80508	Warner Robins	90.8	73 490	471	809.4	54.9	39.6	0.8	3.6	0.3	7.2	6.3
15 00000	HAWAII..................	16 634.5	1 431 603	X	86.1	42.6	3.4	2.4	56.4	25.7	9.6	17.9
15 06290	East Honolulu CDP	59.6	NA	1 430	NA	40.7	1.1	1.6	66.2	13.3	4.1	14.4
15 14650	Hilo CDP....................	138.3	NA	1 430	NA	45.7	1.6	3.0	61.4	40.4	10.6	7.2
15 22700	Kahului CDP................	37.4	NA	1 430	NA	26.7	2.2	3.1	71.0	30.5	10.0	32.8
15 23150	Kailua CDP (Honolulu County)......................	20.1	NA	1 430	NA	66.4	1.7	2.2	40.5	21.7	7.5	8.4
15 28250	Kaneohe CDP	16.9	NA	1 430	NA	44.4	1.6	2.8	64.1	30.7	7.4	7.9
15 51050	Mililani Town CDP........	10.4	NA	1 430	NA	44.2	3.8	2.5	67.6	24.6	10.3	10.5
15 62600	Pearl City CDP	23.6	NA	1 430	NA	31.4	3.5	1.3	72.2	21.1	9.6	13.2
15 71550	Urban Honolulu CDP	156.8	352 769	55	2 249.8	30.3	3.3	1.8	67.1	18.4	5.9	27.5
15 79700	Waipahu CDP	7.2	NA	1 430	NA	14.2	1.7	1.5	78.5	23.3	7.9	38.1
16 00000	IDAHO..................	214 044.7	1 654 930	X	7.7	94.1	1.1	2.4	2.0	0.3	11.7	6.0
16 08830	Boise City	205.6	218 281	99	1 061.7	92.2	2.2	1.9	4.9	0.4	7.7	7.3
16 12250	Caldwell.....................	57.1	51 686	731	905.2	93.2	1.0	1.6	2.1	0.3	34.9	10.9
16 16750	Coeur d'Alene..............	40.3	49 122	769	1 218.9	96.2	0.7	2.5	2.2	0.1	5.2	3.0
16 39700	Idaho Falls..................	57.9	59 184	621	1 022.2	92.8	1.4	2.0	1.3	0.1	12.5	5.8
16 46540	Lewiston	44.6	32 544	1 157	729.7	96.1	0.9	3.0	1.4	0.2	3.2	1.9
16 52120	Meridian.....................	69.4	90 739	346	1 307.5	96.2	1.5	0.5	2.7	0.4	7.1	4.9
16 56260	Nampa.......................	80.8	89 839	351	1 111.9	91.5	1.4	2.2	1.6	0.5	23.4	8.4
16 64090	Pocatello....................	83.5	54 441	687	652.0	94.4	1.6	2.9	2.7	0.5	7.9	4.0
16 64810	Post Falls...................	36.5	30 453	1 228	834.3	96.9	1.6	2.3	2.3	0.6	3.9	1.8
16 67420	Rexburg	25.3	27 663	1 333	1 093.4	96.3	1.1	0.9	2.1	0.7	4.6	4.5
16 82810	Twin Falls	46.9	47 468	798	1 012.1	92.3	1.2	2.3	3.0	0.5	16.1	9.4
17 00000	ILLINOIS..................	143 793.4	12 859 995	X	89.4	74.4	15.3	0.7	5.5	0.1	16.3	13.9
17 00243	Addison	25.3	37 208	1 015	1 470.7	85.4	4.3	0.4	5.9	0.0	40.2	33.1
17 00685	Algonquin	31.7	30 571	1 221	964.4	89.3	2.4	0.6	8.3	0.0	6.7	12.4
17 01114	Alton	40.1	27 003	1 359	673.4	73.7	26.6	1.9	1.0	0.0	2.5	1.1
17 02154	Arlington Heights..........	43.0	75 926	450	1 765.7	88.3	2.1	0.4	8.6	0.1	6.1	17.5
17 03012	Aurora	116.4	200 661	114	1 723.9	58.3	11.6	1.2	7.9	0.1	42.7	25.7
17 04013	Bartlett	40.5	41 545	900	1 025.8	79.0	2.4	0.7	15.6	0.0	11.5	19.4
17 04078	Batavia	25.0	26 495	1 379	1 059.8	94.0	2.7	0.7	2.2	0.0	7.0	5.2
17 04845	Belleville	58.9	42 034	888	713.7	73.8	25.2	1.0	2.8	0.1	3.2	2.3
17 05092	Belvidere	31.3	25 132	1 416	802.9	87.2	4.5	0.2	1.4	0.2	30.4	15.7
17 05573	Berwyn	10.1	56 368	657	5 581.0	70.3	8.2	1.1	3.0	0.0	59.1	25.7
17 06613	Bloomington	70.5	78 292	432	1 110.5	79.6	12.4	0.5	8.2	0.0	5.6	9.6
17 07133	Bolingbrook	62.3	74 306	462	1 192.7	56.6	24.0	0.9	11.4	0.1	23.7	20.4
17 09447	Buffalo Grove	24.6	41 503	901	1 687.1	78.7	2.4	0.6	18.8	0.2	3.9	28.5

1. Dry land or land partially or temporarily covered by water.   2. May be of any race.

Table D. Cities — **Population**

City	Age of population (percent), 2010-2014									Median age 2010–2014	Percent female 2010–2014	Population Census counts		Percent change	
	Under 5 years	5 to 17 years	18 to 24 years	25 to 34 years	35 to 44 years	45 to 54 years	55 to 64 years	65 to 74 years	75 years and over			2000	2010	2000–2010	2010–2015
	12	13	14	15	16	17	18	19	20	21	22	23	24	25	26
GEORGIA	6.8	18.3	10.2	13.7	14.0	14.1	11.5	6.9	4.6	35.7	51.1	8 186 453	9 687 653	18.3	5.4
Albany	7.8	17.8	13.6	14.3	11.7	11.9	10.8	6.4	5.6	32.3	53.9	76 939	77 434	0.6	-3.3
Alpharetta	7.9	21.5	6.8	12.0	15.5	16.5	11.6	4.5	3.7	36.4	50.2	34 854	57 551	65.1	10.8
Athens-Clarke County	5.9	11.5	29.7	16.8	10.3	8.8	8.2	5.0	3.8	26.2	52.4	101 489	115 452	15.1	6.2
Atlanta	6.2	12.3	14.7	20.0	14.8	12.3	9.7	5.7	4.3	33.2	50.0	416 474	420 003	0.8	10.4
Augusta-Richmond County	7.2	17.0	12.0	15.9	11.4	12.8	11.8	6.9	5.0	33.2	51.6	199 775	195 844	0.3	0.7
Columbus	7.5	17.5	11.8	15.6	12.3	12.8	11.0	6.1	5.3	33.3	51.2	186 291	189 885	1.9	5.3
Dalton	8.4	19.7	10.8	14.1	13.1	12.3	9.5	6.1	6.1	32.5	53.2	27 912	33 128	18.7	2.3
Douglasville	8.3	21.9	9.6	14.4	15.8	13.7	8.3	5.0	2.9	32.0	55.2	20 065	30 961	54.3	6.3
Duluth	7.8	16.5	5.8	17.3	17.0	16.5	10.8	4.6	3.8	36.7	56.0	22 122	26 600	20.2	9.7
Dunwoody	6.9	17.0	5.8	18.1	17.4	12.3	10.1	7.4	5.1	36.4	50.5	32 808	46 267	41.0	5.3
East Point	8.6	17.3	10.9	13.3	14.8	12.3	13.3	6.0	3.5	35.0	52.4	39 595	33 712	-14.9	5.2
Gainesville	8.6	20.9	12.7	15.6	11.8	10.0	8.7	5.8	5.9	30.4	50.0	25 578	33 804	32.2	9.7
Hinesville	10.5	18.6	15.9	19.6	11.0	10.3	8.9	3.8	1.4	26.8	51.6	30 392	33 437	10.0	-0.1
Johns Creek	6.4	23.2	7.1	7.6	17.5	18.1	11.7	5.6	2.7	39.2	50.9	NA	76 728	NA	8.6
Kennesaw	5.9	17.9	10.6	16.9	16.6	14.5	8.3	4.4	4.9	34.6	52.8	21 675	29 783	37.4	9.8
LaGrange	8.5	18.7	12.2	14.7	11.4	12.2	10.0	6.9	5.4	32.2	52.8	25 998	29 588	13.8	4.3
Lawrenceville	7.4	21.5	10.9	10.7	14.2	13.7	10.5	5.6	5.4	34.7	50.9	22 397	28 546	27.5	7.4
Macon	8.7	18.0	12.2	13.9	11.2	12.4	11.3	6.2	6.1	32.8	54.5	97 255	91 348	-6.1	-1.2
Marietta	6.9	15.3	12.4	18.1	16.9	12.0	8.2	6.0	4.3	33.2	51.5	58 748	56 579	-3.7	4.3
Milton	5.3	23.8	6.1	9.3	18.7	17.5	11.5	4.7	3.1	37.4	51.2	NA	32 661	NA	14.8
Newnan	8.2	21.0	7.2	13.7	17.4	12.4	9.6	6.6	3.7	34.9	54.8	16 242	33 039	103.4	12.4
Peachtree City	4.4	21.9	8.2	8.9	11.5	17.2	14.2	8.9	5.0	42.0	51.5	31 580	34 364	8.8	2.5
Rome	8.7	15.8	10.7	15.4	11.0	13.0	10.5	8.4	6.4	34.5	52.1	34 980	36 303	3.8	-0.6
Roswell	6.4	18.2	6.8	13.1	15.5	16.4	12.2	6.8	4.6	38.9	50.0	79 334	88 346	11.4	7.0
Sandy Springs	6.8	15.8	7.5	19.6	14.5	14.0	10.5	6.2	5.3	35.2	52.2	85 781	93 853	9.4	12.2
Savannah	6.8	15.4	15.5	16.5	11.0	11.6	10.7	6.7	5.8	31.9	52.6	131 510	136 286	3.6	6.9
Smyrna	8.5	13.7	7.6	22.0	18.3	13.5	8.3	4.9	3.2	34.3	52.7	40 999	51 271	25.1	9.5
Statesboro	4.0	9.2	49.8	11.8	5.4	7.1	5.1	3.6	3.9	22.1	52.9	22 698	28 422	25.2	8.1
Stockbridge	6.4	23.5	10.4	9.9	18.9	12.9	10.0	4.0	3.9	34.8	54.6	9 853	25 636	160.2	7.2
Valdosta	7.9	14.0	25.3	15.5	9.2	9.5	8.6	5.6	4.5	26.6	51.3	43 724	54 518	24.7	1.8
Warner Robins	8.7	19.4	10.2	18.2	12.5	12.7	8.8	5.1	4.3	31.1	51.9	48 804	66 588	36.4	7.2
HAWAII	6.5	15.5	9.8	14.3	12.5	13.3	12.9	8.1	7.0	38.2	49.7	1 211 537	1 360 301	12.3	5.2
East Honolulu CDP	3.9	14.7	6.4	8.6	13.4	14.5	14.4	13.5	10.8	47.2	51.7	NA	NA	NA	NA
Hilo CDP	4.5	15.3	10.5	13.1	9.8	12.8	15.3	9.3	9.4	41.3	50.5	40 759	43 263	6.1	NA
Kahului CDP	5.5	16.3	9.8	15.0	13.1	14.1	10.0	9.0	7.4	38.1	50.7	20 146	26 337	30.7	NA
Kailua CDP (Honolulu County)	4.5	16.2	7.4	13.3	11.9	14.4	16.1	8.6	7.5	42.0	51.3	36 513	38 635	5.8	NA
Kaneohe CDP	5.1	12.4	8.3	14.5	11.4	15.7	12.6	10.6	9.4	42.9	50.8	34 970	34 597	-1.1	NA
Mililani Town CDP	4.7	15.9	10.2	13.2	12.2	13.5	15.1	10.1	5.1	40.1	49.0	28 608	27 629	-3.4	NA
Pearl City CDP	6.9	15.2	9.2	13.4	11.4	12.0	11.9	10.1	9.8	40.5	47.0	30 976	47 698	54.0	NA
Urban Honolulu CDP	5.4	12.4	10.2	14.9	12.6	13.5	13.0	8.3	9.6	40.5	50.6	NA	337 256	NA	4.6
Waipahu CDP	6.5	15.6	10.3	14.6	11.7	13.4	11.6	8.0	8.3	37.7	50.6	33 108	38 216	15.4	NA
IDAHO	7.2	19.5	9.8	13.2	12.2	12.7	12.1	7.7	5.6	35.2	49.9	1 293 953	1 567 582	21.1	5.6
Boise City	5.9	16.0	11.2	15.4	13.3	13.9	12.6	6.5	5.2	36.0	50.5	185 787	205 671	10.7	5.9
Caldwell	10.1	20.2	11.3	16.7	12.5	9.8	8.8	6.2	4.4	29.8	50.3	25 967	46 237	78.1	11.6
Coeur d'Alene	7.5	16.4	11.7	14.4	11.2	12.1	12.5	7.6	6.8	35.1	50.0	34 514	44 137	27.9	11.3
Idaho Falls	9.1	19.7	9.0	15.3	11.6	11.2	11.8	6.4	6.0	33.1	51.3	50 730	56 813	12.0	4.0
Lewiston	5.9	15.3	10.8	12.6	11.0	13.5	12.5	9.1	9.2	39.6	50.9	30 904	31 894	3.2	2.0
Meridian	8.2	24.1	7.1	13.3	14.9	12.6	9.4	5.8	4.5	33.2	51.8	34 919	75 092	115.0	20.8
Nampa	8.0	24.6	9.8	13.8	12.9	11.3	8.1	7.1	4.3	30.4	51.0	51 867	81 557	57.2	9.9
Pocatello	7.4	18.3	13.7	16.8	10.3	11.6	11.1	5.7	4.9	31.2	50.3	51 466	54 255	5.4	0.4
Post Falls	8.6	19.9	6.5	16.8	14.4	10.8	11.5	6.2	5.3	33.6	53.7	17 247	27 574	59.9	10.4
Rexburg	9.1	13.5	43.0	16.6	5.6	4.3	3.4	2.5	2.0	22.6	52.1	17 257	25 484	47.7	8.6
Twin Falls	7.8	19.6	11.4	15.2	12.7	9.6	10.1	6.8	6.7	32.4	50.4	34 469	44 125	28.0	7.1
ILLINOIS	6.3	17.5	9.7	13.8	13.2	14.2	12.2	7.2	6.0	37.0	50.9	12 419 293	12 830 632	3.3	0.2
Addison	7.8	18.7	9.4	15.5	11.7	13.3	12.1	7.1	4.4	33.8	52.1	35 914	36 942	2.9	0.7
Algonquin	5.6	20.6	7.5	9.6	16.8	16.2	14.0	6.5	3.2	39.9	50.2	23 276	30 046	29.1	1.7
Alton	7.4	16.4	8.3	18.5	10.7	12.4	11.8	8.1	6.4	34.7	51.6	30 496	27 865	-8.6	-3.3
Arlington Heights	5.6	15.5	6.8	12.4	12.5	16.2	12.9	9.1	9.0	42.9	51.7	76 031	75 101	-1.2	1.1
Aurora	7.7	22.5	9.2	15.2	16.1	13.4	8.7	4.4	2.8	32.1	50.6	142 990	197 899	38.4	1.4
Bartlett	5.2	20.2	6.1	11.8	14.3	18.3	13.4	6.1	4.6	40.0	48.9	36 706	41 208	12.3	0.8
Batavia	5.8	21.3	6.9	9.6	13.8	17.7	14.3	5.7	4.9	39.9	53.1	23 866	26 045	9.1	1.3
Belleville	5.4	16.6	8.8	15.5	13.8	15.5	11.9	5.8	6.7	36.8	52.6	41 410	44 478	7.4	-4.6
Belvidere	5.7	23.8	10.7	10.2	16.2	13.1	9.0	6.0	5.2	34.7	51.8	20 820	25 585	22.9	-1.8
Berwyn	7.4	20.4	9.3	14.9	16.0	12.5	10.2	5.0	4.3	33.5	51.5	54 016	56 657	4.9	-0.5
Bloomington	7.1	17.5	11.2	15.7	14.0	12.7	11.4	5.0	5.4	33.9	51.5	64 808	76 610	18.2	2.2
Bolingbrook	8.0	20.4	9.7	13.1	17.8	12.5	10.6	5.3	2.6	34.0	50.6	56 321	73 366	30.3	1.3
Buffalo Grove	5.2	18.3	6.0	10.5	15.0	16.8	15.8	7.1	5.4	42.3	51.8	42 909	41 496	-3.3	0.2

Table D. Cities — Households, Group Quarters, Crime, and Education

City	Households, 2010-2014 Number	Persons per house-hold	Percent Female family house-holder[1]	One-person	Persons in group quarters, 2010 Total	Institutional Total	Persons in nursing facilities	Non-institu-tional	Serious crimes known to police,[2] 2014 Total Number	Rate[3]	Rate[3] Violent	Property	Population age 25 and older	High school graduate or less	Bachelor's degree or more
	27	28	29	30	31	32	33	34	35	36	37	38	39	40	41
GEORGIA..................	3 540 690	2.80	15.4	26.7	253 199	144 545	34 738	108 654	369 413	3 659	377	3 281	6 410 416	43.5	28.3
Albany.......................	28 979	2.66	27.0	33.4	4 288	1 421	400	2 867	4 971	6 553	1 022	5 531	46 553	49.7	16.7
Alpharetta.................	22 200	2.74	9.1	25.6	69	57	19	12	1 292	2 035	60	1 975	39 036	14.0	62.4
Athens-Clarke County......	42 107	2.84	12.9	33.9	9 183	779	348	8 404	4 164	3 427	306	3 121	63 733	36.6	39.3
Atlanta......................	181 681	2.43	15.4	46.4	29 484	6 756	1 626	22 728	31 691	6 975	1 227	5 747	293 395	31.3	47.1
Augusta-Richmond County	71 776	2.80	21.9	34.0	10 508	3 907	1 137	6 601	3 224	1 626	127	1 499	128 220	47.8	20.4
Columbus...................	72 556	2.73	21.1	30.4	7 017	3 486	898	3 531	14 479	7 004	533	6 472	125 771	42.2	23.7
Dalton.......................	11 446	2.91	15.6	28.0	904	754	340	150	1 332	3 980	269	3 711	20 336	60.8	18.4
Douglasville...............	11 597	2.72	24.9	28.9	937	826	0	111	2 241	6 979	579	6 399	19 759	37.7	27.9
Duluth.......................	10 558	2.64	13.6	26.9	34	0	0	34	624	2 163	94	2 069	18 868	34.6	41.1
Dunwoody..................	19 344	2.44	5.5	36.1	154	0	0	154	2 244	4 683	121	4 562	32 891	16.7	66.4
East Point.................	12 745	2.75	26.8	35.8	420	44	27	376	4 220	11 745	1 291	10 454	22 512	44.8	25.0
Gainesville................	11 339	3.08	18.4	29.8	1 713	649	434	1 064	1 623	4 512	364	4 148	19 944	55.6	23.7
Hinesville..................	12 747	2.69	17.6	20.2	310	263	0	47	1 599	4 631	469	4 162	19 397	38.7	20.5
Johns Creek...............	26 501	3.06	8.0	16.9	0	0	0	0	622	738	33	705	51 649	14.3	63.8
Kennesaw..................	12 126	2.59	15.6	30.9	244	244	99	0	545	1 681	114	1 566	20 204	29.8	38.0
LaGrange..................	10 713	2.81	28.9	30.6	1 242	627	381	615	1 903	6 203	411	5 792	17 990	54.0	20.8
Lawrenceville.............	9 679	3.03	19.0	25.0	268	238	238	30	957	3 166	175	2 991	17 915	48.1	20.3
Macon......................	56 567	2.74	21.1	31.7	4 292	2 026	680	2 266	NA	NA	NA	NA	99 216	49.9	23.4
Marietta....................	22 261	2.63	15.0	33.1	1 769	758	730	1 011	2 957	4 956	508	4 448	38 414	35.0	36.1
Milton.......................	12 119	2.88	9.9	15.8	4	0	0	4	372	1 014	19	994	22 624	11.1	66.8
Newnan.....................	12 697	2.71	17.7	28.6	518	518	135	0	1 202	3 412	483	2 929	21 156	42.3	29.7
Peachtree City............	12 633	2.75	7.9	22.0	118	118	118	0	453	1 295	29	1 266	22 795	19.7	53.5
Rome........................	13 577	2.66	17.4	34.5	1 606	1 409	447	197	2 442	6 806	672	6 135	23 049	53.8	20.9
Roswell.....................	34 408	2.68	9.7	27.5	516	356	305	160	1 899	1 991	115	1 876	63 923	22.3	55.4
Sandy Springs............	42 196	2.33	9.1	37.6	327	205	205	122	2 904	2 870	157	2 713	69 457	19.6	58.3
Savannah..................	52 264	2.70	20.7	35.1	10 014	4 499	584	5 515	9 434	3 986	392	3 594	87 393	43.4	26.9
Smyrna.....................	23 305	2.27	13.7	36.2	279	269	112	10	1 707	3 163	287	2 876	37 084	24.8	51.5
Statesboro.................	10 127	2.93	18.6	26.9	4 290	266	266	4 024	1 166	3 848	271	3 578	11 071	39.8	28.3
Stockbridge...............	9 473	2.85	26.2	20.8	8	0	0	8	NA	NA	NA	NA	16 515	34.7	30.7
Valdosta....................	21 199	2.66	20.4	31.5	4 122	1 147	444	2 975	3 492	6 141	329	5 812	30 026	45.3	24.4
Warner Robins............	26 574	2.69	17.8	32.0	338	223	208	115	4 853	6 610	448	6 162	43 994	42.9	21.4
HAWAII....................	450 299	3.09	12.3	23.9	42 880	11 306	5 198	31 574	46 977	3 309	259	3 050	950 863	37.4	30.5
East Honolulu CDP........	17 048	2.87	9.4	16.4	235	160	160	75	NA	NA	NA	NA	36 670	20.0	54.2
Hilo CDP...................	15 091	2.95	13.8	29.0	1 648	605	575	1 043	NA	NA	NA	NA	30 019	39.6	28.8
Kahului CDP...............	7 016	3.90	19.5	20.0	1 740	1 296	564	444	NA	NA	NA	NA	18 469	54.7	17.2
Kailua CDP (Honolulu County)...	12 962	3.04	12.6	18.6	119	30	8	89	NA	NA	NA	NA	28 619	24.6	46.2
Kaneohe CDP..............	10 763	3.11	14.7	17.0	643	411	411	232	NA	NA	NA	NA	24 317	36.6	33.8
Mililani Town CDP.........	9 014	3.13	11.1	15.5	0	0	0	0	NA	NA	NA	NA	19 197	29.1	33.8
Pearl City CDP............	14 004	3.38	13.6	18.8	3 694	165	156	3 529	NA	NA	NA	NA	32 777	37.9	28.3
Urban Honolulu CDP......	127 929	2.70	11.8	33.3	13 052	4 247	1 823	8 805	NA	NA	NA	NA	249 862	36.5	35.2
Waipahu CDP..............	8 310	4.88	18.5	13.8	910	390	369	520	NA	NA	NA	NA	27 099	54.0	14.8
IDAHO......................	585 259	2.73	9.6	24.4	28 951	17 076	4 820	11 875	33 784	2 067	212	1 855	1 015 487	38.6	25.4
Boise City..................	86 642	2.44	9.5	30.9	3 717	1 762	548	1 955	5 137	2 375	289	2 087	140 925	26.6	39.1
Caldwell....................	15 641	3.08	13.3	25.7	1 532	913	149	619	1 541	3 107	325	2 782	27 525	51.2	14.3
Coeur d'Alene.............	18 860	2.43	12.0	31.6	1 215	813	428	402	2 067	4 402	513	3 889	29 785	37.5	23.7
Idaho Falls.................	20 846	2.78	12.6	25.2	1 011	477	72	534	1 627	2 776	215	2 561	36 134	37.3	25.5
Lewiston....................	13 361	2.41	11.0	31.2	966	594	385	372	1 193	3 668	172	3 496	22 093	40.9	22.2
Meridian....................	28 431	2.85	9.7	19.3	307	126	103	181	1 308	1 526	89	1 437	50 684	29.0	33.3
Nampa......................	28 098	3.01	14.6	23.6	1 751	540	360	1 211	2 806	3 198	320	2 878	49 072	47.0	17.4
Pocatello...................	20 379	2.67	10.5	30.1	1 519	630	307	889	1 359	2 500	258	2 242	32 633	34.7	29.9
Post Falls..................	11 202	2.57	18.3	22.3	84	42	42	42	903	3 033	171	2 861	18 733	36.1	20.1
Rexburg....................	7 238	3.63	4.9	11.2	1 027	127	44	900	277	1 035	34	1 001	9 119	12.7	38.6
Twin Falls..................	16 412	2.76	13.0	24.9	897	592	314	305	1 586	3 421	255	3 167	27 612	43.7	17.5
ILLINOIS....................	4 778 633	2.69	12.7	28.7	301 773	159 989	81 516	141 784	315 048	2 446	370	2 076	8 560 555	39.4	31.9
Addison.....................	12 302	3.03	15.6	19.3	112	46	0	66	677	1 806	173	1 633	24 098	52.9	20.8
Algonquin..................	10 393	2.90	7.7	15.5	0	0	0	0	465	1 521	59	1 462	19 708	23.1	44.4
Alton........................	11 737	2.34	18.0	35.4	518	356	202	162	1 383	5 093	545	4 548	18 649	43.1	17.6
Arlington Heights.........	30 283	2.50	6.2	29.4	723	545	538	178	786	1 031	56	975	54 356	23.2	54.0
Aurora......................	61 506	3.25	13.8	19.9	2 477	751	577	1 726	3 540	1 766	278	1 488	119 243	44.5	31.2
Bartlett.....................	13 797	3.01	6.7	16.1	58	58	58	0	250	598	34	565	27 635	27.1	43.7
Batavia.....................	9 471	2.74	8.5	23.7	157	148	148	9	408	1 543	136	1 407	17 181	19.7	50.9
Belleville...................	17 652	2.45	16.7	35.3	1 246	1 167	740	79	1 731	4 063	422	3 640	29 689	37.5	23.0
Belvidere...................	8 810	2.92	14.6	23.7	230	221	150	9	481	1 902	182	1 720	15 730	58.4	12.2
Berwyn......................	18 401	3.08	17.1	24.0	52	17	14	35	1 290	2 272	224	2 048	36 090	50.4	20.3
Bloomington...............	30 558	2.55	10.2	31.7	2 234	566	280	1 668	2 029	2 554	419	2 135	49 674	28.8	45.2
Bolingbrook................	22 124	3.35	13.3	15.8	279	279	279	0	1 142	1 542	211	1 332	45 725	36.1	34.5
Buffalo Grove..............	16 276	2.56	7.2	24.7	118	112	112	6	299	715	24	691	29 691	15.2	63.7

1. No spouse present.   2. Data for serious crimes have not been adjusted for underreporting. This may affect comparability between geographic areas and over time.   3. Per 100,000 population estimated by the FBI.   4. Persons 25 years old and over.

City	Money income, 2010–2014					Housing units, 2010			Occupied housing units 2010–2014				
		Households									Owner-occupied		Median owner costs as a percent of income
	Per capita income[1] (dollars)	Median income	Percent with income of $200,000 or more	Percent with income of less than $25,000	Families with income below poverty (percent)	Total	Percent change, 2000–2010	Vacant units for sale or rent[2]	Total	Percent	Median value[3] (dollars)	With a mortgage[4]	Without a mortgage[5]
	42	43	44	45	46	47	48	49	50	51	52	53	54
GEORGIA	25 427	49 342	4.1	25.7	14.2	4 088 801	24.6	503 217	3 540 690	64.2	148 000	23.4	11.6
Albany	17 064	28 303	1.3	44.9	30.1	33 436	3.9	3 655	28 979	38.9	97 800	23.9	13.8
Alpharetta	42 644	87 837	13.4	11.4	4.6	23 029	57.2	1 287	22 200	63.5	316 800	21.5	10.0
Athens-Clarke County	19 333	33 430	2.8	40.7	20.8	51 068	21.2	5 654	42 107	42.6	152 700	22.9	11.4
Atlanta	35 719	46 439	8.3	31.0	19.9	224 573	20.1	39 431	181 681	44.1	205 000	24.0	13.7
Augusta-Richmond County	20 549	37 704	1.7	34.4	20.8	86 331	4.9	9 407	71 776	53.3	100 400	23.0	12.3
Columbus	23 209	41 362	2.9	30.5	16.3	82 690	8.5	8 609	72 556	50.8	134 200	23.5	11.6
Dalton	20 180	35 530	3.3	35.4	22.8	13 378	29.8	2 041	11 446	44.6	125 300	22.9	10.0
Douglasville	23 244	47 563	3.5	24.1	18.3	13 163	66.4	1 536	11 597	47.3	139 500	25.2	10.5
Duluth	28 477	56 849	3.6	20.3	13.2	11 313	23.6	758	10 558	53.4	174 200	23.7	10.0
Dunwoody	44 521	78 063	12.0	12.8	7.9	21 671	48.4	1 727	19 344	54.1	354 800	22.7	12.3
East Point	19 076	37 646	1.2	33.3	23.4	17 225	11.1	3 892	12 745	43.9	94 300	26.8	14.7
Gainesville	19 792	39 791	4.4	31.0	24.7	12 967	45.5	1 694	11 339	36.0	150 700	25.2	12.0
Hinesville	21 264	44 896	1.6	23.7	13.2	14 653	24.4	2 329	12 747	46.3	127 000	24.3	11.2
Johns Creek	43 998	108 114	18.8	8.5	4.4	27 744	NA	1 478	26 501	79.1	324 400	21.3	10.4
Kennesaw	28 601	58 483	2.4	17.5	9.6	12 328	40.7	915	12 126	62.4	157 100	24.0	10.5
LaGrange	18 783	34 056	2.4	39.9	27.1	12 846	16.7	1 603	10 713	39.6	114 700	23.5	12.7
Lawrenceville	19 178	42 459	1.2	29.3	18.4	11 187	45.8	1 214	9 679	52.6	119 400	23.9	13.3
Macon	21 293	36 671	2.8	36.7	22.4	42 794	-3.8	7 191	56 567	53.8	122 000	24.0	12.0
Marietta	24 980	42 688	3.6	27.0	17.0	26 918	6.0	3 853	22 261	42.9	206 300	23.3	10.0
Milton	54 139	110 891	24.9	8.2	4.1	12 338	NA	669	12 119	68.6	451 100	21.0	10.0
Newnan	24 927	50 175	2.8	25.5	17.3	13 860	108.6	1 421	12 697	54.0	178 100	22.7	12.0
Peachtree City	38 599	86 352	9.7	10.4	5.9	13 538	17.8	812	12 633	72.7	271 700	21.4	10.0
Rome	20 041	33 787	2.7	37.7	21.0	15 797	9.3	1 912	13 577	46.4	122 900	24.9	13.0
Roswell	42 383	79 359	13.9	12.5	5.3	36 344	15.8	2 399	34 408	67.1	289 500	21.3	10.0
Sandy Springs	50 387	63 401	14.6	18.0	8.5	46 955	9.9	4 621	42 196	46.2	419 100	21.2	10.6
Savannah	20 284	36 628	1.8	35.6	20.5	61 883	7.6	9 338	52 264	45.0	143 200	26.7	13.3
Smyrna	37 844	61 333	7.3	18.0	10.6	25 745	30.6	2 743	23 305	50.2	208 500	20.2	10.0
Statesboro	12 077	22 196	0.7	54.9	31.8	11 602	25.3	1 395	10 127	22.8	115 500	21.5	11.7
Stockbridge	22 945	54 864	1.3	16.8	10.9	10 312	NA	813	9 473	58.5	124 200	24.4	12.8
Valdosta	17 769	29 828	1.9	41.1	25.0	22 709	19.5	2 238	21 199	38.8	127 800	25.8	11.7
Warner Robins	20 838	44 661	0.8	28.4	20.9	29 084	33.2	2 948	26 574	56.0	109 800	20.7	10.6
HAWAII	29 552	68 201	6.1	16.7	7.8	519 508	12.8	64 170	450 299	57.1	504 500	28.7	10.0
East Honolulu CDP	48 119	111 582	18.2	7.2	2.5	18 774	NA	1 090	17 048	82.8	788 400	28.2	10.0
Hilo CDP	24 384	52 563	2.4	26.3	13.0	16 905	5.5	1 422	15 091	64.1	301 300	24.0	10.0
Kahului CDP	22 016	62 038	3.8	17.7	9.2	7 773	28.6	662	7 016	55.1	485 000	29.6	10.0
Kailua CDP (Honolulu County)	44 224	104 911	15.8	8.4	3.7	13 650	6.9	729	12 962	72.4	813 600	27.5	10.0
Kaneohe CDP	32 666	81 907	7.9	10.9	4.1	11 553	0.7	415	10 763	69.4	627 500	28.9	10.0
Mililani Town CDP	35 441	94 410	7.6	6.7	3.8	9 272	0.0	234	9 014	76.5	551 900	25.2	10.0
Pearl City CDP	31 203	82 895	6.9	10.9	4.6	14 622	60.5	354	14 004	72.3	578 700	24.8	10.0
Urban Honolulu CDP	31 146	60 548	5.7	19.4	7.7	143 173	NA	13 765	127 929	43.1	565 000	28.4	11.6
Waipahu CDP	20 761	68 352	7.1	18.4	11.6	8 850	10.2	467	8 310	57.0	510 100	25.7	10.0
IDAHO	23 087	47 334	2.4	24.3	11.0	667 796	26.5	88 388	585 259	69.2	160 500	23.4	10.0
Boise City	28 956	49 209	4.3	23.9	9.6	92 700	18.9	6 996	86 642	59.6	175 800	21.5	10.0
Caldwell	16 237	41 368	1.0	30.4	16.3	16 323	68.4	1 428	15 641	65.5	103 000	24.7	10.1
Coeur d'Alene	23 040	41 336	2.0	28.0	10.9	20 219	36.8	1 824	18 860	57.2	168 100	23.5	11.8
Idaho Falls	22 839	45 680	2.6	25.6	12.5	22 977	15.9	1 774	20 846	67.6	140 000	20.9	10.0
Lewiston	24 443	45 148	0.9	24.8	7.9	14 057	5.0	733	13 361	68.0	165 400	22.8	12.9
Meridian	26 738	63 225	2.9	13.6	6.4	26 674	117.1	1 372	28 431	75.2	186 400	22.3	10.0
Nampa	16 427	40 083	0.3	29.0	17.6	30 507	56.2	2 778	28 098	63.2	109 900	24.9	11.7
Pocatello	21 326	40 792	1.4	30.4	12.6	22 404	8.3	1 572	20 379	63.6	132 500	21.7	10.3
Post Falls	24 305	49 736	1.8	19.2	10.5	11 150	66.7	887	11 202	67.7	162 900	24.4	10.0
Rexburg	12 914	25 606	1.2	48.4	33.9	7 617	69.2	438	7 238	33.1	172 300	23.2	10.0
Twin Falls	19 552	41 880	1.5	26.5	13.9	18 033	27.4	1 289	16 412	59.3	142 600	23.8	10.0
ILLINOIS	30 019	57 166	5.6	21.8	10.5	5 296 715	8.4	459 743	4 778 633	66.9	175 700	24.2	13.5
Addison	24 695	53 469	3.9	20.8	12.4	12 581	7.3	641	12 302	67.7	228 700	27.9	17.7
Algonquin	39 797	100 534	12.9	7.5	2.2	10 727	33.4	480	10 393	88.5	242 200	23.1	14.2
Alton	20 515	36 076	0.7	35.1	19.5	13 266	-4.5	1 532	11 737	59.1	82 300	22.8	12.6
Arlington Heights	41 994	78 865	10.7	12.6	2.8	32 795	3.4	1 876	30 283	75.9	317 600	24.8	14.9
Aurora	26 527	63 569	5.6	15.8	11.5	67 273	37.5	4 709	61 506	67.5	174 000	25.7	14.0
Bartlett	36 544	94 919	8.6	8.6	3.1	14 509	17.4	436	13 797	88.9	260 400	26.6	15.7
Batavia	40 811	92 015	11.0	14.6	5.0	10 042	13.9	488	9 471	78.5	272 800	23.1	13.3
Belleville	24 970	46 558	1.2	27.8	13.1	21 099	9.4	2 304	17 652	62.0	103 600	21.9	12.8
Belvidere	20 063	49 423	1.2	23.8	14.3	9 565	20.5	762	8 810	74.0	111 500	24.4	14.0
Berwyn	22 180	54 392	1.4	21.8	13.0	20 719	0.1	1 809	18 401	60.3	173 200	29.3	17.4
Bloomington	33 279	62 046	6.4	20.3	7.9	34 339	20.4	2 676	30 558	62.2	162 500	19.8	12.3
Bolingbrook	28 049	78 230	4.8	11.8	7.6	23 141	29.2	929	22 124	82.0	209 500	26.7	13.7
Buffalo Grove	46 517	96 768	13.9	10.6	3.1	17 034	6.9	828	16 276	80.2	295 500	24.1	14.7

1. Based on population estimated by the American Community Survey.   2. Includes units rented or sold but not occupied.   3. Specified owner-occupied units; $1,000,000 represents $1,000,000 or more   4. 50.0 represents 50 percent or more.   5. 10.0 represents 10 percent or less.

Table D. Cities — Housing, Labor Force, and Employment

City	Occupied housing units, 2010–2014 (cont.)				Migration, 2010–2014		Civilian labor force, 2015		Unemployment		Civilian employment[4], 2010–2014			
	Percent renter occupied	Median gross rent[1]	Median gross rent as a percent of income[2]	Percent with no vehicle available	Percent who lived in the same house one year ago	Percent who lived outside current city one year ago	Total	Percent change, 2014–2015	Total	Rate[3]	Population age 16 and older	In labor force	Civilian full-year full-time workers	Households with no workers (percent)
	55	56	57	58	59	60	61	62	63	64	65	66	67	68
GEORGIA...............	35.8	874	31.8	6.9	83.8	13.0	4 770 873	0.4	279 942	5.9	7 693 577	63.3	39.6	26.1
Albany	61.1	693	35.3	14.9	81.4	8.1	30 770	-1.9	2 421	7.9	59 163	57.5	32.2	38.0
Alpharetta	36.5	1 142	25.0	4.5	84.3	13.3	33 703	1.3	1 465	4.3	44 810	70.0	49.8	14.7
Athens-Clarke County ...	57.4	790	38.1	7.3	74.3	14.0	56 558	0.6	3 317	5.9	100 565	57.7	28.9	29.4
Atlanta	55.9	969	31.9	17.4	76.4	12.0	233 306	0.7	14 604	6.3	365 230	64.8	39.7	28.1
Augusta-Richmond County ...	46.7	785	33.2	9.9	81.0	9.4	84 209	-0.5	6 146	7.3	157 529	59.7	33.4	31.5
Columbus	49.2	826	31.2	10.5	75.5	12.6	79 038	-2.2	5 827	7.4	154 637	62.9	34.9	29.5
Dalton	55.4	663	31.0	11.7	79.7	9.7	14 202	-0.1	962	6.8	24 495	65.3	42.8	25.4
Douglasville	52.7	925	29.7	6.2	77.5	16.5	16 152	0.8	1 087	6.7	23 320	65.4	40.0	22.0
Duluth	46.6	1 013	29.6	2.6	87.6	10.8	15 311	0.9	826	5.4	21 370	69.9	47.3	21.4
Dunwoody	45.9	1 170	26.9	4.1	84.4	13.2	25 828	1.1	1 132	4.4	36 335	69.6	49.9	20.2
East Point	56.1	903	36.1	19.6	79.2	15.9	16 808	0.4	1 438	8.6	27 625	66.0	36.4	29.4
Gainesville	64.0	816	30.7	14.7	77.3	14.2	16 605	2.3	885	5.3	25 335	65.7	40.3	24.2
Hinesville	53.7	892	28.6	5.9	73.2	22.0	14 723	-1.3	863	5.9	25 331	70.4	37.9	17.9
Johns Creek	20.9	1 353	25.8	1.5	87.9	10.2	42 825	1.4	1 891	4.4	59 830	70.0	49.9	14.1
Kennesaw	37.6	1 107	30.9	4.9	80.5	16.0	18 566	0.9	1 016	5.5	24 305	75.6	48.4	16.1
LaGrange	60.4	755	32.4	15.6	73.8	13.7	14 972	-0.6	1 015	6.8	23 074	58.8	37.3	31.6
Lawrenceville	47.4	876	36.9	6.8	83.3	13.9	14 351	0.7	955	6.7	22 001	64.9	38.8	24.0
Macon	46.2	742	36.8	11.9	82.0	6.3	68 327	-1.0	4 484	6.6	119 829	56.8	33.7	34.4
Marietta	57.1	888	32.6	9.5	70.5	19.9	34 180	0.9	1 827	5.3	46 721	70.6	40.2	19.1
Milton	31.4	1 220	21.8	1.3	87.1	12.2	NA	NA	NA	NA	25 501	67.1	48.6	13.6
Newnan	46.0	932	29.9	7.2	81.2	14.2	16 326	1.1	941	5.8	25 074	63.9	43.7	27.3
Peachtree City............	27.3	1 218	25.5	2.4	86.1	9.6	17 656	1.1	830	4.7	26 893	65.4	41.5	23.1
Rome	53.6	680	31.5	14.8	78.9	11.0	15 075	-1.5	1 118	7.4	28 261	56.7	32.5	37.1
Roswell.....................	32.9	1 021	29.7	5.3	87.2	9.5	51 666	1.4	2 233	4.3	72 466	70.6	50.1	18.2
Sandy Springs.............	53.8	1 010	27.8	7.3	78.5	17.2	59 522	1.2	2 683	4.5	79 192	73.5	49.4	18.7
Savannah.................	55.0	891	35.2	13.1	79.2	12.0	65 081	0.9	4 138	6.4	113 633	61.0	35.7	30.0
Smyrna.....................	49.8	936	28.3	3.8	75.3	20.0	33 082	1.2	1 625	4.9	41 597	77.8	54.8	15.4
Statesboro................	77.2	756	45.3	9.8	65.8	24.6	13 561	0.6	1 048	7.7	25 870	52.0	21.3	27.0
Stockbridge..............	41.5	996	28.5	2.2	84.3	14.2	13 275	0.6	990	7.5	20 200	67.5	44.2	19.8
Valdosta	61.2	763	34.6	9.6	72.4	13.0	25 320	-0.4	1 582	6.2	44 823	62.7	30.1	29.2
Warner Robins	44.0	855	30.1	4.8	82.2	10.9	31 144	-1.3	1 946	6.2	52 840	65.4	40.0	24.4
HAWAII....................	42.9	1 417	33.5	8.7	85.0	11.3	677 439	1.4	24 500	3.6	1 118 419	65.4	39.9	22.8
East Honolulu CDP.......	17.2	2 000	29.6	4.1	92.2	5.4	NA	NA	NA	NA	40 843	64.0	44.7	24.7
Hilo CDP	35.9	850	35.6	6.7	89.6	5.8	NA	NA	NA	NA	36 104	56.2	34.3	32.5
Kahului CDP...............	44.9	1 099	30.3	10.5	81.7	10.7	NA	NA	NA	NA	21 920	64.2	36.6	21.7
Kailua CDP (Honolulu County)	27.6	2 000	30.0	3.6	87.5	9.2	NA	NA	NA	NA	32 441	67.4	41.6	19.6
Kaneohe CDP	30.6	1 820	34.7	4.6	88.0	9.2	NA	NA	NA	NA	28 018	65.0	41.9	20.4
Mililani Town CDP........	23.5	1 854	34.2	2.6	90.0	8.2	NA	NA	NA	NA	22 824	66.8	43.2	19.3
Pearl City CDP	27.7	1 773	34.0	6.4	86.8	11.6	NA	NA	NA	NA	38 404	63.1	38.3	23.6
Urban Honolulu CDP	56.9	1 297	32.3	17.8	84.7	7.9	NA	NA	NA	NA	290 697	64.0	41.1	24.6
Waipahu CDP	43.0	1 186	32.9	10.4	90.2	7.0	NA	NA	NA	NA	32 555	63.6	39.4	20.0
IDAHO.....................	30.8	738	29.7	4.6	82.7	11.6	797 475	2.1	33 012	4.1	1 216 172	63.2	37.4	27.3
Boise City	40.4	793	29.8	6.5	78.9	9.8	117 934	2.4	4 187	3.6	170 196	68.4	40.7	24.7
Caldwell	34.5	711	29.7	6.0	82.0	11.1	22 867	1.9	1 241	5.4	34 509	64.9	37.3	27.1
Coeur d'Alene	42.8	783	35.1	6.7	77.4	13.2	24 007	2.3	1 203	5.0	36 357	62.1	33.6	31.2
Idaho Falls..................	32.4	683	29.7	6.2	82.7	9.1	28 207	3.0	1 016	3.6	43 090	64.4	39.4	25.8
Lewiston	32.0	651	27.2	6.6	84.7	7.3	17 495	1.8	614	3.5	26 221	64.0	38.2	31.0
Meridian	24.8	1 016	30.0	2.8	86.0	8.9	42 406	2.6	1 489	3.5	58 045	68.8	47.4	20.2
Nampa.......................	36.8	793	32.1	6.0	78.8	13.4	38 831	2.1	1 970	5.1	59 965	63.3	36.3	27.7
Pocatello	36.4	625	30.8	6.6	78.3	9.2	28 659	1.3	1 128	3.9	41 787	66.6	35.7	26.5
Post Falls	32.3	843	27.1	4.3	84.5	10.2	15 555	1.9	732	4.7	21 240	69.5	43.6	24.4
Rexburg	66.9	640	44.0	3.1	49.7	30.9	14 004	3.9	387	2.8	20 755	60.6	19.5	18.0
Twin Falls	40.7	691	29.4	6.3	77.3	11.4	22 937	3.3	822	3.6	34 203	64.7	39.8	23.7
ILLINOIS..................	33.1	903	30.7	10.8	86.8	7.9	6 512 386	0.0	386 079	5.9	10 170 489	66.1	40.6	25.8
Addison	32.3	916	33.4	4.2	84.4	9.5	19 483	-0.2	1 059	5.4	28 334	70.5	42.2	20.3
Algonquin	11.5	1 521	24.3	1.6	91.8	7.2	16 937	0.3	821	4.8	23 312	75.3	48.9	14.8
Alton	40.9	721	32.7	10.5	87.1	7.5	11 753	0.1	1 011	8.6	21 650	59.6	33.9	36.3
Arlington Heights..........	24.1	1 172	27.3	6.3	89.1	8.8	41 031	0.2	1 781	4.3	61 233	67.4	43.6	24.5
Aurora	32.5	1 057	31.7	5.1	85.8	7.3	101 988	0.3	5 878	5.8	144 689	73.1	46.3	15.3
Bartlett	11.1	1 295	33.3	3.2	92.1	5.0	23 357	0.1	1 085	4.6	32 017	73.9	48.4	14.1
Batavia	21.5	1 030	33.5	4.9	92.9	5.3	13 788	0.5	693	5.0	19 894	71.4	44.9	23.3
Belleville	38.0	717	30.3	7.8	88.9	7.9	22 496	0.2	1 476	6.6	35 068	64.1	42.7	28.2
Belvidere	26.0	713	28.8	6.9	86.3	5.9	11 776	-0.2	945	8.0	19 325	66.4	39.4	26.3
Berwyn	39.7	916	29.7	11.2	87.9	8.0	27 859	-0.3	1 778	6.4	43 155	68.9	42.3	22.6
Bloomington	37.8	768	25.1	8.5	82.4	9.9	41 271	0.0	2 066	5.0	60 919	70.8	46.8	21.5
Bolingbrook	18.0	1 163	38.6	2.7	92.6	5.3	40 033	-0.3	2 209	5.5	55 238	72.1	47.1	12.0
Buffalo Grove	19.8	1 290	24.6	4.7	89.4	9.1	24 503	0.5	1 095	4.5	33 355	73.4	50.5	18.4

1. $2,000 represents $2,000 or more.   2. 50.0 represents 50 percent or more.   3. Percent of civilian labor force.   4. Persons 16 years old and over.

Table D. Cities — Construction, Wholesale Trade, and Retail Trade

City	Value of residential construction authorized by building permits, 2015			Wholesale trade,[1] 2012				Retail trade,[2] 2012			
	New construction ($1,000)	Number of housing units	Percent single family	Number of establishments	Number of employees	Sales (mil dol)	Annual payroll (mil dol)	Number of establishments	Number of employees	Sales (mil dol)	Annual payroll (mil dol)
	69	70	71	72	73	74	75	76	77	78	79
GEORGIA	7 955 101	45 549	71.6	10 637	150 168	143 645.3	8 476.3	33 426	433 840	119 801.5	10 290.1
Albany	7 853	86	57.0	111	1 406	824.7	63.5	458	6 179	1 449.6	129.6
Alpharetta	186 814	777	34.2	161	3 714	5 088.0	345.2	372	7 362	1 931.3	170.7
Athens-Clarke County	72 380	642	13.9	99	1 801	1 947.0	85.0	516	6 963	1 684.2	145.6
Atlanta	953 259	6 697	11.3	698	11 556	9 224.9	748.9	1 875	24 977	6 088.3	633.1
Augusta-Richmond County	84 568	699	57.4	182	1 856	864.7	81.5	812	10 830	2 627.3	229.5
Columbus	90 085	616	47.1	157	1 843	1 550.1	80.6	796	11 371	2 847.8	250.2
Dalton	NA	NA	NA	108	1 489	756.2	57.6	259	2 644	678.8	59.3
Douglasville	17 480	55	100.0	20	146	65.8	7.0	253	4 228	922.8	82.2
Duluth	13 605	47	100.0	127	3 067	2 088.3	243.7	199	2 792	1 032.1	82.9
Dunwoody	31 817	56	100.0	60	978	713.5	98.7	250	5 168	916.8	106.9
East Point	7 452	83	68.7	30	640	501.8	29.6	90	1 196	267.7	23.2
Gainesville	74 061	436	93.6	92	D	D	D	299	3 927	1 007.8	95.0
Hinesville	47 562	220	64.5	6	D	D	D	127	1 682	402.9	35.9
Johns Creek	71 852	292	100.0	67	231	116.5	17.8	149	1 831	395.3	40.8
Kennesaw	6 683	29	100.0	80	1 153	832.4	62.3	189	3 621	840.4	78.5
LaGrange	9 069	34	100.0	32	609	287.4	18.2	184	2 600	738.7	64.3
Lawrenceville	16 137	72	100.0	115	1 926	1 257.1	109.0	309	3 550	882.0	81.9
Macon	19 148	113	100.0	122	D	D	D	629	7 527	1 820.1	166.1
Marietta	34 802	128	100.0	275	3 494	2 618.4	199.5	447	6 196	1 976.9	173.8
Milton	70 247	317	100.0	20	147	118.9	9.7	56	916	187.9	18.3
Newnan	118 697	549	61.2	33	D	D	D	200	3 261	798.6	73.3
Peachtree City	13 446	36	100.0	75	1 037	874.5	65.6	145	2 641	617.7	55.5
Rome	NA	NA	NA	54	693	605.1	29.3	283	3 352	840.9	76.5
Roswell	98 204	258	100.0	177	1 786	1 397.9	140.4	324	5 202	1 762.9	163.1
Sandy Springs	76 006	312	43.9	147	3 515	7 647.4	330.3	252	3 933	1 342.8	131.9
Savannah	84 104	328	100.0	180	1 884	3 630.1	102.2	869	11 121	2 862.9	260.4
Smyrna	36 932	190	100.0	73	2 229	2 185.5	138.4	189	2 894	1 028.8	79.6
Statesboro	8 819	70	40.0	23	141	152.5	6.2	202	2 828	655.9	59.1
Stockbridge	NA	NA	NA	11	38	9.7	0.9	95	1 819	443.8	43.5
Valdosta	10 411	83	80.7	85	822	1 113.3	32.0	370	4 978	1 314.1	109.7
Warner Robins	48 181	411	51.3	22	221	71.1	7.5	291	4 392	1 107.7	98.9
HAWAII	1 582 395	5 422	43.5	1 561	16 686	9 608.0	724.5	4 643	68 360	18 901.7	1 835.0
East Honolulu CDP	NA	NA	NA	33	65	22.5	2.4	55	962	343.3	27.9
Hilo CDP	NA	NA	NA	71	839	328.1	31.4	228	3 849	969.6	101.6
Kahului CDP	NA	NA	NA	52	637	513.5	31.8	194	4 127	1 252.3	124.8
Kailua CDP (Honolulu County)	NA	NA	NA	17	62	21.4	2.8	96	1 388	322.1	32.7
Kaneohe CDP	NA	NA	NA	12	19	11.5	1.0	119	1 597	481.5	46.5
Mililani Town CDP	NA	NA	NA	9	16	2.9	0.5	34	974	253.0	25.5
Pearl City CDP	NA	NA	NA	38	463	261.9	19.3	65	2 081	672.5	49.9
Urban Honolulu CDP	NA	NA	NA	782	9 002	5 712.8	399.8	1 851	26 485	7 684.2	748.6
Waipahu CDP	NA	NA	NA	56	790	292.5	35.1	106	2 248	866.1	76.8
IDAHO	1 934 066	9 954	78.2	1 739	21 470	17 906.0	960.8	5 815	72 980	20 444.3	1 794.0
Boise City	237 012	1 419	47.6	376	5 188	5 866.3	287.1	916	13 392	3 485.8	335.1
Caldwell	57 933	444	100.0	29	299	130.4	10.6	121	1 512	430.0	38.0
Coeur d'Alene	72 394	427	67.2	50	612	398.5	26.2	309	4 575	1 433.8	118.5
Idaho Falls	24 949	314	46.5	114	1 210	2 531.3	62.0	362	5 209	1 529.1	119.4
Lewiston	17 199	108	29.6	37	472	314.2	18.8	191	2 163	670.5	54.6
Meridian	298 238	1 470	71.8	93	2 282	1 086.7	100.6	246	4 537	1 648.6	139.2
Nampa	54 501	375	95.2	78	939	707.4	44.7	300	5 210	1 634.4	136.4
Pocatello	8 429	73	97.3	69	656	473.3	25.4	219	2 935	848.4	69.2
Post Falls	68 719	435	60.9	27	143	72.8	7.4	99	1 762	600.9	48.3
Rexburg	36 253	222	35.1	20	285	157.5	8.4	105	1 542	358.6	32.7
Twin Falls	49 788	286	78.3	75	810	336.8	31.3	314	4 308	1 122.4	102.5
ILLINOIS	4 136 596	19 571	51.5	16 036	255 531	295 457.0	15 973.3	39 947	592 942	166 634.5	14 576.1
Addison	1 225	4	100.0	198	3 798	2 418.5	282.6	96	1 807	709.5	72.4
Algonquin	27 946	210	11.4	23	95	69.6	7.5	158	3 492	706.1	66.4
Alton	895	6	100.0	27	284	219.5	14.5	150	2 233	500.2	51.8
Arlington Heights	46 331	148	94.6	151	3 104	2 632.1	263.1	203	3 354	749.7	97.9
Aurora	95 051	422	22.5	150	2 943	26 798.1	179.4	566	9 344	2 025.3	191.3
Bartlett	1 310	4	100.0	57	751	578.0	41.7	41	615	138.7	13.2
Batavia	7 387	16	100.0	78	799	539.8	49.0	90	1 634	394.1	34.5
Belleville	2 070	11	100.0	42	549	330.1	27.1	188	2 333	577.7	60.5
Belvidere	0	0	0.0	12	91	101.2	4.5	86	1 140	354.8	27.0
Berwyn	0	0	0.0	12	37	10.8	1.4	112	836	226.5	21.8
Bloomington	21 667	177	55.9	73	D	D	D	360	5 463	1 396.1	120.9
Bolingbrook	20 283	124	100.0	103	3 334	3 837.2	212.6	214	5 088	1 377.5	135.6
Buffalo Grove	9 356	23	100.0	122	2 672	2 796.2	181.6	128	1 340	381.3	40.2

1. Merchant wholesalers except manufacturers' sales branches and offices.   2. Establishments with payroll.

Table D. Cities — Real Estate, Professional Services, and Manufacturing

City	Real estate and rental and leasing, 2012				Professional, scientific, and technical services,[1] 2012				Manufacturing, 2012			
	Number of establishments	Number of employees	Receipts (mil dol)	Annual payroll (mil dol)	Number of establishments	Number of employees	Receipts (mil dol)	Annual payroll (mil dol)	Number of establishments	Number of employees	Receipts (mil dol)	Annual payroll (mil dol)
	80	81	82	83	84	85	86	87	88	89	90	91
GEORGIA	10 484	55 551	14 232.4	2 703.7	28 018	239 289	41 359.0	15 587.7	7 456	333 837	155 836.8	15 316.6
Albany	130	493	87.1	15.3	197	D	D	D	60	2 943	D	172.1
Alpharetta	203	1 412	723.0	90.7	847	13 182	2 303.2	1 072.3	21	412	D	27.7
Athens-Clarke County	190	926	140.6	27.0	300	D	D	D	78	5 115	2 004.8	229.5
Atlanta	1 121	9 940	2 333.2	660.6	3 501	52 799	12 632.0	4 945.1	295	7 404	3 609.7	356.0
Augusta-Richmond County	201	1 069	248.9	37.9	473	D	D	D	111	7 884	5 452.2	451.0
Columbus	237	1 461	258.1	55.7	346	D	D	D	122	6 977	1 937.2	297.0
Dalton	41	158	35.4	5.2	123	D	D	D	147	10 548	4 437.1	403.8
Douglasville	50	204	53.1	5.6	113	604	56.4	22.1	20	D	69.0	D
Duluth	98	459	112.5	23.3	279	2 539	420.2	172.3	39	1 549	553.4	127.0
Dunwoody	123	1 450	871.4	84.1	572	6 017	1 408.3	415.3	14	54	9.2	1.8
East Point	33	301	93.9	11.3	51	D	D	D	24	648	348.8	32.4
Gainesville	71	254	69.6	10.5	178	D	D	D	86	8 909	4 539.2	335.2
Hinesville	41	159	23.1	4.8	41	D	D	D	4	D	D	D
Johns Creek	99	D	D	D	580	D	D	D	14	D	D	D
Kennesaw	43	220	61.9	8.7	145	980	130.0	42.9	51	1 225	550.7	60.0
LaGrange	42	193	28.8	5.2	65	746	40.9	19.9	57	5 180	2 151.0	258.5
Lawrenceville	71	367	85.4	15.0	231	D	D	D	67	2 258	1 017.4	99.4
Macon	126	575	116.3	18.0	284	D	D	D	71	D	929.5	161.1
Marietta	186	884	174.8	41.4	557	D	D	D	109	3 408	1 129.4	161.1
Milton	24	D	D	D	205	4 498	264.7	132.2	6	16	D	0.6
Newnan	68	185	39.4	6.8	92	514	49.6	22.3	31	1 019	330.9	40.1
Peachtree City	74	158	32.4	7.0	172	D	D	D	39	1 864	789.3	97.9
Rome	61	202	33.1	6.2	146	700	85.0	31.2	61	3 069	2 196.8	142.6
Roswell	179	787	172.4	34.4	750	D	D	D	57	636	113.0	30.6
Sandy Springs	334	2 561	796.8	127.6	970	15 638	2 999.5	1 194.6	30	529	156.7	22.9
Savannah	246	1 266	247.7	38.9	496	D	D	D	104	3 234	1 475.3	166.2
Smyrna	87	297	62.2	12.4	280	8 545	575.5	275.5	40	1 132	208.7	40.4
Statesboro	56	266	44.6	6.7	87	D	D	D	26	1 163	359.6	43.1
Stockbridge	38	151	35.8	4.6	73	454	64.7	16.6	12	D	21.3	D
Valdosta	100	1 363	89.3	24.2	172	D	D	D	65	2 208	2 117.3	89.1
Warner Robins	79	303	50.0	7.6	158	D	D	D	25	519	D	28.4
HAWAII	1 919	11 369	3 411.2	483.9	3 188	20 998	3 229.4	1 225.0	796	11 440	D	465.0
East Honolulu CDP	49	105	18.6	4.2	110	282	33.8	12.2	3	9	1.6	0.4
Hilo CDP	80	358	59.7	9.4	98	D	D	D	46	425	D	16.8
Kahului CDP	52	535	142.3	21.3	43	258	27.7	9.5	18	95	17.3	3.1
Kailua CDP (Honolulu County)	54	176	31.5	7.2	95	D	D	D	13	47	5.7	1.5
Kaneohe CDP	26	89	11.6	3.0	50	D	D	D	15	120	16.9	4.1
Mililani Town CDP	6	28	3.2	0.7	17	D	D	D	NA	NA	NA	NA
Pearl City CDP	21	101	22.5	4.4	36	224	27.6	10.3	12	171		6.6
Urban Honolulu CDP	825	5 335	1 834.2	255.2	1 694	14 113	2 397.4	907.6	351	5 599	1 152.7	200.0
Waipahu CDP	34	182	27.7	5.7	20	226	15.2	5.4	20	359	128.8	13.0
IDAHO	2 033	6 268	1 039.9	184.2	4 177	D	D	D	1 759	52 084	20 201.4	2 445.5
Boise City	452	1 905	341.1	61.6	1 150	9 739	1 465.6	588.0	216	12 584	D	855.5
Caldwell	36	183	17.7	4.2	49	D	D	D	53	D	579.1	63.7
Coeur d'Alene	103	404	92.6	13.1	244	2 077	149.0	74.7	63	1 116	D	47.4
Idaho Falls	101	366	67.8	11.7	282	D	D	D	80	1 528	472.1	54.6
Lewiston	35	D	D	D	77	D	D	D	27	D	D	D
Meridian	101	236	40.4	10.5	197	1 595	242.0	88.2	55	1 143	D	46.4
Nampa	77	186	21.2	4.6	141	798	73.2	31.0	78	3 627	1 102.2	140.3
Pocatello	69	D	D	D	138	D	D	D	33	1 499	D	61.6
Post Falls	33	91	10.5	2.3	57	275	44.3	11.2	49	1 109	320.4	44.4
Rexburg	46	149	22.5	2.6	58	D	D	D	18	415	55.6	13.7
Twin Falls	87	259	45.4	7.1	174	D	D	D	59	1 669	683.0	64.1
ILLINOIS	12 035	76 794	23 649.1	3 816.1	38 540	355 434	68 675.2	27 645.3	13 868	542 004	281 037.8	28 413.7
Addison	42	347	75.6	16.6	94	455	89.2	21.9	310	5 793	1 395.5	279.1
Algonquin	23	D	D	D	111	340	48.7	17.3	23	391	84.6	20.1
Alton	34	109	15.7	3.5	63	D	D	D	22	1 105	442.7	50.3
Arlington Heights	96	633	105.7	32.7	488	D	D	D	71	1 902	980.2	109.7
Aurora	130	676	147.4	22.5	450	2 399	351.6	125.4	138	8 689	4 775.2	512.4
Bartlett	22	61	10.8	1.9	148	319	58.9	19.0	29	999	273.5	53.2
Batavia	26	100	13.6	3.2	138	D	D	D	88	3 758	1 380.5	182.1
Belleville	55	169	31.9	5.4	153	D	D	D	38	1 347	380.4	61.5
Belvidere	15	45	6.4	1.1	31	D	D	D	39	6 985	5 764.7	374.7
Berwyn	27	68	14.4	1.6	71	1 276	49.3	27.9	15	486	D	28.0
Bloomington	95	439	107.7	14.1	238	D	D	D	49	1 525	554.8	71.0
Bolingbrook	39	190	34.0	6.3	154	1 517	178.4	76.7	54	3 763	1 169.0	181.2
Buffalo Grove	47	261	56.0	11.4	313	3 419	392.2	178.1	53	3 097	1 205.8	154.6

1. Establishments subject to federal tax.

City	Accommodation and food services, 2012				Arts, entertainment, and recreation,[1] 2012				Health care and social assistance,[1] 2012			
	Number of establish-ments	Number of employees	Sales (mil dol)	Annual payroll (mil dol)	Number of establish-ments	Number of employees	Receipts (mil dol)	Annual payroll (mil dol)	Number of establish-ments	Number of employees	Receipts (mil dol)	Annual payroll (mil dol)
	92	93	94	95	96	97	98	99	100	101	102	103
GEORGIA	18 815	353 638	18 976.6	5 173.4	2 232	28 800	2 877.8	953.0	20 166	256 945	28 196.2	11 171.4
Albany	211	D	D	D	15	D	D	D	238	D	D	D
Alpharetta	286	6 486	342.2	98.9	33	D	D	D	389	3 667	556.5	236.2
Athens-Clarke County	342	6 927	307.6	83.9	27	354	20.5	5.5	394	D	D	D
Atlanta	1 618	42 124	3 023.4	844.6	272	3 724	871.2	309.6	1 336	17 100	2 332.0	908.9
Augusta-Richmond County	424	9 448	447.0	125.6	28	D	D	D	577	9 118	1 230.5	456.4
Columbus	442	10 453	519.3	149.2	30	427	26.0	6.5	520	6 215	649.7	261.6
Dalton	120	D	D	D	7	D	D	D	122	D	D	D
Douglasville	129	2 867	130.6	36.6	4	D	D	D	115	1 033	118.2	46.4
Duluth	144	1 624	82.0	22.3	19	D	D	D	166	D	D	D
Dunwoody	141	3 952	244.2	73.0	17	D	D	D	202	3 057	258.8	98.0
East Point	72	1 504	97.0	26.8	14	D	D	D	83	1 789	177.9	59.5
Gainesville	151	2 837	163.0	43.3	15	D	D	D	271	D	D	D
Hinesville	80	1 307	68.7	14.9	3	D	D	D	49	525	40.8	18.1
Johns Creek	137	2 100	98.6	30.2	20	557	47.0	15.0	158	D	D	D
Kennesaw	111	2 319	109.7	31.5	15	D	D	D	85	D	D	D
LaGrange	86	1 738	76.2	21.7	7	D	D	D	79	D	D	D
Lawrenceville	128	2 022	107.6	29.9	15	D	D	D	262	D	D	D
Macon	266	4 795	207.3	58.8	11	D	D	D	365	D	D	D
Marietta	289	4 708	264.5	74.0	24	174	19.7	3.8	392	D	D	D
Milton	44	635	34.6	9.8	17	171	13.5	3.2	28	D	D	D
Newnan	112	2 784	129.1	37.1	7	189	9.1	2.2	93	D	D	D
Peachtree City	100	2 410	112.6	35.3	20	D	D	D	119	D	D	D
Rome	138	3 070	136.6	40.0	11	D	D	D	215	D	D	D
Roswell	237	4 531	234.3	68.0	51	D	D	D	352	5 025	553.5	202.6
Sandy Springs	266	4 373	280.1	75.7	33	577	39.2	11.4	640	8 319	1 459.9	597.1
Savannah	571	12 766	759.1	203.0	40	D	D	D	486	8 390	1 182.6	453.3
Smyrna	161	2 788	152.3	41.7	19	291	13.0	4.8	208	1 508	188.3	61.4
Statesboro	124	D	D	D	4	D	D	D	148	D	D	D
Stockbridge	83	1 205	57.8	14.1	8	D	D	D	143	D	D	D
Valdosta	214	4 519	199.0	53.2	13	D	D	D	275	D	D	D
Warner Robins	157	3 608	168.4	44.7	11	234	7.1	2.4	179	D	D	D
HAWAII	3 518	98 364	9 536.7	2 536.0	398	7 327	571.1	168.2	2 794	26 788	3 180.4	1 347.2
East Honolulu CDP	65	D	D	D	12	D	D	D	64	548	56.6	19.3
Hilo CDP	146	2 239	133.8	33.2	6	D	D	D	176	2 291	225.8	99.0
Kahului CDP	84	1 703	123.3	31.2	10	D	D	D	75	704	99.2	42.4
Kailua CDP (Honolulu County)	86	1 446	81.3	20.9	9	D	D	D	113	D	D	D
Kaneohe CDP	74	1 140	76.8	17.5	12	D	D	D	81	725	78.1	31.0
Mililani Town CDP	41	1 055	60.1	15.0	3	119	8.8	1.8	19	180	19.9	10.1
Pearl City CDP	74	1 346	79.7	19.3	3	146	11.9	2.5	76	785	82.2	31.8
Urban Honolulu CDP	1 471	38 426	3 944.0	955.4	103	1 558	117.6	31.5	1 262	11 394	1 445.9	615.3
Waipahu CDP	77	1 007	64.5	15.0	3	5	0.7	0.1	86	749	74.2	28.6
IDAHO	3 564	54 257	2 680.2	726.1	573	6 755	355.9	102.6	4 271	49 613	4 281.1	1 636.4
Boise City	617	11 334	523.9	154.0	56	1 166	44.4	12.3	793	D	D	D
Caldwell	65	1 007	46.6	12.2	5	D	D	D	93	1 484	160.5	55.9
Coeur d'Alene	184	3 531	181.2	51.4	28	244	18.5	5.6	274	D	D	D
Idaho Falls	191	3 578	159.1	46.2	13	D	D	D	416	D	D	D
Lewiston	95	D	D	D	13	D	D	D	119	1 820	167.6	56.4
Meridian	178	3 513	161.9	44.2	25	439	19.6	5.9	279	D	D	D
Nampa	159	2 965	122.8	34.2	16	D	D	D	197	3 419	215.1	99.1
Pocatello	151	2 633	111.4	30.7	17	D	D	D	245	D	D	D
Post Falls	57	735	34.0	9.7	8	65	4.8	1.2	83	1 406	124.7	47.3
Rexburg	48	840	30.4	8.5	7	60	1.8	0.5	84	D	D	D
Twin Falls	140	2 486	123.3	32.4	23	D	D	D	235	D	D	D
ILLINOIS	27 117	469 870	27 937.4	7 707.1	3 564	49 286	5 591.9	1 678.3	27 624	383 980	39 270.3	16 150.8
Addison	73	D	D	D	8	D	D	D	50	969	81.3	41.9
Algonquin	82	1 821	81.9	26.2	16	D	D	D	89	733	76.2	36.1
Alton	92	1 842	85.5	26.3	11	D	D	D	92	D	D	D
Arlington Heights	148	2 732	161.0	45.4	29	274	16.7	5.1	351	D	D	D
Aurora	257	4 005	227.2	56.8	34	973	161.4	29.9	304	4 552	575.3	222.8
Bartlett	36	460	24.8	6.5	7	D	D	D	49	D	D	D
Batavia	63	1 094	50.3	15.2	5	D	D	D	57	D	D	D
Belleville	142	D	D	D	14	D	D	D	159	4 006	362.8	191.6
Belvidere	49	D	D	D	5	D	D	D	45	D	D	D
Berwyn	86	D	D	D	6	42	2.7	0.7	130	3 811	433.8	197.0
Bloomington	223	4 927	234.3	67.4	33	601	18.3	6.0	204	2 790	335.9	142.6
Bolingbrook	154	3 230	173.5	49.0	19	569	17.7	8.6	138	D	D	D
Buffalo Grove	101	1 514	92.8	28.1	14	D	D	D	172	1 506	181.5	64.6

1. Establishments subject to federal tax.

City	Other services[1], 2012				Government employment and payroll, 2012								
					Full-time equivalent employees	March payroll							
							Percent of total for:						
	Number of establish-ments	Number of employees	Receipts (mil dol)	Annual payroll (mil dol)		Total (dollars)	Adminis-tration, judicial, and legal	Police and Corrections	Fire Protection	Highways and trans-portation	Health and welfare	Natural resources and utilities	Education and libraries
	104	105	106	107	108	109	110	111	112	113	114	115	116
GEORGIA..............	11 682	71 989	6 311.9	1 949.9	X	X	X	X	X	X	X	X	X
Albany	113	D	D	D	1 213	4 293 454	11.1	19.0	17.2	7.2	2.0	31.0	0.0
Alpharetta..................	138	D	D	D	443	2 007 691	5.5	32.0	22.6	9.9	0.0	9.9	0.0
Athens-Clarke County ...	153	929	66.0	21.6	1 759	6 225 567	17.5	31.3	12.0	9.2	0.6	19.8	3.4
Atlanta	879	8 945	574.9	212.4	8 214	31 551 612	15.9	34.2	13.9	16.0	0.2	18.5	0.0
Augusta-Richmond County	220	1 531	148.4	44.6	2 708	8 108 733	23.7	31.7	13.0	8.3	1.7	16.6	2.0
Columbus	259	1 902	157.2	51.1	3 147	10 081 635	11.8	34.7	14.0	7.5	4.7	18.9	2.8
Dalton	57	D	D	D	692	2 865 431	2.7	12.6	11.3	8.7	0.3	61.7	0.0
Douglasville	80	369	35.4	10.7	232	792 422	15.8	53.4	0.0	14.1	0.0	8.0	0.0
Duluth........................	133	785	73.7	21.0	140	565 431	33.5	44.9	0.0	10.3	0.0	10.1	0.0
Dunwoody	73	435	28.6	8.8	67	294 800	23.0	77.0	0.0	0.0	0.0	0.0	0.0
East Point..................	38	747	41.5	13.4	535	1 898 606	17.4	33.8	15.0	2.6	0.0	22.3	0.0
Gainesville.................	86	398	34.2	9.9	670	2 183 927	9.3	16.9	16.0	8.4	2.2	43.8	0.0
Hinesville	39	208	14.9	4.4	201	695 457	7.4	56.2	19.8	0.0	3.5	2.5	0.0
Johns Creek	78	D	D	D	8	41 438	87.5	12.5	0.0	0.0	0.0	0.0	0.0
Kennesaw	99	963	111.3	41.3	205	735 014	16.6	34.2	0.0	9.0	2.2	24.9	0.0
LaGrange	45	D	D	D	408	1 594 338	6.9	28.0	14.4	4.1	0.7	29.6	0.0
Lawrenceville..............	135	767	85.7	27.2	246	987 618	20.7	41.4	0.0	4.4	0.0	30.9	0.0
Macon........................	145	839	91.3	25.4	1 169	3 501 960	8.9	33.1	34.1	4.1	1.9	14.4	0.0
Marietta.....................	220	1 340	152.1	45.4	734	3 368 637	23.6	11.1	12.3	4.3	11.8	24.4	0.0
Milton	30	D	D	D	121	520 911	22.5	27.5	44.2	3.3	0.0	2.5	0.0
Newnan	69	308	24.4	6.4	267	989 419	6.4	31.3	19.7	8.0	0.0	19.0	0.6
Peachtree City..............	86	758	53.4	17.9	270	1 079 307	11.4	29.0	29.7	14.7	0.0	5.3	3.6
Rome	62	429	39.4	10.8	589	1 937 155	8.3	18.6	26.8	11.5	0.6	25.2	0.0
Roswell......................	200	1 408	111.7	41.6	741	2 812 794	17.5	29.3	11.9	8.4	0.0	29.5	0.0
Sandy Springs..............	170	D	D	D	295	1 455 396	3.8	60.7	34.3	0.0	0.0	0.0	0.0
Savannah	221	1 473	144.6	43.6	2 548	9 836 488	9.9	34.9	11.9	8.9	2.7	25.8	0.0
Smyrna	102	452	41.9	12.4	391	1 523 989	10.9	37.3	23.1	6.6	3.6	14.0	2.3
Statesboro..................	55	288	21.2	5.4	279	845 101	12.3	28.4	12.3	12.1	0.0	32.0	0.0
Stockbridge	38	175	12.6	3.1	68	227 107	32.1	0.0	0.0	21.8	0.0	33.5	0.0
Valdosta.....................	92	512	31.4	8.5	574	1 813 002	8.4	32.3	17.3	9.7	3.4	24.8	0.0
Warner Robins	81	473	34.5	10.5	536	1 642 600	10.8	31.9	21.3	10.1	3.3	20.5	0.0
HAWAII......................	1 519	11 014	877.5	279.0	X	X	X	X	X	X	X	X	X
East Honolulu CDP......	24	101	4.3	1.6	NA	NA	NA	NA	NA	NA	NA	NA	NA
Hilo CDP	68	351	30.2	8.4	NA	NA	NA	NA	NA	NA	NA	NA	NA
Kahului CDP...............	53	471	34.8	11.6	NA	NA	NA	NA	NA	NA	NA	NA	NA
Kailua CDP (Honolulu County)	47	196	15.1	4.7	NA	NA	NA	NA	NA	NA	NA	NA	NA
Kaneohe CDP..............	38	268	20.0	7.2	NA	NA	NA	NA	NA	NA	NA	NA	NA
Mililani Town CDP........	15	93	5.1	2.0	NA	NA	NA	NA	NA	NA	NA	NA	NA
Pearl City CDP.............	43	187	21.3	6.1	NA	NA	NA	NA	NA	NA	NA	NA	NA
Urban Honolulu CDP	721	6 242	481.7	157.1	NA	NA	NA	NA	NA	NA	NA	NA	NA
Waipahu CDP	53	276	23.2	6.9	NA	NA	NA	NA	NA	NA	NA	NA	NA
IDAHO	2 055	9 826	849.8	240.9	X	X	X	X	X	X	X	X	X
Boise City	371	2 083	162.4	51.1	1 617	7 522 788	17.0	29.2	23.6	4.2	0.9	17.7	4.2
Caldwell.....................	46	290	30.2	8.4	228	861 823	8.7	36.4	24.0	12.2	0.0	13.3	3.2
Coeur d'Alene	82	447	32.5	10.0	318	1 619 497	16.8	30.1	21.9	7.8	0.2	19.0	3.2
Idaho Falls.................	92	448	42.2	11.5	659	2 848 455	10.4	20.7	20.0	4.4	0.0	33.4	2.9
Lewiston	65	381	28.8	8.9	314	1 377 725	8.6	24.1	24.4	12.2	3.9	16.1	2.7
Meridian	90	556	37.4	13.7	343	1 643 338	14.3	34.7	25.5	8.1	0.0	15.4	0.0
Nampa	100	578	47.8	14.8	565	2 435 649	5.6	35.1	21.4	3.5	2.1	14.7	2.4
Pocatello....................	76	416	39.1	9.5	561	2 333 293	10.6	25.9	18.5	10.3	1.9	26.0	2.6
Post Falls	48	236	18.4	5.5	169	673 051	14.6	40.3	0.0	12.1	1.2	22.8	0.0
Rexburg	25	D	D	D	115	440 960	21.3	29.6	8.0	11.5	0.8	17.1	0.0
Twin Falls	87	614	50.1	14.4	284	1 088 260	9.5	36.0	16.2	11.3	4.2	14.9	5.2
ILLINOIS....................	18 681	117 388	10 571.7	3 334.1	X	X	X	X	X	X	X	X	X
Addison	113	775	89.8	27.4	245	1 559 535	9.6	44.1	0.0	4.2	9.2	20.0	8.6
Algonquin	66	364	22.1	7.5	143	751 901	11.3	26.1	0.0	11.5	0.3	33.9	0.0
Alton	46	251	16.2	5.6	230	1 141 005	7.5	40.6	24.3	8.2	1.8	13.2	0.0
Arlington Heights.........	138	912	99.9	29.3	594	3 727 355	11.4	27.0	22.6	8.1	2.6	6.6	15.0
Aurora.......................	159	1 044	120.6	29.7	1 402	8 465 715	9.4	32.8	18.5	7.5	8.1	14.5	5.4
Bartlett	33	142	18.3	4.9	166	992 280	14.8	48.1	0.0	13.2	11.3	12.4	0.0
Batavia	55	509	52.3	18.0	160	528 428	11.6	29.4	18.9	8.0	7.5	24.3	0.0
Belleville	96	635	49.6	15.9	345	1 469 633	6.3	35.6	25.0	5.2	0.0	14.8	4.1
Belvidere	30	231	17.9	6.1	125	645 335	6.9	38.7	26.4	8.1	0.0	13.1	4.0
Berwyn	53	214	19.6	4.7	402	2 004 230	7.2	46.5	25.8	5.7	1.5	5.4	6.1
Bloomington	127	1 022	74.9	28.0	723	3 168 188	7.2	25.0	19.2	14.3	0.0	27.5	5.8
Bolingbrook	79	424	31.8	10.7	391	2 517 306	8.3	44.4	26.4	8.1	0.0	9.5	0.0
Buffalo Grove	77	463	37.9	11.1	255	1 764 688	6.4	35.2	28.3	6.6	3.6	14.2	0.0

1. Establishments subject to federal tax.

Table D. Cities — **City Government Finances**

City	City government finances, 2012									
	General revenue							General expenditure		
	Intergovernmental			Taxes					Per capita[1] (dollars)	
					Per capita[1] (dollars)					
	Total (mil dol)	Total (mil dol)	Percent from state government	Total (mil dol)	Total	Property	Sales and gross receipts	Total (mil dol)	Total	Capital outlays
	117	118	119	120	121	122	123	124	125	126
GEORGIA............	X	X	X	X	X	X	X	X	X	X
Albany	124.2	55.1	36.8	24.1	312	164	148	134.7	1 739	76
Alpharetta	73.1	15.6	8.8	42.0	678	393	285	72.3	1 166	291
Athens-Clarke County ...	206.5	69.1	26.0	71.2	598	405	191	249.4	2 095	484
Atlanta	1 789.4	282.2	8.0	521.0	1 173	704	465	1 567.5	3 530	1 093
Augusta-Richmond County	364.7	133.0	12.9	103.4	524	291	230	341.5	1 731	350
Columbus	354.1	116.0	29.3	135.0	675	498	175	364.1	1 820	349
Dalton	69.4	16.5	0.3	14.2	427	283	144	82.6	2 478	515
Douglasville	27.0	7.1	10.3	13.8	441	190	246	34.0	1 088	313
Duluth	24.7	9.0	7.9	11.7	419	226	192	21.2	761	234
Dunwoody	20.5	0.6	15.1	17.6	372	123	247	26.5	560	185
East Point	49.3	11.3	1.5	20.7	582	366	216	55.0	1 547	287
Gainesville	78.3	19.3	20.5	21.8	626	363	263	70.8	2 035	502
Hinesville	30.4	10.9	1.3	9.9	287	163	124	30.3	873	89
Johns Creek	48.5	16.3	1.2	29.0	352	203	148	41.5	504	64
Kennesaw	26.5	5.0	1.3	14.0	449	296	154	24.9	796	112
LaGrange	35.7	9.6	8.9	4.7	155	1	153	44.0	1 454	186
Lawrenceville...........	22.3	5.6	4.6	5.4	185	59	120	28.0	952	219
Macon	105.9	49.5	9.0	37.3	239	126	113	116.6	748	73
Marietta	82.2	22.8	7.9	30.6	524	231	293	98.4	1 683	284
Milton	21.7	4.6	14.9	15.2	433	294	139	20.2	577	192
Newnan	30.9	10.4	1.6	10.9	320	137	184	29.9	875	209
Peachtree City.........	37.7	9.3	2.0	19.4	559	360	199	41.6	1 200	340
Rome	65.6	22.8	6.9	19.0	526	247	230	61.5	1 706	503
Roswell	94.1	26.7	5.7	44.7	478	286	192	94.3	1 006	196
Sandy Springs.........	95.9	28.3	2.8	60.0	604	296	307	75.2	757	151
Savannah	345.6	126.6	7.8	105.1	739	418	308	307.5	2 161	358
Smyrna	56.3	11.1	0.4	27.0	513	327	184	52.4	994	224
Statesboro	31.5	5.9	3.1	9.5	316	131	185	31.3	1 045	125
Stockbridge	16.8	7.3	22.1	4.0	149	1	148	12.9	481	83
Valdosta	56.4	22.7	6.1	17.4	302	105	197	59.7	1 036	254
Warner Robins	55.2	4.5	3.8	28.0	390	229	159	54.2	755	88
HAWAII.................	X	X	X	X	X	X	X	X	X	X
East Honolulu CDP	NA	NA	NA	NA	NA	NA	NA	NA	NA	NA
Hilo CDP	NA	NA	NA	NA	NA	NA	NA	NA	NA	NA
Kahului CDP.............	NA	NA	NA	NA	NA	NA	NA	NA	NA	NA
Kailua CDP (Honolulu County)	NA	NA	NA	NA	NA	NA	NA	NA	NA	NA
Kaneohe CDP	NA	NA	NA	NA	NA	NA	NA	NA	NA	NA
Mililani Town CDP........	NA	NA	NA	NA	NA	NA	NA	NA	NA	NA
Pearl City CDP	NA	NA	NA	NA	NA	NA	NA	NA	NA	NA
Urban Honolulu CDP	NA	NA	NA	NA	NA	NA	NA	NA	NA	NA
Waipahu CDP	NA	NA	NA	NA	NA	NA	NA	NA	NA	NA
IDAHO	X	X	X	X	X	X	X	X	X	X
Boise City	272.0	25.8	66.8	117.7	555	507	48	267.8	1 262	173
Caldwell..................	38.9	8.0	82.7	14.3	300	279	21	36.7	769	225
Coeur d'Alene	48.9	9.7	58.0	22.9	502	399	102	55.8	1 224	307
Idaho Falls..............	69.3	13.2	98.9	29.0	500	478	22	71.2	1 228	104
Lewiston	41.1	7.7	98.7	16.4	511	463	48	40.2	1 252	159
Meridian	53.9	9.9	100.0	23.3	290	242	48	42.4	528	89
Nampa....................	96.5	19.8	60.9	39.9	476	446	30	87.0	1 036	141
Pocatello.................	63.5	14.4	48.1	27.0	493	456	37	67.9	1 239	121
Post Falls	27.0	5.7	100.0	8.8	307	307	0	21.0	732	124
Rexburg	28.6	9.7	87.9	4.9	188	131	58	28.9	1 102	434
Twin Falls	39.5	5.6	70.4	19.5	433	398	35	33.6	747	116
ILLINOIS.................	X	X	X	X	X	X	X	X	X	X
Addison	44.5	12.7	100.0	22.1	594	338	250	39.8	1 067	5
Algonquin	27.6	11.4	100.0	12.4	415	200	215	21.1	704	36
Alton	40.8	15.1	100.0	14.7	535	282	253	34.8	1 267	124
Arlington Heights.........	98.7	20.5	94.8	68.0	897	574	324	81.7	1 078	28
Aurora	238.0	71.0	89.2	134.1	671	453	211	225.1	1 127	121
Bartlett...................	31.0	7.0	96.0	17.3	415	315	93	29.2	703	48
Batavia	30.0	8.1	95.0	13.2	500	278	223	38.7	1 468	511
Belleville	58.9	17.0	97.2	27.8	641	477	164	95.3	2 198	622
Belvidere	21.8	7.4	92.3	8.4	331	227	105	17.2	679	20
Berwyn	69.4	14.0	73.5	38.6	679	499	163	80.9	1 425	107
Bloomington	114.7	26.3	94.5	54.8	704	308	396	104.9	1 349	122
Bolingbrook	85.6	23.0	91.1	43.5	588	210	348	83.2	1 124	65
Buffalo Grove	47.2	12.4	82.1	22.3	535	338	184	50.5	1 215	102

1. Based on population estimated as of July 1 of the year shown.

City	Public welfare	Highways	Parking facilities	Education	Health and hospitals	Police protection	Sewerage and sanitation	Parks and recreation	Housing and community development	Interest on debt
	127	128	129	130	131	132	133	134	135	136
GEORGIA................	X	X	X	X	X	X	X	X	X	X
Albany	0.0	4.9	0.0	0.0	0.0	11.4	15.9	5.6	5.6	1.4
Alpharetta	0.0	23.5	0.0	0.0	0.0	19.9	4.3	8.5	0.0	1.8
Athens-Clarke County ...	0.2	4.4	1.6	0.0	5.2	11.0	11.5	5.5	1.8	0.4
Atlanta	1.2	2.2	0.0	1.3	0.1	11.0	13.8	4.1	1.0	10.4
Augusta-Richmond County	0.2	6.6	0.1	0.0	6.2	11.7	18.1	4.9	6.5	1.3
Columbus	0.0	10.1	0.0	0.0	8.2	13.4	10.9	3.8	2.8	2.7
Dalton	0.8	5.6	0.0	0.0	0.0	10.7	27.0	11.8	0.1	2.3
Douglasville	0.0	4.7	0.0	0.0	0.0	25.3	15.3	31.6	0.8	3.5
Duluth	0.0	21.9	0.5	0.0	0.0	31.7	0.0	12.3	0.9	2.1
Dunwoody	0.0	22.3	0.0	0.0	0.0	22.3	2.5	23.3	8.6	0.3
East Point	0.0	6.9	0.0	0.0	0.0	25.4	20.7	2.7	3.3	3.1
Gainesville	4.3	4.3	0.0	0.0	0.0	12.4	22.0	12.2	0.9	2.6
Hinesville	0.0	11.7	0.0	0.0	0.0	23.7	19.6	1.5	4.0	1.6
Johns Creek	0.0	20.6	0.0	0.0	0.0	21.0	0.0	3.6	6.9	0.5
Kennesaw	0.0	17.6	0.0	0.0	0.0	21.1	7.9	9.3	2.7	4.0
LaGrange	0.0	12.7	0.0	0.0	0.5	20.4	32.2	2.5	1.6	0.5
Lawrenceville...............	0.0	16.5	0.0	0.0	0.0	37.1	18.1	0.0	1.5	0.0
Macon	0.0	2.6	0.1	0.0	0.4	20.4	8.6	5.0	5.9	1.3
Marietta	5.6	11.8	0.0	0.0	0.0	14.3	14.3	5.3	3.3	4.2
Milton	0.0	25.7	0.0	0.0	0.7	15.0	0.0	2.8	3.7	0.3
Newnan	0.0	11.4	0.0	0.0	0.2	21.1	23.1	3.7	1.2	0.0
Peachtree City............	0.3	7.9	0.0	0.0	0.7	16.0	2.6	8.7	0.1	1.9
Rome........................	0.0	8.7	0.8	0.1	0.0	12.5	22.9	2.5	2.4	0.5
Roswell.....................	0.0	12.1	0.0	0.0	0.0	17.7	10.8	11.8	2.1	1.2
Sandy Springs..............	0.0	27.3	0.0	0.0	0.0	23.0	1.9	6.3	1.1	0.3
Savannah	0.3	4.5	2.1	0.0	0.0	20.3	17.7	6.9	10.8	1.5
Smyrna	0.0	22.7	0.0	0.0	0.0	14.8	15.7	4.7	0.3	3.6
Statesboro	0.0	8.4	0.0	0.0	0.3	19.2	31.7	2.2	2.0	0.1
Stockbridge	0.0	17.1	0.0	0.0	0.0	8.4	17.0	3.3	1.1	5.7
Valdosta	0.0	12.1	0.0	0.0	0.0	21.5	25.4	2.4	1.0	0.2
Warner Robins	0.2	11.8	0.0	0.0	0.8	25.1	22.9	3.7	3.1	0.0
HAWAII.....................	X	X	X	X	X	X	X	X	X	X
East Honolulu CDP.......	NA	NA	NA	NA	NA	NA	NA	NA	NA	NA
Hilo CDP	NA	NA	NA	NA	NA	NA	NA	NA	NA	NA
Kahului CDP...............	NA	NA	NA	NA	NA	NA	NA	NA	NA	NA
Kailua CDP (Honolulu County)	NA	NA	NA	NA	NA	NA	NA	NA	NA	NA
Kaneohe CDP	NA	NA	NA	NA	NA	NA	NA	NA	NA	NA
Mililani Town CDP........	NA	NA	NA	NA	NA	NA	NA	NA	NA	NA
Pearl City CDP.............	NA	NA	NA	NA	NA	NA	NA	NA	NA	NA
Urban Honolulu CDP	NA	NA	NA	NA	NA	NA	NA	NA	NA	NA
Waipahu CDP	NA	NA	NA	NA	NA	NA	NA	NA	NA	NA
IDAHO......................	X	X	X	X	X	X	X	X	X	X
Boise City	0.0	0.9	0.0	0.0	0.0	16.9	19.6	7.6	2.4	0.6
Caldwell....................	0.0	10.3	0.0	0.0	0.0	19.7	16.9	5.7	0.0	1.3
Coeur d'Alene	0.0	10.0	0.3	0.0	0.0	18.0	32.7	5.5	0.2	1.6
Idaho Falls.................	0.0	6.6	0.0	0.0	4.4	14.1	16.6	12.8	0.0	0.1
Lewiston	0.0	13.4	0.0	0.0	0.0	15.9	27.8	7.7	3.2	0.7
Meridian	0.0	0.0	0.0	0.0	0.0	26.6	23.6	9.0	0.4	0.3
Nampa	0.0	7.3	0.1	0.0	0.6	21.3	17.3	14.0	0.9	3.1
Pocatello...................	0.0	9.8	0.0	0.0	4.3	16.7	12.7	5.2	1.4	1.8
Post Falls	0.0	12.2	0.0	0.0	0.0	22.6	27.3	8.3	0.0	3.4
Rexburg	0.0	9.2	0.0	0.0	0.7	6.6	16.2	20.9	2.6	1.0
Twin Falls	0.0	14.4	0.2	0.0	1.0	21.5	19.5	6.3	1.9	0.8
ILLINOIS...................	X	X	X	X	X	X	X	X	X	X
Addison	0.0	16.5	0.0	0.0	0.0	38.7	13.7	0.0	0.0	6.6
Algonquin	0.0	19.0	0.0	0.0	0.0	39.5	10.4	8.0	0.0	0.9
Alton	0.0	13.1	0.0	0.0	0.5	25.5	14.9	8.3	0.0	2.0
Arlington Heights...........	0.0	12.4	1.5	0.0	1.8	26.6	1.9	0.9	0.4	2.9
Aurora.......................	0.0	10.8	0.6	0.0	0.4	28.0	2.2	3.8	2.0	11.6
Bartlett	0.0	16.3	0.7	0.0	0.0	37.2	10.5	8.1	0.0	7.2
Batavia	0.0	37.4	0.0	0.0	0.0	19.8	6.2	0.0	0.0	1.8
Belleville	0.0	8.5	0.0	0.0	0.0	9.1	31.1	1.7	0.0	4.9
Belvidere	0.0	14.5	0.0	0.0	0.1	33.8	11.9	1.0	0.0	2.3
Berwyn	0.3	11.0	0.1	0.0	0.0	26.6	8.8	2.9	4.0	5.8
Bloomington	0.0	5.5	0.9	0.0	0.0	14.8	15.4	16.9	0.6	2.8
Bolingbrook	0.0	14.2	0.0	0.0	0.0	22.2	9.2	11.1	0.3	10.3
Buffalo Grove	0.0	6.9	0.3	0.0	0.0	24.6	16.7	6.1	0.0	0.4

Table D. Cities — City Government Finances, City Government Employment, and Climate

City	City government finances, 2012 (cont.)			Climate[2]						
	Debt outstanding			Average daily temperature (degrees Fahrenheit)						
				Mean		Limits				
	Total (mil dol)	Per capita[1] (dollars)	Debt issued during year	January	July	January[3]	July[4]	Annual precipitation (inches)	Heating degree days	Cooling degree days
	137	138	139	140	141	142	143	144	145	146
GEORGIA	X	X	X	X	X	X	X	X	X	X
Albany	71.8	926	16.6	47.5	81.4	35.1	92.5	53.40	2 106	2 264
Alpharetta	54.6	880	29.0	39.5	77.2	29.1	87.5	51.82	3 490	1 327
Athens-Clarke County	263.4	2 214	18.1	42.2	79.8	32.9	90.2	47.83	2 861	1 785
Atlanta	7 446.5	16 770	997.4	41.7	79.5	31.3	90.6	49.10	3 004	1 679
Augusta-Richmond County	619.6	3 141	0.0	44.8	80.8	33.1	92.0	44.58	2 525	1 986
Columbus	514.9	2 574	66.6	46.8	82.0	36.6	91.7	48.57	2 154	2 296
Dalton	51.3	1 540	0.5	39.4	78.0	28.8	89.8	53.64	3 534	1 393
Douglasville	43.7	1 399	13.4	NA	NA	NA	NA	NA	NA	NA
Duluth	10.1	363	0.0	NA	NA	NA	NA	NA	NA	NA
Dunwoody	7.3	154	5.2	NA	NA	NA	NA	NA	NA	NA
East Point	99.0	2 784	0.0	42.7	80.0	33.5	89.4	50.20	2 827	1 810
Gainesville	711.3	20 464	0.0	36.0	72.9	24.7	84.0	58.19	4 421	752
Hinesville	24.5	706	1.8	51.6	82.6	40.7	93.3	48.32	1 551	2 539
Johns Creek	3.2	39	0.2	NA	NA	NA	NA	NA	NA	NA
Kennesaw	25.6	819	0.0	NA	NA	NA	NA	NA	NA	NA
LaGrange	38.1	1 257	0.0	42.2	78.7	31.3	89.3	53.38	3 078	1 551
Lawrenceville	0.0	0	0.0	NA	NA	NA	NA	NA	NA	NA
Macon	46.4	298	19.4	45.5	81.1	34.5	91.8	45.00	2 364	2 115
Marietta	100.1	1 712	0.0	39.4	77.9	28.5	89.3	54.43	3 505	1 403
Milton	1.1	32	0.0	NA	NA	NA	NA	NA	NA	NA
Newnan	38.2	1 119	0.0	NA	NA	NA	NA	NA	NA	NA
Peachtree City	15.8	457	0.0	42.6	79.4	31.8	90.5	50.10	2 958	1 679
Rome	63.5	1 764	0.0	39.4	77.5	29.1	87.7	56.16	3 510	1 360
Roswell	12.2	130	1.7	39.5	77.2	29.1	87.5	51.82	3 490	1 327
Sandy Springs	2.8	29	0.0	NA	NA	NA	NA	NA	NA	NA
Savannah	184.3	1 296	0.0	49.2	82.1	38.0	92.3	49.58	1 799	2 454
Smyrna	50.4	956	0.0	42.7	80.0	33.5	89.4	50.20	2 827	1 810
Statesboro	18.7	623	0.1	NA	NA	NA	NA	NA	NA	NA
Stockbridge	17.6	656	0.4	NA	NA	NA	NA	NA	NA	NA
Valdosta	48.0	832	12.1	50.0	80.9	38.0	92.0	53.06	1 782	2 319
Warner Robins	39.6	552	31.7	45.5	81.1	34.5	91.8	45.00	2 364	2 115
HAWAII	X	X	X	X	X	X	X	X	X	X
East Honolulu CDP	NA	NA	NA	NA	NA	NA	NA	NA	NA	NA
Hilo CDP	NA	NA	NA	NA	NA	NA	NA	NA	NA	NA
Kahului CDP	NA	NA	NA	NA	NA	NA	NA	NA	NA	NA
Kailua CDP (Honolulu County)	NA	NA	NA	NA	NA	NA	NA	NA	NA	NA
Kaneohe CDP	NA	NA	NA	NA	NA	NA	NA	NA	NA	NA
Mililani Town CDP	NA	NA	NA	NA	NA	NA	NA	NA	NA	NA
Pearl City CDP	NA	NA	NA	NA	NA	NA	NA	NA	NA	NA
Urban Honolulu CDP	NA	NA	NA	NA	NA	NA	NA	NA	NA	NA
Waipahu CDP	NA	NA	NA	NA	NA	NA	NA	NA	NA	NA
IDAHO	X	X	X	X	X	X	X	X	X	X
Boise City	79.7	375	36.5	30.2	74.7	23.6	89.2	12.19	5 727	807
Caldwell	12.5	263	0.0	29.3	68.8	19.6	85.7	10.90	6 749	410
Coeur d'Alene	31.6	692	7.6	28.4	68.7	22.1	82.6	26.07	6 540	426
Idaho Falls	21.5	370	1.6	19.3	68.4	11.1	85.9	11.02	7 917	322
Lewiston	6.6	205	0.0	33.7	73.5	28.0	87.6	12.74	5 220	792
Meridian	1.3	17	1.3	29.4	71.8	22.1	89.2	9.94	5 752	579
Nampa	58.7	700	6.7	28.9	73.3	20.8	90.5	11.37	5 873	692
Pocatello	24.5	448	0.0	24.4	69.2	16.3	87.5	12.58	7 109	387
Post Falls	11.1	387	0.0	NA	NA	NA	NA	NA	NA	NA
Rexburg	14.4	549	10.0	NA	NA	NA	NA	NA	NA	NA
Twin Falls	43.5	967	0.0	28.2	72.2	19.7	87.9	9.42	6 300	587
ILLINOIS	X	X	X	X	X	X	X	X	X	X
Addison	59.7	1 602	6.8	22.0	73.3	14.3	83.5	36.27	6 498	830
Algonquin	13.6	453	0.1	NA	NA	NA	NA	NA	NA	NA
Alton	20.7	752	0.0	27.7	78.4	19.4	88.1	38.54	5 149	1 354
Arlington Heights	53.7	709	19.6	22.0	73.3	14.3	83.5	36.27	6 498	830
Aurora	553.2	2 769	9.1	20.0	72.4	10.5	84.2	38.39	6 859	661
Bartlett	54.9	1 320	13.6	19.3	72.6	10.9	83.0	37.22	6 975	679
Batavia	54.8	2 077	1.0	NA	NA	NA	NA	NA	NA	NA
Belleville	71.6	1 652	32.1	30.9	78.1	22.1	89.6	39.37	4 612	1 339
Belvidere	5.1	199	0.0	NA	NA	NA	NA	NA	NA	NA
Berwyn	97.3	1 712	7.4	25.8	75.3	17.3	86.2	40.96	5 555	1 027
Bloomington	96.3	1 238	12.7	22.4	75.2	13.7	85.6	37.45	6 190	998
Bolingbrook	272.1	3 679	5.0	23.1	74.8	14.2	86.8	37.94	6 053	942
Buffalo Grove	2.2	52	0.0	18.4	72.1	9.6	82.3	36.56	7 149	624

1. Based on the population estimated as of July 1 of the year shown.   2. Represents normal values based on the 30-year period, 1971–2000.   3. Average daily minimum.   4. Average daily maximum.

Table D. Cities — **Land Area and Population**

STATE Place code	City	Land area,[1] 2010 (sq km)	Total persons	Rank	Per square kilometer	White	Black	American Indian, Alaska Native	Asian	Hawaiian Pacific Islander	Percent Hispanic or Latino[2] 2010-2014	Percent foreign born 2010-2014
		1	2	3	4	5	6	7	8	9	10	11
	ILLINOIS—Cont'd											
17 09642	Burbank.................	10.8	29 128	1 273	2 697.0	84.6	2.1	0.6	3.8	0.1	27.8	30.4
17 10487	Calumet City...............	18.6	37 031	1 019	1 990.9	25.3	71.8	1.3	0.5	0.0	14.9	8.3
17 11163	Carbondale.................	44.3	26 399	1 384	595.9	66.2	28.0	1.3	7.6	0.1	6.7	9.8
17 11332	Carol Stream.............	23.6	40 356	931	1 710.0	74.6	5.7	0.4	17.4	0.0	13.9	21.5
17 11358	Carpentersville	20.5	38 512	971	1 878.6	65.4	7.5	0.8	4.8	0.0	50.9	30.4
17 12385	Champaign.................	58.1	86 096	379	1 481.9	70.7	17.1	0.3	12.9	0.0	5.8	13.9
17 14000	Chicago...................	589.6	2 720 546	3	4 614.2	50.1	32.8	0.7	6.5	0.1	28.9	20.9
17 14026	Chicago Heights..........	26.1	30 284	1 235	1 160.3	43.9	43.5	0.7	0.2	0.0	33.4	11.8
17 14351	Cicero...................	15.2	83 886	392	5 518.8	45.1	4.5	1.3	0.5	0.1	87.7	41.0
17 15599	Collinsville	38.0	24 754	1 425	651.4	88.3	12.1	0.6	0.9	0.1	4.0	1.8
17 17887	Crystal Lake................	47.5	40 448	927	851.5	93.1	2.0	0.2	3.8	0.1	11.0	10.8
17 18563	Danville...................	46.3	32 108	1 177	693.5	64.2	32.8	1.0	2.0	0.2	6.2	3.9
17 18823	Decatur...................	109.4	73 254	473	669.6	75.7	24.8	2.1	1.6	0.0	2.3	2.4
17 19161	DeKalb...................	38.0	43 211	864	1 137.1	75.4	15.2	0.3	4.7	0.0	13.2	8.8
17 19642	Des Plaines.................	37.0	58 677	630	1 585.9	77.9	1.9	0.5	13.8	0.0	17.7	29.7
17 20591	Downers Grove............	37.1	49 732	755	1 340.5	89.6	3.0	0.3	7.2	0.0	4.6	9.7
17 22255	East St. Louis.............	36.2	26 790	1 367	740.1	2.1	97.7	0.4	0.5	0.0	0.5	0.4
17 23074	Elgin	96.3	112 111	251	1 164.2	67.6	8.0	0.8	6.7	0.1	44.4	26.0
17 23256	Elk Grove Village	29.4	33 238	1 130	1 130.5	83.4	1.0	0.5	11.8	0.2	10.0	18.6
17 23620	Elmhurst..................	26.6	45 957	822	1 727.7	90.6	2.2	0.3	6.6	0.0	6.7	8.8
17 24582	Evanston..................	20.2	75 527	452	3 739.0	71.1	19.2	0.9	10.4	0.1	10.1	19.0
17 27884	Freeport..................	30.5	24 476	1 429	802.5	80.4	19.7	0.5	1.5	0.3	5.2	1.9
17 28326	Galesburg.................	46.0	31 273	1 189	679.8	82.3	14.2	0.6	1.6	0.0	7.6	3.2
17 29730	Glendale Heights..........	13.9	34 435	1 091	2 477.3	65.8	7.4	0.9	24.9	0.3	31.2	36.8
17 29756	Glen Ellyn................	17.1	28 201	1 309	1 649.2	87.7	4.1	0.8	8.9	0.1	4.5	11.8
17 29938	Glenview..................	36.1	47 446	799	1 314.3	85.6	1.7	0.4	13.2	0.1	8.3	21.8
17 30926	Granite City...............	50.0	29 054	1 275	581.1	93.0	6.5	0.7	1.3	0.1	4.9	2.0
17 32018	Gurnee...................	35.0	31 056	1 194	887.3	77.7	10.5	1.0	12.3	0.2	12.1	15.1
17 32746	Hanover Park.............	16.4	38 333	978	2 337.4	54.0	9.3	0.3	16.4	0.1	37.5	34.8
17 33383	Harvey...................	16.3	25 194	1 414	1 545.6	13.6	77.1	1.2	0.5	0.1	18.5	7.6
17 34722	Highland Park.............	31.6	29 743	1 254	941.2	94.5	2.7	0.1	3.4	0.0	7.2	12.5
17 35411	Hoffman Estates..........	53.9	52 138	724	967.3	60.8	5.4	0.7	26.0	0.0	15.6	30.0
17 38570	Joliet....................	160.9	147 861	176	919.0	70.9	17.2	0.9	2.6	0.1	27.7	15.1
17 38934	Kankakee	36.6	26 676	1 372	728.9	56.7	39.5	0.9	0.9	0.1	18.0	9.9
17 41183	Lake in the Hills	26.9	29 024	1 276	1 079.0	92.0	2.2	0.1	5.8	0.8	11.9	10.6
17 42028	Lansing..................	17.6	28 349	1 298	1 610.7	58.9	35.5	0.4	1.2	0.0	14.1	7.5
17 44407	Lombard	26.6	43 797	854	1 646.5	84.8	5.3	1.4	9.8	0.1	7.9	11.6
17 45694	McHenry	38.2	26 657	1 374	697.8	91.3	0.8	1.6	2.8	0.0	13.4	8.9
17 48242	Melrose Park.............	11.0	25 379	1 411	2 307.2	53.7	5.8	0.6	1.2	0.1	73.9	38.7
17 49867	Moline...................	42.6	42 681	876	1 001.9	87.3	5.8	1.1	2.8	0.1	15.8	9.4
17 51089	Mount Prospect..........	26.8	54 747	684	2 042.8	74.9	2.6	1.1	12.6	0.1	17.0	32.3
17 51349	Mundelein................	24.8	31 582	1 182	1 273.5	85.0	2.2	0.3	9.6	0.0	30.8	28.9
17 51622	Naperville	100.4	147 100	179	1 465.1	76.7	5.7	0.8	18.2	0.1	6.3	18.1
17 53000	Niles....................	15.1	29 876	1 248	1 978.5	77.4	2.3	0.7	18.5	0.2	11.3	43.5
17 53234	Normal...................	47.5	54 373	689	1 144.7	86.4	9.2	0.6	4.6	0.1	5.2	5.1
17 53481	Northbrook...............	34.2	33 663	1 114	984.3	86.9	1.3	0.3	13.0	0.0	2.7	19.1
17 53559	North Chicago............	20.5	29 491	1 261	1 438.6	55.5	30.9	2.1	6.2	0.4	28.5	16.4
17 54638	Oak Forest	15.4	28 074	1 315	1 823.0	89.6	5.6	1.8	2.4	0.0	12.8	9.0
17 54820	Oak Lawn.................	22.3	56 781	654	2 546.2	88.0	5.6	0.6	2.5	0.0	16.6	15.3
17 54885	Oak Park.................	12.2	52 287	720	4 285.8	70.5	22.7	0.5	6.9	0.1	7.2	10.8
17 55249	O'Fallon	37.2	29 002	1 277	779.6	81.6	16.4	0.7	4.3	0.2	3.1	3.9
17 56640	Orland Park..............	56.7	58 619	631	1 033.8	89.6	2.5	0.9	7.5	0.1	6.4	13.2
17 56887	Oswego..................	40.2	33 955	1 104	844.7	86.1	9.2	0.2	5.7	0.0	10.3	4.9
17 57225	Palatine	35.3	69 308	502	1 963.4	74.3	3.7	0.4	15.6	0.1	17.1	25.2
17 57875	Park Ridge	18.4	37 757	997	2 052.0	94.2	1.3	0.1	4.4	0.0	6.5	15.0
17 58447	Pekin....................	37.7	33 223	1 131	881.2	97.1	2.9	0.5	0.6	0.1	2.1	1.4
17 59000	Peoria...................	124.3	115 070	241	925.7	66.1	28.8	1.0	5.7	0.2	5.5	7.8
17 60287	Plainfield.................	60.2	42 527	879	706.4	82.2	7.2	0.7	10.0	0.1	10.5	11.5
17 62367	Quincy...................	41.2	40 780	916	989.8	91.6	7.2	0.8	1.4	0.1	1.6	1.8
17 65000	Rockford..................	158.2	148 278	175	937.3	71.0	23.8	1.1	3.3	0.0	17.1	11.1
17 65078	Rock Island	43.6	38 620	969	885.8	76.4	20.7	1.5	2.4	0.1	10.9	6.4
17 65442	Romeoville...............	47.8	39 719	943	830.9	69.1	10.3	1.5	9.4	0.0	31.8	20.7
17 66040	Round Lake Beach	13.1	27 852	1 326	2 126.1	87.0	3.5	1.1	4.2	0.0	48.5	29.4
17 66703	St. Charles...............	37.8	33 460	1 123	885.2	90.9	2.5	0.6	3.5	0.1	8.9	11.0
17 68003	Schaumburg..............	49.8	74 693	459	1 499.9	71.9	4.1	0.4	21.2	0.1	9.6	26.4
17 70122	Skokie...................	26.1	64 821	550	2 483.6	64.7	7.3	0.6	28.1	0.3	10.5	41.6
17 72000	Springfield................	154.1	116 565	236	756.4	76.8	21.0	0.7	2.9	0.1	2.4	4.4
17 73157	Streamwood	20.2	40 554	923	2 007.6	62.0	3.4	0.3	16.4	0.0	29.8	30.4
17 75484	Tinley Park...............	41.5	57 143	646	1 376.9	88.8	4.1	0.1	4.6	0.1	9.9	9.8
17 77005	Urbana...................	30.2	42 311	882	1 401.0	64.4	17.7	0.6	19.4	0.1	4.9	19.1
17 77694	Vernon Hills................	20.0	26 314	1 386	1 315.7	77.5	2.0	0.4	22.7	0.3	11.6	29.9

1. Dry land or land partially or temporarily covered by water.   2. May be of any race.

Table D. Cities — **Population**

City	\multicolumn{9}{c}{Age of population (percent), 2010-2014}	Median age 2010–2014	Percent female 2010–2014	\multicolumn{2}{c}{Census counts}	\multicolumn{2}{c}{Percent change}
	Under 5 years	5 to 17 years	18 to 24 years	25 to 34 years	35 to 44 years	45 to 54 years	55 to 64 years	65 to 74 years	75 years and over			2000	2010	2000–2010	2010–2015
	12	13	14	15	16	17	18	19	20	21	22	23	24	25	26
ILLINOIS—Cont'd															
Burbank	5.6	18.4	10.7	13.0	12.0	15.3	11.6	7.2	6.2	37.0	51.1	27 902	28 925	3.7	0.7
Calumet City	5.6	22.8	8.5	13.3	14.2	13.2	10.6	7.1	4.7	34.9	53.5	39 071	37 042	-5.2	0.0
Carbondale	4.9	9.4	43.4	15.4	8.0	7.0	5.0	2.9	4.0	22.9	49.4	20 681	25 902	25.2	-0.2
Carol Stream	4.5	17.8	10.8	14.2	12.8	17.7	12.5	5.1	4.6	37.4	51.2	40 438	39 711	-1.8	1.6
Carpentersville	8.6	25.8	10.3	15.5	14.3	14.5	6.6	3.0	1.4	29.1	49.9	30 586	37 691	23.2	2.2
Champaign	5.1	11.8	29.0	17.4	9.9	9.2	9.5	4.5	3.6	27.1	48.9	67 518	81 055	20.0	6.0
Chicago	6.8	15.6	10.9	19.2	14.2	12.4	10.3	5.9	4.8	33.5	51.4	2 896 016	2 695 598	-6.9	0.9
Chicago Heights	7.5	19.5	10.5	14.7	12.0	14.2	9.8	5.4	6.5	33.5	50.6	32 776	30 276	-7.6	-0.1
Cicero	8.9	24.6	11.2	16.6	16.1	9.3	7.6	3.3	2.3	28.5	49.8	85 616	83 891	-2.0	-0.4
Collinsville	6.9	14.7	10.4	13.4	14.7	15.3	11.3	8.1	5.2	38.3	52.5	24 707	25 579	3.5	-3.1
Crystal Lake	5.8	20.7	7.8	13.0	13.4	16.3	11.6	6.5	4.9	36.9	51.7	38 000	40 743	7.2	-0.9
Danville	6.8	18.4	10.6	12.2	12.0	12.0	12.2	8.4	7.4	37.1	50.8	33 904	33 027	-2.6	-2.8
Decatur	6.1	15.9	10.4	12.6	10.7	13.2	13.6	8.3	9.1	39.3	52.8	81 860	76 122	-7.0	-3.8
DeKalb	6.4	12.9	33.1	14.7	9.0	8.4	6.7	4.6	4.2	24.0	51.9	39 018	43 862	12.4	-2.1
Des Plaines	6.1	14.0	7.2	13.8	12.3	13.7	15.1	8.6	9.2	42.4	50.7	58 720	58 364	-0.6	0.5
Downers Grove	5.7	16.9	7.2	10.4	12.3	17.7	14.2	8.7	6.9	43.4	51.2	48 724	47 833	-1.8	1.8
East St. Louis	8.4	19.3	10.8	12.1	9.2	13.8	13.2	7.2	6.1	34.6	54.8	31 542	27 006	-14.4	-0.5
Elgin	9.2	20.0	9.6	15.6	14.3	12.4	9.8	5.3	3.8	32.4	50.0	94 487	108 188	14.5	3.7
Elk Grove Village	5.8	15.5	6.9	11.9	13.0	17.2	14.5	7.9	7.3	42.5	52.3	34 727	33 127	-4.6	0.3
Elmhurst	5.4	20.5	9.3	8.3	13.9	15.5	12.2	6.8	8.1	40.3	50.6	42 762	44 121	3.2	4.1
Evanston	6.5	14.1	16.4	13.9	13.1	11.9	11.5	6.4	6.2	34.2	52.2	74 239	74 486	0.3	1.4
Freeport	6.5	16.1	8.7	9.5	13.0	12.8	14.3	7.3	11.8	42.6	53.0	26 443	25 638	-3.0	-4.5
Galesburg	5.4	14.0	12.4	13.5	10.3	12.8	12.8	9.0	9.9	39.7	50.8	33 706	32 195	-4.5	-2.8
Glendale Heights	7.9	15.5	11.2	16.9	15.1	14.7	10.5	5.8	2.4	33.9	47.8	31 765	34 208	7.7	0.7
Glen Ellyn	6.4	19.9	6.5	9.6	14.9	15.5	14.3	5.7	7.3	40.8	52.5	26 999	27 450	1.7	1.6
Glenview	5.5	18.8	5.6	7.8	12.4	14.3	15.1	9.1	11.3	44.9	52.2	41 847	44 692	6.8	6.2
Granite City	4.8	17.6	10.0	12.8	11.0	14.1	13.7	7.9	8.1	39.3	49.2	31 301	29 849	-4.6	-2.7
Gurnee	4.6	21.9	8.1	8.7	16.5	19.3	11.3	5.4	4.3	38.6	51.9	28 834	31 295	8.5	-0.6
Hanover Park	6.7	22.1	8.9	15.6	14.7	15.1	10.2	4.5	2.2	33.0	50.1	38 278	37 973	-0.8	1.0
Harvey	7.6	18.0	11.3	12.3	12.5	14.4	10.8	8.1	5.1	35.8	52.7	30 000	25 282	-15.7	-0.2
Highland Park	5.9	20.6	5.6	6.4	11.9	15.0	14.6	10.6	9.5	44.8	50.1	31 365	29 763	-5.1	0.1
Hoffman Estates	5.4	18.6	7.8	14.3	12.6	15.7	15.0	6.7	3.9	38.3	50.6	49 495	51 895	4.8	0.5
Joliet	8.3	21.4	9.3	14.9	15.9	13.1	8.5	4.5	4.1	32.4	50.8	106 221	147 433	38.8	0.2
Kankakee	8.9	21.1	7.9	13.5	13.4	12.0	9.7	7.2	6.4	34.0	48.5	27 491	27 537	0.2	-3.1
Lake in the Hills	7.0	22.4	7.4	14.0	17.8	16.2	8.3	3.8	3.1	34.6	48.8	23 152	28 965	25.1	0.0
Lansing	5.1	18.1	8.4	12.2	10.8	15.3	13.4	8.9	7.8	41.0	51.8	28 332	28 331	0.0	0.0
Lombard	4.1	15.3	8.7	13.4	13.2	16.6	12.6	6.8	9.3	42.0	53.4	42 322	43 165	2.0	0.9
McHenry	6.4	18.5	8.8	13.6	11.8	17.8	10.9	6.2	6.0	38.2	50.0	21 501	26 992	25.5	-1.3
Melrose Park	9.3	21.0	11.0	14.8	14.8	10.1	9.8	5.3	4.1	31.0	49.5	23 171	25 411	9.7	-0.1
Moline	5.9	16.7	7.9	13.9	12.4	12.6	14.5	7.9	8.3	39.4	50.6	43 768	43 483	-0.7	-1.8
Mount Prospect	5.8	17.3	6.9	14.5	14.0	15.9	11.4	7.2	7.0	39.3	50.8	56 265	54 167	-3.7	0.9
Mundelein	6.8	18.1	9.1	12.8	15.6	14.8	13.7	6.0	3.2	36.8	50.0	30 935	31 064	0.4	1.8
Naperville	5.4	21.9	9.0	9.9	14.0	17.2	12.0	6.3	4.3	38.1	50.9	128 358	141 853	10.5	3.5
Niles	5.0	11.7	5.5	13.5	9.6	14.0	15.0	10.7	14.9	49.1	54.9	30 068	29 803	-0.9	0.2
Normal	4.8	12.6	35.2	12.2	9.0	10.3	7.5	4.8	3.6	23.6	51.7	45 386	52 497	15.7	3.5
Northbrook	4.7	20.0	5.0	4.0	12.8	16.8	13.3	11.6	11.8	47.2	51.5	33 435	33 170	-0.8	1.3
North Chicago	7.6	13.2	34.4	18.2	9.2	6.7	5.7	2.9	2.0	23.7	41.6	35 918	32 574	-9.3	-9.5
Oak Forest	6.5	15.0	10.6	14.8	12.1	14.3	14.6	7.6	4.5	38.3	51.4	28 051	27 962	-0.3	0.3
Oak Lawn	6.0	15.4	8.0	14.4	10.2	16.0	12.5	7.1	10.5	41.1	52.3	55 245	56 690	2.6	0.2
Oak Park	6.2	18.1	5.8	13.7	15.9	16.1	13.4	6.6	4.3	39.1	53.9	52 524	51 878	-1.2	0.8
O'Fallon	5.9	22.3	8.9	10.7	16.6	14.9	10.3	6.3	4.0	36.5	51.5	21 910	28 281	29.1	1.1
Orland Park	4.5	14.7	8.5	8.9	11.2	17.1	13.9	11.2	10.1	46.1	53.2	51 077	56 767	11.1	3.5
Oswego	6.9	25.8	6.1	11.7	20.0	15.4	8.1	3.6	2.4	34.6	50.0	13 326	30 355	127.8	11.9
Palatine	7.6	17.5	7.1	15.4	14.1	14.8	12.4	7.0	4.1	36.9	51.3	65 479	68 557	4.7	1.1
Park Ridge	5.4	19.9	6.5	7.4	12.5	16.9	14.2	8.6	8.6	44.0	53.2	37 775	37 480	-0.8	0.7
Pekin	5.7	16.1	8.3	14.8	13.3	13.1	12.6	7.7	8.5	39.0	50.8	33 857	34 094	0.7	-2.6
Peoria	7.1	18.3	11.9	15.1	11.8	11.3	11.4	6.8	6.4	33.1	52.5	112 936	115 007	1.8	0.0
Plainfield	6.9	28.2	6.7	9.4	19.5	15.7	8.2	3.7	1.6	34.0	51.7	13 038	39 581	203.6	6.7
Quincy	7.0	15.9	9.1	13.9	11.3	12.0	12.6	8.3	9.8	38.1	52.6	40 366	40 633	0.7	0.4
Rockford	7.5	18.7	9.1	13.8	11.7	13.0	11.8	7.1	7.3	35.7	51.6	150 115	152 871	1.8	-3.1
Rock Island	6.9	16.7	13.1	12.8	9.8	13.1	12.0	7.7	8.0	35.4	52.8	39 684	39 018	-1.7	-1.0
Romeoville	6.0	24.1	11.9	14.0	15.8	13.0	7.3	4.9	3.1	31.7	52.0	21 153	39 680	87.6	0.3
Round Lake Beach	7.5	22.3	10.9	13.1	17.5	14.6	7.6	3.5	3.1	32.0	48.4	25 859	28 175	9.0	-0.9
St. Charles	3.8	18.6	5.8	11.7	13.8	15.5	15.1	7.5	8.2	42.5	50.7	27 896	32 974	18.2	1.6
Schaumburg	7.6	13.0	6.4	20.1	13.4	13.0	14.1	7.2	5.3	37.2	51.4	75 386	74 227	-1.5	0.6
Skokie	5.3	15.7	6.7	11.4	12.2	14.1	16.9	9.2	8.5	43.7	53.1	63 348	64 784	2.3	0.1
Springfield	6.3	15.9	9.8	13.5	11.6	14.1	13.7	7.6	7.5	38.9	51.9	111 454	116 250	4.3	0.1
Streamwood	6.0	21.0	8.0	16.7	13.8	15.5	9.5	6.0	3.5	33.8	49.3	36 407	39 858	9.5	1.7
Tinley Park	5.9	17.1	7.5	14.5	11.4	16.2	13.4	8.4	5.5	39.2	52.2	48 401	56 703	17.2	0.7
Urbana	4.4	7.4	42.2	16.2	7.3	6.5	8.0	3.1	4.8	23.8	51.1	36 395	41 250	13.3	2.0
Vernon Hills	6.2	19.5	7.2	11.3	16.6	18.0	10.9	5.1	5.1	37.7	50.1	20 120	25 113	24.8	5.2

City	Households, 2010-2014				Persons in group quarters, 2010				Serious crimes known to police,[2] 2014				Educational attainment, 2010–2014		
			Percent			Institutional			Total		Rate[3]			Attainment[4] (percent)	
	Number	Persons per house-hold	Female family house-holder[1]	One-person	Total	Total	Persons in nursing facilities	Non-institu-tional	Number	Rate[3]	Violent	Property	Population age 25 and older	High school graduate or less	Bachelor's degree or more
	27	28	29	30	31	32	33	34	35	36	37	38	39	40	41
ILLINOIS—Cont'd															
Burbank	8 795	3.31	12.8	19.6	242	186	186	56	445	1 520	150	1 370	18 953	62.9	12.3
Calumet City	14 127	2.63	23.6	36.0	24	4	0	20	1 752	4 699	515	4 184	23 562	41.7	15.8
Carbondale	9 416	2.80	12.7	43.0	3 600	359	193	3 241	1 078	4 088	523	3 565	11 122	23.6	46.0
Carol Stream	14 735	2.72	9.4	27.0	44	44	44	0	427	1 053	109	945	26 781	31.3	37.7
Carpentersville	10 987	3.47	15.0	14.2	5	0	0	5	622	1 621	86	1 535	22 153	52.9	20.9
Champaign	32 734	2.53	9.3	37.3	8 514	392	341	8 122	3 064	3 648	770	2 878	44 887	22.8	50.3
Chicago	1 028 829	2.64	17.1	36.2	60 246	27 250	14 382	32 996	109 484	4 019	886	3 133	1 807 376	41.6	34.9
Chicago Heights	10 341	2.94	22.0	29.8	644	507	502	137	1 114	3 658	653	3 004	18 604	53.7	14.2
Cicero	21 792	3.87	19.5	15.2	196	173	173	23	2 128	2 529	385	2 144	47 255	73.1	7.6
Collinsville	10 723	2.36	13.1	32.1	65	59	59	6	805	3 228	208	3 019	16 889	39.0	26.7
Crystal Lake	14 491	2.80	10.6	22.2	267	163	163	104	894	2 219	129	2 090	26 804	28.5	40.4
Danville	12 446	2.61	20.4	36.0	2 422	2 243	159	179	2 226	6 870	1 074	5 796	20 678	53.6	15.3
Decatur	31 481	2.39	14.4	37.4	3 918	1 908	1 005	2 010	2 580	3 469	477	2 992	50 496	47.6	21.0
DeKalb	14 937	2.95	12.9	32.6	6 292	363	363	5 929	1 345	3 071	409	2 663	20 231	30.8	35.0
Des Plaines	22 418	2.62	8.1	30.3	888	822	702	66	771	1 306	90	1 216	42 980	37.7	35.2
Downers Grove	19 018	2.60	8.9	27.1	548	176	153	372	683	1 370	62	1 308	34 179	21.5	53.4
East St. Louis	10 368	2.57	37.6	38.6	433	109	90	324	2 062	7 774	3 646	4 128	16 348	54.4	8.0
Elgin	34 755	3.19	12.2	23.4	1 953	1 041	699	912	2 217	2 005	199	1 806	68 766	47.9	24.0
Elk Grove Village	13 393	2.49	8.8	31.2	132	96	96	36	529	1 580	63	1 517	24 054	30.8	36.4
Elmhurst	15 655	2.88	8.3	24.3	1 298	373	373	925	526	1 146	44	1 102	29 024	18.7	57.7
Evanston	28 939	2.60	10.2	36.7	7 024	1 297	1 150	5 727	2 051	2 705	199	2 506	47 745	16.9	66.4
Freeport	10 541	2.39	15.2	37.2	754	613	468	141	686	2 756	193	2 563	17 399	47.7	17.0
Galesburg	13 082	2.44	13.2	40.6	3 771	2 468	485	1 303	1 161	3 681	400	3 282	22 012	53.7	16.4
Glendale Heights	11 351	3.03	11.2	23.3	1	0	0	1	537	1 547	78	1 469	21 880	43.3	29.0
Glen Ellyn	10 443	2.62	7.3	27.9	5	0	0	5	366	1 314	83	1 231	18 307	18.0	61.4
Glenview	16 801	2.70	6.2	27.2	642	606	606	36	404	886	39	847	32 044	19.4	61.1
Granite City	12 423	2.40	14.7	33.8	256	158	158	98	NA	NA	NA	NA	20 581	56.7	13.3
Gurnee	11 603	2.69	10.7	26.2	89	61	61	28	1 420	4 541	106	4 435	20 553	24.7	47.4
Hanover Park	11 134	3.44	14.8	13.2	0	0	0	0	378	978	106	872	23 746	50.4	21.7
Harvey	8 647	2.92	28.9	37.3	252	192	192	60	1 539	6 065	1 296	4 768	15 541	63.8	9.2
Highland Park	11 549	2.58	7.3	24.6	255	183	173	72	354	1 183	64	1 120	20 548	13.3	69.5
Hoffman Estates	17 731	2.95	11.0	17.3	435	172	172	263	608	1 158	95	1 063	35 142	27.9	45.9
Joliet	46 992	3.14	14.1	22.3	2 945	2 185	1 189	760	3 483	2 356	335	2 021	89 754	45.8	23.4
Kankakee	9 455	2.87	22.9	33.0	1 810	921	305	889	1 453	5 376	818	4 559	16 726	56.5	11.3
Lake in the Hills	9 925	2.91	11.1	18.5	0	0	0	0	157	543	59	484	18 297	33.7	31.3
Lansing	11 221	2.54	17.9	32.7	91	83	83	8	1 262	4 421	319	4 102	19 380	42.8	19.3
Lombard	17 781	2.47	10.2	31.8	502	288	288	214	908	2 062	70	1 992	31 104	26.6	42.5
McHenry	10 194	2.63	9.4	26.6	194	186	186	8	356	1 339	90	1 249	18 058	40.7	24.8
Melrose Park	7 555	3.38	18.2	22.4	52	0	0	52	413	1 617	106	1 511	15 271	66.5	10.4
Moline	18 114	2.38	12.3	34.4	322	280	280	42	1 603	3 726	363	3 364	29 564	41.1	25.5
Mount Prospect	20 288	2.69	6.9	25.7	121	0	0	121	608	1 108	44	1 064	38 232	35.4	38.0
Mundelein	10 808	2.91	7.6	20.3	203	0	0	203	277	880	57	823	21 139	33.3	41.3
Naperville	49 741	2.90	7.5	19.5	2 489	1 188	1 108	1 301	1 747	1 201	78	1 123	92 759	14.8	66.1
Niles	11 398	2.63	11.0	30.7	1 118	1 100	1 100	18	727	2 418	90	2 328	23 158	46.3	28.5
Normal	18 877	2.86	8.6	29.0	8 332	391	377	7 941	1 160	2 102	185	1 917	25 745	25.5	51.5
Northbrook	12 287	2.72	5.9	21.7	678	611	611	67	363	1 077	21	1 056	23 676	13.0	68.9
North Chicago	6 765	4.55	22.5	25.6	12 741	196	0	12 545	381	1 293	343	951	13 646	47.0	19.4
Oak Forest	10 145	2.77	10.6	24.5	43	5	5	38	362	1 281	92	1 189	19 349	41.1	25.5
Oak Lawn	21 701	2.63	11.5	30.6	493	479	479	14	1 101	1 926	157	1 769	40 288	43.0	26.7
Oak Park	21 658	2.40	10.8	34.8	383	255	224	128	1 667	3 199	198	3 001	36 201	12.5	67.1
O'Fallon	10 525	2.76	10.6	25.1	0	0	0	0	512	1 750	140	1 610	18 418	20.1	48.8
Orland Park	21 678	2.67	9.1	25.1	464	451	451	13	1 315	2 227	37	2 189	41 176	30.6	41.3
Oswego	9 999	3.17	10.5	13.8	52	47	47	5	524	1 607	80	1 528	19 505	23.2	44.1
Palatine	26 163	2.64	9.4	28.2	168	134	134	34	659	948	52	896	47 124	27.9	48.5
Park Ridge	14 138	2.65	10.1	25.0	492	434	399	58	463	1 221	32	1 189	26 075	21.8	54.0
Pekin	13 912	2.44	13.3	31.6	2 042	1 933	281	109	832	2 441	282	2 160	23 530	47.2	18.6
Peoria	47 286	2.45	16.8	35.0	3 832	1 313	1 109	2 519	5 617	4 804	649	4 155	73 001	37.8	33.1
Plainfield	11 973	3.39	9.1	12.3	109	109	109	0	357	846	76	770	24 005	21.3	48.8
Quincy	16 810	2.43	13.4	35.5	2 087	1 378	1 015	709	1 553	3 790	464	3 327	27 532	45.5	22.0
Rockford	58 746	2.58	18.7	32.6	4 179	2 881	1 728	1 298	8 306	5 553	1 245	4 307	98 074	48.5	21.0
Rock Island	15 422	2.52	15.2	37.1	2 441	685	452	1 756	1 036	2 667	409	2 258	25 002	44.4	21.9
Romeoville	11 747	3.38	12.1	16.4	1 188	0	0	1 188	679	1 713	119	1 594	23 481	40.6	25.4
Round Lake Beach	8 087	3.47	12.9	16.1	139	139	139	0	697	2 483	125	2 359	16 654	59.5	15.3
St. Charles	12 880	2.59	8.0	26.4	1 211	1 121	161	90	510	1 530	60	1 470	23 422	26.9	48.8
Schaumburg	30 389	2.45	9.0	32.1	414	374	374	40	1 943	2 589	97	2 491	54 087	27.3	44.8
Skokie	22 532	2.89	12.6	23.6	706	494	475	212	1 502	2 301	265	2 036	46 481	28.6	46.9
Springfield	50 732	2.30	13.6	37.3	3 396	1 489	831	1 907	6 783	5 791	1 065	4 725	79 408	35.6	34.9
Streamwood	13 041	3.12	11.3	19.7	288	268	160	20	705	1 743	101	1 641	27 107	42.3	31.2
Tinley Park	21 058	2.71	10.3	25.0	45	0	0	45	975	1 698	80	1 618	39 569	32.9	34.9
Urbana	15 803	2.64	8.4	39.0	7 050	781	339	6 269	1 597	3 820	311	3 509	19 330	23.9	53.6
Vernon Hills	9 430	2.71	7.2	26.4	43	43	43	0	518	2 011	35	1 976	17 055	19.9	59.6

1. No spouse present.   2. Data for serious crimes have not been adjusted for underreporting. This may affect comparability between geographic areas and over time.   3. Per 100,000 population estimated by the FBI.   4. Persons 25 years old and over.

Table D. Cities — Income, Poverty, and Housing

City	Money income, 2010–2014 Per capita income[1] (dollars)	Households Median income	Households Percent with income of $200,000 or more	Households Percent with income of less than $25,000	Families with income below poverty (percent)	Housing units, 2010 Total	Housing units, 2010 Percent change, 2000–2010	Vacant units for sale or rent[2]	Occupied housing units 2010–2014 Total	Owner-occupied Percent	Owner-occupied Median value[3] (dollars)	Median owner costs as a percent of income With a mortgage[4]	Median owner costs as a percent of income Without a mortgage[5]
	42	43	44	45	46	47	48	49	50	51	52	53	54
ILLINOIS—Cont'd													
Burbank	21 500	56 869	1.5	18.6	9.8	9 721	2.0	434	8 795	80.1	184 400	29.1	15.2
Calumet City	20 066	39 530	0.7	32.1	18.9	15 646	-1.8	1 668	14 127	58.2	105 100	31.0	15.1
Carbondale	14 302	17 677	1.1	58.9	31.0	12 419	12.7	1 384	9 416	25.9	113 300	20.3	11.2
Carol Stream	30 679	74 026	3.5	15.0	6.7	15 050	6.2	786	14 735	67.0	229 100	24.4	14.1
Carpentersville	21 749	57 978	3.8	18.2	13.7	11 583	29.6	731	10 987	72.5	155 100	26.5	14.7
Champaign	25 651	42 077	4.7	33.9	12.4	34 434	20.4	2 227	32 734	47.6	148 400	19.8	11.1
Chicago	28 623	47 831	5.5	28.8	18.7	1 194 337	3.6	148 777	1 028 829	44.7	225 700	27.5	15.5
Chicago Heights	19 213	44 272	1.5	32.3	24.1	11 060	-3.7	1 473	10 341	58.9	111 400	23.8	16.1
Cicero	14 624	41 882	0.8	24.2	19.7	24 329	-1.3	2 228	21 792	50.9	131 800	35.2	14.1
Collinsville	27 041	52 821	2.1	25.8	12.4	11 891	7.1	964	10 723	61.5	123 300	21.0	12.8
Crystal Lake	34 041	80 136	6.2	11.2	4.4	15 176	13.6	755	14 491	76.6	204 700	23.5	16.1
Danville	18 925	35 581	1.6	38.5	26.0	14 719	-1.0	1 876	12 446	58.0	66 000	19.5	12.4
Decatur	22 788	39 588	1.5	32.7	18.4	36 134	-3.0	3 790	31 481	61.7	81 200	19.0	12.5
DeKalb	19 088	38 357	1.6	36.1	20.0	16 436	21.4	1 050	14 937	43.0	162 200	25.1	13.8
Des Plaines	31 299	65 953	4.6	15.1	4.6	24 075	4.9	1 375	22 418	79.9	236 800	27.4	16.4
Downers Grove	42 538	85 020	12.9	14.3	3.5	20 478	4.9	1 291	19 018	76.9	332 800	23.1	12.9
East St. Louis	12 060	19 856	0.1	59.5	43.8	12 055	-6.6	1 936	10 368	45.1	57 000	40.5	15.8
Elgin	23 532	59 832	2.8	18.0	11.3	37 848	15.7	2 754	34 755	67.9	171 000	27.2	14.7
Elk Grove Village	33 423	68 188	4.1	16.0	5.1	13 905	3.3	598	13 393	74.4	261 600	26.7	14.2
Elmhurst	45 515	95 240	15.8	11.2	2.4	16 590	2.1	825	15 655	81.0	366 900	24.4	14.2
Evanston	41 340	69 347	13.2	19.9	6.3	33 181	7.7	3 134	28 939	55.4	342 800	24.5	15.8
Freeport	20 847	36 250	0.7	35.4	15.8	12 396	-0.7	1 364	10 541	62.5	76 500	20.6	13.0
Galesburg	20 025	33 360	1.1	38.5	17.7	14 280	1.2	1 272	13 082	58.5	73 500	19.7	12.6
Glendale Heights	23 931	60 879	2.3	13.7	9.6	11 864	7.3	607	11 351	68.7	173 900	29.8	14.6
Glen Ellyn	52 486	91 051	20.6	15.4	4.4	11 051	4.3	627	10 443	75.0	386 400	23.3	15.0
Glenview	52 326	92 304	21.2	11.0	2.2	17 746	12.2	963	16 801	81.6	469 200	24.7	16.1
Granite City	22 397	43 759	0.6	30.4	14.8	13 578	-3.9	1 364	12 423	67.3	82 000	19.1	11.8
Gurnee	37 710	85 141	9.5	12.6	3.8	12 031	11.2	495	11 603	72.7	254 800	24.1	14.6
Hanover Park	22 989	66 359	4.1	13.4	11.5	11 483	0.7	562	11 134	77.3	179 400	27.9	14.6
Harvey	13 481	25 074	0.2	49.9	28.5	9 805	-3.6	1 858	8 647	45.4	81 000	33.0	18.1
Highland Park	68 688	115 382	27.6	10.7	4.2	12 256	2.8	846	11 549	81.7	511 500	24.4	16.5
Hoffman Estates	36 015	83 518	9.0	9.9	4.3	18 970	8.5	838	17 731	75.2	255 200	24.1	12.9
Joliet	24 461	62 008	3.0	17.8	10.3	51 285	34.3	3 266	46 992	71.5	166 200	26.0	14.0
Kankakee	16 077	32 265	0.5	39.4	27.9	10 935	-0.1	1 289	9 455	49.5	96 500	27.7	14.7
Lake in the Hills	33 134	83 149	6.0	8.8	3.3	9 885	25.8	341	9 925	89.9	205 100	26.0	15.0
Lansing	25 296	49 684	1.9	23.0	10.7	11 741	0.1	784	11 221	71.3	134 600	28.1	14.9
Lombard	34 551	70 415	4.4	12.6	3.5	18 454	8.9	1 049	17 781	73.8	235 300	26.0	14.2
McHenry	29 893	62 580	3.3	19.2	7.0	10 741	32.1	666	10 194	75.0	177 700	26.7	13.7
Melrose Park	18 394	45 697	1.2	24.2	15.0	8 525	7.2	567	7 555	50.6	173 800	31.7	16.4
Moline	27 458	50 209	2.6	21.5	8.3	19 856	1.9	1 283	18 114	66.7	112 800	21.3	12.1
Mount Prospect	33 983	69 155	6.3	11.5	2.3	21 836	-1.1	1 272	20 288	71.4	290 800	26.6	16.9
Mundelein	33 296	78 635	7.3	11.5	5.8	10 992	8.3	485	10 808	75.8	225 000	24.9	16.1
Naperville	46 620	109 512	18.9	8.8	3.2	52 270	14.7	2 261	49 741	75.7	377 900	23.4	12.0
Niles	27 030	48 666	2.8	22.2	7.8	12 572	1.9	666	11 398	75.4	257 100	29.7	17.8
Normal	24 881	52 134	2.8	28.3	7.4	18 816	20.3	823	18 877	57.8	160 900	20.3	10.0
Northbrook	58 154	115 085	23.7	10.9	3.0	13 434	7.6	792	12 287	87.6	522 300	24.5	15.0
North Chicago	17 093	41 866	1.0	29.2	22.2	7 745	-7.3	1 125	6 765	37.4	120 000	33.4	16.1
Oak Forest	30 113	71 082	2.4	14.4	3.8	10 672	6.8	464	10 145	79.8	191 200	23.9	13.8
Oak Lawn	28 551	57 567	2.9	19.5	6.9	23 517	2.6	1 156	21 701	81.3	190 600	27.1	16.6
Oak Park	47 573	78 895	14.8	15.7	6.1	24 519	3.4	1 849	21 658	59.7	354 400	24.2	15.1
O'Fallon	36 234	79 795	7.5	15.8	6.3	11 414	32.7	667	10 525	70.4	193 300	19.4	11.6
Orland Park	40 244	79 334	9.6	11.9	3.7	22 443	17.6	804	21 678	89.1	275 700	25.7	15.5
Oswego	33 114	97 323	7.3	7.7	3.6	10 388	125.0	453	9 999	84.3	227 100	24.9	12.7
Palatine	35 904	72 180	7.2	14.4	7.1	28 621	9.2	1 745	26 163	68.5	269 200	25.5	14.8
Park Ridge	45 635	87 626	14.0	11.2	2.9	15 030	2.8	912	14 138	82.6	388 900	25.6	16.8
Pekin	24 931	48 544	1.2	23.0	9.6	14 714	5.1	894	13 912	68.6	99 200	19.5	11.3
Peoria	27 546	46 042	3.6	28.7	16.6	52 621	7.3	5 469	47 286	55.6	122 200	20.4	12.0
Plainfield	36 007	111 536	10.6	5.7	2.8	12 532	174.2	612	11 973	85.7	289 300	24.6	12.8
Quincy	22 995	40 886	1.6	29.3	13.9	18 655	3.7	1 504	16 810	63.5	98 900	20.4	10.7
Rockford	21 615	38 231	2.4	34.5	21.0	66 700	4.9	6 727	58 746	55.8	97 700	23.6	13.9
Rock Island	22 722	40 654	2.5	30.3	17.1	17 422	-0.5	1 492	15 422	67.2	98 000	21.6	14.1
Romeoville	22 695	66 705	1.2	9.9	6.7	12 623	71.3	636	11 747	85.2	167 300	28.6	14.6
Round Lake Beach	20 116	61 113	1.4	18.3	13.0	8 587	13.5	532	8 087	80.3	131 000	27.5	14.2
St. Charles	45 270	83 997	13.8	10.1	2.1	13 157	18.9	733	12 880	71.7	277 800	23.6	15.2
Schaumburg	35 925	72 745	5.3	12.7	4.9	33 610	1.6	2 071	30 389	63.1	240 200	26.2	14.2
Skokie	31 844	66 586	8.0	18.4	8.9	25 066	5.8	1 535	22 532	72.9	280 400	28.6	15.9
Springfield	29 621	48 848	3.9	26.7	13.7	55 729	3.4	5 015	50 732	63.1	116 600	19.3	11.1
Streamwood	28 916	72 720	4.9	9.7	3.4	13 629	10.0	595	13 041	86.2	181 800	26.5	15.2
Tinley Park	34 165	75 991	4.6	13.1	6.4	22 491	24.7	825	21 058	84.4	225 200	24.5	15.6
Urbana	20 057	30 834	2.4	43.0	15.3	19 090	25.2	2 129	15 803	36.4	148 600	21.3	10.3
Vernon Hills	42 846	89 667	14.5	9.5	2.1	9 956	25.2	439	9 430	71.5	315 900	25.3	15.9

1. Based on population estimated by the American Community Survey.   2. Includes units rented or sold but not occupied.   3. Specified owner-occupied units; $1,000,000 represents $1,000,000 or more   4. 50.0 represents 50 percent or more.   5. 10.0 represents 10 percent or less.

Table D. Cities — Housing, Labor Force, and Employment

City	Occupied housing units, 2010–2014 (cont.) Percent renter occupied	Median gross rent[1]	Median gross rent as a percent of income[2]	Percent with no vehicle available	Migration, 2010–2014 Percent who lived in the same house one year ago	Percent who lived outside current city one year ago	Civilian labor force, 2015 Total	Percent change, 2014–2015	Unemployment Total	Rate[3]	Civilian employment[4], 2010–2014 Population age 16 and older	In labor force	Civilian full-year full-time workers	Households with no workers (percent)
	55	56	57	58	59	60	61	62	63	64	65	66	67	68
ILLINOIS—Cont'd														
Burbank	19.9	1 021	27.7	7.9	91.5	7.6	14 306	-0.5	871	6.1	22 678	63.6	39.0	24.1
Calumet City	41.8	900	34.8	15.9	88.0	9.9	16 549	-0.9	1 526	9.2	27 987	66.1	35.4	33.1
Carbondale	74.1	684	50.0	20.0	62.2	21.9	11 945	1.2	731	6.1	23 020	52.3	16.9	41.4
Carol Stream	33.0	1 018	33.0	6.2	89.1	8.4	23 945	0.5	1 156	4.8	32 146	77.5	48.7	17.0
Carpentersville	27.5	969	34.1	4.4	87.6	7.5	19 233	0.6	1 393	7.2	26 804	75.1	47.3	12.9
Champaign	52.4	837	36.9	14.2	67.5	19.4	42 667	0.6	2 209	5.2	70 240	64.1	34.2	23.5
Chicago	55.3	963	31.8	26.9	83.6	5.0	1 361 418	-0.1	87 691	6.4	2 168 489	66.3	40.2	26.3
Chicago Heights	41.1	844	38.0	13.8	90.3	7.1	13 174	-0.6	1 232	9.4	23 223	62.4	33.9	31.2
Cicero	49.1	851	31.3	10.8	89.2	4.7	37 095	-0.5	2 405	6.5	59 282	67.3	39.5	18.5
Collinsville	38.5	813	28.0	7.8	86.2	10.2	12 910	0.4	780	6.0	20 119	66.9	40.1	28.7
Crystal Lake	23.4	1 139	28.4	4.0	89.7	6.1	22 608	0.2	1 122	5.0	31 515	72.8	45.2	17.2
Danville	42.0	664	34.5	15.8	83.8	8.2	13 174	-0.1	1 022	7.8	24 933	54.2	30.9	38.0
Decatur	38.3	659	30.6	12.7	79.8	7.6	33 128	-1.0	2 610	7.9	60 160	61.5	34.0	34.1
DeKalb	57.0	818	40.8	10.9	65.8	18.9	22 841	0.6	1 328	5.8	36 308	65.2	28.5	26.8
Des Plaines	20.1	1 013	28.9	6.7	91.5	6.4	32 730	0.0	1 675	5.1	48 381	66.6	42.8	25.8
Downers Grove	23.1	1 103	27.4	5.9	89.8	8.0	27 265	0.4	1 138	4.2	39 221	68.3	44.0	23.8
East St. Louis	54.9	574	34.8	30.1	87.7	6.5	9 113	-0.4	1 065	11.7	19 837	47.0	24.8	46.7
Elgin	32.1	971	33.0	5.3	86.6	5.6	57 023	0.0	3 945	6.9	82 355	71.0	44.2	18.8
Elk Grove Village	25.6	1 020	31.7	5.2	90.9	7.2	19 289	0.4	961	5.0	27 181	69.7	47.1	22.7
Elmhurst	19.0	1 378	27.4	5.0	89.8	8.0	23 110	0.3	1 021	4.4	34 270	65.7	41.0	22.8
Evanston	44.6	1 197	34.6	16.4	78.1	14.4	39 533	0.1	1 934	4.9	61 830	64.5	38.4	24.8
Freeport	37.5	605	32.9	15.1	82.1	7.2	10 618	-3.1	815	7.7	20 176	60.1	32.5	38.1
Galesburg	41.5	586	30.4	12.5	85.9	7.5	13 010	-1.9	844	6.5	26 569	50.9	29.4	41.2
Glendale Heights	31.3	1 043	29.7	4.6	84.9	9.7	19 376	0.1	1 056	5.5	26 630	75.1	46.8	13.5
Glen Ellyn	25.0	962	30.3	7.0	88.6	9.3	14 017	0.6	646	4.6	21 055	67.6	41.7	24.9
Glenview	18.4	1 732	33.9	6.8	90.8	7.3	22 695	0.6	993	4.4	35 848	61.2	41.0	27.5
Granite City	32.7	658	32.0	9.3	87.0	7.1	13 423	1.0	1 062	7.9	24 063	59.2	35.6	35.0
Gurnee	27.3	1 112	30.8	4.5	88.0	10.1	17 266	0.5	837	4.8	24 224	72.4	47.0	17.2
Hanover Park	22.7	1 153	31.5	2.7	87.7	9.5	20 828	-0.1	1 261	6.1	28 642	73.2	46.8	14.4
Harvey	54.6	822	49.4	21.9	90.3	5.7	8 411	-1.8	969	11.5	18 699	54.3	28.0	45.9
Highland Park	18.3	1 490	31.6	3.5	90.6	6.8	15 065	0.5	619	4.1	23 105	62.7	39.7	26.0
Hoffman Estates	24.8	1 086	27.4	3.2	87.8	9.3	30 117	0.2	1 333	4.4	40 813	74.8	49.5	12.6
Joliet	28.5	894	32.2	7.0	87.4	6.7	74 742	-0.6	5 546	7.4	109 423	70.3	43.2	20.2
Kankakee	50.5	735	35.2	15.6	84.0	8.5	11 278	-1.1	1 063	9.4	20 170	58.1	31.0	36.6
Lake in the Hills	10.1	1 335	24.7	0.9	92.3	6.8	16 067	0.0	812	5.1	21 308	78.1	52.4	10.9
Lansing	28.7	955	35.0	4.9	92.6	5.9	14 492	-0.2	972	6.7	22 991	67.1	40.1	29.9
Lombard	26.2	1 182	27.7	4.4	88.6	9.0	25 093	0.2	1 153	4.6	36 314	69.8	43.2	23.7
McHenry	25.0	990	36.9	5.9	89.3	7.2	14 060	0.1	779	5.5	21 040	72.2	43.3	24.3
Melrose Park	49.4	877	32.1	9.3	86.8	9.1	12 060	0.3	781	6.5	18 651	69.4	42.0	21.2
Moline	33.3	691	26.0	7.2	88.1	7.2	21 995	-0.9	1 360	6.2	34 539	65.5	41.0	28.5
Mount Prospect	28.6	973	27.6	5.2	89.5	7.9	29 575	0.1	1 283	4.3	43 328	68.8	46.9	21.1
Mundelein	24.2	1 112	27.7	2.8	88.2	8.7	18 087	0.2	911	5.0	24 414	74.3	46.6	15.6
Naperville	24.3	1 290	26.6	3.2	87.6	8.6	77 333	0.3	3 499	4.5	110 281	70.1	46.2	15.0
Niles	24.6	996	39.0	11.2	90.7	7.1	13 928	0.0	718	5.2	25 333	55.1	33.8	34.6
Normal	42.2	780	37.3	6.1	68.7	20.2	28 980	0.1	1 379	4.8	45 479	67.7	32.9	20.5
Northbrook	12.4	1 900	36.0	4.1	91.1	7.2	16 231	0.4	696	4.3	26 541	58.8	38.4	28.1
North Chicago	62.6	1 063	32.4	10.7	58.4	36.8	9 215	-0.5	679	7.4	24 496	77.0	21.6	26.0
Oak Forest	20.2	935	31.6	4.5	92.4	5.1	15 248	-0.2	881	5.8	23 129	71.5	42.7	21.5
Oak Lawn	18.7	997	33.6	7.7	92.6	5.7	28 814	-0.2	1 647	5.7	46 489	63.6	38.6	30.0
Oak Park	40.3	1 021	28.6	13.1	86.0	10.6	29 394	0.3	1 396	4.7	40 563	72.9	47.4	21.2
O'Fallon	29.6	1 009	29.6	3.6	85.5	12.4	13 741	0.7	763	5.6	21 816	68.6	42.0	18.5
Orland Park	10.9	1 089	27.6	3.7	92.2	6.3	30 180	0.0	1 462	4.8	47 506	64.1	39.5	27.3
Oswego	15.7	1 535	27.7	1.1	91.7	5.7	18 004	0.2	869	4.8	22 672	76.5	50.9	12.0
Palatine	31.5	1 130	27.9	3.9	86.6	8.9	39 457	0.2	1 895	4.8	54 094	72.5	47.6	18.2
Park Ridge	17.4	1 181	28.1	4.7	93.1	4.9	19 553	0.1	866	4.4	29 799	63.8	40.7	25.5
Pekin	31.4	650	24.3	7.5	85.4	8.2	16 123	-0.5	1 224	7.6	27 040	61.3	40.5	29.5
Peoria	44.4	717	30.2	13.0	80.2	8.6	54 817	-1.1	3 853	7.0	89 632	63.4	37.1	29.1
Plainfield	14.3	1 465	24.2	2.8	90.5	8.2	21 940	0.0	1 165	5.3	28 324	76.5	52.4	9.1
Quincy	36.5	598	30.9	9.7	86.6	5.0	19 406	-0.4	1 040	5.4	32 195	64.3	40.6	32.5
Rockford	44.2	730	32.9	12.0	82.9	6.8	67 740	-0.3	5 649	8.3	115 905	62.8	33.6	33.8
Rock Island	32.8	686	33.5	12.3	83.7	8.4	18 413	-0.8	1 239	6.7	30 958	61.4	33.7	35.1
Romeoville	14.8	1 321	31.9	2.8	89.9	8.1	19 871	-1.0	1 287	6.5	29 088	70.2	44.8	17.4
Round Lake Beach	19.7	999	30.7	4.6	91.5	6.8	14 982	-0.3	1 112	7.4	20 416	73.0	44.4	14.2
St. Charles	28.3	1 061	27.2	5.5	87.5	8.1	18 758	0.7	859	4.6	26 941	69.0	46.0	20.3
Schaumburg	36.9	1 227	25.3	5.5	83.7	13.1	44 137	0.1	2 023	4.6	60 858	71.7	48.9	19.8
Skokie	27.1	1 123	36.1	8.6	91.8	5.0	32 998	0.1	1 590	4.8	53 330	63.3	38.0	25.1
Springfield	36.9	727	31.3	9.4	81.8	9.0	59 645	0.2	3 346	5.6	93 455	65.4	40.9	29.5
Streamwood	13.8	1 444	31.5	1.6	91.7	6.8	23 483	-0.2	1 263	5.4	31 692	76.1	50.0	14.7
Tinley Park	15.6	1 008	28.8	3.2	90.7	7.3	32 176	-0.1	1 596	5.0	45 836	69.4	43.5	22.6
Urbana	63.6	782	39.8	20.9	58.8	30.1	21 169	0.5	1 176	5.6	37 572	59.7	23.0	27.1
Vernon Hills	28.5	1 381	31.5	6.8	86.8	9.3	14 682	0.7	645	4.4	19 568	73.0	48.7	16.4

1. $2,000 represents $2,000 or more.   2. 50.0 represents 50 percent or more.   3. Percent of civilian labor force.   4. Persons 16 years old and over.

Table D. Cities — Construction, Wholesale Trade, and Retail Trade

City	Value of residential construction authorized by building permits, 2015			Wholesale trade,[1] 2012				Retail trade,[2] 2012			
	New construction ($1,000)	Number of housing units	Percent single family	Number of establish-ments	Number of employees	Sales (mil dol)	Annual payroll (mil dol)	Number of establish-ments	Number of employees	Sales (mil dol)	Annual payroll (mil dol)
	69	70	71	72	73	74	75	76	77	78	79
ILLINOIS—Cont'd											
Burbank	1 942	14	85.7	6	25	6.3	0.6	90	1 363	370.6	25.7
Calumet City	0	0	0.0	12	D	D	D	173	2 769	550.6	57.6
Carbondale	881	33	3.0	10	108	32.8	4.7	157	2 760	760.2	56.4
Carol Stream	1 788	15	66.7	109	2 642	3 245.6	162.4	91	1 508	606.1	43.9
Carpentersville	0	0	0.0	14	D	D	D	52	882	251.1	19.5
Champaign	89 395	831	9.9	66	1 267	670.3	52.9	394	6 538	1 496.1	132.6
Chicago	1 097 463	5 750	8.7	2 310	37 189	33 135.0	2 291.0	7 285	85 388	22 627.3	2 221.8
Chicago Heights	0	0	0.0	37	1 028	850.8	52.8	68	758	172.0	15.8
Cicero	0	0	0.0	37	638	460.5	29.8	134	2 028	638.7	46.1
Collinsville	2 629	12	100.0	27	201	135.3	10.1	89	1 754	465.6	39.7
Crystal Lake	530	2	100.0	68	662	565.9	35.7	210	3 601	940.5	83.8
Danville	477	3	100.0	42	D	D	D	150	2 342	537.7	50.3
Decatur	920	6	100.0	83	1 104	2 699.4	56.1	296	4 330	1 204.4	106.5
DeKalb	1 145	5	100.0	15	D	D	D	133	2 587	508.9	50.7
Des Plaines	2 366	8	100.0	138	2 522	3 236.9	181.8	171	3 047	972.2	96.9
Downers Grove	29 836	76	100.0	113	2 190	3 356.2	202.4	227	4 336	1 393.7	112.5
East St. Louis	23 565	197	1.5	20	201	462.1	8.2	61	378	91.2	9.3
Elgin	45 329	272	100.0	193	3 654	3 558.4	242.5	240	3 813	1 223.6	105.5
Elk Grove Village	485	1	100.0	447	7 000	5 203.5	432.9	116	2 416	692.4	70.3
Elmhurst	114 936	330	41.8	130	3 294	1 738.7	321.0	158	2 107	726.8	65.1
Evanston	11 561	47	36.2	53	529	468.7	33.7	213	3 480	940.1	95.6
Freeport	0	0	0.0	22	161	104.1	5.8	111	1 665	380.4	36.5
Galesburg	0	0	0.0	23	362	188.5	15.0	153	3 184	717.4	70.5
Glendale Heights	0	0	0.0	66	1 605	1 089.3	101.3	68	1 459	410.3	38.7
Glen Ellyn	20 330	40	100.0	32	340	188.3	19.0	95	1 154	271.5	25.2
Glenview	54 746	192	81.8	100	1 478	1 320.7	86.2	159	3 471	1 344.4	153.0
Granite City	836	7	100.0	27	311	290.1	14.0	88	1 361	376.4	36.8
Gurnee	175	1	100.0	64	869	752.5	45.7	255	4 991	1 080.4	98.3
Hanover Park	221	1	100.0	29	1 122	1 993.0	59.8	68	872	216.5	19.1
Harvey	0	0	0.0	22	320	102.2	15.7	64	362	108.6	8.2
Highland Park	17 030	18	100.0	48	172	715.5	14.9	166	2 543	1 008.3	82.9
Hoffman Estates	7 420	31	100.0	80	1 536	1 900.4	178.6	116	2 421	792.2	78.3
Joliet	40 533	210	68.1	93	1 662	1 981.6	93.5	408	6 796	1 819.2	161.5
Kankakee	850	6	100.0	31	591	442.4	22.2	84	1 152	292.6	26.5
Lake in the Hills	2 015	6	100.0	21	D	D	D	43	708	221.3	19.9
Lansing	0	0	0.0	31	310	117.6	20.6	103	1 840	430.2	44.8
Lombard	36 566	200	9.5	106	1 333	3 230.1	72.3	239	4 273	911.9	91.9
McHenry	5 821	64	12.5	50	2 143	975.7	109.9	130	1 633	406.3	38.1
Melrose Park	7 215	38	0.0	59	1 157	832.9	67.1	100	2 887	931.5	73.3
Moline	3 387	43	34.9	34	D	D	D	259	4 706	1 022.6	104.8
Mount Prospect	2 452	6	100.0	81	1 167	1 546.9	87.3	162	3 666	4 621.7	110.6
Mundelein	2 877	19	52.6	69	698	552.8	45.2	110	1 413	332.5	32.4
Naperville	105 939	337	97.3	224	2 764	3 346.8	193.6	518	9 553	4 083.3	277.8
Niles	3 472	7	100.0	100	2 067	1 060.5	148.9	273	6 549	1 744.6	155.6
Normal	11 228	137	50.4	24	D	D	D	131	2 949	701.4	59.6
Northbrook	21 678	38	100.0	188	3 410	5 037.6	390.6	259	4 718	1 282.0	139.8
North Chicago	0	0	0.0	11	415	352.7	29.2	35	124	69.5	3.0
Oak Forest	439	3	100.0	21	89	40.6	3.4	59	630	184.5	14.8
Oak Lawn	1 745	10	100.0	28	89	34.9	3.0	162	3 509	1 151.6	95.4
Oak Park	5 977	29	100.0	22	46	58.3	2.3	154	1 491	311.4	31.7
O'Fallon	36 980	134	100.0	15	68	64.4	3.1	84	2 087	860.4	62.7
Orland Park	47 547	307	45.3	51	350	129.1	17.4	371	8 020	1 924.8	186.5
Oswego	13 073	70	100.0	25	117	64.1	6.6	94	2 158	463.8	44.6
Palatine	14 079	47	66.0	69	446	414.6	20.3	186	3 623	853.2	84.9
Park Ridge	18 553	49	100.0	52	191	275.6	12.6	93	1 009	340.9	32.3
Pekin	5 354	34	100.0	15	D	D	D	125	2 127	574.9	51.7
Peoria	12 839	49	100.0	150	2 501	1 151.3	116.8	502	7 845	1 927.7	188.2
Plainfield	47 794	151	92.1	28	361	318.9	29.1	97	1 781	459.8	37.4
Quincy	9 764	64	100.0	71	1 290	693.4	52.9	256	4 452	985.0	94.2
Rockford	5 280	30	60.0	187	2 468	1 826.9	122.4	551	8 326	2 140.2	193.8
Rock Island	4 516	22	63.6	64	1 280	853.6	61.3	79	969	240.6	25.4
Romeoville	3 144	21	90.5	67	1 833	5 959.8	104.7	59	1 194	330.6	23.6
Round Lake Beach	0	0	0.0	6	18	5.0	0.8	54	1 518	323.6	32.1
St. Charles	7 119	35	77.1	102	1 005	1 648.1	55.9	160	3 016	906.6	82.0
Schaumburg	21 308	200	1.0	270	4 850	6 838.8	373.8	483	11 457	2 790.9	301.5
Skokie	6 965	10	100.0	122	D	D	D	334	5 566	1 148.2	125.8
Springfield	29 986	152	50.7	130	2 845	2 386.0	122.5	586	10 451	2 625.3	242.6
Streamwood	0	0	0.0	21	83	41.8	3.7	88	1 637	374.7	37.3
Tinley Park	4 831	26	84.6	64	739	394.4	38.2	157	3 495	1 195.9	93.4
Urbana	13 514	145	14.5	27	D	D	D	83	1 532	423.9	38.8
Vernon Hills	10 511	49	34.7	68	2 464	2 447.8	174.3	214	5 361	2 085.3	149.8

1. Merchant wholesalers except manufacturers' sales branches and offices.   2. Establishments with payroll.

Table D. Cities — Real Estate, Professional Services, and Manufacturing

City	Real estate and rental and leasing, 2012				Professional, scientific, and technical services,[1] 2012				Manufacturing, 2012			
	Number of establishments	Number of employees	Receipts (mil dol)	Annual payroll (mil dol)	Number of establishments	Number of employees	Receipts (mil dol)	Annual payroll (mil dol)	Number of establishments	Number of employees	Receipts (mil dol)	Annual payroll (mil dol)
	80	81	82	83	84	85	86	87	88	89	90	91
ILLINOIS—Cont'd												
Burbank	7	19	2.6	0.4	28	92	6.9	2.3	6	47	D	2.4
Calumet City	17	95	27.8	2.4	30	D	D	D	10	485	231.5	25.8
Carbondale	51	287	40.7	5.9	59	D	D	D	13	276	D	12.3
Carol Stream	36	267	56.9	10.0	90	494	86.9	25.8	95	4 421	1 452.3	237.5
Carpentersville	22	91	13.0	3.4	36	D	D	D	24	1 720	538.9	114.1
Champaign	108	1 117	307.5	45.4	245	D	D	D	55	1 692	656.3	86.6
Chicago	3 076	23 960	7 312.7	1 464.7	10 102	147 767	36 711.4	14 148.1	1 870	58 435	26 503.4	2 891.9
Chicago Heights	15	164	58.8	9.0	26	149	10.4	4.9	52	2 462	1 775.4	143.8
Cicero	14	70	16.4	2.7	36	206	15.0	4.4	70	2 847	818.5	144.4
Collinsville	26	158	27.4	6.2	83	621	69.6	28.3	11	98	D	3.6
Crystal Lake	44	197	33.9	7.5	204	763	190.2	44.2	76	2 902	770.8	138.0
Danville	31	114	16.2	2.8	59	349	40.9	15.0	48	3 425	1 654.4	180.8
Decatur	73	432	89.0	11.4	126	1 036	119.8	45.4	81	7 384	13 124.3	380.7
DeKalb	41	340	84.7	10.6	48	146	18.8	4.1	27	987	D	42.6
Des Plaines	82	1 134	1 241.2	67.9	273	D	D	D	127	5 811	1 498.2	300.7
Downers Grove	104	504	124.9	26.5	343	3 641	798.1	288.8	62	3 257	808.2	202.8
East St. Louis	14	45	15.3	1.8	13	D	D	D	11	169	61.6	8.2
Elgin	78	298	75.2	13.2	275	1 441	213.8	73.2	182	7 541	2 914.3	396.1
Elk Grove Village	59	695	109.0	32.2	179	1 872	339.1	146.4	406	13 764	3 678.1	712.1
Elmhurst	65	367	99.6	17.0	244	1 290	193.2	85.6	75	1 574	427.8	95.0
Evanston	106	443	91.9	18.5	412	D	D	D	48	1 051	255.0	51.9
Freeport	20	68	8.6	1.8	59	345	38.1	14.7	36	1 727	402.7	89.4
Galesburg	27	107	14.9	2.4	56	285	26.1	10.1	30	732	D	29.5
Glendale Heights	15	151	97.0	5.6	43	142	16.6	5.9	47	3 195	845.5	177.9
Glen Ellyn	44	278	247.0	19.2	180	484	128.6	26.7	9	D	2.3	D
Glenview	85	475	446.8	31.4	280	2 042	250.5	161.9	47	635	165.2	37.8
Granite City	30	150	19.6	4.9	32	214	26.6	10.4	30	4 619	2 895.2	320.6
Gurnee	37	175	52.1	8.6	126	488	59.5	21.2	67	2 485	890.5	140.1
Hanover Park	13	D	D	D	38	151	26.7	5.4	11	645	217.1	31.4
Harvey	9	63	19.7	3.2	8	48	2.3	1.0	22	1 384	771.4	75.1
Highland Park	61	186	88.8	10.9	232	D	D	D	24	115	12.3	3.4
Hoffman Estates	32	123	49.8	6.7	223	1 756	291.5	133.3	25	824	290.7	67.3
Joliet	83	400	66.1	14.4	235	D	D	D	73	3 592	2 050.1	225.9
Kankakee	26	75	13.1	2.6	53	D	D	D	29	1 347	1 122.5	83.6
Lake in the Hills	10	22	3.6	0.4	53	236	48.9	14.7	18	133	D	6.1
Lansing	25	95	15.1	3.8	46	169	21.1	7.6	29	1 427	348.7	60.1
Lombard	76	2 385	474.0	96.8	222	2 198	376.2	172.9	58	895	170.8	44.5
McHenry	31	D	D	D	77	D	D	D	58	1 296	242.2	60.0
Melrose Park	20	106	26.8	4.9	23	83	8.2	2.1	97	4 615	1 763.8	222.9
Moline	56	286	74.2	8.4	112	D	D	D	39	2 353	1 518.8	140.6
Mount Prospect	45	235	50.8	15.4	176	2 613	107.1	270.5	39	1 541	536.1	97.6
Mundelein	23	66	11.9	2.4	107	590	108.0	47.9	59	1 625	451.6	80.5
Naperville	207	731	212.6	33.0	1 076	D	D	D	82	1 751	570.1	88.3
Niles	46	319	45.9	11.5	89	472	65.9	22.7	55	1 914	667.9	113.0
Normal	34	256	37.5	7.9	68	D	D	D	16	1 881	D	110.0
Northbrook	152	2 172	237.2	61.1	578	D	D	D	79	2 299	514.6	113.0
North Chicago	4	29	4.8	0.8	16	D	D	D	15	6 797	2 649.0	D
Oak Forest	14	64	7.2	2.9	48	131	20.5	5.8	14	366	D	16.0
Oak Lawn	38	162	27.7	5.8	95	D	D	D	27	436	128.7	21.9
Oak Park	83	352	86.0	14.7	288	D	D	D	18	158	21.7	5.4
O'Fallon	37	143	25.6	6.3	85	1 347	224.8	91.9	11	276	143.6	10.8
Orland Park	74	201	68.1	8.1	237	1 155	156.2	64.1	33	414	146.6	18.0
Oswego	25	D	D	D	71	D	D	D	23	477	D	21.9
Palatine	72	198	39.9	7.0	349	1 385	221.4	84.5	43	1 882	566.4	85.8
Park Ridge	68	D	D	D	252	874	133.5	45.1	10	358	80.9	10.7
Pekin	20	57	9.2	1.3	41	251	21.0	9.2	30	1 003	960.8	60.6
Peoria	152	778	137.6	26.5	356	D	D	D	84	3 270	3 634.4	162.3
Plainfield	29	128	38.7	7.4	134	801	113.1	58.2	21	620	D	39.0
Quincy	50	201	30.4	5.6	116	693	66.3	25.0	45	1 744	651.1	85.8
Rockford	144	1 187	133.5	34.0	418	2 844	539.9	150.2	340	15 649	5 385.6	961.7
Rock Island	22	66	12.2	2.0	112	D	D	D	39	1 390	455.3	64.7
Romeoville	22	435	71.1	23.9	38	346	43.1	12.5	50	1 642	564.9	85.4
Round Lake Beach	9	25	5.3	0.6	20	74	5.0	2.4	7	67	D	1.9
St. Charles	79	456	262.5	22.0	213	D	D	D	93	5 614	1 569.4	280.4
Schaumburg	148	1 064	356.5	64.7	713	10 430	2 509.6	777.0	151	3 929	1 699.7	201.9
Skokie	103	670	179.7	36.8	383	D	D	D	134	5 070	1 263.7	258.2
Springfield	152	676	136.6	22.0	414	3 918	504.4	206.6	66	2 116	497.3	107.6
Streamwood	21	247	67.4	13.8	81	236	22.9	7.3	34	764	188.1	37.3
Tinley Park	35	135	46.3	4.5	140	990	136.0	48.8	38	1 063	253.5	56.4
Urbana	31	1 483	202.8	62.7	72	D	D	D	21	D	320.6	50.9
Vernon Hills	24	D	D	D	160	1 632	384.7	139.2	24	1 696	622.7	133.0

1. Establishments subject to federal tax.

City	Accommodation and food services, 2012				Arts, entertainment, and recreation,[1] 2012				Health care and social assistance,[1] 2012			
	Number of establishments	Number of employees	Sales (mil dol)	Annual payroll (mil dol)	Number of establishments	Number of employees	Receipts (mil dol)	Annual payroll (mil dol)	Number of establishments	Number of employees	Receipts (mil dol)	Annual payroll (mil dol)
	92	93	94	95	96	97	98	99	100	101	102	103
ILLINOIS—Cont'd												
Burbank	50	742	37.9	10.4	3	D	D	D	36	D	D	D
Calumet City	79	1 238	63.8	16.5	3	37	2.1	0.6	58	798	48.1	23.9
Carbondale	95	D	D	D	4	D	D	D	90	D	D	D
Carol Stream	76	991	58.0	13.5	9	62	3.5	0.8	56	456	43.3	17.0
Carpentersville	37	859	34.9	10.1	4	D	D	D	20	D	D	D
Champaign	301	6 636	298.9	82.6	23	D	D	D	155	D	D	D
Chicago	6 022	115 965	8 996.4	2 481.8	716	11 186	2 159.3	742.9	5 253	73 916	6 786.9	2 549.9
Chicago Heights	46	576	26.8	8.0	1	D	D	D	52	713	57.4	23.5
Cicero	86	1 040	64.0	16.5	5	34	3.0	0.5	60	505	41.7	14.5
Collinsville	67	1 471	64.6	18.7	9	D	D	D	50	D	D	D
Crystal Lake	120	2 615	143.7	41.2	18	106	6.5	1.3	185	2 021	186.4	82.5
Danville	87	1 544	65.9	18.9	7	55	2.8	0.8	77	1 103	96.0	44.9
Decatur	179	3 415	152.1	43.8	13	279	8.2	4.1	206	D	D	D
DeKalb	99	1 677	69.6	19.5	3	D	D	D	53	D	D	D
Des Plaines	163	2 001	135.4	30.3	14	D	D	D	211	2 857	244.0	99.0
Downers Grove	154	3 004	175.7	52.0	16	208	8.5	2.6	215	D	D	D
East St. Louis	35	D	D	D	1	D	D	D	29	D	D	D
Elgin	185	3 061	147.6	41.1	19	D	D	D	246	2 757	302.9	148.7
Elk Grove Village	114	1 739	121.7	33.6	14	D	D	D	130	D	D	D
Elmhurst	108	1 721	92.5	25.7	17	117	7.6	1.9	219	D	D	D
Evanston	238	3 779	274.7	77.2	42	393	24.7	8.6	259	4 212	630.9	389.4
Freeport	64	889	41.2	10.4	8	D	D	D	62	D	D	D
Galesburg	92	1 464	65.9	18.5	3	24	0.8	0.2	67	1 761	183.4	64.6
Glendale Heights	45	706	42.6	10.1	9	D	D	D	33	D	D	D
Glen Ellyn	61	959	51.4	13.8	9	D	D	D	92	1 095	190.8	87.2
Glenview	158	2 761	163.8	52.1	34	328	45.9	20.6	254	3 243	317.0	133.0
Granite City	67	1 011	46.0	12.7	6	D	D	D	67	D	D	D
Gurnee	136	3 217	166.2	47.8	15	D	D	D	166	1 442	196.1	77.9
Hanover Park	36	446	26.2	5.9	3	73	3.6	0.8	32	286	24.4	8.9
Harvey	40	744	41.1	12.3	NA	NA	NA	NA	42	D	D	D
Highland Park	90	1 506	91.0	28.9	30	393	19.9	9.5	155	D	D	D
Hoffman Estates	117	1 993	130.7	36.7	15	D	D	D	226	D	D	D
Joliet	235	5 812	555.9	117.0	16	277	67.5	9.0	337	4 717	581.8	230.6
Kankakee	53	D	D	D	5	D	D	D	71	D	D	D
Lake in the Hills	29	524	25.4	7.8	8	D	D	D	51	583	38.8	16.8
Lansing	62	1 206	57.9	15.9	6	D	D	D	57	504	38.4	15.2
Lombard	148	3 359	210.1	62.0	14	320	14.7	4.6	147	2 367	232.5	95.6
McHenry	83	1 267	53.3	15.2	7	55	4.6	1.2	91	D	D	D
Melrose Park	72	D	D	D	6	D	D	D	106	D	D	D
Moline	156	2 771	128.6	36.9	11	D	D	D	163	2 283	237.6	107.0
Mount Prospect	112	1 568	86.8	23.9	8	D	D	D	118	2 071	159.2	61.2
Mundelein	75	1 082	53.2	13.5	12	D	D	D	48	296	26.4	10.5
Naperville	361	7 975	472.3	129.5	58	730	82.7	29.4	589	D	D	D
Niles	135	D	D	D	9	D	D	D	147	2 732	262.6	89.7
Normal	106	2 742	132.3	36.2	10	D	D	D	74	1 254	119.4	45.5
Northbrook	96	2 082	140.2	46.3	33	D	D	D	269	3 224	294.6	125.2
North Chicago	31	390	19.8	4.9	NA	NA	NA	NA	8	D	D	D
Oak Forest	37	593	28.3	7.6	4	D	D	D	45	869	44.4	23.5
Oak Lawn	108	2 406	172.7	39.1	12	144	7.9	1.8	239	D	D	D
Oak Park	101	1 703	86.0	26.0	25	275	23.2	5.9	262	4 148	374.6	171.8
O'Fallon	69	D	D	D	8	D	D	D	69	D	D	D
Orland Park	170	4 254	207.9	61.7	20	D	D	D	293	4 528	413.6	185.3
Oswego	60	1 375	66.7	19.5	10	108	5.4	1.2	70	D	D	D
Palatine	111	1 558	80.0	22.1	18	D	D	D	134	1 711	101.3	39.2
Park Ridge	66	887	51.4	13.9	11	D	D	D	242	D	D	D
Pekin	86	1 460	62.7	17.3	9	D	D	D	68	926	65.6	30.9
Peoria	326	6 429	294.4	84.8	27	955	36.5	13.6	334	6 614	826.5	352.7
Plainfield	85	1 610	75.6	19.6	7	D	D	D	115	D	D	D
Quincy	126	2 186	98.8	28.2	11	D	D	D	97	2 168	334.1	112.8
Rockford	336	7 122	344.0	97.8	28	317	17.3	4.8	365	5 805	856.7	340.5
Rock Island	62	1 356	157.5	22.1	7	D	D	D	75	D	D	D
Romeoville	61	1 259	58.0	17.6	10	420	22.6	6.8	31	D	D	D
Round Lake Beach	31	484	31.5	8.2	7	87	5.3	1.3	26	D	D	D
St. Charles	114	2 960	140.1	44.4	17	D	D	D	149	1 471	169.2	71.4
Schaumburg	265	7 508	488.2	150.8	31	777	47.5	11.9	261	3 141	316.3	118.4
Skokie	155	3 453	232.9	63.6	22	D	D	D	346	3 873	352.6	149.3
Springfield	402	8 032	383.4	114.2	43	D	D	D	286	9 744	1 233.0	436.3
Streamwood	64	991	53.1	13.9	3	15	0.9	0.3	52	1 247	126.7	50.0
Tinley Park	130	2 621	147.9	38.4	18	216	30.4	5.9	162	2 257	259.1	86.1
Urbana	108	1 781	84.3	23.4	11	D	D	D	45	D	D	D
Vernon Hills	95	1 717	103.9	30.6	16	D	D	D	106	1 089	161.7	55.2

1. Establishments subject to federal tax.

Table D. Cities — Other Services and Government Employment and Payroll

City	Other services[1], 2012				Government employment and payroll, 2012								
					Full-time equivalent employees	March payroll							
						Total (dollars)	Percent of total for:						
	Number of establishments	Number of employees	Receipts (mil dol)	Annual payroll (mil dol)			Administration, judicial, and legal	Police and Corrections	Fire Protection	Highways and transportation	Health and welfare	Natural resources and utilities	Education and libraries
	104	105	106	107	108	109	110	111	112	113	114	115	116
ILLINOIS—Cont'd													
Burbank	39	134	11.1	3.7	134	786 445	7.6	47.7	28.5	12.5	0.0	0.0	0.0
Calumet City	34	108	11.2	3.2	270	1 459 484	9.0	47.4	26.2	6.4	3.6	3.2	4.2
Carbondale	42	152	13.2	3.2	243	1 024 650	20.3	36.8	14.6	7.4	0.7	17.5	0.0
Carol Stream	59	257	23.2	7.0	178	1 066 716	18.8	48.5	0.0	9.7	2.2	4.7	13.5
Carpentersville	30	124	8.9	2.6	197	1 212 358	9.8	38.1	25.5	7.4	4.7	10.2	0.0
Champaign	103	766	51.3	17.7	613	3 303 325	9.3	26.5	21.3	13.7	2.4	1.6	17.9
Chicago	3 455	21 793	1 817.1	565.1	25 630	175 627 618	2.8	74.4	7.6	3.4	2.3	5.3	1.0
Chicago Heights	40	189	15.1	5.0	294	1 453 188	3.9	43.8	28.2	5.0	0.3	9.0	5.7
Cicero	71	248	23.0	5.9	584	2 867 400	8.1	39.8	18.0	10.1	11.3	7.3	1.8
Collinsville	38	200	17.5	5.2	169	956 282	5.4	39.2	23.4	8.4	4.4	16.9	0.0
Crystal Lake	109	730	55.8	17.6	309	1 877 299	13.5	27.5	25.3	5.8	2.7	10.3	9.1
Danville	49	270	24.0	6.7	294	1 321 594	8.4	29.2	21.7	13.2	2.3	14.1	5.3
Decatur	102	865	126.6	28.1	554	2 990 379	8.4	39.2	24.9	9.4	4.8	6.5	5.6
DeKalb	43	312	15.5	5.5	198	1 271 653	11.8	36.9	32.8	11.6	1.9	5.0	0.0
Des Plaines	142	940	130.6	36.5	446	2 438 468	5.2	30.6	34.3	7.1	3.0	5.9	10.5
Downers Grove	115	1 076	103.5	31.9	390	2 164 897	16.2	30.8	26.2	1.6	2.8	10.9	8.4
East St. Louis	16	108	5.7	1.8	189	693 926	9.2	35.2	34.7	6.6	4.3	0.0	2.0
Elgin	143	1 294	139.9	49.7	718	4 472 423	10.3	39.1	24.6	3.4	0.0	18.7	0.0
Elk Grove Village	106	964	120.0	35.0	298	2 048 828	10.7	36.3	32.2	8.8	6.0	5.0	0.0
Elmhurst	94	781	68.0	22.5	587	3 047 235	10.6	25.1	12.8	8.0	0.0	13.7	21.9
Evanston	113	739	46.4	16.6	756	4 935 582	8.8	31.1	21.1	2.8	8.4	20.2	3.5
Freeport	46	195	13.7	3.9	191	868 424	5.9	37.1	28.7	6.7	0.0	12.7	3.3
Galesburg	53	D	D	D	284	1 182 039	9.7	30.8	19.6	8.9	4.7	17.2	4.2
Glendale Heights	39	299	36.2	11.3	240	1 253 066	11.8	42.0	0.0	9.8	5.4	20.6	0.0
Glen Ellyn	48	261	20.7	6.6	170	812 456	21.3	30.1	0.0	7.6	0.0	23.8	11.9
Glenview	126	726	57.9	19.6	368	2 419 770	8.4	26.3	34.2	5.3	3.0	8.4	10.8
Granite City	48	394	45.7	14.2	233	1 173 888	7.7	32.1	27.6	12.2	4.4	14.0	0.0
Gurnee	64	491	47.5	14.0	198	1 570 289	5.9	45.6	29.7	8.4	0.0	3.7	0.0
Hanover Park	34	330	19.3	6.6	207	1 331 356	9.4	44.7	23.0	7.5	3.0	8.6	0.0
Harvey	19	77	6.6	1.6	195	871 135	8.5	48.6	27.8	8.3	0.3	6.5	0.0
Highland Park	101	582	48.4	15.2	227	1 445 604	8.6	30.8	26.4	9.8	1.3	11.6	0.0
Hoffman Estates	59	416	19.3	8.7	347	2 420 731	11.8	35.1	29.9	4.6	1.4	10.1	0.0
Joliet	151	1 366	144.2	44.6	941	6 790 745	6.4	38.7	25.4	6.8	1.3	12.5	3.8
Kankakee	41	246	22.9	6.8	264	1 273 939	5.5	35.8	24.1	7.9	6.7	10.1	4.5
Lake in the Hills	43	168	14.6	4.0	131	726 848	15.2	43.1	0.0	11.6	4.1	15.1	0.0
Lansing	48	561	57.3	16.4	200	1 054 688	6.3	47.0	25.7	7.3	0.0	5.9	5.3
Lombard	107	701	75.0	22.0	289	1 794 844	9.3	33.8	26.1	6.4	0.8	8.5	8.0
McHenry	72	377	28.3	8.4	136	766 529	11.7	38.7	0.0	16.4	0.0	26.3	0.0
Melrose Park	42	D	D	D	274	1 377 728	3.3	43.1	26.6	6.0	1.7	8.5	5.6
Moline	84	478	32.8	10.5	392	2 247 548	10.9	28.1	19.6	8.6	0.7	17.4	6.2
Mount Prospect	81	458	39.5	12.0	445	2 620 859	6.5	27.8	21.6	6.5	3.5	10.4	15.1
Mundelein	71	374	31.2	9.8	167	523 415	11.5	34.6	14.6	10.6	0.0	10.8	0.0
Naperville	249	1 950	138.1	45.2	1 141	6 999 358	11.3	27.3	20.8	10.0	0.0	21.1	9.4
Niles	74	463	36.0	10.0	277	1 803 453	9.8	28.4	25.4	11.8	9.9	11.0	0.0
Normal	49	391	26.9	9.3	426	2 272 555	9.0	24.8	18.8	7.7	0.7	25.9	7.3
Northbrook	87	584	39.7	14.6	275	2 019 890	9.3	35.9	30.6	13.5	2.9	7.8	0.0
North Chicago	10	D	D	D	176	982 302	7.8	51.2	16.6	5.2	4.6	10.0	4.6
Oak Forest	38	172	15.2	3.9	137	814 381	8.2	43.6	26.4	10.5	0.1	10.0	0.0
Oak Lawn	91	709	57.2	17.9	421	2 260 980	6.9	39.4	25.9	7.3	0.7	8.8	7.3
Oak Park	100	582	47.7	14.0	450	2 566 842	9.0	37.0	19.6	5.0	4.3	3.8	10.5
O'Fallon	47	304	27.7	8.3	177	876 752	17.3	46.2	0.5	7.4	7.7	15.6	4.9
Orland Park	121	1 053	78.1	27.9	409	2 080 080	14.2	43.9	0.0	6.5	0.0	22.3	8.2
Oswego	58	331	28.0	9.2	107	609 946	20.4	64.0	0.0	0.0	0.0	15.5	0.0
Palatine	135	781	61.8	19.8	348	2 424 446	10.2	40.9	30.9	4.8	1.1	3.4	0.0
Park Ridge	61	352	31.7	10.3	255	1 549 856	7.5	29.7	26.8	7.3	4.0	6.5	14.1
Pekin	58	255	15.5	5.3	259	1 110 590	5.2	29.2	27.7	6.0	1.0	5.6	4.2
Peoria	158	3 995	358.2	183.6	831	4 963 632	9.9	36.9	26.3	5.9	1.3	5.1	5.3
Plainfield	61	426	29.8	9.2	131	858 893	12.3	62.1	0.0	9.7	0.0	13.1	0.0
Quincy	88	476	38.8	11.9	391	1 653 065	8.8	30.0	19.6	12.1	0.3	15.1	5.2
Rockford	242	1 586	154.2	43.7	1 085	6 113 597	5.6	33.3	36.5	5.3	7.4	4.8	4.2
Rock Island	50	370	31.5	9.6	372	1 377 794	14.6	16.8	10.5	8.7	9.2	29.1	7.6
Romeoville	40	474	48.6	14.5	297	1 580 154	8.8	38.4	18.0	2.8	3.6	17.7	0.0
Round Lake Beach	26	118	7.7	2.5	90	514 049	11.2	62.5	0.0	8.6	4.5	13.1	0.0
St. Charles	85	647	44.9	15.4	264	1 823 844	18.8	26.0	21.1	7.0	0.0	19.6	0.0
Schaumburg	197	1 612	162.4	51.5	536	3 458 405	11.4	32.6	25.6	5.7	7.4	8.7	0.0
Skokie	157	1 128	107.7	36.5	593	3 361 285	7.8	29.7	23.3	2.7	5.7	10.6	14.6
Springfield	184	1 494	123.1	38.3	1 621	10 142 573	6.4	16.0	12.6	5.8	1.5	56.2	1.6
Streamwood	55	288	22.7	6.3	179	1 160 444	8.6	42.2	27.2	3.9	3.6	10.8	0.0
Tinley Park	57	343	25.6	8.5	346	1 824 694	11.4	45.9	13.6	6.6	0.8	8.0	9.0
Urbana	33	193	14.3	4.6	302	1 464 071	11.1	26.0	23.5	13.2	5.3	4.2	11.9
Vernon Hills	34	373	21.8	8.8	101	697 505	10.9	66.3	0.0	16.7	0.0	0.0	0.0

1. Establishments subject to federal tax.

Table D. Cities — **City Government Finances**

City	City government finances, 2012									
	General revenue							General expenditure		
		Intergovernmental		Taxes					Per capita[1] (dollars)	
					Per capita[1] (dollars)					
	Total (mil dol)	Total (mil dol)	Percent from state government	Total (mil dol)	Total	Property	Sales and gross receipts	Total (mil dol)	Total	Capital outlays
	117	118	119	120	121	122	123	124	125	126
ILLINOIS—Cont'd										
Burbank	19.3	6.5	97.7	12.0	410	185	219	17.0	584	9
Calumet City	50.9	11.6	90.1	34.2	919	681	229	45.9	1 232	103
Carbondale	32.4	10.9	88.9	14.1	533	69	464	31.8	1 202	47
Carol Stream	28.1	11.1	91.6	10.1	252	15	219	25.3	631	60
Carpentersville	32.2	12.8	86.2	12.7	332	234	98	36.5	955	239
Champaign	100.8	38.9	81.8	49.4	597	285	312	101.7	1 229	343
Chicago	6 690.6	1 758.6	65.4	2 526.4	930	327	547	7 439.1	2 740	425
Chicago Heights	44.6	13.6	76.8	22.9	750	593	155	45.7	1 500	202
Cicero	111.4	23.7	88.5	72.9	863	556	300	108.6	1 285	185
Collinsville	30.2	11.1	94.1	12.0	478	200	278	29.1	1 154	106
Crystal Lake	53.2	19.4	99.7	23.3	576	375	201	54.2	1 341	305
Danville	42.4	15.6	82.1	19.3	590	227	363	42.8	1 309	210
Decatur	75.9	32.1	85.6	34.5	458	179	279	89.1	1 182	206
DeKalb	53.3	19.6	68.3	26.9	614	331	283	45.2	1 031	260
Des Plaines	103.1	31.2	96.3	57.8	982	617	358	92.0	1 563	249
Downers Grove	65.8	18.9	98.8	39.1	793	447	346	58.7	1 190	157
East St. Louis	38.6	19.9	85.1	15.8	592	444	148	38.3	1 439	101
Elgin	136.9	44.5	93.0	66.3	605	479	126	125.2	1 141	155
Elk Grove Village	60.1	13.5	93.1	37.1	1 113	630	466	64.9	1 946	411
Elmhurst	70.4	17.9	99.2	36.4	806	479	320	65.4	1 450	192
Evanston	123.4	24.9	70.5	64.7	858	533	298	116.5	1 544	176
Freeport	29.6	13.3	99.7	8.0	317	186	130	28.8	1 144	64
Galesburg	39.9	19.3	93.4	14.5	455	218	236	38.4	1 207	64
Glendale Heights	35.6	10.2	99.2	15.9	460	241	210	43.0	1 246	422
Glen Ellyn	37.6	7.6	88.9	16.6	602	374	215	32.5	1 176	174
Glenview	101.0	27.2	76.5	62.0	1 377	1 042	336	95.5	2 120	282
Granite City	40.9	13.0	100.0	18.6	629	472	157	45.0	1 521	211
Gurnee	38.2	22.9	85.8	9.6	307	0	307	34.9	1 121	11
Hanover Park	38.2	10.2	89.4	21.6	563	376	180	53.4	1 392	426
Harvey	23.0	6.4	100.0	13.8	543	424	119	25.1	990	34
Highland Park	56.2	12.1	93.3	29.2	978	521	419	47.5	1 591	94
Hoffman Estates	82.1	13.5	91.6	51.3	982	736	239	64.6	1 237	110
Joliet	202.1	70.4	93.0	72.3	488	283	198	177.8	1 199	22
Kankakee	60.8	25.8	88.2	20.1	735	562	173	66.7	2 438	258
Lake in the Hills	20.2	7.5	78.9	9.1	314	217	97	18.0	620	82
Lansing	33.0	8.0	94.6	18.5	649	445	203	35.4	1 241	283
Lombard	90.1	27.3	90.2	20.3	464	194	270	97.6	2 231	83
McHenry	24.8	12.3	96.4	6.7	249	217	33	23.4	873	150
Melrose Park	43.6	13.9	98.6	23.4	918	732	185	48.9	1 914	285
Moline	72.2	20.2	84.2	35.3	819	413	405	74.2	1 720	148
Mount Prospect	70.6	19.0	93.5	43.9	805	533	265	70.0	1 283	142
Mundelein	36.2	9.6	91.1	18.0	577	372	205	32.6	1 046	94
Naperville	169.6	55.1	89.1	79.8	555	355	183	143.7	999	101
Niles	48.5	18.9	99.5	23.3	776	251	518	41.3	1 378	19
Normal	80.5	31.2	99.5	31.3	581	208	372	77.3	1 435	387
Northbrook	51.6	18.4	98.1	23.9	715	481	233	52.8	1 578	131
North Chicago	26.1	8.5	79.5	13.3	441	299	138	26.6	885	25
Oak Forest	21.4	5.3	98.7	12.5	444	315	129	20.9	744	55
Oak Lawn	62.1	19.1	99.2	28.3	496	394	96	68.1	1 194	211
Oak Park	89.0	14.1	80.8	58.0	1 115	815	268	90.4	1 737	226
O'Fallon	33.2	13.4	98.6	10.8	370	237	133	31.4	1 072	258
Orland Park	85.4	30.2	96.4	33.9	592	346	245	81.3	1 420	303
Oswego	21.0	9.6	98.5	6.3	198	46	152	17.5	553	6
Palatine	81.2	22.0	76.2	45.6	660	486	175	87.2	1 262	293
Park Ridge	46.1	10.0	100.0	30.9	818	523	283	47.4	1 255	36
Pekin	40.2	14.5	81.3	13.8	404	189	215	48.4	1 417	388
Peoria	185.6	76.4	95.2	81.2	702	306	396	173.5	1 500	288
Plainfield	34.8	10.0	90.4	14.1	348	155	193	27.5	680	54
Quincy	46.5	24.3	86.8	13.5	330	59	271	36.7	898	111
Rockford	205.7	107.8	79.0	75.0	497	396	100	178.2	1 180	127
Rock Island	69.8	23.7	74.6	23.3	601	427	175	75.1	1 934	393
Romeoville	58.3	11.7	84.0	28.8	726	381	336	58.2	1 465	267
Round Lake Beach	17.9	8.1	98.7	8.5	305	231	74	22.5	802	338
St. Charles	51.7	14.2	98.9	26.8	807	424	383	54.5	1 637	225
Schaumburg	155.0	40.4	92.8	70.0	937	341	596	138.1	1 847	106
Skokie	104.2	37.0	66.4	60.5	929	512	413	82.4	1 265	140
Springfield	137.9	49.3	90.7	68.8	587	235	353	135.8	1 159	63
Streamwood	29.9	8.7	93.2	15.7	390	250	135	26.2	650	57
Tinley Park	70.3	22.1	99.9	36.1	632	519	114	61.1	1 069	254
Urbana	47.8	17.7	62.5	22.2	531	252	279	48.4	1 159	285
Vernon Hills	21.2	13.2	99.1	5.7	222	0	222	18.9	740	29

1. Based on population estimated as of July 1 of the year shown.

Table D. Cities — City Government Finances

City	City government finances, 2012 (cont.)									
	General expenditure (cont.)									
	Percent of total for:									
	Public welfare	Highways	Parking facilities	Education	Health and hospitals	Police protection	Sewerage and sanitation	Parks and recreation	Housing and community development	Interest on debt
	127	128	129	130	131	132	133	134	135	136
ILLINOIS—Cont'd										
Burbank	0.0	11.1	0.0	0.0	0.0	42.1	0.0	0.0	0.0	2.8
Calumet City	0.0	11.2	0.0	0.0	1.3	21.0	3.8	0.0	0.3	4.9
Carbondale	0.0	7.9	0.6	0.0	0.0	26.7	11.0	1.0	10.1	4.7
Carol Stream	0.0	12.8	0.0	0.0	0.0	46.9	11.5	0.0	0.0	1.4
Carpentersville	0.0	38.6	0.0	0.0	0.0	24.1	5.9	0.7	0.0	5.8
Champaign	0.3	8.8	2.1	0.0	0.0	19.0	14.5	0.0	0.8	3.1
Chicago	4.6	9.7	0.1	0.0	2.5	18.0	5.3	0.5	4.4	12.5
Chicago Heights	0.0	5.4	0.0	0.0	0.0	23.2	9.3	0.0	6.0	4.9
Cicero	0.3	10.4	0.0	0.0	1.4	22.1	4.8	0.3	1.6	5.0
Collinsville	0.0	8.9	0.0	0.0	0.6	27.3	16.9	0.0	0.0	5.9
Crystal Lake	0.0	25.3	0.0	0.0	0.2	19.8	6.0	1.9	0.0	2.7
Danville	0.0	17.2	0.0	0.0	0.0	16.9	12.9	5.0	1.7	1.3
Decatur	0.0	29.1	0.0	0.0	0.0	25.2	3.2	0.1	2.3	5.8
DeKalb	0.0	13.3	0.0	0.0	0.0	23.6	3.7	0.6	0.6	2.7
Des Plaines	0.0	20.8	0.2	0.0	0.0	21.7	6.9	0.0	0.3	2.6
Downers Grove	0.0	18.1	1.8	0.0	0.0	24.0	7.0	0.0	0.0	5.8
East St. Louis	0.0	6.6	0.0	0.0	0.0	18.9	0.4	0.0	6.8	5.2
Elgin	0.0	11.0	0.0	0.0	0.0	27.7	8.5	13.6	1.2	2.1
Elk Grove Village	0.0	19.6	0.0	0.0	0.0	23.4	3.9	0.0	0.0	5.1
Elmhurst	0.0	18.1	1.0	0.0	0.4	21.5	11.4	1.7	0.0	4.4
Evanston	1.7	7.6	6.0	0.0	2.3	18.5	5.9	10.8	6.7	7.0
Freeport	0.0	13.2	0.0	0.0	0.3	14.5	17.8	0.4	0.0	4.6
Galesburg	0.0	25.9	0.0	0.0	0.0	14.5	5.0	7.5	0.0	3.6
Glendale Heights	0.0	11.3	0.0	0.0	0.0	37.4	2.1	17.7	0.0	7.1
Glen Ellyn	0.0	21.1	0.6	0.0	0.0	22.1	17.3	8.7	0.0	1.6
Glenview	0.0	8.2	0.3	0.0	0.0	12.5	5.1	0.0	0.0	5.3
Granite City	0.0	20.6	0.0	0.0	0.0	20.0	15.5	0.0	0.0	3.9
Gurnee	0.0	13.7	0.0	0.0	0.0	33.2	3.7	0.6	0.0	1.0
Hanover Park	0.0	10.2	0.9	0.0	0.0	43.0	3.1	0.0	0.0	2.1
Harvey	0.0	17.0	0.7	0.0	0.0	22.3	4.4	0.3	0.0	8.0
Highland Park	0.0	10.3	2.4	0.0	0.0	27.0	7.1	5.1	0.0	3.1
Hoffman Estates	0.0	14.7	0.0	0.0	0.9	25.3	5.6	4.4	0.0	8.8
Joliet	0.0	9.3	0.7	0.0	0.0	20.1	10.8	4.0	1.9	1.3
Kankakee	0.0	10.0	0.0	0.0	0.0	14.5	21.2	0.0	1.5	5.0
Lake in the Hills	0.0	10.4	0.0	0.0	0.0	38.8	0.0	8.9	0.0	1.8
Lansing	0.0	15.2	0.0	0.0	0.0	25.7	5.9	0.0	0.0	2.9
Lombard	0.0	4.1	0.1	0.0	0.0	13.3	3.6	0.0	0.0	8.5
McHenry	0.0	14.9	0.0	0.0	0.0	39.0	22.4	8.5	0.0	2.9
Melrose Park	0.0	8.0	0.0	0.0	0.0	22.1	4.8	2.9	0.0	7.5
Moline	0.0	12.6	0.3	0.0	0.0	17.7	10.4	7.3	0.0	5.5
Mount Prospect	1.4	12.6	0.5	0.0	0.2	19.8	8.5	0.5	1.3	1.5
Mundelein	0.0	20.8	0.1	0.0	0.0	30.0	6.2	0.0	0.0	3.3
Naperville	0.0	19.4	0.7	0.0	0.0	24.1	7.8	5.9	0.0	3.5
Niles	0.0	16.1	0.0	0.0	0.0	31.3	5.8	3.8	0.0	1.7
Normal	0.0	7.7	0.0	0.0	0.0	14.0	6.7	12.9	0.2	5.5
Northbrook	0.0	16.7	0.3	0.0	0.0	24.8	2.5	0.0	0.0	5.0
North Chicago	0.0	8.1	0.0	0.0	0.0	30.4	1.8	0.0	1.3	5.2
Oak Forest	0.0	17.8	1.0	0.0	0.0	37.1	4.8	0.0	0.0	2.4
Oak Lawn	0.3	14.0	0.1	0.0	0.0	20.6	8.3	0.6	0.3	5.5
Oak Park	0.0	7.1	4.0	0.0	1.3	20.3	6.0	0.0	4.7	3.1
O'Fallon	0.1	13.1	0.0	0.0	0.0	15.5	10.4	15.1	0.0	9.0
Orland Park	0.0	27.8	0.4	0.0	0.0	21.1	12.3	10.6	0.0	3.0
Oswego	0.0	11.6	0.0	0.0	0.0	45.1	16.3	0.0	0.0	9.0
Palatine	0.0	7.7	0.6	0.0	0.0	41.7	6.7	0.0	0.2	6.5
Park Ridge	0.0	7.0	0.8	0.0	0.0	19.5	10.4	0.0	0.0	3.3
Pekin	0.0	9.3	0.0	0.0	0.0	17.4	28.2	0.0	1.1	3.9
Peoria	0.0	15.7	1.7	0.0	0.0	20.6	1.4	1.5	2.0	5.8
Plainfield	0.0	20.5	0.0	0.0	0.0	39.3	16.5	0.0	0.0	10.9
Quincy	0.0	11.6	0.0	0.0	0.3	22.6	10.1	1.7	2.9	2.4
Rockford	9.5	16.5	0.7	0.0	0.0	25.1	3.9	0.0	5.8	2.4
Rock Island	0.0	8.4	0.2	0.0	0.0	15.4	24.0	9.0	0.4	0.8
Romeoville	0.0	11.3	0.0	0.0	0.0	20.1	10.5	6.5	0.0	8.6
Round Lake Beach	0.0	7.7	0.0	0.0	0.0	28.5	0.0	0.6	0.0	4.2
St. Charles	0.0	20.9	0.0	0.0	1.2	19.4	13.9	0.0	0.0	9.3
Schaumburg	0.8	12.2	0.1	0.0	0.5	18.6	4.6	1.6	0.3	10.1
Skokie	0.0	10.7	0.1	0.0	1.7	19.6	5.0	2.4	1.0	3.2
Springfield	0.0	12.3	1.1	0.0	0.0	27.2	4.0	0.0	3.0	2.0
Streamwood	0.0	17.6	0.0	0.0	0.0	33.2	9.7	1.3	0.0	1.6
Tinley Park	0.0	17.1	0.9	0.0	0.0	26.6	4.6	0.0	0.0	3.6
Urbana	0.3	29.3	1.4	0.0	0.0	17.9	3.0	0.3	7.3	1.1
Vernon Hills	0.0	21.7	0.0	0.0	0.0	46.0	0.0	4.1	0.0	7.1

City	City government finances, 2012 (cont.) Debt outstanding Total (mil dol)	Per capita[1] (dollars)	Debt issued during year	Climate[2] Average daily temperature (degrees Fahrenheit) Mean January	July	Limits January[3]	July[4]	Annual precipitation (inches)	Heating degree days	Cooling degree days
	137	138	139	140	141	142	143	144	145	146
ILLINOIS—Cont'd										
Burbank	10.1	346	0.0	23.5	75.5	16.2	84.7	38.35	6 083	1 001
Calumet City	52.6	1 413	0.0	22.0	74.2	14.8	83.7	38.65	6 355	866
Carbondale	33.7	1 276	6.6	NA	NA	NA	NA	NA	NA	NA
Carol Stream	7.2	180	0.0	23.1	74.8	14.2	86.8	37.94	6 053	942
Carpentersville	49.4	1 295	0.0	19.3	72.6	10.9	83.0	37.22	6 975	679
Champaign	74.8	904	0.0	33.7	79.0	25.0	89.5	47.93	4 183	1 501
Chicago	21 209.6	7 811	2 295.0	25.3	75.4	18.3	84.4	38.01	5 787	994
Chicago Heights	67.7	2 223	46.7	22.0	74.2	14.8	83.7	38.65	6 355	866
Cicero	108.3	1 282	0.0	22.0	73.3	14.3	83.5	36.27	6 498	830
Collinsville	47.8	1 894	0.0	NA	NA	NA	NA	NA	NA	NA
Crystal Lake	42.4	1 049	0.0	28.6	76.3	19.0	87.2	46.96	5 168	1 112
Danville	12.0	367	4.4	25.8	75.3	17.3	86.2	40.96	5 555	1 027
Decatur	96.9	1 286	1.9	25.8	76.2	17.1	87.8	39.74	5 458	1 142
DeKalb	29.2	667	1.0	18.5	73.1	10.3	83.6	37.38	6 979	736
Des Plaines	71.7	1 218	4.0	22.0	73.3	14.3	83.5	36.27	6 498	830
Downers Grove	80.1	1 623	0.0	23.1	74.8	14.2	86.8	37.94	6 053	942
East St. Louis	25.4	954	0.0	29.1	78.6	20.0	88.7	40.33	4 826	1 378
Elgin	106.3	969	10.2	19.3	72.6	10.9	83.0	37.22	6 975	679
Elk Grove Village	52.6	1 579	0.3	22.0	73.3	14.3	83.5	36.27	6 498	830
Elmhurst	61.9	1 371	0.0	23.1	74.8	14.2	86.8	37.94	6 053	942
Evanston	237.9	3 154	19.4	22.0	72.9	13.7	83.2	36.80	6 630	702
Freeport	32.6	1 295	0.0	17.2	71.9	9.0	82.0	34.79	7 317	611
Galesburg	27.4	863	7.9	21.3	74.9	13.5	84.5	37.22	6 347	941
Glendale Heights	49.6	1 437	0.0	22.0	73.3	14.3	83.5	36.27	6 498	830
Glen Ellyn	13.3	482	0.0	21.7	74.4	12.2	85.7	38.58	6 359	888
Glenview	137.4	3 052	11.0	22.0	73.3	14.3	83.5	36.27	6 498	830
Granite City	30.0	1 015	2.2	27.7	78.4	19.4	88.1	38.54	5 149	1 354
Gurnee	16.1	518	10.0	19.9	72.2	12.1	82.2	35.50	6 955	634
Hanover Park	24.0	625	7.0	18.4	72.1	9.6	82.3	36.56	7 149	624
Harvey	50.8	2 004	0.0	22.0	74.2	14.8	83.7	38.65	6 355	866
Highland Park	44.8	1 503	4.6	22.0	72.9	13.7	83.2	36.80	6 630	702
Hoffman Estates	193.6	3 703	2.5	18.4	72.1	9.6	82.3	36.56	7 149	624
Joliet	61.9	417	12.6	21.7	73.7	13.5	84.6	36.96	6 464	809
Kankakee	78.1	2 856	8.7	21.7	74.4	12.2	85.7	38.58	6 359	888
Lake in the Hills	7.6	261	0.0	NA	NA	NA	NA	NA	NA	NA
Lansing	20.8	728	1.5	21.7	74.4	12.2	85.7	38.58	6 359	888
Lombard	219.0	5 007	0.0	23.1	74.8	14.2	86.8	37.94	6 053	942
McHenry	17.9	668	0.0	NA	NA	NA	NA	NA	NA	NA
Melrose Park	80.3	3 147	11.7	NA	NA	NA	NA	NA	NA	NA
Moline	79.9	1 853	18.2	21.8	76.4	13.3	85.1	35.10	6 179	1 100
Mount Prospect	40.7	745	9.3	22.0	73.3	14.3	83.5	36.27	6 498	830
Mundelein	21.6	693	0.0	18.4	72.1	9.6	82.3	36.56	7 149	624
Naperville	178.8	1 244	25.1	23.1	74.8	14.2	86.8	37.94	6 053	942
Niles	18.8	626	4.4	22.0	73.3	14.3	83.5	36.27	6 498	830
Normal	87.9	1 632	0.0	25.8	76.2	17.1	87.8	39.74	5 458	1 142
Northbrook	72.5	2 166	3.0	22.0	72.9	13.7	83.2	36.80	6 630	702
North Chicago	31.9	1 060	2.1	20.3	71.5	12.0	81.7	34.09	7 031	613
Oak Forest	30.0	1 067	0.0	22.0	74.2	14.8	83.7	38.65	6 355	866
Oak Lawn	87.5	1 535	9.2	23.5	75.5	16.2	84.7	38.35	6 083	1 001
Oak Park	104.7	2 013	11.4	22.0	73.3	14.3	83.5	36.27	6 498	830
O'Fallon	47.3	1 618	0.0	NA	NA	NA	NA	NA	NA	NA
Orland Park	81.7	1 427	10.0	23.5	75.5	16.2	84.7	38.35	6 083	1 001
Oswego	34.4	1 087	4.1	NA	NA	NA	NA	NA	NA	NA
Palatine	119.0	1 722	8.2	18.4	72.1	9.6	82.3	36.56	7 149	624
Park Ridge	45.7	1 210	7.5	22.0	73.3	14.3	83.5	36.27	6 498	830
Pekin	49.3	1 445	2.2	24.4	75.8	15.7	87.4	35.71	5 695	1 088
Peoria	222.0	1 920	9.4	22.5	75.1	14.3	85.7	36.03	6 097	998
Plainfield	63.7	1 575	8.4	NA	NA	NA	NA	NA	NA	NA
Quincy	20.2	494	0.0	24.9	76.8	16.0	88.0	35.63	5 707	1 117
Rockford	164.6	1 090	17.5	19.0	72.9	10.8	83.1	36.63	6 933	768
Rock Island	36.5	939	12.7	21.8	76.4	13.3	85.1	35.10	6 179	1 100
Romeoville	169.7	4 271	2.3	NA	NA	NA	NA	NA	NA	NA
Round Lake Beach	25.1	897	4.0	19.9	72.2	12.1	82.2	35.50	6 955	634
St. Charles	142.6	4 289	12.8	19.3	72.6	10.9	83.0	37.22	6 975	679
Schaumburg	302.1	4 043	23.0	18.4	72.1	9.6	82.3	36.56	7 149	624
Skokie	66.5	1 022	0.0	22.0	73.3	14.3	83.5	36.27	6 498	830
Springfield	703.4	6 000	0.3	25.1	76.3	17.1	86.5	35.56	5 596	1 165
Streamwood	10.0	249	0.0	19.3	72.6	10.9	83.0	37.22	6 975	679
Tinley Park	45.9	803	5.2	21.8	76.4	13.3	85.1	35.10	6 179	1 100
Urbana	11.4	273	0.0	20.7	73.2	12.4	83.7	34.47	6 606	774
Vernon Hills	24.7	969	9.5	NA	NA	NA	NA	NA	NA	NA

1. Based on the population estimated as of July 1 of the year shown.   2. Represents normal values based on the 30-year period, 1971–2000.   3. Average daily minimum.
4. Average daily maximum.

Table D. Cities — **Land Area and Population**

STATE Place code	City	Land area,[1] 2010 (sq km)	Total persons	Rank	Per square kilometer	White	Black	American Indian, Alaska Native	Asian	Hawaiian Pacific Islander	Percent Hispanic or Latino[2] 2010-2014	Percent foreign born 2010-2014
			Population, 2015			Race alone or in combination (percent), 2010-2014						
		1	2	3	4	5	6	7	8	9	10	11
	ILLINOIS—Cont'd											
17 79293	Waukegan	61.3	88 475	358	1 443.3	62.2	19.7	0.9	5.7	0.3	53.4	30.7
17 80060	West Chicago	38.3	27 447	1 341	716.6	84.1	2.6	0.2	6.6	0.0	51.2	33.0
17 81048	Wheaton	29.1	53 715	695	1 845.9	89.4	4.4	0.5	7.4	0.1	4.9	10.7
17 81087	Wheeling	22.5	38 079	984	1 692.4	68.4	2.0	0.4	15.9	0.1	32.6	41.7
17 82075	Wilmette	14.0	27 413	1 343	1 958.1	85.5	1.2	0.5	13.6	0.1	4.6	17.7
17 83245	Woodridge	24.4	33 370	1 129	1 367.6	75.0	10.2	0.4	13.0	0.3	13.0	21.1
18 00000	**INDIANA**	92 789.2	6 619 680	X	71.3	86.3	10.2	0.9	2.2	0.1	6.3	4.8
18 01468	Anderson	107.2	55 305	679	515.9	83.5	15.1	1.6	0.9	0.0	5.0	2.9
18 05860	Bloomington	60.0	84 067	391	1 401.1	84.9	5.6	1.4	10.3	0.1	4.1	12.2
18 10342	Carmel	122.9	88 713	354	721.8	86.3	3.5	0.5	11.0	0.1	3.5	11.9
18 14734	Columbus	71.2	46 690	812	655.8	87.0	4.0	0.7	7.9	0.1	4.5	10.6
18 16138	Crown Point	45.9	28 879	1 281	629.2	87.3	8.0	0.3	2.4	0.1	6.7	4.4
18 19486	East Chicago	36.5	28 699	1 289	786.3	29.7	40.8	0.9	0.3	0.0	50.0	8.7
18 20728	Elkhart	60.7	52 348	718	862.4	75.7	15.8	1.5	2.0	0.1	23.8	14.1
18 22000	Evansville	114.4	119 943	228	1 048.5	85.2	14.4	0.7	1.1	0.2	3.1	2.3
18 23278	Fishers	87.0	88 658	355	1 019.1	88.9	5.9	0.5	6.5	0.1	3.3	7.9
18 25000	Fort Wayne	286.5	260 326	77	908.6	77.2	18.0	1.1	4.2	0.1	8.1	7.5
18 27000	Gary	129.2	77 156	437	597.2	13.5	84.4	0.6	0.6	0.2	5.5	1.8
18 28386	Goshen	42.0	32 983	1 141	785.3	86.9	5.6	0.8	1.5	0.4	28.0	15.7
18 29898	Greenwood	55.0	55 586	670	1 010.7	89.8	4.2	0.8	5.6	0.1	4.9	7.1
18 31000	Hammond	59.0	77 614	435	1 315.5	55.0	23.2	1.6	1.4	0.0	36.0	11.6
18 34114	Hobart	68.2	28 404	1 296	416.5	87.6	6.8	1.1	1.2	0.1	13.3	4.4
18 36000	Indianapolis	949.1	853 173	14	911.4	64.7	29.3	0.9	2.8	0.1	9.6	8.6
18 38358	Jeffersonville	88.2	46 960	804	532.4	84.5	15.6	0.9	2.1	0.2	3.9	3.8
18 40392	Kokomo	47.9	57 995	640	1 210.8	86.9	11.7	0.9	1.7	0.1	3.5	2.7
18 40788	Lafayette	71.9	71 111	490	989.0	88.0	8.9	0.7	2.5	0.1	12.6	7.8
18 42426	Lawrence	52.1	47 809	793	917.6	70.7	26.9	1.7	1.7	0.1	12.3	7.4
18 46908	Marion	40.7	29 081	1 274	714.5	84.2	17.3	0.6	1.2	0.1	5.8	2.4
18 48528	Merrillville	86.0	35 224	1 071	409.6	45.7	49.4	1.2	1.6	0.0	13.6	5.9
18 48798	Michigan City	50.7	31 459	1 186	620.5	70.2	30.2	0.8	1.5	0.1	6.2	3.8
18 49932	Mishawaka	44.0	48 261	785	1 096.8	88.4	7.6	0.7	3.6	0.1	5.8	6.1
18 51876	Muncie	70.4	70 087	497	995.6	88.1	10.1	3.6	2.0	0.1	2.4	2.8
18 52326	New Albany	38.7	36 732	1 027	949.1	89.7	10.4	0.9	0.7	0.0	4.1	2.2
18 54180	Noblesville	81.3	59 093	623	726.9	92.3	5.9	0.4	2.6	0.2	4.6	4.2
18 60246	Plainfield	57.7	30 590	1 218	530.2	86.4	8.1	0.6	4.8	0.0	4.1	6.9
18 61092	Portage	66.4	36 738	1 025	553.3	88.5	9.4	0.2	1.6	0.2	17.2	4.5
18 64260	Richmond	61.9	35 854	1 054	579.2	89.0	10.5	1.0	1.7	0.1	4.2	3.4
18 68220	Schererville	38.1	28 791	1 284	755.7	86.3	5.9	0.3	3.6	0.0	11.8	9.7
18 71000	South Bend	107.4	101 516	296	945.2	67.2	29.8	1.5	1.7	0.1	12.6	7.3
18 75428	Terre Haute	89.5	60 825	594	679.6	86.7	12.3	1.0	2.0	0.2	3.3	3.5
18 78326	Valparaiso	40.2	32 626	1 153	811.6	92.6	4.7	0.8	2.6	0.0	8.0	6.0
18 82700	Westfield	69.5	36 738	1 025	528.6	91.0	5.6	0.7	3.8	0.0	3.8	4.9
18 82862	West Lafayette	19.7	45 550	826	2 312.2	76.4	3.9	0.7	21.2	0.2	3.3	23.0
19 00000	**IOWA**	144 669.3	3 123 899	X	21.6	93.2	4.0	0.9	2.3	0.1	5.3	4.7
19 01855	Ames	62.7	65 060	546	1 037.6	86.8	4.3	0.5	10.1	0.1	3.2	11.8
19 02305	Ankeny	76.0	56 764	655	746.9	96.1	1.6	0.9	3.1	0.0	2.0	3.4
19 06355	Bettendorf	55.0	35 505	1 065	645.5	91.3	3.7	0.5	4.9	0.0	3.2	5.4
19 09550	Burlington	37.5	25 410	1 410	677.6	90.8	10.1	1.0	0.4	0.0	3.4	1.4
19 11755	Cedar Falls	74.5	41 255	906	553.8	94.0	2.7	0.4	3.2	0.0	1.8	4.8
19 12000	Cedar Rapids	183.4	130 405	203	711.0	89.9	8.3	1.0	2.6	0.0	3.5	3.4
19 14430	Clinton	91.1	26 064	1 395	286.1	92.3	6.6	1.0	1.4	0.1	3.0	2.8
19 16860	Council Bluffs	106.1	62 597	574	590.0	95.5	3.1	1.5	1.0	0.1	9.1	4.0
19 19000	Davenport	163.0	102 582	293	629.3	84.2	13.6	1.3	2.7	0.0	8.2	3.9
19 21000	Des Moines	209.5	210 330	104	1 004.0	80.5	13.0	1.2	5.5	0.2	12.3	11.3
19 22395	Dubuque	77.6	58 799	628	757.7	95.5	3.5	2.5	1.8	0.5	2.2	2.8
19 28515	Fort Dodge	41.6	24 649	1 427	592.5	91.3	7.8	1.0	1.4	0.1	5.0	2.9
19 38595	Iowa City	64.8	74 220	463	1 145.4	83.5	7.2	1.0	8.6	0.3	5.2	13.4
19 49485	Marion	41.6	37 330	1 012	897.4	95.1	2.5	0.3	2.9	0.1	1.5	3.9
19 49755	Marshalltown	49.9	27 620	1 337	553.5	82.6	3.1	0.9	3.8	0.1	25.9	16.9
19 50160	Mason City	72.0	27 366	1 347	380.1	96.1	2.8	0.6	1.5	0.0	4.7	2.1
19 60465	Ottumwa	41.1	24 624	1 428	599.1	92.7	2.6	0.8	1.2	0.0	11.7	9.7
19 73335	Sioux City	148.5	82 821	400	557.7	84.9	5.0	3.3	3.5	0.1	17.6	10.7
19 79950	Urbandale	56.8	44 062	848	775.7	93.9	3.9	0.5	3.7	0.0	2.8	7.8
19 82425	Waterloo	159.0	68 460	511	430.6	80.7	17.6	0.7	2.0	0.1	5.9	6.3
19 83910	West Des Moines	99.9	64 113	561	641.8	88.3	4.5	0.8	6.9	0.2	5.9	11.1

1. Dry land or land partially or temporarily covered by water.   2. May be of any race.

City	Age of population (percent), 2010-2014									Median age 2010–2014	Percent female 2010–2014	Population			
												Census counts		Percent change	
	Under 5 years	5 to 17 years	18 to 24 years	25 to 34 years	35 to 44 years	45 to 54 years	55 to 64 years	65 to 74 years	75 years and over			2000	2010	2000–2010	2010–2015
	12	13	14	15	16	17	18	19	20	21	22	23	24	25	26
ILLINOIS—Cont'd															
Waukegan	7.8	20.7	11.8	15.7	12.4	13.3	10.1	4.2	3.9	31.0	49.9	87 901	89 078	1.3	-0.7
West Chicago	11.0	23.0	9.9	14.4	14.3	12.3	8.6	4.9	1.6	28.9	48.9	23 469	27 086	15.4	0.9
Wheaton	6.1	17.7	10.7	12.6	11.5	15.0	13.1	6.9	6.3	38.0	51.6	55 416	52 894	-4.6	1.4
Wheeling	7.2	14.1	7.2	17.4	14.3	13.0	13.1	6.7	7.0	38.1	53.5	34 496	37 648	9.1	1.2
Wilmette	6.0	24.8	5.3	4.3	13.4	15.3	13.4	10.0	7.5	42.8	49.9	27 651	27 087	-2.0	1.2
Woodridge	5.3	15.1	9.6	15.6	14.3	14.3	14.9	8.0	3.0	38.5	47.8	30 934	32 971	6.6	1.2
INDIANA	6.5	17.8	10.1	12.8	12.7	14.1	12.5	7.5	6.1	37.2	50.8	6 080 485	6 483 802	6.6	2.1
Anderson	5.8	17.0	11.5	13.3	11.7	12.7	11.9	8.1	8.1	37.0	52.4	59 734	56 129	-6.0	-1.6
Bloomington	4.3	7.2	44.4	14.5	8.8	6.5	6.0	4.2	4.2	23.3	49.9	69 291	80 405	16.0	4.7
Carmel	6.0	22.3	5.7	10.1	15.7	16.3	12.6	7.0	4.2	38.9	51.8	37 733	79 191	109.9	12.0
Columbus	6.3	18.6	8.1	14.8	14.3	12.9	10.1	7.4	7.5	36.2	51.0	39 059	44 061	12.8	5.9
Crown Point	4.0	15.8	7.0	13.8	14.1	14.9	13.4	8.3	8.7	41.2	50.7	19 806	27 317	37.9	3.7
East Chicago	9.2	22.3	10.7	13.2	10.7	11.7	10.8	6.0	5.3	30.5	53.6	32 414	29 698	-8.4	-3.4
Elkhart	8.4	19.5	10.3	14.6	12.9	13.0	10.1	5.1	6.0	33.1	52.0	51 874	50 949	-1.8	1.4
Evansville	6.8	15.2	10.9	15.4	10.7	13.9	12.1	7.4	7.6	36.6	52.8	121 582	117 429	-3.4	-0.1
Fishers	8.1	24.2	6.0	14.0	18.1	16.0	7.6	3.6	2.4	33.7	51.2	37 835	76 794	103.0	15.3
Fort Wayne	7.5	18.4	10.3	13.8	12.5	13.0	11.8	6.6	6.1	35.0	51.8	205 727	253 691	23.3	2.6
Gary	7.3	20.2	9.2	11.4	10.7	12.7	13.3	8.1	7.2	36.8	55.2	102 746	80 294	-21.9	-3.9
Goshen	9.2	17.2	9.9	15.8	11.4	10.5	10.6	7.1	8.4	33.0	51.2	29 383	31 719	8.0	2.7
Greenwood	8.1	16.3	8.9	16.2	13.1	14.4	10.6	6.7	5.7	35.2	51.5	36 037	49 791	38.2	8.6
Hammond	7.9	19.9	10.5	14.5	12.0	15.2	10.2	5.1	4.8	32.9	51.0	83 048	80 830	-2.7	-4.0
Hobart	6.5	15.8	9.2	13.1	13.0	13.5	14.9	7.6	6.4	39.2	51.0	25 363	29 059	14.6	-3.2
Indianapolis	7.5	17.3	10.3	16.5	13.0	13.4	11.3	5.9	4.9	33.9	51.7	791 926	820 445	4.9	4.0
Jeffersonville	7.1	15.9	8.7	13.7	15.2	12.4	14.1	7.3	5.7	38.1	52.2	27 362	44 953	64.3	4.3
Kokomo	7.2	16.0	8.4	13.5	11.7	13.2	13.2	8.9	7.8	38.9	52.0	46 113	45 468	-1.4	-0.1
Lafayette	7.9	16.2	13.6	18.3	11.8	11.2	10.2	5.4	5.6	31.1	52.1	56 397	67 140	19.0	3.3
Lawrence	7.9	20.6	7.0	15.8	11.8	15.6	11.1	5.3	4.7	33.7	51.1	38 915	46 001	18.2	3.9
Marion	6.2	13.1	17.7	11.5	10.6	13.0	11.2	7.7	9.0	37.0	55.5	31 320	29 948	-4.4	-2.8
Merrillville	6.2	19.0	7.5	14.4	14.4	12.2	13.5	6.7	6.1	37.2	49.9	30 560	35 246	15.3	0.7
Michigan City	7.0	15.4	10.7	13.3	12.5	14.9	12.0	8.0	6.3	37.9	49.8	32 900	31 479	-4.3	-0.1
Mishawaka	7.5	15.8	12.8	15.6	12.8	12.5	10.1	6.0	6.8	33.4	52.7	46 557	48 252	3.6	0.0
Muncie	4.7	11.6	29.2	11.9	8.6	10.2	10.1	7.3	6.4	27.9	53.2	67 430	70 085	3.9	-0.2
New Albany	6.5	15.2	10.7	14.6	12.5	12.5	13.0	7.9	7.0	37.8	51.7	37 603	36 372	-3.3	1.1
Noblesville	8.3	20.3	6.4	15.9	16.1	12.2	10.2	5.9	4.6	34.4	50.6	28 590	51 969	81.8	13.2
Plainfield	5.8	16.8	8.5	14.9	14.8	13.5	12.1	6.8	6.7	38.0	49.9	18 396	27 631	50.2	10.7
Portage	5.9	18.3	10.0	14.2	12.4	13.7	12.7	7.9	4.9	36.6	51.9	33 496	36 828	9.9	-0.2
Richmond	6.9	14.3	11.9	12.6	11.4	13.6	12.5	8.8	8.0	38.6	51.7	39 124	36 812	-5.9	-2.6
Schererville	5.5	14.9	8.0	11.3	14.4	14.3	15.8	9.0	6.9	42.0	52.1	24 851	29 243	17.7	-1.5
South Bend	7.9	18.6	9.4	15.7	11.9	11.7	12.2	5.9	6.7	34.1	50.9	107 789	101 168	-6.1	0.5
Terre Haute	6.0	13.5	19.0	15.0	12.1	11.6	10.0	6.7	6.1	32.5	48.7	59 614	60 785	2.0	0.1
Valparaiso	5.0	16.4	14.3	15.8	12.9	11.2	10.7	5.4	8.3	33.6	50.2	27 428	31 730	15.7	2.8
Westfield	8.6	23.2	7.0	14.2	15.6	16.9	7.3	4.4	2.8	33.5	52.0	9 293	30 068	223.6	22.1
West Lafayette	3.2	8.9	47.9	11.5	6.9	7.0	5.9	3.0	5.7	22.9	45.2	28 778	29 596	2.8	8.4
IOWA	6.3	17.2	10.2	12.6	11.8	13.7	12.9	7.8	7.5	38.1	50.4	2 926 324	3 046 355	4.1	2.5
Ames	3.6	9.6	43.0	13.8	7.5	7.6	7.0	4.0	3.8	23.4	47.5	50 731	58 965	16.2	10.3
Ankeny	8.6	18.1	9.7	19.7	14.4	10.2	10.4	5.1	3.8	32.4	49.8	27 117	45 582	68.1	24.5
Bettendorf	6.3	17.3	6.0	10.9	13.8	16.1	13.5	8.6	7.5	41.6	51.5	31 275	33 217	6.2	6.9
Burlington	5.7	17.1	7.6	11.2	11.2	14.8	13.8	8.6	9.9	42.2	52.3	26 839	25 663	-4.4	-0.8
Cedar Falls	5.5	12.6	29.3	11.7	9.2	9.5	10.5	5.4	6.4	26.5	52.3	36 145	39 260	8.6	5.1
Cedar Rapids	6.9	16.2	12.2	14.2	12.4	12.8	12.1	6.6	6.6	35.4	51.1	120 758	126 326	4.6	3.2
Clinton	6.9	16.3	9.5	13.0	11.3	12.5	13.0	8.0	9.5	39.4	50.4	27 772	26 885	-3.2	-3.1
Council Bluffs	6.4	17.1	10.8	14.0	11.8	13.8	12.5	6.9	6.8	36.4	51.2	58 268	62 230	6.8	0.6
Davenport	7.2	17.0	10.3	15.6	12.2	12.8	12.4	6.5	6.1	35.0	50.9	98 359	99 685	1.3	2.9
Des Moines	8.0	17.1	10.5	17.0	12.8	12.8	10.9	6.0	5.0	33.2	50.7	198 682	203 433	2.4	3.0
Dubuque	5.6	14.8	13.0	13.3	10.5	13.3	12.6	7.5	9.3	38.2	52.0	57 686	57 637	-0.1	2.1
Fort Dodge	5.3	15.0	11.7	13.2	11.4	12.8	12.9	8.7	8.9	39.0	48.7	25 136	25 206	0.3	-2.2
Iowa City	4.9	10.7	32.7	16.3	8.7	9.2	8.7	4.7	4.2	25.6	49.9	62 220	67 862	9.1	9.3
Marion	6.4	20.2	6.4	14.9	14.1	14.2	10.1	7.4	6.2	36.7	50.6	26 294	34 768	32.2	7.4
Marshalltown	8.0	18.7	8.8	14.0	9.8	11.8	11.9	8.1	8.9	35.4	51.6	26 009	27 552	5.9	0.2
Mason City	4.5	16.3	9.4	10.6	12.2	15.0	13.6	8.6	9.8	43.4	50.7	29 172	28 079	-3.7	-2.5
Ottumwa	6.6	16.9	11.0	12.3	12.8	12.0	12.4	7.3	8.7	37.3	52.0	24 998	25 023	0.1	-1.6
Sioux City	7.8	18.0	11.1	13.7	11.8	12.6	11.9	6.0	6.0	34.4	50.7	85 013	82 684	-2.7	-0.0
Urbandale	6.2	19.9	6.5	12.1	15.3	15.7	12.3	6.9	5.0	38.8	52.4	29 072	39 463	35.7	11.7
Waterloo	7.0	16.1	11.3	14.6	10.9	12.1	12.5	7.7	7.7	35.7	50.8	68 747	68 406	-0.5	0.1
West Des Moines	7.7	16.6	9.5	19.3	14.7	11.3	10.7	5.2	5.0	33.3	49.1	46 403	56 609	22.0	13.1

Table D. Cities — **Households, Group Quarters, Crime, and Education**

City	Households, 2010-2014				Persons in group quarters, 2010				Serious crimes known to police,[2] 2014				Educational attainment, 2010–2014		
			Percent			Institutional			Total		Rate[3]			Attainment[4] (percent)	
	Number	Persons per house-hold	Female family house-holder[1]	One-person	Total	Total	Persons in nursing facilities	Non-institu-tional	Number	Rate[3]	Violent	Property	Population age 25 and older	High school graduate or less	Bachelor's degree or more
	27	28	29	30	31	32	33	34	35	36	37	38	39	40	41
ILLINOIS—Cont'd															
Waukegan	28 725	3.09	19.4	23.7	2 077	1 586	842	491	2 966	3 342	439	2 903	52 540	57.7	18.7
West Chicago	7 743	3.54	10.0	14.8	333	325	325	8	371	1 342	90	1 252	16 253	53.2	24.7
Wheaton	19 194	2.78	6.7	25.4	3 379	1 395	578	1 984	398	740	52	688	34 825	16.6	61.1
Wheeling	14 334	2.64	9.2	28.8	465	461	461	4	546	1 433	118	1 315	26 562	39.6	35.9
Wilmette	9 604	2.85	8.2	20.5	126	69	69	57	362	1 320	36	1 283	17 999	6.9	81.1
Woodridge	12 935	2.57	8.9	27.5	88	86	0	2	410	1 224	110	1 113	22 865	24.5	47.3
INDIANA	2 492 183	2.63	12.4	27.8	186 923	95 336	41 158	91 587	198 875	3 015	365	2 649	4 287 819	47.3	23.6
Anderson	23 132	2.41	17.4	36.1	2 401	910	527	1 491	2 680	4 825	342	4 483	36 789	55.6	14.1
Bloomington	30 085	2.72	9.3	40.0	14 669	543	282	14 126	2 760	3 322	354	2 968	36 920	21.4	56.4
Carmel	30 594	2.73	6.8	20.2	600	579	470	21	828	946	14	932	54 941	12.1	68.8
Columbus	18 420	2.47	11.4	31.3	870	704	450	166	2 046	4 429	97	4 332	30 620	39.5	34.5
Crown Point	10 773	2.62	10.5	29.0	1 863	1 839	338	24	NA	NA	NA	NA	20 407	43.6	31.3
East Chicago	9 890	2.97	32.2	29.3	178	98	92	80	1 471	5 057	856	4 201	16 712	63.7	7.5
Elkhart	19 064	2.70	18.2	31.3	915	611	611	304	2 929	5 702	1 258	4 445	31 684	61.4	13.5
Evansville	51 335	2.34	16.3	37.0	4 727	2 103	1 194	2 624	7 506	6 236	518	5 718	80 315	49.4	18.8
Fishers	28 216	2.87	8.0	21.1	27	27	27	0	832	972	21	951	50 086	14.0	61.1
Fort Wayne	101 549	2.52	15.1	32.7	5 356	2 680	1 643	2 676	9 168	3 565	317	3 248	162 405	41.3	25.8
Gary	30 746	2.57	30.0	34.6	708	261	237	447	4 764	6 107	913	5 194	50 545	53.1	13.1
Goshen	11 946	2.70	18.1	26.8	1 467	808	411	659	1 276	3 946	111	3 835	20 093	56.4	21.3
Greenwood	20 807	2.54	12.1	28.6	481	456	405	25	2 112	3 886	351	3 535	34 793	42.4	26.1
Hammond	28 678	2.78	19.3	29.4	975	82	71	893	3 478	4 429	811	3 618	50 171	57.8	13.2
Hobart	11 542	2.52	10.7	29.7	144	1	0	143	1 823	6 422	292	6 129	20 250	51.0	15.8
Indianapolis	332 300	2.54	16.9	34.1	16 040	8 750	4 382	7 290	52 162	6 078	1 255	4 823	548 475	44.3	27.7
Jeffersonville	17 650	2.60	13.1	28.7	878	535	109	343	1 708	3 704	579	3 125	31 703	44.1	21.4
Kokomo	24 823	2.29	13.7	37.3	722	532	426	190	2 236	3 929	285	3 645	38 853	51.3	16.8
Lafayette	29 448	2.38	14.3	34.3	1 433	1 058	477	375	3 777	5 339	496	4 842	44 203	44.1	25.5
Lawrence	17 316	2.70	18.3	27.0	333	289	223	44	NA	NA	NA	NA	29 531	36.4	32.5
Marion	11 952	2.46	17.5	39.0	3 364	797	481	2 567	1 341	4 550	299	4 251	18 893	58.3	16.3
Merrillville	13 225	2.67	16.4	33.1	455	366	362	89	1 349	3 777	333	3 444	23 103	44.0	20.2
Michigan City	12 718	2.47	18.5	35.0	2 670	2 506	234	164	1 482	4 704	317	4 386	21 250	54.5	15.7
Mishawaka	20 544	2.34	13.4	37.6	1 013	212	83	801	2 458	5 128	221	4 907	31 273	46.8	24.0
Muncie	27 662	2.53	14.2	34.5	8 508	1 267	744	7 241	3 176	4 515	394	4 121	38 100	48.7	22.4
New Albany	15 312	2.38	18.4	34.6	1 008	724	429	284	2 165	5 866	244	5 622	24 720	53.4	16.6
Noblesville	20 952	2.70	10.4	24.7	661	632	316	29	NA	NA	NA	NA	36 184	25.0	45.7
Plainfield	10 494	2.78	13.5	27.2	2 615	2 595	145	20	947	3 082	179	2 903	19 772	42.5	27.5
Portage	13 992	2.64	16.8	26.0	255	233	233	22	846	2 299	163	2 136	24 903	53.0	15.4
Richmond	15 288	2.39	17.2	34.8	2 292	1 198	561	1 094	NA	NA	NA	NA	24 139	54.9	17.8
Schererville	11 528	2.52	8.6	28.2	120	63	0	57	150	518	14	504	20 524	37.9	32.8
South Bend	39 866	2.52	19.4	35.1	2 692	1 697	773	995	5 435	5 389	685	4 704	63 997	47.1	23.5
Terre Haute	21 812	2.80	14.6	35.8	8 875	4 173	589	4 702	3 210	5 255	324	4 931	37 766	48.6	20.0
Valparaiso	12 092	2.63	12.2	35.6	2 936	1 070	546	1 866	654	2 020	108	1 912	19 875	33.5	35.9
Westfield	11 491	2.82	8.6	19.6	139	99	99	40	457	1 336	105	1 230	19 801	17.5	57.8
West Lafayette	11 924	2.59	4.0	38.8	3 069	155	155	2 914	381	1 221	103	1 119	11 773	15.8	69.7
IOWA	1 232 228	2.50	9.3	28.8	98 112	43 282	26 871	54 830	73 553	2 367	273	2 094	2 038 942	41.2	26.4
Ames	23 566	2.60	4.3	30.4	7 767	294	181	7 473	1 192	1 907	120	1 787	27 391	14.5	62.8
Ankeny	19 324	2.56	7.1	23.6	663	174	146	489	748	1 409	115	1 294	31 666	20.0	45.2
Bettendorf	13 623	2.51	7.2	29.2	176	172	158	4	513	1 464	148	1 315	23 712	23.4	48.3
Burlington	10 882	2.35	15.1	32.1	495	367	235	128	1 038	4 029	633	3 396	17 483	43.7	20.9
Cedar Falls	14 290	2.80	5.8	27.5	4 574	354	354	4 220	840	2 055	122	1 932	21 270	27.2	44.6
Cedar Rapids	53 125	2.41	11.0	32.3	3 518	1 561	769	1 957	5 431	4 213	301	3 912	83 621	33.8	30.9
Clinton	11 239	2.37	11.3	34.0	713	379	347	334	1 386	5 255	626	4 629	18 417	48.2	18.4
Council Bluffs	24 769	2.51	14.7	31.0	1 908	964	440	944	4 459	7 208	548	6 660	40 696	48.0	17.5
Davenport	40 912	2.48	13.6	33.2	3 111	1 247	751	1 864	4 831	4 703	619	4 084	66 527	39.2	27.3
Des Moines	81 239	2.54	15.3	31.6	6 104	1 641	1 005	4 463	10 148	4 873	613	4 260	132 557	44.1	24.7
Dubuque	24 025	2.42	11.3	33.5	4 027	1 133	806	2 894	1 665	2 850	248	2 602	38 813	43.5	28.9
Fort Dodge	10 169	2.44	14.1	39.3	2 509	1 651	345	858	1 398	5 701	689	5 011	16 518	42.0	20.8
Iowa City	28 843	2.45	8.7	35.2	6 585	296	168	6 289	1 969	2 715	294	2 421	36 819	17.6	58.8
Marion	14 590	2.45	10.3	28.6	292	214	210	78	585	1 604	134	1 469	24 203	30.2	33.7
Marshalltown	10 054	2.76	11.4	29.5	1 190	1 040	985	150	958	3 432	552	2 880	17 945	49.9	20.1
Mason City	12 873	2.16	9.6	40.3	856	448	344	408	969	3 509	94	3 414	19 062	40.2	20.9
Ottumwa	10 253	2.42	14.2	31.5	826	371	248	455	1 147	4 626	290	4 336	16 555	55.5	15.0
Sioux City	31 419	2.63	13.8	29.9	2 565	743	437	1 822	3 479	4 224	353	3 870	51 962	49.6	20.5
Urbandale	16 289	2.53	7.2	24.5	234	230	222	4	781	1 845	198	1 646	28 071	22.9	48.4
Waterloo	28 834	2.37	14.1	36.3	1 165	687	515	478	3 336	4 880	958	3 922	44 912	49.2	20.2
West Des Moines	25 261	2.37	8.1	30.6	273	262	262	11	1 694	2 717	186	2 531	40 400	19.9	52.4

1. No spouse present.　2. Data for serious crimes have not been adjusted for underreporting. This may affect comparability between geographic areas and over time.　3. Per 100,000 population estimated by the FBI.　4. Persons 25 years old and over.

Table D. Cities — Income, Poverty, and Housing

City	Money income, 2010–2014					Housing units, 2010			Occupied housing units 2010–2014			Median owner costs as a percent of income	
	Per capita income[1] (dollars)	Households			Families with income below poverty (percent)	Total	Percent change, 2000–2010	Vacant units for sale or rent[2]	Total	Owner-occupied		With a mortgage[4]	Without a mortgage[5]
		Median income	Percent with income of $200,000 or more	Percent with income of less than $25,000						Percent	Median value[3] (dollars)		
	42	43	44	45	46	47	48	49	50	51	52	53	54
ILLINOIS—Cont'd													
Waukegan	20 333	45 983	2.3	26.4	18.7	30 746	5.1	2 667	28 725	51.0	130 900	27.8	14.1
West Chicago	25 995	69 252	8.5	11.0	10.3	7 763	15.2	433	7 743	66.9	226 500	27.8	12.4
Wheaton	42 106	84 833	12.8	11.5	4.5	20 112	1.1	921	19 194	72.1	336 500	23.3	14.1
Wheeling	28 235	57 543	3.9	19.6	9.6	15 397	12.5	936	14 334	63.6	178 000	29.2	14.9
Wilmette	67 116	126 471	31.6	7.5	2.3	10 290	-0.4	548	9 604	85.6	609 200	25.3	15.1
Woodridge	38 990	77 164	8.6	9.0	3.6	13 392	14.6	746	12 935	65.5	252 300	25.1	13.5
INDIANA	24 953	48 737	2.7	24.3	11.3	2 795 541	10.4	293 387	2 492 183	69.5	122 700	20.4	10.9
Anderson	18 366	33 854	0.5	38.8	21.0	27 953	1.3	4 393	23 132	57.0	73 000	21.8	13.6
Bloomington	19 600	28 660	3.4	44.8	20.9	33 239	17.2	1 814	30 085	34.3	170 900	20.2	10.0
Carmel	52 207	107 916	18.9	8.4	2.6	30 738	117.0	1 741	30 594	78.5	297 600	18.5	10.0
Columbus	29 396	55 288	4.0	22.0	9.2	19 700	14.9	1 913	18 420	62.1	143 300	18.9	11.6
Crown Point	31 673	64 250	4.5	16.8	4.3	10 976	36.0	582	10 773	77.1	171 400	20.6	11.5
East Chicago	13 868	27 215	0.2	46.7	34.3	12 958	-2.3	2 234	9 890	43.4	83 000	25.2	12.9
Elkhart	17 365	35 505	1.2	33.3	23.4	22 699	4.9	3 438	19 064	51.0	84 100	22.1	13.5
Evansville	20 951	35 996	1.3	32.8	15.5	57 799	1.2	7 211	51 335	53.3	90 000	21.8	12.6
Fishers	38 600	91 646	9.3	6.5	2.1	28 511	82.0	1 293	28 216	83.1	210 800	19.6	10.0
Fort Wayne	23 607	43 994	2.2	26.5	14.8	113 541	24.9	11 956	101 549	63.2	99 800	19.5	10.0
Gary	15 983	27 458	0.5	46.8	33.3	39 531	-9.4	8 151	30 746	51.7	65 500	24.6	13.8
Goshen	18 811	40 259	0.9	30.7	19.4	12 631	12.2	1 287	11 946	57.0	111 400	21.2	12.7
Greenwood	26 813	52 621	2.2	19.9	11.2	21 339	33.6	1 724	20 807	61.5	131 700	19.8	10.0
Hammond	18 460	39 771	0.7	30.7	20.0	32 945	-3.5	2 996	28 678	61.8	90 200	22.2	12.3
Hobart	26 172	55 840	1.4	18.4	7.6	12 399	20.6	749	11 542	71.9	132 600	22.0	13.9
Indianapolis	24 227	42 169	2.5	29.3	16.9	384 414	7.6	48 228	332 300	54.7	117 600	21.2	11.4
Jeffersonville	25 712	51 706	1.9	21.9	7.7	19 991	60.9	1 411	17 650	69.5	125 400	20.7	11.8
Kokomo	22 102	35 690	1.2	33.8	16.3	23 010	3.0	3 162	24 823	61.7	83 100	19.5	11.0
Lafayette	21 431	39 378	1.4	31.1	15.8	31 260	22.4	2 715	29 448	48.4	102 000	19.6	10.5
Lawrence	23 801	49 849	2.2	22.5	13.6	19 515	19.9	1 651	17 316	68.3	123 700	20.8	14.4
Marion	18 479	32 334	1.2	39.1	23.0	13 715	-0.6	1 887	11 952	58.5	65 500	21.2	12.4
Merrillville	22 729	49 711	0.6	23.4	9.7	14 842	19.8	1 146	13 225	63.3	127 600	24.7	10.8
Michigan City	18 990	35 710	1.5	36.9	26.1	14 435	1.5	2 299	12 718	54.4	93 300	21.0	12.9
Mishawaka	20 998	37 542	1.1	31.1	17.5	24 088	11.4	2 745	20 544	49.7	92 700	20.8	12.1
Muncie	16 986	30 570	0.7	42.5	19.4	31 958	5.8	4 236	27 662	50.4	70 400	20.9	12.7
New Albany	21 866	40 061	1.2	32.8	18.1	17 315	1.5	1 740	15 312	55.5	112 300	22.4	12.1
Noblesville	31 738	67 939	5.5	14.1	5.9	21 121	86.3	2 041	20 952	70.8	170 400	20.9	10.1
Plainfield	25 448	58 625	2.0	15.7	7.2	10 386	38.3	639	10 494	73.7	145 400	20.7	11.6
Portage	23 812	51 180	0.7	24.6	11.9	14 807	11.1	815	13 992	73.4	135 300	20.0	13.9
Richmond	18 481	29 802	0.9	42.7	23.8	17 649	-0.4	2 551	15 288	55.9	79 500	21.7	11.9
Schererville	34 563	69 011	5.0	11.4	3.7	12 393	24.0	510	11 528	75.2	209 500	21.1	10.5
South Bend	19 818	34 656	1.8	36.0	22.8	46 324	0.2	6 564	39 866	58.7	83 100	21.9	11.1
Terre Haute	17 758	33 317	1.2	37.7	19.0	25 518	-0.3	2 873	21 812	53.7	75 900	19.7	12.1
Valparaiso	25 002	49 656	2.3	26.0	10.5	13 506	15.8	896	12 092	57.7	165 500	21.0	11.5
Westfield	36 951	85 071	8.1	9.9	5.0	11 209	NA	719	11 491	79.5	219 300	19.8	10.5
West Lafayette	21 875	28 507	4.1	44.5	8.4	12 591	16.5	646	11 924	31.2	177 300	18.3	10.0
IOWA	27 621	52 716	3.0	22.0	8.2	1 336 417	8.4	114 841	1 232 228	71.8	126 300	20.0	11.5
Ames	24 082	42 373	2.9	33.7	7.6	23 876	27.6	1 117	23 566	41.5	172 600	19.2	10.0
Ankeny	33 555	75 069	3.9	10.8	3.1	18 339	69.8	906	19 324	74.9	172 700	20.3	11.9
Bettendorf	38 191	74 529	7.8	14.4	4.1	14 437	10.6	756	13 623	76.5	177 000	19.2	10.0
Burlington	21 866	37 223	1.5	31.7	17.0	11 899	-1.0	961	10 882	67.9	83 300	22.8	14.0
Cedar Falls	25 850	52 678	3.1	23.1	7.3	15 477	16.4	869	14 290	64.3	167 700	19.0	10.0
Cedar Rapids	29 506	54 465	3.1	21.5	7.7	57 217	9.7	3 981	53 125	69.3	134 600	20.0	12.6
Clinton	25 313	41 848	1.9	29.8	13.4	12 202	-1.8	956	11 239	68.0	92 100	19.7	13.9
Council Bluffs	23 665	45 204	1.8	26.0	12.0	26 594	9.1	1 801	24 769	63.6	111 000	21.9	12.7
Davenport	24 864	45 424	1.7	26.3	13.1	44 087	6.6	3 467	40 912	61.5	121 200	20.8	12.5
Des Moines	23 989	46 430	2.1	25.9	15.1	88 729	4.3	7 360	81 239	61.7	117 600	22.1	12.9
Dubuque	25 148	46 806	2.0	24.3	10.1	25 029	5.1	1 523	24 025	64.2	131 400	19.9	12.2
Fort Dodge	22 434	38 380	1.5	34.0	13.5	11 215	0.1	940	10 169	60.9	79 700	19.5	11.1
Iowa City	27 336	42 119	4.8	33.6	10.3	29 270	12.4	1 613	28 843	48.1	185 500	21.2	10.4
Marion	31 037	62 532	3.6	17.7	3.5	15 064	37.2	956	14 590	75.3	146 800	20.3	11.9
Marshalltown	22 512	48 750	1.9	22.5	10.6	11 171	2.9	836	10 054	66.7	98 000	20.6	12.2
Mason City	26 065	42 009	2.6	28.9	9.6	13 352	2.3	986	12 873	66.6	98 300	19.6	12.9
Ottumwa	20 694	38 095	1.3	33.8	15.7	11 257	2.6	1 006	10 253	68.0	70 700	19.9	13.2
Sioux City	22 395	43 629	1.8	26.9	12.4	33 425	-1.1	1 854	31 419	64.2	94 800	20.3	11.4
Urbandale	41 328	79 909	9.1	9.5	4.4	16 319	37.7	723	16 289	81.6	192 700	19.5	10.0
Waterloo	22 628	41 461	1.2	28.3	14.8	30 723	4.2	2 116	28 834	64.2	101 900	20.2	11.9
West Des Moines	39 353	70 882	7.1	13.5	5.7	26 219	26.2	1 908	25 261	60.3	186 300	19.1	10.2

1. Based on population estimated by the American Community Survey.   2. Includes units rented or sold but not occupied.   3. Specified owner-occupied units; $1,000,000 represents $1,000,000 or more   4. 50.0 represents 50 percent or more.   5. 10.0 represents 10 percent or less.

Table D. Cities — Housing, Labor Force, and Employment

City	Occupied housing units, 2010–2014 (cont.)				Migration, 2010–2014		Civilian labor force, 2015		Unemployment		Civilian employment[4], 2010–2014	Percent		
	Percent renter occupied	Median gross rent[1]	Median gross rent as a percent of income[2]	Percent with no vehicle available	Percent who lived in the same house one year ago	Percent who lived outside current city one year ago	Total	Percent change, 2014–2015	Total	Rate[3]	Population age 16 and older	In labor force	Civilian full-year full-time workers	Households with no workers (percent)
	55	56	57	58	59	60	61	62	63	64	65	66	67	68
ILLINOIS—Cont'd														
Waukegan	49.0	875	31.7	10.3	82.5	8.2	44 958	-0.2	3 225	7.2	65 979	69.3	40.3	22.8
West Chicago	33.1	928	35.5	3.7	90.4	5.5	14 412	0.2	856	5.9	20 241	73.0	44.0	12.7
Wheaton	27.9	1 218	29.2	4.6	83.8	11.6	28 852	0.3	1 229	4.3	42 789	67.7	41.7	21.4
Wheeling	36.4	1 054	29.3	6.0	87.0	10.4	22 352	0.0	1 048	4.7	30 278	74.3	50.2	17.7
Wilmette	14.4	1 779	24.7	4.2	90.5	6.8	12 845	0.3	543	4.2	20 415	60.7	39.1	23.2
Woodridge	34.5	1 103	26.5	2.4	87.7	10.4	20 041	0.0	885	4.4	26 782	76.8	51.8	13.6
INDIANA	30.5	741	30.1	6.9	85.0	9.5	3 265 761	1.2	156 544	4.8	5 131 317	64.1	39.6	27.4
Anderson	43.0	691	33.6	13.6	77.7	8.3	23 387	0.9	1 454	6.2	44 627	55.8	29.9	42.2
Bloomington	65.7	798	44.9	12.4	54.4	25.6	37 021	-0.5	1 933	5.2	73 329	55.7	23.2	33.0
Carmel	21.5	1 118	23.1	2.5	86.2	10.2	46 256	2.1	1 512	3.3	62 671	70.9	48.6	16.9
Columbus	37.9	818	26.8	6.9	82.6	8.6	24 998	2.6	878	3.5	35 563	65.4	43.4	28.4
Crown Point	22.9	944	27.3	6.0	87.0	10.0	14 587	-0.2	835	5.7	23 091	61.8	39.1	25.6
East Chicago	56.6	668	34.4	20.6	83.7	9.2	10 193	-0.8	917	9.0	21 123	54.6	27.8	41.7
Elkhart	49.0	684	29.0	12.7	77.8	10.6	24 453	2.1	1 174	4.8	37 807	65.1	38.6	29.2
Evansville	46.7	707	30.7	11.1	81.2	6.9	58 950	0.1	2 671	4.5	95 675	62.4	39.7	30.3
Fishers	16.9	1 071	25.6	1.6	88.5	9.4	47 317	2.1	1 519	3.2	57 358	76.2	53.8	11.1
Fort Wayne	36.8	661	28.2	4.9	84.0	4.9	123 223	1.7	5 934	4.8	195 831	65.8	40.6	27.5
Gary	48.3	724	40.7	18.9	85.0	5.6	27 519	-0.8	2 692	9.8	59 997	51.7	26.5	43.7
Goshen	43.0	719	32.9	11.6	80.9	10.1	16 001	2.3	595	3.7	24 233	62.7	37.1	28.2
Greenwood	38.5	823	30.2	5.0	82.0	12.4	28 237	1.9	1 193	4.2	41 115	68.3	43.3	23.3
Hammond	38.2	814	32.1	10.0	86.9	8.4	34 934	-0.2	2 450	7.0	61 063	61.4	34.2	29.7
Hobart	28.1	840	25.6	5.1	89.1	7.5	15 011	-0.4	1 123	7.5	23 208	68.4	42.5	26.7
Indianapolis	45.3	784	32.7	9.7	82.7	5.8	433 264	1.2	21 812	5.0	656 307	67.5	40.6	26.3
Jeffersonville	30.5	739	27.8	6.0	89.7	6.2	24 096	2.1	922	3.8	36 384	67.3	43.8	26.3
Kokomo	38.3	645	32.3	10.1	79.6	7.5	24 767	0.0	1 215	4.9	45 310	59.0	33.3	38.2
Lafayette	51.6	766	31.7	8.7	76.5	12.3	37 575	1.3	1 589	4.2	55 068	69.8	41.6	25.1
Lawrence	31.7	804	29.0	6.3	86.0	11.2	25 577	1.3	1 157	4.5	34 483	74.9	44.2	21.2
Marion	41.5	596	28.6	13.4	80.2	8.8	12 909	-1.0	847	6.6	24 252	53.8	29.0	42.4
Merrillville	36.7	929	33.9	8.3	82.9	14.5	17 042	-0.2	1 169	6.9	27 229	64.4	39.5	29.0
Michigan City	45.6	706	34.2	11.3	80.6	11.1	12 908	-0.3	913	7.1	25 404	57.1	31.2	33.0
Mishawaka	50.3	714	28.3	7.6	80.4	13.6	24 878	1.3	1 156	4.6	38 214	67.8	39.1	27.2
Muncie	49.6	690	39.5	11.2	63.3	18.2	31 625	1.7	1 915	6.1	59 570	57.4	25.0	36.0
New Albany	44.5	699	30.0	11.6	82.3	9.7	18 314	1.8	881	4.8	29 480	64.5	39.6	30.1
Noblesville	29.2	912	26.7	3.1	84.0	12.0	31 715	1.9	1 083	3.4	41 922	74.1	50.8	16.0
Plainfield	26.3	919	29.3	2.2	82.5	13.9	14 676	1.9	631	4.3	23 157	60.9	42.3	22.2
Portage	26.6	827	30.5	5.0	86.0	8.5	17 761	-0.2	1 122	6.3	29 225	62.5	38.7	29.1
Richmond	44.1	610	32.2	16.6	78.0	10.1	14 946	-1.0	865	5.8	29 226	54.0	29.6	37.6
Schererville	24.8	867	27.6	3.6	90.1	8.2	16 004	0.2	796	5.0	23 494	68.8	46.6	22.6
South Bend	41.3	711	32.3	12.9	80.0	9.9	46 523	1.3	2 641	5.7	76 037	65.2	34.9	31.5
Terre Haute	46.3	664	32.8	10.8	78.7	11.9	25 579	-1.2	1 660	6.5	50 389	54.6	27.9	33.2
Valparaiso	42.3	840	29.0	8.5	80.1	14.0	15 843	0.3	800	5.0	25 600	60.9	35.5	28.7
Westfield	20.5	896	23.5	4.3	88.8	8.7	19 186	2.2	596	3.1	23 003	74.8	53.7	10.8
West Lafayette	68.8	854	50.0	13.0	55.8	30.0	14 810	1.7	547	3.7	27 685	50.0	19.4	36.9
IOWA	28.2	689	27.7	5.7	84.9	9.3	1 701 329	0.2	62 461	3.7	2 434 242	67.9	44.2	25.5
Ames	58.5	774	38.6	7.1	58.0	22.6	39 026	1.3	851	2.2	54 030	66.4	30.3	21.2
Ankeny	25.1	822	24.3	3.5	81.7	11.7	31 044	0.3	711	2.3	37 367	77.8	55.2	15.2
Bettendorf	23.5	812	28.8	4.7	85.9	10.5	17 732	-1.5	618	3.5	26 542	66.0	45.0	25.4
Burlington	32.1	653	29.6	9.7	82.9	6.8	12 926	0.2	629	4.9	20 167	61.0	36.3	34.1
Cedar Falls	35.7	754	35.8	5.7	76.0	14.4	22 577	-2.2	670	3.0	33 998	68.9	34.5	25.5
Cedar Rapids	30.7	702	27.7	6.9	82.8	8.9	71 536	-0.9	2 688	3.8	101 857	70.9	46.4	22.9
Clinton	32.0	595	29.6	9.2	85.1	5.0	12 775	-0.9	663	5.2	21 456	62.1	38.5	33.4
Council Bluffs	36.4	763	29.0	8.3	82.8	8.0	32 281	0.1	1 198	3.7	48 988	67.5	45.1	26.3
Davenport	38.5	693	29.0	7.5	84.3	6.7	50 864	-1.5	2 552	5.0	79 788	65.9	41.2	26.5
Des Moines	38.3	751	30.9	9.0	78.1	9.4	110 861	-0.1	4 721	4.3	159 353	70.3	44.9	24.1
Dubuque	35.8	695	31.2	8.9	82.2	9.2	33 281	0.3	1 146	3.4	47 479	67.1	40.5	26.7
Fort Dodge	39.1	562	28.6	9.6	80.9	11.9	12 925	2.2	553	4.3	20 291	60.3	34.5	33.2
Iowa City	51.9	861	42.7	9.8	63.3	18.5	42 754	-0.2	1 065	2.5	60 878	66.6	33.8	22.8
Marion	24.7	625	26.3	5.3	85.9	9.7	19 784	-0.9	603	3.0	27 408	72.0	49.7	21.6
Marshalltown	33.3	645	25.2	8.3	81.9	7.4	12 644	-1.7	693	5.5	21 179	63.0	40.3	29.4
Mason City	33.4	611	27.6	9.2	86.2	5.8	14 573	-0.6	567	3.9	22 648	67.3	41.5	29.3
Ottumwa	32.0	618	32.0	8.6	82.6	5.6	12 315	-0.9	629	5.1	19 843	63.1	37.3	31.0
Sioux City	35.8	662	29.5	8.9	81.3	7.2	44 800	-0.1	1 669	3.7	63 570	69.3	43.7	24.6
Urbandale	18.4	818	26.4	2.7	90.3	8.0	25 133	0.4	655	2.6	31 651	75.4	54.5	16.7
Waterloo	35.8	669	31.6	8.5	84.8	6.5	34 734	-2.3	1 847	5.3	53 652	66.4	42.0	31.4
West Des Moines	39.7	900	24.5	3.3	79.2	15.5	38 058	0.2	950	2.5	47 626	76.6	54.4	17.4

1. $2,000 represents $2,000 or more. 2. 50.0 represents 50 percent or more. 3. Percent of civilian labor force. 4. Persons 16 years old and over.

Table D. Cities — Construction, Wholesale Trade, and Retail Trade

City	Value of residential construction authorized by building permits, 2015			Wholesale trade,[1] 2012				Retail trade,[2] 2012			
	New construction ($1,000)	Number of housing units	Percent single family	Number of establishments	Number of employees	Sales (mil dol)	Annual payroll (mil dol)	Number of establishments	Number of employees	Sales (mil dol)	Annual payroll (mil dol)
	69	70	71	72	73	74	75	76	77	78	79
ILLINOIS—Cont'd											
Waukegan	6 708	44	63.6	65	1 228	1 089.5	83.7	209	3 534	1 105.5	133.6
West Chicago	678	3	100.0	61	1 725	746.3	91.4	77	1 098	360.6	32.2
Wheaton	13 310	45	100.0	50	D	D	D	176	2 564	508.7	50.3
Wheeling	28 744	244	0.8	143	2 705	1 386.7	156.5	90	1 437	387.8	41.5
Wilmette	30 402	48	100.0	33	69	103.7	4.1	98	1 255	245.6	33.2
Woodridge	27 359	160	41.3	64	2 715	1 589.2	157.6	98	2 039	526.8	51.5
INDIANA	3 737 044	18 483	68.4	6 460	91 474	81 173.4	4 650.5	21 601	309 552	85 858.0	7 078.7
Anderson	3 987	27	77.8	36	D	D	D	234	3 713	1 008.3	83.7
Bloomington	NA	NA	NA	40	444	172.5	22.8	386	6 729	1 480.9	132.7
Carmel	227 171	1 643	16.7	135	1 253	1 277.1	106.2	289	5 860	1 749.0	168.1
Columbus	NA	NA	NA	53	895	681.4	49.3	193	3 316	829.1	75.4
Crown Point	59 235	245	80.0	38	D	D	D	75	895	236.8	22.0
East Chicago	326	1	100.0	35	D	D	D	47	356	120.1	7.8
Elkhart	1 500	12	100.0	144	2 148	1 552.6	109.2	258	3 871	1 039.2	93.7
Evansville	7 459	64	84.4	219	4 224	2 315.7	264.0	730	11 717	2 871.9	268.3
Fishers	192 102	764	65.8	83	1 279	847.7	83.2	185	3 340	974.1	83.5
Fort Wayne	NA	NA	NA	412	5 926	6 481.8	278.0	1 096	18 193	4 689.3	426.8
Gary	939	5	100.0	44	928	661.1	43.3	173	1 321	596.3	26.9
Goshen	6 442	42	95.2	30	825	530.5	32.8	162	2 853	779.2	65.8
Greenwood	52 076	281	98.9	45	1 444	883.1	87.1	327	6 283	1 488.0	138.5
Hammond	8 900	88	0.0	81	D	D	D	196	3 401	1 185.3	79.1
Hobart	7 741	32	100.0	26	D	D	D	224	4 767	1 210.7	105.5
Indianapolis	540 200	1 716	43.3	1 210	22 417	17 495.9	1 279.5	2 725	42 887	13 502.0	1 070.3
Jeffersonville	20 971	150	82.0	49	686	899.7	38.8	120	1 524	415.4	38.2
Kokomo	24 404	241	35.3	50	498	469.3	28.2	297	4 441	1 060.7	94.2
Lafayette	12 817	92	73.9	81	1 088	600.2	46.6	416	7 125	1 844.9	158.1
Lawrence	12 147	68	100.0	45	780	664.6	40.1	120	1 957	467.6	43.6
Marion	8 734	49	24.5	21	206	95.7	7.4	176	2 595	668.9	55.6
Merrillville	4 932	33	81.8	37	D	D	D	204	3 524	1 049.1	88.4
Michigan City	13 050	62	19.4	36	448	266.0	19.3	250	3 669	736.3	67.8
Mishawaka	31 140	237	45.6	61	679	706.9	35.2	371	6 956	1 843.0	151.6
Muncie	1 349	7	100.0	53	551	381.5	19.7	355	5 605	1 266.9	117.5
New Albany	5 088	35	100.0	48	509	301.0	21.0	144	2 129	508.3	50.0
Noblesville	170 268	971	52.3	68	634	325.3	35.9	231	4 179	1 028.1	93.8
Plainfield	55 292	419	39.9	32	2 638	2 509.8	127.5	135	2 794	782.2	64.2
Portage	3 115	22	100.0	24	481	501.3	27.5	91	1 828	490.5	39.4
Richmond	7 319	71	11.3	38	352	241.7	16.5	208	3 244	850.5	72.5
Schererville	17 023	66	75.8	19	130	51.7	6.1	105	2 289	598.8	55.5
South Bend	NA	NA	NA	154	2 577	1 673.0	124.2	315	5 010	1 310.0	127.9
Terre Haute	9 831	106	15.1	77	971	395.4	37.9	330	4 709	998.1	92.0
Valparaiso	59 983	335	30.4	42	550	236.6	28.3	193	3 356	854.6	76.4
Westfield	159 455	598	95.2	30	722	804.8	55.3	85	1 872	467.8	42.5
West Lafayette	7 007	36	100.0	5	15	2.2	0.3	61	1 350	300.6	25.6
IOWA	2 243 252	12 097	61.4	4 302	58 872	62 318.3	2 841.8	12 046	174 556	44 905.6	3 865.3
Ames	73 110	450	20.2	35	204	102.0	9.8	212	4 054	937.4	86.2
Ankeny	232 069	1 061	83.9	40	1 385	1 852.5	76.7	142	3 622	1 175.9	94.1
Bettendorf	41 894	161	100.0	42	466	570.2	23.8	95	1 525	358.6	39.9
Burlington	4 689	31	100.0	24	377	939.4	17.8	114	1 524	307.2	32.6
Cedar Falls	31 467	163	65.6	48	961	646.7	49.7	154	2 884	678.7	60.5
Cedar Rapids	33 126	354	80.5	219	3 999	2 352.7	219.9	489	11 220	3 525.8	272.5
Clinton	5 266	22	27.3	22	155	188.1	5.7	127	2 161	509.2	45.4
Council Bluffs	18 886	87	95.4	67	1 010	1 416.1	50.6	236	5 340	1 462.8	116.1
Davenport	27 946	233	32.6	180	2 928	1 425.4	139.1	478	8 922	2 337.4	209.0
Des Moines	139 922	966	19.2	270	4 570	3 586.5	243.0	647	9 121	2 190.1	215.3
Dubuque	12 032	76	100.0	81	883	870.3	39.7	336	6 175	1 355.8	127.8
Fort Dodge	702	3	100.0	36	544	228.3	29.6	151	2 488	569.8	52.6
Iowa City	92 333	688	21.9	34	676	502.3	27.6	247	4 188	927.7	101.9
Marion	38 008	441	40.8	29	257	106.8	10.9	120	1 894	456.6	41.3
Marshalltown	4 149	17	76.5	23	346	225.9	19.4	125	1 923	405.0	41.2
Mason City	4 955	19	100.0	45	584	587.7	27.6	179	3 317	753.3	71.5
Ottumwa	845	5	100.0	24	177	281.4	7.1	119	2 164	488.7	46.0
Sioux City	29 499	211	32.2	129	2 034	1 640.3	91.5	388	6 950	1 675.3	148.6
Urbandale	69 997	281	70.1	96	1 331	1 041.5	81.9	148	2 686	1 017.6	92.9
Waterloo	11 805	102	82.4	80	1 370	961.3	60.8	300	5 413	1 274.6	120.3
West Des Moines	121 594	532	43.0	63	723	1 145.8	42.9	389	8 652	1 620.3	164.8

1. Merchant wholesalers except manufacturers' sales branches and offices.   2. Establishments with payroll.

Table D. Cities — **Real Estate, Professional Services, and Manufacturing**

City	Real estate and rental and leasing, 2012				Professional, scientific, and technical services,[1] 2012				Manufacturing, 2012			
	Number of establishments	Number of employees	Receipts (mil dol)	Annual payroll (mil dol)	Number of establishments	Number of employees	Receipts (mil dol)	Annual payroll (mil dol)	Number of establishments	Number of employees	Receipts (mil dol)	Annual payroll (mil dol)
	80	81	82	83	84	85	86	87	88	89	90	91
ILLINOIS—Cont'd												
Waukegan	52	239	61.7	8.2	162	D	D	D	81	4 911	1 775.3	314.4
West Chicago	19	129	44.2	8.8	78	800	255.7	58.8	94	4 848	2 358.0	245.6
Wheaton	66	209	51.0	8.1	413	D	D	D	21	440	D	11.9
Wheeling	30	116	28.1	4.2	124	976	245.8	57.2	141	7 219	2 463.4	346.7
Wilmette	38	D	D	D	174	390	77.3	26.0	11	95	13.4	3.1
Woodridge	31	303	62.1	11.4	115	924	133.2	66.7	40	1 714	481.7	77.3
INDIANA	5 729	31 715	6 547.9	1 171.7	12 780	99 322	14 627.5	5 453.3	8 141	452 513	242 763.8	23 041.3
Anderson	58	276	42.1	7.7	107	513	42.1	13.9	48	982	383.8	48.4
Bloomington	134	709	132.7	22.7	219	D	D	D	40	1 182	241.2	D
Carmel	200	1 684	1 226.0	116.1	575	3 523	604.7	250.0	61	827	D	40.4
Columbus	60	218	38.5	7.2	137	D	D	D	100	10 319	5 398.3	500.9
Crown Point	32	105	15.4	2.8	102	724	104.2	33.1	36	838	D	35.7
East Chicago	12	173	50.5	9.5	16	193	24.4	13.4	42	7 628	5 950.8	662.5
Elkhart	76	452	90.7	16.9	136	D	D	D	314	16 342	4 442.2	707.8
Evansville	178	1 359	201.9	40.1	355	D	D	D	173	7 490	2 730.9	322.8
Fishers	86	267	80.1	12.2	340	D	D	D	37	685	185.6	42.0
Fort Wayne	307	1 715	327.5	60.5	719	D	D	D	352	14 791	4 689.3	736.2
Gary	40	347	61.9	9.3	44	D	D	D	42	6 100	4 920.5	465.3
Goshen	36	126	18.2	3.3	67	397	35.4	12.0	103	14 551	4 138.7	617.4
Greenwood	67	247	68.4	7.6	121	819	94.6	30.4	41	1 175	496.5	70.8
Hammond	38	284	60.7	13.8	92	D	D	D	59	3 013	2 166.5	170.1
Hobart	22	79	14.1	2.3	44	D	D	D	19	816	D	31.4
Indianapolis	1 177	11 003	2 038.4	451.9	2 572	31 210	5 676.0	2 251.5	813	41 099	27 082.4	2 493.8
Jeffersonville	41	313	57.6	11.4	100	642	81.8	24.1	77	5 491	1 891.2	249.7
Kokomo	64	300	49.5	8.7	100	600	57.6	21.5	62	D	D	D
Lafayette	103	496	99.6	16.6	177	D	D	D	81	11 970	11 260.2	713.8
Lawrence	40	217	36.3	8.8	100	1 046	175.5	60.2	25	363	D	14.9
Marion	29	121	14.4	2.9	54	292	26.1	8.6	38	3 034	1 474.2	200.8
Merrillville	66	525	67.7	18.5	179	1 403	137.5	58.3	25	452	D	16.8
Michigan City	29	131	30.0	3.4	61	333	37.9	11.7	59	2 978	1 323.9	145.8
Mishawaka	56	374	68.2	12.6	109	D	D	D	85	2 618	1 071.2	119.6
Muncie	71	314	54.3	9.6	124	D	D	D	64	1 955	638.9	86.2
New Albany	35	133	17.1	3.6	117	D	D	D	83	4 966	1 660.8	246.4
Noblesville	57	170	50.0	6.5	182	708	90.1	32.6	46	2 056	753.2	95.0
Plainfield	30	252	25.8	8.5	51	387	47.2	16.3	21	582	205.4	24.2
Portage	30	140	24.9	5.4	40	239	24.9	10.8	20	2 252	2 221.9	151.4
Richmond	38	158	31.0	5.0	62	323	23.8	8.9	70	4 238	1 843.2	185.9
Schererville	34	201	46.0	7.4	88	D	D	D	12	374	D	19.1
South Bend	107	659	100.9	22.8	269	D	D	D	164	7 099	2 747.8	370.2
Terre Haute	72	414	69.8	14.9	163	1 035	102.5	38.7	74	6 131	1 922.0	300.0
Valparaiso	62	346	53.3	9.7	150	850	100.6	37.4	46	1 909	959.1	107.0
Westfield	24	131	15.0	4.0	72	234	25.1	9.7	19	1 092	234.3	44.2
West Lafayette	36	182	25.6	5.1	59	D	D	D	15	488	116.3	27.2
IOWA	2 742	12 031	2 268.3	425.9	6 169	48 261	6 396.9	2 454.9	3 598	203 722	116 668.8	10 021.2
Ames	72	364	55.3	11.2	135	D	D	D	43	3 163	2 048.5	180.0
Ankeny	58	148	31.5	4.9	91	463	55.4	23.8	27	3 429	3 100.7	185.8
Bettendorf	45	D	D	D	103	431	48.8	16.2	27	3 277	1 415.5	207.7
Burlington	25	623	110.3	24.4	45	238	25.6	8.8	26	2 687	913.6	110.1
Cedar Falls	49	224	50.1	6.5	98	2 726	150.9	151.5	43	1 523	393.3	69.6
Cedar Rapids	159	744	172.7	28.1	360	3 991	504.1	239.3	120	15 535	8 635.1	1 164.2
Clinton	26	89	14.9	2.9	47	221	17.0	6.7	30	2 803	4 090.3	156.2
Council Bluffs	70	329	51.2	8.3	103	D	D	D	39	3 878	D	167.8
Davenport	121	566	155.1	21.9	271	1 963	252.4	86.8	98	6 751	4 872.0	387.3
Des Moines	212	1 470	302.4	56.6	550	6 032	895.0	375.5	155	6 111	4 837.8	293.4
Dubuque	80	318	61.8	10.7	130	D	D	D	87	3 472	1 283.3	159.6
Fort Dodge	35	D	D	D	64	1 039	34.0	52.4	33	1 006	D	53.5
Iowa City	75	326	63.0	11.7	148	D	D	D	42	2 852	2 889.9	132.3
Marion	24	D	D	D	55	357	46.9	21.3	39	633	123.6	28.6
Marshalltown	27	D	D	D	37	306	46.3	11.9	30	4 891	D	241.9
Mason City	44	116	21.6	3.1	60	D	D	D	37	2 333	1 240.8	109.0
Ottumwa	20	86	12.2	2.9	41	D	D	D	17	D	D	D
Sioux City	83	496	61.9	12.7	176	D	D	D	77	4 428	2 997.7	172.8
Urbandale	43	245	52.4	7.0	178	1 832	517.5	150.7	35	1 403	548.8	83.4
Waterloo	83	387	67.2	10.9	114	D	D	D	98	11 343	9 231.0	577.4
West Des Moines	120	906	193.1	50.2	359	4 625	709.2	247.2	32	1 031	238.7	49.4

1. Establishments subject to federal tax.

Table D. Cities — Accommodation and Food Services, Arts, Entertainment, and Recreation, and Health Care and Social Assistance

City	Accommodation and food services, 2012				Arts, entertainment, and recreation,[1] 2012				Health care and social assistance,[1] 2012			
	Number of establishments	Number of employees	Sales (mil dol)	Annual payroll (mil dol)	Number of establishments	Number of employees	Receipts (mil dol)	Annual payroll (mil dol)	Number of establishments	Number of employees	Receipts (mil dol)	Annual payroll (mil dol)
	92	93	94	95	96	97	98	99	100	101	102	103
ILLINOIS—Cont'd												
Waukegan	133	1 955	117.5	30.2	13	228	14.6	3.3	102	2 622	313.1	118.7
West Chicago	46	567	27.5	7.3	8	104	6.4	1.7	39	463	43.9	15.0
Wheaton	111	1 954	95.4	29.0	19	D	D	D	173	2 236	205.0	92.6
Wheeling	57	D	D	D	3	31	1.9	0.6	69	897	57.7	26.2
Wilmette	50	D	D	D	17	D	D	D	117	1 034	80.0	32.5
Woodridge	55	965	50.5	14.1	12	231	12.5	4.0	78	443	46.8	18.2
INDIANA	13 057	255 223	13 076.6	3 432.7	1 559	23 917	3 152.7	761.2	12 360	206 531	21 191.4	8 625.9
Anderson	148	2 940	123.6	36.2	19	D	D	D	137	2 075	182.3	76.1
Bloomington	340	7 466	320.5	87.5	15	D	D	D	237	4 035	430.7	181.7
Carmel	185	3 477	180.6	55.8	53	590	40.5	11.1	391	D	D	D
Columbus	167	3 488	160.7	43.7	13	148	5.0	1.5	157	D	D	D
Crown Point	69	1 271	51.6	14.7	10	D	D	D	90	1 145	161.3	56.8
East Chicago	39	D	D	D	1	D	D	D	25	D	D	D
Elkhart	161	3 011	128.0	35.9	9	102	4.4	1.9	129	2 634	317.3	126.3
Evansville	403	9 956	511.6	133.5	39	847	67.1	10.5	405	6 878	732.3	335.7
Fishers	175	3 719	185.5	48.2	34	D	D	D	208	D	D	D
Fort Wayne	614	14 022	590.8	175.7	69	D	D	D	691	18 728	1 992.0	878.5
Gary	87	1 078	119.7	22.5	6	D	D	D	88	1 360	86.0	35.2
Goshen	88	1 742	78.3	20.9	5	D	D	D	82	1 106	106.4	53.7
Greenwood	152	4 007	177.8	52.2	13	D	D	D	159	D	D	D
Hammond	145	D	D	D	9	D	D	D	86	D	D	D
Hobart	73	1 440	66.3	18.9	12	D	D	D	58	D	D	D
Indianapolis	1 988	45 071	2 532.3	704.9	221	D	D	D	1 867	36 083	4 152.6	1 810.4
Jeffersonville	90	D	D	D	10	D	D	D	113	D	D	D
Kokomo	175	3 811	157.7	45.4	17	D	D	D	180	D	D	D
Lafayette	222	4 819	220.1	61.7	19	300	7.8	2.4	237	4 108	437.4	191.0
Lawrence	81	D	D	D	12	D	D	D	54	D	D	D
Marion	84	1 540	67.8	18.3	4	D	D	D	117	D	D	D
Merrillville	132	3 016	167.2	45.4	10	213	9.5	3.1	238	D	D	D
Michigan City	100	3 199	274.3	57.2	3	40	1.7	0.4	82	D	D	D
Mishawaka	200	4 928	221.2	62.2	17	D	D	D	153	D	D	D
Muncie	171	3 804	149.0	42.5	17	163	5.6	1.7	213	D	D	D
New Albany	85	D	D	D	8	D	D	D	146	D	D	D
Noblesville	107	2 503	119.1	34.3	21	D	D	D	128	D	D	D
Plainfield	89	1 947	96.7	26.6	7	D	D	D	46	D	D	D
Portage	81	1 687	81.6	20.3	10	D	D	D	69	976	86.3	32.1
Richmond	119	2 480	107.7	31.2	8	49	1.8	0.6	105	D	D	D
Schererville	96	2 116	88.9	27.7	6	D	D	D	81	670	59.9	25.5
South Bend	234	4 026	180.5	52.6	14	D	D	D	238	5 356	735.7	255.2
Terre Haute	231	4 616	201.8	58.6	14	D	D	D	210	3 875	484.6	171.0
Valparaiso	117	2 468	107.6	31.2	10	D	D	D	152	2 234	223.6	93.3
Westfield	63	1 494	64.3	18.4	14	D	D	D	52	D	D	D
West Lafayette	129	2 599	113.0	30.0	6	D	D	D	46	D	D	D
IOWA	7 047	115 134	5 468.7	1 466.6	993	13 165	1 305.5	255.5	5 582	78 961	7 151.2	3 356.8
Ames	195	3 976	160.9	45.2	15	308	12.5	4.4	96	1 702	217.7	103.8
Ankeny	100	2 414	109.4	31.1	13	150	6.4	2.3	88	925	74.7	32.2
Bettendorf	70	1 919	134.2	30.7	10	D	D	D	108	2 123	185.4	93.7
Burlington	80	1 689	71.7	21.2	9	D	D	D	56	D	D	D
Cedar Falls	110	2 719	94.9	30.9	15	D	D	D	70	D	D	D
Cedar Rapids	372	7 177	316.2	94.2	36	915	31.4	8.9	302	4 513	532.9	246.0
Clinton	76	1 377	93.3	20.1	7	D	D	D	65	987	85.4	33.0
Council Bluffs	159	4 908	393.2	86.2	13	D	D	D	143	D	D	D
Davenport	285	6 066	266.6	78.3	27	60	D	D	241	3 098	348.5	158.8
Des Moines	537	9 062	464.2	133.8	57	601	36.0	10.3	366	7 237	912.1	461.0
Dubuque	181	3 760	145.4	43.6	30	1 253	135.0	29.9	154	2 900	320.2	179.6
Fort Dodge	79	1 347	60.6	16.5	10	31	2.3	0.5	70	D	D	D
Iowa City	214	D	D	D	19	D	D	D	145	1 949	198.8	81.8
Marion	53	880	36.2	10.1	8	D	D	D	50	721	47.7	20.7
Marshalltown	79	1 049	43.7	11.9	4	D	D	D	36	D	D	D
Mason City	83	1 464	60.4	16.8	10	D	D	D	67	D	D	D
Ottumwa	71	1 188	46.2	13.1	9	D	D	D	63	D	D	D
Sioux City	232	D	D	D	26	D	D	D	190	2 778	287.8	121.9
Urbandale	81	1 762	88.7	23.4	19	D	D	D	73	1 189	68.9	30.2
Waterloo	169	3 684	214.3	51.0	21	179	11.7	3.4	154	2 109	227.0	109.8
West Des Moines	214	4 793	244.9	74.5	26	D	D	D	257	3 685	465.1	241.5

1. Establishments subject to federal tax.

City	Other services[1], 2012				Government employment and payroll, 2012								
					Full-time equivalent employees	March payroll	Percent of total for:						
	Number of establishments	Number of employees	Receipts (mil dol)	Annual payroll (mil dol)		Total (dollars)	Administration, tration, judicial, and legal	Police and Corrections	Fire Protection	Highways and transportation	Health and welfare	Natural resources and utilities	Education and libraries
	104	105	106	107	108	109	110	111	112	113	114	115	116
ILLINOIS—Cont'd													
Waukegan	90	374	30.5	9.1	502	3 187 722	12.7	40.5	27.8	4.1	1.1	8.7	5.1
West Chicago	41	238	37.0	10.5	117	799 988	15.4	54.5	0.0	9.6	0.7	18.2	0.0
Wheaton	86	578	31.9	12.0	437	2 488 726	8.6	34.0	12.7	8.3	0.0	11.5	18.2
Wheeling	63	347	44.9	9.4	232	1 575 381	12.4	38.6	25.9	1.8	8.3	8.9	0.0
Wilmette	59	364	33.8	10.9	220	1 531 248	12.5	32.9	25.0	14.4	0.9	11.8	0.0
Woodridge	42	429	12.7	12.4	165	972 329	16.5	46.7	0.0	5.4	0.0	13.1	14.2
INDIANA	8 429	54 735	5 020.8	1 548.5	X	X	X	X	X	X	X	X	X
Anderson	85	519	38.8	12.0	638	2 851 826	7.5	21.3	15.8	10.2	3.5	35.9	0.0
Bloomington	117	1 148	86.0	27.5	814	3 124 701	11.6	21.8	16.1	13.9	5.2	29.9	0.0
Carmel	145	861	63.7	22.3	467	2 600 210	3.5	30.7	43.9	10.0	0.0	10.1	0.0
Columbus	72	502	46.4	13.8	432	1 650 956	6.5	22.9	26.7	7.3	1.6	34.1	0.0
Crown Point	73	560	52.3	16.4	201	804 519	8.2	32.5	18.8	9.5	0.4	23.3	0.0
East Chicago	23	128	12.0	3.5	698	2 567 542	8.3	26.6	16.1	7.5	4.7	36.8	0.0
Elkhart	102	757	71.7	22.9	536	2 197 116	9.6	30.1	28.2	10.0	0.6	18.8	0.0
Evansville	234	2 033	185.2	56.8	1 278	5 214 822	2.6	31.8	24.3	11.2	3.0	24.8	0.0
Fishers	97	503	32.5	10.3	389	1 761 025	11.8	31.1	35.0	5.2	0.0	6.0	0.0
Fort Wayne	462	3 446	282.9	96.5	2 016	8 885 678	3.7	33.2	19.0	14.2	5.3	20.6	0.0
Gary	67	396	46.9	12.4	1 123	2 786 750	11.6	16.2	20.1	6.3	10.1	27.4	0.0
Goshen	54	D	D	D	227	709 892	8.9	38.2	24.5	7.4	0.8	13.4	0.0
Greenwood	101	880	101.2	32.1	279	1 071 961	16.9	33.3	24.5	11.2	0.0	12.1	0.0
Hammond	107	762	80.9	23.2	849	3 866 970	4.7	34.3	24.6	4.0	3.3	25.4	0.0
Hobart	62	410	42.4	12.6	245	963 819	14.4	31.6	27.9	6.1	0.0	15.8	0.0
Indianapolis	1 040	10 121	1 009.7	343.3	12 328	49 785 804	10.1	20.7	10.8	4.3	40.3	12.3	0.0
Jeffersonville	66	556	87.2	16.9	348	1 320 589	10.0	25.0	25.4	9.1	2.7	26.2	0.0
Kokomo	100	D	D	D	458	1 913 705	2.4	27.7	28.3	8.2	3.0	16.6	0.0
Lafayette	147	919	77.8	25.0	727	2 921 411	4.8	26.6	23.4	22.4	1.3	19.2	0.0
Lawrence	58	217	23.6	6.3	310	1 228 922	6.9	27.5	42.0	4.8	1.5	16.4	0.0
Marion	48	255	24.2	7.2	258	851 770	12.9	39.0	29.5	14.0	1.8	2.1	0.0
Merrillville	65	497	47.3	14.9	123	450 414	14.0	61.3	1.8	18.1	0.0	2.7	0.0
Michigan City	51	258	17.2	5.5	429	1 619 412	5.6	25.8	23.0	10.4	1.1	32.5	0.0
Mishawaka	92	578	41.4	14.5	503	2 151 708	6.9	27.5	24.4	4.6	0.7	31.4	0.0
Muncie	100	658	53.2	16.5	505	1 776 621	4.8	23.6	21.0	18.0	2.0	19.4	0.0
New Albany	66	330	28.2	7.9	265	917 338	5.7	32.4	36.7	5.6	3.3	8.7	0.0
Noblesville	75	484	34.1	10.6	368	1 696 635	8.6	26.2	41.3	9.3	0.0	13.7	0.0
Plainfield	49	570	37.3	14.9	268	950 626	7.8	22.5	43.0	4.3	0.0	21.5	0.0
Portage	48	374	27.4	9.2	254	948 853	7.5	31.0	27.5	15.8	0.6	16.7	0.0
Richmond	44	180	12.4	3.9	513	1 860 795	5.6	18.1	16.9	7.3	0.0	51.7	0.0
Schererville	62	588	52.8	16.0	180	726 293	13.7	41.3	15.8	13.1	0.0	16.0	0.0
South Bend	167	1 443	141.4	42.6	1 318	5 351 987	3.8	29.1	24.4	12.9	2.3	21.5	0.0
Terre Haute	91	666	55.3	17.5	615	2 301 273	8.2	27.5	28.9	17.6	1.5	14.9	0.0
Valparaiso	87	594	43.2	16.2	288	1 148 922	5.9	21.1	26.3	6.8	0.0	39.9	0.0
Westfield	43	296	23.5	7.3	176	867 739	19.6	28.0	32.8	8.5	1.6	9.5	0.0
West Lafayette	24	197	10.2	3.7	229	856 416	6.6	32.8	21.3	4.1	5.3	24.8	0.0
IOWA	4 687	23 537	2 103.6	598.9	X	X	X	X	X	X	X	X	X
Ames	69	451	33.2	10.8	616	2 954 800	12.2	13.1	10.5	21.5	2.3	30.9	5.6
Ankeny	64	D	D	D	283	1 240 311	16.5	23.8	24.3	9.4	0.0	18.9	4.5
Bettendorf	53	297	15.9	5.6	243	1 226 060	11.1	23.4	12.3	14.0	5.9	13.4	10.5
Burlington	47	248	20.8	6.4	239	935 691	5.6	25.4	21.5	13.3	0.5	20.2	7.2
Cedar Falls	51	454	36.1	12.0	478	2 270 443	8.5	9.9	7.7	7.0	0.6	57.2	2.9
Cedar Rapids	209	1 602	138.5	47.7	1 296	6 423 374	10.4	21.6	12.8	16.4	1.8	24.1	3.3
Clinton	47	172	15.3	4.4	210	897 240	6.0	29.8	22.4	15.6	2.5	17.4	5.3
Council Bluffs	102	553	47.5	14.5	471	2 609 951	9.1	27.0	20.1	6.8	10.1	21.8	5.0
Davenport	162	1 345	100.9	34.1	906	4 276 351	9.9	26.0	20.2	14.2	1.5	17.2	5.2
Des Moines	289	2 035	156.6	53.2	1 956	10 193 831	8.0	24.9	16.0	11.6	5.0	26.6	3.2
Dubuque	124	804	67.4	20.0	645	3 046 153	13.2	22.4	16.1	21.5	5.8	14.0	4.4
Fort Dodge	36	286	34.2	9.2	118	524 670	9.2	38.3	26.4	3.8	0.0	16.1	6.2
Iowa City	90	577	45.4	14.4	20	1 762 642	14.5	13.9	9.2	13.9	4.6	17.2	6.5
Marion	47	242	23.0	6.9	184	916 685	6.3	31.1	21.9	10.4	6.4	17.3	6.7
Marshalltown	41	238	19.3	4.7	231	825 058	5.3	30.0	16.7	12.6	5.2	25.4	4.7
Mason City	58	375	29.2	9.1	326	1 435 146	5.2	16.5	11.1	10.8	8.2	18.1	25.1
Ottumwa	32	185	14.3	5.3	247	856 818	6.4	16.0	15.1	23.1	5.3	28.1	3.8
Sioux City	120	879	56.6	19.4	794	3 661 919	9.1	25.7	18.3	17.6	2.2	19.7	3.4
Urbandale	61	470	34.2	12.7	223	998 550	11.0	20.8	15.3	12.5	1.1	26.9	9.6
Waterloo	97	708	57.5	17.4	603	2 720 527	5.5	26.6	21.7	9.9	2.6	18.8	4.1
West Des Moines	89	585	36.6	14.7	435	2 294 576	8.6	23.7	13.4	9.2	16.6	19.7	4.4

1. Establishments subject to federal tax.

Table D. Cities — City Government Finances

City	City government finances, 2012									
	General revenue							General expenditure		
		Intergovernmental		Taxes					Per capita¹ (dollars)	
					Per capita¹ (dollars)					
	Total (mil dol)	Total (mil dol)	Percent from state government	Total (mil dol)	Total	Property	Sales and gross receipts	Total (mil dol)	Total	Capital outlays
	117	118	119	120	121	122	123	124	125	126
ILLINOIS—Cont'd										
Waukegan	87.3	16.1	90.5	46.7	525	307	218	72.7	819	47
West Chicago	29.0	8.4	99.1	8.9	324	172	153	28.0	1 022	227
Wheaton	56.0	12.7	96.7	32.9	616	438	167	46.6	872	33
Wheeling	45.9	10.7	93.0	29.0	765	553	212	45.1	1 188	197
Wilmette	38.5	7.6	85.0	22.4	821	509	287	38.9	1 425	199
Woodridge	30.1	9.8	82.4	14.4	434	225	199	26.2	789	18
INDIANA	X	X	X	X	X	X	X	X	X	X
Anderson	84.2	19.0	48.2	36.3	652	443	39	65.2	1 172	281
Bloomington	85.2	17.5	64.4	44.3	539	434	15	72.9	886	129
Carmel	111.9	17.9	66.3	72.8	871	597	53	93.8	1 122	60
Columbus	72.5	21.0	50.2	29.8	657	647	11	59.6	1 314	244
Crown Point	35.9	4.6	85.5	17.3	616	580	36	21.8	773	94
East Chicago	103.6	44.0	82.6	50.0	1 697	1 676	21	63.2	2 147	65
Elkhart	70.5	21.2	34.3	30.9	606	596	10	59.6	1 167	88
Evansville	183.6	54.1	55.1	68.3	568	460	15	192.0	1 598	442
Fishers	58.2	7.3	74.3	35.2	430	286	25	55.3	676	109
Fort Wayne	289.9	59.4	54.7	141.1	554	423	16	257.6	1 011	147
Gary	181.4	65.4	74.4	81.4	1 028	1 008	20	145.6	1 839	385
Goshen	35.1	9.7	53.7	14.5	454	447	7	47.8	1 498	416
Greenwood	47.0	10.2	33.2	19.8	376	365	12	34.0	645	24
Hammond	192.8	73.8	83.1	63.5	797	775	22	155.5	1 953	159
Hobart	40.0	5.7	88.9	23.0	794	772	22	36.0	1 242	112
Indianapolis	2 604.6	712.4	81.1	887.7	1 064	601	112	3 151.6	3 777	1 038
Jeffersonville	55.6	10.3	33.9	27.6	605	592	13	57.7	1 264	472
Kokomo	76.1	16.8	67.8	44.3	777	655	2	63.7	1 118	63
Lafayette	99.8	25.3	67.7	44.5	637	508	7	75.9	1 086	2
Lawrence	36.4	5.3	60.9	19.2	411	308	19	34.5	739	4
Marion	32.5	6.6	85.0	19.7	665	514	11	37.1	1 252	46
Merrillville	30.3	3.8	91.0	20.7	587	559	28	18.3	518	137
Michigan City	59.4	25.0	70.4	17.2	553	532	21	50.5	1 621	213
Mishawaka	83.6	10.9	75.5	54.8	1 142	914	13	78.3	1 630	554
Muncie	72.4	20.0	73.9	29.0	414	346	11	72.9	1 040	117
New Albany	59.3	15.9	55.8	20.6	564	548	16	50.5	1 385	371
Noblesville	84.0	18.9	89.5	45.5	823	556	66	67.7	1 226	347
Plainfield	48.8	11.2	29.1	24.9	854	718	136	35.1	1 203	268
Portage	42.2	5.4	93.6	22.3	604	531	19	46.8	1 270	181
Richmond	48.2	15.7	58.1	13.4	368	357	11	46.4	1 269	343
Schererville	33.2	3.7	90.7	21.3	734	702	32	19.4	667	73
South Bend	201.3	37.3	61.0	106.9	1 060	823	30	141.5	1 404	147
Terre Haute	82.6	28.3	35.8	31.8	519	512	8	64.3	1 051	189
Valparaiso	44.4	6.4	59.9	22.8	713	632	30	35.7	1 116	232
Westfield	33.7	3.8	75.3	18.3	572	359	56	25.9	808	40
West Lafayette	32.5	8.8	47.0	12.7	416	322	9	24.7	808	153
IOWA	X	X	X	X	X	X	X	X	X	X
Ames	250.4	24.1	59.9	29.1	475	382	93	219.0	3 578	476
Ankeny	57.6	6.0	79.4	32.3	658	584	74	69.7	1 421	618
Bettendorf	52.9	7.7	67.3	30.2	883	675	208	55.4	1 617	483
Burlington	34.5	5.6	56.2	17.9	700	447	253	35.7	1 395	364
Cedar Falls	77.7	19.4	43.0	31.2	783	598	185	81.6	2 049	977
Cedar Rapids	405.0	168.3	22.7	115.9	905	655	249	457.5	3 573	2 065
Clinton	48.5	10.4	28.4	20.3	761	562	198	67.1	2 521	1 417
Council Bluffs	118.7	29.8	38.3	61.1	983	702	281	111.9	1 801	467
Davenport	165.6	37.9	52.7	84.9	837	610	227	177.4	1 749	508
Des Moines	404.2	93.7	24.5	156.5	757	643	114	460.9	2 228	484
Dubuque	135.5	48.8	22.7	45.3	780	520	260	160.4	2 763	1 348
Fort Dodge	36.9	6.2	50.6	17.7	717	531	186	39.3	1 589	605
Iowa City	138.3	36.0	53.0	63.8	906	715	191	128.1	1 819	366
Marion	36.5	5.5	81.7	22.6	630	474	156	37.9	1 056	306
Marshalltown	34.2	10.2	31.7	16.6	595	411	184	35.1	1 262	431
Mason City	52.9	17.0	23.3	20.8	748	531	218	45.1	1 625	357
Ottumwa	40.4	7.9	63.1	16.8	679	503	177	37.3	1 505	459
Sioux City	139.6	32.9	58.3	63.3	766	553	213	143.7	1 737	477
Urbandale	41.8	4.8	80.6	29.6	721	645	76	40.8	995	315
Waterloo	115.1	25.8	46.6	59.1	865	644	221	119.5	1 749	524
West Des Moines	100.9	15.8	70.7	63.9	1 076	976	100	85.4	1 439	353

1. Based on population estimated as of July 1 of the year shown.

City	Public welfare	Highways	Parking facilities	Education	Health and hospitals	Police protection	Sewerage and sanitation	Parks and recreation	Housing and community development	Interest on debt
	127	128	129	130	131	132	133	134	135	136

City government finances, 2012 (cont.) — General expenditure (cont.) — Percent of total for:

City	Public welfare	Highways	Parking facilities	Education	Health and hospitals	Police protection	Sewerage and sanitation	Parks and recreation	Housing and community development	Interest on debt
ILLINOIS—Cont'd										
Waukegan	0.0	11.3	0.5	0.0	0.0	30.6	9.2	0.0	1.6	5.9
West Chicago	0.0	15.8	0.4	0.0	0.0	30.2	28.0	0.7	0.0	2.8
Wheaton	0.0	14.4	1.4	0.0	0.0	27.1	7.8	1.1	0.0	4.7
Wheeling	0.0	15.8	0.1	0.0	0.0	27.4	4.3	0.0	0.0	7.2
Wilmette	0.0	14.4	0.8	0.0	0.6	24.7	15.4	0.0	0.0	5.9
Woodridge	0.0	11.2	0.0	0.0	0.0	36.6	9.9	0.1	0.0	4.4
INDIANA	X	X	X	X	X	X	X	X	X	X
Anderson	0.0	5.6	0.1	0.0	0.3	14.5	38.2	1.7	3.5	2.5
Bloomington	0.0	7.2	2.0	0.0	1.5	13.2	15.3	10.4	1.4	3.6
Carmel	0.0	9.2	0.0	0.0	0.0	16.1	5.8	3.9	6.8	11.8
Columbus	0.0	3.5	0.0	0.0	0.5	9.2	28.6	6.4	0.8	4.1
Crown Point	0.0	12.6	0.0	0.0	0.3	15.8	28.1	3.3	0.0	1.9
East Chicago	0.0	1.5	0.0	0.0	4.1	14.6	18.5	4.4	3.2	0.9
Elkhart	0.0	9.1	0.0	0.0	0.0	15.2	19.4	5.4	1.3	2.0
Evansville	0.0	4.5	0.1	0.0	0.4	13.7	25.8	6.1	1.4	1.4
Fishers	0.0	15.5	0.0	0.0	0.0	12.7	15.0	1.2	0.0	7.5
Fort Wayne	0.0	6.4	0.2	0.0	0.9	19.3	29.0	5.5	5.1	2.8
Gary	0.0	2.5	0.0	0.0	2.6	8.6	23.7	5.0	3.3	1.1
Goshen	0.0	13.7	1.0	0.0	0.0	8.2	27.0	2.5	1.1	7.9
Greenwood	0.0	14.9	0.0	0.0	0.0	16.9	24.3	2.9	0.0	3.6
Hammond	0.0	2.9	0.0	0.0	0.0	16.8	11.7	12.4	3.7	2.7
Hobart	0.0	12.7	0.0	0.0	0.1	10.5	26.5	4.8	0.0	0.9
Indianapolis	0.0	1.2	0.4	0.0	35.8	6.6	8.7	11.7	4.3	10.4
Jeffersonville	0.0	1.9	0.0	0.0	0.6	13.1	50.7	3.9	2.0	4.1
Kokomo	0.0	6.8	0.0	0.0	0.0	19.6	18.4	4.5	3.7	1.9
Lafayette	0.0	6.9	0.0	0.0	0.0	16.5	15.5	7.3	3.9	5.6
Lawrence	0.0	3.7	0.0	0.0	2.8	16.4	18.9	3.1	0.0	1.4
Marion	0.0	5.7	0.0	0.0	0.0	20.7	14.4	2.8	0.0	1.5
Merrillville	0.0	6.0	0.0	0.0	0.0	21.1	8.9	0.9	0.0	4.6
Michigan City	0.0	3.1	0.0	0.0	0.5	13.7	18.8	10.2	2.7	3.3
Mishawaka	0.0	3.8	0.0	0.0	1.4	11.5	26.4	3.8	0.9	3.5
Muncie	0.0	3.7	0.1	0.0	0.3	11.3	46.5	1.9	1.2	2.0
New Albany	0.0	2.5	0.9	0.0	0.8	9.6	21.0	4.4	6.5	5.0
Noblesville	0.0	5.0	0.2	0.0	0.2	11.2	32.6	4.6	0.0	13.9
Plainfield	0.0	3.4	0.0	0.0	0.0	12.1	14.0	10.2	0.0	3.2
Portage	0.0	7.4	0.0	0.0	0.2	9.3	26.6	6.0	0.0	5.4
Richmond	0.0	3.5	0.1	0.0	1.1	13.2	43.5	6.3	0.0	2.2
Schererville	0.0	8.6	0.0	0.0	0.3	23.5	39.5	5.2	0.0	2.5
South Bend	0.0	5.8	0.5	0.0	0.3	16.8	22.7	12.5	1.8	5.0
Terre Haute	0.0	7.4	0.0	0.0	0.4	14.5	16.6	4.9	14.2	3.8
Valparaiso	0.0	12.1	0.1	0.0	0.0	9.7	21.3	7.1	0.0	3.4
Westfield	0.0	6.4	0.0	0.0	0.0	16.6	19.5	1.9	0.0	6.9
West Lafayette	0.0	12.3	0.0	0.0	0.0	16.7	38.4	6.0	2.0	4.7
IOWA	X	X	X	X	X	X	X	X	X	X
Ames	0.5	2.1	0.3	0.0	72.3	3.5	4.7	2.0	0.3	2.0
Ankeny	0.4	27.0	0.0	0.0	3.9	9.7	21.2	8.8	0.0	7.2
Bettendorf	0.0	12.9	0.0	0.0	0.0	11.1	12.3	17.3	0.9	8.1
Burlington	0.0	6.6	0.2	0.0	2.2	14.7	12.6	9.1	0.0	6.4
Cedar Falls	0.0	13.0	0.2	0.0	0.3	5.2	6.7	5.8	2.0	1.5
Cedar Rapids	0.0	7.6	0.9	0.0	0.2	7.2	13.4	2.0	1.6	3.1
Clinton	0.0	10.7	0.1	0.0	2.5	7.2	48.1	3.5	1.1	3.6
Council Bluffs	0.0	3.7	0.1	0.0	2.9	13.5	11.9	3.6	1.1	1.9
Davenport	0.0	4.9	0.6	0.0	0.0	13.1	17.7	6.8	6.3	6.4
Des Moines	2.3	11.4	1.8	0.0	0.0	12.6	19.8	4.9	6.4	5.1
Dubuque	0.3	10.6	1.2	0.0	1.4	7.8	26.9	4.5	3.9	3.8
Fort Dodge	0.8	9.9	0.4	0.0	0.1	9.5	14.8	11.3	1.5	5.7
Iowa City	0.0	8.1	3.7	0.0	0.5	8.4	16.3	4.9	8.7	4.8
Marion	0.0	7.5	0.0	0.0	0.1	13.8	13.7	4.6	1.9	5.3
Marshalltown	0.1	16.2	0.1	0.0	4.0	15.0	32.3	6.4	5.1	2.3
Mason City	1.7	6.4	0.2	0.0	4.0	12.0	17.3	4.5	0.0	4.0
Ottumwa	0.3	19.9	0.0	0.0	1.4	12.0	30.9	4.9	0.0	2.4
Sioux City	0.0	5.9	1.1	0.0	0.4	12.2	17.1	8.9	5.9	5.4
Urbandale	0.0	28.4	0.0	0.0	0.1	15.2	5.4	9.9	1.4	4.5
Waterloo	0.2	14.3	0.3	0.0	1.7	13.5	9.5	5.5	7.5	3.5
West Des Moines	1.3	14.3	0.0	0.0	5.2	10.7	16.9	5.3	0.9	4.8

City	City government finances, 2012 (cont.) Debt outstanding Total (mil dol)	Per capita[1] (dollars)	Debt issued during year	Climate[2] Average daily temperature (degrees Fahrenheit) Mean January	July	Limits January[3]	July[4]	Annual precipitation (inches)	Heating degree days	Cooling degree days
	137	138	139	140	141	142	143	144	145	146
ILLINOIS—Cont'd										
Waukegan	133.5	1 504	26.6	20.3	71.5	12.0	81.7	34.09	7 031	613
West Chicago	20.8	757	0.0	NA	NA	NA	NA	NA	NA	NA
Wheaton	45.4	849	0.0	23.1	74.8	14.2	86.8	37.94	6 053	942
Wheeling	84.5	2 228	8.5	18.4	72.1	9.6	82.3	36.56	7 149	624
Wilmette	76.2	2 790	14.3	22.0	73.3	14.3	83.5	36.27	6 498	830
Woodridge	24.8	746	3.3	23.1	74.8	14.2	86.8	37.94	6 053	942
INDIANA	X	X	X	X	X	X	X	X	X	X
Anderson	127.1	2 286	25.5	25.7	74.0	18.4	83.8	39.82	5 807	872
Bloomington	159.2	1 937	55.7	27.9	75.4	19.3	86.0	44.91	5 348	1 017
Carmel	367.8	4 400	0.0	25.3	74.2	17.0	84.5	42.85	5 901	873
Columbus	109.4	2 413	0.0	27.9	75.9	19.1	86.4	41.94	5 367	1 059
Crown Point	22.4	795	1.9	NA	NA	NA	NA	NA	NA	NA
East Chicago	42.0	1 427	0.0	23.7	74.0	15.3	84.8	38.13	6 055	887
Elkhart	28.7	562	0.0	22.8	72.1	14.3	83.3	38.56	6 487	663
Evansville	274.1	2 281	67.7	33.2	79.6	24.8	90.5	45.76	4 140	1 616
Fishers	131.1	1 603	33.0	25.3	74.2	17.0	84.5	42.85	5 901	873
Fort Wayne	435.4	1 708	0.0	23.6	73.4	16.1	84.3	36.55	6 205	830
Gary	85.2	1 076	21.7	22.2	73.5	13.9	83.9	38.02	6 497	776
Goshen	101.3	3 178	9.3	24.3	73.7	17.0	84.5	36.59	6 075	826
Greenwood	30.0	570	0.0	25.7	74.7	18.0	84.0	40.24	5 783	942
Hammond	112.1	1 407	0.0	22.2	73.5	13.9	83.9	38.02	6 497	776
Hobart	25.7	886	0.0	22.2	73.5	13.9	83.9	38.02	6 497	776
Indianapolis	6 001.3	7 191	2 503.6	26.5	75.4	18.5	85.6	40.95	5 521	1 042
Jeffersonville	54.0	1 182	0.0	31.3	75.8	21.4	88.5	45.47	4 829	1 079
Kokomo	32.5	570	0.0	22.8	73.0	15.0	84.1	41.54	6 368	771
Lafayette	133.7	1 913	0.0	23.0	73.5	14.3	84.5	36.90	6 206	842
Lawrence	27.5	589	0.0	25.7	74.7	18.0	84.0	40.24	5 783	942
Marion	11.4	385	0.0	24.2	73.8	16.3	84.5	39.01	6 143	819
Merrillville	22.7	644	0.2	21.1	72.7	12.1	83.6	40.04	6 642	734
Michigan City	54.0	1 733	7.8	23.4	73.0	15.7	83.1	39.70	6 294	812
Mishawaka	117.0	2 436	0.0	24.3	73.7	17.0	84.5	36.59	6 075	826
Muncie	33.5	478	0.0	24.4	72.5	15.9	83.9	41.23	6 215	717
New Albany	61.3	1 681	0.0	31.3	75.8	21.4	88.5	45.47	4 829	1 079
Noblesville	240.4	4 350	12.0	25.3	74.2	17.0	84.5	42.85	5 901	873
Plainfield	56.2	1 924	0.0	NA	NA	NA	NA	NA	NA	NA
Portage	59.2	1 607	0.0	22.9	73.0	15.5	83.1	40.06	6 270	745
Richmond	34.6	947	0.0	25.7	73.1	17.2	84.6	39.55	5 942	769
Schererville	18.2	626	0.0	NA	NA	NA	NA	NA	NA	NA
South Bend	230.5	2 286	60.5	23.4	73.0	15.7	83.1	39.70	6 294	812
Terre Haute	52.7	860	0.0	26.5	76.2	17.7	87.3	42.47	5 433	1 107
Valparaiso	56.6	1 769	9.8	22.9	73.0	15.5	83.1	40.06	6 270	745
Westfield	55.7	1 737	0.0	NA	NA	NA	NA	NA	NA	NA
West Lafayette	40.9	1 338	2.5	25.2	75.5	17.2	86.3	36.32	5 732	1 024
IOWA	X	X	X	X	X	X	X	X	X	X
Ames	127.9	2 091	71.7	18.5	73.8	9.6	84.3	34.07	6 791	830
Ankeny	178.3	3 634	21.3	18.2	74.8	8.7	85.8	33.38	6 961	881
Bettendorf	119.0	3 478	20.8	21.1	76.2	13.2	85.4	34.11	6 246	1 072
Burlington	62.6	2 447	19.5	22.8	76.3	15.1	85.4	37.94	5 948	1 095
Cedar Falls	86.6	2 177	4.4	16.1	73.6	6.3	85.0	33.15	7 348	758
Cedar Rapids	538.7	4 206	127.7	19.9	74.8	11.5	85.3	36.62	6 488	910
Clinton	83.3	3 130	29.0	20.4	74.7	12.5	85.0	35.68	6 416	915
Council Bluffs	125.8	2 024	15.1	21.1	76.2	10.4	87.7	33.25	6 323	1 057
Davenport	324.8	3 202	66.5	21.1	76.2	13.2	85.4	34.11	6 246	1 072
Des Moines	556.3	2 689	43.7	20.4	76.1	11.7	86.0	34.72	6 436	1 052
Dubuque	185.8	3 199	67.9	17.8	75.1	8.7	85.4	33.96	6 891	908
Fort Dodge	80.9	3 272	8.5	15.4	73.1	5.8	84.3	34.39	7 513	746
Iowa City	187.9	2 668	19.6	21.7	76.9	13.4	87.5	37.27	6 052	1 134
Marion	67.4	1 881	13.8	16.8	73.9	7.1	84.4	36.40	7 191	787
Marshalltown	31.2	1 121	12.4	16.8	73.9	7.1	84.4	36.40	7 191	787
Mason City	60.3	2 170	1.5	13.9	72.4	5.1	83.3	34.48	7 765	655
Ottumwa	37.1	1 498	13.2	NA	NA	NA	NA	NA	NA	NA
Sioux City	249.2	3 013	42.4	18.6	74.6	8.5	86.2	25.99	6 900	914
Urbandale	55.3	1 347	9.4	20.4	76.1	11.7	86.0	34.72	6 436	1 052
Waterloo	115.2	1 686	21.4	16.1	73.6	6.3	85.0	33.15	7 348	758
West Des Moines	136.6	2 302	44.3	20.4	76.1	11.7	86.0	34.72	6 436	1 052

1. Based on the population estimated as of July 1 of the year shown.   2. Represents normal values based on the 30-year period, 1971–2000.   3. Average daily minimum.
4. Average daily maximum.

Table D. Cities — **Land Area and Population**

STATE Place code	City	Land area,[1] 2010 (sq km)	Total persons	Rank	Per square kilometer	White	Black	American Indian, Alaska Native	Asian	Hawaiian Pacific Islander	Percent Hispanic or Latino,[2] 2010-2014	Percent foreign born 2010-2014
		Population, 2015				Race alone or in combination (percent), 2010-2014						
		1	2	3	4	5	6	7	8	9	10	11
20 00000	KANSAS.................	211 754.1	2 911 641	X	13.8	88.2	7.2	2.2	3.1	0.2	11.0	6.8
20 18250	Dodge City..............	37.4	27 912	1 322	746.3	88.3	3.1	1.4	2.1	0.1	60.0	30.8
20 25325	Garden City.............	22.8	27 005	1 358	1 184.4	80.4	4.5	1.4	5.1	0.1	50.0	22.1
20 33625	Hutchinson..............	58.8	41 569	898	707.0	91.0	5.9	2.3	1.0	0.1	11.4	3.3
20 36000	Kansas City.............	323.3	151 306	171	468.0	62.5	28.1	1.7	3.6	0.2	28.2	15.8
20 38900	Lawrence...............	86.9	93 917	329	1 080.7	86.9	6.7	4.4	6.2	0.2	6.5	7.9
20 39000	Leavenworth............	62.3	35 980	1 051	577.5	80.5	16.9	2.1	2.9	0.4	8.3	4.7
20 39075	Leawood................	39.0	34 579	1 088	886.6	94.3	1.6	1.0	4.5	0.0	1.9	5.2
20 39350	Lenexa.................	88.3	52 490	715	594.5	89.0	4.7	1.0	4.7	0.2	8.0	8.8
20 44250	Manhattan..............	48.6	56 308	658	1 158.6	86.4	7.7	1.9	6.8	0.4	6.3	7.9
20 52575	Olathe.................	154.5	134 305	194	869.3	88.6	6.3	0.9	5.7	0.2	10.8	10.9
20 53775	Overland Park...........	193.8	186 515	128	962.4	87.1	6.1	0.9	7.6	0.1	6.5	9.9
20 62700	Salina.................	65.0	47 813	792	735.6	89.7	5.6	1.9	3.2	0.1	11.3	6.1
20 64500	Shawnee................	108.4	65 046	547	600.1	91.2	6.6	2.2	3.0	0.2	6.7	5.3
20 71000	Topeka.................	155.8	127 265	215	816.8	82.7	14.1	3.1	2.3	0.3	13.6	5.6
20 79000	Wichita................	412.6	389 965	48	945.1	79.1	13.6	2.7	5.6	0.1	15.7	10.2
21 00000	KENTUCKY.............	102 269.1	4 425 092	X	43.3	89.5	9.0	0.7	1.6	0.1	3.2	3.4
21 08902	Bowling Green...........	97.9	63 616	566	649.8	76.1	15.4	0.5	4.9	0.5	6.6	12.7
21 17848	Covington..............	34.2	40 997	912	1 198.7	86.5	13.9	0.7	0.5	0.1	3.8	2.0
21 24274	Elizabethtown...........	65.7	29 678	1 255	451.7	83.8	13.4	1.3	4.2	0.2	3.7	5.1
21 27982	Florence...............	26.7	32 227	1 170	1 207.0	89.4	7.0	0.6	4.4	0.0	2.0	6.8
21 28900	Frankfort..............	37.1	27 830	1 327	750.1	78.2	18.9	0.8	1.9	0.0	4.7	4.7
21 30700	Georgetown.............	41.0	32 356	1 164	789.2	88.9	9.0	0.3	1.6	0.1	4.2	3.2
21 35866	Henderson..............	39.6	28 890	1 280	729.5	86.1	13.6	0.7	0.6	0.0	2.4	1.4
21 37918	Hopkinsville............	79.4	32 205	1 172	405.6	69.1	30.1	1.7	1.5	0.3	5.6	2.9
21 40222	Jeffersontown...........	25.7	26 946	1 362	1 048.5	83.2	15.0	0.5	2.4	0.1	5.0	7.4
21 46027	Lexington-Fayette........	734.7	314 488	61	428.0	78.5	16.2	0.9	4.1	0.1	6.8	9.1
21 48003	Louisville/Jefferson County...............	842.4	615 366	30	730.5	75.7	22.6	0.8	2.9	0.1	4.6	6.7
21 56136	Nicholasville...........	33.7	29 754	1 252	882.9	93.4	5.7	1.2	0.3	0.0	3.5	2.4
21 58620	Owensboro..............	49.5	59 042	625	1 192.8	90.8	9.4	0.5	1.1	0.0	3.1	2.5
21 58836	Paducah................	51.5	24 864	1 421	482.8	77.0	23.6	1.2	0.8	0.0	2.4	2.0
21 65226	Richmond...............	59.1	33 533	1 121	567.4	88.3	10.3	1.4	2.4	0.1	2.0	2.1
22 00000	LOUISIANA.............	111 897.6	4 670 724	X	41.7	64.3	33.0	1.3	1.9	0.1	4.6	3.9
22 00975	Alexandria.............	73.6	47 889	790	650.7	36.8	60.2	0.9	2.8	0.1	1.2	3.4
22 05000	Baton Rouge............	199.3	228 590	97	1 147.0	40.1	56.1	0.9	3.8	0.1	3.3	5.3
22 08920	Bossier City............	109.7	68 094	514	620.7	68.7	27.8	1.1	3.1	0.2	7.4	5.1
22 13960	Central................	161.2	28 295	1 303	175.5	89.3	10.6	0.5	0.8	0.1	1.5	1.0
22 36255	Houma.................	37.3	34 287	1 096	919.2	67.8	25.3	5.7	1.5	0.0	5.0	4.6
22 39475	Kenner................	38.5	67 091	525	1 742.6	68.7	22.3	1.0	4.3	0.0	22.3	18.1
22 40735	Lafayette..............	127.5	127 657	214	1 001.2	65.7	32.2	1.0	2.4	0.0	4.6	5.6
22 41155	Lake Charles............	108.9	76 070	448	698.5	47.9	50.6	1.1	2.3	0.1	3.2	3.5
22 51410	Monroe................	75.7	49 598	759	655.2	33.7	64.9	0.8	1.3	0.0	1.6	2.0
22 54035	New Iberia.............	28.9	30 754	1 208	1 064.2	56.1	41.6	0.8	3.3	0.0	5.1	4.5
22 55000	New Orleans............	438.8	389 617	49	887.9	35.4	60.5	0.8	3.3	0.1	5.4	6.0
22 70000	Shreveport.............	272.9	197 204	120	722.6	41.5	56.0	0.8	1.7	0.1	2.7	2.6
22 70805	Slidell................	38.4	27 942	1 321	727.7	78.9	18.6	1.6	0.9	0.3	6.2	4.3
23 00000	MAINE................	79 882.8	1 329 328	X	16.6	96.9	1.6	1.6	1.5	0.1	1.4	3.5
23 02795	Bangor.................	88.7	32 391	1 161	365.2	94.6	2.2	1.5	2.4	0.0	2.1	3.7
23 38740	Lewiston...............	88.4	36 202	1 041	409.5	94.2	5.5	4.1	1.8	0.2	2.9	4.5
23 60545	Portland...............	55.2	66 881	529	1 211.6	87.9	8.5	1.1	4.4	0.0	3.4	13.2
23 71990	South Portland..........	31.0	25 556	1 406	824.4	93.2	2.9	1.0	4.5	0.0	1.8	7.0
24 00000	MARYLAND............	25 141.6	6 006 401	X	238.9	60.4	31.1	1.0	6.8	0.2	8.8	14.2
24 01600	Annapolis..............	18.6	39 474	952	2 122.3	64.1	25.0	0.2	2.4	0.0	18.4	15.0
24 04000	Baltimore..............	209.6	621 849	29	2 966.8	31.9	64.6	1.1	3.0	0.1	4.5	7.5
24 08775	Bowie..................	47.7	58 025	639	1 216.5	45.4	49.7	1.3	5.4	0.2	6.7	13.0
24 18750	College Park............	14.6	32 301	1 166	2 212.4	63.6	18.8	0.6	14.9	0.3	10.7	18.7
24 30325	Frederick..............	57.0	69 479	499	1 218.9	68.7	21.3	1.5	7.4	0.3	16.3	19.3
24 31175	Gaithersburg...........	26.4	67 456	521	2 555.2	54.0	18.2	1.3	20.4	0.0	24.1	40.2
24 36075	Hagerstown.............	30.5	40 432	928	1 325.6	77.4	23.0	1.5	2.8	0.1	5.9	6.8
24 45900	Laurel.................	11.1	26 215	1 392	2 361.7	34.0	52.3	1.2	8.2	0.1	17.8	24.4
24 67675	Rockville..............	35.0	66 980	526	1 913.7	64.7	9.6	0.7	21.8	0.4	16.0	34.5
24 69925	Salisbury..............	34.7	32 899	1 142	948.1	60.0	37.0	0.8	3.3	0.4	6.5	11.5
25 00000	MASSACHUSETTS ...	20 202.1	6 794 422	X	336.3	82.5	8.5	0.7	6.5	0.1	10.2	15.3
25 00840	Agawam Town	60.4	28 839	1 283	477.5	94.3	1.5	1.0	2.4	0.2	5.6	8.0
25 02690	Attleboro..............	69.4	44 284	844	638.1	88.4	6.1	0.5	5.1	0.2	6.6	9.3
25 03690	Barnstable Town	154.9	44 331	842	286.2	93.5	4.5	1.2	1.0	0.1	3.6	10.0

1. Dry land or land partially or temporarily covered by water.   2. May be of any race.

Table D. Cities — **Population**

City	Age of population (percent), 2010-2014									Median age 2010–2014	Percent female 2010–2014	Population			
												Census counts		Percent change	
	Under 5 years	5 to 17 years	18 to 24 years	25 to 34 years	35 to 44 years	45 to 54 years	55 to 64 years	65 to 74 years	75 years and over			2000	2010	2000–2010	2010–2015
	12	13	14	15	16	17	18	19	20	21	22	23	24	25	26
KANSAS	7.0	18.1	10.3	13.4	12.0	13.4	12.2	7.2	6.5	36.0	50.3	2 688 418	2 853 118	6.1	2.1
Dodge City	10.7	21.5	12.0	15.7	12.3	11.2	8.7	4.0	3.8	28.6	47.7	25 176	27 340	8.6	2.1
Garden City	10.1	21.1	10.6	15.3	11.5	11.5	9.9	5.3	4.6	30.3	48.7	28 451	26 658	-6.3	1.1
Hutchinson	7.0	15.9	9.6	13.1	11.9	12.9	13.1	8.0	8.5	38.3	50.7	40 787	42 080	3.2	-1.5
Kansas City	8.6	19.9	9.4	15.1	12.6	12.7	10.9	6.2	4.7	33.0	50.5	146 866	145 786	-0.7	3.8
Lawrence	5.2	12.2	28.7	17.2	10.1	9.5	8.7	4.4	4.1	27.0	50.3	80 098	87 643	9.4	7.2
Leavenworth	8.5	18.0	10.1	14.7	15.4	12.2	10.5	6.1	4.4	34.3	46.5	35 420	35 251	-0.5	2.1
Leawood	5.0	21.4	4.6	4.0	14.1	17.1	15.9	10.4	7.5	45.6	51.6	27 656	31 867	15.2	8.5
Lenexa	7.2	18.1	7.8	14.4	14.5	13.1	13.8	6.0	5.2	36.6	51.6	40 238	48 190	19.8	8.9
Manhattan	5.6	9.3	37.1	19.5	7.8	6.8	6.9	3.4	3.7	24.4	48.4	44 831	52 281	16.6	7.7
Olathe	8.0	21.3	7.9	14.3	16.1	14.0	10.4	4.9	3.1	34.2	50.2	92 962	125 872	35.4	6.7
Overland Park	6.3	17.6	7.5	15.6	12.4	14.7	12.6	6.8	6.3	37.3	51.6	149 080	173 372	16.3	7.6
Salina	7.4	17.6	10.5	13.0	12.0	13.2	11.4	7.9	6.9	36.1	50.7	45 679	47 707	4.4	0.2
Shawnee	6.4	20.8	7.9	13.0	14.9	15.9	10.5	5.8	4.7	36.5	51.5	47 996	62 209	29.6	4.6
Topeka	7.6	16.5	9.8	14.4	11.5	13.1	12.4	7.3	7.4	36.6	52.1	122 377	127 473	4.2	-0.2
Wichita	8.0	18.3	10.0	14.8	12.2	13.1	11.6	6.3	5.6	34.1	50.5	344 284	382 368	11.1	2.0
KENTUCKY	6.3	16.9	9.7	12.9	12.9	14.3	12.9	8.1	5.9	38.4	50.8	4 041 769	4 339 367	7.4	2.0
Bowling Green	6.8	14.1	24.3	14.5	10.9	10.4	8.3	5.4	5.3	27.5	51.9	49 296	58 067	17.8	8.0
Covington	7.4	15.7	10.5	14.7	13.8	15.5	11.4	5.7	5.3	35.8	51.5	43 370	40 640	-6.3	1.2
Elizabethtown	6.3	18.9	11.4	12.9	11.5	15.2	10.9	6.1	6.8	35.4	50.3	22 542	28 531	26.6	3.8
Florence	8.8	17.0	9.0	13.4	15.7	11.3	10.0	8.3	6.4	36.3	50.5	23 551	29 951	27.2	7.6
Frankfort	5.5	14.2	12.7	13.7	13.9	11.1	14.2	8.3	6.2	37.1	50.8	27 741	25 527	-8.0	2.1
Georgetown	7.7	19.3	11.4	16.4	15.3	12.3	9.2	4.8	3.5	32.0	51.6	18 080	29 098	60.9	11.1
Henderson	6.1	16.5	8.1	14.3	12.5	14.8	11.9	9.0	6.8	38.9	53.5	27 373	28 757	5.1	0.3
Hopkinsville	8.0	14.4	11.6	15.6	11.2	13.3	11.9	7.0	6.9	35.3	51.0	30 089	31 577	4.9	0.5
Jeffersontown	6.5	16.7	8.3	14.1	15.3	13.8	12.2	8.4	4.7	37.2	51.8	26 633	26 595	-0.1	1.3
Lexington-Fayette	6.3	14.8	14.4	16.1	13.3	12.9	11.3	6.2	4.8	34.0	50.9	260 512	295 803	13.5	6.3
Louisville/Jefferson County	6.7	16.7	9.4	14.3	12.8	14.2	12.8	7.0	6.2	37.4	51.7	693 604	597 337	7.9	NA
Nicholasville	8.1	18.7	8.0	15.8	14.9	13.6	10.0	6.4	4.4	34.4	51.7	19 680	28 015	42.4	6.1
Owensboro	7.5	17.0	8.4	12.7	12.0	14.6	11.1	8.1	8.4	38.5	52.7	54 067	57 265	5.9	2.8
Paducah	7.1	12.9	8.0	14.8	9.8	14.4	13.6	9.4	10.0	42.6	54.7	26 307	25 024	-4.9	-0.7
Richmond	5.5	13.1	28.3	13.3	10.4	10.2	8.9	4.7	5.5	26.6	51.6	27 152	31 364	15.5	6.9
LOUISIANA	6.8	17.5	10.3	14.1	12.3	13.8	12.4	7.4	5.5	36.0	51.1	4 468 976	4 533 372	1.4	3.0
Alexandria	7.1	20.6	8.7	12.8	10.8	13.7	12.6	7.1	6.7	35.7	52.1	46 342	47 723	3.0	0.6
Baton Rouge	6.5	14.8	18.7	15.8	10.1	11.4	10.8	6.5	5.5	30.8	52.2	227 818	229 493	0.7	-0.4
Bossier City	7.8	17.3	11.6	16.2	12.7	11.6	10.3	6.1	6.4	32.6	52.9	56 461	61 315	8.6	10.5
Central	6.7	15.9	8.1	12.6	11.6	13.2	15.3	10.0	6.5	40.5	52.0	NA	26 864	NA	5.3
Houma	6.9	18.9	8.4	15.1	12.5	13.0	12.9	7.1	5.1	35.8	49.8	32 393	33 727	4.1	1.7
Kenner	6.2	14.8	9.2	15.7	10.8	15.0	13.1	9.1	6.1	38.6	52.7	70 517	66 702	-5.4	0.6
Lafayette	5.5	16.0	14.7	15.4	11.7	13.2	11.5	6.6	5.4	33.7	51.3	110 257	120 623	9.4	5.3
Lake Charles	6.9	16.3	12.8	13.6	10.4	13.5	12.8	7.2	6.6	35.7	51.7	71 757	71 993	0.3	5.6
Monroe	8.4	19.3	14.3	12.9	9.7	10.9	11.5	6.1	7.0	31.2	56.2	53 107	48 815	-8.1	0.9
New Iberia	8.2	20.5	8.4	13.1	9.9	13.6	11.9	8.5	6.0	34.9	54.3	32 623	30 617	-6.1	0.4
New Orleans	6.3	14.5	11.2	17.9	12.4	13.5	12.8	6.5	4.9	35.0	51.9	484 674	343 829	-29.1	13.3
Shreveport	7.4	17.7	10.3	15.3	11.3	12.9	12.2	6.7	6.3	34.6	52.9	200 145	199 311	-0.4	-1.6
Slidell	6.0	20.0	8.1	13.0	12.8	15.3	9.8	8.1	6.9	37.8	53.1	25 695	27 068	5.3	3.2
MAINE	4.9	15.0	8.7	11.1	12.2	15.8	15.2	9.4	7.6	43.6	51.0	1 274 923	1 328 361	4.2	0.1
Bangor	4.7	13.7	15.5	15.7	10.5	12.7	12.6	7.4	7.2	35.3	52.4	31 473	33 039	5.0	-2.0
Lewiston	5.8	13.5	12.9	13.1	10.5	13.9	13.1	8.9	8.3	40.6	51.7	35 690	36 592	2.5	-1.1
Portland	4.9	11.8	10.5	19.9	13.6	14.7	12.0	6.0	6.6	37.2	50.5	64 249	66 194	3.0	1.0
South Portland	5.2	14.7	10.0	12.8	14.8	14.5	13.1	8.5	6.4	40.4	55.1	23 324	25 002	7.2	2.2
MARYLAND	6.2	16.6	9.6	13.6	13.2	15.2	12.5	7.3	5.7	38.1	51.6	5 296 486	5 773 552	9.0	4.0
Annapolis	7.9	13.4	10.5	16.8	14.7	11.5	12.2	8.1	4.9	36.2	51.0	35 838	38 394	7.1	3.1
Baltimore	6.7	14.4	11.8	17.7	12.0	13.6	11.8	6.5	5.4	34.5	52.9	651 154	620 961	-4.6	0.1
Bowie	6.2	17.0	9.1	10.9	14.6	18.0	12.6	6.3	5.3	40.0	52.2	50 269	54 727	8.9	5.6
College Park	3.0	5.0	58.8	12.9	4.1	4.6	6.3	3.0	2.3	21.4	46.5	24 657	30 413	23.3	6.2
Frederick	7.1	15.8	9.9	17.0	14.0	13.6	11.3	6.2	5.1	35.2	51.8	52 767	65 239	23.6	6.4
Gaithersburg	8.1	17.7	6.5	18.5	14.6	13.2	11.1	5.6	4.7	34.7	51.8	52 613	59 933	13.9	12.6
Hagerstown	7.2	18.5	8.1	17.1	13.5	13.3	10.1	5.9	6.4	34.2	52.1	36 687	39 662	8.1	1.8
Laurel	9.8	14.7	6.9	19.1	18.0	14.2	9.8	5.2	2.1	34.6	53.7	19 960	25 115	25.8	4.4
Rockville	6.4	14.0	7.2	14.1	15.6	14.8	12.1	8.4	7.3	40.4	51.1	47 388	61 209	29.2	9.3
Salisbury	7.8	14.2	23.3	12.5	10.0	11.5	9.9	5.5	5.3	28.5	52.4	23 743	30 343	27.8	8.3
MASSACHUSETTS	5.5	15.6	10.4	13.4	12.8	15.1	12.8	7.6	6.8	39.3	51.6	6 349 097	6 547 629	3.1	3.8
Agawam Town	5.2	15.2	8.4	11.0	11.7	16.2	15.4	7.9	9.1	44.0	52.2	28 144	28 438	1.0	1.4
Attleboro	6.6	15.6	7.4	12.8	14.7	16.1	13.0	8.1	5.7	40.6	51.7	42 068	43 593	3.6	1.6
Barnstable Town	4.2	12.6	7.6	9.8	10.0	14.2	19.0	12.0	10.6	48.9	51.2	47 821	45 193	-5.5	-1.9

City	Households, 2010-2014 Number	Persons per house-hold	Percent Female family house-holder[1]	Percent One-person	Persons in group quarters, 2010 Total	Institutional Total	Persons in nursing facilities	Non-institu-tional	Serious crimes known to police,[2] 2014 Total Number	Total Rate[3]	Rate[3] Violent	Property	Population age 25 and older	High school graduate or less	Bachelor's degree or more
	27	28	29	30	31	32	33	34	35	36	37	38	39	40	41
KANSAS	1 112 335	2.59	10.4	28.5	79 074	41 393	20 672	37 681	89 554	3 084	349	2 735	1 861 894	37.2	30.7
Dodge City	8 695	3.21	14.6	21.1	596	363	207	233	895	3 160	420	2 740	15 870	58.0	15.9
Garden City	9 361	2.88	13.0	23.7	548	231	96	317	976	3 613	611	3 003	15 737	54.6	17.8
Hutchinson	16 868	2.49	12.8	32.5	2 850	2 402	447	448	1 916	4 583	490	4 093	28 329	40.0	19.6
Kansas City	53 802	2.74	19.2	29.7	1 109	815	421	294	8 376	5 618	711	4 907	91 767	54.7	15.5
Lawrence	34 926	2.58	8.5	31.8	7 984	430	270	7 554	2 128	2 325	231	2 095	48 204	21.6	53.4
Leavenworth	12 347	2.89	12.6	30.4	4 031	3 352	72	679	1 427	3 962	694	3 268	22 992	38.5	30.3
Leawood	12 306	2.67	4.7	19.5	11	0	0	11	432	1 299	69	1 229	22 176	7.3	74.3
Lenexa	19 694	2.52	9.7	25.7	348	327	325	21	870	1 710	110	1 600	33 660	17.8	54.3
Manhattan	20 476	2.69	7.2	33.0	6 227	401	306	5 826	NA	NA	NA	NA	26 403	19.1	51.7
Olathe	45 166	2.88	9.1	20.8	1 418	789	661	629	1 847	1 385	76	1 309	80 833	23.9	45.0
Overland Park	74 058	2.42	9.5	31.0	1 343	1 215	1 040	128	3 360	1 835	179	1 656	122 790	16.2	57.4
Salina	19 393	2.47	13.7	31.2	1 435	545	377	890	2 028	4 238	403	3 835	31 038	44.9	23.9
Shawnee	23 688	2.68	9.2	23.3	406	384	384	22	1 173	1 809	163	1 646	41 364	25.6	43.1
Topeka	53 411	2.39	13.5	36.0	4 083	2 648	1 246	1 435	6 911	5 413	510	4 903	84 156	42.9	27.5
Wichita	150 282	2.57	12.9	32.5	6 420	3 555	1 666	2 865	21 240	5 481	758	4 723	244 805	39.3	28.8
KENTUCKY	1 702 235	2.58	12.8	28.1	125 870	70 779	26 044	55 091	108 506	2 459	212	2 247	2 939 709	50.3	21.8
Bowling Green	23 153	2.62	14.5	33.7	6 147	1 173	492	4 974	3 160	5 087	335	4 752	33 390	46.2	26.4
Covington	16 863	2.41	17.9	39.3	1 406	946	420	460	1 888	4 597	497	4 100	27 350	50.4	19.0
Elizabethtown	11 765	2.50	14.2	34.1	1 075	995	284	80	1 113	3 684	136	3 549	19 241	41.7	27.0
Florence	12 684	2.45	13.0	32.5	268	265	265	3	1 548	4 873	195	4 678	20 742	41.5	26.6
Frankfort	12 099	2.26	15.4	38.4	1 644	648	188	996	1 126	4 096	338	3 758	18 644	47.9	25.5
Georgetown	11 270	2.69	14.9	25.0	1 284	211	136	1 073	1 005	3 213	205	3 008	18 806	43.7	25.6
Henderson	12 405	2.32	16.2	36.5	1 162	806	262	356	1 052	3 647	236	3 412	20 006	51.8	16.7
Hopkinsville	13 064	2.49	18.1	34.0	1 425	1 204	348	221	1 133	3 465	315	3 150	21 420	48.8	17.5
Jeffersontown	10 721	2.51	9.0	28.6	351	351	351	0	675	2 489	129	2 360	18 762	32.0	35.9
Lexington-Fayette	124 101	2.45	12.4	32.6	12 804	3 996	1 092	8 808	13 251	4 249	337	3 912	196 497	31.9	40.2
Louisville/Jefferson County	306 511	2.45	14.7	33.0	14 153	8 529	4 831	5 624	32 453	4 789	592	4 196	511 378	39.3	30.8
Nicholasville	10 767	2.65	17.2	20.8	312	269	80	43	1 135	3 929	183	3 745	18 390	49.4	21.2
Owensboro	23 761	2.44	14.2	34.0	1 817	1 025	806	792	2 385	4 066	210	3 856	38 825	50.3	19.0
Paducah	11 317	2.21	15.3	41.8	1 090	1 024	510	66	1 448	5 788	324	5 464	17 856	42.2	22.7
Richmond	12 760	2.56	13.9	37.0	4 344	480	207	3 864	1 366	4 161	308	3 853	17 391	40.5	30.0
LOUISIANA	1 718 876	2.68	16.9	28.7	127 427	88 104	24 524	39 323	184 758	3 974	515	3 459	3 010 828	51.1	22.1
Alexandria	17 237	2.78	23.3	35.3	2 356	1 611	531	745	4 619	9 501	1 765	7 736	30 627	52.7	20.0
Baton Rouge	88 576	2.59	19.2	35.1	9 554	3 531	1 129	6 023	12 390	5 401	924	4 477	136 941	40.0	32.7
Bossier City	24 933	2.60	16.9	33.2	1 614	811	671	803	3 637	5 391	642	4 749	41 285	41.8	26.1
Central	10 097	2.72	11.3	19.4	59	0	0	59	NA	NA	NA	NA	18 791	45.8	20.2
Houma	12 297	2.75	18.0	27.1	212	134	114	78	1 601	4 691	618	4 073	21 994	59.6	16.1
Kenner	24 704	2.71	14.4	29.0	422	319	303	103	2 577	3 844	236	3 608	46 234	48.3	22.4
Lafayette	49 556	2.49	14.8	35.2	4 509	1 775	613	2 734	7 614	6 085	651	5 435	79 000	38.6	33.3
Lake Charles	29 705	2.47	20.7	34.0	3 149	2 018	596	1 131	3 733	5 013	690	4 323	46 746	46.6	23.6
Monroe	18 390	2.69	26.9	36.7	3 273	1 229	663	2 044	6 385	12 796	2 579	10 216	28 973	48.1	27.1
New Iberia	11 409	2.70	21.3	30.8	433	367	367	66	NA	NA	NA	NA	19 210	60.2	15.9
New Orleans	150 409	2.45	19.6	40.2	13 165	5 509	1 509	7 656	20 152	5 206	974	4 232	250 155	39.2	34.4
Shreveport	77 726	2.58	22.6	34.7	5 574	3 588	1 975	1 986	10 648	5 319	721	4 598	130 248	45.9	25.3
Slidell	10 091	2.71	14.8	22.4	315	286	286	29	1 553	5 622	300	5 321	18 792	43.6	23.2
MAINE	553 086	2.40	9.6	29.1	35 545	12 409	7 878	23 136	28 121	2 114	128	1 986	947 959	42.2	28.4
Bangor	14 287	2.30	10.4	38.8	2 690	854	561	1 836	1 733	5 318	169	5 149	21 799	40.2	28.0
Lewiston	15 497	2.35	16.1	34.7	2 117	365	344	1 752	986	2 709	231	2 478	24 310	52.5	15.7
Portland	30 107	2.20	10.4	39.1	2 613	1 065	592	1 548	2 292	3 453	238	3 215	47 614	28.5	45.6
South Portland	10 852	2.32	14.6	32.5	636	195	73	441	840	3 317	154	3 163	17 859	29.4	40.2
MARYLAND	2 155 983	2.73	14.6	26.9	138 375	66 838	28 001	71 537	176 520	2 954	446	2 508	3 973 193	36.7	37.3
Annapolis	15 781	2.45	13.8	36.4	603	143	143	460	1 143	2 946	500	2 446	26 552	31.3	45.7
Baltimore	242 212	2.57	22.9	39.0	25 199	9 951	3 793	15 248	37 766	6 057	1 339	4 718	416 974	48.8	27.7
Bowie	19 402	2.90	14.2	23.4	255	148	145	107	921	1 610	133	1 478	37 902	23.2	48.0
College Park	6 580	4.77	6.6	30.2	11 535	0	0	11 535	NA	NA	NA	NA	10 623	30.8	50.0
Frederick	26 157	2.55	13.2	31.4	1 785	803	803	982	1 845	2 743	430	2 314	44 960	33.2	37.6
Gaithersburg	22 818	2.78	14.3	25.5	547	372	366	175	NA	NA	NA	NA	43 074	26.8	51.6
Hagerstown	16 295	2.47	18.7	34.3	806	546	508	260	1 741	4 269	650	3 619	26 339	51.9	17.1
Laurel	9 934	2.58	17.9	35.3	183	0	0	183	1 068	4 115	593	3 522	17 708	35.8	39.4
Rockville	24 567	2.58	10.5	26.6	1 103	833	665	270	NA	NA	NA	NA	45 517	20.4	62.3
Salisbury	11 635	2.69	19.6	34.4	1 391	155	135	1 236	2 121	6 674	900	5 774	16 982	45.1	27.8
MASSACHUSETTS	2 538 485	2.62	12.6	28.8	238 882	74 667	43 833	164 215	151 666	2 248	391	1 857	4 561 346	36.0	40.0
Agawam Town	11 495	2.49	10.3	30.2	677	669	669	8	426	1 481	181	1 300	20 610	40.5	27.8
Attleboro	16 619	2.63	10.8	26.3	564	451	429	113	953	2 162	243	1 919	30 210	42.1	30.2
Barnstable Town	19 262	2.32	9.2	32.2	363	106	79	257	1 365	3 058	632	2 426	33 564	31.7	37.5

1. No spouse present. 2. Data for serious crimes have not been adjusted for underreporting. This may affect comparability between geographic areas and over time. 3. Per 100,000 population estimated by the FBI. 4. Persons 25 years old and over.

Table D. Cities — Income, Poverty, and Housing

City	Per capita income[1] (dollars)	Median income	Percent with income of $200,000 or more	Percent with income of less than $25,000	Families with income below poverty (percent)	Total	Percent change, 2000–2010	Vacant units for sale or rent[2]	Total	Percent	Median value[3] (dollars)	With a mortgage[4]	Without a mortgage[5]
	42	43	44	45	46	47	48	49	50	51	52	53	54
KANSAS...................	27 367	51 872	3.5	22.3	9.4	1 233 215	9.0	121 119	1 112 335	67.1	129 400	21.0	11.9
Dodge City	19 196	49 083	2.6	21.0	16.2	9 378	4.3	601	8 695	61.0	90 800	20.9	12.3
Garden City	21 652	46 611	2.3	16.4	13.0	9 656	-1.7	585	9 361	61.0	110 500	23.4	12.7
Hutchinson	22 451	41 677	1.4	27.5	10.5	18 580	5.1	1 599	16 868	61.4	91 000	21.0	13.0
Kansas City	18 425	38 073	0.9	32.3	20.7	61 969	0.8	8 044	53 802	58.5	88 600	24.6	16.0
Lawrence....................	25 989	46 929	3.5	28.4	8.3	37 502	14.4	2 532	34 926	45.6	177 900	21.7	11.6
Leavenworth................	23 781	52 022	2.0	23.4	10.6	13 670	5.9	1 414	12 347	49.9	117 000	21.2	12.3
Leawood.....................	76 304	133 702	30.8	8.1	2.4	12 384	22.2	603	12 306	93.0	388 100	19.5	10.6
Lenexa......................	38 390	75 400	7.1	12.5	5.1	20 832	27.4	1 544	19 694	62.6	221 400	20.5	10.0
Manhattan	24 323	43 275	3.3	29.1	6.1	21 619	22.1	1 611	20 476	38.9	182 800	21.5	10.7
Olathe.......................	31 724	76 519	5.0	12.5	4.8	46 851	40.6	2 344	45 166	71.8	195 500	20.9	10.0
Overland Park	40 065	72 231	8.6	13.4	3.9	76 280	21.7	4 837	74 058	64.2	225 000	21.0	10.1
Salina	24 435	44 398	2.2	27.8	14.2	20 803	6.1	1 412	19 393	63.8	115 100	22.2	12.3
Shawnee....................	33 859	74 992	6.5	12.9	4.9	24 954	30.6	1 303	23 688	72.1	195 300	20.8	11.5
Topeka	24 155	41 412	1.8	28.3	15.7	59 582	5.5	5 639	53 411	56.8	95 400	20.3	12.7
Wichita......................	24 921	45 907	2.8	26.0	13.0	167 310	10.0	15 492	150 282	60.6	118 400	21.2	11.8
KENTUCKY	23 741	43 342	2.5	29.9	14.4	1 927 164	10.1	207 199	1 702 235	67.7	121 600	21.2	10.9
Bowling Green.............	19 489	34 036	1.6	37.8	22.1	24 712	16.6	1 977	23 153	38.8	134 500	22.2	10.0
Covington...................	20 548	35 460	1.0	37.2	21.0	20 053	-1.9	3 020	16 863	50.3	98 100	22.2	12.6
Elizabethtown..............	25 926	42 735	3.1	27.6	13.3	12 664	26.3	953	11 765	51.4	151 500	19.4	10.0
Florence	27 818	52 878	2.8	23.2	7.7	13 447	31.2	954	12 684	50.9	136 500	20.8	10.0
Frankfort....................	24 059	40 622	1.2	28.3	16.8	12 938	-3.4	1 798	12 099	49.4	129 300	21.4	10.0
Georgetown.................	24 237	56 854	1.1	19.2	10.2	11 957	66.8	1 224	11 270	64.3	149 100	19.4	10.0
Henderson..................	20 841	35 725	1.2	36.6	17.0	13 171	4.0	1 080	12 405	54.9	95 000	22.6	11.1
Hopkinsville................	20 688	34 670	1.9	35.9	18.8	14 318	7.8	1 464	13 064	49.6	112 600	20.9	10.5
Jeffersontown	30 696	60 251	3.4	15.4	6.3	11 800	5.5	735	10 721	64.6	162 300	19.3	10.0
Lexington-Fayette.........	29 168	48 667	4.4	27.1	12.2	135 160	16.3	12 117	124 101	54.9	166 000	20.3	10.0
Louisville/Jefferson County	28 464	47 692	4.2	26.2	12.3	337 616	NA	28 441	306 511	62.2	149 900	21.2	11.5
Nicholasville...............	20 802	44 213	1.2	27.9	17.2	11 405	47.0	913	10 767	55.0	138 700	22.7	11.3
Owensboro..................	21 343	38 213	1.5	33.1	15.6	26 072	7.0	1 857	23 761	57.7	104 400	21.2	11.0
Paducah.....................	24 938	31 338	2.2	40.6	22.1	12 851	-2.5	1 389	11 317	49.8	97 500	20.8	11.2
Richmond...................	17 850	30 295	1.0	43.4	23.1	13 788	16.5	1 353	12 760	38.8	132 000	22.9	12.2
LOUISIANA	24 775	44 991	3.4	29.7	15.1	1 964 981	6.4	236 621	1 718 876	66.3	140 400	20.9	10.0
Alexandria	20 149	35 263	2.4	37.3	21.8	20 366	2.4	2 094	17 237	54.2	123 200	24.8	11.0
Baton Rouge	23 990	38 790	3.7	35.0	16.9	100 801	3.6	9 327	88 576	50.1	154 000	22.0	10.1
Bossier City................	25 617	47 103	3.4	25.2	14.5	25 579	11.7	1 713	24 933	55.4	144 400	20.4	10.0
Central......................	30 408	66 778	4.8	16.9	6.8	10 574	NA	395	10 097	85.3	176 000	20.6	10.0
Houma.......................	23 882	47 212	3.7	29.5	16.4	13 924	12.1	1 173	12 297	64.3	150 100	19.9	10.0
Kenner.......................	26 255	49 771	4.6	24.4	11.3	28 076	2.5	3 232	24 704	59.6	171 000	23.9	10.0
Lafayette....................	28 845	45 682	5.1	30.2	13.1	53 356	13.9	3 912	49 556	55.5	171 700	21.0	10.3
Lake Charles...............	23 475	35 830	3.4	36.2	18.7	32 469	3.7	3 529	29 705	53.7	124 800	21.6	10.0
Monroe......................	20 571	28 565	4.5	45.0	28.9	20 570	-3.5	2 125	18 390	45.5	125 700	20.8	11.5
New Iberia	21 135	40 117	1.5	34.2	19.3	13 059	1.1	1 353	11 409	59.3	103 400	19.7	10.0
New Orleans	27 255	36 964	4.7	37.2	22.7	189 896	-11.7	47 738	150 409	46.9	184 100	26.3	14.1
Shreveport..................	24 202	38 413	3.4	33.9	18.5	88 253	1.5	7 602	77 726	56.0	125 600	21.0	10.5
Slidell.......................	24 550	50 432	2.3	20.2	11.6	11 155	10.4	1 105	10 091	69.9	153 900	22.9	11.3
MAINE	27 332	48 804	2.9	25.1	9.4	721 830	10.7	164 611	553 086	71.4	173 600	23.6	14.0
Bangor.......................	23 977	36 272	2.5	34.2	16.6	15 674	7.5	1 199	14 287	44.2	147 400	23.7	14.8
Lewiston....................	21 668	36 696	1.0	37.0	20.7	16 731	1.6	1 464	15 497	47.4	147 500	25.2	17.2
Portland.....................	29 445	45 865	3.3	29.9	15.7	33 836	6.2	3 111	30 107	43.7	236 000	25.4	15.0
South Portland	31 164	53 614	2.8	20.4	9.6	11 484	11.0	607	10 852	59.8	221 700	25.1	14.1
MARYLAND	36 670	74 149	9.1	15.4	6.9	2 378 814	10.9	222 403	2 155 983	67.1	287 500	24.0	12.1
Annapolis...................	43 590	75 320	9.8	17.4	7.1	17 845	10.2	1 709	15 781	51.6	374 500	24.4	12.4
Baltimore	25 062	41 819	3.2	32.7	19.5	296 685	-1.3	46 782	242 210	47.2	155 000	25.3	14.9
Bowie........................	42 544	106 396	12.4	5.8	1.5	20 687	11.1	737	19 402	85.0	297 700	24.6	10.0
College Park................	17 809	56 736	5.7	29.5	6.2	8 212	31.4	1 455	6 580	46.8	256 100	25.1	11.7
Frederick	32 751	65 967	5.0	14.4	7.1	27 559	25.0	2 207	26 157	53.6	242 100	24.4	13.1
Gaithersburg...............	39 846	78 441	11.1	11.8	7.4	23 337	13.5	1 337	22 818	55.3	363 800	24.0	10.5
Hagerstown	20 812	38 080	1.0	36.1	22.6	18 682	9.5	2 233	16 295	38.9	151 000	24.6	14.0
Laurel	34 257	68 230	5.1	12.3	7.8	11 397	19.4	899	9 934	46.8	233 500	27.4	10.0
Rockville....................	49 246	98 530	15.5	9.5	4.2	25 199	41.6	1 513	24 567	59.5	479 100	23.2	10.9
Salisbury....................	21 763	37 131	2.5	34.4	21.5	13 401	37.2	1 418	11 635	33.3	151 900	24.8	13.4
MASSACHUSETTS ...	36 441	67 846	8.5	20.0	8.3	2 808 254	7.1	261 179	2 538 485	62.3	329 900	24.6	14.9
Agawam Town	30 482	63 561	2.9	20.6	6.7	12 139	4.1	475	11 495	74.9	228 500	23.6	14.0
Attleboro....................	31 032	65 141	4.2	19.5	6.5	18 022	8.9	1 138	16 619	63.6	273 600	25.5	14.1
Barnstable Town	36 139	58 933	5.4	22.6	7.3	26 343	5.3	7 118	19 262	74.9	341 100	29.0	17.0

1. Based on population estimated by the American Community Survey.   2. Includes units rented or sold but not occupied.   3. Specified owner-occupied units; $1,000,000 represents $1,000,000 or more   4. 50.0 represents 50 percent or more.   5. 10.0 represents 10 percent or less.

Table D. Cities — Housing, Labor Force, and Employment

City	Occupied housing units, 2010–2014 (cont.)				Migration, 2010–2014		Civilian labor force, 2015				Civilian employment[4], 2010–2014			
									Unemployment			Percent		
	Percent renter occupied	Median gross rent[1]	Median gross rent as a percent of income[2]	Percent with no vehicle available	Percent who lived in the same house one year ago	Percent who lived outside current city one year ago	Total	Percent change, 2014–2015	Total	Rate[3]	Population age 16 and older	In labor force	Civilian full-year full-time workers	Households with no workers (percent)
	55	56	57	58	59	60	61	62	63	64	65	66	67	68
KANSAS	32.9	748	28.2	5.4	83.4	9.7	1 499 009	0.3	63 125	4.2	2 236 421	67.4	43.5	24.2
Dodge City	39.0	611	22.9	5.6	86.8	5.5	14 553	0.1	523	3.6	19 996	70.7	47.4	18.1
Garden City	39.0	696	22.6	4.5	84.1	7.0	14 758	0.0	544	3.7	19 536	73.4	51.0	13.1
Hutchinson	38.6	668	26.8	6.1	78.1	11.3	19 690	-0.8	903	4.6	33 392	60.8	40.1	29.8
Kansas City	41.5	767	33.1	10.2	82.7	7.6	69 808	0.6	4 295	6.2	109 895	65.7	38.7	28.4
Lawrence	54.4	852	33.1	6.1	67.9	13.6	52 222	0.8	1 921	3.7	75 810	69.9	36.4	18.7
Leavenworth	50.1	864	25.2	6.0	69.2	23.7	13 936	1.1	710	5.1	27 277	57.6	30.8	27.1
Leawood	7.0	1 161	28.7	2.7	90.0	8.6	17 310	1.2	522	3.0	24 787	65.4	44.2	21.8
Lenexa	37.4	960	26.9	4.4	81.9	15.0	29 817	1.4	1 057	3.5	38 726	74.1	50.4	16.6
Manhattan	61.1	855	32.9	7.1	72.3	17.5	31 296	2.9	937	3.0	47 833	65.7	31.9	21.0
Olathe	28.2	895	29.5	3.6	84.7	9.3	75 726	1.2	2 489	3.3	95 688	77.1	51.8	14.9
Overland Park	35.8	974	26.2	4.0	83.6	10.2	105 129	1.1	3 643	3.5	140 560	71.8	49.1	20.1
Salina	36.2	680	30.2	6.9	83.7	7.3	26 353	0.9	1 040	3.9	37 137	68.7	44.4	23.4
Shawnee	27.9	825	28.0	2.6	86.0	10.0	35 805	1.1	1 287	3.6	48 017	72.3	49.3	16.9
Topeka	43.2	708	30.2	9.6	79.9	7.1	63 827	-0.5	2 955	4.6	99 908	64.0	40.4	30.7
Wichita	39.4	708	29.3	7.1	82.7	5.6	188 731	0.3	9 452	5.0	294 461	67.3	42.7	25.0
KENTUCKY	32.3	667	29.5	7.9	84.7	10.7	1 953 393	-2.6	105 455	5.4	3 476 701	59.8	37.1	32.6
Bowling Green	61.2	665	32.2	10.8	65.3	19.7	29 349	-2.5	1 440	4.9	49 473	63.9	32.5	29.9
Covington	49.7	674	33.0	17.3	79.5	12.6	18 094	-2.4	974	5.4	32 138	62.1	36.7	32.6
Elizabethtown	48.6	698	27.9	8.8	75.1	16.2	13 302	-0.9	665	5.0	23 205	62.3	37.4	26.7
Florence	49.1	855	26.8	8.3	78.9	16.2	15 477	-1.6	783	5.1	23 996	68.7	45.3	24.1
Frankfort	50.6	676	30.1	7.3	74.1	12.8	13 618	-2.0	597	4.4	22 640	62.4	37.6	32.0
Georgetown	35.7	739	25.9	7.4	79.8	11.1	16 157	-1.1	689	4.3	22 900	71.8	48.9	21.3
Henderson	45.1	599	31.2	12.3	81.7	9.6	12 559	-2.8	651	5.2	23 255	60.6	36.0	36.1
Hopkinsville	50.4	622	29.8	10.5	79.2	11.8	12 308	-1.0	867	7.0	25 569	56.8	32.6	36.5
Jeffersontown	35.4	831	26.3	2.2	80.6	15.2	14 765	-1.6	620	4.2	21 359	74.2	47.6	19.2
Lexington-Fayette	45.1	766	31.0	8.5	75.7	9.7	164 121	-1.7	6 433	3.9	246 175	68.4	41.6	23.6
Louisville/Jefferson County	37.8	734	29.2	10.1	85.3	7.0	370 336	-1.9	18 143	4.9	597 548	65.8	41.0	28.7
Nicholasville	45.0	794	29.2	6.8	75.4	11.8	14 094	-1.5	635	4.5	21 755	67.4	42.1	24.7
Owensboro	42.3	637	29.1	8.2	83.6	7.1	25 428	-2.5	1 272	5.0	45 424	59.1	36.7	34.8
Paducah	50.2	573	29.2	12.9	82.7	9.8	10 088	-3.5	663	6.6	20 353	53.6	34.1	40.0
Richmond	61.2	608	32.5	8.3	69.5	18.0	17 283	-1.6	880	5.1	27 593	62.4	29.4	32.0
LOUISIANA	33.7	786	32.0	8.6	86.0	9.7	2 160 195	0.2	135 093	6.3	3 610 029	61.1	39.5	28.3
Alexandria	45.8	769	36.3	13.7	85.5	5.9	20 245	0.5	1 410	7.0	36 507	55.1	35.6	34.9
Baton Rouge	49.9	787	35.0	10.0	80.7	9.2	117 782	1.6	7 064	6.0	185 351	64.0	36.8	27.1
Bossier City	44.6	862	30.1	7.8	80.7	12.9	30 566	-0.5	1 723	5.6	49 931	67.6	42.7	23.6
Central	14.7	778	30.8	2.1	91.8	5.8	15 386	1.4	684	4.4	21 938	65.9	43.3	23.5
Houma	35.7	753	28.5	12.8	84.8	8.9	16 199	-3.1	978	6.0	26 129	60.5	39.9	29.2
Kenner	40.4	946	31.9	7.4	89.0	7.3	34 100	0.8	1 809	5.3	54 276	66.4	42.5	24.6
Lafayette	44.5	786	31.7	8.3	80.5	10.6	64 627	-2.6	3 656	5.7	99 937	66.4	40.6	23.5
Lake Charles	46.3	743	30.8	10.1	75.8	10.9	37 616	3.7	2 073	5.5	57 881	62.1	33.6	29.7
Monroe	54.5	612	34.5	15.4	85.4	6.3	20 897	0.0	1 589	7.6	37 392	57.6	35.3	32.5
New Iberia	40.7	685	29.1	14.2	83.8	8.1	12 427	-1.3	1 102	8.9	22 984	60.7	35.6	30.6
New Orleans	53.1	927	37.2	18.7	82.5	7.3	180 778	0.6	11 680	6.5	299 971	62.1	37.9	31.3
Shreveport	44.0	761	32.1	12.0	83.4	6.0	87 474	-0.8	6 247	7.1	156 622	60.9	39.5	28.1
Slidell	30.1	1 014	32.9	5.6	84.0	9.0	12 769	0.8	871	6.8	21 664	62.9	40.2	27.2
MAINE	28.6	772	31.0	7.5	86.1	11.2	679 756	-2.4	29 901	4.4	1 095 219	63.9	38.4	30.8
Bangor	55.8	742	34.9	16.0	76.8	16.2	16 684	-2.6	670	4.0	27 523	62.0	35.7	32.0
Lewiston	52.6	684	31.0	18.6	80.8	10.0	17 024	-2.7	746	4.4	29 652	61.3	35.6	36.3
Portland	56.3	932	31.5	18.6	74.9	14.5	37 310	-1.7	1 235	3.3	56 198	70.1	42.2	28.1
South Portland	40.2	1 019	29.7	6.9	80.9	13.5	14 152	-1.8	474	3.3	20 687	71.6	44.2	23.3
MARYLAND	32.9	1 218	30.9	9.4	86.7	10.2	3 151 929	0.8	163 828	5.2	4 695 768	68.9	45.4	21.9
Annapolis	48.4	1 402	28.4	10.4	83.7	12.4	21 843	0.8	945	4.3	30 976	70.9	48.0	22.3
Baltimore	52.8	944	32.9	30.0	82.8	6.2	295 482	0.4	22 726	7.7	503 884	62.1	37.9	32.7
Bowie	15.0	1 764	27.9	3.2	90.2	8.4	32 961	0.9	1 419	4.3	44 485	74.2	50.9	16.5
College Park	53.2	1 471	47.4	11.9	61.8	32.0	14 644	0.8	964	6.6	29 053	51.8	20.6	24.7
Frederick	46.4	1 236	30.9	9.9	80.5	11.8	36 780	0.8	1 765	4.8	52 247	74.0	48.1	19.5
Gaithersburg	44.7	1 504	30.9	7.5	83.8	11.9	35 877	0.7	1 404	3.9	48 835	74.3	50.2	14.5
Hagerstown	61.1	809	31.5	18.5	76.3	12.7	19 689	-0.4	1 415	7.2	30 731	65.9	39.7	31.6
Laurel	53.2	1 383	28.9	8.1	79.2	15.5	15 460	1.1	743	4.8	20 123	78.5	57.0	13.0
Rockville	40.5	1 784	29.8	9.1	84.5	11.9	36 545	0.9	1 312	3.6	51 512	72.7	49.8	18.5
Salisbury	66.7	994	35.3	14.8	69.0	18.5	15 332	1.1	1 184	7.7	24 857	60.9	33.8	28.9
MASSACHUSETTS	37.7	1 088	30.3	12.6	86.8	9.1	3 569 956	0.4	177 849	5.0	5 427 407	67.6	40.8	26.0
Agawam Town	25.1	885	29.5	6.7	91.7	6.1	15 766	0.0	781	5.0	23 647	67.3	41.5	28.7
Attleboro	36.4	971	29.3	7.7	88.4	6.4	23 898	-0.1	1 187	5.0	34 882	70.2	44.6	23.6
Barnstable Town	25.1	1 106	33.9	8.3	90.7	5.9	23 531	0.1	1 314	5.6	38 055	61.9	35.3	33.2

1. $2,000 represents $2,000 or more. 2. 50.0 represents 50 percent or more. 3. Percent of civilian labor force. 4. Persons 16 years old and over.

Table D. Cities — Construction, Wholesale Trade, and Retail Trade

City	Value of residential construction authorized by building permits, 2015			Wholesale trade,[1] 2012				Retail trade,[2] 2012			
	New construction ($1,000)	Number of housing units	Percent single family	Number of establishments	Number of employees	Sales (mil dol)	Annual payroll (mil dol)	Number of establishments	Number of employees	Sales (mil dol)	Annual payroll (mil dol)
	69	70	71	72	73	74	75	76	77	78	79
KANSAS	1 646 377	8 644	58.6	3 790	52 168	60 226.3	3 055.4	10 548	145 480	38 276.5	3 325.0
Dodge City	3 630	21	100.0	44	535	470.1	27.0	108	1 697	469.2	38.7
Garden City	17 570	129	50.4	27	199	227.0	9.5	149	2 259	538.9	49.9
Hutchinson	10 583	120	16.7	50	630	742.0	25.0	202	2 967	705.3	66.8
Kansas City	28 240	154	87.0	197	4 909	4 507.3	256.9	405	6 193	1 594.1	155.6
Lawrence	111 980	786	40.6	53	413	168.8	16.7	333	5 800	1 253.6	118.2
Leavenworth	1 895	11	100.0	9	D	D	D	110	1 589	405.0	34.5
Leawood	17 381	62	100.0	34	407	217.0	33.5	137	2 931	520.8	74.5
Lenexa	83 940	289	86.2	289	4 625	2 981.9	267.5	200	3 850	2 504.9	122.2
Manhattan	50 347	279	54.1	31	480	144.0	19.7	260	5 438	1 031.9	111.4
Olathe	184 819	675	73.8	154	3 054	3 163.4	177.9	336	6 935	2 223.4	179.6
Overland Park	283 039	1 486	26.0	248	7 767	18 445.8	776.3	739	13 517	3 011.8	310.8
Salina	10 891	65	87.7	72	898	704.3	43.4	243	3 949	1 112.7	86.1
Shawnee	58 338	190	81.6	58	805	700.8	45.9	175	3 243	761.8	72.7
Topeka	15 533	93	100.0	120	1 342	845.1	62.1	574	8 921	2 185.9	197.4
Wichita	197 845	1 242	45.7	515	7 443	7 544.6	436.2	1 477	24 136	6 284.9	572.7
KENTUCKY	1 467 802	10 566	62.5	3 690	57 630	71 745.9	3 090.3	15 224	202 615	54 870.0	4 619.2
Bowling Green	51 517	704	22.6	108	1 303	2 669.4	65.2	449	6 831	1 634.5	150.6
Covington	351	2	100.0	26	D	D	D	121	1 297	396.0	33.7
Elizabethtown	7 184	57	75.4	36	319	194.9	14.2	264	4 076	1 089.3	97.1
Florence	NA	NA	NA	40	D	D	D	295	6 297	1 571.5	138.6
Frankfort	1 245	5	100.0	22	D	D	D	137	1 965	476.8	42.0
Georgetown	NA	NA	NA	18	D	D	D	107	1 687	510.4	35.6
Henderson	4 128	106	14.2	34	D	D	D	152	2 089	665.2	51.4
Hopkinsville	5 810	57	61.4	50	739	958.0	28.8	169	2 369	717.7	61.0
Jeffersontown	4 238	29	100.0	163	2 822	1 782.0	150.6	145	2 960	1 005.9	85.4
Lexington-Fayette	137 582	1 342	46.9	352	7 283	4 517.8	527.7	1 192	19 820	4 994.8	466.9
Louisville/Jefferson County	284 211	2 051	44.9	1 006	15 867	13 048.4	836.7	2 659	41 294	10 964.4	1 004.0
Nicholasville	14 618	110	89.1	27	D	D	D	117	1 996	741.7	56.1
Owensboro	32 855	241	95.9	67	943	527.4	41.0	336	4 944	1 209.2	111.0
Paducah	24 292	325	8.6	72	D	D	D	320	5 210	1 415.2	120.6
Richmond	12 613	196	53.6	18	99	134.9	3.7	199	2 976	712.7	59.7
LOUISIANA	2 777 014	13 830	89.1	4 823	64 259	68 012.8	3 260.2	16 743	220 257	61 396.4	5 334.6
Alexandria	6 619	24	100.0	73	914	443.7	37.0	385	5 698	1 633.6	142.8
Baton Rouge	75 617	371	94.9	306	3 894	2 296.2	192.8	1 146	16 570	4 262.5	409.4
Bossier City	40 055	250	100.0	77	1 165	822.5	55.7	379	5 660	1 621.7	137.8
Central	38 262	168	100.0	9	33	250.0	3.7	40	867	203.6	18.8
Houma	NA	NA	NA	68	686	325.7	42.9	167	2 292	639.3	51.6
Kenner	11 273	35	100.0	113	883	385.7	48.5	266	4 356	1 554.2	130.9
Lafayette	NA	NA	NA	276	3 728	1 815.8	182.4	808	12 699	3 434.7	316.5
Lake Charles	72 917	492	52.0	72	847	764.6	33.7	442	6 000	1 812.8	143.5
Monroe	26 502	146	68.5	81	1 211	1 198.0	53.9	400	5 914	1 452.5	131.1
New Iberia	5 680	38	55.3	54	695	330.9	34.5	208	2 791	743.1	68.9
New Orleans	72 830	496	25.6	256	3 794	2 687.0	191.5	1 275	12 371	3 245.1	337.8
Shreveport	73 064	314	96.2	294	D	D	D	875	12 231	3 645.9	311.7
Slidell	2 612	19	100.0	27	158	337.9	7.3	282	4 263	1 096.7	96.6
MAINE	683 014	3 699	77.1	1 344	14 753	12 961.3	691.5	6 351	80 155	21 521.7	1 884.6
Bangor	5 871	28	42.9	63	849	463.0	41.9	310	6 147	1 819.4	136.7
Lewiston	1 534	6	100.0	37	657	300.1	30.0	157	1 935	710.1	46.6
Portland	21 379	151	21.2	174	2 511	1 899.3	129.6	395	4 893	1 551.1	135.3
South Portland	3 983	35	77.1	50	811	2 204.9	43.1	244	4 606	1 131.5	98.7
MARYLAND	3 080 620	17 057	65.1	4 768	73 369	60 734.2	4 378.5	18 179	281 678	76 379.7	7 168.5
Annapolis	8 842	55	76.4	62	404	423.4	22.4	488	7 230	1 508.1	172.2
Baltimore	205 977	1 293	16.9	544	8 592	7 954.3	495.2	1 839	15 747	3 647.7	379.0
Bowie	NA	NA	NA	14	168	62.8	11.9	149	3 864	884.7	82.7
College Park	NA	NA	NA	11	55	15.5	4.5	69	1 686	494.9	46.8
Frederick	61 751	383	46.0	78	844	448.2	45.2	320	5 293	1 594.9	145.0
Gaithersburg	24 486	161	100.0	76	1 339	619.5	79.4	337	6 863	2 146.6	197.4
Hagerstown	3 209	22	100.0	51	463	287.1	20.7	207	4 043	1 212.7	101.4
Laurel	269	1	100.0	11	195	101.4	9.1	138	2 078	542.5	48.4
Rockville	10 115	55	12.7	74	1 661	4 078.6	182.6	321	5 420	1 877.2	162.5
Salisbury	3 762	47	6.4	58	707	461.6	31.3	234	4 178	987.1	91.9
MASSACHUSETTS	3 980 521	17 424	39.7	6 619	114 195	123 904.4	8 035.1	24 311	351 598	92 915.4	9 161.7
Agawam Town	4 730	32	37.5	49	729	819.9	46.1	75	922	262.8	26.5
Attleboro	12 921	94	100.0	32	496	227.5	26.1	134	2 277	638.5	51.3
Barnstable Town	17 322	72	88.9	47	444	185.9	22.3	384	4 724	1 267.9	127.6

1. Merchant wholesalers except manufacturers' sales branches and offices.   2. Establishments with payroll.

Table D. Cities — Real Estate, Professional Services, and Manufacturing

City	Real estate and rental and leasing, 2012				Professional, scientific, and technical services,[1] 2012				Manufacturing, 2012			
	Number of establishments	Number of employees	Receipts (mil dol)	Annual payroll (mil dol)	Number of establishments	Number of employees	Receipts (mil dol)	Annual payroll (mil dol)	Number of establishments	Number of employees	Receipts (mil dol)	Annual payroll (mil dol)
	80	81	82	83	84	85	86	87	88	89	90	91
KANSAS	2 999	14 256	2 743.1	507.6	7 071	60 615	8 562.6	3 577.1	2 875	152 423	86 076.3	7 578.3
Dodge City	21	D	D	D	42	D	D	D	17	D	D	D
Garden City	26	69	13.5	2.3	54	D	D	D	12	D	D	7.6
Hutchinson	52	145	22.9	3.9	82	D	D	D	41	1 579	441.5	70.9
Kansas City	128	519	107.4	18.4	173	D	D	D	161	10 043	10 883.2	640.0
Lawrence	141	D	D	D	249	D	D	D	45	2 467	957.6	103.4
Leavenworth	25	130	39.4	3.8	73	D	D	D	17	685	178.8	28.4
Leawood	102	D	D	D	236	D	D	D	14	189	26.4	9.8
Lenexa	105	588	133.8	31.5	319	D	D	D	135	6 020	2 108.2	298.4
Manhattan	102	D	D	D	117	D	D	D	34	673	137.0	28.9
Olathe	131	585	134.3	24.4	342	1 676	199.2	77.5	100	5 995	1 402.8	337.4
Overland Park	362	2 042	672.6	98.2	1 219	D	D	D	84	2 007	667.9	95.7
Salina	59	199	48.3	6.0	101	D	D	D	55	3 944	1 128.0	159.4
Shawnee	77	306	61.9	10.1	168	929	127.9	46.9	46	1 586	D	105.0
Topeka	173	803	124.1	24.6	382	D	D	D	84	4 722	2 456.0	220.0
Wichita	478	3 607	493.4	121.0	1 002	8 827	1 463.6	506.0	442	25 801	10 181.7	1 336.6
KENTUCKY	3 534	18 250	4 845.5	637.3	8 064	62 431	7 746.8	2 799.3	3 782	213 545	129 284.4	10 140.1
Bowling Green	102	363	73.7	10.4	181	D	D	D	95	7 873	5 079.8	402.6
Covington	32	203	62.0	10.6	124	D	D	D	28	746	215.7	33.6
Elizabethtown	61	304	42.3	7.6	110	D	D	D	51	4 727	2 009.7	220.6
Florence	49	260	71.8	7.9	102	1 559	106.1	43.1	38	3 293	1 633.6	176.6
Frankfort	27	154	13.2	3.5	102	714	77.5	30.0	15	550	104.0	23.3
Georgetown	32	D	D	D	53	261	31.3	12.5	22	7 150	D	502.3
Henderson	36	D	D	D	62	364	31.7	11.1	54	2 214	1 110.0	98.3
Hopkinsville	44	124	19.1	3.1	58	D	D	D	49	4 305	D	191.7
Jeffersontown	85	586	185.4	19.1	180	3 598	284.8	154.5	93	3 786	999.1	163.6
Lexington-Fayette	431	2 128	442.3	76.6	1 067	10 048	1 438.1	560.1	224	8 005	2 922.0	351.1
Louisville/Jefferson County	926	7 168	2 895.1	289.1	2 191	21 986	3 257.7	1 129.8	718	40 666	28 642.1	2 159.3
Nicholasville	21	87	10.8	2.2	52	286	63.6	15.3	51	2 245	588.9	79.9
Owensboro	63	427	57.1	11.7	128	D	D	D	64	3 644	2 865.5	159.3
Paducah	58	252	47.8	8.1	140	D	D	D	36	D	D	D
Richmond	42	150	29.2	4.2	77	D	D	D	32	1 896	D	83.4
LOUISIANA	4 500	31 298	7 486.4	1 461.4	11 669	87 367	13 417.4	4 986.5	3 308	136 327	271 191.1	8 489.3
Alexandria	98	472	76.2	15.2	202	1 325	163.5	55.0	37	1 826	753.8	99.6
Baton Rouge	339	1 827	382.5	71.7	1 144	D	D	D	185	4 968	D	343.8
Bossier City	79	508	104.5	16.1	116	D	D	D	47	1 018	D	47.8
Central	15	42	5.7	0.8	25	75	9.7	3.2	21	155	D	5.6
Houma	61	589	138.9	37.8	145	925	121.6	47.4	32	1 045	228.4	59.8
Kenner	86	622	156.8	20.9	159	1 862	349.7	122.5	54	1 074	182.8	43.0
Lafayette	334	2 352	623.9	122.8	1 009	7 293	1 312.5	444.7	129	3 831	1 042.7	171.7
Lake Charles	117	480	85.9	16.5	275	1 775	214.0	77.5	39	1 224	1 251.5	76.1
Monroe	119	811	137.7	26.1	292	D	D	D	41	1 356	455.0	66.4
New Iberia	56	311	60.9	12.3	100	400	51.5	15.9	49	1 703	566.7	100.5
New Orleans	379	2 156	411.6	79.1	1 421	D	D	D	144	6 049	4 352.7	335.6
Shreveport	285	2 266	439.8	90.1	574	D	D	D	145	4 796	3 670.1	251.9
Slidell	37	365	116.2	26.1	139	583	62.2	21.6	26	1 895	D	115.8
MAINE	1 580	6 242	1 100.4	220.6	3 457	21 188	3 061.0	1 134.1	1 650	49 238	16 044.5	2 424.3
Bangor	90	404	80.3	14.5	157	D	D	D	37	775	167.2	34.7
Lewiston	48	222	31.1	6.6	83	D	D	D	65	1 507	430.2	65.7
Portland	226	1 453	291.5	56.6	586	5 193	1 044.1	380.9	101	2 425	747.5	112.2
South Portland	48	459	93.8	16.4	101	686	96.6	37.9	33	1 452	247.9	86.6
MARYLAND	6 001	42 838	13 410.1	2 253.2	19 529	D	D	D	3 096	100 079	39 533.0	5 908.9
Annapolis	98	449	115.3	25.7	371	D	D	D	37	324	65.5	14.9
Baltimore	596	4 055	883.7	187.6	1 524	20 740	4 544.9	1 808.5	409	11 748	5 043.3	574.0
Bowie	28	170	59.1	7.0	167	D	D	D	6	19	2.6	0.7
College Park	19	77	10.8	2.5	75	D	D	D	6	101	D	4.3
Frederick	99	462	123.1	23.3	369	D	D	D	59	2 045	D	129.9
Gaithersburg	95	514	181.9	30.3	415	D	D	D	35	1 039	397.5	72.6
Hagerstown	65	251	58.6	8.6	113	1 009	111.0	43.9	61	3 335	1 870.3	199.2
Laurel	42	655	104.1	25.6	74	930	154.4	60.6	12	115	D	8.2
Rockville	131	1 785	1 087.7	198.4	861	18 500	3 927.4	1 747.3	61	1 516	348.0	107.9
Salisbury	77	478	55.7	16.0	156	D	D	D	46	2 713	882.7	109.7
MASSACHUSETTS	6 485	42 788	13 628.4	2 357.9	21 203	243 993	57 979.0	22 938.7	6 806	234 168	81 927.8	14 395.3
Agawam Town	20	77	20.6	3.4	65	707	80.2	36.0	54	2 280	779.8	112.5
Attleboro	26	115	23.8	5.4	59	342	38.7	16.0	88	3 518	926.6	223.9
Barnstable Town	70	227	72.0	9.2	201	D	D	D	46	897	215.2	51.6

1. Establishments subject to federal tax.

Table D. Cities — Accommodation and Food Services, Arts, Entertainment, and Recreation, and Health Care and Social Assistance

City	Accommodation and food services, 2012				Arts, entertainment, and recreation,[1] 2012				Health care and social assistance,[1] 2012			
	Number of establishments	Number of employees	Sales (mil dol)	Annual payroll (mil dol)	Number of establishments	Number of employees	Receipts (mil dol)	Annual payroll (mil dol)	Number of establishments	Number of employees	Receipts (mil dol)	Annual payroll (mil dol)
	92	93	94	95	96	97	98	99	100	101	102	103
KANSAS.................	5 943	106 850	4 873.4	1 342.9	668	9 807	615.7	170.2	5 977	93 121	9 677.8	3 955.4
Dodge City	71	D	D	D	5	D	D	D	53	D	D	D
Garden City	66	1 333	67.5	17.5	4	37	0.8	0.3	68	981	66.9	26.7
Hutchinson	99	1 867	82.0	23.3	1	D	D	D	103	1 783	206.1	89.5
Kansas City...............	227	4 773	254.8	69.8	24	D	D	D	224	D	D	D
Lawrence...................	270	6 211	249.2	69.3	22	327	36.2	3.7	203	2 798	242.1	93.0
Leavenworth...............	59	974	43.6	11.6	6	39	1.0	0.2	65	D	D	D
Leawood...................	73	2 185	96.2	31.7	14	D	D	D	158	1 906	259.5	108.9
Lenexa........................	106	1 884	94.5	28.0	18	D	D	D	144	4 505	700.3	214.6
Manhattan	168	3 912	150.0	41.4	8	D	D	D	132	1 402	163.2	57.6
Olathe.......................	234	5 437	245.6	70.9	32	D	D	D	244	D	D	D
Overland Park	456	10 355	538.6	162.8	71	1 583	78.0	25.7	664	12 623	1 736.3	705.9
Salina.......................	132	2 986	115.8	31.0	10	D	D	D	137	2 391	231.7	93.3
Shawnee	109	2 166	95.9	27.2	12	D	D	D	121	1 609	123.8	58.3
Topeka.......................	330	6 636	291.1	80.0	32	D	D	D	358	5 825	699.8	308.8
Wichita......................	962	19 526	918.8	255.2	78	1 300	48.4	18.5	977	18 132	2 250.5	883.1
KENTUCKY..............	7 678	156 965	7 500.1	2 083.5	931	11 322	862.3	237.6	9 449	127 446	11 985.2	5 178.2
Bowling Green..............	243	5 498	255.4	68.2	15	425	12.3	4.3	289	D	D	D
Covington	125	1 793	117.0	29.4	9	D	D	D	39	D	D	D
Elizabethtown	112	2 798	132.4	37.0	9	115	5.2	1.4	204	D	D	D
Florence	161	3 755	201.4	55.7	21	500	20.0	5.8	136	2 375	210.7	92.3
Frankfort	88	1 698	83.5	22.2	6	D	D	D	109	1 198	100.9	45.0
Georgetown	80	D	D	D	5	D	D	D	93	D	D	D
Henderson..................	81	1 388	64.2	16.5	9	D	D	D	105	D	D	D
Hopkinsville	77	1 524	67.6	19.2	5	39	1.9	0.6	120	1 151	111.2	36.4
Jeffersontown	108	2 931	141.4	41.9	18	397	13.0	4.8	101	2 692	165.9	77.6
Lexington-Fayette.........	772	17 490	939.4	270.7	91	1 469	110.6	37.9	895	12 181	1 255.7	587.7
Louisville/Jefferson County	1 651	39 711	2 006.3	572.1	220	3 486	288.7	88.2	2 072	32 822	3 186.5	1 478.1
Nicholasville	53	D	D	D	9	D	D	D	67	551	35.4	17.4
Owensboro	134	3 481	150.9	44.1	13	D	D	D	235	D	D	D
Paducah	174	3 615	161.2	46.8	10	D	D	D	187	D	D	D
Richmond	113	2 762	121.8	33.3	11	D	D	D	134	1 421	115.1	50.1
LOUISIANA	9 019	193 928	11 697.9	3 110.7	1 085	18 036	2 224.7	606.4	10 240	167 792	15 869.9	6 156.9
Alexandria	165	3 114	158.9	43.1	11	D	D	D	277	5 734	754.5	262.4
Baton Rouge	699	15 983	881.3	244.6	65	1 706	232.9	31.8	746	12 755	1 183.1	497.2
Bossier City................	202	7 287	643.8	129.8	23	935	126.5	17.7	153	2 187	184.1	66.4
Central	15	363	12.6	3.5	4	D	D	D	36	473	33.6	14.0
Houma	90	1 690	114.5	33.7	9	78	3.3	1.2	145	D	D	D
Kenner......................	184	3 718	210.3	58.3	20	D	D	D	149	1 864	186.3	74.9
Lafayette	542	12 372	689.9	202.6	50	D	D	D	756	14 701	1 619.6	624.3
Lake Charles	197	6 132	579.2	125.3	24	D	D	D	314	5 528	599.3	241.0
Monroe	167	3 761	170.7	46.2	17	310	15.7	2.3	346	5 454	463.4	179.3
New Iberia	81	D	D	D	10	D	D	D	157	D	D	D
New Orleans	1 300	35 510	2 765.4	764.7	129	3 024	367.8	140.6	628	8 481	1 013.6	371.5
Shreveport	460	12 644	750.2	196.0	43	D	D	D	687	D	D	D
Slidell	180	3 220	150.4	41.0	4	D	D	D	196	D	D	D
MAINE......................	3 958	49 672	2 901.3	850.8	585	4 484	368.2	96.3	3 071	41 700	3 486.8	1 613.4
Bangor......................	139	3 366	222.7	58.4	8	D	D	D	211	4 175	353.1	166.6
Lewiston	74	1 015	51.8	14.3	11	D	D	D	98	1 182	131.6	53.6
Portland	330	5 887	312.7	99.7	39	404	34.3	8.7	278	4 363	470.5	216.3
South Portland	124	2 729	137.4	41.5	11	D	D	D	106	1 379	150.4	64.4
MARYLAND	11 344	204 222	12 516.8	3 410.5	1 561	24 878	2 726.9	806.3	13 217	168 241	18 823.4	7 784.6
Annapolis...................	194	4 975	299.5	91.6	NA	NA	NA	NA	143	1 523	189.2	69.3
Baltimore	1 541	21 832	1 607.8	435.6	NA	NA	NA	NA	1 069	16 427	1 991.0	827.4
Bowie.......................	72	1 969	110.3	30.4	NA	NA	NA	NA	188	1 744	157.8	67.7
College Park................	111	1 966	116.5	30.5	NA	NA	NA	NA	29	175	16.3	7.5
Frederick	218	4 153	220.7	64.6	NA	NA	NA	NA	318	4 441	550.3	212.9
Gaithersburg...............	204	3 774	267.0	71.0	NA	NA	NA	NA	170	1 725	182.4	60.5
Hagerstown	127	2 416	121.7	34.9	NA	NA	NA	NA	132	1 703	199.8	82.6
Laurel	79	1 725	94.2	26.6	NA	NA	NA	NA	94	1 192	123.7	48.6
Rockville	252	4 133	278.5	76.7	NA	NA	NA	NA	278	4 285	845.6	434.3
Salisbury...................	143	2 552	128.3	31.6	NA	NA	NA	NA	161	2 553	311.6	133.3
MASSACHUSETTS ...	16 898	273 185	17 509.0	5 019.8	2 277	35 108	3 412.3	1 261.8	13 136	237 631	26 639.0	12 209.0
Agawam Town	58	618	30.0	7.9	9	D	D	D	53	1 341	109.3	47.0
Attleboro....................	83	D	D	D	9	102	3.7	1.9	90	2 274	169.0	83.7
Barnstable Town	196	2 834	192.1	58.4	21	136	11.2	2.6	157	2 523	267.3	130.6

1. Establishments subject to federal tax.

City	Other services[1], 2012				Government employment and payroll, 2012								
						March payroll							
							Percent of total for:						
	Number of establishments	Number of employees	Receipts (mil dol)	Annual payroll (mil dol)	Full-time equivalent employees	Total (dollars)	Administration, judicial, and legal	Police and Corrections	Fire Protection	Highways and transportation	Health and welfare	Natural resources and utilities	Education and libraries
	104	105	106	107	108	109	110	111	112	113	114	115	116
KANSAS................	3 957	21 148	1 920.4	560.0	X	X	X	X	X	X	X	X	X
Dodge City..............	37	229	22.9	5.6	249	803 190	14.8	27.3	12.1	6.2	2.3	27.5	6.6
Garden City..............	35	D	D	D	310	1 086 046	12.7	30.4	12.2	6.7	0.7	30.7	0.0
Hutchinson..............	66	343	20.9	7.2	392	1 720 937	8.7	26.7	25.6	7.2	2.1	25.6	0.0
Kansas City..............	157	827	89.5	25.3	2 707	14 492 572	12.6	24.6	15.1	5.6	5.3	29.9	0.0
Lawrence..............	117	713	43.2	14.4	1 978	10 089 159	4.2	10.8	8.9	2.8	58.2	13.8	0.0
Leavenworth..............	44	255	17.7	5.7	268	973 969	12.2	33.1	20.9	8.2	4.8	17.2	0.0
Leawood..............	48	451	48.8	18.0	262	1 218 472	17.8	32.5	22.4	11.6	1.7	11.1	0.0
Lenexa..............	68	538	49.5	18.3	414	1 898 039	18.6	33.0	22.5	12.1	0.0	11.7	0.0
Manhattan..............	72	D	D	D	362	1 385 412	18.7	0.0	25.9	14.5	5.9	32.8	0.0
Olathe..............	158	1 168	93.9	28.8	826	3 674 590	18.5	24.2	20.1	16.9	2.0	17.6	0.0
Overland Park..............	304	1 696	122.8	39.0	899	4 414 214	19.0	34.6	19.7	13.5	0.9	8.8	0.0
Salina..............	87	D	D	D	484	1 858 261	10.4	24.5	22.0	12.0	3.3	23.9	0.0
Shawnee..............	76	534	37.2	13.3	287	1 666 597	13.6	38.1	23.7	12.5	0.8	9.1	0.0
Topeka..............	190	1 382	108.7	34.1	1 062	3 978 506	7.7	32.8	28.1	11.7	1.6	15.4	0.0
Wichita..............	560	4 092	364.5	115.2	2 864	12 396 633	10.7	30.7	18.5	13.7	3.8	15.4	2.9
KENTUCKY..............	4 793	31 452	2 830.7	850.2	X	X	X	X	X	X	X	X	X
Bowling Green..............	137	784	69.1	19.1	699	2 772 912	7.1	20.2	19.5	5.5	2.9	30.0	0.0
Covington..............	74	318	25.9	8.4	421	1 788 490	6.5	36.3	30.5	3.6	11.9	5.7	0.0
Elizabethtown..............	66	436	37.9	11.0	289	996 440	11.3	24.1	21.7	8.8	0.0	27.7	0.0
Florence..............	67	538	35.4	12.7	198	919 937	6.2	36.7	28.5	4.6	0.0	11.5	0.0
Frankfort..............	38	233	14.8	4.7	530	2 153 521	5.6	15.6	18.6	4.9	2.2	22.3	0.0
Georgetown..............	38	166	11.3	3.2	179	621 131	11.9	34.9	35.4	6.1	0.0	6.7	0.0
Henderson..............	41	D	D	D	454	1 639 406	10.9	14.7	13.1	5.8	6.0	45.6	0.0
Hopkinsville..............	39	229	21.7	5.9	398	1 517 254	6.4	20.1	21.3	2.1	5.3	33.5	0.0
Jeffersontown..............	78	735	118.2	28.7	108	518 932	9.2	65.9	0.0	12.9	5.5	1.6	1.2
Lexington-Fayette..........	393	3 062	238.3	81.6	3 926	16 180 537	10.0	31.5	18.1	5.0	11.0	15.2	3.0
Louisville/Jefferson County	1 023	8 809	890.5	254.0	8 264	32 734 538	10.3	29.9	8.6	12.9	15.7	14.6	2.2
Nicholasville..............	46	174	21.5	4.3	214	748 387	13.4	32.1	20.0	4.1	0.0	17.4	0.0
Owensboro..............	90	706	49.6	17.4	840	3 418 017	7.9	17.9	10.1	5.1	3.1	53.8	0.0
Paducah..............	76	584	48.2	13.4	537	2 054 380	7.5	18.4	12.7	12.4	7.8	37.6	0.0
Richmond..............	48	242	17.3	4.8	264	708 015	11.1	30.0	21.4	6.8	9.1	12.4	0.0
LOUISIANA..............	5 092	36 098	3 916.0	1 216.5	X	X	X	X	X	X	X	X	X
Alexandria..............	89	539	45.5	13.2	858	3 139 622	13.3	29.0	18.9	9.8	0.4	22.4	0.0
Baton Rouge..............	392	4 825	381.6	214.7	7 745	28 842 476	18.7	20.3	13.5	8.8	15.7	11.6	4.2
Bossier City..............	98	634	55.2	15.9	738	2 695 669	13.1	32.2	30.2	2.8	1.1	15.5	0.0
Central..............	24	115	12.9	4.0	11	24 511	92.3	7.7	0.0	0.0	0.0	0.0	0.0
Houma..............	57	527	77.3	29.1	2 552	9 484 779	6.9	16.5	2.3	2.5	60.4	8.0	3.4
Kenner..............	107	759	114.6	27.1	633	2 227 138	15.0	42.0	19.4	6.5	3.2	7.8	0.0
Lafayette..............	232	2 047	253.7	62.1	3 047	10 656 600	18.8	30.9	10.4	8.4	1.8	24.1	2.4
Lake Charles..............	98	793	74.7	23.3	1 030	3 427 311	10.3	24.5	19.4	6.9	0.4	29.2	0.0
Monroe..............	65	549	40.9	12.8	1 137	2 092 527	21.1	3.5	2.5	12.5	15.1	42.2	0.0
New Iberia..............	69	388	35.3	10.7	222	646 974	12.2	1.2	36.3	13.5	4.6	27.2	0.0
New Orleans..............	364	2 537	210.4	62.9	6 570	26 033 023	13.9	33.2	9.9	2.7	8.0	23.7	1.6
Shreveport..............	252	2 069	184.1	54.8	2 841	10 287 795	8.1	28.1	26.4	6.9	2.4	18.7	7.2
Slidell..............	83	392	28.4	8.2	294	1 068 129	19.4	46.5	0.0	11.4	0.0	18.5	0.0
MAINE..............	2 041	9 424	881.5	242.9	X	X	X	X	X	X	X	X	X
Bangor..............	71	499	47.6	12.4	1 172	4 803 542	4.3	9.1	8.0	17.8	2.9	5.2	50.9
Lewiston..............	60	355	30.1	8.5	1 063	4 275 573	4.7	10.1	8.1	4.7	0.9	4.1	64.8
Portland..............	167	1 005	87.6	26.5	2 667	11 280 661	5.1	9.2	9.4	4.1	13.4	3.5	50.8
South Portland..............	63	561	29.1	10.6	774	2 806 318	7.4	11.7	11.2	5.1	0.2	9.9	54.4
MARYLAND..............	7 877	57 077	5 195.8	1 677.9	X	X	X	X	X	X	X	X	X
Annapolis..............	153	1 410	122.6	50.1	620	3 140 557	12.6	28.5	24.6	16.2	0.0	13.6	0.0
Baltimore..............	682	6 054	643.0	173.9	26 392	122 552 640	6.0	16.4	7.7	3.4	7.5	8.8	48.9
Bowie..............	43	274	19.4	6.5	332	1 491 481	15.5	19.2	0.0	6.4	9.8	36.4	0.0
College Park..............	45	300	26.5	9.3	308	540 180	25.6	19.0	0.0	6.4	12.3	21.9	0.0
Frederick..............	147	996	81.8	25.1	560	2 537 922	10.7	39.5	0.0	8.4	5.7	23.2	0.0
Gaithersburg..............	133	875	110.8	28.8	303	1 564 921	28.1	25.0	0.0	16.4	6.3	21.9	0.0
Hagerstown..............	81	428	34.6	11.4	445	2 038 054	10.3	26.5	16.9	6.9	0.7	32.9	0.0
Laurel..............	51	465	33.5	12.3	197	975 036	19.1	49.9	0.0	7.4	0.0	18.1	0.0
Rockville..............	185	1 289	135.0	38.5	652	3 046 807	18.3	18.4	0.0	9.1	8.6	45.6	0.0
Salisbury..............	83	757	60.2	19.3	375	1 345 111	6.4	35.5	18.2	7.5	4.4	26.4	0.0
MASSACHUSETTS ...	11 154	67 531	5 985.4	1 892.2	X	X	X	X	X	X	X	X	X
Agawam Town..............	46	197	22.9	5.6	958	3 825 533	4.3	9.2	8.3	3.0	2.5	2.9	64.5
Attleboro..............	67	272	24.0	6.7	1 376	5 707 365	4.1	9.4	7.8	1.4	1.4	7.2	68.0
Barnstable Town..........	119	629	54.1	17.3	1 040	5 101 618	12.3	17.0	0.0	7.1	2.3	6.5	50.4

1. Establishments subject to federal tax.

City	General revenue Total (mil dol)	Intergovernmental Total (mil dol)	Intergovernmental Percent from state government	Taxes Total (mil dol)	Taxes Per capita Total	Taxes Per capita Property	Taxes Per capita Sales and gross receipts	General expenditure Total (mil dol)	General expenditure Per capita Total	General expenditure Per capita Capital outlays
	117	118	119	120	121	122	123	124	125	126
KANSAS..................	X	X	X	X	X	X	X	X	X	X
Dodge City	42.1	4.4	73.2	19.0	676	272	403	61.8	2 199	497
Garden City	32.6	5.3	13.6	13.7	508	224	285	32.2	1 196	137
Hutchinson	47.8	10.1	16.6	24.0	572	287	285	36.3	867	15
Kansas City	345.7	20.8	59.0	197.9	1 342	609	724	304.9	2 068	35
Lawrence	300.0	35.4	66.1	51.1	569	251	318	265.3	2 952	315
Leavenworth	35.9	6.9	24.9	18.7	523	329	194	39.7	1 108	180
Leawood	52.4	9.2	26.4	36.5	1 121	518	604	38.2	1 173	233
Lenexa	84.1	15.1	53.5	48.4	979	537	442	101.5	2 056	664
Manhattan	75.3	14.5	19.2	38.3	675	346	329	70.4	1 243	66
Olathe	165.1	23.5	34.3	90.7	697	288	410	149.2	1 147	163
Overland Park	224.8	42.2	25.4	90.5	506	129	377	208.7	1 166	223
Salina	68.5	10.3	26.4	25.7	535	240	295	75.4	1 572	264
Shawnee	54.4	10.0	26.2	38.6	607	330	277	48.9	769	62
Topeka	206.4	27.9	31.8	106.8	835	320	515	153.6	1 201	139
Wichita	562.5	102.8	20.6	167.5	435	306	129	543.6	1 410	223
KENTUCKY	X	X	X	X	X	X	X	X	X	X
Bowling Green..............	98.4	10.3	24.6	55.7	916	177	90	76.0	1 251	71
Covington	71.2	13.5	27.4	40.2	989	171	183	54.8	1 350	183
Elizabethtown	45.8	8.2	36.9	25.3	863	132	268	37.6	1 280	347
Florence	43.3	5.6	79.1	28.8	928	238	141	28.8	926	346
Frankfort	67.6	2.6	55.3	25.5	937	148	150	57.0	2 091	104
Georgetown	46.6	3.3	36.0	15.8	523	64	100	38.6	1 277	68
Henderson	46.8	13.7	10.5	17.3	597	254	172	40.9	1 415	213
Hopkinsville	42.0	7.0	7.7	23.2	702	139	127	37.4	1 128	88
Jeffersontown	25.4	1.1	76.1	17.1	637	144	99	23.6	876	92
Lexington-Fayette.........	544.8	60.2	29.6	318.9	1 045	282	143	440.5	1 443	142
Louisville/Jefferson County	935.3	222.4	25.0	456.1	753	225	93	992.9	1 640	335
Nicholasville	20.8	2.5	72.9	13.4	473	139	110	18.1	638	35
Owensboro	98.3	27.0	14.9	35.0	602	166	123	105.2	1 812	630
Paducah	63.2	11.9	37.1	32.6	1 297	237	164	49.1	1 954	263
Richmond	34.6	1.4	35.9	20.5	631	93	132	25.5	785	137
LOUISIANA	X	X	X	X	X	X	X	X	X	X
Alexandria	82.5	13.7	28.9	53.7	1 121	153	967	92.8	1 936	198
Baton Rouge	959.1	199.4	55.2	458.1	1 992	692	1 300	1 203.6	5 233	1 750
Bossier City	108.4	8.2	55.5	71.3	1 090	181	909	129.1	1 975	823
Central	9.1	0.3	100.0	8.6	313	0	313	4.7	169	2
Houma......................	411.9	103.8	73.9	117.3	3 483	1 624	1 859	430.0	12 764	2 321
Kenner......................	77.5	40.2	21.3	22.2	332	125	207	70.3	1 050	164
Lafayette....................	402.4	70.2	47.1	201.1	1 631	828	803	443.4	3 597	882
Lake Charles	116.9	27.3	9.2	70.1	952	108	845	117.0	1 590	348
Monroe	129.3	28.8	34.5	77.5	1 564	218	1 346	140.8	2 843	755
New Iberia	32.2	4.6	29.3	21.4	693	131	562	42.4	1 376	297
New Orleans	1 505.1	535.6	44.1	499.4	1 349	692	647	1 604.4	4 334	1 371
Shreveport.................	369.6	59.6	35.0	209.5	1 037	312	725	315.2	1 560	169
Slidell	55.2	15.5	65.5	27.4	1 001	202	798	55.1	2 012	612
MAINE	X	X	X	X	X	X	X	X	X	X
Bangor......................	131.1	38.3	93.4	54.2	1 653	1 624	29	165.2	5 035	1 527
Lewiston	117.7	52.6	84.0	49.4	1 355	1 342	13	112.8	3 095	292
Portland....................	318.6	71.3	78.7	144.3	2 178	2 129	49	329.4	4 972	746
South Portland	82.8	11.7	92.5	61.0	2 430	2 411	20	82.1	3 270	347
MARYLAND	X	X	X	X	X	X	X	X	X	X
Annapolis...................	82.8	14.6	35.6	43.3	1 125	985	140	65.6	1 703	14
Baltimore	3 407.6	1 720.1	81.7	1 238.8	1 989	1 226	267	3 659.5	5 874	527
Bowie.......................	46.8	10.8	16.7	27.6	491	444	47	42.1	748	0
College Park................	15.3	2.1	19.1	9.8	315	239	76	14.1	451	4
Frederick	90.8	14.2	14.9	46.5	700	655	45	84.6	1 273	9
Gaithersburg	54.0	13.4	7.5	31.2	495	390	104	49.4	783	40
Hagerstown	57.3	7.1	21.8	26.1	645	527	114	50.2	1 239	16
Laurel	29.2	4.0	20.5	20.5	800	757	43	25.4	992	3
Rockville....................	92.8	17.8	12.0	40.8	644	553	86	94.1	1 486	5
Salisbury	51.7	5.3	32.3	22.5	725	675	49	39.7	1 279	49
MASSACHUSETTS ...	X	X	X	X	X	X	X	X	X	X
Agawam Town	84.8	27.5	99.5	50.0	1 745	1 720	26	102.8	3 589	65
Attleboro....................	126.9	47.0	97.8	61.9	1 412	1 380	32	113.5	2 593	116
Barnstable Town	177.7	41.0	87.9	109.9	2 458	2 319	139	175.2	3 917	633

1. Based on population estimated as of July 1 of the year shown.

Table D. Cities — City Government Finances

City	Public welfare	Highways	Parking facilities	Education	Health and hospitals	Police protection	Sewerage and sanitation	Parks and recreation	Housing and community development	Interest on debt
	127	128	129	130	131	132	133	134	135	136
KANSAS..................	X	X	X	X	X	X	X	X	X	X
Dodge City	0.0	1.2	0.0	0.0	0.8	7.8	35.2	17.9	0.0	16.3
Garden City	0.0	11.0	0.0	0.0	0.0	19.9	11.8	14.6	0.0	1.0
Hutchinson	0.0	4.4	0.0	0.0	1.3	22.1	23.3	12.7	0.0	3.8
Kansas City	0.0	2.6	0.2	0.0	3.4	15.9	7.5	2.3	1.5	23.3
Lawrence	0.0	2.7	0.5	0.0	59.4	5.5	8.3	3.1	1.3	2.8
Leavenworth	0.0	10.0	0.0	0.0	0.0	17.1	12.8	5.5	9.0	2.9
Leawood	0.0	22.0	0.0	0.0	0.0	21.4	0.0	17.6	0.0	6.5
Lenexa.....................	0.0	20.0	0.0	0.0	0.0	12.2	3.8	8.5	0.0	16.9
Manhattan	0.0	6.3	0.0	0.0	1.1	17.5	8.4	8.0	1.8	12.6
Olathe.....................	0.0	15.8	0.0	0.0	0.2	13.0	15.5	3.6	0.0	9.4
Overland Park	0.0	21.1	0.0	0.0	0.0	14.4	2.5	5.2	0.0	25.8
Salina	0.0	9.2	0.0	0.0	1.6	11.2	10.5	9.0	5.0	11.5
Shawnee	0.0	12.9	0.0	0.0	0.0	24.3	6.3	9.2	0.0	18.0
Topeka	1.1	9.1	1.4	0.0	0.0	20.4	12.2	10.5	1.5	7.1
Wichita....................	0.0	13.4	0.0	0.0	0.7	13.7	8.7	4.9	0.0	31.2
KENTUCKY...............	X	X	X	X	X	X	X	X	X	X
Bowling Green	0.0	9.4	0.0	0.0	0.0	12.0	10.5	10.4	6.4	20.5
Covington	0.0	7.9	3.6	0.0	0.0	19.6	4.0	2.4	21.8	12.5
Elizabethtown	0.0	9.8	0.1	0.0	0.0	10.7	9.3	8.0	0.0	3.4
Florence	0.0	44.2	0.0	0.0	0.0	16.0	5.1	0.0	0.0	10.7
Frankfort	0.0	3.8	0.0	0.0	5.8	7.9	12.9	5.0	0.0	2.6
Georgetown	0.2	3.1	0.0	0.0	0.0	7.8	10.8	2.3	1.1	49.3
Henderson	0.0	5.4	0.0	0.0	0.0	9.2	27.0	2.5	13.3	1.8
Hopkinsville	0.7	5.7	0.0	0.0	0.0	20.8	13.6	1.2	13.7	14.5
Jeffersontown	0.0	9.1	0.0	0.0	0.0	23.5	4.4	2.6	2.8	37.7
Lexington-Fayette........	2.0	2.5	0.3	0.0	3.6	10.8	15.8	4.0	1.1	4.1
Louisville/Jefferson County	1.2	6.8	7.9	5.7	3.3	10.2	1.5	5.7	6.5	9.9
Nicholasville	0.0	18.8	0.0	0.0	0.0	22.5	18.6	0.0	0.0	5.0
Owensboro	0.0	5.3	0.2	0.0	0.0	7.1	17.8	7.1	27.9	10.8
Paducah	0.0	8.5	0.0	3.6	0.0	12.3	6.2	4.9	18.9	2.5
Richmond	0.0	3.7	0.0	0.0	0.0	13.5	29.4	8.7	7.4	15.3
LOUISIANA	X	X	X	X	X	X	X	X	X	X
Alexandria	0.0	13.7	0.0	0.0	0.0	18.0	11.3	3.8	8.9	3.0
Baton Rouge	0.2	8.7	0.1	1.3	8.7	10.5	28.4	2.0	5.2	5.2
Bossier City	0.0	1.7	0.0	0.0	0.4	15.1	16.6	5.5	6.7	5.7
Central....................	0.0	4.9	0.0	0.0	2.1	3.8	0.0	0.0	0.0	0.0
Houma.....................	0.4	4.2	0.0	0.0	41.2	6.3	5.5	2.3	1.7	1.6
Kenner....................	0.0	19.8	0.0	0.0	0.2	23.7	14.3	6.4	1.0	2.8
Lafayette	0.2	7.6	0.2	0.0	1.4	12.7	9.1	6.0	5.0	8.8
Lake Charles.............	0.7	13.5	0.0	0.0	0.5	14.4	17.5	8.9	13.5	3.4
Monroe	0.1	4.4	0.0	0.0	0.0	13.1	9.8	5.7	17.4	5.8
New Iberia	0.4	16.2	0.0	0.0	0.0	14.0	25.5	5.1	10.0	4.0
New Orleans	0.2	7.6	0.1	0.0	0.8	8.9	13.7	5.5	15.5	5.9
Shreveport	0.0	4.5	0.2	0.0	0.0	18.2	14.6	9.9	7.6	4.3
Slidell.....................	0.0	11.7	0.0	0.0	0.7	14.9	13.3	2.9	10.4	1.7
MAINE	X	X	X	X	X	X	X	X	X	X
Bangor.....................	0.0	0.0	0.4	26.4	2.3	4.8	3.0	22.8	0.9	2.0
Lewiston	0.9	3.4	0.0	49.5	0.0	5.9	6.7	0.6	1.5	5.2
Portland...................	7.7	5.4	0.6	30.3	1.3	4.1	8.1	2.0	1.0	5.2
South Portland	0.3	4.6	0.0	52.3	0.0	5.4	11.2	4.3	0.0	1.6
MARYLAND	X	X	X	X	X	X	X	X	X	X
Annapolis..................	0.0	7.2	2.3	0.0	0.0	25.6	12.0	5.3	0.0	5.0
Baltimore	0.0	5.7	0.8	38.4	3.3	10.2	6.6	1.6	2.1	1.4
Bowie......................	0.0	11.4	0.0	0.0	0.5	17.6	23.4	16.4	0.1	1.5
College Park.............	0.0	22.3	1.0	0.0	0.6	7.3	18.8	9.4	1.5	2.1
Frederick	0.0	10.8	3.8	0.0	0.0	30.2	13.3	9.7	0.6	5.8
Gaithersburg	0.0	8.4	0.0	0.0	1.2	15.6	4.7	20.3	1.6	11.6
Hagerstown	0.0	5.9	1.4	0.0	0.0	23.0	29.3	6.2	1.0	2.0
Laurel	0.0	4.9	0.0	0.0	0.0	34.6	4.6	9.1	0.2	1.9
Rockville..................	0.0	12.9	2.9	0.0	0.4	17.1	13.5	19.7	4.1	4.0
Salisbury..................	0.0	9.1	1.5	0.0	0.5	25.3	23.5	5.2	2.1	3.6
MASSACHUSETTS ...	X	X	X	X	X	X	X	X	X	X
Agawam Town	0.1	2.9	0.0	52.9	1.8	4.2	4.3	0.8	0.0	0.8
Attleboro	0.6	3.1	0.0	63.9	0.2	5.5	8.6	1.4	0.5	2.3
Barnstable Town	0.2	2.3	0.0	45.7	0.6	6.2	4.5	2.8	0.2	2.5

Table D. Cities — City Government Finances, City Government Employment, and Climate

City	City government finances, 2012 (cont.)			Climate[2]						
	Debt outstanding			Average daily temperature (degrees Fahrenheit)						
				Mean		Limits				
	Total (mil dol)	Per capita[1] (dollars)	Debt issued during year	January	July	January[3]	July[4]	Annual precipitation (inches)	Heating degree days	Cooling degree days
	137	138	139	140	141	142	143	144	145	146
KANSAS..............................	X	X	X	X	X	X	X	X	X	X
Dodge City..............................	220.7	7 857	12.2	30.1	79.8	18.7	92.8	22.35	5 037	1 481
Garden City..............................	42.2	1 564	3.5	28.6	77.8	14.7	92.1	18.77	5 423	1 191
Hutchinson..............................	54.3	1 294	5.6	28.5	79.9	17.0	92.7	30.32	5 146	1 454
Kansas City..............................	1 786.2	12 115	126.8	29.1	79.0	19.9	89.4	40.17	4 847	1 406
Lawrence..............................	287.4	3 197	46.3	29.9	80.2	20.5	90.6	39.78	4 685	1 582
Leavenworth..............................	32.8	917	10.5	26.6	79.1	16.4	89.8	40.94	5 331	1 356
Leawood..............................	60.6	1 863	5.3	29.1	79.0	19.9	89.4	40.17	4 847	1 406
Lenexa..............................	280.1	5 672	46.2	29.1	79.0	19.9	89.4	40.17	4 847	1 406
Manhattan..............................	344.8	6 084	41.3	27.8	79.9	16.1	92.5	34.80	5 120	1 465
Olathe..............................	1 141.4	8 779	55.5	29.1	79.0	19.9	89.4	40.17	4 847	1 406
Overland Park..............................	1 428.3	7 983	15.2	29.1	79.0	19.9	89.4	40.17	4 847	1 406
Salina..............................	168.5	3 513	22.8	29.0	81.3	18.8	93.3	32.19	4 952	1 600
Shawnee..............................	215.7	3 390	22.2	29.1	79.0	19.9	89.4	40.17	4 847	1 406
Topeka..............................	364.4	2 850	72.6	27.2	78.4	17.2	89.1	35.64	5 225	1 357
Wichita..............................	3 471.3	9 003	335.8	30.2	81.0	20.3	92.9	30.38	4 765	1 658
KENTUCKY..............................	X	X	X	X	X	X	X	X	X	X
Bowling Green..............................	283.6	4 667	7.1	34.2	78.5	25.4	89.2	51.63	4 243	1 413
Covington..............................	162.2	3 993	3.6	32.0	76.1	24.1	85.9	45.91	4 713	1 154
Elizabethtown..............................	55.2	1 880	18.5	NA	NA	NA	NA	NA	NA	NA
Florence..............................	69.3	2 230	3.1	NA	NA	NA	NA	NA	NA	NA
Frankfort..............................	46.6	1 711	0.0	30.3	75.2	20.8	86.9	43.56	5 129	994
Georgetown..............................	473.4	15 642	0.0	NA	NA	NA	NA	NA	NA	NA
Henderson..............................	50.4	1 744	15.8	32.6	77.6	23.6	88.4	44.77	4 374	1 344
Hopkinsville..............................	170.2	5 136	12.2	33.2	78.2	24.4	88.5	50.92	4 298	1 433
Jeffersontown..............................	160.3	5 960	0.0	33.0	78.4	24.9	87.0	44.54	4 352	1 443
Lexington-Fayette..............................	1 000.4	3 277	37.3	31.6	75.9	22.5	86.3	46.39	4 769	1 094
Louisville/Jefferson County..............................	1 594.3	2 633	310.5	NA	NA	NA	NA	NA	NA	NA
Nicholasville..............................	32.1	1 130	3.5	NA	NA	NA	NA	NA	NA	NA
Owensboro..............................	399.8	6 888	55.2	33.5	79.2	24.4	90.7	46.53	4 159	1 565
Paducah..............................	39.7	1 583	6.6	35.2	79.9	27.2	90.8	46.04	3 893	1 635
Richmond..............................	104.2	3 208	2.7	34.7	75.8	25.6	87.0	47.33	4 231	1 150
LOUISIANA..............................	X	X	X	X	X	X	X	X	X	X
Alexandria..............................	94.9	1 980	2.6	48.1	83.3	38.0	92.8	61.44	1 908	2 602
Baton Rouge..............................	1 639.8	7 130	219.4	50.1	81.7	40.2	90.7	63.08	1 689	2 628
Bossier City..............................	360.5	5 513	5.7	48.3	81.0	37.4	91.0	61.06	1 981	2 220
Central..............................	0.0	0	0.0	NA	NA	NA	NA	NA	NA	NA
Houma..............................	213.1	6 326	64.3	53.1	82.5	43.4	90.7	63.67	1 346	2 804
Kenner..............................	61.5	919	19.6	52.6	82.7	43.4	91.1	64.16	1 417	2 773
Lafayette..............................	1 132.6	9 186	183.7	51.3	82.2	41.6	91.2	60.54	1 531	2 671
Lake Charles..............................	92.3	1 253	3.7	50.9	82.6	41.2	91.0	57.19	1 546	2 705
Monroe..............................	177.3	3 581	34.9	44.6	83.0	33.5	94.1	58.04	2 399	2 311
New Iberia..............................	38.7	1 257	24.3	51.3	82.3	41.4	91.1	60.89	1 544	2 680
New Orleans..............................	2 018.9	5 454	51.5	52.7	82.2	43.3	90.9	65.15	1 416	2 686
Shreveport..............................	540.8	2 676	85.6	46.4	83.4	36.5	93.3	51.30	2 251	2 405
Slidell..............................	25.1	916	0.0	50.7	82.1	40.2	91.1	62.66	1 652	2 548
MAINE..............................	X	X	X	X	X	X	X	X	X	X
Bangor..............................	109.4	3 335	32.1	18.0	69.2	8.3	79.6	39.57	7 676	313
Lewiston..............................	152.4	4 182	7.6	20.5	71.4	11.5	81.5	45.79	7 107	465
Portland..............................	423.0	6 384	38.7	21.7	68.7	12.5	78.8	45.83	7 318	347
South Portland..............................	50.1	1 994	30.0	NA	NA	NA	NA	NA	NA	NA
MARYLAND..............................	X	X	X	X	X	X	X	X	X	X
Annapolis..............................	96.8	2 513	0.0	32.8	77.5	23.8	87.7	44.78	4 695	1 162
Baltimore..............................	2 621.6	4 208	13.3	36.8	81.7	29.4	90.6	43.59	4 720	1 147
Bowie..............................	18.0	320	0.1	31.8	75.2	21.2	87.1	44.66	4 970	917
College Park..............................	8.4	269	0.0	NA	NA	NA	NA	NA	NA	NA
Frederick..............................	224.2	3 375	31.4	33.3	77.9	25.1	88.9	40.64	4 430	1 272
Gaithersburg..............................	142.6	2 261	0.0	31.8	75.3	23.8	85.4	43.08	4 990	983
Hagerstown..............................	66.0	1 630	7.9	29.3	75.2	20.8	86.1	39.45	5 249	902
Laurel..............................	10.1	396	0.1	NA	NA	NA	NA	NA	NA	NA
Rockville..............................	135.9	2 144	40.7	31.8	75.3	23.8	85.4	43.08	4 990	983
Salisbury..............................	70.9	2 286	15.2	NA	NA	NA	NA	NA	NA	NA
MASSACHUSETTS..............................	X	X	X	X	X	X	X	X	X	X
Agawam Town..............................	25.0	871	6.2	NA	NA	NA	NA	NA	NA	NA
Attleboro..............................	72.7	1 660	1.5	27.4	72.2	17.8	83.0	48.34	6 012	558
Barnstable Town..............................	131.5	2 941	18.5	29.2	70.5	21.2	77.8	43.03	6 026	413

1. Based on the population estimated as of July 1 of the year shown.   2. Represents normal values based on the 30-year period, 1971–2000.   3. Average daily minimum.
4. Average daily maximum.

Table D. Cities — **Land Area and Population**

STATE Place code	City	Land area,[1] 2010 (sq km)	Total persons	Rank	Per square kilometer	White	Black	American Indian, Alaska Native	Asian	Hawaiian Pacific Islander	Percent Hispanic or Latino[2], 2010-2014	Percent foreign born 2010–2014
		1	2	3	4	5	6	7	8	9	10	11
	MASSACHUSETTS—Cont'd											
25 05595	Beverly	39.1	41 186	907	1 053.4	95.4	2.1	0.6	2.4	0.0	3.5	6.3
25 07000	Boston	125.0	667 137	23	5 337.1	57.2	28.2	0.9	10.1	0.2	18.4	27.0
25 07740	Braintree Town	35.6	37 497	1 006	1 053.3	86.1	5.7	0.3	8.3	0.3	2.7	13.2
25 09000	Brockton	55.2	95 314	318	1 726.7	50.5	42.1	1.0	2.2	0.5	10.0	25.2
25 11000	Cambridge	16.5	110 402	259	6 691.0	71.0	12.7	1.0	16.9	0.2	7.4	28.1
25 13205	Chelsea	5.7	39 398	956	6 911.9	80.5	36.9	0.4	3.6	0.1	62.8	44.4
25 13660	Chicopee	59.1	56 741	656	960.1	88.3	4.5	0.5	1.7	0.0	16.7	8.8
25 21990	Everett	8.9	46 050	820	5 174.2	71.7	21.6	0.6	4.6	0.1	20.8	40.6
25 23000	Fall River	85.8	88 777	353	1 034.7	89.2	5.2	1.7	2.6	0.3	8.6	19.1
25 23875	Fitchburg	72.1	40 545	924	562.3	82.3	6.0	0.8	5.0	0.1	23.9	11.5
25 25172	Franklin Town	69.0	33 147	1 135	480.4	94.5	1.7	0.3	4.6	0.1	3.1	6.4
25 26150	Gloucester	67.9	29 781	1 251	438.6	97.0	1.4	0.7	0.9	0.0	2.9	8.5
25 29405	Haverhill	85.4	62 765	572	735.0	85.7	3.9	0.5	1.6	0.0	17.4	9.0
25 30840	Holyoke	55.1	40 684	919	738.4	82.5	5.4	0.8	1.8	0.0	47.0	6.1
25 34550	Lawrence	17.9	80 231	417	4 482.2	40.0	8.5	0.8	3.4	0.1	75.7	38.3
25 35075	Leominster	74.6	41 569	898	557.2	85.7	7.2	0.8	3.3	0.0	15.1	12.7
25 37000	Lowell	35.2	110 699	256	3 144.9	59.7	8.3	0.7	22.0	0.1	18.2	25.2
25 37490	Lynn	27.8	92 457	340	3 325.8	58.7	16.5	0.9	8.2	0.2	34.2	32.0
25 37875	Malden	13.1	61 068	591	4 661.7	59.7	15.0	1.4	25.4	0.1	11.1	42.4
25 38715	Marlborough	54.0	39 818	940	737.4	90.5	11.3	0.8	5.4	0.0	12.8	21.6
25 39835	Medford	21.0	57 403	643	2 733.5	81.9	10.6	0.6	8.6	0.1	4.6	21.1
25 40115	Melrose	12.1	27 997	1 318	2 313.8	93.0	3.0	0.1	4.8	0.1	3.9	12.2
25 40710	Methuen Town	57.6	49 660	757	862.2	80.6	3.9	0.7	3.5	0.1	21.4	15.0
25 45000	New Bedford	51.8	94 958	322	1 833.2	76.9	9.8	1.0	1.5	0.2	17.5	19.7
25 45560	Newton	46.2	88 817	352	1 922.4	81.9	4.2	0.3	15.4	0.2	5.4	20.9
25 46330	Northampton	88.7	28 540	1 293	321.8	88.3	3.8	0.5	7.3	0.1	7.6	9.5
25 52490	Peabody	42.0	52 504	713	1 250.1	90.3	3.2	0.4	2.7	0.0	7.8	15.6
25 53960	Pittsfield	104.8	43 303	863	413.2	90.6	8.2	0.9	2.1	0.3	5.3	6.3
25 55745	Quincy	42.9	93 618	331	2 182.2	67.1	6.5	0.8	26.6	0.3	3.1	29.4
25 56585	Revere	14.7	53 422	700	3 634.1	80.3	8.9	0.4	6.5	0.1	26.2	33.1
25 59105	Salem	21.4	42 869	873	2 003.2	84.0	8.4	1.1	2.9	0.1	16.0	14.8
25 62535	Somerville	10.7	80 318	416	7 506.4	79.3	8.8	0.4	11.1	0.1	9.5	24.3
25 67000	Springfield	82.5	154 341	163	1 870.8	57.0	24.3	1.2	2.6	0.2	41.4	10.8
25 69170	Taunton	121.0	56 789	653	469.3	90.3	6.9	0.7	1.3	0.1	6.6	11.3
25 72600	Waltham	33.0	63 378	568	1 920.5	77.4	7.0	0.3	13.2	0.3	14.1	26.5
25 73440	Watertown Town	10.3	34 319	1 095	3 331.9	86.6	3.7	0.7	8.8	0.1	8.4	23.8
25 76030	Westfield	120.0	41 690	897	347.4	91.4	2.6	0.6	3.1	0.3	8.5	9.5
25 77890	West Springfield Town	43.3	28 693	1 290	662.7	86.3	1.6	0.8	4.9	0.0	9.7	15.0
25 78972	Weymouth Town	43.5	55 957	664	1 286.4	89.9	4.4	0.7	6.3	0.6	2.5	9.9
25 81035	Woburn	32.7	39 555	948	1 209.6	87.0	5.3	0.1	7.1	0.3	4.3	15.9
25 82000	Worcester	96.8	184 815	130	1 909.2	76.0	15.0	1.0	7.4	0.2	20.5	21.4
26 00000	MICHIGAN	146 435.1	9 922 576	X	67.8	81.4	15.3	1.4	3.2	0.1	4.6	6.2
26 01380	Allen Park	18.1	27 425	1 342	1 515.2	96.3	3.2	0.9	0.3	0.0	8.6	4.9
26 03000	Ann Arbor	72.1	117 070	234	1 623.7	75.8	9.4	1.2	16.7	0.0	4.6	17.7
26 05920	Battle Creek	110.4	51 589	734	467.3	76.0	21.8	2.0	3.1	0.1	7.5	5.5
26 06020	Bay City	26.3	33 917	1 107	1 289.6	94.7	5.2	1.6	0.7	0.0	8.7	1.3
26 12060	Burton	60.5	28 788	1 285	475.8	93.0	7.2	1.8	0.8	0.1	3.6	1.4
26 21000	Dearborn	62.7	95 171	319	1 517.9	93.4	4.1	0.5	4.4	0.3	3.5	26.5
26 21020	Dearborn Heights	30.4	56 145	660	1 846.9	87.4	9.2	1.1	3.6	0.1	4.3	18.3
26 22000	Detroit	359.4	677 116	21	1 884.0	14.0	82.5	1.1	1.5	0.1	7.3	5.2
26 24120	East Lansing	35.2	48 471	783	1 377.0	79.6	10.1	1.1	12.5	0.1	3.6	15.2
26 24290	Eastpointe	13.3	32 657	1 151	2 455.4	57.3	40.3	1.3	1.8	0.0	3.3	3.3
26 27440	Farmington Hills	86.2	81 330	408	943.5	69.3	19.9	0.8	11.9	0.0	3.1	18.4
26 29000	Flint	86.6	98 310	309	1 135.2	42.6	58.0	2.1	0.6	0.1	3.8	1.1
26 31420	Garden City	15.2	26 920	1 363	1 771.1	96.0	2.7	1.3	0.9	0.0	2.7	3.2
26 34000	Grand Rapids	115.0	195 097	122	1 696.5	72.0	24.0	1.5	2.8	0.1	15.7	9.9
26 38640	Holland	43.0	33 742	1 113	784.7	85.7	5.7	1.4	4.5	0.2	24.5	11.4
26 40680	Inkster	16.2	24 672	1 426	1 523.0	19.7	78.9	1.5	1.4	0.1	2.2	2.8
26 41420	Jackson	28.1	33 133	1 136	1 179.1	75.1	26.0	0.9	0.9	0.1	5.6	1.8
26 42160	Kalamazoo	63.9	76 041	449	1 190.0	74.0	23.7	2.0	3.3	0.1	6.8	6.1
26 42820	Kentwood	54.1	51 357	738	949.3	72.4	19.8	1.9	8.9	0.1	8.6	16.4
26 46000	Lansing	93.4	115 056	242	1 231.9	68.7	27.5	3.1	5.4	0.2	12.6	8.1
26 47800	Lincoln Park	15.3	37 012	1 020	2 419.1	86.8	7.2	1.1	0.4	0.0	16.6	7.4
26 49000	Livonia	92.5	94 635	324	1 023.1	93.5	3.5	0.6	3.5	0.1	2.4	6.9
26 50560	Madison Heights	18.4	30 198	1 238	1 641.2	87.2	8.4	2.2	5.2	0.1	1.0	16.0
26 53780	Midland	87.3	42 200	883	483.4	92.1	2.5	1.0	4.6	0.1	2.4	6.5
26 56020	Mount Pleasant	20.1	26 060	1 396	1 296.5	90.0	5.8	3.8	4.5	0.0	3.2	6.0
26 56320	Muskegon	36.8	38 401	975	1 043.5	65.0	36.4	2.8	0.7	0.0	7.3	2.4
26 59440	Novi	78.4	58 723	629	749.0	73.9	8.1	0.4	18.7	0.2	2.8	18.8

1. Dry land or land partially or temporarily covered by water.   2. May be of any race.

Table D. Cities — **Population**

City	Under 5 years	5 to 17 years	18 to 24 years	25 to 34 years	35 to 44 years	45 to 54 years	55 to 64 years	65 to 74 years	75 years and over	Median age 2010–2014	Percent female 2010–2014	Census counts 2000	Census counts 2010	Percent change 2000–2010	Percent change 2010–2015
	12	13	14	15	16	17	18	19	20	21	22	23	24	25	26
MASSACHUSETTS— Cont'd															
Beverly	5.3	13.8	13.3	11.7	12.9	14.2	14.1	7.9	6.7	39.4	53.4	39 862	39 502	-0.9	4.3
Boston	5.4	11.3	17.4	22.2	12.4	11.3	9.6	5.6	4.9	31.4	52.2	589 141	617 594	4.8	8.0
Braintree Town	5.0	16.4	9.4	12.5	12.3	14.9	13.7	6.5	9.2	41.1	51.6	33 698	35 744	6.1	4.9
Brockton	7.6	18.5	9.2	13.0	13.0	14.2	11.3	7.1	6.1	36.1	52.0	94 304	93 810	-0.5	1.6
Cambridge	4.0	7.3	21.0	27.9	11.8	8.9	8.7	5.9	4.6	30.4	51.8	101 355	105 162	3.8	4.9
Chelsea	9.5	15.8	9.7	20.9	14.9	13.6	6.8	4.9	4.0	31.7	49.4	35 080	35 177	0.3	12.0
Chicopee	5.5	14.0	9.2	15.3	11.5	14.3	12.9	9.2	8.1	40.3	50.9	54 653	55 298	1.2	2.6
Everett	5.0	15.3	9.7	16.2	15.8	15.6	9.6	5.7	7.1	37.3	50.8	38 037	41 667	9.5	10.5
Fall River	6.4	15.2	9.3	14.3	12.7	15.2	10.9	8.4	7.6	38.6	53.3	91 938	88 857	-3.4	-0.1
Fitchburg	6.5	15.2	13.7	14.0	11.4	14.1	11.3	7.1	6.8	35.7	49.5	39 102	40 318	3.1	0.6
Franklin Town	5.7	20.5	9.5	9.6	13.7	16.7	11.7	6.6	6.0	39.7	51.0	29 560	31 635	7.0	4.8
Gloucester	4.7	13.7	7.4	10.6	10.7	16.6	17.6	10.0	8.7	47.0	53.7	30 273	28 789	-4.9	3.4
Haverhill	7.2	15.2	8.8	13.4	13.9	16.3	12.8	6.1	6.5	39.5	52.4	58 969	60 879	3.2	3.1
Holyoke	7.3	17.6	10.1	14.0	12.3	14.4	10.3	5.6	8.3	35.7	52.3	39 838	39 880	0.1	2.0
Lawrence	8.6	19.4	13.1	15.1	12.6	11.9	10.4	4.6	4.5	30.5	52.5	72 043	76 377	6.0	5.0
Leominster	4.9	15.1	8.5	12.3	13.5	17.5	13.3	7.4	7.5	42.2	51.4	41 303	40 759	-1.3	2.0
Lowell	6.9	15.6	12.8	17.9	12.1	13.5	10.6	5.6	5.0	33.0	50.2	105 167	106 519	1.3	3.9
Lynn	8.0	18.2	9.8	16.7	12.3	13.6	10.4	6.2	4.8	33.5	51.6	89 050	90 329	1.4	2.4
Malden	5.9	13.3	11.2	19.0	14.5	14.2	11.3	5.4	5.2	35.4	51.8	56 340	59 450	5.5	2.7
Marlborough	7.9	14.4	7.5	15.4	15.2	14.9	13.0	5.6	6.2	38.9	49.4	36 255	38 499	6.2	3.4
Medford	5.6	9.7	12.7	19.4	13.0	12.7	12.0	7.0	7.8	36.5	52.7	55 765	56 173	0.7	2.0
Melrose	7.0	14.3	5.2	12.8	18.1	15.7	11.7	8.5	6.7	41.3	51.5	27 134	26 983	-0.6	3.8
Methuen Town	6.4	17.6	7.6	11.6	14.7	14.9	12.8	8.1	6.4	39.6	50.2	43 789	47 255	7.9	5.1
New Bedford	6.3	15.8	9.5	15.3	12.8	13.1	12.0	7.2	8.0	37.1	52.3	93 768	95 072	1.4	-0.1
Newton	5.7	16.1	12.4	9.3	13.5	13.7	13.1	8.6	7.5	40.1	52.8	83 829	85 146	1.6	4.3
Northampton	3.8	12.9	15.6	12.9	11.6	14.1	13.5	8.5	7.1	39.0	55.8	28 978	28 549	-1.5	0.0
Peabody	4.5	13.9	8.6	11.0	12.1	15.9	13.5	9.0	11.4	45.0	52.3	48 129	51 251	6.5	2.4
Pittsfield	5.6	13.7	8.6	12.5	11.4	14.1	15.2	9.8	9.1	43.7	52.4	45 793	44 737	-2.3	-3.2
Quincy	6.2	10.5	9.1	19.4	12.6	15.6	11.4	7.2	7.9	38.5	51.1	88 025	92 271	4.8	1.5
Revere	5.7	13.2	7.3	17.2	16.6	14.9	11.6	7.2	6.4	39.5	47.5	47 283	51 755	9.5	3.3
Salem	5.1	11.9	13.3	15.2	12.2	14.7	14.1	6.9	6.5	38.2	53.9	40 407	41 340	2.3	3.7
Somerville	5.2	8.2	13.8	31.2	14.7	10.1	7.1	5.1	4.6	31.5	50.9	77 478	75 754	-2.2	6.2
Springfield	7.1	19.5	13.3	13.8	11.8	12.5	10.8	6.2	5.1	32.5	52.2	152 082	153 060	0.6	0.7
Taunton	6.0	14.6	9.1	12.7	13.7	16.5	13.8	7.0	6.7	40.9	51.4	55 976	55 874	-0.2	1.6
Waltham	5.0	8.9	16.7	20.7	13.9	12.1	10.6	6.4	5.7	33.9	52.4	59 226	60 632	2.4	4.5
Watertown Town	6.0	9.5	5.3	22.7	15.1	15.2	10.3	9.6	6.3	38.3	51.2	32 986	31 915	-3.2	7.5
Westfield	6.4	14.5	16.7	10.7	11.0	13.9	13.2	7.6	6.1	37.0	51.0	40 072	41 094	2.6	1.5
West Springfield Town	5.7	16.0	10.5	14.2	11.7	13.7	13.2	7.6	7.4	38.0	51.7	27 899	28 391	1.8	1.1
Weymouth Town	4.5	16.0	6.9	10.5	14.6	16.7	14.7	8.6	7.5	43.3	52.6	53 988	53 743	-0.5	4.1
Woburn	6.7	13.1	6.2	19.1	12.7	14.2	13.6	7.0	7.5	39.0	49.9	37 258	38 120	2.3	3.7
Worcester	6.8	15.1	14.8	15.4	12.0	13.0	10.9	6.1	5.9	33.3	52.2	172 648	181 045	4.9	2.1
MICHIGAN	5.8	17.1	10.1	11.9	12.4	14.7	13.4	8.0	6.5	39.4	50.9	9 938 444	9 883 640	-0.6	0.4
Allen Park	5.4	15.7	8.8	10.7	13.1	15.9	13.8	7.4	9.2	42.4	52.8	29 376	28 210	-4.0	-2.8
Ann Arbor	4.2	10.0	30.0	17.4	9.5	9.2	9.5	5.5	4.7	27.7	49.9	114 024	113 934	-0.1	2.7
Battle Creek	7.7	18.2	9.6	13.6	12.4	13.1	11.5	7.2	6.8	35.5	52.3	53 364	52 347	-1.9	-1.4
Bay City	7.4	17.4	11.1	13.4	12.1	14.2	12.2	6.1	6.0	35.5	51.4	36 817	34 932	-5.1	-2.9
Burton	5.6	18.3	8.3	11.9	12.2	17.1	12.6	6.9	7.2	39.7	50.3	30 308	29 999	-1.0	-4.0
Dearborn	8.3	21.6	10.0	13.1	12.3	11.5	11.5	5.3	6.4	32.4	51.2	97 775	98 153	0.4	-3.0
Dearborn Heights	7.0	17.7	9.0	12.8	12.1	13.5	12.8	6.6	8.5	38.2	51.5	58 264	57 774	-0.8	-2.8
Detroit	7.1	18.4	12.1	12.3	12.4	13.2	12.3	6.7	5.5	35.1	52.5	951 270	713 777	-25.0	-5.1
East Lansing	2.3	5.8	60.5	10.2	5.0	4.0	5.6	3.1	3.4	21.4	48.8	46 525	48 579	4.4	-0.2
Eastpointe	6.0	20.2	9.9	11.4	14.6	14.2	11.7	6.4	5.6	36.3	52.8	34 077	32 442	-4.8	0.7
Farmington Hills	4.8	15.0	7.6	12.1	13.2	14.2	15.4	8.7	9.0	42.9	52.8	82 111	79 740	-2.9	2.0
Flint	7.6	18.2	11.1	13.5	12.1	13.9	11.9	6.4	5.2	34.6	51.5	124 943	102 434	-18.0	-4.0
Garden City	6.6	14.7	8.1	13.4	12.4	17.3	13.4	7.1	6.9	40.8	50.2	30 047	27 692	-7.8	-2.8
Grand Rapids	7.9	16.4	14.2	17.5	11.8	10.9	10.0	5.2	6.2	31.1	51.3	197 800	188 040	-4.9	3.7
Holland	8.2	17.0	19.1	13.1	10.9	10.2	9.8	4.5	7.3	29.6	51.4	35 048	33 051	-5.7	1.9
Inkster	8.5	21.3	10.3	12.4	12.7	12.8	11.4	6.0	4.6	32.8	53.2	30 115	25 369	-15.8	-2.7
Jackson	9.2	20.7	9.8	16.1	11.3	11.0	11.0	5.9	4.2	31.0	54.2	36 316	33 534	-7.7	-1.2
Kalamazoo	5.5	14.6	28.3	13.6	10.9	8.8	8.8	4.2	5.4	25.7	49.7	77 145	74 262	-3.7	2.4
Kentwood	6.8	16.4	11.8	16.3	12.3	14.9	9.8	5.9	5.8	33.8	52.6	45 255	48 707	7.6	5.4
Lansing	7.7	15.7	13.5	16.9	12.4	12.2	11.5	5.7	4.5	32.0	52.5	119 128	114 297	-4.1	0.7
Lincoln Park	6.6	17.1	9.0	14.0	13.6	14.1	14.5	5.3	5.7	37.4	52.3	40 008	38 144	-4.7	-3.0
Livonia	4.6	15.3	7.5	11.3	11.7	16.7	15.2	8.8	9.1	44.7	50.9	100 545	96 942	-3.6	-2.4
Madison Heights	7.2	12.1	9.0	18.0	13.1	14.4	12.1	7.1	7.0	37.6	51.3	31 101	29 694	-4.5	1.7
Midland	5.8	16.9	10.3	13.1	11.6	14.3	12.3	6.7	9.1	37.9	51.9	41 685	41 863	0.4	0.8
Mount Pleasant	3.2	8.5	49.7	12.0	6.0	7.1	6.2	3.7	3.7	22.2	54.2	25 946	26 016	0.3	0.2
Muskegon	6.9	14.9	12.5	15.0	11.8	14.9	12.1	5.7	6.4	35.7	47.9	40 105	38 401	-4.2	0.0
Novi	5.2	18.8	7.3	10.8	15.7	16.9	11.9	6.3	7.1	40.8	51.6	47 386	55 224	16.5	6.3

Table D. Cities — Households, Group Quarters, Crime, and Education

City	Households, 2010-2014				Persons in group quarters, 2010				Serious crimes known to police,[2] 2014				Educational attainment, 2010–2014		
			Percent			Institutional			Total		Rate[3]			Attainment[4] (percent)	
	Number	Persons per house-hold	Female family house-holder[1]	One-person	Total	Total	Persons in nursing facilities	Non-institu-tional	Number	Rate[3]	Violent	Property	Population age 25 and older	High school graduate or less	Bachelor's degree or more
	27	28	29	30	31	32	33	34	35	36	37	38	39	40	41
MASSACHUSETTS—Cont'd															
Beverly	15 925	2.54	10.4	31.4	2 514	533	369	1 981	552	1 346	190	1 155	27 701	29.0	45.4
Boston	251 212	2.55	16.9	37.4	46 214	6 697	3 280	39 517	22 018	3 365	726	2 639	421 038	37.1	44.6
Braintree Town	13 226	2.76	11.7	25.0	545	524	514	21	890	2 401	237	2 164	25 320	35.2	37.0
Brockton	32 966	2.86	24.1	26.9	1 768	1 088	790	680	3 900	4 130	1 052	3 079	60 335	53.7	18.1
Cambridge	44 013	2.43	8.3	41.3	17 102	324	277	16 778	2 912	2 691	279	2 412	72 099	15.4	74.7
Chelsea	11 862	3.13	23.0	28.1	682	570	570	112	1 483	3 862	1 112	2 750	23 875	66.8	16.4
Chicopee	22 921	2.43	14.6	32.7	1 155	341	231	814	1 693	3 032	385	2 647	38 946	53.4	17.8
Everett	15 350	2.79	20.6	24.5	191	150	150	41	1 045	2 410	404	2 006	29 028	58.0	16.1
Fall River	38 655	2.30	19.0	36.1	1 735	1 071	994	664	3 229	3 632	1 167	2 464	61 571	61.3	13.8
Fitchburg	14 782	2.73	16.9	27.1	2 538	669	356	1 869	1 491	3 682	815	2 867	25 701	50.0	20.6
Franklin Town	10 992	2.95	8.0	20.9	875	79	72	796	110	335	15	320	20 471	25.7	51.5
Gloucester	12 201	2.40	10.9	30.5	450	230	216	220	331	1 118	307	810	21 863	40.6	32.7
Haverhill	23 529	2.63	16.2	29.0	1 300	671	618	629	1 839	2 940	699	2 241	42 358	40.8	28.7
Holyoke	15 599	2.57	25.9	30.2	1 385	1 086	934	299	2 643	6 552	967	5 586	26 234	51.0	23.2
Lawrence	26 328	2.94	31.7	24.1	902	542	310	360	2 897	3 706	1 094	2 612	46 025	63.5	11.9
Leominster	16 751	2.44	10.6	30.1	327	251	224	76	1 442	3 502	658	2 844	29 139	45.0	26.4
Lowell	38 639	2.81	19.4	29.1	4 346	1 112	1 101	3 234	3 399	3 098	546	2 552	70 313	54.9	21.6
Lynn	32 764	2.79	23.4	28.3	835	284	263	551	2 999	3 255	777	2 478	58 557	54.1	19.3
Malden	22 851	2.64	13.5	28.1	373	116	116	257	1 327	2 178	359	1 819	42 204	45.0	31.7
Marlborough	15 740	2.49	8.8	32.3	661	286	253	375	829	2 086	340	1 746	28 072	39.8	39.2
Medford	22 126	2.58	9.8	26.6	1 959	479	465	1 480	957	1 663	184	1 479	41 120	33.1	45.0
Melrose	11 304	2.43	7.9	29.8	267	229	223	38	296	1 059	111	948	20 275	24.2	50.5
Methuen Town	17 584	2.74	13.8	25.8	420	277	232	143	883	1 804	194	1 610	32 691	42.9	28.7
New Bedford	39 088	2.43	20.8	34.1	1 966	1 415	1 196	551	4 564	4 786	1 258	3 527	64 299	61.0	15.3
Newton	31 175	2.79	8.2	24.9	7 103	483	474	6 620	811	912	68	845	56 779	12.5	75.9
Northampton	11 637	2.46	10.8	37.1	3 156	846	527	2 310	825	2 898	464	2 435	19 462	23.9	56.0
Peabody	21 686	2.39	10.6	33.2	520	397	389	123	1 028	1 963	267	1 696	38 178	43.8	28.8
Pittsfield	19 541	2.26	16.0	36.9	1 184	894	501	290	1 539	3 506	444	3 062	32 081	43.9	26.0
Quincy	39 643	2.34	10.7	36.5	1 400	729	698	671	1 894	2 014	419	1 595	69 016	37.6	40.0
Revere	20 110	2.65	17.1	32.0	280	228	228	52	1 389	2 553	557	1 996	39 105	56.5	19.0
Salem	18 148	2.33	15.7	37.5	1 770	167	156	1 603	1 311	3 060	359	2 700	29 030	34.0	38.1
Somerville	31 784	2.44	10.2	32.1	2 269	37	22	2 232	1 437	1 801	267	1 534	55 835	31.1	55.5
Springfield	56 130	2.74	27.9	29.1	5 677	954	553	4 723	7 585	4 933	1 091	3 842	92 450	55.0	17.9
Taunton	21 859	2.56	14.8	28.7	784	574	406	210	845	1 502	371	1 130	39 287	53.7	18.5
Waltham	23 873	2.59	9.2	34.6	6 686	308	287	6 378	872	1 390	196	1 194	42 039	34.4	48.4
Watertown Town	14 449	2.28	7.4	34.4	234	104	0	130	470	1 409	93	1 316	25 447	24.9	57.7
Westfield	14 909	2.77	13.9	27.9	2 976	359	294	2 617	618	1 495	208	1 287	25 788	39.0	30.2
West Springfield Town	11 400	2.50	15.4	31.6	170	120	120	50	1 414	4 915	431	4 484	19 602	42.3	28.5
Weymouth Town	22 559	2.43	12.8	33.2	460	373	373	87	812	1 450	239	1 211	39 989	37.6	32.0
Woburn	14 914	2.60	10.7	29.3	323	238	238	85	586	1 487	180	1 307	28 558	40.4	35.3
Worcester	68 000	2.68	17.8	32.5	12 152	2 093	1 845	10 059	7 380	4 027	965	3 063	116 083	45.2	30.1
MICHIGAN	3 827 880	2.58	12.8	28.9	229 068	109 867	42 473	119 201	244 895	2 471	427	2 044	6 619 834	40.9	26.4
Allen Park	10 956	2.54	13.0	28.0	171	138	132	33	610	2 214	189	2 025	19 767	42.2	22.9
Ann Arbor	46 497	2.49	6.6	37.9	11 840	78	61	11 762	2 410	2 046	166	1 881	65 148	11.4	70.9
Battle Creek	20 502	2.53	18.1	33.9	1 399	862	228	537	2 835	4 630	786	3 845	33 896	43.9	21.3
Bay City	14 134	2.45	16.4	34.5	515	180	0	335	1 187	3 460	531	2 929	22 670	50.1	16.2
Burton	11 643	2.53	16.3	27.8	111	0	0	111	1 360	4 690	476	4 214	20 178	48.5	15.0
Dearborn	31 647	3.06	10.9	28.7	226	195	180	31	3 482	3 650	359	3 292	58 491	41.4	29.2
Dearborn Heights	20 984	2.72	12.9	29.8	602	504	344	98	1 423	2 525	380	2 145	38 065	47.7	20.6
Detroit	254 197	2.74	29.0	38.1	14 759	6 541	3 365	8 218	46 617	6 808	1 990	4 819	434 788	54.6	13.1
East Lansing	13 705	3.55	5.3	37.8	15 701	193	193	15 508	839	1 728	284	1 444	14 622	11.7	69.8
Eastpointe	12 399	2.62	24.5	30.8	21	0	0	21	1 295	3 963	826	3 137	20 755	50.1	13.4
Farmington Hills	34 219	2.36	8.7	32.9	319	319	251	374	1 085	1 328	116	1 212	58 175	21.5	52.8
Flint	40 509	2.48	26.8	37.0	3 193	988	85	2 205	5 588	5 635	1 709	3 926	62 902	53.0	11.3
Garden City	10 279	2.66	13.7	26.6	54	0	0	54	443	1 639	215	1 424	19 182	53.1	11.8
Grand Rapids	72 536	2.63	16.1	32.7	8 260	3 298	2 011	4 962	6 555	3 390	714	2 675	117 051	39.5	30.7
Holland	11 452	2.91	13.6	25.8	2 723	283	273	2 440	1 149	3 421	426	2 995	18 867	42.6	30.4
Inkster	9 466	2.65	30.2	36.2	230	18	3	212	1 070	4 324	1 229	3 096	15 256	51.2	10.4
Jackson	12 851	2.59	24.4	34.0	773	468	263	305	1 727	5 170	895	4 275	20 209	49.2	14.9
Kalamazoo	28 064	2.68	15.5	35.1	7 462	1 126	489	6 336	3 791	4 998	1 165	3 832	38 737	31.2	33.1
Kentwood	19 708	2.52	15.8	28.1	395	246	114	149	1 651	3 262	358	2 904	32 301	37.4	33.1
Lansing	48 288	2.37	17.6	36.8	1 181	273	120	908	4 865	4 271	1 119	3 153	72 116	37.8	25.1
Lincoln Park	14 659	2.57	16.5	31.8	64	13	0	51	1 428	3 846	587	3 259	25 269	59.4	8.2
Livonia	37 262	2.57	8.7	27.7	1 366	791	764	575	1 899	2 002	125	1 877	69 482	30.9	35.8
Madison Heights	12 945	2.32	12.3	37.8	156	149	149	7	779	2 566	231	2 335	21 331	45.7	21.8
Midland	17 603	2.39	10.3	32.2	1 159	489	352	670	598	1 415	118	1 297	27 909	27.0	42.2
Mount Pleasant	8 116	3.22	9.5	33.3	6 365	442	286	5 923	557	2 124	248	1 876	9 947	28.2	40.8
Muskegon	13 825	2.74	22.6	37.2	5 199	4 459	426	740	2 077	5 619	822	4 797	24 527	57.1	11.4
Novi	23 001	2.47	7.6	31.8	360	316	316	44	899	1 533	78	1 454	38 766	19.9	55.9

1. No spouse present.   2. Data for serious crimes have not been adjusted for underreporting. This may affect comparability between geographic areas and over time.   3. Per 100,000 population estimated by the FBI.   4. Persons 25 years old and over.

City	Per capita income[1] (dollars) (42)	Median income (43)	Percent with income of $200,000 or more (44)	Percent with income of less than $25,000 (45)	Families with income below poverty (percent) (46)	Total (47)	Percent change, 2000–2010 (48)	Vacant units for sale or rent[2] (49)	Total (50)	Percent (51)	Median value[3] (dollars) (52)	With a mortgage[4] (53)	Without a mortgage[5] (54)
MASSACHUSETTS— Cont'd													
Beverly	39 471	73 980	8.1	18.8	5.4	16 641	2.2	791	15 925	61.0	366 500	25.0	13.8
Boston	34 770	54 485	7.7	29.2	17.1	272 481	8.2	19 782	251 212	34.2	379 500	25.1	14.5
Braintree Town	37 301	87 500	8.7	12.7	4.3	14 302	10.7	566	13 226	71.2	368 100	24.3	13.9
Brockton	22 466	48 569	2.0	27.6	15.1	35 552	2.1	2 249	32 966	55.9	221 200	29.0	16.9
Cambridge	48 446	75 909	12.9	20.1	10.2	47 291	5.7	3 259	44 013	36.1	552 600	22.2	12.3
Chelsea	21 523	48 725	2.3	28.4	20.0	12 621	2.3	790	11 862	28.0	261 200	29.4	18.5
Chicopee	25 251	47 276	1.2	25.2	9.4	25 140	2.9	1 401	22 921	56.9	174 300	22.5	15.5
Everett	23 419	51 056	2.0	23.2	12.2	16 715	5.1	1 172	15 350	38.9	311 900	33.0	15.6
Fall River	21 201	33 763	0.9	38.8	19.6	42 750	2.1	4 293	38 655	35.8	234 500	27.8	17.4
Fitchburg	22 720	46 628	1.3	30.1	14.3	17 117	7.0	1 952	14 782	54.7	185 900	25.1	18.2
Franklin Town	42 444	101 980	15.1	11.0	2.6	11 394	10.3	399	10 992	79.3	381 600	22.1	13.9
Gloucester	37 005	60 229	6.3	21.5	6.3	14 557	4.3	2 071	12 201	62.4	362 200	28.9	17.1
Haverhill	30 348	61 208	4.4	20.3	10.1	25 657	8.1	1 507	23 529	61.8	256 600	24.8	14.3
Holyoke	21 671	35 550	2.2	39.3	27.1	16 384	1.1	1 023	15 599	40.2	186 100	23.9	13.7
Lawrence	17 295	34 496	1.3	37.7	26.1	27 137	6.0	1 956	26 328	28.0	211 900	30.2	14.2
Leominster	30 055	59 263	2.6	23.3	9.1	17 873	5.3	1 106	16 751	54.6	232 000	25.1	15.1
Lowell	23 046	49 164	2.3	27.8	16.1	41 431	5.0	2 961	38 639	44.4	228 000	26.8	14.3
Lynn	23 457	47 195	2.9	29.1	17.9	35 776	3.1	2 466	32 764	45.6	251 000	27.6	17.1
Malden	26 760	55 523	3.3	24.0	12.7	25 161	6.5	1 488	22 851	41.4	328 800	27.7	13.7
Marlborough	37 368	71 424	6.8	15.0	5.0	16 416	10.2	1 021	15 740	55.9	299 400	24.1	14.8
Medford	36 636	77 868	5.9	14.9	6.7	24 046	6.0	1 236	22 126	57.5	392 700	27.4	16.1
Melrose	43 866	86 409	9.6	12.8	2.2	11 751	4.5	538	11 304	67.2	423 500	23.6	14.3
Methuen Town	31 023	68 587	5.2	17.2	6.7	18 340	8.6	811	17 584	71.2	279 100	23.8	14.6
New Bedford	21 181	36 813	0.9	36.0	20.6	42 933	3.4	4 172	39 088	42.5	210 200	28.8	17.4
Newton	64 475	118 639	28.7	11.0	3.9	32 648	1.7	1 480	31 175	69.7	715 000	22.7	13.8
Northampton	35 516	58 179	6.0	22.9	8.4	12 728	2.6	728	11 637	57.2	280 300	24.5	14.6
Peabody	34 316	62 234	4.5	19.1	5.5	22 220	17.6	907	21 686	63.8	331 000	26.4	15.3
Pittsfield	26 913	43 489	2.7	30.3	14.1	21 487	0.6	1 834	19 541	60.7	172 500	23.4	15.6
Quincy	33 932	62 710	4.5	20.1	7.6	42 838	6.8	2 180	39 643	47.6	342 600	27.1	16.8
Revere	26 269	50 900	2.5	25.9	13.2	22 100	9.5	1 646	20 110	49.4	305 500	31.8	19.9
Salem	31 965	59 044	4.1	25.5	11.8	19 130	5.3	1 288	18 148	49.2	303 100	26.9	19.8
Somerville	36 229	66 866	6.2	19.0	9.9	33 720	3.8	1 615	31 784	34.3	449 100	26.0	17.8
Springfield	18 435	34 731	1.4	39.5	25.6	61 706	0.9	4 954	56 130	47.8	146 500	25.6	16.5
Taunton	26 461	52 225	2.2	23.9	9.5	23 896	4.3	1 564	21 859	63.4	239 500	26.8	15.7
Waltham	35 642	73 162	6.8	18.2	7.1	24 926	4.4	1 236	23 873	49.3	411 400	24.6	15.5
Watertown Town	45 822	86 461	9.8	13.8	4.8	15 584	3.8	875	14 449	52.5	438 900	24.7	15.6
Westfield	27 664	60 845	4.0	21.1	6.5	16 075	4.1	740	14 909	67.3	221 800	22.8	14.5
West Springfield Town	27 356	52 806	2.3	25.4	8.6	12 697	3.6	573	11 400	60.3	200 000	23.4	16.7
Weymouth Town	35 162	69 099	4.2	15.1	4.8	23 480	4.0	1 045	22 559	66.9	316 200	25.6	15.9
Woburn	35 767	77 883	5.1	14.0	5.5	16 309	6.0	785	14 914	61.4	365 500	24.0	14.7
Worcester	24 447	46 105	3.1	30.9	17.4	74 645	5.5	6 032	68 000	44.0	210 200	25.9	14.6
MICHIGAN	26 143	49 087	3.3	25.2	12.1	4 532 233	7.0	659 725	3 827 880	71.5	120 200	22.6	13.4
Allen Park	28 866	60 655	2.3	17.8	4.7	12 206	-0.4	626	10 956	86.2	94 300	19.8	13.3
Ann Arbor	36 074	56 835	7.4	23.7	7.2	49 789	5.5	2 729	46 497	45.7	231 700	21.8	12.3
Battle Creek	22 010	37 885	2.3	32.2	17.5	24 277	3.1	3 159	20 502	60.7	81 300	22.6	13.8
Bay City	19 616	36 179	0.8	34.4	17.6	15 923	-2.1	1 487	14 134	69.1	68 800	22.6	13.9
Burton	22 013	42 002	1.4	28.8	15.8	13 075	5.9	1 111	11 643	73.2	69 500	24.1	13.6
Dearborn	21 311	46 776	2.7	28.4	23.5	37 871	-2.8	3 529	31 647	68.3	102 800	24.2	14.9
Dearborn Heights	21 753	44 440	1.5	28.2	16.2	24 068	0.6	1 802	20 984	74.8	81 900	24.3	14.4
Detroit	14 984	26 095	0.7	48.5	34.8	349 170	-6.9	79 725	254 197	50.7	45 100	28.6	17.4
East Lansing	19 256	33 064	6.0	41.6	10.6	15 787	3.1	1 013	13 705	34.8	174 100	21.4	10.4
Eastpointe	19 090	40 997	0.5	31.3	19.7	13 796	-1.2	1 239	12 399	70.8	58 800	25.9	16.3
Farmington Hills	41 340	71 061	8.8	15.9	6.0	36 178	3.8	2 619	34 219	62.1	200 100	21.6	12.4
Flint	14 527	24 679	0.4	50.6	36.0	51 321	-7.5	10 849	40 509	55.5	36 700	26.6	15.9
Garden City	23 333	51 461	0.6	21.0	8.6	11 616	-0.9	722	10 279	81.5	80 100	22.3	14.0
Grand Rapids	20 542	39 913	1.4	31.5	19.2	80 619	3.4	8 493	72 536	55.1	107 800	22.0	12.6
Holland	21 044	44 619	1.9	23.8	13.0	13 212	5.2	1 191	11 452	63.9	115 800	22.5	12.9
Inkster	15 277	27 849	0.0	45.6	32.3	11 647	-3.0	1 826	9 466	51.2	51 700	26.6	16.9
Jackson	15 570	27 342	0.6	45.9	33.4	15 457	1.4	2 163	12 851	51.2	65 100	22.8	14.7
Kalamazoo	19 064	32 959	1.8	38.5	22.3	32 433	2.0	3 292	28 064	45.5	98 000	22.4	13.9
Kentwood	25 256	49 201	1.9	23.3	11.5	21 584	10.7	1 843	19 708	59.1	125 400	22.3	14.9
Lansing	19 430	35 675	0.6	35.4	23.5	54 181	1.8	5 731	48 288	51.6	79 600	23.4	14.5
Lincoln Park	19 681	39 871	0.3	29.3	16.9	16 530	-1.7	1 606	14 659	71.1	58 700	23.2	14.6
Livonia	32 520	69 386	3.6	13.2	3.5	40 401	4.5	1 687	37 262	84.8	153 800	21.1	12.3
Madison Heights	22 740	40 820	1.3	29.9	15.1	13 685	0.5	973	12 945	62.4	80 300	22.5	13.6
Midland	30 715	50 433	5.9	25.5	10.6	18 578	4.7	1 072	17 603	63.4	137 900	19.4	11.7
Mount Pleasant	16 254	29 107	2.6	46.0	21.1	8 981	0.8	605	8 116	35.1	123 200	19.8	11.8
Muskegon	14 533	25 989	0.4	48.3	31.4	16 105	0.5	2 138	13 825	49.6	63 300	24.0	13.1
Novi	44 800	80 299	12.5	11.5	4.1	24 226	23.2	1 968	23 001	65.9	235 600	20.0	13.2

1. Based on population estimated by the American Community Survey.   2. Includes units rented or sold but not occupied.   3. Specified owner-occupied units; $1,000,000 represents $1,000,000 or more.   4. 50.0 represents 50 percent or more.   5. 10.0 represents 10 percent or less.

Table D. Cities — **Housing, Labor Force, and Employment**

City	Occupied housing units, 2010–2014 (cont.)				Migration, 2010–2014		Civilian labor force, 2015		Unemployment		Civilian employment[4], 2010–2014		Percent	
	Percent renter occupied	Median gross rent[1]	Median gross rent as a percent of income[2]	Percent with no vehicle available	Percent who lived in the same house one year ago	Percent who lived outside current city one year ago	Total	Percent change, 2014–2015	Total	Rate[3]	Population age 16 and older	In labor force	Civilian full-year full-time workers	Households with no workers (percent)
	55	56	57	58	59	60	61	62	63	64	65	66	67	68
MASSACHUSETTS—Cont'd														
Beverly	39.0	1 068	28.9	9.9	87.1	9.4	22 568	-0.3	1 005	4.5	33 831	68.3	41.2	27.2
Boston	65.8	1 298	30.9	35.5	78.2	11.0	358 648	0.7	16 376	4.6	545 208	68.2	39.9	27.2
Braintree Town	28.8	1 324	31.6	8.2	91.1	6.3	20 215	0.6	904	4.5	29 385	69.9	42.7	22.6
Brockton	44.1	1 039	35.9	17.0	86.1	6.2	47 037	0.2	3 284	7.0	72 801	66.5	36.7	28.7
Cambridge	63.9	1 656	29.1	31.2	73.1	19.4	63 861	0.9	2 014	3.2	95 376	67.6	40.7	25.6
Chelsea	72.0	1 165	30.4	30.1	85.2	8.2	19 388	0.6	977	5.0	28 344	71.8	41.0	25.1
Chicopee	43.1	814	29.4	11.2	87.1	7.8	27 378	-0.3	1 810	6.6	45 746	63.4	37.9	33.9
Everett	61.1	1 210	33.5	16.9	87.3	9.7	24 540	0.1	1 133	4.6	34 565	72.5	42.5	22.7
Fall River	64.2	722	31.1	19.3	83.8	6.9	39 583	-0.7	3 493	8.8	72 165	59.7	33.2	40.3
Fitchburg	45.3	860	32.9	14.4	82.0	10.5	19 264	-0.3	1 331	6.9	32 419	64.2	34.8	31.1
Franklin Town	20.7	1 087	24.8	6.0	91.4	7.0	17 457	0.7	711	4.1	24 810	72.7	45.2	18.5
Gloucester	37.6	975	28.3	9.6	90.0	5.8	15 459	0.2	1 022	6.6	24 735	65.5	35.2	30.0
Haverhill	38.2	1 042	32.9	10.1	86.4	6.5	34 032	1.3	1 825	5.4	49 245	68.5	41.8	25.5
Holyoke	59.8	697	31.6	24.7	84.4	8.2	16 128	-0.5	1 305	8.1	31 510	58.7	31.4	38.6
Lawrence	72.0	998	34.1	25.0	83.6	6.6	35 530	0.6	3 395	9.6	58 303	63.5	35.0	29.1
Leominster	45.4	902	28.5	11.0	87.9	6.8	21 737	0.0	1 286	5.9	33 599	69.2	39.4	27.6
Lowell	55.6	1 005	31.5	16.7	83.2	8.4	54 118	0.5	3 508	6.5	86 973	66.9	37.6	28.5
Lynn	54.4	987	32.9	22.2	84.2	6.5	46 546	0.2	2 609	5.6	71 012	67.1	41.4	28.2
Malden	58.6	1 264	31.7	20.6	82.3	13.3	33 041	0.3	1 522	4.6	50 339	70.9	42.4	23.6
Marlborough	44.1	1 142	26.9	7.5	85.4	9.0	23 202	0.2	969	4.2	32 143	74.9	47.7	20.0
Medford	42.5	1 464	27.9	10.4	83.7	12.4	33 193	0.6	1 344	4.0	49 197	69.6	45.0	22.0
Melrose	32.8	1 118	26.0	8.3	87.8	9.0	15 920	0.6	597	3.8	22 385	71.8	47.4	23.3
Methuen Town	28.8	1 026	31.6	7.1	90.8	5.8	26 487	1.4	1 445	5.5	38 150	70.4	44.2	25.8
New Bedford	57.5	769	31.0	19.6	86.2	4.5	46 974	0.0	4 112	8.8	75 587	62.2	33.1	36.0
Newton	30.3	1 672	29.3	6.6	85.2	11.2	46 041	0.5	1 721	3.7	69 875	67.2	42.8	22.3
Northampton	42.8	965	30.2	10.2	82.5	11.3	15 908	0.0	590	3.7	24 616	67.8	35.6	24.5
Peabody	36.2	1 241	32.7	11.0	90.2	6.2	28 515	-0.4	1 297	4.5	43 195	65.4	41.2	31.6
Pittsfield	39.3	762	31.1	14.7	86.3	5.6	21 889	-0.3	1 294	5.9	36 436	64.7	34.3	34.8
Quincy	52.4	1 235	28.8	15.8	83.4	10.9	52 638	0.7	2 560	4.9	79 171	70.4	43.9	24.8
Revere	50.6	1 176	33.6	19.1	85.8	9.5	28 456	0.5	1 420	5.0	44 198	68.5	41.0	26.2
Salem	50.8	1 082	29.5	16.8	81.4	11.9	23 600	-0.5	1 208	5.1	35 607	68.8	41.6	28.5
Somerville	65.7	1 470	27.4	24.9	76.7	17.0	49 395	0.8	1 644	3.3	68 182	74.4	47.6	19.7
Springfield	52.2	813	37.6	23.3	82.8	6.9	63 426	-0.7	5 910	9.3	117 536	58.3	30.1	37.8
Taunton	36.6	912	31.4	10.3	88.3	6.0	29 526	-0.2	1 787	6.1	45 503	66.3	39.7	30.1
Waltham	50.7	1 358	28.0	10.6	81.7	14.1	36 823	0.9	1 440	3.9	53 780	68.3	42.5	22.4
Watertown Town	47.5	1 530	24.8	9.3	83.8	12.9	21 137	0.6	719	3.4	28 249	76.2	52.0	19.0
Westfield	32.7	848	31.8	8.3	85.9	9.2	20 989	0.0	1 218	5.8	33 783	64.8	37.5	27.5
West Springfield Town	39.7	836	27.8	9.6	85.4	11.4	14 468	0.0	803	5.6	23 274	66.0	39.5	28.3
Weymouth Town	33.1	1 138	29.9	8.9	91.4	6.1	30 138	0.6	1 536	5.1	45 117	70.1	42.9	26.5
Woburn	38.6	1 292	27.9	7.8	87.9	8.0	22 364	0.5	968	4.3	32 035	71.7	45.5	21.9
Worcester	56.0	935	32.1	17.6	84.5	7.5	90 301	-0.3	5 455	6.0	147 274	62.6	36.6	30.2
MICHIGAN	28.5	780	32.3	8.0	85.3	11.2	4 750 627	-0.1	257 638	5.4	7 893 971	61.5	35.0	32.1
Allen Park	13.8	932	30.0	4.1	92.0	6.1	13 469	-0.5	641	4.8	23 017	62.4	36.7	32.1
Ann Arbor	54.3	1 042	32.6	12.7	64.6	20.4	63 414	1.2	1 840	2.9	101 651	61.9	32.4	26.9
Battle Creek	39.3	703	32.4	12.0	80.6	10.4	23 676	0.2	1 361	5.7	40 240	60.1	34.0	35.7
Bay City	30.9	551	34.6	12.8	83.5	7.7	16 525	-2.0	1 176	7.1	26 948	61.5	32.8	36.2
Burton	26.8	759	33.6	7.5	86.5	9.3	13 413	-1.1	786	5.9	23 676	59.9	32.4	37.3
Dearborn	31.7	984	37.8	8.3	86.8	6.2	36 765	-0.6	1 758	4.8	70 956	55.2	30.5	32.3
Dearborn Heights	25.2	954	36.3	6.8	88.9	8.1	23 903	-0.8	1 285	5.4	44 548	57.7	31.9	34.1
Detroit	49.3	756	43.2	24.6	83.7	4.3	240 000	-3.3	29 758	12.4	539 755	53.3	23.9	46.0
East Lansing	65.2	876	50.0	10.6	44.3	37.2	23 650	0.8	745	3.2	45 360	52.1	15.6	30.0
Eastpointe	29.2	1 011	34.8	7.7	81.5	15.8	14 874	-1.3	1 311	8.8	25 056	64.0	34.3	35.2
Farmington Hills	37.9	1 019	27.5	5.5	83.8	13.0	42 246	0.7	1 361	3.2	66 124	65.3	42.7	25.2
Flint	44.5	684	46.1	18.8	77.7	8.6	34 555	-2.7	3 605	10.4	77 313	50.3	21.0	50.5
Garden City	18.5	1 008	32.6	5.5	88.3	9.7	14 088	-0.6	699	5.0	22 222	64.3	37.0	29.5
Grand Rapids	44.9	777	33.9	13.7	76.6	12.2	101 115	1.3	4 816	4.8	147 885	66.7	35.3	29.8
Holland	36.1	779	32.0	9.0	75.0	16.7	17 378	1.6	692	4.0	26 100	63.6	33.7	26.4
Inkster	48.8	739	42.6	14.6	80.6	14.8	8 608	-2.7	923	10.7	18 579	57.0	27.0	41.7
Jackson	48.8	635	34.6	17.9	76.2	11.2	13 943	-1.5	1 174	8.4	24 484	60.5	30.8	39.1
Kalamazoo	54.5	721	35.9	13.5	65.3	20.1	36 998	0.6	1 910	5.2	61 922	63.9	28.3	31.5
Kentwood	40.9	787	27.3	9.0	81.4	14.8	29 411	1.8	995	3.4	39 626	69.5	42.0	23.6
Lansing	48.4	743	34.3	12.1	77.0	12.1	57 862	-0.5	3 653	6.3	89 908	65.8	33.4	31.6
Lincoln Park	28.9	804	35.5	9.2	84.5	10.9	16 518	-0.9	925	5.6	29 449	59.5	33.1	33.6
Livonia	15.2	981	26.9	4.2	90.9	6.4	49 282	0.0	1 602	3.3	79 166	64.0	39.8	29.2
Madison Heights	37.6	763	33.1	12.6	85.4	10.8	15 035	-0.6	1 069	7.1	24 995	65.1	37.6	31.8
Midland	36.6	731	30.4	7.1	81.2	12.0	21 324	0.0	800	3.8	33 704	60.8	35.7	31.4
Mount Pleasant	64.9	701	42.8	12.6	51.3	30.3	13 089	0.0	603	4.6	23 543	58.9	18.6	28.4
Muskegon	50.4	630	39.1	19.7	73.4	16.7	14 340	-1.2	1 335	9.3	30 210	50.9	23.2	42.8
Novi	34.1	1 053	24.4	3.8	86.2	11.3	30 659	0.6	1 034	3.4	44 651	69.3	47.1	22.4

1. $2,000 represents $2,000 or more.   2. 50.0 represents 50 percent or more.   3. Percent of civilian labor force.   4. Persons 16 years old and over.

Table D. Cities — Construction, Wholesale Trade, and Retail Trade

City	Value of residential construction authorized by building permits, 2015			Wholesale trade,[1] 2012				Retail trade,[2] 2012			
	New construction ($1,000)	Number of housing units	Percent single family	Number of establishments	Number of employees	Sales (mil dol)	Annual payroll (mil dol)	Number of establishments	Number of employees	Sales (mil dol)	Annual payroll (mil dol)
	69	70	71	72	73	74	75	76	77	78	79
MASSACHUSETTS— Cont'd											
Beverly	2 725	10	100.0	41	274	134.9	14.2	139	2 099	690.4	75.2
Boston	1 164 407	4 955	1.0	517	9 559	7 074.8	716.3	2 161	28 148	7 885.6	807.6
Braintree Town	2 604	16	6.3	62	1 246	1 014.3	92.0	283	5 695	1 394.2	140.3
Brockton	9 257	67	91.0	60	1 117	2 195.0	66.9	331	4 816	1 305.4	128.6
Cambridge	127 175	535	7.3	75	2 383	1 696.9	498.0	455	6 195	1 366.5	153.5
Chelsea	23 856	223	0.4	83	D	D	D	95	1 884	485.7	43.8
Chicopee	4 784	25	100.0	36	1 193	1 014.4	57.3	158	2 538	728.7	63.1
Everett	18 029	164	3.7	46	1 375	1 194.3	76.1	118	1 880	451.8	43.4
Fall River	5 955	52	88.5	67	1 218	454.9	57.8	284	3 310	811.3	83.8
Fitchburg	3 026	20	100.0	34	292	146.2	13.0	114	1 234	318.6	30.9
Franklin Town	11 486	37	100.0	45	1 609	1 499.3	91.0	106	1 651	413.7	42.4
Gloucester	15 148	33	87.9	47	385	675.1	24.3	129	1 514	344.3	37.0
Haverhill	13 677	105	21.9	48	626	261.0	36.0	146	2 420	677.7	59.5
Holyoke	885	6	33.3	25	483	149.6	23.2	229	4 017	717.2	79.8
Lawrence	2 044	18	44.4	57	1 311	899.2	103.3	196	1 593	486.4	47.3
Leominster	10 850	92	44.6	45	541	290.1	30.7	234	4 584	1 004.1	91.2
Lowell	5 709	58	55.2	58	945	501.5	51.4	225	2 474	725.6	63.0
Lynn	3 044	20	100.0	38	381	402.6	21.4	221	2 345	668.2	65.5
Malden	1 103	10	100.0	36	398	295.8	23.5	133	1 280	330.2	30.2
Marlborough	3 588	27	100.0	79	1 587	1 340.6	120.7	221	3 452	800.8	76.1
Medford	1 391	12	33.3	44	789	301.8	41.7	163	2 317	692.4	61.9
Melrose	6 325	40	27.5	4	D	D	D	57	664	178.2	19.3
Methuen Town	34 885	116	98.3	33	D	D	D	110	2 240	530.3	52.5
New Bedford	2 476	24	100.0	98	1 933	1 299.7	92.6	287	3 185	792.3	71.4
Newton	12 203	27	100.0	102	1 642	1 542.7	136.1	322	4 523	1 111.1	136.8
Northampton	10 046	37	89.2	26	D	D	D	176	2 277	548.9	59.6
Peabody	5 368	24	100.0	59	1 497	5 754.2	116.6	298	5 204	1 256.0	134.2
Pittsfield	1 359	6	100.0	54	655	284.0	28.6	186	2 985	789.5	73.5
Quincy	22 344	208	5.3	65	1 188	592.7	97.2	234	4 022	1 113.6	107.2
Revere	8 635	53	11.3	25	D	D	D	117	1 717	422.0	35.8
Salem	2 300	11	100.0	36	274	147.9	14.3	164	2 242	469.6	51.4
Somerville	101 877	604	0.7	39	489	246.5	25.9	183	3 203	759.4	74.0
Springfield	9 431	44	100.0	105	1 487	1 386.7	90.4	468	5 777	1 384.6	134.6
Taunton	9 445	56	69.6	59	2 147	1 566.7	127.8	220	3 261	718.4	76.7
Waltham	14 999	43	65.1	94	D	D	D	232	3 100	1 041.0	97.7
Watertown Town	69 511	389	1.0	31	391	146.2	20.1	144	2 660	889.9	84.5
Westfield	4 732	22	90.9	43	1 006	1 897.0	45.0	123	1 944	450.2	43.8
West Springfield Town	1 635	12	50.0	58	830	295.0	44.8	194	3 483	1 249.9	105.2
Weymouth Town	19 963	102	24.5	51	343	386.3	19.0	198	2 472	757.5	74.1
Woburn	13 600	43	100.0	201	4 360	2 476.5	299.1	185	3 843	1 053.8	112.2
Worcester	22 110	174	24.7	178	2 454	1 098.5	118.1	564	7 853	1 991.5	198.9
MICHIGAN	3 850 470	18 226	73.5	9 392	132 490	115 704.9	7 474.6	34 858	441 190	119 302.0	10 527.3
Allen Park	0	0	0.0	15	145	113.7	7.8	110	1 877	387.3	37.8
Ann Arbor	6 130	17	100.0	77	452	227.3	27.9	507	8 042	1 758.5	184.5
Battle Creek	2 120	11	100.0	31	440	468.0	21.3	247	3 200	796.6	70.2
Bay City	50	1	100.0	36	614	222.7	22.1	145	1 187	251.0	27.4
Burton	5 875	34	82.4	24	723	162.7	44.1	153	2 299	505.4	52.4
Dearborn	4 926	16	100.0	140	1 314	1 896.2	82.7	539	6 554	1 568.3	147.9
Dearborn Heights	3 106	17	52.9	44	157	69.3	7.1	181	1 602	400.2	33.3
Detroit	79 707	631	4.9	409	7 378	7 269.3	430.5	2 092	11 850	3 196.3	251.5
East Lansing	842	7	100.0	8	45	29.6	3.1	85	1 293	303.8	24.7
Eastpointe	5 478	49	2.0	14	47	9.6	1.2	126	1 120	304.3	35.7
Farmington Hills	6 571	21	100.0	182	2 605	2 587.7	175.7	298	4 091	1 269.7	118.6
Flint	0	0	0.0	62	885	587.8	37.2	377	3 419	740.2	73.0
Garden City	250	1	100.0	12	D	D	D	103	906	326.1	27.0
Grand Rapids	83 422	455	17.8	218	5 550	4 778.9	303.7	545	6 140	1 672.6	164.4
Holland	2 619	14	100.0	36	373	403.2	25.1	158	2 040	571.4	47.2
Inkster	0	0	0.0	5	D	D	D	53	278	74.9	5.5
Jackson	0	0	0.0	58	1 008	615.9	47.2	173	1 735	398.3	41.7
Kalamazoo	6 980	32	56.3	86	1 218	600.9	63.3	271	2 495	586.6	64.1
Kentwood	9 330	93	94.6	128	2 727	1 345.8	152.5	284	4 399	894.9	89.8
Lansing	87 579	461	8.5	107	1 728	2 126.3	82.5	430	6 033	1 623.4	150.3
Lincoln Park	0	0	0.0	10	D	D	D	123	1 315	320.8	29.8
Livonia	9 877	37	100.0	244	3 484	4 012.5	211.0	467	7 544	1 929.3	190.0
Madison Heights	795	8	100.0	107	1 638	1 062.7	88.5	178	3 280	1 059.3	85.0
Midland	8 086	60	63.3	29	219	674.5	13.8	241	3 558	887.7	77.5
Mount Pleasant	4 407	62	9.7	24	292	227.4	10.2	114	2 381	556.0	52.0
Muskegon	3 834	33	100.0	34	808	291.0	37.8	126	1 911	518.1	48.5
Novi	51 201	289	59.9	147	2 514	4 754.7	173.2	355	6 929	1 800.8	168.0

1. Merchant wholesalers except manufacturers' sales branches and offices. 2. Establishments with payroll.

City	Real estate and rental and leasing, 2012				Professional, scientific, and technical services,[1] 2012				Manufacturing, 2012			
	Number of establishments	Number of employees	Receipts (mil dol)	Annual payroll (mil dol)	Number of establishments	Number of employees	Receipts (mil dol)	Annual payroll (mil dol)	Number of establishments	Number of employees	Receipts (mil dol)	Annual payroll (mil dol)
	80	81	82	83	84	85	86	87	88	89	90	91
MASSACHUSETTS—Cont'd												
Beverly	40	226	65.8	9.7	175	1 223	238.9	90.9	56	2 099	594.9	156.1
Boston	1 030	10 940	3 760.4	812.7	3 017	57 617	17 290.7	6 428.1	284	6 965	3 334.5	386.6
Braintree Town	73	1 395	247.5	74.4	206	D	D	D	27	1 842	450.2	140.9
Brockton	51	183	48.0	7.8	133	D	D	D	68	2 022	421.8	87.6
Cambridge	159	983	360.7	52.3	892	24 581	7 324.8	3 022.0	68	1 810	464.6	113.9
Chelsea	33	184	26.2	6.5	33	1 405	47.5	25.6	37	1 604	391.5	69.8
Chicopee	43	164	29.6	4.8	47	544	46.8	19.2	70	3 014	938.8	169.4
Everett	23	85	13.8	3.5	31	D	D	D	45	705	151.2	33.6
Fall River	75	292	51.5	11.1	149	D	D	D	133	4 419	894.1	182.1
Fitchburg	29	98	16.1	3.2	46	227	27.2	11.3	58	1 701	509.9	90.9
Franklin Town	29	123	55.0	8.3	106	944	96.4	50.7	55	3 313	4 723.8	197.9
Gloucester	28	D	D	D	83	D	D	D	47	2 248	D	171.1
Haverhill	46	263	51.1	11.6	91	621	81.2	29.0	82	2 653	719.3	132.3
Holyoke	39	316	32.4	11.8	67	D	D	D	63	1 672	353.9	82.6
Lawrence	42	220	43.9	8.8	69	D	D	D	91	4 080	813.6	189.4
Leominster	43	298	52.5	14.5	96	554	77.1	29.0	88	2 714	1 094.8	142.2
Lowell	68	315	64.8	11.6	132	D	D	D	76	3 530	1 396.0	263.6
Lynn	47	222	58.0	8.5	82	D	D	D	36	3 277	D	241.3
Malden	46	174	44.4	8.5	64	300	35.7	15.4	40	1 439	436.5	64.4
Marlborough	51	206	63.9	9.2	198	D	D	D	66	3 867	1 795.8	295.1
Medford	34	148	53.8	11.0	119	497	67.5	32.1	39	450	77.5	23.5
Melrose	20	72	25.3	3.3	75	253	35.9	14.8	9	84	D	4.4
Methuen Town	38	D	D	D	85	374	54.6	17.4	42	1 448	635.2	85.2
New Bedford	81	296	63.8	12.1	160	D	D	D	109	4 990	1 543.5	202.6
Newton	155	2 297	2 336.2	131.9	607	D	D	D	51	685	D	47.9
Northampton	36	108	218.4	3.4	125	D	D	D	27	1 072	527.1	52.0
Peabody	41	393	75.7	16.1	101	1 263	182.3	85.7	58	2 187	1 063.9	159.0
Pittsfield	40	244	27.7	7.7	133	D	D	D	51	2 555	506.3	168.8
Quincy	84	455	91.4	25.9	266	D	D	D	42	593	D	33.0
Revere	18	219	29.4	6.9	46	146	14.2	4.9	12	D	D	D
Salem	42	206	55.0	8.4	167	D	D	D	33	734	133.0	33.9
Somerville	63	267	60.7	12.9	174	D	D	D	53	1 142	375.5	80.2
Springfield	109	658	100.7	25.0	325	D	D	D	98	4 029	1 528.2	237.0
Taunton	36	109	22.0	4.0	101	1 018	163.9	62.1	49	4 336	1 714.7	436.9
Waltham	106	894	257.3	51.8	385	11 201	2 336.7	1 198.6	95	4 122	1 130.4	244.5
Watertown Town	31	183	55.0	11.5	135	D	D	D	46	1 161	363.5	89.8
Westfield	32	144	31.4	5.0	59	640	85.4	34.6	92	3 103	858.0	169.0
West Springfield Town	34	90	18.2	3.4	78	498	75.3	27.3	59	1 657	439.0	81.8
Weymouth Town	46	182	44.7	10.3	120	1 165	207.3	88.8	33	495	177.0	25.2
Woburn	84	859	163.1	50.3	302	D	D	D	131	4 341	2 050.1	347.5
Worcester	152	707	200.3	28.7	419	D	D	D	163	7 061	2 300.6	426.2
MICHIGAN	7 826	48 706	11 974.5	1 806.9	21 532	238 884	34 273.5	15 936.8	12 444	514 058	238 892.4	27 611.4
Allen Park	21	399	37.1	12.9	55	593	77.8	25.3	19	158	17.2	5.1
Ann Arbor	146	1 591	367.8	76.4	634	5 588	925.1	397.5	66	1 132	201.1	53.4
Battle Creek	42	247	38.5	7.5	93	D	D	D	57	7 973	4 180.7	449.3
Bay City	24	113	12.3	2.3	91	650	61.7	29.7	50	1 974	589.5	118.2
Burton	21	98	15.2	3.2	42	240	33.2	7.1	32	334	106.0	15.6
Dearborn	95	D	D	D	267	11 832	664.8	1 048.8	79	9 205	D	660.1
Dearborn Heights	46	D	D	D	75	257	20.1	8.3	24	172	34.3	8.4
Detroit	266	1 293	212.4	45.8	682	15 164	3 821.7	1 259.7	382	17 613	19 668.1	1 008.9
East Lansing	54	D	D	D	129	D	D	D	5	D	D	0.7
Eastpointe	13	49	6.9	1.7	31	D	D	D	14	137	17.6	4.3
Farmington Hills	168	3 544	490.9	133.8	734	D	D	D	88	1 849	495.7	106.3
Flint	67	440	64.4	15.1	134	D	D	D	70	6 444	D	486.1
Garden City	11	D	D	D	20	103	8.8	3.7	18	204	31.2	9.5
Grand Rapids	194	1 027	162.3	43.8	569	D	D	D	293	17 974	7 029.5	968.4
Holland	46	225	51.8	7.0	82	D	D	D	96	7 866	2 614.0	331.6
Inkster	13	D	D	D	11	D	D	D	14	185	37.6	9.1
Jackson	31	150	23.1	4.0	91	D	D	D	92	2 477	709.6	122.5
Kalamazoo	82	669	66.4	17.7	200	D	D	D	107	3 950	1 417.5	215.2
Kentwood	48	254	101.3	10.2	124	1 622	303.9	103.1	122	9 987	2 414.6	441.7
Lansing	94	511	84.1	20.5	240	D	D	D	90	4 856	3 904.7	289.1
Lincoln Park	11	D	D	D	26	237	17.0	6.5	15	178	D	6.3
Livonia	105	607	124.1	21.4	376	D	D	D	251	9 447	3 667.7	504.5
Madison Heights	41	489	100.2	28.3	109	2 800	341.5	147.8	156	3 674	881.6	195.9
Midland	52	242	34.2	8.1	112	D	D	D	47	5 897	3 495.9	454.0
Mount Pleasant	32	980	57.2	24.5	67	D	D	D	24	434	D	18.6
Muskegon	18	121	14.3	2.7	79	D	D	D	63	3 241	931.9	148.9
Novi	81	388	98.6	16.0	314	4 877	715.8	271.8	73	1 726	450.0	99.4

1. Establishments subject to federal tax.

Table D. Cities — Accommodation and Food Services, Arts, Entertainment, and Recreation, and Health Care and Social Assistance

City	Accommodation and food services, 2012				Arts, entertainment, and recreation,[1] 2012				Health care and social assistance,[1] 2012			
	Number of establishments	Number of employees	Sales (mil dol)	Annual payroll (mil dol)	Number of establishments	Number of employees	Receipts (mil dol)	Annual payroll (mil dol)	Number of establishments	Number of employees	Receipts (mil dol)	Annual payroll (mil dol)
	92	93	94	95	96	97	98	99	100	101	102	103
MASSACHUSETTS—Cont'd												
Beverly	115	D	D	D	20	D	D	D	128	D	D	D
Boston	2 276	52 474	4 409.2	1 271.2	215	D	D	D	935	18 605	3 118.9	1 413.4
Braintree Town	124	2 474	142.7	42.4	18	D	D	D	86	2 494	250.8	104.6
Brockton	153	2 206	123.9	36.4	10	166	6.5	1.8	193	5 657	650.7	302.7
Cambridge	466	9 912	784.2	227.4	46	771	164.9	19.5	226	3 649	628.1	254.3
Chelsea	71	746	46.9	11.9	2	D	D	D	35	629	48.9	22.2
Chicopee	115	1 553	79.4	22.2	5	55	4.4	1.1	45	1 055	113.9	43.4
Everett	91	D	D	D	5	109	5.6	1.7	38	D	D	D
Fall River	182	D	D	D	12	120	7.1	1.8	196	5 222	598.4	259.4
Fitchburg	83	1 145	56.0	14.9	3	D	D	D	68	1 217	113.4	45.8
Franklin Town	68	1 532	90.2	24.5	14	D	D	D	54	779	75.9	31.3
Gloucester	117	1 078	72.4	21.0	13	93	12.1	4.1	60	687	65.7	29.6
Haverhill	131	1 829	100.6	28.9	23	551	30.4	10.5	103	2 729	284.2	119.1
Holyoke	92	1 516	77.7	21.2	11	154	5.0	2.0	77	1 518	115.5	58.1
Lawrence	119	D	D	D	4	83	1.9	0.7	82	1 243	149.0	68.2
Leominster	107	2 048	93.9	28.3	16	D	D	D	91	1 667	171.2	69.6
Lowell	218	D	D	D	14	128	8.9	2.5	133	3 122	284.3	143.1
Lynn	140	D	D	D	16	74	3.8	1.2	99	2 137	142.9	73.1
Malden	95	1 129	65.6	19.1	5	D	D	D	81	3 105	759.8	393.0
Marlborough	133	2 397	139.9	39.1	17	374	22.9	6.0	77	1 549	133.4	57.5
Medford	102	1 323	95.0	24.2	12	D	D	D	94	1 788	210.8	94.1
Melrose	40	467	25.4	6.4	6	34	2.2	0.8	74	D	D	D
Methuen Town	104	1 800	96.9	27.4	11	234	10.6	3.6	92	2 434	285.6	124.6
New Bedford	216	D	D	D	17	196	10.9	3.1	137	2 981	245.8	115.8
Newton	191	4 920	381.6	109.6	47	703	86.8	41.7	354	5 904	636.5	291.6
Northampton	105	1 982	92.3	30.0	18	244	11.3	3.2	116	1 464	160.8	76.5
Peabody	141	2 605	154.7	46.5	7	20	2.1	0.4	107	2 241	326.5	148.1
Pittsfield	141	1 849	90.2	26.8	19	236	14.2	3.4	143	1 881	179.7	82.1
Quincy	241	3 168	205.7	55.1	25	252	23.6	6.8	216	5 889	618.3	243.1
Revere	96	1 142	79.0	17.9	8	D	D	D	45	D	D	D
Salem	132	1 707	116.4	31.4	18	D	D	D	101	D	D	D
Somerville	195	2 436	167.1	49.0	16	122	9.6	2.4	83	1 859	219.9	94.5
Springfield	268	4 663	236.2	65.1	15	126	10.0	2.6	301	7 082	910.0	482.5
Taunton	111	D	D	D	6	D	D	D	93	1 312	137.9	60.8
Waltham	304	3 249	244.9	68.9	23	496	33.8	7.2	135	1 854	207.3	102.0
Watertown Town	84	996	61.7	16.6	17	D	D	D	69	764	93.8	34.9
Westfield	78	1 356	61.7	18.4	9	95	3.6	1.1	67	758	74.6	33.8
West Springfield Town	105	2 119	109.8	31.3	9	D	D	D	68	1 694	109.4	58.5
Weymouth Town	102	1 520	73.7	19.1	12	D	D	D	135	D	D	D
Woburn	102	2 048	148.1	39.2	24	346	15.8	4.5	119	3 488	393.7	153.8
Worcester	441	6 201	342.0	95.4	26	420	21.3	7.0	395	12 907	1 671.6	839.6
MICHIGAN	19 491	347 337	17 962.4	4 871.7	2 706	32 268	2 881.5	1 119.9	21 447	270 655	27 434.6	11 943.9
Allen Park	68	1 258	61.4	18.3	8	D	D	D	72	752	78.4	32.4
Ann Arbor	381	8 311	467.1	131.5	37	156	10.6	3.3	307	D	D	D
Battle Creek	140	D	D	D	12	128	4.6	1.3	147	1 939	187.9	82.0
Bay City	102	1 744	59.5	19.7	15	D	D	D	104	1 410	154.2	66.0
Burton	56	1 191	53.5	14.3	8	D	D	D	83	D	D	D
Dearborn	257	4 444	236.5	67.6	18	D	D	D	368	3 186	479.1	179.2
Dearborn Heights	97	1 408	65.6	17.2	5	79	5.2	1.6	94	D	D	D
Detroit	933	20 452	2 237.3	495.8	49	2 577	500.3	295.9	668	21 711	2 848.7	1 101.4
East Lansing	121	2 411	100.0	26.3	5	28	0.9	0.3	109	2 481	410.1	139.5
Eastpointe	47	704	33.1	9.1	5	D	D	D	81	D	D	D
Farmington Hills	175	2 826	137.7	40.1	25	480	16.2	6.2	395	5 861	509.0	236.8
Flint	179	2 260	102.2	25.3	5	D	D	D	148	2 244	254.3	97.4
Garden City	46	740	28.2	7.6	2	D	D	D	73	D	D	D
Grand Rapids	408	8 881	448.6	130.1	56	1 134	38.9	11.2	393	7 651	938.5	470.8
Holland	79	1 893	78.4	24.5	5	178	5.2	1.8	106	1 892	160.2	79.9
Inkster	22	187	13.4	3.1	NA	NA	NA	NA	16	63	4.7	1.5
Jackson	96	1 480	65.6	17.9	9	D	D	D	134	1 613	206.7	111.5
Kalamazoo	210	4 849	194.0	61.6	27	397	17.4	6.2	168	2 775	310.1	160.3
Kentwood	106	2 408	117.2	32.5	16	D	D	D	99	2 708	326.4	158.6
Lansing	233	4 028	181.5	50.1	24	449	82.3	10.9	213	2 226	253.4	123.9
Lincoln Park	67	895	45.1	10.9	4	16	0.8	0.2	45	D	D	D
Livonia	259	5 903	276.8	81.4	23	D	D	D	448	4 931	510.1	217.3
Madison Heights	101	1 743	87.2	23.8	13	116	6.0	1.8	93	1 696	141.7	72.2
Midland	111	2 562	122.9	37.3	14	305	14.1	4.9	166	D	D	D
Mount Pleasant	73	D	D	D	4	D	D	D	103	D	D	D
Muskegon	72	1 276	57.1	16.1	9	201	10.7	3.5	91	D	D	D
Novi	161	3 802	205.2	60.5	20	D	D	D	227	2 509	311.6	114.5

1. Establishments subject to federal tax.

Table D. Cities — Other Services and Government Employment and Payroll

City	Other services[1], 2012 Number of establishments	Number of employees	Receipts (mil dol)	Annual payroll (mil dol)	Full-time equivalent employees	Government employment and payroll, 2012 — March payroll Total (dollars)	Percent of total for: Administration, judicial, and legal	Police and Corrections	Fire Protection	Highways and transportation	Health and welfare	Natural resources and utilities	Education and libraries
	104	105	106	107	108	109	110	111	112	113	114	115	116
MASSACHUSETTS— Cont'd													
Beverly	63	329	28.7	8.5	996	4 817 626	4.0	11.2	9.0	4.5	1.8	2.6	66.3
Boston	1 253	9 009	772.9	242.2	19 230	112 444 857	3.5	18.3	12.2	2.2	8.9	3.5	49.1
Braintree Town	91	1 006	75.5	22.8	1 198	6 476 545	2.5	10.2	9.4	2.2	1.8	15.8	58.0
Brockton	146	1 021	74.7	25.7	3 168	15 359 504	2.3	8.6	7.5	1.3	0.8	2.7	75.2
Cambridge	153	1 154	107.3	39.0	5 751	29 806 492	5.4	9.0	6.6	1.8	37.9	3.3	26.6
Chelsea	36	251	36.9	7.1	1 195	6 010 338	2.8	12.8	10.5	1.7	2.0	0.7	68.2
Chicopee	72	406	28.9	9.7	1 968	9 607 115	2.4	8.9	8.8	2.2	1.0	8.2	68.6
Everett	74	439	37.2	11.3	1 148	6 059 197	2.8	14.5	12.3	1.2	2.1	1.4	63.1
Fall River	150	728	56.9	17.6	2 306	10 353 050	2.4	15.4	12.8	3.5	0.6	2.2	61.8
Fitchburg	50	241	23.4	6.3	1 151	5 547 200	3.4	9.4	7.3	2.6	1.4	5.1	70.3
Franklin Town	58	546	44.2	13.5	966	4 884 796	3.9	7.4	6.9	0.9	1.2	3.4	75.4
Gloucester	53	223	18.9	5.7	1 097	5 414 614	3.5	6.3	6.5	1.4	2.1	2.0	78.1
Haverhill	84	417	36.6	12.5	1 832	8 913 896	3.7	7.9	7.8	2.3	3.5	5.7	67.6
Holyoke	46	229	15.1	4.7	1 884	8 334 885	2.7	13.7	8.2	1.9	1.5	16.1	55.4
Lawrence	88	567	48.9	15.2	537	3 239 260	9.3	38.4	19.3	2.8	4.3	18.5	2.0
Leominster	67	278	23.7	6.4	1 158	5 702 455	3.5	8.2	8.6	2.7	4.5	1.1	71.5
Lowell	142	671	60.4	19.1	2 860	17 379 993	21.6	7.8	6.2	1.2	1.9	2.6	57.2
Lynn	98	492	40.5	12.2	3 200	15 232 790	2.0	9.3	9.0	0.6	2.4	2.0	71.9
Malden	96	609	50.6	17.0	1 385	7 796 658	4.0	11.7	8.4	1.5	2.2	1.1	67.0
Marlborough	68	703	100.0	29.9	1 155	5 341 768	2.6	10.8	7.8	2.2	2.8	3.2	68.1
Medford	110	657	57.4	19.1	1 214	5 909 654	4.2	14.6	12.9	2.3	1.5	3.3	61.4
Melrose	42	212	18.3	6.1	763	3 328 642	4.7	9.6	9.5	2.3	3.8	3.1	64.8
Methuen Town	57	326	24.1	8.9	1 087	7 336 774	2.5	10.2	7.0	2.2	1.2	5.3	71.1
New Bedford	137	787	79.6	21.8	2 769	11 838 508	3.4	15.9	8.7	0.5	2.2	2.3	64.5
Newton	178	1 202	106.0	36.3	2 832	16 441 085	4.0	8.3	7.3	3.8	2.0	4.3	68.5
Northampton	60	325	25.5	8.5	1 315	6 640 659	6.9	16.3	15.0	3.3	4.8	8.4	45.1
Peabody	116	626	68.0	15.6	1 445	6 993 068	3.9	10.1	8.5	2.0	3.4	9.6	59.9
Pittsfield	73	363	30.8	10.9	1 418	6 191 800	2.1	11.1	7.7	3.1	2.0	2.3	70.3
Quincy	182	1 019	102.2	29.6	2 107	11 341 562	3.7	14.1	12.3	2.7	1.9	3.4	58.4
Revere	76	312	30.3	7.5	1 148	6 190 389	2.9	10.4	9.9	1.4	2.2	0.9	70.9
Salem	92	548	44.5	13.3	1 293	5 566 047	3.8	10.4	7.7	2.3	1.1	2.1	70.6
Somerville	109	1 376	119.9	44.1	1 637	10 044 072	4.6	10.5	15.6	1.3	3.6	1.4	56.7
Springfield	183	1 829	123.1	43.5	6 400	28 244 315	2.7	10.9	5.2	0.8	1.6	1.8	75.7
Taunton	80	381	28.6	8.7	1 574	7 371 663	2.8	12.1	9.6	1.1	6.5	4.4	62.0
Waltham	135	747	59.8	21.5	1 543	7 799 064	4.9	13.2	11.2	3.6	1.6	2.7	59.4
Watertown Town	77	1 305	112.4	47.4	718	3 483 060	6.4	20.3	14.0	1.6	1.6	4.8	50.1
Westfield	57	288	29.1	10.3	1 493	7 020 504	2.4	7.7	7.1	1.5	0.9	11.5	68.2
West Springfield Town	63	469	44.3	12.1	976	3 909 287	3.2	12.1	9.7	5.8	0.8	0.5	65.8
Weymouth Town	110	532	44.7	13.4	1 151	5 346 322	0.0	0.0	0.0	0.0	0.0	0.0	100.0
Woburn	102	D	D	D	1 052	4 899 436	3.8	10.6	8.5	4.3	1.8	2.5	67.9
Worcester	254	1 668	157.3	46.3	5 736	34 255 682	3.1	10.9	7.3	1.4	1.6	2.9	72.6
MICHIGAN	13 062	75 714	6 509.2	1 982.4	X	X	X	X	X	X	X	X	X
Allen Park	43	278	19.6	4.6	145	695 062	17.1	36.5	23.7	3.5	2.1	12.0	1.1
Ann Arbor	148	945	71.1	25.5	1 014	4 848 561	15.1	39.8	10.1	6.4	0.3	20.8	0.0
Battle Creek	75	D	D	D	520	2 297 856	15.9	27.9	16.4	20.0	2.1	17.3	0.0
Bay City	61	390	30.3	10.7	307	1 423 139	12.6	19.6	15.4	7.2	3.8	41.4	0.0
Burton	55	260	23.3	7.6	88	380 820	19.8	42.5	6.3	13.2	3.7	10.2	0.0
Dearborn	192	864	64.3	17.4	923	3 654 827	12.9	29.4	13.1	4.0	5.7	11.8	4.5
Dearborn Heights	83	282	25.1	6.7	306	1 426 569	13.6	40.6	19.1	3.5	0.6	11.8	3.5
Detroit	609	3 355	261.9	82.4	12 364	57 433 160	8.6	36.8	19.2	8.8	3.7	16.3	1.7
East Lansing	25	167	11.3	3.3	396	1 817 436	16.7	32.0	14.5	2.5	2.2	20.9	4.6
Eastpointe	54	259	22.1	6.3	180	830 736	14.8	39.6	19.5	6.0	0.0	11.0	3.5
Farmington Hills	155	1 573	97.8	33.6	445	2 178 404	16.2	39.5	19.9	10.2	0.0	13.4	0.0
Flint	105	665	52.6	13.9	3 484	16 192 746	3.4	5.1	4.1	1.1	80.7	4.6	0.0
Garden City	51	249	19.2	5.3	125	1 093 459	18.2	37.0	20.6	11.9	0.0	10.8	1.6
Grand Rapids	229	1 640	123.7	40.7	1 502	7 515 829	14.9	31.3	17.1	6.5	4.9	18.7	5.4
Holland	60	528	48.1	16.3	501	2 186 069	19.7	18.0	6.4	11.0	2.5	31.8	8.0
Inkster	15	74	2.7	1.8	210	862 765	16.2	39.6	11.9	3.5	10.7	10.1	0.0
Jackson	55	448	37.4	11.5	317	1 468 468	14.1	26.2	16.9	10.7	9.1	20.9	0.0
Kalamazoo	135	1 028	100.7	33.6	737	3 816 582	9.9	48.7	0.0	14.8	4.0	21.7	0.0
Kentwood	68	759	66.8	26.7	223	1 105 109	17.7	43.8	20.2	4.1	0.4	7.1	0.0
Lansing	145	D	D	D	1 615	8 042 053	9.4	18.0	12.0	4.6	2.5	31.5	0.0
Lincoln Park	60	339	32.7	10.6	136	745 448	11.3	45.2	24.4	3.7	3.5	7.7	0.1
Livonia	212	1 646	201.4	50.7	675	3 250 072	15.0	29.9	18.3	6.5	2.1	12.7	4.9
Madison Heights	86	577	55.1	18.3	168	954 270	18.4	39.5	19.8	4.4	6.9	6.2	3.1
Midland	83	593	47.7	13.7	384	1 817 246	18.5	13.7	13.1	13.3	3.3	24.4	7.5
Mount Pleasant	43	302	15.7	4.7	138	584 882	17.9	28.1	11.5	10.7	3.3	20.6	0.0
Muskegon	43	230	20.5	5.8	249	1 066 412	10.8	37.4	17.3	11.3	4.4	11.2	0.0
Novi	95	941	74.1	26.9	303	1 465 600	14.7	34.8	16.3	10.0	0.9	6.5	8.2

1. Establishments subject to federal tax.

Table D. Cities — City Government Finances

City	General revenue Total (mil dol)	Intergovernmental Total (mil dol)	Intergovernmental Percent from state government	Taxes Total (mil dol)	Taxes Per capita (dollars) Total	Taxes Per capita (dollars) Property	Taxes Sales and gross receipts	General expenditure Total (mil dol)	General expenditure Per capita (dollars) Total	General expenditure Per capita (dollars) Capital outlays
	117	118	119	120	121	122	123	124	125	126
MASSACHUSETTS— Cont'd										
Beverly	134.3	32.2	93.2	84.0	2 083	2 032	50	122.1	3 027	262
Boston	3 134.7	946.2	90.8	1 822.2	2 844	2 612	231	3 160.4	4 932	468
Braintree Town	122.1	30.7	98.2	76.9	2 110	2 032	78	126.4	3 467	261
Brockton	341.1	188.9	94.9	118.0	1 255	1 218	36	341.2	3 628	290
Cambridge	1 412.6	295.2	74.5	338.8	3 195	2 843	352	1 310.4	12 357	887
Chelsea	149.1	80.2	94.0	48.9	1 320	1 254	66	146.8	3 958	166
Chicopee	183.1	93.0	88.2	72.3	1 298	1 255	43	183.1	3 289	279
Everett	159.8	65.9	97.2	88.8	2 084	2 072	12	163.2	3 832	25
Fall River	291.2	173.4	87.5	84.8	956	911	46	273.3	3 082	273
Fitchburg	133.3	69.5	95.2	44.8	1 108	1 068	40	123.9	3 067	250
Franklin Town	113.1	39.1	99.7	62.6	1 932	1 864	68	108.1	3 337	214
Gloucester	108.7	22.2	85.3	70.1	2 398	2 265	133	118.1	4 041	621
Haverhill	179.2	72.3	95.2	91.2	1 477	1 436	41	178.9	2 897	125
Holyoke	180.1	108.6	96.0	51.5	1 283	1 249	34	193.1	4 810	387
Lawrence	293.4	219.3	93.9	57.3	741	711	30	270.5	3 497	39
Leominster	137.6	72.2	98.2	57.3	1 401	1 379	22	130.9	3 200	778
Lowell	379.7	222.6	91.4	119.6	1 102	1 055	47	358.5	3 303	268
Lynn	304.3	187.6	95.4	107.6	1 179	1 155	24	313.0	3 429	13
Malden	196.5	94.6	92.6	74.5	1 234	1 215	19	199.3	3 301	386
Marlborough	132.1	30.2	96.1	91.0	2 319	2 265	54	126.8	3 229	96
Medford	142.6	31.8	91.0	94.1	1 650	1 604	46	142.2	2 492	58
Melrose	82.1	18.2	97.0	52.8	1 924	1 914	10	86.2	3 141	285
Methuen Town	133.7	50.8	97.6	70.6	1 469	1 434	35	135.9	2 829	221
New Bedford	342.6	197.7	87.3	103.4	1 091	1 041	50	319.6	3 371	394
Newton	352.9	45.9	82.2	268.4	3 076	2 977	99	348.0	3 989	200
Northampton	93.2	21.7	85.3	47.2	1 647	1 575	72	100.6	3 506	673
Peabody	155.1	38.9	89.5	98.2	1 894	1 799	95	155.3	2 995	158
Pittsfield	156.1	75.8	92.6	70.5	1 592	1 549	43	180.6	4 076	509
Quincy	303.7	68.6	83.6	184.2	1 983	1 919	64	317.7	3 420	279
Revere	167.2	86.7	75.9	74.7	1 396	1 343	53	159.6	2 981	128
Salem	150.4	51.6	89.1	76.8	1 818	1 779	39	149.1	3 528	208
Somerville	214.8	65.2	90.3	115.7	1 489	1 387	102	222.7	2 865	243
Springfield	710.6	501.8	92.6	183.4	1 192	1 136	56	702.0	4 562	459
Taunton	200.1	101.1	96.2	78.0	1 394	1 336	58	198.2	3 540	473
Waltham	215.4	26.2	94.8	161.6	2 606	2 487	119	206.3	3 326	185
Watertown Town	111.0	16.6	95.8	77.8	2 365	2 342	23	108.0	3 282	224
Westfield	141.0	61.2	91.3	63.5	1 541	1 514	27	132.3	3 207	439
West Springfield Town	111.8	41.7	97.5	63.7	2 226	2 135	90	122.2	4 273	802
Weymouth Town	149.6	43.6	97.1	86.4	1 571	1 532	40	133.5	2 426	127
Woburn	134.2	22.5	96.5	94.7	2 436	2 328	108	140.9	3 624	251
Worcester	673.9	351.9	90.1	250.3	1 373	1 328	45	681.7	3 738	461
MICHIGAN	X	X	X	X	X	X	X	X	X	X
Allen Park	38.0	4.5	94.9	19.7	707	622	85	43.2	1 545	192
Ann Arbor	205.6	39.3	54.4	89.8	775	705	70	199.0	1 717	426
Battle Creek	117.1	35.5	38.6	47.3	913	607	16	105.6	2 035	231
Bay City	52.3	16.3	64.9	12.8	371	359	12	52.6	1 522	200
Burton	18.2	5.5	93.6	4.3	148	132	16	18.3	623	116
Dearborn	175.2	29.5	56.1	86.0	888	866	22	163.2	1 685	219
Dearborn Heights	74.1	29.6	29.1	28.0	490	465	25	61.3	1 071	5
Detroit	2 146.1	681.0	63.6	750.8	1 078	381	362	2 248.4	3 227	289
East Lansing	62.4	13.1	74.3	22.1	455	428	27	63.0	1 296	67
Eastpointe	33.6	7.4	68.2	15.1	466	436	30	35.4	1 090	71
Farmington Hills	79.0	13.9	86.1	37.4	463	453	10	81.3	1 007	37
Flint	502.1	117.5	72.0	32.2	321	147	26	538.2	5 357	401
Garden City	29.5	6.1	87.6	10.9	398	370	28	24.0	874	14
Grand Rapids	321.9	89.0	37.4	121.3	637	264	15	325.6	1 709	174
Holland	45.8	12.0	77.2	16.8	504	489	15	51.4	1 542	413
Inkster	43.4	14.9	32.0	13.5	537	526	11	41.5	1 654	64
Jackson	52.5	18.8	34.8	18.5	555	325	11	61.6	1 847	294
Kalamazoo	130.6	43.5	46.0	43.7	580	555	25	121.7	1 617	207
Kentwood	37.6	7.9	86.2	20.9	420	392	28	37.4	753	60
Lansing	199.5	45.8	54.5	68.7	601	343	13	191.2	1 673	175
Lincoln Park	33.8	9.0	78.1	15.8	418	401	17	38.4	1 019	22
Livonia	124.8	25.5	60.0	56.3	586	566	21	115.2	1 199	38
Madison Heights	38.4	6.7	70.4	20.2	674	650	24	43.5	1 448	121
Midland	69.8	10.8	85.7	36.7	874	857	17	61.2	1 460	164
Mount Pleasant	19.8	5.1	79.3	8.1	309	295	14	19.6	748	41
Muskegon	40.9	9.9	74.7	17.3	468	235	33	46.3	1 248	68
Novi	64.1	7.6	98.2	31.7	557	530	26	58.8	1 034	128

1. Based on population estimated as of July 1 of the year shown.

City	Public welfare	Highways	Parking facilities	Education	Health and hospitals	Police protection	Sewerage and sanitation	Parks and recreation	Housing and community development	Interest on debt
	127	128	129	130	131	132	133	134	135	136
MASSACHUSETTS— Cont'd										
Beverly	0.3	3.4	0.0	51.9	0.4	5.3	7.8	1.4	0.2	2.4
Boston	1.5	1.6	0.1	34.9	9.0	10.0	7.1	2.1	3.3	1.8
Braintree Town	0.2	4.6	0.0	56.1	0.2	6.0	1.8	2.0	0.0	0.6
Brockton	0.3	2.4	0.1	69.7	0.2	5.1	4.9	0.4	0.7	0.6
Cambridge	0.1	0.8	0.1	15.3	59.9	2.3	2.5	1.4	0.7	2.6
Chelsea	0.4	1.5	0.0	55.8	0.0	5.6	1.8	0.1	1.3	0.9
Chicopee	0.5	2.5	0.0	55.4	0.2	5.1	10.9	1.4	1.6	1.4
Everett	0.3	4.8	0.3	53.5	0.9	5.4	1.6	0.1	0.5	1.6
Fall River	1.1	2.7	0.1	60.7	1.7	6.0	7.2	0.5	2.1	2.7
Fitchburg	0.4	3.8	0.1	55.3	0.5	5.0	7.7	0.4	1.1	1.6
Franklin Town	0.2	3.8	0.0	62.7	0.2	4.0	5.2	0.4	0.0	1.5
Gloucester	0.3	1.0	0.0	46.4	0.3	4.3	12.1	0.2	0.8	2.6
Haverhill	0.4	2.6	0.0	57.9	0.5	4.9	6.4	0.2	0.8	1.7
Holyoke	3.6	2.3	0.1	57.6	0.3	6.1	4.9	0.6	1.3	0.8
Lawrence	0.2	1.0	0.1	69.2	0.0	4.2	3.9	0.2	0.5	1.9
Leominster	0.3	5.4	0.0	62.2	0.3	4.8	12.4	0.5	0.4	0.5
Lowell	0.3	1.5	0.8	55.4	0.5	6.0	5.9	0.7	2.2	2.0
Lynn	0.3	2.2	0.3	60.6	0.0	5.4	1.5	0.1	1.5	1.0
Malden	0.1	1.8	0.0	51.9	0.3	4.9	1.7	0.4	2.1	1.9
Marlborough	0.1	6.3	0.0	59.3	0.3	5.4	5.3	0.2	0.3	0.9
Medford	0.2	2.1	0.0	42.8	0.3	7.6	4.1	0.4	1.6	0.9
Melrose	0.5	2.1	0.0	46.0	1.6	4.2	1.7	2.4	0.1	2.2
Methuen Town	0.4	4.2	0.0	68.1	0.5	6.5	5.7	0.1	0.7	1.2
New Bedford	1.1	1.1	0.2	57.4	1.0	6.6	5.2	0.4	1.7	2.7
Newton	0.1	2.9	0.0	59.6	0.6	4.5	3.4	1.2	1.0	2.4
Northampton	0.8	3.6	0.4	37.7	1.9	16.0	5.4	0.3	2.0	2.3
Peabody	0.1	2.7	0.0	56.3	0.7	5.9	2.5	1.9	2.2	0.9
Pittsfield	0.3	5.5	0.6	46.8	0.5	4.6	5.2	1.1	1.2	1.6
Quincy	0.5	2.3	0.0	39.4	0.6	6.9	3.3	0.7	2.0	1.2
Revere	0.7	1.0	0.1	51.2	0.2	5.2	7.3	0.3	0.7	1.4
Salem	0.2	3.0	0.5	53.2	0.3	5.4	2.7	1.9	0.9	1.3
Somerville	0.2	2.5	0.0	35.0	0.5	6.5	3.8	0.4	2.1	1.0
Springfield	0.4	1.8	0.0	65.3	0.2	5.5	1.3	1.2	0.9	1.9
Taunton	4.3	2.3	0.0	50.4	0.4	5.5	8.7	0.5	0.9	1.4
Waltham	0.2	3.7	0.1	36.6	0.4	6.4	4.4	0.7	0.6	1.4
Watertown Town	0.1	3.1	0.0	42.6	0.5	6.9	4.0	0.5	0.0	1.3
Westfield	0.5	3.3	0.0	62.6	1.6	4.9	3.8	1.5	0.2	1.7
West Springfield Town	0.5	8.0	0.0	57.3	1.3	5.5	3.0	0.4	0.7	0.9
Weymouth Town	0.4	2.0	0.0	50.6	0.4	6.9	5.0	0.4	0.7	1.5
Woburn	0.3	2.9	0.0	54.1	0.4	6.0	2.5	0.5	0.0	1.5
Worcester	0.0	3.3	0.2	50.4	0.0	6.0	6.2	0.7	1.5	4.3
MICHIGAN	X	X	X	X	X	X	X	X	X	X
Allen Park	0.0	6.4	0.0	0.0	0.0	14.5	38.3	2.2	0.9	7.5
Ann Arbor	0.0	12.0	16.4	0.0	0.0	13.0	19.6	7.4	7.6	4.1
Battle Creek	0.0	15.2	1.0	0.0	0.0	14.4	15.7	5.1	11.4	2.5
Bay City	0.0	12.0	0.0	0.0	0.0	11.7	20.5	1.6	9.1	4.9
Burton	0.0	14.3	0.0	0.0	2.0	21.7	30.0	0.2	0.0	1.5
Dearborn	0.0	11.9	0.7	0.0	0.0	20.4	25.1	8.8	1.7	3.2
Dearborn Heights	0.0	9.4	0.0	0.0	0.0	18.9	29.2	1.7	1.5	3.4
Detroit	0.3	4.1	0.2	2.6	3.2	16.5	19.9	1.5	2.3	14.4
East Lansing	0.0	8.7	6.6	0.0	0.1	13.6	17.4	9.9	5.3	4.2
Eastpointe	0.0	7.5	0.0	0.0	0.0	24.2	26.9	3.0	5.4	0.5
Farmington Hills	0.0	12.0	0.0	0.0	0.0	23.0	18.5	10.0	0.4	1.0
Flint	0.0	2.0	0.0	0.0	71.4	4.3	4.8	0.9	4.2	1.0
Garden City	0.0	11.4	0.0	0.0	0.2	16.2	27.1	1.4	0.6	2.6
Grand Rapids	0.0	8.3	1.9	0.0	0.0	14.7	16.6	1.9	16.1	6.7
Holland	0.2	23.5	0.0	0.0	0.6	14.8	25.5	11.0	1.1	2.2
Inkster	0.0	5.5	0.0	0.0	0.0	15.9	18.5	2.0	23.8	3.0
Jackson	0.0	33.1	0.4	0.0	0.0	12.4	10.4	5.3	12.6	2.4
Kalamazoo	0.0	11.0	0.0	0.0	0.0	27.5	24.5	3.5	2.8	2.5
Kentwood	0.0	17.7	0.0	0.0	0.0	26.5	9.2	5.2	0.1	2.3
Lansing	0.0	9.1	3.2	0.0	0.0	16.0	13.6	7.6	1.0	5.1
Lincoln Park	0.0	8.0	0.0	0.0	0.0	21.1	23.4	1.1	2.1	1.9
Livonia	0.0	11.9	0.0	0.0	0.0	19.1	24.0	8.3	8.3	1.5
Madison Heights	0.0	12.4	0.0	0.0	0.0	20.1	32.9	1.9	4.4	0.4
Midland	0.0	14.5	0.2	0.0	0.0	11.9	18.0	11.9	1.8	1.5
Mount Pleasant	0.0	13.1	1.1	0.0	0.0	24.5	10.3	7.8	4.3	1.3
Muskegon	0.0	13.1	0.0	0.0	0.0	19.8	27.3	2.8	7.1	1.1
Novi	0.0	18.7	0.0	0.0	0.0	19.2	17.0	6.8	0.0	4.0

Table D. Cities — City Government Finances, City Government Employment, and Climate

City	City government finances, 2012 (cont.) Debt outstanding			Climate[2] Average daily temperature (degrees Fahrenheit)						
				Mean		Limits				
	Total (mil dol)	Per capita[1] (dollars)	Debt issued during year	January	July	January[3]	July[4]	Annual precipitation (inches)	Heating degree days	Cooling degree days
	137	138	139	140	141	142	143	144	145	146
MASSACHUSETTS—Cont'd										
Beverly	89.1	2 208	0.0	28.8	72.6	20.4	82.1	45.51	5 704	582
Boston	1 572.5	2 454	245.5	29.3	73.9	22.1	82.2	42.53	5 630	777
Braintree Town	145.9	4 001	8.7	NA	NA	NA	NA	NA	NA	NA
Brockton	242.9	2 583	12.5	27.9	72.1	17.8	83.2	48.25	6 008	529
Cambridge	340.3	3 209	55.5	29.3	73.9	22.1	82.2	42.53	5 630	777
Chelsea	35.1	947	2.0	29.3	73.9	22.1	82.2	42.53	5 630	777
Chicopee	51.4	924	11.0	21.5	68.9	10.4	81.7	48.07	7 312	287
Everett	61.8	1 452	1.4	29.3	73.9	22.1	82.2	42.53	5 630	777
Fall River	271.7	3 064	39.8	28.5	74.2	20.0	83.1	50.77	5 734	740
Fitchburg	74.6	1 846	20.7	24.2	71.9	15.2	81.0	49.13	6 576	548
Franklin Town	55.4	1 710	16.4	NA	NA	NA	NA	NA	NA	NA
Gloucester	137.0	4 689	26.4	28.8	72.6	20.4	82.1	45.51	5 704	582
Haverhill	94.2	1 525	3.0	25.3	72.2	15.6	83.5	46.88	6 435	550
Holyoke	104.5	2 604	16.8	21.5	68.9	10.4	81.7	48.07	7 312	287
Lawrence	148.3	1 917	0.0	24.5	71.8	14.5	82.9	44.09	6 539	510
Leominster	58.1	1 421	13.9	24.2	71.9	15.2	81.0	49.13	6 576	548
Lowell	256.6	2 363	32.8	23.6	72.4	14.1	84.5	43.14	6 575	532
Lynn	67.5	740	0.0	29.3	73.9	22.1	82.2	42.53	5 630	777
Malden	106.3	1 761	5.1	29.3	73.9	22.1	82.2	42.53	5 630	777
Marlborough	60.4	1 537	31.1	25.9	73.4	16.2	84.0	45.87	6 060	651
Medford	45.4	795	34.5	29.3	73.9	22.1	82.2	42.53	5 630	777
Melrose	63.4	2 311	5.5	29.3	73.9	22.1	82.2	42.53	5 630	777
Methuen Town	66.0	1 374	0.5	24.5	71.8	14.5	82.9	44.09	6 539	510
New Bedford	257.5	2 716	19.6	28.5	74.2	20.0	83.1	50.77	5 734	740
Newton	217.6	2 495	9.9	25.9	73.4	16.2	84.0	45.87	6 060	651
Northampton	81.7	2 847	20.6	22.3	71.2	11.2	83.2	45.57	6 856	452
Peabody	45.3	874	10.0	28.8	72.6	20.4	82.1	45.51	5 704	582
Pittsfield	87.1	1 966	7.2	19.9	67.6	11.2	77.5	48.71	7 689	222
Quincy	211.7	2 279	14.8	26.0	71.6	18.1	81.2	51.19	6 371	558
Revere	59.8	1 117	0.2	29.3	73.9	22.1	82.2	42.53	5 630	777
Salem	62.2	1 472	6.0	28.8	72.6	20.4	82.1	45.51	5 704	582
Somerville	99.6	1 281	18.7	29.3	73.9	22.1	82.2	42.53	5 630	777
Springfield	260.5	1 693	0.0	25.7	73.7	17.2	84.9	46.16	6 104	759
Taunton	120.6	2 154	0.7	27.4	72.2	17.8	83.0	48.34	6 012	558
Waltham	106.4	1 717	23.1	25.4	71.5	15.7	82.7	46.95	6 370	485
Watertown Town	44.3	1 348	4.0	29.3	73.9	22.1	82.2	42.53	5 630	777
Westfield	98.9	2 398	0.0	21.5	68.9	10.4	81.7	48.07	7 312	287
West Springfield Town	43.5	1 522	0.0	NA	NA	NA	NA	NA	NA	NA
Weymouth Town	91.2	1 657	25.5	NA	NA	NA	NA	NA	NA	NA
Woburn	86.3	2 221	30.5	25.5	71.5	15.7	82.5	48.31	6 401	472
Worcester	657.7	3 607	57.8	23.6	70.1	15.8	79.3	49.05	6 831	371
MICHIGAN	X	X	X	X	X	X	X	X	X	X
Allen Park	85.9	3 076	3.7	24.5	73.5	17.8	83.4	32.89	6 422	736
Ann Arbor	244.9	2 113	25.9	23.4	72.6	16.6	83.0	35.35	6 503	691
Battle Creek	87.6	1 690	0.0	23.1	71.0	15.3	82.5	35.15	6 742	559
Bay City	72.6	2 101	3.7	21.0	71.5	13.8	81.5	31.25	7 106	545
Burton	12.1	411	3.5	21.3	70.6	13.3	82.0	31.61	7 005	555
Dearborn	274.1	2 831	7.6	24.7	73.7	16.1	85.7	33.58	6 224	788
Dearborn Heights	58.1	1 016	3.6	24.7	73.7	16.1	85.7	33.58	6 224	788
Detroit	8 166.1	11 720	1 166.2	24.7	73.7	16.1	85.7	33.58	6 224	788
East Lansing	60.8	1 250	0.0	21.6	70.3	13.9	82.1	31.53	7 098	558
Eastpointe	15.3	472	0.4	25.3	73.6	18.8	83.3	33.97	6 160	757
Farmington Hills	17.7	219	0.0	24.7	73.7	16.1	85.7	33.58	6 224	788
Flint	170.4	1 696	13.5	21.3	70.6	13.3	82.0	31.61	7 005	555
Garden City	50.5	1 842	12.9	24.7	73.7	16.1	85.7	33.58	6 224	788
Grand Rapids	552.9	2 902	23.4	22.4	71.4	15.6	82.3	37.13	6 896	613
Holland	47.8	1 433	12.8	24.4	71.4	17.6	82.5	36.25	6 589	611
Inkster	48.3	1 924	9.7	24.5	73.5	17.8	83.4	32.89	6 422	736
Jackson	42.3	1 268	13.0	22.2	71.3	14.7	82.7	30.67	6 873	570
Kalamazoo	453.2	6 023	117.6	24.3	73.2	17.0	84.2	37.41	6 235	773
Kentwood	20.1	405	0.0	22.4	71.4	15.6	82.3	37.13	6 896	613
Lansing	693.1	6 066	30.4	21.6	70.3	13.9	82.1	31.53	7 098	558
Lincoln Park	16.7	443	0.0	24.5	73.5	17.8	83.4	32.89	6 422	736
Livonia	52.7	549	0.0	24.7	73.7	16.1	85.7	33.58	6 224	788
Madison Heights	14.5	483	0.0	24.7	73.7	16.1	85.7	33.58	6 224	788
Midland	35.9	855	4.6	22.9	72.7	16.2	83.8	30.69	6 645	679
Mount Pleasant	13.0	496	1.5	20.7	70.6	13.5	82.2	31.57	7 329	492
Muskegon	30.6	826	6.5	23.5	69.9	17.1	80.0	32.88	6 943	487
Novi	48.0	844	0.0	22.1	71.0	14.3	81.7	29.28	6 989	550

1. Based on the population estimated as of July 1 of the year shown.   2. Represents normal values based on the 30-year period, 1971–2000.   3. Average daily minimum.
4. Average daily maximum.

Table D. Cities — **Land Area and Population**

STATE Place code	City	Land area,[1] 2010 (sq km)	Population, 2015			Race alone or in combination (percent), 2010-2014					Percent Hispanic or Latino[2], 2010-2014	Percent foreign born 2010–2014
			Total persons	Rank	Per square kilometer	White	Black	American Indian, Alaska Native	Asian	Hawaiian Pacific Islander		
		1	2	3	4	5	6	7	8	9	10	11
	MICHIGAN—Cont'd											
26 59920	Oak Park	13.4	29 752	1 253	2 220.3	36.8	62.9	3.5	2.4	0.0	1.3	10.5
26 65440	Pontiac	51.7	59 917	611	1 158.9	43.8	55.8	1.8	2.9	0.1	16.6	7.2
26 65560	Portage	83.5	48 177	786	577.0	89.8	7.1	1.2	3.9	0.1	3.0	4.6
26 65820	Port Huron	20.9	29 330	1 264	1 403.3	89.7	11.1	2.1	1.6	0.0	4.7	3.4
26 69035	Rochester Hills	85.0	73 424	472	863.8	83.5	6.2	0.9	10.9	0.4	3.3	14.8
26 69800	Roseville	25.5	47 637	795	1 868.1	81.3	15.5	1.8	2.4	0.4	2.7	4.3
26 70040	Royal Oak	30.5	59 008	626	1 934.7	93.5	3.6	0.3	3.8	0.0	2.5	7.6
26 70520	Saginaw	44.9	49 347	763	1 099.0	50.4	47.4	1.6	0.8	0.2	14.5	1.7
26 70760	St. Clair Shores	30.1	59 903	612	1 990.1	93.4	5.3	1.0	1.4	0.1	2.1	4.7
26 74900	Southfield	68.1	73 156	474	1 074.2	27.4	71.8	1.5	2.3	0.0	1.3	10.2
26 74960	Southgate	17.7	29 293	1 266	1 655.0	90.8	6.2	1.0	2.2	0.4	6.5	5.9
26 76460	Sterling Heights	94.6	132 052	201	1 395.9	87.3	6.2	0.6	7.7	0.2	2.0	25.2
26 79000	Taylor	61.1	61 568	586	1 007.7	79.2	17.9	1.8	2.0	0.1	6.1	4.5
26 80700	Troy	86.7	83 280	396	960.6	73.3	4.5	0.6	22.7	0.1	2.2	27.7
26 84000	Warren	89.1	135 358	193	1 519.2	78.0	16.5	1.0	6.4	0.0	1.9	11.5
26 86000	Westland	52.9	82 000	405	1 550.1	76.1	19.8	1.5	4.1	0.1	2.6	6.6
26 88900	Wyandotte	13.7	25 156	1 415	1 836.2	96.4	1.4	0.9	0.6	0.1	5.1	2.6
26 88940	Wyoming	63.8	75 275	454	1 179.9	85.5	7.4	2.2	3.7	0.1	19.6	10.4
27 00000	MINNESOTA	206 232.3	5 489 594	X	26.6	87.5	6.5	1.9	5.0	0.1	4.9	7.5
27 01486	Andover	87.7	32 213	1 171	367.3	95.7	2.1	1.1	3.6	0.1	2.0	3.3
27 01900	Apple Valley	43.7	51 221	740	1 172.1	87.8	7.9	1.4	6.6	0.2	4.2	9.3
27 06382	Blaine	87.7	62 124	583	708.4	85.4	5.1	1.4	9.3	0.1	3.1	10.0
27 06616	Bloomington	89.8	86 435	376	962.5	82.4	9.5	1.1	7.5	0.3	7.2	11.5
27 07948	Brooklyn Center	20.6	30 770	1 207	1 493.7	51.9	31.9	1.7	15.7	0.0	8.9	23.2
27 07966	Brooklyn Park	67.5	79 149	426	1 172.6	56.1	28.3	0.7	15.8	0.1	7.4	21.6
27 08794	Burnsville	64.5	61 481	587	953.2	77.4	13.6	1.1	5.7	0.1	8.9	13.4
27 13114	Coon Rapids	58.6	62 240	580	1 062.1	89.4	7.0	1.7	3.9	0.0	3.7	7.6
27 13456	Cottage Grove	87.1	35 918	1 052	412.4	88.8	4.1	1.0	7.5	0.1	3.9	6.0
27 17000	Duluth	175.6	86 110	378	490.4	93.4	3.9	3.3	2.3	0.2	1.7	2.8
27 17288	Eagan	80.6	66 286	537	822.4	83.4	7.1	1.1	9.1	0.3	4.7	11.9
27 18116	Eden Prairie	84.0	63 496	567	755.9	82.3	6.3	1.1	11.9	0.3	3.1	13.9
27 18188	Edina	40.0	50 138	751	1 253.5	89.0	2.7	1.1	8.0	0.2	3.2	10.5
27 22814	Fridley	26.3	27 713	1 332	1 053.7	76.4	15.8	2.2	7.1	0.0	6.1	10.9
27 31076	Inver Grove Heights	71.9	34 857	1 077	484.8	86.3	5.4	1.5	5.0	0.2	9.9	7.7
27 35180	Lakeville	93.4	60 633	597	649.2	91.7	2.7	0.1	5.6	0.1	3.6	6.3
27 39878	Mankato	46.4	41 044	911	884.6	92.4	5.0	0.9	3.7	0.1	3.1	5.3
27 40166	Maple Grove	84.5	68 385	512	809.3	88.9	4.5	0.4	7.8	0.1	2.1	9.1
27 40382	Maplewood	44.0	40 567	922	922.0	75.9	9.2	1.4	15.6	0.2	5.8	12.4
27 43000	Minneapolis	139.8	410 939	46	2 939.5	70.5	20.6	3.0	6.9	0.3	9.8	15.1
27 43252	Minnetonka	69.7	51 669	732	741.3	90.8	5.4	0.6	5.1	0.1	2.4	8.5
27 43864	Moorhead	51.3	42 005	890	818.8	93.4	2.8	2.6	3.0	0.4	4.8	4.3
27 47680	Oakdale	28.4	28 080	1 314	988.7	82.4	10.5	1.0	8.2	0.1	3.6	7.4
27 49300	Owatonna	37.6	25 725	1 401	684.2	92.0	4.6	0.5	1.5	0.1	7.9	4.9
27 51730	Plymouth	84.7	75 907	451	896.2	85.8	6.2	0.9	9.0	0.0	3.6	12.0
27 54214	Richfield	17.8	36 216	1 039	2 034.6	75.6	12.8	1.9	7.1	0.2	19.4	21.1
27 54880	Rochester	141.4	112 225	250	793.7	85.1	7.8	0.6	8.3	0.1	5.4	12.6
27 55852	Roseville	33.7	35 580	1 063	1 055.8	84.0	7.8	1.2	8.8	0.1	5.8	11.9
27 56896	St. Cloud	103.7	67 109	524	647.1	86.9	10.1	1.3	3.5	0.4	2.4	6.8
27 57220	St. Louis Park	27.6	48 171	787	1 745.3	85.7	9.5	1.1	4.9	0.3	4.4	10.1
27 58000	St. Paul	134.6	300 851	64	2 235.1	64.3	18.2	2.6	16.9	0.1	9.5	18.2
27 58738	Savage	40.5	30 391	1 231	750.4	86.5	5.6	1.3	8.6	0.2	2.7	10.4
27 59350	Shakopee	72.5	39 991	936	551.5	78.9	6.7	2.3	12.2	0.2	9.3	16.0
27 59998	Shoreview	27.9	26 477	1 380	949.0	89.7	3.5	0.4	8.8	0.1	2.3	9.5
27 71032	Winona	48.8	27 094	1 354	555.2	94.6	2.6	0.7	2.8	0.1	0.6	3.6
27 71428	Woodbury	90.0	67 855	516	753.9	84.4	7.0	1.0	10.0	0.2	4.6	10.5
28 00000	MISSISSIPPI	121 530.7	2 992 333	X	24.6	60.3	37.9	0.8	1.1	0.1	2.8	2.2
28 06220	Biloxi	99.0	45 637	824	461.0	70.2	24.4	1.3	6.0	0.2	7.3	7.7
28 14420	Clinton	108.3	25 254	1 412	233.2	54.6	40.2	0.4	4.9	0.1	3.0	5.8
28 29180	Greenville	69.7	32 156	1 174	461.3	20.7	78.0	0.4	0.9	0.0	1.1	1.8
28 29700	Gulfport	144.0	71 856	484	499.0	61.3	37.5	0.9	1.9	0.1	5.9	3.9
28 31020	Hattiesburg	138.3	46 805	808	338.4	43.9	53.9	0.4	2.1	0.0	2.9	3.7
28 33700	Horn Lake	41.5	26 915	1 364	648.6	62.3	36.9	0.5	1.4	0.0	6.5	3.9
28 36000	Jackson	287.6	170 674	148	593.4	18.8	80.5	0.4	0.4	0.0	1.6	1.7
28 46640	Meridian	139.2	39 661	946	284.9	37.2	62.1	0.3	1.0	0.0	2.0	1.6
28 54040	Olive Branch	95.1	36 010	1 049	378.7	71.9	26.5	1.0	1.6	0.1	4.8	4.6
28 55760	Pearl	61.1	26 462	1 383	433.1	74.0	23.5	0.1	1.3	0.0	5.9	3.8
28 69280	Southaven	106.8	52 589	711	492.4	72.3	25.3	0.5	2.6	0.2	5.1	3.5
28 74840	Tupelo	132.5	35 680	1 059	269.3	59.5	40.1	0.2	0.9	0.0	3.7	2.7

1. Dry land or land partially or temporarily covered by water.   2. May be of any race.

Table D. Cities — **Population**

City	Under 5 years	5 to 17 years	18 to 24 years	25 to 34 years	35 to 44 years	45 to 54 years	55 to 64 years	65 to 74 years	75 years and over	Median age 2010–2014	Percent female 2010–2014	Census counts 2000	Census counts 2010	Percent change 2000–2010	Percent change 2010–2015
	12	13	14	15	16	17	18	19	20	21	22	23	24	25	26
MICHIGAN—Cont'd															
Oak Park	6.2	18.2	12.3	11.4	14.9	12.8	11.4	6.1	6.6	36.5	53.9	29 793	29 319	-1.6	1.5
Pontiac	7.4	18.8	12.0	13.7	12.9	12.9	11.8	5.7	4.8	33.4	52.1	66 337	59 515	-10.3	0.7
Portage	8.0	16.3	10.3	13.6	13.1	13.6	11.7	7.8	5.6	36.6	52.4	44 897	46 292	3.1	4.1
Port Huron	6.0	18.2	10.6	13.3	11.7	13.6	12.0	8.6	6.0	36.7	50.7	32 338	30 184	-6.7	-2.8
Rochester Hills	5.8	16.9	7.2	11.9	13.0	15.5	15.3	7.8	6.6	42.1	50.9	68 825	70 995	3.2	3.4
Roseville	6.0	17.1	9.0	14.7	13.8	14.4	12.4	6.0	6.5	37.3	50.8	48 129	47 299	-1.7	0.7
Royal Oak	5.1	11.3	8.1	22.0	14.6	13.4	12.9	6.0	6.7	37.0	50.9	60 062	57 236	-4.7	3.1
Saginaw	7.1	20.3	12.2	11.2	12.3	13.4	12.0	5.6	5.9	34.2	52.0	61 799	51 508	-16.7	-4.2
St. Clair Shores	4.5	14.2	6.7	14.3	10.8	16.5	14.6	8.1	10.2	44.5	52.1	63 096	59 715	-5.4	0.3
Southfield	5.8	15.2	9.0	10.7	12.6	14.3	14.4	9.6	8.5	42.6	55.2	78 296	71 739	-8.4	2.0
Southgate	4.0	14.9	10.4	11.8	15.1	13.5	14.7	8.2	7.2	41.8	52.6	30 136	30 047	-0.3	-2.5
Sterling Heights	5.0	16.0	8.8	12.3	13.7	14.8	13.2	8.7	7.4	41.3	50.3	124 471	129 699	4.2	1.8
Taylor	6.3	17.4	9.6	12.5	12.8	15.6	11.3	7.9	6.5	38.4	52.1	65 868	63 131	-4.2	-2.5
Troy	5.2	17.8	7.4	11.0	13.8	15.9	14.0	9.0	6.0	41.6	51.5	80 959	80 980	0.0	2.8
Warren	6.2	16.0	9.8	12.3	12.8	14.4	12.7	7.4	8.4	39.7	51.6	138 247	134 056	-3.0	1.0
Westland	6.5	14.3	10.1	14.5	12.7	14.6	12.7	7.7	6.8	38.3	53.3	86 602	84 094	-2.9	-2.5
Wyandotte	5.3	14.4	8.7	14.4	14.0	16.9	12.5	7.5	6.5	40.9	50.9	28 006	25 883	-7.6	-2.8
Wyoming	7.7	16.9	10.8	17.8	12.8	13.2	11.8	5.4	3.6	33.1	49.0	69 368	72 125	4.0	4.4
MINNESOTA	6.5	17.3	9.4	13.7	12.4	14.6	12.6	7.3	6.3	37.6	50.3	4 919 479	5 303 925	7.8	3.5
Andover	4.4	24.3	9.0	9.3	14.7	18.4	12.3	5.6	2.0	37.6	49.6	26 588	30 598	15.1	5.3
Apple Valley	7.2	17.6	8.5	13.5	12.9	16.5	12.8	7.1	3.9	37.5	49.9	45 527	49 084	7.8	4.4
Blaine	8.4	19.3	6.9	14.7	15.4	14.1	12.2	5.5	3.6	35.4	50.3	44 942	57 186	27.2	8.7
Bloomington	5.6	13.8	6.8	14.1	12.1	14.2	13.9	9.5	9.9	43.0	51.6	85 172	82 893	-2.7	4.3
Brooklyn Center	8.1	18.0	8.4	17.2	14.6	12.8	9.8	5.2	6.0	33.3	53.2	29 172	30 104	3.2	2.1
Brooklyn Park	7.6	19.3	10.1	15.9	12.4	14.6	11.1	5.9	3.0	33.0	50.0	67 388	75 781	12.5	4.4
Burnsville	5.9	16.5	8.9	16.0	12.9	14.7	12.3	7.1	5.8	37.2	51.1	60 220	60 306	0.1	1.9
Coon Rapids	6.9	16.2	9.5	15.2	12.6	14.9	12.7	5.2	5.2	36.8	50.7	61 607	61 476	-0.2	1.2
Cottage Grove	6.8	21.9	7.2	13.3	14.3	16.8	10.0	5.2	4.4	35.4	50.5	30 582	34 589	13.1	3.8
Duluth	5.7	13.2	20.0	13.2	9.9	11.9	11.9	6.9	7.3	33.1	50.1	86 918	86 265	-0.8	-0.2
Eagan	7.0	18.2	7.8	14.7	12.7	18.0	12.8	5.7	3.2	37.0	50.1	63 557	64 206	1.0	3.2
Eden Prairie	6.9	19.1	6.8	14.4	13.6	16.8	13.6	5.5	3.4	37.4	50.3	54 901	60 797	10.7	4.5
Edina	5.5	19.2	5.0	9.9	11.4	15.4	13.9	8.5	11.1	44.3	52.4	47 425	47 941	1.1	4.6
Fridley	7.7	14.2	9.8	16.0	11.9	14.8	11.6	7.7	6.4	37.4	50.5	27 449	27 208	-0.9	1.9
Inver Grove Heights	6.1	18.1	10.8	11.2	11.5	16.5	12.0	8.4	5.3	38.1	51.9	29 751	33 880	13.9	2.9
Lakeville	7.2	23.4	6.5	12.1	16.4	17.9	9.9	2.7	2.7	35.4	50.9	43 128	55 954	29.7	8.4
Mankato	5.7	10.2	32.2	15.1	9.1	8.5	8.4	4.9	5.9	25.9	50.4	32 427	39 309	21.2	3.3
Maple Grove	7.1	19.1	5.3	14.1	15.5	15.9	13.9	5.6	3.3	37.7	52.0	50 365	61 567	22.2	11.1
Maplewood	6.0	17.3	6.9	14.1	10.8	15.7	13.8	7.4	8.0	40.6	52.5	34 947	38 018	8.8	6.7
Minneapolis	6.9	13.4	14.1	21.4	13.3	11.9	10.4	4.8	3.6	31.8	49.5	382 618	382 578	0.0	7.4
Minnetonka	5.3	15.5	6.1	13.0	10.8	14.9	17.5	8.9	8.1	44.3	52.8	51 301	49 734	-3.1	3.9
Moorhead	7.0	13.3	23.2	14.8	9.9	10.6	10.1	4.8	6.3	29.2	51.3	32 177	38 065	18.3	6.5
Oakdale	5.4	17.8	11.3	12.2	10.6	17.9	12.1	7.6	5.1	38.1	51.7	26 653	27 378	2.7	2.6
Owatonna	7.7	18.6	7.8	12.6	13.3	13.8	11.2	7.9	7.1	38.5	50.7	22 434	25 599	14.1	0.5
Plymouth	6.0	16.9	6.0	15.3	13.5	15.7	13.7	7.2	5.7	40.1	51.5	65 894	70 576	7.1	7.6
Richfield	7.4	12.8	7.0	20.0	13.4	12.7	11.6	6.9	8.2	36.7	50.5	34 439	35 228	2.3	2.8
Rochester	7.4	17.1	8.5	16.5	12.5	13.4	11.3	6.9	6.6	35.4	51.5	85 806	106 769	24.4	5.1
Roseville	4.5	12.9	11.7	14.8	10.0	13.7	11.1	10.0	11.3	41.5	50.3	33 690	33 660	-0.1	5.7
St. Cloud	6.5	13.9	22.0	16.5	9.4	12.0	9.4	5.2	5.1	28.7	47.2	59 107	65 842	11.4	1.8
St. Louis Park	6.0	13.3	7.8	22.7	14.8	12.4	9.6	6.1	7.2	35.1	51.1	44 126	45 250	2.5	6.5
St. Paul	7.8	17.4	13.1	17.3	12.5	12.0	10.7	4.9	4.2	31.3	50.7	287 151	285 068	-0.7	5.5
Savage	7.0	23.6	6.7	13.0	15.9	18.9	8.5	3.9	2.6	34.8	49.8	21 115	26 911	27.4	12.9
Shakopee	8.5	20.7	7.6	17.5	19.2	12.1	7.6	3.9	2.9	32.8	49.8	20 568	37 076	80.3	7.8
Shoreview	5.4	16.2	5.9	11.5	12.1	15.2	17.7	9.8	6.3	44.1	53.4	25 924	25 043	-3.4	5.7
Winona	3.4	8.8	32.7	11.1	7.3	11.1	11.3	7.0	7.3	28.7	52.5	27 069	27 592	1.9	-1.8
Woodbury	7.4	20.8	6.5	13.1	15.2	16.1	11.4	5.9	3.6	36.2	52.6	46 463	61 961	33.4	9.5
MISSISSIPPI	6.8	18.1	10.5	12.8	12.6	13.5	12.2	7.7	5.7	36.4	51.4	2 844 658	2 967 297	4.3	0.8
Biloxi	6.6	15.0	14.8	14.6	12.1	13.4	11.3	5.5	6.8	34.4	47.7	50 644	44 054	-13.0	3.6
Clinton	5.9	17.6	11.5	13.5	11.8	14.7	10.4	7.8	6.8	36.0	52.3	23 347	25 216	8.0	0.2
Greenville	7.8	18.9	9.3	12.9	12.0	13.9	12.6	7.3	5.4	36.1	53.2	41 633	34 400	-17.4	-6.6
Gulfport	7.9	16.4	10.5	14.7	12.9	13.5	11.3	7.2	5.6	35.2	50.7	71 127	67 793	-4.7	6.0
Hattiesburg	6.6	12.6	23.4	17.6	10.9	9.4	8.6	5.5	5.5	28.2	52.5	44 779	45 989	2.7	2.3
Horn Lake	9.4	22.0	7.4	16.9	14.6	12.0	10.1	5.2	2.6	32.6	51.6	14 099	26 066	84.9	3.2
Jackson	7.5	19.2	12.4	15.3	11.7	12.2	11.1	5.8	4.6	31.6	53.8	184 256	173 514	-5.8	-1.7
Meridian	7.4	19.3	10.3	14.0	11.4	11.3	12.9	6.8	6.4	33.9	53.7	39 968	41 148	3.0	-3.6
Olive Branch	5.2	20.2	10.6	9.8	16.0	16.8	10.0	6.9	4.5	37.5	52.0	21 054	33 484	59.0	7.5
Pearl	7.4	17.7	11.7	14.8	13.1	13.1	9.1	8.2	4.9	34.4	53.5	21 961	25 092	14.3	3.0
Southaven	6.5	21.6	8.3	14.6	14.7	13.8	9.6	6.4	4.5	34.5	53.3	28 977	48 982	69.0	7.4
Tupelo	8.6	19.6	7.3	13.9	12.4	13.0	10.5	7.5	7.2	35.5	51.1	34 211	34 546	1.0	3.3

Table D. Cities — Households, Group Quarters, Crime, and Education

City	Households, 2010-2014				Persons in group quarters, 2010				Serious crimes known to police,[2] 2014				Educational attainment, 2010-2014		
			Percent			Institutional			Total		Rate[3]			Attainment[4] (percent)	
	Number	Persons per household	Female family householder[1]	One-person	Total	Total	Persons in nursing facilities	Non-institutional	Number	Rate[3]	Violent	Property	Population age 25 and older	High school graduate or less	Bachelor's degree or more
	27	28	29	30	31	32	33	34	35	36	37	38	39	40	41
MICHIGAN—Cont'd															
Oak Park	11 385	2.60	21.0	29.9	58	0	0	58	655	2 185	337	1 848	19 295	33.8	28.6
Pontiac	23 238	2.57	27.0	33.6	2 563	1 586	102	977	NA	NA	NA	NA	36 105	56.6	11.0
Portage	19 293	2.44	10.1	30.7	156	111	111	45	1 573	3 289	157	3 133	31 081	26.0	40.2
Port Huron	12 106	2.44	17.6	33.5	761	235	228	526	1 066	3 658	762	2 896	19 376	46.3	16.0
Rochester Hills	27 790	2.60	7.8	26.1	1 181	507	507	674	NA	NA	NA	NA	50 022	20.1	52.4
Roseville	19 669	2.41	19.0	34.0	245	148	148	97	2 080	4 368	449	3 919	32 289	53.9	10.4
Royal Oak	28 269	2.07	6.1	40.9	404	249	225	155	672	1 132	130	1 002	44 246	21.7	51.1
Saginaw	19 376	2.62	26.9	35.7	1 693	876	346	817	2 067	4 132	1 689	2 443	31 681	57.0	11.4
St. Clair Shores	26 663	2.25	11.5	35.5	277	248	248	29	883	1 468	193	1 275	44 551	38.7	23.7
Southfield	31 930	2.27	19.1	39.4	1 189	453	451	736	2 356	3 213	280	2 934	51 821	27.8	36.5
Southgate	12 749	2.33	12.7	35.4	117	88	88	29	999	3 402	310	3 092	21 382	47.4	16.3
Sterling Heights	49 387	2.64	10.4	26.6	772	566	554	206	2 234	1 698	160	1 537	91 942	42.3	26.7
Taylor	23 553	2.65	19.9	28.4	673	540	512	133	2 142	3 481	559	2 922	41 412	55.8	9.6
Troy	30 635	2.68	7.5	23.1	310	117	117	193	1 418	1 703	61	1 641	57 048	20.7	57.7
Warren	52 936	2.54	16.2	30.0	1 248	945	945	303	4 090	3 028	478	2 550	90 725	51.6	16.8
Westland	34 002	2.45	16.2	35.0	1 034	779	548	255	2 212	2 689	364	2 326	57 363	46.1	17.7
Wyandotte	10 611	2.40	12.4	35.3	88	0	0	88	616	2 456	175	2 281	18 484	48.3	16.5
Wyoming	27 253	2.69	13.5	25.9	358	149	149	209	1 808	2 423	389	2 035	46 785	48.0	20.4
MINNESOTA	2 115 337	2.55	9.6	28.2	135 395	56 308	32 989	79 087	137 882	2 527	229	2 297	3 599 228	34.1	33.2
Andover	10 131	3.09	7.2	13.7	39	0	0	39	NA	NA	NA	NA	19 489	28.7	32.7
Apple Valley	19 284	2.59	11.0	23.9	316	198	189	118	1 084	2 148	83	2 065	33 616	21.9	44.4
Blaine	21 881	2.71	10.8	21.4	147	71	31	76	1 884	3 079	72	3 007	39 721	31.3	32.0
Bloomington	36 608	2.33	9.1	33.0	991	489	481	502	3 359	3 854	180	3 674	62 806	28.9	39.7
Brooklyn Center	11 135	2.74	18.0	28.3	182	93	86	89	1 315	4 261	324	3 937	19 567	47.5	19.8
Brooklyn Park	26 345	2.94	17.1	22.5	209	17	8	192	2 678	3 390	386	3 004	47 837	34.7	30.0
Burnsville	24 445	2.50	11.5	28.9	443	294	287	149	1 770	2 869	115	2 754	41 030	29.3	35.6
Coon Rapids	23 730	2.60	11.0	25.7	359	205	201	154	1 624	2 609	133	2 476	41 937	35.0	25.6
Cottage Grove	11 923	2.95	9.3	16.1	64	13	7	51	694	1 951	56	1 894	22 414	32.2	31.2
Duluth	35 548	2.43	11.3	34.7	6 640	1 416	924	5 224	3 959	4 598	359	4 239	52 993	32.6	32.7
Eagan	25 919	2.51	9.4	25.6	197	61	61	136	1 201	1 827	36	1 790	44 126	19.5	50.4
Eden Prairie	24 088	2.58	8.0	24.3	208	127	112	81	871	1 382	35	1 347	41 696	13.3	60.7
Edina	20 833	2.35	5.7	33.1	190	112	100	78	916	1 842	54	1 788	34 582	11.8	67.9
Fridley	11 054	2.49	14.1	29.5	131	48	48	83	1 357	4 885	245	4 640	18 473	38.7	26.3
Inver Grove Heights	13 640	2.51	12.5	26.3	193	154	140	39	748	2 171	200	1 971	22 941	34.2	33.2
Lakeville	19 314	2.99	9.4	14.1	46	14	6	32	704	1 189	42	1 147	36 330	23.3	46.3
Mankato	15 351	2.60	6.5	32.4	4 347	324	239	4 023	1 536	3 750	261	3 489	20 731	30.9	34.3
Maple Grove	24 397	2.64	8.1	20.6	50	4	4	46	1 204	1 815	35	1 780	43 849	19.9	49.4
Maplewood	15 168	2.59	12.1	32.1	1 131	800	362	331	1 976	4 904	151	4 752	27 018	38.5	30.2
Minneapolis	166 824	2.36	11.4	40.3	18 066	3 896	2 814	14 170	23 216	5 740	1 012	4 728	259 273	28.1	47.0
Minnetonka	22 306	2.28	7.8	31.3	380	292	209	88	814	1 572	46	1 526	37 620	16.5	55.7
Moorhead	14 454	2.70	10.3	30.4	3 650	344	263	3 306	897	2 259	176	2 083	21 975	32.1	34.0
Oakdale	10 859	2.55	14.3	27.2	177	7	2	170	1 262	4 528	187	4 342	18 180	31.3	30.6
Owatonna	10 214	2.50	9.5	30.7	531	321	203	210	655	2 564	141	2 423	16 972	42.6	27.6
Plymouth	29 597	2.46	7.8	26.0	1 128	730	229	398	1 113	1 487	72	1 415	51 578	15.8	57.3
Richfield	14 689	2.44	10.1	34.7	347	112	110	235	955	2 623	214	2 409	25 340	36.1	33.4
Rochester	43 651	2.50	9.8	30.6	2 615	1 760	646	855	2 428	2 173	184	1 990	73 660	27.0	42.2
Roseville	14 797	2.34	6.6	37.7	1 426	342	292	1 084	1 899	5 375	127	5 247	24 362	26.7	46.5
St. Cloud	25 279	2.61	11.2	30.2	5 615	1 690	448	3 925	2 771	4 175	393	3 782	38 572	33.8	28.4
St. Louis Park	22 056	2.11	8.4	40.9	755	633	630	122	1 369	2 855	136	2 719	33 899	19.2	54.5
St. Paul	112 407	2.60	14.6	35.3	11 438	2 351	1 608	9 087	12 357	4 147	662	3 484	179 486	35.5	38.6
Savage	9 316	3.01	6.7	17.4	6	4	0	2	624	2 147	93	2 054	17 818	23.7	42.6
Shakopee	12 981	2.97	10.3	20.2	884	843	167	41	825	2 082	144	1 938	24 013	32.2	38.5
Shoreview	10 910	2.35	7.7	29.6	204	9	0	195	306	1 168	61	1 106	18 659	20.9	53.5
Winona	10 219	2.69	6.7	38.8	4 223	376	324	3 847	97	352	91	261	15 267	36.8	31.8
Woodbury	23 659	2.73	9.4	20.5	286	161	161	125	1 213	1 823	54	1 769	42 064	16.8	57.2
MISSISSIPPI	1 092 627	2.73	18.5	27.3	91 964	55 135	16 496	36 829	95 800	3 200	278	2 921	1 929 591	48.3	20.4
Biloxi	17 619	2.53	15.6	34.6	3 065	209	158	2 856	2 936	6 523	478	6 046	28 468	40.1	23.8
Clinton	9 092	2.80	13.9	24.5	397	265	265	132	NA	NA	NA	NA	16 323	25.2	41.5
Greenville	12 228	2.74	28.7	30.0	432	370	254	62	2 450	7 443	295	7 148	21 276	50.0	20.0
Gulfport	27 335	2.56	21.5	31.5	1 984	1 222	278	762	3 706	5 161	199	4 961	45 121	46.2	20.1
Hattiesburg	18 033	2.59	21.2	36.9	3 529	832	468	2 697	2 855	5 957	198	5 758	26 160	40.0	32.2
Horn Lake	9 225	2.87	21.5	24.4	56	56	56	0	571	2 133	112	2 021	16 125	50.6	11.9
Jackson	62 417	2.78	28.0	32.1	6 035	1 419	998	4 616	11 975	6 947	924	6 023	104 982	41.3	26.0
Meridian	15 959	2.56	26.9	34.6	1 678	1 161	268	517	2 242	5 485	587	4 898	26 072	43.9	21.5
Olive Branch	12 844	2.69	14.4	21.3	0	0	0	0	1 038	2 939	255	2 684	22 464	39.0	26.7
Pearl	10 179	2.56	20.1	25.4	70	57	57	13	64	243	27	216	16 669	42.7	19.1
Southaven	17 986	2.80	15.3	22.5	264	264	264	0	1 596	3 101	272	2 829	31 872	39.0	21.0
Tupelo	13 261	2.67	21.4	28.5	895	834	471	61	NA	NA	NA	NA	22 586	39.0	28.5

1. No spouse present. 2. Data for serious crimes have not been adjusted for underreporting. This may affect comparability between geographic areas and over time. 3. Per 100,000 population estimated by the FBI. 4. Persons 25 years old and over.

Table D. Cities — Income, Poverty, and Housing

City	Money income, 2010–2014 Per capita income[1] (dollars)	Households Median income	Households Percent with income of $200,000 or more	Households Percent with income of less than $25,000	Families with income below poverty (percent)	Housing units, 2010 Total	Percent change, 2000–2010	Vacant units for sale or rent[2]	Occupied housing units 2010–2014 Total	Owner-occupied Percent	Median value[3] (dollars)	Median owner costs as a percent of income With a mortgage[4]	Without a mortgage[5]
	42	43	44	45	46	47	48	49	50	51	52	53	54
MICHIGAN—Cont'd													
Oak Park	22 143	47 292	0.8	26.7	15.9	12 782	12.4	1 063	11 385	57.3	79 800	23.3	13.7
Pontiac	15 518	27 632	0.1	45.9	33.4	27 084	2.8	4 864	23 238	44.4	55 300	25.6	17.8
Portage	29 906	55 050	4.2	21.9	8.7	20 559	8.9	1 360	19 293	67.8	147 300	21.0	12.9
Port Huron	18 265	32 888	1.1	40.9	24.2	13 871	-0.9	1 694	12 106	55.3	77 100	24.0	14.7
Rochester Hills	39 394	80 806	9.6	13.2	4.2	29 494	8.1	1 916	27 790	75.5	215 200	20.6	12.1
Roseville	20 611	40 646	0.3	29.8	14.7	21 260	3.6	1 707	19 669	65.1	62 300	24.5	13.8
Royal Oak	39 676	64 873	4.4	17.0	4.4	30 207	0.9	2 144	28 269	67.0	159 000	20.3	14.0
Saginaw	15 127	29 049	0.5	43.9	31.1	23 574	-8.1	3 775	19 376	60.9	46 800	24.2	14.5
St. Clair Shores	29 338	53 252	1.4	20.5	7.6	28 467	0.9	1 882	26 663	78.4	92 100	21.1	13.6
Southfield	29 045	49 548	2.7	24.7	12.4	35 986	0.8	4 208	31 930	49.8	104 100	23.6	15.3
Southgate	26 048	48 924	0.8	23.4	7.9	13 933	4.3	871	12 749	63.9	85 900	20.9	14.0
Sterling Heights	27 375	58 800	2.6	19.1	10.5	52 190	9.8	2 739	49 387	73.1	143 500	22.1	12.6
Taylor	20 246	41 742	0.7	29.1	18.5	26 422	2.0	2 052	23 553	66.5	73 900	23.1	14.1
Troy	39 781	84 325	10.7	13.8	5.5	32 907	6.6	2 204	30 635	73.5	220 100	21.1	11.4
Warren	21 762	43 500	0.8	28.2	15.9	57 938	1.2	4 496	52 936	72.4	86 200	23.3	15.3
Westland	24 123	43 903	1.0	27.4	11.7	39 201	3.0	3 315	34 002	59.4	88 200	22.0	13.4
Wyandotte	26 560	51 074	1.6	24.7	9.3	12 081	-1.8	1 090	10 611	73.6	85 100	21.3	13.9
Wyoming	21 379	46 672	1.0	22.0	12.4	28 983	5.4	2 013	27 253	65.3	98 900	22.1	11.6
MINNESOTA	31 642	60 828	5.0	19.1	7.5	2 347 201	13.6	259 974	2 115 337	72.1	185 200	22.5	11.5
Andover	36 364	93 314	7.2	6.1	3.1	10 091	23.0	280	10 131	93.1	234 700	22.9	10.0
Apple Valley	38 444	80 609	7.7	10.2	4.2	19 600	18.5	725	19 284	79.5	215 700	21.4	10.0
Blaine	33 224	73 496	4.0	10.7	3.4	21 921	35.6	844	21 881	86.4	179 900	22.0	12.2
Bloomington	36 430	63 053	5.3	15.5	5.2	37 641	1.5	1 736	36 608	68.9	210 100	22.6	11.6
Brooklyn Center	20 822	45 198	0.9	23.6	17.1	11 640	0.4	884	11 135	61.6	134 600	25.0	13.3
Brooklyn Park	26 508	62 656	3.8	15.9	10.0	27 841	12.1	1 612	26 345	70.0	178 700	23.6	10.1
Burnsville	31 911	63 997	4.6	16.4	7.9	25 759	6.2	1 476	24 445	65.4	211 100	23.1	11.8
Coon Rapids	30 652	64 694	3.5	14.5	6.0	24 462	7.3	930	23 730	77.4	165 500	22.4	11.2
Cottage Grove	31 724	82 485	4.4	8.3	4.5	12 102	20.8	383	11 923	88.6	204 600	22.7	10.3
Duluth	25 715	43 518	2.8	30.8	12.3	38 208	3.3	2 503	35 548	59.8	145 900	22.0	11.9
Eagan	41 037	80 247	9.2	10.4	4.3	26 414	8.3	1 165	25 919	70.4	245 000	20.2	10.0
Eden Prairie	50 435	95 697	17.3	9.2	3.9	25 075	19.3	1 145	24 088	73.7	301 200	21.1	10.0
Edina	61 438	86 968	19.8	13.1	2.3	22 560	4.2	1 888	20 833	73.1	393 100	22.0	13.3
Fridley	26 931	54 509	1.9	17.9	9.8	11 760	2.2	650	11 054	64.3	167 900	22.9	12.2
Inver Grove Heights	35 212	64 635	6.0	15.3	6.9	14 062	22.8	586	13 640	70.9	205 100	23.4	11.1
Lakeville	37 110	94 635	9.7	8.1	4.2	19 456	41.0	773	19 314	88.1	243 000	22.1	10.0
Mankato	23 249	42 929	2.3	31.2	12.5	15 784	24.0	933	15 351	54.1	151 100	22.1	10.5
Maple Grove	43 833	92 267	11.4	8.4	4.4	23 626	33.2	759	24 397	85.0	242 200	21.5	10.0
Maplewood	29 864	60 323	2.8	16.8	6.3	15 561	11.1	679	15 168	72.0	185 900	23.2	12.0
Minneapolis	32 232	50 767	5.3	27.2	16.1	178 287	5.7	14 747	166 824	48.6	205 200	23.2	13.6
Minnetonka	48 600	80 068	12.0	11.5	2.8	23 294	4.8	1 393	22 306	72.2	289 000	22.3	13.0
Moorhead	23 436	49 514	1.9	26.5	8.9	15 274	25.5	970	14 454	61.2	153 300	21.5	11.3
Oakdale	31 869	67 822	3.2	12.5	5.6	11 388	9.5	440	10 859	75.2	188 500	21.4	10.0
Owatonna	27 467	52 790	2.8	22.8	9.9	10 724	20.0	656	10 214	72.4	146 400	21.8	10.9
Plymouth	46 375	84 321	13.1	11.2	4.8	29 982	18.7	1 319	29 597	72.1	291 800	20.9	10.8
Richfield	28 089	52 484	2.7	20.8	9.3	15 735	2.5	917	14 689	63.5	184 800	23.0	14.3
Rochester	33 625	63 472	5.6	17.2	5.3	45 683	29.7	2 658	43 651	69.6	163 400	20.6	10.0
Roseville	34 934	62 464	4.2	18.9	5.7	15 490	3.8	867	14 797	64.4	217 500	21.7	10.0
St. Cloud	23 078	44 485	2.5	29.1	13.8	27 338	17.8	1 899	25 279	53.4	144 300	22.6	10.9
St. Louis Park	39 502	65 151	5.1	15.8	7.0	23 285	10.2	1 542	22 056	57.2	228 900	22.1	13.3
St. Paul	26 268	48 258	3.7	27.8	17.5	120 795	4.4	9 794	112 407	49.4	175 000	23.1	11.8
Savage	36 932	94 432	9.2	6.7	3.8	9 429	34.5	313	9 316	87.9	246 700	21.3	10.0
Shakopee	31 965	79 670	5.4	9.7	5.0	13 339	71.2	567	12 981	77.1	210 700	20.8	10.0
Shoreview	44 033	79 485	10.5	11.1	3.1	10 826	5.2	424	10 910	81.7	232 400	20.8	11.8
Winona	21 847	40 113	1.8	33.0	6.0	10 989	3.1	540	10 219	61.7	138 000	23.9	10.0
Woodbury	44 047	98 974	13.9	7.9	2.4	23 568	34.4	974	23 659	77.9	267 500	20.7	10.0
MISSISSIPPI	20 956	39 464	2.2	33.2	17.7	1 274 719	9.7	158 951	1 092 627	68.9	100 800	22.6	11.9
Biloxi	23 155	39 374	2.2	31.5	19.2	21 278	-3.9	4 174	17 619	46.9	144 600	23.4	10.5
Clinton	27 407	60 161	4.5	19.6	7.4	10 359	16.2	593	9 092	70.2	150 100	19.5	10.0
Greenville	16 937	30 096	2.3	44.8	30.8	14 561	-10.5	1 883	12 228	52.9	76 200	22.8	13.1
Gulfport	20 340	36 658	1.5	34.6	22.4	31 602	6.8	5 295	27 335	51.6	120 600	25.9	12.3
Hattiesburg	19 338	27 827	2.3	46.3	29.4	21 381	11.5	2 880	18 033	37.3	111 000	23.3	12.5
Horn Lake	18 940	45 817	0.2	22.6	11.8	9 705	90.4	653	9 225	62.4	94 900	20.1	10.5
Jackson	19 042	33 080	2.4	38.8	25.0	74 537	-1.5	10 014	62 417	52.4	89 200	23.4	11.2
Meridian	20 933	29 531	2.7	44.1	30.3	18 591	3.6	2 082	15 959	51.6	85 300	24.1	12.4
Olive Branch	27 672	64 253	1.7	14.5	6.3	12 942	60.6	864	12 844	76.1	163 100	22.8	10.9
Pearl	21 058	41 326	1.0	25.4	11.2	10 396	14.6	604	10 179	61.2	110 600	21.8	10.0
Southaven	24 944	58 712	2.4	17.5	7.6	19 101	66.3	1 132	17 986	68.8	137 800	21.1	10.0
Tupelo	23 825	41 979	4.0	32.2	22.9	15 371	5.0	1 769	13 261	61.8	120 600	23.3	10.1

1. Based on population estimated by the American Community Survey.   2. Includes units rented or sold but not occupied.   3. Specified owner-occupied units; $1,000,000 represents $1,000,000 or more   4. 50.0 represents 50 percent or more.   5. 10.0 represents 10 percent or less.

City	Occupied housing units, 2010–2014 (cont.)				Migration, 2010–2014		Civilian labor force, 2015				Civilian employment[4], 2010–2014			
									Unemployment			Percent		
	Percent renter occupied	Median gross rent[1]	Median gross rent as a percent of income[2]	Percent with no vehicle available	Percent who lived in the same house one year ago	Percent who lived outside current city one year ago	Total	Percent change, 2014–2015	Total	Rate[3]	Population age 16 and older	In labor force	Civilian full-year full-time workers	Households with no workers (percent)
	55	56	57	58	59	60	61	62	63	64	65	66	67	68
MICHIGAN—Cont'd														
Oak Park	42.7	993	33.0	8.7	85.8	11.0	13 920	-1.0	1 157	8.3	23 373	64.1	35.0	27.5
Pontiac	55.6	730	36.6	18.1	74.5	11.5	24 484	-2.1	2 834	11.6	45 160	60.9	27.3	37.8
Portage	32.2	725	30.5	5.8	84.8	11.1	24 623	1.1	933	3.8	36 650	67.9	42.5	27.4
Port Huron	44.7	682	34.1	16.1	80.3	10.0	12 405	-2.0	1 195	9.6	22 981	60.7	29.5	38.9
Rochester Hills	24.5	1 093	28.0	4.8	87.2	9.6	37 124	0.4	1 542	4.2	57 267	66.9	42.9	24.7
Roseville	34.9	877	33.8	10.0	84.2	11.4	22 392	-0.9	1 739	7.8	37 810	63.3	36.4	33.7
Royal Oak	33.0	901	23.5	5.2	83.9	12.0	36 381	0.7	1 122	3.1	50 074	74.7	50.8	22.7
Saginaw	39.1	661	43.1	18.0	82.2	9.0	19 593	-2.2	1 870	9.5	38 993	55.8	25.8	42.4
St. Clair Shores	21.6	921	30.0	6.1	89.2	7.7	30 110	-0.3	1 763	5.9	49 793	63.2	38.8	33.2
Southfield	50.2	972	34.0	10.0	81.1	13.3	33 483	-0.6	2 393	7.1	59 724	60.3	36.4	34.7
Southgate	36.1	792	27.6	6.1	85.7	11.3	14 868	-0.4	644	4.3	25 209	61.1	36.1	33.9
Sterling Heights	26.9	888	29.4	5.1	88.2	8.6	63 842	-0.3	3 686	5.8	107 272	63.7	37.5	27.1
Taylor	33.5	795	33.7	8.0	83.4	12.4	27 425	-1.4	1 990	7.3	48 951	61.0	31.7	34.7
Troy	26.5	1 036	24.3	4.7	87.4	10.0	41 096	0.4	1 696	4.1	65 663	64.8	41.4	22.7
Warren	27.6	836	35.8	9.1	86.5	9.4	61 099	-0.8	4 449	7.3	107 234	60.7	34.6	33.8
Westland	40.6	794	32.9	9.4	84.0	12.4	41 353	-0.7	2 121	5.1	67 986	64.4	37.5	32.4
Wyandotte	26.4	731	33.8	8.2	88.6	8.3	12 657	-0.6	633	5.0	21 061	64.2	37.5	33.3
Wyoming	34.7	730	28.9	6.9	83.4	12.9	43 531	1.6	1 705	3.9	56 583	72.7	43.3	22.0
MINNESOTA	27.9	835	29.6	7.3	85.5	10.2	3 010 367	0.9	111 503	3.7	4 247 699	70.1	43.5	24.1
Andover	6.9	1 483	39.2	2.9	92.6	6.9	18 310	0.7	544	3.0	23 412	77.4	50.6	12.3
Apple Valley	20.5	1 120	29.4	3.4	86.7	9.7	29 126	0.9	903	3.1	38 999	75.7	50.2	16.8
Blaine	13.6	1 043	30.5	3.5	89.8	7.6	34 951	1.0	1 210	3.5	45 427	75.7	49.5	17.2
Bloomington	31.1	956	29.5	6.8	86.5	9.6	46 710	0.6	1 583	3.4	70 591	68.3	43.0	26.9
Brooklyn Center	38.4	885	39.4	8.6	83.0	14.7	15 319	0.8	678	4.4	22 938	67.3	42.8	24.9
Brooklyn Park	30.0	849	33.8	7.8	86.2	11.0	41 737	0.6	1 616	3.9	57 483	73.5	47.7	16.6
Burnsville	34.6	978	28.2	5.3	82.7	12.6	35 837	0.9	1 231	3.4	48 681	73.3	45.6	21.0
Coon Rapids	22.6	1 004	31.1	5.0	86.3	9.9	35 273	0.9	1 293	3.7	48 944	74.2	46.2	20.7
Cottage Grove	11.4	1 098	31.3	2.2	91.9	5.4	19 882	0.8	631	3.2	26 213	75.9	50.7	16.4
Duluth	40.2	726	34.6	13.4	76.4	10.8	45 379	-1.4	1 707	3.8	72 344	64.5	33.1	29.7
Eagan	29.6	998	24.6	3.8	85.0	11.4	39 586	0.8	1 151	2.9	51 089	77.5	52.8	15.9
Eden Prairie	26.3	1 154	23.9	3.1	86.2	10.1	35 868	0.8	1 002	2.8	47 596	74.7	50.4	16.2
Edina	26.9	1 145	25.2	6.4	88.0	10.4	24 709	0.9	694	2.8	38 578	62.7	40.8	30.8
Fridley	35.7	876	28.5	8.7	77.7	17.5	14 797	0.7	568	3.8	21 738	69.2	44.0	24.9
Inver Grove Heights	29.1	975	29.7	4.8	86.0	10.9	19 501	0.8	669	3.4	27 332	73.2	46.8	21.8
Lakeville	11.9	1 121	28.7	2.3	91.0	7.6	33 845	0.8	998	2.9	42 102	78.8	52.2	13.7
Mankato	45.9	730	35.2	9.0	76.4	15.2	24 772	1.0	769	3.1	33 862	71.1	35.2	24.9
Maple Grove	15.0	1 286	31.1	2.6	90.8	7.6	38 983	0.9	1 122	2.9	49 013	77.1	53.2	14.6
Maplewood	28.0	926	34.3	9.4	85.8	12.5	20 502	0.6	748	3.6	31 178	66.0	41.6	26.4
Minneapolis	51.4	854	30.2	18.6	75.0	13.0	232 315	0.7	7 768	3.3	322 431	73.3	42.5	22.8
Minnetonka	27.8	1 130	25.5	4.4	84.8	13.2	29 369	0.7	862	2.9	41 843	70.0	46.8	23.3
Moorhead	38.8	718	36.2	8.0	77.8	14.2	23 437	1.6	623	2.7	31 678	71.7	40.3	23.1
Oakdale	24.8	986	33.5	5.2	87.9	9.5	16 113	0.8	552	3.4	21 976	74.3	47.2	21.2
Owatonna	27.6	719	33.7	9.4	85.8	6.3	14 840	-0.5	518	3.5	19 777	69.7	44.5	28.5
Plymouth	27.9	1 150	28.0	3.0	86.0	11.7	42 480	0.8	1 255	3.0	58 167	71.7	48.8	20.3
Richfield	36.5	841	32.5	10.6	86.0	10.6	20 097	0.6	614	3.1	28 976	72.7	45.1	26.5
Rochester	30.4	801	29.4	7.5	84.5	7.8	61 366	0.2	1 846	3.0	84 952	71.8	46.2	21.4
Roseville	35.6	904	26.5	8.7	84.6	13.2	18 928	0.7	563	3.0	29 029	64.0	40.0	32.5
St. Cloud	46.6	708	32.0	9.1	69.1	19.2	36 780	0.7	1 501	4.1	54 649	69.4	34.6	25.5
St. Louis Park	42.8	971	25.6	8.3	80.2	15.1	29 750	0.9	867	2.9	38 659	75.6	50.3	19.6
St. Paul	50.6	823	31.6	15.0	77.9	11.2	153 855	0.8	5 734	3.7	225 983	70.5	39.9	24.1
Savage	12.1	1 063	30.2	1.7	91.9	7.6	17 185	0.8	503	2.9	20 531	79.9	53.8	9.8
Shakopee	22.9	1 047	27.6	4.0	87.9	8.2	22 533	0.8	707	3.1	28 286	78.6	54.6	11.8
Shoreview	18.3	1 102	24.9	4.3	89.8	9.0	14 640	0.9	425	2.9	20 969	67.3	46.0	25.4
Winona	38.3	615	30.5	11.2	75.6	12.9	16 079	0.5	580	3.6	24 395	69.6	30.9	27.1
Woodbury	22.1	1 344	23.8	2.2	87.7	9.9	37 636	1.0	997	2.6	48 076	75.1	52.5	15.7
MISSISSIPPI	31.1	714	32.0	6.9	86.0	10.3	1 272 657	1.9	83 011	6.5	2 323 223	58.4	36.9	31.9
Biloxi	53.1	796	31.3	7.4	75.7	18.0	19 617	0.7	1 234	6.3	35 678	68.0	36.4	27.5
Clinton	29.8	910	30.5	4.1	90.2	7.2	13 185	3.2	591	4.5	20 175	65.8	44.1	22.7
Greenville	47.1	627	37.6	15.0	81.3	6.2	12 315	-0.7	1 278	10.4	25 585	59.5	32.1	35.4
Gulfport	48.4	840	35.9	5.9	74.3	15.1	29 756	0.5	2 146	7.2	54 257	62.7	35.6	29.5
Hattiesburg	62.7	709	36.8	11.5	71.0	15.0	21 957	2.9	1 632	7.4	38 143	63.4	30.3	30.2
Horn Lake	37.6	964	32.0	3.8	81.7	14.4	12 461	2.7	629	5.0	19 466	72.4	48.6	18.8
Jackson	47.6	753	36.8	9.5	83.8	5.5	75 521	2.2	4 865	6.4	131 955	62.0	38.7	29.1
Meridian	48.4	654	31.3	10.3	82.0	8.2	15 795	-2.4	1 305	8.3	31 434	59.3	38.2	33.4
Olive Branch	23.9	1 053	26.0	2.6	87.5	8.6	18 492	3.4	874	4.7	26 736	72.7	50.1	17.8
Pearl	38.8	806	31.2	3.3	79.6	12.8	12 684	3.3	549	4.3	20 384	65.5	46.1	24.5
Southaven	31.2	936	28.4	2.0	83.0	11.4	25 977	3.1	1 156	4.5	37 487	71.5	50.7	18.2
Tupelo	38.2	699	31.9	7.1	85.1	9.1	16 281	3.1	1 065	6.5	26 542	60.4	38.7	28.3

1. $2,000 represents $2,000 or more.   2. 50.0 represents 50 percent or more.   3. Percent of civilian labor force.   4. Persons 16 years old and over.

City	Value of residential construction authorized by building permits, 2015			Wholesale trade,[1] 2012				Retail trade,[2] 2012			
	New construction ($1,000)	Number of housing units	Percent single family	Number of establishments	Number of employees	Sales (mil dol)	Annual payroll (mil dol)	Number of establishments	Number of employees	Sales (mil dol)	Annual payroll (mil dol)
	69	70	71	72	73	74	75	76	77	78	79
MICHIGAN—Cont'd											
Oak Park	229	1	100.0	63	600	307.9	37.6	121	980	220.7	22.4
Pontiac	894	8	100.0	43	D	D	D	190	1 572	414.7	39.7
Portage	21 208	96	52.1	46	903	352.9	70.5	302	5 471	1 137.7	105.7
Port Huron	1 316	6	100.0	20	194	120.3	10.2	115	1 145	299.2	29.2
Rochester Hills	33 785	90	100.0	89	959	865.6	77.0	247	5 126	1 393.8	127.7
Roseville	5 235	41	2.4	45	593	670.2	34.0	250	4 380	1 170.5	99.1
Royal Oak	42 876	160	100.0	55	590	1 218.9	36.5	224	2 496	634.0	65.1
Saginaw	6 906	55	9.1	35	544	276.8	28.0	146	874	188.6	18.5
St. Clair Shores	2 719	16	100.0	38	187	95.9	9.2	174	2 098	565.5	55.8
Southfield	3 582	9	100.0	149	2 717	3 983.5	188.2	421	5 634	2 009.7	163.2
Southgate	3 794	14	100.0	7	D	D	D	130	2 593	740.5	64.9
Sterling Heights	53 887	268	60.8	151	1 914	845.2	111.2	449	7 490	1 976.7	186.4
Taylor	7 393	29	86.2	66	1 096	783.5	53.2	326	5 342	1 360.1	125.1
Troy	52 901	254	52.8	331	6 106	4 293.4	363.9	550	10 978	3 608.5	299.7
Warren	5 957	49	67.3	165	3 181	1 893.9	188.7	460	5 305	1 498.3	137.6
Westland	7 555	65	87.7	51	477	258.8	24.8	305	4 569	1 094.1	99.9
Wyandotte	466	3	100.0	14	D	D	D	86	467	127.7	11.2
Wyoming	9 291	62	96.8	166	3 842	3 083.0	206.9	257	4 053	1 114.2	115.0
MINNESOTA	4 135 089	19 545	55.8	6 569	108 467	104 485.1	7 170.1	19 109	288 888	78 898.2	6 857.5
Andover	21 576	74	100.0	11	36	15.8	1.4	37	601	140.2	11.3
Apple Valley	55 571	400	30.0	22	83	37.5	3.8	119	3 499	924.7	85.0
Blaine	88 955	301	100.0	72	1 059	555.4	53.8	222	4 265	966.4	92.8
Bloomington	3 716	16	100.0	193	5 005	5 106.6	355.4	522	12 250	3 007.9	330.6
Brooklyn Center	1 159	10	100.0	25	508	285.1	24.1	72	1 863	658.2	55.7
Brooklyn Park	32 612	134	100.0	80	1 488	1 018.1	85.7	155	3 311	979.3	87.7
Burnsville	10 763	49	100.0	159	D	D	D	333	5 998	1 506.7	163.7
Coon Rapids	7 523	29	100.0	24	331	107.0	15.7	180	4 610	1 314.0	113.7
Cottage Grove	20 858	65	100.0	11	D	D	D	48	956	236.4	21.0
Duluth	47 834	397	7.3	93	1 063	531.9	52.7	427	6 141	1 384.7	130.1
Eagan	17 048	49	100.0	143	2 815	1 679.9	184.4	163	3 258	1 040.7	81.2
Eden Prairie	23 959	73	100.0	177	2 957	5 430.6	223.2	242	5 876	2 684.5	201.2
Edina	142 540	492	23.6	129	1 086	1 118.7	75.6	299	6 044	1 173.2	135.4
Fridley	519	4	100.0	70	9 569	5 882.7	1 457.6	86	2 040	591.5	53.8
Inver Grove Heights	11 372	33	100.0	20	D	D	D	69	1 520	766.8	54.1
Lakeville	126 950	420	98.6	45	D	D	D	120	2 125	664.4	53.6
Mankato	51 796	540	14.4	55	980	715.9	48.6	271	5 743	1 334.6	122.3
Maple Grove	85 732	397	48.4	86	935	601.4	53.7	183	4 073	1 016.9	91.2
Maplewood	2 249	11	100.0	38	425	219.9	23.7	229	4 308	1 218.2	110.9
Minneapolis	311 473	1 489	8.2	483	7 802	6 079.5	477.3	1 123	14 533	4 070.0	397.3
Minnetonka	57 583	262	18.3	131	3 457	2 016.4	204.4	294	5 982	1 771.5	167.8
Moorhead	65 552	507	39.3	31	433	356.1	22.1	113	1 992	471.4	42.2
Oakdale	2 503	11	100.0	40	480	579.2	33.5	64	1 514	365.5	31.7
Owatonna	8 336	50	28.0	22	323	216.3	18.5	103	2 096	469.4	45.5
Plymouth	133 379	455	65.5	203	5 086	4 243.4	356.7	183	3 279	1 175.4	96.4
Richfield	1 526	6	100.0	15	285	69.5	19.1	116	2 488	3 045.5	74.6
Rochester	221 188	1 466	24.5	71	905	471.2	44.1	507	9 720	2 224.4	213.7
Roseville	5 336	15	100.0	68	1 075	796.5	59.0	304	6 393	1 200.6	130.6
St. Cloud	26 284	267	17.2	75	2 002	970.1	92.7	326	6 280	1 548.2	141.3
St. Louis Park	74 797	389	7.5	108	1 486	781.5	92.4	205	4 325	1 292.0	127.0
St. Paul	139 731	923	6.5	270	4 879	3 332.8	295.3	739	9 230	1 959.9	208.7
Savage	29 146	85	100.0	33	594	1 002.6	30.7	83	1 069	286.1	23.5
Shakopee	25 865	147	40.1	54	1 186	939.9	83.8	116	2 294	688.9	52.2
Shoreview	4 654	19	100.0	23	D	D	D	38	696	153.6	16.7
Winona	6 286	58	10.3	33	354	200.2	15.4	113	2 298	532.8	46.8
Woodbury	117 470	417	61.6	38	D	D	D	232	4 979	1 005.9	93.7
MISSISSIPPI	1 078 138	6 845	81.9	2 484	30 351	28 303.0	1 373.6	11 594	136 032	37 053.2	2 968.4
Biloxi	23 958	104	100.0	37	417	188.9	14.3	209	2 470	542.5	51.4
Clinton	18 069	81	100.0	13	96	44.1	3.6	84	960	240.7	21.9
Greenville	121	1	100.0	40	333	825.3	15.5	168	1 891	405.4	36.0
Gulfport	16 427	111	100.0	84	869	392.0	41.4	385	5 435	1 432.3	123.6
Hattiesburg	5 337	178	52.2	85	866	532.1	33.8	453	7 195	4 103.8	149.6
Horn Lake	6 353	71	100.0	17	D	D	D	70	1 069	266.2	24.0
Jackson	3 749	21	100.0	244	3 355	2 146.6	162.5	700	9 327	2 606.3	236.8
Meridian	3 144	13	100.0	58	1 362	1 511.3	61.2	344	4 598	1 193.9	104.4
Olive Branch	35 584	297	100.0	51	1 000	862.2	45.5	122	1 896	646.7	50.2
Pearl	3 726	21	100.0	68	1 095	777.5	59.8	115	1 947	483.3	48.5
Southaven	39 506	295	96.6	38	1 464	2 194.9	63.9	214	3 945	1 123.1	94.4
Tupelo	8 151	53	100.0	113	1 169	819.3	48.5	374	6 061	1 350.0	127.5

1. Merchant wholesalers except manufacturers' sales branches and offices.   2. Establishments with payroll.

Table D. Cities — Real Estate, Professional Services, and Manufacturing

City	Real estate and rental and leasing, 2012				Professional, scientific, and technical services,[1] 2012				Manufacturing, 2012			
	Number of establishments	Number of employees	Receipts (mil dol)	Annual payroll (mil dol)	Number of establishments	Number of employees	Receipts (mil dol)	Annual payroll (mil dol)	Number of establishments	Number of employees	Receipts (mil dol)	Annual payroll (mil dol)
	80	81	82	83	84	85	86	87	88	89	90	91
MICHIGAN—Cont'd												
Oak Park	30	D	D	D	39	317	71.7	23.1	45	812	154.8	42.8
Pontiac	45	221	36.5	8.3	41	370	46.4	19.0	43	984	615.6	61.1
Portage	52	1 240	93.4	41.2	139	1 131	176.4	60.9	56	6 306	D	415.8
Port Huron	23	71	10.2	1.7	66	D	D	D	45	2 633	1 562.4	130.0
Rochester Hills	48	199	31.4	6.2	250	2 652	439.3	181.0	97	4 059	1 368.3	215.9
Roseville	46	301	54.9	12.4	52	288	18.1	9.4	128	3 854	761.8	216.3
Royal Oak	65	284	39.1	11.7	289	D	D	D	66	1 118	412.6	54.1
Saginaw	20	61	10.5	1.9	81	D	D	D	57	2 770	948.9	155.1
St. Clair Shores	41	130	23.1	3.4	161	781	90.7	36.7	39	1 191	382.1	60.6
Southfield	219	3 050	707.3	151.1	731	13 009	2 655.0	1 221.5	72	3 434	D	207.9
Southgate	21	D	D	D	32	230	21.4	8.4	7	D	D	D
Sterling Heights	93	549	121.6	19.3	265	D	D	D	254	15 436	10 090.2	1 077.1
Taylor	45	312	76.9	9.5	93	D	D	D	80	2 506	817.5	133.8
Troy	152	1 427	287.5	58.2	869	16 374	2 482.5	1 139.0	251	5 912	2 053.0	308.7
Warren	99	605	130.0	25.9	192	13 153	410.5	1 111.3	320	13 623	9 322.0	847.9
Westland	52	D	D	D	64	308	35.0	11.0	67	1 690	441.3	78.6
Wyandotte	9	D	D	D	43	138	19.8	7.1	31	1 430	716.3	142.2
Wyoming	73	669	147.0	27.6	108	D	D	D	155	6 340	1 682.6	298.2
MINNESOTA	6 300	34 499	7 827.9	1 396.0	16 260	D	D	D	7 313	297 884	123 076.3	15 822.6
Andover	45	162	19.1	3.6	64	129	16.1	5.4	12	165	D	6.4
Apple Valley	53	201	46.9	5.4	162	D	D	D	13	506	D	32.0
Blaine	61	190	57.9	6.1	112	D	D	D	160	2 730	1 018.4	138.7
Bloomington	199	4 195	904.5	204.9	564	D	D	D	120	4 999	1 673.6	314.9
Brooklyn Center	32	131	30.4	5.6	60	438	76.7	30.4	26	1 719	335.2	99.3
Brooklyn Park	55	299	48.8	11.3	129	1 205	373.8	58.3	113	5 330	1 491.8	294.6
Burnsville	118	503	114.9	18.3	289	1 438	260.1	94.4	94	3 051	850.4	163.6
Coon Rapids	62	199	43.3	8.6	113	842	138.1	49.1	50	2 992	990.6	184.4
Cottage Grove	21	D	D	D	33	94	8.7	3.3	11	1 173	D	82.1
Duluth	120	657	103.9	19.7	229	D	D	D	89	2 381	D	124.9
Eagan	106	799	163.5	35.3	337	D	D	D	86	3 073	1 166.7	165.1
Eden Prairie	124	916	692.7	60.9	430	4 020	819.8	326.0	110	7 861	2 647.8	545.5
Edina	195	1 617	290.7	80.5	492	D	D	D	62	3 155	866.6	221.5
Fridley	36	D	D	D	77	302	72.0	17.1	113	5 972	1 933.4	340.2
Inver Grove Heights	27	168	19.7	4.2	84	398	60.9	24.1	27	832	321.3	40.5
Lakeville	64	122	33.5	4.6	167	523	86.0	25.8	55	2 932	760.7	133.7
Mankato	70	539	63.0	12.9	117	D	D	D	49	2 644	3 469.1	126.6
Maple Grove	86	191	43.4	7.3	275	1 183	202.1	76.0	95	6 410	1 689.4	404.0
Maplewood	43	176	29.9	4.4	93	374	47.5	14.0	24	541	183.8	26.2
Minneapolis	684	4 056	764.1	195.6	2 338	31 241	6 957.8	2 808.4	427	12 837	3 944.2	689.5
Minnetonka	140	1 091	307.6	73.9	438	D	D	D	81	4 523	2 144.7	354.0
Moorhead	30	145	16.3	3.2	48	D	D	D	21	699	D	29.4
Oakdale	27	D	D	D	87	877	157.0	64.4	28	673	151.6	31.2
Owatonna	20	235	15.2	4.4	46	158	15.3	5.1	36	4 139	D	188.5
Plymouth	137	710	405.0	39.0	500	6 498	990.9	362.5	167	10 038	3 905.4	684.6
Richfield	27	384	36.7	8.3	100	450	58.9	26.5	15	46	D	1.2
Rochester	149	676	134.6	21.4	226	D	D	D	56	7 887	2 962.0	543.3
Roseville	53	352	106.4	17.5	213	2 187	545.6	150.0	56	1 644	616.8	91.4
St. Cloud	104	478	87.5	16.4	149	D	D	D	59	4 810	1 515.6	204.2
St. Louis Park	131	2 014	235.5	66.1	370	D	D	D	64	1 517	330.8	77.5
St. Paul	349	2 485	1 113.1	125.8	868	6 532	1 088.9	446.2	225	6 867	2 018.1	380.6
Savage	41	81	24.2	3.4	109	D	D	D	42	1 165	349.1	59.2
Shakopee	44	110	30.7	3.8	120	D	D	D	43	2 790	1 493.2	194.6
Shoreview	25	D	D	D	112	340	52.2	19.4	34	1 368	400.8	92.0
Winona	33	100	15.4	1.9	61	D	D	D	65	3 317	1 069.7	162.6
Woodbury	74	D	D	D	266	1 287	179.2	68.3	22	686	279.7	42.6
MISSISSIPPI	2 374	10 235	1 709.3	334.1	4 727	30 071	4 009.1	1 443.3	2 252	132 789	66 441.6	5 919.1
Biloxi	69	279	64.1	9.7	135	D	D	D	20	265	D	8.5
Clinton	33	D	D	D	58	353	36.9	13.5	8	D	D	6.4
Greenville	35	127	17.5	4.3	57	D	D	D	23	740	526.6	35.6
Gulfport	121	598	110.4	18.6	185	D	D	D	57	1 788	D	82.3
Hattiesburg	99	424	91.7	15.3	187	D	D	D	57	2 861	825.1	105.4
Horn Lake	22	106	22.8	3.1	14	102	6.4	2.4	14	683	D	35.3
Jackson	232	1 458	313.1	65.5	552	D	D	D	103	2 717	855.6	132.7
Meridian	69	242	54.7	7.4	118	D	D	D	46	1 331	448.3	47.5
Olive Branch	19	56	13.8	2.3	40	176	15.0	5.0	54	1 854	742.3	86.4
Pearl	43	218	25.5	6.6	30	169	31.9	6.3	25	628	156.7	25.9
Southaven	40	135	42.9	5.3	75	538	57.3	14.6	15	D	142.1	D
Tupelo	77	343	64.5	11.0	162	1 025	104.0	44.4	72	3 811	1 605.0	172.4

1. Establishments subject to federal tax.

Table D. Cities — Accommodation and Food Services, Arts, Entertainment, and Recreation, and Health Care and Social Assistance

City	Accommodation and food services, 2012				Arts, entertainment, and recreation,[1] 2012				Health care and social assistance,[1] 2012			
	Number of establish-ments	Number of employees	Sales (mil dol)	Annual payroll (mil dol)	Number of establish-ments	Number of employees	Receipts (mil dol)	Annual payroll (mil dol)	Number of establish-ments	Number of employees	Receipts (mil dol)	Annual payroll (mil dol)
	92	93	94	95	96	97	98	99	100	101	102	103
MICHIGAN—Cont'd												
Oak Park	43	D	D	D	1	D	D	D	80	555	41.2	16.1
Pontiac	102	1 226	76.3	18.3	9	96	8.4	1.6	114	1 294	156.3	59.4
Portage	142	D	D	D	14	76	4.1	0.9	160	1 924	167.2	75.6
Port Huron	64	1 016	39.8	11.6	11	132	5.3	1.5	127	1 263	153.2	78.4
Rochester Hills	105	2 490	109.1	33.8	20	D	D	D	290	3 201	358.3	139.4
Roseville	109	2 763	116.3	33.6	9	133	4.3	1.4	102	D	D	D
Royal Oak	157	3 304	170.7	49.2	15	D	D	D	175	D	D	D
Saginaw	76	948	44.7	12.0	2	D	D	D	111	1 788	193.9	83.0
St. Clair Shores	116	D	D	D	22	D	D	D	203	D	D	D
Southfield	240	4 113	234.8	65.0	21	256	17.6	7.1	692	8 755	934.5	419.4
Southgate	92	2 179	99.8	29.7	4	D	D	D	75	835	90.1	34.6
Sterling Heights	226	4 510	191.9	55.7	27	D	D	D	349	3 546	324.1	132.3
Taylor	143	2 257	103.7	28.0	15	D	D	D	121	1 790	160.6	65.4
Troy	269	6 231	342.7	102.3	34	D	D	D	477	D	D	D
Warren	296	5 058	236.0	66.5	23	D	D	D	338	D	D	D
Westland	151	2 695	119.6	32.6	16	D	D	D	120	1 569	132.3	54.9
Wyandotte	60	604	28.1	7.7	4	D	D	D	46	D	D	D
Wyoming	128	2 271	99.7	27.0	11	D	D	D	102	D	D	D
MINNESOTA	11 345	221 859	11 722.6	3 238.0	1 927	27 308	2 355.8	917.7	11 233	189 308	15 774.4	7 258.9
Andover	19	339	15.5	4.0	6	50	2.1	0.7	43	559	40.0	16.5
Apple Valley	72	1 751	80.2	22.9	10	D	D	D	113	1 128	115.6	47.6
Blaine	109	2 569	117.6	34.4	23	D	D	D	100	1 342	135.0	48.8
Bloomington	266	8 597	540.8	163.0	25	D	D	D	221	3 751	287.0	122.0
Brooklyn Center	48	1 089	53.9	12.7	5	D	D	D	75	963	59.8	29.6
Brooklyn Park	84	1 407	61.5	17.2	17	D	D	D	102	2 753	156.1	60.5
Burnsville	129	2 756	129.5	38.5	30	560	19.8	5.8	209	D	D	D
Coon Rapids	110	2 581	128.3	36.6	15	314	17.3	4.4	127	D	D	D
Cottage Grove	32	652	27.9	8.1	5	59	2.2	0.8	44	D	D	D
Duluth	227	5 656	250.0	71.8	28	286	10.4	3.7	263	5 585	485.0	214.0
Eagan	153	3 503	216.5	51.8	16	D	D	D	164	2 756	242.0	94.3
Eden Prairie	149	3 143	165.8	49.4	31	D	D	D	147	2 642	494.2	125.1
Edina	104	2 811	161.3	46.9	26	D	D	D	365	D	D	D
Fridley	48	D	D	D	8	D	D	D	77	D	D	D
Inver Grove Heights	52	971	43.3	13.0	6	60	3.4	1.0	59	944	58.2	28.1
Lakeville	65	1 687	69.7	20.5	13	D	D	D	102	D	D	D
Mankato	140	3 421	138.6	37.9	9	171	6.6	1.5	123	2 577	231.0	109.7
Maple Grove	113	3 337	169.1	48.5	14	D	D	D	150	2 340	223.3	94.4
Maplewood	108	2 244	104.6	30.3	16	D	D	D	155	2 048	258.9	103.9
Minneapolis	1 141	27 424	1 646.9	469.0	169	2 816	501.8	258.8	818	16 746	1 296.2	670.3
Minnetonka	112	2 594	147.1	44.7	29	D	D	D	167	2 597	499.3	141.1
Moorhead	57	1 584	59.7	18.0	7	D	D	D	79	1 420	94.8	40.5
Oakdale	40	963	68.0	16.0	12	D	D	D	42	522	41.1	13.4
Owatonna	66	1 448	54.8	15.6	8	D	D	D	72	D	D	D
Plymouth	131	2 863	137.0	41.4	21	384	25.4	6.2	198	2 705	421.0	189.0
Richfield	62	1 172	66.6	20.0	6	23	1.8	0.6	76	1 832	107.1	50.3
Rochester	292	7 130	374.5	106.7	28	613	20.9	6.9	260	6 019	558.8	248.2
Roseville	118	3 330	164.7	51.5	14	D	D	D	142	3 636	299.1	147.0
St. Cloud	163	3 714	163.6	44.9	28	359	23.8	5.7	166	5 141	424.5	257.6
St. Louis Park	96	2 413	135.1	40.2	28	D	D	D	198	D	D	D
St. Paul	599	11 383	589.0	173.3	84	1 613	203.0	98.9	685	15 640	1 017.7	535.3
Savage	43	D	D	D	9	203	14.3	3.9	47	428	34.8	14.0
Shakopee	78	D	D	D	17	D	D	D	72	695	58.6	29.0
Shoreview	30	629	27.3	7.8	9	42	4.1	1.1	68	703	56.7	26.4
Winona	88	1 902	68.3	18.3	12	154	6.9	2.7	43	D	D	D
Woodbury	114	2 800	133.5	38.7	22	D	D	D	188	2 604	312.7	125.7
MISSISSIPPI	5 177	116 238	6 999.2	1 765.0	467	6 178	453.1	115.8	5 149	84 441	8 730.7	3 450.8
Biloxi	127	10 835	1 089.8	266.2	21	1 448	114.4	27.6	128	D	D	D
Clinton	56	1 270	60.0	14.3	9	D	D	D	48	834	57.9	22.5
Greenville	71	1 709	115.4	27.9	5	D	D	D	110	D	D	D
Gulfport	197	5 065	345.8	81.8	12	D	D	D	209	D	D	D
Hattiesburg	232	5 570	248.9	68.4	16	D	D	D	199	5 424	709.3	332.0
Horn Lake	52	1 260	59.3	15.3	5	D	D	D	17	D	D	D
Jackson	370	7 443	378.2	103.7	22	449	42.9	10.6	515	10 396	1 297.0	513.0
Meridian	154	3 512	168.4	44.0	8	48	2.5	0.6	169	D	D	D
Olive Branch	70	1 581	77.6	19.9	10	D	D	D	54	333	42.0	12.4
Pearl	73	1 563	86.6	21.6	5	D	D	D	31	333	42.0	12.4
Southaven	125	3 105	149.8	39.2	8	D	D	D	137	D	D	D
Tupelo	165	4 002	173.2	47.7	11	D	D	D	188	D	D	D

1. Establishments subject to federal tax.

Table D. Cities — **Other Services and Government Employment and Payroll**

City	Other services[1], 2012				Government employment and payroll, 2012								
						March payroll							
							Percent of total for:						
	Number of establishments	Number of employees	Receipts (mil dol)	Annual payroll (mil dol)	Full-time equivalent employees	Total (dollars)	Adminis- tration, judicial, and legal	Police and Corrections	Fire Protection	Highways and trans- portation	Health and welfare	Natural resources and utilities	Education and libraries
	104	105	106	107	108	109	110	111	112	113	114	115	116
MICHIGAN—Cont'd													
Oak Park	34	197	21.9	6.4	185	937 924	18.6	60.3	0.0	10.5	1.9	3.7	3.3
Pontiac	58	439	46.2	13.5	430	1 925 926	17.1	26.9	21.9	5.4	1.8	16.6	1.4
Portage	89	659	53.5	16.1	226	1 051 828	15.4	37.7	18.1	12.3	4.6	4.9	0.0
Port Huron	34	193	10.0	3.1	265	1 254 174	10.2	26.7	19.4	6.8	0.5	25.3	0.0
Rochester Hills	83	472	31.1	9.7	212	1 126 747	28.0	1.5	20.1	6.3	0.0	29.2	0.0
Roseville	76	425	36.9	10.6	272	1 442 763	17.1	38.9	18.8	5.1	2.8	6.5	2.7
Royal Oak	118	650	59.8	17.3	321	1 931 268	16.4	25.4	37.1	2.0	1.2	5.2	3.3
Saginaw	45	245	21.6	5.7	613	1 804 633	11.1	28.9	17.4	6.3	2.1	29.3	0.0
St. Clair Shores	98	577	33.0	10.4	289	1 541 860	15.0	42.8	21.6	1.7	0.7	11.6	5.1
Southfield	115	631	59.1	16.2	690	3 446 012	19.1	28.8	18.1	5.7	1.0	8.4	6.3
Southgate	53	532	55.1	15.3	177	773 845	14.0	43.0	18.7	6.4	1.2	9.7	2.6
Sterling Heights	175	950	85.3	27.6	579	3 290 094	12.5	40.0	22.0	5.0	1.9	8.5	3.7
Taylor	103	974	88.6	37.0	369	1 754 345	13.6	40.4	19.0	6.4	4.2	14.1	0.3
Troy	178	1 647	169.1	58.1	515	2 464 478	14.8	42.0	3.2	8.2	0.0	17.1	6.8
Warren	214	1 570	191.9	60.4	409	1 654 082	24.5	41.8	6.8	11.2	1.1	10.9	0.0
Westland	110	720	74.4	21.5	341	1 711 074	17.2	33.4	26.3	2.7	4.2	10.7	4.8
Wyandotte	35	171	15.2	4.9	264	1 258 764	6.9	21.7	11.9	10.2	0.2	39.9	0.0
Wyoming	110	771	68.1	21.3	303	1 910 038	15.8	32.7	7.9	12.1	3.7	22.2	0.0
MINNESOTA	8 286	51 746	4 542.3	1 382.9	X	X	X	X	X	X	X	X	X
Andover	33	253	11.5	4.8	57	306 532	24.8	0.0	6.4	37.0	5.8	20.9	0.0
Apple Valley	57	492	35.1	12.2	229	1 179 963	20.1	31.5	5.2	9.3	0.0	23.8	0.0
Blaine	116	899	89.2	27.5	193	1 113 430	14.4	41.7	4.5	11.3	3.0	15.1	0.0
Bloomington	150	1 477	137.0	42.8	580	3 330 394	17.4	31.1	1.2	8.0	13.9	19.4	0.0
Brooklyn Center	20	99	4.8	1.7	190	907 979	13.2	39.3	1.8	9.0	0.9	16.1	0.0
Brooklyn Park	80	457	34.6	12.1	439	1 758 756	8.0	36.5	10.9	10.9	10.0	15.7	0.0
Burnsville	117	802	66.9	22.7	283	1 681 229	9.1	34.0	19.2	3.9	1.0	16.7	0.0
Coon Rapids	75	502	44.9	12.5	274	1 545 147	17.1	30.9	13.2	6.2	5.6	15.0	0.0
Cottage Grove	38	203	11.3	4.1	144	711 248	12.8	41.8	9.7	7.9	5.8	15.7	0.0
Duluth	124	909	75.2	20.9	1 045	5 036 775	9.3	20.6	16.0	20.5	3.8	18.3	4.0
Eagan	111	1 396	130.4	45.7	268	1 561 646	13.0	28.8	3.4	11.0	7.1	30.5	0.0
Eden Prairie	117	971	89.6	26.0	328	1 743 608	14.5	34.2	4.6	8.2	2.3	23.7	0.0
Edina	90	1 073	83.2	30.7	352	1 123 601	13.6	25.8	14.8	13.3	1.1	27.2	0.0
Fridley	46	383	32.9	12.9	159	814 545	21.9	36.8	8.3	11.3	0.0	18.0	0.0
Inver Grove Heights	43	276	24.6	8.0	165	851 190	11.3	30.5	5.7	13.8	7.8	30.9	0.0
Lakeville	77	546	41.2	13.2	211	1 082 740	14.0	36.0	3.4	11.5	2.5	18.7	0.0
Mankato	71	547	40.6	13.8	247	1 231 381	15.7	27.7	8.8	14.5	6.7	19.1	0.0
Maple Grove	104	862	68.6	24.4	296	1 469 495	14.2	34.1	4.5	6.8	2.2	24.2	0.0
Maplewood	70	359	31.7	10.1	213	1 114 986	14.1	35.4	13.8	12.7	0.3	17.3	0.0
Minneapolis	680	5 266	422.1	142.9	5 068	26 103 507	17.5	27.4	10.3	12.5	9.5	21.9	0.0
Minnetonka	96	717	40.5	15.2	278	1 451 759	17.2	30.1	6.4	12.6	6.1	22.6	0.0
Moorhead	62	311	23.5	7.3	325	1 425 672	7.7	22.3	13.7	9.6	0.7	41.4	0.0
Oakdale	34	D	D	D	111	601 791	15.3	41.9	9.3	5.0	3.9	15.6	0.0
Owatonna	52	278	35.4	7.6	211	1 033 223	2.7	19.8	4.9	11.0	1.6	48.8	5.9
Plymouth	94	765	62.7	24.2	284	1 540 683	14.5	33.6	5.5	10.0	5.3	23.7	0.0
Richfield	51	337	26.5	10.6	152	758 629	14.7	33.6	0.0	13.7	5.8	23.9	0.0
Rochester	145	1 329	90.8	32.3	902	4 970 436	6.7	22.3	13.1	9.3	0.0	38.4	6.2
Roseville	88	825	60.5	20.8	191	1 032 673	11.9	37.1	9.1	3.6	4.1	15.9	0.0
St. Cloud	98	941	91.9	28.1	476	2 084 342	8.3	31.7	16.1	9.7	5.9	21.3	0.0
St. Louis Park	109	545	35.9	12.0	270	1 697 664	10.1	28.0	11.9	8.0	13.9	19.8	0.0
St. Paul	371	2 885	226.3	78.2	3 092	18 028 194	10.8	29.1	17.9	10.0	8.1	20.1	4.0
Savage	53	500	26.3	9.9	118	627 032	15.4	38.4	2.4	14.5	0.0	16.4	0.0
Shakopee	59	314	34.7	9.9	200	1 024 903	11.0	30.0	5.6	7.6	0.0	27.1	0.0
Shoreview	19	D	D	D	99	459 573	15.0	0.0	37.1	15.7	12.0	15.7	0.0
Winona	41	230	21.4	6.2	178	771 072	9.5	27.9	14.3	9.5	3.1	24.9	4.4
Woodbury	84	800	48.3	18.2	208	1 116 340	7.1	20.7	13.8	10.0	0.0	38.6	5.6
MISSISSIPPI	2 801	15 027	1 359.2	402.3	X	X	X	X	X	X	X	X	X
Biloxi	44	285	23.6	7.4	618	2 485 229	7.2	33.9	31.9	11.2	2.3	9.3	0.0
Clinton	28	135	13.3	3.9	200	583 437	12.6	31.2	23.8	11.1	0.0	20.4	0.0
Greenville	45	366	32.0	9.5	418	1 079 087	14.6	25.9	20.6	12.0	0.0	22.1	0.0
Gulfport	102	537	46.0	14.7	2 468	12 266 312	2.9	7.1	4.8	1.2	81.1	1.5	0.0
Hattiesburg	84	551	43.3	12.9	695	1 732 465	13.4	28.5	23.1	10.4	3.7	17.8	0.0
Horn Lake	20	107	13.7	3.6	207	963 937	6.8	40.4	27.4	12.4	0.0	9.9	0.0
Jackson	192	1 476	118.0	40.1	1 879	5 259 822	12.8	36.0	22.9	4.9	6.7	16.7	0.0
Meridian	85	D	D	D	506	1 342 577	12.8	26.9	25.1	9.4	2.6	19.3	0.0
Olive Branch	48	280	22.9	6.8	339	1 161 405	13.8	24.1	23.4	3.7	6.6	20.3	0.0
Pearl	42	214	24.6	7.2	218	812 891	8.6	31.3	29.5	10.4	2.5	17.7	0.0
Southaven	52	328	24.4	8.1	376	1 251 638	8.3	38.8	36.0	1.8	0.0	15.2	0.0
Tupelo	83	809	70.2	31.0	513	1 717 455	12.7	24.9	21.1	9.8	0.0	29.0	0.0

1. Establishments subject to federal tax.

Table D. Cities — **City Government Finances**

City	General revenue							General expenditure		
	Intergovernmental			Taxes					Per capita[1] (dollars)	
					Per capita[1] (dollars)					
	Total (mil dol)	Total (mil dol)	Percent from state government	Total (mil dol)	Total	Property	Sales and gross receipts	Total (mil dol)	Total	Capital outlays
	117	118	119	120	121	122	123	124	125	126
MICHIGAN—Cont'd										
Oak Park	34.3	6.1	77.1	15.3	515	501	14	32.4	1 094	25
Pontiac	80.8	29.4	48.1	29.2	491	278	50	91.7	1 541	157
Portage	42.4	7.6	94.6	24.0	508	481	26	39.8	842	89
Port Huron	56.4	17.9	36.7	21.0	712	492	23	60.3	2 048	427
Rochester Hills	71.4	14.4	64.9	31.6	437	403	34	59.2	819	60
Roseville	60.4	8.9	82.4	25.0	527	511	16	53.3	1 126	43
Royal Oak	80.5	15.1	59.4	31.4	537	481	56	82.6	1 412	97
Saginaw	92.8	33.0	36.6	21.3	420	150	24	92.8	1 827	78
St. Clair Shores	68.3	10.3	86.2	32.7	546	515	32	62.0	1 037	61
Southfield	103.2	22.5	49.8	64.7	892	863	29	95.5	1 316	49
Southgate	30.9	6.3	84.0	16.4	550	533	17	30.8	1 034	2
Sterling Heights	116.0	21.5	85.9	55.5	426	408	17	126.6	970	137
Taylor	98.5	28.2	37.2	43.0	688	652	36	96.7	1 549	17
Troy	91.2	12.7	89.5	49.2	600	579	21	79.5	969	131
Warren	142.5	27.4	77.3	78.9	588	570	18	136.7	1 019	40
Westland	82.4	25.5	58.5	27.2	327	312	14	78.6	943	2
Wyandotte	44.6	7.8	56.0	16.7	656	640	16	53.7	2 107	160
Wyoming	74.0	21.7	50.6	26.8	365	333	32	64.1	874	19
MINNESOTA	X	X	X	X	X	X	X	X	X	X
Andover	22.9	1.9	92.9	12.6	406	393	12	18.3	588	147
Apple Valley	46.2	2.4	99.7	25.9	518	476	43	38.3	766	170
Blaine	45.6	3.0	81.8	23.5	396	359	37	44.2	746	172
Bloomington	120.6	11.3	85.5	69.9	812	609	203	137.2	1 595	316
Brooklyn Center	39.3	5.0	72.8	18.2	595	514	59	39.3	1 280	319
Brooklyn Park	79.5	9.0	54.3	44.0	566	543	23	69.8	898	50
Burnsville	55.1	4.0	78.6	33.5	547	501	46	54.1	885	185
Coon Rapids	50.6	4.4	75.2	28.1	453	367	86	69.6	1 124	385
Cottage Grove	32.6	4.1	86.1	13.7	391	358	32	30.2	858	186
Duluth	206.7	90.6	73.8	42.1	488	216	272	223.1	2 586	972
Eagan	55.0	3.8	90.8	28.6	442	413	29	57.4	885	201
Eden Prairie	70.0	5.2	80.2	37.9	610	555	54	67.1	1 079	147
Edina	63.6	3.2	88.7	32.5	663	592	70	63.8	1 301	290
Fridley	25.2	2.5	85.3	13.4	485	445	39	22.0	798	53
Inver Grove Heights	31.7	4.0	89.5	15.9	466	442	24	53.2	1 557	670
Lakeville	38.7	2.8	74.0	25.0	436	404	32	42.0	732	180
Mankato	77.8	20.6	42.2	21.6	539	345	195	74.6	1 863	805
Maple Grove	94.0	6.8	98.0	34.4	534	494	40	87.7	1 362	607
Maplewood	49.5	5.8	59.6	18.9	481	447	34	51.2	1 300	407
Minneapolis	1 017.5	148.8	51.2	459.8	1 170	858	312	1 439.6	3 663	222
Minnetonka	66.8	15.6	62.1	35.1	686	601	85	65.7	1 286	502
Moorhead	71.8	30.0	77.2	8.2	210	171	39	91.5	2 342	1 042
Oakdale	20.9	1.3	73.5	10.5	379	346	33	27.2	981	403
Owatonna	26.3	7.8	88.0	10.8	426	355	71	25.3	995	237
Plymouth	77.8	8.1	86.5	32.3	443	399	45	66.3	909	162
Richfield	43.3	7.0	35.4	22.3	617	560	57	42.6	1 180	117
Rochester	216.6	36.4	96.7	62.4	572	415	158	238.9	2 190	743
Roseville	33.7	3.3	86.1	17.5	506	445	61	34.0	981	217
St. Cloud	89.0	22.7	89.2	36.3	550	348	201	105.0	1 592	659
St. Louis Park	76.4	3.2	86.2	35.3	760	659	101	77.7	1 676	320
St. Paul	510.2	119.9	59.1	175.4	602	412	190	504.8	1 733	219
Savage	32.0	3.4	94.3	16.3	584	537	46	22.4	802	183
Shakopee	36.9	5.1	99.9	15.9	410	373	37	36.0	928	217
Shoreview	25.3	1.3	99.9	11.3	441	424	17	23.1	899	137
Winona	24.8	11.9	97.0	7.9	284	213	71	23.2	837	90
Woodbury	61.1	3.7	75.8	30.7	475	432	44	55.7	863	229
MISSISSIPPI	X	X	X	X	X	X	X	X	X	X
Biloxi	102.9	58.6	70.6	23.1	518	393	125	110.6	2 484	715
Clinton	22.4	8.4	97.4	8.5	332	293	39	20.7	810	145
Greenville	30.6	10.5	67.0	12.3	368	293	75	32.5	970	190
Gulfport	510.2	92.4	40.6	32.6	466	348	117	508.4	7 267	1 373
Hattiesburg	68.9	33.4	74.6	25.2	537	368	168	64.6	1 378	307
Horn Lake	18.5	4.3	95.2	7.0	264	233	31	15.9	598	35
Jackson	222.7	65.9	65.5	79.3	452	389	63	212.1	1 210	208
Meridian	43.9	15.5	100.0	18.6	456	387	69	39.7	973	158
Olive Branch	42.4	15.2	100.0	15.0	434	379	55	33.8	978	185
Pearl	24.5	10.5	91.4	6.9	263	226	37	32.5	1 241	187
Southaven	49.4	12.7	100.0	25.8	512	457	55	48.7	966	118
Tupelo	65.5	32.8	96.4	15.7	442	418	24	62.2	1 751	529

1. Based on population estimated as of July 1 of the year shown.

Table D. Cities — **City Government Finances**

	City government finances, 2012 (cont.)									
	General expenditure (cont.)									
	Percent of total for:									
City	Public welfare	Highways	Parking facilities	Education	Health and hospitals	Police protection	Sewerage and sanitation	Parks and recreation	Housing and community development	Interest on debt
	127	128	129	130	131	132	133	134	135	136
MICHIGAN—Cont'd										
Oak Park	0.0	4.6	0.0	0.0	0.0	26.1	25.4	3.4	1.7	4.4
Pontiac	0.0	7.1	0.9	0.0	0.0	12.5	18.4	0.4	15.4	3.8
Portage	0.3	15.3	0.0	0.0	0.0	16.1	25.8	5.4	0.7	6.0
Port Huron	0.0	9.9	0.2	0.0	0.0	12.5	24.6	6.6	19.9	4.4
Rochester Hills	0.0	16.6	0.0	0.0	0.0	14.1	16.0	17.9	0.0	1.7
Roseville	0.0	9.7	0.0	0.0	0.0	22.0	20.2	4.1	2.4	0.9
Royal Oak	0.0	8.3	2.6	0.0	0.9	15.6	28.0	4.9	2.8	4.3
Saginaw	0.0	6.8	0.3	0.0	0.0	19.4	19.6	0.4	17.3	1.0
St. Clair Shores	0.0	8.8	0.0	0.0	0.0	18.5	24.7	7.1	0.1	3.1
Southfield	0.0	8.3	0.0	0.0	0.0	25.8	3.3	9.2	0.8	2.2
Southgate	0.0	10.8	0.0	0.0	0.0	19.5	14.2	3.9	0.7	2.6
Sterling Heights	0.0	9.6	0.0	0.0	0.0	23.7	27.1	2.0	0.7	0.9
Taylor	0.0	6.6	0.0	0.0	0.0	13.8	11.6	3.9	20.5	5.2
Troy	0.0	17.7	0.0	0.0	0.0	27.5	18.5	11.2	0.2	3.2
Warren	0.0	10.2	0.0	0.0	0.0	25.5	15.8	5.4	3.9	3.3
Westland	0.0	7.6	0.0	0.0	0.0	18.9	22.4	3.3	2.0	0.4
Wyandotte	0.0	10.3	0.0	0.0	0.0	12.1	10.3	3.8	0.0	1.2
Wyoming	0.0	10.0	0.0	0.0	0.0	23.8	19.2	7.1	14.4	1.7
MINNESOTA	X	X	X	X	X	X	X	X	X	X
Andover	0.0	21.8	0.0	0.0	0.1	14.3	10.5	11.4	13.2	10.2
Apple Valley	0.0	23.5	0.0	0.0	0.1	20.0	12.9	18.3	1.6	4.4
Blaine	0.0	19.5	0.0	0.0	0.0	20.6	22.6	3.2	4.5	4.2
Bloomington	0.0	15.1	0.0	0.0	4.6	18.4	9.8	10.4	0.3	2.3
Brooklyn Center	0.0	19.6	0.0	0.0	0.0	18.2	16.1	7.6	5.8	2.3
Brooklyn Park	0.0	12.2	0.0	0.0	0.0	24.2	11.5	13.9	1.1	5.9
Burnsville	0.0	20.0	0.0	0.0	0.0	22.5	13.2	12.7	0.0	4.0
Coon Rapids	0.0	11.5	0.9	0.0	0.1	12.5	11.3	29.9	4.5	4.1
Cottage Grove	0.0	33.1	0.0	0.0	3.9	16.5	6.7	11.5	4.3	12.1
Duluth	0.0	10.1	0.4	0.0	0.0	13.3	14.3	13.0	4.6	4.5
Eagan	0.0	20.7	0.0	0.0	0.0	19.5	13.7	14.3	0.0	5.8
Eden Prairie	1.2	12.6	0.0	0.0	0.2	17.7	14.4	15.9	4.9	12.0
Edina	0.0	27.8	0.0	0.0	0.8	13.8	14.5	20.4	1.1	3.7
Fridley	0.0	16.8	0.0	0.0	0.0	23.9	27.0	6.0	5.6	0.1
Inver Grove Heights	0.0	24.4	0.0	0.0	0.0	10.4	20.8	20.6	1.3	4.3
Lakeville	0.0	25.3	0.0	0.0	0.0	21.3	9.7	9.7	1.2	8.8
Mankato	0.0	18.4	5.3	0.0	0.0	11.5	15.6	4.6	16.8	3.8
Maple Grove	0.0	38.8	0.0	0.0	0.0	10.9	8.6	15.2	1.5	5.0
Maplewood	0.0	30.5	0.0	0.0	0.3	15.2	9.0	8.7	0.7	17.9
Minneapolis	0.0	6.6	3.3	0.0	1.1	10.1	41.6	7.3	9.6	8.6
Minnetonka	0.0	31.5	0.0	0.0	0.5	16.6	9.2	10.9	8.2	3.8
Moorhead	0.0	11.8	0.0	0.0	0.4	8.0	8.7	5.0	1.2	11.2
Oakdale	0.0	28.1	0.0	0.0	0.0	15.5	10.8	5.0	0.0	3.0
Owatonna	0.0	25.9	0.0	0.0	0.0	16.3	14.0	13.5	3.4	3.0
Plymouth	0.0	16.9	0.0	0.0	0.0	14.7	11.2	18.8	2.0	8.3
Richfield	0.0	7.8	0.0	0.0	0.3	17.0	11.9	11.5	23.0	12.9
Rochester	0.0	14.1	1.4	0.0	0.1	8.6	5.1	7.5	0.2	27.8
Roseville	0.0	14.4	0.0	0.0	0.0	18.2	17.2	12.1	4.2	1.3
St. Cloud	0.0	11.6	1.2	0.0	0.9	15.3	22.1	22.3	1.4	4.9
St. Louis Park	0.0	9.2	0.0	0.0	0.0	9.0	10.3	10.9	1.1	25.9
St. Paul	0.0	12.4	1.3	0.0	0.7	17.5	8.3	15.6	9.7	6.3
Savage	0.0	30.8	0.0	0.0	0.0	19.3	12.0	7.6	0.9	11.4
Shakopee	0.0	22.2	0.0	0.0	0.0	18.6	16.8	12.4	0.0	13.3
Shoreview	0.0	15.7	0.0	0.0	0.0	7.9	23.0	26.0	3.7	6.4
Winona	0.0	12.5	0.0	0.0	0.5	18.9	18.0	13.8	3.7	0.8
Woodbury	0.0	22.0	2.9	0.0	3.0	20.7	11.9	11.7	3.2	3.7
MISSISSIPPI	X	X	X	X	X	X	X	X	X	X
Biloxi	1.0	7.1	0.0	0.0	0.2	13.5	15.9	12.3	0.7	2.1
Clinton	0.0	13.3	0.0	0.0	0.0	19.0	28.7	7.7	0.0	3.8
Greenville	0.4	16.8	0.0	0.0	0.9	22.4	13.5	2.6	0.0	1.1
Gulfport	0.0	5.6	0.0	0.0	72.1	4.7	4.9	3.1	2.1	1.8
Hattiesburg	0.0	16.5	0.3	0.0	1.6	16.2	16.4	6.6	2.8	2.3
Horn Lake	0.0	6.3	0.0	0.0	0.7	27.6	15.3	6.7	0.7	6.2
Jackson	0.5	9.5	0.0	0.0	0.5	15.4	16.2	6.3	0.9	4.0
Meridian	0.0	13.7	0.4	0.0	0.0	18.3	14.0	5.1	2.6	5.1
Olive Branch	0.0	10.9	0.0	0.0	2.5	22.3	22.4	4.0	0.0	5.9
Pearl	0.0	22.1	0.0	0.0	1.4	19.0	18.3	4.3	0.0	6.3
Southaven	0.0	2.9	0.0	0.0	0.6	21.9	9.2	9.5	0.0	8.5
Tupelo	0.0	24.5	0.0	0.0	0.0	16.4	11.5	9.2	0.1	4.2

	City government finances, 2012 (cont.)			Climate[2]						
	Debt outstanding			Average daily temperature (degrees Fahrenheit)						
				Mean		Limits				
City	Total (mil dol)	Per capita[1] (dollars)	Debt issued during year	January	July	January[3]	July[4]	Annual precipitation (inches)	Heating degree days	Cooling degree days
	137	138	139	140	141	142	143	144	145	146
MICHIGAN—Cont'd										
Oak Park	45.1	1 521	0.0	24.7	73.7	16.1	85.7	33.58	6 224	788
Pontiac	80.8	1 357	5.6	22.9	71.9	15.9	82.3	30.03	6 680	626
Portage	90.1	1 908	15.0	24.3	73.2	17.0	84.2	37.41	6 235	773
Port Huron	122.4	4 160	21.5	22.8	72.2	15.1	81.9	31.39	6 845	626
Rochester Hills	31.9	441	5.0	22.0	70.6	13.7	82.7	35.74	7 046	523
Roseville	13.3	282	0.3	25.3	73.6	18.8	83.3	33.97	6 160	757
Royal Oak	117.8	2 013	0.0	24.7	73.7	16.1	85.7	33.58	6 224	788
Saginaw	81.9	1 612	13.5	21.4	71.2	14.9	81.9	31.61	7 099	548
St. Clair Shores	53.2	890	9.1	25.3	73.6	18.8	83.3	33.97	6 160	757
Southfield	64.8	893	0.0	24.7	73.7	16.1	85.7	33.58	6 224	788
Southgate	22.5	757	0.3	24.5	73.5	17.8	83.4	32.89	6 422	736
Sterling Heights	63.9	490	13.6	24.4	71.9	18.0	81.8	32.24	6 620	597
Taylor	147.4	2 362	1.4	24.5	73.5	17.8	83.4	32.89	6 422	736
Troy	55.0	669	0.0	22.9	71.9	15.9	82.3	30.03	6 680	626
Warren	159.2	1 186	8.8	24.7	73.7	16.1	85.7	33.58	6 224	788
Westland	12.4	149	0.8	24.6	73.9	17.6	84.7	32.80	6 167	828
Wyandotte	63.3	2 483	0.8	24.5	73.5	17.8	83.4	32.89	6 422	736
Wyoming	117.0	1 595	7.3	22.4	71.4	15.6	82.3	37.13	6 896	613
MINNESOTA	X	X	X	X	X	X	X	X	X	X
Andover	55.4	1 776	0.3	10.9	70.4	1.8	80.5	31.36	8 367	500
Apple Valley	71.3	1 426	9.2	9.2	69.4	-1.1	80.5	29.19	8 805	416
Blaine	51.9	874	1.6	10.9	70.4	1.8	80.5	31.36	8 367	500
Bloomington	158.7	1 844	27.0	13.1	73.2	4.3	83.3	29.41	7 876	699
Brooklyn Center	47.5	1 549	0.0	13.0	71.4	2.8	82.8	30.50	7 983	587
Brooklyn Park	95.6	1 229	16.1	13.0	71.4	2.8	82.8	30.50	7 983	587
Burnsville	62.7	1 026	8.4	13.8	74.0	3.4	85.8	30.44	7 549	803
Coon Rapids	87.0	1 407	9.1	13.0	71.4	2.8	82.8	30.50	7 983	587
Cottage Grove	57.0	1 618	0.0	12.0	72.1	2.5	82.6	29.95	8 032	617
Duluth	251.3	2 914	21.9	8.4	65.5	-1.2	76.3	31.00	9 724	189
Eagan	61.1	943	0.0	13.1	73.2	4.3	83.3	29.41	7 876	699
Eden Prairie	202.7	3 258	11.3	10.2	71.4	-0.3	82.2	28.82	8 429	567
Edina	119.7	2 440	15.0	13.8	74.0	3.4	85.8	30.44	7 549	803
Fridley	14.9	541	0.0	10.9	70.4	1.8	80.5	31.36	8 367	500
Inver Grove Heights	55.6	1 626	4.6	10.1	71.0	0.0	81.3	34.60	8 345	533
Lakeville	90.0	1 570	4.3	13.1	72.2	3.8	83.6	31.43	7 773	658
Mankato	117.0	2 921	4.6	12.5	72.1	2.4	83.4	33.42	8 029	650
Maple Grove	207.8	3 225	5.4	13.0	71.4	2.8	82.8	30.50	7 983	587
Maplewood	157.8	4 004	10.0	14.5	73.0	6.2	83.2	32.59	7 606	715
Minneapolis	3 439.9	8 754	233.0	13.1	73.2	4.3	83.3	29.41	7 876	699
Minnetonka	91.2	1 784	0.0	13.1	73.2	4.3	83.3	29.41	7 876	699
Moorhead	252.1	6 451	10.0	3.8	69.8	-7.1	81.5	21.56	9 628	478
Oakdale	31.2	1 124	10.6	14.5	73.0	6.2	83.2	32.59	7 606	715
Owatonna	49.7	1 954	8.3	NA	NA	NA	NA	NA	NA	NA
Plymouth	108.6	1 490	0.0	13.0	71.4	2.8	82.8	30.50	7 983	587
Richfield	105.3	2 917	11.9	13.1	73.2	4.3	83.3	29.41	7 876	699
Rochester	2 086.4	19 128	285.0	9.8	70.0	0.0	80.9	29.10	8 703	474
Roseville	20.1	581	10.0	14.5	73.0	6.2	83.2	32.59	7 606	715
St. Cloud	413.3	6 266	35.1	8.8	69.8	-1.2	81.7	27.13	8 815	443
St. Louis Park	499.7	10 778	0.0	13.0	71.4	2.8	82.8	30.50	7 983	587
St. Paul	770.7	2 646	98.7	14.5	73.0	6.2	83.2	32.59	7 606	715
Savage	84.5	3 021	10.7	NA	NA	NA	NA	NA	NA	NA
Shakopee	92.8	2 394	0.0	NA	NA	NA	NA	NA	NA	NA
Shoreview	51.1	1 990	8.6	14.5	73.0	6.2	83.2	32.59	7 606	715
Winona	7.0	254	0.0	17.6	75.8	9.2	85.3	34.20	6 839	990
Woodbury	92.0	1 427	1.5	11.5	72.1	1.9	81.9	29.92	8 104	621
MISSISSIPPI	X	X	X	X	X	X	X	X	X	X
Biloxi	68.0	1 528	0.5	50.7	81.7	43.5	88.5	64.84	1 645	2 517
Clinton	36.4	1 422	1.7	NA	NA	NA	NA	NA	NA	NA
Greenville	22.8	681	10.5	42.3	82.6	33.0	92.6	54.20	2 715	2 216
Gulfport	212.6	3 038	5.0	51.6	82.6	42.6	91.3	65.20	1 514	2 679
Hattiesburg	89.3	1 904	5.4	47.9	81.7	36.0	92.1	62.47	2 024	2 327
Horn Lake	35.8	1 350	0.0	NA	NA	NA	NA	NA	NA	NA
Jackson	322.3	1 839	62.9	45.0	81.4	35.0	91.4	55.95	2 401	2 264
Meridian	61.0	1 493	9.3	46.1	81.7	34.7	92.9	58.65	2 352	2 173
Olive Branch	57.9	1 676	15.0	NA	NA	NA	NA	NA	NA	NA
Pearl	99.8	3 814	6.4	NA	NA	NA	NA	NA	NA	NA
Southaven	96.2	1 909	8.0	37.9	80.4	27.8	90.3	55.06	3 442	1 749
Tupelo	82.1	2 311	14.6	40.4	80.6	30.5	91.4	55.86	3 086	1 884

1. Based on the population estimated as of July 1 of the year shown. 2. Represents normal values based on the 30-year period, 1971–2000. 3. Average daily minimum.
4. Average daily maximum.

Table D. Cities — **Land Area and Population**

STATE Place code	City	Land area,[1] 2010 (sq km)	Population, 2015			Race alone or in combination (percent), 2010-2014					Percent Hispanic or Latino[2], 2010-2014	Percent foreign born 2010–2014
			Total persons	Rank	Per square kilometer	White	Black	American Indian, Alaska Native	Asian	Hawaiian Pacific Islander		
		1	2	3	4	5	6	7	8	9	10	11
29 00000	MISSOURI................	178 039.7	6 083 672	X	34.2	85.0	12.6	1.3	2.2	0.2	3.8	3.9
29 03160	Ballwin	23.3	30 577	1 220	1 312.3	90.8	2.9	1.0	7.4	0.2	1.8	7.3
29 06652	Blue Springs	57.7	54 148	692	938.4	89.2	9.0	1.5	2.2	0.0	4.2	2.4
29 11242	Cape Girardeau	73.6	39 462	954	536.2	83.3	14.4	0.9	2.8	0.5	2.4	4.1
29 13600	Chesterfield	82.3	47 864	791	581.6	86.1	4.3	0.2	10.0	0.0	3.5	11.3
29 15670	Columbia	163.4	119 108	229	728.9	82.3	12.6	1.9	6.4	0.0	3.4	7.8
29 24778	Florissant.....................	32.5	52 268	721	1 608.2	69.7	30.8	1.7	2.2	0.0	1.4	2.6
29 27190	Gladstone	20.9	26 861	1 366	1 285.2	92.2	5.9	2.3	1.1	0.0	6.4	5.0
29 31276	Hazelwood....................	41.5	25 661	1 404	618.3	62.5	35.4	1.1	3.8	0.0	3.1	6.3
29 35000	Independence...............	200.9	117 255	233	583.6	86.6	8.4	1.4	1.6	0.6	8.8	4.4
29 37000	Jefferson City	93.1	43 169	866	463.7	78.1	18.8	1.2	2.2	0.3	2.0	3.6
29 37592	Joplin...........................	92.1	51 818	728	562.6	91.9	5.1	4.0	2.1	0.4	3.8	2.5
29 38000	Kansas City	815.7	475 378	36	582.8	62.5	31.1	1.6	3.1	0.5	10.1	7.6
29 39044	Kirkwood......................	23.7	27 750	1 331	1 170.9	91.6	7.5	0.9	1.7	0.0	2.3	2.9
29 41348	Lee's Summit	164.1	95 094	321	579.5	86.6	10.0	0.6	3.0	0.0	3.9	3.8
29 42032	Liberty..........................	75.2	30 450	1 229	404.9	93.9	4.9	0.9	1.4	0.0	3.4	2.8
29 46586	Maryland Heights	56.5	27 389	1 346	484.8	74.1	14.0	2.1	11.6	0.4	6.6	15.0
29 54074	O'Fallon	75.6	85 040	385	1 124.9	91.8	5.2	0.6	3.9	0.0	2.0	3.7
29 60788	Raytown	25.7	29 401	1 263	1 144.0	67.5	30.7	1.1	1.2	0.4	6.2	2.0
29 64082	St. Charles	61.3	68 796	507	1 122.3	89.0	8.1	1.0	3.0	0.1	4.3	6.0
29 64550	St. Joseph	113.9	76 596	441	672.5	91.4	8.0	1.4	1.5	0.4	6.2	4.0
29 65000	St. Louis	160.3	315 685	60	1 969.3	47.7	49.5	1.0	3.6	0.1	3.7	6.8
29 65126	St. Peters	57.9	56 971	651	984.0	92.7	4.8	0.4	2.5	0.0	3.6	3.6
29 70000	Springfield	211.7	166 810	150	788.0	92.0	5.2	1.8	2.5	0.4	4.1	3.9
29 75220	University City	15.3	35 058	1 073	2 291.4	57.0	39.4	1.5	4.3	0.2	4.4	7.2
29 78442	Wentzville	51.7	35 603	1 062	688.6	94.5	5.6	1.5	0.9	0.0	2.3	1.2
29 79820	Wildwood......................	172.0	35 899	1 053	208.7	94.0	1.9	0.6	4.0	0.1	2.4	6.3
30 00000	MONTANA	376 961.9	1 032 949	X	2.7	91.8	0.9	8.0	1.2	0.2	3.2	2.0
30 06550	Billings	112.4	110 263	261	981.0	92.0	1.3	5.9	1.4	0.1	5.5	1.9
30 08950	Bozeman	49.5	43 405	860	876.9	95.3	1.0	2.5	3.5	0.3	3.0	4.3
30 11390	Butte-Silver Bow...........	1 855.1	33 922	1 106	18.3	96.7	0.7	3.1	0.8	0.1	3.9	1.8
30 32800	Great Falls	56.4	59 638	616	1 057.4	91.4	2.2	8.0	1.6	0.1	4.0	2.2
30 35600	Helena..........................	42.3	30 581	1 219	723.0	95.2	1.4	4.4	1.3	0.2	2.4	1.7
30 50200	Missoula	71.3	71 022	493	996.1	95.1	1.1	4.1	2.3	0.2	3.3	2.9
31 00000	NEBRASKA...............	198 973.7	1 896 190	X	9.5	90.2	5.6	1.7	2.4	0.2	9.7	6.5
31 03950	Bellevue.......................	41.1	55 510	674	1 350.6	88.0	8.0	2.0	3.1	0.6	13.4	8.6
31 17670	Fremont........................	22.8	26 474	1 382	1 161.1	97.1	0.8	1.2	1.0	0.6	13.7	7.2
31 19595	Grand Island................	73.6	51 440	736	698.9	92.9	2.9	1.0	1.7	0.0	28.0	15.8
31 25055	Kearney	33.1	33 021	1 139	997.6	94.1	1.7	0.8	2.5	0.2	8.1	4.3
31 28000	Lincoln	230.8	277 348	72	1 201.7	89.5	5.5	1.5	4.7	0.2	6.7	7.9
31 37000	Omaha..........................	329.2	443 885	43	1 348.4	79.5	14.5	1.8	3.4	0.1	13.3	9.8
32 00000	NEVADA	284 331.9	2 890 845	X	10.2	73.5	9.7	1.9	9.4	1.3	27.2	19.1
32 09700	Carson City	374.7	54 521	686	145.5	86.0	2.5	3.5	3.2	0.4	22.2	11.7
32 31900	Henderson....................	279.0	285 667	67	1 023.9	81.7	7.0	1.0	9.8	0.9	14.9	12.1
32 40000	Las Vegas	351.8	623 747	28	1 773.0	69.2	13.1	1.4	8.3	1.2	32.2	21.3
32 51800	North Las Vegas	262.5	234 807	95	894.5	56.4	22.2	1.4	7.9	1.8	38.9	21.7
32 60600	Reno.............................	266.8	241 445	87	905.0	82.8	3.9	2.1	8.0	1.3	24.7	16.4
32 68400	Sparks	92.6	96 094	317	1 037.7	82.6	3.2	2.3	7.8	1.5	28.2	16.9
33 00000	NEW HAMPSHIRE.....	23 187.3	1 330 608	X	57.4	95.5	1.9	0.8	2.9	0.1	3.1	5.6
33 14200	Concord........................	166.4	42 620	877	256.1	93.7	3.4	0.8	3.8	0.0	1.9	6.4
33 18820	Dover............................	69.2	30 880	1 203	446.2	94.1	2.7	1.5	4.9	0.0	1.6	6.5
33 45140	Manchester...................	85.7	110 229	262	1 286.2	88.1	5.8	1.0	5.5	0.0	8.1	13.2
33 50260	Nashua.........................	79.9	87 970	365	1 101.0	88.4	4.8	0.9	7.6	0.3	11.1	13.4
33 65140	Rochester.....................	117.6	30 038	1 243	255.4	97.3	1.3	0.7	1.9	0.7	1.7	2.6
34 00000	NEW JERSEY..........	19 047.3	8 958 013	X	470.3	70.6	14.7	0.7	9.6	0.1	18.6	21.5
34 02080	Atlantic City	27.8	39 260	958	1 412.2	36.8	42.9	1.5	17.0	0.3	25.1	31.4
34 03580	Bayonne.......................	15.0	66 311	536	4 420.7	76.2	11.6	0.9	9.2	0.3	21.0	27.9
34 05170	Bergenfield	7.5	27 621	1 336	3 682.8	49.9	7.3	0.5	25.3	0.3	30.3	40.7
34 07600	Bridgeton......................	16.0	25 031	1 418	1 564.4	37.7	37.2	2.9	0.6	0.1	48.7	23.9
34 10000	Camden........................	23.1	76 119	447	3 295.2	15.3	51.3	1.6	3.1	0.2	48.0	12.6
34 13690	Clifton	29.2	86 334	377	2 956.6	73.6	5.6	0.7	10.3	0.1	34.7	35.7
34 19390	East Orange.................	10.2	64 949	549	6 367.5	5.1	90.1	0.7	1.0	0.0	8.2	24.5
34 21000	Elizabeth......................	31.9	129 007	210	4 044.1	52.0	20.4	0.6	2.7	0.1	62.8	47.1
34 21480	Englewood....................	12.7	28 539	1 294	2 247.2	43.9	35.4	0.7	11.4	0.3	21.0	32.2
34 22470	Fair Lawn	13.3	33 597	1 117	2 526.1	80.8	3.2	0.5	13.5	0.1	13.5	30.4
34 24420	Fort Lee........................	6.6	36 672	1 028	5 556.4	54.8	2.8	0.7	41.6	0.1	12.9	51.6

1. Dry land or land partially or temporarily covered by water.   2. May be of any race.

Table D. Cities — **Population**

City	Age of population (percent), 2010-2014									Median age 2010–2014	Percent female 2010–2014	Population			
	Under 5 years	5 to 17 years	18 to 24 years	25 to 34 years	35 to 44 years	45 to 54 years	55 to 64 years	65 to 74 years	75 years and over			Census counts		Percent change	
												2000	2010	2000–2010	2010–2015
	12	13	14	15	16	17	18	19	20	21	22	23	24	25	26
MISSOURI	6.3	17.0	9.9	13.2	12.2	14.2	12.7	8.0	6.6	38.1	51.0	5 595 211	5 988 927	7.0	1.6
Ballwin	5.5	19.2	8.8	10.1	13.2	14.6	13.6	8.9	6.1	39.4	53.3	31 283	30 404	-2.8	0.5
Blue Springs	6.8	21.1	7.4	13.9	13.8	13.7	12.9	6.1	4.3	35.6	51.3	48 080	52 575	9.3	2.9
Cape Girardeau	6.1	13.5	18.7	14.6	9.1	11.6	11.2	6.9	8.3	32.4	52.5	35 349	37 941	7.3	3.9
Chesterfield	4.9	18.1	6.2	8.6	10.9	16.5	14.1	10.9	9.7	45.8	51.8	46 802	47 484	1.5	0.8
Columbia	6.2	13.0	26.9	16.4	10.0	9.9	8.8	4.4	4.4	26.7	52.0	84 531	108 500	28.4	9.2
Florissant	6.9	17.9	8.5	12.6	12.7	13.6	11.1	7.1	9.5	38.0	53.6	50 497	52 158	3.3	-0.1
Gladstone	8.2	12.6	8.2	14.4	10.8	14.1	13.7	9.0	8.9	40.9	52.7	26 365	25 410	-3.6	5.5
Hazelwood	5.9	16.9	12.1	13.0	12.2	14.9	12.8	5.5	6.7	35.9	50.5	26 206	25 703	-1.9	-0.2
Independence	6.6	15.1	8.1	14.0	11.3	14.2	13.2	9.2	8.3	40.8	52.8	113 288	116 830	3.1	0.4
Jefferson City	6.4	15.1	9.6	16.4	11.7	14.1	12.2	7.4	7.1	37.2	48.6	39 636	43 079	8.7	0.2
Joplin	6.6	15.4	12.4	14.2	12.6	12.2	11.7	7.5	7.4	35.7	50.6	45 504	50 150	10.2	2.0
Kansas City	7.2	16.4	9.7	16.6	13.2	13.6	11.8	6.4	5.2	35.0	51.4	441 545	459 787	4.1	3.4
Kirkwood	6.6	14.9	5.4	13.6	11.9	14.1	15.2	9.0	9.2	43.1	55.1	27 324	27 540	0.8	0.8
Lee's Summit	6.9	21.0	7.0	12.6	13.8	15.1	11.6	6.0	5.9	36.7	52.3	70 700	91 364	29.2	4.1
Liberty	4.7	21.1	11.3	10.5	15.3	13.7	11.4	6.8	5.3	36.3	49.7	26 232	29 149	11.1	4.4
Maryland Heights	7.6	12.8	9.7	18.9	13.6	12.6	12.2	7.7	4.8	35.8	49.8	25 756	27 472	6.7	-0.3
O'Fallon	7.1	21.9	7.4	13.7	16.2	14.8	9.3	5.1	4.5	34.9	50.3	46 169	79 329	71.8	6.8
Raytown	6.8	18.9	9.2	9.7	14.0	14.9	11.5	7.3	7.7	40.0	49.8	30 388	29 526	-2.8	-0.3
St. Charles	5.4	14.2	14.6	14.4	11.4	14.4	11.8	6.8	6.9	35.9	51.0	60 321	65 794	9.1	4.5
St. Joseph	7.3	16.1	11.4	14.2	12.0	13.5	11.8	7.0	6.7	35.7	50.4	73 990	76 780	3.8	-0.3
St. Louis	6.7	13.9	11.4	19.0	12.6	13.4	12.0	5.8	5.2	34.4	51.7	348 189	319 294	-8.3	-1.2
St. Peters	7.1	15.5	8.3	15.0	12.5	15.2	14.0	6.9	5.6	38.5	53.2	51 381	52 575	2.3	8.2
Springfield	6.2	11.9	19.1	15.8	10.9	10.7	10.6	7.2	7.5	32.9	51.9	151 580	159 498	5.2	4.6
University City	6.1	11.9	11.4	16.4	12.7	12.3	12.6	8.2	8.4	38.9	53.6	37 428	35 371	-5.5	-0.9
Wentzville	8.7	22.7	5.2	15.5	17.8	10.3	10.1	6.4	3.4	34.2	51.4	6 896	29 070	321.5	21.3
Wildwood	5.9	23.9	6.2	6.4	11.7	20.7	15.1	6.6	3.6	42.2	50.0	32 884	35 517	8.0	1.0
MONTANA	6.0	16.2	9.9	12.5	11.3	13.8	14.7	8.8	6.8	39.8	49.8	902 195	989 415	9.7	4.4
Billings	6.6	16.0	9.8	14.5	12.0	13.3	12.9	7.8	7.2	37.4	52.0	89 847	104 170	15.9	5.7
Bozeman	5.3	9.1	29.3	20.3	11.8	8.2	8.1	3.9	3.9	27.7	47.6	27 509	37 280	35.5	16.4
Butte-Silver Bow	5.1	15.3	11.4	11.3	11.2	14.8	14.1	9.1	7.6	41.4	49.5	34 606	33 525	-1.1	1.2
Great Falls	7.3	15.3	9.7	14.4	10.7	13.6	12.6	8.1	8.3	37.9	51.0	56 690	58 505	3.2	0.9
Helena	6.3	12.4	11.1	13.1	12.0	13.6	15.0	8.6	7.8	40.0	50.5	25 780	28 190	9.3	8.4
Missoula	5.4	12.1	19.5	17.3	11.8	11.6	10.5	6.1	5.8	32.1	50.3	57 053	66 788	17.1	6.2
NEBRASKA	7.0	17.9	10.1	13.5	12.0	13.4	12.3	7.1	6.7	36.2	50.3	1 711 263	1 826 341	6.7	3.8
Bellevue	7.2	19.5	9.3	14.2	12.0	14.1	11.4	7.5	4.8	34.8	51.2	44 382	50 137	13.0	7.7
Fremont	7.1	17.5	9.3	14.1	12.6	12.0	11.3	7.3	8.8	36.0	51.7	25 174	26 397	4.9	0.2
Grand Island	8.0	19.0	9.0	14.0	12.9	12.8	11.4	6.2	6.7	35.0	50.1	42 940	48 520	13.0	5.7
Kearney	7.8	14.0	21.3	14.9	9.7	10.8	9.9	6.5	5.1	28.9	50.8	27 431	30 787	12.2	7.2
Lincoln	7.0	15.7	15.9	15.6	12.0	11.7	11.0	6.0	5.3	32.0	49.9	225 581	258 379	14.5	7.3
Omaha	7.4	17.5	10.4	16.2	12.3	13.1	11.5	6.2	5.5	34.0	51.1	390 007	408 958	4.9	2.8
NEVADA	6.6	17.4	9.2	14.2	13.8	13.7	12.0	8.1	5.0	36.9	49.6	1 998 257	2 700 551	35.1	7.0
Carson City	5.3	16.2	8.3	12.3	12.1	13.9	14.0	10.0	7.9	42.0	48.8	52 457	55 274	5.4	-1.4
Henderson	5.1	17.0	7.9	12.2	14.0	14.8	12.7	10.2	6.2	40.8	52.3	175 381	257 729	47.0	11.0
Las Vegas	6.8	17.8	9.0	14.2	14.2	13.6	11.3	7.7	5.5	36.6	49.5	478 434	583 756	22.0	6.7
North Las Vegas	8.2	23.1	9.9	15.4	15.3	11.9	8.6	5.2	2.5	30.6	49.8	115 488	216 961	87.9	8.4
Reno	6.7	16.4	11.7	15.9	12.4	13.1	11.5	7.2	5.1	34.5	49.1	180 480	225 221	24.8	6.8
Sparks	7.0	17.3	8.4	13.4	14.4	13.3	12.7	8.5	4.9	37.7	51.3	66 346	90 264	36.1	6.5
NEW HAMPSHIRE	5.0	15.8	9.5	11.2	12.7	16.7	14.4	8.3	6.4	41.9	50.7	1 235 786	1 316 470	6.5	1.1
Concord	5.6	14.5	8.8	14.8	13.9	15.1	13.0	7.1	7.2	40.2	51.5	40 687	42 695	4.9	-0.2
Dover	5.7	14.5	12.0	15.2	12.8	13.8	12.5	6.6	7.0	37.3	51.0	26 884	29 987	11.5	3.0
Manchester	5.6	14.8	10.6	16.4	14.0	13.8	11.8	7.0	6.0	36.7	50.0	107 006	109 565	2.4	0.6
Nashua	7.2	15.4	8.9	15.1	13.3	15.6	11.7	6.8	6.1	37.5	51.1	86 605	86 494	-0.1	1.7
Rochester	6.3	12.5	9.7	14.3	13.2	15.2	12.8	9.3	6.6	40.9	53.5	28 461	29 752	4.5	1.0
NEW JERSEY	6.0	16.9	8.9	12.8	13.5	15.4	12.5	7.5	6.5	39.3	51.2	8 414 350	8 791 894	4.5	1.9
Atlantic City	8.3	17.2	10.2	13.1	10.8	15.6	11.5	6.8	6.4	36.0	51.8	40 517	39 558	-2.4	-0.8
Bayonne	6.6	14.9	8.2	14.6	15.8	14.2	12.3	7.0	6.3	38.7	51.4	61 842	63 024	1.9	5.2
Bergenfield	5.3	17.0	8.7	11.8	16.0	14.3	12.6	7.2	7.1	39.9	50.7	26 247	26 764	2.0	3.2
Bridgeton	9.6	17.6	11.7	20.5	15.3	11.6	6.4	4.7	2.7	30.5	41.2	22 771	25 349	11.3	-1.3
Camden	8.8	23.0	11.9	15.3	12.5	11.7	9.0	5.1	2.7	29.1	52.3	79 904	77 344	-3.2	-1.6
Clifton	6.6	15.6	9.4	15.3	13.8	13.8	12.1	6.9	6.4	37.1	49.7	78 672	84 136	6.9	2.6
East Orange	6.7	16.4	10.4	13.3	13.9	13.9	12.2	7.7	5.4	37.4	56.6	69 824	64 270	-8.0	1.3
Elizabeth	9.3	18.4	10.5	16.4	14.1	12.5	9.1	5.6	4.0	31.9	51.9	120 568	124 969	3.7	3.2
Englewood	6.9	15.4	7.8	14.8	15.9	12.9	11.9	8.7	5.6	37.6	53.1	26 203	27 147	3.6	5.2
Fair Lawn	5.1	16.4	6.3	12.5	14.7	13.2	16.0	8.1	7.6	41.8	51.7	31 637	32 457	2.6	3.5
Fort Lee	4.7	10.6	4.8	12.6	15.8	12.1	15.5	11.3	12.5	46.5	54.4	35 461	35 345	-0.3	3.8

Table D. Cities — Households, Group Quarters, Crime, and Education

City	Households, 2010-2014				Persons in group quarters, 2010				Serious crimes known to police,[2] 2014				Educational attainment, 2010-2014		
			Percent			Institutional			Total		Rate[3]			Attainment[4] (percent)	
	Number	Persons per house-hold	Female family house-holder[1]	One-person	Total	Total	Persons in nursing facilities	Non-institu-tional	Number	Rate[3]	Violent	Property	Population age 25 and older	High school graduate or less	Bachelor's degree or more
	27	28	29	30	31	32	33	34	35	36	37	38	39	40	41
MISSOURI...................	2 361 232	2.55	12.1	29.1	174 142	93 274	44 866	80 868	203 093	3 349	443	2 906	4 028 930	43.4	26.7
Ballwin........................	11 498	2.65	9.9	18.5	2	0	0	2	218	714	26	688	21 158	18.9	53.6
Blue Springs	19 353	2.74	13.2	20.3	218	182	182	36	1 456	2 725	157	2 567	34 471	34.9	30.3
Cape Girardeau	15 279	2.53	11.7	33.5	3 466	789	712	2 677	2 019	5 175	579	4 596	23 879	38.9	32.7
Chesterfield.....................	19 196	2.48	8.0	25.3	934	925	925	9	764	1 598	71	1 527	33 985	13.9	64.0
Columbia........................	44 378	2.55	9.2	31.6	8 804	1 146	624	7 658	4 398	3 764	351	3 413	60 698	21.0	55.9
Florissant	21 305	2.46	16.6	31.7	788	668	542	120	1 010	1 928	187	1 741	35 461	39.7	23.1
Gladstone......................	10 848	2.40	12.4	29.6	42	36	36	6	812	3 084	277	2 807	18 499	41.1	25.7
Hazelwood......................	10 799	2.38	17.9	33.9	140	0	0	140	899	3 503	273	3 230	17 059	39.4	25.4
Independence	48 170	2.43	13.6	33.5	1 225	1 048	982	177	7 058	6 016	406	5 610	81 099	50.7	17.5
Jefferson City.................	16 829	2.57	14.7	33.5	4 964	3 990	456	974	1 464	3 375	307	3 069	29 612	38.1	33.2
Joplin.............................	20 914	2.43	12.4	32.6	1 988	743	653	1 245	4 226	8 327	516	7 811	33 368	46.0	22.2
Kansas City...................	192 799	2.41	15.6	36.7	8 812	4 192	2 499	4 620	28 668	6 120	1 258	4 862	309 930	38.1	31.6
Kirkwood........................	12 011	2.30	6.9	34.2	257	223	218	34	521	1 887	127	1 760	19 965	15.9	61.8
Lee's Summit	33 785	2.75	10.9	22.0	714	626	573	88	1 879	2 008	88	1 920	60 534	24.8	42.6
Liberty	10 779	2.77	9.9	22.2	1 358	585	277	773	614	2 025	211	1 814	19 076	33.3	37.7
Maryland Heights.............	11 641	2.36	10.8	33.2	559	522	473	37	567	2 067	222	1 845	19 080	29.2	40.0
O'Fallon........................	29 130	2.81	10.3	20.7	294	254	247	40	1 139	1 363	72	1 291	51 714	30.5	37.5
Raytown.........................	11 513	2.56	16.3	31.2	559	401	395	158	1 361	4 613	400	4 213	19 576	41.1	23.6
St. Charles	26 604	2.51	13.6	30.9	4 623	917	508	3 706	1 837	2 703	184	2 519	43 973	35.1	34.9
St. Joseph	28 825	2.67	13.8	33.3	4 493	3 104	673	1 389	4 645	6 011	454	5 557	50 446	51.5	19.5
St. Louis........................	139 594	2.28	18.1	44.2	11 978	4 822	2 060	7 156	25 267	7 931	1 679	6 253	216 807	41.0	30.4
St. Peters	21 539	2.52	8.9	27.0	203	184	184	19	1 219	2 202	170	2 032	37 597	31.9	34.2
Springfield.....................	70 788	2.29	11.5	37.6	10 739	3 302	1 443	7 437	14 599	8 833	1 186	7 646	101 527	40.7	26.6
University City................	15 837	2.22	13.3	37.2	232	200	169	32	1 532	4 365	544	3 821	25 007	21.9	52.6
Wentzville......................	10 557	2.99	9.9	17.4	137	133	133	4	543	1 632	129	1 502	19 513	33.4	30.9
Wildwood	12 082	2.95	5.6	13.2	66	62	40	4	NA	NA	NA	NA	23 011	11.5	65.8
MONTANA...................	407 797	2.47	8.8	30.2	28 849	11 929	5 200	16 920	28 625	2 797	324	2 473	683 960	37.4	29.1
Billings..........................	44 208	2.42	10.9	33.1	3 351	1 750	753	1 601	5 381	4 881	381	4 500	72 317	36.0	30.5
Bozeman........................	16 073	2.43	6.3	33.0	3 030	199	145	2 831	1 194	2 946	188	2 759	21 881	14.3	54.4
Butte-Silver Bow	15 275	2.26	11.7	35.9	998	610	276	388	1 643	4 740	355	4 385	23 285	45.8	23.5
Great Falls	25 127	2.35	11.4	34.4	1 263	798	482	465	2 738	4 602	274	4 328	40 309	38.6	25.5
Helena	12 881	2.26	10.1	40.3	1 682	432	191	1 250	1 302	4 350	535	3 816	20 369	24.6	44.8
Missoula........................	29 266	2.34	9.7	33.7	3 519	766	374	2 753	3 147	4 517	327	4 190	42 569	23.5	45.7
NEBRASKA	731 347	2.54	10.0	28.7	51 165	23 633	13 519	27 532	52 754	2 804	280	2 523	1 205 229	37.3	29.0
Bellevue	20 105	2.62	14.3	24.1	74	31	15	43	1 003	1 849	96	1 753	34 307	34.9	28.1
Fremont.........................	10 668	2.48	11.0	27.1	832	468	386	364	686	2 606	220	2 386	17 479	49.7	19.5
Grand Island	18 702	2.68	13.4	28.2	1 058	781	546	277	2 354	4 616	257	4 359	31 851	49.8	17.2
Kearney.........................	12 351	2.57	8.8	28.7	2 002	390	284	1 612	761	2 341	258	2 082	18 326	29.8	35.9
Lincoln..........................	106 512	2.50	10.4	30.7	13 579	4 236	1 001	9 343	10 000	3 687	338	3 349	163 055	29.8	36.2
Omaha...........................	172 034	2.53	13.7	33.0	11 183	4 676	2 002	6 507	21 511	4 906	561	4 345	280 756	35.2	33.8
NEVADA.....................	1 005 958	2.75	12.9	27.7	36 154	25 835	5 005	10 319	92 583	3 261	636	2 625	1 847 920	43.8	22.5
Carson City....................	21 225	2.57	12.5	31.3	3 625	3 560	313	65	1 035	1 906	295	1 611	38 327	42.8	20.4
Henderson	102 051	2.61	11.4	26.1	1 104	787	585	317	5 875	2 143	165	1 978	187 165	33.8	30.7
Las Vegas	213 037	2.80	15.1	28.3	9 482	6 514	1 628	2 968	57 630	3 764	841	2 923	396 060	46.2	21.6
North Las Vegas.............	68 001	3.28	16.3	21.2	2 441	2 167	683	274	7 290	3 177	777	2 401	133 166	52.3	15.2
Reno..............................	91 133	2.54	11.8	34.7	4 583	1 679	323	2 904	7 945	3 380	488	2 892	151 169	37.6	29.4
Sparks...........................	34 750	2.65	13.0	27.2	321	256	256	65	2 801	2 979	327	2 653	61 752	42.6	21.9
NEW HAMPSHIRE.......	519 580	2.54	9.6	25.4	40 104	13 113	7 767	26 991	28 643	2 159	196	1 963	919 033	37.1	34.4
Concord	17 141	2.48	11.7	33.8	2 903	2 282	454	621	1 058	2 498	203	2 295	29 845	33.6	35.0
Dover	12 586	2.41	10.4	29.4	896	789	358	107	503	1 642	134	1 508	20 658	29.3	39.7
Manchester	44 973	2.45	13.5	30.7	2 578	1 547	662	1 031	4 691	4 243	620	3 623	76 416	45.6	26.4
Nashua..........................	34 403	2.52	12.1	28.0	1 685	546	505	1 139	2 059	2 359	234	2 125	59 663	36.3	35.0
Rochester.......................	12 715	2.35	13.3	30.2	240	192	181	48	1 386	4 659	407	4 253	21 191	49.9	20.2
NEW JERSEY	3 188 498	2.78	13.5	25.8	186 876	100 621	45 512	86 255	178 339	1 995	261	1 734	6 052 621	40.4	36.4
Atlantic City....................	15 847	2.49	23.9	40.0	802	186	186	616	2 973	7 518	1 323	6 196	25 654	63.2	15.6
Bayonne.........................	25 292	2.56	18.7	29.7	276	0	0	276	951	1 449	226	1 224	45 098	48.9	30.6
Bergenfield.....................	9 112	2.98	13.0	19.3	38	0	0	38	127	465	40	425	18 873	40.4	36.8
Bridgeton........................	5 937	4.25	30.6	24.4	4 276	4 257	0	19	1 236	4 896	1 022	3 874	15 256	76.6	5.9
Camden..........................	25 189	3.07	36.5	29.4	3 321	2 229	290	1 092	4 395	5 716	2 016	3 700	43 365	69.5	8.2
Clifton............................	28 652	2.97	12.6	26.5	254	192	182	62	1 613	1 879	217	1 663	57 787	45.1	30.4
East Orange....................	25 594	2.52	26.4	41.2	1 235	780	716	455	1 558	2 406	707	1 699	43 065	52.0	16.2
Elizabeth........................	39 273	3.23	24.1	24.0	2 545	1 833	398	712	4 988	3 886	890	2 997	78 977	66.9	11.8
Englewood......................	10 462	2.62	15.5	30.7	164	136	136	28	588	2 125	278	1 847	19 525	34.7	46.9
Fair Lawn	11 807	2.79	11.5	21.1	187	152	152	35	356	1 073	75	998	23 475	27.3	52.2
Fort Lee.........................	16 604	2.17	8.6	40.3	7	0	0	7	273	754	47	707	28 104	28.2	54.1

1. No spouse present.   2. Data for serious crimes have not been adjusted for underreporting. This may affect comparability between geographic areas and over time.   3. Per 100,000 population estimated by the FBI.   4. Persons 25 years old and over.

Table D. Cities — Income, Poverty, and Housing

City	Money income, 2010–2014				Housing units, 2010			Occupied housing units 2010–2014				
		Households							Owner-occupied		Median owner costs as a percent of income	
	Per capita income[1] (dollars)	Median income	Percent with income of $200,000 or more	Percent with income of less than $25,000	Families with income below poverty (percent)	Total	Percent change, 2000–2010	Vacant units for sale or rent[2]	Total	Percent	Median value[3] (dollars)	With a mortgage[4]	Without a mortgage[5]
	42	43	44	45	46	47	48	49	50	51	52	53	54
MISSOURI...............	26 006	47 764	3.1	25.5	11.1	2 712 729	11.1	337 118	2 361 232	67.9	136 700	21.6	11.8
Ballwin......................	40 300	82 685	9.3	10.3	1.9	12 435	3.2	561	11 498	80.0	237 000	19.9	11.4
Blue Springs................	28 211	63 850	3.4	15.3	7.2	20 643	16.0	1 121	19 353	68.0	143 600	22.3	10.7
Cape Girardeau............	22 629	40 077	2.1	33.0	14.1	16 760	6.0	1 555	15 279	54.3	129 700	20.2	11.6
Chesterfield	52 010	94 263	15.8	11.4	3.5	20 393	8.5	1 169	19 196	77.0	329 900	19.9	12.4
Columbia	26 203	43 776	4.0	31.2	11.1	46 758	30.0	3 693	44 378	48.3	175 900	20.7	10.0
Florissant...................	25 656	51 415	1.1	19.6	5.7	22 632	8.0	1 385	21 305	71.9	99 500	21.6	12.0
Gladstone	26 939	52 783	1.8	20.5	7.9	12 148	1.8	966	10 848	68.3	129 500	22.1	13.8
Hazelwood..................	25 050	44 855	1.1	20.9	10.1	11 730	2.9	797	10 799	63.1	105 900	23.4	11.9
Independence.............	23 390	44 038	1.2	27.4	12.7	53 834	7.3	5 092	48 170	64.7	98 800	22.2	13.3
Jefferson City	25 349	47 901	2.2	24.8	11.2	18 852	10.9	1 574	16 829	59.0	139 200	18.9	10.0
Joplin........................	23 043	37 899	2.2	31.7	12.7	23 322	9.2	2 462	20 914	57.2	103 300	21.8	12.6
Kansas City................	27 282	45 376	3.1	27.8	14.8	221 860	9.7	29 454	192 799	55.4	133 600	22.0	13.3
Kirkwood....................	46 273	77 420	12.1	14.6	3.6	12 895	4.6	1 001	12 011	77.0	242 600	20.8	11.4
Lee's Summit	34 153	78 186	6.2	12.9	5.0	36 679	33.9	2 250	33 785	76.0	188 200	21.0	10.8
Liberty.......................	30 593	65 106	4.1	14.0	6.2	11 284	14.5	702	10 779	75.5	164 700	20.5	12.8
Maryland Heights	30 511	58 744	3.0	16.7	7.6	13 092	10.7	912	11 641	57.3	155 100	20.6	12.4
O'Fallon	31 809	78 634	4.5	10.5	4.2	29 376	84.8	1 142	29 130	80.4	192 300	20.5	10.6
Raytown	23 506	49 442	1.0	20.1	9.1	13 276	-0.2	1 172	11 513	68.3	98 300	22.6	13.5
St. Charles	29 645	56 622	4.1	17.7	8.8	28 590	13.4	1 875	26 604	64.3	173 300	19.9	13.0
St. Joseph	22 144	42 042	1.6	31.6	15.1	33 189	4.7	3 462	28 825	60.0	100 500	19.8	11.7
St. Louis....................	23 244	34 800	2.1	38.0	22.0	176 002	-0.2	33 945	139 594	44.2	118 600	23.0	14.1
St. Peters	32 380	69 854	3.1	11.5	2.5	21 717	15.5	856	21 539	81.1	168 100	21.0	10.3
Springfield	20 540	32 473	1.5	38.0	18.8	77 620	11.1	7 866	70 788	47.2	106 900	22.0	10.6
University City	38 933	53 667	9.2	23.2	11.1	18 021	3.0	1 867	15 837	57.0	200 100	21.3	14.4
Wentzville	28 192	72 095	3.3	10.1	3.9	10 305	NA	538	10 557	85.7	187 300	23.2	12.2
Wildwood...................	51 614	123 578	22.3	6.4	2.7	12 604	11.5	492	12 082	91.9	351 400	20.2	10.1
MONTANA	25 977	46 766	2.7	25.8	10.0	482 825	17.0	73 218	407 797	67.7	187 600	23.3	11.3
Billings......................	28 364	49 265	3.3	24.4	10.0	46 317	18.3	2 372	44 208	63.0	185 900	21.7	10.9
Bozeman	26 350	46 422	3.0	28.1	7.2	17 464	50.0	1 689	16 073	45.5	256 300	25.3	11.0
Butte-Silver Bow...........	23 698	37 503	1.7	32.9	13.9	16 717	3.3	1 785	15 275	64.0	122 100	19.6	11.4
Great Falls.................	24 733	43 374	1.9	27.7	11.9	26 854	6.3	1 553	25 127	61.8	158 900	21.6	10.4
Helena	29 594	50 311	3.0	24.7	9.1	13 457	11.0	677	12 881	56.6	201 000	21.9	10.0
Missoula....................	25 275	41 968	2.4	30.7	10.8	30 682	22.3	1 601	29 266	48.1	236 800	24.1	12.3
NEBRASKA...............	27 339	52 400	3.2	21.9	8.9	796 793	10.3	75 663	731 347	66.5	130 100	20.7	12.2
Bellevue....................	26 527	59 123	2.3	16.8	8.4	20 591	18.0	1 449	20 105	66.9	135 300	20.6	11.9
Fremont.....................	22 776	47 239	1.1	24.0	9.6	11 427	8.0	702	10 668	60.7	113 200	18.8	13.8
Grand Island..............	23 221	46 527	1.9	24.6	14.3	19 426	11.7	1 100	18 702	60.8	113 500	21.3	12.6
Kearney	24 918	48 433	2.0	24.8	9.0	12 738	15.7	537	12 351	57.8	143 900	20.0	11.3
Lincoln......................	26 574	49 794	3.0	23.9	10.3	110 546	16.1	7 000	106 512	56.8	144 900	20.5	11.3
Omaha......................	27 226	48 751	3.5	24.7	12.2	177 518	7.1	14 891	172 034	58.1	134 700	21.5	13.1
NEVADA...................	26 515	52 205	3.4	21.9	11.5	1 173 814	41.9	167 564	1 005 958	55.7	167 100	25.5	10.8
Carson City	25 893	50 108	2.2	24.1	12.7	23 534	10.6	2 107	21 225	58.2	188 000	24.3	12.1
Henderson..................	33 238	63 830	5.5	16.0	7.2	113 586	59.0	12 272	102 051	62.0	207 500	25.3	10.0
Las Vegas..................	25 555	50 903	3.5	23.4	13.2	243 701	27.7	32 012	213 037	52.5	161 600	25.8	10.9
North Las Vegas..........	21 003	53 105	1.8	19.8	13.7	76 073	107.9	9 574	68 001	55.2	138 700	26.3	10.0
Reno.........................	26 352	46 489	3.4	28.1	13.1	102 582	28.9	11 658	91 133	46.6	200 800	24.8	11.5
Sparks	26 185	53 481	2.3	20.0	9.8	36 455	39.8	2 953	34 750	58.1	176 500	26.4	10.9
NEW HAMPSHIRE.....	33 821	65 986	5.7	16.7	5.7	614 754	12.4	95 781	519 580	71.0	237 400	25.2	16.6
Concord.....................	30 043	54 182	4.0	20.0	7.9	18 852	11.7	1 260	17 141	54.7	210 800	24.7	18.1
Dover........................	32 315	60 038	4.3	18.6	5.5	13 685	14.8	858	12 586	50.7	238 700	26.2	17.3
Manchester.................	28 189	55 306	2.4	21.8	10.8	49 288	7.4	3 522	44 973	48.5	209 900	26.6	15.1
Nashua......................	32 842	66 818	5.1	19.1	7.5	37 168	5.0	2 124	34 403	56.7	234 000	24.2	16.0
Rochester..................	27 346	48 114	1.7	22.3	13.4	13 372	13.0	994	12 715	64.0	168 900	26.6	19.2
NEW JERSEY...........	36 359	72 062	9.8	17.3	8.1	3 553 562	7.3	339 202	3 188 498	65.0	319 900	27.5	18.4
Atlantic City	18 282	26 936	1.5	47.4	32.9	20 013	-1.0	4 509	15 847	29.6	201 600	47.5	21.8
Bayonne....................	28 595	55 224	3.4	22.2	13.0	27 799	3.6	2 562	25 292	37.5	324 400	34.0	22.8
Bergenfield	32 853	80 365	8.3	15.8	7.7	9 200	0.6	348	9 112	67.8	341 400	29.1	19.3
Bridgeton...................	13 730	35 352	1.8	37.3	33.6	6 782	-0.2	517	5 937	40.2	108 100	26.3	19.6
Camden......................	13 597	26 201	0.7	48.5	36.3	28 358	-4.7	3 883	25 189	39.3	86 000	28.3	17.7
Clifton.......................	31 073	68 096	5.7	17.1	7.2	31 946	2.9	1 285	28 652	61.8	338 800	30.8	22.9
East Orange...............	21 713	36 978	1.2	36.3	18.7	28 803	1.1	3 858	25 594	26.8	217 800	37.9	19.8
Elizabeth....................	19 069	43 966	2.1	26.5	17.0	45 516	6.3	3 920	39 273	27.1	271 400	36.1	24.3
Englewood..................	45 506	73 249	13.2	17.5	8.0	10 695	11.2	638	10 462	51.3	390 500	30.3	22.6
Fair Lawn...................	41 400	100 755	10.9	12.0	3.4	12 266	2.2	336	11 807	78.2	391 200	27.3	18.5
Fort Lee.....................	42 311	67 119	9.7	20.9	9.2	17 818	2.1	1 447	16 604	57.6	328 800	28.9	17.5

1. Based on population estimated by the American Community Survey. 2. Includes units rented or sold but not occupied. 3. Specified owner-occupied units; $1,000,000 represents $1,000,000 or more. 4. 50.0 represents 50 percent or more. 5. 10.0 represents 10 percent or less.

City	Occupied housing units, 2010–2014 (cont.)				Migration, 2010–2014		Civilian labor force, 2015				Civilian employment[4], 2010–2014			
									Unemployment			Percent		
	Percent renter occupied	Median gross rent[1]	Median gross rent as a percent of income[2]	Percent with no vehicle available	Percent who lived in the same house one year ago	Percent who lived outside current city one year ago	Total	Percent change, 2014–2015	Total	Rate[3]	Population age 16 and older	In labor force	Civilian full-year full-time workers	Households with no workers (percent)
	55	56	57	58	59	60	61	62	63	64	65	66	67	68
MISSOURI	32.1	740	29.8	7.4	83.9	11.2	3 113 760	2.0	155 584	5.0	4 781 853	63.9	40.2	28.6
Ballwin	20.0	1 030	27.4	1.7	87.7	10.2	17 309	2.4	584	3.4	24 222	69.2	44.6	20.6
Blue Springs	32.0	921	26.9	1.9	87.9	7.3	30 681	3.0	1 373	4.5	40 424	69.9	47.1	20.6
Cape Girardeau	45.7	665	31.8	8.8	75.6	14.3	20 203	0.9	900	4.5	32 171	62.9	36.0	29.8
Chesterfield	23.0	1 050	30.0	3.2	88.1	9.6	25 290	2.5	851	3.4	38 738	62.7	41.0	25.8
Columbia	51.7	804	35.4	7.4	67.8	15.8	67 818	2.6	2 269	3.3	93 811	68.1	38.0	22.2
Florissant	28.1	867	28.5	6.3	85.7	10.9	28 864	1.9	1 369	4.7	41 450	68.6	43.7	25.6
Gladstone	31.7	812	27.2	4.8	83.8	13.3	14 882	2.6	718	4.8	21 213	66.0	42.7	28.1
Hazelwood	36.9	796	30.7	8.8	83.6	15.1	14 185	1.9	731	5.2	20 287	70.4	45.8	23.6
Independence	35.3	761	31.3	7.1	89.0	6.5	59 482	2.6	3 334	5.6	93 366	61.8	40.2	31.8
Jefferson City	41.0	577	26.5	9.4	79.4	10.8	21 289	0.5	846	4.0	34 964	59.4	42.3	27.2
Joplin	42.8	684	29.5	9.0	79.3	10.2	26 394	1.7	1 079	4.1	40 679	66.2	40.9	29.9
Kansas City	44.6	796	30.4	11.1	80.2	9.3	257 631	2.6	14 289	5.5	365 716	68.5	44.0	25.8
Kirkwood	23.0	1 053	29.6	4.9	88.7	9.2	16 059	2.5	537	3.3	22 107	66.7	46.6	26.7
Lee's Summit	24.0	997	30.9	5.4	88.4	7.5	54 316	3.0	2 061	3.8	69 711	72.3	49.6	20.4
Liberty	24.5	770	29.2	4.1	83.6	12.6	16 327	3.0	716	4.4	23 401	67.4	42.6	24.4
Maryland Heights	42.7	869	23.4	4.0	79.9	16.4	16 569	2.4	664	4.0	22 326	72.9	48.0	19.4
O'Fallon	19.6	965	27.4	3.8	89.0	8.9	47 783	2.4	1 579	3.3	60 261	75.2	52.3	17.0
Raytown	31.7	914	29.6	6.0	88.5	8.3	15 882	2.6	1 035	6.5	22 710	66.0	44.0	27.5
St. Charles	35.7	833	28.3	5.7	82.2	13.0	38 369	2.3	1 553	4.0	55 215	67.8	43.3	25.0
St. Joseph	40.0	681	31.4	10.8	77.5	10.4	39 487	1.1	1 832	4.6	60 724	63.6	38.8	29.7
St. Louis	55.8	742	33.1	21.9	78.5	9.4	163 001	1.6	9 862	6.1	260 306	65.1	38.2	32.3
St. Peters	18.9	867	25.1	3.7	89.9	7.5	33 933	2.4	1 260	3.7	43 355	73.1	49.6	20.2
Springfield	52.8	668	32.8	8.9	73.3	12.9	87 710	2.7	3 737	4.3	136 136	62.3	34.0	30.9
University City	43.0	926	30.7	12.3	82.2	14.0	19 280	2.1	860	4.5	29 203	66.1	43.4	29.2
Wentzville	14.3	946	29.3	4.1	89.8	8.0	18 520	2.5	592	3.2	22 137	74.8	50.5	15.2
Wildwood	8.1	1 112	24.6	1.6	91.6	6.5	19 397	2.7	668	3.4	26 734	69.7	47.1	15.8
MONTANA	32.3	696	28.6	5.2	83.5	11.1	522 727	1.3	21 541	4.1	807 917	64.3	38.3	28.5
Billings	37.0	740	28.8	6.3	81.0	9.3	57 357	2.4	1 865	3.3	84 688	67.9	42.7	25.2
Bozeman	54.5	849	31.0	6.3	65.3	22.4	26 419	4.5	692	2.6	33 745	72.1	36.5	19.8
Butte-Silver Bow	36.0	595	30.0	10.2	81.2	8.5	17 315	1.1	738	4.3	28 145	62.3	37.2	33.1
Great Falls	38.2	610	27.2	8.4	80.3	8.6	28 638	1.0	1 130	3.9	47 491	63.8	37.2	29.5
Helena	43.4	724	28.5	9.7	75.2	12.1	16 671	-0.6	525	3.1	24 388	65.7	42.6	28.4
Missoula	51.9	765	33.0	7.4	73.8	12.6	38 742	1.3	1 375	3.5	57 400	70.2	36.3	25.4
NEBRASKA	33.5	721	27.2	5.6	83.5	8.8	1 012 973	-0.1	30 266	3.0	1 442 692	70.5	46.6	22.9
Bellevue	33.1	842	27.0	4.4	81.7	12.7	27 271	0.2	778	2.9	40 720	71.3	45.5	23.2
Fremont	39.3	708	25.5	5.7	82.6	7.2	13 717	-0.3	416	3.0	20 577	67.0	43.0	25.1
Grand Island	39.2	653	26.1	7.3	80.7	7.9	26 317	-1.9	994	3.8	37 913	72.1	46.6	23.2
Kearney	42.2	713	28.3	5.4	73.2	13.4	18 772	-0.8	410	2.2	25 454	74.9	45.9	18.2
Lincoln	43.2	727	29.6	7.0	76.7	8.4	151 547	-0.1	3 813	2.5	211 284	72.0	45.0	21.6
Omaha	41.9	797	29.7	8.5	81.2	6.7	232 675	0.3	7 249	3.1	337 606	70.8	45.1	23.1
NEVADA	44.3	980	30.5	7.9	77.8	13.6	1 425 711	1.7	96 159	6.7	2 175 721	65.1	39.0	26.4
Carson City	41.8	837	29.0	7.3	76.7	11.6	25 103	-0.1	1 821	7.3	44 409	60.4	33.9	35.6
Henderson	38.0	1 155	28.7	4.0	82.2	10.3	145 972	2.1	9 756	6.7	213 949	65.1	40.8	26.0
Las Vegas	47.5	983	31.3	10.0	76.1	11.2	299 563	2.2	20 883	7.0	467 890	64.5	37.8	27.6
North Las Vegas	44.8	1 116	32.2	6.4	75.5	14.9	108 153	2.1	8 065	7.5	162 635	67.3	41.1	20.2
Reno	53.4	862	31.5	10.6	75.6	10.9	123 011	1.9	7 687	6.2	183 922	66.7	39.1	27.2
Sparks	41.9	949	30.3	7.8	77.4	13.9	49 377	2.1	3 202	6.5	72 465	68.3	41.9	25.2
NEW HAMPSHIRE	29.0	1 001	29.8	5.3	86.5	10.3	741 192	0.1	25 465	3.4	1 080 795	68.7	43.3	24.0
Concord	45.3	961	29.9	9.6	81.8	10.8	22 241	-0.2	686	3.1	34 931	65.2	41.8	25.9
Dover	49.3	997	29.9	6.2	79.1	14.8	17 721	0.5	503	2.8	24 755	72.8	45.7	22.2
Manchester	51.5	1 002	30.4	10.1	80.6	8.2	61 760	0.2	2 273	3.7	90 663	69.6	45.3	25.1
Nashua	43.3	1 110	29.3	8.1	83.4	8.4	48 665	0.0	1 951	4.0	69 377	71.3	45.3	23.5
Rochester	36.0	915	32.8	7.0	84.4	9.3	16 892	0.3	554	3.3	24 820	65.9	43.0	30.4
NEW JERSEY	35.0	1 188	32.2	11.7	90.1	7.6	4 543 777	0.7	254 952	5.6	7 080 181	66.3	42.0	24.6
Atlantic City	70.4	844	37.6	46.1	85.8	6.7	15 913	-4.6	2 094	13.2	30 593	60.4	30.9	38.5
Bayonne	62.5	1 133	28.5	22.5	94.0	4.1	33 537	0.7	1 985	5.9	52 528	62.4	44.8	26.5
Bergenfield	32.2	1 198	32.1	9.9	91.8	6.0	14 868	1.2	628	4.2	22 176	68.3	46.3	19.2
Bridgeton	59.8	969	40.1	18.9	82.6	10.4	8 401	-0.3	839	10.0	18 850	50.9	26.9	32.3
Camden	60.7	872	41.2	33.7	82.9	6.7	27 095	0.4	3 001	11.1	55 062	57.1	29.8	41.9
Clifton	38.2	1 261	33.0	8.8	92.8	5.2	45 731	0.8	2 668	5.8	67 906	67.2	46.5	21.0
East Orange	73.2	993	34.4	32.9	84.8	8.4	30 367	-0.4	2 599	8.6	51 327	67.4	37.4	34.1
Elizabeth	72.9	1 069	33.5	23.4	85.2	7.0	63 866	-0.1	4 589	7.2	95 174	70.7	44.3	23.1
Englewood	48.7	1 335	31.2	15.4	89.2	8.4	14 808	1.1	748	5.1	21 933	68.4	49.1	21.5
Fair Lawn	21.8	1 413	28.1	5.7	91.8	6.4	18 533	1.5	840	4.5	26 478	69.5	47.0	19.9
Fort Lee	42.4	1 464	32.2	13.5	90.7	7.2	19 321	1.3	680	3.5	30 682	60.9	41.9	31.0

1. $2,000 represents $2,000 or more.   2. 50.0 represents 50 percent or more.   3. Percent of civilian labor force.   4. Persons 16 years old and over.

Table D. Cities — **Construction, Wholesale Trade, and Retail Trade**

City	Value of residential construction authorized by building permits, 2015			Wholesale trade,[1] 2012				Retail trade,[2] 2012			
	New construction ($1,000)	Number of housing units	Percent single family	Number of establish-ments	Number of employees	Sales (mil dol)	Annual payroll (mil dol)	Number of establish-ments	Number of employees	Sales (mil dol)	Annual payroll (mil dol)
	69	70	71	72	73	74	75	76	77	78	79
MISSOURI................	3 146 410	18 344	56.4	6 557	96 683	91 916.4	4 978.9	21 456	302 568	90 546.6	7 278.2
Ballwin.....................	5 145	17	100.0	16	49	57.5	2.5	88	1 585	644.5	47.4
Blue Springs.............	20 676	184	84.8	42	304	280.9	17.1	160	3 296	929.4	76.1
Cape Girardeau...........	17 114	102	41.2	88	1 141	655.7	47.6	299	4 617	1 240.7	101.1
Chesterfield	NA	NA	NA	146	2 241	1 231.8	161.8	315	5 198	1 093.6	112.9
Columbia...................	203 026	1 170	44.1	98	1 158	461.5	55.6	537	10 468	3 251.6	254.7
Florissant...................	200	1	100.0	18	55	27.7	2.0	176	3 083	789.0	73.0
Gladstone..................	18 591	74	37.8	16	43	19.5	1.9	82	1 845	489.2	45.3
Hazelwood.................	1 372	10	100.0	53	1 573	1 366.0	87.1	142	3 422	2 338.6	137.3
Independence............	19 947	107	72.0	71	473	165.7	20.6	456	8 382	2 068.8	196.1
Jefferson City	8 942	62	67.7	60	2 030	915.7	58.0	258	4 881	1 191.7	110.5
Joplin........................	25 893	274	77.4	99	1 568	691.6	60.1	378	6 152	1 819.7	135.3
Kansas City	381 321	3 129	24.8	614	10 628	14 577.6	675.7	1 458	24 531	7 537.3	620.8
Kirkwood...................	23 742	65	100.0	35	228	105.1	13.6	128	2 693	738.1	66.5
Lee's Summit	116 868	522	60.0	98	1 351	799.3	72.6	290	5 326	1 337.8	126.7
Liberty......................	4 401	22	100.0	23	235	216.3	13.1	86	1 299	300.9	31.6
Maryland Heights	0	0	0.0	235	5 339	4 493.9	360.0	117	2 674	4 687.1	107.1
O'Fallon....................	78 020	550	68.7	72	D	D	D	199	3 400	962.6	85.0
Raytown	374	3	100.0	22	162	69.0	9.5	92	1 528	364.0	35.7
St. Charles................	51 893	172	91.9	82	1 620	1 102.6	100.2	257	4 047	1 085.4	92.7
St. Joseph.................	20 654	171	31.6	92	1 627	1 421.4	72.0	321	5 412	1 353.4	119.5
St. Louis	87 445	548	13.7	452	7 692	5 916.4	423.3	923	9 422	2 471.9	231.1
St. Peters..................	46 934	200	76.0	74	D	D	D	325	6 097	1 695.3	149.1
Springfield	65 716	1 087	14.2	328	6 097	4 390.8	269.4	967	16 828	4 329.5	388.8
University City	2 381	6	100.0	23	298	226.8	20.4	86	781	156.9	18.2
Wentzville..................	168 852	664	92.8	26	D	D	D	100	2 179	583.1	58.2
Wildwood...................	NA	NA	NA	30	82	30.8	4.5	35	452	97.4	10.8
MONTANA	827 389	4 826	62.0	1 288	13 034	12 645.8	577.1	4 831	55 418	15 623.6	1 346.5
Billings.....................	149 201	871	73.6	236	3 832	2 734.4	190.2	618	9 047	2 761.8	240.4
Bozeman	130 863	780	36.8	60	549	286.0	20.8	357	5 153	1 192.1	120.8
Butte-Silver Bow...........	5 009	72	40.3	37	348	189.3	14.3	172	2 203	610.1	51.7
Great Falls................	19 873	111	35.1	92	1 011	847.3	45.7	314	4 496	1 268.2	109.5
Helena......................	30 093	170	44.7	49	425	295.9	17.8	220	3 292	803.0	77.6
Missoula....................	30 106	424	44.1	104	1 372	1 023.3	63.8	476	6 831	1 677.6	153.7
NEBRASKA................	1 317 315	8 096	64.2	2 720	34 409	42 619.0	1 675.4	7 279	105 953	30 470.7	2 440.4
Bellevue....................	36 348	133	97.0	15	68	28.8	4.3	110	2 318	661.9	55.4
Fremont.....................	9 221	36	100.0	30	395	566.6	20.6	131	2 220	1 026.6	56.2
Grand Island..............	32 077	211	63.0	75	1 089	707.6	56.0	273	4 710	1 198.9	107.1
Kearney....................	28 197	164	75.0	46	698	816.6	34.0	190	3 245	756.9	69.9
Lincoln......................	337 502	2 353	38.0	242	3 927	2 924.6	159.2	946	16 644	4 184.1	375.6
Omaha......................	307 638	2 633	56.9	667	10 205	12 272.0	565.0	1 634	33 150	8 083.1	793.0
NEVADA...................	2 141 757	14 083	74.0	2 501	27 649	19 841.7	1 516.2	8 135	129 977	38 234.2	3 454.1
Carson City	9 311	43	90.7	89	519	276.4	25.2	212	3 139	918.2	92.6
Henderson.................	280 809	2 165	78.3	196	1 314	776.5	92.8	721	13 600	5 601.8	398.5
Las Vegas	331 250	1 666	99.8	431	3 801	2 620.7	222.9	1 705	29 614	8 550.0	770.5
North Las Vegas	100 100	696	90.5	160	2 944	2 079.2	157.1	291	6 155	1 725.4	147.9
Reno.........................	328 256	1 654	63.8	302	4 234	3 320.6	229.2	975	15 952	4 519.4	438.6
Sparks......................	170 051	851	77.8	227	3 506	2 699.0	172.5	304	4 346	1 158.3	106.8
NEW HAMPSHIRE.....	736 931	3 763	64.4	1 543	21 140	18 029.2	1 307.9	6 127	95 660	26 018.2	2 403.6
Concord.....................	19 150	177	20.9	53	934	600.2	49.4	279	5 383	1 391.2	125.3
Dover........................	16 238	82	95.1	34	445	170.6	26.2	96	1 391	339.4	38.6
Manchester.................	42 169	286	35.0	192	3 297	2 037.3	253.4	464	7 470	2 173.8	198.4
Nashua......................	18 455	130	47.7	127	1 591	1 231.6	105.3	455	9 973	2 735.4	244.2
Rochester..................	11 872	119	44.5	14	D	D	D	123	2 506	621.8	67.2
NEW JERSEY..........	4 051 996	30 560	34.4	12 760	208 830	288 467.8	14 976.8	31 722	436 299	133 665.7	12 676.0
Atlantic City	8 567	55	30.9	12	388	95.8	12.0	330	3 060	641.0	61.1
Bayonne....................	21 820	188	23.4	48	1 157	1 944.2	72.5	190	1 864	467.1	43.6
Bergenfield	4 709	23	100.0	32	202	122.1	10.5	88	702	178.8	19.5
Bridgeton...................	1 146	14	100.0	18	249	68.3	7.1	92	842	337.1	24.3
Camden.....................	8 984	249	8.0	53	1 070	711.4	56.4	211	1 129	305.5	28.3
Clifton.......................	9 271	79	43.0	181	2 492	1 275.3	140.4	281	4 593	1 260.5	121.2
East Orange...............	1 779	37	13.5	16	169	350.2	9.0	133	1 073	310.1	25.7
Elizabeth....................	11 040	188	1.1	118	3 077	2 824.0	198.0	540	6 663	1 489.2	132.4
Englewood..................	3 779	43	2.3	88	1 119	577.9	65.1	163	1 915	1 037.0	93.1
Fair Lawn	5 990	71	15.5	51	376	180.0	18.7	94	1 142	482.4	42.5
Fort Lee.....................	15 885	116	16.4	147	950	13 212.0	91.3	127	917	350.4	26.8

1. Merchant wholesalers except manufacturers' sales branches and offices. 2. Establishments with payroll.

Table D. Cities — Real Estate, Professional Services, and Manufacturing

City	Real estate and rental and leasing, 2012				Professional, scientific, and technical services,[1] 2012				Manufacturing, 2012			
	Number of establishments	Number of employees	Receipts (mil dol)	Annual payroll (mil dol)	Number of establishments	Number of employees	Receipts (mil dol)	Annual payroll (mil dol)	Number of establishments	Number of employees	Receipts (mil dol)	Annual payroll (mil dol)
	80	81	82	83	84	85	86	87	88	89	90	91
MISSOURI	6 165	33 447	6 730.0	1 297.9	13 221	136 446	24 006.6	8 518.4	6 097	243 208	111 535.4	11 920.8
Ballwin	22	57	11.2	2.1	66	132	15.3	6.0	7	50	D	D
Blue Springs	69	199	31.6	5.7	110	564	65.7	25.8	35	905	196.0	41.5
Cape Girardeau	89	263	49.1	7.5	108	D	D	D	40	1 959	2 326.0	110.1
Chesterfield	129	673	162.9	27.9	394	13 252	2 523.7	849.6	57	1 345	376.0	76.5
Columbia	192	852	153.7	27.5	346	3 314	396.5	148.0	72	2 930	1 280.6	123.0
Florissant	28	170	23.7	4.5	56	318	20.4	9.0	10	49	3.1	D
Gladstone	48	345	35.2	11.9	75	D	D	D	7	D	D	D
Hazelwood	29	193	34.5	5.5	46	D	D	D	35	3 589	1 384.6	228.3
Independence	105	593	138.5	20.2	225	1 035	89.4	34.3	72	4 011	1 235.8	227.1
Jefferson City	54	207	42.2	6.3	203	D	D	D	35	2 574	2 091.7	122.0
Joplin	77	407	68.1	11.4	146	D	D	D	83	2 217.7	227.6	
Kansas City	578	4 517	1 142.9	221.8	1 507	D	D	D	374	17 035	8 635.1	935.0
Kirkwood	43	D	D	D	133	613	98.8	33.0	28	643	173.8	32.9
Lee's Summit	120	370	82.9	14.6	305	D	D	D	71	D	482.1	101.9
Liberty	35	160	25.8	3.9	114	D	D	D	22	927	D	40.6
Maryland Heights	57	371	130.2	19.0	157	3 597	566.4	254.7	107	3 658	1 408.7	207.4
O'Fallon	80	339	58.9	11.6	124	791	323.9	65.9	56	4 204	985.7	204.9
Raytown	23	108	16.0	2.8	58	318	30.4	13.6	26	302	38.8	13.6
St. Charles	104	519	285.3	25.8	245	3 406	195.4	81.6	66	1 654	463.4	84.7
St. Joseph	92	323	58.8	9.8	145	D	D	D	88	D	D	474.4
St. Louis	411	2 432	1 003.0	102.5	1 003	D	D	D	484	17 422	10 737.0	975.2
St. Peters	64	235	46.8	7.4	140	755	82.9	31.0	49	1 365	1 527.5	64.4
Springfield	342	2 232	308.2	65.4	665	D	D	D	239	10 927	4 323.9	478.9
University City	39	404	55.6	13.4	86	241	28.4	10.3	13	112	D	6.0
Wentzville	12	44	8.4	1.3	40	159	15.9	6.2	21	2 315	D	183.2
Wildwood	29	D	D	D	112	364	57.0	18.1	4	12	D	D
MONTANA	1 726	5 207	835.4	162.3	3 501	16 363	2 160.8	784.0	1 237	15 729	11 535.2	714.5
Billings	231	828	152.5	28.0	518	3 166	554.9	178.6	128	2 078	D	127.4
Bozeman	162	420	78.0	14.0	409	1 609	218.3	81.0	79	932	223.2	38.3
Butte-Silver Bow	47	137	15.1	3.2	107	654	73.9	30.8	35	492	D	31.5
Great Falls	104	296	49.0	8.2	171	D	D	D	43	832	D	40.7
Helena	79	265	60.0	10.0	197	1 490	191.1	76.7	38	380	D	17.1
Missoula	158	818	113.4	27.1	415	2 625	305.0	129.2	64	573	160.4	D
NEBRASKA	2 001	10 068	1 732.0	388.5	4 426	74 339	5 705.2	3 628.5	1 844	92 409	57 499.2	4 002.8
Bellevue	50	167	37.5	5.0	85	D	D	D	13	578	126.4	22.9
Fremont	33	167	22.7	4.1	38	152	15.7	5.8	35	1 126	990.8	45.2
Grand Island	73	293	54.1	9.0	99	D	D	D	58	6 981	5 695.9	270.6
Kearney	50	146	37.2	4.2	80	536	65.9	24.4	29	710	130.2	28.7
Lincoln	323	1 561	243.8	53.6	783	8 731	1 254.8	444.0	210	11 045	5 711.5	557.2
Omaha	605	5 464	926.8	248.9	1 472	54 641	3 129.5	2 713.5	381	16 879	9 325.5	718.3
NEVADA	3 866	22 412	4 981.2	814.7	8 076	47 386	7 722.2	2 813.8	1 706	38 123	14 719.1	1 979.3
Carson City	111	304	51.7	9.5	292	D	D	D	122	2 798	634.0	162.7
Henderson	395	1 468	332.9	63.9	929	3 835	633.2	229.3	122	3 591	1 459.3	170.9
Las Vegas	904	5 221	900.9	202.0	2 331	13 142	2 330.1	827.8	197	2 631	896.8	127.8
North Las Vegas	103	630	126.9	24.9	136	D	D	D	107	3 260	856.0	139.6
Reno	454	2 345	523.8	86.2	1 172	7 000	1 131.1	437.9	231	7 327	3 300.4	385.2
Sparks	108	561	102.9	20.7	146	D	D	D	171	5 510	2 459.4	391.3
NEW HAMPSHIRE	1 338	7 044	1 593.1	309.7	3 794	29 853	3 910.7	1 678.8	1 851	66 636	18 895.6	3 923.8
Concord	66	330	74.2	13.3	224	D	D	D	63	1 332	330.9	62.2
Dover	35	358	42.1	10.5	103	D	D	D	44	919	141.4	44.7
Manchester	132	1 348	276.1	69.3	438	D	D	D	116	5 175	1 189.9	263.6
Nashua	109	414	94.6	17.1	324	D	D	D	117	8 970	D	801.7
Rochester	22	75	12.0	2.2	39	389	32.2	14.6	34	1 135	248.3	59.6
NEW JERSEY	8 749	53 751	17 327.6	2 813.1	29 289	305 648	58 415.3	23 862.4	7 758	230 697	108 855.0	14 094.8
Atlantic City	47	475	111.2	15.8	68	D	D	D	6	54	D	1.0
Bayonne	40	203	36.6	7.8	83	685	72.3	36.4	32	931	528.6	53.4
Bergenfield	15	24	5.6	1.2	46	154	20.4	6.1	17	158	D	7.5
Bridgeton	13	109	15.1	2.4	31	142	13.2	5.0	11	627	D	33.3
Camden	37	D	D	D	49	D	D	D	47	1 487	488.4	119.5
Clifton	95	586	117.1	25.7	253	1 866	281.3	114.1	144	5 418	1 781.7	339.4
East Orange	59	323	55.6	8.7	40	D	D	D	12	112	D	4.1
Elizabeth	98	447	216.1	19.7	116	D	D	D	69	2 138	935.4	106.5
Englewood	67	538	192.2	31.5	117	650	136.9	44.5	54	1 240	667.7	61.3
Fair Lawn	35	D	D	D	197	1 219	374.1	71.3	35	1 421	529.1	93.8
Fort Lee	118	499	133.9	21.1	269	1 142	480.9	92.0	14	203	D	8.2

1. Establishments subject to federal tax.

City	Accommodation and food services, 2012				Arts, entertainment, and recreation,[1] 2012				Health care and social assistance,[1] 2012			
	Number of establish-ments	Number of employees	Sales (mil dol)	Annual payroll (mil dol)	Number of establish-ments	Number of employees	Receipts (mil dol)	Annual payroll (mil dol)	Number of establish-ments	Number of employees	Receipts (mil dol)	Annual payroll (mil dol)
	92	93	94	95	96	97	98	99	100	101	102	103
MISSOURI	12 459	239 264	12 430.3	3 409.2	1 626	26 954	3 047.3	1 099.3	14 644	184 918	17 917.0	7 524.7
Ballwin	42	774	31.8	8.9	11	D	D	D	41	D	D	D
Blue Springs	114	2 209	103.1	28.4	24	D	D	D	129	D	D	D
Cape Girardeau	123	3 435	142.1	40.4	14	134	31.8	7.6	227	3 601	404.0	160.5
Chesterfield	175	4 601	217.4	66.7	31	303	18.5	5.2	260	D	D	D
Columbia	367	8 566	354.6	99.6	38	D	D	D	436	5 081	598.8	232.3
Florissant	108	2 211	103.2	28.2	9	179	6.5	1.8	178	2 003	180.9	83.4
Gladstone	41	756	33.9	10.5	5	D	D	D	69	508	44.4	18.4
Hazelwood	69	1 138	60.5	14.5	7	D	D	D	69	616	49.4	20.5
Independence	223	5 275	236.3	71.0	18	D	D	D	243	5 483	603.8	221.8
Jefferson City	152	3 034	126.0	37.8	16	D	D	D	175	3 035	336.4	152.1
Joplin	194	4 298	199.8	56.2	10	82	5.0	1.4	235	D	D	D
Kansas City	1 098	25 669	1 630.0	452.9	129	3 506	747.5	292.7	1 153	15 415	1 821.9	778.3
Kirkwood	65	1 509	68.4	21.0	13	84	5.9	1.9	100	700	105.4	39.1
Lee's Summit	183	3 599	156.7	47.1	25	371	19.3	3.6	270	D	D	D
Liberty	63	1 380	57.8	18.0	9	89	2.7	0.8	110	D	D	D
Maryland Heights	94	3 434	445.0	76.8	11	D	D	D	65	2 502	451.7	108.7
O'Fallon	155	D	D	D	24	D	D	D	179	D	D	D
Raytown	47	658	29.3	8.7	4	D	D	D	47	837	44.3	18.0
St. Charles	209	5 808	481.2	101.0	27	D	D	D	194	2 341	235.7	101.5
St. Joseph	177	3 925	175.6	47.4	12	D	D	D	242	D	D	D
St. Louis	1 036	22 069	1 255.7	371.4	81	4 971	819.6	293.0	927	11 437	1 124.3	388.0
St. Peters	181	3 751	163.4	47.8	27	514	18.2	6.3	231	2 273	249.7	105.0
Springfield	646	13 397	578.7	172.8	58	D	D	D	577	9 875	1 108.5	556.9
University City	82	1 295	66.4	19.4	6	D	D	D	163	1 216	57.8	24.6
Wentzville	73	D	D	D	4	D	D	D	75	824	63.4	28.0
Wildwood	28	D	D	D	6	288	4.9	1.0	58	652	56.1	25.0
MONTANA	3 458	46 251	2 420.5	649.5	899	8 346	676.6	130.3	2 545	24 420	2 508.0	1 040.9
Billings	346	7 362	421.5	113.8	89	847	119.0	13.9	412	5 194	686.5	303.8
Bozeman	190	3 550	160.6	45.5	46	715	36.9	10.1	220	1 633	174.1	72.1
Butte-Silver Bow	147	2 244	102.4	28.7	29	214	19.0	2.8	111	1 672	143.0	71.5
Great Falls	210	3 656	182.1	48.7	61	D	D	D	187	2 481	314.9	109.4
Helena	149	2 758	126.5	35.9	38	D	D	D	183	1 477	147.6	60.3
Missoula	275	5 444	282.1	75.2	60	656	56.0	9.2	341	4 181	428.3	166.2
NEBRASKA	4 326	70 128	3 094.5	855.4	557	7 147	471.2	110.6	4 282	57 239	5 706.7	2 397.7
Bellevue	104	1 961	88.7	25.9	10	D	D	D	94	D	D	D
Fremont	75	1 208	50.1	14.0	5	D	D	D	81	D	D	D
Grand Island	139	2 398	107.7	31.3	21	356	24.2	5.8	147	2 176	206.4	88.1
Kearney	123	2 815	107.4	30.4	12	D	D	D	123	D	D	D
Lincoln	635	12 813	573.3	149.5	78	D	D	D	761	10 250	1 055.7	489.8
Omaha	1 164	23 447	1 115.1	325.7	123	2 255	138.6	36.4	1 308	D	D	D
NEVADA	5 815	296 762	27 481.5	8 555.6	1 179	25 232	3 507.5	732.8	5 766	77 665	9 936.7	3 598.2
Carson City	159	2 740	133.4	41.2	43	1 064	94.0	27.2	198	2 390	334.4	123.6
Henderson	478	14 087	1 083.9	313.2	132	2 709	246.3	66.1	715	D	D	D
Las Vegas	1 140	40 393	2 979.2	962.3	260	4 052	877.0	165.9	1 677	23 573	3 082.1	1 070.0
North Las Vegas	224	7 028	515.5	157.2	27	D	D	D	195	D	D	D
Reno	697	21 617	1 436.8	452.8	105	1 995	139.2	39.9	815	10 429	1 415.2	595.9
Sparks	193	4 855	313.9	92.6	30	926	49.7	15.0	166	2 231	218.6	76.3
NEW HAMPSHIRE	3 606	54 047	2 942.3	890.9	536	10 803	681.9	192.0	2 775	35 400	4 001.6	1 769.7
Concord	120	2 629	122.9	41.6	15	227	11.6	3.5	158	2 713	340.2	176.7
Dover	88	1 552	78.5	23.4	7	29	2.3	0.3	111	D	D	D
Manchester	304	5 518	290.4	87.8	34	879	85.2	38.3	274	3 595	423.1	222.6
Nashua	232	4 426	224.1	68.4	28	534	27.4	7.4	270	3 480	458.1	196.6
Rochester	80	969	51.8	13.8	2	D	D	D	61	627	83.9	34.7
NEW JERSEY	20 127	291 933	19 673.6	5 386.8	2 821	39 560	3 690.4	1 238.1	23 088	297 847	32 634.9	13 027.7
Atlantic City	228	38 593	3 539.1	1 154.8	13	D	D	D	45	D	D	D
Bayonne	125	1 247	72.0	18.6	9	D	D	D	153	1 338	140.8	57.1
Bergenfield	42	284	18.5	4.4	2	D	D	D	64	527	47.5	16.0
Bridgeton	41	364	17.4	4.4	NA	NA	NA	NA	28	230	20.9	9.3
Camden	87	723	46.7	11.5	5	D	D	D	70	2 037	176.9	98.4
Clifton	159	2 027	125.1	31.3	18	D	D	D	367	3 382	338.6	131.9
East Orange	44	593	35.2	8.0	3	D	D	D	103	1 643	123.2	52.2
Elizabeth	249	2 725	206.5	52.3	10	D	D	D	201	2 087	165.7	69.3
Englewood	63	787	54.2	14.2	17	D	D	D	209	D	D	D
Fair Lawn	65	673	49.4	10.9	13	191	9.2	2.6	174	1 903	217.8	88.3
Fort Lee	116	1 113	88.2	18.7	14	37	4.5	1.2	190	D	D	D

1. Establishments subject to federal tax.

Table D. Cities — Other Services and Government Employment and Payroll

City	Other services[1], 2012				Government employment and payroll, 2012								
					Full-time equivalent employees	March payroll							
						Total (dollars)	Percent of total for:						
	Number of establishments	Number of employees	Receipts (mil dol)	Annual payroll (mil dol)			Administration, judicial, and legal	Police and Corrections	Fire Protection	Highways and transportation	Health and welfare	Natural resources and utilities	Education and libraries
	104	105	106	107	108	109	110	111	112	113	114	115	116
MISSOURI	8 441	49 408	4 235.2	1 361.6	X	X	X	X	X	X	X	X	X
Ballwin	42	351	20.0	7.0	0	0	0.0	0.0	0.0	0.0	0.0	0.0	0.0
Blue Springs	80	447	37.2	11.3	262	1 043 733	19.7	47.3	0.0	9.7	0.9	18.0	0.0
Cape Girardeau	86	502	37.7	12.2	634	1 734 259	10.2	18.8	19.9	13.6	0.0	29.9	5.9
Chesterfield	104	824	48.3	20.3	272	943 362	17.5	48.7	0.0	16.3	0.0	12.9	0.0
Columbia	211	1 418	87.7	32.1	1 462	5 497 108	19.3	10.6	11.4	6.9	6.7	33.2	0.0
Florissant	81	495	46.3	15.9	357	1 267 576	12.1	34.2	0.4	11.1	12.2	29.7	0.0
Gladstone	46	241	19.1	6.4	214	773 534	15.6	32.5	18.4	8.2	3.9	21.3	0.0
Hazelwood	38	323	41.2	10.4	195	925 216	9.7	45.0	25.1	8.3	0.5	6.9	0.0
Independence	153	825	65.0	20.0	1 064	6 218 560	8.1	26.4	15.4	4.9	2.8	41.9	0.0
Jefferson City	87	566	39.6	12.1	415	1 606 150	17.3	28.1	18.7	13.4	4.3	18.2	0.0
Joplin	111	749	48.9	16.7	548	1 718 395	9.6	29.9	20.7	11.8	6.0	12.5	4.3
Kansas City	634	4 554	358.7	119.1	6 482	21 087 489	9.4	47.9	29.2	7.6	1.6	0.9	0.0
Kirkwood	48	369	30.9	11.0	247	1 279 082	4.4	28.6	22.0	4.0	0.0	32.0	0.0
Lee's Summit	135	732	56.2	16.9	662	3 026 236	14.1	26.0	24.8	12.2	1.2	15.7	0.0
Liberty	46	301	25.2	7.0	236	903 212	17.2	26.6	21.9	6.0	2.2	21.9	0.0
Maryland Heights	44	455	39.8	16.5	213	1 068 259	19.4	51.3	0.0	8.8	0.8	12.2	0.0
O'Fallon	118	905	70.2	23.2	411	1 761 725	11.2	39.0	0.0	8.3	0.2	28.0	0.0
Raytown	48	344	41.1	11.9	163	693 572	15.3	25.3	23.0	16.1	0.7	19.6	0.0
St. Charles	132	941	76.1	24.6	509	2 509 796	9.9	33.7	23.0	9.7	0.0	13.6	0.0
St. Joseph	125	D	D	D	663	2 327 632	8.6	25.3	21.9	12.5	6.9	20.6	0.0
St. Louis	462	2 903	291.4	85.6	6 234	25 364 525	13.6	42.1	13.8	12.2	1.8	10.5	0.0
St. Peters	137	949	82.4	23.7	494	2 194 343	14.2	29.0	0.0	11.7	1.0	34.9	0.0
Springfield	408	2 992	241.6	75.3	2 692	13 095 113	4.7	15.6	8.4	9.6	2.7	34.5	0.0
University City	50	496	44.1	17.7	298	1 365 064	15.3	34.6	18.6	11.0	0.0	13.0	5.7
Wentzville	54	351	32.5	10.2	193	721 735	12.9	42.6	0.0	13.1	0.0	18.1	0.0
Wildwood	25	124	5.2	1.8	22	125 285	42.6	1.4	0.0	18.0	0.0	3.7	0.0
MONTANA	1 583	7 375	732.0	192.6	X	X	X	X	X	X	X	X	X
Billings	235	1 446	135.1	38.4	872	4 012 052	9.7	22.7	20.9	15.3	1.0	18.6	2.7
Bozeman	89	485	35.9	11.5	338	1 647 964	17.1	21.0	15.4	5.9	2.9	25.5	4.6
Butte-Silver Bow	57	228	22.8	6.3	430	1 750 790	15.7	24.3	18.9	14.2	2.0	21.6	0.0
Great Falls	87	593	44.9	14.1	488	2 209 954	12.9	30.2	16.9	10.2	6.8	19.7	3.2
Helena	67	355	29.9	8.9	301	1 298 064	13.5	27.1	14.7	7.9	4.9	23.7	0.0
Missoula	155	1 073	81.3	28.1	447	1 919 831	13.5	30.6	24.9	10.1	1.2	12.0	0.0
NEBRASKA	3 155	16 918	1 516.3	447.6	X	X	X	X	X	X	X	X	X
Bellevue	71	407	32.4	10.8	265	938 368	6.4	36.6	4.0	16.6	2.5	17.7	7.0
Fremont	51	D	D	D	278	1 259 723	10.6	16.8	8.8	6.2	0.0	47.0	2.3
Grand Island	102	D	D	D	596	2 645 689	9.6	16.2	16.0	8.3	0.3	43.9	3.6
Kearney	62	354	32.6	9.7	270	1 071 385	12.0	30.1	5.2	9.0	0.0	29.1	4.9
Lincoln	426	2 442	167.1	57.2	2 609	13 359 820	7.8	16.2	13.7	9.9	9.9	36.2	2.7
Omaha	770	6 202	489.2	176.4	2 835	15 258 712	6.3	39.2	26.1	8.5	2.6	11.0	3.8
NEVADA	2 935	20 584	1 790.5	543.2	X	X	X	X	X	X	X	X	X
Carson City	95	552	42.3	14.2	599	3 175 867	20.0	28.1	15.2	8.9	6.6	14.1	2.2
Henderson	315	2 190	175.4	53.3	2 239	13 759 509	18.4	29.3	14.7	1.2	2.0	25.6	0.0
Las Vegas	661	5 005	401.8	125.7	2 582	17 371 881	20.0	12.6	31.6	6.1	2.8	17.6	0.0
North Las Vegas	126	1 726	146.2	47.7	1 363	9 456 660	14.1	46.1	18.2	3.1	4.2	11.5	1.3
Reno	357	2 581	191.6	64.3	1 190	7 727 021	13.9	33.3	27.4	3.9	0.0	11.5	0.0
Sparks	153	958	119.1	35.2	500	2 883 097	19.7	31.5	22.6	3.6	0.0	21.4	0.0
NEW HAMPSHIRE	2 267	12 435	1 111.0	350.4	X	X	X	X	X	X	X	X	X
Concord	114	604	51.3	16.7	511	2 745 870	14.5	22.9	23.9	13.9	5.1	10.5	4.7
Dover	57	336	22.4	7.3	877	3 404 621	4.9	9.4	7.4	1.9	0.4	5.5	67.4
Manchester	216	1 767	144.0	51.4	3 353	14 363 066	3.8	12.5	9.5	7.7	2.7	7.3	55.0
Nashua	150	1 349	117.8	41.6	2 841	11 458 659	3.6	11.3	8.2	3.9	1.1	3.4	67.9
Rochester	44	232	20.0	6.0	998	3 938 623	4.0	9.1	4.3	1.9	0.5	3.1	75.7
NEW JERSEY	15 754	89 543	7 479.9	2 333.1	X	X	X	X	X	X	X	X	X
Atlantic City	50	743	49.3	16.0	1 521	8 728 573	8.1	41.3	24.3	1.3	7.3	9.0	1.9
Bayonne	110	457	28.1	8.9	2 167	12 420 526	2.7	16.8	11.4	3.3	4.4	2.0	58.3
Bergenfield	51	132	11.9	2.8	255	1 134 735	8.1	48.9	3.6	7.5	2.5	16.0	6.5
Bridgeton	22	89	9.0	2.2	17	61 842	0.0	0.0	0.0	0.0	100.0	0.0	0.0
Camden	54	388	28.9	9.9	98	380 956	0.0	0.0	0.0	0.0	100.0	0.0	0.0
Clifton	158	743	68.1	21.7	557	3 601 939	8.2	40.5	27.4	6.6	4.9	6.5	4.0
East Orange	57	D	D	D	2 832	17 819 602	3.5	12.8	6.9	1.2	5.1	2.4	67.4
Elizabeth	189	1 214	102.9	54.0	1 367	7 810 360	7.8	38.8	26.4	7.8	8.7	0.5	1.8
Englewood	86	425	36.5	11.9	885	5 644 368	2.5	19.1	9.9	1.8	4.0	3.8	56.7
Fair Lawn	82	345	40.2	12.5	256	1 498 256	15.9	40.2	1.4	5.4	2.1	22.3	7.1
Fort Lee	89	263	26.0	7.0	326	1 959 502	8.0	51.4	17.5	5.4	6.0	4.7	4.2

1. Establishments subject to federal tax.

City	General revenue — Total (mil dol)	Intergovernmental — Total (mil dol)	Intergovernmental — Percent from state government	Taxes — Total (mil dol)	Taxes — Per capita (dollars) — Total	Taxes — Per capita (dollars) — Property	Sales and gross receipts	General expenditure — Total (mil dol)	General expenditure — Per capita (dollars) — Total	Capital outlays
	117	118	119	120	121	122	123	124	125	126
MISSOURI.................	X	X	X	X	X	X	X	X	X	X
Ballwin.......................	18.7	9.4	1.9	5.3	173	15	159	18.7	613	106
Blue Springs.................	53.1	13.3	54.5	24.5	462	193	260	57.4	1 082	459
Cape Girardeau.............	57.8	5.4	100.0	35.6	921	61	860	52.2	1 349	435
Chesterfield..................	34.7	22.0	9.0	9.6	202	20	182	34.5	723	209
Columbia.....................	138.4	19.3	25.9	63.8	563	95	468	212.6	1 877	640
Florissant....................	33.1	18.3	15.6	8.4	161	11	147	32.8	626	96
Gladstone....................	29.7	4.2	55.7	15.5	597	132	465	27.7	1 069	194
Hazelwood...................	38.3	16.6	5.6	17.5	683	419	264	41.8	1 627	196
Independence...............	188.3	31.9	65.8	87.8	748	125	624	191.9	1 636	278
Jefferson City	59.3	4.3	100.0	36.2	838	120	718	57.9	1 340	163
Joplin........................	79.1	7.5	60.0	45.9	914	50	864	75.9	1 511	421
Kansas City..................	1 256.7	117.6	15.8	742.9	1 599	266	877	1 156.0	2 489	448
Kirkwood.....................	31.5	7.3	39.6	15.7	568	296	272	30.7	1 115	279
Lee's Summit	126.6	6.4	34.2	72.9	788	290	499	116.7	1 263	277
Liberty........................	33.0	1.0	69.8	19.8	663	218	445	32.0	1 073	157
Maryland Heights	47.8	14.1	52.2	24.5	891	113	778	36.8	1 340	394
O'Fallon......................	65.0	5.7	97.0	39.2	478	97	381	58.2	710	117
Raytown......................	24.5	1.7	100.0	13.8	468	60	405	23.7	802	108
St. Charles...................	85.0	6.1	40.0	58.8	884	225	659	87.4	1 314	334
St. Joseph...................	112.7	24.2	75.0	53.0	685	173	513	85.5	1 107	153
St. Louis.....................	986.4	175.2	99.4	544.6	1 706	233	878	1 082.7	3 391	490
St. Peters	69.7	8.7	23.6	38.5	712	244	469	72.3	1 337	393
Springfield...................	302.8	56.5	34.5	151.6	934	123	811	276.2	1 702	333
University City	39.5	14.2	32.7	14.1	401	174	227	40.5	1 149	172
Wentzville....................	32.7	2.6	11.6	20.8	663	174	488	39.1	1 245	374
Wildwood....................	13.3	6.4	6.0	5.9	164	64	100	11.4	318	100
MONTANA	X	X	X	X	X	X	X	X	X	X
Billings.......................	139.3	26.8	53.7	38.1	356	286	52	121.4	1 134	258
Bozeman.....................	47.2	7.7	100.0	17.3	446	415	31	47.1	1 218	295
Butte-Silver Bow...........	75.8	25.6	85.0	27.7	820	793	27	64.6	1 913	455
Great Falls...................	59.8	11.2	86.2	17.7	300	264	36	59.2	1 004	125
Helena........................	39.8	8.5	54.5	9.3	320	301	19	38.1	1 306	175
Missoula	74.2	24.8	96.6	28.9	422	381	42	74.8	1 093	151
NEBRASKA...............	X	X	X	X	X	X	X	X	X	X
Bellevue......................	47.3	5.6	93.3	31.0	589	275	302	46.0	874	117
Fremont......................	32.4	11.1	42.3	11.6	439	202	237	26.6	1 007	230
Grand Island.................	57.1	7.8	100.0	23.4	468	139	329	52.8	1 053	87
Kearney......................	41.2	6.7	95.0	15.3	478	83	395	40.5	1 270	296
Lincoln........................	295.4	84.6	29.9	137.0	516	178	338	277.5	1 045	307
Omaha........................	610.0	80.9	60.1	392.9	903	317	586	580.3	1 333	325
NEVADA...................	X	X	X	X	X	X	X	X	X	X
Carson City	111.3	36.0	61.3	38.3	701	418	283	103.8	1 902	301
Henderson...................	402.5	181.2	47.5	129.1	487	256	231	422.6	1 594	454
Las Vegas....................	801.6	407.6	63.4	200.6	336	186	150	876.8	1 470	462
North Las Vegas	281.9	110.2	80.4	84.1	377	246	131	281.1	1 260	340
Reno...........................	315.2	72.0	57.4	121.3	526	255	271	287.2	1 245	153
Sparks........................	93.5	28.6	69.1	34.8	378	260	118	85.8	933	92
NEW HAMPSHIRE.....	X	X	X	X	X	X	X	X	X	X
Concord.......................	62.7	3.7	75.0	39.6	931	895	36	59.6	1 402	31
Dover..........................	105.4	21.2	95.8	64.9	2 139	2 120	18	90.6	2 982	200
Manchester...................	391.9	151.9	74.0	152.0	1 379	1 330	50	436.7	3 964	479
Nashua........................	282.0	81.9	99.2	176.1	2 033	2 010	23	264.6	3 055	177
Rochester....................	102.0	39.7	96.1	54.8	1 835	1 692	143	100.7	3 371	643
NEW JERSEY...........	X	X	X	X	X	X	X	X	X	X
Atlantic City	265.6	40.5	25.2	197.6	4 993	4 875	117	225.7	5 703	269
Bayonne......................	247.8	88.4	85.4	137.0	2 113	2 095	18	277.8	4 287	148
Bergenfield	32.3	2.9	94.6	28.1	1 033	1 005	28	28.7	1 057	46
Bridgeton.....................	34.1	9.2	55.7	12.4	491	454	37	34.9	1 382	155
Camden.......................	232.9	174.8	71.9	30.2	391	338	53	160.2	2 073	195
Clifton	115.4	15.5	73.5	84.3	990	936	54	103.5	1 216	37
East Orange.................	399.7	273.1	95.8	111.4	1 730	1 712	17	362.6	5 630	108
Elizabeth.....................	263.2	59.9	65.7	151.2	1 191	1 058	134	254.8	2 007	251
Englewood...................	130.4	25.5	71.3	98.9	3 607	3 555	52	132.8	4 840	411
Fair Lawn....................	44.1	4.4	97.6	38.3	1 166	1 116	50	39.3	1 195	65
Fort Lee......................	75.6	8.8	24.0	61.9	1 726	1 666	61	78.8	2 198	328

1. Based on population estimated as of July 1 of the year shown.

City	City government finances, 2012 (cont.)									
	General expenditure (cont.)									
	Percent of total for:									
	Public welfare	Highways	Parking facilities	Education	Health and hospitals	Police protection	Sewerage and sanitation	Parks and recreation	Housing and community development	Interest on debt
	127	128	129	130	131	132	133	134	135	136
MISSOURI..............	X	X	X	X	X	X	X	X	X	X
Ballwin......................	0.0	26.8	0.0	0.0	0.0	25.3	1.6	20.8	0.0	6.3
Blue Springs................	0.0	4.3	0.0	0.0	0.0	16.3	33.2	7.3	0.0	6.1
Cape Girardeau.............	0.0	23.1	0.0	0.0	0.6	13.1	19.5	15.6	0.7	2.2
Chesterfield	0.0	20.9	0.0	0.0	0.0	22.6	0.8	28.1	0.0	8.7
Columbia	0.3	9.2	2.5	0.0	2.7	7.7	25.4	7.7	0.9	2.5
Florissant	0.0	13.2	0.0	0.0	1.9	30.6	0.5	18.0	2.8	1.4
Gladstone	0.0	11.8	0.0	0.0	0.8	18.2	17.1	13.9	1.8	5.2
Hazelwood..................	0.0	0.9	0.0	0.0	0.0	19.1	0.3	8.1	0.0	2.2
Independence..............	1.9	13.2	0.0	0.0	1.6	15.3	15.0	3.9	0.4	8.1
Jefferson City	0.0	20.0	1.2	0.0	1.0	18.7	8.8	13.4	0.7	3.2
Joplin	0.3	11.6	0.1	0.0	3.2	12.8	22.9	7.3	2.2	0.8
Kansas City................	0.5	13.1	0.4	0.0	4.6	17.1	7.8	4.6	3.5	8.1
Kirkwood....................	0.0	5.0	0.0	0.0	0.0	21.3	10.0	12.4	0.0	1.8
Lee's Summit	0.0	15.2	0.0	0.0	0.0	15.6	11.5	6.5	1.2	3.3
Liberty	0.0	13.8	0.0	0.0	0.0	14.6	20.9	11.7	4.7	6.1
Maryland Heights	0.9	36.0	0.0	0.0	0.0	26.9	8.2	10.0	3.4	3.1
O'Fallon.....................	0.0	16.9	0.0	0.0	0.0	20.3	13.7	13.5	0.3	7.4
Raytown	0.0	5.9	0.0	0.0	0.0	28.8	18.1	6.2	2.8	11.3
St. Charles	0.0	22.9	0.1	0.0	0.0	21.1	5.4	10.0	0.6	8.9
St. Joseph	2.1	11.2	0.4	0.0	5.5	11.2	14.3	7.0	1.5	5.9
St. Louis	0.0	2.3	0.9	0.0	3.6	23.2	1.7	2.2	2.7	8.4
St. Peters	0.0	24.8	0.0	0.0	0.7	19.4	20.1	17.9	0.2	4.6
Springfield	0.4	10.7	0.1	0.0	2.9	23.9	12.1	10.6	0.9	5.3
University City	0.0	18.3	0.5	0.0	0.0	18.1	6.7	8.2	3.5	2.0
Wentzville	0.0	14.6	0.0	0.0	0.0	18.0	37.0	7.4	0.0	5.5
Wildwood....................	0.0	34.1	0.0	0.0	0.0	26.6	0.1	4.4	0.0	1.4
MONTANA	X	X	X	X	X	X	X	X	X	X
Billings......................	0.0	16.9	1.9	0.0	0.6	16.1	21.3	3.4	2.8	1.8
Bozeman....................	11.0	10.4	0.8	0.0	0.0	20.0	29.4	0.9	0.2	3.2
Butte-Silver Bow...........	0.2	7.2	0.2	0.0	7.7	10.3	23.9	4.7	0.4	2.6
Great Falls..................	0.0	12.3	1.1	0.0	0.0	20.7	22.3	10.6	4.0	2.1
Helena	0.0	10.7	5.1	0.0	0.4	18.4	19.1	15.1	0.1	3.1
Missoula	0.2	13.6	1.8	0.0	1.9	17.8	14.7	6.3	1.4	3.5
NEBRASKA..............	X	X	X	X	X	X	X	X	X	X
Bellevue.....................	0.0	10.3	0.0	0.0	0.0	34.9	13.4	5.1	0.4	3.6
Fremont......................	0.0	16.1	0.0	0.0	0.0	16.9	17.3	8.7	9.2	1.3
Grand Island...............	0.0	12.5	0.1	0.0	0.0	16.4	18.8	8.4	1.9	2.1
Kearney.....................	0.0	21.9	0.1	0.0	0.0	16.5	18.4	15.8	3.0	0.7
Lincoln	2.3	19.2	1.4	0.0	4.4	12.9	12.2	4.2	3.8	1.5
Omaha.......................	0.3	10.5	0.8	0.0	0.0	16.3	19.0	13.1	0.3	7.2
NEVADA..................	X	X	X	X	X	X	X	X	X	X
Carson City	2.3	10.5	0.0	0.0	4.2	15.9	10.8	10.1	1.5	9.1
Henderson..................	0.0	1.7	0.0	0.0	0.0	17.2	10.2	28.6	2.7	2.3
Las Vegas	0.1	6.9	0.4	0.0	0.4	14.6	13.4	11.0	2.7	3.5
North Las Vegas	0.0	13.1	0.0	0.0	0.0	26.3	10.0	10.6	2.4	3.8
Reno.........................	0.0	9.4	0.0	0.0	0.0	18.6	14.1	3.8	6.8	15.2
Sparks	0.0	7.6	0.0	0.0	0.0	23.2	17.6	6.4	0.6	13.5
NEW HAMPSHIRE.....	X	X	X	X	X	X	X	X	X	X
Concord......................	1.8	11.5	1.5	0.0	0.3	16.9	15.6	4.2	0.0	4.5
Dover.........................	0.9	5.5	0.4	50.9	0.0	7.9	7.8	2.6	0.3	5.1
Manchester..................	0.3	5.2	0.6	39.2	1.3	7.0	4.3	1.3	0.9	5.3
Nashua	0.3	2.6	0.0	55.6	0.3	6.6	7.7	1.0	0.5	4.0
Rochester...................	0.6	7.4	0.0	57.0	0.0	6.1	4.6	0.7	0.3	2.9
NEW JERSEY...........	X	X	X	X	X	X	X	X	X	X
Atlantic City	0.6	1.1	0.0	0.0	1.7	16.6	1.7	3.0	11.8	1.9
Bayonne	0.0	0.6	0.5	41.0	0.5	9.0	4.6	1.2	21.6	4.2
Bergenfield	0.0	7.1	0.0	0.0	1.5	23.3	16.4	2.7	0.0	1.9
Bridgeton....................	0.0	3.9	0.0	0.0	0.4	15.8	23.3	1.5	13.4	0.5
Camden......................	0.0	2.8	0.0	0.0	1.1	17.8	5.7	1.0	24.6	2.6
Clifton........................	0.1	2.8	0.0	0.0	1.0	20.0	12.8	1.5	3.1	2.4
East Orange................	0.0	0.5	0.1	63.0	1.4	7.5	2.7	0.7	4.4	0.7
Elizabeth....................	0.0	2.3	0.8	0.0	2.2	17.0	12.9	4.9	15.8	1.7
Englewood...................	0.0	2.1	0.0	52.5	0.6	9.2	4.3	0.7	5.2	1.0
Fair Lawn	0.2	2.9	0.0	0.0	1.8	20.0	13.4	4.5	0.0	3.4
Fort Lee.....................	0.3	3.2	1.7	0.0	1.8	18.2	8.2	2.4	8.3	3.6

City	City government finances, 2012 (cont.)			Climate[2]						
	Debt outstanding			Average daily temperature (degrees Fahrenheit)						
				Mean		Limits				
	Total (mil dol)	Per capita[1] (dollars)	Debt issued during year	January	July	January[3]	July[4]	Annual precipitation (inches)	Heating degree days	Cooling degree days
	137	138	139	140	141	142	143	144	145	146
MISSOURI	X	X	X	X	X	X	X	X	X	X
Ballwin	17.1	563	0.0	27.5	78.1	17.3	89.2	38.00	5 199	1 293
Blue Springs	129.0	2 432	12.5	24.6	76.6	14.9	87.2	41.18	5 623	1 137
Cape Girardeau	56.2	1 453	14.5	32.4	79.5	24.0	90.1	46.54	4 344	1 515
Chesterfield	69.9	1 467	0.0	27.5	78.1	17.3	89.2	38.00	5 199	1 293
Columbia	354.5	3 130	121.7	27.8	77.4	18.2	88.6	40.28	5 177	1 246
Florissant	22.1	421	7.2	29.6	80.2	21.2	89.8	38.75	4 758	1 561
Gladstone	41.1	1 585	0.0	29.3	81.3	20.7	90.5	35.51	4 734	1 676
Hazelwood	43.7	1 703	7.9	29.6	80.2	21.2	89.8	38.75	4 758	1 561
Independence	427.5	3 645	74.2	26.6	77.1	17.1	87.5	43.14	5 373	1 176
Jefferson City	62.3	1 443	0.0	28.2	77.9	17.7	89.4	39.59	5 158	1 261
Joplin	15.0	299	1.4	33.1	79.9	23.7	90.4	46.07	4 253	1 555
Kansas City	2 948.0	6 347	651.3	29.3	81.3	20.7	90.5	35.51	4 734	1 676
Kirkwood	23.0	833	0.0	29.6	80.2	21.2	89.8	38.75	4 758	1 561
Lee's Summit	98.3	1 064	7.9	24.6	76.6	14.9	87.2	41.18	5 623	1 137
Liberty	47.2	1 585	5.9	26.6	77.1	17.1	87.5	43.14	5 373	1 176
Maryland Heights	17.8	647	0.0	29.5	80.7	21.2	90.5	38.84	4 650	1 633
O'Fallon	231.0	2 818	8.6	28.3	79.0	19.0	90.2	38.28	5 020	1 399
Raytown	54.1	1 832	0.0	24.6	76.6	14.9	87.2	41.18	5 623	1 137
St. Charles	217.8	3 273	9.9	27.5	78.1	17.3	89.2	38.00	5 199	1 293
St. Joseph	532.1	6 888	30.2	26.4	78.7	15.9	89.9	35.24	5 345	1 339
St. Louis	1 862.1	5 832	143.8	29.5	80.7	21.2	90.5	38.84	4 650	1 633
St. Peters	126.3	2 335	11.7	28.3	79.0	19.0	90.2	38.28	5 020	1 399
Springfield	1 021.0	6 292	42.8	31.7	78.5	21.8	89.9	44.97	4 602	1 366
University City	13.5	382	6.6	29.5	80.7	21.2	90.5	38.84	4 650	1 633
Wentzville	64.6	2 058	31.8	NA	NA	NA	NA	NA	NA	NA
Wildwood	5.1	142	0.0	27.5	78.1	17.3	89.2	38.00	5 199	1 293
MONTANA	X	X	X	X	X	X	X	X	X	X
Billings	108.2	1 011	7.4	24.0	72.0	15.1	85.8	14.77	7 006	583
Bozeman	35.1	906	4.1	22.6	65.3	12.0	81.8	16.45	7 984	216
Butte-Silver Bow	42.1	1 246	15.8	17.6	62.7	5.4	79.8	12.78	9 399	127
Great Falls	39.4	668	0.9	21.7	66.2	11.3	82.0	14.89	7 828	288
Helena	45.1	1 546	0.5	20.2	67.8	9.9	83.4	11.32	7 975	277
Missoula	84.9	1 240	6.4	23.5	66.9	16.2	83.6	13.82	7 622	256
NEBRASKA	X	X	X	X	X	X	X	X	X	X
Bellevue	65.0	1 234	8.2	21.7	76.7	11.6	87.4	30.22	6 311	1 095
Fremont	38.9	1 473	4.0	21.1	76.2	10.4	87.7	29.80	6 444	1 004
Grand Island	50.6	1 010	9.3	22.4	75.8	12.2	87.1	25.89	6 385	1 027
Kearney	40.8	1 277	10.8	22.4	74.7	11.0	85.7	25.20	6 652	852
Lincoln	1 294.9	4 876	354.0	22.4	77.8	11.5	89.6	28.37	6 242	1 154
Omaha	1 049.9	2 411	111.5	21.7	76.7	11.6	87.4	30.22	6 311	1 095
NEVADA	X	X	X	X	X	X	X	X	X	X
Carson City	282.0	5 168	35.1	33.7	70.0	21.7	89.2	10.36	5 661	419
Henderson	308.8	1 165	35.1	47.0	91.2	36.8	104.1	4.49	2 239	3 214
Las Vegas	637.5	1 069	51.5	47.0	91.2	36.8	104.1	4.49	2 239	3 214
North Las Vegas	473.2	2 122	27.1	47.0	91.2	36.8	104.1	4.49	2 239	3 214
Reno	1 243.0	5 389	55.4	33.6	71.3	21.8	91.2	7.48	5 600	493
Sparks	243.8	2 649	0.0	33.6	71.3	21.8	91.2	7.48	5 600	493
NEW HAMPSHIRE	X	X	X	X	X	X	X	X	X	X
Concord	67.0	1 577	8.1	20.1	70.0	9.7	82.9	37.60	7 478	442
Dover	72.6	2 392	9.7	23.3	70.7	13.1	83.2	42.80	6 748	427
Manchester	566.8	5 145	160.3	18.8	68.4	5.2	82.1	39.82	7 742	263
Nashua	156.2	1 803	14.8	22.8	70.8	12.1	82.5	45.43	6 834	445
Rochester	80.7	2 701	11.6	23.3	70.7	13.1	83.2	42.80	6 748	427
NEW JERSEY	X	X	X	X	X	X	X	X	X	X
Atlantic City	164.0	4 143	51.6	35.2	75.2	29.0	80.6	38.37	4 480	951
Bayonne	460.2	7 102	0.0	31.3	77.2	24.4	85.2	46.25	4 843	1 220
Bergenfield	14.8	544	0.0	28.6	75.0	19.5	85.5	51.50	5 522	824
Bridgeton	15.0	593	0.0	NA	NA	NA	NA	NA	NA	NA
Camden	77.8	1 007	0.0	32.3	76.3	23.2	87.8	48.25	4 801	1 054
Clifton	71.7	842	15.7	28.6	75.0	19.5	85.5	51.50	5 522	824
East Orange	100.2	1 556	0.0	31.3	77.2	24.4	85.2	46.25	4 843	1 220
Elizabeth	124.1	978	19.1	29.6	74.5	19.8	85.7	50.94	5 450	787
Englewood	44.8	1 633	0.0	29.6	75.3	22.7	82.5	46.33	5 367	882
Fair Lawn	38.7	1 176	0.0	28.6	75.0	19.5	85.5	51.50	5 522	824
Fort Lee	62.2	1 736	14.1	29.6	75.3	22.7	82.5	46.33	5 367	882

1. Based on the population estimated as of July 1 of the year shown.   2. Represents normal values based on the 30-year period, 1971–2000.   3. Average daily minimum.
4. Average daily maximum.

Table D. Cities — **Land Area and Population**

STATE Place code	City	Land area,[1] 2010 (sq km)	Population, 2015 Total persons	Rank	Per square kilometer	Race alone or in combination (percent), 2010-2014 White	Black	American Indian, Alaska Native	Asian	Hawaiian Pacific Islander	Percent Hispanic or Latino[2], 2010-2014	Percent foreign born 2010-2014
		1	2	3	4	5	6	7	8	9	10	11
	NEW JERSEY— Cont'd											
34 25770	Garfield	5.4	31 802	1 179	5 889.3	87.6	6.6	0.3	2.9	0.2	34.0	44.3
34 28680	Hackensack	10.8	44 834	835	4 151.3	44.9	24.0	0.7	11.0	0.0	33.9	39.1
34 32250	Hoboken	3.3	53 635	697	16 253.0	87.5	4.4	0.3	9.7	0.1	17.0	16.0
34 36000	Jersey City	38.3	264 290	75	6 900.5	36.9	26.9	0.8	26.1	0.2	27.4	39.8
34 36510	Kearny	22.7	42 137	886	1 856.3	64.6	3.9	0.5	5.1	0.0	44.9	41.0
34 40350	Linden	27.7	42 021	889	1 517.0	59.1	29.8	0.6	2.9	0.0	27.9	33.0
34 41310	Long Branch	13.7	30 941	1 201	2 258.5	76.0	15.5	1.9	3.1	0.0	29.6	30.1
34 46680	Millville	108.8	28 230	1 305	259.5	72.6	22.9	1.0	1.2	0.0	16.3	3.5
34 51000	Newark	62.6	281 944	70	4 503.9	28.4	53.9	1.5	2.2	0.2	34.8	27.9
34 51210	New Brunswick	13.5	57 035	648	4 224.8	69.8	14.7	0.7	8.6	0.0	55.6	38.6
34 55950	Paramus	27.1	26 974	1 361	995.4	69.9	2.3	0.2	26.4	0.1	8.3	30.6
34 56550	Passaic	8.2	71 085	491	8 668.9	49.9	13.1	2.9	3.4	0.3	71.7	43.3
34 57000	Paterson	21.8	147 754	177	6 777.7	47.9	37.5	0.7	4.0	0.3	58.4	33.1
34 58200	Perth Amboy	12.2	52 682	710	4 318.2	79.1	10.3	0.4	2.1	0.1	80.0	39.1
34 59190	Plainfield	15.6	51 217	741	3 283.1	16.7	43.9	0.6	1.9	0.3	38.9	39.2
34 61530	Rahway	10.1	29 508	1 259	2 921.6	50.7	33.3	0.2	5.0	0.0	25.8	23.1
34 65790	Sayreville	41.0	44 920	833	1 095.6	67.3	13.6	0.4	18.5	0.0	12.7	27.1
34 74000	Trenton	19.8	84 225	389	4 253.8	33.8	52.3	1.2	1.3	0.1	34.0	23.6
34 74630	Union City	3.3	69 156	504	20 956.4	68.1	5.7	0.8	3.4	0.0	85.0	57.8
34 76070	Vineland	177.2	60 818	595	343.2	66.4	17.7	1.5	1.7	0.2	37.2	12.6
34 79040	Westfield	17.4	30 548	1 222	1 755.6	88.3	4.0	0.5	6.3	0.0	7.0	10.7
34 79610	West New York	2.6	53 366	701	20 525.4	63.7	4.9	1.9	5.3	0.3	78.5	57.7
35 00000	**NEW MEXICO**	314 160.8	2 085 109	X	6.6	75.7	2.8	10.3	2.1	0.2	47.0	9.9
35 01780	Alamogordo	55.5	30 753	1 209	554.1	81.6	7.3	2.8	3.4	0.2	33.6	9.6
35 02000	Albuquerque	486.2	559 121	32	1 150.0	74.9	4.4	5.5	3.9	0.3	47.3	10.7
35 12150	Carlsbad	74.9	28 957	1 278	386.6	90.5	2.3	1.5	0.9	0.0	44.3	4.3
35 16420	Clovis	58.8	39 480	951	671.4	72.7	8.5	2.6	2.5	0.1	41.3	8.2
35 25800	Farmington	81.6	42 871	872	525.4	68.0	2.4	25.2	0.9	0.5	23.2	4.6
35 32520	Hobbs	62.0	38 416	974	619.6	89.1	7.0	1.3	0.4	0.0	53.3	16.9
35 39380	Las Cruces	198.1	101 643	295	513.1	89.9	2.5	2.7	2.6	0.2	56.7	10.7
35 63460	Rio Rancho	267.7	94 171	327	351.8	85.5	4.8	3.7	2.8	0.3	38.9	5.9
35 64930	Roswell	77.3	48 544	781	628.0	80.0	2.9	2.3	1.5	0.1	55.7	13.3
35 70500	Santa Fe	119.1	84 099	390	706.1	87.4	1.7	2.9	2.4	0.1	48.6	12.9
36 00000	**NEW YORK**	122 056.8	19 795 791	X	162.2	67.1	17.0	1.0	8.6	0.1	18.2	22.3
36 01000	Albany	55.4	98 469	305	1 777.4	59.6	34.4	0.9	7.1	0.1	9.2	11.2
36 03078	Auburn	21.6	26 985	1 360	1 249.3	88.4	11.3	1.1	1.3	0.2	3.7	3.1
36 06607	Binghamton	27.2	46 032	821	1 692.4	79.9	15.1	1.3	6.2	0.1	6.8	9.7
36 11000	Buffalo	104.6	258 071	78	2 467.2	52.2	39.9	1.4	4.7	0.1	10.0	8.6
36 24229	Elmira	18.8	28 213	1 307	1 500.7	85.3	18.8	0.9	0.5	0.0	4.8	2.0
36 27485	Freeport	12.0	43 334	862	3 611.2	46.9	38.4	5.9	2.9	0.0	42.5	32.9
36 29113	Glen Cove	17.2	27 400	1 345	1 593.0	66.8	8.0	0.8	4.1	0.0	30.6	34.6
36 32402	Harrison	43.4	28 348	1 299	653.2	81.8	4.2	0.4	7.8	0.1	16.6	25.2
36 33139	Hempstead	9.5	55 547	671	5 847.1	20.0	51.0	1.1	2.4	0.1	41.2	38.1
36 38077	Ithaca	14.0	30 788	1 205	2 199.1	72.8	9.0	0.6	19.5	0.0	8.0	17.6
36 38264	Jamestown	23.1	30 075	1 241	1 301.9	90.9	6.8	1.4	0.7	0.1	9.0	1.6
36 42554	Lindenhurst	9.7	27 277	1 350	2 812.1	93.6	1.8	0.7	2.0	0.0	13.1	15.5
36 43335	Long Beach	5.7	33 550	1 120	5 886.0	83.5	6.8	1.2	4.0	0.0	18.7	18.5
36 47042	Middletown	13.2	27 812	1 328	2 107.0	51.2	24.3	1.4	4.0	0.2	38.5	21.0
36 49121	Mount Vernon	11.4	68 628	508	6 020.0	26.3	66.2	1.4	2.8	0.3	14.7	33.4
36 50034	Newburgh	9.9	28 290	1 304	2 857.6	38.2	33.7	1.9	0.7	0.3	49.3	24.2
36 50617	New Rochelle	26.8	79 846	421	2 979.3	68.3	21.5	0.6	4.8	0.1	26.9	28.2
36 51000	New York	783.8	8 550 405	1	10 908.9	45.8	26.3	0.9	14.3	0.2	28.8	37.1
36 51055	Niagara Falls	36.5	48 916	773	1 340.2	74.2	24.9	1.8	1.3	0.3	2.2	4.7
36 53682	North Tonawanda	26.2	30 785	1 206	1 175.0	96.6	2.1	0.5	1.2	0.2	1.9	2.9
36 55530	Ossining	8.2	25 441	1 409	3 102.6	48.0	16.1	2.6	5.5	0.0	49.1	39.6
36 59223	Port Chester	6.0	29 620	1 257	4 936.7	47.8	7.6	0.7	1.8	0.0	61.3	45.3
36 59641	Poughkeepsie	13.3	30 371	1 232	2 283.5	51.0	39.2	1.4	3.1	0.1	21.4	21.8
36 63000	Rochester	92.7	209 802	105	2 263.2	48.2	44.1	1.8	4.0	0.2	17.2	9.1
36 63418	Rome	193.7	32 573	1 156	168.2	89.9	7.2	1.2	1.6	0.1	6.1	3.5
36 65255	Saratoga Springs	72.7	27 765	1 330	381.9	94.5	3.2	1.0	3.2	0.1	4.0	6.4
36 65508	Schenectady	27.9	65 305	544	2 340.7	65.3	24.0	1.7	6.8	0.2	11.2	13.3
36 70420	Spring Valley	5.2	32 598	1 155	6 268.8	30.6	40.5	0.6	4.0	0.5	29.7	44.5
36 73000	Syracuse	64.9	144 142	182	2 221.0	59.4	32.8	2.3	7.2	0.2	8.0	11.8
36 75484	Troy	26.8	49 906	753	1 862.2	80.3	18.2	2.3	4.7	0.2	8.5	8.3
36 76540	Utica	43.4	61 100	590	1 407.8	71.4	19.0	1.2	9.6	0.1	10.5	18.2
36 76705	Valley Stream	9.0	37 962	990	4 218.0	49.7	19.4	0.3	15.9	0.0	30.1	33.7
36 78608	Watertown	23.4	26 780	1 368	1 144.4	88.6	8.9	1.2	2.6	0.5	5.7	4.6
36 81677	White Plains	25.3	58 459	635	2 310.6	66.1	15.8	1.4	7.9	0.1	34.0	32.2

1. Dry land or land partially or temporarily covered by water.   2. May be of any race.

Table D. Cities — **Population**

City	Age of population (percent), 2010-2014									Median age 2010–2014	Percent female 2010–2014	Population			
												Census counts		Percent change	
	Under 5 years	5 to 17 years	18 to 24 years	25 to 34 years	35 to 44 years	45 to 54 years	55 to 64 years	65 to 74 years	75 years and over			2000	2010	2000–2010	2010–2015
	12	13	14	15	16	17	18	19	20	21	22	23	24	25	26
NEW JERSEY— Cont'd															
Garfield	8.1	14.7	10.2	16.2	13.4	15.9	9.7	5.7	6.0	35.4	51.3	29 786	30 487	2.4	4.3
Hackensack	6.8	11.0	9.8	16.0	16.3	14.4	12.3	7.5	5.9	38.6	48.6	42 677	43 010	0.8	4.2
Hoboken	6.6	6.7	11.1	37.8	17.2	8.8	5.2	3.1	3.4	31.1	50.2	38 577	50 005	29.6	7.3
Jersey City	7.0	13.5	9.3	22.8	15.0	12.6	10.0	5.8	4.0	33.6	50.7	240 055	247 597	3.1	6.7
Kearny	6.9	17.3	8.9	13.9	15.8	14.8	11.8	6.2	4.4	37.0	48.5	40 513	40 684	0.4	3.6
Linden	5.1	14.6	9.7	15.6	13.3	15.7	13.2	6.8	6.0	38.8	51.8	39 394	40 499	2.8	3.8
Long Branch	7.8	17.0	9.8	15.9	13.3	13.5	11.1	7.2	5.2	35.3	51.8	31 340	30 719	-2.0	0.7
Millville	8.0	16.7	10.2	13.5	11.6	11.9	14.5	7.6	6.1	36.4	53.2	26 847	28 400	5.8	-0.6
Newark	7.7	17.9	11.6	16.8	14.4	13.9	9.2	5.0	3.5	32.4	49.9	273 546	277 140	1.3	1.7
New Brunswick	8.3	14.7	30.8	17.4	12.0	6.6	5.5	2.5	2.1	23.2	50.0	48 573	55 181	13.6	4.5
Paramus	4.7	14.7	6.8	8.3	12.4	15.3	15.9	9.1	12.8	47.4	52.1	25 737	26 342	2.4	2.4
Passaic	9.8	23.3	10.4	16.0	13.8	11.1	8.2	3.9	3.7	29.7	49.9	67 861	69 781	2.8	1.9
Paterson	8.1	18.8	12.2	14.3	13.2	14.0	9.6	6.1	3.6	32.5	52.6	149 222	146 199	-2.0	1.1
Perth Amboy	8.0	18.1	10.9	15.4	13.5	13.9	9.9	5.5	4.8	33.4	50.8	47 303	50 814	7.4	3.7
Plainfield	6.9	16.5	12.2	17.0	14.4	13.4	10.2	4.9	4.5	33.4	48.8	47 829	49 808	4.1	2.8
Rahway	6.2	16.7	8.1	14.7	14.1	16.0	10.8	6.3	7.0	38.3	49.8	26 500	27 346	3.2	7.9
Sayreville	5.8	15.7	8.3	13.7	13.9	16.3	12.9	7.7	5.6	39.6	49.9	40 377	42 704	5.8	5.2
Trenton	7.6	17.7	11.0	16.8	15.0	13.9	9.9	4.7	3.5	33.6	49.2	85 403	84 913	-0.6	-0.8
Union City	6.6	16.2	10.8	17.3	14.4	14.6	10.1	6.1	3.9	34.4	48.4	67 088	66 455	-0.9	4.1
Vineland	6.5	19.1	8.7	12.6	12.4	14.1	12.1	7.8	6.6	37.7	53.1	56 271	60 724	7.9	0.2
Westfield	6.0	22.4	5.2	8.1	15.9	16.4	14.1	5.0	6.9	41.1	51.1	29 644	30 316	2.3	0.8
West New York	7.9	13.0	9.2	20.8	17.7	12.0	8.4	5.1	5.8	34.5	50.2	45 768	49 708	8.6	7.4
NEW MEXICO	6.7	17.8	10.2	13.1	11.9	13.3	12.8	8.2	6.0	36.8	50.4	1 819 046	2 059 179	13.2	1.3
Alamogordo	7.4	16.7	8.8	15.6	10.5	12.8	11.8	9.4	7.0	35.9	51.0	35 582	30 403	-14.6	1.1
Albuquerque	6.7	16.8	10.1	15.6	12.7	13.3	12.0	7.1	5.8	35.6	51.4	448 607	545 852	21.7	2.3
Carlsbad	6.1	19.8	8.2	11.7	13.4	13.1	12.6	7.7	7.3	37.6	49.6	25 625	26 138	2.0	10.6
Clovis	8.9	18.3	12.0	15.7	11.8	11.3	10.7	6.2	5.1	30.8	49.3	32 667	37 775	15.6	4.4
Farmington	7.3	19.7	9.2	15.5	11.7	12.8	11.8	6.7	5.3	33.6	50.4	37 844	45 877	21.2	-6.7
Hobbs	9.6	20.1	10.3	15.4	12.9	11.7	10.0	5.3	4.6	31.3	48.2	28 657	34 122	19.1	12.6
Las Cruces	8.0	17.3	15.4	14.8	10.8	11.2	9.5	7.0	6.1	31.1	50.5	74 267	97 618	31.4	4.1
Rio Rancho	6.7	20.8	8.2	12.8	13.5	14.4	11.5	7.2	4.9	36.4	51.1	51 765	87 521	69.1	7.8
Roswell	8.3	19.8	10.8	13.4	10.8	11.0	11.4	7.7	6.9	33.1	51.4	45 293	48 366	6.8	0.3
Santa Fe	5.1	14.0	7.3	12.3	12.1	13.5	16.3	11.4	8.1	44.5	53.5	62 203	67 947	9.2	3.6
NEW YORK	6.0	15.8	10.0	14.1	13.0	14.5	12.4	7.5	6.5	38.1	51.5	18 976 457	19 378 102	2.1	2.2
Albany	5.6	12.0	21.1	16.2	10.4	11.1	11.2	6.3	6.1	31.4	52.4	95 658	97 856	2.3	0.6
Auburn	5.8	13.4	11.3	13.7	12.9	14.6	11.7	7.1	9.5	40.5	49.4	28 574	27 687	-3.1	-2.5
Binghamton	5.2	12.6	17.2	13.7	10.2	12.9	11.5	7.7	9.1	36.6	50.7	47 380	47 376	0.0	-2.8
Buffalo	6.5	16.3	13.7	15.8	11.5	12.8	12.0	5.7	5.7	33.3	52.0	292 648	261 310	-10.7	-1.2
Elmira	7.3	16.6	14.0	14.6	13.1	13.3	10.8	5.6	4.9	33.8	48.3	30 940	29 200	-5.6	-3.5
Freeport	7.7	16.2	8.8	13.7	14.8	14.7	11.3	7.2	5.5	37.5	51.2	43 783	42 860	-2.1	1.1
Glen Cove	5.5	14.3	9.0	16.1	12.9	12.3	12.0	8.6	9.3	39.0	50.0	26 622	26 964	1.3	1.6
Harrison	2.8	18.0	19.6	8.6	11.3	15.8	10.5	6.9	6.4	36.0	51.0	24 154	27 472	13.7	3.2
Hempstead	8.2	16.3	10.6	16.5	14.9	13.4	10.0	5.3	4.7	33.8	49.7	56 554	53 891	-4.7	3.1
Ithaca	3.4	6.3	54.5	14.0	6.3	4.5	5.7	1.7	3.5	21.9	49.2	29 287	30 014	2.5	2.6
Jamestown	6.7	18.8	8.5	13.4	12.1	14.1	12.1	6.4	7.9	36.9	51.1	31 730	31 146	-1.8	-3.4
Lindenhurst	4.0	15.9	10.1	13.4	12.2	17.7	14.0	6.8	5.9	40.7	51.9	27 819	27 253	-2.0	0.1
Long Beach	3.6	11.8	6.9	16.8	13.6	18.6	12.2	9.2	7.4	43.7	54.8	35 462	33 275	-6.2	0.8
Middletown	7.0	18.2	12.6	16.6	13.2	12.7	10.0	4.6	5.1	31.8	50.1	25 388	28 086	10.6	-1.0
Mount Vernon	7.7	15.5	9.3	13.9	14.0	14.2	11.7	7.4	6.2	37.9	54.6	68 381	67 292	-1.6	2.0
Newburgh	9.6	22.8	14.9	14.5	11.4	10.5	8.9	4.1	3.4	27.8	51.2	28 259	28 866	2.1	-2.0
New Rochelle	5.8	16.1	10.2	12.5	11.8	14.8	13.8	7.1	7.9	39.4	50.6	72 182	77 062	6.8	3.6
New York	6.6	14.8	10.1	17.4	14.0	13.3	11.2	6.8	5.7	35.7	52.3	8 008 278	8 175 133	2.1	4.6
Niagara Falls	5.7	15.7	9.9	13.1	11.2	15.3	13.6	7.6	7.9	40.1	51.7	55 593	50 193	-9.7	-2.5
North Tonawanda	5.6	13.9	9.5	13.4	10.8	16.0	15.2	6.9	8.6	41.6	52.3	33 262	31 568	-5.1	-2.5
Ossining	6.0	16.8	7.1	16.8	16.5	15.9	11.8	4.0	5.1	37.2	46.3	24 010	25 060	4.4	1.5
Port Chester	6.1	15.7	8.9	18.7	16.1	13.8	10.6	4.8	5.4	35.4	47.8	27 867	28 967	3.9	2.3
Poughkeepsie	5.9	16.3	11.2	15.0	12.2	12.3	12.5	7.9	6.7	36.8	51.2	29 871	32 736	9.6	-1.7
Rochester	7.0	17.2	13.2	18.0	11.7	12.6	10.4	5.6	4.2	31.0	51.4	219 773	210 565	-4.2	-0.5
Rome	6.1	14.4	7.6	14.1	12.7	13.7	14.4	8.6	8.4	40.8	48.3	34 950	33 725	-3.5	-3.4
Saratoga Springs	4.5	12.9	15.5	14.1	11.2	12.3	12.3	8.8	8.4	37.8	50.0	26 186	26 586	1.5	4.5
Schenectady	6.6	16.0	13.5	14.9	12.4	13.3	11.2	6.5	5.6	34.2	51.2	61 821	66 135	7.0	-1.3
Spring Valley	11.2	22.2	11.3	18.0	12.0	10.0	8.5	4.5	2.4	27.7	49.4	25 464	31 347	23.1	4.2
Syracuse	7.1	15.7	18.9	15.4	9.9	11.6	10.3	5.6	5.6	29.7	52.8	147 306	145 170	-1.5	-0.7
Troy	6.0	13.2	21.7	16.0	11.4	11.2	9.3	5.5	5.7	30.3	50.6	49 170	50 129	2.0	-0.4
Utica	7.6	17.6	12.3	13.1	10.3	12.7	11.6	6.8	8.0	34.6	51.0	60 651	62 235	2.6	-1.8
Valley Stream	7.5	16.7	7.9	14.2	12.8	14.3	13.4	7.0	6.2	38.0	50.3	36 368	37 511	3.1	1.1
Watertown	10.3	13.8	13.8	18.1	10.8	10.3	9.8	6.4	6.6	30.6	51.3	26 705	27 023	1.2	-0.1
White Plains	6.2	14.3	8.9	15.1	15.1	12.6	12.0	7.8	8.0	38.3	52.1	53 077	56 853	7.1	2.8

City	Households, 2010-2014				Persons in group quarters, 2010				Serious crimes known to police[2] 2014				Educational attainment, 2010–2014		
			Percent			Institutional			Total		Rate[3]			Attainment[4] (percent)	
	Number	Persons per household	Female family householder[1]	One-person	Total	Total	Persons in nursing facilities	Non-institutional	Number	Rate[3]	Violent	Property	Population age 25 and older	High school graduate or less	Bachelor's degree or more
	27	28	29	30	31	32	33	34	35	36	37	38	39	40	41
NEW JERSEY—Cont'd															
Garfield	10 673	2.90	20.9	22.1	32	0	0	32	721	2 295	207	2 088	20 859	59.6	18.9
Hackensack	18 345	2.39	14.6	36.6	1 301	985	172	316	732	1 647	202	1 444	31 929	44.5	32.5
Hoboken	24 330	2.14	8.3	38.3	1 574	0	0	1 574	1 182	2 218	280	1 938	39 318	16.5	74.3
Jersey City	96 634	2.65	17.6	29.3	2 843	984	914	1 859	5 621	2 162	531	1 631	177 924	38.4	42.5
Kearny	13 691	3.03	16.2	19.1	2 570	2 501	167	69	985	2 347	207	2 140	27 976	55.3	21.0
Linden	14 400	2.85	19.1	26.3	245	242	214	3	1 232	2 965	366	2 599	28 965	54.2	18.0
Long Branch	11 883	2.57	14.7	33.6	184	75	70	109	838	2 765	320	2 445	20 615	50.1	28.3
Millville	10 258	2.79	18.7	28.4	212	117	117	95	2 133	7 417	692	6 725	18 711	57.2	15.9
Newark	91 771	3.04	29.1	30.1	16 367	8 545	1 015	7 822	10 967	3 929	1 078	2 851	174 844	63.9	13.3
New Brunswick	13 866	4.02	22.0	25.5	7 745	182	147	7 563	2 000	3 559	744	2 815	25 480	65.5	20.5
Paramus	8 435	3.15	9.3	17.6	1 165	1 110	521	55	1 219	4 550	86	4 464	19 464	30.7	48.3
Passaic	20 044	3.52	27.1	23.6	458	232	224	226	1 601	2 248	651	1 596	40 220	69.8	14.3
Paterson	43 462	3.37	31.1	22.7	2 628	1 353	212	1 275	5 048	3 456	816	2 640	88 997	67.9	10.7
Perth Amboy	16 306	3.17	24.2	22.5	667	445	445	222	1 234	2 358	472	1 886	32 574	65.4	14.8
Plainfield	14 518	3.47	26.3	21.8	732	342	327	390	1 572	3 092	710	2 382	33 014	59.2	18.2
Rahway	10 577	2.65	16.0	30.0	124	109	109	15	365	1 273	181	1 092	19 472	45.1	26.0
Sayreville	15 811	2.78	12.9	22.7	200	193	193	7	501	1 115	80	1 035	31 021	38.9	33.0
Trenton	27 998	3.02	26.3	31.2	5 123	4 250	1 166	873	2 960	3 510	1 104	2 406	53 741	67.6	10.7
Union City	22 786	2.98	24.7	24.9	649	342	341	307	1 425	2 072	347	1 724	45 286	63.3	17.4
Vineland	20 966	2.91	19.4	24.6	1 491	897	593	594	2 510	4 107	437	3 670	40 244	59.6	16.3
Westfield	10 327	2.97	6.0	19.5	220	204	204	16	293	945	61	883	20 171	17.5	66.4
West New York	19 034	2.71	18.4	27.6	14	0	0	14	717	1 358	290	1 068	36 333	55.9	24.3
NEW MEXICO	764 684	2.72	14.1	28.9	42 629	25 266	5 567	17 363	86 336	4 140	597	3 542	1 360 013	42.4	26.1
Alamogordo	12 470	2.50	14.5	30.3	611	515	278	96	1 061	3 363	295	3 069	21 264	43.4	17.3
Albuquerque	222 868	2.48	14.4	32.7	7 659	2 897	1 712	4 762	35 371	6 329	883	5 446	367 227	34.2	33.2
Carlsbad	10 068	2.68	14.0	29.0	533	470	217	63	1 370	4 886	510	4 376	17 373	50.9	18.4
Clovis	14 618	2.68	14.4	29.9	597	503	188	94	2 461	6 180	362	5 819	24 113	43.5	20.6
Farmington	15 255	2.97	14.1	25.9	1 465	979	164	486	1 822	4 023	665	3 358	28 318	42.8	19.9
Hobbs	11 128	3.18	14.5	22.5	1 494	1 316	146	178	1 828	5 002	673	4 329	21 066	56.2	14.4
Las Cruces	38 670	2.60	15.6	29.9	1 610	1 186	251	424	4 909	4 807	289	4 519	60 605	34.0	33.6
Rio Rancho	32 574	2.78	12.1	23.1	197	141	141	56	1 989	2 140	188	1 951	58 573	32.1	28.6
Roswell	17 731	2.74	18.7	28.4	1 489	452	216	1 037	3 429	7 050	765	6 285	29 957	47.0	18.6
Santa Fe	31 498	2.20	11.5	39.8	1 119	270	247	849	3 261	4 630	346	4 283	51 070	30.5	44.0
NEW YORK	7 255 528	2.70	14.8	29.6	585 678	231 163	116 558	354 515	414 680	2 100	382	1 718	13 329 734	41.6	33.7
Albany	39 903	2.46	15.4	43.9	10 248	1 452	941	8 796	4 668	4 735	803	3 931	59 590	38.2	36.3
Auburn	11 119	2.46	15.1	40.5	2 328	2 139	370	189	1 078	3 947	454	3 493	19 130	48.6	17.7
Binghamton	19 902	2.35	15.0	40.2	1 262	846	458	416	2 355	5 094	664	4 430	29 916	49.2	23.0
Buffalo	111 444	2.33	22.2	39.2	9 371	2 530	1 201	6 841	15 622	6 045	1 228	4 817	165 318	44.7	24.7
Elmira	10 826	2.68	19.5	34.8	3 458	2 380	296	1 078	1 045	3 628	281	3 347	18 350	55.2	14.1
Freeport	13 557	3.18	21.9	23.1	574	354	346	220	1 000	2 313	352	1 961	29 022	51.3	24.1
Glen Cove	9 531	2.85	12.1	27.1	723	404	396	319	103	378	22	356	19 221	45.9	34.9
Harrison	8 299	3.35	8.9	17.9	4 285	0	0	4 285	135	480	21	459	16 475	30.6	50.0
Hempstead	16 233	3.38	26.1	24.5	1 306	686	678	620	1 446	2 595	863	1 732	34 998	59.6	15.9
Ithaca	9 489	3.20	7.3	42.7	7 701	179	172	7 522	1 221	3 985	144	3 842	10 629	17.5	64.3
Jamestown	13 108	2.35	17.7	35.9	1 134	399	353	735	1 510	4 927	728	4 200	20 071	48.8	18.4
Lindenhurst	9 012	3.03	14.2	18.7	29	0	0	29	NA	NA	NA	NA	19 271	48.0	23.9
Long Beach	14 418	2.33	12.2	38.5	1 094	920	822	174	339	1 009	128	881	25 572	29.9	45.1
Middletown	9 976	2.80	19.2	33.1	489	190	181	299	953	3 440	451	2 989	17 743	51.3	18.4
Mount Vernon	25 762	2.64	24.2	33.5	833	429	418	404	1 526	2 230	722	1 508	45 803	45.0	27.3
Newburgh	8 762	3.27	26.0	28.6	945	24	0	921	1 285	4 528	1 476	3 052	15 353	66.7	11.2
New Rochelle	28 251	2.78	13.0	28.6	3 277	1 256	999	2 021	1 396	1 744	229	1 516	52 932	38.6	41.0
New York	3 095 931	2.70	18.5	32.5	185 530	70 041	45 516	115 489	186 311	2 199	597	1 602	5 723 275	44.4	35.0
Niagara Falls	21 300	2.33	19.9	37.6	376	159	157	217	3 228	6 548	1 189	5 359	33 819	52.9	16.5
North Tonawanda	13 939	2.24	10.0	36.8	142	74	70	68	530	1 710	155	1 556	22 517	42.1	25.0
Ossining	7 449	3.39	14.8	23.8	1 858	1 830	102	28	266	1 045	216	829	17 399	51.8	30.7
Port Chester	9 251	3.16	18.6	21.6	465	154	154	311	563	1 908	213	1 694	20 194	59.1	21.4
Poughkeepsie	12 018	2.56	22.1	36.1	2 904	921	540	1 983	978	3 201	894	2 307	20 273	48.3	24.0
Rochester	86 025	2.45	24.0	40.4	10 200	3 657	1 960	6 543	10 643	5 060	850	4 210	131 362	48.0	24.4
Rome	13 249	2.50	13.2	36.1	2 882	2 581	462	301	658	2 017	101	1 916	23 550	48.6	19.5
Saratoga Springs	11 590	2.33	5.2	39.8	2 510	445	352	2 065	655	2 382	236	2 146	18 840	25.2	49.6
Schenectady	24 557	2.69	16.7	39.9	3 470	677	296	2 793	3 068	4 660	870	3 790	42 282	51.9	20.1
Spring Valley	8 604	3.72	21.6	19.7	216	0	0	216	524	1 608	408	1 200	18 227	57.3	17.4
Syracuse	55 279	2.62	21.4	39.8	12 782	2 332	1 523	10 450	6 927	4 793	811	3 982	84 171	47.0	26.0
Troy	19 962	2.50	19.6	37.3	4 508	493	202	4 015	2 561	5 127	759	4 368	29 858	43.6	25.4
Utica	23 828	2.60	19.8	36.8	3 076	1 171	983	1 905	2 788	4 518	653	3 865	38 746	53.5	16.6
Valley Stream	11 422	3.31	13.5	17.4	41	0	0	41	NA	NA	NA	NA	25 401	39.8	32.6
Watertown	11 865	2.33	13.2	37.4	905	667	473	238	1 449	5 173	546	4 627	17 334	43.2	21.5
White Plains	22 033	2.61	11.5	33.4	1 755	704	460	1 051	1 150	1 979	179	1 800	40 946	33.7	47.7

1. No spouse present. 2. Data for serious crimes have not been adjusted for underreporting. This may affect comparability between geographic areas and over time. 3. Per 100,000 population estimated by the FBI. 4. Persons 25 years old and over.

Table D. Cities — Income, Poverty, and Housing

City	Money income, 2010–2014					Housing units, 2010			Occupied housing units 2010–2014				
		Households			Families with income below poverty (percent)					Owner-occupied		Median owner costs as a percent of income	
	Per capita income[1] (dollars)	Median income	Percent with income of $200,000 or more	Percent with income of less than $25,000		Total	Percent change, 2000–2010	Vacant units for sale or rent[2]	Total	Percent	Median value[3] (dollars)	With a mortgage[4]	Without a mortgage[5]
	42	43	44	45	46	47	48	49	50	51	52	53	54
NEW JERSEY—Cont'd													
Garfield	21 397	46 499	2.2	25.3	12.4	11 788	0.8	715	10 673	35.7	334 300	40.1	25.3
Hackensack	31 135	53 338	3.9	22.5	14.9	19 375	2.3	1 233	18 345	35.5	284 300	32.6	21.5
Hoboken	69 476	106 875	21.8	14.1	10.1	26 855	34.3	1 814	24 330	31.0	563 300	22.6	17.2
Jersey City	32 791	58 907	8.2	24.9	16.2	108 720	16.1	11 861	96 634	29.9	323 800	30.3	20.1
Kearny	26 281	63 093	3.3	17.0	8.4	14 180	2.2	718	13 691	45.7	311 200	30.2	20.2
Linden	27 057	62 778	2.7	20.1	8.8	15 872	2.0	963	14 400	57.8	270 900	32.6	22.0
Long Branch	29 478	48 736	6.6	25.1	14.1	14 170	1.3	2 417	11 883	41.4	329 700	32.8	15.5
Millville	23 892	50 787	1.8	26.2	13.8	11 435	7.4	787	10 258	63.6	164 600	26.6	16.1
Newark	16 828	34 012	1.1	38.3	26.9	109 520	9.4	14 978	91 771	22.3	229 600	38.5	23.0
New Brunswick	14 119	38 399	1.9	32.4	25.4	15 053	8.3	934	13 866	21.0	240 700	35.1	17.6
Paramus	41 157	96 454	14.9	9.0	1.8	8 915	8.6	285	8 435	87.9	554 400	28.1	17.9
Passaic	15 193	33 081	1.4	39.4	29.9	20 432	1.2	1 021	20 044	24.1	309 300	40.9	19.9
Paterson	16 259	33 964	1.2	37.4	26.1	47 946	1.6	3 617	43 462	27.3	262 200	43.9	22.2
Perth Amboy	19 217	45 276	0.9	30.7	20.9	16 556	8.7	1 137	16 306	33.6	245 600	30.5	23.9
Plainfield	22 541	53 099	4.1	25.7	20.1	16 621	2.7	1 441	14 518	48.5	246 500	31.8	20.7
Rahway	28 994	59 076	3.5	19.7	7.6	11 300	8.9	767	10 577	58.8	279 900	32.3	23.7
Sayreville	34 685	81 136	6.3	11.6	4.2	16 393	7.6	757	15 811	68.4	305 500	27.3	18.4
Trenton	17 021	35 647	1.4	38.0	24.4	33 035	-2.6	4 457	27 998	38.0	113 100	28.1	18.9
Union City	19 834	40 939	2.0	31.3	22.5	24 931	5.0	2 117	22 786	18.7	293 200	37.5	32.8
Vineland	24 598	50 690	3.2	25.2	14.0	22 661	8.1	1 211	20 966	66.9	168 500	25.7	17.6
Westfield	64 374	138 165	34.2	6.6	1.1	10 950	1.2	384	10 327	79.9	653 900	23.3	16.6
West New York	26 081	45 412	4.7	29.3	19.2	20 018	15.3	1 166	19 034	20.3	320 200	30.7	26.4
NEW MEXICO	23 948	44 968	2.9	28.9	16.1	901 388	15.5	109 993	764 684	68.2	159 300	23.2	10.0
Alamogordo	22 768	43 460	2.2	28.6	14.7	14 052	-11.2	1 289	12 470	58.3	112 100	22.1	10.0
Albuquerque	26 876	47 413	3.2	26.9	14.8	239 166	20.4	14 836	222 868	59.3	185 100	23.4	10.0
Carlsbad	24 472	48 058	2.1	27.8	11.2	11 243	-2.4	986	10 068	70.0	107 300	17.6	10.4
Clovis	22 351	40 136	1.4	31.5	17.1	15 573	8.9	1 285	14 618	60.4	132 300	20.4	10.0
Farmington	26 003	55 810	3.8	22.9	13.4	17 548	16.6	1 102	15 255	68.4	177 200	21.1	10.0
Hobbs	22 115	53 750	3.1	24.1	16.2	12 900	7.5	1 271	11 128	66.8	104 900	18.6	10.0
Las Cruces	21 782	40 658	2.0	33.6	17.1	42 370	33.9	2 937	38 670	56.0	149 700	22.7	10.0
Rio Rancho	27 400	59 243	3.2	16.9	8.3	33 964	68.3	2 072	32 574	78.6	172 400	24.9	10.0
Roswell	20 104	38 919	1.0	29.8	18.7	19 743	2.4	2 089	17 731	61.5	97 400	20.4	10.0
Santa Fe	33 967	50 213	5.2	25.3	12.8	37 200	22.0	5 305	31 498	61.0	276 500	27.6	10.0
NEW YORK	32 829	58 687	7.3	22.9	12.0	8 108 103	5.6	790 348	7 255 528	53.8	283 700	25.3	14.9
Albany	24 342	41 099	1.6	34.0	18.7	46 362	2.4	5 205	39 903	38.1	173 500	23.0	13.4
Auburn	20 678	38 399	0.8	34.7	14.3	12 639	0.0	948	11 119	47.8	95 900	19.9	14.1
Binghamton	19 946	30 828	1.7	42.9	24.1	23 842	-0.5	2 692	19 902	46.6	85 700	22.7	14.4
Buffalo	20 726	31 668	1.5	41.4	26.2	133 444	-8.3	20 908	111 444	41.6	67 800	21.6	13.2
Elmira	17 460	29 865	1.2	42.2	27.4	12 313	-4.5	1 322	10 826	46.6	68 200	19.0	13.6
Freeport	28 120	67 056	7.6	20.3	12.2	13 865	0.3	586	13 557	66.2	323 000	33.3	20.0
Glen Cove	36 141	65 267	11.2	18.5	10.3	10 352	6.3	588	9 531	52.1	470 900	29.9	24.7
Harrison	61 059	111 122	26.2	11.5	6.2	8 956	3.5	581	8 299	64.4	786 800	29.2	19.1
Hempstead	21 691	51 714	3.3	25.7	17.3	16 034	3.0	800	16 233	42.7	320 100	35.8	20.6
Ithaca	16 718	30 318	2.2	44.2	17.3	10 950	2.2	542	9 489	27.5	205 700	23.1	13.3
Jamestown	18 825	31 128	0.7	40.6	25.4	14 738	-1.9	1 616	13 108	50.8	64 200	19.6	13.3
Lindenhurst	33 254	84 414	7.2	10.7	3.7	9 665	4.1	349	9 012	79.1	347 100	32.7	19.8
Long Beach	45 749	83 396	9.6	14.7	7.3	16 450	2.0	1 641	14 418	55.2	464 200	29.6	19.0
Middletown	22 949	50 584	2.1	26.5	17.3	10 866	7.1	890	9 976	51.1	200 100	30.8	18.1
Mount Vernon	27 059	49 268	4.4	26.1	12.7	28 990	7.2	2 730	25 750	38.8	372 100	32.9	21.0
Newburgh	16 114	33 125	0.9	38.6	33.2	10 505	0.2	1 475	8 762	32.0	172 200	29.0	20.0
New Rochelle	40 791	68 270	12.8	17.9	7.7	29 586	9.6	1 633	28 251	49.8	551 400	28.2	19.3
New York	32 459	52 737	7.4	27.2	17.5	3 371 062	5.3	261 278	3 095 931	31.9	490 700	29.6	14.5
Niagara Falls	20 643	33 009	1.3	38.7	20.5	26 220	-5.8	3 617	21 300	56.3	67 600	19.8	15.2
North Tonawanda	28 959	47 604	1.7	24.8	7.7	14 757	2.3	753	13 939	66.8	105 600	20.1	15.0
Ossining	27 746	68 533	7.7	17.4	15.2	8 862	4.1	518	7 449	47.4	394 400	32.0	17.9
Port Chester	26 256	56 134	5.3	18.7	12.4	10 046	2.8	806	9 251	43.6	440 800	34.5	19.6
Poughkeepsie	23 923	38 973	3.2	34.1	19.5	13 984	6.3	1 584	12 018	38.7	211 400	29.2	22.0
Rochester	19 180	30 784	1.3	42.3	31.0	97 158	-2.7	10 131	86 025	38.2	76 600	23.0	13.5
Rome	24 475	44 694	2.1	25.7	11.5	14 893	-8.6	1 367	13 249	56.7	89 700	21.4	13.0
Saratoga Springs	39 395	67 303	7.6	19.4	2.2	12 936	11.7	1 624	11 590	54.1	310 200	23.6	12.0
Schenectady	20 652	38 916	1.3	33.8	20.3	30 095	-0.8	3 462	24 557	47.9	116 700	25.1	16.7
Spring Valley	19 256	46 142	3.1	25.3	24.1	9 374	20.2	619	8 604	29.7	270 900	33.0	14.7
Syracuse	19 283	31 566	1.6	41.5	28.2	64 356	-5.6	7 001	55 279	38.5	87 800	21.2	13.6
Troy	21 635	39 526	0.7	33.3	23.0	23 474	1.6	2 969	19 962	38.6	142 900	23.5	14.1
Utica	17 897	31 173	0.8	41.5	25.9	28 166	-3.4	3 261	23 828	47.2	89 400	22.2	15.3
Valley Stream	32 214	88 145	7.8	11.7	7.0	12 625	-0.6	436	11 422	79.0	371 000	30.7	21.1
Watertown	22 187	41 197	1.3	31.2	17.5	12 562	0.9	1 153	11 865	39.7	119 800	20.6	13.0
White Plains	46 673	81 743	14.7	15.6	7.0	24 382	13.0	1 472	22 033	51.5	507 800	25.0	17.4

1. Based on population estimated by the American Community Survey.　2. Includes units rented or sold but not occupied.　3. Specified owner-occupied units; $1,000,000 represents $1,000,000 or more.　4. 50.0 represents 50 percent or more.　5. 10.0 represents 10 percent or less.

Table D. Cities — Housing, Labor Force, and Employment

City	Occupied housing units, 2010–2014 (cont.)				Migration, 2010–2014		Civilian labor force, 2015		Unemployment		Civilian employment[4], 2010–2014			
	Percent renter occupied	Median gross rent[1]	Median gross rent as a percent of income[2]	Percent with no vehicle available	Percent who lived in the same house one year ago	Percent who lived outside current city one year ago	Total	Percent change, 2014–2015	Total	Rate[3]	Population age 16 and older	In labor force	Civilian full-year full-time workers	Households with no workers (percent)
	55	56	57	58	59	60	61	62	63	64	65	66	67	68
NEW JERSEY— Cont'd														
Garfield	64.3	1 196	35.6	11.6	95.4	3.2	16 084	0.2	1 195	7.4	24 490	64.3	43.7	22.8
Hackensack	64.5	1 258	32.0	16.8	85.1	10.3	24 451	1.0	1 343	5.5	36 722	66.6	49.2	22.5
Hoboken	69.0	1 829	23.7	33.5	76.3	14.3	36 515	1.5	999	2.7	45 499	78.0	62.4	14.8
Jersey City	70.1	1 187	29.0	38.0	85.4	7.3	140 658	0.8	7 474	5.3	208 208	68.8	46.5	20.4
Kearny	54.3	1 181	29.8	13.2	89.4	5.9	20 960	1.0	1 350	6.4	33 212	69.0	46.2	20.2
Linden	42.2	1 165	30.0	9.5	88.7	7.5	21 921	0.4	1 433	6.5	33 818	67.7	42.1	25.5
Long Branch	58.6	1 221	36.2	14.3	85.0	7.7	16 214	1.2	927	5.7	24 094	68.1	38.4	25.4
Millville	36.4	910	35.6	12.1	86.0	6.6	13 373	0.4	1 180	8.8	22 185	65.5	35.4	32.3
Newark	77.7	978	34.2	39.5	86.2	5.6	118 426	-0.5	10 387	8.8	214 879	63.3	33.9	31.2
New Brunswick	79.0	1 370	41.1	32.5	73.0	13.6	27 236	1.2	1 387	5.1	44 162	60.0	33.1	22.4
Paramus	12.1	1 874	50.0	5.5	94.7	4.4	12 938	1.0	585	4.5	22 012	57.3	37.3	27.9
Passaic	75.9	1 076	39.9	38.3	95.8	2.2	30 394	0.3	2 428	8.0	50 174	59.5	37.2	27.3
Paterson	72.7	1 116	40.6	30.2	90.1	3.1	62 637	-0.1	6 352	10.1	110 949	57.2	38.7	31.6
Perth Amboy	66.4	1 167	35.1	23.2	93.3	4.2	25 304	0.8	2 350	9.3	39 118	60.3	43.8	23.5
Plainfield	51.5	1 167	40.0	17.3	84.1	6.3	27 400	-0.1	2 018	7.4	39 737	75.0	43.3	22.5
Rahway	41.2	1 222	35.6	14.0	91.7	5.9	14 595	0.2	966	6.6	22 625	69.2	41.9	26.3
Sayreville	31.6	1 142	26.8	5.3	94.2	4.2	24 293	1.3	1 226	5.0	35 702	67.3	44.2	18.8
Trenton	62.0	991	37.0	30.4	84.0	7.7	39 087	1.7	3 145	8.0	65 487	61.6	33.9	34.7
Union City	81.3	1 095	33.8	43.8	87.4	6.3	35 075	0.4	2 241	6.4	54 409	68.2	40.6	22.1
Vineland	33.1	996	36.2	9.7	90.9	4.6	28 298	-0.3	2 346	8.3	47 739	63.1	38.3	28.9
Westfield	20.1	1 669	26.5	3.7	90.7	6.9	14 554	0.6	514	3.5	23 056	67.8	44.8	18.1
West New York	79.7	1 157	31.7	37.8	83.1	10.1	28 375	0.7	1 520	5.4	41 892	71.3	42.9	23.7
NEW MEXICO	31.8	774	30.5	5.7	85.5	8.6	919 889	-0.2	60 647	6.6	1 625 155	60.2	37.0	29.9
Alamogordo	41.7	689	26.9	7.1	80.3	11.3	12 937	-0.1	708	5.5	24 948	56.6	29.3	34.9
Albuquerque	40.7	798	31.4	6.9	83.1	6.6	267 231	-0.1	15 263	5.7	436 720	65.3	41.3	27.1
Carlsbad	30.0	740	24.6	4.3	83.5	8.9	14 411	1.4	683	4.7	20 260	63.0	43.7	28.1
Clovis	39.6	693	31.3	7.4	77.1	11.1	17 156	0.3	833	4.9	29 658	64.4	40.1	27.3
Farmington	31.6	798	30.0	5.5	86.0	9.5	21 292	0.3	1 219	5.7	33 575	63.4	40.7	22.6
Hobbs	33.2	844	23.6	3.2	87.3	8.0	15 205	-3.8	944	6.2	25 438	61.8	40.5	20.4
Las Cruces	44.0	750	34.1	6.3	76.2	10.4	45 025	-0.3	2 777	6.2	78 681	61.9	35.3	30.4
Rio Rancho	21.4	1 043	30.7	2.6	87.6	7.5	42 358	-0.4	2 592	6.1	68 651	64.1	43.3	24.6
Roswell	38.5	700	29.8	5.9	81.8	8.9	20 194	1.5	1 313	6.5	36 463	59.7	36.7	29.7
Santa Fe	39.0	950	31.4	6.2	80.5	10.5	34 782	0.1	1 778	5.1	57 511	64.5	39.0	31.7
NEW YORK	46.2	1 117	32.1	29.3	88.9	6.3	9 679 321	0.9	513 075	5.3	15 832 743	63.5	40.2	27.1
Albany	61.9	862	32.8	25.9	79.9	11.7	47 414	0.6	2 472	5.2	83 030	61.0	36.9	31.1
Auburn	52.2	635	28.9	20.9	80.7	10.6	12 085	0.0	768	6.4	22 449	58.1	30.2	36.9
Binghamton	53.4	660	37.2	23.5	79.6	11.5	18 615	-1.6	1 227	6.6	38 849	54.2	27.4	40.3
Buffalo	58.4	696	33.2	29.3	82.3	7.6	111 383	-0.3	7 865	7.1	207 494	59.8	32.5	37.1
Elmira	53.4	647	36.5	26.4	77.7	12.8	10 431	-0.8	787	7.5	23 014	50.4	28.9	37.1
Freeport	33.8	1 312	39.0	14.8	93.5	3.9	22 619	1.2	1 229	5.4	34 103	67.9	42.7	24.4
Glen Cove	47.9	1 632	35.7	12.5	90.6	6.9	13 997	1.4	638	4.6	21 967	64.1	44.0	24.8
Harrison	35.6	1 897	29.5	6.5	85.1	11.3	13 292	1.7	635	4.8	22 563	60.7	36.5	19.2
Hempstead	57.3	1 311	39.4	29.2	88.5	7.5	27 451	0.9	1 556	5.7	42 176	67.7	40.3	23.9
Ithaca	72.5	989	47.2	32.0	55.1	28.1	14 425	0.9	665	4.6	28 060	47.6	17.1	39.8
Jamestown	49.2	597	33.1	20.8	80.8	9.7	12 324	-1.2	775	6.3	24 031	59.6	32.7	39.7
Lindenhurst	20.9	1 420	29.0	7.2	94.2	5.1	15 292	1.1	730	4.8	22 910	67.9	42.5	20.0
Long Beach	44.8	1 651	28.9	14.3	86.8	8.4	19 593	1.2	820	4.2	29 099	69.0	48.8	22.7
Middletown	48.9	1 124	38.0	19.9	87.8	6.5	13 602	1.5	715	5.3	21 817	67.4	40.5	26.6
Mount Vernon	61.2	1 197	36.0	28.0	89.6	5.3	33 261	1.1	2 067	6.2	53 974	67.9	42.1	25.8
Newburgh	68.0	1 065	48.3	33.5	86.1	5.0	12 243	1.3	743	6.1	20 382	62.7	36.9	31.3
New Rochelle	50.2	1 348	34.1	18.4	87.4	7.2	39 046	1.7	2 059	5.3	63 299	65.0	41.3	24.4
New York	68.1	1 234	32.2	55.4	89.0	3.2	4 197 279	1.3	237 381	5.7	6 768 448	63.4	41.0	26.5
Niagara Falls	43.7	637	34.1	20.2	90.4	3.7	21 653	-0.2	1 670	7.7	40 229	57.9	32.7	39.8
North Tonawanda	33.2	666	29.1	8.2	88.1	6.2	15 831	-0.2	849	5.4	26 017	66.2	40.1	31.6
Ossining	52.6	1 427	36.2	12.9	90.0	4.0	13 170	1.4	513	3.9	20 133	70.7	41.5	16.4
Port Chester	56.4	1 422	37.2	18.9	84.5	7.9	16 628	2.0	642	3.9	23 510	73.9	42.1	18.0
Poughkeepsie	61.3	1 022	38.5	26.9	82.3	8.9	13 337	0.3	749	5.6	24 409	64.1	35.2	32.4
Rochester	61.8	764	38.0	25.9	76.6	8.3	91 242	-0.5	6 450	7.1	164 701	61.2	33.5	35.5
Rome	43.3	710	26.7	14.0	82.8	9.6	13 564	-0.3	752	5.5	27 423	55.6	36.0	34.0
Saratoga Springs	45.9	988	27.3	9.5	81.2	13.8	13 741	1.0	583	4.2	23 098	63.4	36.7	28.0
Schenectady	52.1	817	34.3	20.5	88.1	6.3	30 456	0.5	1 778	5.8	52 038	63.2	37.7	32.4
Spring Valley	70.3	1 177	38.3	20.8	85.0	7.5	14 802	1.8	635	4.3	22 274	72.1	39.4	19.2
Syracuse	61.5	719	34.9	28.2	74.3	11.8	59 191	-0.4	3 881	6.6	115 193	56.5	30.2	36.4
Troy	61.4	832	32.1	22.5	75.2	14.1	23 372	0.5	1 401	6.0	40 927	62.4	34.2	32.5
Utica	52.8	672	34.1	24.0	80.2	8.3	23 900	-0.8	1 529	6.4	48 154	56.8	30.0	39.4
Valley Stream	21.0	1 547	31.9	7.0	92.6	5.3	19 550	1.1	924	4.7	30 133	69.3	42.6	21.0
Watertown	60.3	790	27.9	17.9	70.0	19.0	11 225	0.1	659	5.9	21 549	64.4	33.9	31.3
White Plains	48.5	1 544	32.9	16.9	86.9	8.2	31 672	1.7	1 211	3.8	46 952	70.2	45.0	21.3

1. $2,000 represents $2,000 or more.   2. 50.0 represents 50 percent or more.   3. Percent of civilian labor force.   4. Persons 16 years old and over.

City	Value of residential construction authorized by building permits, 2015			Wholesale trade,[1] 2012				Retail trade,[2] 2012			
	New construction ($1,000)	Number of housing units	Percent single family	Number of establish-ments	Number of employees	Sales (mil dol)	Annual payroll (mil dol)	Number of establish-ments	Number of employees	Sales (mil dol)	Annual payroll (mil dol)
	69	70	71	72	73	74	75	76	77	78	79
NEW JERSEY— Cont'd											
Garfield	4 298	50	62.0	42	407	223.0	18.5	81	825	213.1	20.6
Hackensack	6 829	154	6.5	182	1 678	1 878.3	95.9	259	3 895	1 208.7	112.4
Hoboken	189 324	743	0.1	48	269	396.8	14.6	164	1 297	314.1	30.6
Jersey City	343 519	2 658	12.7	191	4 740	12 481.7	338.8	807	2 568.1	2 568.1	241.5
Kearny	0	0	0.0	75	1 611	2 672.4	112.5	104	1 643	402.9	43.2
Linden	14 305	341	8.8	119	1 875	2 144.0	104.5	183	2 770	843.2	66.8
Long Branch	13 008	94	36.2	20	113	73.3	3.7	89	1 000	268.7	28.6
Millville	2 524	27	100.0	27	468	282.8	28.1	88	1 798	460.5	41.2
Newark	33 609	275	0.4	335	5 162	5 373.5	322.4	913	5 918	2 173.9	173.8
New Brunswick	186 564	1 033	0.7	60	839	751.1	41.8	121	736	179.5	15.9
Paramus	10 418	28	92.9	112	2 436	2 254.0	277.8	618	15 076	3 833.9	364.1
Passaic	4 798	77	7.8	80	768	311.9	30.2	260	2 083	541.7	49.8
Paterson	4 350	23	82.6	194	2 269	1 075.2	105.3	541	3 169	849.8	74.6
Perth Amboy	11 464	114	9.6	34	1 109	1 079.3	85.1	208	1 281	324.3	30.8
Plainfield	1 981	6	100.0	25	D	D	D	125	633	210.9	17.7
Rahway	3 728	117	5.1	67	808	1 282.7	55.6	70	651	321.8	21.9
Sayreville	1 852	149	0.7	57	511	562.7	31.4	104	1 185	406.6	29.1
Trenton	55	40	0.0	49	733	745.6	37.2	242	1 208	341.6	27.9
Union City	12 504	94	0.0	48	203	107.7	8.7	270	1 209	340.8	27.0
Vineland	7 242	75	100.0	78	1 429	1 467.9	65.5	271	3 918	1 066.4	95.1
Westfield	30 685	90	100.0	23	D	D	D	131	1 394	262.4	28.2
West New York	33 079	385	0.0	33	D	D	D	213	1 141	288.9	27.1
NEW MEXICO	872 141	4 599	85.3	1 646	17 448	10 720.4	814.6	6 590	90 792	25 179.3	2 214.5
Alamogordo	NA	NA	NA	11	D	D	D	136	1 966	525.3	46.6
Albuquerque	206 166	1 142	85.2	700	8 712	4 784.9	429.6	1 885	31 702	9 067.4	817.5
Carlsbad	19 902	121	100.0	21	148	74.1	6.9	118	1 753	476.4	44.9
Clovis	14 397	58	93.1	30	297	117.0	9.6	176	2 391	596.7	54.0
Farmington	13 615	60	100.0	103	921	466.2	48.5	319	4 848	1 378.0	123.9
Hobbs	42 090	420	41.7	69	877	465.5	45.0	146	2 271	749.8	57.5
Las Cruces	76 501	413	90.1	66	473	224.5	22.7	398	6 973	1 719.0	150.3
Rio Rancho	141 128	775	91.7	24	D	D	D	115	2 593	732.5	62.1
Roswell	7 773	47	100.0	33	336	163.5	12.4	211	2 992	863.1	69.9
Santa Fe	26 627	110	100.0	81	683	606.3	29.8	714	7 979	2 063.4	225.7
NEW YORK	10 826 337	74 611	13.5	28 853	325 663	341 735.0	19 833.3	77 463	905 325	251 167.7	23 641.2
Albany	39 672	242	2.1	115	1 234	2 016.9	65.1	477	7 460	1 710.7	170.1
Auburn	5 724	29	3.4	20	209	353.0	9.3	130	2 095	501.8	45.0
Binghamton	1 890	10	0.0	61	658	687.6	26.4	183	2 279	563.7	48.1
Buffalo	16 335	105	42.9	253	3 776	2 011.9	178.1	939	10 760	1 972.0	200.0
Elmira	0	0	0.0	38	448	194.6	19.4	86	1 051	308.2	27.3
Freeport	4 375	14	100.0	75	737	348.1	31.7	192	1 963	803.0	63.3
Glen Cove	591	3	33.3	36	140	173.8	6.6	115	1 192	534.5	42.8
Harrison	26 065	33	100.0	58	1 192	4 816.8	148.3	53	423	82.1	12.0
Hempstead	940	5	100.0	31	297	136.8	16.5	198	1 830	893.6	56.3
Ithaca	7 697	68	2.9	13	98	23.2	3.5	177	3 072	729.8	71.0
Jamestown	468	1	100.0	39	221	130.7	8.2	126	1 462	391.5	36.0
Lindenhurst	612	3	100.0	39	D	D	D	118	804	306.8	27.2
Long Beach	3 200	16	100.0	30	443	225.2	23.6	85	629	171.5	17.1
Middletown	14 968	62	100.0	25	247	257.0	9.5	133	2 251	591.3	51.0
Mount Vernon	650	7	42.9	91	1 605	896.2	71.5	227	2 427	597.7	59.4
Newburgh	1 130	9	100.0	47	378	849.8	15.9	114	2 067	558.2	48.1
New Rochelle	1 394	17	5.9	85	821	611.8	64.9	252	2 869	1 150.2	95.9
New York	570 944	4 682	0.1	15 124	148 956	173 797.8	9 474.6	34 215	318 004	92 265.0	9 163.8
Niagara Falls	3 349	23	13.0	30	D	D	D	261	3 751	843.2	67.1
North Tonawanda	1 690	8	100.0	27	640	159.4	27.3	80	804	210.8	21.0
Ossining	200	1	100.0	14	70	102.9	4.5	78	542	156.6	16.1
Port Chester	3 053	15	60.0	44	428	189.0	22.5	140	1 997	624.4	58.8
Poughkeepsie	0	0	0.0	23	D	D	D	158	2 246	497.8	50.0
Rochester	33 518	413	15.7	279	3 486	1 528.7	175.7	783	7 561	1 414.1	161.5
Rome	4 983	39	59.0	20	148	56.4	6.1	134	2 050	539.5	47.8
Saratoga Springs	31 609	198	28.8	28	278	260.8	18.0	154	2 059	575.3	48.7
Schenectady	3 720	38	5.3	34	354	306.2	15.9	203	1 642	460.5	43.9
Spring Valley	3 280	18	22.2	52	259	388.1	14.1	102	1 146	265.5	24.8
Syracuse	19 634	303	3.6	145	2 316	1 344.5	108.7	573	7 928	1 726.2	168.5
Troy	1 150	13	7.7	30	D	D	D	148	1 648	487.5	44.5
Utica	0	0	0.0	63	877	636.7	41.8	180	2 547	686.9	58.7
Valley Stream	668	1	100.0	68	432	395.6	27.0	203	2 570	654.1	55.4
Watertown	0	0	0.0	21	290	143.2	11.7	185	3 253	858.3	71.7
White Plains	2 920	7	100.0	100	1 551	4 084.6	159.5	422	7 482	1 956.9	204.0

1. Merchant wholesalers except manufacturers' sales branches and offices.   2. Establishments with payroll.

Table D. Cities — Real Estate, Professional Services, and Manufacturing

City	Real estate and rental and leasing, 2012				Professional, scientific, and technical services,[1] 2012				Manufacturing, 2012			
	Number of establish-ments	Number of employees	Receipts (mil dol)	Annual payroll (mil dol)	Number of establish-ments	Number of employees	Receipts (mil dol)	Annual payroll (mil dol)	Number of establish-ments	Number of employees	Receipts (mil dol)	Annual payroll (mil dol)
	80	81	82	83	84	85	86	87	88	89	90	91
NEW JERSEY—Cont'd												
Garfield	12	110	9.9	3.2	35	183	14.2	5.1	56	576	146.0	27.2
Hackensack	126	573	206.3	27.3	425	D	D	D	83	1 190	233.2	55.4
Hoboken	81	472	108.6	17.5	209	1 148	266.1	80.8	22	184	33.9	9.7
Jersey City	233	1 129	301.2	53.8	587	D	D	D	99	2 493	857.6	101.8
Kearny	34	227	68.4	12.1	47	227	34.4	11.0	47	1 272	617.1	73.7
Linden	34	187	51.6	9.4	53	1 152	166.5	92.7	105	3 184	14 465.7	223.0
Long Branch	29	76	32.3	3.2	46	183	19.2	10.7	17	250	D	12.2
Millville	12	51	10.6	1.7	44	213	24.5	6.3	43	2 425	450.4	104.5
Newark	214	2 108	518.5	77.8	407	6 545	1 896.8	727.0	251	6 686	3 139.4	358.9
New Brunswick	46	263	166.0	12.3	130	D	D	D	52	842	381.4	46.7
Paramus	73	692	725.3	60.1	216	D	D	D	17	265	78.2	15.9
Passaic	44	124	26.7	4.2	60	360	31.9	10.3	101	1 388	226.0	55.4
Paterson	70	382	54.5	12.6	75	D	D	D	225	4 649	1 167.9	222.8
Perth Amboy	30	135	33.1	4.9	47	D	D	D	37	1 099	579.3	52.3
Plainfield	18	60	12.9	2.2	38	192	21.7	9.4	23	390	D	12.7
Rahway	20	257	35.9	14.9	29	264	29.6	15.4	40	3 169	425.3	361.1
Sayreville	20	95	22.3	3.6	103	857	120.9	64.8	32	1 262	1 031.9	87.6
Trenton	52	352	273.6	16.9	112	D	D	D	53	1 273	D	65.2
Union City	50	147	27.0	3.5	87	314	48.3	10.8	42	339	58.8	10.0
Vineland	76	276	62.5	10.6	119	D	D	D	86	3 864	1 553.6	169.0
Westfield	29	119	56.6	5.4	153	830	170.9	56.6	7	85	11.1	2.2
West New York	57	405	135.5	19.3	70	167	22.7	6.2	40	188	23.2	6.3
NEW MEXICO	2 369	9 754	1 960.4	368.7	4 634	42 423	7 376.4	2 677.8	1 389	26 731	29 102.4	1 349.2
Alamogordo	43	136	17.5	3.3	48	219	17.0	7.1	10	118	D	3.1
Albuquerque	851	4 012	782.3	141.7	2 015	D	D	D	482	10 810	D	522.8
Carlsbad	28	142	33.8	7.5	46	D	D	D	16	252	D	13.8
Clovis	57	204	30.2	5.5	68	439	36.7	14.2	17	120	D	D
Farmington	82	592	167.0	28.6	174	D	D	D	46	519	124.8	27.3
Hobbs	59	459	169.8	36.5	56	403	52.4	23.0	29	479	D	D
Las Cruces	160	563	89.5	15.5	257	D	D	D	55	948	D	30.1
Rio Rancho	58	157	35.2	6.9	100	D	D	D	29	3 562	D	235.3
Roswell	71	201	30.5	5.7	94	954	166.4	62.9	25	95	D	4.0
Santa Fe	229	847	162.7	33.7	477	D	D	D	87	456	D	18.4
NEW YORK	32 033	166 315	56 409.8	8 654.4	58 867	557 669	127 952.2	47 330.7	16 475	426 621	148 879.9	22 073.3
Albany	146	951	161.4	32.4	418	5 267	1 121.9	408.4	63	1 500	684.8	67.5
Auburn	40	121	21.6	3.1	54	D	D	D	49	2 185	858.0	115.1
Binghamton	61	245	29.4	5.9	121	D	D	D	49	1 261	603.4	55.5
Buffalo	257	2 117	240.0	61.9	662	D	D	D	321	11 225	5 260.6	600.2
Elmira	34	137	30.1	7.5	50	D	D	D	29	1 823	385.6	86.9
Freeport	38	176	24.9	6.9	119	447	66.6	20.2	77	1 736	324.3	69.5
Glen Cove	24	93	20.6	4.5	87	335	57.3	20.8	22	254	D	9.6
Harrison	80	718	256.3	48.2	186	D	D	D	7	54	6.5	1.8
Hempstead	51	275	67.0	9.0	96	D	D	D	19	221	D	11.0
Ithaca	53	372	54.2	11.4	123	D	D	D	32	397	63.9	19.9
Jamestown	26	D	D	D	64	D	D	D	62	1 733	251.3	68.4
Lindenhurst	13	54	7.2	2.0	67	221	25.6	8.5	37	368	96.7	17.4
Long Beach	49	129	42.9	5.6	102	203	31.3	9.6	6	15	2.6	0.6
Middletown	26	76	15.8	1.9	50	209	24.6	11.2	29	685	166.3	30.5
Mount Vernon	133	468	86.2	18.4	101	D	D	D	99	2 363	676.9	99.6
Newburgh	27	127	17.9	3.9	60	D	D	D	47	696	109.9	26.9
New Rochelle	202	770	265.6	32.8	228	D	D	D	46	744	159.1	41.2
New York	19 341	107 333	42 465.9	6 213.2	26 420	321 736	92 285.6	32 985.0	5 572	68 953	14 816.3	2 898.8
Niagara Falls	44	223	38.4	7.2	84	D	D	D	43	1 662	1 071.8	116.3
North Tonawanda	12	48	4.6	1.3	35	429	45.3	12.2	62	1 440	437.1	66.3
Ossining	21	60	21.5	2.4	56	228	31.7	12.4	5	D	D	D
Port Chester	40	119	33.4	5.7	61	187	27.4	9.5	33	874	130.1	36.0
Poughkeepsie	61	263	48.3	7.7	131	D	D	D	27	2 474	D	238.8
Rochester	261	2 499	291.6	92.4	639	7 429	1 143.0	421.6	417	19 217	7 492.3	1 164.8
Rome	41	152	24.5	4.6	75	D	D	D	37	1 439	957.7	75.1
Saratoga Springs	51	209	51.4	7.5	153	D	D	D	22	1 441	561.2	73.4
Schenectady	55	225	49.9	7.2	148	D	D	D	53	2 742	1 093.1	193.2
Spring Valley	65	212	37.0	5.2	71	167	74.5	32.1	20	159	29.9	6.4
Syracuse	258	2 011	311.6	91.5	473	D	D	D	111	3 772	1 656.4	181.3
Troy	45	214	42.4	6.9	110	D	D	D	32	620	88.8	24.3
Utica	52	213	27.6	4.7	135	D	D	D	68	1 708	322.2	73.4
Valley Stream	48	218	54.2	10.0	146	1 088	128.2	54.0	25	92	15.2	3.6
Watertown	43	232	46.9	6.4	57	D	D	D	15	818	D	47.7
White Plains	187	892	374.9	59.3	632	5 332	1 359.2	492.6	33	338	56.4	14.5

1. Establishments subject to federal tax.

City	Accommodation and food services, 2012				Arts, entertainment, and recreation,[1] 2012				Health care and social assistance,[1] 2012			
	Number of establish-ments	Number of employees	Sales (mil dol)	Annual payroll (mil dol)	Number of establish-ments	Number of employees	Receipts (mil dol)	Annual payroll (mil dol)	Number of establish-ments	Number of employees	Receipts (mil dol)	Annual payroll (mil dol)
	92	93	94	95	96	97	98	99	100	101	102	103
NEW JERSEY—Cont'd												
Garfield	43	343	28.9	7.8	1	D	D	D	29	313	13.6	6.1
Hackensack	120	D	D	D	12	D	D	D	342	D	D	D
Hoboken	219	D	D	D	24	D	D	D	125	2 091	237.4	98.6
Jersey City	471	4 941	422.5	97.5	47	484	52.6	13.9	439	6 026	521.3	210.3
Kearny	56	532	33.2	8.7	3	D	D	D	68	D	D	D
Linden	95	986	62.1	14.7	6	74	3.8	1.1	63	1 413	115.3	44.9
Long Branch	93	1 567	88.5	25.3	6	137	4.3	1.2	84	D	D	D
Millville	56	673	42.5	8.7	3	D	D	D	59	939	73.2	33.9
Newark	536	7 920	582.4	146.1	15	D	D	D	310	4 836	383.4	162.7
New Brunswick	161	2 009	127.1	35.8	4	D	D	D	80	D	D	D
Paramus	156	3 372	221.9	58.6	22	D	D	D	199	2 320	258.7	100.4
Passaic	115	674	46.1	9.7	12	100	4.7	1.4	103	D	D	D
Paterson	232	D	D	D	12	D	D	D	156	1 927	192.0	71.6
Perth Amboy	102	614	41.5	8.7	3	D	D	D	66	1 254	70.5	30.2
Plainfield	75	613	33.5	7.8	1	D	D	D	71	947	78.0	32.2
Rahway	53	524	34.2	8.4	3	D	D	D	39	D	D	D
Sayreville	82	677	37.9	9.2	10	203	15.2	5.0	50	D	D	D
Trenton	140	D	D	D	6	D	D	D	94	1 646	147.3	64.5
Union City	126	831	53.8	12.9	5	D	D	D	156	1 745	91.7	40.7
Vineland	128	2 165	98.9	26.5	7	D	D	D	164	2 173	268.1	95.2
Westfield	74	D	D	D	11	218	10.1	4.2	150	1 979	178.7	81.2
West New York	87	669	42.8	11.0	9	D	D	D	95	D	D	D
NEW MEXICO	4 177	82 601	4 349.7	1 250.4	488	10 536	1 207.2	219.7	3 970	67 477	6 071.0	2 449.7
Alamogordo	75	D	D	D	7	D	D	D	67	801	75.0	26.8
Albuquerque	1 281	29 238	1 579.0	454.3	138	D	D	D	1 468	25 832	2 659.8	1 045.2
Carlsbad	69	1 320	78.4	20.0	4	D	D	D	52	1 124	152.2	54.9
Clovis	78	1 927	77.4	21.9	7	42	1.6	0.5	94	D	D	D
Farmington	129	3 091	150.4	41.9	11	D	D	D	193	D	D	D
Hobbs	98	1 703	110.1	24.6	7	D	D	D	68	D	D	D
Las Cruces	276	6 189	262.7	72.6	18	383	9.9	2.9	379	8 409	840.8	336.9
Rio Rancho	91	2 066	90.2	26.7	15	D	D	D	122	1 646	119.9	51.6
Roswell	119	2 281	106.2	28.0	5	D	D	D	134	3 029	289.8	111.6
Santa Fe	349	7 896	532.7	158.5	58	186	28.8	8.2	362	3 454	397.5	170.6
NEW YORK	49 731	679 146	49 285.5	13 734.3	9 600	103 072	16 431.7	4 940.4	43 548	540 067	55 599.5	22 400.9
Albany	453	5 990	373.4	98.6	21	730	12.9	4.8	216	3 700	522.7	199.4
Auburn	94	1 291	54.4	15.1	11	61	3.8	1.2	101	1 097	105.3	48.2
Binghamton	171	3 078	154.7	38.0	12	D	D	D	103	1 390	167.0	74.4
Buffalo	660	11 300	510.5	158.3	44	820	185.7	95.7	363	7 108	684.7	361.8
Elmira	63	995	42.7	10.7	7	137	7.2	1.5	70	794	85.7	36.4
Freeport	95	638	48.3	12.2	20	92	18.8	2.7	109	1 395	96.8	41.3
Glen Cove	82	D	D	D	10	135	15.3	3.2	118	D	D	D
Harrison	67	D	D	D	25	197	12.4	4.6	87	D	D	D
Hempstead	121	983	63.5	14.5	5	D	D	D	115	1 342	148.1	53.1
Ithaca	203	2 774	153.0	43.5	10	67	6.9	1.8	68	669	57.7	22.6
Jamestown	72	733	37.0	8.9	10	D	D	D	55	543	54.4	18.6
Lindenhurst	80	893	52.0	12.7	8	D	D	D	52	555	46.4	18.9
Long Beach	91	1 052	61.6	17.7	11	97	8.0	1.8	94	D	D	D
Middletown	67	616	30.1	8.4	5	D	D	D	71	2 591	332.5	147.7
Mount Vernon	104	692	49.5	11.4	15	159	13.2	5.3	111	927	75.2	29.0
Newburgh	87	1 121	79.9	18.1	5	D	D	D	76	887	81.0	32.2
New Rochelle	208	1 949	139.6	37.0	35	D	D	D	234	3 089	327.0	117.8
New York	21 506	304 855	27 452.9	7 757.8	4 956	50 582	11 117.6	3 322.1	18 267	234 221	22 637.1	8 976.3
Niagara Falls	171	5 873	883.7	134.7	13	D	D	D	68	1 178	67.5	32.2
North Tonawanda	55	642	27.4	8.3	7	50	2.7	0.7	53	301	22.2	9.5
Ossining	44	417	28.0	10.4	6	31	4.9	1.4	33	337	27.3	11.1
Port Chester	98	948	70.4	20.3	8	D	D	D	39	469	77.9	30.2
Poughkeepsie	126	D	D	D	5	7	0.7	0.2	103	2 052	299.4	131.4
Rochester	570	7 114	366.7	105.5	64	1 228	62.6	20.8	264	5 172	420.6	192.5
Rome	81	D	D	D	15	66	3.3	1.0	85	1 234	94.7	41.1
Saratoga Springs	170	3 198	196.3	57.3	39	949	162.4	34.0	109	1 410	158.0	74.2
Schenectady	182	1 857	93.1	25.5	8	402	80.7	11.6	138	1 958	182.0	82.2
Spring Valley	46	D	D	D	4	D	D	D	40	509	41.2	14.9
Syracuse	386	6 146	311.3	92.3	29	162	13.8	4.3	316	4 768	625.4	249.8
Troy	146	1 747	95.0	28.2	7	D	D	D	107	1 509	139.2	62.8
Utica	158	D	D	D	8	52	2.6	0.7	143	2 547	301.7	130.7
Valley Stream	82	1 147	66.7	17.9	14	62	7.4	1.9	134	954	157.5	46.6
Watertown	105	2 206	96.5	28.7	10	50	2.6	0.7	96	1 331	140.6	63.4
White Plains	203	3 100	235.8	75.9	31	233	28.3	5.7	348	5 680	639.1	303.9

1. Establishments subject to federal tax.

City	Other services[1], 2012				Government employment and payroll, 2012								
					Full-time equivalent employees	March payroll							
						Total (dollars)	Percent of total for:						
	Number of establishments	Number of employees	Receipts (mil dol)	Annual payroll (mil dol)			Administration, judicial, and legal	Police and Corrections	Fire Protection	Highways and transportation	Health and welfare	Natural resources and utilities	Education and libraries
	104	105	106	107	108	109	110	111	112	113	114	115	116
NEW JERSEY— Cont'd													
Garfield	65	268	29.8	8.1	172	1 065 564	10.9	55.4	1.4	9.0	14.1	5.5	3.1
Hackensack	117	757	63.8	20.3	540	2 983 931	6.1	38.2	33.3	3.4	8.9	5.9	3.9
Hoboken	118	D	D	D	712	4 180 854	7.4	42.5	22.9	2.8	7.1	10.6	3.1
Jersey City	318	1 625	144.0	44.1	2 936	18 762 329	8.1	43.6	27.3	3.2	7.6	6.7	2.0
Kearny	58	241	26.5	6.9	326	2 506 387	6.0	43.9	30.5	0.2	2.6	7.9	1.8
Linden	101	647	63.6	20.9	585	3 237 694	11.7	49.9	25.1	3.6	5.9	2.5	0.8
Long Branch	52	195	11.3	3.2	338	2 021 115	9.6	41.0	10.8	0.7	12.9	21.3	3.7
Millville	32	147	9.8	3.3	210	1 102 759	14.1	44.9	6.7	4.0	8.6	14.2	0.0
Newark	425	4 834	339.5	123.8	3 857	25 580 741	14.8	36.1	19.3	0.6	13.6	10.8	2.2
New Brunswick	74	535	49.5	15.3	1 983	11 480 514	2.4	14.2	6.5	0.7	1.8	3.7	67.3
Paramus	63	494	49.3	22.3	293	1 879 108	9.0	31.6	18.6	10.8	1.2	13.4	8.4
Passaic	90	251	20.0	5.3	563	3 095 395	9.0	45.4	25.9	6.9	9.0	1.7	2.3
Paterson	183	1 164	94.0	28.2	1 472	8 450 610	6.5	42.6	30.2	1.1	8.2	5.3	1.6
Perth Amboy	89	736	67.5	23.4	401	2 317 835	10.2	44.0	15.6	5.1	10.9	6.6	1.8
Plainfield	75	266	22.3	6.6	551	3 548 125	11.6	36.0	23.0	0.9	9.8	7.5	2.9
Rahway	42	162	19.7	5.2	277	1 741 702	7.4	40.4	21.7	9.0	8.1	6.9	4.4
Sayreville	87	372	38.5	11.7	240	1 549 628	10.5	59.2	0.8	2.5	2.2	9.8	4.9
Trenton	83	359	27.6	7.6	2 747	16 968 078	3.1	14.5	9.4	0.5	3.5	5.2	60.7
Union City	105	233	17.4	4.5	2 174	11 223 072	2.5	14.9	0.8	0.1	2.4	3.3	73.7
Vineland	108	538	44.6	12.1	718	3 828 158	13.3	30.7	5.0	1.6	10.8	34.6	2.3
Westfield	83	465	40.5	11.7	238	1 357 302	9.1	33.5	21.3	15.6	9.8	5.2	5.0
West New York	75	228	17.6	4.0	1 416	9 134 998	2.4	10.3	4.4	1.4	1.5	0.3	79.2
NEW MEXICO	2 182	12 810	1 115.9	349.7	X	X	X	X	X	X	X	X	X
Alamogordo	38	202	14.8	4.1	280	741 098	18.0	39.9	1.3	4.0	10.8	22.4	3.5
Albuquerque	718	4 969	379.7	125.0	6 438	33 331 138	10.6	29.5	14.1	15.4	8.8	17.0	1.5
Carlsbad	39	195	24.0	6.2	381	1 625 310	11.0	22.8	19.6	11.1	0.7	23.8	1.9
Clovis	55	332	26.5	7.3	383	1 169 467	11.4	25.1	25.2	9.8	5.3	18.8	2.8
Farmington	116	973	105.0	36.0	882	3 555 193	11.2	22.9	12.7	4.9	2.4	35.0	4.8
Hobbs	62	571	72.3	23.8	403	1 643 293	10.3	27.3	18.4	9.1	3.7	22.7	2.5
Las Cruces	138	753	51.6	16.6	1 337	4 708 150	16.1	21.4	12.0	10.4	4.2	18.4	1.9
Rio Rancho	67	437	31.6	12.0	606	2 382 289	13.5	29.4	20.0	10.8	8.8	12.6	4.3
Roswell	46	222	19.0	5.4	548	1 751 942	8.5	26.4	20.7	10.4	1.6	25.5	3.2
Santa Fe	162	866	71.7	23.4	1 540	6 258 370	13.8	15.1	12.9	7.7	6.4	28.1	2.3
NEW YORK	34 948	168 002	14 493.2	4 209.4	X	X	X	X	X	X	X	X	X
Albany	146	825	81.6	24.9	1 455	6 784 879	6.9	38.4	23.1	4.0	10.7	16.1	0.0
Auburn	53	242	19.2	5.0	306	1 503 241	6.8	27.5	30.2	4.3	6.2	19.5	0.0
Binghamton	81	439	34.3	10.7	581	2 791 570	8.2	32.5	25.6	1.7	4.0	21.6	0.0
Buffalo	301	1 577	149.1	47.0	8 627	45 770 501	2.5	13.0	9.3	1.2	2.8	5.8	63.6
Elmira	29	155	12.6	3.8	297	1 470 047	6.0	34.4	27.9	5.6	6.2	16.6	0.0
Freeport	95	491	40.6	11.1	414	2 410 577	14.5	41.4	0.5	2.6	0.9	35.0	0.0
Glen Cove	71	259	21.8	5.5	313	2 051 266	16.9	46.0	2.4	7.0	7.0	17.7	0.0
Harrison	44	D	D	D	272	1 502 544	14.2	43.3	8.0	7.9	2.8	13.9	7.7
Hempstead	97	562	59.8	16.0	437	2 884 577	9.4	54.8	2.8	5.5	2.5	17.0	3.8
Ithaca	42	274	21.6	6.5	454	2 158 827	9.3	24.0	19.7	8.1	0.9	28.6	0.0
Jamestown	44	211	19.7	5.0	658	3 048 026	3.6	13.9	18.8	8.5	1.7	2.6	51.0
Lindenhurst	102	289	31.4	6.7	72	206 485	20.7	0.0	5.1	24.6	6.2	32.4	0.0
Long Beach	54	178	8.6	2.4	484	2 657 473	9.3	32.7	12.4	11.0	4.5	25.8	0.0
Middletown	54	376	29.6	8.9	283	1 449 586	12.4	41.3	15.8	7.3	3.0	20.2	0.0
Mount Vernon	128	768	87.4	28.0	873	4 489 959	6.4	36.3	23.8	1.9	2.2	13.5	2.9
Newburgh	62	479	52.2	12.3	258	1 411 393	6.5	44.1	27.5	10.5	1.6	9.6	0.0
New Rochelle	157	669	59.3	15.7	652	4 204 505	7.5	35.0	29.4	4.5	9.0	14.1	0.0
New York	15 271	69 456	5 597.1	1 634.2	404 260	2 380 283 176	3.2	19.0	5.4	13.7	18.1	4.4	34.0
Niagara Falls	62	323	23.2	6.3	687	3 126 887	0.0	30.2	23.2	0.0	6.6	0.0	0.0
North Tonawanda	56	153	11.3	3.0	281	1 334 637	8.0	28.4	16.0	17.6	0.8	25.8	0.0
Ossining	38	109	10.2	2.8	186	1 201 283	12.6	41.7	0.4	13.3	0.9	24.9	0.0
Port Chester	73	282	34.4	9.6	227	2 070 548	10.9	52.5	7.8	6.0	2.3	13.1	0.0
Poughkeepsie	71	288	25.8	7.1	365	2 055 377	6.9	43.5	19.1	6.3	5.4	15.8	0.0
Rochester	274	1 741	176.4	53.9	9 049	47 150 145	2.7	13.0	6.6	0.8	3.9	4.3	67.0
Rome	56	208	21.1	5.3	373	1 669 365	8.0	27.2	30.1	12.6	4.5	16.3	0.0
Saratoga Springs	49	232	18.3	5.5	349	1 565 062	9.5	32.3	19.4	23.7	4.3	7.4	0.0
Schenectady	90	526	61.4	17.3	637	3 109 293	5.4	38.3	21.7	5.1	10.0	14.6	0.0
Spring Valley	36	94	11.3	1.8	298	901 316	12.0	64.5	0.6	10.1	7.0	0.4	0.0
Syracuse	198	1 576	131.3	43.9	5 644	31 187 441	1.4	12.0	7.9	4.1	2.4	3.2	68.9
Troy	55	398	31.1	12.3	598	3 268 327	9.0	41.8	17.7	4.1	9.7	13.5	0.0
Utica	75	516	35.6	12.4	614	2 894 903	5.7	39.6	26.6	3.3	11.4	9.1	0.0
Valley Stream	116	1 253	73.5	22.6	225	1 128 453	12.8	3.8	0.6	18.2	0.6	37.3	6.6
Watertown	47	259	24.6	6.6	370	1 573 042	9.1	22.3	27.5	9.6	5.8	20.8	2.5
White Plains	141	958	83.4	26.2	1 041	6 536 682	8.4	25.5	18.2	8.2	6.7	11.5	3.6

1. Establishments subject to federal tax.

Table D. Cities — **City Government Finances**

City	City government finances, 2012									
	General revenue							General expenditure		
		Intergovernmental		Taxes					Per capita[1] (dollars)	
					Per capita[1] (dollars)					
	Total (mil dol)	Total (mil dol)	Percent from state government	Total (mil dol)	Total	Property	Sales and gross receipts	Total (mil dol)	Total	Capital outlays
	117	118	119	120	121	122	123	124	125	126
NEW JERSEY— Cont'd										
Garfield..................	35.0	4.4	66.3	24.7	798	774	23	30.5	985	29
Hackensack..............	89.8	9.7	58.1	74.7	1 693	1 640	53	81.7	1 851	0
Hoboken..................	112.1	26.1	53.1	59.5	1 137	1 071	66	110.1	2 106	65
Jersey City	597.9	170.1	64.9	235.7	918	842	76	580.2	2 260	102
Kearny....................	76.1	28.2	95.1	41.5	994	966	27	71.6	1 713	127
Linden....................	93.5	30.9	71.2	55.1	1 345	1 310	36	93.7	2 288	123
Long Branch.............	71.9	21.4	25.7	37.9	1 241	1 202	40	74.6	2 445	343
Millville..................	50.7	12.0	68.9	21.9	765	691	74	49.8	1 738	61
Newark	845.2	438.4	36.2	305.9	1 099	784	156	860.7	3 093	368
New Brunswick...........	273.2	161.6	90.4	60.6	1 087	1 034	52	308.3	5 532	930
Paramus.................	60.6	4.7	91.3	49.5	1 859	1 738	120	49.8	1 869	77
Passaic..................	116.8	43.8	42.5	59.3	840	818	22	115.2	1 634	39
Paterson.................	273.4	94.3	64.3	140.1	959	943	17	265.5	1 818	72
Perth Amboy	99.9	23.5	45.3	58.9	1 136	1 119	17	92.3	1 780	148
Plainfield.................	100.9	20.9	40.2	54.9	1 089	1 063	26	102.8	2 039	6
Rahway	52.2	8.2	52.9	35.2	1 263	1 210	53	40.3	1 445	119
Sayreville................	48.5	12.4	79.2	29.1	663	632	31	48.1	1 097	44
Trenton	505.3	395.0	94.6	79.2	938	887	51	482.0	5 714	70
Union City................	355.1	263.5	96.4	81.0	1 184	1 161	23	313.3	4 583	154
Vineland	73.4	16.1	56.5	36.7	602	549	53	67.7	1 110	67
Westfield.................	37.4	4.0	79.9	29.6	967	909	57	39.3	1 283	88
West New York	209.6	134.4	93.8	51.2	986	966	20	216.0	4 160	249
NEW MEXICO..........	X	X	X	X	X	X	X	X	X	X
Alamogordo..............	41.0	11.2	83.4	17.7	560	107	454	39.0	1 236	363
Albuquerque..............	951.2	282.5	80.4	367.8	663	244	419	827.4	1 491	292
Carlsbad.................	58.1	6.7	35.3	37.8	1 412	97	1 316	48.5	1 811	487
Clovis....................	56.3	14.0	34.5	27.9	706	44	662	57.5	1 457	483
Farmington	92.1	35.8	11.0	27.5	600	38	562	99.0	2 161	207
Hobbs....................	89.8	35.4	93.8	38.4	1 098	56	1 042	69.8	1 994	1 088
Las Cruces................	182.5	39.2	26.8	96.3	953	139	815	144.3	1 429	190
Rio Rancho	95.2	13.7	34.9	54.3	599	175	424	87.0	959	166
Roswell..................	55.1	34.8	96.0	9.3	192	110	82	56.9	1 173	255
Santa Fe.................	162.5	78.1	73.2	35.9	518	123	395	178.9	2 584	479
NEW YORK..............	X	X	X	X	X	X	X	X	X	X
Albany	252.8	90.3	28.3	61.5	625	548	77	277.7	2 820	454
Auburn	42.1	14.9	40.5	12.2	447	408	39	47.1	1 722	251
Binghamton	80.6	30.7	45.7	35.7	765	729	37	75.4	1 615	190
Buffalo	1 438.1	1 151.5	83.0	149.0	573	504	69	1 532.1	5 896	790
Elmira	41.8	23.4	53.0	11.6	398	367	31	41.7	1 427	358
Freeport..................	62.3	3.3	46.3	42.5	985	940	44	67.6	1 566	34
Glen Cove	53.4	17.4	54.0	30.6	1 125	1 054	71	56.1	2 063	478
Harrison..................	13.5	1.5	60.8	10.7	385	338	47	12.1	434	112
Hempstead................	71.2	3.7	54.3	55.6	1 013	971	42	80.4	1 463	51
Ithaca...................	58.8	12.2	65.1	33.1	1 088	633	455	57.2	1 881	235
Jamestown...............	70.2	29.9	76.1	15.0	487	459	28	77.7	2 528	164
Lindenhurst...............	11.6	1.7	75.6	7.0	257	207	50	11.3	413	55
Long Beach	66.7	9.4	52.8	33.6	1 002	859	144	74.0	2 210	91
Middletown...............	41.5	13.3	24.7	19.0	681	633	47	38.9	1 397	51
Mount Vernon.............	96.7	15.2	70.5	70.8	1 042	724	319	104.4	1 537	169
Newburgh................	57.5	23.9	52.4	21.2	742	667	74	56.9	1 989	235
New Rochelle.............	134.5	29.2	42.3	80.1	1 022	628	394	133.3	1 700	146
New York................	85 078.0	30 398.8	83.5	42 476.1	5 077	2 176	970	81 160.8	9 701	1 196
Niagara Falls.............	98.1	50.3	53.9	40.9	824	581	243	127.6	2 570	657
North Tonawanda.........	43.9	17.1	37.3	18.6	596	510	86	41.6	1 330	104
Ossining	33.4	8.9	10.1	20.3	805	760	45	37.3	1 479	39
Port Chester..............	36.3	5.3	14.4	23.6	808	753	54	37.3	1 275	86
Poughkeepsie..............	58.3	29.4	22.7	19.2	624	566	58	54.6	1 777	206
Rochester.................	1 215.0	931.5	73.2	180.9	859	798	61	1 222.9	5 805	517
Rome....................	49.4	15.0	77.6	25.0	760	462	298	50.7	1 538	140
Saratoga Springs	48.9	5.5	67.4	32.2	1 193	719	474	43.3	1 605	81
Schenectady..............	89.2	31.5	44.8	29.9	453	405	48	98.0	1 484	180
Spring Valley	34.8	11.4	13.6	21.9	684	651	33	34.7	1 083	29
Syracuse	822.4	598.0	72.4	96.4	668	613	55	858.4	5 950	640
Troy	90.3	48.5	30.6	21.6	433	387	47	91.3	1 830	238
Utica....................	93.1	41.6	48.0	37.0	597	363	234	94.1	1 521	162
Valley Stream.............	33.6	2.5	57.9	27.0	716	656	60	37.3	987	118
Watertown	42.6	26.8	23.3	8.9	316	265	50	49.0	1 746	140
White Plains	165.8	12.3	50.2	108.8	1 897	862	1 035	178.6	3 112	124

1. Based on population estimated as of July 1 of the year shown.

Table D. Cities — **City Government Finances**

	City government finances, 2012 (cont.)									
	General expenditure (cont.)									
	Percent of total for:									
City	Public welfare	Highways	Parking facilities	Education	Health and hospitals	Police protection	Sewerage and sanitation	Parks and recreation	Housing and community development	Interest on debt
	127	128	129	130	131	132	133	134	135	136
NEW JERSEY— Cont'd										
Garfield	0.0	4.9	0.0	0.0	1.2	28.2	11.9	2.8	13.2	2.5
Hackensack	0.3	1.3	0.4	0.0	1.2	17.9	12.8	1.5	6.5	1.4
Hoboken	0.0	2.5	7.0	0.0	0.5	13.9	4.0	1.6	15.2	3.1
Jersey City	0.0	2.1	1.3	0.0	2.2	16.2	14.1	1.4	13.6	4.6
Kearny	0.0	7.5	0.1	0.0	1.0	20.6	13.2	0.8	0.0	3.6
Linden	0.8	2.4	0.6	0.0	0.9	15.3	6.7	2.6	6.2	1.7
Long Branch	0.0	2.4	0.0	0.0	1.1	15.9	20.9	1.9	20.8	3.0
Millville	0.0	2.0	0.0	0.0	0.0	13.2	16.0	1.1	16.4	2.3
Newark	0.3	0.7	0.4	0.2	4.3	15.3	9.7	2.5	24.4	3.2
New Brunswick	0.0	1.0	16.5	54.0	0.2	6.3	3.2	1.5	2.1	2.1
Paramus	0.1	3.7	0.0	0.0	3.0	23.8	11.3	5.3	0.0	2.7
Passaic	0.0	2.5	0.6	0.0	2.3	17.6	7.6	3.5	20.1	0.7
Paterson	0.0	3.0	1.9	0.0	4.0	17.4	9.1	2.0	10.5	1.2
Perth Amboy	0.1	2.3	0.6	0.0	0.6	15.2	8.7	1.9	19.0	3.0
Plainfield	0.0	6.3	0.0	0.0	0.6	15.9	18.4	1.4	13.0	1.7
Rahway	0.0	12.8	2.0	0.0	0.8	23.3	11.5	1.3	12.1	2.9
Sayreville	0.0	4.9	0.0	0.0	0.6	24.7	13.2	3.4	5.0	3.8
Trenton	0.0	0.8	0.8	58.2	0.5	6.3	3.8	0.3	4.5	2.6
Union City	0.0	2.3	0.7	64.8	0.6	6.4	1.9	0.7	4.1	0.9
Vineland	0.0	5.5	0.0	0.0	6.5	25.3	10.8	1.0	11.4	1.3
Westfield	0.0	5.2	0.5	0.0	2.2	16.1	8.8	2.6	0.0	1.6
West New York	0.0	1.4	0.6	65.2	0.6	5.6	1.5	0.6	5.1	1.0
NEW MEXICO	X	X	X	X	X	X	X	X	X	X
Alamogordo	3.1	26.7	0.0	0.0	0.0	16.5	10.5	11.1	3.1	3.2
Albuquerque	3.0	8.8	0.6	0.0	3.4	19.6	11.0	13.3	4.4	3.2
Carlsbad	0.0	11.5	0.0	0.0	1.6	17.0	21.2	11.8	0.0	0.8
Clovis	0.0	8.5	0.0	0.0	0.2	12.6	18.1	12.9	5.5	1.0
Farmington	0.0	12.8	0.0	0.0	1.2	15.7	9.6	13.8	1.3	0.6
Hobbs	0.0	29.3	0.0	0.0	1.5	6.2	12.9	10.4	0.0	0.0
Las Cruces	0.0	12.7	0.0	0.0	0.2	17.7	14.3	7.1	8.6	3.4
Rio Rancho	0.5	17.8	0.0	1.7	0.0	19.1	15.5	6.6	0.4	4.5
Roswell	0.0	8.7	0.0	0.0	0.0	19.1	9.7	11.3	0.0	1.5
Santa Fe	2.8	5.9	2.5	0.0	1.6	12.5	12.4	13.0	6.7	6.9
NEW YORK	X	X	X	X	X	X	X	X	X	X
Albany	0.0	5.6	0.0	0.0	0.2	17.8	5.3	1.6	23.5	17.5
Auburn	0.0	13.1	0.7	0.0	0.1	17.6	14.0	3.7	9.5	4.2
Binghamton	0.0	7.1	1.1	0.0	0.2	14.2	12.9	3.0	6.5	4.6
Buffalo	0.0	2.4	0.1	58.2	0.1	5.2	5.6	0.8	7.1	2.0
Elmira	0.0	21.6	0.6	0.0	0.5	16.9	2.2	3.1	4.9	2.6
Freeport	0.0	3.4	0.1	0.0	0.0	22.9	5.8	6.0	1.8	4.8
Glen Cove	0.0	9.1	0.0	0.0	0.6	22.5	4.1	13.1	9.0	6.4
Harrison	0.0	7.9	0.0	0.0	0.0	4.4	33.2	0.4	0.0	15.8
Hempstead	0.0	2.8	0.3	0.0	0.0	25.2	3.6	3.9	1.3	2.5
Ithaca	0.0	9.6	2.5	0.0	0.1	13.5	10.9	10.1	0.0	4.4
Jamestown	0.0	6.4	0.1	44.5	0.1	7.1	9.8	2.5	0.0	1.1
Lindenhurst	0.0	23.9	0.2	0.0	0.0	0.7	5.7	10.7	1.3	4.1
Long Beach	0.0	0.4	0.0	0.0	0.0	16.1	15.3	10.1	0.0	2.7
Middletown	0.0	5.3	0.0	0.0	0.0	19.0	11.9	6.4	5.3	3.9
Mount Vernon	0.0	2.6	0.1	0.0	0.4	19.2	7.2	5.0	2.7	3.0
Newburgh	0.0	3.7	0.2	0.0	0.1	24.8	13.6	2.8	1.7	4.8
New Rochelle	0.0	5.4	1.6	0.0	0.3	22.3	5.0	4.2	10.9	6.0
New York	15.7	1.8	0.1	27.7	10.4	6.2	5.6	1.3	5.8	5.3
Niagara Falls	0.0	16.1	0.0	0.0	0.1	14.7	2.8	4.1	5.6	2.1
North Tonawanda	0.0	12.9	0.0	0.0	0.1	13.1	15.2	4.4	0.0	1.2
Ossining	0.0	7.2	0.1	0.0	0.3	20.5	6.4	6.1	8.8	5.0
Port Chester	0.0	4.5	0.2	0.0	0.7	20.4	7.3	4.6	1.8	9.9
Poughkeepsie	0.0	9.9	0.9	0.0	0.2	23.5	8.9	1.2	1.5	3.8
Rochester	0.0	1.8	0.6	55.2	0.1	6.7	2.7	1.4	7.0	0.4
Rome	0.0	13.1	0.6	0.0	0.1	12.0	8.8	4.1	5.0	4.1
Saratoga Springs	0.0	10.1	0.2	0.0	0.1	23.1	9.2	8.2	0.6	3.2
Schenectady	0.0	7.4	0.7	0.0	0.1	16.3	15.5	2.0	4.8	6.5
Spring Valley	0.0	3.7	0.1	0.0	0.1	24.6	0.3	1.4	24.9	4.1
Syracuse	0.0	4.0	0.0	53.9	0.1	5.2	1.8	0.9	7.1	6.5
Troy	0.0	7.6	0.0	0.0	0.2	18.6	6.2	3.0	21.6	5.7
Utica	0.0	8.1	0.5	0.0	0.8	16.1	5.0	3.3	19.4	5.5
Valley Stream	0.0	15.7	0.7	0.0	0.4	0.6	12.9	12.6	0.0	5.6
Watertown	0.0	10.7	0.1	0.0	0.0	15.9	10.4	3.1	0.9	3.8
White Plains	0.0	8.2	7.1	0.0	0.0	18.6	5.2	4.4	3.7	1.8

1088   NJ(Garfield)—NY(White Plains)   Items 127—136

Table D. Cities — City Government Finances, City Government Employment, and Climate

City	City government finances, 2012 (cont.)			Climate[2]						
	Debt outstanding			Average daily temperature (degrees Fahrenheit)						
				Mean		Limits				
	Total (mil dol)	Per capita[1] (dollars)	Debt issued during year	January	July	January[3]	July[4]	Annual precipitation (inches)	Heating degree days	Cooling degree days
	137	138	139	140	141	142	143	144	145	146
NEW JERSEY—Cont'd										
Garfield	21.5	693	2.6	28.6	75.0	19.5	85.5	51.50	5 522	824
Hackensack	36.0	817	0.0	28.6	75.0	19.5	85.5	51.50	5 522	824
Hoboken	101.0	1 932	0.0	29.6	75.3	22.7	82.5	46.33	5 367	882
Jersey City	847.1	3 300	36.1	29.6	75.3	22.7	82.5	46.33	5 367	882
Kearny	83.3	1 995	9.1	31.3	77.2	24.4	85.2	46.25	4 843	1 220
Linden	46.6	1 137	15.0	28.5	74.0	18.2	85.8	51.61	5 595	757
Long Branch	70.9	2 322	0.0	31.7	74.1	22.8	82.6	48.63	5 168	750
Millville	39.9	1 390	9.2	32.7	76.3	24.1	85.9	43.20	4 835	1 009
Newark	658.6	2 366	2.2	31.3	77.2	24.4	85.2	46.25	4 843	1 220
New Brunswick	406.3	7 289	53.2	29.7	74.8	21.1	85.4	48.78	5 346	816
Paramus	39.3	1 477	0.0	28.6	75.0	19.5	85.5	51.50	5 522	824
Passaic	18.9	269	0.0	28.6	75.0	19.5	85.5	51.50	5 522	824
Paterson	119.6	819	5.1	28.6	75.0	19.5	85.5	51.50	5 522	824
Perth Amboy	91.3	1 761	13.7	29.7	74.8	21.1	85.4	48.78	5 346	816
Plainfield	48.0	952	0.1	30.0	74.9	21.5	86.6	49.63	5 266	854
Rahway	64.7	2 321	0.0	29.6	74.5	19.8	85.7	50.94	5 450	787
Sayreville	53.0	1 208	6.3	29.7	74.8	21.1	85.4	48.78	5 346	816
Trenton	390.2	4 626	34.2	30.4	75.2	21.3	86.9	44.83	5 262	903
Union City	82.9	1 213	0.0	29.6	75.3	22.7	82.5	46.33	5 367	882
Vineland	133.2	2 183	0.0	26.7	70.4	16.8	81.7	53.28	6 281	438
Westfield	20.7	675	0.0	30.0	74.9	21.5	86.6	49.63	5 266	854
West New York	52.4	1 010	0.0	29.6	75.3	22.7	82.5	46.33	5 367	882
NEW MEXICO	X	X	X	X	X	X	X	X	X	X
Alamogordo	58.7	1 859	25.6	42.2	79.7	28.9	93.0	13.20	31	1 715
Albuquerque	2 091.8	3 769	165.1	35.7	78.5	23.8	92.3	9.47	4 281	1 290
Carlsbad	40.7	1 520	8.7	42.7	81.7	27.5	95.8	14.15	2 823	2 029
Clovis	25.6	649	13.2	37.9	77.5	25.0	91.0	18.50	3 955	1 305
Farmington	1 802.6	39 348	11.1	29.8	74.9	17.9	90.7	8.39	5 508	805
Hobbs	58.7	1 677	0.0	42.9	80.1	29.1	93.5	18.15	2 849	1 842
Las Cruces	152.7	1 512	18.5	39.0	78.7	21.1	94.9	11.44	3 818	1 364
Rio Rancho	236.5	2 609	12.4	33.8	73.9	19.7	90.0	9.28	4 981	773
Roswell	18.0	371	0.0	40.0	80.8	24.4	94.8	13.34	3 332	1 814
Santa Fe	381.4	5 509	62.7	29.3	69.8	15.5	85.6	14.22	6 073	414
NEW YORK	X	X	X	X	X	X	X	X	X	X
Albany	773.1	7 851	27.8	22.2	71.1	13.3	82.2	38.60	6 860	544
Auburn	52.9	1 933	0.0	23.7	71.2	16.0	81.5	36.98	6 694	528
Binghamton	115.0	2 462	10.4	21.7	68.7	15.0	78.1	38.65	7 237	396
Buffalo	609.4	2 345	116.7	24.5	70.8	17.8	79.6	40.54	6 692	548
Elmira	36.3	1 243	8.5	23.9	70.3	15.0	82.3	34.95	6 806	446
Freeport	138.4	3 205	19.4	30.7	73.8	24.2	81.0	42.97	5 504	779
Glen Cove	81.8	3 010	11.6	31.9	74.2	25.4	82.8	46.36	5 231	839
Harrison	65.6	2 358	21.0	NA	NA	NA	NA	NA	NA	NA
Hempstead	47.9	872	0.0	31.9	74.2	25.4	82.8	46.36	5 231	839
Ithaca	76.9	2 530	0.0	22.6	68.7	13.9	80.1	36.71	7 182	312
Jamestown	36.2	1 179	4.0	22.3	69.2	14.1	80.1	45.68	7 048	389
Lindenhurst	5.9	218	0.0	30.7	73.8	24.2	81.0	42.97	5 504	779
Long Beach	54.6	1 631	2.5	31.8	74.8	24.7	82.9	42.46	4 947	949
Middletown	84.2	3 024	23.7	26.5	73.0	17.5	84.0	44.00	5 820	674
Mount Vernon	56.4	831	0.0	29.7	74.2	20.1	86.0	46.46	5 400	770
Newburgh	100.8	3 527	0.0	26.6	74.3	17.1	84.9	45.79	5 813	790
New Rochelle	141.5	1 805	20.0	29.7	74.2	20.1	86.0	46.46	5 400	770
New York	131 462.0	15 714	16 736.2	32.1	76.5	26.2	84.2	49.69	4 754	1 151
Niagara Falls	72.6	1 461	7.4	24.2	71.4	16.8	81.8	33.93	6 752	508
North Tonawanda	13.9	445	3.3	24.2	71.4	16.8	81.8	33.93	6 752	508
Ossining	25.9	1 027	2.3	NA	NA	NA	NA	NA	NA	NA
Port Chester	50.5	1 727	13.4	28.4	73.8	21.0	82.5	50.45	5 660	716
Poughkeepsie	86.8	2 825	12.4	24.5	71.9	14.7	83.6	44.12	6 438	550
Rochester	496.9	2 359	124.1	23.9	70.7	16.6	81.4	33.98	6 728	576
Rome	46.6	1 415	0.8	20.8	70.2	11.9	81.3	46.27	7 146	416
Saratoga Springs	36.7	1 362	3.4	20.9	71.2	11.6	83.0	43.31	6 904	477
Schenectady	159.7	2 417	13.3	22.2	71.1	13.3	82.2	38.60	6 860	544
Spring Valley	16.9	528	0.2	27.3	73.1	18.2	83.8	51.01	5 809	642
Syracuse	1 117.3	7 744	121.3	22.7	70.9	14.0	81.7	40.05	6 803	551
Troy	99.0	1 985	0.0	22.2	71.1	13.3	82.2	38.60	6 860	544
Utica	95.0	1 535	6.0	22.2	70.5	12.6	83.2	41.90	6 855	441
Valley Stream	28.5	756	3.5	22.2	70.5	12.6	83.2	41.90	6 855	441
Watertown	24.2	862	0.0	18.6	70.2	9.1	79.4	42.57	7 517	421
White Plains	106.6	1 858	45.7	29.7	74.2	20.1	86.0	46.46	5 400	770

1. Based on the population estimated as of July 1 of the year shown. 2. Represents normal values based on the 30-year period, 1971–2000. 3. Average daily minimum.
4. Average daily maximum.

Table D. Cities — Land Area and Population

STATE Place code	City	Land area,[1] 2010 (sq km)	Population, 2015 Total persons	Rank	Per square kilometer	Race alone or in combination (percent), 2010-2014 White	Black	American Indian, Alaska Native	Asian	Hawaiian Pacific Islander	Percent Hispanic or Latino[2], 2010-2014	Percent foreign born 2010–2014
		1	2	3	4	5	6	7	8	9	10	11
	NEW YORK—Cont'd											
36 84000	Yonkers	46.7	201 116	112	4 306.6	58.8	18.6	0.7	7.8	0.1	35.6	31.2
37 00000	NORTH CAROLINA ...	125 919.8	10 042 802	X	79.8	71.5	22.7	1.9	2.9	0.1	8.7	7.6
37 01520	Apex	39.8	45 585	825	1 145.4	82.5	9.9	0.9	7.3	0.0	7.6	10.1
37 02080	Asheboro..................	48.0	26 103	1 394	543.8	80.4	13.3	0.9	1.1	0.1	25.8	15.9
37 02140	Asheville..................	116.4	88 512	356	760.4	83.9	13.6	0.9	2.3	0.1	6.1	7.1
37 09060	Burlington	65.2	52 472	717	804.8	61.5	30.4	1.3	2.8	0.3	13.0	9.4
37 10740	Cary	140.8	159 769	158	1 134.7	74.1	8.8	1.1	15.2	0.0	8.9	19.8
37 11800	Chapel Hill..............	54.7	59 568	617	1 089.0	77.0	9.3	0.6	14.2	0.2	5.9	16.7
37 12000	Charlotte..................	771.0	827 097	17	1 072.8	54.1	36.6	1.2	6.2	0.1	13.4	15.3
37 14100	Concord..................	156.1	87 696	367	561.8	73.4	19.5	0.7	3.9	0.1	12.4	10.3
37 19000	Durham....................	278.1	257 636	79	926.4	49.1	41.8	1.2	5.7	0.1	13.9	14.5
37 22920	Fayetteville	377.7	201 963	110	534.7	51.1	44.4	2.7	4.2	0.7	10.9	6.5
37 25480	Garner	38.2	28 053	1 316	734.4	57.5	38.6	1.5	2.1	0.0	7.5	6.7
37 25580	Gastonia	130.8	74 543	460	569.9	64.4	29.2	1.2	1.7	0.1	10.7	8.2
37 26880	Goldsboro	72.9	35 826	1 056	491.4	40.1	57.3	0.6	2.1	0.2	5.0	4.6
37 28000	Greensboro	327.7	285 342	68	870.7	51.3	42.6	1.1	4.5	0.1	7.4	10.8
37 28080	Greenville	89.6	90 597	348	1 011.1	57.6	38.0	0.7	3.7	0.1	4.3	5.4
37 31060	Hickory	76.9	40 374	930	525.0	76.3	14.8	0.6	3.4	0.1	11.9	9.4
37 31400	High Point................	139.4	110 268	260	791.0	55.3	34.9	1.1	8.1	0.0	8.6	11.9
37 33120	Huntersville..............	102.6	52 704	709	513.7	87.0	10.4	1.1	2.8	0.4	5.1	5.9
37 33560	Indian Trail	56.2	37 073	1 018	659.7	80.9	15.0	1.2	2.5	0.0	9.8	8.2
37 34200	Jacksonville..............	120.5	67 357	522	559.0	69.4	24.5	1.3	4.5	0.7	14.7	5.0
37 35200	Kannapolis	82.7	46 144	819	558.0	72.4	22.1	1.3	1.7	0.0	11.5	6.9
37 41960	Matthews	44.3	30 678	1 214	692.5	83.5	11.5	0.7	3.9	0.0	5.0	8.6
37 43920	Monroe	77.1	34 623	1 085	449.1	65.1	25.0	0.6	2.0	0.0	28.6	19.7
37 44220	Mooresville	54.2	36 009	1 050	664.4	83.0	11.7	0.9	4.4	0.1	6.0	6.7
37 46340	New Bern	73.1	30 070	1 242	411.4	59.6	33.6	2.6	6.3	0.0	5.1	7.4
37 55000	Raleigh	370.1	451 066	42	1 218.8	62.7	30.0	0.8	5.0	0.1	10.9	13.3
37 57500	Rocky Mount............	113.4	55 806	665	492.1	33.4	64.1	1.5	1.6	0.0	3.3	3.3
37 58860	Salisbury.................	57.4	34 017	1 102	592.6	55.9	39.9	1.5	2.0	0.1	8.2	4.7
37 59280	Sanford	69.4	29 144	1 271	419.9	62.7	26.7	1.5	1.8	0.1	23.4	14.6
37 67420	Thomasville	43.4	27 061	1 355	623.5	74.5	21.6	0.4	1.3	0.0	14.6	8.6
37 70540	Wake Forest..............	39.1	38 199	981	977.0	79.1	17.3	0.4	3.8	0.0	6.4	7.5
37 74440	Wilmington	133.4	115 933	238	869.1	77.0	20.2	0.5	1.8	0.1	5.8	6.4
37 74540	Wilson	74.5	49 643	758	666.3	44.6	48.8	1.2	1.7	0.3	8.8	6.9
37 75000	Winston-Salem	343.0	241 218	88	703.3	59.0	35.9	0.7	2.4	0.1	15.3	10.8
38 00000	NORTH DAKOTA......	178 711.2	756 927	X	4.2	91.2	2.1	6.4	1.5	0.2	2.6	2.9
38 07200	Bismarck..................	79.9	71 167	489	890.7	94.0	1.5	5.0	1.1	0.2	1.7	1.8
38 25700	Fargo	126.5	118 523	231	936.9	91.5	3.9	2.6	3.5	0.0	2.8	7.0
38 32060	Grand Forks	51.6	57 011	649	1 104.9	91.2	3.5	4.4	3.1	0.2	2.8	4.5
38 53380	Minot......................	45.1	49 450	762	1 096.5	93.0	4.0	3.9	1.7	0.4	3.4	3.5
38 84780	West Fargo	37.4	33 597	1 117	898.3	93.0	4.6	1.5	2.7	0.5	1.0	5.1
39 00000	OHIO	105 828.7	11 613 423	X	109.7	84.8	13.6	0.8	2.2	0.1	3.3	4.1
39 01000	Akron......................	160.7	197 542	119	1 229.3	65.9	33.4	1.2	3.3	0.1	2.1	4.6
39 03828	Barberton.................	23.4	26 234	1 390	1 121.1	92.7	8.8	1.0	0.3	0.0	1.7	2.6
39 04720	Beavercreek	68.4	46 277	818	676.6	91.0	3.5	0.8	6.7	0.0	3.0	7.5
39 07972	Bowling Green...........	32.5	31 246	1 190	961.4	90.1	6.6	0.8	1.8	0.1	6.2	5.0
39 09680	Brunswick................	33.5	34 689	1 083	1 035.5	98.2	1.8	0.2	0.7	0.0	2.8	2.7
39 12000	Canton	66.0	71 885	483	1 089.2	75.4	29.0	1.6	0.7	0.0	2.6	2.2
39 15000	Cincinnati.................	201.9	298 550	66	1 478.7	52.9	45.6	1.0	2.4	0.1	3.0	5.1
39 16000	Cleveland	201.2	388 072	51	1 928.8	42.9	54.3	1.1	2.2	0.1	10.0	4.7
39 16014	Cleveland Heights	21.0	44 962	832	2 141.0	53.0	43.0	0.8	5.2	0.2	1.9	8.1
39 18000	Columbus	562.5	850 106	15	1 511.3	65.0	30.4	1.2	5.2	0.1	5.7	11.3
39 19778	Cuyahoga Falls	66.4	49 146	768	740.2	95.1	3.7	0.5	1.7	0.1	2.5	3.4
39 21000	Dayton	144.1	140 599	187	975.7	56.1	43.3	1.1	1.4	0.1	3.4	4.0
39 21434	Delaware	49.1	37 995	988	773.8	94.0	5.5	1.0	0.9	0.0	1.5	2.8
39 22694	Dublin	63.3	45 098	831	712.4	81.1	2.5	0.3	17.3	0.4	4.5	16.1
39 25256	Elyria	53.3	53 775	694	1 008.9	83.3	18.2	2.1	1.3	0.5	5.1	1.5
39 25704	Euclid.....................	27.5	47 676	794	1 733.7	42.2	58.5	0.7	0.6	0.1	1.5	3.0
39 25914	Fairborn	34.1	33 452	1 124	981.0	85.9	10.9	1.2	4.9	0.3	3.2	5.4
39 25970	Fairfield	54.2	42 767	874	789.1	81.6	16.3	1.0	1.7	0.1	5.8	8.0
39 27048	Findlay	49.6	41 149	909	829.6	93.8	3.5	0.4	2.9	0.2	6.3	3.6
39 29106	Gahanna	32.2	34 590	1 087	1 074.2	84.2	13.4	0.6	2.8	0.0	1.4	5.6
39 29428	Garfield Heights	18.7	28 097	1 313	1 502.5	58.2	42.0	0.5	2.1	0.0	2.6	3.4
39 31860	Green	83.0	25 898	1 399	312.0	96.9	2.4	0.5	1.6	0.0	1.0	2.7
39 32592	Grove City	42.0	39 388	957	937.8	95.2	3.6	0.3	2.2	0.0	2.0	2.6

1. Dry land or land partially or temporarily covered by water.   2. May be of any race.

Table D. Cities — **Population**

City	Age of population (percent), 2010-2014									Median age 2010–2014	Percent female 2010–2014	Population			
	Under 5 years	5 to 17 years	18 to 24 years	25 to 34 years	35 to 44 years	45 to 54 years	55 to 64 years	65 to 74 years	75 years and over			Census counts		Percent change	
												2000	2010	2000–2010	2010–2015
	12	13	14	15	16	17	18	19	20	21	22	23	24	25	26
NEW YORK—Cont'd															
Yonkers	6.8	15.7	9.2	14.4	13.0	13.9	11.8	8.0	7.2	37.6	52.9	196 086	195 976	-0.1	2.6
NORTH CAROLINA	6.3	17.1	10.0	12.9	13.5	14.0	12.3	8.0	5.8	37.8	51.3	8 049 313	9 535 483	18.5	5.3
Apex	6.6	24.3	6.8	9.9	20.6	16.9	8.7	4.0	2.3	37.3	52.1	20 212	37 476	85.4	21.4
Asheboro	8.4	19.6	9.8	12.2	14.4	11.4	10.9	6.9	6.3	34.9	52.6	21 672	25 012	15.4	2.8
Asheville	6.5	13.2	10.2	16.7	12.9	11.8	12.3	8.4	7.9	37.2	52.9	68 889	83 393	21.1	6.1
Burlington	6.5	16.5	9.5	13.6	11.2	12.4	14.0	8.2	8.1	38.9	53.7	44 917	49 963	11.2	3.0
Cary	7.1	19.9	6.6	13.7	16.6	16.2	10.6	5.6	3.8	36.9	50.6	94 536	135 234	43.1	18.0
Chapel Hill	3.4	12.9	33.6	11.5	10.0	10.5	8.7	4.9	4.4	25.1	53.5	48 715	57 233	17.5	4.1
Charlotte	7.4	17.6	9.9	17.4	15.5	13.3	10.0	5.1	3.8	33.6	52.0	540 828	731 424	35.2	12.4
Concord	7.0	20.3	8.4	12.8	16.8	14.3	9.3	6.6	4.5	35.7	51.3	55 977	79 066	41.2	10.7
Durham	7.5	14.9	12.1	19.6	14.3	12.0	10.3	5.4	4.0	32.7	52.7	187 035	228 330	22.1	12.8
Fayetteville	8.4	16.8	13.6	17.9	11.6	11.5	9.8	5.7	4.7	30.3	51.1	121 015	200 564	65.7	0.7
Garner	6.3	18.4	7.3	14.4	14.4	15.1	10.9	8.0	5.2	38.2	59.1	17 757	25 745	45.0	8.9
Gastonia	8.1	18.7	9.6	11.5	13.6	14.1	11.7	7.1	5.6	36.5	52.2	66 277	71 741	8.2	3.9
Goldsboro	9.1	14.9	10.7	17.4	9.0	12.4	12.5	7.0	7.0	33.6	51.7	39 043	36 437	-6.7	0.9
Greensboro	6.5	15.7	13.6	15.5	12.8	12.9	11.1	6.5	5.5	34.1	52.7	223 891	269 666	20.4	6.1
Greenville	5.6	13.2	28.6	16.2	11.4	8.4	8.7	4.3	3.7	25.9	55.1	60 476	84 554	39.8	7.1
Hickory	6.1	17.2	10.8	12.5	14.7	12.7	11.2	7.5	7.3	37.4	53.9	37 222	40 010	7.5	0.8
High Point	6.7	17.5	10.5	13.3	14.8	13.5	11.4	6.7	5.7	36.3	53.2	85 839	104 371	21.6	5.6
Huntersville	7.6	20.6	5.7	15.3	19.1	16.2	7.6	5.3	2.5	35.3	48.5	24 960	46 773	87.4	12.7
Indian Trail	7.1	25.0	9.1	10.3	17.8	13.8	7.9	6.1	3.0	34.0	52.8	11 905	33 518	181.5	10.3
Jacksonville	10.8	14.9	30.4	18.0	6.9	6.9	5.3	3.8	2.9	23.2	42.4	66 715	70 145	5.1	-4.0
Kannapolis	6.5	18.6	8.0	14.4	13.4	15.0	11.9	7.4	4.8	36.8	52.0	36 910	42 625	15.5	8.3
Matthews	4.2	19.3	8.6	10.3	12.4	16.4	14.0	8.7	6.2	41.3	52.8	22 127	27 198	22.9	12.8
Monroe	8.8	21.4	8.2	14.2	15.8	12.2	9.3	5.6	4.7	33.7	51.0	26 228	32 797	25.0	5.5
Mooresville	5.1	22.8	8.7	13.5	17.4	13.9	9.4	4.8	4.5	34.9	49.6	18 823	32 711	73.8	7.0
New Bern	7.7	17.0	10.2	14.3	10.7	11.3	11.5	8.3	9.0	35.7	53.3	23 128	29 524	27.7	1.8
Raleigh	6.9	16.0	13.6	18.1	15.2	12.3	9.1	4.9	3.9	32.6	51.9	276 093	403 892	46.3	11.6
Rocky Mount	6.3	18.3	9.6	11.6	12.4	13.1	12.6	8.8	7.3	38.8	53.3	55 893	57 477	2.8	-3.3
Salisbury	7.4	16.4	11.4	13.8	11.5	12.4	9.9	8.3	8.9	36.3	52.1	26 462	33 662	27.2	1.5
Sanford	7.8	20.3	9.7	12.1	13.1	13.9	10.1	7.1	5.9	35.2	51.5	23 220	28 094	21.0	3.6
Thomasville	9.8	18.0	9.7	12.5	12.5	13.2	9.0	7.3	8.0	34.9	52.6	19 788	26 757	35.2	1.1
Wake Forest	9.1	23.6	5.5	12.9	17.7	14.6	7.4	6.2	3.0	34.5	48.5	12 588	30 117	139.3	26.9
Wilmington	4.9	13.1	16.9	15.6	11.6	12.1	12.1	7.5	6.3	34.7	52.9	75 838	106 476	40.4	8.9
Wilson	7.2	17.7	10.3	11.9	11.7	13.5	12.4	8.3	7.0	37.3	54.5	44 405	49 167	10.7	1.0
Winston-Salem	7.3	17.2	12.0	14.1	12.7	12.9	11.0	6.8	6.0	34.6	53.0	185 776	229 617	23.6	5.0
NORTH DAKOTA	6.6	15.7	12.6	14.0	11.0	13.2	12.5	7.1	7.2	35.9	49.1	642 200	672 591	4.7	12.5
Bismarck	6.4	14.8	10.6	16.1	10.9	12.8	12.9	7.7	7.9	36.7	51.9	55 532	61 272	10.3	16.0
Fargo	6.4	13.3	19.9	17.6	11.1	10.9	10.2	4.8	5.7	30.4	50.2	90 599	105 549	16.5	12.3
Grand Forks	5.8	12.4	25.7	15.3	8.9	11.0	10.1	5.6	5.2	28.5	48.7	49 321	52 838	7.1	7.8
Minot	7.0	14.4	15.5	16.0	11.3	11.9	10.4	6.2	7.3	33.0	48.7	36 567	40 888	11.8	20.7
West Fargo	8.0	17.0	9.0	18.7	14.1	13.1	10.8	5.9	3.3	33.1	48.3	14 940	25 830	72.9	30.1
OHIO	6.0	17.1	9.6	12.4	12.4	14.5	13.3	8.0	6.8	39.2	51.1	11 353 140	11 536 504	1.6	0.7
Akron	7.0	15.4	12.8	13.6	11.8	13.2	13.1	7.1	6.1	36.1	52.0	217 074	199 110	-8.3	-0.8
Barberton	5.7	16.9	8.0	13.8	11.4	14.1	12.6	8.6	8.8	40.7	54.0	27 899	26 550	-4.8	-1.3
Beavercreek	4.7	17.2	8.2	12.9	12.3	14.3	14.6	9.4	6.4	40.9	50.5	37 984	45 193	19.0	2.4
Bowling Green	5.1	9.0	42.0	11.5	7.5	7.5	8.9	4.4	4.0	23.0	53.1	29 636	30 028	1.3	4.0
Brunswick	4.7	17.3	9.2	13.0	14.0	16.4	12.6	8.0	4.8	39.4	51.6	33 388	34 255	2.6	1.2
Canton	7.9	17.6	9.6	13.7	11.0	13.0	13.2	6.5	7.6	36.2	55.0	80 806	73 007	-9.7	-1.6
Cincinnati	7.4	14.7	14.2	17.3	11.4	12.6	11.3	6.0	5.2	32.4	52.2	331 285	296 943	-10.4	0.5
Cleveland	6.6	16.5	11.5	14.2	11.7	14.6	12.5	6.6	5.8	36.0	52.1	478 403	396 815	-17.1	-2.2
Cleveland Heights	6.6	16.8	10.7	16.8	11.2	10.9	13.2	7.8	5.9	34.3	55.2	49 958	46 121	-7.7	-2.8
Columbus	7.7	15.4	12.7	19.6	13.5	12.2	10.1	5.0	3.9	31.9	51.2	711 470	787 033	10.6	7.8
Cuyahoga Falls	5.7	14.6	7.5	15.5	13.2	13.6	14.8	7.3	7.7	39.9	51.0	49 374	49 652	0.6	-0.9
Dayton	6.4	14.8	16.9	13.9	11.7	12.0	12.2	6.4	5.6	33.5	51.1	166 179	141 527	-14.8	-0.8
Delaware	7.1	17.2	12.8	15.0	14.1	12.9	9.2	6.2	5.5	33.7	51.4	25 243	34 753	37.7	9.3
Dublin	6.8	24.0	4.8	9.3	15.7	17.2	12.9	6.4	2.9	38.6	52.1	31 392	41 751	33.0	9.1
Elyria	7.0	15.3	10.4	14.0	12.9	13.3	13.0	7.4	6.7	37.6	53.0	55 953	54 533	-2.5	-1.4
Euclid	5.5	16.7	7.8	11.7	12.3	16.5	14.1	6.8	8.4	41.4	54.2	52 717	48 920	-7.2	-2.5
Fairborn	6.5	12.9	17.2	14.6	10.5	13.0	11.3	6.9	7.2	34.0	50.9	32 052	32 352	0.9	2.1
Fairfield	5.5	15.9	8.0	14.9	12.9	14.3	14.7	7.7	6.0	39.3	50.3	42 097	42 510	1.0	0.6
Findlay	6.2	15.4	13.5	13.8	11.8	12.2	12.0	8.0	7.0	35.6	52.7	38 967	41 202	5.7	-0.1
Gahanna	5.1	18.6	10.2	11.9	12.1	17.0	13.5	5.7	5.9	38.4	51.3	32 636	33 248	1.9	4.1
Garfield Heights	6.0	16.8	9.3	12.0	12.2	14.9	12.5	7.4	8.8	39.7	54.9	30 734	28 849	-6.1	-2.6
Green	3.5	17.9	9.3	10.0	10.8	17.2	14.7	10.2	6.4	43.9	49.5	22 817	25 699	12.6	0.6
Grove City	6.5	17.0	6.9	14.0	13.0	15.8	12.9	8.3	5.7	39.2	52.0	27 075	35 575	31.4	10.7

Table D. Cities — Households, Group Quarters, Crime, and Education

City	Households, 2010-2014 Number (27)	Persons per house-hold (28)	Percent Female family house-holder[1] (29)	One-person (30)	Persons in group quarters, 2010 Total (31)	Institutional Total (32)	Persons in nursing facilities (33)	Non-institutional (34)	Serious crimes Total Number (35)	Rate[3] (36)	Violent (37)	Property (38)	Population age 25 and older (39)	High school graduate or less (40)	Bachelor's degree or more (41)
NEW YORK—Cont'd															
Yonkers	73 357	2.71	18.2	31.3	3 286	1 099	864	2 187	2 986	1 488	487	1 001	136 334	45.0	30.7
NORTH CAROLINA	3 742 514	2.61	13.8	27.9	257 246	113 296	46 638	143 950	318 464	3 203	330	2 873	6 495 047	41.4	27.8
Apex	13 811	2.94	10.9	19.2	121	98	97	23	490	1 129	64	1 064	24 919	11.5	60.9
Asheboro	10 012	2.55	20.3	32.8	665	565	357	100	1 628	6 243	261	5 982	16 234	58.2	16.5
Asheville	37 709	2.27	11.3	39.7	4 249	2 292	1 047	1 957	4 778	5 418	568	4 850	61 269	27.6	45.0
Burlington	21 873	2.37	17.5	33.7	906	464	445	442	2 416	4 680	682	3 998	35 272	46.2	22.2
Cary	53 975	2.71	8.0	22.8	260	211	193	49	1 809	1 167	63	1 104	97 337	16.4	61.8
Chapel Hill	20 271	2.88	7.4	33.3	9 003	258	227	8 745	1 433	2 381	143	2 238	29 959	11.4	74.0
Charlotte	298 815	2.59	15.8	31.2	13 369	5 104	2 595	8 265	35 619	4 157	590	3 567	504 765	31.3	40.7
Concord	29 228	2.81	13.7	25.7	893	797	431	96	2 504	2 961	114	2 848	52 596	37.1	30.1
Durham	98 318	2.44	15.9	33.3	9 936	1 962	1 136	7 974	12 919	5 173	734	4 439	157 011	29.0	47.3
Fayetteville	77 935	2.60	18.5	30.4	8 841	1 253	689	7 588	11 563	5 632	506	5 126	123 641	33.3	25.2
Garner	10 322	2.59	16.3	29.5	284	243	232	41	1 264	4 682	189	4 493	18 338	33.4	32.3
Gastonia	26 895	2.70	18.6	28.1	1 745	1 149	691	596	4 172	5 670	658	5 013	46 648	45.0	22.0
Goldsboro	14 095	2.55	23.0	36.2	2 422	1 606	394	816	2 537	6 954	899	6 055	23 194	45.3	19.8
Greensboro	113 232	2.44	16.6	34.5	11 389	2 110	1 407	9 279	11 506	4 077	477	3 600	178 085	34.8	36.3
Greenville	34 741	2.52	17.2	34.4	5 858	760	734	5 098	4 153	4 604	519	4 085	46 360	31.2	37.9
Hickory	15 991	2.51	15.9	31.5	1 351	312	312	1 039	2 053	5 077	391	4 687	26 621	40.1	31.6
High Point	40 988	2.61	19.2	30.0	3 577	940	599	2 637	4 368	4 024	465	3 559	68 692	39.0	29.7
Huntersville	18 181	2.71	7.4	23.2	268	260	260	8	1 063	2 069	113	1 956	32 740	19.7	53.7
Indian Trail	11 209	3.12	11.2	12.6	0	0	0	0	NA	NA	NA	NA	20 972	32.5	35.4
Jacksonville	21 112	3.28	16.0	23.8	16 413	825	379	15 588	NA	NA	NA	NA	31 090	33.5	22.1
Kannapolis	16 020	2.74	17.0	27.8	330	303	278	27	1 042	2 327	179	2 148	28 547	47.6	18.0
Matthews	10 907	2.63	9.2	23.8	269	259	254	10	796	2 660	150	2 509	19 344	21.2	49.8
Monroe	11 069	3.03	19.5	19.3	379	273	248	106	1 945	5 679	455	5 223	20 656	57.0	16.2
Mooresville	12 237	2.82	12.1	25.2	372	252	252	120	1 112	3 161	225	2 936	21 560	30.4	31.9
New Bern	12 320	2.45	15.8	36.7	753	618	433	135	1 389	4 573	402	4 172	19 464	41.6	26.2
Raleigh	166 316	2.55	14.0	33.9	19 526	5 387	1 443	14 139	5 183	1 182	152	1 030	269 334	25.4	47.6
Rocky Mount	22 614	2.52	22.9	33.5	1 597	906	377	691	3 277	5 774	939	4 835	38 038	51.8	18.9
Salisbury	12 428	2.70	19.7	34.4	3 775	2 057	622	1 718	1 968	5 852	711	5 142	21 895	45.3	23.5
Sanford	10 029	2.87	16.9	28.0	858	684	289	174	1 093	3 667	265	3 402	18 003	48.5	21.2
Thomasville	10 593	2.55	16.3	31.4	390	315	275	75	1 160	4 294	374	3 920	17 569	55.9	13.1
Wake Forest	11 510	2.89	8.4	19.9	303	138	138	165	794	2 208	156	2 053	20 901	21.5	50.5
Wilmington	47 528	2.32	12.6	35.6	5 118	430	382	4 688	5 938	5 236	675	4 560	71 388	30.5	39.8
Wilson	19 581	2.52	20.4	32.2	1 534	1 003	756	531	2 166	4 355	533	3 823	32 412	49.5	23.6
Winston-Salem	92 567	2.53	16.1	34.9	9 431	2 480	1 268	6 951	14 592	6 129	712	5 417	148 872	39.8	32.7
NORTH DAKOTA	292 616	2.41	7.8	31.2	25 056	9 675	6 433	15 381	17 565	2 375	265	2 110	458 527	36.1	27.3
Bismarck	28 550	2.28	10.2	33.1	1 815	1 371	534	444	1 892	2 762	270	2 492	44 227	31.4	34.0
Fargo	48 958	2.26	8.1	37.8	4 924	1 011	678	3 913	3 478	3 006	359	2 648	67 160	25.1	38.6
Grand Forks	22 844	2.37	8.3	36.3	3 754	478	285	3 276	1 685	3 039	240	2 800	30 135	30.4	34.9
Minot	18 226	2.44	8.6	33.3	1 524	527	421	997	1 367	2 867	325	2 542	27 632	35.7	26.1
West Fargo	11 125	2.55	7.5	25.9	51	0	0	51	611	1 973	194	1 779	18 403	25.1	35.7
OHIO	4 570 015	2.53	12.9	29.8	306 266	166 042	83 019	140 224	357 558	3 084	285	2 799	7 781 111	45.6	25.6
Akron	83 021	2.39	19.1	37.1	6 133	1 981	878	4 152	10 489	5 300	690	4 610	129 208	49.0	20.5
Barberton	10 603	2.49	19.1	32.3	371	259	259	112	1 072	4 078	259	3 820	18 091	63.7	12.0
Beavercreek	18 423	2.48	6.5	26.5	278	257	257	21	1 037	2 262	55	2 208	32 120	22.4	50.0
Bowling Green	11 007	2.85	7.8	35.5	5 632	503	278	5 129	675	2 100	118	1 982	13 764	33.3	42.1
Brunswick	13 351	2.58	11.1	25.1	200	147	147	53	325	939	55	884	23 444	46.4	21.1
Canton	29 874	2.43	20.8	36.1	3 102	1 256	701	1 846	4 659	6 436	1 008	5 427	46 746	55.4	13.8
Cincinnati	131 160	2.27	19.0	43.7	14 443	4 531	2 199	9 912	19 399	6 517	913	5 604	189 480	41.1	32.3
Cleveland	166 650	2.35	24.1	41.6	13 742	6 258	3 062	7 484	26 421	6 798	1 339	5 459	254 947	55.6	15.2
Cleveland Heights	19 530	2.34	15.1	37.0	738	118	118	620	1 325	2 931	234	2 696	30 782	22.5	51.1
Columbus	329 994	2.46	16.1	35.8	21 099	6 086	3 236	15 013	40 184	4 837	558	4 278	521 137	37.8	33.4
Cuyahoga Falls	21 811	2.26	12.0	35.7	530	345	345	185	1 150	2 338	100	2 238	35 343	39.8	30.6
Dayton	57 367	2.47	21.6	42.3	9 365	2 099	773	7 266	9 238	6 450	864	5 587	88 451	49.1	16.7
Delaware	13 858	2.61	10.4	32.3	2 041	572	377	1 469	861	2 336	174	2 163	22 646	36.0	33.3
Dublin	15 068	2.81	6.3	18.6	127	127	127	0	482	1 091	18	1 073	27 604	9.0	73.7
Elyria	22 646	2.39	17.7	29.0	1 040	881	430	159	NA	NA	NA	NA	36 225	49.9	14.7
Euclid	22 191	2.18	21.1	43.2	675	489	391	186	125	261	25	236	33 299	45.3	19.4
Fairborn	14 149	2.34	14.9	34.4	275	229	229	46	1 043	3 134	144	2 990	20 913	41.9	24.7
Fairfield	17 315	2.46	13.7	26.9	506	404	384	102	1 355	3 177	230	2 947	29 608	41.1	26.9
Findlay	17 451	2.37	13.5	33.7	1 506	504	383	1 002	1 556	3 739	192	3 547	27 191	43.2	26.4
Gahanna	12 931	2.61	10.6	25.2	171	166	158	5	670	1 956	70	1 886	22 751	25.9	45.8
Garfield Heights	11 422	2.49	21.3	32.5	391	308	265	83	1 001	3 540	382	3 158	19 197	55.0	13.5
Green	10 411	2.48	7.5	27.4	141	133	130	8	NA	NA	NA	NA	18 232	38.0	33.1
Grove City	14 233	2.60	11.1	25.0	282	248	165	34	1 452	3 827	100	3 726	25 203	37.9	28.3

1. No spouse present. 2. Data for serious crimes have not been adjusted for underreporting. This may affect comparability between geographic areas and over time. 3. Per 100,000 population estimated by the FBI. 4. Persons 25 years old and over.

Table D. Cities — Income, Poverty, and Housing

City	Money income, 2010–2014 — Per capita income[1] (dollars)	Households — Median income	Households — Percent with income of $200,000 or more	Households — Percent with income of less than $25,000	Families with income below poverty (percent)	Housing units, 2010 — Total	Housing units, 2010 — Percent change, 2000–2010	Housing units, 2010 — Vacant units for sale or rent[2]	Occupied housing units 2010–2014 — Total	Occupied housing units 2010–2014 — Owner-occupied Percent	Occupied housing units 2010–2014 — Median value[3] (dollars)	Median owner costs as a percent of income — With a mortgage[4]	Median owner costs as a percent of income — Without a mortgage[5]
	42	43	44	45	46	47	48	49	50	51	52	53	54
NEW YORK—Cont'd													
Yonkers	30 114	61 132	5.9	22.9	12.8	80 389	3.6	5 839	73 357	48.4	394 500	28.0	18.7
NORTH CAROLINA	25 608	46 693	3.4	26.3	13.0	4 327 528	22.8	582 373	3 742 514	65.8	153 600	22.6	11.9
Apex	35 852	89 392	8.1	8.1	3.1	13 922	72.9	697	13 811	71.2	265 500	18.7	10.0
Asheboro	17 411	31 652	0.9	39.4	24.5	11 158	16.7	1 278	10 012	52.0	112 000	26.7	13.0
Asheville	28 106	44 077	3.1	28.3	11.9	41 626	23.9	4 246	37 709	50.8	198 400	24.2	13.1
Burlington	23 388	37 316	2.4	34.0	17.2	23 414	19.9	2 782	21 873	55.8	122 800	23.4	12.4
Cary	41 785	91 481	12.2	10.6	5.0	55 303	50.1	3 512	53 975	68.7	301 600	18.8	10.0
Chapel Hill	36 928	62 620	14.3	24.0	7.2	22 254	16.6	1 690	20 271	48.6	379 900	21.7	10.0
Charlotte	31 844	53 274	6.4	22.2	13.7	319 918	38.8	30 058	298 815	55.4	170 200	22.2	11.7
Concord	25 987	52 901	3.8	19.5	10.0	32 130	43.1	2 993	29 228	67.3	167 800	22.8	11.9
Durham	29 051	49 585	4.4	25.1	13.8	103 221	27.6	9 780	98 318	49.9	178 200	21.5	10.9
Fayetteville	23 843	44 514	2.0	25.4	15.8	87 005	62.7	8 731	77 935	48.6	127 700	23.5	11.4
Garner	27 436	58 107	1.5	15.6	9.0	10 993	51.9	786	10 322	64.2	163 700	21.6	11.6
Gastonia	21 524	39 578	1.9	32.6	18.9	31 238	12.2	3 468	26 895	55.4	135 100	24.4	12.8
Goldsboro	20 730	35 086	1.2	37.0	21.1	16 824	2.3	1 859	14 095	38.0	111 000	25.6	12.6
Greensboro	25 729	41 518	3.1	29.5	14.6	124 074	25.2	12 343	113 232	51.8	147 500	22.9	11.6
Greenville	22 867	35 225	3.0	37.4	17.2	40 564	43.5	4 493	34 741	37.1	145 700	22.0	13.0
Hickory	26 190	42 393	4.1	27.9	15.1	18 719	12.0	2 105	15 991	53.5	155 800	20.9	10.9
High Point	23 077	43 015	2.1	28.4	17.2	46 677	29.9	5 765	40 988	56.5	144 000	24.6	12.6
Huntersville	39 446	85 258	10.1	11.5	3.8	18 477	87.2	1 054	18 181	74.4	246 900	19.4	11.6
Indian Trail	26 272	67 338	3.0	8.9	4.5	11 700	166.4	579	11 209	83.7	170 400	22.3	11.0
Jacksonville	21 212	41 293	1.0	23.0	11.8	21 135	15.2	1 150	21 112	35.0	155 400	23.7	12.0
Kannapolis	21 149	41 453	1.6	29.8	14.7	18 645	17.4	2 270	16 020	58.5	124 600	24.4	14.5
Matthews	35 191	71 361	7.5	11.8	4.4	11 021	33.2	495	10 907	73.9	215 600	19.8	10.5
Monroe	18 981	43 328	1.5	28.2	19.2	12 375	27.4	1 255	11 069	58.1	142 500	24.1	13.1
Mooresville	26 936	61 458	3.3	18.6	6.2	13 655	74.1	1 281	12 237	67.6	186 100	22.3	12.3
New Bern	23 335	41 238	2.1	31.0	15.4	14 471	31.0	1 701	12 320	50.9	146 900	24.9	14.8
Raleigh	31 169	54 581	5.5	20.0	11.8	176 124	45.9	13 125	166 316	53.2	205 200	21.8	10.0
Rocky Mount	20 236	36 724	1.8	36.1	19.6	26 953	11.1	3 856	22 614	53.6	107 400	23.8	15.0
Salisbury	19 745	34 230	2.2	38.8	22.1	14 626	28.5	2 059	12 428	50.0	120 900	24.0	12.7
Sanford	19 937	44 391	1.1	32.3	19.3	11 411	23.1	953	10 029	53.9	134 900	21.4	12.3
Thomasville	18 012	35 127	0.6	35.5	21.6	11 870	39.2	1 333	10 593	59.9	107 500	24.8	12.6
Wake Forest	33 124	77 173	6.2	12.4	5.3	11 370	123.8	849	11 510	73.7	259 000	21.2	10.0
Wilmington	29 225	42 130	4.5	31.7	16.2	53 400	38.3	6 452	47 528	45.1	224 100	24.1	13.9
Wilson	21 845	38 030	1.6	33.8	21.5	21 870	17.1	2 285	19 581	50.9	132 800	25.3	15.5
Winston-Salem	24 800	40 480	3.8	30.8	17.9	103 974	25.8	11 637	92 567	55.7	139 700	22.5	11.5
NORTH DAKOTA	30 894	55 579	4.1	21.1	7.3	317 498	9.6	36 306	292 616	65.1	142 000	18.9	10.0
Bismarck	32 702	57 660	3.7	19.3	5.9	28 648	18.6	1 385	28 550	64.8	169 600	19.5	10.0
Fargo	29 986	46 311	3.8	24.3	8.1	49 956	21.0	3 165	48 958	44.3	162 000	20.3	10.1
Grand Forks	26 968	44 134	3.6	30.3	10.8	23 449	12.6	1 189	22 844	46.7	156 600	19.5	10.5
Minot	29 957	57 248	2.9	18.1	6.7	18 744	13.7	881	18 226	60.7	167 200	20.4	10.0
West Fargo	32 129	69 104	4.2	13.6	6.6	10 760	83.8	412	11 125	68.6	164 100	20.2	11.9
OHIO	26 520	48 849	3.2	25.5	11.7	5 127 508	7.2	524 073	4 570 015	66.9	129 600	21.9	12.6
Akron	20 245	34 139	1.4	37.7	20.7	96 288	-1.0	12 576	83 021	53.3	82 600	22.6	13.4
Barberton	20 208	37 965	0.6	31.3	15.0	12 191	0.2	1 137	10 603	63.2	85 400	21.1	13.6
Beavercreek	39 325	79 243	7.1	10.2	2.6	19 449	31.1	1 254	18 423	71.7	174 200	20.1	11.8
Bowling Green	19 778	34 202	2.1	37.9	16.5	12 301	15.9	1 013	11 007	41.1	154 300	20.4	10.4
Brunswick	28 306	62 417	2.2	14.7	5.6	13 600	10.9	633	13 351	74.0	156 600	21.1	10.3
Canton	16 769	29 980	0.9	42.8	26.7	34 571	-2.6	4 866	29 874	51.5	74 300	22.7	12.4
Cincinnati	25 256	34 002	3.3	40.2	25.1	161 095	-2.9	27 675	131 160	39.4	121 900	23.1	13.7
Cleveland	17 436	26 179	1.1	48.2	31.1	207 536	-3.8	40 046	166 650	43.5	73 100	25.3	14.7
Cleveland Heights	31 744	53 155	5.5	25.9	12.4	22 465	2.9	2 508	19 530	56.9	129 200	23.5	13.2
Columbus	24 721	44 774	2.0	27.9	17.4	370 965	13.3	39 363	329 994	45.9	128 900	22.6	12.7
Cuyahoga Falls	26 859	49 188	1.3	23.5	9.2	23 859	4.9	1 609	21 811	61.0	119 700	21.4	13.0
Dayton	16 673	28 174	0.7	45.3	29.2	74 065	-4.2	15 661	57 367	49.3	68 200	23.9	14.2
Delaware	27 421	54 683	2.2	19.6	7.3	14 192	37.9	939	13 858	62.3	157 200	22.2	12.4
Dublin	54 045	117 860	21.7	4.7	2.2	15 779	31.1	795	15 068	79.1	334 900	21.7	10.0
Elyria	21 638	42 272	0.6	29.0	16.3	25 085	5.2	2 685	22 646	60.4	96 000	22.1	13.9
Euclid	22 354	36 128	1.1	35.9	16.4	26 037	-0.3	3 352	22 191	50.4	85 300	22.6	15.0
Fairborn	23 450	42 545	1.3	32.5	19.1	15 893	10.3	1 587	14 149	48.9	106 600	22.0	10.6
Fairfield	28 660	55 803	2.5	16.6	6.3	18 803	5.7	1 388	17 315	62.7	144 400	20.6	11.1
Findlay	24 986	43 948	2.4	29.0	16.1	19 318	12.5	1 964	17 451	61.2	121 800	20.1	11.4
Gahanna	36 472	73 583	6.2	10.8	2.6	13 577	9.9	540	12 931	73.4	186 800	21.7	13.1
Garfield Heights	20 645	41 171	1.0	28.0	13.6	13 125	1.6	1 434	11 422	70.0	80 700	25.4	14.1
Green	32 721	61 665	4.9	15.8	4.8	10 858	18.3	788	10 411	77.4	175 500	22.2	11.2
Grove City	30 165	66 964	2.1	13.7	5.6	14 720	38.2	774	14 233	69.3	160 100	21.5	14.6

1. Based on population estimated by the American Community Survey. 2. Includes units rented or sold but not occupied. 3. Specified owner-occupied units; $1,000,000 represents $1,000,000 or more. 4. 50.0 represents 50 percent or more. 5. 10.0 represents 10 percent or less.

City	Occupied housing units, 2010–2014 (cont.)				Migration, 2010–2014		Civilian labor force, 2015		Unemployment		Civilian employment[4], 2010–2014	Percent		
	Percent renter occupied	Median gross rent[1]	Median gross rent as a percent of income[2]	Percent with no vehicle available	Percent who lived in the same house one year ago	Percent who lived outside current city one year ago	Total	Percent change, 2014–2015	Total	Rate[3]	Population age 16 and older	In labor force	Civilian full-year full-time workers	Households with no workers (percent)
	55	56	57	58	59	60	61	62	63	64	65	66	67	68
NEW YORK—Cont'd														
Yonkers	51.6	1 211	32.7	25.4	89.4	5.0	95 213	1.6	5 295	5.6	159 133	62.6	41.0	27.0
NORTH CAROLINA	34.2	790	30.6	6.5	84.7	10.7	4 769 245	1.7	273 772	5.7	7 717 630	63.2	38.2	28.5
Apex	28.8	1 045	24.0	1.6	85.8	12.0	23 600	3.4	884	3.7	28 913	76.9	51.4	11.8
Asheboro	48.0	627	32.1	10.1	83.6	8.3	11 146	1.8	652	5.8	19 015	58.7	34.3	38.1
Asheville	49.2	852	28.6	10.4	77.5	13.7	47 207	2.8	1 956	4.1	71 091	64.4	37.2	31.8
Burlington	44.2	738	33.6	8.6	83.4	8.6	25 122	0.5	1 321	5.3	41 282	62.9	37.3	32.9
Cary	31.3	1 006	25.7	2.7	82.8	12.7	85 773	3.6	3 287	3.8	111 202	72.4	49.9	15.1
Chapel Hill	51.4	982	35.4	8.6	63.9	23.2	29 520	2.3	1 531	5.2	50 394	57.4	29.7	25.4
Charlotte	44.6	902	29.7	7.9	79.1	8.2	446 584	3.2	22 077	4.9	601 694	72.1	44.9	20.1
Concord	32.7	809	29.1	5.5	84.9	9.3	43 012	3.4	1 836	4.3	62 459	68.5	42.5	22.3
Durham	50.1	871	30.7	9.9	75.7	11.8	134 430	2.3	6 250	4.6	190 650	68.8	43.6	22.4
Fayetteville	51.4	883	29.5	6.6	75.9	14.3	74 401	0.3	4 919	6.6	157 188	65.8	31.7	25.4
Garner	35.8	942	26.8	3.0	85.2	12.4	15 544	3.2	665	4.3	20 874	70.6	46.3	20.5
Gastonia	44.6	762	34.2	8.6	83.5	7.6	34 846	3.1	2 158	6.2	55 346	63.3	36.3	29.2
Goldsboro	62.0	728	31.1	16.3	73.2	17.0	12 558	0.5	989	7.9	27 970	56.8	29.0	38.4
Greensboro	48.2	751	30.6	8.4	83.6	8.0	141 977	1.6	8 095	5.7	221 741	65.0	39.2	26.4
Greenville	62.9	743	34.8	9.3	69.1	16.9	46 206	0.7	2 663	5.8	72 916	66.5	35.2	24.7
Hickory	46.5	677	26.7	7.1	83.3	9.0	19 477	0.7	1 044	5.4	31 847	63.2	40.0	27.6
High Point	43.5	778	32.1	10.1	82.6	8.7	52 850	1.2	3 106	5.9	82 770	66.0	38.5	27.0
Huntersville	25.6	1 071	24.6	2.1	85.7	10.4	29 740	3.6	1 141	3.8	36 770	75.5	52.1	15.5
Indian Trail	16.3	1 103	30.3	0.6	86.8	11.0	18 916	3.4	763	4.0	24 793	75.3	48.9	13.7
Jacksonville	65.0	1 025	32.8	6.6	66.6	25.5	19 301	0.6	1 352	7.0	53 568	75.2	21.6	19.2
Kannapolis	41.5	792	31.2	7.4	88.5	7.3	21 190	2.9	1 219	5.8	33 515	65.0	38.5	28.2
Matthews	26.1	969	34.7	3.5	87.9	10.0	16 294	3.5	728	4.5	22 453	68.9	43.0	21.4
Monroe	41.9	785	34.2	7.7	82.5	10.6	16 535	3.3	894	5.4	24 369	67.1	41.8	23.6
Mooresville	32.4	928	26.1	3.6	83.7	11.4	18 646	3.4	959	5.1	26 071	70.0	45.2	23.2
New Bern	49.1	862	31.1	14.7	79.9	13.2	12 352	1.2	684	5.5	23 276	63.6	32.4	34.8
Raleigh	46.8	914	30.1	6.3	78.9	10.5	239 363	3.4	10 930	4.6	336 474	70.9	46.2	18.9
Rocky Mount	46.4	748	36.3	12.2	82.2	7.5	24 074	-0.2	2 128	8.8	45 313	58.2	32.9	36.1
Salisbury	50.0	725	33.6	11.6	77.6	16.2	13 543	2.7	917	6.8	26 626	50.7	27.8	40.2
Sanford	46.1	679	28.1	10.8	81.2	9.0	12 230	4.2	862	7.0	21 594	64.4	38.9	29.1
Thomasville	40.1	592	30.7	9.4	82.9	8.7	12 198	1.2	717	5.9	20 646	64.6	37.3	30.6
Wake Forest	26.3	966	25.3	4.9	85.3	11.5	18 805	3.8	706	3.8	23 658	70.2	44.8	20.1
Wilmington	54.9	850	33.4	8.6	75.7	13.1	58 882	2.9	3 067	5.2	92 552	65.2	34.6	29.4
Wilson	49.1	739	32.3	12.6	80.7	7.8	21 436	-1.9	2 141	10.0	38 533	59.9	36.5	33.4
Winston-Salem	44.3	722	32.0	10.1	80.8	7.9	113 998	1.5	6 290	5.5	183 069	63.4	36.9	28.6
NORTH DAKOTA	34.9	676	25.3	5.5	82.5	11.3	414 344	-0.2	11 286	2.7	563 755	70.5	46.5	22.1
Bismarck	35.2	719	23.9	5.8	83.0	9.4	36 916	2.4	833	2.3	52 437	71.4	49.7	22.3
Fargo	55.7	690	26.8	8.4	72.9	14.2	65 665	2.3	1 424	2.2	90 700	75.7	47.0	18.8
Grand Forks	53.3	717	31.4	8.4	74.6	13.8	30 909	0.8	688	2.2	45 182	71.4	39.8	21.4
Minot	39.3	786	26.2	5.2	76.0	12.3	25 040	-0.5	761	3.0	35 650	72.7	46.2	20.1
West Fargo	31.4	722	23.7	3.6	85.0	12.4	18 773	2.3	395	2.1	21 687	78.8	57.2	14.6
OHIO	33.1	729	29.9	8.4	85.4	9.7	5 700 344	0.0	277 325	4.9	9 197 668	63.6	39.1	29.7
Akron	46.7	682	34.0	15.4	85.0	6.5	91 228	0.1	5 188	5.7	158 874	62.4	35.0	34.2
Barberton	36.8	655	29.2	10.6	88.9	7.1	12 680	0.3	679	5.4	20 883	63.4	36.7	32.7
Beavercreek	28.3	1 100	23.1	3.2	86.3	10.1	22 758	0.7	879	3.9	37 483	64.4	42.5	23.6
Bowling Green	58.9	638	37.7	9.1	57.1	25.1	16 716	0.6	760	4.5	27 656	64.8	25.7	25.2
Brunswick	26.0	818	27.8	4.1	91.5	5.3	19 721	-0.7	771	3.9	27 578	71.8	45.1	21.2
Canton	48.5	601	32.3	17.1	81.7	8.8	31 862	-1.1	1 950	6.1	55 402	61.5	32.2	36.5
Cincinnati	60.6	653	32.2	21.6	75.5	10.1	142 309	0.2	7 072	5.0	238 302	64.7	36.2	33.4
Cleveland	56.5	661	34.8	25.3	79.8	7.9	158 985	-1.3	10 095	6.3	310 651	58.9	30.5	40.6
Cleveland Heights	43.1	853	30.6	12.5	83.1	12.9	22 845	-0.8	973	4.3	36 841	65.6	41.4	27.0
Columbus	54.1	822	29.7	9.9	77.0	10.0	444 237	1.0	18 149	4.1	641 663	69.8	44.2	23.8
Cuyahoga Falls	39.0	758	25.9	7.2	90.1	6.9	26 536	0.3	1 193	4.5	40 108	66.8	45.7	27.7
Dayton	50.7	640	36.8	20.1	74.8	11.2	58 158	-0.1	3 445	5.9	114 004	57.5	27.8	40.0
Delaware	37.7	830	29.5	6.1	82.3	10.8	20 119	1.2	737	3.7	27 981	66.9	46.9	22.7
Dublin	20.9	1 178	19.4	2.5	88.1	8.9	23 937	1.3	741	3.1	31 121	72.5	52.2	12.3
Elyria	39.6	716	30.4	9.6	82.4	9.6	26 901	-0.9	1 449	5.4	43 342	65.4	37.8	31.2
Euclid	49.6	734	34.8	16.3	84.8	9.4	22 666	-1.2	1 324	5.8	38 433	63.5	38.9	35.8
Fairborn	51.1	776	30.9	6.5	82.5	11.4	16 668	0.6	730	4.4	26 819	64.8	34.0	29.5
Fairfield	37.3	842	26.0	3.5	84.8	10.3	24 031	0.4	1 026	4.3	34 457	71.8	46.7	21.3
Findlay	38.8	658	29.3	9.3	79.0	11.1	21 403	0.7	813	3.8	33 446	64.7	37.4	32.4
Gahanna	26.6	981	28.2	4.7	87.4	8.5	19 637	1.1	693	3.5	26 830	72.7	48.2	18.5
Garfield Heights	30.0	772	33.2	10.2	87.3	9.4	13 659	-1.4	753	5.5	22 569	63.4	37.1	31.8
Green	22.6	804	26.8	2.9	92.2	6.0	13 954	0.5	617	4.4	21 185	66.8	44.0	26.6
Grove City	30.7	875	26.7	3.5	88.5	8.3	20 825	1.1	779	3.7	29 153	69.4	48.7	20.9

1. $2,000 represents $2,000 or more.   2. 50.0 represents 50 percent or more.   3. Percent of civilian labor force.   4. Persons 16 years old and over.

Table D. Cities — **Construction, Wholesale Trade, and Retail Trade**

City	Value of residential construction authorized by building permits, 2015			Wholesale trade,[1] 2012				Retail trade,[2] 2012			
	New construction ($1,000)	Number of housing units	Percent single family	Number of establishments	Number of employees	Sales (mil dol)	Annual payroll (mil dol)	Number of establishments	Number of employees	Sales (mil dol)	Annual payroll (mil dol)
	69	70	71	72	73	74	75	76	77	78	79
NEW YORK—Cont'd											
Yonkers	63 735	222	7.2	161	1 348	852.6	72.2	657	9 473	2 708.5	250.0
NORTH CAROLINA	9 707 931	54 757	71.1	9 713	136 174	105 275.6	7 853.7	34 288	446 373	120 691.0	10 421.2
Apex	139 666	683	100.0	44	753	621.3	39.8	131	2 427	657.6	56.1
Asheboro	3 428	38	100.0	33	313	180.7	11.8	196	2 375	556.5	48.5
Asheville	69 783	327	82.6	155	1 477	883.6	71.4	776	11 310	2 822.0	265.2
Burlington	27 042	243	78.6	81	1 025	423.2	40.9	367	5 655	1 236.2	120.3
Cary	229 294	1 058	98.9	144	1 776	2 938.5	134.8	495	9 194	2 877.2	229.4
Chapel Hill	65 833	361	10.8	27	141	176.5	7.7	199	2 833	684.1	72.3
Charlotte	NA	NA	NA	1 540	25 446	19 884.6	1 617.4	2 600	39 240	10 901.0	960.8
Concord	NA	NA	NA	113	1 941	1 285.3	92.3	489	9 070	2 228.3	189.2
Durham	325 303	2 907	49.5	173	5 168	4 131.5	426.0	871	13 896	3 313.6	317.4
Fayetteville	134 080	724	40.3	104	2 032	663.0	79.3	825	12 882	3 625.9	311.0
Garner	24 907	311	20.3	57	1 381	1 135.3	57.4	112	1 911	490.5	42.2
Gastonia	95 950	363	100.0	86	848	328.4	34.2	378	5 774	1 341.6	125.3
Goldsboro	6 853	41	90.2	56	1 306	1 019.9	54.9	311	4 058	1 143.7	90.6
Greensboro	135 810	898	64.6	541	7 993	9 675.9	453.6	1 232	19 426	4 950.9	488.9
Greenville	39 694	375	51.5	70	700	350.5	35.0	421	6 355	1 589.1	141.5
Hickory	NA	NA	NA	129	4 126	3 196.1	196.6	454	6 897	1 934.2	165.6
High Point	82 649	449	60.8	298	4 852	3 737.6	268.8	410	4 792	1 347.0	114.9
Huntersville	NA	NA	NA	66	621	341.0	41.8	161	2 686	782.3	65.0
Indian Trail	NA	NA	NA	84	838	379.9	44.2	91	1 494	468.6	42.2
Jacksonville	9 615	78	61.5	26	109	73.0	4.5	340	5 936	1 691.7	141.4
Kannapolis	NA	NA	NA	25	178	118.1	8.3	158	1 596	398.1	36.6
Matthews	NA	NA	NA	53	549	204.2	31.8	170	3 135	1 099.4	85.6
Monroe	17 843	152	100.0	76	1 328	647.5	58.3	230	3 076	861.7	68.7
Mooresville	NA	NA	NA	81	690	499.8	38.7	226	3 734	1 130.1	84.1
New Bern	23 496	226	46.9	33	D	D	D	248	3 073	834.7	72.9
Raleigh	578 240	3 958	32.0	570	8 627	5 399.8	577.4	1 698	27 148	7 268.5	688.9
Rocky Mount	2 560	32	100.0	74	1 406	1 071.4	63.1	331	4 143	1 014.0	89.4
Salisbury	NA	NA	NA	47	945	612.8	38.8	203	2 948	832.5	70.1
Sanford	7 816	36	100.0	22	D	D	D	192	2 658	706.4	58.3
Thomasville	6 632	33	75.8	30	453	211.9	22.1	128	1 458	354.7	31.5
Wake Forest	90 489	754	71.6	26	139	96.6	7.8	87	1 725	489.2	43.6
Wilmington	NA	NA	NA	139	1 191	570.6	58.3	764	10 389	3 009.5	261.3
Wilson	19 963	64	100.0	76	742	444.0	30.7	263	3 268	899.3	76.9
Winston-Salem	73 549	703	77.8	239	3 943	2 266.4	189.6	1 008	15 129	4 067.8	365.3
NORTH DAKOTA	953 024	6 256	55.0	1 430	18 880	28 150.8	1 078.2	3 185	47 186	15 519.8	1 204.4
Bismarck	93 955	664	55.9	115	1 967	1 346.8	106.9	357	6 779	1 948.7	175.8
Fargo	190 178	1 428	36.8	251	5 114	4 124.9	288.3	518	11 065	3 299.9	266.9
Grand Forks	60 764	433	35.3	59	965	697.8	50.3	279	5 654	1 501.8	126.4
Minot	36 869	252	48.0	68	1 285	2 418.1	80.1	250	5 160	1 686.7	149.6
West Fargo	118 072	614	77.5	41	477	194.6	23.5	91	1 133	373.8	27.1
OHIO	3 982 890	20 047	67.5	11 744	182 791	155 426.0	9 627.2	36 531	549 152	153 554.0	13 099.3
Akron	NA	NA	NA	217	2 998	1 695.8	153.6	612	7 731	1 906.6	185.0
Barberton	810	6	100.0	22	523	113.2	17.8	71	780	171.4	15.5
Beavercreek	NA	NA	NA	23	167	327.3	9.5	216	4 600	941.1	87.2
Bowling Green	NA	NA	NA	15	116	109.0	6.5	99	1 599	368.3	34.6
Brunswick	11 545	75	100.0	48	532	238.0	27.5	93	1 759	727.5	48.8
Canton	1 105	11	100.0	89	1 263	770.9	58.2	249	3 432	823.7	73.9
Cincinnati	29 076	216	44.4	358	5 890	6 371.5	337.1	941	13 549	3 977.7	350.4
Cleveland	7 907	172	75.6	577	9 142	5 475.0	465.9	1 206	10 637	2 764.9	244.1
Cleveland Heights	412	1	100.0	8	43	11.8	1.6	97	1 340	294.9	32.8
Columbus	516 166	3 915	18.6	807	17 060	14 346.8	1 005.3	2 566	46 211	13 114.2	1 178.1
Cuyahoga Falls	NA	NA	NA	39	573	243.9	26.5	171	3 313	1 015.8	79.1
Dayton	8 518	66	90.9	158	3 063	12 234.4	182.6	375	3 791	870.1	88.8
Delaware	40 744	202	89.1	14	120	40.6	6.4	118	1 738	539.0	44.8
Dublin	48 895	120	98.3	88	1 426	1 730.1	115.1	118	2 215	997.6	79.5
Elyria	4 557	48	66.7	56	309	150.4	12.6	219	3 567	887.5	79.0
Euclid	300	2	100.0	34	533	206.2	25.9	84	993	235.3	22.0
Fairborn	17 589	129	24.8	11	330	338.2	17.0	78	1 061	300.0	22.6
Fairfield	2 342	11	100.0	72	1 793	1 060.2	92.0	175	3 937	1 355.5	133.3
Findlay	5 800	27	77.8	40	638	483.4	29.8	205	3 287	823.7	72.0
Gahanna	17 692	109	25.7	38	619	358.8	28.4	87	1 378	475.2	39.6
Garfield Heights	0	0	0.0	27	404	152.7	15.1	78	960	211.5	18.5
Green	NA	NA	NA	31	457	465.3	45.9	55	1 490	706.3	46.3
Grove City	40 605	182	100.0	32	869	592.4	38.9	121	3 256	1 130.1	76.0

1. Merchant wholesalers except manufacturers' sales branches and offices.   2. Establishments with payroll.

Table D. Cities — **Real Estate, Professional Services, and Manufacturing**

City	Real estate and rental and leasing, 2012				Professional, scientific, and technical services,[1] 2012				Manufacturing, 2012			
	Number of establish-ments	Number of employees	Receipts (mil dol)	Annual payroll (mil dol)	Number of establish-ments	Number of employees	Receipts (mil dol)	Annual payroll (mil dol)	Number of establish-ments	Number of employees	Receipts (mil dol)	Annual payroll (mil dol)
	80	81	82	83	84	85	86	87	88	89	90	91
NEW YORK—Cont'd												
Yonkers	363	1 099	341.3	42.1	254	D	D	D	88	2 755	984.9	141.4
NORTH CAROLINA	10 140	47 155	9 301.7	1 942.6	22 730	190 441	30 520.8	12 461.5	8 953	403 593	202 344.6	18 191.2
Apex	27	74	12.0	2.8	158	611	83.3	27.8	34	1 042	1 399.5	63.7
Asheboro	38	152	34.8	4.5	76	358	28.0	10.0	63	6 915	3 002.3	245.9
Asheville	244	785	163.3	26.3	575	D	D	D	130	4 595	983.8	224.4
Burlington	66	419	106.4	18.7	107	828	75.6	33.9	92	3 671	855.4	141.8
Cary	218	681	151.2	29.9	903	D	D	D	68	1 693	696.0	79.4
Chapel Hill	88	381	67.0	13.7	293	D	D	D	17	D	7.4	D
Charlotte	1 372	8 759	2 045.6	494.7	3 202	D	D	D	643	21 152	9 376.1	1 164.0
Concord	103	464	88.7	13.4	207	D	D	D	87	4 261	1 352.5	190.7
Durham	275	1 601	337.0	66.8	973	D	D	D	144	7 368	4 773.1	499.7
Fayetteville	264	1 622	314.8	54.9	443	D	D	D	63	2 169	616.0	109.6
Garner	33	128	39.8	4.6	76	558	63.6	21.5	22	684	611.1	39.6
Gastonia	90	546	125.8	21.3	170	D	D	D	104	5 248	1 597.3	223.9
Goldsboro	44	216	23.0	6.0	104	614	61.0	22.9	49	3 089	808.7	137.0
Greensboro	455	3 181	525.0	135.4	936	D	D	D	308	16 855	22 411.9	1 025.3
Greenville	125	546	86.3	17.7	228	D	D	D	35	424	84.9	15.1
Hickory	100	324	88.9	9.9	199	1 198	602.5	54.9	161	5 444	1 261.8	195.0
High Point	115	754	127.8	25.4	273	D	D	D	241	12 901	3 676.7	541.1
Huntersville	62	160	42.1	8.0	183	856	120.2	52.3	25	706	209.7	35.8
Indian Trail	21	55	11.9	2.1	59	174	17.3	6.4	53	830	197.3	35.3
Jacksonville	100	390	73.2	12.0	152	D	D	D	12	D	D	D
Kannapolis	33	142	18.6	4.1	56	D	D	D	28	468	101.5	22.4
Matthews	50	236	32.3	7.5	144	690	89.7	35.9	34	713	296.9	38.6
Monroe	43	135	28.6	5.4	90	422	47.5	18.4	89	6 657	2 763.7	321.8
Mooresville	64	191	45.4	7.3	147	1 618	202.9	72.6	73	2 277	825.9	109.7
New Bern	51	223	29.9	7.0	111	D	D	D	34	2 008	683.6	100.2
Raleigh	735	5 229	1 173.6	305.0	2 185	22 893	4 304.5	1 706.4	267	5 229	1 842.0	270.5
Rocky Mount	77	357	54.8	12.0	125	803	83.1	33.8	43	4 002	940.1	217.5
Salisbury	44	205	18.3	4.3	97	529	64.3	20.7	66	1 904	585.2	84.1
Sanford	38	144	26.2	5.2	66	D	D	D	44	4 754	1 224.1	195.9
Thomasville	24	D	D	D	44	141	15.6	3.5	86	2 096	642.1	79.0
Wake Forest	33	76	17.9	3.2	116	D	D	D	14	111	18.0	6.2
Wilmington	249	1 574	260.9	58.6	652	D	D	D	91	3 247	1 623.2	250.0
Wilson	65	229	41.2	5.8	97	D	D	D	59	6 692	12 784.2	334.9
Winston-Salem	293	1 575	276.0	58.3	672	D	D	D	200	8 322	4 017.0	410.7
NORTH DAKOTA	912	5 157	1 445.1	247.5	1 706	13 633	1 836.9	732.4	745	23 541	14 427.4	1 042.8
Bismarck	122	389	101.5	13.2	274	D	D	D	57	824	D	35.8
Fargo	238	1 613	286.7	62.0	411	D	D	D	126	6 087	2 601.4	278.6
Grand Forks	73	481	83.5	14.3	117	D	D	D	42	2 015	564.1	73.6
Minot	68	D	D	D	119	D	D	D	26	346	110.3	13.9
West Fargo	21	D	D	D	38	D	D	D	42	2 294	791.0	109.1
OHIO	9 932	60 966	16 132.7	2 441.8	23 851	228 728	35 259.4	13 870.3	14 482	627 124	313 630.0	33 135.4
Akron	167	1 062	182.7	40.1	449	D	D	D	269	8 672	3 477.8	461.5
Barberton	6	19	1.9	0.4	27	D	D	D	50	1 938	530.0	97.4
Beavercreek	46	176	56.2	4.8	188	D	D	D	28	D	76.3	D
Bowling Green	38	159	21.8	4.3	49	D	D	D	35	1 906	729.3	87.6
Brunswick	22	92	17.7	2.3	56	390	35.0	12.3	49	969	204.1	45.2
Canton	71	248	39.3	8.2	155	D	D	D	136	8 020	6 885.8	429.7
Cincinnati	405	2 489	609.1	120.1	1 118	19 286	3 946.0	1 410.5	363	12 881	7 058.1	760.4
Cleveland	349	3 895	816.6	177.7	1 159	17 004	3 382.2	1 318.3	805	22 075	7 794.7	1 192.0
Cleveland Heights	50	166	27.9	4.4	104	D	D	D	8	46	6.3	1.5
Columbus	904	6 933	1 893.8	317.8	2 055	D	D	D	518	19 881	9 829.7	1 036.6
Cuyahoga Falls	42	197	26.6	5.6	108	867	73.7	33.2	76	2 565	857.7	128.3
Dayton	136	713	118.0	24.4	306	D	D	D	266	9 794	2 940.7	467.6
Delaware	36	117	25.0	5.8	54	355	48.7	14.7	38	2 755	2 055.5	169.2
Dublin	75	673	434.5	29.4	369	3 381	496.2	250.6	33	1 051	404.2	58.3
Elyria	48	223	34.8	7.1	79	D	D	D	100	4 869	1 604.5	260.5
Euclid	49	355	51.3	9.7	42	361	39.4	16.1	75	5 059	1 704.4	368.8
Fairborn	35	161	23.0	4.0	76	D	D	D	12	443	85.9	22.3
Fairfield	50	299	94.5	11.8	82	D	D	D	82	3 088	880.8	140.4
Findlay	50	382	46.4	12.4	108	649	87.7	34.2	56	5 654	2 137.3	287.6
Gahanna	40	159	35.3	6.3	143	973	120.1	46.4	27	754	235.0	32.9
Garfield Heights	20	69	10.8	2.8	48	360	46.8	20.8	18	838	186.7	40.7
Green	22	176	38.5	6.0	77	958	102.9	39.9	37	1 479	458.4	66.2
Grove City	34	164	36.7	6.5	46	389	52.7	14.4	29	1 545	393.2	70.7

1. Establishments subject to federal tax.

Table D. Cities — Accommodation and Food Services, Arts, Entertainment, and Recreation, and Health Care and Social Assistance

City	Accommodation and food services, 2012				Arts, entertainment, and recreation,[1] 2012				Health care and social assistance,[1] 2012			
	Number of establishments	Number of employees	Sales (mil dol)	Annual payroll (mil dol)	Number of establishments	Number of employees	Receipts (mil dol)	Annual payroll (mil dol)	Number of establishments	Number of employees	Receipts (mil dol)	Annual payroll (mil dol)
	92	93	94	95	96	97	98	99	100	101	102	103
NEW YORK—Cont'd												
Yonkers	351	3 484	259.8	65.3	46	1 168	286.4	45.1	403	4 301	453.0	184.7
NORTH CAROLINA	19 496	358 602	18 622.3	5 040.6	2 696	37 335	3 805.3	1 167.0	19 152	292 709	27 305.8	11 432.3
Apex	90	1 635	79.2	21.5	10	D	D	D	104	D	D	D
Asheboro	102	1 875	87.1	22.8	8	D	D	D	121	D	D	D
Asheville	541	11 795	698.6	201.3	64	1 459	103.0	35.1	530	7 203	898.5	383.9
Burlington	188	4 010	175.6	50.4	16	D	D	D	208	3 755	374.2	204.6
Cary	372	7 249	386.6	114.4	56	956	57.7	17.6	471	4 842	566.0	221.9
Chapel Hill	220	4 078	221.9	63.0	29	97	12.9	4.1	209	D	D	D
Charlotte	1 888	40 752	2 413.6	659.0	231	5 691	619.8	322.6	1 739	25 574	3 149.2	1 263.4
Concord	233	6 309	337.1	89.4	46	2 034	599.3	132.0	197	3 012	361.3	155.4
Durham	645	12 968	767.1	209.7	64	731	58.8	11.4	604	8 801	935.0	342.0
Fayetteville	480	10 965	516.5	143.3	42	D	D	D	597	9 245	705.4	309.7
Garner	66	1 528	68.1	18.8	4	D	D	D	83	934	84.4	31.8
Gastonia	191	3 998	199.4	51.2	20	224	11.9	2.6	270	D	D	D
Goldsboro	144	2 625	129.6	33.4	13	128	5.8	1.4	156	2 442	232.0	104.5
Greensboro	789	16 835	856.6	237.3	72	1 183	77.5	21.7	723	12 951	1 352.5	583.9
Greenville	288	6 910	313.5	85.4	23	D	D	D	332	D	D	D
Hickory	219	4 748	210.4	59.0	12	130	7.0	2.3	237	D	D	D
High Point	229	D	D	D	20	234	18.3	2.9	235	4 742	580.3	213.0
Huntersville	99	2 246	118.5	33.8	28	703	130.4	49.4	145	D	D	D
Indian Trail	55	887	41.7	10.8	11	114	7.9	1.7	43	337	33.1	11.5
Jacksonville	219	4 593	257.1	60.9	15	203	9.4	2.8	179	D	D	D
Kannapolis	74	D	D	D	10	D	D	D	48	934	81.5	36.3
Matthews	104	2 147	103.8	28.4	22	250	19.1	4.6	129	D	D	D
Monroe	105	1 927	91.2	24.5	8	D	D	D	116	D	D	D
Mooresville	159	2 948	149.8	40.0	44	D	D	D	147	2 454	339.9	123.9
New Bern	123	2 528	108.2	30.7	15	213	8.3	2.6	147	D	D	D
Raleigh	1 145	24 150	1 237.1	348.9	135	4 102	350.3	97.6	1 291	18 328	1 959.5	866.1
Rocky Mount	146	3 442	150.4	41.8	20	D	D	D	192	3 250	310.3	125.0
Salisbury	138	2 714	123.3	34.0	13	85	5.4	1.7	157	D	D	D
Sanford	92	1 665	77.3	20.9	6	D	D	D	123	2 042	213.9	78.1
Thomasville	72	D	D	D	7	D	D	D	35	745	46.6	21.9
Wake Forest	57	1 050	47.5	14.0	17	195	9.0	2.3	93	1 027	78.7	31.8
Wilmington	440	9 326	440.1	124.0	48	544	29.8	8.0	547	8 125	895.9	369.0
Wilson	124	2 521	133.0	32.7	11	D	D	D	151	D	D	D
Winston-Salem	539	11 157	564.9	159.4	56	548	32.9	8.9	510	9 646	868.9	430.6
NORTH DAKOTA	1 935	35 698	2 045.1	521.3	259	2 153	145.3	34.2	1 235	15 038	1 809.1	775.9
Bismarck	162	4 873	236.6	69.4	23	D	D	D	196	D	D	D
Fargo	316	8 386	389.1	114.6	52	662	51.3	10.4	284	5 329	931.1	386.1
Grand Forks	174	4 076	173.4	51.4	24	D	D	D	97	D	D	D
Minot	150	3 741	203.9	56.9	19	D	D	D	102	D	D	D
West Fargo	38	D	D	D	6	D	D	D	39	D	D	D
OHIO	23 432	437 293	20 652.8	5 742.7	2 869	36 390	3 903.5	1 464.8	22 945	393 909	34 637.9	15 470.9
Akron	407	5 634	257.4	69.3	31	310	42.4	9.4	351	7 424	853.5	418.3
Barberton	46	D	D	D	3	D	D	D	75	2 196	237.1	87.3
Beavercreek	105	2 738	140.8	37.8	4	D	D	D	121	D	D	D
Bowling Green	117	2 586	89.2	23.7	10	D	D	D	75	D	D	D
Brunswick	63	1 072	50.8	13.5	9	D	D	D	51	762	51.6	27.8
Canton	170	2 652	119.8	31.6	14	123	7.4	1.6	154	3 277	373.8	185.5
Cincinnati	738	15 321	858.6	247.4	82	1 803	462.6	323.2	652	15 018	2 070.9	917.9
Cleveland	980	16 885	950.9	254.3	63	2 425	509.8	290.4	402	7 946	537.2	237.2
Cleveland Heights	80	1 005	55.6	16.3	9	51	2.1	0.6	85	1 247	77.8	38.2
Columbus	1 959	42 063	2 259.0	637.6	152	3 969	354.9	122.1	1 620	31 398	3 077.4	1 331.6
Cuyahoga Falls	119	2 339	111.2	32.1	9	D	D	D	130	2 582	252.4	100.3
Dayton	276	4 570	206.8	57.9	17	210	23.6	5.6	285	5 572	659.7	342.5
Delaware	87	1 313	62.5	17.1	8	D	D	D	92	1 626	86.5	40.9
Dublin	123	3 294	167.6	52.9	27	D	D	D	195	D	D	D
Elyria	118	2 230	96.8	26.9	8	74	2.5	1.0	115	D	D	D
Euclid	71	D	D	D	7	D	D	D	98	2 556	121.2	62.9
Fairborn	74	1 535	71.9	20.2	7	D	D	D	39	D	D	D
Fairfield	104	1 990	100.4	25.7	9	D	D	D	136	D	D	D
Findlay	147	3 530	146.5	42.1	8	51	1.6	0.4	125	D	D	D
Gahanna	104	1 861	89.4	24.3	12	D	D	D	140	2 473	261.4	110.1
Garfield Heights	46	654	29.6	7.2	4	10	0.8	0.2	62	614	63.7	33.4
Green	54	949	45.3	12.2	10	106	6.9	2.1	67	D	D	D
Grove City	110	2 387	130.7	34.8	14	D	D	D	94	1 147	128.8	47.1

1. Establishments subject to federal tax.

Table D. Cities — **Other Services and Government Employment and Payroll**

City	Other services[1], 2012				Government employment and payroll, 2012								
						March payroll							
							Percent of total for:						
	Number of establishments	Number of employees	Receipts (mil dol)	Annual payroll (mil dol)	Full-time equivalent employees	Total (dollars)	Administration, judicial, and legal	Police and Corrections	Fire Protection	Highways and transportation	Health and welfare	Natural resources and utilities	Education and libraries
	104	105	106	107	108	109	110	111	112	113	114	115	116
NEW YORK—Cont'd													
Yonkers	305	1 248	129.1	34.1	5 538	39 341 604	3.2	17.5	10.4	1.0	2.7	6.0	58.2
NORTH CAROLINA	11 506	64 643	5 548.4	1 664.9	X	X	X	X	X	X	X	X	X
Apex	64	436	30.8	10.3	344	1 509 120	15.4	23.1	14.9	7.4	4.6	28.3	0.0
Asheboro	43	265	27.2	7.5	349	1 396 592	5.9	23.8	15.1	5.8	2.2	22.5	0.0
Asheville	214	1 148	87.1	27.3	1 057	3 889 185	9.1	23.7	24.5	5.3	3.3	19.0	0.0
Burlington	86	514	39.3	11.9	628	2 130 883	10.7	32.6	15.8	5.7	0.1	29.4	0.0
Cary	196	1 880	141.3	54.1	1 135	5 112 012	14.8	23.3	19.4	15.6	0.0	21.6	0.0
Chapel Hill	59	545	34.2	13.1	840	3 017 788	12.7	26.8	15.1	19.0	2.7	8.1	3.9
Charlotte	1 161	9 188	865.2	265.7	7 449	34 348 745	9.7	36.0	16.2	12.9	2.2	17.0	0.0
Concord	134	672	60.1	15.6	923	3 576 064	7.2	20.8	21.3	7.1	4.4	23.7	0.0
Durham	306	2 624	221.3	72.2	1 086	4 030 398	25.2	0.0	0.0	16.5	6.6	47.8	0.0
Fayetteville	256	1 445	107.3	33.2	1 960	7 748 728	4.9	24.8	14.8	6.6	0.8	30.0	0.0
Garner	52	338	30.0	8.8	177	821 893	16.4	47.7	0.0	3.4	1.0	15.0	0.0
Gastonia	122	742	51.1	16.1	935	3 494 489	15.2	23.5	14.9	10.2	1.1	28.7	0.0
Goldsboro	73	484	38.1	11.4	449	1 502 437	12.1	25.9	19.1	3.7	0.8	27.4	0.0
Greensboro	413	2 580	239.4	71.4	3 098	11 503 988	8.8	28.2	17.9	6.9	2.9	20.8	2.5
Greenville	103	692	52.0	14.4	1 347	5 208 426	6.5	18.6	12.5	6.2	2.4	34.6	0.0
Hickory	105	824	63.2	18.2	636	2 107 555	11.1	23.4	23.3	9.5	0.2	23.5	3.6
High Point	150	1 094	111.3	31.0	1 446	5 797 223	10.4	32.4	13.1	5.0	2.2	31.9	3.2
Huntersville	71	360	27.5	8.2	161	688 375	25.1	57.8	0.0	7.5	0.0	9.6	0.0
Indian Trail	60	283	24.5	6.8	48	144 392	56.2	0.0	0.0	9.0	0.0	9.0	0.0
Jacksonville	109	795	48.3	16.8	542	2 172 480	13.1	25.3	14.1	6.1	0.2	19.4	0.0
Kannapolis	48	D	D	D	289	1 109 005	13.6	30.3	23.4	4.8	0.0	27.8	0.0
Matthews	66	310	21.4	6.9	163	577 637	14.5	49.3	6.0	9.7	1.3	6.1	0.0
Monroe	82	392	37.1	11.2	511	1 971 029	15.1	20.8	15.3	6.0	0.0	37.8	0.0
Mooresville	81	506	50.3	12.2	760	1 406 044	10.4	25.8	21.5	3.5	0.0	23.4	4.8
New Bern	54	280	22.6	6.9	449	1 701 922	12.5	25.9	16.3	4.6	1.3	33.6	0.0
Raleigh	712	5 192	401.9	131.8	3 936	15 850 858	10.6	25.2	16.4	6.4	0.7	28.5	0.0
Rocky Mount	89	D	D	D	1 002	3 610 762	13.3	21.6	15.9	8.8	1.5	39.0	0.0
Salisbury	41	338	22.5	8.0	458	1 569 483	17.2	19.6	16.0	10.0	0.7	25.8	0.0
Sanford	52	284	18.9	6.3	345	1 295 948	13.5	31.2	15.8	6.0	2.5	21.9	0.0
Thomasville	45	207	22.4	5.7	377	1 184 674	5.8	27.3	23.1	5.5	0.0	20.8	0.0
Wake Forest	46	310	31.0	9.2	200	792 417	16.8	36.0	0.0	10.9	6.1	19.0	0.0
Wilmington	240	1 326	102.4	32.2	949	3 706 301	13.1	34.8	22.0	7.7	2.3	17.8	0.0
Wilson	74	D	D	D	776	2 938 961	12.7	19.6	12.6	8.5	5.3	36.1	0.0
Winston-Salem	276	1 682	131.3	43.3	2 489	8 460 457	12.1	31.4	15.9	7.1	5.7	23.1	0.0
NORTH DAKOTA	1 296	6 652	721.6	189.3	X	X	X	X	X	X	X	X	X
Bismarck	138	D	D	D	605	2 280 206	9.2	23.4	16.3	8.9	10.4	15.3	4.2
Fargo	226	1 642	138.6	44.9	836	3 889 052	10.7	22.5	14.1	18.2	12.7	15.1	3.8
Grand Forks	99	642	52.1	15.8	549	2 249 631	11.5	21.4	13.7	14.6	8.9	22.9	0.0
Minot	84	521	48.4	14.6	348	1 359 688	12.5	26.4	15.9	13.9	0.0	20.0	3.8
West Fargo	52	313	35.3	9.8	120	521 710	16.1	47.5	0.0	0.0	0.0	30.4	6.0
OHIO	15 038	99 624	8 638.0	2 607.8	X	X	X	X	X	X	X	X	X
Akron	272	1 576	104.3	34.7	1 872	8 159 087	15.0	31.5	21.9	4.1	0.5	18.7	0.0
Barberton	36	195	19.1	6.4	256	1 078 359	17.1	23.7	20.5	6.9	9.7	22.1	0.0
Beavercreek	54	443	31.1	9.3	144	794 411	6.5	49.4	0.0	17.6	4.9	14.0	0.0
Bowling Green	40	190	9.6	3.5	302	1 389 538	15.6	20.6	19.6	2.1	0.6	31.6	0.0
Brunswick	59	422	39.6	12.5	156	716 777	14.6	38.7	22.6	9.5	2.3	6.8	0.0
Canton	115	597	54.1	15.3	914	3 932 055	14.5	23.0	20.1	7.9	7.6	22.3	0.0
Cincinnati	415	3 189	264.2	77.6	5 222	26 843 252	9.4	25.7	17.7	5.4	8.4	28.9	0.0
Cleveland	546	3 780	261.7	90.6	7 389	33 318 506	12.7	29.1	13.0	9.9	7.8	25.3	0.0
Cleveland Heights	52	306	27.0	8.7	461	2 098 391	11.2	30.1	23.8	3.9	3.6	16.1	0.0
Columbus	916	8 412	668.6	217.0	8 035	42 573 757	14.7	32.2	23.9	4.3	5.7	16.8	0.0
Cuyahoga Falls	92	522	39.1	12.7	489	2 562 538	13.6	24.8	17.8	10.3	2.3	25.4	0.0
Dayton	176	1 277	133.1	38.3	1 940	9 617 585	13.2	22.8	17.4	11.8	4.6	25.3	0.0
Delaware	33	D	D	D	269	1 371 645	23.1	26.5	19.6	10.0	0.0	17.2	0.0
Dublin	34	D	D	D	836	2 882 615	15.9	35.7	0.0	4.5	15.6	11.3	0.0
Elyria	56	340	58.0	8.9	532	2 415 086	14.1	27.3	15.3	5.3	6.2	26.7	0.0
Euclid	50	149	11.5	3.3	454	1 882 329	12.3	36.1	22.3	4.1	5.6	15.3	0.0
Fairborn	38	187	15.5	4.8	222	557 607	20.8	22.1	26.3	4.5	1.3	11.4	0.0
Fairfield	82	590	60.6	17.0	340	1 631 218	20.0	30.2	17.2	8.1	0.0	22.3	0.0
Findlay	81	587	46.9	15.2	325	1 499 497	13.1	24.6	25.6	9.6	3.8	22.6	0.0
Gahanna	58	676	49.3	18.0	274	1 378 735	13.1	50.2	0.0	7.2	1.6	18.8	0.0
Garfield Heights	32	205	11.2	3.5	204	993 260	15.9	40.2	25.6	1.0	4.0	2.4	0.0
Green	41	531	92.4	27.9	131	615 958	19.2	0.0	49.5	27.4	0.0	2.9	0.0
Grove City	57	1 019	73.6	25.3	169	893 462	12.9	61.0	0.0	6.2	0.0	15.6	0.0

1. Establishments subject to federal tax.

Table D. Cities — City Government Finances

City	City government finances, 2012									
	General revenue							General expenditure		
		Intergovernmental		Taxes					Per capita[1] (dollars)	
					Per capita[1] (dollars)					
	Total (mil dol)	Total (mil dol)	Percent from state government	Total (mil dol)	Total	Property	Sales and gross receipts	Total (mil dol)	Total	Capital outlays
	117	118	119	120	121	122	123	124	125	126
NEW YORK—Cont'd										
Yonkers	973.8	463.3	98.2	426.2	2 146	1 487	460	967.5	4 872	267
NORTH CAROLINA ...	X	X	X	X	X	X	X	X	X	X
Apex	41.1	5.4	89.2	23.2	575	413	161	41.1	1 016	152
Asheboro	28.8	4.7	94.5	15.9	623	480	143	29.2	1 140	28
Asheville...................	115.3	28.1	51.3	66.5	775	542	233	121.5	1 415	244
Burlington	64.2	9.0	59.4	35.6	695	482	213	62.8	1 224	7
Cary..........................	187.2	16.9	75.1	100.1	687	482	205	218.0	1 496	577
Chapel Hill.................	80.0	23.1	43.6	48.5	826	614	212	68.9	1 174	154
Charlotte	1 401.8	250.6	43.7	622.1	803	489	314	1 294.8	1 671	438
Concord.....................	109.3	19.4	51.2	56.1	682	525	158	107.7	1 311	79
Durham.......................	303.7	47.0	61.0	171.9	717	538	179	302.6	1 262	129
Fayetteville	208.3	50.9	51.4	95.2	472	298	174	235.1	1 166	340
Garner	26.6	2.9	28.3	20.3	760	553	207	24.8	926	110
Gastonia	81.0	9.5	71.1	46.3	636	418	218	85.6	1 176	76
Goldsboro	41.9	6.6	92.5	22.8	633	417	216	47.0	1 303	68
Greensboro	371.9	60.4	63.7	196.6	711	528	183	412.3	1 492	244
Greenville	116.0	31.1	70.0	46.0	525	360	165	107.6	1 228	125
Hickory	61.0	10.1	62.0	33.9	844	579	265	60.2	1 500	170
High Point..................	158.5	22.3	59.1	81.9	768	572	196	167.5	1 571	282
Huntersville...............	34.2	5.5	74.2	22.2	450	329	122	35.6	722	217
Indian Trail	10.0	2.4	32.5	6.4	182	142	41	7.7	220	16
Jacksonville	66.3	10.7	56.8	31.8	458	272	186	75.1	1 079	221
Kannapolis..................	41.5	5.6	64.3	25.1	572	425	147	48.1	1 099	338
Matthews	20.9	3.5	73.5	14.5	506	361	145	19.8	691	109
Monroe	55.3	6.6	75.2	24.8	738	578	160	69.9	2 080	827
Mooresville	65.3	6.7	75.3	35.6	1 034	845	189	71.2	2 068	563
New Bern	44.8	7.8	87.0	19.3	636	440	196	43.0	1 416	135
Raleigh	555.4	92.1	53.9	287.3	679	448	231	527.4	1 245	199
Rocky Mount	82.1	24.8	46.4	31.3	549	385	164	81.9	1 437	161
Salisbury....................	55.5	5.3	90.5	21.9	656	510	146	64.5	1 931	175
Sanford	35.2	4.6	61.9	18.2	628	419	210	34.4	1 189	24
Thomasville	26.0	4.5	82.6	14.1	525	395	129	26.2	973	39
Wake Forest................	31.1	3.1	92.3	26.4	802	585	216	34.4	1 042	231
Wilmington..................	128.8	25.2	52.9	76.2	693	481	212	132.5	1 206	224
Wilson........................	71.8	10.0	67.7	27.6	557	410	147	70.7	1 427	69
Winston-Salem	293.3	50.8	63.3	139.2	594	431	163	303.3	1 294	272
NORTH DAKOTA.......	X	X	X	X	X	X	X	X	X	X
Bismarck.....................	128.3	46.0	40.5	37.1	571	261	310	118.8	1 827	623
Fargo	237.9	83.4	99.5	72.5	658	188	465	229.3	2 080	749
Grand Forks	100.1	20.7	28.9	38.0	709	279	430	59.4	1 106	129
Minot..........................	75.0	19.3	56.5	37.3	849	247	603	44.2	1 005	135
West Fargo..................	34.8	5.1	100.0	10.6	384	237	147	41.1	1 488	814
OHIO	X	X	X	X	X	X	X	X	X	X
Akron..........................	350.3	65.6	64.3	174.5	879	131	9	337.8	1 701	101
Barberton....................	31.7	6.9	86.9	14.0	533	53	31	30.8	1 170	202
Beavercreek	25.7	8.8	100.0	12.8	279	249	24	26.8	583	125
Bowling Green..............	36.0	6.4	100.0	21.2	667	71	53	36.9	1 161	103
Brunswick....................	26.4	4.7	51.4	15.9	463	47	13	22.8	662	108
Canton........................	118.3	36.4	85.3	46.7	642	37	21	113.3	1 558	208
Cincinnati....................	947.1	392.8	17.6	415.4	1 400	180	74	783.9	2 641	864
Cleveland	897.0	231.8	58.8	419.1	1 071	143	124	897.7	2 294	222
Cleveland Heights	55.8	10.6	84.0	31.9	699	210	54	57.2	1 254	119
Columbus	1 434.3	260.4	47.1	776.6	958	53	57	1 353.3	1 670	431
Cuyahoga Falls	65.4	9.3	91.5	31.4	637	219	19	59.4	1 207	245
Dayton........................	304.4	74.9	66.0	118.0	832	117	10	297.8	2 099	314
Delaware.....................	45.0	6.0	28.6	20.7	578	47	21	56.6	1 578	458
Dublin	103.4	5.5	100.0	74.6	1 739	85	61	90.8	2 117	497
Elyria	65.0	18.3	87.1	27.5	508	62	44	62.4	1 153	112
Euclid.........................	62.8	10.1	90.8	28.1	581	104	4	73.1	1 514	131
Fairborn......................	38.1	6.6	99.9	16.6	498	73	74	37.4	1 124	168
Fairfield......................	52.2	6.6	100.0	29.3	686	121	80	61.3	1 438	11
Findlay........................	47.4	7.7	100.0	24.9	599	67	8	43.6	1 050	149
Gahanna......................	35.0	5.1	65.6	19.0	562	61	37	38.9	1 150	171
Garfield Heights	34.7	4.5	59.7	21.3	748	365	31	32.2	1 130	3
Green	27.4	4.6	79.0	20.6	800	59	29	25.0	969	123
Grove City	38.4	8.3	45.2	24.0	651	84	43	33.8	917	213

1. Based on population estimated as of July 1 of the year shown.

City	City government finances, 2012 (cont.)									
	General expenditure (cont.)									
	Percent of total for:									
	Public welfare	Highways	Parking facilities	Education	Health and hospitals	Police protection	Sewerage and sanitation	Parks and recreation	Housing and community development	Interest on debt
	127	128	129	130	131	132	133	134	135	136
NEW YORK—Cont'd										
Yonkers	0.0	0.9	0.5	52.5	0.1	8.5	2.4	1.0	0.9	3.4
NORTH CAROLINA	X	X	X	X	X	X	X	X	X	X
Apex	0.0	9.5	0.0	0.0	2.8	16.4	27.0	10.3	2.5	2.0
Asheboro	0.0	8.3	0.0	0.0	0.1	21.9	25.3	5.2	4.4	0.7
Asheville	0.0	11.4	6.4	0.0	0.1	18.3	8.4	17.4	4.6	1.0
Burlington	0.0	3.6	0.0	0.0	0.0	23.7	18.2	9.5	2.5	2.6
Cary	0.0	5.6	0.0	0.0	0.0	10.3	37.2	10.3	1.6	2.8
Chapel Hill	0.0	7.2	2.8	0.0	0.0	17.7	7.9	9.7	8.4	3.6
Charlotte	0.0	9.3	0.1	0.0	0.0	19.2	21.6	2.2	6.0	10.5
Concord	0.0	5.4	0.0	0.0	0.0	16.5	22.1	5.5	14.1	2.4
Durham	0.0	10.6	0.6	0.0	0.0	20.7	18.7	6.5	7.1	5.9
Fayetteville	0.0	4.9	1.7	0.0	0.0	18.9	35.9	6.3	3.1	2.1
Garner	0.0	19.6	0.0	0.0	0.0	27.7	7.0	11.0	3.5	2.1
Gastonia	0.0	10.5	1.2	0.0	0.0	19.9	26.7	5.9	5.3	3.9
Goldsboro	0.0	9.3	0.0	0.0	0.0	21.0	16.1	5.8	8.1	2.6
Greensboro	0.0	9.9	0.4	0.0	0.1	17.5	24.6	17.5	4.9	2.7
Greenville	0.0	8.9	0.1	0.0	0.0	22.4	22.7	8.4	5.4	2.9
Hickory	0.0	10.0	0.0	0.0	0.1	18.2	21.0	5.9	0.9	0.8
High Point	0.0	8.3	0.2	0.0	0.0	15.8	29.1	8.4	4.3	4.7
Huntersville	0.0	24.6	0.0	0.0	1.1	36.8	1.5	16.6	4.1	3.6
Indian Trail	0.0	12.0	0.0	0.0	0.2	17.8	38.0	0.6	12.1	1.2
Jacksonville	0.0	5.6	0.0	0.0	0.0	20.5	39.6	8.4	2.4	3.8
Kannapolis	0.0	7.6	0.0	0.0	0.0	14.6	9.5	9.7	2.7	4.1
Matthews	0.0	12.0	0.0	0.0	0.0	32.5	9.0	16.0	2.3	1.5
Monroe	0.0	3.6	0.0	0.0	0.1	13.8	9.2	5.7	1.3	0.9
Mooresville	0.0	5.1	0.0	0.0	0.0	9.5	29.1	9.2	9.4	12.4
New Bern	0.0	7.7	0.0	0.0	0.0	30.7	26.9	5.0	4.4	3.1
Raleigh	0.2	6.1	1.7	0.0	0.0	19.1	14.8	23.5	4.8	5.4
Rocky Mount	0.0	9.3	0.0	0.0	0.0	18.5	26.3	9.8	4.8	1.0
Salisbury	0.0	7.1	0.0	0.0	0.0	10.8	24.8	3.7	1.0	4.6
Sanford	0.0	6.4	0.0	0.0	0.2	24.4	26.0	2.5	7.0	4.5
Thomasville	0.0	7.7	0.0	0.0	0.1	20.4	26.1	8.1	3.0	3.4
Wake Forest	0.0	17.8	0.0	0.0	0.0	19.6	7.2	10.3	0.0	2.7
Wilmington	0.0	10.5	2.9	0.0	0.0	20.7	15.0	8.1	1.1	7.7
Wilson	0.6	5.3	0.2	0.0	0.0	18.4	20.5	7.6	5.6	3.2
Winston-Salem	0.0	6.9	0.9	0.0	0.0	21.2	27.1	7.5	5.2	7.0
NORTH DAKOTA	X	X	X	X	X	X	X	X	X	X
Bismarck	0.0	24.2	0.9	0.0	2.1	9.9	17.2	6.8	0.7	2.1
Fargo	4.1	24.0	0.3	0.0	0.0	12.3	6.2	5.9	0.9	7.6
Grand Forks	0.0	6.9	0.6	0.0	2.9	14.2	20.7	2.9	5.6	13.8
Minot	0.0	12.9	0.3	0.0	0.0	16.1	18.8	4.7	0.0	1.5
West Fargo	0.0	39.8	0.0	0.0	0.0	11.7	25.6	0.8	0.0	9.2
OHIO	X	X	X	X	X	X	X	X	X	X
Akron	0.0	2.5	1.8	0.0	1.6	10.0	12.3	1.6	3.3	7.7
Barberton	0.0	7.0	0.0	0.0	0.0	16.3	30.7	3.3	3.5	1.0
Beavercreek	0.0	39.4	0.0	0.0	0.6	27.4	0.0	12.8	2.3	3.6
Bowling Green	0.0	18.5	0.0	0.0	0.2	14.7	20.9	5.0	0.0	3.1
Brunswick	0.0	16.1	0.0	0.0	0.4	28.0	10.3	6.3	1.3	1.4
Canton	0.0	11.9	0.3	0.0	5.6	18.0	15.3	1.7	0.0	0.9
Cincinnati	0.0	7.1	1.4	0.0	3.5	14.5	34.1	4.3	5.1	2.9
Cleveland	1.2	3.1	0.7	0.0	4.6	19.2	6.3	4.4	9.1	9.8
Cleveland Heights	0.0	12.2	1.9	0.0	2.4	15.6	7.3	6.2	7.6	1.5
Columbus	0.0	9.9	0.2	0.0	2.8	18.9	20.2	10.2	2.3	6.4
Cuyahoga Falls	0.0	8.0	0.0	0.0	0.0	15.5	16.0	12.1	2.4	2.6
Dayton	0.8	8.7	0.0	0.0	0.0	14.5	12.3	2.9	7.3	0.8
Delaware	0.0	8.1	0.1	0.0	0.0	10.0	11.3	20.5	0.8	7.8
Dublin	0.0	5.5	0.0	0.0	0.3	11.4	6.9	18.8	0.0	2.5
Elyria	0.0	9.1	0.0	0.0	5.9	20.7	28.4	3.7	2.1	2.2
Euclid	0.0	2.8	0.0	0.0	0.5	15.6	17.9	2.5	1.4	1.9
Fairborn	0.0	14.7	0.0	0.0	0.0	15.7	20.6	0.7	1.8	2.3
Fairfield	0.0	27.4	0.0	0.0	0.0	16.3	11.4	7.3	0.0	2.2
Findlay	0.0	12.0	0.2	0.0	4.9	14.8	17.2	3.5	0.0	3.6
Gahanna	0.0	13.2	0.2	0.0	2.8	22.0	20.7	10.3	0.0	2.6
Garfield Heights	0.8	3.9	0.0	0.0	1.6	0.6	19.0	5.9	2.2	0.4	4.5
Green	0.0	27.0	0.0	0.0	3.3	7.4	0.7	5.3	0.0	7.8
Grove City	0.0	24.3	0.0	0.0	0.0	28.2	2.0	7.8	0.0	4.8

Table D. Cities — **City Government Finances, City Government Employment, and Climate**

City	City government finances, 2012 (cont.) Debt outstanding Total (mil dol)	Per capita[1] (dollars)	Debt issued during year	Climate[2] Average daily temperature (degrees Fahrenheit) Mean January	July	Limits January[3]	July[4]	Annual precipitation (inches)	Heating degree days	Cooling degree days
	137	138	139	140	141	142	143	144	145	146
NEW YORK—Cont'd										
Yonkers	757.7	3 815	113.7	29.7	74.2	20.1	86.0	46.46	5 400	770
NORTH CAROLINA	NA	NA	NA	X	X	X	X	X	X	X
Apex	63.3	1 566	35.0	NA	NA	NA	NA	NA	NA	NA
Asheboro	9.3	363	0.0	NA	NA	NA	NA	NA	NA	NA
Asheville	110.4	1 286	39.2	36.4	73.9	26.6	84.3	37.32	4 237	877
Burlington	62.0	1 208	18.4	38.7	79.3	27.6	90.6	45.08	3 588	1 489
Cary	243.8	1 672	11.3	39.5	78.7	30.1	87.9	46.49	3 431	1 456
Chapel Hill	60.5	1 030	33.5	38.5	79.4	27.8	88.6	48.04	3 650	1 491
Charlotte	3 227.6	4 165	470.5	41.7	80.3	32.1	90.1	43.51	3 162	1 681
Concord	100.3	1 221	19.4	39.4	79.2	27.9	90.3	47.30	3 463	1 540
Durham	398.4	1 661	15.6	39.7	78.8	29.6	89.1	43.05	3 465	1 521
Fayetteville	204.6	1 014	10.6	41.7	80.4	31.1	90.4	46.78	3 097	1 721
Garner	13.9	520	0.0	NA	NA	NA	NA	NA	NA	NA
Gastonia	94.3	1 295	6.0	42.0	79.9	31.7	89.9	49.19	3 009	1 701
Goldsboro	50.9	1 411	14.3	43.4	81.2	33.0	91.4	49.84	2 771	1 922
Greensboro	443.1	1 603	48.7	39.7	78.6	29.0	88.9	42.89	3 443	1 438
Greenville	143.1	1 633	4.3	42.0	78.8	31.9	88.4	49.30	3 113	1 516
Hickory	38.0	947	3.4	39.0	77.7	29.2	87.8	48.98	3 608	1 333
High Point	267.0	2 504	53.4	39.7	78.2	29.6	89.0	46.19	3 399	1 424
Huntersville	41.4	839	24.3	NA	NA	NA	NA	NA	NA	NA
Indian Trail	2.4	69	0.0	NA	NA	NA	NA	NA	NA	NA
Jacksonville	103.2	1 484	51.6	44.7	80.2	33.9	89.5	54.07	2 656	1 832
Kannapolis	67.9	1 550	17.0	39.4	79.2	27.9	90.3	47.30	3 463	1 540
Matthews	6.0	211	0.0	NA	NA	NA	NA	NA	NA	NA
Monroe	59.6	1 773	2.8	41.5	79.0	31.0	89.7	48.73	3 125	1 538
Mooresville	220.0	6 392	65.4	NA	NA	NA	NA	NA	NA	NA
New Bern	76.1	2 504	3.5	NA	NA	NA	NA	NA	NA	NA
Raleigh	1 004.7	2 373	218.5	39.1	79.4	28.1	89.9	45.70	3 514	1 550
Rocky Mount	10.0	175	2.4	41.1	79.2	30.8	89.7	46.51	3 215	1 518
Salisbury	81.1	2 426	8.3	40.2	78.7	29.5	89.5	42.86	3 356	1 466
Sanford	51.3	1 774	0.0	NA	NA	NA	NA	NA	NA	NA
Thomasville	42.9	1 594	11.3	NA	NA	NA	NA	NA	NA	NA
Wake Forest	32.8	993	6.3	NA	NA	NA	NA	NA	NA	NA
Wilmington	205.6	1 872	30.7	44.8	80.1	33.3	90.0	58.44	2 606	1 791
Wilson	113.0	2 279	12.2	40.4	79.2	29.5	90.2	47.18	3 328	1 575
Winston-Salem	727.7	3 105	38.5	39.7	78.2	29.6	89.0	46.19	3 399	1 424
NORTH DAKOTA	X	X	X	X	X	X	X	X	X	X
Bismarck	97.9	1 506	12.3	10.2	70.4	-0.6	84.5	16.84	8 802	471
Fargo	566.3	5 136	79.8	6.8	70.6	-2.3	82.2	21.19	9 092	533
Grand Forks	382.8	7 136	24.1	5.3	69.4	-4.3	81.9	19.60	9 489	420
Minot	41.8	952	7.0	7.5	68.4	-1.8	80.4	18.65	9 479	422
West Fargo	120.7	4 372	17.9	NA	NA	NA	NA	NA	NA	NA
OHIO	X	X	X	X	X	X	X	X	X	X
Akron	794.0	3 998	96.9	27.2	74.1	20.1	83.9	36.07	5 752	856
Barberton	16.6	631	0.0	29.1	73.6	20.3	85.0	39.16	5 348	813
Beavercreek	12.0	260	4.2	27.6	73.1	19.5	83.5	40.06	5 531	768
Bowling Green	24.2	761	3.4	23.1	72.9	15.2	84.2	33.18	6 492	690
Brunswick	11.1	322	0.4	25.7	71.9	18.8	81.4	38.71	6 121	702
Canton	20.1	276	0.0	25.2	71.8	17.4	82.3	38.47	6 154	678
Cincinnati	917.4	3 091	175.8	30.6	76.8	22.7	86.8	39.57	4 841	1 210
Cleveland	2 530.4	6 465	194.4	25.7	71.9	18.8	81.4	38.71	6 121	702
Cleveland Heights	18.6	407	0.0	25.7	71.9	18.8	81.4	38.71	6 121	702
Columbus	2 555.4	3 153	190.4	28.3	74.7	20.2	85.6	40.03	5 349	935
Cuyahoga Falls	55.8	1 133	3.3	29.1	73.6	20.3	85.0	39.16	5 348	813
Dayton	131.3	926	0.2	26.3	74.3	19.0	84.2	39.58	5 690	935
Delaware	89.4	2 492	2.2	25.1	73.0	16.6	84.6	37.58	6 178	739
Dublin	57.2	1 334	0.0	28.3	74.7	20.2	85.6	40.03	5 349	935
Elyria	50.5	934	13.2	27.1	73.8	19.3	85.0	38.02	5 731	818
Euclid	40.5	839	19.4	23.0	68.8	14.3	80.0	47.33	6 956	372
Fairborn	21.9	657	0.0	27.9	77.0	20.6	87.2	39.41	5 343	1 214
Fairfield	32.0	750	0.0	28.7	76.6	19.9	88.1	43.36	5 261	1 135
Findlay	18.2	439	2.7	24.5	73.6	17.4	83.5	36.91	6 194	809
Gahanna	26.3	777	5.8	28.3	75.1	20.3	85.3	38.52	5 492	951
Garfield Heights	27.3	959	0.0	25.7	71.9	18.8	81.4	38.71	6 121	702
Green	58.3	2 261	7.2	NA	NA	NA	NA	NA	NA	NA
Grove City	35.9	973	0.0	28.3	74.7	20.2	85.6	40.03	5 349	935

1. Based on the population estimated as of July 1 of the year shown.   2. Represents normal values based on the 30-year period, 1971–2000.   3. Average daily minimum.
4. Average daily maximum.

Table D. Cities — Land Area and Population

STATE Place code	City	Land area,[1] 2010 (sq km)	Population, 2015			Race alone or in combination (percent), 2010-2014					Percent Hispanic or Latino,[2] 2010-2014	Percent foreign born 2010-2014
			Total persons	Rank	Per square kilometer	White	Black	American Indian, Alaska Native	Asian	Hawaiian Pacific Islander		
		1	2	3	4	5	6	7	8	9	10	11
	OHIO—Cont'd											
39 33012	Hamilton	55.9	62 407	577	1 116.4	88.7	10.4	0.8	0.7	0.0	5.5	3.6
39 35476	Hilliard	34.1	33 649	1 115	986.8	90.7	3.6	0.4	6.7	0.2	1.9	6.1
39 36610	Huber Heights	57.7	38 176	982	661.6	83.6	16.1	1.7	2.8	0.3	3.6	3.5
39 39872	Kent	23.8	29 810	1 250	1 252.5	83.7	13.2	0.5	6.1	0.1	1.8	6.5
39 40040	Kettering	48.4	55 525	673	1 147.2	94.6	3.8	0.5	2.3	0.0	2.2	3.4
39 41664	Lakewood	14.3	50 656	744	3 542.4	90.9	9.6	0.8	2.1	0.2	4.1	8.1
39 41720	Lancaster	48.8	39 766	942	814.9	97.4	1.8	0.9	0.9	0.0	1.6	1.5
39 43554	Lima	35.1	37 873	995	1 079.0	71.5	30.3	1.3	0.6	0.0	2.9	1.0
39 44856	Lorain	61.3	63 647	565	1 038.3	76.3	20.5	1.8	1.6	0.1	26.7	3.0
39 47138	Mansfield	80.0	46 830	807	585.4	77.5	25.1	2.2	0.5	0.1	2.2	1.5
39 47754	Marion	30.4	36 363	1 033	1 196.2	87.6	11.5	1.1	0.6	0.0	3.2	1.4
39 48188	Mason	48.3	32 662	1 150	676.2	84.2	5.0	0.7	11.1	0.0	4.6	11.2
39 48244	Massillon	48.1	32 252	1 168	670.5	91.1	11.3	0.4	0.2	0.0	2.4	1.1
39 48790	Medina	30.0	26 339	1 385	878.0	93.9	5.2	0.6	1.6	0.1	1.7	2.5
39 49056	Mentor	69.0	46 901	806	679.7	96.8	1.8	0.3	1.6	0.0	1.0	3.7
39 49840	Middletown	67.8	48 760	777	719.2	85.1	13.2	1.3	1.7	0.1	4.3	3.2
39 54040	Newark	54.1	47 986	788	887.0	95.4	5.9	1.7	0.9	0.0	1.3	1.2
39 56882	North Olmsted	30.2	32 004	1 178	1 059.7	93.6	3.2	0.6	3.5	0.0	4.0	8.1
39 56966	North Ridgeville	60.7	32 483	1 158	535.1	96.0	2.1	0.3	1.7	0.0	3.7	4.6
39 57008	North Royalton	55.2	30 311	1 234	549.1	94.4	2.5	0.5	3.8	0.0	1.9	9.5
39 61000	Parma	51.9	79 937	420	1 540.2	94.3	3.6	0.8	2.3	0.1	5.1	10.1
39 66390	Reynoldsburg	28.9	37 158	1 016	1 285.7	71.7	26.8	0.8	4.0	0.3	4.5	6.8
39 67468	Riverside	25.2	24 972	1 420	991.0	91.4	7.0	1.0	2.2	0.0	3.5	3.1
39 70380	Sandusky	25.2	25 212	1 413	1 000.5	75.5	25.9	1.5	0.6	0.4	5.6	2.3
39 71682	Shaker Heights	16.3	27 646	1 335	1 696.1	57.8	36.4	1.1	7.7	0.0	2.5	8.9
39 74118	Springfield	65.5	59 680	615	911.1	78.9	21.9	1.0	1.0	0.1	3.2	2.5
39 74944	Stow	44.3	34 797	1 079	785.5	95.4	3.0	0.5	2.6	0.1	1.2	4.2
39 75098	Strongsville	63.8	44 668	837	700.1	90.9	3.4	0.3	5.4	0.2	2.6	7.8
39 77000	Toledo	209.0	279 789	71	1 338.7	68.8	29.7	1.2	1.7	0.2	7.6	3.4
39 77588	Troy	30.4	25 659	1 405	844.0	92.7	6.0	0.8	3.0	0.0	2.1	3.0
39 79002	Upper Arlington	25.5	34 907	1 074	1 368.9	93.8	1.7	0.4	5.6	0.0	2.8	7.6
39 80892	Warren	41.8	40 245	933	962.8	68.2	33.9	0.7	0.5	0.0	2.6	1.8
39 83342	Westerville	32.3	38 384	976	1 188.4	89.5	9.0	0.3	3.9	0.1	2.0	5.4
39 83622	Westlake	41.3	32 428	1 160	785.2	91.8	2.9	0.1	6.8	0.0	3.4	9.4
39 86548	Wooster	42.2	26 749	1 369	633.9	92.9	5.2	1.0	2.6	0.2	2.5	4.1
39 86772	Xenia	34.4	25 976	1 398	755.1	84.0	17.1	1.2	1.1	0.1	1.5	1.7
39 88000	Youngstown	87.9	64 628	553	735.2	52.7	47.0	1.5	0.8	0.1	10.0	4.2
39 88084	Zanesville	30.5	25 498	1 408	836.0	91.8	12.5	1.9	0.2	0.1	1.0	1.1
40 00000	OKLAHOMA	177 660.0	3 911 338	X	22.0	80.4	8.9	13.3	2.4	0.2	9.4	5.6
40 04450	Bartlesville	58.9	36 595	1 029	621.3	85.6	4.5	12.6	2.2	0.0	5.9	4.1
40 09050	Broken Arrow	159.5	106 563	279	668.1	86.9	5.9	10.2	4.2	0.2	6.9	5.8
40 23200	Edmond	219.4	90 092	350	410.6	86.2	7.1	5.5	4.5	0.4	5.0	6.6
40 23950	Enid	190.8	51 776	729	271.4	85.5	5.2	4.0	1.5	2.5	11.5	8.1
40 41850	Lawton	209.9	96 655	313	460.5	67.3	24.5	8.1	4.7	1.1	14.0	6.4
40 48350	Midwest City	63.2	57 249	644	905.8	72.3	23.1	8.1	2.7	0.4	6.7	3.8
40 49200	Moore	56.5	60 451	603	1 069.9	86.9	6.6	10.0	4.0	0.4	10.4	5.0
40 50050	Muskogee	109.8	38 456	973	350.2	67.5	18.2	19.7	1.2	0.0	7.4	4.0
40 52500	Norman	463.0	120 284	226	259.8	86.4	5.4	7.3	5.0	0.3	6.5	6.5
40 55000	Oklahoma City	1 570.6	631 346	27	402.0	72.9	17.0	7.7	4.9	0.2	18.0	12.4
40 56650	Owasso	42.2	34 542	1 089	818.5	85.4	3.7	13.1	3.2	0.0	6.7	3.8
40 59850	Ponca City	47.6	24 758	1 424	520.1	85.2	4.6	14.0	1.2	0.1	7.0	2.9
40 66800	Shawnee	114.3	31 286	1 188	273.7	80.1	5.8	19.7	1.3	0.1	5.9	2.2
40 70300	Stillwater	76.5	48 967	772	640.1	83.7	6.3	7.6	7.7	0.1	4.6	8.8
40 75000	Tulsa	509.6	403 505	47	791.8	72.0	17.9	9.5	3.1	0.2	14.8	10.1
41 00000	OREGON	248 607.8	4 028 977	X	16.2	88.6	2.6	2.9	5.2	0.7	12.1	9.8
41 01000	Albany	45.4	52 175	723	1 149.2	92.2	1.5	3.1	3.4	0.3	12.0	5.9
41 05350	Beaverton	48.5	96 577	314	1 991.3	76.7	3.3	1.9	14.4	0.9	15.8	20.4
41 05800	Bend	85.5	87 014	375	1 017.7	94.2	1.3	1.2	2.7	0.6	8.2	5.1
41 15800	Corvallis	36.6	55 780	666	1 524.0	88.3	1.7	1.4	9.9	0.5	7.7	11.5
41 23850	Eugene	113.2	163 460	154	1 444.0	90.0	2.6	2.9	6.2	0.9	8.4	8.1
41 30550	Grants Pass	28.2	37 088	1 017	1 315.2	95.1	0.9	3.4	2.1	0.7	9.8	3.2
41 31250	Gresham	60.1	110 553	257	1 839.5	82.8	5.1	2.6	6.1	2.0	19.0	17.6
41 34100	Hillsboro	61.9	102 347	294	1 653.4	77.4	2.8	3.0	10.9	1.7	24.1	19.6
41 38500	Keizer	18.4	37 895	993	2 059.5	91.1	1.6	3.3	2.4	0.7	20.4	9.5
41 40550	Lake Oswego	27.7	38 496	972	1 389.7	91.0	1.0	0.9	8.3	0.5	4.0	11.3
41 45000	McMinnville	27.4	33 892	1 109	1 236.9	87.3	2.4	2.8	3.2	0.4	21.8	12.6
41 47000	Medford	66.7	79 805	423	1 196.5	94.3	1.7	2.5	2.8	1.0	13.4	7.0
41 55200	Oregon City	23.5	35 831	1 055	1 524.7	93.4	1.2	2.2	2.4	0.1	9.2	5.7
41 59000	Portland	345.6	632 309	26	1 829.6	81.4	7.5	2.4	9.3	0.8	9.6	14.0

1. Dry land or land partially or temporarily covered by water.   2. May be of any race.

Table D. Cities — **Population**

City	Age of population (percent), 2010-2014									Median age 2010–2014	Percent female 2010–2014	Population			
	Under 5 years	5 to 17 years	18 to 24 years	25 to 34 years	35 to 44 years	45 to 54 years	55 to 64 years	65 to 74 years	75 years and over			Census counts		Percent change	
												2000	2010	2000–2010	2010–2015
	12	13	14	15	16	17	18	19	20	21	22	23	24	25	26
OHIO—Cont'd															
Hamilton	8.0	16.5	9.2	14.4	12.3	14.6	12.2	6.1	6.7	37.0	54.1	60 690	62 477	2.9	0.2
Hilliard	6.3	23.5	6.3	11.6	14.5	17.8	10.0	5.5	4.6	37.3	52.0	24 230	28 435	17.4	19.2
Huber Heights	7.4	19.2	7.6	14.8	11.7	13.6	12.1	8.7	4.9	35.6	52.6	38 212	38 101	-0.3	0.2
Kent	4.0	10.1	42.6	13.2	6.8	6.8	8.2	4.5	3.7	23.0	52.6	27 906	28 904	3.6	3.1
Kettering	5.2	16.3	7.9	14.3	11.3	14.5	12.9	8.7	9.0	40.6	51.9	57 502	56 163	-2.3	-1.1
Lakewood	5.8	13.5	9.2	21.4	12.8	14.0	11.9	5.7	5.7	35.0	51.7	56 646	52 131	-8.0	-2.8
Lancaster	6.1	17.0	9.7	13.8	12.2	12.8	12.5	8.1	7.7	38.2	52.0	35 335	38 780	9.7	2.5
Lima	7.5	18.8	14.1	13.3	11.2	12.8	11.3	5.9	5.3	32.4	47.8	40 081	38 771	-3.3	-2.2
Lorain	5.9	19.9	8.7	11.4	12.6	14.6	11.9	7.8	7.1	37.9	53.5	68 652	64 097	-6.6	-0.7
Mansfield	6.1	14.4	9.5	14.8	12.5	13.3	12.3	8.2	8.9	39.0	47.0	49 346	47 821	-3.1	-2.1
Marion	6.4	14.5	10.3	14.9	14.2	15.1	12.0	6.9	5.8	38.4	41.6	35 318	36 837	4.3	-1.3
Mason	5.5	23.8	5.7	9.8	14.0	18.5	10.6	6.7	5.3	39.9	53.1	22 016	30 712	39.5	5.8
Massillon	6.6	16.1	8.5	13.7	10.1	13.1	15.3	8.1	8.5	40.8	50.5	31 325	32 149	2.6	0.2
Medina	7.2	21.3	8.0	10.0	14.9	15.8	10.8	5.2	6.8	37.6	53.3	25 139	26 678	6.1	-1.2
Mentor	5.6	14.9	6.4	10.5	11.8	17.9	15.8	9.7	7.4	45.9	51.6	50 278	47 159	-6.2	-0.5
Middletown	8.1	15.9	9.9	13.2	11.1	13.9	12.6	9.1	6.3	37.5	51.7	51 605	48 694	-5.6	0.2
Newark	7.4	17.9	8.9	13.5	12.7	13.2	11.9	8.1	6.6	36.8	52.0	46 279	47 573	2.8	0.9
North Olmsted	5.0	16.3	6.2	10.9	12.4	15.0	15.3	10.3	8.7	44.5	51.4	34 113	32 718	-4.1	-2.2
North Ridgeville	7.5	15.3	5.1	11.9	13.9	15.6	13.6	10.9	6.1	41.5	49.7	22 338	29 465	31.9	10.2
North Royalton	3.9	16.8	6.1	12.6	12.5	17.7	14.7	7.4	8.4	43.8	51.5	28 648	30 444	6.3	-0.4
Parma	5.7	14.2	9.8	12.5	11.4	15.4	13.0	8.4	9.5	42.2	51.8	85 655	81 601	-4.7	-2.0
Reynoldsburg	5.9	18.7	10.5	13.5	12.7	15.0	11.7	7.2	4.9	36.3	52.0	32 069	35 893	11.9	3.5
Riverside	6.6	17.8	10.8	13.6	12.4	13.4	11.9	6.7	6.8	36.1	48.9	23 545	25 201	7.0	-0.9
Sandusky	6.4	14.7	8.2	16.2	8.9	14.1	14.8	9.0	7.7	39.2	51.1	27 844	25 793	-7.4	-2.7
Shaker Heights	6.0	19.3	6.5	11.0	13.3	13.9	13.9	7.9	8.0	41.3	54.3	29 405	28 448	-3.3	-2.8
Springfield	7.5	17.3	11.4	12.3	10.7	12.6	12.9	7.7	7.5	36.6	52.6	65 358	60 608	-7.3	-1.5
Stow	5.6	16.4	7.7	13.9	11.7	14.5	14.2	8.1	7.8	40.8	53.7	32 139	34 837	8.4	-0.1
Strongsville	4.9	17.5	6.2	9.1	12.4	16.8	15.2	9.7	8.2	44.9	51.2	43 858	44 750	2.0	-0.2
Toledo	6.9	16.4	12.1	14.3	11.9	13.7	12.0	6.5	6.2	35.3	51.0	313 619	287 208	-8.4	-2.6
Troy	4.7	19.0	7.9	14.2	14.1	13.6	12.0	8.7	5.8	39.1	51.1	21 999	25 058	13.9	1.7
Upper Arlington	6.5	19.7	5.1	11.1	13.6	14.5	13.8	8.1	7.5	41.2	51.7	33 686	33 771	0.3	3.6
Warren	6.6	16.5	9.1	13.0	11.7	14.1	11.9	8.4	8.7	39.5	52.7	46 832	41 557	-11.3	-3.2
Westerville	4.4	16.6	11.7	8.8	13.5	14.9	14.6	8.6	6.9	41.3	52.7	35 318	36 120	2.3	6.3
Westlake	5.1	17.5	4.6	10.4	13.2	15.1	15.0	8.9	10.2	44.1	53.8	31 719	32 729	3.2	-0.9
Wooster	6.8	12.9	17.7	13.8	10.2	9.8	11.9	9.6	7.4	34.3	51.9	24 811	26 119	5.3	2.4
Xenia	7.9	18.9	6.3	16.7	11.8	11.4	11.4	8.3	7.3	35.2	52.7	24 164	25 719	6.4	1.2
Youngstown	6.6	15.9	11.6	11.5	11.4	13.7	13.8	6.6	8.9	39.4	51.4	82 026	66 982	-18.3	-3.5
Zanesville	8.7	17.4	9.5	15.9	9.1	13.7	10.7	7.6	7.3	33.5	50.9	25 586	25 487	-0.4	0.1
OKLAHOMA	6.9	17.7	10.2	13.6	12.2	13.2	12.1	7.9	6.1	36.2	50.5	3 450 654	3 751 351	8.7	4.3
Bartlesville	7.2	16.6	9.4	12.5	11.8	11.8	13.0	9.3	8.4	38.5	52.3	34 748	35 750	2.9	2.4
Broken Arrow	7.1	19.3	8.1	13.2	13.8	14.8	12.5	6.8	4.5	36.9	50.8	74 859	98 850	32.0	7.8
Edmond	6.1	18.4	11.8	12.5	12.2	14.6	12.2	7.3	4.8	35.8	50.7	68 315	81 405	19.2	10.7
Enid	7.9	16.6	9.6	14.7	10.6	13.0	12.1	7.7	7.9	36.2	51.2	47 045	49 379	5.0	4.9
Lawton	8.2	16.6	15.2	17.9	11.7	11.5	9.3	5.3	4.4	30.1	47.8	92 757	96 867	4.4	-0.2
Midwest City	6.4	17.8	9.5	14.7	13.0	13.6	11.5	6.6	6.9	36.1	52.5	54 088	54 371	0.5	5.3
Moore	7.4	19.3	10.2	18.8	12.4	13.7	9.8	5.3	3.1	32.2	51.8	41 138	55 081	33.9	9.7
Muskogee	7.8	18.5	10.1	12.8	10.9	12.6	12.3	8.1	6.8	35.7	53.1	38 310	39 223	2.4	-2.0
Norman	5.7	14.2	21.3	15.1	11.0	10.8	10.4	6.5	4.9	30.4	50.0	95 694	110 925	15.9	8.4
Oklahoma City	8.0	17.7	9.7	16.6	12.6	12.7	11.5	6.2	5.0	33.6	50.7	506 132	579 999	14.6	8.9
Owasso	5.8	23.3	8.3	13.3	17.4	13.1	8.9	5.7	4.1	34.6	50.8	18 502	28 915	56.3	16.2
Ponca City	7.6	18.3	8.9	12.2	10.9	12.2	12.5	8.4	8.9	37.2	50.8	25 919	25 387	-2.1	-2.5
Shawnee	8.8	16.3	14.1	12.4	11.1	11.6	11.4	7.3	7.1	33.6	52.0	28 692	29 857	4.1	4.8
Stillwater	5.3	10.6	38.4	13.7	8.0	8.1	7.1	4.7	4.1	23.7	50.1	39 065	45 688	17.0	7.2
Tulsa	7.6	16.9	10.6	15.2	12.0	13.0	12.0	6.8	6.0	34.9	51.5	393 049	391 906	-0.3	3.0
OREGON	6.0	16.1	9.4	13.6	13.0	13.4	13.7	8.5	6.4	38.9	50.5	3 421 399	3 831 074	12.0	5.2
Albany	6.8	18.5	8.8	15.1	13.2	12.5	12.0	7.7	5.5	35.6	49.6	40 852	50 158	22.8	4.0
Beaverton	6.3	17.1	8.7	18.0	15.0	12.9	11.2	6.2	4.6	35.0	51.6	76 129	89 803	18.0	7.5
Bend	6.6	16.7	7.8	14.5	14.2	13.1	12.7	8.0	6.4	38.4	50.9	52 029	76 639	47.3	13.5
Corvallis	4.4	10.2	32.2	12.9	9.9	9.6	9.9	5.4	5.6	27.0	49.2	49 322	54 462	10.4	2.4
Eugene	4.7	12.8	20.0	13.7	11.9	11.3	12.1	7.2	6.2	34.1	50.8	137 893	156 185	13.3	4.5
Grants Pass	6.9	16.6	8.6	11.7	10.3	13.8	11.8	9.3	11.2	40.9	53.3	23 003	34 533	50.1	3.4
Gresham	7.7	18.6	10.2	14.6	12.2	14.0	11.2	5.9	5.6	34.4	50.3	90 205	105 594	17.1	4.7
Hillsboro	8.5	18.0	8.6	18.8	15.9	12.6	9.2	5.1	3.2	32.7	51.7	70 186	91 611	30.5	11.1
Keizer	7.5	19.0	8.8	15.5	11.1	12.3	11.3	7.6	6.8	34.6	51.8	32 203	36 478	13.3	3.9
Lake Oswego	4.5	17.4	6.1	8.9	13.3	15.1	16.6	10.6	7.4	44.9	52.9	35 278	36 619	3.8	5.0
McMinnville	7.1	19.4	11.9	11.9	10.9	11.9	10.7	7.8	8.4	34.9	53.2	26 499	32 187	21.5	5.3
Medford	7.3	16.1	9.4	14.6	11.1	12.8	11.8	7.7	9.1	37.4	50.4	63 154	74 907	18.6	6.5
Oregon City	6.0	19.6	8.1	13.2	14.6	16.0	11.9	6.5	4.0	37.5	50.4	25 754	31 859	23.7	9.8
Portland	5.8	12.8	9.0	19.7	16.7	12.9	12.2	6.3	4.7	36.4	50.5	529 121	583 776	10.3	8.3

Table D. Cities — Households, Group Quarters, Crime, and Education

City	Households, 2010-2014				Persons in group quarters, 2010				Serious crimes known to police,[2] 2014				Educational attainment, 2010–2014		
			Percent			Institutional			Total		Rate[3]			Attainment[4] (percent)	
	Number	Persons per house-hold	Female family house-holder[1]	One-person	Total	Total	Persons in nursing facilities	Non-institu-tional	Number	Rate[3]	Violent	Property	Population age 25 and older	High school graduate or less	Bachelor's degree or more
	27	28	29	30	31	32	33	34	35	36	37	38	39	40	41

OHIO—Cont'd

City	27	28	29	30	31	32	33	34	35	36	37	38	39	40	41
Hamilton	24 168	2.58	17.6	30.7	1 663	1 354	436	309	1 168	1 877	169	1 708	41 087	59.3	15.1
Hilliard	10 937	2.82	9.1	20.9	155	155	155	0	NA	NA	NA	NA	19 706	25.7	47.9
Huber Heights	15 159	2.54	15.8	26.7	184	64	64	120	1 235	3 238	197	3 042	25 878	37.4	23.4
Kent	9 839	2.98	12.8	27.8	6 067	81	81	5 986	654	2 007	233	1 774	12 835	29.6	42.3
Kettering	25 340	2.22	11.1	37.3	427	304	304	123	1 132	2 029	95	1 934	40 107	32.9	31.3
Lakewood	24 573	2.09	10.9	45.1	370	304	303	66	824	1 618	130	1 489	36 287	29.6	41.5
Lancaster	16 186	2.42	12.9	34.2	871	692	383	179	1 858	4 709	276	4 433	26 422	55.0	16.2
Lima	14 125	2.72	23.3	34.4	4 300	3 401	279	899	2 221	5 804	923	4 882	22 958	57.7	10.8
Lorain	25 562	2.50	21.0	32.2	662	444	423	218	2 876	4 521	384	4 137	41 715	55.7	12.1
Mansfield	18 179	2.59	16.5	39.3	6 594	5 881	519	713	3 421	7 414	466	6 948	33 125	57.9	12.9
Marion	12 536	2.93	16.0	30.7	5 267	5 112	363	155	1 666	4 531	286	4 246	25 056	60.8	9.8
Mason	11 112	2.82	8.0	21.9	186	76	76	110	393	1 251	35	1 216	20 019	23.6	54.5
Massillon	13 127	2.45	13.8	33.4	951	683	348	268	1 197	3 718	267	3 451	22 137	54.0	15.7
Medina	10 266	2.59	12.3	28.2	361	345	186	16	72	153	6	147	16 894	36.8	32.3
Mentor	19 230	2.44	9.1	26.9	403	381	381	22	118	251	6	245	34 472	35.5	31.3
Middletown	19 631	2.46	15.9	32.7	573	472	399	101	4 088	8 411	638	7 773	32 010	59.2	16.0
Newark	19 719	2.42	15.0	33.6	1 011	750	486	261	2 361	4 939	153	4 786	31 467	53.5	16.7
North Olmsted	13 462	2.40	10.0	30.2	323	264	264	59	NA	NA	NA	NA	24 031	35.2	30.5
North Ridgeville	11 954	2.57	9.2	25.4	225	213	213	12	237	747	35	713	21 651	38.3	27.6
North Royalton	12 511	2.43	7.9	29.6	247	226	226	21	NA	NA	NA	NA	22 480	34.2	36.0
Parma	33 400	2.42	12.9	32.7	1 063	897	792	166	1 293	1 613	85	1 528	56 985	47.7	19.6
Reynoldsburg	14 216	2.56	15.3	27.7	25	0	0	25	1 208	3 294	155	3 139	23 599	37.0	29.6
Riverside	10 213	2.46	15.4	29.4	0	0	0	0	632	2 521	203	2 318	16 666	48.0	15.7
Sandusky	11 432	2.24	17.6	41.0	579	305	240	274	1 120	4 438	289	4 149	17 531	55.5	15.2
Shaker Heights	11 447	2.45	13.7	30.0	156	119	44	37	272	978	32	945	19 331	14.5	65.8
Springfield	24 449	2.46	18.9	35.9	2 497	1 128	854	1 369	4 680	7 947	751	7 196	38 502	55.5	15.3
Stow	13 978	2.49	7.8	28.5	454	405	405	49	687	1 977	69	1 908	24 113	30.6	40.5
Strongsville	17 403	2.57	6.7	25.5	304	277	264	27	782	1 748	92	1 657	31 824	28.5	43.9
Toledo	117 785	2.41	19.3	36.4	8 475	2 987	1 239	5 488	8 708	3 097	1 091	2 006	182 725	49.1	17.7
Troy	10 415	2.43	13.2	29.6	420	263	163	157	934	3 663	161	3 502	17 589	48.4	22.0
Upper Arlington	13 369	2.56	6.4	25.3	254	254	254	0	411	1 188	12	1 176	23 648	10.4	74.2
Warren	16 991	2.41	20.5	39.3	2 517	2 302	525	215	1 838	4 528	448	4 080	27 174	62.6	11.7
Westerville	13 827	2.68	7.1	26.2	1 685	454	454	1 231	849	2 244	74	2 170	24 785	22.7	52.6
Westlake	13 547	2.40	5.3	34.8	871	830	830	41	400	1 234	37	1 197	23 842	21.6	53.6
Wooster	10 639	2.48	12.0	35.1	2 381	387	230	1 994	981	3 708	276	3 432	16 843	47.6	27.7
Xenia	10 588	2.45	16.7	36.8	925	700	312	225	893	3 444	216	3 228	17 415	49.3	18.7
Youngstown	26 477	2.49	24.6	39.7	5 831	3 929	644	1 902	3 623	5 602	660	4 942	43 970	59.4	11.5
Zanesville	10 830	2.35	19.0	35.7	582	514	290	68	1 597	6 284	405	5 878	17 003	62.3	11.5
OKLAHOMA	1 450 117	2.63	12.5	28.1	112 017	64 411	21 678	47 606	131 726	3 397	406	2 991	2 489 023	45.0	23.8
Bartlesville	15 057	2.40	12.2	32.2	658	256	145	402	1 001	2 753	228	2 524	24 436	38.8	30.4
Broken Arrow	36 731	2.77	10.9	20.9	468	466	466	2	1 864	1 782	142	1 641	66 047	32.1	31.7
Edmond	31 792	2.68	9.1	23.4	1 586	313	268	1 273	1 619	1 832	92	1 740	53 610	19.9	51.9
Enid	19 445	2.58	14.1	28.3	1 824	1 005	593	819	2 234	4 377	370	4 007	32 717	50.1	20.8
Lawton	34 320	2.85	17.0	30.3	10 143	3 772	523	6 371	5 401	5 570	921	4 649	59 275	44.7	19.3
Midwest City	22 812	2.45	17.0	31.8	285	260	235	25	2 778	4 847	323	4 524	36 839	40.2	20.4
Moore	21 226	2.71	14.0	22.1	309	179	179	130	1 603	2 708	132	2 577	36 881	40.8	22.2
Muskogee	15 083	2.58	17.3	31.3	1 353	834	430	519	1 956	5 047	1 102	3 945	24 727	49.4	19.8
Norman	44 637	2.59	10.0	30.8	6 757	1 124	566	5 633	3 435	2 864	160	2 703	67 279	27.8	42.9
Oklahoma City	230 517	2.61	13.4	30.7	12 144	6 609	2 521	5 535	32 040	5 185	774	4 411	389 574	40.4	28.5
Owasso	11 630	2.73	10.8	22.4	242	214	173	28	538	1 623	157	1 466	19 949	33.4	30.0
Ponca City	10 114	2.47	12.3	33.7	700	433	245	267	1 472	5 943	787	5 156	16 278	44.5	21.6
Shawnee	11 858	2.58	16.8	31.7	1 670	468	249	1 202	2 067	6 617	836	5 782	18 858	45.8	22.5
Stillwater	18 202	2.57	7.7	36.1	6 945	367	180	6 578	1 477	3 106	320	2 786	21 260	22.7	48.5
Tulsa	163 519	2.42	15.4	35.1	8 386	4 284	2 033	4 102	23 521	5 887	805	5 082	257 507	38.6	30.1
OREGON	1 522 988	2.56	10.6	27.9	86 642	36 612	11 491	50 030	123 529	3 111	232	2 879	2 677 376	35.1	30.1
Albany	19 512	2.62	14.5	27.3	824	560	256	264	1 717	3 309	81	3 228	33 616	35.7	23.5
Beaverton	37 028	2.50	11.1	30.1	945	460	393	485	1 648	1 745	135	1 611	62 962	26.7	43.5
Bend	32 442	2.46	9.1	29.7	578	183	157	395	2 312	2 805	144	2 661	55 300	22.8	39.0
Corvallis	21 251	2.58	7.5	32.3	4 899	116	74	4 783	1 813	3 264	131	3 133	29 028	15.8	58.5
Eugene	65 924	2.40	9.9	32.5	7 249	1 131	585	6 118	7 224	4 518	367	4 151	98 778	25.1	39.9
Grants Pass	13 943	2.50	14.6	35.1	1 051	627	355	424	2 163	6 146	372	5 774	22 922	42.9	15.9
Gresham	38 556	2.81	15.3	25.8	1 514	553	491	961	5 710	5 178	498	4 680	70 006	45.2	18.6
Hillsboro	33 559	2.85	12.7	24.8	1 528	989	220	539	2 391	2 424	189	2 236	61 515	34.0	33.7
Keizer	13 830	2.67	15.3	23.0	364	190	190	174	867	2 331	175	2 157	23 795	37.8	24.6
Lake Oswego	16 004	2.33	6.2	30.4	222	187	148	35	535	1 414	50	1 364	26 964	12.1	65.2
McMinnville	11 644	2.82	12.5	25.3	1 716	396	183	1 320	981	2 940	165	2 775	20 267	46.5	21.1
Medford	29 695	2.58	13.2	29.4	1 553	691	450	862	5 546	7 078	482	6 596	51 436	40.2	24.2
Oregon City	12 639	2.68	12.8	23.4	650	555	157	95	844	2 404	85	2 318	22 794	35.0	22.7
Portland	252 185	2.39	9.9	34.5	17 754	4 821	2 160	12 933	35 140	5 708	473	5 235	434 638	26.1	44.4

1. No spouse present.   2. Data for serious crimes have not been adjusted for underreporting. This may affect comparability between geographic areas and over time.   3. Per 100,000 population estimated by the FBI.   4. Persons 25 years old and over.

City	Money income, 2010–2014					Housing units, 2010			Occupied housing units 2010–2014				
		Households							Owner-occupied			Median owner costs as a percent of income	
	Per capita income[1] (dollars)	Median income	Percent with income of $200,000 or more	Percent with income of less than $25,000	Families with income below poverty (percent)	Total	Percent change, 2000–2010	Vacant units for sale or rent[2]	Total	Percent	Median value[3] (dollars)	With a mortgage[4]	Without a mortgage[5]
	42	43	44	45	46	47	48	49	50	51	52	53	54
OHIO—Cont'd													
Hamilton	20 844	40 080	0.9	30.9	17.5	27 878	7.5	3 220	24 168	56.4	100 200	21.7	11.8
Hilliard	36 688	88 203	8.2	9.7	3.7	10 637	19.6	439	10 937	77.7	207 100	21.7	13.1
Huber Heights	25 555	51 938	1.9	19.3	9.4	15 875	6.2	1 155	15 159	70.5	106 000	22.1	12.4
Kent	19 207	35 210	1.7	39.6	21.3	11 174	6.8	886	9 839	38.5	139 000	18.4	10.6
Kettering	29 833	49 790	3.0	22.9	8.9	27 602	2.5	2 175	25 340	61.6	127 800	21.7	13.2
Lakewood	28 806	45 098	2.3	27.0	13.4	28 498	0.3	3 224	24 573	44.2	128 700	22.5	14.1
Lancaster	22 324	37 494	1.3	34.1	15.2	17 685	11.6	1 637	16 186	54.4	116 100	22.1	10.6
Lima	15 264	28 901	0.5	45.6	28.4	16 784	-5.0	2 563	14 125	44.8	70 600	20.4	13.0
Lorain	19 240	35 330	1.0	37.0	23.2	29 144	3.3	3 615	25 562	58.2	90 700	21.9	12.8
Mansfield	17 852	32 225	1.0	37.8	20.2	22 022	-1.4	3 326	18 179	54.7	79 400	22.6	12.4
Marion	16 140	33 423	1.0	37.7	20.3	15 066	2.3	2 198	12 536	58.4	75 800	21.9	12.2
Mason	37 459	83 466	11.8	9.3	2.0	11 471	41.1	455	11 112	81.0	214 600	21.3	11.7
Massillon	21 261	39 390	0.7	32.1	13.5	14 497	7.1	1 357	13 127	65.5	96 800	21.4	13.1
Medina	27 402	53 425	3.3	20.7	10.0	11 152	13.9	770	10 266	65.1	159 600	21.2	10.4
Mentor	33 136	67 983	3.8	13.8	4.9	20 218	4.8	1 052	19 230	85.1	166 900	20.7	11.6
Middletown	20 345	35 828	1.6	34.3	20.7	23 296	0.5	3 058	19 631	55.8	95 500	24.1	14.1
Newark	21 388	36 679	1.4	35.5	18.3	21 976	6.3	2 136	19 719	54.1	112 700	20.3	11.8
North Olmsted	30 820	60 136	2.0	13.8	4.4	14 500	3.1	855	13 462	76.7	145 700	22.4	14.5
North Ridgeville	30 209	66 746	2.7	11.0	4.3	12 109	41.0	609	11 954	85.6	157 800	21.9	13.1
North Royalton	35 938	69 126	6.5	14.6	2.8	13 710	16.6	766	12 511	71.8	193 500	21.8	13.6
Parma	24 828	49 568	1.1	22.5	8.9	36 608	0.5	2 119	33 400	74.6	112 300	21.8	14.0
Reynoldsburg	28 510	60 183	2.5	18.2	8.8	15 611	15.9	1 224	14 216	59.9	143 200	22.1	14.3
Riverside	21 816	41 734	0.7	26.8	12.4	11 304	8.8	1 020	10 213	54.5	89 000	21.5	13.0
Sandusky	21 725	34 377	1.6	37.1	17.3	13 386	0.4	2 304	11 432	52.2	82 400	21.4	13.6
Shaker Heights	49 650	75 177	16.9	17.9	5.2	13 318	2.5	1 478	11 447	62.8	217 600	21.4	14.0
Springfield	18 699	31 327	1.4	40.5	23.5	28 437	-2.9	3 978	24 449	49.8	80 100	21.1	12.3
Stow	32 098	64 073	3.4	14.1	4.6	15 141	17.8	915	13 978	71.0	164 300	20.9	11.8
Strongsville	37 990	77 849	6.6	13.1	3.1	18 476	9.6	817	17 403	80.6	192 700	21.1	12.3
Toledo	19 113	33 485	0.8	39.1	22.7	138 039	-1.3	18 309	117 785	54.6	80 600	22.9	13.7
Troy	24 632	47 517	0.7	24.4	12.0	11 166	17.1	813	10 415	60.7	123 200	19.8	11.0
Upper Arlington	53 970	100 736	19.7	9.3	2.8	14 544	0.8	790	13 369	82.4	317 200	21.1	12.5
Warren	17 079	29 249	0.8	43.8	29.1	20 384	-4.5	3 381	16 991	53.3	63 700	20.5	14.3
Westerville	38 181	81 763	10.0	12.0	3.5	14 467	10.1	608	13 827	75.3	205 400	19.9	10.0
Westlake	46 435	76 250	11.1	11.5	3.2	14 883	8.4	973	13 547	74.5	226 900	20.7	11.5
Wooster	23 610	41 143	2.2	30.3	14.9	11 822	10.0	1 089	10 639	57.6	124 100	22.5	11.6
Xenia	20 508	37 153	0.6	34.0	20.9	11 424	15.4	1 034	10 588	62.0	97 500	23.2	13.2
Youngstown	14 742	24 361	0.3	51.2	31.2	33 123	-10.9	6 284	26 477	57.7	45 400	23.3	13.7
Zanesville	16 622	26 240	0.6	48.3	26.7	12 385	5.4	1 521	10 830	44.5	74 600	23.2	13.9
OKLAHOMA	24 695	46 235	2.9	26.5	12.6	1 664 378	9.9	203 928	1 450 117	66.5	115 000	20.9	10.8
Bartlesville	28 029	48 862	4.2	24.9	11.6	16 768	4.1	1 791	15 057	69.0	109 400	19.5	10.1
Broken Arrow	29 802	66 250	4.3	13.1	5.2	38 013	40.2	1 872	36 731	77.1	152 000	20.8	10.1
Edmond	38 298	71 825	9.6	16.6	6.0	33 178	25.8	1 703	31 792	69.6	196 400	20.1	10.0
Enid	24 076	44 266	2.6	23.6	10.8	21 936	3.2	2 210	19 445	61.9	91 700	21.0	10.5
Lawton	21 486	43 263	1.8	27.5	16.6	39 409	8.2	4 508	34 320	49.2	105 300	21.4	10.0
Midwest City	23 073	45 196	1.1	24.3	12.2	24 723	3.9	1 997	22 812	59.9	99 500	21.0	11.6
Moore	25 321	58 542	1.6	15.7	8.4	21 444	34.8	998	21 226	72.0	121 700	21.0	11.6
Muskogee	19 380	36 322	0.7	35.9	20.9	18 055	2.8	2 351	15 083	58.4	83 500	19.8	10.5
Norman	28 273	50 714	3.8	26.0	10.3	47 965	15.5	3 304	44 637	55.6	154 700	20.4	10.0
Oklahoma City	26 275	47 004	3.6	25.3	14.1	256 930	12.6	26 697	230 517	58.8	135 200	22.1	11.5
Owasso	27 800	65 550	2.5	14.5	5.6	11 346	64.9	657	11 630	67.2	149 800	20.2	10.4
Ponca City	22 411	40 089	1.8	31.4	13.7	11 950	0.5	1 555	10 114	66.5	80 100	20.0	12.3
Shawnee	21 063	38 001	2.4	33.9	18.0	13 205	4.0	1 586	11 858	56.7	95 300	21.1	11.7
Stillwater	20 046	32 255	3.1	41.5	15.5	19 753	17.5	1 812	18 202	38.1	147 200	24.1	10.4
Tulsa	27 313	41 957	4.1	29.0	16.1	185 127	3.1	21 152	163 519	52.9	123 100	21.9	11.8
OREGON	27 173	50 521	3.5	24.2	11.5	1 675 562	15.3	156 624	1 522 988	61.5	234 100	25.5	12.7
Albany	22 128	45 478	1.2	27.5	16.9	20 979	20.6	1 274	19 512	59.0	173 800	23.8	12.3
Beaverton	30 326	57 068	3.5	19.7	10.8	39 500	21.5	2 287	37 028	47.8	277 500	24.7	13.2
Bend	30 946	52 471	4.3	22.7	8.9	36 110	60.5	4 320	32 442	58.3	256 400	25.0	13.3
Corvallis	25 002	40 425	3.7	35.9	11.9	23 423	12.1	1 140	21 251	44.3	265 400	21.1	10.4
Eugene	26 313	42 715	3.0	32.0	12.3	69 951	14.1	3 532	65 924	48.9	237 000	25.2	13.0
Grants Pass	20 402	33 240	1.9	36.4	18.3	15 561	57.8	1 248	13 943	50.1	178 900	26.9	14.2
Gresham	21 634	47 706	1.2	25.3	17.7	41 015	16.2	2 311	38 556	52.3	210 600	26.5	13.3
Hillsboro	27 943	66 668	3.8	16.5	11.0	35 487	30.5	2 198	33 559	53.5	238 300	24.5	11.8
Keizer	23 990	50 897	1.5	20.8	13.5	14 445	13.1	742	13 830	60.4	195 300	25.4	11.4
Lake Oswego	57 359	84 244	16.9	13.7	4.8	16 995	8.5	1 102	16 004	67.2	478 400	23.9	11.5
McMinnville	20 936	44 451	1.7	25.6	15.7	12 389	26.0	715	11 644	55.9	192 500	23.5	13.6
Medford	23 097	42 366	2.2	28.0	16.9	32 430	23.3	2 351	29 695	51.2	201 500	27.0	13.1
Oregon City	26 831	59 429	1.9	18.4	9.3	12 900	26.9	927	12 639	65.4	248 400	26.2	12.5
Portland	32 438	53 230	5.3	24.1	12.1	265 439	11.9	16 893	252 185	52.8	285 300	25.4	14.1

1. Based on population estimated by the American Community Survey.   2. Includes units rented or sold but not occupied.   3. Specified owner-occupied units; $1,000,000 represents $1,000,000 or more.   4. 50.0 represents 50 percent or more.   5. 10.0 represents 10 percent or less.

Table D. Cities — Housing, Labor Force, and Employment

City	Occupied housing units, 2010–2014 (cont.)				Migration, 2010–2014		Civilian labor force, 2015		Unemployment		Civilian employment[4], 2010–2014	Percent		
	Percent renter occupied	Median gross rent[1]	Median gross rent as a percent of income[2]	Percent with no vehicle available	Percent who lived in the same house one year ago	Percent who lived outside current city one year ago	Total	Percent change, 2014–2015	Total	Rate[3]	Population age 16 and older	In labor force	Civilian full-year full-time workers	Households with no workers (percent)
	55	56	57	58	59	60	61	62	63	64	65	66	67	68
OHIO—Cont'd														
Hamilton	43.6	725	31.6	11.2	82.7	9.5	27 791	0.1	1 416	5.1	48 325	61.0	37.1	33.1
Hilliard	22.3	1 005	27.2	4.5	88.2	9.5	17 666	1.3	603	3.4	22 641	74.3	52.2	18.7
Huber Heights	29.5	872	30.8	4.0	84.1	9.6	18 028	0.1	889	4.9	29 979	64.8	40.5	27.6
Kent	61.5	734	41.3	8.7	62.1	22.8	16 643	0.4	754	4.5	25 442	69.6	28.1	25.8
Kettering	38.4	726	27.2	7.1	83.9	10.5	28 918	0.2	1 184	4.1	45 473	65.5	40.6	30.6
Lakewood	55.8	702	26.1	13.5	78.6	13.6	29 945	-0.8	1 157	3.9	42 611	73.6	47.6	23.1
Lancaster	45.6	732	34.1	11.1	78.7	9.4	17 885	0.6	862	4.8	30 925	59.6	35.3	36.2
Lima	55.2	614	35.5	15.7	74.2	12.4	14 786	-0.8	867	5.9	29 340	59.3	28.0	36.2
Lorain	41.8	659	33.6	12.3	83.1	7.1	27 211	-1.2	1 924	7.1	49 254	60.4	34.7	36.7
Mansfield	45.3	578	29.1	14.0	77.5	11.0	17 802	-1.7	1 112	6.2	38 439	49.4	26.2	40.0
Marion	41.6	682	34.9	10.9	75.7	12.2	13 749	0.2	806	5.9	29 766	48.3	28.1	34.6
Mason	19.0	1 023	28.7	2.0	89.8	7.3	16 004	0.7	595	3.7	22 870	68.9	47.9	16.6
Massillon	34.5	643	29.7	10.3	86.2	9.0	15 255	-1.0	872	5.7	26 039	61.8	35.1	36.2
Medina	34.9	808	31.3	8.4	85.7	9.9	13 226	-0.9	518	3.9	20 002	68.6	42.8	24.4
Mentor	14.9	879	32.2	4.7	93.3	5.5	26 085	-0.9	998	3.8	38 953	67.9	45.3	24.5
Middletown	44.2	748	33.7	9.0	80.6	8.8	20 722	-0.1	1 185	5.7	37 822	61.2	33.9	36.5
Newark	45.9	678	33.4	10.5	78.9	9.9	23 287	0.7	1 089	4.7	37 175	63.1	36.9	33.3
North Olmsted	23.3	872	25.2	4.7	91.0	7.3	17 396	-0.9	713	4.1	26 922	67.1	42.5	27.0
North Ridgeville	14.4	1 005	30.1	3.5	91.5	5.8	16 846	-0.8	688	4.1	24 386	67.9	41.6	25.5
North Royalton	28.2	772	22.0	4.1	91.0	6.3	17 329	-0.7	716	4.1	25 395	68.2	46.2	24.3
Parma	25.4	742	29.9	6.5	88.9	7.6	42 031	-1.0	1 964	4.7	66 699	65.4	39.9	29.8
Reynoldsburg	40.1	881	27.7	5.6	82.8	11.0	20 292	0.9	810	4.0	28 362	72.1	46.9	23.2
Riverside	45.5	759	27.0	6.7	79.0	16.2	10 714	0.3	597	5.6	20 056	63.1	35.8	32.7
Sandusky	47.8	624	28.2	13.4	81.3	8.3	11 635	-1.7	692	5.9	20 475	62.4	34.8	35.1
Shaker Heights	37.2	929	29.1	8.3	89.1	8.2	14 184	-0.8	574	4.0	21 849	65.8	44.9	24.8
Springfield	50.2	645	33.1	14.8	78.0	8.2	25 631	-1.3	1 387	5.4	46 841	58.1	31.5	37.7
Stow	29.0	888	25.1	4.5	92.4	5.7	18 692	0.3	796	4.3	28 069	66.8	46.6	22.9
Strongsville	19.4	841	26.9	3.9	90.9	7.1	24 125	-0.8	946	3.9	36 089	67.7	44.4	23.7
Toledo	45.4	638	33.8	14.2	80.7	6.5	128 667	0.1	7 474	5.8	224 060	62.3	33.0	36.0
Troy	39.3	733	27.3	6.3	81.1	9.9	13 408	0.5	568	4.2	20 316	66.4	43.2	27.6
Upper Arlington	17.6	997	25.1	3.6	89.5	8.1	18 067	1.2	588	3.3	26 319	67.6	45.5	22.9
Warren	46.7	602	35.9	12.7	83.0	8.3	14 642	-1.5	1 074	7.3	31 864	49.9	27.4	43.7
Westerville	24.7	935	27.7	5.7	86.4	11.1	21 066	1.2	743	3.5	29 792	68.9	44.8	20.1
Westlake	25.5	982	24.0	6.3	89.3	9.1	16 939	-0.7	648	3.8	26 307	65.7	45.0	24.5
Wooster	42.4	655	29.5	11.1	74.5	13.7	13 623	0.5	532	3.9	21 536	59.9	34.0	31.8
Xenia	38.0	678	33.9	11.0	85.2	8.1	11 047	-0.1	562	5.1	20 059	56.2	34.1	37.6
Youngstown	42.3	612	38.5	18.4	82.7	9.3	23 136	-1.3	1 780	7.7	53 228	50.1	22.6	45.3
Zanesville	55.5	608	33.2	16.9	78.1	10.9	9 708	-1.3	640	6.6	19 761	52.6	28.4	42.9
OKLAHOMA	33.5	717	28.5	5.7	82.5	10.6	1 842 049	2.5	78 205	4.2	2 977 835	61.9	41.1	28.0
Bartlesville	31.0	674	28.2	6.3	81.1	10.5	17 444	0.8	658	3.8	28 519	59.6	40.6	32.1
Broken Arrow	22.9	951	27.1	2.6	86.2	9.3	55 845	2.2	1 752	3.1	77 678	71.1	50.0	18.0
Edmond	30.4	909	30.5	4.2	81.5	12.7	46 787	2.6	1 314	2.8	66 163	68.1	45.1	20.7
Enid	38.1	681	23.2	5.3	75.9	11.2	23 720	1.2	912	3.8	38 918	64.1	39.8	25.6
Lawton	50.8	773	28.0	8.2	67.7	18.6	37 522	1.7	1 519	4.0	75 702	65.1	33.6	24.8
Midwest City	40.1	778	28.5	6.3	83.1	10.4	26 982	2.3	1 115	4.1	43 357	68.3	42.4	29.1
Moore	28.0	911	28.5	2.6	82.6	11.8	30 605	2.6	1 004	3.3	43 647	70.5	48.6	18.7
Muskogee	41.6	626	32.0	11.7	80.7	8.3	16 673	1.9	739	4.4	29 703	57.7	36.5	36.3
Norman	44.4	780	31.8	4.9	73.0	14.2	61 085	2.3	1 874	3.1	95 337	64.3	39.7	23.2
Oklahoma City	41.2	763	29.9	7.0	79.6	9.2	311 587	2.5	10 963	3.5	462 537	67.0	44.5	24.1
Owasso	32.8	885	28.0	3.9	82.1	13.2	17 910	2.4	563	3.1	23 804	73.0	50.1	15.6
Ponca City	33.5	659	27.3	7.4	79.7	8.7	10 557	0.3	541	5.1	19 251	59.9	39.1	33.8
Shawnee	43.3	657	28.7	8.2	79.5	11.3	14 584	2.5	570	3.9	23 705	61.2	38.5	29.8
Stillwater	61.9	720	41.8	6.7	63.2	20.5	23 950	0.4	701	2.9	40 237	61.0	27.8	27.1
Tulsa	47.1	738	29.3	8.3	79.5	7.7	197 890	2.0	7 660	3.9	308 077	65.6	43.1	26.8
OREGON	38.5	894	32.5	8.0	81.8	12.2	1 969 466	1.6	112 352	5.7	3 139 152	62.5	35.0	30.5
Albany	41.0	791	35.8	8.0	81.0	10.3	24 226	1.1	1 515	6.3	39 371	61.9	33.6	33.7
Beaverton	52.2	1 012	29.6	8.7	78.2	15.8	52 520	2.0	2 338	4.5	73 297	70.6	42.3	21.1
Bend	41.7	947	32.0	6.0	78.9	9.8	44 967	4.0	2 154	4.8	63 483	66.4	36.7	29.0
Corvallis	55.7	850	42.3	11.0	71.1	18.4	28 919	1.8	1 233	4.3	47 662	58.7	25.4	32.0
Eugene	51.1	877	39.1	11.4	71.7	13.4	79 066	1.4	4 282	5.4	133 182	60.4	29.1	32.8
Grants Pass	49.9	823	37.6	10.2	80.0	10.0	14 327	1.3	1 013	7.1	27 149	51.9	28.1	44.1
Gresham	47.7	898	34.2	10.2	81.7	13.1	53 833	1.8	3 003	5.6	83 797	65.3	35.4	28.1
Hillsboro	46.5	1 090	28.4	7.2	79.2	13.6	52 744	2.1	2 433	4.6	72 746	70.9	44.1	17.3
Keizer	39.6	823	31.2	6.5	81.1	14.4	18 400	1.8	1 061	5.8	28 336	64.5	38.8	27.2
Lake Oswego	32.8	1 273	33.0	5.7	82.1	12.5	19 863	2.1	858	4.3	30 213	64.2	38.6	28.1
McMinnville	44.1	853	32.5	8.5	82.6	11.3	15 943	1.7	846	5.3	25 564	60.3	32.0	34.1
Medford	48.8	871	36.6	10.1	78.3	10.9	37 194	1.0	2 378	6.4	60 656	61.8	32.2	33.2
Oregon City	34.6	974	34.3	6.9	82.8	11.3	17 966	1.6	990	5.5	26 275	65.3	39.7	26.0
Portland	47.2	945	32.6	15.0	79.3	9.5	349 764	1.9	16 896	4.8	500 472	69.4	39.2	24.9

1. $2,000 represents $2,000 or more.   2. 50.0 represents 50 percent or more.   3. Percent of civilian labor force.   4. Persons 16 years old and over.

Table D. Cities — Construction, Wholesale Trade, and Retail Trade

City	Value of residential construction authorized by building permits, 2015			Wholesale trade,[1] 2012				Retail trade,[2] 2012			
	New construction ($1,000)	Number of housing units	Percent single family	Number of establishments	Number of employees	Sales (mil dol)	Annual payroll (mil dol)	Number of establishments	Number of employees	Sales (mil dol)	Annual payroll (mil dol)
	69	70	71	72	73	74	75	76	77	78	79
OHIO—Cont'd											
Hamilton	2 648	20	100.0	43	800	635.4	43.1	213	3 262	733.6	69.0
Hilliard	51 679	418	30.4	51	700	448.5	36.9	85	1 405	382.8	40.2
Huber Heights	NA	NA	NA	20	394	270.8	20.8	98	2 020	476.1	41.0
Kent	19 691	183	6.6	13	D	D	D	78	1 344	404.7	34.2
Kettering	574	3	100.0	26	D	D	D	158	3 328	803.7	80.7
Lakewood	425	2	100.0	22	D	D	D	110	1 149	255.6	26.5
Lancaster	6 582	33	87.9	27	368	75.2	14.9	235	3 240	641.9	66.5
Lima	420	3	100.0	49	663	431.3	30.2	125	1 634	463.2	39.7
Lorain	12 738	127	100.0	27	786	333.4	26.3	121	1 836	361.1	39.0
Mansfield	1 950	11	100.0	56	1 001	369.2	44.1	185	2 073	465.0	50.1
Marion	150	2	100.0	18	286	403.2	12.9	112	1 762	446.2	42.3
Mason	31 622	137	96.4	51	1 783	1 023.7	132.9	105	1 864	428.8	46.5
Massillon	8 809	96	43.8	29	419	241.8	21.5	119	2 488	617.7	55.3
Medina	728	3	100.0	50	526	371.0	23.6	111	1 813	384.7	33.8
Mentor	19 171	84	100.0	97	944	439.1	43.2	303	5 884	1 498.9	130.9
Middletown	8 740	120	20.0	33	D	D	D	153	3 372	1 461.3	86.1
Newark	NA	NA	NA	34	514	459.8	22.8	145	1 825	498.5	41.2
North Olmsted	1 260	5	100.0	22	166	188.0	13.3	250	4 827	1 176.4	114.5
North Ridgeville	31 844	246	80.5	30	442	254.5	18.4	58	647	169.3	14.5
North Royalton	13 771	52	100.0	52	478	357.7	33.4	63	484	112.9	13.8
Parma	80	1	100.0	44	851	314.7	32.4	270	3 793	913.3	76.8
Reynoldsburg	8 484	57	57.9	8	D	D	D	119	2 127	1 053.8	79.5
Riverside	NA	NA	NA	9	D	D	D	57	516	144.4	11.9
Sandusky	2 105	5	100.0	31	380	220.9	16.7	101	1 277	330.6	28.8
Shaker Heights	1 000	2	100.0	10	20	7.1	0.9	47	494	109.2	11.9
Springfield	1 710	13	84.6	50	1 628	2 331.3	82.1	221	3 643	1 118.8	88.4
Stow	9 817	35	100.0	47	590	462.9	34.7	102	2 184	514.7	44.8
Strongsville	35 065	96	100.0	70	1 636	877.5	91.3	240	4 775	1 004.1	95.1
Toledo	2 428	23	78.3	249	3 832	2 592.8	188.6	935	13 004	2 837.1	282.7
Troy	NA	NA	NA	18	253	388.6	11.2	79	1 695	411.5	39.9
Upper Arlington	10 409	14	100.0	14	D	D	D	85	891	192.1	19.3
Warren	0	0	0.0	28	712	772.8	36.5	155	1 907	605.4	48.8
Westerville	13 551	120	7.5	52	494	190.6	21.8	108	1 683	454.8	41.0
Westlake	12 619	23	100.0	82	1 308	830.6	74.6	161	2 377	540.9	50.0
Wooster	8 155	46	56.5	36	476	552.5	19.5	165	2 606	597.9	55.4
Xenia	NA	NA	NA	14	263	285.6	12.0	79	1 259	331.7	32.5
Youngstown	NA	NA	NA	89	1 488	734.0	70.3	219	2 454	473.8	48.8
Zanesville	75	1	100.0	24	251	96.6	8.8	210	3 093	751.9	64.3
OKLAHOMA	2 216 234	11 545	82.9	3 909	50 660	71 892.9	2 718.6	13 051	168 839	50 256.2	4 055.1
Bartlesville	8 433	44	81.8	21	D	D	D	161	D	D	D
Broken Arrow	93 953	422	100.0	125	1 347	691.5	71.5	253	4 115	1 357.3	103.9
Edmond	184 595	544	97.4	96	D	D	D	327	4 505	1 154.8	107.5
Enid	15 981	72	100.0	58	690	1 312.1	33.5	251	3 289	894.8	81.6
Lawton	7 416	44	100.0	49	378	119.1	12.1	352	4 956	1 340.6	112.7
Midwest City	16 752	106	100.0	19	D	D	D	176	4 097	1 280.7	111.1
Moore	54 672	274	100.0	33	D	D	D	147	2 442	638.3	53.5
Muskogee	8 955	63	100.0	45	806	353.8	38.1	215	2 855	806.8	68.8
Norman	132 241	641	74.4	59	746	476.1	39.7	419	7 006	2 124.7	174.3
Oklahoma City	651 543	3 387	92.7	1 025	17 349	43 266.0	1 022.8	2 186	31 326	10 272.1	844.2
Owasso	66 529	537	38.0	15	D	D	D	115	2 434	618.1	50.9
Ponca City	2 395	12	66.7	23	157	74.9	5.5	126	1 576	431.5	37.3
Shawnee	7 292	42	100.0	29	D	D	D	191	2 675	676.9	59.0
Stillwater	56 722	496	25.8	22	158	163.5	7.5	202	3 157	739.2	66.5
Tulsa	119 340	564	61.0	770	11 810	11 596.9	716.4	1 708	26 411	7 542.2	665.1
OREGON	3 591 958	17 510	58.6	4 393	59 523	48 325.3	3 233.0	13 879	187 402	49 481.1	4 831.5
Albany	35 113	155	96.1	39	369	307.0	16.1	187	2 812	741.1	70.0
Beaverton	84 730	539	23.9	185	2 640	2 230.6	185.4	391	7 600	2 759.6	241.8
Bend	297 275	1 569	57.3	136	908	621.5	43.0	503	6 406	1 741.9	171.3
Corvallis	22 220	88	95.5	26	D	D	D	212	3 138	676.7	75.6
Eugene	67 330	316	71.2	241	3 013	1 585.8	151.3	726	10 971	2 487.2	271.9
Grants Pass	29 641	173	63.0	25	307	270.2	13.0	241	3 637	872.6	94.9
Gresham	73 801	398	45.7	55	1 615	854.4	73.4	270	3 677	1 087.3	95.5
Hillsboro	130 582	807	23.7	99	1 315	1 047.6	79.5	303	5 624	1 666.9	151.8
Keizer	46 060	287	37.3	11	25	18.9	1.4	83	1 213	255.2	24.0
Lake Oswego	45 739	95	93.7	94	1 457	781.5	136.0	126	D	D	D
McMinnville	25 593	113	92.9	20	111	68.0	5.4	144	2 005	510.0	49.7
Medford	69 290	329	73.9	112	1 139	543.6	46.9	479	7 401	1 965.9	194.4
Oregon City	37 071	130	100.0	14	163	69.3	8.4	98	1 607	448.7	39.4
Portland	689 257	4 411	19.9	1 139	20 024	20 321.0	1 195.1	2 527	32 426	8 508.3	886.3

1. Merchant wholesalers except manufacturers' sales branches and offices. 2. Establishments with payroll.

Table D. Cities — Real Estate, Professional Services, and Manufacturing

City	Real estate and rental and leasing, 2012				Professional, scientific, and technical services,[1] 2012				Manufacturing, 2012			
	Number of establishments	Number of employees	Receipts (mil dol)	Annual payroll (mil dol)	Number of establishments	Number of employees	Receipts (mil dol)	Annual payroll (mil dol)	Number of establishments	Number of employees	Receipts (mil dol)	Annual payroll (mil dol)
	80	81	82	83	84	85	86	87	88	89	90	91
OHIO—Cont'd												
Hamilton	31	165	34.3	5.3	96	D	D	D	69	1 827	509.6	115.7
Hilliard	39	256	40.3	9.1	85	778	123.9	56.4	28	1 506	436.3	73.5
Huber Heights	25	124	26.4	4.4	32	495	53.8	19.5	31	2 494	1 089.2	237.9
Kent	22	93	11.3	2.9	44	D	D	D	59	1 435	369.6	65.5
Kettering	57	197	60.6	6.9	110	D	D	D	45	1 601	D	73.3
Lakewood	58	322	63.1	12.5	116	388	49.3	20.4	33	587	204.9	30.5
Lancaster	54	215	27.1	4.3	70	D	D	D	45	2 844	864.5	145.2
Lima	29	186	18.9	5.7	73	D	D	D	37	1 724	D	123.5
Lorain	36	118	18.8	3.4	51	D	D	D	40	2 533	D	169.7
Mansfield	58	295	31.0	5.8	117	668	73.7	27.1	96	5 359	2 170.7	257.6
Marion	25	93	14.2	2.1	41	D	D	D	31	2 001	1 291.7	90.7
Mason	30	86	21.6	2.7	110	587	89.7	32.2	32	3 399	1 492.0	197.9
Massillon	24	88	19.8	3.6	44	236	21.2	8.8	60	5 519	1 962.7	218.7
Medina	30	110	24.7	4.1	109	531	55.5	23.3	61	3 036	1 320.6	144.5
Mentor	49	163	47.0	5.1	169	899	118.2	45.6	213	8 675	2 501.6	449.4
Middletown	53	219	40.4	5.9	63	579	51.3	23.3	53	4 040	D	250.4
Newark	42	158	22.9	4.0	82	D	D	D	41	2 302	688.0	103.5
North Olmsted	36	156	28.8	6.1	68	2 306	60.4	33.2	16	208	44.8	8.0
North Ridgeville	12	46	5.2	0.8	43	240	22.5	9.7	42	1 305	318.8	57.3
North Royalton	26	141	38.7	10.6	93	308	44.0	14.6	73	779	113.7	37.3
Parma	57	314	47.8	9.6	91	638	78.4	22.3	32	1 923	692.1	132.2
Reynoldsburg	39	185	42.9	6.5	74	464	40.2	15.9	15	243	D	12.1
Riverside	16	82	23.1	2.5	37	D	D	D	5	90	D	3.1
Sandusky	35	135	19.9	4.1	56	D	D	D	41	1 644	424.9	85.1
Shaker Heights	36	D	D	D	94	D	D	D	NA	NA	NA	NA
Springfield	58	324	35.3	9.3	101	D	D	D	79	2 767	793.4	127.3
Stow	38	169	31.6	4.4	100	864	96.2	42.2	47	1 336	230.6	74.1
Strongsville	53	439	89.0	16.3	121	402	51.7	17.6	72	2 434	685.3	137.3
Toledo	237	1 823	2 219.2	127.8	448	D	D	D	295	11 821	11 102.3	734.4
Troy	21	105	18.5	3.6	59	411	50.8	19.5	49	5 461	2 360.9	285.1
Upper Arlington	42	D	D	D	117	D	D	D	11	61	D	1.5
Warren	32	175	18.6	3.6	97	D	D	D	45	5 428	1 836.3	422.8
Westerville	54	D	D	D	206	2 231	328.1	141.2	34	1 218	354.1	56.2
Westlake	64	258	70.7	11.4	230	1 534	375.8	109.8	49	1 200	295.1	58.0
Wooster	31	107	22.8	3.7	76	746	91.7	33.1	36	3 603	1 406.3	188.9
Xenia	16	43	6.4	1.7	29	118	8.2	2.6	27	493	100.1	27.1
Youngstown	54	357	37.7	7.2	115	D	D	D	90	3 310	719.4	182.1
Zanesville	29	170	24.2	5.0	68	D	D	D	28	D	430.8	46.6
OKLAHOMA	4 000	21 261	4 269.6	898.0	9 428	71 303	10 915.0	4 080.1	3 610	133 064	74 295.4	6 416.0
Bartlesville	39	D	D	D	79	D	D	D	25	D	200.7	D
Broken Arrow	92	227	34.8	7.2	228	1 457	241.0	105.0	132	5 570	1 953.3	332.2
Edmond	181	642	256.3	35.0	430	2 414	312.1	106.9	38	410	78.6	15.7
Enid	72	312	50.1	10.7	107	563	78.8	27.9	50	2 172	D	78.6
Lawton	118	D	D	D	128	D	D	D	39	3 367	D	178.3
Midwest City	74	374	80.1	10.3	93	D	D	D	12	280	83.8	12.8
Moore	47	172	39.0	8.1	64	412	28.4	12.7	25	808	191.2	25.9
Muskogee	48	196	26.7	5.5	75	D	D	D	46	3 200	1 371.0	157.9
Norman	210	975	134.7	35.4	451	D	D	D	69	2 255	1 077.8	101.1
Oklahoma City	893	5 794	1 255.5	266.3	2 357	D	D	D	645	21 675	8 249.8	979.6
Owasso	40	125	20.4	4.6	83	452	38.5	13.8	23	633	D	26.1
Ponca City	27	97	18.0	3.1	67	377	43.2	17.4	34	1 373	488.9	60.8
Shawnee	33	139	21.6	3.8	83	D	D	D	30	2 564	1 032.2	118.3
Stillwater	66	263	46.1	7.3	101	D	D	D	28	946	343.2	37.1
Tulsa	715	5 522	899.2	224.1	1 871	16 400	3 016.5	1 025.7	629	22 012	11 517.9	1 180.7
OREGON	5 644	26 016	4 649.6	902.8	11 564	82 456	11 167.3	5 723.4	5 289	D	D	D
Albany	58	203	31.8	6.6	99	D	D	D	61	D	528.4	D
Beaverton	208	904	162.5	30.0	450	D	D	D	115	6 475	2 817.0	442.4
Bend	257	701	116.7	24.4	500	D	D	D	162	2 444	524.2	117.1
Corvallis	86	D	D	D	208	D	D	D	47	974	235.3	43.4
Eugene	286	1 256	197.0	36.9	673	D	D	D	263	5 512	1 384.9	254.1
Grants Pass	72	248	35.1	6.7	89	D	D	D	68	1 632	318.2	66.0
Gresham	119	445	65.2	11.1	128	D	D	D	73	4 848	1 275.2	291.1
Hillsboro	116	914	467.6	34.3	216	D	D	D	149	D	D	D
Keizer	36	218	22.4	4.3	43	207	22.7	7.9	7	46	6.2	1.5
Lake Oswego	127	627	148.0	38.3	372	3 174	583.8	237.4	36	674	D	54.2
McMinnville	35	120	15.8	2.6	86	D	D	D	63	1 915	776.4	85.2
Medford	145	642	102.9	17.5	242	D	D	D	91	1 599	380.2	66.1
Oregon City	37	109	23.2	4.1	93	D	D	D	47	586	113.8	28.0
Portland	1 221	8 268	1 479.3	357.0	3 434	29 338	5 410.0	2 066.2	978	26 432	8 768.5	1 300.8

1. Establishments subject to federal tax.

Table D. Cities — Accommodation and Food Services, Arts, Entertainment, and Recreation, and Health Care and Social Assistance

City	Accommodation and food services, 2012				Arts, entertainment, and recreation,[1] 2012				Health care and social assistance,[1] 2012			
	Number of establishments	Number of employees	Sales (mil dol)	Annual payroll (mil dol)	Number of establishments	Number of employees	Receipts (mil dol)	Annual payroll (mil dol)	Number of establishments	Number of employees	Receipts (mil dol)	Annual payroll (mil dol)
	92	93	94	95	96	97	98	99	100	101	102	103
OHIO—Cont'd												
Hamilton	129	2 433	124.0	31.5	6	40	3.8	0.7	111	1 417	122.6	51.6
Hilliard	70	1 572	72.2	20.5	14	224	14.1	4.6	92	D	D	D
Huber Heights	78	1 638	79.2	22.6	6	D	D	D	67	D	D	D
Kent	89	1 426	84.5	18.3	5	D	D	D	38	518	32.6	15.1
Kettering	107	D	D	D	12	413	16.7	6.3	170	D	D	D
Lakewood	115	1 820	86.4	27.6	11	79	4.3	1.0	104	1 259	97.6	40.3
Lancaster	108	2 393	99.5	29.4	10	66	4.6	0.9	146	D	D	D
Lima	77	1 196	63.9	15.8	2	D	D	D	129	2 405	308.3	168.9
Lorain	71	1 107	50.0	12.8	14	104	5.7	1.7	100	1 278	150.0	64.6
Mansfield	111	2 022	86.2	23.9	8	60	2.2	0.5	178	D	D	D
Marion	66	1 259	56.5	14.2	4	D	D	D	108	D	D	D
Mason	98	2 588	129.5	35.3	18	1 038	130.5	32.4	117	1 503	122.9	51.1
Massillon	79	1 175	54.7	14.4	2	D	D	D	70	2 249	205.4	75.4
Medina	59	1 182	50.2	14.5	6	D	D	D	75	D	D	D
Mentor	174	3 813	162.3	46.2	10	D	D	D	155	2 340	211.0	89.2
Middletown	91	2 064	96.7	26.8	6	68	2.6	0.9	117	D	D	D
Newark	97	1 672	72.0	20.0	10	D	D	D	126	3 126	271.2	124.2
North Olmsted	119	2 387	112.3	30.9	7	58	3.3	0.9	72	1 135	77.4	31.0
North Ridgeville	43	611	25.9	6.9	6	64	3.4	1.1	39	521	35.4	13.3
North Royalton	39	398	13.7	3.6	8	D	D	D	59	691	49.7	19.7
Parma	163	2 484	110.1	28.3	11	D	D	D	184	3 232	293.7	139.9
Reynoldsburg	74	D	D	D	7	47	1.9	0.6	104	D	D	D
Riverside	51	D	D	D	3	D	D	D	28	D	D	D
Sandusky	72	865	81.7	13.6	16	D	D	D	58	607	81.9	37.3
Shaker Heights	33	362	19.8	5.2	10	105	6.0	2.1	51	938	50.8	25.1
Springfield	154	3 174	149.7	40.3	12	82	3.9	1.3	188	3 381	255.6	114.1
Stow	86	1 724	78.0	21.0	19	D	D	D	63	1 145	88.2	37.7
Strongsville	122	2 951	127.8	36.6	14	192	30.1	6.8	98	1 391	125.2	54.7
Toledo	632	11 286	485.9	141.1	61	786	167.8	28.9	528	8 914	904.1	446.6
Troy	75	1 906	81.6	23.6	8	D	D	D	74	D	D	D
Upper Arlington	66	1 333	60.8	18.2	6	10	1.0	0.2	70	1 120	86.0	44.6
Warren	89	6 193	301.0	97.1	8	D	D	D	154	D	D	D
Westerville	102	D	D	D	7	D	D	D	222	3 299	342.2	164.6
Westlake	99	2 797	127.0	39.5	10	368	8.6	3.3	236	4 021	374.4	172.0
Wooster	85	1 683	75.0	21.6	5	D	D	D	91	1 529	140.0	69.5
Xenia	50	1 003	42.7	11.1	5	D	D	D	55	485	48.0	17.6
Youngstown	117	D	D	D	9	D	D	D	124	4 127	396.0	180.4
Zanesville	100	2 215	103.0	29.1	7	83	2.8	0.8	117	D	D	D
OKLAHOMA	7 403	143 561	7 121.2	1 908.3	816	22 012	2 526.6	578.2	8 868	128 437	13 382.5	4 996.4
Bartlesville	100	D	D	D	8	D	D	D	119	D	D	D
Broken Arrow	169	D	D	D	25	D	D	D	191	2 529	176.7	71.3
Edmond	202	4 394	197.9	54.0	33	D	D	D	403	3 669	450.9	150.6
Enid	120	2 183	111.9	26.6	11	69	5.8	1.0	172	2 734	250.9	88.2
Lawton	195	4 445	207.1	62.1	17	D	D	D	210	D	D	D
Midwest City	121	2 544	125.1	34.9	11	60	4.2	0.9	188	3 214	418.2	136.1
Moore	105	2 398	117.7	30.2	5	D	D	D	95	D	D	D
Muskogee	106	2 011	88.5	23.5	8	D	D	D	177	D	D	D
Norman	312	7 292	325.2	93.0	41	D	D	D	393	3 976	397.6	155.8
Oklahoma City	1 361	30 537	1 510.0	413.0	141	2 398	459.8	136.5	1 969	31 146	4 098.3	1 466.1
Owasso	76	1 812	82.7	24.2	12	D	D	D	85	D	D	D
Ponca City	54	932	45.7	11.3	3	21	0.7	0.2	81	1 264	109.1	40.3
Shawnee	98	2 180	95.0	25.3	7	D	D	D	99	1 508	120.2	55.9
Stillwater	146	3 143	134.8	36.7	8	D	D	D	98	1 494	114.9	44.2
Tulsa	1 099	D	D	D	114	D	D	D	1 387	22 659	3 105.8	1 205.0
OREGON	10 610	150 482	8 466.8	2 438.5	1 190	16 916	1 176.8	415.8	9 829	105 341	11 016.4	4 533.8
Albany	119	1 905	87.6	24.4	12	D	D	D	98	D	D	D
Beaverton	317	5 077	279.4	81.1	45	564	69.0	13.4	360	3 703	381.2	140.5
Bend	303	4 684	255.1	74.6	44	1 231	47.0	13.8	384	D	D	D
Corvallis	179	2 837	131.5	37.8	14	D	D	D	175	D	D	D
Eugene	526	8 479	417.8	124.4	44	574	25.5	6.4	586	D	D	D
Grants Pass	145	2 089	100.1	29.4	15	D	D	D	178	2 519	235.5	81.6
Gresham	221	3 294	181.5	49.0	21	374	19.7	6.3	284	3 040	247.1	100.5
Hillsboro	237	3 789	222.3	61.7	20	265	13.3	3.5	248	D	D	D
Keizer	56	D	D	D	10	117	5.6	1.9	60	D	D	D
Lake Oswego	113	1 928	111.3	33.3	19	156	10.0	3.4	186	1 643	156.1	60.1
McMinnville	86	1 138	56.6	16.1	6	D	D	D	111	D	D	D
Medford	262	4 049	204.4	59.8	26	355	23.4	5.9	303	D	D	D
Oregon City	79	1 044	55.6	15.6	7	D	D	D	105	D	D	D
Portland	2 522	38 496	2 261.7	671.0	274	3 542	436.5	185.9	1 963	D	D	D

1. Establishments subject to federal tax.

Table D. Cities — **Other Services and Government Employment and Payroll**

City	Other services[1], 2012				Government employment and payroll, 2012								
						March payroll							
							Percent of total for:						
	Number of establishments	Number of employees	Receipts (mil dol)	Annual payroll (mil dol)	Full-time equivalent employees	Total (dollars)	Administration, judicial, and legal	Police and Corrections	Fire Protection	Highways and transportation	Health and welfare	Natural resources and utilities	Education and libraries
	104	105	106	107	108	109	110	111	112	113	114	115	116
OHIO—Cont'd													
Hamilton	73	417	41.3	11.8	648	3 715 041	12.3	21.8	20.8	4.6	2.2	31.0	0.0
Hilliard	43	287	30.7	9.1	138	630 071	19.0	53.4	0.0	3.8	0.0	18.6	0.0
Huber Heights	50	279	20.4	6.7	178	969 065	15.5	36.2	31.4	11.5	0.0	0.2	0.0
Kent	43	273	18.6	6.8	203	1 021 262	8.2	30.7	21.0	16.4	6.0	15.0	0.0
Kettering	72	623	28.5	9.9	489	2 337 531	21.1	27.0	15.6	13.9	0.8	14.6	0.0
Lakewood	55	417	19.5	6.9	462	2 388 158	12.9	31.2	24.7	3.8	7.9	16.6	0.0
Lancaster	61	400	36.0	11.3	414	1 841 272	17.3	24.9	20.9	5.2	0.7	29.3	0.9
Lima	52	297	19.1	5.3	375	1 604 715	20.6	25.2	20.8	9.0	2.6	21.4	0.0
Lorain	58	401	30.2	8.5	466	2 344 000	9.9	33.0	23.6	4.0	5.6	19.7	4.2
Mansfield	87	577	42.8	13.0	423	1 865 914	20.0	26.6	23.0	4.6	1.3	17.6	0.0
Marion	40	285	18.1	5.7	241	1 067 754	11.2	34.1	23.1	9.9	0.0	17.7	0.0
Mason	38	237	13.8	5.4	266	1 194 447	18.2	24.2	20.0	7.6	0.0	21.7	0.0
Massillon	54	340	31.7	10.7	321	1 362 818	15.6	16.2	16.6	5.0	6.2	34.1	0.0
Medina	63	487	36.1	11.8	221	904 261	23.8	27.5	4.7	5.0	3.8	26.8	0.0
Mentor	120	838	57.7	21.3	500	2 127 362	11.3	29.5	28.5	14.3	5.5	10.9	0.0
Middletown	62	465	41.4	13.1	404	1 752 509	12.7	30.0	25.2	6.7	4.9	15.7	0.0
Newark	56	410	27.1	10.1	384	1 681 225	15.2	30.1	24.2	8.0	3.0	18.9	0.0
North Olmsted	100	676	54.7	16.5	255	1 250 704	8.6	28.1	19.4	3.8	2.7	29.3	0.0
North Ridgeville	46	193	19.3	5.1	199	885 287	13.3	28.1	21.5	10.7	2.1	18.6	0.0
North Royalton	58	292	26.0	8.6	185	949 689	9.7	32.8	24.0	9.0	2.8	17.2	0.0
Parma	129	828	74.7	22.5	468	1 957 354	15.6	32.5	28.4	11.6	3.1	4.2	0.0
Reynoldsburg	41	229	17.2	6.2	136	685 686	14.7	61.7	0.0	5.3	1.2	11.6	0.0
Riverside	18	74	5.3	1.7	85	380 891	12.2	46.1	28.8	12.4	0.0	0.0	0.0
Sandusky	33	122	10.0	3.0	231	1 023 311	17.4	23.9	23.6	4.8	2.8	23.4	0.0
Shaker Heights	18	81	5.9	1.7	356	1 867 638	14.5	30.2	20.9	14.6	4.9	6.2	0.0
Springfield	93	634	55.9	15.3	591	2 580 272	18.3	27.7	26.1	4.8	3.8	16.2	0.0
Stow	59	406	27.2	9.1	268	1 324 714	23.7	25.9	29.3	6.1	0.7	9.3	0.0
Strongsville	74	755	53.2	18.6	365	1 769 488	7.3	33.1	24.7	16.5	5.3	11.6	0.0
Toledo	356	2 384	178.0	57.2	2 146	10 282 276	15.9	23.9	36.8	7.3	1.5	13.8	0.0
Troy	48	279	18.0	5.7	184	972 285	13.3	25.7	22.4	11.8	1.3	24.4	0.0
Upper Arlington	29	239	15.7	5.7	239	1 342 741	13.2	27.2	31.7	10.1	4.0	11.5	0.0
Warren	60	319	22.3	6.7	445	1 785 083	16.7	23.0	19.1	3.3	3.9	30.7	0.0
Westerville	63	D	D	D	484	2 542 559	12.4	27.1	26.3	4.3	0.0	26.7	0.0
Westlake	71	678	39.2	14.8	288	1 367 977	13.6	30.0	24.5	2.8	3.2	21.7	0.0
Wooster	44	291	21.3	6.8	879	3 824 028	2.0	5.4	6.8	4.2	78.8	2.8	0.0
Xenia	33	164	12.2	3.6	219	1 060 316	20.5	35.1	21.7	3.3	0.9	13.1	0.0
Youngstown	78	358	25.6	9.2	757	3 252 504	14.0	28.1	18.4	6.3	4.9	27.3	0.0
Zanesville	65	633	43.5	13.4	297	1 096 683	10.0	29.7	21.1	6.3	2.8	25.1	0.0
OKLAHOMA	4 369	26 154	2 610.1	707.1	X	X	X	X	X	X	X	X	X
Bartlesville	51	373	28.3	9.4	344	1 284 794	8.5	23.4	23.5	6.4	0.4	26.0	5.4
Broken Arrow	136	834	88.2	22.0	618	2 786 415	13.1	30.6	27.6	5.5	0.0	17.1	0.0
Edmond	157	902	68.3	20.1	688	3 323 448	15.6	22.5	27.9	6.2	1.5	21.4	0.0
Enid	91	468	48.5	11.7	477	1 757 022	12.4	27.9	23.3	7.6	2.5	18.8	2.4
Lawton	98	659	52.1	17.1	892	3 414 778	14.9	29.7	19.3	9.4	2.0	20.6	1.8
Midwest City	52	415	26.1	8.2	494	2 315 063	15.2	28.4	24.6	3.8	4.3	18.9	0.0
Moore	60	D	D	D	275	1 722 367	12.5	35.2	32.5	2.3	5.4	6.1	0.0
Muskogee	55	470	44.3	11.5	497	1 548 570	8.5	26.0	24.8	12.1	0.0	24.8	0.0
Norman	132	769	56.0	16.9	3 161	15 136 504	3.2	7.5	5.5	2.7	74.3	5.6	0.0
Oklahoma City	835	6 134	660.7	173.6	4 418	24 268 820	9.9	32.6	28.7	9.3	4.5	15.0	0.0
Owasso	44	155	13.3	3.2	219	910 478	15.5	28.5	31.9	5.8	0.7	11.3	0.0
Ponca City	34	192	19.0	4.9	400	1 441 141	9.1	18.8	20.4	7.8	0.7	35.3	2.6
Shawnee	45	248	17.3	5.3	279	1 055 211	16.1	30.3	23.8	5.8	1.6	22.2	0.0
Stillwater	58	D	D	D	1 308	5 630 416	4.6	9.5	6.8	1.6	62.0	12.2	1.1
Tulsa	686	4 968	482.3	149.2	3 932	16 951 552	11.3	27.1	20.9	14.4	1.8	12.8	0.0
OREGON	5 258	28 203	2 519.4	794.3	X	X	X	X	X	X	X	X	X
Albany	63	412	25.0	9.0	389	2 123 666	12.9	24.2	24.6	13.2	0.1	18.7	3.7
Beaverton	180	1 217	116.1	37.3	488	2 217 436	38.8	23.9	0.0	5.4	0.0	10.8	12.0
Bend	159	822	64.7	20.0	432	2 556 081	14.4	29.2	23.0	5.2	3.3	12.8	0.0
Corvallis	75	389	24.1	8.5	430	2 437 922	9.9	21.5	18.9	5.8	8.1	18.9	8.1
Eugene	251	1 832	146.3	47.3	1 983	11 796 504	9.0	18.2	12.2	8.0	1.2	26.1	3.1
Grants Pass	59	285	22.5	6.6	214	1 160 951	18.8	44.3	16.7	2.1	0.0	13.1	0.0
Gresham	117	495	40.4	13.3	515	3 198 886	13.0	29.6	21.1	3.3	0.6	22.0	0.0
Hillsboro	119	947	121.9	49.5	759	4 281 252	14.6	24.9	17.5	3.5	0.0	24.7	6.8
Keizer	34	166	11.3	3.7	89	489 891	18.6	57.2	0.0	2.5	4.8	16.6	0.0
Lake Oswego	74	318	23.2	7.1	325	1 928 696	17.6	21.1	21.4	8.6	1.3	17.6	6.5
McMinnville	40	165	12.8	4.0	252	1 307 113	16.9	18.4	16.1	4.8	2.3	34.2	4.5
Medford	125	860	71.7	26.4	452	2 575 154	14.2	34.5	21.7	15.1	0.1	9.8	0.0
Oregon City	49	254	20.5	7.5	159	835 368	19.0	32.4	0.0	14.2	0.0	19.2	5.8
Portland	1 246	8 014	781.3	237.5	5 804	35 656 383	18.1	25.5	15.0	10.2	0.9	27.3	0.0

1. Establishments subject to federal tax.

Table D. Cities — **City Government Finances**

City	City government finances, 2012									
	General revenue							General expenditure		
		Intergovernmental		Taxes					Per capita[1] (dollars)	
					Per capita[1] (dollars)					
	Total (mil dol)	Total (mil dol)	Percent from state government	Total (mil dol)	Total	Property	Sales and gross receipts	Total (mil dol)	Total	Capital outlays
	117	118	119	120	121	122	123	124	125	126
OHIO—Cont'd										
Hamilton	89.3	12.8	82.9	38.5	618	143	14	83.9	1 348	178
Hilliard	35.0	7.3	60.4	23.3	762	41	50	31.8	1 040	211
Huber Heights	30.3	5.3	52.2	16.8	442	90	32	34.7	911	258
Kent	26.7	4.8	93.2	14.4	488	94	24	31.0	1 046	271
Kettering	81.4	18.4	94.3	48.4	863	160	8	83.8	1 495	462
Lakewood	61.0	11.1	71.9	35.2	685	265	25	53.0	1 032	61
Lancaster	74.4	14.1	95.8	19.9	511	72	1	62.8	1 614	139
Lima	73.9	31.0	93.2	18.5	482	32	28	56.9	1 483	345
Lorain	67.9	22.6	96.7	25.7	402	58	34	56.8	890	61
Mansfield	55.9	12.3	51.1	27.7	588	43	15	51.8	1 101	78
Marion	39.4	10.3	100.0	13.8	375	33	10	36.5	989	43
Mason	54.1	7.0	87.3	29.3	937	192	66	56.2	1 798	343
Massillon	35.7	5.9	26.8	17.4	540	50	45	33.4	1 036	44
Medina	27.0	2.3	92.3	16.9	636	121	21	24.7	931	114
Mentor	61.5	10.0	90.4	40.5	862	94	40	59.9	1 274	0
Middletown	84.2	23.4	47.0	24.4	501	100	5	78.5	1 612	138
Newark	52.3	16.1	92.8	22.0	462	55	6	52.1	1 091	140
North Olmsted	41.3	6.2	95.2	23.4	724	285	44	35.0	1 082	136
North Ridgeville	32.6	5.0	88.6	15.8	516	189	54	29.7	972	100
North Royalton	28.1	4.2	100.0	16.8	554	150	19	25.8	852	47
Parma	80.5	21.4	100.0	48.3	599	109	29	75.6	937	31
Reynoldsburg	27.3	3.4	100.0	14.8	406	60	10	25.5	702	31
Riverside	11.8	3.1	96.7	6.6	263	93	1	11.2	447	11
Sandusky	39.2	10.7	84.2	17.6	686	79	317	32.3	1 262	169
Shaker Heights	52.5	8.5	41.5	33.5	1 195	272	23	57.7	2 057	258
Springfield	86.7	27.8	35.7	38.2	635	49	32	79.9	1 328	177
Stow	35.8	7.4	100.0	21.6	623	215	21	32.9	950	128
Strongsville	63.9	10.5	39.1	39.3	881	209	21	66.8	1 498	383
Toledo	451.3	105.2	62.6	175.0	618	42	23	399.2	1 408	377
Troy	33.3	3.4	70.1	17.1	674	74	29	30.1	1 187	140
Upper Arlington	43.7	6.5	59.0	27.9	815	255	41	52.7	1 538	476
Warren	62.9	13.4	36.4	19.8	486	36	24	56.8	1 394	127
Westerville	85.6	17.7	81.5	50.6	1 359	332	29	96.9	2 605	855
Westlake	58.8	5.1	53.1	39.7	1 222	403	54	49.3	1 518	310
Wooster	134.0	6.0	94.8	14.0	532	83	27	128.8	4 877	371
Xenia	28.5	5.5	95.4	13.4	514	62	40	28.4	1 089	214
Youngstown	104.6	20.7	41.1	54.6	826	37	116	89.8	1 358	37
Zanesville	44.9	17.1	96.5	17.8	701	46	54	34.3	1 347	67
OKLAHOMA	X	X	X	X	X	X	X	X	X	X
Bartlesville	40.2	4.0	79.0	22.5	619	96	523	44.1	1 213	354
Broken Arrow	90.6	4.1	24.8	53.9	528	119	409	91.4	896	239
Edmond	93.1	6.8	73.5	55.3	651	0	651	115.9	1 364	281
Enid	67.3	6.0	81.8	38.4	769	57	712	80.2	1 606	728
Lawton	96.6	12.3	38.3	56.7	575	41	534	92.9	943	108
Midwest City	69.8	4.9	68.6	36.3	646	46	600	62.1	1 107	89
Moore	45.7	1.5	65.9	32.5	561	58	503	41.5	717	95
Muskogee	130.4	3.3	45.2	28.4	729	5	724	134.9	3 462	322
Norman	443.4	6.4	56.7	79.6	687	68	619	422.1	3 646	294
Oklahoma City	1 107.5	90.6	50.5	601.9	1 003	139	865	835.1	1 392	272
Owasso	32.7	0.8	93.6	20.7	658	0	658	29.0	924	98
Ponca City	41.3	2.3	61.5	16.3	655	21	635	56.7	2 278	730
Shawnee	34.1	5.6	40.8	20.1	656	2	653	30.7	1 003	220
Stillwater	49.0	2.9	45.6	29.0	622	29	593	48.2	1 033	155
Tulsa	741.9	77.4	11.3	340.0	862	161	701	712.6	1 806	561
OREGON	X	X	X	X	X	X	X	X	X	X
Albany	59.2	9.0	56.9	32.7	638	505	133	56.1	1 094	127
Beaverton	79.4	16.3	57.8	44.0	475	344	131	78.1	842	126
Bend	88.7	15.0	54.7	44.0	558	331	227	81.1	1 029	162
Corvallis	71.4	12.8	43.7	35.6	647	446	202	62.4	1 135	94
Eugene	265.1	45.3	46.0	119.6	757	620	138	254.5	1 612	275
Grants Pass	36.2	6.8	64.2	20.5	589	453	136	35.8	1 028	164
Gresham	102.2	33.7	52.1	39.5	363	243	120	106.4	979	155
Hillsboro	134.5	12.8	83.8	79.4	832	541	291	124.8	1 309	91
Keizer	21.2	3.3	99.7	10.7	290	216	74	18.1	490	50
Lake Oswego	80.7	14.9	44.5	43.4	1 164	919	245	69.2	1 857	263
McMinnville	37.5	4.1	96.1	15.2	459	360	99	30.1	909	86
Medford	102.4	14.5	49.3	58.0	758	455	303	104.2	1 361	306
Oregon City	52.1	16.8	99.0	19.9	594	337	257	43.8	1 308	472
Portland	1 298.8	266.5	44.2	612.5	1 016	708	308	1 280.8	2 124	548

1. Based on population estimated as of July 1 of the year shown.

City	Public welfare	Highways	Parking facilities	Education	Health and hospitals	Police protection	Sewerage and sanitation	Parks and recreation	Housing and community development	Interest on debt
	127	128	129	130	131	132	133	134	135	136
OHIO—Cont'd										
Hamilton	0.0	6.1	0.5	0.0	1.5	24.9	20.3	0.9	3.4	4.7
Hilliard	0.0	24.2	0.0	0.0	0.5	19.2	1.2	7.4	0.0	8.3
Huber Heights	0.0	13.8	0.0	0.0	0.0	17.2	7.9	12.9	4.7	5.3
Kent	0.4	5.1	0.0	0.0	3.0	20.7	13.4	5.7	2.8	0.8
Kettering	0.0	11.2	0.0	0.0	0.0	17.2	0.0	14.9	1.4	0.8
Lakewood	3.1	12.4	0.5	0.0	0.8	19.5	15.5	4.3	5.6	4.7
Lancaster	0.0	5.4	0.0	0.0	0.4	12.7	21.9	2.9	0.9	23.9
Lima	0.0	16.0	0.0	0.0	0.0	15.9	21.7	1.8	6.7	2.8
Lorain	1.5	5.3	0.0	0.0	2.1	22.9	25.4	0.6	7.9	2.8
Mansfield	0.0	13.1	0.0	1.8	0.0	16.3	8.4	0.5	3.4	0.6
Marion	0.0	8.9	0.0	0.0	1.3	18.4	33.3	2.5	0.0	2.0
Mason	0.0	17.2	0.0	0.0	0.0	10.0	9.1	17.8	0.0	7.0
Massillon	0.0	11.0	0.1	0.0	1.8	14.9	25.5	10.7	0.9	5.3
Medina	0.0	17.5	8.9	0.0	0.0	17.4	12.9	13.7	0.0	1.6
Mentor	0.0	24.6	0.0	0.0	0.0	19.1	0.0	11.9	0.8	2.7
Middletown	0.0	12.5	0.0	0.0	1.0	10.4	16.2	3.7	18.8	2.3
Newark	0.0	9.2	0.0	0.0	0.0	16.1	17.8	0.0	0.0	2.0
North Olmsted	0.9	13.9	0.0	0.0	0.0	15.9	22.0	12.1	0.5	5.6
North Ridgeville	0.0	12.1	0.0	0.0	8.5	17.4	25.4	1.3	4.6	3.6
North Royalton	0.0	20.6	0.0	0.0	0.7	23.5	21.0	1.5	2.7	1.6
Parma	0.0	5.8	0.0	0.0	0.4	40.5	0.5	5.1	11.3	1.6
Reynoldsburg	0.0	5.9	0.0	0.0	0.8	30.8	31.8	3.9	0.0	1.4
Riverside	0.0	14.6	0.0	0.0	0.0	41.2	0.0	0.4	0.0	0.8
Sandusky	0.0	8.5	0.0	0.0	0.0	15.5	25.9	1.2	2.8	6.9
Shaker Heights	0.0	7.5	0.0	0.0	1.0	20.4	8.3	8.9	8.8	1.6
Springfield	0.0	3.0	0.0	0.0	0.0	15.5	8.1	0.0	5.0	1.9
Stow	0.0	10.2	0.0	0.0	0.9	18.9	2.2	7.6	0.0	3.2
Strongsville	0.0	30.1	0.0	0.0	0.5	17.2	11.8	7.8	0.0	4.3
Toledo	0.4	8.8	0.2	0.0	3.7	23.7	22.4	1.8	3.2	5.8
Troy	0.0	7.4	0.4	0.0	1.1	12.4	14.3	12.0	6.3	2.2
Upper Arlington	0.0	34.9	0.0	0.0	0.4	13.2	6.2	6.9	2.2	3.4
Warren	0.0	8.6	0.2	0.0	1.6	12.9	18.9	4.3	7.2	1.3
Westerville	0.0	2.3	0.0	0.0	0.0	14.8	10.3	17.5	0.0	1.5
Westlake	0.0	17.5	0.0	0.0	0.0	13.8	11.8	6.6	0.0	1.6
Wooster	0.0	1.4	0.0	0.0	76.3	4.9	6.2	1.1	0.2	0.4
Xenia	0.0	1.1	0.3	0.0	0.0	19.2	20.9	0.6	1.7	1.4
Youngstown	0.0	6.3	0.1	0.0	1.5	22.0	27.0	2.7	6.8	1.8
Zanesville	0.0	10.9	0.0	0.0	1.2	22.8	24.7	2.4	0.0	3.0
OKLAHOMA	X	X	X	X	X	X	X	X	X	X
Bartlesville	0.0	15.9	0.0	0.0	0.0	12.6	20.7	12.2	2.0	1.5
Broken Arrow	0.0	7.8	0.0	0.0	0.8	18.6	18.5	7.7	0.8	5.5
Edmond	1.6	24.4	0.0	0.0	1.5	11.6	15.1	8.3	0.6	0.3
Enid	0.3	12.1	0.0	0.0	5.1	10.6	19.3	6.6	17.6	0.7
Lawton	0.0	9.4	0.0	5.7	0.9	21.2	15.2	1.3	1.1	1.4
Midwest City	0.0	8.1	0.0	0.0	0.0	23.9	12.5	4.6	7.6	6.6
Moore	0.0	14.8	0.0	0.0	0.0	23.2	14.3	3.7	3.2	1.9
Muskogee	0.0	3.1	0.0	0.0	65.8	5.4	5.9	4.1	0.6	0.1
Norman	0.0	6.6	0.0	0.0	68.5	5.5	5.8	1.8	0.4	3.1
Oklahoma City	0.0	8.8	0.7	2.5	0.9	18.5	8.3	17.3	3.5	5.8
Owasso	0.0	4.3	0.0	0.0	4.7	22.5	13.0	6.5	1.6	5.2
Ponca City	0.0	7.2	0.0	0.0	1.8	11.7	12.2	6.8	1.4	3.7
Shawnee	0.0	12.2	0.0	0.0	0.0	22.5	9.6	3.8	2.4	0.3
Stillwater	0.4	18.2	0.0	0.0	0.2	21.6	13.9	8.0	0.0	2.1
Tulsa	2.1	19.7	1.1	0.0	8.8	12.2	19.9	4.8	0.0	6.0
OREGON	X	X	X	X	X	X	X	X	X	X
Albany	0.0	7.1	0.0	0.0	3.9	21.6	16.2	10.8	0.1	1.7
Beaverton	0.0	7.6	0.0	0.0	0.0	31.5	10.8	0.2	1.1	0.8
Bend	0.0	12.0	0.8	0.0	0.0	21.4	12.9	0.0	4.1	3.6
Corvallis	0.0	5.9	0.2	0.0	0.0	20.1	18.1	9.1	2.8	3.7
Eugene	0.0	2.5	1.5	0.0	0.0	18.2	14.0	9.7	2.9	0.9
Grants Pass	0.0	8.4	0.0	0.0	0.0	30.5	11.8	5.8	3.1	1.3
Gresham	0.0	10.0	0.0	0.0	0.0	20.1	23.2	3.0	1.4	3.3
Hillsboro	0.0	8.1	0.1	0.0	0.0	20.0	22.0	13.5	1.2	2.5
Keizer	0.0	10.4	0.0	0.0	0.0	28.9	33.1	2.7	4.7	7.4
Lake Oswego	0.0	4.0	0.0	0.0	0.0	13.3	14.8	11.9	0.0	6.6
McMinnville	0.0	5.9	0.0	0.0	10.6	19.5	16.7	11.4	0.0	3.2
Medford	0.0	12.8	0.4	0.0	0.0	19.0	14.3	5.7	5.9	15.0
Oregon City	0.0	35.9	0.8	0.0	0.0	15.8	13.8	8.7	1.1	3.8
Portland	0.0	13.9	0.6	0.0	0.0	13.5	20.3	7.8	7.5	7.6

City	City government finances, 2012 (cont.)			Climate[2]						
	Debt outstanding			Average daily temperature (degrees Fahrenheit)						
				Mean		Limits				
	Total (mil dol)	Per capita[1] (dollars)	Debt issued during year	January	July	January[3]	July[4]	Annual precipitation (inches)	Heating degree days	Cooling degree days
	137	138	139	140	141	142	143	144	145	146
OHIO—Cont'd										
Hamilton	315.7	5 070	50.5	28.7	76.6	19.9	88.1	43.36	5 261	1 135
Hilliard	62.6	2 046	8.0	NA	NA	NA	NA	NA	NA	NA
Huber Heights	57.3	1 501	0.6	27.9	77.0	20.6	87.2	39.41	5 343	1 214
Kent	19.1	645	0.0	27.2	74.1	20.1	83.9	36.07	5 752	856
Kettering	18.1	324	0.0	27.9	77.0	20.6	87.2	39.41	5 343	1 214
Lakewood	92.2	1 795	12.3	25.7	71.9	18.8	81.4	38.71	6 121	702
Lancaster	375.7	9 659	0.2	26.5	73.1	17.8	84.4	36.55	5 887	764
Lima	36.5	953	1.1	25.5	73.6	18.1	84.0	37.20	5 932	835
Lorain	48.2	755	6.9	27.1	73.8	19.3	85.0	38.02	5 731	818
Mansfield	9.9	210	0.4	24.3	71.0	16.2	81.8	43.24	6 364	653
Marion	44.8	1 215	0.0	24.5	72.7	16.0	83.7	38.35	6 300	703
Mason	120.3	3 846	16.6	NA	NA	NA	NA	NA	NA	NA
Massillon	22.4	697	0.1	25.2	71.8	17.4	82.3	38.47	6 154	678
Medina	45.6	1 720	0.0	23.7	71.3	16.2	82.0	38.34	6 525	558
Mentor	34.9	742	4.4	23.0	68.8	14.3	80.0	47.33	6 956	372
Middletown	241.5	4 959	0.3	27.5	74.2	18.3	86.3	39.54	5 609	879
Newark	24.5	514	2.9	25.8	72.7	17.3	83.8	41.62	6 084	687
North Olmsted	38.8	1 199	1.4	25.7	71.9	18.8	81.4	38.71	6 121	702
North Ridgeville	34.1	1 115	4.1	NA	NA	NA	NA	NA	NA	NA
North Royalton	40.3	1 328	15.0	25.7	71.9	18.8	81.4	38.71	6 121	702
Parma	37.5	465	0.0	25.7	71.9	18.8	81.4	38.71	6 121	702
Reynoldsburg	22.9	631	0.0	28.3	75.1	20.3	85.3	38.52	5 492	951
Riverside	2.0	79	0.0	NA	NA	NA	NA	NA	NA	NA
Sandusky	27.6	1 078	4.1	25.6	73.8	18.9	81.8	34.46	6 065	785
Shaker Heights	27.3	972	0.3	25.7	71.9	18.8	81.4	38.71	6 121	702
Springfield	42.8	711	0.0	26.1	73.5	18.2	83.8	37.70	5 921	796
Stow	28.9	832	0.0	27.2	74.1	20.1	83.9	36.07	5 752	856
Strongsville	60.3	1 353	10.7	25.7	71.9	18.8	81.4	38.71	6 121	702
Toledo	357.2	1 260	8.3	27.5	77.6	21.7	87.1	33.52	5 464	1 257
Troy	19.5	768	0.0	NA	NA	NA	NA	NA	NA	NA
Upper Arlington	51.9	1 515	6.0	28.3	75.1	20.3	85.3	38.52	5 492	951
Warren	33.9	832	0.0	24.0	70.2	15.3	82.4	37.80	6 678	458
Westerville	75.5	2 027	10.0	27.7	74.4	19.7	85.4	39.35	5 434	924
Westlake	43.8	1 350	7.4	27.1	73.8	19.3	85.0	38.02	5 731	818
Wooster	10.1	381	0.0	NA	NA	NA	NA	NA	NA	NA
Xenia	7.4	286	1.1	NA	NA	NA	NA	NA	NA	NA
Youngstown	32.0	483	0.0	24.9	69.9	17.4	81.0	38.02	6 451	552
Zanesville	6.6	261	0.0	24.3	68.4	16.3	78.7	36.91	6 639	373
OKLAHOMA	X	X	X	X	X	X	X	X	X	X
Bartlesville	60.7	1 673	0.0	35.4	82.2	23.7	94.5	38.99	3 743	1 894
Broken Arrow	183.9	1 802	48.4	34.8	81.3	23.5	92.9	40.46	3 917	1 746
Edmond	136.7	1 609	0.0	36.7	82.0	26.2	93.1	35.85	3 663	1 907
Enid	78.5	1 572	17.0	33.1	82.6	21.9	94.4	34.25	4 269	1 852
Lawton	141.0	1 431	38.0	38.2	84.2	26.4	95.7	31.64	3 326	2 199
Midwest City	106.7	1 901	73.2	36.7	82.0	26.2	93.1	35.85	3 663	1 907
Moore	71.4	1 232	25.2	36.7	82.0	26.2	93.1	35.85	3 663	1 907
Muskogee	44.3	1 136	5.0	36.1	82.1	25.2	93.1	43.77	3 667	1 858
Norman	372.5	3 217	23.4	35.8	82.1	23.2	93.9	41.65	3 713	1 906
Oklahoma City	1 318.9	2 199	185.3	36.7	82.0	26.2	93.1	35.85	3 663	1 907
Owasso	39.4	1 254	0.0	NA	NA	NA	NA	NA	NA	NA
Ponca City	59.4	2 385	24.9	33.8	82.9	23.8	94.1	36.41	4 053	1 964
Shawnee	23.5	767	3.5	37.3	83.0	25.5	94.5	40.87	3 460	2 024
Stillwater	38.1	817	4.6	34.5	82.3	21.9	93.6	36.71	3 899	1 881
Tulsa	1 254.1	3 179	126.1	37.4	81.9	27.1	92.2	45.10	3 413	1 905
OREGON	X	X	X	X	X	X	X	X	X	X
Albany	122.1	2 381	0.0	40.3	66.5	33.6	81.2	43.66	4 715	247
Beaverton	26.4	285	0.0	40.0	66.8	33.8	79.2	39.95	4 723	287
Bend	92.3	1 171	10.9	31.2	63.5	22.6	80.7	11.73	7 042	147
Corvallis	59.4	1 080	0.0	38.1	63.8	31.6	77.4	67.76	5 501	139
Eugene	418.2	2 649	112.5	39.8	66.2	33.0	81.5	50.90	4 786	242
Grants Pass	12.2	350	0.0	NA	NA	NA	NA	NA	NA	NA
Gresham	82.4	758	3.0	40.0	68.3	33.5	81.5	45.70	4 491	450
Hillsboro	62.2	652	0.0	40.5	67.6	35.1	80.4	38.19	4 532	323
Keizer	28.7	779	0.0	40.3	66.8	33.5	81.5	40.00	4 784	257
Lake Oswego	156.3	4 196	37.7	41.8	69.3	35.7	82.6	46.05	4 132	475
McMinnville	22.1	668	5.6	39.6	66.6	33.0	81.9	41.66	4 815	288
Medford	380.1	4 966	26.6	39.1	72.7	30.9	90.2	18.37	4 539	711
Oregon City	33.8	1 009	0.0	41.8	69.3	35.7	82.6	46.05	4 132	475
Portland	3 381.1	5 608	353.6	41.8	69.3	35.7	82.6	46.05	4 132	475

1. Based on the population estimated as of July 1 of the year shown.   2. Represents normal values based on the 30-year period, 1971–2000.   3. Average daily minimum.
4. Average daily maximum.

Table D. Cities — Land Area and Population

STATE Place code	City	Land area,[1] 2010 (sq km)	Population, 2015 Total persons	Rank	Per square kilometer	Race alone or in combination (percent), 2010-2014 White	Black	American Indian, Alaska Native	Asian	Hawaiian Pacific Islander	Percent Hispanic or Latino[2], 2010-2014	Percent foreign born 2010–2014
		1	2	3	4	5	6	7	8	9	10	11
	OREGON—Cont'd											
41 61200	Redmond	43.5	28 654	1 291	658.7	95.7	0.9	2.2	1.6	1.3	13.1	6.4
41 64900	Salem	124.1	164 549	152	1 325.9	84.1	2.2	4.2	4.2	1.5	21.3	12.0
41 69600	Springfield	40.8	60 870	593	1 491.9	93.2	1.4	3.9	2.8	0.6	11.8	5.3
41 73650	Tigard	30.6	51 253	739	1 674.9	86.8	2.1	1.6	8.6	0.7	11.3	13.5
41 74950	Tualatin	21.3	27 154	1 353	1 274.8	92.4	2.6	2.2	3.2	0.6	18.5	12.2
41 80150	West Linn	19.1	26 593	1 376	1 392.3	92.4	1.1	0.8	6.9	0.8	4.6	9.1
42 00000	PENNSYLVANIA	115 883.1	12 802 503	X	110.5	83.6	12.1	0.7	3.4	0.1	6.1	6.1
42 02000	Allentown	45.4	120 207	227	2 647.7	65.9	16.4	1.1	2.3	0.3	46.0	15.5
42 02184	Altoona	25.7	45 344	828	1 764.4	95.8	4.6	0.6	1.1	0.0	1.0	1.3
42 06064	Bethel Park	30.2	32 118	1 175	1 063.5	96.0	2.7	0.4	1.8	0.1	0.9	2.5
42 06088	Bethlehem	49.5	74 892	457	1 513.0	81.0	10.5	1.3	3.3	0.1	25.5	8.4
42 13208	Chester	12.5	34 092	1 100	2 727.4	20.9	75.5	0.8	0.8	0.2	10.1	4.3
42 21648	Easton	10.6	26 915	1 364	2 539.2	73.5	22.9	2.1	3.3	0.2	21.7	12.2
42 24000	Erie	49.4	99 475	304	2 013.7	78.8	19.6	0.7	2.8	0.1	6.7	6.6
42 32800	Harrisburg	21.1	49 081	770	2 326.1	38.2	54.2	1.9	4.5	0.2	19.5	9.8
42 33408	Hazleton	15.6	24 825	1 422	1 591.3	75.8	7.7	2.1	1.0	0.1	46.2	26.1
42 41216	Lancaster	18.7	59 339	619	3 173.2	63.3	19.6	1.0	3.8	0.3	39.7	9.2
42 42168	Lebanon	10.8	25 534	1 407	2 364.3	70.1	6.0	0.8	1.0	0.2	38.1	6.7
42 50528	Monroeville	51.1	28 176	1 310	551.4	81.6	15.0	0.6	5.5	0.1	1.4	7.0
42 54656	Norristown	9.1	34 412	1 092	3 781.5	57.1	38.5	1.2	2.6	0.8	24.8	18.3
42 60000	Philadelphia	347.3	1 567 442	5	4 513.2	43.5	44.7	1.0	7.3	0.3	13.0	12.5
42 61000	Pittsburgh	143.4	304 391	63	2 122.7	69.2	26.6	1.2	5.6	0.2	2.7	7.5
42 61536	Plum	74.0	27 505	1 339	371.7	95.6	3.7	0.6	1.0	0.1	1.5	1.5
42 63624	Reading	25.6	87 879	366	3 432.8	63.2	17.7	6.3	1.1	0.5	60.0	18.5
42 69000	Scranton	65.6	77 118	438	1 175.6	87.3	8.1	0.5	4.1	0.1	10.9	9.0
42 73808	State College	11.8	42 161	885	3 573.0	84.3	5.1	0.5	11.0	0.0	4.2	11.6
42 85152	Wilkes-Barre	18.1	40 780	916	2 253.0	80.2	15.7	0.8	1.7	0.1	13.3	6.1
42 85312	Williamsport	22.6	29 201	1 268	1 292.1	82.8	17.7	0.4	1.0	0.1	3.8	1.7
42 87048	York	13.7	43 992	849	3 211.1	60.8	32.7	1.0	1.2	0.0	28.5	7.0
44 00000	RHODE ISLAND	2 677.6	1 056 298	X	394.5	83.5	7.8	1.2	3.7	0.2	13.3	13.1
44 19180	Cranston	73.4	81 073	410	1 104.5	84.8	6.2	1.2	6.1	0.1	11.5	13.0
44 22960	East Providence	34.3	47 408	800	1 382.2	86.5	10.2	1.7	2.8	0.2	5.3	15.5
44 54640	Pawtucket	22.5	71 591	485	3 181.8	67.0	20.6	1.2	2.1	0.3	20.6	23.7
44 59000	Providence	47.7	179 207	135	3 757.0	53.6	18.6	2.2	7.0	0.5	40.4	29.8
44 74300	Warwick	90.8	81 699	406	899.8	93.5	2.1	0.8	3.2	0.0	4.4	6.7
44 80780	Woonsocket	20.0	41 475	902	2 073.8	82.4	9.6	0.5	7.9	0.0	14.2	10.8
45 00000	SOUTH CAROLINA	77 856.8	4 896 146	X	62.9	68.8	28.7	0.9	1.7	0.1	5.3	4.8
45 00550	Aiken	53.6	30 604	1 217	571.0	67.7	29.9	0.7	2.9	0.0	4.8	5.0
45 01360	Anderson	37.8	27 335	1 348	723.1	61.9	37.1	0.7	1.2	0.0	4.0	3.4
45 13330	Charleston	282.3	132 609	199	469.7	73.1	25.5	0.8	1.8	0.2	2.8	3.9
45 16000	Columbia	342.4	133 803	195	390.8	53.4	43.4	1.1	2.7	0.3	5.3	5.4
45 25810	Florence	54.1	38 228	980	706.6	51.6	47.2	0.6	1.7	0.0	2.1	2.3
45 29815	Goose Creek	103.8	40 633	921	391.5	72.9	20.6	1.3	6.6	0.4	5.6	5.8
45 30850	Greenville	74.3	64 579	555	869.2	66.7	30.7	0.7	2.3	0.2	5.5	7.0
45 30985	Greer	53.5	28 365	1 297	530.2	74.8	20.3	1.2	2.8	0.0	17.4	11.9
45 34045	Hilton Head Island	107.1	40 512	925	378.3	82.7	8.9	0.6	1.0	0.0	14.1	14.6
45 48535	Mount Pleasant	116.8	81 317	409	696.2	93.6	4.8	0.3	2.4	0.3	2.8	4.6
45 49075	Myrtle Beach	60.4	31 035	1 195	513.8	78.7	12.9	1.6	2.0	0.8	13.3	16.8
45 50875	North Charleston	189.6	108 304	271	571.2	46.4	49.7	1.0	2.9	0.1	10.2	8.6
45 61405	Rock Hill	92.5	71 548	487	773.5	56.7	40.8	0.9	3.1	0.1	4.8	4.8
45 68290	Spartanburg	51.2	37 867	996	739.6	50.2	48.0	0.8	1.9	0.3	2.6	3.8
45 70270	Summerville	46.7	48 848	775	1 046.0	78.6	21.2	0.7	1.7	0.1	4.3	3.5
45 70405	Sumter	83.1	40 816	915	491.2	48.7	49.4	0.7	1.9	0.0	4.1	3.9
46 00000	SOUTH DAKOTA	196 349.6	858 469	X	4.4	87.7	2.1	10.3	1.4	0.1	3.2	2.9
46 00100	Aberdeen	40.2	28 102	1 312	699.1	92.2	1.5	4.9	2.1	0.0	2.1	3.4
46 52980	Rapid City	143.5	73 569	470	512.7	86.0	2.9	14.9	1.9	0.1	5.2	1.8
46 59020	Sioux Falls	189.0	171 544	145	907.6	88.2	5.6	3.5	2.5	0.1	4.8	7.1
47 00000	TENNESSEE	106 797.9	6 600 299	X	61.8	79.7	17.6	1.0	1.9	0.1	4.8	4.7
47 03440	Bartlett	69.0	58 579	632	849.0	77.1	19.7	0.5	3.2	0.2	2.8	4.0
47 08280	Brentwood	106.7	41 763	896	391.4	89.2	4.6	0.5	7.3	0.1	2.6	8.0
47 08540	Bristol	83.7	26 666	1 373	318.6	95.0	3.1	0.3	0.7	0.0	2.2	2.1
47 14000	Chattanooga	355.2	176 588	137	497.2	61.5	35.0	0.8	2.6	0.2	5.5	5.4
47 15160	Clarksville	252.8	149 176	173	590.1	70.9	25.7	2.0	3.5	0.7	10.2	6.4
47 15400	Cleveland	69.7	43 898	852	629.8	88.0	9.2	0.9	2.0	0.4	8.8	8.2
47 16420	Collierville	75.9	48 863	774	643.8	79.2	13.7	1.2	7.0	0.0	2.9	6.4

1. Dry land or land partially or temporarily covered by water.   2. May be of any race.

Table D. Cities — **Population**

City	Age of population (percent), 2010-2014									Median age 2010–2014	Percent female 2010–2014	Population			
												Census counts		Percent change	
	Under 5 years	5 to 17 years	18 to 24 years	25 to 34 years	35 to 44 years	45 to 54 years	55 to 64 years	65 to 74 years	75 years and over			2000	2010	2000–2010	2010–2015
	12	13	14	15	16	17	18	19	20	21	22	23	24	25	26
OREGON—Cont'd															
Redmond	7.0	19.2	9.9	13.1	11.8	10.2	13.7	8.1	6.9	36.3	52.9	13 481	26 215	94.5	9.3
Salem	7.4	18.0	10.5	14.1	12.9	12.5	11.7	7.1	5.9	35.0	50.9	136 924	154 637	12.9	6.3
Springfield	6.9	16.8	11.3	15.0	12.8	13.2	13.3	5.9	4.8	35.0	51.5	52 864	59 403	12.4	2.5
Tigard	5.9	16.7	9.0	13.8	14.4	14.4	13.2	7.0	5.5	38.2	50.4	41 223	48 035	16.5	6.6
Tualatin	7.3	18.9	8.1	13.2	17.0	13.4	14.1	4.8	3.2	36.2	51.3	22 791	26 054	14.3	4.3
West Linn	3.8	19.2	6.9	8.2	12.8	19.1	15.8	8.6	5.5	44.4	49.1	22 261	25 109	12.8	5.9
PENNSYLVANIA	5.6	15.8	9.9	12.4	12.2	14.7	13.5	8.3	7.7	40.4	51.2	12 281 054	12 702 379	3.4	0.8
Allentown	7.5	18.6	12.4	14.5	12.7	12.4	10.3	5.6	6.1	32.9	51.6	106 632	118 032	10.7	1.7
Altoona	6.6	16.3	9.8	12.4	12.2	12.6	13.6	8.8	7.8	39.0	50.1	49 523	46 320	-6.5	-2.1
Bethel Park	5.0	16.0	5.5	11.5	11.6	17.1	13.2	9.4	10.6	45.5	53.2	33 556	32 313	-3.7	-0.6
Bethlehem	4.8	14.8	15.3	14.3	11.3	12.4	11.7	7.6	7.9	35.7	51.1	71 329	74 982	5.1	-0.1
Chester	6.7	16.0	17.2	13.9	11.2	11.0	11.8	7.5	4.7	30.9	52.7	36 854	33 972	-7.8	0.4
Easton	6.6	15.5	17.0	15.3	12.6	11.6	10.2	5.9	5.3	32.3	52.0	26 263	26 800	2.0	0.4
Erie	7.0	15.7	13.3	15.1	11.5	12.8	11.4	6.6	6.6	34.2	50.8	103 717	101 786	-1.9	-2.3
Harrisburg	8.6	18.4	11.0	15.4	13.8	11.5	11.7	5.5	4.1	32.5	52.4	48 950	49 528	1.2	-0.9
Hazleton	7.5	17.0	12.2	13.0	11.3	14.5	10.0	6.8	7.8	35.5	50.2	23 329	25 340	8.6	-2.0
Lancaster	7.7	17.9	14.0	18.2	11.9	12.3	9.4	4.9	3.6	30.5	52.1	56 348	59 322	5.3	0.0
Lebanon	7.3	19.7	10.2	12.4	12.1	13.4	11.4	6.6	6.8	35.4	51.3	24 461	25 477	4.2	0.2
Monroeville	4.5	13.0	6.0	14.6	11.1	13.0	15.7	9.5	12.6	46.1	52.6	29 349	28 386	-3.3	-0.6
Norristown	7.7	15.5	11.2	18.1	14.3	12.7	10.7	5.3	4.5	33.8	48.7	31 282	34 324	9.7	0.3
Philadelphia	6.9	15.4	12.4	17.2	12.2	12.6	11.1	6.5	5.8	33.6	52.8	1 517 550	1 526 006	0.6	2.7
Pittsburgh	5.0	11.1	17.4	18.8	10.4	11.4	11.9	6.7	7.2	33.5	51.6	334 563	305 704	-8.6	-0.4
Plum	5.2	17.2	6.6	10.0	12.2	18.0	12.2	9.4	9.2	44.1	51.8	26 940	27 126	0.7	1.4
Reading	8.9	21.5	12.4	14.2	12.3	12.1	8.8	5.0	4.7	29.6	50.8	81 207	88 082	8.5	-0.2
Scranton	6.0	14.4	14.7	12.9	9.8	13.3	12.2	7.7	9.1	37.4	52.3	76 415	76 089	-0.4	1.4
State College	2.0	2.6	69.2	10.4	4.1	4.0	3.4	1.9	2.3	21.5	46.5	38 420	42 034	9.4	0.3
Wilkes-Barre	6.5	16.9	14.6	14.0	10.9	11.2	11.0	7.2	7.8	33.0	50.7	43 123	41 498	-3.8	-1.7
Williamsport	7.2	14.6	18.6	15.3	10.3	12.3	10.8	5.8	5.1	30.9	50.8	30 706	29 381	-4.3	-0.6
York	9.0	19.0	11.7	16.5	11.9	12.2	10.8	5.3	3.6	30.6	52.0	40 862	43 718	7.0	0.4
RHODE ISLAND	5.2	15.4	11.4	12.5	12.3	15.0	13.1	7.7	7.3	39.7	51.6	1 048 319	1 052 567	0.4	0.3
Cranston	6.0	14.2	10.0	12.4	13.0	16.7	12.8	7.2	7.8	40.9	49.9	79 269	80 387	1.4	0.9
East Providence	6.9	14.3	6.7	14.2	12.3	15.2	12.3	7.9	10.1	40.9	54.7	48 688	47 037	-3.4	0.8
Pawtucket	6.9	15.9	9.3	16.1	12.9	14.1	12.7	6.4	5.7	36.5	50.7	72 958	71 148	-2.5	0.6
Providence	5.9	17.0	19.6	16.7	12.1	11.1	8.9	4.5	4.1	28.9	51.3	173 618	178 042	2.5	0.7
Warwick	4.9	14.1	7.0	13.0	13.0	15.5	14.9	8.8	8.9	43.7	52.8	85 808	82 672	-3.7	-1.2
Woonsocket	7.2	15.2	8.7	15.1	11.9	14.9	12.3	7.3	7.4	37.8	50.0	43 224	41 186	-4.7	0.7
SOUTH CAROLINA	6.2	16.6	10.3	12.8	12.6	13.8	13.0	8.8	5.9	38.4	51.4	4 012 012	4 625 364	15.3	5.9
Aiken	5.0	13.7	13.0	9.1	8.6	11.8	15.7	12.4	10.6	45.5	55.7	25 337	29 524	16.5	3.5
Anderson	6.8	16.9	11.9	11.4	12.8	12.8	9.3	8.5	9.5	37.7	54.1	25 514	26 686	4.6	3.6
Charleston	6.2	11.5	15.4	18.7	12.1	11.6	11.7	7.5	5.3	33.9	52.8	96 650	120 083	24.2	10.3
Columbia	5.8	11.5	26.6	17.0	10.7	10.6	8.7	4.7	4.4	27.8	47.9	116 278	129 272	11.2	2.8
Florence	6.6	18.3	6.7	13.9	12.9	13.0	13.9	8.7	6.0	38.8	55.1	30 248	37 056	22.5	2.2
Goose Creek	7.5	16.9	15.9	15.6	11.9	14.4	9.8	5.7	2.3	30.4	46.7	29 208	35 938	23.0	12.4
Greenville	6.4	14.0	12.2	18.4	13.4	12.3	11.4	6.5	5.3	34.4	50.1	56 002	58 409	4.3	9.2
Greer	8.1	17.6	9.7	17.0	13.5	12.8	10.4	6.0	4.9	33.5	51.8	16 843	25 515	51.5	10.7
Hilton Head Island	3.0	11.9	5.0	9.5	10.1	13.1	15.5	18.4	13.3	53.1	49.3	33 862	37 099	9.6	9.2
Mount Pleasant	5.5	18.7	6.4	14.0	15.2	13.8	12.6	7.5	6.2	38.2	51.8	47 609	67 843	42.5	19.8
Myrtle Beach	6.0	10.3	7.0	16.0	13.5	13.1	15.9	10.6	7.6	42.0	51.3	22 759	27 109	19.1	14.5
North Charleston	8.6	15.8	12.0	19.6	11.9	12.9	10.6	5.3	3.2	31.2	50.5	79 641	97 471	22.4	10.9
Rock Hill	7.0	16.6	14.7	16.0	12.4	11.8	10.5	5.7	5.2	32.0	52.3	49 765	66 154	32.9	7.5
Spartanburg	8.1	13.7	15.6	11.2	11.4	13.0	11.5	7.6	7.8	36.5	56.7	39 673	37 013	-6.7	3.0
Summerville	7.6	19.4	9.6	12.6	14.9	14.2	10.3	5.8	5.6	35.4	53.1	27 752	43 392	56.4	14.7
Sumter	6.2	17.3	12.3	14.1	11.2	13.2	10.7	7.3	7.6	35.0	54.0	39 643	40 524	2.2	0.7
SOUTH DAKOTA	7.1	17.5	10.1	13.1	11.4	13.4	12.8	7.4	7.1	36.8	49.8	754 844	814 180	7.9	5.4
Aberdeen	7.4	15.5	12.0	15.3	10.5	11.5	11.9	6.7	9.2	34.8	51.8	24 658	26 091	5.8	7.7
Rapid City	7.9	15.9	10.0	14.8	11.3	12.3	12.7	7.5	7.5	35.9	50.2	59 607	67 956	14.0	7.4
Sioux Falls	8.2	16.1	10.0	17.4	12.6	12.9	11.8	5.9	5.3	33.9	50.2	123 975	153 888	24.1	11.4
TENNESSEE	6.2	16.9	9.7	13.0	13.1	14.1	12.8	8.3	5.9	38.3	51.2	5 689 283	6 346 105	11.5	4.0
Bartlett	6.5	19.6	7.4	10.2	13.9	14.9	14.0	7.8	5.7	39.6	51.2	40 543	54 613	34.7	2.9
Brentwood	5.7	24.7	5.2	5.9	14.4	18.5	14.1	7.5	4.1	41.6	50.6	23 445	37 060	58.1	12.7
Bristol	5.0	14.7	10.0	11.3	13.2	13.4	14.8	9.7	7.8	41.4	50.6	24 821	26 702	7.6	-0.2
Chattanooga	6.3	15.0	11.2	14.7	12.3	12.9	12.9	7.7	7.1	37.0	51.9	155 554	167 674	7.8	3.7
Clarksville	9.2	18.5	13.6	19.6	13.3	10.9	7.7	4.2	2.8	28.7	50.5	103 455	132 929	28.5	12.2
Cleveland	6.4	17.1	14.7	13.5	12.0	12.2	9.9	6.9	7.2	33.3	50.6	37 192	41 285	11.0	6.3
Collierville	5.6	22.9	7.1	9.5	14.1	18.0	12.8	6.1	3.9	38.7	52.3	31 872	43 965	37.9	7.1

Table D. Cities — Households, Group Quarters, Crime, and Education

City	Households, 2010-2014				Persons in group quarters, 2010				Serious crimes known to police,[2] 2014				Educational attainment, 2010–2014		
		Percent				Institutional			Total		Rate[3]			Attainment[4] (percent)	
	Number	Persons per household	Female family householder[1]	One-person	Total	Total	Persons in nursing facilities	Non-institutional	Number	Rate[3]	Violent	Property	Population age 25 and older	High school graduate or less	Bachelor's degree or more
	27	28	29	30	31	32	33	34	35	36	37	38	39	40	41
OREGON—Cont'd															
Redmond	10 156	2.66	15.8	24.2	300	181	181	119	1 076	3 880	328	3 552	17 122	40.7	18.7
Salem	57 925	2.73	12.8	29.8	8 635	5 610	639	3 025	7 583	4 680	314	4 367	102 388	39.0	26.9
Springfield	23 648	2.53	15.0	28.5	587	181	140	406	2 950	4 886	353	4 533	38 756	44.5	15.2
Tigard	19 694	2.52	9.4	27.0	347	111	78	236	1 445	2 832	149	2 683	34 392	24.1	41.4
Tualatin	10 677	2.49	9.5	28.1	87	45	45	42	787	2 906	103	2 803	17 874	26.1	41.8
West Linn	9 902	2.60	8.4	21.7	127	63	63	60	260	992	31	962	17 986	14.5	54.1
PENNSYLVANIA	4 957 736	2.57	12.0	29.6	426 113	197 112	87 775	229 001	287 180	2 246	314	1 932	8 764 740	47.8	28.1
Allentown	41 537	2.86	23.3	30.0	5 070	2 089	885	2 981	4 432	3 733	515	3 219	72 784	58.2	16.2
Altoona	18 755	2.45	14.5	33.8	1 189	452	443	737	1 049	2 297	348	1 949	31 038	60.0	16.2
Bethel Park	13 198	2.45	7.9	27.5	217	184	184	33	288	889	77	812	23 709	31.7	44.8
Bethlehem	29 359	2.56	15.2	34.9	6 265	955	882	5 310	2 034	2 711	281	2 430	48 339	46.9	26.5
Chester	12 068	2.82	31.5	36.9	3 151	1 328	143	1 823	1 699	4 989	1 536	3 453	20 353	66.6	9.5
Easton	9 513	2.84	19.5	31.2	3 087	1 093	311	1 994	713	2 627	298	2 328	16 599	56.4	17.9
Erie	40 825	2.47	17.5	36.9	5 244	1 578	715	3 666	3 046	3 034	404	2 629	64 084	55.5	21.2
Harrisburg	20 346	2.42	25.7	37.8	987	265	89	722	2 375	4 836	1 114	3 722	30 242	57.9	18.4
Hazleton	9 068	2.78	23.6	29.7	410	384	218	26	694	2 773	476	2 298	15 733	64.7	11.5
Lancaster	21 825	2.72	19.1	34.7	3 189	1 214	121	1 975	2 694	4 541	679	3 862	36 001	60.0	18.8
Lebanon	9 956	2.57	21.3	34.5	364	106	102	258	700	2 741	309	2 432	16 040	69.7	10.9
Monroeville	12 594	2.25	10.3	35.5	520	457	457	63	597	2 101	341	1 760	21 635	34.1	37.8
Norristown	12 735	2.71	20.2	33.2	947	224	224	723	1 139	3 306	746	2 560	22 270	58.3	18.3
Philadelphia	580 297	2.67	20.6	39.5	57 383	19 376	7 877	38 007	68 741	4 409	1 021	3 388	1 009 812	52.9	24.5
Pittsburgh	132 379	2.31	14.3	41.2	24 329	6 967	2 242	17 362	12 338	4 011	798	3 213	202 690	38.1	37.2
Plum	10 867	2.52	7.0	26.9	132	132	122	0	323	1 171	275	895	19 420	36.4	33.8
Reading	30 435	2.89	27.1	29.2	2 545	485	265	2 060	3 309	3 767	865	2 902	50 053	72.6	8.3
Scranton	28 924	2.62	15.0	34.9	5 472	2 380	1 444	3 092	2 318	3 060	285	2 775	49 222	53.6	21.4
State College	12 106	3.47	4.3	37.1	13 071	194	155	12 877	658	1 164	46	1 118	11 006	16.2	67.1
Wilkes-Barre	15 808	2.61	19.1	38.0	3 065	1 115	420	1 950	1 628	3 969	436	3 533	25 720	57.5	15.3
Williamsport	10 756	2.73	19.5	31.4	2 896	408	143	2 488	1 143	3 896	450	3 446	17 032	53.3	18.2
York	16 482	2.66	25.7	33.4	1 121	113	0	1 008	1 832	4 168	883	3 285	25 962	70.5	10.7
RHODE ISLAND	409 569	2.57	13.8	30.2	42 663	12 932	8 420	29 731	25 248	2 393	219	2 174	716 161	42.0	31.4
Cranston	30 536	2.64	12.0	29.9	4 523	4 004	224	519	1 703	2 105	133	1 971	57 016	44.2	29.6
East Providence	19 896	2.37	17.1	34.2	800	759	680	41	701	1 480	112	1 369	34 201	47.8	25.9
Pawtucket	28 124	2.54	19.6	32.8	524	357	335	167	2 328	3 259	291	2 967	48 247	55.1	17.4
Providence	60 967	2.93	22.0	30.9	15 086	1 200	1 152	13 886	7 793	4 362	522	3 840	102 934	49.9	28.6
Warwick	35 156	2.33	10.3	32.3	660	502	494	158	1 952	2 377	102	2 275	61 031	37.9	30.3
Woonsocket	16 979	2.42	16.8	35.7	802	568	568	234	1 336	3 247	532	2 715	28 078	57.2	14.0
SOUTH CAROLINA	1 795 715	2.63	15.2	27.8	139 154	63 765	19 020	75 389	191 269	3 958	498	3 460	3 163 095	45.0	25.3
Aiken	12 374	2.42	13.3	35.4	1 382	469	427	913	1 620	5 319	348	4 971	20 600	30.6	43.1
Anderson	10 851	2.47	20.1	38.0	1 751	716	577	1 035	2 429	8 953	992	7 962	17 381	50.6	20.6
Charleston	52 150	2.41	11.9	35.4	5 770	300	291	5 470	3 257	2 508	210	2 298	83 494	24.6	49.2
Columbia	44 992	2.92	16.2	38.8	29 919	7 777	920	22 142	8 280	6 173	772	5 401	74 696	33.3	40.1
Florence	14 870	2.52	23.1	30.4	654	389	384	265	3 128	8 242	843	7 399	24 934	40.3	29.3
Goose Creek	12 984	2.97	13.4	19.7	2 322	0	0	2 322	988	2 425	248	2 177	22 877	34.7	25.9
Greenville	26 161	2.32	12.9	42.9	5 129	1 393	208	3 736	3 397	5 486	809	4 677	40 689	34.3	41.5
Greer	10 067	2.64	15.7	29.1	272	130	130	142	903	3 279	356	2 923	17 357	41.5	30.2
Hilton Head Island	16 805	2.29	6.5	28.2	202	202	202	0	NA	NA	NA	NA	30 514	26.3	47.2
Mount Pleasant	29 101	2.49	8.4	27.2	568	544	544	24	1 502	1 958	180	1 778	50 595	15.2	58.4
Myrtle Beach	12 222	2.33	12.7	35.4	217	22	22	195	5 171	17 419	1 438	15 981	20 786	44.3	27.8
North Charleston	36 913	2.77	20.4	30.5	3 859	2 139	283	1 720	6 538	6 192	724	5 468	63 654	48.5	19.6
Rock Hill	26 635	2.56	18.5	31.5	3 005	612	442	2 393	2 733	3 918	515	3 403	41 927	39.5	27.9
Spartanburg	15 332	2.43	23.8	36.9	2 489	302	175	2 187	2 806	7 424	960	6 464	23 257	43.4	27.4
Summerville	16 542	2.70	14.5	26.3	318	251	160	67	1 773	3 788	299	3 489	28 810	34.0	30.8
Sumter	16 001	2.55	21.1	31.9	1 790	364	330	1 426	2 253	5 450	779	4 671	25 609	41.0	25.3
SOUTH DAKOTA	327 101	2.55	9.6	29.5	34 050	14 797	7 005	19 253	18 688	2 190	327	1 864	544 604	40.8	26.7
Aberdeen	11 363	2.37	11.1	36.0	1 191	433	351	758	623	2 255	279	1 976	17 314	43.1	26.5
Rapid City	28 244	2.48	11.6	33.1	2 471	1 331	491	1 140	3 140	4 393	599	3 794	46 536	36.0	29.2
Sioux Falls	64 197	2.51	11.6	30.4	6 085	3 336	982	2 749	5 694	3 403	445	2 958	105 130	36.5	32.5
TENNESSEE	2 487 349	2.59	13.5	28.1	153 472	84 371	33 041	69 101	240 295	3 669	608	3 061	4 336 243	48.1	24.4
Bartlett	19 683	2.94	11.4	17.6	703	688	244	15	1 155	1 973	268	1 705	38 458	31.4	35.5
Brentwood	12 486	3.13	4.9	9.2	349	312	275	37	376	923	47	876	25 082	12.7	67.9
Bristol	11 292	2.36	12.4	33.4	833	226	218	607	1 094	4 112	459	3 654	18 960	49.6	22.4
Chattanooga	69 890	2.46	16.8	35.4	7 562	3 067	1 212	4 495	12 697	7 278	973	6 306	116 077	42.7	26.3
Clarksville	50 351	2.79	16.2	22.3	2 921	904	419	2 017	5 255	3 633	671	2 963	82 124	37.8	23.6
Cleveland	15 671	2.70	13.2	31.4	2 703	786	430	1 917	2 960	6 862	858	6 004	26 618	45.2	24.3
Collierville	15 370	3.04	9.1	14.3	62	62	62	0	857	1 795	157	1 637	29 969	19.8	52.7

1. No spouse present.   2. Data for serious crimes have not been adjusted for underreporting. This may affect comparability between geographic areas and over time.   3. Per 100,000 population estimated by the FBI.   4. Persons 25 years old and over.

Table D. Cities — Income, Poverty, and Housing

City	Per capita income[1] (dollars)	Median income	Percent with income of $200,000 or more	Percent with income of less than $25,000	Families with income below poverty (percent)	Total	Percent change, 2000–2010	Vacant units for sale or rent[2]	Total	Percent	Median value[3] (dollars)	With a mortgage[4]	Without a mortgage[5]
	42	43	44	45	46	47	48	49	50	51	52	53	54
OREGON—Cont'd													
Redmond	18 723	39 008	0.1	31.7	19.5	10 965	92.8	1 018	10 156	54.2	155 800	28.3	12.1
Salem	23 201	46 273	2.1	25.5	14.7	61 276	14.0	3 986	57 925	53.5	181 500	25.1	12.7
Springfield	19 571	39 355	0.7	30.8	16.9	24 809	15.0	1 144	23 648	52.5	164 700	26.8	15.4
Tigard	33 884	60 849	5.1	16.8	7.4	20 068	15.4	911	19 694	61.1	294 000	24.4	11.1
Tualatin	34 502	65 903	6.8	19.6	8.7	10 528	14.2	528	10 677	56.2	310 400	22.8	11.5
West Linn	41 622	83 933	10.8	11.1	3.6	10 035	14.8	512	9 902	76.3	377 700	24.8	12.5
PENNSYLVANIA	28 912	53 115	4.4	23.2	9.3	5 567 315	6.0	548 411	4 957 736	69.5	164 900	22.7	13.5
Allentown	17 483	36 578	1.0	34.5	21.8	46 921	2.1	4 117	41 537	46.2	128 700	26.7	16.2
Altoona	19 962	36 258	1.4	35.2	14.3	21 179	-2.3	1 878	18 755	66.3	84 500	20.2	12.9
Bethel Park	35 292	70 102	4.5	12.2	2.4	14 311	3.2	652	13 198	78.7	158 700	19.9	12.9
Bethlehem	24 244	46 902	2.1	27.5	15.0	31 221	5.4	1 856	29 359	51.0	171 300	24.6	14.8
Chester	15 516	28 607	0.9	43.6	27.3	13 745	-8.2	2 083	12 068	39.7	67 200	26.5	14.0
Easton	19 731	39 773	1.6	33.4	19.6	10 356	-1.8	1 049	9 513	47.6	130 700	26.7	15.4
Erie	18 877	33 007	0.8	38.7	21.6	44 790	-0.4	3 877	40 825	51.4	84 700	22.1	14.0
Harrisburg	18 559	32 476	0.8	40.2	29.0	24 269	-0.3	3 664	20 346	38.6	84 100	23.8	13.9
Hazleton	16 781	30 947	1.0	36.3	24.0	11 409	-1.0	1 611	9 068	50.7	83 700	26.4	16.9
Lancaster	16 884	33 772	0.6	37.9	23.9	23 377	1.5	1 584	21 825	42.9	107 900	24.6	13.2
Lebanon	18 454	35 313	0.7	38.6	23.7	11 278	0.5	920	9 956	44.3	89 400	19.7	13.1
Monroeville	32 647	56 554	3.7	20.0	4.7	13 496	2.6	884	12 594	65.4	129 800	20.4	11.4
Norristown	21 369	42 296	1.3	29.6	18.8	13 420	-0.8	1 457	12 735	39.3	153 300	24.8	15.9
Philadelphia	22 542	37 460	2.6	35.8	21.2	670 171	1.2	70 435	580 297	52.9	143 200	25.0	15.3
Pittsburgh	27 435	40 009	3.9	33.9	16.2	156 165	-4.4	19 948	132 379	48.8	91 500	19.7	13.1
Plum	30 971	67 639	3.5	14.8	3.4	11 494	8.2	608	10 867	81.5	139 700	20.1	11.6
Reading	13 339	26 867	0.5	46.8	37.2	34 208	-0.3	4 229	30 435	42.8	67 500	27.2	15.4
Scranton	20 351	37 551	1.4	34.2	16.1	33 853	-4.2	3 784	28 924	51.9	107 400	22.5	16.2
State College	15 915	26 627	2.4	46.5	11.9	13 007	4.2	397	12 106	21.0	278 100	19.6	10.0
Wilkes-Barre	17 329	31 361	0.7	41.4	23.3	19 595	-3.4	2 721	15 808	47.2	79 500	22.1	14.3
Williamsport	18 162	33 537	1.6	37.1	24.4	12 864	-4.9	1 218	10 756	43.7	101 000	22.7	14.4
York	14 872	28 819	0.4	45.1	34.4	18 496	-0.2	2 243	16 482	41.3	82 500	26.7	16.2
RHODE ISLAND	30 765	56 423	5.1	23.4	10.0	463 388	5.4	49 788	409 569	60.3	241 200	25.8	15.6
Cranston	29 878	58 684	4.5	20.7	7.2	33 117	3.3	2 105	30 536	65.5	217 100	26.2	17.9
East Providence	28 446	51 077	3.1	25.9	9.2	21 440	0.6	1 239	19 896	55.6	216 000	26.1	17.1
Pawtucket	21 239	40 578	0.9	33.1	16.2	32 055	0.7	3 033	28 124	43.7	174 100	29.4	17.6
Providence	21 924	37 514	4.0	37.3	24.5	71 530	5.3	8 812	60 967	35.0	186 000	28.0	15.5
Warwick	33 889	62 803	4.2	19.3	4.8	37 730	1.7	2 496	35 156	71.5	198 200	25.6	15.2
Woonsocket	21 716	35 216	1.6	36.8	22.6	19 214	2.4	2 152	16 979	39.2	168 200	28.0	18.0
SOUTH CAROLINA	24 222	45 033	2.7	28.1	13.9	2 137 683	21.9	336 502	1 795 715	68.6	137 600	22.5	11.3
Aiken	30 773	53 489	4.1	25.9	10.4	14 162	25.3	1 389	12 374	69.3	174 000	20.1	10.0
Anderson	18 974	28 987	1.3	44.6	24.3	12 938	7.3	1 858	10 851	50.0	122 200	22.7	10.8
Charleston	33 117	52 971	6.6	25.3	12.6	59 522	34.8	7 181	52 150	52.5	248 200	24.4	13.0
Columbia	24 723	41 454	4.3	31.9	17.4	52 471	13.9	6 805	44 992	45.9	159 600	21.6	12.1
Florence	25 420	43 007	3.4	30.7	14.7	16 665	27.5	1 686	14 870	59.2	151 500	20.3	10.0
Goose Creek	26 032	62 107	2.3	15.8	9.7	13 484	42.4	1 128	12 984	64.8	167 600	21.9	10.0
Greenville	31 043	41 147	5.9	32.6	16.6	29 418	7.5	3 819	26 161	43.6	207 200	21.6	11.6
Greer	24 874	44 111	2.2	28.4	16.0	11 127	48.5	1 115	10 067	57.2	139 200	22.3	10.4
Hilton Head Island	45 116	68 437	10.8	15.2	5.4	33 306	35.0	16 771	16 805	72.4	447 400	30.8	12.6
Mount Pleasant	42 485	76 202	10.4	12.9	5.6	30 674	52.4	2 932	29 101	71.6	351 500	24.6	11.2
Myrtle Beach	26 949	37 064	4.0	34.9	18.7	23 262	59.2	11 149	12 222	51.8	167 000	29.2	11.1
North Charleston	19 820	39 446	1.1	32.3	19.5	42 219	25.5	5 304	36 913	46.5	142 000	25.5	14.4
Rock Hill	22 460	40 718	1.4	30.7	13.9	29 159	42.4	3 193	26 635	50.7	131 400	23.0	13.1
Spartanburg	20 858	34 092	2.5	40.3	24.1	17 516	-1.1	2 332	15 332	50.8	121 700	23.3	11.9
Summerville	25 808	55 290	2.5	19.1	10.2	18 557	64.9	1 691	16 542	63.2	179 000	22.3	12.3
Sumter	22 141	39 072	2.2	31.2	17.7	18 150	12.6	2 517	16 001	51.7	133 000	22.3	11.8
SOUTH DAKOTA	26 311	50 338	3.0	22.9	9.2	363 438	12.4	41 156	327 101	68.0	135 700	21.0	10.9
Aberdeen	25 468	47 540	2.4	25.9	6.1	12 158	8.1	740	11 363	63.5	133 300	20.1	13.1
Rapid City	25 983	46 392	3.1	24.6	9.7	30 254	20.4	1 668	28 244	58.8	153 900	22.7	12.4
Sioux Falls	28 120	52 607	3.3	19.8	8.9	66 283	28.1	4 576	64 197	60.8	155 200	21.1	10.0
TENNESSEE	24 811	44 621	3.1	28.0	13.4	2 812 133	15.3	318 581	2 487 349	67.1	139 900	22.7	11.0
Bartlett	32 392	80 240	4.5	8.6	3.3	20 143	43.9	687	19 683	82.7	172 900	21.7	10.6
Brentwood	58 745	138 395	32.6	4.3	2.3	12 577	58.5	407	12 486	91.5	487 900	20.3	10.0
Bristol	21 859	35 959	2.0	36.0	15.0	12 773	10.9	1 317	11 292	68.7	103 100	23.0	12.5
Chattanooga	24 134	39 683	2.7	32.6	17.1	79 607	10.4	8 858	69 890	53.3	141 300	23.0	11.8
Clarksville	21 395	47 489	1.4	23.4	14.6	54 815	36.9	5 376	50 351	55.0	135 500	22.2	10.2
Cleveland	23 066	37 325	2.7	35.6	19.9	17 841	8.4	1 734	15 671	49.2	156 500	23.4	10.5
Collierville	41 346	106 783	13.8	6.5	2.9	15 781	46.7	602	15 370	85.7	273 500	22.4	10.0

1. Based on population estimated by the American Community Survey. 2. Includes units rented or sold but not occupied. 3. Specified owner-occupied units; $1,000,000 represents $1,000,000 or more 4. 50.0 represents 50 percent or more. 5. 10.0 represents 10 percent or less.

Table D. Cities — Housing, Labor Force, and Employment

City	Occupied housing units, 2010–2014 (cont.)				Migration, 2010–2014		Civilian labor force, 2015		Unemployment		Civilian employment[4], 2010–2014	Percent		
	Percent renter occupied	Median gross rent[1]	Median gross rent as a percent of income[2]	Percent with no vehicle available	Percent who lived in the same house one year ago	Percent who lived outside current city one year ago	Total	Percent change, 2014–2015	Total	Rate[3]	Population age 16 and older	In labor force	Civilian full-year full-time workers	Households with no workers (percent)
	55	56	57	58	59	60	61	62	63	64	65	66	67	68
OREGON—Cont'd														
Redmond	45.8	876	37.2	6.7	78.2	11.9	11 540	3.9	726	6.3	20 340	61.2	28.9	39.7
Salem	46.5	788	32.6	9.2	78.2	11.7	75 593	2.2	4 538	6.0	123 125	61.6	33.7	30.3
Springfield	47.5	799	31.6	8.4	75.8	13.4	29 691	1.0	1 846	6.2	47 481	65.3	35.2	29.1
Tigard	38.9	959	31.0	5.2	83.6	13.8	28 496	2.2	1 249	4.4	40 172	70.7	42.2	22.9
Tualatin	43.8	976	31.5	6.8	87.1	10.2	14 556	2.4	670	4.6	21 109	72.5	45.3	21.0
West Linn	23.7	1 244	30.6	2.8	86.4	11.3	14 112	1.8	606	4.3	20 653	65.5	38.9	23.3
PENNSYLVANIA	30.5	832	30.4	11.5	88.0	8.9	6 423 903	0.5	330 045	5.1	10 351 296	62.9	39.3	29.4
Allentown	53.8	882	37.8	20.5	77.0	10.1	53 831	0.5	3 974	7.4	90 905	62.8	34.1	32.1
Altoona	33.7	563	31.1	13.7	87.8	4.5	20 684	0.1	1 152	5.6	36 602	59.2	35.4	35.3
Bethel Park	21.3	875	27.0	5.2	92.1	6.8	17 274	0.7	726	4.2	26 417	66.8	44.7	25.3
Bethlehem	49.0	929	32.6	13.9	79.2	11.3	37 025	0.5	2 137	5.8	62 305	58.7	35.6	33.8
Chester	60.3	810	35.6	33.8	85.1	9.1	13 285	-0.3	1 175	8.8	26 856	53.7	27.0	40.2
Easton	52.4	914	33.0	19.0	71.2	16.0	11 919	0.4	790	6.6	21 798	58.5	33.1	27.3
Erie	48.6	641	33.3	20.4	81.0	8.6	45 649	0.1	2 754	6.0	79 919	60.5	33.6	34.6
Harrisburg	61.4	769	33.4	29.4	78.6	10.6	21 574	0.8	1 463	6.8	36 973	62.3	36.2	35.4
Hazleton	49.3	699	31.5	18.6	82.9	8.1	11 586	-1.7	1 077	9.3	19 396	61.4	33.9	34.8
Lancaster	57.1	778	36.2	21.9	81.4	11.5	26 848	0.8	1 608	6.0	45 995	63.1	34.7	29.3
Lebanon	55.7	664	33.8	21.3	80.3	8.5	11 708	-0.4	805	6.9	19 389	65.0	37.2	35.4
Monroeville	34.6	875	27.2	6.8	88.5	9.2	14 722	0.2	676	4.6	23 951	61.6	40.5	31.1
Norristown	60.7	990	35.7	25.0	86.9	7.6	17 988	0.8	900	5.0	26 619	69.4	41.8	25.4
Philadelphia	47.1	915	34.7	32.8	85.8	4.6	696 194	0.8	47 914	6.9	1 239 760	59.2	34.4	35.4
Pittsburgh	51.2	794	30.3	24.7	79.1	11.8	157 832	0.2	8 012	5.1	262 136	61.9	36.6	31.7
Plum	18.5	869	25.7	4.4	92.9	5.5	15 017	0.3	681	4.5	22 249	67.2	45.2	26.0
Reading	57.2	732	39.5	29.1	77.6	8.3	34 262	0.4	2 519	7.4	64 269	60.4	28.8	37.7
Scranton	48.1	705	29.7	15.6	82.3	9.2	35 714	-0.5	2 193	6.1	62 156	57.5	34.7	34.9
State College	79.0	947	50.0	23.2	43.5	37.3	16 549	0.1	764	4.6	40 159	43.7	15.6	31.6
Wilkes-Barre	52.8	642	31.2	21.6	78.5	13.3	18 458	-0.6	1 311	7.1	33 446	56.7	31.4	36.2
Williamsport	56.3	691	31.9	18.3	78.7	11.6	14 247	-1.2	932	6.5	23 494	60.9	30.4	31.1
York	58.7	698	38.8	26.7	74.2	11.2	17 789	-0.2	1 503	8.4	32 814	60.7	30.1	38.8
RHODE ISLAND	39.7	923	30.9	9.8	86.6	9.5	554 558	-0.3	33 124	6.0	862 851	65.9	38.5	28.5
Cranston	34.5	980	32.0	6.3	89.8	7.3	41 368	-0.3	2 450	5.9	66 989	64.1	38.7	28.2
East Providence	44.4	888	28.1	9.6	86.5	7.4	24 279	-0.5	1 541	6.3	38 455	65.7	40.1	32.7
Pawtucket	56.3	827	30.3	16.7	84.7	8.9	36 332	-0.8	2 480	6.8	56 662	67.3	38.3	31.4
Providence	65.0	910	32.6	19.3	77.7	11.3	86 585	-0.5	6 157	7.1	143 441	64.2	32.9	30.1
Warwick	28.5	1 052	31.1	6.5	90.6	5.1	46 122	-0.1	2 397	5.2	68 882	68.4	42.3	28.4
Woonsocket	60.8	805	31.4	17.9	90.5	4.8	19 027	-0.5	1 477	7.8	32 229	58.8	37.2	36.1
SOUTH CAROLINA	31.4	784	31.6	7.0	84.5	12.9	2 257 077	1.8	134 504	6.0	3 768 421	61.2	37.4	30.6
Aiken	30.7	847	33.4	8.5	82.9	11.7	13 148	1.0	796	6.1	24 668	53.2	33.1	40.2
Anderson	50.0	630	35.5	14.7	77.2	13.6	11 613	2.3	686	5.9	21 174	54.4	30.0	40.9
Charleston	47.5	989	33.9	9.8	77.0	14.6	70 671	2.7	3 128	4.4	104 674	66.4	42.7	25.2
Columbia	54.1	833	32.6	11.5	64.8	26.1	59 597	1.8	3 661	6.1	111 984	64.3	31.4	27.4
Florence	40.8	664	31.8	11.2	84.6	8.3	18 614	1.6	1 089	5.9	28 868	65.5	41.2	29.2
Goose Creek	35.2	1 094	33.0	2.3	74.8	20.9	18 673	2.3	922	4.9	29 645	71.8	42.0	17.0
Greenville	56.4	774	29.3	11.8	76.2	17.1	32 694	2.7	1 559	4.8	49 916	65.6	38.7	28.9
Greer	42.8	751	27.7	6.5	79.8	13.8	14 509	2.5	631	4.3	20 714	69.0	42.9	23.5
Hilton Head Island	27.6	1 096	29.3	5.6	83.7	11.4	17 866	3.2	800	4.5	33 276	54.5	32.1	42.1
Mount Pleasant	28.4	1 257	31.0	3.1	81.0	10.5	42 450	2.8	1 627	3.8	56 871	71.4	48.9	21.1
Myrtle Beach	48.2	822	34.3	10.5	82.3	10.9	14 648	1.8	1 060	7.2	23 978	65.0	35.2	32.9
North Charleston	53.5	883	34.5	11.3	74.6	16.4	51 398	2.6	2 837	5.5	78 343	68.4	41.5	22.9
Rock Hill	49.3	786	33.3	8.2	78.4	10.8	36 652	2.2	2 203	6.0	53 993	68.3	40.9	25.8
Spartanburg	49.2	677	32.4	17.8	78.4	12.8	16 629	1.8	1 067	6.4	29 540	58.2	30.9	37.2
Summerville	36.8	977	32.4	4.8	78.1	16.4	22 617	2.7	1 160	5.1	34 303	66.8	43.0	24.9
Sumter	48.3	728	29.6	12.8	79.4	13.2	16 118	0.5	1 053	6.5	31 711	60.9	34.1	31.6
SOUTH DAKOTA	32.0	648	26.2	5.3	83.7	9.7	452 300	0.8	14 223	3.1	651 429	69.1	46.1	23.8
Aberdeen	36.5	576	25.9	7.8	79.8	10.7	15 269	0.3	440	2.9	21 291	70.7	46.7	23.5
Rapid City	41.2	779	28.9	6.4	77.1	10.0	35 411	0.2	1 265	3.6	55 048	67.8	40.7	26.7
Sioux Falls	39.2	713	26.7	6.3	81.9	6.6	98 044	1.8	2 723	2.8	125 269	74.7	52.0	19.3
TENNESSEE	32.9	757	30.9	6.4	84.6	10.1	3 062 775	0.5	176 751	5.8	5 125 250	61.4	38.7	29.8
Bartlett	17.3	1 197	29.5	2.7	91.1	6.5	29 669	0.0	1 540	5.2	44 777	67.9	47.1	17.9
Brentwood	8.5	1 964	26.8	1.7	90.1	7.8	20 061	1.8	843	4.2	29 039	65.3	43.7	14.5
Bristol	31.3	612	29.3	7.5	82.3	10.7	11 518	-1.7	686	6.0	21 919	55.7	33.9	38.2
Chattanooga	46.7	745	30.9	11.9	80.7	9.3	79 151	1.1	4 768	6.0	139 250	61.6	37.5	31.9
Clarksville	45.0	855	28.9	5.1	73.1	15.2	58 255	0.9	3 561	6.1	105 166	66.4	34.4	22.2
Cleveland	50.8	695	32.7	9.5	76.4	11.5	20 047	-0.6	1 146	5.7	33 677	59.7	33.3	30.7
Collierville	14.3	1 135	25.6	1.0	89.6	8.2	24 128	0.1	1 123	4.7	35 305	70.5	47.3	13.5

1. $2,000 represents $2,000 or more. 2. 50.0 represents 50 percent or more. 3. Percent of civilian labor force. 4. Persons 16 years old and over.

Table D. Cities — Construction, Wholesale Trade, and Retail Trade

City	Value of residential construction authorized by building permits, 2015			Wholesale trade,[1] 2012				Retail trade,[2] 2012			
	New construction ($1,000)	Number of housing units	Percent single family	Number of establishments	Number of employees	Sales (mil dol)	Annual payroll (mil dol)	Number of establishments	Number of employees	Sales (mil dol)	Annual payroll (mil dol)
	69	70	71	72	73	74	75	76	77	78	79
OREGON—Cont'd											
Redmond	45 225	198	96.5	33	206	78.9	8.4	113	1 962	532.5	50.2
Salem	92 691	440	61.6	141	1 652	1 862.8	77.8	604	9 646	2 535.4	252.4
Springfield	21 748	96	94.8	39	873	433.4	35.3	209	3 545	812.2	79.1
Tigard	42 840	249	32.5	148	2 255	2 065.8	150.7	327	7 093	1 827.1	198.3
Tualatin	18 399	121	19.0	107	1 685	785.6	90.2	109	1 837	478.3	43.0
West Linn	17 437	50	100.0	29	93	66.9	5.2	54	473	129.1	12.1
PENNSYLVANIA	4 406 389	22 854	67.5	12 568	195 004	191 170.1	11 203.8	43 952	643 903	178 794.9	15 330.6
Allentown	856	10	100.0	144	2 072	1 088.9	87.3	366	5 377	1 387.1	125.7
Altoona	701	7	28.6	47	803	355.3	36.0	248	4 693	1 095.5	94.3
Bethel Park	9 343	29	100.0	32	257	115.6	12.3	109	2 824	628.3	62.0
Bethlehem	3 446	28	100.0	59	D	D	D	214	3 511	919.0	79.5
Chester	0	0	0.0	18	163	78.1	8.3	61	340	119.5	10.6
Easton	295	4	100.0	28	D	D	D	143	1 730	423.5	39.8
Erie	410	5	100.0	110	1 629	679.5	74.2	374	5 516	1 018.6	108.5
Harrisburg	0	0	0.0	58	1 349	1 837.2	89.7	233	2 682	613.8	56.3
Hazleton	0	0	0.0	33	499	151.6	22.7	112	1 124	275.4	22.1
Lancaster	333	2	100.0	60	719	491.1	29.5	364	5 382	1 100.3	117.8
Lebanon	1 543	6	100.0	18	D	D	D	107	1 260	296.1	31.2
Monroeville	1 303	6	100.0	46	520	195.8	25.6	276	5 452	1 635.0	131.3
Norristown	1 400	18	55.6	43	732	456.5	38.6	92	614	134.5	16.5
Philadelphia	690 914	3 666	22.4	1 047	16 940	13 181.9	973.0	4 506	50 185	12 241.3	1 165.5
Pittsburgh	116 724	1 270	6.5	399	6 843	7 437.6	393.2	1 202	17 411	4 107.1	410.7
Plum	7 405	57	100.0	29	227	104.4	9.9	51	658	149.3	15.9
Reading	514	2	100.0	47	973	490.8	50.7	227	3 321	1 085.9	88.0
Scranton	93 880	414	100.0	96	1 385	963.1	62.1	340	4 493	1 127.2	102.9
State College	0	0	0.0	9	51	16.6	2.5	138	1 883	299.4	33.7
Wilkes-Barre	625	5	100.0	46	546	167.9	19.5	260	5 744	4 517.9	139.9
Williamsport	210	2	100.0	40	1 077	638.3	38.4	109	1 683	386.8	38.3
York	0	0	0.0	60	1 005	845.5	38.2	138	2 077	555.9	53.9
RHODE ISLAND	211 614	998	84.3	1 158	15 697	22 310.4	1 000.2	3 795	47 688	12 063.9	1 206.6
Cranston	6 021	50	100.0	129	D	D	D	288	4 488	1 135.5	124.6
East Providence	0	0	0.0	81	D	D	D	150	1 954	561.3	50.6
Pawtucket	1 205	8	100.0	64	D	D	D	176	1 604	456.3	41.9
Providence	10 904	91	16.5	184	1 942	1 475.2	102.4	646	6 835	1 448.7	156.4
Warwick	5 952	43	86.0	140	1 919	909.2	104.8	429	7 656	1 960.7	188.2
Woonsocket	985	9	100.0	33	D	D	D	129	1 366	328.2	35.2
SOUTH CAROLINA	6 242 696	31 030	78.4	4 337	54 949	45 520.9	2 806.2	17 586	220 438	58 093.8	4 954.6
Aiken	21 139	121	100.0	19	92	158.2	4.2	233	3 420	774.1	68.4
Anderson	5 027	39	100.0	35	253	105.4	9.3	279	4 031	819.8	84.6
Charleston	123 139	1 045	62.3	137	1 331	1 032.0	80.8	733	10 061	2 642.6	246.2
Columbia	57 204	508	43.3	206	3 094	2 469.9	181.7	657	10 186	2 631.1	231.5
Florence	NA	NA	NA	59	973	545.1	45.0	382	5 058	1 162.9	107.6
Goose Creek	31 777	180	100.0	9	D	D	D	74	1 511	387.6	34.0
Greenville	258 115	2 036	12.4	173	2 302	2 438.0	117.4	777	12 402	3 109.2	298.0
Greer	61 911	291	100.0	42	309	134.3	13.1	138	2 345	786.4	63.9
Hilton Head Island	51 487	93	100.0	54	188	132.4	9.7	259	2 750	645.8	67.0
Mount Pleasant	370 205	1 341	70.1	69	388	149.9	24.7	360	5 269	1 145.8	115.5
Myrtle Beach	131 125	474	84.0	82	616	281.5	26.0	683	9 822	2 163.0	206.7
North Charleston	56 682	483	100.0	219	3 399	1 876.0	177.0	580	8 363	2 269.3	203.1
Rock Hill	103 911	545	42.9	68	1 091	556.9	57.5	322	4 914	1 279.3	106.0
Spartanburg	4 729	20	100.0	63	508	352.6	26.2	355	5 853	1 418.3	130.5
Summerville	50 659	231	100.0	39	339	279.2	12.0	196	3 764	909.6	82.7
Sumter	NA	NA	NA	31	278	96.0	11.7	289	3 599	754.7	69.1
SOUTH DAKOTA	740 741	4 482	64.0	1 317	15 827	20 411.1	756.9	3 843	49 867	13 791.8	1 127.3
Aberdeen	11 529	154	40.9	42	698	1 225.2	35.3	176	2 778	751.1	70.2
Rapid City	58 359	414	49.3	139	1 600	1 109.9	69.4	475	7 691	2 110.4	183.0
Sioux Falls	225 125	1 562	47.2	324	5 257	3 108.2	267.7	751	14 515	4 340.9	342.0
TENNESSEE	5 596 464	32 219	67.2	5 828	92 537	111 718.4	4 863.3	22 615	306 078	91 641.6	7 420.3
Bartlett	47 729	221	100.0	64	1 097	755.5	62.6	124	2 019	889.8	54.7
Brentwood	95 323	240	100.0	59	785	1 413.2	49.0	175	3 254	1 076.3	102.5
Bristol	19 491	320	13.1	40	394	123.1	12.5	118	1 872	597.2	51.0
Chattanooga	100 507	610	74.8	374	4 859	2 711.5	249.6	1 123	16 813	4 359.1	419.3
Clarksville	84 569	756	91.0	68	952	553.2	43.2	489	7 756	1 983.0	188.4
Cleveland	33 437	375	21.9	41	D	D	D	297	4 319	1 150.0	103.0
Collierville	65 090	280	57.1	50	671	518.5	41.7	213	3 540	852.9	76.9

1. Merchant wholesalers except manufacturers' sales branches and offices. 2. Establishments with payroll.

Table D. Cities — **Real Estate, Professional Services, and Manufacturing**

City	Real estate and rental and leasing, 2012				Professional, scientific, and technical services,[1] 2012				Manufacturing, 2012			
	Number of establish-ments	Number of employees	Receipts (mil dol)	Annual payroll (mil dol)	Number of establish-ments	Number of employees	Receipts (mil dol)	Annual payroll (mil dol)	Number of establish-ments	Number of employees	Receipts (mil dol)	Annual payroll (mil dol)
	80	81	82	83	84	85	86	87	88	89	90	91
OREGON—Cont'd												
Redmond	42	164	23.8	5.5	43	D	D	D	59	951	221.6	36.9
Salem	271	1 130	173.7	40.0	494	3 110	381.0	145.7	182	5 324	1 708.8	217.6
Springfield	64	274	54.2	8.4	87	572	49.3	20.0	85	2 380	1 240.8	126.6
Tigard	121	615	219.5	27.6	362	D	D	D	93	1 716	D	D
Tualatin	59	595	125.1	23.3	107	D	D	D	121	6 893	2 103.6	410.6
West Linn	41	172	16.9	4.9	122	290	44.4	15.5	10	264	D	D
PENNSYLVANIA	9 438	58 585	13 364.0	2 617.5	29 113	310 692	54 014.0	22 242.0	13 988	543 641	231 396.2	28 057.8
Allentown	95	498	93.0	16.6	214	D	D	D	140	2 442	687.5	115.1
Altoona	41	193	30.0	6.0	87	D	D	D	45	1 006	293.8	39.6
Bethel Park	30	104	32.6	5.2	92	391	69.9	25.5	30	441	82.1	18.1
Bethlehem	62	306	167.0	13.3	176	1 009	152.0	61.7	53	3 306	1 017.5	188.3
Chester	15	D	D	D	14	D	D	D	26	1 401	929.4	99.3
Easton	21	D	D	D	87	369	59.0	15.1	26	505	233.3	22.1
Erie	66	427	61.9	15.9	196	D	D	D	148	5 832	1 842.9	298.2
Harrisburg	44	381	206.6	40.2	256	D	D	D	32	1 432	666.1	84.0
Hazleton	19	51	9.6	1.5	54	472	70.1	11.7	47	2 606	1 393.1	105.5
Lancaster	48	394	65.3	13.7	222	D	D	D	74	3 363	1 357.6	168.3
Lebanon	27	128	17.6	3.8	53	D	D	D	55	1 140	342.7	44.0
Monroeville	58	546	99.3	21.3	100	1 194	155.2	84.5	17	549	D	30.5
Norristown	29	108	36.4	3.7	94	D	D	D	16	470	D	19.6
Philadelphia	1 079	8 856	1 951.0	443.5	2 793	44 342	10 124.7	4 075.8	765	22 558	19 718.6	1 198.5
Pittsburgh	473	3 628	816.9	179.9	1 505	D	D	D	295	7 303	2 054.6	372.7
Plum	17	57	12.4	1.9	37	539	145.0	54.7	26	320	145.4	14.0
Reading	60	436	61.7	14.1	129	D	D	D	94	7 270	3 814.0	457.0
Scranton	54	333	56.8	10.3	205	D	D	D	77	2 100	660.4	91.6
State College	56	401	91.1	15.9	90	D	D	D	5	169	D	10.4
Wilkes-Barre	34	237	58.7	10.4	119	D	D	D	26	1 099	279.5	48.4
Williamsport	28	204	38.7	8.0	75	1 194	86.8	37.2	51	3 612	1 461.4	168.1
York	36	297	39.9	11.4	137	D	D	D	76	3 422	1 334.4	192.6
RHODE ISLAND	1 058	5 615	1 119.8	218.5	2 980	20 991	3 316.8	1 300.2	1 509	39 608	11 262.2	2 076.5
Cranston	66	366	67.9	14.3	222	1 893	287.4	103.5	156	4 275	1 845.9	211.8
East Providence	57	376	165.0	17.0	129	1 318	191.7	68.9	89	2 304	654.6	112.1
Pawtucket	55	311	38.2	12.4	106	D	D	D	132	3 327	733.0	169.5
Providence	208	1 126	227.9	50.4	790	D	D	D	217	3 165	628.4	135.4
Warwick	111	1 102	223.1	42.2	344	D	D	D	130	3 281	1 227.7	199.0
Woonsocket	40	131	18.0	4.5	44	262	40.2	12.7	43	853	178.8	39.5
SOUTH CAROLINA	4 692	23 189	4 334.4	825.9	9 688	79 433	12 645.3	4 789.2	3 854	207 396	99 160.8	10 082.1
Aiken	42	168	27.9	5.6	125	D	D	D	22	1 506	518.0	70.2
Anderson	47	178	34.4	4.7	133	D	D	D	50	1 956	626.4	79.9
Charleston	278	1 716	249.2	57.6	660	D	D	D	77	1 335	521.0	64.7
Columbia	227	1 594	529.1	96.6	838	D	D	D	69	1 172	D	60.3
Florence	79	398	74.6	14.9	132	D	D	D	20	1 773	1 034.8	117.6
Goose Creek	22	90	33.1	3.4	60	1 152	218.9	65.3	13	755	845.2	47.1
Greenville	243	1 308	310.1	54.5	809	D	D	D	104	3 863	1 260.2	160.8
Greer	35	146	25.9	4.9	66	334	57.7	16.7	39	849	372.9	42.0
Hilton Head Island	223	1 158	179.3	45.4	245	1 028	167.3	70.0	28	186	19.7	6.3
Mount Pleasant	183	384	93.3	15.5	415	D	D	D	35	D	D	D
Myrtle Beach	211	2 259	251.5	66.6	218	1 141	152.1	54.1	27	758	D	35.5
North Charleston	148	1 039	209.0	39.9	345	D	D	D	122	11 200	3 422.0	655.8
Rock Hill	77	319	47.2	10.9	160	D	D	D	60	2 691	1 154.2	153.3
Spartanburg	82	404	69.7	18.0	192	D	D	D	32	1 002	296.2	47.6
Summerville	67	248	43.1	8.3	116	D	D	D	27	1 055	374.8	46.2
Sumter	57	208	22.0	5.3	99	517	44.6	11.9	29	D	214.6	D
SOUTH DAKOTA	962	3 526	582.8	105.7	1 806	11 083	1 310.0	479.5	1 025	41 931	16 882.6	1 764.7
Aberdeen	55	D	D	D	67	378	47.4	16.1	31	2 351	873.4	93.8
Rapid City	141	528	92.4	15.1	270	D	D	D	93	1 766	D	74.6
Sioux Falls	236	1 231	268.4	47.6	473	4 266	497.7	210.2	147	9 836	3 126.3	436.3
TENNESSEE	5 470	30 593	6 178.4	1 220.0	10 815	D	D	D	5 823	293 646	139 960.5	14 180.5
Bartlett	35	145	109.4	4.8	104	921	103.5	41.7	34	920	260.5	44.4
Brentwood	94	D	D	D	306	D	D	D	18	173	D	6.9
Bristol	34	93	17.4	2.7	64	569	80.2	34.0	47	2 255	1 512.1	212.0
Chattanooga	290	1 898	384.3	91.1	621	6 999	979.3	362.0	323	18 889	10 598.1	1 048.6
Clarksville	137	605	100.4	18.4	157	D	D	D	45	3 378	1 142.0	159.0
Cleveland	55	254	33.6	7.2	125	786	71.4	30.7	80	5 481	4 457.4	229.6
Collierville	41	149	32.4	5.0	105	416	54.5	25.9	38	2 236	1 536.9	100.0

1. Establishments subject to federal tax.

Table D. Cities — Accommodation and Food Services, Arts, Entertainment, and Recreation, and Health Care and Social Assistance

City	Accommodation and food services, 2012				Arts, entertainment, and recreation,[1] 2012				Health care and social assistance,[1] 2012			
	Number of establishments	Number of employees	Sales (mil dol)	Annual payroll (mil dol)	Number of establishments	Number of employees	Receipts (mil dol)	Annual payroll (mil dol)	Number of establishments	Number of employees	Receipts (mil dol)	Annual payroll (mil dol)
	92	93	94	95	96	97	98	99	100	101	102	103
OREGON—Cont'd												
Redmond	93	1 231	64.1	18.9	5	D	D	D	80	D	D	D
Salem	405	6 360	318.8	92.9	30	515	29.4	8.7	502	6 639	715.7	304.0
Springfield	168	2 503	136.0	36.9	20	D	D	D	147	D	D	D
Tigard	167	2 707	155.8	44.5	15	D	D	D	200	2 120	229.1	90.6
Tualatin	80	1 542	78.3	23.3	11	D	D	D	126	1 520	216.2	83.7
West Linn	45	645	34.3	10.2	11	69	2.9	0.7	92	D	D	D
PENNSYLVANIA	27 646	439 159	23 504.2	6 377.4	3 117	67 396	6 763.8	2 052.6	27 983	433 818	43 779.7	19 364.3
Allentown	255	3 394	173.8	50.0	18	184	25.4	5.1	283	4 491	471.4	222.0
Altoona	137	2 176	97.5	27.2	9	D	D	D	157	2 596	276.1	123.2
Bethel Park	65	1 589	63.9	19.8	10	D	D	D	110	1 593	127.4	59.1
Bethlehem	217	4 921	636.2	121.2	9	D	D	D	186	2 369	251.4	124.0
Chester	40	D	D	D	3	D	D	D	44	1 671	222.3	122.8
Easton	110	1 447	71.7	19.1	4	D	D	D	58	653	46.2	22.0
Erie	222	3 551	151.0	40.4	29	D	D	D	285	5 043	619.6	320.3
Harrisburg	183	2 537	136.0	35.5	12	D	D	D	97	1 657	184.2	81.9
Hazleton	60	553	25.4	6.4	4	D	D	D	84	1 485	122.1	50.1
Lancaster	162	2 948	174.5	51.3	12	D	D	D	138	D	D	D
Lebanon	58	609	28.1	6.9	4	43	3.1	0.8	66	D	D	D
Monroeville	128	2 852	150.0	40.8	11	190	5.1	2.3	193	3 252	412.6	162.2
Norristown	59	D	D	D	5	1	0.5	0.1	71	787	84.8	43.2
Philadelphia	3 669	53 533	3 551.7	982.4	208	13 373	1 333.2	697.1	2 647	47 119	5 255.8	2 270.4
Pittsburgh	1 234	22 377	1 306.2	375.3	92	D	D	D	963	19 796	2 162.6	1 330.0
Plum	36	527	24.5	6.9	8	D	D	D	20	112	6.8	3.0
Reading	149	1 822	98.4	24.9	7	236	13.1	5.0	99	2 195	189.6	82.5
Scranton	217	2 965	136.3	35.6	17	367	18.8	4.6	227	5 785	719.2	314.6
State College	135	3 042	126.0	34.8	7	70	5.4	1.5	90	D	D	D
Wilkes-Barre	126	2 784	133.9	37.5	7	D	D	D	111	3 579	442.0	167.6
Williamsport	101	1 570	90.5	24.1	6	44	4.7	1.0	83	1 902	166.3	109.0
York	113	1 581	76.0	22.3	6	D	D	D	57	D	D	D
RHODE ISLAND	2 973	44 063	2 481.3	705.9	406	6 108	593.5	150.4	2 470	35 597	3 467.0	1 535.8
Cranston	182	D	D	D	28	D	D	D	231	2 679	227.2	111.4
East Providence	114	1 746	82.6	21.8	20	D	D	D	141	2 850	305.9	155.3
Pawtucket	139	1 384	74.6	20.0	16	129	16.1	5.1	136	2 049	180.2	81.1
Providence	566	9 893	584.0	169.8	35	1 396	85.4	23.1	415	5 910	770.3	358.2
Warwick	248	4 910	262.4	74.2	31	357	24.5	6.8	303	4 416	385.9	170.1
Woonsocket	93	1 218	57.8	15.7	4	52	2.2	0.6	75	2 245	236.0	95.3
SOUTH CAROLINA	9 828	185 282	9 763.8	2 650.5	1 226	17 936	1 471.4	318.4	8 346	132 360	13 822.7	5 385.0
Aiken	134	3 030	118.0	34.6	19	311	17.8	6.3	153	3 760	381.8	139.0
Anderson	165	3 355	147.6	42.8	10	31	1.2	0.4	162	D	D	D
Charleston	517	11 876	786.3	216.0	67	722	63.0	13.2	423	4 151	582.4	230.9
Columbia	505	11 042	560.3	153.4	30	D	D	D	447	7 578	925.6	362.0
Florence	192	3 845	192.1	51.2	11	264	6.4	3.5	230	D	D	D
Goose Creek	69	1 254	57.0	15.1	6	121	4.0	1.3	44	D	D	D
Greenville	448	10 151	539.9	148.8	50	743	34.0	10.5	436	6 515	671.2	316.3
Greer	74	1 172	55.8	15.5	8	D	D	D	79	949	79.1	32.7
Hilton Head Island	226	5 252	388.2	111.7	53	1 045	73.5	20.5	149	1 681	275.2	72.5
Mount Pleasant	220	4 417	229.8	62.5	39	516	25.3	7.8	316	4 075	548.0	169.8
Myrtle Beach	546	13 643	869.7	232.6	78	1 575	151.3	34.2	219	2 882	566.6	167.6
North Charleston	322	6 364	364.7	92.2	14	1 218	19.2	6.3	282	6 172	858.2	285.2
Rock Hill	196	4 123	200.9	52.8	9	52	4.6	1.0	231	5 653	666.2	221.2
Spartanburg	200	4 453	213.9	61.2	13	D	D	D	168	3 712	492.0	227.8
Summerville	146	2 968	134.8	39.0	11	D	D	D	133	D	D	D
Sumter	128	2 635	112.9	31.4	4	68	3.1	1.3	144	2 705	239.6	100.7
SOUTH DAKOTA	2 363	37 974	1 873.7	514.2	526	4 636	352.8	73.0	1 544	20 514	2 023.2	829.8
Aberdeen	90	1 833	77.5	22.9	22	121	14.3	1.8	81	D	D	D
Rapid City	247	5 808	296.8	84.8	66	D	D	D	265	3 417	424.3	155.5
Sioux Falls	409	10 412	491.0	147.6	118	D	D	D	358	6 363	680.4	300.1
TENNESSEE	12 004	241 348	12 499.0	3 546.5	1 931	20 971	2 793.2	934.8	12 286	220 313	24 541.3	9 564.0
Bartlett	84	1 282	62.5	15.3	10	D	D	D	115	2 716	316.5	97.5
Brentwood	92	1 834	107.5	27.5	55	500	59.6	22.7	220	3 698	460.8	224.1
Bristol	83	1 431	58.5	16.3	11	D	D	D	114	D	D	D
Chattanooga	651	14 791	763.5	220.8	63	1 040	59.8	17.2	661	11 426	1 520.4	604.5
Clarksville	319	5 879	285.5	77.3	14	D	D	D	281	4 771	469.8	173.3
Cleveland	163	D	D	D	8	167	5.9	2.3	169	D	D	D
Collierville	97	2 332	105.5	30.6	12	D	D	D	103	D	D	D

1. Establishments subject to federal tax.

Table D. Cities — Other Services and Government Employment and Payroll

City	Other services[1], 2012				Government employment and payroll, 2012							
						March payroll						
							Percent of total for:					
	Number of establishments	Number of employees	Receipts (mil dol)	Annual payroll (mil dol)	Full-time equivalent employees	Total (dollars)	Administration, judicial, and legal	Police and Corrections	Fire Protection	Highways and transportation	Health and welfare	Natural resources and utilities	Education and libraries
	104	105	106	107	108	109	110	111	112	113	114	115	116
OREGON—Cont'd													
Redmond	41	161	19.9	5.4	145	696 980	14.3	31.9	0.0	20.4	5.5	20.4	0.0
Salem	221	1 161	86.8	28.8	1 201	6 557 144	12.3	26.5	18.4	2.9	8.3	17.5	2.8
Springfield	79	375	36.9	11.1	535	3 245 769	12.3	22.4	20.4	10.8	4.0	18.1	2.0
Tigard	107	696	75.5	25.0	286	1 551 160	26.2	36.8	0.0	7.7	0.0	11.2	12.8
Tualatin	79	509	42.7	13.8	147	818 379	22.2	35.7	0.0	9.0	1.8	13.6	10.1
West Linn	37	171	8.2	3.3	104	541 464	20.2	40.2	0.0	4.2	0.0	22.8	12.6
PENNSYLVANIA	20 247	114 850	10 517.4	3 078.9	X	X	X	X	X	X	X	X	X
Allentown	196	1 384	115.2	37.0	870	4 561 766	8.4	33.3	19.8	5.0	8.9	19.7	0.0
Altoona	104	579	37.6	12.7	242	1 031 472	8.7	39.4	29.9	15.7	4.9	1.4	0.0
Bethel Park	80	610	37.9	13.3	127	577 790	11.9	56.2	0.0	16.0	0.0	15.3	0.0
Bethlehem	103	892	72.1	26.8	680	3 090 583	7.7	30.1	17.3	3.5	8.2	18.8	0.0
Chester	33	214	16.3	4.7	305	1 818 516	31.3	36.7	17.7	3.5	2.3	3.4	0.0
Easton	51	249	21.3	6.6	246	1 153 107	13.0	32.8	24.1	5.8	1.5	12.2	0.0
Erie	158	727	55.7	16.7	656	3 187 505	6.2	34.9	25.5	9.0	2.8	15.7	0.0
Harrisburg	73	320	28.9	9.4	534	2 458 452	13.1	41.4	17.4	3.7	6.0	16.7	0.0
Hazleton	40	119	9.2	2.8	93	424 630	10.3	46.4	20.8	13.6	6.5	0.6	0.0
Lancaster	94	499	32.6	11.6	519	2 372 327	5.8	43.9	17.4	3.9	3.7	21.3	0.0
Lebanon	51	208	18.1	5.2	153	662 861	5.0	39.2	17.2	5.8	2.6	30.3	0.0
Monroeville	82	503	30.5	10.6	148	872 947	9.5	53.2	0.0	15.7	2.8	6.5	6.5
Norristown	43	188	24.6	7.4	170	899 425	10.6	61.2	15.6	6.4	0.0	0.7	0.0
Philadelphia	1 947	10 726	869.3	257.8	29 409	148 399 324	18.0	39.0	9.6	3.4	11.1	15.4	1.7
Pittsburgh	589	4 360	396.7	123.0	4 176	16 527 485	9.4	38.3	25.1	11.2	8.9	5.4	0.0
Plum	40	182	17.4	4.7	67	358 089	66.3	0.0	0.0	0.0	0.0	0.0	0.0
Reading	80	473	47.4	14.7	730	12 558 088	5.8	44.6	24.9	0.6	5.6	13.5	1.3
Scranton	123	595	42.9	12.5	484	2 233 185	4.0	40.2	30.7	5.1	1.7	7.2	6.5
State College	41	285	15.2	6.1	165	866 140	14.2	48.6	0.0	13.8	4.0	4.8	0.0
Wilkes-Barre	70	349	30.5	8.2	284	1 342 714	13.0	34.7	27.3	0.0	8.1	12.4	0.0
Williamsport	51	390	28.4	8.2	201	913 971	5.1	32.7	21.3	35.2	1.9	3.5	0.0
York	54	510	48.9	14.2	379	1 772 634	9.4	43.1	18.8	1.0	6.2	13.8	0.0
RHODE ISLAND	1 838	9 862	884.8	273.4	X	X	X	X	X	X	X	X	X
Cranston	157	971	86.9	28.6	2 144	11 389 033	1.9	8.5	6.8	1.5	0.6	0.6	78.6
East Providence	91	431	50.1	14.8	1 234	5 386 925	3.6	8.7	7.8	3.2	0.6	4.6	71.2
Pawtucket	106	623	61.0	18.7	1 817	9 164 839	2.7	8.8	7.2	0.8	1.4	4.4	72.6
Providence	290	1 961	165.9	50.3	5 219	27 174 708	5.3	17.6	13.9	1.5	0.0	6.7	54.9
Warwick	173	1 135	94.7	30.2	2 400	12 798 555	2.8	10.0	12.2	1.9	0.5	3.3	67.2
Woonsocket	60	274	30.1	8.6	1 167	6 516 930	2.3	7.1	7.8	1.5	0.3	1.7	77.9
SOUTH CAROLINA	5 482	34 926	3 006.7	1 000.9	X	X	X	X	X	X	X	X	X
Aiken	48	279	21.0	6.0	346	1 255 386	18.9	27.9	10.5	14.5	0.0	24.7	0.0
Anderson	67	428	30.2	9.8	420	924 851	13.0	31.8	14.8	8.6	2.0	25.1	0.0
Charleston	187	1 286	81.0	28.8	2 045	7 787 974	9.2	27.1	16.5	1.2	1.0	37.8	0.0
Columbia	179	1 789	129.9	41.8	2 261	7 098 669	11.6	20.9	23.5	2.0	2.7	24.7	0.0
Florence	64	571	35.9	10.4	510	1 554 745	9.4	29.2	16.4	5.2	3.3	35.0	0.0
Goose Creek	42	220	15.4	4.7	271	928 636	14.9	34.9	20.4	3.8	0.0	23.9	0.0
Greenville	208	1 367	89.8	31.4	1 049	3 701 819	9.4	20.4	14.8	5.7	1.5	42.0	0.0
Greer	41	195	15.1	4.9	189	659 763	25.5	37.5	20.6	2.5	0.0	13.8	0.0
Hilton Head Island	97	396	33.3	11.0	242	1 283 504	30.6	57.1	4.6	0.0	0.0	0.5	0.0
Mount Pleasant	120	838	59.9	22.1	569	1 912 550	16.4	33.5	20.8	2.0	0.8	24.2	0.0
Myrtle Beach	122	653	47.9	15.1	889	3 176 078	16.3	31.5	18.5	3.8	0.5	25.7	1.3
North Charleston	192	1 544	152.2	49.9	1 049	3 596 992	11.5	39.1	21.3	5.5	0.4	16.7	0.0
Rock Hill	89	787	71.8	22.4	836	2 857 047	21.2	21.2	14.2	3.9	6.3	29.3	0.0
Spartanburg	90	737	58.3	15.4	616	2 210 757	10.5	25.6	11.1	4.0	2.5	41.1	0.0
Summerville	91	560	40.0	14.3	357	1 158 866	7.9	29.3	23.7	1.9	0.0	33.0	0.0
Sumter	73	D	D	D	550	1 497 205	11.8	29.7	18.8	1.8	1.1	29.5	0.0
SOUTH DAKOTA	1 363	6 155	578.2	152.9	X	X	X	X	X	X	X	X	X
Aberdeen	43	198	16.7	4.5	287	1 030 395	10.5	20.7	18.3	13.5	0.0	31.3	4.3
Rapid City	176	1 034	84.9	26.0	868	1 798 797	7.6	17.7	12.4	6.9	0.0	24.6	3.9
Sioux Falls	265	1 851	149.3	47.4	1 148	5 118 747	9.5	24.6	18.4	10.7	7.0	21.1	5.6
TENNESSEE	6 521	44 354	3 896.0	1 201.1	X	X	X	X	X	X	X	X	X
Bartlett	62	614	45.6	14.5	511	2 039 502	14.7	30.7	21.1	6.5	0.0	20.1	0.0
Brentwood	58	427	38.4	11.5	256	1 094 815	19.4	23.6	26.3	6.2	0.0	13.8	5.5
Bristol	47	307	29.4	9.1	919	3 282 369	4.6	12.4	6.6	3.8	0.6	7.7	61.5
Chattanooga	346	2 676	264.2	76.0	3 133	11 941 830	7.9	16.8	12.6	11.2	5.0	42.3	2.0
Clarksville	164	931	71.3	19.9	1 114	3 666 316	6.5	29.4	19.3	13.3	0.6	26.7	0.0
Cleveland	64	748	59.6	18.9	1 030	3 567 674	2.1	10.1	17.6	4.9	1.2	2.8	59.7
Collierville	58	525	30.7	11.5	435	1 694 955	11.6	31.7	20.1	7.3	1.0	19.2	0.0

1. Establishments subject to federal tax.

Table D. Cities — **City Government Finances**

City	City government finances, 2012									
	General revenue							General expenditure		
	Intergovernmental			Taxes					Per capita[1] (dollars)	
					Per capita[1] (dollars)					
	Total (mil dol)	Total (mil dol)	Percent from state government	Total (mil dol)	Total	Property	Sales and gross receipts	Total (mil dol)	Total	Capital outlays
	117	118	119	120	121	122	123	124	125	126
OREGON—Cont'd										
Redmond	35.3	5.9	60.8	13.4	502	328	174	32.9	1 229	258
Salem	251.3	76.0	63.8	101.3	642	489	153	240.9	1 527	209
Springfield	103.6	9.1	99.1	32.9	549	452	97	90.7	1 514	262
Tigard	45.1	9.8	49.5	26.0	522	305	217	43.3	870	90
Tualatin	29.9	5.6	64.3	13.3	498	310	188	27.4	1 025	191
West Linn	24.0	5.0	70.0	11.3	439	271	168	22.2	865	100
PENNSYLVANIA	X	X	X	X	X	X	X	X	X	X
Allentown	129.2	30.4	47.0	56.8	477	247	115	175.0	1 471	88
Altoona	29.3	7.5	47.2	17.6	381	194	73	27.1	587	40
Bethel Park	24.5	2.7	71.8	13.8	427	131	46	25.6	790	60
Bethlehem	101.1	27.5	100.0	47.5	632	280	117	89.6	1 193	0
Chester	47.9	12.2	79.6	19.2	563	252	84	45.6	1 340	83
Easton	52.4	14.3	75.3	14.8	546	331	69	53.4	1 967	129
Erie	113.3	23.8	46.1	46.9	464	337	53	105.0	1 039	74
Harrisburg	93.9	6.2	90.0	30.4	616	345	171	78.7	1 595	121
Hazleton	18.6	7.2	55.0	8.3	329	113	39	13.3	528	65
Lancaster	69.1	11.7	71.8	31.0	522	384	54	87.4	1 472	261
Lebanon	21.7	10.2	34.6	8.3	325	116	37	26.5	1 036	259
Monroeville	23.1	1.7	95.3	19.7	695	159	284	30.1	1 058	116
Norristown	28.2	3.4	47.9	21.6	627	320	95	30.2	875	85
Philadelphia	6 411.8	2 254.7	74.3	3 239.1	2 089	323	474	5 483.2	3 537	209
Pittsburgh	607.0	163.6	87.2	357.2	1 166	443	419	548.9	1 791	25
Plum	13.3	1.8	85.5	9.6	352	192	32	13.6	498	25
Reading	139.8	30.8	89.3	42.9	488	220	111	135.9	1 543	96
Scranton	67.6	10.7	95.5	45.2	593	179	69	70.2	923	3
State College	36.3	5.5	55.6	11.4	272	114	42	35.4	843	78
Wilkes-Barre	52.9	20.4	46.2	24.1	583	208	78	57.3	1 386	201
Williamsport	41.3	20.3	45.8	15.5	526	329	123	30.5	1 035	151
York	68.7	9.7	51.4	24.7	566	395	110	63.2	1 448	39
RHODE ISLAND	X	X	X	X	X	X	X	X	X	X
Cranston	282.2	60.2	92.5	187.4	2 322	2 290	32	256.9	3 184	42
East Providence	148.4	43.6	95.5	91.6	1 942	1 918	24	155.3	3 292	150
Pawtucket	197.7	91.3	77.8	95.5	1 339	1 328	10	192.3	2 697	24
Providence	747.8	292.1	91.6	325.5	1 822	1 765	57	715.3	4 004	160
Warwick	318.8	59.3	98.4	219.5	2 682	2 607	74	303.4	3 707	110
Woonsocket	147.2	67.5	95.5	57.6	1 401	1 352	50	147.3	3 584	80
SOUTH CAROLINA	X	X	X	X	X	X	X	X	X	X
Aiken	42.7	5.6	22.9	23.7	790	330	460	40.3	1 341	206
Anderson	40.2	4.0	38.2	19.7	735	460	275	43.2	1 613	63
Charleston	207.6	27.8	72.1	132.3	1 053	446	607	178.8	1 424	222
Columbia	222.0	28.7	56.5	95.1	721	383	339	189.3	1 435	255
Florence	47.5	3.6	40.8	22.6	603	96	506	40.8	1 086	63
Goose Creek	19.6	0.7	100.0	11.6	298	47	251	20.5	528	67
Greenville	95.3	5.9	100.0	64.6	1 066	598	468	99.6	1 643	290
Greer	28.9	2.8	31.9	15.7	593	370	223	45.5	1 711	36
Hilton Head Island	89.1	35.5	16.2	48.4	1 261	625	586	94.8	2 471	1 299
Mount Pleasant	114.5	34.1	60.2	59.9	833	385	448	106.8	1 486	667
Myrtle Beach	161.3	12.2	83.8	82.5	2 918	878	2 040	123.3	4 360	375
North Charleston	122.2	14.2	23.7	93.4	915	471	408	119.1	1 168	208
Rock Hill	88.3	12.8	15.4	35.8	525	351	174	102.2	1 502	271
Spartanburg	53.3	13.1	6.6	33.4	895	449	446	42.1	1 130	160
Summerville	29.5	3.1	88.8	21.9	494	238	255	26.9	608	53
Sumter	43.8	6.9	24.7	24.0	587	218	369	40.1	980	178
SOUTH DAKOTA	X	X	X	X	X	X	X	X	X	X
Aberdeen	39.6	5.1	70.4	24.2	900	292	609	38.1	1 414	18
Rapid City	138.0	19.9	85.8	75.4	1 077	309	768	126.9	1 813	706
Sioux Falls	226.3	20.3	62.2	149.5	933	282	651	225.7	1 408	474
TENNESSEE	X	X	X	X	X	X	X	X	X	X
Bartlett	55.6	18.3	51.6	21.0	361	305	56	47.7	820	25
Brentwood	49.5	19.7	38.7	18.1	463	278	185	45.0	1 153	330
Bristol	75.0	35.6	60.9	26.6	999	899	101	74.6	2 797	336
Chattanooga	485.4	165.9	19.7	139.3	809	668	141	396.3	2 300	197
Clarksville	137.4	38.8	51.1	37.5	262	197	65	103.9	725	103
Cleveland	109.5	65.6	56.3	19.7	464	400	64	96.6	2 278	237
Collierville	56.6	15.9	37.4	25.4	547	460	87	51.4	1 107	164

1. Based on population estimated as of July 1 of the year shown.

Table D. Cities — **City Government Finances**

City	Public welfare	Highways	Parking facilities	Education	Health and hospitals	Police protection	Sewerage and sanitation	Parks and recreation	Housing and community development	Interest on debt
	127	128	129	130	131	132	133	134	135	136
OREGON—Cont'd										
Redmond	0.0	21.1	0.0	0.0	0.0	15.5	10.0	8.1	3.5	10.2
Salem	0.0	14.5	0.7	0.0	0.5	13.9	12.1	3.7	13.0	8.7
Springfield	0.0	5.4	0.0	0.0	5.6	16.9	38.3	0.0	1.1	4.0
Tigard	0.3	7.7	0.0	0.0	0.0	32.1	6.0	8.9	0.0	3.8
Tualatin	0.0	6.8	0.1	0.0	0.0	16.5	24.6	7.3	13.2	1.4
West Linn	0.0	8.3	0.0	0.0	0.0	26.6	11.1	13.8	0.0	1.9
PENNSYLVANIA	X	X	X	X	X	X	X	X	X	X
Allentown	0.0	8.9	0.0	0.0	3.5	18.4	23.6	4.4	6.1	2.8
Altoona	0.0	14.2	0.0	0.0	0.0	19.2	3.2	1.2	0.4	4.1
Bethel Park	0.0	22.7	0.0	0.0	0.0	23.6	35.2	3.1	0.5	0.9
Bethlehem	0.0	9.0	0.0	0.0	4.0	14.3	14.7	6.1	3.7	7.6
Chester	0.0	7.2	0.0	0.0	1.1	32.8	3.0	11.5	2.2	2.3
Easton	0.0	6.5	0.4	0.0	0.1	15.5	18.0	5.8	18.7	5.4
Erie	0.0	11.3	0.0	0.0	0.0	14.0	14.2	2.1	11.8	7.3
Harrisburg	0.0	7.4	0.0	0.0	0.2	24.9	23.4	3.9	8.6	3.8
Hazleton	0.0	13.4	0.0	0.0	1.1	27.9	2.4	0.8	7.7	3.1
Lancaster	0.0	5.5	0.0	0.0	0.0	20.9	23.8	6.2	5.6	9.3
Lebanon	0.0	53.3	0.1	0.0	0.7	15.7	0.8	1.4	6.1	0.1
Monroeville	0.0	20.1	0.0	0.0	0.3	34.5	4.7	6.1	1.2	3.1
Norristown	0.0	15.4	0.0	0.0	1.6	24.2	5.2	2.1	0.0	4.5
Philadelphia	10.4	2.1	0.0	1.4	24.8	11.1	7.0	1.5	3.5	3.9
Pittsburgh	0.0	0.6	0.0	0.0	2.5	14.1	2.8	3.0	16.9	6.6
Plum	0.0	28.0	0.0	0.0	0.0	29.8	11.8	0.2	0.0	4.0
Reading	0.0	8.0	0.0	0.0	2.7	20.8	21.1	2.8	14.3	8.1
Scranton	0.0	4.2	3.7	0.0	2.3	23.1	4.8	1.1	0.2	11.1
State College	0.0	15.4	4.9	0.0	0.9	24.5	27.4	3.1	3.2	2.6
Wilkes-Barre	0.0	23.8	0.5	0.0	4.6	16.0	7.5	7.7	7.2	7.7
Williamsport	0.0	28.5	0.0	0.0	0.0	21.9	14.1	2.4	3.5	1.1
York	0.0	6.2	0.9	0.0	3.2	15.4	23.5	4.9	6.1	8.0
RHODE ISLAND	X	X	X	X	X	X	X	X	X	X
Cranston	0.0	6.7	0.0	55.8	1.1	9.1	6.7	0.9	0.6	2.1
East Providence	0.0	3.8	0.0	57.0	0.3	7.9	7.4	1.5	0.8	1.9
Pawtucket	0.0	1.0	0.0	62.2	0.0	8.3	1.9	0.8	1.8	1.1
Providence	0.0	1.4	0.0	53.6	0.0	11.5	1.4	1.2	2.1	5.7
Warwick	0.4	2.3	0.0	56.7	0.1	6.4	4.3	0.7	0.4	1.6
Woonsocket	0.2	1.6	0.0	53.4	0.1	6.0	10.2	0.1	1.1	8.0
SOUTH CAROLINA	X	X	X	X	X	X	X	X	X	X
Aiken	0.0	7.0	0.0	0.0	0.0	22.5	13.8	12.3	1.7	0.1
Anderson	0.0	8.9	1.2	0.0	0.0	14.1	22.7	7.2	3.6	9.8
Charleston	0.4	3.1	5.1	0.0	0.0	22.4	4.6	13.3	3.8	1.7
Columbia	0.0	4.0	1.7	0.0	0.7	13.1	43.5	7.0	3.2	2.4
Florence	0.0	6.9	0.0	0.0	0.1	23.0	19.5	15.0	6.8	1.0
Goose Creek	0.0	12.8	0.0	0.0	0.0	27.9	5.4	24.9	0.0	0.3
Greenville	0.0	7.1	3.2	0.0	0.5	18.3	13.4	14.0	4.6	2.4
Greer	0.0	2.8	0.0	0.0	0.0	10.2	60.8	3.3	1.8	7.7
Hilton Head Island	0.0	1.9	0.0	0.0	0.0	6.5	2.0	0.0	30.1	4.5
Mount Pleasant	0.0	41.5	0.0	0.0	0.0	10.2	14.4	4.9	1.7	4.1
Myrtle Beach	0.0	3.8	1.5	0.0	0.0	16.0	11.8	19.5	3.8	7.6
North Charleston	0.0	4.5	0.5	0.0	0.0	25.1	8.9	5.1	1.0	5.2
Rock Hill	0.0	2.7	0.0	0.0	0.0	13.2	22.9	12.5	2.9	3.6
Spartanburg	0.0	6.2	2.3	0.0	0.0	22.3	4.7	7.7	4.1	5.1
Summerville	0.0	11.9	0.0	0.0	0.0	23.8	8.6	7.7	0.1	1.8
Sumter	0.0	1.7	0.0	0.0	0.0	23.3	16.2	12.9	8.3	0.8
SOUTH DAKOTA	X	X	X	X	X	X	X	X	X	X
Aberdeen	0.0	29.4	0.0	0.0	3.2	9.7	7.1	15.7	0.0	2.8
Rapid City	0.6	19.1	0.5	0.0	2.8	10.2	14.4	12.7	1.8	3.0
Sioux Falls	0.0	19.1	0.9	0.0	4.2	12.3	22.3	14.2	2.2	3.2
TENNESSEE	X	X	X	X	X	X	X	X	X	X
Bartlett	0.7	8.5	0.0	0.0	5.6	26.6	15.0	11.0	0.0	2.2
Brentwood	0.0	19.3	0.0	0.5	0.2	13.3	16.6	5.6	0.0	3.8
Bristol	0.0	4.9	0.0	54.1	0.0	9.0	9.0	5.1	0.9	1.0
Chattanooga	3.7	5.6	0.4	0.0	0.6	13.8	18.8	6.1	2.6	4.4
Clarksville	0.0	10.6	0.3	0.0	0.0	22.6	26.1	6.1	1.6	6.6
Cleveland	0.0	6.0	0.0	47.1	0.6	9.4	11.6	2.5	1.3	2.9
Collierville	0.7	12.6	0.0	0.0	1.6	20.1	14.9	7.5	0.0	2.6

Table D. Cities — City Government Finances, City Government Employment, and Climate

City	City government finances, 2012 (cont.)			Climate[2]						
	Debt outstanding			Average daily temperature (degrees Fahrenheit)						
				Mean		Limits				
	Total (mil dol)	Per capita[1] (dollars)	Debt issued during year	January	July	January[3]	July[4]	Annual precipitation (inches)	Heating degree days	Cooling degree days
	137	138	139	140	141	142	143	144	145	146
OREGON—Cont'd										
Redmond	73.6	2 750	12.3	NA	NA	NA	NA	NA	NA	NA
Salem	711.5	4 509	94.7	40.3	66.8	33.5	81.5	40.00	4 784	257
Springfield	151.8	2 534	3.8	39.8	66.2	33.0	81.5	50.90	4 786	242
Tigard	131.8	2 649	100.1	40.0	66.8	33.8	79.2	39.95	4 723	287
Tualatin	14.5	544	0.0	NA	NA	NA	NA	NA	NA	NA
West Linn	21.7	847	8.5	NA	NA	NA	NA	NA	NA	NA
PENNSYLVANIA	X	X	X	X	X	X	X	X	X	X
Allentown	119.4	1 003	11.6	27.1	73.3	19.1	83.9	45.17	5 830	787
Altoona	38.9	844	1.0	26.5	71.1	18.2	81.9	42.69	6 055	546
Bethel Park	4.8	147	0.0	28.6	73.1	19.8	84.5	37.78	5 727	709
Bethlehem	228.4	3 041	27.6	27.1	73.3	19.1	83.9	45.17	5 830	787
Chester	8.1	239	0.0	33.7	78.7	27.9	87.5	40.66	4 469	1 333
Easton	33.9	1 250	7.7	27.1	73.3	19.1	83.9	45.17	5 830	787
Erie	189.6	1 876	47.4	26.9	72.1	20.3	80.4	42.77	6 243	620
Harrisburg	110.0	2 230	0.0	30.3	75.9	23.1	85.7	41.45	5 201	955
Hazleton	11.6	460	5.6	NA	NA	NA	NA	NA	NA	NA
Lancaster	221.6	3 732	38.9	29.1	74.4	20.7	84.7	43.47	5 448	809
Lebanon	0.3	12	0.0	NA	NA	NA	NA	NA	NA	NA
Monroeville	30.2	1 064	7.5	28.6	73.1	19.8	84.5	37.78	5 727	709
Norristown	23.9	694	0.0	30.2	75.1	20.4	86.6	43.87	5 174	884
Philadelphia	7 729.2	4 985	667.1	32.3	77.6	25.5	85.5	42.05	4 759	1 235
Pittsburgh	704.7	2 300	0.0	27.5	72.6	19.9	82.7	37.85	5 829	726
Plum	50.0	1 825	11.3	28.6	73.1	19.8	84.5	37.78	5 727	709
Reading	256.9	2 918	24.4	27.1	73.6	19.1	83.8	45.28	5 876	723
Scranton	61.9	814	0.0	26.3	72.1	18.5	82.6	37.56	6 234	611
State College	28.2	673	0.0	25.4	71.2	18.3	80.7	39.76	6 345	538
Wilkes-Barre	73.4	1 775	9.2	21.5	67.7	13.2	77.4	47.89	7 466	234
Williamsport	5.4	183	2.3	25.5	72.4	17.9	83.2	41.59	6 063	709
York	128.7	2 949	22.1	30.0	74.6	20.9	86.5	43.00	5 233	862
RHODE ISLAND	X	X	X	X	X	X	X	X	X	X
Cranston	88.4	1 096	19.4	28.7	73.3	20.3	82.6	46.45	5 754	714
East Providence	75.2	1 595	23.3	28.7	73.3	20.3	82.6	46.45	5 754	714
Pawtucket	159.7	2 239	9.4	28.7	73.3	20.3	82.6	46.45	5 754	714
Providence	735.9	4 120	5.4	28.7	73.3	20.3	82.6	46.45	5 754	714
Warwick	170.1	2 078	2.4	28.7	73.3	20.3	82.6	46.45	5 754	714
Woonsocket	202.3	4 921	1.0	25.4	72.3	13.3	84.3	48.75	6 302	534
SOUTH CAROLINA	X	X	X	X	X	X	X	X	X	X
Aiken	2.8	92	0.0	45.6	81.7	33.4	93.7	52.43	2 413	2 081
Anderson	125.4	4 687	53.2	41.7	79.7	31.3	90.5	46.67	3 087	1 700
Charleston	74.3	592	0.0	49.8	82.8	42.4	88.5	46.39	1 755	2 473
Columbia	505.3	3 832	205.7	47.3	83.6	36.5	95.2	47.14	2 044	2 475
Florence	139.9	3 725	7.4	45.0	81.2	35.2	90.7	44.76	2 523	2 029
Goose Creek	1.4	36	0.0	47.9	81.7	36.9	90.9	51.53	2 005	2 306
Greenville	94.3	1 556	17.3	40.8	78.8	31.4	88.8	50.24	3 272	1 526
Greer	93.7	3 527	1.7	NA	NA	NA	NA	NA	NA	NA
Hilton Head Island	127.7	3 326	46.9	47.9	80.5	37.3	88.2	52.52	2 128	2 012
Mount Pleasant	99.4	1 383	0.0	47.1	81.1	37.5	88.5	49.38	2 260	2 124
Myrtle Beach	216.4	7 653	27.5	NA	NA	NA	NA	NA	NA	NA
North Charleston	186.0	1 823	52.5	47.9	81.7	36.9	90.9	51.53	2 005	2 306
Rock Hill	186.9	2 745	54.5	42.2	80.1	32.5	90.1	48.32	2 934	1 721
Spartanburg	205.6	5 518	0.0	42.1	79.3	30.1	91.1	49.95	3 080	1 591
Summerville	7.9	179	0.0	49.1	81.8	38.0	91.8	48.24	1 907	2 251
Sumter	45.0	1 100	4.2	44.9	80.7	33.6	91.8	48.65	2 577	1 913
SOUTH DAKOTA	X	X	X	X	X	X	X	X	X	X
Aberdeen	63.9	2 375	5.3	NA	NA	NA	NA	NA	NA	NA
Rapid City	113.7	1 624	24.2	22.3	70.2	10.3	82.7	18.45	7 623	480
Sioux Falls	307.2	1 916	24.4	14.0	73.0	2.9	85.6	24.69	7 812	747
TENNESSEE	X	X	X	X	X	X	X	X	X	X
Bartlett	40.8	701	9.5	37.3	79.6	27.3	89.9	55.09	3 665	1 635
Brentwood	29.8	765	16.6	NA	NA	NA	NA	NA	NA	NA
Bristol	50.2	1 884	3.1	NA	NA	NA	NA	NA	NA	NA
Chattanooga	733.3	4 256	51.6	39.4	79.6	29.9	89.8	54.52	3 427	1 608
Clarksville	870.1	6 075	29.2	35.2	79.0	25.0	90.4	51.78	4 058	1 512
Cleveland	130.0	3 067	3.1	38.0	77.5	27.7	88.5	55.42	3 782	1 333
Collierville	60.9	1 313	5.0	37.9	81.1	28.2	91.1	53.63	3 491	1 838

1. Based on the population estimated as of July 1 of the year shown.   2. Represents normal values based on the 30-year period, 1971–2000.   3. Average daily minimum.
4. Average daily maximum.

Table D. Cities — **Land Area and Population**

STATE Place code	City	Land area,[1] 2010 (sq km)	Population, 2015			Race alone or in combination (percent), 2010-2014					Percent Hispanic or Latino[2], 2010-2014	Percent foreign born 2010–2014
			Total persons	Rank	Per square kilometer	White	Black	American Indian, Alaska Native	Asian	Hawaiian Pacific Islander		
		1	2	3	4	5	6	7	8	9	10	11
	TENNESSEE— Cont'd											
47 16540	Columbia	81.7	36 800	1 024	450.4	78.3	21.2	0.7	1.1	0.0	7.8	4.9
47 16920	Cookeville	84.6	32 113	1 176	379.6	92.9	4.7	1.2	2.7	0.3	6.2	8.0
47 27740	Franklin	106.8	72 639	476	680.1	88.2	6.6	0.4	5.3	0.0	6.7	9.5
47 28540	Gallatin	80.8	34 334	1 094	424.9	82.2	14.4	0.6	1.7	0.3	8.8	6.6
47 28960	Germantown	51.7	39 240	960	759.0	88.4	5.2	0.4	6.8	0.0	3.0	7.1
47 33280	Hendersonville	81.3	56 018	663	689.0	87.7	9.0	0.7	2.6	0.0	3.6	4.8
47 37640	Jackson	139.2	66 975	527	481.1	52.1	46.4	0.5	1.8	0.2	4.6	4.3
47 38320	Johnson City	111.2	66 027	539	593.8	89.5	8.6	0.8	2.8	0.2	4.2	5.2
47 39560	Kingsport	129.0	53 014	705	411.0	93.7	4.6	1.4	1.6	0.3	2.7	2.2
47 40000	Knoxville	255.2	185 291	129	726.1	78.7	18.9	1.1	2.2	0.1	4.7	5.6
47 41200	La Vergne	64.6	34 794	1 081	538.6	74.3	21.8	1.7	3.0	0.1	19.3	13.2
47 41520	Lebanon	100.1	30 262	1 236	302.3	80.1	13.3	0.4	2.3	0.2	7.3	6.6
47 46380	Maryville	43.5	28 464	1 295	654.3	95.5	2.9	0.5	2.3	0.0	2.6	3.5
47 48000	Memphis	816.0	655 770	24	803.6	31.7	63.9	0.7	2.1	0.2	6.5	6.2
47 50280	Morristown	72.3	29 478	1 262	407.7	85.6	8.6	1.2	1.1	0.0	20.1	10.8
47 51560	Murfreesboro	143.4	126 118	219	879.5	78.4	17.6	1.1	4.5	0.2	5.2	6.7
47 52004	Nashville-Davidson	1 230.6	654 610	25	531.9	64.1	28.8	0.8	3.8	0.1	9.8	11.8
47 55120	Oak Ridge	220.8	29 302	1 265	132.7	87.0	11.1	1.4	3.4	0.1	5.0	6.7
47 69420	Smyrna	76.7	46 607	813	607.7	81.7	14.0	1.3	3.8	0.1	9.0	8.3
47 70580	Spring Hill	70.1	36 055	1 048	514.3	91.8	5.1	0.8	1.3	0.0	7.5	4.3
48 00000	TEXAS	676 587.0	27 469 114	X	40.6	76.8	12.7	1.2	4.7	0.2	38.2	16.5
48 01000	Abilene	276.6	121 721	223	440.1	81.1	11.4	1.2	2.5	0.1	25.6	5.9
48 01924	Allen	68.1	98 143	310	1 441.2	75.8	9.3	1.3	15.1	0.1	10.8	17.1
48 03000	Amarillo	257.6	198 645	117	771.1	85.8	8.0	1.4	4.1	0.4	30.0	10.5
48 04000	Arlington	248.3	388 125	50	1 563.1	68.3	20.8	1.1	7.8	0.2	28.7	19.7
48 05000	Austin	771.6	931 830	11	1 207.7	77.2	9.0	1.2	7.6	0.2	34.8	18.4
48 06128	Baytown	91.8	76 335	445	831.5	68.6	18.2	1.2	1.4	0.2	43.7	17.9
48 07000	Beaumont	214.5	118 129	232	550.7	44.7	49.1	0.7	3.5	0.1	13.8	9.9
48 07132	Bedford	25.9	49 337	764	1 904.9	84.3	7.3	0.8	5.7	0.9	12.7	8.6
48 08236	Big Spring	49.5	28 862	1 282	583.1	82.7	8.7	1.9	1.6	0.4	44.0	12.1
48 10768	Brownsville	342.7	183 887	131	536.6	93.5	0.5	0.2	1.0	0.1	93.7	29.7
48 10912	Bryan	115.0	82 118	404	714.1	67.2	18.4	1.6	2.4	0.0	38.1	15.0
48 11428	Burleson	67.4	43 625	857	647.3	94.9	4.1	0.5	0.7	0.2	12.4	2.5
48 13024	Carrollton	94.0	133 168	197	1 416.7	71.3	10.0	1.4	14.7	0.2	32.4	26.2
48 13492	Cedar Hill	92.8	48 507	782	522.7	41.7	53.9	0.8	3.6	0.1	20.0	9.7
48 13552	Cedar Park	59.2	65 945	540	1 113.9	84.1	6.3	1.0	9.5	0.6	16.0	11.8
48 15364	Cleburne	76.6	30 020	1 244	391.9	91.5	4.6	1.4	0.9	1.8	25.4	11.3
48 15976	College Station	128.1	107 889	273	842.2	80.8	8.0	0.9	10.2	0.1	14.3	13.1
48 16432	Conroe	136.5	68 602	509	502.6	84.8	10.8	0.5	1.4	0.1	37.7	21.5
48 16612	Coppell	37.3	41 159	908	1 103.5	73.0	5.5	0.7	21.0	0.1	11.3	20.8
48 16624	Copperas Cove	46.7	33 081	1 138	708.4	74.2	20.2	1.9	3.5	1.6	15.2	7.4
48 17000	Corpus Christi	416.0	324 074	58	779.0	87.0	5.1	1.1	2.4	0.2	60.8	8.1
48 19000	Dallas	881.9	1 300 092	9	1 474.2	59.9	25.5	1.1	3.4	0.1	41.7	24.2
48 19624	Deer Park	27.1	33 806	1 112	1 247.5	90.9	1.8	1.7	1.7	0.0	29.0	7.5
48 19792	Del Rio	52.2	36 153	1 043	692.6	93.2	1.5	0.7	0.6	0.1	84.1	24.8
48 19972	Denton	227.8	131 044	202	575.3	80.9	12.5	1.7	5.3	0.4	22.2	13.5
48 20092	DeSoto	56.0	52 486	716	937.3	27.4	70.0	1.3	0.6	0.1	13.2	5.1
48 21628	Duncanville	29.1	39 826	938	1 368.6	59.0	32.4	0.7	1.6	0.2	36.5	14.2
48 21892	Eagle Pass	24.8	28 765	1 287	1 159.9	94.5	0.5	0.5	0.4	0.0	95.5	32.7
48 22660	Edinburg	97.5	84 497	388	866.6	89.9	1.8	0.4	3.1	0.1	88.2	19.7
48 24000	El Paso	661.1	681 124	20	1 030.3	84.6	4.1	1.0	1.9	0.3	79.7	24.9
48 24768	Euless	42.0	54 219	691	1 290.9	68.6	12.5	1.3	12.7	2.4	19.9	19.3
48 25452	Farmers Branch	30.6	32 689	1 148	1 068.3	83.0	4.6	1.1	5.8	0.1	40.8	23.3
48 26232	Flower Mound	107.2	71 253	488	664.7	85.3	4.2	1.2	10.1	0.2	8.5	11.4
48 27000	Fort Worth	880.1	833 319	16	946.8	67.8	20.1	1.4	4.6	0.3	34.2	17.5
48 27648	Friendswood	53.7	38 800	966	722.5	90.6	3.9	1.3	5.4	0.0	14.9	8.7
48 27684	Frisco	160.1	154 407	162	964.4	77.7	8.6	1.0	13.6	0.3	13.1	15.9
48 28068	Galveston	106.8	50 180	749	469.9	73.4	20.6	1.0	4.8	0.1	30.0	14.8
48 29000	Garland	147.9	236 897	91	1 601.7	51.5	15.6	3.3	11.5	0.2	40.1	27.4
48 29336	Georgetown	124.0	63 716	563	513.8	93.0	4.3	1.0	1.0	0.0	24.0	10.3
48 30464	Grand Prairie	186.8	187 809	127	1 005.4	64.7	21.9	0.9	6.9	0.2	43.3	21.4
48 30644	Grapevine	82.7	51 404	737	621.6	86.5	2.5	1.7	5.3	0.1	19.6	12.9
48 30920	Greenville	84.5	26 515	1 378	313.8	67.0	15.8	1.3	2.1	0.0	24.1	10.9
48 31928	Haltom City	32.0	44 206	846	1 381.4	74.7	6.9	1.5	6.8	0.1	40.9	23.2
48 32312	Harker Heights	39.3	29 142	1 272	741.5	74.8	19.8	1.6	7.3	1.1	21.8	10.0
48 32372	Harlingen	103.1	65 774	542	638.0	93.9	1.8	0.9	1.1	0.0	79.6	16.2
48 35000	Houston	1 552.9	2 296 224	4	1 478.7	59.3	23.9	0.9	7.0	0.1	43.9	28.4
48 35528	Huntsville	92.9	40 938	914	440.7	68.3	27.7	1.0	1.9	0.1	19.6	8.2
48 35576	Hurst	25.7	39 016	963	1 518.1	86.7	6.6	0.9	3.0	0.1	21.5	12.2

1. Dry land or land partially or temporarily covered by water.   2. May be of any race.

Table D. Cities — **Population**

City	Age of population (percent), 2010-2014									Median age 2010–2014	Percent female 2010–2014	Population — Census counts		Population — Percent change	
	Under 5 years	5 to 17 years	18 to 24 years	25 to 34 years	35 to 44 years	45 to 54 years	55 to 64 years	65 to 74 years	75 years and over			2000	2010	2000–2010	2010–2015
	12	13	14	15	16	17	18	19	20	21	22	23	24	25	26
TENNESSEE—Cont'd															
Columbia	8.0	17.6	9.3	13.8	11.0	12.0	13.4	7.1	7.8	36.0	54.0	33 055	34 681	4.9	6.1
Cookeville	4.9	13.9	23.3	15.1	10.0	10.2	10.2	6.6	5.9	29.0	52.3	23 923	30 435	27.2	3.1
Franklin	5.7	20.6	6.9	11.5	16.5	15.1	12.9	5.2	5.5	38.4	51.9	41 842	62 487	49.3	16.0
Gallatin	7.2	15.9	8.6	17.0	11.1	13.9	12.2	7.9	6.0	36.1	52.2	23 230	30 278	30.3	13.2
Germantown	5.9	18.4	6.2	6.9	12.8	15.6	16.9	10.3	7.0	44.8	50.0	37 348	38 844	4.0	1.0
Hendersonville	5.4	19.5	7.9	11.2	15.5	15.3	11.6	7.8	5.9	39.4	51.6	40 620	51 372	26.5	9.1
Jackson	7.3	17.2	13.1	13.5	11.0	13.0	11.6	7.2	6.3	34.2	53.8	59 643	65 211	9.3	0.1
Johnson City	4.6	14.1	16.0	13.3	12.0	12.2	12.4	9.0	6.5	37.2	52.4	55 469	63 152	13.9	4.0
Kingsport	5.7	15.6	7.3	10.4	13.1	13.9	12.7	11.2	10.1	43.8	53.2	44 905	48 205	7.3	0.4
Knoxville	6.1	11.6	17.3	16.5	11.4	12.0	11.0	7.7	6.4	33.9	51.8	173 890	178 874	2.9	3.7
La Vergne	8.1	22.7	7.2	16.2	18.2	13.1	8.9	3.6	2.0	33.1	48.8	18 687	32 588	74.4	6.8
Lebanon	6.8	16.9	9.4	13.3	14.6	12.8	11.2	8.3	6.6	37.0	51.3	20 235	26 190	29.4	15.7
Maryville	5.1	18.4	11.0	9.5	14.5	13.4	11.7	8.1	8.4	40.0	52.8	23 120	27 465	18.8	3.6
Memphis	7.6	17.6	11.6	15.6	12.4	12.9	11.9	5.9	4.7	33.2	52.4	650 100	646 889	-0.5	0.6
Morristown	7.3	17.5	7.8	16.7	12.7	12.6	9.9	7.4	8.1	35.4	53.1	24 965	29 137	16.7	1.7
Murfreesboro	6.8	15.3	18.2	17.4	13.2	11.0	8.7	5.5	3.9	30.2	50.2	68 816	108 755	58.0	15.7
Nashville-Davidson	7.1	14.6	11.0	19.0	13.8	12.9	11.1	5.8	4.6	33.8	51.6	569 891	601 222	10.2	8.5
Oak Ridge	5.9	16.4	9.6	11.4	12.0	13.9	13.2	8.7	8.9	40.7	51.5	27 387	29 330	7.1	-0.1
Smyrna	8.0	20.7	9.0	15.2	15.7	12.8	10.0	5.4	3.2	33.0	52.7	25 569	39 974	56.3	16.5
Spring Hill	9.4	23.4	5.6	15.9	18.2	15.6	6.3	4.6	0.9	32.8	51.4	7 715	29 036	276.4	24.2
TEXAS	7.4	19.4	10.3	14.4	13.6	13.2	10.8	6.3	4.6	33.9	50.3	20 851 820	25 145 561	20.6	9.2
Abilene	7.4	15.5	16.3	15.8	11.1	11.8	9.7	6.5	5.9	31.1	48.3	115 930	117 063	1.0	3.6
Allen	7.9	23.4	6.8	11.1	17.9	17.3	8.8	4.1	2.6	35.4	52.9	43 554	84 246	93.4	16.4
Amarillo	7.9	19.5	9.5	15.5	12.3	12.0	10.9	6.5	5.8	33.3	51.2	173 627	190 695	9.8	4.2
Arlington	8.0	19.0	11.3	15.5	13.8	13.7	9.9	5.4	3.4	32.2	50.9	332 969	365 438	9.8	6.2
Austin	6.8	14.9	12.8	21.3	15.4	12.1	9.3	4.2	3.1	31.9	49.7	656 562	790 390	20.4	14.8
Baytown	8.8	21.3	9.4	14.7	12.2	12.8	11.0	4.4	5.3	31.7	51.0	66 430	71 802	8.1	6.2
Beaumont	7.4	17.2	11.5	14.6	11.3	12.9	11.8	6.9	6.3	34.5	52.3	113 866	118 296	3.9	0.7
Bedford	5.8	13.6	7.9	15.4	13.4	14.7	13.7	8.4	7.1	40.6	51.1	47 152	46 979	-0.4	5.0
Big Spring	6.5	15.2	11.4	15.8	15.1	13.6	10.8	5.9	5.6	35.5	41.9	25 233	27 282	8.1	5.8
Brownsville	8.8	24.1	10.7	12.9	12.8	11.7	8.8	5.7	4.6	30.3	52.3	139 722	175 023	25.3	5.1
Bryan	7.5	16.7	16.5	17.7	12.0	10.8	8.6	5.2	4.9	29.8	48.4	65 660	76 201	16.1	7.7
Burleson	7.8	23.2	7.4	14.9	14.1	12.5	9.7	6.7	3.6	33.2	52.9	20 976	36 690	74.9	18.9
Carrollton	6.2	18.4	8.7	15.3	14.1	16.5	11.9	5.8	3.2	36.1	50.6	109 576	119 097	8.7	11.8
Cedar Hill	7.5	22.6	7.6	12.5	16.2	14.2	12.3	4.9	2.4	34.9	54.1	32 093	45 028	40.3	7.7
Cedar Park	6.5	22.5	8.5	14.0	17.3	14.0	10.2	4.3	2.7	34.2	51.1	26 049	48 937	87.9	27.4
Cleburne	9.6	20.0	11.1	12.6	12.3	12.8	9.3	6.3	6.1	32.2	51.5	26 005	29 337	12.8	0.9
College Station	4.8	10.9	45.3	14.3	8.0	6.4	5.5	3.3	1.7	22.5	49.1	67 890	93 857	38.2	14.7
Conroe	8.8	18.9	10.2	16.3	15.3	11.1	9.1	5.5	4.9	32.5	52.7	36 811	56 207	52.7	20.4
Coppell	5.5	23.5	6.4	9.4	16.3	20.2	12.2	4.2	2.3	38.4	50.6	35 958	38 659	7.5	6.5
Copperas Cove	8.2	20.9	9.6	17.6	13.1	13.1	7.7	6.2	3.7	31.4	52.4	29 592	32 032	8.2	2.8
Corpus Christi	6.7	18.8	10.5	14.3	12.3	13.2	12.0	6.8	5.5	34.7	51.0	277 454	305 215	10.0	6.2
Dallas	8.1	17.7	10.4	18.5	14.0	12.4	9.8	5.1	4.0	32.2	49.9	1 188 580	1 197 816	0.8	8.5
Deer Park	7.9	18.1	9.7	14.7	15.1	13.2	12.0	5.6	3.8	34.6	51.5	28 520	32 010	12.2	5.6
Del Rio	9.2	20.5	9.9	13.5	11.7	12.0	9.6	6.7	6.9	32.6	50.0	33 867	35 591	5.1	0.6
Denton	5.5	14.9	23.7	16.6	11.3	10.8	8.4	5.9	3.0	27.7	51.9	80 537	113 383	40.8	12.7
DeSoto	4.7	19.1	9.1	10.3	13.2	15.2	15.3	7.9	5.4	40.4	53.3	37 646	49 047	30.3	7.1
Duncanville	8.1	18.5	9.1	12.2	13.7	13.2	12.1	8.1	5.0	36.4	52.7	36 081	38 524	6.8	3.3
Eagle Pass	9.3	22.5	10.1	11.5	12.5	11.6	9.6	6.9	5.9	31.8	50.4	22 413	26 248	17.1	9.6
Edinburg	9.6	20.7	14.0	16.5	13.1	11.4	6.7	4.1	3.8	28.0	50.3	48 465	77 100	59.1	13.4
El Paso	7.9	20.2	11.3	14.1	12.5	12.5	10.0	6.2	5.3	32.2	51.7	563 662	649 121	15.2	4.9
Euless	6.3	18.1	10.2	17.1	15.6	13.8	10.5	5.3	2.9	33.6	50.5	46 005	51 277	11.5	5.7
Farmers Branch	6.5	18.8	8.4	14.6	14.1	14.0	10.9	6.2	6.6	36.8	52.5	27 508	28 616	4.0	14.2
Flower Mound	5.9	24.8	6.6	7.2	17.9	21.0	10.7	4.1	1.9	38.7	50.5	50 702	64 669	27.5	10.2
Fort Worth	8.6	20.4	10.0	16.2	14.3	12.5	9.3	4.8	3.7	31.7	51.4	534 694	741 206	38.6	12.2
Friendswood	4.3	21.2	8.3	10.3	12.0	18.1	12.7	8.9	4.2	40.3	49.2	29 037	35 805	23.3	8.4
Frisco	8.0	25.1	6.1	11.6	22.1	13.2	7.2	4.5	2.1	34.5	49.6	33 714	116 989	247.0	31.9
Galveston	5.5	13.7	13.0	15.6	10.7	14.4	13.1	7.4	6.5	36.8	51.2	57 247	47 743	-16.6	5.1
Garland	8.0	21.5	9.6	13.4	14.0	13.8	10.2	5.6	3.9	33.2	51.1	215 768	226 876	5.1	4.4
Georgetown	5.4	15.1	6.2	11.2	11.1	8.6	13.6	16.4	12.3	46.4	51.6	28 339	47 400	67.3	34.2
Grand Prairie	7.9	21.9	9.9	15.4	14.9	14.1	9.2	4.5	2.3	32.0	50.2	127 427	175 396	37.6	7.0
Grapevine	6.2	19.6	7.0	13.2	15.6	17.6	12.3	5.2	3.3	37.4	52.4	42 059	46 334	10.2	10.9
Greenville	8.9	16.2	9.2	15.1	12.6	11.2	11.9	7.1	7.8	35.4	53.4	23 960	25 557	6.7	3.7
Haltom City	7.6	19.5	11.2	12.6	13.4	14.9	9.7	7.3	3.9	34.5	49.5	39 018	42 409	8.7	4.2
Harker Heights	8.1	22.5	10.9	14.2	16.0	12.7	8.2	4.4	3.0	31.8	49.9	17 308	26 700	54.3	9.1
Harlingen	9.5	22.3	9.2	12.2	13.8	10.5	10.2	6.5	5.9	31.8	50.7	57 564	64 849	12.7	1.3
Houston	7.8	17.6	10.6	17.8	14.0	12.6	10.2	5.5	4.0	32.6	49.9	1 953 631	2 099 451	7.5	8.9
Huntsville	4.8	9.0	27.3	18.3	14.1	11.5	7.7	3.9	3.3	29.2	38.7	35 078	38 548	9.9	6.2
Hurst	7.0	17.1	9.6	13.2	12.3	12.9	11.7	9.1	7.1	37.4	50.1	36 273	37 337	2.9	4.5

Table D. Cities — Households, Group Quarters, Crime, and Education

City	Households, 2010-2014				Persons in group quarters, 2010				Serious crimes known to police,[2] 2014				Educational attainment, 2010–2014		
			Percent			Institutional			Total		Rate[3]			Attainment[4] (percent)	
	Number	Persons per house-hold	Female family house-holder[1]	One-person	Total	Total	Persons in nursing facilities	Non-institu-tional	Number	Rate[3]	Violent	Property	Population age 25 and older	High school graduate or less	Bachelor's degree or more
	27	28	29	30	31	32	33	34	35	36	37	38	39	40	41
TENNESSEE—Cont'd															
Columbia	13 838	2.54	18.2	33.3	863	795	462	68	1 452	4 060	624	3 437	22 732	51.4	16.9
Cookeville	12 738	2.43	13.8	34.1	2 410	431	201	1 979	1 525	4 879	400	4 479	18 076	48.0	27.1
Franklin	25 740	2.59	8.6	27.3	795	792	491	3	1 101	1 562	139	1 423	43 930	19.5	56.1
Gallatin	11 892	2.67	16.8	25.6	890	870	308	20	570	1 740	317	1 423	20 986	46.5	20.8
Germantown	14 585	2.69	5.7	19.1	43	43	43	0	480	1 215	81	1 134	27 765	11.9	65.1
Hendersonville	20 333	2.62	12.4	23.2	139	128	128	11	853	1 559	181	1 378	35 847	35.9	32.5
Jackson	24 804	2.71	18.8	32.3	4 297	1 456	557	2 841	3 802	5 602	1 083	4 519	42 337	44.6	27.9
Johnson City	27 460	2.35	11.4	33.6	3 936	750	626	3 186	2 611	3 984	366	3 618	41 771	35.3	38.9
Kingsport	23 497	2.25	13.5	34.0	887	744	660	143	2 957	5 578	604	4 975	37 849	46.7	25.4
Knoxville	82 079	2.21	12.1	44.0	10 048	1 723	1 287	8 325	13 656	7 407	875	6 532	116 778	40.7	29.9
La Vergne	10 651	3.16	17.0	19.1	5	0	0	5	768	2 231	502	1 728	19 939	52.1	18.6
Lebanon	10 328	2.70	15.9	31.9	1 101	609	375	492	1 175	4 057	763	3 294	18 111	54.4	21.7
Maryville	10 572	2.63	12.4	31.2	1 644	886	529	758	706	2 511	135	2 376	18 250	35.8	35.1
Memphis	248 320	2.64	24.2	34.5	16 536	10 165	2 710	6 371	50 683	7 739	1 744	5 995	414 853	46.1	24.7
Morristown	11 028	2.64	17.9	29.0	903	763	487	140	1 666	5 666	653	5 013	19 227	60.7	16.4
Murfreesboro	43 431	2.64	12.6	27.8	4 434	1 348	458	3 086	4 630	3 891	535	3 355	68 123	30.8	37.0
Nashville-Davidson	259 557	2.50	14.6	35.4	25 870	9 226	2 169	16 644	30 909	4 772	1 125	3 647	436 824	37.7	36.5
Oak Ridge	12 391	2.36	11.3	35.5	483	226	218	257	NA	NA	NA	NA	20 323	30.2	40.8
Smyrna	15 367	2.75	13.5	28.2	365	353	215	12	1 290	2 944	331	2 613	26 689	43.5	23.6
Spring Hill	10 401	3.03	7.8	18.0	47	30	0	17	376	1 123	111	1 013	19 307	25.6	42.8
TEXAS	9 013 582	2.89	14.4	24.9	581 139	375 392	94 278	205 747	923 348	3 425	406	3 019	16 426 730	43.7	27.1
Abilene	42 491	2.84	13.9	28.6	9 592	5 306	816	4 286	5 915	4 901	473	4 428	73 705	45.5	22.6
Allen	29 344	3.06	10.9	15.0	171	171	164	0	1 201	1 279	78	1 201	55 887	17.3	52.6
Amarillo	74 457	2.62	14.3	28.9	1 881	1 419	1 019	462	10 742	5 433	684	4 749	123 148	41.5	22.5
Arlington	133 601	2.81	15.5	26.0	3 132	1 061	1 053	2 071	15 316	3 999	484	3 515	231 191	38.8	28.9
Austin	344 289	2.51	11.8	34.0	20 261	4 199	1 869	16 062	41 025	4 539	396	4 142	564 388	29.5	46.0
Baytown	24 771	2.99	18.9	24.4	601	507	507	94	3 398	4 456	316	4 140	45 109	51.6	13.5
Beaumont	45 301	2.59	20.4	33.3	5 133	2 634	513	2 499	6 580	5 581	891	4 690	75 055	47.1	22.3
Bedford	21 136	2.28	10.7	34.3	331	325	287	6	1 540	3 144	457	2 687	34 893	26.1	35.3
Big Spring	8 025	3.46	15.8	31.0	6 080	5 768	280	312	1 549	5 466	762	4 704	18 483	54.7	13.1
Brownsville	50 207	3.58	24.1	17.3	1 637	963	671	674	8 063	4 396	304	4 091	100 185	58.9	17.2
Bryan	28 265	2.77	15.8	29.9	3 097	2 822	361	275	2 859	3 607	426	3 180	46 337	50.3	25.7
Burleson	14 018	2.81	10.6	21.1	108	108	108	0	983	2 355	165	2 190	24 693	37.6	24.1
Carrollton	44 394	2.80	12.5	22.1	376	350	350	26	2 950	2 294	129	2 165	83 013	34.0	36.5
Cedar Hill	15 833	2.93	18.4	22.5	293	171	171	122	1 532	3 256	198	3 058	28 488	31.1	30.1
Cedar Park	19 667	2.95	12.0	20.5	137	107	107	30	1 032	1 621	105	1 515	36 749	21.7	44.1
Cleburne	10 495	2.84	14.3	23.6	876	794	316	82	1 079	3 629	256	3 373	18 312	53.7	15.7
College Station	35 032	2.81	8.4	27.7	10 347	201	201	10 146	2 534	2 497	188	2 309	39 007	19.3	55.1
Conroe	21 234	2.89	16.4	27.6	2 263	2 088	291	175	2 463	3 822	321	3 501	38 499	51.3	20.0
Coppell	14 309	2.80	8.7	18.7	3	0	0	3	518	1 271	56	1 215	26 102	14.5	63.2
Copperas Cove	11 323	2.92	13.6	21.9	284	174	174	110	1 069	3 204	336	2 868	20 317	32.2	20.1
Corpus Christi	113 376	2.76	17.7	25.0	5 640	3 199	1 344	2 441	16 204	5 076	656	4 420	200 105	46.1	21.2
Dallas	467 501	2.65	16.3	34.4	18 725	12 739	3 693	5 986	54 126	4 254	665	3 589	790 484	47.8	29.7
Deer Park	11 139	2.96	13.9	16.9	109	87	87	22	730	2 178	137	2 040	20 762	38.8	19.6
Del Rio	11 368	3.17	14.3	24.6	1 373	1 347	203	26	975	2 742	135	2 607	22 083	60.5	16.4
Denton	42 961	2.86	12.0	27.9	8 976	1 646	391	7 330	3 388	2 705	270	2 435	68 982	30.0	38.3
DeSoto	18 720	2.72	19.9	27.0	304	275	275	29	1 920	3 690	282	3 407	33 929	31.2	28.6
Duncanville	13 812	2.85	20.6	23.7	176	165	165	11	1 531	3 841	314	3 527	25 413	42.5	26.0
Eagle Pass	8 543	3.21	21.8	19.3	342	311	59	31	875	3 121	128	2 993	16 244	57.3	17.5
Edinburg	23 575	3.35	17.7	17.8	4 072	3 008	169	1 064	4 716	5 727	359	5 367	43 249	44.2	28.1
El Paso	218 490	3.07	19.8	23.1	9 414	5 777	1 482	3 637	17 241	2 534	393	2 142	406 790	46.8	22.7
Euless	21 315	2.47	13.3	31.8	109	99	99	10	1 313	2 446	119	2 327	35 451	31.9	31.9
Farmers Branch	11 091	2.73	13.5	28.4	103	0	0	103	1 000	3 079	188	2 891	19 964	40.4	33.3
Flower Mound	21 952	3.08	8.2	12.4	159	155	110	4	691	993	55	939	42 710	14.4	57.6
Fort Worth	268 884	2.90	16.1	27.2	13 977	8 117	2 410	5 860	36 693	4 559	558	4 001	475 701	44.2	26.7
Friendswood	13 032	2.84	7.7	20.5	207	201	201	6	350	921	55	866	24 454	20.6	48.3
Frisco	43 491	3.00	8.9	15.6	225	225	225	0	2 653	1 869	83	1 786	80 357	15.1	58.4
Galveston	20 401	2.38	15.2	40.6	2 477	1 261	86	1 216	2 310	4 718	523	4 195	32 724	45.3	27.4
Garland	74 989	3.10	16.7	20.4	567	478	463	89	8 339	3 527	272	3 255	143 303	48.3	21.6
Georgetown	20 769	2.55	8.1	28.9	2 499	1 436	389	1 063	785	1 382	118	1 264	37 303	29.1	42.9
Grand Prairie	58 531	3.09	16.7	21.4	257	188	188	69	5 117	2 762	260	2 502	108 915	47.0	23.0
Grapevine	19 349	2.52	11.3	27.1	242	226	226	16	1 265	2 474	121	2 353	32 932	25.8	45.6
Greenville	9 575	2.70	13.5	34.9	678	604	316	74	1 336	5 142	550	4 591	16 764	52.4	17.3
Haltom City	15 049	2.87	14.5	29.4	96	96	96	0	1 314	2 996	246	2 750	26 684	59.6	12.3
Harker Heights	8 901	3.12	15.1	19.9	166	166	166	0	886	3 111	267	2 844	16 575	33.7	29.3
Harlingen	20 562	3.19	19.5	22.3	1 070	457	415	613	2 205	3 351	222	3 129	39 721	53.7	18.9
Houston	792 763	2.73	16.3	32.2	37 071	18 243	4 778	18 828	126 205	5 685	991	4 694	1 387 729	46.5	29.8
Huntsville	10 617	3.75	16.4	31.8	11 239	8 489	190	2 750	1 167	2 913	527	2 386	22 992	51.6	18.6
Hurst	14 578	2.62	15.2	27.7	245	239	224	6	1 848	4 774	369	4 405	26 028	40.5	25.9

1. No spouse present. 2. Data for serious crimes have not been adjusted for underreporting. This may affect comparability between geographic areas and over time. 3. Per 100,000 population estimated by the FBI. 4. Persons 25 years old and over.

Table D. Cities — Income, Poverty, and Housing

City	Money income, 2010–2014					Housing units, 2010			Occupied housing units 2010–2014				
	Per capita income[1] (dollars)	Households			Families with income below poverty (percent)	Total	Percent change, 2000–2010	Vacant units for sale or rent[2]	Owner-occupied			Median owner costs as a percent of income	
		Median income	Percent with income of $200,000 or more	Percent with income of less than $25,000					Total	Percent	Median value[3] (dollars)	With a mortgage[4]	Without a mortgage[5]
	42	43	44	45	46	47	48	49	50	51	52	53	54
TENNESSEE— Cont'd													
Columbia	19 012	34 325	1.3	37.4	18.7	15 906	10.7	1 894	13 838	57.9	116 000	25.4	13.5
Cookeville	21 104	29 240	1.9	45.1	24.6	13 706	26.9	1 235	12 738	42.5	157 800	22.0	10.9
Franklin	40 447	81 432	10.6	13.4	6.1	25 586	48.6	1 546	25 740	68.3	312 400	22.2	10.0
Gallatin	25 755	46 279	3.0	22.7	11.4	13 093	35.8	1 222	11 892	55.6	161 700	21.8	11.7
Germantown	52 763	110 169	19.6	6.8	1.7	15 536	13.4	626	14 585	86.7	282 100	20.9	10.6
Hendersonville	32 988	61 514	6.1	17.9	7.1	21 543	30.6	1 432	20 333	70.8	197 300	23.2	10.0
Jackson	22 964	37 988	3.2	33.3	18.4	28 052	9.8	2 861	24 804	56.5	118 700	23.3	12.8
Johnson City	27 619	39 121	4.5	34.8	16.1	30 583	19.5	3 566	27 460	55.1	154 500	20.9	10.0
Kingsport	25 687	38 333	2.6	33.9	16.0	23 784	9.0	2 495	23 497	64.2	134 000	20.6	10.0
Knoxville	23 177	33 494	2.2	36.6	17.3	88 009	3.7	9 961	82 079	48.0	116 500	23.3	13.0
La Vergne	21 130	53 672	1.2	13.3	9.4	11 612	66.3	696	10 651	75.6	127 700	23.7	10.0
Lebanon	22 277	41 051	3.1	30.2	14.9	11 030	26.1	900	10 328	56.7	169 800	23.4	11.5
Maryville	27 057	52 120	4.1	24.8	9.8	11 629	19.1	917	10 572	64.5	189 100	22.5	10.0
Memphis	21 909	37 099	2.6	35.0	22.6	291 883	7.4	41 539	248 320	49.9	95 400	25.3	13.5
Morristown	17 879	31 082	1.6	42.4	27.0	12 705	15.2	1 293	11 028	52.2	112 400	22.9	13.1
Murfreesboro	25 789	50 337	2.7	23.6	10.5	45 500	57.2	3 560	43 431	51.8	177 200	22.2	10.0
Nashville-Davidson	28 971	47 434	4.3	25.3	14.2	283 978	12.3	24 479	259 557	54.0	167 400	23.6	11.5
Oak Ridge	31 491	52 534	4.1	27.5	12.6	14 494	8.0	1 722	12 391	60.0	152 000	19.3	10.0
Smyrna	24 562	52 516	2.3	19.6	12.1	15 787	57.9	980	15 367	65.2	149 000	21.8	10.0
Spring Hill	28 763	76 840	2.9	8.1	3.7	10 569	NA	708	10 401	78.2	198 200	20.8	10.0
TEXAS	26 513	52 576	5.0	23.4	13.7	9 977 436	22.3	1 054 503	9 013 582	62.7	131 400	22.2	11.9
Abilene	21 095	42 766	1.8	28.1	14.0	47 783	4.8	4 171	42 491	55.3	95 000	20.3	11.7
Allen	40 741	102 120	14.3	7.0	4.6	28 877	89.4	1 007	29 344	76.8	207 400	20.7	10.0
Amarillo	24 904	47 053	2.6	25.6	13.3	80 298	11.0	6 380	74 457	61.3	114 800	20.8	11.4
Arlington	25 236	53 055	3.2	21.6	13.5	144 805	10.7	11 733	133 601	56.7	129 800	22.5	11.7
Austin	32 672	55 216	6.3	21.8	13.3	354 241	28.1	29 349	344 289	44.8	227 800	23.3	12.6
Baytown	21 429	46 776	2.3	25.9	18.2	28 998	10.2	4 043	24 771	60.0	94 500	22.6	11.9
Beaumont	23 925	39 191	3.5	34.2	19.1	50 689	3.8	5 041	45 301	57.8	96 700	22.4	12.3
Bedford	34 530	60 373	4.0	17.8	6.5	22 301	5.5	1 285	21 136	56.7	161 700	21.6	10.8
Big Spring	18 431	43 750	1.6	26.1	14.3	9 640	-2.4	1 373	8 025	61.2	68 500	17.5	11.3
Brownsville	14 124	32 288	1.5	40.7	31.6	53 936	28.8	4 065	50 207	62.4	81 900	25.6	13.7
Bryan	20 499	39 231	2.6	32.4	18.7	30 582	18.6	2 857	28 265	47.6	114 900	23.1	12.3
Burleson	28 396	69 088	3.7	11.7	6.3	13 591	74.5	703	14 018	72.1	126 300	19.6	13.0
Carrollton	32 336	69 282	5.7	11.4	7.7	45 508	12.3	2 209	44 394	61.6	168 600	21.7	11.3
Cedar Hill	28 210	67 913	3.6	12.7	7.7	16 338	47.0	832	15 833	71.5	130 700	23.6	12.3
Cedar Park	33 632	79 323	7.4	10.8	4.8	18 726	108.8	909	19 667	69.1	206 500	23.1	11.9
Cleburne	21 418	48 260	1.2	24.8	14.3	11 418	14.5	979	10 495	59.9	94 700	21.7	12.5
College Station	21 310	33 434	4.2	40.4	15.0	37 226	43.1	2 189	35 032	34.3	180 100	21.4	11.5
Conroe	23 362	46 109	3.7	27.2	16.6	22 215	54.5	2 198	21 234	48.8	133 100	23.7	12.6
Coppell	49 098	111 325	19.1	6.8	3.1	14 343	14.2	537	14 309	71.3	291 700	20.3	10.7
Copperas Cove	22 927	52 948	1.4	17.2	7.1	13 094	16.7	1 236	11 323	59.2	99 000	20.1	10.5
Corpus Christi	25 203	49 675	3.1	24.9	13.7	125 469	16.3	12 674	113 376	56.7	113 700	22.2	12.1
Dallas	27 917	43 359	5.9	28.3	20.6	516 639	6.7	58 582	467 501	43.0	130 900	24.5	13.5
Deer Park	30 582	77 612	4.4	12.0	5.6	11 742	18.6	609	11 139	73.1	133 900	19.1	10.0
Del Rio	18 301	41 110	1.5	31.7	16.6	12 958	9.5	1 359	11 368	64.5	94 400	21.5	13.1
Denton	24 348	48 518	3.5	27.2	11.3	46 211	41.1	3 576	42 961	48.5	149 200	22.4	12.6
DeSoto	27 576	56 911	2.7	20.1	9.2	19 488	38.1	1 278	18 720	64.8	142 300	25.9	13.0
Duncanville	23 907	55 100	2.3	17.9	10.3	14 011	5.6	731	13 812	67.4	113 800	24.2	12.0
Eagle Pass	16 830	35 590	1.6	37.7	21.8	9 019	17.6	747	8 543	62.6	108 300	26.0	14.1
Edinburg	17 388	42 498	1.4	32.6	22.1	25 167	57.8	2 068	23 575	55.6	100 900	21.7	12.9
El Paso	20 050	42 037	2.5	30.1	18.5	227 605	17.5	10 711	218 490	59.3	117 800	23.0	11.1
Euless	29 651	54 619	3.5	17.8	11.1	23 447	16.8	1 916	21 315	43.1	146 600	21.1	10.6
Farmers Branch	28 738	58 666	4.6	16.4	8.9	11 549	13.0	752	11 091	59.1	144 700	22.5	13.2
Flower Mound	45 981	121 549	17.5	4.6	2.0	21 570	27.1	559	21 952	89.3	269 800	20.3	10.7
Fort Worth	24 726	52 492	3.7	24.1	15.2	291 086	37.8	28 434	268 884	57.7	122 100	22.8	12.8
Friendswood	42 963	95 120	17.4	9.2	3.7	13 254	28.3	528	13 032	79.9	228 800	20.6	10.6
Frisco	43 595	112 155	15.0	6.0	3.4	42 306	209.0	2 405	43 491	74.8	261 900	20.5	10.7
Galveston	26 164	38 008	4.3	34.2	17.5	32 368	8.0	12 425	20 401	45.1	136 700	24.7	13.2
Garland	21 661	51 997	2.3	19.0	13.6	80 834	7.4	5 138	74 989	63.9	115 800	24.4	12.6
Georgetown	31 505	62 219	4.1	16.6	6.9	20 037	81.6	1 207	20 769	71.4	197 600	23.4	11.8
Grand Prairie	23 101	55 336	2.4	19.1	12.9	62 424	34.9	4 253	58 531	61.7	124 600	23.9	12.1
Grapevine	40 574	75 931	9.8	13.1	9.2	19 685	19.2	1 183	19 349	57.9	233 200	21.0	11.1
Greenville	20 338	36 960	0.8	32.3	20.1	10 838	9.3	1 122	9 575	53.7	84 000	21.9	12.4
Haltom City	20 322	43 792	1.0	24.8	14.4	16 626	5.0	1 357	15 049	55.9	86 700	22.1	13.1
Harker Heights	25 581	63 878	3.3	17.9	12.6	10 347	51.2	859	8 901	60.9	162 800	19.9	10.0
Harlingen	17 253	34 868	2.2	37.5	25.4	25 585	10.1	3 940	20 562	58.8	78 500	22.3	12.2
Houston	27 938	45 728	6.2	27.9	19.6	892 646	14.1	110 003	792 763	44.5	125 400	23.0	12.3
Huntsville	11 825	29 257	1.4	46.0	26.6	12 853	12.7	1 062	10 617	35.3	134 800	20.0	14.5
Hurst	28 413	53 488	3.9	19.5	10.9	15 761	6.8	1 109	14 578	65.6	139 600	21.4	12.8

1. Based on population estimated by the American Community Survey. 2. Includes units rented or sold but not occupied. 3. Specified owner-occupied units; $1,000,000 represents $1,000,000 or more   4. 50.0 represents 50 percent or more. 5. 10.0 represents 10 percent or less.

Table D. Cities — Housing, Labor Force, and Employment

City	Occupied housing units, 2010–2014 (cont.)				Migration, 2010–2014		Civilian labor force, 2015		Unemployment		Civilian employment[4], 2010–2014	Percent		
	Percent renter occupied	Median gross rent[1]	Median gross rent as a percent of income[2]	Percent with no vehicle available	Percent who lived in the same house one year ago	Percent who lived outside current city one year ago	Total	Percent change, 2014–2015	Total	Rate[3]	Population age 16 and older	In labor force	Civilian full-year full-time workers	Households with no workers (percent)
	55	56	57	58	59	60	61	62	63	64	65	66	67	68
TENNESSEE—Cont'd														
Columbia	42.1	668	31.4	8.8	81.4	9.8	16 336	1.5	976	6.0	26 649	61.5	37.0	31.1
Cookeville	57.5	609	35.6	5.3	77.8	13.1	12 962	0.8	828	6.4	26 163	53.3	29.5	38.3
Franklin	31.7	1 097	28.0	3.5	81.4	12.5	38 497	1.8	1 479	3.8	50 778	70.8	47.8	18.2
Gallatin	44.4	836	27.8	6.5	78.2	14.4	16 632	2.2	852	5.1	24 357	62.5	41.1	26.6
Germantown	13.3	1 442	25.5	2.4	91.1	7.8	19 230	0.1	857	4.5	31 283	63.6	44.4	21.9
Hendersonville	29.2	924	29.9	4.0	84.3	10.4	29 541	1.7	1 282	4.3	41 332	69.9	47.3	20.2
Jackson	43.5	763	37.1	9.6	82.9	8.0	30 793	0.1	1 991	6.5	53 010	60.2	36.3	31.1
Johnson City	44.9	667	32.9	8.1	81.1	10.0	30 492	-0.2	1 810	5.9	53 400	59.9	36.5	32.2
Kingsport	35.8	578	30.8	9.7	83.7	9.4	22 355	-1.2	1 334	6.0	43 254	54.3	33.5	41.9
Knoxville	52.0	745	32.5	10.9	81.7	8.6	93 074	0.8	5 002	5.4	151 951	61.0	37.0	32.4
La Vergne	24.4	1 046	27.0	2.1	86.1	9.8	17 668	1.6	873	4.9	23 789	74.5	53.4	12.5
Lebanon	43.3	786	34.3	7.8	79.1	13.9	13 396	2.0	746	5.6	21 565	61.5	38.1	31.1
Maryville	35.5	784	29.8	5.6	83.6	11.8	13 214	0.7	700	5.3	22 049	59.2	35.8	31.4
Memphis	50.1	831	35.6	12.3	80.2	5.4	287 431	-0.5	20 951	7.3	508 815	64.0	38.4	28.3
Morristown	47.8	645	33.9	10.2	83.5	9.4	11 190	0.0	789	7.1	22 568	54.8	33.4	37.0
Murfreesboro	48.2	864	31.3	4.8	73.1	14.8	65 295	2.0	3 092	4.7	91 568	68.8	42.2	22.0
Nashville-Davidson	46.0	859	30.7	7.5	79.4	8.6	364 254	1.9	16 259	4.5	520 729	69.0	43.9	22.6
Oak Ridge	40.0	738	29.2	7.1	82.2	11.6	13 903	0.6	733	5.3	23 537	61.3	38.3	31.4
Smyrna	34.8	856	27.7	4.4	81.8	13.2	23 891	1.9	1 110	4.6	31 276	71.6	47.1	20.6
Spring Hill	21.8	1 079	28.6	1.3	86.9	11.1	17 868	2.1	759	4.2	21 554	75.1	53.5	14.2
TEXAS	37.3	870	29.5	5.9	83.0	10.3	13 078 304	0.4	583 954	4.5	19 858 082	64.9	42.9	21.9
Abilene	44.7	775	30.7	6.1	73.4	11.5	54 278	-1.2	2 035	3.7	95 997	60.1	36.1	25.0
Allen	23.2	1 233	25.8	1.2	87.0	9.7	51 196	2.1	1 714	3.3	65 200	75.9	53.3	9.4
Amarillo	38.7	751	28.6	6.4	80.9	6.3	99 848	-0.5	3 047	3.1	147 189	67.8	47.5	22.8
Arlington	43.3	861	31.5	4.7	79.9	9.7	202 116	0.1	8 144	4.0	285 564	71.1	46.8	18.0
Austin	55.2	1 012	30.6	6.7	74.3	10.5	539 664	2.2	16 072	3.0	692 902	73.2	47.9	16.9
Baytown	40.0	839	30.9	7.4	79.5	8.5	33 661	0.2	2 308	6.9	54 507	60.9	38.4	26.5
Beaumont	42.2	758	34.0	11.5	84.4	6.4	52 370	-1.4	3 184	6.1	92 093	59.9	37.4	32.0
Bedford	43.3	898	29.1	5.2	82.6	12.9	28 578	0.0	1 079	3.8	39 670	71.0	49.8	20.7
Big Spring	38.8	738	25.3	9.1	78.8	11.5	9 680	-2.3	481	5.0	22 034	47.9	32.1	30.3
Brownsville	37.6	632	33.6	10.5	88.3	4.1	74 266	-1.3	5 198	7.0	126 888	57.5	34.9	25.9
Bryan	52.4	789	31.4	9.8	72.6	16.4	40 163	1.7	1 415	3.5	60 740	66.5	38.2	25.6
Burleson	27.9	1 116	27.4	2.4	83.8	9.7	21 765	0.4	766	3.5	28 894	73.4	52.4	17.2
Carrollton	38.4	1 005	26.4	2.6	85.1	9.3	75 208	1.9	2 663	3.5	97 245	75.4	52.1	12.9
Cedar Hill	28.5	1 157	30.6	4.2	88.5	8.8	26 017	1.6	1 210	4.7	34 328	74.3	50.6	15.1
Cedar Park	30.9	1 089	28.9	2.0	80.9	15.8	34 254	2.2	1 037	3.0	42 834	72.5	50.4	14.0
Cleburne	40.1	813	28.2	4.4	78.0	11.8	13 201	0.5	623	4.7	22 374	60.9	40.3	26.3
College Station	65.7	914	50.0	5.7	60.2	23.8	52 743	1.4	1 716	3.3	84 748	60.2	28.0	23.2
Conroe	51.2	869	29.6	6.7	79.6	12.7	32 062	0.6	1 226	3.8	46 678	64.0	40.5	21.9
Coppell	28.7	1 183	23.5	1.7	85.7	10.2	22 897	2.0	821	3.6	30 150	73.3	52.8	9.9
Copperas Cove	40.8	903	26.0	4.0	80.2	14.6	12 964	0.5	560	4.3	24 520	63.1	36.2	22.5
Corpus Christi	43.3	872	29.8	8.7	79.6	7.7	151 192	-0.8	7 053	4.7	242 032	65.0	42.8	23.4
Dallas	57.0	852	29.3	10.0	80.8	8.1	643 737	1.9	26 672	4.1	948 542	67.8	45.1	21.4
Deer Park	26.9	1 007	28.3	3.9	85.0	11.4	17 076	0.0	775	4.5	24 833	67.7	47.8	20.0
Del Rio	35.5	625	26.9	8.1	85.5	6.7	14 401	0.5	875	6.1	26 492	60.7	37.8	27.9
Denton	51.5	877	36.3	5.6	69.3	17.4	68 536	2.2	2 302	3.4	101 110	67.6	36.9	21.4
DeSoto	35.2	930	33.3	6.5	89.0	8.1	27 313	1.7	1 449	5.3	39 909	68.2	45.9	23.7
Duncanville	32.6	975	29.1	5.2	90.1	8.3	20 126	1.8	979	4.9	29 875	68.1	45.7	20.8
Eagle Pass	37.4	569	26.2	9.8	89.0	5.2	12 359	0.2	1 406	11.4	19 677	58.5	35.3	28.3
Edinburg	44.4	682	30.6	5.8	81.8	9.1	37 448	0.0	1 894	5.1	57 383	64.9	39.4	19.0
El Paso	40.7	747	30.0	8.4	84.6	6.1	286 847	-0.2	13 675	4.8	504 140	60.7	36.8	24.2
Euless	56.9	961	26.3	3.8	79.3	15.0	30 202	0.0	1 140	3.8	41 112	75.4	50.9	15.3
Farmers Branch	40.9	1 071	25.4	2.6	82.1	13.5	17 207	2.0	651	3.8	23 691	69.2	44.0	19.8
Flower Mound	10.7	1 584	23.2	1.1	88.9	8.3	38 215	2.3	1 262	3.3	49 887	74.1	54.3	11.7
Fort Worth	42.3	878	30.2	6.5	81.8	9.1	391 626	0.3	16 271	4.2	574 986	67.2	45.0	20.7
Friendswood	20.1	1 147	28.5	2.1	87.7	8.7	19 518	0.1	745	3.8	28 896	64.9	45.3	18.1
Frisco	25.2	1 244	25.3	1.4	84.7	11.3	78 569	2.2	2 298	2.9	91 682	76.1	55.4	10.4
Galveston	54.9	830	33.7	14.1	70.7	16.3	24 070	0.0	1 187	4.9	40 303	59.8	35.2	30.9
Garland	36.1	941	32.0	4.6	84.7	8.4	120 847	1.8	5 082	4.2	173 477	70.5	46.7	17.7
Georgetown	28.6	996	31.0	4.2	83.8	11.4	24 230	2.0	939	3.9	42 345	50.5	33.7	41.9
Grand Prairie	38.3	896	30.1	3.5	86.4	9.0	94 169	1.2	3 862	4.1	132 824	71.8	49.4	15.1
Grapevine	42.1	1 075	26.6	2.9	81.1	12.3	30 280	0.2	992	3.3	37 926	76.2	53.6	14.0
Greenville	46.3	747	33.9	10.0	77.8	13.0	10 790	1.8	541	5.0	19 678	58.7	37.3	33.5
Haltom City	44.1	811	28.1	2.5	80.8	16.4	22 007	0.3	939	4.3	32 587	68.0	46.0	19.4
Harker Heights	39.1	849	26.2	2.3	77.8	16.4	11 736	0.9	554	4.7	20 309	64.9	39.1	21.4
Harlingen	41.2	713	30.4	8.8	89.1	5.6	24 417	-1.2	1 450	5.9	47 841	51.2	34.7	33.9
Houston	55.5	862	29.8	9.6	79.4	7.7	1 137 653	0.3	48 881	4.3	1 675 069	68.1	44.4	19.9
Huntsville	64.7	775	42.5	7.2	72.6	20.7	11 396	-1.6	628	5.5	34 674	34.7	18.0	29.8
Hurst	34.4	814	30.3	2.1	83.6	13.3	20 031	0.1	819	4.1	29 906	68.1	45.1	22.7

1. $2,000 represents $2,000 or more.   2. 50.0 represents 50 percent or more.   3. Percent of civilian labor force.   4. Persons 16 years old and over.

Table D. Cities — Construction, Wholesale Trade, and Retail Trade

City	Value of residential construction authorized by building permits, 2015			Wholesale trade,[1] 2012				Retail trade,[2] 2012			
	New construction ($1,000)	Number of housing units	Percent single family	Number of establish-ments	Number of employees	Sales (mil dol)	Annual payroll (mil dol)	Number of establish-ments	Number of employees	Sales (mil dol)	Annual payroll (mil dol)
	69	70	71	72	73	74	75	76	77	78	79
TENNESSEE— Cont'd											
Columbia	21 883	157	100.0	39	496	223.7	30.5	221	2 817	845.7	69.4
Cookeville	23 902	202	34.2	50	887	260.9	35.3	274	4 064	1 040.3	88.8
Franklin	238 295	864	81.3	134	1 764	8 777.6	126.9	477	8 372	2 529.1	225.5
Gallatin	98 904	490	85.3	37	530	497.6	26.2	144	2 057	620.6	54.0
Germantown	NA	NA	NA	33	D	D	D	140	1 977	349.6	39.7
Hendersonville	45 079	246	100.0	50	D	D	D	198	2 898	686.8	66.5
Jackson	27 500	160	95.0	117	1 383	688.7	61.0	426	6 689	1 806.3	155.1
Johnson City	47 891	366	72.4	93	1 048	664.6	41.7	436	7 306	1 780.5	155.2
Kingsport	19 017	78	100.0	75	904	642.3	38.8	337	5 487	1 293.3	119.1
Knoxville	68 725	494	48.6	411	5 879	3 451.0	312.1	1 326	22 849	6 049.5	553.2
La Vergne	10 454	59	100.0	74	4 419	12 983.0	187.8	61	667	261.9	18.8
Lebanon	71 175	416	75.5	42	1 219	891.1	66.2	213	2 781	782.1	67.1
Maryville	23 545	119	100.0	29	271	793.8	13.6	174	2 749	605.8	57.1
Memphis	NA	NA	NA	980	20 551	28 725.9	1 109.3	2 365	35 878	18 848.9	999.6
Morristown	6 517	34	100.0	42	D	D	D	248	3 728	961.9	90.9
Murfreesboro	325 984	2 305	47.0	88	925	706.0	48.5	554	8 860	2 448.0	197.9
Nashville-Davidson	1 317 216	8 103	46.1	923	17 595	17 607.0	1 115.0	2 575	37 506	10 138.3	989.0
Oak Ridge	7 610	32	100.0	21	D	D	D	107	1 720	397.7	37.9
Smyrna	48 714	568	41.9	31	831	1 062.2	40.8	149	2 386	592.6	54.0
Spring Hill	119 572	537	100.0	11	423	184.9	14.1	64	1 105	256.0	23.6
TEXAS	29 086 961	175 443	60.1	27 752	408 692	691 242.6	24 826.1	78 281	1 150 148	356 116.4	28 835.5
Abilene	80 316	531	56.3	131	1 619	1 861.9	79.7	533	7 619	2 087.4	181.6
Allen	170 423	796	58.5	58	D	D	D	281	5 344	1 113.8	105.1
Amarillo	159 119	804	62.4	216	3 356	2 985.1	174.7	841	12 920	4 067.9	311.0
Arlington	111 587	821	46.2	333	5 752	4 034.0	317.8	1 147	17 817	5 419.7	452.1
Austin	1 372 412	10 104	28.2	942	19 901	55 702.0	1 417.1	3 091	49 905	14 738.2	1 363.0
Baytown	29 445	190	100.0	41	460	164.0	19.0	276	4 460	1 572.2	105.0
Beaumont	40 035	261	70.9	180	2 151	1 889.9	117.4	611	9 166	2 511.7	234.4
Bedford	6 631	29	100.0	33	211	113.2	15.0	119	1 747	556.4	46.5
Big Spring	9 543	95	100.0	21	D	D	D	99	1 309	383.9	30.9
Brownsville	54 589	565	91.9	175	1 681	891.1	53.2	563	8 869	2 169.6	181.8
Bryan	60 257	406	66.7	83	1 126	864.9	58.7	299	3 842	1 271.3	93.6
Burleson	86 126	405	99.0	22	138	52.2	5.2	154	3 015	885.6	73.7
Carrollton	133 645	345	100.0	394	6 422	5 487.6	365.5	406	4 850	2 173.2	156.5
Cedar Hill	28 462	99	100.0	12	94	65.0	4.7	146	3 056	602.7	57.9
Cedar Park	129 955	909	48.3	44	D	D	D	232	3 735	835.7	75.7
Cleburne	8 969	52	100.0	35	498	315.7	25.1	155	2 084	584.0	51.3
College Station	188 557	1 210	71.1	34	344	235.6	15.6	309	5 876	1 375.4	111.6
Conroe	315 543	2 374	27.3	111	1 352	5 498.0	69.0	382	6 345	2 214.1	171.2
Coppell	71 361	203	100.0	70	2 125	1 442.5	167.5	75	1 605	713.9	59.3
Copperas Cove	28 550	212	58.5	1	D	D	D	70	1 004	278.4	21.5
Corpus Christi	187 661	1 089	98.9	326	4 376	4 143.7	229.2	1 043	16 278	4 939.2	401.2
Dallas	1 235 369	13 085	11.1	1 934	28 244	22 578.0	1 572.1	4 022	57 240	16 889.0	1 603.0
Deer Park	22 442	98	100.0	40	898	466.1	61.6	57	1 014	283.4	22.7
Del Rio	6 889	53	100.0	21	D	D	D	142	1 984	573.3	43.6
Denton	219 518	1 153	66.0	93	1 231	1 208.9	51.8	399	6 463	1 802.7	149.9
DeSoto	60 957	274	100.0	25	368	220.3	22.3	80	1 395	410.9	34.7
Duncanville	3 999	16	100.0	16	D	D	D	130	1 521	558.9	44.0
Eagle Pass	10 007	95	83.2	38	D	D	D	150	2 425	565.9	47.7
Edinburg	72 440	552	65.8	73	1 425	688.7	46.3	216	3 856	1 371.8	91.3
El Paso	579 648	4 251	53.7	884	9 548	6 348.6	404.9	2 064	32 405	8 445.4	706.3
Euless	61 924	166	100.0	48	418	306.6	25.7	135	1 595	641.0	46.0
Farmers Branch	105 952	1 061	1.5	207	5 093	3 422.1	356.4	150	2 360	772.0	79.2
Flower Mound	245 051	801	57.4	58	698	790.8	40.4	153	2 668	625.3	60.6
Fort Worth	1 014 267	6 094	56.1	696	16 814	17 624.0	1 062.3	2 047	31 491	10 333.5	866.2
Friendswood	59 962	152	100.0	15	D	D	D	96	1 743	480.3	37.4
Frisco	769 313	3 800	60.0	96	D	D	D	437	9 421	2 468.7	229.1
Galveston	46 407	179	100.0	36	D	D	D	208	2 523	615.4	55.4
Garland	38 639	162	100.0	184	2 917	1 771.9	143.2	608	9 210	2 725.4	226.9
Georgetown	304 772	1 279	99.1	33	D	D	D	190	3 460	1 234.9	95.6
Grand Prairie	221 676	1 375	34.4	267	5 982	5 073.0	337.2	343	5 605	2 050.9	146.2
Grapevine	38 501	113	96.5	93	1 933	1 902.9	109.6	315	4 979	1 563.4	128.1
Greenville	17 759	58	100.0	23	249	275.3	9.1	139	2 206	636.5	65.5
Haltom City	918	8	100.0	96	1 072	473.3	51.8	144	1 370	509.3	40.0
Harker Heights	48 171	215	98.1	4	24	7.6	0.8	58	1 136	296.4	23.4
Harlingen	18 041	142	100.0	75	738	585.5	27.3	298	4 835	1 183.7	111.2
Houston	2 139 027	15 216	33.6	4 501	77 057	322 772.6	5 461.8	8 592	130 540	41 589.4	3 488.6
Huntsville	10 774	51	100.0	22	D	D	D	138	2 258	696.9	48.1
Hurst	1 908	12	50.0	37	234	154.5	11.8	282	5 108	1 292.0	117.4

1. Merchant wholesalers except manufacturers' sales branches and offices. 2. Establishments with payroll.

City	Real estate and rental and leasing, 2012				Professional, scientific, and technical services,[1] 2012				Manufacturing, 2012			
	Number of establish-ments	Number of employees	Receipts (mil dol)	Annual payroll (mil dol)	Number of establish-ments	Number of employees	Receipts (mil dol)	Annual payroll (mil dol)	Number of establish-ments	Number of employees	Receipts (mil dol)	Annual payroll (mil dol)
	80	81	82	83	84	85	86	87	88	89	90	91
TENNESSEE—Cont'd												
Columbia	50	175	29.4	4.6	70	D	D	D	40	856	187.7	38.2
Cookeville	54	156	31.0	4.2	114	D	D	D	76	2 976	912.5	119.6
Franklin	120	753	357.2	45.0	373	3 940	700.5	271.3	68	1 770	474.7	74.7
Gallatin	38	456	83.3	30.3	53	D	D	D	61	2 257	985.0	92.1
Germantown	42	D	D	D	115	418	67.3	24.9	9	D	3.6	D
Hendersonville	68	251	51.2	8.8	120	D	D	D	48	810	147.5	37.5
Jackson	90	431	68.9	14.1	157	D	D	D	77	7 033	3 426.0	317.7
Johnson City	99	494	80.6	15.0	170	D	D	D	74	3 902	1 278.7	149.8
Kingsport	59	264	46.2	8.5	143	966	104.2	41.9	38	10 628	D	D
Knoxville	396	2 635	470.7	97.2	719	D	D	D	208	D	2 070.7	D
La Vergne	17	136	33.7	6.9	18	233	15.2	15.6	46	3 289	D	167.8
Lebanon	58	228	57.3	9.1	86	D	D	D	47	2 115	1 015.7	111.6
Maryville	32	88	19.0	2.5	97	D	D	D	31	3 037	2 235.1	173.7
Memphis	745	5 964	1 152.7	263.4	1 305	D	D	D	450	18 847	18 372.5	1 096.2
Morristown	49	162	32.5	4.5	60	D	D	D	84	8 441	3 203.3	350.6
Murfreesboro	134	715	238.3	31.7	226	D	D	D	99	5 030	2 935.5	226.9
Nashville-Davidson	897	6 348	1 410.7	284.0	1 922	24 110	4 015.2	1 637.4	552	18 154	7 319.4	851.8
Oak Ridge	42	152	31.4	5.8	143	D	D	D	44	5 527	1 166.0	445.1
Smyrna	26	111	31.0	4.5	53	650	88.2	43.0	31	6 099	7 170.4	405.2
Spring Hill	18	64	16.5	2.9	27	89	12.5	3.4	9	D	D	D
TEXAS	26 639	169 941	38 757.4	7 751.8	62 085	632 486	120 954.5	46 783.6	19 782	767 024	702 603.1	42 529.8
Abilene	162	881	149.9	27.0	255	D	D	D	83	1 991	898.3	84.5
Allen	77	413	84.0	17.6	280	1 169	204.3	83.0	27	987	334.1	64.8
Amarillo	272	1 247	244.3	42.2	463	D	D	D	159	12 263	D	755.5
Arlington	379	1 915	398.2	74.6	736	D	D	D	224	9 679	15 060.3	518.9
Austin	1 548	10 167	2 332.9	520.7	4 826	56 872	11 692.9	4 737.1	616	20 866	11 413.4	1 356.9
Baytown	79	444	84.3	17.5	97	2 249	182.6	303.9	55	5 545	D	545.5
Beaumont	176	1 179	231.5	49.4	370	4 918	871.7	338.4	103	4 671	D	349.7
Bedford	55	209	46.8	9.2	162	805	100.1	37.5	13	111	11.2	4.0
Big Spring	37	146	29.4	4.3	34	169	16.5	6.3	16	495	D	33.4
Brownsville	142	537	63.8	13.2	263	D	D	D	103	2 705	1 215.2	123.5
Bryan	92	558	75.5	16.4	189	D	D	D	69	3 967	928.5	149.1
Burleson	32	106	21.7	3.5	77	321	37.4	9.5	32	920	178.9	38.8
Carrollton	143	1 629	302.6	85.9	407	3 355	571.1	209.8	187	11 424	3 739.1	564.1
Cedar Hill	23	69	14.7	1.6	55	D	D	D	27	782	151.6	27.9
Cedar Park	65	185	68.5	6.1	155	912	142.0	51.6	39	1 200	384.8	75.0
Cleburne	37	120	21.7	3.8	72	434	40.1	18.2	32	1 433	599.9	75.8
College Station	120	638	132.9	20.1	165	D	D	D	13	241	D	13.6
Conroe	83	578	111.4	26.6	203	D	D	D	104	3 733	1 763.5	194.3
Coppell	47	482	113.4	25.0	208	2 604	562.9	231.0	35	1 485	297.0	66.8
Copperas Cove	29	D	D	D	31	138	10.6	3.8	4	7	D	D
Corpus Christi	370	2 602	623.1	121.9	786	5 700	840.3	306.1	168	5 412	D	357.1
Dallas	2 162	20 336	4 905.7	1 160.5	5 407	67 331	14 598.6	5 688.9	1 125	42 824	17 731.3	2 126.8
Deer Park	32	421	104.1	22.0	51	1 007	175.6	55.4	41	4 605	28 034.8	485.4
Del Rio	32	114	16.5	2.7	37	D	D	D	15	176	D	5.0
Denton	149	585	125.7	19.9	260	D	D	D	93	5 210	4 794.0	277.2
DeSoto	39	162	31.9	5.6	48	199	16.9	6.8	27	733	120.5	39.8
Duncanville	38	173	19.2	5.5	54	196	21.3	8.4	22	1 137	223.0	39.0
Eagle Pass	26	71	12.5	1.9	36	D	D	D	14	339	49.0	9.0
Edinburg	60	205	41.5	6.1	148	D	D	D	29	625	215.0	22.9
El Paso	671	2 969	548.7	101.9	1 119	D	D	D	432	11 607	13 170.8	487.1
Euless	40	267	50.6	8.9	86	D	D	D	37	832	197.2	39.3
Farmers Branch	70	929	144.0	47.3	308	4 575	1 077.9	470.0	80	2 707	910.5	117.6
Flower Mound	66	400	66.6	17.0	271	D	D	D	20	636	212.3	36.7
Fort Worth	704	4 977	1 106.6	228.7	1 652	D	D	D	645	39 747	D	2 369.4
Friendswood	44	314	23.4	8.1	128	447	58.6	21.0	16	175	D	7.2
Frisco	135	672	165.1	27.0	552	4 343	778.7	263.7	36	533	233.7	29.2
Galveston	75	403	76.2	15.5	106	D	D	D	29	948	D	48.9
Garland	173	1 113	183.7	33.5	280	3 620	463.2	299.6	264	9 585	5 396.6	427.2
Georgetown	63	228	62.7	13.0	161	616	86.9	30.9	48	1 541	344.6	63.4
Grand Prairie	126	1 945	355.9	83.2	169	1 299	174.6	65.1	181	12 084	4 512.7	758.4
Grapevine	77	785	328.6	40.5	219	1 265	198.4	76.2	43	1 942	D	95.9
Greenville	38	115	20.4	3.3	47	281	49.8	10.4	39	6 681	2 783.6	523.9
Haltom City	38	350	82.6	19.8	56	687	53.9	22.5	90	2 612	684.3	107.5
Harker Heights	32	127	18.7	4.0	28	138	9.6	3.5	4	23	2.6	D
Harlingen	97	443	80.5	9.8	146	D	D	D	49	903	D	40.8
Houston	3 435	28 791	7 005.4	1 456.0	9 252	158 979	38 304.1	14 658.9	2 436	86 899	53 787.1	4 791.2
Huntsville	48	175	42.9	6.1	68	393	27.6	9.8	17	347	D	21.3
Hurst	52	240	72.6	8.6	167	1 037	134.3	59.3	31	467	127.0	22.8

1. Establishments subject to federal tax.

Table D. Cities — Accommodation and Food Services, Arts, Entertainment, and Recreation, and Health Care and Social Assistance

City	Accommodation and food services, 2012				Arts, entertainment, and recreation,[1] 2012				Health care and social assistance,[1] 2012			
	Number of establish-ments	Number of employees	Sales (mil dol)	Annual payroll (mil dol)	Number of establish-ments	Number of employees	Receipts (mil dol)	Annual payroll (mil dol)	Number of establish-ments	Number of employees	Receipts (mil dol)	Annual payroll (mil dol)
	92	93	94	95	96	97	98	99	100	101	102	103
TENNESSEE—Cont'd												
Columbia	101	1 771	81.2	22.3	7	D	D	D	136	D	D	D
Cookeville	137	D	D	D	10	D	D	D	173	D	D	D
Franklin	281	6 519	337.0	97.6	95	D	D	D	285	4 901	744.3	269.8
Gallatin	58	905	44.3	12.2	6	D	D	D	84	D	D	D
Germantown	70	1 454	82.7	22.4	13	130	5.8	1.9	191	D	D	D
Hendersonville	112	2 638	113.7	34.6	26	D	D	D	142	2 039	249.7	85.2
Jackson	210	4 703	220.3	62.4	17	D	D	D	261	D	D	D
Johnson City	239	5 668	249.2	72.7	16	D	D	D	252	D	D	D
Kingsport	193	4 387	199.6	58.9	19	D	D	D	228	3 761	503.7	220.1
Knoxville	714	17 958	865.1	267.4	47	548	34.6	9.6	755	16 303	2 046.1	772.1
La Vergne	29	412	20.6	5.3	NA	NA	NA	NA	15	143	7.3	3.6
Lebanon	108	2 239	98.8	28.6	8	D	D	D	136	2 476	294.2	114.8
Maryville	94	1 644	75.5	22.0	13	D	D	D	140	1 629	171.3	82.1
Memphis	1 243	28 822	1 503.9	425.7	82	1 976	210.8	102.7	1 415	26 987	2 964.4	1 216.1
Morristown	106	D	D	D	9	D	D	D	123	2 306	227.8	96.0
Murfreesboro	314	7 922	356.0	105.3	21	D	D	D	327	6 004	576.4	262.1
Nashville-Davidson	1 714	40 106	2 573.8	759.3	665	4 720	1 476.9	524.5	1 467	30 924	4 176.2	1 568.7
Oak Ridge	74	1 604	76.3	21.4	6	101	4.6	1.6	101	D	D	D
Smyrna	109	2 367	112.1	32.0	6	D	D	D	117	D	D	D
Spring Hill	57	1 188	45.9	14.2	9	19	3.6	0.5	35	D	D	D
TEXAS	48 721	976 390	54 480.8	14 743.8	4 966	83 587	7 770.7	2 523.6	55 176	945 659	93 988.1	36 493.1
Abilene	284	D	D	D	34	258	21.1	4.0	316	7 710	657.8	271.4
Allen	170	3 771	194.3	56.4	24	462	25.4	8.1	259	D	D	D
Amarillo	500	10 147	514.1	139.7	52	687	38.7	11.3	567	10 579	1 228.0	437.8
Arlington	684	15 492	910.8	233.2	67	3 881	616.2	255.2	865	15 821	1 542.7	638.3
Austin	2 517	55 702	3 474.7	962.5	317	4 559	468.8	144.0	2 329	37 842	4 746.7	1 859.6
Baytown	174	3 836	193.7	52.2	12	D	D	D	213	D	D	D
Beaumont	283	6 727	320.7	88.3	35	D	D	D	501	D	D	D
Bedford	93	1 993	98.5	27.8	9	D	D	D	191	D	D	D
Big Spring	71	1 057	61.0	13.8	3	D	D	D	57	D	D	D
Brownsville	299	5 246	244.3	65.5	26	D	D	D	418	13 860	789.1	346.9
Bryan	139	2 436	115.0	32.5	13	D	D	D	186	2 546	275.6	118.1
Burleson	105	2 511	112.7	31.4	8	D	D	D	95	1 020	82.2	34.5
Carrollton	244	3 204	187.6	49.4	27	D	D	D	328	3 721	410.7	148.7
Cedar Hill	86	2 068	97.8	25.6	6	D	D	D	79	1 220	84.9	30.5
Cedar Park	137	2 517	119.2	31.5	20	D	D	D	163	D	D	D
Cleburne	81	1 365	63.3	18.1	7	68	3.7	0.6	99	D	D	D
College Station	287	6 966	327.7	88.0	21	330	14.7	5.0	136	D	D	D
Conroe	164	3 450	175.2	48.5	10	125	11.6	1.4	200	D	D	D
Coppell	73	1 538	93.3	22.2	9	159	6.8	2.3	106	D	D	D
Copperas Cove	50	934	42.1	10.8	3	D	D	D	27	426	22.3	10.3
Corpus Christi	749	15 806	825.4	223.7	57	D	D	D	907	17 743	1 577.5	620.5
Dallas	2 687	59 649	3 851.5	1 087.3	283	4 840	477.0	208.1	3 535	56 873	8 201.1	3 427.0
Deer Park	44	769	46.6	11.2	2	D	D	D	45	D	D	D
Del Rio	87	1 613	76.2	19.5	7	41	1.1	0.5	84	D	D	D
Denton	283	5 961	277.1	75.9	20	291	15.1	4.0	390	6 232	770.2	285.0
DeSoto	60	1 240	63.9	17.8	5	89	5.7	2.1	165	3 622	236.3	105.8
Duncanville	60	1 406	69.0	19.1	5	101	5.7	1.5	101	2 187	105.2	47.1
Eagle Pass	65	D	D	D	7	D	D	D	81	D	D	D
Edinburg	120	1 970	102.3	25.9	12	D	D	D	331	9 143	433.5	212.2
El Paso	1 362	27 187	1 310.8	354.0	89	D	D	D	1 300	26 860	2 875.1	1 005.3
Euless	89	1 538	76.0	20.2	5	D	D	D	77	D	D	D
Farmers Branch	99	1 493	83.9	25.9	6	D	D	D	136	2 292	285.2	112.7
Flower Mound	118	2 866	157.4	42.2	23	411	26.0	7.3	178	1 971	257.9	91.6
Fort Worth	1 288	28 324	1 609.5	440.5	134	2 108	225.1	46.6	1 602	24 161	2 738.6	1 078.8
Friendswood	70	1 121	55.0	14.1	11	D	D	D	111	D	D	D
Frisco	254	6 182	360.8	100.4	41	1 555	148.3	83.1	394	D	D	D
Galveston	212	6 605	391.2	110.0	22	480	35.2	7.9	85	D	D	D
Garland	309	5 540	286.8	79.7	31	504	40.5	9.4	414	7 134	439.2	187.8
Georgetown	103	2 188	109.6	30.5	14	D	D	D	152	2 278	225.8	90.9
Grand Prairie	216	3 855	221.9	54.6	21	D	D	D	234	2 519	181.0	66.5
Grapevine	175	7 278	628.9	152.0	17	379	26.3	5.7	186	D	D	D
Greenville	68	1 304	65.2	17.1	4	D	D	D	110	D	D	D
Haltom City	72	735	37.6	9.0	7	49	4.1	0.5	35	D	D	D
Harker Heights	63	951	37.1	10.2	15	D	D	D	34	D	D	D
Harlingen	170	3 749	203.8	57.5	16	D	D	D	334	11 017	834.5	354.0
Houston	5 645	122 643	7 746.6	2 082.8	442	10 362	1 681.5	523.7	6 526	105 192	11 479.2	4 372.6
Huntsville	94	D	D	D	3	D	D	D	78	D	D	D
Hurst	103	2 129	126.6	32.5	14	182	9.7	2.5	130	D	D	D

1. Establishments subject to federal tax.

Table D. Cities — Other Services and Government Employment and Payroll

City	Other services[1], 2012				Government employment and payroll, 2012								
						March payroll							
							Percent of total for:						
	Number of establish-ments	Number of employees	Receipts (mil dol)	Annual payroll (mil dol)	Full-time equivalent employees	Total (dollars)	Adminis-tration, judicial, and legal	Police and Corrections	Fire Protection	Highways and trans-portation	Health and welfare	Natural resources and utilities	Education and libraries
	104	105	106	107	108	109	110	111	112	113	114	115	116
TENNESSEE— Cont'd													
Columbia	57	381	30.1	9.6	492	1 828 149	7.0	18.8	18.5	8.4	0.0	42.6	0.0
Cookeville	80	413	34.4	9.2	2 260	9 757 664	1.2	3.6	1.9	1.3	85.3	5.8	0.0
Franklin	133	1 096	75.2	26.9	635	2 507 514	14.1	24.5	24.1	7.9	2.9	21.9	0.0
Gallatin	46	230	20.9	6.9	429	1 515 188	8.8	22.7	17.5	5.7	0.0	40.3	0.0
Germantown	51	506	24.7	9.6	286	1 166 262	0.4	46.4	32.0	8.9	0.0	6.3	0.0
Hendersonville	78	421	27.5	8.9	317	1 225 951	9.7	37.8	33.9	3.9	0.4	5.6	0.0
Jackson	91	D	D	D	732	2 706 306	10.3	39.0	26.4	6.9	0.2	15.5	0.0
Johnson City	104	D	D	D	2 069	7 207 080	4.3	9.1	5.7	7.6	0.0	24.2	46.3
Kingsport	83	531	48.6	15.0	2 088	7 112 728	4.6	8.2	5.7	3.4	0.1	9.0	66.2
Knoxville	392	3 196	242.1	83.5	2 544	10 707 196	7.3	20.0	11.8	5.2	1.3	49.6	0.0
La Vergne	24	794	124.4	25.1	165	495 446	15.9	42.8	0.0	4.2	0.0	26.3	4.3
Lebanon	56	657	63.8	20.5	337	1 064 568	9.9	34.9	13.8	8.3	1.8	27.1	0.0
Maryville	50	266	19.8	6.8	929	3 586 065	5.2	6.5	5.0	4.0	0.0	15.5	63.0
Memphis	712	5 678	522.2	172.5	24 196	79 305 378	2.0	15.7	10.1	4.9	0.8	25.5	40.2
Morristown	49	245	21.5	6.7	417	1 625 386	6.0	20.1	18.2	6.1	0.3	38.5	0.0
Murfreesboro	167	1 164	91.2	29.6	2 265	7 333 077	3.8	13.4	9.7	3.3	0.2	20.3	45.7
Nashville-Davidson	868	8 126	726.0	233.6	21 697	83 700 973	6.4	13.3	7.5	1.1	9.0	11.1	49.9
Oak Ridge	44	D	D	D	1 132	4 632 934	5.5	7.1	8.2	4.8	1.0	10.3	62.3
Smyrna	46	442	34.2	16.1	426	1 763 154	14.1	27.9	24.5	2.1	0.0	27.9	0.0
Spring Hill	26	136	10.8	3.2	153	514 319	5.2	29.3	24.9	4.9	0.0	23.4	4.4
TEXAS	28 255	216 219	21 861.4	6 765.6	X	X	X	X	X	X	X	X	X
Abilene	162	1 407	104.9	34.0	1 115	4 154 689	10.5	32.0	23.1	4.8	5.7	16.9	2.3
Allen	81	693	53.5	17.3	662	2 925 255	11.5	28.9	20.0	3.9	2.3	27.3	4.5
Amarillo	296	2 035	192.1	55.1	2 117	7 521 677	9.3	27.1	24.7	8.3	4.8	19.1	2.1
Arlington	374	2 410	207.6	61.6	2 551	12 130 944	13.1	38.1	20.5	5.1	4.7	13.8	2.7
Austin	1 319	11 317	1 060.8	331.5	12 580	64 599 610	10.4	24.1	13.4	7.1	8.1	30.6	1.9
Baytown	87	779	71.7	24.8	748	3 193 832	12.8	28.9	19.0	2.5	7.2	18.6	3.5
Beaumont	178	1 744	180.5	55.1	1 387	7 544 738	11.5	29.5	22.1	6.9	9.1	14.8	1.6
Bedford	55	334	28.4	8.5	396	1 910 062	12.2	44.6	25.8	2.3	0.9	11.0	3.3
Big Spring	28	D	D	D	255	860 648	10.2	23.3	19.7	6.6	10.8	21.6	2.2
Brownsville	98	498	35.4	11.2	1 660	6 576 268	6.3	28.3	16.9	10.1	3.1	22.4	2.2
Bryan	120	727	64.4	18.2	926	4 516 110	3.1	19.6	11.5	1.8	0.7	38.5	3.0
Burleson	66	364	26.8	8.7	314	1 837 857	11.3	27.1	16.3	3.9	5.4	20.8	2.6
Carrollton	168	1 866	164.0	66.9	750	3 791 660	11.3	30.8	28.1	4.7	3.6	12.4	3.2
Cedar Hill	35	227	19.1	5.7	345	1 415 937	9.4	29.5	24.7	6.8	4.1	17.5	2.3
Cedar Park	105	720	53.2	19.3	366	1 608 634	12.6	30.9	18.4	2.3	0.5	20.7	3.2
Cleburne	51	317	28.3	8.6	331	1 384 254	10.9	25.9	23.1	7.1	3.7	23.7	1.6
College Station	75	549	34.1	11.0	818	3 487 614	20.0	22.9	18.5	6.9	0.0	27.4	0.0
Conroe	104	679	59.5	17.1	506	2 148 894	13.0	28.8	20.3	9.4	1.3	18.9	0.0
Coppell	48	964	119.8	36.7	374	2 007 729	18.0	24.0	25.7	6.8	0.9	15.3	4.2
Copperas Cove	42	228	21.2	5.7	265	875 963	7.7	30.2	19.1	1.6	1.2	17.4	2.0
Corpus Christi	358	3 496	346.7	116.1	2 747	10 789 288	5.1	28.6	19.2	4.2	3.3	21.1	1.6
Dallas	1 450	12 565	1 440.8	409.3	14 235	67 511 933	7.3	31.8	17.3	19.3	4.4	14.9	1.2
Deer Park	58	906	130.9	49.5	328	1 382 968	18.7	32.7	5.3	2.7	0.0	31.9	2.9
Del Rio	32	D	D	D	479	1 348 047	13.5	25.7	21.8	5.8	8.4	17.9	0.0
Denton	150	972	89.5	27.1	1 265	6 238 827	15.5	19.1	17.6	2.9	1.6	38.3	2.8
DeSoto	39	154	15.1	4.3	317	1 509 174	9.4	33.2	25.8	4.2	5.1	12.0	3.0
Duncanville	63	321	32.4	8.9	262	1 180 545	13.5	32.0	24.0	4.8	0.9	15.2	3.2
Eagle Pass	29	126	7.5	2.1	351	916 457	7.8	31.5	17.9	15.9	3.9	20.4	1.6
Edinburg	69	313	21.9	6.5	687	2 190 991	12.2	35.3	5.2	5.7	1.0	33.1	3.3
El Paso	714	4 354	334.6	101.8	5 996	23 812 936	7.0	28.9	21.6	16.9	1.4	12.9	2.2
Euless	59	D	D	D	434	2 144 456	12.6	34.2	21.4	3.9	1.0	17.4	4.5
Farmers Branch	53	615	61.6	17.3	372	1 986 448	11.5	30.7	24.2	3.4	5.2	21.2	0.0
Flower Mound	88	931	73.4	25.9	440	1 883 026	25.4	26.1	22.5	3.5	4.1	11.7	3.5
Fort Worth	700	6 296	605.7	172.5	6 536	32 292 472	9.5	36.9	20.2	4.1	1.8	17.7	2.4
Friendswood	57	303	22.4	7.9	194	961 732	21.4	48.5	0.4	6.3	7.0	10.9	5.4
Frisco	142	1 037	80.7	26.6	594	2 715 180	9.9	30.4	23.9	5.3	1.2	19.8	3.8
Galveston	64	301	25.2	8.2	808	3 423 101	7.9	29.1	17.6	21.5	3.7	16.9	0.0
Garland	230	1 159	100.6	32.4	1 920	9 882 194	9.5	22.2	17.3	5.1	4.8	30.5	2.2
Georgetown	75	446	37.7	12.4	540	2 310 226	14.5	21.6	17.8	5.7	3.2	24.6	2.8
Grand Prairie	143	1 111	98.2	32.3	1 169	5 599 824	10.7	29.3	27.8	5.1	5.9	13.3	1.6
Grapevine	69	662	56.1	18.8	572	2 942 808	10.6	24.3	22.7	7.0	1.2	13.7	2.9
Greenville	36	211	16.2	5.5	403	1 671 286	7.6	21.2	16.8	3.9	1.7	41.0	1.8
Haltom City	65	D	D	D	281	1 111 357	13.5	36.6	17.0	6.0	1.5	13.9	4.9
Harker Heights	32	151	9.1	2.7	218	830 934	17.0	29.4	23.6	4.0	1.0	16.2	3.2
Harlingen	91	501	34.2	10.3	751	2 448 262	8.2	27.6	19.8	7.2	2.5	27.1	1.8
Houston	3 244	31 771	3 283.0	1 045.9	21 007	99 616 057	8.7	36.5	20.9	7.6	4.6	8.9	1.5
Huntsville	41	244	21.2	5.3	308	1 115 825	24.2	27.0	5.3	6.6	0.0	23.7	2.4
Hurst	71	450	31.1	10.3	371	1 783 347	13.7	36.1	21.5	5.6	0.0	15.6	6.0

1. Establishments subject to federal tax.

Table D. Cities — **City Government Finances**

City	General revenue Total (mil dol)	Intergovernmental Total (mil dol)	Intergovernmental Percent from state government	Taxes Total (mil dol)	Taxes Per capita (dollars) Total	Taxes Per capita (dollars) Property	Sales and gross receipts	General expenditure Total (mil dol)	General expenditure Per capita (dollars) Total	Capital outlays
	117	118	119	120	121	122	123	124	125	126
TENNESSEE—Cont'd										
Columbia	41.4	15.4	53.0	12.6	360	269	88	40.7	1 166	252
Cookeville	277.1	19.0	22.5	9.4	303	201	101	277.4	8 954	919
Franklin	87.6	39.1	37.2	24.4	368	176	192	85.2	1 285	230
Gallatin	34.4	11.7	42.9	11.9	376	302	74	33.1	1 045	154
Germantown	61.8	21.1	73.1	24.7	627	570	58	65.4	1 661	429
Hendersonville	35.8	16.0	45.5	13.8	260	194	66	34.8	655	51
Jackson	87.7	28.3	31.7	40.9	609	491	118	83.5	1 243	137
Johnson City	163.0	78.4	55.6	47.4	732	608	124	167.9	2 594	204
Kingsport	166.0	83.1	48.9	57.0	1 080	915	166	164.5	3 118	644
Knoxville	351.6	81.3	38.7	163.6	898	585	313	318.2	1 747	425
La Vergne	25.4	7.8	50.3	10.3	306	225	80	18.7	553	55
Lebanon	28.1	13.4	31.2	6.1	218	112	106	31.0	1 113	106
Maryville	74.6	37.7	68.6	28.4	1 027	932	95	71.2	2 571	85
Memphis	2 270.7	1 329.3	61.2	520.3	789	551	237	2 276.9	3 451	425
Morristown	51.1	16.0	22.3	12.8	440	314	127	46.1	1 582	230
Murfreesboro	157.1	75.8	58.2	48.0	422	310	112	168.1	1 476	135
Nashville-Davidson	2 398.7	624.4	98.0	1 220.6	1 952	1 260	691	2 431.3	3 888	403
Oak Ridge	134.1	83.4	33.6	34.7	1 182	710	463	107.5	3 666	210
Smyrna	53.2	16.9	24.7	11.2	269	186	83	50.3	1 205	109
Spring Hill	19.8	7.0	49.1	5.7	182	127	55	26.7	857	343
TEXAS	X	X	X	X	X	X	X	X	X	X
Abilene	137.0	15.0	30.9	83.5	697	279	418	116.5	972	130
Allen	117.2	4.4	12.3	78.6	873	457	416	125.1	1 390	272
Amarillo	243.2	33.1	39.3	120.2	614	172	442	262.0	1 339	339
Arlington	460.5	35.2	25.8	242.5	644	301	343	480.0	1 275	145
Austin	1 410.8	92.8	27.1	613.6	709	410	298	1 511.5	1 746	382
Baytown	105.9	8.6	14.0	43.5	589	251	339	126.1	1 710	339
Beaumont	168.9	28.1	23.8	91.4	782	377	405	178.4	1 526	395
Bedford	41.1	0.8	100.0	27.1	562	290	272	42.9	889	121
Big Spring	26.6	1.5	86.7	14.4	521	200	321	29.9	1 081	134
Brownsville	224.1	50.4	11.0	74.7	415	197	218	175.9	976	181
Bryan	85.5	6.5	55.6	40.7	522	297	225	96.3	1 235	236
Burleson	54.3	0.2	84.0	35.0	897	409	488	43.5	1 115	101
Carrollton	128.2	6.2	86.1	88.8	708	435	273	119.3	951	184
Cedar Hill	54.5	2.8	12.5	34.8	748	403	345	54.1	1 163	158
Cedar Park	71.9	5.6	100.0	42.4	732	349	383	67.0	1 156	349
Cleburne	51.2	3.4	11.5	26.3	884	463	421	43.9	1 472	106
College Station	94.1	3.3	25.7	53.8	549	255	294	101.4	1 036	172
Conroe	70.6	1.0	16.8	50.6	824	235	589	74.4	1 211	375
Coppell	72.0	0.3	100.0	58.2	1 451	828	624	65.6	1 638	306
Copperas Cove	25.8	0.6	100.0	14.2	425	258	167	73.0	2 187	1 475
Corpus Christi	357.9	29.6	42.3	191.7	614	280	333	389.3	1 246	290
Dallas	2 544.8	172.7	56.8	1 084.4	872	545	327	2 543.0	2 045	435
Deer Park	42.3	0.3	34.3	19.4	585	370	215	36.3	1 097	77
Del Rio	34.7	4.3	47.7	15.1	418	189	229	37.0	1 026	201
Denton	169.7	11.5	79.7	94.5	765	357	408	149.1	1 207	175
DeSoto	50.0	1.3	100.0	32.7	640	413	227	48.8	954	113
Duncanville	37.1	1.0	60.3	22.7	573	320	253	42.9	1 085	220
Eagle Pass	32.1	2.3	62.3	10.6	387	159	228	32.6	1 184	237
Edinburg	72.5	6.4	81.8	40.8	518	269	249	71.1	903	197
El Paso	743.5	92.0	24.8	386.6	572	287	285	621.6	920	181
Euless	66.2	1.7	13.5	42.6	806	223	583	61.4	1 162	109
Farmers Branch	55.4	0.8	73.5	41.0	1 395	732	663	53.3	1 813	185
Flower Mound	74.2	2.2	6.5	54.3	800	457	343	76.4	1 125	247
Fort Worth	1 108.5	81.2	53.9	609.6	783	466	317	1 116.7	1 434	341
Friendswood	32.1	3.1	8.8	20.8	562	394	168	35.6	963	285
Frisco	214.9	32.8	2.5	125.6	977	507	469	202.2	1 572	466
Galveston	180.4	62.3	54.6	58.9	1 217	502	716	182.3	3 769	1 529
Garland	228.5	19.9	12.3	106.8	457	312	145	234.9	1 004	127
Georgetown	65.1	3.9	87.5	35.5	675	289	386	70.7	1 345	298
Grand Prairie	252.2	40.5	30.9	131.5	723	393	330	217.4	1 195	147
Grapevine	125.9	3.7	100.0	94.8	1 953	609	1 344	92.9	1 916	312
Greenville	39.6	2.4	41.3	19.8	762	371	392	43.8	1 690	468
Haltom City	42.3	2.2	23.7	24.5	565	230	336	38.1	878	131
Harker Heights	24.0	0.5	27.3	15.5	558	324	234	26.5	951	239
Harlingen	87.2	13.1	29.3	40.5	615	250	365	112.2	1 703	650
Houston	3 667.9	315.0	27.9	1 921.4	888	474	414	3 697.9	1 708	274
Huntsville	32.1	1.0	50.9	14.9	376	122	253	30.5	766	52
Hurst	51.1	2.4	26.0	34.8	911	328	583	49.1	1 285	225

1. Based on population estimated as of July 1 of the year shown.

City	City government finances, 2012 (cont.)									
	General expenditure (cont.)									
	Percent of total for:									
	Public welfare	Highways	Parking facilities	Education	Health and hospitals	Police protection	Sewerage and sanitation	Parks and recreation	Housing and community development	Interest on debt
	127	128	129	130	131	132	133	134	135	136
TENNESSEE— Cont'd										
Columbia	0.0	10.7	0.0	0.0	0.0	16.5	23.4	4.1	0.0	2.9
Cookeville	0.0	1.2	0.0	0.0	84.6	2.6	1.6	1.0	0.0	1.2
Franklin	0.0	10.0	0.0	0.0	0.0	16.6	17.5	4.0	0.2	6.0
Gallatin	0.0	5.6	0.0	0.0	0.4	19.4	17.8	11.9	0.0	1.4
Germantown	0.0	27.4	0.0	0.0	0.5	17.1	10.4	14.4	2.9	1.4
Hendersonville	0.0	12.3	0.0	0.0	0.0	27.4	13.2	7.3	0.0	1.2
Jackson	0.0	14.0	0.0	0.0	0.2	25.1	12.3	11.3	3.2	3.2
Johnson City	0.5	5.3	0.0	40.8	0.0	8.8	12.9	8.4	0.3	4.0
Kingsport	0.0	3.2	0.0	40.7	0.0	7.2	9.4	4.1	0.3	3.0
Knoxville	0.0	3.1	0.3	0.0	0.0	15.7	31.2	5.9	3.8	8.0
La Vergne	0.7	9.0	0.0	0.0	0.1	30.0	21.7	6.8	0.0	2.9
Lebanon	0.0	8.4	0.0	0.0	0.0	25.7	25.8	7.6	0.0	1.0
Maryville	0.0	3.8	0.0	66.8	0.3	6.3	5.5	2.0	0.0	3.6
Memphis	0.0	1.2	0.0	52.3	0.0	9.9	4.8	1.6	6.4	4.4
Morristown	0.6	10.0	0.0	0.0	0.0	15.5	27.8	3.8	1.6	1.5
Murfreesboro	0.1	11.1	0.1	38.8	0.0	13.6	8.2	6.7	0.8	2.6
Nashville-Davidson	1.3	1.6	0.0	34.8	9.5	8.0	6.5	3.3	0.0	7.0
Oak Ridge	0.0	2.3	0.0	52.8	0.0	6.5	10.1	3.7	0.6	3.4
Smyrna	0.5	5.1	0.0	0.0	0.0	18.7	11.2	12.4	0.3	2.6
Spring Hill	0.0	9.8	0.0	0.0	0.0	14.6	51.6	2.8	0.0	0.9
TEXAS	X	X	X	X	X	X	X	X	X	X
Abilene	0.0	7.3	0.0	0.0	3.8	18.8	16.3	6.3	1.0	2.9
Allen	0.0	4.2	0.0	0.0	0.2	15.6	11.7	22.6	1.0	5.9
Amarillo	0.0	6.1	0.0	0.0	6.0	13.9	17.9	6.7	4.4	2.1
Arlington	0.1	9.3	0.0	0.0	0.9	17.6	13.8	7.7	1.1	26.6
Austin	0.0	7.5	0.0	0.0	6.9	17.8	18.1	8.2	3.3	5.9
Baytown	0.0	9.2	0.0	0.0	3.4	15.7	9.1	9.2	2.3	5.4
Beaumont	0.0	21.9	0.0	0.0	5.1	21.4	8.4	9.5	1.2	4.0
Bedford	0.0	4.8	0.0	0.0	0.8	24.7	12.9	6.3	0.0	5.0
Big Spring	0.0	5.1	0.0	0.0	7.7	15.7	16.2	15.7	0.0	2.1
Brownsville	1.3	7.1	0.3	0.0	1.0	18.2	22.3	5.7	1.0	5.9
Bryan	0.0	9.9	0.0	0.0	0.0	16.0	19.2	3.8	1.3	6.5
Burleson	0.0	9.7	0.0	0.0	1.7	16.8	16.6	12.8	0.0	9.0
Carrollton	0.0	12.5	0.0	0.0	2.0	17.5	10.3	7.8	2.6	6.3
Cedar Hill	0.1	6.3	0.0	0.0	0.3	19.0	15.2	8.6	0.0	7.0
Cedar Park	0.0	19.4	0.0	0.0	0.4	11.4	13.6	7.0	0.0	10.8
Cleburne	0.0	5.5	0.0	0.0	1.7	16.6	19.7	9.4	3.6	4.0
College Station	0.0	15.6	1.2	0.0	0.0	13.7	18.3	9.5	1.4	5.1
Conroe	0.0	11.1	0.0	0.0	0.0	18.9	12.0	15.3	0.4	6.4
Coppell	0.0	7.8	0.0	0.0	0.5	14.6	6.7	17.0	0.0	5.6
Copperas Cove	0.0	63.3	0.0	0.0	0.5	6.3	7.5	2.6	0.0	4.4
Corpus Christi	0.0	10.6	0.1	0.0	1.8	18.9	23.2	9.8	3.9	3.6
Dallas	0.7	5.5	0.0	0.0	1.0	14.0	11.3	7.1	1.9	16.7
Deer Park	0.0	3.7	0.0	0.0	0.6	17.6	14.8	15.5	0.0	4.5
Del Rio	3.2	16.9	0.0	0.0	1.4	17.0	15.7	4.1	0.0	4.6
Denton	0.0	8.4	0.0	0.0	0.6	14.7	25.1	9.1	1.2	4.9
DeSoto	0.0	7.2	0.0	0.0	1.1	16.2	19.1	6.8	0.0	10.7
Duncanville	0.0	7.7	0.0	0.0	0.7	17.1	17.5	22.4	0.0	2.2
Eagle Pass	0.0	20.2	0.0	0.0	0.2	16.0	19.6	9.2	0.0	4.5
Edinburg	0.0	4.6	0.0	0.0	2.0	17.8	26.4	14.6	1.5	3.2
El Paso	0.4	3.1	0.0	0.0	3.3	18.8	16.2	4.6	2.2	8.5
Euless	0.0	6.2	0.0	0.0	0.5	16.4	4.4	12.4	0.1	3.2
Farmers Branch	0.0	11.0	0.0	0.0	1.5	20.8	10.8	13.5	0.0	2.3
Flower Mound	0.2	27.9	0.0	0.0	1.1	16.1	10.1	9.8	0.1	4.3
Fort Worth	0.0	9.2	0.3	0.0	1.3	21.0	19.0	7.6	3.1	5.7
Friendswood	0.0	4.5	0.0	0.0	3.2	21.8	12.3	5.4	1.7	2.4
Frisco	0.0	14.8	0.0	4.9	0.6	9.4	9.2	9.5	0.2	12.3
Galveston	0.0	12.7	0.0	0.0	0.3	9.8	11.8	9.1	14.0	5.5
Garland	0.0	6.6	0.0	0.0	1.3	19.5	18.2	8.0	6.9	6.4
Georgetown	0.0	19.8	0.0	0.0	0.9	12.7	17.5	8.6	0.0	5.3
Grand Prairie	0.0	8.1	0.0	0.0	0.7	16.1	13.9	10.7	14.8	6.4
Grapevine	0.0	8.5	0.0	0.0	0.0	14.9	6.7	16.5	0.0	4.9
Greenville	0.0	8.7	0.0	0.0	0.0	15.0	24.1	3.8	3.9	3.5
Haltom City	0.0	7.6	0.0	0.0	0.9	19.6	15.2	2.7	0.0	5.1
Harker Heights	0.0	3.6	0.0	0.0	0.0	18.2	17.1	6.8	0.0	4.4
Harlingen	0.0	5.5	0.0	0.0	0.6	11.9	13.7	4.7	0.7	3.1
Houston	0.0	10.0	0.2	0.0	3.0	16.1	6.5	2.7	2.5	13.3
Huntsville	0.0	8.0	0.0	0.0	1.5	17.2	34.7	4.6	0.0	4.1
Hurst	0.0	11.9	0.0	0.0	2.5	22.9	10.3	15.1	0.0	3.7

Table D. Cities — City Government Finances, City Government Employment, and Climate

City	City government finances, 2012 (cont.) Debt outstanding Total (mil dol)	Per capita[1] (dollars)	Debt issued during year	Climate[2] Average daily temperature (degrees Fahrenheit) Mean January	July	Limits January[3]	July[4]	Annual precipitation (inches)	Heating degree days	Cooling degree days
	137	138	139	140	141	142	143	144	145	146
TENNESSEE—Cont'd										
Columbia	73.5	2 105	17.0	35.6	77.2	25.0	88.5	56.13	4 183	1 267
Cookeville	143.9	4 643	5.1	NA	NA	NA	NA	NA	NA	NA
Franklin	172.8	2 606	19.4	35.1	77.4	25.2	88.9	54.33	4 199	1 294
Gallatin	47.2	1 492	8.7	NA	NA	NA	NA	NA	NA	NA
Germantown	32.1	815	6.0	37.9	81.1	28.2	91.1	53.63	3 491	1 838
Hendersonville	11.8	222	0.3	36.8	79.1	27.9	88.7	48.11	3 677	1 652
Jackson	119.1	1 772	10.0	37.1	79.6	28.2	89.4	54.86	3 649	1 648
Johnson City	422.8	6 531	15.0	34.2	74.2	24.3	84.8	41.33	4 445	956
Kingsport	225.1	4 268	41.5	35.6	76.2	26.2	86.9	44.44	4 178	1 139
Knoxville	920.7	5 055	198.0	38.5	78.7	30.3	88.2	48.22	3 531	1 527
La Vergne	25.9	769	1.0	NA	NA	NA	NA	NA	NA	NA
Lebanon	61.0	2 191	5.9	NA	NA	NA	NA	NA	NA	NA
Maryville	130.5	4 709	0.0	NA	NA	NA	NA	NA	NA	NA
Memphis	2 500.9	3 791	107.2	39.9	82.5	31.3	92.1	54.65	3 041	2 187
Morristown	126.8	4 355	37.3	NA	NA	NA	NA	NA	NA	NA
Murfreesboro	318.3	2 795	1.6	35.4	78.1	25.3	89.1	54.98	4 107	1 388
Nashville-Davidson	4 895.0	7 828	800.3	36.8	79.1	27.9	88.7	48.11	3 677	1 652
Oak Ridge	170.4	5 812	11.1	36.6	77.3	27.2	88.1	55.05	3 993	1 301
Smyrna	71.6	1 717	2.4	36.8	79.1	27.9	88.7	48.11	3 677	1 652
Spring Hill	21.6	692	10.8	NA	NA	NA	NA	NA	NA	NA
TEXAS	NA	NA	NA	X	X	X	X	X	X	X
Abilene	132.7	1 106	22.6	43.5	83.5	31.8	94.8	23.78	2 659	2 386
Allen	179.7	1 997	8.8	41.8	82.4	31.1	92.7	41.01	2 843	2 060
Amarillo	366.9	1 876	40.4	35.8	78.2	22.6	91.0	19.71	4 318	1 344
Arlington	2 154.5	5 724	564.5	44.1	85.0	34.0	95.4	34.73	2 370	2 568
Austin	5 572.8	6 438	681.1	50.2	84.2	40.0	95.0	33.65	1 648	2 974
Baytown	189.8	2 575	22.4	51.6	83.6	41.9	91.6	53.75	1 471	2 841
Beaumont	353.3	3 022	53.2	51.1	83.1	41.1	92.7	57.38	1 548	2 734
Bedford	61.2	1 268	14.8	44.1	85.0	34.0	95.4	34.73	2 370	2 568
Big Spring	23.3	843	0.0	42.7	82.7	29.6	94.3	20.12	2 724	2 243
Brownsville	528.4	2 931	23.6	59.6	83.9	50.5	92.4	27.55	644	3 874
Bryan	362.9	4 655	34.6	50.2	84.6	39.8	95.6	39.67	1 616	2 938
Burleson	130.3	3 340	17.8	NA	NA	NA	NA	NA	NA	NA
Carrollton	168.5	1 343	0.0	44.1	85.0	34.0	95.4	34.73	2 370	2 568
Cedar Hill	156.9	3 375	18.0	43.7	84.3	33.2	94.9	34.54	2 437	2 508
Cedar Park	214.5	3 700	8.4	47.2	83.8	35.1	95.7	36.42	1 998	2 584
Cleburne	132.4	4 443	26.5	45.9	84.5	34.0	97.0	36.25	2 158	2 604
College Station	242.2	2 475	47.0	50.2	84.6	39.8	95.6	39.67	1 616	2 938
Conroe	196.2	3 194	37.9	50.3	83.7	40.0	94.3	49.32	1 647	2 793
Coppell	93.5	2 332	21.3	44.1	85.0	34.0	95.4	34.73	2 370	2 568
Copperas Cove	98.1	2 937	52.5	46.0	83.5	34.0	95.3	32.88	2 190	2 477
Corpus Christi	1 152.6	3 689	80.5	56.1	83.8	46.2	93.2	32.26	950	3 497
Dallas	7 943.6	6 389	1 246.4	45.9	86.5	36.4	96.1	37.05	2 219	2 878
Deer Park	44.9	1 359	0.0	54.3	84.5	45.2	93.6	53.96	1 174	3 179
Del Rio	64.8	1 795	0.1	51.3	85.3	39.7	96.2	18.80	1 417	3 226
Denton	501.7	4 062	45.1	42.7	83.6	32.0	94.1	37.79	2 650	2 269
DeSoto	130.8	2 556	20.2	46.0	84.6	35.0	96.0	38.81	2 130	2 608
Duncanville	19.1	483	6.9	45.9	86.5	36.4	96.1	37.05	2 219	2 878
Eagle Pass	61.2	2 224	14.7	NA	NA	NA	NA	NA	NA	NA
Edinburg	98.1	1 246	24.2	58.7	85.1	48.2	95.5	22.61	719	3 898
El Paso	1 534.1	2 270	166.5	45.1	83.3	32.9	94.5	9.43	2 543	2 254
Euless	51.8	980	9.6	44.1	85.0	34.0	95.4	34.73	2 370	2 568
Farmers Branch	24.3	827	0.0	45.9	86.5	36.4	96.1	37.05	2 219	2 878
Flower Mound	129.5	1 908	3.6	44.1	85.0	34.0	95.4	34.73	2 370	2 568
Fort Worth	2 401.8	3 084	394.8	43.3	84.5	31.4	96.6	34.01	2 509	2 466
Friendswood	66.6	1 804	17.5	54.3	84.5	45.2	93.6	53.96	1 174	3 179
Frisco	640.8	4 982	148.2	41.8	82.4	31.1	92.7	41.01	2 843	2 060
Galveston	316.3	6 539	9.9	55.8	84.3	49.7	88.7	43.84	1 008	3 268
Garland	905.7	3 873	152.4	45.9	86.5	36.4	96.1	37.05	2 219	2 878
Georgetown	168.4	3 205	21.7	47.2	83.8	35.1	95.7	36.42	1 998	2 584
Grand Prairie	447.1	2 458	34.9	44.1	85.0	34.0	95.4	34.73	2 370	2 568
Grapevine	142.7	2 942	0.0	42.4	84.0	30.8	95.5	34.66	2 649	2 340
Greenville	148.3	5 723	11.5	NA	NA	NA	NA	NA	NA	NA
Haltom City	60.4	1 392	15.4	43.0	84.1	31.4	95.7	34.12	2 608	2 358
Harker Heights	50.6	1 819	8.0	NA	NA	NA	NA	NA	NA	NA
Harlingen	118.7	1 803	50.3	58.6	84.4	48.4	94.5	28.13	737	3 736
Houston	13 983.7	6 459	2 478.6	54.3	84.5	45.2	93.6	53.96	1 174	3 179
Huntsville	38.9	977	5.0	48.5	83.2	39.0	93.8	48.51	1 835	2 600
Hurst	57.6	1 508	9.1	44.1	85.0	34.0	95.4	34.73	2 370	2 568

1. Based on the population estimated as of July 1 of the year shown.   2. Represents normal values based on the 30-year period, 1971–2000.   3. Average daily minimum.
4. Average daily maximum.

STATE Place code	City	Land area,[1] 2010 (sq km)	Population, 2015			Race alone or in combination (percent), 2010-2014					Percent Hispanic or Latino[2] 2010-2014	Percent foreign born 2010-2014
			Total persons	Rank	Per square kilometer	White	Black	American Indian, Alaska Native	Asian	Hawaiian Pacific Islander		
		1	2	3	4	5	6	7	8	9	10	11
	TEXAS—Cont'd											
48 37000	Irving	173.6	236 607	93	1 362.9	59.7	13.9	1.0	16.2	0.2	41.7	34.2
48 38632	Keller	47.8	45 758	823	957.3	91.1	2.6	0.6	5.6	0.4	7.2	6.7
48 39148	Killeen	138.8	140 806	186	1 014.5	52.4	37.7	2.3	5.7	1.8	24.4	8.8
48 39352	Kingsville	35.8	26 225	1 391	732.5	87.1	5.2	0.7	3.0	0.1	73.2	7.2
48 39952	Kyle	49.4	35 733	1 058	723.3	78.4	7.8	1.0	1.7	0.2	46.6	8.3
48 40588	Lake Jackson	50.4	27 533	1 338	546.3	83.0	8.1	1.0	4.2	0.0	23.2	7.3
48 41212	Lancaster	78.4	38 801	965	494.9	30.8	67.6	0.6	0.2	0.1	20.9	7.3
48 41440	La Porte	48.3	35 148	1 072	727.7	85.5	6.2	2.0	1.7	0.4	30.4	8.7
48 41464	Laredo	230.3	255 473	82	1 109.3	94.3	0.5	0.5	0.7	0.0	95.3	27.2
48 41980	League City	132.8	98 312	308	740.3	83.5	8.5	1.1	6.8	0.0	18.9	9.4
48 42016	Leander	59.2	37 889	994	640.0	90.3	5.7	0.8	4.3	0.1	30.3	8.2
48 42508	Lewisville	94.3	104 039	288	1 103.3	78.7	11.3	2.0	8.9	0.5	30.2	19.8
48 43012	Little Elm	37.7	38 341	977	1 017.0	74.4	16.8	0.9	3.4	0.1	23.7	13.5
48 43888	Longview	144.2	82 287	403	570.6	73.3	23.0	1.1	1.4	0.3	19.2	9.8
48 45000	Lubbock	317.0	249 042	83	785.6	80.3	9.1	1.3	3.1	0.2	33.2	5.9
48 45072	Lufkin	86.4	36 333	1 034	420.5	66.3	29.3	0.4	1.3	0.0	23.8	10.7
48 45384	McAllen	125.2	140 269	188	1 120.4	89.7	1.2	0.6	3.0	0.1	85.0	28.6
48 45744	McKinney	161.1	162 898	155	1 011.2	81.6	12.5	0.9	5.6	0.2	19.3	12.3
48 46452	Mansfield	94.2	64 274	556	682.3	77.2	17.2	1.0	5.1	0.0	13.4	9.1
48 47892	Mesquite	119.2	144 788	181	1 214.7	68.4	25.1	1.0	3.7	0.1	34.5	16.2
48 48072	Midland	186.7	132 950	198	712.1	82.5	8.8	1.1	1.8	0.1	40.4	9.9
48 48768	Mission	88.0	83 298	395	946.6	93.1	0.7	0.3	1.3	0.0	86.1	27.4
48 48804	Missouri City	73.6	74 139	465	1 007.3	35.2	44.4	0.9	16.6	0.4	17.2	22.3
48 50256	Nacogdoches	70.1	33 894	1 108	483.5	64.4	30.9	1.2	2.3	0.0	18.7	10.9
48 50820	New Braunfels	113.6	70 543	495	621.0	93.0	2.8	0.4	1.3	0.2	35.7	7.1
48 52356	North Richland Hills	47.1	69 204	503	1 469.3	86.9	4.8	1.4	4.7	0.5	17.9	9.6
48 53388	Odessa	108.7	118 968	230	1 094.5	86.1	7.6	1.7	1.6	0.1	52.8	13.1
48 55080	Paris	94.5	24 782	1 423	262.2	74.3	24.5	2.7	1.5	0.6	5.2	3.7
48 56000	Pasadena	110.8	153 784	164	1 387.9	78.8	3.2	2.0	2.5	0.2	63.8	25.4
48 56348	Pearland	121.8	108 821	268	893.4	65.3	17.0	0.8	14.8	0.0	21.3	16.5
48 57176	Pflugerville	57.8	57 122	647	988.3	72.6	16.7	1.2	10.2	0.4	27.4	15.3
48 57200	Pharr	60.7	76 538	442	1 260.9	94.8	0.3	0.3	0.6	0.1	93.7	32.4
48 58016	Plano	185.4	283 558	69	1 529.4	71.5	8.4	1.0	19.6	0.2	14.7	24.1
48 58820	Port Arthur	199.2	55 340	678	277.8	50.7	38.3	1.0	7.5	0.1	31.1	20.7
48 61796	Richardson	74.0	110 815	255	1 497.5	70.0	9.3	1.7	17.1	0.5	16.6	23.0
48 62828	Rockwall	71.7	42 566	878	593.7	89.0	6.9	1.5	3.2	0.9	17.0	9.1
48 63284	Rosenberg	58.2	35 510	1 064	610.1	79.5	11.7	0.5	2.9	0.0	59.0	18.9
48 63500	Round Rock	88.4	115 997	237	1 312.2	81.7	10.3	1.3	6.7	0.2	29.9	13.6
48 63572	Rowlett	51.5	60 236	608	1 169.6	74.2	16.2	1.0	8.7	0.1	20.5	13.4
48 64472	San Angelo	147.3	100 450	300	681.9	86.8	5.6	1.1	1.8	0.1	39.9	6.7
48 65000	San Antonio	1 193.8	1 469 845	7	1 231.2	79.3	7.8	1.4	3.1	0.3	63.3	14.2
48 65516	San Juan	29.7	36 556	1 030	1 230.8	96.4	0.3	0.0	0.1	0.0	97.9	30.1
48 65600	San Marcos	78.3	60 684	596	775.0	83.9	5.6	1.5	2.5	0.5	40.3	5.5
48 66128	Schertz	73.6	37 938	991	515.5	82.7	11.8	0.8	4.7	0.2	26.6	7.4
48 66644	Seguin	89.3	27 864	1 325	312.0	80.5	9.8	1.1	1.6	0.1	51.6	9.1
48 67496	Sherman	107.2	40 667	920	379.4	79.2	12.8	2.3	2.3	0.2	21.7	10.7
48 68636	Socorro	57.1	33 222	1 132	581.8	78.3	0.9	2.3	0.4	0.3	96.7	36.1
48 69032	Southlake	56.7	29 941	1 246	528.1	89.1	3.3	0.5	8.2	0.0	6.0	9.4
48 70808	Sugar Land	83.9	88 156	363	1 050.7	53.6	7.5	0.8	38.3	0.1	11.1	34.0
48 72176	Temple	178.7	72 277	478	404.5	77.5	17.3	0.6	3.9	0.3	23.3	8.3
48 72368	Texarkana	75.2	37 280	1 014	495.7	57.7	39.9	0.9	2.0	0.1	7.3	5.3
48 72392	Texas City	165.3	47 618	796	288.1	70.3	27.3	0.9	0.5	0.0	28.3	6.6
48 72530	The Colony	36.3	41 779	894	1 150.9	80.9	9.2	1.0	9.1	0.0	18.0	14.6
48 74144	Tyler	139.5	103 700	289	743.4	70.2	24.7	0.7	2.7	0.3	22.7	12.0
48 75428	Victoria	91.9	67 574	520	735.3	85.8	8.4	2.5	1.8	0.0	48.9	6.4
48 76000	Waco	230.4	132 356	200	574.5	70.9	22.3	0.9	2.1	0.1	31.7	11.2
48 76816	Waxahachie	123.4	33 384	1 128	270.5	76.6	16.3	2.8	0.7	0.2	24.2	7.8
48 76864	Weatherford	64.4	28 742	1 288	446.3	92.3	3.4	3.0	1.3	0.1	16.8	5.7
48 77272	Weslaco	38.1	39 474	952	1 036.1	91.1	0.5	0.4	1.1	0.0	84.2	21.1
48 79000	Wichita Falls	186.8	104 710	285	560.5	80.7	13.8	1.6	3.5	0.2	20.4	8.2
48 80356	Wylie	54.5	46 708	811	857.0	77.8	14.2	0.9	6.4	0.3	16.7	11.6
49 00000	UTAH	212 818.3	2 995 919	X	14.1	90.2	1.6	1.7	3.0	1.4	13.3	8.4
49 01310	American Fork	23.8	28 326	1 302	1 190.2	95.2	0.9	1.5	2.3	1.7	6.6	4.2
49 07690	Bountiful	34.8	43 784	855	1 258.2	95.0	1.0	0.9	2.6	0.8	6.0	3.9
49 11320	Cedar City	95.4	30 184	1 240	316.4	93.4	0.9	3.4	1.9	0.9	8.0	4.2
49 13850	Clearfield	19.7	30 653	1 216	1 556.0	87.3	4.4	1.4	3.3	0.9	16.1	5.9
49 16270	Cottonwood Heights	22.9	34 343	1 093	1 499.7	92.0	0.9	1.1	7.2	1.0	4.6	7.8
49 20170	Draper	77.9	46 774	809	600.4	93.0	1.2	1.4	3.2	0.6	7.6	6.9
49 36070	Holladay	20.5	30 864	1 204	1 505.6	95.1	1.2	0.3	2.2	1.6	5.3	6.2

1. Dry land or land partially or temporarily covered by water.   2. May be of any race.

Table D. Cities — **Population**

City	Under 5 years	5 to 17 years	18 to 24 years	25 to 34 years	35 to 44 years	45 to 54 years	55 to 64 years	65 to 74 years	75 years and over	Median age 2010–2014	Percent female 2010–2014	Census counts 2000	Census counts 2010	Percent change 2000–2010	Percent change 2010–2015
	12	13	14	15	16	17	18	19	20	21	22	23	24	25	26
TEXAS—Cont'd															
Irving	8.9	17.5	9.1	20.0	16.2	12.6	8.2	4.2	3.1	31.9	50.4	191 615	216 290	12.9	9.4
Keller	4.9	25.1	6.0	7.9	16.0	18.0	12.1	6.5	3.4	40.0	50.2	27 345	39 627	44.9	15.5
Killeen	10.4	20.4	12.7	19.8	13.8	10.7	6.7	3.5	2.0	27.8	50.7	86 911	127 921	47.2	10.1
Kingsville	7.6	17.6	21.8	14.4	10.4	8.2	8.7	5.9	5.3	26.5	47.7	25 575	26 213	2.5	0.0
Kyle	9.4	26.1	7.2	17.3	19.1	10.5	6.0	2.7	1.7	30.1	51.3	5 314	28 016	427.2	27.5
Lake Jackson	5.6	20.7	9.3	13.1	12.8	15.6	11.4	5.9	5.5	36.1	51.1	26 386	26 849	1.8	2.6
Lancaster	8.2	23.3	8.9	11.9	16.7	13.6	9.1	4.4	3.8	32.8	54.1	25 894	36 361	40.4	5.9
La Porte	6.9	19.5	9.4	13.5	14.4	14.6	12.6	5.8	3.4	35.4	48.0	31 880	33 800	6.0	4.0
Laredo	9.8	24.5	11.1	13.7	13.8	10.9	7.9	4.7	3.6	28.6	51.3	176 576	236 091	33.7	8.2
League City	7.3	19.4	8.0	14.6	15.1	16.3	10.7	5.4	3.4	35.4	50.3	45 444	83 560	83.9	17.7
Leander	9.1	25.3	6.1	12.1	21.3	13.9	6.3	4.2	1.7	33.1	51.6	7 596	26 521	249.1	44.3
Lewisville	7.7	19.3	8.8	19.3	16.3	12.7	8.3	4.8	2.7	32.4	51.5	77 737	95 290	22.6	9.1
Little Elm	10.7	23.5	3.8	19.0	20.3	10.8	7.3	2.8	1.7	31.2	49.0	3 646	25 898	610.3	48.6
Longview	7.6	18.1	10.6	14.1	12.2	12.8	11.1	6.6	7.0	34.8	50.8	73 344	80 455	9.7	2.3
Lubbock	7.1	16.8	18.9	15.1	10.5	11.1	9.5	5.8	5.2	29.2	50.8	199 564	229 573	15.0	8.6
Lufkin	7.5	19.3	11.7	12.0	10.8	11.8	12.0	6.0	8.9	34.6	51.1	32 709	35 067	7.2	3.6
McAllen	7.5	21.3	10.7	13.8	13.9	11.8	10.1	6.4	4.6	32.7	51.0	106 414	129 877	22.0	7.7
McKinney	8.4	22.6	7.9	13.6	17.4	13.9	8.3	4.6	3.4	33.7	50.2	54 369	131 117	141.2	24.3
Mansfield	7.3	23.6	7.0	11.2	16.8	16.3	9.6	5.6	2.7	35.9	49.4	28 031	56 368	101.1	14.0
Mesquite	8.2	21.5	10.1	14.6	13.3	13.6	10.1	4.8	3.8	31.9	53.1	124 523	139 824	12.3	3.7
Midland	8.5	18.9	10.6	15.9	12.0	12.2	11.0	5.4	5.5	31.9	51.3	94 996	111 147	17.0	19.6
Mission	9.0	25.4	9.7	11.1	14.0	11.6	7.8	7.0	4.5	30.2	51.5	45 408	77 058	69.7	7.3
Missouri City	4.8	18.7	10.0	10.5	13.3	16.2	15.1	7.5	4.0	39.8	52.3	52 913	67 358	27.3	10.9
Nacogdoches	7.1	12.9	30.0	12.8	9.8	9.5	7.4	5.2	5.4	25.0	55.4	29 914	32 996	10.3	3.0
New Braunfels	7.3	20.7	8.2	15.4	13.1	11.6	9.9	7.3	6.6	33.9	51.3	36 494	57 740	58.2	22.2
North Richland Hills	6.8	16.9	9.5	14.9	11.8	15.2	12.6	6.1	6.3	36.8	51.5	55 635	63 343	13.9	9.3
Odessa	8.7	19.8	11.0	16.6	11.9	11.8	10.6	4.8	4.9	31.1	49.7	90 943	99 940	9.9	19.1
Paris	8.0	16.7	10.7	12.9	11.5	13.1	10.7	9.5	7.0	36.3	55.0	25 898	25 171	-2.8	-1.5
Pasadena	8.1	21.9	11.3	14.4	12.8	12.5	10.4	4.7	4.0	30.8	50.0	141 674	149 043	5.2	3.0
Pearland	8.2	20.7	8.0	13.5	17.1	13.8	9.7	4.7	4.2	34.8	50.8	37 640	91 252	142.4	21.0
Pflugerville	8.2	21.0	6.9	11.1	15.8	17.4	12.1	5.1	2.4	37.1	51.3	16 335	46 936	187.3	18.1
Pharr	9.6	25.9	10.6	14.2	13.5	8.6	7.5	4.7	5.3	28.0	52.1	46 660	70 400	50.9	8.6
Plano	6.2	19.1	7.5	13.3	15.3	16.3	12.0	6.6	3.7	37.8	50.5	222 030	259 841	17.0	9.1
Port Arthur	8.8	19.9	9.8	13.3	11.8	13.4	11.2	5.4	6.5	33.4	49.9	57 755	53 818	-6.8	1.8
Richardson	6.2	16.7	10.5	13.0	14.8	14.4	11.5	7.2	5.7	37.3	49.7	91 802	99 223	8.1	11.7
Rockwall	5.0	23.3	7.4	12.0	14.9	14.4	11.4	7.7	4.0	36.5	51.8	17 976	37 490	108.6	13.2
Rosenberg	9.6	21.3	12.2	15.3	16.2	10.2	7.9	5.6	4.3	28.8	52.2	24 043	30 618	27.3	13.2
Round Rock	9.9	21.4	9.3	15.9	16.2	13.6	7.4	4.2	2.0	31.4	51.8	61 136	99 887	63.4	16.0
Rowlett	4.8	20.6	9.8	9.5	15.5	18.5	11.5	6.2	3.6	37.9	50.3	44 503	56 199	26.3	7.1
San Angelo	7.3	16.1	14.9	15.1	9.8	11.8	10.8	7.5	6.7	32.3	51.0	88 439	93 200	5.4	7.7
San Antonio	7.4	18.8	11.3	15.5	13.0	12.9	10.2	6.1	4.9	32.8	51.2	1 144 646	1 327 407	16.0	10.7
San Juan	9.6	24.3	10.9	13.6	13.5	10.0	9.2	4.9	3.9	28.7	51.5	26 229	33 856	29.1	8.0
San Marcos	4.6	10.1	41.8	17.0	8.5	6.2	5.2	3.7	3.1	23.5	50.9	34 733	44 894	29.3	34.6
Schertz	7.0	18.9	9.2	13.8	13.0	15.5	11.1	6.7	4.7	35.8	51.3	18 694	31 465	68.3	19.3
Seguin	6.3	19.3	12.9	11.1	11.7	12.6	10.0	7.7	8.4	35.4	50.5	22 011	25 175	14.4	8.8
Sherman	6.7	17.7	13.8	14.0	11.3	12.2	11.5	6.5	6.4	33.1	51.6	35 082	38 521	9.8	6.1
Socorro	7.3	23.3	11.8	11.4	13.8	11.4	11.6	6.2	3.3	31.3	50.2	27 152	32 013	17.9	3.7
Southlake	4.4	28.6	3.8	4.3	13.7	22.3	14.4	4.4	4.1	42.5	49.7	21 519	26 575	23.5	12.7
Sugar Land	5.1	17.9	8.1	10.0	13.3	17.0	16.5	7.5	4.5	41.8	51.1	63 328	78 817	24.5	12.2
Temple	7.6	17.7	8.2	16.2	11.6	12.5	12.0	7.3	7.0	35.4	51.0	54 514	66 102	21.3	9.0
Texarkana	7.9	16.9	10.3	13.9	11.9	12.4	12.5	7.0	7.1	35.5	52.4	34 782	36 411	4.7	2.4
Texas City	8.4	18.4	8.2	14.6	12.4	11.7	13.2	7.3	5.8	35.3	51.0	41 521	45 099	8.6	5.6
The Colony	6.9	16.8	10.0	17.3	15.8	15.4	11.5	3.8	2.5	34.4	49.6	26 531	36 328	36.9	15.1
Tyler	6.2	16.9	14.1	14.4	11.5	11.0	10.8	7.1	8.0	33.7	53.6	83 650	96 900	15.8	7.0
Victoria	7.3	18.9	9.9	13.5	11.8	13.2	11.7	7.3	6.4	35.3	51.0	60 603	62 592	3.3	7.9
Waco	8.1	16.4	19.5	13.6	10.7	10.8	9.4	5.2	6.2	29.1	51.7	113 726	124 805	9.7	6.0
Waxahachie	7.7	21.4	9.9	15.0	13.0	11.7	11.0	5.7	4.7	31.6	52.3	21 426	29 621	38.2	12.8
Weatherford	7.5	19.9	9.8	13.8	13.2	12.0	9.2	7.9	6.9	34.6	53.7	19 000	25 250	32.9	13.3
Weslaco	9.1	22.7	7.0	12.1	12.1	10.3	9.6	9.2	8.0	33.8	53.2	26 935	35 670	32.4	7.2
Wichita Falls	6.3	16.3	15.3	14.8	11.3	12.5	10.6	6.6	6.2	32.7	47.6	104 197	104 553	0.3	0.0
Wylie	6.9	23.4	8.6	12.7	20.9	13.0	7.8	3.9	2.7	33.8	51.7	15 132	41 427	173.8	12.8
UTAH	9.0	22.1	11.4	15.5	12.6	10.7	9.2	5.4	4.1	29.9	49.7	2 233 169	2 763 885	23.8	8.4
American Fork	8.5	27.3	11.3	11.3	13.8	10.0	7.5	5.3	5.0	27.9	49.6	21 941	26 263	19.7	6.9
Bountiful	7.5	21.2	9.0	13.1	11.0	12.0	9.5	7.1	9.6	34.2	52.2	41 301	42 552	3.0	2.8
Cedar City	10.2	17.5	21.2	15.6	9.4	8.9	7.8	5.2	4.1	25.5	51.5	20 527	28 857	40.6	4.6
Clearfield	10.6	24.5	10.8	18.5	12.8	9.5	7.4	3.6	2.4	27.9	48.8	25 974	30 112	15.9	2.4
Cottonwood Heights	5.9	16.5	11.0	15.3	11.8	13.1	12.7	8.7	5.0	35.9	51.5	27 569	33 433	21.3	2.3
Draper	9.6	24.4	6.9	14.6	17.0	12.8	8.9	3.7	2.1	30.9	47.5	25 220	42 274	67.6	10.7
Holladay	5.5	17.8	6.4	14.6	11.7	12.1	13.3	9.5	9.3	40.1	51.6	14 561	26 472	81.8	2.4

Table D. Cities — **Households, Group Quarters, Crime, and Education**

City	Households, 2010-2014 Number	Persons per house-hold	Percent Female family house-holder[1]	Percent One-person	Persons in group quarters, 2010 Total	Institutional Total	Persons in nursing facilities	Non-institutional	Serious crimes known to police,[2] 2014 Total Number	Rate[3]	Rate[3] Violent	Property	Population age 25 and older	Attainment[4] (percent) High school graduate or less	Bachelor's degree or more
	27	28	29	30	31	32	33	34	35	36	37	38	39	40	41
TEXAS—Cont'd															
Irving	82 817	2.72	13.8	29.7	873	393	393	480	6 803	2 936	221	2 715	143 339	41.5	33.8
Keller	14 170	2.96	6.2	15.5	251	251	251	0	398	911	55	856	27 061	15.5	56.8
Killeen	45 383	2.95	18.2	23.6	179	97	60	82	5 549	3 986	608	3 378	76 019	35.5	17.8
Kingsville	9 195	2.87	17.5	25.0	1 791	293	173	1 498	1 168	4 436	725	3 711	14 141	47.0	25.8
Kyle	9 271	3.31	11.2	14.2	391	388	0	3	584	1 789	205	1 584	17 862	34.5	28.5
Lake Jackson	9 984	2.73	11.3	25.3	57	56	56	1	570	2 070	127	1 943	17 912	29.9	29.6
Lancaster	12 840	2.94	22.4	26.5	360	359	359	1	1 387	3 612	276	3 336	22 574	44.8	18.4
La Porte	11 606	2.97	13.4	17.8	64	46	46	18	654	1 877	201	1 676	22 036	46.1	14.7
Laredo	65 014	3.77	22.5	15.1	3 479	2 014	367	1 465	10 663	4 248	389	3 859	133 498	57.6	17.6
League City	31 666	2.81	9.0	21.0	471	471	368	0	1 905	2 053	106	1 947	57 606	25.4	41.2
Leander	9 122	3.29	12.3	14.5	0	0	0	0	403	1 217	115	1 102	18 272	31.4	30.1
Lewisville	38 272	2.59	13.4	29.2	399	286	264	113	2 806	2 739	196	2 543	64 465	35.6	30.8
Little Elm	9 378	3.22	14.6	13.7	0	0	0	0	330	954	118	835	18 385	31.2	30.5
Longview	30 535	2.69	17.4	29.4	3 690	1 913	767	1 777	3 982	4 876	460	4 416	52 247	43.8	20.6
Lubbock	90 394	2.62	14.4	30.0	9 933	2 400	1 214	7 533	12 701	5 252	862	4 390	136 044	38.5	29.5
Lufkin	13 252	2.70	19.3	26.7	1 239	823	536	416	2 173	5 982	432	5 550	22 474	49.7	20.0
McAllen	42 040	3.21	18.0	20.4	1 110	899	890	211	5 128	3 713	131	3 582	82 077	46.3	27.7
McKinney	47 490	3.03	12.0	16.8	2 192	1 454	439	738	3 071	2 010	147	1 863	88 283	24.2	45.1
Mansfield	19 744	3.03	10.6	16.1	363	355	159	8	991	1 600	95	1 505	37 154	26.6	41.1
Mesquite	47 927	2.97	20.2	22.0	663	644	644	19	6 278	4 348	299	4 049	85 999	47.7	18.1
Midland	42 010	2.84	14.3	24.2	1 567	684	362	883	3 673	2 884	320	2 565	74 204	40.0	25.5
Mission	23 478	3.43	16.9	15.8	179	162	162	17	2 500	3 054	116	2 938	45 321	52.6	23.6
Missouri City	22 430	3.08	16.1	16.7	180	138	138	42	1 288	1 818	178	1 640	45 335	25.2	43.0
Nacogdoches	11 941	2.81	16.7	35.1	5 025	632	428	4 393	1 331	3 904	323	3 581	16 203	41.4	28.9
New Braunfels	21 827	2.83	14.8	23.6	940	666	411	274	2 283	3 533	282	3 251	39 547	37.6	28.1
North Richland Hills	24 853	2.65	10.8	25.6	294	267	267	27	1 662	2 433	176	2 257	43 477	32.8	30.5
Odessa	38 130	2.81	16.3	25.3	2 143	1 285	437	858	5 285	4 652	940	3 712	64 305	50.9	17.3
Paris	10 056	2.49	19.0	33.5	614	406	258	208	1 226	4 935	559	4 375	16 401	50.5	14.9
Pasadena	48 526	3.14	16.4	23.6	884	737	547	147	5 221	3 400	385	3 016	90 062	59.0	14.0
Pearland	33 112	2.94	11.7	18.4	318	312	299	6	2 228	2 173	156	2 017	61 590	25.0	45.7
Pflugerville	17 968	2.90	14.6	19.3	183	131	131	52	913	1 657	111	1 546	33 517	27.4	36.2
Pharr	19 971	3.66	24.5	14.3	19	15	0	4	2 676	3 589	390	3 199	40 401	65.0	13.1
Plano	102 182	2.65	10.1	24.4	859	791	733	68	5 967	2 148	165	1 983	183 045	19.7	54.6
Port Arthur	20 283	2.70	20.8	34.5	687	515	501	172	2 472	4 563	629	3 933	34 114	61.0	10.4
Richardson	39 576	2.62	10.9	25.4	931	517	501	414	2 584	2 444	169	2 274	69 675	23.8	51.2
Rockwall	13 722	2.91	12.5	17.4	325	325	158	0	802	1 924	98	1 825	25 797	28.6	38.2
Rosenberg	10 855	3.02	21.1	22.9	134	129	129	5	817	2 432	274	2 158	19 706	60.9	12.7
Round Rock	35 338	3.03	11.4	21.3	454	398	251	56	2 329	2 076	125	1 951	65 418	29.0	37.3
Rowlett	18 251	3.15	12.2	12.4	335	335	334	0	878	1 502	127	1 375	36 978	33.2	31.3
San Angelo	36 157	2.66	13.8	31.4	4 858	788	365	4 070	4 191	4 256	332	3 924	59 764	48.9	21.6
San Antonio	484 219	2.86	17.7	28.3	27 800	11 979	5 617	15 821	85 096	5 957	539	5 418	866 335	44.4	24.9
San Juan	8 908	3.95	23.0	12.1	121	112	112	9	1 335	3 710	542	3 168	18 751	70.0	10.3
San Marcos	18 782	2.73	11.6	32.8	6 202	729	300	5 473	1 933	3 414	318	3 096	21 833	37.5	32.2
Schertz	12 273	2.86	11.1	19.6	188	188	188	0	719	1 945	176	1 769	22 831	32.1	31.4
Seguin	9 382	2.80	17.6	32.4	1 644	881	396	763	1 083	4 007	351	3 655	16 789	58.6	15.4
Sherman	14 640	2.67	15.6	28.8	1 368	509	285	859	1 292	3 269	359	2 910	24 209	45.5	19.1
Socorro	9 037	3.61	25.9	12.4	25	0	0	25	427	1 309	129	1 180	18 705	69.5	6.8
Southlake	8 808	3.15	5.3	10.9	0	0	0	0	421	1 470	24	1 446	17 423	9.7	68.5
Sugar Land	26 635	3.09	7.9	14.9	1 413	1 245	313	168	1 499	1 762	116	1 646	55 924	19.8	54.2
Temple	24 696	2.79	13.6	29.4	1 613	989	908	624	2 630	3 702	251	3 451	45 489	43.8	26.3
Texarkana	13 931	2.66	20.9	33.6	1 641	1 469	554	172	2 718	7 212	862	6 350	24 095	42.9	26.0
Texas City	16 570	2.76	21.4	26.1	937	916	470	21	1 802	3 894	324	3 570	29 961	48.9	12.5
The Colony	13 978	2.77	10.2	26.1	0	0	0	0	439	1 091	134	957	24 700	29.9	33.4
Tyler	37 996	2.61	16.3	32.7	3 647	1 709	893	1 938	4 557	4 513	463	4 051	62 401	37.1	29.5
Victoria	23 649	2.72	17.6	27.6	1 324	1 053	478	271	2 649	4 030	516	3 515	40 553	49.3	17.6
Waco	45 874	2.79	16.6	32.4	8 019	3 026	1 488	4 993	5 585	4 298	443	3 855	70 940	49.1	21.3
Waxahachie	10 684	2.91	16.7	22.8	1 209	715	232	494	1 013	3 160	90	3 070	18 844	43.3	23.9
Weatherford	9 934	2.67	11.6	29.0	1 077	845	450	232	740	2 698	171	2 527	16 719	36.0	25.8
Weslaco	11 570	3.18	22.9	20.4	637	590	488	47	3 105	8 289	1 207	7 083	22 383	59.5	16.8
Wichita Falls	37 108	2.82	14.7	31.6	11 889	5 334	1 072	6 555	4 684	4 463	406	4 057	64 648	45.9	22.2
Wylie	13 675	3.18	12.6	15.8	155	155	155	0	548	1 209	108	1 101	26 256	31.7	34.7
UTAH	896 194	3.19	9.6	19.5	46 152	22 161	5 854	23 991	91 057	3 094	216	2 878	1 642 728	32.2	30.6
American Fork	7 471	3.66	8.9	16.1	283	72	62	211	842	2 192	55	2 137	14 278	24.3	33.5
Bountiful	14 018	3.06	8.6	18.0	330	318	318	12	884	2 050	90	1 960	26 684	21.9	40.1
Cedar City	9 478	3.08	9.2	21.7	986	259	83	727	845	2 892	267	2 625	14 712	29.7	33.6
Clearfield	9 767	3.11	14.1	22.1	1 263	144	96	1 119	686	2 247	128	2 119	16 278	40.6	19.7
Cottonwood Heights	12 042	2.82	9.3	19.5	14	0	0	14	801	2 326	122	2 204	22 457	20.6	46.8
Draper	12 287	3.63	8.7	11.8	3 960	3 960	71	0	1 221	2 653	156	2 496	26 611	22.1	39.8
Holladay	10 054	2.68	7.6	27.6	166	160	160	6	NA	NA	NA	NA	18 186	17.3	51.5

1. No spouse present.　2. Data for serious crimes have not been adjusted for underreporting. This may affect comparability between geographic areas and over time.　3. Per 100,000 population estimated by the FBI.　4. Persons 25 years old and over.

Table D. Cities — Income, Poverty, and Housing

City	Money income, 2010–2014					Housing units, 2010			Occupied housing units 2010–2014				
	Households				Families with income below poverty (percent)				Owner-occupied			Median owner costs as a percent of income	
	Per capita income[1] (dollars)	Median income	Percent with income of $200,000 or more	Percent with income of less than $25,000		Total	Percent change, 2000–2010	Vacant units for sale or rent[2]	Total	Percent	Median value[3] (dollars)	With a mortgage[4]	Without a mortgage[5]
	42	43	44	45	46	47	48	49	50	51	52	53	54
TEXAS—Cont'd													
Irving..................	26 959	50 942	4.5	21.1	13.9	91 128	13.5	8 590	82 817	38.7	138 900	23.8	11.7
Keller..................	45 415	114 266	16.8	9.2	3.1	14 051	52.9	537	14 170	84.0	285 200	21.6	12.4
Killeen...............	20 709	48 283	1.1	22.1	12.9	53 913	52.8	5 861	45 383	48.4	116 400	23.9	10.5
Kingsville............	17 656	36 500	1.7	37.8	21.8	10 354	-0.6	1 259	9 195	46.7	75 100	21.2	11.7
Kyle....................	24 869	75 182	1.7	8.6	4.8	9 226	NA	467	9 271	78.8	147 200	22.3	12.9
Lake Jackson.........	32 589	72 645	5.9	13.0	5.3	11 149	6.3	830	9 984	67.3	143 500	18.6	10.0
Lancaster.............	20 222	49 590	0.8	23.3	14.7	13 622	41.7	1 102	12 840	65.4	100 600	26.0	13.7
La Porte..............	27 186	67 806	1.7	15.0	8.0	12 875	10.2	985	11 606	74.4	121 600	19.3	11.0
Laredo	15 127	39 408	2.0	33.4	26.9	68 610	36.2	5 065	65 014	61.8	110 700	26.0	14.2
League City............	37 953	90 972	8.3	8.6	3.2	32 119	86.3	1 927	31 666	71.6	182 000	20.8	12.1
Leander...............	28 445	75 983	4.5	8.1	4.2	8 949	NA	392	9 122	77.9	154 500	22.4	13.5
Lewisville..............	28 630	58 559	2.6	15.0	8.7	39 967	26.0	2 471	38 272	44.6	156 100	21.3	11.2
Little Elm.............	28 052	81 866	2.9	9.2	5.5	8 581	NA	421	9 378	80.3	159 200	24.4	10.1
Longview..............	23 792	43 767	2.9	29.1	15.2	32 751	6.8	2 189	30 535	56.5	129 300	20.9	11.4
Lubbock................	24 168	44 139	3.2	29.3	14.0	95 926	14.2	7 420	90 394	53.6	111 900	21.4	12.0
Lufkin..................	23 103	39 606	2.7	31.0	15.3	14 183	5.9	1 255	13 252	53.5	93 900	19.5	12.3
McAllen................	21 410	43 476	4.0	32.2	23.4	45 862	21.0	4 289	42 040	60.3	112 200	22.2	13.2
McKinney..............	33 941	82 988	8.8	10.8	6.4	47 915	146.7	3 562	47 490	68.7	192 900	22.2	12.5
Mansfield.............	36 265	89 774	8.5	11.4	4.7	19 106	103.0	801	19 744	79.0	182 700	22.5	12.9
Mesquite.............	21 788	49 837	1.5	20.4	13.2	51 952	11.9	3 562	47 927	58.8	108 900	23.1	11.3
Midland...............	34 949	67 144	8.5	16.6	8.7	44 708	12.3	2 821	42 010	64.8	162 600	19.9	10.0
Mission................	17 614	43 592	2.7	30.7	22.5	27 291	54.0	4 174	23 478	71.0	96 100	23.6	12.6
Missouri City........	34 336	84 662	9.0	9.0	4.9	23 374	34.0	998	22 430	84.3	156 900	21.8	11.0
Nacogdoches	17 921	31 442	1.8	41.6	22.2	13 635	10.3	1 403	11 941	38.9	125 200	21.8	13.0
New Braunfels........	26 181	59 083	2.5	17.0	8.2	23 381	55.7	2 122	21 827	65.1	167 400	21.0	11.6
North Richland Hills	30 804	62 927	4.4	13.8	6.1	26 395	22.8	1 541	24 853	63.2	151 300	21.6	12.1
Odessa.................	26 794	56 119	4.0	21.9	11.5	39 806	4.8	3 198	38 130	61.0	109 500	18.8	10.1
Paris	19 411	33 557	1.1	37.4	21.4	11 883	1.0	1 577	10 056	53.1	73 100	20.1	13.3
Pasadena..............	20 590	46 585	2.6	26.7	18.2	53 899	6.9	5 428	48 526	55.6	101 000	22.6	11.4
Pearland...............	38 608	94 653	9.1	8.8	3.3	33 169	138.7	1 947	33 112	78.5	179 600	21.5	10.8
Pflugerville............	30 514	74 196	4.8	13.5	7.9	16 418	209.9	629	17 968	77.3	168 500	22.5	10.9
Pharr..................	13 568	34 655	0.8	39.6	31.7	22 796	37.4	3 097	19 971	60.5	72 900	26.1	12.5
Plano..................	41 902	82 944	11.5	10.9	5.4	103 672	20.4	4 541	102 182	63.1	222 800	21.3	10.7
Port Arthur............	18 382	31 736	1.1	40.0	27.6	23 577	-4.6	3 394	20 283	57.8	66 200	23.4	12.0
Richardson	35 584	70 959	7.6	15.3	5.4	40 630	11.7	1 916	39 576	60.4	190 400	20.7	12.6
Rockwall...............	34 789	86 627	5.9	11.1	4.6	13 957	96.1	745	13 722	74.0	188 500	20.6	14.4
Rosenberg.............	20 008	44 318	1.9	26.7	17.5	11 162	32.2	999	10 855	51.2	114 900	23.3	12.3
Round Rock............	30 605	70 952	5.2	12.2	6.4	37 223	71.9	2 173	35 338	60.0	172 500	21.2	10.6
Rowlett................	30 386	83 442	5.1	8.2	4.3	18 969	30.1	598	18 251	86.0	159 400	22.8	13.1
San Angelo............	23 884	42 855	2.6	28.8	13.2	39 548	4.8	3 431	36 157	59.0	99 000	21.1	11.8
San Antonio..............	22 784	46 317	3.0	26.9	16.0	524 246	21.0	44 604	484 219	55.0	114 600	22.2	11.9
San Juan...............	13 188	34 518	1.8	34.8	28.6	9 740	25.8	858	8 908	75.6	78 300	26.7	13.9
San Marcos............	16 270	27 261	1.3	44.3	17.5	18 179	36.8	1 148	18 782	27.2	134 800	24.6	15.0
Schertz................	30 578	72 463	3.9	11.8	6.6	12 047	74.5	668	12 273	77.4	168 300	20.4	10.6
Seguin.................	19 853	36 755	2.1	35.7	18.4	9 714	18.7	920	9 382	63.8	101 200	23.1	14.5
Sherman...............	21 853	42 820	2.2	28.4	15.2	16 404	10.0	1 599	14 640	54.8	96 200	22.0	12.9
Socorro................	11 845	30 416	0.3	40.3	31.7	9 313	28.0	521	9 037	75.8	83 000	29.0	12.9
Southlake.............	74 380	170 742	42.5	7.0	2.4	8 494	28.7	301	8 808	92.4	530 300	23.5	11.9
Sugar Land..............	45 611	105 400	19.7	7.5	4.0	27 727	31.0	1 018	26 635	82.1	263 700	21.7	11.0
Temple................	25 554	47 962	3.7	24.5	11.7	28 422	21.2	2 309	24 696	57.5	117 900	19.3	12.1
Texarkana.............	23 973	38 810	3.0	35.3	21.1	16 115	6.5	1 693	13 931	55.8	100 000	22.8	12.1
Texas City............	21 303	44 659	1.4	27.6	16.8	18 773	12.6	2 145	16 570	60.0	95 300	21.9	10.9
The Colony...............	33 165	71 425	4.8	10.0	3.7	14 052	59.0	884	13 978	63.5	144 500	20.6	11.9
Tyler	26 132	42 752	4.4	28.8	13.5	41 742	17.4	3 846	37 996	53.5	130 800	22.5	12.2
Victoria	24 294	46 745	2.8	27.2	15.7	25 660	6.1	2 239	23 649	58.3	114 800	21.1	12.8
Waco	18 623	32 864	1.9	39.3	21.0	51 452	12.2	5 050	45 874	46.1	92 500	23.6	13.3
Waxahachie............	23 061	53 336	2.2	21.8	12.4	11 554	47.0	1 097	10 684	56.1	130 900	20.9	13.4
Weatherford............	25 637	52 532	3.5	20.2	8.6	10 853	31.3	1 083	9 934	61.5	135 400	22.4	11.2
Weslaco................	15 676	37 057	1.3	36.1	23.1	14 394	41.0	3 182	11 570	63.7	71 700	23.2	13.1
Wichita Falls............	22 768	43 751	2.6	28.3	14.4	43 632	4.3	5 178	37 108	57.5	92 000	21.7	12.6
Wylie..................	28 869	83 594	3.4	8.3	4.4	13 840	162.5	603	13 675	84.5	154 600	21.9	16.2
UTAH................	24 312	59 846	3.9	17.8	9.4	979 709	27.5	102 017	896 194	69.7	212 500	23.5	10.0
American Fork............	21 371	66 687	3.5	17.0	10.5	7 598	24.2	324	7 471	72.6	217 000	23.4	10.0
Bountiful	28 789	64 630	5.9	13.6	5.6	15 193	10.1	689	14 018	73.4	243 700	23.0	10.0
Cedar City.............	17 737	40 061	1.7	32.7	21.0	10 860	52.2	1 391	9 478	52.4	172 000	24.3	10.0
Clearfield...............	19 043	48 158	1.2	22.4	12.1	10 062	19.7	701	9 767	53.2	152 600	22.7	10.0
Cottonwood Heights......	38 477	76 630	10.8	8.8	4.0	13 194	33.2	735	12 042	71.7	305 700	22.4	10.0
Draper	34 083	94 852	11.5	8.1	3.2	12 125	84.3	581	12 287	79.0	372 600	23.9	10.0
Holladay	40 211	72 827	10.3	15.0	3.8	10 537	99.0	610	10 054	74.9	352 600	22.5	10.1

1. Based on population estimated by the American Community Survey.   2. Includes units rented or sold but not occupied.   3. Specified owner-occupied units; $1,000,000 represents $1,000,000 or more   4. 50.0 represents 50 percent or more.   5. 10.0 represents 10 percent or less.

Table D. Cities — **Housing, Labor Force, and Employment**

City	Occupied housing units, 2010–2014 (cont.)				Migration, 2010–2014		Civilian labor force, 2015		Unemployment		Civilian employment[4], 2010–2014		Percent	
	Percent renter occupied	Median gross rent[1]	Median gross rent as a percent of income[2]	Percent with no vehicle available	Percent who lived in the same house one year ago	Percent who lived outside current city one year ago	Total	Percent change, 2014–2015	Total	Rate[3]	Population age 16 and older	In labor force	Civilian full-year full-time workers	Households with no workers (percent)
	55	56	57	58	59	60	61	62	63	64	65	66	67	68
TEXAS—Cont'd														
Irving	61.3	906	26.5	5.6	77.2	11.9	125 153	2.0	4 809	3.8	168 543	73.4	50.6	14.1
Keller	16.0	1 186	32.6	2.0	86.7	10.7	22 411	0.4	768	3.4	31 320	66.8	46.1	17.8
Killeen	51.6	866	28.1	5.4	70.9	17.4	53 413	0.5	2 632	4.9	96 668	70.9	37.0	18.1
Kingsville	53.3	734	30.5	9.7	79.7	8.5	11 688	-6.0	670	5.7	20 294	60.9	31.3	27.2
Kyle	21.2	1 280	27.1	1.9	81.0	14.3	17 058	2.3	427	2.5	20 971	74.7	56.9	9.3
Lake Jackson	32.7	854	27.5	3.9	83.1	10.7	13 977	0.0	587	4.2	21 375	64.6	46.4	19.1
Lancaster	34.6	889	33.4	5.4	88.7	9.5	18 144	1.1	1 056	5.8	27 118	66.9	46.6	21.4
La Porte	25.6	1 040	28.1	3.7	86.4	9.8	18 627	0.1	880	4.7	26 692	70.0	46.9	18.0
Laredo	38.2	750	34.7	8.3	84.8	3.6	107 014	1.0	4 639	4.3	169 544	58.6	38.3	20.4
League City	28.4	1 181	23.5	2.1	85.4	11.0	52 484	0.3	1 928	3.7	66 706	73.1	54.1	13.9
Leander	22.1	1 316	29.2	2.3	80.3	16.2	17 531	2.4	501	2.9	21 018	77.7	51.3	9.4
Lewisville	55.4	961	27.3	4.1	75.3	16.0	61 835	2.1	2 052	3.3	76 018	78.3	55.2	13.6
Little Elm	19.7	1 433	27.9	1.6	87.1	11.0	17 921	2.3	489	2.7	20 674	75.9	54.3	10.2
Longview	43.5	773	31.0	7.7	78.6	10.1	38 909	-2.9	1 887	4.8	63 290	62.6	40.5	26.8
Lubbock	46.4	816	34.0	5.6	73.0	11.8	124 286	0.3	4 151	3.3	186 787	66.9	41.2	22.8
Lufkin	46.5	784	34.1	5.7	76.2	10.8	15 650	-1.1	847	5.4	27 536	61.6	37.8	30.6
McAllen	39.7	726	30.9	6.3	85.8	7.6	62 662	0.0	3 121	5.0	100 535	61.3	38.7	22.6
McKinney	31.3	1 112	27.6	3.4	84.2	10.5	81 619	2.1	2 908	3.6	103 684	71.3	52.9	13.1
Mansfield	21.0	1 162	27.4	2.3	88.6	9.3	32 768	0.2	1 127	3.4	43 510	73.2	51.6	13.8
Mesquite	41.2	972	31.4	4.4	83.4	10.5	75 129	1.8	3 215	4.3	105 005	71.4	49.2	16.2
Midland	35.2	1 042	27.0	4.5	82.4	8.6	72 505	-2.8	2 428	3.3	89 669	70.1	50.6	16.1
Mission	29.0	717	32.7	6.7	91.1	5.7	32 852	-0.1	2 036	6.2	55 960	57.8	36.0	26.3
Missouri City	15.7	1 388	27.7	1.5	91.6	7.0	38 586	0.2	1 741	4.5	53 924	70.4	49.5	14.7
Nacogdoches	61.1	731	34.1	12.5	68.5	17.1	14 453	-1.7	678	4.7	26 964	57.4	32.4	30.9
New Braunfels	34.9	988	29.4	3.8	81.1	11.5	33 347	0.9	980	2.9	46 351	66.9	45.4	22.8
North Richland Hills	36.8	948	29.0	4.1	83.5	13.0	38 061	0.1	1 369	3.6	51 997	71.1	49.4	18.8
Odessa	39.0	890	24.9	5.1	80.3	9.9	61 052	-3.3	2 522	4.1	79 495	68.0	47.9	19.1
Paris	46.9	653	32.4	11.9	76.5	9.7	10 804	0.8	537	5.0	19 776	58.8	35.7	36.5
Pasadena	44.4	795	30.4	6.1	80.3	10.1	68 953	0.2	3 840	5.6	112 125	64.5	41.3	22.3
Pearland	21.5	1 158	25.6	1.9	89.9	8.8	56 840	0.4	1 965	3.5	71 871	73.7	55.0	12.8
Pflugerville	22.7	1 110	34.8	3.0	89.8	8.3	30 327	2.1	886	2.9	38 824	74.5	54.0	14.1
Pharr	39.5	688	33.5	7.0	88.0	8.2	28 763	0.1	1 996	6.9	49 896	58.7	35.1	27.7
Plano	36.9	1 115	26.4	3.4	86.6	9.2	154 716	2.1	5 680	3.7	212 112	71.5	51.0	14.6
Port Arthur	42.2	689	30.5	12.2	85.3	6.7	22 420	-1.7	2 214	9.9	41 113	58.6	34.8	34.1
Richardson	39.6	1 081	27.6	3.8	82.4	12.5	58 620	2.1	2 165	3.7	83 516	69.0	47.2	19.2
Rockwall	26.0	1 228	27.3	3.6	85.5	11.0	21 215	2.2	767	3.6	29 721	69.2	49.6	18.2
Rosenberg	48.8	905	31.6	8.2	82.1	9.4	16 703	0.7	712	4.3	24 474	64.1	46.7	19.0
Round Rock	40.0	1 028	28.1	3.3	76.9	16.9	60 641	2.0	1 968	3.2	77 618	74.1	51.0	11.2
Rowlett	14.0	1 372	28.2	1.4	92.0	7.0	32 282	1.9	1 278	4.0	45 232	71.6	49.8	12.4
San Angelo	41.0	730	30.0	6.5	73.4	14.1	45 633	-0.4	1 874	4.1	76 023	63.8	37.7	27.2
San Antonio	45.0	840	30.0	9.3	80.5	6.5	676 424	1.0	24 928	3.7	1 063 972	64.6	41.1	23.6
San Juan	24.4	574	30.7	7.3	90.3	7.1	14 493	0.0	1 060	7.3	23 451	58.9	36.9	23.5
San Marcos	72.8	919	47.1	5.8	59.2	24.6	29 999	2.1	1 046	3.5	44 442	62.3	26.8	24.4
Schertz	22.6	1 038	25.2	2.4	86.5	11.5	17 326	1.0	569	3.3	26 816	67.1	44.2	21.4
Seguin	36.2	701	29.0	10.7	85.5	7.1	12 255	1.0	463	3.8	20 886	60.8	37.7	29.6
Sherman	45.2	807	28.9	7.2	75.6	12.3	19 185	0.2	752	3.9	30 291	63.4	39.6	29.1
Socorro	24.2	615	33.4	6.0	91.7	6.8	13 223	-0.5	708	5.4	23 732	58.0	31.8	25.7
Southlake	7.6	1 425	37.3	1.9	90.9	7.5	13 541	0.3	493	3.6	19 966	63.3	45.0	15.3
Sugar Land	17.9	1 514	26.0	2.2	89.4	8.8	45 433	0.4	1 612	3.5	65 453	65.0	46.1	13.8
Temple	42.5	803	29.4	7.8	83.6	9.1	33 342	0.9	1 245	3.7	52 923	62.0	43.4	28.4
Texarkana	44.2	701	32.4	12.6	85.6	9.5	15 452	-0.7	740	4.8	28 890	57.2	37.2	34.2
Texas City	40.0	823	33.4	8.2	78.1	11.5	21 120	-0.3	1 307	6.2	35 311	59.6	36.1	28.6
The Colony	36.5	1 170	28.5	1.4	82.7	13.5	25 980	2.0	890	3.4	29 891	79.8	56.7	11.8
Tyler	46.5	828	32.2	7.3	76.0	13.2	48 913	0.3	2 081	4.3	78 399	62.8	38.8	26.7
Victoria	41.7	791	31.1	6.8	79.6	8.9	33 047	-0.7	1 360	4.1	49 266	65.2	42.8	25.3
Waco	53.9	747	35.5	10.0	74.7	12.1	56 846	-0.4	2 461	4.3	99 583	58.8	33.9	29.0
Waxahachie	43.9	931	31.1	6.4	76.7	11.8	16 201	2.1	599	3.7	23 331	66.9	43.5	21.4
Weatherford	38.5	917	29.3	6.4	79.7	13.5	12 449	0.4	516	4.1	20 065	62.0	40.3	27.6
Weslaco	36.3	653	30.1	8.3	84.7	8.7	14 208	-1.1	927	6.5	26 588	55.4	33.2	35.4
Wichita Falls	42.5	731	28.9	7.1	79.0	12.6	43 166	-1.4	1 874	4.3	83 469	62.4	35.9	26.5
Wylie	15.5	1 129	26.7	1.3	87.0	10.9	24 792	2.2	840	3.4	31 225	74.3	53.8	10.2
UTAH	30.3	875	29.4	4.6	82.8	12.4	1 464 404	2.3	51 931	3.5	2 057 591	68.0	40.8	19.5
American Fork	27.4	1 025	31.5	2.9	86.2	11.6	12 697	4.0	450	3.5	18 110	66.1	39.4	17.6
Bountiful	26.6	894	26.4	4.1	85.8	10.7	20 252	2.3	684	3.4	32 042	62.6	38.2	24.9
Cedar City	47.6	638	31.2	5.5	79.6	11.6	13 056	2.1	575	4.4	21 743	64.7	30.1	24.8
Clearfield	46.8	913	30.9	6.5	78.2	18.7	13 982	2.5	571	4.1	20 420	72.6	44.1	18.3
Cottonwood Heights	28.3	998	23.9	2.7	86.1	11.8	19 448	1.8	614	3.2	26 720	70.3	44.9	16.1
Draper	21.0	1 194	26.9	1.6	84.5	12.2	21 549	1.9	694	3.2	31 096	64.7	44.1	9.5
Holladay	25.1	1 005	26.4	2.7	87.0	10.9	13 744	2.0	458	3.3	20 662	63.2	39.2	26.1

1. $2,000 represents $2,000 or more. 2. 50.0 represents 50 percent or more. 3. Percent of civilian labor force. 4. Persons 16 years old and over.

Table D. Cities — Construction, Wholesale Trade, and Retail Trade

City	Value of residential construction authorized by building permits, 2015			Wholesale trade,[1] 2012				Retail trade,[2] 2012			
	New construction ($1,000)	Number of housing units	Percent single family	Number of establishments	Number of employees	Sales (mil dol)	Annual payroll (mil dol)	Number of establishments	Number of employees	Sales (mil dol)	Annual payroll (mil dol)
	69	70	71	72	73	74	75	76	77	78	79
TEXAS—Cont'd											
Irving..........................	308 447	1 655	32.6	356	11 506	13 262.4	880.3	606	11 927	4 776.3	357.3
Keller..........................	71 322	218	100.0	26	93	84.4	4.7	104	1 435	420.6	32.8
Killeen........................	136 987	1 060	76.8	22	D	D	D	402	6 119	1 679.6	138.6
Kingsville....................	8 105	55	80.0	4	D	D	D	100	1 397	494.1	32.1
Kyle............................	89 084	912	57.3	8	63	27.8	5.8	111	2 489	604.1	54.6
Lake Jackson	5 836	25	100.0	12	63	27.8	5.8	111	2 489	604.1	54.6
Lancaster....................	32 487	155	100.0	18	D	D	D	63	995	235.8	21.5
La Porte......................	11 097	87	100.0	50	833	392.3	45.3	70	508	217.3	14.1
Laredo	201 418	1 848	55.8	356	D	D	D	782	D	D	D
League City.................	232 488	1 210	93.8	47	D	D	D	181	3 492	1 319.5	103.4
Leander	377 473	1 420	83.0	9	D	D	D	36	807	246.9	18.7
Lewisville	81 539	395	84.1	105	2 322	1 992.2	147.4	411	7 286	2 343.5	193.5
Little Elm	404 779	1 354	81.4	8	D	D	D	31	585	177.9	12.9
Longview.....................	27 478	179	100.0	170	2 233	1 211.0	114.1	508	7 547	2 082.8	192.5
Lubbock.......................	290 069	1 771	50.2	317	4 844	4 623.3	239.3	946	15 727	4 583.3	388.0
Lufkin.........................	4 745	33	100.0	47	684	310.6	30.4	271	4 094	1 148.9	100.2
McAllen.......................	167 935	1 038	49.6	348	3 131	2 539.6	124.1	870	14 085	3 716.8	301.9
McKinney.....................	899 932	4 235	49.4	93	771	705.9	43.3	330	6 634	2 507.3	187.9
Mansfield.....................	111 884	320	100.0	65	1 523	681.2	70.7	141	2 807	785.5	61.8
Mesquite......................	16 470	182	14.8	63	674	656.6	34.7	431	7 326	2 015.8	180.2
Midland.......................	204 438	1 025	74.2	164	2 436	2 268.9	136.4	453	7 059	2 661.1	201.3
Mission.......................	38 270	302	100.0	68	410	205.9	12.7	231	3 721	1 110.8	85.5
Missouri City................	72 866	276	92.0	52	316	225.2	16.6	147	2 936	757.1	60.7
Nacogdoches	2 227	21	61.9	34	D	D	D	210	2 763	824.0	66.9
New Braunfels..............	215 284	1 001	92.8	58	D	D	D	276	4 435	1 585.3	125.1
North Richland Hills	40 544	152	100.0	29	188	82.9	9.7	150	3 641	1 423.3	108.1
Odessa........................	111 046	612	76.5	184	2 717	1 951.1	189.8	401	6 849	2 658.0	208.0
Paris	1 998	32	37.5	34	D	D	D	178	2 252	628.8	53.7
Pasadena	35 162	298	39.9	137	1 665	979.4	92.2	440	6 288	1 733.4	146.8
Pearland......................	337 255	1 776	78.0	59	481	302.0	23.9	262	5 120	1 244.6	111.1
Pflugerville..................	96 541	851	50.2	41	511	243.6	29.2	86	1 515	416.4	35.3
Pharr..........................	29 717	431	49.0	142	1 208	876.6	51.4	179	2 374	622.6	62.7
Plano	275 942	2 416	19.0	420	7 367	4 626.3	589.3	1 064	20 770	7 683.0	624.0
Port Arthur...................	17 829	153	100.0	24	D	D	D	187	3 169	865.8	71.9
Richardson	186 697	1 531	7.4	220	8 348	31 123.6	713.3	353	4 650	1 846.0	154.0
Rockwall	88 128	388	100.0	41	D	D	D	202	3 754	1 268.6	97.4
Rosenberg	79 918	403	92.3	23	498	260.2	26.9	161	2 925	954.5	75.2
Round Rock	153 498	1 419	25.7	104	D	D	D	398	8 410	4 317.2	253.1
Rowlett	96 364	773	25.6	33	123	63.4	5.9	92	1 508	409.1	36.6
San Angelo..................	46 508	236	100.0	94	853	407.1	45.4	398	5 806	1 771.6	145.5
San Antonio.................	521 850	2 993	74.1	1 287	D	D	D	4 211	72 437	23 870.2	1 785.6
San Juan.....................	8 193	104	88.5	15	D	D	D	60	887	311.7	23.2
San Marcos..................	37 700	277	100.0	26	D	D	D	405	7 099	1 501.9	128.8
Schertz.......................	137 540	575	100.0	56	D	D	D	50	1 220	362.5	24.4
Seguin........................	45 269	325	64.3	25	D	D	D	139	1 826	516.0	45.2
Sherman......................	19 873	134	95.5	47	425	653.6	17.9	207	3 645	1 048.3	86.8
Socorro........................	11 390	130	96.9	14	140	148.7	6.1	58	695	219.3	13.8
Southlake.....................	199 438	273	100.0	59	591	528.1	40.5	229	5 140	1 760.0	142.1
Sugar Land...................	60 541	143	100.0	164	1 983	3 499.2	101.2	475	8 226	2 057.7	173.9
Temple	84 436	554	81.2	59	1 974	3 323.9	110.3	286	4 130	1 179.3	95.8
Texarkana....................	11 216	193	8.8	57	742	2 243.1	30.4	309	5 047	1 276.2	120.7
Texas City	25 236	177	100.0	28	211	113.5	12.0	186	1 575	517.8	49.6
The Colony...................	130 429	292	100.0	17	D	D	D	69	987	282.7	23.2
Tyler...........................	100 311	309	90.3	114	1 433	533.3	66.2	632	9 824	2 734.3	243.4
Victoria	20 794	136	100.0	82	1 085	557.4	58.6	353	5 240	1 563.4	134.0
Waco...........................	166 539	1 286	29.5	130	2 062	1 025.9	88.1	589	7 888	2 154.0	176.1
Waxahachie..................	59 556	347	100.0	31	D	D	D	138	2 364	623.9	53.6
Weatherford..................	41 596	205	97.1	25	274	362.1	10.5	198	3 255	1 372.8	96.3
Weslaco.......................	27 158	333	47.7	37	417	228.7	13.5	160	2 807	818.9	63.1
Wichita Falls................	13 861	58	100.0	116	981	508.4	46.0	434	6 851	1 830.0	154.1
Wylie..........................	108 873	523	100.0	14	D	D	D	62	1 258	340.1	30.4
UTAH........................	3 851 184	18 297	68.4	3 015	43 523	30 927.9	2 364.4	9 095	133 535	38 024.5	3 334.9
American Fork..............	31 406	126	88.9	28	439	166.3	17.1	137	2 331	737.3	56.8
Bountiful	21 788	76	40.8	42	263	209.0	14.9	146	1 951	614.2	49.5
Cedar City	37 076	181	70.7	24	183	140.2	7.3	140	1 698	505.3	39.8
Clearfield.....................	7 591	61	100.0	21	302	360.7	12.2	58	549	136.4	11.3
Cottonwood Heights......	10 194	23	100.0	41	914	513.9	135.6	70	1 589	1 291.6	68.7
Draper	70 158	258	85.3	51	772	303.2	47.8	186	3 580	1 289.4	117.5
Holladay	14 160	33	100.0	25	189	47.0	6.5	75	784	122.9	15.3

1. Merchant wholesalers except manufacturers' sales branches and offices.   2. Establishments with payroll.

Table D. Cities — Real Estate, Professional Services, and Manufacturing

City	Real estate and rental and leasing, 2012				Professional, scientific, and technical services,[1] 2012				Manufacturing, 2012			
	Number of establish-ments	Number of employees	Receipts (mil dol)	Annual payroll (mil dol)	Number of establish-ments	Number of employees	Receipts (mil dol)	Annual payroll (mil dol)	Number of establish-ments	Number of employees	Receipts (mil dol)	Annual payroll (mil dol)
	80	81	82	83	84	85	86	87	88	89	90	91
TEXAS—Cont'd												
Irving	339	4 857	1 213.8	191.9	1 008	D	D	D	160	6 926	3 150.8	425.8
Keller	35	219	78.0	9.7	152	562	116.2	28.5	17	87	16.4	3.7
Killeen	144	580	88.7	19.5	105	1 036	114.2	42.8	15	94	16.0	3.5
Kingsville	26	D	D	D	29	160	13.9	3.5	13	D	D	D
Kyle	13	16	5.9	0.6	12	34	3.2	0.8	7	353	D	20.9
Lake Jackson	21	113	28.2	4.2	46	D	D	D	3	10	D	0.7
Lancaster	20	75	17.6	3.2	17	D	D	D	24	949	341.2	37.1
La Porte	38	469	146.7	27.1	55	1 954	348.4	145.0	39	2 483	4 902.1	214.8
Laredo	199	692	132.4	22.0	316	D	D	D	68	D	D	D
League City	60	182	34.9	6.6	175	1 646	189.3	79.6	26	113	D	5.8
Leander	14	36	6.3	1.0	36	D	D	D	17	174	D	8.6
Lewisville	112	551	139.1	19.7	215	D	D	D	99	2 046	462.9	93.5
Little Elm	7	23	3.1	0.7	26	64	6.6	2.4	7	188	D	D
Longview	149	792	175.3	33.3	313	2 706	390.9	157.3	120	8 520	4 525.5	450.7
Lubbock	367	1 524	263.7	48.2	573	3 620	441.8	164.5	197	4 181	1 348.7	177.3
Lufkin	67	299	48.1	9.5	121	642	77.4	29.0	43	3 980	1 126.2	144.2
McAllen	206	810	213.5	27.2	455	D	D	D	96	2 207	729.1	100.2
McKinney	121	1 027	144.3	33.5	348	D	D	D	70	5 938	4 106.2	469.4
Mansfield	39	140	33.6	6.6	116	545	64.2	24.1	82	2 745	1 053.8	132.4
Mesquite	97	413	84.6	12.7	106	764	62.1	23.1	66	2 300	1 044.8	109.1
Midland	225	1 243	347.7	62.0	445	D	D	D	77	D	393.9	D
Mission	55	219	36.2	6.1	75	438	47.6	17.6	26	312	65.3	8.6
Missouri City	41	93	17.5	3.7	131	D	D	D	26	550	134.5	26.6
Nacogdoches	49	154	27.8	4.1	78	D	D	D	43	3 753	1 244.6	109.5
New Braunfels	101	423	63.9	11.7	153	670	74.9	25.1	60	2 039	587.1	86.6
North Richland Hills	66	280	42.8	9.3	141	D	D	D	20	1 003	409.0	44.1
Odessa	136	815	318.2	40.4	180	D	D	D	122	2 282	780.5	128.0
Paris	43	152	20.0	3.5	46	D	D	D	35	2 757	1 905.5	148.0
Pasadena	128	762	165.0	28.1	157	D	D	D	102	4 633	10 180.0	344.0
Pearland	86	418	104.1	16.1	189	D	D	D	62	1 502	D	81.1
Pflugerville	17	59	14.4	2.2	59	185	16.0	6.4	19	389	78.4	26.2
Pharr	41	264	37.9	6.8	60	770	34.2	14.3	25	333	95.0	12.4
Plano	398	3 742	744.5	192.9	1 492	D	D	D	150	4 601	1 698.4	277.0
Port Arthur	35	282	49.1	10.7	48	471	42.4	19.7	40	4 687	D	447.9
Richardson	172	756	194.7	32.3	682	9 109	2 070.8	693.6	138	7 059	2 336.5	546.5
Rockwall	52	D	D	D	155	D	D	D	41	936	241.2	48.1
Rosenberg	36	123	34.0	4.5	38	D	D	D	22	823	583.8	42.7
Round Rock	119	402	100.1	14.8	311	1 693	252.5	100.6	77	2 828	923.9	159.5
Rowlett	25	52	9.9	1.6	76	502	41.5	11.9	42	592	D	22.5
San Angelo	127	D	D	D	192	D	D	D	88	3 166	1 205.4	123.9
San Antonio	1 500	10 878	2 522.4	478.0	3 338	33 837	5 854.7	2 108.0	742	27 947	14 068.1	1 370.3
San Juan	10	38	3.4	1.4	12	46	4.4	0.9	9	99	D	2.1
San Marcos	75	338	87.0	9.8	96	823	54.9	19.6	40	D	687.6	D
Schertz	27	D	D	D	31	275	29.9	8.7	25	773	165.8	25.2
Seguin	34	192	36.9	7.6	49	198	16.6	6.5	48	3 995	2 029.9	180.9
Sherman	50	178	29.5	4.9	114	395	50.0	17.5	46	4 317	D	191.4
Socorro	8	33	10.2	1.2	7	41	1.7	0.5	14	79	16.7	2.2
Southlake	92	599	98.4	25.3	229	1 624	250.9	81.1	28	295	81.4	14.1
Sugar Land	167	483	155.5	20.7	521	4 603	724.3	604.4	57	3 099	1 374.8	159.4
Temple	80	409	65.1	12.8	117	D	D	D	59	4 222	1 611.1	180.0
Texarkana	78	385	79.6	15.3	123	D	D	D	26	814	276.8	36.9
Texas City	34	281	66.9	11.7	43	D	D	D	25	4 126	40 766.1	498.9
The Colony	17	177	41.1	4.0	51	276	36.3	10.4	NA	NA	NA	NA
Tyler	208	953	217.8	39.9	458	D	D	D	88	4 002	4 317.4	201.7
Victoria	110	714	492.3	39.4	142	D	D	D	55	1 062	D	D
Waco	162	1 293	245.6	55.7	272	D	D	D	134	12 060	5 828.2	576.4
Waxahachie	46	149	31.1	4.7	63	D	D	D	54	3 534	1 293.8	154.3
Weatherford	37	174	24.8	5.4	86	D	D	D	31	825	177.4	40.7
Weslaco	49	201	35.0	4.1	59	D	D	D	12	92	11.7	4.3
Wichita Falls	153	759	153.6	28.2	208	D	D	D	97	3 045	724.1	148.2
Wylie	17	54	11.1	1.6	49	153	14.8	6.1	32	1 788	653.8	75.9
UTAH	4 446	16 197	3 226.1	604.8	8 961	75 648	10 415.5	3 860.6	3 163	108 264	50 046.4	5 762.6
American Fork	60	167	27.7	5.1	118	1 593	235.8	76.3	27	591	D	31.7
Bountiful	81	170	19.1	6.0	192	D	D	D	42	797	1 594.5	52.5
Cedar City	57	140	26.1	4.5	83	385	54.8	14.5	57	1 212	639.8	51.5
Clearfield	25	102	31.3	3.3	59	1 259	142.0	70.8	47	5 724	1 740.4	267.2
Cottonwood Heights	232	745	127.3	30.7	210	1 225	192.1	76.0	23	250	D	14.9
Draper	104	334	55.2	12.8	245	1 348	180.2	73.3	41	1 216	362.4	69.8
Holladay	80	D	D	D	159	D	D	D	11	445	D	22.1

1. Establishments subject to federal tax.

Table D. Cities — Accommodation and Food Services, Arts, Entertainment, and Recreation, and Health Care and Social Assistance

City	Accommodation and food services, 2012				Arts, entertainment, and recreation,[1] 2012				Health care and social assistance,[1] 2012			
	Number of establishments	Number of employees	Sales (mil dol)	Annual payroll (mil dol)	Number of establishments	Number of employees	Receipts (mil dol)	Annual payroll (mil dol)	Number of establishments	Number of employees	Receipts (mil dol)	Annual payroll (mil dol)
	92	93	94	95	96	97	98	99	100	101	102	103
TEXAS—Cont'd												
Irving	545	11 557	795.8	219.0	41	882	308.9	194.8	524	9 189	1 018.6	422.2
Keller	81	1 232	64.1	17.2	10	D	D	D	116	D	D	D
Killeen	248	5 406	275.3	73.2	20	D	D	D	162	D	D	D
Kingsville	70	D	D	D	4	27	1.9	0.7	49	D	D	D
Kyle	39	461	26.7	7.0	5	D	D	D	42	D	D	D
Lake Jackson	58	1 421	67.1	18.7	6	180	4.8	2.3	127	D	D	D
Lancaster	32	646	34.6	10.3	2	D	D	D	42	882	44.4	19.0
La Porte	68	1 241	60.2	17.1	4	4	0.1	0.1	39	D	D	D
Laredo	388	D	D	D	29	D	D	D	495	D	D	D
League City	121	2 047	101.4	28.6	19	D	D	D	147	D	D	D
Leander	27	405	20.0	5.0	4	D	D	D	37	D	D	D
Lewisville	232	4 707	268.4	69.0	29	D	D	D	235	4 569	466.8	185.6
Little Elm	23	D	D	D	4	85	4.4	1.3	18	160	9.8	3.7
Longview	239	5 463	255.8	71.5	18	233	14.7	4.0	330	D	D	D
Lubbock	597	13 817	697.7	186.1	56	966	44.5	14.4	681	12 591	1 244.5	475.9
Lufkin	122	2 852	129.3	36.8	11	84	4.1	1.0	206	4 992	368.7	159.6
McAllen	402	8 909	434.2	116.1	27	298	31.6	5.0	737	15 849	1 434.3	538.1
McKinney	229	4 652	233.6	66.7	28	756	34.3	12.7	340	5 253	601.0	220.2
Mansfield	118	D	D	D	16	D	D	D	177	1 699	177.1	68.4
Mesquite	217	5 218	270.6	75.1	22	324	22.3	4.3	309	D	D	D
Midland	279	6 352	431.1	102.8	24	D	D	D	319	D	D	D
Mission	135	2 294	119.2	28.9	11	239	10.1	3.2	262	D	D	D
Missouri City	101	1 540	82.2	20.4	10	D	D	D	163	1 529	104.2	40.9
Nacogdoches	105	2 457	96.1	27.0	9	D	D	D	172	2 233	248.4	76.5
New Braunfels	228	4 685	247.9	66.5	27	D	D	D	214	D	D	D
North Richland Hills	127	2 539	118.8	33.0	20	D	D	D	129	2 717	342.9	117.9
Odessa	230	5 893	377.8	90.6	23	239	15.9	2.6	273	5 379	633.2	215.6
Paris	93	1 462	67.5	18.9	8	D	D	D	153	3 443	310.7	115.6
Pasadena	202	3 882	206.4	54.8	10	D	D	D	307	6 675	807.2	289.9
Pearland	180	4 226	212.0	58.5	15	D	D	D	242	2 374	209.8	83.3
Pflugerville	61	1 266	61.4	17.6	7	100	6.1	1.7	59	D	D	D
Pharr	92	1 721	102.4	22.5	10	95	5.8	1.3	141	3 312	128.5	68.5
Plano	681	14 581	846.9	241.8	63	1 334	112.0	25.0	1 326	16 372	2 368.0	869.3
Port Arthur	102	1 890	86.4	24.4	8	D	D	D	111	D	D	D
Richardson	322	5 202	307.9	82.9	31	427	31.0	10.6	479	5 290	475.4	182.8
Rockwall	124	3 006	154.6	46.0	16	D	D	D	168	2 085	270.0	90.3
Rosenberg	92	1 713	89.5	25.8	2	D	D	D	52	D	D	D
Round Rock	278	6 112	340.4	92.7	29	D	D	D	288	D	D	D
Rowlett	70	990	49.9	14.0	9	D	D	D	100	1 983	246.4	72.1
San Angelo	210	4 220	211.7	57.1	22	264	15.8	3.7	225	3 970	425.1	200.0
San Antonio	3 209	79 964	4 616.3	1 242.7	255	D	D	D	3 448	74 255	8 556.3	3 003.7
San Juan	28	363	19.3	4.6	3	D	D	D	52	942	37.0	17.6
San Marcos	212	4 456	215.6	59.6	6	D	D	D	119	D	D	D
Schertz	58	1 287	62.4	17.5	4	D	D	D	44	681	61.7	24.3
Seguin	81	1 368	73.6	17.3	5	D	D	D	89	D	D	D
Sherman	102	2 593	124.4	35.3	13	171	6.6	1.6	208	4 944	426.2	184.1
Socorro	24	263	12.7	3.0	1	D	D	D	12	303	7.1	3.8
Southlake	111	D	D	D	21	D	D	D	193	2 328	300.7	102.7
Sugar Land	328	7 038	377.8	109.4	27	772	63.8	17.7	563	D	D	D
Temple	170	3 451	159.8	44.4	17	136	8.5	2.0	157	D	D	D
Texarkana	134	3 369	158.4	46.2	18	169	6.4	2.4	215	4 013	462.8	181.8
Texas City	74	1 229	55.7	15.6	3	D	D	D	92	2 400	223.0	86.3
The Colony	47	1 083	50.1	14.3	10	136	11.6	2.8	47	D	D	D
Tyler	310	7 298	339.0	97.3	33	D	D	D	465	11 350	1 145.8	482.2
Victoria	176	3 538	182.8	48.4	27	D	D	D	254	D	D	D
Waco	350	7 672	380.5	106.7	29	338	20.8	5.4	317	6 697	512.1	245.1
Waxahachie	80	1 902	85.0	25.3	3	D	D	D	86	D	D	D
Weatherford	116	2 114	98.8	28.6	6	D	D	D	128	1 988	207.2	79.7
Weslaco	84	1 781	86.0	21.4	10	D	D	D	174	D	D	D
Wichita Falls	236	5 370	249.6	76.2	20	D	D	D	305	5 113	540.1	185.9
Wylie	42	D	D	D	5	42	3.6	0.8	50	D	D	D
UTAH	5 108	95 933	4 789.3	1 362.9	790	17 988	982.5	330.3	6 601	77 036	8 253.6	3 016.8
American Fork	82	1 558	69.8	18.5	7	D	D	D	129	D	D	D
Bountiful	69	D	D	D	10	D	D	D	209	D	D	D
Cedar City	82	1 224	57.5	14.8	9	D	D	D	117	D	D	D
Clearfield	32	611	23.0	6.5	5	D	D	D	44	D	D	D
Cottonwood Heights	54	799	43.5	11.6	13	D	D	D	120	D	D	D
Draper	94	1 494	72.3	21.8	15	D	D	D	132	997	104.1	37.5
Holladay	51	578	30.2	8.2	11	D	D	D	96	972	85.2	33.2

1. Establishments subject to federal tax.

	Other services[1], 2012				Government employment and payroll, 2012							
						March payroll						
							Percent of total for:					
City	Number of establish-ments	Number of employees	Receipts (mil dol)	Annual payroll (mil dol)	Full-time equivalent employees	Total (dollars)	Adminis-tration, judicial, and legal	Police and Corrections	Fire Protection	Highways and trans-portation	Health and welfare	Natural resources and utilities	Education and libraries
	104	105	106	107	108	109	110	111	112	113	114	115	116
TEXAS—Cont'd													
Irving	239	2 926	307.3	114.7	1 743	8 046 007	11.8	31.8	18.7	7.1	2.9	19.2	3.6
Keller	55	377	31.5	9.8	322	1 442 647	19.7	27.3	24.3	2.1	4.2	18.4	3.8
Killeen	150	974	79.5	24.9	1 394	4 447 306	9.5	31.5	19.2	10.2	0.6	25.4	2.0
Kingsville	31	D	D	D	241	740 345	13.5	34.2	17.7	5.2	3.4	18.4	2.6
Kyle	18	91	7.2	2.0	143	570 004	14.8	39.7	0.0	1.7	5.7	18.1	3.7
Lake Jackson	28	191	12.6	4.6	223	1 137 302	14.0	31.7	0.5	2.3	1.6	37.2	0.0
Lancaster	24	150	17.5	5.4	197	872 132	6.8	31.3	33.7	2.6	3.3	16.0	2.4
La Porte	42	5 934	655.6	342.7	386	1 606 505	14.9	33.6	6.2	5.1	7.8	22.0	0.0
Laredo	175	975	90.0	24.7	2 366	9 931 436	6.8	30.9	24.7	11.9	8.6	14.4	1.1
League City	93	670	50.8	15.5	495	2 096 779	14.9	38.2	2.0	7.5	5.2	20.9	5.0
Leander	26	146	11.5	3.6	176	773 154	15.8	34.3	18.9	9.2	0.8	16.9	0.0
Lewisville	150	1 053	116.4	32.6	702	3 410 758	13.2	32.7	24.8	4.3	1.7	15.0	2.1
Little Elm	12	44	4.1	1.4	174	691 106	17.2	23.6	29.0	9.8	0.8	13.6	2.1
Longview	155	1 278	152.8	44.8	813	3 225 874	7.0	26.2	26.9	3.4	3.3	21.3	2.7
Lubbock	338	2 485	217.7	69.3	2 120	8 958 861	10.0	27.2	23.3	4.5	2.1	29.5	1.5
Lufkin	75	615	135.8	27.5	429	1 543 350	10.3	27.6	23.6	6.7	2.2	23.4	1.9
McAllen	145	1 046	142.4	30.6	1 664	5 174 843	11.6	30.2	15.6	10.8	1.0	24.6	3.0
McKinney	132	1 023	89.8	27.9	813	4 047 327	14.6	26.8	24.0	4.8	0.1	11.7	2.8
Mansfield	67	D	D	D	451	2 111 359	10.1	41.1	18.9	1.8	1.4	11.7	1.5
Mesquite	122	946	102.3	28.3	1 105	5 253 222	10.9	34.0	25.7	3.7	4.0	15.6	2.0
Midland	157	D	D	D	894	4 038 726	12.2	27.1	26.9	7.2	3.1	13.6	0.0
Mission	72	434	36.4	9.7	597	1 943 490	10.4	37.6	17.4	3.6	1.5	22.5	3.1
Missouri City	68	415	28.1	9.5	283	1 318 714	9.4	42.4	22.9	9.3	0.0	4.5	0.0
Nacogdoches	49	298	23.9	7.2	302	1 195 157	10.1	30.1	23.9	1.7	1.3	26.6	1.9
New Braunfels	105	1 334	54.3	37.3	732	3 498 442	7.2	20.5	22.3	4.6	3.6	21.9	2.5
North Richland Hills	73	459	48.3	13.6	574	2 442 427	13.2	35.1	19.1	9.2	9.3	9.3	4.0
Odessa	149	1 399	178.1	47.0	873	3 249 214	13.9	28.3	26.0	7.1	3.0	16.3	0.0
Paris	58	301	28.1	7.8	203	911 303	16.1	38.4	1.6	2.6	5.8	17.2	7.9
Pasadena	135	1 402	179.6	68.1	960	4 082 891	10.8	48.1	2.1	4.7	5.5	18.7	2.8
Pearland	129	906	77.4	25.7	598	2 337 139	14.4	37.4	8.4	4.4	15.8	16.8	0.0
Pflugerville	51	308	28.6	10.5	253	1 010 931	16.1	44.8	0.0	8.0	1.3	21.6	3.5
Pharr	52	340	29.9	8.1	558	1 780 708	10.5	35.0	15.9	8.1	1.9	18.2	3.4
Plano	419	3 683	759.6	161.0	2 089	10 395 648	9.8	32.0	22.2	2.2	0.0	14.1	5.2
Port Arthur	36	162	11.7	3.2	668	2 985 904	7.8	28.2	20.4	6.1	9.3	23.9	1.7
Richardson	146	1 302	141.4	44.2	1 085	4 745 385	14.8	25.0	17.8	5.0	3.3	20.5	3.5
Rockwall	55	559	27.7	10.4	286	1 221 546	32.3	33.7	9.6	3.1	0.0	16.3	0.0
Rosenberg	53	230	30.8	8.3	213	967 179	15.7	34.7	16.7	5.1	5.0	18.2	0.0
Round Rock	147	1 405	151.8	46.8	471	2 565 694	21.2	46.9	28.7	0.0	0.0	0.7	2.5
Rowlett	74	396	34.4	11.4	332	1 590 040	18.8	30.9	25.7	4.7	2.6	10.7	1.9
San Angelo	161	867	85.1	23.1	915	3 145 374	16.7	27.8	25.3	3.8	3.2	19.2	0.0
San Antonio	1 694	12 508	1 000.7	326.7	15 382	70 371 976	6.9	20.9	12.5	5.3	3.5	46.3	2.1
San Juan	14	D	D	D	204	595 583	10.6	35.0	12.1	4.4	4.5	31.9	0.4
San Marcos	73	D	D	D	528	2 976 832	13.7	28.7	14.8	4.1	4.9	21.3	2.7
Schertz	36	342	28.5	9.8	292	1 152 930	17.4	24.7	12.8	2.8	16.4	9.2	3.8
Seguin	47	323	25.3	7.7	907	3 729 350	5.2	8.3	6.1	1.8	68.5	7.0	0.7
Sherman	43	375	37.8	16.0	387	1 528 362	13.7	25.7	23.1	4.3	3.0	22.7	2.2
Socorro	24	112	8.0	1.6	92	274 728	24.8	59.5	0.0	13.4	2.2	0.0	0.0
Southlake	68	D	D	D	274	1 309 065	24.1	24.8	21.4	7.0	0.0	20.0	2.7
Sugar Land	128	947	72.3	23.2	631	3 018 681	23.4	31.1	19.1	10.0	1.3	10.4	0.0
Temple	104	933	55.9	26.2	731	2 585 537	12.4	26.7	22.3	6.4	2.4	25.4	2.6
Texarkana	91	661	56.2	17.8	562	2 018 866	13.1	24.0	17.3	8.1	4.9	29.4	1.7
Texas City	38	241	27.2	9.5	481	1 954 986	8.1	29.3	20.9	5.9	1.6	25.9	2.0
The Colony	32	157	11.7	3.1	311	1 270 659	11.9	29.0	21.2	3.8	7.3	20.1	4.5
Tyler	170	1 478	125.2	57.0	778	3 106 473	9.1	34.9	25.5	3.1	3.1	18.2	1.7
Victoria	103	D	D	D	566	2 159 618	10.1	31.7	22.5	6.4	0.0	22.4	3.2
Waco	177	1 205	90.1	28.9	1 507	5 739 695	9.4	29.8	17.3	5.4	5.9	25.5	2.4
Waxahachie	42	262	29.4	6.8	264	1 145 356	12.3	28.0	25.5	3.4	3.0	21.1	0.0
Weatherford	63	579	42.4	15.3	345	1 550 071	17.4	23.4	20.0	5.7	2.6	21.9	3.2
Weslaco	45	347	28.5	7.3	368	1 252 682	6.2	31.0	27.7	5.1	2.2	17.8	3.2
Wichita Falls	142	835	70.0	20.7	1 213	4 712 736	7.8	25.5	27.3	8.3	5.3	16.8	1.2
Wylie	33	172	13.3	4.5	191	622 464	4.4	29.0	33.5	4.3	0.0	22.4	6.3
UTAH	3 631	21 705	1 875.3	549.2	X	X	X	X	X	X	X	X	X
American Fork	55	448	23.4	5.8	215	711 482	13.8	21.8	14.3	3.1	1.3	25.9	5.2
Bountiful	72	572	38.0	11.3	195	922 673	14.7	32.2	0.0	14.9	0.0	37.8	0.0
Cedar City	43	174	14.8	3.9	172	568 537	11.0	28.7	7.6	11.9	1.2	27.7	2.2
Clearfield	34	194	11.7	4.6	150	543 342	19.4	32.7	17.0	4.0	0.9	22.9	0.0
Cottonwood Heights	25	150	5.7	1.9	68	323 642	24.8	70.5	0.0	4.6	0.0	0.0	0.0
Draper	78	494	43.8	10.8	152	605 204	26.7	28.9	0.0	17.1	3.4	14.1	0.0
Holladay	40	158	11.1	3.1	18	69 533	64.5	0.0	0.0	0.0	22.6	12.9	0.0

1. Establishments subject to federal tax.

Table D. Cities — **City Government Finances**

	City government finances, 2012								
	General revenue						General expenditure		
		Intergovernmental		Taxes				Per capita[1] (dollars)	
					Per capita[1] (dollars)				
City	Total (mil dol)	Total (mil dol)	Percent from state government	Total (mil dol)	Total	Property	Sales and gross receipts	Total (mil dol)	Total	Capital outlays
	117	118	119	120	121	122	123	124	125	126
TEXAS—Cont'd										
Irving	281.4	21.9	71.5	189.3	839	427	411	289.2	1 281	200
Keller	52.3	5.6	60.6	32.1	765	471	294	46.9	1 117	201
Killeen	120.2	5.4	5.6	62.9	466	248	219	125.1	928	204
Kingsville	22.9	0.6	12.6	12.2	464	228	236	21.7	825	89
Kyle	18.5	1.7	25.7	10.7	346	201	145	21.9	709	200
Lake Jackson	29.0	0.4	54.4	14.7	543	207	335	25.6	942	152
Lancaster	48.5	11.5	23.8	24.6	649	359	290	46.9	1 238	111
La Porte	56.7	0.9	100.0	26.5	769	497	272	48.6	1 407	246
Laredo	394.6	81.6	35.0	126.6	516	281	235	350.9	1 429	400
League City	86.5	3.8	100.0	58.1	658	411	247	73.3	829	130
Leander	26.5	2.2	9.7	17.9	606	377	229	29.0	981	234
Lewisville	95.9	2.2	49.8	62.5	628	286	342	100.9	1 013	207
Little Elm	30.5	4.2	98.1	18.2	629	354	275	39.3	1 357	641
Longview	103.8	12.8	28.3	64.9	798	306	492	94.8	1 166	149
Lubbock	270.7	38.4	30.0	127.0	538	245	293	310.3	1 313	386
Lufkin	50.9	0.7	59.9	25.8	716	272	443	52.9	1 468	203
McAllen	185.3	20.0	21.5	98.4	727	242	485	201.4	1 488	430
McKinney	171.7	14.0	23.8	109.6	764	437	327	184.3	1 284	234
Mansfield	76.9	0.3	100.0	53.1	894	514	381	67.5	1 136	167
Mesquite	149.0	15.9	19.4	81.9	571	255	316	164.5	1 147	212
Midland	147.3	7.4	38.3	94.6	790	273	516	126.0	1 052	145
Mission	73.0	7.2	12.2	38.7	478	266	212	68.7	850	112
Missouri City	57.5	9.1	36.1	36.0	524	363	161	66.1	963	354
Nacogdoches	37.5	1.3	98.2	17.4	514	223	291	34.0	1 005	86
New Braunfels	75.8	2.4	48.3	46.1	754	263	491	79.1	1 294	279
North Richland Hills	83.8	11.2	100.0	46.1	705	344	361	93.1	1 424	490
Odessa	103.9	3.9	38.2	61.7	580	196	384	93.2	877	116
Paris	30.9	2.2	100.0	18.1	722	303	419	29.3	1 166	79
Pasadena	146.5	20.4	12.6	75.9	497	217	280	138.9	910	167
Pearland	113.9	0.6	58.8	76.6	794	500	295	118.6	1 230	308
Pflugerville	42.9	1.9	93.4	26.5	509	326	184	44.6	858	248
Pharr	63.4	5.8	5.1	30.9	422	211	211	59.7	815	150
Plano	386.2	19.2	55.2	247.7	907	528	380	338.6	1 240	181
Port Arthur	104.3	23.2	53.0	35.6	652	306	346	92.8	1 701	263
Richardson	156.9	3.8	94.5	105.8	1 020	591	428	174.7	1 684	269
Rockwall	44.0	0.7	30.2	36.4	910	434	476	49.9	1 249	367
Rosenberg	36.1	5.0	24.6	21.6	665	231	434	29.5	906	207
Round Rock	146.3	3.6	66.0	112.0	1 050	315	735	119.5	1 120	243
Rowlett	58.1	2.1	65.8	33.9	587	420	167	55.7	965	142
San Angelo	93.6	7.0	10.4	55.3	575	299	276	98.6	1 026	216
San Antonio	1 748.6	300.5	51.3	740.3	534	275	253	1 743.3	1 258	188
San Juan	18.0	1.1	32.3	9.7	275	168	107	18.5	524	97
San Marcos	67.7	3.7	100.0	38.5	769	285	485	82.3	1 643	440
Schertz	37.4	1.3	65.0	21.3	611	306	305	31.5	902	81
Seguin	116.5	6.1	85.0	13.9	529	240	289	116.4	4 428	511
Sherman	47.8	2.7	3.7	27.5	704	182	522	48.9	1 254	120
Socorro	7.7	0.5	0.0	6.1	185	124	61	9.8	298	92
Southlake	68.2	0.6	38.4	54.7	1 972	1 139	834	66.5	2 398	864
Sugar Land	160.2	31.2	93.8	77.6	948	347	601	161.5	1 972	729
Temple	85.5	3.7	93.7	46.0	666	317	349	91.2	1 319	299
Texarkana	47.9	0.8	78.3	31.7	853	368	485	49.1	1 322	277
Texas City	68.4	8.3	43.2	43.1	944	451	493	58.5	1 280	147
The Colony	38.4	2.1	73.4	25.5	652	384	268	46.1	1 181	397
Tyler	128.9	15.0	13.7	61.9	623	142	481	120.1	1 209	168
Victoria	78.7	5.7	39.9	49.8	773	320	453	89.3	1 386	576
Waco	359.0	127.8	9.2	97.3	762	414	348	344.8	2 700	343
Waxahachie	40.4	0.2	100.0	28.8	928	477	451	33.9	1 090	82
Weatherford	34.6	3.2	80.9	20.7	782	306	475	43.0	1 627	441
Weslaco	37.6	0.7	25.3	22.1	599	267	332	35.9	972	114
Wichita Falls	120.3	13.6	34.0	66.3	633	276	357	114.0	1 088	129
Wylie	43.1	1.6	92.9	30.5	688	467	221	53.2	1 199	374
UTAH	X	X	X	X	X	X	X	X	X	X
American Fork	30.4	2.8	100.0	13.6	497	205	291	29.8	1 092	170
Bountiful	25.9	3.0	48.4	13.7	320	93	227	21.6	504	27
Cedar City	26.1	3.3	64.2	13.5	465	185	280	21.4	736	103
Clearfield	27.3	4.4	91.5	11.8	387	164	223	21.4	704	59
Cottonwood Heights	14.9	1.2	96.8	12.7	374	206	168	16.8	494	109
Draper	36.2	2.5	98.9	24.0	544	247	297	32.8	742	114
Holladay	17.7	2.0	70.1	11.7	434	197	236	15.0	555	0

1. Based on population estimated as of July 1 of the year shown.

Table D. Cities — **City Government Finances**

City	City government finances, 2012 (cont.)									
	General expenditure (cont.)									
	Percent of total for:									
	Public welfare	Highways	Parking facilities	Education	Health and hospitals	Police protection	Sewerage and sanitation	Parks and recreation	Housing and community development	Interest on debt
	127	128	129	130	131	132	133	134	135	136
TEXAS—Cont'd										
Irving	0.0	6.3	0.0	0.0	0.3	18.5	10.7	16.0	1.7	6.2
Keller	0.0	17.7	0.0	0.0	0.0	17.1	7.0	11.8	0.0	10.1
Killeen	0.2	9.1	0.0	0.0	0.4	19.5	23.3	5.7	0.3	4.1
Kingsville	0.0	9.8	0.0	0.0	1.5	31.1	19.6	0.9	0.0	1.3
Kyle	0.0	2.5	0.0	0.0	0.7	17.1	24.0	10.5	0.0	11.7
Lake Jackson	0.0	11.4	0.0	0.0	3.4	18.2	19.4	20.7	0.0	5.0
Lancaster	0.0	1.7	0.0	0.0	0.3	12.2	16.8	4.5	18.4	8.3
La Porte	0.0	8.4	0.0	0.0	0.0	21.8	10.5	11.3	0.0	3.9
Laredo	0.2	2.1	0.4	0.0	4.1	15.0	11.2	3.3	3.8	5.2
League City	0.0	10.6	0.0	0.0	3.9	20.7	11.4	6.2	0.2	5.1
Leander	0.0	21.6	0.0	0.0	0.6	14.8	12.0	7.8	0.0	17.7
Lewisville	0.0	16.6	0.0	0.0	1.2	21.6	6.1	10.4	2.2	6.4
Little Elm	0.0	4.0	0.0	0.0	0.3	8.7	13.3	2.7	0.0	4.5
Longview	0.0	10.3	0.0	0.0	1.5	21.3	12.6	8.8	7.2	2.4
Lubbock	0.0	7.3	0.0	0.0	1.8	16.3	18.4	5.2	1.4	10.2
Lufkin	0.0	14.7	0.0	0.0	1.2	15.2	18.1	7.6	0.3	13.8
McAllen	0.6	11.5	0.4	0.0	0.8	16.5	22.1	10.4	1.7	2.6
McKinney	0.0	8.4	0.0	0.0	0.8	10.9	11.9	6.8	0.3	6.0
Mansfield	0.0	9.9	0.0	0.0	0.6	14.5	12.1	8.2	0.0	8.1
Mesquite	0.0	6.4	0.0	0.0	0.8	18.5	13.6	7.0	8.4	4.2
Midland	0.0	5.4	0.0	0.0	3.3	17.0	15.9	13.4	0.6	2.3
Mission	0.0	8.3	0.0	0.0	0.5	20.0	10.6	12.1	1.7	18.9
Missouri City	0.0	12.6	0.0	0.0	0.3	16.3	9.7	12.1	0.5	7.8
Nacogdoches	0.0	4.3	0.0	0.0	0.0	20.6	28.3	4.4	0.0	1.2
New Braunfels	0.0	16.3	0.0	0.0	0.9	17.7	16.5	7.8	0.3	6.0
North Richland Hills	0.0	7.5	0.0	0.0	0.9	17.6	8.3	14.6	0.0	2.6
Odessa	0.1	14.4	0.0	0.0	0.7	18.6	16.0	6.7	2.6	1.6
Paris	0.0	12.8	0.0	0.0	10.9	19.7	12.9	3.9	4.1	2.1
Pasadena	0.3	19.6	0.0	0.0	2.5	30.9	13.9	6.5	7.8	3.5
Pearland	0.0	21.9	0.0	0.0	3.6	13.1	14.4	6.1	0.0	12.2
Pflugerville	0.0	14.9	0.0	0.0	0.0	22.4	18.1	6.3	0.0	7.6
Pharr	0.0	17.9	0.0	0.0	3.4	23.5	9.1	9.1	2.3	3.4
Plano	0.0	5.1	0.0	0.0	1.0	16.3	18.5	12.9	0.8	4.2
Port Arthur	2.1	10.7	0.0	0.0	3.3	19.4	20.8	2.7	3.2	3.5
Richardson	0.0	11.9	0.0	0.0	1.1	13.7	17.6	8.7	0.0	6.6
Rockwall	0.0	20.4	0.0	0.0	1.1	16.8	11.8	16.8	0.0	11.1
Rosenberg	0.0	19.1	0.0	0.0	0.8	23.4	17.4	3.5	0.0	6.0
Round Rock	0.0	13.0	0.0	0.0	0.7	19.5	9.2	7.3	0.4	5.1
Rowlett	0.0	13.1	0.0	0.0	1.6	18.1	14.7	6.6	0.0	6.4
San Angelo	0.0	7.5	0.0	0.0	3.5	15.8	10.8	5.9	3.1	4.7
San Antonio	7.8	6.4	0.3	0.0	1.9	17.7	19.6	7.8	2.9	1.6
San Juan	0.0	7.7	0.0	0.0	0.0	18.3	23.7	7.5	0.0	4.2
San Marcos	0.0	3.2	0.0	0.0	2.0	17.4	16.7	3.5	0.8	8.8
Schertz	0.0	7.2	0.0	0.0	12.4	14.7	16.9	4.0	0.0	6.6
Seguin	0.0	2.2	0.0	0.0	64.9	4.6	5.0	2.7	0.0	6.7
Sherman	0.1	14.6	0.0	0.0	1.2	15.7	18.0	4.8	0.6	2.0
Socorro	0.0	16.3	0.0	0.0	4.1	19.1	0.0	1.1	2.7	3.8
Southlake	0.0	16.1	0.0	0.0	0.0	12.5	7.7	19.6	0.0	8.2
Sugar Land	0.0	21.1	0.0	0.0	0.4	10.2	11.7	4.0	0.2	5.9
Temple	0.0	5.4	0.0	0.0	0.9	17.8	21.2	9.8	0.0	5.0
Texarkana	0.0	16.5	0.0	0.0	1.7	19.3	24.5	4.0	0.9	4.9
Texas City	0.0	17.5	0.0	0.0	0.7	18.1	12.1	12.9	0.8	4.6
The Colony	0.0	20.7	0.0	0.0	0.0	26.6	8.9	7.9	0.0	5.3
Tyler	0.0	11.3	0.0	0.0	0.0	18.5	17.1	3.5	6.7	14.7
Victoria	0.0	29.4	0.0	0.0	0.0	15.1	11.6	3.8	1.2	5.0
Waco	0.0	2.2	0.0	0.0	2.2	10.3	12.3	7.5	1.0	48.3
Waxahachie	0.0	7.3	0.0	0.0	2.2	18.4	13.9	8.1	0.0	10.0
Weatherford	0.0	29.0	0.0	0.0	0.1	15.8	13.4	5.2	0.0	6.7
Weslaco	0.0	3.7	0.0	0.0	1.2	15.5	23.6	1.3	0.0	10.1
Wichita Falls	0.0	8.9	0.0	0.0	4.1	17.6	17.4	5.8	5.2	1.7
Wylie	0.0	21.8	0.0	0.0	0.5	9.5	11.2	16.0	0.0	9.1
UTAH	X	X	X	X	X	X	X	X	X	X
American Fork	0.0	15.1	0.0	0.0	4.9	14.4	17.4	12.8	0.9	3.0
Bountiful	0.0	19.3	0.0	0.0	0.0	26.9	15.0	11.0	3.2	0.7
Cedar City	0.0	17.1	0.0	0.0	0.0	18.7	14.8	18.3	3.1	4.1
Clearfield	0.0	8.5	0.0	0.0	0.0	19.0	14.3	16.1	2.4	4.6
Cottonwood Heights	0.0	31.0	0.0	0.0	0.0	0.9	1.2	1.1	0.0	0.0
Draper	0.0	22.1	0.0	0.0	0.6	12.1	7.5	9.8	9.4	3.2
Holladay	0.0	9.9	0.0	0.0	0.0	21.1	1.5	5.1	20.2	6.0

Table D. Cities — **City Government Finances, City Government Employment, and Climate**

City	City government finances, 2012 (cont.) Debt outstanding — Total (mil dol)	Per capita[1] (dollars)	Debt issued during year	Climate[2] Average daily temperature (degrees Fahrenheit) Mean January	July	Limits January[3]	July[4]	Annual precipitation (inches)	Heating degree days	Cooling degree days
	137	138	139	140	141	142	143	144	145	146
TEXAS—Cont'd										
Irving	567.8	2 515	137.2	45.9	86.5	36.4	96.1	37.05	2 219	2 878
Keller	128.2	3 054	0.0	43.0	84.1	31.4	95.7	34.12	2 608	2 358
Killeen	238.9	1 773	75.1	46.0	83.5	34.0	95.3	32.88	2 190	2 477
Kingsville	28.3	1 072	10.0	55.9	84.3	43.4	95.5	29.03	1 001	3 404
Kyle	69.4	2 246	7.7	NA	NA	NA	NA	NA	NA	NA
Lake Jackson	42.1	1 549	0.0	54.0	83.7	45.4	90.2	50.66	1 234	3 003
Lancaster	96.3	2 540	0.0	44.4	84.0	33.3	95.7	38.69	2 380	2 452
La Porte	45.1	1 307	0.0	51.6	83.6	41.9	91.6	53.75	1 471	2 841
Laredo	576.1	2 347	109.7	55.6	88.5	43.7	101.6	21.53	931	4 213
League City	210.1	2 379	39.8	52.7	82.7	43.1	91.2	51.73	1 365	2 815
Leander	176.0	5 952	0.0	NA	NA	NA	NA	NA	NA	NA
Lewisville	244.1	2 452	15.1	42.7	83.6	32.0	94.1	37.79	2 650	2 269
Little Elm	74.2	2 564	0.0	NA	NA	NA	NA	NA	NA	NA
Longview	160.6	1 975	39.2	45.4	83.4	33.7	94.5	49.06	2 319	2 355
Lubbock	1 342.1	5 681	257.0	38.1	79.8	24.4	91.9	18.69	3 508	1 769
Lufkin	179.5	4 983	21.3	48.6	82.6	37.9	93.5	46.62	1 900	2 480
McAllen	182.6	1 349	18.6	58.7	85.1	48.2	95.5	22.61	719	3 898
McKinney	313.4	2 184	16.9	41.8	82.4	31.1	92.7	41.01	2 843	2 060
Mansfield	183.2	3 084	26.8	43.7	84.3	33.2	94.9	34.54	2 437	2 508
Mesquite	242.0	1 687	42.9	45.9	86.5	36.4	96.1	37.05	2 219	2 878
Midland	125.3	1 046	6.0	44.5	81.8	29.5	95.6	14.84	2 479	2 241
Mission	387.2	4 787	51.7	58.8	86.3	47.5	97.7	22.13	740	4 128
Missouri City	174.1	2 535	5.1	51.8	84.1	41.6	93.7	49.34	1 475	2 950
Nacogdoches	62.8	1 856	1.7	46.5	83.9	36.4	93.5	48.36	2 150	2 555
New Braunfels	122.5	2 004	19.1	48.6	82.7	35.5	94.7	35.74	1 840	2 545
North Richland Hills	95.6	1 463	9.4	44.1	85.0	34.0	95.4	34.73	2 370	2 568
Odessa	124.0	1 168	0.0	43.2	81.7	29.6	94.3	14.80	2 716	2 139
Paris	25.2	1 004	0.0	40.6	83.1	29.9	94.3	47.82	2 972	2 197
Pasadena	223.9	1 467	34.6	54.3	84.5	45.2	93.6	53.96	1 174	3 179
Pearland	497.5	5 162	21.5	54.3	84.5	45.2	93.6	53.96	1 174	3 179
Pflugerville	167.6	3 224	21.9	NA	NA	NA	NA	NA	NA	NA
Pharr	103.3	1 410	2.2	60.1	85.9	50.3	96.1	22.96	624	4 181
Plano	352.8	1 293	21.4	44.1	85.0	34.0	95.4	34.73	2 370	2 568
Port Arthur	88.1	1 615	9.5	52.2	82.7	42.9	91.6	59.89	1 447	2 823
Richardson	311.9	3 007	21.2	45.9	86.5	36.4	96.1	37.05	2 219	2 878
Rockwall	163.4	4 091	17.3	NA	NA	NA	NA	NA	NA	NA
Rosenberg	52.3	1 608	15.4	NA	NA	NA	NA	NA	NA	NA
Round Rock	260.2	2 439	16.1	47.2	83.8	35.1	95.7	36.42	1 998	2 584
Rowlett	119.6	2 070	9.2	42.1	82.8	30.8	94.2	40.06	2 710	2 212
San Angelo	234.6	2 440	163.8	44.9	82.4	31.8	94.4	20.91	2 396	2 383
San Antonio	8 830.9	6 374	589.4	50.3	84.3	38.6	94.6	32.92	1 573	3 038
San Juan	24.6	697	5.9	60.1	85.9	50.3	96.1	22.96	624	4 181
San Marcos	264.7	5 283	17.2	49.9	84.4	38.6	95.1	37.19	1 629	2 913
Schertz	73.9	2 118	13.8	NA	NA	NA	NA	NA	NA	NA
Seguin	172.6	6 568	18.6	NA	NA	NA	NA	NA	NA	NA
Sherman	23.5	602	0.0	41.5	82.8	32.2	92.7	42.04	2 850	2 137
Socorro	12.3	374	8.1	44.9	83.6	29.2	98.7	9.71	2 557	2 372
Southlake	179.6	6 478	11.1	NA	NA	NA	NA	NA	NA	NA
Sugar Land	363.3	4 437	130.2	51.8	84.1	41.6	93.7	49.34	1 475	2 950
Temple	177.8	2 572	24.1	46.1	83.7	34.9	95.0	35.81	2 191	2 551
Texarkana	69.8	1 880	0.0	41.6	82.6	30.7	93.1	51.24	2 893	2 138
Texas City	91.3	1 997	31.9	55.8	84.3	49.7	88.7	43.84	1 008	3 268
The Colony	97.6	2 499	7.6	42.7	83.6	32.0	94.1	37.79	2 650	2 269
Tyler	428.2	4 307	9.4	47.5	83.4	37.7	93.6	45.27	1 958	2 521
Victoria	179.1	2 780	9.7	53.2	84.2	43.6	93.4	40.10	1 248	3 203
Waco	8 413.1	65 880	7.3	46.1	85.4	35.1	96.7	33.34	2 164	2 840
Waxahachie	170.0	5 475	0.0	NA	NA	NA	NA	NA	NA	NA
Weatherford	117.6	4 447	33.5	NA	NA	NA	NA	NA	NA	NA
Weslaco	115.6	3 134	11.5	58.6	84.5	47.7	95.4	25.37	755	3 791
Wichita Falls	168.4	1 607	0.0	40.5	84.8	28.9	97.2	28.83	3 024	2 396
Wylie	119.8	2 699	5.4	NA	NA	NA	NA	NA	NA	NA
UTAH	X	X	X	X	X	X	X	X	X	X
American Fork	62.3	2 284	1.7	NA	NA	NA	NA	NA	NA	NA
Bountiful	18.1	421	0.0	29.1	75.8	21.6	88.4	22.40	5 937	861
Cedar City	21.1	725	0.0	NA	NA	NA	NA	NA	NA	NA
Clearfield	24.6	809	0.0	27.6	74.2	18.6	89.9	20.75	6 142	746
Cottonwood Heights	0.0	0	0.0	NA	NA	NA	NA	NA	NA	NA
Draper	33.1	749	0.0	31.6	78.0	22.0	95.3	15.76	5 251	1 172
Holladay	20.8	770	9.2	NA	NA	NA	NA	NA	NA	NA

1. Based on the population estimated as of July 1 of the year shown.   2. Represents normal values based on the 30-year period, 1971–2000.   3. Average daily minimum.
4. Average daily maximum.

Table D. Cities — **Land Area and Population**

STATE Place code	City	Land area,[1] 2010 (sq km)	Total persons	Rank	Per square kilometer	White	Black	American Indian, Alaska Native	Asian	Hawaiian Pacific Islander	Percent Hispanic or Latino[2] 2010-2014	Percent foreign born 2010-2014
		1	2	3	4	5	6	7	8	9	10	11
	UTAH—Cont'd											
49 40360	Kaysville	27.1	30 472	1 226	1 124.4	97.1	0.9	0.6	1.4	0.1	3.8	2.3
49 43660	Layton	57.0	74 143	464	1 300.8	91.4	2.1	1.4	4.0	1.2	11.1	6.6
49 44320	Lehi	68.2	58 486	634	857.6	95.2	0.3	0.7	1.7	1.3	7.8	4.2
49 45860	Logan	46.5	50 371	746	1 083.2	87.8	1.5	1.3	4.4	0.8	14.9	11.2
49 49710	Midvale	15.4	32 613	1 154	2 117.7	86.7	3.1	1.0	4.1	1.5	23.9	15.2
49 53230	Murray	31.8	49 250	767	1 548.7	91.5	2.5	1.3	1.8	1.2	10.8	7.5
49 55980	Ogden	70.2	85 444	382	1 217.2	83.3	2.6	2.1	2.4	0.5	29.8	12.8
49 57300	Orem	47.4	94 457	326	1 992.8	91.6	1.7	1.3	2.9	1.7	15.6	10.8
49 60930	Pleasant Grove	23.7	38 052	986	1 605.6	97.6	0.6	0.9	1.5	0.5	8.5	3.8
49 62470	Provo	107.9	115 264	240	1 068.2	90.5	1.3	1.1	3.9	2.1	16.8	11.1
49 64340	Riverton	32.7	41 900	892	1 281.3	95.8	0.8	0.4	1.9	1.2	5.6	2.8
49 65110	Roy	20.5	37 964	989	1 851.9	91.8	1.6	1.1	2.4	1.1	15.2	5.9
49 65330	St. George	182.3	80 202	418	439.9	93.4	1.3	2.0	1.5	1.2	13.0	8.5
49 67000	Salt Lake City	287.8	192 672	124	669.5	76.7	3.5	2.2	6.2	2.3	20.9	17.5
49 67440	Sandy	59.2	93 613	332	1 581.3	93.0	1.0	0.5	4.1	1.0	8.2	6.9
49 70850	South Jordan	57.1	66 648	532	1 167.2	95.0	0.9	0.4	3.8	1.7	5.1	4.5
49 71290	Spanish Fork	39.9	37 935	992	950.8	96.5	0.9	1.3	0.5	0.7	10.1	6.2
49 72280	Springville	37.3	32 286	1 167	865.6	94.6	0.5	2.2	2.6	1.3	9.5	6.8
49 75360	Taylorsville	28.1	60 514	601	2 153.5	84.4	3.1	1.5	4.5	2.6	20.5	14.3
49 76680	Tooele	55.6	33 157	1 134	596.3	92.4	1.4	2.8	1.2	0.9	13.7	3.4
49 82950	West Jordan	84.1	111 946	253	1 331.1	89.6	1.9	2.0	3.2	2.0	18.8	9.6
49 83470	West Valley City	92.1	136 208	192	1 478.9	72.0	2.9	1.8	6.5	4.7	36.0	22.0
50 00000	**VERMONT**	23 871.0	626 042	X	26.2	96.9	1.6	1.2	1.8	0.1	1.6	4.2
50 10675	Burlington	26.7	42 452	880	1 590.0	89.7	4.7	1.3	6.4	0.2	2.7	10.2
51 00000	**VIRGINIA**	102 278.9	8 382 993	X	82.0	71.9	20.8	1.0	7.0	0.2	8.4	11.6
51 01000	Alexandria	38.9	153 511	166	3 946.3	67.3	23.2	1.0	8.0	0.1	16.5	26.6
51 07784	Blacksburg	51.5	44 215	845	858.5	81.5	5.7	0.7	13.5	0.1	4.1	17.0
51 14968	Charlottesville	26.5	46 597	814	1 758.4	72.5	20.6	0.4	8.1	0.2	4.9	11.8
51 16000	Chesapeake	882.7	235 429	94	266.7	64.9	31.2	1.1	4.5	0.3	4.9	4.7
51 21344	Danville	111.2	42 082	887	378.4	48.6	49.8	0.5	1.3	0.1	3.1	3.4
51 35000	Hampton	133.2	136 454	191	1 024.4	45.3	52.1	1.3	3.3	0.1	5.0	4.9
51 35624	Harrisonburg	45.1	52 538	712	1 164.9	87.3	8.6	0.6	4.7	0.1	17.3	15.5
51 44984	Leesburg	32.1	51 209	742	1 595.3	76.8	9.3	0.2	10.4	0.2	19.1	22.5
51 47672	Lynchburg	127.2	79 812	422	627.5	67.4	30.3	0.9	3.3	0.0	3.2	5.1
51 48952	Manassas	25.6	41 764	895	1 631.4	76.5	17.0	0.8	6.3	0.0	32.5	26.9
51 56000	Newport News	178.0	182 385	132	1 024.6	54.0	42.8	1.7	4.2	0.5	8.0	7.7
51 57000	Norfolk	140.2	246 393	86	1 757.4	50.7	44.7	1.3	4.5	0.5	7.1	6.8
51 61832	Petersburg	59.4	32 477	1 159	546.8	19.8	79.0	0.9	1.3	0.4	4.1	3.6
51 64000	Portsmouth	87.2	96 201	316	1 103.2	43.4	54.8	1.2	1.8	0.2	3.5	2.6
51 67000	Richmond	154.9	220 289	98	1 422.1	46.4	51.2	1.9	2.9	0.1	6.4	7.0
51 68000	Roanoke	110.2	99 897	302	906.5	68.0	30.4	1.3	2.5	0.2	5.7	7.3
51 76432	Suffolk	1 036.4	88 161	362	85.1	54.9	44.3	1.4	2.5	0.2	3.3	3.3
51 82000	Virginia Beach	645.0	452 745	41	701.9	71.8	21.7	1.2	8.1	0.4	7.2	8.9
51 86720	Winchester	23.9	27 284	1 349	1 141.6	83.1	12.4	1.3	2.9	0.1	16.0	11.2
53 00000	**WASHINGTON**	172 119.0	7 170 351	X	41.7	82.5	5.1	3.0	9.5	1.1	11.7	13.3
53 03180	Auburn	76.7	77 006	440	1 004.0	75.5	8.0	4.1	12.0	2.4	14.6	18.3
53 05210	Bellevue	82.8	139 820	189	1 688.6	65.0	3.5	1.1	32.3	0.6	6.6	34.6
53 05280	Bellingham	70.1	85 146	384	1 214.6	89.3	2.4	3.0	7.4	0.3	8.3	10.2
53 07380	Bothell	31.4	42 939	870	1 367.5	82.6	2.4	1.3	15.4	0.3	7.5	16.7
53 07695	Bremerton	73.6	39 520	949	537.0	81.0	8.3	4.7	6.5	1.7	11.7	8.0
53 08850	Burien	19.2	50 467	745	2 628.5	71.5	10.0	4.1	12.9	2.1	23.6	24.0
53 17635	Des Moines	16.8	31 221	1 191	1 858.4	69.5	10.3	3.0	17.0	2.1	16.6	24.0
53 20750	Edmonds	23.1	41 375	903	1 791.1	86.0	3.4	1.0	11.6	0.7	4.5	13.9
53 22640	Everett	86.6	108 010	272	1 247.2	81.5	7.0	3.1	10.2	1.6	16.1	18.1
53 23515	Federal Way	57.7	95 171	319	1 649.4	66.6	13.2	2.9	17.3	2.3	17.3	23.7
53 33805	Issaquah	29.5	36 081	1 047	1 223.1	80.2	4.0	0.7	18.2	0.6	5.8	19.2
53 35275	Kennewick	69.8	78 896	428	1 130.3	78.1	3.1	1.7	3.5	0.4	24.6	12.3
53 35415	Kent	74.1	126 952	216	1 713.3	62.8	12.5	2.0	20.6	3.8	15.9	26.7
53 35940	Kirkland	27.9	87 281	370	3 128.4	83.0	2.9	1.8	16.0	0.4	6.4	20.0
53 36745	Lacey	41.6	46 409	816	1 115.6	77.6	8.4	2.6	12.5	2.7	8.2	11.6
53 37900	Lake Stevens	23.0	30 886	1 202	1 342.9	93.2	1.3	3.0	4.9	0.7	8.7	6.3
53 38038	Lakewood	44.5	59 829	614	1 344.5	69.6	13.8	4.2	12.0	4.0	16.8	15.9
53 40245	Longview	37.5	36 848	1 023	982.6	93.7	1.8	4.3	3.5	1.1	9.0	5.7
53 40840	Lynnwood	20.3	36 997	1 021	1 822.5	68.8	7.2	3.3	20.8	1.0	13.3	28.4
53 43955	Marysville	53.6	66 773	531	1 245.8	86.7	3.2	2.7	8.4	1.6	9.7	9.6
53 47560	Mount Vernon	31.9	34 053	1 101	1 067.5	83.1	1.1	1.7	3.8	0.5	34.3	17.5
53 51300	Olympia	46.2	50 302	747	1 088.8	89.2	2.2	2.2	7.5	0.8	7.8	8.3

1. Dry land or land partially or temporarily covered by water.   2. May be of any race.

Table D. Cities — **Population**

City	Under 5 years	5 to 17 years	18 to 24 years	25 to 34 years	35 to 44 years	45 to 54 years	55 to 64 years	65 to 74 years	75 years and over	Median age 2010–2014	Percent female 2010–2014	Census counts 2000	Census counts 2010	Percent change 2000–2010	Percent change 2010–2015
	12	13	14	15	16	17	18	19	20	21	22	23	24	25	26
UTAH—Cont'd															
Kaysville	9.2	27.0	8.9	12.1	14.7	12.0	9.4	3.8	2.9	29.4	50.4	20 351	27 300	34.1	10.4
Layton	9.8	21.7	10.8	16.4	12.7	10.6	10.2	4.3	3.5	29.6	49.4	58 474	67 311	15.1	9.8
Lehi	13.9	29.5	8.7	15.8	14.3	7.3	5.6	2.9	2.0	23.8	48.7	19 028	47 407	149.1	22.5
Logan	9.3	15.0	30.8	19.1	8.7	5.9	5.2	2.9	3.3	23.9	51.5	42 670	48 174	12.9	4.5
Midvale	6.5	17.9	10.7	23.4	12.8	10.0	8.8	5.3	4.5	30.9	51.3	27 029	27 964	3.5	16.5
Murray	5.8	15.7	11.5	16.2	12.8	11.4	12.6	7.0	7.1	35.5	50.6	34 024	46 746	37.4	5.4
Ogden	9.6	17.9	12.2	18.4	11.5	10.9	9.6	5.1	4.8	30.3	48.8	77 226	82 825	7.3	3.2
Orem	10.8	19.4	16.9	17.3	9.3	9.0	8.6	5.0	3.5	26.6	50.3	84 324	88 328	4.7	6.9
Pleasant Grove	11.8	26.8	12.1	14.0	13.5	9.3	6.0	3.8	2.6	24.6	50.4	23 468	33 509	42.8	13.4
Provo	8.7	14.7	34.7	18.0	7.5	5.4	5.2	2.7	3.0	23.6	50.4	105 166	112 488	7.0	2.5
Riverton	11.1	26.0	8.2	15.8	13.3	11.8	8.2	3.2	2.5	28.7	50.0	25 011	38 753	54.9	7.9
Roy	8.6	23.2	7.8	15.9	14.7	11.7	8.0	5.7	4.5	31.3	50.0	32 885	36 884	12.2	3.0
St. George	7.8	20.6	10.7	12.4	10.2	9.2	10.3	9.7	9.2	33.7	51.2	49 663	72 897	46.8	10.2
Salt Lake City	7.4	14.7	13.2	20.8	13.4	11.2	9.5	5.2	4.7	31.7	48.5	181 743	186 440	2.6	3.3
Sandy	7.1	21.2	8.6	13.3	13.7	13.0	12.5	6.9	3.6	34.8	49.9	88 418	87 461	-1.1	5.5
South Jordan	8.4	25.3	8.7	14.8	13.6	11.7	9.7	4.6	3.3	30.1	49.4	29 437	50 418	71.3	32.0
Spanish Fork	10.6	29.3	10.3	17.8	12.4	8.8	5.0	3.3	2.4	24.9	48.9	20 246	34 691	71.3	9.2
Springville	12.4	24.3	13.2	14.6	12.4	8.3	6.8	4.0	4.1	25.1	49.4	20 424	29 466	44.3	9.5
Taylorsville	9.3	18.7	9.5	17.6	12.4	11.2	11.2	6.1	3.8	31.6	51.3	57 439	58 652	2.1	3.1
Tooele	8.8	25.0	8.9	14.6	14.7	10.7	9.3	4.6	3.4	30.3	50.7	22 502	31 605	40.5	4.9
West Jordan	9.8	23.9	10.0	15.7	15.3	11.7	8.2	3.4	2.0	29.6	49.5	68 336	103 712	51.8	8.0
West Valley City	9.7	22.5	10.0	16.9	13.9	11.2	8.7	4.6	2.4	29.9	49.7	108 896	129 480	18.9	5.2
VERMONT	4.9	15.0	10.6	11.3	11.9	15.5	15.1	8.9	6.8	42.2	50.7	608 827	625 741	2.8	0.0
Burlington	3.2	8.9	34.0	16.6	9.2	9.3	8.4	5.1	5.3	26.9	50.1	38 889	42 417	9.1	0.1
VIRGINIA	6.2	16.5	10.1	13.9	13.4	14.7	12.3	7.5	5.4	37.6	50.9	7 078 515	8 001 024	13.0	4.8
Alexandria	7.4	10.1	6.4	24.4	17.9	13.4	10.9	5.6	3.9	35.8	51.5	128 283	139 966	9.1	9.6
Blacksburg	3.2	6.4	57.6	11.9	5.9	5.4	4.6	2.7	2.3	21.9	44.9	39 573	42 620	7.7	3.8
Charlottesville	5.4	9.7	25.1	20.0	11.3	9.7	9.7	5.1	4.1	29.0	51.7	45 049	43 475	-3.5	7.3
Chesapeake	6.3	18.7	9.4	13.3	13.4	15.8	11.9	6.5	4.6	36.6	51.2	199 184	222 209	11.6	5.9
Danville	6.8	15.0	9.7	11.7	10.2	13.3	14.4	9.3	9.6	41.8	54.3	48 411	43 055	-11.1	-2.3
Hampton	6.2	15.9	12.5	14.5	11.1	14.4	12.4	7.3	5.6	35.6	51.9	146 437	137 436	-6.1	-0.8
Harrisonburg	4.8	10.9	38.2	14.6	9.3	7.6	7.0	3.7	4.0	22.8	53.0	40 468	48 914	20.9	7.4
Leesburg	7.4	21.7	7.9	15.0	15.6	16.8	9.3	3.7	2.7	33.8	50.5	28 311	42 616	50.5	20.2
Lynchburg	6.1	13.6	23.8	12.9	9.0	10.8	10.2	6.8	7.0	29.2	52.8	65 269	75 568	15.8	5.6
Manassas	8.4	19.1	10.2	16.5	13.3	15.0	9.4	5.1	3.1	32.7	50.9	35 135	37 821	7.6	10.4
Newport News	7.5	16.3	13.1	16.4	11.7	13.3	10.6	6.2	5.0	32.7	51.7	180 150	180 719	0.3	0.8
Norfolk	6.9	13.6	19.3	18.1	11.2	11.6	9.8	5.1	4.5	29.9	47.9	234 403	242 803	3.6	1.5
Petersburg	8.1	13.1	11.1	13.2	10.7	15.1	13.8	8.1	6.8	39.9	53.7	33 740	32 420	-3.9	0.2
Portsmouth	7.6	16.0	10.9	15.7	11.4	13.3	11.8	7.1	6.3	34.9	51.7	100 565	95 535	-5.0	0.7
Richmond	6.4	12.2	15.3	19.2	11.5	12.4	11.7	6.0	5.3	32.7	52.4	197 790	204 214	3.2	7.9
Roanoke	7.3	14.5	8.7	15.3	13.0	13.9	13.1	7.3	6.9	38.0	52.3	94 911	97 032	2.2	3.1
Suffolk	6.7	18.7	9.0	12.0	13.8	15.6	12.1	7.1	4.9	38.2	51.8	63 677	84 585	32.8	4.2
Virginia Beach	6.7	16.7	10.6	16.2	13.1	14.2	11.2	6.5	4.9	34.9	50.9	425 257	437 994	3.0	3.4
Winchester	6.7	16.2	11.8	14.8	11.8	13.1	11.6	7.1	6.9	35.4	50.6	23 585	26 203	11.1	4.1
WASHINGTON	6.4	16.6	9.7	14.1	13.2	13.9	12.8	7.6	5.6	37.4	50.1	5 894 121	6 724 540	14.1	6.6
Auburn	6.9	17.3	9.9	13.2	14.5	13.1	12.9	6.5	5.7	37.0	51.6	40 314	70 180	74.1	9.7
Bellevue	6.0	14.3	6.8	17.6	15.2	14.1	12.1	7.1	6.9	37.9	48.5	109 569	122 363	11.7	9.3
Bellingham	5.4	11.0	23.9	15.3	10.3	9.3	11.9	6.7	6.2	31.0	51.0	67 171	80 885	20.4	5.3
Bothell	5.5	16.6	7.3	12.0	17.6	15.5	12.4	7.2	6.1	40.2	50.9	30 150	33 505	11.1	11.1
Bremerton	7.2	11.9	17.9	19.6	11.2	10.8	10.3	6.6	4.5	30.8	46.0	37 259	37 729	1.3	4.5
Burien	7.3	16.3	9.0	13.8	12.7	16.0	11.6	8.1	5.3	38.4	49.0	31 881	33 313	4.5	5.0
Des Moines	5.9	14.1	11.0	17.6	11.5	13.6	12.5	5.9	7.8	36.2	48.2	29 267	29 673	1.4	5.2
Edmonds	5.1	12.1	6.9	10.3	11.9	14.7	19.1	10.6	9.3	48.1	53.2	39 515	39 709	0.5	4.2
Everett	7.5	14.4	11.1	17.2	13.2	14.7	11.2	5.9	4.8	34.9	48.9	91 488	103 019	12.6	4.8
Federal Way	6.8	17.5	11.2	13.5	12.6	14.9	11.8	6.3	5.4	35.8	51.2	83 259	89 306	7.3	6.6
Issaquah	7.5	17.4	5.5	15.4	16.0	17.0	9.7	4.9	6.4	37.5	52.2	11 212	30 434	171.4	18.6
Kennewick	8.2	19.3	10.2	14.6	13.1	12.5	10.5	6.1	5.5	33.2	50.1	54 693	73 917	35.1	6.8
Kent	7.6	18.3	9.7	16.0	14.1	14.3	10.4	5.7	3.8	33.9	49.4	79 524	92 411	16.2	7.0
Kirkland	6.9	15.2	6.8	17.6	15.3	15.1	12.0	6.8	4.2	37.2	51.0	45 054	48 787	8.3	8.3
Lacey	7.5	16.7	9.7	17.0	14.6	9.6	10.4	7.1	7.5	33.9	51.2	31 226	42 393	35.8	9.5
Lake Stevens	8.0	20.1	7.9	14.3	17.1	14.3	10.3	4.7	3.4	34.8	48.5	6 361	28 069	341.3	10.1
Lakewood	6.9	14.2	10.0	16.0	10.5	13.9	13.9	7.7	6.8	37.3	51.5	58 211	58 163	-0.1	2.9
Longview	5.7	16.1	7.3	13.0	11.8	13.7	14.1	9.5	8.9	41.6	52.1	34 660	36 648	5.7	0.0
Lynnwood	4.3	16.7	9.2	16.4	13.5	13.0	12.7	6.8	7.4	37.4	48.4	33 847	35 836	5.9	3.2
Marysville	8.3	18.7	9.2	15.4	14.1	13.6	10.4	5.6	4.7	34.0	49.6	25 315	60 020	137.1	11.2
Mount Vernon	8.9	20.2	11.7	11.9	12.3	11.1	10.2	7.0	6.6	33.0	49.7	26 232	31 743	21.0	7.2
Olympia	5.7	13.6	11.7	15.2	13.7	13.8	12.7	7.1	6.5	37.3	52.2	42 514	46 478	9.3	7.3

Table D. Cities — Households, Group Quarters, Crime, and Education

City	Households, 2010-2014 Number	Persons per house-hold	Female family house-holder[1] Percent	One-person Percent	Persons in group quarters, 2010 Total	Institutional Total	Persons in nursing facilities	Non-institu-tional	Serious crimes known to police,[2] 2014 Total Number	Rate[3]	Violent	Property	Population age 25 and older	High school graduate or less	Bachelor's degree or more
	27	28	29	30	31	32	33	34	35	36	37	38	39	40	41
UTAH—Cont'd															
Kaysville	7 868	3.62	6.9	12.3	24	0	0	24	210	719	51	667	15 229	19.3	45.7
Layton	21 838	3.18	10.6	15.5	44	26	0	18	1 596	2 228	123	2 105	39 834	27.2	31.8
Lehi	13 355	3.89	7.4	9.3	107	16	16	91	749	1 336	68	1 268	25 426	21.0	39.1
Logan	15 839	3.09	8.6	21.2	3 529	502	160	3 027	819	1 670	71	1 598	22 200	29.0	36.9
Midvale	11 434	2.62	13.1	29.4	85	10	0	75	NA	NA	NA	NA	19 492	40.2	23.8
Murray	18 646	2.57	12.1	28.2	175	124	97	51	2 644	5 387	454	4 932	31 818	30.2	30.0
Ogden	29 454	2.84	14.7	27.1	2 061	1 421	260	640	4 169	4 930	538	4 392	50 454	47.5	18.6
Orem	25 884	3.50	11.0	14.8	1 790	461	301	1 329	1 992	2 156	43	2 112	47 291	25.0	35.6
Pleasant Grove	9 539	3.65	9.7	12.9	51	42	42	9	275	779	42	736	17 588	22.9	37.0
Provo	32 332	3.55	7.2	14.7	10 353	1 037	223	9 316	2 388	2 038	131	1 907	47 989	23.6	39.9
Riverton	11 044	3.65	7.9	8.6	45	14	14	31	NA	NA	NA	NA	22 725	24.2	31.4
Roy	12 345	3.04	10.3	19.7	124	115	93	9	806	2 125	111	2 015	22 473	39.6	19.8
St. George	25 736	2.93	8.5	22.3	1 053	648	303	405	1 631	2 095	145	1 950	46 445	32.4	28.1
Salt Lake City	74 652	2.54	9.6	36.3	4 795	822	539	3 973	17 728	9 216	755	8 461	121 718	30.7	42.1
Sandy	28 478	3.14	8.9	17.0	365	287	287	78	2 714	2 987	175	2 812	56 212	24.8	38.7
South Jordan	15 713	3.60	5.8	11.8	7	7	7	0	1 424	2 312	78	2 234	32 484	20.6	38.7
Spanish Fork	9 411	3.86	7.8	12.5	832	813	27	19	497	1 327	24	1 303	18 350	30.6	27.8
Springville	8 773	3.49	7.9	12.9	119	119	55	0	650	2 057	108	1 950	15 745	25.3	36.5
Taylorsville	19 570	3.06	13.4	22.9	112	82	82	30	NA	NA	NA	NA	37 730	38.8	20.5
Tooele	10 294	3.12	11.3	19.3	243	237	103	6	1 469	4 520	314	4 206	18 737	41.2	17.4
West Jordan	31 116	3.47	11.6	15.5	502	394	162	108	2 288	2 050	191	1 859	60 921	36.0	23.5
West Valley City	36 946	3.58	15.6	15.8	193	158	77	35	6 620	4 919	473	4 446	76 576	54.8	12.7
VERMONT	257 252	2.43	9.2	28.5	25 329	5 571	3 588	19 758	10 173	1 624	99	1 524	434 995	38.9	35.2
Burlington	16 337	2.59	8.6	36.1	7 060	539	476	6 521	1 455	3 444	137	3 306	23 074	29.2	49.1
VIRGINIA	3 041 710	2.69	12.4	26.5	239 834	101 333	30 324	138 501	177 060	2 127	196	1 930	5 501 125	37.1	35.8
Alexandria	65 916	2.22	8.1	42.7	1 827	974	506	853	3 263	2 160	185	1 975	111 478	20.6	61.5
Blacksburg	13 581	3.18	4.1	29.7	8 718	150	134	8 568	424	967	73	894	14 467	13.9	69.3
Charlottesville	17 604	2.53	10.4	37.0	2 438	228	167	2 210	1 550	3 477	431	3 047	26 533	33.5	49.3
Chesapeake	80 388	2.84	15.5	20.9	3 721	3 258	650	463	7 428	3 195	430	2 765	149 636	36.1	29.4
Danville	18 520	2.31	21.0	35.9	1 483	987	558	496	1 965	4 577	447	4 129	29 264	49.9	17.2
Hampton	52 700	2.60	18.2	30.9	4 454	902	516	3 552	4 790	3 507	256	3 251	89 527	37.5	23.3
Harrisonburg	15 881	3.20	9.4	26.3	7 583	681	378	6 902	1 257	2 416	198	2 218	23 420	43.3	35.6
Leesburg	15 098	3.06	10.8	18.7	256	247	247	9	788	1 611	121	1 490	29 015	28.0	49.4
Lynchburg	28 424	2.73	15.5	34.7	10 198	1 534	863	8 664	2 372	3 016	472	2 545	43 722	38.3	32.3
Manassas	12 274	3.29	14.5	20.3	46	0	0	46	866	2 031	326	1 705	25 239	44.3	29.1
Newport News	68 987	2.63	17.8	31.5	7 499	1 555	633	5 944	6 334	3 473	429	3 044	114 288	39.3	24.1
Norfolk	86 397	2.83	18.2	32.6	32 780	2 746	924	30 034	10 981	4 444	520	3 924	147 486	40.3	25.6
Petersburg	12 515	2.59	25.4	35.2	1 058	587	273	471	1 036	3 183	593	2 590	22 015	57.4	14.9
Portsmouth	36 764	2.61	21.8	30.4	3 416	2 541	454	875	5 451	5 653	610	5 043	63 228	46.5	19.5
Richmond	85 913	2.46	18.6	41.4	12 725	2 884	1 312	9 841	NA	NA	NA	NA	139 277	40.7	35.4
Roanoke	42 549	2.30	16.9	37.4	2 126	1 083	517	1 043	4 476	4 524	344	4 180	68 034	47.0	24.1
Suffolk	30 798	2.78	17.0	22.6	1 128	1 029	267	99	2 485	2 890	272	2 618	56 441	40.9	26.1
Virginia Beach	165 296	2.70	13.9	23.9	9 253	2 961	1 520	6 292	10 532	2 335	148	2 187	294 652	29.3	33.5
Winchester	10 692	2.53	13.2	33.2	976	157	125	819	1 171	4 261	313	3 948	17 755	47.2	28.1
WASHINGTON	2 645 396	2.61	10.3	27.8	139 375	57 844	22 156	81 531	281 842	3 991	285	3 706	4 645 804	33.2	32.3
Auburn	27 371	2.68	14.3	26.7	668	289	228	379	4 900	6 446	397	6 048	47 104	41.7	22.5
Bellevue	53 231	2.48	7.3	26.8	1 110	154	154	956	4 750	3 507	106	3 401	95 034	15.9	62.1
Bellingham	33 847	2.43	10.4	33.7	5 172	1 065	570	4 107	4 934	5 941	270	5 671	49 071	25.7	40.7
Bothell	13 922	2.51	6.9	26.9	321	188	188	133	1 130	3 131	72	3 059	24 690	23.0	45.5
Bremerton	15 347	2.52	12.2	38.0	4 255	428	350	3 827	2 025	5 145	528	4 616	24 678	35.2	19.4
Burien	18 266	2.70	12.4	29.2	300	209	119	91	2 632	5 234	511	4 723	33 062	42.9	23.1
Des Moines	11 347	2.68	12.2	30.4	596	382	382	214	1 274	4 120	388	3 731	21 433	41.8	23.0
Edmonds	17 440	2.31	8.9	30.9	476	220	220	256	1 231	3 004	134	2 870	30 341	19.6	47.1
Everett	41 500	2.52	12.0	36.6	4 145	1 706	404	2 439	7 311	6 903	344	6 559	70 026	39.6	21.0
Federal Way	34 064	2.69	15.3	25.0	831	445	421	386	5 944	6 354	386	5 968	59 568	37.8	25.7
Issaquah	13 869	2.35	8.1	30.9	443	242	242	201	1 103	3 209	52	3 157	23 217	12.0	60.1
Kennewick	27 250	2.79	12.8	27.6	1 081	930	200	151	2 617	3 382	246	3 136	47 068	41.4	22.3
Kent	42 457	2.89	14.5	26.5	1 390	888	86	502	6 634	5 272	288	4 984	77 924	41.6	24.3
Kirkland	34 762	2.40	7.4	29.9	630	175	150	455	2 122	2 486	100	2 387	60 180	15.7	55.6
Lacey	17 346	2.54	12.1	28.8	998	207	204	791	1 507	3 310	182	3 128	29 530	30.5	31.0
Lake Stevens	10 026	2.92	12.9	18.7	29	5	5	24	830	2 731	165	2 567	18 418	35.7	22.2
Lakewood	24 107	2.44	12.3	36.9	1 268	992	152	276	2 860	4 822	644	4 178	39 927	39.1	21.3
Longview	15 266	2.40	12.5	35.5	962	769	389	193	2 453	6 728	365	6 363	25 802	41.6	15.5
Lynnwood	13 919	2.61	12.1	30.7	618	237	195	381	2 654	7 245	273	6 972	25 230	37.8	26.4
Marysville	22 456	2.78	11.1	23.5	600	225	191	375	2 897	4 522	175	4 347	40 473	39.0	18.1
Mount Vernon	11 308	2.86	16.0	24.4	639	399	173	240	1 595	4 862	265	4 597	19 507	44.7	20.3
Olympia	20 657	2.32	11.2	37.1	1 283	942	415	341	2 389	4 899	410	4 489	33 262	24.2	43.4

1. No spouse present. 2. Data for serious crimes have not been adjusted for underreporting. This may affect comparability between geographic areas and over time. 3. Per 100,000 population estimated by the FBI. 4. Persons 25 years old and over.

Table D. Cities — Income, Poverty, and Housing

City	Money income, 2010–2014					Housing units, 2010			Occupied housing units 2010–2014				
	Per capita income[1] (dollars)	Households			Families with income below poverty (percent)	Total	Percent change, 2000–2010	Vacant units for sale or rent[2]	Owner-occupied			Median owner costs as a percent of income	
		Median income	Percent with income of $200,000 or more	Percent with income of less than $25,000					Total	Percent	Median value[3] (dollars)	With a mortgage[4]	Without a mortgage[5]
	42	43	44	45	46	47	48	49	50	51	52	53	54
UTAH—Cont'd													
Kaysville	27 702	86 982	5.9	11.2	6.1	7 700	35.3	176	7 868	86.3	268 900	22.2	10.0
Layton	25 984	66 665	3.9	14.0	7.5	22 356	16.8	981	21 838	74.9	200 200	21.8	10.0
Lehi	22 510	74 200	3.5	9.1	5.6	13 064	146.5	662	13 355	80.9	242 900	23.7	10.0
Logan	17 438	35 770	1.9	33.1	17.7	16 790	14.0	962	15 839	42.3	163 600	24.2	10.0
Midvale	23 716	51 077	1.9	22.2	13.5	11 764	9.6	851	11 434	45.2	194 200	25.4	11.1
Murray	29 013	53 797	3.7	21.1	9.3	19 181	44.1	955	18 646	63.9	225 300	22.9	10.0
Ogden	19 475	40 937	1.7	28.0	17.4	32 482	9.1	2 851	29 454	54.9	131 200	24.1	10.1
Orem	20 621	54 048	2.9	20.4	13.4	26 970	11.6	1 154	25 884	60.9	202 000	22.9	10.0
Pleasant Grove	20 257	62 660	2.3	14.4	8.6	9 841	55.1	460	9 539	67.3	221 400	23.8	10.0
Provo	17 539	40 359	2.4	31.3	20.3	33 212	9.2	1 688	32 332	42.1	200 300	24.0	10.0
Riverton	28 093	84 718	6.3	4.3	2.1	10 810	63.9	350	11 044	89.0	269 600	24.3	10.0
Roy	22 114	60 100	0.9	14.5	8.4	12 599	14.3	425	12 345	84.4	159 300	23.2	10.0
St. George	22 230	48 188	3.0	23.1	11.1	32 089	52.2	6 569	25 736	64.7	212 000	26.7	10.0
Salt Lake City	28 428	45 833	5.0	28.4	14.5	80 724	4.8	6 211	74 652	48.4	235 200	23.3	10.0
Sandy	31 552	78 048	7.2	11.4	6.0	29 501	10.8	1 205	28 478	77.0	272 300	22.5	10.0
South Jordan	29 964	91 228	8.0	5.5	2.9	14 943	92.5	610	15 713	81.3	324 100	23.2	10.0
Spanish Fork	19 133	63 376	1.5	11.7	4.8	9 440	62.3	371	9 411	77.3	191 800	23.9	10.0
Springville	20 510	59 375	2.0	13.2	5.3	8 927	42.7	396	8 773	70.5	195 300	24.9	10.0
Taylorsville	23 224	57 779	1.9	17.4	9.7	20 671	7.8	910	19 570	69.0	186 700	23.0	10.0
Tooele	21 596	56 370	1.2	14.7	7.7	10 646	33.6	687	10 294	74.9	160 400	23.1	10.0
West Jordan	22 808	69 404	1.7	11.4	7.7	31 366	60.2	1 517	31 116	76.4	220 900	24.0	10.0
West Valley City	18 179	52 814	1.3	18.7	17.0	38 978	16.4	1 839	36 946	68.8	167 300	24.5	10.0
VERMONT	29 535	54 447	3.6	21.8	7.8	322 539	9.6	66 097	257 252	70.9	216 200	24.9	16.7
Burlington	25 234	42 745	3.1	31.7	12.9	16 897	3.1	778	16 337	40.6	256 700	24.4	16.6
VIRGINIA	33 958	64 792	8.0	18.3	8.2	3 364 939	15.9	308 881	3 041 710	66.7	243 500	23.2	10.8
Alexandria	54 597	87 319	14.5	10.6	6.6	72 376	12.6	4 294	65 916	42.7	494 400	22.2	11.6
Blacksburg	18 323	29 271	4.3	46.4	12.8	15 342	12.5	887	13 581	28.3	266 900	19.4	10.0
Charlottesville	28 285	47 218	4.9	30.2	11.4	19 189	9.1	1 411	17 604	41.6	283 100	21.8	13.2
Chesapeake	29 735	70 176	4.5	14.8	7.6	83 196	14.5	3 622	80 388	71.7	254 900	25.8	12.4
Danville	20 569	32 173	1.7	39.5	21.0	22 438	-2.9	3 607	18 520	54.1	88 300	22.5	11.9
Hampton	25 131	49 879	1.8	23.8	12.1	59 566	3.9	4 535	52 700	58.8	191 800	25.0	13.0
Harrisonburg	17 919	38 807	1.8	32.2	12.0	17 444	27.4	1 456	15 881	35.7	200 700	22.1	10.2
Leesburg	39 533	101 719	13.0	6.8	4.3	15 119	41.7	678	15 098	68.2	377 100	23.6	10.0
Lynchburg	21 236	39 391	2.4	33.5	17.2	31 992	15.7	3 516	28 424	52.1	147 900	22.9	11.9
Manassas	28 646	71 215	6.2	12.8	10.2	13 123	8.3	596	12 274	64.7	257 500	23.5	12.6
Newport News	25 408	51 000	2.4	22.2	12.0	76 198	2.8	5 534	68 987	50.6	194 600	24.4	12.5
Norfolk	24 252	44 150	2.5	27.9	15.8	95 018	0.6	8 533	86 397	43.7	196 700	27.7	14.0
Petersburg	18 535	33 927	0.5	38.3	22.4	16 326	2.3	2 692	12 515	44.6	114 100	25.0	13.1
Portsmouth	23 219	46 239	1.7	26.4	14.5	40 806	-1.9	3 482	36 764	55.8	173 700	27.6	15.8
Richmond	27 860	41 331	4.2	32.4	20.0	98 349	6.6	11 198	85 913	42.7	195 000	25.7	15.0
Roanoke	23 565	39 530	1.7	31.8	16.6	47 453	4.9	4 741	42 549	54.5	135 600	24.1	13.6
Suffolk	30 021	66 822	4.6	17.2	8.5	33 035	33.7	2 167	30 798	71.6	240 200	25.6	11.9
Virginia Beach	32 477	67 001	5.0	13.2	6.6	177 879	9.6	12 790	165 296	64.1	263 200	25.8	11.9
Winchester	26 624	44 731	4.3	26.7	10.2	11 872	12.1	1 265	10 692	47.7	219 700	23.2	13.0
WASHINGTON	31 233	60 294	5.2	19.4	9.1	2 885 677	17.7	265 601	2 645 396	62.7	257 200	24.9	12.0
Auburn	26 918	57 635	2.9	19.6	11.6	27 834	66.3	1 776	27 371	59.7	231 200	25.7	14.7
Bellevue	50 405	92 524	15.3	11.4	5.3	55 551	15.0	5 196	53 231	56.4	538 300	24.4	13.0
Bellingham	24 864	42 440	2.1	31.2	14.0	36 760	24.9	2 089	33 847	45.7	287 100	25.5	11.9
Bothell	38 841	75 643	8.3	13.5	5.0	14 255	15.3	758	13 922	66.1	344 600	23.6	13.5
Bremerton	24 451	43 527	1.4	28.1	15.1	17 273	3.9	2 341	15 347	41.9	184 100	25.8	11.3
Burien	26 015	52 140	3.0	23.6	14.4	14 322	2.1	1 069	18 266	52.3	273 800	28.0	12.2
Des Moines	27 933	58 308	3.7	17.8	10.5	12 588	6.2	924	11 347	58.3	247 000	27.4	13.7
Edmonds	42 433	72 926	9.3	14.5	5.5	18 378	4.9	997	17 440	68.7	381 500	25.8	13.2
Everett	25 981	48 562	2.0	24.9	14.0	44 609	15.6	3 297	41 500	45.1	230 800	26.8	14.3
Federal Way	27 145	54 186	3.3	20.9	12.5	35 444	8.8	2 256	34 064	55.0	242 800	26.1	13.0
Issaquah	49 532	88 770	14.5	12.0	2.7	13 914	173.6	1 073	13 869	59.7	449 800	24.1	15.6
Kennewick	25 088	51 739	3.4	24.4	13.6	28 507	29.3	1 241	27 250	61.5	168 200	19.9	10.0
Kent	25 497	57 490	2.7	20.3	15.0	36 424	12.0	2 380	42 457	53.8	251 000	26.0	12.4
Kirkland	48 902	90 611	12.2	10.6	3.8	24 345	11.0	1 900	34 762	63.6	424 700	25.9	12.5
Lacey	27 135	59 885	1.1	15.2	7.7	18 493	41.4	1 544	17 346	53.8	224 400	26.0	11.3
Lake Stevens	28 000	70 345	2.7	13.0	6.7	10 414	NA	604	10 026	71.7	245 300	27.0	15.3
Lakewood	25 607	44 667	2.8	29.0	14.2	26 548	4.7	2 479	24 107	46.0	217 200	25.8	12.3
Longview	22 196	37 827	1.6	36.0	17.2	16 380	7.7	1 099	15 266	55.0	167 700	25.9	13.3
Lynnwood	25 797	50 562	2.3	24.6	10.9	14 939	8.5	832	13 919	51.5	273 800	26.2	15.2
Marysville	27 159	64 328	1.4	15.1	5.8	22 363	130.6	1 144	22 456	68.9	229 400	27.2	13.1
Mount Vernon	21 623	44 404	1.7	26.0	16.6	12 058	24.0	716	11 308	55.0	210 700	26.2	13.7
Olympia	30 206	52 834	3.4	24.7	11.4	22 086	12.1	1 325	20 657	49.0	240 800	23.8	12.8

1. Based on population estimated by the American Community Survey. 2. Includes units rented or sold but not occupied. 3. Specified owner-occupied units; $1,000,000 represents $1,000,000 or more 4. 50.0 represents 50 percent or more. 5. 10.0 represents 10 percent or less.

Table D. Cities — Housing, Labor Force, and Employment

City	Occupied housing units, 2010–2014 (cont.) Percent renter occupied	Median gross rent[1]	Median gross rent as a percent of income[2]	Percent with no vehicle available	Migration, 2010–2014 Percent who lived in the same house one year ago	Percent who lived outside current city one year ago	Civilian labor force, 2015 Total	Percent change, 2014–2015	Unemployment Total	Rate[3]	Civilian employment[4], 2010–2014 Population age 16 and older	Percent In labor force	Civilian full-year full-time workers	Households with no workers (percent)
	55	56	57	58	59	60	61	62	63	64	65	66	67	68
UTAH—Cont'd														
Kaysville	13.7	744	28.1	2.5	89.1	9.0	13 477	2.5	409	3.0	18 772	68.9	42.2	14.6
Layton	25.1	857	28.8	4.9	83.7	12.5	36 250	2.5	1 266	3.5	49 536	69.0	43.5	16.0
Lehi	19.1	1 202	31.5	2.2	86.1	11.0	23 731	3.9	752	3.2	31 050	69.6	42.6	13.4
Logan	57.7	645	30.3	6.3	67.0	19.0	26 833	2.0	809	3.0	37 946	69.3	31.3	17.7
Midvale	54.8	947	27.8	8.2	77.6	18.1	19 001	1.9	680	3.6	23 713	74.3	48.8	16.6
Murray	36.1	919	32.5	5.9	81.1	16.5	28 493	1.7	975	3.4	37 918	70.3	44.5	21.8
Ogden	45.1	729	30.4	9.5	77.8	11.8	39 869	2.3	1 823	4.6	62 790	65.6	36.9	25.2
Orem	39.1	888	31.6	3.8	79.7	14.2	46 107	4.1	1 457	3.2	65 740	67.0	35.2	18.8
Pleasant Grove	32.7	1 032	30.2	3.1	77.6	17.9	17 642	4.0	550	3.1	22 811	69.6	39.2	13.2
Provo	57.9	734	32.7	4.8	60.8	22.2	63 117	4.0	1 921	3.0	91 124	68.3	24.2	16.9
Riverton	11.0	1 110	24.9	1.8	90.1	8.5	22 311	1.6	632	2.8	27 345	76.3	50.9	8.1
Roy	15.6	921	25.2	2.8	87.4	10.4	18 567	2.3	766	4.1	26 668	68.4	44.6	21.5
St. George	35.3	873	31.7	4.4	79.9	10.8	33 155	3.6	1 282	3.9	56 830	57.0	30.8	35.9
Salt Lake City	51.6	807	30.3	12.6	77.7	12.7	107 749	1.8	3 488	3.2	151 683	70.1	41.2	23.1
Sandy	23.0	1 123	28.4	3.4	87.5	9.9	50 065	1.7	1 611	3.2	66 575	70.8	44.9	16.6
South Jordan	18.7	1 401	26.6	2.2	84.0	13.5	31 463	2.0	1 011	3.2	39 529	70.2	45.9	13.2
Spanish Fork	22.7	928	27.8	1.8	82.8	11.9	16 436	4.0	547	3.3	23 175	68.2	41.1	13.3
Springville	29.5	937	25.1	2.5	83.6	12.6	15 107	3.9	488	3.2	20 284	69.9	42.5	14.1
Taylorsville	31.0	900	31.2	4.3	84.3	13.2	33 480	1.5	1 160	3.5	45 003	73.0	45.6	18.5
Tooele	25.1	886	28.4	3.8	84.2	9.4	15 578	1.3	672	4.3	22 476	67.3	43.1	19.7
West Jordan	23.6	1 064	30.3	2.2	87.1	9.9	59 841	1.7	1 941	3.2	75 499	76.1	50.3	11.3
West Valley City	31.2	928	34.2	3.8	82.0	12.2	68 809	1.6	2 537	3.7	92 923	72.8	45.6	16.0
VERMONT	29.1	889	31.2	6.7	86.7	11.2	344 414	-1.0	12 590	3.7	517 411	67.2	40.7	26.7
Burlington	59.4	1 011	36.0	16.1	67.5	19.3	24 092	-0.5	668	2.8	37 606	64.7	31.9	27.8
VIRGINIA	33.3	1 108	30.0	6.4	84.7	11.6	4 240 470	-0.4	188 562	4.4	6 531 424	66.4	43.2	23.4
Alexandria	57.3	1 520	28.1	9.1	78.2	15.9	93 782	-0.1	3 094	3.3	122 705	79.2	58.5	13.4
Blacksburg	71.7	893	50.0	7.5	55.1	26.4	20 529	0.0	1 111	5.4	39 467	51.2	21.0	28.0
Charlottesville	58.4	1 015	31.4	11.6	72.8	18.2	24 613	1.2	909	3.7	38 471	61.9	37.3	25.6
Chesapeake	28.3	1 163	31.0	4.3	85.9	9.7	116 597	-0.9	5 302	4.5	178 039	67.6	43.8	18.5
Danville	45.9	595	29.7	16.0	82.3	8.5	19 010	-2.6	1 393	7.3	34 402	55.8	31.3	41.0
Hampton	41.2	1 005	35.8	8.4	84.1	8.5	65 159	-1.0	3 891	6.0	109 998	64.9	38.1	26.3
Harrisonburg	64.3	843	33.4	9.4	67.3	23.4	24 034	-1.1	1 272	5.3	43 598	57.8	29.9	22.6
Leesburg	31.8	1 369	30.1	4.0	84.6	11.4	26 802	-0.3	926	3.5	34 062	77.7	55.2	8.3
Lynchburg	47.9	759	33.8	14.8	74.2	15.0	35 740	-1.1	1 987	5.6	64 099	58.4	30.6	32.1
Manassas	35.3	1 334	35.6	5.5	84.4	9.4	22 087	-0.5	913	4.1	30 526	75.1	50.7	13.9
Newport News	49.4	975	30.3	9.1	76.4	12.8	90 051	-1.1	4 866	5.4	142 696	69.5	40.2	23.8
Norfolk	56.3	965	33.7	12.5	77.3	11.9	111 318	-1.0	6 211	5.6	199 157	68.8	34.9	25.2
Petersburg	55.4	845	35.0	17.2	81.2	8.8	13 811	-0.2	1 247	9.0	26 319	55.5	33.1	38.1
Portsmouth	44.2	967	33.3	11.0	81.1	9.1	44 656	-1.3	2 781	6.2	75 643	63.7	38.2	27.9
Richmond	57.3	893	33.1	16.9	76.4	11.6	113 384	0.5	5 888	5.2	175 279	65.1	37.9	29.5
Roanoke	45.5	719	29.4	13.3	81.0	8.5	49 475	-1.6	2 404	4.9	78 578	63.5	40.8	30.3
Suffolk	28.4	1 022	32.6	6.1	86.7	7.5	42 106	-1.0	2 089	5.0	65 953	67.8	42.7	22.6
Virginia Beach	35.9	1 239	31.5	3.9	82.0	9.1	230 434	-0.9	9 869	4.3	352 991	70.7	43.9	19.5
Winchester	52.3	919	34.6	11.8	78.1	15.8	14 519	0.2	630	4.3	21 525	63.6	39.8	28.6
WASHINGTON	37.3	995	30.3	7.0	82.6	12.4	3 544 242	1.5	200 250	5.7	5 488 038	64.7	38.7	26.4
Auburn	40.3	1 013	33.3	8.4	82.5	11.8	38 725	1.4	1 905	4.9	56 626	65.6	40.4	24.4
Bellevue	43.6	1 451	24.5	6.9	79.1	14.7	75 163	1.4	2 993	4.0	108 531	66.6	44.2	20.7
Bellingham	54.3	901	34.9	10.8	75.8	12.4	42 906	1.7	2 397	5.6	70 492	64.9	30.8	29.0
Bothell	33.9	1 308	32.2	5.3	83.0	13.5	20 540	1.6	932	4.5	28 121	70.3	44.8	21.0
Bremerton	58.1	864	32.2	14.5	70.2	18.9	16 086	1.3	1 067	6.6	32 258	65.2	31.8	32.4
Burien	47.7	1 004	32.7	8.4	81.7	13.1	26 292	1.4	1 175	4.5	38 523	66.3	40.4	25.7
Des Moines	41.7	1 066	29.8	6.8	83.4	12.9	16 243	1.3	860	5.3	24 726	64.3	39.4	25.9
Edmonds	31.3	1 091	28.9	3.8	88.0	9.7	22 206	1.2	983	4.4	34 038	63.6	40.7	27.7
Everett	54.9	965	31.2	11.4	78.4	14.1	54 430	1.2	2 945	5.4	83 376	68.6	38.9	26.0
Federal Way	45.0	1 032	33.3	8.7	80.2	12.0	48 064	1.3	2 516	5.2	72 523	66.8	40.5	23.3
Issaquah	40.3	1 469	26.6	5.9	78.7	15.8	18 899	1.5	720	3.8	25 492	70.4	48.4	23.3
Kennewick	38.5	799	31.6	6.2	80.1	12.1	38 020	1.9	2 431	6.4	56 621	64.2	40.9	25.4
Kent	46.2	1 012	34.1	7.6	82.0	12.2	63 656	1.4	3 352	5.3	94 356	67.2	41.2	20.9
Kirkland	36.4	1 398	26.9	4.2	81.7	13.6	50 387	1.3	1 872	3.7	67 944	72.3	48.1	18.2
Lacey	46.2	1 107	30.1	5.5	76.2	19.4	19 075	2.1	1 246	6.5	34 936	62.2	35.0	27.7
Lake Stevens	28.3	1 247	29.9	2.6	85.7	10.9	15 515	1.4	492	3.2	21 446	72.2	43.9	17.8
Lakewood	54.0	844	34.9	9.0	76.5	17.3	25 144	1.7	1 663	6.6	47 641	60.2	31.8	32.7
Longview	45.0	709	37.6	13.2	78.5	9.7	15 031	1.6	1 152	7.7	29 320	53.8	28.5	42.9
Lynnwood	48.5	979	33.2	9.9	83.6	10.9	19 365	1.3	979	5.1	29 854	64.8	38.7	28.5
Marysville	31.1	1 152	32.2	4.0	83.4	11.8	32 760	1.5	1 355	4.1	47 987	68.8	41.9	24.1
Mount Vernon	45.0	906	34.6	7.0	80.2	10.7	14 596	1.1	1 025	7.0	24 240	61.5	33.5	30.6
Olympia	51.0	926	31.6	11.6	78.1	15.0	25 189	2.0	1 341	5.3	39 405	66.0	38.7	28.8

1. $2,000 represents $2,000 or more.   2. 50.0 represents 50 percent or more.   3. Percent of civilian labor force.   4. Persons 16 years old and over.

Table D. Cities — **Construction, Wholesale Trade, and Retail Trade**

City	Value of residential construction authorized by building permits, 2015			Wholesale trade,[1] 2012				Retail trade,[2] 2012			
	New construction ($1,000)	Number of housing units	Percent single family	Number of establishments	Number of employees	Sales (mil dol)	Annual payroll (mil dol)	Number of establishments	Number of employees	Sales (mil dol)	Annual payroll (mil dol)
	69	70	71	72	73	74	75	76	77	78	79
UTAH—Cont'd											
Kaysville	61 059	198	100.0	22	269	117.4	11.7	62	707	169.1	17.7
Layton	78 668	449	58.8	47	321	117.8	10.7	295	4 761	1 123.0	106.0
Lehi	165 030	713	74.8	22	303	180.4	15.0	144	2 159	637.8	63.4
Logan	15 161	136	64.7	67	606	435.2	23.7	248	3 710	725.7	71.2
Midvale	40 547	229	30.1	48	604	354.9	25.5	149	2 153	554.8	53.1
Murray	15 470	69	82.6	109	1 032	520.2	54.1	353	5 656	1 921.1	161.3
Ogden	43 699	396	24.7	100	1 412	949.3	67.5	344	3 839	1 121.8	93.9
Orem	133 772	937	14.9	102	1 421	658.4	62.1	451	7 296	1 843.7	165.6
Pleasant Grove	50 895	201	94.0	19	75	28.7	2.6	65	675	219.9	21.0
Provo	34 740	217	47.9	55	1 506	1 153.2	99.6	317	4 334	1 205.9	98.9
Riverton	68 112	296	82.8	21	76	42.2	2.7	68	1 184	261.9	25.9
Roy	2 950	22	100.0	7	D	D	D	72	906	236.3	19.3
St. George	124 720	768	95.8	106	D	D	D	425	5 477	1 468.9	126.9
Salt Lake City	145 553	1 206	3.0	603	12 541	10 292.8	748.3	918	14 096	4 071.1	374.7
Sandy	76 642	675	11.0	130	1 173	847.6	59.8	382	6 580	2 199.2	187.0
South Jordan	190 097	765	98.2	38	1 231	900.5	73.8	112	2 249	662.1	55.5
Spanish Fork	66 678	229	97.4	19	186	106.2	7.3	88	1 077	204.4	19.6
Springville	34 725	204	35.3	25	639	228.5	25.2	74	1 095	301.6	23.9
Taylorsville	11 644	49	100.0	18	76	41.8	2.9	101	1 695	375.1	36.2
Tooele	15 808	132	68.9	7	D	D	D	75	1 334	361.7	31.4
West Jordan	127 631	640	57.8	76	1 201	1 118.5	66.9	207	3 971	945.0	84.5
West Valley City	33 403	269	83.6	143	2 669	1 906.8	143.3	280	5 549	1 457.0	157.9
VERMONT	333 954	1 998	46.8	696	9 464	6 450.1	464.4	3 509	38 910	9 933.8	967.1
Burlington	11 549	81	6.2	48	539	327.8	37.4	224	3 271	610.2	75.9
VIRGINIA	4 724 305	28 469	69.8	6 232	88 353	86 613.6	4 983.1	27 415	410 918	110 002.4	10 007.9
Alexandria	42 764	193	100.0	82	1 139	502.8	61.6	480	7 180	2 416.0	222.6
Blacksburg	31 312	233	99.1	14	D	D	D	97	1 363	284.4	22.3
Charlottesville	38 149	231	28.6	48	513	183.3	23.7	331	3 925	747.9	82.8
Chesapeake	256 186	1 325	82.8	239	3 447	2 225.2	169.7	789	15 088	4 114.9	336.7
Danville	1 279	13	100.0	50	545	285.2	24.5	306	4 165	965.0	87.2
Hampton	10 384	162	100.0	71	886	344.7	39.3	436	6 791	1 512.5	148.3
Harrisonburg	9 598	63	92.1	57	1 006	405.9	43.2	334	5 664	1 519.8	144.6
Leesburg	NA	NA	NA	27	366	172.4	19.0	266	5 403	1 388.7	124.5
Lynchburg	33 142	281	27.4	69	877	509.0	39.0	385	7 371	1 995.2	178.2
Manassas	19 308	137	100.0	41	D	D	D	194	2 778	895.3	86.1
Newport News	25 033	512	20.9	110	1 438	851.3	72.7	686	9 879	2 480.8	229.7
Norfolk	80 752	931	43.5	209	3 287	3 195.3	161.6	867	12 440	2 683.2	281.6
Petersburg	4 631	85	5.9	21	570	560.1	16.2	145	1 426	334.5	33.0
Portsmouth	12 830	94	100.0	48	688	249.5	32.0	273	3 081	699.5	71.1
Richmond	52 933	523	49.3	269	3 767	3 288.5	201.3	808	8 666	1 955.2	206.1
Roanoke	21 498	155	9.0	180	2 727	1 398.0	130.3	535	9 912	2 461.0	230.1
Suffolk	85 380	798	45.4	54	961	666.0	49.8	226	3 536	958.9	79.1
Virginia Beach	175 889	1 493	46.6	391	6 893	8 187.6	477.1	1 500	22 723	5 671.5	521.6
Winchester	2 968	13	100.0	39	677	286.8	26.1	283	4 126	888.5	94.4
WASHINGTON	8 518 859	40 374	49.0	7 733	103 307	83 313.4	5 789.8	21 588	307 089	118 924.0	8 722.5
Auburn	80 581	226	100.0	174	3 739	4 631.5	198.0	281	4 676	1 475.0	140.8
Bellevue	214 356	911	27.7	324	4 333	5 128.3	368.3	673	12 225	4 113.9	412.6
Bellingham	89 017	590	23.7	147	D	D	D	532	8 805	2 243.5	206.9
Bothell	76 916	310	35.8	63	1 357	1 465.7	112.4	100	1 451	363.3	41.6
Bremerton	30 907	162	54.9	27	191	83.1	9.6	134	1 704	572.5	55.8
Burien	49 188	298	21.5	23	138	33.0	4.7	163	2 013	573.1	58.3
Des Moines	8 095	30	53.3	15	116	91.7	10.1	38	360	93.3	10.2
Edmonds	22 762	53	100.0	39	201	177.8	12.4	133	1 449	448.2	43.9
Everett	43 897	309	52.4	134	2 108	1 355.6	129.1	449	6 782	2 023.4	194.6
Federal Way	109 902	744	5.4	54	450	250.1	22.5	257	4 441	1 184.1	118.0
Issaquah	143 512	608	37.2	44	272	372.7	17.3	136	3 108	2 801.7	110.1
Kennewick	89 416	451	61.4	67	659	927.9	31.5	378	6 113	1 620.4	148.4
Kent	83 123	381	49.6	430	8 772	6 803.7	509.9	340	4 711	1 447.3	137.9
Kirkland	165 777	313	100.0	104	1 023	656.4	81.0	216	4 128	1 776.8	148.9
Lacey	78 376	308	100.0	23	493	421.0	24.6	148	3 567	869.8	92.1
Lake Stevens	52 148	192	100.0	6	40	15.9	1.2	45	848	219.2	20.3
Lakewood	12 984	48	95.8	67	834	1 407.2	41.8	227	2 725	701.2	69.7
Longview	2 692	12	100.0	39	637	712.5	30.9	175	3 043	796.3	78.7
Lynnwood	45 030	326	5.5	95	794	407.1	44.8	425	7 823	2 042.0	210.1
Marysville	30 391	116	100.0	34	236	117.4	12.5	172	3 450	933.4	88.4
Mount Vernon	21 687	132	100.0	32	385	219.6	18.1	135	2 017	491.7	53.0
Olympia	33 797	138	89.9	39	390	461.9	24.3	367	5 515	1 396.7	142.3

1. Merchant wholesalers except manufacturers' sales branches and offices.   2. Establishments with payroll.

City	Real estate and rental and leasing, 2012				Professional, scientific, and technical services,[1] 2012				Manufacturing, 2012			
	Number of establish-ments	Number of employees	Receipts (mil dol)	Annual payroll (mil dol)	Number of establish-ments	Number of employees	Receipts (mil dol)	Annual payroll (mil dol)	Number of establish-ments	Number of employees	Receipts (mil dol)	Annual payroll (mil dol)
	80	81	82	83	84	85	86	87	88	89	90	91
UTAH—Cont'd												
Kaysville	36	77	11.5	2.4	90	647	74.6	35.3	15	180	37.4	7.1
Layton	111	313	69.3	9.9	177	D	D	D	43	870	372.5	39.8
Lehi	58	70	17.2	3.3	173	D	D	D	32	518	198.1	27.0
Logan	108	396	57.3	14.3	179	D	D	D	112	7 049	2 431.3	301.9
Midvale	69	468	105.0	25.5	92	D	D	D	34	435	D	18.9
Murray	134	1 271	154.0	51.4	300	2 624	380.0	136.7	118	1 590	320.6	65.0
Ogden	100	413	51.5	10.6	245	D	D	D	134	7 939	3 135.1	383.0
Orem	185	566	108.3	15.8	358	7 806	401.3	195.9	122	2 729	780.8	124.9
Pleasant Grove	48	98	13.9	3.4	99	670	83.9	32.6	30	238	D	9.1
Provo	120	569	85.7	13.1	346	D	D	D	81	1 908	376.7	96.3
Riverton	41	95	15.9	2.7	89	191	14.6	4.9	8	D	D	0.7
Roy	19	54	5.6	1.0	29	249	16.2	8.5	17	65	8.1	D
St. George	218	541	77.1	14.8	324	D	D	D	87	1 376	322.3	55.1
Salt Lake City	528	3 093	878.2	142.4	1 434	16 666	3 114.5	1 238.7	457	24 316	11 969.2	1 556.7
Sandy	202	654	157.6	28.0	443	2 500	324.0	131.8	103	2 619	891.9	137.8
South Jordan	93	253	42.3	10.3	230	1 478	223.0	60.7	23	D	D	D
Spanish Fork	29	60	12.7	2.1	80	381	36.1	9.2	39	1 771	671.8	94.5
Springville	19	21	2.9	0.6	66	320	29.0	10.5	46	3 092	1 538.7	143.1
Taylorsville	48	157	20.9	4.6	85	D	D	D	17	601	85.8	26.6
Tooele	19	61	8.5	1.3	32	165	13.4	6.1	19	729	343.7	D
West Jordan	82	181	30.4	5.2	153	D	D	D	106	2 439	895.2	116.7
West Valley City	73	525	111.5	24.5	118	D	D	D	156	4 762	2 397.5	240.5
VERMONT	741	3 092	509.9	103.6	2 093	15 781	1 762.8	730.9	1 013	31 487	9 315.5	1 594.3
Burlington	61	347	91.9	15.5	267	D	D	D	24	613	192.2	30.9
VIRGINIA	8 862	54 246	11 758.9	2 378.3	29 176	416 651	90 042.2	35 093.6	5 101	228 197	96 389.9	11 586.1
Alexandria	240	1 475	524.1	76.6	1 228	16 537	3 436.0	1 497.8	72	1 332	273.0	57.9
Blacksburg	50	393	73.4	14.9	153	D	D	D	20	1 473	514.6	99.8
Charlottesville	99	502	107.6	19.7	316	D	D	D	46	455	98.7	21.6
Chesapeake	273	1 227	291.6	52.9	509	7 649	1 029.3	412.6	130	3 965	1 504.2	211.6
Danville	64	339	48.7	9.1	72	D	D	D	46	4 635	1 703.0	223.7
Hampton	114	750	117.3	23.7	273	D	D	D	68	2 189	508.3	114.9
Harrisonburg	72	351	75.9	10.9	137	D	D	D	46	2 556	832.6	99.4
Leesburg	64	288	136.2	14.5	302	D	D	D	11	347	D	D
Lynchburg	109	447	79.9	14.5	199	D	D	D	83	8 339	2 749.6	504.3
Manassas	52	229	64.0	11.4	212	D	D	D	32	4 012	1 365.7	366.4
Newport News	254	1 672	276.5	60.3	361	D	D	D	91	26 503	5 578.9	1 558.5
Norfolk	291	2 496	430.8	127.7	700	D	D	D	130	6 866	1 812.5	328.2
Petersburg	32	223	27.2	5.8	34	D	D	D	28	1 646	D	91.0
Portsmouth	71	332	52.6	9.7	144	D	D	D	56	2 196	447.1	97.6
Richmond	258	1 539	304.3	67.1	844	10 249	2 511.6	888.8	187	5 882	16 885.9	386.3
Roanoke	155	950	141.8	31.0	326	D	D	D	100	3 869	1 629.7	174.8
Suffolk	67	243	37.5	8.1	121	D	D	D	46	1 996	1 521.0	103.6
Virginia Beach	649	6 165	902.5	210.7	1 391	17 195	3 883.4	1 188.8	207	5 616	1 954.2	255.1
Winchester	59	260	56.4	8.0	130	D	D	D	23	2 197	866.2	117.6
WASHINGTON	9 913	45 209	9 695.5	1 895.1	19 882	D	D	D	6 992	248 192	131 530.6	14 461.8
Auburn	86	344	96.7	13.9	120	D	D	D	159	9 859	1 243.4	582.0
Bellevue	517	3 594	974.9	195.2	1 260	14 873	2 735.3	1 204.9	115	1 733	621.1	87.9
Bellingham	199	847	193.4	27.6	432	D	D	D	126	3 061	D	129.2
Bothell	75	269	75.9	9.9	201	D	D	D	38	3 273	1 724.1	260.6
Bremerton	67	218	38.4	6.6	83	D	D	D	21	578	D	27.2
Burien	72	226	38.4	6.5	95	477	40.2	15.8	28	82	D	2.8
Des Moines	16	36	6.0	1.1	32	106	9.0	3.5	6	18	3.2	0.8
Edmonds	76	205	46.1	10.6	174	755	109.3	45.1	19	214	D	9.2
Everett	168	1 056	172.8	36.9	312	D	D	D	134	43 136	D	3 324.1
Federal Way	101	442	92.4	15.2	167	1 491	176.7	97.4	25	347	D	12.5
Issaquah	77	311	89.4	14.5	189	1 046	145.5	96.2	27	1 407	505.4	96.3
Kennewick	117	683	123.7	19.6	202	D	D	D	45	714	293.9	37.4
Kent	155	866	200.1	36.9	217	1 766	282.1	127.2	247	14 012	7 642.4	924.1
Kirkland	182	867	643.3	64.0	457	D	D	D	50	668	146.4	34.4
Lacey	54	210	45.1	6.0	74	2 388	319.2	147.8	17	415	D	19.8
Lake Stevens	30	D	D	D	20	69	7.1	2.5	12	D	5.4	D
Lakewood	102	445	85.3	12.9	111	544	55.3	21.0	36	585	D	24.6
Longview	55	208	34.2	5.8	83	D	D	D	37	2 469	1 391.6	203.7
Lynnwood	90	307	99.0	13.1	155	D	D	D	48	675	213.4	31.0
Marysville	63	218	67.8	9.8	60	336	31.8	8.4	55	1 672	340.2	68.8
Mount Vernon	56	143	24.1	4.4	117	512	64.3	22.6	32	673	328.2	26.9
Olympia	114	428	88.3	14.2	280	1 524	210.6	88.8	32	514	205.9	24.6

1. Establishments subject to federal tax.

Table D. Cities — Accommodation and Food Services, Arts, Entertainment, and Recreation, and Health Care and Social Assistance

City	Accommodation and food services, 2012				Arts, entertainment, and recreation,[1] 2012				Health care and social assistance,[1] 2012			
	Number of establishments	Number of employees	Sales (mil dol)	Annual payroll (mil dol)	Number of establishments	Number of employees	Receipts (mil dol)	Annual payroll (mil dol)	Number of establishments	Number of employees	Receipts (mil dol)	Annual payroll (mil dol)
	92	93	94	95	96	97	98	99	100	101	102	103
UTAH—Cont'd												
Kaysville	16	354	11.4	3.4	6	239	14.9	3.3	52	D	D	D
Layton	149	3 414	138.2	40.9	19	D	D	D	156	2 734	304.0	116.0
Lehi	50	1 117	48.2	12.4	17	D	D	D	62	D	D	D
Logan	120	2 287	98.7	26.6	19	244	10.7	1.9	175	D	D	D
Midvale	94	1 572	73.1	21.6	6	D	D	D	53	D	D	D
Murray	113	2 538	120.0	40.6	13	D	D	D	298	D	D	D
Ogden	184	3 206	124.0	36.2	14	D	D	D	270	D	D	D
Orem	152	3 262	148.0	43.6	43	D	D	D	238	4 058	391.5	134.5
Pleasant Grove	29	280	12.9	3.1	11	35	4.6	0.8	60	D	D	D
Provo	186	3 335	143.9	40.6	32	387	25.6	7.2	285	D	D	D
Riverton	48	758	32.8	9.6	5	10	0.8	0.2	79	D	D	D
Roy	40	661	29.6	7.4	5	55	1.5	0.6	53	D	D	D
St. George	216	3 957	197.1	55.1	30	393	13.9	4.6	383	D	D	D
Salt Lake City	735	16 057	961.6	277.0	77	1 617	227.7	90.4	587	5 979	775.9	270.9
Sandy	188	3 696	173.1	49.7	28	D	D	D	272	D	D	D
South Jordan	68	1 569	65.6	20.3	13	D	D	D	123	D	D	D
Spanish Fork	40	664	28.4	7.4	7	D	D	D	59	644	44.7	15.2
Springville	39	D	D	D	7	26	1.6	0.3	63	D	D	D
Taylorsville	83	1 618	80.8	21.1	11	D	D	D	100	1 045	93.1	34.5
Tooele	45	755	33.8	8.9	6	60	3.3	1.1	58	D	D	D
West Jordan	116	2 362	125.2	32.2	13	D	D	D	170	2 883	365.1	92.4
West Valley City	179	2 987	161.6	43.4	18	D	D	D	101	D	D	D
VERMONT	1 920	31 365	1 564.3	494.0	286	5 468	233.6	73.7	1 370	14 976	1 297.2	578.2
Burlington	151	2 846	172.1	51.6	12	107	7.2	2.0	96	1 655	135.2	70.7
VIRGINIA	16 832	320 514	17 795.9	4 908.6	1 970	35 718	2 993.0	875.7	16 070	236 459	25 556.4	10 868.1
Alexandria	387	8 051	647.5	180.7	41	606	45.8	15.2	343	3 739	466.5	194.6
Blacksburg	100	2 054	91.4	25.1	7	D	D	D	93	1 512	197.5	73.2
Charlottesville	293	5 199	293.3	75.9	25	D	D	D	121	D	D	D
Chesapeake	466	10 267	447.6	121.1	42	D	D	D	456	6 275	637.4	290.0
Danville	139	2 850	120.4	33.6	11	D	D	D	175	3 730	374.9	152.4
Hampton	250	5 380	249.0	72.2	23	D	D	D	217	3 137	322.2	134.7
Harrisonburg	186	4 468	216.0	58.8	11	D	D	D	128	2 006	163.9	75.6
Leesburg	118	2 305	135.4	37.9	11	D	D	D	166	1 736	209.9	92.8
Lynchburg	215	5 071	216.4	61.0	21	243	10.2	3.1	205	D	D	D
Manassas	109	1 587	91.4	24.7	10	116	4.8	1.4	157	D	D	D
Newport News	386	6 621	323.8	87.6	28	D	D	D	327	6 977	693.3	380.1
Norfolk	593	11 264	547.1	148.4	41	504	37.2	10.7	422	6 733	776.7	359.3
Petersburg	79	885	39.1	10.2	6	D	D	D	103	3 619	364.2	135.7
Portsmouth	172	2 624	107.1	29.3	17	119	10.7	2.2	166	3 362	274.4	117.8
Richmond	618	11 470	576.5	184.1	53	896	52.7	10.8	441	11 147	1 922.8	628.0
Roanoke	320	6 509	308.1	94.4	17	188	7.9	2.6	228	4 017	462.5	191.5
Suffolk	147	2 477	122.9	30.6	12	D	D	D	155	2 625	273.4	125.1
Virginia Beach	1 153	21 910	1 202.7	324.3	153	1 714	129.4	31.6	919	12 464	1 177.1	571.3
Winchester	130	2 518	119.1	33.1	12	D	D	D	226	D	D	D
WASHINGTON	16 333	234 145	14 297.3	4 159.7	2 029	41 184	4 079.6	1 177.3	16 888	194 136	20 414.0	8 703.2
Auburn	145	1 859	107.0	30.9	28	D	D	D	163	2 421	232.0	100.8
Bellevue	432	8 993	618.4	184.7	63	1 856	151.9	47.0	887	8 423	958.7	398.7
Bellingham	325	5 589	277.4	84.5	50	434	20.2	6.1	423	4 236	422.2	171.3
Bothell	140	1 982	120.6	32.9	7	D	D	D	152	1 457	128.3	50.7
Bremerton	108	1 440	88.2	22.7	6	76	2.2	0.9	110	2 072	208.8	76.9
Burien	103	1 221	61.3	17.6	11	D	D	D	182	1 404	166.8	67.1
Des Moines	55	744	42.8	12.0	2	D	D	D	55	475	34.1	14.8
Edmonds	113	1 426	83.1	23.3	11	346	20.8	6.3	210	D	D	D
Everett	343	4 457	265.2	72.9	27	364	18.6	6.4	362	5 867	622.3	298.1
Federal Way	221	3 085	182.5	51.8	16	325	14.1	6.6	320	4 356	425.8	144.9
Issaquah	109	1 729	107.2	31.5	8	260	12.5	4.3	200	2 294	388.2	126.9
Kennewick	195	3 554	183.4	51.8	17	575	22.9	8.5	246	3 243	314.4	114.6
Kent	272	3 198	179.9	50.2	21	308	22.3	8.6	283	2 592	199.0	79.1
Kirkland	191	2 958	187.3	57.6	44	801	33.4	12.5	324	D	D	D
Lacey	122	1 852	101.8	28.7	11	D	D	D	114	D	D	D
Lake Stevens	42	621	39.4	9.0	4	145	3.7	1.0	39	276	28.1	10.4
Lakewood	179	2 433	132.6	35.9	16	599	28.9	13.6	192	2 524	199.3	92.3
Longview	104	1 490	63.4	19.3	12	D	D	D	131	1 795	161.7	68.4
Lynnwood	204	3 092	189.1	53.0	9	D	D	D	193	2 322	158.2	62.4
Marysville	104	1 365	81.6	21.4	8	D	D	D	118	1 282	114.0	49.3
Mount Vernon	83	915	52.0	14.4	6	167	6.6	2.4	114	D	D	D
Olympia	215	3 316	166.4	52.7	12	152	7.7	2.3	400	4 538	594.5	232.9

1. Establishments subject to federal tax.

Table D. Cities — Other Services and Government Employment and Payroll

City	Other services[1], 2012				Full-time equivalent employees	Government employment and payroll, 2012 March payroll	Percent of total for:						
	Number of establishments	Number of employees	Receipts (mil dol)	Annual payroll (mil dol)		Total (dollars)	Administration, judicial, and legal	Police and Corrections	Fire Protection	Highways and transportation	Health and welfare	Natural resources and utilities	Education and libraries
	104	105	106	107	108	109	110	111	112	113	114	115	116
UTAH—Cont'd													
Kaysville	27	134	9.5	2.7	134	462 338	10.8	22.9	9.0	7.6	0.0	39.1	0.0
Layton	108	729	48.9	13.9	349	1 449 599	18.3	33.6	21.9	4.9	0.0	21.4	0.0
Lehi	36	203	13.8	4.1	336	1 214 483	12.5	20.4	13.7	4.2	0.0	36.3	4.1
Logan	86	509	36.2	11.4	471	1 727 277	13.4	20.5	14.4	3.6	0.0	36.1	3.5
Midvale	60	338	31.1	8.2	75	305 262	65.6	0.0	0.0	6.5	2.9	20.3	0.0
Murray	138	886	86.2	27.3	431	1 925 114	16.4	23.1	16.8	2.6	0.0	30.9	3.1
Ogden	134	957	76.3	22.7	634	2 507 571	18.7	28.7	20.1	7.0	5.2	16.9	0.0
Orem	137	740	53.8	15.5	516	2 194 808	19.2	27.2	17.2	4.8	2.4	19.7	7.3
Pleasant Grove	38	138	13.3	3.4	245	686 046	17.4	27.3	9.0	3.6	2.6	26.1	8.0
Provo	118	749	59.2	17.7	702	2 815 201	17.2	23.0	14.4	5.6	1.8	29.5	4.4
Riverton	36	173	15.0	3.8	91	415 613	39.8	2.6	0.0	25.0	0.6	22.8	0.0
Roy	38	172	11.7	3.2	176	633 604	20.3	31.4	22.5	4.2	0.0	16.1	0.0
St. George	118	695	59.3	16.2	700	2 450 568	9.2	24.3	5.4	10.7	2.4	44.2	0.0
Salt Lake City	459	4 071	340.1	115.3	2 853	13 446 478	15.0	21.7	15.0	20.9	2.4	14.9	4.1
Sandy	118	785	56.3	19.2	496	2 122 916	21.0	24.1	15.6	9.8	7.5	20.1	0.0
South Jordan	52	295	22.6	6.9	333	1 224 842	20.3	19.7	17.6	6.1	2.9	18.3	0.0
Spanish Fork	38	236	17.2	5.4	215	776 827	12.0	18.4	0.0	6.4	4.3	34.7	2.8
Springville	33	124	10.2	2.2	213	858 647	17.7	20.4	1.6	8.5	0.6	42.5	4.7
Taylorsville	37	220	19.4	5.4	122	499 977	35.5	62.2	0.0	0.0	0.4	0.3	0.0
Tooele	33	D	D	D	184	603 981	20.7	27.5	3.3	5.6	6.8	29.9	3.6
West Jordan	93	670	67.8	22.8	409	1 901 684	7.2	32.4	23.5	4.1	0.0	8.0	0.0
West Valley City	123	642	71.8	20.9	699	2 859 122	17.7	37.1	17.3	7.1	8.8	9.1	0.0
VERMONT	1 057	4 255	398.4	109.0	X	X	X	X	X	X	X	X	X
Burlington	65	361	25.2	9.7	741	3 858 642	9.5	18.3	12.6	11.2	3.0	32.5	2.0
VIRGINIA	11 654	76 041	6 881.1	2 289.3	X	X	X	X	X	X	X	X	X
Alexandria	241	2 374	213.3	75.6	5 221	27 072 935	10.0	12.5	7.7	2.6	12.6	6.5	44.7
Blacksburg	45	D	D	D	360	1 254 541	15.3	27.9	0.6	24.0	1.6	12.0	0.0
Charlottesville	100	817	69.3	23.2	2 140	8 097 522	10.3	6.1	3.5	6.3	5.6	8.0	55.6
Chesapeake	361	2 768	291.0	89.0	9 069	32 784 817	5.1	11.5	6.3	2.1	5.7	4.5	62.1
Danville	84	466	34.2	8.7	2 451	7 816 325	9.2	11.3	5.7	3.0	5.2	9.6	51.6
Hampton	153	854	66.1	21.4	6 070	20 036 058	6.9	11.2	6.1	1.0	5.7	6.3	61.8
Harrisonburg	101	595	47.0	15.8	1 474	5 157 943	4.1	7.6	6.7	5.8	0.3	15.0	53.6
Leesburg	78	478	39.0	13.4	378	1 973 445	18.8	28.6	0.0	10.5	0.0	34.5	1.1
Lynchburg	130	929	73.3	24.1	3 057	9 313 489	8.7	9.6	8.0	2.9	8.1	7.5	52.5
Manassas	121	713	75.6	20.4	1 551	7 149 920	5.0	8.7	4.1	2.5	3.1	8.0	67.1
Newport News	251	1 757	157.4	53.0	8 390	34 469 339	6.2	10.2	4.6	1.3	4.5	9.2	63.2
Norfolk	287	2 254	192.7	73.6	11 723	42 393 144	6.3	13.5	5.5	3.7	10.1	7.2	51.8
Petersburg	63	508	33.1	13.2	1 422	4 584 024	6.0	20.2	8.9	4.5	6.2	4.0	47.4
Portsmouth	128	1 019	117.8	35.7	4 082	15 197 404	6.6	10.7	7.0	0.8	8.6	5.3	58.8
Richmond	370	2 708	213.2	75.5	8 746	33 243 527	9.0	18.5	6.0	1.8	8.7	7.9	42.5
Roanoke	207	1 415	111.5	37.8	3 839	13 972 707	8.1	12.9	8.3	1.7	8.0	2.4	56.6
Suffolk	84	551	35.7	12.1	3 545	11 901 204	10.3	7.7	9.6	2.9	3.6	6.8	58.2
Virginia Beach	724	4 164	320.0	99.7	18 286	64 539 702	3.7	9.5	3.6	0.3	6.6	7.3	60.5
Winchester	69	422	29.0	9.2	1 441	5 056 458	6.8	23.0	6.6	2.0	4.0	7.0	48.8
WASHINGTON	9 852	54 069	4 710.4	1 503.1	X	X	X	X	X	X	X	X	X
Auburn	143	808	83.2	28.8	428	2 532 346	24.2	34.3	0.0	15.0	4.6	18.9	0.0
Bellevue	332	2 177	173.9	64.4	1 278	8 997 838	17.4	19.2	22.6	7.6	8.6	23.3	0.0
Bellingham	201	1 185	106.1	34.2	813	4 462 504	14.2	23.4	26.3	8.6	0.9	16.4	3.3
Bothell	64	407	39.1	10.4	290	2 203 744	15.3	29.0	30.7	8.0	5.8	5.8	0.0
Bremerton	60	300	27.1	8.7	363	2 283 752	11.7	25.1	21.9	5.4	0.6	29.5	0.0
Burien	98	471	39.1	11.3	70	380 590	32.7	0.0	0.0	22.6	20.3	22.5	0.0
Des Moines	23	D	D	D	130	840 420	26.3	37.5	0.0	7.8	4.0	18.8	0.0
Edmonds	59	325	27.2	9.0	206	1 296 656	16.1	35.4	0.0	8.9	4.8	28.4	0.0
Everett	192	1 194	118.6	38.2	1 193	7 513 828	9.0	22.1	21.2	14.6	2.1	22.6	3.2
Federal Way	136	668	49.6	16.5	338	1 899 108	20.8	52.5	0.0	7.2	0.0	15.6	0.0
Issaquah	76	D	D	D	241	1 458 971	48.2	24.1	0.0	5.7	0.0	22.0	0.0
Kennewick	114	736	52.9	17.4	365	2 339 914	19.2	32.4	27.2	7.2	0.0	14.0	0.0
Kent	221	1 354	135.1	42.8	659	3 957 128	25.4	33.2	0.0	11.4	1.3	24.6	0.0
Kirkland	151	703	57.2	18.9	575	3 364 380	21.8	25.2	24.8	2.6	0.0	12.1	0.0
Lacey	71	423	34.4	11.2	244	1 204 776	6.5	40.8	0.0	5.7	7.4	37.2	0.0
Lake Stevens	27	111	6.8	2.1	60	371 914	10.4	53.2	0.0	21.3	10.4	0.0	0.0
Lakewood	130	607	54.2	18.0	252	1 631 866	29.1	53.0	0.0	11.9	1.0	3.8	0.0
Longview	72	459	34.1	10.9	291	1 531 626	13.5	28.3	20.6	13.2	0.0	18.9	5.5
Lynnwood	134	974	87.8	27.1	514	3 172 400	18.5	30.1	20.2	2.4	0.0	17.3	0.0
Marysville	103	496	52.8	13.3	244	1 573 886	23.0	37.9	0.0	9.3	0.0	24.8	0.0
Mount Vernon	55	271	22.6	7.3	209	1 138 810	14.6	30.5	21.7	3.5	0.0	18.1	5.0
Olympia	130	638	50.1	16.9	524	3 201 082	31.0	21.7	21.0	4.7	0.3	21.2	0.0

1. Establishments subject to federal tax.

Table D. Cities — **City Government Finances**

City	City government finances, 2012									
	General revenue							General expenditure		
	Intergovernmental			Taxes					Per capita[1] (dollars)	
					Per capita[1] (dollars)					
	Total (mil dol)	Total (mil dol)	Percent from state government	Total (mil dol)	Total	Property	Sales and gross receipts	Total (mil dol)	Total	Capital outlays
	117	118	119	120	121	122	123	124	125	126
UTAH—Cont'd										
Kaysville	15.6	1.7	75.8	6.7	236	50	186	10.3	364	62
Layton	45.3	3.8	61.6	25.7	375	112	263	40.3	587	14
Lehi	47.8	1.8	100.0	28.4	552	308	244	36.9	718	82
Logan	58.6	7.2	21.6	20.1	408	111	297	49.7	1 011	194
Midvale	17.3	1.8	50.9	11.1	368	138	230	17.2	568	9
Murray	52.5	4.5	36.2	29.2	604	209	395	48.5	1 005	89
Ogden	102.4	13.2	30.0	48.5	578	280	298	114.7	1 367	205
Orem	78.3	6.3	49.6	38.7	427	131	296	65.7	725	49
Pleasant Grove	23.6	2.0	81.2	9.0	261	99	162	21.4	621	39
Provo	87.3	11.8	35.6	39.2	339	125	214	98.1	850	250
Riverton	19.6	1.5	82.4	10.7	264	47	217	34.9	864	199
Roy	21.0	1.5	77.3	10.5	279	86	193	16.4	436	23
St. George	76.3	3.8	65.5	38.0	504	165	340	76.8	1 020	221
Salt Lake City	529.4	30.7	31.4	201.1	1 062	642	419	382.9	2 021	145
Sandy	79.3	5.3	56.3	44.9	502	168	334	64.8	724	74
South Jordan	55.2	2.4	79.1	34.3	614	349	265	50.1	895	75
Spanish Fork	37.6	1.4	82.8	10.0	277	75	202	31.9	880	170
Springville	25.9	1.1	90.9	10.0	325	103	223	30.3	989	165
Taylorsville	24.7	2.8	76.1	17.3	287	79	208	28.5	473	69
Tooele	20.4	1.8	85.9	11.5	358	130	227	20.7	645	92
West Jordan	65.0	6.3	62.5	35.7	329	119	210	59.0	544	60
West Valley City	134.8	12.6	33.4	67.2	507	262	245	154.8	1 168	359
VERMONT	X	X	X	X	X	X	X	X	X	X
Burlington	110.0	17.7	38.0	38.4	908	674	234	92.8	2 192	417
VIRGINIA	X	X	X	X	X	X	X	X	X	X
Alexandria	694.5	112.0	62.0	498.6	3 394	2 493	843	697.3	4 746	514
Blacksburg	40.4	14.5	48.6	16.4	382	130	252	36.6	855	218
Charlottesville	233.9	98.5	67.6	93.0	2 089	1 298	743	229.9	5 163	617
Chesapeake	886.7	369.8	97.8	422.6	1 852	1 303	538	865.4	3 792	475
Danville	173.3	85.4	95.4	50.7	1 186	638	544	179.2	4 189	318
Hampton	525.3	220.7	90.2	218.7	1 599	1 068	519	516.8	3 777	217
Harrisonburg	165.0	51.6	74.2	63.4	1 238	628	603	166.3	3 246	275
Leesburg	59.3	13.1	95.3	31.9	693	279	414	58.7	1 273	249
Lynchburg	266.8	110.8	87.0	117.5	1 510	897	597	268.3	3 449	589
Manassas	181.8	62.5	84.3	83.5	2 049	1 559	467	169.8	4 168	200
Newport News	774.9	330.7	85.5	322.2	1 785	1 271	515	806.2	4 467	333
Norfolk	1 105.0	447.5	74.8	416.3	1 691	1 027	664	1 153.5	4 686	548
Petersburg	125.4	70.3	87.3	45.2	1 406	1 038	357	129.9	4 039	140
Portsmouth	430.0	216.4	85.2	161.2	1 669	1 218	439	514.7	5 331	1 170
Richmond	1 063.0	471.0	79.9	412.6	1 951	1 242	709	1 029.3	4 866	638
Roanoke	385.6	172.3	96.1	172.9	1 766	1 081	685	378.3	3 865	222
Suffolk	304.8	145.8	82.7	134.3	1 577	1 160	411	324.3	3 808	436
Virginia Beach	1 602.6	600.6	84.2	810.1	1 817	1 221	583	1 799.1	4 036	628
Winchester	116.1	39.1	89.9	61.6	2 267	1 283	983	112.7	4 147	231
WASHINGTON	X	X	X	X	X	X	X	X	X	X
Auburn	109.0	17.7	41.8	43.9	598	200	378	107.6	1 464	393
Bellevue	284.5	33.1	23.5	153.0	1 157	275	833	257.3	1 947	276
Bellingham	120.9	15.0	39.1	67.7	825	212	593	118.7	1 446	280
Bothell	54.5	14.0	63.8	29.4	848	273	531	61.1	1 763	521
Bremerton	57.7	6.4	49.1	25.4	646	218	419	58.3	1 484	236
Burien	28.1	4.7	75.2	18.7	378	142	222	34.9	705	215
Des Moines	29.2	4.6	73.5	12.6	412	142	257	26.8	881	214
Edmonds	45.6	4.4	75.7	28.0	693	332	334	42.6	1 054	137
Everett	182.2	16.6	67.5	108.1	1 033	367	650	170.4	1 629	324
Federal Way	65.3	12.0	93.7	40.0	435	107	311	59.1	643	167
Issaquah	59.7	10.5	71.1	31.0	949	250	650	53.3	1 633	344
Kennewick	68.6	6.5	69.3	41.7	550	142	391	69.4	914	179
Kent	137.7	20.6	82.9	62.9	511	157	335	140.6	1 143	354
Kirkland	106.7	9.7	53.2	61.0	731	262	428	105.7	1 267	159
Lacey	56.2	9.1	68.1	26.8	611	136	454	60.0	1 365	347
Lake Stevens	14.7	2.9	47.3	9.7	333	139	178	9.2	318	2
Lakewood	45.5	9.7	66.3	28.3	480	104	367	49.0	831	168
Longview	58.1	10.3	61.4	25.0	685	222	460	58.2	1 593	375
Lynnwood	66.8	5.6	76.9	38.6	1 065	319	731	58.4	1 610	230
Marysville	60.6	3.7	74.9	30.1	483	246	222	58.8	943	114
Mount Vernon	38.0	3.3	70.9	17.8	552	222	318	33.3	1 033	107
Olympia	99.6	9.9	54.8	50.0	1 045	267	761	116.3	2 434	673

1. Based on population estimated as of July 1 of the year shown.

City	City government finances, 2012 (cont.)									
	General expenditure (cont.)									
	Percent of total for:									
	Public welfare	Highways	Parking facilities	Education	Health and hospitals	Police protection	Sewerage and sanitation	Parks and recreation	Housing and community development	Interest on debt
	127	128	129	130	131	132	133	134	135	136
UTAH—Cont'd										
Kaysville	0.0	10.3	0.0	0.0	0.0	7.6	51.5	11.5	0.0	0.4
Layton	0.0	16.8	0.0	0.0	0.0	26.0	19.4	9.8	1.1	0.5
Lehi	0.0	39.4	0.0	0.0	0.0	13.0	21.2	1.1	0.0	4.8
Logan	0.0	14.4	0.0	0.0	0.0	16.5	26.1	11.6	5.4	0.7
Midvale	0.0	9.4	0.0	0.0	0.0	30.1	15.3	2.0	3.5	7.1
Murray	0.0	15.6	0.0	0.0	0.0	19.8	13.0	13.4	2.1	1.2
Ogden	0.0	4.7	0.0	0.0	0.0	14.8	16.3	5.7	17.8	2.5
Orem	0.0	11.1	0.0	0.0	0.0	20.7	17.2	10.0	3.7	2.9
Pleasant Grove	0.0	3.1	0.0	0.0	0.0	20.0	22.6	14.2	0.0	8.8
Provo	0.0	10.5	0.0	0.0	0.0	15.5	9.1	27.2	5.6	4.5
Riverton	0.0	25.5	0.0	0.0	0.0	7.2	8.5	5.8	2.0	36.7
Roy	0.0	7.7	0.0	0.0	0.0	26.4	11.6	13.2	2.1	0.2
St. George	0.0	18.8	0.0	0.0	0.0	16.5	19.8	18.3	1.4	6.6
Salt Lake City	0.0	10.9	0.0	0.0	0.0	14.9	5.8	5.6	9.0	3.8
Sandy	0.0	7.4	0.0	0.0	0.0	18.4	13.6	11.7	1.0	5.4
South Jordan	0.0	14.1	0.0	0.0	0.0	10.9	6.1	12.5	9.7	3.6
Spanish Fork	0.0	10.9	0.0	0.0	0.0	11.9	16.0	20.8	0.0	2.7
Springville	0.0	7.8	0.0	0.0	0.9	12.7	15.8	12.5	0.0	5.5
Taylorsville	0.0	10.3	0.0	0.0	0.0	27.4	1.8	1.8	4.8	1.3
Tooele	0.0	12.0	0.0	0.0	0.0	16.2	9.4	17.6	12.8	5.1
West Jordan	0.0	17.8	0.0	0.0	0.0	22.3	18.1	4.0	3.7	2.0
West Valley City	0.0	7.4	0.0	0.0	1.1	13.1	5.3	16.7	25.5	4.1
VERMONT	X	X	X	X	X	X	X	X	X	X
Burlington	0.0	9.2	5.2	0.0	0.0	11.3	8.3	8.8	5.6	3.9
VIRGINIA	X	X	X	X	X	X	X	X	X	X
Alexandria	6.3	3.7	0.0	34.5	6.0	9.6	6.1	3.7	2.0	2.8
Blacksburg	0.0	22.9	0.0	0.0	1.6	19.2	16.1	5.9	6.9	2.2
Charlottesville	11.0	6.3	0.1	31.0	8.0	7.1	5.8	5.3	2.3	1.6
Chesapeake	3.3	5.6	0.0	54.2	3.3	4.6	3.4	2.3	0.4	2.3
Danville	4.2	5.7	0.0	41.3	2.3	5.5	6.6	2.2	2.3	1.7
Hampton	5.7	1.3	0.1	45.5	0.8	5.2	4.9	6.8	8.5	3.2
Harrisonburg	1.8	11.3	0.1	38.9	0.7	4.7	9.4	3.1	0.3	18.0
Leesburg	0.0	9.2	0.0	0.0	0.0	19.2	10.4	11.6	0.0	4.3
Lynchburg	7.1	2.8	0.1	35.8	0.7	6.4	15.5	2.2	2.9	2.8
Manassas	0.7	6.2	0.1	54.0	2.2	7.8	7.8	0.2	2.3	3.2
Newport News	5.1	3.9	0.0	42.3	8.5	5.7	4.8	3.1	5.8	3.6
Norfolk	6.6	4.6	1.0	36.0	3.2	5.9	5.3	4.1	9.5	3.1
Petersburg	11.4	4.7	0.0	40.0	1.0	9.0	4.0	1.3	1.0	1.0
Portsmouth	5.0	1.3	0.2	33.2	2.1	6.8	5.2	2.1	6.8	2.7
Richmond	1.6	2.7	0.0	31.6	4.5	8.9	10.5	2.5	9.1	0.8
Roanoke	15.3	3.5	0.4	39.4	0.9	6.1	2.2	2.5	6.6	3.1
Suffolk	4.4	6.8	0.0	45.2	0.2	6.3	2.0	1.6	1.2	2.8
Virginia Beach	3.8	4.8	0.1	46.8	3.0	5.0	7.1	5.9	1.4	3.0
Winchester	6.4	5.0	0.8	43.4	1.0	6.4	10.1	2.6	1.9	4.9
WASHINGTON	X	X	X	X	X	X	X	X	X	X
Auburn	0.0	19.6	0.0	0.0	0.5	15.0	33.6	9.0	0.2	2.2
Bellevue	0.0	15.0	0.0	0.0	6.3	11.9	18.4	15.2	5.3	2.8
Bellingham	0.0	10.0	1.2	0.0	7.0	13.4	14.1	16.3	1.8	1.6
Bothell	0.0	30.3	0.0	0.0	0.2	16.3	12.8	2.0	1.6	0.9
Bremerton	0.0	5.7	0.8	0.0	4.2	18.7	14.8	21.3	1.8	3.3
Burien	0.0	31.7	0.0	0.0	3.0	27.1	2.7	8.9	2.0	2.6
Des Moines	0.1	19.9	0.0	0.0	0.8	24.9	4.7	24.1	0.0	1.4
Edmonds	0.0	7.5	0.0	0.0	0.1	18.8	16.6	11.8	0.0	2.5
Everett	0.2	7.5	0.1	0.0	4.4	15.4	24.4	7.7	1.3	4.0
Federal Way	0.2	28.9	0.0	0.0	1.1	27.6	4.7	10.0	2.0	1.0
Issaquah	0.0	14.9	0.0	0.0	0.0	8.3	20.1	9.3	2.9	3.0
Kennewick	0.0	11.4	0.0	0.0	5.3	18.7	4.5	20.4	0.8	2.9
Kent	0.2	5.1	0.0	0.0	1.2	15.6	40.1	11.7	2.0	3.1
Kirkland	0.0	10.8	0.1	0.0	0.7	17.1	22.2	8.0	0.0	2.1
Lacey	0.0	19.2	0.0	0.0	2.9	14.1	25.7	13.0	0.0	1.6
Lake Stevens	0.2	13.5	0.0	0.0	0.4	40.6	12.7	1.9	2.0	3.5
Lakewood	1.0	17.8	0.0	0.0	0.6	40.2	7.5	3.3	4.9	0.3
Longview	0.2	8.3	0.0	0.0	0.0	15.9	40.1	5.9	2.7	1.2
Lynnwood	0.0	8.5	0.0	0.0	7.2	19.4	9.5	17.2	1.2	1.4
Marysville	0.0	17.7	0.0	0.0	4.9	14.4	17.3	5.1	0.0	5.8
Mount Vernon	0.0	9.6	0.0	0.0	0.5	19.0	29.6	4.4	0.0	2.1
Olympia	0.0	6.3	0.0	0.0	1.9	9.4	24.8	12.3	0.4	3.4

Table D. Cities — City Government Finances, City Government Employment, and Climate

City	City government finances, 2012 (cont.) — Debt outstanding — Total (mil dol)	Per capita[1] (dollars)	Debt issued during year	Climate[2] — Average daily temperature (degrees Fahrenheit) — Mean — January	July	Limits — January[3]	July[4]	Annual precipitation (inches)	Heating degree days	Cooling degree days
	137	138	139	140	141	142	143	144	145	146
UTAH—Cont'd										
Kaysville	2.6	91	0.0	NA	NA	NA	NA	NA	NA	NA
Layton	4.9	71	0.0	27.6	74.2	18.6	89.9	20.75	6 142	746
Lehi	97.2	1 889	0.7	NA	NA	NA	NA	NA	NA	NA
Logan	43.8	891	0.0	21.8	71.6	12.7	88.3	17.86	7 174	522
Midvale	50.8	1 678	1.5	30.4	78.5	22.1	90.9	26.19	5 441	1 197
Murray	36.9	765	6.1	29.2	77.0	21.3	90.6	16.50	5 631	1 066
Ogden	115.6	1 378	7.1	28.1	76.6	20.1	90.0	23.67	5 868	980
Orem	67.1	740	4.3	28.6	76.5	20.3	92.3	12.84	5 564	1 016
Pleasant Grove	62.2	1 801	22.8	NA	NA	NA	NA	NA	NA	NA
Provo	115.1	997	34.5	30.9	76.9	22.5	93.4	20.13	5 264	1 028
Riverton	482.2	11 921	4.6	31.6	78.0	22.0	95.3	15.76	5 251	1 172
Roy	7.2	193	0.6	27.6	74.2	18.6	89.9	20.75	6 142	746
St. George	157.4	2 090	6.1	41.8	86.3	28.9	102.8	8.77	3 103	2 471
Salt Lake City	393.2	2 075	81.7	32.0	78.1	25.4	89.0	17.75	5 095	1 190
Sandy	93.6	1 045	8.3	30.4	78.5	22.1	90.9	26.19	5 441	1 197
South Jordan	71.6	1 279	6.9	31.6	78.0	22.0	95.3	15.76	5 251	1 172
Spanish Fork	24.7	681	0.0	NA	NA	NA	NA	NA	NA	NA
Springville	37.6	1 229	0.0	NA	NA	NA	NA	NA	NA	NA
Taylorsville	10.9	182	0.7	29.2	77.0	21.3	90.6	16.50	5 631	1 066
Tooele	36.8	1 147	15.2	NA	NA	NA	NA	NA	NA	NA
West Jordan	23.2	214	3.3	30.4	78.5	22.1	90.9	26.19	5 441	1 197
West Valley City	149.0	1 125	33.1	29.2	77.0	21.3	90.6	16.50	5 631	1 066
VERMONT	X	X	X	X	X	X	X	X	X	X
Burlington	192.6	4 550	24.3	18.0	70.6	9.3	81.4	36.05	7 665	489
VIRGINIA	X	X	X	X	X	X	X	X	X	X
Alexandria	580.7	3 952	133.6	34.9	79.2	27.3	88.3	39.35	4 055	1 531
Blacksburg	23.1	541	9.5	30.9	71.1	20.6	82.5	42.63	5 559	533
Charlottesville	117.7	2 645	34.1	35.5	76.9	26.2	88.0	48.87	4 103	1 212
Chesapeake	635.5	2 785	137.5	40.1	79.1	32.3	86.8	45.74	3 368	1 612
Danville	152.0	3 554	3.9	36.6	78.8	25.8	90.0	44.98	3 970	1 418
Hampton	359.9	2 630	78.5	39.4	78.5	32.0	85.2	47.90	3 535	1 432
Harrisonburg	500.6	9 773	28.6	30.5	73.5	20.4	85.3	36.12	5 333	758
Leesburg	126.9	2 753	33.9	31.5	75.2	20.8	87.1	43.21	5 031	911
Lynchburg	330.4	4 247	7.0	34.5	75.1	24.5	86.4	43.31	4 354	1 075
Manassas	130.5	3 202	0.0	31.7	75.7	21.9	87.4	41.80	4 925	1 075
Newport News	797.6	4 419	228.9	41.2	80.3	33.8	87.9	43.53	3 179	1 682
Norfolk	1 752.2	7 119	414.1	40.1	79.1	32.3	86.8	45.74	3 368	1 612
Petersburg	34.6	1 076	1.5	39.7	79.6	29.2	91.0	45.26	3 334	1 619
Portsmouth	519.2	5 378	88.9	40.1	79.1	32.3	86.8	45.74	3 368	1 612
Richmond	1 340.2	6 336	260.0	36.4	77.9	27.6	87.5	43.91	3 919	1 435
Roanoke	544.5	5 563	52.3	35.8	76.2	26.6	87.5	42.49	4 284	1 134
Suffolk	538.4	6 320	114.6	39.6	78.5	30.3	88.1	48.71	3 467	1 427
Virginia Beach	1 698.8	3 811	173.0	40.7	78.8	32.2	86.9	44.50	3 336	1 482
Winchester	201.0	7 395	51.9	NA	NA	NA	NA	NA	NA	NA
WASHINGTON	X	X	X	X	X	X	X	X	X	X
Auburn	68.3	929	0.0	40.8	66.4	34.6	77.4	39.59	4 624	219
Bellevue	176.9	1 338	0.0	41.5	65.5	36.0	74.5	38.25	4 615	192
Bellingham	92.2	1 124	49.1	40.5	63.3	34.8	72.5	34.84	4 980	68
Bothell	43.3	1 251	30.0	40.8	65.2	35.2	75.0	35.96	4 756	174
Bremerton	75.6	1 923	12.7	40.1	64.6	34.7	75.2	53.96	4 994	158
Burien	33.0	667	8.6	40.9	65.3	35.9	75.3	37.07	4 797	173
Des Moines	14.4	471	2.0	40.9	65.3	35.9	75.3	37.07	4 797	173
Edmonds	37.6	929	13.8	40.8	65.2	35.2	75.0	35.96	4 756	174
Everett	252.3	2 410	52.2	39.7	63.6	33.6	73.0	37.54	5 199	121
Federal Way	13.7	149	0.0	41.0	65.6	35.1	76.1	38.95	4 650	167
Issaquah	38.5	1 180	5.4	NA	NA	NA	NA	NA	NA	NA
Kennewick	63.3	834	5.4	34.2	75.2	28.0	89.3	8.01	4 731	909
Kent	164.6	1 338	0.0	40.8	66.4	34.6	77.4	39.59	4 624	219
Kirkland	53.5	641	8.3	40.8	65.2	35.2	75.0	35.96	4 756	174
Lacey	24.6	561	1.6	38.1	62.8	31.8	76.1	50.79	5 531	97
Lake Stevens	22.3	768	0.0	NA	NA	NA	NA	NA	NA	NA
Lakewood	12.0	203	1.3	41.0	65.6	35.1	76.1	38.95	4 650	167
Longview	34.6	948	15.4	39.9	64.5	33.8	76.5	48.02	4 900	148
Lynnwood	46.2	1 274	6.4	40.8	65.2	35.2	75.0	35.96	4 756	174
Marysville	92.8	1 487	4.8	39.7	63.6	33.6	73.0	37.54	5 199	121
Mount Vernon	37.4	1 161	0.0	39.9	62.3	34.1	73.0	32.70	5 197	47
Olympia	95.1	1 989	3.4	38.1	62.8	31.8	76.1	50.79	5 531	97

1. Based on the population estimated as of July 1 of the year shown.   2. Represents normal values based on the 30-year period, 1971–2000.   3. Average daily minimum.
4. Average daily maximum.

Table D. Cities — **Land Area and Population**

STATE Place code	City	Land area,[1] 2010 (sq km)	Total persons	Rank	Per square kilometer	White	Black	American Indian, Alaska Native	Asian	Hawaiian Pacific Islander	Percent Hispanic or Latino[2], 2010-2014	Percent foreign born 2010–2014
		Population, 2015				Race alone or in combination (percent), 2010-2014						
		1	2	3	4	5	6	7	8	9	10	11
	WASHINGTON— Cont'd											
53 53545	Pasco	79.0	69 451	500	879.1	67.3	3.0	1.3	2.8	0.1	55.5	25.7
53 56625	Pullman	25.6	32 816	1 145	1 281.9	83.6	3.9	1.8	14.0	0.8	6.4	14.0
53 56695	Puyallup	36.1	39 659	947	1 098.6	88.9	5.9	2.1	6.5	0.5	8.4	6.5
53 57535	Redmond	42.2	60 598	599	1 436.0	66.1	2.2	1.1	31.9	0.4	9.3	37.3
53 57745	Renton	59.9	100 242	301	1 673.5	59.1	13.0	2.5	25.0	1.3	13.6	28.5
53 58235	Richland	92.5	54 248	690	586.5	88.1	2.2	2.6	6.8	0.4	9.0	8.1
53 61115	Sammamish	47.2	52 253	722	1 107.1	77.4	1.6	1.0	23.0	0.4	4.1	24.7
53 62288	SeaTac	26.0	28 215	1 306	1 085.2	55.0	24.7	3.3	16.9	3.4	19.6	37.6
53 63000	Seattle	217.4	684 451	18	3 148.3	74.9	9.0	2.2	17.2	1.0	6.4	18.0
53 63960	Shoreline	30.2	55 439	675	1 835.7	74.3	6.9	3.2	16.5	1.4	8.1	19.7
53 67000	Spokane	153.5	213 272	101	1 389.4	91.0	4.3	3.7	4.1	0.6	5.7	7.0
53 67167	Spokane Valley	97.8	94 919	323	970.5	93.7	2.3	2.5	3.2	0.9	4.7	4.7
53 70000	Tacoma	128.8	207 948	106	1 614.5	72.8	14.6	3.3	11.6	2.2	11.0	13.4
53 73465	University Place	21.8	32 842	1 144	1 506.5	78.7	10.6	3.3	12.6	2.0	7.8	13.0
53 74060	Vancouver	120.3	172 860	144	1 436.9	83.8	5.0	2.6	7.4	2.3	11.2	13.1
53 75775	Walla Walla	33.2	32 237	1 169	971.0	86.4	3.7	3.7	3.6	0.6	22.3	12.3
53 77105	Wenatchee	20.1	33 636	1 116	1 673.4	90.5	1.3	2.7	2.1	0.8	31.1	12.9
53 80010	Yakima	70.4	93 701	330	1 331.0	74.5	2.1	3.6	2.0	0.3	44.0	17.4
54 00000	**WEST VIRGINIA**	62 258.7	1 844 128	X	29.6	95.5	4.1	1.1	0.9	0.1	1.3	1.5
54 14600	Charleston	81.6	49 736	754	609.5	87.3	11.8	4.8	3.1	0.3	1.5	3.0
54 39460	Huntington	42.0	48 638	779	1 158.0	90.4	10.7	1.1	1.4	0.1	1.2	2.6
54 55756	Morgantown	26.3	30 708	1 211	1 167.6	89.2	7.0	0.8	4.7	0.0	2.6	5.7
54 62140	Parkersburg	30.6	30 991	1 196	1 012.8	97.4	2.8	1.2	0.6	0.0	0.9	0.6
54 86452	Wheeling	35.7	27 648	1 334	774.5	92.8	6.7	0.9	1.3	0.0	1.2	1.5
55 00000	**WISCONSIN**	140 268.1	5 771 337	X	41.1	88.6	7.2	1.6	2.8	0.1	6.2	4.7
55 02375	Appleton	63.0	74 139	465	1 176.8	89.7	2.6	1.3	6.4	0.2	5.5	6.6
55 06500	Beloit	45.0	36 891	1 022	819.8	84.4	13.7	3.5	1.5	0.0	18.9	9.3
55 10025	Brookfield	70.2	38 025	987	541.7	93.5	1.6	0.3	5.5	0.0	2.6	6.7
55 22300	Eau Claire	83.0	67 778	517	816.6	94.2	1.9	0.9	5.0	0.1	2.4	3.5
55 25950	Fitchburg	90.6	27 996	1 319	309.0	71.4	13.1	1.7	6.5	0.2	19.6	16.9
55 26275	Fond du Lac	48.8	42 933	871	879.8	92.4	3.5	1.6	2.2	0.0	6.6	5.1
55 27300	Franklin	89.6	36 222	1 037	404.3	87.7	6.0	1.6	7.2	0.1	4.2	7.4
55 31000	Green Bay	117.8	105 207	283	893.1	84.9	5.4	5.1	4.5	0.0	12.8	8.2
55 31175	Greenfield	29.8	37 349	1 011	1 253.3	90.4	3.2	1.2	5.4	0.1	9.6	8.7
55 37825	Janesville	87.7	64 123	560	731.2	95.6	2.7	2.3	2.1	0.0	5.1	3.6
55 39225	Kenosha	69.8	99 858	303	1 430.6	85.3	11.8	1.2	2.1	0.1	16.6	7.6
55 40775	La Crosse	53.1	52 306	719	985.0	91.9	3.2	1.1	4.6	0.1	2.0	3.1
55 48000	Madison	198.9	248 951	84	1 251.6	82.3	9.1	1.2	9.0	0.1	6.6	10.7
55 48500	Manitowoc	45.7	33 010	1 140	722.3	92.7	1.0	0.9	5.7	0.2	5.0	3.4
55 51000	Menomonee Falls	85.3	36 119	1 044	423.4	92.0	2.8	0.5	5.2	0.0	2.4	5.4
55 53000	Milwaukee	249.0	600 155	31	2 410.3	49.9	41.5	1.8	4.2	0.1	17.7	9.8
55 54875	Mount Pleasant	87.4	26 272	1 389	300.6	88.4	7.3	1.1	2.5	0.2	8.9	5.2
55 55750	Neenah	23.9	25 792	1 400	1 079.2	93.0	1.8	1.5	3.4	0.0	4.9	3.3
55 56375	New Berlin	94.4	39 825	939	421.9	94.4	1.2	0.6	5.0	0.1	2.8	5.3
55 58800	Oak Creek	73.7	35 243	1 069	478.2	90.9	2.9	1.3	4.8	0.2	8.5	6.7
55 60500	Oshkosh	66.3	66 555	533	1 003.8	93.9	4.0	1.2	2.6	0.1	3.0	2.5
55 66000	Racine	40.1	77 742	434	1 938.7	69.1	24.1	1.3	1.5	0.0	21.7	7.7
55 72975	Sheboygan	36.2	48 797	776	1 348.0	85.7	2.9	0.8	10.3	0.1	10.6	10.4
55 77200	Stevens Point	41.3	26 604	1 375	644.2	92.6	2.0	1.3	4.6	0.0	3.0	4.0
55 78600	Sun Prairie	31.7	32 365	1 163	1 021.0	89.5	7.3	0.2	4.1	0.2	3.6	4.3
55 78650	Superior	95.7	26 579	1 377	277.7	95.1	2.5	3.5	1.7	0.0	1.0	2.6
55 84250	Waukesha	64.3	71 970	481	1 119.3	89.8	3.9	0.8	4.4	0.1	12.4	7.8
55 84475	Wausau	48.6	39 094	962	804.4	83.8	3.4	1.7	14.7	0.0	4.0	7.9
55 84675	Wauwatosa	34.3	47 614	797	1 388.2	92.1	5.3	0.6	3.6	0.1	2.9	4.5
55 85300	West Allis	29.5	60 620	598	2 054.9	90.1	5.3	2.0	3.1	0.1	10.5	5.4
55 85350	West Bend	37.7	31 695	1 181	840.7	95.6	1.9	0.7	1.8	0.0	3.7	2.8
56 00000	**WYOMING**	251 470.1	586 107	X	2.3	93.4	1.6	3.8	1.3	0.2	9.4	3.4
56 13150	Casper	69.7	60 285	607	864.9	94.9	2.8	2.9	1.3	0.3	7.8	2.4
56 13900	Cheyenne	63.5	63 335	569	997.4	88.5	4.8	2.4	2.6	0.3	15.0	2.9
56 31855	Gillette	49.1	32 649	1 152	664.9	94.0	1.3	1.9	0.9	0.1	10.0	4.3
56 45050	Laramie	45.9	32 158	1 173	700.6	92.0	2.1	1.3	4.2	0.1	9.6	5.9

1. Dry land or land partially or temporarily covered by water.　　2. May be of any race.

Table D. Cities — **Population**

City	Age of population (percent), 2010-2014									Median age 2010– 2014	Percent female 2010– 2014	Population — Census counts		Population — Percent change	
	Under 5 years	5 to 17 years	18 to 24 years	25 to 34 years	35 to 44 years	45 to 54 years	55 to 64 years	65 to 74 years	75 years and over			2000	2010	2000– 2010	2010– 2015
	12	13	14	15	16	17	18	19	20	21	22	23	24	25	26
WASHINGTON— Cont'd															
Pasco	10.7	24.3	10.1	16.9	12.9	10.4	7.6	4.0	3.2	28.1	49.4	32 066	59 781	86.4	13.7
Pullman	3.7	7.7	53.7	14.3	6.5	4.8	4.8	2.2	2.3	22.0	49.2	24 675	29 799	20.8	10.1
Puyallup	5.5	15.3	11.2	15.0	13.1	13.0	14.6	6.5	5.9	38.2	49.2	33 011	37 022	12.2	6.5
Redmond	7.7	13.9	7.1	23.3	17.3	12.4	9.4	4.3	4.6	34.1	48.9	45 256	54 144	19.6	11.6
Renton	7.6	15.4	7.5	17.7	17.1	13.8	11.1	5.1	4.7	36.0	50.6	50 052	90 927	81.7	9.1
Richland	7.2	18.3	8.5	13.4	11.2	14.5	12.1	8.8	6.0	37.3	49.5	38 708	48 058	24.2	12.8
Sammamish	7.2	25.1	5.4	7.5	19.2	18.6	10.8	4.2	2.0	38.2	50.2	34 104	45 780	34.2	11.7
SeaTac	7.6	14.6	11.2	17.8	13.9	13.5	10.8	6.7	3.9	34.2	45.8	25 496	26 909	5.5	4.9
Seattle	5.3	10.5	11.2	21.6	15.7	12.7	11.7	6.4	4.9	35.9	50.2	563 374	608 660	8.0	12.5
Shoreline	4.5	14.6	8.6	14.1	13.4	14.1	13.8	8.6	8.3	41.2	51.0	53 025	53 007	0.0	4.5
Spokane	7.1	15.0	11.8	15.7	11.9	12.4	12.1	7.2	6.9	35.3	51.0	195 629	208 916	6.8	1.8
Spokane Valley	5.5	17.4	8.4	14.0	12.2	14.9	12.8	8.1	6.8	38.9	49.3	NA	89 755	NA	5.8
Tacoma	6.8	15.8	10.7	15.5	13.4	13.6	11.9	6.7	5.5	35.8	50.8	193 556	198 397	2.5	4.8
University Place	6.1	19.0	10.8	11.3	12.8	12.9	13.3	6.8	6.9	36.8	52.9	29 933	31 144	4.0	5.4
Vancouver	6.8	16.8	9.0	15.2	14.1	12.9	11.9	7.5	5.9	36.7	51.1	143 560	161 791	12.7	6.4
Walla Walla	4.7	16.3	14.6	12.8	13.9	12.5	11.3	6.9	7.0	36.3	46.9	29 686	31 731	6.9	1.6
Wenatchee	9.4	18.8	8.6	16.7	8.6	12.4	11.2	5.8	8.4	31.9	52.0	27 856	31 925	14.6	4.7
Yakima	8.9	18.4	11.1	14.8	11.7	11.1	10.4	7.0	6.5	32.8	50.0	71 845	91 067	26.8	2.7
WEST VIRGINIA	5.5	15.1	9.3	11.8	12.6	14.2	14.7	9.4	7.3	41.6	50.7	1 808 344	1 852 994	2.5	-0.5
Charleston	5.6	14.7	9.2	13.3	11.4	14.5	14.4	8.8	8.1	41.2	51.4	53 421	51 400	-3.8	-3.1
Huntington	5.2	12.8	16.7	14.2	10.7	11.4	13.9	7.9	7.3	35.8	52.3	51 475	49 138	-4.5	-1.0
Morgantown	2.5	6.9	43.7	16.9	7.3	6.4	8.2	3.5	4.7	23.8	44.1	26 809	29 660	10.6	7.3
Parkersburg	6.0	14.9	8.9	11.0	11.9	16.1	13.1	9.2	8.9	42.8	54.1	33 099	31 492	-4.9	-1.2
Wheeling	6.2	12.7	8.4	10.6	10.5	13.6	16.5	10.2	11.3	46.7	51.4	31 419	28 486	-9.3	-2.8
WISCONSIN	6.1	16.9	9.7	12.7	12.3	14.8	13.1	7.7	6.7	38.9	50.4	5 363 675	5 686 986	6.0	1.5
Appleton	6.5	18.3	9.8	14.5	13.3	14.6	11.5	6.0	5.6	35.7	51.1	70 087	72 623	3.6	2.1
Beloit	6.3	19.5	13.1	11.8	12.6	13.0	11.0	6.2	6.5	34.4	52.7	35 775	36 966	3.3	-0.3
Brookfield	4.0	18.3	6.5	6.6	12.0	16.3	15.3	9.6	11.4	47.2	53.9	38 649	37 920	-1.9	0.2
Eau Claire	4.9	14.6	21.3	15.2	10.4	11.5	10.4	6.1	5.6	30.6	51.8	61 704	65 883	6.8	2.4
Fitchburg	7.2	18.2	7.6	19.8	15.3	11.1	11.4	6.7	2.7	33.5	46.7	20 501	25 260	23.2	11.3
Fond du Lac	6.5	15.0	9.8	13.7	13.8	13.4	12.4	7.3	8.1	38.2	51.1	42 203	43 021	1.9	-0.2
Franklin	5.2	16.7	7.5	12.6	14.7	14.9	14.6	6.9	6.8	40.7	48.0	29 494	35 451	20.2	2.2
Green Bay	7.7	16.0	11.1	16.3	11.8	13.3	11.7	5.8	6.3	34.0	51.0	102 313	104 057	1.7	1.2
Greenfield	5.6	11.1	6.6	15.7	11.6	13.1	16.3	8.6	11.3	44.3	53.1	35 476	36 720	3.5	1.6
Janesville	7.1	17.5	8.4	14.6	13.0	14.3	11.1	7.5	6.6	36.8	51.2	59 498	63 575	6.9	0.8
Kenosha	7.0	19.7	10.5	13.6	13.7	14.2	10.3	5.5	5.5	34.4	51.3	90 352	99 218	9.8	0.6
La Crosse	4.6	11.1	27.6	13.2	9.0	11.5	10.3	5.5	7.2	29.1	51.8	51 818	51 320	-1.0	1.9
Madison	5.7	11.6	20.5	19.5	11.5	11.2	10.1	5.3	4.7	30.9	50.7	208 054	233 209	12.1	6.8
Manitowoc	6.6	15.7	8.1	11.5	11.0	13.7	14.2	7.8	11.5	42.8	52.4	34 053	33 736	-0.9	-2.2
Menomonee Falls	5.3	16.5	6.9	10.1	11.4	16.7	14.1	9.2	9.9	44.9	51.6	32 647	35 626	9.1	1.4
Milwaukee	7.8	18.9	12.9	16.7	12.4	11.9	10.0	4.8	4.5	30.9	51.9	596 974	594 833	-0.4	0.9
Mount Pleasant	6.3	15.1	6.6	10.1	11.3	15.3	16.0	9.6	9.7	45.5	51.7	NA	26 197	NA	0.3
Neenah	5.7	18.9	8.8	12.9	13.0	16.1	11.6	6.0	7.1	37.8	52.8	24 507	25 501	4.1	1.1
New Berlin	4.1	16.7	6.8	9.6	11.7	17.8	15.6	8.8	8.9	46.1	51.0	38 220	39 584	3.6	0.6
Oak Creek	7.6	15.5	7.3	15.3	15.2	16.2	12.1	6.6	4.2	38.0	51.3	28 456	34 451	21.1	2.3
Oshkosh	5.1	13.9	19.8	13.8	11.8	12.5	10.3	6.3	6.7	33.2	48.0	62 916	66 083	5.0	0.7
Racine	7.3	20.4	9.9	13.3	14.2	12.9	10.8	6.1	5.2	34.0	52.3	81 855	78 860	-3.7	-1.4
Sheboygan	7.1	17.5	8.6	15.3	11.9	14.4	10.9	7.5	6.8	36.3	51.2	50 792	49 288	-3.0	-1.0
Stevens Point	3.6	11.6	31.0	14.4	7.6	11.0	9.2	6.1	5.5	26.4	52.3	24 551	26 717	8.8	-0.4
Sun Prairie	8.8	20.2	7.6	15.4	14.8	13.3	10.6	5.9	3.6	33.8	52.4	20 369	29 364	44.2	9.6
Superior	5.9	14.9	12.4	15.0	11.0	13.6	13.8	7.1	6.2	36.4	51.3	27 368	27 244	-0.5	-2.4
Waukesha	7.2	15.5	11.0	17.3	13.5	12.9	11.4	5.9	5.3	34.1	50.1	64 825	70 718	9.1	1.8
Wausau	7.6	15.5	8.4	14.4	10.0	14.5	12.5	7.4	9.6	39.4	51.5	38 426	39 106	1.8	-0.1
Wauwatosa	7.1	15.2	5.9	16.1	12.7	13.5	13.8	6.8	9.0	39.3	52.4	47 271	46 396	-1.9	2.5
West Allis	6.6	13.9	8.4	18.3	11.5	14.9	12.1	6.2	8.1	37.3	50.5	61 254	60 411	-1.4	0.3
West Bend	6.1	18.8	7.2	14.8	13.9	13.8	11.5	6.7	7.3	36.6	50.1	28 152	31 078	10.4	1.6
WYOMING	6.7	17.2	9.9	14.0	12.0	13.5	13.7	7.5	5.4	36.8	49.0	493 782	563 626	14.1	4.0
Casper	6.8	16.9	9.9	16.2	11.7	12.5	13.2	6.6	6.2	35.2	49.7	49 644	55 316	11.4	9.0
Cheyenne	6.4	17.8	9.6	15.8	12.3	12.3	12.6	7.1	6.1	35.6	50.8	53 011	59 466	12.2	6.2
Gillette	9.7	20.1	10.2	17.9	13.9	11.1	11.2	3.7	2.3	30.4	47.6	19 646	29 087	48.1	9.5
Laramie	5.4	11.2	32.9	17.5	10.0	7.5	9.1	3.4	3.1	25.2	47.5	27 204	30 816	13.3	4.4

Table D. Cities — **Households, Group Quarters, Crime, and Education**

City	Households, 2010-2014 Number	Persons per house-hold	Percent Female family house-holder[1]	One-person	Persons in group quarters, 2010 Total	Institutional Total	Persons in nursing facilities	Non-institu-tional	Serious crimes known to police,[2] 2014 Total Number	Rate[3]	Rate[3] Violent	Property	Population age 25 and older	Attainment[4] (percent) High school graduate or less	Bachelor's degree or more
	27	28	29	30	31	32	33	34	35	36	37	38	39	40	41
WASHINGTON—Cont'd															
Pasco	19 055	3.46	18.1	18.8	385	276	98	109	1 657	2 397	255	2 143	36 452	55.9	15.5
Pullman	10 536	2.93	6.5	29.8	5 788	18	18	5 770	550	1 729	211	1 518	10 957	13.5	65.0
Puyallup	14 966	2.55	14.7	29.4	710	443	403	267	2 901	7 435	282	7 153	25 430	40.0	24.6
Redmond	23 520	2.41	5.8	30.7	274	171	171	103	1 788	3 066	57	3 010	40 562	13.7	62.4
Renton	37 207	2.57	11.5	31.3	685	263	191	422	5 459	5 557	233	5 324	66 464	36.0	31.7
Richland	20 401	2.51	10.6	28.7	285	163	163	122	1 307	2 446	170	2 275	33 910	22.8	43.7
Sammamish	15 820	3.10	5.1	9.3	99	0	0	99	394	772	16	757	30 439	7.9	72.5
SeaTac	9 945	2.78	13.2	32.3	1 014	905	74	109	1 682	5 985	637	5 348	18 728	49.9	18.8
Seattle	290 822	2.19	6.9	41.1	24 925	4 904	2 588	20 021	44 776	6 749	604	6 146	466 943	18.1	57.9
Shoreline	21 360	2.54	10.4	30.8	1 415	581	578	834	1 778	3 221	170	3 050	39 765	25.2	43.2
Spokane	87 235	2.41	12.9	34.1	6 949	1 972	1 236	4 977	19 218	9 107	548	8 559	138 956	34.0	28.6
Spokane Valley	36 802	2.47	11.4	28.9	802	439	418	363	5 542	6 065	325	5 740	62 103	37.3	20.9
Tacoma	78 761	2.56	13.4	33.5	6 693	4 084	1 392	2 609	14 412	7 040	798	6 242	135 199	40.8	25.5
University Place	12 806	2.47	12.5	28.0	206	118	118	88	785	2 433	214	2 219	20 948	26.6	34.9
Vancouver	65 666	2.52	13.3	30.2	2 056	1 192	429	864	5 840	3 462	344	3 118	111 506	37.4	25.1
Walla Walla	11 614	2.75	11.1	38.4	3 651	2 600	190	1 051	1 668	5 240	330	4 910	20 746	38.5	23.1
Wenatchee	11 586	2.82	10.8	29.7	582	402	88	180	1 220	3 717	192	3 525	20 740	45.8	24.2
Yakima	33 023	2.81	15.6	29.4	2 448	1 841	650	607	5 042	5 383	438	4 945	57 966	53.0	17.3
WEST VIRGINIA	742 359	2.50	11.3	29.9	49 382	28 323	9 748	21 059	43 236	2 337	302	2 035	1 298 614	56.5	18.7
Charleston	22 919	2.22	12.3	41.2	1 940	675	220	1 265	3 985	7 861	1 243	6 618	36 023	35.8	39.3
Huntington	21 148	2.32	14.7	40.1	3 012	676	412	2 336	0	0	0	0	31 784	42.4	28.7
Morgantown	10 055	3.00	6.5	45.0	5 636	86	19	5 550	894	2 874	260	2 614	14 112	28.6	47.8
Parkersburg	13 314	2.34	13.6	37.7	547	341	326	206	1 160	3 725	286	3 439	21 906	53.6	14.5
Wheeling	12 738	2.21	13.4	42.1	1 436	523	413	913	929	3 331	782	2 549	20 272	44.6	28.0
WISCONSIN	2 293 250	2.50	10.1	29.0	150 214	74 295	33 808	75 919	136 952	2 379	290	2 088	3 850 995	41.6	27.4
Appleton	28 741	2.54	11.0	30.1	2 429	864	487	1 565	1 603	2 171	269	1 901	47 461	36.2	31.9
Beloit	14 140	2.61	19.5	30.0	1 553	242	242	1 311	1 388	3 764	404	3 360	22 691	57.2	15.4
Brookfield	14 557	2.61	4.7	22.4	513	460	460	53	1 034	2 720	58	2 662	26 919	18.1	57.7
Eau Claire	27 255	2.46	9.2	34.1	4 536	613	256	3 923	1 837	2 704	162	2 542	39 655	31.3	32.6
Fitchburg	10 407	2.50	12.3	29.1	822	815	0	7	486	1 822	277	1 544	17 868	30.6	45.9
Fond du Lac	18 271	2.35	12.3	34.5	2 087	1 481	480	606	1 344	3 129	328	2 801	29 334	45.8	22.1
Franklin	13 126	2.74	7.0	26.1	1 982	1 908	42	74	788	2 158	55	2 103	25 732	33.7	34.1
Green Bay	42 358	2.47	12.6	33.6	3 206	1 362	617	1 844	2 836	2 701	497	2 204	67 407	46.4	23.1
Greenfield	16 661	2.22	8.6	39.6	821	728	728	93	1 015	2 724	150	2 574	28 327	43.3	26.7
Janesville	25 581	2.49	13.2	28.4	930	756	309	174	2 238	3 503	254	3 250	42 488	45.5	21.5
Kenosha	37 305	2.67	16.5	28.8	3 488	1 620	736	1 868	2 701	2 700	288	2 412	63 112	45.0	23.0
La Crosse	20 749	2.50	9.6	35.6	4 681	827	540	3 854	1 638	3 177	202	2 975	29 201	35.0	30.6
Madison	103 169	2.32	8.2	35.7	10 740	2 171	1 173	8 569	7 835	3 188	344	2 844	148 209	20.2	55.0
Manitowoc	14 839	2.25	8.9	37.2	956	532	524	424	1 003	3 017	223	2 794	23 557	49.2	21.8
Menomonee Falls	14 539	2.46	6.4	28.0	217	202	202	15	451	1 253	22	1 231	25 582	31.7	40.8
Milwaukee	230 181	2.60	22.2	35.0	18 401	5 302	2 512	13 099	36 461	6 073	1 485	4 588	360 444	48.4	22.8
Mount Pleasant	11 053	2.37	7.8	29.9	290	268	265	22	811	3 092	61	3 031	19 082	35.5	33.0
Neenah	10 798	2.38	8.8	31.5	277	233	211	44	514	1 978	142	1 835	17 309	39.1	29.3
New Berlin	16 612	2.39	5.3	29.1	161	125	125	36	NA	NA	NA	NA	29 320	28.8	40.6
Oak Creek	14 140	2.46	7.4	29.8	125	0	0	125	1 015	2 889	125	2 763	23 992	37.2	29.1
Oshkosh	25 987	2.56	11.1	35.2	7 520	4 056	974	3 464	1 588	2 371	233	2 139	40 819	45.2	24.8
Racine	29 979	2.61	17.7	33.1	1 548	1 276	152	272	3 040	3 895	406	3 488	48 780	51.2	17.2
Sheboygan	20 151	2.43	11.9	32.2	953	766	472	187	1 422	2 926	317	2 609	32 365	52.0	18.5
Stevens Point	10 529	2.54	8.6	34.8	3 330	178	94	3 152	595	2 231	158	2 074	14 404	34.6	34.2
Sun Prairie	12 029	2.54	12.5	24.5	102	82	82	20	767	2 455	90	2 366	19 994	25.0	42.5
Superior	11 669	2.31	13.0	37.6	1 191	393	234	798	1 813	6 771	276	6 494	18 134	38.3	22.4
Waukesha	28 466	2.50	10.5	30.6	2 911	892	228	2 019	1 296	1 823	129	1 694	46 539	32.2	34.4
Wausau	16 562	2.37	12.4	37.1	1 100	820	526	280	851	2 162	221	1 941	26 356	44.3	25.1
Wauwatosa	20 515	2.28	8.4	36.0	871	732	615	139	1 604	3 391	159	3 232	33 591	18.9	55.8
West Allis	27 294	2.22	10.8	40.0	829	591	583	238	2 936	4 832	360	4 471	43 420	45.1	22.4
West Bend	13 009	2.42	8.6	29.2	530	429	215	101	955	3 018	164	2 853	21 460	38.4	26.1
WYOMING	225 514	2.55	8.8	27.7	13 712	6 701	2 450	7 011	12 619	2 160	195	1 965	381 098	37.1	25.1
Casper	23 535	2.46	10.8	29.5	1 125	548	483	577	1 716	2 824	138	2 685	37 968	33.9	22.9
Cheyenne	25 007	2.46	11.8	31.6	865	636	330	229	1 884	2 983	141	2 842	40 586	32.4	27.7
Gillette	11 342	2.74	11.5	23.0	422	260	123	162	1 008	3 123	158	2 965	18 738	43.8	19.0
Laramie	12 992	2.43	6.0	32.4	2 176	78	70	2 098	753	2 350	150	2 201	16 229	18.5	51.4

1. No spouse present.   2. Data for serious crimes have not been adjusted for underreporting. This may affect comparability between geographic areas and over time.   3. Per 100,000 population estimated by the FBI.   4. Persons 25 years old and over.

Table D. Cities — Income, Poverty, and Housing

City	Money income, 2010–2014					Housing units, 2010			Occupied housing units 2010–2014				
	Households				Families with income below poverty (percent)					Owner-occupied		Median owner costs as a percent of income	
	Per capita income[1] (dollars)	Median income	Percent with income of $200,000 or more	Percent with income of less than $25,000		Total	Percent change, 2000–2010	Vacant units for sale or rent[2]	Total	Percent	Median value[3] (dollars)	With a mortgage[4]	Without a mortgage[5]
	42	43	44	45	46	47	48	49	50	51	52	53	54
WASHINGTON— Cont'd													
Pasco	19 175	54 700	1.5	23.0	17.4	18 782	81.7	799	19 055	66.3	159 900	22.8	10.0
Pullman	17 651	24 487	4.2	51.0	17.6	11 966	27.4	937	10 536	28.4	219 700	19.9	10.0
Puyallup	30 948	63 009	3.7	17.8	5.6	16 171	20.8	1 221	14 966	50.7	251 300	23.8	12.5
Redmond	50 787	99 586	15.2	10.9	5.4	24 177	19.1	1 627	23 520	50.9	462 200	21.4	10.1
Renton	32 136	65 223	5.0	16.8	9.1	38 930	71.5	2 921	37 207	53.2	282 400	26.4	12.5
Richland	36 298	69 372	7.1	16.8	7.3	20 876	26.9	1 169	20 401	66.1	200 800	18.6	10.0
Sammamish	56 662	144 775	29.3	4.9	2.4	15 736	34.7	582	15 820	87.6	586 400	22.6	10.0
SeaTac	21 185	45 573	0.9	23.1	18.2	10 360	3.3	827	9 945	51.6	224 600	28.1	15.1
Seattle	44 167	67 365	9.6	19.0	7.6	308 516	14.0	25 006	290 822	46.2	437 400	24.2	13.0
Shoreline	34 111	64 096	5.4	18.2	5.5	22 787	6.8	1 226	21 360	64.2	330 200	26.4	13.6
Spokane	24 511	42 814	2.3	29.9	13.1	94 291	7.0	7 020	87 235	56.2	157 900	23.9	12.0
Spokane Valley	23 892	48 274	1.1	24.0	10.5	38 851	NA	2 293	36 802	62.2	169 400	24.2	11.0
Tacoma	26 805	51 269	2.8	24.3	13.1	85 786	5.9	7 245	78 761	51.1	207 000	26.3	13.6
University Place	32 104	59 164	5.3	19.9	8.2	13 573	6.8	754	12 806	55.3	282 200	24.8	12.2
Vancouver	26 365	50 379	2.8	21.7	11.8	70 005	16.6	4 314	65 666	50.3	196 700	25.1	11.1
Walla Walla	20 962	42 348	1.9	31.0	14.9	12 514	9.3	977	11 614	56.8	171 600	24.5	12.9
Wenatchee	23 922	47 168	2.7	24.2	10.0	13 175	14.6	796	11 586	56.2	199 200	24.5	10.5
Yakima	20 736	40 189	2.0	30.5	17.7	34 829	21.2	1 755	33 023	53.8	157 300	23.4	12.0
WEST VIRGINIA	23 237	41 576	2.0	31.4	13.1	881 917	4.4	118 086	742 359	73.0	100 200	19.4	10.0
Charleston	34 944	48 959	6.6	28.3	13.6	26 205	-3.2	2 752	22 919	60.1	142 800	18.3	10.0
Huntington	21 173	28 673	2.6	46.2	21.8	25 146	-3.0	3 372	21 148	51.6	89 100	20.8	10.9
Morgantown	21 405	32 400	3.5	45.0	13.8	12 664	7.2	963	10 055	41.6	169 600	16.7	10.0
Parkersburg	20 564	33 247	1.0	38.5	18.3	15 562	-3.2	1 755	13 314	60.8	86 700	19.8	10.9
Wheeling	24 831	36 085	1.8	34.6	13.9	14 661	-6.2	1 845	12 738	62.0	96 800	18.2	10.0
WISCONSIN	27 907	52 738	3.1	22.0	8.9	2 624 358	13.1	344 590	2 293 250	67.7	165 900	23.2	13.7
Appleton	27 548	53 439	3.0	20.9	8.8	30 348	9.7	1 474	28 741	67.9	137 900	21.9	13.7
Beloit	18 798	36 384	1.0	32.1	20.5	15 177	6.5	1 396	14 140	59.1	85 500	24.3	14.5
Brookfield	47 205	91 485	14.6	9.5	2.6	15 317	7.5	741	14 557	88.4	282 300	21.6	13.3
Eau Claire	23 792	43 295	1.5	28.3	8.8	28 134	13.7	1 331	27 255	53.4	138 600	21.3	13.0
Fitchburg	34 836	62 832	6.7	17.1	12.0	10 668	23.2	713	10 407	50.3	268 500	22.6	12.2
Fond du Lac	24 854	45 914	1.3	25.5	11.5	19 181	9.2	1 239	18 271	56.9	123 500	21.8	14.5
Franklin	34 377	73 122	5.5	14.8	4.7	14 356	31.0	714	13 126	77.6	226 500	23.0	13.6
Green Bay	23 907	43 063	2.4	27.3	14.2	45 241	4.8	2 997	42 358	57.5	128 000	22.4	13.2
Greenfield	29 934	50 311	1.9	22.6	6.6	17 790	9.9	930	16 661	57.9	173 500	24.1	17.9
Janesville	25 181	49 372	1.9	23.0	11.5	27 996	11.7	2 168	25 581	66.9	129 200	22.6	12.0
Kenosha	23 287	48 181	2.0	27.4	15.6	40 643	12.4	3 267	37 305	57.8	143 900	24.7	14.4
La Crosse	21 723	40 340	1.6	30.0	9.1	22 628	1.9	1 200	20 749	50.2	129 000	22.7	14.2
Madison	31 659	53 933	4.1	23.1	9.8	108 843	17.9	6 327	103 169	48.7	211 600	23.6	12.2
Manitowoc	25 249	41 280	1.6	27.3	8.6	15 955	6.4	1 332	14 839	66.8	107 000	21.3	13.5
Menomonee Falls	36 386	73 936	6.8	14.5	3.1	15 142	15.1	575	14 539	75.2	227 100	21.8	14.2
Milwaukee	19 636	35 489	1.3	36.4	25.3	255 569	2.5	25 348	230 181	43.0	121 600	26.4	16.5
Mount Pleasant	34 630	65 347	4.3	14.3	4.4	11 827	NA	691	11 053	77.9	183 000	22.8	14.5
Neenah	29 454	52 271	3.6	20.0	7.9	11 313	11.2	619	10 798	66.9	132 900	21.6	12.2
New Berlin	39 339	74 203	6.7	11.5	2.7	16 829	12.7	537	16 612	76.0	236 700	22.2	14.0
Oak Creek	31 976	64 570	3.0	15.6	4.8	14 754	24.0	690	14 140	60.6	205 500	23.0	14.9
Oshkosh	22 367	42 860	1.2	28.8	10.1	28 179	11.1	2 041	25 987	54.6	115 300	22.1	14.2
Racine	20 429	39 623	0.9	32.2	18.9	33 887	1.3	3 357	29 979	56.0	114 800	24.1	16.0
Sheboygan	21 879	43 107	0.9	26.3	11.2	22 339	2.4	2 031	20 151	61.7	111 800	21.9	15.3
Stevens Point	21 320	40 081	1.1	32.1	11.2	11 220	15.0	622	10 529	49.0	113 600	22.2	12.3
Sun Prairie	30 905	66 956	2.7	12.8	6.2	12 413	53.0	777	12 029	58.7	203 300	23.6	12.6
Superior	23 114	39 503	1.4	30.7	17.2	12 328	1.0	658	11 669	55.7	113 300	22.0	13.2
Waukesha	28 866	58 126	2.3	19.5	8.8	29 843	11.1	1 548	28 466	58.9	194 400	23.4	14.1
Wausau	24 459	40 464	1.8	32.0	15.7	18 154	8.8	1 667	16 562	58.9	113 800	22.6	14.3
Wauwatosa	38 253	69 467	5.3	15.6	3.1	21 520	2.9	1 085	20 515	64.3	222 500	22.2	12.8
West Allis	25 021	44 475	0.7	27.7	10.5	29 353	2.2	1 899	27 294	55.1	145 500	24.9	16.5
West Bend	28 017	56 829	2.1	18.2	6.3	13 546	13.7	777	13 009	65.7	165 600	22.8	15.4
WYOMING	29 381	58 252	3.2	19.4	8.0	261 868	17.0	34 989	225 514	69.3	189 300	21.1	10.0
Casper	30 624	57 511	4.0	17.5	7.0	24 536	11.6	1 742	23 535	65.2	182 000	21.0	10.0
Cheyenne	28 485	54 845	2.5	20.1	8.7	27 283	14.6	1 726	25 007	62.4	179 600	21.3	10.0
Gillette	32 361	73 426	4.0	14.5	8.4	12 153	52.3	1 178	11 342	68.9	202 200	19.6	10.0
Laramie	22 097	38 451	1.5	36.6	15.8	14 307	19.2	913	12 992	43.9	193 200	22.4	10.0

1. Based on population estimated by the American Community Survey.　2. Includes units rented or sold but not occupied.　3. Specified owner-occupied units; $1,000,000 represents $1,000,000 or more.　4. 50.0 represents 50 percent or more.　5. 10.0 represents 10 percent or less.

City	Occupied housing units, 2010–2014 (cont.)				Migration, 2010–2014		Civilian labor force, 2015		Unemployment		Civilian employment[4], 2010–2014		Percent	
	Percent renter occupied	Median gross rent[1]	Median gross rent as a percent of income[2]	Percent with no vehicle available	Percent who lived in the same house one year ago	Percent who lived outside current city one year ago	Total	Percent change, 2014–2015	Total	Rate[3]	Population age 16 and older	In labor force	Civilian full-year full-time workers	Households with no workers (percent)
	55	56	57	58	59	60	61	62	63	64	65	66	67	68
WASHINGTON— Cont'd														
Pasco	33.7	782	28.9	6.3	83.7	7.6	31 057	2.5	2 401	7.7	45 192	67.6	42.5	19.4
Pullman	71.6	705	50.0	10.6	51.1	27.5	15 465	2.7	732	4.7	27 682	55.1	18.7	28.3
Puyallup	49.3	1 023	30.3	8.5	79.2	16.1	20 302	1.8	1 198	5.9	30 985	67.3	40.1	24.4
Redmond	49.1	1 445	23.0	6.7	76.3	18.0	34 244	1.5	1 326	3.9	44 982	71.2	50.0	16.8
Renton	46.8	1 165	29.7	7.2	78.6	14.6	55 588	1.5	2 345	4.2	76 114	71.7	48.3	20.5
Richland	33.9	888	27.0	4.9	81.8	12.3	26 437	1.9	1 497	5.7	39 719	64.5	42.8	26.3
Sammamish	12.4	1 824	23.0	1.1	90.6	7.4	26 016	1.4	1 037	4.0	34 717	68.8	48.8	11.1
SeaTac	48.4	930	33.0	9.4	77.3	16.7	14 277	1.5	790	5.5	22 217	63.7	36.3	23.2
Seattle	53.8	1 131	28.7	16.3	77.2	11.2	417 992	1.5	16 936	4.1	547 635	72.4	44.9	21.8
Shoreline	35.8	1 124	31.7	8.1	84.8	13.0	29 684	1.2	1 296	4.4	45 534	66.0	38.6	25.3
Spokane	43.8	747	32.6	10.9	81.0	9.1	100 004	1.2	6 552	6.6	168 740	61.4	34.8	31.3
Spokane Valley	37.8	787	31.6	6.5	84.6	10.0	44 858	1.4	3 003	6.7	72 060	63.1	37.7	30.6
Tacoma	48.9	933	31.8	9.7	80.5	11.0	98 015	1.9	6 546	6.7	162 086	64.6	37.9	28.2
University Place	44.7	940	31.1	4.4	83.7	13.9	15 943	1.9	842	5.3	25 047	67.2	38.5	26.1
Vancouver	49.7	923	30.5	7.7	80.0	11.7	81 399	2.1	5 361	6.6	131 126	64.6	37.5	28.2
Walla Walla	43.2	721	32.1	12.5	80.9	10.7	14 031	-1.0	888	6.3	25 976	54.8	31.0	36.0
Wenatchee	43.8	788	28.4	10.1	87.0	7.2	18 652	3.0	1 042	5.6	24 632	61.2	38.7	30.5
Yakima	46.2	772	33.8	9.3	79.1	8.6	45 400	2.2	3 097	6.8	69 832	62.0	35.6	31.0
WEST VIRGINIA	27.0	630	29.1	8.7	88.3	9.7	785 049	-0.6	52 903	6.7	1 513 749	54.3	35.0	37.0
Charleston	39.9	673	26.4	14.6	82.6	9.9	23 942	-1.7	1 343	5.6	41 740	61.9	41.2	32.0
Huntington	48.4	609	35.2	19.6	78.0	12.3	20 259	-1.2	1 161	5.7	41 074	52.5	29.0	41.3
Morgantown	58.4	692	46.2	14.0	63.6	26.5	14 547	1.0	799	5.5	27 976	53.9	23.2	32.3
Parkersburg	39.2	604	34.5	13.4	88.2	7.8	12 763	-0.9	890	7.0	25 325	55.7	34.0	41.4
Wheeling	38.0	544	30.6	16.8	86.5	7.4	12 749	-1.2	769	6.0	23 286	57.6	35.5	38.4
WISCONSIN	32.3	772	29.3	7.1	85.8	8.9	3 095 376	0.3	142 579	4.6	4 561 244	67.4	41.5	26.5
Appleton	32.1	667	26.0	5.9	85.4	10.4	40 051	0.6	1 627	4.1	57 198	69.9	44.2	22.5
Beloit	40.9	723	33.8	8.9	83.2	7.8	17 179	1.4	1 126	6.6	28 295	63.6	32.7	32.9
Brookfield	11.6	1 291	28.5	2.4	91.7	6.6	19 220	0.2	714	3.7	30 446	63.1	40.4	28.9
Eau Claire	46.6	733	31.9	7.0	77.2	10.7	39 695	0.2	1 531	3.9	55 646	71.3	37.7	23.4
Fitchburg	49.7	872	29.2	6.5	77.7	18.7	15 546	1.3	498	3.2	20 453	73.8	48.0	17.5
Fond du Lac	43.1	681	27.8	9.4	82.1	7.0	23 111	0.2	1 012	4.4	34 365	66.9	40.9	29.1
Franklin	22.4	948	29.0	2.8	83.9	14.9	18 446	0.3	823	4.5	29 091	61.4	41.0	26.5
Green Bay	42.5	656	29.0	8.6	82.9	8.5	54 663	0.3	2 523	4.6	81 849	67.0	40.9	27.6
Greenfield	42.1	855	26.5	6.2	88.4	8.7	19 892	-0.4	934	4.7	31 177	63.1	41.2	32.4
Janesville	33.1	744	30.7	6.1	82.7	7.0	33 198	1.4	1 732	5.2	49 365	67.3	40.2	29.3
Kenosha	42.2	806	33.4	8.7	82.6	8.5	49 727	0.3	2 826	5.7	76 561	66.4	37.8	27.6
La Crosse	49.8	704	32.2	8.2	71.2	14.3	29 864	-0.1	1 252	4.2	44 557	66.6	33.4	26.2
Madison	51.3	922	32.6	12.6	71.9	13.7	151 208	1.3	4 734	3.1	201 152	72.5	41.0	20.4
Manitowoc	33.2	610	27.1	8.9	91.4	3.7	16 370	-1.5	892	5.4	27 283	64.1	38.9	31.3
Menomonee Falls	24.8	914	29.8	4.8	89.9	8.0	19 781	0.0	736	3.7	28 976	67.1	44.7	27.3
Milwaukee	57.0	784	34.9	18.4	78.9	6.0	282 662	-0.6	18 934	6.7	455 573	65.1	36.1	29.4
Mount Pleasant	22.1	779	23.6	4.5	89.8	8.5	14 163	-0.1	705	5.0	21 513	64.8	42.6	28.6
Neenah	33.1	675	27.1	6.7	84.7	9.5	13 943	-0.4	581	4.2	20 211	69.5	47.0	24.3
New Berlin	24.0	1 053	28.5	4.3	91.1	8.0	21 881	0.0	844	3.9	32 900	67.6	45.1	27.0
Oak Creek	39.4	951	24.7	3.1	88.6	9.1	20 297	0.1	850	4.2	27 589	72.0	49.3	22.0
Oshkosh	45.4	660	28.5	8.8	78.9	11.4	34 830	-0.2	1 600	4.6	55 412	63.3	36.5	26.9
Racine	44.0	739	32.5	13.3	86.9	4.9	36 116	-1.0	2 553	7.1	58 615	64.6	37.8	31.4
Sheboygan	38.3	622	26.3	9.2	83.6	6.0	25 192	-0.1	1 055	4.2	38 140	69.4	40.2	27.9
Stevens Point	51.0	659	33.1	9.2	68.3	18.5	15 111	1.3	671	4.4	23 016	67.4	29.3	28.3
Sun Prairie	41.3	1 003	27.3	3.8	84.3	10.1	18 987	1.1	609	3.2	23 018	76.6	51.6	18.2
Superior	44.3	686	31.4	12.0	81.9	9.7	14 654	-1.2	650	4.4	21 857	66.5	36.7	29.7
Waukesha	41.1	841	28.3	7.7	81.9	11.5	41 468	0.1	1 706	4.1	56 353	73.1	46.1	23.2
Wausau	41.1	653	31.5	9.4	79.5	9.3	19 989	0.6	868	4.3	31 177	66.2	36.7	29.5
Wauwatosa	35.7	930	27.8	7.8	86.6	9.9	26 855	0.3	993	3.7	37 647	71.4	49.2	23.6
West Allis	44.9	768	30.8	12.1	86.3	10.1	33 925	-0.2	1 876	5.5	49 301	69.5	43.6	27.2
West Bend	34.3	797	27.4	7.1	85.7	7.7	17 066	0.1	700	4.1	24 509	70.8	43.6	26.1
WYOMING	30.7	778	25.7	3.8	81.6	11.9	306 012	-0.3	12 750	4.2	453 096	68.4	44.8	22.7
Casper	34.8	837	26.2	4.6	81.1	9.1	31 680	-1.5	1 298	4.1	45 717	69.9	46.3	23.1
Cheyenne	37.6	762	26.8	5.7	79.0	11.5	31 874	0.2	1 184	3.7	48 142	68.0	45.1	23.8
Gillette	31.1	913	26.8	4.6	78.1	9.6	16 663	-1.7	543	3.3	22 712	76.4	54.1	13.9
Laramie	56.1	727	39.7	4.8	64.7	19.3	17 530	1.7	495	2.8	26 936	66.0	35.3	20.3

1. $2,000 represents $2,000 or more.   2. 50.0 represents 50 percent or more.   3. Percent of civilian labor force.   4. Persons 16 years old and over.

Table D. Cities — Construction, Wholesale Trade, and Retail Trade

City	Value of residential construction authorized by building permits, 2015			Wholesale trade,[1] 2012				Retail trade,[2] 2012			
	New construction ($1,000)	Number of housing units	Percent single family	Number of establishments	Number of employees	Sales (mil dol)	Annual payroll (mil dol)	Number of establishments	Number of employees	Sales (mil dol)	Annual payroll (mil dol)
	69	70	71	72	73	74	75	76	77	78	79
WASHINGTON—Cont'd											
Pasco	73 337	305	100.0	77	939	595.5	46.6	157	2 051	722.8	67.7
Pullman	27 854	174	28.7	11	177	182.1	9.0	51	1 027	222.7	20.4
Puyallup	54 494	213	77.5	39	652	343.0	27.6	239	5 078	1 686.5	152.9
Redmond	156 542	896	22.3	173	3 101	4 143.8	257.7	251	3 923	947.4	105.4
Renton	95 979	454	48.0	110	3 308	2 769.4	197.3	264	5 284	1 831.9	165.6
Richland	76 647	235	100.0	19	186	192.6	7.6	143	2 531	680.0	60.7
Sammamish	84 661	192	100.0	31	52	46.8	2.9	47	413	129.3	12.6
SeaTac	3 165	15	66.7	19	177	146.3	10.2	71	943	213.9	18.1
Seattle	1 900 449	11 340	7.1	1 093	16 045	12 790.5	1 049.7	2 530	34 652	40 037.9	1 230.2
Shoreline	19 099	47	100.0	33	135	57.2	5.6	121	2 364	835.7	75.9
Spokane	136 996	823	41.1	249	3 330	1 686.8	158.8	862	13 166	3 132.8	341.2
Spokane Valley	52 336	371	44.2	202	2 963	1 772.5	140.6	476	7 626	1 987.3	207.5
Tacoma	72 414	373	56.0	210	2 967	2 750.1	151.2	744	11 177	3 036.6	314.9
University Place	3 200	14	85.7	12	75	49.4	4.1	51	728	154.9	19.8
Vancouver	90 585	1 087	33.7	185	2 441	2 580.9	139.4	555	10 131	2 863.9	278.6
Walla Walla	19 022	87	79.3	54	483	437.5	18.3	150	1 667	386.1	40.7
Wenatchee	16 201	84	83.3	52	587	710.1	27.7	185	2 635	615.3	68.3
Yakima	29 690	140	97.9	108	2 196	1 875.8	100.9	346	5 078	1 334.7	134.8
WEST VIRGINIA	417 183	2 814	72.1	1 334	16 906	14 295.4	761.9	6 393	85 305	22 637.9	1 908.5
Charleston	4 089	16	100.0	121	1 588	1 059.8	78.1	358	5 805	1 495.4	134.6
Huntington	50	4	0.0	73	1 250	511.6	62.2	211	2 788	670.4	66.6
Morgantown	7 873	161	11.8	26	142	47.8	5.3	260	4 385	1 081.4	86.6
Parkersburg	713	10	100.0	40	338	134.5	12.1	203	3 074	791.4	68.8
Wheeling	13 031	57	100.0	62	D	D	D	142	1 690	380.3	37.4
WISCONSIN	3 078 382	16 793	58.3	5 990	97 040	77 066.9	5 253.6	19 272	296 956	78 201.8	6 835.0
Appleton	33 999	308	18.8	98	1 432	5 759.6	66.1	291	4 865	1 306.6	111.5
Beloit	1 001	9	77.8	19	456	292.8	25.0	115	1 756	481.9	40.3
Brookfield	17 530	36	100.0	108	1 733	686.6	105.7	301	5 576	1 022.7	117.4
Eau Claire	33 038	230	40.4	79	1 509	961.9	64.8	340	6 565	1 419.6	131.8
Fitchburg	39 707	346	10.4	25	967	1 149.6	59.0	58	614	173.3	16.1
Fond du Lac	4 704	27	85.2	41	812	610.4	46.3	211	3 688	959.5	81.9
Franklin	12 969	37	89.2	35	402	292.7	23.6	75	2 107	614.6	52.0
Green Bay	17 937	98	72.4	106	2 190	1 714.9	122.4	340	5 909	1 595.9	134.6
Greenfield	4 604	20	90.0	14	192	128.7	7.3	149	3 100	932.8	80.5
Janesville	17 203	75	84.0	75	1 941	1 843.2	96.1	276	5 678	1 422.0	144.0
Kenosha	13 574	134	19.4	56	763	769.3	42.7	295	5 162	1 369.5	114.4
La Crosse	7 935	123	10.6	61	1 690	2 434.7	78.4	251	4 879	976.7	97.7
Madison	275 499	1 665	18.0	270	4 849	2 859.6	252.1	972	17 918	4 804.9	409.1
Manitowoc	5 481	68	23.5	27	461	211.0	23.9	146	2 436	555.8	53.0
Menomonee Falls	52 326	314	28.7	89	1 425	651.3	89.4	126	2 741	700.4	63.1
Milwaukee	60 539	355	6.8	485	11 513	8 694.3	908.5	1 368	15 652	3 894.9	360.3
Mount Pleasant	10 933	48	91.7	21	346	145.5	14.4	64	1 331	441.7	31.9
Neenah	14 508	124	47.6	24	278	252.6	13.1	82	1 520	436.6	34.5
New Berlin	8 726	25	84.0	119	2 332	1 178.0	137.1	96	2 375	579.0	64.6
Oak Creek	49 306	399	8.5	32	1 429	891.0	89.5	80	2 059	718.9	43.7
Oshkosh	20 397	275	6.2	50	1 198	517.4	48.5	250	4 856	1 205.0	107.7
Racine	210	1	100.0	42	448	225.6	22.3	281	3 410	622.1	61.4
Sheboygan	1 539	8	100.0	41	451	304.5	18.9	197	3 362	758.9	74.1
Stevens Point	5 300	23	73.9	32	332	270.7	14.4	120	2 003	470.3	39.3
Sun Prairie	39 000	170	94.1	33	822	362.4	38.0	70	1 155	305.8	25.6
Superior	1 750	8	75.0	39	669	817.8	31.9	113	1 835	541.2	45.8
Waukesha	13 052	65	100.0	115	2 148	1 126.3	119.0	213	4 314	1 601.4	120.4
Wausau	4 838	20	100.0	44	817	375.7	36.8	187	4 576	1 239.9	101.2
Wauwatosa	34 376	339	0.9	56	1 033	652.0	55.5	293	5 436	1 107.9	113.4
West Allis	774	4	100.0	107	1 830	975.2	99.4	243	4 249	1 154.4	102.4
West Bend	8 272	54	53.7	25	201	93.9	8.1	120	2 163	553.4	46.4
WYOMING	607 666	1 903	88.3	709	7 003	5 597.9	398.7	2 681	30 088	9 446.0	796.0
Casper	27 429	121	63.6	80	841	1 414.8	51.5	299	4 299	1 244.2	116.3
Cheyenne	46 310	281	81.5	93	782	336.4	52.5	321	4 632	1 561.0	112.7
Gillette	34 489	77	100.0	49	813	462.8	41.3	160	2 202	757.5	62.0
Laramie	10 726	85	76.5	19	95	127.6	4.0	131	1 671	470.8	35.7

1. Merchant wholesalers except manufacturers' sales branches and offices.   2. Establishments with payroll.

City	Real estate and rental and leasing, 2012				Professional, scientific, and technical services,[1] 2012				Manufacturing, 2012			
	Number of establish-ments	Number of employees	Receipts (mil dol)	Annual payroll (mil dol)	Number of establish-ments	Number of employees	Receipts (mil dol)	Annual payroll (mil dol)	Number of establish-ments	Number of employees	Receipts (mil dol)	Annual payroll (mil dol)
	80	81	82	83	84	85	86	87	88	89	90	91
WASHINGTON— Cont'd												
Pasco	46	224	39.2	6.8	61	369	37.2	16.4	37	D	D	59.8
Pullman	40	180	19.4	4.4	36	304	40.0	17.3	12	D	D	D
Puyallup	86	417	83.6	13.0	119	627	65.7	26.1	43	954	240.9	43.2
Redmond	128	1 207	288.5	71.4	385	D	D	D	127	6 634	3 469.5	443.1
Renton	115	610	212.1	29.7	208	2 109	213.2	103.7	71	13 466	D	994.5
Richland	89	268	46.3	9.2	181	D	D	D	39	1 839	D	119.8
Sammamish	41	D	D	D	197	405	85.7	26.5	6	14	2.5	0.6
SeaTac	40	312	71.5	11.6	17	243	32.8	13.3	15	130	D	6.0
Seattle	1 966	11 652	2 431.3	587.9	4 631	50 113	10 321.5	4 432.8	859	20 323	5 200.2	1 054.2
Shoreline	70	282	64.4	11.6	113	D	D	D	17	147	29.9	5.9
Spokane	281	1 580	283.9	57.9	741	D	D	D	200	4 292	1 101.4	202.5
Spokane Valley	147	814	146.0	26.8	189	1 245	123.8	51.5	189	6 500	2 048.1	324.3
Tacoma	297	1 748	304.2	64.2	504	D	D	D	194	6 347	1 923.4	338.4
University Place	55	D	D	D	66	251	29.2	11.6	17	87	D	2.9
Vancouver	273	1 384	225.1	51.1	570	D	D	D	182	6 379	2 585.4	336.6
Walla Walla	42	128	17.4	4.0	79	356	36.7	14.4	83	1 043	221.4	46.9
Wenatchee	61	211	32.7	5.9	101	D	D	D	23	401	71.9	14.9
Yakima	146	587	81.6	16.1	211	D	D	D	99	2 981	838.8	122.6
WEST VIRGINIA	1 405	6 011	1 255.8	203.8	2 918	23 115	2 804.7	1 053.4	1 245	48 686	24 553.1	2 603.9
Charleston	135	663	154.9	22.9	385	D	D	D	39	528	148.4	22.8
Huntington	74	259	50.9	9.4	135	D	D	D	52	3 170	1 697.1	206.5
Morgantown	79	435	64.2	10.7	126	D	D	D	22	446	D	23.3
Parkersburg	53	239	52.6	7.4	89	D	D	D	25	657	134.7	26.1
Wheeling	49	D	D	D	136	D	D	D	37	D	D	D
WISCONSIN	4 509	23 762	4 358.9	801.1	11 253	98 507	15 028.9	5 701.2	8 995	436 777	177 728.9	21 879.3
Appleton	60	D	D	D	193	1 791	315.2	106.8	104	7 600	D	409.2
Beloit	17	88	66.4	4.6	38	212	20.4	9.2	52	2 599	1 801.2	132.8
Brookfield	94	1 075	88.2	31.8	306	3 589	744.8	278.8	56	1 544	368.5	79.4
Eau Claire	94	462	72.5	14.0	145	1 527	188.2	78.6	79	3 823	1 148.1	170.4
Fitchburg	42	247	46.1	7.9	85	556	90.6	34.8	30	3 154	1 287.1	205.2
Fond du Lac	31	144	25.7	3.7	91	1 050	125.8	63.4	72	4 252	1 894.6	202.1
Franklin	25	127	25.8	3.3	58	424	80.7	23.0	52	3 383	1 221.8	176.4
Green Bay	94	610	93.9	21.6	226	D	D	D	130	10 215	6 399.1	513.4
Greenfield	38	182	31.6	6.8	80	589	63.7	26.0	17	106	D	4.8
Janesville	53	260	74.1	12.6	107	624	70.8	24.5	82	3 985	1 600.9	187.1
Kenosha	67	289	44.5	7.3	125	816	73.3	33.0	99	2 044	738.6	95.7
La Crosse	74	475	70.7	12.9	171	D	D	D	93	4 666	1 527.4	195.8
Madison	369	2 871	759.2	115.5	1 019	13 787	2 399.8	978.8	182	8 788	2 798.2	467.9
Manitowoc	19	D	D	D	58	453	68.2	16.7	75	6 299	1 804.1	295.0
Menomonee Falls	20	260	33.5	14.7	91	1 294	253.1	76.0	176	8 361	3 503.9	464.3
Milwaukee	460	3 036	618.5	127.5	1 091	D	D	D	540	22 779	8 678.9	1 199.8
Mount Pleasant	20	80	9.6	2.8	50	387	38.9	19.2	35	2 073	3 299.8	155.3
Neenah	17	142	151.8	6.5	51	476	60.8	31.5	60	5 008	2 079.0	262.2
New Berlin	27	263	44.5	7.7	109	2 193	348.9	102.6	130	6 222	2 305.6	359.7
Oak Creek	38	405	92.1	16.3	35	414	32.6	12.5	55	3 412	1 390.3	196.4
Oshkosh	53	306	43.0	8.3	100	D	D	D	115	11 025	6 369.1	607.7
Racine	37	121	31.0	3.8	118	D	D	D	143	4 602	1 264.5	245.5
Sheboygan	31	181	41.8	8.1	94	D	D	D	89	6 676	2 068.9	311.6
Stevens Point	19	D	D	D	57	635	57.0	23.5	30	1 791	570.9	73.8
Sun Prairie	25	70	13.3	2.1	60	404	50.5	20.4	29	1 020	283.2	48.2
Superior	34	106	14.5	2.4	55	323	35.1	14.3	40	1 200	D	77.6
Waukesha	56	321	69.7	10.8	188	1 794	285.7	100.4	142	9 474	4 144.2	668.2
Wausau	39	D	D	D	130	D	D	D	64	4 486	1 177.6	184.4
Wauwatosa	45	268	89.0	13.0	236	D	D	D	51	3 718	1 267.0	356.5
West Allis	43	293	77.6	14.4	86	925	100.6	52.4	92	3 448	743.0	196.1
West Bend	18	D	D	D	49	D	D	D	52	1 779	409.9	79.6
WYOMING	1 076	4 546	1 259.1	215.6	2 132	D	D	D	553	10 094	10 783.8	630.6
Casper	124	649	182.3	31.4	216	1 146	166.8	64.1	27	471	91.8	25.8
Cheyenne	112	390	89.7	14.4	414	D	D	D	51	1 132	2 542.4	75.4
Gillette	61	265	72.1	9.9	94	D	D	D	27	482	D	30.7
Laramie	50	132	20.2	3.0	95	D	D	D	21	141	D	5.5

1. Establishments subject to federal tax.

Table D. Cities — Accommodation and Food Services, Arts, Entertainment, and Recreation, and Health Care and Social Assistance

City	Accommodation and food services, 2012				Arts, entertainment, and recreation,[1] 2012				Health care and social assistance,[1] 2012			
	Number of establishments	Number of employees	Sales (mil dol)	Annual payroll (mil dol)	Number of establishments	Number of employees	Receipts (mil dol)	Annual payroll (mil dol)	Number of establishments	Number of employees	Receipts (mil dol)	Annual payroll (mil dol)
	92	93	94	95	96	97	98	99	100	101	102	103
WASHINGTON—Cont'd												
Pasco	88	1 288	71.1	19.4	10	D	D	D	82	712	67.0	23.5
Pullman	103	1 302	55.6	15.4	4	93	5.0	1.8	58	D	D	D
Puyallup	151	2 421	134.5	41.0	11	149	7.2	2.1	186	D	D	D
Redmond	244	4 597	340.1	100.7	32	D	D	D	210	2 496	242.3	95.7
Renton	241	3 787	253.7	71.3	19	D	D	D	293	3 016	379.9	154.7
Richland	127	2 055	108.4	31.6	13	460	16.3	6.3	213	2 156	238.8	113.7
Sammamish	30	488	26.5	7.7	17	D	D	D	67	452	49.3	20.3
SeaTac	96	2 996	251.0	72.1	2	D	D	D	29	860	20.9	11.6
Seattle	2 823	45 976	3 164.1	970.4	323	4 218	540.3	224.9	2 101	24 068	3 408.6	1 564.3
Shoreline	100	1 054	55.9	15.9	21	698	31.6	10.1	181	1 928	148.4	64.8
Spokane	601	10 256	549.0	165.9	58	883	47.7	12.4	722	13 373	1 618.3	684.5
Spokane Valley	216	3 468	180.3	51.5	23	D	D	D	305	5 354	479.1	203.9
Tacoma	501	7 220	387.9	118.9	45	1 749	231.4	53.3	561	8 906	951.2	503.6
University Place	41	459	25.8	7.3	7	89	4.9	1.1	87	D	D	D
Vancouver	428	6 939	364.3	111.0	38	578	31.7	9.0	514	7 399	755.8	370.4
Walla Walla	114	1 746	83.9	25.4	12	77	4.2	1.7	96	D	D	D
Wenatchee	112	1 622	84.5	25.0	9	74	4.4	1.2	120	D	D	D
Yakima	239	3 527	183.5	53.1	20	491	18.5	7.1	291	4 885	631.0	234.6
WEST VIRGINIA	3 629	66 302	4 036.3	975.9	631	6 055	550.1	98.9	3 734	57 400	5 125.5	2 107.5
Charleston	225	4 651	253.2	69.2	20	267	22.8	5.6	318	4 136	555.2	230.6
Huntington	172	2 964	141.0	38.8	18	D	D	D	176	3 266	356.7	167.6
Morgantown	207	4 596	190.5	52.1	23	182	10.0	2.7	89	D	D	D
Parkersburg	130	2 121	97.5	29.0	21	D	D	D	158	1 922	235.2	94.9
Wheeling	103	2 033	181.0	33.4	27	D	D	D	152	D	D	D
WISCONSIN	14 137	221 567	10 303.3	2 764.3	1 966	28 433	2 548.1	826.1	11 460	175 153	16 357.2	7 784.6
Appleton	211	4 363	168.4	47.9	12	262	8.6	2.9	209	3 503	485.0	217.5
Beloit	90	1 338	63.4	17.0	5	D	D	D	43	D	D	D
Brookfield	124	3 114	159.0	44.7	22	358	14.6	5.7	306	D	D	D
Eau Claire	229	D	D	D	26	411	25.7	5.0	217	5 434	656.6	349.8
Fitchburg	43	930	42.0	12.0	15	D	D	D	35	D	D	D
Fond du Lac	125	2 424	86.8	25.7	18	200	21.7	3.5	139	D	D	D
Franklin	60	768	43.4	10.9	11	D	D	D	91	D	D	D
Green Bay	272	5 414	234.0	68.2	23	D	D	D	204	4 567	663.1	285.6
Greenfield	72	D	D	D	17	D	D	D	134	3 258	279.4	127.6
Janesville	162	3 046	132.5	37.4	15	197	9.0	2.7	104	D	D	D
Kenosha	235	3 801	160.5	45.2	22	D	D	D	282	3 366	297.5	140.4
La Crosse	222	3 923	155.1	45.9	24	D	D	D	100	1 197	86.8	36.7
Madison	743	15 474	718.3	209.5	73	1 144	96.4	19.6	443	10 016	1 248.6	619.4
Manitowoc	86	1 544	57.0	16.8	10	94	9.3	1.6	90	D	D	D
Menomonee Falls	66	1 248	56.4	15.1	11	D	D	D	68	D	D	D
Milwaukee	1 106	D	D	D	87	D	D	D	1 135	18 188	1 518.5	812.0
Mount Pleasant	56	1 290	57.7	16.9	6	D	D	D	82	886	83.4	37.3
Neenah	70	1 153	48.7	13.4	10	D	D	D	85	1 134	170.1	69.1
New Berlin	65	1 345	56.6	15.0	16	D	D	D	84	1 074	99.6	47.1
Oak Creek	68	1 366	75.1	18.9	13	D	D	D	53	580	45.6	19.9
Oshkosh	187	3 495	136.7	39.0	16	147	7.1	2.1	142	2 244	240.8	121.8
Racine	161	D	D	D	29	190	13.5	3.2	139	1 401	91.3	43.1
Sheboygan	132	1 976	79.9	21.5	9	110	5.6	1.5	155	3 073	286.6	143.0
Stevens Point	112	1 748	69.1	18.9	10	D	D	D	81	D	D	D
Sun Prairie	50	844	36.4	9.5	7	D	D	D	52	761	65.7	30.0
Superior	107	1 625	60.4	16.8	13	D	D	D	46	963	50.5	22.5
Waukesha	153	3 185	142.4	42.7	22	321	11.9	3.3	193	2 607	288.5	147.1
Wausau	111	1 690	73.6	21.1	14	137	5.1	1.9	164	D	D	D
Wauwatosa	142	3 107	158.9	47.0	13	D	D	D	329	5 474	602.4	307.0
West Allis	159	D	D	D	13	250	10.5	3.2	159	3 183	277.0	141.5
West Bend	66	1 326	52.2	14.2	11	D	D	D	98	1 085	79.5	33.4
WYOMING	1 799	27 580	1 644.8	468.7	317	2 922	168.9	57.1	1 457	13 706	1 486.2	607.7
Casper	158	3 224	170.2	49.2	17	D	D	D	239	D	D	D
Cheyenne	176	3 518	200.9	53.0	11	D	D	D	237	2 779	258.7	113.1
Gillette	94	1 529	86.2	24.3	8	81	2.7	1.1	80	D	D	D
Laramie	103	1 976	73.8	22.0	9	62	1.7	0.5	99	D	D	D

1. Establishments subject to federal tax.

Table D. Cities — Other Services and Government Employment and Payroll

City	Other services[1], 2012				Government employment and payroll, 2012								
						March payroll							
							Percent of total for:						
	Number of establishments	Number of employees	Receipts (mil dol)	Annual payroll (mil dol)	Full-time equivalent employees	Total (dollars)	Administration, judicial, and legal	Police and Corrections	Fire Protection	Highways and transportation	Health and welfare	Natural resources and utilities	Education and libraries
	104	105	106	107	108	109	110	111	112	113	114	115	116
WASHINGTON— Cont'd													
Pasco	63	308	34.5	8.6	285	1 601 010	14.1	30.2	22.2	7.6	4.6	21.0	0.0
Pullman	25	D	D	D	232	989 864	6.3	23.6	22.8	32.0	0.0	11.6	3.7
Puyallup	85	763	64.8	21.2	469	3 001 181	14.9	30.0	21.9	6.7	0.0	16.4	3.2
Redmond	130	892	98.9	30.0	679	4 387 058	20.9	18.6	29.5	4.1	1.4	18.8	0.0
Renton	148	854	76.7	27.0	825	5 336 014	10.3	32.9	23.1	6.5	6.4	17.5	0.0
Richland	68	522	42.4	14.8	499	3 031 486	16.6	16.7	14.9	6.2	1.1	33.3	2.9
Sammamish	31	180	11.4	4.1	85	514 186	26.6	1.0	0.0	28.1	16.1	22.8	0.0
SeaTac	48	687	63.2	17.1	162	1 068 652	30.3	0.6	37.3	13.7	1.2	5.9	0.0
Seattle	1 302	8 892	755.8	250.0	10 193	71 586 796	7.4	21.3	13.4	5.8	3.3	38.0	3.4
Shoreline	63	326	25.3	7.4	222	1 123 950	28.0	39.9	0.0	5.5	0.6	22.6	0.0
Spokane	349	2 163	171.0	52.9	2 161	12 463 086	15.6	21.9	20.6	8.3	0.4	26.4	3.2
Spokane Valley	177	1 222	110.3	35.5	92	466 469	31.8	0.0	0.0	24.5	34.4	9.2	0.0
Tacoma	330	2 444	223.1	75.5	3 458	23 314 293	11.1	13.2	14.4	8.2	0.5	43.6	2.1
University Place	46	293	20.0	7.5	48	264 084	30.6	4.5	0.0	30.0	14.8	9.6	0.0
Vancouver	300	1 562	120.8	37.4	1 018	5 857 054	12.9	26.3	24.0	6.1	0.0	21.4	0.0
Walla Walla	42	240	16.7	6.0	251	1 313 753	15.6	33.8	26.5	0.9	0.3	16.4	3.3
Wenatchee	65	228	21.7	6.0	185	996 105	13.5	30.6	19.2	10.0	2.0	19.4	0.0
Yakima	140	736	62.9	17.7	615	3 330 932	12.9	39.5	16.4	10.4	0.9	18.9	0.0
WEST VIRGINIA	2 003	12 728	1 246.8	343.2	X	X	X	X	X	X	X	X	X
Charleston	110	979	56.3	17.8	826	2 940 542	13.0	28.6	24.9	0.8	1.4	16.3	0.0
Huntington	67	434	39.9	11.4	338	1 166 129	8.3	42.3	27.9	4.5	2.5	8.5	0.0
Morgantown	56	D	D	D	442	1 584 824	7.6	19.5	12.7	10.7	0.3	38.5	4.0
Parkersburg	64	446	33.0	10.3	347	1 079 226	8.0	24.0	18.5	10.1	1.5	34.7	0.0
Wheeling	66	715	76.6	19.2	828	2 250 153	5.6	14.0	15.9	7.2	0.0	55.8	0.0
WISCONSIN	8 338	47 662	4 015.9	1 242.4	X	X	X	X	X	X	X	X	X
Appleton	127	972	89.6	27.8	663	3 090 024	10.6	24.2	16.9	8.2	4.8	15.8	6.5
Beloit	48	195	14.1	4.2	368	1 795 646	10.7	25.3	19.5	14.3	3.6	17.7	4.9
Brookfield	101	1 064	92.4	31.2	333	1 844 609	12.7	28.6	21.1	12.3	0.0	14.9	6.1
Eau Claire	125	901	62.1	19.6	608	2 643 962	9.0	24.0	17.4	10.5	10.6	15.3	5.6
Fitchburg	30	289	28.3	9.4	168	745 550	17.6	38.6	15.3	7.5	2.7	10.2	0.8
Fond du Lac	89	610	40.0	14.2	344	1 652 329	8.9	25.7	21.9	14.0	1.9	15.0	6.8
Franklin	47	329	29.9	10.1	218	1 131 749	9.5	36.1	24.9	12.6	2.8	4.7	5.0
Green Bay	146	913	67.4	21.0	860	4 043 340	7.5	30.8	25.6	11.5	1.1	19.5	0.0
Greenfield	65	456	26.6	10.5	217	1 158 811	11.1	38.6	26.7	12.0	3.2	3.7	3.2
Janesville	99	626	36.7	12.8	482	2 513 217	10.6	24.7	21.6	15.6	3.3	16.1	7.3
Kenosha	147	915	66.9	20.6	811	3 859 872	5.8	28.1	22.1	10.6	2.7	18.1	7.7
La Crosse	93	681	44.6	17.3	567	2 357 551	9.7	24.1	19.2	17.7	2.0	14.4	9.6
Madison	349	2 839	212.6	76.1	3 036	14 945 308	10.6	21.2	12.9	22.9	2.3	18.7	5.5
Manitowoc	55	273	19.5	5.7	355	1 875 536	6.3	20.8	18.2	15.1	0.0	32.1	5.9
Menomonee Falls	63	563	52.2	15.9	252	1 124 295	9.0	39.6	11.5	12.7	2.5	9.8	5.9
Milwaukee	623	4 127	367.3	126.6	6 455	32 385 292	9.5	39.7	17.4	3.2	7.3	12.0	3.2
Mount Pleasant	34	232	17.6	5.4	206	856 388	12.7	34.6	41.4	6.6	0.0	4.6	0.0
Neenah	49	366	27.3	10.1	272	1 262 394	8.6	24.1	29.0	10.9	5.7	15.3	6.4
New Berlin	69	664	69.6	27.6	254	1 283 876	12.9	39.3	15.4	12.5	0.0	11.2	4.4
Oak Creek	42	439	49.7	12.3	266	1 412 700	9.6	31.2	21.6	13.5	2.3	15.7	2.7
Oshkosh	80	687	53.0	18.2	576	2 558 304	7.2	22.6	21.9	15.9	6.5	17.9	5.9
Racine	110	731	40.6	14.4	815	4 196 517	6.8	33.8	20.0	8.7	5.3	19.5	3.6
Sheboygan	83	518	26.7	9.1	431	1 929 836	9.1	27.3	17.8	18.6	2.9	13.8	7.8
Stevens Point	54	298	29.0	8.2	194	851 692	9.1	29.9	22.2	24.4	3.2	11.3	0.0
Sun Prairie	35	202	18.0	4.1	223	1 003 694	14.5	33.1	0.0	9.8	7.1	24.8	7.1
Superior	53	351	28.1	9.0	255	1 159 999	11.2	29.7	15.8	11.8	0.7	18.3	5.6
Waukesha	117	872	73.3	23.8	566	2 950 957	10.7	28.4	19.7	16.3	0.3	16.6	5.6
Wausau	55	328	31.9	9.2	306	1 383 873	11.0	27.3	21.3	24.5	3.8	8.0	0.0
Wauwatosa	68	639	52.4	18.0	414	2 166 975	10.9	28.6	27.5	10.0	3.1	9.0	5.3
West Allis	114	604	68.2	17.0	541	2 746 980	10.4	30.7	21.8	7.9	7.6	15.5	3.5
West Bend	76	464	30.9	10.2	261	1 244 682	11.9	33.2	19.5	9.0	0.0	16.8	5.0
WYOMING	998	5 095	660.2	169.6	X	X	X	X	X	X	X	X	X
Casper	106	687	82.8	22.0	563	2 490 135	12.1	24.0	15.7	5.9	2.6	30.8	0.0
Cheyenne	102	561	47.1	14.6	655	2 479 867	12.4	24.6	20.1	11.9	5.3	17.8	0.0
Gillette	77	512	63.1	17.6	278	1 359 171	21.1	29.1	0.0	9.2	3.7	24.3	0.0
Laramie	56	D	D	D	282	1 207 422	11.8	25.1	22.5	5.3	8.5	26.7	0.0

1. Establishments subject to federal tax.

Table D. Cities — **City Government Finances**

City	General revenue							General expenditure		
		Intergovernmental		Taxes					Per capita[1] (dollars)	
					Per capita[1] (dollars)					
	Total (mil dol)	Total (mil dol)	Percent from state government	Total (mil dol)	Total	Property	Sales and gross receipts	Total (mil dol)	Total	Capital outlays
	117	118	119	120	121	122	123	124	125	126
WASHINGTON— Cont'd										
Pasco	56.3	7.4	83.9	27.7	414	100	307	43.0	644	84
Pullman	28.8	6.2	79.9	14.1	450	166	280	23.2	740	102
Puyallup	56.2	6.0	83.5	28.9	756	220	514	45.2	1 184	149
Redmond......................	132.9	19.1	27.4	73.4	1 298	388	860	135.8	2 399	780
Renton.........................	182.1	40.0	23.2	80.9	844	338	484	161.6	1 687	421
Richland	85.1	16.9	69.5	35.1	682	273	382	81.3	1 579	382
Sammamish	38.6	2.0	89.9	31.3	638	438	144	30.6	623	115
SeaTac	44.1	5.0	93.3	33.9	1 224	437	770	38.5	1 392	195
Seattle	1 849.1	193.2	68.5	913.5	1 438	626	809	1 658.2	2 611	430
Shoreline	64.6	27.8	75.5	28.7	527	212	300	61.5	1 129	532
Spokane	360.6	46.8	62.8	134.2	641	291	339	346.3	1 653	310
Spokane Valley	47.6	9.5	74.7	34.3	379	118	250	44.6	492	104
Tacoma	497.4	82.6	61.5	160.2	792	300	477	525.2	2 597	668
University Place	20.3	3.7	81.0	12.2	386	120	255	19.2	607	164
Vancouver	216.2	36.9	48.3	102.8	622	244	361	188.0	1 138	228
Walla Walla	47.0	7.8	77.4	16.3	512	186	320	48.0	1 505	391
Wenatchee	35.6	3.6	70.5	20.4	627	183	433	31.6	972	109
Yakima	108.8	28.2	59.7	50.2	539	163	367	101.0	1 085	250
WEST VIRGINIA	X	X	X	X	X	X	X	X	X	X
Charleston...................	119.9	8.4	43.3	74.5	1 461	237	1 224	118.2	2 318	327
Huntington	66.4	5.5	20.3	27.6	561	105	408	69.9	1 422	172
Morgantown.................	47.5	3.6	18.6	18.2	602	114	488	57.9	1 916	338
Parkersburg.................	38.3	2.2	14.9	16.0	512	159	345	37.9	1 214	142
Wheeling	68.9	4.3	9.3	21.9	776	214	556	77.9	2 759	267
WISCONSIN............	X	X	X	X	X	X	X	X	X	X
Appleton	105.8	35.3	66.9	40.0	547	511	29	95.4	1 306	185
Beloit	62.8	26.8	88.2	19.9	542	506	31	62.9	1 709	281
Brookfield	58.1	9.5	75.4	37.1	977	878	98	58.2	1 531	164
Eau Claire	86.2	27.3	65.5	36.1	536	481	48	88.9	1 320	274
Fitchburg	30.2	5.5	88.9	18.6	718	696	22	39.3	1 517	661
Fond du Lac.................	60.5	20.6	71.8	21.1	490	445	41	63.0	1 465	223
Franklin.......................	41.4	6.9	92.4	26.8	747	678	68	36.9	1 030	91
Green Bay	138.7	46.3	79.3	53.7	512	485	22	133.7	1 276	218
Greenfield....................	36.7	6.5	88.9	20.6	556	518	38	41.0	1 106	190
Janesville....................	81.1	21.4	60.8	31.0	488	455	30	86.4	1 359	476
Kenosha	136.7	40.5	74.7	66.5	666	635	29	121.2	1 213	141
La Crosse	96.0	32.3	81.3	41.7	801	727	63	83.2	1 597	241
Madison	476.1	163.1	64.2	192.4	802	725	69	469.3	1 956	262
Manitowoc	48.5	17.0	90.1	15.7	469	434	32	54.5	1 630	246
Menomonee Falls..........	46.2	6.0	94.8	25.0	698	656	42	54.6	1 523	188
Milwaukee	1 070.1	483.1	64.8	302.6	505	483	22	1 000.4	1 671	211
Mount Pleasant	34.1	6.0	62.3	15.7	601	545	49	36.3	1 387	0
Neenah........................	34.2	7.5	78.2	17.5	681	647	32	35.3	1 374	110
New Berlin	42.8	4.9	98.3	23.5	591	549	41	43.8	1 103	116
Oak Creek....................	39.6	9.3	95.7	20.6	591	532	53	40.8	1 169	139
Oshkosh	88.9	26.0	83.5	36.9	554	503	47	92.9	1 393	336
Racine	138.3	56.9	78.9	49.1	627	593	33	139.8	1 787	186
Sheboygan	64.8	24.2	81.4	26.8	549	494	49	58.7	1 204	114
Stevens Point..............	34.5	13.5	80.1	14.0	519	471	42	34.2	1 272	140
Sun Prairie	36.3	6.6	89.6	21.4	700	647	49	33.4	1 092	159
Superior......................	47.8	19.7	86.8	13.1	488	414	69	43.1	1 604	221
Waukesha	94.8	23.2	75.8	53.6	753	709	40	92.3	1 297	257
Wausau	59.2	21.8	72.8	26.1	667	628	35	52.5	1 340	306
Wauwatosa	76.5	14.7	62.5	41.9	891	830	51	68.2	1 451	107
West Allis	89.6	27.7	67.2	39.6	652	626	24	88.3	1 455	97
West Bend...................	37.8	8.6	79.5	22.6	714	667	45	36.4	1 152	223
WYOMING	X	X	X	X	X	X	X	X	X	X
Casper.........................	90.9	48.4	57.4	10.7	185	79	91	91.8	1 586	372
Cheyenne.....................	102.2	45.4	60.0	14.2	231	86	144	84.7	1 372	240
Gillette........................	102.0	79.8	46.5	4.1	129	81	48	73.4	2 334	563
Laramie	40.4	21.5	68.2	5.1	162	66	95	47.7	1503	636

1. Based on population estimated as of July 1 of the year shown.

City	City government finances, 2012 (cont.)									
	General expenditure (cont.)									
	Percent of total for:									
	Public welfare	Highways	Parking facilities	Education	Health and hospitals	Police protection	Sewerage and sanitation	Parks and recreation	Housing and community development	Interest on debt
	127	128	129	130	131	132	133	134	135	136
WASHINGTON—Cont'd										
Pasco	0.0	12.0	0.0	0.0	5.4	17.4	11.1	11.5	2.3	5.8
Pullman	0.0	11.6	0.0	0.0	6.2	18.7	14.9	9.3	0.0	0.8
Puyallup	0.0	14.1	0.0	0.0	0.3	25.3	23.3	8.8	1.9	6.7
Redmond	0.1	20.2	0.0	0.0	3.2	9.2	16.1	13.1	0.8	2.8
Renton	0.0	13.1	0.0	0.0	0.2	11.9	18.6	6.2	1.5	5.1
Richland	0.0	12.0	0.0	0.0	3.2	11.2	16.4	9.6	5.1	3.3
Sammamish	0.0	22.0	0.0	0.0	0.5	13.9	5.2	17.5	3.3	0.4
SeaTac	0.0	17.5	0.0	0.0	0.0	22.5	3.5	7.6	3.2	0.3
Seattle	6.2	11.8	0.5	0.3	1.1	10.5	29.3	9.1	1.8	4.1
Shoreline	0.0	46.6	0.0	0.0	0.0	16.3	3.4	7.7	2.4	3.0
Spokane	1.1	10.6	0.1	0.0	0.1	12.3	34.0	5.6	2.9	2.6
Spokane Valley	0.0	29.1	0.0	0.0	0.7	37.4	3.1	8.3	3.7	0.9
Tacoma	1.2	12.1	1.0	0.0	2.6	11.0	24.3	5.6	2.6	4.8
University Place	0.0	26.2	0.0	0.0	0.9	17.4	7.1	4.1	4.1	14.1
Vancouver	0.0	18.7	0.7	0.0	0.1	13.2	12.4	8.6	1.9	4.8
Walla Walla	0.0	9.6	0.0	0.0	5.4	12.5	19.2	5.1	0.0	3.1
Wenatchee	0.0	8.3	0.0	0.0	0.6	18.3	19.6	9.2	4.5	4.1
Yakima	0.0	18.3	0.0	0.0	0.4	19.6	13.4	5.3	3.1	2.2
WEST VIRGINIA	X	X	X	X	X	X	X	X	X	X
Charleston	0.0	12.8	2.4	0.0	0.0	18.6	20.7	8.7	3.5	3.1
Huntington	1.1	3.4	1.2	0.0	0.5	17.3	19.7	5.0	6.2	1.0
Morgantown	0.0	7.3	3.3	0.0	0.1	10.7	27.2	11.8	9.3	1.9
Parkersburg	0.1	17.9	0.6	0.0	0.0	14.6	24.6	1.3	3.6	0.4
Wheeling	0.3	8.2	0.9	0.0	0.0	10.7	13.4	47.9	2.8	1.1
WISCONSIN	X	X	X	X	X	X	X	X	X	X
Appleton	0.5	20.7	1.8	0.0	1.3	17.2	14.6	5.8	1.5	8.6
Beloit	0.0	15.7	0.0	0.0	2.0	18.6	18.7	5.0	1.7	7.4
Brookfield	0.0	16.4	0.0	0.0	5.1	16.4	24.7	6.6	0.0	4.2
Eau Claire	0.0	26.3	0.5	0.0	7.7	17.5	7.2	8.4	1.3	5.0
Fitchburg	0.0	15.1	0.0	0.0	1.4	15.9	6.7	4.4	0.0	3.0
Fond du Lac	0.0	15.2	1.0	0.0	7.9	15.6	15.7	3.3	5.5	12.5
Franklin	0.0	12.4	0.0	0.0	6.0	25.2	13.8	0.9	1.9	3.9
Green Bay	0.0	15.6	1.6	0.0	0.1	19.6	17.1	7.5	0.1	7.7
Greenfield	0.0	24.5	0.0	0.0	6.1	25.0	12.3	4.7	0.0	3.4
Janesville	1.0	12.8	0.1	0.0	3.5	15.3	28.2	6.8	4.9	2.7
Kenosha	0.0	15.3	0.0	0.0	8.7	23.0	12.6	7.0	3.3	5.4
La Crosse	0.1	15.0	1.9	0.1	0.2	14.5	10.0	13.5	2.4	5.6
Madison	0.0	12.8	1.8	0.0	2.2	14.5	7.9	12.6	8.8	4.6
Manitowoc	0.0	15.2	0.1	0.0	0.4	14.2	10.4	6.0	0.2	12.4
Menomonee Falls	0.0	15.5	0.0	0.0	0.2	16.2	20.2	2.6	0.0	7.8
Milwaukee	0.0	12.7	2.5	0.0	2.4	25.6	14.5	0.3	4.2	5.0
Mount Pleasant	0.0	17.1	0.0	0.0	4.2	20.6	21.1	0.8	0.0	5.8
Neenah	0.0	16.2	0.6	0.0	1.9	17.0	13.8	6.1	0.8	10.8
New Berlin	0.0	19.7	0.0	0.0	2.8	23.9	21.2	4.8	0.0	3.7
Oak Creek	0.0	19.5	0.0	0.0	14.6	24.8	12.2	3.6	0.0	2.2
Oshkosh	0.0	23.8	0.5	0.0	2.4	13.2	11.8	12.9	0.2	8.2
Racine	0.0	14.3	1.2	0.0	5.6	23.4	15.4	8.0	2.0	7.2
Sheboygan	0.0	14.8	0.7	0.0	0.9	20.3	13.9	5.4	6.3	5.0
Stevens Point	0.0	23.7	0.0	0.0	4.9	16.2	9.8	7.6	0.0	4.2
Sun Prairie	0.0	21.7	0.0	0.0	4.2	20.7	12.6	6.0	0.0	10.6
Superior	0.0	18.0	0.0	0.0	0.4	17.5	22.0	4.7	2.4	3.9
Waukesha	0.0	16.2	0.8	0.0	2.6	18.4	16.2	9.4	0.3	5.9
Wausau	0.0	21.0	3.6	0.0	5.0	16.8	11.2	7.1	1.6	3.1
Wauwatosa	0.0	13.3	0.0	0.0	8.5	23.5	12.9	2.4	2.5	4.8
West Allis	0.0	15.5	0.1	0.0	4.5	22.8	11.5	0.5	5.7	4.1
West Bend	0.0	15.4	0.3	0.0	1.8	22.0	12.1	9.0	0.5	10.6
WYOMING	X	X	X	X	X	X	X	X	X	X
Casper	2.2	10.7	0.0	0.0	1.5	13.9	20.6	12.8	0.5	0.4
Cheyenne	1.4	15.7	0.8	0.0	2.2	15.2	14.6	13.7	0.4	1.9
Gillette	0.0	29.3	0.0	0.0	0.8	10.9	11.6	5.5	1.5	0.5
Laramie	0.0	22.8	0.0	0.0	3.0	15.4	15.8	9.0	1.0	1.4

City	City government finances, 2012 (cont.) Debt outstanding — Total (mil dol)	Per capita[1] (dollars)	Debt issued during year	Climate[2] — Average daily temperature (degrees Fahrenheit) Mean — January	Mean — July	Limits — January[3]	Limits — July[4]	Annual precipitation (inches)	Heating degree days	Cooling degree days
	137	138	139	140	141	142	143	144	145	146
WASHINGTON—Cont'd										
Pasco	48.6	727	4.2	34.2	75.2	28.0	89.3	8.01	4 731	909
Pullman	7.0	224	0.3	NA	NA	NA	NA	NA	NA	NA
Puyallup	75.3	1 972	2.6	39.9	64.9	32.9	77.8	40.51	4 991	153
Redmond	82.8	1 463	8.0	25.1	55.0	20.0	65.0	82.86	9 630	12
Renton	184.1	1 921	26.1	40.9	65.3	35.9	75.3	37.07	4 797	173
Richland	147.2	2 861	0.3	33.0	73.2	26.0	87.9	7.55	5 133	739
Sammamish	7.7	157	0.0	40.8	65.2	35.2	75.0	35.96	4 756	174
SeaTac	5.8	208	0.0	40.9	65.3	35.9	75.3	37.07	4 797	173
Seattle	4 163.6	6 556	431.3	41.5	65.5	36.0	74.5	38.25	4 615	192
Shoreline	38.3	704	0.0	40.8	65.2	35.2	75.0	35.96	4 756	174
Spokane	189.9	906	0.0	27.3	68.6	21.7	82.5	16.67	6 820	394
Spokane Valley	7.9	88	0.0	NA	NA	NA	NA	NA	NA	NA
Tacoma	1 587.6	7 849	58.5	41.0	65.6	35.1	76.1	38.95	4 650	167
University Place	55.9	1 770	5.9	41.0	65.6	35.1	76.1	38.95	4 650	167
Vancouver	263.9	1 597	10.6	39.0	65.4	32.4	77.3	41.92	4 990	197
Walla Walla	62.5	1 959	0.0	34.7	75.3	28.8	89.9	20.88	4 882	957
Wenatchee	42.9	1 318	18.9	29.2	74.4	23.2	87.8	9.12	5 533	832
Yakima	60.7	653	2.8	29.1	69.1	20.5	87.2	8.26	6 104	431
WEST VIRGINIA	X	X	X	X	X	X	X	X	X	X
Charleston	118.0	2 315	9.2	33.4	73.9	24.2	84.9	44.05	4 644	978
Huntington	44.1	897	2.3	32.1	76.3	23.5	87.1	41.74	4 737	1 128
Morgantown	120.1	3 972	3.8	30.8	73.5	22.3	83.4	43.30	5 174	815
Parkersburg	67.9	2 176	4.9	30.7	75.4	22.3	85.8	40.69	5 091	1 038
Wheeling	49.6	1 759	8.3	29.6	74.8	21.4	85.2	40.34	5 313	926
WISCONSIN	X	X	X	X	X	X	X	X	X	X
Appleton	159.0	2 176	6.9	16.0	71.6	7.8	81.4	30.16	7 721	572
Beloit	93.8	2 547	28.1	19.1	72.4	11.6	82.5	35.25	6 969	664
Brookfield	66.3	1 745	9.1	20.0	74.3	11.5	85.1	32.09	6 886	791
Eau Claire	99.4	1 476	8.5	11.9	71.4	2.5	82.6	32.12	8 196	554
Fitchburg	29.6	1 143	6.6	NA	NA	NA	NA	NA	NA	NA
Fond du Lac	203.2	4 724	19.8	16.6	71.8	9.1	81.1	30.15	7 534	586
Franklin	32.5	906	0.0	20.7	72.0	13.4	81.1	34.81	7 087	616
Green Bay	209.5	1 998	5.7	15.6	69.9	7.1	81.2	29.19	7 963	463
Greenfield	32.8	886	7.3	19.9	73.8	12.7	81.9	33.86	6 847	764
Janesville	106.9	1 682	22.1	17.7	72.1	8.6	83.8	32.78	7 238	629
Kenosha	179.5	1 797	26.2	20.8	71.3	13.2	78.7	34.74	6 999	549
La Crosse	98.7	1 894	17.8	15.9	74.0	6.3	85.2	32.36	7 340	775
Madison	526.8	2 195	99.4	17.3	71.6	9.3	82.1	32.95	7 493	582
Manitowoc	154.4	4 618	11.6	18.7	69.9	10.8	79.6	30.49	7 563	425
Menomonee Falls	94.1	2 625	18.0	16.5	69.3	8.1	80.2	33.45	7 832	407
Milwaukee	1 306.0	2 181	454.0	20.0	74.3	11.5	85.1	32.09	6 886	791
Mount Pleasant	47.2	1 806	5.6	NA	NA	NA	NA	NA	NA	NA
Neenah	75.6	2 939	5.0	NA	NA	NA	NA	NA	NA	NA
New Berlin	45.0	1 133	6.4	19.9	73.8	12.7	81.9	33.86	6 847	764
Oak Creek	112.6	3 230	18.5	20.7	72.0	13.4	81.1	34.81	7 087	616
Oshkosh	221.7	3 326	42.5	16.1	72.0	7.8	81.8	31.57	7 639	591
Racine	233.6	2 986	30.0	20.7	71.3	13.3	78.6	35.35	7 032	567
Sheboygan	62.5	1 281	1.4	20.9	71.4	13.2	81.4	31.90	7 056	559
Stevens Point	44.4	1 651	18.4	NA	NA	NA	NA	NA	NA	NA
Sun Prairie	70.0	2 289	0.0	NA	NA	NA	NA	NA	NA	NA
Superior	54.2	2 019	18.4	12.1	66.6	3.4	76.2	30.78	9 006	241
Waukesha	127.7	1 793	19.3	19.5	73.8	11.4	84.2	34.64	6 893	784
Wausau	50.1	1 279	7.7	13.0	70.1	3.6	80.8	33.36	8 237	464
Wauwatosa	100.8	2 142	19.5	20.0	74.3	11.5	85.1	32.09	6 886	791
West Allis	78.5	1 294	5.9	19.9	73.8	12.7	81.9	33.86	6 847	764
West Bend	79.7	2 525	6.8	18.4	70.6	10.7	81.3	32.85	7 371	502
WYOMING	X	X	X	X	X	X	X	X	X	X
Casper	19.5	338	0.1	22.3	70.0	12.2	86.8	13.03	7 571	428
Cheyenne	86.1	1 395	14.1	25.9	67.7	14.8	81.9	15.45	7 388	273
Gillette	91.7	2 916	2.2	NA	NA	NA	NA	NA	NA	NA
Laramie	44.3	1 394	0.5	20.3	62.9	7.8	79.4	11.19	9 233	75

1. Based on the population estimated as of July 1 of the year shown.   2. Represents normal values based on the 30-year period, 1971–2000.   3. Average daily minimum.
4. Average daily maximum.

Congressional Districts of the 114th Congress

(For explanation of symbols, see page viii)

Congressional District Highlights and Rankings

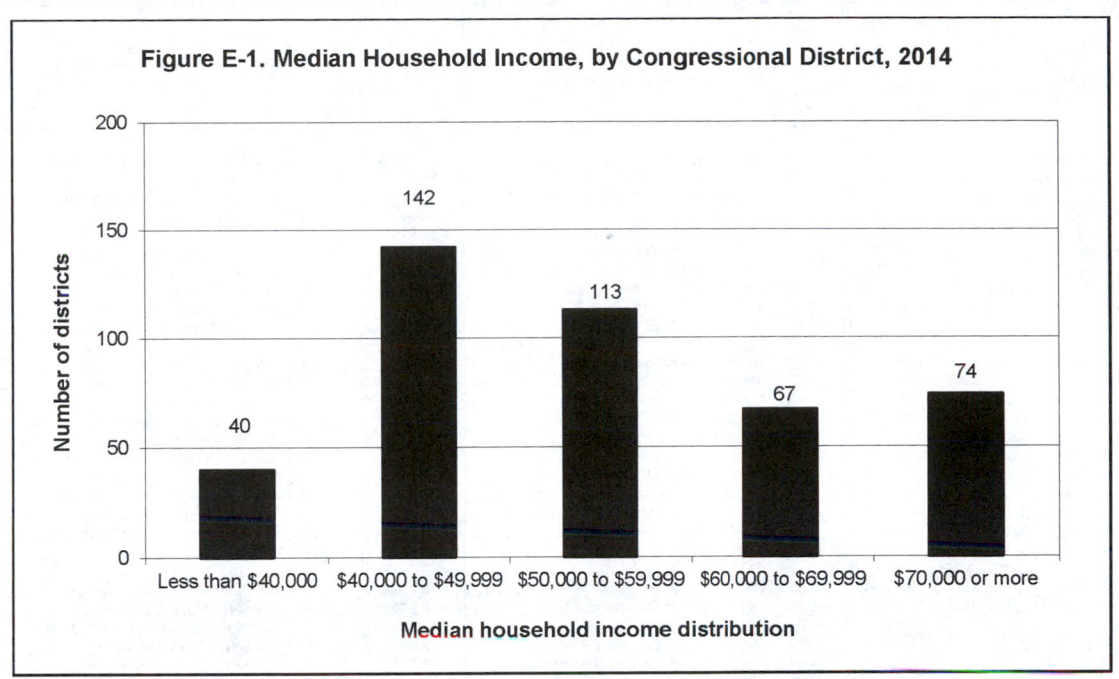

Figure E-1. Median Household Income, by Congressional District, 2014

Every 10 years, the Census Bureau conducts a count to reapportion the seats in the U.S. House of Representatives. The House's 435 seats are divided among the 50 states. (The District of Columbia has no representative in Congress, although it has a nonvoting delegate.) The seats are reapportioned according to the population measured on April 1 of the census year in order to account for population changes among the states over the previous decade. The number of districts within a state may change after each decennial census, and the districts' boundaries may change more than once during a decade. The 114th Congress which convened in 2015 was the second to reflect the new boundaries based on the 2010 census. The data in Table E were assembled for the districts of the 114th Congress. The Representatives of the 114th Congress are listed. There were no boundary changes between the 113th and the 114th Congress.

As the state with the largest population, California had the most representatives with 53. Texas (36) and New York (27) were second and third largest, respectively. There were 7 states with just 1 representative: Alaska, Delaware, Montana, North Dakota, South Dakota, Vermont, and Wyoming. These states' representatives were considered 'At Large,' as they represented an entire state instead of a specific congressional district within the state.

Because the number of representatives is limited to 435, states with larger population growth add seats, while states with little or no growth lose seats. When the 113th Congress convened in January 2013, eight states had more representatives in congress and 10 states had fewer. Based on the 2010 census, Texas gained 4 seats, Florida gained 2, while Washington, Nevada, Utah, Arizona, Georgia, and South Carolina each gained one seat. New York and Ohio each lost two seats, while Massachusetts, New Jersey, Pennsylvania, Michigan, Illinois, Iowa, Missouri, and Louisiana each lost a seat.

As each decade progresses, population shifts alter the size of districts, leading up to the reapportionment of the next census. After the 2000 census, the population of each congressional district was about 645,000. Based on the 2014 population estimates, the new congressional districts average over 731,000 people. Montana's

at-large congressional district had over a million people, while Delaware and South Dakota also had at-large seats with above average populations. Idaho's 1st district is the largest apportioned congressional district in the United States with a population over 834,000 in 2014. Rhode Island's two congressional districts have the smallest populations at 523,028 and 532,145. Congressional districts in Nebraska and West Virginia also have smaller populations. For years, Louisiana's 2nd district was the least populous congressional district in the nation due to outmigration after Hurricane Katrina.

While most of the congressional districts had about the same population size, they varied widely in other characteristics. In Colorado's 2nd district, 96.0 percent of the residents were high school graduates, compared with just 51.5 percent in California's 40th district and 58.5 percent in California's 21st district. California's 21st district had the lowest proportion of college graduates, with only 7.1 percent of its residents holding a bachelor's degree, followed by Texas' 33rd district at 8.9 percent, Texas' 29th district at 9.1 percent and California's 40th district at 9.2 percent. In New York's 12th district, 71.8 percent of residents were college graduates.

The highest unemployment rates were found in Michigan's 13th district at 15.7 percent and Illinois' 2nd district at 15.4 percent. Two districts each from California, Illinois, and Michigan along with one district each from Pennsylvania, Mississippi, Georgia, and Ohio ranked among the 10 highest. Eighty-four congressional districts had 20 percent or more of their populations living in poverty. New York's 15th district had the highest poverty rate in the nation at 41.0 percent and the lowest median household income at $24,429 in 2014. In Virginia's 10th district, the median household income was $115,291, the highest in the nation. Fifty-one congressional districts had median household incomes exceeding $75,000 per year, while forty districts had median household incomes below $40,000. The U.S. median household income in 2014 was $53,657.

Congressional Districts of the 114th Congress of the United States
Selected Rankings

Population, 2014			Land area, 2010			Population density, 2014		
Popu-lation rank	State congressional district Representative	Population [col 2]	Land area rank	State congressional district Representative	Land area (square kilometers) [col 1]	Density rank	State congressional district Representative	Population density (per square kilometer) [col 3]
1	MT At-Large Ryan K. Zinke (R)	1 023 579	1	AK At-Large: Don Young (R)	1 477 953	1	NY 13th: Charles B. Rangel (D)	28 970
2	DE At-Large: John C. Carney (D)	935 614	2	MT At-Large Ryan K. Zinke (R)	376 962	2	NY 10th: Jerrold Nadler (D)	19 919
3	SD At-Large: Kristi Noem (R)	853 175	3	WY At-Large Cynthia M. Lummis (R)	251 470	3	NY 15th: José E. Serrano (D)	19 761
4	ID 1st: Raul Labrador (R)	834 295	4	SD At-Large: Kristi Noem (R)	196 350	4	NY 12th: Carolyn B. Maloney (D)	19 191
5	TX 22nd: Pete Olson (R)	814 594	5	NM 2nd: Steve Pearce (R)	185 804	5	NY 9th: Yvette D. Clarke (D)	18 877
6	OR 3rd: Earl Blumenauer (D)	806 382	6	OR 2nd: Greg Walden (R)	179 856	6	NY 7th: Nydia M. Velázquez (D)	17 430
7	NC 9th: Robert Pittenger (R)	805 960	7	ND-At Large Kevin Cramer (R)	178 711	7	NY 14th: Joseph Crowley (D)	10 306
8	OR 1st: Suzanne Bonamici (D)	805 943	8	NE 3rd: Adrian Smith (R)	174 657	8	NY 8th: Hakeem S. Jeffries (D)	9 851
9	VA10th Barbara Comstock (R)	802 127	9	TX 23rd: Will Hurd (R)	150 373	9	NY 6th: Grace Meng (D)	9 525
10	IA 3rd: David Young (R)	801 039	10	NV 2nd: Mark E. Amodei (R)	144 598	10	CA 12th:Nancy Pelosi (D)	7 288
11	ID 2nd: Michael K. Simpson (R)	800 169	11	AZ 1st: Ann Kirkpatrick (D)	142 552	11	CA 34th: Xavier Becerra (D)	5 857
12	OR 5th: Kurt Schrader (D)	798 185	12	KS 1st: Tim Huelskamp (R)	136 084	12	NY 5th: Gregory W. Meeks (D)	5 675
13	LA 1st: Steve Scalise (R)	796 858	13	NV 4th: Cresent Hardy (R)	132 084	13	NJ 8th: Albio Sires (D)	5 368
14	OK 5th: Steve Russell (R)	796 326	14	CO 3rd: Scott R. Tipton (R)	128 805	14	IL 4th:Luis V. Gutierrez (D)	5 335
15	NC 4th: David E. Price (D)	795 798	15	NM 3rd: Ben Ray Luján (D)	116 442	15	CA 37th: Karen Bass (D)	5 061
16	TX 3rd: Sam Johnson (R)	792 608	16	ID 2nd: Michael K. Simpson (R)	111 952	16	CA 40th: Lucille Roybal-Allard (D)	4 792
17	LA 6th: Garret Graves (R)	791 864	17	UT 2nd: Chris Stewart (R)	103 568	17	MA 7th: Michael E. Capuano (D)	4 753
18	CO 1st: Diana DeGette (D)	788 664	18	ID 1st: Raul Labrador (R)	102 092	18	IL 7th: Danny K. Davis (D)	4 491
19	OR 2nd: Greg Walden (R)	784 114	19	TX 13th: Mac Thornberry (R)	99 324	19	NY 11th: Daniel M. Donovan Jr. (R)	4 251
20	TX 26th: Michael C. Burgess (R)	783 257	20	CO 4th: Ken Buck (R)	98 685	20	DC At Large: Eleanor Holmes Norton (D)	4 170
21	VA11th Gerald E. Connolly (D)	782 204	21	OK 3rd: Frank D. Lucas (R)	88 362	21	CA 46th: Loretta Sanchez (D)	3 929
22	NY 13th: Charles B. Rangel (D)	782 199	22	MN 6th: Collin C. Peterson (D)	86 582	22	CA 43rd: Maxine Waters (D)	3 914
23	AZ 5th: Matt Salmon (R)	781 441	23	AZ 4th: Paul A. Gosar (R)	85 986	23	NJ 10th: Donald M. Payne, Jr. (D)	3 771
24	OK 1st: Jim Bridenstine (R)	781 067	24	CA 8th: Paul Cook (R)	85 126	24	PA 2nd: Chaka Fattah (D)	3 734
25	NC 12th: Alma S. Adams (D)	778 251	25	CA 1st: Doug LaMalfa (D)	72 751	25	NY 16th: Eliot L. Engel (D)	3 608
26	LA 3rd: Charles W. Boustany Jr. (R)	777 665	26	MN 7th: Richard M. Nolan (D)	72 282	26	PA 1st: Robert A. Brady (D)	3 545
27	OK 3rd: Frank D. Lucas (R)	776 896	27	TX 11th K. Michael Conaway (R)	72 085	27	CA 44th: Janice Hahn (D)	3 525
28	IA 2nd: David Loebsack (D)	776 785	28	ME 2nd: Bruce Poliquin (R)	71 373	28	NJ 9th: Bill Pascrell, Jr. (D)	3 074
29	TX 31st: John R. Carter (R)	776 518	29	TX 19th: Randy Neugebauer (R)	66 914	29	CA 29th: Tony Cárdenas (D)	3 020
30	LA 2nd: Cedric Richmond (D)	775 807	30	MI 1st: Dan Benishek (R)	64 822	30	CA 13th:Barbara Lee (D)	2 961
31	OR 4th: Peter A. DeFazio (D)	775 615	31	WI 7th: Sean P. Duffy (R)	59 666	31	IL 5th: Michael Quigley (D)	2 894
32	NC 2nd: Renee Ellmers (R)	774 723	32	IA 4th: Steve King (R)	58 940	32	CA 38th: Linda T. Sánchez (D)	2 738
33	VA 8th Donald S. Beyer, Jr. (D)	774 065	33	AR 2nd: Bruce Westerman (R)	57 855	33	FL 24th: Frederica S. Wilson (D)	2 698
34	OK 4th: Tom Cole (R)	773 994	34	OK 2nd: Markwayne Mullin (R)	54 378	34	IL 9th: Janice D. Schakowsky (D)	2 602
35	CO 6th: Mike Coffman (R)	772 966	35	UT 3rd: Jason Chaffetz (R)	51 982	35	NV 1st: Dina Titus (D)	2 560
36	NC 13th: George Holding (R)	772 469	36	MO 8th: Jason T. Smith (R)	51 544	36	NY 4th: Kathleen M. Rice (D)	2 515
37	NC 7th: David Rouzer (R)	772 311	37	UT 1st: Rob Bishop (R)	50 662	37	CA 32nd: Grace F. Napolitano (D)	2 286
38	TX 9th: Al Green (D)	772 152	38	AR 1st: Eric A. "Rick" Crawford (R)	50 034	38	WI 4th: Gwen Moore (D)	2 162
39	CO 7th: Ed Perlmutter (D)	771 211	39	WA 1st: Dan Newsome (R)	49 858	39	CA 53rd: Susan A. Davis (D)	2 148
40	TX 10th: Michael T. McCaul (R)	771 009	40	MO 6th: Sam Graves (R)	47 134	40	CA 30th: Brad Sherman (D)	2 143
41	TX 7th: John Abney Culberson (R)	770 950	41	OR 4th: Peter A. DeFazio (D)	44 740	41	MN 5th: Keith Ellison (D)	2 013
42	IA 1st: Rod Blum (R)	770 612	42	AZ 3rd: Raul M. Grijalva (D)	40 634	42	VA 8th Donald S. Beyer, Jr. (D)	2 000
43	VA 1st Robert J. Wittman (R)	770 044	43	MS 2nd: Bennie G. Thompson (D)	40 278	43	WA 7th: Jim McDermott (D)	1 964
44	VA 7th Dave Brat (R)	769 995	44	WA 5th: Cathy McMorris Rodgers (R)	40 075	44	CA 48th: Dana Rohrabacher (R)	1 927
45	FL 9th: Alan Grayson (D)	769 993	45	NY 21st: Elise M. Stefanik (R)	39 147	45	TX 7th: John Abney Culberson (R)	1 840
46	MA 7th: Michael E. Capuano (D)	769 929	46	IL 15th: John Shimkus (R)	38 062	46	PA 13th: Brendan F. Boyle (D)	1 804
47	MD 3rd: John P. Sarbanes (D)	768 378	47	LA 5th: Ralph Lee Abraham (R)	37 433	47	TX 9th: Al Green (D)	1 800
48	CO 4th: Ken Buck (R)	768 242	48	MO 4th: Vicky Hartzler (R)	37 299	48	AZ 9th: Kyrsten Sinema (D)	1 745
49	AR 2nd: Steve Womack (R)	767 904	49	KS 4th: Mike Pompeo (R)	37 077	49	CA 35th Norma J. Torres (D)	1 677
50	TX 35th: Lloyd Doggett (D)	767 436	50	KS 2nd: Lynn Jenkins (R)	36 631	50	FL 23rd: Debbie Wasserman Schultz (D)	1 667
51	TX 8th: Kevin Brady (R)	767 431	51	CA 2nd:Jared Huffman (D)	33 546	51	VA11th Gerald E. Connolly (D)	1 633
52	MO 3rd: Blaine Luetkemeyer (R)	766 993	52	CA 4th:Tom McClintock (R)	33 246	52	FL 22nd: Lois Frankel (D)	1 632
53	TX 21st: Lamar Smith (R)	766 190	53	MS 3rd: Gregg Harper (R)	33 034	53	CA 6th: Doris O. Matsui (D)	1 628
54	CO: 2nd: Jared Polis (D)	765 721	54	LA 4th: John Fleming (R)	32 207	54	CO 1st: Diana DeGette (D)	1 606
55	MO 7th: Bill Long (R)	765 669	55	IA 2nd: David Loebsack (D)	31 758	55	CA 17th: Michael M. Honda (D)	1 580
56	TX 15th: Rubén Hinojosa (D)	764 850	56	KY 1st: Ed Whitfield (R)	31 286	56	TX 32nd: Pete Sessions (R)	1 554
57	UT 4th: Mia B. Love (R)	764 474	57	IA 1st: Rod Blum (R)	31 206	57	TX 29th: Gene Green (D)	1 544
58	CA 45th: Mimi Walters (R)	763 368	58	MN 1st: Timothy J. Walz (D)	31 012	58	NY 2nd: Peter T. King (R)	1 538
59	AZ 7th: Ruben Gallego (D)	763 089	59	KY 5th: Harold Rogers (R)	29 099	59	MI 9th: Sander M. Levin (D)	1 517
60	MO 4th: Vicky Hartzler (R)	763 003	60	WI 3rd: Ron Kind (D)	28 779	60	WA 9th: Adam Smith (D)	1 498
61	TX 20th: Joaquin Castro (D)	762 801	61	PA 5th: Glenn Thompson (R)	27 742	61	TX 20th: Joaquin Castro (D)	1 475
62	NJ 8th: Albio Sires (D)	762 249	62	MS 1st: Trent Kelly (R)	27 383	62	FL 13th: David W. Jolly (R)	1 468
63	MS 4th: Steven Palazzo (R)	761 734	63	IL 18th: Darin LaHood (R)	27 236	63	AZ 7th: Ruben Gallego (D)	1 437
64	AZ 8th: Trent Franks (R)	760 904	64	AL 7th: Terri A. Sewell (D)	26 304	64	MI 13th: John Conyers Jr. (D)	1 435
65	NY 5th: Gregory W. Meeks (D)	760 487	65	AL 2nd: Martha Roby (R)	26 267	65	MI 14th: Brenda L. Lawrence (D)	1 430
66	FL 27th: Ileana Ros-Lehtinen (R)	760 443	66	TX 4th: John Ratcliffe (R)	26 218	66	FL 27th: Ileana Ros-Lehtinen (R)	1 406
67	MO 6th: Sam Graves (R)	760 291	67	VA 5th Robert Hurt (R)	25 977	67	IL 8th: Tammy Duckworth (D)	1 363
68	MS 1st: Trent Kelly (R)	760 275	68	CA 23rd: Kevin McCarthy (R)	25 636	68	CA 39th: Edward R. Royce (R)	1 355
69	CO 5th: Doug Lamborn (R)	759 664	69	OK 4th: Tom Cole (R)	25 323	69	TX 33rd: Marc A. Veasey (D)	1 353
70	NC 3rd: Walter B. Jones (R)	759 653	70	WV 3rd: Evan H. Jenkins (R)	25 240	70	NJ 6th: Frank Pallone Jr. (D)	1 342
71	CA 52nd: Scott H. Peters (D)	759 602	71	GA 2nd: Sanford D. Bishop Jr. (D)	24 932	71	CA 31st:Pete Aguilar (D)	1 307
72	NJ 9th: Bill Pascrell, Jr. (D)	759 352	72	TX 28th: Henry Cuellar (D)	24 290	72	HI 1st: Mark Takai (D)	1 305
73	TX 24th: Kenny Marchant (R)	759 022	73	VT At-Large: Peter Welch (D)	23 871	73	PA 14th: Michael F. Doyle (D)	1 294
74	IA 4th: Steve King (R)	758 690	74	TN 7th: Marsha Blackburn (R)	23 725	74	CA 47th: Alan S. Lowenthal (D)	1 284
75	NY 8th: Hakeem S. Jeffries (D)	758 543	75	TX 27th: Blake Farenthold (R)	23 642	75	OH 3rd: Joyce Beatty (D)	1 278

Congressional Districts of the 114th Congress of the United States
Selected Rankings

Percent Non-Hispanic White alone, 2014			Percent Black alone, 2014			Percent American Indian, Alaska Native alone, 2014		
Non-Hispanic White alone rank	State congressional district Representative	Percent white [col 11]	Black rank	State congressional district Representative	Percent black [col 5]	American Indian Alaska Native rank	State congressional district Representative	Percent American Indian Alaska Native [col 6]
1	KY 5th: Harold Rogers (R)	96.1	1	MS 2nd: Bennie G. Thompson (D)	66.2	1	AZ 1st: Ann Kirkpatrick (D)	23.5
2	OH 6th: Bill Johnson (R)	94.7	2	TN 9th: Steve Cohen (D)	65.7	2	NM 3rd: Ben Ray Luján (D)	18.5
3	ME 2nd: Bruce Poliquin (R)	94.3	3	AL 7th: Terri A. Sewell (D)	63.9	3	OK 2nd: Markwayne Mullin (R)	17.3
4	WV 1st: David McKinley (R)	93.7	4	LA 2nd: Cedric Richmond (D)	62.3	4	AK: At-Large Don Young (R)	14.0
5	VT At-Large: Peter Welch (D)	93.2	5	GA 5th: John Lewis (D)	58.1	5	SD At-Large: Kristi Noem (R)	8.4
5	WV 3rd: Evan H. Jenkins (R)	93.2	6	PA 2nd: Chaka Fattah (D)	58.0	6	NC 8th: Richard Hudson (R)	7.0
7	ME 1st: Chellie Pingree (D)	93.0	7	FL 24th: Frederica S. Wilson (D)	57.6	7	MT At-Large Ryan K. Zinke (R)	6.8
7	PA 9th: Bill Shuster (R)	93.0	8	GA 4th: Henry C. "Hank" Johnson Jr. (D)	57.2	8	OK 3rd: Frank D. Lucas (R)	6.0
9	PA 18th: Tim Murphy (R)	92.9	9	VA 3rd Robert C. "Bobby" Scott (D)	57.1	9	NM 2nd: Steve Pearce (R)	5.7
10	PA 5th: Glenn Thompson (R)	92.4	10	GA 13th: David Scott (D)	56.7	10	ND-At Large Kevin Cramer (R)	5.4
10	WI 3rd: Ron Kind (D)	92.4	10	SC 6th: James E. Clyburn (D)	56.7	10	OK 1st: Jim Bridenstine (R)	5.4
12	IN 6th: Luke Messer (R)	92.1	12	MI 14th: Brenda L. Lawrence (D)	56.6	12	OK 4th: Tom Cole (R)	4.7
12	OH 16th: James B. Renacci (R)	92.1	13	IL 2nd: Robin L. Kelly (D)	55.6	13	NM 1st: Michelle Lujan Grisham (D)	4.4
12	WI 7th: Sean P. Duffy (R)	92.1	14	MI 13th: John Conyers Jr. (D)	55.1	14	OK 5th: Steve Russell (R)	4.3
15	MN 7th: Richard M. Nolan (D)	92.0	15	NY 8th: Hakeem S. Jeffries (D)	55.0	15	AZ 3rd: Raul M. Grijalva (D)	3.7
15	PA 12th: Keith J. Rothfus (R)	92.0	16	OH 11th: Marcia L. Fudge (D)	54.3	16	AZ 9th: Kyrsten Sinema (D)	2.9
17	MI 4th: John L. Moolenar (R)	91.8	17	MD 7th: Elijah E. Cummings (D)	53.7	17	WA 4th: Dan Newsome (R)	2.7
17	TN 1st: David P. Roe (R)	91.8	17	NJ 10th: Donald M. Payne, Jr. (D)	53.7	18	AZ 7th: Ruben Gallego (D)	2.6
19	IL 15th: John Shimkus (R)	91.3	19	NC 1st: G. K. Butterfield (D)	53.5	18	MN 6th: Collin C. Peterson (D)	2.6
19	NH 2nd: Ann M. Kuster (D)	91.3	20	FL 5th: Corrine Brown (D)	52.9	18	MN 7th: Richard M. Nolan (D)	2.6
19	NY 27th: Chris Collins (R)	91.3	21	MD 4th: Donna F. Edwards (D)	52.6	18	WY At-Large Cynthia M. Lummis (R)	2.6
22	MI 1st: Dan Benishek (R)	91.2	22	FL 20th: Alcee L. Hastings (D)	51.9	22	WI 8th: Reid J. Ribble (R)	2.4
23	IN 8th: Larry Bucshon (R)	91.1	23	GA 2nd: Sanford D. Bishop Jr. (D)	51.5	23	CO 3rd: Scott R. Tipton (R)	2.3
24	NH 1st: Frank C. Guinta (R)	91.0	24	NY 5th: Gregory W. Meeks (D)	51.2	23	MI 1st: Dan Benishek (R)	2.3
25	MO 3rd: Blaine Luetkemeyer (R)	90.9	25	IL 1st: Bobby L. Rush (D)	51.1	25	NV 2nd: Mark E. Amodei (R)	2.2
25	OH 7th: Bob Gibbs (R)	90.9	25	NC 12th: Alma S. Adams (D)	51.1	26	CA 2nd: Jared Huffman (D)	2.1
25	WV 2nd: Alexander X. Mooney (R)	90.9	27	IL 7th: Danny K. Davis (D)	49.7	27	CA 1st: Doug LaMalfa (R)	2.0
28	KY 4th: Thomas Massie (R)	90.7	28	NY 9th: Yvette D. Clarke (D)	49.6	27	WI 7th: Sean P. Duffy (R)	2.0
28	MI 10th: Candice S. Miller (R)	90.7	29	MO 1st: William Lacy Clay (D)	49.2	29	AZ 4th: Paul A. Gosar (R)	1.9
30	MO 8th: Jason T. Smith (R)	90.4	30	DC At Large: Eleanor Holmes Norton (D)	48.8	29	NC 7th: David Rouzer (R)	1.9
30	PA 3rd: Mike Kelly (R)	90.4	31	TX 30th: Eddie Bernice Johnson (D)	43.1	31	CA 37th: Karen Bass (D)	1.8
32	MN 5th: Tom Emmer (R)	90.1	32	TX 18th: Sheila Jackson-Lee (D)	39.3	31	OR 2nd: Greg Walden (R)	1.8
32	PA 10th: Tom Marino (R)	90.1	33	TX 9th: Al Green (D)	38.5	31	WA 5th: Cathy McMorris Rodgers (R)	1.8
34	WI 6th: Glen Grothman (R)	90.0	34	MD 5th: Steny H. Hoyer (D)	37.6	31	WA 6th: Derek Kilmer (D)	1.8
35	NY 21st: Elise M. Stefanik (R)	89.9	35	PA 1st: Robert A. Brady (D)	36.4	35	WA 10th: Denny Heck (D)	1.7
36	IN 9th: Todd C. Young (R)	89.8	36	GA 12th: Rick W. Allen (R)	35.7	36	AZ 2nd: Martha McSally (R)	1.6
36	MN 6th: Collin C. Peterson (D)	89.8	37	LA 5th: Ralph Lee Abraham (R)	35.6	36	NC 11th: Mark Meadows (R)	1.6
38	VA 9th Morgan Griffith (R)	89.7	38	MS 3rd: Gregg Harper (R)	35.3	36	UT 3rd: Jason Chaffetz (R)	1.6
39	IA 1st: Rod Blum (R)	89.4	39	NY 15th: José E. Serrano (D)	34.3	39	CA 8th: Paul Cook (R)	1.5
39	OH 5th: Robert E. Latta (R)	89.4	40	WI 4th: Gwen Moore (D)	34.2	39	WA 2nd Rick Larsen (D)	1.5
41	IL 18th: Darin LaHood (R)	89.3	41	MD 2nd: C. A. Dutch Ruppersberger (D)	33.9	41	AZ 6th: David Schweikert (R)	1.4
41	OH 14th: David P. Joyce (R)	89.3	42	LA 4th: John Fleming (R)	33.6	41	CO 7th: Ed Perlmutter (D)	1.4
43	OH 15th: Steve Stivers (R)	89.2	43	OH 3rd: Joyce Beatty (D)	32.5	41	ID 1st: Raul Labrador (R)	1.4
44	TN 6th: Diane Black (R)	89.0	44	VA 4th J. Randy Forbes (R)	31.7	41	KS 2nd: Lynn Jenkins (R)	1.4
45	MO 7th: Bill Long (R)	88.7	45	AL 2nd: Martha Roby (R)	30.9	41	LA 1st: Steve Scalise (R)	1.4
46	NY 23rd: Tom Reed (R)	88.6	45	GA 8th: Austin Scott (R)	30.9	46	AZ 5th: Matt Salmon (R)	1.3
47	IA 4th: Steve King (R)	88.5	47	NY 16th: Eliot L. Engel (D)	30.6	46	CA 5th: Mike Thompson (D)	1.3
47	MO 6th: Sam Graves (R)	88.5	48	NY 13th: Charles B. Rangel (D)	30.0	46	ID 2nd: Michael K. Simpson (R)	1.3
49	MI 7th: Tim Walberg (R)	88.3	49	GA 1st: Earl L. "Buddy" Carter (R)	29.8	46	OR 4th: Peter A. DeFazio (D)	1.3
50	NY 22nd: Richard L. Hanna (R)	88.1	49	IN 7th: André Carson (D)	29.8	50	CA 21st: David G. Valadao (R)	1.2
51	OH 4th: Jim Jordan (R)	88.0	49	NC 4th: David E. Price (D)	29.8	50	CA 23rd: Kevin McCarthy (R)	1.2
51	WI 5th: F. James Sensenbrenner Jr. (R)	88.0	52	SC 7th: Tom Rice (R)	29.3	50	NE 1st: Jeff Fortenberry (R)	1.2
53	WI 8th: Reid J. Ribble (R)	87.7	53	AL 1st: Bradley Byrne (R)	27.9	53	AR 2nd: Steve Womack (R)	1.1
54	KY 1st: Ed Whitfield (R)	87.5	54	MS 1st: Trent Kelly (R)	27.3	53	CA 4th: Tom McClintock (R)	1.1
54	KY 2nd: Brett Guthrie (R)	87.5	55	SC 5th: Mick Mulvaney (R)	26.9	53	CA 36th: Raul Ruiz (D)	1.1
56	MO 2nd: Ann Wagner (R)	87.2	56	GA 10th: Jody B. Hice (R)	26.7	53	KS 4th: Mike Pompeo (R)	1.1
57	OH 12th: Patrick J. Tiberi (R)	87.0	57	AL 3rd: Mike Rogers (R)	26.0	53	NV 4th: Cresent Hardy (R)	1.1
58	MO 4th: Vicky Hartzler (R)	86.9	58	FL 14th: Kathy Castor (D)	25.2	53	UT 1st: Rob Bishop (R)	1.1
59	MA 9th: William R. Keating (D)	86.8	59	FL 2nd: Gwen Graham (D)	25.0	53	UT 2nd: Chris Stewart (R)	1.1
59	ND-At Large Kevin Cramer (R)	86.8	59	LA 3rd: Charles W. Boustany Jr. (R)	25.0	60	CA 13th: Barbara Lee (D)	1.0
61	MN 1st: Timothy J. Walz (D)	86.7	61	MA 7th: Michael E. Capuano (D)	24.9	60	CA 41st: Mark Takano (D)	1.0
61	MT At-Large Ryan K. Zinke (R)	86.7	61	TN 5th: Jim Cooper (D)	24.9	60	CO 1st: Diana DeGette (D)	1.0
63	OH 8th: Vacancy	86.5	63	LA 6th: Garret Graves (R)	24.5	60	MN 5th: Keith Ellison (D)	1.0
63	PA 11th: Lou Barletta (R)	86.5	64	GA 3rd: Lynn A. Westmoreland (R)	24.4	60	OR 5th: Kurt Schrader (D)	1.0
65	IA 2nd: David Loebsack (D)	86.4	65	CA 43rd: Maxine Waters (D)	23.9	60	WA 9th: Adam Smith (D)	1.0
65	TN 2nd: John J. Duncan Jr. (R)	86.4	65	MS 4th: Steven Palazzo (R)	23.9	66	CA 3rd: John Garamendi (D)	0.9
67	NC 11th: Mark Meadows (R)	86.3	67	MD 3rd: John P. Sarbanes (D)	23.5	66	CA 22nd: Devin Nunes (R)	0.9
68	OH 2nd: Brad R. Wenstrup (R)	86.0	68	SC 2nd: Joe Wilson (R)	23.2	66	CA 26th: Julia Brownley (D)	0.9
69	IN 4th: Todd Rokita (R)	85.7	69	CA 37th: Karen Bass (D)	22.3	66	CA 35th Norma J. Torres (D)	0.9
70	NY 19th: Christopher P. Gibson (R)	85.2	70	AR 2nd: J. French Hill (R)	22.2	66	CA 50th: Duncan Hunter (R)	0.9
71	ID 1st: Raul Labrador (R)	85.1	70	MO 5th: Emanuel Cleaver (D)	22.2	66	MO 7th: Bill Long (R)	0.9
72	NE 3rd: Adrian Smith (R)	85.0	72	OH 1st: Steve Chabot (R)	22.1	66	NE 3rd: Adrian Smith (R)	0.9
72	PA 7th: Patrick Meehan (R)	85.0	73	DE At-Large: John C. Carney (D)	21.7	66	NY 21st: Elise M. Stefanik (R)	0.9
74	OR 4th: Peter A. DeFazio (D)	84.9	73	KY 3rd: John A. Yarmuth (D)	21.7	66	NC 2nd: Renee Ellmers (R)	0.9
75	MA 4th: Joseph P. Kennedy III (D)	84.8	75	VA 2nd Scott Rigell (R)	21.6	66	OR 3rd: Earl Blumenauer (D)	0.9

Congressional Districts of the 114th Congress of the United States
Selected Rankings

Asian or Pacific Islander rank	Percent Asian or Pacific Islander alone, 2014 State congressional district Representative	Percent Asian or Pacific Islander [col 7]	Hispanic rank	Percent Hispanic or Latino,[1] 2014 State congressional district Representative	Percent Hispanic [col 10]	Foreign-born rank	Percent foreign born, 2014 State congressional district Representative	Percent foreign born [col 13]
1	HI 1st: Mark Takai (D)	58.7	1	CA 40th: Lucille Roybal-Allard (D)	86.9	1	FL 27th: Ileana Ros-Lehtinen (R)	55.4
2	CA 17th: Michael M. Honda (D)	52.7	2	TX 34th: Filemon Vela (D)	83.8	2	FL 25th: Mario Diaz-Balart (R)	52.5
3	NY 6th: Grace Meng (D)	39.8	3	TX 15th: Rubén Hinojosa (D)	81.4	3	NY 6th: Grace Meng (D)	51.5
4	CA 27th: Judy Chu (D)	38.4	4	TX 16th: Beto O'Rourke (D)	79.2	4	CA 34th: Xavier Becerra (D)	49.0
5	HI 2nd: Tulsi Gabbard (D)	37.4	5	TX 29th: Gene Green (D)	77.0	5	CA 17th: Michael M. Honda (D)	47.3
6	CA 14th: Jackie Speier (D)	34.3	6	TX 28th: Henry Cuellar (D)	76.9	6	FL 25th: Carlos Curbelo (R)	47.0
7	CA 15th: Eric Swalwell (D)	33.5	7	FL 27th: Ileana Ros-Lehtinen (R)	76.1	7	NY 14th: Joseph Crowley (D)	46.2
8	CA 12th: Nancy Pelosi (D)	32.5	8	CA 21st: David G. Valadao (R)	73.9	8	NJ 8th: Albio Sires (D)	43.8
9	CA 39th: Edward R. Royce (R)	29.6	9	CA 51st: Juan Vargas (D)	70.9	9	CA 29th: Tony Cárdenas (D)	43.4
10	CA 19th: Zoe Lofgren (D)	27.7	10	FL 25th: Mario Diaz-Balart (R)	70.8	10	NY 5th: Gregory W. Meeks (D)	42.5
11	WA 9th: Adam Smith (D)	25.3	11	IL 4th: Luis V. Gutierrez (D)	70.6	11	CA 40th: Lucille Roybal-Allard (D)	42.4
12	CA 47th: Alan S. Lowenthal (D)	23.9	12	CA 35th Norma J. Torres (D)	70.5	12	CA 28th: Adam B. Schiff (D)	41.3
13	CA 18th: Anna G. Eshoo (D)	22.7	12	CA 44th: Janice Hahn (D)	70.5	13	CA 46th: Loretta Sanchez (D)	40.5
14	CA 45th: Mimi Walters (R)	21.8	14	CA 29th: Tony Cárdenas (D)	69.1	14	NY 9th: Yvette D. Clarke (D)	39.4
15	CA 34th: Xavier Becerra (D)	20.9	15	FL 26th: Carlos Curbelo (R)	68.8	15	FL 24th: Frederica S. Wilson (D)	39.3
16	CA 13th: Barbara Lee (D)	20.2	15	TX 20th: Joaquin Castro (D)	68.8	16	CA 27th: Judy Chu (D)	38.7
17	NY 7th: Nydia M. Velázquez (D)	19.6	17	TX 23rd: Will Hurd (R)	67.7	17	CA 14th: Jackie Speier (D)	37.8
18	CA 52nd: Scott H. Peters (D)	19.5	18	CA 46th: Loretta Sanchez (D)	66.8	18	FL 23rd: Debbie Wasserman Schultz (D)	37.7
19	NJ 6th: Frank Pallone Jr. (D)	18.8	19	NY 15th: José E. Serrano (D)	65.3	19	NY 7th: Nydia M. Velázquez (D)	36.8
20	CA 48th: Dana Rohrabacher (R)	18.7	20	CA 34th: Xavier Becerra (D)	64.8	20	NY 13th: Charles B. Rangel (D)	36.6
21	CA 32nd: Grace F. Napolitano (D)	18.5	21	AZ 7th: Ruben Gallego (D)	64.0	21	CA 19th: Zoe Lofgren (D)	36.2
22	NY 10th: Jerrold Nadler (D)	18.4	22	TX 33rd: Marc A. Veasey (D)	63.2	22	CA 32nd: Grace F. Napolitano (D)	35.7
23	TX 22nd: Pete Olson (R)	17.8	23	CA 38th: Linda T. Sánchez (D)	63.1	22	NJ 9th: Bill Pascrell, Jr. (D)	35.7
24	VA 11th Gerald E. Connolly (D)	17.6	24	CA 32nd: Grace F. Napolitano (D)	62.0	24	CA 44th: Janice Hahn (D)	35.5
25	CA 6th: Doris O. Matsui (D)	17.3	25	AZ 3rd: Raul M. Grijalva (D)	61.6	24	NY 15th: José E. Serrano (D)	35.5
26	NY 14th: Joseph Crowley (D)	17.0	26	TX 35th: Lloyd Doggett (D)	60.9	26	TX 9th: Al Green (D)	34.8
27	NJ 12th: Bonnie Watson Coleman (D)	16.6	27	CA 16th: Jim Costa (D)	59.1	27	IL 4th: Luis V. Gutierrez (D)	34.1
28	CA 7th: Ami Bera (D)	15.6	28	CA 41st: Mark Takano (D)	58.9	28	CA 51st: Juan Vargas (D)	34.0
29	CA 38th: Linda T. Sánchez (D)	15.5	29	NJ 8th: Albio Sires (D)	54.9	29	CA 15th: Eric Swalwell (D)	33.7
30	NY 3rd: Steve Israel (D)	15.0	30	NY 13th: Charles B. Rangel (D)	54.5	29	NY 8th: Hakeem S. Jeffries (D)	33.7
31	CA 9th: Jerry McNerney (D)	14.9	31	NM 2nd: Steve Pearce (R)	53.4	31	CA 30th: Brad Sherman (D)	33.6
32	CA 53rd: Susan A. Davis (D)	14.7	32	CA 20th: Sam Farr (D)	52.4	32	TX 29th: Gene Green (D)	33.4
33	CA 33rd: Ted Lieu (D)	14.2	33	TX 27th: Blake Farenthold (R)	51.5	33	CA 12th: Nancy Pelosi (D)	33.3
34	CA 28th: Adam B. Schiff (D)	13.9	34	CA 31st: Pete Aguilar (D)	51.1	34	CA 37th: Karen Bass (D)	32.8
35	NV 3rd: Joseph J. Heck (R)	13.8	35	CA 36th: Raul Ruiz (D)	49.1	35	FL 20th: Alcee L. Hastings (D)	32.6
35	NY 5th: Gregory W. Meeks (D)	13.8	36	NM 1st: Michelle Lujan Grisham (D)	48.8	36	NY 10th: Jerrold Nadler (D)	32.1
35	TX 3rd: Sam Johnson (R)	13.8	37	NY 14th: Joseph Crowley (D)	47.9	37	CA 39th: Edward R. Royce (R)	32.0
38	CA 11th: Mark Desaulnier (D)	13.7	38	FL 9th: Alan Grayson (D)	47.4	38	TX 33rd: Marc A. Veasey (D)	31.9
38	VA 10th Barbara Comstock (R)	13.7	39	CA 22nd: Devin Nunes (R)	46.7	39	MA 7th: Michael E. Capuano (D)	30.9
40	IL 8th: Tammy Duckworth (D)	13.4	40	CA 43rd: Maxine Waters (D)	45.8	39	VA 11th Gerald E. Connolly (D)	30.9
41	IL 9th: Janice D. Schakowsky (D)	13.3	41	CA 26th: Julia Brownley (D)	44.7	41	CA 47th: Alan S. Lowenthal (D)	30.7
41	NY 12th: Carolyn B. Maloney (D)	13.3	42	NV 1st: Dina Titus (D)	44.0	42	CA 38th: Linda T. Sánchez (D)	30.6
43	CA 46th: Loretta Sanchez (D)	13.2	43	CA 10th: Jeff Denham (R)	42.3	43	NV 1st: Dina Titus (D)	30.3
44	NY 11th: Daniel M. Donovan Jr. (R)	13.1	44	CA 19th: Zoe Lofgren (D)	41.6	44	CA 43rd: Maxine Waters (D)	29.9
45	GA 7th: Robert Woodall (R)	13.0	45	TX 18th: Sheila Jackson-Lee (D)	41.2	45	CA 35th Norma J. Torres (D)	29.8
46	TX 24th: Kenny Marchant (R)	12.7	46	NM 3rd: Ben Ray Luján (D)	40.7	46	NY 16th: Eliot L. Engel (D)	29.6
47	NJ 9th: Bill Pascrell, Jr. (D)	12.5	46	NY 7th: Nydia M. Velázquez (D)	40.7	47	NY 11th: Daniel M. Donovan Jr. (R)	29.5
47	TX 9th: Al Green (D)	12.5	48	FL 23rd: Debbie Wasserman Schultz (D)	40.0	47	WA 9th: Adam Smith (D)	29.5
49	CA 30th: Brad Sherman (D)	12.2	49	CA 8th: Paul Cook (R)	39.4	49	IL 8th: Tammy Duckworth (D)	29.1
49	VA 8th Donald S. Beyer, Jr. (D)	12.2	50	CA 37th: Karen Bass (D)	39.3	50	CA 18th: Anna G. Eshoo (D)	28.9
51	MN 4th: Betty McCollum (D)	12.1	51	TX 30th: Eddie Bernice Johnson (D)	39.0	50	TX 7th: John Abney Culberson (R)	28.9
52	CA 3rd: John Garamendi (D)	11.8	52	WA 4th: Dan Newsome (R)	38.1	52	VA 8th Donald S. Beyer, Jr. (D)	28.8
53	CA 43rd: Maxine Waters (D)	11.7	53	CA 23rd: Kevin McCarthy (R)	38.0	53	CA 45th: Mimi Walters (R)	28.5
54	CA 5th: Mike Thompson (D)	11.5	54	TX 9th: Al Green (D)	37.7	54	CA 21st: David G. Valadao (R)	28.1
54	MA 5th: Katherine Clark (D)	11.5	55	CA 25th: Stephen Knight (R)	37.5	54	NJ 6th: Frank Pallone Jr. (D)	28.1
56	MD 6th: John K. Delaney (D)	10.9	55	CA 42nd: Ken Calvert (R)	37.5	56	NJ 12th: Bonnie Watson Coleman (D)	28.0
56	NJ 5th: Scott Garrett (R)	10.9	55	TX 11th K. Michael Conaway (R)	37.5	57	AZ 7th: Ruben Gallego (D)	27.4
56	WA 7th: Jim McDermott (D)	10.9	58	CA 9th: Jerry McNerney (D)	37.1	57	NY 10th: Donald M. Payne, Jr. (D)	27.4
59	TX 7th: John Abney Culberson (R)	10.8	59	NJ 9th: Bill Pascrell, Jr. (D)	36.1	59	CA 13th: Barbara Lee (D)	27.3
60	CA 37th: Karen Bass (D)	10.6	60	CA 24th: Lois Capps (D)	35.6	60	FL 21st: Theodore E. Deutch (D)	26.8
61	GA 6th: Tom Price (R)	10.5	60	TX 19th: Randy Neugebauer (R)	35.6	61	NY 12th: Carolyn B. Maloney (D)	26.7
62	IL 10th: Robert J. Dold (R)	10.2	62	CA 47th: Alan S. Lowenthal (D)	34.3	62	CA 20th: Sam Farr (D)	26.2
63	NJ 11th: Rodney P. Frelinghuysen (R)	10.0	63	CA 39th: Edward R. Royce (R)	34.2	63	IL 9th: Janice D. Schakowsky (D)	25.9
64	MA 7th: Michael E. Capuano (D)	9.9	64	CA 53rd: Susan A. Davis (D)	33.4	64	CA 11th: Mark Desaulnier (D)	25.7
65	NJ 7th: Leonard Lance (R)	9.8	65	FL 24th: Frederica S. Wilson (D)	32.1	65	FL 22nd: Lois Frankel (D)	24.8
66	IL 6th: Peter J. Roskam (R)	9.6	66	TX 7th: John Abney Culberson (R)	31.4	65	IL 10th: Robert J. Dold (R)	24.8
66	NJ 8th: Albio Sires (D)	9.6	67	CA 50th: Duncan Hunter (R)	31.2	67	CA 16th: Jim Costa (D)	24.6
66	WA 1st Suzan K. DelBene (D)	9.6	68	IL 3rd: Daniel Lipinski (D)	31.1	67	CA 41st: Mark Takano (D)	24.6
69	MD 8th: Chris Van Hollen (D)	9.5	69	TX 2nd: Ted Poe (R)	30.7	67	CA 48th: Dana Rohrabacher (R)	24.6
69	PA 13th: Brendan F. Boyle (D)	9.5	70	TX 21st: Lamar Smith (R)	30.1	67	TX 16th: Beto O'Rourke (D)	24.6
71	WA 2nd Rick Larsen (D)	9.4	71	NV 4th: Cresent Hardy (R)	29.2	71	GA 7th: Robert Woodall (R)	24.5
72	MI 11th: David A. Trott (R)	9.2	72	CA 3rd: John Garamendi (D)	29.0	72	MD 8th: Chris Van Hollen (D)	24.2
73	CA 16th: Jim Costa (D)	9.1	72	CA 6th: Doris O. Matsui (D)	29.0	73	NY 17th: Nita M. Lowey (D)	23.6
74	NV 1st: Dina Titus (D)	8.9	72	FL 14th: Kathy Castor (D)	29.0	74	NY 3rd: Steve Israel (D)	23.4
75	CA 25th: Stephen Knight (R)	8.8	75	IL 8th: Tammy Duckworth (D)	28.6	75	TX 22nd: Pete Olson (R)	23.3

Congressional Districts of the 114th Congress of the United States
Selected Rankings

Under 18 years old rank	Percent under 18 years old, 2014 — State congressional district Representative	Percent under 18 years old [col 15 and 16]	65 years old and over rank	Percent 65 years old and over, 2014 — State congressional district Representative	Percent 65 years old and over [col 22 and 23]	College graduates rank	Percent college graduates (bachelor's degree or more), 2014 — State congressional district Representative	Percent college graduates [col 27]
1	UT 4th: Mia B. Love (R)	32.3	1	FL 11th: Richard B. Nugent (R)	32.9	1	NY 12th: Carolyn B. Maloney (D)	71.8
2	TX 15th: Rubén Hinojosa (D)	32.0	2	FL 16th: Vern Buchanan (R)	30.0	2	CA 33rd:Ted Lieu (D)	64.0
3	AZ 7th: Ruben Gallego (D)	31.8	3	FL 19th: Curt Clawson (R)	29.3	3	VA 8th Donald S. Beyer, Jr. (D)	61.3
4	TX 33rd: Marc A. Veasey (D)	31.3	4	FL 17th: Thomas J. Rooney (R)	26.6	4	NY 10th: Jerrold Nadler (D)	60.1
4	UT 1st: Rob Bishop (R)	31.3	5	AZ 4th: Paul A. Gosar (R)	26.0	5	CA 18th: Anna G. Eshoo (D)	59.7
6	CA 21st: David G. Valadao (R)	31.0	6	FL 18th: Patrick Murphy (D)	24.2	6	GA 6th: Tom Price (R)	58.0
7	TX 28th: Henry Cuellar (D)	30.9	7	FL 8th: Bill Posey (R)	24.0	7	CA 52nd: Scott H. Peters (D)	57.9
8	TX 29th: Gene Green (D)	30.6	8	FL 6th: Ron DeSantis (R)	23.7	8	WA 7th: Jim McDermott (D)	57.3
8	UT 3rd: Jason Chaffetz (R)	30.6	9	FL 13th: David W. Jolly (R)	23.6	9	CA 12th:Nancy Pelosi (D)	55.6
10	CA 16th:Jim Costa (D)	30.3	10	FL 21st: Theodore E. Deutch (D)	23.3	10	VA10th Barbara Comstock (R)	55.2
11	CA 40th: Lucille Roybal-Allard (D)	29.7	11	FL 12th: Gus M. Bilirakis (R)	21.5	11	DC At Large: Eleanor Holmes Norton (D)	55.0
12	TX 34th: Filemon Vela (D)	29.6	12	FL 22nd: Lois Frankel (D)	21.4	12	CA 17th: Michael M. Honda (D)	54.3
13	TX 23rd: Will Hurd (R)	29.0	13	MI 1st: Dan Benishek (R)	21.1	13	MD 8th: Chris Van Hollen (D)	54.1
14	WA 4th: Dan Newsome (R)	28.9	13	NC 11th: Mark Meadows (R)	21.1	13	MA 5th: Katherine Clark (D)	54.1
15	CA 22nd: Devin Nunes (R)	28.8	15	AZ 8th: Trent Franks (R)	20.4	15	VA11th Gerald E. Connolly (D)	53.3
16	UT 2nd: Chris Stewart (R)	28.7	16	MA 9th: William R. Keating (D)	20.2	16	IL 5th: Michael Quigley (D)	52.9
17	TX 22nd: Pete Olson (R)	28.4	17	PA 12th: Keith J. Rothfus (R)	20.0	17	IL 9th: Janice D. Schakowsky (D)	52.8
18	CA 23rd: Kevin McCarthy (R)	28.3	18	AZ 2nd: Martha McSally (R)	19.6	18	CO: 2nd: Jared Polis (D)	52.7
18	TX 30th: Eddie Bernice Johnson (D)	28.3	18	CA 1st: Doug LaMalfa (R)	19.6	19	NJ 11th: Rodney P. Frelinghuysen (R)	52.3
20	CA 44th: Janice Hahn (D)	28.2	20	CA 36th: Raul Ruiz (D)	19.5	20	TX 3rd: Sam Johnson (R)	52.2
21	NY 15th: José E. Serrano (D)	28.1	21	OR 4th: Peter A. DeFazio (D)	19.2	21	NJ 7th: Leonard Lance (R)	52.1
22	AZ 5th: Matt Salmon (R)	27.9	22	CA 4th:Tom McClintock (R)	19.1	22	CA 45th: Mimi Walters (R)	51.6
22	GA 13th: David Scott (D)	27.9	22	OR 2nd: Greg Walden (R)	19.1	23	NY 3rd: Steve Israel (D)	50.9
24	CA 41st: Mark Takano (D)	27.8	22	PA 9th: Bill Shuster (R)	19.1	24	IL 6th: Peter J. Roskam (R)	50.8
25	CA 8th: Paul Cook (R)	27.6	25	FL 10th: Daniel Webster (R)	19.0	25	NC 9th: Robert Pittenger (R)	49.3
25	CA 31st:Pete Aguilar (D)	27.6	25	PA 18th: Tim Murphy (R)	19.0	26	CT 4th: James A. Himes (D)	49.1
25	TX 16th: Beto O'Rourke (D)	27.6	27	TN 1st: David P. Roe (R)	18.9	27	MA 4th:Joseph P. Kennedy III (D)	48.7
28	AZ 3rd: Raul M. Grijalva (D)	27.5	28	ME 2nd: Bruce Poliquin (R)	18.6	28	MO 2nd: Ann Wagner (R)	48.0
28	CA 10th: Jeff Denham (R)	27.5	28	MN 7th: Richard M. Nolan (D)	18.6	29	MN 3rd: Erik Paulsen (R)	47.8
28	ID 2nd: Michael K. Simpson (R)	27.5	28	VA 9th Morgan Griffith (R)	18.6	30	TX 7th: John Abney Culberson (R)	47.2
31	CA 25th: Stephen Knight (R)	27.4	31	MN 6th: Collin C. Peterson (D)	18.5	31	MD 3rd: John P. Sarbanes (D)	46.8
31	TX 26th: Michael C. Burgess (R)	27.4	31	NY 3rd: Steve Israel (D)	18.5	32	NY 17th: Nita M. Lowey (D)	46.2
33	CA 9th:Jerry McNerney (D)	27.3	31	PA 10th: Tom Marino (R)	18.5	33	CA 13th:Barbara Lee (D)	45.7
33	TX 18th: Sheila Jackson-Lee (D)	27.3	31	VA 5th Robert Hurt (R)	18.5	33	MI 11th: David A.Trott (R)	45.7
33	VA10th Barbara Comstock (R)	27.3	31	WV 3rd: Evan H. Jenkins (R)	18.5	35	CA 14th:Jackie Speier (D)	45.3
36	GA 7th: Robert Woodall (R)	27.1	31	WI 7th: Sean P. Duffy (R)	18.5	36	KS 3rd: Kevin Yoder (R)	45.1
37	CA 35th Norma J. Torres (D)	27.0	37	NJ 3rd: Thomas MacArthur (R)	18.4	37	NJ 5th: Scott Garrett (R)	44.7
37	TX 6th: Joe Barton (R)	27.0	37	SC 7th: Tom Rice (R)	18.4	37	TX 21st: Lamar Smith (R)	44.7
39	TX 3rd: Sam Johnson (R)	26.9	39	NE 3rd: Adrian Smith (R)	18.3	39	TX 22nd: Pete Olson (R)	44.5
40	IL 11th: Bill Foster (D)	26.8	40	PA 17th: Matt Cartwright (D)	18.2	40	CO 1st: Diana DeGette (D)	44.3
40	TX 31st: John R. Carter (R)	26.8	41	OH 14th: David P. Joyce (R)	18.1	41	MA 8th: Stephen F. Lynch (D)	44.2
42	CA 42nd: Ken Calvert (R)	26.7	41	WA 6th: Derek Kilmer (D)	18.1	42	CA 49th: Darrell E. Issa (R)	44.0
42	IL 4th:Luis V. Gutierrez (D)	26.7	43	NY 19th: Christopher P. Gibson (R)	18.0	42	IL 10th: Robert J. Dold (R)	44.0
44	TX 20th: Joaquin Castro (D)	26.5	43	OH 6th: Bill Johnson (R)	18.0	44	CA 48th: Dana Rohrabacher (R)	43.9
45	CA 46th: Loretta Sanchez (D)	26.4	45	CA 2nd:Jared Huffman (D)	17.9	44	IN 5th: Susan W. Brooks (R)	43.9
45	CO 6th: Mike Coffman (R)	26.4	45	ME 1st: Chellie Pingree (D)	17.9	46	CA 28th: Adam B. Schiff (D)	43.7
45	TX 5th: Jeb Hensarling (R)	26.4	45	OH 16th: James B. Renacci (R)	17.9	47	TX 24th: Kenny Marchant (R)	43.6
45	TX 9th: Al Green (D)	26.4	45	PA 11th: Lou Barletta (R)	17.9	48	MN 5th: Keith Ellison (D)	43.5
45	TX 10th: Michael T. McCaul (R)	26.4	49	MO 8th: Jason T. Smith (R)	17.8	48	NJ 12th: Bonnie Watson Coleman (D)	43.5
50	NE 2nd: Brad Ashford (D)	26.3	49	PA 3rd: Mike Kelly (R)	17.8	50	MA 7th: Michael E. Capuano (D)	43.0
50	TX 35th: Lloyd Doggett (D)	26.3	51	AR 2nd: Bruce Westerman (R)	17.7	51	MA 6th: Seth Moulton (D)	42.9
52	CA 51st: Juan Vargas (D)	26.2	51	NJ 4th: Christopher H. Smith (R)	17.7	52	TX 32nd: Pete Sessions (R)	42.7
53	WA 8th: David G. Reichert (R)	26.1	51	OH 13th: Tim Ryan (D)	17.7	53	MN 4th: Betty McCollum (D)	42.6
54	CO 4th: Ken Buck (R)	26.0	51	OK 2nd: Markwayne Mullin (R)	17.7	54	CA 30th: Brad Sherman (D)	42.5
54	KS 3rd: Kevin Yoder (R)	26.0	55	WV 1st: David McKinley (R)	17.6	54	PA 6th: Ryan A. Costello (R)	42.5
54	MN 5th: Tom Emmer (R)	26.0	56	IA 4th: Steve King (R)	17.5	56	AZ 6th: David Schweikert (R)	42.4
57	IL 14th: Randy Hultgren (R)	25.9	56	MO 2nd: Ann Wagner (R)	17.5	57	CO 6th: Mike Coffman (R)	42.0
57	TX 7th: John Abney Culberson (R)	25.9	58	AR 1st: Eric A. "Rick" Crawford (R)	17.4	57	PA 7th: Patrick Meehan (R)	42.0
59	GA 4th: Henry C. "Hank" Johnson Jr. (D)	25.8	58	MI 4th: John L. Moolenar (R)	17.4	59	MD 6th: John K. Delaney (D)	41.6
59	IN 3rd: Marlin Stutzman (R)	25.8	58	WV 2nd: Alexander X. Mooney (R)	17.4	60	CA 11th:Mark Desaulnier (D)	41.5
59	KS 4th: Mike Pompeo (R)	25.8	61	IL 15th: John Shimkus (R)	17.3	61	WA 1st Suzan K. DelBene (D)	41.3
62	IN 7th: André Carson (D)	25.7	61	PA 5th: Glenn Thompson (R)	17.3	62	NC 4th: David E. Price (D)	41.0
62	NC 9th: Robert Pittenger (R)	25.7	61	SC 3rd: Jeff Duncan (R)	17.3	63	TX 26th: Michael C. Burgess (R)	40.9
64	NC 2nd: Renee Ellmers (R)	25.6	61	TN 6th: Diane Black (R)	17.3	63	WI 2nd: Mark Pocan (D)	40.9
65	MN 2nd: John Kline (R)	25.5	65	GA 9th: Doug Collins (R)	17.2	65	CA 27th: Judy Chu (D)	40.8
65	OK 5th: Steve Russell (R)	25.5	65	IL 17th: Cheri Bustos (D)	17.2	66	CA 15th: Eric Swalwell (D)	40.4
65	TX 36th: Brian Babin (R)	25.5	65	MD 1st: Andrew Harris (R)	17.2	66	NC 13th: George Holding (R)	40.4
68	GA 14th: Tom Graves (R)	25.4	65	NC 7th: David Rouzer (R)	17.2	66	OH 12th: Patrick J. Tiberi (R)	40.4
68	ID 1st: Raul Labrador (R)	25.4	65	OH 7th: Bob Gibbs (R)	17.2	69	WA 9th: Adam Smith (D)	40.2
68	NC 13th: George Holding (R)	25.4	65	VA 6th Bob Goodlatte (R)	17.2	70	GA 5th: John Lewis (D)	40.1
68	OK 1st: Jim Bridenstine (R)	25.4	71	AL 4th: Robert B. Aderholt (R)	17.1	70	NY 4th: Kathleen M. Rice (D)	40.1
68	WI 4th: Gwen Moore (D)	25.4	71	HI 1st: Mark Takai (D)	17.1	72	VA 7th Dave Brat (R)	39.9
73	AK: At-Large Don Young (R)	25.3	71	NJ 11th: Rodney P. Frelinghuysen (R)	17.1	73	CA 2nd:Jared Huffman (D)	39.7
73	CA 6th: Doris O. Matsui (D)	25.3	71	NC 10th: Patrick T. McHenry (R)	17.1	73	CA 39th: Edward R. Royce (R)	39.7
73	MS 2nd: Bennie G. Thompson (D)	25.3	75	FL 3rd: Ted S. Yoho (R)	17.0	75	TX 2nd: Ted Poe (R)	39.5

Congressional Districts of the 114th Congress of the United States
Selected Rankings

Median value of owner-occupied housing units, 2014

Median value rank	State congressional district Representative	Median value (dollars) [col 43]
1	CA 33rd:Ted Lieu (D)	1 000 000
2	CA 18th: Anna G. Eshoo (D)	990 900
3	NY 10th: Jerrold Nadler (D)	869 700
4	NY 12th: Carolyn B. Maloney (D)	867 600
5	CA 12th:Nancy Pelosi (D)	860 300
6	CA 14th:Jackie Speier (D)	773 000
7	CA 17th: Michael M. Honda (D)	708 400
8	CA 28th: Adam B. Schiff (D)	681 000
9	CA 48th: Dana Rohrabacher (R)	663 200
10	CA 45th: Mimi Walters (R)	648 700
11	CA 19th: Zoe Lofgren (D)	619 500
12	CA 27th: Judy Chu (D)	611 300
13	CA 49th: Darrell E. Issa (R)	609 500
14	CA 52nd: Scott H. Peters (D)	608 800
15	CA 15th: Eric Swalwell (D)	606 700
16	CA 37th: Karen Bass (D)	604 700
17	NY 7th: Nydia M. Velázquez (D)	597 800
18	HI 1st: Mark Takai (D)	585 100
19	CA 39th: Edward R. Royce (R)	571 200
20	CA 30th: Brad Sherman (D)	569 200
21	CA 13th:Barbara Lee (D)	562 800
22	NY 3rd: Steve Israel (D)	552 900
23	NY 9th: Yvette D. Clarke (D)	545 500
24	CA 11th:Mark Desaulnier (D)	530 300
25	CA 2nd:Jared Huffman (D)	512 600
26	VA 8th Donald S. Beyer, Jr. (D)	499 800
27	NY 6th: Grace Meng (D)	493 900
28	CT 4th: James A. Himes (D)	490 500
29	CA 26th: Julia Brownley (D)	487 700
30	DC At Large: Eleanor Holmes Norton (D)	486 900
31	CA 47th: Alan S. Lowenthal (D)	481 500
32	NY 8th: Hakeem S. Jeffries (D)	476 500
33	CA 24th: Lois Capps (D)	466 600
34	NY 11th: Daniel M. Donovan Jr. (R)	465 600
35	CA 20th: Sam Farr (D)	464 200
36	HI 2nd: Tulsi Gabbard (D)	464 000
37	VA10th Barbara Comstock (R)	461 300
38	WA 7th: Jim McDermott (D)	455 000
39	CA 34th: Xavier Becerra (D)	454 100
40	MA 5th: Katherine Clark (D)	452 200
41	NY 17th: Nita M. Lowey (D)	449 500
42	VA11th Gerald E. Connolly (D)	444 200
43	NY 14th: Joseph Crowley (D)	438 700
44	NY 16th: Eliot L. Engel (D)	436 000
45	CA 53rd: Susan A. Davis (D)	432 400
46	NY 4th: Kathleen M. Rice (D)	424 800
47	CA 46th: Loretta Sanchez (D)	423 800
48	MD 8th: Chris Van Hollen (D)	423 000
49	NJ 11th: Rodney P. Frelinghuysen (R)	420 100
50	NY 13th: Charles B. Rangel (D)	418 100
51	CA 43rd: Maxine Waters (D)	415 800
52	NJ 7th: Leonard Lance (R)	415 100
53	CA 38th: Linda T. Sánchez (D)	413 200
54	CA 5th: Mike Thompson (D)	404 800
55	CA 50th: Duncan Hunter (R)	399 200
56	NY 5th: Gregory W. Meeks (D)	397 400
57	NJ 5th: Scott Garrett (R)	395 000
58	CA 32nd: Grace F. Napolitano (D)	390 100
59	MA 4th:Joseph P. Kennedy III (D)	388 000
60	MA 7th: Michael E. Capuano (D)	385 100
61	MA 6th: Seth Moulton (D)	384 100
62	CA 29th: Tony Cárdenas (D)	379 500
63	MA 8th: Stephen F. Lynch (D)	371 500
64	WA 1st Suzan K. DelBene (D)	366 800
65	NY 1st: Lee M. Zeldin (R)	363 400
66	CA 25th: Stephen Knight (R)	360 400
67	NY 2nd: Peter T. King (R)	356 400
68	NJ 9th: Bill Pascrell, Jr. (D)	351 600
69	CA 4th:Tom McClintock (R)	350 700
70	CA 42nd: Ken Calvert (R)	350 600
71	NY 15th: José E. Serrano (D)	346 800
72	CA 40th: Lucille Roybal-Allard (D)	344 500
73	WA 9th: Adam Smith (D)	342 900
74	NJ 4th: Christopher H. Smith (R)	340 200
75	CO: 2nd: Jared Polis (D)	336 100

Percent female-headed family households, 2014

Female house-holder rank	State congressional district Representative	Percent with female house-holder [col 32]
1	NY 15th: José E. Serrano (D)	37.8
2	NY 13th: Charles B. Rangel (D)	27.5
3	CA 40th: Lucille Roybal-Allard (D)	26.1
4	TN 9th: Steve Cohen (D)	25.3
5	MS 2nd: Bennie G. Thompson (D)	24.7
6	AL 7th: Terri A. Sewell (D)	24.5
7	NY 8th: Hakeem S. Jeffries (D)	24.4
8	CA 44th: Janice Hahn (D)	23.9
9	FL 24th: Frederica S. Wilson (D)	23.6
9	MI 13th: John Conyers Jr. (D)	23.6
11	NY 5th: Gregory W. Meeks (D)	23.4
12	FL 5th: Corrine Brown (D)	23.1
13	NJ 10th: Donald M. Payne, Jr. (D)	23.0
14	FL 20th: Alcee L. Hastings (D)	22.8
14	NY 9th: Yvette D. Clarke (D)	22.8
16	TX 30th: Eddie Bernice Johnson (D)	22.3
17	TX 33rd: Marc A. Veasey (D)	22.2
18	GA 2nd: Sanford D. Bishop Jr. (D)	22.0
18	IL 2nd: Robin L. Kelly (D)	22.0
20	GA 13th: David Scott (D)	21.9
20	TX 34th: Filemon Vela (D)	21.9
22	CA 43rd: Maxine Waters (D)	21.7
23	PA 2nd: Chaka Fattah (D)	21.6
23	VA 3rd Robert C. "Bobby" Scott (D)	21.6
25	OH 11th: Marcia L. Fudge (D)	21.5
26	CA 16th:Jim Costa (D)	21.4
26	GA 4th: Henry C. "Hank" Johnson Jr. (D)	21.4
28	AZ 7th: Ruben Gallego (D)	21.3
29	IL 1st: Bobby L. Rush (D)	21.2
30	NC 12th: Alma S. Adams (D)	20.9
31	CA 51st: Juan Vargas (D)	20.7
31	LA 2nd: Cedric Richmond (D)	20.7
33	NC 1st: G. K. Butterfield (D)	20.6
33	SC 6th: James E. Clyburn (D)	20.6
35	WI 4th: Gwen Moore (D)	20.5
36	TX 18th: Sheila Jackson-Lee (D)	20.4
37	MD 7th: Elijah E. Cummings (D)	20.2
38	CA 21st: David G. Valadao (R)	20.1
39	MI 14th: Brenda L. Lawrence (D)	20.0
40	CA 35th Norma J. Torres (D)	19.9
41	TX 29th: Gene Green (D)	19.8
42	TX 9th: Al Green (D)	19.7
42	TX 28th: Henry Cuellar (D)	19.7
44	TX 15th: Rubén Hinojosa (D)	19.5
45	IL 7th: Danny K. Davis (D)	19.4
45	PA 1st: Robert A. Brady (D)	19.4
47	OH 3rd: Joyce Beatty (D)	19.3
48	MD 4th: Donna F. Edwards (D)	19.2
49	TX 20th: Joaquin Castro (D)	19.1
50	MO 1st: William Lacy Clay (D)	18.9
50	TX 16th: Beto O'Rourke (D)	18.9
52	NJ 8th: Albio Sires (D)	18.7
53	NY 16th: Eliot L. Engel (D)	18.5
54	IN 7th: André Carson (D)	18.3
55	CA 34th: Xavier Becerra (D)	18.1
55	CA 46th: Loretta Sanchez (D)	18.1
57	MA 7th: Michael E. Capuano (D)	17.7
57	NY 7th: Nydia M. Velázquez (D)	17.7
57	TX 35th: Lloyd Doggett (D)	17.7
60	GA 5th: John Lewis (D)	17.6
61	LA 5th: Ralph Lee Abraham (R)	17.5
62	CA 41st: Mark Takano (D)	17.3
62	FL 14th: Kathy Castor (D)	17.3
62	GA 12th: Rick W. Allen (R)	17.3
62	IL 4th:Luis V. Gutierrez (D)	17.3
66	AZ 3rd: Raul M. Grijalva (D)	17.2
66	CA 29th: Tony Cárdenas (D)	17.2
66	FL 27th: Ileana Ros-Lehtinen (R)	17.2
69	AL 3rd: Mike Rogers (R)	17.1
70	CA 38th: Linda T. Sánchez (D)	16.8
70	MD 2nd: C. A. Dutch Ruppersberger (D)	16.8
72	FL 26th: Carlos Curbelo (R)	16.7
72	GA 8th: Austin Scott (R)	16.7
72	MS 4th: Steven Palazzo (R)	16.7
75	FL 25th: Mario Diaz-Balart (R)	16.6

Percent of households with one person, 2014

One-person house-hold rank	State congressional district Representative	Percent one-person house-holds [col 33]
1	NY 12th: Carolyn B. Maloney (D)	47.8
2	DC At Large: Eleanor Holmes Norton (D)	44.6
3	GA 5th: John Lewis (D)	43.6
4	PA 2nd: Chaka Fattah (D)	41.1
5	NY 10th: Jerrold Nadler (D)	41.0
6	OH 11th: Marcia L. Fudge (D)	40.2
6	PA 14th: Michael F. Doyle (D)	40.2
8	CA 12th:Nancy Pelosi (D)	40.1
9	IL 7th: Danny K. Davis (D)	39.7
10	MO 1st: William Lacy Clay (D)	39.3
11	FL 13th: David W. Jolly (R)	38.7
12	MN 5th: Keith Ellison (D)	38.3
13	FL 22nd: Lois Frankel (D)	38.1
14	WA 7th: Jim McDermott (D)	38.0
15	PA 1st: Robert A. Brady (D)	37.5
16	CO 1st: Diana DeGette (D)	37.0
17	NY 26th: Brian Higgins (D)	36.8
18	MO 5th: Emanuel Cleaver (D)	36.7
19	LA 2nd: Cedric Richmond (D)	36.5
20	OH 9th: Marcy Kaptur (D)	36.0
21	MI 13th: John Conyers Jr. (D)	35.9
21	MI 14th: Brenda L. Lawrence (D)	35.9
23	IL 5th: Michael Quigley (D)	35.1
24	AZ 9th: Kyrsten Sinema (D)	34.9
24	CA 28th: Adam B. Schiff (D)	34.9
24	VA 3rd Robert C. "Bobby" Scott (D)	34.9
27	IL 9th: Janice D. Schakowsky (D)	34.8
27	VA 8th Donald S. Beyer, Jr. (D)	34.8
29	WI 4th: Gwen Moore (D)	34.7
30	CT 3rd: Rosa L. DeLauro (D)	34.5
31	KY 3rd: John A. Yarmuth (D)	34.4
32	CA 33rd:Ted Lieu (D)	34.1
32	MA 7th: Michael E. Capuano (D)	34.1
34	NY 13th: Charles B. Rangel (D)	34.0
34	NY 25th: Louise McIntosh Slaughter (D)	34.0
36	OH 10th: Michael R. Turner (R)	33.9
37	CA 37th: Karen Bass (D)	33.8
38	SC 6th: James E. Clyburn (D)	33.7
39	NV 1st: Dina Titus (D)	33.6
39	OH 3rd: Joyce Beatty (D)	33.6
41	FL 14th: Kathy Castor (D)	33.5
41	IN 7th: André Carson (D)	33.5
41	OH 13th: Tim Ryan (D)	33.5
41	TN 5th: Jim Cooper (D)	33.5
41	TN 9th: Steve Cohen (D)	33.5
46	NY 20th: Paul Tonko (D)	33.3
47	NC 12th: Alma S. Adams (D)	33.2
48	AZ 2nd: Martha McSally (R)	33.1
48	MI 9th: Sander M. Levin (D)	33.1
48	NC 4th: David E. Price (D)	33.1
51	IL 13th: Rodney Davis (R)	33.0
51	NC 1st: G. K. Butterfield (D)	33.0
53	AL 7th: Terri A. Sewell (D)	32.9
53	NJ 10th: Donald M. Payne, Jr. (D)	32.9
55	IL 1st: Bobby L. Rush (D)	32.7
55	TX 21st: Lamar Smith (R)	32.7
57	FL 23rd: Debbie Wasserman Schultz (D)	32.3
58	IL 17th: Cheri Bustos (D)	32.0
59	MA 8th: Stephen F. Lynch (D)	31.9
59	NY 8th: Hakeem S. Jeffries (D)	31.9
61	IL 12th: Mike Bost (R)	31.7
61	MN 1st: Dan Benishek (R)	31.7
63	NM 1st: Michelle Lujan Grisham (D)	31.6
64	CA 2nd:Jared Huffman (D)	31.5
64	FL 5th: Corrine Brown (D)	31.5
64	OH 1st: Steve Chabot (R)	31.5
67	IL 2nd: Robin L. Kelly (D)	31.4
68	MN 4th: Betty McCollum (D)	31.3
69	CA 13th:Barbara Lee (D)	31.2
69	MT At-Large Ryan K. Zinke (R)	31.2
69	OK 5th: Steve Russell (R)	31.2
69	VA 9th Morgan Griffith (R)	31.2
73	NY 9th: Yvette D. Clarke (D)	31.1
74	FL 18th: Patrick Murphy (D)	31.0
74	LA 4th: John Fleming (R)	31.0

Congressional Districts of the 114th Congress of the United States

Selected Rankings

Median household income, 2014				Percent of persons below 65 years with no health insurance, 2014				Percent of persons below the poverty level, 2014			
Median income rank	State congressional district Representative	Median income (dollars) [col 47]		No health insurance rank	State congressional district Representative	Percent with no health insurance [col 59]		Poverty rate rank	State congressional district Representative	Poverty rate [col 49]	
1	VA10th Barbara Comstock (R)	115 291		1	TX 33rd: Marc A. Veasey (D)	35.5		1	NY 15th: José E. Serrano (D)	41.0	
2	CA 18th: Anna G. Eshoo (D)	105 872		2	TX 29th: Gene Green (D)	34.6		2	AZ 7th: Ruben Gallego (D)	35.3	
3	NJ 7th: Leonard Lance (R)	105 386		3	TX 34th: Filemon Vela (D)	33.1		3	CA 21st: David G. Valadao (R)	33.8	
4	CA 17th: Michael M. Honda (D)	103 316		4	TX 15th: Rubén Hinojosa (D)	31.0		4	MI 13th: John Conyers Jr. (D)	32.3	
5	CA 33rd:Ted Lieu (D)	101 573		5	FL 24th: Frederica S. Wilson (D)	29.2		5	TX 34th: Filemon Vela (D)	31.1	
6	NY 3rd: Steve Israel (D)	100 835		6	TX 9th: Al Green (D)	28.4		6	CA 16th:Jim Costa (D)	30.6	
7	VA11th Gerald E. Connolly (D)	100 361		7	TX 28th: Henry Cuellar (D)	28.3		7	NY 13th: Charles B. Rangel (D)	29.8	
8	VA 8th Donald S. Beyer, Jr. (D)	99 094		8	CA 34th: Xavier Becerra (D)	27.6		8	CA 34th: Xavier Becerra (D)	29.5	
9	NJ 11th: Rodney P. Frelinghuysen (R)	98 964		9	FL 20th: Alcee L. Hastings (D)	26.4		9	TN 9th: Steve Cohen (D)	29.3	
10	CA 14th:Jackie Speier (D)	95 972		10	FL 25th: Mario Diaz-Balart (R)	26.3		10	KY 5th: Harold Rogers (R)	29.2	
11	NY 12th: Carolyn B. Maloney (D)	94 127		11	NV 1st: Dina Titus (D)	26.0		10	TX 15th: Rubén Hinojosa (D)	29.2	
12	MD 8th: Chris Van Hollen (D)	94 004		11	TX 18th: Sheila Jackson-Lee (D)	26.0		12	AL 7th: Terri A. Sewell (D)	29.0	
13	NY 4th: Kathleen M. Rice (D)	92 472		11	TX 35th: Lloyd Doggett (D)	26.0		13	CA 40th: Lucille Roybal-Allard (D)	28.5	
14	CA 45th: Mimi Walters (R)	91 848		14	CA 40th: Lucille Roybal-Allard (D)	25.3		13	FL 5th: Corrine Brown (D)	28.5	
15	NJ 5th: Scott Garrett (R)	91 749		15	TX 5th: Jeb Hensarling (R)	24.9		13	TX 33rd: Marc A. Veasey (D)	28.5	
16	CA 15th: Eric Swalwell (D)	91 265		16	AZ 7th: Ruben Gallego (D)	24.8		16	MS 2nd: Bennie G. Thompson (D)	28.2	
17	NY 17th: Nita M. Lowey (D)	91 073		17	FL 27th: Ileana Ros-Lehtinen (R)	24.7		16	OH 11th: Marcia L. Fudge (D)	28.2	
18	TX 22nd: Pete Olson (R)	89 689		18	TX 30th: Eddie Bernice Johnson (D)	24.5		18	GA 2nd: Sanford D. Bishop Jr. (D)	28.1	
19	MD 5th: Steny H. Hoyer (D)	89 671		19	TX 16th: Beto O'Rourke (D)	24.1		19	PA 2nd: Chaka Fattah (D)	27.3	
20	IL 6th: Peter J. Roskam (R)	88 574		20	NJ 8th: Albio Sires (D)	23.9		20	TX 28th: Henry Cuellar (D)	27.1	
21	CT 4th: James A. Himes (D)	88 279		21	OK 2nd: Markwayne Mullin (R)	23.5		21	LA 5th: Ralph Lee Abraham (R)	26.1	
22	MA 4th:Joseph P. Kennedy III (D)	87 957		22	FL 9th: Alan Grayson (D)	23.3		22	SC 6th: James E. Clyburn (D)	26.0	
23	TX 3rd: Sam Johnson (R)	86 846		22	TX 1st: Louie Gohmert (R)	23.3		22	WI 4th: Gwen Moore (D)	26.0	
24	NY 2nd: Peter T. King (R)	86 442		24	IL 4th:Luis V. Gutierrez (D)	23.1		24	TX 30th: Eddie Bernice Johnson (D)	25.8	
25	IL 14th: Randy Hultgren (R)	86 124		24	TX 11th K. Michael Conaway (R)	23.1		25	NC 12th: Alma S. Adams (D)	25.7	
26	CA 12th:Nancy Pelosi (D)	85 370		26	FL 17th: Thomas J. Rooney (R)	22.9		26	AZ 3rd: Raul M. Grijalva (D)	25.5	
27	CA 52nd: Scott H. Peters (D)	85 121		27	FL 19th: Curt Clawson (R)	22.5		27	TX 35th: Lloyd Doggett (D)	25.3	
28	NY 1st: Lee M. Zeldin (R)	84 668		28	TX 23rd: Will Hurd (R)	21.5		28	LA 2nd: Cedric Richmond (D)	25.2	
29	WA 1st Suzan K. DelBene (D)	84 419		29	CA 29th: Tony Cárdenas (D)	21.4		28	PA 1st: Robert A. Brady (D)	25.2	
30	CA 19th: Zoe Lofgren (D)	83 701		30	CA 36th: Raul Ruiz (D)	21.3		30	NY 7th: Nydia M. Velázquez (D)	25.1	
31	CA 48th: Dana Rohrabacher (R)	83 425		30	FL 26th: Carlos Curbelo (R)	21.3		30	NC 1st: G. K. Butterfield (D)	25.1	
32	MA 5th: Katherine Clark (D)	81 376		32	CA 44th: Janice Hahn (D)	21.1		32	FL 24th: Frederica S. Wilson (D)	25.0	
33	NY 10th: Jerrold Nadler (D)	81 267		32	TX 14th: Randy K. Weber, Sr. (R)	21.1		32	IL 7th: Danny K. Davis (D)	25.0	
34	MA 6th: Seth Moulton (D)	81 137		34	GA 2nd: Sanford D. Bishop Jr. (D)	21.0		34	NM 2nd: Steve Pearce (R)	24.5	
35	MD 3rd: John P. Sarbanes (D)	81 015		35	TX 27th: Blake Farenthold (R)	20.9		35	CA 44th: Janice Hahn (D)	24.2	
36	MN 3rd: Erik Paulsen (R)	79 965		36	FL 11th: Richard B. Nugent (R)	20.8		36	CA 51st: Juan Vargas (D)	24.1	
37	GA 6th: Tom Price (R)	79 510		37	CA 46th: Loretta Sanchez (D)	20.7		37	MI 14th: Brenda L. Lawrence (D)	24.0	
38	TX 26th: Michael C. Burgess (R)	78 796		37	LA 5th: Ralph Lee Abraham (R)	20.7		37	NY 8th: Hakeem S. Jeffries (D)	24.0	
39	PA 7th: Patrick Meehan (R)	78 058		39	TX 36th: Brian Babin (R)	20.5		39	GA 5th: John Lewis (D)	23.9	
40	PA 8th: Michael G. Fitzpatrick (R)	77 735		40	CA 51st: Juan Vargas (D)	20.4		40	TX 29th: Gene Green (D)	23.8	
41	NJ 12th: Bonnie Watson Coleman (D)	77 694		41	FL 22nd: Lois Frankel (D)	20.3		41	IN 7th: André Carson (D)	23.7	
42	MA 8th: Stephen F. Lynch (D)	77 203		41	GA 4th: Henry C. "Hank" Johnson Jr. (D)	20.3		42	GA 12th: Rick W. Allen (R)	23.5	
43	NJ 6th: Frank Pallone Jr. (D)	77 184		41	TX 19th: Randy Neugebauer (R)	20.3		42	OH 3rd: Joyce Beatty (D)	23.5	
43	VA 1st Robert J. Wittman (R)	77 184		41	TX 24th: Kenny Marchant (R)	20.3		44	GA 8th: Austin Scott (R)	23.3	
45	NY 18th: Sean Patrick Maloney (D)	77 110		45	FL 10th: Daniel Webster (R)	20.2		44	VA 3rd Robert C. "Bobby" Scott (D)	23.3	
46	CA 49th: Darrell E. Issa (R)	77 025		45	GA 8th: Austin Scott (R)	20.2		46	CA 6th: Doris O. Matsui (D)	23.2	
47	CA 39th: Edward R. Royce (R)	76 910		47	GA 9th: Doug Collins (R)	20.1		46	CA 8th: Paul Cook (R)	23.2	
48	MN 2nd: John Kline (R)	76 409		48	TX 13th: Mac Thornberry (R)	20.0		46	CA 37th: Karen Bass (D)	23.2	
49	NJ 4th: Christopher H. Smith (R)	75 857		49	AZ 3rd: Raul M. Grijalva (D)	19.9		49	FL 20th: Alcee L. Hastings (D)	22.7	
50	NJ 3rd: Thomas MacArthur (R)	75 658		49	FL 14th: Kathy Castor (D)	19.9		50	TX 9th: Al Green (D)	22.3	
51	CA 11th:Mark Desaulnier (D)	75 036		51	NY 14th: Joseph Crowley (D)	19.8		51	CA 29th: Tony Cárdenas (D)	22.2	
52	MO 2nd: Ann Wagner (R)	74 868		52	FL 6th: Ron DeSantis (R)	19.6		51	TX 16th: Beto O'Rourke (D)	22.2	
53	CA 26th: Julia Brownley (D)	74 758		52	FL 16th: Vern Buchanan (R)	19.6		53	IL 4th:Luis V. Gutierrez (D)	22.1	
54	MI 11th: David A.Trott (R)	74 527		52	TX 20th: Joaquin Castro (D)	19.6		53	LA 4th: John Fleming (R)	22.1	
55	IL 10th: Robert J. Dold (R)	74 174		55	TX 4th: John Ratcliffe (R)	19.5		53	NV 1st: Dina Titus (D)	22.1	
56	VA 7th Dave Brat (R)	74 162		56	FL 5th: Corrine Brown (D)	19.4		53	TX 18th: Sheila Jackson-Lee (D)	22.1	
57	PA 6th: Ryan A. Costello (R)	74 128		57	CA 21st: David G. Valadao (R)	19.3		57	MA 7th: Michael E. Capuano (D)	22.0	
58	WA 8th: David G. Reichert (R)	74 078		57	CA 41st: Mark Takano (D)	19.3		58	AZ 1st: Ann Kirkpatrick (D)	21.9	
59	MD 6th: John K. Delaney (D)	73 980		57	NC 12th: Alma S. Adams (D)	19.3		58	AR 1st: Eric A. "Rick" Crawford (R)	21.9	
60	NC 9th: Robert Pittenger (R)	73 755		57	OK 5th: Steve Russell (R)	19.3		60	FL 14th: Kathy Castor (D)	21.8	
61	HI 1st: Mark Takai (D)	73 008		61	FL 23rd: Debbie Wasserman Schultz (D)	19.0		61	OH 9th: Marcy Kaptur (D)	21.6	
62	TX 2nd: Ted Poe (R)	72 369		61	TX 32nd: Pete Sessions (R)	19.0		62	CA 22nd: Devin Nunes (R)	21.5	
63	WA 7th: Jim McDermott (D)	72 279		63	AK: At-Large Don Young (R)	18.8		62	CA 23rd: Kevin McCarthy (R)	21.5	
64	MD 4th: Donna F. Edwards (D)	72 035		63	FL 18th: Patrick Murphy (D)	18.8		62	CA 31st:Pete Aguilar (D)	21.5	
65	CA 42nd: Ken Calvert (R)	71 902		63	LA 2nd: Cedric Richmond (D)	18.8		65	WV 3rd: Evan H. Jenkins (R)	21.1	
66	IL 5th: Michael Quigley (D)	71 833		63	SC 7th: Tom Rice (R)	18.8		66	AR 2nd: Bruce Westerman (R)	21.0	
67	DC At Large: Eleanor Holmes Norton (D)	71 648		67	CA 35th Norma J. Torres (D)	18.7		66	IL 2nd: Robin L. Kelly (D)	21.0	
68	MN 5th: Tom Emmer (R)	71 604		67	GA 5th: John Lewis (D)	18.7		66	MI 5th: Daniel T. Kildee (D)	21.0	
69	AK: At-Large Don Young (R)	71 583		67	TN 9th: Steve Cohen (D)	18.7		66	SC 7th: Tom Rice (R)	21.0	
70	CO 6th: Mike Coffman (R)	71 518		70	FL 8th: Bill Posey (R)	18.6		70	CA 9th:Jerry McNerney (D)	20.9	
71	TX 7th: John Abney Culberson (R)	71 321		70	GA 1st: Earl L. "Buddy" Carter (R)	18.6		71	OK 2nd: Markwayne Mullin (R)	20.8	
72	CT 2nd: Joe Courtney (D)	70 992		70	UT 2nd: Chris Stewart (R)	18.6		72	AL 3rd: Mike Rogers (R)	20.7	
73	CA 25th: Stephen Knight (R)	70 727		73	NM 3rd: Ben Ray Luján (D)	18.5		72	CA 36th: Raul Ruiz (D)	20.7	
74	CO: 2nd: Jared Polis (D)	70 322		74	MS 4th: Steven Palazzo (R)	18.4		72	GA 4th: Henry C. "Hank" Johnson Jr. (D)	20.7	
75	CA 30th: Brad Sherman (D)	69 353		74	SC 6th: James E. Clyburn (D)	18.4		72	MS 3rd: Gregg Harper (R)	20.7	

Table E. Congressional Districts 114th Congress — Land Area and Population Characteristics

STATE District	Representative, 114th Congress	Land area,[1] 2010 (sq km)	Population and population characteristics, 2014												
							Percent								
						Race alone									
			Total persons	Per square kilometer	White	Black	American Indian, Alaska Native	Asian and Pacific Islander	Some other race	Two or more races	Hispanic or Latino[2]	Non-Hispanic White alone	Female	Foreign-born	Born in state of residence
		1	2	3	4	5	6	7	8	9	10	11	12	13	14

1. Dry land or land partially or temporarily covered by water. 2. May be of any race.

Table E. Congressional Districts 114th Congress — Age and Education

STATE District	Population and population characteristics, 2014 (cont.)											Education, 2014		
	Age (percent)											Attainment[2] (percent)		
	Under 5 years	5 to 17 years	18 to 24 years	25 to 34 years	35 to 44 years	45 to 54 years	55 to 64 years	65 to 74 years	75 years and over	Median age		Total Enrollment[1]	High school graduate or more	Bachelor's degree or more
	15	16	17	18	19	20	21	22	23	24		25	26	27

1. All persons 3 years old and over enrolled in nursery school through college and graduate or professional school. 2. Persons 25 years old and over.

Table E. Congressional Districts 114th Congress — Households and Group Quarters

STATE District	Households, 2014						Group quarters, 2010					
	Number	Average household size	Family households (percent)	Married-couple family (percent)	Female family householder[1]	One person households (percent)	Total in group quarters, 2014	Percent 65 years and over	Persons in correctional institutions	Persons in nursing facilities	Persons in college dormitories	Persons in military quarters
	28	29	30	31	32	33	34	35	36	37	38	39

1. No spouse present.

Table E. Congressional Districts 114th Congress — Housing and Money Income

STATE District	Housing units, 2014						Money income, 2014		
		Occupied units						Households	
			Owner-occupied			Renter-occupied			
	Total	Occupied units as a percent of all units	Owner-occupied units as a percent of occupied units	Median value[1] (dollars)	Percent valued at $500,000 or more	Median rent[2]	Per capita income (dollars)	Median income (dollars)	Percent with income of $100,000 or more
	40	41	42	43	44	45	46	47	48

1. Specified owner-occupied units; $1,000,000 represents $1,000,000 or more. 2. Specified renter-occupied units.

Table E. Congressional Districts 114th Congress — **Poverty, Labor Force, Employment, and Social Security**

STATE District	Poverty, 2014			Civilian labor force, 2014			Civilian employment,[2] 2014					Social Security beneficiaries, December 2014		Supplemental Security Income recipients, December 2014
					Unemployment			Percent						
	Persons below poverty level (percent)	Families below poverty level (percent)	Percent of households receiving food stamps in past 12 months	Total	Total	Rate[1]	Total	Manage-ment, business, science and arts occupa-tions	Service, sales, and office	Con-struction and production	Persons under age 65 with no health insurance, 2014 (percent)	Number	Rate[3]	
	49	50	51	52	53	54	55	56	57	58	59	60	61	62

1. Percent of civilian labor force.　　2. Persons 16 years old and over.　　3. Per 1,000 resident population estimated in the 2014 American Community Survey.

Table E. Congressional Districts 114th Congress — **Agriculture**

STATE District	Agriculture, 2012									
	Land in farms			Value of products sold				Government payments		
	Number of farms	Acres	Average size of farm (acres)	Irrigated land (acres)	Total ($1,000)	Average per farm (dollars)	Percent from crops	Percent from livestock and poultry products	Total ($1,000)	Average per farm receiving payments (dollars)
	63	64	65	66	67	68	69	70	71	72

Table E. Congressional Districts 114th Congress — **Nonfarm Employment and Payroll**

STATE District	Private nonfarm employment and payroll, 2014													
	Employment												Annual payroll	
		Percent by selected industries												
	Number of establish-ments	Total	Manufact-uring	Construc-tion	Wholesale trade	Retail trade	Health care and social assistance	Finance and Insurance	Real estate and rental and leasing	Professio-nal, scientific, and technical services	Information		Total (mil dol)	Average per employee dollars
	73	74	75	76	77	78	79	80	81	82	83		84	85

Table E. Congressional Districts 114th Congress — **Land Area and Population Characteristics**

STATE District	Representative, 114th Congress	Land area,[1] 2010 (sq km)	Population and population characteristics, 2014: Total persons	Per square kilometer	Percent: Race alone: White	Black	American Indian, Alaska Native	Asian and Pacific Islander	Some other race	Two or more races	Hispanic or Latino[2]	Non-Hispanic White alone	Female	Foreign-born	Born in state of residence
		1	2	3	4	5	6	7	8	9	10	11	12	13	14
UNITED STATES....		9 147 593	318 857 056	34.9	73.4	12.7	0.8	5.4	4.7	3.0	17.3	61.9	50.8	13.3	58.7
ALABAMA		131 171	4 849 377	37.0	68.5	26.6	0.5	1.2	1.4	1.8	4.0	66.1	51.6	3.2	70.3
District 1	Bradley Byrne (R)	15 713	696 783	44.3	67.2	27.9	0.8	1.4	1.0	1.7	3.1	65.3	51.6	3.0	68.6
District 2	Martha Roby (R)	26 267	678 622	25.8	65.4	30.9	0.5	1.1	0.8	1.3	3.2	63.3	51.2	2.6	69.1
District 3	Mike Rogers (R)	19 539	706 574	36.2	69.7	26.0	0.3	1.5	0.8	1.8	3.0	67.7	51.0	3.0	66.2
District 4	Robert B. Aderholt (R)	23 022	683 372	29.7	87.3	6.9	0.7	0.5	2.6	2.0	6.0	84.0	50.9	3.4	75.9
District 5	Mo Brooks (R)	9 524	706 373	74.2	76.8	17.2	0.6	1.5	1.0	2.9	5.0	73.1	51.4	4.2	60.6
District 6	Gary J. Palmer (R)	10 802	696 788	64.5	79.3	14.5	0.3	1.9	2.7	1.3	4.9	77.2	51.3	4.4	71.2
District 7	Terri A. Sewell (D)	26 304	680 865	25.9	32.9	63.9	0.1	0.6	1.2	1.2	2.6	31.5	53.6	2.1	81.0
ALASKA		1 477 953	736 732	0.5	65.6	3.4	14.0	7.1	1.4	8.5	6.7	61.8	47.7	7.4	41.3
At Large	Don Young (R)	1 477 953	736 732	0.5	65.6	3.4	14.0	7.1	1.4	8.5	6.7	61.8	47.7	7.4	41.3
ARIZONA		294 207	6 731 484	22.9	78.3	4.2	4.4	3.3	6.4	3.3	30.5	56.1	50.3	13.7	39.0
District 1	Ann Kirkpatrick (D)	142 552	739 373	5.2	65.8	2.5	23.5	1.8	3.4	3.2	21.8	49.7	49.7	6.4	52.2
District 2	Martha McSally (R)	20 301	713 036	35.1	81.4	3.6	1.6	3.3	5.6	4.5	27.6	61.9	50.3	11.4	37.2
District 3	Raul M. Grijalva (D)	40 634	757 119	18.6	74.3	4.5	3.7	1.7	12.1	3.8	61.6	28.1	49.8	21.0	48.2
District 4	Paul A. Gosar (R)	85 986	734 258	8.5	88.6	1.8	1.9	1.5	3.8	2.4	18.0	75.3	49.4	9.1	27.5
District 5	Matt Salmon (R)	760	781 441	1 028.2	85.8	2.7	1.3	4.8	2.4	3.0	18.6	70.8	51.0	9.7	37.0
District 6	David Schweikert (R)	1 619	737 185	455.3	85.9	2.2	1.4	5.2	2.6	2.6	15.9	73.4	51.5	13.7	30.5
District 7	Ruben Gallego (D)	531	763 089	1 437.1	63.0	9.5	2.6	3.4	17.7	3.9	64.0	20.2	50.1	27.4	47.4
District 8	Trent Franks (R)	1 398	760 904	544.3	84.1	5.1	0.7	3.6	3.4	3.0	19.1	69.4	52.9	9.0	33.0
District 9	Kyrsten Sinema (D)	427	745 079	1 744.9	76.4	5.5	2.9	4.8	6.8	3.6	27.2	57.2	48.3	14.9	37.2
ARKANSAS............		134 771	2 966 369	22.0	78.3	15.8	0.6	1.5	1.7	2.2	6.9	73.4	50.9	4.7	61.1
District 1	Eric A. "Rick" Crawford (R)	50 034	723 492	14.5	78.9	18.3	0.4	0.4	0.4	1.6	3.1	76.5	50.8	1.8	65.4
District 2	J. French Hill (R)	12 893	756 326	58.7	73.0	22.2	0.2	1.4	0.8	2.3	5.1	69.0	51.6	4.2	66.6
District 3	Steve Womack (R)	13 988	767 904	54.9	86.1	3.1	1.1	3.4	3.2	3.1	13.8	76.1	50.6	9.4	48.2
District 4	Bruce Westerman (R)	57 855	718 647	12.4	74.9	20.0	0.6	0.6	2.3	1.6	5.5	71.9	50.6	3.3	64.7
CALIFORNIA..........		403 466	38 802 500	96.2	61.4	5.8	0.7	14.3	13.2	4.6	38.6	38.3	50.4	27.1	55.0
District 1	Doug LaMalfa (R)	72 751	710 428	9.8	85.8	1.5	2.0	2.6	2.8	5.2	13.4	77.1	49.8	6.3	69.4
District 2	Jared Huffman (D)	33 546	720 049	21.5	79.7	1.6	2.1	4.1	7.8	4.6	17.9	70.8	50.3	14.2	59.8
District 3	John Garamendi (D)	16 015	720 104	45.0	65.4	6.0	0.9	11.8	10.1	5.8	29.0	48.8	50.1	18.6	60.5
District 4	Tom McClintock (R)	33 246	719 688	21.6	86.2	1.2	1.1	5.4	2.4	3.7	12.8	76.8	49.9	9.4	65.0
District 5	Mike Thompson (D)	4 483	722 814	161.2	64.8	6.7	1.3	11.5	9.8	6.0	27.6	50.1	51.7	20.2	60.2
District 6	Doris O. Matsui (D)	453	737 671	1 628.4	51.4	13.2	0.7	17.3	10.8	6.6	29.0	36.1	51.1	23.0	59.4
District 7	Ami Bera (D)	1 421	736 555	518.3	66.1	7.2	0.8	15.6	4.1	6.2	16.5	56.0	51.2	18.0	61.5
District 8	Paul Cook (R)	85 126	715 953	8.4	75.6	8.2	1.5	3.7	7.3	3.8	39.4	45.5	50.5	13.2	64.9
District 9	Jerry McNerney (D)	3 225	738 320	228.9	54.6	9.8	0.6	14.9	11.7	8.3	37.1	35.4	50.3	21.8	64.1
District 10	Jeff Denham (R)	4 711	732 084	155.4	73.4	2.5	0.8	7.8	10.5	5.0	42.3	43.8	50.5	21.1	64.3
District 11	Mark Desaulnier (D)	1 278	739 693	578.8	62.0	7.6	0.5	13.7	10.1	6.0	26.7	47.3	51.4	25.7	53.5
District 12	Nancy Pelosi (D)	101	736 123	7 288.3	49.9	5.3	0.3	32.5	7.1	5.0	14.8	43.3	48.9	33.3	39.5
District 13	Barbara Lee (D)	251	743 310	2 961.4	44.6	17.4	1.0	20.2	10.3	6.5	22.4	35.2	51.9	27.3	48.6
District 14	Jackie Speier (D)	672	753 002	1 120.5	46.2	3.4	0.3	34.3	10.8	4.9	24.2	34.8	50.8	37.8	47.0
District 15	Eric Swalwell (D)	1 553	753 911	485.5	47.8	6.5	0.3	33.5	6.1	5.8	22.8	33.0	50.2	33.7	50.6
District 16	Jim Costa (D)	7 354	718 849	97.7	56.9	5.9	0.6	9.1	23.3	4.2	59.1	24.0	50.2	24.6	64.3
District 17	Michael M. Honda (D)	479	756 995	1 580.4	33.1	2.7	0.3	52.7	6.8	4.3	16.1	25.4	50.1	47.3	39.7
District 18	Anna G. Eshoo (D)	1 803	734 378	407.3	65.2	2.3	0.2	22.7	5.2	4.4	16.7	54.6	49.8	28.9	46.8
District 19	Zoe Lofgren (D)	2 371	746 211	314.7	47.2	2.8	0.7	27.7	16.7	4.9	41.6	25.5	49.6	36.2	50.6
District 20	Sam Farr (D)	12 624	732 074	58.0	77.8	1.9	0.7	5.7	10.0	4.0	52.4	37.4	49.5	26.2	57.2
District 21	David G. Valadao (R)	17 430	712 295	40.9	71.3	3.7	1.2	3.6	17.2	3.0	73.9	17.2	47.5	28.1	62.6
District 22	Devin Nunes (R)	3 018	739 418	245.0	72.8	3.6	0.9	8.2	10.6	3.9	46.7	39.4	50.3	18.1	68.5
District 23	Kevin McCarthy (R)	25 636	747 914	29.2	75.8	7.3	1.2	5.0	6.3	4.4	38.0	46.5	49.8	13.3	70.0
District 24	Lois Capps (D)	17 828	726 519	40.8	81.1	1.9	0.6	4.6	7.4	4.4	35.6	55.1	49.8	17.9	60.5
District 25	Stephen Knight (R)	4 378	718 796	164.2	63.3	8.3	0.5	8.8	13.8	5.4	37.5	42.1	51.3	20.9	61.9
District 26	Julia Brownley (D)	2 432	725 795	298.4	80.4	1.7	0.9	6.6	5.7	4.6	44.7	44.3	50.5	23.2	58.1
District 27	Judy Chu (D)	1 813	714 911	394.3	39.6	4.1	0.4	38.4	14.1	3.5	28.1	27.3	51.3	38.7	48.0
District 28	Adam B. Schiff (D)	566	721 435	1 274.6	66.8	2.2	0.4	13.9	12.7	4.0	26.6	54.4	50.1	41.3	37.0
District 29	Tony Cárdenas (D)	238	718 633	3 019.5	55.5	3.8	0.6	7.7	30.3	2.1	69.1	18.3	49.4	43.4	46.2
District 30	Brad Sherman (D)	352	754 331	2 143.0	66.7	5.4	0.5	12.2	10.9	4.2	26.9	52.1	50.3	33.6	45.1
District 31	Pete Aguilar (D)	565	738 321	1 306.8	61.8	10.4	0.8	8.6	14.5	3.9	51.1	27.7	51.0	23.2	62.5
District 32	Grace F. Napolitano (D)	322	735 945	2 285.5	45.3	3.3	0.6	18.5	28.6	3.7	62.0	15.5	50.7	35.7	56.5
District 33	Ted Lieu (D)	747	714 411	956.4	74.6	2.1	0.4	14.2	2.5	6.2	12.9	66.0	51.4	22.3	46.9
District 34	Xavier Becerra (D)	123	720 406	5 857.0	42.7	4.0	0.5	20.9	29.7	2.2	64.8	9.5	49.4	49.0	41.8
District 35	Norma J. Torres (D)	437	732 845	1 677.0	47.9	6.2	0.9	6.4	34.9	3.8	70.5	15.2	49.4	29.8	60.6
District 36	Raul Ruiz (D)	15 314	746 522	48.7	68.2	4.2	1.1	3.7	19.4	3.4	49.1	40.7	50.2	22.8	55.1
District 37	Karen Bass (D)	143	723 724	5 061.0	44.7	22.3	1.8	10.6	17.4	3.2	39.3	25.5	51.9	32.8	47.0
District 38	Linda T. Sánchez (D)	263	720 208	2 738.4	49.5	3.6	0.6	15.5	27.1	3.6	63.1	16.4	51.1	30.6	60.4
District 39	Edward R. Royce (R)	529	716 854	1 355.1	53.2	2.4	0.4	29.6	10.3	4.1	34.2	31.4	50.9	32.0	54.5
District 40	Lucille Roybal-Allard (D)	149	713 940	4 791.5	54.2	4.9	0.7	3.5	35.0	1.8	86.9	4.7	50.6	42.4	52.9
District 41	Mark Takano (D)	820	739 287	901.6	53.0	8.4	1.0	6.9	26.5	4.1	58.9	23.1	50.3	24.6	61.7
District 42	Ken Calvert (R)	2 424	754 191	311.1	67.3	6.4	0.7	8.4	12.0	5.2	37.5	44.7	50.4	19.6	60.3
District 43	Maxine Waters (D)	187	731 916	3 914.0	37.6	23.9	0.6	11.7	18.7	7.4	45.8	15.1	52.1	29.9	55.6
District 44	Janice Hahn (D)	206	726 147	3 525.0	45.3	15.8	0.8	6.5	27.7	3.9	70.5	6.1	50.4	35.5	56.6
District 45	Mimi Walters (R)	856	763 368	891.8	63.6	2.0	0.4	21.8	7.3	4.9	20.0	52.4	51.3	28.5	49.3
District 46	Loretta Sanchez (D)	186	730 783	3 928.9	60.5	1.4	0.4	13.2	21.9	2.6	66.8	17.2	49.2	40.5	50.6
District 47	Alan S. Lowenthal (D)	560	718 747	1 283.5	57.0	7.1	0.6	23.9	7.5	3.9	34.3	32.6	50.9	30.7	53.8
District 48	Dana Rohrabacher (R)	377	726 491	1 927.0	65.2	1.1	0.5	18.7	10.0	4.4	21.4	55.3	50.5	24.6	52.5
District 49	Darrell E. Issa (R)	1 432	728 456	508.7	80.0	2.4	0.4	7.2	5.7	4.4	24.6	62.6	49.4	16.9	50.4
District 50	Duncan Hunter (R)	7 219	737 332	102.1	77.6	2.8	0.9	6.6	6.5	5.7	31.2	55.6	49.8	19.5	54.9
District 51	Juan Vargas (D)	12 410	720 935	58.1	64.4	7.0	0.7	7.9	15.8	4.2	70.9	13.0	49.4	34.0	52.5
District 52	Scott H. Peters (D)	692	759 602	1 097.7	68.9	3.1	0.3	19.5	2.8	5.3	14.5	58.6	49.6	22.8	42.6
District 53	Susan A. Davis (D)	351	753 810	2 147.6	65.3	7.8	0.5	14.7	5.6	6.2	33.4	40.6	50.9	22.7	50.6

1. Dry land or land partially or temporarily covered by water. 2. May be of any race.

Table E. Congressional Districts 114th Congress — **Age and Education**

STATE District	Population and population characteristics, 2014 (cont.)											Education, 2014		
	Age (percent)												Attainment[2] (percent)	
	Under 5 years	5 to 17 years	18 to 24 years	25 to 34 years	35 to 44 years	45 to 54 years	55 to 64 years	65 to 74 years	75 years and over	Median age	Total Enrollment[1]	High school graduate or more	Bachelor's degree or more
	15	16	17	18	19	20	21	22	23	24	25	26	27
UNITED STATES..............	6.2	16.9	9.9	13.5	12.8	13.6	12.6	8.3	6.2	37.7	82 063 714	86.9	30.1
ALABAMA	6.0	16.8	10.0	12.7	12.6	13.4	13.0	8.9	6.4	38.6	1 190 580	84.7	23.5
District 1.............................	6.1	17.3	8.9	12.3	12.2	13.7	13.3	9.5	6.7	39.5	164 033	86.5	23.1
District 2.............................	6.1	17.0	10.2	12.7	12.7	13.0	12.7	8.9	6.6	38.0	166 147	83.6	21.6
District 3.............................	5.8	16.5	11.4	12.3	13.3	13.0	12.7	8.9	6.0	38.0	186 914	83.5	20.4
District 4.............................	5.8	17.4	8.5	11.3	12.7	13.9	13.3	10.0	7.1	40.9	155 496	80.8	16.3
District 5.............................	5.7	16.8	9.4	13.0	12.3	14.8	13.0	8.6	6.4	39.4	173 665	86.0	29.5
District 6.............................	6.0	17.3	7.9	13.3	13.6	13.4	13.2	8.9	6.3	39.3	168 462	89.0	34.6
District 7.............................	6.5	15.7	13.5	14.0	11.7	12.2	12.8	7.7	5.8	35.2	175 863	83.4	17.9
ALASKA	7.2	18.1	11.5	15.5	12.7	13.1	12.5	6.3	3.2	33.3	195 830	92.9	28.0
At Large	7.2	18.1	11.5	15.5	12.7	13.1	12.5	6.3	3.2	33.3	195 830	92.9	28.0
ARIZONA	6.4	17.6	10.0	13.3	12.5	12.4	11.8	9.3	6.7	36.9	1 757 664	86.1	27.6
District 1.............................	6.7	18.2	10.8	11.9	11.9	11.7	12.6	10.2	6.2	37.0	196 852	85.0	23.2
District 2.............................	5.8	14.9	10.2	12.4	11.3	12.3	13.5	11.0	8.6	40.9	170 160	91.1	33.4
District 3.............................	7.0	20.5	13.9	14.0	12.7	11.4	9.8	6.5	4.2	31.0	236 386	73.9	16.1
District 4.............................	5.1	14.9	7.1	10.4	10.5	11.3	14.6	15.1	10.9	47.2	152 296	86.7	19.0
District 5.............................	7.3	20.6	7.6	12.0	13.4	13.2	10.5	8.7	6.8	36.5	221 585	92.5	33.6
District 6.............................	5.7	14.9	7.4	13.9	13.2	14.6	13.5	10.1	6.6	41.4	163 443	92.5	42.4
District 7.............................	9.3	22.5	11.8	15.9	13.4	11.5	8.5	4.5	2.4	28.8	223 730	67.8	13.9
District 8.............................	5.5	16.7	7.6	11.7	12.6	12.9	12.7	11.1	9.3	42.0	184 895	92.4	27.4
District 9.............................	5.4	15.3	13.7	17.5	13.0	12.9	10.8	6.4	5.1	33.6	208 317	87.9	35.4
ARKANSAS.....................	6.4	17.4	9.8	12.7	12.7	12.8	12.5	9.1	6.6	37.8	746 254	85.3	21.4
District 1.............................	6.3	17.0	9.2	11.9	12.7	12.9	12.7	10.0	7.4	39.6	174 315	83.5	15.7
District 2.............................	6.6	17.2	10.0	14.2	12.9	12.8	12.3	8.2	5.9	36.6	195 363	89.9	28.3
District 3.............................	6.6	18.4	10.7	13.6	12.9	12.7	11.4	7.9	5.7	35.4	204 005	84.1	24.9
District 4.............................	6.2	17.0	9.4	11.2	12.0	13.0	13.5	10.2	7.5	40.0	172 571	83.7	16.5
CALIFORNIA...................	6.5	17.1	10.3	14.7	13.3	13.4	11.6	7.3	5.5	36.0	10 531 321	82.1	31.7
District 1.............................	5.1	14.8	10.4	12.0	10.3	12.7	15.1	11.3	8.3	42.6	170 900	89.6	23.9
District 2.............................	5.0	15.0	8.3	11.4	12.3	14.3	15.7	10.9	7.0	43.4	169 175	90.1	39.7
District 3.............................	5.9	17.5	12.5	13.8	11.9	13.6	11.9	7.4	5.5	35.2	211 281	83.2	24.2
District 4.............................	4.8	16.5	7.5	10.6	11.9	14.5	15.1	11.4	7.7	44.1	171 445	92.6	32.0
District 5.............................	5.9	15.9	9.4	13.5	12.1	13.3	13.9	9.4	6.5	39.5	180 509	86.6	31.7
District 6.............................	7.4	17.9	10.6	16.7	13.2	12.1	10.8	6.5	4.8	33.5	206 412	83.1	26.1
District 7.............................	6.3	17.6	8.4	13.9	12.7	14.2	12.8	7.9	6.2	37.9	192 965	90.5	32.7
District 8.............................	8.0	19.6	10.6	12.9	11.8	12.5	11.9	7.7	5.1	34.2	196 987	82.4	15.8
District 9.............................	6.7	20.6	10.2	12.7	12.6	13.5	11.4	7.1	5.2	34.8	215 647	79.7	19.8
District 10...........................	7.3	20.2	10.2	13.8	13.3	13.0	10.8	6.6	4.8	33.7	212 973	79.4	17.7
District 11...........................	5.8	16.4	8.5	12.9	13.6	14.2	13.6	8.7	6.4	39.5	187 620	88.0	41.5
District 12...........................	4.5	8.4	7.2	23.3	16.6	13.6	11.9	7.7	6.9	38.6	133 587	88.3	55.6
District 13...........................	5.8	13.6	11.6	17.0	14.5	13.0	11.9	7.3	5.2	36.2	200 204	84.7	45.7
District 14...........................	5.8	14.6	8.3	14.9	14.6	14.5	12.9	8.1	6.3	39.1	189 147	87.6	45.3
District 15...........................	6.4	17.5	7.4	14.3	15.0	15.0	12.0	7.2	5.3	37.9	190 730	88.8	40.4
District 16...........................	8.6	21.7	11.9	14.4	12.5	11.5	9.3	6.0	4.3	30.0	214 402	66.1	12.0
District 17...........................	7.1	15.9	7.2	17.6	16.3	13.6	10.6	6.5	4.9	36.3	193 771	91.0	54.3
District 18...........................	5.8	16.8	7.3	13.1	14.3	15.6	12.8	7.8	6.6	40.3	195 045	93.9	59.7
District 19...........................	6.3	17.0	10.4	14.4	14.3	14.5	11.5	6.8	4.9	36.2	205 475	79.9	32.9
District 20...........................	7.1	17.6	12.6	14.1	12.5	12.6	11.9	6.8	5.0	34.1	210 155	75.2	27.0
District 21...........................	8.3	22.7	11.9	16.0	12.6	11.9	8.7	4.6	3.3	29.3	221 048	58.5	7.1
District 22...........................	8.1	20.7	10.9	13.9	12.1	11.9	10.7	6.7	4.9	32.4	225 583	80.4	23.2
District 23...........................	8.3	20.0	9.9	14.6	12.5	12.3	10.9	6.6	5.0	32.9	205 953	83.3	19.3
District 24...........................	5.9	14.8	15.9	12.7	11.1	11.9	12.5	8.5	6.9	35.6	212 828	84.2	32.8
District 25...........................	6.4	21.0	9.2	12.5	13.5	15.0	11.9	6.6	4.0	35.7	215 837	85.2	26.2
District 26...........................	6.7	18.0	10.1	13.3	12.3	14.0	12.1	7.5	6.1	36.7	194 494	82.4	32.1
District 27...........................	5.5	13.5	9.2	13.7	13.8	14.7	13.4	8.8	7.4	41.0	175 905	85.0	40.8
District 28...........................	4.6	11.2	8.3	20.1	15.1	14.4	11.9	8.1	6.3	38.7	151 054	87.4	43.7
District 29...........................	6.8	17.3	11.9	16.6	13.7	13.6	10.1	5.8	4.2	33.2	193 559	67.4	17.9
District 30...........................	5.8	14.1	9.4	14.9	14.4	13.9	12.8	7.8	6.8	39.2	185 209	88.2	42.5
District 31...........................	7.0	20.6	11.2	15.6	12.9	12.5	10.3	5.9	3.8	31.8	238 533	79.6	23.0
District 32...........................	6.4	17.1	11.2	13.8	13.6	13.2	11.7	7.6	5.4	36.1	206 079	73.5	20.0
District 33...........................	4.5	13.5	9.0	14.9	13.4	15.6	12.4	8.9	7.8	41.2	178 377	95.6	64.0
District 34...........................	6.3	15.9	10.7	17.5	15.9	12.8	10.2	5.9	5.0	34.7	190 359	64.8	24.1
District 35...........................	6.9	20.1	12.8	15.1	14.0	13.3	9.5	4.8	3.4	31.3	226 288	69.6	13.9
District 36...........................	6.4	18.1	8.6	12.0	11.6	12.4	11.3	10.5	9.0	38.9	188 327	79.7	20.8
District 37...........................	6.1	13.5	11.7	17.2	14.6	13.1	11.3	6.8	5.5	35.8	183 492	80.1	37.1
District 38...........................	6.5	16.6	10.8	14.2	13.5	13.5	11.6	7.2	6.2	36.3	198 849	77.4	20.9
District 39...........................	6.3	16.6	10.5	13.2	13.2	14.4	12.4	7.3	6.2	37.7	206 365	89.2	39.7
District 40...........................	8.3	21.4	11.3	15.2	14.1	12.5	9.3	4.4	3.4	30.6	221 376	51.5	9.2
District 41...........................	7.3	20.5	13.2	14.7	13.1	12.0	10.0	5.5	3.6	30.7	227 107	74.9	15.0
District 42...........................	6.6	20.1	9.9	13.5	13.6	14.2	10.7	6.6	4.8	34.9	226 426	85.2	24.2
District 43...........................	7.2	17.2	10.7	15.7	13.8	13.4	10.9	6.4	4.8	34.4	204 785	77.3	24.2
District 44...........................	7.8	20.4	12.2	15.9	12.7	13.0	9.5	4.9	3.5	30.6	220 043	61.5	11.1
District 45...........................	6.3	16.7	9.2	13.6	13.8	14.9	12.2	7.3	6.0	38.1	213 544	92.5	51.6
District 46...........................	7.7	18.7	12.3	16.5	14.1	12.8	9.2	5.2	3.6	31.6	213 938	66.9	17.8
District 47...........................	6.0	16.4	10.2	14.6	13.8	15.1	11.6	7.0	5.4	37.1	194 526	81.9	29.7
District 48...........................	4.8	14.4	8.7	14.4	12.8	15.3	13.6	9.3	6.6	41.1	174 072	89.4	43.9
District 49...........................	6.3	17.1	10.4	13.1	13.7	13.7	11.7	7.8	6.4	37.4	185 385	90.6	44.0
District 50...........................	6.5	17.4	9.9	13.4	12.4	14.0	12.5	8.2	5.8	37.2	197 978	85.8	28.1
District 51...........................	7.4	18.8	12.9	16.0	13.0	11.5	9.8	5.9	4.7	31.6	207 164	69.2	14.0
District 52...........................	6.1	14.3	10.5	17.6	13.4	13.7	11.8	7.1	5.6	36.2	198 577	95.4	57.9
District 53...........................	6.5	13.7	11.2	18.2	13.2	13.3	11.4	6.7	5.8	35.2	199 831	87.7	35.8

1. All persons 3 years old and over enrolled in nursery school through college and graduate or professional school.   2. Persons 25 years old and over.

Table E. Congressional Districts 114th Congress — Households and Group Quarters

STATE District	Households, 2014						Group quarters, 2010					
	Number	Average household size	Family households (percent)	Married-couple family (percent)	Female family householder[1]	One person households (percent)	Total in group quarters, 2014	Percent 65 years and over	Persons in correctional institutions	Persons in nursing facilities	Persons in college dormitories	Persons in military quarters
	28	29	30	31	32	33	34	35	36	37	38	39
UNITED STATES	117 259 427	2.65	65.8	47.9	13.0	27.8	8 064 161	18.3	2 263 602	1 502 264	2 521 090	338 191
ALABAMA	1 841 217	2.57	66.9	47.3	15.5	28.8	118 470	18.7	41 177	22 995	36 341	2 152
District 1	255 303	2.66	67.3	48.5	15.1	29.0	17 324	19.1	5 651	2 671	2 579	0
District 2	258 138	2.56	65.7	45.3	16.3	30.0	18 909	15.4	13 081	3 727	3 107	1 274
District 3	270 971	2.54	67.5	46.6	17.1	27.2	19 476	15.9	7 014	3 016	6 949	0
District 4	259 439	2.60	69.6	52.8	11.8	27.2	8 070	39.0	2 922	3 652	791	0
District 5	274 891	2.51	66.9	50.6	12.4	29.1	16 158	17.5	5 087	2 879	5 347	823
District 6	265 000	2.58	69.5	54.2	11.4	26.6	12 679	23.8	4 884	2 733	2 830	0
District 7	257 475	2.54	62.0	32.3	24.5	32.9	25 854	15.1	2 538	4 317	14 738	55
ALASKA	249 659	2.84	66.1	49.7	10.5	25.6	28 311	5.9	4 206	1 626	1 872	5 055
At Large	249 659	2.84	66.1	49.7	10.5	25.6	28 311	5.9	4 206	1 626	1 872	5 055
ARIZONA	2 428 743	2.71	65.0	47.0	12.5	27.6	151 403	12.2	67 767	13 819	27 987	5 172
District 1	249 074	2.84	68.4	48.4	14.2	25.4	32 644	4.2	15 071	816	7 630	0
District 2	292 370	2.37	59.0	44.0	11.2	33.1	21 214	19.9	7 538	2 914	118	3 352
District 3	234 874	3.12	72.0	46.6	17.2	21.4	25 181	5.3	11 711	863	6 913	0
District 4	282 598	2.51	66.6	52.7	9.8	26.9	26 216	6.9	19 869	1 431	1 213	1 164
District 5	269 256	2.89	72.2	56.4	10.5	22.3	3 108	55.3	11	859	346	0
District 6	299 053	2.45	61.5	47.6	9.8	29.9	4 820	53.4	10	1 594	274	0
District 7	224 388	3.35	66.4	35.1	21.3	25.6	12 216	5.2	8 915	840	1 162	0
District 8	284 913	2.63	69.2	55.1	10.5	26.2	11 141	30.5	4 624	2 809	861	656
District 9	292 217	2.50	52.9	35.4	11.2	34.9	14 863	12.2	18	1 693	9 470	0
ARKANSAS	1 131 288	2.55	66.5	48.3	13.4	28.6	82 184	21.7	25 844	18 532	24 144	619
District 1	282 699	2.46	66.7	46.7	14.7	28.8	27 894	20.6	15 495	5 770	2 669	0
District 2	285 873	2.59	64.7	45.9	14.1	30.2	16 766	20.1	3 461	3 521	6 184	616
District 3	283 989	2.65	67.4	52.1	10.6	26.6	16 646	21.3	1 599	3 663	9 499	0
District 4	278 727	2.50	67.2	48.5	14.4	28.8	20 878	24.7	5 289	5 578	5 792	3
CALIFORNIA	12 758 648	2.98	68.7	48.9	13.7	24.0	817 130	15.4	256 807	111 884	172 843	57 628
District 1	273 795	2.51	62.2	47.7	9.9	29.9	23 988	14.1	11 908	2 834	2 728	5
District 2	280 016	2.50	60.9	45.9	9.8	31.5	19 871	13.5	9 975	2 246	2 645	393
District 3	245 160	2.85	69.6	50.5	12.9	22.8	22 102	9.1	12 154	1 728	4 981	1 321
District 4	267 604	2.64	68.5	56.7	8.3	25.5	13 592	15.3	8 633	1 677	458	0
District 5	265 421	2.68	66.2	47.9	12.9	27.1	12 676	22.6	1 940	3 657	3 581	0
District 6	264 422	2.75	61.8	39.3	16.2	29.7	10 804	19.4	2 254	1 789	1 493	0
District 7	258 041	2.80	70.4	50.9	14.6	23.6	14 241	23.1	6 682	1 704	22	0
District 8	231 229	3.03	73.0	50.4	15.4	22.1	15 832	10.8	6 717	1 325	117	4 748
District 9	230 743	3.15	74.1	50.4	16.5	20.1	12 458	21.5	1 358	2 403	2 194	0
District 10	228 743	3.16	74.6	54.3	14.2	19.2	8 925	24.1	4 848	2 580	584	0
District 11	268 357	2.72	67.4	51.3	12.0	25.8	8 626	35.3	865	3 004	1 568	0
District 12	318 240	2.26	43.5	31.9	7.9	40.1	17 125	18.3	1 573	2 810	5 993	0
District 13	282 191	2.56	57.1	39.3	13.4	31.2	20 769	13.2	1 044	2 600	11 927	661
District 14	249 842	2.97	68.5	52.8	10.9	23.5	10 873	29.2	1 090	1 939	2 487	0
District 15	245 929	3.02	76.3	59.0	11.1	18.3	11 764	23.6	5 669	2 136	1 076	0
District 16	207 675	3.36	74.2	44.5	21.4	20.8	20 813	11.0	12 113	2 113	1 443	0
District 17	248 336	3.01	74.6	60.1	9.9	19.0	10 537	20.8	2 564	1 666	2 592	0
District 18	269 816	2.67	67.5	56.1	7.9	24.6	15 141	24.9	4	2 889	6 712	5
District 19	221 998	3.31	73.3	52.9	13.4	19.8	12 392	11.7	1 448	916	3 356	0
District 20	222 810	3.15	70.7	50.2	14.3	22.4	30 227	8.9	11 516	2 072	8 411	2 504
District 21	181 929	3.68	81.1	52.9	20.1	13.9	43 019	4.1	44 549	1 252	239	2 038
District 22	235 530	3.11	73.8	50.4	15.2	20.9	7 729	28.5	1 349	1 709	1 566	0
District 23	240 106	3.03	73.4	50.0	15.1	21.2	20 083	9.1	17 160	2 293	560	329
District 24	248 895	2.78	63.4	47.6	10.9	26.2	35 822	7.2	11 387	1 805	15 714	475
District 25	220 969	3.21	77.3	56.3	14.5	18.1	10 206	5.7	7 129	251	1 775	0
District 26	228 883	3.12	74.0	55.5	12.7	20.6	11 562	18.2	1 535	1 644	2 316	1 349
District 27	239 911	2.92	69.4	50.4	13.5	24.3	13 450	25.4	331	3 659	5 809	0
District 28	292 855	2.43	53.3	37.3	11.1	34.9	10 438	32.8	183	3 356	647	0
District 29	201 576	3.53	71.8	44.9	17.2	21.5	6 608	35.7	307	2 842	151	0
District 30	276 791	2.69	63.0	45.6	11.8	28.4	10 104	41.0	20	2 996	2 746	0
District 31	217 372	3.30	72.8	49.4	15.9	21.5	21 967	15.4	5 464	2 391	2 739	0
District 32	198 676	3.65	78.1	53.3	16.4	17.0	11 714	29.1	74	2 895	3 298	0
District 33	297 852	2.33	54.7	43.4	8.4	34.1	20 370	11.2	98	1 851	14 107	0
District 34	239 711	2.90	60.1	33.9	18.1	30.6	24 897	11.7	8 722	3 270	2 438	0
District 35	185 910	3.81	79.6	51.5	19.9	15.4	24 462	11.5	6 996	2 041	1 948	0
District 36	261 820	2.80	64.7	46.3	12.4	29.1	12 200	16.9	9 107	1 504	70	0
District 37	271 981	2.60	54.1	33.3	15.5	33.8	16 126	14.0	155	2 263	7 976	0
District 38	203 362	3.49	78.2	53.4	16.8	18.2	10 711	26.5	156	2 794	3 305	0
District 39	219 406	3.23	79.4	59.8	12.9	15.8	7 804	26.5	2	1 230	2 630	0
District 40	179 453	3.96	81.9	44.7	26.1	13.6	3 262	37.5	7	1 571	5	0
District 41	191 499	3.79	79.2	52.5	17.3	15.2	13 287	11.9	1 171	1 826	7 379	0
District 42	219 885	3.40	78.8	62.1	11.3	16.7	6 266	10.4	5 652	440	161	0
District 43	240 996	2.99	68.6	38.8	21.7	26.0	10 306	27.0	120	2 478	3 293	0
District 44	184 112	3.90	79.3	46.1	23.9	16.6	8 300	16.1	2 843	1 687	587	20
District 45	265 906	2.82	71.7	57.6	10.3	22.0	12 367	22.2	534	789	5 705	0
District 46	187 247	3.81	77.2	50.4	18.1	16.3	16 795	19.0	4 906	2 887	1 967	0
District 47	242 825	2.92	66.5	44.3	16.2	26.3	10 221	31.5	235	2 931	2 040	2
District 48	268 779	2.68	65.0	49.8	10.4	26.3	5 635	30.5	13	1 555	1 249	14
District 49	251 417	2.81	70.8	56.7	9.6	21.7	22 087	6.5	782	1 612	7 910	16 563
District 50	239 592	3.04	75.7	57.4	12.9	18.7	8 816	26.3	889	1 975	757	0
District 51	194 825	3.55	75.4	46.8	20.7	19.4	29 771	11.0	17 756	1 059	0	11 846
District 52	282 394	2.60	61.6	48.9	8.9	28.1	24 731	8.6	2 774	1 881	4 151	15 213
District 53	265 815	2.79	62.1	44.5	11.8	26.2	13 258	28.3	46	3 059	3 237	142

1. No spouse present.

Table E. Congressional Districts 114th Congress — **Housing and Money Income**

STATE District	Housing units, 2014						Money income, 2014		
	Total	Occupied units					Households		
		Occupied units as a percent of all units	Owner-occupied			Renter-occupied	Per capita income (dollars)	Median income (dollars)	Percent with income of $100,000 or more
			Owner-occupied units as a percent of occupied units	Median value[1] (dollars)	Percent valued at $500,000 or more	Median rent[2]			
	40	41	42	43	44	45	46	47	48
UNITED STATES.............	133 962 970	87.5	63.1	181 200	11.2	934	28 889	53 657	23.6
ALABAMA	2 208 030	83.4	67.7	125 600	3.1	717	23 606	42 830	16.2
District 1	328 532	77.7	68.0	132 300	3.6	802	23 297	44 030	16.3
District 2	309 169	83.5	66.3	117 700	2.1	720	22 565	42 628	14.9
District 3	324 122	83.6	67.3	116 900	2.2	683	22 331	40 896	14.1
District 4	311 200	83.4	71.5	97 300	2.5	599	20 625	39 246	12.0
District 5	310 432	88.6	69.1	147 700	2.4	674	27 772	49 202	21.6
District 6	298 431	88.8	73.7	171 100	6.8	900	30 022	58 073	25.1
District 7	326 144	78.9	57.6	90 800	1.5	714	18 385	31 563	9.0
ALASKA	308 571	80.9	62.5	254 500	7.1	1 183	33 062	71 583	33.9
At Large	308 571	80.9	62.5	254 500	7.1	1 183	33 062	71 583	33.9
ARIZONA	2 909 336	83.5	61.1	176 700	7.8	916	25 715	50 068	19.9
District 1	331 747	75.1	67.3	151 100	5.9	851	21 522	47 618	17.2
District 2	345 434	84.6	59.7	164 400	6.1	808	28 066	47 586	18.6
District 3	269 999	87.0	58.3	122 000	2.1	854	17 237	40 734	11.1
District 4	384 567	73.5	71.5	156 000	4.6	874	23 475	43 771	13.5
District 5	310 218	86.8	70.7	229 000	7.1	1 123	29 311	65 129	30.1
District 6	350 948	85.2	63.3	297 600	23.8	1 008	39 032	61 389	29.6
District 7	261 283	85.9	41.1	112 100	1.6	795	14 629	34 881	9.4
District 8	326 564	87.2	70.2	195 500	4.3	1 136	29 111	59 512	24.5
District 9	328 576	88.9	45.1	219 700	10.4	908	29 386	51 106	20.9
ARKANSAS.......................	1 341 081	84.4	65.8	112 500	2.3	683	22 883	41 262	14.0
District 1	338 438	83.5	65.9	92 900	1.3	624	20 268	37 247	10.4
District 2	335 178	85.3	63.2	136 600	2.6	756	25 706	46 361	17.3
District 3	324 420	87.5	64.1	140 900	3.5	707	25 078	45 351	17.4
District 4	343 045	81.3	70.1	84 600	1.8	616	20 201	37 793	10.8
CALIFORNIA.....................	13 901 594	91.8	53.7	412 700	38.9	1 268	30 441	61 933	30.1
District 1	324 834	84.3	65.8	236 400	9.8	884	26 074	45 923	18.3
District 2	320 423	87.4	60.1	512 600	51.1	1 274	40 888	64 958	32.8
District 3	264 765	92.6	58.8	266 700	12.9	1 103	26 241	56 275	24.9
District 4	353 558	75.7	73.3	350 700	22.9	1 166	34 720	68 539	32.0
District 5	287 407	92.4	58.8	404 800	32.1	1 331	33 080	65 520	29.8
District 6	286 820	92.2	44.6	236 900	9.9	959	24 495	46 805	19.2
District 7	274 333	94.1	62.5	307 300	13.7	1 111	30 890	66 104	31.2
District 8	308 186	75.0	59.7	183 100	6.7	977	20 396	45 873	16.5
District 9	246 207	93.7	56.6	265 200	12.9	1 065	24 224	54 491	24.9
District 10	243 718	93.9	56.9	245 700	8.4	1 004	22 928	54 681	22.2
District 11	281 591	95.3	60.9	530 300	52.4	1 378	42 160	75 036	38.4
District 12	350 084	90.9	35.4	860 300	85.6	1 570	53 975	85 370	44.1
District 13	300 263	94.0	42.8	562 800	56.7	1 266	36 851	62 811	33.7
District 14	265 184	94.2	57.2	773 000	84.3	1 779	44 477	95 972	48.3
District 15	254 808	96.5	61.8	606 700	64.4	1 588	38 260	91 265	46.0
District 16	226 066	91.9	46.0	162 600	4.0	833	16 064	36 780	12.6
District 17	260 541	95.3	54.5	708 400	77.9	1 938	43 259	103 316	53.2
District 18	285 121	94.6	60.2	990 900	88.1	1 795	59 396	105 872	53.0
District 19	229 697	96.6	58.1	619 500	68.8	1 594	33 912	83 701	42.7
District 20	247 741	89.9	51.9	464 200	45.3	1 312	27 365	60 076	27.4
District 21	195 325	93.1	49.3	153 000	2.5	798	13 730	36 972	10.9
District 22	251 110	93.8	58.0	219 500	7.4	943	23 314	52 172	21.8
District 23	270 707	88.7	60.1	209 000	4.7	923	23 698	55 195	24.2
District 24	277 637	89.6	55.1	466 600	46.1	1 330	30 677	63 704	28.9
District 25	235 324	93.9	67.0	360 400	26.7	1 451	28 778	70 727	32.2
District 26	241 663	94.7	62.2	487 700	48.0	1 499	32 245	74 758	35.1
District 27	257 231	93.3	53.6	611 300	66.3	1 307	33 372	66 454	33.3
District 28	318 123	92.1	34.0	681 000	72.8	1 302	37 764	57 782	29.0
District 29	209 616	96.2	42.6	379 500	17.6	1 158	18 931	47 499	17.5
District 30	290 214	95.4	52.3	569 200	58.6	1 464	38 659	69 353	34.9
District 31	233 311	93.2	52.9	292 100	13.9	1 161	21 996	52 396	23.8
District 32	209 870	94.7	59.9	390 100	23.4	1 247	22 020	57 177	25.8
District 33	328 288	90.7	48.9	1 000 000	87.4	1 831	65 486	101 573	51.1
District 34	257 743	93.0	21.0	454 100	41.7	1 013	19 341	35 691	12.6
District 35	195 747	95.0	55.2	296 500	7.1	1 189	17 883	53 318	19.8
District 36	349 892	74.8	62.9	213 800	11.5	1 012	23 656	44 446	17.7
District 37	289 749	93.9	35.0	604 700	61.0	1 288	31 152	49 669	23.6
District 38	214 707	94.7	61.8	413 200	28.2	1 285	23 489	61 537	26.4
District 39	228 508	96.0	64.7	571 200	61.1	1 486	32 086	76 910	38.5
District 40	188 054	95.4	33.3	344 500	13.9	1 044	13 851	39 199	10.2
District 41	207 336	92.4	57.5	259 400	7.1	1 216	19 173	55 255	20.3
District 42	233 095	94.3	70.0	350 600	17.5	1 447	26 580	71 902	32.7
District 43	254 377	94.7	40.2	415 800	32.8	1 160	23 201	48 361	20.3
District 44	193 694	95.1	47.3	322 700	10.6	1 088	16 758	45 678	16.6
District 45	277 017	96.0	64.1	648 700	71.7	1 819	42 672	91 848	46.8
District 46	193 810	96.6	42.3	423 800	28.3	1 369	18 988	55 073	20.8
District 47	255 020	95.2	46.4	481 500	45.9	1 222	28 045	58 787	28.0
District 48	289 122	93.0	58.4	663 200	70.4	1 702	44 445	83 425	41.7
District 49	275 385	91.3	59.8	609 500	60.6	1 610	39 856	77 025	39.5
District 50	258 043	92.8	61.3	399 200	27.7	1 266	27 786	65 009	29.0
District 51	220 996	88.2	42.2	264 900	6.3	1 048	17 061	41 561	15.1
District 52	303 518	93.0	52.2	608 800	64.4	1 681	43 395	85 121	43.0
District 53	286 014	92.9	49.9	432 400	34.2	1 342	30 686	65 226	28.8

1. Specified owner-occupied units; $1,000,000 represents $1,000,000 or more.   2. Specified renter-occupied units.

Table E. Congressional Districts 114th Congress — Poverty, Labor Force, Employment, and Social Security

STATE District	Poverty, 2014			Civilian labor force, 2014			Civilian employment,[2] 2014					Social Security beneficiaries, December 2014		Supplemental Security Income recipients, December 2014
					Unemployment			Percent						
	Persons below poverty level (percent)	Families below poverty level (percent)	Percent of households receiving food stamps in past 12 months	Total	Total	Rate[1]	Total	Management, business, science and arts occupations	Service, sales, and office	Construction and production	Persons under age 65 with no health insurance, 2014 (percent)	Number	Rate[3]	
	49	50	51	52	53	54	55	56	57	58	59	60	61	62
UNITED STATES	15.5	11.3	13.2	159 550 452	11 530 544	7.2	148 019 908	36.9	41.9	21.2	13.5	57 499 952	180.3	8 334 413
ALABAMA	19.3	15.0	15.8	2 220 715	190 233	8.6	2 030 482	32.9	41.2	26.0	14.2	1 095 925	226.0	174 524
District 1	17.9	14.0	14.4	310 102	25 734	8.3	284 368	31.5	44.0	24.5	16.2	160 696	230.6	22 768
District 2	19.9	15.7	17.1	304 679	27 955	9.2	276 724	31.6	42.2	26.1	14.0	155 698	229.4	28 328
District 3	20.7	15.5	16.4	323 831	29 524	9.1	294 307	30.8	40.7	28.5	12.7	160 666	227.4	24 164
District 4	19.9	14.8	15.9	292 929	22 341	7.6	270 588	28.1	38.8	33.1	16.3	179 732	263.0	26 036
District 5	15.8	12.0	13.6	343 484	26 057	7.6	317 427	38.4	38.6	23.0	13.9	144 427	204.5	16 939
District 6	12.1	9.5	8.1	345 645	21 473	6.2	324 172	40.6	39.4	20.1	10.9	138 457	198.7	11 902
District 7	29.0	24.8	25.7	300 045	37 149	12.4	262 896	26.9	45.1	28.0	15.8	156 249	229.5	44 387
ALASKA	11.2	7.9	10.3	381 695	29 164	7.6	352 531	35.8	39.7	24.6	18.8	89 047	120.9	12 399
At Large	11.2	7.9	10.3	381 695	29 164	7.6	352 531	35.8	39.7	24.6	18.8	89 047	120.9	12 399
ARIZONA	18.2	13.2	13.1	3 113 634	247 005	7.9	2 866 629	35.1	45.9	19.0	16.0	1 207 102	179.3	119 510
District 1	21.9	15.9	16.0	304 618	32 405	10.6	272 213	33.0	45.9	21.2	16.5	140 530	190.1	18 446
District 2	15.5	10.5	12.1	329 346	26 110	7.9	303 236	37.9	46.9	15.2	13.5	160 723	225.4	13 755
District 3	25.5	20.5	22.3	347 862	35 511	10.2	312 351	25.1	47.9	27.0	19.9	104 068	137.5	18 563
District 4	16.0	10.7	12.4	276 364	25 896	9.4	250 468	29.9	47.2	22.8	17.0	198 212	269.9	11 714
District 5	10.3	7.7	6.9	366 457	22 286	6.1	344 171	40.8	43.6	15.6	10.1	124 104	158.8	6 554
District 6	12.2	8.4	7.5	392 444	24 579	6.3	367 865	44.4	42.8	12.8	12.6	135 221	183.4	8 129
District 7	35.3	31.0	29.1	326 966	33 668	10.3	293 298	21.4	49.6	29.0	24.8	80 224	105.1	23 604
District 8	10.3	7.0	7.9	345 853	20 655	6.0	325 198	38.5	44.6	16.8	10.4	164 540	216.2	8 253
District 9	17.3	12.0	9.5	423 724	25 895	6.1	397 829	39.3	45.8	14.9	17.6	99 480	133.5	10 492
ARKANSAS	18.9	13.8	14.4	1 361 069	91 977	6.8	1 269 092	32.4	41.4	26.3	13.9	673 193	226.9	111 482
District 1	21.9	16.2	18.2	311 435	22 479	7.2	288 956	29.1	40.6	30.3	13.0	184 366	254.8	35 947
District 2	15.2	11.0	11.7	366 272	23 051	6.3	343 221	37.3	43.1	19.6	13.5	154 201	203.9	26 367
District 3	17.7	12.5	11.2	367 327	19 635	5.3	347 692	33.7	41.5	24.8	14.6	149 115	194.2	17 892
District 4	21.0	15.7	16.4	316 035	26 812	8.5	289 223	28.3	39.9	31.9	14.3	185 511	258.1	31 276
CALIFORNIA	16.4	12.2	9.5	19 276 719	1 638 567	8.5	17 638 152	37.6	42.1	20.3	14.0	5 538 810	142.7	1 304 400
District 1	16.7	9.1	9.9	309 279	28 403	9.2	280 876	33.5	46.2	20.4	13.4	177 834	250.3	32 543
District 2	13.1	7.4	7.4	370 408	25 500	6.9	344 908	42.5	41.1	16.4	12.0	146 441	203.4	19 343
District 3	16.5	11.3	9.6	333 051	31 235	9.4	301 816	34.1	42.6	23.3	11.2	118 433	164.5	23 376
District 4	10.1	6.8	6.3	336 148	26 416	7.9	309 732	40.1	45.0	14.9	9.6	160 319	222.8	13 208
District 5	11.8	8.6	7.0	371 947	28 152	7.6	343 795	36.2	43.3	20.5	11.6	133 418	184.6	18 098
District 6	23.2	17.7	15.5	351 414	36 915	10.5	314 499	35.1	46.2	18.7	13.2	108 024	146.4	45 321
District 7	13.2	9.4	8.6	363 115	33 865	9.3	329 250	40.9	43.8	15.3	9.9	118 310	160.6	23 076
District 8	23.2	18.2	18.5	292 598	38 496	13.2	254 102	29.1	45.5	25.4	12.9	120 234	167.9	28 464
District 9	20.9	16.2	13.9	335 764	37 591	11.2	298 173	29.6	42.6	27.8	12.7	110 984	150.3	30 035
District 10	16.0	13.4	14.6	342 527	43 045	12.6	299 482	26.8	41.3	31.9	11.1	110 893	151.5	26 260
District 11	11.7	8.1	7.0	381 554	30 781	8.1	350 773	42.8	42.2	15.0	10.7	121 585	164.4	20 822
District 12	12.4	6.9	4.4	459 202	26 290	5.7	432 912	55.6	35.8	8.5	8.3	102 619	139.4	39 641
District 13	17.7	11.6	8.8	404 477	29 712	7.3	374 765	48.4	36.9	14.6	10.3	101 725	136.9	33 414
District 14	7.6	4.1	4.0	421 521	23 685	5.6	397 836	44.4	41.8	13.9	8.3	110 144	146.3	15 457
District 15	8.0	5.6	5.5	391 490	24 048	6.1	367 442	46.0	37.9	16.1	7.8	91 950	122.0	16 425
District 16	30.6	26.4	27.1	299 658	36 874	12.3	262 784	21.7	41.9	36.4	16.6	90 470	125.9	38 411
District 17	6.8	3.9	3.2	402 774	22 033	5.5	380 741	56.9	29.8	13.3	5.9	80 674	106.6	15 378
District 18	6.9	4.0	3.1	389 191	21 395	5.5	367 796	58.5	31.5	10.0	6.9	101 916	138.8	11 812
District 19	10.7	7.6	8.2	401 664	28 689	7.1	372 975	38.6	41.0	20.5	10.2	87 390	117.1	26 429
District 20	17.7	12.8	8.5	343 887	23 537	6.8	320 350	31.7	40.1	28.2	15.6	104 554	142.8	15 728
District 21	33.8	29.7	25.1	282 366	37 298	13.2	245 068	15.7	36.2	48.1	19.3	76 799	107.8	26 895
District 22	21.5	15.7	16.5	335 644	30 543	9.1	305 101	31.3	42.8	26.0	12.8	106 474	144.0	26 483
District 23	21.5	16.7	14.7	320 836	29 331	9.1	291 505	32.3	40.4	27.3	12.1	110 023	147.1	27 185
District 24	16.7	9.5	7.1	356 327	22 686	6.4	333 641	35.6	44.4	20.0	15.7	128 013	176.2	14 300
District 25	14.6	10.9	7.4	341 133	30 087	8.8	311 046	39.3	42.0	18.7	11.7	92 817	129.1	22 701
District 26	11.9	8.7	7.2	370 757	30 687	8.3	340 070	36.1	41.1	22.8	13.8	112 635	155.2	14 634
District 27	13.6	10.2	4.5	366 696	21 722	5.9	344 974	44.3	41.8	13.9	12.1	108 159	151.3	30 281
District 28	16.4	12.2	6.7	425 647	35 052	8.2	390 595	48.8	39.4	11.7	16.4	88 190	122.2	45 368
District 29	22.2	19.1	12.6	382 050	38 525	10.1	343 525	23.8	47.9	28.3	21.4	73 903	102.8	33 534
District 30	12.4	7.7	5.3	416 987	33 632	8.1	383 355	46.4	40.9	12.7	13.9	105 713	140.1	22 276
District 31	21.5	16.6	16.1	339 050	36 677	10.8	302 373	32.4	42.1	25.6	15.1	90 001	121.9	28 446
District 32	15.0	11.0	8.4	363 204	31 993	8.8	331 211	27.7	46.4	25.9	18.0	97 917	133.0	27 273
District 33	9.6	5.3	1.5	397 050	25 969	6.5	371 081	62.4	30.9	6.7	7.1	112 388	157.3	12 216
District 34	29.5	26.5	13.5	373 931	32 929	8.8	341 002	27.2	47.2	25.6	27.6	74 781	103.8	44 227
District 35	19.2	15.8	16.0	344 062	37 180	10.8	306 882	22.7	43.8	33.5	18.7	74 346	101.4	22 971
District 36	20.7	16.7	13.1	314 280	35 325	11.2	278 955	24.4	51.9	23.7	21.3	153 722	205.9	23 658
District 37	23.2	18.6	9.7	392 247	34 956	8.9	357 291	41.4	44.1	14.5	17.5	91 229	126.1	31 097
District 38	11.5	9.0	9.1	346 100	24 357	7.0	321 743	30.6	45.4	24.0	17.8	105 271	146.2	27 133
District 39	11.1	7.7	4.9	364 669	23 734	6.5	340 935	44.0	41.7	14.3	12.1	100 191	139.8	16 820
District 40	28.5	26.5	19.7	332 591	34 020	10.2	298 571	16.6	44.9	38.5	25.3	66 856	93.6	26 854
District 41	20.6	15.7	13.0	354 846	47 298	13.3	307 548	24.1	45.3	30.6	19.3	83 182	112.5	25 231
District 42	11.4	8.9	7.7	354 696	38 425	10.8	316 271	34.0	45.7	20.3	13.1	98 850	131.1	11 785
District 43	19.5	16.2	11.6	380 444	39 836	10.5	340 608	29.1	49.7	21.2	17.4	90 944	124.3	33 187
District 44	24.2	21.3	17.1	346 906	40 172	11.6	306 734	18.3	46.8	34.9	21.1	82 358	113.4	36 617
District 45	9.1	5.7	3.6	406 248	24 549	6.0	381 699	51.6	38.6	9.7	8.7	102 621	134.4	9 833
District 46	19.9	16.4	14.6	369 516	26 632	7.2	342 884	22.6	49.8	27.6	20.7	71 575	99.7	27 427
District 47	18.0	13.1	10.1	372 957	29 965	8.0	342 992	36.7	43.3	20.0	14.1	93 220	129.7	33 556
District 48	10.6	7.4	4.8	399 702	24 292	6.1	375 410	45.4	41.8	12.8	11.5	116 617	160.5	10 688
District 49	10.5	7.4	3.1	343 398	19 485	5.7	323 913	44.4	40.4	15.2	11.0	108 174	148.5	8 586
District 50	15.0	11.1	8.6	360 617	28 401	7.9	332 216	35.8	44.0	20.2	16.0	114 460	155.2	15 793
District 51	24.1	21.1	16.7	316 735	42 566	13.4	274 169	21.4	52.6	26.0	20.4	106 877	148.2	39 679
District 52	9.4	5.4	2.2	403 027	23 318	5.8	379 709	57.0	33.5	9.4	8.4	102 943	135.5	14 354
District 53	14.2	9.4	7.2	400 331	30 263	7.6	370 068	42.5	43.5	14.1	13.7	99 644	132.2	20 071

1. Percent of civilian labor force.   2. Persons 16 years old and over.   3. Per 1,000 resident population estimated in the 2014 American Community Survey.

STATE District	Land in farms				Value of products sold				Government payments	
	Number of farms	Acres	Average size of farm (acres)	Irrigated land (acres)	Total ($1,000)	Average per farm (dollars)	Percent from crops	Percent from livestock and poultry products	Total ($1,000)	Average per farm receiving payments (dollars)
	63	64	65	66	67	68	69	70	71	72
UNITED STATES..............	2 109 303	914 527 657	434	55 822 231	394 644 481	187 097	53.8	46.2	8 053 346	9 925
ALABAMA	43 223	8 902 654	206	113 008	5 571 173	128 894	23.6	76.4	88 145	6 802
District 1	3 041	621 188	204	11 518	337 273	110 909	78.6	21.4	9 284	10 125
District 2	8 890	2 339 433	263	40 808	1 477 342	166 180	24.7	75.3	29 691	6 929
District 3	5 244	1 101 850	210	15 725	685 901	130 797	22.0	78.0	7 690	7 180
District 4	12 450	1 691 155	136	11 693	1 879 383	150 954	9.7	90.3	15 683	5 528
District 5	6 283	1 043 516	166	19 334	507 359	80 751	46.8	53.2	12 988	6 559
District 6	2 759	414 441	150	2 353	211 764	76 754	16.5	83.5	2 073	5 498
District 7	4 556	1 691 071	371	11 577	472 151	103 633	16.9	83.1	10 736	7 201
ALASKA	762	833 861	1 094	2 451	58 925	77 329	42.2	57.8	2 432	12 472
At Large	762	833 861	1 094	2 451	58 925	77 329	42.2	57.8	2 432	12 473
ARIZONA	20 005	26 249 195	1 312	880 613	3 732 113	186 559	55.6	44.4	31 329	10 245
District 1	13 505	20 238 604	1 499	274 134	1 189 607	88 086	41.3	58.7	15 323	6 574
District 2	1 452	981 592	676	67 103	170 117	117 161	D	D	2 662	13 513
District 3	1 467	3 206 653	2 186	220 098	1 051 870	717 021	57.8	42.2	5 901	23 892
District 4	1 851	1 618 174	874	236 656	927 038	500 831	65.5	34.5	4 673	26 551
District 5	559	39 587	71	22 692	123 985	221 798	26.0	74.0	945	26 995
District 6	459	105 916	231	16 105	77 337	168 490	D	D	295	12 303
District 7	173	D	D	22 562	110 396	638 125	D	D	911	70 065
District 8	455	D	D	16 399	60 936	133 925	70.4	29.6	541	18 664
District 9	84	7 562	90	4 864	20 827	247 937	95.6	4.4	78	12 964
ARKANSAS........................	45 071	13 810 786	306	4 803 902	9 775 758	216 897	49.5	50.5	262 967	20 013
District 1	14 422	7 829 889	543	4 372 332	4 886 232	338 804	87.6	12.4	213 501	29 087
District 2	5 715	1 031 106	180	81 263	377 217	66 005	25.3	74.7	10 237	9 418
District 3	9 735	1 617 495	166	9 975	1 696 333	174 251	2.7	97.3	12 498	6 975
District 4	15 199	3 332 296	219	340 332	2 815 976	185 274	14.7	85.3	26 731	9 151
CALIFORNIA........................	77 857	25 569 001	328	7 861 964	42 627 472	547 510	71.2	28.8	146 919	19 349
District 1	8 970	3 605 203	402	823 662	1 598 258	178 178	80.2	19.8	20 753	19 414
District 2	5 047	2 066 839	410	103 785	1 213 224	240 385	57.7	42.3	5 084	16 453
District 3	6 350	2 502 923	394	1 126 206	2 636 257	415 159	91.0	9.0	44 654	27 770
District 4	5 257	1 451 586	276	204 969	866 959	164 915	81.3	18.7	3 025	15 672
District 5	3 592	544 785	152	92 050	851 570	237 074	89.4	10.6	1 043	10 032
District 6	171	23 658	138	9 578	16 301	95 328	89.6	10.4	240	21 799
District 7	814	154 475	190	34 153	158 078	194 199	55.6	44.4	846	14 582
District 8	1 016	451 523	444	63 093	298 555	293 853	16.4	83.6	379	17 209
District 9	3 238	689 573	213	404 975	1 895 907	585 518	74.5	25.5	4 447	15 548
District 10	4 768	895 191	188	411 475	2 605 175	546 387	51.5	48.5	8 320	16 030
District 11	327	112 764	345	18 602	54 849	167 734	78.3	21.7	219	10 418
District 12	X	X	X	X	X	X	X	X	X	X
District 13	32	D	D	25	1 386	43 320	34.8	65.2	4	1 300
District 14	180	24 402	136	1 370	59 526	330 702	97.6	2.4	116	12 909
District 15	395	122 196	309	8 413	47 578	120 450	83.5	16.5	44	2 921
District 16	4 025	1 389 192	345	718 961	4 429 651	1 100 534	52.4	47.6	11 620	17 396
District 17	74	13 886	188	993	10 881	147 042	93.7	6.3	4	1 466
District 18	523	80 723	154	10 387	186 955	357 466	96.2	3.8	66	13 263
District 19	736	204 524	278	10 694	176 147	239 330	95.6	4.4	6	802
District 20	2 323	1 938 924	835	309 691	3 603 918	1 551 407	97.3	2.7	822	6 273
District 21	5 300	2 806 804	530	1 670 398	9 238 009	1 743 021	61.6	38.4	22 328	21 449
District 22	3 817	673 040	176	413 405	2 735 381	716 631	50.6	49.4	8 027	19 158
District 23	3 373	2 214 121	656	465 834	2 351 633	697 193	84.5	15.5	4 352	13 068
District 24	4 487	2 092 601	466	195 967	2 176 789	485 132	95.4	4.6	4 079	15 162
District 25	505	58 321	115	29 580	80 815	160 030	D	D	186	5 806
District 26	1 885	231 273	123	69 082	1 105 491	586 467	99.5	0.5	134	3 612
District 27	154	4 357	28	1 448	24 375	158 280	99.0	1.0	7	1 167
District 28	133	3 668	28	46	1 907	14 339	33.0	67.0	47	15 759
District 29	59	1 703	29	245	8 994	152 438	99.1	0.9	0	0
District 30	51	2 077	41	592	3 853	75 553	95.5	4.5	8	2 733
District 31	181	3 547	20	2 222	5 777	31 918	96.2	3.8	10	3 386
District 32	58	767	13	128	13 127	226 320	99.9	0.1	0	0
District 33	133	8 247	62	1 982	6 266	47 110	93.0	7.0	D	D
District 34	X	X	X	X	X	X	X	X	X	X
District 35	195	7 032	36	1 442	311 590	1 597 900	7.8	92.2	569	21 901
District 36	1 148	201 280	175	111 349	734 534	639 838	78.6	21.4	1 447	16 439
District 37	23	448	19	439	2 725	118 471	D	D	0	0
District 38	30	1 770	59	108	6 575	219 161	100.0	0.0	0	0
District 39	115	1 527	13	657	9 804	85 251	96.0	4.0	D	D
District 40	16	128	8	95	1 450	90 631	D	D	0	0
District 41	426	30 431	71	8 036	43 767	102 739	D	D	181	9 037
District 42	1 314	106 046	81	20 049	225 256	171 428	41.9	58.1	548	18 880
District 43	46	712	15	132	8 896	193 384	99.4	0.6	0	0
District 44	56	521	9	152	13 299	237 477	0.0	0.0	0	0
District 45	114	48 582	426	5 163	96 549	846 923	98.7	1.3	10	1 615
District 46	41	1 137	28	111	5 239	127 776	99.1	0.9	24	7 942
District 47	43	D	D	944	3 623	84 263	96.6	3.4	D	D
District 48	37	3 114	84	1 638	39 131	1 057 588	D	D	D	D
District 49	935	D	D	6 737	137 991	147 584	81.4	18.6	71	4 730
District 50	4 302	160 752	37	36 291	529 777	123 147	90.8	9.2	388	4 844
District 51	721	557 584	773	462 112	1 955 250	2 711 858	70.3	29.7	2 789	21 790
District 52	227	6 597	29	2 203	31 502	138 777	98.3	1.7	D	D
District 53	84	1 594	19	290	6 909	82 246	99.2	0.8	0	0

Private nonfarm employment and payroll, 2014

STATE District	Number of establish-ments	Total	Manufact-uring	Construc-tion	Wholesale trade	Retail trade	Health care and social assistance	Finance and Insurance	Real estate and rental and leasing	Professio-nal, scientific, and technical services	Information	Total (mil dol)	Average per employee dollars
	73	74	75	76	77	78	79	80	81	82	83	84	85
UNITED STATES.............	7 563 085	121 079 879	9.4	4.7	4.9	12.7	15.6	5.0	1.7	7.1	2.8	5 940 443	49 062
ALABAMA.......................	97 714	1 604 016	15.2	4.8	4.5	14.2	14.8	4.4	1.4	5.8	2.1	64 292	40 082
District 1..........................	15 101	222 746	12.8	5.6	4.2	16.8	12.9	3.5	2.1	5.0	1.7	8 411	37 759
District 2..........................	14 270	215 248	12.4	4.2	4.9	15.9	16.5	3.6	1.4	4.7	1.6	7 744	35 978
District 3..........................	11 156	166 526	21.7	3.9	3.3	15.8	15.4	2.7	1.0	2.8	1.3	5 631	33 815
District 4..........................	12 463	179 660	26.7	4.0	3.5	15.1	16.3	3.3	1.0	2.0	1.1	6 125	34 092
District 5..........................	14 851	252 133	15.8	4.3	4.1	14.0	14.6	2.7	1.1	14.7	2.4	10 887	43 181
District 6..........................	15 760	244 871	6.4	6.3	4.8	16.2	12.0	8.6	1.5	5.1	4.3	11 046	45 108
District 7..........................	13 729	291 057	16.8	5.4	5.8	9.6	17.5	5.1	1.8	3.9	1.7	13 443	46 187
ALASKA.........................	20 752	266 886	4.8	7.6	3.6	12.6	17.7	2.8	1.7	7.1	2.5	15 275	57 235
At Large	20 752	266 886	4.8	7.6	3.6	12.6	17.7	2.8	1.7	7.1	2.5	15 275	57 235
ARIZONA.......................	134 434	2 241 077	6.3	5.9	4.1	13.7	14.5	6.1	1.9	6.4	2.1	96 796	43 192
District 1..........................	11 466	157 456	9.1	6.1	2.1	17.7	16.6	1.8	1.5	2.9	2.1	5 952	37 799
District 2..........................	15 490	209 228	2.9	4.6	1.5	17.7	19.5	4.9	2.2	7.7	1.7	7 506	35 877
District 3..........................	9 585	159 583	10.0	6.6	5.0	14.4	17.7	2.4	1.5	3.5	2.2	6 202	38 862
District 4..........................	12 371	135 676	6.7	6.7	3.1	20.7	18.9	2.4	1.6	2.8	1.3	4 385	32 320
District 5..........................	13 387	173 083	0.0	7.7	2.0	20.2	15.0	4.6	1.8	5.4	1.2	7 189	41 538
District 6..........................	23 999	360 238	3.6	6.1	2.8	12.9	12.2	10.7	2.4	7.9	2.8	17 344	48 147
District 7..........................	13 760	373 352	9.8	6.5	8.7	7.5	12.0	5.8	1.5	4.7	1.6	18 135	48 572
District 8..........................	10 965	142 821	3.0	6.3	1.7	23.3	22.2	3.3	1.7	3.2	0.8	4 779	33 462
District 9..........................	22 925	442 490	6.0	5.4	5.1	10.8	13.1	9.2	2.8	10.7	3.2	22 084	49 908
ARKANSAS...................	64 670	992 201	15.5	4.2	4.4	14.2	17.2	3.7	1.4	3.8	2.6	38 335	38 636
District 1..........................	13 861	191 477	19.1	3.4	4.7	16.4	19.5	3.1	1.0	2.2	3.4	6 108	31 898
District 2..........................	18 662	291 920	7.4	4.8	5.1	14.0	19.9	5.3	1.4	5.0	4.3	11 983	41 050
District 3..........................	18 030	310 866	16.6	3.9	4.4	12.9	13.6	2.8	1.6	4.3	1.5	13 544	43 569
District 4..........................	13 848	188 350	23.4	4.5	2.6	15.4	17.3	3.2	1.2	2.6	0.9	6 333	33 622
CALIFORNIA..................	889 646	13 838 702	8.3	4.7	6.1	11.8	13.1	4.2	2.0	8.9	4.7	797 046	57 595
District 1..........................	15 268	163 696	7.6	5.1	3.1	18.2	21.7	3.7	1.7	4.4	1.5	6 010	36 713
District 2..........................	21 452	217 627	7.6	5.6	4.3	16.0	15.8	4.2	2.2	6.8	2.9	10 472	48 120
District 3..........................	11 542	157 345	9.4	5.8	5.6	17.6	17.8	3.2	1.8	4.0	1.8	6 669	42 386
District 4..........................	18 023	206 851	4.2	7.4	2.6	16.0	14.8	6.4	2.7	6.5	2.1	9 441	45 639
District 5..........................	16 620	225 949	12.4	6.4	4.3	14.7	18.4	3.3	1.6	4.5	1.3	11 099	49 120
District 6..........................	15 122	250 821	4.7	5.7	5.9	11.9	18.9	3.6	2.4	7.6	2.7	12 128	48 353
District 7..........................	13 055	194 774	5.1	6.0	5.4	15.4	16.0	8.9	1.9	7.7	3.6	10 247	52 610
District 8..........................	9 024	107 447	4.7	5.9	1.6	20.3	15.4	2.0	2.3	3.6	1.2	3 446	32 070
District 9..........................	10 525	154 688	9.1	6.1	5.4	15.1	17.7	4.0	1.7	2.8	1.0	6 627	42 843
District 10........................	11 604	177 831	13.9	5.2	6.2	17.4	16.0	2.3	1.4	3.6	1.0	7 329	41 212
District 11........................	16 479	216 313	4.4	6.2	3.4	15.2	17.7	7.7	2.1	7.7	2.3	12 144	56 140
District 12........................	31 647	560 641	1.3	3.1	2.5	7.5	10.6	8.4	2.5	17.1	10.1	52 517	93 673
District 13........................	18 631	286 671	6.7	5.2	5.0	10.1	16.8	3.2	2.1	8.5	3.9	17 696	61 730
District 14........................	18 887	346 162	0.0	5.1	6.7	9.9	9.1	5.3	1.9	9.2	11.3	36 262	104 755
District 15........................	16 241	270 457	8.3	6.4	10.0	11.2	12.1	4.0	1.7	10.8	5.7	19 333	71 484
District 16........................	8 879	144 660	16.5	4.9	6.7	13.4	17.7	1.8	1.5	3.1	2.3	5 585	38 606
District 17........................	20 770	543 339	15.1	3.7	15.4	6.2	6.0	D	1.0	15.7	6.3	62 516	115 060
District 18........................	21 728	362 591	3.8	3.0	3.6	10.2	17.4	3.2	1.6	13.0	13.7	37 577	103 634
District 19........................	13 444	192 660	7.0	7.8	5.0	11.9	10.9	5.1	1.9	10.4	5.3	11 522	59 803
District 20........................	15 920	189 278	7.4	4.9	5.7	17.6	15.8	2.5	1.7	5.6	1.5	7 966	42 085
District 21........................	6 742	100 576	17.7	5.0	9.1	17.8	12.0	1.2	1.4	1.5	0.0	3 793	37 709
District 22........................	13 889	201 048	7.6	5.2	3.7	17.8	18.6	4.7	1.9	4.8	1.0	7 674	38 169
District 23........................	11 945	183 836	4.1	7.4	4.1	14.0	18.7	3.6	2.0	7.0	1.8	8 025	43 653
District 24........................	19 818	236 350	8.5	6.0	3.5	15.0	15.4	2.8	2.1	6.3	3.5	10 634	44 995
District 25........................	11 813	162 984	12.3	5.5	4.0	16.9	11.6	4.0	1.7	8.4	1.8	7 081	43 444
District 26........................	18 344	237 859	9.7	4.9	6.2	14.9	13.1	5.4	2.1	9.3	2.6	12 976	54 555
District 27........................	21 167	251 542	2.8	2.2	3.0	12.5	18.3	7.0	1.9	10.1	1.8	11 831	47 034
District 28........................	23 795	487 645	3.3	1.6	1.6	7.4	11.4	1.7	1.7	0.0	9.1	23 981	49 178
District 29........................	11 557	161 620	16.1	6.8	8.4	13.0	19.0	1.7	2.8	3.4	1.9	7 291	45 110
District 30........................	29 183	378 910	5.2	3.1	3.3	10.5	13.7	6.4	2.3	10.2	17.7	18 819	49 667
District 31........................	12 531	229 413	8.0	5.0	5.4	13.7	20.4	3.1	1.5	4.1	0.0	9 341	40 718
District 32........................	14 707	242 676	16.5	4.4	9.9	13.5	13.1	3.1	1.3	4.2	1.3	10 373	42 746
District 33........................	39 189	483 758	6.4	1.7	2.6	10.9	11.2	4.6	3.2	14.4	9.7	34 143	70 578
District 34........................	23 072	320 138	8.1	1.4	10.8	6.5	15.1	8.1	2.4	10.4	2.1	19 101	59 665
District 35........................	13 018	252 571	12.6	6.5	11.6	12.9	11.5	1.8	1.2	1.9	1.2	10 972	43 440
District 36........................	12 069	160 372	3.3	5.5	1.9	20.1	15.8	1.8	3.0	2.7	1.8	5 419	33 791
District 37........................	20 348	311 004	2.8	1.6	3.0	8.7	9.5	3.9	2.6	8.9	25.5	18 671	60 033
District 38........................	14 479	235 805	13.7	5.5	14.1	13.4	13.5	2.2	1.5	3.2	1.5	9 912	42 034
District 39........................	18 604	245 727	11.1	7.3	11.5	12.8	8.4	5.9	1.5	5.6	1.2	10 981	44 687
District 40........................	11 104	214 302	22.9	2.2	16.6	10.5	11.1	1.2	1.2	1.8	0.8	8 662	40 419
District 41........................	9 626	167 760	9.1	7.7	5.8	15.8	15.5	2.3	1.5	3.2	1.4	6 343	37 809
District 42........................	11 115	144 655	12.7	13.6	6.4	16.0	11.5	2.0	1.6	4.6	1.1	5 621	38 858
District 43........................	14 822	277 580	11.4	2.8	6.5	10.2	12.1	2.1	2.4	5.7	1.9	13 740	49 498
District 44........................	8 578	164 791	21.0	5.3	12.2	9.9	8.4	1.0	1.0	2.1	0.0	7 260	44 056
District 45........................	24 755	388 813	10.3	4.8	8.7	8.8	9.4	7.8	4.5	12.8	5.2	26 074	67 060
District 46........................	17 579	384 764	10.9	6.3	5.8	8.0	12.8	4.8	1.9	4.7	1.2	17 345	45 078
District 47........................	15 238	241 853	8.3	5.3	4.8	11.6	14.8	4.4	1.8	6.1	1.9	12 019	49 696
District 48........................	24 509	317 610	7.8	4.4	5.4	14.0	11.5	8.1	3.7	10.6	1.4	18 593	58 542
District 49........................	20 798	258 966	11.4	4.9	6.5	13.3	11.7	2.9	2.2	11.5	2.2	13 593	52 488
District 50........................	15 532	193 291	7.4	11.3	4.0	18.0	10.8	2.0	1.8	3.6	1.1	7 204	37 268
District 51........................	10 011	135 263	12.1	3.6	6.8	24.1	14.0	2.5	1.7	2.7	1.6	4 613	34 107
District 52........................	28 489	516 152	7.6	4.3	6.0	8.8	7.3	5.9	2.7	16.0	4.2	31 287	60 616
District 53........................	15 672	223 164	3.2	4.5	2.0	13.0	27.3	4.2	2.5	7.5	1.0	9 803	43 927

1. Specified owner-occupied units; $1,000,000 represents $1,000,000 or more.   2. Specified renter-occupied units.

Table E. Congressional Districts 114th Congress — **Land Area and Population Characteristics**

STATE District	Representative, 114th Congress	Land area,[1] 2010 (sq km)	Total persons	Per square kilometer	White	Black	American Indian, Alaska Native	Asian and Pacific Islander	Some other race	Two or more races	Hispanic or Latino[2]	Non-Hispanic White alone	Female	Foreign-born	Born in state of residence
		1	2	3	4	5	6	7	8	9	10	11	12	13	14
COLORADO		268 431	5 355 866	20.0	84.4	4.0	1.0	3.1	4.0	3.4	21.2	68.8	49.7	10.0	42.9
District 1	Diana DeGette (D)	491	788 694	1 606.3	79.9	8.3	1.0	3.7	3.8	3.3	28.2	57.2	50.0	15.6	41.4
District 2	Jared Polis (D)	19 516	765 721	39.2	90.8	0.9	0.6	3.2	1.9	2.5	10.2	83.5	49.1	7.4	36.0
District 3	Scott R. Tipton (R)	128 805	729 368	5.7	88.2	0.9	2.3	0.9	5.5	2.3	24.8	70.6	49.9	6.8	49.2
District 4	Ken Buck (R)	98 685	768 242	7.8	89.0	1.6	0.8	1.9	3.6	3.1	21.7	72.4	49.6	8.1	48.7
District 5	Doug Lamborn (R)	18 818	759 664	40.4	80.8	5.3	0.6	2.8	4.7	5.8	15.4	72.0	49.1	6.3	34.1
District 6	Mike Coffman (R)	1 229	772 966	628.9	74.4	9.1	0.8	5.4	6.2	4.1	20.0	62.1	50.6	15.2	39.5
District 7	Ed Perlmutter (D)	886	771 211	870.4	88.1	1.6	1.4	3.5	2.4	3.0	27.9	64.5	49.9	10.6	51.5
CONNECTICUT		12 542	3 596 677	286.8	76.8	10.3	0.2	4.2	5.5	2.9	15.0	68.6	51.2	13.7	55.4
District 1	John B. Larson (D)	1 749	711 205	406.6	70.7	15.3	0.2	4.9	5.7	3.2	16.2	62.3	51.8	14.7	58.6
District 2	Joe Courtney (D)	5 148	710 798	138.1	86.2	4.3	0.3	3.0	2.8	3.4	7.9	82.0	50.2	7.1	57.0
District 3	Rosa L. DeLauro (D)	1 218	720 986	591.9	74.8	13.2	0.1	4.0	5.3	2.6	14.4	66.9	52.2	11.6	62.6
District 4	James A. Himes (D)	1 193	740 215	620.5	72.5	12.1	0.2	5.5	7.5	2.2	19.0	62.1	51.2	21.5	42.0
District 5	Elizabeth H. Esty (D)	3 233	713 473	220.7	80.3	6.7	0.1	3.7	6.2	3.0	17.6	69.7	50.7	13.2	57.3
DELAWARE		5 047	935 614	185.4	69.2	21.7	0.4	3.9	2.2	2.6	8.9	63.5	51.5	8.6	45.6
At Large	John C. Carney (D)	5 047	935 614	185.4	69.2	21.7	0.4	3.9	2.2	2.6	8.9	63.5	51.5	8.6	45.6
DISTRICT OF COLUMBIA		158	658 893	4 170.2	40.2	48.8	0.3	3.8	4.4	2.5	10.4	35.7	52.6	14.0	36.2
Delegate District (At Large)	Eleanor Holmes Norton (D)	158	658 893	4 170.2	40.2	48.8	0.3	3.8	4.4	2.5	10.4	35.7	52.6	14.0	36.2
FLORIDA		138 887	19 893 297	143.2	76.0	16.2	0.3	2.7	2.5	2.4	24.1	55.6	51.1	20.0	36.1
District 1	Jeff Miller (R)	10 402	743 897	71.5	76.9	13.5	0.6	2.9	2.1	4.1	6.2	73.6	49.3	5.5	39.4
District 2	Gwen Graham (D)	22 309	711 296	31.9	69.3	25.0	0.5	2.2	0.6	2.3	5.8	64.7	49.4	5.1	53.9
District 3	Ted S. Yoho (R)	18 923	716 034	37.8	80.1	12.6	0.3	3.0	1.0	3.0	9.1	72.6	50.0	7.1	49.6
District 4	Ander Crenshaw (R)	4 859	714 880	147.1	77.6	13.6	0.2	4.6	1.2	2.8	8.2	71.2	50.8	10.3	45.7
District 5	Corrine Brown (D)	3 510	742 217	211.5	38.7	52.9	0.1	2.6	3.0	2.5	12.9	30.4	52.6	12.8	55.2
District 6	Ron DeSantis (R)	6 493	736 069	113.4	85.3	9.2	0.3	2.0	1.3	1.9	7.8	79.0	51.0	8.0	35.3
District 7	John L. Mica (R)	1 330	735 643	553.1	80.1	10.5	0.3	3.7	2.3	3.2	21.2	62.6	50.9	11.7	39.2
District 8	Bill Posey (R)	4 538	715 672	157.7	83.3	10.4	0.3	2.3	1.3	2.5	10.0	75.6	51.3	9.0	32.6
District 9	Alan Grayson (D)	4 422	769 993	174.1	73.9	10.5	0.3	4.8	7.7	2.9	47.4	36.5	51.0	21.1	26.4
District 10	Daniel Webster (R)	2 925	758 350	259.3	78.0	11.8	0.3	4.2	2.9	2.8	18.5	63.4	51.0	14.4	35.5
District 11	Richard B. Nugent (R)	6 501	728 133	112.0	86.5	8.6	0.2	1.3	1.3	2.2	9.3	78.8	51.6	7.1	32.6
District 12	Gus M. Bilirakis (R)	2 289	729 937	318.9	88.0	5.2	0.2	2.9	1.3	2.4	13.0	77.0	51.8	10.7	31.2
District 13	David W. Jolly (R)	482	707 503	1 467.8	86.3	6.0	0.3	3.4	1.1	2.9	9.6	78.2	51.4	12.0	31.0
District 14	Kathy Castor (D)	687	757 963	1 103.3	62.6	25.2	0.4	3.6	5.1	3.0	29.0	40.7	51.7	17.8	42.0
District 15	Dennis A. Ross (R)	2 120	724 176	341.6	74.4	14.2	0.3	3.0	5.3	2.9	18.1	62.2	51.3	10.9	45.4
District 16	Vern Buchanan (R)	2 267	744 076	328.2	88.5	6.7	0.2	1.9	1.0	1.7	12.0	78.1	52.0	12.1	27.2
District 17	Thomas J. Rooney (R)	16 498	725 251	44.0	83.9	8.9	0.4	1.7	3.3	1.8	19.2	68.9	49.7	10.9	36.2
District 18	Patrick Murphy (D)	3 917	731 704	186.8	80.8	12.9	0.2	1.8	2.2	2.1	14.9	68.8	51.9	15.8	31.9
District 19	Curt Clawson (R)	1 943	753 542	387.8	86.6	8.1	0.3	1.5	2.0	1.6	19.1	70.6	51.9	17.0	24.2
District 20	Alcee L. Hastings (D)	6 287	745 656	118.6	41.3	51.9	0.3	2.2	1.6	2.7	21.5	22.8	51.4	32.6	40.3
District 21	Theodore E. Deutch (D)	676	742 664	1 098.6	78.1	12.8	0.2	3.8	2.9	2.2	22.0	59.1	51.9	26.8	26.3
District 22	Lois Frankel (D)	448	731 165	1 632.1	80.1	12.5	0.1	2.9	2.1	2.2	20.9	62.1	49.6	24.8	28.1
District 23	Debbie Wasserman Schultz (D)	438	730 033	1 666.7	77.4	11.8	0.3	3.4	4.1	2.9	40.0	43.6	51.3	37.7	30.6
District 24	Frederica S. Wilson (D)	275	741 950	2 698.0	35.9	57.6	0.2	1.6	2.7	2.0	32.1	10.6	52.2	39.3	44.6
District 25	Mario Diaz-Balart (R)	8 373	745 358	89.0	85.5	7.3	0.2	2.3	3.3	1.4	70.8	20.5	50.9	52.5	26.5
District 26	Carlos Curbelo (R)	5 435	749 692	137.9	86.3	9.4	0.1	1.8	1.0	1.3	68.8	20.1	50.9	47.0	34.6
District 27	Ileana Ros-Lehtinen (R)	541	760 443	1 405.6	87.3	7.2	0.1	1.8	2.4	1.3	76.1	16.1	51.5	55.4	30.2
GEORGIA		148 959	10 097 343	67.8	59.9	31.3	0.3	3.7	2.8	2.0	9.1	54.2	51.3	9.9	55.6
District 1	Earl L. "Buddy" Carter (R)	20 675	729 328	35.3	62.3	29.8	0.5	2.2	2.6	2.6	6.2	59.5	50.7	5.5	57.0
District 2	Sanford D. Bishop Jr. (D)	24 932	685 342	27.5	42.9	51.5	0.1	1.1	2.0	2.3	5.0	40.2	50.8	3.7	73.1
District 3	Lynn A. Westmoreland (R)	9 941	725 530	73.0	69.4	24.4	0.2	2.1	1.5	2.3	5.2	66.1	51.3	5.2	62.2
District 4	Henry C. "Hank" Johnson Jr. (D)	1 286	728 367	566.4	31.3	57.2	0.4	5.4	3.4	2.2	10.2	25.9	51.9	16.9	46.3
District 5	John Lewis (D)	686	738 016	1 075.8	33.1	58.1	0.2	4.4	2.1	2.0	6.6	29.3	52.0	8.6	52.5
District 6	Tom Price (R)	774	732 089	945.9	70.8	13.7	0.4	10.5	2.5	2.0	12.4	61.3	50.5	19.1	34.8
District 7	Robert Woodall (R)	1 017	752 996	740.4	58.8	18.8	0.4	13.0	6.4	2.5	18.3	47.8	51.0	24.5	35.0
District 8	Austin Scott (R)	22 563	705 698	31.3	64.6	30.9	0.2	1.2	1.3	1.8	5.9	60.5	51.2	4.1	70.0
District 9	Doug Collins (R)	13 496	717 371	53.2	86.5	7.4	0.4	1.0	2.8	1.9	12.5	77.5	50.8	8.1	62.1
District 10	Jody B. Hice (R)	18 379	713 570	38.8	68.6	26.7	0.1	2.1	0.9	1.5	4.9	64.9	51.8	5.2	65.3
District 11	Barry Loudermilk (R)	2 775	725 169	261.3	73.1	17.6	0.1	3.4	3.6	2.1	10.8	67.2	51.1	12.3	44.8
District 12	Rick W. Allen (R)	21 200	701 628	33.1	58.7	35.7	0.2	1.7	1.9	1.8	5.7	55.4	50.7	4.4	67.4
District 13	David Scott (D)	1 852	741 383	400.3	34.2	56.7	0.1	2.4	4.9	1.8	12.4	28.0	52.8	11.7	51.6
District 14	Tom Graves (R)	9 384	700 856	74.7	85.0	9.7	0.2	1.0	2.9	1.1	11.0	77.4	51.0	7.2	59.5
HAWAII		16 635	1 419 561	85.3	25.4	2.2	0.2	48.0	1.0	23.3	10.1	22.9	49.5	17.6	53.1
District 1	Mark Takai (D)	542	707 541	1 305.4	18.5	2.3	0.1	58.7	0.9	19.4	8.0	16.9	49.6	21.8	52.6
District 2	Tulsi Gabbard (D)	16 093	712 020	44.2	32.2	2.0	0.2	37.4	1.0	27.2	12.2	28.9	49.4	13.5	53.6
IDAHO		214 045	1 634 464	7.6	91.7	0.7	1.3	1.6	2.2	2.5	12.0	82.8	50.0	6.0	48.5
District 1	Raul Labrador (R)	102 092	834 295	8.2	93.3	0.4	1.4	1.3	1.3	2.4	10.4	85.1	50.0	4.5	45.7
District 2	Michael K. Simpson (R)	111 952	800 169	7.1	90.0	1.0	1.3	1.9	3.2	2.6	13.8	80.3	49.6	7.4	51.4
ILLINOIS		143 793	12 880 580	89.6	72.1	14.3	0.2	5.2	5.9	2.3	16.7	62.2	50.9	13.9	67.3
District 1	Bobby L. Rush (D)	669	717 741	1 072.9	41.0	51.1	0.2	1.6	4.0	2.1	9.9	36.1	52.8	6.6	77.4
District 2	Robin L. Kelly (D)	2 799	707 817	252.9	39.0	55.6	0.1	0.7	2.9	1.6	13.2	29.6	53.1	6.9	75.2

1. Dry land or land partially or temporarily covered by water. 2. May be of any race.

Table E. Congressional Districts 114th Congress — **Age and Education**

STATE District	Age (percent) Under 5 years	5 to 17 years	18 to 24 years	25 to 34 years	35 to 44 years	45 to 54 years	55 to 64 years	65 to 74 years	75 years and over	Median age	Total Enrollment[1]	High school graduate or more	Bachelor's degree or more
	15	16	17	18	19	20	21	22	23	24	25	26	27
COLORADO	6.2	17.0	9.8	14.9	13.6	13.3	12.6	7.7	5.0	36.3	1 404 518	90.5	38.3
District 1	6.7	14.2	8.7	20.9	15.2	12.2	11.1	6.5	4.5	34.8	186 552	86.8	44.3
District 2	5.0	15.0	13.4	13.5	12.8	13.1	14.0	8.5	4.7	37.5	216 270	96.0	52.7
District 3	5.6	16.7	9.4	13.0	12.2	12.8	14.5	9.5	6.4	38.9	176 981	89.6	30.7
District 4	6.6	19.4	9.0	12.4	13.6	14.1	12.2	7.5	5.0	36.8	212 157	90.5	32.8
District 5	6.5	17.4	10.7	14.8	12.4	13.3	12.2	7.7	5.0	35.3	208 824	92.6	34.6
District 6	6.6	19.8	8.1	14.1	15.1	13.9	11.3	6.8	4.3	35.8	212 080	91.6	42.0
District 7	6.4	16.9	9.2	15.4	13.3	13.6	12.4	7.2	5.4	36.3	191 654	87.3	30.6
CONNECTICUT	5.3	16.3	9.7	12.2	12.3	15.3	13.5	8.5	7.0	40.5	928 526	90.1	38.0
District 1	5.3	16.0	9.0	12.6	12.0	15.2	13.9	8.7	7.4	40.9	177 981	89.3	36.1
District 2	4.7	15.3	11.4	11.2	11.6	15.8	14.0	9.2	6.9	41.9	178 489	91.9	33.9
District 3	5.1	15.1	10.7	13.9	11.9	14.1	13.4	8.4	7.3	39.4	189 263	90.2	35.9
District 4	5.9	18.3	8.8	11.7	13.3	15.4	12.9	7.4	6.4	38.9	203 552	90.1	49.1
District 5	5.2	16.6	8.8	11.7	12.6	15.9	13.7	8.7	6.9	41.5	179 241	89.0	35.1
DELAWARE	6.0	15.8	9.8	13.0	12.0	13.7	13.4	9.8	6.6	39.6	235 650	89.0	30.6
At Large	6.0	15.8	9.8	13.0	12.0	13.7	13.4	9.8	6.6	39.6	235 650	89.0	30.6
DISTRICT OF COLUMBIA	6.5	11.0	12.2	22.8	14.0	11.7	10.5	6.4	4.9	33.8	164 598	90.2	55.0
Delegate District (At Large)	6.5	11.0	12.2	22.8	14.0	11.7	10.5	6.4	4.9	33.8	164 598	90.2	55.0
FLORIDA	5.4	14.9	9.0	12.6	12.2	13.8	12.9	10.5	8.6	41.6	4 674 255	87.2	27.3
District 1	5.8	15.7	10.9	14.1	11.7	13.4	12.9	9.2	6.5	38.2	183 553	90.5	27.1
District 2	5.4	14.2	14.5	13.7	12.1	12.8	12.7	8.7	5.8	36.8	200 400	86.4	26.8
District 3	5.2	14.9	13.1	12.5	11.4	13.0	12.8	10.2	6.8	38.8	189 870	88.0	24.5
District 4	6.0	15.8	9.2	15.4	12.6	14.2	12.6	8.6	5.7	38.1	171 946	91.4	30.5
District 5	7.6	16.9	11.1	15.6	12.4	13.0	12.1	6.5	5.0	34.0	192 007	82.2	16.1
District 6	4.6	13.9	7.8	10.4	10.7	13.7	15.3	13.3	10.4	46.8	153 614	89.6	27.2
District 7	5.2	15.9	11.9	14.0	12.4	14.0	12.6	8.1	5.9	37.4	216 854	93.0	33.6
District 8	4.5	13.8	7.5	10.3	10.3	14.2	15.2	12.7	11.3	47.7	148 859	90.8	27.0
District 9	6.0	18.9	10.1	14.4	15.5	13.5	10.1	6.9	4.6	35.4	215 618	86.8	24.3
District 10	5.7	15.3	8.1	13.6	12.6	13.6	12.1	11.3	7.7	41.0	167 766	88.8	29.1
District 11	4.0	12.6	6.4	8.7	9.5	11.5	14.6	18.7	14.2	52.8	126 122	87.0	18.9
District 12	4.9	15.7	6.8	10.5	12.6	14.6	13.4	11.5	10.0	44.6	162 306	90.0	28.2
District 13	4.5	11.9	7.1	11.2	11.3	14.8	15.5	12.7	10.9	47.9	132 592	90.0	28.7
District 14	6.7	15.5	9.5	16.7	14.0	13.3	11.7	7.2	5.5	36.1	182 130	84.7	27.0
District 15	5.9	17.1	11.2	13.1	12.0	13.9	12.3	8.6	6.0	37.4	193 404	88.2	26.2
District 16	4.3	12.8	6.6	9.0	10.0	12.6	14.7	15.8	14.2	51.1	135 896	91.4	31.5
District 17	4.6	15.1	7.1	10.0	10.6	11.7	14.0	14.2	12.4	47.2	145 831	83.4	19.1
District 18	4.6	13.8	6.9	10.6	11.3	14.3	14.4	12.5	11.7	47.2	151 693	88.9	27.4
District 19	4.6	12.5	6.9	10.2	9.9	12.2	14.5	16.3	13.0	50.0	140 349	87.5	31.3
District 20	6.7	16.3	9.9	14.7	12.9	13.4	12.1	7.5	6.6	36.6	190 870	79.9	17.9
District 21	4.8	16.3	7.7	10.4	11.4	14.1	12.0	10.9	12.4	44.4	185 714	91.8	35.2
District 22	4.8	12.3	7.1	13.6	12.5	14.3	14.0	11.1	10.3	44.8	145 184	88.8	37.7
District 23	5.8	15.1	8.0	12.6	14.3	15.9	12.1	8.7	7.6	41.2	178 673	90.2	36.3
District 24	6.7	16.0	10.4	15.7	13.9	14.1	11.2	7.0	5.0	35.8	205 300	80.2	20.2
District 25	5.5	16.2	9.1	12.8	14.2	15.5	11.0	8.5	7.3	39.5	181 818	81.1	26.6
District 26	5.4	14.6	10.1	13.4	13.0	14.6	13.1	8.6	7.2	40.1	191 050	83.5	26.3
District 27	6.1	14.5	8.9	13.4	14.8	14.6	11.3	8.5	7.9	39.9	184 836	79.8	29.2
GEORGIA	6.5	18.2	10.2	13.6	13.8	13.7	11.7	7.6	4.8	36.1	2 780 545	85.6	29.1
District 1	7.1	17.1	11.1	14.8	12.4	12.8	11.7	8.0	5.2	35.0	194 438	87.7	25.0
District 2	7.0	17.3	11.5	13.6	11.9	12.8	12.2	8.4	5.5	35.6	186 244	80.4	17.5
District 3	6.0	19.1	10.5	12.2	13.0	14.0	11.7	8.4	5.2	37.0	196 397	85.6	24.5
District 4	6.7	19.1	9.2	13.9	14.2	14.6	12.1	6.7	3.5	35.7	209 130	87.4	30.1
District 5	7.1	13.9	12.8	19.1	13.9	12.3	10.4	6.6	3.9	33.5	205 101	87.3	40.1
District 6	6.7	18.5	6.8	13.9	16.1	15.4	11.5	6.5	4.5	37.5	192 465	93.5	58.0
District 7	6.6	20.5	8.5	13.6	15.5	15.6	10.6	5.8	3.1	35.5	220 866	89.0	39.3
District 8	6.1	18.0	10.7	12.9	12.9	13.0	12.1	8.5	5.7	36.6	190 558	82.6	20.3
District 9	5.5	18.1	9.1	11.2	12.9	13.2	12.6	10.6	6.6	39.7	178 829	81.5	20.7
District 10	5.7	18.1	12.0	11.5	13.3	13.4	12.1	8.5	5.4	37.1	209 453	84.2	24.2
District 11	6.4	17.7	9.7	14.8	14.3	14.5	11.6	7.0	3.9	35.9	196 166	89.1	38.8
District 12	6.5	17.2	12.5	13.8	12.1	12.7	12.1	7.9	5.3	35.0	191 974	83.1	20.1
District 13	6.9	21.0	9.3	12.6	15.3	14.1	11.1	6.0	3.6	35.1	227 101	86.5	26.4
District 14	6.4	19.0	9.3	12.7	13.7	13.8	11.7	8.1	5.4	37.2	181 823	80.0	17.4
HAWAII	6.4	15.3	9.6	14.8	12.4	12.6	12.7	8.9	7.1	38.1	335 539	91.7	31.0
District 1	6.0	14.1	9.6	15.6	12.7	12.8	12.0	9.0	8.1	38.6	170 286	91.1	33.3
District 2	6.8	16.5	9.6	14.1	12.1	12.4	13.4	8.9	6.1	37.5	165 253	92.4	28.6
IDAHO	6.8	19.6	9.7	12.9	12.4	12.0	12.2	8.6	5.8	35.9	445 627	90.1	25.0
District 1	6.2	19.2	8.9	12.3	12.5	12.7	12.7	9.7	5.9	37.9	216 644	90.7	23.0
District 2	7.5	20.0	10.5	13.5	12.3	11.4	11.7	7.6	5.6	34.1	228 983	89.5	27.3
ILLINOIS	6.1	17.0	9.8	13.8	13.1	13.7	12.6	7.8	6.1	37.5	3 379 651	88.2	32.8
District 1	5.9	17.2	10.3	13.0	12.0	13.9	13.1	8.2	6.5	38.1	201 302	88.7	27.7
District 2	6.3	18.0	9.6	12.3	12.3	14.4	13.4	7.8	5.9	38.2	187 837	87.2	22.7

1. All persons 3 years old and over enrolled in nursery school through college and graduate or professional school.   2. Persons 25 years old and over.

Table E. Congressional Districts 114th Congress — **Households and Group Quarters**

STATE District	Households, 2014						Group quarters, 2010					
	Number	Average household size	Family households (percent)	Married-couple family (percent)	Female family householder[1]	One person households (percent)	Total in group quarters, 2014	Percent 65 years and over	Persons in correctional institutions	Persons in nursing facilities	Persons in college dormitories	Persons in military quarters
	28	29	30	31	32	33	34	35	36	37	38	39
COLORADO..................	2 039 592	2.57	64.5	49.3	10.3	27.5	117 480	14.3	40 568	18 079	29 952	10 945
District 1	332 241	2.33	51.5	36.7	10.6	37.0	16 068	12.3	3 960	2 592	4 940	0
District 2	300 661	2.48	62.8	51.6	7.1	25.9	20 242	11.6	1 634	2 213	11 841	0
District 3	282 857	2.52	64.9	50.4	10.0	27.9	17 418	20.4	3 982	3 460	5 041	0
District 4	272 870	2.75	71.8	56.3	10.1	22.2	18 504	12.8	13 075	2 577	3 993	0
District 5	283 910	2.57	68.6	52.6	11.0	25.4	29 229	6.9	12 094	2 245	2 580	10 678
District 6	277 454	2.76	70.7	53.5	11.9	23.3	5 813	32.7	3 009	2 128	0	267
District 7	289 599	2.63	63.9	46.6	11.7	28.6	10 206	28.1	2 814	2 864	1 557	0
CONNECTICUT	1 355 817	2.57	65.4	48.0	12.7	28.9	118 226	20.9	20 059	26 371	48 537	3 977
District 1	279 974	2.48	64.6	44.8	14.8	30.1	17 032	33.0	1 335	6 778	5 649	0
District 2	267 479	2.50	66.7	50.1	11.2	26.8	42 913	10.7	12 975	4 306	16 779	3 977
District 3	278 098	2.50	59.5	43.4	12.2	34.5	26 506	17.9	902	5 257	16 566	0
District 4	262 907	2.76	69.9	52.4	13.0	24.9	14 193	31.6	1 159	4 719	5 030	0
District 5	267 359	2.60	66.9	49.7	12.1	28.0	17 582	28.1	3 688	5 311	4 513	0
DELAWARE	349 743	2.60	66.6	47.3	14.1	27.5	25 510	16.8	6 457	4 591	10 184	283
At Large	349 743	2.60	66.6	47.3	14.1	27.5	25 510	16.8	6 457	4 591	10 184	283
DISTRICT OF COLUMBIA	277 378	2.23	42.5	23.9	15.2	44.6	40 293	7.8	3 598	3 064	24 087	1 504
Delegate District (At Large) ..	277 378	2.23	42.5	23.9	15.2	44.6	40 293	7.8	3 598	3 064	24 087	1 504
FLORIDA..........................	7 328 046	2.66	64.0	46.1	13.1	29.1	431 463	17.5	167 453	73 372	85 243	14 612
District 1	271 005	2.62	64.4	47.9	11.6	28.7	33 436	8.8	10 881	2 652	4 832	8 580
District 2	262 789	2.52	61.1	43.4	12.5	29.9	50 077	6.9	32 671	3 280	10 370	513
District 3	261 176	2.58	64.5	47.9	12.0	27.7	41 066	9.3	21 156	3 439	9 235	0
District 4	272 496	2.57	63.3	46.8	12.0	30.0	15 692	18.0	2 597	2 852	2 776	4 662
District 5	260 285	2.78	61.4	32.6	23.1	31.5	17 925	10.6	10 195	2 281	1 357	0
District 6	286 085	2.53	64.7	51.4	9.3	28.5	12 601	20.3	4 351	3 572	5 748	4
District 7	256 554	2.78	62.3	47.1	11.1	29.8	22 964	15.3	757	3 056	13 306	0
District 8	285 836	2.48	63.8	48.0	11.6	30.3	7 676	27.2	3 105	2 612	1 259	182
District 9	245 209	3.11	71.5	50.3	15.3	21.7	6 353	24.1	3 819	1 838	245	0
District 10	280 952	2.67	67.0	52.2	10.6	26.3	7 989	16.2	3 929	2 605	315	0
District 11	297 719	2.37	65.0	51.6	9.6	29.2	22 596	15.3	16 221	2 953	312	0
District 12	281 737	2.56	65.8	50.9	10.4	27.8	9 031	40.5	1 981	2 902	1 050	0
District 13	310 672	2.23	53.0	39.6	9.1	38.7	13 368	35.3	3 506	5 478	1 751	0
District 14	290 566	2.56	56.3	33.3	17.3	33.5	13 557	18.8	3 483	3 007	3 375	324
District 15	255 190	2.78	67.7	49.2	13.6	25.5	15 125	15.6	854	2 303	7 847	0
District 16	311 660	2.36	63.6	51.0	9.0	29.7	9 740	38.1	2 011	3 857	1 569	0
District 17	275 502	2.55	66.3	50.8	10.7	28.9	21 917	15.9	12 761	3 312	606	0
District 18	292 179	2.48	62.8	49.1	10.0	31.0	8 203	25.5	3 930	1 838	339	2
District 19	303 652	2.44	63.9	49.6	10.7	30.2	12 970	26.8	2 727	2 860	2 688	9
District 20	244 629	2.97	65.2	36.2	22.8	27.8	18 235	18.4	10 719	3 611	214	0
District 21	275 199	2.69	67.3	50.9	12.0	27.6	2 372	52.8	619	1 396	19	0
District 22	307 349	2.35	51.8	37.5	9.7	38.1	9 914	29.7	1 291	3 658	3 672	0
District 23	278 160	2.61	61.4	43.6	12.9	32.3	4 909	23.7	938	1 239	1 463	59
District 24	230 890	3.15	63.6	33.1	23.6	30.5	15 657	21.9	3 004	2 733	3 132	0
District 25	223 881	3.28	77.5	54.2	16.6	17.6	10 777	12.7	5 752	717	596	0
District 26	218 812	3.35	74.8	51.9	16.7	20.4	17 266	17.9	4 186	1 100	2 657	277
District 27	247 862	3.03	68.5	44.7	17.2	25.7	10 047	24.6	9	2 221	4 510	0
GEORGIA	3 587 521	2.74	67.6	47.2	15.7	26.9	261 656	12.5	104 012	34 738	72 288	16 072
District 1	264 770	2.65	67.3	48.3	14.7	26.9	27 128	10.4	10 733	3 028	5 798	5 069
District 2	245 947	2.63	64.7	37.4	22.0	30.9	37 451	8.4	17 145	3 559	7 343	5 167
District 3	257 294	2.77	71.2	51.9	14.7	25.2	12 532	20.6	4 777	2 837	4 020	64
District 4	251 970	2.86	68.1	40.7	21.4	26.3	6 967	17.9	4 367	1 472	653	0
District 5	287 587	2.42	47.3	25.4	17.6	43.6	41 535	5.3	6 731	2 500	22 635	78
District 6	275 326	2.65	66.7	52.2	8.9	27.6	2 854	49.0	89	1 109	620	0
District 7	242 595	3.08	75.7	57.3	13.0	20.0	5 311	18.9	4 093	1 167	0	0
District 8	254 286	2.69	69.1	48.0	16.7	26.4	22 853	13.4	13 355	4 044	5 390	401
District 9	251 634	2.80	71.5	54.3	11.8	24.0	13 544	17.7	4 824	2 514	4 115	44
District 10	243 617	2.83	68.8	49.9	14.7	24.6	24 789	12.0	10 678	2 840	9 699	74
District 11	270 931	2.64	69.5	52.8	12.4	23.5	10 549	14.1	3 520	1 539	4 296	36
District 12	244 477	2.71	66.3	44.2	17.3	28.5	38 079	10.7	15 029	3 980	5 294	5 139
District 13	248 292	2.96	71.3	44.2	21.9	24.1	5 580	21.4	3 437	1 322	0	0
District 14	248 795	2.77	73.4	55.6	12.9	22.4	12 484	21.5	5 234	2 827	2 425	0
HAWAII	450 769	3.05	69.7	51.5	12.4	23.6	44 216	12.2	5 673	5 198	7 540	12 551
District 1	231 099	2.96	67.6	50.0	12.0	26.1	23 047	13.3	3 581	2 672	4 641	5 332
District 2	219 670	3.14	71.9	53.1	12.8	21.0	21 169	10.9	2 092	2 526	2 899	7 219
IDAHO.............................	591 587	2.71	68.9	54.9	9.3	25.6	29 601	16.9	11 275	4 820	7 223	466
District 1	304 513	2.68	68.8	54.5	9.5	25.6	17 566	15.4	7 951	2 375	4 359	0
District 2	287 074	2.75	68.9	55.3	9.2	25.5	12 035	19.2	3 324	2 445	2 864	466
ILLINOIS	4 772 421	2.64	64.9	47.6	12.6	28.9	300 410	22.6	70 828	81 516	92 960	12 483
District 1	265 021	2.66	63.0	35.0	21.2	32.7	12 302	21.7	0	4 063	5 957	0
District 2	258 513	2.69	64.8	37.9	22.0	31.4	11 413	31.1	685	5 037	2 054	0

1. No spouse present.

Table E. Congressional Districts 114th Congress — Housing and Money Income

STATE District	Housing units, 2014						Money income, 2014		
	Occupied units						Households		
			Owner-occupied			Renter-occupied			
	Total	Occupied units as a percent of all units	Owner-occupied units as a percent of occupied units	Median value[1] (dollars)	Percent valued at $500,000 or more	Median rent[2]	Per capita income (dollars)	Median income (dollars)	Percent with income of $100,000 or more
	40	41	42	43	44	45	46	47	48
COLORADO..............	2 276 280	89.6	63.9	255 200	13.6	1 020	32 357	61 303	27.3
District 1...............	351 177	94.6	51.4	282 900	17.6	998	36 736	57 347	26.4
District 2...............	368 687	81.5	66.1	336 100	25.9	1 159	37 696	70 322	33.0
District 3...............	357 512	79.1	67.5	203 200	12.2	836	26 918	49 885	19.1
District 4...............	293 140	93.1	71.4	245 800	11.3	988	31 224	65 595	29.6
District 5...............	314 604	90.2	64.8	222 500	8.3	955	28 796	56 789	23.7
District 6...............	290 406	95.5	65.6	277 800	12.0	1 137	34 607	71 518	33.5
District 7...............	300 754	96.3	62.7	237 900	7.3	1 057	30 102	61 426	25.7
CONNECTICUT..............	1 493 632	90.8	66.4	267 200	16.0	1 076	39 373	70 048	34.1
District 1...............	303 974	92.1	64.8	229 200	5.3	991	35 215	65 352	31.0
District 2...............	301 250	88.8	72.6	240 000	8.1	985	34 533	70 992	32.2
District 3...............	302 123	92.0	62.1	249 700	7.7	1 118	34 430	61 574	30.4
District 4...............	283 579	92.7	65.4	490 500	49.0	1 398	55 765	88 279	44.9
District 5...............	302 706	88.3	67.3	264 800	11.9	980	36 328	67 929	32.5
DELAWARE..............	417 413	83.8	70.3	230 500	6.9	1 024	30 488	59 716	26.3
At Large.................	417 413	83.8	70.3	230 500	6.9	1 024	30 488	59 716	26.3
DISTRICT OF COLUMBIA	306 184	90.6	40.6	486 900	48.3	1 360	45 877	71 648	36.7
Delegate District (At Large)..	306 184	90.6	40.6	486 900	48.3	1 360	45 877	71 648	36.7
FLORIDA..............	9 144 650	80.1	64.1	162 700	7.2	1 003	26 582	47 463	18.7
District 1...............	354 090	76.5	64.1	152 200	5.9	946	26 693	50 926	18.7
District 2...............	340 451	77.2	61.2	152 700	3.7	884	23 286	43 045	17.0
District 3...............	309 080	84.5	68.4	130 000	2.6	877	23 322	45 273	16.2
District 4...............	313 316	87.0	62.5	163 200	6.3	1 039	30 109	54 281	22.7
District 5...............	315 342	82.5	49.0	91 500	1.0	851	17 143	32 781	8.1
District 6...............	372 846	76.7	71.6	168 500	6.8	953	27 353	48 408	19.0
District 7...............	301 228	85.2	66.1	170 200	5.3	1 051	28 029	51 288	21.7
District 8...............	355 549	80.4	70.2	153 600	4.6	924	28 449	47 676	17.8
District 9...............	316 665	77.4	55.9	151 600	1.5	1 096	20 619	45 204	14.3
District 10...............	346 066	81.2	65.5	164 700	6.4	1 027	28 028	51 609	20.3
District 11...............	369 455	80.6	78.6	126 200	1.9	823	23 416	41 172	11.0
District 12...............	342 946	82.2	71.7	156 400	4.8	980	28 088	50 835	21.5
District 13...............	391 351	79.4	63.5	145 200	7.0	965	29 258	45 071	17.0
District 14...............	335 762	86.5	48.3	138 300	7.0	940	25 703	43 758	16.7
District 15...............	294 163	86.8	64.4	148 900	2.8	931	24 934	49 681	19.5
District 16...............	407 974	76.4	70.0	182 900	10.1	1 007	32 059	51 985	21.4
District 17...............	360 575	76.4	75.2	113 100	2.6	822	22 635	42 179	13.0
District 18...............	366 911	79.6	74.6	175 800	10.1	1 149	32 760	52 400	22.0
District 19...............	455 732	66.6	68.8	200 500	15.1	977	33 889	51 834	21.3
District 20...............	295 695	82.7	51.6	115 300	1.6	1 029	17 877	38 582	10.4
District 21...............	332 001	82.9	73.6	218 900	9.0	1 306	31 819	57 016	25.6
District 22...............	405 133	75.9	61.0	244 500	18.7	1 182	39 051	53 536	25.8
District 23...............	379 265	73.3	60.7	243 500	16.5	1 291	32 190	54 650	25.6
District 24...............	277 982	83.1	45.7	157 000	6.3	1 025	18 757	36 660	13.0
District 25...............	264 980	84.5	61.9	212 300	7.2	1 163	22 240	49 544	19.8
District 26...............	259 096	84.5	67.3	231 400	7.5	1 256	22 873	53 204	21.9
District 27...............	280 996	88.2	48.3	265 800	22.3	1 062	27 564	43 957	21.0
GEORGIA..............	4 151 387	86.4	62.2	147 900	5.6	882	25 615	49 321	20.1
District 1...............	314 752	84.1	59.7	143 100	5.0	893	23 861	48 091	17.8
District 2...............	298 934	82.3	54.2	97 600	1.8	687	19 285	34 707	10.3
District 3...............	286 599	89.8	65.3	155 100	4.1	863	24 900	49 833	19.4
District 4...............	280 930	89.7	61.3	122 100	2.1	936	22 724	46 792	16.4
District 5...............	354 402	81.1	45.9	155 200	12.3	936	29 972	44 411	20.5
District 6...............	298 471	92.2	61.8	309 800	17.6	1 129	42 518	79 510	39.9
District 7...............	259 690	93.4	66.2	203 200	5.6	1 061	29 086	64 255	29.3
District 8...............	299 346	84.9	62.8	106 100	1.9	691	20 847	39 646	13.5
District 9...............	320 370	78.5	72.1	148 700	5.3	790	22 306	46 213	16.1
District 10...............	292 764	83.2	67.2	149 300	4.6	775	22 499	47 191	18.4
District 11...............	289 679	93.5	62.8	191 000	11.3	1 007	34 491	65 837	29.8
District 12...............	294 385	83.0	63.5	106 900	1.8	725	20 058	38 144	12.9
District 13...............	280 844	88.4	62.7	121 000	1.8	956	22 852	51 358	18.2
District 14...............	280 221	88.8	68.4	119 600	2.0	695	22 064	46 170	15.5
HAWAII..............	530 118	85.0	56.7	528 000	53.3	1 448	29 736	69 592	31.5
District 1...............	258 008	89.6	53.5	585 100	61.5	1 526	31 570	73 008	33.7
District 2...............	272 110	80.7	60.0	464 000	45.5	1 338	27 913	66 042	29.2
IDAHO..............	685 098	86.4	68.0	165 300	4.8	755	23 938	47 861	16.5
District 1...............	353 223	86.2	70.1	171 400	4.7	791	24 241	48 523	16.4
District 2...............	331 875	86.5	65.9	158 900	4.8	730	23 621	47 234	16.6
ILLINOIS..............	5 307 508	89.9	65.5	171 900	7.8	905	30 417	57 444	25.6
District 1...............	304 253	87.1	59.5	170 300	3.4	881	24 955	48 557	19.7
District 2...............	303 071	85.3	61.5	123 900	1.3	883	22 891	45 505	17.3

1. Specified owner-occupied units; $1,000,000 represents $1,000,000 or more.   2. Specified renter-occupied units.

Table E. Congressional Districts 114th Congress — Poverty, Labor Force, Employment, and Social Security

STATE District	Poverty, 2014			Civilian labor force, 2014	Unemployment		Civilian employment,[2] 2014	Percent			Persons under age 65 with no health insurance, 2014 (percent)	Social Security beneficiaries, December 2014		Supplemental Security Income recipients, December 2014
	Persons below poverty level (percent)	Families below poverty level (percent)	Percent of households receiving food stamps in past 12 months	Total	Total	Rate[1]	Total	Management, business, science and arts occupations	Service, sales, and office	Construction and production		Number	Rate[3]	
	49	50	51	52	53	54	55	56	57	58	59	60	61	62
COLORADO	12.0	8.0	8.9	2 854 920	155 638	5.5	2 699 282	40.3	40.9	18.9	11.6	794 937	148.4	72 872
District 1	14.6	10.8	10.1	449 862	21 009	4.7	428 853	43.8	39.9	16.3	13.0	101 513	128.7	15 986
District 2	11.3	5.1	5.0	434 925	20 957	4.8	413 968	46.7	39.0	14.4	8.4	109 929	143.6	4 959
District 3	15.0	10.3	11.7	370 108	24 933	6.7	345 175	33.1	42.6	24.3	15.9	140 402	192.5	13 941
District 4	9.8	6.8	8.1	396 154	20 333	5.1	375 821	37.6	39.9	22.5	9.6	113 077	147.2	9 018
District 5	12.2	8.7	10.4	358 938	25 715	7.2	333 223	39.7	42.7	17.6	10.7	120 255	158.3	10 282
District 6	10.9	7.8	7.8	419 281	21 548	5.1	397 733	42.3	40.4	17.3	11.5	96 400	124.7	8 955
District 7	10.5	7.0	9.1	425 652	21 143	5.0	404 509	37.0	42.2	20.8	12.7	113 361	147.0	9 731
CONNECTICUT	10.8	7.5	12.8	1 952 827	154 069	7.9	1 798 758	42.5	40.4	17.1	8.0	654 533	182.0	63 259
District 1	11.7	9.1	14.9	388 241	35 662	9.2	352 579	43.5	39.6	16.9	6.5	138 580	194.9	16 626
District 2	9.0	5.9	10.9	389 284	24 762	6.4	364 522	40.3	41.1	18.6	5.5	136 341	191.8	8 256
District 3	11.8	8.2	13.5	397 137	32 019	8.1	365 118	41.9	40.3	17.8	7.0	132 329	183.5	14 043
District 4	9.0	6.4	10.0	396 839	33 594	8.5	363 245	45.9	40.8	13.3	12.0	113 992	154.0	10 248
District 5	12.2	8.2	14.4	381 326	28 032	7.4	353 294	40.8	40.0	19.2	8.8	133 291	186.8	14 086
DELAWARE	12.5	8.5	12.9	472 991	31 847	6.7	441 144	38.8	41.7	19.4	9.2	192 187	205.4	16 687
At Large	12.5	8.5	12.9	472 991	31 847	6.7	441 144	38.8	41.7	19.4	9.2	192 187	205.4	16 687
DISTRICT OF COLUMBIA	17.7	14.2	14.1	379 186	33 594	8.9	345 592	60.0	33.2	6.7	5.8	79 716	121.0	26 782
Delegate District (At Large)	17.7	14.2	14.1	379 186	33 594	8.9	345 592	60.0	33.2	6.7	5.8	79 716	121.0	26 782
FLORIDA	16.5	12.0	14.8	9 503 651	764 681	8.0	8 738 970	34.2	47.6	18.3	20.1	4 223 274	212.3	561 125
District 1	13.1	9.6	13.9	343 635	23 830	6.9	319 805	35.2	45.8	19.0	16.0	156 717	210.7	17 135
District 2	19.8	12.1	16.3	335 989	33 854	10.1	302 135	37.1	45.6	17.3	15.8	135 939	191.1	20 847
District 3	18.8	12.9	15.3	313 348	32 183	10.3	281 165	36.4	44.8	18.8	17.1	152 545	213.0	16 732
District 4	12.7	9.2	12.2	365 418	25 138	6.9	340 280	38.3	45.1	16.7	14.9	126 476	176.9	15 193
District 5	28.5	23.3	28.3	359 396	44 065	12.3	315 331	25.5	52.9	21.6	19.4	130 928	176.4	32 128
District 6	13.5	8.4	11.1	324 561	21 021	6.5	303 540	35.1	45.7	19.2	19.6	203 145	276.0	14 478
District 7	14.3	9.6	9.9	370 434	25 337	6.8	345 097	40.1	45.9	14.0	16.1	128 852	175.2	12 387
District 8	14.5	10.2	11.5	321 616	29 411	9.1	292 205	38.1	44.7	17.2	18.6	199 101	278.2	14 449
District 9	19.0	15.0	18.2	383 126	32 241	8.4	350 885	30.5	50.9	18.6	23.3	126 757	164.6	22 625
District 10	13.4	9.6	11.0	368 726	27 458	7.4	341 268	37.9	45.7	16.5	20.2	159 224	210.0	18 076
District 11	16.0	11.1	13.1	262 357	23 434	8.9	238 923	27.0	52.4	20.5	20.8	271 819	373.3	17 181
District 12	12.0	8.5	11.8	328 382	21 187	6.5	307 195	39.7	45.0	15.3	15.7	178 878	245.1	13 713
District 13	14.2	8.9	11.4	346 789	22 063	6.4	324 726	36.6	46.8	16.6	18.2	180 900	255.7	14 661
District 14	21.8	17.9	20.7	392 573	32 235	8.2	360 338	33.7	47.7	18.6	19.9	127 750	168.5	33 968
District 15	16.8	11.2	12.9	357 961	29 250	8.2	328 711	36.5	43.0	20.4	16.4	134 725	186.0	18 890
District 16	12.0	7.7	9.1	322 828	18 278	5.7	304 550	33.8	49.0	17.2	19.6	217 184	291.9	10 649
District 17	16.6	12.2	14.0	289 403	30 032	10.4	259 371	29.8	45.7	24.5	22.9	203 226	280.2	15 070
District 18	12.6	9.0	8.2	347 439	25 027	7.2	322 412	36.0	47.1	16.8	18.8	180 748	247.0	11 696
District 19	14.5	9.6	9.7	329 860	20 637	6.3	309 223	32.1	50.6	17.3	22.5	201 032	266.8	12 180
District 20	22.7	18.7	23.4	386 717	44 221	11.4	342 496	23.4	54.1	22.5	26.4	120 057	161.0	25 000
District 21	11.0	8.4	8.9	364 298	25 459	7.0	338 839	37.4	48.8	13.8	18.0	161 321	217.2	9 102
District 22	14.8	10.4	10.3	388 944	28 622	7.4	360 322	39.3	45.5	15.3	20.3	152 897	209.1	14 889
District 23	13.6	10.2	12.3	381 957	26 625	7.0	355 332	39.2	46.6	14.2	19.0	116 671	159.8	15 367
District 24	25.0	21.7	27.0	374 242	45 181	12.1	329 061	28.1	51.9	20.0	29.2	105 967	142.8	45 524
District 25	18.6	15.1	23.5	369 468	24 263	6.6	345 205	29.0	46.6	24.4	26.3	116 575	156.4	33 890
District 26	15.0	12.0	18.7	382 697	23 019	6.0	359 678	33.0	49.1	17.9	21.3	115 596	154.2	32 387
District 27	20.3	16.7	27.8	391 487	30 610	7.8	360 877	32.0	47.1	20.8	24.7	118 244	155.5	52 908
GEORGIA	18.3	14.1	15.7	4 869 705	403 398	8.3	4 466 307	36.1	41.7	22.2	17.9	1 676 778	166.1	256 314
District 1	17.4	13.8	15.3	334 316	27 105	8.1	307 211	32.9	42.9	24.2	18.6	126 049	172.8	17 998
District 2	28.1	23.6	25.2	289 773	38 750	13.4	251 023	29.4	45.0	25.6	21.0	137 995	201.4	32 610
District 3	17.8	13.8	14.9	338 654	29 416	8.7	309 238	32.0	42.8	25.2	15.4	137 009	188.8	17 888
District 4	20.7	16.1	19.4	379 598	42 053	11.1	337 545	34.5	43.8	21.7	20.3	103 086	141.5	21 114
District 5	23.9	18.9	20.0	387 880	42 765	11.0	345 115	46.7	38.9	14.4	18.7	98 692	133.7	25 663
District 6	9.6	6.3	5.4	401 466	18 085	4.5	383 381	52.7	36.9	10.4	14.2	88 973	121.5	5 452
District 7	10.6	8.5	8.8	392 781	20 499	5.2	372 282	40.7	40.2	19.0	18.3	82 088	109.0	8 824
District 8	23.3	19.0	20.1	304 908	25 578	8.4	279 330	30.5	43.5	26.0	20.2	135 713	192.3	23 686
District 9	17.1	12.0	13.1	322 450	18 770	5.8	303 680	29.5	40.0	30.5	20.1	159 205	221.9	15 328
District 10	20.2	13.8	15.9	317 430	25 700	8.1	291 730	34.9	42.5	22.6	14.9	132 866	186.2	18 300
District 11	11.5	8.6	9.5	393 299	24 983	6.4	368 316	40.6	42.1	17.3	16.7	102 168	140.9	9 763
District 12	23.5	17.4	19.3	301 092	29 258	9.7	271 834	31.5	43.4	25.1	17.2	131 138	186.9	24 398
District 13	17.5	15.2	17.6	368 758	35 785	9.7	332 973	33.3	43.1	23.6	18.3	104 499	141.0	18 026
District 14	17.1	13.9	15.5	337 300	24 651	7.3	312 649	27.2	40.6	32.2	17.5	137 297	195.9	17 264
HAWAII	11.4	7.8	11.7	702 065	37 885	5.4	664 180	34.2	47.9	17.9	6.1	251 591	177.2	25 235
District 1	9.8	6.6	9.5	360 094	16 123	4.5	343 971	36.0	47.2	16.8	5.8	125 953	178.0	12 263
District 2	12.9	9.0	14.0	341 971	21 762	6.4	320 209	32.2	48.6	19.2	6.4	125 638	176.5	12 972
IDAHO	14.8	10.2	11.8	769 337	42 569	5.5	726 768	33.4	41.8	24.8	15.7	306 264	187.4	30 493
District 1	14.0	9.0	11.3	385 405	22 557	5.9	362 848	33.0	41.5	25.5	15.9	168 132	201.5	15 395
District 2	15.8	11.5	12.3	383 932	20 012	5.2	363 920	33.8	42.2	24.1	15.5	138 132	172.6	15 098
ILLINOIS	14.4	10.5	13.7	6 681 866	538 437	8.1	6 143 429	37.1	41.7	21.2	11.1	2 155 290	167.3	275 671
District 1	20.1	15.0	21.7	352 309	48 536	13.8	303 773	34.4	46.4	19.2	11.6	123 902	172.6	25 992
District 2	21.0	16.4	22.8	345 097	53 129	15.4	291 968	28.7	46.3	25.0	12.6	130 029	183.7	28 962

1. Percent of civilian labor force. 2. Persons 16 years old and over. 3. Per 1,000 resident population estimated in the 2014 American Community Survey.

Table E. Congressional Districts 114th Congress — **Agriculture**

STATE District	Land in farms				Value of products sold				Government payments	
	Number of farms	Acres	Average size of farm (acres)	Irrigated land (acres)	Total ($1,000)	Average per farm (dollars)	Percent from crops	Percent from livestock and poultry products	Total ($1,000)	Average per farm receiving payments (dollars)
	63	64	65	66	67	68	69	70	71	72
COLORADO	36 180	31 886 676	881	2 516 785	7 780 874	215 060	31.3	68.7	165 576	14 897
District 1	24	1 065	44	74	D	D	D	D	0	0
District 2	3 055	926 007	303	116 782	177 941	58 246	47.7	52.3	1 675	5 511
District 3	13 954	8 837 850	633	1 062 127	970 501	69 550	53.5	46.5	18 852	8 360
District 4	15 949	20 596 438	1 291	1 293 158	6 460 512	405 073	26.6	73.4	141 885	17 318
District 5	2 520	1 237 551	491	36 488	83 271	33 044	0.0	0.0	1 745	7 897
District 6	357	220 448	618	4 345	D	D	D	D	1 001	9 351
District 7	321	67 317	210	3 811	40 961	127 603	91.2	8.8	D	D
CONNECTICUT	5 977	436 539	73	9 272	550 620	92 123	70.7	29.3	4 841	9 328
District 1	826	46 562	56	4 128	106 344	128 745	96.7	3.3	325	5 908
District 2	2 762	200 857	73	3 001	272 398	98 624	57.4	42.6	2 729	10 579
District 3	579	35 645	62	1 080	34 176	59 026	78.6	21.4	238	5 409
District 4	348	53 930	155	319	30 068	86 401	55.1	44.9	78	6 487
District 5	1 462	99 545	68	744	107 634	73 621	80.5	19.5	1 471	9 808
DELAWARE	2 451	508 652	208	127 272	1 274 014	519 794	33.7	66.3	9 677	10 553
At Large	2 451	508 652	208	127 272	1 274 014	519 794	33.7	66.3	9 677	10 553
DISTRICT OF COLUMBIA	X	X	X	X	X	X	X	X	X	X
Delegate District (At Large)	X	X	X	X	X	X	X	X	X	X
FLORIDA	47 740	9 548 342	200	1 493 320	7 701 532	161 322	77.5	22.5	40 164	10 158
District 1	3 181	469 042	147	9 215	169 985	53 438	74.9	25.1	6 426	7 377
District 2	4 105	794 768	194	33 990	256 516	62 489	75.0	25.0	5 840	5 720
District 3	8 862	1 290 144	146	107 825	975 689	110 098	34.1	65.9	6 700	7 718
District 4	1 114	95 293	86	781	31 667	28 426	29.1	70.9	242	6 916
District 5	1 419	112 887	80	5 257	243 410	171 536	89.5	10.5	183	5 709
District 6	1 811	228 498	126	29 595	233 438	128 900	93.7	6.3	1 729	12 264
District 7	473	33 415	71	4 545	59 629	126 065	96.9	3.1	43	4 825
District 8	1 122	399 784	356	73 129	203 360	181 248	85.8	14.2	959	29 963
District 9	578	578 346	1 001	32 362	130 432	225 662	67.3	32.7	328	19 265
District 10	2 017	221 769	110	26 061	198 780	98 552	94.9	5.1	366	14 635
District 11	4 978	441 454	89	14 700	170 324	34 215	45.3	54.7	881	8 476
District 12	1 298	182 782	141	7 371	82 447	63 519	45.0	55.0	427	12 948
District 13	87	847	10	101	1 856	21 332	89.1	10.9	D	D
District 14	232	56 265	243	2 466	57 548	248 052	67.4	32.6	D	D
District 15	2 141	222 673	104	19 924	237 271	110 823	82.9	17.1	569	12 116
District 16	670	141 262	211	9 799	90 251	134 703	84.6	15.4	394	39 408
District 17	6 479	2 668 107	412	382 609	1 799 624	277 763	73.4	26.6	4 283	17 132
District 18	1 341	462 571	345	169 758	540 342	402 940	85.8	14.2	1 316	18 533
District 19	480	48 914	102	11 239	73 268	152 643	96.4	3.6	31	3 924
District 20	674	563 547	836	336 357	791 626	1 174 519	98.0	2.0	1 483	23 917
District 21	554	57 082	103	35 053	223 947	404 237	96.2	3.8	547	20 272
District 22	133	2 812	21	355	8 918	67 056	81.5	18.5	46	5 072
District 23	432	6 315	15	1 372	27 072	62 667	88.8	11.2	52	17 176
District 24	40	1 870	47	53	518	12 949	68.9	31.1	D	D
District 25	695	390 142	561	134 835	486 358	699 796	97.0	3.0	344	14 964
District 26	2 382	59 843	25	35 808	551 229	231 415	96.3	3.7	6 009	27 691
District 27	442	17 910	41	8 760	56 027	126 758	97.9	2.1	876	31 299
GEORGIA	42 257	9 620 836	228	1 125 355	9 255 125	219 020	39.7	60.3	142 322	9 793
District 1	2 069	417 353	202	37 955	290 617	140 462	58.1	41.9	4 870	7 356
District 2	5 559	2 470 948	444	D	1 887 305	339 504	70.0	30.0	49 436	14 669
District 3	3 475	447 816	129	6 652	357 673	102 928	12.5	87.5	1 939	4 683
District 4	248	18 707	75	45	2 149	8 664	52.8	47.2	20	997
District 5	30	2 801	93	D	211	7 025	90.0	10.0	12	2 007
District 6	105	7 064	67	245	1 378	13 119	60.5	39.5	28	3 540
District 7	209	13 328	64	81	10 188	48 748	72.3	27.7	37	2 651
District 8	6 419	2 068 738	322	343 268	1 501 791	233 960	71.7	28.3	40 267	11 375
District 9	7 080	666 984	94	4 291	2 135 687	301 651	2.4	97.6	4 110	4 160
District 10	5 566	1 082 225	194	39 355	784 526	140 950	22.5	77.5	9 360	6 138
District 11	936	88 216	94	2 474	140 080	149 658	15.8	84.2	1 056	9 183
District 12	6 035	1 793 019	297	163 770	1 211 704	200 779	61.3	38.7	26 685	8 290
District 13	342	24 390	71	279	5 701	16 671	70.3	29.7	128	3 464
District 14	4 184	519 247	124	4 551	926 116	221 347	5.7	94.3	4 374	7 112
HAWAII	7 000	1 129 317	161	81 813	661 347	94 478	81.5	18.5	5 228	8 325
District 1	291	21 133	73	3 760	28 230	97 009	82.6	17.4	101	5 617
District 2	6 709	1 108 184	165	78 053	633 117	94 368	81.4	18.6	5 127	8 405
IDAHO	24 816	11 760 109	474	3 365 292	7 801 446	314 372	44.1	55.9	99 789	10 673
District 1	11 404	4 227 137	371	612 775	1 790 850	157 037	48.6	51.4	33 991	9 847
District 2	13 412	7 532 972	562	2 752 517	6 010 597	448 151	42.8	57.2	65 798	11 156
ILLINOIS	75 087	26 937 721	359	522 479	17 187 052	228 895	82.3	17.7	553 300	9 829
District 1	191	66 255	347	387	47 865	250 604	91.7	8.3	923	10 487
District 2	1 204	451 866	375	14 622	367 131	304 926	90.6	9.4	7 554	8 898

Table E. Congressional Districts 114th Congress — **Nonfarm Employment and Payroll**

Private nonfarm employment and payroll, 2014

STATE District	Number of establish-ments	Employment Total	Manufact-uring	Construc-tion	Wholesale trade	Retail trade	Health care and social assistance	Finance and Insurance	Real estate and rental and leasing	Professio-nal, scientific, and technical services	Information	Annual payroll Total (mil dol)	Average per employee dollars
	73	74	75	76	77	78	79	80	81	82	83	84	85
COLORADO....................	158 064	2 181 455	5.5	6.2	4.3	12.0	12.8	4.7	1.9	8.9	3.8	112 194	51 431
District 1..........................	28 251	475 845	4.3	4.7	5.1	8.2	12.9	5.5	2.3	9.7	3.6	27 635	58 075
District 2..........................	28 672	345 627	9.6	4.7	4.5	12.7	11.6	3.3	2.1	13.2	3.7	18 234	52 756
District 3..........................	25 238	242 381	4.5	9.2	3.0	15.5	16.9	3.1	2.6	4.2	1.7	9 503	39 208
District 4..........................	18 756	223 548	9.3	8.9	3.9	15.8	13.1	4.7	1.2	6.4	4.9	10 891	48 720
District 5..........................	18 885	243 167	4.9	5.3	2.5	14.1	15.1	4.6	1.8	8.9	4.0	10 308	42 391
District 6..........................	19 139	291 859	2.4	5.6	5.8	12.3	13.7	8.0	1.8	8.9	7.8	16 529	56 634
District 7..........................	18 591	256 120	6.6	10.0	5.4	14.3	12.2	4.4	1.7	8.0	2.1	11 739	45 833
CONNECTICUT	88 555	1 485 426	10.2	3.5	4.8	12.5	18.6	7.6	1.3	6.9	2.8	87 867	59 152
District 1..........................	18 249	364 788	10.8	3.9	5.0	11.2	18.2	11.1	1.1	7.5	3.2	21 562	59 107
District 2..........................	14 194	214 204	12.8	3.3	3.8	16.0	17.7	3.1	0.9	5.4	1.8	9 383	43 803
District 3..........................	16 373	307 075	12.9	3.4	4.8	11.2	20.8	3.6	1.4	4.5	1.9	15 390	50 118
District 4..........................	21 843	321 681	4.4	2.5	6.3	11.3	15.6	11.3	1.4	9.7	4.3	27 026	84 016
District 5..........................	17 505	260 503	11.8	4.5	3.5	15.5	22.1	5.5	1.6	5.1	2.0	13 285	50 998
DELAWARE	24 312	391 636	6.6	4.7	4.1	13.9	16.4	10.0	1.6	8.5	2.1	20 919	53 414
At Large	24 312	391 636	6.6	4.7	4.1	13.9	16.4	10.0	1.6	8.5	2.1	20 919	53 414
DISTRICT OF COLUMBIA	22 210	495 453	0.2	1.8	0.9	4.3	13.4	3.5	2.2	20.2	4.5	36 953	74 585
Delegate District (At Large) ..	22 210	495 453	0.2	1.8	0.9	4.3	13.4	3.5	2.2	20.2	4.5	36 953	74 585
FLORIDA.........................	519 875	7 441 584	3.9	4.5	4.2	13.8	13.8	4.6	2.1	6.3	2.3	312 960	42 056
District 1..........................	16 349	198 521	3.8	6.2	2.8	18.5	17.7	4.8	2.3	7.5	1.4	7 168	36 107
District 2..........................	15 854	195 689	5.5	5.0	3.1	17.8	18.2	3.7	2.2	8.0	4.1	6 947	35 501
District 3..........................	12 608	153 714	5.0	5.7	2.1	18.0	25.0	4.0	1.7	5.0	1.9	5 432	35 338
District 4..........................	20 469	330 920	4.5	4.7	4.3	12.6	14.9	11.9	1.6	6.1	1.9	15 363	46 426
District 5..........................	15 888	272 722	7.1	6.4	7.4	16.2	13.0	3.6	3.0	5.1	4.3	11 519	42 236
District 6..........................	18 133	191 053	5.5	5.1	2.9	18.2	17.7	3.4	2.4	5.2	1.6	6 537	34 218
District 7..........................	20 987	278 679	2.7	6.3	3.4	13.6	12.4	8.6	2.5	9.1	5.3	12 840	46 075
District 8..........................	17 599	207 298	9.2	5.4	2.6	17.4	18.1	3.3	1.7	6.5	1.6	8 297	40 023
District 9..........................	13 078	200 174	4.4	5.1	4.1	17.5	11.1	1.6	4.4	2.6	1.3	7 371	36 825
District 10........................	21 716	391 501	3.9	3.6	2.0	12.0	12.6	2.5	2.8	6.7	2.4	15 001	38 317
District 11........................	13 533	155 082	5.7	6.6	3.3	20.8	23.4	2.7	2.0	4.2	1.2	5 147	33 190
District 12........................	15 965	159 560	4.1	6.6	3.0	19.1	18.2	4.8	1.9	8.4	1.6	5 528	34 648
District 13........................	20 383	276 098	9.0	4.2	4.5	14.3	17.5	6.6	1.9	6.9	2.8	11 557	41 859
District 14........................	23 963	450 767	3.3	4.7	5.2	10.3	12.8	9.0	2.1	10.6	3.7	21 738	48 224
District 15........................	14 234	208 178	6.6	5.6	5.7	14.5	18.3	6.4	1.5	4.9	3.1	8 593	41 277
District 16........................	21 195	221 355	6.4	6.8	3.1	18.3	19.0	3.6	2.5	5.9	1.7	8 286	37 432
District 17........................	11 574	121 417	4.7	5.6	3.1	20.6	21.2	6.3	1.7	3.3	0.8	4 037	33 250
District 18........................	20 258	202 986	3.8	5.6	3.0	18.4	16.1	3.7	2.1	7.2	1.8	8 550	42 123
District 19........................	24 276	279 935	2.4	8.5	4.4	19.4	16.6	3.0	2.4	5.1	2.0	10 856	38 781
District 20........................	16 696	233 289	5.5	6.7	7.8	14.4	16.7	3.5	2.1	6.9	3.9	10 420	44 665
District 21........................	18 417	159 080	2.6	5.7	5.3	20.6	15.2	3.9	2.0	6.2	1.7	5 669	35 634
District 22........................	36 638	392 120	2.5	4.1	3.7	13.6	14.0	5.5	3.2	10.8	2.5	19 237	49 059
District 23........................	27 044	301 762	1.8	3.0	4.2	19.8	13.1	4.2	4.0	5.5	2.5	12 836	42 535
District 24........................	18 292	255 513	3.5	2.3	7.8	11.0	16.6	4.9	2.0	7.0	3.0	13 340	52 209
District 25........................	22 597	260 831	5.5	5.2	14.6	13.6	9.8	4.0	1.7	4.5	3.3	10 830	41 520
District 26........................	15 849	131 974	2.1	5.5	5.3	19.2	15.4	4.8	2.8	5.5	1.5	4 376	33 159
District 27........................	25 422	283 011	2.6	3.0	4.1	16.1	18.2	6.7	3.1	9.1	2.0	13 592	48 027
GEORGIA	220 605	3 551 163	9.9	4.4	5.6	12.8	13.0	4.7	1.7	7.0	3.3	163 852	46 140
District 1..........................	15 275	218 672	11.9	4.1	3.6	15.4	15.2	2.5	1.5	4.1	1.3	8 252	37 735
District 2..........................	13 016	204 557	13.3	3.6	4.7	13.6	19.3	9.3	1.3	4.0	1.4	7 522	36 771
District 3..........................	14 067	215 751	16.0	4.6	4.0	16.4	14.9	3.7	1.1	2.8	2.0	7 678	35 585
District 4..........................	10 871	144 010	11.8	8.6	5.4	16.3	14.4	2.1	1.9	4.5	2.1	5 378	37 343
District 5..........................	21 121	495 572	3.5	2.4	4.6	6.7	11.8	4.2	2.2	8.9	4.3	29 580	59 688
District 6..........................	27 569	451 957	1.7	2.5	5.8	9.2	9.9	8.9	2.2	14.1	9.0	29 599	65 490
District 7..........................	23 572	344 473	7.7	6.7	11.1	13.7	8.8	4.6	1.4	8.3	5.0	16 501	47 902
District 8..........................	13 118	179 785	12.8	3.7	4.0	17.0	18.1	3.8	1.6	4.3	1.2	5 767	32 075
District 9..........................	14 076	181 368	24.8	4.6	4.2	15.9	12.9	2.8	0.8	2.8	1.1	6 594	36 355
District 10........................	12 593	150 051	12.0	4.8	3.6	17.0	17.0	2.9	1.6	4.1	1.2	4 934	32 881
District 11........................	20 395	337 112	0.0	6.6	7.4	12.2	9.3	6.3	2.2	9.4	2.8	18 880	56 006
District 12........................	13 006	202 175	13.0	4.3	3.8	15.3	21.1	2.8	1.1	4.2	1.8	7 386	36 532
District 13........................	10 974	165 846	6.3	5.9	7.8	18.0	15.8	2.6	0.0	2.6	1.3	6 209	37 436
District 14........................	10 376	168 619	28.4	3.6	5.1	14.4	12.8	2.2	0.8	2.5	1.3	5 931	35 175
HAWAII	31 801	519 130	2.3	5.4	3.7	13.6	13.2	3.7	2.3	4.5	1.6	20 847	40 158
District 1..........................	18 046	315 467	2.8	6.0	4.6	13.0	13.7	5.0	2.3	5.3	2.0	13 734	43 536
District 2..........................	13 599	180 153	1.8	4.8	2.4	16.5	14.0	1.7	2.7	3.4	1.0	6 303	34 985
IDAHO............................	43 816	530 490	10.4	6.1	5.6	15.0	16.6	4.3	1.3	6.4	2.3	20 015	37 730
District 1..........................	20 561	223 984	11.8	8.2	4.9	16.1	16.0	4.5	1.4	4.8	1.8	7 793	34 790
District 2..........................	23 009	297 096	9.7	4.7	5.9	14.6	17.5	4.1	1.3	7.8	2.6	11 914	40 102
ILLINOIS	316 120	5 312 290	10.2	3.4	5.9	11.4	14.8	6.2	1.4	7.9	2.4	273 438	51 473
District 1..........................	11 822	188 991	6.7	4.3	3.7	16.2	20.7	2.7	1.3	2.8	1.0	7 744	40 973
District 2..........................	10 359	163 559	17.2	4.1	6.0	13.3	21.7	2.6	1.3	2.4	1.6	6 576	40 203

---

1. Specified owner-occupied units; $1,000,000 represents $1,000,000 or more.   2. Specified renter-occupied units.

Table E. Congressional Districts 114th Congress — **Land Area and Population Characteristics**

STATE District	Representative, 114th Congress	Land area,[1] 2010 (sq km)	Total persons	Per square kilometer	White	Black	American Indian, Alaska Native	Asian and Pacific Islander	Some other race	Two or more races	Hispanic or Latino[2]	Non-Hispanic White alone	Female	Foreign-born	Born in state of residence
		1	2	3	4	5	6	7	8	9	10	11	12	13	14
ILLINOIS—Cont'd															
District 3	Daniel Lipinski (D)	614	730 269	1 189.4	76.7	4.2	0.3	4.7	12.2	1.9	31.1	59.0	51.1	21.5	69.4
District 4	Luis V. Gutierrez (D)	136	725 616	5 335.4	58.5	4.8	0.5	3.4	30.3	2.6	70.6	20.7	49.4	34.1	53.9
District 5	Michael Quigley (D)	248	717 666	2 893.8	81.6	2.7	0.2	6.5	5.9	3.2	19.0	69.7	50.9	20.8	55.4
District 6	Peter J. Roskam (R)	981	734 700	748.9	83.5	2.8	0.1	9.6	2.3	1.7	9.5	76.7	50.5	15.2	65.2
District 7	Danny K. Davis (D)	162	727 478	4 490.6	33.4	49.7	0.2	7.4	7.1	2.0	14.8	27.0	52.0	13.6	63.6
District 8	Tammy Duckworth (D)	532	725 320	1 363.4	68.0	4.1	0.5	13.4	11.7	2.4	28.6	52.5	50.0	29.1	58.4
District 9	Janice D. Schakowsky (D)	273	710 295	2 601.8	72.5	9.2	0.1	13.3	2.5	2.4	10.8	64.6	51.4	25.9	52.9
District 10	Robert J. Dold (R)	776	711 698	917.1	77.2	6.5	0.2	10.2	3.3	2.6	23.2	57.9	50.4	24.8	55.6
District 11	Bill Foster (D)	728	712 657	978.9	63.6	12.0	0.3	6.9	13.8	3.5	26.6	52.1	51.4	18.3	65.4
District 12	Mike Bost (R)	12 971	701 698	54.1	78.9	16.8	0.1	1.1	0.7	2.3	3.4	76.5	50.8	2.0	69.7
District 13	Rodney Davis (R)	15 005	715 374	47.7	81.3	11.7	0.2	3.6	0.6	2.6	3.4	78.7	51.3	4.7	75.4
District 14	Randy Hultgren (R)	4 138	725 522	175.3	87.5	3.0	0.1	4.7	2.7	2.1	11.9	78.8	50.2	9.5	71.1
District 15	John Shimkus (R)	38 062	705 504	18.5	93.2	4.3	0.2	0.7	0.4	1.2	2.4	91.3	49.7	1.6	76.2
District 16	Adam Kinzinger (R)	20 506	699 582	34.1	90.5	4.0	0.2	1.6	2.0	1.7	8.4	84.5	50.8	4.9	76.3
District 17	Cheri Bustos (D)	17 957	701 014	39.0	81.7	11.1	0.2	1.1	2.7	3.2	9.2	75.9	50.6	5.0	72.4
District 18	Darin LaHood (R)	27 236	710 629	26.1	91.3	3.4	0.1	2.7	0.7	1.8	2.7	89.3	50.2	3.5	79.4
INDIANA		92 789	6 596 855	71.1	84.1	9.3	0.2	2.0	2.2	2.2	6.4	80.2	50.8	4.8	68.3
District 1	Peter J. Visclosky (D)	2 997	718 064	239.6	69.9	19.4	0.3	1.3	6.5	2.6	15.0	62.9	51.1	6.1	59.2
District 2	Jackie Walorski (R)	10 253	721 627	70.4	86.5	6.8	0.3	1.2	2.5	2.7	9.1	80.5	50.7	5.3	68.5
District 3	Marlin Stutzman (R)	10 827	734 384	67.8	87.1	6.0	0.2	2.2	1.7	2.9	5.8	83.6	50.6	4.2	72.3
District 4	Todd Rokita (R)	16 453	742 958	45.2	89.8	3.7	0.2	2.7	1.7	2.0	5.9	85.7	50.0	5.2	70.8
District 5	Susan W. Brooks (R)	4 985	743 454	149.1	85.8	7.5	0.1	3.5	0.9	2.3	3.8	83.1	51.5	5.4	64.8
District 6	Luke Messer (R)	16 076	720 106	44.8	93.3	2.9	0.2	1.3	1.1	1.4	2.2	92.1	50.6	2.4	70.3
District 7	André Carson (D)	787	756 223	960.9	60.8	29.8	0.2	2.6	3.9	2.6	11.0	54.1	51.6	9.2	67.8
District 8	Larry Bucshon (R)	18 791	723 064	38.5	92.2	4.1	0.2	1.1	0.7	1.7	1.9	91.1	50.2	1.9	76.8
District 9	Todd C. Young (R)	11 621	736 975	63.4	92.0	2.9	0.2	2.3	0.8	1.9	3.2	89.8	51.0	3.7	64.7
IOWA		144 669	3 107 126	21.5	91.3	3.1	0.3	2.3	1.0	1.9	5.5	87.1	50.3	4.9	71.2
District 1	Rod Blum (R)	31 206	770 612	24.7	91.5	3.5	0.3	1.8	1.3	1.6	3.7	89.4	50.6	3.7	75.5
District 2	David Loebsack (D)	31 758	776 785	24.5	90.4	3.8	0.3	2.4	1.0	2.2	5.2	86.4	50.0	4.9	68.8
District 3	David Young (R)	22 765	801 039	35.2	90.1	4.0	0.2	3.0	0.5	2.2	6.6	84.5	50.7	6.4	68.1
District 4	Steve King (R)	58 940	758 690	12.9	93.4	1.3	0.6	1.9	1.2	1.7	6.5	88.5	49.8	4.6	72.6
KANSAS		211 754	2 904 021	13.7	84.9	5.9	0.8	2.7	2.2	3.4	11.3	76.7	50.2	7.0	58.6
District 1	Tim Huelskamp (R)	136 084	718 346	5.3	87.5	3.1	0.7	1.6	4.2	3.0	15.5	77.2	49.3	7.9	63.4
District 2	Lynn Jenkins (R)	36 631	715 446	19.5	87.5	4.8	1.4	1.5	0.7	4.2	6.3	83.0	50.2	3.0	63.7
District 3	Kevin Yoder (R)	1 961	749 250	382.1	81.5	8.6	0.3	4.4	1.9	3.3	11.6	72.6	51.0	10.1	42.2
District 4	Mike Pompeo (R)	37 077	720 979	19.4	83.3	7.1	1.1	3.3	2.0	3.2	11.8	74.3	50.4	7.0	65.9
KENTUCKY		102 269	4 413 457	43.2	87.4	7.9	0.2	1.3	1.0	2.1	3.3	85.4	50.7	3.7	69.6
District 1	Ed Whitfield (R)	31 286	724 041	23.1	89.2	7.0	0.3	0.5	0.9	2.1	2.9	87.5	50.4	1.9	69.2
District 2	Brett Guthrie (R)	18 589	742 858	40.0	89.4	5.2	0.1	1.4	1.2	2.7	3.3	87.5	50.9	3.6	71.4
District 3	John A. Yarmuth (D)	827	736 532	890.6	72.1	21.7	0.2	2.6	0.5	2.9	4.9	68.5	51.8	7.6	69.3
District 4	Thomas Massie (R)	11 350	748 191	65.9	92.5	3.2	0.1	0.9	1.2	2.0	3.0	90.7	50.5	2.9	62.2
District 5	Harold Rogers (R)	29 099	712 274	24.5	96.7	1.6	0.2	0.4	0.4	0.8	0.9	96.1	50.0	0.8	78.0
District 6	Garland "Andy" Barr (R)	11 118	749 561	67.4	84.9	8.8	0.4	1.8	1.7	2.3	4.6	82.5	50.9	5.1	68.2
LOUISIANA		111 898	4 649 676	41.6	62.8	32.3	0.6	1.8	0.9	1.7	4.8	59.2	51.1	4.2	77.7
District 1	Steve Scalise (R)	10 438	796 858	76.3	79.1	13.6	1.4	2.6	1.4	2.0	9.1	71.9	51.4	7.5	73.3
District 2	Cedric Richmond (D)	3 285	775 807	236.2	32.1	62.3	0.2	2.4	1.5	1.4	5.6	28.6	51.8	5.6	78.2
District 3	Charles W. Boustany Jr. (R)	18 087	777 665	43.0	70.8	25.0	0.3	1.5	0.5	1.9	3.6	68.0	51.2	3.2	83.0
District 4	John Fleming (R)	32 207	756 663	23.5	61.2	33.6	0.7	1.0	1.1	2.2	4.0	58.7	50.6	2.4	74.2
District 5	Ralph Lee Abraham (R)	37 433	750 819	20.1	61.6	35.6	0.4	0.7	0.3	1.3	2.0	60.1	50.3	1.9	80.5
District 6	Garret Graves (R)	10 448	791 864	75.8	71.1	24.5	0.3	2.2	0.6	1.3	4.3	67.5	51.5	4.3	77.3
MAINE		79 883	1 330 089	16.7	94.8	1.2	0.6	1.1	0.2	2.1	1.5	93.7	51.3	3.7	63.3
District 1	Chellie Pingree (D)	8 509	673 835	79.2	94.5	1.7	0.4	1.4	0.3	1.8	1.7	93.0	51.5	4.9	56.7
District 2	Bruce Poliquin (R)	71 373	656 254	9.2	95.1	0.8	0.8	0.8	0.2	2.4	1.2	94.3	51.1	2.6	70.2
MARYLAND		25 142	5 976 407	237.7	57.4	29.7	0.2	6.2	3.5	2.9	9.3	52.4	51.5	14.9	47.5
District 1	Andrew Harris (R)	10 301	728 405	70.7	82.8	12.2	0.1	2.5	0.7	1.6	3.6	80.2	50.9	5.2	61.3
District 2	C. A. Dutch Ruppersberger (D)	904	743 321	822.3	55.6	33.9	0.2	5.3	2.0	3.0	6.6	51.9	51.9	11.9	61.7
District 3	John P. Sarbanes (D)	788	768 378	975.1	63.1	23.5	0.1	7.6	2.4	3.2	8.5	58.1	52.9	16.3	49.9
District 4	Donna F. Edwards (D)	771	742 761	963.4	34.2	52.6	0.2	2.8	7.9	2.2	15.7	26.9	52.0	18.9	30.7
District 5	Steny H. Hoyer (D)	3 836	753 079	196.3	51.7	37.6	0.3	4.3	2.3	3.7	8.0	46.8	50.5	11.3	38.0
District 6	John K. Delaney (D)	5 051	755 369	149.5	68.0	12.3	0.4	10.9	4.4	4.0	12.8	60.9	50.2	20.5	43.7
District 7	Elijah E. Cummings (D)	1 264	738 431	584.2	35.9	53.7	0.3	6.7	1.1	2.4	4.0	33.5	52.0	10.5	62.6
District 8	Chris Van Hollen (D)	2 227	746 663	335.3	68.2	12.1	0.2	9.5	7.2	2.8	15.0	61.4	51.9	24.2	32.8
MASSACHUSETTS		20 202	6 745 408	333.9	79.3	7.1	0.2	6.1	4.1	3.1	10.8	73.8	51.5	15.7	61.8
District 1	Richard E. Neal (D)	6 087	733 426	120.5	83.8	6.4	0.3	1.9	5.2	2.3	16.7	73.5	52.1	7.4	67.0
District 2	James P. McGovern (D)	4 216	736 475	174.7	84.8	5.0	0.2	5.3	1.6	3.1	9.3	78.7	50.7	12.0	65.3
District 3	Niki Tsongas (D)	1 963	755 778	385.0	76.7	2.6	0.4	7.4	9.8	3.1	19.1	69.1	50.7	16.1	61.5
District 4	Joseph P. Kennedy III (D)	1 731	748 190	432.2	87.4	2.9	0.1	5.8	1.4	2.5	4.2	84.8	51.7	12.7	60.0
District 5	Katherine Clark (D)	687	755 944	1 100.4	78.4	5.3	0.0	11.5	2.0	2.7	8.7	72.3	51.7	23.2	53.8
District 6	Seth Moulton (D)	1 364	757 309	555.2	85.6	3.0	0.2	4.1	4.7	2.3	8.2	82.9	51.6	13.1	69.6
District 7	Michael E. Capuano (D)	162	769 929	4 752.6	51.3	24.9	0.3	9.9	6.5	7.1	20.8	42.2	51.5	30.9	41.8
District 8	Stephen F. Lynch (D)	845	751 768	889.7	78.0	9.9	0.2	7.5	1.9	2.4	5.3	75.1	51.8	16.2	66.4
District 9	William R. Keating (D)	3 146	736 589	234.1	88.5	3.2	0.3	1.4	4.1	2.5	4.8	86.8	52.0	9.1	71.5

1. Dry land or land partially or temporarily covered by water.   2. May be of any race.

Table E. Congressional Districts 114th Congress — **Age and Education**

STATE District	Population and population characteristics, 2014 (cont.)										Education, 2014		
	Age (percent)											Attainment[2] (percent)	
	Under 5 years	5 to 17 years	18 to 24 years	25 to 34 years	35 to 44 years	45 to 54 years	55 to 64 years	65 to 74 years	75 years and over	Median age	Total Enrollment[1]	High school graduate or more	Bachelor's degree or more
	15	16	17	18	19	20	21	22	23	24	25	26	27
ILLINOIS—Cont'd													
District 3	6.4	17.3	9.6	13.2	13.8	13.5	12.6	7.8	5.8	37.5	195 552	84.8	26.2
District 4	7.4	19.3	10.2	18.3	14.6	11.5	9.7	4.9	3.9	31.9	203 564	69.1	21.6
District 5	6.8	12.4	9.0	21.8	14.6	12.8	10.7	6.2	5.6	35.0	159 181	91.4	52.9
District 6	5.3	18.3	7.8	11.4	12.6	16.6	14.0	8.3	5.6	41.2	193 582	94.4	50.8
District 7	6.5	14.6	11.7	19.6	13.2	11.9	10.9	6.9	4.6	33.6	188 768	84.1	39.4
District 8	6.7	17.2	8.6	15.0	14.6	13.8	12.1	7.2	4.9	36.7	180 620	85.3	32.5
District 9	5.5	15.3	8.0	14.5	13.9	14.1	12.7	8.2	7.7	39.7	178 535	92.2	52.8
District 10	6.3	18.7	9.4	11.9	13.3	14.3	12.8	7.3	6.0	38.1	191 996	88.6	44.0
District 11	6.9	19.9	9.9	13.5	15.0	13.7	11.5	5.7	4.0	34.9	202 761	86.4	35.0
District 12	6.0	16.2	9.8	13.1	12.1	13.9	13.3	8.5	7.0	39.3	176 129	88.6	21.0
District 13	5.6	15.0	15.4	12.9	11.6	11.9	12.5	8.2	6.9	35.9	214 561	91.1	29.8
District 14	5.5	20.4	8.2	10.1	14.0	16.3	13.0	7.8	4.7	39.5	209 737	93.6	39.3
District 15	5.8	16.8	9.1	11.9	11.6	13.4	13.9	9.2	8.1	40.5	167 377	88.8	18.2
District 16	5.6	16.8	9.9	11.6	11.8	14.3	13.5	9.2	7.4	40.3	180 637	90.5	21.8
District 17	6.1	16.7	9.7	11.8	12.1	12.8	13.5	9.5	7.7	39.7	171 233	87.5	18.4
District 18	5.6	16.6	9.6	12.0	12.0	13.9	13.7	9.0	7.7	40.4	176 279	93.3	31.9
INDIANA	6.3	17.7	10.2	12.8	12.6	13.5	12.7	8.2	6.2	37.4	1 727 143	88.4	24.7
District 1	6.1	17.7	9.0	12.4	12.9	13.6	13.5	8.3	6.3	38.9	185 382	88.2	22.0
District 2	6.5	18.5	9.7	12.3	12.3	13.1	12.9	8.1	6.6	37.1	183 116	86.5	20.9
District 3	6.9	18.9	9.3	12.3	12.4	13.0	12.8	8.0	6.2	37.0	190 041	87.8	23.0
District 4	5.7	17.4	12.4	12.2	12.5	13.1	12.3	8.0	6.2	37.0	209 465	90.1	24.6
District 5	6.6	18.4	7.8	13.4	13.9	14.1	12.3	7.7	5.8	37.9	189 471	92.9	43.9
District 6	5.6	16.9	10.3	11.4	12.3	14.0	13.3	9.3	6.9	40.0	182 144	89.4	20.4
District 7	7.6	18.1	10.4	16.3	12.8	13.0	11.2	6.1	4.4	33.4	205 238	82.4	21.8
District 8	5.9	16.7	10.1	12.2	12.1	13.5	13.5	9.0	6.9	39.3	181 042	89.0	19.3
District 9	6.0	16.3	12.2	12.4	12.2	13.6	12.6	8.6	6.0	37.6	201 244	89.7	25.2
IOWA	6.2	17.1	10.3	12.6	11.8	13.2	13.1	8.3	7.5	38.2	804 095	92.1	27.7
District 1	6.1	16.9	10.3	12.3	11.4	13.4	13.2	8.6	7.9	38.6	194 141	92.7	26.0
District 2	6.1	16.6	10.9	12.4	11.9	13.2	13.2	8.6	7.2	38.4	204 940	92.3	28.2
District 3	6.9	18.2	8.5	14.0	13.1	13.5	12.2	7.5	6.0	37.0	204 714	92.3	32.2
District 4	5.8	16.9	11.5	11.4	10.8	12.5	13.7	8.6	8.9	39.1	200 300	91.2	23.9
KANSAS	6.9	18.0	10.3	13.3	12.1	12.6	12.4	7.8	6.6	36.2	785 489	90.3	31.5
District 1	7.0	17.2	12.6	13.0	10.9	11.6	12.2	8.0	7.6	35.1	195 307	87.5	24.3
District 2	6.3	17.0	11.7	12.4	11.6	12.6	13.1	8.6	6.9	37.2	197 463	91.7	27.4
District 3	7.0	19.0	8.1	14.3	13.6	13.5	12.0	7.1	5.3	36.2	198 827	92.2	45.1
District 4	7.1	18.7	9.1	13.5	12.1	12.5	12.8	7.7	6.5	36.4	193 892	89.6	28.3
KENTUCKY	6.2	16.8	9.8	12.8	12.7	13.9	13.1	8.7	6.1	38.5	1 078 943	84.5	22.2
District 1	6.4	16.6	9.8	11.9	11.7	13.3	13.4	9.6	7.1	39.5	167 343	82.7	15.5
District 2	6.2	17.6	10.2	12.3	12.5	14.1	12.5	8.6	5.9	37.7	191 901	85.6	18.9
District 3	6.4	16.1	9.0	14.5	12.8	13.4	13.3	8.2	6.4	37.7	180 386	88.2	31.0
District 4	6.5	18.2	8.3	12.7	12.9	14.6	13.1	8.3	5.4	38.2	184 611	88.0	25.5
District 5	5.6	16.0	9.0	12.0	12.9	14.3	13.8	9.9	6.4	41.0	156 592	74.4	11.6
District 6	6.2	16.1	12.2	13.1	13.2	13.6	12.6	7.9	5.2	36.9	198 110	87.7	30.6
LOUISIANA	6.6	17.4	10.2	14.2	12.5	13.0	12.6	8.0	5.6	36.1	1 179 507	83.6	22.9
District 1	6.1	17.1	9.5	14.3	12.3	13.4	13.2	8.4	5.8	37.3	202 668	87.1	29.1
District 2	6.6	16.2	10.1	16.1	12.8	13.2	12.8	7.5	4.7	35.7	193 532	82.5	22.4
District 3	6.8	18.4	9.8	14.4	12.1	13.0	12.5	7.6	5.4	35.4	197 237	81.5	20.4
District 4	7.0	17.8	9.9	13.3	12.3	12.5	12.3	8.5	6.2	36.3	187 411	83.5	18.6
District 5	6.4	17.5	10.6	12.7	12.4	12.8	12.7	8.6	6.3	37.1	185 352	79.8	17.2
District 6	6.5	17.7	11.3	14.3	12.8	12.9	12.3	7.5	4.9	35.2	213 307	86.8	29.1
MAINE	4.7	14.7	8.5	11.5	11.8	15.1	15.5	10.5	7.7	44.1	296 931	91.7	29.4
District 1	4.7	14.7	8.4	11.8	12.0	15.3	15.1	10.3	7.6	43.7	149 989	93.2	36.2
District 2	4.7	14.5	8.6	11.1	11.5	15.0	15.9	10.8	7.8	44.6	146 942	90.2	22.3
MARYLAND	6.1	16.4	9.4	13.8	12.9	14.7	12.8	8.0	5.7	38.3	1 563 158	89.6	38.2
District 1	5.2	16.5	9.6	11.0	11.3	15.1	14.1	10.2	7.0	42.1	178 484	90.2	30.3
District 2	6.6	16.3	10.1	15.2	12.9	13.9	12.4	7.3	5.2	36.1	188 861	87.7	29.4
District 3	6.1	15.3	9.4	16.5	12.8	13.4	12.5	7.7	6.2	36.9	204 879	92.2	46.8
District 4	6.9	16.6	8.8	14.9	14.2	14.3	12.1	7.3	4.8	36.9	188 136	85.9	31.3
District 5	5.7	17.5	10.4	12.8	12.7	16.2	12.8	7.7	4.4	38.3	210 481	91.4	33.9
District 6	6.8	16.9	8.4	13.2	13.7	15.8	12.3	7.6	5.5	38.7	198 037	90.3	41.6
District 7	6.0	15.8	10.6	14.6	12.1	14.2	12.7	7.9	5.9	37.4	199 194	88.3	37.4
District 8	5.8	16.8	7.9	12.5	13.5	14.5	13.6	8.4	7.0	40.4	195 086	90.7	54.1
MASSACHUSETTS	5.4	15.2	10.4	13.7	12.4	14.6	13.1	8.4	6.7	39.4	1 737 678	89.7	41.2
District 1	5.3	15.8	10.3	12.1	11.5	14.3	14.2	9.2	7.2	41.0	182 783	86.8	28.7
District 2	5.2	15.3	13.0	12.1	11.7	14.9	13.6	7.9	6.3	39.1	204 942	90.4	36.8
District 3	6.2	17.0	9.2	12.7	13.0	15.7	12.9	7.9	5.5	38.7	195 317	87.7	37.0
District 4	5.2	17.4	9.7	10.8	13.0	16.0	13.6	8.3	6.2	41.0	202 110	92.8	48.7
District 5	6.0	14.1	9.4	15.3	13.8	14.0	12.4	8.0	6.9	38.7	194 339	92.8	54.1
District 6	5.1	15.6	8.8	11.6	11.9	16.2	14.6	8.7	7.6	42.7	182 611	92.4	42.9
District 7	5.8	12.1	16.3	22.6	12.8	11.1	9.5	5.5	4.2	31.3	233 254	83.3	43.0
District 8	5.4	14.5	8.1	16.0	12.8	14.1	12.9	8.8	7.3	39.7	178 307	91.6	44.2
District 9	4.7	15.1	8.5	10.3	11.4	15.2	14.8	11.2	9.0	45.1	164 015	89.1	34.3

1. All persons 3 years old and over enrolled in nursery school through college and graduate or professional school.   2. Persons 25 years old and over.

Table E. Congressional Districts 114th Congress — **Households and Group Quarters**

STATE District	Households, 2014						Group quarters, 2010					
	Number	Average household size	Family households (percent)	Married-couple family (percent)	Female family householder[1]	One person households (percent)	Total in group quarters, 2014	Percent 65 years and over	Persons in correctional institutions	Persons in nursing facilities	Persons in college dormitories	Persons in military quarters
	28	29	30	31	32	33	34	35	36	37	38	39
ILLINOIS—Cont'd												
District 3	245 112	2.93	71.2	52.2	12.7	23.9	11 082	30.2	3 160	3 740	1 890	0
District 4	223 752	3.22	68.5	42.4	17.3	22.7	4 063	34.4	1	1 268	285	0
District 5	294 812	2.39	52.9	41.4	7.9	35.1	11 617	32.7	0	3 882	4 823	0
District 6	265 609	2.73	73.6	62.9	7.4	22.0	8 996	36.8	786	4 034	3 517	0
District 7	286 948	2.44	52.2	27.7	19.4	39.7	27 298	6.3	11 612	3 240	7 992	16
District 8	253 238	2.84	70.1	53.6	11.5	24.3	4 899	45.7	0	2 564	744	0
District 9	280 810	2.45	58.1	46.5	8.2	34.8	22 793	27.4	31	8 543	8 803	0
District 10	244 599	2.82	72.6	57.5	11.0	23.6	20 946	19.5	704	5 665	2 088	12 155
District 11	236 716	2.98	73.1	55.2	13.2	21.7	6 722	33.9	1 085	2 891	1 495	0
District 12	273 446	2.48	63.0	44.9	14.0	31.7	22 226	22.6	10 700	5 209	3 332	307
District 13	285 134	2.37	58.0	42.8	11.1	33.0	40 937	12.5	5 125	5 481	27 454	0
District 14	252 091	2.86	74.9	62.3	8.3	20.5	4 633	33.0	1 364	1 562	158	0
District 15	274 400	2.48	66.3	50.3	10.6	28.7	26 242	23.2	12 642	6 376	3 900	0
District 16	268 332	2.54	66.1	51.1	10.7	27.8	18 909	26.0	6 821	5 619	6 178	0
District 17	280 965	2.41	62.0	43.5	13.7	32.0	23 197	21.2	8 864	5 921	5 835	0
District 18	282 923	2.43	65.2	53.1	8.4	29.2	22 135	27.7	7 248	6 421	6 455	5
INDIANA	2 502 739	2.56	66.2	48.7	12.7	27.7	189 082	20.5	48 694	41 158	75 434	228
District 1	265 908	2.63	68.9	46.5	16.4	26.2	17 482	19.0	7 380	3 116	3 194	0
District 2	268 091	2.61	68.0	51.1	12.7	26.6	21 682	20.0	5 936	4 482	8 659	0
District 3	278 743	2.58	69.3	52.9	12.0	26.5	13 980	33.2	2 229	4 852	3 948	0
District 4	277 447	2.57	66.7	51.2	11.0	26.1	29 317	15.3	7 233	4 934	15 651	0
District 5	290 210	2.51	67.0	53.2	10.4	27.5	15 785	25.1	4 416	4 444	5 257	0
District 6	280 605	2.49	67.5	50.4	11.1	26.7	21 333	23.8	5 096	5 532	8 541	178
District 7	282 965	2.62	58.0	33.7	18.3	33.5	15 385	18.3	3 216	3 152	5 162	0
District 8	281 213	2.46	65.2	49.7	10.8	29.1	30 178	19.4	10 561	5 980	10 509	50
District 9	277 557	2.57	65.6	49.8	11.6	26.9	23 940	17.9	2 627	4 666	14 513	0
IOWA	1 241 471	2.42	64.6	51.3	8.9	28.7	99 927	26.1	13 309	26 871	44 574	3
District 1	311 138	2.39	65.8	52.6	8.9	28.4	26 709	26.1	2 415	7 519	13 934	3
District 2	308 412	2.44	63.1	49.8	8.9	29.7	25 226	21.8	5 185	5 702	11 804	0
District 3	312 956	2.50	66.3	51.7	9.8	27.1	17 186	27.7	3 690	5 218	5 248	0
District 4	308 965	2.36	63.0	51.0	8.0	29.8	30 806	29.1	2 019	8 432	13 588	0
KANSAS	1 109 280	2.55	65.7	50.9	10.1	28.9	79 124	24.4	18 009	20 672	27 754	3 943
District 1	274 215	2.51	65.0	50.6	9.4	29.5	29 081	23.2	5 306	7 084	10 873	3 425
District 2	277 280	2.48	64.0	50.1	9.6	29.9	29 094	17.4	7 436	5 478	12 652	192
District 3	285 307	2.60	67.7	52.5	10.5	26.8	6 231	49.6	1 355	3 598	544	0
District 4	272 478	2.59	66.0	50.4	11.0	29.5	14 718	29.4	3 912	4 512	3 685	326
KENTUCKY	1 712 094	2.50	65.7	48.4	12.6	28.5	130 347	19.2	41 122	26 044	36 340	5 856
District 1	282 156	2.48	67.5	51.2	11.7	28.9	25 270	20.4	7 869	5 548	4 101	3 843
District 2	277 832	2.60	69.7	53.5	11.9	25.7	21 175	21.3	4 501	4 378	7 527	2 013
District 3	300 489	2.40	58.3	39.3	13.9	34.4	16 668	30.7	2 662	4 723	3 307	0
District 4	275 723	2.65	68.4	52.4	11.2	25.9	17 701	21.9	9 255	3 657	1 768	0
District 5	278 624	2.47	68.1	48.8	14.3	27.6	24 427	15.1	12 451	4 570	5 039	0
District 6	297 270	2.44	62.8	46.1	12.7	27.8	25 106	12.1	4 384	3 168	14 598	0
LOUISIANA	1 718 194	2.63	64.8	43.2	16.2	29.7	128 560	16.7	60 804	24 524	24 891	2 861
District 1	294 038	2.66	66.9	48.3	13.1	27.2	13 596	24.4	1 182	2 957	5 469	57
District 2	292 635	2.58	57.3	30.9	20.7	36.5	19 449	12.0	11 687	3 058	4 007	138
District 3	286 954	2.67	65.5	44.9	15.5	28.6	12 616	26.9	4 329	4 273	2 935	0
District 4	276 860	2.66	64.7	42.6	16.6	31.0	21 383	18.4	13 410	5 425	2 390	2 524
District 5	271 296	2.58	66.0	43.4	17.5	29.6	50 605	11.6	28 559	5 925	6 333	142
District 6	296 411	2.63	68.2	48.9	13.9	25.5	10 911	23.4	1 637	2 886	3 757	0
MAINE	549 841	2.35	62.7	48.0	10.0	29.4	35 630	22.5	3 679	7 878	17 251	131
District 1	279 939	2.35	63.2	48.2	10.0	28.4	16 971	24.5	2 708	4 128	7 433	119
District 2	269 902	2.36	62.2	47.7	10.0	30.5	18 659	20.4	971	3 750	9 818	12
MARYLAND	2 165 438	2.70	66.8	47.2	14.7	26.9	139 814	19.4	35 832	28 001	48 141	7 534
District 1	268 746	2.64	70.6	55.8	10.3	24.7	17 997	20.6	5 648	3 465	5 803	7
District 2	273 842	2.64	64.3	41.9	16.8	28.2	19 249	17.1	7 411	3 533	3 971	2 113
District 3	290 531	2.58	62.8	45.5	13.4	29.5	18 020	19.9	583	3 399	6 910	4 515
District 4	263 670	2.80	66.5	40.3	19.2	28.2	5 226	42.2	1 149	2 597	410	115
District 5	255 049	2.87	71.7	51.2	15.0	22.5	21 067	11.8	1 111	2 598	14 602	387
District 6	269 094	2.73	68.8	52.7	12.1	25.3	20 791	17.6	12 569	3 716	2 766	93
District 7	270 119	2.64	61.3	36.4	20.2	30.7	26 420	14.8	6 305	4 677	10 895	0
District 8	274 387	2.68	68.7	54.0	10.5	25.8	11 044	37.8	1 056	4 016	2 784	304
MASSACHUSETTS	2 549 336	2.55	63.2	46.4	12.5	29.0	247 801	17.7	24 683	43 833	135 773	498
District 1	285 689	2.48	63.5	42.5	15.9	30.2	24 998	20.9	1 897	5 855	13 226	0
District 2	271 530	2.56	64.1	48.4	11.4	28.5	41 440	13.9	1 576	5 572	26 184	0
District 3	270 944	2.72	68.9	50.0	13.7	24.8	19 432	19.7	6 829	3 823	4 944	0
District 4	273 453	2.64	68.9	56.9	9.0	24.5	26 963	19.7	2 520	4 914	15 480	0
District 5	291 331	2.49	60.2	47.6	8.9	30.5	29 205	16.5	771	4 440	18 907	25
District 6	286 188	2.58	67.3	52.8	10.7	27.4	17 645	28.9	2 014	4 919	5 965	113
District 7	281 429	2.54	50.9	28.1	17.7	34.1	55 073	4.7	1 895	2 728	42 309	73
District 8	294 978	2.49	59.4	42.7	12.8	31.9	17 322	35.8	3 879	6 322	3 522	261
District 9	293 794	2.45	66.0	49.2	12.7	28.9	15 723	30.2	3 302	5 260	5 236	26

1. No spouse present.

1202   IL(District 3)—MA(District 9)   Items 28—39

STATE District	Total	Occupied units as a percent of all units	Owner-occupied units as a percent of occupied units	Median value[1] (dollars)	Percent valued at $500,000 or more	Median rent[2]	Per capita income (dollars)	Median income (dollars)	Percent with income of $100,000 or more
	Housing units, 2014						**Money income, 2014**		
		Occupied units						**Households**	
			Owner-occupied			**Renter-occupied**			
	40	41	42	43	44	45	46	47	48
ILLINOIS—Cont'd									
District 3	264 675	92.6	74.2	205 400	5.9	937	27 574	60 637	26.4
District 4	251 320	89.0	44.6	188 600	4.4	887	19 593	43 947	16.3
District 5	318 333	92.6	54.3	312 800	23.5	1 174	44 090	71 833	35.6
District 6	279 793	94.9	79.8	293 300	18.6	1 205	43 526	88 574	44.8
District 7	339 562	84.5	42.1	241 400	17.6	1 053	33 802	51 311	25.7
District 8	268 662	94.3	66.2	201 700	4.1	1 101	28 637	64 560	26.3
District 9	310 715	90.4	59.9	305 900	20.9	1 043	38 585	64 804	31.8
District 10	265 247	92.2	70.4	250 600	21.9	1 062	39 145	74 174	37.4
District 11	252 741	93.7	70.4	194 200	5.3	1 120	29 742	67 898	31.9
District 12	319 289	85.6	65.9	102 600	1.3	687	24 564	44 940	17.0
District 13	319 169	89.3	63.9	114 400	1.8	721	25 828	47 026	17.1
District 14	266 222	94.7	80.7	238 400	7.8	1 113	37 691	86 124	41.3
District 15	315 465	87.0	74.1	95 900	1.0	623	24 515	48 615	16.2
District 16	297 404	90.2	71.9	129 700	1.5	741	27 057	54 155	21.6
District 17	321 126	87.5	65.9	96 900	1.2	638	23 867	44 735	14.4
District 18	310 461	91.1	75.2	137 900	2.2	709	30 765	58 821	24.2
INDIANA	2 829 630	88.4	68.6	124 300	2.4	753	25 140	49 446	17.4
District 1	303 811	87.5	70.6	142 100	1.9	820	25 591	51 887	20.0
District 2	306 940	87.3	70.0	115 300	1.8	697	23 133	47 178	14.2
District 3	314 418	88.7	73.0	116 200	2.3	662	24 654	50 078	14.8
District 4	309 346	89.7	68.8	129 800	1.1	772	24 678	51 370	17.9
District 5	317 665	91.4	71.2	167 200	7.0	866	34 779	63 471	28.7
District 6	312 312	89.8	71.4	114 900	1.5	718	24 198	47 327	16.2
District 7	333 640	84.8	52.2	103 500	1.3	775	20 163	39 238	11.4
District 8	317 760	88.5	70.5	110 200	1.8	681	24 115	45 635	15.3
District 9	313 738	88.5	69.7	136 000	2.3	781	24 925	50 321	17.5
IOWA	1 362 034	91.1	70.9	133 100	2.4	711	28 361	53 712	20.1
District 1	337 117	92.3	73.5	136 700	2.6	678	28 600	55 648	20.0
District 2	338 446	91.1	70.6	127 900	2.8	722	27 400	51 019	18.5
District 3	339 874	92.1	68.6	153 500	2.5	782	31 240	59 460	25.3
District 4	346 597	89.1	70.8	111 900	1.6	639	26 062	49 623	16.6
KANSAS	1 248 861	88.8	66.6	132 100	2.8	773	27 870	52 504	20.5
District 1	317 108	86.5	66.5	101 000	1.4	704	24 449	47 985	14.8
District 2	315 760	87.8	66.8	116 400	1.3	735	25 056	49 435	16.9
District 3	305 290	93.5	66.5	195 700	6.6	916	35 328	64 949	30.5
District 4	310 703	87.7	66.8	119 800	2.0	731	26 322	51 538	19.5
KENTUCKY	1 950 504	87.8	66.1	123 800	2.7	678	23 684	42 958	15.6
District 1	332 284	84.9	67.3	99 000	1.4	611	20 874	38 507	11.2
District 2	318 253	87.3	68.9	125 400	1.8	671	22 429	45 757	15.3
District 3	333 978	90.0	60.2	149 400	3.7	742	28 410	47 228	18.6
District 4	306 845	89.9	70.0	155 800	4.6	718	27 094	54 214	22.9
District 5	329 516	84.6	70.5	75 200	0.8	564	17 136	30 267	7.3
District 6	329 628	90.2	60.4	147 200	3.6	711	25 818	47 057	18.1
LOUISIANA	2 011 037	85.4	64.4	143 600	3.4	801	24 800	44 555	19.0
District 1	332 907	88.3	69.1	182 400	5.9	894	29 547	54 764	24.0
District 2	350 321	83.5	52.9	148 400	3.8	860	22 971	36 297	14.6
District 3	329 317	87.1	66.7	123 200	2.7	752	25 172	47 095	20.3
District 4	340 258	81.4	64.6	112 600	1.9	751	22 511	40 576	15.6
District 5	329 546	82.3	64.5	99 000	1.5	665	19 495	35 169	13.6
District 6	328 688	90.2	68.7	163 800	4.1	859	28 671	56 102	25.3
MAINE	727 693	75.6	71.3	174 800	6.0	776	27 978	49 462	18.1
District 1	351 630	79.6	70.7	224 700	9.3	865	32 249	56 043	23.3
District 2	376 063	71.8	71.9	138 300	2.6	676	23 592	42 623	12.7
MARYLAND	2 422 317	89.4	65.9	288 500	18.1	1 242	36 338	73 971	36.1
District 1	338 413	79.4	76.2	264 500	12.0	1 021	32 928	68 386	31.9
District 2	302 093	90.6	59.2	218 800	4.8	1 155	29 834	60 941	27.8
District 3	315 879	92.0	64.8	304 500	20.3	1 349	40 315	81 015	40.1
District 4	284 673	92.6	61.0	274 900	14.5	1 285	34 335	72 035	34.0
District 5	274 055	93.1	75.2	297 000	10.9	1 433	36 348	89 671	43.9
District 6	297 669	90.4	68.2	295 700	22.5	1 216	36 772	73 980	36.3
District 7	319 108	84.6	56.2	244 900	21.7	1 032	31 936	58 093	27.3
District 8	290 427	94.5	67.0	423 000	37.7	1 599	47 943	94 004	47.4
MASSACHUSETTS	2 828 592	90.1	61.6	338 900	23.3	1 107	37 288	69 160	34.4
District 1	319 385	89.4	62.9	210 700	6.0	827	28 299	50 966	22.0
District 2	297 227	91.4	62.5	255 700	7.8	946	31 253	63 721	30.3
District 3	291 341	93.0	62.5	303 400	18.9	1 039	35 330	68 401	34.7
District 4	290 181	94.2	71.5	388 000	33.6	1 175	45 287	87 957	44.3
District 5	308 341	94.5	59.3	452 200	40.5	1 384	45 074	81 376	41.6
District 6	303 080	94.4	69.4	384 100	28.1	1 154	41 513	81 137	40.8
District 7	303 572	92.7	33.1	385 100	31.0	1 317	31 852	54 152	27.6
District 8	314 300	93.9	62.1	371 500	25.8	1 323	41 720	77 203	37.4
District 9	401 165	73.2	70.9	330 600	20.5	853	34 978	63 304	30.7

1. Specified owner-occupied units; $1,000,000 represents $1,000,000 or more. 2. Specified renter-occupied units.

Table E. Congressional Districts 114th Congress — **Poverty, Labor Force, Employment, and Social Security**

STATE District	Poverty, 2014			Civilian labor force, 2014			Civilian employment,[2] 2014				Persons under age 65 with no health insurance, 2014 (percent)	Social Security beneficiaries, December 2014		Supplemental Security Income recipients, December 2014
	Persons below poverty level (percent)	Families below poverty level (percent)	Percent of households receiving food stamps in past 12 months	Total	Unemployment Total	Rate[1]	Total	Management, business, science and arts occupations	Service, sales, and office	Construction and production		Number	Rate[3]	
	49	50	51	52	53	54	55	56	57	58	59	60	61	62
ILLINOIS—Cont'd														
District 3	12.8	9.6	12.2	371 466	30 387	8.2	341 079	31.5	43.4	25.2	13.2	114 430	156.7	12 542
District 4	22.1	20.2	22.3	372 555	33 743	9.1	338 812	24.8	44.6	30.7	23.1	74 904	103.2	19 525
District 5	10.4	7.1	6.6	434 270	23 172	5.3	411 098	49.4	37.2	13.4	11.0	96 337	134.2	12 638
District 6	5.7	3.9	4.9	404 081	19 705	4.9	384 376	48.2	37.8	14.0	6.2	109 553	149.1	4 367
District 7	25.0	19.7	23.6	372 723	46 643	12.5	326 080	43.9	43.0	13.2	13.8	98 495	135.4	35 330
District 8	10.1	8.0	9.6	406 691	30 631	7.5	376 060	32.8	42.9	24.4	14.4	101 010	139.3	8 619
District 9	11.0	7.5	9.9	380 560	25 376	6.7	355 184	48.6	37.9	13.5	10.3	122 168	172.0	19 661
District 10	9.8	7.9	10.6	363 593	22 496	6.2	341 097	42.8	40.2	17.1	11.8	105 994	148.9	9 425
District 11	11.1	8.2	12.2	382 888	25 995	6.8	356 893	36.3	39.9	23.7	11.8	94 897	133.2	8 245
District 12	19.2	14.0	17.6	325 203	25 491	7.8	299 712	31.9	43.6	24.5	9.8	144 069	205.3	20 703
District 13	19.1	12.6	13.2	365 366	25 290	6.9	340 076	36.9	44.5	18.6	8.2	135 003	188.7	15 440
District 14	5.7	3.9	6.3	396 172	20 650	5.2	375 522	40.9	42.0	17.1	5.7	107 508	148.2	4 388
District 15	15.2	11.0	14.9	343 345	26 494	7.7	316 851	28.6	41.0	30.4	9.4	154 265	218.7	14 438
District 16	12.3	8.5	11.6	359 053	30 282	8.4	328 771	32.0	40.4	27.6	8.8	143 645	205.3	8 354
District 17	18.2	13.6	17.4	341 678	29 599	8.7	312 079	28.0	43.0	29.0	9.5	154 042	219.7	18 589
District 18	10.3	6.1	9.4	364 816	20 818	5.7	343 998	40.0	39.2	20.9	6.8	145 039	204.1	8 453
INDIANA	15.2	10.9	12.8	3 321 845	234 575	7.1	3 087 270	32.9	39.9	27.2	13.8	1 286 099	195.0	127 957
District 1	16.2	13.0	14.8	350 854	35 140	10.0	315 714	31.8	42.2	26.0	13.3	141 571	197.2	16 275
District 2	15.3	11.3	13.0	361 261	23 889	6.6	337 372	28.7	39.0	32.3	16.6	143 479	198.8	13 330
District 3	13.7	9.8	11.4	373 097	23 222	6.2	349 875	30.3	38.7	31.0	16.1	142 243	193.7	12 637
District 4	13.8	8.7	10.2	371 052	22 963	6.2	348 089	32.5	38.2	29.3	12.9	139 677	188.0	9 931
District 5	10.2	7.1	8.7	391 689	20 748	5.3	370 941	47.4	37.5	15.1	9.5	131 517	176.9	9 815
District 6	15.0	10.7	13.0	360 690	23 644	6.6	337 046	30.9	39.0	30.1	12.9	162 114	225.1	14 736
District 7	23.7	18.7	21.7	385 586	39 377	10.2	346 209	28.4	45.6	26.0	17.5	120 664	159.6	23 638
District 8	14.8	10.7	12.2	352 189	20 370	5.8	331 819	29.1	39.5	31.4	12.8	156 359	216.2	15 102
District 9	14.4	9.0	10.0	375 427	25 222	6.7	350 205	35.1	39.8	25.0	12.5	148 475	201.5	12 493
IOWA	12.2	7.9	11.9	1 667 252	73 662	4.4	1 593 590	35.1	39.4	25.5	7.2	616 301	198.4	51 227
District 1	10.8	7.4	10.7	415 462	16 411	4.0	399 051	33.6	39.0	27.4	6.3	158 932	206.2	12 830
District 2	13.8	8.6	12.3	406 581	19 546	4.8	387 035	34.9	39.9	25.3	7.7	154 582	199.0	15 137
District 3	12.0	8.6	13.6	441 243	20 451	4.6	420 792	38.2	41.2	20.7	6.9	139 454	174.1	13 106
District 4	12.4	7.0	11.2	403 966	17 254	4.3	386 712	33.3	37.6	29.0	8.1	163 333	215.3	10 154
KANSAS	13.6	9.2	9.5	1 474 596	76 742	5.2	1 397 854	36.9	39.2	23.8	11.8	521 955	179.7	48 920
District 1	15.0	9.7	10.4	361 720	18 688	5.2	343 032	32.0	37.9	30.1	11.8	133 240	185.5	10 073
District 2	15.6	9.6	9.9	355 557	18 770	5.3	336 787	35.7	40.0	24.3	11.4	145 083	202.8	15 249
District 3	10.3	7.4	7.1	399 114	19 436	4.9	379 678	43.5	40.1	16.4	10.9	110 930	148.1	9 326
District 4	13.7	10.1	10.8	358 205	19 848	5.5	338 357	35.9	38.8	25.3	13.3	132 702	184.1	14 272
KENTUCKY	19.1	14.5	17.5	2 067 812	158 108	7.6	1 909 704	32.9	40.4	26.7	9.8	954 284	216.2	188 401
District 1	19.8	14.5	17.7	313 913	26 061	8.3	287 852	28.0	39.6	32.4	11.0	175 843	242.9	29 806
District 2	16.2	11.8	15.3	352 769	24 172	6.9	328 597	29.9	39.7	30.4	9.5	158 552	213.4	24 756
District 3	17.1	12.1	15.4	385 731	26 390	6.8	359 341	36.3	41.1	22.7	9.0	143 829	195.3	25 749
District 4	14.2	10.9	13.0	366 126	23 380	6.4	342 746	35.4	40.9	23.7	9.1	139 414	186.3	19 099
District 5	29.2	23.9	27.6	264 186	29 591	11.2	234 595	27.0	41.9	31.1	10.0	193 499	271.7	64 558
District 6	18.8	13.4	16.0	385 087	28 514	7.4	356 573	37.7	39.7	22.7	10.5	143 147	191.0	24 433
LOUISIANA	19.8	14.9	15.7	2 180 626	162 602	7.5	2 018 024	32.3	43.3	24.4	17.0	854 211	183.7	181 279
District 1	14.2	10.2	10.1	399 661	25 950	6.5	373 711	36.3	42.1	21.7	15.7	146 286	183.6	19 444
District 2	25.2	19.9	21.7	377 152	35 084	9.3	342 068	30.5	47.6	21.9	18.8	135 904	175.2	42 500
District 3	17.6	13.3	15.8	378 538	25 478	6.7	353 060	29.2	43.1	27.8	16.1	141 797	182.3	25 953
District 4	22.1	17.0	16.5	319 610	25 845	8.1	293 765	31.2	43.0	25.8	16.6	148 780	196.6	33 169
District 5	26.1	20.2	18.9	301 728	28 077	9.3	273 651	28.6	44.9	26.4	20.7	153 663	204.7	40 533
District 6	14.7	10.1	11.6	403 937	22 168	5.5	381 769	36.3	39.8	23.9	14.3	127 781	161.4	19 680
MAINE	14.1	9.7	16.9	693 848	40 659	5.9	653 189	35.8	42.3	21.8	12.3	325 496	244.7	37 591
District 1	11.4	7.6	12.5	369 793	17 925	4.8	351 868	38.8	42.4	18.7	10.5	157 934	234.4	14 796
District 2	16.9	11.9	21.4	324 055	22 734	7.0	301 321	32.4	42.3	25.4	14.2	167 562	255.3	22 795
MARYLAND	10.1	7.1	11.6	3 225 569	231 268	7.2	2 994 301	44.7	39.1	16.2	8.9	936 372	156.7	118 184
District 1	9.7	7.3	11.1	379 739	18 666	4.9	361 073	38.3	40.9	20.8	7.1	152 330	209.1	11 320
District 2	13.0	9.6	13.9	389 500	30 217	7.8	359 283	38.6	42.9	18.5	9.0	121 215	163.1	16 680
District 3	8.6	6.2	9.9	435 351	26 977	6.2	408 374	51.4	36.6	12.0	8.2	113 488	147.7	16 190
District 4	9.4	6.7	11.6	418 669	35 464	8.5	383 205	37.8	43.4	18.8	14.0	97 593	131.4	11 015
District 5	7.6	5.1	9.1	410 669	31 515	7.7	379 154	43.5	38.3	18.3	7.6	102 580	136.2	9 165
District 6	9.4	6.5	11.2	402 278	27 518	6.8	374 760	46.9	37.3	15.8	8.5	113 592	150.4	13 433
District 7	16.8	11.4	19.9	371 551	34 484	9.3	337 067	45.5	41.0	13.5	7.7	125 045	169.3	32 541
District 8	6.7	4.3	5.7	417 812	26 427	6.3	391 385	54.3	33.3	12.4	9.0	110 529	148.0	7 840
MASSACHUSETTS	11.6	8.3	13.0	3 720 446	249 791	6.7	3 470 655	44.7	39.7	15.7	3.8	1 224 469	181.5	188 726
District 1	15.5	11.8	19.3	385 302	34 085	8.8	351 217	36.5	44.5	19.0	4.0	162 522	221.6	37 138
District 2	12.7	8.3	13.6	403 030	27 817	6.9	375 213	41.9	40.6	17.5	3.2	132 423	179.8	20 350
District 3	12.3	9.6	15.2	402 481	27 221	6.8	375 260	43.7	36.9	19.4	3.9	127 141	168.2	24 377
District 4	6.5	4.0	7.9	416 459	22 883	5.5	393 576	49.1	37.3	13.7	3.1	129 089	172.5	11 215
District 5	9.2	6.0	7.1	428 687	22 133	5.2	406 554	53.8	35.5	10.7	3.2	120 559	159.5	11 898
District 6	7.2	5.0	9.3	425 219	24 330	5.7	400 889	44.7	39.5	15.9	3.4	143 760	189.8	14 217
District 7	22.0	17.0	20.6	440 901	36 967	8.4	403 934	45.8	41.6	12.6	5.4	90 954	118.1	34 328
District 8	9.4	7.2	11.8	429 429	29 788	6.9	399 641	46.9	39.2	13.9	3.2	134 741	179.2	16 162
District 9	10.2	7.8	12.1	388 938	24 567	6.3	364 371	37.8	42.7	19.5	4.5	183 280	248.8	19 041

1. Percent of civilian labor force.   2. Persons 16 years old and over.   3. Per 1,000 resident population estimated in the 2014 American Community Survey.

Table E. Congressional Districts 114th Congress — **Agriculture**

STATE District		Land in farms			Value of products sold				Government payments	
	Number of farms	Acres	Average size of farm (acres)	Irrigated land (acres)	Total ($1,000)	Average per farm (dollars)	Percent from crops	Percent from livestock and poultry products	Total ($1,000)	Average per farm receiving payments (dollars)
	63	64	65	66	67	68	69	70	71	72
ILLINOIS—Cont'd										
District 3	97	13 188	136	326	8 734	90 045	0.0	0.0	212	8 140
District 4	X	X	X	X	X	X	X	X	X	X
District 5	21	349	17	D	D	D	D	D	D	D
District 6	187	17 561	94	462	30 306	162 064	95.9	4.1	420	9 765
District 7	X	X	X	X	X	X	X	X	X	X
District 8	21	4 457	212	D	3 655	174 060	99.7	0.3	D	D
District 9	X	X	X	X	X	X	X	X	X	X
District 10	141	8 223	58	407	13 357	94 727	95.6	4.4	126	8 421
District 11	131	31 383	240	D	23 965	182 943	95.8	4.2	559	9 172
District 12	6 959	1 905 115	274	15 491	688 176	98 890	85.7	14.3	29 651	6 488
District 13	7 760	2 974 971	383	13 854	1 842 362	237 418	88.1	11.9	53 882	9 103
District 14	2 132	625 197	293	18 015	560 569	262 931	83.2	16.8	13 128	13 274
District 15	22 203	7 559 605	340	102 777	3 613 564	162 751	78.7	21.3	155 644	8 968
District 16	10 468	4 292 328	410	48 782	3 466 237	331 127	84.7	15.3	92 879	11 381
District 17	9 730	3 458 529	355	118 763	2 861 291	294 069	75.5	24.5	85 811	11 696
District 18	13 826	5 528 495	400	187 608	3 658 219	264 590	84.0	16.0	112 453	10 343
INDIANA	58 695	14 720 396	251	437 445	11 210 818	191 001	67.2	32.8	267 287	8 331
District 1	1 212	348 046	287	38 398	300 726	248 123	D	D	6 174	9 752
District 2	7 547	1 747 268	232	183 555	1 685 428	223 324	61.1	38.9	32 668	8 128
District 3	11 801	1 957 311	166	53 255	1 877 293	159 079	54.8	45.2	38 957	6 794
District 4	8 570	3 273 095	382	47 054	2 697 593	314 772	72.4	27.6	59 486	10 747
District 5	2 682	803 313	300	5 904	690 258	257 367	89.1	10.9	13 671	8 507
District 6	10 531	2 532 278	240	20 206	1 686 224	160 120	69.8	30.2	50 568	8 006
District 7	185	17 001	92	163	26 173	141 475	D	D	201	6 708
District 8	9 529	2 812 457	295	79 188	1 677 310	176 022	65.2	34.8	45 753	8 707
District 9	6 638	1 229 627	185	9 722	569 814	85 841	61.2	38.8	19 809	6 733
IOWA	88 637	30 622 731	345	171 656	30 821 532	347 728	56.3	43.7	782 290	11 262
District 1	22 478	6 620 256	295	D	6 557 733	291 740	57.8	42.2	197 364	10 957
District 2	20 546	5 960 872	290	24 598	4 317 514	210 139	60.7	39.3	168 748	11 138
District 3	12 191	4 565 364	374	D	2 960 578	242 849	69.2	30.8	94 951	10 699
District 4	33 422	13 476 239	403	125 421	16 980 000	508 219	52.5	47.6	321 228	11 713
KANSAS	61 773	46 137 295	747	2 881 292	18 460 564	298 845	37.8	62.2	442 090	10 426
District 1	30 489	30 369 854	996	2 320 029	14 300 000	469 295	32.3	67.8	306 513	12 602
District 2	19 808	7 356 986	371	50 780	1 835 532	92 666	60.9	39.1	69 467	6 390
District 3	1 013	195 215	193	2 877	47 298	46 691	73.0	27.0	1 567	5 458
District 4	10 463	8 215 240	785	507 606	2 269 393	216 897	53.7	46.3	64 543	9 324
KENTUCKY	77 064	13 049 347	169	73 573	5 067 334	65 755	45.0	55.0	169 821	5 087
District 1	22 897	4 970 288	217	46 542	2 738 196	119 588	47.8	52.2	88 556	6 975
District 2	19 734	3 055 139	155	14 508	1 059 346	53 681	48.6	51.4	44 239	5 052
District 3	223	13 572	61	101	5 973	26 784	82.2	17.8	184	4 611
District 4	11 411	1 595 512	140	6 248	311 349	27 285	62.8	37.2	13 820	3 421
District 5	11 144	1 522 271	137	1 494	277 300	24 883	32.6	67.4	8 668	2 468
District 6	11 655	1 892 565	162	4 680	675 171	57 930	24.4	75.6	14 353	3 310
LOUISIANA	28 093	7 900 864	281	1 092 881	3 809 401	135 600	73.1	26.9	138 164	14 625
District 1	1 386	376 150	271	1 242	101 752	73 414	48.0	52.0	291	4 037
District 2	404	234 199	580	1 175	103 689	256 656	95.7	4.3	277	6 915
District 3	5 363	1 709 327	319	246 622	646 950	120 632	83.8	16.2	23 708	11 824
District 4	7 545	1 535 386	203	104 062	737 447	97 740	29.8	70.2	19 192	11 980
District 5	11 106	3 503 066	315	730 933	1 891 903	170 350	84.7	15.3	90 840	16 970
District 6	2 289	542 736	237	8 847	327 660	143 146	83.0	17.0	3 857	10 285
MAINE	8 173	1 454 104	178	30 887	763 062	93 364	62.1	37.9	10 162	7 629
District 1	2 650	234 530	89	2 884	91 532	34 540	66.5	33.5	1 525	6 809
District 2	5 523	1 219 574	221	28 003	671 531	121 588	61.5	38.5	8 637	7 795
MARYLAND	12 256	2 030 745	166	104 910	2 271 397	185 329	46.3	53.7	36 024	7 784
District 1	5 451	1 180 832	217	97 880	1 731 665	317 678	41.3	58.7	25 698	8 696
District 2	115	7 376	64	182	5 909	51 381	89.3	10.7	304	17 878
District 3	204	20 466	100	112	27 937	136 945	86.8	13.2	118	7 345
District 4	114	7 095	62	628	11 343	99 500	98.2	1.8	38	2 916
District 5	1 850	198 919	108	1 755	70 566	38 144	87.3	12.7	2 074	5 171
District 6	2 360	341 624	145	1 644	199 544	84 552	49.6	50.4	3 123	5 385
District 7	604	69 173	115	305	53 048	87 827	D	D	673	5 342
District 8	1 558	205 260	132	2 404	171 386	110 004	D	D	3 997	7 686
MASSACHUSETTS	7 755	523 517	68	23 433	492 211	63 470	77.8	22.2	8 124	10 415
District 1	2 043	189 425	93	1 513	72 106	35 294	56.3	43.7	2 293	10 059
District 2	1 832	142 899	78	3 554	125 634	68 578	75.5	24.5	1 671	8 033
District 3	936	37 576	40	1 304	40 736	43 522	71.8	28.2	565	8 972
District 4	750	33 528	45	2 149	41 671	55 562	88.0	12.0	467	6 578
District 5	196	6 332	32	700	43 367	221 262	99.3	0.7	D	D
District 6	464	18 673	40	464	20 476	44 129	74.9	25.1	174	9 141
District 7	23	282	12	30	164	7 113	86.0	13.4	D	D
District 8	162	5 471	34	612	9 196	56 763	66.6	33.4	120	7 031
District 9	1 349	89 331	66	13 107	138 861	102 936	84.1	15.9	2 740	18 269

Table E. Congressional Districts 114th Congress — Nonfarm Employment and Payroll

Private nonfarm employment and payroll, 2014

STATE District	Number of establish-ments	Employment Total	Manufact-uring	Construc-tion	Wholesale trade	Retail trade	Health care and social assistance	Finance and Insurance	Real estate and rental and leasing	Professio-nal, scientific, and technical services	Information	Annual payroll Total (mil dol)	Average per employee dollars
	73	74	75	76	77	78	79	80	81	82	83	84	85
ILLINOIS—Cont'd													
District 3	15 180	215 053	12.6	5.0	5.3	13.4	14.5	2.9	1.2	4.7	1.0	9 492	44 140
District 4	10 570	151 846	13.1	2.8	7.0	14.7	13.6	2.6	1.0	3.1	0.8	5 426	35 732
District 5	22 510	365 849	8.4	3.2	5.5	10.6	13.2	3.9	2.3	5.3	2.3	18 002	49 206
District 6	24 952	374 918	8.7	4.0	6.4	11.5	12.8	7.1	1.3	7.4	2.5	20 151	53 747
District 7	29 317	772 498	2.8	1.4	2.6	4.7	14.9	15.4	2.1	17.9	5.5	60 000	77 671
District 8	23 815	449 503	12.4	5.0	11.1	10.0	7.3	4.5	1.7	6.2	3.3	24 136	53 695
District 9	20 282	278 640	6.7	2.7	4.9	11.5	23.9	3.4	1.9	6.1	2.3	14 417	51 741
District 10	21 430	373 362	11.7	2.6	11.5	10.2	11.3	6.3	1.1	11.2	1.1	27 030	72 396
District 11	16 126	276 654	10.2	2.9	8.1	14.3	13.6	3.3	1.3	4.9	2.8	12 057	43 580
District 12	14 700	212 934	12.4	4.8	3.6	16.3	19.4	3.2	1.1	4.6	1.1	8 069	37 893
District 13	15 566	241 020	7.5	4.3	4.1	14.0	21.6	4.5	1.7	4.4	2.4	9 117	37 829
District 14	17 151	186 136	15.0	6.5	6.3	16.3	11.6	3.2	1.2	5.4	1.2	7 677	41 244
District 15	15 387	196 486	19.6	4.4	5.6	13.6	18.1	3.9	1.0	2.3	1.3	7 107	36 171
District 16	15 114	217 834	19.8	3.2	4.8	14.9	16.0	3.7	1.1	2.9	1.2	8 724	40 050
District 17	15 060	267 562	16.6	3.1	3.9	11.4	18.1	3.7	0.7	3.8	1.4	12 901	48 218
District 18	16 181	255 652	10.6	4.2	6.5	15.9	13.8	12.5	0.9	3.3	1.5	10 701	41 859
INDIANA	143 826	2 602 895	18.3	4.4	4.5	12.1	15.5	3.8	1.2	4.2	1.7	107 452	41 282
District 1	14 633	239 408	15.1	6.1	3.6	14.8	18.1	2.4	1.3	3.5	1.0	10 085	42 124
District 2	15 551	301 386	32.4	3.1	4.9	10.8	13.1	2.5	0.9	2.7	1.3	11 661	38 692
District 3	17 399	310 154	27.0	3.7	5.3	11.8	15.4	3.7	1.0	2.6	1.5	12 370	39 883
District 4	14 744	245 969	22.6	4.2	4.0	14.5	14.1	2.7	1.0	2.4	1.0	9 061	36 838
District 5	21 078	361 978	6.2	4.0	4.8	12.1	16.4	7.0	1.7	7.8	2.8	16 690	46 107
District 6	14 093	232 076	21.9	3.8	3.2	12.7	16.0	3.5	0.8	4.8	0.9	8 885	38 283
District 7	14 792	355 595	9.4	5.2	5.3	8.1	15.7	4.1	2.0	6.5	2.9	17 856	50 214
District 8	16 143	276 841	20.2	5.6	4.5	13.0	16.8	3.1	1.0	3.2	1.5	10 913	39 420
District 9	14 927	227 436	17.7	5.0	3.6	15.8	17.0	3.0	1.2	3.2	1.3	7 997	35 160
IOWA	80 466	1 316 447	15.9	4.5	5.1	13.7	16.4	6.9	0.9	3.9	2.3	52 563	39 928
District 1	19 519	342 265	18.8	4.3	4.6	13.2	16.2	5.9	0.8	4.2	2.4	13 670	39 941
District 2	18 783	316 696	19.5	4.4	4.0	14.0	17.8	3.2	0.9	3.0	2.0	11 886	37 532
District 3	19 894	356 411	8.5	4.6	5.2	13.7	14.4	13.7	1.2	5.2	2.8	16 170	45 368
District 4	21 993	283 929	18.7	5.3	6.6	14.7	18.5	3.8	0.8	3.0	2.1	10 128	35 669
KANSAS	74 055	1 178 062	14.0	5.3	5.5	12.8	16.6	5.3	1.3	5.4	2.9	49 713	42 199
District 1	20 129	248 293	17.2	5.5	5.7	14.8	18.3	3.9	1.0	3.0	1.9	8 335	33 569
District 2	15 926	233 208	13.8	5.5	3.0	13.4	21.6	4.5	1.1	4.3	2.6	8 328	35 712
District 3	20 756	392 572	8.4	5.0	7.4	11.6	13.4	7.4	1.5	8.2	4.7	19 961	50 847
District 4	16 882	283 939	20.1	5.6	4.1	12.9	16.2	4.0	1.4	4.2	1.8	12 145	42 773
KENTUCKY	91 418	1 535 417	14.8	4.1	4.5	13.3	16.1	4.7	1.2	4.6	2.4	60 162	39 183
District 1	14 374	213 655	23.0	4.0	3.8	14.7	16.4	3.0	0.9	2.7	1.2	7 551	35 340
District 2	14 494	225 171	19.4	4.5	3.0	14.0	16.7	3.9	1.1	3.3	3.0	7 758	34 452
District 3	19 242	401 941	10.4	4.0	4.9	10.5	15.3	6.9	1.4	6.1	2.2	18 465	45 939
District 4	14 161	230 053	15.0	4.1	6.0	13.4	14.5	5.5	1.2	3.7	1.3	9 390	40 819
District 5	11 903	162 036	10.5	2.9	3.7	17.9	21.6	3.5	1.1	3.8	4.5	5 244	32 360
District 6	16 865	277 502	14.8	4.8	4.8	13.9	16.0	3.2	1.2	6.1	2.7	11 037	39 772
LOUISIANA	104 976	1 717 797	7.6	8.4	4.5	13.4	16.8	3.7	2.0	5.9	1.5	76 731	44 668
District 1	20 767	319 784	6.2	6.0	5.3	14.3	17.3	4.6	2.3	5.4	1.3	14 863	46 478
District 2	15 643	288 688	9.3	5.3	3.8	10.2	12.9	3.3	1.5	7.2	1.4	14 127	48 937
District 3	19 900	302 575	9.9	5.9	5.5	13.7	16.4	2.8	3.5	5.5	1.3	13 856	45 792
District 4	15 082	222 494	8.4	6.3	4.4	15.2	20.9	3.3	1.7	4.0	1.6	8 162	36 684
District 5	15 247	208 805	7.9	5.7	3.8	16.2	26.5	4.5	1.4	3.6	2.6	7 189	34 431
District 6	17 930	329 751	5.4	19.8	3.9	13.7	13.3	4.3	1.5	7.0	1.3	15 720	47 671
MAINE	40 369	492 690	9.9	4.6	3.6	16.6	21.8	5.3	1.3	4.8	2.3	19 632	39 846
District 1	22 872	286 131	8.8	4.4	3.7	15.8	21.6	5.8	1.4	5.4	2.4	12 150	42 463
District 2	17 267	204 058	11.5	4.9	3.3	17.8	22.3	4.4	1.1	3.7	2.2	7 303	35 787
MARYLAND	136 501	2 216 867	4.4	6.5	3.9	13.2	16.3	4.5	2.0	12.6	2.5	114 338	51 576
District 1	17 763	195 773	8.9	6.8	3.8	17.9	18.0	3.0	1.3	4.5	1.4	7 252	37 044
District 2	16 074	323 523	8.6	7.1	6.8	14.7	11.4	3.9	1.7	11.5	2.0	16 288	50 345
District 3	20 818	371 388	3.2	4.9	4.4	11.9	16.7	4.3	2.0	12.1	3.3	19 698	53 040
District 4	12 277	188 669	2.2	8.4	4.5	16.2	12.6	2.5	2.7	12.9	2.1	8 240	43 672
District 5	13 996	204 000	2.2	12.3	3.7	15.6	14.1	2.1	2.1	15.0	1.7	9 487	46 507
District 6	18 540	284 868	6.5	6.9	3.5	15.7	14.4	5.5	1.7	12.9	2.8	13 546	47 551
District 7	15 505	290 194	2.1	2.8	2.1	9.0	27.1	6.8	2.1	10.7	2.0	16 819	57 958
District 8	21 101	329 287	2.0	6.3	2.0	9.6	16.2	5.5	2.3	17.3	3.4	21 114	64 121
MASSACHUSETTS	173 575	3 087 030	7.2	3.7	4.4	11.7	19.7	5.8	1.5	8.5	3.6	185 353	60 042
District 1	16 178	246 877	11.5	3.8	3.6	14.6	22.6	4.8	1.2	4.0	1.6	10 458	42 361
District 2	16 494	279 179	9.1	3.3	4.2	14.0	25.0	5.2	1.0	5.5	1.6	12 104	43 355
District 3	16 038	266 218	15.8	4.0	7.0	11.0	18.3	3.4	0.9	8.8	3.8	15 769	59 233
District 4	20 587	321 848	8.3	3.6	5.9	14.3	16.8	3.8	1.8	7.1	2.6	18 137	56 352
District 5	20 646	376 949	4.2	3.7	4.0	9.8	14.8	4.2	1.3	11.5	5.8	24 776	65 727
District 6	20 797	342 092	11.1	4.7	5.6	14.0	18.0	3.3	1.1	8.3	5.3	19 926	58 248
District 7	16 476	480 239	2.1	1.9	2.6	6.8	21.5	7.0	1.9	10.6	4.0	35 326	73 559
District 8	23 754	499 321	3.9	4.1	4.0	9.6	21.8	12.3	2.0	10.6	4.3	36 045	72 188
District 9	22 142	241 384	6.7	6.2	3.7	18.1	20.7	3.1	1.4	5.0	1.7	10 604	43 929

1. Specified owner-occupied units; $1,000,000 represents $1,000,000 or more.   2. Specified renter-occupied units.

Table E. Congressional Districts 114th Congress — **Land Area and Population Characteristics**

STATE District	Representative, 114th Congress	Land area,[1] 2010 (sq km)	Total persons	Per square kilometer	White	Black	American Indian, Alaska Native	Asian and Pacific Islander	Some other race	Two or more races	Hispanic or Latino[2]	Non-Hispanic White alone	Female	Foreign-born	Born in state of residence
		1	2	3	4	5	6	7	8	9	10	11	12	13	14
MICHIGAN		146 435	9 909 877	67.7	78.9	13.9	0.6	2.9	1.2	2.6	4.8	75.7	50.9	6.4	76.7
District 1	Dan Benishek (R)	64 822	703 687	10.9	92.4	1.7	2.3	0.7	0.3	2.7	1.7	91.2	49.1	1.9	79.1
District 2	Bill Huizenga (R)	8 498	724 843	85.3	85.0	6.0	0.5	2.2	3.0	3.4	9.4	79.4	51.1	5.7	79.2
District 3	Justin Amash (R)	6 808	725 487	106.6	84.1	8.9	0.6	1.9	2.0	2.5	7.0	79.9	50.1	4.9	78.8
District 4	John L. Moolenar (R)	21 906	702 630	32.1	94.1	1.8	0.8	1.0	0.3	2.0	3.1	91.8	50.0	2.0	86.2
District 5	Daniel T. Kildee (D)	6 083	687 292	113.0	77.4	17.3	0.4	1.0	1.0	2.9	4.8	74.0	51.8	2.4	83.6
District 6	Fred Upton (R)	9 186	712 100	77.5	84.9	8.4	0.6	1.7	1.4	3.1	5.9	81.1	51.0	4.3	70.5
District 7	Tim Walberg (R)	10 950	702 894	64.2	91.4	4.1	0.4	0.9	1.0	2.2	4.4	88.3	49.8	2.5	74.5
District 8	Mike Bishop (R)	3 893	725 201	186.3	85.4	5.9	0.3	4.3	1.2	2.9	4.8	82.3	51.0	7.1	75.3
District 9	Sander M. Levin (D)	475	720 485	1 516.8	79.6	13.2	0.3	3.9	0.5	2.4	2.1	78.1	51.3	10.8	76.7
District 10	Candice S. Miller (R)	10 724	706 525	65.9	93.1	2.5	0.3	1.7	0.5	2.0	3.2	90.7	50.3	5.7	83.7
District 11	David A.Trott (R)	1 086	718 435	661.5	82.6	5.3	0.2	9.2	0.8	2.0	3.5	79.9	50.8	12.6	70.6
District 12	Debbie Dingell (D)	1 044	705 207	675.5	78.6	10.6	0.3	5.5	1.9	3.2	5.8	74.8	51.0	12.0	68.7
District 13	John Conyers Jr. (D)	479	687 170	1 434.6	38.5	55.1	0.6	1.3	2.6	2.0	6.8	34.3	52.5	6.9	76.3
District 14	Brenda L. Lawrence (D)	481	687 921	1 430.2	34.5	56.6	0.2	4.7	0.9	3.1	4.7	31.1	53.0	11.1	70.1
MINNESOTA		206 232	5 457 173	26.5	84.4	5.7	1.0	4.6	1.6	2.6	5.1	81.3	50.3	7.8	68.2
District 1	Timothy J. Walz (D)	31 012	666 946	21.5	91.6	2.9	0.3	2.7	1.2	1.4	6.2	86.7	50.3	5.8	68.4
District 2	John Kline (R)	6 314	689 759	109.2	85.2	4.4	0.5	4.5	2.7	2.6	5.6	82.6	50.6	7.8	68.3
District 3	Erik Paulsen (R)	1 365	685 736	502.4	81.2	6.6	0.2	7.8	1.2	2.9	4.5	78.3	51.5	11.7	62.6
District 4	Betty McCollum (D)	861	695 920	808.3	72.1	9.6	0.7	12.1	1.7	3.7	6.5	68.2	51.3	12.9	61.8
District 5	Keith Ellison (D)	351	706 584	2 013.1	69.4	16.5	1.0	5.8	3.6	3.7	9.1	64.4	50.2	14.8	55.9
District 6	Tom Emmer (R)	7 465	684 784	91.7	91.6	2.7	0.4	2.2	0.6	2.5	2.6	90.1	49.4	4.4	77.3
District 7	Collin C. Peterson (D)	86 582	662 682	7.7	92.5	1.4	2.6	0.8	1.0	1.7	4.3	89.8	49.8	3.0	73.3
District 8	Richard M. Nolan (D)	72 282	664 762	9.2	93.1	1.0	2.6	0.7	0.3	2.3	1.6	92.0	49.3	1.6	79.2
MISSISSIPPI		121 531	2 994 079	24.6	58.8	37.8	0.4	0.8	0.8	1.3	2.7	57.2	51.3	2.2	71.5
District 1	Trent Kelly (R)	27 383	760 275	27.8	69.5	27.3	0.1	0.7	1.0	1.5	3.0	67.6	51.5	2.2	63.8
District 2	Bennie G. Thompson (D)	40 278	722 640	17.9	31.5	66.2	0.4	0.4	0.9	0.6	2.1	30.7	52.0	1.7	83.9
District 3	Gregg Harper (R)	33 034	749 430	22.7	61.4	35.3	0.8	1.1	0.5	0.9	2.0	60.1	51.1	2.0	76.0
District 4	Steven Palazzo (R)	20 835	761 734	36.6	71.6	23.9	0.4	1.1	1.0	2.0	3.6	69.2	50.7	2.8	63.0
MISSOURI..............		178 040	6 063 589	34.1	82.3	11.7	0.4	1.8	1.2	2.5	3.8	79.9	51.0	3.7	66.1
District 1	William Lacy Clay (D)	584	744 782	1 275.3	44.2	49.2	0.2	2.6	1.0	2.8	2.8	42.2	52.6	5.1	69.7
District 2	Ann Wagner (R)	1 206	758 288	628.8	89.6	3.4	0.1	4.7	0.5	1.6	3.0	87.2	52.0	7.2	65.4
District 3	Blaine Luetkemeyer (R)	17 745	766 993	43.2	92.5	3.7	0.4	0.7	0.9	1.9	2.2	90.9	50.3	2.1	75.6
District 4	Vicky Hartzler (R)	37 299	763 003	20.5	88.8	4.9	0.5	1.5	0.9	3.4	3.5	86.9	50.2	2.8	62.6
District 5	Emanuel Cleaver (D)	6 280	758 442	120.8	67.3	22.2	0.5	1.9	4.8	3.4	8.9	64.0	51.6	5.3	61.4
District 6	Sam Graves (R)	47 134	760 291	16.1	90.9	4.3	0.4	1.2	0.7	2.5	3.7	88.5	50.2	2.8	64.3
District 7	Bill Long (R)	16 247	765 669	47.1	92.5	2.1	0.9	1.3	0.7	2.5	4.8	88.7	50.9	3.0	57.5
District 8	Jason T. Smith (R)	51 544	746 121	14.5	91.7	4.9	0.5	0.8	0.3	1.8	1.8	90.4	50.2	1.4	72.4
MONTANA		376 962	1 023 579	2.7	89.4	0.6	6.8	0.8	0.3	2.1	3.4	86.7	49.8	2.3	54.3
At Large.................	Ryan K. Zinke (R)	376 962	1 023 579	2.7	89.4	0.6	6.8	0.8	0.3	2.1	3.4	86.7	49.8	2.3	54.3
NEBRASKA.............		198 974	1 881 503	9.5	88.3	4.7	1.0	2.1	1.6	2.3	10.1	80.4	50.2	6.7	65.2
District 1	Jeff Fortenberry (R)	22 997	634 290	27.6	89.5	3.0	1.2	2.6	1.2	2.6	8.3	83.2	50.2	6.4	67.0
District 2	Brad Ashford (D)	1 320	641 045	485.6	82.0	9.8	0.8	3.0	1.6	2.8	11.0	73.4	50.4	8.2	60.3
District 3	Adrian Smith (R)	174 657	606 168	3.5	93.7	1.2	0.9	0.7	2.0	1.6	11.1	85.0	50.1	5.3	68.7
NEVADA.................		284 332	2 839 099	10.0	68.0	8.6	1.1	8.5	9.5	4.4	27.8	51.3	49.7	19.4	25.8
District 1	Dina Titus (D)	271	693 623	2 559.5	54.9	11.6	0.5	8.9	20.3	3.8	44.0	33.5	48.4	30.3	22.6
District 2	Mark E. Amodei (R)	144 598	697 426	4.8	83.2	1.6	2.2	4.4	5.1	3.5	21.8	67.6	49.3	12.5	31.2
District 3	Joseph J. Heck (R)	7 379	734 973	99.6	68.0	6.5	0.5	13.8	5.3	5.8	17.0	58.1	50.5	18.9	22.9
District 4	Cresent Hardy (R)	132 084	713 077	5.4	66.0	14.5	1.1	6.4	7.5	4.5	29.2	45.8	50.7	16.1	26.7
NEW HAMPSHIRE..		23 187	1 326 813	57.2	93.4	1.3	0.2	2.6	0.5	2.1	3.2	91.2	50.6	6.0	42.7
District 1	Frank C. Guinta (R)	6 381	665 612	104.3	93.4	1.3	0.1	2.6	0.4	2.3	3.2	91.0	50.9	5.8	42.0
District 2	Ann M. Kuster (D)	16 806	661 201	39.3	93.5	1.2	0.2	2.6	0.6	1.9	3.2	91.3	50.4	6.2	43.4
NEW JERSEY........		19 047	8 938 175	469.3	67.7	13.6	0.2	9.3	6.9	2.3	19.3	56.6	51.2	21.9	52.7
District 1	Donald Norcross (D)	907	732 232	807.3	67.5	17.5	0.2	5.0	8.0	1.9	13.1	63.9	51.7	9.2	55.3
District 2	Frank A. LoBiondo (R)	5 419	733 973	135.4	74.4	13.1	0.2	4.0	5.0	3.3	15.9	65.7	50.7	11.1	61.2
District 3	Thomas MacArthur (R)	2 330	734 551	315.3	80.4	10.2	0.1	3.7	2.2	3.4	7.7	75.5	50.9	9.0	59.9
District 4	Christopher H. Smith (R)	1 792	748 864	417.9	85.6	6.6	0.0	3.9	1.6	2.2	9.8	78.2	51.9	11.5	59.9
District 5	Scott Garrett (R)	2 567	745 147	290.3	77.5	5.4	0.1	10.9	4.5	1.6	13.6	69.2	50.9	21.1	51.2
District 6	Frank Pallone Jr. (D)	558	748 924	1 342.2	63.6	10.2	0.1	18.8	5.3	2.0	21.7	48.4	50.8	28.1	50.3
District 7	Leonard Lance (R)	2 513	748 182	297.7	80.0	5.0	0.1	9.8	3.8	1.3	12.2	71.9	51.3	18.7	56.1
District 8	Albio Sires (D)	142	762 249	5 368.0	57.4	10.2	0.1	9.6	20.0	2.7	54.9	24.8	49.3	43.8	37.4
District 9	Bill Pascrell, Jr. (D)	247	759 352	3 074.3	57.4	10.3	0.5	12.5	16.0	3.3	36.1	40.4	51.5	35.7	44.4
District 10	Donald M. Payne, Jr. (D)	197	742 855	3 770.8	29.0	53.7	0.3	6.4	8.8	1.9	18.9	20.5	52.6	27.4	52.2
District 11	Rodney P. Frelinghuysen (R)	1 308	739 014	565.0	82.1	3.8	0.1	10.0	2.1	1.9	10.6	74.2	51.9	18.5	57.9
District 12	Bonnie Watson Coleman (D)	1 068	742 832	695.5	58.5	17.1	0.2	16.6	5.6	2.1	16.2	48.1	50.8	28.0	47.3
NEW MEXICO........		314 161	2 085 572	6.6	73.1	2.0	9.5	1.5	10.8	3.0	47.7	38.7	50.5	9.9	52.9
District 1	Michelle Lujan Grisham (D)	11 914	699 493	58.7	72.5	2.6	4.4	2.3	13.7	4.5	48.8	40.7	51.2	10.5	53.1
District 2	Steve Pearce (R)	185 804	699 424	3.8	82.2	1.9	5.7	1.0	7.0	2.2	53.4	37.7	49.9	12.1	49.3

1. Dry land or land partially or temporarily covered by water.   2. May be of any race.

STATE District	Population and population characteristics, 2014 (cont.)										Education, 2014		
	Age (percent)											Attainment[2] (percent)	
	Under 5 years	5 to 17 years	18 to 24 years	25 to 34 years	35 to 44 years	45 to 54 years	55 to 64 years	65 to 74 years	75 years and over	Median age	Total Enrollment[1]	High school graduate or more	Bachelor's degree or more
	15	16	17	18	19	20	21	22	23	24	25	26	27
MICHIGAN	5.7	16.7	10.1	12.1	12.0	14.1	13.8	8.8	6.6	39.6	2 555 615	89.9	27.4
District 1	4.6	14.4	9.0	10.3	10.5	13.8	16.3	12.0	9.1	46.0	151 178	91.8	23.9
District 2	6.5	17.8	11.0	12.6	11.6	13.4	12.9	8.0	6.1	36.6	193 352	89.2	25.6
District 3	6.5	18.0	9.3	13.6	12.5	13.8	12.6	7.9	5.9	37.1	189 889	90.3	29.0
District 4	5.2	15.8	12.0	10.8	11.1	13.8	14.0	10.0	7.4	40.9	185 672	90.6	20.9
District 5	5.9	16.7	8.9	11.7	11.9	13.8	14.2	9.5	7.4	40.9	164 701	88.3	19.3
District 6	5.9	17.0	11.0	12.0	11.4	13.6	13.5	9.0	6.6	38.5	187 830	90.2	26.6
District 7	5.3	16.9	8.8	11.1	12.1	14.9	14.5	9.5	6.7	41.9	169 684	90.9	22.4
District 8	5.5	17.3	13.1	11.0	12.1	14.7	13.3	8.0	5.0	37.7	220 354	94.4	38.3
District 9	4.9	15.7	8.9	13.7	12.8	14.7	13.7	8.4	7.2	40.4	171 743	89.4	29.4
District 10	5.4	16.9	8.1	10.5	12.2	15.7	14.7	9.7	6.8	42.8	171 910	90.6	23.0
District 11	5.6	17.2	7.5	12.2	13.4	15.5	14.2	8.2	6.2	41.1	183 781	94.5	45.7
District 12	6.1	15.8	13.3	13.9	12.3	12.8	12.4	7.5	6.0	35.7	212 788	89.3	33.4
District 13	7.1	17.5	11.2	13.2	12.3	13.2	12.6	7.2	5.7	35.8	179 439	81.5	13.9
District 14	5.9	16.6	9.9	12.3	12.0	13.8	13.9	8.7	6.8	39.5	173 294	86.1	30.3
MINNESOTA	6.4	17.1	9.2	13.7	12.3	14.0	13.1	7.9	6.4	37.8	1 398 073	92.6	34.3
District 1	6.3	16.9	10.0	12.9	11.5	13.1	13.3	8.2	7.9	38.5	176 632	91.0	26.8
District 2	6.5	19.0	8.6	12.6	13.4	15.4	12.4	7.1	5.0	37.5	184 710	94.2	37.8
District 3	6.1	17.7	6.7	13.1	12.9	15.1	14.4	7.9	6.1	40.1	171 849	95.6	47.8
District 4	6.7	17.0	10.0	15.5	11.9	13.2	12.5	7.3	5.8	35.5	185 858	91.5	42.6
District 5	6.9	14.2	11.0	19.9	13.5	12.3	11.0	6.1	5.0	33.8	181 766	90.7	43.5
District 6	6.5	19.5	9.5	12.9	13.5	15.3	11.8	6.6	4.3	36.1	188 699	94.4	30.0
District 7	6.3	17.0	9.2	11.3	10.6	13.2	14.1	9.5	9.0	40.8	154 466	90.8	21.3
District 8	5.5	16.0	8.4	11.3	11.1	13.7	15.2	10.5	8.1	43.1	154 093	92.3	22.9
MISSISSIPPI	6.4	18.1	10.4	12.8	12.9	12.7	12.4	8.3	6.0	36.7	806 652	82.8	21.1
District 1	6.0	18.3	10.1	12.6	13.2	13.0	12.1	8.5	6.1	37.1	208 473	82.8	19.2
District 2	6.8	18.5	10.8	13.0	12.7	12.2	12.6	7.6	5.7	35.6	199 357	78.9	18.8
District 3	6.2	17.5	10.4	12.7	12.7	12.6	12.8	8.5	6.5	37.5	199 023	84.3	25.2
District 4	6.6	17.8	10.2	13.1	12.9	12.9	12.5	8.4	5.7	36.7	199 799	84.8	20.9
MISSOURI	6.1	16.8	9.8	13.1	12.1	13.5	13.0	8.7	6.7	38.5	1 537 651	88.9	27.5
District 1	6.7	15.5	10.9	16.0	12.3	13.1	13.1	7.0	5.4	35.6	195 422	88.1	31.0
District 2	5.6	16.6	7.1	12.6	11.9	14.6	14.1	9.3	8.2	42.2	187 968	94.8	48.0
District 3	6.0	18.0	9.0	12.5	12.5	14.5	12.9	8.7	5.8	38.5	192 549	89.7	23.8
District 4	6.0	16.9	13.0	12.4	11.5	12.6	12.4	8.9	6.4	36.7	212 024	88.2	24.1
District 5	6.8	16.8	9.0	15.0	12.2	13.2	12.7	7.7	6.4	36.9	183 155	89.2	26.4
District 6	6.1	17.5	9.4	12.2	12.8	13.9	13.0	8.6	6.5	38.9	194 860	91.3	26.5
District 7	6.1	16.7	10.8	12.7	11.9	13.1	12.6	9.2	7.1	38.3	200 261	87.6	22.9
District 8	5.9	16.6	9.2	11.5	11.6	13.6	13.8	10.2	7.6	41.1	171 412	81.7	16.2
MONTANA	5.8	16.1	10.1	12.6	11.2	12.8	14.8	9.7	6.9	39.6	236 766	92.6	29.3
At Large	5.8	16.1	10.1	12.6	11.2	12.8	14.8	9.7	6.9	39.6	236 766	92.6	29.3
NEBRASKA	6.9	17.9	10.0	13.6	12.1	12.6	12.5	7.7	6.7	36.2	501 598	90.3	29.5
District 1	6.8	17.4	11.9	13.3	12.0	12.3	12.3	7.7	6.2	35.4	175 445	91.9	30.0
District 2	7.6	18.7	9.0	16.0	13.1	12.9	11.5	6.3	4.8	34.0	177 383	89.6	37.7
District 3	6.3	17.6	9.2	11.3	11.2	12.6	13.8	9.2	9.1	40.3	148 770	89.3	20.7
NEVADA	6.2	17.1	9.1	14.3	13.6	13.5	12.1	8.8	5.3	37.4	699 683	85.1	23.1
District 1	6.4	16.8	10.0	15.8	12.6	13.8	11.9	7.8	5.0	35.8	156 890	77.0	15.2
District 2	5.8	16.6	9.4	13.5	11.7	14.0	13.5	9.8	5.7	38.7	177 155	87.1	25.3
District 3	5.7	17.0	7.3	14.7	15.4	13.4	12.0	8.9	5.5	38.5	182 864	91.9	31.8
District 4	6.8	18.2	9.6	13.2	14.3	12.9	11.3	8.8	5.0	36.6	182 774	83.7	19.1
NEW HAMPSHIRE	4.9	15.2	9.7	11.7	12.0	15.8	15.0	9.2	6.5	42.5	314 674	92.2	35.0
District 1	5.2	15.0	9.5	12.4	11.8	15.6	14.9	9.1	6.4	42.3	157 894	92.4	36.0
District 2	4.6	15.5	9.9	10.9	12.2	15.9	15.0	9.3	6.7	42.6	156 780	92.0	34.0
NEW JERSEY	6.0	16.6	8.9	12.9	13.2	14.9	12.9	8.2	6.5	39.4	2 272 659	89.1	37.4
District 1	6.1	16.7	9.0	13.6	12.5	14.3	13.3	8.2	6.3	38.7	186 150	89.4	30.4
District 2	5.9	16.2	8.9	11.9	12.2	14.6	13.7	9.7	7.0	41.4	173 937	85.1	23.4
District 3	4.9	16.0	8.4	11.3	12.1	15.1	13.8	9.9	8.5	43.0	175 220	93.0	33.5
District 4	6.7	17.4	8.0	10.7	11.0	14.9	13.4	9.3	8.4	41.6	196 864	92.0	38.7
District 5	5.0	17.2	8.7	9.9	12.4	16.9	14.1	8.9	6.8	43.0	193 831	93.1	44.7
District 6	5.9	16.3	10.7	14.1	13.6	14.9	11.9	7.3	5.1	36.9	202 849	88.7	38.6
District 7	5.0	18.6	8.3	9.0	13.1	17.4	14.0	8.3	6.3	42.4	199 121	94.4	52.1
District 8	7.0	14.3	9.3	20.5	15.5	13.3	9.9	5.7	4.4	34.4	181 061	79.5	30.7
District 9	6.6	16.8	8.6	14.4	14.3	13.6	12.0	7.5	6.2	37.2	188 404	84.9	32.6
District 10	7.3	16.4	10.6	14.7	14.1	13.6	12.0	6.5	4.6	35.6	202 623	86.0	27.4
District 11	5.0	16.6	7.8	10.4	13.0	16.3	13.7	9.1	8.0	43.2	185 958	94.1	52.3
District 12	5.8	16.2	8.7	13.1	14.1	14.3	13.3	7.8	6.7	39.5	186 641	88.6	43.5
NEW MEXICO	6.5	17.4	10.1	13.2	11.8	12.7	13.0	8.9	6.3	37.2	560 799	84.2	26.4
District 1	6.1	16.4	9.8	14.5	12.2	13.2	13.0	8.7	6.2	37.7	186 001	87.5	31.8
District 2	7.0	18.2	11.3	12.4	11.0	12.2	12.2	9.1	6.5	36.1	192 995	79.9	21.1

1. All persons 3 years old and over enrolled in nursery school through college and graduate or professional school.   2. Persons 25 years old and over.

Table E. Congressional Districts 114th Congress — **Households and Group Quarters**

STATE District	Households, 2014						Group quarters, 2010					
	Number	Average household size	Family households (percent)	Married-couple family (percent)	Female family householder[1]	One person households (percent)	Total in group quarters, 2014	Percent 65 years and over	Persons in correctional institutions	Persons in nursing facilities	Persons in college dormitories	Persons in military quarters
	28	29	30	31	32	33	34	35	36	37	38	39
MICHIGAN	3 834 574	2.53	64.8	47.3	12.7	29.1	226 720	19.8	62 083	42 473	78 033	214
District 1.............................	287 370	2.35	62.8	50.3	8.2	31.7	28 397	20.2	12 990	4 884	5 714	129
District 2.............................	268 751	2.62	69.8	53.0	12.2	24.5	19 556	17.4	5 021	2 948	6 414	0
District 3.............................	267 811	2.64	66.8	50.6	11.6	26.4	17 638	18.1	7 012	3 695	5 151	82
District 4.............................	269 433	2.51	66.2	51.7	9.9	26.9	26 689	13.6	9 024	3 606	13 524	0
District 5.............................	281 383	2.41	63.8	42.5	15.9	30.2	9 679	33.6	1 630	3 103	1 303	3
District 6.............................	276 704	2.51	66.0	50.0	11.5	26.6	17 399	22.3	1 476	3 141	6 864	0
District 7.............................	272 507	2.49	68.2	52.4	11.0	26.6	23 337	15.0	14 438	2 638	4 594	0
District 8.............................	272 435	2.58	65.9	51.9	10.0	26.9	21 514	10.0	988	1 873	16 015	0
District 9.............................	298 688	2.39	60.5	41.4	14.0	33.1	6 289	50.7	1 143	3 267	0	0
District 10...........................	269 546	2.59	69.6	56.7	9.4	25.7	9 083	36.3	3 120	2 375	0	0
District 11...........................	274 567	2.59	68.7	56.0	8.7	26.2	6 265	45.5	183	2 598	1 581	0
District 12...........................	269 662	2.54	61.0	43.7	12.8	30.5	19 769	11.9	387	2 155	13 873	0
District 13...........................	257 008	2.64	58.9	27.9	23.6	35.9	9 865	21.2	114	2 806	2 287	0
District 14...........................	268 709	2.52	59.3	34.0	20.0	35.9	11 240	23.4	4 557	3 384	713	0
MINNESOTA.......................	2 129 195	2.50	64.3	50.5	9.6	28.7	134 875	24.9	20 397	32 989	50 444	0
District 1.............................	261 328	2.46	65.5	52.4	8.8	27.9	23 494	23.9	4 808	5 137	9 723	0
District 2.............................	254 262	2.67	70.4	57.1	9.4	24.5	10 632	25.8	1 042	2 781	4 486	0
District 3.............................	268 815	2.53	66.9	54.2	9.3	26.9	4 691	38.8	551	1 864	644	0
District 4.............................	267 760	2.53	60.8	44.5	12.1	31.3	19 527	16.8	3 286	3 540	9 958	0
District 5.............................	293 412	2.33	49.2	34.7	10.4	38.3	22 621	20.9	876	5 425	8 740	0
District 6.............................	242 232	2.77	73.7	59.0	9.5	20.3	14 836	19.1	3 328	2 246	5 885	0
District 7.............................	267 071	2.41	65.3	53.1	8.0	29.4	18 482	40.1	1 022	7 051	6 518	0
District 8.............................	274 315	2.35	65.4	51.9	8.9	29.1	20 592	25.9	5 484	4 945	4 490	0
MISSISSIPPI......................	1 095 823	2.64	67.4	44.0	18.3	28.6	96 334	16.0	34 273	16 496	26 472	3 938
District 1.............................	282 173	2.63	69.5	48.1	15.9	27.1	18 068	22.9	2 943	4 381	7 786	0
District 2.............................	255 841	2.70	66.4	36.3	24.7	30.9	32 229	11.7	14 994	4 226	8 476	8
District 3.............................	280 938	2.58	66.2	45.3	16.5	29.4	25 977	18.4	9 560	4 625	5 828	601
District 4.............................	276 871	2.68	67.4	45.6	16.7	27.2	20 060	14.6	6 776	3 264	4 382	3 329
MISSOURI	2 354 809	2.50	64.1	47.8	11.9	29.8	174 872	22.7	41 956	44 866	52 869	10 217
District 1.............................	307 630	2.36	53.8	30.6	18.9	39.3	19 474	17.6	1 344	4 741	9 050	0
District 2.............................	297 764	2.51	67.8	54.8	9.0	27.6	11 452	55.7	2 300	7 231	1 046	0
District 3.............................	283 399	2.64	71.0	56.1	9.8	23.9	18 469	19.1	6 107	3 662	5 666	0
District 4.............................	283 862	2.56	65.6	51.2	10.1	27.0	36 304	13.4	6 015	5 555	11 262	10 217
District 5.............................	307 730	2.42	56.1	37.0	14.5	36.7	13 456	31.8	1 420	5 172	2 626	0
District 6.............................	285 617	2.56	67.4	53.8	9.5	27.3	29 549	20.5	11 433	6 573	8 326	0
District 7.............................	299 852	2.49	65.3	50.3	10.9	27.6	20 500	22.7	2 358	4 919	9 841	0
District 8.............................	288 955	2.49	66.7	50.2	12.0	28.0	25 668	23.9	10 979	7 013	5 052	0
MONTANA	410 962	2.42	61.1	48.5	8.2	31.2	28 887	19.2	5 338	5 200	8 332	678
At Large	410 962	2.42	61.1	48.5	8.2	31.2	28 887	19.2	5 338	5 200	8 332	678
NEBRASKA.........................	740 765	2.47	64.8	50.2	10.5	28.6	52 101	24.4	8 084	13 519	22 073	443
District 1.............................	249 406	2.47	65.1	50.5	10.7	27.7	19 441	19.1	3 362	4 124	10 719	443
District 2.............................	243 695	2.58	63.5	46.7	12.2	29.1	13 026	17.6	2 325	2 632	4 750	0
District 3.............................	247 664	2.37	65.9	53.3	8.8	28.9	19 634	35.5	2 397	6 763	6 604	0
NEVADA	1 021 519	2.74	62.9	43.8	12.5	29.2	36 558	15.2	19 891	5 005	3 336	1 022
District 1.............................	245 248	2.79	58.2	34.7	15.5	33.6	9 332	11.3	4 771	954	1 211	0
District 2.............................	262 993	2.61	62.7	47.1	10.1	29.3	11 561	12.8	6 685	1 334	2 125	166
District 3.............................	274 521	2.67	64.3	47.3	10.8	27.5	2 226	58.1	352	1 044	0	0
District 4.............................	238 757	2.93	66.3	45.4	14.1	26.4	13 439	14.2	8 083	1 673	0	856
NEW HAMPSHIRE	519 756	2.47	66.6	52.1	9.8	25.4	40 523	19.5	4 851	7 767	22 820	454
District 1.............................	262 564	2.46	65.0	50.8	9.6	26.3	18 758	21.5	1 640	3 963	10 357	454
District 2.............................	257 192	2.49	68.1	53.5	9.9	24.6	21 765	17.9	3 211	3 804	12 463	0
NEW JERSEY.....................	3 194 844	2.74	69.0	50.3	13.8	25.9	185 527	23.7	44 468	45 512	55 483	1 452
District 1.............................	271 572	2.66	66.9	46.0	15.8	27.5	10 825	33.0	2 221	3 995	2 424	0
District 2.............................	268 122	2.65	68.1	46.6	15.8	26.0	23 578	17.9	11 704	4 360	2 376	768
District 3.............................	274 785	2.62	70.8	54.7	12.0	24.3	15 223	26.5	6 383	4 169	0	360
District 4.............................	270 829	2.74	68.1	55.3	9.3	27.2	7 610	50.3	1 319	4 614	1 306	254
District 5.............................	264 036	2.77	73.9	58.9	10.1	22.4	14 846	39.2	1 041	5 005	4 364	0
District 6.............................	250 583	2.87	71.5	53.3	13.7	23.6	28 810	12.3	2 976	3 169	15 266	70
District 7.............................	264 239	2.79	73.2	61.6	8.8	23.5	12 143	37.9	2 789	3 543	129	0
District 8.............................	276 592	2.73	61.9	35.8	18.7	27.9	7 867	22.0	3 043	2 492	1 409	0
District 9.............................	261 555	2.88	70.9	48.7	16.6	24.6	5 706	26.3	1 068	1 145	468	0
District 10...........................	263 010	2.75	61.8	32.7	23.0	32.9	20 767	11.0	7 245	2 896	6 771	0
District 11...........................	263 467	2.74	71.2	58.8	9.1	24.3	15 928	30.3	411	5 741	9 278	0
District 12...........................	266 054	2.71	69.8	52.2	12.6	25.9	22 224	16.9	4 268	4 383	11 692	0
NEW MEXICO	760 916	2.68	64.3	44.8	14.0	29.9	43 150	14.3	17 907	5 567	8 478	1 789
District 1.............................	270 360	2.55	62.1	41.8	14.1	31.6	10 721	15.9	4 489	1 768	2 750	530
District 2.............................	248 398	2.73	67.2	47.4	14.9	27.5	20 144	11.7	9 874	2 334	3 613	815

1. No spouse present.

STATE District	Housing units, 2014						Money income, 2014		
	Total	Occupied units					Households		
			Owner-occupied			Renter-occupied			
	Total	Occupied units as a percent of all units	Owner-occupied units as a percent of occupied units	Median value[1] (dollars)	Percent valued at $500,000 or more	Median rent[2]	Per capita income (dollars)	Median income (dollars)	Percent with income of $100,000 or more
	40	41	42	43	44	45	46	47	48
MICHIGAN	4 540 088	84.5	70.2	125 700	3.0	788	26 613	49 847	19.4
District 1	443 848	64.7	78.7	119 600	4.1	677	24 837	44 265	13.1
District 2	313 719	85.7	72.9	125 700	1.8	740	23 580	49 175	16.1
District 3	295 974	90.5	71.1	137 600	2.5	780	26 028	52 809	19.8
District 4	344 608	78.2	76.3	111 900	0.9	679	23 455	44 572	14.8
District 5	329 603	85.4	69.5	89 700	0.8	697	23 138	41 597	12.9
District 6	325 708	85.0	69.7	130 900	3.7	701	24 668	46 697	17.0
District 7	304 753	89.4	76.6	130 600	2.2	749	26 935	53 554	20.4
District 8	295 594	92.2	72.2	176 900	4.7	854	32 126	63 645	29.7
District 9	322 836	92.5	67.3	121 100	3.4	880	29 718	50 706	20.3
District 10	305 706	88.2	79.7	154 400	2.0	816	27 981	58 479	23.3
District 11	292 518	93.9	76.1	196 200	7.1	962	38 098	74 527	36.2
District 12	290 736	92.8	63.9	122 200	3.7	904	28 544	52 569	21.9
District 13	339 393	75.7	53.6	59 800	0.4	737	17 115	31 887	8.5
District 14	335 092	80.2	54.5	90 100	3.4	858	25 665	41 516	17.2
MINNESOTA......................	2 385 261	89.3	71.7	188 300	5.8	859	32 638	61 481	26.9
District 1	285 084	91.7	73.7	152 700	3.0	701	29 231	57 321	21.3
District 2	266 439	95.4	76.9	225 900	5.9	973	35 653	76 409	35.9
District 3	281 573	95.5	75.2	251 100	14.5	1 097	43 833	79 965	39.5
District 4	281 445	95.1	63.0	215 000	7.0	897	33 737	61 244	28.9
District 5	313 138	93.7	53.8	193 800	6.3	887	32 474	52 447	23.9
District 6	260 310	93.1	80.8	198 300	4.0	852	31 806	71 604	32.0
District 7	327 413	81.6	76.3	138 400	2.9	654	26 998	51 880	17.2
District 8	369 859	74.2	76.6	156 200	3.3	719	26 884	51 322	17.6
MISSISSIPPI......................	1 294 738	84.6	67.7	104 000	1.7	711	21 036	39 680	13.6
District 1	323 162	87.3	68.9	106 100	1.6	711	21 358	41 448	13.4
District 2	310 126	82.5	62.7	81 900	0.6	644	17 222	32 701	10.4
District 3	329 850	85.2	71.8	113 200	2.7	722	24 387	41 762	17.5
District 4	331 600	83.5	66.8	118 000	1.5	769	21 035	41 944	12.7
MISSOURI	2 735 803	86.1	66.9	138 500	3.5	754	26 126	48 363	18.0
District 1	370 871	82.9	51.0	102 000	3.2	798	24 466	40 843	13.6
District 2	315 314	94.4	79.4	214 400	9.7	953	41 147	74 868	35.9
District 3	335 146	84.6	77.1	157 700	2.3	778	26 614	58 204	21.0
District 4	344 251	82.5	66.7	131 800	1.8	733	22 549	45 674	14.5
District 5	354 606	86.8	56.6	114 600	2.3	788	25 183	43 513	14.9
District 6	327 132	87.3	71.3	141 400	3.0	713	26 625	54 389	20.7
District 7	348 845	86.0	65.5	122 400	2.4	698	22 183	41 004	12.8
District 8	339 638	85.1	69.3	105 300	1.9	615	20 170	38 400	10.6
MONTANA	491 515	83.6	66.4	196 800	7.1	711	25 989	46 328	17.0
At Large	491 515	83.6	66.4	196 800	7.1	711	25 989	46 328	17.0
NEBRASKA......................	814 957	90.9	65.9	133 800	2.7	742	27 446	52 686	20.1
District 1	268 041	93.0	65.0	141 200	2.5	741	27 562	54 310	20.5
District 2	262 055	93.0	62.8	149 700	3.1	835	29 037	56 867	24.7
District 3	284 861	86.9	70.0	102 800	2.5	635	25 641	48 359	15.3
NEVADA	1 198 969	85.2	53.6	192 100	6.3	955	25 773	51 450	18.9
District 1	301 626	81.3	39.4	130 200	3.4	837	19 672	37 724	9.9
District 2	299 015	88.0	61.1	211 900	7.7	872	27 250	53 070	20.6
District 3	317 951	86.3	55.5	239 500	9.8	1 170	32 230	62 934	26.0
District 4	280 377	85.2	57.9	174 100	2.9	997	23 609	52 378	17.9
NEW HAMPSHIRE	619 865	83.8	70.2	236 400	6.9	994	34 691	66 532	30.4
District 1	316 142	83.1	69.6	242 900	7.4	1 002	35 431	67 083	32.2
District 2	303 723	84.7	70.8	229 400	6.3	986	33 945	65 933	28.6
NEW JERSEY......................	3 591 847	88.9	63.3	313 200	20.1	1 202	36 593	71 919	36.0
District 1	297 501	91.3	68.8	193 500	3.2	994	31 715	64 464	30.4
District 2	384 623	69.7	70.6	218 100	9.9	1 016	29 364	57 765	25.7
District 3	312 039	88.1	80.2	252 500	8.2	1 317	36 702	75 658	36.3
District 4	299 770	90.3	74.8	340 200	23.7	1 272	39 120	75 857	39.1
District 5	283 618	93.1	74.6	395 000	31.7	1 271	43 366	91 749	46.3
District 6	273 497	91.6	61.6	322 500	15.0	1 320	34 127	77 184	37.5
District 7	281 504	93.9	77.2	415 100	36.1	1 360	51 247	105 386	53.0
District 8	304 819	90.7	27.8	307 400	18.5	1 169	29 182	53 397	24.3
District 9	283 719	92.2	45.9	351 600	20.0	1 257	30 330	60 540	30.5
District 10	302 278	87.0	37.7	263 600	11.6	1 071	26 025	47 363	20.9
District 11	279 324	94.3	75.8	420 100	35.6	1 392	49 017	98 964	49.6
District 12	289 155	92.0	64.2	321 000	20.6	1 248	39 034	77 694	39.7
NEW MEXICO	912 910	83.4	66.9	158 400	5.4	777	23 683	44 803	17.0
District 1	301 123	89.8	62.1	180 200	4.8	800	26 206	46 267	19.6
District 2	304 327	81.6	68.4	118 600	3.1	713	20 281	41 013	13.2

1. Specified owner-occupied units; $1,000,000 represents $1,000,000 or more.   2. Specified renter-occupied units.

Table E. Congressional Districts 114th Congress — Poverty, Labor Force, Employment, and Social Security

STATE District	Poverty, 2014 Persons below poverty level (percent)	Families below poverty level (percent)	Percent of households receiving food stamps in past 12 months	Civilian labor force, 2014 Total	Unemployment Total	Rate[1]	Civilian employment,[2] 2014 Total	Percent Management, business, science and arts occupations	Service, sales, and office	Construction and production	Persons under age 65 with no health insurance, 2014 (percent)	Social Security beneficiaries, December 2014 Number	Rate[3]	Supplemental Security Income recipients, December 2014
	49	50	51	52	53	54	55	56	57	58	59	60	61	62
MICHIGAN	16.2	11.4	16.2	4 848 831	400 797	8.3	4 448 034	35.2	41.0	23.8	10.0	2 121 776	214.1	277 309
District 1	14.5	9.2	13.7	323 399	25 163	7.8	298 236	30.8	44.4	24.8	12.3	200 557	285.0	15 626
District 2	15.1	10.3	15.7	362 634	26 688	7.4	335 946	32.3	38.5	29.2	9.3	148 791	205.3	16 192
District 3	15.1	9.8	14.3	364 637	24 033	6.6	340 604	34.6	39.7	25.7	9.9	138 392	190.8	18 485
District 4	17.9	11.3	14.9	325 528	25 405	7.8	300 123	31.2	42.2	26.6	10.4	171 810	244.5	16 857
District 5	21.0	16.4	22.9	304 309	34 754	11.4	269 555	30.2	44.8	25.0	8.6	172 824	251.5	29 657
District 6	16.8	11.8	15.0	355 424	24 604	6.9	330 820	32.1	39.2	28.7	10.2	153 230	215.2	17 643
District 7	11.5	8.3	13.1	341 568	22 950	6.7	318 618	32.1	40.3	27.6	9.1	158 423	225.4	13 652
District 8	11.7	6.5	10.2	377 504	24 336	6.4	353 168	42.9	39.5	17.6	7.4	128 230	176.8	11 544
District 9	14.9	11.8	15.6	375 533	28 573	7.6	346 960	37.6	41.7	20.8	10.4	151 063	209.7	19 276
District 10	9.7	6.4	11.3	350 966	24 054	6.9	326 912	33.3	39.5	27.2	8.9	156 056	220.9	12 432
District 11	6.5	4.6	6.4	382 597	21 261	5.6	361 336	49.4	35.9	14.7	7.2	133 866	186.3	7 853
District 12	16.7	11.5	14.2	353 754	27 623	7.8	326 131	40.5	38.9	20.6	8.3	131 943	187.1	16 517
District 13	32.3	26.3	35.0	307 673	48 323	15.7	259 350	24.4	47.3	28.3	14.7	134 669	196.0	42 140
District 14	24.0	20.1	25.0	323 305	43 030	13.3	280 275	36.2	45.3	18.4	14.0	141 922	206.3	39 435
MINNESOTA	11.5	7.5	9.2	3 005 705	141 188	4.7	2 864 517	40.4	38.9	20.7	6.8	965 018	176.8	94 207
District 1	12.3	7.8	8.6	363 954	15 355	4.2	348 599	36.9	37.7	20.9	6.8	131 597	197.3	9 200
District 2	7.4	5.1	5.8	394 392	14 819	3.8	379 573	41.5	39.1	19.4	5.6	102 791	149.0	6 772
District 3	6.4	3.9	5.5	385 478	13 272	3.4	372 206	47.6	38.3	14.1	5.5	112 437	164.0	7 032
District 4	13.9	10.4	13.1	377 744	21 701	5.7	356 043	46.1	38.1	15.8	6.7	109 260	157.0	18 134
District 5	18.7	12.6	13.9	416 686	26 558	6.4	390 128	46.1	39.2	14.7	9.4	95 218	134.8	22 629
District 6	7.6	4.8	7.2	387 862	18 169	4.7	369 693	37.4	40.0	22.6	4.7	103 193	150.7	6 911
District 7	12.3	7.9	8.6	348 991	12 953	3.7	336 038	32.5	38.0	29.6	7.8	149 594	225.7	10 500
District 8	13.2	8.5	10.3	330 598	18 361	5.6	312 237	32.9	41.4	25.7	7.7	160 928	242.1	13 029
MISSISSIPPI	21.5	16.5	18.1	1 339 521	130 935	9.8	1 208 586	31.1	41.4	27.6	16.8	640 772	214.0	125 595
District 1	18.6	13.7	16.1	351 931	31 261	8.9	320 670	30.3	38.3	31.5	16.4	167 280	220.0	25 679
District 2	28.2	22.5	23.5	308 884	43 662	14.1	265 222	28.7	44.2	27.2	18.2	158 096	218.8	47 444
District 3	20.7	15.4	14.8	342 122	23 903	7.0	318 219	36.2	39.2	24.6	14.2	156 805	209.2	27 838
District 4	19.1	14.9	18.4	336 584	32 109	9.5	304 475	28.7	44.5	26.8	18.4	158 591	208.2	24 634
MISSOURI	15.5	10.7	12.8	3 009 857	204 211	6.8	2 805 646	36.0	42.6	21.4	13.7	1 246 269	205.5	142 768
District 1	20.1	14.6	19.6	393 758	42 436	10.8	351 322	37.9	46.4	15.7	15.4	134 535	180.6	30 610
District 2	6.0	4.0	4.1	400 065	16 848	4.2	383 217	50.8	37.6	11.7	7.1	149 030	196.5	5 830
District 3	11.6	7.9	9.4	391 053	22 529	5.8	368 524	33.1	42.5	24.4	10.9	155 606	202.9	10 777
District 4	17.5	12.1	12.9	353 400	22 775	6.4	330 625	34.1	41.8	24.1	14.9	157 015	205.8	15 708
District 5	17.2	12.2	14.0	390 776	26 880	6.9	363 896	34.6	44.3	21.1	15.4	144 942	191.1	19 728
District 6	12.6	8.4	10.4	385 575	19 995	5.2	365 580	34.3	41.7	24.0	11.6	147 841	194.5	12 290
District 7	18.4	12.7	12.8	369 913	24 431	6.6	345 482	32.6	44.4	23.0	16.8	171 629	224.2	18 183
District 8	20.6	14.8	18.6	325 317	28 317	8.7	297 000	28.6	42.4	29.0	17.3	185 671	248.8	29 642
MONTANA	15.4	9.5	11.1	520 318	25 696	4.9	494 622	36.1	41.1	22.8	16.9	212 535	207.6	18 248
At Large	15.4	9.5	11.1	520 318	25 696	4.9	494 622	36.1	41.1	22.8	16.9	212 535	207.6	18 248
NEBRASKA	12.4	8.7	9.4	1 024 201	42 752	4.2	981 449	36.0	40.5	23.4	11.2	326 078	173.3	27 719
District 1	11.9	8.0	8.5	349 834	13 779	3.9	336 055	35.7	40.4	23.9	10.1	106 038	167.2	8 508
District 2	12.5	8.6	9.9	352 645	17 514	5.0	335 131	40.1	42.3	17.6	11.7	91 890	143.3	10 543
District 3	13.0	9.5	9.8	321 722	11 459	3.6	310 263	32.0	38.8	29.2	11.8	128 150	211.4	8 668
NEVADA	15.2	11.0	12.3	1 425 975	127 154	8.9	1 298 821	27.6	54.4	18.0	17.4	475 811	167.6	50 919
District 1	22.1	18.1	20.3	352 662	40 169	11.4	312 493	17.5	63.6	18.9	26.0	104 209	150.2	16 842
District 2	15.5	9.7	10.2	350 533	26 784	7.6	323 749	32.0	45.8	22.2	15.1	133 093	190.8	10 392
District 3	9.1	6.4	6.5	387 435	27 535	7.1	359 900	33.8	53.7	12.5	12.5	120 059	163.4	8 150
District 4	14.6	11.0	13.1	335 345	32 666	9.7	302 679	26.0	54.8	19.2	16.2	118 450	166.1	15 535
NEW HAMPSHIRE	9.2	6.0	7.9	742 710	37 863	5.1	704 847	39.4	40.4	20.2	10.8	283 983	214.0	19 671
District 1	9.5	6.3	8.0	377 126	19 682	5.2	357 444	39.4	41.4	19.2	11.3	139 773	210.0	9 952
District 2	8.8	5.7	7.8	365 584	18 181	5.0	347 403	39.4	39.4	21.2	10.2	144 210	218.1	9 719
NEW JERSEY	11.1	8.3	9.2	4 725 817	355 865	7.5	4 369 952	41.2	41.1	17.7	12.6	1 568 016	175.4	181 606
District 1	12.0	8.8	11.7	390 161	31 947	8.2	358 214	39.3	42.2	18.5	11.2	139 217	190.1	20 225
District 2	14.0	10.6	12.6	371 801	34 794	9.4	337 007	31.7	47.0	21.3	12.9	160 469	218.6	17 894
District 3	7.2	5.0	6.0	380 871	30 935	8.1	349 936	39.6	43.7	16.8	8.4	168 148	228.9	9 728
District 4	10.6	7.5	7.1	370 559	23 438	6.3	347 121	42.8	40.5	16.7	9.2	155 525	207.7	9 037
District 5	5.4	3.3	4.1	403 487	22 816	5.7	380 671	45.4	39.3	15.4	8.8	132 629	178.0	8 142
District 6	9.5	7.0	7.5	394 222	26 504	6.7	367 718	42.3	38.1	19.7	12.9	112 773	150.6	12 528
District 7	4.9	3.2	3.3	408 536	20 982	5.1	387 554	50.9	36.1	12.9	6.7	120 976	161.7	6 011
District 8	18.3	15.7	16.2	432 509	36 553	8.5	395 956	32.1	42.9	25.0	23.9	89 479	117.4	25 795
District 9	17.3	13.9	14.1	381 675	22 237	5.8	359 438	35.6	42.0	22.3	18.2	118 629	156.2	19 384
District 10	19.8	17.1	17.5	387 390	51 608	13.3	335 782	34.5	46.6	18.9	17.0	106 972	144.0	31 371
District 11	4.2	2.4	2.8	402 837	24 837	6.2	378 000	50.6	38.1	11.3	6.9	135 722	183.7	6 655
District 12	9.7	7.5	7.5	401 769	29 214	7.3	372 555	47.4	38.4	14.2	12.5	127 477	171.6	14 836
NEW MEXICO	21.3	16.5	15.5	958 074	83 321	8.7	874 753	35.2	44.2	20.6	16.8	399 987	191.8	64 059
District 1	19.9	16.0	13.9	343 066	28 475	8.3	314 591	39.7	43.3	17.1	14.7	128 075	183.1	18 880
District 2	24.5	19.3	18.5	301 359	26 770	8.9	274 589	28.5	46.8	24.7	17.3	137 844	197.1	23 760

1. Percent of civilian labor force.   2. Persons 16 years old and over.   3. Per 1,000 resident population estimated in the 2014 American Community Survey.

Table E. Congressional Districts 114th Congress — **Agriculture**

STATE District	Agriculture, 2012 Land in farms — Number of farms	Acres	Average size of farm (acres)	Irrigated land (acres)	Value of products sold — Total ($1,000)	Average per farm (dollars)	Percent from crops	Percent from livestock and poultry products	Government payments — Total ($1,000)	Average per farm receiving payments (dollars)
	63	64	65	66	67	68	69	70	71	72
MICHIGAN	52 194	9 948 564	191	592 243	8 678 050	166 265	63.5	36.5	155 919	7 567
District 1	7 028	1 174 716	167	17 529	304 476	43 323	55.8	44.2	12 542	7 241
District 2	3 913	596 787	153	48 685	927 761	237 097	58.1	41.9	7 836	8 257
District 3	4 328	804 218	186	32 235	865 263	199 922	45.6	54.4	13 587	7 922
District 4	10 328	2 076 879	201	100 624	1 711 590	165 723	58.5	41.5	29 973	6 191
District 5	2 837	598 773	211	9 459	462 461	163 011	87.4	12.6	9 239	6 103
District 6	6 072	1 155 210	190	289 103	1 603 431	264 070	63.2	36.8	18 373	9 379
District 7	8 650	1 623 909	188	76 959	991 129	114 581	77.1	22.9	34 636	8 108
District 8	2 057	316 696	154	3 079	200 689	97 564	76.9	23.1	4 270	10 363
District 9	26	D	D	13	1 700	65 380	94.0	6.0	D	D
District 10	6 328	1 559 304	246	13 305	1 561 544	246 767	65.2	34.8	25 149	8 030
District 11	191	8 146	43	513	13 673	71 587	94.7	5.3	21	1 935
District 12	379	30 066	79	562	30 614	80 777	98.6	1.4	282	4 780
District 13	44	2 399	55	173	3 605	81 921	99.6	0.4	6	1 443
District 14	13	D	D	4	115	8 857	100.0	0.0	D	D
MINNESOTA	74 542	26 035 838	349	524 016	21 280 184	285 479	65.2	34.8	467 867	8 962
District 1	19 041	6 309 496	331	22 341	7 132 552	374 589	58.9	41.1	133 151	8 920
District 2	4 642	1 121 134	242	58 464	1 146 580	247 001	62.6	37.4	21 757	7 489
District 3	699	78 393	112	625	65 380	93 534	81.2	18.8	1 223	4 703
District 4	372	34 196	92	1 069	37 456	100 689	92.5	7.5	448	4 766
District 5	32	1 477	46	26	4 610	144 055	99.7	0.3	9	2 266
District 6	5 739	1 084 584	189	69 319	939 820	163 760	57.5	42.5	18 404	5 481
District 7	33 431	15 157 479	453	276 423	11 010 000	329 444	71.8	28.3	276 140	10 362
District 8	10 586	2 249 079	212	95 749	940 152	88 811	45.7	54.3	16 736	4 177
MISSISSIPPI	38 076	10 931 080	287	1 651 978	6 441 025	169 162	46.2	53.8	181 205	10 983
District 1	10 989	2 650 855	241	41 049	785 235	71 456	59.0	41.0	32 055	5 487
District 2	10 256	5 182 018	505	1 580 386	2 848 319	277 722	79.4	20.6	124 539	19 898
District 3	10 656	2 250 486	211	25 717	2 096 730	196 765	7.7	92.3	17 972	5 567
District 4	6 175	847 721	137	4 826	710 741	115 100	12.0	88.0	6 640	5 680
MISSOURI	99 171	28 266 137	285	1 180 886	9 164 886	92 415	49.8	50.2	323 953	7 834
District 1	60	6 587	110	218	3 893	64 882	92.6	7.4	62	3 422
District 2	209	28 798	138	300	17 733	84 847	98.2	1.8	285	6 059
District 3	11 580	2 688 776	232	19 373	684 080	59 074	41.2	58.8	19 580	4 688
District 4	23 699	6 461 439	273	50 614	1 917 653	80 917	37.2	62.8	54 640	6 422
District 5	3 727	1 121 876	301	13 153	444 240	119 195	75.8	24.2	14 699	6 789
District 6	27 780	9 406 377	339	66 257	2 807 585	101 065	60.0	40.0	160 256	8 483
District 7	12 894	2 269 377	176	11 727	1 301 247	100 919	7.6	92.4	9 439	4 762
District 8	19 222	6 282 907	327	1 019 244	1 988 454	103 447	72.0	28.0	64 993	11 677
MONTANA	28 008	59 758 917	2 134	1 903 019	4 230 083	151 031	53.3	46.7	209 846	16 865
At Large	28 008	59 758 917	2 134	1 903 019	4 230 083	151 031	53.3	46.7	209 846	16 865
NEBRASKA	49 969	45 331 783	907	8 296 573	23 068 756	461 661	49.3	50.7	392 428	11 436
District 1	13 381	5 484 143	410	1 187 864	5 270 537	393 882	46.5	53.5	90 779	9 562
District 2	738	169 478	230	28 590	115 796	156 905	83.2	16.8	2 519	6 845
District 3	35 850	39 678 162	1 107	7 080 119	17 680 000	493 234	49.9	50.1	299 130	12 232
NEVADA	4 137	5 913 761	1 429	687 790	764 144	184 710	47.9	52.1	3 253	9 568
District 1	X	X	X	X	X	X	X	X	X	X
District 2	2 991	5 105 484	1 707	528 164	552 567	184 743	49.0	51.0	2 568	9 303
District 3	66	6 105	93	D	D	D	D	D	D	D
District 4	1 074	802 153	747	159 045	210 323	195 831	44.9	55.1	D	D
NEW HAMPSHIRE	4 391	474 065	108	2 630	190 907	43 477	52.8	47.2	3 472	7 435
District 1	1 576	118 543	75	1 011	42 022	26 664	58.4	41.6	1 110	7 761
District 2	2 815	355 522	126	1 619	148 885	52 890	51.2	48.8	2 362	7 290
NEW JERSEY	9 071	715 057	79	88 376	1 006 936	111 006	88.5	11.5	7 596	7 332
District 1	357	21 147	59	5 235	39 064	109 422	96.3	3.7	226	8 707
District 2	2 409	235 314	98	57 342	482 153	200 147	93.7	6.3	2 652	7 245
District 3	860	94 990	110	13 112	101 201	117 676	95.4	4.6	1 939	17 315
District 4	906	45 690	50	4 542	93 422	103 115	82.2	17.8	296	4 479
District 5	1 571	109 563	70	1 993	97 306	61 939	58.1	41.9	884	5 357
District 6	122	6 224	51	606	12 143	99 531	79.7	20.3	5	752
District 7	2 154	155 495	72	2 042	114 738	53 267	86.0	14.0	1 142	4 989
District 8	X	X	X	X	X	X	X	X	X	X
District 9	11	D	D	D	D	D	D	D	D	D
District 10	X	X	X	X	X	X	X	X	X	X
District 11	264	11 276	43	286	24 624	93 272	D	D	5	1 176
District 12	416	35 112	84	3 207	41 520	99 808	92.7	7.3	447	7 320
NEW MEXICO	24 721	43 201 023	1 748	680 318	2 550 147	103 157	24.2	75.8	70 588	12 830
District 1	1 868	2 249 327	1 204	33 967	73 029	39 095	44.7	55.3	3 559	14 829
District 2	10 130	21 702 074	2 142	369 030	1 599 576	157 905	27.4	72.6	37 277	16 257

Table E. Congressional Districts 114th Congress — Nonfarm Employment and Payroll

Private nonfarm employment and payroll, 2014

STATE District	Number of establish-ments	Total	Employment — Percent by selected industries — Manufact-uring	Construc-tion	Wholesale trade	Retail trade	Health care and social assistance	Finance and Insurance	Real estate and rental and leasing	Professio-nal, scientific, and technical services	Information	Annual payroll Total (mil dol)	Average per employee dollars
	73	74	75	76	77	78	79	80	81	82	83	84	85
MICHIGAN	218 282	3 620 465	14.9	3.3	4.7	12.6	16.7	4.2	1.4	6.9	1.9	165 700	45 768
District 1	19 674	203 329	12.7	5.6	2.9	17.8	20.1	3.6	1.2	3.3	1.6	7 332	36 057
District 2	16 142	300 116	26.5	3.6	6.2	12.9	11.9	2.6	1.2	3.1	0.9	11 990	39 951
District 3	15 316	304 752	19.1	3.3	6.1	8.8	19.6	4.2	1.1	4.6	1.7	13 231	43 415
District 4	13 485	183 872	16.7	4.6	3.6	17.8	16.6	3.6	1.6	2.4	1.3	7 196	39 136
District 5	13 742	208 633	11.3	3.1	4.1	15.8	24.1	3.2	1.2	3.4	1.5	8 134	38 985
District 6	14 365	225 930	21.1	3.6	4.3	12.9	15.9	3.7	1.5	3.9	1.0	9 662	42 764
District 7	12 582	194 425	21.3	2.9	3.5	13.9	14.6	4.0	0.9	4.4	1.7	8 011	41 203
District 8	15 686	215 923	11.9	4.2	3.5	15.2	17.7	6.3	1.5	6.1	1.6	8 865	41 057
District 9	17 392	262 703	15.3	3.0	4.7	12.8	19.3	3.0	2.5	10.7	1.9	12 224	46 531
District 10	14 552	194 945	26.4	5.1	3.3	16.4	12.9	2.4	0.9	6.2	0.8	8 096	41 528
District 11	23 641	439 473	9.3	3.5	7.2	12.5	11.0	5.1	1.3	14.3	2.7	25 103	57 122
District 12	15 082	276 825	11.2	2.2	4.2	13.9	20.8	3.8	1.4	8.2	2.7	14 293	51 631
District 13	9 910	199 300	13.3	2.3	4.4	8.9	23.0	1.4	1.1	2.5	1.3	9 360	46 964
District 14	16 226	316 413	5.2	2.5	4.7	7.7	17.2	9.4	2.6	11.5	4.7	19 225	60 760
MINNESOTA	147 483	2 566 086	11.6	4.1	5.2	11.6	17.3	5.9	1.4	6.5	2.4	126 186	49 175
District 1	16 858	281 602	17.6	3.6	3.5	13.6	19.8	3.5	0.9	10.3	2.2	11 328	40 227
District 2	16 644	266 586	12.0	5.8	5.5	12.5	13.3	4.9	1.3	4.9	4.6	12 418	46 583
District 3	23 041	444 514	13.2	3.5	7.4	12.0	10.5	7.1	2.6	8.5	2.4	26 110	58 738
District 4	17 266	353 538	7.6	3.6	4.6	10.2	19.6	6.6	1.3	4.9	2.5	18 004	52 622
District 5	20 758	520 639	6.2	2.3	5.1	6.5	18.6	9.2	1.6	9.0	2.5	31 283	60 086
District 6	16 220	216 146	15.6	8.2	4.7	15.1	17.1	3.0	1.0	3.1	1.4	8 634	39 947
District 7	19 188	239 232	19.0	5.4	6.3	15.0	21.1	3.4	0.6	2.8	1.4	8 381	35 034
District 8	17 075	211 522	9.2	4.8	2.7	15.6	25.1	3.7	1.0	3.5	1.5	7 699	36 400
MISSISSIPPI	58 541	912 014	15.4	4.7	3.9	15.4	17.9	3.7	1.1	3.4	1.5	32 777	35 939
District 1	14 146	218 626	22.5	3.4	4.4	15.9	14.8	3.1	0.9	2.5	0.9	7 301	33 394
District 2	12 716	192 033	15.0	4.6	3.9	15.0	19.0	3.0	1.0	2.2	1.5	6 490	33 797
District 3	17 260	260 746	10.7	5.3	4.6	15.5	20.5	5.2	1.4	4.5	2.2	9 969	38 234
District 4	14 142	223 995	15.3	4.8	2.5	16.4	17.0	3.1	1.2	4.0	1.3	8 447	37 709
MISSOURI	153 945	2 404 701	10.3	4.5	5.2	12.9	16.8	5.4	1.4	6.6	2.4	104 218	43 339
District 1	22 052	427 938	9.7	4.0	7.0	6.9	14.7	4.7	1.3	6.5	2.4	23 171	54 147
District 2	24 285	417 609	3.8	4.3	4.1	13.6	16.0	7.8	1.9	9.4	2.7	21 104	50 536
District 3	17 325	224 616	14.1	6.8	4.7	16.3	15.0	4.5	1.1	4.4	2.0	8 355	37 198
District 4	15 996	199 677	12.5	4.7	3.1	17.6	20.3	5.9	1.2	4.0	1.6	6 474	32 422
District 5	20 252	387 416	9.6	4.9	7.3	10.7	15.8	6.6	1.4	10.1	3.4	19 189	49 531
District 6	16 245	206 983	13.5	5.0	4.3	16.7	16.8	4.2	1.4	3.5	1.9	7 292	35 232
District 7	18 929	290 487	12.3	3.7	4.9	14.6	17.6	3.8	1.8	4.2	2.3	10 360	35 665
District 8	18 422	210 269	15.9	4.0	4.1	16.1	24.8	3.5	1.1	3.4	1.4	6 498	30 905
MONTANA	36 791	363 650	4.8	6.4	4.3	16.2	18.8	4.4	1.5	4.9	2.6	13 367	36 758
At Large	36 791	363 650	4.8	6.4	4.3	16.2	18.8	4.4	1.5	4.9	2.6	13 367	36 758
NEBRASKA	52 991	851 128	10.9	4.8	5.0	12.9	14.6	7.1	1.3	11.5	2.4	34 953	41 067
District 1	16 446	232 854	14.4	5.4	4.5	14.6	16.6	6.0	1.2	5.5	2.6	8 823	37 892
District 2	17 524	336 708	6.8	5.3	5.2	12.5	14.6	10.9	1.8	6.6	3.3	15 979	47 457
District 3	18 760	205 456	17.9	5.2	6.8	16.6	17.6	4.5	0.7	2.5	1.4	6 962	33 887
NEVADA	61 625	1 090 071	3.8	5.4	3.2	12.9	10.0	3.1	2.6	5.2	1.5	43 673	40 065
District 1	17 992	411 129	1.2	3.9	1.8	11.4	9.9	1.9	2.6	4.0	0.9	15 606	37 959
District 2	18 061	255 794	8.8	5.7	4.9	13.2	12.0	3.0	1.9	5.2	1.8	11 082	43 326
District 3	16 327	266 374	3.5	6.3	2.9	14.5	7.9	4.9	3.5	7.1	1.7	10 844	40 710
District 4	8 917	133 893	3.6	8.3	4.4	14.6	12.1	3.6	2.1	5.4	2.6	5 171	38 624
NEW HAMPSHIRE	37 396	563 323	11.7	4.1	4.3	17.3	15.6	5.2	1.3	5.3	2.5	26 937	47 817
District 1	19 391	280 404	9.8	4.2	4.3	17.3	15.1	7.1	1.6	5.6	3.1	13 634	48 623
District 2	17 704	260 739	14.8	4.4	4.2	18.7	17.5	3.1	1.1	4.5	2.0	11 986	45 969
NEW JERSEY	230 600	3 526 716	6.3	3.9	7.3	12.9	15.9	5.5	1.5	9.0	2.6	202 658	57 464
District 1	15 912	244 027	7.3	4.8	6.3	16.2	20.9	2.4	1.5	5.9	2.0	10 781	44 179
District 2	17 266	229 944	6.8	4.9	4.6	16.4	17.3	2.7	1.3	3.6	1.1	8 821	38 361
District 3	16 798	244 614	6.2	4.2	5.2	16.7	19.1	7.6	1.8	8.7	1.9	11 577	47 329
District 4	20 930	275 223	5.5	5.8	3.9	16.6	19.7	4.3	2.0	8.0	3.5	12 775	46 418
District 5	23 364	303 894	6.2	3.9	7.8	17.3	19.8	3.7	1.2	6.5	2.2	17 514	57 633
District 6	18 593	302 644	5.9	3.8	9.6	11.1	14.1	3.6	1.6	14.0	2.6	17 771	58 720
District 7	23 720	366 618	6.0	4.2	5.2	13.8	15.3	5.5	1.2	10.4	0.0	26 314	71 776
District 8	15 082	243 151	5.6	3.0	6.2	10.9	13.4	15.5	1.4	3.9	2.4	15 931	65 518
District 9	20 680	294 469	10.2	4.8	11.3	11.5	13.8	2.8	2.4	6.8	2.8	16 301	55 357
District 10	13 417	189 959	6.9	3.2	5.5	10.4	20.6	5.2	2.3	4.5	2.5	10 320	54 325
District 11	25 598	414 285	5.7	3.6	8.4	10.8	13.3	6.7	1.6	14.7	2.6	28 851	69 641
District 12	18 717	323 491	6.1	2.6	11.3	9.6	13.4	6.5	1.1	13.3	2.5	20 984	64 866
NEW MEXICO	43 748	602 632	4.4	6.3	3.6	15.9	19.2	3.7	1.7	7.7	1.9	23 629	39 210
District 1	16 214	248 787	5.0	6.6	4.6	14.8	19.6	4.3	1.8	7.9	2.6	9 673	38 881
District 2	12 821	169 680	4.1	7.4	2.8	16.7	19.5	3.0	1.9	5.3	1.1	6 346	37 398

1. Specified owner-occupied units; $1,000,000 represents $1,000,000 or more.   2. Specified renter-occupied units.

STATE District	Representative, 114th Congress	Land area,[1] 2010 (sq km)	Total persons	Per square kilometer	White	Black	American Indian, Alaska Native	Asian and Pacific Islander	Some other race	Two or more races	Hispanic or Latino[2]	Non-Hispanic White alone	Female	Foreign-born	Born in state of residence
		1	2	3	4	5	6	7	8	9	10	11	12	13	14
NEW MEXICO— Cont'd															
District 3	Ben Ray Luján (D)	116 442	686 655	5.9	64.5	1.5	18.5	1.3	11.7	2.4	40.7	37.7	50.3	6.9	56.5
NEW YORK		122 057	19 746 227	161.8	64.0	15.7	0.4	8.2	8.8	2.9	18.6	56.3	51.5	22.6	63.3
District 1	Lee M. Zeldin (R)	1 684	725 932	431.1	86.7	5.3	0.4	3.9	1.7	2.0	12.8	76.6	50.8	12.2	78.3
District 2	Peter T. King (R)	471	724 171	1 537.5	76.5	10.1	0.1	2.5	7.6	3.1	22.0	64.1	51.1	16.9	76.4
District 3	Steve Israel (D)	660	718 780	1 089.1	75.1	2.8	0.2	15.0	5.2	1.7	12.3	68.1	51.1	23.4	68.7
District 4	Kathleen M. Rice (D)	287	721 920	2 515.4	65.9	14.6	0.3	6.4	8.1	4.8	20.1	57.8	51.7	22.5	70.0
District 5	Gregory W. Meeks (D)	134	760 487	5 675.3	17.4	51.2	0.4	13.8	13.3	3.9	18.4	10.4	52.8	42.5	49.1
District 6	Grace Meng (D)	77	733 419	9 524.9	45.0	3.7	0.3	39.8	8.7	2.6	19.6	35.0	52.0	51.5	43.5
District 7	Nydia M. Velázquez (D)	42	732 079	17 430.5	48.0	11.9	0.5	19.6	16.5	3.6	40.7	30.2	51.1	36.8	45.7
District 8	Hakeem S. Jeffries (D)	77	758 543	9 851.2	29.1	55.0	0.3	5.0	8.1	2.5	18.2	22.4	53.9	33.7	52.5
District 9	Yvette D. Clarke (D)	40	755 073	18 876.8	34.4	49.6	0.3	7.1	6.4	2.1	11.5	31.4	54.1	39.4	47.8
District 10	Jerrold Nadler (D)	37	736 997	19 918.8	69.0	3.6	0.4	18.4	6.0	2.6	12.5	63.3	51.0	32.1	44.3
District 11	Daniel M. Donovan Jr. (R)	171	726 893	4 250.8	72.0	7.4	0.2	13.1	4.6	2.8	17.1	61.4	51.8	29.5	63.0
District 12	Carolyn B. Maloney (D)	38	729 253	19 190.9	73.3	5.1	0.2	13.3	4.9	3.0	14.2	65.1	52.5	26.7	41.7
District 13	Charles B. Rangel (D)	27	782 199	28 970.3	24.2	30.0	0.8	5.1	33.6	6.3	54.5	12.7	52.7	36.6	45.6
District 14	Joseph Crowley (D)	73	752 344	10 306.1	48.3	11.3	0.5	17.0	20.2	2.8	47.9	23.9	49.4	46.2	44.3
District 15	José E. Serrano (D)	38	750 915	19 760.9	12.5	34.3	0.6	1.7	48.6	2.4	65.3	2.0	53.7	35.5	52.5
District 16	Eliot L. Engel (D)	203	732 521	3 608.5	49.7	30.6	0.3	5.5	10.3	3.6	24.1	39.0	52.5	29.6	57.5
District 17	Nita M. Lowey (D)	991	739 263	746.0	69.6	10.8	0.7	5.9	10.5	2.6	22.5	59.8	51.4	23.6	62.2
District 18	Sean Patrick Maloney (D)	3 505	720 115	205.5	76.4	9.6	0.4	3.1	7.3	3.2	16.5	69.2	50.1	12.1	70.7
District 19	Christopher P. Gibson (R)	20 557	708 116	34.4	89.7	4.6	0.1	1.7	1.6	2.4	6.9	85.2	50.3	6.8	74.8
District 20	Paul Tonko (D)	3 189	727 913	228.3	80.7	8.9	0.1	4.7	1.9	3.6	6.1	77.7	51.4	7.9	76.0
District 21	Elise M. Stefanik (R)	39 147	713 276	18.2	91.7	3.1	0.9	1.1	1.2	2.0	3.4	89.9	48.7	3.7	77.1
District 22	Richard L. Hanna (R)	13 151	709 851	54.0	90.2	3.9	0.4	2.7	0.9	1.9	3.5	88.1	50.7	5.1	81.0
District 23	Tom Reed (R)	19 092	715 663	37.5	91.0	3.0	0.7	2.4	0.6	2.3	3.7	88.6	50.2	3.8	74.9
District 24	John Katko (R)	6 186	715 188	115.6	84.5	8.5	0.5	2.6	1.1	2.8	4.1	82.3	51.1	5.7	79.4
District 25	Louise McIntosh Slaughter (D)	1 321	721 227	546.0	75.7	15.6	0.6	3.4	1.6	3.1	8.1	70.9	51.8	8.2	74.8
District 26	Brian Higgins (D)	568	717 332	1 262.9	71.9	18.2	0.5	4.2	2.7	2.6	5.8	69.9	51.7	8.1	79.0
District 27	Chris Collins (R)	10 290	716 757	69.7	92.8	3.0	0.6	0.9	1.1	1.6	3.0	91.3	50.7	3.2	84.6
NORTH CAROLINA		125 920	9 943 964	79.0	69.1	21.7	1.1	2.5	3.2	2.4	9.0	64.0	51.3	7.7	57.5
District 1	G. K. Butterfield (D)	14 230	742 851	52.2	39.2	53.5	0.7	1.5	3.2	2.0	8.3	34.6	52.4	6.4	70.2
District 2	Renee Ellmers (R)	8 409	774 723	92.1	71.6	16.9	0.9	4.1	2.8	3.6	10.9	65.0	50.3	8.4	51.8
District 3	Walter B. Jones (R)	20 228	759 653	37.6	73.7	19.0	0.4	0.9	3.0	3.1	7.9	69.8	49.3	3.9	52.6
District 4	David E. Price (D)	2 707	795 798	294.0	56.9	29.8	0.5	5.9	3.4	3.5	11.9	49.4	51.3	13.7	45.6
District 5	Virginia Foxx (R)	9 251	750 233	81.1	81.5	12.9	0.2	1.4	2.6	1.4	8.8	75.5	51.5	6.5	65.6
District 6	Mark Walker (R)	9 517	755 280	79.4	77.1	15.7	0.2	2.6	2.5	1.8	7.2	72.9	52.0	6.8	62.5
District 7	David Rouzer (R)	15 959	772 311	48.4	74.8	17.4	1.9	0.8	3.0	2.2	9.1	69.5	51.2	5.8	59.9
District 8	Richard Hudson (R)	11 688	746 671	63.9	66.8	19.2	7.0	1.3	3.8	1.8	9.3	61.5	50.7	6.3	68.8
District 9	Robert Pittenger (R)	2 219	805 960	363.2	77.2	12.6	0.4	4.6	2.3	2.9	8.5	71.6	51.8	9.9	40.2
District 10	Patrick T. McHenry (R)	6 670	744 808	111.7	81.5	11.9	0.3	1.5	3.1	1.8	5.9	78.8	51.8	4.9	65.6
District 11	Mark Meadows (R)	17 711	744 956	42.1	89.2	3.7	1.6	1.5	2.3	1.6	5.9	86.3	51.0	4.5	60.2
District 12	Alma S. Adams (D)	1 424	778 251	546.5	36.1	51.1	0.3	4.2	5.8	2.5	13.7	28.5	52.0	14.0	53.6
District 13	George Holding (R)	5 907	772 469	130.8	73.1	17.7	0.3	2.4	4.2	2.3	8.5	69.2	51.5	8.0	53.8
NORTH DAKOTA		178 711	739 482	4.1	88.5	2.0	5.4	1.2	0.6	2.3	2.8	86.8	49.1	3.3	65.0
At Large	Kevin Cramer (R)	178 711	739 482	4.1	88.5	2.0	5.4	1.2	0.6	2.3	2.8	86.8	49.1	3.3	65.0
OHIO		105 829	11 594 163	109.6	82.1	12.2	0.2	2.0	0.9	2.6	3.4	80.0	51.0	4.2	75.1
District 1	Steve Chabot (R)	1 779	729 726	410.2	71.4	22.1	0.1	3.0	1.2	2.2	2.9	69.8	51.0	5.2	72.3
District 2	Brad R. Wenstrup (R)	8 344	724 587	86.8	87.3	8.5	0.1	1.5	0.7	1.9	2.0	86.0	51.3	2.9	73.6
District 3	Joyce Beatty (D)	591	755 499	1 278.3	57.1	32.5	0.1	3.6	1.8	4.7	6.2	53.5	51.9	11.5	65.7
District 4	Jim Jordan (R)	12 082	709 882	58.8	89.7	5.1	0.3	0.9	1.1	3.0	3.1	88.0	49.9	1.7	82.0
District 5	Robert E. Latta (R)	14 572	730 503	50.1	92.4	2.9	0.2	1.3	1.2	2.1	4.8	89.4	51.1	2.8	78.9
District 6	Bill Johnson (R)	18 687	713 457	38.2	95.4	2.4	0.1	0.5	0.2	1.4	0.9	94.7	50.2	1.0	70.7
District 7	Bob Gibbs (R)	10 010	725 548	72.5	92.3	3.8	0.1	0.6	0.7	2.4	2.3	90.9	50.8	1.8	82.9
District 8	Vacancy	6 347	722 889	113.9	88.7	6.3	0.3	1.9	0.8	2.0	3.3	86.5	50.9	3.9	75.2
District 9	Marcy Kaptur (D)	1 203	709 813	590.0	75.2	15.5	0.4	1.4	2.6	4.9	11.0	69.4	51.5	4.2	76.7
District 10	Michael R. Turner (R)	2 926	720 794	246.3	77.0	17.2	0.3	2.2	0.6	2.7	2.6	75.3	51.5	4.3	68.7
District 11	Marcia L. Fudge (D)	633	699 736	1 105.4	39.6	54.3	0.3	2.3	1.0	2.6	3.7	37.7	53.0	5.3	73.4
District 12	Patrick J. Tiberi (R)	5 884	755 978	128.5	88.7	3.9	0.1	3.5	0.5	3.3	2.3	87.0	50.2	4.6	73.2
District 13	Tim Ryan (D)	2 316	707 940	305.7	82.9	11.9	0.1	1.9	0.6	2.5	3.1	80.9	51.5	3.3	76.9
District 14	David P. Joyce (R)	5 059	722 474	142.8	91.5	4.1	0.2	2.1	0.4	1.8	2.8	89.3	51.2	5.1	76.6
District 15	Steve Stivers (R)	12 274	740 854	60.4	90.6	4.1	0.3	2.5	0.4	2.1	2.0	89.2	49.4	3.6	77.5
District 16	James B. Renacci (R)	3 122	724 483	232.1	93.6	2.1	0.3	2.2	0.4	1.4	2.2	92.1	51.4	4.9	78.3
OKLAHOMA		177 660	3 878 051	21.8	72.9	7.4	7.5	2.1	2.4	7.7	9.8	67.0	50.5	5.8	60.8
District 1	Jim Bridenstine (R)	4 226	781 067	184.8	71.9	8.5	5.4	2.4	3.5	8.2	10.7	65.6	51.2	7.5	57.8
District 2	Markwayne Mullin (R)	54 378	749 768	13.8	66.9	3.6	17.3	0.7	1.5	10.1	5.0	64.6	50.3	2.1	61.7
District 3	Frank D. Lucas (R)	88 362	776 896	8.8	79.8	4.1	6.0	1.7	3.0	5.4	9.2	74.6	49.7	4.4	64.6
District 4	Tom Cole (R)	25 323	773 994	30.6	76.1	7.1	4.7	2.3	1.7	8.1	8.4	71.2	50.1	4.5	60.8
District 5	Steve Russell (R)	5 371	796 326	148.3	69.7	13.5	4.3	3.2	2.5	6.7	15.3	58.9	51.1	10.5	59.4
OREGON		248 608	3 970 239	16.0	84.6	1.8	1.2	4.4	3.6	4.5	12.5	76.9	50.5	9.9	46.0
District 1	Suzanne Bonamici (D)	7 788	805 943	103.5	81.1	1.6	0.8	7.7	4.3	4.3	14.3	72.3	50.8	14.1	44.3
District 2	Greg Walden (R)	179 856	784 114	4.4	89.3	0.5	1.8	1.1	3.5	3.7	13.6	80.1	50.4	6.6	44.5

1. Dry land or land partially or temporarily covered by water.   2. May be of any race.

Table E. Congressional Districts 114th Congress — **Age and Education**

STATE District	Population and population characteristics, 2014 (cont.)											Education, 2014		
	Age (percent)												Attainment[2] (percent)	
	Under 5 years	5 to 17 years	18 to 24 years	25 to 34 years	35 to 44 years	45 to 54 years	55 to 64 years	65 to 74 years	75 years and over	Median age	Total Enrollment[1]	High school graduate or more	Bachelor's degree or more
	15	16	17	18	19	20	21	22	23	24	25	26	27
NEW MEXICO—Cont'd													
District 3	6.4	17.9	9.4	12.8	12.1	12.5	13.6	8.9	6.3	38.0	181 803	84.9	26.0
NEW YORK	6.0	15.4	10.0	14.4	12.7	14.1	12.7	8.1	6.5	38.2	4 874 923	85.7	34.5
District 1	5.5	16.3	9.3	10.7	12.4	15.8	13.7	9.5	6.9	41.8	181 702	92.1	34.9
District 2	5.4	17.1	9.6	12.7	12.5	16.2	13.0	7.6	6.0	39.1	182 299	88.1	28.9
District 3	4.6	17.0	8.2	9.3	11.7	16.6	14.1	9.2	9.3	44.4	182 494	91.5	50.9
District 4	6.0	16.2	9.2	12.3	12.8	14.5	13.2	8.4	7.3	40.3	183 599	89.9	40.1
District 5	6.6	16.1	10.1	13.9	12.8	14.7	12.5	7.5	5.6	37.4	205 449	80.3	23.7
District 6	5.9	12.3	7.5	15.0	14.7	14.9	14.0	8.5	7.3	41.3	154 851	84.6	34.3
District 7	7.5	14.6	10.3	20.4	14.9	12.4	10.1	5.2	4.5	33.4	172 828	71.9	31.5
District 8	6.9	15.5	10.6	15.6	13.1	13.0	11.7	7.7	5.9	35.8	193 702	81.8	29.3
District 9	7.5	15.4	8.8	17.0	14.1	12.7	11.5	7.4	5.5	35.7	186 814	84.8	35.7
District 10	6.9	13.2	8.2	20.3	14.6	12.2	10.9	8.2	5.6	35.7	175 205	87.7	60.1
District 11	6.3	15.8	8.6	13.9	13.1	14.1	13.3	8.4	6.6	39.3	182 250	85.2	33.4
District 12	4.8	7.7	8.5	28.1	15.2	11.0	10.5	7.7	6.5	35.5	130 297	93.5	71.8
District 13	6.7	14.4	11.5	18.3	14.0	13.2	10.9	6.0	5.0	34.4	195 809	72.8	28.8
District 14	6.2	14.4	9.5	19.1	14.9	13.3	10.7	6.7	5.4	35.5	174 868	74.0	25.9
District 15	8.4	19.7	12.8	15.4	12.2	13.2	9.1	5.6	3.7	30.6	220 897	63.0	12.6
District 16	6.2	16.6	9.3	12.5	13.1	14.4	12.2	8.0	7.6	38.9	188 467	85.0	38.6
District 17	6.2	18.4	9.1	11.3	12.4	14.2	12.9	8.2	6.9	39.1	199 727	87.6	46.2
District 18	5.7	17.9	10.5	10.6	12.4	15.6	13.0	8.1	6.0	39.6	195 840	90.1	35.0
District 19	4.5	14.6	10.2	10.8	10.8	15.7	15.2	10.5	7.5	44.3	161 297	89.1	27.2
District 20	5.3	15.0	12.1	12.8	12.1	13.8	13.6	8.5	6.8	39.1	182 988	92.6	36.9
District 21	5.6	15.1	11.0	12.6	11.7	14.6	13.6	9.0	7.0	40.3	162 505	88.5	23.6
District 22	5.2	15.3	11.8	11.4	10.9	14.4	13.9	9.2	7.8	41.4	171 868	89.2	23.3
District 23	5.4	15.0	12.9	11.8	10.6	13.6	14.0	9.3	7.4	40.0	180 204	89.6	25.4
District 24	5.7	16.1	10.8	12.6	11.3	14.5	13.6	8.6	6.9	39.4	182 102	89.4	30.0
District 25	5.8	15.7	10.8	13.9	11.4	13.9	13.1	8.5	7.0	38.8	186 147	90.3	36.0
District 26	5.8	14.3	11.0	14.8	10.9	13.0	13.4	8.8	7.9	38.9	174 158	89.1	29.6
District 27	4.4	16.5	8.8	10.7	11.6	16.2	15.2	9.3	7.3	43.7	166 556	92.2	27.2
NORTH CAROLINA	6.0	17.0	10.0	12.9	13.3	13.7	12.5	8.7	6.0	38.3	2 556 055	86.4	28.7
District 1	6.5	15.7	11.4	13.4	11.8	12.7	13.3	8.8	6.5	37.6	189 551	80.4	19.6
District 2	7.0	18.6	9.0	13.5	13.6	13.8	11.1	8.1	5.4	36.4	203 119	87.1	29.9
District 3	6.5	15.4	14.5	13.7	11.9	11.7	11.8	8.7	5.8	34.8	197 630	87.9	22.9
District 4	6.1	15.9	13.8	17.0	14.5	12.2	10.1	6.3	4.4	33.1	243 713	89.2	41.0
District 5	5.2	16.6	10.7	11.2	12.5	14.3	13.3	9.4	6.8	40.3	193 101	85.1	26.0
District 6	5.2	16.1	8.9	11.2	12.8	14.7	14.5	9.5	7.2	42.1	176 284	87.3	28.3
District 7	5.5	17.4	8.2	11.0	12.9	14.1	13.7	10.8	6.4	41.4	183 857	85.4	23.7
District 8	6.2	18.1	8.8	12.4	13.4	13.8	12.3	9.0	5.9	39.0	189 614	83.3	18.2
District 9	6.4	19.3	6.9	12.9	15.7	15.1	11.8	7.3	4.7	38.3	216 993	93.7	49.3
District 10	5.5	16.2	8.7	11.4	12.9	14.4	13.6	10.0	7.1	41.9	171 668	84.6	23.4
District 11	4.9	14.5	8.7	10.3	12.4	13.8	14.4	12.3	8.8	44.4	159 240	85.5	23.8
District 12	7.3	17.3	12.9	16.9	13.6	12.8	9.9	5.8	3.7	32.2	223 890	82.8	24.6
District 13	6.2	19.2	7.4	12.0	14.5	15.2	12.5	8.0	5.0	39.0	207 395	90.7	40.4
NORTH DAKOTA	6.8	15.9	12.6	14.6	11.2	12.4	12.6	7.4	6.8	35.1	182 606	92.2	27.4
At Large	6.8	15.9	12.6	14.6	11.2	12.4	12.6	7.4	6.8	35.1	182 606	92.2	27.4
OHIO	5.9	16.8	9.5	12.6	12.3	13.8	13.6	8.7	6.8	39.4	2 901 361	89.4	26.6
District 1	6.6	18.0	9.9	13.3	12.3	14.1	12.6	7.3	6.0	36.6	196 686	89.8	33.0
District 2	6.1	16.8	8.0	13.4	12.6	13.8	13.9	8.6	6.7	39.4	166 648	89.7	30.2
District 3	7.6	17.0	11.8	18.3	13.1	12.3	10.3	5.7	3.9	31.9	214 747	86.1	27.3
District 4	5.8	16.7	9.0	11.7	12.3	13.9	14.3	9.0	7.4	40.9	169 792	89.2	16.5
District 5	5.5	17.2	10.3	11.4	11.8	13.6	14.1	9.0	6.9	39.9	192 821	92.5	26.2
District 6	5.3	16.1	8.1	11.2	12.0	13.9	15.2	10.2	7.8	43.1	155 296	87.7	16.0
District 7	5.9	17.3	9.1	11.1	11.3	14.1	13.8	9.8	7.4	41.0	173 435	86.8	18.5
District 8	6.2	17.6	10.1	11.6	12.1	13.7	13.3	8.7	6.6	38.8	187 451	89.0	23.0
District 9	6.2	16.6	9.9	13.6	12.7	13.6	12.9	7.8	6.6	38.1	176 102	86.2	21.6
District 10	6.1	16.0	10.2	13.0	11.4	13.5	13.4	9.0	7.4	39.4	189 342	90.3	28.0
District 11	6.4	16.0	10.7	13.4	11.5	12.7	14.1	7.9	7.1	38.1	182 472	85.1	26.2
District 12	6.4	18.2	8.3	12.6	14.1	14.0	13.0	7.9	5.5	38.3	201 815	92.9	40.4
District 13	5.1	15.2	10.6	12.6	11.4	13.3	14.2	9.4	8.3	41.2	173 528	89.2	21.5
District 14	5.0	17.1	7.9	10.1	11.8	15.4	14.7	10.0	8.1	43.8	166 640	91.3	33.2
District 15	5.5	16.3	10.0	13.4	13.4	14.2	12.8	8.3	6.0	38.6	188 307	90.6	30.7
District 16	5.3	16.2	8.1	11.5	11.8	14.3	15.1	9.9	8.0	42.9	166 279	92.6	32.7
OKLAHOMA	6.8	17.8	10.2	13.6	12.3	12.6	12.2	8.3	6.2	36.2	997 987	87.3	24.2
District 1	7.2	18.2	9.1	14.2	12.9	12.8	12.3	7.6	5.8	36.0	200 517	88.9	29.5
District 2	6.0	17.6	9.3	11.5	11.7	13.0	13.1	10.5	7.2	40.1	177 553	84.3	16.1
District 3	6.6	17.7	11.2	12.9	11.7	12.8	12.2	8.4	6.5	36.2	200 904	88.0	22.0
District 4	6.5	17.5	12.0	14.0	12.3	12.4	11.8	7.7	5.8	35.0	212 586	88.7	23.6
District 5	7.7	17.8	9.5	15.3	12.7	12.4	11.8	7.4	5.5	34.8	206 427	86.5	29.4
OREGON	5.7	15.9	9.2	13.6	13.2	12.8	13.7	9.5	6.5	39.3	956 494	89.7	30.8
District 1	6.2	17.2	8.2	14.4	14.8	13.5	12.6	7.8	5.2	37.5	195 723	90.1	38.1
District 2	5.8	16.3	8.1	12.0	12.0	12.2	14.6	11.1	8.0	41.7	173 913	87.7	23.4

1. All persons 3 years old and over enrolled in nursery school through college and graduate or professional school. 2. Persons 25 years old and over.

STATE District	Number	Average household size	Family households (percent)	Married-couple family (percent)	Female family householder[1]	One person households (percent)	Total in group quarters, 2014	Percent 65 years and over	Persons in correctional institutions	Persons in nursing facilities	Persons in college dormitories	Persons in military quarters
	28	29	30	31	32	33	34	35	36	37	38	39
NEW MEXICO—Cont'd												
District 3	242 158	2.78	64.0	45.4	13.0	30.4	12 285	17.2	3 544	1 465	2 115	444
NEW YORK	7 282 398	2.63	63.5	43.6	14.8	29.7	581 178	19.7	95 306	116 558	218 960	8 100
District 1	249 690	2.81	71.9	57.2	10.6	23.4	23 105	20.6	1 648	4 504	9 203	6
District 2	225 524	3.18	76.9	57.3	14.2	18.4	6 899	46.7	6	2 952	720	4
District 3	247 359	2.85	75.1	63.2	8.4	22.0	13 701	41.2	10	5 607	3 982	4
District 4	231 363	3.07	75.3	57.8	12.8	20.8	12 308	28.5	1 657	4 200	4 748	0
District 5	227 580	3.28	74.2	43.7	23.4	21.9	14 519	30.2	234	5 713	2 367	0
District 6	269 779	2.70	66.2	47.5	13.0	28.6	6 274	62.0	17	4 179	812	0
District 7	254 793	2.82	60.8	37.4	17.7	27.0	14 274	12.2	3 636	1 600	1 803	0
District 8	281 396	2.63	62.0	31.5	24.4	31.9	17 546	26.0	256	4 120	2 056	0
District 9	280 103	2.66	61.9	33.3	22.8	31.1	9 039	27.0	0	2 585	611	0
District 10	310 947	2.30	48.3	38.1	6.7	41.0	20 476	10.2	165	2 076	16 711	0
District 11	258 510	2.78	70.8	52.0	14.4	25.2	8 220	36.4	924	3 540	1 457	60
District 12	367 878	1.91	38.3	30.3	5.9	47.8	27 755	10.4	414	3 896	16 755	0
District 13	291 316	2.64	56.9	23.3	27.5	34.0	14 352	29.6	334	5 101	1 924	0
District 14	249 345	2.95	65.3	40.6	15.9	26.8	16 681	21.9	11 095	5 195	2 355	0
District 15	247 735	2.96	67.5	21.3	37.8	29.5	17 774	8.9	981	2 145	2 352	0
District 16	263 056	2.72	66.0	41.6	18.5	29.9	16 722	41.8	0	7 221	5 113	0
District 17	242 676	2.95	73.1	58.9	10.2	22.9	22 886	23.3	3 245	4 756	8 571	0
District 18	244 301	2.84	70.0	55.0	10.6	25.1	26 369	14.3	8 143	3 627	7 046	4 409
District 19	268 269	2.49	64.4	49.3	10.6	29.0	39 573	13.1	9 986	4 771	12 644	3
District 20	287 521	2.42	58.1	42.4	12.1	33.3	31 580	16.3	1 298	4 651	18 920	0
District 21	271 972	2.47	65.7	49.9	11.1	26.8	42 130	10.4	18 001	3 692	11 032	3 614
District 22	275 383	2.45	62.5	45.8	11.9	29.9	34 029	18.0	6 104	6 243	17 830	0
District 23	281 202	2.39	61.6	44.8	11.2	30.3	42 802	13.9	6 988	5 257	23 896	0
District 24	280 593	2.44	62.9	43.9	13.3	30.2	29 351	17.7	4 484	4 882	14 806	0
District 25	287 527	2.42	59.0	41.0	13.7	34.0	25 601	20.7	1 499	4 931	14 361	0
District 26	306 964	2.27	56.2	35.7	16.0	36.8	20 478	20.0	926	3 778	11 661	0
District 27	279 616	2.47	66.1	51.6	10.2	28.2	26 734	20.3	13 255	5 336	5 224	0
NORTH CAROLINA	3 790 620	2.56	65.7	47.6	13.6	28.4	253 987	16.6	61 680	46 638	89 795	26 326
District 1	286 254	2.49	60.7	34.7	20.6	33.0	31 344	15.6	13 922	6 285	10 496	594
District 2	283 123	2.68	69.8	52.0	13.3	25.7	15 151	21.8	1 132	3 214	1 773	5 949
District 3	286 013	2.54	66.2	49.8	12.1	27.2	34 110	6.2	6 616	2 817	8 725	19 749
District 4	308 881	2.46	57.0	38.8	13.7	33.1	36 308	7.0	5 518	2 406	22 784	0
District 5	291 365	2.51	64.8	48.3	12.2	29.6	19 149	18.3	2 268	3 598	10 492	0
District 6	297 049	2.48	67.1	50.5	12.3	28.5	19 748	23.6	2 493	3 811	6 738	0
District 7	297 924	2.56	67.8	51.5	12.3	26.7	10 757	29.2	5 511	3 495	9	33
District 8	273 964	2.66	70.5	49.9	15.4	25.4	16 685	17.1	8 325	3 469	3 449	0
District 9	303 975	2.63	68.7	55.9	9.7	25.6	5 231	45.8	50	2 736	2 155	1
District 10	283 641	2.58	66.7	48.8	13.0	27.7	13 953	30.8	2 503	4 741	4 033	0
District 11	296 292	2.45	65.5	51.0	10.0	29.9	19 073	23.1	5 915	4 622	4 965	0
District 12	292 966	2.57	58.3	31.8	20.9	33.2	25 853	10.1	4 648	3 049	13 560	0
District 13	289 173	2.65	72.3	55.6	12.3	23.5	6 625	28.6	2 779	2 395	616	0
NORTH DAKOTA	305 431	2.33	61.5	48.8	8.1	30.8	26 637	25.3	2 489	6 433	10 570	1 380
At Large	305 431	2.33	61.5	48.8	8.1	30.8	26 637	25.3	2 489	6 433	10 570	1 380
OHIO	4 593 172	2.46	63.6	45.8	13.2	30.4	311 030	25.3	76 590	83 019	106 042	571
District 1	285 010	2.48	61.9	42.8	14.9	31.5	21 728	17.7	6 431	4 486	7 060	0
District 2	291 964	2.45	63.7	46.7	11.8	30.3	10 081	55.0	880	5 887	712	0
District 3	296 151	2.48	57.7	32.8	19.3	33.6	22 115	10.7	2 353	2 793	11 851	0
District 4	277 572	2.46	66.1	48.3	13.2	28.5	27 130	17.6	15 892	5 563	5 261	0
District 5	288 070	2.47	65.2	51.7	8.9	28.3	18 610	31.9	971	6 014	8 367	0
District 6	278 327	2.48	67.2	50.9	11.8	28.2	22 347	30.8	9 881	6 354	3 595	0
District 7	277 654	2.56	68.8	53.1	11.1	26.4	15 705	35.8	795	6 223	5 129	0
District 8	273 993	2.58	67.8	50.5	11.9	26.8	17 030	24.8	1 369	4 682	8 537	0
District 9	293 191	2.37	56.9	35.8	16.0	36.0	14 151	26.5	1 894	4 930	5 512	0
District 10	295 834	2.35	61.1	42.0	14.4	33.9	25 281	21.5	1 997	5 845	12 267	547
District 11	298 796	2.26	53.8	27.3	21.5	40.2	23 382	21.5	3 906	6 243	7 446	0
District 12	285 099	2.59	66.8	54.2	9.2	26.7	17 999	19.4	6 071	3 929	6 352	0
District 13	297 444	2.31	60.1	39.3	15.6	33.5	21 036	20.6	5 134	5 394	10 204	0
District 14	287 411	2.47	68.1	53.5	10.3	27.0	12 500	40.5	2 076	5 260	1 338	24
District 15	280 269	2.53	67.0	52.2	10.6	26.4	31 403	11.1	16 670	3 476	9 591	0
District 16	286 387	2.49	67.8	54.6	9.1	27.4	10 532	51.7	270	5 940	2 820	0
OKLAHOMA	1 459 759	2.58	66.2	48.7	12.5	28.2	110 052	24.0	40 562	21 678	30 148	7 203
District 1	305 903	2.52	65.1	47.3	12.9	29.1	9 463	28.8	2 371	3 656	2 981	0
District 2	280 477	2.59	68.6	50.3	12.8	26.9	23 704	19.9	9 915	5 506	4 623	0
District 3	285 371	2.62	68.1	52.6	10.8	26.7	29 275	13.8	15 091	4 818	10 089	463
District 4	284 755	2.62	67.1	50.4	11.9	26.6	28 004	12.1	7 991	3 797	7 490	6 740
District 5	303 253	2.56	62.5	43.4	14.0	31.2	19 606	18.8	5 194	3 901	4 965	0
OREGON	1 535 511	2.53	62.9	47.6	10.7	28.1	86 917	18.0	22 203	11 491	23 704	178
District 1	305 696	2.59	65.9	50.7	10.6	27.0	14 554	20.7	4 641	1 964	3 338	127
District 2	302 941	2.52	63.9	48.3	10.7	28.9	20 888	19.0	8 762	2 660	1 775	13

1. No spouse present.

Table E. Congressional Districts 114th Congress — **Housing and Money Income**

STATE District	Housing units, 2014						Money income, 2014		
		Occupied units						Households	
		Owner-occupied				Renter-occupied			
	Total	Occupied units as a percent of all units	Owner-occupied units as a percent of occupied units	Median value[1] (dollars)	Percent valued at $500,000 or more	Median rent[2]	Per capita income (dollars)	Median income (dollars)	Percent with income of $100,000 or more
	40	41	42	43	44	45	46	47	48
NEW MEXICO—Cont'd									
District 3	307 460	78.8	70.8	170 900	8.2	822	24 579	47 785	17.9
NEW YORK	8 191 528	88.9	53.0	279 100	23.3	1 148	33 095	58 878	28.1
District 1	308 215	81.0	79.0	363 400	24.0	1 589	38 425	84 668	42.2
District 2	241 254	93.5	78.0	356 400	14.2	1 597	33 120	86 442	43.4
District 3	264 312	93.6	80.7	552 900	56.4	1 751	50 114	100 835	50.7
District 4	246 424	93.9	78.4	424 800	31.4	1 598	40 009	92 472	47.0
District 5	244 124	93.2	54.4	397 400	20.9	1 265	24 295	59 420	26.7
District 6	289 505	93.2	46.2	493 900	49.3	1 387	29 321	58 933	26.9
District 7	274 845	92.7	21.7	597 800	60.2	1 251	29 097	48 113	24.7
District 8	311 229	90.4	32.4	476 500	45.1	1 103	24 648	42 242	20.2
District 9	300 391	93.2	28.2	545 500	54.5	1 234	28 007	49 193	21.2
District 10	358 347	86.8	30.7	869 700	79.4	1 690	62 462	81 267	43.0
District 11	281 155	91.9	56.5	465 600	42.8	1 228	30 174	62 756	30.2
District 12	420 598	87.5	26.8	867 600	79.6	1 931	78 605	94 127	48.0
District 13	311 203	93.6	8.8	418 100	39.3	1 096	22 295	37 546	14.1
District 14	267 535	93.2	28.9	438 700	39.0	1 367	23 211	51 650	19.3
District 15	261 761	94.6	8.6	346 800	14.9	992	13 309	24 429	5.8
District 16	284 688	92.4	48.4	436 000	40.9	1 258	38 367	63 143	31.9
District 17	258 232	94.0	66.3	449 500	40.1	1 420	43 247	91 073	46.4
District 18	273 831	89.2	71.7	287 800	16.7	1 183	35 914	77 110	37.9
District 19	362 881	73.9	71.7	195 000	6.7	922	29 457	56 626	23.5
District 20	325 554	88.3	60.7	197 500	3.8	918	32 274	61 584	27.0
District 21	368 555	73.8	69.7	138 800	4.2	789	25 456	51 653	18.0
District 22	320 683	85.9	68.1	110 000	1.4	721	24 891	48 538	16.8
District 23	340 391	82.6	68.9	99 500	2.3	722	24 666	46 797	15.9
District 24	313 716	89.4	66.9	125 800	2.0	756	27 370	51 649	20.1
District 25	312 169	92.1	63.9	137 000	2.0	822	29 489	50 888	21.0
District 26	344 704	89.1	58.9	110 500	1.6	740	26 583	43 365	16.2
District 27	305 226	91.6	77.6	142 000	2.3	734	30 325	59 377	24.7
NORTH CAROLINA	4 452 464	85.1	64.2	155 000	5.3	803	25 774	46 556	17.8
District 1	336 393	85.1	54.1	104 000	1.6	710	19 015	33 955	9.2
District 2	322 074	87.9	65.9	157 900	4.4	845	25 858	50 390	20.4
District 3	377 057	75.9	62.5	156 800	4.3	851	23 429	46 272	14.1
District 4	342 252	90.2	49.9	181 700	8.5	901	28 821	47 954	20.7
District 5	352 324	82.7	67.6	145 800	3.5	716	24 054	44 546	14.8
District 6	334 901	88.7	71.5	153 900	4.4	782	27 125	48 558	19.6
District 7	369 467	80.6	69.8	151 800	4.6	779	24 642	44 557	17.6
District 8	313 858	87.3	67.8	124 300	1.9	697	21 156	42 357	13.5
District 9	326 055	93.2	70.6	233 300	14.2	1 047	40 079	73 755	35.1
District 10	336 118	84.4	68.3	137 200	5.1	696	23 609	42 820	13.9
District 11	395 432	74.9	71.2	154 400	4.3	688	22 673	40 963	11.9
District 12	328 293	89.2	43.5	117 900	1.4	809	20 055	38 564	10.2
District 13	318 240	90.9	72.9	201 600	7.5	902	33 217	64 299	29.7
NORTH DAKOTA	350 534	87.1	63.8	161 800	3.6	728	33 071	59 029	24.4
At Large	350 534	87.1	63.8	161 800	3.6	728	33 071	59 029	24.4
OHIO	5 147 282	89.2	65.3	129 100	2.5	735	26 937	49 308	19.1
District 1	318 883	89.4	59.6	147 500	4.2	715	28 436	52 182	22.7
District 2	325 455	89.7	66.2	137 600	4.6	705	29 684	51 937	21.8
District 3	338 665	87.4	44.1	113 700	1.7	811	22 622	41 684	13.9
District 4	308 515	90.0	69.6	114 300	1.7	690	23 629	47 253	14.7
District 5	310 674	92.7	71.4	124 600	1.7	683	27 955	52 896	19.8
District 6	322 005	86.4	73.8	99 700	1.0	629	23 045	43 492	14.2
District 7	305 686	90.8	72.3	128 300	1.2	690	24 047	48 962	16.0
District 8	301 411	90.9	68.5	133 600	1.5	748	26 058	51 699	20.0
District 9	351 035	83.5	58.5	95 600	1.7	682	23 469	40 137	12.9
District 10	334 060	88.6	61.6	117 800	1.9	743	26 519	45 749	18.3
District 11	365 350	81.8	48.9	92 300	3.2	690	23 740	33 113	12.9
District 12	307 084	92.8	71.2	185 600	5.4	856	35 025	68 142	32.0
District 13	336 217	88.5	63.6	95 800	0.7	681	23 277	41 498	12.0
District 14	309 442	92.9	75.6	165 200	3.8	842	32 978	61 602	26.7
District 15	307 857	91.0	67.7	155 200	2.9	825	28 585	56 396	23.3
District 16	304 943	93.9	75.1	158 600	2.2	793	31 329	60 543	26.0
OKLAHOMA	1 699 556	85.9	65.1	119 800	2.7	737	25 229	47 529	17.5
District 1	340 569	89.8	62.8	138 100	3.3	784	28 304	51 271	20.0
District 2	352 474	79.6	70.4	92 600	2.1	631	20 684	38 723	11.6
District 3	334 939	85.2	68.9	108 600	2.0	696	24 420	48 959	17.0
District 4	326 343	87.3	66.6	127 700	2.3	767	25 550	52 243	18.9
District 5	345 231	87.8	57.7	132 500	4.2	764	26 968	46 954	19.5
OREGON	1 700 611	90.3	60.7	239 800	10.4	924	27 646	51 075	20.2
District 1	328 332	93.1	60.0	283 000	14.7	1 055	32 087	62 883	27.6
District 2	356 040	85.1	63.5	198 600	8.2	812	24 229	44 269	14.8

1. Specified owner-occupied units; $1,000,000 represents $1,000,000 or more.   2. Specified renter-occupied units.

Items 40—48

STATE District	Poverty, 2014			Civilian labor force, 2014			Civilian employment,[2] 2014				Persons under age 65 with no health insurance, 2014 (percent)	Social Security beneficiaries, December 2014		Supplemental Security Income recipients, December 2014
					Unemployment			Percent						
	Persons below poverty level (percent)	Families below poverty level (percent)	Percent of households receiving food stamps in past 12 months	Total	Total	Rate[1]	Total	Management, business, science and arts occupations	Service, sales, and office	Construction and production		Number	Rate[3]	
	49	50	51	52	53	54	55	56	57	58	59	60	61	62
NEW MEXICO—Cont'd														
District 3	19.6	14.1	14.4	313 649	28 076	9.0	285 573	36.8	42.6	20.6	18.5	134 068	195.2	21 419
NEW YORK	15.9	12.2	15.6	10 085 377	731 222	7.3	9 354 155	39.6	43.6	16.8	10.0	3 482 978	176.4	653 601
District 1	7.0	4.3	6.8	374 938	20 974	5.6	353 964	39.5	42.4	18.1	7.9	146 447	201.7	9 768
District 2	7.2	5.3	7.8	390 199	22 080	5.7	368 119	33.4	45.6	20.9	9.0	130 880	180.7	10 075
District 3	6.5	4.6	3.5	359 570	18 157	5.0	341 413	50.3	37.7	12.0	6.1	145 067	201.8	7 306
District 4	7.6	5.4	5.7	381 662	21 843	5.7	359 819	41.5	43.1	15.4	8.4	133 939	185.5	10 356
District 5	13.3	10.4	18.3	387 920	37 817	9.7	350 103	29.2	51.7	19.1	12.5	102 527	134.8	27 403
District 6	14.7	12.7	10.5	379 213	24 683	6.5	354 530	38.2	46.4	15.3	15.8	112 626	153.6	22 933
District 7	25.1	22.3	25.2	382 436	30 228	7.9	352 208	38.2	45.5	16.3	15.2	83 727	114.4	35 325
District 8	24.0	19.9	25.9	369 768	36 287	9.8	333 481	35.2	49.2	15.6	10.5	105 883	139.6	53 234
District 9	20.0	16.4	22.8	378 872	32 964	8.7	345 908	41.3	45.1	13.6	12.0	96 830	128.2	36 237
District 10	16.9	13.5	12.1	406 031	21 160	5.2	384 871	59.1	32.4	8.6	7.9	100 602	136.5	22 667
District 11	16.8	13.6	15.6	346 889	23 297	6.7	323 592	39.3	44.1	16.5	9.3	126 841	174.5	28 614
District 12	11.7	7.1	6.3	473 195	25 294	5.3	447 901	65.4	30.0	4.6	8.4	105 476	144.6	14 622
District 13	29.8	26.1	31.1	392 583	45 367	11.6	347 216	33.9	52.2	13.9	13.3	104 624	133.8	64 580
District 14	17.6	14.9	17.4	396 012	31 354	7.9	364 658	27.7	49.4	22.9	19.8	93 138	123.8	20 138
District 15	41.0	38.1	48.5	308 384	38 369	12.4	270 015	17.6	60.1	22.3	17.1	88 527	117.9	66 634
District 16	13.9	10.6	14.3	372 297	33 228	8.9	339 069	41.8	44.2	14.1	10.7	124 250	169.6	22 042
District 17	11.0	7.6	7.9	386 324	23 053	6.0	363 271	46.8	40.4	12.9	9.9	126 727	171.4	10 273
District 18	10.9	7.5	8.5	365 437	24 793	6.8	340 644	38.2	44.8	16.9	7.8	129 428	179.7	11 578
District 19	11.8	7.3	11.3	358 122	25 802	7.2	332 320	37.0	41.4	21.6	8.8	162 363	229.3	15 598
District 20	12.7	8.4	12.9	388 269	23 562	6.1	364 707	43.6	40.9	15.5	6.3	146 102	200.7	18 651
District 21	14.9	10.2	15.6	333 361	25 136	7.5	308 225	33.6	43.9	22.5	8.6	164 197	230.2	19 719
District 22	16.0	11.4	16.9	343 649	22 573	6.6	321 076	35.0	43.2	21.8	6.7	165 007	232.5	21 771
District 23	17.2	12.0	15.1	341 629	23 942	7.0	317 687	34.2	40.5	25.3	8.8	162 565	227.2	20 008
District 24	16.1	11.8	15.1	359 264	28 432	7.9	330 832	37.3	43.3	19.4	7.0	152 335	213.0	20 453
District 25	14.5	10.8	14.9	376 738	27 380	7.3	349 358	42.6	42.6	14.8	5.7	150 700	208.9	25 027
District 26	18.8	14.1	20.8	359 461	23 370	6.5	336 091	36.9	45.4	17.8	6.5	157 698	219.8	28 365
District 27	9.8	6.5	9.9	373 154	20 077	5.4	353 077	35.9	41.3	22.7	6.3	164 472	229.5	10 224
NORTH CAROLINA	17.2	12.8	14.4	4 849 396	404 407	8.3	4 444 989	36.1	41.3	22.5	15.2	1 948 531	196.0	235 300
District 1	25.1	19.6	23.8	333 690	39 272	11.8	294 418	31.8	42.4	25.7	18.0	161 884	217.9	38 863
District 2	15.6	12.1	14.1	352 867	26 594	7.5	326 273	38.2	39.0	22.8	13.7	138 722	179.1	15 469
District 3	16.3	12.4	14.6	350 022	36 165	10.3	313 857	32.2	44.5	23.3	15.0	145 412	191.4	16 948
District 4	18.1	13.3	12.2	420 690	28 008	6.7	392 682	42.2	42.4	15.4	15.4	108 119	135.9	16 621
District 5	19.1	13.0	12.6	367 040	33 934	9.2	333 106	34.1	41.5	24.4	14.3	164 726	219.6	14 040
District 6	13.7	9.5	12.0	372 011	25 422	6.8	346 589	37.1	40.7	22.2	13.2	166 391	220.3	14 096
District 7	19.5	13.6	15.6	359 383	27 378	7.6	332 005	33.3	40.9	25.8	16.7	173 772	225.0	19 713
District 8	19.5	15.0	17.6	353 935	36 450	10.3	317 485	30.1	41.3	28.6	16.7	154 555	207.0	22 195
District 9	8.3	6.7	5.5	436 455	28 379	6.5	408 076	48.8	38.5	12.7	10.5	114 294	141.8	6 596
District 10	16.7	13.1	15.6	352 398	29 756	8.4	322 642	31.6	40.4	28.0	15.5	172 382	231.4	19 690
District 11	16.8	12.1	13.8	340 643	24 005	7.0	316 638	29.7	43.5	26.8	17.6	203 552	273.2	16 849
District 12	25.7	21.0	22.9	407 125	46 014	11.3	361 111	29.9	44.6	25.4	19.3	115 566	148.5	25 252
District 13	10.6	7.9	7.6	403 137	23 030	5.7	380 107	44.6	38.6	16.9	12.4	129 156	167.2	8 968
NORTH DAKOTA	11.5	7.4	8.2	403 774	12 130	3.0	391 644	35.9	38.7	25.4	9.0	124 372	168.2	8 224
At Large	11.5	7.4	8.2	403 774	12 130	3.0	391 644	35.9	38.7	25.4	9.0	124 372	168.2	8 224
OHIO	15.8	11.6	14.9	5 858 014	420 481	7.2	5 437 533	35.6	40.9	23.5	9.8	2 267 508	195.6	313 259
District 1	15.9	11.4	14.3	370 740	32 080	8.7	338 660	39.6	41.4	19.0	9.1	123 812	169.7	20 117
District 2	15.0	11.0	14.0	365 634	24 890	6.8	340 744	38.9	40.1	21.0	10.3	143 617	198.2	21 547
District 3	23.5	19.8	21.9	403 748	29 727	7.4	374 021	34.2	46.1	19.6	13.5	102 306	135.4	29 347
District 4	15.7	11.4	13.3	349 166	23 824	6.8	325 342	27.2	38.4	34.4	9.0	149 244	210.2	15 352
District 5	12.7	7.9	10.7	377 429	19 245	5.1	358 184	32.5	38.6	28.9	7.0	146 059	199.9	10 840
District 6	16.9	12.4	17.6	329 888	27 040	8.2	302 848	28.4	41.3	30.3	10.9	169 591	237.7	25 664
District 7	14.4	10.2	13.3	357 672	22 055	6.2	335 617	29.2	39.6	31.2	12.4	152 496	210.2	13 636
District 8	14.5	10.2	13.7	368 057	23 942	6.5	344 115	33.2	40.0	26.7	8.9	141 856	196.2	14 763
District 9	21.6	17.0	21.4	356 790	33 515	9.4	323 275	31.6	43.0	25.4	10.1	140 139	197.4	31 374
District 10	18.2	14.5	14.8	353 494	29 464	8.3	324 030	37.1	42.2	20.6	10.7	144 673	200.7	19 734
District 11	28.2	22.7	27.5	339 611	47 013	13.8	292 598	37.0	45.4	17.5	10.7	136 763	195.4	41 733
District 12	10.3	6.3	9.2	396 472	18 354	4.6	378 118	46.3	36.8	16.9	7.1	127 940	169.2	12 983
District 13	18.2	14.6	17.7	352 668	27 337	7.8	325 331	29.8	44.4	25.8	10.5	159 138	224.8	24 961
District 14	9.4	6.1	8.3	378 448	19 972	5.3	358 476	40.9	38.8	20.3	8.9	150 735	208.6	9 989
District 15	12.2	8.5	12.4	373 199	22 636	6.1	350 563	40.5	39.1	20.4	8.2	128 490	173.4	13 733
District 16	7.6	5.6	7.1	384 998	19 387	5.0	365 611	40.1	39.6	20.2	8.7	150 649	207.9	7 480
OKLAHOMA	16.6	12.2	13.8	1 840 095	104 334	5.7	1 735 761	34.1	40.9	25.1	17.8	749 794	193.3	96 975
District 1	14.1	11.0	12.4	402 206	20 591	5.1	381 615	37.1	41.3	21.6	16.6	140 624	180.0	17 161
District 2	20.8	15.4	18.0	313 421	21 021	6.7	292 400	29.4	40.3	30.3	23.5	182 412	243.3	28 042
District 3	14.9	10.3	11.1	365 516	18 796	5.1	346 720	31.8	39.5	28.7	15.5	149 306	192.2	14 572
District 4	14.1	10.2	12.4	365 262	19 157	5.2	346 105	34.2	41.2	24.6	14.6	142 285	183.8	16 010
District 5	19.1	14.1	15.1	393 690	24 769	6.3	368 921	36.6	41.8	21.6	19.3	135 167	169.7	21 190
OREGON	16.6	11.0	18.9	1 972 039	153 954	7.8	1 818 085	37.1	41.9	21.0	11.5	798 156	201.0	85 136
District 1	13.1	9.0	13.8	420 441	28 926	6.9	391 515	42.2	39.7	18.1	10.8	128 274	159.2	11 717
District 2	18.4	12.4	21.1	355 357	27 510	7.7	327 847	31.5	43.1	25.4	13.6	191 740	244.5	17 812

1. Percent of civilian labor force.　2. Persons 16 years old and over.　3. Per 1,000 resident population estimated in the 2014 American Community Survey.

STATE District	Land in farms				Value of products sold				Government payments	
	Number of farms	Acres	Average size of farm (acres)	Irrigated land (acres)	Total ($1,000)	Average per farm (dollars)	Percent from crops	Percent from livestock and poultry products	Total ($1,000)	Average per farm receiving payments (dollars)
	63	64	65	66	67	68	69	70	71	72
NEW MEXICO—Cont'd										
District 3	12 723	19 249 622	1 513	277 321	877 541	68 973	16.6	83.4	29 752	10 021
NEW YORK	35 537	7 183 576	202	59 807	5 415 125	152 380	41.5	58.5	74 511	7 955
District 1	499	27 475	55	8 672	196 009	392 803	83.0	17.0	605	15 508
District 2	39	1 088	28	265	4 469	114 580	98.0	2.0	D	D
District 3	112	10 121	90	2 954	45 149	403 114	88.6	11.4	185	61 793
District 4	10	20	2	14	492	49 170	D	D	0	0
District 5	X	X	X	X	X	X	X	X	X	X
District 6	X	X	X	X	X	X	X	X	X	X
District 7	X	X	X	X	X	X	X	X	X	X
District 8	X	X	X	X	X	X	X	X	X	X
District 9	X	X	X	X	X	X	X	X	X	X
District 10	X	X	X	X	X	X	X	X	X	X
District 11	X	X	X	X	X	X	X	X	X	X
District 12	X	X	X	X	X	X	X	X	X	X
District 13	X	X	X	X	X	X	X	X	X	X
District 14	X	X	X	X	X	X	X	X	X	X
District 15	X	X	X	X	X	X	X	X	X	X
District 16	10	1 017	102	9	828	82 774	91.8	8.2	0	0
District 17	70	2 001	29	113	6 584	94 053	62.7	37.3	D	D
District 18	871	110 109	126	3 066	113 514	130 326	71.9	28.1	2 102	10 778
District 19	5 314	957 846	180	8 894	462 961	87 121	44.3	55.7	8 095	6 581
District 20	1 181	161 612	137	804	113 423	96 040	44.2	55.8	1 111	5 142
District 21	6 108	1 496 682	245	2 668	977 396	160 019	23.1	76.9	15 284	9 983
District 22	4 770	941 790	197	2 123	493 919	103 547	26.9	73.1	10 122	7 174
District 23	8 716	1 667 821	191	5 848	1 054 998	121 042	39.1	60.9	14 867	6 541
District 24	2 712	603 589	223	3 754	667 658	246 187	46.4	53.6	6 666	8 199
District 25	364	56 344	155	810	47 235	129 766	88.4	11.6	760	9 266
District 26	58	10 225	176	38	8 791	151 564	99.2	0.8	D	D
District 27	4 674	1 135 393	243	19 756	1 218 619	260 723	46.4	53.6	14 616	9 351
NORTH CAROLINA	50 218	8 414 756	168	174 526	12 588 142	250 670	34.2	65.8	120 129	8 332
District 1	3 457	1 267 552	367	37 421	1 411 910	408 421	48.5	51.5	29 500	13 176
District 2	4 319	540 316	125	9 955	794 538	183 963	20.7	79.3	6 417	7 902
District 3	3 115	1 258 856	404	23 466	1 667 112	535 188	52.2	47.8	25 085	13 663
District 4	1 051	113 099	108	2 044	117 955	112 231	33.8	66.2	1 419	5 609
District 5	7 523	782 829	104	3 009	863 937	114 839	22.6	77.4	4 295	3 873
District 6	6 051	744 474	123	12 316	442 156	73 072	44.1	55.9	6 752	4 271
District 7	5 330	1 205 092	226	46 178	3 720 633	698 055	21.0	79.0	19 390	8 106
District 8	5 065	901 322	178	11 176	1 694 602	334 571	21.9	78.1	9 344	7 205
District 9	1 068	128 936	121	1 065	282 689	264 690	68.8	31.2	819	7 805
District 10	4 082	385 987	95	1 696	307 645	75 366	22.2	77.8	2 462	3 558
District 11	6 428	461 764	72	8 510	305 338	47 501	65.3	34.7	6 241	6 125
District 12	483	49 775	103	918	36 733	76 052	71.7	28.3	289	3 849
District 13	2 246	574 754	256	16 772	942 895	419 811	54.3	45.7	8 114	8 058
NORTH DAKOTA	30 961	39 262 613	1 268	218 407	10 950 680	353 693	88.3	11.7	381 710	15 398
At Large	30 961	39 262 613	1 268	218 407	10 950 680	353 693	88.3	11.7	381 710	15 398
OHIO	75 462	13 960 604	185	46 569	10 064 085	133 366	65.6	34.4	228 858	6 603
District 1	1 200	124 692	104	970	80 571	67 142	89.9	10.1	1 194	4 593
District 2	6 107	983 627	161	1 478	373 277	61 123	82.8	17.2	17 161	5 529
District 3	92	16 593	180	144	19 539	212 376	94.4	5.6	120	4 435
District 4	9 348	2 307 012	247	6 343	1 844 009	197 262	76.8	23.2	45 190	6 949
District 5	10 792	2 847 931	264	6 809	2 386 632	221 148	70.5	29.5	61 441	7 107
District 6	11 766	1 584 934	135	4 365	426 139	36 218	46.0	54.0	10 048	4 426
District 7	9 520	1 354 995	142	6 634	1 072 386	112 646	50.5	49.5	15 873	5 529
District 8	6 055	1 174 229	194	5 577	1 371 101	226 441	43.7	56.3	23 599	6 752
District 9	506	76 485	151	1 354	82 288	162 624	97.9	2.1	1 493	4 993
District 10	1 898	378 015	199	1 868	254 837	134 266	86.2	13.8	6 374	6 612
District 11	81	2 497	31	197	3 575	44 131	94.0	6.0	37	7 391
District 12	4 307	712 235	165	1 331	536 943	124 668	67.4	32.6	9 618	6 438
District 13	1 038	107 448	104	184	57 947	55 825	69.0	31.0	962	4 413
District 14	3 053	342 898	112	2 734	265 078	86 825	77.1	22.9	2 865	4 783
District 15	6 879	1 598 791	232	5 392	850 104	123 580	83.2	16.8	27 660	8 745
District 16	2 820	348 222	123	1 189	439 660	155 908	32.6	67.4	5 223	7 048
OKLAHOMA	80 245	34 356 110	428	479 750	7 129 584	88 848	26.3	73.7	256 845	8 634
District 1	3 160	575 332	182	D	99 709	31 553	42.0	58.0	2 618	4 392
District 2	29 692	8 013 419	270	38 897	2 053 254	69 152	16.2	83.8	37 636	5 317
District 3	30 326	19 992 205	659	395 097	4 172 753	137 597	30.6	69.4	182 507	10 572
District 4	13 283	5 059 287	381	33 614	711 085	53 533	28.0	72.0	31 371	7 483
District 5	3 784	715 867	189	D	92 783	24 520	28.2	71.8	2 714	4 391
OREGON	35 439	16 301 578	460	1 629 735	4 883 674	137 805	66.5	33.5	85 840	16 054
District 1	4 759	400 597	84	46 715	584 568	122 834	84.9	15.1	4 343	6 861
District 2	13 284	13 924 323	1 048	1 349 942	2 419 047	182 102	58.7	41.3	72 580	21 038

Private nonfarm employment and payroll, 2014

| STATE District | Number of establishments | Total | Employment — Percent by selected industries | | | | | | | | | Annual payroll | |
			Manufacturing	Construction	Wholesale trade	Retail trade	Health care and social assistance	Finance and Insurance	Real estate and rental and leasing	Professional, scientific, and technical services	Information	Total (mil dol)	Average per employee dollars
	73	74	75	76	77	78	79	80	81	82	83	84	85
NEW MEXICO—Cont'd													
District 3	14 451	174 959	4.0	5.2	2.7	17.5	19.4	3.3	1.6	8.8	1.7	7 093	40 539
NEW YORK	536 890	7 858 425	5.4	4.0	4.7	11.9	18.6	6.8	2.2	8.0	3.6	492 706	62 698
District 1	22 767	233 301	7.6	7.9	6.2	17.3	20.2	0.0	1.2	7.5	1.6	11 679	50 060
District 2	20 592	245 044	12.2	8.9	8.9	14.3	14.5	2.7	1.3	6.5	2.4	11 129	45 417
District 3	29 626	372 327	3.3	3.9	7.2	11.1	21.7	7.4	2.0	8.9	3.1	22 216	59 668
District 4	24 390	264 728	3.5	5.3	3.9	15.1	19.1	6.1	1.6	8.8	1.9	12 319	46 534
District 5	10 759	149 822	2.1	5.1	2.4	12.7	18.2	1.3	1.9	2.2	0.8	6 191	41 323
District 6	17 936	163 398	2.6	6.7	3.4	14.3	37.2	3.6	2.7	3.6	1.6	6 303	38 572
District 7	21 284	206 451	5.5	6.0	6.8	11.4	22.3	3.9	2.8	4.8	1.7	8 023	38 861
District 8	10 888	127 556	3.4	2.8	4.1	15.0	28.0	2.7	2.5	3.0	0.0	4 935	38 689
District 9	12 238	113 626	1.0	2.3	1.8	14.2	45.2	1.7	3.3	3.1	0.0	4 313	37 960
District 10	40 341	774 277	1.6	1.9	3.3	7.4	13.1	13.8	2.7	12.2	6.9	71 453	92 283
District 11	15 713	150 503	1.1	6.6	2.0	16.5	35.4	2.7	1.9	3.6	1.6	5 616	37 313
District 12	70 941	1 498 495	1.3	2.4	5.2	6.7	9.2	13.0	3.3	14.1	7.5	164 802	109 978
District 13	9 875	139 273	0.3	1.3	0.5	10.7	0.0	1.5	3.7	2.0	1.2	7 305	52 448
District 14	12 177	144 583	3.5	9.5	5.1	11.6	24.9	2.3	2.4	1.9	2.1	6 843	47 326
District 15	8 917	117 976	3.9	4.4	8.7	13.7	32.4	1.2	3.8	1.8	0.0	5 002	42 401
District 16	16 176	170 504	3.9	8.0	2.9	16.6	23.3	2.5	3.6	3.3	2.0	7 641	44 812
District 17	25 672	328 255	3.8	4.8	5.5	12.1	21.4	6.3	1.8	7.6	2.8	21 491	65 470
District 18	18 988	220 482	6.8	4.3	5.2	18.1	19.1	3.0	1.4	6.9	2.0	9 770	44 311
District 19	16 697	162 413	8.4	5.1	3.3	17.8	21.8	3.8	1.3	3.2	1.7	5 771	35 531
District 20	18 850	325 613	6.9	4.2	4.1	13.5	20.0	5.9	1.4	8.2	2.8	14 694	45 126
District 21	15 507	179 679	11.2	4.4	2.8	20.2	20.9	2.5	1.1	2.9	2.1	6 355	35 366
District 22	14 318	226 350	13.4	3.1	3.7	15.1	20.4	5.2	0.9	4.2	2.4	8 209	36 268
District 23	14 587	224 635	15.3	3.3	2.7	15.2	17.5	2.5	1.1	4.1	1.5	8 455	37 639
District 24	16 574	274 892	10.8	4.4	5.6	14.3	18.6	4.7	1.6	6.3	2.0	11 451	41 655
District 25	16 960	338 514	10.3	3.3	4.4	12.3	18.8	3.6	1.7	6.7	2.8	14 699	43 423
District 26	17 652	350 472	8.9	2.9	4.9	12.4	18.5	7.5	1.5	7.5	2.1	14 901	42 516
District 27	15 875	203 226	17.7	5.6	5.0	18.3	15.1	2.8	1.1	3.4	1.2	7 852	38 637
NORTH CAROLINA	219 897	3 560 448	11.5	4.7	4.9	13.2	15.7	4.8	1.4	5.7	2.3	155 372	43 638
District 1	15 632	280 719	13.2	3.7	3.8	12.4	23.6	3.1	0.9	3.5	1.8	11 116	39 599
District 2	14 889	215 157	16.1	4.9	3.8	14.6	17.4	2.6	1.3	5.2	2.6	7 875	36 601
District 3	15 669	174 699	6.8	6.3	2.7	20.3	15.2	3.2	2.9	5.2	1.4	5 822	33 326
District 4	19 425	372 458	5.0	4.4	6.3	11.6	16.3	5.1	1.6	13.6	5.0	20 586	55 272
District 5	16 218	265 627	15.0	4.0	3.3	13.6	20.4	3.4	1.1	3.1	0.9	10 644	40 072
District 6	16 033	248 459	14.6	5.8	4.5	14.6	16.7	4.1	1.5	3.8	2.2	10 208	41 087
District 7	14 962	181 363	16.6	6.4	3.7	17.8	17.0	2.9	1.5	3.4	1.9	6 270	34 574
District 8	13 228	185 313	19.1	6.5	4.0	15.7	17.6	2.3	0.9	2.3	0.8	6 269	33 837
District 9	22 067	325 137	6.6	4.6	6.1	12.3	16.9	6.0	1.8	7.4	1.8	16 653	51 219
District 10	17 567	263 983	18.2	3.9	5.2	12.4	19.8	2.1	1.5	2.9	1.2	9 695	36 724
District 11	15 228	189 476	20.5	5.3	3.0	16.7	17.4	2.2	1.1	2.5	1.2	6 238	32 924
District 12	20 616	483 597	8.1	4.1	7.2	9.0	7.3	11.8	1.6	7.0	3.2	26 530	54 859
District 13	17 822	240 879	7.0	5.8	4.8	15.4	13.9	5.6	1.6	8.1	3.1	10 843	45 013
NORTH DAKOTA	24 698	360 970	6.9	6.7	6.6	14.2	16.5	4.9	1.5	4.3	1.9	17 363	48 100
At Large	24 698	360 970	6.9	6.7	6.6	14.2	16.5	4.9	1.5	4.3	1.9	17 363	48 100
OHIO	250 535	4 636 844	13.9	3.7	5.0	12.1	17.7	5.4	1.4	5.2	1.9	203 868	43 967
District 1	16 650	386 318	9.0	4.1	5.4	9.4	19.2	6.7	1.4	7.3	2.4	21 022	54 416
District 2	15 654	260 192	10.0	4.2	5.7	14.5	16.9	6.2	1.4	7.5	2.3	11 561	44 431
District 3	14 813	361 248	6.0	3.7	5.1	10.8	19.3	8.9	1.7	5.7	2.6	17 654	48 871
District 4	14 467	262 519	28.6	3.7	4.4	11.9	15.8	2.2	0.8	3.8	1.0	10 587	40 329
District 5	16 277	296 360	21.4	3.6	3.8	12.8	13.9	3.0	1.1	4.0	1.0	11 231	37 896
District 6	13 006	173 214	14.8	5.4	3.6	15.3	21.7	2.9	1.0	2.3	1.0	6 121	35 339
District 7	14 246	214 946	23.5	5.6	4.4	14.5	16.9	3.2	0.8	2.6	1.1	8 010	37 265
District 8	13 626	233 349	19.4	4.2	7.5	13.8	13.9	5.4	1.0	2.6	0.9	9 246	39 622
District 9	13 389	241 037	16.5	3.3	4.8	11.7	17.7	3.4	1.5	3.3	1.8	10 265	42 589
District 10	15 045	284 204	11.2	3.2	3.9	13.4	20.3	4.4	1.3	7.6	3.4	12 108	42 604
District 11	18 512	420 744	8.7	2.9	4.6	6.8	27.9	6.4	2.0	7.4	1.9	22 438	53 329
District 12	16 885	313 609	8.3	3.3	3.0	11.2	18.4	11.2	1.0	5.8	3.1	15 063	48 032
District 13	15 022	255 090	15.4	4.1	4.8	15.2	18.5	2.1	1.8	3.6	1.4	9 902	38 818
District 14	20 377	326 860	18.8	3.4	7.9	11.9	12.2	6.2	2.0	5.3	1.7	15 125	46 274
District 15	13 738	219 177	11.9	3.5	5.5	15.8	14.9	4.2	1.5	5.2	2.2	8 512	38 836
District 16	18 204	282 656	14.0	4.1	5.1	16.4	17.1	4.2	1.2	4.3	1.8	11 106	39 290
OKLAHOMA	92 430	1 359 851	10.0	5.1	4.5	13.3	15.9	4.3	1.7	5.2	2.2	58 150	42 762
District 1	21 261	371 347	12.3	4.7	5.0	11.7	14.7	4.4	1.9	6.2	3.3	17 840	48 042
District 2	13 100	160 894	14.9	4.4	3.4	16.2	23.8	3.9	1.0	2.5	1.1	5 235	32 535
District 3	17 426	202 651	12.1	7.2	4.4	15.0	13.5	3.7	1.9	3.6	1.5	7 863	38 803
District 4	16 524	209 802	8.7	5.7	2.8	16.6	17.7	4.2	1.8	4.8	1.6	7 370	35 127
District 5	23 759	377 224	6.4	4.9	5.6	12.2	15.7	4.9	1.7	6.3	2.3	17 642	46 768
OREGON	109 875	1 444 041	11.2	5.3	5.1	13.6	15.8	4.2	1.9	5.9	2.6	65 715	45 508
District 1	22 271	343 315	14.6	5.6	6.0	12.4	12.0	4.4	2.0	7.7	3.6	19 653	57 245
District 2	22 551	235 346	10.8	5.0	3.6	17.3	18.6	3.3	1.6	3.6	2.2	8 531	36 250

1. Specified owner-occupied units; $1,000,000 represents $1,000,000 or more. 2. Specified renter-occupied units.

Table E. Congressional Districts 114th Congress — **Land Area and Population Characteristics**

STATE District	Representative, 114th Congress	Land area,[1] 2010 (sq km)	Total persons	Per square kilometer	White	Black	American Indian, Alaska Native	Asian and Pacific Islander	Some other race	Two or more races	Hispanic or Latino[2]	Non-Hispanic White alone	Female	Foreign-born	Born in state of residence
		1	2	3	4	5	6	7	8	9	10	11	12	13	14
OREGON—Cont'd															
District 3	Earl Blumenauer (D)	2 783	806 382	289.8	78.2	4.9	0.9	6.9	3.8	5.2	11.1	72.0	50.2	13.5	43.9
District 4	Peter A. DeFazio (D)	44 740	775 615	17.3	89.8	0.8	1.3	2.5	1.6	4.0	7.2	84.9	50.5	5.0	46.0
District 5	Kurt Schrader (D)	13 441	798 185	59.4	84.8	1.1	1.0	3.5	4.4	5.2	16.2	75.5	50.8	10.1	51.3
PENNSYLVANIA		115 883	12 787 209	110.3	81.4	11.1	0.2	3.2	1.9	2.3	6.5	77.7	51.1	6.4	73.4
District 1	Robert A. Brady (D)	202	716 072	3 544.9	49.0	36.4	0.4	6.6	4.9	2.6	16.4	39.8	51.4	13.3	67.3
District 2	Chaka Fattah (D)	192	716 892	3 733.8	31.8	58.0	0.4	5.0	2.0	2.9	6.2	28.8	54.9	8.2	69.3
District 3	Mike Kelly (R)	9 974	702 323	70.4	91.6	4.7	0.1	1.0	0.5	2.1	2.1	90.4	50.8	2.8	81.5
District 4	Scott Perry (R)	3 931	719 504	183.0	85.2	7.8	0.0	2.2	2.1	2.7	6.9	81.2	50.7	5.0	66.6
District 5	Glenn Thompson (R)	27 742	700 531	25.3	93.6	2.5	0.3	1.6	0.4	1.6	2.0	92.4	49.1	3.7	79.6
District 6	Ryan A. Costello (R)	2 229	716 612	321.5	86.9	4.7	0.0	4.1	2.1	2.2	6.0	83.8	51.0	7.2	71.8
District 7	Patrick Meehan (R)	2 234	714 577	319.9	87.5	5.7	0.1	4.6	0.4	1.6	3.3	85.0	51.6	7.5	73.9
District 8	Michael G. Fitzpatrick (R)	1 831	713 387	389.6	88.2	3.9	0.1	5.2	0.9	1.7	5.0	84.3	50.9	8.2	68.5
District 9	Bill Shuster (R)	14 841	694 973	46.8	94.6	2.9	0.2	0.6	0.3	1.4	2.1	93.0	50.7	1.6	80.9
District 10	Tom Marino (R)	21 699	696 416	32.1	92.7	3.7	0.2	0.9	1.0	1.5	4.0	90.1	49.7	2.9	69.2
District 11	Lou Barletta (R)	8 693	700 342	80.6	89.6	5.4	0.1	1.6	1.6	1.6	5.6	86.5	50.4	4.7	77.5
District 12	Keith J. Rothfus (R)	5 602	704 560	125.8	92.7	3.3	0.1	1.6	0.4	1.9	1.2	92.0	51.0	2.8	82.9
District 13	Brendan F. Boyle (D)	402	725 185	1 803.9	65.4	17.5	0.3	9.5	4.5	2.6	11.5	59.6	51.3	17.4	67.5
District 14	Michael F. Doyle (D)	542	701 362	1 294.0	71.4	21.5	0.2	3.3	0.6	3.0	2.3	70.0	52.1	5.2	79.7
District 15	Charles W. Dent (R)	3 328	722 560	217.1	83.5	4.8	0.3	2.4	6.2	2.9	15.3	76.3	51.4	7.2	67.7
District 16	Joseph R. Pitts (R)	2 584	722 837	279.7	80.6	7.1	0.6	2.1	4.5	5.2	17.7	72.3	50.9	8.3	69.8
District 17	Matt Cartwright (D)	4 489	707 062	157.5	88.8	6.0	0.2	2.1	1.1	1.8	8.1	82.6	50.8	5.7	68.3
District 18	Tim Murphy (R)	5 368	712 014	132.6	93.8	2.5	0.1	2.1	0.3	1.3	1.4	92.9	51.1	3.4	80.7
RHODE ISLAND		2 678	1 055 173	394.0	81.3	6.7	0.5	3.4	5.4	2.6	14.0	74.1	51.5	13.4	58.3
District 1	David Cicilline (D)	695	532 145	765.7	78.2	8.6	0.6	3.0	6.4	3.1	17.3	69.0	51.2	15.6	52.5
District 2	James R. Langevin (D)	1 982	523 028	263.9	84.5	4.7	0.4	3.8	4.5	2.1	10.7	79.2	51.8	11.1	64.1
SOUTH CAROLINA		77 857	4 832 482	62.1	67.3	27.3	0.3	1.5	1.4	2.1	5.3	63.8	51.3	4.7	57.7
District 1	Mark Sanford (R)	4 009	728 626	181.7	75.5	18.4	0.2	2.0	1.4	2.5	6.5	70.7	51.4	5.8	44.5
District 2	Joe Wilson (R)	7 827	686 952	87.8	70.7	23.2	0.3	2.0	1.5	2.3	5.4	67.0	51.4	5.1	54.0
District 3	Jeff Duncan (R)	13 645	666 489	48.8	77.0	18.4	0.2	0.8	1.6	2.0	4.3	74.7	50.9	3.3	66.1
District 4	Trey Gowdy (R)	3 365	703 720	209.1	74.8	19.5	0.2	2.2	1.3	2.0	8.3	68.3	51.5	7.0	56.3
District 5	Mick Mulvaney (R)	14 259	684 083	48.0	67.9	26.9	0.3	1.0	1.2	2.6	3.8	65.5	51.1	3.6	58.5
District 6	James E. Clyburn (D)	20 883	673 637	32.3	38.3	56.7	0.2	1.3	1.5	1.9	4.8	35.5	51.1	4.3	69.0
District 7	Tom Rice (R)	13 868	688 975	49.7	66.2	29.3	0.6	0.9	1.5	1.4	3.9	64.0	51.9	3.9	56.9
SOUTH DAKOTA		196 350	853 175	4.3	84.9	1.7	8.4	1.3	0.8	2.8	3.4	83.2	49.9	2.9	65.1
At Large	Kristi Noem (R)	196 350	853 175	4.3	84.9	1.7	8.4	1.3	0.8	2.8	3.4	83.2	49.9	2.9	65.1
TENNESSEE		106 798	6 549 352	61.3	77.6	16.9	0.3	1.6	1.5	2.1	4.9	74.5	51.3	4.9	60.9
District 1	David P. Roe (R)	10 728	713 317	66.5	93.9	2.2	0.2	0.6	1.2	1.9	3.5	91.8	51.1	2.6	61.7
District 2	John J. Duncan Jr. (R)	6 011	726 315	120.8	89.2	6.6	0.4	1.6	0.7	1.6	3.8	86.4	51.4	4.5	59.8
District 3	Chuck Fleischmann (R)	11 837	716 365	60.5	85.1	11.2	0.2	1.2	0.3	1.9	3.5	82.4	51.2	3.4	64.3
District 4	Scott DesJarlais (R)	15 501	747 195	48.2	85.0	8.1	0.3	1.5	1.6	3.6	5.8	81.1	51.1	4.9	61.2
District 5	Jim Cooper (D)	3 234	751 222	232.3	66.0	24.9	0.3	2.9	3.5	2.4	9.1	60.7	51.9	11.6	53.6
District 6	Diane Black (R)	16 768	733 467	43.7	91.1	4.4	0.3	1.1	1.4	1.7	3.7	89.0	50.8	3.3	63.0
District 7	Marsha Blackburn (R)	23 725	743 173	31.3	84.6	10.5	0.2	1.8	0.6	2.3	4.9	80.8	50.3	4.2	53.1
District 8	Stephen Lee Fincher (R)	17 743	710 910	40.1	76.0	19.4	0.2	1.9	0.8	1.6	3.3	73.8	51.3	3.2	66.3
District 9	Steve Cohen (D)	1 252	707 388	565.0	26.8	65.7	0.2	1.9	3.5	2.0	6.6	24.0	52.6	6.3	65.8
TEXAS		676 587	26 956 958	39.8	75.2	12.0	0.5	4.4	5.5	2.5	38.6	43.4	50.3	16.8	60.1
District 1	Louie Gohmert (R)	20 354	712 779	35.0	76.8	18.6	0.4	1.2	1.9	1.1	16.8	62.6	50.8	7.7	71.8
District 2	Ted Poe (R)	800	737 492	921.9	70.6	9.6	0.4	7.0	9.7	2.6	30.7	50.7	49.8	21.5	49.9
District 3	Sam Johnson (R)	1 245	792 608	636.6	71.0	9.1	0.4	13.8	2.6	3.2	14.7	59.6	51.0	20.4	44.2
District 4	John Ratcliffe (R)	26 218	719 372	27.4	80.9	10.3	0.6	0.9	4.5	2.8	13.6	72.4	50.5	6.7	66.9
District 5	Jeb Hensarling (R)	13 064	734 553	56.2	74.7	15.7	0.4	2.5	4.2	2.4	27.6	52.2	49.3	14.2	65.2
District 6	Joe Barton (R)	5 564	737 480	132.5	68.3	19.6	0.9	4.3	3.4	3.5	22.6	51.4	51.6	12.6	59.5
District 7	John Abney Culberson (R)	419	770 950	1 840.0	69.0	13.3	0.1	10.8	4.4	2.4	31.4	43.2	51.0	28.9	45.3
District 8	Kevin Brady (R)	15 679	767 431	48.9	83.2	8.0	0.2	3.0	3.0	2.4	20.9	66.1	49.6	11.3	59.7
District 9	Al Green (D)	429	772 152	1 799.9	34.8	38.5	0.2	12.5	11.9	2.1	37.7	10.5	51.0	34.8	49.0
District 10	Michael T. McCaul (R)	13 134	771 009	58.7	77.1	9.8	0.4	5.2	5.1	2.5	27.8	55.5	50.2	16.0	58.9
District 11	K. Michael Conaway (R)	72 085	741 069	10.3	86.5	3.8	0.4	1.1	6.0	2.1	37.5	56.6	49.5	9.1	70.6
District 12	Kay Granger (R)	3 733	750 952	201.2	79.3	9.0	0.5	3.6	5.0	2.7	22.6	62.5	51.1	10.3	61.1
District 13	Mac Thornberry (R)	99 324	707 803	7.1	85.1	5.4	0.9	2.0	3.3	3.3	26.4	64.1	48.6	8.8	67.0
District 14	Randy K. Weber, Sr. (R)	6 323	724 881	114.6	72.3	20.0	0.2	3.1	2.1	2.2	23.8	51.6	49.6	10.9	67.0
District 15	Rubén Hinojosa (D)	20 212	764 850	37.8	88.6	1.9	0.3	1.1	7.1	1.0	81.4	15.3	50.6	22.3	65.4
District 16	Beto O'Rourke (D)	1 840	735 246	399.6	82.5	4.3	0.5	1.3	9.0	2.2	79.2	14.7	50.7	24.6	56.0
District 17	Bill Flores (R)	19 816	740 151	37.4	74.5	13.3	0.3	4.5	4.6	2.8	24.6	55.8	50.4	12.0	67.2
District 18	Sheila Jackson-Lee (D)	609	750 812	1 232.9	44.8	39.3	0.4	3.3	10.4	1.7	41.2	15.5	49.7	21.1	61.0
District 19	Randy Neugebauer (R)	66 914	719 594	10.8	80.7	6.2	0.8	1.4	7.8	3.0	35.6	55.3	49.2	8.4	72.7
District 20	Joaquin Castro (D)	517	762 801	1 475.4	80.4	5.5	0.6	3.4	7.1	3.0	68.8	21.4	50.9	14.5	65.2
District 21	Lamar Smith (R)	15 335	766 190	50.0	88.0	3.2	0.5	3.2	2.6	2.5	30.1	61.8	49.9	9.3	59.5
District 22	Pete Olson (R)	2 675	814 594	304.5	62.5	13.6	0.4	17.8	3.5	2.2	24.5	42.7	50.5	23.3	51.5
District 23	Will Hurd (R)	150 373	743 201	4.9	85.4	3.4	0.6	1.3	7.5	1.8	67.7	26.6	49.9	16.8	64.5
District 24	Kenny Marchant (R)	681	759 022	1 114.6	67.3	11.0	0.3	12.7	5.5	3.3	24.2	49.7	50.9	22.6	44.3
District 25	Roger Williams (R)	19 738	748 022	37.9	83.1	7.1	0.5	3.1	2.6	3.7	18.3	68.6	51.1	8.4	57.4

1. Dry land or land partially or temporarily covered by water.   2. May be of any race.

Table E. Congressional Districts 114th Congress — **Age and Education**

STATE District	Under 5 years (15)	5 to 17 years (16)	18 to 24 years (17)	25 to 34 years (18)	35 to 44 years (19)	45 to 54 years (20)	55 to 64 years (21)	65 to 74 years (22)	75 years and over (23)	Median age (24)	Total Enrollment[1] (25)	High school graduate or more (26)	Bachelor's degree or more (27)
OREGON—Cont'd													
District 3	5.8	14.3	8.7	17.6	15.4	12.9	12.6	7.6	5.0	37.2	194 386	90.7	37.4
District 4	4.8	14.4	11.7	11.8	10.9	12.4	15.0	11.4	7.8	42.0	194 205	90.6	26.0
District 5	6.0	17.5	9.2	12.2	12.5	12.9	13.5	9.5	6.6	39.3	198 267	89.3	28.7
PENNSYLVANIA	5.6	15.5	9.6	12.8	11.9	14.1	13.9	9.0	7.7	40.7	3 011 245	89.4	29.0
District 1	7.3	15.8	9.5	19.0	12.9	12.7	11.3	6.6	5.0	34.1	174 781	82.9	26.1
District 2	6.7	14.5	14.5	17.1	10.9	11.2	11.8	7.4	5.9	32.9	209 597	86.3	33.3
District 3	5.3	15.6	9.4	11.2	11.5	14.5	14.6	9.5	8.3	42.6	159 303	90.5	24.6
District 4	5.6	16.4	9.1	12.3	12.4	14.5	13.7	8.9	7.1	40.9	167 780	88.9	25.9
District 5	4.9	13.9	13.3	11.7	11.1	13.6	14.1	9.6	7.7	40.9	174 915	90.5	23.1
District 6	5.9	16.9	8.8	11.6	12.7	15.0	13.6	8.3	7.3	40.8	177 407	92.4	42.5
District 7	5.7	16.7	8.8	11.3	11.4	15.3	13.9	8.9	8.0	41.8	174 418	92.1	42.0
District 8	4.8	16.6	8.1	11.0	12.1	15.9	14.9	9.1	7.4	43.2	170 422	93.6	37.9
District 9	5.2	15.1	9.6	10.8	11.7	13.9	14.6	10.3	8.8	43.0	148 421	87.4	17.6
District 10	4.7	15.7	9.3	11.1	11.2	14.8	14.7	10.3	8.2	43.6	152 771	87.4	20.0
District 11	5.2	14.9	9.2	11.8	12.2	14.2	14.6	10.0	7.9	42.4	155 395	89.5	24.0
District 12	5.2	15.4	6.7	11.2	11.6	14.2	15.7	10.6	9.4	45.0	148 040	93.0	31.1
District 13	6.1	16.2	8.2	14.7	12.7	13.9	12.8	8.0	7.2	38.6	174 849	86.4	33.2
District 14	5.0	12.3	11.9	16.6	10.9	12.6	14.4	8.1	8.2	38.7	164 379	92.1	31.3
District 15	5.5	16.2	9.8	12.2	12.1	13.9	13.9	9.0	7.5	40.7	172 692	89.3	27.5
District 16	6.7	17.9	9.5	12.9	12.0	13.5	12.3	8.1	7.1	37.6	176 073	84.1	25.0
District 17	5.2	15.5	9.3	11.6	12.1	14.5	13.6	9.8	8.4	42.5	161 651	88.8	21.3
District 18	5.0	14.5	7.8	12.0	11.8	14.9	15.0	10.3	8.7	44.2	148 351	94.0	34.7
RHODE ISLAND	5.2	14.9	11.1	13.0	12.0	14.4	13.4	8.5	7.3	39.8	267 358	85.8	30.4
District 1	5.7	15.5	10.8	13.8	12.3	14.0	12.9	7.9	7.3	38.2	137 276	84.0	30.8
District 2	4.6	14.4	11.3	12.4	11.6	15.0	13.9	9.2	7.4	41.5	130 082	87.5	30.1
SOUTH CAROLINA	5.9	16.5	10.1	12.8	12.5	13.4	13.1	9.7	6.1	38.8	1 207 095	86.1	26.3
District 1	6.0	15.9	8.5	14.6	13.0	13.3	12.4	10.3	6.1	38.7	177 368	92.6	37.5
District 2	6.1	17.1	9.9	12.9	13.0	13.7	13.2	8.6	5.6	38.1	174 840	89.2	33.3
District 3	5.6	16.3	10.4	11.6	12.1	13.4	13.4	10.5	6.8	40.3	167 899	83.0	20.4
District 4	6.3	17.1	10.1	13.1	12.7	13.6	12.5	8.6	6.0	37.8	176 051	86.9	29.4
District 5	5.9	17.2	9.3	11.3	13.6	14.1	13.1	9.6	5.8	39.9	165 976	83.4	21.9
District 6	5.9	15.9	13.8	14.4	11.1	12.3	12.5	8.7	5.4	35.0	188 121	81.7	19.4
District 7	5.6	15.8	8.9	11.7	11.8	13.4	14.4	11.7	6.7	41.9	156 840	85.2	20.6
SOUTH DAKOTA	7.1	17.6	10.2	13.1	11.3	12.5	13.0	8.1	7.1	36.6	223 281	91.7	27.8
At Large	7.1	17.6	10.2	13.1	11.3	12.5	13.0	8.1	7.1	36.6	223 281	91.7	27.8
TENNESSEE	6.1	16.8	9.6	13.1	12.9	13.7	12.9	9.0	6.1	38.6	1 589 191	85.8	25.3
District 1	5.0	15.2	8.6	11.5	12.4	14.2	14.2	11.3	7.6	43.1	156 291	83.6	19.9
District 2	5.5	15.5	10.9	12.4	12.5	13.5	13.0	9.9	6.8	39.9	171 279	87.5	29.4
District 3	5.5	15.6	8.8	12.0	12.7	14.1	14.2	9.9	7.1	41.4	156 887	85.0	23.1
District 4	5.9	17.7	10.5	12.6	13.4	13.3	12.0	8.7	5.6	37.2	191 953	84.5	21.2
District 5	6.9	15.0	10.1	18.4	13.7	12.8	11.7	6.6	4.7	34.8	180 539	86.2	34.9
District 6	5.8	16.8	8.5	11.5	12.7	14.1	13.2	10.6	6.7	40.9	171 077	85.6	20.4
District 7	6.5	18.6	9.1	12.2	13.4	14.1	12.2	8.5	5.5	37.9	188 988	87.2	26.9
District 8	5.8	18.5	8.8	10.9	12.8	14.1	13.4	9.4	6.4	39.7	182 175	88.4	29.4
District 9	7.8	17.3	11.4	15.8	12.4	12.6	11.9	6.2	4.4	33.6	190 002	84.2	22.2
TEXAS	7.2	19.2	10.2	14.4	13.6	12.8	11.0	6.8	4.7	34.3	7 467 266	82.2	27.8
District 1	6.8	17.8	11.1	12.2	11.6	12.2	12.3	9.0	7.0	36.6	184 847	83.3	20.4
District 2	7.2	16.8	8.8	17.3	13.6	14.2	12.2	6.4	3.6	35.0	196 075	88.3	39.5
District 3	6.3	20.6	7.9	13.2	16.5	15.2	10.6	6.3	3.4	36.2	229 542	94.1	52.2
District 4	6.1	18.5	8.8	11.4	12.8	13.7	12.8	9.3	6.8	39.3	181 847	85.6	19.7
District 5	7.3	19.1	9.0	13.7	13.3	13.1	11.6	7.6	5.2	35.6	191 344	80.3	20.0
District 6	6.4	20.6	10.3	13.0	14.0	13.7	11.6	6.4	4.0	34.7	214 249	88.4	28.8
District 7	6.9	19.0	8.9	16.0	15.6	12.4	11.6	5.5	4.2	34.5	216 207	88.5	47.2
District 8	6.1	19.2	9.8	12.3	13.9	13.9	12.1	7.8	4.9	36.6	200 246	85.6	29.9
District 9	8.1	18.3	11.3	17.1	13.6	12.2	10.5	5.6	3.1	32.2	214 765	75.7	24.6
District 10	7.4	19.0	8.3	13.9	14.6	13.9	11.4	7.2	4.4	36.0	204 053	88.1	37.8
District 11	7.0	17.6	10.3	14.0	11.5	11.9	12.3	8.4	6.9	35.8	176 414	82.0	20.4
District 12	7.3	17.8	9.6	15.2	13.1	13.3	11.3	7.3	5.1	35.1	195 719	87.6	29.7
District 13	6.8	18.3	10.0	13.6	12.1	12.7	12.3	7.9	6.3	36.0	179 950	84.2	19.8
District 14	6.5	17.7	9.5	13.5	12.9	13.8	12.9	7.7	5.4	36.9	182 043	84.6	22.2
District 15	8.9	23.1	10.8	13.6	13.4	11.2	8.4	6.2	4.4	30.3	242 989	69.2	19.7
District 16	8.2	19.4	11.9	14.5	12.7	11.7	10.1	6.0	5.3	32.1	223 621	77.9	23.1
District 17	6.5	16.7	16.1	14.6	12.6	11.7	10.3	6.6	4.8	32.3	231 277	85.3	28.5
District 18	7.6	19.7	10.7	17.5	14.2	11.9	9.6	5.2	3.5	31.8	225 140	76.9	21.6
District 19	6.9	18.2	13.7	14.5	11.2	11.8	10.8	7.3	6.0	32.9	207 306	81.0	21.4
District 20	7.6	18.9	12.0	17.0	13.0	11.8	9.7	5.9	4.4	31.5	226 964	80.1	22.9
District 21	5.3	15.1	10.6	15.2	12.8	12.9	12.8	8.9	6.3	37.8	195 532	93.0	44.7
District 22	7.1	21.3	8.0	12.8	16.0	14.2	11.0	6.1	3.6	35.5	247 419	90.3	44.5
District 23	7.8	21.2	10.3	13.2	12.9	12.3	10.1	7.5	4.8	32.8	212 505	75.0	21.3
District 24	6.9	16.9	7.7	17.6	14.6	15.1	11.0	6.2	3.9	35.6	189 193	90.1	43.6
District 25	6.6	17.8	10.0	14.5	13.4	12.9	12.2	7.6	4.9	35.8	207 618	88.7	35.3

1. All persons 3 years old and over enrolled in nursery school through college and graduate or professional school.   2. Persons 25 years old and over.

Table E. Congressional Districts 114th Congress — Households and Group Quarters

STATE District	Number	Average household size	Family households (percent)	Married-couple family (percent)	Female family householder[1]	One person households (percent)	Total in group quarters, 2014	Percent 65 years and over	Persons in correctional institutions	Persons in nursing facilities	Persons in college dormitories	Persons in military quarters
	28	29	30	31	32	33	34	35	36	37	38	39
OREGON—Cont'd												
District 3	317 520	2.48	57.5	42.0	10.9	30.1	18 164	15.5	2 065	2 399	6 604	0
District 4	313 058	2.42	60.6	46.3	10.0	28.6	17 805	16.5	1 354	2 067	8 825	21
District 5	296 296	2.64	67.1	50.9	11.3	25.7	15 506	19.1	5 381	2 401	3 162	17
PENNSYLVANIA	4 945 972	2.50	64.4	47.8	12.0	29.6	430 836	21.0	97 820	87 775	177 332	259
District 1	266 461	2.62	54.8	29.3	19.4	37.5	19 263	9.2	10 896	2 024	7 108	14
District 2	269 128	2.53	50.7	25.2	21.6	41.1	36 726	13.8	680	4 909	23 446	0
District 3	283 310	2.38	65.5	49.0	11.7	28.7	27 227	19.5	6 328	5 188	11 315	11
District 4	280 428	2.49	67.8	52.4	10.7	26.0	20 968	20.4	6 485	3 922	7 205	37
District 5	269 986	2.42	64.4	50.9	8.9	28.5	47 872	11.4	14 533	5 088	23 276	0
District 6	267 004	2.61	69.8	56.2	9.2	24.3	19 836	24.0	3 336	4 461	7 424	0
District 7	260 127	2.66	70.0	56.8	9.8	25.5	23 434	21.2	5 890	5 118	10 160	0
District 8	263 799	2.67	70.3	57.6	9.1	24.3	9 859	46.3	1 039	4 098	1 569	0
District 9	275 792	2.43	65.2	49.7	10.2	29.9	23 812	23.8	6 117	5 134	8 771	0
District 10	265 081	2.52	66.9	51.8	10.4	27.9	29 098	15.5	11 878	4 486	10 876	0
District 11	279 363	2.41	65.1	48.8	11.0	28.7	27 608	22.1	7 333	6 231	9 991	6
District 12	287 682	2.39	67.9	54.2	9.8	28.2	16 068	32.7	4 480	4 694	3 073	6
District 13	269 264	2.65	65.5	44.7	15.0	29.5	11 222	57.8	2	6 384	1 329	121
District 14	311 663	2.16	51.0	32.5	14.4	40.2	28 387	15.0	4 663	4 194	15 905	0
District 15	273 061	2.55	66.9	51.2	11.8	27.0	25 597	21.1	1 424	5 210	13 039	63
District 16	262 000	2.68	69.5	52.2	12.8	24.4	20 689	27.5	1 132	5 327	9 156	0
District 17	268 401	2.54	64.4	47.9	11.4	29.9	24 989	25.7	7 876	6 346	7 783	1
District 18	293 422	2.36	65.2	51.9	9.7	29.5	18 181	30.3	3 728	4 961	5 906	0
RHODE ISLAND	409 654	2.47	62.8	43.7	14.1	29.7	41 534	18.5	3 783	8 420	24 687	1 385
District 1	205 292	2.49	62.0	41.7	15.1	30.2	21 421	21.3	350	4 996	13 035	1 385
District 2	204 362	2.46	63.5	45.8	13.0	29.2	20 113	15.5	3 433	3 424	11 652	0
SOUTH CAROLINA	1 826 914	2.57	65.8	46.4	14.8	28.8	136 745	13.0	41 649	19 020	46 463	19 413
District 1	279 589	2.57	66.3	51.4	11.8	27.6	10 118	15.4	531	1 662	2 560	4 436
District 2	260 687	2.56	65.4	48.1	13.2	29.2	18 427	12.8	1 458	2 391	823	11 567
District 3	254 391	2.53	66.6	48.4	13.0	27.6	22 185	14.3	7 044	3 116	9 817	0
District 4	264 315	2.60	67.3	48.6	14.3	27.9	17 565	14.5	3 776	2 832	9 668	0
District 5	255 114	2.63	67.7	47.4	15.1	28.0	12 473	20.0	5 318	2 792	3 289	611
District 6	242 578	2.60	60.0	34.0	20.6	33.7	43 070	6.5	18 400	3 087	17 383	2 799
District 7	270 240	2.50	66.7	45.7	16.3	28.1	12 907	22.4	5 122	3 140	2 923	0
SOUTH DAKOTA	334 475	2.45	63.2	49.5	9.3	30.7	33 981	21.1	6 327	7 005	10 248	597
At Large	334 475	2.45	63.2	49.5	9.3	30.7	33 981	21.1	6 327	7 005	10 248	597
TENNESSEE	2 509 665	2.55	66.2	47.9	13.6	28.3	154 597	19.8	46 957	33 041	53 136	1 544
District 1	292 994	2.38	65.2	48.4	11.4	29.8	16 430	26.7	4 577	4 466	4 176	0
District 2	284 921	2.49	64.8	49.6	10.6	29.2	17 861	19.1	1 901	3 686	10 443	0
District 3	277 570	2.51	65.1	48.8	12.4	30.0	19 117	23.8	4 913	4 071	4 884	3
District 4	277 263	2.64	68.9	50.2	13.8	25.6	15 536	21.1	3 301	3 584	6 619	0
District 5	297 372	2.45	58.1	39.5	14.8	33.5	23 046	9.0	6 769	2 588	13 660	0
District 6	280 870	2.57	70.7	54.9	11.3	24.5	10 730	36.4	2 385	3 730	2 283	0
District 7	268 304	2.71	73.4	57.8	11.3	22.7	17 150	21.2	8 311	3 918	2 350	1 250
District 8	265 181	2.61	71.0	54.4	12.4	25.0	18 767	21.3	7 494	4 158	4 748	10
District 9	265 190	2.61	59.0	28.0	25.3	33.5	15 960	14.0	7 306	2 840	3 973	281
TEXAS	9 277 197	2.84	69.1	49.6	14.3	25.3	595 855	14.9	267 405	94 278	119 834	35 260
District 1	255 970	2.68	68.5	49.5	14.0	27.6	25 675	17.3	8 132	5 093	9 123	0
District 2	269 587	2.71	67.4	51.8	10.8	25.5	8 166	18.4	2 441	1 873	2 921	0
District 3	283 000	2.79	73.1	59.7	9.8	22.3	3 202	31.9	1 061	1 326	387	0
District 4	255 142	2.75	72.6	55.5	13.1	23.1	17 371	25.8	8 850	5 078	2 237	0
District 5	249 636	2.85	71.4	49.9	15.2	24.2	23 927	14.9	17 768	3 964	938	0
District 6	255 443	2.86	72.0	54.0	13.6	22.8	6 551	32.8	689	2 419	2 137	0
District 7	293 681	2.62	63.9	48.1	11.4	30.4	1 398	58.1	3	774	5	0
District 8	257 776	2.84	71.8	57.6	9.8	23.2	34 546	8.5	23 107	2 021	2 615	0
District 9	261 388	2.94	65.7	39.1	19.7	28.4	3 168	32.7	154	1 629	1 520	0
District 10	271 381	2.80	67.7	53.2	10.5	26.0	12 219	25.7	2 453	3 156	4 344	0
District 11	267 234	2.69	67.1	50.6	11.7	28.0	21 719	18.3	9 050	3 721	3 615	1 924
District 12	271 290	2.71	66.3	50.8	11.9	27.7	15 968	20.3	5 807	3 540	3 405	202
District 13	256 294	2.62	68.1	51.2	12.3	27.6	36 221	11.8	17 511	4 208	2 479	5 487
District 14	266 576	2.60	67.6	47.6	15.0	27.5	32 972	9.5	22 748	2 861	2 869	40
District 15	217 726	3.44	81.1	55.4	19.5	15.8	16 381	14.6	8 632	2 035	1 514	0
District 16	229 932	3.13	73.2	48.3	18.9	23.3	15 412	9.8	6 076	1 482	491	5 683
District 17	273 445	2.60	61.3	44.4	13.0	28.7	28 975	11.1	8 355	3 792	14 831	0
District 18	260 178	2.80	61.8	34.9	20.4	31.0	23 421	3.8	12 624	783	5 661	0
District 19	257 049	2.64	67.8	49.4	12.9	25.4	41 788	10.0	19 845	4 073	10 748	621
District 20	248 715	3.01	67.0	43.0	19.1	25.8	13 446	11.9	4	2 081	4 846	9 322
District 21	306 367	2.44	58.1	45.7	8.7	32.7	17 184	19.9	600	4 024	7 505	3 793
District 22	263 321	3.07	78.8	63.9	11.1	17.7	6 569	21.6	4 494	1 409	4	0
District 23	226 174	3.20	76.2	55.4	15.6	20.5	19 902	7.6	16 613	1 566	193	877
District 24	304 192	2.49	63.1	47.3	11.7	30.6	2 912	65.8	53	1 913	480	0
District 25	266 438	2.68	69.8	55.2	10.8	23.1	34 201	9.6	11 967	3 274	10 926	2 822

1. No spouse present.

STATE District	Housing units, 2014						Money income, 2014		
		Occupied units						Households	
			Owner-occupied			Renter-occupied			
	Total	Occupied units as a percent of all units	Owner-occupied units as a percent of occupied units	Median value[1] (dollars)	Percent valued at $500,000 or more	Median rent[2]	Per capita income (dollars)	Median income (dollars)	Percent with income of $100,000 or more
	40	41	42	43	44	45	46	47	48
OREGON—Cont'd									
District 3	336 887	94.3	55.0	283 300	13.6	984	29 980	53 293	22.8
District 4	347 465	90.1	62.4	201 000	6.0	850	24 192	43 696	14.3
District 5	331 887	89.3	63.1	239 900	10.2	880	27 518	53 287	21.7
PENNSYLVANIA	5 590 712	88.5	68.8	165 400	5.5	848	29 220	53 234	22.4
District 1	305 016	87.4	55.5	136 300	4.5	951	23 922	41 704	15.8
District 2	324 153	83.0	49.0	145 800	12.1	921	27 712	38 136	17.4
District 3	318 291	89.0	71.1	121 700	3.0	676	26 113	47 498	17.8
District 4	300 921	93.2	71.5	171 500	2.7	859	29 320	58 161	22.8
District 5	340 403	79.3	72.1	114 900	2.5	712	23 534	46 418	15.1
District 6	280 285	95.3	74.4	257 700	13.4	1 098	38 393	74 128	36.5
District 7	271 756	95.7	78.4	277 500	14.2	1 094	38 934	78 058	38.3
District 8	279 237	94.5	74.8	304 400	14.6	1 126	38 725	77 735	38.1
District 9	319 108	86.4	71.9	113 700	2.2	668	23 126	44 107	13.4
District 10	343 734	77.1	74.4	154 900	3.2	737	24 602	48 233	16.3
District 11	322 060	86.7	71.9	151 400	2.4	777	26 818	51 849	19.0
District 12	320 084	89.9	77.2	143 200	2.9	687	31 737	57 323	23.7
District 13	289 911	92.9	62.4	221 500	6.3	1 029	30 101	57 051	25.4
District 14	359 588	86.7	55.6	93 600	1.8	754	27 005	42 155	14.7
District 15	290 299	94.1	68.8	190 900	5.1	895	30 165	60 009	24.2
District 16	284 556	92.1	64.7	180 700	4.4	877	26 523	54 817	21.9
District 17	322 319	83.3	70.4	136 800	1.3	767	24 476	48 356	17.2
District 18	318 991	92.0	75.2	157 300	3.5	768	34 229	60 233	27.2
RHODE ISLAND	462 630	88.5	58.8	236 000	8.8	934	30 830	54 891	25.3
District 1	229 718	89.4	52.8	239 100	10.6	919	30 499	51 860	24.5
District 2	232 912	87.7	64.8	233 500	7.3	955	31 166	57 924	26.1
SOUTH CAROLINA	2 188 258	83.5	68.0	140 000	5.4	791	24 596	45 238	16.6
District 1	335 444	83.3	67.5	220 100	15.1	1 044	32 685	60 832	25.7
District 2	296 386	88.0	72.1	146 100	4.7	833	28 143	54 287	22.0
District 3	300 902	84.5	72.0	116 500	2.9	667	21 518	40 778	12.5
District 4	295 072	89.6	64.3	144 700	4.3	755	25 568	46 442	17.0
District 5	294 163	86.7	71.8	124 100	3.6	739	23 599	44 361	16.2
District 6	294 791	82.3	58.6	93 600	3.1	780	17 894	32 935	9.3
District 7	371 500	72.7	69.7	131 400	3.3	737	22 031	40 729	12.3
SOUTH DAKOTA	376 347	88.9	68.2	142 300	2.9	647	26 959	50 979	17.7
At Large	376 347	88.9	68.2	142 300	2.9	647	26 959	50 979	17.7
TENNESSEE	2 869 419	87.5	66.1	142 900	4.8	770	24 922	44 361	16.5
District 1	347 048	84.4	69.7	123 700	2.7	632	21 979	37 298	10.9
District 2	325 031	87.7	68.6	157 000	5.0	758	26 617	45 474	17.5
District 3	323 216	85.9	68.7	138 300	4.6	708	24 125	43 701	15.8
District 4	307 659	90.1	67.5	136 600	2.7	763	23 293	45 739	15.3
District 5	326 334	91.1	54.6	169 500	8.1	881	28 577	47 842	18.9
District 6	313 797	89.5	72.6	153 400	3.6	707	24 447	45 975	15.7
District 7	312 592	85.8	72.6	155 800	8.8	789	26 864	49 336	20.6
District 8	298 101	89.0	73.2	151 300	5.6	720	28 244	52 532	23.3
District 9	315 641	84.0	47.9	91 000	1.5	840	19 907	35 043	11.3
TEXAS	10 426 760	89.0	61.2	139 600	4.9	896	27 125	53 035	23.6
District 1	305 038	83.9	66.7	109 500	2.6	767	22 484	44 168	15.6
District 2	288 898	93.3	61.3	174 500	6.7	1 072	37 960	72 369	35.1
District 3	297 549	95.1	64.9	241 900	7.6	1 114	41 309	86 846	44.3
District 4	302 255	84.4	71.2	111 600	2.1	756	23 455	48 654	18.5
District 5	286 691	87.1	62.9	110 300	2.1	810	22 401	45 949	17.0
District 6	276 650	92.3	64.3	145 300	1.8	942	27 414	61 209	26.0
District 7	319 976	91.8	50.3	217 000	23.8	1 042	44 861	71 321	37.0
District 8	295 237	87.3	71.0	166 500	8.1	977	30 053	62 743	29.1
District 9	287 117	91.0	44.6	109 200	0.6	852	20 405	42 661	14.9
District 10	305 006	89.0	68.4	185 200	8.7	1 061	33 977	66 236	32.1
District 11	325 575	82.1	67.6	113 300	3.8	893	28 541	51 266	22.7
District 12	298 938	90.8	61.4	148 800	5.0	969	30 150	60 846	25.5
District 13	303 657	84.4	67.0	99 900	1.7	732	24 636	48 594	18.5
District 14	309 903	86.0	64.4	122 200	2.0	826	27 272	51 585	24.1
District 15	249 713	87.2	66.9	90 000	2.3	698	16 937	40 614	14.4
District 16	258 285	89.0	59.5	120 600	0.8	747	19 186	41 347	14.4
District 17	310 017	88.2	54.8	138 600	2.4	883	24 447	48 600	18.6
District 18	292 735	88.9	45.9	107 900	4.4	845	23 238	42 166	17.5
District 19	296 216	86.8	61.0	94 600	1.4	779	23 286	45 428	16.3
District 20	270 784	91.8	55.3	116 500	1.3	867	20 947	46 345	16.8
District 21	341 995	89.6	58.0	229 600	11.0	1 054	35 186	60 971	28.9
District 22	277 521	94.9	74.9	206 900	6.3	1 117	38 407	89 689	44.7
District 23	261 100	86.6	71.3	106 000	4.3	795	23 890	51 528	22.4
District 24	322 952	94.2	49.1	213 900	11.1	989	39 073	63 409	31.6
District 25	302 058	88.2	67.8	189 700	14.4	998	32 315	61 319	28.4

1. Specified owner-occupied units; $1,000,000 represents $1,000,000 or more. 2. Specified renter-occupied units.

Table E. Congressional Districts 114th Congress — Poverty, Labor Force, Employment, and Social Security

STATE District	Poverty, 2014			Civilian labor force, 2014	Unemployment		Civilian employment,[2] 2014	Percent			Persons under age 65 with no health insurance, 2014 (percent)	Social Security beneficiaries, December 2014		Supplemental Security Income recipients, December 2014
	Persons below poverty level (percent)	Families below poverty level (percent)	Percent of households receiving food stamps in past 12 months	Total	Total	Rate[1]	Total	Manage-ment, business, science and arts occupa-tions	Service, sales, and office	Con-struction and production		Number	Rate[3]	
	49	50	51	52	53	54	55	56	57	58	59	60	61	62
OREGON—Cont'd														
District 3	18.2	12.1	20.3	445 307	34 152	7.7	411 155	41.5	40.2	18.2	10.8	123 419	153.1	20 498
District 4	19.3	11.8	20.9	360 357	32 048	8.9	328 309	32.8	44.8	22.4	11.0	192 055	247.6	20 412
District 5	13.9	9.8	18.5	390 577	31 318	8.0	359 259	35.5	42.5	22.0	11.4	162 668	203.8	14 697
PENNSYLVANIA	13.6	9.4	13.0	6 503 715	457 791	7.0	6 045 924	36.9	41.3	21.8	10.0	2 722 892	212.9	374 111
District 1	25.2	20.4	24.9	347 221	41 453	11.9	305 768	36.4	45.1	18.6	15.1	109 942	153.5	43 438
District 2	27.3	20.6	25.0	336 081	45 805	13.6	290 276	44.2	44.8	11.0	11.7	126 113	175.9	49 122
District 3	13.3	9.6	14.4	344 472	21 416	6.2	323 056	33.4	42.1	24.5	10.0	168 728	240.2	24 296
District 4	11.5	8.2	11.0	378 213	22 239	5.9	355 974	34.0	40.9	25.1	8.5	148 668	206.6	13 870
District 5	15.7	9.7	12.4	330 905	20 251	6.1	310 654	34.0	39.7	26.3	8.9	161 731	230.9	17 999
District 6	7.4	4.4	6.1	395 609	21 327	5.4	374 282	45.2	38.1	16.7	6.7	134 835	188.2	7 443
District 7	6.6	4.3	5.4	375 755	21 001	5.6	354 754	43.6	40.3	16.0	8.3	138 539	193.9	5 833
District 8	6.6	4.5	5.6	397 231	23 792	6.0	373 439	42.8	39.3	17.9	6.1	142 482	199.7	7 869
District 9	15.5	10.7	15.1	328 933	21 217	6.5	307 716	28.6	41.5	29.9	11.7	173 355	249.4	24 932
District 10	13.8	9.8	11.9	331 724	22 056	6.6	309 668	29.3	41.3	29.3	12.3	168 597	242.1	15 175
District 11	12.3	8.0	12.0	352 035	19 546	5.6	332 489	33.3	41.1	25.6	9.9	164 433	234.8	16 769
District 12	9.3	6.8	10.4	354 213	20 602	5.8	333 611	39.7	40.5	19.8	6.7	174 284	247.4	16 778
District 13	13.6	10.2	13.5	384 910	30 131	7.8	354 779	37.9	43.2	18.9	12.2	127 536	175.9	31 302
District 14	19.7	14.6	18.1	374 979	31 060	8.3	343 919	39.8	44.5	15.7	9.8	152 546	217.5	30 213
District 15	11.1	7.7	11.1	380 076	28 432	7.5	351 644	35.0	42.4	22.6	10.1	153 244	212.1	16 808
District 16	14.3	10.4	13.9	373 288	24 672	6.6	348 616	32.1	38.6	29.3	14.7	141 481	195.7	19 151
District 17	14.0	10.3	14.6	345 538	25 964	7.5	319 574	30.8	42.9	26.3	10.7	166 912	236.1	19 804
District 18	8.3	5.9	8.9	372 532	16 827	4.5	355 705	40.8	39.5	19.7	6.2	169 466	238.0	13 309
RHODE ISLAND	14.3	10.0	17.5	561 526	43 662	7.8	517 864	36.3	44.6	19.1	8.7	216 029	204.7	33 280
District 1	16.9	12.5	20.1	277 514	21 982	7.9	255 532	36.6	44.6	18.8	9.0	106 951	201.0	18 585
District 2	11.8	7.5	14.9	284 012	21 680	7.6	262 332	35.9	44.6	19.4	8.3	109 078	208.6	14 695
SOUTH CAROLINA	18.0	13.2	14.3	2 314 815	187 866	8.1	2 126 949	33.0	43.4	23.6	16.0	1 040 971	215.4	118 354
District 1	11.3	7.5	7.1	370 488	21 129	5.7	349 359	39.6	42.6	17.8	13.6	140 419	192.7	8 824
District 2	14.1	9.9	10.7	351 366	21 099	6.0	330 267	37.7	41.9	20.4	14.5	130 436	189.9	12 163
District 3	18.9	13.6	15.2	302 779	25 022	8.3	277 757	30.7	39.5	29.8	16.4	162 599	244.0	15 260
District 4	16.2	12.2	12.5	347 466	22 649	6.5	324 817	35.2	40.8	24.0	15.5	142 776	202.9	15 704
District 5	19.3	14.6	14.9	322 151	31 431	9.8	290 720	30.6	42.3	27.1	15.1	148 370	216.9	17 321
District 6	26.0	20.6	23.1	302 879	35 159	11.6	267 720	25.5	49.6	24.9	18.4	138 750	206.0	27 252
District 7	21.0	15.4	17.8	317 686	31 377	9.9	286 309	28.9	48.1	23.0	18.8	177 621	257.8	21 830
SOUTH DAKOTA	14.2	9.4	10.9	460 449	17 960	3.9	442 489	36.4	40.2	23.4	11.4	165 499	194.0	14 905
At Large	14.2	9.4	10.9	460 449	17 960	3.9	442 489	36.4	40.2	23.4	11.4	165 499	194.0	14 905
TENNESSEE	18.3	13.7	17.6	3 156 636	245 980	7.8	2 910 656	33.3	41.9	24.8	14.1	1 371 542	209.4	183 890
District 1	20.0	14.9	18.9	326 494	27 227	8.3	299 267	29.5	45.0	25.5	15.8	193 879	271.8	23 266
District 2	17.6	12.5	16.2	351 328	24 553	7.0	326 775	36.3	42.2	21.4	12.6	160 063	220.4	18 774
District 3	16.8	12.7	17.8	337 536	27 374	8.1	310 162	33.3	40.9	25.8	13.4	171 111	238.9	22 629
District 4	17.7	13.0	17.1	364 029	27 698	7.6	336 331	29.7	39.2	31.0	13.8	149 508	200.1	17 554
District 5	19.2	15.2	15.9	414 480	27 012	6.5	387 468	38.2	42.6	19.3	16.6	114 677	152.7	17 674
District 6	14.8	10.6	15.9	348 934	24 579	7.0	324 355	30.0	41.6	28.4	13.0	171 819	234.3	17 306
District 7	15.3	11.4	15.5	330 870	26 878	8.1	303 992	36.5	40.1	23.3	12.3	145 368	195.6	15 932
District 8	14.5	10.7	15.1	334 707	23 442	7.0	311 265	36.9	39.8	23.3	10.1	152 535	214.6	18 342
District 9	29.3	24.7	26.2	348 258	37 217	10.7	311 041	28.0	45.6	26.4	18.7	112 602	159.2	32 413
TEXAS	17.2	13.4	13.1	13 210 842	799 519	6.1	12 411 323	35.3	41.8	22.8	21.3	3 842 249	142.5	666 301
District 1	18.3	13.6	14.1	323 517	21 793	6.7	301 724	30.1	41.3	28.6	23.3	142 817	200.4	21 326
District 2	11.9	9.4	6.5	407 088	18 809	4.6	388 279	45.0	38.0	16.9	17.8	86 799	117.7	11 530
District 3	7.1	5.4	3.0	436 720	21 697	5.0	415 023	54.3	36.5	9.2	11.7	83 052	104.8	7 007
District 4	16.9	13.1	14.3	329 821	24 140	7.3	305 681	31.4	40.2	28.4	19.5	149 523	207.9	20 218
District 5	17.9	14.3	15.4	344 121	22 893	6.7	321 228	29.9	43.3	26.8	24.9	123 146	167.6	16 906
District 6	13.4	9.6	10.2	383 350	20 749	5.4	362 601	36.8	41.1	22.1	16.7	101 804	138.0	12 094
District 7	13.1	10.9	6.2	417 797	16 652	4.0	401 145	46.5	37.5	16.0	18.3	78 456	101.8	9 539
District 8	12.6	8.5	7.7	355 729	15 436	4.3	340 293	36.1	42.8	21.1	16.0	118 297	154.1	13 089
District 9	22.3	18.8	18.2	407 041	34 495	8.5	372 546	27.6	47.0	25.4	28.4	81 303	105.3	26 779
District 10	11.7	8.1	8.4	394 662	18 616	4.7	376 046	42.7	39.3	18.0	15.3	101 562	131.7	10 827
District 11	13.3	10.1	10.1	351 880	14 841	4.2	337 039	30.9	38.6	30.6	23.1	136 415	184.1	16 783
District 12	12.3	8.4	9.4	384 846	22 131	5.8	362 715	36.9	41.3	21.8	17.4	110 552	147.2	12 592
District 13	15.4	11.4	11.7	338 654	15 553	4.6	323 101	30.8	42.7	26.5	20.0	125 192	176.9	13 933
District 14	16.2	13.3	14.6	339 309	20 216	6.0	319 093	33.7	41.9	24.4	21.1	121 140	167.1	19 239
District 15	29.2	25.4	26.7	319 817	26 646	8.3	293 171	29.0	47.4	23.6	31.0	100 068	130.8	32 894
District 16	22.2	19.7	21.6	319 714	24 053	7.5	295 661	31.1	49.2	19.7	24.1	107 063	145.6	26 453
District 17	19.3	12.2	11.2	371 304	17 678	4.8	353 626	35.7	42.4	21.9	18.1	106 689	144.1	16 809
District 18	22.1	18.9	18.3	374 885	26 684	7.1	348 201	28.7	44.4	26.9	26.0	90 766	120.9	28 669
District 19	16.9	12.6	12.3	342 571	16 674	4.9	325 897	31.0	42.9	26.2	20.3	119 396	165.9	17 599
District 20	20.7	16.6	16.3	374 208	28 587	7.6	345 621	31.8	47.9	20.3	19.6	107 160	140.5	23 737
District 21	13.4	7.9	5.8	407 034	20 854	5.1	386 180	47.4	40.4	12.3	14.6	128 520	167.7	11 809
District 22	8.7	6.3	7.2	405 343	16 147	4.0	389 196	51.5	32.4	16.1	12.8	84 483	103.7	10 074
District 23	18.2	15.3	17.2	332 734	23 035	6.9	309 699	30.0	42.4	27.7	21.5	116 998	157.4	24 104
District 24	10.6	9.0	6.0	439 229	22 130	5.0	417 099	43.6	40.2	16.2	20.3	83 058	109.4	7 101
District 25	13.5	9.6	10.0	353 930	21 759	6.1	332 171	44.0	37.9	18.1	15.4	117 251	156.7	10 898

1. Percent of civilian labor force.   2. Persons 16 years old and over.   3. Per 1,000 resident population estimated in the 2014 American Community Survey.

STATE District	Agriculture, 2012 Land in farms — Number of farms (63)	Acres (64)	Average size of farm (acres) (65)	Irrigated land (acres) (66)	Value of products sold — Total ($1,000) (67)	Average per farm (dollars) (68)	Percent from crops (69)	Percent from livestock and poultry products (70)	Government payments — Total ($1,000) (71)	Average per farm receiving payments (dollars) (72)
OREGON—Cont'd										
District 3	2 500	86 297	35	12 384	210 983	84 393	85.5	14.5	448	6 395
District 4	8 820	1 301 199	148	95 961	646 366	73 284	67.3	32.7	3 986	7 157
District 5	6 076	589 162	97	124 733	1 022 711	168 320	70.1	29.9	4 483	7 038
PENNSYLVANIA	59 309	7 704 444	130	38 990	7 400 781	124 783	37.6	62.4	86 359	5 395
District 1	X	X	X	X	X	X	X	X	X	X
District 2	17	548	32	17	330	19 408	90.6	9.4	0	0
District 3	5 489	808 725	147	1 426	353 468	64 396	55.9	44.1	7 271	4 835
District 4	3 470	442 692	128	3 131	445 123	128 277	60.2	39.8	4 659	5 508
District 5	7 119	1 025 582	144	3 772	448 440	62 992	39.2	60.8	10 295	5 589
District 6	1 821	161 792	89	1 708	433 872	238 260	45.4	54.6	2 446	7 109
District 7	2 521	214 656	85	2 080	682 479	270 718	64.7	35.3	2 325	5 033
District 8	1 048	75 181	72	922	74 095	70 701	74.0	26.0	D	D
District 9	7 608	1 178 741	155	5 850	886 733	116 553	27.1	72.9	12 005	5 333
District 10	10 157	1 530 318	151	3 931	1 036 895	102 087	22.8	77.2	21 819	6 165
District 11	5 191	681 540	131	3 494	535 209	103 103	42.4	57.6	8 608	4 435
District 12	2 312	289 072	125	639	128 146	55 427	44.2	55.8	2 453	4 576
District 13	60	1 550	26	74	2 026	33 774	97.6	2.4	D	D
District 14	52	3 737	72	14	679	13 064	86.6	13.4	D	D
District 15	2 654	327 761	123	2 862	600 645	226 317	27.8	72.2	4 326	5 769
District 16	5 054	416 310	82	6 010	1 498 795	296 556	25.2	74.8	5 716	6 226
District 17	1 388	170 812	123	1 943	198 442	142 969	51.0	49.0	2 205	4 641
District 18	3 340	375 166	112	1 112	74 892	22 423	53.2	46.8	1 538	3 395
RHODE ISLAND	1 243	69 589	56	3 954	59 652	47 990	82.1	17.9	2 345	12 342
District 1	344	15 923	46	647	19 582	56 923	80.6	19.4	875	13 059
District 2	899	53 666	60	3 307	40 070	44 572	82.9	17.1	1 470	11 955
SOUTH CAROLINA	25 266	4 971 244	197	159 239	3 040 069	120 323	42.6	57.4	46 616	6 867
District 1	544	82 106	151	4 774	39 179	72 021	95.4	4.6	310	4 996
District 2	3 158	453 236	144	24 868	388 653	123 069	30.6	69.4	3 820	5 343
District 3	6 630	878 661	133	14 298	540 476	81 520	19.8	80.2	5 673	6 107
District 4	1 912	135 628	71	2 756	42 760	22 364	61.8	38.2	898	7 240
District 5	4 848	858 012	177	17 565	683 746	141 037	26.1	73.9	6 325	6 164
District 6	4 690	1 601 949	342	74 041	713 033	152 033	67.5	32.5	16 616	7 434
District 7	3 484	961 652	276	20 937	632 221	181 464	54.3	45.7	12 974	7 645
SOUTH DAKOTA	31 989	43 257 079	1 352	378 678	10 170 227	317 929	59.7	40.3	283 797	12 451
At Large	31 989	43 257 079	1 352	378 678	10 170 000	317 929	59.7	40.3	283 797	12 451
TENNESSEE	68 050	10 867 812	160	146 442	3 611 037	53 064	57.8	42.2	67 665	4 184
District 1	9 853	905 084	92	D	255 474	25 929	24.2	75.8	3 479	1 706
District 2	5 214	522 807	100	1 856	168 328	32 284	54.7	45.3	1 492	1 565
District 3	5 665	627 645	111	826	240 743	42 497	9.6	90.4	1 616	2 726
District 4	10 696	1 649 872	154	14 838	625 877	58 515	35.3	64.7	5 744	3 258
District 5	1 918	237 050	124	881	35 345	18 428	64.2	35.8	335	1 573
District 6	13 698	1 963 227	143	7 539	601 843	43 937	53.2	46.8	9 216	3 391
District 7	13 249	2 330 708	176	10 200	433 743	32 738	58.1	41.9	11 722	3 232
District 8	7 529	2 581 642	343	103 713	1 227 122	162 986	87.4	12.6	33 653	7 990
District 9	228	49 777	218	D	22 562	98 957	95.9	4.1	408	7 425
TEXAS	248 809	130 153 438	523	4 489 163	25 375 581	101 988	29.0	71.0	643 993	12 293
District 1	12 033	1 894 203	157	7 229	1 248 621	103 766	9.3	90.7	2 219	5 604
District 2	277	26 687	96	696	24 812	89 575	93.6	6.4	135	8 991
District 3	1 239	181 470	146	1 483	49 687	40 103	63.7	36.3	1 063	10 738
District 4	23 397	4 272 976	183	35 066	1 185 301	50 660	25.1	74.9	18 210	6 358
District 5	12 498	1 955 349	156	9 102	447 708	35 822	44.0	56.0	3 504	8 505
District 6	5 164	1 029 961	199	1 486	161 229	31 222	63.1	36.9	5 425	6 082
District 7	145	22 255	153	613	1 872	12 911	64.6	35.5	237	9 112
District 8	9 297	2 007 965	216	12 705	286 726	30 841	39.9	60.1	4 791	7 557
District 9	138	14 387	104	19	1 778	12 886	62.3	37.7	98	6 540
District 10	14 453	2 579 215	178	39 297	388 941	26 911	48.1	51.9	12 664	6 758
District 11	21 093	15 735 425	746	231 436	1 140 013	54 047	30.5	69.5	71 961	11 722
District 12	5 466	663 119	121	2 653	92 035	16 838	24.2	75.8	459	2 871
District 13	20 372	22 410 589	1 100	1 321 922	8 593 468	421 827	16.1	83.9	142 997	14 697
District 14	3 818	1 023 671	268	43 308	144 002	37 717	57.4	42.6	9 058	19 231
District 15	8 704	4 303 286	494	154 612	506 516	58 193	67.4	32.6	17 789	9 165
District 16	370	120 411	325	10 427	23 588	63 753	94.9	5.1	409	14 114
District 17	16 124	4 032 650	250	59 093	1 003 696	62 249	27.5	72.5	21 247	9 123
District 18	119	4 478	38	28	3 789	31 843	10.5	89.5	20	4 904
District 19	15 781	1 471 4 801	932	1 783 134	5 205 921	329 885	27.7	72.3	191 903	17 292
District 20	221	18 965	86	770	1 394	6 306	62.3	37.6	35	2 345
District 21	7 738	2 997 190	387	7 650	103 517	13 378	30.3	69.7	4 697	5 820
District 22	1 965	414 170	211	12 771	128 234	65 259	86.2	13.8	4 359	10 209
District 23	9 377	28 460 973	3 035	314 787	966 721	103 095	51.4	48.6	35 825	16 647
District 24	158	10 534	67	93	3 807	24 094	92.4	7.6	61	8 648
District 25	13 361	3 908 812	293	11 239	538 906	40 334	39.2	60.8	9 765	5 694

Table E. Congressional Districts 114th Congress — Nonfarm Employment and Payroll

Private nonfarm employment and payroll, 2014

STATE District	Number of establishments	Employment Total	Manufacturing	Construction	Wholesale trade	Retail trade	Health care and social assistance	Finance and Insurance	Real estate and rental and leasing	Professional, scientific, and technical services	Information	Annual payroll Total (mil dol)	Average per employee dollars
	73	74	75	76	77	78	79	80	81	82	83	84	85
OREGON—Cont'd													
District 3	24 782	368 099	7.7	5.3	5.8	10.4	15.0	5.1	2.1	7.3	2.8	18 069	49 089
District 4	19 002	230 643	12.4	4.6	3.7	15.8	18.8	3.7	1.7	4.2	2.4	8 559	37 108
District 5	20 915	255 272	11.4	6.2	5.4	15.1	17.2	3.7	1.9	4.9	1.4	10 257	40 182
PENNSYLVANIA	298 297	5 255 409	10.4	4.2	4.7	12.6	18.5	5.1	1.2	6.1	2.2	248 561	47 296
District 1	14 229	267 167	5.7	2.8	4.0	10.5	18.8	4.8	2.0	4.8	1.9	12 831	48 026
District 2	14 057	343 509	0.9	1.0	1.1	5.7	25.5	6.9	1.5	11.0	3.2	21 371	62 215
District 3	16 662	267 388	16.0	3.6	4.0	13.6	22.1	3.8	0.9	4.5	1.5	10 140	37 921
District 4	15 602	290 559	14.3	4.4	5.2	13.1	16.3	5.5	1.1	5.5	1.5	12 289	42 295
District 5	15 603	218 267	20.3	3.6	2.6	16.1	17.8	2.5	1.2	3.2	1.6	7 914	36 256
District 6	19 787	347 762	9.0	3.3	6.7	14.2	13.8	9.3	1.1	8.3	3.0	21 156	60 836
District 7	17 724	305 023	8.1	5.8	4.1	9.6	15.5	7.2	1.3	9.2	5.5	18 418	60 384
District 8	20 952	279 765	12.6	6.0	7.1	14.6	15.7	3.5	1.4	6.2	2.3	12 351	44 146
District 9	14 395	208 346	14.4	4.6	3.8	16.1	18.4	2.7	0.7	3.1	1.5	7 337	35 216
District 10	15 850	216 316	16.5	4.4	3.2	17.1	18.9	3.2	1.2	2.7	1.1	7 632	35 281
District 11	14 437	254 259	12.7	3.1	4.5	12.8	19.1	4.8	0.8	4.5	1.7	10 502	41 304
District 12	16 671	245 726	12.2	5.3	3.9	14.3	19.1	3.2	1.0	6.0	1.9	10 424	42 419
District 13	17 575	324 910	6.2	4.0	6.6	15.4	21.2	4.6	1.4	7.2	2.6	17 410	53 585
District 14	19 682	470 808	4.8	3.3	3.5	9.0	19.5	8.7	1.3	8.7	2.7	24 600	52 251
District 15	15 726	305 854	12.8	3.5	6.1	12.7	18.9	3.4	0.9	3.8	1.6	14 546	47 559
District 16	15 458	292 296	15.9	6.7	5.6	12.5	18.4	3.2	0.9	4.6	1.1	12 459	42 624
District 17	14 974	255 791	11.4	2.9	4.4	14.7	21.2	3.8	0.8	3.6	2.3	9 367	36 621
District 18	18 342	302 639	8.1	8.6	5.3	13.2	16.4	2.8	1.3	5.0	1.8	13 861	45 800
RHODE ISLAND	28 132	421 578	9.3	3.8	4.9	11.6	20.4	6.3	1.3	5.3	1.8	19 511	46 281
District 1	13 322	204 541	9.3	3.9	4.7	9.4	19.9	6.2	1.3	4.7	1.4	9 511	46 498
District 2	14 590	213 951	9.4	3.7	4.8	13.9	21.3	6.4	1.3	5.5	2.1	9 798	45 798
SOUTH CAROLINA	102 297	1 617 249	13.6	4.4	4.3	14.2	13.7	4.2	1.5	5.2	2.1	62 406	38 588
District 1	17 902	215 912	4.8	4.6	2.3	19.0	13.1	4.0	2.4	6.0	2.7	7 814	36 190
District 2	12 994	202 759	9.8	5.0	4.3	16.4	13.3	6.6	1.1	5.3	1.0	7 854	38 734
District 3	11 104	168 981	25.8	4.1	3.7	13.9	13.7	2.0	0.8	3.0	0.9	6 009	35 562
District 4	17 503	326 155	15.0	4.1	5.5	11.8	12.2	3.0	1.1	6.2	2.7	13 506	41 410
District 5	11 625	173 825	20.1	4.8	4.6	15.1	12.1	4.5	0.9	3.0	2.5	6 488	37 324
District 6	14 848	270 510	14.0	4.6	5.3	10.3	17.8	5.2	1.6	7.2	3.0	11 648	43 060
District 7	15 909	218 117	11.1	4.2	3.2	18.0	15.5	4.2	2.7	3.3	1.3	7 155	32 802
SOUTH DAKOTA	26 198	347 819	12.7	5.3	5.3	15.0	18.8	7.6	1.1	3.4	2.0	13 161	37 839
At Large	26 198	347 819	12.7	5.3	5.3	15.0	18.8	7.6	1.1	3.4	2.0	13 161	37 839
TENNESSEE	131 504	2 453 470	12.6	4.2	4.6	12.9	16.0	4.5	1.3	4.7	1.9	103 559	42 209
District 1	13 459	232 605	19.2	3.9	2.6	16.0	18.4	3.3	1.3	2.9	1.8	8 290	35 641
District 2	15 368	279 430	8.4	3.9	5.5	14.5	15.8	4.9	1.5	4.9	2.2	11 078	39 644
District 3	14 090	270 106	19.3	3.9	2.9	12.0	14.2	5.2	0.9	6.6	1.4	10 954	40 553
District 4	12 596	227 000	21.6	6.0	5.0	14.5	12.3	4.1	0.9	2.1	1.4	8 638	38 055
District 5	19 900	436 237	5.5	4.2	4.8	9.7	18.4	5.0	1.6	7.7	3.0	21 259	48 732
District 6	13 019	187 921	19.4	4.6	4.4	15.5	15.2	3.4	1.2	4.0	1.4	6 803	36 203
District 7	14 469	214 768	11.4	4.3	2.9	15.1	16.8	6.8	1.1	5.3	3.0	9 751	45 401
District 8	14 739	243 550	13.0	4.0	3.9	13.7	20.0	4.9	1.4	3.7	1.3	10 190	41 838
District 9	13 404	315 845	7.1	3.7	7.9	11.3	14.1	2.7	1.5	3.2	1.4	14 909	47 203
TEXAS	557 721	9 920 214	8.1	6.1	5.2	12.5	14.2	5.0	1.9	6.7	2.3	501 457	50 549
District 1	16 819	261 409	13.8	5.4	3.9	13.8	18.9	4.3	1.6	4.3	1.5	10 468	40 044
District 2	19 267	361 672	11.4	9.1	7.9	11.2	7.4	4.1	2.0	6.7	1.7	22 285	61 616
District 3	19 452	343 261	4.8	4.1	4.6	13.3	12.1	12.0	1.9	11.0	3.7	20 333	59 236
District 4	13 418	191 142	18.9	4.9	3.3	16.3	19.6	3.5	1.0	2.6	1.2	6 727	35 193
District 5	12 279	175 290	12.9	9.3	5.2	16.9	15.1	2.4	1.7	3.9	0.8	6 197	35 353
District 6	13 549	220 688	13.8	5.9	6.2	14.9	13.2	4.5	1.4	3.4	1.4	8 410	38 107
District 7	24 619	451 037	2.6	5.8	3.8	11.0	10.3	6.3	2.9	12.6	2.5	34 490	76 469
District 8	13 811	185 622	9.4	6.4	4.3	15.8	11.8	3.5	1.7	6.8	1.2	9 965	53 685
District 9	12 695	318 337	5.2	4.2	5.0	7.5	31.9	2.1	1.5	9.8	2.1	18 235	57 282
District 10	18 677	278 048	9.4	6.6	4.2	15.5	11.4	4.4	1.9	8.3	3.5	13 412	48 237
District 11	18 921	266 800	6.7	7.6	6.2	13.8	13.0	2.9	2.1	3.9	1.3	13 852	51 919
District 12	16 780	308 726	11.8	5.2	4.0	12.2	14.3	6.2	1.3	5.2	2.2	15 836	51 295
District 13	16 608	223 809	13.3	5.8	5.4	15.2	17.1	4.0	1.4	3.0	1.5	8 750	39 097
District 14	13 399	223 431	13.3	10.6	3.4	14.5	15.9	3.3	1.4	4.8	1.0	10 759	48 155
District 15	11 937	180 117	6.8	4.2	4.6	19.1	24.8	3.4	1.5	3.3	1.2	5 585	31 008
District 16	13 075	212 749	6.2	4.3	4.4	17.0	18.5	2.9	1.8	4.5	4.1	6 691	31 448
District 17	14 135	244 710	11.9	6.5	4.6	13.1	14.7	3.9	1.8	4.4	3.9	9 852	40 261
District 18	16 327	406 755	8.7	5.9	10.4	6.0	7.5	4.3	1.6	9.5	2.7	31 975	78 609
District 19	16 554	235 620	6.3	5.7	5.4	15.5	19.0	4.6	1.5	3.1	2.0	8 584	36 433
District 20	11 146	247 544	3.4	3.0	2.5	14.8	16.6	14.5	1.8	7.4	1.9	10 499	42 413
District 21	25 023	400 438	2.7	6.0	4.0	10.8	15.5	5.2	2.3	10.1	3.5	19 388	48 417
District 22	14 385	191 372	7.3	4.8	3.4	20.9	16.8	2.7	1.5	5.7	2.0	8 070	42 171
District 23	10 991	168 019	5.6	12.9	3.4	17.2	12.8	4.1	1.3	2.4	1.7	6 584	39 186
District 24	26 875	659 675	4.4	4.7	6.7	7.9	7.9	8.7	2.8	10.5	4.8	40 137	60 843
District 25	16 818	212 077	6.6	5.9	4.5	14.0	17.4	4.2	2.4	8.1	2.4	10 573	49 857

1. Specified owner-occupied units; $1,000,000 represents $1,000,000 or more.   2. Specified renter-occupied units.

STATE District	Representative, 114th Congress	Land area,[1] 2010 (sq km)	Total persons	Per square kilometer	White	Black	Amer-ican Indian, Alaska Native	Asian and Pacific Islander	Some other race	Two or more races	Hispanic or Latino[2]	Non-Hispanic White alone	Female	Foreign-born	Born in state of resi-dence
		1	2	3	4	5	6	7	8	9	10	11	12	13	14
TEXAS—Cont'd															
District 26	Michael C. Burgess (R)	2 350	783 257	333.3	80.9	6.4	0.4	5.6	3.2	3.5	17.8	67.0	50.6	12.1	51.1
District 27	Blake Farenthold (R)	23 642	726 394	30.7	86.8	5.4	0.3	1.6	3.6	2.3	51.5	40.3	50.5	8.0	76.1
District 28	Henry Cuellar (D)	24 290	725 977	29.9	88.3	4.1	0.2	1.0	4.5	1.9	76.9	17.3	51.5	21.3	64.6
District 29	Gene Green (D)	485	749 098	1 544.5	73.4	11.4	0.9	1.3	11.7	1.2	77.0	10.0	49.7	33.4	56.3
District 30	Eddie Bernice Johnson (D)	923	744 247	806.3	48.0	43.1	0.2	2.1	4.5	2.2	39.0	14.8	52.0	17.6	64.1
District 31	John R. Carter (R)	5 580	776 518	139.2	76.2	11.3	0.6	5.0	3.4	3.5	23.8	57.7	50.2	10.7	51.4
District 32	Pete Sessions (R)	481	747 437	1 553.9	70.1	12.2	0.3	7.7	6.4	3.3	25.8	51.7	50.6	21.2	50.7
District 33	Marc A. Veasey (D)	549	742 701	1 352.8	67.0	17.1	0.6	2.4	10.7	2.1	63.2	16.3	49.6	31.9	55.7
District 34	Filemon Vela (D)	21 213	717 582	33.8	92.6	1.3	0.3	0.6	4.4	0.9	83.8	14.2	50.3	21.3	68.8
District 35	Lloyd Doggett (D)	1 538	767 436	499.0	77.4	10.3	0.6	1.3	7.8	2.7	60.9	26.1	50.2	17.0	63.3
District 36	Brian Babin (R)	18 456	731 297	39.6	82.5	9.1	0.4	2.0	3.7	2.3	24.2	62.5	49.8	10.1	68.0
UTAH		212 818	2 942 902	13.8	87.3	1.1	1.1	3.1	4.7	2.7	13.5	79.2	49.7	8.5	62.2
District 1	Rob Bishop (R)	50 662	727 828	14.4	90.0	1.0	1.1	1.9	3.1	2.7	12.0	81.8	49.4	6.1	65.3
District 2	Chris Stewart (R)	103 568	729 552	7.0	82.9	1.1	1.1	3.7	8.4	2.7	16.1	76.0	49.1	10.4	58.6
District 3	Jason Chaffetz (R)	51 982	721 048	13.9	90.7	0.8	1.6	2.7	1.6	2.6	9.8	83.0	49.9	7.1	59.7
District 4	Mia B. Love (R)	6 605	764 474	115.7	85.5	1.6	0.6	4.1	5.7	2.6	15.9	76.1	50.4	10.3	64.8
VERMONT		23 871	626 562	26.2	94.5	1.0	0.4	1.6	0.5	2.1	1.7	93.2	50.8	4.1	52.3
At Large	Peter Welch (D)	23 871	626 562	26.2	94.5	1.0	0.4	1.6	0.5	2.1	1.7	93.2	50.8	4.1	52.3
VIRGINIA		102 279	8 326 289	81.4	68.9	19.2	0.3	6.2	2.1	3.3	8.8	63.0	50.8	12.1	49.2
District 1	Robert J. Wittman (R)	9 542	770 044	80.7	72.6	16.8	0.4	3.7	2.4	4.1	9.3	66.6	50.7	9.5	45.7
District 2	Scott Rigell (R)	2 568	732 346	285.2	67.1	21.6	0.3	5.1	1.9	4.0	7.5	62.6	50.1	7.9	42.7
District 3	Robert C. "Bobby" Scott (D)	2 453	753 380	307.1	35.0	57.1	0.5	2.2	1.7	3.5	6.1	31.6	51.9	6.0	60.5
District 4	J. Randy Forbes (R)	11 164	746 976	66.9	61.2	31.7	0.2	2.6	1.4	2.9	5.4	57.9	50.2	4.6	60.9
District 5	Robert Hurt (R)	25 977	733 330	28.2	74.5	20.0	0.3	1.6	1.6	2.0	3.6	72.6	51.4	4.5	64.0
District 6	Bob Goodlatte (R)	15 359	746 357	48.6	83.7	11.0	0.1	1.9	1.3	1.9	4.8	80.5	51.4	5.3	64.2
District 7	Dave Brat (R)	7 191	769 995	107.1	75.4	14.9	0.2	5.0	1.7	2.9	5.9	71.6	51.8	9.5	54.5
District 8	Donald S. Beyer, Jr. (D)	387	774 065	2 000.2	64.6	13.6	0.1	12.2	5.2	4.2	19.1	51.8	50.8	28.8	23.3
District 9	Morgan Griffith (R)	23 605	715 465	30.3	91.1	5.7	0.3	1.1	0.5	1.4	2.0	89.7	50.2	2.5	64.8
District 10	Barbara Comstock (R)	3 554	802 127	225.7	73.3	6.9	0.2	13.7	1.7	4.3	12.6	63.2	50.2	20.9	36.0
District 11	Gerald E. Connolly (D)	479	782 204	1 633.0	60.9	12.9	0.3	17.6	3.4	4.8	19.0	47.0	50.6	30.9	28.4
WASHINGTON		172 119	7 061 530	41.0	77.7	3.6	1.4	8.5	3.5	5.4	12.2	70.3	50.0	13.4	47.7
District 1	Suzan K. DelBene (D)	16 023	713 399	44.5	81.5	1.1	0.9	9.6	2.6	4.4	8.8	76.1	50.3	15.0	50.1
District 2	Rick Larsen (D)	2 629	708 323	269.4	78.4	2.8	1.5	9.4	2.5	5.4	10.8	71.4	50.1	13.7	48.6
District 3	Jaime Herrera Beutler (R)	23 605	697 884	29.6	86.4	1.4	0.8	3.6	3.0	4.9	9.0	80.9	50.2	8.4	42.0
District 4	Dan Newsome (R)	49 858	704 219	14.1	78.1	1.1	2.7	1.6	13.2	3.3	38.1	55.0	49.5	16.4	55.0
District 5	Cathy McMorris Rodgers (R)	40 075	690 518	17.2	88.3	1.6	1.8	2.6	1.5	4.3	6.2	84.4	50.3	5.7	52.7
District 6	Derek Kilmer (D)	17 878	676 910	37.9	82.2	3.8	1.8	4.7	1.7	5.8	7.7	77.1	49.4	7.1	48.5
District 7	Jim McDermott (D)	373	732 733	1 964.4	76.4	4.2	0.6	10.9	1.6	6.4	7.6	71.7	49.3	14.9	40.9
District 8	David G. Reichert (R)	19 062	711 629	37.3	80.3	3.2	0.8	8.5	2.2	5.0	10.3	73.1	50.6	12.8	52.8
District 9	Adam Smith (D)	475	711 466	1 497.8	52.1	10.4	1.0	25.3	4.2	7.1	12.1	46.1	49.9	29.5	38.6
District 10	Denny Heck (D)	2 141	714 449	333.7	74.0	5.9	1.7	8.0	2.7	7.7	11.0	67.5	50.5	9.8	47.8
WEST VIRGINIA		62 259	1 850 326	29.7	93.6	3.7	0.2	0.6	0.2	1.7	1.3	92.6	50.6	1.4	70.2
District 1	David McKinley (R)	16 254	616 232	37.9	94.7	2.6	0.2	1.0	0.3	1.3	1.3	93.7	50.3	1.6	69.3
District 2	Alexander X. Mooney (R)	20 765	628 276	30.3	92.2	4.6	0.1	0.6	0.2	2.3	1.7	90.9	50.6	1.6	63.4
District 3	Evan H. Jenkins (R)	25 240	605 818	24.0	93.9	3.9	0.3	0.4	0.2	1.4	0.9	93.2	50.8	0.8	78.2
WISCONSIN		140 268	5 757 564	41.0	86.3	6.3	0.9	2.6	1.8	2.1	6.4	82.2	50.4	4.9	71.2
District 1	Paul Ryan (R)	4 475	712 072	159.1	88.2	5.7	0.4	1.8	1.6	2.3	9.5	81.1	51.0	5.3	66.6
District 2	Mark Pocan (D)	11 750	740 988	63.1	86.3	4.4	0.3	4.1	2.1	2.9	6.3	82.9	50.3	6.7	64.7
District 3	Ron Kind (D)	28 779	718 518	25.0	93.9	1.0	0.6	2.4	0.6	1.5	2.4	92.4	49.7	2.8	71.3
District 4	Gwen Moore (D)	332	717 657	2 161.6	52.9	34.2	0.6	3.7	5.6	3.0	16.3	43.3	51.6	9.2	66.1
District 5	F. James Sensenbrenner Jr. (R)	4 897	722 537	147.5	92.2	1.9	0.4	2.7	1.0	1.9	5.8	88.0	50.8	5.0	77.4
District 6	Glen Grothman (R)	12 739	712 031	55.9	93.1	1.6	0.4	2.4	1.0	1.4	4.4	90.0	49.5	3.8	78.6
District 7	Sean P. Duffy (R)	59 666	711 006	11.9	93.5	0.6	2.0	1.7	0.4	1.8	2.1	92.1	49.7	2.1	67.9
District 8	Reid J. Ribble (R)	17 629	722 755	41.0	90.0	1.3	2.4	2.2	2.3	1.9	4.9	87.7	50.2	4.1	77.1
WYOMING		251 470	584 153	2.3	91.0	1.1	2.6	1.1	2.0	2.2	9.8	84.0	49.1	3.8	41.0
At Large	Cynthia M. Lummis (R)	251 470	584 153	2.3	91.0	1.1	2.6	1.1	2.0	2.2	9.8	84.0	49.1	3.8	41.0

1. Dry land or land partially or temporarily covered by water.   2. May be of any race.

Table E. Congressional Districts 114th Congress — Age and Education

STATE District	Population and population characteristics, 2014 (cont.) — Age (percent)											Education, 2014 — Attainment[2] (percent)	
	Under 5 years	5 to 17 years	18 to 24 years	25 to 34 years	35 to 44 years	45 to 54 years	55 to 64 years	65 to 74 years	75 years and over	Median age	Total Enrollment[1]	High school graduate or more	Bachelor's degree or more
	15	16	17	18	19	20	21	22	23	24	25	26	27
TEXAS—Cont'd													
District 26	7.0	20.4	9.1	13.8	15.7	14.8	10.1	6.1	3.0	34.8	232 772	92.3	40.9
District 27	6.7	18.5	9.4	13.9	12.1	12.5	12.7	8.3	6.0	36.3	177 127	80.9	19.2
District 28	8.9	22.0	10.9	13.0	13.1	11.7	9.8	6.2	4.5	31.5	216 565	70.9	16.6
District 29	9.5	21.1	11.0	16.0	14.2	11.4	9.0	4.7	3.0	30.4	212 940	58.8	9.1
District 30	7.6	20.7	10.0	14.6	14.0	13.0	10.7	5.4	3.7	33.0	210 272	74.7	18.3
District 31	7.1	19.7	9.3	14.8	15.1	13.0	9.9	6.6	4.3	34.4	219 668	91.4	34.0
District 32	6.3	17.2	9.7	15.0	14.4	14.0	11.6	6.9	4.8	36.4	190 634	85.6	42.7
District 33	9.1	22.2	10.9	16.2	13.8	11.5	8.7	4.4	3.1	29.8	213 333	58.6	8.9
District 34	8.1	21.5	11.0	12.3	12.5	11.4	9.9	7.1	6.1	32.5	208 509	66.1	15.5
District 35	7.6	18.7	12.3	16.9	14.1	11.8	9.8	5.1	3.6	31.4	218 990	75.8	18.3
District 36	6.1	19.4	9.0	13.0	12.9	13.4	12.8	8.4	5.0	36.7	189 591	84.3	18.8
UTAH	8.5	22.3	11.3	14.9	13.2	10.5	9.5	5.9	4.2	30.5	953 887	91.4	31.1
District 1	8.2	23.1	10.7	14.4	12.9	10.8	9.8	5.9	4.1	30.6	237 256	92.4	29.0
District 2	7.9	20.8	11.0	15.6	12.9	10.3	9.8	6.9	4.8	31.6	224 689	89.5	29.3
District 3	8.5	22.1	14.7	13.3	12.3	10.0	9.5	5.4	4.0	28.4	255 504	94.0	38.8
District 4	9.3	23.0	8.9	15.9	14.5	10.7	8.6	5.2	3.7	30.7	236 438	90.1	28.0
VERMONT	4.9	14.5	10.6	11.7	11.6	14.4	15.4	10.0	7.0	42.8	146 261	92.0	34.9
At Large	4.9	14.5	10.6	11.7	11.6	14.4	15.4	10.0	7.0	42.8	146 261	92.0	34.9
VIRGINIA	6.1	16.4	10.0	14.0	13.2	14.1	12.5	8.2	5.6	37.7	2 168 651	88.5	36.7
District 1	6.3	18.4	9.6	11.9	13.3	14.8	12.2	8.2	5.5	37.9	211 257	91.7	36.5
District 2	6.4	15.1	11.6	16.5	12.5	13.3	11.8	7.4	5.4	35.2	188 650	91.4	32.4
District 3	6.9	15.2	13.7	17.2	11.4	12.2	11.5	6.7	5.1	32.9	206 895	84.1	22.6
District 4	5.8	17.7	9.5	12.9	13.3	14.8	12.9	8.3	4.8	38.3	196 727	87.9	25.4
District 5	4.8	15.4	10.0	11.3	11.5	14.0	14.5	10.7	7.8	42.8	179 987	84.6	25.9
District 6	5.5	14.6	12.8	12.0	11.2	13.2	13.4	9.6	7.6	39.8	191 436	87.0	27.1
District 7	5.6	17.7	7.8	12.7	13.5	14.7	13.2	8.8	6.0	40.0	194 133	91.0	39.9
District 8	7.3	13.6	7.3	21.0	16.1	13.6	10.8	6.3	4.1	35.4	177 331	90.1	61.3
District 9	4.5	14.3	12.0	11.3	11.7	13.7	13.9	10.7	7.9	42.0	175 544	82.4	19.8
District 10	7.0	20.3	7.4	11.8	15.1	15.9	11.6	7.1	3.9	37.6	227 716	91.7	55.2
District 11	6.8	17.0	9.3	15.2	15.4	14.3	11.7	6.2	4.1	36.1	218 975	91.2	53.3
WASHINGTON	6.3	16.4	9.6	14.4	13.1	13.4	12.9	8.4	5.7	37.5	1 725 154	90.4	33.1
District 1	6.3	18.0	7.6	14.1	14.2	14.3	13.2	7.7	4.5	37.8	177 463	93.3	41.3
District 2	5.9	15.3	10.6	13.7	12.7	13.5	13.2	9.0	6.1	38.3	168 874	91.5	29.4
District 3	6.0	17.8	8.3	11.9	13.0	13.4	13.5	9.7	6.2	39.6	173 384	90.1	22.9
District 4	8.1	20.8	10.0	12.8	12.2	11.9	11.3	7.7	5.1	33.6	187 212	78.2	19.1
District 5	5.9	15.9	12.1	13.3	11.3	12.6	13.5	9.2	6.3	37.4	186 875	91.9	27.7
District 6	5.2	14.9	8.9	12.9	11.3	13.6	15.2	11.0	7.1	42.1	146 716	91.4	29.0
District 7	5.4	10.3	10.3	20.3	15.5	13.0	12.2	7.5	5.3	37.2	161 085	94.8	57.3
District 8	6.9	19.2	8.2	12.5	13.4	14.9	13.1	7.2	4.8	37.4	184 400	91.5	32.5
District 9	6.2	15.3	9.0	16.8	14.3	13.6	11.7	7.1	5.9	37.0	164 043	88.0	40.2
District 10	7.0	16.6	10.4	15.0	12.7	12.6	12.2	7.9	5.5	35.8	175 102	91.7	26.4
WEST VIRGINIA	5.5	15.1	9.2	11.9	12.3	13.6	14.6	10.3	7.5	41.9	411 243	85.2	19.2
District 1	5.3	14.3	11.1	12.3	11.9	13.3	14.3	10.1	7.5	41.3	144 790	87.9	21.6
District 2	5.6	16.3	8.1	11.5	12.7	14.1	14.4	10.2	7.2	42.1	138 895	85.8	20.6
District 3	5.8	15.0	8.5	11.7	12.3	13.2	14.9	10.7	7.8	42.5	127 558	81.9	15.2
WISCONSIN	5.9	16.7	9.7	12.7	12.0	14.2	13.6	8.4	6.8	39.2	1 451 402	91.4	28.4
District 1	5.6	17.5	8.5	12.0	12.7	15.1	13.9	8.4	6.4	40.3	177 687	91.3	28.1
District 2	5.9	15.8	11.7	14.4	12.8	13.4	12.8	7.6	5.6	36.5	201 043	93.3	40.9
District 3	5.6	15.8	13.1	11.7	10.9	13.5	13.3	8.8	7.3	38.3	191 271	91.9	24.5
District 4	7.7	17.7	11.8	16.1	12.7	12.3	11.0	5.9	5.0	32.8	207 754	84.7	27.4
District 5	5.6	16.8	8.2	12.4	12.1	14.7	14.0	8.6	7.6	40.9	178 519	93.7	35.3
District 6	5.5	16.1	8.8	12.0	11.7	14.8	14.5	9.0	7.7	41.9	167 059	92.1	24.7
District 7	5.4	16.4	7.3	10.8	11.4	14.7	15.3	10.3	8.2	43.9	152 072	91.7	21.7
District 8	5.8	17.3	8.3	12.2	12.0	15.1	13.8	8.7	6.7	40.0	175 997	91.7	24.4
WYOMING	6.5	17.1	9.8	14.3	12.2	12.4	14.0	8.4	5.4	36.6	144 582	92.6	26.6
At Large	6.5	17.1	9.8	14.3	12.2	12.4	14.0	8.4	5.4	36.6	144 582	92.6	26.6

1. All persons 3 years old and over enrolled in nursery school through college and graduate or professional school.   2. Persons 25 years old and over.

STATE District	Households, 2014						Group quarters, 2010					
	Number	Average household size	Family households (percent)	Married-couple family (percent)	Female family householder[1]	One person households (percent)	Total in group quarters, 2014	Percent 65 years and over	Persons in correctional institutions	Persons in nursing facilities	Persons in college dormitories	Persons in military quarters
	28	29	30	31	32	33	34	35	36	37	38	39
TEXAS—Cont'd												
District 26	266 038	2.90	74.6	59.1	11.5	18.9	12 063	14.1	1 179	1 636	6 475	0
District 27	259 534	2.75	69.6	49.0	13.8	25.1	12 369	31.7	3 832	4 197	1 365	103
District 28	208 891	3.44	78.2	52.6	19.7	18.6	6 873	32.3	3 252	2 888	740	146
District 29	224 503	3.33	73.6	45.4	19.8	22.1	2 323	36.1	31	1 008	0	0
District 30	249 315	2.91	66.6	37.7	22.3	28.0	19 986	9.2	11 108	2 286	2 507	0
District 31	267 991	2.85	71.0	54.2	12.2	23.9	13 706	16.1	3 442	2 183	2 041	4 084
District 32	286 216	2.59	62.7	47.4	10.7	29.5	5 156	38.4	22	2 226	2 437	0
District 33	223 616	3.29	72.1	41.4	22.2	22.6	5 903	19.3	2 147	1 389	534	0
District 34	211 742	3.30	77.3	49.9	21.9	20.1	19 029	13.7	13 244	2 881	2 180	41
District 35	254 107	2.94	62.2	37.1	17.7	28.2	19 211	9.9	7 971	2 563	5 761	115
District 36	257 309	2.78	68.8	50.8	12.4	26.4	15 942	16.7	12 140	2 926	0	0
UTAH	918 370	3.16	75.3	61.7	9.5	19.3	44 655	10.4	12 666	5 854	15 666	523
District 1	232 907	3.09	76.8	64.0	9.1	18.5	9 050	10.6	1 892	1 190	3 227	488
District 2	236 700	3.03	70.8	57.9	8.8	22.9	12 483	12.1	3 459	1 763	3 443	35
District 3	213 752	3.31	78.8	67.1	7.7	15.6	14 197	7.5	441	1 279	8 960	0
District 4	235 011	3.21	75.1	58.4	12.0	19.7	8 925	12.4	6 874	1 622	36	0
VERMONT	257 229	2.34	63.0	48.9	9.6	28.6	25 356	15.0	1 592	3 588	16 895	5
At Large	257 229	2.34	63.0	48.9	9.6	28.6	25 356	15.0	1 592	3 588	16 895	5
VIRGINIA	3 083 820	2.62	66.8	50.1	12.4	27.0	240 917	12.0	1 592	30 324	84 048	37 568
District 1	268 803	2.79	73.5	58.5	11.2	21.2	19 188	13.8	4 215	2 568	6 380	3 351
District 2	274 587	2.55	66.5	49.2	12.7	27.2	31 738	11.2	1 685	2 534	7 086	7 370
District 3	286 632	2.52	57.3	30.3	21.6	34.9	31 020	5.4	6 045	3 045	11 014	24 287
District 4	265 513	2.69	72.8	51.7	16.2	23.2	32 815	10.2	19 352	2 662	2 942	316
District 5	289 733	2.43	66.1	49.0	12.6	28.1	28 793	13.8	10 972	4 052	12 206	0
District 6	290 076	2.45	64.1	47.8	12.3	29.1	35 313	12.6	4 623	4 349	19 615	1 398
District 7	286 332	2.65	71.1	56.0	10.9	24.2	10 876	19.8	4 500	2 649	3 721	0
District 8	308 510	2.49	55.1	42.5	8.9	34.8	6 581	28.6	944	2 026	1 084	846
District 9	284 490	2.41	63.0	48.2	10.2	31.2	30 826	13.1	10 091	4 288	14 085	0
District 10	263 798	3.02	77.3	65.4	8.7	18.5	5 789	18.7	1 606	907	1 068	0
District 11	265 346	2.92	70.3	55.1	10.7	22.6	7 978	13.6	1 207	1 244	4 847	0
WASHINGTON	2 679 601	2.58	64.4	49.6	10.3	27.7	140 967	18.6	31 960	22 156	35 534	12 385
District 1	259 859	2.71	71.6	59.5	8.3	21.7	8 302	23.7	2 676	1 313	620	0
District 2	275 308	2.52	63.2	48.7	9.5	28.1	13 272	20.5	1 754	2 323	3 862	2 504
District 3	264 592	2.61	67.9	52.0	10.9	25.5	6 921	35.8	1 539	1 617	0	14
District 4	235 617	2.94	71.3	51.8	13.7	23.9	10 537	25.7	4 028	2 246	382	4
District 5	267 126	2.47	63.6	48.4	10.9	28.7	29 520	11.8	5 656	2 927	13 048	513
District 6	265 236	2.48	63.9	50.0	9.8	29.1	18 572	16.0	8 063	3 211	1 022	5 694
District 7	328 789	2.16	47.7	38.2	7.0	38.0	21 724	13.6	1 851	2 700	10 456	362
District 8	254 292	2.77	70.7	56.5	9.7	22.4	6 649	24.8	839	1 305	2 155	0
District 9	267 150	2.62	63.9	47.2	11.4	28.7	11 161	26.9	3 031	2 422	1 348	0
District 10	261 632	2.68	65.3	47.4	12.6	27.5	14 309	17.9	2 523	2 092	2 641	3 294
WEST VIRGINIA	735 375	2.45	64.3	48.4	11.4	29.6	49 490	18.9	16 591	9 748	17 113	79
District 1	242 233	2.46	62.2	48.0	9.7	30.8	21 385	15.8	6 965	3 632	10 300	0
District 2	247 865	2.49	66.1	49.2	12.0	28.1	11 357	23.6	2 583	2 791	3 447	79
District 3	245 277	2.40	64.6	47.9	12.5	30.1	16 748	20.1	7 043	3 325	3 366	0
WISCONSIN	2 307 685	2.43	64.4	49.1	10.3	28.5	148 985	23.1	38 102	33 808	56 773	132
District 1	272 387	2.56	68.7	51.5	11.3	25.7	14 829	21.6	6 723	3 632	2 368	0
District 2	302 685	2.39	60.8	46.5	9.4	29.6	17 957	19.7	2 269	2 791	8 805	0
District 3	282 399	2.43	64.4	51.5	8.1	26.7	31 986	15.5	6 311	3 325	18 297	122
District 4	281 593	2.48	57.2	30.6	20.5	34.7	18 466	17.5	2 539	3 173	9 814	0
District 5	291 080	2.43	65.7	53.6	8.2	28.4	15 063	33.1	1 490	4 832	5 703	0
District 6	287 900	2.39	64.7	52.1	8.5	28.9	23 952	20.2	12 174	5 078	6 097	0
District 7	298 690	2.34	67.0	53.6	8.1	27.1	12 155	42.6	3 541	5 073	1 198	0
District 8	290 951	2.43	66.8	53.1	9.0	26.7	14 577	31.5	3 055	4 742	4 491	10
WYOMING	232 594	2.45	64.1	50.3	8.5	28.8	14 257	18.4	3 576	2 450	4 443	503
At Large	232 594	2.45	64.1	50.3	8.5	28.8	14 257	18.4	3 576	2 450	4 443	503

1. No spouse present.

Table E. Congressional Districts 114th Congress — Housing and Money Income

STATE District	Housing units, 2014						Money income, 2014		
		Occupied units					Households		
			Owner-occupied			Renter-occupied			
	Total	Occupied units as a percent of all units	Owner-occupied units as a percent of occupied units	Median value[1] (dollars)	Percent valued at $500,000 or more	Median rent[2]	Per capita income (dollars)	Median income (dollars)	Percent with income of $100,000 or more
	40	41	42	43	44	45	46	47	48
TEXAS—Cont'd									
District 26	279 494	95.2	69.8	197 500	5.8	1 067	35 013	78 796	38.2
District 27	309 361	83.9	63.5	114 900	2.2	852	25 453	50 656	20.6
District 28	238 252	87.7	67.7	103 200	1.0	768	18 184	43 999	16.3
District 29	246 164	91.2	50.3	87 900	0.3	799	16 416	39 580	10.5
District 30	274 649	90.8	52.3	102 600	1.1	881	19 731	40 536	14.1
District 31	296 027	90.5	62.1	185 300	3.1	941	29 341	62 772	27.2
District 32	312 995	91.4	57.0	178 300	14.8	1 016	40 278	65 082	31.9
District 33	246 860	90.6	46.6	81 400	0.5	784	14 527	35 311	7.1
District 34	256 405	82.6	68.1	74 700	1.2	655	16 208	35 451	13.9
District 35	280 250	90.7	49.3	114 600	1.1	891	18 965	40 856	12.0
District 36	300 437	85.6	69.2	116 900	1.3	866	26 203	54 560	23.3
UTAH	1 022 593	89.8	69.2	223 200	7.8	886	24 877	60 922	23.8
District 1	269 093	86.6	72.9	197 700	6.7	817	25 114	62 017	23.7
District 2	275 514	85.9	64.7	206 800	6.9	848	23 668	53 651	19.0
District 3	233 515	91.5	69.6	263 800	12.9	909	26 286	65 144	29.4
District 4	244 471	96.1	69.7	229 600	5.0	966	24 474	63 365	23.9
VERMONT	325 774	79.0	70.0	214 600	6.4	917	29 178	54 166	20.8
At Large	325 774	79.0	70.0	214 600	6.4	917	29 178	54 166	20.8
VIRGINIA	3 446 585	89.5	65.3	247 800	17.3	1 116	34 052	64 902	30.9
District 1	304 779	88.2	72.9	294 100	13.1	1 241	34 701	77 184	37.4
District 2	308 304	89.1	61.6	236 500	9.9	1 113	30 557	61 484	25.2
District 3	322 684	88.8	44.3	166 600	3.0	923	22 859	40 679	13.3
District 4	290 795	91.3	70.3	214 100	4.4	1 046	27 308	60 950	25.6
District 5	346 726	83.6	70.1	172 000	9.5	821	27 324	48 179	18.6
District 6	330 414	87.8	65.1	182 300	3.9	804	25 404	49 724	17.4
District 7	310 783	92.1	72.6	246 700	10.4	1 116	36 851	74 162	34.8
District 8	333 194	92.6	51.5	499 800	50.0	1 706	52 357	99 094	49.5
District 9	342 477	83.1	70.2	117 700	2.7	630	22 125	39 872	12.6
District 10	277 560	95.0	78.2	461 300	44.4	1 509	48 404	115 291	57.9
District 11	278 869	95.2	64.6	444 200	40.5	1 751	43 791	100 361	50.3
WASHINGTON	2 963 293	90.4	61.7	266 200	16.0	1 032	31 841	61 366	27.3
District 1	284 841	91.2	71.4	366 900	28.6	1 328	38 534	84 419	41.1
District 2	307 937	89.4	59.7	285 000	12.7	1 074	29 687	59 385	24.7
District 3	291 304	90.8	64.3	216 300	5.4	925	27 159	54 561	21.0
District 4	260 944	90.3	65.7	170 200	4.0	805	22 763	50 705	17.5
District 5	299 216	89.3	62.8	178 700	4.5	787	25 018	47 973	17.0
District 6	315 203	84.1	64.9	239 700	10.4	954	30 238	55 338	22.6
District 7	349 848	94.0	49.3	455 000	42.5	1 223	45 322	72 279	36.9
District 8	280 491	90.7	72.8	294 600	18.7	1 105	33 679	74 078	34.7
District 9	287 342	93.0	54.1	342 900	27.1	1 154	37 493	67 261	32.3
District 10	286 167	91.4	56.6	231 200	4.9	1 048	27 642	58 252	22.4
WEST VIRGINIA	884 574	83.1	72.2	103 900	1.5	656	22 714	41 059	13.3
District 1	289 575	83.7	70.1	104 900	1.6	653	23 194	41 825	13.6
District 2	295 466	83.9	73.6	124 900	1.8	705	24 463	46 370	15.9
District 3	299 533	81.9	72.8	86 200	1.1	609	20 411	35 217	10.3
WISCONSIN	2 648 342	87.1	66.6	164 700	3.5	782	28 213	52 622	20.1
District 1	302 906	89.9	70.0	181 000	3.4	838	28 804	58 345	24.4
District 2	323 122	93.7	61.1	206 800	5.6	871	31 533	58 205	24.2
District 3	321 123	87.9	69.0	146 200	2.4	725	25 785	49 915	17.2
District 4	311 611	90.4	45.3	126 200	3.5	805	22 730	38 200	13.0
District 5	307 379	94.7	69.4	211 400	5.2	867	34 100	62 606	27.5
District 6	322 862	89.2	70.4	151 500	3.6	702	28 782	53 257	19.2
District 7	416 006	71.8	75.9	149 200	2.8	680	26 401	50 060	16.0
District 8	343 333	84.7	71.3	153 100	2.2	686	27 423	53 871	19.2
WYOMING	268 205	86.7	66.9	201 000	7.2	792	29 698	57 055	23.9
At Large	268 205	86.7	66.9	201 000	7.2	792	29 698	57 055	23.9

1. Specified owner-occupied units; $1,000,000 represents $1,000,000 or more.   2. Specified renter-occupied units.

Table E. Congressional Districts 114th Congress — **Poverty, Labor Force, Employment, and Social Security**

STATE District	Poverty, 2014			Civilian labor force, 2014			Civilian employment,[2] 2014					Social Security beneficiaries, December 2014		
					Unemployment			Percent						
	Persons below poverty level (percent)	Families below poverty level (percent)	Percent of households receiving food stamps in past 12 months	Total	Total	Rate[1]	Total	Manage-ment, business, science and arts occupa-tions	Service, sales, and office	Con-struction and production	Persons under age 65 with no health insurance, 2014 (percent)	Number	Rate[3]	Supple-mental Security Income recipients, December 2014
	49	50	51	52	53	54	55	56	57	58	59	60	61	62
TEXAS—Cont'd														
District 26	8.5	5.6	5.7	427 169	20 642	4.8	406 527	45.4	39.3	15.2	13.5	84 379	107.7	6 181
District 27	16.0	12.7	15.2	352 622	23 155	6.6	329 467	29.3	41.4	29.3	20.9	133 420	183.7	22 891
District 28	27.1	22.1	24.1	308 888	22 268	7.2	286 620	26.9	47.4	25.8	28.3	105 027	144.7	30 968
District 29	23.8	21.0	20.4	360 452	26 974	7.5	333 478	17.7	40.9	41.5	34.6	74 036	98.8	23 160
District 30	25.8	22.3	21.6	351 550	28 190	8.0	323 360	27.1	45.9	27.0	24.5	99 527	133.7	32 978
District 31	10.6	8.0	8.9	388 267	21 975	5.7	366 292	40.7	41.7	17.7	13.1	106 692	137.4	11 179
District 32	12.4	9.3	9.0	418 784	24 634	5.9	394 150	43.0	39.7	17.2	19.0	93 854	125.6	11 865
District 33	28.5	25.6	25.4	347 793	30 568	8.8	317 225	15.0	44.8	40.2	35.5	79 093	106.5	24 390
District 34	31.1	26.4	24.8	285 691	22 600	7.9	263 091	26.7	48.3	25.0	33.1	111 171	154.9	38 703
District 35	25.3	21.1	20.2	382 493	25 737	6.7	356 756	27.4	46.8	25.8	26.0	101 026	131.6	25 489
District 36	14.6	11.4	12.8	331 829	20 508	6.2	311 321	31.0	39.3	29.7	20.5	132 514	181.2	16 488
UTAH	11.7	8.5	8.1	1 435 751	71 359	5.0	1 364 392	36.9	41.5	21.6	13.8	365 730	124.3	31 212
District 1	10.7	8.2	7.9	350 152	17 680	5.0	332 472	36.0	39.3	24.7	11.0	88 053	121.0	7 600
District 2	14.1	9.3	9.2	354 229	22 505	6.4	331 724	34.0	43.1	22.9	18.6	107 561	147.4	8 996
District 3	12.1	8.0	6.0	351 548	15 715	4.5	335 833	42.1	40.5	17.4	12.5	85 686	118.8	6 294
District 4	10.1	8.3	9.2	379 822	15 459	4.1	364 363	35.6	42.8	21.6	13.5	84 430	110.4	8 322
VERMONT	12.2	8.7	14.3	343 957	18 746	5.5	325 211	40.2	38.4	21.4	5.9	140 634	224.5	15 783
At Large	12.2	8.7	14.3	343 957	18 746	5.5	325 211	40.2	38.4	21.4	5.9	140 634	224.5	15 783
VIRGINIA	11.8	8.3	9.9	4 300 221	260 537	6.1	4 039 684	42.9	39.1	18.0	12.5	1 415 661	170.0	155 501
District 1	7.4	5.1	7.3	386 401	20 071	5.2	366 330	41.9	40.2	17.8	10.2	124 974	162.3	7 848
District 2	9.5	7.1	8.4	364 746	22 181	6.1	342 565	37.6	43.2	19.2	12.6	117 726	160.8	10 889
District 3	23.3	18.4	18.8	380 703	38 739	10.2	341 964	31.8	45.2	23.0	17.2	128 402	170.4	30 807
District 4	12.1	8.8	12.3	368 316	28 471	7.7	339 845	35.8	41.6	22.6	11.5	134 315	179.8	15 325
District 5	15.8	11.0	13.8	349 661	19 745	5.6	329 916	36.7	39.9	23.4	14.4	173 964	237.2	18 254
District 6	15.2	9.7	11.3	377 289	20 684	5.5	356 605	34.1	41.8	24.1	13.9	164 185	220.0	16 775
District 7	7.5	5.0	6.4	417 181	21 792	5.2	395 389	44.8	38.9	16.3	8.7	134 546	174.7	7 993
District 8	9.1	7.0	5.0	465 815	19 673	4.2	446 142	57.8	31.7	10.5	13.1	73 370	94.8	7 689
District 9	19.5	13.1	15.4	313 100	24 611	7.9	288 489	33.5	42.2	24.3	13.6	197 606	276.2	25 589
District 10	5.2	3.7	4.4	430 996	21 164	4.9	409 832	55.1	34.0	10.9	9.6	88 987	110.9	5 546
District 11	7.1	4.7	4.9	446 013	23 406	5.2	422 607	52.1	35.6	12.3	12.8	77 586	99.2	8 786
WASHINGTON	13.2	8.8	14.1	3 564 013	232 125	6.5	3 331 888	39.4	39.5	21.0	10.6	1 230 039	174.2	151 262
District 1	8.7	5.2	9.1	374 556	22 521	6.0	352 035	44.9	37.1	18.0	7.8	106 833	149.8	7 739
District 2	12.7	8.0	13.3	367 136	25 323	6.9	341 813	36.8	41.4	21.7	11.4	126 270	178.3	14 248
District 3	12.4	8.4	17.5	332 596	27 437	8.2	305 159	32.6	41.3	26.0	11.2	144 720	207.4	16 564
District 4	18.1	13.6	19.3	321 908	20 086	6.2	301 822	28.8	35.8	35.3	16.8	117 815	167.3	17 182
District 5	17.6	11.5	18.8	320 989	21 066	6.6	299 923	34.9	44.5	20.6	9.9	141 797	205.3	19 160
District 6	14.0	9.6	15.3	310 742	23 530	7.6	287 212	36.1	42.3	21.6	10.6	156 813	231.7	18 608
District 7	12.3	6.3	8.9	442 961	19 194	4.3	423 767	55.2	34.7	10.2	7.1	103 575	141.4	13 062
District 8	10.4	6.7	10.5	361 146	22 300	6.2	338 846	39.6	38.3	22.2	9.4	107 315	150.8	10 549
District 9	12.9	9.2	14.7	389 148	23 201	6.0	365 947	42.0	40.2	17.8	11.0	98 443	138.4	17 737
District 10	13.3	9.5	15.2	342 831	27 467	8.0	315 364	35.9	41.7	22.3	11.4	126 458	177.0	16 413
WEST VIRGINIA	18.3	13.1	16.4	803 400	55 257	6.9	748 143	31.8	43.7	24.4	10.4	464 823	251.2	77 715
District 1	18.0	11.8	13.7	280 061	16 727	6.0	263 334	31.6	43.1	25.4	10.5	146 580	237.9	20 548
District 2	15.8	11.7	14.8	285 759	20 359	7.1	265 400	34.9	42.4	22.6	9.5	150 263	239.2	21 266
District 3	21.1	15.7	20.6	237 580	18 171	7.6	219 409	28.4	46.1	25.5	11.3	167 980	277.3	35 901
WISCONSIN	13.2	9.0	13.1	3 080 347	163 484	5.3	2 916 863	35.0	39.6	25.4	8.6	1 153 149	200.3	117 679
District 1	11.7	8.4	12.6	376 772	21 314	5.7	355 458	34.9	40.3	24.8	8.7	141 508	198.7	13 400
District 2	13.5	8.3	12.2	425 797	21 347	5.0	404 450	43.8	37.7	18.5	7.4	125 380	169.2	11 346
District 3	13.8	7.6	11.2	382 680	16 863	4.4	365 817	31.3	40.0	28.7	9.3	152 339	212.0	12 855
District 4	26.0	21.8	27.0	360 373	35 645	9.9	324 728	33.8	44.2	22.1	12.8	112 115	156.2	39 607
District 5	8.3	5.4	8.2	397 939	17 095	4.3	380 844	40.7	38.1	21.2	5.8	145 418	201.3	7 201
District 6	9.8	6.2	10.9	383 367	16 426	4.3	366 941	31.3	38.9	29.8	7.2	153 626	215.8	9 721
District 7	11.2	8.0	12.1	367 937	18 437	5.0	349 500	31.0	38.8	30.2	9.9	174 271	245.1	12 286
District 8	11.0	8.0	11.1	385 482	16 357	4.2	369 125	31.8	39.3	29.0	7.5	148 492	205.5	11 263
WYOMING	11.2	7.4	6.7	312 702	13 477	4.3	299 225	32.7	39.0	28.2	13.7	101 296	173.4	6 786
At Large	11.2	7.4	6.7	312 702	13 477	4.3	299 225	32.7	39.0	28.2	13.7	101 296	173.4	6 786

1. Percent of civilian labor force.   2. Persons 16 years old and over.   3. Per 1,000 resident population estimated in the 2014 American Community Survey.

Table E. Congressional Districts 114th Congress — **Agriculture**

STATE District	Agriculture, 2012									
	Land in farms				Value of products sold				Government payments	
	Number of farms	Acres	Average size of farm (acres)	Irrigated land (acres)	Total ($1,000)	Average per farm (dollars)	Percent from crops	Percent from livestock and poultry products	Total ($1,000)	Average per farm receiving payments (dollars)
	63	64	65	66	67	68	69	70	71	72
TEXAS—Cont'd										
District 26	3 302	378 816	115	3 483	144 039	43 622	28.8	71.2	1 060	4 400
District 27	12 248	4 802 357	392	136 796	1 227 580	100 227	54.0	46.0	42 540	14 347
District 28	7 794	5 145 001	660	79 700	406 827	52 197	36.3	63.7	11 471	7 439
District 29	100	3 742	37	9	1 099	10 995	81.8	18.3	0	0
District 30	387	38 849	100	1 212	24 876	64 280	95.4	4.6	135	4 657
District 31	4 996	953 480	191	4 435	212 132	42 460	62.2	37.8	5 772	5 305
District 32	220	28 677	130	58	9 079	41 269	40.2	59.8	108	6 012
District 33	107	8 001	75	27	7 499	70 083	96.0	3.9	2	300
District 34	8 326	4 632 760	556	174 856	931 238	111 847	44.1	55.9	17 803	9 825
District 35	1 133	250 124	221	1 547	39 002	34 423	73.0	27.0	873	6 616
District 36	6 888	1 108 089	161	25 421	119 925	17 411	53.7	46.3	5 295	17 534
UTAH	18 027	10 974 396	609	1 104 257	1 816 147	100 746	31.6	68.4	23 898	8 584
District 1	7 334	5 425 669	740	500 075	568 013	77 449	37.1	62.9	12 472	9 805
District 2	4 911	2 536 753	517	404 236	897 850	182 824	24.8	75.2	6 598	7 558
District 3	3 651	2 577 805	706	127 071	205 267	56 222	42.2	57.8	2 877	6 851
District 4	2 131	434 169	204	72 875	145 017	68 051	37.3	62.7	1 950	8 906
VERMONT	7 338	1 251 713	171	3 565	776 105	105 765	22.9	77.1	13 930	8 929
At Large	7 338	1 251 713	171	3 565	776 105	105 765	22.9	77.1	13 930	8 929
VIRGINIA	46 030	8 302 444	180	68 651	3 753 287	81 540	36.2	63.8	82 318	7 719
District 1	2 338	522 532	223	10 540	215 529	92 185	87.3	12.7	8 842	14 495
District 2	567	157 025	277	11 243	280 070	493 951	48.3	51.7	4 246	19 478
District 3	369	104 848	284	3 470	64 905	175 894	81.9	18.1	2 661	19 423
District 4	3 003	766 641	255	7 971	473 780	157 769	61.3	38.7	19 465	14 735
District 5	12 069	2 441 870	202	15 716	613 975	50 872	40.7	59.3	18 392	5 929
District 6	8 195	1 297 577	158	11 153	1 271 186	155 117	9.9	90.1	7 944	6 576
District 7	3 265	523 003	160	4 983	242 528	74 281	68.7	31.3	5 367	10 713
District 8	33	1 227	37	15	1 611	48 818	D	D	D	D
District 9	13 389	2 166 935	162	2 506	487 735	36 428	17.9	82.1	14 226	4 245
District 10	2 775	318 962	115	1 050	100 953	36 379	61.2	38.8	1 150	5 478
District 11	27	1 824	68	4	1 014	37 546	D	D	D	D
WASHINGTON	37 249	14 748 107	396	1 633 571	9 120 749	244 859	71.2	28.8	159 269	22 014
District 1	3 651	215 635	59	44 402	568 090	155 598	45.9	54.1	4 361	10 794
District 2	1 660	124 240	75	19 235	251 457	151 480	61.8	38.2	1 391	10 303
District 3	5 698	888 616	156	53 077	379 033	66 520	44.4	55.6	5 823	11 418
District 4	10 221	7 236 719	708	1 287 721	6 100 198	596 830	73.0	27.0	64 825	25 302
District 5	7 733	5 665 632	733	112 588	1 151 558	148 915	92.9	7.1	79 599	24 364
District 6	2 533	197 926	78	15 406	86 682	34 221	D	D	390	4 432
District 7	196	2 185	11	195	D	D	D	D	38	5 463
District 8	3 967	349 188	88	95 859	413 543	104 246	70.5	29.5	2 648	11 220
District 9	115	1 916	17	282	D	D	D	D	29	4 767
District 10	1 475	66 050	45	4 806	130 983	88 802	43.3	56.7	166	8 316
WEST VIRGINIA	21 489	3 606 674	168	2 064	806 775	37 544	17.2	82.8	7 034	3 203
District 1	8 458	1 305 274	154	D	D	D	D	D	1 923	3 162
District 2	7 563	1 366 085	181	1 238	473 385	62 592	16.2	83.8	3 203	3 632
District 3	5 468	935 315	171	D	D	D	D	D	1 909	2 703
WISCONSIN	69 754	14 568 926	209	421 721	11 744 476	168 370	39.2	60.8	237 304	6 093
District 1	2 667	563 204	211	12 892	485 265	181 952	D	D	D	D
District 2	9 962	2 127 676	214	42 496	1 553 585	155 951	38.1	61.9	44 895	6 876
District 3	19 895	4 295 732	216	218 340	2 936 452	147 597	45.4	54.6	61 572	5 263
District 4	37	455	12	23	4 098	110 746	D	D	D	D
District 5	3 462	635 541	184	11 247	611 624	176 668	43.5	56.5	12 337	6 184
District 6	8 882	1 813 360	204	52 490	1 824 851	205 455	38.0	62.0	34 602	6 824
District 7	16 175	3 418 268	211	70 755	2 438 450	150 754	36.2	63.8	39 552	5 465
District 8	8 674	1 714 690	198	13 478	1 890 152	217 910	28.1	71.9	32 326	6 516
WYOMING	11 736	3 036 3 641	2 587	1 435 710	1 689 416	143 952	26.0	74.0	28 146	10 027
At Large	11 736	3 036 3 641	2 587	1 435 710	1 689 416	143 952	26.0	74.0	28 146	10 027

Table E. Congressional Districts 114th Congress — Nonfarm Employment and Payroll

Private nonfarm employment and payroll, 2014

STATE District	Number of establishments	Employment Total	Percent by selected industries — Manufacturing	Construction	Wholesale trade	Retail trade	Health care and social assistance	Finance and Insurance	Real estate and rental and leasing	Professional, scientific, and technical services	Information	Annual payroll Total (mil dol)	Average per employee dollars
	73	74	75	76	77	78	79	80	81	82	83	84	85
TEXAS—Cont'd													
District 26	13 784	213 626	5.8	4.9	5.0	15.0	11.2	9.1	1.7	5.0	1.8	9 165	42 903
District 27	15 645	242 554	9.6	8.0	4.9	14.8	18.0	2.8	2.3	4.0	1.2	10 336	42 614
District 28	10 864	164 633	2.4	4.6	4.0	18.4	21.5	3.4	1.8	2.7	4.0	5 600	34 013
District 29	10 509	214 369	16.6	11.9	7.8	11.7	5.6	2.3	1.6	4.7	0.0	10 806	50 407
District 30	13 177	309 743	6.9	3.9	4.8	8.8	18.4	6.1	2.5	9.5	3.4	19 781	63 862
District 31	14 041	219 296	6.8	6.1	2.9	16.7	18.5	5.0	1.6	6.6	2.7	9 456	43 121
District 32	20 945	322 529	0.0	3.7	3.9	12.3	16.2	7.8	3.4	10.1	3.4	17 792	55 165
District 33	12 222	266 369	15.9	8.2	11.3	9.8	10.2	1.8	1.8	4.3	0.0	12 024	45 139
District 34	10 569	161 299	4.7	3.3	3.3	17.0	29.8	3.1	1.8	2.9	1.8	4 847	30 052
District 35	14 915	277 097	7.9	6.8	7.3	13.5	12.3	3.2	1.9	5.4	2.3	11 105	40 075
District 36	12 622	239 786	18.3	10.5	3.6	11.3	10.7	2.1	1.5	8.1	0.6	13 075	54 526
UTAH	73 375	1 148 251	10.0	5.9	4.8	12.4	11.2	5.2	1.7	8.0	3.6	47 913	41 727
District 1	17 224	224 252	17.0	6.7	3.5	15.0	11.8	3.8	2.0	7.3	1.3	8 244	36 764
District 2	20 068	348 636	10.1	4.8	5.8	10.7	11.4	5.9	1.5	7.3	3.2	16 136	46 283
District 3	17 977	237 062	6.3	5.4	3.8	14.0	12.6	4.7	1.7	6.7	4.5	9 284	39 161
District 4	17 725	282 342	9.4	8.2	6.1	13.6	11.5	6.6	1.9	9.0	5.9	12 197	43 198
VERMONT	21 041	261 058	11.4	5.2	4.3	14.8	17.9	3.5	1.3	6.9	2.7	10 180	38 994
At Large	21 041	261 058	11.4	5.2	4.3	14.8	17.9	3.5	1.3	6.9	2.7	10 180	38 994
VIRGINIA	195 639	3 160 539	7.4	5.4	3.2	13.3	13.5	5.0	1.7	13.8	3.0	159 145	50 354
District 1	16 264	209 716	3.8	8.5	3.0	18.5	13.3	4.2	1.3	9.9	1.7	8 042	38 347
District 2	16 592	243 989	4.7	4.9	2.5	15.0	15.5	5.4	2.9	10.8	2.1	9 519	39 014
District 3	15 721	319 510	15.4	4.7	4.3	9.6	18.5	5.0	1.6	7.3	2.0	15 393	48 176
District 4	14 367	217 014	10.5	8.1	4.3	16.4	12.0	3.6	1.4	6.3	2.1	8 415	38 775
District 5	16 599	200 115	11.0	6.6	3.0	16.1	18.5	3.7	1.4	5.2	1.8	7 643	38 191
District 6	17 857	299 257	14.4	5.0	3.1	14.8	16.5	4.5	1.3	4.2	1.7	11 309	37 790
District 7	20 098	320 039	3.7	5.2	5.1	14.9	14.6	11.0	1.9	7.2	2.3	15 153	47 349
District 8	20 150	358 977	1.0	4.3	1.6	10.0	9.2	3.1	2.2	25.9	3.1	23 026	64 144
District 9	14 407	209 313	19.0	4.0	3.9	17.1	17.0	2.8	1.0	3.9	1.7	7 476	35 716
District 10	21 378	310 361	5.7	7.8	3.3	12.4	10.2	2.7	1.4	19.8	4.1	18 052	58 165
District 11	21 697	431 458	0.8	2.8	1.7	10.4	9.8	5.9	2.0	31.0	6.9	32 228	74 696
WASHINGTON	179 012	2 528 874	10.2	5.9	5.0	12.7	15.2	3.9	1.8	7.7	5.0	141 278	55 866
District 1	18 459	256 375	9.8	8.5	5.1	9.5	9.3	2.3	1.5	8.4	19.1	20 759	80 972
District 2	19 222	261 442	23.6	6.8	3.4	16.4	13.1	4.1	1.4	4.1	2.1	12 176	46 573
District 3	15 332	178 883	13.6	7.9	4.6	14.6	17.5	3.4	1.6	5.6	2.2	7 919	44 271
District 4	13 697	178 452	12.6	5.8	6.5	15.9	16.9	2.5	1.5	5.7	1.4	7 404	41 489
District 5	16 588	219 548	9.3	5.1	5.5	15.0	19.9	5.8	1.8	4.9	1.9	9 005	41 014
District 6	16 617	187 522	4.8	5.2	2.4	16.9	26.0	3.9	1.8	5.1	1.4	7 373	39 316
District 7	27 596	430 185	4.0	3.9	3.6	9.2	14.6	5.0	2.5	12.9	6.3	30 409	70 688
District 8	14 723	161 939	10.6	9.1	7.4	15.4	11.8	2.0	1.4	3.5	2.2	7 530	46 496
District 9	21 975	421 147	10.9	4.6	6.9	9.4	13.4	4.1	2.2	6.3	5.2	27 140	64 442
District 10	14 337	195 537	7.2	6.8	5.1	16.2	17.3	4.4	2.0	4.9	2.3	7 860	40 197
WEST VIRGINIA	37 354	575 228	8.6	4.4	3.7	14.9	23.1	3.1	1.1	4.6	1.8	22 100	38 420
District 1	13 162	212 628	10.2	3.9	2.7	14.5	24.0	2.7	1.3	4.5	1.6	8 253	38 812
District 2	12 512	189 793	8.5	5.5	4.6	14.5	20.7	4.1	1.1	4.9	1.9	7 273	38 322
District 3	11 433	166 796	7.0	3.7	3.6	16.4	25.3	2.5	0.9	3.2	2.0	6 220	37 291
WISCONSIN	138 221	2 450 254	18.1	4.0	4.7	12.5	15.8	5.6	1.0	4.2	2.2	106 791	43 584
District 1	14 859	235 920	20.8	3.5	5.2	16.2	14.3	2.6	0.9	2.8	1.3	9 602	40 700
District 2	18 642	342 316	11.3	4.4	4.8	12.8	16.2	7.4	1.3	6.6	4.7	16 012	46 775
District 3	16 775	270 210	17.7	3.5	4.0	14.4	17.2	5.4	0.9	3.1	1.9	9 971	36 903
District 4	13 118	316 778	10.2	1.8	4.4	7.3	20.6	9.7	1.2	5.3	2.3	16 819	53 093
District 5	21 021	395 981	18.1	4.2	6.2	12.1	14.6	4.7	1.1	4.9	2.6	18 288	46 183
District 6	16 597	300 333	26.8	5.5	3.7	12.1	13.9	3.8	0.7	3.3	1.0	12 688	42 245
District 7	18 788	241 948	22.6	4.2	3.9	15.8	18.0	4.1	0.7	2.7	1.1	8 926	36 891
District 8	18 023	318 768	21.4	4.8	4.4	12.3	13.5	5.2	0.9	3.3	2.1	13 284	41 674
WYOMING	20 807	219 857	4.6	9.1	3.9	14.4	14.5	3.0	2.3	4.6	1.9	10 376	47 192
At Large	20 807	219 857	4.6	9.1	3.9	14.4	14.5	3.0	2.3	4.6	1.9	10 376	47 192

1. Specified owner-occupied units; $1,000,000 represents $1,000,000 or more.   2. Specified renter-occupied units.

APPENDIX A
GEOGRAPHIC CONCEPTS AND CODES

GEOGRAPHIC AREAS COVERED

County and City Extra presents data for states (Table A), states and counties (Table B), metropolitan areas (Table C), cities with populations of 25,000 or more in 2010 (Table D), and congressional districts (Table E).

STATES AND COUNTIES

Data are presented for each of the 50 states, the District of Columbia, and the United States as a whole. The states are arranged alphabetically and counties in Table B are arranged alphabetically within each state. Data are presented for 3,143 counties and county equivalents.

County equivalents

In Louisiana, the primary divisions of the state are known as parishes rather than counties. In Alaska, the county equivalents are the organized boroughs, together with the census areas that were developed for general statistical purposes by the state of Alaska and the U.S. Census Bureau. Four states—Maryland, Missouri, Nevada, and Virginia—have one or more incorporated places that are legally independent of any county and thus constitute primary divisions of their states. Within each state, independent cities are listed alphabetically following the list of counties. The District of Columbia is not divided into counties or county equivalents—data for the entire district are presented as a county equivalent. New York City contains five counties: Bronx, Kings, New York, Queens, and Richmond.

County changes since the 2010 census

- The independent city of Bedford, Virginia changed to town status and was added to Bedford County effective July 1, 2013. Both entities are retained in this book because most data sources have not made the change.
- Wade Hampton Census Area, AK (02-270) changed its name and FIPS code to Kusilvak Census Area (02-158), effective July 1, 2015.
- Shannon County, SD (46-113) changed its name and FIPS code to Oglala Lakota County (46-102), effective May 1, 2015.
- Petersburg Borough, AK was created from part of Petersburg Census Area and part of Hoonah-Angoon Census Area. Petersburg Borough retains the FIPS code 02-195, formerly used by Petersburg Census Area, effective January 3, 2013.
- Prince of Wales-Hyder Census Area added part of the former Petersburg Census Area, effective January 3, 2013.

County changes since the 2000 census

- Broomfield County, CO, was created from parts of Adams, Boulder, Jefferson, and Weld Counties, effective November 15, 2001. The boundaries of Broomfield County reflect the boundaries of Broomfield city legally in effect on that date.
- Clifton Forge city, VA, formerly an independent city, became a town within Alleghany County, effective July 1, 2001.
- Effective June 20, 2007, the Skagway-Hoonah-Angoon Census Area in Alaska was divided into the Skagway Municipality and the Hoonah-Angoon Census Area.
- In May and June 2008, the Wrangell-Petersburg and Prince of Wales-Outer Ketchikan Census Areas were dissolved and replaced by Wrangell City and Borough, Petersburg Census Area, and Prince of Wales Census Area. Some territory from the Prince of Wales Outer Ketchikan Census Area became part of the existing Ketchikan Gateway Borough.

METROPOLITAN AREAS

Table C presents data for 381 metropolitan statistical areas and 31 metropolitan divisions, which are located within the 11 largest metropolitan statistical areas. The metropolitan statistical areas are listed alphabetically, and the metropolitan divisions are listed alphabetically under the metropolitan statistical area of which they are components.

The U.S. Office of Management and Budget (OMB) defines metropolitan and micropolitan statistical areas according to published standards. The major purpose of defining these areas is to enable all U.S. government agencies to use the same geographic definitions in tabulating and publishing data. The general concept of a metropolitan or micropolitan statistical area is that of a core area containing a substantial population nucleus, together with adjacent communities that have a high degree of economic and social integration with the core.

New delineations of these Core Based Statistical Areas (CBSAs) based on the 2010 census were released in February 2013 and most federal agencies now use these new definitions. Table C in this book uses these delineations for metropolitan areas and metropolitan divisions. Micropolitan areas are not included in Table C. A few of the data items in Table C were released under the old scheme but have been aggregated from county data to the newly defined metropolitan areas. This results in a higher level of data suppression for those items. New delineations were released in July 2015, mainly affecting micropolitan areas, but they have not yet been used for any of the data sources in this book.

Appendix B lists the metropolitan areas and metropolitan divisions with their component counties and 2010 census populations. Appendix C lists the metropolitan and micropolitan areas, together with their 2010 census populations and their 2015 estimated populations.

Standard definitions of metropolitan areas were first issued in 1949 by the Bureau of the Budget (the predecessor of OMB), under the designation ''standard metropolitan area'' (SMA). The term was changed to ''standard metropolitan statistical area'' (SMSA) in 1959, and to ''metropolitan statistical area'' (MSA) in 1983. The term ''metropolitan area'' (MA) was adopted in

1990 and referred collectively to metropolitan statistical areas (MSAs), consolidated metropolitan statistical areas (CMSAs), and primary metropolitan statistical areas (PMSAs). The term ''core based statistical area'' (CBSA) became effective in 2000 and refers collectively to metropolitan and micropolitan statistical areas.

The 2010 standards provide that each CBSA must contain at least one urban area of 10,000 or more population. Each metropolitan statistical area must have at least one urbanized area of 50,000 or more inhabitants. Each micropolitan statistical area must have at least one urban cluster of at least 10,000 but less than 50,000 people.

Under the standards, a metro area contains a core urban area of 50,000 or more population, and a micro area contains an urban core of at least 10,000 (but less than 50,000) population. Each metro or micro area consists of one or more counties and includes the counties containing the core urban area, as well as any adjacent counties that have a high degree of social and economic integration (as measured by commuting to work) with the urban core.

If specified criteria are met, a metropolitan statistical area containing a single core with a population of 2.5 million or more may be subdivided to form smaller groupings of counties referred to as ''metropolitan divisions.''

As of February 28, 2013, there were 381 metropolitan statistical areas and 541 micropolitan statistical areas in the United States. Table C includes the 381 metropolitan statistical areas and the 31 metropolitan divisions. The metropolitan areas and metropolitan divisions are listed in Appendix B with their 2010 census population counts. The metropolitan areas, metropolitan divisions, and micropolitan areas are listed in Appendix C with their 2010 census populations and their 2015 estimated populations.

The largest city in each metropolitan or micropolitan statistical area is designated a ''principal city.'' Additional cities qualify if specified requirements are met concerning population size and employment. The title of each metropolitan or micropolitan statistical area consists of the names of up to three of its principal cities and the name of each state into which the metropolitan or micropolitan statistical area extends. Titles of metropolitan divisions also typically are based on principal city names, but in certain cases consist of county names. The principal city need not be an incorporated place if it meets the requirements of population size and employment. Usually such a principal city is a census designated place in decennial census data, but it is not included in most other data sources and is not in Table D (cities) in this volume.

In view of the importance of cities and towns in New England, the 2010 standards also provide for a set of geographic areas that are defined using cities and towns in the six New England states. These New England city and town areas (NECTAs) are not included in this volume.

Appendix B lists the 381 metropolitan statistical areas, together with their component metropolitan divisions, where appropriate, the component counties of each area, and their 2010 census populations Appendix C provides the same information for the 381 metropolitan areas, and it also includes the 541 micropolitan statistical areas. Maps showing the metropolitan and micropolitan areas within each state can be found in Appendix D.

CITIES

Table D presents data for 1,436 cities with 2010 census populations of 25,000 or more. Corresponding data for states are also provided. The states are arranged alphabetically, and the cities are ordered alphabetically within each state.

As used in this volume, the term *city* refers to places that have been incorporated as cities, boroughs, towns, or villages under the laws of their respective states. Towns in the New England states and New York are treated as minor civil divisions (MCDs) and are not included in the cities database. For Hawaii, data for the census designated places (CDPs) are included in the cities table, since the Census Bureau does not recognize any incorporated places in Hawaii. CDPs are delineated by the Census Bureau, in cooperation with states and localities, as statistical counterparts of incorporated places for purposes of the decennial census. CDPs comprise densely settled concentrations of population that are identifiable by name but are not legally incorporated as places.

Appendix E lists the 1,436 cities followed by the county where each city is located. If a city includes portions of more than one county, the population in each part is specified.

A consolidated city is an incorporated place that has combined its government functions with a county or subcounty entity but contains one or more other semi-independent incorporated places that continue to function as local governments within the consolidated government. Each consolidated city contains a core city, the area of a consolidated city not included in another separately incorporated place. The census geographic term for this core is the ''balance'' of the consolidated city. Thus the ''balance'' is essentially the core city of the consolidated government. This volume includes the consolidated city data where possible, but some data sources include numbers only for the ''balance,'' and others do not specify which entity is represented.

Consolidated cities included in this volume are Milford, CT; Athens-Clarke County, GA; Augusta-Richmond County, GA; Indianapolis, IN; Louisville-Jefferson County, KY; Butte-Silver Bow, MT; and Nashville-Davidson, TN.

Appendix E lists these seven consolidated cities, followed by the component places and their 2010 census populations.

On January 1, 2014, Macon, Georgia consolidated with Bibb county. A small portion of Macon that was in Jones county was de-annexed. The total population for 2015 is the only data yet available for the new entity. This book includes Macon city, but the 2015 population is for Macon-Bibb County.

CONGRESSIONAL DISTRICTS

The congressional districts shown in this volume are the districts used for the election of the 114th Congress, which convened in January 2015. These are the districts that were established following the 2010 Census and are based on population data from that census. Data are shown for the 435 regular districts plus the District of Columbia, which has a non-voting delegate, but no representative. Corresponding data for each state also are included. States are listed alphabetically and districts numerically within each state. A map showing congressional districts for the 113th Congress is included in Appendix D.

GEOGRAPHIC CODES

Tables A, B, C, and D provide, in one or more columns at the beginning of the table, a geographic code or codes for each area.

In Table B (states and counties), a five-digit state and county code is given for each state and county. The first two digits indicate the state; the remaining three represent the county. Within each state, the counties are listed in order, beginning with 001, with even numbers usually omitted. Independent cities follow the counties and begin with the number 510. In the second column of Table B, a five-digit core based statistical area (CBSA) code is given for those counties that are within metropolitan and micropolitan areas. In Table A, a two-digit state code is provided. The state code is a sequential numbering, with some gaps, of the states and the District of Columbia in alphabetical order from Alabama (01) to Wyoming (56).

These codes have been established by the U.S. government as Federal Information Processing Standards and are often referred to as *FIPS codes*. They are used by U.S. government agencies and many other organizations for data presentation. The codes are provided in this volume for use in matching the data given here with other data sources in which counties are identified by FIPS code. The metro area codes will also enable the user to identify the metro area of which a county is a component. Table C (metropolitan areas) provides the same metro area codes for each metropolitan area, as well as metropolitan division codes where appropriate.

Table D (cities) provides, in the first column, a seven-digit state and place code. The first two digits identify the state and are the same as the FIPS codes described above. The remaining five digits are the place FIPS codes established by the U.S. government.

INDEPENDENT CITIES

The following independent cities are not included in any county; their data are presented separately in this volume.

MARYLAND
Baltimore (separate from Baltimore County)

MISSOURI
St. Louis (separate from St. Louis County)

NEVADA
Carson City

VIRGINIA

Alexandria	Manassas
Bedford[1]	Manassas Park
Bristol	Martinsville
Buena Vista	Newport News
Charlottesville	Norfolk
Chesapeake	Norton
Colonial Heights	Petersburg
Covington	Poquoson
Danville	Portsmouth
Emporia	Radford
Fairfax	Richmond
Falls Church	Roanoke
Franklin	Salem
Fredericksburg	Staunton
Galax	Suffolk
Hampton	Virginia Beach
Harrisonburg	Waynesboro
Hopewell	Williamsburg
Lexington	Winchester
Lynchburg	

COUNTY TYPE

Table B (states and counties) provides, in the third column, a *county type* code that identifies each county by its metropolitan/nonmetropolitan status and its size. These are the "rural-urban continuum codes" developed by the Economic Research Service of the U.S. Department of Agriculture.

The 2003 rural-urban continuum codes form a classification scheme that distinguishes metropolitan counties by size and nonmetropolitan counties by degree of urbanization and proximity to metro areas. The standard OMB metro and nonmetro categories have been subdivided into three metro and six nonmetro categories, resulting in a nine-part county codification. This scheme was originally developed in 1974. The codes were updated in 1983 and 1993, and slightly revised in 1988. The 1988 revision was first published in 1990. This scheme allows researchers to break county data into finer residential groups, beyond metro and nonmetro, particularly for the analysis of trends in nonmetro areas that are related to population density and metro influence. The 2003 rural-urban continuum codes are not directly comparable with the codes from previous years because of the new methodology used in developing the 2003 metropolitan areas.

Metropolitan counties
1. Counties in metro areas of 1 million population or more.
2. Counties in metro areas of 250,000 to 1 million population.
3. Counties in metro areas of fewer than 250,000 population.

Nonmetropolitan counties
4. Urban population of 20,000 or more, adjacent to a metro area.
5. Urban population of 20,000 or more, not adjacent to a metro area.
6. Urban population of 2,500 to 19,999, adjacent to a metro area.
7. Urban population of 2,500 to 19,999, not adjacent to a metro area.
8. Completely rural or less than 2,500 urban population, adjacent to a metro area.
9. Completely rural or less than 2,500 urban population, not adjacent to a metro area.

---

[1] Bedford city became a town within Bedford county on July 1, 2013. Most of the data in this book, however, continues to reference the independent city.

APPENDIX B
METROPOLITAN STATISTICAL AREAS, METROPOLITAN DIVISIONS, AND COMPONENTS
(as defined February 2013)

Core based statistical area	State/County FIPS code	Title and Geographic Components	2010 Census Population	Core based statistical area	State/County FIPS code	Title and Geographic Components	2010 Census Population
10180		Abilene, TX..	165 252	11540		Appleton, WI.......................................	225 666
	48 059	Callahan County	13 544		55 015	Calumet County................................	48 971
	48 253	Jones County	20 202		55 087	Outagamie County............................	176 695
	48 441	Taylor County	131 506	11700		Asheville, NC.....................................	424 858
10420		Akron, OH...	703 200		37 021	Buncombe County	238 318
	39 133	Portage County	161 419		37 087	Haywood County	59 036
	39 153	Summit County	541 781		37 089	Henderson County............................	106 740
10500		Albany, GA..	157 308		37 115	Madison County................................	20 764
	13 007	Baker County	3 451	12020		Athens-Clarke County, GA................	192 541
	13 095	Dougherty County	94 565		13 059	Clarke County..................................	116 714
	13 177	Lee County	28 298		13 195	Madison County................................	28 120
	13 273	Terrell County	9 315		13 219	Oconee County................................	32 808
	13 321	Worth County...................................	21 679		13 221	Oglethorpe County...........................	14 899
10540		Albany, OR..	116 672	12060		Atlanta-Sandy Springs-Roswell, GA	5 286 728
	41 043	Linn County......................................	116 672		13 013	Barrow County	69 367
10580		Albany-Schenectady-Troy, NY	870 716		13 015	Bartow County	100 157
	36 001	Albany County	304 204		13 035	Butts County	23 655
	36 083	Rensselaer County	159 429		13 045	Carroll County	110 527
	36 091	Saratoga County..............................	219 607		13 057	Cherokee County..............................	214 346
	36 093	Schenectady County........................	154 727		13 063	Clayton County	259 424
	36 095	Schoharie County............................	32 749		13 067	Cobb County	688 078
10740		Albuquerque, NM	887 077		13 077	Coweta County.................................	127 317
	35 001	Bernalillo County..............................	662 564		13 085	Dawson County................................	22 330
	35 043	Sandoval County	131 561		13 089	DeKalb County.................................	691 893
	35 057	Torrance County	16 383		13 097	Douglas County	132 403
	35 061	Valencia County...............................	76 569		13 113	Fayette County	106 567
10780		Alexandria, LA..................................	153 922		13 117	Forsyth County.................................	175 511
	22 043	Grant Parish....................................	22 309		13 121	Fulton County	920 581
	22 079	Rapides Parish	131 613		13 135	Gwinnett County	805 321
10900		Allentown-Bethlehem-Easton, PA-NJ...............	821 173		13 143	Haralson County	28 780
	34 041	Warren County.................................	108 692		13 149	Heard County	11 834
	42 025	Carbon County.................................	65 249		13 151	Henry County	203 922
	42 077	Lehigh County..................................	349 497		13 159	Jasper County..................................	13 900
	42 095	Northampton County........................	297 735		13 171	Lamar County	18 317
11020		Altoona, PA	127 089		13 199	Meriwether County...........................	21 992
	42 013	Blair County	127 089		13 211	Morgan County	17 868
11100		Amarillo, TX......................................	251 933		13 217	Newton County	99 958
	48 011	Armstrong County	1 901		13 223	Paulding County	142 324
	48 065	Carson County	6 182		13 227	Pickens County................................	29 431
	48 359	Oldham County................................	2 052		13 231	Pike County	17 869
	48 375	Potter County...................................	121 073		13 247	Rockdale County..............................	85 215
	48 381	Randall County................................	120 725		13 255	Spalding County	64 073
11180		Ames, IA...	89 542		13 297	Walton County..................................	83 768
	19 169	Story County....................................	89 542	12100		Atlantic City-Hammonton, NJ............	274 549
11260		Anchorage, AK..................................	380 821		34 001	Atlantic County.................................	274 549
	02 020	Anchorage Municipality....................	291 826	12220		Auburn-Opelika, AL..........................	140 247
	02 170	Matanuska-Susitna Borough	88 995		01 081	Lee County.......................................	140 247
11460		Ann Arbor, MI...................................	344 791	12260		Augusta-Richmond County, GA-SC...............	564 873
	26 161	Washtenaw County...........................	344 791		13 033	Burke County	23 316
11500		Anniston-Oxford-Jacksonville, AL	118 572		13 073	Columbia County	124 053
	01 015	Calhoun County................................	118 572		13 181	Lincoln County	7 996
					13 189	McDuffie County...............................	21 875
					13 245	Richmond County	200 549
					45 003	Aiken County	160 099
					45 037	Edgefield County..............................	26 985

Metropolitan Statistical Areas, Metropolitan Divisions, and Components (as defined February 2013)–*Continued*

Core based statistical area	State/ County FIPS code	Title and Geographic Components	2010 Census Population	Core based statistical area	State/ County FIPS code	Title and Geographic Components	2010 Census Population
12420		Austin-Round Rock, TX................................	1716 289	13780		Binghamton, NY	251 725
	48 021	Bastrop County...............................	74 171		36 007	Broome County................................	200 600
	48 055	Caldwell County..............................	38 066		36 107	Tioga County	51 125
	48 209	Hays County	157 107	13820		Birmingham-Hoover, AL	1128 047
	48 453	Travis County................................	1024 266		01 007	Bibb County	22 915
	48 491	Williamson County	422 679		01 009	Blount County	57 322
12540		Bakersfield, CA................................	839 631		01 021	Chilton County	43 643
	06 029	Kern County	839 631		01 073	Jefferson County................................	658 466
12580		Baltimore-Columbia-Towson, MD	2710 489		01 115	St. Clair County	83 593
	24 003	Anne Arundel County	537 656		01 117	Shelby County	195 085
	24 005	Baltimore County	805 029		01 127	Walker County	67 023
	24 013	Carroll County...............................	167 134	13900		Bismarck, ND	114 778
	24 025	Harford County	244 826		38 015	Burleigh County	81 308
	24 027	Howard County	287 085		38 059	Morton County	27 471
	24 035	Queen Anne's County	47 798		38 065	Oliver County	1 846
	24 510	Baltimore city................................	620 961		38 085	Sioux County	4 153
12620		Bangor, ME	153 923	13980		Blacksburg-Christiansburg-Radford, VA	178 237
	23 019	Penobscot County	153 923		51 063	Floyd County	15 279
12700		Barnstable Town, MA............................	215 888		51 071	Giles County	17 286
	25 001	Barnstable County	215 888		51 121	Montgomery County	94 392
12940		Baton Rouge, LA...............................	802 484		51 155	Pulaski County................................	34 872
	22 005	Ascension Parish.............................	107 215		51 750	Radford city................................	16 408
	22 033	East Baton Rouge Parish	440 171	14010		Bloomington, IL	186 133
	22 037	East Feliciana Parish.........................	20 267		17 039	De Witt County	16 561
	22 047	Iberville Parish	33 387		17 113	McLean County................................	169 572
	22 063	Livingston Parish	128 026	14020		Bloomington, IN................................	159 549
	22 077	Pointe Coupee Parish.........................	22 802		18 105	Monroe County	137 974
	22 091	St. Helena Parish............................	11 203		18 119	Owen County	21 575
	22 121	West Baton Rouge Parish	23 788	14100		Bloomsburg-Berwick, PA................................	85 562
	22 125	West Feliciana Parish	15 625		42 037	Columbia County	67 295
12980		Battle Creek, MI	136 146		42 093	Montour County	18 267
	26 025	Calhoun County	136 146	14260		Boise City, ID	616 561
13020		Bay City, MI..................................	107 771		16 001	Ada County	392 365
	26 017	Bay County	107 771		16 015	Boise County	7 028
13140		Beaumont-Port Arthur, TX........................	403 190		16 027	Canyon County	188 923
	48 199	Hardin County	54 635		16 045	Gem County	16 719
	48 245	Jefferson County.............................	252 273		16 073	Owyhee County	11 526
	48 351	Newton County	14 445	14460		Boston-Cambridge-Newton, MA-NH	4552 402
	48 361	Orange County	81 837			Boston, MA Div 14454	1887 792
13220		Beckley, WV..................................	124 898		25 021	Norfolk County	670 850
	54 019	Fayette County	46 039		25 023	Plymouth County................................	494 919
	54 081	Raleigh County	78 859		25 025	Suffolk County	722 023
13380		Bellingham, WA................................	201 140			Cambridge-Newton-Framingham, MA Div 15764	2246 244
	53 073	Whatcom County	201 140		25 009	Essex County	743 159
13460		Bend-Redmond, OR.............................	157 733		25 017	Middlesex County................................	1503 085
	41 017	Deschutes County	157 733			Rockingham County-Strafford County, NH Div 40484	418 366
13740		Billings, MT..................................	158 934		33 015	Rockingham County................................	295 223
	30 009	Carbon County	10 078		33 017	Strafford County	123 143
	30 037	Golden Valley County.........................	884	14500		Boulder, CO................................	294 567
	30 111	Yellowstone County...........................	147 972		08 013	Boulder County	294 567

Metropolitan Statistical Areas, Metropolitan Divisions, and Components (as defined February 2013)–*Continued*

Core based statistical area	State/ County FIPS code	Title and Geographic Components	2010 Census Population	Core based statistical area	State/ County FIPS code	Title and Geographic Components	2010 Census Population
14540		Bowling Green, KY	158 599	16580		Champaign-Urbana, IL	231 891
	21 003	Allen County	19 956		17 019	Champaign County	201 081
	21 031	Butler County	12 690		17 053	Ford County	14 081
	21 061	Edmonson County	12 161		17 147	Piatt County	16 729
	21 227	Warren County	113 792				
				16620		Charleston, WV	227 078
14740		Bremerton-Silverdale, WA	251 133		54 005	Boone County	24 629
	53 035	Kitsap County	251 133		54 015	Clay County	9 386
					54 039	Kanawha County	193 063
14860		Bridgeport-Stamford-Norwalk, CT	916 829	16700		Charleston-North Charleston, SC	664 607
	09 001	Fairfield County	916 829		45 015	Berkeley County	177 843
15180		Brownsville-Harlingen, TX	406 220		45 019	Charleston County	350 209
	48 061	Cameron County	406 220		45 035	Dorchester County	136 555
15260		Brunswick, GA	112 370	16740		Charlotte-Concord-Gastonia, NC-SC	2217 012
	13 025	Brantley County	18 411		37 025	Cabarrus County	178 011
	13 127	Glynn County	79 626		37 071	Gaston County	206 086
	13 191	McIntosh County	14 333		37 097	Iredell County	159 437
					37 109	Lincoln County	78 265
15380		Buffalo-Cheektowaga-Niagara Falls, NY	1135 509		37 119	Mecklenburg County	919 628
	36 029	Erie County	919 040		37 159	Rowan County	138 428
	36 063	Niagara County	216 469		37 179	Union County	201 292
					45 023	Chester County	33 140
15500		Burlington, NC	151 131		45 057	Lancaster County	76 652
	37 001	Alamance County	151 131		45 091	York County	226 073
15540		Burlington-South Burlington, VT	211 261	16820		Charlottesville, VA	218 705
	50 007	Chittenden County	156 545		51 003	Albemarle County	98 970
	50 011	Franklin County	47 746		51 029	Buckingham County	17 146
	50 013	Grand Isle County	6 970		51 065	Fluvanna County	25 691
					51 079	Greene County	18 403
15680		California-Lexington Park, MD	105 151		51 125	Nelson County	15 020
	24 037	St. Mary's County	105 151		51 540	Charlottesville city	43 475
15940		Canton-Massillon, OH	404 422	16860		Chattanooga, TN-GA	528 143
	39 019	Carroll County	28 836		13 047	Catoosa County	63 942
	39 151	Stark County	375 586		13 083	Dade County	16 633
					13 295	Walker County	68 756
15980		Cape Coral-Fort Myers, FL	618 754		47 065	Hamilton County	336 463
	12 071	Lee County	618 754		47 115	Marion County	28 237
					47 153	Sequatchie County	14 112
16020		Cape Girardeau, MO-IL	96 275				
	17 003	Alexander County	8 238	16940		Cheyenne, WY	91 738
	29 017	Bollinger County	12 363		56 021	Laramie County	91 738
	29 031	Cape Girardeau County	75 674				
16060		Carbondale-Marion, IL	126 575				
	17 077	Jackson County	60 218				
	17 199	Williamson County	66 357				
16180		Carson City, NV	55 274				
	32 510	Carson City	55 274				
16220		Casper, WY	75 450				
	56 025	Natrona County	75 450				
16300		Cedar Rapids, IA	257 940				
	19 011	Benton County	26 076				
	19 105	Jones County	20 638				
	19 113	Linn County	211 226				
16540		Chambersburg-Waynesboro, PA	149 618				
	42 055	Franklin County	149 618				

Metropolitan Statistical Areas, Metropolitan Divisions, and Components (as defined February 2013)–*Continued*

Core based statistical area	State/ County FIPS code	Title and Geographic Components	2010 Census Population	Core based statistical area	State/ County FIPS code	Title and Geographic Components	2010 Census Population
16980		Chicago-Naperville-Elgin, IL-IN-WI	9461 105	17780		College Station-Bryan, TX.............................	228 660
		Chicago-Naperville-Arlington Heights, IL			48 041	Brazos County	194 851
		Div 16974...	7262 718		48 051	Burleson County	17 187
	17 031	Cook County	5194 675		48 395	Robertson County	16 622
	17 043	DuPage County..............................	916 924				
	17 063	Grundy County	50 063	17820		Colorado Springs, CO	645 613
	17 093	Kendall County	114 736		08 041	El Paso County	622 263
	17 111	McHenry County	308 760		08 119	Teller County	23 350
	17 197	Will County	677 560				
		Elgin, IL Div 20994	620 429	17860		Columbia, MO	162 642
	17 037	DeKalb County	105 160		29 019	Boone County	162 642
	17 089	Kane County	515 269				
		Gary, IN Div 23844	708 070	17900		Columbia, SC	767 598
	18 073	Jasper County	33 478		45 017	Calhoun County............................	15 175
	18 089	Lake County	496 005		45 039	Fairfield County	23 956
	18 111	Newton County.............................	14 244		45 055	Kershaw County	61 697
	18 127	Porter County	164 343		45 063	Lexington County	262 391
		Lake County-Kenosha County, IL-WI Div			45 079	Richland County	384 504
		29404	869 888		45 081	Saluda County	19 875
	17 097	Lake County	703 462				
	55 059	Kenosha County............................	166 426	17980		Columbus, GA-AL	294 865
					01 113	Russell County.............................	52 947
17020		Chico, CA	220 000		13 053	Chattahoochee County	11 267
	06 007	Butte County	220 000		13 145	Harris County	32 024
17140		Cincinnati, OH-KY-IN	2114 580		13 197	Marion County	8 742
	18 029	Dearborn County	50 047		13 215	Muscogee County	189 885
	18 115	Ohio County.................................	6 128	18020		Columbus, IN...	76 794
	18 161	Union County	7 516		18 005	Bartholomew County	76 794
	21 015	Boone County	118 811				
	21 023	Bracken County	8 488	18140		Columbus, OH	1901 974
	21 037	Campbell County	90 336		39 041	Delaware County	174 214
	21 077	Gallatin County	8 589		39 045	Fairfield County	146 156
	21 081	Grant County	24 662		39 049	Franklin County	1163 414
	21 117	Kenton County	159 720		39 073	Hocking County	29 380
	21 191	Pendleton County	14 877		39 089	Licking County	166 492
	39 015	Brown County	44 846		39 097	Madison County	43 435
	39 017	Butler County	368 130		39 117	Morrow County	34 827
	39 025	Clermont County	197 363		39 127	Perry County	36 058
	39 061	Hamilton County	802 374		39 129	Pickaway County	55 698
	39 165	Warren County	212 693		39 159	Union County	52 300
17300		Clarksville, TN-KY	260 625	18580		Corpus Christi, TX..	428 185
	21 047	Christian County	73 955		48 007	Aransas County	23 158
	21 221	Trigg County	14 339		48 355	Nueces County	340 223
	47 125	Montgomery County	172 331		48 409	San Patricio County........................	64 804
17420		Cleveland, TN...............................	115 788	18700		Corvallis, OR	85 579
	47 011	Bradley County	98 963		41 003	Benton County..............................	85 579
	47 139	Polk County	16 825				
				18880		Crestview-Fort Walton Beach-Destin, FL.........	235 865
17460		Cleveland-Elyria, OH......................	2077 240		12 091	Okaloosa County	180 822
	39 035	Cuyahoga County...........................	1280 122		12 131	Walton County..............................	55 043
	39 055	Geauga County..............................	93 389				
	39 085	Lake County	230 041	19060		Cumberland, MD-WV	103 299
	39 093	Lorain County	301 356		24 001	Allegany County............................	75 087
	39 103	Medina County..............................	172 332		54 057	Mineral County.............................	28 212
17660		Coeur d'Alene, ID...........................	138 494				
	16 055	Kootenai County	138 494				

Metropolitan Statistical Areas,
Metropolitan Divisions,
and Components
(as defined February 2013)–*Continued*

Core based statistical area	State/ County FIPS code	Title and Geographic Components	2010 Census Population	Core based statistical area	State/ County FIPS code	Title and Geographic Components	2010 Census Population
19100		Dallas-Fort Worth-Arlington, TX	6426 214	19780		Des Moines-West Des Moines, IA	569 633
		Dallas-Plano-Irving, TX Div 19124	4230 520		19 049	Dallas County	66 135
	48 085	Collin County..	782 341		19 077	Guthrie County..	10 954
	48 113	Dallas County..	2368 139		19 121	Madison County	15 679
	48 121	Denton County	662 614		19 153	Polk County	430 640
	48 139	Ellis County	149 610		19 181	Warren County	46 225
	48 231	Hunt County	86 129				
	48 257	Kaufman County	103 350	19820		Detroit-Warren-Dearborn, MI........................	4296 250
	48 397	Rockwall County	78 337			Detroit-Dearborn-Livonia, MI Div 19804.......	1820 584
		Fort Worth-Arlington, TX Div 23104	2195 694		26 163	Wayne County	1820 584
	48 221	Hood County	51 182			Warren-Troy-Farmington Hills, MI 47664	2475 666
	48 251	Johnson County	150 934		26 087	Lapeer County	88 319
	48 367	Parker County	116 927		26 093	Livingston County...	180 967
	48 425	Somervell County	8 490		26 099	Macomb County	840 978
	48 439	Tarrant County	1809 034		26 125	Oakland County	1202 362
	48 497	Wise County	59 127		26 147	St. Clair County..	163 040
19140		Dalton, GA..	142 227	20020		Dothan, AL	145 639
	13 213	Murray County	39 628		01 061	Geneva County..	26 790
	13 313	Whitfield County...	102 599		01 067	Henry County	17 302
					01 069	Houston County...	101 547
19180		Danville, IL...	81 625				
	17 183	Vermilion County	81 625	20100		Dover, DE..	162 310
					10 001	Kent County	162 310
19300		Daphne-Fairhope-Foley, AL..........................	182 265				
	01 003	Baldwin County..	182 265	20220		Dubuque, IA	93 653
					19 061	Dubuque County..	93 653
19340		Davenport-Moline-Rock Island, IA-IL	379 690				
	17 073	Henry County	50 486	20260		Duluth, MN-WI...	279 771
	17 131	Mercer County	16 434		27 017	Carlton County...	35 386
	17 161	Rock Island County	147 546		27 137	St. Louis County	200 226
	19 163	Scott County	165 224		55 031	Douglas County...	44 159
19380		Dayton, OH..	799 232	20500		Durham-Chapel Hill, NC................................	504 357
	39 057	Greene County	161 573		37 037	Chatham County..	63 505
	39 109	Miami County	102 506		37 063	Durham County..	267 587
	39 113	Montgomery County	535 153		37 135	Orange County	133 801
					37 145	Person County	39 464
19460		Decatur, AL	153 829				
	01 079	Lawrence County..	34 339	20700		East Stroudsburg, PA...................................	169 842
	01 103	Morgan County	119 490		42 089	Monroe County	169 842
19500		Decatur, IL...	110 768	20740		Eau Claire, WI...	161 151
	17 115	Macon County..	110 768		55 017	Chippewa County	62 415
					55 035	Eau Claire County	98 736
19660		Deltona-Daytona Beach-Ormond Beach, FL ...	590 289				
	12 035	Flagler County	95 696	20940		El Centro, CA	174 528
	12 127	Volusia County	494 593		06 025	Imperial County...	174 528
19740		Denver-Aurora-Lakewood, CO.......................	2543 482	21060		Elizabethtown-Fort Knox, KY	148 338
	08 001	Adams County	441 603		21 093	Hardin County...	105 543
	08 005	Arapahoe County	572 003		21 123	Larue County	14 193
	08 014	Broomfield County..	55 889		21 163	Meade County	28 602
	08 019	Clear Creek County	9 088				
	08 031	Denver County	600 158	21140		Elkhart-Goshen, IN.......................................	197 559
	08 035	Douglas County	285 465		18 039	Elkhart County	197 559
	08 039	Elbert County	23 086				
	08 047	Gilpin County	5 441	21300		Elmira, NY	88 830
	08 059	Jefferson County..	534 543		36 015	Chemung County...	88 830
	08 093	Park County...	16 206				
				21340		El Paso, TX	804 123
					48 141	El Paso County..	800 647
					48 229	Hudspeth County	3 476

Metropolitan Statistical Areas, Metropolitan Divisions, and Components (as defined February 2013)–*Continued*

Core based statistical area	State/ County FIPS code	Title and Geographic Components	2010 Census Population	Core based statistical area	State/ County FIPS code	Title and Geographic Components	2010 Census Population
21500		Erie, PA	280 566	23420		Fresno, CA	930 450
	42 049	Erie County	280 566		06 019	Fresno County	930 450
21660		Eugene, OR	351 715	23460		Gadsden, AL	104 430
	41 039	Lane County	351 715		01 055	Etowah County	104 430
21780		Evansville, IN-KY	311 552	23540		Gainesville, FL	264 275
	18 129	Posey County	25 910		12 001	Alachua County	247 336
	18 163	Vanderburgh County	179 703		12 041	Gilchrist County	16 939
	18 173	Warrick County	59 689	23580		Gainesville, GA	179 684
	21 101	Henderson County	46 250		13 139	Hall County	179 684
21820		Fairbanks, AK	97 581				
	02 090	Fairbanks North Star Borough	97 581	23900		Gettysburg, PA	101 407
					42 001	Adams County	101 407
22020		Fargo, ND-MN	208 777				
	27 027	Clay County	58 999	24020		Glens Falls, NY	128 923
	38 017	Cass County	149 778		36 113	Warren County	65 707
					36 115	Washington County	63 216
22140		Farmington, NM	130 044				
	35 045	San Juan County	130 044	24140		Goldsboro, NC	122 623
					37 191	Wayne County	122 623
22180		Fayetteville, NC	366 383				
	37 051	Cumberland County	319 431	24220		Grand Forks, ND-MN	98 461
	37 093	Hoke County	46 952		27 119	Polk County	31 600
					38 035	Grand Forks County	66 861
22220		Fayetteville-Springdale-Rogers, AR-MO	463 204				
	05 007	Benton County	221 339	24260		Grand Island, NE	81 850
	05 087	Madison County	15 717		31 079	Hall County	58 607
	05 143	Washington County	203 065		31 081	Hamilton County	9 124
	29 119	McDonald County	23 083		31 093	Howard County	6 274
					31 121	Merrick County	7 845
22380		Flagstaff, AZ	134 421				
	04 005	Coconino County	134 421	24300		Grand Junction, CO	146 723
					08 077	Mesa County	146 723
22420		Flint, MI	425 790				
	26 049	Genesee County	425 790	24340		Grand Rapids-Wyoming, MI	988 938
					26 015	Barry County	59 173
22500		Florence, SC	205 566		26 081	Kent County	602 622
	45 031	Darlington County	68 681		26 117	Montcalm County	63 342
	45 041	Florence County	136 885		26 139	Ottawa County	263 801
22520		Florence-Muscle Shoals, AL	147 137	24420		Grants Pass, OR	82 713
	01 033	Colbert County	54 428		41 033	Josephine County	82 713
	01 077	Lauderdale County	92 709				
				24500		Great Falls, MT	81 327
22540		Fond du Lac, WI	101 633		30 013	Cascade County	81 327
	55 039	Fond du Lac County	101 633				
				24540		Greeley, CO	252 825
22660		Fort Collins, CO	299 630		08 123	Weld County	252 825
	08 069	Larimer County	299 630				
				24580		Green Bay, WI	306 241
22900		Fort Smith, AR-OK	280 467		55 009	Brown County	248 007
	05 033	Crawford County	61 948		55 061	Kewaunee County	20 574
	05 131	Sebastian County	125 744		55 083	Oconto County	37 660
	40 079	Le Flore County	50 384				
	40 135	Sequoyah County	42 391	24660		Greensboro-High Point, NC	723 801
					37 081	Guilford County	488 406
23060		Fort Wayne, IN	416 257		37 151	Randolph County	141 752
	18 003	Allen County	355 329		37 157	Rockingham County	93 643
	18 179	Wells County	27 636				
	18 183	Whitley County	33 292	24780		Greenville, NC	168 148
					37 147	Pitt County	168 148

Metropolitan Statistical Areas, Metropolitan Divisions, and Components (as defined February 2013)–*Continued*

Core based statistical area	State/ County FIPS code	Title and Geographic Components	2010 Census Population	Core based statistical area	State/ County FIPS code	Title and Geographic Components	2010 Census Population
24860		Greenville-Anderson-Mauldin, SC	824 112	26420		Houston-The Woodlands-Sugar Land, TX	5920 416
	45 007	Anderson County	187 126		48 015	Austin County	28 417
	45 045	Greenville County	451 225		48 039	Brazoria County	313 166
	45 059	Laurens County	66 537		48 071	Chambers County	35 096
	45 077	Pickens County	119 224		48 157	Fort Bend County	585 375
					48 167	Galveston County	291 309
25060		Gulfport-Biloxi-Pascagoula, MS	370 702		48 201	Harris County	4092 459
	28 045	Hancock County	43 929		48 291	Liberty County	75 643
	28 047	Harrison County	187 105		48 339	Montgomery County	455 746
	28 059	Jackson County	139 668		48 473	Waller County	43 205
25180		Hagerstown-Martinsburg, MD-WV	251 599	26580		Huntington-Ashland, WV-KY-OH	364 908
	24 043	Washington County	147 430		21 019	Boyd County	49 542
	54 003	Berkeley County	104 169		21 089	Greenup County	36 910
					39 087	Lawrence County	62 450
25220		Hammond, LA	121 097		54 011	Cabell County	96 319
	22 105	Tangipahoa Parish	121 097		54 043	Lincoln County	21 720
					54 079	Putnam County	55 486
25260		Hanford-Corcoran, CA	152 982		54 099	Wayne County	42 481
	06 031	Kings County	152 982				
				26620		Huntsville, AL	417 593
25420		Harrisburg-Carlisle, PA	549 475		01 083	Limestone County	82 782
	42 041	Cumberland County	235 406		01 089	Madison County	334 811
	42 043	Dauphin County	268 100				
	42 099	Perry County	45 969	26820		Idaho Falls, ID	133 265
					16 019	Bonneville County	104 234
25500		Harrisonburg, VA	125 228		16 023	Butte County	2 891
	51 165	Rockingham County	76 314		16 051	Jefferson County	26 140
	51 660	Harrisonburg city	48 914				
				26900		Indianapolis-Carmel-Anderson, IN	1887 877
25540		Hartford-West Hartford-East Hartford, CT	1212 381		18 011	Boone County	56 640
	09 003	Hartford County	894 014		18 013	Brown County	15 242
	09 007	Middlesex County	165 676		18 057	Hamilton County	274 569
	09 013	Tolland County	152 691		18 059	Hancock County	70 002
					18 063	Hendricks County	145 448
25620		Hattiesburg, MS	142 842		18 081	Johnson County	139 654
	28 035	Forrest County	74 934		18 095	Madison County	131 636
	28 073	Lamar County	55 658		18 097	Marion County	903 393
	28 111	Perry County	12 250		18 109	Morgan County	68 894
					18 133	Putnam County	37 963
25860		Hickory-Lenoir-Morganton, NC	365 497		18 145	Shelby County	44 436
	37 003	Alexander County	37 198				
	37 023	Burke County	90 912	26980		Iowa City, IA	152 586
	37 027	Caldwell County	83 029		19 103	Johnson County	130 882
	37 035	Catawba County	154 358		19 183	Washington County	21 704
25940		Hilton Head Island-Bluffton-Beaufort, NC	187 010	27060		Ithaca, NY	101 564
	45 013	Beaufort County	162 233		36 109	Tompkins County	101 564
	45 053	Jasper County	24 777				
				27100		Jackson, MI	160 248
25980		Hinesville, GA	77 917		26 075	Jackson County	160 248
	13 179	Liberty County	63 453				
	13 183	Long County	14 464	27140		Jackson, MS	567 122
					28 029	Copiah County	29 449
26140		Homosassa Springs, FL	141 236		28 049	Hinds County	245 285
	12 017	Citrus County	141 236		28 089	Madison County	95 203
					28 121	Rankin County	141 617
26300		Hot Springs, AR	96 024		28 127	Simpson County	27 503
	05 051	Garland County	96 024		28 163	Yazoo County	28 065
26380		Houma-Thibodaux, LA	208 178	27180		Jackson, TN	130 011
	22 057	Lafourche Parish	96 318		47 023	Chester County	17 131
	22 109	Terrebonne Parish	111 860		47 033	Crockett County	14 586
					47 113	Madison County	98 294

Core based statistical area	State/County FIPS code	Title and Geographic Components	2010 Census Population	Core based statistical area	State/County FIPS code	Title and Geographic Components	2010 Census Population
27260		Jacksonville, FL	1345 596	28420		Kennewick-Richland, WA	253 340
	12 003	Baker County	27 115		53 005	Benton County	175 177
	12 019	Clay County	190 865		53 021	Franklin County	78 163
	12 031	Duval County	864 263				
	12 089	Nassau County	73 314	28660		Killeen-Temple, TX	405 300
	12 109	St. Johns County	190 039		48 027	Bell County	310 235
					48 099	Coryell County	75 388
27340		Jacksonville, NC	177 772		48 281	Lampasas County	19 677
	37 133	Onslow County	177 772				
				28700		Kingsport-Bristol-Bristol, TN-VA	309 544
27500		Janesville-Beloit, WI	160 331		47 073	Hawkins County	56 833
	55 105	Rock County	160 331		47 163	Sullivan County	156 823
					51 169	Scott County	23 177
27620		Jefferson City, MO	149 807		51 191	Washington County	54 876
	29 027	Callaway County	44 332		51 520	Bristol city	17 835
	29 051	Cole County	75 990				
	29 135	Moniteau County	15 607	28740		Kingston, NY	182 493
	29 151	Osage County	13 878		36 111	Ulster County	182 493
27740		Johnson City, TN	198 716	28940		Knoxville, TN	837 571
	47 019	Carter County	57 424		47 001	Anderson County	75 129
	47 171	Unicoi County	18 313		47 009	Blount County	123 010
	47 179	Washington County	122 979		47 013	Campbell County	40 716
					47 057	Grainger County	22 657
27780		Johnstown, PA	143 679		47 093	Knox County	432 226
	42 021	Cambria County	143 679		47 105	Loudon County	48 556
					47 129	Morgan County	21 987
27860		Jonesboro, AR	121 026		47 145	Roane County	54 181
	05 031	Craighead County	96 443		47 173	Union County	19 109
	05 111	Poinsett County	24 583				
				29020		Kokomo, IN	82 752
27900		Joplin, MO	175 518		18 067	Howard County	82 752
	29 097	Jasper County	117 404				
	29 145	Newton County	58 114	29100		La Crosse-Onalaska, WI-MN	133 665
					27 055	Houston County	19 027
27980		Kahului-Wailuku-Lahaina, HI	154 924		55 063	La Crosse County	114 638
	15 005	Kalawao County	90				
	15 009	Maui County	154 834	29180		Lafayette, LA	466 750
					22 001	Acadia Parish	61 773
					22 045	Iberia Parish	73 240
28020		Kalamazoo-Portage, MI	326 589		22 055	Lafayette Parish	221 578
	26 077	Kalamazoo County	250 331		22 099	St. Martin Parish	52 160
	26 159	Van Buren County	76 258		22 113	Vermilion Parish	57 999
28100		Kankakee, IL	113 449			Lafayette-West Lafayette, IN	201 789
	17 091	Kankakee County	113 449	29200			
					18 007	Benton County	8 854
28140		Kansas City, MO-KS	2009 342		18 015	Carroll County	20 155
	20 091	Johnson County	544 179		18 157	Tippecanoe County	172 780
	20 103	Leavenworth County	76 227				
	20 107	Linn County	9 656	29340		Lake Charles, LA	199 607
	20 121	Miami County	32 787		22 019	Calcasieu Parish	192 768
	20 209	Wyandotte County	157 505		22 023	Cameron Parish	6 839
	29 013	Bates County	17 049				
	29 025	Caldwell County	9 424	29420		Lake Havasu City-Kingman, AZ	200 186
	29 037	Cass County	99 478		04 015	Mohave County	200 186
	29 047	Clay County	221 939				
	29 049	Clinton County	20 743	29460		Lakeland-Winter Haven, FL	602 095
	29 095	Jackson County	674 158		12 105	Polk County	602 095
	29 107	Lafayette County	33 381				
	29 165	Platte County	89 322	29540		Lancaster, PA	519 445
	29 177	Ray County	23 494		42 071	Lancaster County	519 445

Metropolitan Statistical Areas, Metropolitan Divisions, and Components (as defined February 2013)–*Continued*

Core based statistical area	State/County FIPS code	Title and Geographic Components	2010 Census Population	Core based statistical area	State/County FIPS code	Title and Geographic Components	2010 Census Population
29620		Lansing-East Lansing, MI....................	464 036	31020		Longview, WA..................................	102 410
	26 037	Clinton County.......................	75 382		53 015	Cowlitz County................................	102 410
	26 045	Eaton County........................	107 759				
	26 065	Ingham County.......................	280 895	31080		Los Angeles-Long Beach-Anaheim, CA	12828 837
						Anaheim-Santa Ana-Irvine, CA Div 11244...	3010 232
29700		Laredo, TX...................................	250 304		06 059	Orange County................................	3010 232
	48 479	Webb County........................	250 304			Los Angeles-Long Beach-Glendale, CA Div 31084..........................	9818 605
29740		Las Cruces, NM	209 233		06 037	Los Angeles County............................	9818 605
	35 013	Dona Ana County....................	209 233				
				31140		Louisville/Jefferson County, KY-IN..................	1235 708
29820		Las Vegas-Henderson-Paradise, NV	1951 269		18 019	Clark County................................	110 232
	32 003	Clark County.........................	1951 269		18 043	Floyd County................................	74 578
					18 061	Harrison County..............................	39 364
29940		Lawrence, KS................................	110 826		18 143	Scott County................................	24 181
	20 045	Douglas County......................	110 826		18 175	Washington County...........................	28 262
					21 029	Bullitt County................................	74 319
30020		Lawton, OK..................................	130 291		21 103	Henry County................................	15 416
	40 031	Comanche County.....................	124 098		21 111	Jefferson County..............................	741 096
	40 033	Cotton County.......................	6 193		21 185	Oldham County...............................	60 316
					21 211	Shelby County................................	42 074
30140		Lebanon, PA.................................	133 568		21 215	Spencer County...............................	17 061
	42 075	Lebanon County......................	133 568		21 223	Trimble County...............................	8 809
30300		Lewiston, ID-WA.............................	60 888	31180		Lubbock, TX.................................	290 805
	16 069	Nez Perce County....................	39 265		48 107	Crosby County................................	6 059
	53 003	Asotin County........................	21 623		48 303	Lubbock County..............................	278 831
					48 305	Lynn County.................................	5 915
30340		Lewiston-Auburn, ME.........................	107 702				
	23 001	Androscoggin County..................	107 702	31340		Lynchburg, VA................................	252 634
					51 009	Amherst County...............................	32 353
30460		Lexington-Fayette, KY........................	472 099		51 011	Appomattox County...........................	14 973
	21 017	Bourbon County......................	19 985		51 019	Bedford County...............................	68 676
	21 049	Clark County.........................	35 613		51 031	Campbell County.............................	54 842
	21 067	Fayette County.......................	295 803		51 515	Bedford city.................................	6 222
	21 113	Jessamine County....................	48 586		51 680	Lynchburg city...............................	75 568
	21 209	Scott County.........................	47 173				
	21 239	Woodford County.....................	24 939	31420		Macon, GA..................................	232 293
					13 021	Bibb County.................................	155 547
30620		Lima, OH....................................	106 331		13 079	Crawford County..............................	12 630
	39 003	Allen County.........................	106 331		13 169	Jones County................................	28 669
					13 207	Monroe County...............................	26 424
30700		Lincoln, NE..................................	302 157		13 289	Twiggs County...............................	9 023
	31 109	Lancaster County.....................	285 407				
	31 159	Seward County.......................	16 750	31460		Madera, CA.................................	150 865
					06 039	Madera County...............................	150 865
30780		Little Rock-North Little Rock-Conway, AR.......	699 757				
	05 045	Faulkner County.....................	113 237	31540		Madison, WI.................................	605 435
	05 053	Grant County........................	17 853		55 021	Columbia County..............................	56 833
	05 085	Lonoke County.......................	68 356		55 025	Dane County................................	488 073
	05 105	Perry County........................	10 445		55 045	Green County................................	36 842
	05 119	Pulaski County.......................	382 748		55 049	Iowa County.................................	23 687
	05 125	Saline County........................	107 118				
				31700		Manchester-Nashua, NH........................	400 721
30860		Logan, UT-ID................................	125 442		33 011	Hillsborough County...........................	400 721
	16 041	Franklin County......................	12 786				
	49 005	Cache County........................	112 656	31740		Manhattan, KS...............................	92 719
					20 149	Pottawatomie County..........................	21 604
30980		Longview, TX................................	214 369		20 161	Riley County.................................	71 115
	48 183	Gregg County........................	121 730				
	48 401	Rusk County.........................	53 330	31860		Mankato-North Mankato, MN....................	96 740
	48 459	Upshur County.......................	39 309		27 013	Blue Earth County............................	64 013
					27 103	Nicollet County...............................	32 727

Core based statistical area	State/ County FIPS code	Title and Geographic Components	2010 Census Population	Core based statistical area	State/ County FIPS code	Title and Geographic Components	2010 Census Population
31900		Mansfield, OH............................	124 475	33460		Minneapolis-St. Paul-Bloomington, MN	3348 859
	39 139	Richland County	124 475		27 003	Anoka County	330 844
32580		McAllen-Edinburg-Mission, TX	774 769		27 019	Carver County	91 042
	48 215	Hidalgo County	774 769		27 025	Chisago County	53 887
32780		Medford, OR............................	203 206		27 037	Dakota County	398 552
	41 029	Jackson County	203 206		27 053	Hennepin County............................	1152 425
32820		Memphis, TN-MS-AR	1324 829		27 059	Isanti County	37 816
	05 035	Crittenden County............................	50 902		27 079	Le Sueur County	27 703
	28 009	Benton County	8 729		27 095	Mille Lacs County	26 097
	28 033	DeSoto County	161 252		27 123	Ramsey County	508 640
	28 093	Marshall County	37 144		27 139	Scott County	129 928
	28 137	Tate County	28 886		27 141	Sherburne County	88 499
	28 143	Tunica County............................	10 778		27 143	Sibley County	15 226
	47 047	Fayette County	38 413		27 163	Washington County	238 136
	47 157	Shelby County	927 644		27 171	Wright County	124 700
	47 167	Tipton County............................	61 081		55 093	Pierce County	41 019
32900		Merced, CA............................	255 793		55 109	St. Croix County	84 345
	06 047	Merced County	255 793	33540		Missoula, MT............................	109 299
33100		Miami-Fort Lauderdale-West Palm Beach, FL.	5564 635		30 063	Missoula County	109 299
		Fort Lauderdale-Pompano Beach-Deerfield Beach, FL Div 22744............................	1748 066	33660		Mobile, AL............................	412 992
	12 011	Broward County	1748 066		01 097	Mobile County............................	412 992
		Miami-Miami Beach-Kendall, FL Div 33124.	2496 435	33700		Modesto, CA............................	514 453
	12 086	Miami-Dade County	2496 435		06 099	Stanislaus County............................	514 453
		West Palm Beach-Boca Raton-Delray Beach, FL Div 48424............................	1320 134	33740		Monroe, LA............................	176 441
					22 073	Ouachita Parish	153 720
	12 099	Palm Beach County	1320 134		22 111	Union Parish	22 721
33140		Michigan City-La Porte, IN	111 467	33780		Monroe, MI............................	152 021
	18 091	LaPorte County............................	111 467		26 115	Monroe County............................	152 021
33220		Midland, MI............................	83 629	33860		Montgomery, AL............................	374 536
	26 111	Midland County	83 629		01 001	Autauga County............................	54 571
33260		Midland, TX............................	141 671		01 051	Elmore County............................	79 303
	48 317	Martin County	4 799		01 085	Lowndes County............................	11 299
	48 329	Midland County............................	136 872		01 101	Montgomery County	229 363
33340		Milwaukee-Waukesha-West Allis, WI.............	1555 908	34060		Morgantown, WV............................	129 709
	55 079	Milwaukee County	947 735		54 061	Monongalia County............................	96 189
	55 089	Ozaukee County	86 395		54 077	Preston County............................	33 520
	55 131	Washington County	131 887	34100		Morristown, TN............................	113 951
	55 133	Waukesha County	389 891		47 063	Hamblen County............................	62 544
					47 089	Jefferson County............................	51 407
				34580		Mount Vernon-Anacortes, WA	116 901
					53 057	Skagit County	116 901
				34620		Muncie, IN............................	117 671
					18 035	Delaware County	117 671
				34740		Muskegon, MI............................	172 188
					26 121	Muskegon County	172 188
				34820		Myrtle Beach-Conway-North Myrtle Beach, NC-SC	376 722
					37 019	Brunswick County............................	107 431
					45 051	Horry County............................	269 291
				34900		Napa, CA............................	136 484
					06 055	Napa County............................	136 484

Core based statistical area	State/ County FIPS code	Title and Geographic Components	2010 Census Population	Core based statistical area	State/ County FIPS code	Title and Geographic Components	2010 Census Population
34940		Naples-Immokalee-Marco Island, FL	321 520	35620		New York-Newark-Jersey City, NY-NJ-PA	19567 410
	12 021	Collier County	321 520			Dutchess County-Putnam County, NY Div 20524	397 198
34980		Nashville-Davidson—Murfreesboro—Franklin, TN	1670 890		36 027	Dutchess County	297 488
	47 015	Cannon County	13 801		36 079	Putnam County	99 710
	47 021	Cheatham County	39 105			Nassau County-Suffolk County, NY Div 35004	2832 882
	47 037	Davidson County	626 681		36 059	Nassau County	1339 532
	47 043	Dickson County	49 666		36 103	Suffolk County	1493 350
	47 081	Hickman County	24 690			Newark, NJ-PA Div 35084	2471 171
	47 111	Macon County	22 248		34 013	Essex County	783 969
	47 119	Maury County	80 956		34 019	Hunterdon County	128 349
	47 147	Robertson County	66 283		34 027	Morris County	492 276
	47 149	Rutherford County	262 604		34 035	Somerset County	323 444
	47 159	Smith County	19 166		34 037	Sussex County	149 265
	47 165	Sumner County	160 645		34 039	Union County	536 499
	47 169	Trousdale County	7 870		42 103	Pike County	57 369
	47 187	Williamson County	183 182			New York-Jersey City-White Plains, NY-NJ Div 35614	13866 159
	47 189	Wilson County	113 993		34 003	Bergen County	905 116
35100		New Bern, NC	126 802		34 017	Hudson County	634 266
	37 049	Craven County	103 505		34 023	Middlesex County	809 858
	37 103	Jones County	10 153		34 025	Monmouth County	630 380
	37 137	Pamlico County	13 144		34 029	Ocean County	576 567
35300		New Haven-Milford, CT	862 477		34 031	Passaic County	501 226
	09 009	New Haven County	862 477		36 005	Bronx County	1385 108
35380		New Orleans-Metairie, LA	1189 866		36 047	Kings County	2504 700
	22 051	Jefferson Parish	432 552		36 061	New York County	1585 873
	22 071	Orleans Parish	343 829		36 071	Orange County	372 813
	22 075	Plaquemines Parish	23 042		36 081	Queens County	2230 722
	22 087	St. Bernard Parish	35 897		36 085	Richmond County	468 730
	22 089	St. Charles Parish	52 780		36 087	Rockland County	311 687
	22 093	St. James Parish	22 102		36 119	Westchester County	949 113
	22 095	St. John the Baptist Parish	45 924	35660		Niles-Benton Harbor, MI	156 813
	22 103	St. Tammany Parish	233 740		26 021	Berrien County	156 813
				35840		North Port-Sarasota-Bradenton, FL	702 281
					12 081	Manatee County	322 833
					12 115	Sarasota County	379 448
				35980		Norwich-New London, CT	274 055
					09 011	New London County	274 055
				36100		Ocala, FL	331 298
					12 083	Marion County	331 298
				36140		Ocean City, NJ	97 265
					34 009	Cape May County	97 265
				36220		Odessa, TX	137 130
					48 135	Ector County	137 130
				36260		Ogden-Clearfield, UT	597 159
					49 003	Box Elder County	49 975
					49 011	Davis County	306 479
					49 029	Morgan County	9 469
					49 057	Weber County	231 236

Core based statistical area	State/County FIPS code	Title and Geographic Components	2010 Census Population	Core based statistical area	State/County FIPS code	Title and Geographic Components	2010 Census Population
36420		Oklahoma City, OK	1252 987	37980		Philadelphia-Camden-Wilmington, PA-NJ-DE-MD	5965 343
	40 017	Canadian County	115 541			Camden, NJ Div 15804	1250 679
	40 027	Cleveland County	255 755		34 005	Burlington County	448 734
	40 051	Grady County	52 431		34 007	Camden County	513 657
	40 081	Lincoln County	34 273		34 015	Gloucester County	288 288
	40 083	Logan County	41 848			Montgomery County-Bucks County-Chester County, PA Div 33874	1924 009
	40 087	McClain County	34 506				
	40 109	Oklahoma County	718 633		42 017	Bucks County	625 249
36500		Olympia-Tumwater, WA	252 264		42 029	Chester County	498 886
	53 067	Thurston County	252 264		42 091	Montgomery County	799 874
36540		Omaha-Council Bluffs, NE-IA	865 350			Philadelphia, PA Div 37964	2084 985
	19 085	Harrison County	14 928		42 045	Delaware County	558 979
	19 129	Mills County	15 059		42 101	Philadelphia County	1526 006
	19 155	Pottawattamie County	93 158			Wilmington, DE-MD-NJ Div 48864	705 670
	31 025	Cass County	25 241		10 003	New Castle County	538 479
	31 055	Douglas County	517 110		24 015	Cecil County	101 108
	31 153	Sarpy County	158 840		34 033	Salem County	66 083
	31 155	Saunders County	20 780	38060		Phoenix-Mesa-Scottsdale, AZ	4192 887
	31 177	Washington County	20 234		04 013	Maricopa County	3817 117
36740		Orlando-Kissimmee-Sanford, FL	2134 411		04 021	Pinal County	375 770
	12 069	Lake County	297 052	38220		Pine Bluff, AR	100 258
	12 095	Orange County	1145 956		05 025	Cleveland County	8 689
	12 097	Osceola County	268 685		05 069	Jefferson County	77 435
	12 117	Seminole County	422 718		05 079	Lincoln County	14 134
36780		Oshkosh-Neenah, WI	166 994	38300		Pittsburgh, PA	2356 285
	55 139	Winnebago County	166 994		42 003	Allegheny County	1223 348
					42 005	Armstrong County	68 941
36980		Owensboro, KY	114 752		42 007	Beaver County	170 539
	21 059	Daviess County	96 656		42 019	Butler County	183 862
	21 091	Hancock County	8 565		42 051	Fayette County	136 606
	21 149	McLean County	9 531		42 125	Washington County	207 820
37100		Oxnard-Thousand Oaks-Ventura, CA	823 318		42 129	Westmoreland County	365 169
	06 111	Ventura County	823 318	38340		Pittsfield, MA	131 219
37340		Palm Bay-Melbourne-Titusville, FL	543 376		25 003	Berkshire County	131 219
	12 009	Brevard County	543 376	38540		Pocatello, ID	82 839
37460		Panama City, FL	184 715		16 005	Bannock County	82 839
	12 005	Bay County	168 852	38860		Portland-South Portland, ME	514 098
	12 045	Gulf County	15 863		23 005	Cumberland County	281 674
37620		Parkersburg-Vienna, WV	92 673		23 023	Sagadahoc County	35 293
	54 105	Wirt County	5 717		23 031	York County	197 131
	54 107	Wood County	86 956	38900		Portland-Vancouver-Hillsboro, OR-WA	2226 009
					41 005	Clackamas County	375 992
37860		Pensacola-Ferry Pass-Brent, FL	448 991		41 009	Columbia County	49 351
	12 033	Escambia County	297 619		41 051	Multnomah County	735 334
	12 113	Santa Rosa County	151 372		41 067	Washington County	529 710
					41 071	Yamhill County	99 193
37900		Peoria, IL	379 186		53 011	Clark County	425 363
	17 123	Marshall County	12 640		53 059	Skamania County	11 066
	17 143	Peoria County	186 494				
	17 175	Stark County	5 994	38940		Port St. Lucie, FL	424 107
	17 179	Tazewell County	135 394		12 085	Martin County	146 318
	17 203	Woodford County	38 664		12 111	St. Lucie County	277 789
				39140		Prescott, AZ	211 033
					04 025	Yavapai County	211 033

Core based statistical area	State/County FIPS code	Title and Geographic Components	2010 Census Population	Core based statistical area	State/County FIPS code	Title and Geographic Components	2010 Census Population
39300		Providence-Warwick, RI-MA	1600 852	40220		Roanoke, VA	308 707
	25 005	Bristol County	548 285		51 023	Botetourt County	33 148
	44 001	Bristol County	49 875		51 045	Craig County	5 190
	44 003	Kent County	166 158		51 067	Franklin County	56 159
	44 005	Newport County	82 888		51 161	Roanoke County	92 376
	44 007	Providence County	626 667		51 770	Roanoke city	97 032
	44 009	Washington County	126 979		51 775	Salem city	24 802
39340		Provo-Orem, UT	526 810	40340		Rochester, MN	206 877
	49 023	Juab County	10 246		27 039	Dodge County	20 087
	49 049	Utah County	516 564		27 045	Fillmore County	20 866
					27 109	Olmsted County	144 248
39380		Pueblo, CO	159 063		27 157	Wabasha County	21 676
	08 101	Pueblo County	159 063				
				40380		Rochester, NY	1079 671
39460		Punta Gorda, FL	159 978		36 051	Livingston County	65 393
	12 015	Charlotte County	159 978		36 055	Monroe County	744 344
					36 069	Ontario County	107 931
39540		Racine, WI	195 408		36 073	Orleans County	42 883
	55 101	Racine County	195 408		36 117	Wayne County	93 772
					36 123	Yates County	25 348
39580		Raleigh, NC	1130 490				
	37 069	Franklin County	60 619	40420		Rockford, IL	349 431
	37 101	Johnston County	168 878		17 007	Boone County	54 165
	37 183	Wake County	900 993		17 201	Winnebago County	295 266
39660		Rapid City, SD	134 598	40580		Rocky Mount, NC	152 392
	46 033	Custer County	8 216		37 065	Edgecombe County	56 552
	46 093	Meade County	25 434		37 127	Nash County	95 840
	46 103	Pennington County	100 948				
				40660		Rome, GA	96 317
39740		Reading, PA	411 442		13 115	Floyd County	96 317
	42 011	Berks County	411 442				
				40900		Sacramento—Roseville—Arden-Arcade, CA	2149 127
39820		Redding, CA	177 223		06 017	El Dorado County	181 058
	06 089	Shasta County	177 223		06 061	Placer County	348 432
					06 067	Sacramento County	1418 788
39900		Reno, NV	425 417		06 113	Yolo County	200 849
	32 029	Storey County	4 010				
	32 031	Washoe County	421 407	40980		Saginaw, MI	200 169
					26 145	Saginaw County	200 169
40060		Richmond, VA	1208 101				
	51 007	Amelia County	12 690	41060		St. Cloud, MN	189 093
	51 033	Caroline County	28 545		27 009	Benton County	38 451
	51 036	Charles City County	7 256		27 145	Stearns County	150 642
	51 041	Chesterfield County	316 236				
	51 053	Dinwiddie County	28 001	41100		St. George, UT	138 115
	51 075	Goochland County	21 717		49 053	Washington County	138 115
	51 085	Hanover County	99 863				
	51 087	Henrico County	306 935	41140		St. Joseph, MO-KS	127 329
	51 101	King William County	15 935		20 043	Doniphan County	7 945
	51 127	New Kent County	18 429		29 003	Andrew County	17 291
	51 145	Powhatan County	28 046		29 021	Buchanan County	89 201
	51 149	Prince George County	35 725		29 063	DeKalb County	12 892
	51 183	Sussex County	12 087				
	51 570	Colonial Heights city	17 411				
	51 670	Hopewell city	22 591				
	51 730	Petersburg city	32 420				
	51 760	Richmond city	204 214				
40140		Riverside-San Bernardino-Ontario, CA	4224 851				
	06 065	Riverside County	2189 641				
	06 071	San Bernardino County	2035 210				

Core based statistical area	State/ County FIPS code	Title and Geographic Components	2010 Census Population	Core based statistical area	State/ County FIPS code	Title and Geographic Components	2010 Census Population
41180		St. Louis, MO-IL	2787 701	41940		San Jose-Sunnyvale-Santa Clara, CA	1836 911
	17 005	Bond County	17 768		06 069	San Benito County	55 269
	17 013	Calhoun County	5 089		06 085	Santa Clara County	1781 642
	17 027	Clinton County	37 762				
	17 083	Jersey County	22 985	42020		San Luis Obispo-Paso Robles-Arroyo Grande, CA	269 637
	17 117	Macoupin County	47 765		06 079	San Luis Obispo County	269 637
	17 119	Madison County	269 282				
	17 133	Monroe County	32 957	42100		Santa Cruz-Watsonville, CA	262 382
	17 163	St. Clair County	270 056		06 087	Santa Cruz County	262 382
	29 071	Franklin County	101 492				
	29 099	Jefferson County	218 733	42140		Santa Fe, NM	144 170
	29 113	Lincoln County	52 566		35 049	Santa Fe County	144 170
	29 183	St. Charles County	360 485				
	29 189	St. Louis County	998 954	42200		Santa Maria-Santa Barbara, CA	423 895
	29 219	Warren County	32 513		06 083	Santa Barbara County	423 895
	29 510	St. Louis city	319 294				
				42220		Santa Rosa, CA	483 878
41420		Salem, OR	390 738		06 097	Sonoma County	483 878
	41 047	Marion County	315 335				
	41 053	Polk County	75 403	42340		Savannah, GA	347 611
41500		Salinas, CA	415 057		13 029	Bryan County	30 233
	06 053	Monterey County	415 057		13 051	Chatham County	265 128
					13 103	Effingham County	52 250
41540		Salisbury, MD-DE	373 802				
	10 005	Sussex County	197 145	42540		Scranton—Wilkes-Barre—Hazleton, PA	563 631
	24 039	Somerset County	26 470		42 069	Lackawanna County	214 437
	24 045	Wicomico County	98 733		42 079	Luzerne County	320 918
	24 047	Worcester County	51 454		42 131	Wyoming County	28 276
41620		Salt Lake City, UT	1087 873	42660		Seattle-Tacoma-Bellevue, WA	3439 809
	49 035	Salt Lake County	1029 655			Seattle-Bellevue-Everett, WA Div 42644	2644 584
	49 045	Tooele County	58 218		53 033	King County	1931 249
					53 061	Snohomish County	713 335
41660		San Angelo, TX	111 823			Tacoma-Lakewood, WA Div 45104	795 225
	48 235	Irion County	1 599		53 053	Pierce County	795 225
	48 451	Tom Green County	110 224				
				42680		Sebastian-Vero Beach, FL	138 028
41700		San Antonio-New Braunfels, TX	2142 508		12 061	Indian River County	138 028
	48 013	Atascosa County	44 911				
	48 019	Bandera County	20 485	42700		Sebring, FL	98 786
	48 029	Bexar County	1714 773		12 055	Highlands County	98 786
	48 091	Comal County	108 472				
	48 187	Guadalupe County	131 533	43100		Sheboygan, WI	115 507
	48 259	Kendall County	33 410		55 117	Sheboygan County	115 507
	48 325	Medina County	46 006				
	48 493	Wilson County	42 918	43300		Sherman-Denison, TX	120 877
					48 181	Grayson County	120 877
41740		San Diego-Carlsbad, CA	3095 313				
	06 073	San Diego County	3095 313	43340		Shreveport-Bossier City, LA	439 811
					22 015	Bossier Parish	116 979
41860		San Francisco-Oakland-Hayward, CA	4335 391		22 017	Caddo Parish	254 969
		Oakland-Hayward-Berkeley, CA Div 36084	2559 296		22 031	De Soto Parish	26 656
	06 001	Alameda County	1510 271		22 119	Webster Parish	41 207
	06 013	Contra Costa County	1049 025				
		San Francisco-Redwood City-South San Francisco, CA Div 41884	1523 686	43420		Sierra Vista-Douglas, AZ	131 346
	06 075	San Francisco County	805 235		04 003	Cochise County	131 346
	06 081	San Mateo County	718 451				
		San Rafael, CA Div 42034	252 409	43580		Sioux City, IA-NE-SD	168 563
	06 041	Marin County	252 409		19 149	Plymouth County	24 986
					19 193	Woodbury County	102 172
					31 043	Dakota County	21 006
					31 051	Dixon County	6 000
					46 127	Union County	14 399

Core based statistical area	State/ County FIPS code	Title and Geographic Components	2010 Census Population	Core based statistical area	State/ County FIPS code	Title and Geographic Components	2010 Census Population
43620		Sioux Falls, SD......................	228 261	45300		Tampa-St. Petersburg-Clearwater, FL............	2783 243
	46 083	Lincoln County.......................	44 828		12 053	Hernando County........................	172 778
	46 087	McCook County	5 618		12 057	Hillsborough County	1229 226
	46 099	Minnehaha County....................	169 468		12 101	Pasco County	464 697
	46 125	Turner County	8 347		12 103	Pinellas County	916 542
43780		South Bend-Mishawaka, IN-MI	319 224	45460		Terre Haute, IN	172 425
	18 141	St. Joseph County....................	266 931		18 021	Clay County	26 890
	26 027	Cass County	52 293		18 153	Sullivan County	21 475
43900		Spartanburg, SC......................	313 268		18 165	Vermillion County	16 212
	45 083	Spartanburg County..................	284 307		18 167	Vigo County	107 848
	45 087	Union County	28 961	45500		Texarkana, TX-AR.....................	149 198
44060		Spokane-Spokane Valley, WA	527 753		05 081	Little River County	13 171
	53 051	Pend Oreille County	13 001		05 091	Miller County...........................	43 462
	53 063	Spokane County	471 221		48 037	Bowie County..........................	92 565
	53 065	Stevens County	43 531	45540		The Villages, FL	93 420
44100		Springfield, IL	210 170		12 119	Sumter County	93 420
	17 129	Menard County	12 705	45780		Toledo, OH	610 001
	17 167	Sangamon County	197 465		39 051	Fulton County	42 698
44140		Springfield, MA.......................	621 570		39 095	Lucas County..........................	441 815
	25 013	Hampden County	463 490		39 173	Wood County	125 488
	25 015	Hampshire County	158 080	45820		Topeka, KS............................	233 870
44180		Springfield, MO.......................	436 712		20 085	Jackson County	13 462
	29 043	Christian County	77 422		20 087	Jefferson County.......................	19 126
	29 059	Dallas County	16 777		20 139	Osage County	16 295
	29 077	Greene County	275 174		20 177	Shawnee County	177 934
	29 167	Polk County	31 137		20 197	Wabaunsee County	7 053
	29 225	Webster County.......................	36 202	45940		Trenton, NJ............................	366 513
44220		Springfield, OH.......................	138 333		34 021	Mercer County	366 513
	39 023	Clark County	138 333	46060		Tucson, AZ............................	980 263
44300		State College, PA.....................	153 990		04 019	Pima County	980 263
	42 027	Centre County.........................	153 990	46140		Tulsa, OK	937 478
44420		Staunton-Waynesboro, VA..............	118 502		40 037	Creek County..........................	69 967
	51 015	Augusta County	73 750		40 111	Okmulgee County	40 069
	51 790	Staunton city	23 746		40 113	Osage County	47 472
	51 820	Waynesboro city	21 006		40 117	Pawnee County	16 577
44700		Stockton-Lodi, CA.....................	685 306		40 131	Rogers County	86 905
	06 077	San Joaquin County	685 306		40 143	Tulsa County	603 403
44940		Sumter, SC............................	107 456		40 145	Wagoner County	73 085
	45 085	Sumter County	107 456	46220		Tuscaloosa, AL........................	230 162
45060		Syracuse, NY	662 577		01 065	Hale County	15 760
	36 053	Madison County	73 442		01 107	Pickens County	19 746
	36 067	Onondaga County.....................	467 026		01 125	Tuscaloosa County	194 656
	36 075	Oswego County	122 109	46340		Tyler, TX..............................	209 714
45220		Tallahassee, FL.......................	367 413		48 423	Smith County	209 714
	12 039	Gadsden County	46 389	46520		Urban Honolulu, HI....................	953 207
	12 065	Jefferson County......................	14 761		15 003	Honolulu County	953 207
	12 073	Leon County	275 487	46540		Utica-Rome, NY	299 397
	12 129	Wakulla County.......................	30 776		36 043	Herkimer County	64 519
					36 065	Oneida County.........................	234 878

Core based statistical area	State/ County FIPS code	Title and Geographic Components	2010 Census Population	Core based statistical area	State/ County FIPS code	Title and Geographic Components	2010 Census Population
46660		Valdosta, GA	139 588	47900		Washington-Arlington-Alexandria, DC-VA-MD-WV	5636 232
	13 027	Brooks County	16 243			Silver Spring-Frederick-Rockville, MD Div 43524	1205 162
	13 101	Echols County	4 034		24 021	Frederick County	233 385
	13 173	Lanier County	10 078		24 031	Montgomery County	971 777
	13 185	Lowndes County	109 233			Washington-Arlington-Alexandria, DC-VA-MD-WV Div 47894	4431 070
46700		Vallejo-Fairfield, CA...............................	413 344		11 001	District of Columbia	601 723
	06 095	Solano County	413 344		24 009	Calvert County	88 737
47020		Victoria, TX..	94 003		24 017	Charles County	146 551
	48 175	Goliad County	7 210		24 033	Prince George's County	863 420
	48 469	Victoria County	86 793		51 013	Arlington County	207 627
47220		Vineland-Bridgeton, NJ	156 898		51 043	Clarke County	14 034
	34 011	Cumberland County	156 898		51 047	Culpeper County	46 689
47260		Virginia Beach-Norfolk-Newport News, VA-NC	1676 822		51 059	Fairfax County	1081 726
	37 053	Currituck County	23 547		51 061	Fauquier County	65 203
	37 073	Gates County	12 197		51 107	Loudoun County	312 311
	51 073	Gloucester County	36 858		51 153	Prince William County	402 002
	51 093	Isle of Wight County	35 270		51 157	Rappahannock County	7 373
	51 095	James City County	67 009		51 177	Spotsylvania County	122 397
	51 115	Mathews County	8 978		51 179	Stafford County	128 961
	51 199	York County	65 464		51 187	Warren County	37 575
	51 550	Chesapeake city	222 209		51 510	Alexandria city	139 966
	51 650	Hampton city	137 436		51 600	Fairfax city	22 565
	51 700	Newport News city	180 719		51 610	Falls Church city	12 332
	51 710	Norfolk city	242 803		51 630	Fredericksburg city	24 286
	51 735	Poquoson city	12 150		51 683	Manassas city	37 821
	51 740	Portsmouth city	95 535		51 685	Manassas Park city	14 273
	51 800	Suffolk city	84 585		54 037	Jefferson County	53 498
	51 810	Virginia Beach city	437 994	47940		Waterloo-Cedar Falls, IA.......................	167 819
	51 830	Williamsburg city	14 068		19 013	Black Hawk County	131 090
47300		Visalia-Porterville, CA............................	442 179		19 017	Bremer County	24 276
	06 107	Tulare County	442 179		19 075	Grundy County	12 453
47380		Waco, TX..	252 772	48060		Watertown-Fort Drum, NY........................	116 229
	48 145	Falls County	17 866		36 045	Jefferson County	116 229
	48 309	McLennan County	234 906	48140		Wausau, WI..	134 063
47460		Walla Walla, WA	62 859		55 073	Marathon County	134 063
	53 013	Columbia County	4 078	48260		Weirton-Steubenville, WV-OH....................	124 454
	53 071	Walla Walla County	58 781		39 081	Jefferson County	69 709
47580		Warner Robins, GA	179 605		54 009	Brooke County	24 069
	13 153	Houston County	139 900		54 029	Hancock County	30 676
	13 225	Peach County	27 695	48300		Wenatchee, WA	110 884
	13 235	Pulaski County	12 010		53 007	Chelan County	72 453
					53 017	Douglas County	38 431
				48540		Wheeling, WV-OH...................................	147 950
					39 013	Belmont County	70 400
					54 051	Marshall County	33 107
					54 069	Ohio County	44 443
				48620		Wichita, KS..	630 919
					20 015	Butler County	65 880
					20 079	Harvey County	34 684
					20 095	Kingman County	7 858
					20 173	Sedgwick County	498 365
					20 191	Sumner County	24 132

Core based statistical area	State/ County FIPS code	Title and Geographic Components	2010 Census Population	Core based statistical area	State/ County FIPS code	Title and Geographic Components	2010 Census Population
48660		Wichita Falls, TX	151 306	49420		Yakima, WA....................................	243 231
	48 009	Archer County.................................	9 054		53 077	Yakima County	243 231
	48 077	Clay County.....................................	10 752				
	48 485	Wichita County................................	131 500	49620		York-Hanover, PA	434 972
					42 133	York County....................................	434 972
48700		Williamsport, PA............................	116 111				
	42 081	Lycoming County............................	116 111	49660		Youngstown-Warren-Boardman, OH-PA	565 773
					39 099	Mahoning County............................	238 823
48900		Wilmington, NC...............................	254 884		39 155	Trumbull County	210 312
	37 129	New Hanover County	202 667		42 085	Mercer County	116 638
	37 141	Pender County	52 217				
				49700		Yuba City, CA.................................	166 892
49020		Winchester, VA-WV.......................	128 472		06 101	Sutter County..................................	94 737
	51 069	Frederick County	78 305		06 115	Yuba County....................................	72 155
	51 840	Winchester city...............................	26 203				
	54 027	Hampshire County..........................	23 964	49740		Yuma, AZ	195 751
					04 027	Yuma County...................................	195 751
49180		Winston-Salem, NC........................	640 595				
	37 057	Davidson County.............................	162 878				
	37 059	Davie County	41 240				
	37 067	Forsyth County	350 670				
	37 169	Stokes County	47 401				
	37 197	Yadkin County	38 406				
49340		Worcester, MA-CT..........................	916 980				
	09 015	Windham County	118 428				
	25 027	Worcester County...........................	798 552				

APPENDIX C
CORE BASED STATISTICAL AREAS
(Metropolitan and Micropolitan),
METROPOLITAN DIVISIONS, AND COMPONENTS
(as defined February 2013)

Core Based Statistical Area	State/ County FIPS Code	Title and Geographic Components	2010 Census Population	2015 Estimated Population	Core Based Statistical Area	State/ County FIPS Code	Title and Geographic Components	2010 Census Population	2015 Estimated Population
10100		Aberdeen, SD Micro area	40 602	42 784	10820		Alexandria, MN Micro area	36 009	37 075
	46013	Brown County, SD	36 531	38 785		27041	Douglas County, MN	36 009	37 075
	46045	Edmunds County, SD	4 071	3 999	10860		Alice, TX Micro area	40 838	41 382
10140		Aberdeen, WA Micro area	72 797	71 122		48249	Jim Wells County, TX	40 838	41 382
	53027	Grays Harbor County, WA	72 797	71 122	10900		Allentown-Bethlehem-Easton, PA-NJ Metro area	821 173	832 327
10180		Abilene, TX Metro area	165 252	169 578		34041	Warren County, NJ	108 692	106 869
	48059	Callahan County, TX	13 544	13 557		42025	Carbon County, PA	65 249	63 960
	48253	Jones County, TX	20 202	19 970		42077	Lehigh County, PA	349 497	360 685
	48441	Taylor County, TX	131 506	136 051		42095	Northampton County, PA	297 735	300 813
10220		Ada, OK Micro area	37 492	38 194	10940		Alma, MI Micro area	42 476	41 540
	40123	Pontotoc County, OK	37 492	38 194		26057	Gratiot County, MI	42 476	41 540
10300		Adrian, MI Micro area	99 892	98 573	10980		Alpena, MI Micro area	29 598	28 803
	26091	Lenawee County, MI	99 892	98 573		26007	Alpena County, MI	29 598	28 803
10420		Akron, OH Metro area	703 200	704 243	11020		Altoona, PA Metro area	127 089	125 593
	39133	Portage County, OH	161 419	162 275		42013	Blair County, PA	127 089	125 593
	39153	Summit County, OH	541 781	541 968	11060		Altus, OK Micro area	26 446	25 574
10460		Alamogordo, NM Micro area	63 797	64 362		40065	Jackson County, OK	26 446	25 574
	35035	Otero County, NM	63 797	64 362	11100		Amarillo, TX Metro area	251 933	262 056
10500		Albany, GA Metro area	157 308	153 526		48011	Armstrong County, TX	1 901	1 947
	13007	Baker County, GA	3 451	3 180		48065	Carson County, TX	6 182	5 969
	13095	Dougherty County, GA	94 565	91 332		48359	Oldham County, TX	2 052	2 069
	13177	Lee County, GA	28 298	29 202		48375	Potter County, TX	121 073	121 802
	13273	Terrell County, GA	9 315	9 113		48381	Randall County, TX	120 725	130 269
	13321	Worth County, GA	21 679	20 699	11140		Americus, GA Micro area	37 829	35 947
10540		Albany, OR Metro area	116 672	120 547		13249	Schley County, GA	5 010	5 168
	41043	Linn County, OR	116 672	120 547		13261	Sumter County, GA	32 819	30 779
10580		Albany-Schenectady-Troy, NY Metro area	870 716	881 830	11180		Ames, IA Metro area	89 542	96 021
	36001	Albany County, NY	304 204	309 381		19169	Story County, IA	89 542	96 021
	36083	Rensselaer County, NY	159 429	160 266	11220		Amsterdam, NY Micro area	50 219	49 642
	36091	Saratoga County, NY	219 607	226 249		36057	Montgomery County, NY	50 219	49 642
	36093	Schenectady County, NY	154 727	154 604	11260		Anchorage, AK Metro area	380 821	399 790
	36095	Schoharie County, NY	32 749	31 330		02020	Anchorage Municipality, AK	291 826	298 695
10620		Albemarle, NC Micro area	60 585	60 714		02170	Matanuska-Susitna Borough, AK	88 995	101 095
	37167	Stanly County, NC	60 585	60 714	11380		Andrews, TX Micro area	14 786	18 105
10660		Albert Lea, MN Micro area	31 255	30 613		48003	Andrews County, TX	14 786	18 105
	27047	Freeborn County, MN	31 255	30 613	11420		Angola, IN Micro area	34 185	34 372
10700		Albertville, AL Micro area	93 019	94 725		18151	Steuben County, IN	34 185	34 372
	01095	Marshall County, AL	93 019	94 725	11460		Ann Arbor, MI Metro area	344 791	358 880
10740		Albuquerque, NM Metro area	887 077	907 301		26161	Washtenaw County, MI	344 791	358 880
	35001	Bernalillo County, NM	662 564	676 685	11500		Anniston-Oxford-Jacksonville, AL Metro area	118 572	115 620
	35043	Sandoval County, NM	131 561	139 394		01015	Calhoun County, AL	118 572	115 620
	35057	Torrance County, NM	16 383	15 485					
	35061	Valencia County, NM	76 569	75 737					
10780		Alexandria, LA Metro area	153 922	154 484	11540		Appleton, WI Metro area	225 666	233 007
	22043	Grant Parish, LA	22 309	22 343		55015	Calumet County, WI	48 971	49 762
	22079	Rapides Parish, LA	131 613	132 141		55087	Outagamie County, WI	176 695	183 245

Core Based Statistical Area	State/County FIPS Code	Title and Geographic Components	2010 Census Population	2015 Estimated Population	Core Based Statistical Area	State/County FIPS Code	Title and Geographic Components	2010 Census Population	2015 Estimated Population
11580		Arcadia, FL Micro area	34 862	35 458		13199	Meriwether County, GA	21 992	21 190
	12027	DeSoto County, FL	34 862	35 458		13211	Morgan County, GA	17 868	18 046
						13217	Newton County, GA	99 958	105 473
11620		Ardmore, OK Micro area	47 557	48 689		13223	Paulding County, GA	142 324	152 238
	40019	Carter County, OK	47 557	48 689		13227	Pickens County, GA	29 431	30 309
						13231	Pike County, GA	17 869	17 941
11660		Arkadelphia, AR Micro area	22 995	22 633		13247	Rockdale County, GA	85 215	88 856
	05019	Clark County, AR	22 995	22 633		13255	Spalding County, GA	64 073	64 051
						13297	Walton County, GA	83 768	88 399
11680		Arkansas City-Winfield, KS Micro area	36 311	35 788	12100		Atlantic City-Hammonton, NJ Metro area	274 549	274 219
	20035	Cowley County, KS	36 311	35 788		34001	Atlantic County, NJ	274 549	274 219
11700		Asheville, NC Metro area	424 858	446 840	12140		Auburn, IN Micro area	42 223	42 589
	37021	Buncombe County, NC	238 318	253 178		18033	DeKalb County, IN	42 223	42 589
	37087	Haywood County, NC	59 036	59 868	12180		Auburn, NY Micro area	80 026	78 288
	37089	Henderson County, NC	106 740	112 655		36011	Cayuga County, NY	80 026	78 288
	37115	Madison County, NC	20 764	21 139	12220		Auburn-Opelika, AL Metro area	140 247	156 993
11740		Ashland, OH Micro area	53 139	53 213		01081	Lee County, AL	140 247	156 993
	39005	Ashland County, OH	53 139	53 213	12260		Augusta-Richmond County, GA-SC Metro area	564 873	590 146
11780		Ashtabula, OH Micro area	101 497	98 632		13033	Burke County, GA	23 316	22 745
	39007	Ashtabula County, OH	101 497	98 632		13073	Columbia County, GA	124 053	144 052
11820		Astoria, OR Micro area	37 039	37 831		13181	Lincoln County, GA	7 996	7 673
	41007	Clatsop County, OR	37 039	37 831		13189	McDuffie County, GA	21 875	21 540
11860		Atchison, KS Micro area	16 924	16 398		13245	Richmond County, GA	200 549	201 793
	20005	Atchison County, KS	16 924	16 398		45003	Aiken County, SC	160 099	165 829
11900		Athens, OH Micro area	64 757	65 886		45037	Edgefield County, SC	26 985	26 514
	39009	Athens County, OH	64 757	65 886	12300		Augusta-Waterville, ME Micro area	122 151	119 980
11940		Athens, TN Micro area	52 266	52 639		23011	Kennebec County, ME	122 151	119 980
	47107	McMinn County, TN	52 266	52 639	12380		Austin, MN Micro area	39 163	39 116
11980		Athens, TX Micro area	78 532	79 545		27099	Mower County, MN	39 163	39 116
	48213	Henderson County, TX	78 532	79 545	12420		Austin-Round Rock, TX Metro area	1 716 289	2 000 860
12020		Athens-Clarke County, GA Metro area	192 541	203 189		48021	Bastrop County, TX	74 171	80 527
	13059	Clarke County, GA	116 714	123 912		48055	Caldwell County, TX	38 066	40 522
	13195	Madison County, GA	28 120	28 441		48209	Hays County, TX	157 107	194 739
	13219	Oconee County, GA	32 808	35 965		48453	Travis County, TX	1 024 266	1 176 558
	13221	Oglethorpe County, GA	14 899	14 871		48491	Williamson County, TX	422 679	508 514
12060		Atlanta-Sandy Springs-Roswell, GA Metro area	5 286 728	5 710 795	12460		Bainbridge, GA Micro area	27 842	27 174
	13013	Barrow County, GA	69 367	75 370		13087	Decatur County, GA	27 842	27 174
	13015	Bartow County, GA	100 157	102 747	12540		Bakersfield, CA Metro area	839 631	882 176
	13035	Butts County, GA	23 655	23 593		06029	Kern County, CA	839 631	882 176
	13045	Carroll County, GA	110 527	114 545	12580		Baltimore-Columbia-Towson, MD Metro area	2 710 489	2 797 407
	13057	Cherokee County, GA	214 346	235 900		24003	Anne Arundel County, MD	537 656	564 195
	13063	Clayton County, GA	259 424	273 955		24005	Baltimore County, MD	805 029	831 128
	13067	Cobb County, GA	688 078	741 334		24013	Carroll County, MD	167 134	167 627
	13077	Coweta County, GA	127 317	138 427		24025	Harford County, MD	244 826	250 290
	13085	Dawson County, GA	22 330	23 312		24027	Howard County, MD	287 085	313 414
	13089	DeKalb County, GA	691 893	734 871		24035	Queen Anne's County, MD	47 798	48 904
	13097	Douglas County, GA	132 403	140 733		24510	Baltimore city, MD	620 961	621 849
	13113	Fayette County, GA	106 567	110 714	12620		Bangor, ME Metro area	153 923	152 692
	13117	Forsyth County, GA	175 511	212 438		23019	Penobscot County, ME	153 923	152 692
	13121	Fulton County, GA	920 581	1 010 562	12660		Baraboo, WI Micro area	61 976	63 642
	13135	Gwinnett County, GA	805 321	895 823		55111	Sauk County, WI Micro area	61 976	63 642
	13143	Haralson County, GA	28 780	28 854					
	13149	Heard County, GA	11 834	11 539					
	13151	Henry County, GA	203 922	217 739					
	13159	Jasper County, GA	13 900	13 635					
	13171	Lamar County, GA	18 317	18 201					

Core Based Statistical Areas (Metropolitan and Micropolitan), Metropolitan Divisions, and Components (as defined February 2013)–*Continued*

Core Based Statistical Area	State/ County FIPS Code	Title and Geographic Components	2010 Census Population	2015 Estimated Population	Core Based Statistical Area	State/ County FIPS Code	Title and Geographic Components	2010 Census Population	2015 Estimated Population
12680		Bardstown, KY Micro area................	43 437	45 126	13420		Bemidji, MN Micro area	44 442	45 672
	21179	Nelson County, KY.....................	43 437	45 126		27007	Beltrami County, MN..................	44 442	45 672
12700		Barnstable Town, MA Metro area.....	215 888	214 333	13460		Bend-Redmond, OR Metro area.......	157 733	175 268
	25001	Barnstable County, MA	215 888	214 333		41017	Deschutes County, OR	157 733	175 268
12740		Barre, VT Micro area.....................	59 534	58 612	13500		Bennettsville, SC Micro area	28 933	27 494
	50023	Washington County, VT	59 534	58 612		45069	Marlboro County, SC..................	28 933	27 494
12780		Bartlesville, OK Micro area.............	50 976	52 021	13540		Bennington, VT Micro area.............	37 125	36 317
	40147	Washington County, OK................	50 976	52 021		50003	Bennington County, VT	37 125	36 317
12820		Bastrop, LA Micro area..................	27 979	26 395	13620		Berlin, NH-VT Micro area	39 361	37 375
	22067	Morehouse Parish, LA.................	27 979	26 395		33007	Coos County, NH	33 055	31 212
12860		Batavia, NY Micro area..................	60 079	58 937		50009	Essex County, VT	6 306	6 163
	36037	Genesee County, NY	60 079	58 937	13660		Big Rapids, MI Micro area..............	42 798	43 067
12900		Batesville, AR Micro area	36 647	37 052		26107	Mecosta County, MI	42 798	43 067
	05063	Independence County, AR...........	36 647	37 052	13700		Big Spring, TX Micro area	36 238	38 521
12940		Baton Rouge, LA Metro area...........	802 484	830 480		48173	Glasscock County, TX.................	1 226	1 315
	22005	Ascension Parish, LA.................	107 215	119 455		48227	Howard County, TX....................	35 012	37 206
	22033	East Baton Rouge Parish, LA......	440 171	446 753	13720		Big Stone Gap, VA Micro area	61 313	58 772
	22037	East Feliciana Parish, LA............	20 267	19 696		51051	Dickenson County, VA	15 903	15 115
	22047	Iberville Parish, LA	33 387	33 095		51195	Wise County, VA	41 452	39 718
	22063	Livingston Parish, LA	128 026	137 788		51720	Norton city, VA	3 958	3 939
	22077	Pointe Coupee Parish, LA...........	22 802	22 251	13740		Billings, MT Metro area.................	158 934	168 283
	22091	St. Helena Parish, LA.................	11 203	10 567		30009	Carbon County, MT....................	10 078	10 408
	22121	West Baton Rouge Parish, LA......	23 788	25 490		30037	Golden Valley County, MT	884	827
	22125	West Feliciana Parish, LA............	15 625	15 385		30111	Yellowstone County, MT	147 972	157 048
12980		Battle Creek, MI Metro area	136 146	134 314	13780		Binghamton, NY Metro area............	251 725	246 020
	26025	Calhoun County, MI	136 146	134 314		36007	Broome County, NY	200 600	196 567
13020		Bay City, MI Metro area.................	107 771	105 659		36107	Tioga County, NY......................	51 125	49 453
	26017	Bay County, MI.........................	107 771	105 659	13820		Birmingham-Hoover, AL Metro area.	1 128 047	1 145 647
13060		Bay City, TX Micro area.................	36 702	36 770		01007	Bibb County, AL	22 915	22 583
	48321	Matagorda County, TX................	36 702	36 770		01009	Blount County, AL	57 322	57 673
13100		Beatrice, NE Micro area	22 311	21 900		01021	Chilton County, AL	43 643	43 943
	31067	Gage County, NE Micro area.......	22 311	21 900		01073	Jefferson County, AL..................	658 466	660 367
13140		Beaumont-Port Arthur, TX Metro area..............................	403 190	408 419		01115	St. Clair County, AL	83 593	87 074
	48199	Hardin County, TX.....................	54 635	55 865		01117	Shelby County, AL	195 085	208 713
	48245	Jefferson County, TX	252 273	254 308		01127	Walker County, AL	67 023	65 294
	48351	Newton County, TX....................	14 445	13 986	13900		Bismarck, ND Metro area	114 778	129 517
	48361	Orange County, TX....................	81 837	84 260		38015	Burleigh County, ND	81 308	92 991
13180		Beaver Dam, WI Micro area...........	88 759	88 502		38059	Morton County, ND....................	27 471	30 310
	55027	Dodge County, WI......................	88 759	88 502		38065	Oliver County, ND	1 846	1 846
13220		Beckley, WV Metro area................	124 898	122 507		38085	Sioux County, ND......................	4 153	4 370
	54019	Fayette County, WV....................	46 039	44 997	13940		Blackfoot, ID Micro area	45 607	44 990
	54081	Raleigh County, WV....................	78 859	77 510		16011	Bingham County, ID	45 607	44 990
13260		Bedford, IN Micro area	46 134	45 495	13980		Blacksburg-Christiansburg-Radford, VA Metro area.................................	178 237	181 747
	18093	Lawrence County, IN...................	46 134	45 495		51063	Floyd County, VA	15 279	15 651
13300		Beeville, TX Micro area.................	31 861	32 874		51071	Giles County, VA	17 286	16 708
	48025	Bee County, TX.........................	31 861	32 874		51121	Montgomery County, VA...............	94 392	97 653
13340		Bellefontaine, OH Micro area	45 858	45 386		51155	Pulaski County, VA	34 872	34 332
	39091	Logan County, OH	45 858	45 386		51750	Radford city, VA	16 408	17 403
13380		Bellingham, WA Metro area............	201 140	212 284	14010		Bloomington, IL Metro area.............	186 133	189 413
	53073	Whatcom County, WA.................	201 140	212 284		17039	De Witt County, IL	16 561	16 247
						17113	McLean County, IL	169 572	173 166

Core Based Statistical Areas (Metropolitan and Micropolitan), Metropolitan Divisions, and Components (as defined February 2013)–*Continued*

Core Based Statistical Area	State/County FIPS Code	Title and Geographic Components	2010 Census Population	2015 Estimated Population	Core Based Statistical Area	State/County FIPS Code	Title and Geographic Components	2010 Census Population	2015 Estimated Population
14020		Bloomington, IN Metro area............	159 549	165 577	14660		Brainerd, MN Micro area	91 067	92 134
	18105	Monroe County, IN......................	137 974	144 705		27021	Cass County, MN..........................	28 567	28 706
	18119	Owen County, IN.........................	21 575	20 872		27035	Crow Wing County, MN	62 500	63 428
14100		Bloomsburg-Berwick, PA Metro area..	85 562	85 229	14700		Branson, MO Micro area	83 877	85 535
	42037	Columbia County, PA...................	67 295	66 672		29209	Stone County, MO Micro area......	32 202	30 943
	42093	Montour County, PA.....................	18 267	18 557		29213	Taney County, MO Micro area......	51 675	54 592
14140		Bluefield, WV-VA Micro area	107 342	104 063	14720		Breckenridge, CO Micro area...........	27 994	30 257
	51185	Tazewell County, VA....................	45 078	42 899		08117	Summit County, CO......................	27 994	30 257
	54055	Mercer County, WV......................	62 264	61 164	14740		Bremerton-Silverdale, WA Metro area..	251 133	260 131
14180		Blytheville, AR Micro area	46 480	43 738		53035	Kitsap County, WA.......................	251 133	260 131
	05093	Mississippi County, AR	46 480	43 738	14780		Brenham, TX Micro area	33 718	34 765
14220		Bogalusa, LA Micro area	47 168	46 371		48477	Washington County, TX	33 718	34 765
	22117	Washington Parish, LA.................	47 168	46 371	14820		Brevard, NC Micro area...................	33 090	33 211
14260		Boise City, ID Metro area	616 561	676 909		37175	Transylvania County, NC	33 090	33 211
	16001	Ada County, ID............................	392 365	434 211	14860		Bridgeport-Stamford-Norwalk, CT Metro area..	916 829	948 053
	16015	Boise County, ID..........................	7 028	7 058		09001	Fairfield County, CT....................	916 829	948 053
	16027	Canyon County, ID........................	188 923	207 478	15020		Brookhaven, MS Micro area............	34 869	34 649
	16045	Gem County, ID	16 719	16 852		28085	Lincoln County, MS......................	34 869	34 649
	16073	Owyhee County, ID.......................	11 526	11 310	15060		Brookings, OR Micro area	22 364	22 483
14340		Boone, IA Micro area.......................	26 306	26 643		41015	Curry County, OR........................	22 364	22 483
	19015	Boone County, IA........................	26 306	26 643	15100		Brookings, SD Micro area................	31 965	33 897
14380		Boone, NC Micro area.....................	51 079	52 906		46011	Brookings County, SD...................	31 965	33 897
	37189	Watauga County, NC	51 079	52 906	15180		Brownsville-Harlingen, TX Metro area..	406 220	422 156
14420		Borger, TX Micro area	22 150	21 734		48061	Cameron County, TX	406 220	422 156
	48233	Hutchinson County, TX	22 150	21 734	15220		Brownwood, TX Micro area	38 106	37 896
14460		Boston-Cambridge Newton, MA-NH Metro area..	4 552 402	4 774 321		48049	Brown County, TX.......................	38 106	37 896
		Boston, MA Metro Div 14454........	1 887 792	1 984 537	15260		Brunswick, GA Metro area...............	112 370	116 003
	25021	Norfolk County, MA	670 850	696 023		13025	Brantley County, GA	18 411	18 455
	25023	Plymouth County, MA.................	494 919	510 393		13127	Glynn County, GA	79 626	83 579
	25025	Suffolk County, MA.....................	722 023	778 121		13191	McIntosh County, GA...................	14 333	13 969
14460		Cambridge-Newton-Framingham, MA Metro Div 15764	2 246 244	2 361 182	15340		Bucyrus, OH Micro area	43 784	42 306
	25009	Essex County, MA.....................	743 159	776 043		39033	Crawford County, OH...................	43 784	42 306
	25017	Middlesex County, MA...............	1 503 085	1 585 139	15380		Buffalo-Cheektowaga-Niagara Falls, NY Metro area	1 135 509	1 135 230
14460		Rockingham County-Strafford County-NH Metro Div 40484........	418 366	428 602		36029	Erie County, NY	919 040	922 578
	33015	Rockingham County, NH..........	295 223	301 777		36063	Niagara County, NY......................	216 469	212 652
	33017	Strafford County, NH	123 143	126 825	15420		Burley, ID Micro area......................	43 021	43 967
14500		Boulder, CO Metro area	294 567	319 372		16031	Cassia County, ID	22 952	23 506
	08013	Boulder County, CO	294 567	319 372		16067	Minidoka County, ID....................	20 069	20 461
14540		Bowling Green, KY Metro area........	158 599	168 436	15460		Burlington, IA-IL Micro area............	47 656	47 050
	21003	Allen County, KY.........................	19 956	20 640		17071	Henderson County, IL	7 331	6 995
	21031	Butler County, KY........................	12 660	12 938		19057	Des Moines County, IA	40 325	40 055
	21061	Edmonson County, KY..................	12 161	12 007	15500		Burlington, NC Metro area...............	151 131	158 276
	21227	Warren County, KY......................	113 792	122 851		37001	Alamance County, NC...................	151 131	158 276
14580		Bozeman, MT Micro area	89 513	100 739					
	30031	Gallatin County, MT	89 513	100 739					
14620		Bradford, PA Micro area..................	43 450	42 412					
	42083	McKean County, PA......................	43 450	42 412					

Core Based Statistical Areas (Metropolitan and Micropolitan), Metropolitan Divisions, and Components (as defined February 2013)–*Continued*

Core Based Statistical Area	State/County FIPS Code	Title and Geographic Components	2010 Census Population	2015 Estimated Population	Core Based Statistical Area	State/County FIPS Code	Title and Geographic Components	2010 Census Population	2015 Estimated Population
15540		Burlington-South Burlington, VT Metro area............	211 261	217 042	16300		Cedar Rapids, IA Metro area............	257 940	266 040
	50007	Chittenden County, VT................	156 545	161 382		19011	Benton County, IA........................	26 076	25 658
	50011	Franklin County, VT....................	47 746	48 799		19105	Jones County, IA..........................	20 638	20 466
	50013	Grand Isle County, VT	6 970	6 861		19113	Linn County, IA............................	211 226	219 916
15580		Butte-Silver Bow, MT Micro area......	34 200	34 622	16340		Cedartown, GA Micro area..............	41 475	41 524
	30093	Silver Bow County, MT	34 200	34 622		13233	Polk County, GA..........................	41 475	41 524
15620		Cadillac, MI Micro area................	47 584	47 906	16380		Celina, OH Micro area	40 814	40 968
	26113	Missaukee County, MI.................	14 849	14 903		39107	Mercer County, OH	40 814	40 968
	26165	Wexford County, MI	32 735	33 003	16460		Centralia, IL Micro area	39 437	38 339
15660		Calhoun, GA Micro area................	55 186	56 574		17121	Marion County, IL........................	39 437	38 339
	13129	Gordon County, GA......................	55 186	56 574	16500		Centralia, WA Micro area	75 455	75 882
15680		California-Lexington Park, MD Metro area............	105 151	111 413		53041	Lewis County, WA........................	75 455	75 882
	24037	St. Mary's County, MD	105 151	111 413	16540		Chambersburg-Waynesboro, PA Metro area............	149 618	153 638
15700		Cambridge, MD Micro area	32 618	32 384		42055	Franklin County, PA	149 618	153 638
	24019	Dorchester County, MD...............	32 618	32 384	16580		Champaign-Urbana, IL Metro area...	231 891	238 984
15740		Cambridge, OH Micro area............	40 087	39 258		17019	Champaign County, IL	201 081	208 861
	39059	Guernsey County, OH..................	40 087	39 258		17053	Ford County, IL	14 081	13 736
15780		Camden, AR Micro area................	31 488	29 587		17147	Piatt County, IL............................	16 729	16 387
	05013	Calhoun County, AR	5 368	5 229	16620		Charleston, WV Metro area..............	227 078	220 614
	05103	Ouachita County, AR	26 120	24 358		54005	Boone County, WV........................	24 629	23 372
15820		Campbellsville, KY Micro area..........	24 512	25 420		54015	Clay County, WV..........................	9 386	8 910
	21217	Taylor County, KY	24 512	25 420		54039	Kanawha County, WV...................	193 063	188 332
15860		Cañon City, CO Micro area	46 824	46 692	16660		Charleston-Mattoon, IL Micro area...	64 921	63 419
	08043	Fremont County, CO	46 824	46 692		17029	Coles County, IL...........................	53 873	52 521
15900		Canton, IL Micro area	37 069	35 699		17035	Cumberland County, IL	11 048	10 898
	17057	Fulton County, IL..........................	37 069	35 699	16700		Charleston-North Charleston, SC Metro area............	664 607	744 526
15940		Canton-Massillon, OH Metro area....	404 422	402 976		45015	Berkeley County, SC	177 843	202 786
	39019	Carroll County, OH	28 836	27 811		45019	Charleston County, SC	350 209	389 262
	39151	Stark County, OH	375 586	375 165		45035	Dorchester County, SC	136 555	152 478
15980		Cape Coral-Fort Myers, FL Metro area............	618 754	701 982	16740		Charlotte-Concord-Gastonia, NC-SC Metro area............	2 217 012	2 426 363
	12071	Lee County, FL............................	618 754	701 982		37025	Cabarrus County, NC....................	178 011	196 762
16020		Cape Girardeau, MO-IL Metro area .	96 275	97 534		37071	Gaston County, NC.......................	206 086	213 442
	17003	Alexander County, IL....................	8 238	6 780		37097	Iredell County, NC........................	159 437	169 866
	29017	Bollinger County, MO	12 363	12 182		37109	Lincoln County, NC.......................	78 265	81 035
	29031	Cape Girardeau County, MO	75 674	78 572		37119	Mecklenburg County, NC..............	919 628	1 034 070
16060		Carbondale-Marion, IL Metro area ...	126 575	126 828		37159	Rowan County, NC.......................	138 428	139 142
	17077	Jackson County, IL........................	60 218	59 362		37179	Union County, NC.........................	201 292	222 742
	17199	Williamson County, IL	66 357	67 466		45023	Chester County, SC......................	33 140	32 267
16100		Carlsbad-Artesia, NM Micro area	53 829	57 578		45057	Lancaster County, SC...................	76 652	85 842
	35015	Eddy County, NM.........................	53 829	57 578		45091	York County, SC	226 073	251 195
16180		Carson City, NV Metro area	55 274	54 521	16820		Charlottesville, VA Metro area..........	218 705	229 514
	32510	Carson City, NV Metro area..........	55 274	54 521		51003	Albemarle County, VA...................	98 970	105 703
16220		Casper, WY Metro area................	75 450	82 178		51029	Buckingham County, VA	17 146	17 032
	56025	Natrona County, WY	75 450	82 178		51065	Fluvanna County, VA....................	25 691	26 235
16260		Cedar City, UT Micro area..............	46 163	48 368		51079	Greene County, VA.......................	18 403	19 162
	49021	Iron County, UT............................	46 163	48 368		51125	Nelson County, VA.......................	15 020	14 785
						51540	Charlottesville city, VA.................	43 475	46 597
					16860		Chattanooga, TN-GA Metro area	528 143	547 776
						13047	Catoosa County, GA	63 942	66 050
						13083	Dade County, GA.........................	16 633	16 264
						13295	Walker County, GA.......................	68 756	68 066
						47065	Hamilton County, TN.....................	336 463	354 098
						47115	Marion County, TN........................	28 237	28 487
						47153	Sequatchie County, TN.................	14 112	14 811

Core Based Statistical Area	State/County FIPS Code	Title and Geographic Components	2010 Census Population	2015 Estimated Population	Core Based Statistical Area	State/County FIPS Code	Title and Geographic Components	2010 Census Population	2015 Estimated Population
16940		Cheyenne, WY Metro area...............	91 738	97 121	17300		Clarksville, TN-KY Metro area..........	260 625	281 021
	56021	Laramie County, WY.....................	91 738	97 121		21047	Christian County, KY................	73 955	73 309
16980		Chicago-Naperville-Elgin, IL-IN-WI				21221	Trigg County, KY....................	14 339	14 233
		Metro area..	9 461 105	9 551 031		47125	Montgomery County, TN.............	172 331	193 479
		Chicago-Naperville-Arlington							
		Heights, IL Metro Div 16974	7 262 718	7 340 454	17340		Clearlake, CA Micro area	64 665	64 591
	17031	Cook County, IL....................	5 194 675	5 238 216		06033	Lake County, CA......................	64 665	64 591
	17043	DuPage County, IL.................	916 924	933 736					
	17063	Grundy County, IL..................	50 063	50 541	17380		Cleveland, MS Micro area	34 145	33 322
	17093	Kendall County, IL.................	114 736	123 355		28011	Bolivar County, MS	34 145	33 322
	17111	McHenry County, IL................	308 760	307 343					
	17197	Will County, IL.....................	677 560	687 263	17420		Cleveland, TN Metro area	115 788	120 864
						47011	Bradley County, TN..................	98 963	104 091
16980		Elgin, IL Metro Div 20994	620 429	635 199		47139	Polk County, TN.....................	16 825	16 773
	17037	DeKalb County, IL..................	105 160	104 352					
	17089	Kane County, IL....................	515 269	530 847	17460		Cleveland-Elyria, OH Metro area......	2 077 240	2 060 810
						39035	Cuyahoga County, OH...............	1 280 122	1 255 921
16980		Gary, IN Metro Div 23844.............	708 070	703 031		39055	Geauga County, OH.................	93 389	94 102
	18073	Jasper County, IN...................	33 478	33 470		39085	Lake County, OH.....................	230 041	229 245
	18089	Lake County, IN....................	496 005	487 865		39093	Lorain County, OH..................	301 356	305 147
	18111	Newton County, IN	14 244	14 008		39103	Medina County, OH.................	172 332	176 395
	18127	Porter County, IN...................	164 343	167 688					
					17500		Clewiston, FL Micro area	39 140	39 119
16980		Lake County-Kenosha County, IL-WI Metro Div 29404	869 888	872 347		12051	Hendry County, FL...................	39 140	39 119
	17097	Lake County, IL.....................	703 462	703 910	17540		Clinton, IA Micro area	49 116	47 768
	55059	Kenosha County, WI................	166 426	168 437		19045	Clinton County, IA	49 116	47 768
17020		Chico, CA Metro area	220 000	225 411	17580		Clovis, NM Micro area	48 376	50 398
	06007	Butte County, CA	220 000	225 411		35009	Curry County, NM	48 376	50 398
17060		Chillicothe, OH Micro area...............	78 064	77 170	17660		Coeur d'Alene, ID Metro area..........	138 494	150 346
	39141	Ross County, OH	78 064	77 170		16055	Kootenai County, ID.................	138 494	150 346
17140		Cincinnati, OH-KY-IN Metro area	2 114 580	2 157 719	17700		Coffeyville, KS Micro area	35 471	33 314
	18029	Dearborn County, IN	50 047	49 455		20125	Montgomery County, KS.............	35 471	33 314
	18115	Ohio County, IN.....................	6 128	5 938					
	18161	Union County, IN....................	7 516	7 182	17740		Coldwater, MI Micro area	45 248	43 664
	21015	Boone County, KY...................	118 811	127 712		26023	Branch County, MI...................	45 248	43 664
	21023	Bracken County, KY.................	8 488	8 321					
	21037	Campbell County, KY................	90 336	92 066	17780		College Station-Bryan, TX Metro area...	228 660	249 156
	21077	Gallatin County, KY.................	8 589	8 636		48041	Brazos County, TX..................	194 851	215 037
	21081	Grant County, KY....................	24 662	24 757		48051	Burleson County, TX................	17 187	17 460
	21117	Kenton County, KY..................	159 720	165 012		48395	Robertson County, TX...............	16 622	16 659
	21191	Pendleton County, KY..............	14 877	14 408					
	39015	Brown County, OH..................	44 846	43 839	17820		Colorado Springs, CO Metro area.....	645 613	697 856
	39017	Butler County, OH...................	368 130	376 353		08041	El Paso County, CO.................	622 263	674 471
	39025	Clermont County, OH...............	197 363	201 973		08119	Teller County, CO	23 350	23 385
	39061	Hamilton County, OH...............	802 374	807 598	17860		Columbia, MO Metro area	162 642	174 974
	39165	Warren County, OH..................	212 693	224 469		29019	Boone County, MO..................	162 642	174 974
17200		Claremont-Lebanon, NH-VT Micro area...	218 466	216 923	17900		Columbia, SC Metro area	767 598	810 068
	33009	Grafton County, NH.................	89 118	89 320		45017	Calhoun County, SC	15 175	14 781
	33019	Sullivan County, NH................	43 742	42 967		45039	Fairfield County, SC	23 956	22 747
	50017	Orange County, VT..................	28 936	28 899		45055	Kershaw County, SC	61 697	63 603
	50027	Windsor County, VT.................	56 670	55 737		45063	Lexington County, SC	262 391	281 833
						45079	Richland County, SC	384 504	407 051
17220		Clarksburg, WV Micro area	94 196	93 802		45081	Saluda County, SC	19 875	20 053
	54017	Doddridge County, WV.............	8 202	8 176					
	54033	Harrison County, WV	69 099	68 714	17980		Columbus, GA-AL Metro area	294 865	313 749
	54091	Taylor County, WV..................	16 895	16 912		01113	Russell County, AL..................	52 947	59 660
						13053	Chattahoochee County, GA	11 267	11 368
17260		Clarksdale, MS Micro area	26 151	24 620		13145	Harris County, GA..................	32 024	33 381
	28027	Coahoma County, MS...............	26 151	24 620		13197	Marion County, GA.................	8 742	8 761
						13215	Muscogee County, GA..............	189 885	200 579

Core Based Statistical Areas (Metropolitan and Micropolitan), Metropolitan Divisions, and Components (as defined February 2013)–*Continued*

Core Based Statistical Area	State/County FIPS Code	Title and Geographic Components	2010 Census Population	2015 Estimated Population	Core Based Statistical Area	State/County FIPS Code	Title and Geographic Components	2010 Census Population	2015 Estimated Population
18020		Columbus, IN Metro area	76 794	81 162	18860		Crescent City, CA Micro area	28 610	27 254
	18005	Bartholomew County, IN	76 794	81 162		06015	Del Norte County, CA	28 610	27 254
18060		Columbus, MS Micro area	59 779	59 710	18880		Crestview-Fort Walton Beach-Destin, FL Metro area......................	235 865	262 172
	28087	Lowndes County, MS	59 779	59 710		12091	Okaloosa County, FL	180 822	198 664
18100		Columbus, NE Micro area	32 237	32 847		12131	Walton County, FL	55 043	63 508
	31141	Platte County, NE	32 237	32 847	18900		Crossville, TN Micro area	56 053	58 229
18140		Columbus, OH Metro area	1 901 974	2 021 632		47035	Cumberland County, TN	56 053	58 229
	39041	Delaware County, OH	174 214	193 013					
	39045	Fairfield County, OH....................	146 156	151 408	18980		Cullman, AL Micro area	80 406	82 005
	39049	Franklin County, OH	1 163 414	1 251 722		01043	Cullman County, AL	80 406	82 005
	39073	Hocking County, OH	29 380	28 491					
	39089	Licking County, OH	166 492	170 570	19000		Cullowhee, NC Micro area	40 271	41 265
	39097	Madison County, OH	43 435	44 094		37099	Jackson County, NC	40 271	41 265
	39117	Morrow County, OH	34 827	35 074					
	39127	Perry County, OH	36 058	35 985	19060		Cumberland, MD-WV Metro area	103 299	99 979
	39129	Pickaway County, OH	55 698	56 998		24001	Allegany County, MD	75 087	72 528
	39159	Union County, OH	52 300	54 277		54057	Mineral County, WV	28 212	27 451
18180		Concord, NH Micro area..................	146 445	147 994	19100		Dallas-Fort Worth-Arlington, TX Metro area..................................	6 426 214	7 102 796
	33013	Merrimack County, NH.................	146 445	147 994			Dallas-Plano-Irving, TX Metro Div 19124...........................	4 230 520	4 707 151
18220		Connersville, IN Micro area	24 277	23 434		48085	Collin County, TX......................	782 341	914 127
	18041	Fayette County, IN	24 277	23 434		48113	Dallas County, TX.....................	2 368 139	2 553 385
18260		Cookeville, TN Micro area	106 042	108 191		48121	Denton County, TX....................	662 614	780 612
	47087	Jackson County, TN....................	11 638	11 509		48139	Ellis County, TX.......................	149 610	163 632
	47133	Overton County, TN....................	22 083	22 129		48231	Hunt County, TX......................	86 129	89 844
	47141	Putnam County, TN....................	72 321	74 553		48257	Kaufman County, TX..................	103 350	114 690
18300		Coos Bay, OR Micro area	63 043	63 121		48397	Rockwall County, TX	78 337	90 861
	41011	Coos County, OR	63 043	63 121	19100		Fort Worth-Arlington, TX Metro Div 23104	2 195 694	2 395 645
18380		Cordele, GA Micro area	23 439	22 881		48221	Hood County, TX......................	51 182	55 423
	13081	Crisp County, GA	23 439	22 881		48251	Johnson County, TX...................	150 934	159 990
18420		Corinth, MS Micro area...................	37 057	37 388		48367	Parker County, TX.....................	116 927	126 042
	28003	Alcorn County, MS	37 057	37 388		48425	Somervell County, TX..................	8 490	8 739
18460		Cornelia, GA Micro area	43 041	43 996		48439	Tarrant County, TX....................	1 809 034	1 982 498
	13137	Habersham County, GA	43 041	43 996		48497	Wise County, TX......................	59 127	62 953
18500		Corning, NY Micro area	98 990	97 631	19140		Dalton, GA Metro area....................	142 227	143 781
	36101	Steuben County, NY	98 990	97 631		13213	Murray County, GA	39 628	39 565
18580		Corpus Christi, TX Metro area..........	428 185	452 422		13313	Whitfield County, GA	102 599	104 216
	48007	Aransas County, TX....................	23 158	25 350	19180		Danville, IL Metro area....................	81 625	79 282
	48355	Nueces County, TX.....................	340 223	359 715		17183	Vermilion County, IL....................	81 625	79 282
	48409	San Patricio County, TX...............	64 804	67 357	19220		Danville, KY Micro area	53 174	54 272
18620		Corsicana, TX Micro area	47 735	48 323		21021	Boyle County, KY......................	28 432	29 809
	48349	Navarro County, TX	47 735	48 323		21137	Lincoln County, KY.....................	24 742	24 463
18660		Cortland, NY Micro area	49 336	48 494	19260		Danville, VA Micro area	106 561	104 276
	36023	Cortland County, NY	49 336	48 494		51143	Pittsylvania County, VA................	63 506	62 194
18700		Corvallis, OR Metro area	85 579	87 572		51590	Danville city, VA.......................	43 055	42 082
	41003	Benton County, OR.....................	85 579	87 572	19300		Daphne-Fairhope-Foley, AL Metro area.......................................	182 265	203 709
18740		Coshocton, OH Micro area..............	36 901	36 569		01003	Baldwin County, AL....................	182 265	203 709
	39031	Coshocton County, OH	36 901	36 569	19340		Davenport-Moline-Rock Island, IA-IL Metro area.............................	379 690	383 606
18780		Craig, CO Micro area.....................	13 795	12 937		17073	Henry County, IL.......................	50 486	49 489
	08081	Moffat County, CO	13 795	12 937		17131	Mercer County, IL......................	16 434	15 858
18820		Crawfordsville, IN Micro area	38 124	38 227		17161	Rock Island County, IL.................	147 546	146 133
	18107	Montgomery County, IN...............	38 124	38 227		19163	Scott County, IA	165 224	172 126

Core Based Statistical Areas (Metropolitan and Micropolitan), Metropolitan Divisions, and Components (as defined February 2013)–*Continued*

Core Based Statistical Area	State/County FIPS Code	Title and Geographic Components	2010 Census Population	2015 Estimated Population	Core Based Statistical Area	State/County FIPS Code	Title and Geographic Components	2010 Census Population	2015 Estimated Population
19380		Dayton, OH Metro area	799 232	800 909	19860		Dickinson, ND Micro area	24 199	32 154
	39057	Greene County, OH	161 573	164 427		38089	Stark County, ND	24 199	32 154
	39109	Miami County, OH	102 506	104 224					
	39113	Montgomery County, OH	535 153	532 258	19940		Dixon, IL Micro area	36 031	34 584
						17103	Lee County, IL	36 031	34 584
19420		Dayton, TN Micro area	31 809	32 526					
	47143	Rhea County, TN	31 809	32 526	19980		Dodge City, KS Micro area	33 848	34 536
						20057	Ford County, KS	33 848	34 536
19460		Decatur, AL Metro area	153 829	152 680					
	01079	Lawrence County, AL	34 339	33 115	20020		Dothan, AL Metro area	145 639	148 171
	01103	Morgan County, AL	119 490	119 565		01061	Geneva County, AL	26 790	26 777
						01067	Henry County, AL	17 302	17 221
19500		Decatur, IL Metro area	110 768	107 303		01069	Houston County, AL	101 547	104 173
	17115	Macon County, IL	110 768	107 303					
					20060		Douglas, GA Micro area	42 356	43 108
19540		Decatur, IN Micro area	34 387	34 980		13069	Coffee County, GA	42 356	43 108
	18001	Adams County, IN	34 387	34 980					
					20100		Dover, DE Metro area	162 310	173 533
19580		Defiance, OH Micro area	39 037	38 352		10001	Kent County, Delaware	162 310	173 533
	39039	Defiance County, OH	39 037	38 352					
					20140		Dublin, GA Micro area	58 414	57 387
19620		Del Rio, TX Micro area	48 879	48 988		13167	Johnson County, GA	9 980	9 656
	48465	Val Verde County, TX	48 879	48 988		13175	Laurens County, GA	48 434	47 731
19660		Deltona-Daytona Beach-Ormond Beach, FL Metro area	590 289	623 279	20180		DuBois, PA Micro area	81 642	80 994
	12035	Flagler County, FL	95 696	105 392		42033	Clearfield County, PA	81 642	80 994
	12127	Volusia County, FL	494 593	517 887	20220		Dubuque, IA Metro area	93 653	97 125
						19061	Dubuque County, IA	93 653	97 125
19700		Deming, NM Micro area	25 095	24 518					
	35029	Luna County, NM	25 095	24 518	20260		Duluth, MN-WI Metro area	279 771	279 601
						27017	Carlton County, MN	35 386	35 569
19740		Denver-Aurora-Lakewood, CO Metro area	2 543 482	2 814 330		27137	St. Louis County, MN	200 226	200 431
	08001	Adams County, CO	441 603	491 337		55031	Douglas County, WI	44 159	43 601
	08005	Arapahoe County, CO	572 003	631 096	20300		Dumas, TX Micro area	21 904	22 255
	08014	Broomfield County, CO	55 889	65 065		48341	Moore County, TX	21 904	22 255
	08019	Clear Creek County, CO	9 088	9 303					
	08031	Denver County, CO	600 158	682 545	20340		Duncan, OK Micro area	45 048	44 581
	08035	Douglas County, CO	285 465	322 387		40137	Stephens County, OK	45 048	44 581
	08039	Elbert County, CO	23 086	24 735					
	08047	Gilpin County, CO	5 441	5 828	20380		Dunn, NC Micro area	114 678	128 140
	08059	Jefferson County, CO	534 543	565 524		37085	Harnett County, NC	114 678	128 140
	08093	Park County, CO	16 206	16 510					
					20420		Durango, CO Micro area	51 334	54 688
19760		DeRidder, LA Micro area	35 654	36 462		08067	La Plata County, CO	51 334	54 688
	22011	Beauregard Parish, LA	35 654	36 462					
					20460		Durant, OK Micro area	42 416	44 884
19780		Des Moines-West Des Moines, IA Metro area	569 633	622 899		40013	Bryan County, OK	42 416	44 884
	19049	Dallas County, IA	66 135	80 133	20500		Durham-Chapel Hill, NC Metro area	504 357	552 493
	19077	Guthrie County, IA	10 954	10 676		37037	Chatham County, NC	63 505	70 928
	19121	Madison County, IA	15 679	15 753		37063	Durham County, NC	267 587	300 952
	19153	Polk County, IA	430 640	467 711		37135	Orange County, NC	133 801	141 354
	19181	Warren County, IA	46 225	48 626		37145	Person County, NC	39 464	39 259
19820		Detroit-Warren-Dearborn, MI Metro area	4 296 250	4 302 043	20540		Dyersburg, TN Micro area	38 335	37 893
		Detroit-Dearborn-Livonia, MI Metro Div 19804	1 820 584	1 759 335		47045	Dyer County, TN	38 335	37 893
	26163	Wayne County, MI	1 820 584	1 759 335	20580		Eagle Pass, TX Micro area	54 258	57 706
						48323	Maverick County, TX	54 258	57 706
19820		Warren-Troy-Farmington Hills, MI Metro Div 47664	2 475 666	2 542 708	20660		Easton, MD Micro area	37 782	37 512
	26087	Lapeer County, MI	88 319	88 373		24041	Talbot County, MD	37 782	37 512
	26093	Livingston County, MI	180 967	187 316	20700		East Stroudsburg, PA Metro area	169 842	166 397
	26099	Macomb County, MI	840 978	864 840		42089	Monroe County, PA	169 842	166 397
	26125	Oakland County, MI	1 202 362	1 242 304					
	26147	St. Clair County, MI	163 040	159 875					

Core Based Statistical Area	State/ County FIPS Code	Title and Geographic Components	2010 Census Population	2015 Estimated Population	Core Based Statistical Area	State/ County FIPS Code	Title and Geographic Components	2010 Census Population	2015 Estimated Population
20740		Eau Claire, WI Metro area................	161 151	165 636	21580		Española, NM Micro area.................	40 246	39 465
	55017	Chippewa County, WI	62 415	63 531		35039	Rio Arriba County, NM.................	40 246	39 465
	55035	Eau Claire County, WI	98 736	102 105	21660		Eugene, OR Metro area.................	351 715	362 895
20780		Edwards, CO Micro area	52 197	53 605		41039	Lane County, OR	351 715	362 895
	08037	Eagle County, CO	52 197	53 605	21700		Eureka-Arcata-Fortuna, CA Micro area.................	134 623	135 727
20820		Effingham, IL Micro area	34 242	34 371		06023	Humboldt County, CA	134 623	135 727
	17049	Effingham County, IL...............	34 242	34 371					
20900		El Campo, TX Micro area	41 280	41 486	21740		Evanston, WY Micro area...............	21 118	20 822
	48481	Wharton County, TX	41 280	41 486		56041	Uinta County, WY.....................	21 118	20 822
20940		El Centro, CA Metro area.............	174 528	180 191	21780		Evansville, IN-KY Metro area	311 552	315 693
	06025	Imperial County, CA....................	174 528	180 191		18129	Posey County, IN	25 910	25 512
20980		El Dorado, AR Micro area	41 639	40 144		18163	Vanderburgh County, IN	179 703	181 877
	05139	Union County, AR	41 639	40 144		18173	Warrick County, IN	59 689	61 897
21020		Elizabeth City, NC Micro area	64 094	63 578		21101	Henderson County, KY	46 250	46 407
	37029	Camden County, NC	9 980	10 309	21820		Fairbanks, AK Metro area...............	97 581	99 631
	37139	Pasquotank County, NC...............	40 661	39 829		02090	Fairbanks North Star Borough, AK	97 581	99 631
	37143	Perquimans County, NC	13 453	13 440	21840		Fairfield, IA Micro area	16 843	17 555
21060		Elizabethtown-Fort Knox, KY Metro area......................	148 338	148 604		19101	Jefferson County, IA.....................	16 843	17 555
	21093	Hardin County, KY	105 543	106 439	21900		Fairmont, WV Micro area	56 418	56 925
	21123	Larue County, KY.....................	14 193	14 241		54049	Marion County, WV	56 418	56 925
	21163	Meade County, KY...................	28 602	27 924	21980		Fallon, NV Micro area	24 877	24 200
21120		Elk City, OK Micro area	22 119	23 768		32001	Churchill County, NV...................	24 877	24 200
	40009	Beckham County, OK...................	22 119	23 768	22020		Fargo, ND-MN Metro area...............	208 777	233 836
21140		Elkhart-Goshen, IN Metro area........	197 559	203 474		27027	Clay County, MN	58 999	62 324
	18039	Elkhart County, IN.....................	197 559	203 474		38017	Cass County, ND	149 778	171 512
21180		Elkins, WV Micro area	29 405	29 126	22060		Faribault-Northfield, MN Micro area .	64 142	65 400
	54083	Randolph County, WV.................	29 405	29 126		27131	Rice County, MN	64 142	65 400
21220		Elko, NV Micro area.....................	50 805	53 951	22100		Farmington, MO Micro area.............	65 359	66 520
	32007	Elko County, NV	48 818	51 935		29187	St. Francois County, MO...............	65 359	66 520
	32011	Eureka County, NV	1 987	2 016	22140		Farmington, NM Metro area	130 044	118 737
21260		Ellensburg, WA Micro area..............	40 915	43 269		35045	San Juan County, NM..................	130 044	118 737
	53037	Kittitas County, WA	40 915	43 269	22180		Fayetteville, NC Metro area.............	366 383	376 509
21300		Elmira, NY Metro area....................	88 830	87 071		37051	Cumberland County, NC...............	319 431	323 838
	36015	Chemung County, NY	88 830	87 071		37093	Hoke County, NC	46 952	52 671
21340		El Paso, TX Metro area	804 123	838 972	22220		Fayetteville-Springdale-Rogers, AR-MO Metro area....................	463 204	513 559
	48141	El Paso County, TX....................	800 647	835 593		05007	Benton County, AR	221 339	249 672
	48229	Hudspeth County, TX.................	3 476	3 379		05087	Madison County, AR	15 717	15 767
21380		Emporia, KS Micro area	33 690	33 339		05143	Washington County, AR...............	203 065	225 477
	20111	Lyon County, KS	33 690	33 339		29119	McDonald County, MO................	23 083	22 643
21420		Enid, OK Micro area	60 580	63 569	22260		Fergus Falls, MN Micro area	57 303	57 716
	40047	Garfield County, OK....................	60 580	63 569		27111	Otter Tail County, MN	57 303	57 716
21460		Enterprise, AL Micro area	49 948	51 211	22280		Fernley, NV Micro area................	51 980	52 585
	01031	Coffee County, AL.....................	49 948	51 211		32019	Lyon County, NV	51 980	52 585
21500		Erie, PA Metro area......................	280 566	278 045	22300		Findlay, OH Micro area.................	74 782	75 573
	42049	Erie County, PA........................	280 566	278 045		39063	Hancock County, OH	74 782	75 573
21540		Escanaba, MI Micro area...............	37 069	36 377	22340		Fitzgerald, GA Micro area..............	17 634	17 403
	26041	Delta County, MI	37 069	36 377		13017	Ben Hill County, GA...................	17 634	17 403

Core Based Statistical Area	State/County FIPS Code	Title and Geographic Components	2010 Census Population	2015 Estimated Population	Core Based Statistical Area	State/County FIPS Code	Title and Geographic Components	2010 Census Population	2015 Estimated Population
22380		Flagstaff, AZ Metro area.................	134 421	139 097	23340		Fremont, NE Micro area	36 691	36 706
	04005	Coconino County, AZ..................	134 421	139 097		31053	Dodge County, NE	36 691	36 706
22420		Flint, MI Metro area	425 790	410 849	23380		Fremont, OH Micro area................	60 944	59 679
	26049	Genesee County, MI	425 790	410 849		39143	Sandusky County, OH................	60 944	59 679
22500		Florence, SC Metro area	205 566	206 448	23420		Fresno, CA Metro area	930 450	974 861
	45031	Darlington County, SC	68 681	67 548		06019	Fresno County, CA......................	930 450	974 861
	45041	Florence County, SC..................	136 885	138 900	23460		Gadsden, AL Metro area	104 430	103 057
22520		Florence-Muscle Shoals, AL Metro area	147 137	146 950		01055	Etowah County, AL	104 430	103 057
	01033	Colbert County, AL......................	54 428	54 354	23500		Gaffney, SC Micro area	55 342	56 194
	01077	Lauderdale County, AL	92 709	92 596		45021	Cherokee County, SC	55 342	56 194
22540		Fond du Lac, WI Metro area	101 633	101 973	23540		Gainesville, FL Metro area	264 275	277 163
	55039	Fond du Lac County, WI.............	101 633	101 973		12001	Alachua County, FL....................	247 336	259 964
22580		Forest City, NC Micro area..............	67 810	66 390		12041	Gilchrist County, FL...................	16 939	17 199
	37161	Rutherford County, NC................	67 810	66 390	23580		Gainesville, GA Metro area	179 684	193 535
22620		Forrest City, AR Micro area	28 258	26 589		13139	Hall County, GA	179 684	193 535
	05123	St. Francis County, AR	28 258	26 589	23620		Gainesville, TX Micro area	38 437	39 229
22660		Fort Collins, CO Metro area	299 630	333 577		48097	Cooke County, TX......................	38 437	39 229
	08069	Larimer County, CO	299 630	333 577	23660		Galesburg, IL Micro area................	52 919	51 441
22700		Fort Dodge, IA Micro area..............	38 013	37 071		17095	Knox County, IL..........................	52 919	51 441
	19187	Webster County, IA.....................	38 013	37 071	23700		Gallup, NM Micro area...................	71 492	76 708
22780		Fort Leonard Wood, MO Micro area	52 274	53 221		35031	McKinley County, NM.................	71 492	76 708
	29169	Pulaski County, MO....................	52 274	53 221	23780		Garden City, KS Micro area	40 753	41 074
22800		Fort Madison-Keokuk, IA-IL-MO Micro area	62 105	60 433		20055	Finney County, KS	36 776	37 118
	17067	Hancock County, IL.....................	19 104	18 543		20093	Kearny County, KS.....................	3 977	3 956
	19111	Lee County, IA	35 862	35 089	23820		Gardnerville Ranchos, NV Micro area	46 997	47 710
	29045	Clark County, MO.......................	7 139	6 801		32005	Douglas County, NV...................	46 997	47 710
22820		Fort Morgan, CO Micro area	28 159	28 360	23860		Georgetown, SC Micro area	60 158	61 298
	08087	Morgan County, CO	28 159	28 360		45043	Georgetown County, SC	60 158	61 298
22860		Fort Polk South, LA Micro area........	52 334	50 803	23900		Gettysburg, PA Metro area.............	101 407	102 295
	22115	Vernon Parish, LA......................	52 334	50 803		42001	Adams County, PA......................	101 407	102 295
22900		Fort Smith, AR-OK Metro area.........	280 467	280 241	23940		Gillette, WY Micro area...................	46 133	49 220
	05033	Crawford County, AR	61 948	61 703		56005	Campbell County, WY.................	46 133	49 220
	05131	Sebastian County, AR	125 744	127 780	23980		Glasgow, KY Micro area.................	52 272	53 479
	40079	Le Flore County, OK	50 384	49 605		21009	Barren County, KY	42 173	43 570
	40135	Sequoyah County, OK	42 391	41 153		21169	Metcalfe County, KY	10 099	9 909
23060		Fort Wayne, IN Metro area	416 257	429 820	24020		Glens Falls, NY Metro area.............	128 923	126 918
	18003	Allen County, IN	355 329	368 450		36113	Warren County, NY	65 707	64 688
	18179	Wells County, IN	27 636	27 964		36115	Washington County, NY..............	63 216	62 230
	18183	Whitley County, IN	33 292	33 406	24060		Glenwood Springs, CO Micro area...	73 537	75 882
23140		Frankfort, IN Micro area.................	33 224	32 609		08045	Garfield County, CO	56 389	58 095
	18023	Clinton County, IN	33 224	32 609		08097	Pitkin County, CO.......................	17 148	17 787
23180		Frankfort, KY Micro area	70 706	72 354	24100		Gloversville, NY Micro area.............	55 531	53 992
	21005	Anderson County, KY..................	21 421	21 979		36035	Fulton County, NY	55 531	53 992
	21073	Franklin County, KY	49 285	50 375	24140		Goldsboro, NC Metro area.............	122 623	124 132
23240		Fredericksburg, TX Micro area........	24 837	25 963		37191	Wayne County, NC	122 623	124 132
	48171	Gillespie County, TX	24 837	25 963	24220		Grand Forks, ND-MN Metro area.....	98 461	102 449
23300		Freeport, IL Micro area...................	47 711	45 749		27119	Polk County, MN	31 600	31 533
	17177	Stephenson County, IL................	47 711	45 749		38035	Grand Forks County, ND	66 861	70 916

Core Based Statistical Area	State/County FIPS Code	Title and Geographic Components	2010 Census Population	2015 Estimated Population	Core Based Statistical Area	State/County FIPS Code	Title and Geographic Components	2010 Census Population	2015 Estimated Population
24260		Grand Island, NE Metro area	81 850	85 066	24900		Greenwood, MS Micro area..............	42 914	41 242
	31079	Hall County, NE...............	58 607	61 680		28015	Carroll County, MS......................	10 597	10 243
	31081	Hamilton County, NE................	9 124	9 190		28083	Leflore County, MS	32 317	30 999
	31093	Howard County, NE	6 274	6 409					
	31121	Merrick County, NE...................	7 845	7 787	24940		Greenwood, SC Micro area..............	95 078	94 770
24300		Grand Junction, CO Metro area	146 723	148 513		45001	Abbeville County, SC	25 417	24 932
	08077	Mesa County, CO......................	146 723	148 513		45047	Greenwood County, SC	69 661	69 838
24340		Grand Rapids-Wyoming, MI Metro area................	988 938	1 038 583	24980		Grenada, MS Micro area.................	21 906	21 578
						28043	Grenada County, MS	21 906	21 578
	26015	Barry County, MI	59 173	59 314	25060		Gulfport-Biloxi-Pascagoula, MS Metro area................	370 702	389 255
	26081	Kent County, MI	602 622	636 369					
	26117	Montcalm County, MI	63 342	62 945		28045	Hancock County, MS	43 929	46 420
	26139	Ottawa County, MI	263 801	279 955		28047	Harrison County, MS	187 105	201 410
						28059	Jackson County, MS	139 668	141 425
24380		Grants, NM Micro area	27 213	27 329					
	35006	Cibola County, NM......................	27 213	27 329	25100		Guymon, OK Micro area.................	20 640	21 489
24420		Grants Pass, OR Metro area............	82 713	84 745		40139	Texas County, OK........................	20 640	21 489
	41033	Josephine County, OR................	82 713	84 745	25180		Hagerstown-Martinsburg, MD-WV Metro area................	251 599	261 486
24460		Great Bend, KS Micro area	27 674	27 103		24043	Washington County, MD	147 430	149 585
	20009	Barton County, KS	27 674	27 103		54003	Berkeley County, WV	104 169	111 901
24500		Great Falls, MT Metro area	81 327	82 278	25200		Hailey, ID Micro area......................	27 701	27 955
	30013	Cascade County, MT	81 327	82 278		16013	Blaine County, ID	21 376	21 592
24540		Greeley, CO Metro area	252 825	285 174		16025	Camas County, ID	1 117	1 066
	08123	Weld County, CO	252 825	285 174		16063	Lincoln County, ID	5 208	5 297
24580		Green Bay, WI Metro area	306 241	316 519	25220		Hammond, LA Metro area	121 097	128 755
	55009	Brown County, WI	248 007	258 718		22105	Tangipahoa Parish, LA................	121 097	128 755
	55061	Kewaunee County, WI	20 574	20 366	25260		Hanford-Corcoran, CA Metro area ...	152 982	150 965
	55083	Oconto County, WI	37 660	37 435		06031	Kings County, CA........................	152 982	150 965
24620		Greeneville, TN Micro area..............	68 831	68 580	25300		Hannibal, MO Micro area................	38 948	39 076
	47059	Greene County, TN	68 831	68 580		29127	Marion County, MO	28 781	28 880
24640		Greenfield Town, MA Micro area......	71 372	70 601		29173	Ralls County, MO	10 167	10 196
	25011	Franklin County, MA................	71 372	70 601	25420		Harrisburg-Carlisle, PA Metro area ..	549 475	565 006
24660		Greensboro-High Point, NC Metro area................	723 801	752 157		42041	Cumberland County, PA	235 406	246 338
						42043	Dauphin County, PA....................	268 100	272 983
	37081	Guilford County, NC....................	488 406	517 600		42099	Perry County, PA	45 969	45 685
	37151	Randolph County, NC.................	141 752	142 799	25460		Harrison, AR Micro area................	45 233	45 135
	37157	Rockingham County, NC.............	93 643	91 758		05009	Boone County, AR	36 903	37 222
24700		Greensburg, IN Micro area..............	25 740	26 521		05101	Newton County, AR......................	8 330	7 913
	18031	Decatur County, IN.....................	25 740	26 521	25500		Harrisonburg, VA Metro area...........	125 228	131 131
24740		Greenville, MS Micro area	51 137	48 130		51165	Rockingham County, VA	76 314	78 593
	28151	Washington County, MS	51 137	48 130		51660	Harrisonburg city, VA	48 914	52 538
24780		Greenville, NC Metro area...............	168 148	175 842	25540		Hartford-West Hartford-East Hartford, CT Metro area	1 212 381	1 211 324
	37147	Pitt County, NC	168 148	175 842		09003	Hartford County, CT....................	894 014	895 841
24820		Greenville, OH Micro area	52 959	52 076		09007	Middlesex County, CT	165 676	164 063
	39037	Darke County, OH	52 959	52 076		09013	Tolland County, CT	152 691	151 420
24860		Greenville-Anderson-Mauldin, SC Metro area................	824 112	874 869	25580		Hastings, NE Micro area.................	31 364	31 587
						31001	Adams County, NE	31 364	31 587
	45007	Anderson County, SC	187 126	194 692	25620		Hattiesburg, MS Metro area	142 842	148 839
	45045	Greenville County, SC..................	451 225	491 863		28035	Forrest County, MS.....................	74 934	75 944
	45059	Laurens County, SC	66 537	66 623		28073	Lamar County, MS	55 658	60 618
	45077	Pickens County, SC	119 224	121 691		28111	Perry County, MS.......................	12 250	12 277
					25700		Hays, KS Micro area......................	28 452	29 029
						20051	Ellis County, KS	28 452	29 029

Core Based Statistical Areas (Metropolitan and Micropolitan), Metropolitan Divisions, and Components (as defined February 2013)–*Continued*

Core Based Statistical Area	State/County FIPS Code	Title and Geographic Components	2010 Census Population	2015 Estimated Population	Core Based Statistical Area	State/County FIPS Code	Title and Geographic Components	2010 Census Population	2015 Estimated Population
25720		Heber, UT Micro area......................	23 530	29 161	26420		Houston-The Woodlands-Sugar Land, TX Metro area....................	5 920 416	6 656 947
	49051	Wasatch County, UT.................	23 530	29 161		48015	Austin County, TX.....................	28 417	29 563
25740		Helena, MT Micro area..................	74 801	78 063		48039	Brazoria County, TX..................	313 166	346 312
	30043	Jefferson County, MT..............	11 406	11 645		48071	Chambers County, TX...............	35 096	38 863
	30049	Lewis and Clark County, MT........	63 395	66 418		48157	Fort Bend County, TX...............	585 375	716 087
25760		Helena-West Helena, AR Micro area..............................	21 757	19 513		48167	Galveston County, TX...............	291 309	322 225
						48201	Harris County, TX.....................	4 092 459	4 538 028
	05107	Phillips County, AR..................	21 757	19 513		48291	Liberty County, TX...................	75 643	79 654
25780		Henderson, NC Micro area............	45 422	44 568		48339	Montgomery County, TX...........	455 746	537 559
	37181	Vance County, NC....................	45 422	44 568		48473	Waller County, TX....................	43 205	48 656
25820		Hereford, TX Micro area................	19 372	18 952	26460		Hudson, NY Micro area..............	63 096	61 509
	48117	Deaf Smith County, TX............	19 372	18 952		36021	Columbia County, NY................	63 096	61 509
25840		Hermiston-Pendleton, OR Micro area..............................	87 062	87 721	26500		Huntingdon, PA Micro area............	45 913	45 668
						42061	Huntingdon County, PA.............	45 913	45 668
	41049	Morrow County, OR.................	11 173	11 190	26540		Huntington, IN Micro area...............	37 124	36 630
	41059	Umatilla County, OR................	75 889	76 531		18069	Huntington County, IN..............	37 124	36 630
25860		Hickory-Lenoir-Morganton, NC Metro area..........................	365 497	362 510	26580		Huntington-Ashland, WV-KY-OH Metro area..........................	364 908	361 580
	37003	Alexander County, NC..............	37 198	37 325		21019	Boyd County, KY......................	49 542	48 325
	37023	Burke County, NC....................	90 912	88 842		21089	Greenup County, KY.................	36 910	36 068
	37027	Caldwell County, NC................	83 029	81 287		39087	Lawrence County, OH...............	62 450	61 109
	37035	Catawba County, NC................	154 358	155 056		54011	Cabell County, WV...................	96 319	96 844
25880		Hillsdale, MI Micro area..................	46 688	45 941		54043	Lincoln County, WV..................	21 720	21 415
	26059	Hillsdale County, MI.................	46 688	45 941		54079	Putnam County, WV..................	55 486	56 848
25900		Hilo, HI Micro area........................	185 079	196 428		54099	Wayne County, WV...................	42 481	40 971
	15001	Hawaii County, HI....................	185 079	196 428	26620		Huntsville, AL Metro area...............	417 593	444 752
25940		Hilton Head Island-Bluffton-Beaufort, SC Metro area.............	187 010	207 413		01083	Limestone County, AL...............	82 782	91 663
	45013	Beaufort County, SC................	162 233	179 589		01089	Madison County, AL.................	334 811	353 089
	45053	Jasper County, SC...................	24 777	27 824	26660		Huntsville, TX Micro area..............	82 446	85 101
25980		Hinesville, GA Metro area............	77 917	80 198		48455	Trinity County, TX....................	14 585	14 402
	13179	Liberty County, GA..................	63 453	62 467		48471	Walker County, TX...................	67 861	70 699
	13183	Long County, GA.....................	14 464	17 731	26700		Huron, SD Micro area...................	17 398	18 372
26020		Hobbs, NM Micro area.................	64 727	71 180		46005	Beadle County, SD...................	17 398	18 372
	35025	Lea County, NM......................	64 727	71 180	26740		Hutchinson, KS Micro area............	64 511	63 718
26090		Holland, MI Micro area.................	111 408	114 625		20155	Reno County, KS.....................	64 511	63 718
	26005	Allegan County, MI..................	111 408	114 625	26780		Hutchinson, MN Micro area............	36 651	35 932
26140		Homosassa Springs, FL Metro area.	141 236	141 058		27085	McLeod County, MN.................	36 651	35 932
	12017	Citrus County, FL....................	141 236	141 058	26820		Idaho Falls, ID Metro area...............	133 265	139 747
						16019	Bonneville County, ID...............	104 234	110 089
26220		Hood River, OR Micro area............	22 346	23 137		16023	Butte County, ID......................	2 891	2 501
	41027	Hood River County, OR..............	22 346	23 137		16051	Jefferson County, ID.................	26 140	27 157
26300		Hot Springs, AR Metro area............	96 024	97 177	26860		Indiana, PA Micro area.................	88 880	86 966
	05051	Garland County, AR..................	96 024	97 177		42063	Indiana County, PA...................	88 880	86 966
26340		Houghton, MI Micro area................	38 784	38 548	26900		Indianapolis-Carmel-Anderson, IN Metro area..........................	1 887 877	1 988 817
	26061	Houghton County, MI...............	36 628	36 380		18011	Boone County, IN....................	56 640	63 344
	26083	Keweenaw County, MI..............	2 156	2 168		18013	Brown County, IN....................	15 242	14 977
26380		Houma-Thibodaux, LA Metro area ...	208 178	212 297		18057	Hamilton County, IN.................	274 569	309 697
	22057	Lafourche Parish, LA.................	96 318	98 325		18059	Hancock County, IN.................	70 002	72 520
	22109	Terrebonne Parish, LA..............	111 860	113 972		18063	Hendricks County, IN...............	145 448	158 192
						18081	Johnson County, IN.................	139 654	149 633
						18095	Madison County, IN.................	131 636	129 723
						18097	Marion County, IN...................	903 393	939 020
						18109	Morgan County, IN..................	68 894	69 648
						18133	Putnam County, IN..................	37 963	37 585
						18145	Shelby County, IN...................	44 436	44 478

Core Based Statistical Areas (Metropolitan and Micropolitan), Metropolitan Divisions, and Components (as defined February 2013)–*Continued*

Core Based Statistical Area	State/County FIPS Code	Title and Geographic Components	2010 Census Population	2015 Estimated Population	Core Based Statistical Area	State/County FIPS Code	Title and Geographic Components	2010 Census Population	2015 Estimated Population
26940		Indianola, MS Micro area..................	29 450	27 005	27540		Jasper, IN Micro area	54 734	55 055
	28133	Sunflower County, MS	29 450	27 005		18037	Dubois County, IN.........................	41 889	42 461
26960		Ionia, MI Micro area.........................	63 905	64 223		18125	Pike County, IN	12 845	12 594
	26067	Ionia County, MI..............................	63 905	64 223	27600		Jefferson, GA Micro area..................	60 485	63 360
26980		Iowa City, IA Metro area....................	152 586	166 498		13157	Jackson County, GA	60 485	63 360
	19103	Johnson County, IA.......................	130 882	144 251	27620		Jefferson City, MO Metro area	149 807	151 145
	19183	Washington County, IA	21 704	22 247		29027	Callaway County, MO	44 332	44 834
27020		Iron Mountain, MI-WI Micro area......	30 591	30 252		29051	Cole County, MO...........................	75 990	76 720
	26043	Dickinson County, MI......................	26 168	25 788		29135	Moniteau County, MO..................	15 607	15 963
	55037	Florence County, WI	4 423	4 464		29151	Osage County, MO.......................	13 878	13 628
27060		Ithaca, NY Metro area	101 564	104 926	27700		Jesup, GA Micro area.......................	30 099	29 534
	36109	Tompkins County, NY	101 564	104 926		13305	Wayne County, GA	30 099	29 534
27100		Jackson, MI Metro area....................	160 248	159 494	27740		Johnson City, TN Metro area	198 716	200 648
	26075	Jackson County, MI......................	160 248	159 494		47019	Carter County, TN	57 424	56 486
27140		Jackson, MS Metro area..................	567 122	578 777		47171	Unicoi County, TN	18 313	17 860
	28029	Copiah County, MS......................	29 449	28 773		47179	Washington County, TN..............	122 979	126 302
	28049	Hinds County, MS.........................	245 285	242 891	27780		Johnstown, PA Metro area	143 679	136 411
	28089	Madison County, MS.....................	95 203	103 465		42021	Cambria County, PA	143 679	136 411
	28121	Rankin County, MS.......................	141 617	149 039	27860		Jonesboro, AR Metro area	121 026	128 394
	28127	Simpson County, MS.....................	27 503	27 222		05031	Craighead County, AR	96 443	104 354
	28163	Yazoo County, MS........................	28 065	27 387		05111	Poinsett County, AR.....................	24 583	24 040
27160		Jackson, OH Micro area..................	33 225	32 596	27900		Joplin, MO Metro area	175 518	177 211
	39079	Jackson County, OH	33 225	32 596		29097	Jasper County, MO	117 404	118 596
27180		Jackson, TN Metro area	130 011	129 682		29145	Newton County, MO.....................	58 114	58 615
	47023	Chester County, TN	17 131	17 471	27920		Junction City, KS Micro area...........	34 362	37 030
	47033	Crockett County, TN.....................	14 586	14 601		20061	Geary County, KS	34 362	37 030
	47113	Madison County, TN.....................	98 294	97 610	27940		Juneau, AK Micro area....................	31 275	32 756
27220		Jackson, WY-ID Micro area.............	31 464	33 689		02110	Juneau City and Borough, AK	31 275	32 756
	16081	Teton County, ID	10 170	10 564	27980		Kahului-Wailuku-Lahaina, HI Metro area	154 924	164 726
	56039	Teton County, WY........................	21 294	23 125		15005	Kalawao County, HI	90	89
27260		Jacksonville, FL Metro area............	1 345 596	1 449 481		15009	Maui County, HI	154 834	164 637
	12003	Baker County, FL	27 115	27 420	28020		Kalamazoo-Portage, MI Metro area .	326 589	335 340
	12019	Clay County, FL	190 865	203 967		26077	Kalamazoo County, MI.................	250 331	260 263
	12031	Duval County, FL	864 263	913 010		26159	Van Buren County, MI..................	76 258	75 077
	12089	Nassau County, FL	73 314	78 444	28060		Kalispell, MT Micro area..................	90 928	96 165
	12109	St. Johns County, FL	190 039	226 640		30029	Flathead County, MT....................	90 928	96 165
27300		Jacksonville, IL Micro area	40 902	39 920	28100		Kankakee, IL Metro area	113 449	110 879
	17137	Morgan County, IL........................	35 547	34 828		17091	Kankakee County, IL....................	113 449	110 879
	17171	Scott County, IL	5 355	5 092	28140		Kansas City, MO-KS Metro area......	2 009 342	2 087 471
27340		Jacksonville, NC Metro area...........	177 772	186 311		20091	Johnson County, KS	544 179	580 159
	37133	Onslow County, NC.......................	177 772	186 311		20103	Leavenworth County, KS	76 227	79 315
27380		Jacksonville, TX Micro area............	50 845	51 542		20107	Linn County, KS	9 656	9 536
	48073	Cherokee County, TX....................	50 845	51 542		20121	Miami County, KS	32 787	32 553
27420		Jamestown, ND Micro area	21 100	21 103		20209	Wyandotte County, KS.................	157 505	163 369
	38093	Stutsman County, ND	21 100	21 103		29013	Bates County, MO	17 049	16 446
27460		Jamestown-Dunkirk-Fredonia, NY Micro area..	134 905	130 779		29025	Caldwell County, MO...................	9 424	9 014
	36013	Chautauqua County, NY	134 905	130 779		29037	Cass County, MO.........................	99 478	101 603
27500		Janesville-Beloit, WI Metro area.......	160 331	161 448		29047	Clay County, MO..........................	221 939	235 637
	55105	Rock County, WI...........................	160 331	161 448		29049	Clinton County, MO......................	20 743	20 609
						29095	Jackson County, MO....................	674 158	687 623
						29107	Lafayette County, MO..................	33 381	32 701
						29165	Platte County, MO........................	89 322	96 096
						29177	Ray County, MO...........................	23 494	22 810

Core Based Statistical Areas (Metropolitan and Micropolitan), Metropolitan Divisions, and Components (as defined February 2013)–*Continued*

Core Based Statistical Area	State/County FIPS Code	Title and Geographic Components	2010 Census Population	2015 Estimated Population	Core Based Statistical Area	State/County FIPS Code	Title and Geographic Components	2010 Census Population	2015 Estimated Population
28180		Kapaa, HI Micro area	67 091	71 735	28940		Knoxville, TN Metro area	837 571	861 424
	15007	Kauai County, HI	67 091	71 735		47001	Anderson County, TN	75 129	75 749
						47009	Blount County, TN	123 010	127 253
28260		Kearney, NE Micro area	52 591	55 448		47013	Campbell County, TN	40 716	39 752
	31019	Buffalo County, NE	46 102	48 863		47057	Grainger County, TN	22 657	22 846
	31099	Kearney County, NE	6 489	6 585		47093	Knox County, TN	432 226	451 324
						47105	Loudon County, TN	48 556	51 130
28300		Keene, NH Micro area	77 117	75 909		47129	Morgan County, TN	21 987	21 498
	33005	Cheshire County, NH	77 117	75 909		47145	Roane County, TN	54 181	52 753
						47173	Union County, TN	19 109	19 119
28340		Kendallville, IN Micro area	47 536	47 733					
	18113	Noble County, IN	47 536	47 733	29020		Kokomo, IN Metro area	82 752	82 556
						18067	Howard County, IN	82 752	82 556
28380		Kennett, MO Micro area	31 953	30 895					
	29069	Dunklin County, MO	31 953	30 895	29060		Laconia, NH Micro area	60 088	60 641
						33001	Belknap County, NH	60 088	60 641
28420		Kennewick-Richland, WA Metro area	253 340	279 116	29100		La Crosse-Onalaska, WI-MN Metro area	133 665	136 985
	53005	Benton County, WA	175 177	190 309		27055	Houston County, MN	19 027	18 773
	53021	Franklin County, WA	78 163	88 807		55063	La Crosse County, WI	114 638	118 212
28500		Kerrville, TX Micro area	49 625	50 955	29180		Lafayette, LA Metro area	466 750	490 488
	48265	Kerr County, TX	49 625	50 955		22001	Acadia Parish, LA	61 773	62 577
						22045	Iberia Parish, LA	73 240	74 103
28540		Ketchikan, AK Micro area	13 477	13 709		22055	Lafayette Parish, LA	221 578	240 098
	02130	Ketchikan Gateway Borough, AK	13 477	13 709		22099	St. Martin Parish, LA	52 160	53 835
						22113	Vermilion Parish, LA	57 999	59 875
28580		Key West, FL Micro area	73 090	77 482					
	12087	Monroe County, FL	73 090	77 482	29200		Lafayette-West Lafayette, IN Metro area	201 789	214 363
28620		Kill Devil Hills, NC Micro area	38 327	39 733		18007	Benton County, IN	8 854	8 681
	37055	Dare County, NC	33 920	35 663		18015	Carroll County, IN	20 155	19 856
	37177	Tyrrell County, NC	4 407	4 070		18157	Tippecanoe County, IN	172 780	185 826
28660		Killeen-Temple, TX Metro area	405 300	431 032	29260		La Grande, OR Micro area	25 748	25 790
	48027	Bell County, TX	310 235	334 941		41061	Union County, OR	25 748	25 790
	48099	Coryell County, TX	75 388	75 503					
	48281	Lampasas County, TX	19 677	20 588	29300		LaGrange, GA Micro area	67 044	69 763
28700		Kingsport-Bristol-Bristol, TN-VA Metro area	309 544	307 120		13285	Troup County, GA	67 044	69 763
	47073	Hawkins County, TN	56 833	56 471	29340		Lake Charles, LA Metro area	199 607	205 605
	47163	Sullivan County, TN	156 823	156 791		22019	Calcasieu Parish, LA	192 768	198 788
	51169	Scott County, VA	23 177	22 126		22023	Cameron Parish, LA	6 839	6 817
	51191	Washington County, VA	54 876	54 591					
	51520	Bristol city, VA	17 835	17 141	29380		Lake City, FL Micro area	67 531	68 348
						12023	Columbia County, FL	67 531	68 348
28740		Kingston, NY Metro area	182 493	180 143					
	36111	Ulster County, NY	182 493	180 143	29420		Lake Havasu City-Kingman, AZ Metro area	200 186	204 737
28780		Kingsville, TX Micro area	32 477	32 264		04015	Mohave County, AZ	200 186	204 737
	48261	Kenedy County, TX	416	407					
	48273	Kleberg County, TX	32 061	31 857	29460		Lakeland-Winter Haven, FL Metro area	602 095	650 092
28820		Kinston, NC Micro area	59 495	58 106		12105	Polk County, FL	602 095	650 092
	37107	Lenoir County, NC	59 495	58 106					
					29500		Lamesa, TX Micro area	13 833	13 520
28860		Kirksville, MO Micro area	30 038	29 814		48115	Dawson County, TX	13 833	13 520
	29001	Adair County, MO	25 607	25 378					
	29197	Schuyler County, MO	4 431	4 436	29540		Lancaster, PA Metro area	519 445	536 624
						42071	Lancaster County, PA	519 445	536 624
28900		Klamath Falls, OR Micro area	66 380	66 016					
	41035	Klamath County, OR	66 380	66 016	29620		Lansing-East Lansing, MI Metro area	464 036	472 276
						26037	Clinton County, MI	75 382	77 390
						26045	Eaton County, MI	107 759	108 801
						26065	Ingham County, MI	280 895	286 085

Core Based Statistical Areas (Metropolitan and Micropolitan), Metropolitan Divisions, and Components (as defined February 2013)–*Continued*

Core Based Statistical Area	State/County FIPS Code	Title and Geographic Components	2010 Census Population	2015 Estimated Population	Core Based Statistical Area	State/County FIPS Code	Title and Geographic Components	2010 Census Population	2015 Estimated Population
29660		Laramie, WY Micro area..................	36 299	37 956	30580		Liberal, KS Micro area..................	22 952	23 152
	56001	Albany County, WY	36 299	37 956		20175	Seward County, KS...................	22 952	23 152
29700		Laredo, TX Metro area	250 304	269 721	30620		Lima, OH Metro area......................	106 331	104 425
	48479	Webb County, TX.......................	250 304	269 721		39003	Allen County, OH	106 331	104 425
29740		Las Cruces, NM Metro area	209 233	214 295	30660		Lincoln, IL Micro area..................	30 305	29 494
	35013	Doña Ana County, NM.................	209 233	214 295		17107	Logan County, IL......................	30 305	29 494
29780		Las Vegas, NM Micro area..............	29 393	27 967	30700		Lincoln, NE Metro area...................	302 157	323 578
	35047	San Miguel County, NM.................	29 393	27 967		31109	Lancaster County, NE..................	285 407	306 468
29820		Las Vegas-Henderson-Paradise, NV Metro area...............................	1 951 269	2 114 801		31159	Seward County, NE....................	16 750	17 110
	32003	Clark County, NV	1 951 269	2 114 801	30780		Little Rock-North Little Rock-Conway, AR Metro area	699 757	731 612
29860		Laurel, MS Micro area..................	84 823	84 784		05045	Faulkner County, AR...................	113 237	121 552
	28061	Jasper County, MS......................	17 062	16 569		05053	Grant County, AR.......................	17 853	18 102
	28067	Jones County, MS.....................	67 761	68 215		05085	Lonoke County, AR....................	68 356	71 645
29900		Laurinburg, NC Micro area	36 157	35 509		05105	Perry County, AR......................	10 445	10 189
	37165	Scotland County, NC...................	36 157	35 509		05119	Pulaski County, AR....................	382 748	392 664
29940		Lawrence, KS Metro area...............	110 826	118 053		05125	Saline County, AR......................	107 118	117 460
	20045	Douglas County, KS....................	110 826	118 053	30820		Lock Haven, PA Micro area.............	39 238	39 441
29980		Lawrenceburg, TN Micro area	41 869	42 564		42035	Clinton County, PA.....................	39 238	39 441
	47099	Lawrence County, TN	41 869	42 564	30860		Logan, UT-ID Metro area.................	125 442	133 857
30020		Lawton, OK Metro area	130 291	130 644		16041	Franklin County, ID....................	12 786	13 074
	40031	Comanche County, OK.................	124 098	124 648		49005	Cache County, UT......................	112 656	120 783
	40033	Cotton County, OK......................	6 193	5 996	30880		Logan, WV Micro area..................	36 743	34 707
30060		Lebanon, MO Micro area	35 571	35 473		54045	Logan County, WV	36 743	34 707
	29105	Laclede County, MO	35 571	35 473	30900		Logansport, IN Micro area................	38 966	37 979
30140		Lebanon, PA Metro area	133 568	137 067		18017	Cass County, IN.......................	38 966	37 979
	42075	Lebanon County, PA....................	133 568	137 067	30940		London, KY Micro area...................	126 369	127 953
30220		Levelland, TX Micro area...............	22 935	23 433		21121	Knox County, KY.......................	31 883	31 730
	48219	Hockley County, TX	22 935	23 433		21125	Laurel County, KY......................	58 849	60 094
30260		Lewisburg, PA Micro area	44 947	44 954		21235	Whitley County, KY	35 637	36 129
	42119	Union County, PA........................	44 947	44 954	30980		Longview, TX Metro area	214 369	217 781
30280		Lewisburg, TN Micro area	30 617	31 552		48183	Gregg County, TX......................	121 730	124 108
	47117	Marshall County, TN	30 617	31 552		48401	Rusk County, TX.......................	53 330	53 070
30300		Lewiston, ID-WA Metro area	60 888	62 153		48459	Upshur County, TX.....................	39 309	40 603
	16069	Nez Perce County, ID	39 265	40 048	31020		Longview, WA Metro area	102 410	103 468
	53003	Asotin County, WA......................	21 623	22 105		53015	Cowlitz County, WA	102 410	103 468
30340		Lewiston-Auburn, ME Metro area.....	107 702	107 233	31060		Los Alamos, NM Micro area............	17 950	17 785
	23001	Androscoggin County, ME	107 702	107 233		35028	Los Alamos County, NM	17 950	17 785
30380		Lewistown, PA Micro area...............	46 682	46 500	31080		Los Angeles-Long Beach-Anaheim, CA Metro area	12 828 837	13 340 068
	42087	Mifflin County, PA........................	46 682	46 500	31080		Anaheim-Santa Ana-Irvine, CA Metro Div 11244	3 010 232	3 169 776
30420		Lexington, NE Micro area	26 370	25 859		06059	Orange County, CA	3 010 232	3 169 776
	31047	Dawson County, NE....................	24 326	23 886	31080		Los Angeles-Long Beach-Glendale, CA Metro Div 31084	9 818 605	10 170 292
	31073	Gosper County, NE.....................	2 044	1 973		06037	Los Angeles County, CA	9 818 605	10 170 292
30460		Lexington-Fayette, KY Metro area....	472 099	500 535					
	21017	Bourbon County, KY...................	19 985	20 116					
	21049	Clark County, KY.......................	35 613	35 757					
	21067	Fayette County, KY....................	295 803	314 488					
	21113	Jessamine County, KY.................	48 586	51 961					
	21209	Scott County, KY......................	47 173	52 420					
	21239	Woodford County, KY.................	24 939	25 793					

Core Based Statistical Areas (Metropolitan and Micropolitan), Metropolitan Divisions, and Components (as defined February 2013)–*Continued*

Core Based Statistical Area	State/County FIPS Code	Title and Geographic Components	2010 Census Population	2015 Estimated Population	Core Based Statistical Area	State/County FIPS Code	Title and Geographic Components	2010 Census Population	2015 Estimated Population
31140		Louisville/Jefferson County, KY-IN Metro area..............	1 235 708	1 278 413	31700		Manchester-Nashua, NH Metro area	400 721	406 678
	18019	Clark County, IN............................	110 232	115 371		33011	Hillsborough County, NH..............	400 721	406 678
	18043	Floyd County, IN............................	74 578	76 778	31740		Manhattan, KS Metro area	92 719	98 545
	18061	Harrison County, IN........................	39 364	39 578		20149	Pottawatomie County, KS	21 604	23 298
	18143	Scott County, IN	24 181	23 744		20161	Riley County, KS.........................	71 115	75 247
	18175	Washington County, IN	28 262	27 827	31820		Manitowoc, WI Micro area..............	81 442	79 806
	21029	Bullitt County, KY	74 319	78 702		55071	Manitowoc County, WI	81 442	79 806
	21103	Henry County, KY	15 416	15 620	31860		Mankato-North Mankato, MN Metro area..	96 740	99 134
	21111	Jefferson County, KY.....................	741 096	763 623		27013	Blue Earth County, MN	64 013	65 787
	21185	Oldham County, KY	60 316	64 875		27103	Nicollet County, MN	32 727	33 347
	21211	Shelby County, KY	42 074	45 632	31900		Mansfield, OH Metro area..............	124 475	121 707
	21215	Spencer County, KY	17 061	17 894		39139	Richland County, OH	124 475	121 707
	21223	Trimble County, KY	8 809	8 769	31930		Marietta, OH Micro area	61 778	61 112
31180		Lubbock, TX Metro area..................	290 805	311 154		39167	Washington County, OH	61 778	61 112
	48107	Crosby County, TX.........................	6 059	5 977	31940		Marinette, WI-MI Micro area............	65 778	64 432
	48303	Lubbock County, TX........................	278 831	299 453		26109	Menominee County, MI................	24 029	23 548
	48305	Lynn County, TX	5 915	5 724		55075	Marinette County, WI	41 749	40 884
31220		Ludington, MI Micro area................	28 705	28 783	31980		Marion, IN Micro area......................	70 061	67 979
	26105	Mason County, MI..........................	28 705	28 783		18053	Grant County, IN	70 061	67 979
31260		Lufkin, TX Micro area	86 771	88 255	32000		Marion, NC Micro area	44 996	44 989
	48005	Angelina County, TX......................	86 771	88 255		37111	McDowell County, NC	44 996	44 989
31300		Lumberton, NC Micro area	134 168	134 197	32020		Marion, OH Micro area	66 501	65 355
	37155	Robeson County, NC......................	134 168	134 197		39101	Marion County, OH	66 501	65 355
31340		Lynchburg, VA Metro area..............	252 634	259 950	32100		Marquette, MI Micro area	67 077	67 215
	51009	Amherst County, VA.......................	32 353	31 914		26103	Marquette County, MI...................	67 077	67 215
	51011	Appomattox County, VA..................	14 973	15 414	32140		Marshall, MN Micro area	25 857	25 673
	51019	Bedford County, VA	74 866	77 724		27083	Lyon County, MN	25 857	25 673
	51031	Campbell County, VA......................	54 842	55 086	32180		Marshall, MO Micro area	23 370	23 258
	51680	Lynchburg city, VA	75 568	79 812		29195	Saline County, MO.......................	23 370	23 258
31380		Macomb, IL Micro area...................	32 612	31 333	32220		Marshall, TX Micro area	65 631	66 746
	17109	McDonough County, IL...................	32 612	31 333		48203	Harrison County, TX....................	65 631	66 746
31420		Macon, GA Metro area	232 293	230 096	32260		Marshalltown, IA Micro area............	40 648	40 746
	13021	Bibb County, GA	155 547	153 721		19127	Marshall County, IA	40 648	40 746
	13079	Crawford County, GA	12 630	12 388	32280		Martin, TN Micro area......................	35 021	33 960
	13169	Jones County, GA	28 669	28 494		47183	Weakley County, TN	35 021	33 960
	13207	Monroe County, GA	26 424	27 103	32300		Martinsville, VA Micro area.............	67 972	65 526
	13289	Twiggs County, GA	9 023	8 390		51089	Henry County, VA	54 151	51 881
31460		Madera, CA Metro area	150 865	154 998		51690	Martinsville city, VA	13 821	13 645
	06039	Madera County, CA.......................	150 865	154 998	32340		Maryville, MO Micro area.................	23 370	22 810
31500		Madison, IN Micro area...................	32 428	32 416		29147	Nodaway County, MO...................	23 370	22 810
	18077	Jefferson County, IN	32 428	32 416	32380		Mason City, IA Micro area...............	51 749	50 586
31540		Madison, WI Metro area	605 435	641 385		19033	Cerro Gordo County, IA	44 151	43 017
	55021	Columbia County, WI.....................	56 833	56 743		19195	Worth County, IA.........................	7 598	7 569
	55025	Dane County, WI............................	488 073	523 643	32460		Mayfield, KY Micro area..................	37 121	37 421
	55045	Green County, WI	36 842	37 186		21083	Graves County, KY	37 121	37 421
	55049	Iowa County, WI	23 687	23 813	32500		Maysville, KY Micro area.................	17 490	17 099
31580		Madisonville, KY Micro area............	46 920	46 222		21161	Mason County, KY	17 490	17 099
	21107	Hopkins County, KY......................	46 920	46 222					
31620		Magnolia, AR Micro area.................	24 552	24 114					
	05027	Columbia County, AR.....................	24 552	24 114					
31660		Malone, NY Micro area	51 599	50 660					
	36033	Franklin County, NY.....................	51 599	50 660					
31680		Malvern, AR Micro area..................	32 923	33 426					
	05059	Hot Spring County, AR..................	32 923	33 426					

Core Based Statistical Areas (Metropolitan and Micropolitan), Metropolitan Divisions, and Components (as defined February 2013)–*Continued*

Core Based Statistical Area	State/ County FIPS Code	Title and Geographic Components	2010 Census Population	2015 Estimated Population	Core Based Statistical Area	State/ County FIPS Code	Title and Geographic Components	2010 Census Population	2015 Estimated Population
32540		McAlester, OK Micro area	45 837	44 610	33140		Michigan City-La Porte, IN Metro area...	111 467	110 884
	40121	Pittsburg County, OK	45 837	44 610		18091	LaPorte County, IN...............	111 467	110 884
32580		McAllen-Edinburg-Mission, TX Metro area....................................	774 769	842 304	33180		Middlesborough, KY Micro area	28 691	27 337
	48215	Hidalgo County, TX	774 769	842 304		21013	Bell County, KY	28 691	27 337
32620		McComb, MS Micro area.................	53 535	52 530	33220		Midland, MI Metro area	83 629	83 632
	28005	Amite County, MS	13 131	12 574		26111	Midland County, MI	83 629	83 632
	28113	Pike County, MS	40 404	39 956	33260		Midland, TX Metro area	141 671	166 718
32660		McMinnville, TN Micro area..............	39 839	40 435		48317	Martin County, TX	4 799	5 641
	47177	Warren County, TN	39 839	40 435		48329	Midland County, TX	136 872	161 077
32700		McPherson, KS Micro area...............	29 180	28 941	33300		Milledgeville, GA Micro area............	55 149	54 010
	20113	McPherson County, KS	29 180	28 941		13009	Baldwin County, GA	45 720	45 459
32740		Meadville, PA Micro area.................	88 765	86 484		13141	Hancock County, GA....................	9 429	8 551
	42039	Crawford County, PA	88 765	86 484	33340		Milwaukee-Waukesha-West Allis, WI Metro area..................................	1 555 908	1 575 747
32780		Medford, OR Metro area..................	203 206	212 567		55079	Milwaukee County, WI	947 735	957 735
	41029	Jackson County, OR	203 206	212 567		55089	Ozaukee County, WI	86 395	87 850
32820		Memphis, TN-MS-AR Metro area	1 324 829	1 344 127		55131	Washington County, WI	131 887	133 674
	05035	Crittenden County, AR	50 902	48 963		55133	Waukesha County, WI	389 891	396 488
	28009	Benton County, MS	8 729	8 182	33420		Mineral Wells, TX Micro area	28 111	27 895
	28033	DeSoto County, MS	161 252	173 323		48363	Palo Pinto County, TX..................	28 111	27 895
	28093	Marshall County, MS	37 144	35 916	33460		Minneapolis-St. Paul-Bloomington, MN Metro area.................................	3 348 859	3 524 583
	28137	Tate County, MS	28 886	28 296		27003	Anoka County, MN.......................	330 844	344 151
	28143	Tunica County, MS.......................	10 778	10 343		27019	Carver County, MN	91 042	98 741
	47047	Fayette County, TN	38 413	39 165		27025	Chisago County, MN	53 887	54 293
	47157	Shelby County, TN.......................	927 644	938 069		27037	Dakota County, MN......................	398 552	414 686
	47167	Tipton County, TN........................	61 081	61 870		27053	Hennepin County, MN...................	1 152 425	1 223 149
32860		Menomonie, WI Micro area	43 857	44 497		27059	Isanti County, MN........................	37 816	38 429
	55033	Dunn County, WI	43 857	44 497		27079	Le Sueur County, MN	27 703	27 663
32900		Merced, CA Metro area	255 793	268 455		27095	Mille Lacs County, MN	26 097	25 788
	06047	Merced County, CA.......................	255 793	268 455		27123	Ramsey County, MN	508 640	538 133
32940		Meridian, MS Micro area	107 449	104 499		27139	Scott County, MN........................	129 928	141 660
	28023	Clarke County, MS	16 732	16 006		27141	Sherburne County, MN	88 499	91 705
	28069	Kemper County, MS	10 456	9 969		27143	Sibley County, MN.......................	15 226	14 875
	28075	Lauderdale County, MS	80 261	78 524		27163	Washington County, MN	238 136	251 597
32980		Merrill, WI Micro area	28 743	27 980		27171	Wright County, MN......................	124 700	131 311
	55069	Lincoln County, WI	28 743	27 980		55093	Pierce County, WI	41 019	40 889
33020		Mexico, MO Micro area	25 529	26 096		55109	St. Croix County, WI	84 345	87 513
	29007	Audrain County, MO......................	25 529	26 096	33500		Minot, ND Micro area......................	69 540	79 814
33060		Miami, OK Micro area......................	31 848	31 981		38049	McHenry County, ND	5 395	5 968
	40115	Ottawa County, OK	31 848"	31 981		38075	Renville County, ND	2 470	2 571
33100		Miami-Fort Lauderdale-West Palm Beach, FL Metro area.....................	5 564 635	6 012 331		38101	Ward County, ND	61 675	71 275
33100		Fort Lauderdale-Pompano Beach-Deerfield Beach, FL Metro Div 22744..	1 748 066	1 896 425	33540	30063	Missoula, MT Metro area................ Missoula County, MT	109 299 109 299	114 181 114 181
	12011	Broward County, FL................	1 748 066	1 896 425	33580		Mitchell, SD Micro area..................	22 835	23 243
33100		Miami-Miami Beach-Kendall, FL Metro Div 33124	2 496 435	2 693 117		46035	Davison County, SD	19 504	19 858
	12086	Miami-Dade County, FL.............	2 496 435	2 693 117		46061	Hanson County, SD	3 331	3 385
33100		West Palm Beach-Boca Raton-Delray Beach, FL Metro Div 48424..	1 320 134	1 422 789	33620	29175	Moberly, MO Micro area.................. Randolph County, MO..................	25 414 25 414	25 104 25 104
	12099	Palm Beach County, FL	1 320 134	1 422 789	33660	01097	Mobile, AL Metro area .... Mobile County, AL.......................	412 992 412 992	415 395 415 395
					33700	06099	Modesto, CA Metro area .... Stanislaus County, CA	514 453 514 453	538 388 538 388

Core Based Statistical Areas (Metropolitan and Micropolitan), Metropolitan Divisions, and Components (as defined February 2013)–*Continued*

Core Based Statistical Area	State/County FIPS Code	Title and Geographic Components	2010 Census Population	2015 Estimated Population	Core Based Statistical Area	State/County FIPS Code	Title and Geographic Components	2010 Census Population	2015 Estimated Population
33740		Monroe, LA Metro area....................	176 441	179 238	34620		Muncie, IN Metro area.....................	117 671	116 852
	22073	Ouachita Parish, LA....................	153 720	156 761		18035	Delaware County, IN....................	117 671	116 852
	22111	Union Parish, LA........................	22 721	22 477					
					34660		Murray, KY Micro area....................	37 191	38 343
33780		Monroe, MI Metro area....................	152 021	149 568		21035	Calloway County, KY	37 191	38 343
	26115	Monroe County, MI	152 021	149 568					
					34700		Muscatine, IA Micro area.................	42 745	43 011
33860		Montgomery, AL Metro area.............	374 536	373 792		19139	Muscatine County, IA	42 745	43 011
	01001	Autauga County, AL....................	54 571	55 347					
	01051	Elmore County, AL	79 303	81 468	34740		Muskegon, MI Metro area................	172 188	172 790
	01085	Lowndes County, AL	11 299	10 458		26121	Muskegon County, MI	172 188	172 790
	01101	Montgomery County, AL	229 363	226 519					
					34780		Muskogee, OK Micro area..............	70 990	69 699
33940		Montrose, CO Micro area	41 276	40 946		40101	Muskogee County, OK...............	70 990	69 699
	08085	Montrose County, CO	41 276	40 946					
					34820		Myrtle Beach-Conway-North Myrtle Beach, NC-SC Metro area..............	376 722	431 964
33980		Morehead City, NC Micro area........	66 469	68 879		37019	Brunswick County, NC	107 431	122 765
	37031	Carteret County, NC.................	66 469	68 879		45051	Horry County, SC......................	269 291	309 199
34020		Morgan City, LA Micro area.............	54 650	52 810	34860		Nacogdoches, TX Micro area...........	64 524	65 664
	22101	St. Mary Parish, LA......................	54 650	52 810		48347	Nacogdoches County, TX	64 524	65 664
34060		Morgantown, WV Metro area............	129 709	138 176	34900		Napa, CA Metro area.....................	136 484	142 456
	54061	Monongalia County, WV	96 189	104 236		06055	Napa County, CA.......................	136 484	142 456
	54077	Preston County, WV	33 520	33 940					
					34940		Naples-Immokalee-Marco Island, FL Metro area.....................	321 520	357 305
34100		Morristown, TN Metro area..............	113 951	116 642		12021	Collier County, FL	321 520	357 305
	47063	Hamblen County, TN...................	62 544	63 402					
	47089	Jefferson County, TN.................	51 407	53 240	34980		Nashville-Davidson—Murfreesboro—Franklin, TN Metro area..................	1 670 890	1 830 345
						47015	Cannon County, TN	13 801	13 840
34140		Moscow, ID Micro area	37 244	38 778		47021	Cheatham County, TN	39 105	39 741
	16057	Latah County, ID	37 244	38 778		47037	Davidson County, TN	626 681	678 889
						47043	Dickson County, TN	49 666	51 487
34180		Moses Lake, WA Micro area	89 120	93 259		47081	Hickman County, TN	24 690	24 363
	53025	Grant County, WA......................	89 120	93 259		47111	Macon County, TN	22 248	23 177
						47119	Maury County, TN	80 956	87 757
34220		Moultrie, GA Micro area..................	45 498	45 844		47147	Robertson County, TN	66 283	68 570
	13071	Colquitt County, GA	45 498	45 844		47149	Rutherford County, TN	262 604	298 612
						47159	Smith County, TN......................	19 166	19 295
34260		Mountain Home, AR Micro area.......	41 513	41 053		47165	Sumner County, TN	160 645	175 989
	05005	Baxter County, AR	41 513	41 053		47169	Trousdale County, TN	7 870	8 042
						47187	Williamson County, TN................	183 182	211 672
34300		Mountain Home, ID Micro area	27 038	25 876		47189	Wilson County, TN.....................	113 993	128 911
	16039	Elmore County, ID......................	27 038	25 876					
					35020		Natchez, MS-LA Micro area	53 119	51 396
34340		Mount Airy, NC Micro area..............	73 673	72 743		22029	Concordia Parish, LA	20 822	20 142
	37171	Surry County, NC......................	73 673	72 743		28001	Adams County, MS....................	32 297	31 254
34380		Mount Pleasant, MI Micro area	70 311	70 698	35060		Natchitoches, LA Micro area	39 566	39 179
	26073	Isabella County, MI	70 311	70 698		22069	Natchitoches Parish, LA..............	39 566	39 179
34420		Mount Pleasant, TX Micro area........	32 334	32 623	35100		New Bern, NC Metro area................	126 802	126 245
	48449	Titus County, TX	32 334	32 623		37049	Craven County, NC....................	103 505	103 451
						37103	Jones County, NC.....................	10 153	10 013
34460		Mount Sterling, KY Micro area	44 396	46 194		37137	Pamlico County, NC...................	13 144	12 781
	21011	Bath County, KY........................	11 591	12 228					
	21165	Menifee County, KY	6 306	6 358	35140		Newberry, SC Micro area	37 508	38 012
	21173	Montgomery County, KY	26 499	27 608		45071	Newberry County, SC	37 508	38 012
34500		Mount Vernon, IL Micro area...........	38 827	38 353	35220		New Castle, IN Micro area	49 462	48 985
	17081	Jefferson County, IL...................	38 827	38 353		18065	Henry County, IN.......................	49 462	48 985
34540		Mount Vernon, OH Micro area	60 921	61 061	35260		New Castle, PA Micro area	91 108	88 082
	39083	Knox County, OH	60 921	61 061		42073	Lawrence County, PA	91 108	88 082
34580		Mount Vernon-Anacortes, WA Metro area................................	116 901	121 846					
	53057	Skagit County, WA......................	116 901	121 846					

Core Based Statistical Areas (Metropolitan and Micropolitan), Metropolitan Divisions, and Components (as defined February 2013)–*Continued*

Core Based Statistical Area	State/County FIPS Code	Title and Geographic Components	2010 Census Population	2015 Estimated Population
35300		New Haven-Milford, CT Metro area..	862 477	859 470
	09009	New Haven County, CT	862 477	859 470
35380		New Orleans-Metairie, LA Metro area......................	1 189 866	1 262 888
	22051	Jefferson Parish, LA.....................	432 552	436 275
	22071	Orleans Parish, LA.....................	343 829	389 617
	22075	Plaquemines Parish, LA..................	23 042	23 495
	22087	St. Bernard Parish, LA..................	35 897	45 408
	22089	St. Charles Parish, LA..................	52 780	52 812
	22093	St. James Parish, LA	22 102	21 567
	22095	St. John the Baptist Parish, LA.....	45 924	43 626
	22103	St. Tammany Parish, LA................	233 740	250 088
35420		New Philadelphia-Dover, OH Micro area..................	92 582	92 916
	39157	Tuscarawas County, OH..............	92 582	92 916
35440		Newport, OR Micro area..................	46 034	47 038
	41041	Lincoln County, OR.....................	46 034	47 038
35460		Newport, TN Micro area	35 662	35 162
	47029	Cocke County, TN......................	35 662	35 162
35500		Newton, IA Micro area	36 842	36 827
	19099	Jasper County, IA.....................	36 842	36 827
35580		New Ulm, MN Micro area	25 893	25 313
	27015	Brown County, MN......................	25 893	25 313
35620		New York-Newark-Jersey City, NY-NJ-PA Metro area......................	19 567 410	20 182 305
35620		Dutchess County-Putnam County, NY Metro Div 20524....................	397 198	394 796
	36027	Dutchess County, NY	297 488	295 754
	36079	Putnam County, NY	99 710	99 042
35620		Nassau County-Suffolk County, NY Metro Div 35004....................	2 832 882	2 862 937
	36059	Nassau County, NY..................	1 339 532	1 361 350
	36103	Suffolk County, NY..................	1 493 350	1 501 587
35620		Newark, NJ-PA Metro Div 35084..	2 471 171	2 511 493
	34013	Essex County, NJ....................	783 969	797 434
	34019	Hunterdon County, NJ...............	128 349	125 488
	34027	Morris County, NJ...................	492 276	499 509
	34035	Somerset County, NJ	323 444	333 654
	34037	Sussex County, NJ...................	149 265	143 673
	34039	Union County, NJ	536 499	555 786
	42103	Pike County, PA	57 369	55 949
35620		New York-Jersey City-White Plains, NY-NJ Metro Div 35614....	13 866 159	14 413 079
	34003	Bergen County, NJ	905 116	938 506
	34017	Hudson County, NJ..................	634 266	674 836
	34023	Middlesex County, NJ...............	809 858	840 900
	34025	Monmouth County, NJ...............	630 380	628 715
	34029	Ocean County, NJ...................	576 567	588 721
	34031	Passaic County, NJ	501 226	510 916
	36005	Bronx County, NY	1 385 108	1 455 444
	36047	Kings County, NY	2 504 700	2 636 735
	36061	New York County, NY	1 585 873	1 644 518
	36071	Orange County, NY	372 813	377 647
	36081	Queens County, NY.................	2 230 722	2 339 150
	36085	Richmond County, NY	468 730	474 558
	36087	Rockland County, NY	311 687	326 037
	36119	Westchester County, NY	949 113	976 396
35660		Niles-Benton Harbor, MI Metro area	156 813	154 636
	26021	Berrien County, MI	156 813	154 636
35700		Nogales, AZ Micro area..................	47 420	46 461
	04023	Santa Cruz County, AZ................	47 420	46 461
35740		Norfolk, NE Micro area	48 271	48 184
	31119	Madison County, NE	34 876	35 039
	31139	Pierce County, NE....................	7 266	7 208
	31167	Stanton County, NE	6 129	5 937
35820		North Platte, NE Micro area	37 590	36 908
	31111	Lincoln County, NE	36 288	35 656
	31113	Logan County, NE...................	763	777
	31117	McPherson County, NE.................	539	475
35840		North Port-Sarasota-Bradenton, FL Metro area..................	702 281	768 918
	12081	Manatee County, FL....................	322 833	363 369
	12115	Sarasota County, FL.................	379 448	405 549
35860		North Vernon, IN Micro area	28 525	27 897
	18079	Jennings County, IN...................	28 525	27 897
35900		North Wilkesboro, NC Micro area......	69 340	68 502
	37193	Wilkes County, NC..................	69 340	68 502
35940		Norwalk, OH Micro area	59 626	58 469
	39077	Huron County, OH......................	59 626	58 469
35980		Norwich-New London, CT Metro area..................	274 055	271 863
	09011	New London County, CT..............	274 055	271 863
36020		Oak Harbor, WA Micro area	78 506	80 593
	53029	Island County, WA	78 506	80 593
36100		Ocala, FL Metro area....................	331 298	343 254
	12083	Marion County, FL...................	331 298	343 254
36140		Ocean City, NJ Metro area.............	97 265	94 727
	34009	Cape May County, NJ.................	97 265	94 727
36220		Odessa, TX Metro area	137 130	159 436
	48135	Ector County, TX......................	137 130	159 436
36260		Ogden-Clearfield, UT Metro area	597 159	642 850
	49003	Box Elder County, UT	49 975	52 097
	49011	Davis County, UT....................	306 479	336 043
	49029	Morgan County, UT...................	9 469	11 065
	49057	Weber County, UT...................	231 236	243 645
36300		Ogdensburg-Massena, NY Micro area..................	111 944	111 007
	36089	St. Lawrence County, NY.............	111 944	111 007
36340		Oil City, PA Micro area...................	54 984	53 119
	42121	Venango County, PA..................	54 984	53 119
36380		Okeechobee, FL Micro area.............	39 996	39 469
	12093	Okeechobee County, FL..............	39 996	39 469

Core Based Statistical Area	State/County FIPS Code	Title and Geographic Components	2010 Census Population	2015 Estimated Population	Core Based Statistical Area	State/County FIPS Code	Title and Geographic Components	2010 Census Population	2015 Estimated Population
36420		Oklahoma City, OK Metro area	1 252 987	1 358 452	36980		Owensboro, KY Metro area	114 752	117 463
	40017	Canadian County, OK	115 541	133 378		21059	Daviess County, KY	96 656	99 259
	40027	Cleveland County, OK	255 755	274 458		21091	Hancock County, KY	8 565	8 692
	40051	Grady County, OK	52 431	54 648		21149	McLean County, KY	9 531	9 512
	40081	Lincoln County, OK	34 273	35 042					
	40083	Logan County, OK	41 848	45 996	37020		Owosso, MI Micro area	70 648	68 619
	40087	McClain County, OK	34 506	38 066		26155	Shiawassee County, MI	70 648	68 619
	40109	Oklahoma County, OK	718 633	776 864					
					37060		Oxford, MS Micro area	47 351	53 154
36460		Olean, NY Micro area	80 317	77 922		28071	Lafayette County, MS	47 351	53 154
	36009	Cattaraugus County, NY	80 317	77 922					
					37080		Oxford, NC Micro area	59 916	58 674
36500		Olympia-Tumwater, WA Metro area	252 264	269 536		37077	Granville County, NC	59 916	58 674
	53067	Thurston County, WA	252 264	269 536					
					37100		Oxnard-Thousand Oaks-Ventura, CA Metro area	823 318	850 536
36540		Omaha-Council Bluffs, NE-IA Metro area	865 350	915 312		06111	Ventura County, CA	823 318	850 536
	19085	Harrison County, IA	14 928	14 265					
	19129	Mills County, IA	15 059	14 844	37120		Ozark, AL Micro area	50 251	49 565
	19155	Pottawattamie County, IA	93 158	93 671		01045	Dale County, AL	50 251	49 565
	31025	Cass County, NE	25 241	25 512					
	31055	Douglas County, NE	517 110	550 064	37140		Paducah, KY-IL Micro area	98 762	97 312
	31153	Sarpy County, NE	158 840	175 692		17127	Massac County, IL	15 429	14 766
	31155	Saunders County, NE	20 780	21 016		21007	Ballard County, KY	8 249	8 212
	31177	Washington County, NE	20 234	20 248		21139	Livingston County, KY	9 519	9 316
					21145	McCracken County, KY	65 565	65 018
36580		Oneonta, NY Micro area	62 259	60 636					
	36077	Otsego County, NY	62 259	60 636	37220		Pahrump, NV Micro area	43 946	42 477
						32023	Nye County, NV	43 946	42 477
36620		Ontario, OR-ID Micro area	53 936	53 276					
	16075	Payette County, ID	22 623	22 896	37260		Palatka, FL Micro area	74 364	72 023
	41045	Malheur County, OR	31 313	30 380		12107	Putnam County, FL	74 364	72 023
36660		Opelousas, LA Micro area	83 384	83 848	37300		Palestine, TX Micro area	58 458	57 580
	22097	St. Landry Parish, LA	83 384	83 848		48001	Anderson County, TX	58 458	57 580
36700		Orangeburg, SC Micro area	92 501	89 208	37340		Palm Bay-Melbourne-Titusville, FL Metro area	543 376	568 088
	45075	Orangeburg County, SC	92 501	89 208		12009	Brevard County, FL	543 376	568 088
36740		Orlando-Kissimmee-Sanford, FL Metro	2 134 411	2 387 138	37420		Pampa, TX Micro area	22 535	23 210
	12069	Lake County, FL	297 052	325 875		48179	Gray County, TX	22 535	23 210
	12095	Orange County, FL	1 145 956	1 288 126					
	12097	Osceola County, FL	268 685	323 993	37460		Panama City, FL Metro area	184 715	197 506
	12117	Seminole County, FL	422 718	449 144		12005	Bay County, FL	168 852	181 635
					12045	Gulf County, FL	15 863	15 871
36780		Oshkosh-Neenah, WI Metro area	166 994	169 546					
	55139	Winnebago County, WI	166 994	169 546	37500		Paragould, AR Micro area	42 090	44 196
						05055	Greene County, AR	42 090	44 196
36820		Oskaloosa, IA Micro area	22 381	22 324					
	19123	Mahaska County, IA	22 381	22 324	37540		Paris, TN Micro area	32 330	32 147
						47079	Henry County, TN	32 330	32 147
36830		Othello, WA Micro area	18 728	19 254					
	53001	Adams County, WA	18 728	19 254	37580		Paris, TX Micro area	49 793	49 440
						48277	Lamar County, TX	49 793	49 440
36840		Ottawa, KS Micro area	25 992	25 609					
	20059	Franklin County, KS	25 992	25 609	37620		Parkersburg-Vienna, WV Metro area	92 673	92 332
36860		Ottawa-Peru, IL Micro area	154 908	150 564		54105	Wirt County, WV	5 717	5 880
	17011	Bureau County, IL	34 978	33 587		54107	Wood County, WV	86 956	86 452
	17099	LaSalle County, IL	113 924	111 333					
	17155	Putnam County, IL	6 006	5 644	37660		Parsons, KS Micro area	21 607	20 803
						20099	Labette County, KS	21 607	20 803
36900		Ottumwa, IA Micro area	44 378	43 942					
	19051	Davis County, IA	8 753	8 769	37740		Payson, AZ Micro area	53 597	53 159
	19179	Wapello County, IA	35 625	35 173		04007	Gila County, AZ	53 597	53 159
36940		Owatonna, MN Micro area	36 576	36 755	37780		Pecos, TX Micro area	13 783	14 732
	27147	Steele County, MN	36 576	36 755		48389	Reeves County, TX	13 783	14 732

Core Based Statis-tical Area	State/County FIPS Code	Title and Geographic Components	2010 Census Population	2015 Estimated Population	Core Based Statis-tical Area	State/County FIPS Code	Title and Geographic Components	2010 Census Population	2015 Estimated Population
37860		Pensacola-Ferry Pass-Brent, FL Metro area	448 991	478 043	38300		Pittsburgh, PA Metro area	2 356 285	2 353 045
	12033	Escambia County, FL	297 619	311 003		42003	Allegheny County, PA	1 223 348	1 230 459
	12113	Santa Rosa County, FL	151 372	167 040		42005	Armstrong County, PA	68 941	67 052
37900		Peoria, IL Metro area	379 186	378 018		42007	Beaver County, PA	170 539	168 871
	17123	Marshall County, IL	12 640	11 982		42019	Butler County, PA	183 862	186 818
	17143	Peoria County, IL	186 494	186 221		42051	Fayette County, PA	136 606	133 628
	17175	Stark County, IL	5 994	5 788		42125	Washington County, PA	207 820	208 261
	17179	Tazewell County, IL	135 394	134 800		42129	Westmoreland County, PA	365 169	357 956
	17203	Woodford County, IL	38 664	39 227	38340		Pittsfield, MA Metro area	131 219	127 828
37940		Peru, IN Micro area	36 903	35 862		25003	Berkshire County, MA	131 219	127 828
	18103	Miami County, IN	36 903	35 862	38380		Plainview, TX Micro area	36 273	34 360
37980		Philadelphia-Camden-Wilmington, PA-NJ-DE-MD Metro area	5 965 343	6 069 875		48189	Hale County, TX	36 273	34 360
37980		Camden, NJ Metro Div 15804	1 250 679	1 252 628	38420		Platteville, WI Micro area	51 208	52 250
	34005	Burlington County, NJ	448 734	450 226		55043	Grant County, WI	51 208	52 250
	34007	Camden County, NJ	513 657	510 923	38460		Plattsburgh, NY Micro area	82 128	81 251
	34015	Gloucester County, NJ	288 288	291 479		36019	Clinton County, NY	82 128	81 251
37980		Montgomery County-Bucks County-Chester County, PA Metro Div 33874	1 924 009	1 962 570	38500	18099	Plymouth, IN Micro area	47 051	46 857
	42017	Bucks County, PA	625 249	627 367			Marshall County, IN	47 051	46 857
	42029	Chester County, PA	498 886	515 939	38540		Pocatello, ID Metro area	82 839	83 744
	42091	Montgomery County, PA	799 874	819 264		16005	Bannock County, ID	82 839	83 744
37980		Philadelphia, PA Metro Div 37964	2 084 985	2 131 336	38580		Point Pleasant, WV-OH Micro area	58 258	57 179
	42045	Delaware County, PA	558 979	563 894		39053	Gallia County, OH	30 934	30 142
	42101	Philadelphia County, PA	1 526 006	1 567 442		54053	Mason County, WV	27 324	27 037
37980		Wilmington, DE-MD-NJ Metro Div 48864	705 670	723 341	38620		Ponca City, OK Micro area	46 562	45 366
	10003	New Castle County, Delaware	538 479	556 779		40071	Kay County, OK	46 562	45 366
	24015	Cecil County, MD	101 108	102 382	38700		Pontiac, IL Micro area	38 950	36 671
	34033	Salem County, NJ	66 083	64 180		17105	Livingston County, IL	38 950	36 671
38060		Phoenix-Mesa-Scottsdale, AZ Metro area	4 192 887	4 574 531	38740		Poplar Bluff, MO Micro area	42 794	42 951
	04013	Maricopa County, AZ	3 817 117	4 167 947		29023	Butler County, MO	42 794	42 951
	04021	Pinal County, AZ	375 770	406 584	38780		Portales, NM Micro area	19 846	19 120
38100		Picayune, MS Micro area	55 834	55 191		35041	Roosevelt County, NM	19 846	19 120
	28109	Pearl River County, MS	55 834	55 191	38820		Port Angeles, WA Micro area	71 404	73 486
38180		Pierre, SD Micro area	21 361	21 935		53009	Clallam County, WA	71 404	73 486
	46065	Hughes County, SD	17 022	17 555	38840		Port Clinton, OH Micro area	41 428	40 877
	46117	Stanley County, SD	2 966	2 954		39123	Ottawa County, OH	41 428	40 877
	46119	Sully County, SD	1 373	1 426	38860		Portland-South Portland, ME Metro area	514 098	526 295
38220		Pine Bluff, AR Metro area	100 258	93 696		23005	Cumberland County, ME	281 674	289 977
	05025	Cleveland County, AR	8 689	8 311		23023	Sagadahoc County, ME	35 293	35 149
	05069	Jefferson County, AR	77 435	71 565		23031	York County, ME	197 131	201 169
	05079	Lincoln County, AR	14 134	13 820	38900		Portland-Vancouver-Hillsboro, OR-WA Metro area	2 226 009	2 389 228
38240		Pinehurst-Southern Pines, NC Micro area	88 247	94 352		41005	Clackamas County, OR	375 992	401 515
	37125	Moore County, NC	88 247	94 352		41009	Columbia County, OR	49 351	49 600
38260		Pittsburg, KS Micro area	39 134	39 217		41051	Multnomah County, OR	735 334	790 294
	20037	Crawford County, KS	39 134	39 217		41067	Washington County, OR	529 710	574 326
						41071	Yamhill County, OR	99 193	102 659
						53011	Clark County, WA	425 363	459 495
						53059	Skamania County, WA	11 066	11 339
					38920		Port Lavaca, TX Micro area	21 381	21 895
						48057	Calhoun County, TX	21 381	21 895

Core Based Statistical Area	State/County FIPS Code	Title and Geographic Components	2010 Census Population	2015 Estimated Population	Core Based Statistical Area	State/County FIPS Code	Title and Geographic Components	2010 Census Population	2015 Estimated Population
38940		Port St. Lucie, FL Metro area	424 107	454 846	39860		Red Wing, MN Micro area	46 183	46 435
	12085	Martin County, FL	146 318	156 283		27049	Goodhue County, MN	46 183	46 435
	12111	St. Lucie County, FL	277 789	298 563					
					39900		Reno, NV Metro area	425 417	450 890
39020		Portsmouth, OH Micro area	79 499	76 825		32029	Storey County, NV	4 010	3 987
	39145	Scioto County, OH	79 499	76 825		32031	Washoe County, NV	421 407	446 903
39060		Pottsville, PA Micro area	148 289	144 590	39940		Rexburg, ID Micro area	50 778	51 092
	42107	Schuylkill County, PA	148 289	144 590		16043	Fremont County, ID	13 242	12 819
						16065	Madison County, ID	37 536	38 273
39140		Prescott, AZ Metro area	211 033	222 255					
	04025	Yavapai County, AZ	211 033	222 255	39980		Richmond, IN Micro area	68 917	67 001
						18177	Wayne County, IN	68 917	67 001
39220		Price, UT Micro area	21 403	20 479					
	49007	Carbon County, UT	21 403	20 479	40060		Richmond, VA Metro area	1 208 101	1 271 334
						51007	Amelia County, VA	12 690	12 903
39260		Prineville, OR Micro area	20 978	21 630		51033	Caroline County, VA	28 545	29 984
	41013	Crook County, OR	20 978	21 630		51036	Charles City County, VA	7 256	7 040
						51041	Chesterfield County, VA	316 236	335 687
39300		Providence-Warwick, RI-MA Metro area	1 600 852	1 613 070		51053	Dinwiddie County, VA	28 001	27 852
	25005	Bristol County, MA	548 285	556 772		51075	Goochland County, VA	21 717	22 253
	44001	Bristol County, RI	49 875	49 084		51085	Hanover County, VA	99 863	103 227
	44003	Kent County, RI	166 158	164 801		51087	Henrico County, VA	306 935	325 155
	44005	Newport County, RI	82 888	82 423		51101	King William County, VA	15 935	16 269
	44007	Providence County, RI	626 667	633 473		51127	New Kent County, VA	18 429	20 392
	44009	Washington County, RI	126 979	126 517		51145	Powhatan County, VA	28 046	28 031
						51149	Prince George County, VA	35 725	37 862
39340		Provo-Orem, UT Metro area	526 810	585 799		51183	Sussex County, VA	12 087	11 715
	49023	Juab County, UT	10 246	10 594		51570	Colonial Heights city, VA	17 411	17 820
	49049	Utah County, UT	516 564	575 205		51670	Hopewell city, VA	22 591	22 378
						51730	Petersburg city, VA	32 420	32 477
39380		Pueblo, CO Metro area	159 063	163 591		51760	Richmond city, VA	204 214	220 289
	08101	Pueblo County, CO	159 063	163 591	40080		Richmond-Berea, KY Micro area	99 972	104 766
						21151	Madison County, KY	82 916	87 824
39420		Pullman, WA Micro area	44 776	48 177		21203	Rockcastle County, KY	17 056	16 942
	53075	Whitman County, WA	44 776	48 177					
					40100		Rio Grande City, TX Micro area	60 968	63 795
39460		Punta Gorda, FL Metro area	159 978	173 115		48427	Starr County, TX	60 968	63 795
	12015	Charlotte County, FL	159 978	173 115					
					40140		Riverside-San Bernardino-Ontario, CA	4 224 851	4 489 159
39500		Quincy, IL-MO Micro area	77 314	77 220		06065	Riverside County, CA	2 189 641	2 361 026
	17001	Adams County, IL	67 103	67 013		06071	San Bernardino County, CA	2 035 210	2 128 133
	29111	Lewis County, MO	10 211	10 207					
					40180		Riverton, WY Micro area	40 123	40 315
39540		Racine, WI Metro area	195 408	195 080		56013	Fremont County, WY	40 123	40 315
	55101	Racine County, WI	195 408	195 080					
					40220		Roanoke, VA Metro area	308 707	314 560
39580		Raleigh, NC Metro area	1 130 490	1 273 568		51023	Botetourt County, VA	33 148	33 347
	37069	Franklin County, NC	60 619	63 710		51045	Craig County, VA	5 190	5 211
	37101	Johnston County, NC	168 878	185 660		51067	Franklin County, VA	56 159	56 264
	37183	Wake County, NC	900 993	1 024 198		51161	Roanoke County, VA	92 376	94 409
						51770	Roanoke city, VA	97 032	99 897
39660		Rapid City, SD Metro area	134 598	144 134		51775	Salem city, VA	24 802	25 432
	46033	Custer County, SD	8 216	8 446					
	46093	Meade County, SD	25 434	26 986	40260		Roanoke Rapids, NC Micro area	76 790	72 882
	46103	Pennington County, SD	100 948	108 702		37083	Halifax County, NC	54 691	52 456
						37131	Northampton County, NC	22 099	20 426
39700		Raymondville, TX Micro area	22 134	21 903					
	48489	Willacy County, TX	22 134	21 903	40300		Rochelle, IL Micro area	53 497	51 659
						17141	Ogle County, IL	53 497	51 659
39740		Reading, PA Metro area	411 442	415 271					
	42011	Berks County, PA	411 442	415 271	40340		Rochester, MN Metro area	206 877	213 873
						27039	Dodge County, MN	20 087	20 364
39780		Red Bluff, CA Micro area	63 463	63 308		27045	Fillmore County, MN	20 866	20 834
	06103	Tehama County, CA	63 463	63 308		27109	Olmsted County, MN	144 248	151 436
						27157	Wabasha County, MN	21 676	21 239
39820		Redding, CA Metro area	177 223	179 533					
	06089	Shasta County, CA	177 223	179 533					

Core Based Statistical Areas (Metropolitan and Micropolitan), Metropolitan Divisions, and Components (as defined February 2013)–*Continued*

Core Based Statistical Area	State/County FIPS Code	Title and Geographic Components	2010 Census Population	2015 Estimated Population	Core Based Statistical Area	State/County FIPS Code	Title and Geographic Components	2010 Census Population	2015 Estimated Population
40380		Rochester, NY Metro area..............	1 079 671	1 081 954	41180		St. Louis, MO-IL Metro area............	2 787 701	2 811 588
	36051	Livingston County, NY..................	65 393	64 717		17005	Bond County, IL	17 768	16 950
	36055	Monroe County, NY......................	744 344	749 600		17013	Calhoun County, IL	5 089	4 899
	36069	Ontario County, NY......................	107 931	109 561		17027	Clinton County, IL.......................	37 762	37 786
	36073	Orleans County, NY......................	42 883	41 582		17083	Jersey County, IL	22 985	22 372
	36117	Wayne County, NY.......................	93 772	91 446		17117	Macoupin County, IL	47 765	46 045
	36123	Yates County, NY........................	25 348	25 048		17119	Madison County, IL	269 282	266 209
						17133	Monroe County, IL......................	32 957	33 879
40420		Rockford, IL Metro area..................	349 431	340 663		17163	St. Clair County, IL......................	270 056	264 052
	17007	Boone County, IL	54 165	53 585		29071	Franklin County, MO....................	101 492	102 426
	17201	Winnebago County, IL...................	295 266	287 078		29099	Jefferson County, MO..................	218 733	224 124
						29113	Lincoln County, MO.....................	52 566	54 696
40460		Rockingham, NC Micro area	46 639	45 437		29183	St. Charles County, MO................	360 485	385 590
	37153	Richmond County, NC	46 639	45 437		29189	St. Louis County, MO...................	998 954	1 003 362
						29219	Warren County, MO.....................	32 513	33 513
40540		Rock Springs, WY Micro area	43 806	44 626		29510	St. Louis city, MO.......................	319 294	315 685
	56037	Sweetwater County, WY	43 806	44 626						
					41220		St. Marys, GA Micro area	50 513	52 102
40580		Rocky Mount, NC Metro area...........	152 392	148 069		13039	Camden County, GA	50 513	52 102
	37065	Edgecombe County, NC	56 552	54 150						
	37127	Nash County, NC	95 840	93 919	41400		Salem, OH Micro area...................	107 841	104 806
						39029	Columbiana County, OH	107 841	104 806
40620		Rolla, MO Micro area....................	45 156	44 794						
	29161	Phelps County, MO.....................	45 156	44 794	41420		Salem, OR Metro area...................	390 738	410 091
						41047	Marion County, OR	315 335	330 700
40660		Rome, GA Metro area	96 317	96 504		41053	Polk County, OR	75 403	79 391
	13115	Floyd County, GA........................	96 317	96 504						
					41460		Salina, KS Micro area....................	61 697	61 666
40700		Roseburg, OR Micro area...............	107 667	107 685		20143	Ottawa County, KS......................	6 091	5 975
	41019	Douglas County, OR	107 667	107 685		20169	Saline County, KS.......................	55 606	55 691
40740		Roswell, NM Micro area	65 645	65 764	41500		Salinas, CA Metro area	415 057	433 898
	35005	Chaves County, NM	65 645	65 764		06053	Monterey County, CA...................	415 057	433 898
40780		Russellville, AR Micro area.............	83 939	85 103	41540		Salisbury, MD-DE Metro area...........	373 802	395 300
	05115	Pope County, AR	61 754	63 390		10005	Sussex County, DE......................	197 145	215 622
	05149	Yell County, AR.........................	22 185	21 713		24039	Somerset County, MD..................	26 470	25 768
						24045	Wicomico County, MD..................	98 733	102 370
40820		Ruston, LA Micro area...................	46 735	47 774		24047	Worcester County, MD.................	51 454	51 540
	22061	Lincoln Parish, LA	46 735	47 774						
					41620		Salt Lake City, UT Metro area..........	1 087 873	1 170 266
40860		Rutland, VT Micro area...................	61 642	59 736		49035	Salt Lake County, UT...................	1 029 655	1 107 314
	50021	Rutland County, VT.....................	61 642	59 736		49045	Tooele County, UT......................	58 218	62 952
40900		Sacramento—Roseville—Arden-Arcade, CA Metro area....................	2 149 127	2 274 194	41660		San Angelo, TX Metro area.............	111 823	119 659
	06017	El Dorado County, CA...................	181 058	184 452		48235	Irion County, TX	1 599	1 554
	06061	Placer County, CA.......................	348 432	375 391		48451	Tom Green County, TX.................	110 224	118 105
	06067	Sacramento County, CA	1 418 788	1 501 335						
	06113	Yolo County, CA.........................	200 849	213 016	41700		San Antonio-New Braunfels, TX Metro..	2 142 508	2 384 075
						48013	Atascosa County, TX	44 911	48 435
40940		Safford, AZ Micro area	37 220	37 666		48019	Bandera County, TX....................	20 485	21 269
	04009	Graham County, AZ.....................	37 220	37 666		48029	Bexar County, TX........................	1 714 773	1 897 753
						48091	Comal County, TX.......................	108 472	129 048
40980		Saginaw, MI Metro area.................	200 169	193 307		48187	Guadalupe County, TX.................	131 533	151 249
	26145	Saginaw County, MI	200 169	193 307		48259	Kendall County, TX.....................	33 410	40 384
						48325	Medina County, TX	46 006	48 417
41060		St. Cloud, MN Metro area...............	189 093	194 418		48493	Wilson County, TX	42 918	47 520
	27009	Benton County, MN.....................	38 451	39 710						
	27145	Stearns County, MN....................	150 642	154 708	41740		San Diego-Carlsbad, CA Metro area	3 095 313	3 299 521
						06073	San Diego County, CA..................	3 095 313	3 299 521
41100		St. George, UT Metro area..............	138 115	155 602						
	49053	Washington County, UT.................	138 115	155 602	41760		Sandpoint, ID Micro area................	40 877	41 859
						16017	Bonner County, ID.......................	40 877	41 859
41140		St. Joseph, MO-KS Metro area........	127 329	126 880						
	20043	Doniphan County, KS...................	7 945	7 797	41780		Sandusky, OH Micro area	77 079	75 550
	29003	Andrew County, MO.....................	17 291	17 296		39043	Erie County, OH	77 079	75 550
	29021	Buchanan County, MO..................	89 201	89 100						
	29063	DeKalb County, MO	12 892	12 687						

Core Based Statistical Areas (Metropolitan and Micropolitan), Metropolitan Divisions, and Components (as defined February 2013)–*Continued*

Core Based Statistical Area	State/ County FIPS Code	Title and Geographic Components	2010 Census Population	2015 Estimated Population	Core Based Statistical Area	State/ County FIPS Code	Title and Geographic Components	2010 Census Population	2015 Estimated Population
41820		Sanford, NC Micro area...................	57 866	59 660	42620		Searcy, AR Micro area	77 076	79 161
	37105	Lee County, NC...........................	57 866	59 660		05145	White County, AR........................	77 076	79 161
41860		San Francisco-Oakland-Hayward, CA Metro area	4 335 391	4 656 132	42660		Seattle-Tacoma-Bellevue, WA Metro area..	3 439 809	3 733 580
41860		Oakland-Hayward-Berkeley, CA Metro Div 36084	2 559 296	2 764 960	42660		Seattle-Bellevue-Everett, WA Metro Div 42644	2 644 584	2 889 626
	06001	Alameda County, CA................	1 510 271	1 638 215		53033	King County, WA	1 931 249	2 117 125
	06013	Contra Costa County, CA..........	1 049 025	1 126 745		53061	Snohomish County, WA	713 335	772 501
41860		San Francisco-Redwood City-South San Francisco, CA Metro Div 41884	1 523 686	1 629 951	42660		Tacoma-Lakewood, WA Metro Div 45104	795 225	843 954
	06075	San Francisco County, CA........	805 235	864 816		53053	Pierce County, WA	795 225	843 954
	06081	San Mateo County, CA..............	718 451	765 135	42680		Sebastian-Vero Beach, FL Metro area......................................	138 028	147 919
41860		San Rafael, CA Metropolitan Div 42034	252 409	261 221		12061	Indian River County, FL.............	138 028	147 919
	06041	Marin County, CA	252 409	261 221	42700		Sebring, FL Metro area..................	98 786	99 491
41940		San Jose-Sunnyvale-Santa Clara, CA Metro area	1 836 911	1 976 836		12055	Highlands County, FL.................	98 786	99 491
	06069	San Benito County, CA................	55 269	58 792	42740		Sedalia, MO Micro area..................	42 201	42 255
	06085	Santa Clara County, CA..............	1 781 642	1 918 044		29159	Pettis County, MO......................	42 201	42 255
42020		San Luis Obispo-Paso Robles-Arroyo Grande, CA Metro area	269 637	281 401	42780		Selinsgrove, PA Micro area...........	39 702	40 444
	06079	San Luis Obispo County, CA........	269 637	281 401		42109	Snyder County, PA....................	39 702	40 444
42100		Santa Cruz-Watsonville, CA Metro area	262 382	274 146	42820		Selma, AL Micro area	43 820	41 131
	06087	Santa Cruz County, CA..............	262 382	274 146		01047	Dallas County, AL.....................	43 820	41 131
42140		Santa Fe, NM Metro area................	144 170	148 686	42860		Seneca, SC Micro area	74 273	75 713
	35049	Santa Fe County, NM	144 170	148 686		45073	Oconee County, SC	74 273	75 713
42200		Santa Maria-Santa Barbara, CA Metro..	423 895	444 769	42900		Seneca Falls, NY Micro area...........	35 251	34 833
	06083	Santa Barbara County, CA	423 895	444 769		36099	Seneca County, NY......................	35 251	34 833
42220		Santa Rosa, CA Metro area	483 878	502 146	42940		Sevierville, TN Micro area	89 889	95 946
	06097	Sonoma County, CA	483 878	502 146		47155	Sevier County, TN....................	89 889	95 946
42300		Sault Ste. Marie, MI Micro area........	38 520	38 033	42980		Seymour, IN Micro area..................	42 376	44 069
	26033	Chippewa County, MI..................	38 520	38 033		18071	Jackson County, IN....................	42 376	44 069
42340		Savannah, GA Metro area...............	347 611	379 199	43020		Shawano, WI Micro area	46 181	45 877
	13029	Bryan County, GA	30 233	35 137		55078	Menominee County, WI................	4 232	4 573
	13051	Chatham County, GA....................	265 128	286 956		55115	Shawano County, WI	41 949	41 304
	13103	Effingham County, GA	52 250	57 106	43060		Shawnee, OK Micro area................	69 442	71 875
42380		Sayre, PA Micro area	62 622	61 281		40125	Pottawatomie County, OK............	69 442	71 875
	42015	Bradford County, PA....................	62 622	61 281	43100		Sheboygan, WI Metro area..............	115 507	115 569
42420		Scottsbluff, NE Micro area	38 971	38 309		55117	Sheboygan County, WI...............	115 507	115 569
	31007	Banner County, NE	690	788	43140		Shelby, NC Micro area	98 078	96 879
	31157	Scotts Bluff County, NE...............	36 970	36 261		37045	Cleveland County, NC.................	98 078	96 879
	31165	Sioux County, NE.......................	1 311	1 260	43180		Shelbyville, TN Micro area..............	45 058	47 183
42460		Scottsboro, AL Micro area...............	53 227	52 419		47003	Bedford County, TN	45 058	47 183
	01071	Jackson County, AL	53 227	52 419	43220		Shelton, WA Micro area..................	60 699	61 023
42540		Scranton—Wilkes-Barre—Hazleton, PA Metro area................................	563 631	558 166		53045	Mason County, WA	60 699	61 023
	42069	Lackawanna County, PA..............	214 437	211 917	43260		Sheridan, WY Micro area................	29 116	30 009
	42079	Luzerne County, PA....................	320 918	318 449		56033	Sheridan County, WY..................	29 116	30 009
	42131	Wyoming County, PA..................	28 276	27 800	43300		Sherman-Denison, TX Metro area....	120 877	125 467
						48181	Grayson County, TX...................	120 877	125 467
					43320		Show Low, AZ Micro area	107 449	108 277
						04017	Navajo County, AZ....................	107 449	108 277

Core Based Statistical Area	State/County FIPS Code	Title and Geographic Components	2010 Census Population	2015 Estimated Population	Core Based Statistical Area	State/County FIPS Code	Title and Geographic Components	2010 Census Population	2015 Estimated Population
43340		Shreveport-Bossier City, LA Metro area	439 811	443 708	44100		Springfield, IL Metro area	210 170	211 156
	22015	Bossier Parish, LA	116 979	125 175		17129	Menard County, IL	12 705	12 444
	22017	Caddo Parish, LA	254 969	251 460		17167	Sangamon County, IL	197 465	198 712
	22031	De Soto Parish, LA	26 656	27 052	44140		Springfield, MA Metro area	621 570	631 982
	22119	Webster Parish, LA	41 207	40 021		25013	Hampden County, MA	463 490	470 690
43380		Sidney, OH Micro area	49 423	48 901		25015	Hampshire County, MA	158 080	161 292
	39149	Shelby County, OH	49 423	48 901	44180		Springfield, MO Metro area	436 712	456 456
43420		Sierra Vista-Douglas, AZ Metro area	131 346	126 427		29043	Christian County, MO	77 422	83 279
	04003	Cochise County, AZ	131 346	126 427		29059	Dallas County, MO	16 777	16 393
43460		Sikeston, MO Micro area	39 191	39 008		29077	Greene County, MO	275 174	288 072
	29201	Scott County, MO	39 191	39 008		29167	Polk County, MO	31 137	31 229
43500		Silver City, NM Micro area	29 514	28 609		29225	Webster County, MO	36 202	37 483
	35017	Grant County, NM	29 514	28 609	44220		Springfield, OH Metro area	138 333	135 959
43580		Sioux City, IA-NE-SD Metro area	168 563	169 069		39023	Clark County, OH	138 333	135 959
	19149	Plymouth County, IA	24 986	24 800	44260		Starkville, MS Micro area	47 671	49 800
	19193	Woodbury County, IA	102 172	102 782		28105	Oktibbeha County, MS	47 671	49 800
	31043	Dakota County, NE	21 006	20 781	44300		State College, PA Metro area	153 990	160 580
	31051	Dixon County, NE	6 000	5 797		42027	Centre County, PA	153 990	160 580
	46127	Union County, SD	14 399	14 909	44340		Statesboro, GA Micro area	70 217	72 651
43620		Sioux Falls, SD Metro area	228 261	251 854		13031	Bulloch County, GA	70 217	72 651
	46083	Lincoln County, SD	44 828	52 849	44420		Staunton-Waynesboro, VA Metro area	118 502	120 221
	46087	McCook County, SD	5 618	5 599		51015	Augusta County, VA	73 750	74 314
	46099	Minnehaha County, SD	169 468	185 197		51790	Staunton city, VA	23 746	24 416
	46125	Turner County, SD	8 347	8 209		51820	Waynesboro city, VA	21 006	21 491
43660		Snyder, TX Micro area	16 921	17 615	44460		Steamboat Springs, CO Micro area	23 509	24 130
	48415	Scurry County, TX	16 921	17 615		08107	Routt County, CO	23 509	24 130
43700		Somerset, KY Micro area	63 063	63 782	44500		Stephenville, TX Micro area	37 890	41 122
	21199	Pulaski County, KY	63 063	63 782		48143	Erath County, TX	37 890	41 122
43740		Somerset, PA Micro area	77 742	75 522	44540		Sterling, CO Micro area	22 709	22 036
	42111	Somerset County, PA	77 742	75 522		08075	Logan County, CO	22 709	22 036
43760		Sonora, CA Micro area	55 365	53 709	44580		Sterling, IL Micro area	58 498	57 079
	06109	Tuolumne County, CA	55 365	53 709		17195	Whiteside County, IL	58 498	57 079
43780		South Bend-Mishawaka, IN-MI Metro area	319 224	320 098	44620		Stevens Point, WI Micro area	70 019	70 408
	18141	St. Joseph County, IN	266 931	268 441		55097	Portage County, WI	70 019	70 408
	26027	Cass County, MI	52 293	51 657	44660		Stillwater, OK Micro area	77 350	80 850
43900		Spartanburg, SC Metro area	313 268	325 079		40119	Payne County, OK	77 350	80 850
	45083	Spartanburg County, SC	284 307	297 302	44700		Stockton-Lodi, CA Metro area	685 306	726 106
	45087	Union County, SC	28 961	27 777		06077	San Joaquin County, CA	685 306	726 106
43940		Spearfish, SD Micro area	24 097	24 827	44740		Storm Lake, IA Micro area	20 260	20 493
	46081	Lawrence County, SD	24 097	24 827		19021	Buena Vista County, IA	20 260	20 493
43980		Spencer, IA Micro area	16 667	16 507	44780		Sturgis, MI Micro area	61 295	61 018
	19041	Clay County, IA	16 667	16 507		26149	St. Joseph County, MI	61 295	61 018
44020		Spirit Lake, IA Micro area	16 667	17 111	44860		Sulphur Springs, TX Micro area	35 161	36 223
	19059	Dickinson County, IA	16 667	17 111		48223	Hopkins County, TX	35 161	36 223
44060		Spokane-Spokane Valley, WA Metro area	527 753	547 824	44900		Summerville, GA Micro area	26 015	24 922
	53051	Pend Oreille County, WA	13 001	13 088		13055	Chattooga County, GA	26 015	24 922
	53063	Spokane County, WA	471 221	490 945	44920		Summit Park, UT Micro area	36 324	39 633
	53065	Stevens County, WA	43 531	43 791		49043	Summit County, UT	36 324	39 633

Core Based Statistical Area	State/County FIPS Code	Title and Geographic Components	2010 Census Population	2015 Estimated Population	Core Based Statistical Area	State/County FIPS Code	Title and Geographic Components	2010 Census Population	2015 Estimated Population
44940		Sumter, SC Metro area	107 456	107 480	45700		Tifton, GA Micro area	40 118	40 764
	45085	Sumter County, SC	107 456	107 480		13277	Tift County, GA	40 118	40 764
44980		Sunbury, PA Micro area	94 528	93 246	45740		Toccoa, GA Micro area	26 175	25 586
	42097	Northumberland County, PA	94 528	93 246		13257	Stephens County, GA	26 175	25 586
45000		Susanville, CA Micro area	34 895	31 345	45780		Toledo, OH Metro area	610 001	605 956
	06035	Lassen County, CA	34 895	31 345		39051	Fulton County, OH	42 698	42 537
45020		Sweetwater, TX Micro area	15 216	15 107		39095	Lucas County, OH	441 815	433 689
	48353	Nolan County, TX	15 216	15 107		39173	Wood County, OH	125 488	129 730
45060		Syracuse, NY Metro area	662 577	660 458	45820		Topeka, KS Metro area	233 870	233 791
	36053	Madison County, NY	73 442	71 849		20085	Jackson County, KS	13 462	13 338
	36067	Onondaga County, NY	467 026	468 463		20087	Jefferson County, KS	19 126	18 930
	36075	Oswego County, NY	122 109	120 146		20139	Osage County, KS	16 295	15 847
45140		Tahlequah, OK Micro area	46 987	48 447		20177	Shawnee County, KS	177 934	178 725
	40021	Cherokee County, OK	46 987	48 447		20197	Wabaunsee County, KS	7 053	6 951
45180		Talladega-Sylacauga, AL Micro area	93 830	91 586	45860		Torrington, CT Micro area	189 927	183 603
	01037	Coosa County, AL	11 539	10 724		09005	Litchfield County, CT	189 927	183 603
	01121	Talladega County, AL	82 291	80 862	45900		Traverse City, MI Micro area	143 372	148 334
45220		Tallahassee, FL Metro area	367 413	377 924		26019	Benzie County, MI	17 525	17 457
	12039	Gadsden County, FL	46 389	46 036		26055	Grand Traverse County, MI	86 986	91 636
	12065	Jefferson County, FL	14 761	14 081		26079	Kalkaska County, MI	17 153	17 260
	12073	Leon County, FL	275 487	286 272		26089	Leelanau County, MI	21 708	21 981
	12129	Wakulla County, FL	30 776	31 535	45940		Trenton, NJ Metro area	366 513	371 398
45300		Tampa-St. Petersburg-Clearwater, FL Metro area	2 783 243	2 975 225		34021	Mercer County, NJ	366 513	371 398
	12053	Hernando County, FL	172 778	178 439	45980		Troy, AL Micro area	32 899	33 046
	12057	Hillsborough County, FL	1 229 226	1 349 050		01109	Pike County, AL	32 899	33 046
	12101	Pasco County, FL	464 697	497 909	46020		Truckee-Grass Valley, CA Micro area	98 764	98 877
	12103	Pinellas County, FL	916 542	949 827		06057	Nevada County, CA	98 764	98 877
45340		Taos, NM Micro area	32 937	32 907	46060		Tucson, AZ Metro area	980 263	1 010 025
	35055	Taos County, NM	32 937	32 907		04019	Pima County, AZ	980 263	1 010 025
45380		Taylorville, IL Micro area	34 800	33 642	46100		Tullahoma-Manchester, TN Micro area	100 210	102 048
	17021	Christian County, IL	34 800	33 642		47031	Coffee County, TN	52 796	54 277
45460		Terre Haute, IN Metro area	172 425	171 019		47051	Franklin County, TN	41 052	41 449
	18021	Clay County, IN	26 890	26 503		47127	Moore County, TN	6 362	6 322
	18153	Sullivan County, IN	21 475	20 928	46140		Tulsa, OK Metro area	937 478	981 005
	18165	Vermillion County, IN	16 212	15 692		40037	Creek County, OK	69 967	70 892
	18167	Vigo County, IN	107 848	107 896		40111	Okmulgee County, OK	40 069	39 187
45500		Texarkana, TX-AR Metro area	149 198	149 769		40113	Osage County, OK	47 472	47 887
	05081	Little River County, AR	13 171	12 472		40117	Pawnee County, OK	16 577	16 436
	05091	Miller County, AR	43 462	43 908		40131	Rogers County, OK	86 905	90 802
	48037	Bowie County, TX	92 565	93 389		40143	Tulsa County, OK	603 403	639 242
45520		The Dalles, OR Micro area	25 213	25 775		40145	Wagoner County, OK	73 085	76 559
	41065	Wasco County, OR	25 213	25 775	46180		Tupelo, MS Micro area	136 268	139 817
45540		The Villages, FL Metro area	93 420	118 891		28057	Itawamba County, MS	23 401	23 609
	12119	Sumter County, FL	93 420	118 891		28081	Lee County, MS	82 910	85 300
45580		Thomaston, GA Micro area	27 153	26 368		28115	Pontotoc County, MS	29 957	30 908
	13293	Upson County, GA	27 153	26 368	46220		Tuscaloosa, AL Metro area	230 162	239 908
45620		Thomasville, GA Micro area	44 720	45 063		01065	Hale County, AL	15 760	15 068
	13275	Thomas County, GA	44 720	45 063		01107	Pickens County, AL	19 746	20 864
45660		Tiffin, OH Micro area	56 745	55 610		01125	Tuscaloosa County, AL	194 656	203 976
	39147	Seneca County, OH	56 745	55 610	46300		Twin Falls, ID Micro area	99 604	105 189
						16053	Jerome County, ID	22 374	22 814
						16083	Twin Falls County, ID	77 230	82 375

Core Based Statistical Areas (Metropolitan and Micropolitan), Metropolitan Divisions, and Components (as defined February 2013)–*Continued*

Core Based Statistical Area	State/County FIPS Code	Title and Geographic Components	2010 Census Population	2015 Estimated Population
46340		Tyler, TX Metro area.....................	209 714	222 936
	48423	Smith County, TX...................	209 714	222 936
46380		Ukiah, CA Micro area	87 841	87 649
	06045	Mendocino County, CA	87 841	87 649
46460		Union City, TN-KY Micro area	38 620	36 877
	21075	Fulton County, KY.....................	6 813	6 238
	47131	Obion County, TN	31 807	30 639
46500		Urbana, OH Micro area	40 097	38 987
	39021	Champaign County, OH...............	40 097	38 987
46520		Urban Honolulu, HI Metro area	953 207	998 714
	15003	Honolulu County, HI	953 207	998 714
46540		Utica-Rome, NY Metro area	299 397	295 600
	36043	Herkimer County, NY	64 519	63 100
	36065	Oneida County, NY	234 878	232 500
46620		Uvalde, TX Micro area.................	26 405	27 245
	48463	Uvalde County, TX	26 405	27 245
46660		Valdosta, GA Metro area	139 588	142 875
	13027	Brooks County, GA	16 243	15 658
	13101	Echols County, GA.....................	4 034	4 040
	13173	Lanier County, GA.....................	10 078	10 312
	13185	Lowndes County, GA	109 233	112 865
46700		Vallejo-Fairfield, CA Metro area	413 344	436 092
	06095	Solano County, CA	413 344	436 092
46740		Valley, AL Micro area	34 215	34 123
	01017	Chambers County, AL.................	34 215	34 123
46780		Van Wert, OH Micro area	28 744	28 562
	39161	Van Wert County, OH	28 744	28 562
46820		Vermillion, SD Micro area................	13 864	13 964
	46027	Clay County, SD........................	13 864	13 964
46860		Vernal, UT Micro area	32 588	37 928
	49047	Uintah County, UT......................	32 588	37 928
46900		Vernon, TX Micro area	13 535	13 027
	48487	Wilbarger County, TX..................	13 535	13 027
46980		Vicksburg, MS Micro area	58 377	56 635
	28021	Claiborne County, MS.................	9 604	9 150
	28149	Warren County, MS....................	48 773	47 485
47020		Victoria, TX Metro area.................	94 003	99 913
	48175	Goliad County, TX.....................	7 210	7 531
	48469	Victoria County, TX....................	86 793	92 382
47080		Vidalia, GA Micro area.................	36 346	36 192
	13209	Montgomery County, GA..............	9 123	8 951
	13279	Toombs County, GA	27 223	27 241
47180		Vincennes, IN Micro area	38 440	37 927
	18083	Knox County, IN.......................	38 440	37 927
47220		Vineland-Bridgeton, NJ Metro area ..	156 898	155 854
	34011	Cumberland County, NJ................	156 898	155 854
47240		Vineyard Haven, MA Micro area	16 535	17 299
	25007	Dukes County, MA	16 535	17 299
47260		Virginia Beach-Norfolk-Newport News, VA-NC Metro area................	1 676 822	1 724 876
	37053	Currituck County, NC	23 547	25 263
	37073	Gates County, NC......................	12 197	11 431
	51073	Gloucester County, VA.................	36 858	37 143
	51093	Isle of Wight County, VA...............	35 270	36 314
	51095	James City County, VA.................	67 009	73 147
	51115	Mathews County, VA...................	8 978	8 862
	51199	York County, VA.......................	65 464	67 837
	51550	Chesapeake city, VA...................	222 209	235 429
	51650	Hampton city, VA......................	137 436	136 454
	51700	Newport News city, VA................	180 719	182 385
	51710	Norfolk city, VA.......................	242 803	246 393
	51735	Poquoson city, VA.....................	12 150	12 059
	51740	Portsmouth city, VA...................	95 535	96 201
	51800	Suffolk city, VA.......................	84 585	88 161
	51810	Virginia Beach city, VA...............	437 994	452 745
	51830	Williamsburg city, VA	14 068	15 052
47300		Visalia-Porterville, CA Metro area	442 179	459 863
	06107	Tulare County, CA......................	442 179	459 863
47340		Wabash, IN Micro area	32 888	32 138
	18169	Wabash County, IN	32 888	32 138
47380		Waco, TX Metro area	252 772	262 813
	48145	Falls County, TX........................	17 866	17 142
	48309	McLennan County, TX	234 906	245 671
47420		Wahpeton, ND-MN Micro area	22 897	22 798
	27167	Wilkin County, MN......................	6 576	6 396
	38077	Richland County, ND....................	16 321	16 402
47460		Walla Walla, WA Metro area	62 859	64 282
	53013	Columbia County, WA..................	4 078	3 944
	53071	Walla Walla County, WA..............	58 781	60 338
47540		Wapakoneta, OH Micro area	45 949	45 876
	39011	Auglaize County, OH...................	45 949	45 876
47580		Warner Robins, GA Metro area........	179 605	188 149
	13153	Houston County, GA	139 900	150 033
	13225	Peach County, GA	27 695	26 720
	13235	Pulaski County, GA.....................	12 010	11 396
47620		Warren, PA Micro area	41 815	40 396
	42123	Warren County, PA	41 815	40 396
47660		Warrensburg, MO Micro area...........	52 595	53 951
	29101	Johnson County, MO	52 595	53 951
47700		Warsaw, IN Micro area..................	77 358	78 620
	18085	Kosciusko County, IN..................	77 358	78 620
47780		Washington, IN Micro area..............	31 648	32 906
	18027	Daviess County, IN	31 648	32 906
47820		Washington, NC Micro area	47 759	47 651
	37013	Beaufort County, NC...................	47 759	47 651
47900		Washington-Arlington-Alexandria, DC-VA-MD-WV Metro area	5 636 232	6 097 684
47900		Silver Spring-Frederick-Rockville, MD Metro Div 43524...................	1 205 162	1 285 438
	24021	Frederick County, MD..................	233 385	245 322
	24031	Montgomery County, MD..........	971 777	1 040 116

Core Based Statistical Areas (Metropolitan and Micropolitan), Metropolitan Divisions, and Components (as defined February 2013)–*Continued*

Core Based Statistical Area	State/County FIPS Code	Title and Geographic Components	2010 Census Population	2015 Estimated Population	Core Based Statistical Area	State/County FIPS Code	Title and Geographic Components	2010 Census Population	2015 Estimated Population
47900		Washington-Arlington-Alexandria, DC-VA-MD-WV Metro Div 47894..	4 431 070	4 812 246	48460		West Plains, MO Micro area.............	40 400	40 117
	11001	District of Columbia, DC............	601 723	672 228		29091	Howell County, MO......................	40 400	40 117
	24009	Calvert County, MD.................	88 737	90 595	48540		Wheeling, WV-OH Metro area.........	147 950	144 198
	24017	Charles County, MD.................	146 551	156 118		39013	Belmont County, OH....................	70 400	69 154
	24033	Prince George's County, MD.....	863 420	909 535		54051	Marshall County, WV....................	33 107	31 978
	51013	Arlington County, VA................	207 627	229 164		54069	Ohio County, WV........................	44 443	43 066
	51043	Clarke County, VA...................	14 034	14 363					
	51047	Culpeper County, VA...............	46 689	49 432	48580		Whitewater-Elkhorn, WI Micro area..	102 228	102 804
	51059	Fairfax County, VA..................	1 081 726	1 142 234		55127	Walworth County, WI....................	102 228	102 804
	51061	Fauquier County, VA................	65 203	68 782					
	51107	Loudoun County, VA................	312 311	375 629	48620		Wichita, KS Metro area................	630 919	644 610
	51153	Prince William County, VA	402 002	451 721		20015	Butler County, KS........................	65 880	66 741
	51157	Rappahannock County, VA	7 373	7 378		20079	Harvey County, KS......................	34 684	35 073
	51177	Spotsylvania County, VA...........	122 397	130 475		20095	Kingman County, KS...................	7 858	7 687
	51179	Stafford County, VA.................	128 961	142 003		20173	Sedgwick County, KS..................	498 365	511 574
	51187	Warren County, VA..................	37 575	39 083		20191	Sumner County, KS.....................	24 132	23 535
	51510	Alexandria city, VA	139 966	153 511					
	51600	Fairfax city, VA	22 565	24 013	48660		Wichita Falls, TX Metro area...........	151 306	150 780
	51610	Falls Church city, VA	12 332	13 892		48009	Archer County, TX.......................	9 054	8 715
	51630	Fredericksburg city, VA	24 286	28 118		48077	Clay County, TX..........................	10 752	10 360
	51683	Manassas city, VA	37 821	41 764		48485	Wichita County, TX......................	131 500	131 705
	51685	Manassas Park city, VA	14 273	15 726					
	54037	Jefferson County, WV...............	53 498	56 482	48700		Williamsport, PA Metro area............	116 111	116 048
						42081	Lycoming County, PA...................	116 111	116 048
47920		Washington Court House, OH Micro area.............................	29 030	28 679	48780		Williston, ND Micro area................	22 398	35 294
	39047	Fayette County, OH	29 030	28 679		38105	Williams County, ND....................	22 398	35 294
47940		Waterloo-Cedar Falls, IA Metro area	167 819	170 612	48820		Willmar, MN Micro area.................	42 239	42 542
	19013	Black Hawk County, IA	131 090	133 455		27067	Kandiyohi County, MN..................	42 239	42 542
	19017	Bremer County, IA...................	24 276	24 722					
	19075	Grundy County, IA..................	12 453	12 435	48900		Wilmington, NC Metro area	254 884	277 969
						37129	New Hanover County, NC.............	202 667	220 358
47980		Watertown, SD Micro area	27 227	27 939		37141	Pender County, NC.....................	52 217	57 611
	46029	Codington County, SD	27 227	27 939					
					48940		Wilmington, OH Micro area.............	42 040	41 917
48020		Watertown-Fort Atkinson, WI Micro area.............................	83 686	84 559		39027	Clinton County, OH.....................	42 040	41 917
	55055	Jefferson County, WI................	83 686	84 559	48980		Wilson, NC Micro area..................	81 234	81 714
						37195	Wilson County, NC......................	81 234	81 714
48060		Watertown-Fort Drum, NY Metro area.............................	116 229	117 635	49020		Winchester, VA-WV Metro area	128 472	133 836
	36045	Jefferson County, NY................	116 229	117 635		51069	Frederick County, VA...................	78 305	83 199
						51840	Winchester city, VA.....................	26 203	27 284
48100		Wauchula, FL Micro area	27 731	27 502		54027	Hampshire County, WV...............	23 964	23 353
	12049	Hardee County, FL.....................	27 731	27 502					
					49080		Winnemucca, NV Micro area...........	16 528	17 019
48140		Wausau, WI Metro area.................	134 063	135 868		32013	Humboldt County, NV...................	16 528	17 019
	55073	Marathon County, WI................	134 063	135 868					
					49100		Winona, MN Micro area.................	51 461	50 885
48180		Waycross, GA Micro area...............	55 070	54 473		27169	Winona County, MN.....................	51 461	50 885
	13229	Pierce County, GA...................	18 758	19 103					
	13299	Ware County, GA.....................	36 312	35 370	49180		Winston-Salem, NC Metro area........	640 595	659 330
						37057	Davidson County, NC...................	162 878	164 622
48220		Weatherford, OK Micro area............	27 469	29 744		37059	Davie County, NC	41 240	41 753
	40039	Custer County, OK...................	27 469	29 744		37067	Forsyth County, NC.....................	350 670	369 019
						37169	Stokes County, NC......................	47 401	46 351
48260		Weirton-Steubenville, WV-OH Metro area.............................	124 454	120 512		37197	Yadkin County, NC......................	38 406	37 585
	39081	Jefferson County, OH...............	69 709	67 347	49220		Wisconsin Rapids-Marshfield, WI Micro area.............................	74 749	73 435
	54009	Brooke County, WV..................	24 069	23 350		55141	Wood County, WI........................	74 749	73 435
	54029	Hancock County, WV................	30 676	29 815					
					49260		Woodward, OK Micro area	20 081	21 559
48300		Wenatchee, WA Metro area.............	110 884	116 178		40153	Woodward County, OK	20 081	21 559
	53007	Chelan County, WA..................	72 453	75 644					
	53017	Douglas County, WA.................	38 431	40 534	49300		Wooster, OH Micro area.................	114 520	116 063
						39169	Wayne County, OH.....................	114 520	116 063

Core Based Statistical Areas (Metropolitan and Micropolitan), Metropolitan Divisions, and Components (as defined February 2013)–*Continued*

Core Based Statistical Area	State/County FIPS Code	Title and Geographic Components	2010 Census Population	2015 Estimated Population	Core Based Statistical Area	State/County FIPS Code	Title and Geographic Components	2010 Census Population	2015 Estimated Population
49340		Worcester, MA-CT Metro area	916 980	935 536	49700		Yuba City, CA Metro area	166 892	170 955
	09015	Windham County, CT....................	118 428	116 573		06101	Sutter County, CA	94 737	96 463
	25027	Worcester County, MA.................	798 552	818 963		06115	Yuba County, CA	72 155	74 492
49380		Worthington, MN Micro area............	21 378	21 770	49740		Yuma, AZ Metro area	195 751	204 275
	27105	Nobles County, MN	21 378	21 770		04027	Yuma County, AZ.........................	195 751	204 275
49420		Yakima, WA Metro area	243 231	248 830	49780		Zanesville, OH Micro area..............	86 074	86 290
	53077	Yakima County, WA.....................	243 231	248 830		39119	Muskingum County, OH...............	86 074	86 290
49460		Yankton, SD Micro area	22 438	22 702	49820		Zapata, TX Micro area....................	14 018	14 374
	46135	Yankton County, SD.....................	22 438	22 702		48505	Zapata County, TX	14 018	14 374
49620		York-Hanover, PA Metro area	434 972	442 867					
	42133	York County, PA...........................	434 972	442 867					
49660		Youngstown-Warren-Boardman, OH-PA Metro area	565 773	549 885					
	39099	Mahoning County, OH..................	238 823	231 900					
	39155	Trumbull County, OH	210 312	203 751					
	42085	Mercer County, PA.......................	116 638	114 234					

APPENDIX D
MAPS OF CONGRESSIONAL DISTRICTS AND STATES

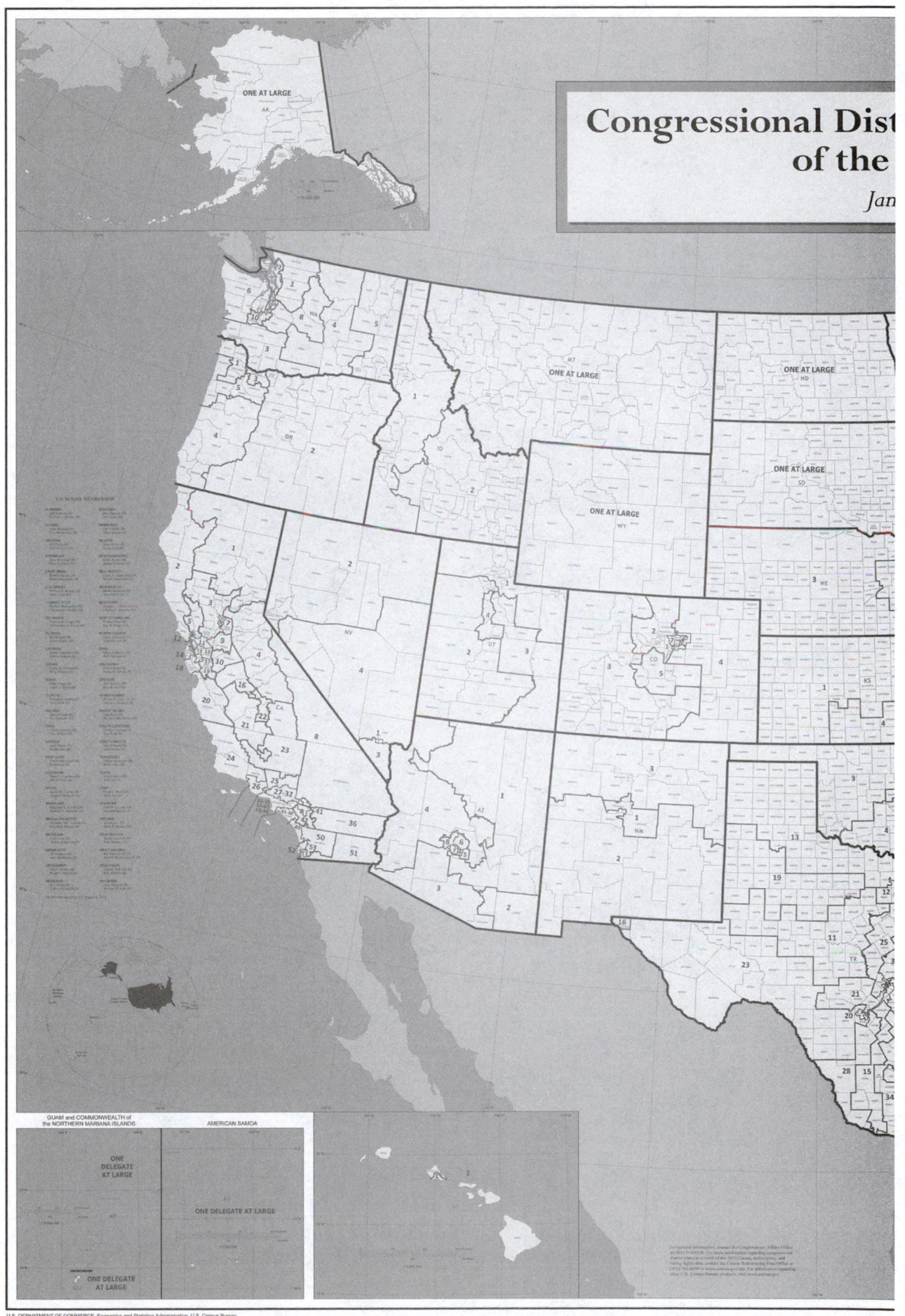

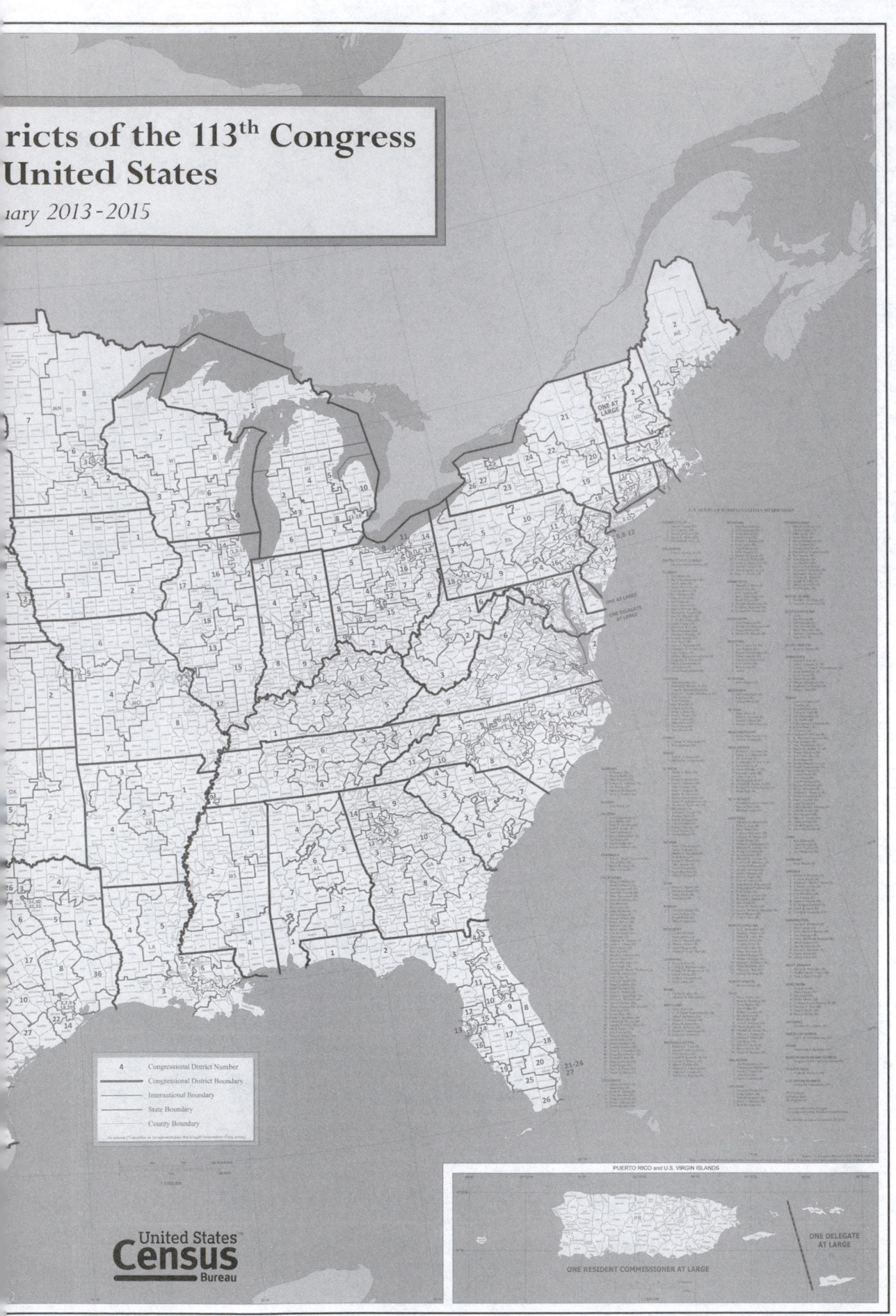

ricts of the 113th Congress
United States

aary 2013-2015

One At Large

Legend:
- 4 — Congressional District Number
- Congressional District Boundary
- International Boundary
- State Boundary
- County Boundary

United States
Census
Bureau

PUERTO RICO and U.S. VIRGIN ISLANDS

PR

ONE DELEGATE AT LARGE

ONE RESIDENT COMMISSIONER AT LARGE

CONGRESSIONAL DISTRICTS OF THE 113TH CONGRESS OF THE UNITED STATES (JANUARY 2013 TO 2015)

ALABAMA - Core Based Statistical Areas (CBSAs) and Counties

N

0 10 20 30 40 Kilometers
0 10 20 30 40 Miles

TENNESSEE

Chattanooga-Cleveland-Dalton

NORTH CAROLINA

Huntsville-Decatur-Albertville

FLORENCE-MUSCLE SHOALS

Lauderdale

Colbert

HUNTSVILLE

Limestone

Madison

Scottsboro

Jackson

DeKalb

Franklin

DECATUR

Lawrence

Morgan

Albertville

Marshall

Cherokee

Marion

Winston

Cullman

CULLMAN

GADSDEN

Etowah

ANNISTON-OXFORD-JACKSONVILLE

Lamar

Fayette

Walker

Blount

St. Clair

Calhoun

Cleburne

GEORGIA

MISSISSIPPI

Pickens

TUSCALOOSA

Tuscaloosa

BIRMINGHAM-HOOVER

Jefferson

Birmingham-Hoover-Talladega

Talladega

Clay

Randolph

Greene

Hale

Bibb

Shelby

Chilton

Talladega-Sylacauga

Coosa

Tallapoosa

Valley

Chambers

COLUMBUS

Harris

Columbus-Auburn-Opelika

Perry

Elmore

MONTGOMERY

Autauga

AUBURN-OPELIKA

Lee

Muscogee

Sumter

Selma

Dallas

Montgomery

Macon

Russell

Chatta-hoochee

Marion

Marengo

Lowndes

Bullock

Choctaw

Wilcox

Butler

Crenshaw

Troy

Pike

Barbour

Clarke

Monroe

Conecuh

Enterprise

Coffee

Ozark

Dale

Henry

Dothan-Enterprise-Ozark

Washington

Escambia

Covington

DOTHAN

Geneva

Houston

MOBILE

Mobile

DAPHNE-FAIRHOPE-FOLEY

Baldwin

FLORIDA

Mobile-Daphne-Fairhope

Gulf of Mexico

LEGEND

Dothan-Enterprise-Ozark — Combined Statistical Area

MOBILE — Metropolitan Statistical Area

Troy — Micropolitan Statistical Area

FLORIDA — State or Statistical Equivalent

Autauga — County or Statistical Equivalent

Gulf of Mexico — Coastline

CBSA boundaries and names are as of February 2013. All other boundaries and names are as of January 1, 2012.

ALASKA - Core Based Statistical Areas (CBSAs) and Counties

CANADA

Prince of Wales-Hyder (pt)

Wrangell

Ketchikan Gateway

Juneau

Juneau

Skagway

Sitka

Petersburg

Prince of Wales-Hyder (pt)

Ketchikan

Haines

Hoonah-Angoon

Yakutat

Southeast Fairbanks

Valdez-Cordova

Anchorage

FAIRBANKS

Denali

ANCHORAGE

Matanuska-Susitna

Kenai Peninsula

Yukon-Koyukuk

Fairbanks North Star

North Slope

Bristol Bay

Kodiak Island

Northwest Arctic

Bethel

Dillingham

Lake and Peninsula

Nome (pt)

Wade Hampton

Nome (pt)

Aleutians East

Aleutians West (pt)

Aleutians West (pt)

Arctic Ocean

Pacific Ocean

RUSSIA

LEGEND

- Metropolitan Statistical Area — FAIRBANKS
- Micropolitan Statistical Area — Juneau
- International — CANADA
- County or Statistical Equivalent — Bethel
- Coastline — *Arctic Ocean*

CBSA boundaries and names are as of February 2013. All other boundaries and names are as of January 1, 2012.

N

0 75 150 225 300 Kilometers
0 75 150 225 300 Miles

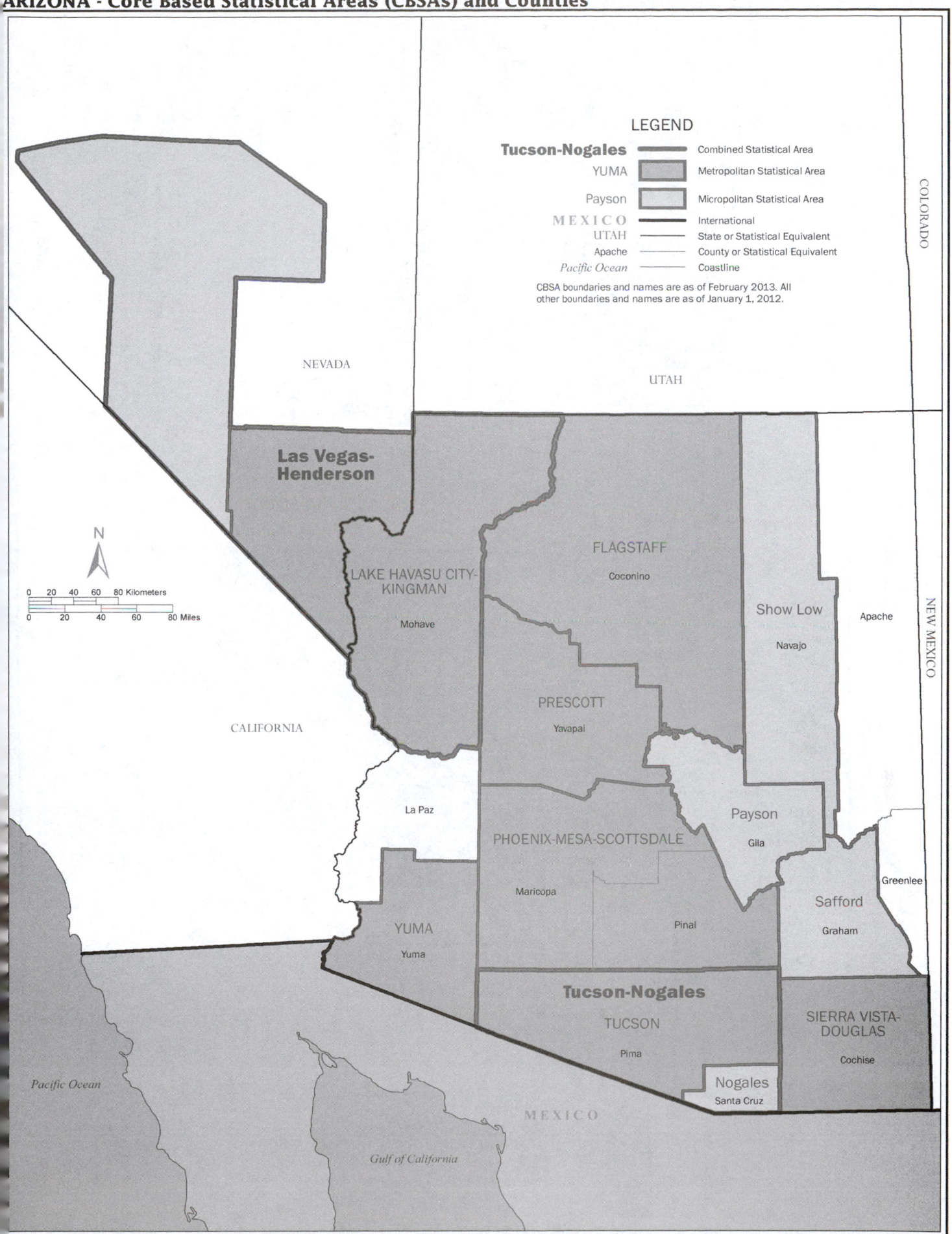

LEGEND

Tucson-Nogales ▬▬▬	Combined Statistical Area
YUMA ▨	Metropolitan Statistical Area
Payson ▢	Micropolitan Statistical Area
MEXICO ▬▬▬	International
UTAH ────	State or Statistical Equivalent
Apache ────	County or Statistical Equivalent
Pacific Ocean ────	Coastline

CBSA boundaries and names are as of February 2013. All other boundaries and names are as of January 1, 2012.

COLORADO

NEVADA

UTAH

NEW MEXICO

N

0 20 40 60 80 Kilometers
0 20 40 60 80 Miles

Las Vegas-Henderson

LAKE HAVASU CITY-KINGMAN

Mohave

FLAGSTAFF

Coconino

Show Low

Apache

CALIFORNIA

PRESCOTT

Yavapai

Navajo

La Paz

PHOENIX-MESA-SCOTTSDALE

Maricopa

Payson

Gila

Safford

Greenlee

Graham

YUMA

Yuma

Pinal

Tucson-Nogales

TUCSON

Pima

SIERRA VISTA-DOUGLAS

Cochise

Nogales

Santa Cruz

Pacific Ocean

MEXICO

Gulf of California

ARKANSAS - Core Based Statistical Areas (CBSAs) and Counties

KENTUCKY

TENNESSEE

MISSOURI

MISSISSIPPI

OKLAHOMA

LOUISIANA

TEXAS

Hot Springs-Malvern

FORT SMITH

Camden

TEXAS

Arkansas

LEGEND

Combined Statistical Area

Metropolitan Statistical Area

Micropolitan Statistical Area

State or Statistical Equivalent

County or Statistical Equivalent

CBSA boundaries and names are as of February 2013. All other boundaries and names are as of January 1, 2012.

N

40 Miles

40 Kilometers

Memphis-Forrest City

MEMPHIS

Benton, Fayette, Marshall, Tipton, Shelby, DeSoto, Tate, Tunica

Blytheville — Mississippi

Paragould — Greene

Jonesboro-Paragould — JONESBORO — Craighead, Poinsett

Clay

Crittenden

Forrest City — St. Francis

Lee

Helena-West Helena — Phillips

Randolph

Lawrence

Jackson

Woodruff

Monroe

Cross

Batesville — Independence

Sharp

Izard

Searcy — White

Prairie

Arkansas

Desha

Chicot

Fulton

Cleburne

Little Rock-North Little Rock

LITTLE ROCK-NORTH LITTLE ROCK-CONWAY

Lonoke

PINE BLUFF — Lincoln

Drew

Ashley

Mountain Home — Baxter

Stone

Faulkner

Pulaski

Jefferson

Cleveland

Bradley

Marion

Searcy

Van Buren

Conway

Saline

Grant

Dallas

Calhoun

Camden — Ouachita

El Dorado — Union

Boone

Harrison — Newton

Pope

Russellville

Perry

HOT SPRINGS — Garland

Hot Springs-Malvern — Malvern — Hot Spring

Arkadelphia — Clark

Nevada

Magnolia — Columbia

Carroll

Madison

Johnson

Logan

Yell

Montgomery

Pike

Hempstead

Lafayette

McDonald

Benton

FAYETTEVILLE-SPRINGDALE-ROGERS — Washington

Crawford

Franklin

Sebastian

Scott

Polk

Howard

Sevier

Little River

Miller

TEXARKANA — Bowie

Sequoyah

FORT SMITH

Le Flore

U.S. DEPARTMENT OF COMMERCE Economics and Statistics Administration U.S. Census Bureau

Appendix D

D-7

CALIFORNIA - Core Based Statistical Areas (CBSAs) and Counties

OREGON

IDAHO

LEGEND

Fresno-Madera	Combined Statistical Area
NAPA	Metropolitan Statistical Area
Ukiah	Micropolitan Statistical Area
San Rafael	Metropolitan Division
M E X I C O	International
NEVADA	State or Statistical Equivalent
Alameda	County or Statistical Equivalent
Pacific Ocean	Coastline

CBSA boundaries and names are as of February 2013. All other boundaries and names are as of January 1, 2012.

Del Norte
Crescent City
Siskiyou
Modoc

Eureka-Arcata-Fortuna

Humboldt
Trinity

REDDING
Shasta
Redding-Red Bluff

Susanville
Lassen

Red Bluff
Tehama

Plumas

Ukiah
Mendocino

CHICO
Glenn
Butte
Sierra

Clear-lake
Lake
Colusa
YUBA CITY
Yuba
Nevada
Placer

Truckee-Grass Valley

SANTA ROSA
Sonoma
NAPA
Napa
Yolo
Sutter
El Dorado

Sacramento-Roseville
SACRAMENTO–ROSEVILLE–ARDEN-ARCADE

San Rafael
Marin
Solano
Sacramento
Amador
Alpine

N

SAN FRANCISCO-OAKLAND-HAYWARD
Contra Costa
San Joaquin
STOCKTON-LODI
Calaveras
Sonora
Tuolumne
NEVADA

0 20 40 60 80 Kilometers
0 20 40 60 80 Miles

San Francisco
San Francisco-Redwood City-South San Francisco
Alameda
MODESTO
Stanislaus
Mariposa
Mono

San Jose-San Francisco-Oakland
Santa Clara
Merced
Modesto-Merced
MERCED
MADERA
Madera

San Mateo
SANTA CRUZ-WATSONVILLE
Santa Cruz
Fresno-Madera

San Benito
FRESNO
Fresno
Inyo

SALINAS
VISALIA-PORTERVILLE

KEY
1 VALLEJO-FAIRFIELD
2 Oakland-Hayward-Berkeley
3 SAN JOSE-SUNNYVALE-SANTA CLARA

Monterey
Kings
Tulare
Visalia-Porterville-Hanford

HANFORD-CORCORAN

ARIZONA

SAN LUIS OBISPO-PASO ROBLES-ARROYO GRANDE

San Luis Obispo
BAKERSFIELD
Kern

Los Angeles-Long Beach

RIVERSIDE-SAN BERNARDINO-ONTARIO
San Bernardino

Santa Barbara
Ventura
Los Angeles-Long Beach-Glendale

LOS ANGELES-LONG BEACH-ANAHEIM

SANTA MARIA-SANTA BARBARA

Los Angeles

Anaheim-Santa Ana-Irvine
Riverside

OXNARD-THOUSAND OAKS-VENTURA

Orange

Pacific Ocean

SAN DIEGO-CARLSBAD
San Diego

EL CENTRO
Imperial

M E X I C O

COLORADO - Core Based Statistical Areas (CBSAs) and Counties

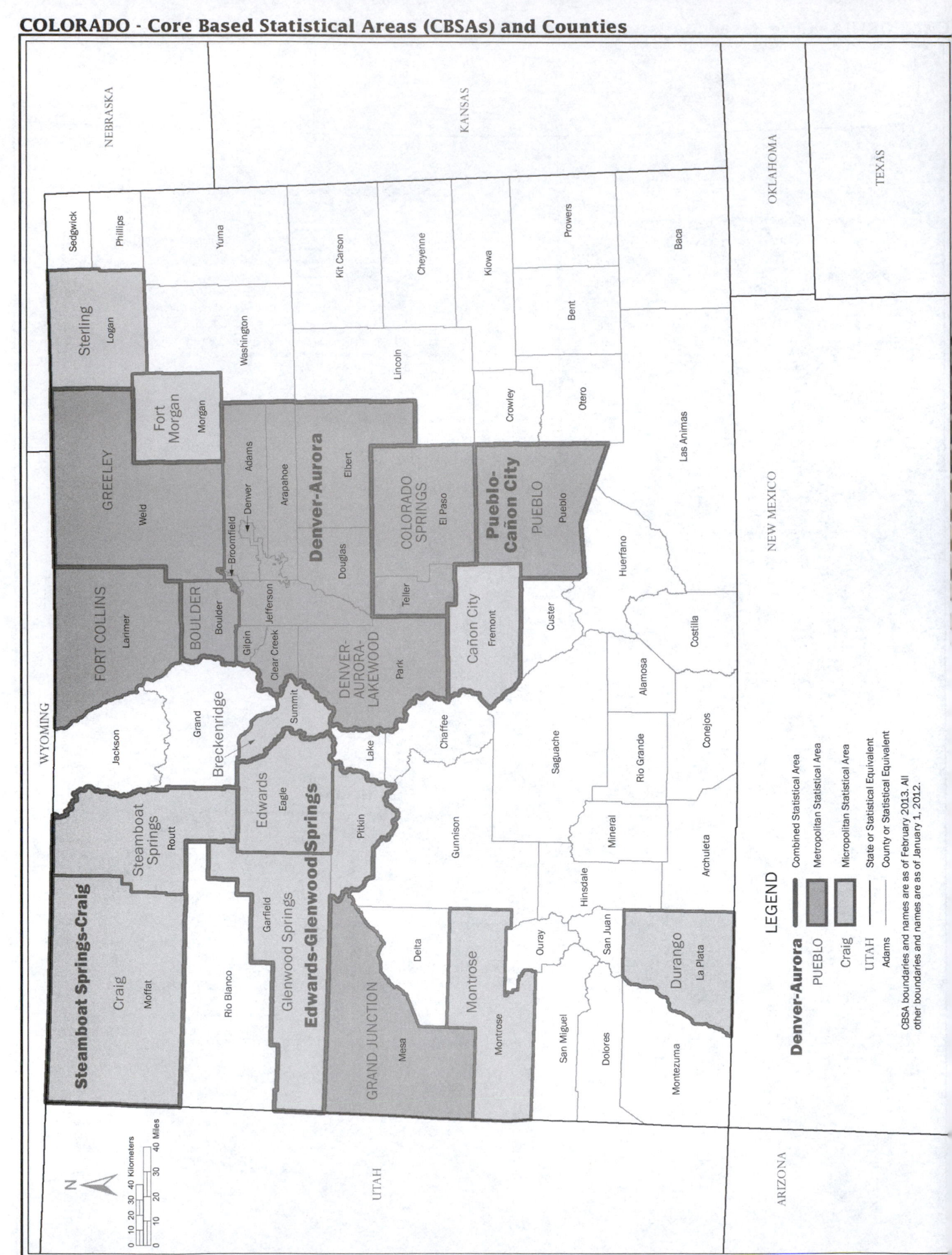

CONNECTICUT - Core Based Statistical Areas (CBSAs) and Counties

Worcester

RHODE ISLAND

MASSACHUSETTS

Boston-Worcester-Providence (pt)

WORCESTER (pt)

Windham

Tolland

NORWICH-NEW LONDON

New London

Hartford-West Hartford

HARTFORD-WEST HARTFORD-EAST HARTFORD

Hartford

Middlesex

NEW HAVEN-MILFORD

New Haven

Long Island Sound

New York-Newark (pt)

Torrington

Litchfield

BRIDGEPORT-STAMFORD-NORWALK

Fairfield

NEW YORK

LEGEND

Combined Statistical Area

Metropolitan Statistical Area

Micropolitan Statistical Area

State or Statistical Equivalent

County or Statistical Equivalent

Coastline

Hartford-West Hartford
NEW HAVEN-MILFORD

Torrington

NEW YORK
Fairfield

Long Island Sound

CBSA boundaries and names are as of February 2013. All other boundaries and names are as of January 1, 2012.

N

0 3 6 9 12 Kilometers
0 3 6 9 12 Miles

DELAWARE - Core Based Statistical Areas (CBSAs) and Counties

Chester

PHILADELPHIA-CAMDEN-WILMINGTON (pt)

Delaware

Philadelphia

Camden

Burlington

PENNSYLVANIA

Wilmington

Gloucester

Philadelphia-Reading-Camden (pt)

Cecil

New Castle

Salem

NEW JERSEY

MARYLAND

DOVER

Kent

Delaware Bay

Atlantic Ocean

Sussex

SALISBURY

Wicomico

Worcester

Somerset

Chesapeake Bay

VIRGINIA

LEGEND

Philadelphia-Reading-Camden	Combined Statistical Area
DOVER	Metropolitan Statistical Area
Wilmington	Metropolitan Division
MARYLAND	State or Statistical Equivalent
Kent	County or Statistical Equivalent
Atlantic Ocean	Coastline

CBSA boundaries and names are as of February 2013. All other boundaries and names are as of January 1, 2012.

N

0 3 6 9 12 Kilometers
0 3 6 9 12 Miles

U.S. DEPARTMENT OF COMMERCE Economics and Statistics Administration U.S. Census Bureau

Appendix D

D-11

DISTRICT OF COLUMBIA - Core Based Statistical Areas (CBSAs) and Counties

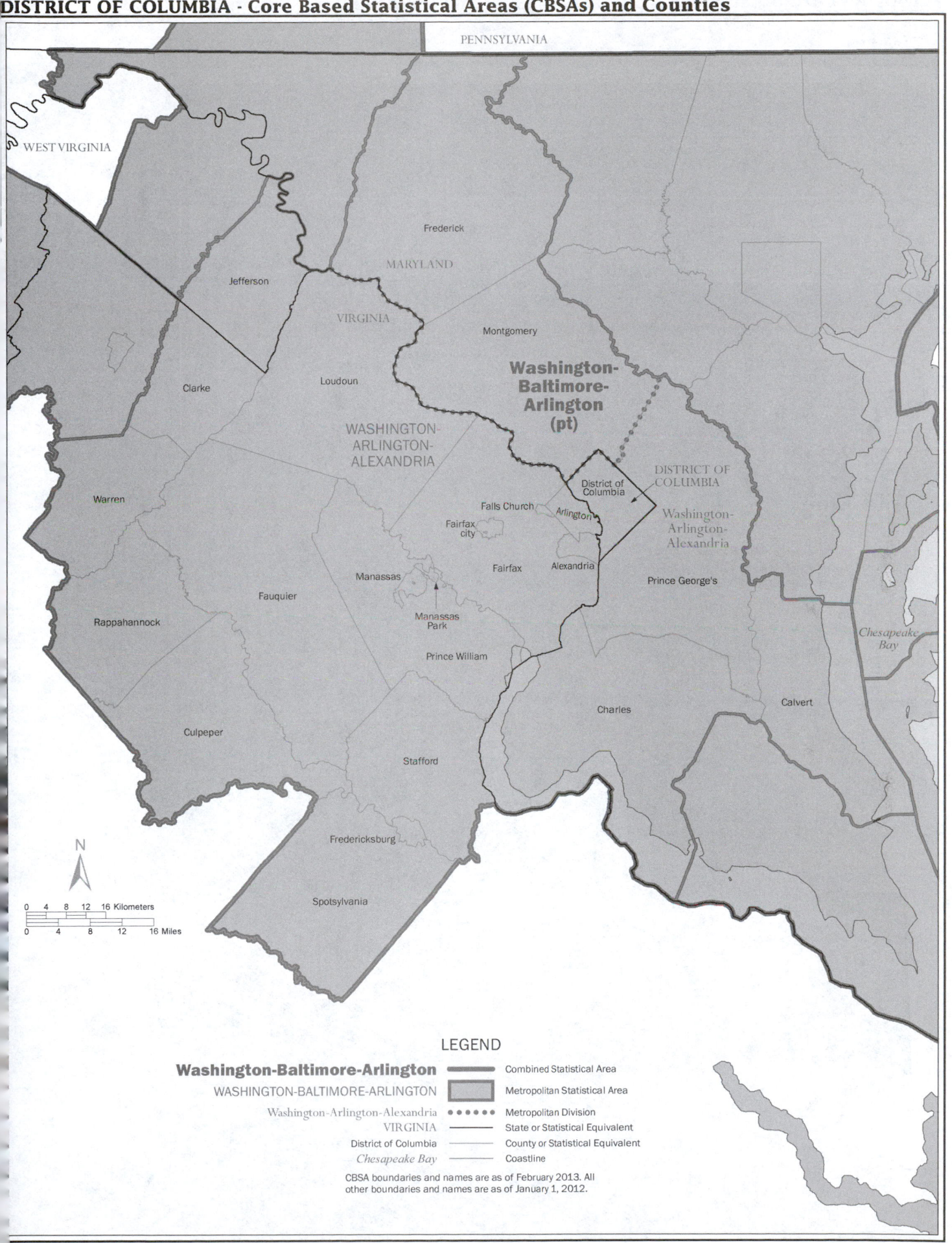

LEGEND

Washington-Baltimore-Arlington ——— Combined Statistical Area

WASHINGTON-BALTIMORE-ARLINGTON ▢ Metropolitan Statistical Area

Washington-Arlington-Alexandria •••••• Metropolitan Division

VIRGINIA ——— State or Statistical Equivalent

District of Columbia ——— County or Statistical Equivalent

Chesapeake Bay ——— Coastline

CBSA boundaries and names are as of February 2013. All
other boundaries and names are as of January 1, 2012.

FLORIDA - Core Based Statistical Areas (CBSAs) and Counties

Atlantic Ocean

Miami-Fort Lauderdale-Port St. Lucie

MIAMI-FORT LAUDERDALE-WEST PALM BEACH

Jacksonville-St. Marys-Palatka

Orlando-Deltona-Daytona Beach

DELTONA-DAYTONA BEACH-ORMOND BEACH

PALM BAY-MELBOURNE-TITUSVILLE

SEBASTIAN-VERO BEACH

PORT ST. LUCIE

West Palm Beach-Boca Raton-Delray Beach

Palm Beach

Fort Lauderdale-Pompano Beach-Deerfield Beach

Broward

Miami-Miami Beach-Kendall

Martin

St. Lucie

Indian River

Brevard

Volusia

Flagler

St. Johns

Duval

Nassau

Clay

Palatka / Putnam

JACKSONVILLE

Baker

Union / Bradford

Columbia

Lake City

GAINESVILLE

Gilchrist

Alachua

OCALA

Marion

THE VILLAGES

Sumter

Lake

Seminole

Orange

ORLANDO-KISSIMMEE-SANFORD

Osceola

Okeechobee

Okeechobee

Highlands

SEBRING

Glades

Clewiston

Hendry

NAPLES-IMMOKALEE-MARCO ISLAND

Collier

Monroe

Key West

Miami-Dade

Gainesville-Lake City

Hamilton

Suwannee

Lafayette

Dixie

Levy

Citrus

HOMOSASSA SPRINGS

Hernando

Pasco

Pinellas

Hillsborough

TAMPA-ST. PETERSBURG-CLEARWATER

Polk

LAKELAND-WINTER HAVEN

Wauchula

Hardee

Arcadia

DeSoto

Manatee

Sarasota

NORTH PORT-SARASOTA-BRADENTON

North Port-Sarasota

PUNTA GORDA

Charlotte

CAPE CORAL-FORT MYERS

Lee

Cape Coral-Fort Myers-Naples

GEORGIA

Madison

Taylor

Jefferson

Leon

TALLAHASSEE

Wakulla

Gadsden

Liberty

Franklin

Calhoun

Gulf

Tallahassee-Bainbridge

Jackson

Holmes

Washington

Bay

PANAMA CITY

Walton

CRESTVIEW-FORT WALTON BEACH-DESTIN

Okaloosa

Santa Rosa

Escambia

PENSACOLA-FERRY PASS-BRENT

ALABAMA

MISSISSIPPI

Gulf of Mexico

LEGEND

North Port-Sarasota Combined Statistical Area

OCALA Metropolitan Statistical Area

Arcadia Micropolitan Statistical Area

Miami-Miami Beach-Kendall Metropolitan Division

GEORGIA State or Statistical Equivalent

Alachua County or Statistical Equivalent

Gulf of Mexico Coastline

CBSA boundaries and names are as of February 2013. All other boundaries and names are as of January 1, 2012.

80 Miles

80 Kilometers

GEORGIA - Core Based Statistical Areas (CBSAs) and Counties

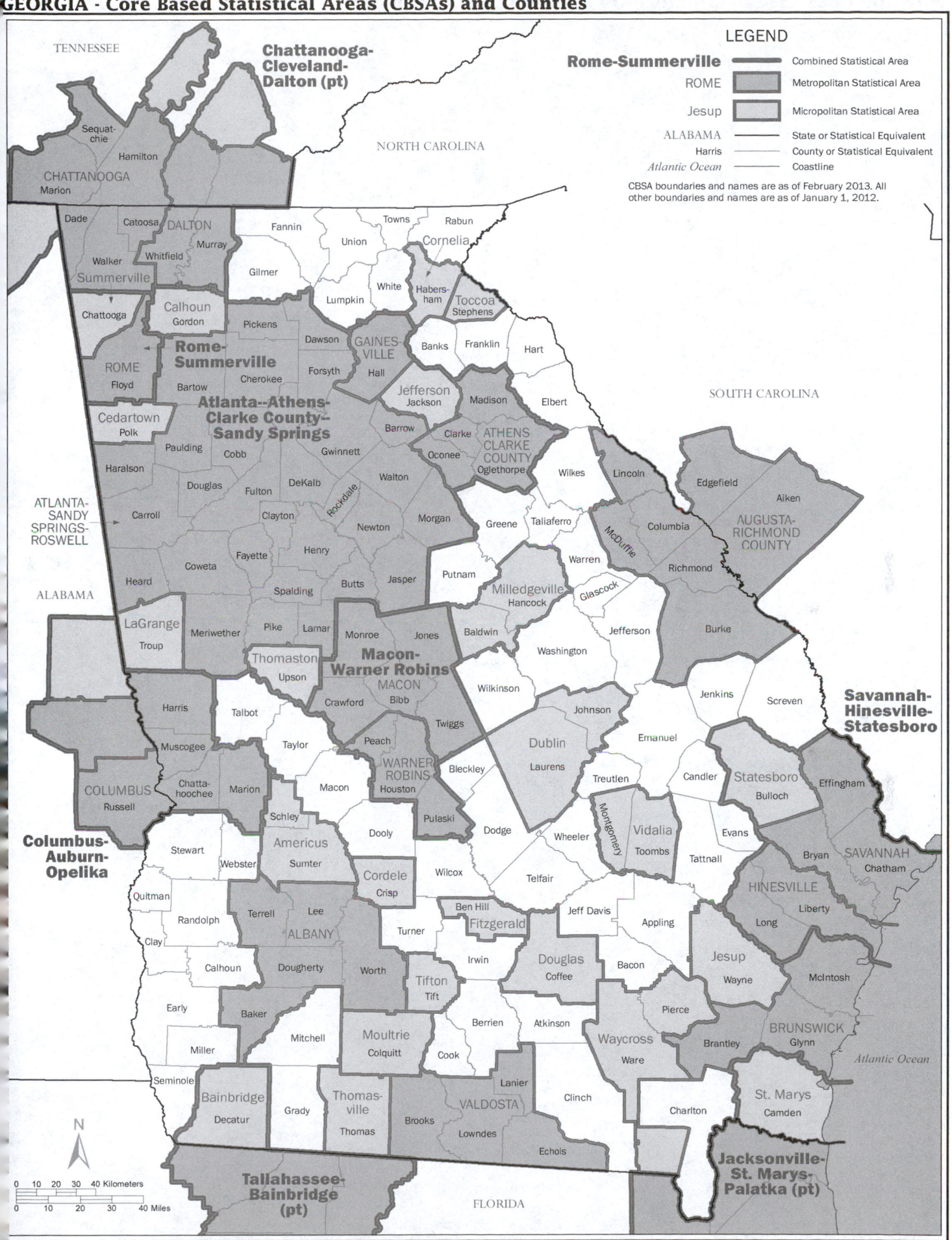

LEGEND

Rome-Summerville	Combined Statistical Area
ROME	Metropolitan Statistical Area
Jesup	Micropolitan Statistical Area
ALABAMA	State or Statistical Equivalent
Harris	County or Statistical Equivalent
Atlantic Ocean	Coastline

CBSA boundaries and names are as of February 2013. All other boundaries and names are as of January 1, 2012.

Pacific Ocean

URBAN HONOLULU
(pt)

Honolulu
(pt)

Kauai

Kapaa

Honolulu
(pt)

URBAN
HONOLULU
(pt)

Kalawao

Maui

KAHULUI-
WAILUKU-
LAHAINA

Hilo
Hawaii

N

0 40 80 120 160 Miles

0 40 80 120 160 Kilometers

LEGEND

URBAN HONOLULU Metropolitan Statistical Area

Hilo Micropolitan Statistical Area

Maui State or Statistical Equivalent

County or Statistical Equivalent

Pacific Ocean Coastline

CBSA boundaries and names are as of February 2013. All
other boundaries and names are as of January 1, 2012.

URBAN
HONOLULU
(pt)

Honolulu
(pt)

MIDWAY
ISLANDS
(U.S.
Unincorporated
Territory)

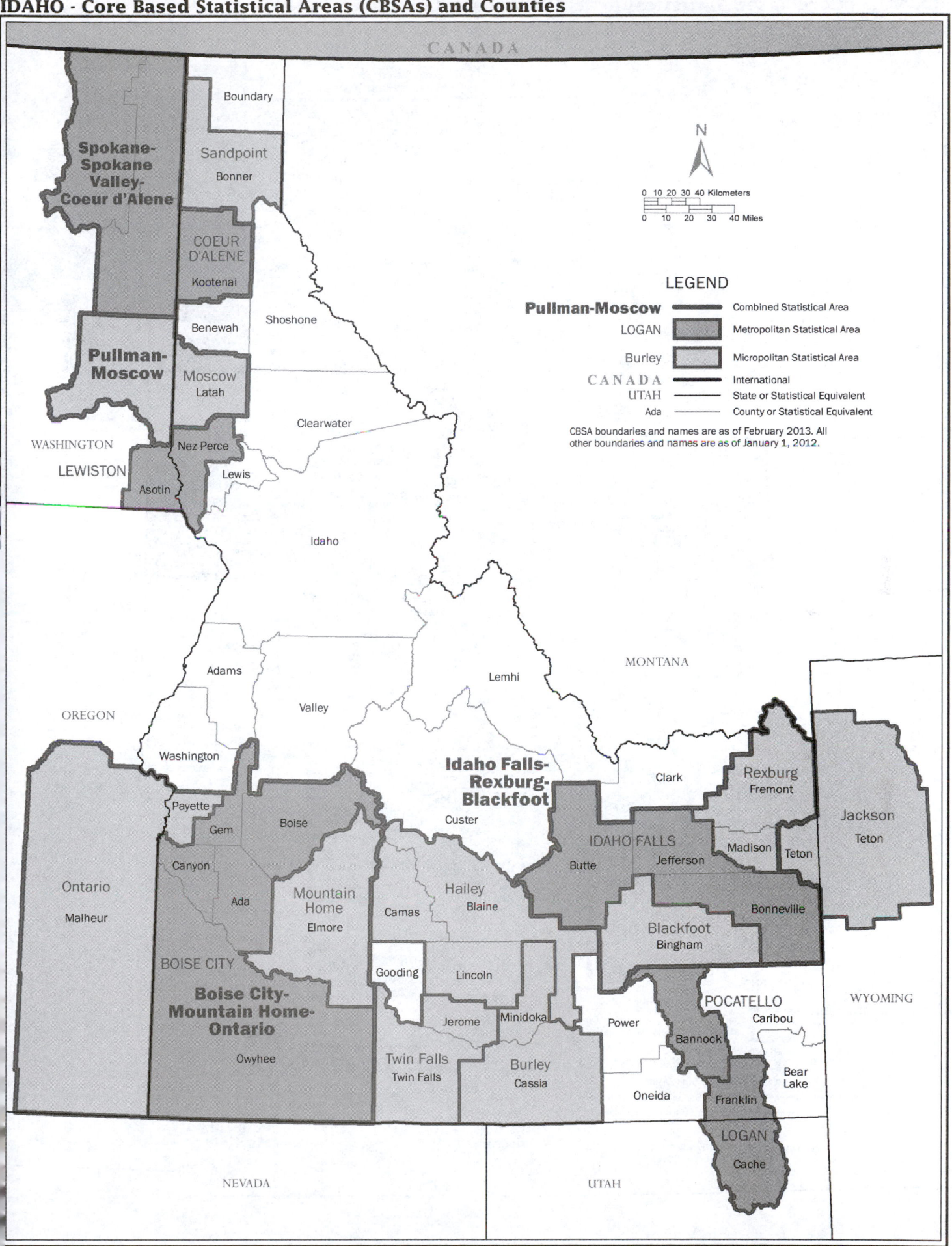

ILLINOIS - Core Based Statistical Areas (CBSAs) and Counties

LEGEND

Peoria-Canton	Combined Statistical Area
PEORIA	Metropolitan Statistical Area
Dixon	Micropolitan Statistical Area
Elgin ••••••	Metropolitan Division
IOWA	State or Statistical Equivalent
Lee	County or Statistical Equivalent
Lake Michigan	Coastline

CBSA boundaries and names are as of February 2013. All other boundaries and names are as of January 1, 2012.

CHICAGO-NAPERVILLE ELGIN (pt)

Lake Michigan

SOUTH BEND-MISHAWAKA

Cass

South Bend-Elkhart-Mishawaka (pt)

MICHIGAN

Lake Erie

DuPage

Cook

Chicago-Naperville (pt)

Will

Lake

Porter

MICHIGAN CITY-LA PORTE

LaPorte

St. Joseph

ELKHART-GOSHEN

Elkhart

LaGrange

Angola

Steuben

Gary

Newton

Jasper

Starke

Plymouth

Marshall

Warsaw

Kosciusko

Kendallville

Noble

Auburn

DeKalb

Fort Wayne-Huntington-Auburn

Pulaski

Fulton

Whitley

Allen

Kokomo-Peru

White

Logansport

Cass

Peru

Miami

Wabash

Wabash

Huntington

Huntington

FORT WAYNE

Decatur

Adams

Wells

Lafayette-West Lafayette-Frankfort

Benton

Carroll

LAFAYETTE-WEST LAFAYETTE

Tippecanoe

KOKOMO

Howard

Marion

Grant

Black-ford

Jay

OHIO

Warren

Frankfort

Clinton

Tipton

Fountain

Crawfords-ville

Montgomery

Boone

Hamilton

Madison

MUNCIE

Delaware

Randolph

ILLINOIS

Vermillion

Parke

Putnam

Hendricks

Marion

New Castle

Henry

Wayne

Richmond

Richmond-Connersville

Indianapolis-Carmel-Muncie

INDIANAPOLIS-CARMEL-ANDERSON

Rush

Fayette

Union

TERRE HAUTE

Vigo

Clay

Owen

Morgan

Johnson

Shelby

Connersville

Franklin

Butler

Warren

BLOOMINGTON

Sullivan

Greensburg

Decatur

CINCINNATI

Hamilton

Clermont

Bloomington-Bedford

Greene

Monroe

Brown

COLUMBUS

Bartholomew

Ripley

Dearborn

Campbell

Brown

North Vernon

Jennings

Ohio

Boone

Kenton

Knox

Daviess

Bedford

Lawrence

Seymour

Jackson

Madison

Jefferson

Switzer-land

Gallatin

Grant

Pendle-ton

Bracken

Vincennes

Washington

Martin

Orange

Scott

Trimble

Gibson

Pike

Jasper

Dubois

Crawford

Washington

Floyd

Clark

Oldham

Henry

Cincinnati-Wilmington-Maysville

Shelby

Posey

Vander-burgh

Warrick

Spencer

Perry

Harrison

Jefferson

Spencer

LOUISVILLE/JEFFERSON COUNTY

EVANSVILLE

Henderson

KENTUCKY

Bullitt

Louisville/Jefferson County--Elizabethtown--Madison

N

0 10 20 30 40 Kilometers
0 10 20 30 40 Miles

LEGEND

Kokomo-Peru — Combined Statistical Area

MUNCIE — Metropolitan Statistical Area

Peru — Micropolitan Statistical Area

Gary ••••• Metropolitan Division

OHIO — State or Statistical Equivalent

Jay — County or Statistical Equivalent

Lake Michigan — Coastline

CBSA boundaries and names are as of February 2013. All other boundaries and names are as of January 1, 2012.

IOWA - Core Based Statistical Areas (CBSAs) and Counties

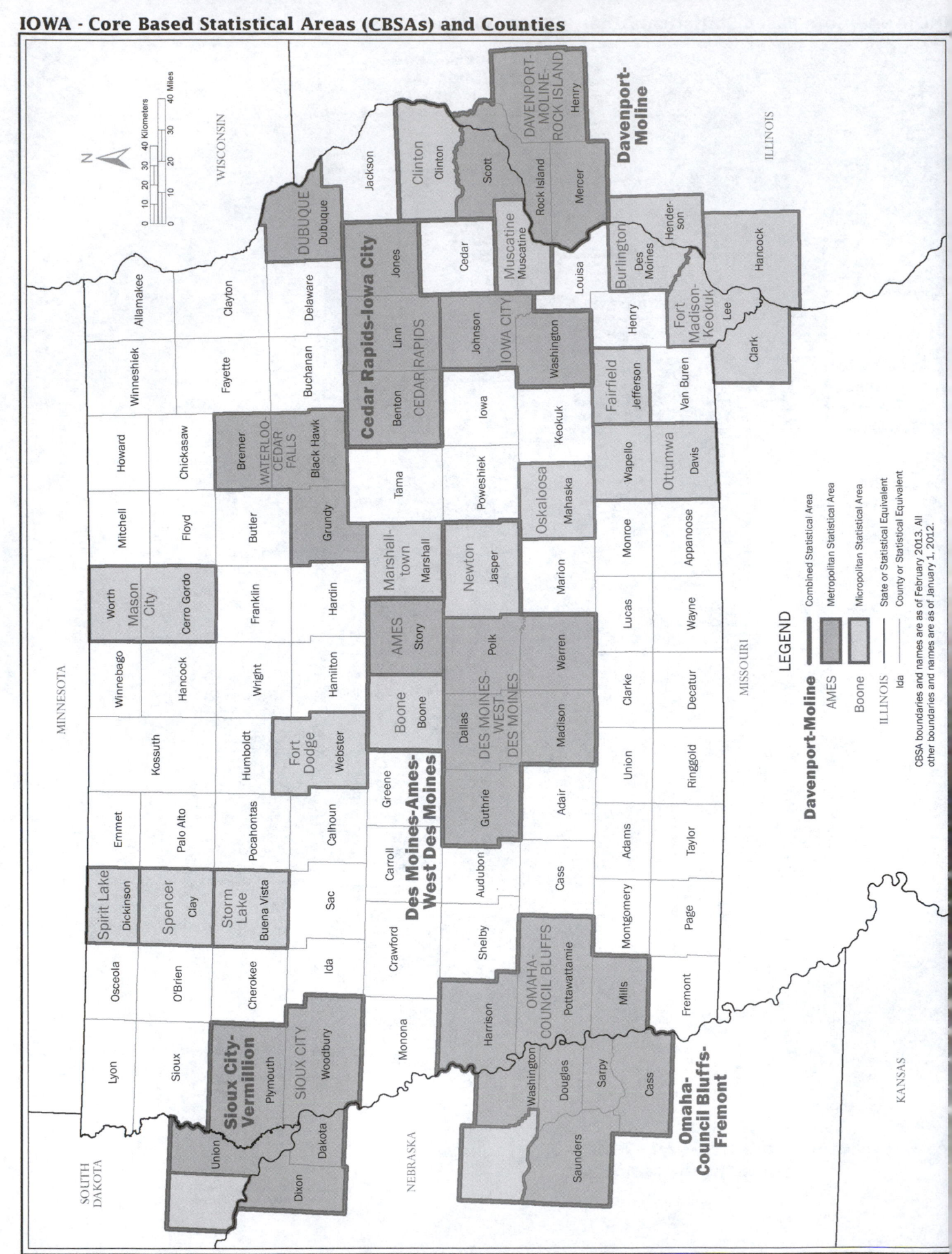

LEGEND

Davenport-Moline Combined Statistical Area

AMES Metropolitan Statistical Area

Boone Micropolitan Statistical Area

ILLINOIS State or Statistical Equivalent

Ida County or Statistical Equivalent

CBSA boundaries and names are as of February 2013. All other boundaries and names are as of January 1, 2012.

Kansas City-
Overland Park-
Kansas City

MISSOURI

IOWA

NEBRASKA

COLORADO

ARKANSAS

OKLAHOMA

TEXAS

Manhattan-Junction City

Manhattan-Junction City
TOPEKA
Hays
MISSOURI
Elk

LEGEND

Combined Statistical Area

Metropolitan Statistical Area

Micropolitan Statistical Area

State or Statistical Equivalent

County or Statistical Equivalent

CBSA boundaries and names are as of February 2013. All other boundaries and names are as of January 1, 2012.

N

0 10 20 30 40 Kilometers
0 10 20 30 40 Miles

Lafayette
Caldwell
Ray
Clinton
ST. JOSEPH
DeKalb
Clay
KANSAS CITY
Jackson
Cass
Bates
Andrew
Buchanan
Platte
Wyandotte
Johnson
Miami
Linn
Bourbon
Pittsburg
Crawford
Cherokee
Doniphan
Leaven-worth
Atchison
Atchison
Jefferson
Douglas
Ottawa
Franklin
Anderson
Allen
Neosho
Parsons
Labette
Brown
Nemaha
Jackson
Shawnee
TOPEKA
Osage
LAWRENCE
Coffey
Woodson
Wilson
Coffeyville
Montgomery
Marshall
Washington
MANHATTAN
Pottawatomie
Wabaunsee
Emporia
Lyon
Greenwood
Elk
Chautauqua
Riley
Geary
Junction City
Morris
Chase
Republic
Clay
Dickinson
Marion
Butler
Arkansas City-Winfield
Cowley
Cloud
Ottawa
Salina
Saline
McPherson
McPherson
Harvey
Sedgwick
WICHITA
Sumner
Jewell
Mitchell
Lincoln
Ellsworth
Rice
Hutchinson
Reno
Kingman
Harper
Smith
Osborne
Russell
Great Bend
Barton
Stafford
Pratt
Barber
Phillips
Rooks
Hays
Ellis
Rush
Pawnee
Edwards
Kiowa
Comanche
Norton
Graham
Trego
Ness
Hodgeman
Dodge City
Ford
Clark
Decatur
Sheridan
Gove
Lane
Gray
Meade
Rawlins
Thomas
Logan
Scott
Garden City
Finney
Haskell
Liberal
Seward
Cheyenne
Sherman
Wallace
Greeley
Wichita
Kearny
Grant
Stevens
Morton
Hamilton
Stanton

Manhattan-Junction City
Wichita-Arkansas City-Winfield

KENTUCKY - Core Based Statistical Areas (CBSAs) and Counties

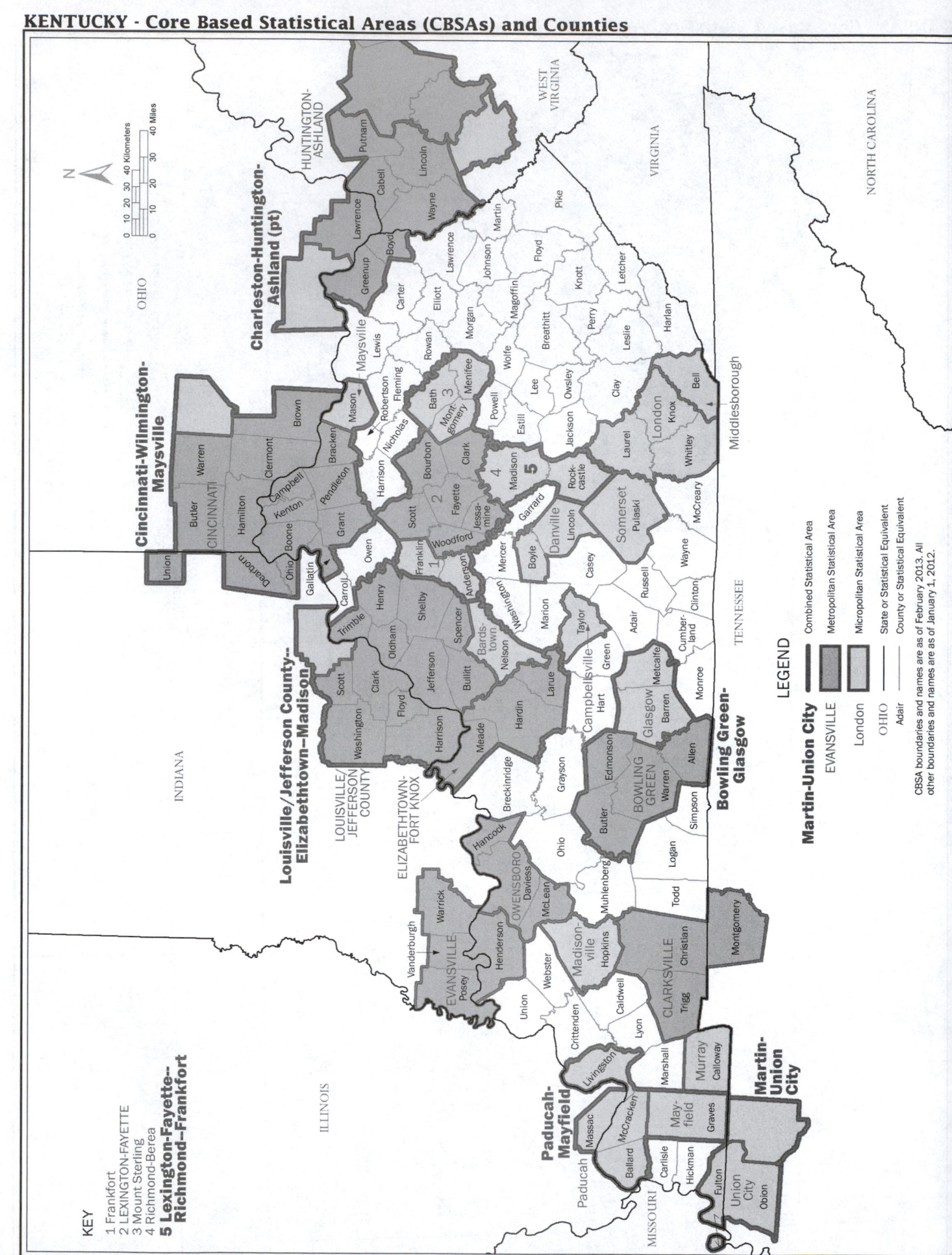

KEY

1 Frankfort
2 LEXINGTON-FAYETTE
3 Mount Sterling
4 Richmond-Berea
5 Lexington-Fayette--Richmond-Frankfort

LEGEND

Combined Statistical Area

Metropolitan Statistical Area

Micropolitan Statistical Area

State or Statistical Equivalent

County or Statistical Equivalent

Martin-Union City
EVANSVILLE

London

OHIO

Adair

CBSA boundaries and names are as of February 2013. All other boundaries and names are as of January 1, 2012.

LOUISIANA - Core Based Statistical Areas (CBSAs) and Counties

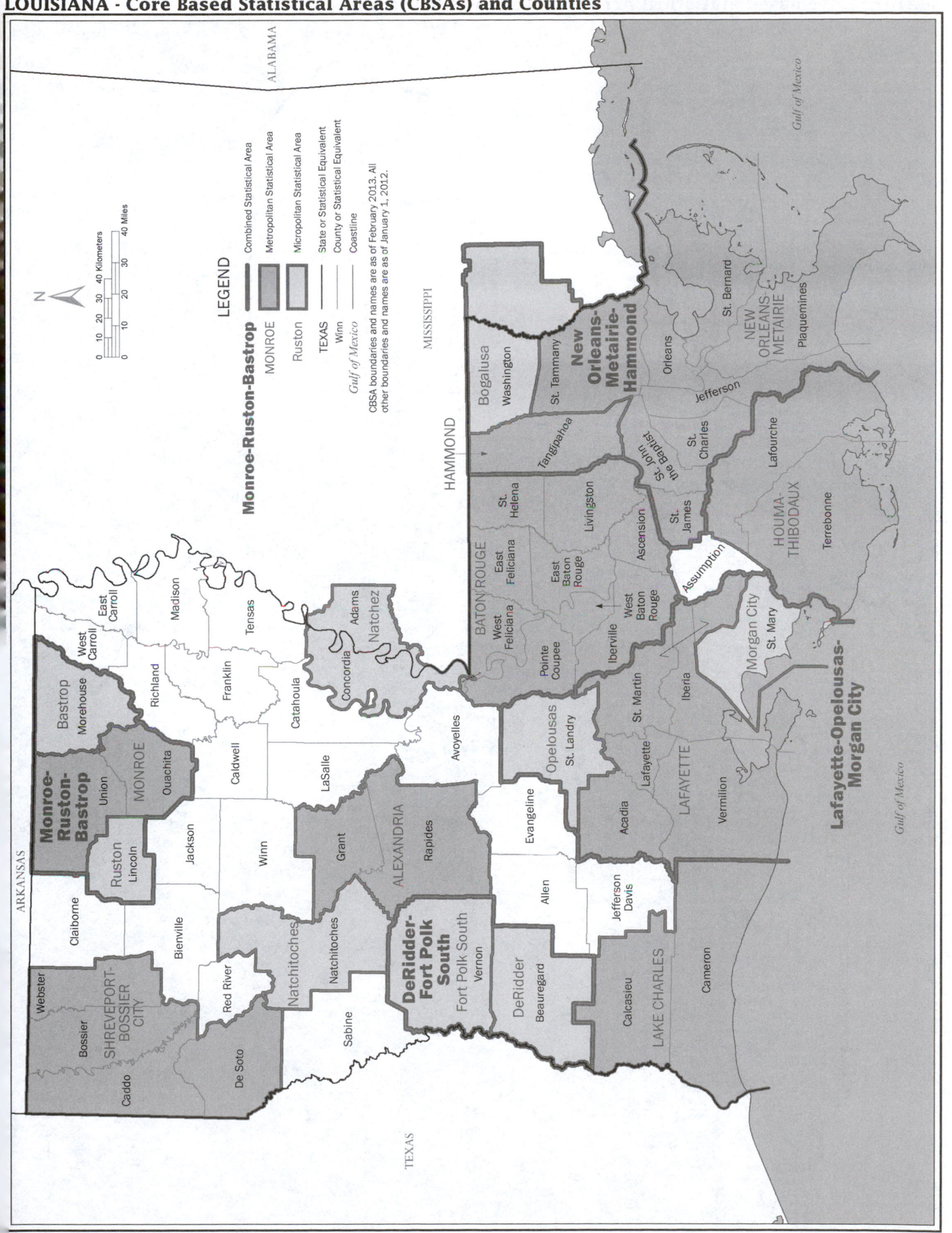

U.S. DEPARTMENT OF COMMERCE Economics and Statistics Administration U.S. Census Bureau

MAINE - Core Based Statistical Areas (CBSAs) and Counties

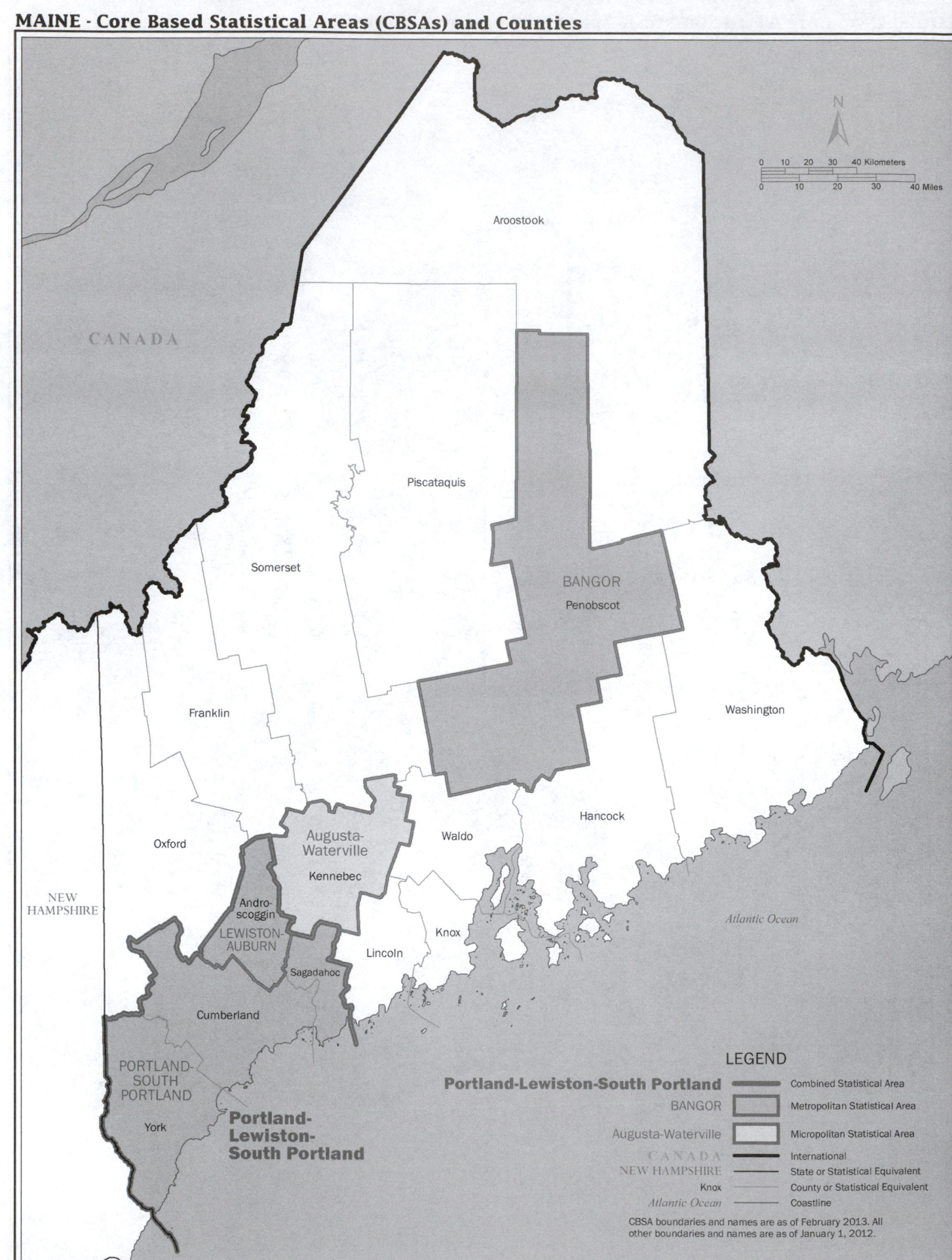

LEGEND

Portland-Lewiston-South Portland	Combined Statistical Area
BANGOR	Metropolitan Statistical Area
Augusta-Waterville	Micropolitan Statistical Area
CANADA	International
NEW HAMPSHIRE	State or Statistical Equivalent
Knox	County or Statistical Equivalent
Atlantic Ocean	Coastline

CBSA boundaries and names are as of February 2013. All other boundaries and names are as of January 1, 2012.

Philadelphia-Reading-Camden (pt)

Washington-Baltimore-Arlington (pt)

PHILADELPHIA-CAMDEN-WILMINGTON (pt)

BALTIMORE-COLUMBIA-TOWSON

WASHINGTON-ARLINGTON-ALEXANDRIA

HAGERSTOWN-MARTINSBURG

CUMBERLAND

SALISBURY

CALIFORNIA-LEXINGTON PARK

Silver Spring-Frederick-Rockville

Easton

NEW JERSEY
DELAWARE

PENNSYLVANIA

WEST VIRGINIA

VIRGINIA

Atlantic Ocean

Chesapeake Bay

Burlington, Camden, Gloucester, Salem, Delaware, New Castle, Chester, Cecil, Kent, Queen Anne's, Caroline, Sussex, Worcester, Wicomico, Somerset, Harford, Baltimore, Baltimore (city), Anne Arundel, Talbot, Easton, Cambridge, Dorchester, St. Mary's, Calvert, Carroll, Howard, Prince George's, Washington-Arlington-Alexandria, Charles, District of Columbia, Montgomery, Frederick, Loudoun, Arlington, Falls Church, Fairfax (city), Alexandria, Fairfax, Manassas Park, Manassas, Prince William, Stafford, Fredericksburg, Spotsylvania, Fauquier, Culpeper, Rappahannock, Warren, Clarke, Jefferson, Berkeley, Washington, Allegany, Mineral, Garrett

LEGEND

	Combined Statistical Area
	Metropolitan Statistical Area
	Micropolitan Statistical Area
•••••	Metropolitan Division
	State or Statistical Equivalent
	County or Statistical Equivalent
	Coastline

Washington-Baltimore-Arlington

SALISBURY

Easton

Silver Spring-Frederick-Rockville

VIRGINIA

Kent

Atlantic Ocean

CBSA boundaries and names are as of February 2013. All other boundaries and names are as of January 1, 2012.

N

0 10 20 30 40 Kilometers
0 10 20 30 40 Miles

U.S. DEPARTMENT OF COMMERCE Economics and Statistics Administration U.S. Census Bureau

Appendix D

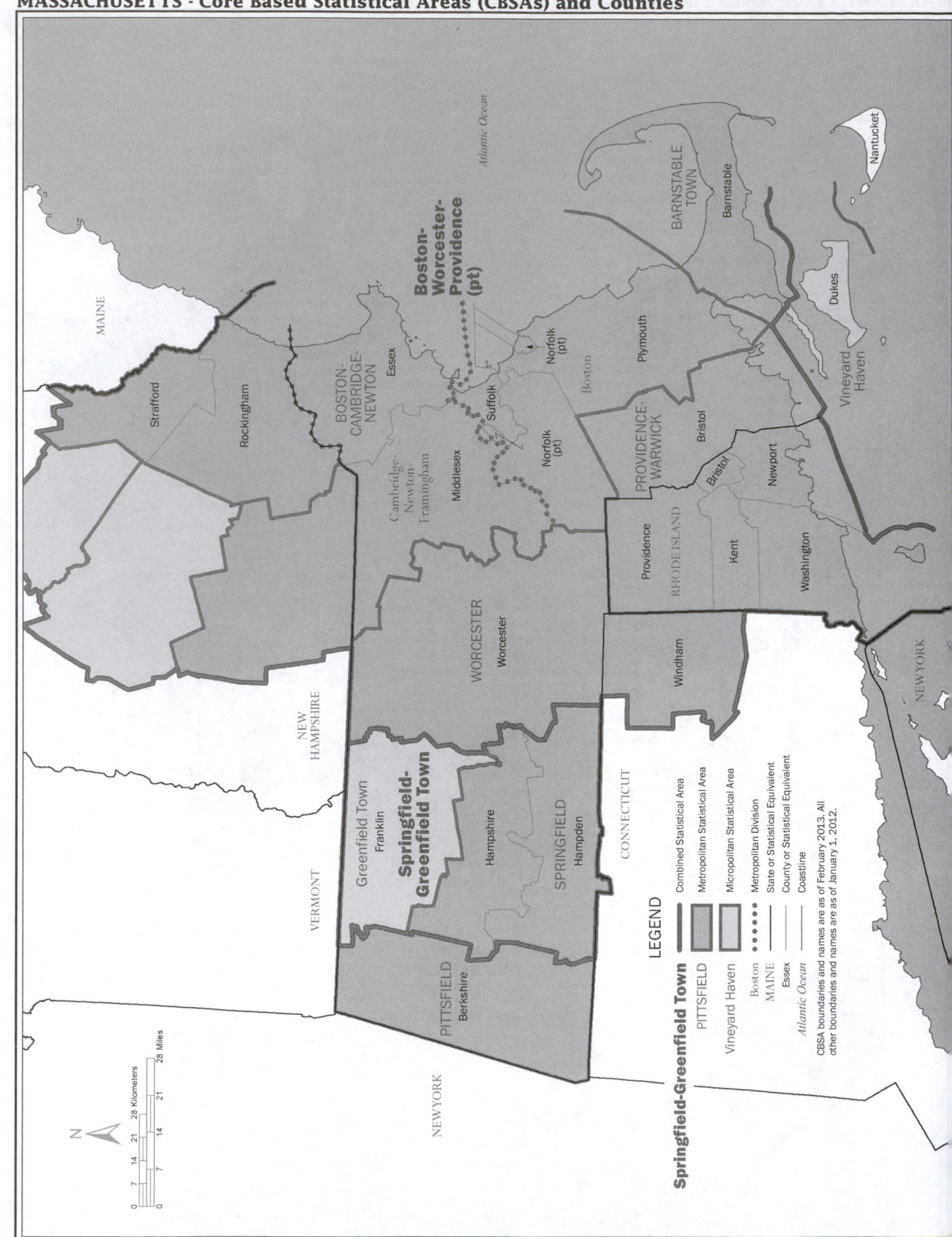

MICHIGAN - Core Based Statistical Areas (CBSAs) and Counties

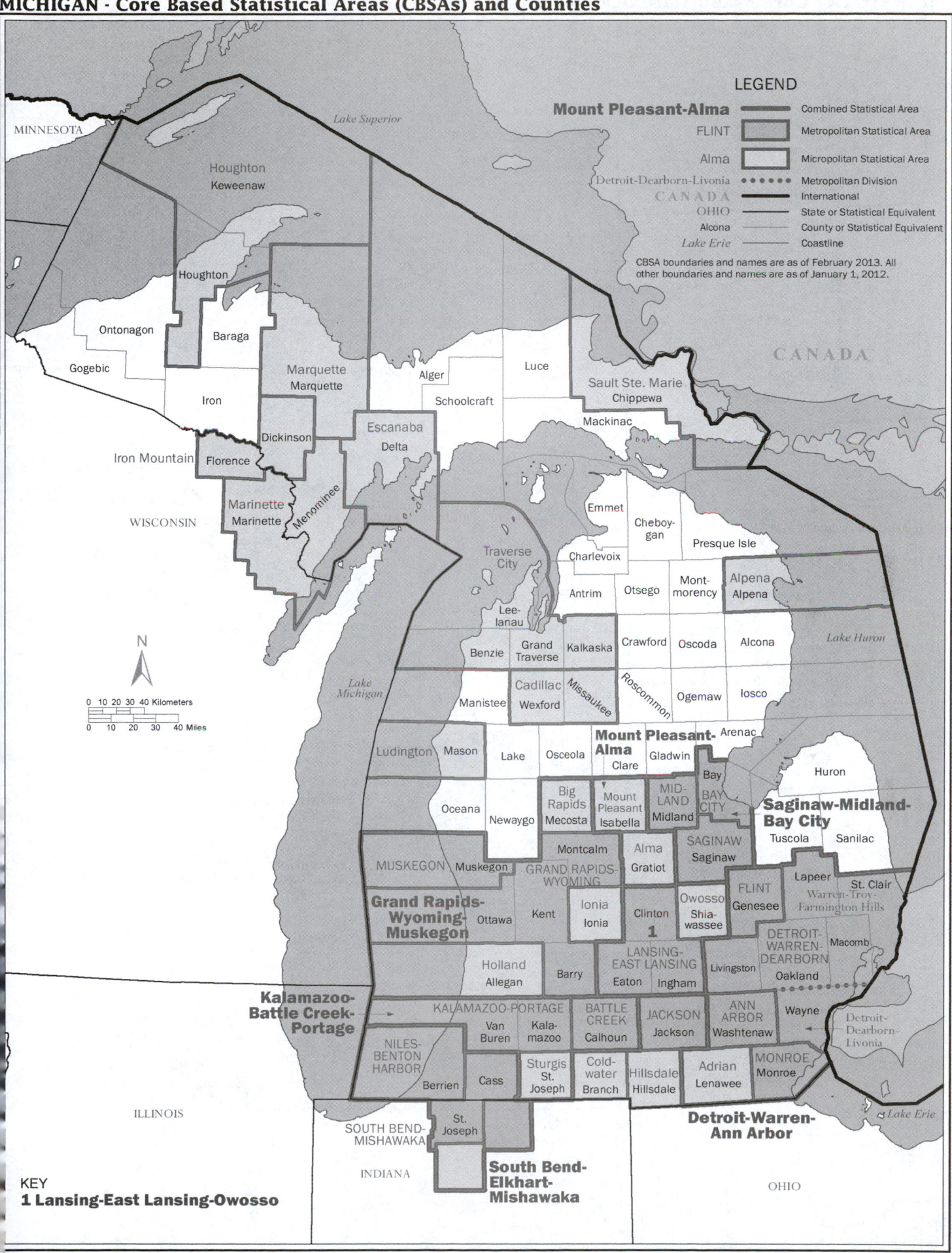

LEGEND

Mount Pleasant-Alma — Combined Statistical Area
FLINT — Metropolitan Statistical Area
Alma — Micropolitan Statistical Area
Detroit-Dearborn-Livonia ••••• Metropolitan Division
—— International
OHIO — State or Statistical Equivalent
Alcona — County or Statistical Equivalent
Lake Erie — Coastline

CBSA boundaries and names are as of February 2013. All other boundaries and names are as of January 1, 2012.

MINNESOTA - Core Based Statistical Areas (CBSAs) and Counties

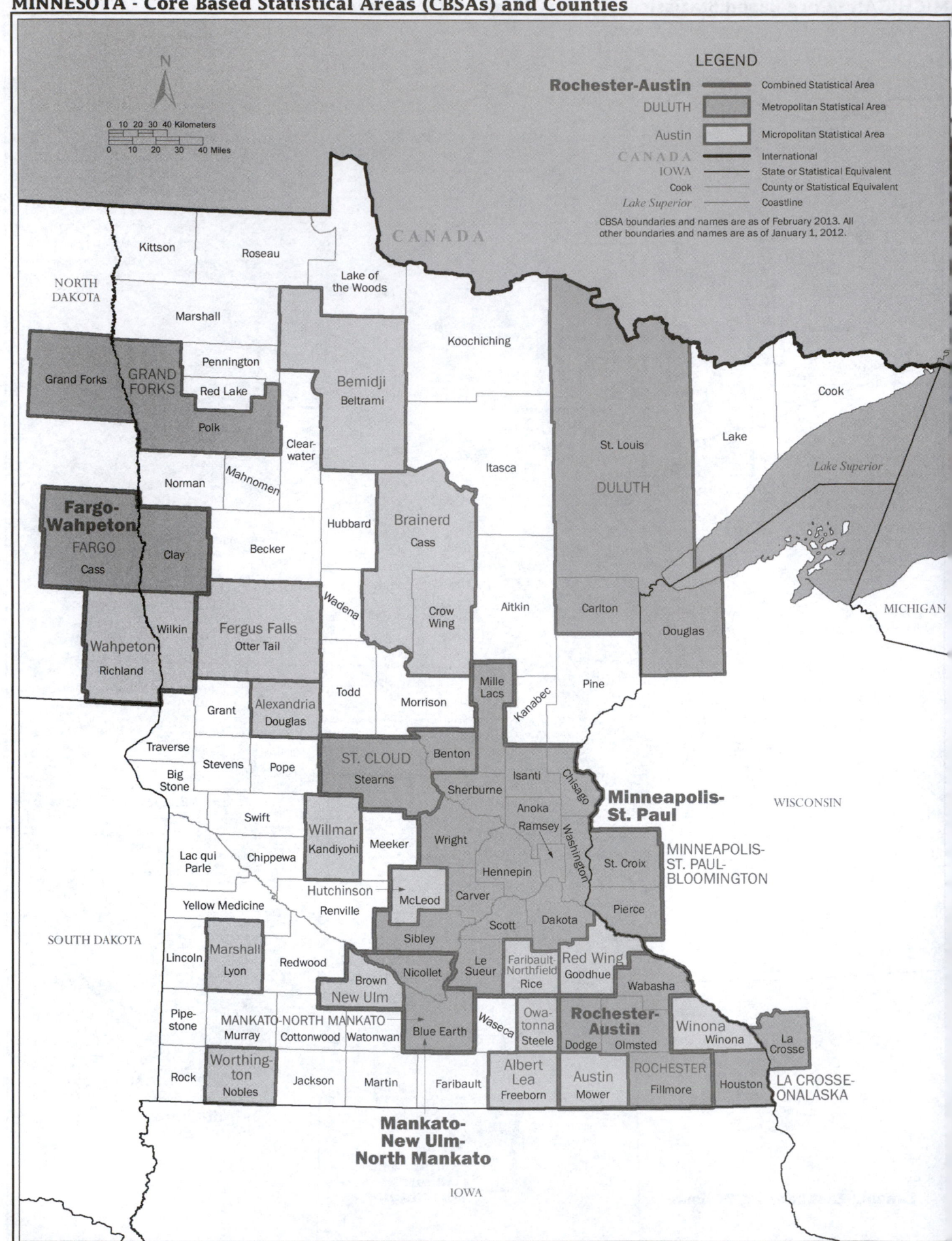

MISSISSIPPI - Core Based Statistical Areas (CBSAs) and Counties

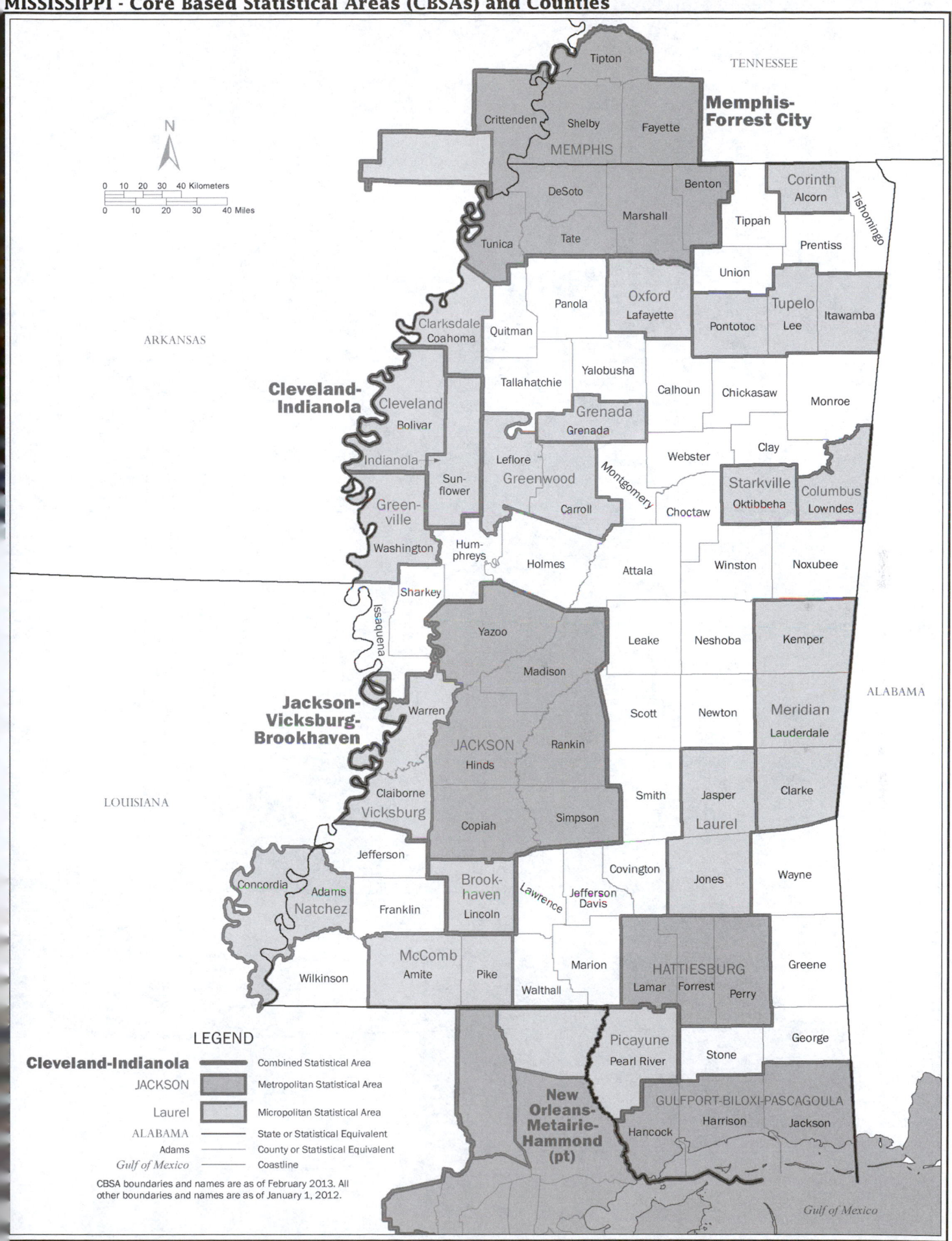

LEGEND

Cleveland-Indianola ━━━ Combined Statistical Area

JACKSON ▢ Metropolitan Statistical Area

Laurel ▢ Micropolitan Statistical Area

ALABAMA ━━━ State or Statistical Equivalent

Adams ─── County or Statistical Equivalent

Gulf of Mexico ─── Coastline

CBSA boundaries and names are as of February 2013. All other boundaries and names are as of January 1, 2012.

U.S. DEPARTMENT OF COMMERCE Economics and Statistics Administration U.S. Census Bureau

MISSOURI - Core Based Statistical Areas (CBSAs) and Counties

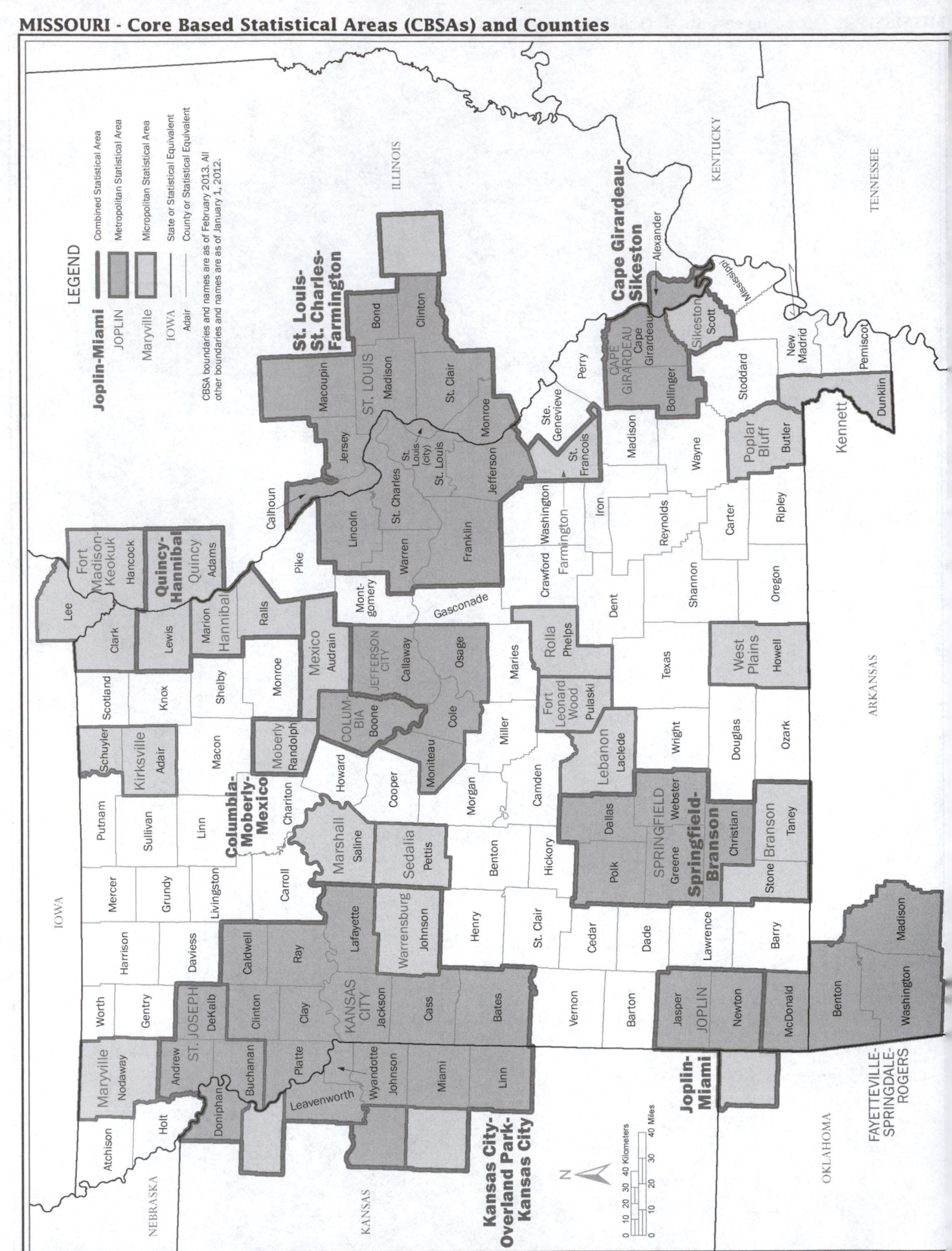

U.S. DEPARTMENT OF COMMERCE Economics and Statistics Administration U.S. Census Bureau

MONTANA - Core Based Statistical Areas (CBSAs) and Counties

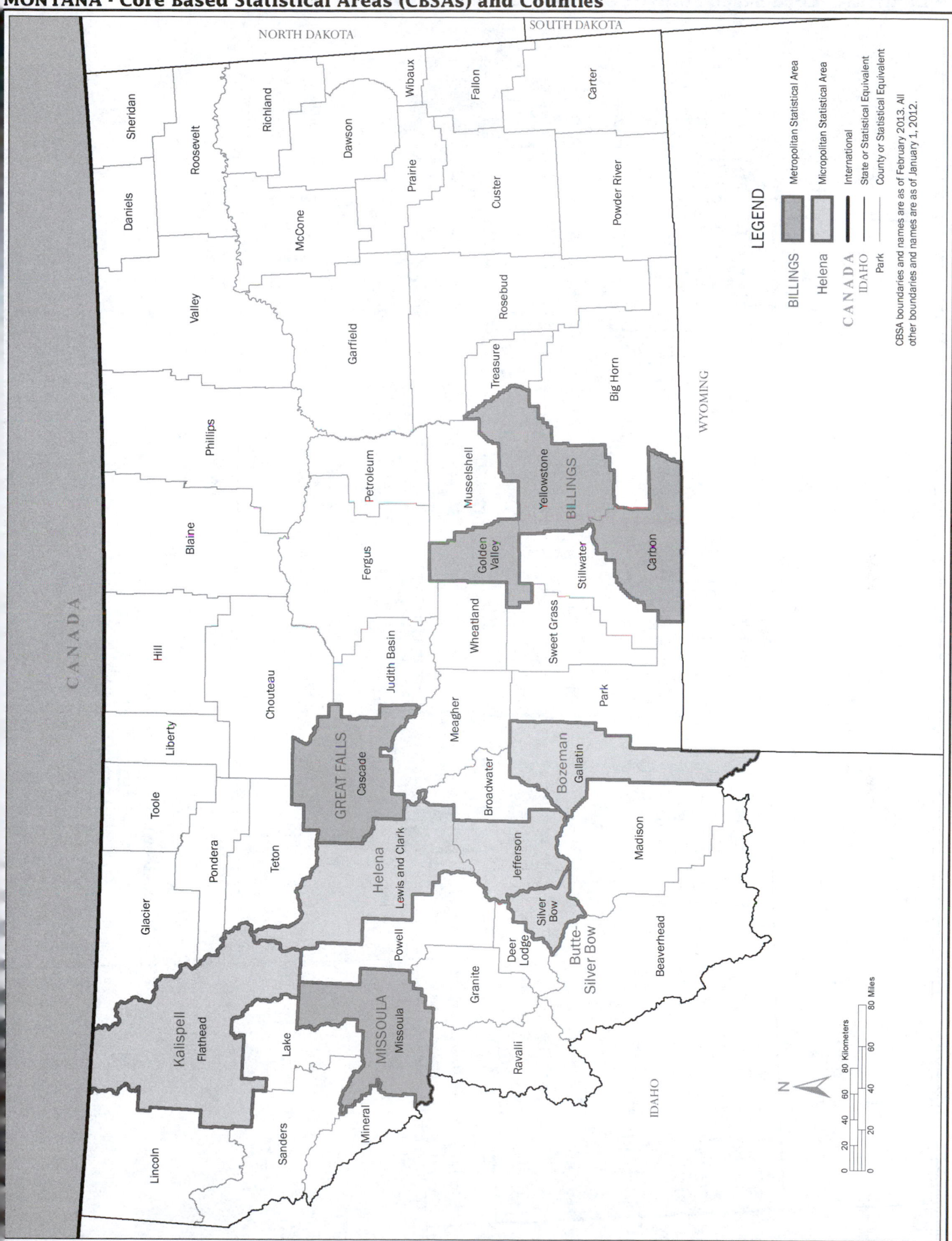

U.S. DEPARTMENT OF COMMERCE Economics and Statistics Administration U.S. Census Bureau

Appendix D

NEBRASKA - Core Based Statistical Areas (CBSAs) and Counties

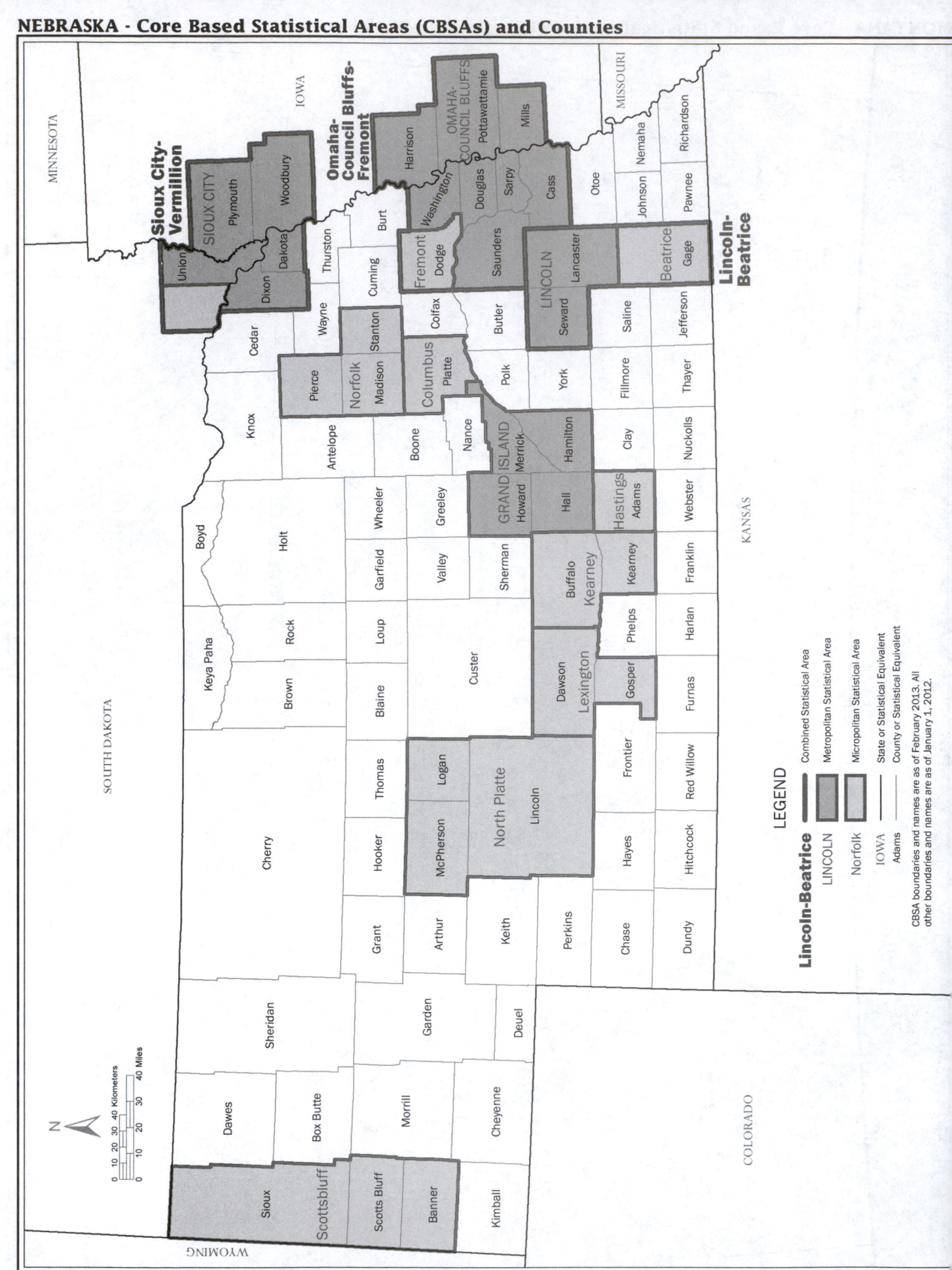

LEGEND

Lincoln-Beatrice — Combined Statistical Area

LINCOLN — Metropolitan Statistical Area

Norfolk — Micropolitan Statistical Area

IOWA — State or Statistical Equivalent

Adams — County or Statistical Equivalent

CBSA boundaries and names are as of February 2013. All other boundaries and names are as of January 1, 2012.

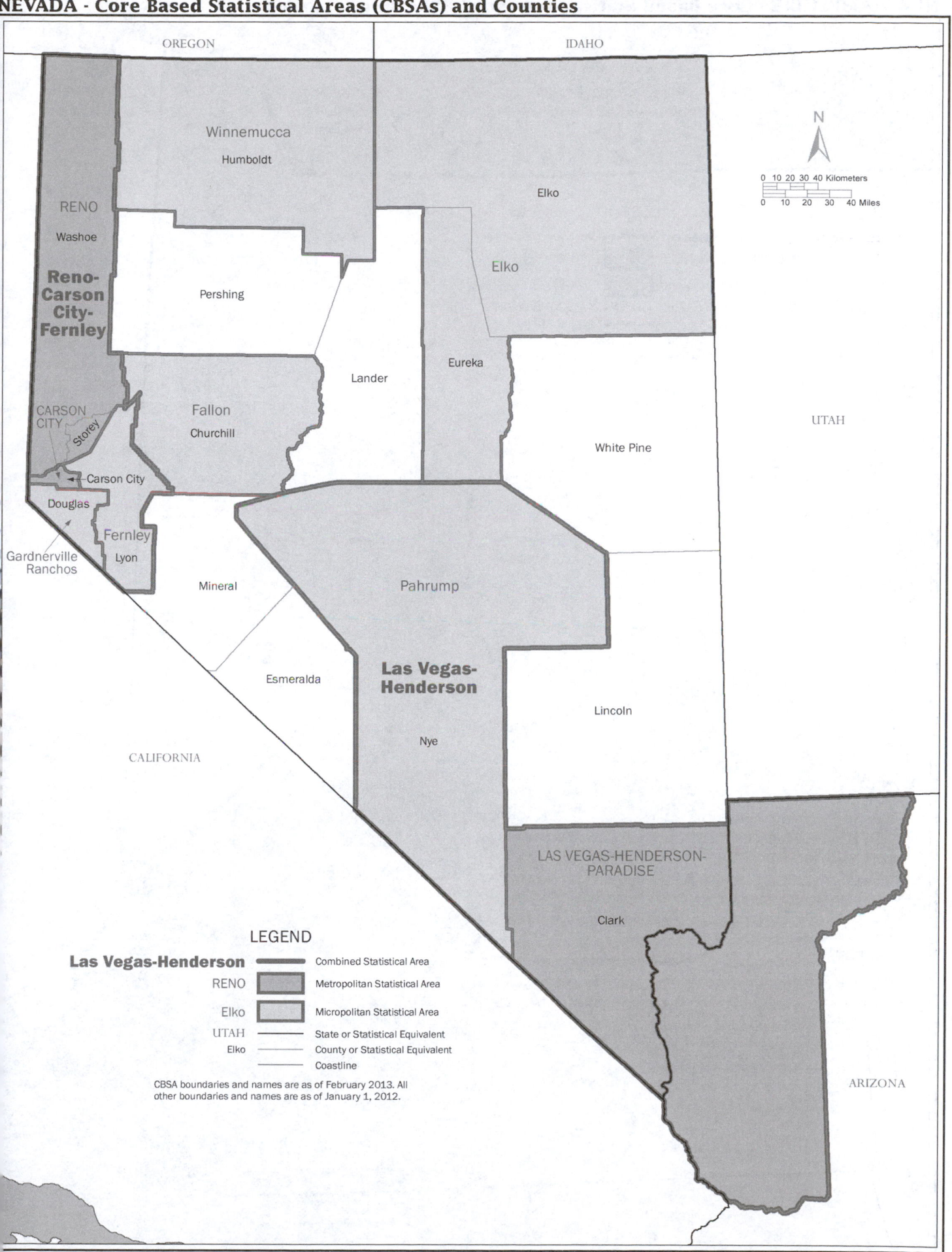

OREGON

IDAHO

N

0 10 20 30 40 Kilometers

0 10 20 30 40 Miles

Winnemucca

Humboldt

Elko

RENO

Washoe

Elko

Reno-
Carson
City-
Fernley

Pershing

Lander

Eureka

UTAH

CARSON
CITY

Storey

White Pine

Fallon

Churchill

Carson City

Douglas

Fernley

Gardnerville
Ranchos

Lyon

Mineral

Pahrump

Esmeralda

Las Vegas-
Henderson

Lincoln

Nye

CALIFORNIA

LAS VEGAS-HENDERSON-
PARADISE

Clark

ARIZONA

LEGEND

Las Vegas-Henderson ━━━ Combined Statistical Area

RENO ▨ Metropolitan Statistical Area

Elko ▢ Micropolitan Statistical Area

UTAH ─── State or Statistical Equivalent

Elko ─── County or Statistical Equivalent

─── Coastline

CBSA boundaries and names are as of February 2013. All
other boundaries and names are as of January 1, 2012.

CANADA

LEGEND

Boston-Providence-Worcester ━━━ Combined Statistical Area

MANCHESTER-NASHUA ▓▓▓ Metropolitan Statistical Area

Berlin ░░░ Micropolitan Statistical Area

Rockingham County-Strafford County •••• Metropolitan Division

CANADA ━━━ International

MAINE ━━━ State or Statistical Equivalent

Belknap ─── County or Statistical Equivalent

Atlantic Ocean ─── Coastline

CBSA boundaries and names are as of February 2013. All other boundaries and names are as of January 1, 2012.

Berlin

Essex

Coos

MAINE

VERMONT

Orange

Grafton

Carroll

Claremont-Lebanon

Windsor

Laconia

Belknap

NEW YORK

Sullivan

Concord

Merrimack

Boston-Worcester-Providence (pt)

Strafford

Rockingham

N

BOSTON-CAMBRIDGE-NEWTON (pt)

Rockingham County-Strafford County

0 5 10 15 20 Kilometers

0 5 10 15 20 Miles

Keene

Cheshire

MANCHESTER-NASHUA

Hillsborough

Atlantic Ocean

MASSACHUSETTS

Essex

Middlesex

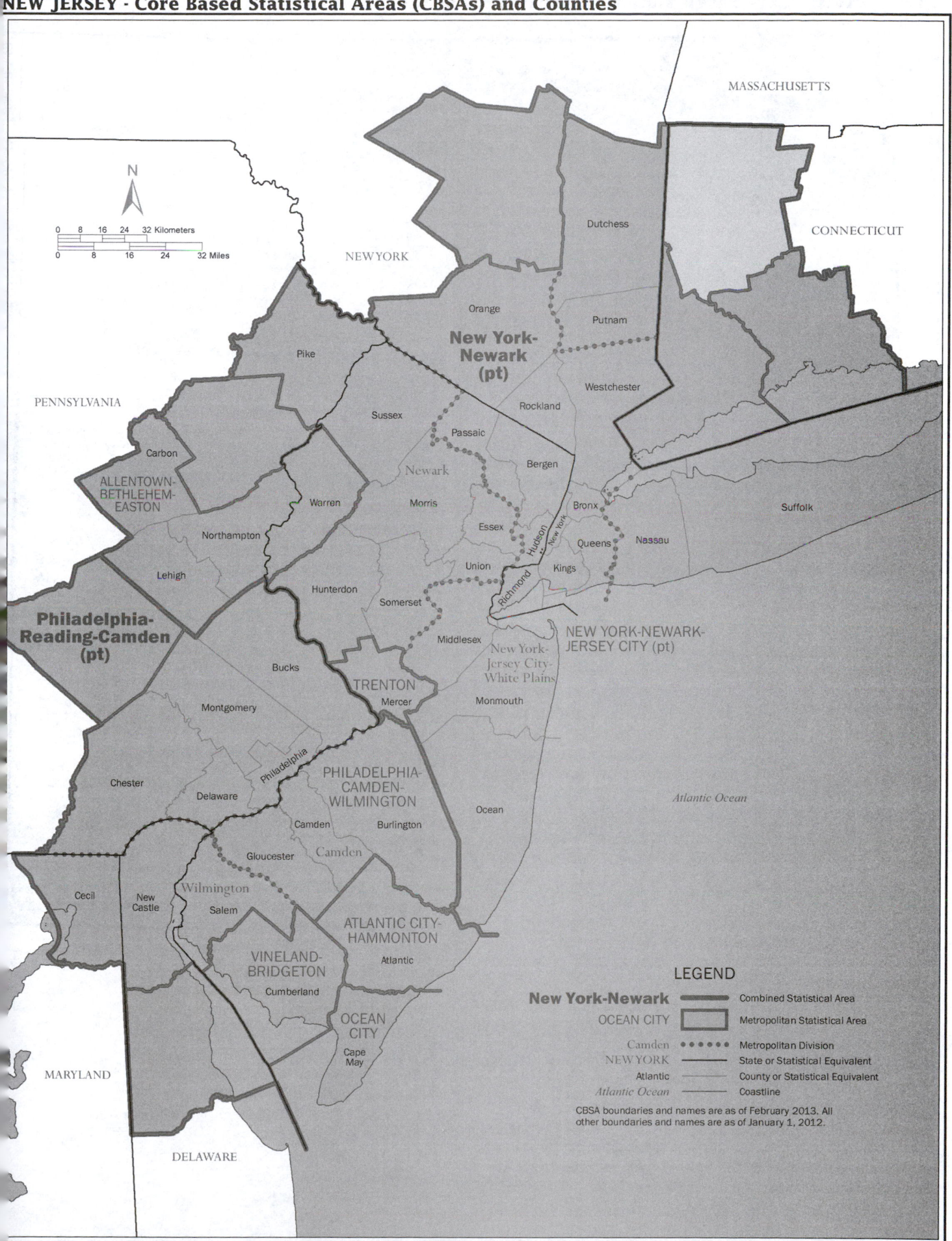

LEGEND

New York-Newark	Combined Statistical Area
OCEAN CITY	Metropolitan Statistical Area
Camden	Metropolitan Division
NEW YORK	State or Statistical Equivalent
Atlantic	County or Statistical Equivalent
Atlantic Ocean	Coastline

CBSA boundaries and names are as of February 2013. All other boundaries and names are as of January 1, 2012.

NEW MEXICO - Core Based Statistical Areas (CBSAs) and Counties

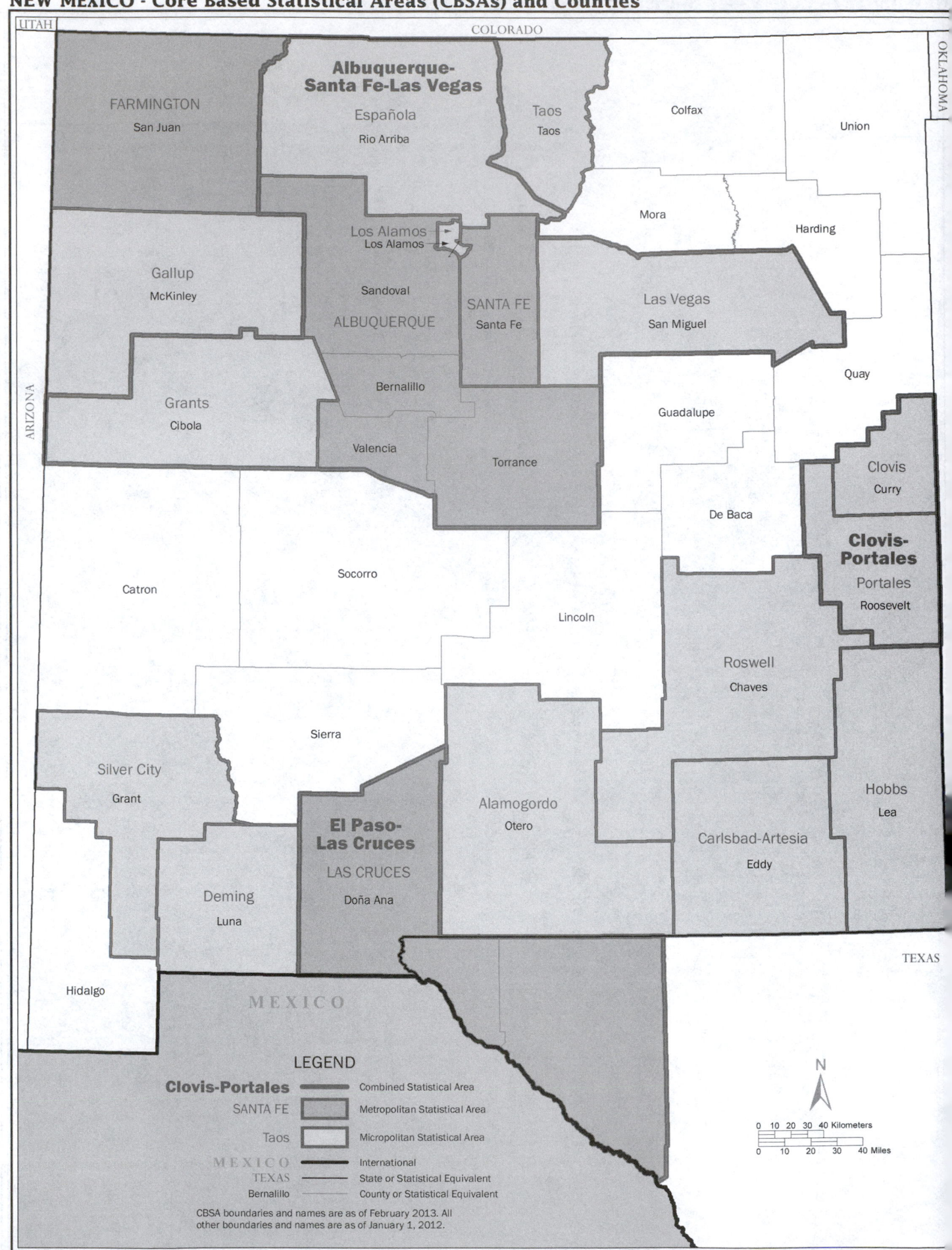

LEGEND

Clovis-Portales	Combined Statistical Area
SANTA FE	Metropolitan Statistical Area
Taos	Micropolitan Statistical Area
MEXICO	International
TEXAS	State or Statistical Equivalent
Bernalillo	County or Statistical Equivalent

CBSA boundaries and names are as of February 2013. All other boundaries and names are as of January 1, 2012.

NEW YORK - Core Based Statistical Areas (CBSAs) and Counties

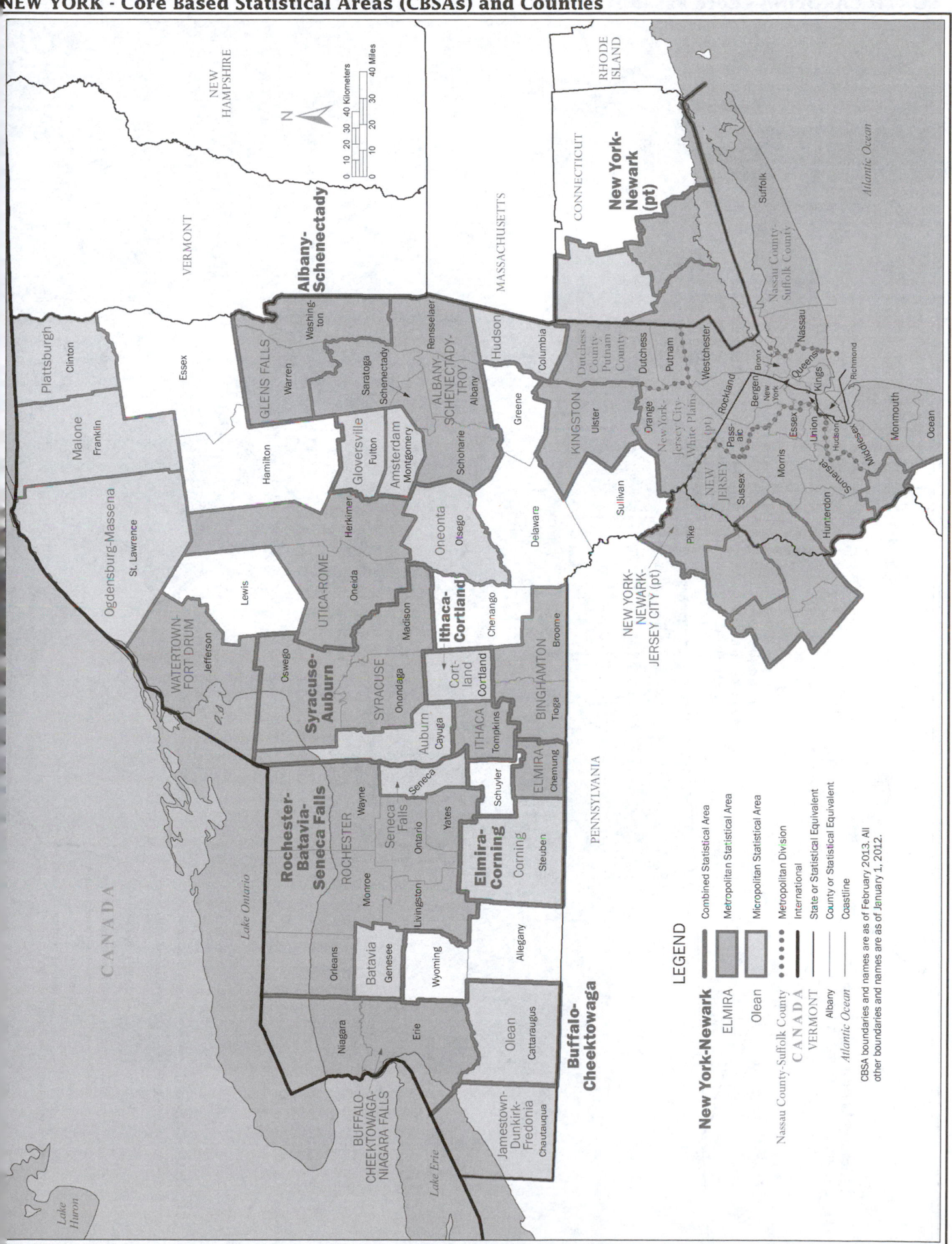

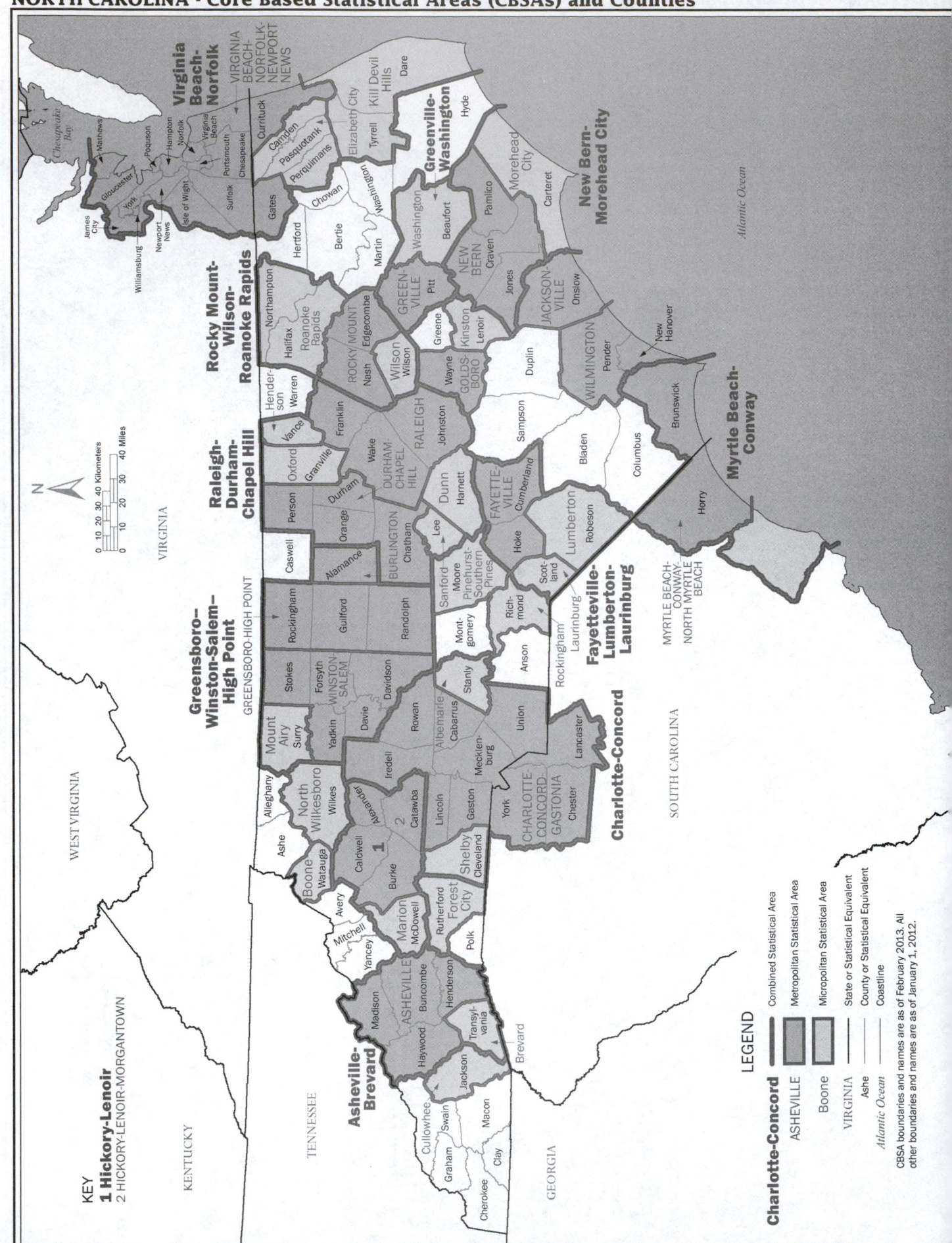

NORTH DAKOTA - Core Based Statistical Areas (CBSAs) and Counties

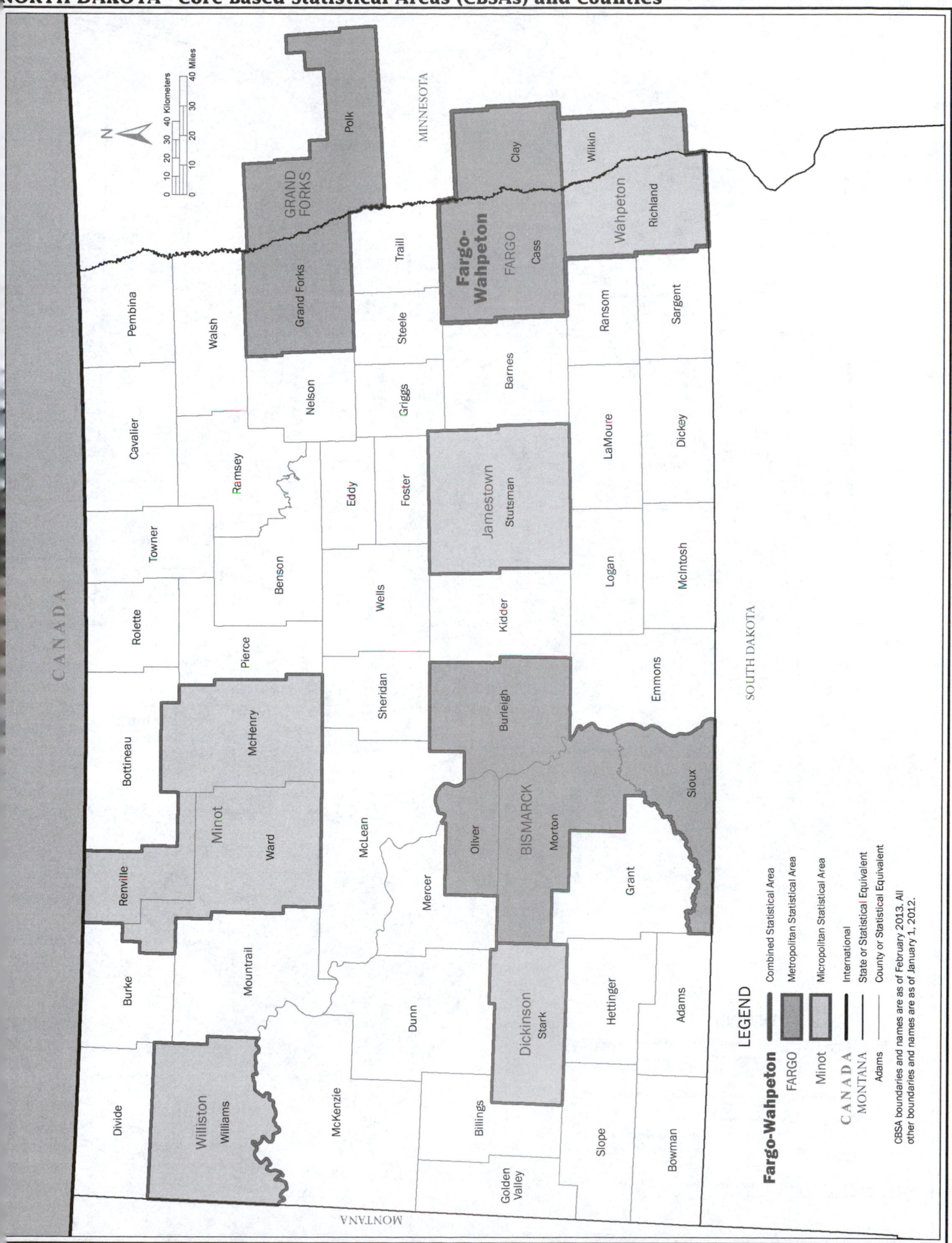

L.S. DEPARTMENT OF COMMERCE Economics and Statistics Administration U.S. Census Bureau

Appendix D

MICHIGAN

CANADA

Lake Erie

PENNSYLVANIA

Toledo-Port Clinton

Williams

Fulton

Lucas

Ottawa

Port Clinton

Erie

Sandusky

Cleveland-Akron-Canton

Lake

Ashtabula
Ashtabula

Geauga

Youngstown-Warren

Defiance
Defiance

Henry

TOLEDO
Wood

Fremont
Sandusky

CLEVELAND-
ELYRIA

Lorain

Cuyahoga

YOUNGSTOWN-WARREN-
BOARDMAN

Trumbull

Mercer

Paulding

Tiffin
Seneca

Norwalk
Huron

**Mansland-
Ashland-
Bucyrus**

Medina

AKRON

Summit

Portage

Mahoning

Putnam

**Findlay-
Tiffin**

Findlay
Hancock

**Lima-
Van Wert-
Celina**

Van Wert
Van Wert

LIMA
Allen

Wyandot

Bucyrus
Crawford

MANS-
FIELD
Richland

Ash-
land
Ashland

Wooster
Wayne

CANTON-
MASSILLON
Stark

Salem
Columbiana

**Pittsburgh-
New Castle
Weirton
(pt)**

INDIANA

Celina
Mercer

Wapakoneta
Auglaize

Hardin

Marion
Marion

Morrow

Holmes

Carroll

Jefferson

WEIRTON-
STEUBENVILLE

Bellefontaine
Logan

Mount
Vernon
Knox

Tuscarawas

New
Philadelphia-
Dover

Harrison

Sidney
Shelby

Urbana
Champaign

Union

Delaware

Coshocton
Coshocton

Greenville
Darke

DAYTON
Miami

SPRINGFIELD
Clark

**Columbus-
Marion-
Zanesville**

COLUMBUS

Licking

Cambridge
Guernsey

WHEELING
Belmont

Ohio

Hancock

Brooke

Preble

Madison

Franklin

Zanesville
Muskingum

Marshall

**Dayton-
Springfield-
Sidney**
Montgomery

Greene

Fairfield

Perry

Noble

Monroe

Union

Washington
Court House
Fayette

Pickaway

Hocking

Morgan

Marietta
Washington

**Cincinnati-
Wilmington-
Maysville**

Butler

Wilmington
Clinton

Warren

Chillicothe
Ross

Vinton

Athens
Athens

**Parkersburg-
Marietta-
Vienna**

Dearborn

CINCINNATI
Hamilton

Highland

Pike

Meigs

Ohio

Boone

Kenton

Campbell

Clermont

Brown

Adams

Jackson
Jackson

Point
Pleasant

WEST VIRGINIA

Gallatin

Pendleton

Bracken

Portsmouth
Scioto

Gallia

Mason

Grant

Lawrence

Greenup

Putnam

KENTUCKY

HUNTINGTON-
ASHLAND

Boyd

Cabell

**Charleston-
Huntington-
Ashland**

Wayne

Lincoln

LEGEND

Findlay-Tiffin ——— Combined Statistical Area

AKRON ▢ Metropolitan Statistical Area

Athens ▢ Micropolitan Statistical Area

CANADA ——— International

INDIANA ——— State or Statistical Equivalent

Adams ——— County or Statistical Equivalent

Lake Erie ——— Coastline

CBSA boundaries and names are as of February 2013. All
other boundaries and names are as of January 1, 2012.

N

0 10 20 30 40 Kilometers
0 10   20   30   40 Miles

VIRGINIA

OKLAHOMA - Core Based Statistical Areas (CBSAs) and Counties

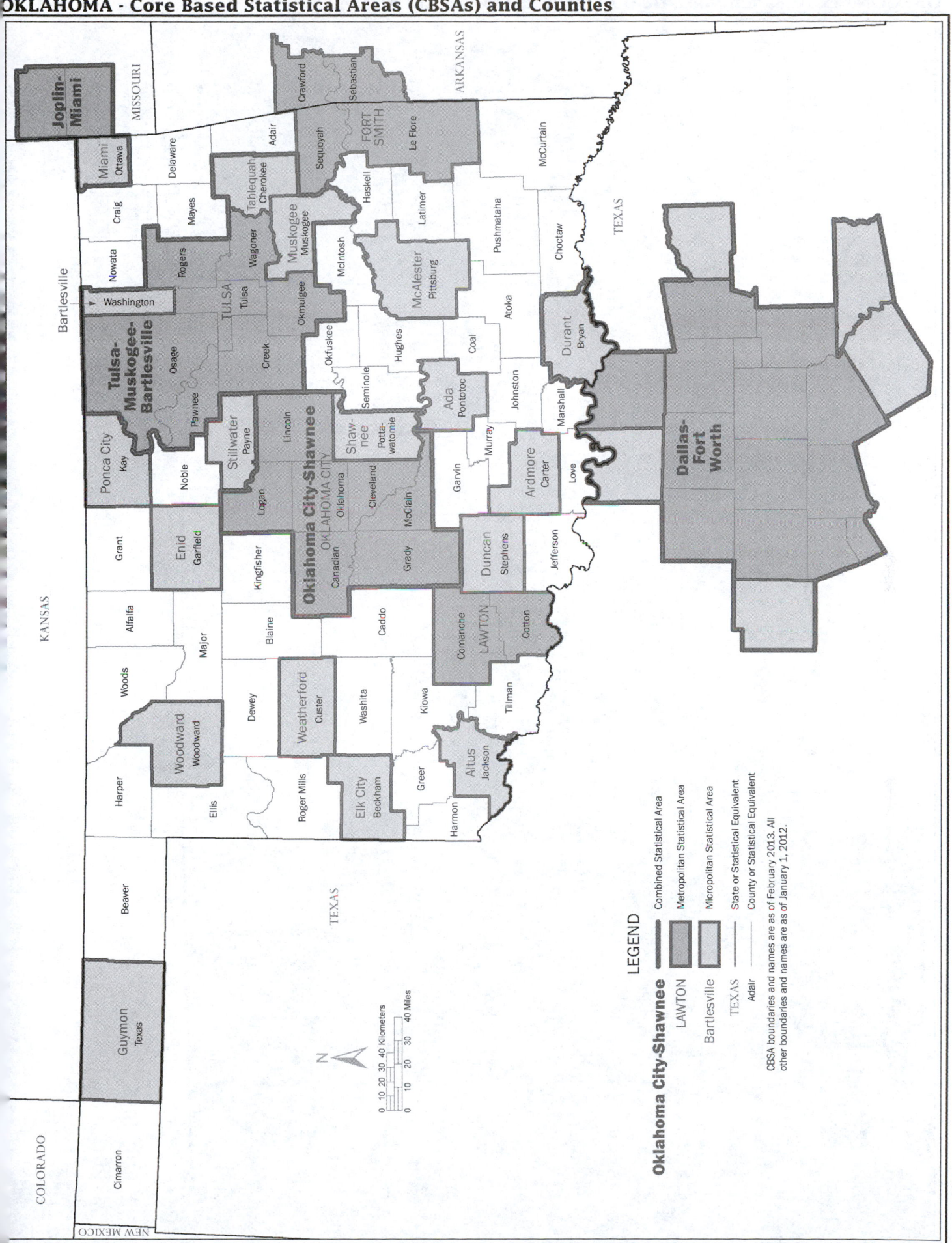

LEGEND

	Combined Statistical Area
	Metropolitan Statistical Area
	Micropolitan Statistical Area
	State or Statistical Equivalent
	County or Statistical Equivalent

Oklahoma City-Shawnee
LAWTON
Bartlesville
TEXAS
Adair

CBSA boundaries and names are as of February 2013. All
other boundaries and names are as of January 1, 2012.

OREGON - Core Based Statistical Areas (CBSAs) and Counties

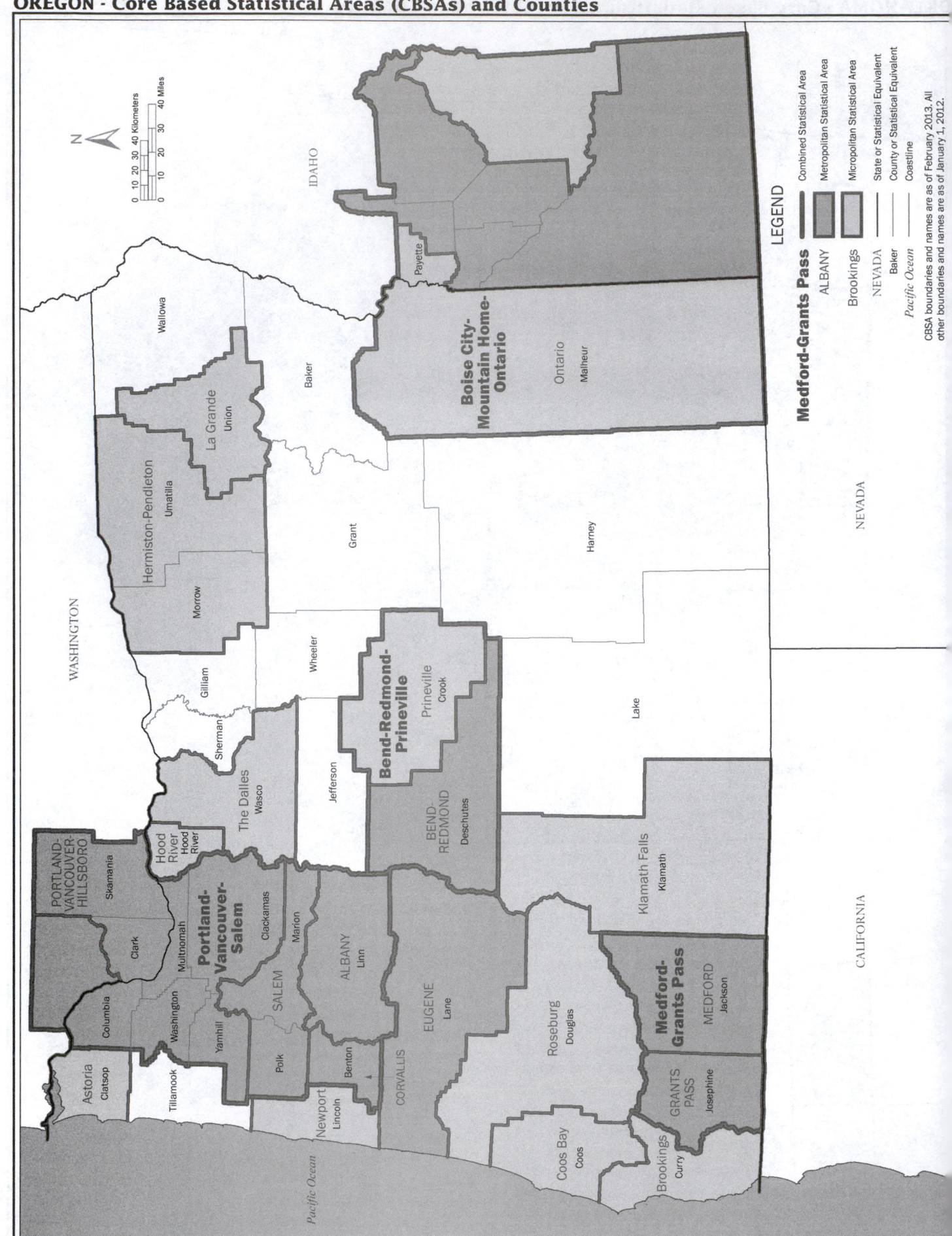

PENNSYLVANIA - Core Based Statistical Areas (CBSAs) and Counties

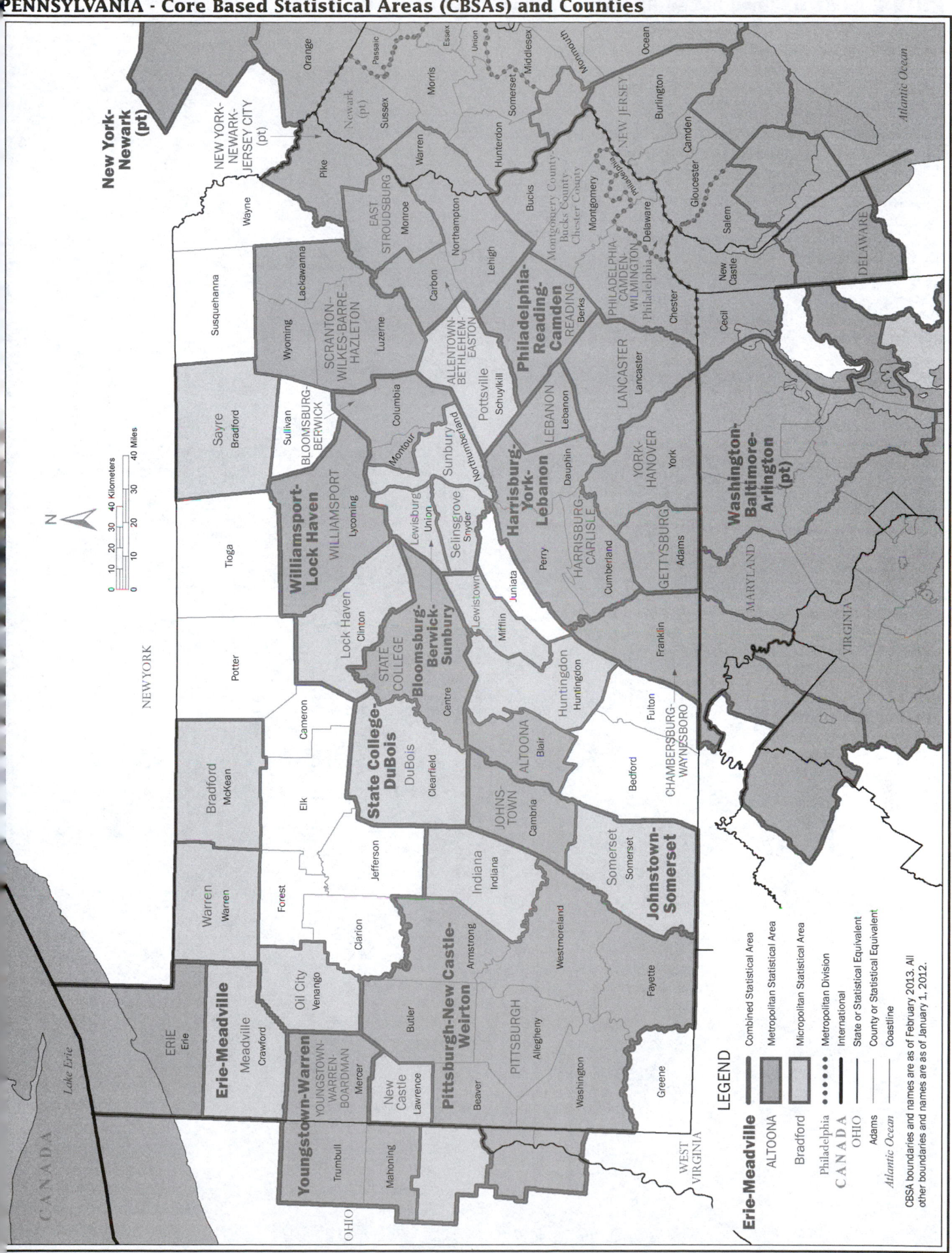

U.S. DEPARTMENT OF COMMERCE Economics and Statistics Administration U.S. Census Bureau

Appendix D

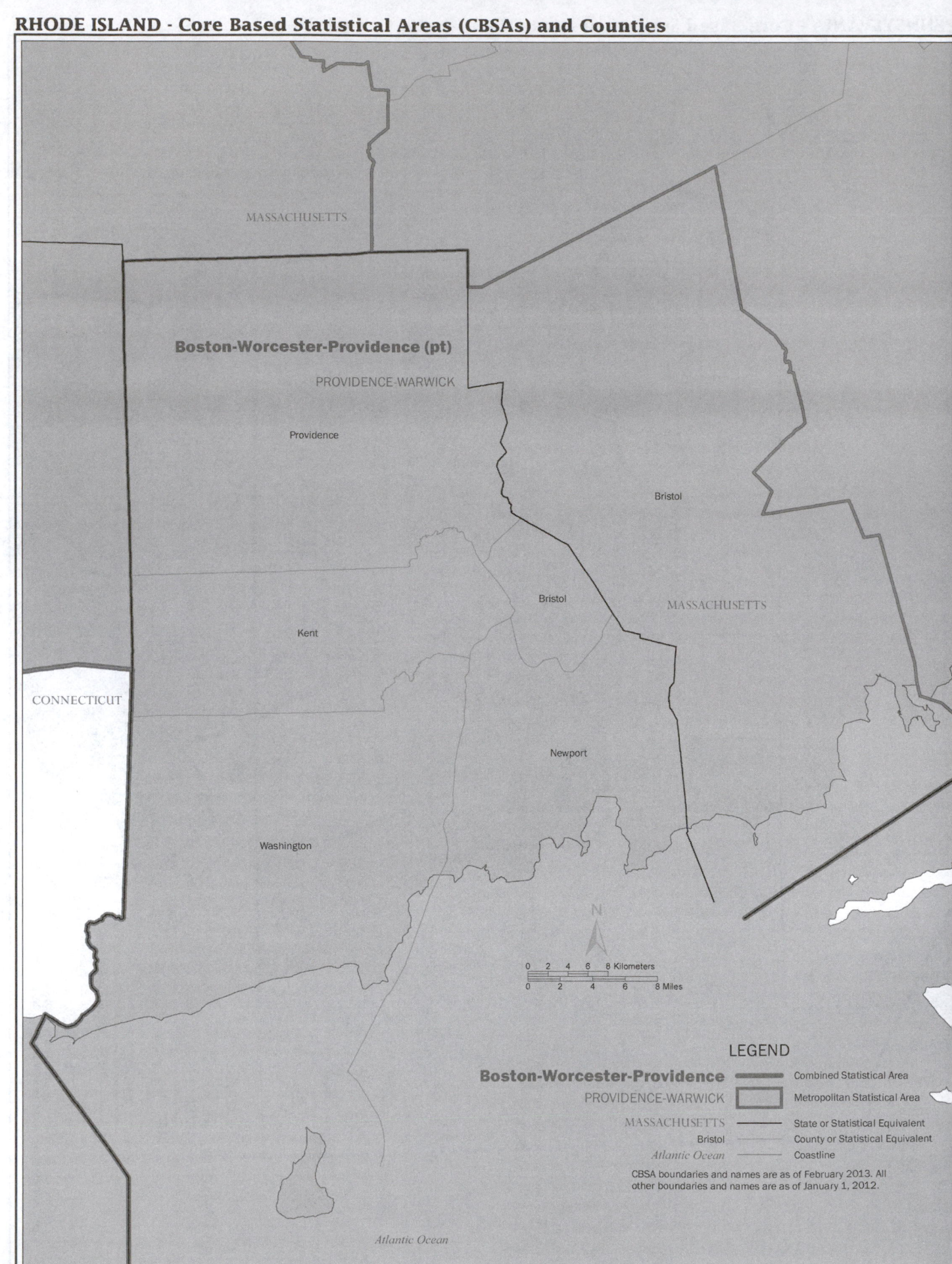

RHODE ISLAND - Core Based Statistical Areas (CBSAs) and Counties

MASSACHUSETTS

Boston-Worcester-Providence (pt)

PROVIDENCE-WARWICK

Providence

Bristol

Bristol

MASSACHUSETTS

CONNECTICUT

Kent

Newport

Washington

N

0   2   4   6   8 Kilometers
0   2   4   6   8 Miles

LEGEND

Boston-Worcester-Providence ⎯⎯⎯ Combined Statistical Area

PROVIDENCE-WARWICK ▭ Metropolitan Statistical Area

MASSACHUSETTS ⎯⎯ State or Statistical Equivalent

Bristol ⎯⎯ County or Statistical Equivalent

Atlantic Ocean ⎯⎯ Coastline

CBSA boundaries and names are as of February 2013. All
other boundaries and names are as of January 1, 2012.

Atlantic Ocean

SOUTH CAROLINA - Core Based Statistical Areas (CBSAs) and Counties

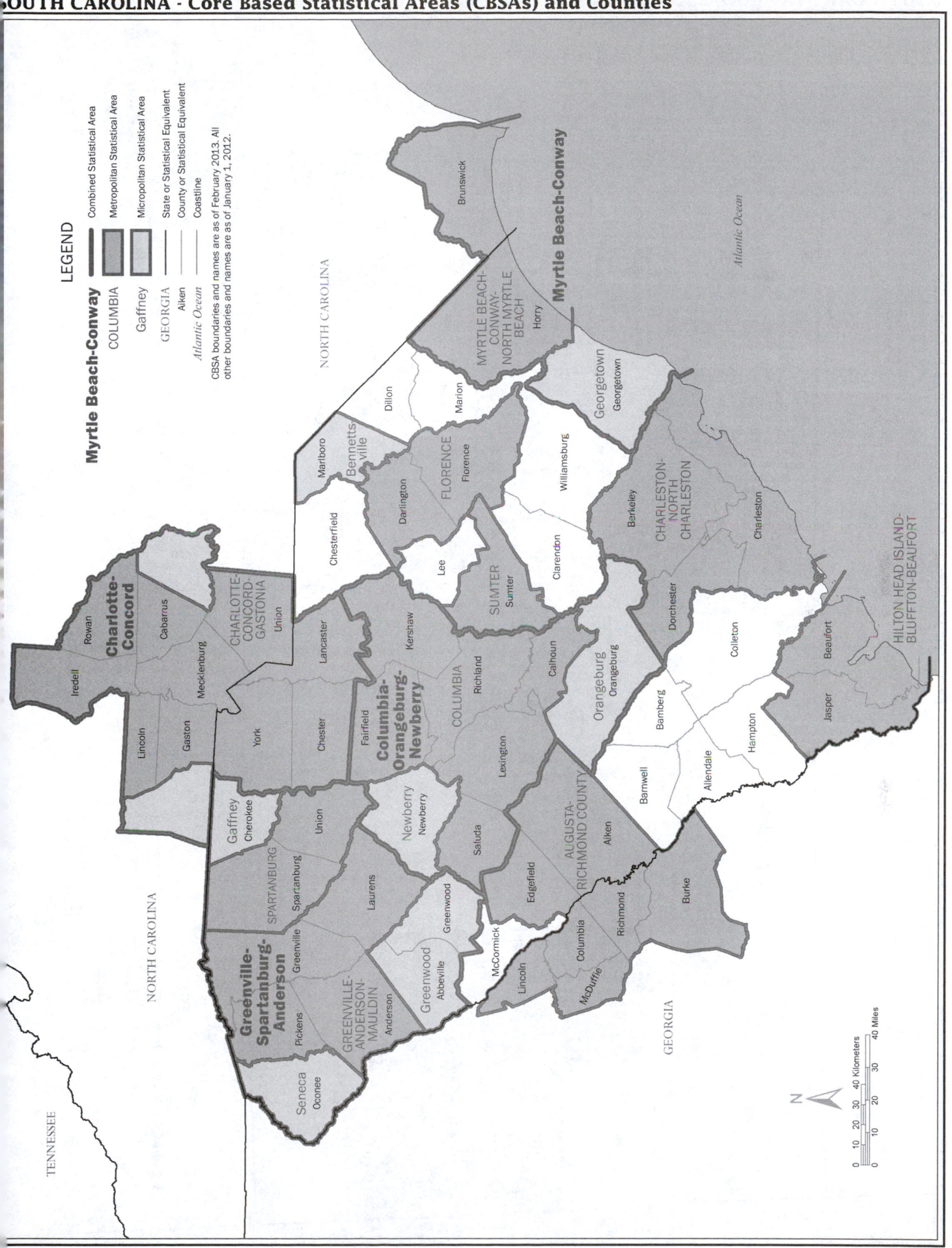

SOUTH DAKOTA - Core Based Statistical Areas (CBSAs) and Counties

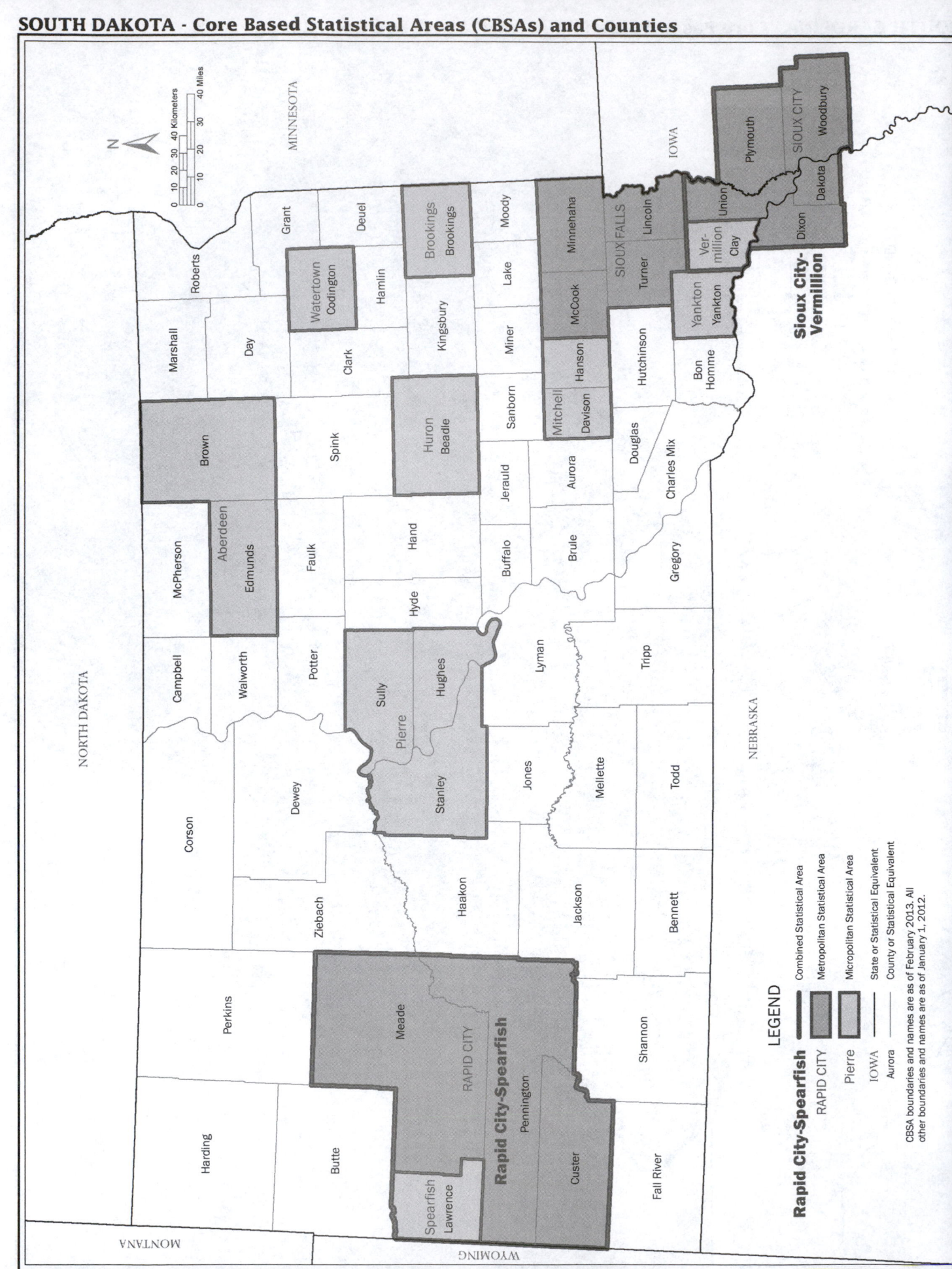

LEGEND

- Combined Statistical Area
- Metropolitan Statistical Area
- Micropolitan Statistical Area
- State or Statistical Equivalent
- County or Statistical Equivalent

Rapid City-Spearfish
RAPID CITY
Pierre
IOWA
Aurora

CBSA boundaries and names are as of February 2013. All other boundaries and names are as of January 1, 2012.

TENNESSEE - Core Based Statistical Areas (CBSAs) and Counties

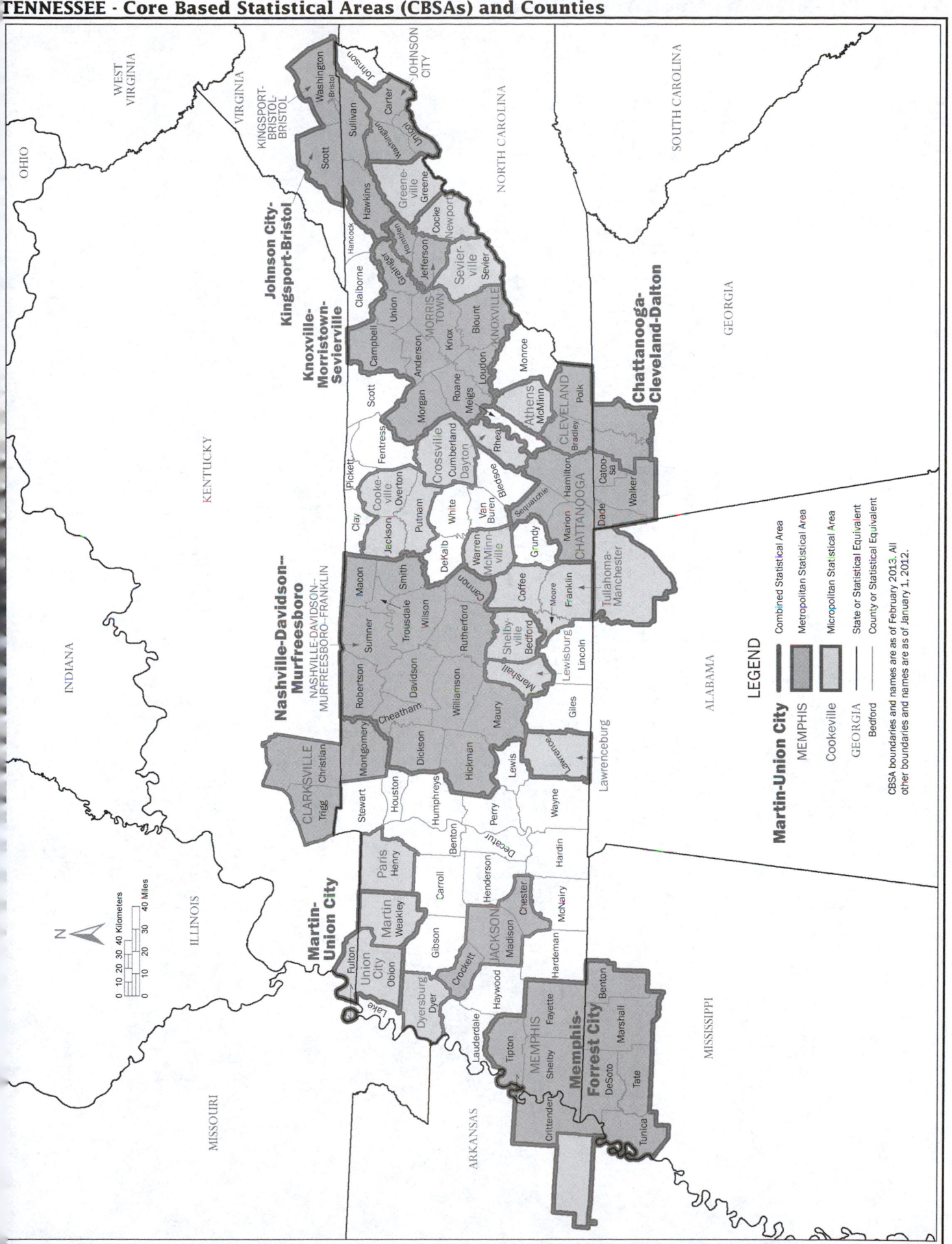

TEXAS - Core Based Statistical Areas (CBSAs) and Counties

ARKANSAS

LOUISIANA

TEXARKANA

KEY
1 DALLAS-FORT WORTH-ARLINGTON
2 Tyler-Jacksonville
3 Jacksonville
4 Nacogdoches

Longview-Marshall

Houston-The Woodlands

Gulf of Mexico

Victoria-Port Lavaca

Corpus Christi-Kingsville-Alice

Brownsville-Harlingen-Raymondville

McAllen-Edinburg

OKLAHOMA

Dallas-Fort Worth

WICHITA FALLS

ABILENE

Amarillo-Borger

Lubbock-Levelland

SAN ANGELO

Midland-Odessa

MEXICO

El Paso-Las Cruces

NEW MEXICO

LEGEND
	Combined Statistical Area
	Metropolitan Statistical Area
	Micropolitan Statistical Area
.....	Metropolitan Division
	International
	State or Statistical Equivalent
	County or Statistical Equivalent
	Coastline

Dallas-Fort Worth Combined Statistical Area
WACO Metropolitan Statistical Area
Alice Micropolitan Statistical Area
Fort Worth-Arlington Metropolitan Division
MEXICO International
OKLAHOMA State or Statistical Equivalent
Harris County or Statistical Equivalent
Gulf of Mexico Coastline

CBSA boundaries and names are as of February 2013. All
other boundaries and names are as of January 1, 2012.

N

0 30 60 90 120 Kilometers
0 30 60 90 120 Miles

UTAH - Core Based Statistical Areas (CBSAs) and Counties

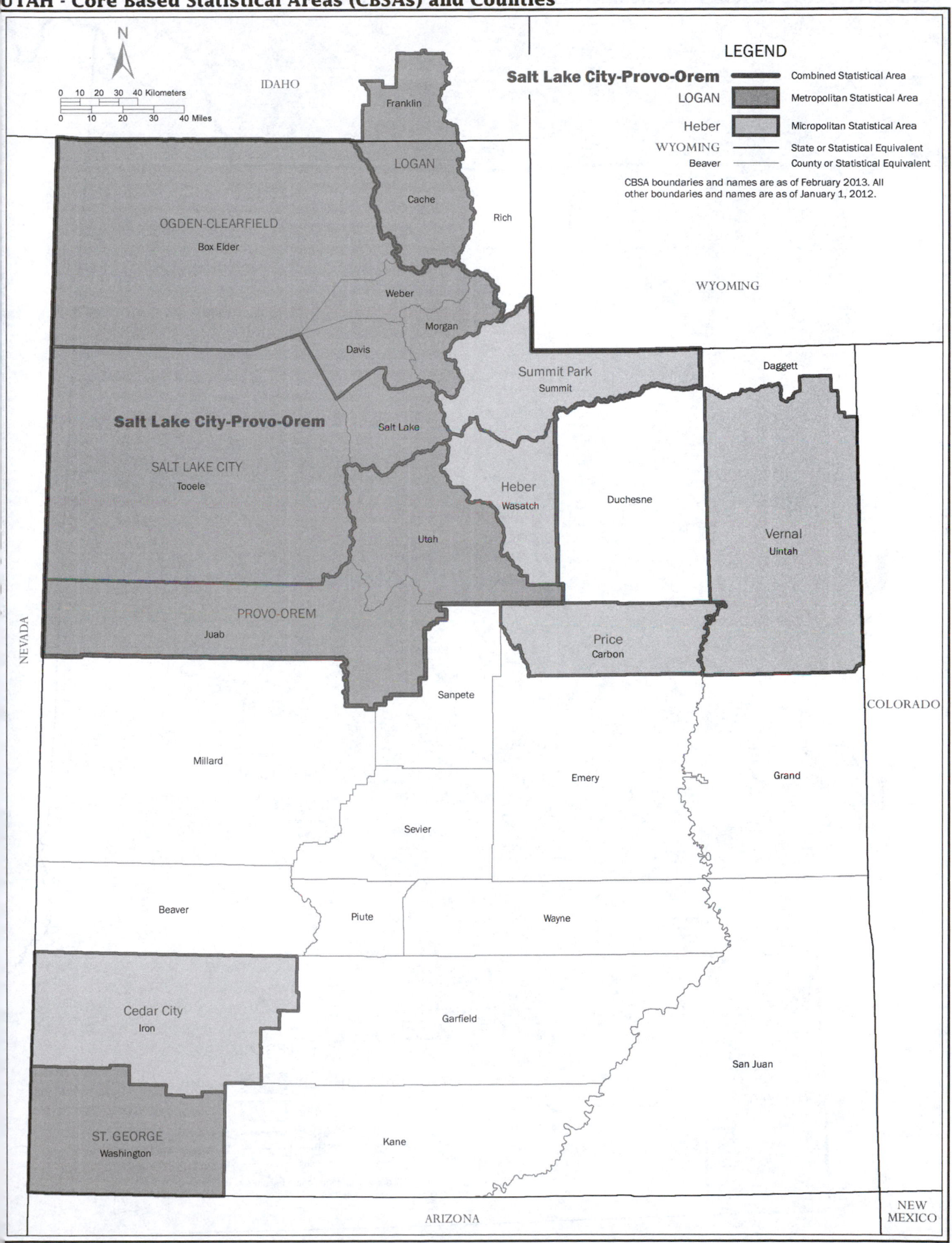

N

0   5   10   15   20 Kilometers

0   5   10   15   20 Miles

CANADA

Grand Isle

Franklin

Orleans

BURLINGTON-
SOUTH BURLINGTON

Essex

Berlin

Coos

Lamoille

Chittenden

Caledonia

MAINE

Barre

Washington

Addison

Orange

Grafton

NEW YORK

Claremont-Lebanon

Rutland

Rutland

Windsor

NEW HAMPSHIRE

Sullivan

Bennington

Bennington

Windham

LEGEND

BURLINGTON-SOUTH BURLINGTON   Metropolitan Statistical Area

Barre   Micropolitan Statistical Area

CANADA   International

NEW HAMPSHIRE   State or Statistical Equivalent

Addison   County or Statistical Equivalent

CBSA boundaries and names are as of February 2013. All
other boundaries and names are as of January 1, 2012.

MASSACHUSETTS

VIRGINIA - Core Based Statistical Areas (CBSAs) and Counties

NEW JERSEY

DELAWARE

MARYLAND

Atlantic Ocean

Accomack

Northampton

Chesapeake Bay

Virginia Beach-Norfolk

Currituck

36

6

35

Gates

NORTH CAROLINA

Washington-Baltimore-Arlington

WASHINGTON-ARLINGTON-ALEXANDRIA

PENNSYLVANIA

Calvert

Prince George's

Charles

Frederick

Montgomery

District of Columbia

DC

Arlington 11

12

Fairfax

Washington-Arlington-Alexandria

22 21

Prince William

Loudoun

Jefferson

Clarke

39

Frederick

Winchester

Hampshire

Warren

Fauquier

Rappa-hannock

Stafford 14

Spot-sylvania

Culpeper

Madison

Orange

Greene 5

Louisa

Shenandoah

Page

HARRISONBURG

17

Rocking-ham

STAUNTON-WAYNESBORO 34

Augusta

37

Albemarle

CHARLOTTESVILLE

Fluvanna

Nelson

Westmore-land

Northumberland

Richmond

Lancaster

Essex

King and Queen

King William

King George

Caroline

Hanover

New Kent

Henrico 31

RICHMOND 7

Goochland

Powhatan

Chesterfield

Amelia

Nottoway

Mathews

Middlesex

Gloucester

York 38

Charles City

Prince George 27

Dinwiddie

18

James City

Surry

Isle of Wight

Southampton

Sussex

Brunswick

Greensville

13

10

VIRGINIA BEACH-NORFOLK-NEWPORT NEWS

Harrisonburg-Staunton-Waynesboro

Highland

Bath

Rockbridge 19

Amherst

Buckingham

Appo-mattox

Campbell

LYNCHBURG

Bedford 2

Cumberland

Prince Edward

Charlotte

Lunenburg

Mecklenburg

Halifax

Danville

Pittsylvania 9

Alleghany 8

Botetourt

Craig

4

Bedford 2

Roanoke 32

ROANOKE

Franklin

33

Giles

Mont-gomery 30

Floyd

Patrick

Henry 23

Martinsville

Danville

WEST VIRGINIA

BLACKSBURG-CHRISTIANSBURG-RADFORD

Pulaski

Carroll

15

Martinsville

Mercer

Bland

Wythe

Grayson

Buchanan

Russell

Tazewell

Bluefield

Smyth

Washington 3

OHIO

Big Stone Gap

Wise 26

Dickenson

Scott

Lee

Sullivan

Hawkins

KINGSPORT-BRISTOL-BRISTOL

KENTUCKY

TENNESSEE

Johnson City-Kingsport-Bristol

LEGEND

Combined Statistical Area

Metropolitan Statistical Area

Micropolitan Statistical Area

Metropolitan Division

State or Statistical Equivalent

County or Statistical Equivalent

Coastline

CBSA boundaries and names are as of February 2013. All other boundaries and names are as of January 1, 2012.

Virginia Beach-Norfolk

RICHMOND

Danville

Washington-Arlington-Alexandria

MARYLAND

Accomack

Atlantic Ocean

Virginia Beach-Norfolk

Johnson City-Kingsport-Bristol

INDEPENDENT CITIES

1 Alexandria
2 Bedford
3 Bristol
4 Buena Vista
5 Charlottesville
6 Chesapeake
7 Colonial Heights
8 Covington
9 Danville
10 Emporia
11 Fairfax
12 Falls Church
13 Franklin
14 Fredericksburg
15 Galax
16 Hampton
17 Harrisonburg
18 Hopewell
19 Lexington
20 Lynchburg
21 Manassas
22 Manassas Park
23 Martinsville
24 Newport News
25 Norfolk
26 Norton
27 Petersburg
28 Poquoson
29 Portsmouth
30 Radford
31 Richmond
32 Roanoke
33 Salem
34 Staunton
35 Suffolk
36 Virginia Beach
37 Waynesboro
38 Williamsburg
39 Winchester

N

0 10 20 30 40 Kilometers

0 10 20 30 40 Miles

CANADA

IDAHO

LEWISTON
Nez Perce

Spokane-Spokane Valley-Coeur d'Alene

Pend Oreille

Stevens

Spokane

SPOKANE-SPOKANE VALLEY

Ferry

Pullman-Moscow

Pullman
Whitman

Garfield

Asotin

WALLA WALLA

Columbia

Walla Walla

Lincoln

Moses Lake-Othello

Othello
Adams

Franklin

Okanogan

WENATCHEE

Douglas

Moses Lake
Grant

KENNEWICK-RICHLAND

Benton

Chelan

Ellensburg
Kittitas

YAKIMA
Yakima

Klickitat

OREGON

LEGEND

Seattle-Tacoma

YAKIMA

Aberdeen

Tacoma-Lakewood

CANADA

OREGON

Adams

Pacific Ocean

Combined Statistical Area
Metropolitan Statistical Area
Micropolitan Statistical Area
Metropolitan Division
International
State or Statistical Equivalent
County or Statistical Equivalent
Coastline

CBSA boundaries and names are as of February 2013. All other boundaries and names are as of January 1, 2012.

BELLINGHAM
Whatcom

MOUNT VERNON-ANACORTES
Skagit

Island

Oak Harbor

Seattle-Tacoma

SEATTLE-TACOMA-BELLEVUE
Snohomish

Seattle-Bellevue-Everett

King

San Juan

BREMERTON-SILVERDALE
Jefferson

Kitsap

Tacoma-Lakewood
Pierce

Centralia
Lewis

PORTLAND-VANCOUVER-HILLSBORO
Skamania

Port Angeles
Clallam

Shelton
Mason

OLYMPIA-TUMWATER
Thurston

LONGVIEW
Cowlitz

Clark

Multnomah

Portland-Vancouver-Salem (pt)
Clackamas

Aberdeen
Grays Harbor

Pacific

Wahkiakum

Columbia

Washington

Yamhill

Pacific Ocean

N

0 10 20 30 40 Kilometers
0 10 20 30 40 Miles

WEST VIRGINIA - Core Based Statistical Areas (CBSAs) and Counties

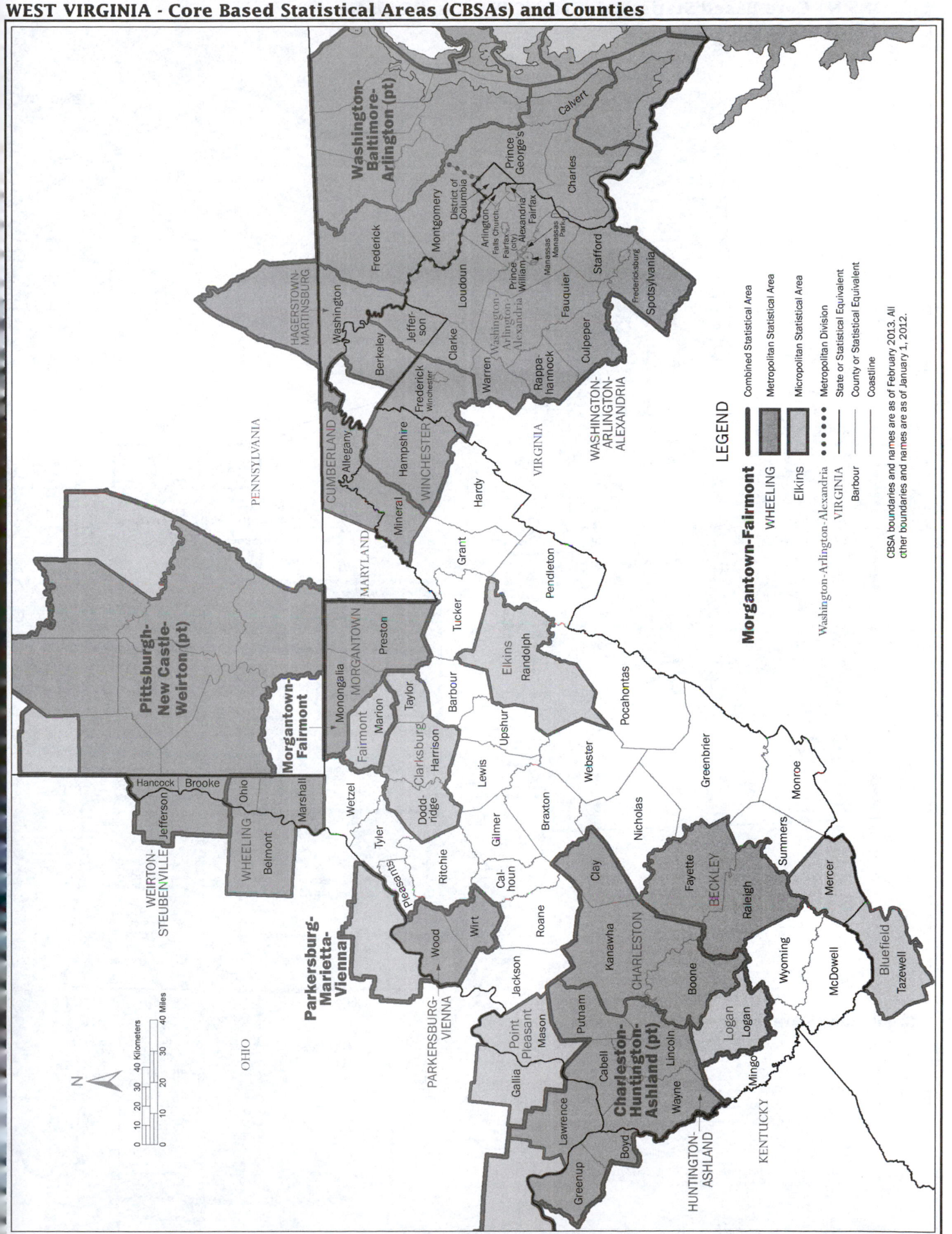

WISCONSIN - Core Based Statistical Areas (CBSAs) and Counties

CANADA

Lake Superior

DULUTH
St. Louis

Carlton

Douglas

Bayfield

Ashland | Iron

MICHIGAN

Iron Mountain
Dickinson

Minneapolis-St. Paul (pt)

Mille Lacs

MINNESOTA

Burnett | Washburn | Sawyer

Vilas

Oneida

Forest

Florence

Isanti

Sherburne

Chisago

Polk

Barron | Rusk

Price

Green Bay-Shawano

Marinette

Menominee

Marinette

Anoka

Wright

Eau Claire-Menomonie

Merrill
Lincoln

Langlade

Hennepin

Ramsey

Washington

St. Croix

Meno-monie
Dunn

EAU CLAIRE
Chippewa

Taylor

Wausau-Stevens Point-Wisconsin Rapids
WAUSAU
Marathon

Menominee

Shawano
Shawano

Oconto

GREEN BAY

Door

Carver

Scott

Dakota

Pierce

Eau Claire

Clark

Wood

Stevens Point

Waupaca

APPLETON
Outagamie

Brown

Kewaunee

Sibley

Pepin

Buffalo

Wisconsin Rapids-Marshfield

Portage

Manitowoc

Le Sueur

Trem-pealeau

Jackson

Appleton-Oshkosh-Neenah
Waushara

OSHKOSH-NEENAH
Winnebago

Calumet

Manitowoc

MINNEAPOLIS-ST. PAUL-BLOOMINGTON

LA CROSSE-ONALASKA
La Crosse

Monroe

Juneau | Adams | Marquette

Green Lake

FOND DU LAC
Fond du Lac

Sheboygan

SHEBOYGAN

Lake Michigan

Houston

Vernon

Richland

Baraboo
Sauk

Columbia

Beaver Dam

Washington

Ozaukee

Milwaukee-Racine-Waukesha

MICHIGAN

Crawford

IOWA

Dodge

Milwaukee

MILWAUKEE-WAUKESHA-WEST ALLIS

Madison-Janesville-Beloit
MADISON
Iowa

Dane

Watertown-Fort Atkinson

Waukesha

Jefferson

Platteville
Grant

Lafayette

Green

JANESVILLE-BELOIT
Rock

Whitewater-Elkhorn
Walworth

RACINE
Racine

Kenosha

Lake County-Kenosha County

ILLINOIS

McHenry | Lake

Chicago-Naperville (pt)

DeKalb | Kane

CHICAGO-NAPERVILLE-ELGIN (pt)
DuPage

Cook

INDIANA

Kendall

Will

Lake | Porter

Grundy

Newton | Jasper

LEGEND

Green Bay-Shawano — Combined Statistical Area
APPLETON — Metropolitan Statistical Area
Baraboo — Micropolitan Statistical Area
Lake County-Kenosha County ···· Metropolitan Division
CANADA — International
ILLINOIS — State or Statistical Equivalent
Adams — County or Statistical Equivalent
Lake Michigan — Coastline

0 10 20 30 40 Kilometers
0 10 20 30 40 Miles

CBSA boundaries and names are as of February 2013. All other boundaries and names are as of January 1, 2012.

WYOMING - Core Based Statistical Areas (CBSAs) and Counties

SOUTH DAKOTA

NEBRASKA

MONTANA

COLORADO

UTAH

IDAHO

Crook

Weston

Niobrara

Goshen

Platte

CHEYENNE
Laramie

Gillette
Campbell

Converse

Laramie
Albany

Sheridan
Sheridan

Johnson

CASPER
Natrona

Carbon

Big Horn

Park

Washakie

Hot Springs

Riverton
Fremont

Rock Springs
Sweetwater

Sublette

Jackson
Teton

Lincoln

Evanston
Uinta

Teton

LEGEND

Metropolitan Statistical Area

Micropolitan Statistical Area

State or Statistical Equivalent

County or Statistical Equivalent

Park

CHEYENNE

Jackson

MONTANA

CBSA boundaries and names are as of February 2013. All other boundaries and names are as of January 1, 2012.

N

0 10 20 30 40 Kilometers
0 10 20 30 40 Miles

APPENDIX E
CITIES BY COUNTY

The following table is arranged alphabetically by state. Under each state heading are listed all cities with a 2010 census population over 25,000 along with their component counties and the population in each component.

State Code	Place Code	County Code	Geographic Area Name	2010 Census Population	State Code	Place Code	County Code	Geographic Area Name	2010 Census Population
01			**ALABAMA**	4 779 736	01	78552		Vestavia Hills city	34 033
01	00820		Alabaster city	30 352	01	78552	073	Jefferson County	34 019
01	00820	117	Shelby County	30 352	01	78552	117	Shelby County	14
01	03076		Auburn city	53 380	02			**ALASKA**	710 231
01	03076	081	Lee County	53 380	02	03000		Anchorage municipality	291 826
01	05980		Bessemer city	27 456	02	03000	020	Anchorage Municipality	291 826
01	05980	073	Jefferson County	27 456	02	24230		Fairbanks city	31 535
01	07000		Birmingham city	212 237	02	24230	090	Fairbanks North Star Borough	31 535
01	07000	073	Jefferson County	210 609	02	36400		Juneau city and borough	31 275
01	07000	117	Shelby County	1 628	02	36400	110	Juneau City and Borough	31 275
01	20104		Decatur city	55 683	04			**ARIZONA**	6 392 017
01	20104	083	Limestone County	84	04	02830		Apache Junction city	35 840
01	20104	103	Morgan County	55 599	04	02830	013	Maricopa County	294
01	21184		Dothan city	65 496	04	02830	021	Pinal County	35 546
01	21184	045	Dale County	887	04	04720		Avondale city	76 238
01	21184	067	Henry County	5	04	04720	013	Maricopa County	76 238
01	21184	069	Houston County	64 604	04	07940		Buckeye town	50 876
01	24184		Enterprise city	26 562	04	07940	013	Maricopa County	50 876
01	24184	031	Coffee County	26 139	04	08220		Bullhead City city	39 540
01	24184	045	Dale County	423	04	08220	015	Mohave County	39 540
01	26896		Florence city	39 319	04	10530		Casa Grande city	48 571
01	26896	077	Lauderdale County	39 319	04	10530	021	Pinal County	48 571
01	28696		Gadsden city	36 856	04	12000		Chandler city	236 123
01	28696	055	Etowah County	36 856	04	12000	013	Maricopa County	236 123
01	35800		Homewood city	25 167	04	22220		El Mirage city	31 797
01	35800	073	Jefferson County	25 167	04	22220	013	Maricopa County	31 797
01	35896		Hoover city	81 619	04	23620		Flagstaff city	65 870
01	35896	073	Jefferson County	58 582	04	23620	005	Coconino County	65 870
01	35896	117	Shelby County	23 037	04	23760		Florence town	25 536
01	37000		Huntsville city	180 105	04	23760	021	Pinal County	25 536
01	37000	083	Limestone County	1 521	04	27400		Gilbert town	208 453
01	37000	089	Madison County	178 584	04	27400	013	Maricopa County	208 453
01	45784		Madison city	42 938	04	27820		Glendale city	226 721
01	45784	083	Limestone County	3 453	04	27820	013	Maricopa County	226 721
01	45784	089	Madison County	39 485	04	28380		Goodyear city	65 275
01	50000		Mobile city	195 111	04	28380	013	Maricopa County	65 275
01	50000	097	Mobile County	195 111	04	37620		Kingman city	28 068
01	51000		Montgomery city	205 764	04	37620	015	Mohave County	28 068
01	51000	101	Montgomery County	205 764	04	39370		Lake Havasu City city	52 527
01	57048		Opelika city	26 477	04	39370	015	Mohave County	52 527
01	57048	081	Lee County	26 477	04	44270		Marana town	34 961
01	59472		Phenix City city	32 822	04	44270	019	Pima County	34 961
01	59472	081	Lee County	4 153	04	44270	021	Pinal County	0
01	59472	113	Russell County	28 669	04	44410		Maricopa city	43 482
01	62328		Prattville city	33 960	04	44410	021	Pinal County	43 482
01	62328	001	Autauga County	32 168	04	46000		Mesa city	439 041
01	62328	051	Elmore County	1 792	04	46000	013	Maricopa County	439 041
01	77256		Tuscaloosa city	90 468					
01	77256	125	Tuscaloosa County	90 468					

State Code	Place Code	County Code	Geographic Area Name	2010 Census Population	State Code	Place Code	County Code	Geographic Area Name	2010 Census Population
04	51600		Oro Valley town	41 011	05	41000		Little Rock city	193 524
04	51600	019	Pima County	41 011	05	41000	119	Pulaski County	193 524
04	54050		Peoria city	154 065	05	50450		North Little Rock city	62 304
04	54050	013	Maricopa County	154 058	05	50450	119	Pulaski County	62 304
04	54050	025	Yavapai County	7					
					05	53390		Paragould city	26 113
04	55000		Phoenix city	1 445 632	05	53390	055	Greene County	26 113
04	55000	013	Maricopa County	1 445 632					
					05	55310		Pine Bluff city	49 083
04	57380		Prescott city	39 843	05	55310	069	Jefferson County	49 083
04	57380	025	Yavapai County	39 843					
					05	60410		Rogers city	55 964
04	57450		Prescott Valley town	38 822	05	60410	007	Benton County	55 964
04	57450	025	Yavapai County	38 822					
					05	61670		Russellville city	27 920
04	58150		Queen Creek town	26 361	05	61670	115	Pope County	27 920
04	58150	013	Maricopa County	25 912					
04	58150	021	Pinal County	449	05	63800		Sherwood city	29 523
					05	63800	119	Pulaski County	29 523
04	62140		Sahuarita town	25 259					
04	62140	019	Pima County	25 259	05	66080		Springdale city	69 797
					05	66080	007	Benton County	6 054
04	63470		San Luis city	25 505	05	66080	143	Washington County	63 743
04	63470	027	Yuma County	25 505					
					05	68810		Texarkana city	29 919
04	65000		Scottsdale city	217 385	05	68810	091	Miller County	29 919
04	65000	013	Maricopa County	217 385					
					05	74540		West Memphis city	26 245
04	66820		Sierra Vista city	43 888	05	74540	035	Crittenden County	26 245
04	66820	003	Cochise County	43 888					
					06			**CALIFORNIA**	37 253 956
04	71510		Surprise city	117 517	06	00296		Adelanto city	31 765
04	71510	013	Maricopa County	117 517	06	00296	071	San Bernardino County	31 765
04	73000		Tempe city	161 719	06	00562		Alameda city	73 812
04	73000	013	Maricopa County	161 719	06	00562	001	Alameda County	73 812
04	77000		Tucson city	520 116	06	00884		Alhambra city	83 089
04	77000	019	Pima County	520 116	06	00884	037	Los Angeles County	83 089
04	85540		Yuma city	93 064	06	00947		Aliso Viejo city	47 823
04	85540	027	Yuma County	93 064	06	00947	059	Orange County	47 823
05			**ARKANSAS**	2 915 918	06	02000		Anaheim city	336 265
05	04840		Bella Vista town	26 461	06	02000	059	Orange County	336 265
05	04840	007	Benton County	26 461					
					06	02252		Antioch city	102 372
05	05290		Benton city	30 681	06	02252	013	Contra Costa County	102 372
05	05290	125	Saline County	30 681					
					06	02364		Apple Valley town	69 135
05	05320		Bentonville city	35 301	06	02364	071	San Bernardino County	69 135
05	05320	007	Benton County	35 301					
					06	02462		Arcadia city	56 364
05	15190		Conway city	58 908	06	02462	037	Los Angeles County	56 364
05	15190	045	Faulkner County	58 908					
					06	03064		Atascadero city	28 310
05	23290		Fayetteville city	73 580	06	03064	079	San Luis Obispo County	28 310
05	23290	143	Washington County	73 580					
					06	03162		Atwater city	28 168
05	24550		Fort Smith city	86 209	06	03162	047	Merced County	28 168
05	24550	131	Sebastian County	86 209					
					06	03386		Azusa city	46 361
05	33400		Hot Springs city	35 193	06	03386	037	Los Angeles County	46 361
05	33400	051	Garland County	35 193					
					06	03526		Bakersfield city	347 483
05	34750		Jacksonville city	28 364	06	03526	029	Kern County	347 483
05	34750	119	Pulaski County	28 364					
					06	03666		Baldwin Park city	75 390
05	35710		Jonesboro city	67 263	06	03666	037	Los Angeles County	75 390
05	35710	031	Craighead County	67 263					

Cities by County–*Continued*

State Code	Place Code	County Code	Geographic Area Name	2010 Census Population	State Code	Place Code	County Code	Geographic Area Name	2010 Census Population
06	03820		Banning city	29 603	06	13214		Chino Hills city	74 799
06	03820	065	Riverside County	29 603	06	13214	071	San Bernardino County	74 799
06	04758		Beaumont city	36 877	06	13392		Chula Vista city	243 916
06	04758	065	Riverside County	36 877	06	13392	073	San Diego County	243 916
06	04870		Bell city	35 477	06	13588		Citrus Heights city	83 301
06	04870	037	Los Angeles County	35 477	06	13588	067	Sacramento County	83 301
06	04982		Bellflower city	76 616	06	13756		Claremont city	34 926
06	04982	037	Los Angeles County	76 616	06	13756	037	Los Angeles County	34 926
06	04996		Bell Gardens city	42 072	06	14218		Clovis city	95 631
06	04996	037	Los Angeles County	42 072	06	14218	019	Fresno County	95 631
06	05108		Belmont city	25 835	06	14260		Coachella city	40 704
06	05108	081	San Mateo County	25 835	06	14260	065	Riverside County	40 704
06	05290		Benicia city	26 997	06	14890		Colton city	52 154
06	05290	095	Solano County	26 997	06	14890	071	San Bernardino County	52 154
06	06000		Berkeley city	112 580	06	15044		Compton city	96 455
06	06000	001	Alameda County	112 580	06	15044	037	Los Angeles County	96 455
06	06308		Beverly Hills city	34 109	06	16000		Concord city	122 067
06	06308	037	Los Angeles County	34 109	06	16000	013	Contra Costa County	122 067
06	08100		Brea city	39 282	06	16350		Corona city	152 374
06	08100	059	Orange County	39 282	06	16350	065	Riverside County	152 374
06	08142		Brentwood city	51 481	06	16532		Costa Mesa city	109 960
06	08142	013	Contra Costa County	51 481	06	16532	059	Orange County	109 960
06	08786		Buena Park city	80 530	06	16742		Covina city	47 796
06	08786	059	Orange County	80 530	06	16742	037	Los Angeles County	47 796
06	08954		Burbank city	103 340	06	17568		Culver City city	38 883
06	08954	037	Los Angeles County	103 340	06	17568	037	Los Angeles County	38 883
06	09066		Burlingame city	28 806	06	17610		Cupertino city	58 302
06	09066	081	San Mateo County	28 806	06	17610	085	Santa Clara County	58 302
06	09710		Calexico city	38 572	06	17750		Cypress city	47 802
06	09710	025	Imperial County	38 572	06	17750	059	Orange County	47 802
06	10046		Camarillo city	65 201	06	17918		Daly City city	101 123
06	10046	111	Ventura County	65 201	06	17918	081	San Mateo County	101 123
06	10345		Campbell city	39 349	06	17946		Dana Point city	33 351
06	10345	085	Santa Clara County	39 349	06	17946	059	Orange County	33 351
06	11194		Carlsbad city	105 328	06	17988		Danville town	42 039
06	11194	073	San Diego County	105 328	06	17988	013	Contra Costa County	42 039
06	11530		Carson city	91 714	06	18100		Davis city	65 622
06	11530	037	Los Angeles County	91 714	06	18100	113	Yolo County	65 622
06	12048		Cathedral City city	51 200	06	18394		Delano city	53 041
06	12048	065	Riverside County	51 200	06	18394	029	Kern County	53 041
06	12524		Ceres city	45 417	06	18996		Desert Hot Springs city	25 938
06	12524	099	Stanislaus County	45 417	06	18996	065	Riverside County	25 938
06	12552		Cerritos city	49 041	06	19192		Diamond Bar city	55 544
06	12552	037	Los Angeles County	49 041	06	19192	037	Los Angeles County	55 544
06	13014		Chico city	86 187	06	19766		Downey city	111 772
06	13014	007	Butte County	86 187	06	19766	037	Los Angeles County	111 772
06	13210		Chino city	77 983	06	20018		Dublin city	46 036
06	13210	071	San Bernardino County	77 983	06	20018	001	Alameda County	46 036

Cities by County–*Continued*

State Code	Place Code	County Code	Geographic Area Name	2010 Census Population	State Code	Place Code	County Code	Geographic Area Name	2010 Census Population
06	20956		East Palo Alto city	28 155	06	32548		Hawthorne city	84 293
06	20956	081	San Mateo County	28 155	06	32548	037	Los Angeles County	84 293
06	21712		El Cajon city	99 478	06	33000		Hayward city	144 186
06	21712	073	San Diego County	99 478	06	33000	001	Alameda County	144 186
06	21782		El Centro city	42 598	06	33182		Hemet city	78 657
06	21782	025	Imperial County	42 598	06	33182	065	Riverside County	78 657
06	22020		Elk Grove city	153 015	06	33434		Hesperia city	90 173
06	22020	067	Sacramento County	153 015	06	33434	071	San Bernardino County	90 173
06	22230		El Monte city	113 475	06	33588		Highland city	53 104
06	22230	037	Los Angeles County	113 475	06	33588	071	San Bernardino County	53 104
06	22300		El Paso de Robles (Paso Robles)	29 793	06	34120		Hollister city	34 928
06	22300	079	San Luis Obispo County	29 793	06	34120	069	San Benito County	34 928
06	22678		Encinitas city	59 518	06	36000		Huntington Beach city	189 992
06	22678	073	San Diego County	59 518	06	36000	059	Orange County	189 992
06	22804		Escondido city	143 911	06	36056		Huntington Park city	58 114
06	22804	073	San Diego County	143 911	06	36056	037	Los Angeles County	58 114
06	23042		Eureka city	27 191	06	36294		Imperial Beach city	26 324
06	23042	023	Humboldt County	27 191	06	36294	073	San Diego County	26 324
06	23182		Fairfield city	105 321	06	36448		Indio city	76 036
06	23182	095	Solano County	105 321	06	36448	065	Riverside County	76 036
06	24638		Folsom city	72 203	06	36546		Inglewood city	109 673
06	24638	067	Sacramento County	72 203	06	36546	037	Los Angeles County	109 673
06	24680		Fontana city	196 069	06	36770		Irvine city	212 375
06	24680	071	San Bernardino County	196 069	06	36770	059	Orange County	212 375
06	25338		Foster City city	30 567	06	39220		Laguna Hills city	30 344
06	25338	081	San Mateo County	30 567	06	39220	059	Orange County	30 344
06	25380		Fountain Valley city	55 313	06	39248		Laguna Niguel city	62 979
06	25380	059	Orange County	55 313	06	39248	059	Orange County	62 979
06	26000		Fremont city	214 089	06	39290		La Habra city	60 239
06	26000	001	Alameda County	214 089	06	39290	059	Orange County	60 239
06	27000		Fresno city	494 665	06	39486		Lake Elsinore city	51 821
06	27000	019	Fresno County	494 665	06	39486	065	Riverside County	51 821
06	28000		Fullerton city	135 161	06	39496		Lake Forest city	77 264
06	28000	059	Orange County	135 161	06	39496	059	Orange County	77 264
06	28168		Gardena city	58 829	06	39892		Lakewood city	80 048
06	28168	037	Los Angeles County	58 829	06	39892	037	Los Angeles County	80 048
06	29000		Garden Grove city	170 883	06	40004		La Mesa city	57 065
06	29000	059	Orange County	170 883	06	40004	073	San Diego County	57 065
06	29504		Gilroy city	48 821	06	40032		La Mirada city	48 527
06	29504	085	Santa Clara County	48 821	06	40032	037	Los Angeles County	48 527
06	30000		Glendale city	191 719	06	40130		Lancaster city	156 633
06	30000	037	Los Angeles County	191 719	06	40130	037	Los Angeles County	156 633
06	30014		Glendora city	50 073	06	40340		La Puente city	39 816
06	30014	037	Los Angeles County	50 073	06	40340	037	Los Angeles County	39 816
06	30378		Goleta city	29 888	06	40354		La Quinta city	37 467
06	30378	083	Santa Barbara County	29 888	06	40354	065	Riverside County	37 467
06	31960		Hanford city	53 967	06	40830		La Verne city	31 063
06	31960	031	Kings County	53 967	06	40830	037	Los Angeles County	31 063

Cities by County—*Continued*

State Code	Place Code	County Code	Geographic Area Name	2010 Census Population	State Code	Place Code	County Code	Geographic Area Name	2010 Census Population
06	40886		Lawndale city	32 769	06	48788		Montclair city	36 664
06	40886	037	Los Angeles County	32 769	06	48788	071	San Bernardino County	36 664
06	41124		Lemon Grove city	25 320	06	48816		Montebello city	62 500
06	41124	073	San Diego County	25 320	06	48816	037	Los Angeles County	62 500
06	41474		Lincoln city	42 819	06	48872		Monterey city	27 810
06	41474	061	Placer County	42 819	06	48872	053	Monterey County	27 810
06	41992		Livermore city	80 968	06	48914		Monterey Park city	60 269
06	41992	001	Alameda County	80 968	06	48914	037	Los Angeles County	60 269
06	42202		Lodi city	62 134	06	49138		Moorpark city	34 421
06	42202	077	San Joaquin County	62 134	06	49138	111	Ventura County	34 421
06	42524		Lompoc city	42 434	06	49270		Moreno Valley city	193 365
06	42524	083	Santa Barbara County	42 434	06	49270	065	Riverside County	193 365
06	43000		Long Beach city	462 257	06	49278		Morgan Hill city	37 882
06	43000	037	Los Angeles County	462 257	06	49278	085	Santa Clara County	37 882
06	43280		Los Altos city	28 976	06	49670		Mountain View city	74 066
06	43280	085	Santa Clara County	28 976	06	49670	085	Santa Clara County	74 066
06	44000		Los Angeles city	3 792 621	06	50076		Murrieta city	103 466
06	44000	037	Los Angeles County	3 792 621	06	50076	065	Riverside County	103 466
06	44028		Los Banos city	35 972	06	50258		Napa city	76 915
06	44028	047	Merced County	35 972	06	50258	055	Napa County	76 915
06	44112		Los Gatos town	29 413	06	50398		National City city	58 582
06	44112	085	Santa Clara County	29 413	06	50398	073	San Diego County	58 582
06	44574		Lynwood city	69 772	06	50916		Newark city	42 573
06	44574	037	Los Angeles County	69 772	06	50916	001	Alameda County	42 573
06	45022		Madera city	61 416	06	51182		Newport Beach city	85 186
06	45022	039	Madera County	61 416	06	51182	059	Orange County	85 186
06	45400		Manhattan Beach city	35 135	06	51560		Norco city	27 063
06	45400	037	Los Angeles County	35 135	06	51560	065	Riverside County	27 063
06	45484		Manteca city	67 096	06	52526		Norwalk city	105 549
06	45484	077	San Joaquin County	67 096	06	52526	037	Los Angeles County	105 549
06	46114		Martinez city	35 824	06	52582		Novato city	51 904
06	46114	013	Contra Costa County	35 824	06	52582	041	Marin County	51 904
06	46492		Maywood city	27 395	06	53000		Oakland city	390 724
06	46492	037	Los Angeles County	27 395	06	53000	001	Alameda County	390 724
06	46842		Menifee city	77 519	06	53070		Oakley city	35 432
06	46842	065	Riverside County	77 519	06	53070	013	Contra Costa County	35 432
06	46870		Menlo Park city	32 026	06	53322		Oceanside city	167 086
06	46870	081	San Mateo County	32 026	06	53322	073	San Diego County	167 086
06	46898		Merced city	78 958	06	53896		Ontario city	163 924
06	46898	047	Merced County	78 958	06	53896	071	San Bernardino County	163 924
06	47766		Milpitas city	66 790	06	53980		Orange city	136 416
06	47766	085	Santa Clara County	66 790	06	53980	059	Orange County	136 416
06	48256		Mission Viejo city	93 305	06	54652		Oxnard city	197 899
06	48256	059	Orange County	93 305	06	54652	111	Ventura County	197 899
06	48354		Modesto city	201 165	06	54806		Pacifica city	37 234
06	48354	099	Stanislaus County	201 165	06	54806	081	San Mateo County	37 234
06	48648		Monrovia city	36 590	06	55156		Palmdale city	152 750
06	48648	037	Los Angeles County	36 590	06	55156	037	Los Angeles County	152 750

Cities by County–*Continued*

State Code	Place Code	County Code	Geographic Area Name	2010 Census Population	State Code	Place Code	County Code	Geographic Area Name	2010 Census Population
06	55184		Palm Desert city	48 445	06	60466		Rialto city	99 171
06	55184	065	Riverside County	48 445	06	60466	071	San Bernardino County	99 171
06	55254		Palm Springs city	44 552	06	60620		Richmond city	103 701
06	55254	065	Riverside County	44 552	06	60620	013	Contra Costa County	103 701
06	55282		Palo Alto city	64 403	06	60704		Ridgecrest city	27 616
06	55282	085	Santa Clara County	64 403	06	60704	029	Kern County	27 616
06	55520		Paradise town	26 218	06	62000		Riverside city	303 871
06	55520	007	Butte County	26 218	06	62000	065	Riverside County	303 871
06	55618		Paramount city	54 098	06	62364		Rocklin city	56 974
06	55618	037	Los Angeles County	54 098	06	62364	061	Placer County	56 974
06	56000		Pasadena city	137 122	06	62546		Rohnert Park city	40 971
06	56000	037	Los Angeles County	137 122	06	62546	097	Sonoma County	40 971
06	56700		Perris city	68 386	06	62896		Rosemead city	53 764
06	56700	065	Riverside County	68 386	06	62896	037	Los Angeles County	53 764
06	56784		Petaluma city	57 941	06	62938		Roseville city	118 788
06	56784	097	Sonoma County	57 941	06	62938	061	Placer County	118 788
06	56924		Pico Rivera city	62 942	06	64000		Sacramento city	466 488
06	56924	037	Los Angeles County	62 942	06	64000	067	Sacramento County	466 488
06	57456		Pittsburg city	63 264	06	64224		Salinas city	150 441
06	57456	013	Contra Costa County	63 264	06	64224	053	Monterey County	150 441
06	57526		Placentia city	50 533	06	65000		San Bernardino city	209 924
06	57526	059	Orange County	50 533	06	65000	071	San Bernardino County	209 924
06	57764		Pleasant Hill city	33 152	06	65028		San Bruno city	41 114
06	57764	013	Contra Costa County	33 152	06	65028	081	San Mateo County	41 114
06	57792		Pleasanton city	70 285	06	65042		San Buenaventura (Ventura)	106 433
06	57792	001	Alameda County	70 285	06	65042	111	Ventura County	106 433
06	58072		Pomona city	149 058	06	65070		San Carlos city	28 406
06	58072	037	Los Angeles County	149 058	06	65070	081	San Mateo County	28 406
06	58240		Porterville city	54 165	06	65084		San Clemente city	63 522
06	58240	107	Tulare County	54 165	06	65084	059	Orange County	63 522
06	58520		Poway city	47 811	06	66000		San Diego city	1 307 402
06	58520	073	San Diego County	47 811	06	66000	073	San Diego County	1 307 402
06	59444		Rancho Cordova city	64 776	06	66070		San Dimas city	33 371
06	59444	067	Sacramento County	64 776	06	66070	037	Los Angeles County	33 371
06	59451		Rancho Cucamonga city	165 269	06	67000		San Francisco city	805 235
06	59451	071	San Bernardino County	165 269	06	67000	075	San Francisco County	805 235
06	59514		Rancho Palos Verdes city	41 643	06	67042		San Gabriel city	39 718
06	59514	037	Los Angeles County	41 643	06	67042	037	Los Angeles County	39 718
06	59587		Rancho Santa Margarita city	47 853	06	67112		San Jacinto city	44 199
06	59587	059	Orange County	47 853	06	67112	065	Riverside County	44 199
06	59920		Redding city	89 861	06	68000		San Jose city	945 942
06	59920	089	Shasta County	89 861	06	68000	085	Santa Clara County	945 942
06	59962		Redlands city	68 747	06	68028		San Juan Capistrano city	34 593
06	59962	071	San Bernardino County	68 747	06	68028	059	Orange County	34 593
06	60018		Redondo Beach city	66 748	06	68084		San Leandro city	84 950
06	60018	037	Los Angeles County	66 748	06	68084	001	Alameda County	84 950
06	60102		Redwood City city	76 815	06	68154		San Luis Obispo city	45 119
06	60102	081	San Mateo County	76 815	06	68154	079	San Luis Obispo County	45 119

Cities by County–*Continued*

State Code	Place Code	County Code	Geographic Area Name	2010 Census Population	State Code	Place Code	County Code	Geographic Area Name	2010 Census Population
06	68196		San Marcos city	83 781	06	75630		Suisun City city	28 111
06	68196	073	San Diego County	83 781	06	75630	095	Solano County	28 111
06	68252		San Mateo city	97 207	06	77000		Sunnyvale city	140 081
06	68252	081	San Mateo County	97 207	06	77000	085	Santa Clara County	140 081
06	68294		San Pablo city	29 139	06	78120		Temecula city	100 097
06	68294	013	Contra Costa County	29 139	06	78120	065	Riverside County	100 097
06	68364		San Rafael city	57 713	06	78148		Temple City city	35 558
06	68364	041	Marin County	57 713	06	78148	037	Los Angeles County	35 558
06	68378		San Ramon city	72 148	06	78582		Thousand Oaks city	126 683
06	68378	013	Contra Costa County	72 148	06	78582	111	Ventura County	126 683
06	69000		Santa Ana city	324 528	06	80000		Torrance city	145 438
06	69000	059	Orange County	324 528	06	80000	037	Los Angeles County	145 438
06	69070		Santa Barbara city	88 410	06	80238		Tracy city	82 922
06	69070	083	Santa Barbara County	88 410	06	80238	077	San Joaquin County	82 922
06	69084		Santa Clara city	116 468	06	80644		Tulare city	59 278
06	69084	085	Santa Clara County	116 468	06	80644	107	Tulare County	59 278
06	69088		Santa Clarita city	176 320	06	80812		Turlock city	68 549
06	69088	037	Los Angeles County	176 320	06	80812	099	Stanislaus County	68 549
06	69112		Santa Cruz city	59 946	06	80854		Tustin city	75 540
06	69112	087	Santa Cruz County	59 946	06	80854	059	Orange County	75 540
06	69196		Santa Maria city	99 553	06	80994		Twentynine Palms city	25 048
06	69196	083	Santa Barbara County	99 553	06	80994	071	San Bernardino County	25 048
06	70000		Santa Monica city	89 736	06	81204		Union City city	69 516
06	70000	037	Los Angeles County	89 736	06	81204	001	Alameda County	69 516
06	70042		Santa Paula city	29 321	06	81344		Upland city	73 732
06	70042	111	Ventura County	29 321	06	81344	071	San Bernardino County	73 732
06	70098		Santa Rosa city	167 815	06	81554		Vacaville city	92 428
06	70098	097	Sonoma County	167 815	06	81554	095	Solano County	92 428
06	70224		Santee city	53 413	06	81666		Vallejo city	115 942
06	70224	073	San Diego County	53 413	06	81666	095	Solano County	115 942
06	70280		Saratoga city	29 926	06	82590		Victorville city	115 903
06	70280	085	Santa Clara County	29 926	06	82590	071	San Bernardino County	115 903
06	70742		Seaside city	33 025	06	82954		Visalia city	124 442
06	70742	053	Monterey County	33 025	06	82954	107	Tulare County	124 442
06	72016		Simi Valley city	124 237	06	82996		Vista city	93 834
06	72016	111	Ventura County	124 237	06	82996	073	San Diego County	93 834
06	72520		Soledad city	25 738	06	83332		Walnut city	29 172
06	72520	053	Monterey County	25 738	06	83332	037	Los Angeles County	29 172
06	73080		South Gate city	94 396	06	83346		Walnut Creek city	64 173
06	73080	037	Los Angeles County	94 396	06	83346	013	Contra Costa County	64 173
06	73220		South Pasadena city	25 619	06	83542		Wasco city	25 545
06	73220	037	Los Angeles County	25 619	06	83542	029	Kern County	25 545
06	73262		South San Francisco city	63 632	06	83668		Watsonville city	51 199
06	73262	081	San Mateo County	63 632	06	83668	087	Santa Cruz County	51 199
06	73962		Stanton city	38 186	06	84200		West Covina city	106 098
06	73962	059	Orange County	38 186	06	84200	037	Los Angeles County	106 098
06	75000		Stockton city	291 707	06	84410		West Hollywood city	34 399
06	75000	077	San Joaquin County	291 707	06	84410	037	Los Angeles County	34 399

Cities by County–*Continued*

State Code	Place Code	County Code	Geographic Area Name	2010 Census Population	State Code	Place Code	County Code	Geographic Area Name	2010 Census Population
06	84550		Westminster city	89 701	08	31660		Grand Junction city	58 566
06	84550	059	Orange County	89 701	08	31660	077	Mesa County	58 566
06	84816		West Sacramento city	48 744	08	32155		Greeley city	92 889
06	84816	113	Yolo County	48 744	08	32155	123	Weld County	92 889
06	85292		Whittier city	85 331	08	43000		Lakewood city	142 980
06	85292	037	Los Angeles County	85 331	08	43000	059	Jefferson County	142 980
06	85446		Wildomar city	32 176	08	45255		Littleton city	41 737
06	85446	065	Riverside County	32 176	08	45255	005	Arapahoe County	39 328
					08	45255	035	Douglas County	28
06	85922		Windsor town	26 801	08	45255	059	Jefferson County	2 381
06	85922	097	Sonoma County	26 801	08	45970		Longmont city	86 270
06	86328		Woodland city	55 468	08	45970	013	Boulder County	86 240
06	86328	113	Yolo County	55 468	08	45970	123	Weld County	30
06	86832		Yorba Linda city	64 234	08	46465		Loveland city	66 859
06	86832	059	Orange County	64 234	08	46465	069	Larimer County	66 859
06	86972		Yuba City city	64 925	08	54330		Northglenn city	35 789
06	86972	101	Sutter County	64 925	08	54330	001	Adams County	35 777
					08	54330	123	Weld County	12
06	87042		Yucaipa city	51 367	08	57630		Parker town	45 297
06	87042	071	San Bernardino County	51 367	08	57630	035	Douglas County	45 297
08			**COLORADO**	5 029 196	08	62000		Pueblo city	106 595
08	03455		Arvada city	106 433	08	62000	101	Pueblo County	106 595
08	03455	001	Adams County	2 849					
08	03455	059	Jefferson County	103 584	08	77290		Thornton city	118 772
					08	77290	001	Adams County	118 772
08	04000		Aurora city	325 078	08	77290	123	Weld County	0
08	04000	001	Adams County	39 871	08	83835		Westminster city	106 114
08	04000	005	Arapahoe County	285 090	08	83835	001	Adams County	63 696
08	04000	035	Douglas County	117	08	83835	059	Jefferson County	42 418
08	07850		Boulder city	97 385	08	84440		Wheat Ridge city	30 166
08	07850	013	Boulder County	97 385	08	84440	059	Jefferson County	30 166
08	08675		Brighton city	33 352	09			**CONNECTICUT**	3 574 097
08	08675	001	Adams County	33 009	09	08000		Bridgeport city	144 229
08	08675	123	Weld County	343	09	08000	001	Fairfield County	144 229
08	09280		Broomfield city	55 889	09	08420		Bristol city	60 477
08	09280	014	Broomfield County	55 889	09	08420	003	Hartford County	60 477
08	12415		Castle Rock town	48 231	09	18430		Danbury city	80 893
08	12415	035	Douglas County	48 231	09	18430	001	Fairfield County	80 893
08	12815		Centennial city	100 377	09	37000		Hartford city	124 775
08	12815	005	Arapahoe County	100 377	09	37000	003	Hartford County	124 775
08	16000		Colorado Springs city	416 427	09	46450		Meriden city	60 868
08	16000	041	El Paso County	416 427	09	46450	009	New Haven County	60 868
08	16495		Commerce City city	45 913	09	47290		Middletown city	47 648
08	16495	001	Adams County	45 913	09	47290	007	Middlesex County	47 648
08	20000		Denver city	600 158	09	49880		Naugatuck borough	31 862
08	20000	031	Denver County	600 158	09	49880	009	New Haven County	31 862
08	24785		Englewood city	30 255	09	50370		New Britain city	73 206
08	24785	005	Arapahoe County	30 255	09	50370	003	Hartford County	73 206
08	27425		Fort Collins city	143 986	09	52000		New Haven city	129 779
08	27425	069	Larimer County	143 986	09	52000	009	New Haven County	129 779
08	27865		Fountain city	25 846	09	52280		New London city	27 620
08	27865	041	El Paso County	25 846	09	52280	011	New London County	27 620

Cities by County–*Continued*

State Code	Place Code	County Code	Geographic Area Name	2010 Census Population	State Code	Place Code	County Code	Geographic Area Name	2010 Census Population
09	55990		Norwalk city	85 603	12	14125		Cooper City city	28 547
09	55990	001	Fairfield County	85 603	12	14125	011	Broward County	28 547
09	56200		Norwich city	40 493	12	14250		Coral Gables city	46 780
09	56200	011	New London County	40 493	12	14250	086	Miami-Dade County	46 780
09	68100		Shelton city	39 559	12	14400		Coral Springs city	121 096
09	68100	001	Fairfield County	39 559	12	14400	011	Broward County	121 096
09	73000		Stamford city	122 643	12	15968		Cutler Bay town	40 286
09	73000	001	Fairfield County	122 643	12	15968	086	Miami-Dade County	40 286
09	76500		Torrington city	36 383	12	16335		Dania Beach city	29 639
09	76500	005	Litchfield County	36 383	12	16335	011	Broward County	29 639
09	80000		Waterbury city	110 366	12	16475		Davie town	91 992
09	80000	009	New Haven County	110 366	12	16475	011	Broward County	91 992
09	82800		West Haven city	55 564	12	16525		Daytona Beach city	61 005
09	82800	009	New Haven County	55 564	12	16525	127	Volusia County	61 005
10			**DELAWARE**	897 934	12	16725		Deerfield Beach city	75 018
10	21200		Dover city	36 047	12	16725	011	Broward County	75 018
10	21200	001	Kent County	36 047					
					12	16875		DeLand city	27 031
10	50670		Newark city	31 454	12	16875	127	Volusia County	27 031
10	50670	003	New Castle County	31 454					
					12	17100		Delray Beach city	60 522
10	77580		Wilmington city	70 851	12	17100	099	Palm Beach County	60 522
10	77580	003	New Castle County	70 851					
					12	17200		Deltona city	85 182
11			**DISTRICT OF COLUMBIA**	601 723	12	17200	127	Volusia County	85 182
11	50000		Washington city	601 723					
11	50000	001	District of Columbia	601 723	12	17935		Doral city	45 704
					12	17935	086	Miami-Dade County	45 704
12			**FLORIDA**	18 801 310					
12	00950		Altamonte Springs city	41 496	12	18575		Dunedin city	35 321
12	00950	117	Seminole County	41 496	12	18575	103	Pinellas County	35 321
12	01700		Apopka city	41 542	12	24000		Fort Lauderdale city	165 521
12	01700	095	Orange County	41 542	12	24000	011	Broward County	165 521
12	02681		Aventura city	35 762	12	24125		Fort Myers city	62 298
12	02681	086	Miami-Dade County	35 762	12	24125	071	Lee County	62 298
12	07300		Boca Raton city	84 392	12	24300		Fort Pierce city	41 590
12	07300	099	Palm Beach County	84 392	12	24300	111	St. Lucie County	41 590
12	07525		Bonita Springs city	43 914	12	25175		Gainesville city	124 354
12	07525	071	Lee County	43 914	12	25175	001	Alachua County	124 354
12	07875		Boynton Beach city	68 217	12	27322		Greenacres city	37 573
12	07875	099	Palm Beach County	68 217	12	27322	099	Palm Beach County	37 573
12	07950		Bradenton city	49 546	12	28452		Hallandale Beach city	37 113
12	07950	081	Manatee County	49 546	12	28452	011	Broward County	37 113
12	10275		Cape Coral city	154 305	12	30000		Hialeah city	224 669
12	10275	071	Lee County	154 305	12	30000	086	Miami-Dade County	224 669
12	11050		Casselberry city	26 241	12	32000		Hollywood city	140 768
12	11050	117	Seminole County	26 241	12	32000	011	Broward County	140 768
12	12875		Clearwater city	107 685	12	32275		Homestead city	60 512
12	12875	103	Pinellas County	107 685	12	32275	086	Miami-Dade County	60 512
12	12925		Clermont city	28 742	12	35000		Jacksonville city	821 784
12	12925	069	Lake County	28 742	12	35000	031	Duval County	821 784
12	13275		Coconut Creek city	52 909	12	35875		Jupiter town	55 156
12	13275	011	Broward County	52 909	12	35875	099	Palm Beach County	55 156

Cities by County–*Continued*

State Code	Place Code	County Code	Geographic Area Name	2010 Census Population	State Code	Place Code	County Code	Geographic Area Name	2010 Census Population
12	36950		Kissimmee city	59 682	12	54075		Palm Beach Gardens city	48 452
12	36950	097	Osceola County	59 682	12	54075	099	Palm Beach County	48 452
12	38250		Lakeland city	97 422	12	54200		Palm Coast city	75 180
12	38250	105	Polk County	97 422	12	54200	035	Flagler County	75 180
12	39075		Lake Worth city	34 910	12	54700		Panama City city	36 484
12	39075	099	Palm Beach County	34 910	12	54700	005	Bay County	36 484
12	39425		Largo city	77 648	12	55775		Pembroke Pines city	154 750
12	39425	103	Pinellas County	77 648	12	55775	011	Broward County	154 750
12	39525		Lauderdale Lakes city	32 593	12	55925		Pensacola city	51 923
12	39525	011	Broward County	32 593	12	55925	033	Escambia County	51 923
12	39550		Lauderhill city	66 887	12	56975		Pinellas Park city	49 079
12	39550	011	Broward County	66 887	12	56975	103	Pinellas County	49 079
12	43125		Margate city	53 284	12	57425		Plantation city	84 955
12	43125	011	Broward County	53 284	12	57425	011	Broward County	84 955
12	43975		Melbourne city	76 068	12	57550		Plant City city	34 721
12	43975	009	Brevard County	76 068	12	57550	057	Hillsborough County	34 721
12	45000		Miami city	399 457	12	58050		Pompano Beach city	99 845
12	45000	086	Miami-Dade County	399 457	12	58050	011	Broward County	99 845
12	45025		Miami Beach city	87 779	12	58575		Port Orange city	56 048
12	45025	086	Miami-Dade County	87 779	12	58575	127	Volusia County	56 048
12	45060		Miami Gardens city	107 167	12	58715		Port St. Lucie city	164 603
12	45060	086	Miami-Dade County	107 167	12	58715	111	St. Lucie County	164 603
12	45100		Miami Lakes town	29 361	12	60975		Riviera Beach city	32 488
12	45100	086	Miami-Dade County	29 361	12	60975	099	Palm Beach County	32 488
12	45975		Miramar city	122 041	12	62100		Royal Palm Beach village	34 140
12	45975	011	Broward County	122 041	12	62100	099	Palm Beach County	34 140
12	49425		North Lauderdale city	41 023	12	62625		St. Cloud city	35 183
12	49425	011	Broward County	41 023	12	62625	097	Osceola County	35 183
12	49450		North Miami city	58 786	12	63000		St. Petersburg city	244 769
12	49450	086	Miami-Dade County	58 786	12	63000	103	Pinellas County	244 769
12	49475		North Miami Beach city	41 523	12	63650		Sanford city	53 570
12	49475	086	Miami-Dade County	41 523	12	63650	117	Seminole County	53 570
12	49675		North Port city	57 357	12	64175		Sarasota city	51 917
12	49675	115	Sarasota County	57 357	12	64175	115	Sarasota County	51 917
12	50575		Oakland Park city	41 363	12	69700		Sunrise city	84 439
12	50575	011	Broward County	41 363	12	69700	011	Broward County	84 439
12	50750		Ocala city	56 315	12	70600		Tallahassee city	181 376
12	50750	083	Marion County	56 315	12	70600	073	Leon County	181 376
12	51075		Ocoee city	35 579	12	70675		Tamarac city	60 427
12	51075	095	Orange County	35 579	12	70675	011	Broward County	60 427
12	53000		Orlando city	238 300	12	71000		Tampa city	335 709
12	53000	095	Orange County	238 300	12	71000	057	Hillsborough County	335 709
12	53150		Ormond Beach city	38 137	12	71900		Titusville city	43 761
12	53150	127	Volusia County	38 137	12	71900	009	Brevard County	43 761
12	53575		Oviedo city	33 342	12	75812		Wellington village	56 508
12	53575	117	Seminole County	33 342	12	75812	099	Palm Beach County	56 508
12	54000		Palm Bay city	103 190	12	76582		Weston city	65 333
12	54000	009	Brevard County	103 190	12	76582	011	Broward County	65 333

Cities by County–*Continued*

State Code	Place Code	County Code	Geographic Area Name	2010 Census Population
12	76600		West Palm Beach city	99 919
12	76600	099	Palm Beach County	99 919
12	78250		Winter Garden city	34 568
12	78250	095	Orange County	34 568
12	78275		Winter Haven city	33 874
12	78275	105	Polk County	33 874
12	78300		Winter Park city	27 852
12	78300	095	Orange County	27 852
12	78325		Winter Springs city	33 282
12	78325	117	Seminole County	33 282
13			**GEORGIA**	9 687 653
13	01052		Albany city	77 434
13	01052	095	Dougherty County	77 434
13	01696		Alpharetta city	57 551
13	01696	121	Fulton County	57 551
13	04000		Atlanta city	420 003
13	04000	089	DeKalb County	28 292
13	04000	121	Fulton County	391 711
13	19000		Columbus city	189 885
13	19000	215	Muscogee County	189 885
13	21380		Dalton city	33 128
13	21380	313	Whitfield County	33 128
13	23900		Douglasville city	30 961
13	23900	097	Douglas County	30 961
13	24600		Duluth city	26 600
13	24600	135	Gwinnett County	26 600
13	24768		Dunwoody city	46 267
13	24768	089	DeKalb County	46 267
13	25720		East Point city	33 712
13	25720	121	Fulton County	33 712
13	31908		Gainesville city	33 804
13	31908	139	Hall County	33 804
13	38964		Hinesville city	33 437
13	38964	179	Liberty County	33 437
13	42425		Johns Creek city	76 728
13	42425	121	Fulton County	76 728
13	43192		Kennesaw city	29 783
13	43192	067	Cobb County	29 783
13	44340		LaGrange city	29 588
13	44340	285	Troup County	29 588
13	45488		Lawrenceville city	28 546
13	45488	135	Gwinnett County	28 546
13	49000		Macon city	91 351
13	49000	021	Bibb County	90 885
13	49000	169	Jones County	466
13	49756		Marietta city	56 579
13	49756	067	Cobb County	56 579
13	51670		Milton city	32 661
13	51670	121	Fulton County	32 661
13	55020		Newnan city	33 039
13	55020	077	Coweta County	33 039
13	59724		Peachtree City city	34 364
13	59724	113	Fayette County	34 364
13	66668		Rome city	36 303
13	66668	115	Floyd County	36 303
13	67284		Roswell city	88 346
13	67284	121	Fulton County	88 346
13	68516		Sandy Springs city	93 853
13	68516	121	Fulton County	93 853
13	69000		Savannah city	136 286
13	69000	051	Chatham County	136 286
13	71492		Smyrna city	51 271
13	71492	067	Cobb County	51 271
13	73256		Statesboro city	28 422
13	73256	031	Bulloch County	28 422
13	73704		Stockbridge city	25 636
13	73704	151	Henry County	25 636
13	78800		Valdosta city	54 518
13	78800	185	Lowndes County	54 518
13	80508		Warner Robins city	66 588
13	80508	153	Houston County	66 22⋯
13	80508	225	Peach County	36⋯
15			**HAWAII**	1 360 30⋯
15	06290		East Honolulu CDP	49 91⋯
15	06290	003	Honolulu County	49 91⋯
15	14650		Hilo CDP	43 26⋯
15	14650	001	Hawaii County	43 26⋯
15	22700		Kahului CDP	26 33⋯
15	22700	009	Maui County	26 33⋯
15	23150		Kailua CDP	38 63⋯
15	23150	003	Honolulu County	38 63⋯
15	28250		Kaneohe CDP	34 59⋯
15	28250	003	Honolulu County	34 59⋯
15	51050		Mililani Town CDP	27 62⋯
15	51050	003	Honolulu County	27 62⋯
15	62600		Pearl City CDP	47 69⋯
15	62600	003	Honolulu County	47 69⋯
15	71550		Urban Honolulu CDP	337 25⋯
15	71550	003	Honolulu County	337 25⋯
15	79700		Waipahu CDP	38 21⋯
15	79700	003	Honolulu County	38 21⋯
16			**IDAHO**	1 567 58⋯
16	08830		Boise City city	205 67⋯
16	08830	001	Ada County	205 67⋯
16	12250		Caldwell city	46 23⋯
16	12250	027	Canyon County	46 23⋯
16	16750		Coeur d'Alene city	44 13⋯
16	16750	055	Kootenai County	44 13⋯

Cities by County–*Continued*

State Code	Place Code	County Code	Geographic Area Name	2010 Census Population	State Code	Place Code	County Code	Geographic Area Name	2010 Census Population
16	39700		Idaho Falls city	56 813	17	09447		Buffalo Grove village	41 496
16	39700	019	Bonneville County	56 813	17	09447	031	Cook County	13 644
					17	09447	097	Lake County	27 852
16	46540		Lewiston city	31 894					
16	46540	069	Nez Perce County	31 894	17	09642		Burbank city	28 925
					17	09642	031	Cook County	28 925
16	52120		Meridian city	75 092					
16	52120	001	Ada County	75 092	17	10487		Calumet City city	37 042
					17	10487	031	Cook County	37 042
16	56260		Nampa city	81 557					
16	56260	027	Canyon County	81 557	17	11163		Carbondale city	25 902
					17	11163	077	Jackson County	25 902
16	64090		Pocatello city	54 255	17	11163	199	Williamson County	0
16	64090	005	Bannock County	54 239					
16	64090	077	Power County	16	17	11332		Carol Stream village	39 711
					17	11332	043	DuPage County	39 711
16	64810		Post Falls city	27 574					
16	64810	055	Kootenai County	27 574	17	11358		Carpentersville village	37 691
					17	11358	089	Kane County	37 691
16	67420		Rexburg city	25 484					
16	67420	065	Madison County	25 484	17	12385		Champaign city	81 055
					17	12385	019	Champaign County	81 055
16	82810		Twin Falls city	44 125					
16	82810	083	Twin Falls County	44 125	17	14000		Chicago city	2 695 598
					17	14000	031	Cook County	2 695 598
17			**ILLINOIS**	12 830 632	17	14000	043	DuPage County	0
17	00243		Addison village	36 942					
17	00243	043	DuPage County	36 942	17	14026		Chicago Heights city	30 276
					17	14026	031	Cook County	30 276
17	00685		Algonquin village	30 046					
17	00685	089	Kane County	8 433	17	14351		Cicero town	83 891
17	00685	111	McHenry County	21 613	17	14351	031	Cook County	83 891
17	01114		Alton city	27 865	17	15599		Collinsville city	25 579
17	01114	119	Madison County	27 865	17	15599	119	Madison County	22 573
					17	15599	163	St. Clair County	3 006
17	02154		Arlington Heights village	75 101					
17	02154	031	Cook County	75 101	17	17887		Crystal Lake city	40 743
17	02154	097	Lake County	0	17	17887	111	McHenry County	40 743
17	03012		Aurora city	197 899	17	18563		Danville city	33 027
17	03012	043	DuPage County	49 433	17	18563	183	Vermilion County	33 027
17	03012	089	Kane County	130 976					
17	03012	093	Kendall County	6 019	17	18823		Decatur city	76 122
17	03012	197	Will County	11 471	17	18823	115	Macon County	76 122
17	04013		Bartlett village	41 208	17	19161		DeKalb city	43 862
17	04013	031	Cook County	16 797	17	19161	037	DeKalb County	43 862
17	04013	043	DuPage County	24 411					
17	04013	089	Kane County	0	17	19642		Des Plaines city	58 364
					17	19642	031	Cook County	58 364
17	04078		Batavia city	26 045					
17	04078	043	DuPage County	0	17	20591		Downers Grove village	47 833
17	04078	089	Kane County	26 045	17	20591	043	DuPage County	47 833
17	04845		Belleville city	44 478	17	22255		East St. Louis city	27 006
17	04845	163	St. Clair County	44 478	17	22255	163	St. Clair County	27 006
17	05092		Belvidere city	25 585	17	23074		Elgin city	108 188
17	05092	007	Boone County	25 585	17	23074	031	Cook County	24 032
					17	23074	089	Kane County	84 156
17	05573		Berwyn city	56 657					
17	05573	031	Cook County	56 657	17	23256		Elk Grove Village village	33 127
					17	23256	031	Cook County	33 127
17	06613		Bloomington city	76 610	17	23256	043	DuPage County	0
17	06613	113	McLean County	76 610					
					17	23620		Elmhurst city	44 121
17	07133		Bolingbrook village	73 366	17	23620	031	Cook County	0
17	07133	043	DuPage County	1 571	17	23620	043	DuPage County	44 121
17	07133	197	Will County	71 795					
					17	24582		Evanston city	74 486
					17	24582	031	Cook County	74 486

Cities by County–*Continued*

State Code	Place Code	County Code	Geographic Area Name	2010 Census Population	State Code	Place Code	County Code	Geographic Area Name	2010 Census Population
17	27884		Freeport city	25 638	17	53234		Normal town	52 497
17	27884	177	Stephenson County	25 638	17	53234	113	McLean County	52 497
17	28326		Galesburg city	32 195	17	53481		Northbrook village	33 170
17	28326	095	Knox County	32 195	17	53481	031	Cook County	33 176
17	29730		Glendale Heights village	34 208	17	53559		North Chicago city	32 574
17	29730	043	DuPage County	34 208	17	53559	097	Lake County	32 574
17	29756		Glen Ellyn village	27 450	17	54638		Oak Forest city	27 962
17	29756	043	DuPage County	27 450	17	54638	031	Cook County	27 962
17	29938		Glenview village	44 692	17	54820		Oak Lawn village	56 690
17	29938	031	Cook County	44 692	17	54820	031	Cook County	56 690
17	30926		Granite City city	29 849	17	54885		Oak Park village	51 878
17	30926	119	Madison County	29 849	17	54885	031	Cook County	51 878
17	32018		Gurnee village	31 295	17	55249		O'Fallon city	28 281
17	32018	097	Lake County	31 295	17	55249	163	St. Clair County	28 281
17	32746		Hanover Park village	37 973	17	56640		Orland Park village	56 767
17	32746	031	Cook County	20 636	17	56640	031	Cook County	56 58
17	32746	043	DuPage County	17 337	17	56640	197	Will County	18
17	33383		Harvey city	25 282	17	56887		Oswego village	30 355
17	33383	031	Cook County	25 282	17	56887	093	Kendall County	30 355
17	34722		Highland Park city	29 763	17	57225		Palatine village	68 55
17	34722	097	Lake County	29 763	17	57225	031	Cook County	68 55
					17	57225	097	Lake County	
17	35411		Hoffman Estates village	51 895					
17	35411	031	Cook County	51 895	17	57875		Park Ridge city	37 48
17	35411	089	Kane County	0	17	57875	031	Cook County	37 48
17	38570		Joliet city	147 433	17	58447		Pekin city	34 09
17	38570	093	Kendall County	9 749	17	58447	143	Peoria County	
17	38570	197	Will County	137 684	17	58447	179	Tazewell County	34 09
17	38934		Kankakee city	27 537	17	59000		Peoria city	115 00
17	38934	091	Kankakee County	27 537	17	59000	143	Peoria County	115 00
17	41183		Lake in the Hills village	28 965	17	60287		Plainfield village	39 58
17	41183	111	McHenry County	28 965	17	60287	093	Kendall County	2 07
					17	60287	197	Will County	37 50
17	42028		Lansing village	28 331					
17	42028	031	Cook County	28 331	17	62367		Quincy city	40 63
					17	62367	001	Adams County	40 63
17	44407		Lombard village	43 165					
17	44407	043	DuPage County	43 165	17	65000		Rockford city	152 87
					17	65000	201	Winnebago County	152 87
17	45694		McHenry city	26 992					
17	45694	111	McHenry County	26 992	17	65078		Rock Island city	39 01
					17	65078	161	Rock Island County	39 01
17	48242		Melrose Park village	25 411					
17	48242	031	Cook County	25 411	17	65442		Romeoville village	39 68
					17	65442	197	Will County	39 68
17	49867		Moline city	43 483					
17	49867	161	Rock Island County	43 483	17	66040		Round Lake Beach village	28 17
					17	66040	097	Lake County	28 17
17	51089		Mount Prospect village	54 167					
17	51089	031	Cook County	54 167	17	66703		St. Charles city	32 97
					17	66703	043	DuPage County	54
17	51349		Mundelein village	31 064	17	66703	089	Kane County	32 43
17	51349	097	Lake County	31 064					
					17	68003		Schaumburg village	74 22
17	51622		Naperville city	141 853	17	68003	031	Cook County	74 22
17	51622	043	DuPage County	94 533	17	68003	043	DuPage County	
17	51622	197	Will County	47 320					
					17	70122		Skokie village	64 78
17	53000		Niles village	29 803	17	70122	031	Cook County	64 78
17	53000	031	Cook County	29 803					

Appendix E

E-13

State Code	Place Code	County Code	Geographic Area Name	2010 Census Population	State Code	Place Code	County Code	Geographic Area Name	2010 Census Population
17	72000		Springfield city	116 250	18	28386		Goshen city	31 719
17	72000	167	Sangamon County	116 250	18	28386	039	Elkhart County	31 719
17	73157		Streamwood village	39 858	18	29898		Greenwood city	49 791
17	73157	031	Cook County	39 858	18	29898	081	Johnson County	49 791
17	75484		Tinley Park village	56 703	18	31000		Hammond city	80 830
17	75484	031	Cook County	49 236	18	31000	089	Lake County	80 830
17	75484	197	Will County	7 467	18	34114		Hobart city	29 059
17	77005		Urbana city	41 250	18	34114	089	Lake County	29 059
17	77005	019	Champaign County	41 250	18	38358		Jeffersonville city	44 953
17	77694		Vernon Hills village	25 113	18	38358	019	Clark County	44 953
17	77694	097	Lake County	25 113	18	40392		Kokomo city	45 468
17	79293		Waukegan city	89 078	18	40392	067	Howard County	45 468
17	79293	097	Lake County	89 078	18	40788		Lafayette city	67 140
17	80060		West Chicago city	27 086	18	40788	157	Tippecanoe County	67 140
17	80060	043	DuPage County	27 086	18	42426		Lawrence city	46 001
17	81048		Wheaton city	52 894	18	42426	097	Marion County	46 001
17	81048	043	DuPage County	52 894	18	46908		Marion city	29 948
17	81087		Wheeling village	37 648	18	46908	053	Grant County	29 948
17	81087	031	Cook County	37 642	18	48528		Merrillville town	35 246
17	81087	097	Lake County	6	18	48528	089	Lake County	35 246
17	82075		Wilmette village	27 087	18	48798		Michigan City city	31 479
17	82075	031	Cook County	27 087	18	48798	091	LaPorte County	31 479
17	83245		Woodridge village	32 971	18	49932		Mishawaka city	48 252
17	83245	031	Cook County	0	18	49932	141	St. Joseph County	48 252
17	83245	043	DuPage County	32 949	18	51876		Muncie city	70 085
17	83245	197	Will County	22	18	51876	035	Delaware County	70 085
18			**INDIANA**	6 483 802	18	52326		New Albany city	36 372
18	01468		Anderson city	56 129	18	52326	043	Floyd County	36 372
18	01468	095	Madison County	56 129	18	54180		Noblesville city	51 969
18	05860		Bloomington city	80 405	18	54180	057	Hamilton County	51 969
18	05860	105	Monroe County	80 405	18	60246		Plainfield town	27 631
18	10342		Carmel city	79 191	18	60246	063	Hendricks County	27 631
18	10342	057	Hamilton County	79 191	18	61092		Portage city	36 828
18	14734		Columbus city	44 061	18	61092	127	Porter County	36 828
18	14734	005	Bartholomew County	44 061	18	64260		Richmond city	36 812
18	16138		Crown Point city	27 317	18	64260	177	Wayne County	36 812
18	16138	089	Lake County	27 317	18	68220		Schererville town	29 243
18	19486		East Chicago city	29 698	18	68220	089	Lake County	29 243
18	19486	089	Lake County	29 698	18	71000		South Bend city	101 168
18	20728		Elkhart city	50 949	18	71000	141	St. Joseph County	101 168
18	20728	039	Elkhart County	50 949	18	75428		Terre Haute city	60 785
18	22000		Evansville city	117 429	18	75428	167	Vigo County	60 785
18	22000	163	Vanderburgh County	117 429	18	78326		Valparaiso city	31 730
18	23278		Fishers town	76 794	18	78326	127	Porter County	31 730
18	23278	057	Hamilton County	76 794	18	82700		Westfield town	30 068
18	25000		Fort Wayne city	253 691	18	82700	057	Hamilton County	30 068
18	25000	003	Allen County	253 691	18	82862		West Lafayette city	29 596
18	27000		Gary city	80 294	18	82862	157	Tippecanoe County	29 596
18	27000	089	Lake County	80 294					

State Code	Place Code	County Code	Geographic Area Name	2010 Census Population
19			**IOWA**	3 046 355
19	01855		Ames city	58 965
19	01855	169	Story County	58 965
19	02305		Ankeny city	45 582
19	02305	153	Polk County	45 582
19	06355		Bettendorf city	33 217
19	06355	163	Scott County	33 217
19	09550		Burlington city	25 663
19	09550	057	Des Moines County	25 663
19	11755		Cedar Falls city	39 260
19	11755	013	Black Hawk County	39 260
19	12000		Cedar Rapids city	126 326
19	12000	113	Linn County	126 326
19	14430		Clinton city	26 885
19	14430	045	Clinton County	26 885
19	16860		Council Bluffs city	62 230
19	16860	155	Pottawattamie County	62 230
19	19000		Davenport city	99 685
19	19000	163	Scott County	99 685
19	21000		Des Moines city	203 433
19	21000	153	Polk County	203 419
19	21000	181	Warren County	14
19	22395		Dubuque city	57 637
19	22395	061	Dubuque County	57 637
19	28515		Fort Dodge city	25 206
19	28515	187	Webster County	25 206
19	38595		Iowa City city	67 862
19	38595	103	Johnson County	67 862
19	49485		Marion city	34 768
19	49485	113	Linn County	34 768
19	49755		Marshalltown city	27 552
19	49755	127	Marshall County	27 552
19	50160		Mason City city	28 079
19	50160	033	Cerro Gordo County	28 079
19	60465		Ottumwa city	25 023
19	60465	179	Wapello County	25 023
19	73335		Sioux City city	82 684
19	73335	149	Plymouth County	6
19	73335	193	Woodbury County	82 678
19	79950		Urbandale city	39 463
19	79950	049	Dallas County	6 337
19	79950	153	Polk County	33 126
19	82425		Waterloo city	68 406
19	82425	013	Black Hawk County	68 406
19	83910		West Des Moines city	56 609
19	83910	049	Dallas County	11 569
19	83910	153	Polk County	44 999
19	83910	181	Warren County	41
20			**KANSAS**	2 853 118
20	18250		Dodge City city	27 340
20	18250	057	Ford County	27 340
20	25325		Garden City city	26 658
20	25325	055	Finney County	26 658
20	33625		Hutchinson city	42 080
20	33625	155	Reno County	42 080
20	36000		Kansas City city	145 786
20	36000	209	Wyandotte County	145 786
20	38900		Lawrence city	87 643
20	38900	045	Douglas County	87 643
20	39000		Leavenworth city	35 251
20	39000	103	Leavenworth County	35 251
20	39075		Leawood city	31 867
20	39075	091	Johnson County	31 867
20	39350		Lenexa city	48 190
20	39350	091	Johnson County	48 190
20	44250		Manhattan city	52 281
20	44250	149	Pottawatomie County	146
20	44250	161	Riley County	52 135
20	52575		Olathe city	125 872
20	52575	091	Johnson County	125 872
20	53775		Overland Park city	173 372
20	53775	091	Johnson County	173 372
20	62700		Salina city	47 707
20	62700	169	Saline County	47 707
20	64500		Shawnee city	62 209
20	64500	091	Johnson County	62 209
20	71000		Topeka city	127 473
20	71000	177	Shawnee County	127 473
20	79000		Wichita city	382 368
20	79000	173	Sedgwick County	382 368
21			**KENTUCKY**	4 339 367
21	08902		Bowling Green city	58 067
21	08902	227	Warren County	58 067
21	17848		Covington city	40 640
21	17848	117	Kenton County	40 640
21	24274		Elizabethtown city	28 531
21	24274	093	Hardin County	28 531
21	27982		Florence city	29 951
21	27982	015	Boone County	29 951
21	28900		Frankfort city	25 527
21	28900	073	Franklin County	25 527
21	30700		Georgetown city	29 098
21	30700	209	Scott County	29 098
21	35866		Henderson city	28 757
21	35866	101	Henderson County	28 757
21	37918		Hopkinsville city	31 577
21	37918	047	Christian County	31 577
21	40222		Jeffersontown city	26 595
21	40222	111	Jefferson County	26 595

Cities by County–*Continued*

State Code	Place Code	County Code	Geographic Area Name	2010 Census Population	State Code	Place Code	County Code	Geographic Area Name	2010 Census Population
21	46027		Lexington-Fayette urban county	295 803	24	04000		Baltimore city	620 961
21	46027	067	Fayette County	295 803	24	04000	510	Baltimore city	620 961
21	56136		Nicholasville city	28 015	24	08775		Bowie city	54 727
21	56136	113	Jessamine County	28 015	24	08775	033	Prince George's County	54 727
21	58620		Owensboro city	57 265	24	18750		College Park city	30 413
21	58620	059	Daviess County	57 265	24	18750	033	Prince George's County	30 413
21	58836		Paducah city	25 024	24	30325		Frederick city	65 239
21	58836	145	McCracken County	25 024	24	30325	021	Frederick County	65 239
21	65226		Richmond city	31 364	24	31175		Gaithersburg city	59 933
21	65226	151	Madison County	31 364	24	31175	031	Montgomery County	59 933
22			**LOUISIANA**	4 533 372	24	36075		Hagerstown city	39 662
22	00975		Alexandria city	47 723	24	36075	043	Washington County	39 662
22	00975	079	Rapides Parish	47 723	24	45900		Laurel city	25 115
22	05000		Baton Rouge city	229 493	24	45900	033	Prince George's County	25 115
22	05000	033	East Baton Rouge Parish	229 493	24	67675		Rockville city	61 209
22	08920		Bossier City city	61 315	24	67675	031	Montgomery County	61 209
22	08920	015	Bossier Parish	61 315	24	69925		Salisbury city	30 343
22	13960		Central city	26 864	24	69925	045	Wicomico County	30 343
22	13960	033	East Baton Rouge Parish	26 864	25			**MASSACHUSETTS**	6 547 629
22	36255		Houma city	33 727	25	00840		Agawam Town city	28 438
22	36255	109	Terrebonne Parish	33 727	25	00840	013	Hampden County	28 438
22	39475		Kenner city	66 702	25	02690		Attleboro city	43 593
22	39475	051	Jefferson Parish	66 702	25	02690	005	Bristol County	43 593
22	40735		Lafayette city	120 623	25	03690		Barnstable Town city	45 193
22	40735	055	Lafayette Parish	120 623	25	03690	001	Barnstable County	45 193
22	41155		Lake Charles city	71 993	25	05595		Beverly city	39 502
22	41155	019	Calcasieu Parish	71 993	25	05595	009	Essex County	39 502
22	51410		Monroe city	48 815	25	07000		Boston city	617 594
22	51410	073	Ouachita Parish	48 815	25	07000	025	Suffolk County	617 594
22	54035		New Iberia city	30 617	25	07740		Braintree Town city	35 744
22	54035	045	Iberia Parish	30 617	25	07740	021	Norfolk County	35 744
22	55000		New Orleans city	343 829	25	09000		Brockton city	93 810
22	55000	071	Orleans Parish	343 829	25	09000	023	Plymouth County	93 810
22	70000		Shreveport city	199 311	25	11000		Cambridge city	105 162
22	70000	015	Bossier Parish	2 702	25	11000	017	Middlesex County	105 162
2	70000	017	Caddo Parish	196 609	25	13205		Chelsea city	35 177
22	70805		Slidell city	27 068	25	13205	025	Suffolk County	35 177
22	70805	103	St. Tammany Parish	27 068	25	13660		Chicopee city	55 298
23			**MAINE**	1 328 361	25	13660	013	Hampden County	55 298
23	02795		Bangor city	33 039	25	21990		Everett city	41 667
23	02795	019	Penobscot County	33 039	25	21990	017	Middlesex County	41 667
23	38740		Lewiston city	36 592	25	23000		Fall River city	88 857
23	38740	001	Androscoggin County	36 592	25	23000	005	Bristol County	88 857
23	60545		Portland city	66 194	25	23875		Fitchburg city	40 318
23	60545	005	Cumberland County	66 194	25	23875	027	Worcester County	40 318
23	71990		South Portland city	25 002	25	25172		Franklin Town city	31 635
23	71990	005	Cumberland County	25 002	25	25172	021	Norfolk County	31 635
24			**MARYLAND**	5 773 552	25	26150		Gloucester city	28 789
24	01600		Annapolis city	38 394	25	26150	009	Essex County	28 789
24	01600	003	Anne Arundel County	38 394					

State Code	Place Code	County Code	Geographic Area Name	2010 Census Population	State Code	Place Code	County Code	Geographic Area Name	2010 Census Population
25	29405		Haverhill city	60 879	25	76030		Westfield city	41 094
25	29405	009	Essex County	60 879	25	76030	013	Hampden County	41 094
25	30840		Holyoke city	39 880	25	77890		West Springfield Town city	28 391
25	30840	013	Hampden County	39 880	25	77890	013	Hampden County	28 391
25	34550		Lawrence city	76 377	25	78972		Weymouth Town city	53 743
25	34550	009	Essex County	76 377	25	78972	021	Norfolk County	53 743
25	35075		Leominster city	40 759	25	81035		Woburn city	38 120
25	35075	027	Worcester County	40 759	25	81035	017	Middlesex County	38 120
25	37000		Lowell city	106 519	25	82000		Worcester city	181 045
25	37000	017	Middlesex County	106 519	25	82000	027	Worcester County	181 045
25	37490		Lynn city	90 329	26			**MICHIGAN**	9 883 640
25	37490	009	Essex County	90 329	26	01380		Allen Park city	28 210
25	37875		Malden city	59 450	26	01380	163	Wayne County	28 210
25	37875	017	Middlesex County	59 450	26	03000		Ann Arbor city	113 934
25	38715		Marlborough city	38 499	26	03000	161	Washtenaw County	113 934
25	38715	017	Middlesex County	38 499	26	05920		Battle Creek city	52 347
25	39835		Medford city	56 173	26	05920	025	Calhoun County	52 347
25	39835	017	Middlesex County	56 173	26	06020		Bay City city	34 932
25	40115		Melrose city	26 983	26	06020	017	Bay County	34 932
25	40115	017	Middlesex County	26 983	26	12060		Burton city	29 999
25	40710		Methuen Town city	47 255	26	12060	049	Genesee County	29 999
25	40710	009	Essex County	47 255	26	21000		Dearborn city	98 153
25	45000		New Bedford city	95 072	26	21000	163	Wayne County	98 153
25	45000	005	Bristol County	95 072	26	21020		Dearborn Heights city	57 774
25	45560		Newton city	85 146	26	21020	163	Wayne County	57 774
25	45560	017	Middlesex County	85 146	26	22000		Detroit city	713 777
25	46330		Northampton city	28 549	26	22000	163	Wayne County	713 777
25	46330	015	Hampshire County	28 549	26	24120		East Lansing city	48 579
25	52490		Peabody city	51 251	26	24120	037	Clinton County	1 969
25	52490	009	Essex County	51 251	26	24120	065	Ingham County	46 610
25	53960		Pittsfield city	44 737	26	24290		Eastpointe city	32 442
25	53960	003	Berkshire County	44 737	26	24290	099	Macomb County	32 442
25	55745		Quincy city	92 271	26	27440		Farmington Hills city	79 740
25	55745	021	Norfolk County	92 271	26	27440	125	Oakland County	79 740
25	56585		Revere city	51 755	26	29000		Flint city	102 434
25	56585	025	Suffolk County	51 755	26	29000	049	Genesee County	102 434
25	59105		Salem city	41 340	26	31420		Garden City city	27 692
25	59105	009	Essex County	41 340	26	31420	163	Wayne County	27 692
25	62535		Somerville city	75 754	26	34000		Grand Rapids city	188 040
25	62535	017	Middlesex County	75 754	26	34000	081	Kent County	188 040
25	67000		Springfield city	153 060	26	38640		Holland city	33 051
25	67000	013	Hampden County	153 060	26	38640	005	Allegan County	7 016
					26	38640	139	Ottawa County	26 035
25	69170		Taunton city	55 874	26	40680		Inkster city	25 369
25	69170	005	Bristol County	55 874	26	40680	163	Wayne County	25 369
25	72600		Waltham city	60 632	26	41420		Jackson city	33 534
25	72600	017	Middlesex County	60 632	26	41420	075	Jackson County	33 534
25	73440		Watertown Town city	31 915	26	42160		Kalamazoo city	74 262
25	73440	017	Middlesex County	31 915	26	42160	077	Kalamazoo County	74 262

Cities by County–*Continued*

State Code	Place Code	County Code	Geographic Area Name	2010 Census Population	State Code	Place Code	County Code	Geographic Area Name	2010 Census Population
26	42820		Kentwood city	48 707	26	84000		Warren city	134 056
26	42820	081	Kent County	48 707	26	84000	099	Macomb County	134 056
26	46000		Lansing city	114 297	26	86000		Westland city	84 094
26	46000	045	Eaton County	4 734	26	86000	163	Wayne County	84 094
26	46000	065	Ingham County	109 563	26	88900		Wyandotte city	25 883
26	47800		Lincoln Park city	38 144	26	88900	163	Wayne County	25 883
26	47800	163	Wayne County	38 144	26	88940		Wyoming city	72 125
26	49000		Livonia city	96 942	26	88940	081	Kent County	72 125
26	49000	163	Wayne County	96 942	27			**MINNESOTA**	5 303 925
26	50560		Madison Heights city	29 694	27	01486		Andover city	30 598
26	50560	125	Oakland County	29 694	27	01486	003	Anoka County	30 598
26	53780		Midland city	41 863	27	01900		Apple Valley city	49 084
26	53780	017	Bay County	157	27	01900	037	Dakota County	49 084
26	53780	111	Midland County	41 706	27	06382		Blaine city	57 186
26	56020		Mount Pleasant city	26 016	27	06382	003	Anoka County	57 186
26	56020	073	Isabella County	26 016	27	06382	123	Ramsey County	0
26	56320		Muskegon city	38 401	27	06616		Bloomington city	82 893
26	56320	121	Muskegon County	38 401	27	06616	053	Hennepin County	82 893
26	59440		Novi city	55 224	27	07948		Brooklyn Center city	30 104
26	59440	125	Oakland County	55 224	27	07948	053	Hennepin County	30 104
26	59920		Oak Park city	29 319	27	07966		Brooklyn Park city	75 781
26	59920	125	Oakland County	29 319	27	07966	053	Hennepin County	75 781
26	65440		Pontiac city	59 515	27	08794		Burnsville city	60 306
26	65440	125	Oakland County	59 515	27	08794	037	Dakota County	60 306
26	65560		Portage city	46 292	27	13114		Coon Rapids city	61 476
26	65560	077	Kalamazoo County	46 292	27	13114	003	Anoka County	61 476
26	65820		Port Huron city	30 184	27	13456		Cottage Grove city	34 589
26	65820	147	St. Clair County	30 184	27	13456	163	Washington County	34 589
26	69035		Rochester Hills city	70 995	27	17000		Duluth city	86 265
26	69035	125	Oakland County	70 995	27	17000	137	St. Louis County	86 265
26	69800		Roseville city	47 299	27	17288		Eagan city	64 206
26	69800	099	Macomb County	47 299	27	17288	037	Dakota County	64 206
26	70040		Royal Oak city	57 236	27	18116		Eden Prairie city	60 797
26	70040	125	Oakland County	57 236	27	18116	053	Hennepin County	60 797
26	70520		Saginaw city	51 508	27	18188		Edina city	47 941
26	70520	145	Saginaw County	51 508	27	18188	053	Hennepin County	47 941
26	70760		St. Clair Shores city	59 715	27	22814		Fridley city	27 208
26	70760	099	Macomb County	59 715	27	22814	003	Anoka County	27 208
26	74900		Southfield city	71 739	27	31076		Inver Grove Heights city	33 880
26	74900	125	Oakland County	71 739	27	31076	037	Dakota County	33 880
26	74960		Southgate city	30 047	27	35180		Lakeville city	55 954
26	74960	163	Wayne County	30 047	27	35180	037	Dakota County	55 954
26	76460		Sterling Heights city	129 699	27	39878		Mankato city	39 309
26	76460	099	Macomb County	129 699	27	39878	013	Blue Earth County	39 305
26	79000		Taylor city	63 131	27	39878	079	Le Sueur County	4
26	79000	163	Wayne County	63 131	27	39878	103	Nicollet County	0
26	80700		Troy city	80 980	27	40166		Maple Grove city	61 567
26	80700	125	Oakland County	80 980	27	40166	053	Hennepin County	61 567
					27	40382		Maplewood city	38 018
					27	40382	123	Ramsey County	38 018

E-18 Appendix E

Cities by County–*Continued*

State Code	Place Code	County Code	Geographic Area Name	2010 Census Population	State Code	Place Code	County Code	Geographic Area Name	2010 Census Population
27	43000		Minneapolis city	382 578	28	36000		Jackson city	173 514
27	43000	053	Hennepin County	382 578	28	36000	049	Hinds County	172 891
					28	36000	089	Madison County	622
27	43252		Minnetonka city	49 734	28	36000	121	Rankin County	1
27	43252	053	Hennepin County	49 734					
					28	46640		Meridian city	41 148
27	43864		Moorhead city	38 065	28	46640	075	Lauderdale County	41 148
27	43864	027	Clay County	38 065					
					28	54040		Olive Branch city	33 484
27	47680		Oakdale city	27 378	28	54040	033	DeSoto County	33 484
27	47680	163	Washington County	27 378					
					28	55760		Pearl city	25 092
27	49300		Owatonna city	25 599	28	55760	121	Rankin County	25 092
27	49300	147	Steele County	25 599					
					28	69280		Southaven city	48 982
27	51730		Plymouth city	70 576	28	69280	033	DeSoto County	48 982
27	51730	053	Hennepin County	70 576					
					28	74840		Tupelo city	34 546
27	54214		Richfield city	35 228	28	74840	081	Lee County	34 546
27	54214	053	Hennepin County	35 228					
					29			**MISSOURI**	5 988 927
27	54880		Rochester city	106 769	29	03160		Ballwin city	30 404
27	54880	109	Olmsted County	106 769	29	03160	189	St. Louis County	30 404
27	55852		Roseville city	33 660	29	06652		Blue Springs city	52 575
27	55852	123	Ramsey County	33 660	29	06652	095	Jackson County	52 575
27	56896		St. Cloud city	65 842	29	11242		Cape Girardeau city	37 941
27	56896	009	Benton County	6 396	29	11242	031	Cape Girardeau County	37 941
27	56896	141	Sherburne County	6 785	29	11242	201	Scott County	0
27	56896	145	Stearns County	52 661					
					29	13600		Chesterfield city	47 484
27	57220		St. Louis Park city	45 250	29	13600	189	St. Louis County	47 484
27	57220	053	Hennepin County	45 250					
					29	15670		Columbia city	108 500
27	58000		St. Paul city	285 068	29	15670	019	Boone County	108 500
27	58000	123	Ramsey County	285 068					
					29	24778		Florissant city	52 158
27	58738		Savage city	26 911	29	24778	189	St. Louis County	52 158
27	58738	139	Scott County	26 911					
					29	27190		Gladstone city	25 410
27	59350		Shakopee city	37 076	29	27190	047	Clay County	25 410
27	59350	139	Scott County	37 076					
					29	31276		Hazelwood city	25 703
27	59998		Shoreview city	25 043	29	31276	189	St. Louis County	25 703
27	59998	123	Ramsey County	25 043					
					29	35000		Independence city	116 830
27	71032		Winona city	27 592	29	35000	047	Clay County	6
27	71032	169	Winona County	27 592	29	35000	095	Jackson County	116 830
27	71428		Woodbury city	61 961	29	37000		Jefferson City city	43 079
27	71428	163	Washington County	61 961	29	37000	027	Callaway County	22
					29	37000	051	Cole County	43 057
28			**MISSISSIPPI**	2 967 297					
28	06220		Biloxi city	44 054	29	37592		Joplin city	50 150
28	06220	047	Harrison County	44 054	29	37592	097	Jasper County	43 955
					29	37592	145	Newton County	6 195
28	14420		Clinton city	25 216					
28	14420	049	Hinds County	25 216	29	38000		Kansas City city	459 787
					29	38000	037	Cass County	197
28	29180		Greenville city	34 400	29	38000	047	Clay County	113 415
28	29180	151	Washington County	34 400	29	38000	095	Jackson County	302 499
					29	38000	165	Platte County	43 676
28	29700		Gulfport city	67 793					
28	29700	047	Harrison County	67 793	29	39044		Kirkwood city	27 540
					29	39044	189	St. Louis County	27 540
28	31020		Hattiesburg city	45 989					
28	31020	035	Forrest County	41 000	29	41348		Lee's Summit city	91 36
28	31020	073	Lamar County	4 989	29	41348	037	Cass County	1 917
					29	41348	095	Jackson County	89 447
28	33700		Horn Lake city	26 066					
28	33700	033	DeSoto County	26 066					

Cities by County–*Continued*

State Code	Place Code	County Code	Geographic Area Name	2010 Census Population	State Code	Place Code	County Code	Geographic Area Name	2010 Census Population
29	42032		Liberty city	29 149	32			**NEVADA**	2 700 551
29	42032	047	Clay County	29 149	32	09700		Carson City	55 274
					32	09700	510	Carson City	55 274
29	46586		Maryland Heights city	27 472					
29	46586	189	St. Louis County	27 472	32	31900		Henderson city	257 729
					32	31900	003	Clark County	257 729
29	54074		O'Fallon city	79 329					
29	54074	183	St. Charles County	79 329	32	40000		Las Vegas city	583 756
					32	40000	003	Clark County	583 756
29	60788		Raytown city	29 526					
29	60788	095	Jackson County	29 526	32	51800		North Las Vegas city	216 961
					32	51800	003	Clark County	216 961
29	64082		St. Charles city	65 794					
29	64082	183	St. Charles County	65 794	32	60600		Reno city	225 221
					32	60600	031	Washoe County	225 221
29	64550		St. Joseph city	76 780					
29	64550	021	Buchanan County	76 780	32	68400		Sparks city	90 264
					32	68400	031	Washoe County	90 264
29	65000		St. Louis city	319 294					
29	65000	510	St. Louis city	319 294	33			**NEW HAMPSHIRE**	1 316 470
					33	14200		Concord city	42 695
29	65126		St. Peters city	52 575	33	14200	013	Merrimack County	42 695
29	65126	183	St. Charles County	52 575					
					33	18820		Dover city	29 987
29	70000		Springfield city	159 498	33	18820	017	Strafford County	29 987
29	70000	043	Christian County	2					
29	70000	077	Greene County	159 496	33	45140		Manchester city	109 565
					33	45140	011	Hillsborough County	109 565
29	75220		University City city	35 371					
29	75220	189	St. Louis County	35 371	33	50260		Nashua city	86 494
					33	50260	011	Hillsborough County	86 494
29	78442		Wentzville city	29 070					
29	78442	183	St. Charles County	29 070	33	65140		Rochester city	29 752
					33	65140	017	Strafford County	29 752
29	79820		Wildwood city	35 517					
29	79820	189	St. Louis County	35 517	34			**NEW JERSEY**	8 791 894
					34	02080		Atlantic City city	39 558
30			**MONTANA**	989 415	34	02080	001	Atlantic County	39 558
30	06550		Billings city	104 170					
30	06550	111	Yellowstone County	104 170	34	03580		Bayonne city	63 024
					34	03580	017	Hudson County	63 024
30	08950		Bozeman city	37 280					
30	08950	031	Gallatin County	37 280	34	05170		Bergenfield borough	26 764
					34	05170	003	Bergen County	26 764
30	32800		Great Falls city	58 505					
30	32800	013	Cascade County	58 505	34	07600		Bridgeton city	25 349
					34	07600	011	Cumberland County	25 349
30	35600		Helena city	28 190					
30	35600	049	Lewis and Clark County	28 190	34	10000		Camden city	77 344
					34	10000	007	Camden County	77 344
30	50200		Missoula city	66 788					
30	50200	063	Missoula County	66 788	34	13690		Clifton city	84 136
					34	13690	031	Passaic County	84 136
31			**NEBRASKA**	1 826 341					
31	03950		Bellevue city	50 137	34	19390		East Orange city	64 270
31	03950	153	Sarpy County	50 137	34	19390	013	Essex County	64 270
31	17670		Fremont city	26 397	34	21000		Elizabeth city	124 969
31	17670	053	Dodge County	26 397	34	21000	039	Union County	124 969
31	19595		Grand Island city	48 520	34	21480		Englewood city	27 147
31	19595	079	Hall County	48 520	34	21480	003	Bergen County	27 147
31	25055		Kearney city	30 787	34	22470		Fair Lawn borough	32 457
31	25055	019	Buffalo County	30 787	34	22470	003	Bergen County	32 457
31	28000		Lincoln city	258 379	34	24420		Fort Lee borough	35 345
31	28000	109	Lancaster County	258 379	34	24420	003	Bergen County	35 345
31	37000		Omaha city	408 958	34	25770		Garfield city	30 487
31	37000	055	Douglas County	408 958	34	25770	003	Bergen County	30 487

State Code	Place Code	County Code	Geographic Area Name	2010 Census Population	State Code	Place Code	County Code	Geographic Area Name	2010 Census Population
34	28680		Hackensack city	43 010	35	16420		Clovis city	37 775
34	28680	003	Bergen County	43 010	35	16420	009	Curry County	37 775
34	32250		Hoboken city	50 005	35	25800		Farmington city	45 877
34	32250	017	Hudson County	50 005	35	25800	045	San Juan County	45 877
34	36000		Jersey City city	247 597	35	32520		Hobbs city	34 122
34	36000	017	Hudson County	247 597	35	32520	025	Lea County	34 122
34	36510		Kearny town	40 684	35	39380		Las Cruces city	97 618
34	36510	017	Hudson County	40 684	35	39380	013	Doña Ana County	97 618
34	40350		Linden city	40 499	35	63460		Rio Rancho city	87 521
34	40350	039	Union County	40 499	35	63460	001	Bernalillo County	130
34	41310		Long Branch city	30 719	35	63460	043	Sandoval County	87 391
34	41310	025	Monmouth County	30 719	35	64930		Roswell city	48 366
34	46680		Millville city	28 400	35	64930	005	Chaves County	48 366
34	46680	011	Cumberland County	28 400	35	70500		Santa Fe city	67 947
34	51000		Newark city	277 140	35	70500	049	Santa Fe County	67 947
34	51000	013	Essex County	277 140	36			**NEW YORK**	19 378 102
34	51210		New Brunswick city	55 181	36	01000		Albany city	97 856
34	51210	023	Middlesex County	55 181	36	01000	001	Albany County	97 856
34	55950		Paramus borough	26 342	36	03078		Auburn city	27 687
34	55950	003	Bergen County	26 342	36	03078	011	Cayuga County	27 687
34	56550		Passaic city	69 781	36	06607		Binghamton city	47 376
34	56550	031	Passaic County	69 781	36	06607	007	Broome County	47 376
34	57000		Paterson city	146 199	36	11000		Buffalo city	261 310
34	57000	031	Passaic County	146 199	36	11000	029	Erie County	261 310
34	58200		Perth Amboy city	50 814	36	24229		Elmira city	29 200
34	58200	023	Middlesex County	50 814	36	24229	015	Chemung County	29 200
34	59190		Plainfield city	49 808	36	27485		Freeport village	42 860
34	59190	039	Union County	49 808	36	27485	059	Nassau County	42 860
34	61530		Rahway city	27 346	36	29113		Glen Cove city	26 964
34	61530	039	Union County	27 346	36	29113	059	Nassau County	26 964
34	65790		Sayreville borough	42 704	36	32402		Harrison village	27 472
34	65790	023	Middlesex County	42 704	36	32402	119	Westchester County	27 472
34	74000		Trenton city	84 913	36	33139		Hempstead village	53 891
34	74000	021	Mercer County	84 913	36	33139	059	Nassau County	53 891
34	74630		Union City city	66 455	36	38077		Ithaca city	30 014
34	74630	017	Hudson County	66 455	36	38077	109	Tompkins County	30 014
34	76070		Vineland city	60 724	36	38264		Jamestown city	31 146
34	76070	011	Cumberland County	60 724	36	38264	013	Chautauqua County	31 146
34	79040		Westfield town	30 316	36	42554		Lindenhurst village	27 253
34	79040	039	Union County	30 316	36	42554	103	Suffolk County	27 253
34	79610		West New York town	49 708	36	43335		Long Beach city	33 275
34	79610	017	Hudson County	49 708	36	43335	059	Nassau County	33 275
35			**NEW MEXICO**	2 059 179	36	47042		Middletown city	28 086
35	01780		Alamogordo city	30 403	36	47042	071	Orange County	28 086
35	01780	035	Otero County	30 403	36	49121		Mount Vernon city	67 292
35	02000		Albuquerque city	545 852	36	49121	119	Westchester County	67 292
35	02000	001	Bernalillo County	545 852	36	50034		Newburgh city	28 866
35	12150		Carlsbad city	26 138	36	50034	071	Orange County	28 866
35	12150	015	Eddy County	26 138					

State Code	Place Code	County Code	Geographic Area Name	2010 Census Population
36	50617		New Rochelle city	77 062
36	50617	119	Westchester County	77 062
36	51000		New York city	8 175 133
36	51000	005	Bronx County	1 385 108
36	51000	047	Kings County	2 504 700
36	51000	061	New York County	1 585 873
36	51000	081	Queens County	2 230 722
36	51000	085	Richmond County	468 730
36	51055		Niagara Falls city	50 193
36	51055	063	Niagara County	50 193
36	53682		North Tonawanda city	31 568
36	53682	063	Niagara County	31 568
36	55530		Ossining village	25 060
36	55530	119	Westchester County	25 060
36	59223		Port Chester village	28 967
36	59223	119	Westchester County	28 967
36	59641		Poughkeepsie city	32 736
36	59641	027	Dutchess County	32 736
36	63000		Rochester city	210 565
36	63000	055	Monroe County	210 565
36	63418		Rome city	33 725
36	63418	065	Oneida County	33 725
36	65255		Saratoga Springs city	26 586
36	65255	091	Saratoga County	26 586
36	65508		Schenectady city	66 135
36	65508	093	Schenectady County	66 135
36	70420		Spring Valley village	31 347
36	70420	087	Rockland County	31 347
36	73000		Syracuse city	145 170
36	73000	067	Onondaga County	145 170
36	75484		Troy city	50 129
36	75484	083	Rensselaer County	50 129
6	76540		Utica city	62 235
6	76540	065	Oneida County	62 235
6	76705		Valley Stream village	37 511
6	76705	059	Nassau County	37 511
6	78608		Watertown city	27 023
6	78608	045	Jefferson County	27 023
6	81677		White Plains city	56 853
6	81677	119	Westchester County	56 853
7			**NORTH CAROLINA**	9 535 483
7	01520		Apex town	37 476
7	01520	183	Wake County	37 476
7	02080		Asheboro city	25 012
7	02080	151	Randolph County	25 012
7	02140		Asheville city	83 393
7	02140	021	Buncombe County	83 393
7	09060		Burlington city	49 963
7	09060	001	Alamance County	49 308
7	09060	081	Guilford County	655
37	10740		Cary town	135 234
37	10740	037	Chatham County	1 422
37	10740	183	Wake County	133 812
37	11800		Chapel Hill town	57 233
37	11800	063	Durham County	2 836
37	11800	135	Orange County	54 397
37	12000		Charlotte city	731 424
37	12000	119	Mecklenburg County	731 424
37	14100		Concord city	79 066
37	14100	025	Cabarrus County	79 066
37	19000		Durham city	228 330
37	19000	063	Durham County	228 300
37	19000	135	Orange County	30
37	19000	183	Wake County	0
37	22920		Fayetteville city	200 564
37	22920	051	Cumberland County	200 564
37	25480		Garner town	25 745
37	25480	183	Wake County	25 745
37	25580		Gastonia city	71 741
37	25580	071	Gaston County	71 741
37	26880		Goldsboro city	36 437
37	26880	191	Wayne County	36 437
37	28000		Greensboro city	269 666
37	28000	081	Guilford County	269 666
37	28080		Greenville city	84 554
37	28080	147	Pitt County	84 554
37	31060		Hickory city	40 010
37	31060	023	Burke County	66
37	31060	027	Caldwell County	18
37	31060	035	Catawba County	39 926
37	31400		High Point city	104 371
37	31400	057	Davidson County	5 310
37	31400	067	Forsyth County	8
37	31400	081	Guilford County	99 042
37	31400	151	Randolph County	11
37	33120		Huntersville town	46 773
37	33120	119	Mecklenburg County	46 773
37	33560		Indian Trail town	33 518
37	33560	179	Union County	33 518
37	34200		Jacksonville city	70 145
37	34200	133	Onslow County	70 145
37	35200		Kannapolis city	42 625
37	35200	025	Cabarrus County	33 194
37	35200	159	Rowan County	9 431
37	41960		Matthews town	27 198
37	41960	119	Mecklenburg County	27 198
37	43920		Monroe city	32 797
37	43920	179	Union County	32 797
37	44220		Mooresville town	32 711
37	44220	097	Iredell County	32 711
37	46340		New Bern city	29 524
37	46340	049	Craven County	29 524

Cities by County–*Continued*

State Code	Place Code	County Code	Geographic Area Name	2010 Census Population	State Code	Place Code	County Code	Geographic Area Name	2010 Census Population
37	55000		Raleigh city	403 892	39	16014		Cleveland Heights city	46 121
37	55000	063	Durham County	1 067	39	16014	035	Cuyahoga County	46 121
37	55000	183	Wake County	402 825					
					39	18000		Columbus city	787 033
37	57500		Rocky Mount city	57 477	39	18000	041	Delaware County	7 245
37	57500	065	Edgecombe County	17 524	39	18000	045	Fairfield County	9 666
37	57500	127	Nash County	39 953	39	18000	049	Franklin County	770 122
37	58860		Salisbury city	33 662	39	19778		Cuyahoga Falls city	49 652
37	58860	159	Rowan County	33 662	39	19778	153	Summit County	49 652
37	59280		Sanford city	28 094	39	21000		Dayton city	141 527
37	59280	105	Lee County	28 094	39	21000	113	Montgomery County	141 527
37	67420		Thomasville city	26 757	39	21434		Delaware city	34 753
37	67420	057	Davidson County	26 493	39	21434	041	Delaware County	34 753
37	67420	151	Randolph County	264					
					39	22694		Dublin city	41 751
37	70540		Wake Forest town	30 117	39	22694	041	Delaware County	4 018
37	70540	069	Franklin County	899	39	22694	049	Franklin County	35 367
37	70540	183	Wake County	29 218	39	22694	159	Union County	2 366
37	74440		Wilmington city	106 476	39	25256		Elyria city	54 533
37	74440	129	New Hanover County	106 476	39	25256	093	Lorain County	54 533
37	74540		Wilson city	49 167	39	25704		Euclid city	48 920
37	74540	195	Wilson County	49 167	39	25704	035	Cuyahoga County	48 920
37	75000		Winston-Salem city	229 617	39	25914		Fairborn city	32 352
37	75000	067	Forsyth County	229 617	39	25914	057	Greene County	32 352
38			**NORTH DAKOTA**	672 591	39	25970		Fairfield city	42 510
38	07200		Bismarck city	61 272	39	25970	017	Butler County	42 510
38	07200	015	Burleigh County	61 272	39	25970	061	Hamilton County	0
38	25700		Fargo city	105 549	39	27048		Findlay city	41 202
38	25700	017	Cass County	105 549	39	27048	063	Hancock County	41 202
38	32060		Grand Forks city	52 838	39	29106		Gahanna city	33 248
38	32060	035	Grand Forks County	52 838	39	29106	049	Franklin County	33 248
38	53380		Minot city	40 888	39	29428		Garfield Heights city	28 849
38	53380	101	Ward County	40 888	39	29428	035	Cuyahoga County	28 849
38	84780		West Fargo city	25 830	39	31860		Green city	25 699
38	84780	017	Cass County	25 830	39	31860	153	Summit County	25 699
39			**OHIO**	11 536 504	39	32592		Grove City city	35 575
39	01000		Akron city	199 110	39	32592	049	Franklin County	35 575
39	01000	153	Summit County	199 110					
					39	33012		Hamilton city	62 477
39	03828		Barberton city	26 550	39	33012	017	Butler County	62 477
39	03828	153	Summit County	26 550					
					39	35476		Hilliard city	28 435
39	04720		Beavercreek city	45 193	39	35476	049	Franklin County	28 435
39	04720	057	Greene County	45 193					
					39	36610		Huber Heights city	38 101
39	07972		Bowling Green city	30 028	39	36610	057	Greene County	0
39	07972	173	Wood County	30 028	39	36610	109	Miami County	959
					39	36610	113	Montgomery County	37 142
39	09680		Brunswick city	34 255					
39	09680	103	Medina County	34 255	39	39872		Kent city	28 904
					39	39872	133	Portage County	28 904
39	12000		Canton city	73 007					
39	12000	151	Stark County	73 007	39	40040		Kettering city	56 163
					39	40040	057	Greene County	467
39	15000		Cincinnati city	296 943	39	40040	113	Montgomery County	55 696
39	15000	061	Hamilton County	296 943					
					39	41664		Lakewood city	52 131
39	16000		Cleveland city	396 815	39	41664	035	Cuyahoga County	52 131
39	16000	035	Cuyahoga County	396 815					

Appendix E

E-23

Cities by County–*Continued*

State Code	Place Code	County Code	Geographic Area Name	2010 Census Population	State Code	Place Code	County Code	Geographic Area Name	2010 Census Population
39	41720		Lancaster city	38 780	39	77588		Troy city	25 058
39	41720	045	Fairfield County	38 780	39	77588	109	Miami County	25 058
39	43554		Lima city	38 771	39	79002		Upper Arlington city	33 771
39	43554	003	Allen County	38 771	39	79002	049	Franklin County	33 771
39	44856		Lorain city	64 097	39	80892		Warren city	41 557
39	44856	093	Lorain County	64 097	39	80892	155	Trumbull County	41 557
39	47138		Mansfield city	47 821	39	83342		Westerville city	36 120
39	47138	139	Richland County	47 821	39	83342	041	Delaware County	7 792
					39	83342	049	Franklin County	28 328
39	47754		Marion city	36 837					
39	47754	101	Marion County	36 837	39	83622		Westlake city	32 729
					39	83622	035	Cuyahoga County	32 729
39	48188		Mason city	30 712					
39	48188	165	Warren County	30 712	39	86548		Wooster city	26 119
					39	86548	169	Wayne County	26 119
39	48244		Massillon city	32 149					
39	48244	151	Stark County	32 149	39	86772		Xenia city	25 719
					39	86772	057	Greene County	25 719
39	48790		Medina city	26 678					
39	48790	103	Medina County	26 678	39	88000		Youngstown city	66 982
					39	88000	099	Mahoning County	66 971
39	49056		Mentor city	47 159	39	88000	155	Trumbull County	11
39	49056	085	Lake County	47 159					
					39	88084		Zanesville city	25 487
39	49840		Middletown city	48 694	39	88084	119	Muskingum County	25 487
39	49840	017	Butler County	45 994					
39	49840	165	Warren County	2 700	40			**OKLAHOMA**	3 751 351
					40	04450		Bartlesville city	35 750
39	54040		Newark city	47 573	40	04450	113	Osage County	3
39	54040	089	Licking County	47 573	40	04450	147	Washington County	35 747
39	56882		North Olmsted city	32 718	40	09050		Broken Arrow city	98 850
39	56882	035	Cuyahoga County	32 718	40	09050	143	Tulsa County	80 634
					40	09050	145	Wagoner County	18 216
39	56966		North Ridgeville city	29 465					
39	56966	093	Lorain County	29 465	40	23200		Edmond city	81 405
					40	23200	109	Oklahoma County	81 405
39	57008		North Royalton city	30 444					
39	57008	035	Cuyahoga County	30 444	40	23950		Enid city	49 379
					40	23950	047	Garfield County	49 379
39	61000		Parma city	81 601					
39	61000	035	Cuyahoga County	81 601	40	41850		Lawton city	96 867
					40	41850	031	Comanche County	96 867
39	66390		Reynoldsburg city	35 893					
39	66390	045	Fairfield County	910	40	48350		Midwest City city	54 371
39	66390	049	Franklin County	26 157	40	48350	109	Oklahoma County	54 371
39	66390	089	Licking County	8 826					
					40	49200		Moore city	55 081
39	67468		Riverside city	25 201	40	49200	027	Cleveland County	55 081
39	67468	113	Montgomery County	25 201					
					40	50050		Muskogee city	39 223
39	70380		Sandusky city	25 793	40	50050	101	Muskogee County	39 223
39	70380	043	Erie County	25 793					
					40	52500		Norman city	110 925
39	71682		Shaker Heights city	28 448	40	52500	027	Cleveland County	110 925
39	71682	035	Cuyahoga County	28 448					
					40	55000		Oklahoma City city	579 999
39	74118		Springfield city	60 608	40	55000	017	Canadian County	44 541
39	74118	023	Clark County	60 608	40	55000	027	Cleveland County	63 723
					40	55000	109	Oklahoma County	471 671
39	74944		Stow city	34 837	40	55000	125	Pottawatomie County	64
39	74944	153	Summit County	34 837					
					40	56650		Owasso city	28 915
39	75098		Strongsville city	44 750	40	56650	131	Rogers County	2 614
39	75098	035	Cuyahoga County	44 750	40	56650	143	Tulsa County	26 301
39	77000		Toledo city	287 208	40	59850		Ponca City city	25 387
39	77000	095	Lucas County	287 208	40	59850	071	Kay County	25 387

State Code	Place Code	County Code	Geographic Area Name	2010 Census Population	State Code	Place Code	County Code	Geographic Area Name	2010 Census Population
40	66800		Shawnee city	29 857	41	74950		Tualatin city	26 054
40	66800	125	Pottawatomie County	29 857	41	74950	005	Clackamas County	2 862
					41	74950	067	Washington County	23 192
40	70300		Stillwater city	45 688					
40	70300	119	Payne County	45 688	41	80150		West Linn city	25 109
					41	80150	005	Clackamas County	25 109
40	75000		Tulsa city	391 906					
40	75000	113	Osage County	6 136	42			**PENNSYLVANIA**	12 702 379
40	75000	131	Rogers County	0	42	02000		Allentown city	118 032
40	75000	143	Tulsa County	385 613	42	02000	077	Lehigh County	118 032
40	75000	145	Wagoner County	157					
					42	02184		Altoona city	46 320
41			**OREGON**	3 831 074	42	02184	013	Blair County	46 320
41	01000		Albany city	50 158					
41	01000	003	Benton County	6 463	42	06064		Bethel Park municipality	32 313
41	01000	043	Linn County	43 695	42	06064	003	Allegheny County	32 313
41	05350		Beaverton city	89 803	42	06088		Bethlehem city	74 982
41	05350	067	Washington County	89 803	42	06088	077	Lehigh County	19 343
					42	06088	095	Northampton County	55 639
41	05800		Bend city	76 639					
41	05800	017	Deschutes County	76 639	42	13208		Chester city	33 972
					42	13208	045	Delaware County	33 972
41	15800		Corvallis city	54 462					
41	15800	003	Benton County	54 462	42	21648		Easton city	26 800
					42	21648	095	Northampton County	26 800
41	23850		Eugene city	156 185					
41	23850	039	Lane County	156 185	42	24000		Erie city	101 786
					42	24000	049	Erie County	101 786
41	30550		Grants Pass city	34 533					
41	30550	033	Josephine County	34 533	42	32800		Harrisburg city	49 528
					42	32800	043	Dauphin County	49 528
41	31250		Gresham city	105 594					
41	31250	051	Multnomah County	105 594	42	33408		Hazleton city	25 340
					42	33408	079	Luzerne County	25 340
41	34100		Hillsboro city	91 611					
41	34100	067	Washington County	91 611	42	41216		Lancaster city	59 322
					42	41216	071	Lancaster County	59 322
41	38500		Keizer city	36 478					
41	38500	047	Marion County	36 478	42	42168		Lebanon city	25 477
					42	42168	075	Lebanon County	25 477
41	40550		Lake Oswego city	36 619					
41	40550	005	Clackamas County	34 066	42	50528		Monroeville municipality	28 386
41	40550	051	Multnomah County	2 544	42	50528	003	Allegheny County	28 386
41	40550	067	Washington County	9					
					42	54656		Norristown borough	34 324
41	45000		McMinnville city	32 187	42	54656	091	Montgomery County	34 324
41	45000	071	Yamhill County	32 187					
					42	60000		Philadelphia city	1 526 006
41	47000		Medford city	74 907	42	60000	101	Philadelphia County	1 526 006
41	47000	029	Jackson County	74 907					
					42	61000		Pittsburgh city	305 704
41	55200		Oregon City city	31 859	42	61000	003	Allegheny County	305 704
41	55200	005	Clackamas County	31 859					
					42	61536		Plum borough	27 126
41	59000		Portland city	583 776	42	61536	003	Allegheny County	27 126
41	59000	005	Clackamas County	744					
41	59000	051	Multnomah County	581 485	42	63624		Reading city	88 082
41	59000	067	Washington County	1 547	42	63624	011	Berks County	88 082
41	61200		Redmond city	26 215	42	69000		Scranton city	76 089
41	61200	017	Deschutes County	26 215	42	69000	069	Lackawanna County	76 089
41	64900		Salem city	154 637	42	73808		State College borough	42 034
41	64900	047	Marion County	130 398	42	73808	027	Centre County	42 034
41	64900	053	Polk County	24 239					
					42	85152		Wilkes-Barre city	41 498
41	69600		Springfield city	59 403	42	85152	079	Luzerne County	41 498
41	69600	039	Lane County	59 403					
					42	85312		Williamsport city	29 381
41	73650		Tigard city	48 035	42	85312	081	Lycoming County	29 381
41	73650	067	Washington County	48 035					

State Code	Place Code	County Code	Geographic Area Name	2010 Census Population	State Code	Place Code	County Code	Geographic Area Name	2010 Census Population
42	87048		York city	43 718	45	70270		Summerville town	43 392
42	87048	133	York County	43 718	45	70270	015	Berkeley County	3 643
					45	70270	019	Charleston County	1 010
44			**RHODE ISLAND**	1 052 567	45	70270	035	Dorchester County	38 739
44	19180		Cranston city	80 387					
44	19180	007	Providence County	80 387	45	70405		Sumter city	40 524
					45	70405	085	Sumter County	40 524
44	22960		East Providence city	47 037					
44	22960	007	Providence County	47 037	46			**SOUTH DAKOTA**	814 180
					46			Aberdeen city	26 091
44	54640		Pawtucket city	71 148	46	00100			
44	54640	007	Providence County	71 148	46	00100	013	Brown County	26 091
44	59000		Providence city	178 042	46	52980		Rapid City city	67 956
44	59000	007	Providence County	178 042	46	52980	103	Pennington County	67 956
44	74300		Warwick city	82 672	46	59020		Sioux Falls city	153 888
44	74300	003	Kent County	82 672	46	59020	083	Lincoln County	21 095
					46	59020	099	Minnehaha County	132 793
44	80780		Woonsocket city	41 186					
44	80780	007	Providence County	41 186	47			**TENNESSEE**	6 346 105
					47			Bartlett city	54 613
45			**SOUTH CAROLINA**	4 625 364	47	03440			
45	00550		Aiken city	29 524	47	03440	157	Shelby County	54 613
45	00550	003	Aiken County	29 524					
					47	08280		Brentwood city	37 060
45	01360		Anderson city	26 686	47	08280	187	Williamson County	37 060
45	01360	007	Anderson County	26 686					
					47	08540		Bristol city	26 702
45	13330		Charleston city	120 083	47	08540	163	Sullivan County	26 702
45	13330	015	Berkeley County	8 095					
45	13330	019	Charleston County	111 988	47	14000		Chattanooga city	167 674
					47	14000	065	Hamilton County	167 674
45	16000		Columbia city	129 272					
45	16000	063	Lexington County	559	47	15160		Clarksville city	132 929
45	16000	079	Richland County	128 713	47	15160	125	Montgomery County	132 929
45	25810		Florence city	37 056	47	15400		Cleveland city	41 285
45	25810	041	Florence County	37 056	47	15400	011	Bradley County	41 285
45	29815		Goose Creek city	35 938	47	16420		Collierville town	43 965
45	29815	015	Berkeley County	35 933	47	16420	047	Fayette County	0
45	29815	019	Charleston County	5	47	16420	157	Shelby County	43 965
45	30850		Greenville city	58 409	47	16540		Columbia city	34 681
45	30850	045	Greenville County	58 409	47	16540	119	Maury County	34 681
45	30985		Greer city	25 515	47	16920		Cookeville city	30 435
45	30985	045	Greenville County	18 635	47	16920	141	Putnam County	30 435
45	30985	083	Spartanburg County	6 880					
					47	27740		Franklin city	62 487
45	34045		Hilton Head Island town	37 099	47	27740	187	Williamson County	62 487
45	34045	013	Beaufort County	37 099					
					47	28540		Gallatin city	30 278
45	48535		Mount Pleasant town	67 843	47	28540	165	Sumner County	30 278
45	48535	019	Charleston County	67 843					
					47	28960		Germantown city	38 844
45	49075		Myrtle Beach city	27 109	47	28960	157	Shelby County	38 844
45	49075	051	Horry County	27 109					
					47	33280		Hendersonville city	51 372
45	50875		North Charleston city	97 471	47	33280	165	Sumner County	51 372
45	50875	015	Berkeley County	0					
45	50875	019	Charleston County	78 393	47	37640		Jackson city	65 211
45	50875	035	Dorchester County	19 078	47	37640	113	Madison County	65 211
45	61405		Rock Hill city	66 154	47	38320		Johnson City city	63 152
45	61405	091	York County	66 154	47	38320	019	Carter County	1 252
					47	38320	163	Sullivan County	367
45	68290		Spartanburg city	37 013	47	38320	179	Washington County	61 533
45	68290	083	Spartanburg County	37 013					
					47	39560		Kingsport city	48 205
					47	39560	073	Hawkins County	2 854
					47	39560	163	Sullivan County	45 351

State Code	Place Code	County Code	Geographic Area Name	2010 Census Population	State Code	Place Code	County Code	Geographic Area Name	2010 Census Population
47	40000		Knoxville city	178 874	48	11428		Burleson city	36 690
47	40000	093	Knox County	178 874	48	11428	251	Johnson County	29 111
					48	11428	439	Tarrant County	7 579
47	41200		La Vergne city	32 588					
47	41200	149	Rutherford County	32 588	48	13024		Carrollton city	119 097
					48	13024	085	Collin County	2
47	41520		Lebanon city	26 190	48	13024	113	Dallas County	49 352
47	41520	189	Wilson County	26 190	48	13024	121	Denton County	69 743
47	46380		Maryville city	27 465	48	13492		Cedar Hill city	45 028
47	46380	009	Blount County	27 465	48	13492	113	Dallas County	44 477
					48	13492	139	Ellis County	551
47	48000		Memphis city	646 889					
47	48000	157	Shelby County	646 889	48	13552		Cedar Park city	48 937
					48	13552	453	Travis County	489
47	50280		Morristown city	29 137	48	13552	491	Williamson County	48 448
47	50280	063	Hamblen County	29 131					
47	50280	089	Jefferson County	6	48	15364		Cleburne city	29 337
					48	15364	251	Johnson County	29 337
47	51560		Murfreesboro city	108 755					
47	51560	149	Rutherford County	108 755	48	15976		College Station city	93 857
					48	15976	041	Brazos County	93 857
47	55120		Oak Ridge city	29 330					
47	55120	001	Anderson County	26 271	48	16432		Conroe city	56 207
47	55120	145	Roane County	3 059	48	16432	339	Montgomery County	56 207
47	69420		Smyrna town	39 974	48	16612		Coppell city	38 659
47	69420	149	Rutherford County	39 974	48	16612	113	Dallas County	37 905
					48	16612	121	Denton County	754
47	70580		Spring Hill city	29 036					
47	70580	119	Maury County	7 023	48	16624		Copperas Cove city	32 032
47	70580	187	Williamson County	22 013	48	16624	027	Bell County	0
					48	16624	099	Coryell County	31 457
48			**TEXAS**	25 145 561	48	16624	281	Lampasas County	575
48	01000		Abilene city	117 063					
48	01000	253	Jones County	5 145	48	17000		Corpus Christi city	305 215
48	01000	441	Taylor County	111 918	48	17000	007	Aransas County	0
					48	17000	273	Kleberg County	0
48	01924		Allen city	84 246	48	17000	355	Nueces County	305 215
48	01924	085	Collin County	84 246	48	17000	409	San Patricio County	0
48	03000		Amarillo city	190 695	48	19000		Dallas city	1 197 816
48	03000	375	Potter County	105 486	48	19000	085	Collin County	46 885
48	03000	381	Randall County	85 209	48	19000	113	Dallas County	1 124 296
					48	19000	121	Denton County	26 579
48	04000		Arlington city	365 438	48	19000	257	Kaufman County	0
48	04000	439	Tarrant County	365 438	48	19000	397	Rockwall County	56
48	05000		Austin city	790 390	48	19624		Deer Park city	32 010
48	05000	209	Hays County	2	48	19624	201	Harris County	32 010
48	05000	453	Travis County	754 691					
48	05000	491	Williamson County	35 697	48	19792		Del Rio city	35 591
					48	19792	465	Val Verde County	35 591
48	06128		Baytown city	71 802					
48	06128	071	Chambers County	4 116	48	19972		Denton city	113 383
48	06128	201	Harris County	67 686	48	19972	121	Denton County	113 383
48	07000		Beaumont city	118 296	48	20092		DeSoto city	49 047
48	07000	245	Jefferson County	118 296	48	20092	113	Dallas County	49 047
48	07132		Bedford city	46 979	48	21628		Duncanville city	38 524
48	07132	439	Tarrant County	46 979	48	21628	113	Dallas County	38 524
48	08236		Big Spring city	27 282	48	21892		Eagle Pass city	26 248
48	08236	227	Howard County	27 282	48	21892	323	Maverick County	26 248
48	10768		Brownsville city	175 023	48	22660		Edinburg city	77 100
48	10768	061	Cameron County	175 023	48	22660	215	Hidalgo County	77 100
48	10912		Bryan city	76 201	48	24000		El Paso city	649 121
48	10912	041	Brazos County	76 201	48	24000	141	El Paso County	649 121

State Code	Place Code	County Code	Geographic Area Name	2010 Census Population	State Code	Place Code	County Code	Geographic Area Name	2010 Census Population
8	24768		Euless city	51 277	48	38632		Keller city	39 627
8	24768	439	Tarrant County	51 277	48	38632	439	Tarrant County	39 627
8	25452		Farmers Branch city	28 616	48	39148		Killeen city	127 921
8	25452	113	Dallas County	28 616	48	39148	027	Bell County	127 921
8	26232		Flower Mound town	64 669	48	39352		Kingsville city	26 213
8	26232	121	Denton County	64 457	48	39352	273	Kleberg County	26 213
8	26232	439	Tarrant County	212					
					48	39952		Kyle city	28 016
8	27000		Fort Worth city	741 206	48	39952	209	Hays County	28 016
8	27000	121	Denton County	7 813					
8	27000	367	Parker County	7	48	40588		Lake Jackson city	26 849
8	27000	439	Tarrant County	733 386	48	40588	039	Brazoria County	26 849
8	27000	497	Wise County	0					
					48	41212		Lancaster city	36 361
8	27648		Friendswood city	35 805	48	41212	113	Dallas County	36 361
8	27648	167	Galveston County	25 510					
8	27648	201	Harris County	10 295	48	41440		La Porte city	33 800
					48	41440	201	Harris County	33 800
8	27684		Frisco city	116 989					
8	27684	085	Collin County	72 489	48	41464		Laredo city	236 091
8	27684	121	Denton County	44 500	48	41464	479	Webb County	236 091
8	28068		Galveston city	47 743	48	41980		League City city	83 560
8	28068	167	Galveston County	47 743	48	41980	167	Galveston County	81 998
					48	41980	201	Harris County	1 562
8	29000		Garland city	226 876					
8	29000	085	Collin County	266	48	42016		Leander city	26 521
8	29000	113	Dallas County	226 608	48	42016	453	Travis County	1 077
8	29000	397	Rockwall County	2	48	42016	491	Williamson County	25 444
8	29336		Georgetown city	47 400	48	42508		Lewisville city	95 290
8	29336	491	Williamson County	47 400	48	42508	113	Dallas County	841
					48	42508	121	Denton County	94 449
8	30464		Grand Prairie city	175 396					
8	30464	113	Dallas County	123 487	48	43012		Little Elm city	25 898
8	30464	139	Ellis County	45	48	43012	121	Denton County	25 898
8	30464	439	Tarrant County	51 864					
					48	43888		Longview city	80 455
8	30644		Grapevine city	46 334	48	43888	183	Gregg County	78 585
8	30644	113	Dallas County	0	48	43888	203	Harrison County	1 870
8	30644	121	Denton County	0					
8	30644	439	Tarrant County	46 334	48	45000		Lubbock city	229 573
					48	45000	303	Lubbock County	229 573
8	30920		Greenville city	25 557					
8	30920	231	Hunt County	25 557	48	45072		Lufkin city	35 067
					48	45072	005	Angelina County	35 067
8	31928		Haltom City city	42 409					
8	31928	439	Tarrant County	42 409	48	45384		McAllen city	129 877
					48	45384	215	Hidalgo County	129 877
8	32312		Harker Heights city	26 700					
8	32312	027	Bell County	26 700	48	45744		McKinney city	131 117
					48	45744	085	Collin County	131 117
8	32372		Harlingen city	64 849					
8	32372	061	Cameron County	64 849	48	46452		Mansfield city	56 368
					48	46452	139	Ellis County	95
8	35000		Houston city	2 099 451	48	46452	251	Johnson County	1 652
8	35000	157	Fort Bend County	38 124	48	46452	439	Tarrant County	54 621
8	35000	201	Harris County	2 057 280					
8	35000	339	Montgomery County	4 047	48	47892		Mesquite city	139 824
					48	47892	113	Dallas County	139 731
8	35528		Huntsville city	38 548	48	47892	257	Kaufman County	93
8	35528	471	Walker County	38 548					
					48	48072		Midland city	111 147
8	35576		Hurst city	37 337	48	48072	317	Martin County	0
8	35576	439	Tarrant County	37 337	48	48072	329	Midland County	111 147
8	37000		Irving city	216 290	48	48768		Mission city	77 058
8	37000	113	Dallas County	216 290	48	48768	215	Hidalgo County	77 058

State Code	Place Code	County Code	Geographic Area Name	2010 Census Population	State Code	Place Code	County Code	Geographic Area Name	2010 Census Population
48	48804		Missouri City city	67 358	48	65600		San Marcos city	44 894
48	48804	157	Fort Bend County	61 755	48	65600	055	Caldwell County	3
48	48804	201	Harris County	5 603	48	65600	187	Guadalupe County	0
					48	65600	209	Hays County	44 891
48	50256		Nacogdoches city	32 996					
48	50256	347	Nacogdoches County	32 996	48	66128		Schertz city	31 465
					48	66128	029	Bexar County	1 157
48	50820		New Braunfels city	57 740	48	66128	091	Comal County	845
48	50820	091	Comal County	47 586	48	66128	187	Guadalupe County	29 463
48	50820	187	Guadalupe County	10 154					
					48	66644		Seguin city	25 175
48	52356		North Richland Hills city	63 343	48	66644	187	Guadalupe County	25 175
48	52356	439	Tarrant County	63 343					
					48	67496		Sherman city	38 521
48	53388		Odessa city	99 940	48	67496	181	Grayson County	38 521
48	53388	135	Ector County	98 270					
48	53388	329	Midland County	1 670	48	68636		Socorro city	32 013
					48	68636	141	El Paso County	32 013
48	55080		Paris city	25 171					
48	55080	277	Lamar County	25 171	48	69032		Southlake city	26 575
					48	69032	121	Denton County	773
48	56000		Pasadena city	149 043	48	69032	439	Tarrant County	25 802
48	56000	201	Harris County	149 043					
					48	70808		Sugar Land city	78 817
48	56348		Pearland city	91 252	48	70808	157	Fort Bend County	78 817
48	56348	039	Brazoria County	86 706					
48	56348	157	Fort Bend County	721	48	72176		Temple city	66 102
48	56348	201	Harris County	3 825	48	72176	027	Bell County	66 102
48	57176		Pflugerville city	46 936	48	72368		Texarkana city	36 411
48	57176	453	Travis County	46 636	48	72368	037	Bowie County	36 411
48	57176	491	Williamson County	300					
					48	72392		Texas City city	45 099
48	57200		Pharr city	70 400	48	72392	071	Chambers County	0
48	57200	215	Hidalgo County	70 400	48	72392	167	Galveston County	45 099
48	58016		Plano city	259 841	48	72530		The Colony city	36 328
48	58016	085	Collin County	254 525	48	72530	121	Denton County	36 328
48	58016	121	Denton County	5 316					
					48	74144		Tyler city	96 900
48	58820		Port Arthur city	53 818	48	74144	423	Smith County	96 900
48	58820	245	Jefferson County	53 814					
48	58820	361	Orange County	4	48	75428		Victoria city	62 592
					48	75428	469	Victoria County	62 592
48	61796		Richardson city	99 223					
48	61796	085	Collin County	28 569	48	76000		Waco city	124 805
48	61796	113	Dallas County	70 654	48	76000	309	McLennan County	124 805
48	62828		Rockwall city	37 490	48	76816		Waxahachie city	29 621
48	62828	397	Rockwall County	37 490	48	76816	139	Ellis County	29 621
48	63284		Rosenberg city	30 618	48	76864		Weatherford city	25 250
48	63284	157	Fort Bend County	30 618	48	76864	367	Parker County	25 250
48	63500		Round Rock city	99 887	48	77272		Weslaco city	35 670
48	63500	453	Travis County	1 362	48	77272	215	Hidalgo County	35 670
48	63500	491	Williamson County	98 525					
					48	79000		Wichita Falls city	104 553
48	63572		Rowlett city	56 199	48	79000	485	Wichita County	104 553
48	63572	113	Dallas County	49 188					
48	63572	397	Rockwall County	7 011	48	80356		Wylie city	41 427
					48	80356	085	Collin County	39 957
48	64472		San Angelo city	93 200	48	80356	113	Dallas County	415
48	64472	451	Tom Green County	93 200	48	80356	397	Rockwall County	1 055
48	65000		San Antonio city	1 327 407	49			**UTAH**	2 763 885
48	65000	029	Bexar County	1 327 381	49	01310		American Fork city	26 263
48	65000	091	Comal County	0	49	01310	049	Utah County	26 263
48	65000	325	Medina County	26					
					49	07690		Bountiful city	42 552
48	65516		San Juan city	33 856	49	07690	011	Davis County	42 552
48	65516	215	Hidalgo County	33 856					

Cities by County–*Continued*

State Code	Place Code	County Code	Geographic Area Name	2010 Census Population	State Code	Place Code	County Code	Geographic Area Name	2010 Census Population
49	11320		Cedar City city	28 857	49	76680		Tooele city	31 605
49	11320	021	Iron County	28 857	49	76680	045	Tooele County	31 605
49	13850		Clearfield city	30 112	49	82950		West Jordan city	103 712
49	13850	011	Davis County	30 112	49	82950	035	Salt Lake County	103 712
49	16270		Cottonwood Heights city	33 433	49	83470		West Valley City city	129 480
49	16270	035	Salt Lake County	33 433	49	83470	035	Salt Lake County	129 480
49	20120		Draper city	42 274	50			**VERMONT**	625 741
49	20120	035	Salt Lake County	40 532	50	10675		Burlington city	42 417
49	20120	049	Utah County	1 742	50	10675	007	Chittenden County	42 417
49	36070		Holladay city	26 472	51			**VIRGINIA**	8 001 024
49	36070	035	Salt Lake County	26 472	51	01000		Alexandria city	139 966
					51	01000	510	Alexandria city	139 966
49	40360		Kaysville city	27 300					
49	40360	011	Davis County	27 300	51	07784		Blacksburg town	42 620
					51	07784	121	Montgomery County	42 620
49	43660		Layton city	67 311					
49	43660	011	Davis County	67 311	51	14968		Charlottesville city	43 475
					51	14968	540	Charlottesville city	43 475
49	44320		Lehi city	47 407					
49	44320	049	Utah County	47 407	51	16000		Chesapeake city	222 209
					51	16000	550	Chesapeake city	222 209
49	45860		Logan city	48 174					
49	45860	005	Cache County	48 174	51	21344		Danville city	43 055
					51	21344	590	Danville city	43 055
49	49710		Midvale city	27 964					
49	49710	035	Salt Lake County	27 964	51	35000		Hampton city	137 436
					51	35000	650	Hampton city	137 436
49	53230		Murray city	46 746					
49	53230	035	Salt Lake County	46 746	51	35624		Harrisonburg city	48 914
					51	35624	660	Harrisonburg city	48 914
49	55980		Ogden city	82 825					
49	55980	057	Weber County	82 825	51	44984		Leesburg town	42 616
					51	44984	107	Loudoun County	42 616
49	57300		Orem city	88 328					
49	57300	049	Utah County	88 328	51	47672		Lynchburg city	75 568
					51	47672	680	Lynchburg city	75 568
49	60930		Pleasant Grove city	33 509					
49	60930	049	Utah County	33 509	51	48952		Manassas city	37 821
					51	48952	683	Manassas city	37 821
49	62470		Provo city	112 488					
49	62470	049	Utah County	112 488	51	56000		Newport News city	180 719
					51	56000	700	Newport News city	180 719
49	64340		Riverton city	38 753					
49	64340	035	Salt Lake County	38 753	51	57000		Norfolk city	242 803
					51	57000	710	Norfolk city	242 803
49	65110		Roy city	36 884					
49	65110	057	Weber County	36 884	51	61832		Petersburg city	32 420
					51	61832	730	Petersburg city	32 420
49	65330		St. George city	72 897					
49	65330	053	Washington County	72 897	51	64000		Portsmouth city	95 535
					51	64000	740	Portsmouth city	95 535
49	67000		Salt Lake City city	186 440					
49	67000	035	Salt Lake County	186 440	51	67000		Richmond city	204 214
					51	67000	760	Richmond city	204 214
49	67440		Sandy city	87 461					
49	67440	035	Salt Lake County	87 461	51	68000		Roanoke city	97 032
					51	68000	770	Roanoke city	97 032
49	70850		South Jordan city	50 418					
49	70850	035	Salt Lake County	50 418	51	76432		Suffolk city	84 585
					51	76432	800	Suffolk city	84 585
49	71290		Spanish Fork city	34 691					
49	71290	049	Utah County	34 691	51	82000		Virginia Beach city	437 994
					51	82000	810	Virginia Beach city	437 994
49	72280		Springville city	29 466					
49	72280	049	Utah County	29 466	51	86720		Winchester city	26 203
					51	86720	840	Winchester city	26 203
49	75360		Taylorsville city	58 652					
49	75360	035	Salt Lake County	58 652					

Appendix E

Cities by County–*Continued*

State Code	Place Code	County Code	Geographic Area Name	2010 Census Population	State Code	Place Code	County Code	Geographic Area Name	2010 Census Population
53			**WASHINGTON**	6 724 540	53	56625		Pullman city	29 799
53	03180		Auburn city	70 180	53	56625	075	Whitman County	29 799
53	03180	033	King County	62 761					
53	03180	053	Pierce County	7 419	53	56695		Puyallup city	37 022
					53	56695	053	Pierce County	37 022
53	05210		Bellevue city	122 363					
53	05210	033	King County	122 363	53	57535		Redmond city	54 144
					53	57535	033	King County	54 144
53	05280		Bellingham city	80 885					
53	05280	073	Whatcom County	80 885	53	57745		Renton city	90 927
					53	57745	033	King County	90 927
53	07380		Bothell city	33 505					
53	07380	033	King County	17 090	53	58235		Richland city	48 058
53	07380	061	Snohomish County	16 415	53	58235	005	Benton County	48 058
53	07695		Bremerton city	37 729	53	61115		Sammamish city	45 780
53	07695	035	Kitsap County	37 729	53	61115	033	King County	45 780
53	08850		Burien city	33 313	53	62288		SeaTac city	26 909
53	08850	033	King County	33 313	53	62288	033	King County	26 909
53	17635		Des Moines city	29 673	53	63000		Seattle city	608 660
53	17635	033	King County	29 673	53	63000	033	King County	608 660
53	20750		Edmonds city	39 709	53	63960		Shoreline city	53 007
53	20750	061	Snohomish County	39 709	53	63960	033	King County	53 007
53	22640		Everett city	103 019	53	67000		Spokane city	208 916
53	22640	061	Snohomish County	103 019	53	67000	063	Spokane County	208 916
53	23515		Federal Way city	89 306	53	67167		Spokane Valley city	89 755
53	23515	033	King County	89 306	53	67167	063	Spokane County	89 755
53	33805		Issaquah city	30 434	53	70000		Tacoma city	198 397
53	33805	033	King County	30 434	53	70000	053	Pierce County	198 397
53	35275		Kennewick city	73 917	53	73465		University Place city	31 144
53	35275	005	Benton County	73 917	53	73465	053	Pierce County	31 144
53	35415		Kent city	92 411	53	74060		Vancouver city	161 791
53	35415	033	King County	92 411	53	74060	011	Clark County	161 791
53	35940		Kirkland city	48 787	53	75775		Walla Walla city	31 731
53	35940	033	King County	48 787	53	75775	071	Walla Walla County	31 731
53	36745		Lacey city	42 393	53	77105		Wenatchee city	31 925
53	36745	067	Thurston County	42 393	53	77105	007	Chelan County	31 925
53	37900		Lake Stevens city	28 069	53	80010		Yakima city	91 067
53	37900	061	Snohomish County	28 069	53	80010	077	Yakima County	91 067
53	38038		Lakewood city	58 163	54			**WEST VIRGINIA**	1 852 994
53	38038	053	Pierce County	58 163	54	14600		Charleston city	51 400
					54	14600	039	Kanawha County	51 400
53	40245		Longview city	36 648					
53	40245	015	Cowlitz County	36 648	54	39460		Huntington city	49 138
					54	39460	011	Cabell County	45 214
53	40840		Lynnwood city	35 836	54	39460	099	Wayne County	3 924
53	40840	061	Snohomish County	35 836					
					54	55756		Morgantown city	29 660
53	43955		Marysville city	60 020	54	55756	061	Monongalia County	29 660
53	43955	061	Snohomish County	60 020					
					54	62140		Parkersburg city	31 492
53	47560		Mount Vernon city	31 743	54	62140	107	Wood County	31 492
53	47560	057	Skagit County	31 743					
					54	86452		Wheeling city	28 486
53	51300		Olympia city	46 478	54	86452	051	Marshall County	276
53	51300	067	Thurston County	46 478	54	86452	069	Ohio County	28 210
53	53545		Pasco city	59 781					
53	53545	021	Franklin County	59 781					

Cities by County–*Continued*

State Code	Place Code	County Code	Geographic Area Name	2010 Census Population	State Code	Place Code	County Code	Geographic Area Name	2010 Census Population
55			**WISCONSIN**	5 686 986	55	72975		Sheboygan city	49 288
55	02375		Appleton city	72 623	55	72975	117	Sheboygan County	49 288
55	02375	015	Calumet County	11 088					
55	02375	087	Outagamie County	60 045	55	77200		Stevens Point city	26 717
55	02375	139	Winnebago County	1 490	55	77200	097	Portage County	26 717
55	06500		Beloit city	36 966	55	78600		Sun Prairie city	29 364
55	06500	105	Rock County	36 966	55	78600	025	Dane County	29 364
55	10025		Brookfield city	37 920	55	78650		Superior city	27 244
55	10025	133	Waukesha County	37 920	55	78650	031	Douglas County	27 244
55	22300		Eau Claire city	65 883	55	84250		Waukesha city	70 718
55	22300	017	Chippewa County	1 981	55	84250	133	Waukesha County	70 718
55	22300	035	Eau Claire County	63 902					
					55	84475		Wausau city	39 106
55	25950		Fitchburg city	25 260	55	84475	073	Marathon County	39 106
55	25950	025	Dane County	25 260					
					55	84675		Wauwatosa city	46 396
55	26275		Fond du Lac city	43 021	55	84675	079	Milwaukee County	46 396
55	26275	039	Fond du Lac County	43 021					
					55	85300		West Allis city	60 411
55	27300		Franklin city	35 451	55	85300	079	Milwaukee County	60 411
55	27300	079	Milwaukee County	35 451					
					55	85350		West Bend city	31 078
55	31000		Green Bay city	104 057	55	85350	131	Washington County	31 078
55	31000	009	Brown County	104 057					
					56			**WYOMING**	563 626
55	31175		Greenfield city	36 720	56	13150		Casper city	55 316
55	31175	079	Milwaukee County	36 720	56	13150	025	Natrona County	55 316
55	37825		Janesville city	63 575	56	13900		Cheyenne city	59 466
55	37825	105	Rock County	63 575	56	13900	021	Laramie County	59 466
55	39225		Kenosha city	99 218	56	31855		Gillette city	29 087
55	39225	059	Kenosha County	99 218	56	31855	005	Campbell County	29 087
55	40775		La Crosse city	51 320	56	45050		Laramie city	30 816
55	40775	063	La Crosse County	51 320	56	45050	001	Albany County	30 816
55	48000		Madison city	233 209					
55	48000	025	Dane County	233 209					
55	48500		Manitowoc city	33 736					
55	48500	071	Manitowoc County	33 736					
55	51000		Menomonee Falls village	35 626					
55	51000	133	Waukesha County	35 626					
55	53000		Milwaukee city	594 833					
55	53000	079	Milwaukee County	594 833					
55	53000	131	Washington County	0					
55	53000	133	Waukesha County	0					
55	54875		Mount Pleasant village	26 197					
55	54875	101	Racine County	26 197					
55	55750		Neenah city	25 501					
55	55750	139	Winnebago County	25 501					
55	56375		New Berlin city	39 584					
55	56375	133	Waukesha County	39 584					
55	58800		Oak Creek city	34 451					
55	58800	079	Milwaukee County	34 451					
55	60500		Oshkosh city	66 083					
55	60500	139	Winnebago County	66 083					
55	66000		Racine city	78 860					
55	66000	101	Racine County	78 860					

The following consolidated cities are included in Table D. They are listed here with their 2010 census populations followed by the separate entities that make up the consolidated city. Data from the American Community Survey include only the "balance," the major city of each consolidated city.

State Code	Place Code	County Code	Geographic Area Name	2010 Census Population	State Code	Place Code	County Code	Geographic Area Name	2010 Census Population
09			**CONNECTICUT**	3 574 097	21	38818		Hurstbourne Acres city	1 811
09	47500		Milford city	52 759	21	39304		Indian Hills city	2 868
			Milford city (balance)	51 271	21	40222		Jeffersontown city	26 595
	88050		Woodmont borough	1 488	21	42598		Kingsley city	381
					21	43900		Langdon Place city	936
13			**GEORGIA**	9 687 653	21	46540		Lincolnshire city	148
13	03436		Athens-Clark county	116 714	21	48006		Louisville/Jefferson County	
13	03440		Athens-Clark county (balance)	115 452				(balance)	597 337
13	09068		Bogart town	140	21	48558		Lyndon city	11 002
13	83728		Winterville city	1 122	21	48648		Lynnview city	914
					21	49800		Manor Creek city	140
13	04200		Augusta-Richmond county	200 549	21	50412		Maryhill Estates city	179
13	04204		Augusta-Richmond county		21	51193		Meadowbrook Farm city	136
			(balance)	195 844	21	51258		Meadow Vale city	736
13	09040		Blythe city	694	21	51294		Meadowview Estates city	363
13	38040		Hephzibah city	4 011	21	51978		Middletown city	7 218
					21	52842		Mockingbird Valley city	167
18			**INDIANA**	6 483 802	21	53328		Moorland city	431
18	36000		Indianapolis city	829 718	21	54660		Murray Hill city	582
18	04204		Beech Grove city	0	21	56550		Norbourne Estates city	441
18	13492		Clermont town	1 356	21	56730		Northfield city	1 020
18	16156		Crows Nest town	73	21	56928		Norwood city	370
18	16336		Cumberland town	2 597	21	57658		Old Brownsboro Place city	353
18	34420		Homecroft town	722	21	59322		Parkway Village city	650
18	36003		Indianapolis city (balance)	820 445	21	61554		Plantation city	832
18	42426		Lawrence city	42	21	62370		Poplar Hills city	362
18	48456		Meridian Hills town	1 616	21	63264		Prospect city	4 636
18	54612		North Crows Nest town	45	21	65208		Richlawn city	405
18	65556		Rocky Ripple town	606	21	65766		Riverwood city	446
18	72232		Spring Hill town	98	21	66486		Rolling Fields city	646
18	80234		Warren Park town	1 480	21	66504		Rolling Hills city	959
18	84374		Williams Creek town	407	21	67944		St. Matthews city	17 472
18	85742		Wynnedale town	231	21	67998		St. Regis Park city	1 454
					21	69384		Seneca Gardens city	696
21			**KENTUCKY**	4 339 367	21	70284		Shively city	15 264
21	46003		Louisville/Jefferson County	741 096	21	72138		South Park View city	7
21	01504		Anchorage city	2 348	21	72770		Spring Mill city	287
21	02656		Audubon Park city	1 473	21	72790		Spring Valley city	654
21	03376		Bancroft city	494	21	74064		Strathmoor Manor city	337
21	03556		Barbourmeade city	1 218	21	74082		Strathmoor Village city	648
21	05068		Beechwood Village city	1 324	21	75190		Sycamore city	160
21	05392		Bellemeade city	865	21	75963		Ten Broeck city	103
21	05464		Bellewood city	321	21	76380		Thornhill city	178
21	07858		Blue Ridge Manor city	767	21	80913		Watterson Park city	976
21	09532		Briarwood city	435	21	81372		Wellington city	565
21	09847		Broeck Pointe city	272	21	81624		West Buechel city	1 230
21	10162		Brownsboro Farm city	648	21	82164		Westwood city	634
21	10198		Brownsboro Village city	319	21	83208		Wildwood city	261
21	12066		Cambridge city	175	21	83784		Windy Hills city	2 385
21	16395		Coldstream city	1 100	21	84486		Woodland Hills city	696
21	18270		Creekside city	305	21	84576		Woodlawn Park city	942
21	18766		Crossgate city	225	21	84891		Worthington Hills city	1 446
21	22204		Douglass Hills city	5 484					
21	22474		Druid Hills city	308	30			**MONTANA**	989 415
21	27262		Fincastle city	817	30	11390		Butte-Silver Bow	34 200
21	28342		Forest Hills city	444	30	11397		Butte-Silver Bow (balance)	33 525
21	31348		Glenview city	531	30	77650		Walkerville town	675
21	31402		Glenview Hills city	319					
21	31420		Glenview Manor city	191	47			**TENNESSEE**	6 346 105
21	31870		Goose Creek city	294	47	52004		Nashville-Davidson	626 681
21	32523		Graymoor-Devondale city	2 870	47	04620		Belle Meade city	2 912
21	32986		Green Spring city	715	47	05140		Berry Hill city	537
21	36102		Heritage Creek city	1 076	47	27020		Forest Hills city	4 812
21	36374		Hickory Hill city	114	47	29920		Goodlettsville city	10 319
21	36865		Hills and Dales city	142	47	40720		Lakewood city	2 302
21	37576		Hollow Creek city	783	47	52006		Nashville-Davidson (balance)	601 222
21	37630		Hollyvilla city	537	47	54780		Oak Hill city	4 529
21	38170		Houston Acres city	507	47	63140		Ridgetop city	48
21	38814		Hurstbourne city	4 216					

APPENDIX F
SOURCE NOTES AND EXPLANATIONS

The following documentation is provided in the order in which items appear in the tables. Internet addresses are provided for the sources of the data. Some of the links refer to the specific data tables. Others provide information about the general data source.

TABLE A—STATES

Table A presents 355 items for the United States as a whole, for each individual state, and for the District of Columbia. The states are presented in alphabetical order.

LAND AREA, Items 1 and 4
Source: U.S. Census Bureau—Decennial Censuses and Population Estimates
http://www.census.gov/2010census/

Land area measurements are shown to the nearest square kilometer. Land area includes dry land and land temporarily or partially covered by water, such as marshlands, swamps, and river floodplains.

POPULATION AND COMPONENTS OF CHANGE, Items 2–4, 31–41
Source: U.S. Census Bureau—Decennial Censuses and Population Estimates
http://www.census.gov/popest/estimates.html
http://www.census.gov/2010census/data/

The population data for 2015 are Census Bureau estimates of the resident population as of July 1, 2015.

The population data for 1990, 2000, and 2010 are from the decennial censuses and represent the resident population as of April 1 of those years.

The change in population between 2010 and 2015 is made up of (a) natural increase—births minus deaths, and (b) net migration—the difference between the number of persons moving into a particular state and the number of persons moving out of the state. Net migration is composed of internal and international migration.

POPULATION AND POPULATION CHARACTERISTICS, Items 5–23 and 45–63
Source: U.S. Census Bureau—Population Estimates and 2014 American Community Survey
http://www.census.gov/popest/estimates.html
http://www.census.gov/acs/www/

Data on age, sex, race, and Hispanic origin are from the Population Estimates program. Data on place of birth are from the 2014 American Community Survey, a nationwide continuous survey designed to replace the long form questionnaire used in previous censuses.

The concept "race alone or in combination " includes people who reported a single race alone (i.e., Asian) and people who reported that race in combination with one or more of the other major race groups (i.e., White, Black or African American, American Indian and Alaska Native, Native Hawaiian and Other Pacific Islander, and Some Other Race). The "race alone or in combination" concept, therefore, represents the maximum number of people who reported as that race group, either alone, or in combination with another race(s).

The sum of the four individual race alone or in combination categories in this book may add to more than the total population because people who reported more than one race were tallied in each race category. In this book, the Asian group has been combined with the Native Hawaiian and Other Pacific Islander group causing double-counting of persons who identify with both groups. This is especially pronounced in Hawaii.

Data on race were derived from answers to the question on race that was asked of all persons. The concept of race, as used by the Census Bureau, reflects self-identification by respondents according to the race or races with which they most closely identify. These categories are sociopolitical constructs and should not be interpreted as being scientific or anthropological in nature. Furthermore, the race categories include both racial and national origin groups.

The **White** population is defined as persons who indicated their race as White, as well as persons who did not classify themselves in one of the specific race categories listed on the questionnaire but entered a nationality such as Irish, German, Italian, Lebanese, Near Easterner, Arab, or Polish.

The **Black** population includes persons who indicated their race as "Black, African Am., or Negro," as well as persons who did not classify themselves in one of the specific race categories but reported entries such as African American, Afro American, Kenyan, Nigerian, or Haitian.

The **American Indian or Alaska Native** population includes persons who indicated their race as American Indian or Alaska Native, as well as persons who did not classify themselves in one of the specific race categories but reported entries such as Canadian Indian, French-American Indian, Spanish-American Indian, Eskimo, Aleut, Alaska Indian, or any of the American Indian or Alaska Native tribes.

The **Asian and Pacific Islander** population combines two census groupings: **Asian** and **Native Hawaiian or Other Pacific Islander**. The **Asian** population includes persons who indicated their race as Asian Indian, Chinese, Filipino, Japanese, Korean, Vietnamese, or "Other Asian," as well as persons who provided write-in entries of such groups as Cambodian, Laotian, Hmong, Pakistani, or Taiwanese. The **Native Hawaiian or Other Pacific Islander** population includes persons who indicated their race as "Native Hawaiian," "Guamanian or Chamorro," "Samoan," or "Other Pacific Islander," as well as persons who reported entries such as Part Hawaiian, American Samoan, Fijian, Melanesian, or Tahitian.

The Hispanic population is based on a question that asked respondents "Is this person Spanish/Hispanic/Latino?" Persons marking any one of the four Hispanic categories (i.e., Mexican, Puerto Rican, Cuban, or other Spanish) are collectively referred to as Hispanic.

Age is defined as age at last birthday (number of completed years since birth), as of April 1 of the census year.

The **median age** is the age that divides the population into two equal-size groups. Half of the population is older than the median age and half is younger. Median age is based on a standard distribution of the population by single years of age and is shown to the nearest tenth of a year.

The **female** population is shown as a percentage of total population.

The **foreign-born** population includes all persons who were not U.S. citizens at birth. Foreign-born persons are those who indicated they were either a U.S. citizen by naturalization or were not a citizen of the United States. Neither the census nor the American Community Survey asked about immigration status. The population surveyed included all persons who indicated that the United States was their usual place of residence. The foreign-born population consists of immigrants (legal permanent residents), temporary migrants (students), humanitarian migrants (refugees), and unauthorized migrants (persons illegally residing in the United States).

Percent born in state of residence is shown as a percentage of total population.

IMMIGRANTS, Item 24

Source: Department of Homeland Security, U.S. Citizenship and Immigration Services
http://www.dhs.gov/yearbook-immigration-statistics

The number of immigrants by state of intended residence is summarized from the administrative records of the Citizenship and Immigration Services. This information is compiled from immigrant visas and forms granting legal permanent resident status.

An **immigrant** is an alien admitted to the United States as a lawful permanent resident. Immigrants are those persons lawfully accorded the privilege of residing permanently in the United States. They may be newly arrived individuals who were issued immigrant visas by the Department of State overseas, or they may be U.S. residents who were admitted to permanent resident status in 2014 by the U.S. Citizenship and Immigration Services.

HOUSEHOLDS, Items 25–30 and 64–68

Source: U.S. Census Bureau—2014 American Community Survey
http://www.census.gov/acs/www/

A **household** includes all of the persons who occupy a housing unit. Persons not living in households are classified as living in group quarters. A housing unit is a house, an apartment, a mobile home, a group of rooms, or a single room occupied (or, if vacant, intended for occupancy) as separate living quarters. Separate living quarters are those in which the occupants live separately from any other persons in the building and have direct access from the outside of the building or through a common hall. The occupants

may be a single family, one person living alone, two or more families living together, or any other group of related or unrelated persons who share living quarters. The number of households is the same as the number of year-round occupied housing units.

The measure of **persons per household** is obtained by dividing the number of persons in households by the number of households or householders. One person in each household is designated as the householder. In most cases, this is the person, (or one of the persons) in whose name the house is owned, being bought, or rented. If there is no such person in the household, any adult household member 15 years old and over can be designated as the householder.

A **family** includes a householder and one or more other persons living in the same household who are related to the householder by birth, marriage, or adoption. All persons in a household who are related to the householder are regarded as members of his or her family. A **family household** may contain persons not related to the householder; thus, family households may include more members than families do. A household can contain only one family for the purposes of census tabulations. Not all households contain families, as a household may comprise a group of unrelated persons or one person living alone. Families are classified by type as either a "married couple" or "other family" according to the presence of a spouse.

The category **female family householder** includes only female-headed family households with no spouse present.

POPULATION PROJECTIONS, Items 42–44

Source: U.S. Census Bureau—Population Projections Branch
http://www.census.gov/population/projections/

Projections are estimates of the population for future dates. They illustrate plausible courses of future population change based on assumptions about future births, deaths, international migration, and domestic migration. Projected numbers are based on an estimated population consistent with the most recent decennial census as enumerated. The Census Bureau does not have a current set of state population projections and currently has no plans to produce them. This volume includes projections released in 2005, based on the 2000 census. The Census Bureau notes that these projections should be used with caution because population trends may have changed substantially since their release.

HOUSING, Items 69–92

Source: U.S. Census Bureau—2010 and 2014 American Community Survey
http://www.census.gov/acs/www/

Housing data for 2010 and 2014 are from the American Community Survey, a nationwide continuous survey designed to replace the long form questionnaire used in previous censuses. A sample of households is surveyed to provide estimates.

A **housing unit** is a house, apartment, mobile home or trailer, group of rooms, or single room occupied or, if vacant, intended for occupancy as separate living quarters. Separate living quarters are those in which the occupants do not live and eat with any other person in the structure and which have direct access from the outside of the building or through a common hall. For vacant units, the criteria of separateness and direct access are applied to the intended occupants whenever possible. If that information cannot be obtained, the criteria are applied to the previous occupants.

The occupants of a housing unit may be a single family, one person living alone, two or more families living together, or any other group of related or unrelated persons who share living arrangements. Both occupied and vacant housing units are included in the housing inventory, although recreational vehicles, tents, caves, boats, railroad cars, and the like are included only if they are occupied as a person's usual place of residence.

A housing unit is classified as **occupied** if it is the usual place of residence of the person or group of persons living in it at the time of enumeration, or if the occupants are only temporarily absent (away on vacation). A household consists of all persons who occupy a housing unit as their usual place of residence.

Housing cost, as a percentage of income, is shown separately for owners with mortgages, owners without mortgages, and renters. Also shown is the percentage of mortgaged owners and renters who pay 30 percent or more of household income on selected monthly costs. Rent as a percent of income is a computed ratio of gross rent and monthly household income (total household income divided by 12). Selected owner costs include utilities and fuels, mortgage payments, insurance, taxes, etc. In each case, the ratio of housing cost to income is computed separately for each housing unit. The housing cost ratios for half of all units are above the median shown in this book, and half are below the median. Median monthly housing costs divides the monthly housing costs distribution into two equal parts, one-half of the cases falling below the median monthly housing costs and one-half above the median.

Median value is the dollar amount that divides the distribution of specified owner-occupied housing units into two equal parts, with half of all units below the median value and half above the median value. Value is defined as the respondent's estimate of what the house would sell for if it were for sale. Data are presented for single-family units on fewer than 10 acres of land that have no business or medical office on the property.

Median rent divides the distribution of renter-occupied housing units into two equal parts. The rent concept used in this volume is gross rent, which includes the amount of cash rent a renter pays (contract rent) plus the estimated average cost of utilities and fuels, if these are paid by the renter. The rent is the amount of rent only for living quarters and excludes any business or other space occupied. Single-family houses on lots of 10 or more acres of land are excluded.

Substandard units are occupied units that are overcrowded or lack complete plumbing facilities. For the purposes of this item, "overcrowded" is defined as having 1.01 persons or more per room. Complete plumbing facilities include hot and cold piped water, a flush toilet, and a bathtub or shower. These facilities must be located inside the housing unit, but do not have to be in the same room.

Different house includes all people 1 year old and over who, a year earlier, lived in a different house or apartment from the one they occupied at the time of interview.

BUILDING PERMITS, Items 93–95
Source: U.S. Census Bureau—Building Permits Survey
http://www.census.gov/construction/bps/

These figures represent private residential construction authorized by building permits in approximately 20,000 places in the United States. Valuation represents the expected cost of construction as recorded on the building permit. This figure usually excludes the cost of on-site and off-site development and improvements, as well as the cost of heating, plumbing, electrical, and elevator installations.

National, state, and county totals were obtained by adding the data for permit-issuing places within each jurisdiction. These totals thus are limited to permits issued in the 20,000 place universe covered by the Census Bureau and may not include all permits issued within a state. Current surveys indicate that construction is undertaken for all but a very small percentage of housing units authorized by building permits.

Residential building permits include buildings with any number of housing units. Housing units exclude group quarters (such as dormitories and rooming houses), transient accommodations (such as transient hotels, motels, and tourist courts), "HUD code" manufactured (mobile) homes, moved or relocated units, and housing units created in an existing residential or nonresidential structure.

MANUFACTURED HOUSING UNITS, Item 96
Source: U.S. Census Bureau—Manufactured Housing Survey
http://www.census.gov/construction/mhs/historicaldata.html

The Manufactured Homes Survey (MHS) is conducted by the U.S. Census Bureau and sponsored by the Department of Housing and Urban Development (HUD). MHS produces monthly regional estimates of the new manufactured home average sales prices and more annual estimates for each state.

A manufactured home is defined as a movable dwelling, 8 feet or more wide and 40 feet or more long, designed to be towed on its own chassis, with transportation gear integral to the unit when it leaves the factory, and without need of a permanent foundation. These manufactured homes include multi-wides and expandable manufactured homes. Excluded are travel trailers, motor homes, and modular housing.

BIRTHS AND DEATHS, Items 97–103
Source: U.S. Centers for Disease Control and Prevention, National Center for Health Statistics
http://www.cdc.gov/nchs/data/nvsr/nvsr64/nvsr6412.pdf
http://www.cdc.gov/nchs/data/nvsr/nvsr64/nvsr6402.pdf

The registration of births, deaths, and other vital events in the United States is primarily a state and local function. The civil laws of every state provide for continuous and permanent birth and death registration systems. Through the National Vital Statistics System, the National Center for Health Statistics (NCHS) obtains data on births and deaths from the registration offices of each state, New York City, and the District of Columbia.

Birth and death statistics are limited to events occurring during the year. The data are by place of residence and exclude events for nonresidents of the United States. Births or deaths occurring outside the United States are excluded.

Birth and death rates represent the number of births and deaths per 1,000 resident population enumerated as of April 1 for decennial census years and estimated as of July 1 for other years.

Figures for infant deaths include deaths of children under 1 year of age but exclude fetal deaths. The infant death rate is per 1,000 live births.

The rates of almost all causes of disease, injury, and death vary by age. Age adjustment is a technique for "removing" the effects of age from crude rates, in order to allow meaningful comparisons across populations with different underlying age structures. For example, comparing the crude death rate in Florida to that of California is misleading, since the relatively older population in Florida will lead to a higher crude death rate. For such a comparison, age-adjusted death rates are preferable.

The population estimates were developed by the Census Bureau's Population Division using a traditional cohort composition method. Starting with a basic population from the 2000 census, each component of population change—births, deaths, domestic migration, and international migration—is estimated separately for each birth cohort by sex, race, and Hispanic or Latino origin.

Age-adjusted rates are calculated by applying the age-specific rates of various populations to a single standard population. In this volume, the standard population is 2000. Beginning in 2003, The Centers for Disease Control and Prevention switched to the year 2000, after many years of using the year 1940 as the standard population for age-adjusted death rates.

PERSONS LACKING HEALTH INSURANCE, Items 104–105
Source: U.S. Census Bureau—American Community Survey
http://www.census.gov/library/publications/2015/demo/p60–253.html

These estimates are from the American Community Survey, an ongoing nationwide survey that is conducted throughout the year. About 250,000 addresses per month receive the ACS. Respondents are asked whether each household member is currently covered (by specific types of health coverage) at the time of interview. The 2013 estimates were the first to use the ACS. Prior year estimates were based on the Annual Social and Economic Supplement (ASEC) of the Current Population Survey (CPS).

Those lacking coverage are the percentage of the population of each state who were not covered by private health plans purchased directly or provided by an employer, Medicaid, Medicare, or military health care.

MEDICARE BENEFICIARIES, Item 106
Source: U.S. Department of Health and Human Services, Centers for Medicare and Medicaid Services
https://www.cms.gov/Research-Statistics-Data-and-Systems/Statistics-Trends-and-Reports/Medicare-Geographic-Variation/GVPUF.html

The Centers for Medicare and Medicaid Services (CMS) administers Medicare, which provides health insurance to persons 65 years old and over, persons with permanent kidney failure, and certain persons with disabilities. Medicare has two parts: Hospital Insurance (Part A) and Supplemental Medical Insurance (Part B). The numbers in Table A include persons 65 and older who were enrolled in either or both parts of the program during the year shown.

CRIME, Items 107–110
Source: U.S. Federal Bureau of Investigation—Uniform Crime Reports
http://www.fbi.gov/ucr/ucr.htm

Crime data are as reported to the Federal Bureau of Investigation (FBI) by law enforcement agencies and have not been adjusted for underreporting. This may affect comparability between geographic areas or over time.

Through the voluntary contribution of crime statistics by law enforcement agencies across the United States, the Uniform Crime Reporting (UCR) Program provides periodic assessments of crime in the nation as measured by offenses that have come to the attention of the law enforcement community. The Committee on Uniform Crime Records of the International Association of Chiefs of Police initiated this voluntary national data-collection effort in 1930. The UCR Program contributors compile and submit their crime data either directly to the FBI or through state-level UCR Programs.

Seven offenses, because of their severity, frequency of occurrence, and likelihood of being reported to police, were initially selected to serve as an index for evaluating fluctuations in the volume of crime. These serious crimes were murder and nonnegligent manslaughter, forcible rape, robbery, aggravated assault, burglary, larceny-theft, and motor vehicle theft. By congressional mandate, arson was added as the eighth index offense in 1979. The totals shown in this volume do not include arson.

In 2004, the FBI discontinued the use of the Crime Index in the UCR Program and its publications, stating that the Crime Index was driven upward by the offense with the highest number of cases (in this case, larceny-theft) creating a bias against jurisdictions with a high number of larceny-thefts but a low number of other serious crimes, such as murder and forcible rape. The FBI is currently publishing a violent crime total and a property crime total until a more viable index is developed.

In 2013, the FBI adopted a new definition of rape. Rape is now defined as, "Penetration, no matter how slight, of the vagina or anus with any body part or object, or oral penetration by a sex organ of another person, without the consent of the victim." The new definition updated the 80-year-old historical definition of rape which was "carnal knowledge of a female forcibly and against her will." Effectively, the revised definition expands rape to include both male and female victims and offenders, and reflects the various forms of sexual penetration understood to be rape, especially non-consenting acts of sodomy, and sexual assaults with objects. **Violent crimes** include four categories of offenses: (1) Murder and non-negligent manslaughter, as defined in the UCR Program, is the willful (non-negligent) killing of one human being by another. This offense excludes deaths caused by negligence, suicide, or accident; justifiable homicides; and attempts to murder or assaults to murder. (2) Rape is the penetration, no matter how slight, of the vagina or anus with any body part or object, or oral penetration by a sex organ of another person, without the consent of the victim. Assaults or attempts to commit rape by force or threat of force are also included; however, statutory rape (without force) and other sex offenses are excluded. (3) Robbery is the taking or attempting to take anything of value from the care, custody, or control of a person or persons by force or threat of force or violence and/or by putting the victim in fear. (4) Aggravated assault is an unlawful attack by one person upon another for the purpose of inflicting severe or aggravated bodily injury. This type of assault is usually accompanied by the use of a weapon or by other means likely to produce death or great bodily harm. Attempts are included, since injury does not necessarily have to result when a gun, knife, or other weapon is used, as these incidents could and probably would result in a serious personal injury if the crime were successfully completed.

Property crimes include three categories: (1) Burglary, or breaking and entering, is the unlawful entry of a structure to commit a felony or theft, even though no force was used to gain entrance. (2) Larceny-theft is the unauthorized taking of the personal property of another, without the use of force. (3) Motor vehicle theft is the unauthorized taking of any motor vehicle.

Rates are based on population estimates provided by the FBI. For some states, reporting is not sufficiently complete to be representative of the state as a whole. The FBI has estimated state totals for those states.

ELEMENTARY AND SECONDARY SCHOOL ENROLLMENT, Items 111 and 112
Source: U.S. Department of Education, National Center for Education Statistics—Common Core of Data
http://nces.ed.gov/ccd/elsi/

Data on public school enrollment is from the Common Core of Data 2013–2014 survey. Public school enrollment includes pre-kindergarten through grade 12 and ungraded students. The student/teacher ratio is calculated by dividing the number of students in all schools by the number of full-time equivalent teachers employed by all schools and agencies.

EDUCATIONAL ATTAINMENT, Items 113–116
Source: U.S. Census Bureau—2010 and 2014 American Community Survey
http://www.census.gov/acs/www/

Data on **educational attainment** are tabulated for the population 25 years old and over. The data were derived from a question that asked respondents for the highest level of school completed or the highest degree received. Persons who had passed a high

school equivalency examination were considered high school graduates. Schooling received in foreign schools was to be reported as the equivalent grade or years in the regular American school system. Vocational and technical training, such as barber school training; business, trade, technical, and vocational schools or other training for a specific trade are specifically excluded.

High school graduate or more. This category includes persons whose highest degree was a high school diploma or its equivalent, and those who reported any level higher than a high school diploma.

Bachelor's degree or more. This category includes persons who have received bachelor's degrees, master's degrees, professional school degrees (such as law school or medical school degrees), and doctoral degrees.

LOCAL GOVERNMENT EDUCATION EXPENDITURES, Items 117 and 118
Source: U.S. Department of Education, National Center for Education Statistics—Common Core of Data
http://nces.ed.gov/ccd/

Total expenditure for education includes provision or support of schools and facilities for elementary and secondary education. It encompasses instructional, support, and auxiliary services (school lunch, student activities, and community service) offered by public school systems. Retirement benefits paid to former education employees and interest payments are not included. Current expenditure includes all components of total expenditure except capital outlay. Expenditure data are obtained by the Census Bureau through its annual survey of government finances and are supplied to the National Center for Education Statistics (NCES). Current expenditure per student is current expenditure divided by the number of students enrolled. The number of students enrolled is based on an annual "membership" count of students on or about October 1.

NCES uses the Common Core of Data (CCD) Survey system to acquire and maintain statistical data from each of the 50 states, the District of Columbia, and the outlying areas. State education agencies compile and submit data for approximately 94,000 schools and 17,000 local school districts. Typically, this results in varying interpretation of NCES definitions and different record keeping systems, leading to large amounts of missing data for several states; this absence is reflected in the data in this publication. The numbers in Table A reflect imputations and adjustments as published in *Revenues and Expenditures for Public Elementary and Secondary Education: School Year 2012–2013 (Fiscal Year 2013)*.

EXPORTS, Items 119–121
Source: U.S. Department of Commerce, International Trade Administration
http://www.census.gov/foreign-trade/statistics/state/originmovement/index.html

The data on exports of goods by state of origin are based on the location of the exporter (the principal party responsible for exportation from the United States). Exporters are often intermedi-ries, so the data do not necessarily represent the states in which the goods were actually produced. The total includes re-exports of foreign goods.

INCOME AND POVERTY, Items 122–133

Source: U.S. Census Bureau—2014 American Community Survey
http://www.census.gov/acs/www/

The data on income were derived from answers to questions which were asked of the population 15 years old and over. **Total income** is the sum of the amounts reported separately for wage or salary income; net self-employment income; interest, dividends, or net rental or royalty income or income from estates and trusts; Social Security or railroad retirement income; Supplemental Security Income (SSI); public assistance or welfare payments; retirement, survivor, or disability pensions; and all other income. Receipts from the following sources are not included as income: capital gains; money received from the sale of property (unless the recipient was engaged in the business of selling such property); the value of income "in kind" from food stamps, public housing subsidies, medical care, employer contributions for individuals, etc.; withdrawal of bank deposits; money borrowed; tax refunds; exchange of money between relatives living in the same household; and gifts and lump-sum inheritances, insurance payments, and other types of lump-sum receipts.

Per capita income is the mean income computed for every man, woman, and child in a particular group. It is derived by dividing the aggregate income of a particular group by the total population in that group. Per capita income is rounded to the nearest whole dollar.

Household income includes the income of the householder and all other individuals 15 years old and over in the household, whether or not they are related to the householder. Since many households consist of only one person, average household income is usually less than average family income. Although the household income statistics cover the past 12 months, the characteristics of individuals and the composition of households refer to the time of enumeration. Thus, the income of the household does not include amounts received by individuals who were members of the household during all or part of the past 12 months if these individuals no longer resided in the household at the time of interview. Similarly, income amounts reported by individuals who did not reside in the household during the past 12 months but who were members of the household at the time of interview are included. However, the composition of most households was the same during the past 12 months as at the time of interview.

Median income divides the income distribution into two equal parts, with half of all cases below the median income level and half of all cases above the median income level. For households and families, the median income is based on the distribution of the total number of households and families, including those with no income. Median income for households is computed on the basis of a standard distribution with a minimum value of less than $2,500 and a maximum value of $200,000 or more and is rounded to the nearest whole dollar.

For **family income**, the incomes of all household members 15 years old and over related to the householder are summed and treated as a single amount. Although the family income statistics cover the past 12 months, the characteristics of individuals and the composition of families refer to the time of interview. Thus, the income of the family does not include amounts received by individuals who were members of the family during all of part of the past 12 months if these individuals no longer resided with the family at the time of interview. Similarly, income amounts reported by individuals who did not reside with the family during the past 12 months but who were members of the family at the time of interview are included. However, the composition of most families was the same during the past 12 months as at the time of interview.

The **poverty status** data were derived from data collected on the number of persons in the household, each person's relationship to the householder, and the income data. The Social Security Administration (SSA) developed the original poverty definition in 1964, which federal interagency committees subsequently revised in 1969 and 1980. The Office of Management and Budget's (OMB) *Directive 14* prescribes the SSA's definition as the official poverty measure for federal agencies to use in their statistical work. Poverty statistics presented in American Community Survey products adhere to the standards defined by OMB in *Directive 14*.

The poverty thresholds vary depending on three criteria: size of family, number of children, and, for one- and two-person families, age of householder. In determining the poverty status of families and unrelated individuals, the Census Bureau uses thresholds (income cutoffs) arranged in a two-dimensional matrix. The matrix consists of family size (from one person to nine or more persons), cross-classified by presence and number of family members under 18 years old (from no children present to eight or more children present). Unrelated individuals and two-person families are further differentiated by age of reference person (under 65 years old and 65 years old and over). To determine a person's poverty status, the person's total family income in the last 12 months is compared to the poverty threshold appropriate for that person's family size and composition. If the total income of that person's family is less than the threshold appropriate for that family, then the person is considered poor or "below the poverty level," together with every member of his or her family. If a person is not living with anyone related by birth, marriage, or adoption, then the person's own income is compared with his or her poverty threshold. The total number of persons below the poverty level is the sum of persons in families and the number of unrelated individuals with incomes below the poverty level in the last 12 months. The average poverty threshold for a four-person family was $24,230 in 2014.

Poverty Thresholds for 2014 by Size of Family and Number of Related Children Under 18 Years

Size of family unit	Weighted average thresholds
One person (unrelated individual)	12,071
Under 65 years	12,316
65 years and over	11,354
Two people	15,379
Householder under 65 years	15,934
Householder 65 years and over	14,326
Three people.................................	18,850
Four people.................................	24,230
Five people.................................	28,695
Six people.................................	32,473
Seven people.................................	36,927
Eight people.................................	40,968
Nine people or more.................................	49,021

Source: U.S. Census Bureau.

The data on **poverty status of households** were derived from answers to the income questions. Since poverty is defined at the family level and not the household level, the poverty status of the household is determined by the poverty status of the householder. Households are classified as poor when the total income of the householder's family in the previous 12 months is below the appropriate poverty threshold. (For nonfamily householders, the person's income is compared with the appropriate threshold.) The income of persons living in the household who are unrelated to the householder is not considered when determining the poverty status of a household, nor does their presence affect the family size in determining the appropriate threshold. The poverty thresholds vary depending upon three criteria: size of family, number of children, and, for one- and two-person families, age of the householder.

Poverty status of children by **family type** is the percentage of children living in that particular type of family that has a family income below the poverty threshold based on family size and composition.

PERSONAL INCOME AND EARNINGS, Items 134–158

Source: U.S. Bureau of Economic Analysis, Regional Economic Accounts
http://www.bea.gov/regional/index.htm#state

Total personal income is the current income received by residents of an area from all sources. It is measured before deductions of income and other personal taxes but after deductions of personal contributions for Social Security, government retirement, and other social insurance programs. It consists of **wage and salary disbursements** (covering all employee earnings, including executive salaries, bonuses, commissions, payments-in-kind, incentive payments, and tips); various types of supplementary earnings, such as employers' contributions to pension funds (termed "other labor income" or "supplements to wages and salaries"); proprietors' income; rental income of persons; dividends; personal interest income; and government and business transfer payments.

Proprietors' income is the monetary income and income-in-kind of proprietorships and partnerships (including the independent professions), and the income of tax-exempt cooperatives. **Dividends** are cash payments by corporations to stockholder who are U.S. residents. **Interest** is the monetary and imputed interest income of persons from all sources. **Rent** is the monetary income of persons from the rental of real property, except the income of persons primarily engaged in the real estate business, the imputed net rental income of owner-occupants of nonfarm dwellings; and the royalties received by persons.

Transfer payments are income for which services are not currently rendered. They consist of both government and business transfer payments. Government transfer payments include payments under the following programs: Federal Old-Age, Survivors, and Disability Insurance ("Social Security"); Medicare and medical vendor payments; unemployment insurance; railroad and government retirement; federal- and state-government-insured workers' compensation; veterans' benefits, including veterans' life insurance; food stamps; black lung payments; Supplemental Security Income; and Temporary Assistance for Needy Families. Government payments to nonprofit institutions, other than for work under research and development contracts, are also included. Business transfer payments consist primarily of liability payments for personal injury and of corporate gifts to nonprofit institutions.

Per capita personal income is based on resident population estimated as of July 1 of the year shown.

Personal tax payments include taxes paid by individuals to federal, state, and local governments. Personal taxes include individual income taxes, estate and gift taxes, motor vehicle license taxes, and personal property taxes. Personal contributions to social insurance ("Social Security taxes") are not included, nor are sales taxes.

Disposable personal income equals personal income less personal tax payments. It is a measure of the income available to persons for spending or saving.

Earnings cover wage and salary disbursements, other labor income, and proprietors' income.

The data for earnings obtained from the Bureau of Economic Analysis (BEA) are based on place of work. In computing personal income, BEA makes an "adjustment for residence" to earnings based on commuting patterns; thus, personal income is presented on a place-of-residence basis.

Farm earnings include the income of farm workers (wages and salaries and other labor income) and farm proprietors. Farm proprietors' income includes only the income of sole proprietorships and partnerships.

Farm earnings estimates are benchmarked to data collected in the Census of Agriculture and the revised Department of Agriculture state totals of income and expense items.

Goods-related industries include mining, construction, and manufacturing. **Service-related** and other industries includes private-sector earnings in forestry, related activities, and other; utilities; transportation and warehousing; information; wholesale trade; retail trade; finance and insurance; real estate and rental and leasing; and services, which includes professional, scientific, and technical services; management of companies and enterprises; administrative and waste services; educational services; health care and social assistance; arts, entertainment, and recreation; accommodation and food services; and other services, except public administration. Government earnings include all levels of government. Industries are categorized under the North American Industry Classification System (NAICS), and are not directly comparable to years prior to 2002.

GROSS STATE PRODUCT, Item 159
Source: U.S. Bureau of Economic Analysis, Regional Economic Accounts
http://www.bea.gov/regional/index.htm#state

Gross state product (GSP) for a state is derived as the sum of gross state product originating in all industries in the state. In concept, an industry's GSP, referred to as its "value added," is equivalent to its gross output (sales or receipts and other operating income, commodity taxes, and inventory changes) minus its intermediate inputs (consumption of goods and services purchased from other industries or imported from other countries). As such, it is often referred to as the state counterpart to the nation's gross domestic product (GDP). In practice, GSP estimates are measured as the sum of distributions by industry of the components of gross domestic income—that is, the sum of the costs incurred (such as compensation of employees, net interest, and indirect business taxes) and the profits earned in production.

SOCIAL SECURITY AND SUPPLEMENTAL SECURITY INCOME, Items 160–162
Source: U.S. Social Security Administration
http://www.ssa.gov/policy/docs/statcomps/oasdisc/
http://www.ssa.gov/policy/docs/statcomps/ssisc/

Social Security beneficiaries are persons receiving benefits under the Old-Age, Survivors, and Disability Insurance Program. These include retired or disabled workers covered by the program, their spouses and dependent children, and the surviving spouses and dependent children of deceased workers.

Supplemental Security Income (SSI) recipients are persons receiving SSI payments. The SSI program is a cash assistance program that provides monthly benefits to low-income aged, blind, or disabled persons.

Data are as of December of the year shown.

CIVILIAN EMPLOYMENT, Items 163–166
Source: U.S. Census Bureau—2014 American Community Survey
http://www.census.gov/acs/www/
http://www2.census.gov/programs-surveys/acs/techdocs/codelists/2014ACSCodeLists.pdf

The data on occupation were derived from answers to questions that were asked of all persons 15 years old and over who had worked in the past 5 years. **Occupation** describes the kind of work the person does on the job. For employed persons, the data refer to the person's job during the previous week. For those who worked two or more jobs, the data refer to the job at which the person worked the greatest number of hours. For unemployed persons, the data refer to their last job. The American Community Survey uses the occupational classification system that was developed for the 2000 census and modified in 2002 and again in 2010. This system consists of 539 specific occupational categories for employed persons arranged into 23 major occupational groups. This classification was developed based on the *Standard Occupational Classification (SOC) Manual: 2010*, published by the Executive Office of the President, Office of Management and Budget.

CIVILIAN LABOR FORCE AND UNEMPLOYMENT, Items 167–171
Source: U.S. Bureau of Labor Statistics—Local Areas Unemployment Statistics
http://www.bls.gov/lau/#tables

Data for the civilian labor force are the product of a federal-state cooperative program in which state employment security agencies prepare labor force and unemployment estimates under concepts, definitions, and technical procedures established by the Bureau of Labor Statistics (BLS). The **civilian labor force** consists of all civilians 16 years old and over who are either employed or unemployed.

Unemployment includes all persons who did not work during the survey week, made specific efforts to find a job during the prior four weeks, and were available for work during the survey week (except for temporary illness). Persons waiting to be called back to a job from which they had been laid off and those waiting to report to a new job within the next 30 days are included in unemployment figures.

PRIVATE NONFARM EMPLOYMENT AND EARNINGS, Items 172–183
Source: U.S. Bureau of Labor Statistics—Current Employment Survey
http://www.bls.gov/ces/#tables

Data for private nonfarm employment and earnings are compiled from payroll information reported monthly on a voluntary basis to the BLS and its cooperating state agencies. More than 350,000 establishments represent all industries except agriculture.

Employment is the annual average of monthly totals of persons who received pay for any part of the pay period including the 12th day of the month. Included are all full-time and part-time workers in nonfarm establishments. Not covered are government employees, proprietors, the self-employed, unpaid volunteers or family workers, farm workers, and domestic workers in households. The data by industry conform to the definitions established in the North American Industry Classification System (NAICS).

Earnings of **production workers** in **manufacturing** industries are derived from reports of gross payrolls and corresponding paid hours. Payroll is reported before deductions of any kinds. Total hours during the pay period include all hours worked (including overtime hours) and hours paid for holidays, vacations, and sick leave.

AGRICULTURE, ITEMS 184–202

Source: U.S. Department of Agriculture, National Agricultural Statistics Service—2012 Census of Agriculture

https://agcensus.usda.gov/Publications/2012/

The Census Bureau took a census of agriculture every 10 years from 1840 to 1920; since 1925, this census has been taken roughly once every 5 years. The 1997 Census of Agriculture was the first one conducted by the National Agricultural Statistics Service of the U.S. Department of Agriculture. Over time, the definition of a farm has varied. For recent censuses (including the 2012 census), a farm has been defined as any place from which $1,000 or more of agricultural products were produced and sold or normally would have been sold during the census year. Dollar figures are expressed in current dollars and have not been adjusted for inflation or deflation.

The term **operator** refers to a person who operates a farm by either doing the work or making day-to-day decisions about such activities as planting, harvesting, feeding, marketing, etc. The operator may be the owner, a member of the owner's household, a salaried manager, a tenant, a renter, or a sharecropper. If a person rents land to others or has land worked on shares by others, he/she is considered the operator only of the land that is retained for his/her own operation. The census collected information on the total number of operators, the total number of women operators, and demographic information for up to three operators per farm.

Government payments consists of direct payments as defined by the 2002 Farm Bill; payments from Conservation Reserve Program (CRP), Wetlands reserve Program (WRP), Farmable Wetlands Program (FWP), and Conservation Reserve Enhancement Program (CREP); loan deficiency payments; disaster payments; other conservation programs; and all other federal farm programs under which payments were made directly to farm operators. Commodity Credit Corporation (CCC) proceeds, amount from state and local federal crop insurance payments were not included in this category.

The acreage designated as **land in farms** consists primarily of agricultural land used for crops, pasture, or grazing. It also includes woodland and wasteland not actually under cultivation or used for pasture or grazing, provided that this land was part of the farm operator's total operation.

Land in farms is an operating-unit concept and includes all land owned and operated, as well as all land rented from others. Land used rent-free is classified as land rented from others. All land in Indian reservations used for growing crops or grazing livestock is classified as land in farms.

Irrigated land includes all land watered by any artificial or controlled means, such as sprinklers, flooding, furrows or ditches, sub-irrigation, and spreader dikes. Included are supplemental, partial, and preplant irrigation. Each acre was counted only once regardless of the number of times it was irrigated or harvested. Livestock lagoon waste water distributed by sprinkler or flood systems was also included.

Total cropland includes cropland harvested, cropland used only for pasture or grazing, cropland on which all crops failed or were abandoned, cropland in cultivated summer fallow, and cropland idle or used for cover crops or soil improvement but not harvested and not pastured or grazed.

Respondents were asked to report their estimate of the current market **value of land and buildings** owned, rented, or leased from others and rented and leased to others. Market value refers to the respondent's estimate of what the land and buildings would sell for under current market conditions.

The **value of machinery and equipment** was estimated by the respondent as the current market value of all cars, trucks, tractors, combines, balers, irrigation equipment, etc., used on the farm. This value is an estimate of what the machinery and equipment would sell for in its present condition and not the replacement of depreciated value. Share interests are reported at full value at the farm where the equipment and machinery are usually kept. Only equipment that was physically located at the farm on December 31, 2012, is included.

Market **value of agricultural products sold** by farms represents the gross market value before taxes and the production expenses of all agricultural products sold or removed from the place in 2012, regardless of who received the payment. It is equivalent to total sales and it includes sales by the operator as well as the value of any share received by partners, landlords, contractors, and others associated with the operation. It includes value of direct sales and the value of commodities placed in the Commodity Credit Corporation (CCC) loan program. Market value of agricultural products sold does not include payments received for participation in other federal farm programs. Also, it does not include income from farm-related sources such as customwork and other agricultural services, or income from non-farm sources.

LAND USE, ITEMS 203 to 205

Source: U.S. Department of Agriculture, Natural Resources Conservation Service—2012 National Resources Inventory

http://www.nrcs.usda.gov/technical/NRI/

The National Resources Inventory (NRI) has been conducted every five years since 1982. It provides updated information on the status, condition, and trends of land, soil, water, and related resources on the Nation's non-federal lands. Non-federal lands include privately owned lands, tribal and trust lands, and land controlled by State and local governments.

The 2012 NRI is based on a sample of about 800,000 locations throughout the United States (excluding Alaska and the District of Columbia). Acreages for federal land and total surface area are established through geospatial processes and administrative records. Total surface area of the contiguous United States is 1,937.7 million acres.

Cropland includes areas used for the production of adapted crops for harvest. Cultivated cropland comprises land in row crops or close-grown crops and also other cultivated cropland, such as hayland or pastureland that is in a rotation with row or close-grown crops. Noncultivated cropland includes permanent hayland and horticultural cropland.

Federally-owned lands include military bases, national forests, wildlife refuges, parks, grassland game preserves, scenic waterways, wilderness areas, monuments, lakeshore, parkways battlefields, Bureau of Land Management lands, and other federal lands.

Developed land includes any built-up area greater than one fourth of an acre. Built-up areas include residential, industrial, commercial, and institutional land; construction sites; public administrative sites; railroad yards; cemeteries; airports; golf courses; sanitary landfills; sewage treatment plants; water control structures and spillways; other land used for such purpose; small parks (fewer than 10 acres of land) within urban and built-up areas; and highways, railroads, and other transportation facilities that are surrounded by urban areas. Also included are tracts of fewer than 10 acres that do not meet the above definition but are completely surrounded by urban and built-up land, as well as all highways, roads, railroads, and associated rights-of-way outside of urban and built-up areas (including private roads to farmsteads or ranch headquarters, logging roads, and other private roads).

WATER CONSUMPTION, Item 206
Source: U.S. Geological Survey, National Water Use Information Program—2010 Water Use Data
http://water.usgs.gov/watuse/

Every five years, the U.S. Geological Survey compiles national water-use estimates. This volume includes the total fresh and saline water withdrawals expressed as million gallons per day. Estimate of withdrawals of ground and surface water are given for the following categories of use: public water supplies, domestic, commercial, irrigation, livestock, industrial, mining, and thermo-electric power.

MANUFACTURES, Items 207–216
Source: U.S. Census Bureau—2014 Annual Survey of Manufactures
http://www.census.gov/manufacturing/asm/

The Annual Survey of Manufactures (ASM) has been conducted annually every year since 1949, except for years ending in ''2'' and ''7,'' at which time ASM data are included in the manufacturing sector of the Economic Census. The ASM provides statistics on employment, payroll, worker hours, payroll supplements, cost of materials, value added by manufacturing, capital expenditures, inventories, and energy consumption. It also provides estimates of value of shipments for over 1,400 classes of manufactured products. The Annual Survey of Manufactures includes approximately 50,000 establishments selected from the census universe of 350,000 manufacturing establishments.

The **all employees** number is the average number of production workers for the payroll periods including the 12th of March, May, August, and November plus the number of other employees in mid-March. Included are all persons on paid sick leave, paid holidays, and paid vacations during the pay period. Officers of corporations are included as employees, while proprietors and partners of unincorporated firms are excluded.

Payroll figures include the gross annual earnings of all employees on the payroll of operating manufacturing establishments. The definition, which is the same as the one used for calculating the federal withholding tax, includes all forms of compensation, such as salaries, wages, commissions, dismissal pay, bonuses, vacation and sick leave pay, and compensation-in-kind, prior to such deductions as employees' Social Security contributions, withholding taxes, group insurance, union dues, and savings bonds. The total includes salaries of officers of corporations; it excludes payments to proprietors or partners of unincorporated concerns. Also excluded are payments to members of armed forces and to pensioners carried on the active payrolls of manufacturing establishments.

Production workers include workers (up through the line-supervisor level) engaged in fabricating, processing, assembling, inspecting, receiving, storing, handling, packing, warehousing, shipping (but not delivering), maintenance, repair, janitorial and guard services, product development, auxiliary production for the plant's own use (for example, power plant), record keeping, and other services closely associated with these production operations at the establishment covered by the report. Employees above the working-supervisor level are excluded.

The number of production workers is the average for the payroll periods including the 12th of March, May, August, and November. Not included in this classification are all other employees, defined as non-production employees, including those engaged in factory supervision above the line-supervisor level.

Production worker hours cover hours worked or paid for at the manufacturing plant, including actual overtime hours (not straight-time equivalent hours). The data exclude hours paid for vacations, holidays, or sick leave when the employee is not at the establishment. Production wages represent all compensation paid to production workers.

Value added by manufacture is derived by subtracting the cost of materials, supplies, containers, fuel, purchased electricity, and contract work from the value of shipments (products manufactured plus receipts for services rendered). The result of this calculation is adjusted by the addition of value added by merchandising operations (the difference between the sales value and the cost of merchandise sold without further manufacture, processing, or assembly) plus the net change in finished goods and work-in-process between the beginning- and end-of-year inventories.

Value of shipments covers the received or receivable net selling values; free on board plant (excluding of freight and taxes), of all products shipped, both primary and secondary; and all miscellaneous receipts, such as receipts for contract work performed for others, installation and repair, sales of scrap, and sales of products bought and sold without further processing. Included are all items made by or for the establishments from material owned by it, whether sold, transferred to other plants of the same company, or shipped on consignment. The net selling value of products made in one plant on a contract basis from materials owned by another was reported by the plant providing the materials.

In the case of multi-unit companies, the manufacturer was asked to report the value of products transferred to other establishments of the same company at full economic or commercial value, including both the direct cost of production and a reasonable proportion of ''all other costs'' (including company overhead) and profit (interplant transfers).

The aggregate of the value of shipments figure for industry groups and for all manufacturing industries includes large amounts of duplications, as the products of some industries are used as materials by others. Estimates as to the overall extent of this duplication indicate that the value of manufactured products exclusive of such duplication (the value of finished manufactures) tends to approximate two-thirds of the total value of products reported in the census of manufactures.

Total cost of materials refers to direct charges actually paid or payable for items consumed or put into production during the year, including freight charges and other direct charges incurred by the establishment in acquiring these materials. It includes the cost of materials or fuel consumed, whether purchased by the individual establishment from other companies, transferred to it from other establishments of the same company, or withdrawn from inventory during the year. Included in this item are cost of parts, components, containers, etc.; cost of products bought and sold in the same condition; cost of fuels consumed for heat and power; cost of purchased electricity; and cost of contract work. Aggregate of total cost of materials and total value of shipments includes extensive duplication, since products of some industries are used as materials of others.

2012 ECONOMIC CENSUS: OVERVIEW, Items 217–308
Source: U.S. Census Bureau
http://www.census.gov/econ/census/about/

The Economic Census provides a detailed portrait of the nation's economy, from the national to the local level, once every five years. The 2012 Economic Census covers nearly all of the U.S. economy in its basic collection of establishment statistics. The 1997 Economic Census was the first major data source to use the North American Industry Classification System (NAICS); therefore, data are not comparable to economic data from prior years, which were based on the Standard Industrial Classification (SIC) system.

NAICS, developed in cooperation with Canada and Mexico, classifies North America's economic activities at two-, three-, four-, and five-digit levels of detail; the U.S. version of NAICS further defines industries to a sixth digit. The Economic Census takes advantage of this hierarchy to publish data at these successive levels of detail: sector (two-digit); subsector (three-digit); industry group (four-digit); industry (five-digit); and U.S. industry (six-digit). Information in Table A is at the two-digit level, with a few three- and four-digit items.

Several key statistics are tabulated for all industries included in this volume: number of establishments (or companies); number of employees; payroll; and a measure of output (sales, receipts, revenue, value of shipments, or value of construction work done).

Number of establishments. An establishment is a single physical location at which business is conducted. It is not necessarily identical with a company or enterprise, which may consist of one establishment or more. Economic Census figures represent a summary of reports for individual establishments rather than companies. For cases in which a census report was received, separate information was obtained for each location where business was conducted. When administrative records of other federal agencies were used instead of a census report, no information was available on the number of locations operated. Each Economic Census establishment was tabulated according to the physical location at which the business was conducted. The count of

establishments represents those in business at any time during 2012.

When two activities or more were carried on at a single location under a single ownership, all activities were generally grouped together as a single establishment. The entire establishment was classified on the basis of its major activity and all of its data were included in that classification. However, when distinct and separate economic activities (for which different industry classification codes were appropriate) were conducted at a single location under a single ownership, separate establishment reports for each of the different activities were obtained in the census.

Number of employees. Paid employees consist of the full time and part-time employees, including salaried officers and executives of corporations. Included are employees on paid sick leave, paid holidays, and paid vacations; not included are proprietors and partners of unincorporated businesses. The definition of paid employees is the same as that used by the Internal Revenue Service (IRS) on form 941.

For some industries, the Economic Census gives codes representing the number of employees as a range of numbers (for example, ''100 to 249 employees'' or ''1,000 to 2,499'' employees). In this volume, those codes have been replaced by the standard suppression code ''D''.

Payroll. Payroll includes all forms of compensation, such as salaries, wages, commissions, dismissal pay, bonuses, vacation allowances, sick-leave pay, and employee contributions to qualified pension plans paid during the year to all employees. For corporations, payroll includes amounts paid to officers and executives; for unincorporated businesses, it does not include profit or other compensation of proprietors or partners. Payroll is reported before deductions for Social Security, income tax, insurance, union dues, etc. This definition of payroll is the same as that used on IRS form 941.

Sales, shipments, receipts, revenue, or business done. This measure includes the total sales, shipments, receipts, revenue, or business done by establishments within the scope of the Economic Census. The definition of each of these items is specific to the economic sector measured.

CONSTRUCTION, Items 217–221
Source: U.S. Census Bureau—2012 Economic Census
(See Overview of 2012 Economic Census prior to Item 217)

The Construction sector (sector 23) comprises establishments primarily engaged in the construction of buildings and other structures, heavy construction (except buildings), additions, alterations, reconstruction, installation, and maintenance and repairs. Establishments engaged in the demolition or wrecking of buildings and other structures, the clearing of building sites, and the sale of materials from demolished structures are also included. This sector also contains those establishments engaged in blasting, test drilling, landfill, leveling, earthmoving, excavating, land drainage, and other land preparation. The industries within the sector have been defined on the basis of their unique production processes. As with all industries, the production processes are distinguished by their use of specialized human resources and specialized physical capital. Construction activities are generally administered or managed at a relatively fixed place of business out the actual construction work can be performed at one or more different project sites. This sector is divided into three subsectors of construction activities: (1) building construction and land subdivision and land development; (2) heavy construction (except buildings), such as highways, power plants, and pipelines; and (3) construction activity by special trade contractors.

WHOLESALE TRADE, Items 222–226

Source: U.S. Census Bureau—2012 Economic Census (See Overview of 2012 Economic Census prior to Item 217)

The Wholesale Trade sector (sector 42) comprises establishments engaged in wholesaling merchandise, generally without transformation, and rendering services incidental to the sale of merchandise. The wholesaling process is an intermediate step in the distribution of merchandise. Wholesalers are organized to sell or arrange the purchase or sale of (1) goods for resale (i.e., goods sold to other wholesalers or retailers), (2) capital or durable nonconsumer goods, and (3) raw and intermediate materials and supplies used in production.

Wholesalers sell merchandise to other businesses and normally operate from a warehouse or office. These warehouses and offices are characterized by having little or no display of merchandise. In addition, neither the design nor the location of the premises is intended to solicit walk-in traffic. Wholesalers do not normally use advertising directed to the general public. Customers are generally first reached via telephone, in-person marketing, or by specialized advertising that may include internet and other electronic means. Follow-up orders are either vendor-initiated or client-initiated, are usually based on previous sales, and typically exhibit strong ties between sellers and buyers. In fact, transactions are often conducted between wholesalers and clients that have long-standing business relationships.

This sector is made up of two main types of wholesalers: those that sell goods on their own account and those that arrange sales and purchases for others for a commission or fee.

(1) Establishments that sell goods on their own account are known as wholesale merchants, distributors, jobbers, drop shippers, import/export merchants, and sales branches. These establishments typically maintain their own warehouse, where they receive and handle goods for their customers. Goods are generally sold without transformation, but may include integral functions, such as sorting, packaging, labeling, and other marketing services.

(2) Establishments arranging for the purchase or sale of goods owned by others or purchasing goods on a commission basis are known as agents and brokers, commission merchants, import/export agents and brokers, auction companies, and manufacturers' representatives. These establishments operate from offices and generally do not own or handle the goods they sell.

Some wholesale establishments may be connected with a single manufacturer and/or promote and sell that particular manufacturer's products to a wide range of other wholesalers or retailers. Other wholesalers may be connected to a retail chain or a limited number of retail chains and only provide a variety of products needed by that particular retail operation(s). These wholesalers may obtain the products from a wide range of manufacturers. Still other wholesalers may not take title to the goods but act as agents and brokers for a commission.

Although, in general, wholesaling normally denotes sales in large volumes, durable nonconsumer goods may be sold in single units. Sales of capital or durable nonconsumer goods used in the production of goods and services, such as farm machinery, medium- and heavy-duty trucks, and industrial machinery, are always included in Wholesale Trade.

RETAIL TRADE, Items 227–235

Source: U.S. Census Bureau—2012 Economic Census (See Overview of 2012 Economic Census prior to Item 217)

The Retail Trade sector (44–45) is made up of establishments engaged in retailing merchandise, generally without transformation, and rendering services incidental to the sale of merchandise.

The retailing process is the final step in the distribution of merchandise; retailers are, therefore, organized to sell merchandise in small quantities to the general public. This sector comprises two main types of retailers: store and nonstore retailers.

Store retailers operate fixed point-of-sale locations, located and designed to attract a high volume of walk-in customers. In general, retail stores have extensive displays of merchandise and use mass-media advertising to attract customers. They typically sell merchandise to the general public for personal or household consumption; some also serve business and institutional clients. These include establishments, such as office supply stores, computer and software stores, building materials dealers, plumbing supply stores, and electrical supply stores. Catalog showrooms, gasoline service stations, automotive dealers, and mobile home dealers are treated as store retailers.

In addition to retailing merchandise, some types of store retailers are also engaged in the provision of after-sales services, such as repair and installation. For example, new automobile dealers, electronic and appliance stores, and musical instrument and supply stores often provide repair services. As a general rule, establishments engaged in retailing merchandise and providing after-sales services are classified in this sector.

Nonstore retailers, like store retailers, are organized to serve the general public, although their retailing methods differ. The establishments of this subsector reach customers and market merchandise with methods, such as the broadcasting of ''infomercials,'' the broadcasting and publishing of direct-response advertising, the publishing of paper and electronic catalogs, door-to-door solicitation, in-home demonstration, selling from portable stalls (street vendors, except food), and distribution through vending machines. Establishments engaged in the direct sale (nonstore) of products, such as home heating oil dealers and home-delivery newspaper routes are included in this sector.

The buying of goods for resale is a characteristic of retail trade establishments that distinguishes them from establishments in the Agriculture, Manufacturing, and Construction sectors. For example, farms that sell their products at or from the point of production are classified in Agriculture instead of in Retail Trade. Similarly, establishments that both manufacture and sell their products to the general public are classified in Manufacturing instead of Retail Trade. However, establishments that engage in processing activities incidental to retailing are classified in retail.

Industries in the **Motor Vehicle and Parts Dealers** subsector (441) retail motor vehicle and parts merchandise from fixed point-of-sale locations. Establishments in this subsector typically operate from a showroom and/or an open lot where the vehicles are on display. The display of vehicles and the related parts require little by way of display equipment. Personnel generally include both sales and sales support staff familiar with the requirements for registering and financing a vehicle as well as a staff of parts experts and mechanics trained to provide vehicle repair and maintenance services. Specific industries have been included in this subsector to identify the type of vehicle being retailed. Sales of capital or durable nonconsumer goods, such as medium and heavy-duty trucks, are always included in the Wholesale Trade sector. These goods are virtually never sold through retail methods.

Industries in the **Food and Beverage Stores** subsector (445) usually retail food and beverage merchandise from fixed point-of-sale locations. Establishments in this subsector have special equipment (e.g., freezers, refrigerated display cases, and refrigerators) for displaying food and beverage goods. They have staff trained in the processing of food products to guarantee the proper storage and sanitary conditions, as mandated by regulatory authority.

Industries in the **Clothing and Clothing Accessories Stores** subsector (448) retail new clothing and clothing accessories merchandise from fixed point-of-sale locations. Establishments in this subsector have similar types of display equipment, as well as employees who are knowledgeable regarding fashion trends and who can match styles, colors, and combinations of clothing and accessories to the characteristics and tastes of the customer.

Industries in the **General Merchandise Stores** subsector (452) retail new general merchandise from fixed point-of-sale locations. Establishments in this subsector are unique in that they have the equipment and staff capable of retailing a large variety of goods from a single location. This includes a variety of display equipment and staff trained to provide information on many lines of products.

INFORMATION, Items 236–246
Source: U.S. Census Bureau—2012 Economic Census (See Overview of 2012 Economic Census prior to Item 217)

The Information sector (51) comprises establishments engaged in the following processes: (1) producing and distributing information and cultural products, (2) providing the means to transmit or distribute these products as well as data or communications, and (3) processing data.

The main components of this sector are the publishing industries, including software publishing; the motion picture and sound recording industries; the broadcasting and telecommunications industries; and the information services and data processing industries.

For the purpose of NAICS, the transformation of information into a commodity that is produced and distributed by a number of growing industries is at issue. The Information sector groups three types of establishments: (1) those engaged in producing and distributing information and cultural products; (2) those that provide the means to transmit or distribute these products as

well as data or communications; and (3) those that process data. Cultural products are those that directly express attitudes, opinions, ideas, values, and artistic creativity; provide entertainment; or offer information and analysis concerning the past and present. Included in this definition are popular, mass-produced products, as well as cultural products that normally have a more limited audience, such as poetry books, literary magazines, or classical records. These activities were formerly classified throughout the existing national classifications. Traditional publishing was in manufacturing; broadcasting in communications; software production in business services; film production in amusement services; and so forth.

Industries in the **Publishing Industries, Except Internet** subsector (511) include establishments engaged in the publishing of newspapers, magazines, other periodicals, and books, as well as database and software publishing. In general, these establishments, which are known as publishers, issue copies of works for which they usually possess copyright. Works may be in one or more formats, including traditional print format, CD-ROM format, or proprietary electronic networks. Publishers may publish works originally created by others for which they have obtained the rights and/or works that they have created in-house. Software publishing is included here because the activity (creation of a copyrighted product and bringing it to market) is equivalent to the creation process for other types of intellectual products.

In NAICS, publishing—the reporting, writing, editing, and other processes that are required to create an edition of a book or a newspaper—is treated as a major economic activity in its own right, rather than as a subsidiary activity to printing, which is a manufacturing activity. Thus, publishing is classified in the Information sector, while printing remains in the NAICS Manufacturing sector. In part, the NAICS classification reflects the fact that publishing increasingly takes place in establishments that are physically separate from the associated printing establishments. More crucially, the NAICS classification of book and newspaper publishing is intended to portray their roles in a modern economy—roles that do not resemble manufacturing activities.

Music publishers are not included in the Publishing Industries subsector, but can be found in the Motion Picture and Sound Recording Industries subsector. Reproduction of prepackaged software is treated in NAICS as a manufacturing activity; online distribution of software products is in the Information sector, and custom design of software to client specifications is included in the Professional, Scientific, and Technical Services sector. These distinctions arise because of the different ways that software is created, reproduced, and distributed.

The Information sector does not include products, such as manifold business forms. Information is not the essential component of these items. Establishments producing these items are included in subsector 323, Printing and Related Support Activities.

Industries in the **Motion Picture and Sound Recording Industries** subsector (512) group establishments involved in the production and distribution of motion pictures and sound recordings. While producers and distributors of motion pictures and sound recordings issue works for sale as traditional publishers do, the processes are different enough to warrant placing the establishments engaged in these activities in separate subsectors. Production is typically a complex process that involves several distinct types of establishments engaged in activities, such as contracting with performers, creating the film or sound content, and providing technical postproduction services. Film distribution is often to exhibitors, such as theaters and broadcasters, rather than to a wholesale or retail distribution chain. When the product is in a mass-produced form, NAICS treats production and distribution as the major economic activity, rather than as a subsidiary activity to the manufacture of such products.

This subsector does not include establishments primarily engaged in the wholesale distribution of video cassettes and sound recordings, such as compact discs and audio tapes; these establishments are included in the Wholesale Trade sector. Reproduction of video cassettes and sound recordings that is carried out separately from establishments engaged in production and distribution is treated in NAICS as a manufacturing activity.

Industries in the **Broadcasting, except Internet** subsector (515) include establishments that create content or acquire the right to distribute and subsequently broadcast content. The industry groups (Radio and Television Broadcasting and Cable and Other Subscription Programming) are based on differences in the methods of communication and the nature of services provided. The Radio and Television Broadcasting industry group includes establishments that operate broadcasting studios and facilities for over-the-air or satellite delivery of radio and television programs, including entertainment, news, and talk programs. These establishments are often engaged in production and purchase of programs and generating revenues from the sale of air time to advertisers, as well as from donations, subsidies, and/or the sale of programs. The Cable and Other Subscription Programming industry group includes establishments that operate studios and facilities for the broadcasting of limited-format programs (such as news, sports, educational, and youth-oriented programs) that are typically narrowly-focused in nature; these programs are usually available on a subscription or fee basis. The distribution of cable and other subscription programming is included in subsector 517, Telecommunications.

Industries in the **Internet Publishing and Broadcasting and Web search portals** subsector (51913) consist of establishments primarily engaged in 1) publishing and/or broadcasting content on the Internet exclusively or 2) operating Web sites that use a search engine to generate and maintain extensive databases of Internet addresses and content in an easily searchable format (and known as Web search portals). The publishing and broadcasting establishments in this industry do not provide traditional (non-Internet) versions of the content that they publish or broadcast. They provide textual, audio, and/or video content of general or specific interest on the Internet exclusively. Establishments known as Web search portals often provide additional Internet services, such as e-mail, connections to other web sites, auctions, news, and other limited content, and serve as a home base for Internet users.

Establishments that are *not* in this group include those primarily engaged in—

Providing wired broadband Internet access using own operated telecommunications infrastructure—these are classified in Wired Telecommunications Carriers;

Providing both Internet publishing and other print or electronic (e.g., CD-ROM, diskette) editions in the same establishment or using proprietary networks to distribute content—these are classified in Publishing Industries (except Internet) based on the materials produced;

- Providing Internet access via client-supplied telecommunications connections—these are classified in All Other Telecommunications;
- Providing streaming services on content owned by others—these are classified in Data Processing, Hosting, and Related Services;
- Wholesaling goods on the Internet—these are classified in Wholesale Trade;
- Retailing goods on the Internet—these are classified in Retail Trade;
- Operating stock brokerages, travel reservation systems, purchasing services, and similar activities using the Internet rather than traditional methods—these are classified with the more traditioal establishments providing these services.

Industries in the **Telecommunications** subsector (517) include establishments that provide telecommunications and services related to that activity (e.g., telephony, including Voice over Internet Protocol (VoIP); cable and satellite television distribution services; Internet access; telecommunications reselling services). The Telecommunications subsector is primarily engaged in operating, maintaining, and/or providing access to facilities for the transmission of voice, data, text, sound, and video. A transmission facility may be based on a single technology or a combination of technologies. Establishments primarily engaged as independent contractors in the maintenance and installation of broadcasting and telecommunications systems are classified in sector 23, Construction.

Industries in the **Data processing, hosting, and related services** subsector (518) are establishments primarily engaged in providing infrastructure for hosting or data processing services. These establishments may provide specialized hosting activities, such as web hosting, streaming services or application hosting; provide application service provisioning; or may provide general time-share mainframe facilities to clients. Data processing establishments provide complete processing and specialized reports from data supplied by clients or provide automated data processing and data entry services.

UTILITIES, Items 247–252
Source: U.S. Census Bureau—2012 Economic Census (See Overview of 2012 Economic Census prior to Item 217)

The Utilities sector (22) comprises establishments engaged in the provision of the following utility services: electric power, natural gas, steam supply, water supply, and sewage removal. Within this sector, the specific activities associated with the utility services provided vary by utility: electric power includes generation, transmission, and distribution; natural gas includes distribution; steam supply includes provision and/or distribution; water supply includes treatment and distribution; and sewage removal includes collection, treatment, and disposal of waste through sewer systems and sewage treatment facilities.

Excluded from this sector are establishments primarily engaged in waste management. These services are classified in subsector 562, Waste Management and Remediation Services, which also collect, treat, and dispose of waste materials; however, establishments in this subsector do not use sewer systems or sewage treatment facilities.

TRANSPORTATION AND WAREHOUSING, Items 252–256

Source: U.S. Census Bureau—2012 Economic Census (See Overview of 2012 Economic Census prior to Item 217)

The Transportation and Warehousing sector (48–49) includes industries that provide transportation of passengers and cargo, warehousing and storage for goods, scenic and sightseeing transportation, and support activities related to modes of transportation. Establishments in these industries use transportation equipment or transportation related facilities as a productive asset. The type of equipment depends on the mode of transportation, which includes air, rail, water, road, and pipeline.

The transportation and warehousing sector distinguishes three basic types of activities: subsectors for each mode of transportation, a subsector for warehousing and storage, and a subsector for establishments providing support activities for transportation. In addition, there are subsectors for establishments that provide passenger transportation for scenic and sightseeing purposes, postal services, and courier services.

FINANCE AND INSURANCE, Items 257–261

Source: U.S. Census Bureau—2012 Economic Census (See Overview of 2012 Economic Census prior to Item 217)

The Finance and Insurance sector (52) comprises establishments primarily engaged in financial transactions (transactions involving the creation, liquidation, or change in ownership of financial assets) and/or in facilitating financial transactions. Three principal types of activities are identified:

(1) Raising funds by taking deposits and/or issuing securities and, in the process, incurring liabilities. Establishments engaged in this activity use raised funds to acquire financial assets by making loans and/or purchasing securities. Putting themselves at risk, they channel funds from lenders to borrowers and transform or repackage the funds with respect to maturity, scale and risk. This activity is known as financial intermediation.

(2) Pooling of risk by underwriting insurance and annuities. Establishments engaged in this activity collect fees, insurance premiums, or annuity considerations; build up reserves; invest those reserves; and make contractual payments. Fees are based on the expected incidence of the insured risk and the expected return on investment.

(3) Providing specialized services facilitating or supporting financial intermediation, insurance, and employee benefit programs.

In addition, monetary authorities charged with monetary control are included in this sector.

REAL ESTATE AND RENTAL AND LEASING, Items 262–266

Source: U.S. Census Bureau—2012 Economic Census (See Overview of 2012 Economic Census prior to Item 217)

The Real Estate and Rental and Leasing sector (53) comprises establishments primarily engaged in renting, leasing, or otherwise allowing the use of tangible or intangible assets, and establishments providing related services. The major portion of this sector comprises establishments that rent, lease, or otherwise allow the use of their own assets by others. The assets may be tangible, such as real estate and equipment, or intangible, such as patents and trademarks.

This sector also includes establishments primarily engaged in managing real estate for others, selling, renting, and/or buying real estate for others, and appraising real estate. These activities are closely related to this sector's main activity. In addition, a substantial proportion of property management is self-performed by lessors.

The main components of this sector are the real estate lessor industries; equipment lessors industries (including motor vehicles, computers, and consumer goods); and lessors of nonfinancial intangible assets (except copyrighted works).

PROFESSIONAL, SCIENTIFIC, AND TECHNICAL SERVICES, Items 267–275

Source: U.S. Census Bureau—2012 Economic Census (See Overview of 2012 Economic Census prior to Item 217)

The Professional, Scientific, and Technical Services sector (54) is made up of establishments that specialize in performing professional, scientific, and technical activities for others. These activities require a high degree of expertise and training. The establishments in this sector specialize according to expertise and provide services to clients in a variety of industries (and, in some cases, to households). Activities performed include legal advice and representation; accounting, bookkeeping, and payroll services; architectural, engineering, and specialized design services; computer services; consulting services; research services; advertising services; photographic services; translation and interpretation services; veterinary services; and other professional, scientific, and technical services.

This sector excludes establishments primarily engaged in providing a range of day-to-day office administrative services, such as financial planning, billing and record keeping, personnel services, and physical distribution and logistics services. These establishments are classified in sector 56, Administrative and Support and Waste Management and Remediation Services.

Legal Services comprises establishments primarily engaged in offering legal services such as offices of lawyers, notaries, title abstract and settlement offices, and all other legal services such as patent agent services, paralegal services, and process serving services.

Accounting, Tax Preparation, Bookkeeping, and Payroll Services comprises establishments primarily engaged in providing services, such as auditing of accounting records, designing accounting systems, preparing financial statements, developing budgets, preparing tax returns, processing payrolls, bookkeeping, and billing.

Architectural, Engineering, and Related Services comprises establishments primarily engaged in offering (1) architectural services for residential, institutional, leisure, commercial, and industrial buildings and structures as well as for landscape purposes; (2) offering engineering services, including drafting services or building inspection services; (3) offering geophysical surveying and mapping services; (4) surveying and mapping services, except geophysical; and (5) offering testing laboratory services except medical and veterinary (the testing can occur in a laboratory or on-site).

Computer Systems Design and Related Services consists of establishments primarily engaged in providing expertise in the field of information technologies through one or more of the following activities: (1) writing, modifying, testing, and supporting software to meet the needs of a particular customer; (2) planning and designing computer systems that integrate computer hardware, software, and communication technologies; (3) on-site management and operation of clients' computer systems and/or data processing facilities; and (4) other professional and technical computer-related advice and services.

HEALTH CARE AND SOCIAL ASSISTANCE, Items 276–289
Source: U.S. Census Bureau—2012 Economic Census (See Overview of 2012 Economic Census prior to Item 217)

The Health Care and Social Assistance sector (62) consists of establishments that provide health care and social assistance services to individuals. The sector includes both health care and social assistance, because it is sometimes difficult to distinguish between the boundaries of these two activities. The industries in this sector are arranged on a continuum starting with those that provide medical care exclusively, continuing with those that provide health care and social assistance, and finishing with those that provide only social assistance. The services provided by establishments in this sector are delivered by trained professionals. All industries in the sector share this commonality of process—namely, labor inputs of health practitioners or social workers with the requisite expertise. Many of the industries in the sector are defined based on the educational degree held by the practitioners included in the industry.

In this volume, taxable and tax-exempt establishments are presented separately.

Excluded from this sector are aerobic classes, which can be found in subsector 713, Amusement, Gambling and Recreation Industries; and nonmedical diet and weight-reducing centers, which can be found in subsector 812, Personal and Laundry Services. Although these can be viewed as health services, they are not typically delivered by health practitioners.

Industries in the **Ambulatory Health Care Services** subsector (621) provide health care services directly or indirectly to ambulatory patients and do not typically provide inpatient services. Health practitioners in this subsector provide outpatient services, and facilities and equipment do not usually play the most significant part in this sector's production process.

Industries in the **Hospitals** subsector (622) provide medical, diagnostic, and treatment services, including physician, nursing, specialized accommodation, and other health services, to inpatients. Hospitals may provide outpatient services as a secondary activity. Many of the services provided by establishments in the Hospitals subsector require the use of specialized facilities and equipment, both of which form a significant and integral part of the production process.

ARTS, ENTERTAINMENT, AND RECREATION, Items 290–294
Source: U.S. Census Bureau—2012 Economic Census (See Overview of 2012 Economic Census prior to Item 217)

The Arts, Entertainment, and Recreation sector (71) includes a wide range of establishments that operate facilities or provide services that meet the diverse cultural, entertainment, and recreational interests of their patrons. This sector is made up of: (1) establishments that are involved in producing, promoting, or participating in live performances, events, or exhibits intended for public viewing; (2) establishments that preserve and exhibit objects and sites of historical, cultural, or educational interest; and (3) establishments that operate facilities or provide services that enable patrons to participate in recreational activities or pursue amusement, hobby, and leisure time interests.

Some establishments that provide cultural, entertainment, or recreational facilities and services are classified in other sectors. Excluded from this sector are: (1) establishments that provide both accommodations and recreational facilities—such as hunting and fishing camps and resort and casino hotels—are classified in subsector 721, Accommodation; (2) restaurants and night clubs that provide live entertainment in addition to the sale of food and beverages are classified in subsector 722, Food Services and Drinking Places; (3) motion picture theaters, libraries and archives, and publishers of newspapers, magazines, books, periodicals, and computer software are classified in sector 51, Information; and (4) establishments that use transportation equipment to provide recreational and entertainment services, such as those operating sightseeing buses, dinner cruises, or helicopter rides, are classified in subsector 487, Scenic and Sightseeing Transportation.

ACCOMMODATION AND FOOD SERVICES, Items 295–300
Source: U.S. Census Bureau—2012 Economic Census (See Overview of 2012 Economic Census prior to Item 217)

The Accommodation and Food Services sector (72) consists of establishments that provide customers with lodging and/or meals, snacks, and beverages for immediate consumption. The sector includes both accommodation and food services establishments because the two activities are often combined at the same establishment. Excluded from this sector are civic and social organizations, amusement and recreation parks, theaters, and other recreation or entertainment facilities providing food and beverage services.

Industries in the **Food Services and Drinking Places** subsector (722) prepare meals, snacks, and beverages to customer order for immediate on-premises and off-premises consumption. There is a wide range of establishments in these industries. Some provide food and drink only; while others provide various combinations of seating space, waiter/waitress services and incidental amenities, such as limited entertainment. The industries in the subsector are grouped based on the type and level of services provided. The industry groups are full-service restaurants; limited-service eating places; special food services, such as food service contractors, caterers, and mobile food services, and drinking places. Food services and drink activities at hotels and motels; amusement parks, theaters, casinos, country clubs, and similar recreational facilities; and civic and social organizations are included in this subsector only if these services are provided by a separate establishment primarily engaged in providing food and beverage services. Excluded from this subsector are establishments operating dinner cruises. These establishments are classified in subsector 487, Scenic and Sightseeing Transportation, because they utilize transportation equipment to provide scenic recreational entertainment.

OTHER SERVICES, EXCEPT PUBLIC ADMINISTRATION Items 301–308

Source: U.S. Census Bureau—2012 Economic Census (See Overview of 2012 Economic Census prior to Item 217)

The Other Services, Except Public Administration sector (81) comprises establishments engaged in providing services not specifically categorized elsewhere in the classification system. Establishments in this sector are primarily engaged in activities such as equipment and machinery repairing, promoting or administering religious activities, grant making, and advocacy; this sector also includes establishments that provide dry-cleaning and laundry services, personal care services, death care services, pet care services, photofinishing services, temporary parking services, and dating services.

Private households that employ workers on or about the premises in activities primarily concerned with the operation of the household are included in this sector.

Excluded from this sector are establishments primarily engaged in retailing new equipment and performing repairs and general maintenance on equipment. These establishments are classified in sector 44–45, Retail Trade.

Industries in the **Repair and Maintenance** subsector (811) restore machinery, equipment, and other products to working order. These establishments also typically provide general or routine maintenance (i.e., servicing) on such products to ensure they work efficiently; this maintenance also helps prevent breakdowns and make certain repairs unnecessary.

The NAICS structure for this subsector brings together most types of repair and maintenance establishments and categorizes them based on production processes (i.e., on the type of repair and maintenance activity performed, and the necessary skills, expertise, and processes required for different repair and maintenance establishments). This NAICS classification does not delineate between repair services provided to businesses versus those provided to households. Although some industries primarily serve either businesses or households, separation by class of customer is limited by the fact that many establishments serve both types. Establishments that repair computers and consumer electronics products are examples of such overlap.

The Repair and Maintenance subsector does not include all establishments engaged in repair and maintenance. For example, a substantial amount of repair is done by establishments that also manufacture machinery, equipment, and other goods. These establishments are included in the Manufacturing sector in NAICS. In addition, the repairing of transportation equipment is often provided by or based at transportation facilities, such as airports and seaports; these activities are included in the Transportation and Warehousing sector.

A particularly unique situation exists with repair of buildings. Plumbing, electrical installation and repair, painting and decorating, and other construction-related establishments are often involved in performing installation or other work on new construction, while also providing repair services on existing structures. Although some establishments do specialize in repair, it is difficult to distinguish between these two types. Thus, all such establishments are included in the Construction sector.

Excluded from this subsector are establishments primarily engaged in rebuilding or remanufacturing machinery and equipment. These are classified in sector 31–33, Manufacturing. Also excluded are retail establishments that provide after-sale services and repair. These are classified in sector 44–45, Retail Trade.

Industries in the **Personal and Laundry Services** subsector (812) include establishments that provide personal and laundry services to individuals, households, and businesses. Services performed include personal care services, death care services, laundry and dry-cleaning services, and a wide range of other personal services, such as pet care (except veterinary) services, photofinishing services, temporary parking services, and dating services.

The Personal and Laundry Services subsector is by no means all-inclusive of the activities that could be termed personal services (i.e., those provided to individuals rather than businesses). There are many other sectors and subsectors that provide services to persons. Establishments providing legal, accounting, tax preparation, architectural, portrait photography, and similar professional services are classified in sector 54, Professional, Scientific and Technical Services; those providing job placement, travel arrangement, home security, interior and exterior house cleaning, exterminating, lawn and garden care, and similar support services are classified in sector 56, Administrative and Support and Waste Management and Remediation Services; those providing health and social services are classified in sector 62, Health Care and Social Assistance; those providing amusement and recreation services are classified in sector 71, Arts, Entertainment and Recreation; those providing educational instruction are classified in sector 61, Educational Services; those providing repair services are classified in subsector 811, Repair and Maintenance; and those providing spiritual, civic, and advocacy services are classified in subsector 813, Religious, Grantmaking, Civic, Professional, and Similar Organizations.

Industries in the **Religious, Grantmaking, Civic, Professional, and Similar Organizations** subsector (813) include establishments that organize and promote religious activities, support various causes through grant making, advocate various social and political causes, and promote and defend the interests of their members. This category includes only tax-exempt establishments.

The industry groups within the subsector are defined in terms of their activities, separately grouping establishments that provide funding for specific causes or for a variety of charitable causes, establishments that advocate and actively promote causes and beliefs for the public good, and establishments that have an active membership structure to promote causes and represent the interests of their members. Establishments in this subsector may publish newsletters, books, and periodicals for distribution to their membership.

GOVERNMENT EMPLOYMENT, Items 309–311

Source: U.S. Bureau of Economic Analysis—Regional Economic Accounts
http://www.bea.gov/regional/index.htm#state

Employment is measured as the average annual sum of full-time and part-time jobs. The estimates are on a place-of-work basis. Data for federal civilian employment include civilian employees of the Department of Defense. Military employment includes all persons on active duty status.

STATE GOVERNMENT EMPLOYMENT AND PAYROLL, Items 312–330

Source: U.S. Census Bureau—Annual Survey of Government Employment and Payroll
http://www.census.gov/govs/apes/index.html

The annual Survey of Government Employment and Payroll measures the number of federal, state, and local civilian government employees and their gross monthly payroll for March of the survey year for state and local governments and for the Federal Government.

The survey provides state and local government data on full-time and part-time employment, part-time hours worked, full-time equivalent employment, and payroll statistics by governmental function (i.e., elementary and secondary education, higher education, police protection, fire protection, financial administration, central staff services, judicial and legal, highways, public welfare, solid waste management, sewerage, parks and recreation, health, hospitals, water supply, electric power, gas supply, transit, natural resources, correction, libraries, air transportation, water transport and terminals, other education, state liquor stores, social insurance administration, and housing and community development).

Data have been collected annually since 1957. A census is conducted every five years (years ending in '2' and '7'). A sample of state and local governments is used to collect data in the intervening years. A new sample is selected every five years (years ending in '4' and '9').

State government employees include all persons paid for personal services performed, including persons paid from federally funded programs, paid elected or appointed officials, persons in paid leave status, and persons paid on a per meeting, annual, semiannual, or quarterly basis. Unpaid officials, pensioners, persons whose work is performed on a fee basis, and contractors and their employees are excluded from the count of employees. **Full-time employees** are persons employed during the pay period

to work the number of hours per week that represents regular full-time employment. Included are full-time temporary or seasonal employees who are working the number of hours that represent full-time employment. **Part-time employees** are persons paid on a part-time basis during the designated pay period. Included are those daily or hourly employees usually engaged for less than the regular full-time workweek, as well as any part-time paid officials. **Full-Time Equivalent employees** is a computed statistic representing the number of full-time employees that could have been employed if the reported number of hours worked by part-time employees had been worked by full-time employees. This statistic is calculated separately for each function of a government by dividing the ''part-time hours paid'' by the standard number of hours for full-time employees in the particular government and then adding the resulting quotient to the number of full-time employees.

Full-time payroll represents gross payroll amounts for the one-month period of March for full-time employees. **Part-time pay** represents gross payroll amounts for the one-month period of March for part-time employees. Gross payroll includes all salaries, wages, fees, commissions, and overtime paid to employees **before** withholdings for taxes, insurance, etc. It also includes incentive payments that are paid at regular pay intervals. It excludes employer share of fringe benefits like retirement, Social Security, health and life insurance, lump sum payments, and so forth.

Administration combines **Financial administration** and **Other government administration**. **Financial administration** includes activities concerned with tax assessment and collection, custody and disbursement of funds, debt management, administration of trust funds, budgeting, and other government-wide financial management activities. This function is not applied to school district or special district governments. **Other government administration** applies to the legislative and government-wide administrative agencies of governments. Included here are overall planning and zoning activities, and central personnel and administrative activities. This function is not applied to school district or special district governments.

Judicial and legal includes all court and court related activities (except probation and parole activities that are included at the ''Correction'' function), court activities of sheriff's offices, prosecuting attorneys' and public defenders' offices, legal departments, and attorneys providing government-wide legal service.

Police includes all activities concerned, with the enforcement of law and order, including coroner's offices, police training academies, investigation bureaus, and local jails, ''lockups'', or other detention facilities not intended to serve as correctional facilities.

Corrections includes activities pertaining to the confinement and correction of adults and minors convicted of criminal offenses. Pardon, probation, and parole activities are also included here.

Highways and transportation includes activities associated with the maintenance and operation of streets, roads, sidewalks, bridges, tunnels, toll roads, and ferries. Snow and ice removal, street lighting, and highway and traffic engineering activities are also included here. Also included are the operation, maintenance, and construction of public mass transit systems, including subways, surface rails, and buses, and the provision, construction, operation, maintenance; support of public waterways, harbors, docks, wharves, and related marine terminal facilities; and activities associated with the operation and support of publicly operated airport facilities.

Public welfare includes the administration of various public assistance programs for the needy, veteran services, operation of nursing homes, indigent care institutions, and programs that provide payments for medical care, handicap transportation, and other services for the needy.

Health includes administration of public health programs, community and visiting nurse services, immunization programs, drug abuse rehabilitation programs, health and food inspection activities, operation of outpatient clinics, and environmental pollution control activities.

Hospitals includes only government operated medical care facilities that provide inpatient care. Employees and payrolls of private corporations that lease and operate government-owned hospital facilities are excluded.

Social insurance administration includes the administration of unemployment compensation systems, public employment services, and the Federal Social Security, Medicare, and Railroad Retirement trusts.

Natural resources and Parks includes activities primarily concerned with the conservation and development of natural resources (soil, water, energy, minerals, etc.) and the regulation of industries that develop, utilize, or affect natural resources, as well as the operation and maintenance of parks, playgrounds, swimming pools, public beaches, auditoriums, public golf courses, museums, marinas, botanical gardens, and zoological parks.

Utilities, sewerage, and waste management includes operation, maintenance, and construction of public water supply systems, including production, acquisition, and distribution of water to general public or to other public or private utilities, for residential, commercial, and industrial use; activities associated with the production or acquisition and distribution of electric power; provision, maintenance, and operation of sanitary and storm sewer systems and sewage disposal and treatment facilities; and refuse collection and disposal, operation of sanitary landfills, and street cleaning activities.

Elementary and secondary education and libraries includes activities associated with the operation of public elementary and secondary schools and locally operated vocational-technical schools. Special education programs operated by elementary and secondary school systems are also included as are all ancillary services associated with the operation of schools, such as pupil transportation and food service. Also included are the establishment and provision of libraries for use by the general public and the technical support of privately operated libraries. This category includes classroom teachers, principals, supervisors of instruction, librarians, teacher aides, library aides, and guidance and psychological personnel as well as school superintendents and other administrative personnel, clerical and secretarial staffs, plant operation and maintenance personnel, health and recreation employees, transportation and food service personnel, and any student employees.

Higher education includes state government degree granting institutions that provide academic training above grade 12. This includes persons engaged in teaching and related academic

research as well as administrative, clerical, custodial, cafeteria, health personnel, noninstructional employees engaged in organized research, law enforcement personnel, and paid student employees.

STATE GOVERNMENT FINANCES, Items 331–350

Source: U.S. Census Bureau—State Government Finances
http://www.census.gov/govs/state/

Data are from an annual survey conducted by the Census Bureau and pertain to state government fiscal years ending on June 30, except for four states with other ending dates: Alabama and Michigan (September 30), New York (March 31), and Texas (August 31).

The state government finance data presented in this publication may differ from data published by state governments because the Census Bureau may be using a different definition of which organizations are covered under the term, "state government."

For the purpose of Census Bureau statistics, the term "state government" refers not only to the executive, legislative, and judicial branches of a given state, but it also includes agencies, institutions, commissions, and public authorities that operate separately or somewhat autonomously from the central state government but where the state government maintains administrative or fiscal control over their activities as defined by the Census Bureau.

Total **general revenue** includes all revenue except utility, liquor stores, and insurance trust revenue. All tax revenue and intergovernmental revenue, even if designated for employee retirement or local utility purpose, are classified as general revenue.

Intergovernmental revenue covers amounts received from the federal government as fiscal aid, reimbursements for performance of general government functions and specific services for the paying government, or in lieu of taxes. It excludes any amounts received from other governments from the sale of property, commodities, and utility services.

Taxes consist of compulsory contributions exacted by governments for public purposes. However, this category excludes employer and employee payments for retirement and social insurance purposes, which are classified as insurance trust revenue; it also excludes special assessments, which are classified as nontax general revenue. Sales and gross receipts taxes do not include dealer discounts, or "commissions" allowed to merchants for collection of taxes from consumers. General sales taxes and selected taxes on sales of motor fuels, tobacco products, and other particular commodities and services are included.

General government expenditure includes capital outlay, a major portion of which is commonly financed by borrowing. Government revenue does not include receipts from borrowing. Among other things, this distorts the relationship between total of revenue and expenditure figures that are presented and renders it useless as a direct measure of the degree of budgetary "balance" (as that term is generally applied).

Direct general expenditure comprises all expenditures of the state governments, excluding utility, liquor stores, insurance trust expenditures, and any intergovernmental payments.

State government expenditure for **education** is mainly for the provision and general support of schools and other educational facilities and services, including those for educational institutions beyond high school. They cover such related services as student transportation; school lunch and other cafeteria operations; school health, recreation, and library services; and dormitories, dining halls, and bookstores operated by public institutions of higher education.

Health and hospitals expenditure includes health research; clinics; nursing; immunization; other categorical, environmental, and general health services provided by health agencies; establishment and operation of hospital facilities; provision of hospital care; and support of other public and private hospitals.

Highways expenditure is for the provision and maintenance of highway facilities, including toll turnpikes, bridges, tunnels, and ferries, as well as regular roads, highways, and streets. Also included are expenditures for street lighting and for snow and ice removal. Not included are highway policing and traffic control, which are considered part of police protection

Public safety expenditure includes police and correctional institution expenditures.

Public welfare expenditure covers support of and assistance to needy persons; this aid is contingent upon the person's needs. Included are cash assistance paid directly to needy persons under categorical (Old Age Assistance, Temporary Assistance for Needy Families, Aid to the Blind, and Aid to the Disabled) and other welfare programs; vendor payments made directly to private purveyors for medical care, burials, and other commodities and services provided under welfare programs; welfare institutions; and any intergovernmental or other direct expenditure for welfare purposes. Pensions to former employees and other benefits not contingent on need are excluded.

Natural resources, parks, and recreation includes expenditures for conservation, promotion, and development of natural resources (soil, water, energy, minerals, etc.) and the regulation of industries which develop, utilize, or affect natural resources. It also includes the provision and support of recreational and cultural-scientific facilities, such as golf courses, playgrounds, tennis courts, public beaches, swimming pools, play fields, parks, camping areas, recreational piers and marinas, galleries, museums, zoos, botanical gardens, auditoriums, stadiums, recreational centers, convention centers, exhibition halls, community music, drama, and celebrations.

Debt outstanding includes all long-term debt obligations of the government and its agencies (exclusive of utility debt) and all interest-bearing, short-term (repayable within one year) debt obligations remaining unpaid at the close of the fiscal year. It includes judgments, mortgages, and revenue bonds, as well as general obligation bonds, notes, and interest-bearing warrants. This category consists of non-interest-bearing, short-term obligations; inter-fund obligations; amounts owed in a trust or agency capacity; advances and contingent loans from other governments; and rights of individuals to benefit from government-administered employee-retirement funds.

VOTING AND REGISTRATION, Items 351 and 352
Source: U.S. Census Bureau—Current Population Survey
http://www.census.gov/topics/public-sector/voting.html

These estimates are based on the November 2014 Voting and Registration Supplement to the Current Population Survey (CPS).

Voting rates are calculated using the voting-age population, which includes both citizens and noncitizens. Statistics from surveys are subject to sampling and nonsampling error. The CPS estimate of overall turnout differs from the ''official'' turnout reported by the Clerk of the House of Representatives.

ELECTION STATISTICS, Items 353–355
Source: Election Data Services, Inc. Washington, DC (copyright)
http://www.electiondataservices.com/

© 2013 Election Data Services, Inc. All rights reserved. This material is proprietary and the subject of copyright protection and other intellectual property rights owned by or licensed to Election Data Services, Inc. The use of this material is subject to the terms of a License Agreement. You will be held liable for any unauthorized copying or disclosure of this material.

Election results show the percentage of the total vote cast for the Democratic and Republican candidates, as well as the combined percentage for all other candidates in the 2012 presidential election.

TABLE B—STATES AND COUNTIES

Table B presents 199 items for the United States as a whole, each individual state, and the District of Columbia; and every county, county equivalent, and independent city. The counties are presented in alphabetical order within each state, and the states are also presented in alphabetical order. Independent cities, which are found in Maryland, Missouri, Nevada, and Virginia, are placed in alphabetical order at the end of the list of counties for those states. The District of Columbia is included in Table B as both a county and a state. It is also included as a city in Table D.

LAND AREA, Items 1 and 4
Source: U.S. Census Bureau—2010 Census of Population and Housing
http://www.census.gov/2010census/data/

Land area measurements are shown to the nearest square kilometer. Land area includes dry land and land temporarily or partially covered by water, such as marshlands, swamps, and river floodplains.

POPULATION, Items 2–4

Source: U.S. Census Bureau—Population Estimates
http://www.census.gov/popest/estimates.html

The population data are Census Bureau estimates of the resident population as of July 1 of the year shown. The ranks are shown for counties (including independent cities and the District of Columbia).

POPULATION AND POPULATION CHARACTERISTICS, Items 5–19

Source: U.S. Census Bureau—Population Estimates
http://www.census.gov/popest/estimates.html

The concept of race, as used by the Census Bureau, reflects self-identification by persons according to the race or races with which they most closely identify. These categories are sociopolitical constructs and should not be interpreted as being scientific or anthropological in nature. Furthermore, race categories include both racial and national origin groups.

Beginning with the 2000 census, respondents were offered the option of selecting one or more races. This option was not available in prior censuses; thus, comparisons between censuses should be made with caution. In Table B, Columns 5 through 8 refer to individuals who identified with each racial category, either alone or in combination with other races. The estimates exclude persons of Hispanic or Latino origin from all race groups.

The sum of the four individual race alone or in combination categories in this book will often add to more than the total population because people who reported more than one race were tallied in each race category. In this book, the Asian group has been combined with the Native Hawaiian and Other Pacific Islander group, causing double-counting of persons who identify with both groups. This is especially pronounced in Hawaii.

The **White** population is defined as persons who indicated their race as White, as well as persons who did not classify themselves in one of the specific race categories listed on the questionnaire but entered a nationality such as Irish, German, Italian, Lebanese, Near Easterner, Arab, or Polish.

The **Black** population includes persons who indicated their race as "Black, African Am., or Negro," as well as persons who did not classify themselves in one of the specific race categories but reported entries such as African American, Afro American, Kenyan, Nigerian, or Haitian.

The **American Indian or Alaska Native** population includes persons who indicated their race as American Indian or Alaska Native, as well as persons who did not classify themselves in one of the specific race categories but reported entries such as Canadian Indian, French-American Indian, Spanish-American Indian, Eskimo, Aleut, Alaska Indian, or any of the American Indian or Alaska Native tribes.

The **Asian and Pacific Islander** population combines two census groupings: **Asian** and **Native Hawaiian or Other Pacific Islander**. The **Asian** population includes persons who indicated their race as Asian Indian, Chinese, Filipino, Japanese, Korean, Vietnamese, or "Other Asian," as well as persons who provided write-in entries of such groups as Cambodian, Laotian, Hmong, Pakistani, or Taiwanese. The **Native Hawaiian or Other Pacific Islander** population includes persons who indicated their race as "Native Hawaiian," "Guamanian or Chamorro," "Samoan," or "Other Pacific Islander," as well as persons who reported entries such as Part Hawaiian, American Samoan, Fijian, Melanesian, or Tahitian.

The **Hispanic population** is based on a question that asked respondents "Is this person Spanish/Hispanic/Latino?" Persons marking any one of the four Hispanic categories (i.e., Mexican, Puerto Rican, Cuban, or other Spanish) are collectively referred to as Hispanic.

In the census, the Hispanic origin question was placed before the race question and specific instructions indicated that both questions should be answered. These changes were designed to improve accuracy and may affect comparability with data prior to the 2000 census.

Age is defined as age at last birthday (number of completed years since birth), as of April 1 of the census year. The census also asked for the specific date of birth of the respondent, and census procedures used the birth date for deriving age data. For this reason, it is likely that the data have fewer problems than data from censuses prior to 2000, such as the tendency of respondents to round ages or to report their ages on the date the questionnaire was filled out rather than on April 1.

The **female** population is shown as a percentage of total population.

POPULATION AND COMPONENTS OF CHANGE, Items 20–26

Source: U.S. Census Bureau—Decennial Censuses and Population Estimates
http://www.census.gov/main/www/cen2000.html
http://www.census.gov/popest/estimates.html
http://www.census.gov/2010census/data/

The population data for 1990, 2000, and 2010 are from the decennial censuses and represent the resident population as of April 1 of those years. The components of change are based on Census Bureau estimates of the resident population as of July 1 2015. The change in population between 2010 and 2015 is made up of (a) natural increase—births minus deaths, and (b) net migration—the difference between the number of persons moving into a particular area and the number of persons moving out of the area. Net migration is composed of internal and international migration

Because the 2015 population estimates are based on a model that begins with a national population estimate, the county components of change do not always exactly add up to the difference between the 2010 census population and the 2015 estimates.

HOUSEHOLDS, Items 27–31

Source: U.S. Census Bureau—American Community Survey
http://www.census.gov/acs/www/

A **household** includes all of the persons who occupy a housing unit. (Persons not living in households are classified as living in group quarters.) A housing unit is a house, an apartment, a mobile home, a group of rooms, or a single room occupied (or, if vacant intended for occupancy) as separate living quarters. Separate living quarters are those in which the occupants live separately from ny other persons in the building and have direct access from the outside of the building or through a common hall. The occupants may be a single family, one person living alone, two or more families living together, or any other group of related or unrelated persons who share living quarters. The number of households is the same as the number of year-round occupied housing units.

A **family** includes a householder and one or more other persons living in the same household who are related to the householder by birth, marriage, or adoption. All persons in a household who are related to the householder are regarded as members of his or her family. A **family household** may contain persons not related to the householder; thus, family households may include more members than families do. A household can contain only one family for the purposes of census tabulations. Not all households contain families, as a household may comprise a group of unrelated persons or of one person living alone. Families are classified by type as either a ''married-couple family'' or ''other family,'' according to the presence or absence of a spouse.

The measure of **persons per household** is obtained by dividing the number of persons by the number of households or householders. One person in each household is designated as the householder. In most cases, this is the person (or one of the persons) in whose name the house is owned, being bought, or rented. If there is no such person in the household, any adult household member 15 years old and over can be designated as the householder.

The category **female family householder** includes only female-headed family households with no spouse present.

GROUP QUARTERS, Item 32
Source:
Source: U.S. Census Bureau—Population Estimates
http://www.census.gov/popest/estimates.html

The Census Bureau classifies all persons not living in households as living in group quarters; this category includes both the institutional and noninstitutional populations. The institutionalized population includes persons under formally authorized, supervised care or custody in institutions, such as correctional institutions, nursing homes, mental (psychiatric) hospitals, and juvenile institutions. The noninstitutionalized population includes persons who live in group quarters other than institutions, such as college dormitories, military quarters, and group homes. This volume includes the total number of persons in group quarters.

DAYTIME POPULATION, Items 33 and 34
Source: U.S. Census Bureau—American Community Survey
http://www.census.gov/acs/www/

Daytime population refers to the number of persons who are present in an area or place during normal business hours, including workers. This can be contrasted with the ''resident'' population, which is present during the evening and nighttime hours. The daytime population estimate is calculated by adding the total resident population and the total workers working in the area/place, and then subtracting the total workers living in the area/place from that result. Information on the expansion or contraction experienced by different communities between their nighttime

and daytime populations is important for many planning purposes, especially those concerning transportation, disaster, and relief operations.

The employment/residence ratio is a measure of the total number of workers working in an area or place, relative to the total number of workers living in the area or place. It is often used as a rough indication of the jobs-workers balance in an area/place, although it does not take into account whether the resident workers possess the skills needed for the jobs available in their particular area/place. The employment/residence ratio is calculated by dividing the number of total workers working in an area/place by the number of total workers residing in the area/place.

BIRTHS AND DEATHS, Items 35–38
Source: U.S. Census Bureau—Population Estimates
http://www.census.gov/popest/estimates.html

The numbers of births and deaths are from the Census Bureau's Population Estimates Program. They represent the total number of live births and deaths occurring to residents of an area as estimated using reports from the National Center for Health Statistics (NCHS) and the Federal-State Cooperative for Population Estimates (FSCPE). The rates measure births and deaths during the specified time period as a proportion of an area's population. Rates are expressed per 1,000 population estimated as of July 1. These numbers and rates do not represent the calendar year, but rather the year-long period ending on July 1.

PERSONS UNDER 65 WITH NO HEALTH INSURANCE, Items 39 and 40
Source: U.S. Census Bureau—Small Area Health Insurance Estimates
http://www.census.gov/did/www/sahie/index.html

The Small Area Health Insurance Estimates (SAHIE) program develops model-based estimates of health insurance coverage for counties and states. This developmental program builds on the work of the Small Area Income and Poverty Estimates (SAIPE) program. The SAHIE program models health insurance coverage by combining survey data with population estimates and administrative records. These estimates combine data from administrative records, postcensal population estimates, and the decennial census with direct estimates from the American Community Survey to provide consistent and reliable single-year estimates. These model-based single-year estimates are more reflective of current conditions than multi-year survey estimates.

MEDICARE ENROLLMENT, Items 41–43
Source: U.S. Department of Health and Human Services, Centers for Medicare and Medicaid Services
https://www.cms.gov/Research-Statistics-Data-and-Systems/Statistics-Trends-and-Reports/Medicare-Geographic-Variation/GVPUF.html

The Centers for Medicare and Medicaid Services (CMS) administers Medicare, which provides health insurance to persons 65 years old and over, persons with permanent kidney failure, and certain persons with disabilities. Original Medicare has two parts: Hospital Insurance and Supplemental Medical Insurance. In recent years, Medicare has been expanded to include two new programs: Medicare Advantage plans and prescription drug coverage. Medicare Advantage Plans are health plan options that are approved by Medicare but run by private companies. Medicare prescription drug plans can be part of Medicare Advantage plans or stand-alone drug plans.

Persons who are eligible for Medicare can enroll in Part A (Hospital Insurance) at no charge, and can choose to pay a monthly premium to enroll in Part B. Most eligible persons are enrolled in Part A, and more than 90 percent of enrollees in Part A are also enrolled in Part B (Supplemental Medical Insurance.) This table includes persons who were enrolled in both Part A and Part B during 2014.

Part B beneficiaries can choose to enroll in **Original Medicare**, a fee-for-service plan administered by the Centers for Medicare and Medicaid Services, or in a **Medicare Advantage** plan. Medicare Advantage plans include private fee-for-service plans, preferred provider organizations, health maintenance organizations, medical savings account plans, demonstration plans, and programs for all-inclusive care for the elderly.

CRIME, Items 44–47
Source: U.S. Federal Bureau of Investigation— Uniform Crime Reports
http://www.fbi.gov/ucr/ucr.htm

Crime data are as reported to the Federal Bureau of Investigation (FBI) by law enforcement agencies and have not been adjusted for underreporting. This may affect comparability between geographic areas or over time.

Through the voluntary contribution of crime statistics by law enforcement agencies across the United States, the Uniform Crime Reporting (UCR) Program provides periodic assessments of crime in the nation as measured by offenses that have come to the attention of the law enforcement community. The Committee on Uniform Crime Records of the International Association of Chiefs of Police initiated this voluntary national data collection effort in 1930. The UCR Program contributors compile and submit their crime data either directly to the FBI or through state-level UCR Programs.

Seven offenses, because of their severity, frequency of occurrence, and likelihood of being reported to police, were initially selected to serve as an index for evaluating fluctuations in the volume of crime. These serious crimes were murder and nonnegligent manslaughter, forcible rape, robbery, aggravated assault, burglary, larceny-theft, and motor vehicle theft. By congressional mandate, arson was added as the eighth index offense in 1979. The totals shown in this volume do not include arson.

In 2004, the FBI discontinued the use of the Crime Index in the UCR Program and its publications, stating that the Crime Index was driven upward by the offense with the highest number of cases (in this case, larceny-theft), creating a bias against jurisdictions with a high number of larceny-thefts but a low number of other serious crimes, such as murder and forcible rape. The FBI is currently publishing a violent crime total and property crime total until a more viable index is developed. This book includes the crime total, as well as violent crime and property crime rates.

In 2013, the FBI adopted a new definition of rape. Rape is now defined as, "Penetration, no matter how slight, of the vagina or anus with any body part or object, or oral penetration by a sex organ of another person, without the consent of the victim." The new definition updated the 80-year-old historical definition of rape which was "carnal knowledge of a female forcibly and against her will." Effectively, the revised definition expands rape to include both male and female victims and offenders, and reflects the various forms of sexual penetration understood to be rape, especially nonconsenting acts of sodomy, and sexual assaults with objects.

Violent crimes include four categories of offenses: (1) Murder and nonnegligent manslaughter, as defined in the UCR Program, is the willful (nonnegligent) killing of one human being by another. This offense excludes deaths caused by negligence, suicide, or accident; justifiable homicides; and attempts to murder or assaults to murder. (2) Rape is the penetration, no matter how slight, of the vagina or anus with any body part or object, or oral penetration by a sex organ of another person, without the consent of the victim. Assaults or attempts to commit rape by force or threat of force are also included; however, statutory rape (without force) and other sex offenses are excluded. (3) Robbery is the taking or attempting to take anything of value from the care, custody, or control of a person or persons by force or threat of force or violence and/or by putting the victim in fear. (4) Aggravated assault is an unlawful attack by one person upon another for the purpose of inflicting severe or aggravated bodily injury. This type of assault is usually accompanied by the use of a weapon or by other means likely to produce death or great bodily harm. Attempts are included, since injury does not necessarily have to result when a gun, knife, or other weapon is used, as these incidents could and probably would result in a serious personal injury if the crime were successfully completed.

Property crimes include three categories: (1) Burglary, or breaking and entering, is the unlawful entry of a structure to commit a felony or theft, even though no force was used to gain entrance. (2) Larceny-theft is the unauthorized taking of the personal property of another, without the use of force. (3) Motor vehicle theft is the unauthorized taking of any motor vehicle.

Rates are based on population estimates provided by the FBI. The county totals published in this volume were obtained by aggregating individual reporting units within each county and MSA. If the population total for the units aggregated was less than 75 percent of the county's population (as estimated by the Census Bureau), the total was not considered representative of the county as a whole and was not published. State and U.S. totals include FBI estimates for those areas. State and U.S. totals in this table are the adjusted totals as published in the FBI's *Crime in the United States*.

EDUCATION—SCHOOL ENROLLMENT AND EDUCATIONAL ATTAINMENT, Items 48–51
Source: U.S. Census Bureau—American Community Survey
http://www.census.gov/acs/www/

Persons were classified as enrolled in school if they reported attending a "regular" public or private school (or college) during the three months preceding the interview. The instructions were to include only nursery school, kindergarten, elementary school, and schooling which would lead to a high school diploma or a college degree as regular school. The Census Bureau defines a public school as "any school or college controlled and supported by a local, county, state, or federal government." Schools primarily supported and controlled by religious organizations or other private groups are defined as private schools.

Data on **educational attainment** are tabulated for the population 25 years old and over. The data were derived from a question that asked respondents for the highest level of school completed or the highest degree received. Persons who had passed a high school equivalency examination were considered high school graduates. Schooling received in foreign schools was to be reported as the equivalent grade or years in the regular American school system.

Vocational and technical training, such as barber school training; business, trade, technical, and vocational schools; or other training for a specific trade are specifically excluded.

High school graduate or less. This category includes persons whose highest degree was a high school diploma or its equivalent, and those who reported any level lower than a high school diploma.

Bachelor's degree or more. This category includes persons who have received bachelor's degrees, master's degrees, professional school degrees (such as law school or medical school degrees), and doctoral degrees.

LOCAL GOVERNMENT EDUCATION EXPENDITURES, Items 52 and 53
Source: U.S. Census Bureau—Annual Survey of
School System Finances
http://www.census.gov/govs/school/

Expenditures are for elementary and secondary Education which includes prekindergarten through twelfth grade regular, special, and vocational education, as well as cocurricular, community service, and adult education programs provided by a public school system. The financial activities of these systems for all instruction, support service, and noninstructional activities are included

Current spending comprises current operation expenditure, payments made by the state government on behalf of school systems, and transfers made by school systems into their own retirement funds. Current operation expenditures include direct expenditure for salaries, employee benefits, purchased professional and technical services, purchased property and other services, and supplies. It includes gross school system expenditure for instruction, support services, and noninstructional functions. It excludes expenditure for debt service, capital outlay, and reimbursement to other governments (including other school systems).

Current expenditure per student is current expenditure divided by the number of students enrolled. The number of students enrolled is based on an annual "membership" count of students on or about October 1, collected by the National Center for Education Statistics on the Common Core of Data (CCD) agency universe file—"Local Education Agency (School District) Universe Survey."

MONEY INCOME, Items 54–57
Source: U.S. Census Bureau—American
CommunitySurvey http://www.census.gov/acs/www/

Total money income is the sum of the amounts reported separately for wage or salary income; net self-employment income; interest, dividends, or net rental or royalty income or income from estates and trusts; Social Security or railroad retirement income; Supplemental Security Income (SSI); public assistance or welfare payments; retirement, survivor, or disability pensions; and all other income. Receipts from the following sources are not included as income: capital gains; money received from the sale of property (unless the recipient was engaged in the business of selling such property); the value of income "in kind" from food stamps, public housing subsidies, medical care, employer contributions for individuals, etc.; withdrawal of bank deposits; money borrowed; tax refunds; exchange of money between relatives living in the same household; and gifts, lump-sum inheritances, insurance payments, and other types of lump-sum receipts.

Money income differs in definition from personal income (item 62). For example, money income does not include the pension rights, employer provided health insurance, food stamps, or Medicare payments that are included in personal income.

Per capita income is the mean income computed for every man, woman, and child in a particular group. It is derived by dividing the aggregate income of a particular group by the resident population in that group as estimated in the American Community Survey. Per capita income is rounded to the nearest whole dollar.

Household income includes the income of the householder and all other individuals 15 years old and over in the household, whether or not they are related to the householder. Since many households consist of only one person, median household income is usually less than median family income. Although the household income statistics cover the 12 months preceding the interview, the characteristics of individuals and the composition of households refer to the date of interview. Thus, the income of the household does not include amounts received by individuals who were no longer residing in the household at the time of interview. Similarly, income amounts reported by individuals who did not reside in the household during all of the past 12 months but who were members of the household at the time of interview are included. However, the composition of most households was the same during those 12 months as it was at the time of interview.

Median income divides the income distribution into two equal parts, with half of all cases below the median income level and half of all cases above the median income level. For households, the median income is based on the distribution of the total number of households, including those with no income. Median income for households is computed on the basis of a standard distribution with a minimum value of less than $2,500 and a maximum value of $200,000 or more and is rounded to the nearest whole dollar. Median income figures are calculated using linear interpolation if the width of the interval containing the estimate is $2,500 or less. If the width of the interval containing the estimate is greater than $2,500, Pareto interpolation is used.

Income amounts have been adjusted for inflation to represent the final year of multi-year estimates, in this case 2010-2014 estimates. The constant-dollar figures are based on an annual average Consumer Price Index from the Bureau of Labor Statistics. Constant-dollar figures are estimates representing an effort to remove the effects of price changes from statistical series reported in dollar terms. However, the estimates do not reflect the price and cost-of-living differences that may exist between areas.

INCOME AND POVERTY, Items 58–61

Source: U.S. Census Bureau—Small Area Income and Poverty Estimates Program
http://www.census.gov/did/www/saipe/index.html

The annual income and poverty estimates by county are constructed from statistical models that relate income and poverty to indicators based on summary data from federal income tax returns, data about participation in the Food Stamp program, and the previous census. A regression model predicts the number of people in poverty using county-level observations from the current year's American Community Survey (ACS) and administrative records and census data as the predictors. The 2005 estimates were the first to use the ACS. Prior year models were based on the Annual Social and Economic Supplement (ASEC) of the Current Population Survey (CPS). The ACS is a much larger survey than the ASEC, permitting income and poverty estimates based on a single year for many counties, Because of the differences between the two surveys, caution should be used when comparing these estimates with those from earlier years.

The **poverty status** data were derived from data collected on the number of persons in a household, each person's relationship to the householder, and income data. The Social Security Administration (SSA) developed the original poverty definition in 1964, which federal interagency committees subsequently revised in 1969 and 1980. The Office of Management and Budget's (OMB) *Directive 14* prescribes the SSA's definition as the official poverty measure for federal agencies to use in their statistical work. Poverty statistics presented in American Community Survey products adhere to the standards defined by OMB in *Directive 14*.

Poverty thresholds vary depending on three criteria: size of family, number of children, and, for one- and two-person families, age of householder. In determining the poverty status of families and unrelated individuals, the Census Bureau uses thresholds (income cutoffs) arranged in a two-dimensional matrix. The matrix consists of family size (from one person to nine or more persons), cross-classified by presence and number of family members under 18 years old (from no children present to eight or more children present). Unrelated individuals and two-person families are further differentiated by age of reference person (under 65 years old and 65 years old and over). To determine a person's poverty status, the person's total family income over the previous 12 months is compared with the poverty threshold appropriate for that person's family size and composition. If the total income of that person's family is less than the threshold appropriate for that family, then the person is considered poor or "below the poverty level," together with every member of his or her family. If a person is not living with anyone related by birth, marriage, or adoption, then the person's own income is compared with his or her poverty threshold. The total number of persons below the poverty level is the sum of persons in families

and the number of unrelated individuals with incomes below the poverty level over the previous12 months.

Poverty Thresholds for 2014 by Size of Family and Number of Related Children Under 18 Years

Size of family unit	Weighted average thresholds
One person (unrelated individual)	12,071
Under 65 years	12,316
65 years and over	11,354
Two people	15,379
Householder under 65 years	15,934
Householder 65 years and over	14,326
Three people...	18,850
Four people...	24,230
Five people	28,695
Six people..	32,473
Seven people	36,927
Eight people..	40,968
Nine people or more.......................................	49,021

Source: U.S. Census Bureau.

PERSONAL INCOME AND EARNINGS, Items 62–83

Source: U.S. Bureau of Economic Analysis, Regional Economic Accounts
http://www.bea.gov/regional/index.htm#state

Total personal income is the current income received by residents of an area from all sources. It is measured before deductions of income and other personal taxes, but after deductions of personal contributions for Social Security, government retirement, and other social insurance programs. It consists of **wage and salary disbursements** (covering all employee earnings, including executive salaries, bonuses, commissions, payments-in-kind, incentive payments, and tips); various types of supplementary earnings, such as employers' contributions to pension funds (termed "other labor income" or "supplements to wages and salaries"); proprietors' income; rental income of persons; dividends; personal interest income; and government and business transfer payments.

Per capita personal income is based on the resident population estimated as of July 1 of the year shown.

Proprietors' income is the monetary income and income-in-kind of proprietorships and partnerships (including the independent professions) and the income of tax-exempt cooperatives.

Dividends are cash payments by corporations to stockholders who are U.S. residents. **Interest** is the monetary and imputed interest income of persons from all sources. **Rent** is the monetary income of persons from the rental of real property, except the income of persons primarily engaged in the real estate business; the imputed net rental income of owner-occupants of nonfarm dwellings; and the royalties received by persons.

Transfer payments are income for which services are not currently rendered. They consist of both government and business transfer payments. Government transfer payments include payments under the following programs: Federal Old-Age, Survivors, and Disability Insurance ("Social Security"); Medicare and medical vendor payments; unemployment insurance; railroad and government retirement; federal- and state-government-insured workers' compensation; veterans' benefits, including veterans' life insurance; food stamps; black lung payments; Supplemental Security Income; and Temporary Assistance for Needy Families. Government payments to nonprofit institutions, other than for work under research and development contracts, are also included. Business transfer payments consist primarily of liability payments for personal injury and of corporate gifts to nonprofit institutions.

Personal income differs in definition from money income (items 54–57). For example, personal income includes pension rights, employer-provided health insurance, food stamps, and Medicare. These are not included in the definition of money income.

Earnings cover wage and salary disbursements, other labor income, and proprietors' income.

The data for earnings obtained from the Bureau of Economic Analysis (BEA) are based on place of work. In computing personal income, BEA makes an "adjustment for residence" to earnings, based on commuting patterns; personal income is thus presented on a place-of-residence basis.

Farm earnings include the income of farm workers (wages and salaries and other labor income) and farm proprietors. Farm proprietors' income includes only the income of sole proprietorships and partnerships. Farm earnings estimates are benchmarked to data collected in the Census of Agriculture and the revised Department of Agriculture statistical totals of income and expense items.

Goods-related industries include mining, construction, and manufacturing. **Service-related** and other industries include private-sector earnings in agricultural services, forestry, and fisheries; transportation and public utilities; wholesale trade; retail trade; finance, insurance, and real estate; and services. Government earnings include all levels of government. Industries are categorized under the North American Industry Classification System (NAICS), and are not comparable to years prior to 2002.

SOCIAL SECURITY AND SUPPLEMENTAL SECURITY INCOME, Items 84–86

Source: U.S. Social Security Administration
http://www.ssa.gov/policy/docs/statcomps/oasdisc/
http://www.ssa.gov/policy/docs/statcomps/ssisc/

Social Security beneficiaries are persons receiving benefits under the Old-Age, Survivors, and Disability Insurance Program. These include retired or disabled workers covered by the program, their spouses and dependent children, and the surviving spouses and dependent children of deceased workers.

Supplemental Security Income (SSI) recipients are persons receiving SSI payments. The SSI program is a cash assistance program that provides monthly benefits to low-income aged, blind, or disabled persons.

Data are as of December of the year shown.

HOUSING, Items 87–96

Source: U.S. Census Bureau—Population Estimates Program
http://www.census.gov/popest/
Source: U.S. Census Bureau—American Community Survey
http://www.census.gov/acs/www/

Housing data for 2014 are from the Population Estimates Program. Housing unit characteristics for 2010-2014 are from the American Community Survey.

A **housing unit** is a house, apartment, mobile home or trailer, group of rooms, or single room occupied or, if vacant, intended for occupancy as separate living quarters. Separate living quarters are those in which the occupants do not live and eat with any other person in the structure and which have direct access from the outside of the building or through a common hall.

The occupants of a housing unit may be a single family, one person living alone, two or more families living together, or any other group of related or unrelated persons who share living quarters. Both occupied and vacant housing units are included in the housing inventory, although recreational vehicles, tents, caves, boats, railroad cars, and the like are included only if they are occupied as a person's usual place of residence.

A housing unit is classified as occupied if it is the usual place of residence of the person or group of persons living in it at the time of enumeration, or if the occupants are only temporarily absent (away on vacation). A household consists of all persons who occupy a housing unit as their usual place of residence. Vacant units for sale or rent include units rented or sold but not occupied and any other units held off the market.

Median value is the dollar amount that divides the distribution of specified owner-occupied housing units into two equal parts, with half of all units below the median value and half of all units above the median value. Value is defined as the respondent's estimate of what the house would sell for if it were for sale. Data are presented for single-family units on fewer than 10 acres of land that have no business or medical offices on the property.

Median rent divides the distribution of renter-occupied housing units into two equal parts. The rent concept used in this volume is gross rent, which includes the amount of cash rent a renter pays (contract rent) plus the estimated average cost of utilities and fuels, if these are paid by the renter. The rent is the amount of rent only for living quarters and excludes amounts paid for any business or other space occupied. Single-family houses on lots of 10 or more acres of land are also excluded.

Housing cost as a percentage of income is shown separately for owners with mortgages, owners without mortgages, and renters. Rent as a percentage of income is a computed ratio of gross rent and monthly household income (total household income in 1999 divided by 12). Selected owner costs include utilities and fuels, mortgage payments, insurance, taxes, etc. In each case, the ratio of housing cost to income is computed separately for each housing unit. The housing cost ratios for half of all units are above the median shown in this book, and half are below the median shown in the book.

The proportion of **Households that have a computer** includes households with desktop or laptop computers, handheld computers, or some other type of computer.

CIVILIAN LABOR FORCE AND UNEMPLOYMENT, Items 97–100

Source: U.S. Bureau of Labor Statistics—Local Area Unemployment Statistics
http://www.bls.gov/lau/#tables

Data for the civilian labor force are the product of a federal-state cooperative program in which state employment security agencies prepare labor force and unemployment estimates under concepts, definitions, and technical procedures established by the Bureau of Labor Statistics (BLS). The civilian labor force consists of all civilians 16 years old and over who are either employed or unemployed.

Unemployment includes all persons who did not work during the survey week, made specific efforts to find a job during the previous four weeks, and were available for work during the survey week (except for temporary illness). Persons waiting to be called back to a job from which they had been laid off and those waiting to report to a new job within the next 30 days are included in unemployment figures.

Table B includes annual average data for the year shown. The Local Area Unemployment Statistics data are periodically updated to reflect revised inputs, reestimation, and controlling to new statewide totals.

CIVILIAN EMPLOYMENT, Items 101–103

Source: U.S. Census Bureau—American Community Survey
http://www.census.gov/acs/www/

Total employment includes all civilians 16 years old and over who were either (1) "at work"—those who did any work at all during the reference week as paid employees, worked in either their own business or profession, worked on their own farm, or worked 15 hours or more as unpaid workers in a family farm or business; or were (2) "with a job, but not at work" —those who had a job but were not at work that week due to illness, weather, industrial dispute, vacation, or other personal reasons.

The **occupational categories** are based on the occupational classification system that was developed for the 2000 census and revised in 2002 and 2010. This system consists of 539 specific occupational categories for employed persons arranged into 23 major occupational groups. This classification was developed based on the *Standard Occupational Classification (SOC) Manual: 2000*, published by the Executive Office of the President, Office of Management and Budget.

PRIVATE NONFARM EMPLOYMENT AND EARNINGS, Items 104–112

Source: U.S. Census Bureau—County Business Patterns
http://www.census.gov/econ/cbp/index.html

Data for private nonfarm employment and earnings are compiled from the payroll information reported monthly in the Census Bureau publication *County Business Patterns*. The estimates are based on surveys conducted by the Census Bureau and administrative records from the Internal Revenue Service (IRS).

The following types of employment are excluded from the tables: government employment, self-employed persons, farm workers, and domestic service workers. Railroad employment jointly covered by Social Security and railroad retirement programs, employment on oceanborne vessels, and employment in foreign countries are also excluded.

Annual payroll is the combined amount of wages paid, tips reported, and other compensation (including salaries, vacation allowances, bonuses, commissions, sick-leave pay, and the value of payments-in-kind such as free meals and lodging) paid to employees before deductions for Social Security, income tax, insurance, union dues, etc. All forms of compensation are included, regardless of whether they are subject to income tax or the Federal Insurance Contributions Act tax, with the exception of annuities, third-party sick pay, and supplemental unemployment compensation benefits (even if income tax was withheld). For corporations, total annual payroll includes compensation paid to officers and executives; for unincorporated businesses, it excludes profit or other compensation of proprietors or partners.

AGRICULTURE, ITEMS 113–132

Source: U.S. Department of Agriculture, National Agricultural Statistics Service—2012 Census of Agriculture
http://agcensus.usda.gov/index.php

Data for the 2012 Census of Agriculture were collected in 2013, but pertain to the year 2012.

The Census Bureau took a census of agriculture every 10 years from 1840 to 1920; since 1925, this census has been taken roughly once every 5 years. The 1997 Census of Agriculture was the first one conducted by the National Agricultural Statistics Service of the U.S. Department of Agriculture. Over time, the definition of a farm has varied. For recent censuses (including the 2012 census), a farm has been defined as any place from which $1,000 or more of agricultural products were produced and sold or normally would have been sold during the census year. Dollar figures are expressed in current dollars and have not been adjusted for inflation or deflation.

The term **operator** refers to a person who operates a farm by either doing the work or making day-to-day decisions about such activities as planting, harvesting, feeding, marketing, etc. The operator may be the owner, a member of the owner's household, a salaried manager, a tenant, a renter, or a sharecropper. If a person rents land to others or has land worked on shares by others, he/she is considered the operator only of the land that is retained for his/her own operation. The census collected information on the total number of operators, the total number of women operators, and demographic information for up to three operators per farm.

The acreage designated as **land in farms** consists primarily of agricultural land used for crops, pasture, or grazing. It also includes woodland and wasteland not actually under cultivation or used for pasture or grazing, provided that this land was part of the farm operator's total operation. Land in farms is an operating-unit concept and includes all land owned and operated, as well as all land rented from others. Land used rent-free is classified as land rented from others. All land in Indian reservations used for growing crops or grazing livestock is classified as land in farms.

Irrigated land includes all land watered by any artificial or controlled means, such as sprinklers, flooding, furrows or ditches, sub-irrigation, and spreader dikes. Included are supplemental, partial, and preplant irrigation. Each acre was counted only once regardless of the number of times it was irrigated or harvested. Livestock lagoon waste water distributed by sprinkler or flood systems was also included.

Total cropland includes cropland harvested, cropland used only for pasture or grazing, cropland on which all crops failed or were abandoned, cropland in cultivated summer fallow, and cropland idle or used for cover crops or soil improvement but not harvested and not pastured or grazed.

Respondents were asked to report their estimate of the current market **value of land and buildings** owned, rented, or leased from others, and rented and leased to others. Market value refers to the respondent's estimate of what the land and buildings would sell for under current market conditions. If the value of land and buildings was not reported, it was estimated during processing by using the average value of land and buildings from similar farms in the same geographic area.

The **value of machinery and equipment** was estimated by the respondent as the current market value of all cars, trucks, tractors, combines, balers, irrigation equipment, etc., used on the farm. This value is an estimate of what the machinery and equipment would sell for in its present condition and not the replacement or depreciated value. Share interests are reported at full value at the farm where the equipment and machinery are usually kept. Only equipment that was physically located at the farm on December 31, 2012, is included.

Market value of agricultural products sold by farms represents the gross market value before taxes and the production expenses of all agricultural products sold or removed from the place in 2012, regardless of who received the payment. It is equivalent to total sales and it includes sales by the operator as well as the value of any share received by partners, landlords, contractors, and others associated with the operation. It includes value of direct sales and the value of commodities placed in the Commodity Credit Corporation (CCC) loan program. Market value of agricultural products sold does not include payments received for participation in other federal farm programs. Also, it does not include income from farm-related sources such as customwork and other agricultural services, or income from non-farm sources.

Government payments consist of direct payments as defined by the 2002 Farm Bill;

payments from Conservation Reserve Program (CRP), Wetlands Reserve Program (WRP), Farmable Wetlands Program (FWP), and Conservation Reserve Enhancement Program (CREP); loan deficiency payments; disaster payments; other conservation programs; and all other federal farm programs under which payments were made directly to farm operators. Commodity Credit Corporation (CCC) proceeds, amount from State and local federal crop insurance payments were not included in this category.

WATER CONSUMPTION, Items 133–134
Source: U.S. Geological Survey, National Water-Use Information Program
http://water.usgs.gov/watuse/

Every five years, the U.S. Geological Survey compiles county-level water-use estimates. This volume includes the total fresh and saline withdrawals expressed as million gallons per day. Estimate of withdrawals of ground and surface water are given for the following categories of use: public water supplies, domestic, commercial, irrigation, livestock, industrial, mining, and thermo-electric power. The number of gallons withdrawn per person is based on the county population but the water is not necessarily used locally, providing an indicator of counties that serve as major water sources.

2012 ECONOMIC CENSUS: OVERVIEW, Items 135–166
Source: U.S. Census Bureau
http://www.census.gov/econ/census07/

The Economic Census provides a detailed portrait of the nation's economy, from the national to the local level, once every five years. The 2012 Economic Census covers nearly all of the U.S. economy in its basic collection of establishment statistics. The 1997 Economic Census was the first major data source to use the new North American Industry Classification System (NAICS); therefore, data from this census are not comparable to economic data from prior years, which were based on the Standard Industrial Classification (SIC) system.

NAICS, developed in cooperation with Canada and Mexico, classifies North America's economic activities at two-, three-, four-, and five-digit levels of detail; the U.S. version of NAICS further defines industries to a sixth digit. The Economic Census takes advantage of this hierarchy to publish data at these successive levels of detail: sector (two-digit), subsector (three-digit), industry group (four-digit), industry (five-digit), and U.S. industry (six-digit). Information in Table A is at the two-digit level, with a few three- and four-digit items. The data in Table B are at the two-digit level.

Several key statistics are tabulated for all industries in this volume, including number of establishments (or companies), number of employees, payroll, and certain measures of output (sales, receipts, revenue, value of shipments, or value of construction work done).

Number of establishments. An establishment is a single physical location at which business is conducted. It is not necessarily identical with a company or enterprise, which may consist of one establishment or more. Economic Census figures represent a summary of reports for individual establishments rather than companies. For cases in which a census report was received, separate information was obtained for each location where business was conducted. When administrative records of other federal agencies were used instead of a census report, no information was available on the number of locations operated. Each Economic Census establishment was tabulated according to the physical location at which the business was conducted. The count of establishments represents those in business at any time during 2012.

When two activities or more were carried on at a single location under a single ownership, all activities were generally grouped together as a single establishment. The entire establishment was classified on the basis of its major activity and all of its data were included in that classification. However, when distinct and separate economic activities (for which different industry classification codes were appropriate) were conducted at a single location under a single ownership, separate establishment reports for each of the different activities were obtained in the census.

Number of employees. Paid employees consist of the full-time and part-time employees, including salaried officers and executives of corporations. Included are employees on paid sick leave, paid holidays, and paid vacations; not included are proprietors and partners of unincorporated businesses. The definition of paid employees is the same as that used by the Internal Revenue Service (IRS) on form 941.

For some industries, the Economic Census gives codes representing the number of employees as a range of numbers (for example, ''100 to 249 employees'' or ''1,000 to 2,499'' employees). In this volume, those codes have been replaced by the standard suppression code ''D''.

Payroll. Payroll includes all forms of compensation, such as salaries, wages, commissions, dismissal pay, bonuses, vacation allowances, sick-leave pay, and employee contributions to qualified pension plans paid during the year to all employees. For corporations, payroll includes amounts paid to officers and executives; for unincorporated businesses, it does not include profit or other compensation of proprietors or partners. Payroll is reported before deductions for Social Security, income tax, insurance, union dues, etc. This definition of payroll is the same as that used by on IRS form 941.

Sales, shipments, receipts, revenue, or business done. This measure includes the total sales, shipments, receipts, revenue, or business done by establishments within the scope of the Economic Census. The definition of each of these items is specific to the economic sector measured.

WHOLESALE TRADE, Items 135–138

Source: U.S. Census Bureau—2012 Economic Census (See Overview of 2012 Economic Census prior to Item 135)

The Wholesale Trade sector (sector 42) comprises establishments engaged in wholesaling merchandise, generally without transformation, and rendering services incidental to the sale of merchandise. The wholesaling process is an intermediate step in the distribution of merchandise.

Wholesalers are organized to sell or arrange the purchase or sale of (1) goods for resale (i.e., goods sold to other wholesalers or retailers), (2) capital or durable nonconsumer goods, and (3) raw and intermediate materials and supplies used in production.

Wholesalers sell merchandise to other businesses and normally operate from a warehouse or office. These warehouses and offices are characterized by having little or no display of merchandise. In addition, neither the design nor the location of the premises is intended to solicit walk-in traffic. Wholesalers do not normally use advertising directed to the general public. In general, customers are initially reached via telephone, in-person marketing, or specialized advertising, which may include the internet and other electronic means. Follow-up orders are either vendor-initiated or client-initiated, are usually based on previous sales, and typically exhibit strong ties between sellers and buyers. In fact, transactions are often conducted between wholesalers and clients that have long-standing business relationships.

This sector is made up of two main types of wholesalers: those that sell goods on their own account and those that arrange sales and purchases for others for a commission or fee.

(1) Establishments that sell goods on their own account are known as wholesale merchants, distributors, jobbers, drop shippers, import/export merchants, and sales branches. These establishments typically maintain their own warehouse, where they receive and handle goods for their customers. Goods are generally sold without transformation, but may include integral functions, such as sorting, packaging, labeling, and other marketing services.

(2) Establishments arranging for the purchase or sale of goods owned by others or purchasing goods on a commission basis are known as agents and brokers, commission merchants, import/export agents and brokers, auction companies, and manufacturers' representatives. These establishments operate from offices and generally do not own or handle the goods they sell.

Some wholesale establishments may be connected with a single manufacturer and promote and sell that particular manufacturer's products to a wide range of other wholesalers or retailers. Other wholesalers may be connected to a retail chain or a limited number of retail chains and only provide the products needed by the particular retail operation(s). These wholesalers may obtain the products from a wide range of manufacturers. Still other wholesalers may not take title to the goods, but act instead as agents and brokers for a commission.

Although wholesaling normally denotes sales in large volumes, durable nonconsumer goods may be sold in single units. Sales of capital or durable nonconsumer goods used in the production of goods and services, such as farm machinery, medium- and heavy-duty trucks, and industrial machinery, are always included in Wholesale Trade.

The county table includes only **Merchant wholesalers, except manufacturers' sales branches and offices,** establishments primarily engaged in buying and selling merchandise on their own account. Included here are such types of establishments as wholesale distributors and jobbers, importers, exporters, own-brand importers/marketers, terminal and country grain elevators, and farm products assemblers.

RETAIL TRADE, Items 139–142

Source: U.S. Census Bureau—2012 Economic Census (See Overview of 2012 Economic Census prior to Item 135)

The Retail Trade sector (44–45) is made up of establishments engaged in retailing merchandise, generally without transformation, and rendering services incidental to the sale of merchandise.

The retailing process is the final step in the distribution of merchandise; retailers are therefore organized to sell merchandise in small quantities to the general public. This sector comprises two main types of retailers: store and nonstore retailers.

Store retailers operate fixed point-of-sale locations, located and designed to attract a high volume of walk-in customers. In general, retail stores have extensive displays of merchandise and use mass-media advertising to attract customers. They typically sell merchandise to the general public for personal or household consumption; some also serve business and institutional clients. These include establishments such as office supply stores, computer and software stores, building materials dealers, plumbing supply stores, and electrical supply stores. Catalog showrooms, gasoline service stations, automotive dealers, and mobile home dealers are treated as store retailers.

In addition to retailing merchandise, some types of store retailers are also engaged in the provision of after-sales services, such as repair and installation. For example, new automobile dealers, electronic and appliance stores, and musical instrument and supply stores often provide repair services. As a general rule, establishments engaged in retailing merchandise and providing after-sales services are classified in this sector.

Nonstore retailers, like store retailers, are organized to serve the general public, although their retailing methods differ. The establishments of this subsector reach customers and market merchandise with methods including the broadcasting of "infomercials," the broadcasting and publishing of direct-response advertising, the publishing of paper and electronic catalogs, door-to-door solicitation, in-home demonstration, selling from portable stalls (street vendors, except food), and distribution through vending machines. Establishments engaged in the direct sale (nonstore) of products, such as home heating oil dealers and home-delivery newspaper routes are included in this sector.

The buying of goods for resale is a characteristic of retail trade establishments that distinguishes them from establishments in the Agriculture, Manufacturing, and Construction sectors. For example, farms that sell their products at or from the point of production are classified in Agriculture instead of in Retail Trade. Similarly, establishments that both manufacture and sell their products to the general public are classified in Manufacturing instead of Retail Trade. However, establishments that engage in processing activities incidental to retailing are classified in Retail Trade.

REAL ESTATE AND RENTAL AND LEASING, Items 143–146
Source: U.S. Census Bureau—2012 Economic Census (See Overview of 2012 Economic Census prior to Item 135)

The Real Estate and Rental and Leasing sector (53) comprises establishments primarily engaged in renting, leasing, or otherwise allowing the use of tangible or intangible assets, and establishments providing related services. The major portion of this sector is made up of establishments that rent, lease, or otherwise allow the use of their own assets by others. The assets may be tangible, such as real estate and equipment, or intangible, such as patents and trademarks.

This sector also includes establishments primarily engaged in managing real estate for others, selling, renting, and/or buying real estate for others, and appraising real estate. These activities are closely related to this sector's main activity. In addition, a substantial proportion of property management is self-performed by lessors.

The main components of this sector are the real estate lessors industries; equipment lessors industries (including motor vehicles,

computers, and consumer goods); and lessors of nonfinancial intangible assets (except copyrighted works).

PROFESSIONAL, SCIENTIFIC, AND TECHNICAL SERVICES, Items 147–150
Source: U.S. Census Bureau—2012 Economic Census (See Overview of 2012 Economic Census prior to Item 135)

The Professional, Scientific, and Technical Services sector (54) is made up of establishments that specialize in performing professional, scientific, and technical activities for others. These activities require a high degree of expertise and training. The establishments in this sector specialize in one or more areas and provide services to clients in a variety of industries (and, in some cases, to households). Activities performed include legal advice and representation; accounting, bookkeeping, and payroll services; architectural, engineering, and specialized design services; computer services; consulting services; research services; advertising services; photographic services; translation and interpretation services; veterinary services; and other professional, scientific, and technical services.

This sector excludes establishments primarily engaged in providing a range of day-to-day office administrative services, such as financial planning, billing and record keeping, personnel services, and physical distribution and logistics services. These establishments are classified in sector 56, Administrative and Support and Waste Management and Remediation Services.

MANUFACTURING, Items 151–154
Source: U.S. Census Bureau—2012 Economic Census (See Overview of 2012 Economic Census prior to Item 135)

The Manufacturing sector (31–33) is made up of establishments engaged in the mechanical, physical, or chemical transformation of materials, substances, or components into new products. The assembling of component parts of manufactured products is considered manufacturing, except in cases in which the activity is appropriately classified in the Construction sector. Establishments in the Manufacturing sector are often described as plants, factories, or mills, and characteristically use power-driven machines and materials-handling equipment. However, establishments that transform materials or substances into new products by hand or in the worker's home, and establishments engaged in selling to the general public products made on the same premises from which they are sold (such as bakeries, candy stores, and custom tailors) may also be included in this sector. Manufacturing establishments may process materials or contract with other establishments to process their materials for them. Both types of establishments are included in the Manufacturing sector.

The materials, substances, or components transformed by manufacturing establishments are raw materials that are products of agriculture, forestry, fishing, mining, or quarrying, or are products of other manufacturing establishments. The materials used may be purchased directly from producers, obtained through customary trade channels, or secured without recourse to the market by transferring the product from one establishment to another, under the same ownership. The new product of a manufacturing establishment may be finished (in the sense that it is ready for utilization or consumption), or it may be semifinished to become an input for an establishment engaged in further manufacturing. For example, the product of the alumina refinery is the input used in the primary production of aluminum; primary aluminum is the input used in an aluminum wire drawing plant; and aluminum wire is the input used in a fabricated wire product manufacturing establishment.

Data are included for counties with 500 or more employees in the Manufacturing sector.

ACCOMMODATION AND FOOD SERVICES, Items 155–158
Source: U.S. Census Bureau—2012 Economic Census (See Overview of 2012 Economic Census prior to Item 135)

The Accommodation and Food Services sector (72) consists of establishments that provide customers with lodging and/or meals, snacks, and beverages for immediate consumption. This sector includes both accommodation and food services establishments because the two activities are often combined at the same establishment.

Excluded from this sector are civic and social organizations, amusement and recreation parks, theaters, and other recreation or entertainment facilities providing food and beverage services.

HEALTH CARE AND SOCIAL ASSISTANCE, Items 159–162
Source: U.S. Census Bureau—2012 Economic Census (See Overview of 2012 Economic Census prior to Item 135)

The Health Care and Social Assistance sector (62) consists of establishments that provide health care and social assistance services to individuals. The sector includes both health care and social assistance because it is sometimes difficult to distinguish between the boundaries of these two activities. The industries in this sector are arranged on a continuum, starting with establishments that provide medical care exclusively, continuing with those that provide health care and social assistance, and finishing with those that provide only social assistance. The services provided by establishments in this sector are delivered by trained professionals. All industries in the sector share this commonality of process—namely, labor inputs of health practitioners or social workers with the requisite expertise. Many of the industries in the sector are defined based on the educational degree held by the practitioners included in the industry.

Excluded from this sector are aerobic classes, which can be found in subsector 713, Amusement, Gambling, and Recreation Industries; and nonmedical diet and weight-reducing centers, which can be found in subsector 812, Personal and Laundry Services. Although these can be viewed as health services, they are not typically delivered by health practitioners.

OTHER SERVICES, EXCEPT PUBLIC ADMINISTRATION Items 163–166
Source: U.S. Census Bureau—2012 Economic Census (See Overview of 2012 Economic Census prior to Item 135)

The Other Services, Except Public Administration sector (81) comprises establishments engaged in providing services not specifically categorized elsewhere in the classification system. Establishments in this sector are primarily engaged in activities such as equipment and machinery repairing, promoting or administering religious activities, grant making, and advocacy; this sector also includes establishments that provide dry-cleaning and laundry services, personal care services, death care services, pet care services, photofinishing services, temporary parking services, and dating services.

Private households that employ workers on or about the premises in activities primarily concerned with the operation of the household are included in this sector.

Excluded from this sector are establishments primarily engaged in retailing new equipment and performing repairs and general maintenance on equipment. These establishments are classified in sector 44–45, Retail Trade.

NONEMPLOYER BUSINESSES, Items 167 and 168
Source: U.S. Census Bureau—Nonemployer Statistics http://www.census.gov/econ/nonemployer/

Nonemployer Statistics is an annual series that provides subnational economic data for businesses that have no paid employees and are subject to federal income tax. The data consist of the number of businesses and total receipts by industry. Most nonemployers are self-employed individuals operating unincorporated businesses (known as sole proprietorships), which may or may not be the owner's principal source of income.

The majority of all business establishments in the United States are nonemployers, yet these firms average less than 4 percent of all sales and receipts nationally. Due to their small economic impact, these firms are excluded from most other Census Bureau business statistics (the primary exception being the Survey of Business Owners). The Nonemployers Statistics series is the primary resource available to study the scope and activities of nonemployers at a detailed geographic level.

BUILDING PERMITS, Items 169 and 170
Source: U.S. Census Bureau—Building Permits Survey http://www.census.gov/construction/bps/

These figures represent private residential construction authorized by building permits in approximately 20,000 places in the United States. Valuation represents the expected cost of construction as recorded on the building permit. This figure usually excludes the cost of on-site and off-site development and improvements, as well as the cost of heating, plumbing, electrical, and elevator installations.

National, state, and county totals were obtained by adding the data for permit-issuing places within each jurisdiction. Not all areas of the country require a building or zoning permit. The statistics only represent those areas that do require a permit. These totals thus are limited to permits issued in the 20,000 place universe covered by the Census Bureau and may not include all permits issued within a state. Current surveys indicate that construction is undertaken for all but a very small percentage of housing units authorized by building permits.

Residential building permits include buildings with any number of housing units. Housing units exclude group quarters (such as dormitories and rooming houses), transient accommodations (such as transient hotels, motels, and tourist courts), "HUD-code" manufactured (mobile) homes, moved or relocated units, and housing units created in an existing residential or nonresidential structure.

COUNTY AREA LOCAL GOVERNMENT EMPLOYMENT AND PAYROLL, Items 171–179

Source: U.S. Census Bureau—2012 Census of Governments
http://www.census.gov/govs/cog2012/

These items include data for all local governments (i.e., counties, municipalities, townships, special districts, and school districts) located within the county. The Census of Governments identifies the scope and nature of the nation's state and local government sector; provides authoritative benchmark figures of public finance and public employment; classifies local government organizations, powers, and activities; and measures federal, state, and local fiscal relationships. The Employment component was mailed March 2012 to collect information on the number of state and local government civilian employees and their payrolls.

Government employees include all persons paid for personal services performed, including persons paid from federally funded programs, paid elected or appointed officials, persons in a paid leave status, and persons paid on a per meeting, annual, semiannual, or quarterly basis. Unpaid officials, pensioners, persons whose work is performed on a fee basis, and contractors and their employees are excluded from the count of employees. **Full-Time Equivalent employees** is a computed statistic representing the number of full-time employees that could have been employed if the reported number of hours worked by part-time employees had been worked by full-time employees. This statistic is calculated separately for each function of a government by dividing the "part-time hours paid" by the standard number of hours for full-time employees in the particular government and then adding the resulting quotient to the number of full-time employees.

March payroll represents gross payroll amounts for the one-month period of March for full-time and part-time employees. Gross payroll includes all salaries, wages, fees, commissions, and overtime paid to employees **before** withholdings for taxes, insurance, etc. It also includes incentive payments that are paid at regular pay intervals. It excludes employer share of fringe benefits like retirement, Social Security, health and life insurance, lump sum payments, and so forth.

Administration and Judicial and Legal combines **Financial administration**, **Other government administration, and Judicial and Legal** activities. **Financial administration** includes activities concerned with tax assessment and collection, custody and disbursement of funds, debt management, administration of trust funds, budgeting, and other government-wide financial management activities. This function is not applied to school district or special district governments. **Other government administration** applies to the legislative and government-wide administrative agencies of governments. Included here are overall planning and zoning activities, and central personnel and administrative activities. This function is not applied to school district or special district governments. **Judicial and legal** includes all court and court related activities (except probation and parole activities that are included at the "Correction" function), court activities of sheriff's offices, prosecuting attorneys' and public defenders' offices, legal departments, and attorneys providing government-wide legal service.

Police and Corrections includes all activities concerned, with the enforcement of law and order, including coroner's offices, police training academies, investigation bureaus, and local jails, "lockups", or other detention facilities not intended to serve as correctional facilities. **Corrections** includes activities pertaining to the confinement and correction of adults and minors convicted of criminal offenses. Pardon, probation, and parole activities are also included here.

Fire protection includes local government fire protection and prevention activities plus any ambulance, rescue, or other auxiliary services provided by a fire protection agency. Volunteer firefighters, if remunerated for their services on a "per fire" or some other basis, are included as part-time employees.

Highways and transportation includes activities associated with the maintenance and operation of streets, roads, sidewalks, bridges, tunnels, toll roads, and ferries. Snow and ice removal, street lighting, and highway and traffic engineering activities are also included here. Also included are the operation, maintenance, and construction of public mass transit systems, including subways, surface rails, and buses, and the provision, construction, operation, maintenance; support of public waterways, harbors, docks, wharves, and related marine terminal facilities; and activities associated with the operation and support of publicly operated airport facilities.

Health and Welfare includes **Health, Hospitals, and Public welfare**. **Health** includes administration of public health programs, community and visiting nurse services, immunization programs, drug abuse rehabilitation programs, health and food inspection activities, operation of outpatient clinics, and environmental pollution control activities. **Hospitals** includes only government operated medical care facilities that provide inpatient care. Employees and payrolls of private corporations that lease and operate government-owned hospital facilities are excluded. **Public Welfare** includes the administration of various public assistance programs for the needy, veteran services, operation of nursing homes, indigent care institutions, and programs that provide payments for medical care, handicap transportation, and other services for the needy.

Natural resources and Utilities includes activities primarily concerned with the conservation and development of natural resources (soil, water, energy, minerals, etc.) and the regulation of industries that develop, utilize, or affect natural resources, as well as the operation and maintenance of **parks**, playgrounds, swimming pools, public beaches, auditoriums, public golf courses, museums, marinas, botanical gardens, and zoological parks. **Utilities, sewerage, and waste management** includes operation, maintenance, and construction of public water supply systems, including production, acquisition, and distribution of water to general public or to other public or private utilities, for residential, commercial, and industrial use; activities associated with the production or acquisition and distribution of electric power; provision, maintenance, and operation of sanitary and storm sewer systems and sewage disposal and treatment facilities; and refuse collection and disposal, operation of sanitary landfills, and street cleaning activities.

Education and libraries includes activities associated with the operation of public elementary and secondary schools and locally operated vocational-technical schools. Special education programs operated by elementary and secondary school systems are also included as are all ancillary services associated with the operation of schools, such as pupil transportation and food service. Also included are the establishment and provision of libraries for use by the general public and the technical support of privately operated libraries. This category includes classroom teachers, principals, supervisors of instruction, librarians, teacher aides, library aides, and guidance and psychological personnel as well as school superintendents and other administrative personnel, clerical and secretarial staffs, plant operation and maintenance personnel, health and recreation employees, transportation and food service personnel, and any student employees. Also included are any degree granting institutions that provide academic training above grade 12.

LOCAL GOVERNMENT FINANCES, Items 180–193

Source: U.S. Census Bureau—2012 Census of Governments
http://www.census.gov/govs/cog/

Data on local government finances are based on result of the 2012 Census of Governments. For each county area, the financial data comprise amounts for all local governments—not only the county government, but also any municipalities, townships, school districts, and special districts within the county. Statistics from governmental units located in two or more county areas are assigned to the county area containing the administrative office.

Revenue and expenditure items include all amounts of money received and paid out, respectively, by a government and its agencies (net of correcting transactions such as recoveries of refunds), with the exception of amounts for debt issuance and retirement and for loan and investment, agency, and private transactions.

Payments among the various funds and agencies of a particular government are excluded from revenue and expenditure items as representing internal transfers. Therefore, a government's contribution to a retirement fund that it administers is not counted as expenditure, nor is the receipt of this contribution by the retirement fund counted as revenue.

Total **general revenue** includes all revenue except utility, liquor stores, and insurance trust revenue. All tax revenue and

intergovernmental revenue, even if designated for employee-retirement or local utility purpose, are classified as general revenue.

Intergovernmental revenue covers amounts received from the federal government as fiscal aid, reimbursements for performance of general government functions and specific services for the paying government, or in lieu of taxes. It excludes any amounts received from other governments from the sale of property, commodities, and utility services.

Taxes consist of compulsory contributions exacted by governments for public purposes. However, this category excludes employer and employee payments for retirement and social insurance purposes, which are classified as insurance trust revenue; it also excludes special assessments, which are classified as nontax general revenue. Property taxes are taxes conditioned on ownership of property and assessed by its value. Sales and gross receipts taxes do not include dealer discounts, or ''commissions'' allowed to merchants for collection of taxes from consumers. General sales taxes and selected taxes on sales of motor fuels, tobacco products, and other particular commodities and services are included.

General government expenditure includes capital outlay, a major portion of which is commonly financed by borrowing. Government revenue does not include receipts from borrowing. Among other things, this distorts the relationship between totals of revenue and expenditure figures that are presented and renders it useless as a direct measure of the degree of budgetary ''balance'' (as that term is generally applied).

Direct general expenditure comprises all expenditures of the local governments, excluding utility, liquor stores, insurance trust expenditures, and any intergovernmental payments.

Local government expenditure for **education** is mainly for the provision and general support of schools and other educational facilities and services, including those for educational institutions beyond high school. They cover such related services as student transportation; school lunch and other cafeteria operations; school health, recreation, and library services; and dormitories, dining halls, and bookstores operated by public institutions of higher education.

Health and hospital expenditure includes health research; clinics; nursing; immunization; other categorical, environmental, and general health services provided by health agencies; establishment and operation of hospital facilities; provision of hospital care; and support of other public and private hospitals.

Police protection expenditure includes police activities such as patrols, communications, custody of persons awaiting trial, and vehicular inspection.

Public welfare expenditure covers support of and assistance to needy persons; this aid is contingent upon the person's needs. Included are cash assistance paid directly to needy persons under categorical (Old Age Assistance, Temporary Assistance for Needy Families, Aid to the Blind, and Aid to the Disabled) and other welfare programs; vendor payments made directly to private purveyors for medical care, burials, and other commodities and services provided under welfare programs; welfare institutions; and any intergovernmental or other direct expenditure for welfare purposes. Pensions to former employees and other benefits not contingent on need are excluded.

Highway expenditure is for the provision and maintenance of highway facilities, including toll turnpikes, bridges, tunnels, and ferries, as well as regular roads, highways, and streets. Also included are expenditures for street lighting and for snow and ice removal. Not included are highway policing and traffic control, which are considered part of police protection

Debt outstanding includes all long-term debt obligations of the government and its agencies (exclusive of utility debt) and all interest-bearing, short-term (repayable within one year) debt obligations remaining unpaid at the close of the fiscal year. It includes judgments, mortgages, and revenue bonds, as well as general obligation bonds, notes, and interest-bearing warrants. This category consists of non-interest-bearing, short-term obligations; inter-fund obligations; amounts owed in a trust or agency capacity; advances and contingent loans from other governments; and rights of individuals to benefit from government-administered employee-retirement funds.

GOVERNMENT EMPLOYMENT, Items 194–196
Source: U.S. Bureau of Economic Analysis—Regional Economic Accounts
http://www.bea.gov/regional/index.htm#state

Employment is measured as the average annual sum of full-time and part-time jobs. The estimates are on a place-of-work basis. State and local government employment includes person employed in all state and local government agencies and enterprises. Data for federal civilian employment include civilian employees of the federal government, including civilian employees of the Department of Defense. Military employment includes all persons on active duty status.

ELECTION STATISTICS, Items 197–199
Source: Election Data Services, Inc. Washington, DC (copyright)
http://www.electiondataservices.com/
index.php?content=elecdata

© 2013 Election Data Services, Inc. All rights reserved. This material is proprietary and the subject of copyright protection and other intellectual property rights owned by or licensed to Election Data Services, Inc. The use of this material is subject to the terms of a License Agreement. You will be held liable for any unauthorized copying or disclosure of this material.

Election results show the percentage of the total vote cast for the Democratic and Republican candidates, as well as the combined percentage for all other candidates in the 2012 presidential election.

TABLE C—METROPOLITAN AREAS

Table C presents 199 items for the 381 metropolitan statistical areas (MSAs) and 31 metropolitan divisions in the United States. The metropolitan areas are presented in alphabetical order, and the metropolitan divisions are presented in alphabetical order within the appropriate metropolitan area. For some data items,

the metropolitan area data have been aggregated from county data sources.

LAND AREA, Items 1 and 4
Source: U.S. Census Bureau—2010 Census of Population and Housing
http://www.census.gov/2010census/data

Land area measurements are shown to the nearest square kilometer. Land area includes dry land and land temporarily or partially covered by water, such as marshlands, swamps, and river floodplains.

POPULATION, Items 2–4
Source: U.S. Census Bureau—Population Estimates
http://www.census.gov/popest/estimates.html

The population data are Census Bureau estimates of the resident population as of July 1 of the year shown. The ranks are shown for metropolitan statistical areas, but exclude metropolitan divisions.

POPULATION AND POPULATION CHARACTERISTICS, Items 5–19
Source: U.S. Census Bureau—Population Estimates
http://www.census.gov/popest/estimates.html

The concept of race, as used by the Census Bureau, reflects self-identification by persons according to the race or races with which they most closely identify. These categories are sociopolitical constructs and should not be interpreted as being scientific or anthropological in nature. Furthermore, race categories include both racial and national origin groups.

Beginning with the 2000 census, respondents were offered the option of selecting one or more races. This option was not available in prior censuses; thus, comparisons between censuses should be made with caution. In Table C, Columns 5 through 8 refer to individuals who identified with each racial category, either alone or in combination with other races. The estimates exclude persons of Hispanic or Latino origin from all race groups. Because respondents could include as many categories as they wished, and because the columns refer to the percentage of the population, the total will often exceed 100 percent.

The **White** population is defined as persons who indicated their race as White, as well as persons who did not classify themselves in one of the specific race categories listed on the questionnaire but entered a nationality such as Irish, German, Italian, Lebanese, Near Easterner, Arab, or Polish.

The **Black** population includes persons who indicated their race as "Black, African Am., or Negro," as well as persons who did not classify themselves in one of the specific race categories but reported entries such as African American, Afro American, Kenyan, Nigerian, or Haitian.

The **American Indian or Alaska Native** population includes persons who indicated their race as American Indian or Alaska Native, as well as persons who did not classify themselves in one of the specific race categories but reported entries such as Canadian Indian, French-American Indian, Spanish-American Indian,

Eskimo, Aleut, Alaska Indian, or any of the American Indian or Alaska Native tribes.

The **Asian and Pacific Islander** population combines two census groupings: **Asian** and **Native Hawaiian or Other Pacific Islander**. The **Asian** population includes persons who indicated their race as Asian Indian, Chinese, Filipino, Japanese, Korean, Vietnamese, or ''Other Asian,'' as well as persons who provided write-in entries of such groups as Cambodian, Laotian, Hmong, Pakistani, or Taiwanese. The **Native Hawaiian or Other Pacific Islander** population includes persons who indicated their race as ''Native Hawaiian,'' ''Guamanian or Chamorro,'' ''Samoan,'' or ''Other Pacific Islander,'' as well as persons who reported entries such as Part Hawaiian, American Samoan, Fijian, Melanesian, or Tahitian.

The sum of the four individual race alone or in combination categories in this book will often add to more than the total population because people who reported more than one race were tallied in each race category. In this book, the Asian group has been combined with the Native Hawaiian and Other Pacific Islander group, causing double-counting of persons who identify with both groups. This is especially pronounced in Hawaii.

The **Hispanic population** is based on a complete-count question that asked respondents ''Is this person Spanish/Hispanic/Latino?'' Persons marking any one of the four Hispanic categories (i.e., Mexican, Puerto Rican, Cuban, or other Spanish) are collectively referred to as Hispanic.

In the 2000 census, the Hispanic origin question was placed before the race question and specific instructions indicated that both questions should be answered. These changes were designed to improve accuracy and may affect comparability with 1990 data.

Age is defined as age at last birthday (number of completed years since birth), as of April 1 of the census year. The 2000 census also asked for the specific date of birth of the respondent, and 2000 census procedures used the birth date for deriving age data. For this reason, it is likely that the 2000 data have fewer problems than data from prior censuses, such as the tendency of respondents to round ages or to report their ages on the date the questionnaire was filled out rather than on April 1.

The **female** population is shown as a percentage of total population.

POPULATION AND COMPONENTS OF CHANGE, Items 20–26
Source: U.S. Census Bureau—Decennial Censuses and Population Estimates
http://www.census.gov/main/www/cen2000.html
http://www.census.gov/popest/estimates.html
http://www.census.gov/2010census/data/

The population data for 2000 and 2010 are from the decennial censuses and represent the resident population as of April 1 of those years. The components of change are based on Census Bureau estimates of the resident population as of July 1 of 2015. The change in population between 2010 and 2015 is made up of (a) natural increase—births minus deaths, and (b) net migration—the difference between the number of persons moving into a particular area and the number of persons moving out of the area. Net migration is composed of internal and international migration.

Because the 2015 population estimates are based on a model that begins with a national population estimate, the county and msa components of change do not always exactly add up to the difference between the 2010 census population and the 2015 estimates.

HOUSEHOLDS, Items 27–31
Source: U.S. Census Bureau—American Community Survey
http://www.census.gov/acs/www/

A **household** includes all of the persons who occupy a housing unit. (Persons not living in households are classified as living in group quarters.) A housing unit is a house, an apartment, a mobile home, a group of rooms, or a single room occupied (or, if vacant, intended for occupancy) as separate living quarters. Separate living quarters are those in which the occupants live separately from any other persons in the building and have direct access from the outside of the building or through a common hall. The occupants may be a single family, one person living alone, two or more families living together, or any other group of related or unrelated persons who share living quarters. The number of households is the same as the number of year-round occupied housing units.

A **family** includes a householder and one or more other persons living in the same household who are related to the householder by birth, marriage, or adoption. All persons in a household who are related to the householder are regarded as members of his or her family. A **family household** may contain persons not related to the householder; thus, family households may include more members than families do. A household can contain only one family for the purposes of census tabulations. Not all households contain families, as a household may comprise a group of unrelated persons or of one person living alone. Families are classified by type as either a ''husband-wife family'' or ''other family,'' according to the presence or absence of a spouse.

The measure of **persons per household** is obtained by dividing the number of persons by the number of households or householders. One person in each household is designated as the householder. In most cases, this is the person (or one of the persons) in whose name the house is owned, being bought, or rented. If there is no such person in the household, any adult household member 15 years old and over can be designated as the householder.

The category **female family householder** includes only female-headed family households with no spouse present.

GROUP QUARTERS, Item 32
Source: U.S. Census Bureau—Population Estimates
http://www.census.gov/popest/estimates.html

The Census Bureau classifies all persons not living in households as living in group quarters; this category includes both the institutional and noninstitutional populations. The institutionalized population includes persons under formally authorized supervised care or custody in institutions, such as correctional institutions, nursing homes, mental (psychiatric) hospitals, and juvenile institutions. The noninstitutionalized population includes persons who live in group quarters other than institutions, such as college dormitories, military quarters, and group homes. This volume includes the total number of persons in group quarters.

DAYTIME POPULATION, Items 33 and 34
Source: U.S. Census Bureau—American Community Survey http://www.census.gov/acs/www/

Daytime population refers to the number of persons who are present in an area or place during normal business hours, including workers. This can be contrasted with the "resident" population, which is present during the evening and nighttime hours. The daytime population estimate is calculated by adding the total resident population and the total workers working in the area/place, and then subtracting the total workers living in the area/place from that result. Information on the expansion or contraction experienced by different communities between their nighttime and daytime populations is important for many planning purposes, especially those concerning transportation, disaster, and relief operations.

The employment/residence ratio is a measure of the total number of workers working in an area or place, relative to the total number of workers living in the area or place. It is often used as a rough indication of the jobs-workers balance in an area/place, although it does not take into account whether the resident workers possess the skills needed for the jobs available in their particular area/place. The employment/residence ratio is calculated by dividing the number of total workers working in an area/place by the number of total workers residing in the area/place.

BIRTHS AND DEATHS, Items 35–38
Source: U.S. Census Bureau—Population Estimates http://www.census.gov/popest/estimates.html

The numbers of births and deaths are from the Census Bureau's Population Estimates Program. They represent the total number of live births and deaths occurring to residents of an area as estimated using reports from the National Center for Health Statistics (NCHS) and the Federal-State Cooperative for Population Estimates (FSCPE). The rates measure births and deaths during the specified time period as a proportion of an area's population. Rates are expressed per 1,000 population estimated as of July 1. These numbers and rates do not represent the calendar year, but rather the year-long period ending on July 1.

PERSONS UNDER 65 WITH NO HEALTH INSURANCE, Items 39 and 40
Source: U.S. Census Bureau—Small Area Health Insurance Estimates http://www.census.gov/did/www/sahie/index.html

The Small Area Health Insurance Estimates (SAHIE) program develops model-based estimates of health insurance coverage for counties and states. This developmental program builds on the work of the Small Area Income and Poverty Estimates (SAIPE) program. The SAHIE program models health insurance coverage by combining survey data with population estimates and administrative records. These estimates combine data from administrative records, postcensal population estimates, and the decennial census

with direct estimates from the American Community Survey to provide consistent and reliable single-year estimates. These model-based single-year estimates are more reflective of current conditions than multi-year survey estimates. The metropolitan area estimates have been aggregated from the county estimates.

MEDICARE ENROLLMENT, Items 41–43
Source: U.S. Department of Health and Human Services, Centers for Medicare and Medicaid Services https://www.cms.gov/Research-Statistics-Data-and-Systems/Statistics-Trends-and-Reports/Medicare-Geographic-Variation/GVPUF.html

The Centers for Medicare and Medicaid Services (CMS) administers Medicare, which provides health insurance to persons 65 years old and over, persons with permanent kidney failure, and certain persons with disabilities. Original Medicare has two parts: Hospital Insurance and Supplemental Medical Insurance. In recent years, Medicare has been expanded to include two new programs: Medicare Advantage plans and prescription drug coverage. Medicare Advantage Plans are health plan options that are approved by Medicare but run by private companies. Medicare prescription drug plans can be part of Medicare Advantage plans or stand-alone drug plans.

Persons who are eligible for Medicare can enroll in Part A (Hospital Insurance) at no charge, and can choose to pay a monthly premium to enroll in Part B. Most eligible persons are enrolled in Part A, and more than 90 percent of enrollees in Part A are also enrolled in Part B (Supplemental Medical Insurance.) This table includes persons who were enrolled in both Part A and Part B during 2014.

Part B beneficiaries can choose to enroll in **Original Medicare**, a fee-for-service plan administered by the Centers for Medicare and Medicaid Services, or in a **Medicare Advantage** plan.

Medicare Advantage plans include private fee-for-service plans, preferred provider organizations, health maintenance organizations, medical savings account plans, demonstration plans, and programs for all-inclusive care for the elderly.

CRIME, Items 44–47
Source: U.S. Federal Bureau of Investigation— Uniform Crime Reports http://www.fbi.gov/ucr/ucr.htm

Crime data are as reported to the Federal Bureau of Investigation (FBI) by law enforcement agencies and have not been adjusted for underreporting. This may affect comparability between geographic areas or over time.

Through the voluntary contribution of crime statistics by law enforcement agencies across the United States, the Uniform Crime Reporting (UCR) Program provides periodic assessments of crime in the nation as measured by offenses that have come to the attention of the law enforcement community. The Committee on Uniform Crime Records of the International Association of Chiefs of Police initiated this voluntary national data collection effort in 1930. The UCR Program contributors compile and submit their crime data either directly to the FBI or through state-level UCR Programs.

Seven offenses, because of their severity, frequency of occurrence, and likelihood of being reported to police, were initially selected to serve as an index for evaluating fluctuations in the volume of crime. These serious crimes were murder and nonnegligent manslaughter, forcible rape, robbery, aggravated assault, burglary, larceny-theft, and motor vehicle theft. By congressional mandate, arson was added as the eighth index offense in 1979. The totals shown in this volume do not include arson.

In 2004, the FBI discontinued the use of the Crime Index in the UCR Program and its publications, stating that the Crime Index was driven upward by the offense with the highest number of cases (in this case, larceny-theft), creating a bias against jurisdictions with a high number of larceny-thefts but a low number of other serious crimes, such as murder and forcible rape. The FBI is currently publishing a violent crime total and property crime total until a more viable index is developed. This book includes the crime total, as well as violent crime and property crime rates.

In 2013, the FBI adopted a new definition of rape. Rape is now defined as, "Penetration, no matter how slight, of the vagina or anus with any body part or object, or oral penetration by a sex organ of another person, without the consent of the victim." The new definition updated the 80-year-old historical definition of rape which was "carnal knowledge of a female forcibly and against her will." Effectively, the revised definition expands rape to include both male and female victims and offenders, and reflects the various forms of sexual penetration understood to be rape, especially nonconsenting acts of sodomy, and sexual assaults with objects.

Violent crimes include four categories of offenses: (1) Murder and nonnegligent manslaughter, as defined in the UCR Program, is the willful (nonnegligent) killing of one human being by another. This offense excludes deaths caused by negligence, suicide, or accident; justifiable homicides; and attempts to murder or assaults to murder. (2) Rape is the penetration, no matter how slight, of the vagina or anus with any body part or object, or oral penetration by a sex organ of another person, without the consent of the victim. Assaults or attempts to commit rape by force or threat of force are also included; however, statutory rape (without force) and other sex offenses are excluded. (3) Robbery is the taking or attempting to take anything of value from the care, custody, or control of a person or persons by force or threat of force or violence and/or by putting the victim in fear. (4) Aggravated assault is an unlawful attack by one person upon another for the purpose of inflicting severe or aggravated bodily injury. This type of assault is usually accompanied by the use of a weapon or by other means likely to produce death or great bodily harm. Attempts are included, since injury does not necessarily have to result when a gun, knife, or other weapon is used, as these incidents could and probably would result in a serious personal injury if the crime were successfully completed.

Property crimes include three categories: (1) Burglary, or breaking and entering, is the unlawful entry of a structure to commit a felony or theft, even though no force was used to gain entrance. (2) Larceny-theft is the unauthorized taking of the personal property of another, without the use of force. (3) Motor vehicle theft is the unauthorized taking of any motor vehicle.

Rates are based on population estimates provided by the FBI. The county totals published in this volume were obtained by aggregating individual reporting units within each county and MSA. If the population total for the units aggregated was less than 75 percent of the county's population (as estimated by the Census Bureau), the total was not considered representative of the county as a whole and was not published. State and U.S. totals include FBI estimates for those areas. State and U.S. totals in this table are the adjusted totals as published in the FBI's *Crime in the United States*.

EDUCATION—SCHOOL ENROLLMENT AND EDUCATIONAL ATTAINMENT, Items 48–51
Source: U.S. Census Bureau—American Community Survey
http://www.census.gov/acs/www/

Data on school enrollment and educational attainment were derived from a sample of the population. Persons were classified as enrolled in school if they reported attending a "regular" public or private school (or college) during the three months prior to the survey. The instructions were to "include only nursery school, kindergarten, elementary school, and schooling which would lead to a high school diploma or a college degree" as regular school. The Census Bureau defines a public school as "any school or college controlled and supported by a local, county, state, or federal government." Schools primarily supported and controlled by religious organizations or other private groups are defined as private schools.

Data on **educational attainment** are tabulated for the population 25 years old and over. The data were derived from a question that asked respondents for the highest level of school completed or the highest degree received. Persons who had passed a high school equivalency examination were considered high school graduates. Schooling received in foreign schools was to be reported as the equivalent grade or years in the regular American school system.

Vocational and technical training, such as barber school training; business, trade, technical, and vocational schools; or other training for a specific trade are specifically excluded.

High school graduate or less. This category includes persons whose highest degree was a high school diploma or its equivalent and those who reported any level lower than a high school diploma.

Bachelor's degree or more. This category includes persons who have received bachelor's degrees, master's degrees, professional school degrees (such as law school or medical school degrees), and doctoral degrees.

LOCAL GOVERNMENT EDUCATION EXPENDITURES, Items 52 and 53
Source: U.S. Census Bureau—Annual Survey of School System Finances
http://www.census.gov/govs/school/

Expenditures are for elementary and secondary Education which includes prekindergarten through twelfth grade regular, special, and vocational education, as well as cocurricular, community service, and adult education programs provided by a public school system. The financial activities of these systems for all instruction, support service, and noninstructional activities are included

Current Spending comprises current operation expenditure, payments made by the state government on behalf of school systems, and transfers made by school systems into their own retirement funds. Current operation expenditures include direct expenditure for salaries, employee benefits, purchased professional and technical services, purchased property and other services, and supplies. It includes gross school system expenditure for instruction, support services, and noninstructional functions. It excludes expenditure for debt service, capital outlay, and reimbursement to other governments (including other school systems).

Current expenditure per student is current expenditure divided by the number of students enrolled. The number of students enrolled is based on an annual ''membership'' count of students on or about October 1.

INCOME AND POVERTY Items 54–61
Source: U.S. Census Bureau—American Community Survey
http://www.census.gov/acs/www/

The data on income were derived from responses of a sample of persons 15 years old and over. **Total money income** is the sum of the amounts reported separately for wage or salary income; net self-employment income; interest, dividends, or net rental or royalty income or income from estates and trusts; Social Security or railroad retirement income; Supplemental Security Income (SSI); public assistance or welfare payments; retirement, survivor, or disability pensions; and all other income. Receipts from the following sources are not included as income: capital gains; money received from the sale of property (unless the recipient was engaged in the business of selling such property); the value of income ''in kind'' from food stamps, public housing subsidies, medical care, employer contributions for individuals, etc.; withdrawal of bank deposits; money borrowed; tax refunds; exchange of money between relatives living in the same household; and gifts, lump-sum inheritances, insurance payments, and other types of lump-sum receipts.

Money income differs in definition from personal income (item 52). For example, money income does not include the pension rights, employer provided health insurance, food stamps, or Medicare payments that are included in personal income.

Per capita income is the mean income computed for every man, woman, and child in a particular group. It is derived by dividing the aggregate income of a particular group by the resident population in that group in the survey year. Per capita income is rounded to the nearest whole dollar.

Household income includes the income of the householder and all other individuals 15 years old and over in the household, whether or not they are related to the householder. Since many households consist of only one person, median household income is usually less than median family income. Although the household income statistics cover the year preceding the survey, the characteristics of individuals and the composition of households refer to the date of the survey. Thus, the income of the household does not include amounts received by individuals who were members of the household during the year if these individuals were no longer residing in the household at the time of the survey. Similarly, income amounts reported by individuals who did not reside in the household during the year but who were members

of the household at the time of the survey are included. However, the composition of most households was the same during the year as it was at the time of the survey.

Mean household income is the amount obtained by dividing the aggregate income of all households by the total number of households. The mean is based on the distribution of the total number of households including those with no income. Mean income is rounded to the nearest whole dollar. Care should be exercised in using and interpreting mean income values for small subgroups of the population. Because the mean is influenced strongly by extreme values in the distribution, it is especially susceptible to the effects of sampling variability, misreporting, and processing errors. The median, which is not affected by extreme values, is, therefore, a better measure than the mean when the population base is small.

Median income divides the income distribution into two equal parts, with half of all cases below the median income level and half of all cases above the median income level. For households, the median income is based on the distribution of the total number of households, including those with no income. Median income for households is computed on the basis of a standard distribution with a minimum value of less than $2,500 and a maximum value of $200,000 or more and is rounded to the nearest whole dollar. Median income figures are calculated using linear interpolation if the width of the interval containing the estimate is $2,500 or less. If the width of the interval containing the estimate is greater than $2,500, Pareto interpolation is used.

Income components were reported for the 12 months preceding the interview month. Monthly Consumer Price Indices (CPI) factors were used to inflation-adjust these components to a reference calendar year (January through December). For example, a household interviewed in March 2012 reports their income for March 2011 through February 2012. Their income is adjusted to the 2012 reference calendar year by multiplying their reported income by 2012 average annual CPI (January-December 2008) and then dividing by the average CPI for March 2011–February 2012. However, the estimates do not reflect the price and cost-of-living differences that may exist between areas.

The **poverty status** data were derived from data collected on the number of persons in a household, each person's relationship to the householder, and income data. The Social Security Administration (SSA) developed the original poverty definition in 1964, which federal interagency committees subsequently revised in 1969 and 1980. The Office of Management and Budget's (OMB) *Directive 14* prescribes the SSA's definition as the official poverty measure for federal agencies to use in their statistical work. Poverty statistics presented in American Community Survey products adhere to the standards defined by OMB in *Directive 14*.

Poverty thresholds vary depending on three criteria: size of family, number of children, and, for one- and two-person families, age of householder. In determining the poverty status of families and unrelated individuals, the Census Bureau uses thresholds (income cutoffs) arranged in a two-dimensional matrix. The matrix consists of family size (from one person to nine or more persons), cross-classified by presence and number of family members under 18 years old (from no children present to eight or more children present). Unrelated individuals and two-person families are further differentiated by age of reference person (under 65 years old and 65 years old and over). To determine a person's poverty status, the person's total family income over the previous 12 months is compared with the poverty threshold appropriate for that person's family size and composition. If the total income of that person's family is less than the threshold appropriate for that family, then the person is considered poor or "below the poverty level," together with every member of his or her family. If a person is not living with anyone related by birth, marriage, or adoption, then the person's own income is compared with his or her poverty threshold. The total number of persons below the poverty level is the sum of persons in families and the number of unrelated individuals with incomes below the poverty level over the previous 12 months.

Poverty Thresholds for 2014 by Size of Family and Number of Related Children Under 18 Years

Size of family unit	Weighted average thresholds
One person (unrelated individual)	12,071
Under 65 years	12,316
65 years and over	11,354
Two people	15,379
Householder under 65 years	15,934
Householder 65 years and over	14,326
Three people...	18,850
Four people...	24,230
Five people	28,695
Six people	32,473
Seven people...	36,927
Eight people...	40,968
Nine people or more..	49,021

Source: U.S. Census Bureau.

PERSONAL INCOME AND EARNINGS, Items 62–83

Source: U.S. Bureau of Economic Analysis, Regional Economic Accounts
http://www.bea.gov/regional/index.htm#state

Total personal income is the current income received by residents of an area from all sources. It is measured before deductions of income and other personal taxes, but after deductions of personal contributions for Social Security, government retirement, and other social insurance programs. It consists of **wage and salary disbursements** (covering all employee earnings, including executive salaries, bonuses, commissions, payments-in-kind, incentive payments, and tips); various types of supplementary earnings, such as employers' contributions to pension funds (termed "other labor income" or "supplements to wages and salaries"); proprietors' income; rental income of persons; dividends; personal interest income; and government and business transfer payments.

Per capita personal income is based on the resident population estimated as of July 1 of the year shown.

Proprietors' income is the monetary income and income-in-kind of proprietorships and partnerships (including the independent professions) and the income of tax-exempt cooperatives. **Dividends** are cash payments by corporations to stockholders who are U.S. residents. **Interest** is the monetary and imputed

interest income of persons from all sources. **Rent** is the monetary income of persons from the rental of real property, except the income of persons primarily engaged in the real estate business; the imputed net rental income of owner-occupants of nonfarm dwellings; and the royalties received by persons.

Transfer payments are income for which services are not currently rendered. They consist of both government and business transfer payments. Government transfer payments include payments under the following programs: Federal Old-Age, Survivors, and Disability Insurance ("Social Security"); Medicare and medical vendor payments; unemployment insurance; railroad and government retirement; federal- and state-government-insured workers' compensation; veterans' benefits, including veterans' life insurance; food stamps; black lung payments; Supplemental Security Income; and Temporary Assistance for Needy Families. Government payments to nonprofit institutions, other than for work under research and development contracts, are also included. Business transfer payments consist primarily of liability payments for personal injury and of corporate gifts to nonprofit institutions.

Personal income differs in definition from money income (items 54–57). For example, personal income includes pension rights, employer-provided health insurance, food stamps, and Medicare. These are not included in the definition of money income.

Earnings cover wage and salary disbursements, other labor income, and proprietors' income.

The data for earnings obtained from the Bureau of Economic Analysis (BEA) are based on place of work. In computing personal income, BEA makes an "adjustment for residence" to earnings, based on commuting patterns; personal income is thus presented on a place-of-residence basis.

Farm earnings include the income of farm workers (wages and salaries and other labor income) and farm proprietors. Farm proprietors' income includes only the income of sole proprietorships and partnerships. Farm earnings estimates are benchmarked to data collected in the Census of Agriculture and the revised Department of Agriculture statistical totals of income and expense items.

Goods-related industries include mining, construction, and manufacturing. **Service-related** and other industries include private-sector earnings in agricultural services, forestry, and fisheries; transportation and public utilities; wholesale trade; retail trade; finance, insurance, and real estate; and services. Government earnings include all levels of government. Industries are categorized under the North American Industry Classification System (NAICS), and are not comparable to years prior to 2002.

SOCIAL SECURITY AND SUPPLEMENTAL SECURITY INCOME, Items 84–86

Source: U.S. Social Security Administration
http://www.ssa.gov/policy/docs/statcomps/oasdisc/
http://www.ssa.gov/policy/docs/statcomps/ssisc/

Social Security beneficiaries are persons receiving benefits under the Old-Age, Survivors, and Disability Insurance Program. These include retired or disabled workers covered by the program, their spouses and dependent children, and the surviving spouses and dependent children of deceased workers.

Supplemental Security Income (SSI) recipients are persons receiving SSI payments. The SSI program is a cash assistance program that provides monthly benefits to low-income aged, blind, or disabled persons.

Data are as of December of the year shown.

HOUSING, Items 87–96
Source: U.S. Census Bureau—Population Estimates Program
http://www.census.gov/popest/
Source: U.S. Census Bureau—American Community Survey
http://www.census.gov/acs/www/

Housing data for 2015 are from the Population Estimates Program. Housing unit characteristics for 2014 are from the American Community Survey.

A **housing unit** is a house, apartment, mobile home or trailer, group of rooms, or single room occupied or, if vacant, intended for occupancy as separate living quarters. Separate living quarters are those in which the occupants do not live and eat with any other person in the structure and which have direct access from the outside of the building through a common hall.

The occupants of a housing unit may be a single family, one person living alone, two or more families living together, or any other group of related or unrelated persons who share living quarters. Both occupied and vacant housing units are included in the housing inventory, although recreational vehicles, tents, caves, boats, railroad cars, and the like are included only if they are occupied as a person's usual place of residence.

A housing unit is classified as occupied if it is the usual place of residence of the person or group of persons living in it at the time of enumeration, or if the occupants are only temporarily absent (away on vacation). A household consists of all persons who occupy a housing unit as their usual place of residence. Vacant units for sale or rent include units rented or sold but not occupied and any other units held off the market.

Median value is the dollar amount that divides the distribution of specified owner-occupied housing units into two equal parts, with half of all units below the median value and half of all units above the median value. Value is defined as the respondent's estimate of what the house would sell for if it were for sale. Data are presented for single-family units on fewer than 10 acres of land that have no business or medical offices on the property.

Median rent divides the distribution of renter-occupied housing units into two equal parts. The rent concept used in this volume is gross rent, which includes the amount of cash rent a renter pays (contract rent) plus the estimated average cost of utilities and fuels, if these are paid by the renter. The rent is the amount of rent only for living quarters and excludes amounts paid for any business or other space occupied. Single-family houses on lots of 10 or more acres of land are also excluded.

Housing cost as a percentage of income is shown separately for owners with mortgages, owners without mortgages, and renters. Rent as a percentage of income is a computed ratio of gross rent and monthly household income (total household income in the past 12 months divided by 12). Selected owner costs include utilities and fuels, mortgage payments, insurance, taxes, etc. In each case, the ratio of housing cost to income is computed separately for each housing unit. The housing cost ratios for half of all units are above the median shown in this book, and half are below the median shown in the book.

Substandard units are occupied units that are overcrowded or lack complete plumbing facilities. For the purposes of this item, "overcrowded" is defined as having 1.01 persons or more per room. Complete plumbing facilities include hot and cold piped water, a flush toilet, and a bathtub or shower. These facilities must be located inside the housing unit, but do not have to be in the same room.

CIVILIAN LABOR FORCE AND UNEMPLOYMENT, Items 97–100
Source: U.S. Bureau of Labor Statistics—Local Area Unemployment Statistics
http://www.bls.gov/lau/#tables

Data for the civilian labor force are the product of a federal-state cooperative program in which state employment security agencies prepare labor force and unemployment estimates under concepts, definitions, and technical procedures established by the Bureau of Labor Statistics (BLS). The civilian labor force consists of all civilians 16 years old and over who are either employed or unemployed.

Unemployment includes all persons who did not work during the survey week, made specific efforts to find a job during the previous four weeks, and were available for work during the survey week (except for temporary illness). Persons waiting to be called back to a job from which they had been laid off and those waiting to report to a new job within the next 30 days are included in unemployment figures.

Table C includes annual average data for the year shown. The Local Area Unemployment Statistics data are periodically updated to reflect revised inputs, reestimation, and controlling to new statewide totals.

CIVILIAN EMPLOYMENT, Items 101–103
Source: U.S. Census Bureau—American Community Survey
http://www.census.gov/acs/www/

Total employment includes all civilians 16 years old and over who were either (1) "at work"—those who did any work at all during the reference week as paid employees, worked in either their own business or profession, worked on their own farm, or worked 15 hours or more as unpaid workers in a family farm or business; or were (2) "with a job, but not at work"—those who had a job but were not at work that week due to illness, weather, industrial dispute, vacation, or other personal reasons.

The **occupational categories** are based on the occupational classification system that was developed for the 2000 census. This system consists of 509 specific occupational categories for employed persons arranged into 23 major occupational groups. This classification was developed based on the *Standard Occupational Classification (SOC) Manual: 2000*, published by the Executive Office of the President, Office of Management and Budget.

PRIVATE NONFARM EMPLOYMENT AND EARNINGS, Items 104–112

Source: U.S. Census Bureau—County Business Patterns
http://www.census.gov/econ/cbp/index.html

Data for private nonfarm employment and earnings are compiled from the payroll information reported monthly in the Census Bureau publication *County Business Patterns*. The estimates are based on surveys conducted by the Census Bureau and administrative records from the Internal Revenue Service (IRS).

The following types of employment are excluded from the tables: government employment, self-employed persons, farm workers, and domestic service workers. Railroad employment jointly covered by Social Security and railroad retirement programs, employment on oceanborne vessels, and employment in foreign countries are also excluded.

Annual payroll is the combined amount of wages paid, tips reported, and other compensation (including salaries, vacation allowances, bonuses, commissions, sick-leave pay, and the value of payments-in-kind such as free meals and lodging) paid to employees before deductions for Social Security, income tax, insurance, union dues, etc. All forms of compensation are included, regardless of whether they are subject to income tax or the Federal Insurance Contributions Act tax, with the exception of annuities, third-party sick pay, and supplemental unemployment compensation benefits (even if income tax was withheld). For corporations, total annual payroll includes compensation paid to officers and executives; for unincorporated businesses, it excludes profit or other compensation of proprietors or partners.

AGRICULTURE, ITEMS 113–132

Source: U.S. Department of Agriculture, National Agricultural Statistics Service—2012 Census of Agriculture
http://agcensus.usda.gov/index.php

Data for the 2012 Census of Agriculture were collected in 2013, but pertain to the year 2012.

The Census Bureau took a census of agriculture every 10 years from 1840 to 1920; since 1925, this census has been taken roughly once every 5 years. The 1997 Census of Agriculture was the first one conducted by the National Agricultural Statistics Service of the U.S. Department of Agriculture. Over time, the definition of a farm has varied. For recent censuses (including the 2012 census), a farm has been defined as any place from which $1,000 or more of agricultural products were produced and sold or normally would have been sold during the census year. Dollar figures are expressed in current dollars and have not been adjusted for inflation or deflation.

The term **operator** refers to a person who operates a farm by either doing the work or making day-to-day decisions about such activities as planting, harvesting, feeding, marketing, etc. The operator may be the owner, a member of the owner's household, a salaried manager, a tenant, a renter, or a sharecropper. If a person rents land to others or has land worked on shares by others, he/she is considered the operator only of the land that is retained for his/her own operation. The census collected information on the total number of operators, the total number of women operators, and demographic information for up to three operators per farm.

The acreage designated as **land in farms** consists primarily of agricultural land used for crops, pasture, or grazing. It also includes woodland and wasteland not actually under cultivation or used for pasture or grazing, provided that this land was part of the farm operator's total operation. Land in farms is an operating-unit concept and includes all land owned and operated, as well as all land rented from others. Land used rent-free is classified as land rented from others. All land in Indian reservations used for growing crops or grazing livestock is classified as land in farms.

Irrigated land includes all land watered by any artificial or controlled means, such as sprinklers, flooding, furrows or ditches, sub-irrigation, and spreader dikes. Included are supplemental, partial, and preplant irrigation. Each acre was counted only once regardless of the number of times it was irrigated or harvested. Livestock lagoon waste water distributed by sprinkler or flood systems was also included.

Total cropland includes cropland harvested, cropland used only for pasture or grazing, cropland on which all crops failed or were abandoned, cropland in cultivated summer fallow, and cropland idle or used for cover crops or soil improvement but not harvested and not pastured or grazed.

Respondents were asked to report their estimate of the current market **value of land and buildings** owned, rented, or leased from others, and rented and leased to others. Market value refers to the respondent's estimate of what the land and buildings would sell for under current market conditions. If the value of land and buildings was not reported, it was estimated during processing by using the average value of land and buildings from similar farms in the same geographic area.

The **value of machinery and equipment** was estimated by the respondent as the current market value of all cars, trucks, tractors, combines, balers, irrigation equipment, etc., used on the farm. This value is an estimate of what the machinery and equipment would sell for in its present condition and not the replacement or depreciated value. Share interests are reported at full value at the farm where the equipment and machinery are usually kept. Only equipment that was physically located at the farm on December 31, 2012, is included.

Market value of agricultural products sold by farms represents the gross market value before taxes and the production expenses of all agricultural products sold or removed from the place in 2012, regardless of who received the payment. It is equivalent to total sales and it includes sales by the operator as well as the value of any share received by partners, landlords, contractors, and others associated with the operation. It includes value of direct sales and the value of commodities placed in the Commodity Credit Corporation (CCC) loan program. Market value of agricultural products sold does not include payments received for participation in other federal farm programs. Also, it does not include income from farm-related sources such as custom work and other agricultural services, or income from nonfarm sources.

Government payments consists of direct payments as defined by the 2002 Farm Bill; payments from Conservation Reserve Program (CRP), Wetlands Reserve Program (WRP), Farmable

Wetlands Program (FWP), and Conservation Reserve Enhancement Program (CREP); loan deficiency payments; disaster payments; other conservation programs; and all other federal farm programs under which payments were made directly to farm operators. Commodity Credit Corporation (CCC) proceeds, amount from State and local federal crop insurance payments were not included in this category.

WATER CONSUMPTION, Items 133–134
Source: U.S. Geological Survey, National Water-Use Information Program
http://water.usgs.gov/watuse/

Every five years, the U.S. Geological Survey compiles county-level water-use estimates. This volume includes the total fresh and saline withdrawals expressed as million gallons per day. Estimate of withdrawals of ground and surface water are given for the following categories of use: public water supplies, domestic, commercial, irrigation, livestock, industrial, mining, and thermo-electric power. The number of gallons withdrawn per person is based on the metropolitan area population but the water is not necessarily used locally, providing an indicator of metropolitan areas that serve as major water sources.

2012 Economic CENSUS: OVERVIEW, Items 135–166
Source: U.S. Census Bureau
http://www.census.gov/econ/census07/

The Economic Census provides a detailed portrait of the nation's economy, from the national to the local level, once every five years. The 2012 Economic Census covers nearly all of the U.S. economy in its basic collection of establishment statistics. The 1997 Economic Census was the first major data source to use the new North American Industry Classification System (NAICS); therefore, data from this census are not comparable to economic data from prior years, which were based on the Standard Industrial Classification (SIC) system.

NAICS, developed in cooperation with Canada and Mexico, classifies North America's economic activities at two-, three-, four-, and five-digit levels of detail; the U.S. version of NAICS further defines industries to a sixth digit. The Economic Census takes advantage of this hierarchy to publish data at these successive levels of detail: sector (two-digit), subsector (three-digit), industry group (four-digit), industry (five-digit), and U.S. industry (six-digit). Information in Table A is at the two-digit level, with a few three- and four-digit items. The data in Tables B and C are at the two-digit level.

Several key statistics are tabulated for all industries in this volume, including number of establishments (or companies), number of employees, payroll, and certain measures of output (sales, receipts, revenue, value of shipments, or value of construction work done).

Number of establishments. An establishment is a single physical location at which business is conducted. It is not necessarily identical with a company or enterprise, which may consist of one establishment or more. Economic Census figures represent a summary of reports for individual establishments rather than companies. For cases in which a census report was received, separate information was obtained for each location where business was conducted. When administrative records of other federal agencies were used instead of a census report, no information was available on the number of locations operated. Each Economic Census establishment was tabulated according to the physical location at which the business was conducted. The count of establishments represents those in business at any time during 2002.

When two activities or more were carried on at a single location under a single ownership, all activities were generally grouped together as a single establishment. The entire establishment was classified on the basis of its major activity and all of its data were included in that classification. However, when distinct and separate economic activities (for which different industry classification codes were appropriate) were conducted at a single location under a single ownership, separate establishment reports for each of the different activities were obtained in the census.

Number of employees. Paid employees consist of the full-time and part-time employees, including salaried officers and executives of corporations. Included are employees on paid sick leave, paid holidays, and paid vacations; not included are proprietors and partners of unincorporated businesses. The definition of paid employees is the same as that used by the Internal Revenue Service (IRS) on form 941.

For some industries, the Economic Census gives codes representing the number of employees as a range of numbers (for example, ''100 to 249 employees'' or ''1,000 to 2,499'' employees). In this volume, those codes have been replaced by the standard suppression code ''D''.

Payroll. Payroll includes all forms of compensation, such as salaries, wages, commissions, dismissal pay, bonuses, vacation allowances, sick-leave pay, and employee contributions to qualified pension plans paid during the year to all employees. For corporations, payroll includes amounts paid to officers and executives; for unincorporated businesses, it does not include profit or other compensation of proprietors or partners. Payroll is reported before deductions for Social Security, income tax, insurance, union dues, etc. This definition of payroll is the same as that used by on IRS form 941.

Sales, shipments, receipts, revenue, or business done. This measure includes the total sales, shipments, receipts, revenue, or business done by establishments within the scope of the Economic Census. The definition of each of these items is specific to the economic sector measured.

WHOLESALE TRADE, Items 135–138
Source: U.S. Census Bureau—2012 Economic Census (See Overview of 2012 Economic Census prior to Item 135)

The Wholesale Trade sector (sector 42) comprises establishments engaged in wholesaling merchandise, generally without transformation, and rendering services incidental to the sale of merchandise. The wholesaling process is an intermediate step in the distribution of merchandise.

Wholesalers are organized to sell or arrange the purchase or sale of (1) goods for resale (i.e., goods sold to other wholesalers or retailers), (2) capital or durable nonconsumer goods, and (3) raw and intermediate materials and supplies used in production.

Wholesalers sell merchandise to other businesses and normally operate from a warehouse or office. These warehouses and offices are characterized by having little or no display of merchandise. In addition, neither the design nor the location of the premises is intended to solicit walk-in traffic. Wholesalers do not normally use advertising directed to the general public. In general, customers are initially reached via telephone, in-person marketing, or specialized advertising, which may include the internet and other electronic means. Follow-up orders are either vendor-initiated or client-initiated, are usually based on previous sales, and typically exhibit strong ties between sellers and buyers. In fact, transactions are often conducted between wholesalers and clients that have long-standing business relationships.

This sector is made up of two main types of wholesalers: those that sell goods on their own account and those that arrange sales and purchases for others for a commission or fee.

(1) Establishments that sell goods on their own account are known as wholesale merchants, distributors, jobbers, drop shippers, import/export merchants, and sales branches. These establishments typically maintain their own warehouse, where they receive and handle goods for their customers. Goods are generally sold without transformation, but may include integral functions, such as sorting, packaging, labeling, and other marketing services.

(2) Establishments arranging for the purchase or sale of goods owned by others or purchasing goods on a commission basis are known as agents and brokers, commission merchants, import/export agents and brokers, auction companies, and manufacturers' representatives. These establishments operate from offices and generally do not own or handle the goods they sell.

Some wholesale establishments may be connected with a single manufacturer and promote and sell that particular manufacturer's products to a wide range of other wholesalers or retailers. Other wholesalers may be connected to a retail chain or a limited number of retail chains and only provide the products needed by the particular retail operation(s). These wholesalers may obtain the products from a wide range of manufacturers. Still other wholesalers may not take title to the goods, but act instead as agents and brokers for a commission.

Although wholesaling normally denotes sales in large volumes, durable nonconsumer goods may be sold in single units. Sales of capital or durable nonconsumer goods used in the production of goods and services, such as farm machinery, medium- and heavy-duty trucks, and industrial machinery, are always included in Wholesale Trade.

The metropolitan area table includes only **Merchant wholesalers, except manufacturers' sales branches and offices,** establishments primarily engaged in buying and selling merchandise on their own account. Included here are such types of establishments as wholesale distributors and jobbers, importers, exporters, own-brand importers/marketers, terminal and country grain elevators, and farm products assemblers.

RETAIL TRADE, Items 139–142
Source: U.S. Census Bureau—2012 Economic Censu
(See Overview of 2012 Economic Census prior to Iter
135)

The Retail Trade sector (44–45) is made up of establishment engaged in retailing merchandise, generally without transforma tion, and rendering services incidental to the sale of merchandis

The retailing process is the final step in the distribution c merchandise; retailers are therefore organized to sell merchandis in small quantities to the general public. This sector comprise two main types of retailers: store and nonstore retailers.

Store retailers operate fixed point-of-sale locations, locate and designed to attract a high volume of walk-in customers. I general, retail stores have extensive displays of merchandise an use mass-media advertising to attract customers. They typicall sell merchandise to the general public for personal or househol consumption; some also serve business and institutional client These include establishments such as office supply stores, com puter and software stores, building materials dealers, plumbin supply stores, and electrical supply stores. Catalog showroom gasoline service stations, automotive dealers, and mobile hom dealers are treated as store retailers.

In addition to retailing merchandise, some types of store retai ers are also engaged in the provision of after-sales services, suc as repair and installation. For example, new automobile dealer electronic and appliance stores, and musical instrument and suppl stores often provide repair services. As a general rule, establish ments engaged in retailing merchandise and providing after-sal services are classified in this sector.

Nonstore retailers, like store retailers, are organized to serv the general public, although their retailing methods differ. Th establishments of this subsector reach customers and market me chandise with methods including the broadcasting of "infome cials," the broadcasting and publishing of direct-response adve tising, the publishing of paper and electronic catalogs, door-tc door solicitation, in-home demonstration, selling from portab stalls (street vendors, except food), and distribution through venc ing machines. Establishments engaged in the direct sale (nonstore of products, such as home heating oil dealers and home-deliver newspaper routes are included in this sector.

The buying of goods for resale is a characteristic of retail trac establishments that distinguishes them from establishments i the Agriculture, Manufacturing, and Construction sectors. Fc example, farms that sell their products at or from the point c production are classified in Agriculture instead of in Retail Trad Similarly, establishments that both manufacture and sell the products to the general public are classified in Manufacturir instead of Retail Trade. However, establishments that engag in processing activities incidental to retailing are classified Retail Trade.

REAL ESTATE AND RENTAL AND LEASING, Items 143–146

Source: U.S. Census Bureau—2012 Economic Census (See Overview of 2012 Economic Census prior to Item 135)

The Real Estate and Rental and Leasing sector (53) comprises establishments primarily engaged in renting, leasing, or otherwise allowing the use of tangible or intangible assets, and establishments providing related services. The major portion of this sector is made up of establishments that rent, lease, or otherwise allow the use of their own assets by others. The assets may be tangible, such as real estate and equipment, or intangible, such as patents and trademarks.

This sector also includes establishments primarily engaged in managing real estate for others, selling, renting, and/or buying real estate for others, and appraising real estate. These activities are closely related to this sector's main activity. In addition, a substantial proportion of property management is self-performed by lessors.

The main components of this sector are the real estate lessors industries; equipment lessors industries (including motor vehicles, computers, and consumer goods); and lessors of nonfinancial intangible assets (except copyrighted works).

PROFESSIONAL, SCIENTIFIC, AND TECHNICAL SERVICES, Items 147–150

Source: U.S. Census Bureau—2012 Economic Census (See Overview of 2012 Economic Census prior to Item 135)

The Professional, Scientific, and Technical Services sector (54) is made up of establishments that specialize in performing professional, scientific, and technical activities for others. These activities require a high degree of expertise and training. The establishments in this sector specialize in one or more areas and provide services to clients in a variety of industries (and, in some cases, to households). Activities performed include legal advice and representation; accounting, bookkeeping, and payroll services; architectural, engineering, and specialized design services; computer services; consulting services; research services; advertising services; photographic services; translation and interpretation services; veterinary services; and other professional, scientific, and technical services.

This sector excludes establishments primarily engaged in providing a range of day-to-day office administrative services, such as financial planning, billing and record keeping, personnel services, and physical distribution and logistics services. These establishments are classified in sector 56, Administrative and Support and Waste Management and Remediation Services.

MANUFACTURING, Items 151–154

Source: U.S. Census Bureau—2012 Economic Census (See Overview of 2012 Economic Census prior to Item 135)

The Manufacturing sector (31–33) is made up of establishments engaged in the mechanical, physical, or chemical transformation of materials, substances, or components into new products. The assembling of component parts of manufactured products is considered manufacturing, except in cases in which the activity is appropriately classified in the Construction sector. Establishments in the Manufacturing sector are often described as plants, factories, or mills, and characteristically use power-driven machines and materials-handling equipment. However, establishments that transform materials or substances into new products by hand or in the worker's home, and establishments engaged in selling to the general public products made on the same premises from which they are sold (such as bakeries, candy stores, and custom tailors) may also be included in this sector. Manufacturing establishments may process materials or contract with other establishments to process their materials for them. Both types of establishments are included in the Manufacturing sector.

The materials, substances, or components transformed by manufacturing establishments are raw materials that are products of agriculture, forestry, fishing, mining, or quarrying, or are products of other manufacturing establishments. The materials used may be purchased directly from producers, obtained through customary trade channels, or secured without recourse to the market by transferring the product from one establishment to another, under the same ownership. The new product of a manufacturing establishment may be finished (in the sense that it is ready for utilization or consumption), or it may be semifinished to become an input for an establishment engaged in further manufacturing. For example, the product of the alumina refinery is the input used in the primary production of aluminum; primary aluminum is the input used in an aluminum wire drawing plant; and aluminum wire is the input used in a fabricated wire product manufacturing establishment.

Data are included for counties with 500 or more employees in the Manufacturing sector.

ACCOMMODATION AND FOOD SERVICES, Items 155–158

Source: U.S. Census Bureau—2012 Economic Census (See Overview of 2012 Economic Census prior to Item 135)

The Accommodation and Food Services sector (72) consists of establishments that provide customers with lodging and/or meals, snacks, and beverages for immediate consumption. This sector includes both accommodation and food services establishments because the two activities are often combined at the same establishment.

Excluded from this sector are civic and social organizations, amusement and recreation parks, theaters, and other recreation or entertainment facilities providing food and beverage services.

HEALTH CARE AND SOCIAL ASSISTANCE, Items 159–162

Source: U.S. Census Bureau—2012 Economic Census (See Overview of 2012 Economic Census prior to Item 135)

The Health Care and Social Assistance sector (62) consists of establishments that provide health care and social assistance services to individuals. The sector includes both health care and social assistance because it is sometimes difficult to distinguish between the boundaries of these two activities. The industries in this sector are arranged on a continuum, starting with establishments that provide medical care exclusively, continuing with those that provide health care and social assistance, and finishing with those that provide only social assistance. The services provided by establishments in this sector are delivered by trained professionals. All industries in the sector share this commonality of process—namely, labor inputs of health practitioners or social workers with the requisite expertise. Many of the industries in the sector are defined based on the educational degree held by the practitioners included in the industry.

Excluded from this sector are aerobic classes, which can be found in subsector 713, Amusement, Gambling, and Recreation Industries; and nonmedical diet and weight-reducing centers, which can be found in subsector 812, Personal and Laundry Services. Although these can be viewed as health services, they are not typically delivered by health practitioners.

OTHER SERVICES, EXCEPT PUBLIC ADMINISTRATION Items 163–166

Source: U.S. Census Bureau—2012 Economic Census (See Overview of 2012 Economic Census prior to Item 135)

The Other Services, Except Public Administration sector (81) comprises establishments engaged in providing services not specifically categorized elsewhere in the classification system. Establishments in this sector are primarily engaged in activities such as equipment and machinery repairing, promoting or administering religious activities, grant making, and advocacy; this sector also includes establishments that provide dry-cleaning and laundry services, personal care services, death care services, pet care services, photofinishing services, temporary parking services, and dating services.

Private households that employ workers on or about the premises in activities primarily concerned with the operation of the household are included in this sector.

Excluded from this sector are establishments primarily engaged in retailing new equipment and performing repairs and general maintenance on equipment. These establishments are classified in sector 44–45, Retail Trade.

NONEMPLOYER BUSINESSES, Items 167 and 168

Source: U.S. Census Bureau—Nonemployer Statistics http://www.census.gov/econ/nonemployer/

Nonemployer Statistics is an annual series that provides subnational economic data for businesses that have no paid employee and are subject to federal income tax. The data consist of the number of businesses and total receipts by industry. Most nonemployers are self-employed individuals operating unincorporated businesses (known as sole proprietorships), which may or may not be the owner's principal source of income.

The majority of all business establishments in the United States are nonemployers, yet these firms average less than 4 percent of all sales and receipts nationally. Due to their small economic impact, these firms are excluded from most other Census Bureau business statistics (the primary exception being the Survey of Business Owners). The Nonemployers Statistics series is the primary resource available to study the scope and activities of nonemployers at a detailed geographic level.

BUILDING PERMITS, Items 169 and 170

Source: U.S. Census Bureau—Building Permits Survey http://www.census.gov/construction/bps/

These figures represent private residential construction authorized by building permits in approximately 20,000 places in the United States. Valuation represents the expected cost of construction as recorded on the building permit. This figure usually excludes the cost of on-site and off-site development and improvements, as well as the cost of heating, plumbing, electrical, and elevator installations.

National, state, and county totals were obtained by adding the data for permit-issuing places within each jurisdiction. Not all areas of the country require a building or zoning permit. The statistics only represent those areas that do require a permit. These totals thus are limited to permits issued in the 20,000 place universe covered by the Census Bureau and may not include all permits issued within a state. Current surveys indicate that construction is undertaken for all but a very small percentage of housing units authorized by building permits.

Residential building permits include buildings with any number of housing units. Housing units exclude group quarters (such as dormitories and rooming houses), transient accommodations (such as transient hotels, motels, and tourist courts), "HUD code" manufactured (mobile) homes, moved or relocated units, and housing units created in an existing residential or nonresidential structure.

METROPOLITAN AREA LOCAL GOVERNMENT EMPLOYMENT AND PAYROLL, Items 171–179

Source: U.S. Census Bureau—2012 Census of Governments
http://www.census.gov/govs/cog2012/

These items include data for all local governments (i.e., counties, municipalities, townships, special districts, and school districts) located within the metropolitan area. The Census of Governments identifies the scope and nature of the nation's state and local government sector; provides authoritative benchmark figures of public finance and public employment; classifies local government organizations, powers, and activities; and measures federal, state, and local fiscal relationships. The Employment component was mailed March 2012 to collect information on the number of state and local government civilian employees and their payrolls.

Government employees include all persons paid for personal services performed, including persons paid from federally funded programs, paid elected or appointed officials, persons in a paid leave status, and persons paid on a per meeting, annual, semiannual, or quarterly basis. Unpaid officials, pensioners, persons whose work is performed on a fee basis, and contractors and their employees are excluded from the count of employees. **Full-Time Equivalent employees** is a computed statistic representing the number of full-time employees that could have been employed if the reported number of hours worked by part-time employees had been worked by full-time employees. This statistic is calculated separately for each function of a government by dividing the "part-time hours paid" by the standard number of hours for full-time employees in the particular government and then adding the resulting quotient to the number of full-time employees.

March payroll represents gross payroll amounts for the one-month period of March for full-time and part-time employees. Gross payroll includes all salaries, wages, fees, commissions, and overtime paid to employees **before** withholdings for taxes, insurance, etc. It also includes incentive payments that are paid at regular pay intervals. It excludes employer share of fringe benefits like retirement, Social Security, health and life insurance, lump sum payments, and so forth.

Administration and Judicial and Legal combines **Financial administration, Other government administration, and Judicial and Legal** activities. **Financial administration** includes activities concerned with tax assessment and collection, custody and disbursement of funds, debt management, administration of trust funds, budgeting, and other government-wide financial management activities. This function is not applied to school district or special district governments. **Other government administration** applies to the legislative and government-wide administrative agencies of governments. Included here are overall planning and zoning activities, and central personnel and administrative activities. This function is not applied to school district or special district governments. **Judicial and legal** includes all court and court related activities (except probation and parole activities that are included at the "Correction" function), court activities of sheriff's offices, prosecuting attorneys' and public defenders' offices, legal departments, and attorneys providing government-wide legal service.

Police and Corrections includes all activities concerned, with the enforcement of law and order, including coroner's offices, police training academies, investigation bureaus, and local jails, "lockups", or other detention facilities not intended to serve as correctional facilities. **Corrections** includes activities pertaining to the confinement and correction of adults and minors convicted of criminal offenses. Pardon, probation, and parole activities are also included here.

Fire protection includes local government fire protection and prevention activities plus any ambulance, rescue, or other auxiliary services provided by a fire protection agency. Volunteer firefighters, if remunerated for their services on a "per fire" or some other basis, are included as part-time employees.

Highways and transportation includes activities associated with the maintenance and operation of streets, roads, sidewalks, bridges, tunnels, toll roads, and ferries. Snow and ice removal, street lighting, and highway and traffic engineering activities are also included here. Also included are the operation, maintenance, and construction of public mass transit systems, including subways, surface rails, and buses, and the provision, construction, operation, maintenance; support of public waterways, harbors, docks, wharves, and related marine terminal facilities; and activities associated with the operation and support of publicly operated airport facilities.

Health and Welfare includes **Health, Hospitals, and Public welfare. Health** includes administration of public health programs, community and visiting nurse services, immunization programs, drug abuse rehabilitation programs, health and food inspection activities, operation of outpatient clinics, and environmental pollution control activities. **Hospitals** includes only government operated medical care facilities that provide inpatient care. Employees and payrolls of private corporations that lease and operate government-owned hospital facilities are excluded. **Public Welfare** includes the administration of various public assistance programs for the needy, veteran services, operation of nursing homes, indigent care institutions, and programs that provide payments for medical care, handicap transportation, and other services for the needy.

Natural resources and Utilities includes activities primarily concerned with the conservation and development of natural resources (soil, water, energy, minerals, etc.) and the regulation of industries that develop, utilize, or affect natural resources, as well as the operation and maintenance of **parks**, playgrounds, swimming pools, public beaches, auditoriums, public golf courses, museums, marinas, botanical gardens, and zoological parks. **Utilities, sewerage, and waste management** includes operation, maintenance, and construction of public water supply systems, including production, acquisition, and distribution of water to general public or to other public or private utilities, for residential, commercial, and industrial use; activities associated with the production or acquisition and distribution of electric power; provision, maintenance, and operation of sanitary and storm sewer systems and sewage disposal and treatment facilities; and refuse collection and disposal, operation of sanitary landfills, and street cleaning activities.

Education and libraries includes activities associated with the operation of public elementary and secondary schools and locally operated vocational-technical schools. Special education programs operated by elementary and secondary school systems are also included as are all ancillary services associated with the operation of schools, such as pupil transportation and food service. Also included are the establishment and provision of libraries for use by the general public and the technical support of privately operated libraries. This category includes classroom teachers, principals, supervisors of instruction, librarians, teacher aides, library aides, and guidance and psychological personnel as well as school superintendents and other administrative personnel, clerical and secretarial staffs, plant operation and maintenance personnel, health and recreation employees, transportation and food service personnel, and any student employees. Also included are any degree granting institutions that provide academic training above grade 12.

LOCAL GOVERNMENT FINANCES, Items 180–193

Source: U.S. Census Bureau—2012 Census of Governments
http://www.census.gov/govs/cog/

Data on local government finances are based on result of the 2012 Census of Governments. For each metropolitan area, the data are aggregated from its component counties, and the financial data comprise amounts for all local governments—not only the county governments, but also any municipalities, townships, school districts, and special districts within the county. Statistics from governmental units located in two or more county areas are assigned to the county area containing the administrative office.

Revenue and expenditure items include all amounts of money received and paid out, respectively, by a government and its agencies (net of correcting transactions such as recoveries of refunds), with the exception of amounts for debt issuance and retirement and for loan and investment, agency, and private transactions.

Payments among the various funds and agencies of a particular government are excluded from revenue and expenditure items as representing internal transfers. Therefore, a government's contribution to a retirement fund that it administers is not counted as expenditure, nor is the receipt of this contribution by the retirement fund counted as revenue.

Total **general revenue** includes all revenue except utility, liquor stores, and insurance trust revenue. All tax revenue and intergovernmental revenue, even if designated for employee-retirement or local utility purpose, are classified as general revenue.

Intergovernmental revenue covers amounts received from the federal government as fiscal aid, reimbursements for performance of general government functions and specific services for the paying government, or in lieu of taxes. It excludes any amounts received from other governments from the sale of property, commodities, and utility services.

Taxes consist of compulsory contributions exacted by governments for public purposes. However, this category excludes employer and employee payments for retirement and social insurance purposes, which are classified as insurance trust revenue; it also excludes special assessments, which are classified as non-tax general revenue. Property taxes are taxes conditioned on ownership of property and assessed by its value. Sales and gross receipts taxes do not include dealer discounts, or "commissions"

allowed to merchants for collection of taxes from consumers. General sales taxes and selected taxes on sales of motor fuels, tobacco products, and other particular commodities and services are included.

General government expenditure includes capital outlay, a major portion of which is commonly financed by borrowing. Government revenue does not include receipts from borrowing. Among other things, this distorts the relationship between totals of revenue and expenditure figures that are presented and renders it useless as a direct measure of the degree of budgetary "balance" (as that term is generally applied).

Direct general expenditure comprises all expenditures of the local governments, excluding utility, liquor stores, insurance trust expenditures, and any intergovernmental payments.

Local government expenditure for **education** is mainly for the provision and general support of schools and other educational facilities and services, including those for educational institutions beyond high school. They cover such related services as student transportation; school lunch and other cafeteria operations; school health, recreation, and library services; and dormitories, dining halls, and bookstores operated by public institutions of higher education.

Health and hospital expenditure includes health research; clinics; nursing; immunization; other categorical, environmental, and general health services provided by health agencies; establishment and operation of hospital facilities; provision of hospital care; and support of other public and private hospitals.

Police protection expenditure includes police activities such as patrols, communications, custody of persons awaiting trial, and vehicular inspection.

Public welfare expenditure covers support of and assistance to needy persons; this aid is contingent upon the person's needs. Included are cash assistance paid directly to needy persons under categorical (Old Age Assistance, Temporary Assistance for Needy Families, Aid to the Blind, and Aid to the Disabled) and other welfare programs; vendor payments made directly to private purveyors for medical care, burials, and other commodities and services provided under welfare programs; welfare institutions; and any intergovernmental or other direct expenditure for welfare purposes. Pensions to former employees and other benefits not contingent on need are excluded.

Highway expenditure is for the provision and maintenance of highway facilities, including toll turnpikes, bridges, tunnels, and ferries, as well as regular roads, highways, and streets. Also included are expenditures for street lighting and for snow and ice removal. Not included are highway policing and traffic control, which are considered part of police protection

Debt outstanding includes all long-term debt obligations of the government and its agencies (exclusive of utility debt) and all interest-bearing, short-term (repayable within one year) debt obligations remaining unpaid at the close of the fiscal year. It includes judgments, mortgages, and revenue bonds, as well as general obligation bonds, notes, and interest-bearing warrants. This category consists of non-interest-bearing, short-term obligations; inter-fund obligations; amounts owed in a trust or agency capacity; advances and contingent loans from other governments; and rights of individuals to benefit from government-administered employee-retirement funds.

GOVERNMENT EMPLOYMENT, Items 194–196

Source: U.S. Bureau of Economic Analysis—Regional Economic Accounts
http://www.bea.gov/regional/index.htm#state

Employment is measured as the average annual sum of full-time and part-time jobs. The estimates are on a place-of-work basis. The estimates are on a place-of-work basis. State and local government employment includes person employed in all state and local government agencies and enterprises. Data for federal civilian employment include civilian employees of the federal government, including civilian employees of the Department of Defense. Military employment includes all persons on active duty status.

ELECTION STATISTICS, Items 197–199

Source: Election Data Services, Inc. Washington, DC (copyright)
http://www.electiondataservices.com/index.php?content = elecdata

Election results show the percentage of the total vote cast for the Democratic and Republican candidates, as well as the combined percentage for all other candidates in the 2012 presidential election.

TABLE D—CITIES

Table D present 146 items of data for cities with populations of 25,000 or more at the time of the 2010 census.

LAND AREA, Items 1 and 4

Source: U.S. Census Bureau—2010 Census of Population and Housing
http://www.census.gov/2010census/data/

Land area measurements are shown to the nearest square kilometer. Land area includes dry land and land temporarily or partially covered by water, such as marshlands, swamps, and river floodplains.

POPULATION, Items 2–4

Source: U.S. Census Bureau—Population Estimates
http://www.census.gov/popest/estimates.html

The population data are Census Bureau estimates of the resident population as of July 1 of the year shown.

POPULATION CHARACTERISTICS, Items 5–22

Source: U.S. Census Bureau—American Community Survey
http://www.census.gov/acs/www/

Data on age, sex, race, and Hispanic origin, and place of birth are from the 2011–2013 American Community Survey, a nationwide continuous survey designed to replace the long form questionnaire used in previous censuses.

Data on race were derived from answers to the question on race that was asked of all persons. The concept of race, as used by the Census Bureau, reflects self-identification by respondents according to the race or races with which they most closely identify. These categories are sociopolitical constructs and should not be interpreted as being scientific or anthropological in nature. Furthermore, the race categories include both racial and national origin groups.

On the American Community Survey, respondents were offered the option of selecting one or more races. This option was not available prior to the 2000 census; thus, comparisons between censuses should be made with caution. In this table, Columns 5 through 9 refer to individuals who identified with each racial category, either alone or in combination with other races. Because respondents could include as many categories as they wished, and because the columns refer to the percentage of the population, the total will often exceed 100 percent.

In this book, the Asian group has been combined with the Native Hawaiian and Other Pacific Islander group, causing double-counting of persons who identify with both groups. This is especially pronounced in Hawaii.

The **White** population is defined as persons who indicated their race as White, as well as persons who did not classify themselves in one of the specific race categories listed on the questionnaire but entered a nationality such as Irish, German, Italian, Lebanese, Near Easterner, Arab, or Polish.

The **Black** population includes persons who indicated their race as ''Black, African Am., or Negro,'' as well as persons who did not classify themselves in one of the specific race categories but reported entries such as African American, Afro American, Kenyan, Nigerian, or Haitian.

The **American Indian or Alaska Native** population includes persons who indicated their race as American Indian or Alaska Native, as well as persons who did not classify themselves in one of the specific race categories but reported entries such as Canadian Indian, French-American Indian, Spanish-American Indian, Eskimo, Aleut, Alaska Indian, or any of the American Indian or Alaska Native tribes.

The **Asian and Pacific Islander** population combines two census groupings: **Asian** and **Native Hawaiian or Other Pacific Islander**. Because two separate groups are combined, this category occasionally represents more than 100 percent of a city's population. The **Asian** population includes persons who indicated their race as Asian Indian, Chinese, Filipino, Japanese, Korean, Vietnamese, or ''Other Asian,'' as well as persons who provided write-in entries of such groups as Cambodian, Laotian, Hmong, Pakistani, or Taiwanese. The **Native Hawaiian or Other Pacific Islander** population includes persons who indicated their race as ''Native Hawaiian,'' ''Guamanian or Chamorro,'' ''Samoan,'' or "Other Pacific Islander," as well as persons who reported entries such as Part Hawaiian, American Samoan, Fijian, Melanesian, or Tahitian.

The **Hispanic population** is based on a separate question that asked respondents "Is this person Spanish/Hispanic/Latino?" Persons marking any one of the four Hispanic categories (i.e., Mexican, Puerto Rican, Cuban, or other Spanish) are collectively referred to as Hispanic.

The Hispanic origin question was placed before the race question and specific instructions indicated that both questions should be answered.

The **foreign-born** population includes all persons who were not U.S. citizens at birth. Foreign-born persons are those who indicated they were either a U.S. citizen by naturalization or were not a citizen of the United States. The foreign-born population consists of immigrants (legal permanent residents), temporary migrants (students), humanitarian migrants (refugees), and unauthorized migrants (persons illegally residing in the United States).

Age is defined as age at last birthday (number of completed years since birth), at the time of the interview. The American Community Survey also asked for the specific date of birth of the respondent. Both age and date of birth are used in combination to calculate the most accurate age at the time of the interview.

The **female** population is shown as a percentage of total population.

POPULATION CHANGE, Items 23–26
Source: U.S. Census Bureau—Decennial Censuses
U.S. Census Bureau—Population Estimates
http://www.census.gov/main/www/cen2000.html
http://www.census.gov/2010census/data/
http://www.census.gov/popest/estimates.html

The population data for 2000 and 2010 are from the decennial censuses and represent the resident population as of April 1 of those years. The data for 2015 are from the Census Bureau's Population Estimates Program and represent the estimated resident population as of July 1.

The change in population from 2010 to 2015 is calculated from census data based on city boundaries as they existed in 2000 and 2010, respectively. No attempt was made to adjust the data to reflect boundary changes.

HOUSEHOLDS, Items 27–30
Source: U.S. Census Bureau—American Community Survey
http://www.census.gov/acs/www/

A **household** includes all of the persons who occupy a housing unit. (Persons not living in households are classified as living in group quarters.) A housing unit is a house, an apartment, a mobile home, a group of rooms, or a single room occupied (or, if vacant, intended for occupancy) as separate living quarters. Separate living quarters are those in which the occupants live separately from any other persons in the building and have direct access from the outside of the building or through a common hall. The occupants may be a single family, one person living alone, two or more families living together, or any other group of related or unrelated

persons who share living quarters. The number of households is the same as the number of year-round occupied housing units.

A **family** includes a householder and one or more other persons living in the same household who are related to the householder by birth, marriage, or adoption. All persons in a household who are related to the householder are regarded as members of his or her family. A **family household** may contain persons not related to the householder; thus, family households may include more members than families do. A household can contain only one family for the purposes of census tabulations. Not all households contain families, as a household may comprise a group of unrelated persons or of one person living alone. Families are classified by type as either a "husband-wife family" or "other family," according to the presence or absence of a spouse.

The measure of **persons per household** is obtained by dividing the number of persons by the number of households or householders. One person in each household is designated as the householder. In most cases, this is the person (or one of the persons) in whose name the house is owned, being bought, or rented. If there is no such person in the household, any adult household member 15 years old and over can be designated as the householder.

The category **female family householder** includes only female-headed family households with no spouse present.

GROUP QUARTERS, Item 31–34
Source: U.S. Census Bureau—2010 Census of Population and Housing
http://www.census.gov/2010census/data/

The Census Bureau classifies all persons not living in households as living in group quarters; this category includes both the institutional and noninstitutional populations. This volume includes the total number of persons in group quarters and in selected types of group quarters.

The **institutionalized population** includes persons who are primarily ineligible, unable, or unlikely to participate in the labor force while residents, including those in correctional institutions, skilled-nursing facilities, mental (psychiatric) hospitals, and juvenile institutions.

Nursing facilities include facilities licensed to provide medical care with 7-day, 24-hour coverage for people requiring long-term non-acute care. People in these facilities require nursing care, regardless of age.. Included in this category are skilled-nursing facilities, intermediate-care facilities, long-term care rooms in wards or buildings on the grounds of hospitals, or long-term care rooms/nursing wings in congregate housing facilities. Also included are nursing, convalescent, and rest homes, such as soldiers', veterans', and fraternal or religious homes for the aged, with or without nursing care.

The **noninstitutionalized population** includes persons who live in group quarters other than institutions, such as college dormitories, military quarters, and group homes.

CRIME, Items 35–38

Source: U.S. Federal Bureau of Investigation—
Uniform Crime Reports
http://www.fbi.gov/ucr/ucr.htm

Crime data are as reported to the Federal Bureau of Investigation (FBI) by law enforcement agencies and have not been adjusted for underreporting. This may affect comparability between geographic areas or over time.

Through the voluntary contribution of crime statistics by law enforcement agencies across the United States, the Uniform Crime Reporting (UCR) Program provides periodic assessments of crime in the nation as measured by offenses that have come to the attention of the law enforcement community. The Committee on Uniform Crime Records of the International Association of Chiefs of Police initiated this voluntary national data collection effort in 1930. The UCR Program contributors compile and submit their crime data either directly to the FBI or through state-level UCR Programs.

Seven offenses, because of their severity, frequency of occurrence, and likelihood of being reported to police, were initially selected to serve as an index for evaluating fluctuations in the volume of crime. These serious crimes were murder and nonnegligent manslaughter, forcible rape, robbery, aggravated assault, burglary, larceny-theft, and motor vehicle theft. By congressional mandate, arson was added as the eighth index offense in 1979. The totals shown in this volume do not include arson.

In 2004, the FBI discontinued the use of the Crime Index in the UCR Program and its publications, stating that the Crime Index was driven upward by the offense with the highest number of cases (in this case, larceny-theft), creating a bias against jurisdictions with a high number of larceny-thefts but a low number of other serious crimes, such as murder and forcible rape. The FBI is currently publishing a violent crime total and property crime total until a more viable index is developed. This book includes the total Crime Index, as well as violent crime and property crime rates.

In 2013, the FBI adopted a new definition of rape. Rape is now defined as, "Penetration, no matter how slight, of the vagina or anus with any body part or object, or oral penetration by a sex organ of another person, without the consent of the victim." The new definition updated the 80-year-old historical definition of rape which was "carnal knowledge of a female forcibly and against her will." Effectively, the revised definition expands rape to include both male and female victims and offenders, and reflects the various forms of sexual penetration understood to be rape, especially nonconsenting acts of sodomy, and sexual assaults with objects.

Violent crimes include four categories of offenses: (1) Murder and nonnegligent manslaughter, as defined in the UCR Program, is the willful (nonnegligent) killing of one human being by another. This offense excludes deaths caused by negligence, suicide, or accident; justifiable homicides; and attempts to murder or assaults to murder. (2)) Rape is the penetration, no matter how slight, of the vagina or anus with any body part or object, or oral penetration by a sex organ of another person, without the consent of the victim Assaults or attempts to commit rape by force or threat of force are also included; however, statutory rape (without force) and other sex offenses are excluded. (3) Robbery is the taking or attempting to take anything of value from the care, custody, or control of a person or persons by force or threat of force or violence and/or by putting the victim in fear. (4) Aggravated assault is an unlawful attack by one person upon another for the purpose of inflicting severe or aggravated bodily injury. This type of assault is usually accompanied by the use of a weapon or by other means likely to produce death or great bodily harm. Attempts are included, since injury does not necessarily have to result when a gun, knife, or other weapon is used, as these incidents could and probably would result in a serious personal injury if the crime were successfully completed.

Property crimes include three categories: (1) Burglary, or breaking and entering, is the unlawful entry of a structure to commit a felony or theft, even though no force was used to gain entrance. (2) Larceny-theft is the unauthorized taking of the personal property of another, without the use of force. (3) Motor vehicle theft is the unauthorized taking of any motor vehicle.

Rates are based on population estimates provided by the FBI. If a city is not in the UCR database, or if the population total for the units aggregated was less than 75 percent of the city's population (as estimated by the Census Bureau), the total was not considered representative of the city as a whole and was not published. State and U.S. totals include FBI estimates for those areas.

EDUCATIONAL ATTAINMENT, Items 39–41

Source: U.S. Census Bureau—American Community Survey
http://www.census.gov/acs/www/

Data on **educational attainment** are tabulated for the population 25 years old and over. The data were derived from a question that asked respondents for the highest level of school completed or the highest degree received. Persons who had passed a high school equivalency examination were considered high school graduates. Schooling received in foreign schools was to be reported as the equivalent grade or years in the regular American school system.

Vocational and technical training, such as barber school training; business, trade, technical, and vocational schools; or other training for a specific trade are specifically excluded.

High school graduate or less. This category includes persons whose highest degree was a high school diploma or its equivalent, and those who reported any level lower than a high school diploma.

Bachelor's degree or more. This category includes persons who have received bachelor's degrees, master's degrees, professional school degrees (such as law school or medical school degrees), and doctoral degrees.

INCOME AND POVERTY, Items 42–46

Source: U.S. Census Bureau—American Community Survey
http://www.census.gov/acs/www/

Total money income is the sum of the amounts reported separately for wage or salary income; net self-employment income; interest, dividends, or net rental or royalty income or income from estates and trusts; Social Security or railroad retirement income; Supplemental Security Income (SSI); public assistance or welfare payments; retirement, survivor, or disability pensions; and all other income. Receipts from the following sources are not included as income: capital gains; money received from the sale of property (unless the recipient was engaged in the business of selling such property); the value of income "in kind" from food stamps, public housing subsidies, medical care, employer contributions for individuals, etc.; withdrawal of bank deposits; money borrowed; tax refunds; exchange of money between relatives living in the same household; and gifts, lump-sum inheritances, insurance payments, and other types of lump-sum receipts.

Per capita income is the mean income computed for every man, woman, and child in a particular group. It is derived by dividing the aggregate income of a particular group by the resident population in that group in the survey year. Per capita income is rounded to the nearest whole dollar.

Household income includes the income of the householder and all other individuals 15 years old and over in the household, whether or not they are related to the householder. Since many households consist of only one person, median household income is usually less than median family income. Although the household income statistics cover the twelve months prior to the survey, the characteristics of individuals and the composition of households refer to the date of the interview. Thus, the income of the household does not include amounts received by individuals who were members of the household during all or part of the year if these individuals were no longer residing in the household at the time of the interview. Similarly, income amounts reported by individuals who did not reside in the household during full year but who were members of the household at the time of the interview are included. However, the composition of most households was the same during the year as it was at the time of the interview.

Median income divides the income distribution into two equal parts, with half of all cases below the median income level and half of all cases above the median income level. For households, the median income is based on the distribution of the total number of households, including those with no income. Median income for households is computed on the basis of a standard distribution with a minimum value of less than $2,500 and a maximum value of $200,000 or more and is rounded to the nearest whole dollar. Median income figures are calculated using linear interpolation if the width of the interval containing the estimate is $2,500 or less. If the width of the interval containing the estimate is greater than $2,500, Pareto interpolation is used.

Income components were reported for the 12 months preceding the interview month. Monthly Consumer Price Index (CPI) factors were used to inflation-adjust these components to a reference calendar year (January through December). For example, a household interviewed in March 2012 reports their income for March 2011 through February 2012. Their income is adjusted to the 2012 reference calendar year by multiplying their reported income by 2012 average annual CPI (January-December 2012) and then dividing by the average CPI for March 2006-February 2012. In addition, the 3-year estimates are inflation-adjusted to the final year. However, the estimates do not reflect the price and cost-of-living differences that may exist between areas.

The **poverty status** data were derived from data collected on the number of persons in a household, each person's relationship to the householder, and each person's income during the past twelve months. The Social Security Administration (SSA) developed the original poverty definition in 1964, which federal interagency committees subsequently revised in 1969 and 1980. The Office of Management and Budget's (OMB) *Directive 14* prescribes the SSA's definition as the official poverty measure for federal agencies to use in their statistical work.

Poverty thresholds vary depending on three criteria: size of family, number of children, and, for one- and two-person families, age of householder. In determining the poverty status of families and unrelated individuals, the Census Bureau uses thresholds (income cutoffs) arranged in a two-dimensional matrix. The matrix consists of family size (from one person to nine or more persons), cross-classified by presence and number of family members under 18 years old (from no children present to eight or more children present). Unrelated individuals and two-person families are further differentiated by age of reference person (under 65 years old and 65 years old and over). To determine a person's poverty status, the person's total family income over the previous 12 months is compared with the poverty threshold appropriate for that person's family size and composition. If the total income of that person's family is less than the threshold appropriate for that family, then the person is considered poor or "below the poverty level," together with every member of his or her family. If a person is not living with anyone related by birth, marriage, or adoption, then the person's own income is compared with his or her poverty threshold. The total number of persons below the poverty level is the sum of persons in families and the number of unrelated individuals with incomes below the poverty level.

Poverty Thresholds for 2014 by Size of Family and Number of Related Children Under 18 Years

Size of family unit	Weighted average thresholds
One person (unrelated individual)	12,071
Under 65 years	12,316
65 years and over	11,354
Two people	15,379
Householder under 65 years	15,934
Householder 65 years and over	14,326
Three people	18,850
Four people	24,230
Five people	28,695
Six people	32,473
Seven people	36,927
Eight people	40,968
Nine people or more	49,021

Source: U.S. Census Bureau.

HOUSING, Items 47–57

Source: U.S. Census Bureau—2010 Census of
Population and Housing
http://www.census.gov/2010census/data/
Source: American Community Survey
http://www.census.gov/acs/www/

The housing unit counts in columns 47 through 49 are from the 2010 census. The characteristics of occupied housing units are from the 2010–2014 American Community Survey.

A **housing unit** is a house, apartment, mobile home or trailer, group of rooms, or single room occupied or, if vacant, intended for occupancy as separate living quarters. Separate living quarters are those in which the occupants do not live and eat with any other person in the structure and which have direct access from the outside of the building through a common hall. For vacant units, the criteria of separateness and direct access are applied to the intended occupants whenever possible. If that information cannot be obtained, the criteria are applied to the previous occupants.

The occupants of a housing unit may be a single family, one person living alone, two or more families living together, or any other group of related or unrelated persons who share living quarters. Both occupied and vacant housing units are included in the housing inventory, although recreational vehicles, tents, caves, boats, railroad cars, and the like are included only if they are occupied as a person's usual place of residence.

A housing unit is classified as occupied if it is the usual place of residence of the person or group of persons living in it at the time of enumeration, or if the occupants are only temporarily absent (away on vacation). A household consists of all persons who occupy a housing unit as their usual place of residence. Vacant units for sale or rent include units rented or sold but not occupied and any other units held off the market.

The percent change represents the difference in the number of total housing units in a specified area from 2000 to 2010.

A housing unit is **owner occupied** if the owner or co-owner lives in the unit, even if it is mortgaged or not fully paid for. The owner or co-owner must live in the unit and is usually the first person listed on the census or ACS questionnaire.

All occupied housing units that are not owner occupied, whether they are rented for cash rent or occupied without payment of cash rent, are classified as **renter occupied**.

Median value is the dollar amount that divides the distribution of specified owner-occupied housing units into two equal parts, with half of all units below the median value and half of all units above the median value. Value is defined as the respondent's estimate of what the house would sell for if it were for sale. Data are presented for single-family units on fewer than 10 acres of land that have no business or medical offices on the property.

Median rent divides the distribution of renter-occupied housing units into two equal parts. The rent concept used in this volume is gross rent, which includes the amount of cash rent a renter pays (contract rent) plus the estimated average cost of utilities and fuels, if these are paid by the renter. The rent is the amount of rent only for living quarters and excludes amounts paid for any business or other space occupied. Single-family houses on lots of 10 or more acres of land are also excluded.

Housing cost as a percentage of income is shown separately for owners with mortgages, owners without mortgages, and renters. Rent as a percentage of income is a computed ratio of gross rent and monthly household income (total household income during the year divided by 12). Selected owner costs include utilities and fuels, mortgage payments, insurance, taxes, etc. In each case, the ratio of housing cost to income is computed separately for each housing unit. The housing cost ratios for half of all units are above the median shown in this book, and half are below the median shown in the book.

PERCENT WITH NO VEHICLES AVAILABLE, Item 58

Source: U.S. Census Bureau—American Community Survey
http://www.census.gov/acs/www/

The data on vehicles available show the number of passenger cars, vans, and pickup or panel trucks of one-ton capacity or less kept at home and available for the use of household members. Vehicles rented or leased for one month or more, company vehicles, and police and government vehicles are included if kept at home and used for non-business purposes. Dismantled or immobile vehicles are excluded. Vehicles kept at home but used only for business purposes also are excluded

MIGRATION, Items 59 and 60

Source: U.S. Census Bureau—American Community Survey
http://www.census.gov/acs/www/

Residence one year ago is used in conjunction with location of current residence to determine the extent of residential mobility of the population and the resulting redistribution of the population across the various states, metropolitan areas, and regions of the country. **Same house** includes all people 1 year old and over who, a year before the survey date, lived in the same house or apartment that they occupied at the time of interview.

The **percent who lived outside this city** includes all persons who did not live in the listed city 1 year before the interview, whether their previous residence was in the same state, a different state, Puerto Rico, or abroad.

CIVILIAN LABOR FORCE AND UNEMPLOYMENT, Items 61–64

Source: U.S. Bureau of Labor Statistics—Local Areas Unemployment Statistics
http://www.bls.gov/lau/#tables

Data for the civilian labor force are the product of a federal-state cooperative program in which state employment security agencies prepare labor force and unemployment estimates under concepts, definitions, and technical procedures established by the Bureau of Labor Statistics (BLS). The civilian labor force consists of all civilians 16 years old and over who are either employed or unemployed.

Unemployment includes all persons who did not work during the survey week, made specific efforts to find a job during the previous four weeks, and were available for work during the survey week (except for temporary illness). Persons waiting to be called back to a job from which they had been laid off and those waiting to report to a new job within the next 30 days are included in unemployment figures.

Table D includes annual average data for the year shown. The Local Area Unemployment Statistics data are periodically updated to reflect revised inputs, reestimation, and controlling to new statewide totals.

CIVILIAN EMPLOYMENT, Items 65–68
Source: U.S. Census Bureau—American Community Survey
http://www.census.gov/acs/www/

The **labor force** includes all persons 16 years old and over who were either (1) "at work"—those who did any work at all during the reference week as paid employees, worked in either their own business or profession, worked on their own farm, or worked 15 hours or more as unpaid workers in a family farm or business; or were (2) "with a job, but not at work" —those who had a job but were not at work that week due to illness, weather, industrial dispute, vacation, or other personal reasons.

Full-year, Full-Time Workers includes all people 16 years old and over who usually worked 35 hours or more per week for 50 to 52 weeks in the past 12 months.

Households with no workers includes households where all members "Did not work in the past 12 months." Workers include all people 16 years old and over who, for one or more weeks, did any work for pay or profit (including paid vacation and paid sick leave) or worked without pay on a family farm or in a family business. Weeks of active service in the Armed Forces are also included.

BUILDING PERMITS, Items 69–71
Source: U.S. Census Bureau—Building Permits Survey
http://www.census.gov/const/www/permitsindex.html

These figures represent private residential construction authorized by building permits in approximately 20,000 places in the United States. Valuation represents the expected cost of construction as recorded on the building permit. This figure usually excludes the cost of on-site and off-site development and improvements, as well as the cost of heating, plumbing, electrical, and elevator installations.

National, state, and county totals were obtained by adding the data for permit-issuing places within each jurisdiction. These totals thus are limited to permits issued in the 20,000 place universe covered by the Census Bureau and may not include all permits issued within a state. Current surveys indicate that construction is undertaken for all but a very small percentage of housing units authorized by building permits.

Residential building permits include buildings with any number of housing units. Housing units exclude group quarters (such as dormitories and rooming houses), transient accommodations (such as transient hotels, motels, and tourist courts), "HUD-code" manufactured (mobile) homes, moved or relocated units, and housing units created in an existing residential or nonresidential structure.

2012 Economic CENSUS: OVERVIEW, Items 72–107
Source: U.S. Census Bureau
http://www.census.gov/econ/census07/

The Economic Census provides a detailed portrait of the nation's economy, from the national to the local level, once every five years. The 2012 Economic Census covers nearly all of the U.S. economy in its basic collection of establishment statistics. The 1997 Economic Census was the first major data source to use the new North American Industry Classification System (NAICS); therefore, data from this census are not comparable to economic data from prior years, which were based on the Standard Industrial Classification (SIC) system.

NAICS, developed in cooperation with Canada and Mexico, classifies North America's economic activities at two-, three-, four-, and five-digit levels of detail; the U.S. version of NAICS further defines industries to a sixth digit. The Economic Census takes advantage of this hierarchy to publish data at these successive levels of detail: sector (two-digit), subsector (three-digit), industry group (four-digit), industry (five-digit), and U.S. industry (six-digit). Information in Table A is at the two-digit level, with a few three- and four-digit items. The data in Table D are at the two-digit level.

Several key statistics are tabulated for all industries in this volume, including number of establishments (or companies), number of employees, payroll, and certain measures of output (sales, receipts, revenue, value of shipments, or value of construction work done).

Number of establishments. An establishment is a single physical location at which business is conducted. It is not necessarily identical with a company or enterprise, which may consist of one establishment or more. Economic Census figures represent a summary of reports for individual establishments rather than companies. For cases in which a census report was received, separate information was obtained for each location where business was conducted. When administrative records of other federal agencies were used instead of a census report, no information was available on the number of locations operated. Each Economic Census establishment was tabulated according to the physical location at which the business was conducted. The count of establishments represents those in business at any time during 2002.

When two activities or more were carried on at a single location under a single ownership, all activities were generally grouped together as a single establishment. The entire establishment was classified on the basis of its major activity and all of its data were included in that classification. However, when distinct and separate economic activities (for which different industry classification codes were appropriate) were conducted at a single location under a single ownership, separate establishment reports for each of the different activities were obtained in the census.

Number of employees. Paid employees consist of the full-time and part-time employees, including salaried officers and executives of corporations. Included are employees on paid sick leave, paid holidays, and paid vacations; not included are proprietors and partners of unincorporated businesses. The definition of paid employees is the same as that used by the Internal Revenue Service (IRS) on form 941. For some industries, the Economic Census gives codes representing the number of employees as a range of numbers (for example, ''100 to 249 employees'' or ''1,000 to 2,499'' employees). In this volume, those codes have been replaced by the standard suppression code ''D''.

Payroll. Payroll includes all forms of compensation, such as salaries, wages, commissions, dismissal pay, bonuses, vacation allowances, sick-leave pay, and employee contributions to qualified pension plans paid during the year to all employees. For corporations, payroll includes amounts paid to officers and executives; for unincorporated businesses, it does not include profit or other compensation of proprietors or partners. Payroll is reported before deductions for Social Security, income tax, insurance, union dues, etc. This definition of payroll is the same as that used by on IRS form 941.

Sales, shipments, receipts, revenue, or business done. This measure includes the total sales, shipments, receipts, revenue, or business done by establishments within the scope of the Economic Census. The definition of each of these items is specific to the economic sector measured.

WHOLESALE TRADE, Items 72–75

Source: U.S. Census Bureau—2012 Economic Census (See Overview of 2012 Economic Census prior to Item 72)

The Wholesale Trade sector (sector 42) comprises establishments engaged in wholesaling merchandise, generally without transformation, and rendering services incidental to the sale of merchandise. The wholesaling process is an intermediate step in the distribution of merchandise.

Wholesalers are organized to sell or arrange the purchase or sale of (1) goods for resale (i.e., goods sold to other wholesalers or retailers), (2) capital or durable nonconsumer goods, and (3) raw and intermediate materials and supplies used in production.

Wholesalers sell merchandise to other businesses and normally operate from a warehouse or office. These warehouses and offices are characterized by having little or no display of merchandise. In addition, neither the design nor the location of the premises is intended to solicit walk-in traffic. Wholesalers do not normally use advertising directed to the general public. In general, customers are initially reached via telephone, in-person marketing, or specialized advertising, which may include the internet and other electronic means. Follow-up orders are either vendor-initiated or client-initiated, are usually based on previous sales, and typically exhibit strong ties between sellers and buyers. In fact, transactions are often conducted between wholesalers and clients that have long-standing business relationships.

This sector is made up of two main types of wholesalers: those that sell goods on their own account and those that arrange sales and purchases for others for a commission or fee.

(1) Establishments that sell goods on their own account are known as wholesale merchants, distributors, jobbers, drop shippers, import/export merchants, and sales branches. These establishments typically maintain their own warehouse, where they receive and handle goods for their customers. Goods are generally sold without transformation, but may include integral functions, such as sorting, packaging, labeling, and other marketing services.

(2) Establishments arranging for the purchase or sale of goods owned by others or purchasing goods on a commission basis are known as agents and brokers, commission merchants, import/export agents and brokers, auction companies, and manufacturers' representatives. These establishments operate from offices and generally do not own or handle the goods they sell.

Some wholesale establishments may be connected with a single manufacturer and promote and sell that particular manufacturer's products to a wide range of other wholesalers or retailers. Other wholesalers may be connected to a retail chain or a limited number of retail chains and only provide the products needed by the particular retail operation(s). These wholesalers may obtain the products from a wide range of manufacturers. Still other wholesalers may not take title to the goods, but act instead as agents and brokers for a commission.

Although wholesaling normally denotes sales in large volumes, durable nonconsumer goods may be sold in single units. Sales of capital or durable nonconsumer goods used in the production of goods and services, such as farm machinery, medium- and heavy-duty trucks, and industrial machinery, are always included in Wholesale Trade.

The city table includes only **Merchant wholesalers, except manufacturers' sales branches and offices,** establishments primarily engaged in buying and selling merchandise on their own account. Included here are such types of establishments as wholesale distributors and jobbers, importers, exporters, own-brand importers/marketers, terminal and country grain elevators, and farm products assemblers.

RETAIL TRADE, Items 76–79

Source: U.S. Census Bureau—2012 Economic Census (See Overview of 2012 Economic Census prior to Item 72)

The Retail Trade sector (44–45) is made up of establishments engaged in retailing merchandise, generally without transformation, and rendering services incidental to the sale of merchandise.

The retailing process is the final step in the distribution of merchandise; retailers are therefore organized to sell merchandise in small quantities to the general public. This sector comprises two main types of retailers: store and nonstore retailers.

Store retailers operate fixed point-of-sale locations, located and designed to attract a high volume of walk-in customers. In general, retail stores have extensive displays of merchandise and use mass-media advertising to attract customers. They typically sell merchandise to the general public for personal or household consumption; some also serve business and institutional clients. These include establishments such as office supply stores, computer and software stores, building materials dealers, plumbing supply stores, and electrical supply stores. Catalog showrooms, gasoline service stations, automotive dealers, and mobile home dealers are treated as store retailers.

In addition to retailing merchandise, some types of store retailers are also engaged in the provision of after-sales services, such as repair and installation. For example, new automobile dealers, electronic and appliance stores, and musical instrument and supply stores often provide repair services. As a general rule, establishments engaged in retailing merchandise and providing after-sales services are classified in this sector.

Nonstore retailers, like store retailers, are organized to serve the general public, although their retailing methods differ. The establishments of this subsector reach customers and market merchandise with methods including the broadcasting of "infomercials," the broadcasting and publishing of direct-response advertising, the publishing of paper and electronic catalogs, door-to-door solicitation, in-home demonstration, selling from portable stalls (street vendors, except food), and distribution through vending machines. Establishments engaged in the direct sale (nonstore) of products, such as home heating oil dealers and home-delivery newspaper routes are included in this sector.

The buying of goods for resale is a characteristic of retail trade establishments that distinguishes them from establishments in the Agriculture, Manufacturing, and Construction sectors. For example, farms that sell their products at or from the point of production are classified in Agriculture instead of in Retail Trade. Similarly, establishments that both manufacture and sell their products to the general public are classified in Manufacturing instead of Retail Trade. However, establishments that engage in processing activities incidental to retailing are classified in Retail Trade.

REAL ESTATE AND RENTAL AND LEASING, Items 80–83

Source: U.S. Census Bureau—2012 Economic Census (See Overview of 2012 Economic Census prior to Item 72)

The Real Estate and Rental and Leasing sector (53) comprises establishments primarily engaged in renting, leasing, or otherwise allowing the use of tangible or intangible assets, and establishments providing related services. The major portion of this sector is made up of establishments that rent, lease, or otherwise allow the use of their own assets by others. The assets may be tangible, such as real estate and equipment, or intangible, such as patents and trademarks.

This sector also includes establishments primarily engaged in managing real estate for others, selling, renting, and/or buying real estate for others, and appraising real estate. These activities are closely related to this sector's main activity. In addition, a substantial proportion of property management is self-performed by lessors.

The main components of this sector are the real estate lessors industries; equipment lessors industries (including motor vehicles, computers, and consumer goods); and lessors of nonfinancial intangible assets (except copyrighted works).

PROFESSIONAL, SCIENTIFIC, AND TECHNICAL SERVICES, Items 84–87

Source: U.S. Census Bureau—2012 Economic Census (See Overview of 2012 Economic Census prior to Item 72)

The Professional, Scientific, and Technical Services sector (54) is made up of establishments that specialize in performing professional, scientific, and technical activities for others. These activities require a high degree of expertise and training. The establishments in this sector specialize in one or more areas and provide services to clients in a variety of industries (and, in some cases, to households). Activities performed include legal advice and representation; accounting, bookkeeping, and payroll services; architectural, engineering, and specialized design services; computer services; consulting services; research services; advertising services; photographic services; translation and interpretation services; veterinary services; and other professional, scientific, and technical services.

Table D includes only those establishments subject to federal income tax.

This sector excludes establishments primarily engaged in providing a range of day-to-day office administrative services, such as financial planning, billing and record keeping, personnel services, and physical distribution and logistics services. These establishments are classified in sector 56, Administrative and Support and Waste Management and Remediation Services.

MANUFACTURING, Items 88–91

Source: U.S. Census Bureau—2012 Economic Census (See Overview of 2012 Economic Census prior to Item 72)

The Manufacturing sector (31–33) is made up of establishments engaged in the mechanical, physical, or chemical transformation of materials, substances, or components into new products. The assembling of component parts of manufactured products is considered manufacturing, except in cases in which the activity is appropriately classified in the Construction sector. Establishments in the Manufacturing sector are often described as plants, factories, or mills, and characteristically use power-driven machines and materials-handling equipment. However, establishments that transform materials or substances into new products by hand or in the worker's home, and establishments engaged in selling to the general public products made on the same premises from which they are sold (such as bakeries, candy stores, and custom tailors) may also be included in this sector. Manufacturing establishments may process materials or contract with other establishments to process their materials for them. Both types of establishments are included in the Manufacturing sector.

The materials, substances, or components transformed by manufacturing establishments are raw materials that are products of agriculture, forestry, fishing, mining, or quarrying, or are products of other manufacturing establishments. The materials used may be purchased directly from producers, obtained through customary trade channels, or secured without recourse to the market by transferring the product from one establishment to another, under the same ownership. The new product of a manufacturing establishment may be finished (in the sense that it is ready for utilization or consumption), or it may be semifinished to become an input for an establishment engaged in further manufacturing. For example, the product of the alumina refinery is the input used in the primary production of aluminum; primary aluminum is the input used in an aluminum wire drawing plant; and aluminum wire is the input used in a fabricated wire product manufacturing establishment.

Data are included for cities with 500 or more employees in the Manufacturing sector.

ACCOMMODATION AND FOOD SERVICES, Items 92–95

Source: U.S. Census Bureau—2012 Economic Census (See Overview of 2012 Economic Census prior to Item 72)

The Accommodation and Food Services sector (72) consists of establishments that provide customers with lodging and/or meals, snacks, and beverages for immediate consumption. This sector includes both accommodation and food services establishments because the two activities are often combined at the same establishment.

Excluded from this sector are civic and social organizations, amusement and recreation parks, theaters, and other recreation or entertainment facilities providing food and beverage services.

ARTS, ENTERTAINMENT, AND RECREATION, Items 96–99

Source: U.S. Census Bureau—2012 Economic Census (See Overview of 2012 Economic Census prior to Item 72)

The Arts, Entertainment, and Recreation sector (71) includes a wide range of establishments that operate facilities or provide services that meet the diverse cultural, entertainment, and recreational interests of their patrons. This sector is made up of: (1) establishments that are involved in producing, promoting, or participating in live performances, events, or exhibits intended for public viewing; (2) establishments that preserve and exhibit objects and sites of historical, cultural, or educational interest; and (3) establishments that operate facilities or provide services that enable patrons to participate in recreational activities or pursue amusement, hobby, and leisure time interests.

Some establishments that provide cultural, entertainment, or recreational facilities and services are classified in other sectors. Excluded from this sector are: (1) establishments that provide both accommodations and recreational facilities—such as hunting and fishing camps and resort and casino hotels—are classified in subsector 721, Accommodation; (2) restaurants and night clubs that provide live entertainment in addition to the sale of food and beverages are classified in subsector 722, Food Services and Drinking Places; (3) motion picture theaters, libraries and archives, and publishers of newspapers, magazines, books, periodicals, and computer software are classified in sector 51, Information; and (4) establishments that use transportation equipment to provide recreational and entertainment services, such as those operating sightseeing buses, dinner cruises, or helicopter rides, are classified in subsector 487, Scenic and Sightseeing Transportation.

Table D includes only those establishments subject to federal tax.

HEALTH CARE AND SOCIAL ASSISTANCE, Items 100–103

Source: U.S. Census Bureau—2012 Economic Census (See Overview of 2012 Economic Census prior to Item 72)

The Health Care and Social Assistance sector (62) consists of establishments that provide health care and social assistance services to individuals. The sector includes both health care and social assistance because it is sometimes difficult to distinguish between the boundaries of these two activities. The industries in this sector are arranged on a continuum, starting with establishments that provide medical care exclusively, continuing with those that provide health care and social assistance, and finishing with those that provide only social assistance. The services provided by establishments in this sector are delivered by trained professionals. All industries in the sector share this commonality of process—namely, labor inputs of health practitioners or social workers with the requisite expertise. Many of the industries in the sector are defined based on the educational degree held by the practitioners included in the industry.

Excluded from this sector are aerobic classes, which can be found in subsector 713, Amusement, Gambling, and Recreation Industries; and nonmedical diet and weight-reducing centers, which can be found in subsector 812, Personal and Laundry Services. Although these can be viewed as health services, they are not typically delivered by health practitioners.

Table D includes only those establishments subject to federal tax.

OTHER SERVICES, EXCEPT PUBLIC ADMINISTRATION Items 104–107

Source: U.S. Census Bureau—2012 Economic Census (See Overview of 2012 Economic Census prior to Item 72)

The Other Services, Except Public Administration sector (81) comprises establishments engaged in providing services not specifically categorized elsewhere in the classification system. Establishments in this sector are primarily engaged in activities such as equipment and machinery repairing, promoting or administering religious activities, grant making, and advocacy; this sector also includes establishments that provide dry-cleaning and laundry services, personal care services, death care services, pet care services, photofinishing services, temporary parking services, and dating services.

Private households that employ workers on or about the premises in activities primarily concerned with the operation of the household are included in this sector.

In Table D, only firms subject to federal tax are included.

Excluded from this sector are establishments primarily engaged in retailing new equipment and performing repairs and general maintenance on equipment. These establishments are classified in sector 44–45, Retail Trade.

CITY GOVERNMENT EMPLOYMENT AND PAYROLL, Items 171–179

Source: U.S. Census Bureau—2012 Census of Governments
http://www.census.gov/govs/cog2012/

These items include data for municipal governments only. They do not include any special district government entities within the city. The Census of Governments identifies the scope and nature of the nation's state and local government sector; provides authoritative benchmark figures of public finance and public employment; classifies local government organizations, powers, and activities; and measures federal, state, and local fiscal relationships. The Employment component was mailed March 2012 to collect information on the number of state and local government civilian employees and their payrolls.

Government employees include all persons paid for personal services performed, including persons paid from federally funded programs, paid elected or appointed officials, persons in a paid leave status, and persons paid on a per meeting, annual, semiannual, or quarterly basis. Unpaid officials, pensioners, persons whose work is performed on a fee basis, and contractors and their employees are excluded from the count of employees. **Full-Time equivalent employees** is a computed statistic representing the number of full-time employees that could have been employed if the reported number of hours worked by part-time employees had been worked by full-time employees. This statistic is calculated separately for each function of a government by dividing the "part-time hours paid" by the standard number of hours for full-time employees in the particular government and then adding the resulting quotient to the number of full-time employees.

March payroll represents gross payroll amounts for the one-month period of March for full-time and part-time employees. Gross payroll includes all salaries, wages, fees, commissions, and overtime paid to employees **before** withholdings for taxes, insurance, etc. It also includes incentive payments that are paid at regular pay intervals. It excludes employer share of fringe benefits like retirement, Social Security, health and life insurance, lump sum payments, and so forth.

Administration and judicial and legal combines **Financial administration**, **Other government administration, and Judicial and legal** activities. **Financial administration** includes activities concerned with tax assessment and collection, custody and disbursement of funds, debt management, administration of trust funds, budgeting, and other government-wide financial management activities. This function is not applied to school district or special district governments. **Other government administration** applies to the legislative and government-wide administrative agencies of governments. Included here are overall planning and zoning activities, and central personnel and administrative activities. This function is not applied to school district or special district governments. **Judicial and legal** includes all court and court related activities (except probation and parole activities that are included at the "Correction" function), court activities of sheriff's offices, prosecuting attorneys' and public defenders' offices, legal departments, and attorneys providing government-wide legal service.

Police and corrections includes all activities concerned, with the enforcement of law and order, including coroner's offices, police training academies, investigation bureaus, and local jails, "lockups", or other detention facilities not intended to serve as correctional facilities. **Corrections** includes activities pertaining to the confinement and correction of adults and minors convicted of criminal offenses. Pardon, probation, and parole activities are also included here.

Fire protection includes local government fire protection and prevention activities plus any ambulance, rescue, or other auxiliary services provided by a fire protection agency. Volunteer firefighters, if remunerated for their services on a "per fire" or some other basis, are included as part-time employees.

Highways and transportation includes activities associated with the maintenance and operation of streets, roads, sidewalks, bridges, tunnels, toll roads, and ferries. Snow and ice removal, street lighting, and highway and traffic engineering activities are also included here. Also included are the operation, maintenance, and construction of public mass transit systems, including subways, surface rails, and buses, and the provision, construction, operation, maintenance; support of public waterways, harbors, docks, wharves, and related marine terminal facilities; and activities associated with the operation and support of publicly operated airport facilities.

Health and welfare includes **Health, hospitals, and public welfare. Health** includes administration of public health programs, community and visiting nurse services, immunization programs, drug abuse rehabilitation programs, health and food inspection activities, operation of outpatient clinics, and environmental pollution control activities. **Hospitals** includes only government operated medical care facilities that provide inpatient care. Employees and payrolls of private corporations that lease and operate government-owned hospital facilities are excluded. **Public welfare** includes the administration of various public assistance programs for the needy, veteran services, operation of nursing homes, indigent care institutions, and programs that provide payments for medical care, handicap transportation, and other services for the needy.

Natural resources and utilities includes activities primarily concerned with the conservation and development of natural resources (soil, water, energy, minerals, etc.) and the regulation of industries that develop, utilize, or affect natural resources, as well as the operation and maintenance of **parks**, playgrounds, swimming pools, public beaches, auditoriums, public golf courses, museums, marinas, botanical gardens, and zoological parks. **Utilities, sewerage, and waste management** include operation, maintenance, and construction of public water supply systems, including production, acquisition, and distribution of water to general public or to other public or private utilities, for residential, commercial, and industrial use; activities associated with the production or acquisition and distribution of electric power; provision, maintenance, and operation of sanitary and storm sewer systems and sewage disposal and treatment facilities; and refuse collection and disposal, operation of sanitary landfills, and street cleaning activities.

Education and libraries includes activities associated with the operation of public elementary and secondary schools and locally operated vocational-technical schools. Special education programs operated by elementary and secondary school systems are also included as are all ancillary services associated with the operation of schools, such as pupil transportation and food service.

Also included are the establishment and provision of libraries for use by the general public and the technical support of privately operated libraries. This category includes classroom teachers, principals, supervisors of instruction, librarians, teacher aides, library aides, and guidance and psychological personnel as well as school superintendents and other administrative personnel, clerical and secretarial staffs, plant operation and maintenance personnel, health and recreation employees, transportation and food service personnel, and any student employees. Also included are any degree granting institutions that provide academic training above grade 12.

CITY GOVERNMENT FINANCES, Items 117–139

Source: U.S. Census Bureau—2012 Census of Governments
http://www.census.gov/govs/cog

Revenue and expenditure data are included in Table D for municipal governments only. The data do not include funds of any special district governments located in the city. For example, if a city's school district is a separate governmental unit, it is not included.

Total **general revenue** includes all revenue except utility, liquor stores, and insurance trust revenue. All tax revenue and intergovernmental revenue, even if designated for employee-retirement or local utility purpose, are classified as general revenue.

Intergovernmental revenue covers amounts received from other governments as fiscal aid in the form of shared revenues and grants-in-aid, as reimbursements for the performance of general government functions and specific services for the paying government (for example, care of prisoners or contractual research), or in lieu of taxes. It excludes any amounts received from other governments from the sale of property, commodities, and utility services. All intergovernmental revenue is classified as general revenue. Intergovernmental revenue from the state governments includes amounts originally from the federal government but channeled through the state.

Taxes consist of compulsory contributions exacted by governments for public purposes. However, this category excludes employer and employee payments for retirement and social insurance purposes, which are classified as insurance trust revenue. All tax revenue is classified as general revenue and comprises amounts received (including interest and penalties, but excluding protested amounts and refunds) from all taxes imposed by a government. Note that local government tax revenue excludes any amounts from shares of state-imposed and collected taxes, which are classified as intergovernmental revenue.

Property taxes are based on ownership of property and measured by its value. They include general property taxes related to property as a whole—real and personal, tangible or intangible—whether taxed at a single rate or at classified rates. Also included are taxes on selected types of property, such as motor vehicles or certain or all intangibles.

Sales and gross receipts taxes include "licenses" at more than nominal rates, based on volume or value of transfers of goods or services; taxes upon gross receipts or upon gross income; and related taxes based upon the use, storage, production (other than the severance of natural resources), importation, or consumption of goods. Dealer discounts "commissions," which are allowed to merchants for the collection of taxes from consumers, are excluded.

Total **general expenditure** includes all city expenditure other than specifically enumerated kinds of expenditure, including utility, liquor store, and employee-retirement and other insurance trust expenditures.

Capital outlays are direct expenditures for contract of force account construction or buildings, roads, and other improvements, and for purchases of equipment, land, and existing structures. They include amounts for additions, replacements, and major alterations to fixed work and structures. Expenditures for repair to such works and structures, however, is classified as current operation expenditure.

A major portion of capital outlay is commonly financed by borrowing, while governmental revenue does not include receipts from borrowing. Among other things, this distorts the relationship between the totals presented for revenue and expenditure and renders this relationship useless as a direct measure of the degree of budgetary "balance" (as that term is generally applied).

Public welfare expenditure covers support of and assistance to needy persons; this aid is contingent upon the person's needs. Included are cash assistance paid directly to needy persons; vendor payments made directly to private purveyors for medical care, burials, and other commodities and services provided under welfare programs; welfare institutions; and any intergovernmental or other direct expenditure for welfare purposes. Pensions to former employees and other benefits not contingent on need are excluded.

Highway expenditure is for the provision and maintenance of highway facilities, including toll turnpikes, bridges, tunnels, and ferries, as well as regular roads, highways, and streets. Also included are expenditures for street lighting and for snow and ice removal. Not included are highway policing and traffic control, which are considered part of police protection

Parking facilities include the construction, purchase, maintenance, and operation of public-use parking lots, garages, parking meters, and other distinctive parking facilities on a commercial basis.

Education is mainly for the provision and general support of schools and other educational facilities and services, including those for educational institutions beyond high school. Elementary and secondary education includes the provision of public kindergarten through high school education by local governments. It encompasses instructional, support, and auxiliary services (school lunch, student activities, and community services) offered by public school systems. Higher education consists of all local institutions of higher education.

Health expenditures include outpatient health services other than hospital care, such as public health administration; research and education; categorical health programs; treatment and immunization clinics; nursing; environmental health activities, such as air and water pollution control; ambulance service if provided separately from fire protection services; and other general public health activities, such as mosquito abatement. School health services provided by health agencies (rather than school agencies) are included here. Not included are sewage treatment operations, which are classified as part of sewerage and sanitation. **Hospital**

expenditures include financing, construction, acquisition, maintenance and operation of hospital facilities, provision of hospital care, and support of public or private hospitals.

Police protection encompasses expenditures for the preservation of law and order, as well as for traffic safety. It includes police patrols and communications, crime prevention activities, detention and custody of persons awaiting trial, traffic safety, and vehicular inspection.

Sewerage and recreation include sanitary and storm sewers, sewage disposal facilities and services, and other government activities for such purposes. Street cleaning and the collection and disposal of garbage and other waste are also included.

Parks and recreation includes cultural and scientific activities, such as museums and art galleries; organized recreation, including playgrounds and playing fields, swimming pools, and bathing beaches; and municipal parks and special recreation facilities, such as auditoriums, stadiums, auto camps, recreation piers, and boat harbors.

Housing and community development includes city housing and redevelopment projects and the regulation, promotion, and support of private housing and redevelopment activities. Data from Arizona, Kentucky, Michigan, New Mexico, New York, and Virginia generally include municipal housing authorities. Housing authorities for other cities are usually classified as independent governments, and data from them are not included.

Interest on debt is the amount paid for the use of borrowed money.

Total **debt outstanding** is the total of debt obligations remaining unpaid on the date specified. **Debt issued during the year** is the amount of the outstanding debt that was recently borrowed.

CLIMATE, Items 140–146
Source: National Oceanic and Atmospheric Administration
https://www.ncdc.noaa.gov/data-access/land-based-station-data/land-based-datasets/climate-normals

All climate data are average values for the 30-year period from 1971 to 2000.

Mean temperatures for January and July were determined by adding the average daily maximum temperatures and the average daily minimum temperatures and dividing by two.

Temperature limits represent average daily minimum for January and average daily maximum for July.

Annual precipitation values are the average annual water equivalent of all precipitation for the 30-year period.

Heating and cooling degree days are used as relative measures of the energy required for heating and cooling buildings. One heating degree day is accumulated for each whole degree that the mean daily temperature is below 65 degrees Fahrenheit (a mean daily temperature of 62 degrees Fahrenheit will produce three heating degree days). Cooling degree days are accumulated in similar fashion for deviations of the mean daily temperature above 65 degrees Fahrenheit.

TABLE E—CONGRESSIONAL DISTRICTS OF THE 113TH CONGRESS

Members of the House of Representatives are for the 114th Congress.

LAND AREA, Items 1 and 3
Source: U.S. Census Bureau—2010 Census of Population and Housing
http://www.census.gov/2010census/data/

Land area measurements are shown to the nearest square kilo meter. Land area includes dry land and land temporarily or partially covered by water, such as marshlands, swamps, and rive floodplains.

POPULATION, Items 2–3
Source: U.S. Census Bureau—American Community Survey
http://www.census.gov/acs/www/

The population data are estimates from the American Community Survey.

POPULATION AND POPULATION CHARACTERISTICS, Items 4–24
Source: U.S. Census Bureau—American Community Survey
http://www.census.gov/acs/www/

Data on age, sex, race, Hispanic origin foreign-born residents and percent born in state of residence are from the 2014 American Community Survey.

Data on race were derived from answers to the question or race that was asked of all respondents. The concept of race, a used by the Census Bureau, reflects self-identification by peopl according to the race or races with which they most closel identify. These categories are sociopolitical constructs and shoul not be interpreted as being scientific or anthropological in nature Furthermore, the race categories include both racial and nationa origin groups.

In Table E, Columns 4 through 8 refer to individuals wh identified with each racial category alone, while column includes persons who identified with two or more races.

The **White** population is defined as persons who indicate their race as White, as well as persons who did not classif themselves in one of the specific race categories listed on th questionnaire but entered a nationality such as Irish, German Italian, Lebanese, Near Easterner, Arab, or Polish.

The **Black** population includes persons who indicated thei race as "Black, African Am., or Negro," as well as persons wh did not classify themselves in one of the specific race categorie but reported entries such as African American, Afro American Kenyan, Nigerian, or Haitian.

The **American Indian or Alaska Native** population include persons who indicated their race as American Indian or Alask Native, as well as persons who did not classify themselves in on of the specific race categories but reported entries such as Canadian Indian, French-American Indian, Spanish-American Indian, Eskimo, Aleut, Alaska Indian, or any of the American Indian or Alaska Native tribes.

The **Asian and Pacific Islander** population combines two census groupings: **Asian** and **Native Hawaiian or Other Pacific Islander**. The **Asian** population includes persons who indicated their race as Asian Indian, Chinese, Filipino, Japanese, Korean, Vietnamese, or "Other Asian," as well as persons who provided write-in entries of such groups as Cambodian, Laotian, Hmong, Pakistani, or Taiwanese. The **Native Hawaiian or Other Pacific Islander** population includes persons who indicated their race as "Native Hawaiian," "Guamanian or Chamorro," "Samoan," or "Other Pacific Islander," as well as persons who reported entries such as Part Hawaiian, American Samoan, Fijian, Melanesian, or Tahitian.

The **Hispanic population** is based on a question that asked respondents "Is this person Spanish/Hispanic/Latino?" Persons marking any one of the four Hispanic categories (i.e., Mexican, Puerto Rican, Cuban, or other Spanish) are collectively referred to as Hispanic.

The **Non-Hispanic White alone** number in Column 11 includes only those persons who were not Hispanic and whose race was "White only."

The **female** population is shown as a percentage of total population.

The **foreign-born** population includes all persons who were not U.S. citizens at birth. Foreign-born persons are those who indicated they were either a U.S. citizen by naturalization or were not a citizen of the United States. The foreign-born population consists of immigrants (legal permanent residents), temporary migrants (students), humanitarian migrants (refugees), and unauthorized migrants (persons illegally residing in the United States).

Percent born in state of residence is shown as a percentage of total population.

Age is defined as age at last birthday (number of completed years since birth).

EDUCATION—SCHOOL ENROLLMENT AND EDUCATIONAL ATTAINMENT, Items 25–27
Source: U.S. Census Bureau—American Community Survey
http://www.census.gov/acs/www/

Data on school enrollment and educational attainment were derived from a sample of the population. Persons were classified as enrolled in school if they reported attending a "regular" public or private school (or college) during the year. The instructions were to "include only nursery school, kindergarten, elementary school, and schooling which would lead to a high school diploma or a college degree" as regular school. The Census Bureau defines a public school as "any school or college controlled and supported by a local, county, state, or federal government." Schools primarily supported and controlled by religious organizations or other private groups are defined as private schools.

Data on **educational attainment** are tabulated for the population 25 years old and over. The data were derived from a question that asked respondents for the highest level of school completed or the highest degree received. Persons who had passed a high

school equivalency examination were considered high school graduates. Schooling received in foreign schools was to be reported as the equivalent grade or years in the regular American school system.

Vocational and technical training, such as barber school training; business, trade, technical, and vocational schools; or other training for a specific trade are specifically excluded.

High school graduate or more. This category includes persons who have received a high school diploma or its equivalent, and those who reported any level higher than a high school diploma.

Bachelor's degree or more. This category includes persons who have received bachelor's degrees, master's degrees, professional school degrees (such as law school or medical school degrees), and doctoral degrees.

HOUSEHOLDS, Items 28–33
Source: U.S. Census Bureau—American Community Survey
http://www.census.gov/acs/www/

A **household** includes all persons who occupy a housing unit. (Persons not living in households are classified as living in group quarters.) A housing unit is a house, an apartment, a mobile home, a group of rooms, or a single room occupied (or, if vacant, intended for occupancy) as separate living quarters. Separate living quarters are those in which the occupants live separately from any other persons in the building and have direct access from the outside of the building or through a common hall. The occupants may be a single family, one person living alone, two or more families living together, or any other group of related or unrelated persons who share living quarters. The number of households is the same as the number of year-round occupied housing units.

A **family** includes a householder and one or more other persons living in the same household who are related to the householder by birth, marriage, or adoption. All persons in a household who are related to the householder are regarded as members of his or her family. A **family household** may contain persons not related to the householder; thus, family households may include more members than families do. A household can contain only one family for the purposes of census tabulations. Not all households contain families, as a household may comprise a group of unrelated persons or of one person living alone. Families are classified by type as either a "husband-wife family" or "other family," according to the presence or absence of a spouse.

The measure of **persons per household** is obtained by dividing the number of persons in households by the number of households or householders. One person in each household is designated as the householder. In most cases, this is the person (or one of the persons) in whose name the house is owned, being bought, or rented. If there is no such person in the household, any adult household member 15 years old and over can be designated as the householder.

The category **female family householder** includes only female-headed family households with no spouse present.

GROUP QUARTERS, Items 34–39

Source: U.S. Census Bureau—American Community Survey
http://www.census.gov/acs/www/

The Census Bureau classifies all people not living in households as living in **group quarters**. There are two types of group quarters: institutional, including **correctional facilities**, **nursing homes**, and mental hospitals; and non-institutional, including **college dormitories**, **military quarters**, group homes, missions, and shelters.

HOUSING, Items 40–45

Source: U.S. Census Bureau—American Community Survey
http://www.census.gov/acs/www/

A **housing unit** is a house, apartment, mobile home or trailer, group of rooms, or single room occupied or, if vacant, intended for occupancy as separate living quarters. Separate living quarters are those in which the occupants do not live and eat with any other person in the structure and which have direct access from the outside of the building or through a common hall. For vacant units, the criteria of separateness and direct access are applied to the intended occupants whenever possible. If that information cannot be obtained, the criteria are applied to the previous occupants.

The occupants of a housing unit may be a single family, one person living alone, two or more families living together, or any other group of related or unrelated persons who share living quarters. Both occupied and vacant housing units are included in the housing inventory, although recreational vehicles, tents, caves, boats, railroad cars, and the like are included only if they are occupied as a person's usual place of residence.

A housing unit is classified as **occupied** if it is the usual place of residence of the person or group of persons living in it at the time of interview, or if the occupants are only temporarily absent (away on vacation). A household consists of all persons who occupy a housing unit as their usual place of residence. Vacant units for sale or rent include units rented or sold but not occupied and any other units held off the market.

A housing unit is **owner occupied** if the owner or co-owner lives in the unit, even if it is mortgaged or not fully paid for. The owner or co-owner must live in the unit and is usually the first person listed on the census questionnaire

All occupied housing units that are not owner occupied, whether they are rented for cash rent or occupied without payment of cash rent, are classified as **renter occupied**.

Median value is the dollar amount that divides the distribution of specified owner-occupied housing units into two equal parts, with half of all units below the median value and half of all units above the median value. Value is defined as the respondent's estimate of what the house would sell for if it was for sale. Data are presented for single-family units on fewer than 10 acres of land that have no business or medical offices on the property.

Median rent divides the distribution of renter-occupied housing units into two equal parts. The rent concept used in this volume is gross rent, which includes the amount of cash rent a renter pays (contract rent) plus the estimated average cost of utilities and fuels, if these are paid by the renter. The rent is the amount of rent only for living quarters and excludes amounts paid for any business or other space occupied. Single-family houses on lots of 10 or more acres of land are also excluded.

Housing cost as a percentage of income is shown separately for owners with mortgages, owners without mortgages, and renters. Rent as a percentage of income is a computed ratio of gross rent and monthly household income (total household income the past 12 months divided by 12). Selected owner costs include utilities and fuels, mortgage payments, insurance, taxes, etc. In each case, the ratio of housing cost to income is computed separately for each housing unit. The housing cost ratios for half of all units are above the median shown in this book, and half are below the median shown in the book.

INCOME AND POVERTY, Items 46–51

Source: U.S. Census Bureau—American Community Survey
http://www.census.gov/acs/www/

The data on income were derived from responses of a sample of persons 15 years old and over. **Total money income** is the sum of the amounts reported separately for wage or salary income; net self-employment income; interest, dividends, or net rental or royalty income or income from estates and trusts; Social Security or railroad retirement income; Supplemental Security Income (SSI); public assistance or welfare payments; retirement, survivor, or disability pensions; and all other income. Receipts from the following sources are not included as income: capital gains; money received from the sale of property (unless the recipient was engaged in the business of selling such property); the value of income ''in kind'' from food stamps, public housing subsidies, medical care, employer contributions for individuals, etc.; withdrawal of bank deposits; money borrowed; tax refunds; exchange of money between relatives living in the same household; and gifts, lump-sum inheritances, insurance payments, and other types of lump-sum receipts.

Per capita income is the mean income computed for every man, woman, and child in a particular group. It is derived by dividing the aggregate income of a particular group by the resident population in that group. Per capita income is rounded to the nearest whole dollar.

Household income includes the income of the householder and all other individuals 15 years old and over in the household, whether or not they are related to the householder. Since many households consist of only one person, median household income is usually less than median family income.

The **poverty status** data were derived from data collected on the number of persons in a household, from questionnaire item 3, which provided data on each person's relationship to the householder, and questionnaire items 41 and 42, which were also used to derive the income data. The Social Security Administration (SSA) developed the original poverty definition in 1964, which federal interagency committees subsequently revised in 1969 and 1980. The Office of Management and Budget's (OMB) *Directive 14* prescribes the SSA's definition as the official poverty measure for federal agencies to use in their statistical work. Poverty statistics presented in American Community Survey products adhere to the standards defined by OMB in *Directive 14.*

Poverty thresholds vary depending on three criteria: size of family, number of children, and, for one- and two-person families, age of householder. In determining the poverty status of families and unrelated individuals, the Census Bureau uses thresholds (income cutoffs) arranged in a two-dimensional matrix. The matrix consists of family size (from one person to nine or more persons), cross-classified by presence and number of family members under 18 years old (from no children present to eight or more children present). Unrelated individuals and two-person families are further differentiated by age of reference person (under 65 years old and 65 years old and over). To determine a person's poverty status, the person's total family income over the previous 12 months is compared with the poverty threshold appropriate for that person's family size and composition. If the total income of that person's family is less than the threshold appropriate for that family, then the person is considered poor or "below the poverty level," together with every member of his or her family. If a person is not living with anyone related by birth, marriage, or adoption, then the person's own income is compared with his or her poverty threshold. The total number of persons below the poverty level is the sum of persons in families and the number of unrelated individuals with incomes below the poverty level over the previous 12 months. The average poverty threshold for a four-person family was $24,230 in 2014.

Poverty Thresholds for 2014 by Size of Family and Number of Related Children Under 18 Years

Size of family unit	Weighted average thresholds
One person (unrelated individual)	12,071
Under 65 years	12,316
65 years and over	11,354
Two people	15,379
Householder under 65 years	15,934
Householder 65 years and over	14,326
Three people..	18,850
Four people..	24,230
Five people..	28,695
Six people..	32,473
Seven people..	36,927
Eight people...	40,968
Nine people or more...	49,021

Source: U.S. Census Bureau.

The data on participation in the Food Stamp Program are designed to identify households in which one or more of the current members received food stamps during the past 12 months. Once a food stamp household was identified, a question was asked about the total value of all food stamps received by the household during that 12-month period. The Food Stamp Act of 1977 defines this federally funded program as one intended to "permit low-income households to obtain a more nutritious diet." From title XIII of P.L. 95–113, The Food Stamp Act of 1977, declaration of policy.) Providing eligible households with coupons that can be used to purchase food increases food purchasing power. The Food and Nutrition Service (FNS) of the U.S. Department of Agriculture (USDA) administers the Food Stamp program through state and local welfare offices. The Food Stamp program

is the major national income support program to which all low-income and low-resource households, regardless of household characteristics, are eligible.

CIVILIAN LABOR FORCE, UNEMPLOYMENT, AND EMPLOYMENT, Items 52–58
Source: U.S. Census Bureau—American Community Survey
http://www.census.gov/acs/www/

The **civilian labor force** consists of all civilians 16 years old and over who are either employed or unemployed.

Unemployment includes all persons who did not work during the survey week, made specific efforts to find a job during the previous four weeks, and were available for work during the survey week (except for temporary illness). Persons waiting to be called back to a job from which they had been laid off and those waiting to report to a new job within the next 30 days are included in unemployment figures.

Total employment includes all civilians 16 years old and over who were either (1) "at work"—those who did any work at all during the reference week as paid employees, worked in either their own business or profession, worked on their own farm, or worked 15 hours or more as unpaid workers in a family farm or business; or were (2) "with a job, but not at work"—those who had a job but were not at work that week due to illness, weather, industrial dispute, vacation, or other personal reasons.

The **occupational categories** are based on the occupational classification system that was developed for the 2000 census. This system consists of 539 specific occupational categories for employed persons arranged into 23 major occupational groups. This classification was developed based on the *Standard Occupational Classification (SOC) Manual: 2010*, published by the Executive Office of the President, Office of Management and Budget.

PERSONS WITH NO HEALTH INSURANCE, Item 59
Source: U.S. Census Bureau—American Community Survey
http://www.census.gov/acs/www/

The percentage of persons under age 65 with no **health insurance** shows the percentage of the population of each congressional district who were not covered by private health plans purchased directly or provided by an employer, Medicaid, Medicare, or military health care.

SOCIAL SECURITY AND SUPPLEMENTAL SECURITY INCOME, Items 60–62
Source: U.S. Social Security Administration
http://www.ssa.gov/policy/docs/factsheets/congstats/

Social Security beneficiaries are persons receiving benefits under the Old-Age, Survivors, and Disability Insurance Program. These include retired or disabled workers covered by the program, their spouses and dependent children, and the surviving spouses and dependent children of deceased workers.

Supplemental Security Income (SSI) recipients are persons receiving SSI payments. The SSI program is a cash assistance program that provides monthly benefits to low-income aged, blind, or disabled persons.

Data are as of December of the year shown.

AGRICULTURE, ITEMS 63–72

Source: U.S. Department of Agriculture, National Agricultural Statistics Service—2012 Census of Agriculture
http://agcensus.usda.gov/index.php

The Census Bureau took a census of agriculture every 10 years from 1840 to 1920; since 1925, this census has been taken roughly once every 5 years. The 1997 Census of Agriculture was the first one conducted by the National Agricultural Statistics Service of the U.S. Department of Agriculture. Over time, the definition of a farm has varied. For recent censuses (including the 2012 census), a farm has been defined as any place from which $1,000 or more of agricultural products were produced and sold or normally would have been sold during the census year. Dollar figures are expressed in current dollars and have not been adjusted for inflation or deflation.

The acreage designated as **land in farms** consists primarily of agricultural land used for crops, pasture, or grazing. It also includes woodland and wasteland not actually under cultivation or used for pasture or grazing, provided that this land was part of the farm operator's total operation.

Land in farms is an operating-unit concept and includes all land owned and operated, as well as all land rented from others. Land used rent-free is classified as land rented from others. All land in Indian reservations used for growing crops or grazing livestock is classified as land in farms.

The **value of farm products sold** by farms represents the gross market value before taxes and the production expenses of all agricultural products sold or removed from the place in 2012, regardless of who received the payment. It includes sales by the operator as well as the value of any share received by partners, landlords, contractors, and others associated with the operation. It represents the sum of all crops, including nursery products sold and livestock and poultry and their products sold.

The value of crops sold in 2012 does not necessarily represent the sales from crops harvested that year. The data include sales from crops produced in earlier years and exclude some crops that were produced in 2012 but held in storage and not sold during the census year. For crops sold through a co-op that made payments in several installments, only the total value received in the census year was reported.

Government payments consists of government payments received from the Conservation Reserve Program (CRP) and Wetlands Reserve Program (WRP), plus government payments received from federal programs other than the CRP, WRP, and Commodity Credit Corporation (CCC).

PRIVATE NONFARM EMPLOYMENT AND EARNINGS, Items 73–85

Source: U.S. Census Bureau—County Business Patterns
http://www.census.gov/econ/cbp/index.html

Data for private nonfarm employment and earnings are compiled from the payroll information reported monthly in the Census Bureau publication *County Business Patterns*. The estimates are based on surveys conducted by the Census Bureau and administrative records from the Internal Revenue Service (IRS).

The following types of employment are excluded from the tables: government employment, self-employed persons, farm workers, and domestic service workers. Railroad employment jointly covered by Social Security and railroad retirement programs, employment on oceanborne vessels, and employment in foreign countries are also excluded.

Annual payroll is the combined amount of wages paid, tips reported, and other compensation (including salaries, vacation allowances, bonuses, commissions, sick-leave pay, and the value of payments-in-kind such as free meals and lodging) paid to employees before deductions for Social Security, income tax, insurance, union dues, etc. All forms of compensation are included, regardless of whether they are subject to income tax or the Federal Insurance Contributions Act tax, with the exception of annuities, third-party sick pay, and supplemental unemployment compensation benefits (even if income tax was withheld). For corporations, total annual payroll includes compensation paid to officers and executives; for unincorporated businesses, it excludes profit or other compensation of proprietors or partners.